2020
Directory of
California
Wholesalers and Service Companies

MERGENT
Exclusive Provider of
Dun & Bradstreet Library Solutions

dun & bradstreet

HOOVERS™

First Research

HARRIS
INFOSOURCE™

Published January 2020 next update January 2021

Publisher

Mergent Inc.

444 Madison Ave

New York, NY 10022

©Mergent Inc All Rights Reserved

2020 Mergent Business Press

ISSN 1080-2614

ISBN 978-1-64141-595-8

MERGENT
BUSINESS PRESS
by FTSE Russell

TABLE OF CONTENTS

Summary of Contents & Explanatory Notes 4

User's Guide to Listings 6

Products & Services Section

SIC Numerical Index 9

SIC Alphabetical Index 11

Firms Listed by SIC...13

Alphabetic Section

Firms listed alphabetically by company name 1155

Geographic Section

County/City Cross-Reference Index...1497

Firms Listed by Location City 1501

SUMMARY OF CONTENTS

Number of Companies 27,313
Number of Decision Makers 69,949
Minimum Number of Employees 50

EXPLANATORY NOTES

How to Cross-Reference in This Directory

Sequential Entry Numbers. Each establishment in the Products & Services Section is numbered sequentially (P-00000). The number assigned to each establishment is referred to as its Entry Number. To make cross-referencing easier, each listing in the Products & Services, Alphabetic and Geographic Sections includes the establishment's entry number. To facilitate locating an entry in the Products & Services Section, the entry numbers for the first listing on the left page and the last listing on the right page are printed at the top of the page next to the Standard Industrial Classification (S.I.C.) description.

Source Suggestions Welcome

Although all known sources were used to compile this directory, it is possible that companies were inadvertently omitted. Your assistance in calling attention to such omissions would be greatly appreciated. A special form on the facing page will help you in the reporting process.

Analysis

Every effort has been made to contact all firms to verify their information. The one exception to this rule is the annual sales figure, which is considered by many companies to be confidential information. Therefore, estimated sales have been calculated by multiplying the nationwide average sales per employee for the firm's major SIC/NAICS code by the firm's number of employees. Nationwide averages for sales per employee by SIC/NAICS codes are provided by the U.S. Department of Commerce and are updated annually. All sales—sales (est)—have been estimated by this method. The exceptions are parent companies (PA), division headquarters (DH) and headquarter locations (HQ) which may include an actual corporate sales figure—sales (corporate-wide) if available.

Types of Companies

Descriptive and statistical data are included for companies in the entire state. These comprise manufacturers, machine shops, fabricators, assemblers and printers. Also identified are corporate offices in the state.

Employment Data

This directory contains companies with 50 or more employees. The employment figure shown in the Products & Services Section includes male and female employees and embraces all levels of the company: administrative, clerical, sales and maintenance. This figure is for the facility listed and does not include other plants or offices. It should be recognized that these figures represent an approximate year-round average. These employment figures are broken into codes A through E and used in the Alphabetic and Geographic Sections to further help you in qualifying a company. Be sure to check the footnotes at the bottom of the page for the code breakdowns.

Standard Industrial Classification (SIC)

The Standard Industrial Classification (SIC) system used in this directory was developed by the federal government for use in classifying establishments by the type of activity they are engaged in. The SIC classifications used in this directory are from the 1987 edition published by the U.S. Government's Office of Management and Budget. The SIC system separates all activities into broad industrial divisions (e.g., manufacturing, mining, retail trade). It further subdivides each division. The range of manufacturing industry classes extends from two-digit codes (major industry group) to four-digit codes (product).

For example:

Industry Breakdown	Code	Industry, Product, etc.
*Major industry group	20	Food and kindred products
Industry group	203	Canned and frozen foods
*Industry	2033	Fruits and vegetables, etc.

*Classifications used in this directory

Only two-digit and four-digit codes are used in this directory.

Arrangement

1. The **Product & Services Section** contains complete in-depth corporate data. This section lists companies under their primary SIC. SIC codes are in numerical order with companies listed alphabetically under each code. A numerical and alphabetical index precedes this section.

IMPORTANT NOTICE: It is a violation of both federal and state law to transmit an unsolicited advertisement to a facsimile machine. Any user of this product that violates such laws may be subject to civil and criminal penalties, which may exceed $500 for each transmission of an unsolicited facsimile. Mergent Inc. provides fax numbers for lawful purposes only and expressly forbids the use of these numbers in any unlawful manner.

2. The **Alphabetic Section** lists all companies with their full physical or mailing addresses and telephone number.

3. The **Geographic Section** is sorted by cities listed in alphabetic order and companies listed alphabetically within each city.

USER'S GUIDE TO LISTINGS

PRODUCT & SERVICES SECTION

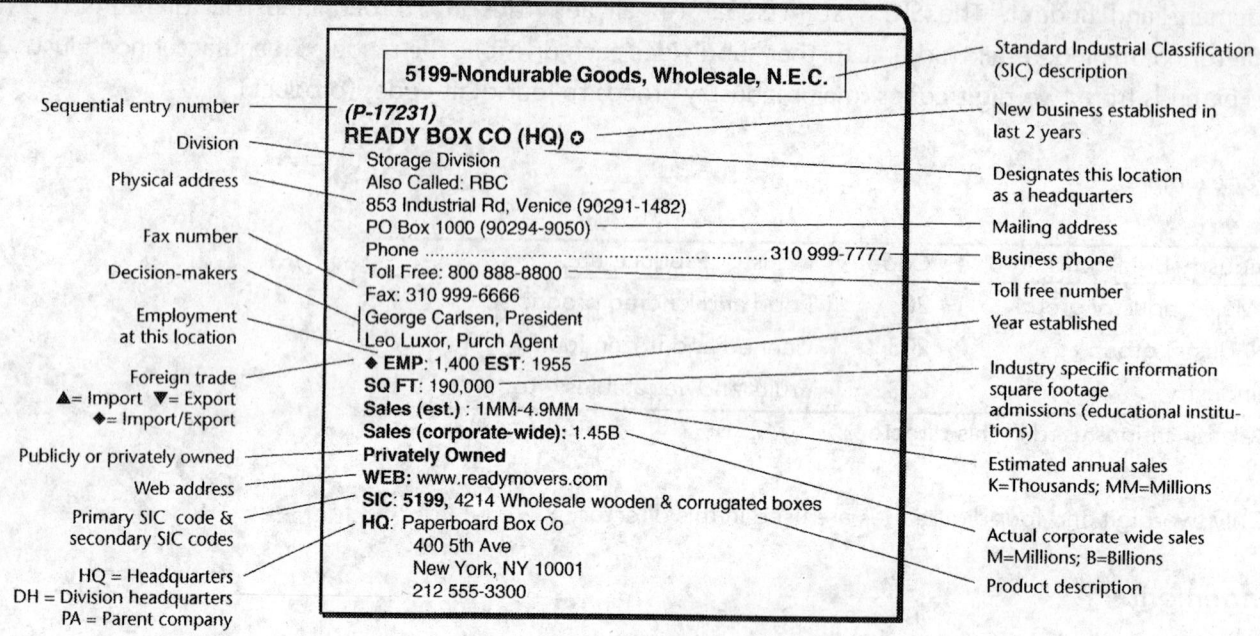

Sequential entry number
Division
Physical address
Fax number
Decision-makers
Employment at this location
Foreign trade
▲= Import ▼= Export
◆= Import/Export
Publicly or privately owned
Web address
Primary SIC code & secondary SIC codes
HQ = Headquarters
DH = Division headquarters
PA = Parent company

5199-Nondurable Goods, Wholesale, N.E.C.

(P-17231)
READY BOX CO (HQ) ⊕
Storage Division
Also Called: RBC
853 Industrial Rd, Venice (90291-1482)
PO Box 1000 (90294-9050)
Phone 310 999-7777
Toll Free: 800 888-8800
Fax: 310 999-6666
George Carlsen, President
Leo Luxor, Purch Agent
◆ **EMP:** 1,400 **EST:** 1955
SQ FT: 190,000
Sales (est.) : 1MM-4.9MM
Sales (corporate-wide): 1.45B
Privately Owned
WEB: www.readymovers.com
SIC: 5199, 4214 Wholesale wooden & corrugated boxes
HQ: Paperboard Box Co
400 5th Ave
New York, NY 10001
212 555-3300

Standard Industrial Classification (SIC) description
New business established in last 2 years
Designates this location as a headquarters
Mailing address
Business phone
Toll free number
Year established
Industry specific information square footage admissions (educational institutions)
Estimated annual sales K=Thousands; MM=Millions
Actual corporate wide sales M=Millions; B=Billions
Product description

ALPHABETIC SECTION

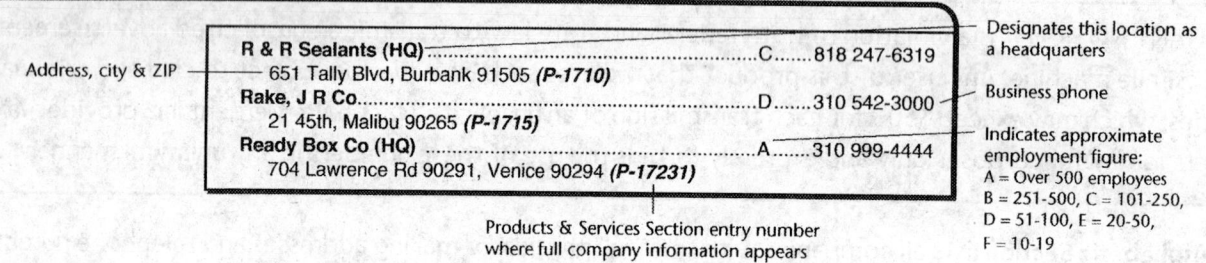

Address, city & ZIP

R & R Sealants (HQ) .... C...... 818 247-6319
651 Tally Blvd, Burbank 91505 *(P-1710)*
Rake, J R Co.... D...... 310 542-3000
21 45th, Malibu 90265 *(P-1715)*
Ready Box Co (HQ) .... A...... 310 999-4444
704 Lawrence Rd 90291, Venice 90294 *(P-17231)*

Designates this location as a headquarters
Business phone
Indicates approximate employment figure:
A = Over 500 employees
B = 251-500, C = 101-250,
D = 51-100, E = 20-50,
F = 10-19

Products & Services Section entry number where full company information appears

GEOGRAPHIC SECTION

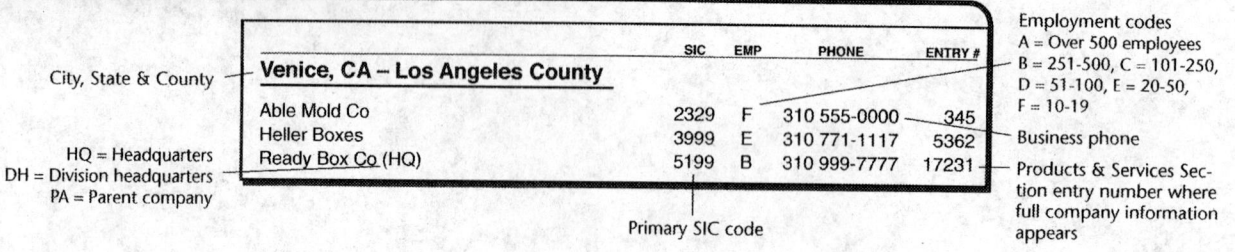

City, State & County

HQ = Headquarters
DH = Division headquarters
PA = Parent company

Venice, CA – Los Angeles County	SIC	EMP	PHONE	ENTRY #
Able Mold Co	2329	F	310 555-0000	345
Heller Boxes	3999	E	310 771-1117	5362
Ready Box Co (HQ)	5199	B	310 999-7777	17231

Employment codes
A = Over 500 employees
B = 251-500, C = 101-250,
D = 51-100, E = 20-50,
F = 10-19
Business phone
Products & Services Section entry number where full company information appears

Primary SIC code

6

NUMERICAL INDEX of SIC DESCRIPTIONS
ALPHABETICAL INDEX of SIC DESCRIPTIONS

PRODUCTS & SERVICES SECTION
Companies listed alphabetically under thier primary SIC
In-depth company data listed

ALPHABETIC SECTION
Company listings in alphabetical order

GEOGRAPHIC INDEX
Companies sorted by city in alphabetical order

SIC INDEX

PRDTS & SVCS

ALPHABETIC

GEOGRAPHIC

California
County Map

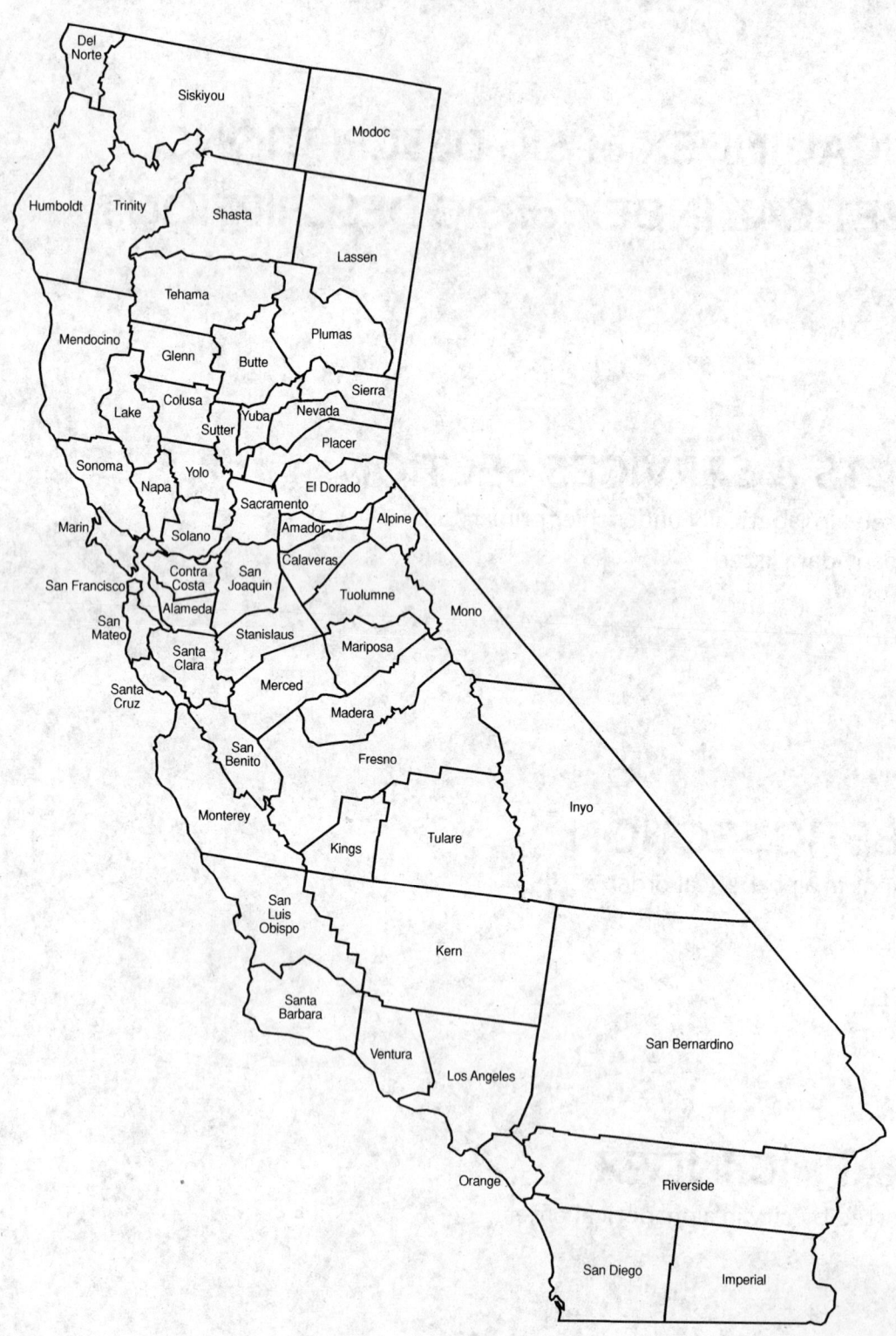

SIC INDEX

Standard Industrial Classification Numerical Index

SIC NO	PRODUCT

01 agricultural production-crops

0111 Wheat
0112 Rice
0115 Corn
0119 Cash Grains, NEC
0131 Cotton
0134 Irish Potatoes
0139 Field Crops, Except Cash Grains, NEC
0161 Vegetables & Melons
0171 Berry Crops
0172 Grapes
0173 Tree Nuts
0174 Citrus Fruits
0175 Deciduous Tree Fruits
0179 Fruits & Tree Nuts, NEC
0181 Ornamental Floriculture & Nursery Prdts
0182 Food Crops Grown Under Cover
0191 Crop Farming, Misc

02 agricultural production-livestock and animal specialties

0211 Beef Cattle Feedlots
0212 Beef Cattle, Except Feedlots
0213 Hogs
0214 Sheep & Goats
0241 Dairy Farms
0252 Chicken Egg Farms
0253 Turkey & Turkey Egg Farms
0254 Poultry Hatcheries
0259 Poultry & Eggs Farms, NEC
0279 Animal Specialties, NEC
0291 Animal Production, NEC

07 agricultural services

0711 Soil Preparation Svcs
0721 Soil Preparation, Planting & Cultivating Svc
0722 Crop Harvesting By Machine
0723 Crop Preparation, Except Cotton Ginning
0724 Cotton Ginning
0741 Veterinary Livestock Svcs
0742 Veterinary Animal Specialties
0751 Livestock Svcs, Except Veterinary
0752 Animal Specialty Svcs, Exc Veterinary
0761 Farm Labor Contractors & Crew Leaders
0762 Farm Management Svcs
0781 Landscape Counseling & Planning
0782 Lawn & Garden Svcs
0783 Ornamental Shrub & Tree Svc

08 forestry

0811 Timber Tracts
0851 Forestry Svcs

09 fishing, hunting, and trapping

0971 Hunting & Trapping

10 metal mining

1041 Gold Ores
1081 Metal Mining Svcs

12 coal mining

1221 Bituminous Coal & Lignite: Surface Mining
1241 Coal Mining Svcs

13 oil and gas extraction

1311 Crude Petroleum & Natural Gas
1381 Drilling Oil & Gas Wells
1382 Oil & Gas Field Exploration Svcs
1389 Oil & Gas Field Svcs, NEC

14 mining and quarrying of nonmetallic minerals, except fuels

1411 Dimension Stone
1422 Crushed & Broken Limestone
1429 Crushed & Broken Stone, NEC
1442 Construction Sand & Gravel
1446 Industrial Sand
1479 Chemical & Fertilizer Mining
1481 Nonmetallic Minerals Svcs, Except Fuels
1499 Miscellaneous Nonmetallic Mining

15 building construction-general contractors and operative builders

1521 General Contractors, Single Family Houses

1522 General Contractors, Residential Other Than Single Family
1531 Operative Builders
1541 General Contractors, Indl Bldgs & Warehouses
1542 General Contractors, Nonresidential & Non-indl Bldgs

16 heavy construction other than building construction-contractors

1611 Highway & Street Construction
1622 Bridge, Tunnel & Elevated Hwy Construction
1623 Water, Sewer & Utility Line Construction
1629 Heavy Construction, NEC

17 construction-special trade contractors

1711 Plumbing, Heating & Air Conditioning Contractors
1721 Painting & Paper Hanging Contractors
1731 Electrical Work
1741 Masonry & Other Stonework
1742 Plastering, Drywall, Acoustical & Insulation Work
1743 Terrazzo, Tile, Marble & Mosaic Work
1751 Carpentry Work
1752 Floor Laying & Other Floor Work, NEC
1761 Roofing, Siding & Sheet Metal Work
1771 Concrete Work
1781 Water Well Drilling
1791 Structural Steel Erection
1793 Glass & Glazing Work
1794 Excavating & Grading Work
1795 Wrecking & Demolition Work
1796 Installation Or Erection Of Bldg Eqpt & Machinery, NEC
1799 Special Trade Contractors, NEC

40 railroad transportation

4011 Railroads, Line-Hauling Operations

41 local and suburban transit and interurban highway passenger transportation

4111 Local & Suburban Transit
4119 Local Passenger Transportation: NEC
4121 Taxi Cabs
4131 Intercity & Rural Bus Transportation
4141 Local Bus Charter Svc
4142 Bus Charter Service, Except Local
4151 School Buses
4173 Bus Terminal & Svc Facilities

42 motor freight transportation and warehousing

4212 Local Trucking Without Storage
4213 Trucking, Except Local
4214 Local Trucking With Storage
4215 Courier Svcs, Except Air
4221 Farm Product Warehousing & Storage
4222 Refrigerated Warehousing & Storage
4225 General Warehousing & Storage
4226 Special Warehousing & Storage, NEC
4231 Terminal & Joint Terminal Maint Facilities

44 water transportation

4412 Deep Sea Foreign Transportation Of Freight
4424 Deep Sea Domestic Transportation Of Freight
4449 Water Transportation Of Freight, NEC
4481 Deep Sea Transportation Of Passengers
4482 Ferries
4489 Water Transport Of Passengers, NEC
4491 Marine Cargo Handling
4492 Towing & Tugboat Svcs
4493 Marinas
4499 Water Transportation Svcs, NEC

45 transportation by air

4512 Air Transportation, Scheduled
4513 Air Courier Svcs
4522 Air Transportation, Nonscheduled
4581 Airports, Flying Fields & Terminal Svcs

46 pipelines, except natural gas

4613 Refined Petroleum Pipelines
4619 Pipelines, NEC

47 transportation services

4724 Travel Agencies
4725 Tour Operators
4729 Passenger Transportation Arrangement, NEC
4731 Freight Forwarding & Arrangement

4741 Railroad Car Rental
4783 Packing & Crating Svcs
4785 Fixed Facilities, Inspection, Weighing Svcs Transptn
4789 Transportation Svcs, NEC

48 communications

4812 Radiotelephone Communications
4813 Telephone Communications, Except Radio
4822 Telegraph & Other Message Communications
4832 Radio Broadcasting Stations
4833 Television Broadcasting Stations
4841 Cable & Other Pay TV Svcs
4899 Communication Svcs, NEC

49 electric, gas, and sanitary services

4911 Electric Svcs
4922 Natural Gas Transmission
4923 Natural Gas Transmission & Distribution
4924 Natural Gas Distribution
4925 Gas Production &/Or Distribution
4931 Electric & Other Svcs Combined
4932 Gas & Other Svcs Combined
4939 Combination Utilities, NEC
4941 Water Sply
4952 Sewerage Systems
4953 Refuse Systems
4959 Sanitary Svcs, NEC
4961 Steam & Air Conditioning Sply
4971 Irrigation Systems

50 wholesale trade¨durable goods

5012 Automobiles & Other Motor Vehicles Wholesale
5013 Motor Vehicle Splys & New Parts Wholesale
5014 Tires & Tubes Wholesale
5015 Motor Vehicle Parts, Used Wholesale
5021 Furniture Wholesale
5023 Home Furnishings Wholesale
5031 Lumber, Plywood & Millwork Wholesale
5032 Brick, Stone & Related Construction Mtrls Wholesale
5033 Roofing, Siding & Insulation Mtrls Wholesale
5039 Construction Materials, NEC Wholesale
5043 Photographic Eqpt & Splys Wholesale
5044 Office Eqpt Wholesale
5045 Computers & Peripheral Eqpt & Software Wholesale
5046 Commercial Eqpt, NEC Wholesale
5047 Medical, Dental & Hospital Eqpt & Splys Wholesale
5048 Ophthalmic Goods Wholesale
5049 Professional Eqpt & Splys, NEC Wholesale
5051 Metals Service Centers
5052 Coal & Other Minerals & Ores Wholesale
5063 Electrl Apparatus, Eqpt, Wiring Splys Wholesale
5064 Electrical Appliances, TV & Radios Wholesale
5065 Electronic Parts & Eqpt Wholesale
5072 Hardware Wholesale
5074 Plumbing & Heating Splys Wholesale
5075 Heating & Air Conditioning Eqpt & Splys Wholesale
5078 Refrigeration Eqpt & Splys Wholesale
5082 Construction & Mining Mach & Eqpt Wholesale
5083 Farm & Garden Mach & Eqpt Wholesale
5084 Industrial Mach & Eqpt Wholesale
5085 Industrial Splys Wholesale
5087 Service Establishment Eqpt & Splys Wholesale
5088 Transportation Eqpt & Splys, Except Motor Vehicles Wholesale
5091 Sporting & Recreational Goods & Splys Wholesale
5092 Toys & Hobby Goods & Splys Wholesale
5093 Scrap & Waste Materials Wholesale
5094 Jewelry, Watches, Precious Stones Wholesale
5099 Durable Goods: NEC Wholesale

51 wholesale trade¨nondurable goods

5111 Printing & Writing Paper Wholesale
5112 Stationery & Office Splys Wholesale
5113 Indl & Personal Svc Paper Wholesale
5122 Drugs, Drug Proprietaries & Sundries Wholesale
5131 Piece Goods, Notions & Dry Goods Wholesale
5136 Men's & Boys' Clothing & Furnishings Wholesale
5137 Women's, Children's & Infants Clothing Wholesale
5139 Footwear Wholesale
5141 Groceries, General Line Wholesale
5142 Packaged Frozen Foods Wholesale
5143 Dairy Prdts, Except Dried Or Canned Wholesale
5144 Poultry & Poultry Prdts Wholesale
5145 Confectionery Wholesale

S I C

SIC NO	PRODUCT

5146 Fish & Seafood Wholesale
5147 Meats & Meat Prdts Wholesale
5148 Fresh Fruits & Vegetables Wholesale
5149 Groceries & Related Prdts, NEC Wholesale
5153 Grain & Field Beans Wholesale
5154 Livestock Wholesale
5159 Farm-Prdt Raw Mtrls, NEC Wholesale
5162 Plastics Materials & Basic Shapes Wholesale
5169 Chemicals & Allied Prdts, NEC Wholesale
5171 Petroleum Bulk Stations & Terminals
5172 Petroleum & Petroleum Prdts Wholesale
5181 Beer & Ale Wholesale
5182 Wine & Distilled Alcoholic Beverages Wholesale
5191 Farm Splys Wholesale
5192 Books, Periodicals & Newspapers Wholesale
5193 Flowers, Nursery Stock & Florists' Splys Wholesale
5194 Tobacco & Tobacco Prdts Wholesale
5198 Paints, Varnishes & Splys Wholesale
5199 Nondurable Goods, NEC Wholesale

60 depository institutions

6011 Federal Reserve Banks
6021 National Commercial Banks
6022 State Commercial Banks
6029 Commercial Banks, NEC
6035 Federal Savings Institutions
6036 Savings Institutions, Except Federal
6061 Federal Credit Unions
6062 State Credit Unions
6081 Foreign Banks, Branches & Agencies
6082 Foreign Trade & Intl Banks
6091 Nondeposit Trust Facilities
6099 Functions Related To Deposit Banking, NEC

61 nondepository credit institutions

6111 Federal Credit Agencies
6141 Personal Credit Institutions
6153 Credit Institutions, Short-Term Business
6159 Credit Institutions, Misc Business
6162 Mortgage Bankers & Loan Correspondents
6163 Loan Brokers

62 security and commodity brokers, dealers, exchanges, and services

6211 Security Brokers & Dealers
6221 Commodity Contracts Brokers & Dealers
6231 Security & Commodity Exchanges
6282 Investment Advice
6289 Security & Commodity Svcs, NEC

63 insurance carriers

6311 Life Insurance Carriers
6321 Accident & Health Insurance
6324 Hospital & Medical Svc Plans Carriers
6331 Fire, Marine & Casualty Insurance
6351 Surety Insurance Carriers
6361 Title Insurance
6371 Pension, Health & Welfare Funds
6399 Insurance Carriers, NEC

64 insurance agents, brokers, and service

6411 Insurance Agents, Brokers & Svc

65 real estate

6512 Operators Of Nonresidential Bldgs
6513 Operators Of Apartment Buildings
6514 Operators Of Dwellings, Except Apartments
6515 Operators Of Residential Mobile Home Sites
6517 Railroad Property Lessors
6519 Lessors Of Real Estate, NEC
6531 Real Estate Agents & Managers
6541 Title Abstract Offices
6552 Land Subdividers & Developers
6553 Cemetery Subdividers & Developers

67 holding and other investment offices

6712 Offices Of Bank Holding Co's
6719 Offices Of Holding Co's, NEC
6722 Management Investment Offices
6726 Unit Investment Trusts, Face-Amount Certificate Offices
6732 Education, Religious & Charitable Trusts
6733 Trusts Except Educational, Religious & Charitable
6794 Patent Owners & Lessors
6798 Real Estate Investment Trusts
6799 Investors, NEC

70 hotels, rooming houses, camps, and other lodging places

7011 Hotels, Motels & Tourist Courts
7021 Rooming & Boarding Houses
7032 Sporting & Recreational Camps
7033 Trailer Parks & Camp Sites
7041 Membership-Basis Hotels

72 personal services

7211 Power Laundries, Family & Commercial
7212 Garment Pressing & Cleaners' Agents
7213 Linen Sply
7215 Coin Operated Laundries & Cleaning
7216 Dry Cleaning Plants, Except Rug Cleaning
7217 Carpet & Upholstery Cleaning
7218 Industrial Launderers
7219 Laundry & Garment Svcs, NEC
7221 Photographic Studios, Portrait
7231 Beauty Shops
7241 Barber Shops
7251 Shoe Repair & Shoeshine Parlors
7261 Funeral Svcs & Crematories
7291 Tax Return Preparation Svcs
7299 Miscellaneous Personal Svcs, NEC

73 business services

7311 Advertising Agencies
7312 Outdoor Advertising Svcs
7313 Radio, TV & Publishers Adv Reps
7319 Advertising, NEC
7322 Adjustment & Collection Svcs
7323 Credit Reporting Svcs
7331 Direct Mail Advertising Svcs
7334 Photocopying & Duplicating Svcs
7335 Commercial Photography
7336 Commercial Art & Graphic Design
7338 Secretarial & Court Reporting Svcs
7342 Disinfecting & Pest Control Svcs
7349 Building Cleaning & Maintenance Svcs, NEC
7352 Medical Eqpt Rental & Leasing
7353 Heavy Construction Eqpt Rental & Leasing
7359 Equipment Rental & Leasing, NEC
7361 Employment Agencies
7363 Help Supply Svcs
7371 Custom Computer Programming Svcs
7372 Prepackaged Software
7373 Computer Integrated Systems Design
7374 Data & Computer Processing & Preparation
7375 Information Retrieval Svcs
7376 Computer Facilities Management Svcs
7377 Computer Rental & Leasing
7378 Computer Maintenance & Repair
7379 Computer Related Svcs, NEC
7381 Detective & Armored Car Svcs
7382 Security Systems Svcs
7383 News Syndicates
7384 Photofinishing Labs
7389 Business Svcs, NEC

75 automotive repair, services, and parking

7513 Truck Rental & Leasing, Without Drivers
7514 Passenger Car Rental
7515 Passenger Car Leasing
7519 Utility Trailers & Recreational Vehicle Rental
7521 Automobile Parking Lots & Garages
7532 Top, Body & Upholstery Repair & Paint Shops
7534 Tire Retreading & Repair Shops
7536 Automotive Glass Replacement Shops
7537 Automotive Transmission Repair Shops
7538 General Automotive Repair Shop
7539 Automotive Repair Shops, NEC
7542 Car Washes
7549 Automotive Svcs, Except Repair & Car Washes

76 miscellaneous repair services

7622 Radio & TV Repair Shops
7623 Refrigeration & Air Conditioning Svc & Repair Shop
7629 Electrical & Elex Repair Shop, NEC
7631 Watch, Clock & Jewelry Repair
7641 Reupholstery & Furniture Repair
7692 Welding Repair
7694 Armature Rewinding Shops
7699 Repair Shop & Related Svcs, NEC

78 motion pictures

7812 Motion Picture & Video Tape Production
7819 Services Allied To Motion Picture Prdtn
7822 Motion Picture & Video Tape Distribution
7829 Services Allied To Motion Picture Distribution
7832 Motion Picture Theaters, Except Drive-In
7833 Drive-In Motion Picture Theaters
7841 Video Tape Rental

79 amusement and recreation services

7911 Dance Studios, Schools & Halls
7922 Theatrical Producers & Misc Theatrical Svcs
7929 Bands, Orchestras, Actors & Entertainers
7933 Bowling Centers
7941 Professional Sports Clubs & Promoters
7948 Racing & Track Operations
7991 Physical Fitness Facilities
7992 Public Golf Courses
7993 Coin-Operated Amusement Devices & Arcades
7996 Amusement Parks
7997 Membership Sports & Recreation Clubs
7999 Amusement & Recreation Svcs, NEC

80 health services

8011 Offices & Clinics Of Doctors Of Medicine
8021 Offices & Clinics Of Dentists
8031 Offices & Clinics Of Doctors Of Osteopathy
8041 Offices & Clinics Of Chiropractors
8042 Offices & Clinics Of Optometrists
8043 Offices & Clinics Of Podiatrists
8049 Offices & Clinics Of Health Practitioners, NEC
8051 Skilled Nursing Facilities
8052 Intermediate Care Facilities
8059 Nursing & Personal Care Facilities, NEC
8062 General Medical & Surgical Hospitals
8063 Psychiatric Hospitals
8069 Specialty Hospitals, Except Psychiatric
8071 Medical Laboratories
8072 Dental Laboratories
8082 Home Health Care Svcs
8092 Kidney Dialysis Centers
8093 Specialty Outpatient Facilities, NEC
8099 Health & Allied Svcs, NEC

81 legal services

8111 Legal Svcs

83 social services

8322 Individual & Family Social Svcs
8331 Job Training & Vocational Rehabilitation Svcs
8351 Child Day Care Svcs
8361 Residential Care
8399 Social Services, NEC

84 museums, art galleries, and botanical and zoological gardens

8412 Museums & Art Galleries
8422 Arboreta, Botanical & Zoological Gardens

86 membership organizations

8611 Business Associations
8621 Professional Membership Organizations
8631 Labor Unions & Similar Organizations
8641 Civic, Social & Fraternal Associations
8651 Political Organizations
8699 Membership Organizations, NEC

87 engineering, accounting, research, management, and related services

8711 Engineering Services
8712 Architectural Services
8713 Surveying Services
8721 Accounting, Auditing & Bookkeeping Svcs
8731 Commercial Physical & Biological Research
8732 Commercial Economic, Sociological & Educational Re-search
8733 Noncommercial Research Organizations
8734 Testing Laboratories
8741 Management Services
8742 Management Consulting Services
8743 Public Relations Svcs
8744 Facilities Support Mgmt Svcs
8748 Business Consulting Svcs, NEC

89 services, not elsewhere classified

8999 Services Not Elsewhere Classified

SIC INDEX

Standard Industrial Classification Alphabetical Index

SIC NO	PRODUCT

A

6321 Accident & Health Insurance
8721 Accounting, Auditing & Bookkeeping Svcs
7322 Adjustment & Collection Svcs
7311 Advertising Agencies
7319 Advertising, NEC
4513 Air Courier Svcs
4522 Air Transportation, Nonscheduled
4512 Air Transportation, Scheduled
4581 Airports, Flying Fields & Terminal Svcs
7999 Amusement & Recreation Svcs, NEC
7996 Amusement Parks
0291 Animal Production, NEC
0279 Animal Specialties, NEC
0752 Animal Specialty Svcs, Exc Veterinary
8422 Arboreta, Botanical & Zoological Gardens
8712 Architectural Services
7694 Armature Rewinding Shops
7521 Automobile Parking Lots & Garages
5012 Automobiles & Other Motor Vehicles Wholesale
7536 Automotive Glass Replacement Shops
7539 Automotive Repair Shops, NEC
7549 Automotive Svcs, Except Repair & Car Washes
7537 Automotive Transmission Repair Shops

B

7929 Bands, Orchestras, Actors & Entertainers
7241 Barber Shops
7231 Beauty Shops
0211 Beef Cattle Feedlots
0212 Beef Cattle, Except Feedlots
5181 Beer & Ale Wholesale
0171 Berry Crops
1221 Bituminous Coal & Lignite: Surface Mining
5192 Books, Periodicals & Newspapers Wholesale
7933 Bowling Centers
5032 Brick, Stone & Related Construction Mtrls Wholesale
1622 Bridge, Tunnel & Elevated Hwy Construction
7349 Building Cleaning & Maintenance Svcs, NEC
4142 Bus Charter Service, Except Local
4173 Bus Terminal & Svc Facilities
8611 Business Associations
8748 Business Consulting Svcs, NEC
7389 Business Svcs, NEC

C

4841 Cable & Other Pay TV Svcs
7542 Car Washes
1751 Carpentry Work
7217 Carpet & Upholstery Cleaning
0119 Cash Grains, NEC
6553 Cemetery Subdividers & Developers
1479 Chemical & Fertilizer Mining
5169 Chemicals & Allied Prdts, NEC Wholesale
0252 Chicken Egg Farms
8351 Child Day Care Svcs
0174 Citrus Fruits
8641 Civic, Social & Fraternal Associations
5052 Coal & Other Minerals & Ores Wholesale
1241 Coal Mining Svcs
7215 Coin Operated Laundries & Cleaning
7993 Coin-Operated Amusement Devices & Arcades
4939 Combination Utilities, NEC
7336 Commercial Art & Graphic Design
6029 Commercial Banks, NEC
8732 Commercial Economic, Sociological & Educational Research
5046 Commercial Eqpt, NEC Wholesale
7335 Commercial Photography
8731 Commercial Physical & Biological Research
6221 Commodity Contracts Brokers & Dealers
4899 Communication Svcs, NEC
7376 Computer Facilities Management Svcs
7373 Computer Integrated Systems Design
7378 Computer Maintenance & Repair
7379 Computer Related Svcs, NEC
7377 Computer Rental & Leasing
5045 Computers & Peripheral Eqpt & Software Wholesale
1771 Concrete Work
5145 Confectionery Wholesale
5082 Construction & Mining Mach & Eqpt Wholesale
5039 Construction Materials, NEC Wholesale
1442 Construction Sand & Gravel

0115 Corn
0131 Cotton
0724 Cotton Ginning
4215 Courier Svcs, Except Air
6159 Credit Institutions, Misc Business
6153 Credit Institutions, Short-Term Business
7323 Credit Reporting Svcs
0191 Crop Farming, Misc
0722 Crop Harvesting By Machine
0723 Crop Preparation, Except Cotton Ginning
1311 Crude Petroleum & Natural Gas
1422 Crushed & Broken Limestone
1429 Crushed & Broken Stone, NEC
7371 Custom Computer Programming Svcs

D

0241 Dairy Farms
5143 Dairy Prdts, Except Dried Or Canned Wholesale
7911 Dance Studios, Schools & Halls
7374 Data & Computer Processing & Preparation
0175 Deciduous Tree Fruits
4424 Deep Sea Domestic Transportation Of Freight
4412 Deep Sea Foreign Transportation Of Freight
4481 Deep Sea Transportation Of Passengers
8072 Dental Laboratories
7381 Detective & Armored Car Svcs
1411 Dimension Stone
7331 Direct Mail Advertising Svcs
7342 Disinfecting & Pest Control Svcs
1381 Drilling Oil & Gas Wells
7833 Drive-In Motion Picture Theaters
5122 Drugs, Drug Proprietaries & Sundries Wholesale
7216 Dry Cleaning Plants, Except Rug Cleaning
5099 Durable Goods: NEC Wholesale

E

6732 Education, Religious & Charitable Trusts
4931 Electric & Other Svcs Combined
4911 Electric Svcs
7629 Electrical & Elex Repair Shop, NEC
5064 Electrical Appliances, TV & Radios Wholesale
1731 Electrical Work
5063 Electrl Apparatus, Eqpt, Wiring Splys Wholesale
5065 Electronic Parts & Eqpt Wholesale
7361 Employment Agencies
8711 Engineering Services
7359 Equipment Rental & Leasing, NEC
1794 Excavating & Grading Work

F

8744 Facilities Support Mgmt Svcs
5083 Farm & Garden Mach & Eqpt Wholesale
0761 Farm Labor Contractors & Crew Leaders
0762 Farm Management Svcs
4221 Farm Product Warehousing & Storage
5191 Farm Splys Wholesale
5159 Farm-Prdt Raw Mtrls, NEC Wholesale
6111 Federal Credit Agencies
6061 Federal Credit Unions
6011 Federal Reserve Banks
6035 Federal Savings Institutions
4482 Ferries
0139 Field Crops, Except Cash Grains, NEC
6331 Fire, Marine & Casualty Insurance
5146 Fish & Seafood Wholesale
4785 Fixed Facilities, Inspection, Weighing Svcs Transptn
1752 Floor Laying & Other Floor Work, NEC
5193 Flowers, Nursery Stock & Florists' Splys Wholesale
0182 Food Crops Grown Under Cover
5139 Footwear Wholesale
6081 Foreign Banks, Branches & Agencies
6082 Foreign Trade & Intl Banks
0851 Forestry Svcs
4731 Freight Forwarding & Arrangement
5148 Fresh Fruits & Vegetables Wholesale
0179 Fruits & Tree Nuts, NEC
6099 Functions Related To Deposit Banking, NEC
7261 Funeral Svcs & Crematories
5021 Furniture Wholesale

G

7212 Garment Pressing & Cleaners' Agents
4932 Gas & Other Svcs Combined
4925 Gas Production &/Or Distribution

7538 General Automotive Repair Shop
1541 General Contractors, Indl Bldgs & Warehouses
1542 General Contractors, Nonresidential & Non-indl Bldgs
1522 General Contractors, Residential Other Than Single Family
1521 General Contractors, Single Family Houses
8062 General Medical & Surgical Hospitals
4225 General Warehousing & Storage
1793 Glass & Glazing Work
1041 Gold Ores
5153 Grain & Field Beans Wholesale
0172 Grapes
5149 Groceries & Related Prdts, NEC Wholesale
5141 Groceries, General Line Wholesale

H

5072 Hardware Wholesale
8099 Health & Allied Svcs, NEC
5075 Heating & Air Conditioning Eqpt & Splys Wholesale
7353 Heavy Construction Eqpt Rental & Leasing
1629 Heavy Construction, NEC
7363 Help Supply Svcs
1611 Highway & Street Construction
0213 Hogs
5023 Home Furnishings Wholesale
8082 Home Health Care Svcs
6324 Hospital & Medical Svc Plans Carriers
7011 Hotels, Motels & Tourist Courts
0971 Hunting & Trapping

I

8322 Individual & Family Social Svcs
5113 Indl & Personal Svc Paper Wholesale
7218 Industrial Launderers
5084 Industrial Mach & Eqpt Wholesale
1446 Industrial Sand
5085 Industrial Splys Wholesale
7375 Information Retrieval Svcs
1796 Installation Or Erection Of Bldg Eqpt & Machinery, NEC
6411 Insurance Agents, Brokers & Svc
6399 Insurance Carriers, NEC
4131 Intercity & Rural Bus Transportation
8052 Intermediate Care Facilities
6282 Investment Advice
6799 Investors, NEC
0134 Irish Potatoes
4971 Irrigation Systems

J

5094 Jewelry, Watches, Precious Stones Wholesale
8331 Job Training & Vocational Rehabilitation Svcs

K

8092 Kidney Dialysis Centers

L

8631 Labor Unions & Similar Organizations
6552 Land Subdividers & Developers
0781 Landscape Counseling & Planning
7219 Laundry & Garment Svcs, NEC
0782 Lawn & Garden Svcs
8111 Legal Svcs
6519 Lessors Of Real Estate, NEC
6311 Life Insurance Carriers
7213 Linen Sply
0751 Livestock Svcs, Except Veterinary
5154 Livestock Wholesale
6163 Loan Brokers
4111 Local & Suburban Transit
4141 Local Bus Charter Svc
4119 Local Passenger Transportation: NEC
4214 Local Trucking With Storage
4212 Local Trucking Without Storage
5031 Lumber, Plywood & Millwork Wholesale

M

8742 Management Consulting Services
6722 Management Investment Offices
8741 Management Services
4493 Marinas
4491 Marine Cargo Handling
1741 Masonry & Other Stonework
5147 Meats & Meat Prdts Wholesale
7352 Medical Eqpt Rental & Leasing
8071 Medical Laboratories

S
I
C

SIC NO	PRODUCT
5047	Medical, Dental & Hospital Eqpt & Splys Wholesale
8699	Membership Organizations, NEC
7997	Membership Sports & Recreation Clubs
7041	Membership-Basis Hotels
5136	Men's & Boys' Clothing & Furnishings Wholesale
1081	Metal Mining Svcs
5051	Metals Service Centers
1499	Miscellaneous Nonmetallic Mining
7299	Miscellaneous Personal Svcs, NEC
6162	Mortgage Bankers & Loan Correspondents
7822	Motion Picture & Video Tape Distribution
7812	Motion Picture & Video Tape Production
7832	Motion Picture Theaters, Except Drive-In
5015	Motor Vehicle Parts, Used Wholesale
5013	Motor Vehicle Splys & New Parts Wholesale
8412	Museums & Art Galleries

N

SIC NO	PRODUCT
6021	National Commercial Banks
4924	Natural Gas Distribution
4922	Natural Gas Transmission
4923	Natural Gas Transmission & Distribution
7383	News Syndicates
8733	Noncommercial Research Organizations
6091	Nondeposit Trust Facilities
5199	Nondurable Goods, NEC Wholesale
1481	Nonmetallic Minerals Svcs, Except Fuels
8059	Nursing & Personal Care Facilities, NEC

O

SIC NO	PRODUCT
5044	Office Eqpt Wholesale
8041	Offices & Clinics Of Chiropractors
8021	Offices & Clinics Of Dentists
8011	Offices & Clinics Of Doctors Of Medicine
8031	Offices & Clinics Of Doctors Of Osteopathy
8049	Offices & Clinics Of Health Practitioners, NEC
8042	Offices & Clinics Of Optometrists
8043	Offices & Clinics Of Podiatrists
6712	Offices Of Bank Holding Co's
6719	Offices Of Holding Co's, NEC
1382	Oil & Gas Field Exploration Svcs
1389	Oil & Gas Field Svcs, NEC
1531	Operative Builders
6513	Operators Of Apartment Buildings
6514	Operators Of Dwellings, Except Apartments
6512	Operators Of Nonresidential Bldgs
6515	Operators of Residential Mobile Home Sites
5048	Ophthalmic Goods Wholesale
0181	Ornamental Floriculture & Nursery Prdts
0783	Ornamental Shrub & Tree Svc
7312	Outdoor Advertising Svcs

P

SIC NO	PRODUCT
5142	Packaged Frozen Foods Wholesale
4783	Packing & Crating Svcs
1721	Painting & Paper Hanging Contractors
5198	Paints, Varnishes & Splys Wholesale
7515	Passenger Car Leasing
7514	Passenger Car Rental
4729	Passenger Transportation Arrangement, NEC
6794	Patent Owners & Lessors
6371	Pension, Health & Welfare Funds
6141	Personal Credit Institutions
5172	Petroleum & Petroleum Prdts Wholesale
5171	Petroleum Bulk Stations & Terminals
7334	Photocopying & Duplicating Svcs
7384	Photofinishing Labs
5043	Photographic Eqpt & Splys Wholesale

SIC NO	PRODUCT
7221	Photographic Studios, Portrait
7991	Physical Fitness Facilities
5131	Piece Goods, Notions & Dry Goods Wholesale
4619	Pipelines, NEC
1742	Plastering, Drywall, Acoustical & Insulation Work
5162	Plastics Materials & Basic Shapes Wholesale
5074	Plumbing & Heating Splys Wholesale
1711	Plumbing, Heating & Air Conditioning Contractors
8651	Political Organizations
0259	Poultry & Eggs Farms, NEC
5144	Poultry & Poultry Prdts Wholesale
0254	Poultry Hatcheries
7211	Power Laundries, Family & Commercial
7372	Prepackaged Software
5111	Printing & Writing Paper Wholesale
5049	Professional Eqpt & Splys, NEC Wholesale
8621	Professional Membership Organizations
7941	Professional Sports Clubs & Promoters
8063	Psychiatric Hospitals
7992	Public Golf Courses
8743	Public Relations Svcs

R

SIC NO	PRODUCT
7948	Racing & Track Operations
7622	Radio & TV Repair Shops
4832	Radio Broadcasting Stations
7313	Radio, TV & Publishers Adv Reps
4812	Radiotelephone Communications
4741	Railroad Car Rental
6517	Railroad Property Lessors
4011	Railroads, Line-Hauling Operations
6531	Real Estate Agents & Managers
6798	Real Estate Investment Trusts
4613	Refined Petroleum Pipelines
4222	Refrigerated Warehousing & Storage
7623	Refrigeration & Air Conditioning Svc & Repair Shop
5078	Refrigeration Eqpt & Splys Wholesale
4953	Refuse Systems
7699	Repair Shop & Related Svcs, NEC
8361	Residential Care
7641	Reupholstery & Furniture Repair
0112	Rice
5033	Roofing, Siding & Insulation Mtrls Wholesale
1761	Roofing, Siding & Sheet Metal Work
7021	Rooming & Boarding Houses

S

SIC NO	PRODUCT
4959	Sanitary Svcs, NEC
6036	Savings Institutions, Except Federal
4151	School Buses
5093	Scrap & Waste Materials Wholesale
7338	Secretarial & Court Reporting Svcs
6231	Security & Commodity Exchanges
6289	Security & Commodity Svcs, NEC
6211	Security Brokers & Dealers
7382	Security Systems Svcs
5087	Service Establishment Eqpt & Splys Wholesale
7829	Services Allied To Motion Picture Distribution
7819	Services Allied To Motion Picture Prdtn
8999	Services Not Elsewhere Classified
4952	Sewerage Systems
0214	Sheep & Goats
7251	Shoe Repair & Shoeshine Parlors
8051	Skilled Nursing Facilities
8399	Social Services, NEC
0711	Soil Preparation Svcs
0721	Soil Preparation, Planting & Cultivating Svc
1799	Special Trade Contractors, NEC

SIC NO	PRODUCT
4226	Special Warehousing & Storage, NEC
8069	Specialty Hospitals, Except Psychiatric
8093	Specialty Outpatient Facilities, NEC
7032	Sporting & Recreational Camps
5091	Sporting & Recreational Goods & Splys Wholesale
6022	State Commercial Banks
6062	State Credit Unions
5112	Stationery & Office Splys Wholesale
4961	Steam & Air Conditioning Sply
1791	Structural Steel Erection
6351	Surety Insurance Carriers
8713	Surveying Services

T

SIC NO	PRODUCT
7291	Tax Return Preparation Svcs
4121	Taxi Cabs
4822	Telegraph & Other Message Communications
4813	Telephone Communications, Except Radio
4833	Television Broadcasting Stations
4231	Terminal & Joint Terminal Maint Facilities
1743	Terrazzo, Tile, Marble & Mosaic Work
8734	Testing Laboratories
7922	Theatrical Producers & Misc Theatrical Svcs
0811	Timber Tracts
7534	Tire Retreading & Repair Shops
5014	Tires & Tubes Wholesale
6541	Title Abstract Offices
6361	Title Insurance
5194	Tobacco & Tobacco Prdts Wholesale
7532	Top, Body & Upholstery Repair & Paint Shops
4725	Tour Operators
4492	Towing & Tugboat Svcs
5092	Toys & Hobby Goods & Splys Wholesale
7033	Trailer Parks & Camp Sites
5088	Transportation Eqpt & Splys, Except Motor Vehicles Wholesale
4789	Transportation Svcs, NEC
4724	Travel Agencies
0173	Tree Nuts
7513	Truck Rental & Leasing, Without Drivers
4213	Trucking, Except Local
6733	Trusts Except Educational, Religious & Charitable
0253	Turkey & Turkey Egg Farms

U

SIC NO	PRODUCT
6726	Unit Investment Trusts, Face-Amount Certificate Offices
7519	Utility Trailers & Recreational Vehicle Rental

V

SIC NO	PRODUCT
0161	Vegetables & Melons
0742	Veterinary Animal Specialties
0741	Veterinary Livestock Svcs
7841	Video Tape Rental

W

SIC NO	PRODUCT
7631	Watch, Clock & Jewelry Repair
4941	Water Sply
4489	Water Transport Of Passengers, NEC
4449	Water Transportation Of Freight, NEC
4499	Water Transportation Svcs, NEC
1781	Water Well Drilling
1623	Water, Sewer & Utility Line Construction
7692	Welding Repair
0111	Wheat
5182	Wine & Distilled Alcoholic Beverages Wholesale
5137	Women's, Children's & Infants Clothing Wholesale
1795	Wrecking & Demolition Work

PRODUCTS & SERVICES SECTION

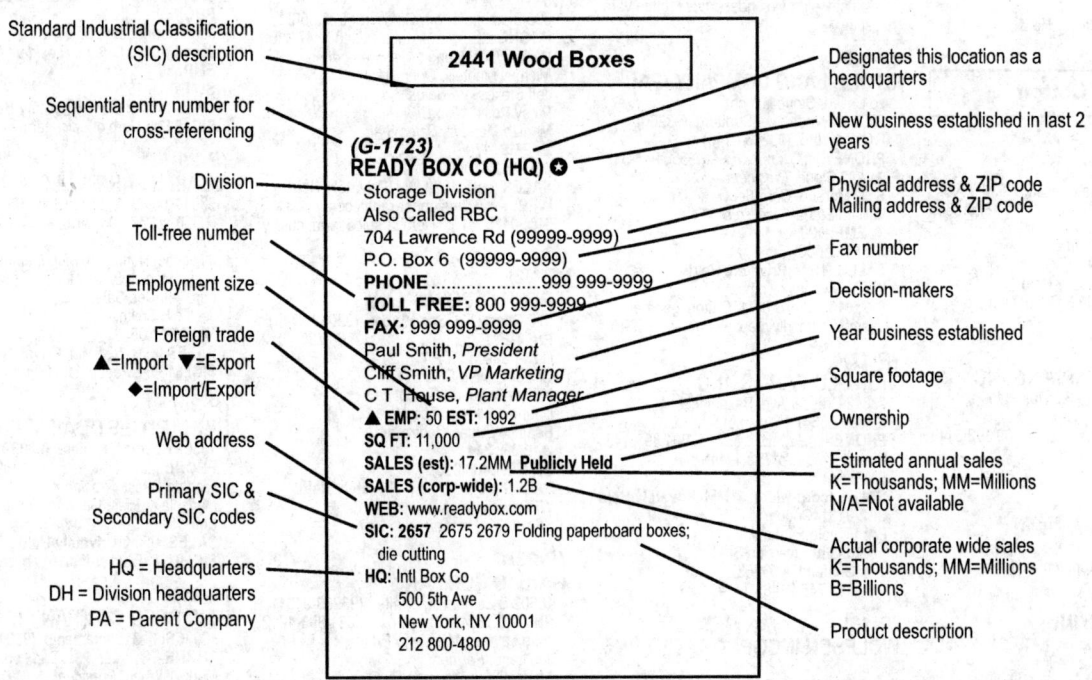

Standard Industrial Classification (SIC) description

Sequential entry number for cross-referencing

Division

Toll-free number

Employment size

Foreign trade
▲=Import ▼=Export
◆=Import/Export

Web address

Primary SIC & Secondary SIC codes

HQ = Headquarters
DH = Division headquarters
PA = Parent Company

2441 Wood Boxes

(G-1723)
READY BOX CO (HQ) ✪
Storage Division
Also Called RBC
704 Lawrence Rd (99999-9999)
P.O. Box 6 (99999-9999)
PHONE 999 999-9999
TOLL FREE: 800 999-9999
FAX: 999 999-9999
Paul Smith, *President*
Cliff Smith, *VP Marketing*
C T House, *Plant Manager*
▲ **EMP:** 50 **EST:** 1992
SQ FT: 11,000
SALES (est): 17.2MM **Publicly Held**
SALES (corp-wide): 1.2B
WEB: www.readybox.com
SIC: 2657 2675 2679 Folding paperboard boxes;
die cutting
HQ: Intl Box Co
500 5th Ave
New York, NY 10001
212 800-4800

Designates this location as a headquarters

New business established in last 2 years

Physical address & ZIP code
Mailing address & ZIP code

Fax number

Decision-makers

Year business established

Square footage

Ownership

Estimated annual sales
K=Thousands; MM=Millions
N/A=Not available

Actual corporate wide sales
K=Thousands; MM=Millions
B=Billions

Product description

- Companies in this section are listed numerically under their primary SIC Companies are in alphabetical order under each code.
- A numerical and alphabetcal index precedes this section.
- **Sequential Entry Numbers.** Each establishment in this section is numbered sequentially. The number assigned to each establishment's Entry Number. To make cross-referencing easier, each listing in the Product's & Services, Alphabetic and Geographical Section includes the establishment's entry number. To facilitate locating an entry in this section, the entry numbers for the first listing on the left page and the last listing on the right page are printed at the top of the page next to the Standard Industrial Classification (SIC) description.
- Further information can be found in the Explanatory Notes starting on page 5.
- See the footnotes for symbols and abbreviations.

IMPORTANT NOTICE: It is a violation of both federal and state law to transmit an unsolicited advertisement to a facsimile machine. Any user of this product that violates such laws may be subject to civil and criminal penalties which may exceed $500 for each transmission of an unsolicited facsimile. Harris InfoSource provides fax numbers for lawful purposes only and expressly forbids the use of these numbers in any unlawful manner.

0111 Wheat

(P-1)
B E GIOVANNETTI & SONS (PA)
Also Called: Half Moon Fruity and Prod Co
403 Court St, Woodland (95695-3421)
PHONE 530 662-1729
Blaise E Giovannetti, *Partner*
John B Giovannetti, *Partner*
Ronald Giovannetti, *Partner*
EMP: 50 **EST:** 1979
SQ FT: 3,000
SALES (est): 4.3MM **Privately Held**
SIC: 0111 0112 0131 0139 Wheat; rice;
cotton; alfalfa farm; vegetables & melons;
melon farms; lettuce & leaf vegetable
farms; walnut grove

(P-2)
MULLER RANCH LLC
15810 County Road 95, Woodland
(95695-9222)
PHONE 530 662-0105
Frank Muller, *Partner*
Thomas Muller, *Partner*
EMP: 85
SALES (est): 12.3MM **Privately Held**
WEB: www.joemuller.com
SIC: 0111 0115 0161 Wheat; corn; tomato
farm

(P-3)
T & P FARMS
1241 Putnam Way, Arbuckle (95912-0738)
P.O. Box 83 (95912-0083)
PHONE 530 476-3038
Perry Charter, *Partner*
Tom Charter, *Partner*
Shelby Nation, *Bookkeeper*
EMP: 100
SALES (est): 16.8MM **Privately Held**
SIC: 0111 0112 0181 0161 Wheat; rice;
seeds, vegetable: growing of; tomato
farm; general farms, primarily crop; food
crops grown under cover

0112 Rice

(P-4)
CATTAIL FARMS INC
3970 Cr95b, Knights Landing (95645)
P.O. Box 1024 (95645-1024)
PHONE 916 207-6580
Sawyer Y Monckton, *CEO*
EMP: 99
SALES (est): 35K **Privately Held**
SIC: 0112 Rice

(P-5)
HALF MOON FRUIT & PRODUCE CO (PA)
Also Called: Giovannetti Equipment Sales
403 Court St, Woodland (95695-3421)
PHONE 530 662-1727
John B Giovannetti, *President*
Harold Dickerson, *Corp Secy*
Ronald Giovannetti, *Vice Pres*
Eric Tenhunfeld, *General Mgr*
EMP: 74
SQ FT: 60,000
SALES (est): 5.6MM **Privately Held**
SIC: 0112 0131 0111 0119 Rice; cotton;
wheat; barley farm; alfalfa farm; lettuce
farm

(P-6)
MCFADDEN FARM
16000 Powerhouse Rd, Potter Valley
(95469-8771)
PHONE 707 743-1122
Eugene McFadden, *Owner*
Andrea Caldwell, *Manager*
EMP: 50
SQ FT: 1,000
SALES: 1.5MM **Privately Held**
WEB: www.mcfaddenfarm.com
SIC: 0112 0172 0139 2099 Rice; grapes;
herb or spice farm; food preparations

(P-7)
SUN WEST WILD RICE FACILITY
Vance Ave, Biggs (95917)
P.O. Box 305 (95917-0305)
PHONE 530 868-5188
Ralph Velasquez, *Manager*
EMP: 50
SALES (est): 1.1MM **Privately Held**
SIC: 0112 Rice

0115 Corn

(P-8)
JOE HEIDRICK ENTERPRISES INC
36826 County Road 24, Woodland
(95695-9355)
PHONE 530 662-2339
Joe Heidrick, *President*
EMP: 50
SQ FT: 1,500
SALES (est): 6.4MM **Privately Held**
SIC: 0115 0111 0161 0139 Corn; wheat;
tomato farm; alfalfa farm

(P-9)
SIMONI & MASSONI FARMS
2510 Taylor Ln, Byron (94514)
P.O. Box 399 (94514-0399)
PHONE 925 634-2304

Diane Simoni, *Partner*
Anthony Massoni, *Partner*
Paul Simoni, *Partner*
EMP: 50
SALES: 5MM **Privately Held**
SIC: 0115 Corn

0131 Cotton

(P-10)
AL BARCELLOS ET
17599 Ward Rd, Los Banos (93635-9595)
PHONE...............................209 826-2636
Aaron Barcellos, *Partner*
Arnold Barcellos, *Partner*
EMP: 50
SALES: 2MM **Privately Held**
SIC: 0131 0161 0139 Cotton; tomato
farm; alfalfa farm

(P-11)
CLARK BROS FARMING INC
19772 State Highway 33, Dos Palos
(93620-9621)
PHONE...............................209 392-6144
Norman L Clark, *Partner*
Allan W Clark, *Partner*
EMP: 50
SQ FT: 5,000
SALES: 8MM **Privately Held**
SIC: 0131 0191 0161 Cotton; general
farms, primarily crop; tomato farm

(P-12)
GILKEY FARMS INC
2411 Whitley Ave, Corcoran (93212-2025)
P.O. Box 426 (93212-0426)
PHONE...............................559 992-2136
Donald Gilkey, *President*
Brent Gilkey, *Vice Pres*
Kirk Gilkey, *Vice Pres*
Matt Gilkey, *Vice Pres*
Ralph Gilkey Jr, *Vice Pres*
EMP: 60
SQ FT: 4,500
SALES (est): 5.1MM **Privately Held**
SIC: 0131 0139 0111 0119 Cotton; alfalfa
farm; hay farm; wheat; safflower farm

(P-13)
J G BOSWELL COMPANY
21101 Bear Mountain Blvd, Bakersfield
(93311-9412)
P.O. Box 9759 (93389-9759)
PHONE...............................661 327-7721
Dave Cosyns, *Manager*
Christina Ortiz, *Admin Asst*
EMP: 200
SALES (corp-wide): 594.5MM **Privately
Held**
SIC: 0131 0111 0724 Cotton; wheat; cotton ginning
PA: J. G. Boswell Company
101 W Walnut St
Pasadena CA 91103
626 583-3000

(P-14)
J G BOSWELL COMPANY
Also Called: Ranching Shop
28001 S Dairy Ave, Corcoran (93212)
P.O. Box 877 (93212-0877)
PHONE...............................559 992-5141
Paul Athorp, *Branch Mgr*
Vern Mullins, *Purch Agent*
EMP: 500
SALES (corp-wide): 594.5MM **Privately
Held**
SIC: 0131 0724 0182 Cotton; cotton ginning; food crops grown under cover
PA: J. G. Boswell Company
101 W Walnut St
Pasadena CA 91103
626 583-3000

(P-15)
OLAM LLC
205 E Rver Pk Cir Ste 310, Fresno (93720)
PHONE...............................559 446-6420
Sandip Sharma, *President*
Munish Minocha, *President*
Ade Adefeko, *Vice Pres*
Carl Askey, *Vice Pres*
Dave Defrank, *Vice Pres*
EMP: 50

SALES (est): 9.3MM **Privately Held**
SIC: 0131 0139 Cotton;
peanuts, machine harvesting services;
tomatoes grown under cover; cotton yarn,
spun

(P-16)
STONE LAND COMPANY (PA)
Also Called: Stone Ranch
28521 Nevada Ave, Stratford (93266)
P.O. Box 146 (93266-0146)
PHONE...............................559 947-3185
Jack G Stone, *President*
Sally Moreno, *Corp Secy*
William Stone, *Vice Pres*
▲ **EMP:** 120
SQ FT: 2,000
SALES: 1MM **Privately Held**
WEB: www.jgslc.com
SIC: 0131 0191 0111 Cotton; general
farms, primarily crop; wheat

(P-17)
VIGNOLO FARMS INC
33342 Dresser Ave, Bakersfield
(93308-9634)
PHONE...............................661 393-1431
Robert J Vignolo, *President*
EMP: 141
SALES (corp-wide): 11MM **Privately Held**
SIC: 0131 Cotton
PA: Vignolo Farms, Inc.
30988 Riverside St
Shafter CA 93263
661 746-2148

(P-18)
WOLFSEN INCORPORATED
Sjr Farming
1269 W I St, Los Banos (93635-3930)
PHONE...............................209 827-7700
Albert Laguna, *Manager*
EMP: 150
SALES (corp-wide): 14.8MM **Privately
Held**
WEB: www.wolfseninc.com
SIC: 0131 Cotton
PA: Wolfsen Incorporated
1269 W I St
Los Banos CA 93635
209 827-7700

0134 Irish Potatoes

(P-19)
GIUMARRA FARMS INC
11220 Edison Hwy, Edison (93220)
PHONE...............................661 395-7000
Salvadore Giumarra, *President*
Jeff Giumarra, *Asst Controller*
EMP: 100
SQ FT: 15,000
SALES (est): 7MM **Privately Held**
SIC: 0134 0174 0161 0175 Irish potatoes; orange grove; carrot farm; plum orchard

---

0139 Field Crops, Except
Cash Grains, NEC

(P-20)
AMERICAN FARMS LLC
1107 Harkins Rd, Salinas (93901-4435)
P.O. Box 599 (93902-0599)
PHONE...............................831 424-1815
David Gill,
Steven Gill,
EMP: 100
SQ FT: 3,000
SALES (est): 23.9MM
SALES (corp-wide): 26.6MM **Privately
Held**
WEB: www.americanfarms.net
SIC: 0139 0161 Feeder crops; lettuce
farm
PA: Mesa Packing Llc
510 Broadway St
King City CA 93930
831 385-9173

(P-21)
**CHRISTOPHER RANCH LLC
(PA)**
305 Bloomfield Ave, Gilroy (95020-9565)
PHONE...............................408 847-1100
William Christopher, *Mng Member*
Michael Mantelli, *Opers Mgr*
Jeff Stokes, *VP Sales*
Patsy Ross, *Mktg Dir*
Maritza Mendez, *Sales Staff*
▲ **EMP:** 170
SQ FT: 220,000
SALES (est): 103.5MM **Privately Held**
WEB: www.christopher-ranch.com
SIC: 0139 0175 Herb or spice farm; cherry
orchard

(P-22)
FRESH ORIGINS LLC
570 Quarry Rd, San Marcos (92069-9744)
PHONE...............................760 736-4072
David Sasuga, *CPA*
Olivier Canler, *CFO*
Norma Stamant, *Executive*
Donna Walker, *Office Mgr*
Beatrice Edgar, *Controller*
▲ **EMP:** 344
SQ FT: 1,400,000
SALES (est): 11.6MM **Privately Held**
WEB: www.freshorigins.com
SIC: 0139 Herb or spice farm

(P-23)
GARLIC COMPANY
18602 S Zerker Rd, Shafter (93263-9101)
PHONE...............................661 393-4212
John Layous, *Managing Prtnr*
Joe Lane, *Partner*
Anthony Kelly, *Human Res Dir*
Bill Lane, *Plant Mgr*
John Merkle, *Plant Mgr*
▲ **EMP:** 125
SQ FT: 150,000
SALES (est): 53.8MM **Privately Held**
WEB: www.thegarliccompany.com
SIC: 0139 2099 0191 Herb or spice farm;
food preparations; general farms, primarily crop

(P-24)
GENE M ACCITO
331 Pelican Pl, Yuba City (95993-7100)
P.O. Box 3322 (95992-3322)
PHONE...............................530 674-3179
Gene M Accito, *Owner*
EMP: 80
SALES (est): 1.5MM **Privately Held**
SIC: 0139 Food crops

(P-25)
HAYDAY FARMS INC
15500 S Commercial St, Blythe
(92225-2750)
P.O. Box 1226 (92226-1226)
PHONE...............................760 922-4713
Atsuya Ichida, *President*
Dale Tyson, *Vice Pres*
◆ **EMP:** 75
SQ FT: 2,160
SALES: 17.4MM **Privately Held**
SIC: 0139 0722 0723 Hay farm; hay, machine harvesting services; field crops, except cash grains, market preparation
services

(P-26)
HERB THYME FARM INC
7909 Crossway Dr, Pico Rivera
(90660-4449)
PHONE...............................603 542-3690
EMP: 70
SALES (est): 1.2MM **Privately Held**
SIC: 0139

(P-27)
**JOHNSON & JOHNSON
PISTACCIOS**
Also Called: Johnson/Johnson
1720 Ben Lomond Dr, Glendale
(91202-1006)
PHONE...............................818 242-7853
Lee Johnson, *President*
EMP: 50
SALES (est): 1.2MM **Privately Held**
SIC: 0139 Peanut farm

(P-28)
MEDTERRA CBD LLC
9801 Research Dr, Irvine (92618-4304)
PHONE...............................800 971-1288
John Hartenbach, *CEO*
John Preston Larsen, *President*
EMP: 89
SQ FT: 29,252
SALES (est): 6MM **Privately Held**
SIC: 0139 Herb or spice farm

(P-29)
QUAIL H FARMS LLC
5301 Robin Ave, Livingston (95334-9317)
P.O. Box 247 (95334-0247)
PHONE...............................209 394-8001
J Michael Hennigan, *Mng Member*
Angie Maciel, *Sales Mgr*
Larelle Miller, *Sales Mgr*
Jackie E Smith,
▼ **EMP:** 505
SALES (est): 52.8MM **Privately Held**
SIC: 0139 Sweet potato farm

(P-30)
RICHARD IEST DAIRY INC
13507 Road 17, Madera (93637-9040)
PHONE...............................559 673-2635
Richard C Iest, *President*
Marisela Macias, *General Mgr*
EMP: 99
SALES: 950K **Privately Held**
SIC: 0139 Field crops, except cash grain

(P-31)
S&W SEED COMPANY (PA)
106 K St Fl 3, Sacramento (95814-3218)
PHONE...............................559 884-2535
Mark W Wong, *President*
Mark J Harvey, *Ch of Bd*
Dennis Jury, *COO*
Matthew K Szot, *CFO*
Grover T Wickersham, *Vice Ch Bd*
◆ **EMP:** 55
SQ FT: 4,885
SALES: 109.7MM **Publicly Held**
WEB: www.swseedco.com
SIC: 0139 0723 Alfalfa farm; seed cleaning

0161 Vegetables & Melons

(P-32)
ABE-EL PRODUCE
42143 Road 120, Orosi (93647-9714)
PHONE...............................559 528-3030
Franklin Abe, *Partner*
Herbert Abe, *Partner*
EMP: 350 **EST:** 1964
SALES (est): 7MM **Privately Held**
SIC: 0161 0174 Vegetables & melons; citrus fruits

(P-33)
ACE TOMATO COMPANY INC
777 N Pershing Ave Ste 1a, Stockton
(95203-2153)
PHONE...............................209 982-0734
Kathleen Lagorio Janssen, *CEO*
Tom McMillen, *CFO*
Dean Janssen, *Corp Secy*
Henry K Cole, *Vice Pres*
EMP: 60
SQ FT: 300,000
SALES (est): 4.2MM **Privately Held**
SIC: 0161 0723 Tomato farm; vegetable
packing services

(P-34)
BALLETTO RANCH INC (PA)
5700 Occidental Rd, Santa Rosa
(95401-5533)
P.O. Box 2579, Sebastopol (95473-2579)
PHONE...............................707 568-2455
John Balletto, *President*
Terri Balletto, *Vice Pres*
Jacqueline Balletto, *Manager*
▲ **EMP:** 70
SALES (est): 9.8MM **Privately Held**
WEB: www.ballettoranch.com
SIC: 0161 Lettuce farm; squash farm

▲ = Import ▼=Export
◆ =Import/Export

(P-35)

BALOIAN PACKING CO INC (PA)
Also Called: Baloian Farm
446 N Blythe Ave, Fresno (93706-1003)
P.O. Box 11337 (93772-1337)
PHONE..................................559 485-9200
Edward Baloian, *Ch of Bd*
Timothy Baloian, *President*
Emily Baloian, *Admin Sec*
Eric Gilmore, *QC Mgr*
Luis Corella, *Sales Mgr*
▲ EMP: 59
SQ FT: 35,000
SALES (est): 26.9MM **Privately Held**
WEB: www.baloianpacking.com
SIC: 0161 0723 Broccoli farm; pepper
farm, sweet & hot (vegetables); cucumber
farm; squash farm; vegetable packing
services

(P-36)

BALOIAN PACKING CO INC
Also Called: Baloian Farms
3138 W Whites Bridge Ave, Fresno
(93706-1125)
PHONE..................................559 441-7043
Glen Yemoto, *Branch Mgr*
EMP: 91
SALES (corp-wide): 26.9MM **Privately
Held**
SIC: 0161 0723 Broccoli farm; pepper
farm, sweet & hot (vegetables); cucumber
farm; squash farm; vegetable packing
services
PA: Baloian Packing Co., Inc.
446 N Blythe Ave
Fresno CA 93706
559 485-9200

(P-37)

**BLACK DOG FARMS OF
CALIFORNIA**
530 W 6th St, Holtville (92250-1023)
P.O. Box 57 (92250-0057)
PHONE..................................760 356-2951
Kenneth Peterson, *President*
Dora Saikhon, *Shareholder*
Carol Saikhon, *Vice Pres*
Carmen Lizaola, *Human Res Dir*
EMP: 150
SQ FT: 4,000
SALES (est): 15.3MM **Privately Held**
WEB: www.blackdogfarms.com
SIC: 0161 Vegetables & melons

(P-38)

BOLTHOUSE FARMS
3200 E Brundage Ln, Bakersfield (93304)
PHONE..................................661 366-7205
William Bolthouse, *Owner*
◆ EMP: 2300
SALES (est): 22.6MM
SALES (corp-wide): 1.1B **Privately Held**
SIC: 0161 Carrot farm
HQ: Wm. Bolthouse Farms, Inc.
7200 E Brundage Ln
Bakersfield CA 93307
661 366-7209

(P-39)

BOSKOVICH FARMS INC
4224 Pleasant Valley Rd, Camarillo
(93012-8533)
P.O. Box 1352, Oxnard (93032-1352)
PHONE..................................805 987-1443
Ken Mumford, *Opers Staff*
Yolanda Erazo, *Receptionist*
EMP: 300
SALES (corp-wide): 76.9MM **Privately
Held**
WEB: www.boskovichfarms.com
SIC: 0161 0115 Vegetables & melons;
corn
PA: Boskovich Farms, Inc.
711 Diaz Ave
Oxnard CA 93030
805 487-2299

(P-40)

C & G FARMS INC
Also Called: AMARAL RANCHES
25453 Iverson Rd, Chualar (93925-9605)
P.O. Box 2216, Gonzales (93926-2216)
PHONE..................................831 679-2978
Carlos Amaral, *President*
George Amaral, *Admin Sec*

▼ EMP: 200 EST: 1996
SQ FT: 2,000
SALES: 52.3MM **Privately Held**
WEB: www.cgfarms.com
SIC: 0161 Lettuce & leaf vegetable farms

(P-41)

**CALIFORNIA WATERCRESS INC
(PA)**
550 E Telegraph Rd, Fillmore (93015-9667)
P.O. Box 874 (93016-0874)
PHONE..................................805 524-4808
Alfred C Beserra, *President*
Teresa Beserra, *Admin Sec*
EMP: 65 EST: 1966
SQ FT: 1,000
SALES: 5MM **Privately Held**
SIC: 0161 Vegetables & melons

(P-42)

CERUTTI BROS INC
26118 Mcclintock Rd, Newman
(95360-9746)
P.O. Box 550 (95360-0550)
PHONE..................................209 862-2249
Patrick Cerutti, *CEO*
EMP: 60
SALES: 950K **Privately Held**
SIC: 0161 Vegetables & melons

(P-43)

CHRISTENSEN & GIANNINI LLC
1588 Moffett St Ste B, Salinas
(93905-3365)
PHONE..................................831 449-2494
Sam Daoro,
Shelley Daroro, *Partner*
Dirk Giannini, *Partner*
Lori Giannini, *Partner*
Renea Wood, *Controller*
EMP: 54
SALES (est): 6.9MM **Privately Held**
SIC: 0161 Vegetables & melons

(P-44)

COSTA SONS
36817 Foothill Rd, Soledad (93960-9656)
PHONE..................................831 678-0799
Tony Costa, *CEO*
David Costa, *Co-Owner*
Diane Costa, *Co-Owner*
Elsie Costa, *Co-Owner*
Michael Costa, *Co-Owner*
EMP: 50 EST: 1958
SALES (est): 2.9MM **Privately Held**
WEB: www.costafarmsinc.com
SIC: 0161 Broccoli farm

(P-45)

DAN AVILA AND SONS
2718 Roberts Rd, Ceres (95307-9627)
PHONE..................................209 495-3899
Daniel Avila, *Owner*
EMP: 60
SALES: 16MM **Privately Held**
SIC: 0161 0139 Watermelon farm; sweet
potato farm

(P-46)

**DARRIGO BROSCOOF
CALIFORNIA (PA)**
Also Called: Andy Boy
21777 Harris Rd, Salinas (93908-8609)
P.O. Box 850 (93902-0850)
PHONE..................................831 455-4500
Andrew A D'Arrigo, *Ch of Bd*
John C D'Arrigo, *President*
E John Culligan, *Corp Secy*
David Martinez, *Vice Pres*
Michelle Penny, *Office Mgr*
EMP: 50
SQ FT: 13,000
SALES (est): 239.1MM **Privately Held**
SIC: 0161 Broccoli farm; carrot farm; let-
tuce farm; celery farm

(P-47)

DIMARE ENTERPRISES INC (PA)
Also Called: Dimare Company
1406 N St, Newman (95360-1309)
P.O. Box 517 (95360-0517)
PHONE..................................209 827-2900
Thomas F Dimare, *President*
Paul J Dimare, *Treasurer*
EMP: 250

SQ FT: 20,000
SALES (est): 51.7MM **Privately Held**
WEB: www.dimare-ca.com
SIC: 0161 0174 Vegetables & melons; cit-
rus fruits

(P-48)

DOBLER & SONS LLC
174 Struve Rd, Moss Landing
(95039-9661)
P.O. Box 1660, Watsonville (95077-1660)
PHONE..................................831 724-6727
Carl Dobler, *Mng Member*
Craig Dobler,
Kenneth Dobler,
Michael Dobler,
Steven Dobler,
EMP: 350
SALES (est): 42MM **Privately Held**
WEB: www.doblerandsons.com
SIC: 0161 Cabbage farm; lettuce farm

(P-49)

**DONALD VALPREDO FARMING
INC**
Also Called: Db Custom Farming
2101 Mttler Frontage Rd E, Bakersfield
(93307-9649)
PHONE..................................661 858-2245
Donald Valpredo, *President*
Susan Gardner, *Human Resources*
EMP: 60
SALES (est): 8.2MM **Privately Held**
WEB: www.valpredofarms.com
SIC: 0161 Tomato farm; onion farm

(P-50)

DRESICK FARMS INC (PA)
19536 Jayne Ave, Huron (93234)
P.O. Box 1260 (93234-1260)
PHONE..................................559 945-2513
Michael L Dresick, *CEO*
Jan Dresick, *Vice Pres*
EMP: 51
SQ FT: 3,500
SALES (est): 32.9MM **Privately Held**
WEB: www.dresickfarms.com
SIC: 0161 Lettuce farm

(P-51)

FREITAS BROTHERS
Hwy 1, Guadalupe (93434)
P.O. Box 895 (93434-0895)
PHONE..................................805 343-3134
Eric Freitas, *Partner*
Jon Freitas, *Partner*
▼ EMP: 50
SQ FT: 1,500
SALES (est): 3.6MM **Privately Held**
WEB: www.freitasfarms.com
SIC: 0161 Vegetables & melons

(P-52)

FRESH FARMS INC
700 Airport Rd, King City (93930-2501)
P.O. Box 1600 (93930-1600)
PHONE..................................831 385-3285
Jerry J Rava II, *President*
▲ EMP: 50 EST: 1994
SALES (est): 2.8MM **Privately Held**
SIC: 0161 Spinach farm

(P-53)

FRESH LEAF FARMS LLC (DH)
1250 Hansen St, Salinas (93901-4552)
PHONE..................................831 422-7405
Mann Packing, *Partner*
Anthony Costa Sons, *Partner*
Joe Nucci, *President*
Tom Koster, *VP Sales*
Alicia Blanco, *Marketing Mgr*
EMP: 50
SALES (est): 20.2MM **Privately Held**
SIC: 0161 Lettuce & leaf vegetable farms
HQ: Mann Packing Co., Inc.
1333 Schilling Pl
Salinas CA 93901
831 422-7405

(P-54)

FRESH VENTURE FARMS LLC
1181 S Wolff Rd, Oxnard (93033-2105)
PHONE..................................805 754-4449
Robert Boelts,
EMP: 80
SQ FT: 4,000

SALES (est): 8MM **Privately Held**
SIC: 0161 0191 Vegetables & melons;
general farms, primarily crop

(P-55)

GEORGE CHIALA FARMS INC
Also Called: Chiala, George Packing
15500 Hill Rd, Morgan Hill (95037-9516)
PHONE..................................408 778-0562
George Chiala Sr, *President*
Alice Chiala, *CFO*
George Chiala Jr, *Vice Pres*
▲ EMP: 120
SQ FT: 14,000
SALES (est): 56.4MM **Privately Held**
WEB: www.gcfarmsinc.com
SIC: 0161 0723 4783 Vegetables & mel-
ons; vegetable crops market preparation
services; containerization of goods for
shipping

(P-56)

GIUSTI FARMS LLC
1800 Higgins Canyon Rd, Half Moon Bay
(94019-2573)
PHONE..................................650 726-9221
Aldo Giusti,
John Giusti,
EMP: 50
SQ FT: 145
SALES (est): 2.1MM **Privately Held**
SIC: 0161 Artichoke farm; pea & bean
farms; brussels sprout farm

(P-57)

GIVENS JOHN
Also Called: Givens Farms
1133 N Fairview Ave, Goleta (93117-1822)
PHONE..................................805 964-4477
John Givens, *Owner*
EMP: 70
SALES (est): 1.9MM **Privately Held**
SIC: 0161 Vegetables & melons

(P-58)

HENRY HIBINO FARMS
106 Rico St, Salinas (93907-2101)
PHONE..................................831 757-3081
Henry Hibino, *Owner*
EMP: 75 EST: 1950
SQ FT: 20,000
SALES (est): 6.8MM **Privately Held**
SIC: 0161 Vegetables & melons

(P-59)

JAY FISHER FARMS INC
2251 W Central Ave, Lompoc (93436)
PHONE..................................805 735-1598
Elmer Fisher, *President*
Patricia Fisher, *Corp Secy*
EMP: 50
SALES (est): 1.8MM **Privately Held**
SIC: 0161 0181 Vegetables & melons;
flowers grown in field nurseries

(P-60)

KELOMAR INC
3949 Austin Rd, Brawley (92227-9702)
PHONE..................................760 344-5253
Michael W Morgan, *President*
Joseph Johnson, *CFO*
EMP: 120
SQ FT: 3,000
SALES (est): 8.3MM **Privately Held**
WEB: www.kelomar.com
SIC: 0161 Vegetables & melons

(P-61)

KONO FARMS INCORPORATED
87481 Avenue 74, Thermal (92274)
PHONE..................................760 397-7110
Emerson Kono, *President*
Barbara Kono, *Treasurer*
Edward Kono, *Vice Pres*
Ronald Kono, *Vice Pres*
Spencer Kono, *Vice Pres*
▲ EMP: 150 EST: 1952
SQ FT: 20,000
SALES: 1.9MM **Privately Held**
SIC: 0161 Vegetables & melons

(P-62)

LA GRANDE FARM
P.O. Box 370 (95987-0370)
PHONE..................................530 473-5923
Ron La Grande, *Partner*

PRODUCTS & SVCS

Mike La Grande, *Partner*
EMP: 70
SQ FT: 8,000
SALES (est): 4.3MM **Privately Held**
SIC: 0161 0191 0111 Tomato farm; general farms, primarily crop; wheat

(P-63)
LUCKY FARMS INC
1194 E Brier Dr, San Bernardino (92408-2838)
P.O. Box 985, Loma Linda (92354-0985)
PHONE....................909 799-6688
Wen S Liaou, *President*
Gary Liaou, *Vice Pres*
▲ **EMP:** 60
SQ FT: 28,000
SALES (est): 8.1MM **Privately Held**
WEB: www.luckyfarms.com
SIC: 0161 Corn farm, sweet

(P-64)
MICHAEL W MORGAN
3949 Austin Rd, Brawley (92227-9702)
PHONE....................760 344-5253
Michael W Morgan, *Owner*
EMP: 50
SALES (est): 2.4MM **Privately Held**
SIC: 0161 Vegetables & melons

(P-65)
MIKAELIAN & SONS INC
10368 Avenue 400, Dinuba (93618-9558)
PHONE....................559 591-6324
Mike Mikaelian, *President*
Carol Mikaelian, *Corp Secy*
EMP: 120 **EST:** 1953
SALES: 1MM **Privately Held**
SIC: 0161 0175 0172 Watermelon farm; deciduous tree fruits; grapes

(P-66)
NEIL BASSETTI FARMS
41715 Espinosa Rd, Greenfield (93927-6101)
P.O. Box 429 (93927-0429)
PHONE....................831 674-2040
Maryanne Martinus, *Partner*
Adrienne Bassetti, *Partner*
Patrick Bassetti, *Partner*
Allison Fierro, *Partner*
Mary Ann Martinus, *Partner*
EMP: 50 **EST:** 1939
SALES (est): 6.3MM **Privately Held**
WEB: www.nbassetti.com
SIC: 0161 Vegetables & melons

(P-67)
OCEAN MIST FARMING COMPANY (PA)
Also Called: Ocean Mist Farms
10855 Ocean Mist Pkwy A, Castroville (95012-3232)
PHONE....................831 633-2144
C Edward Boutonnet, *CEO*
Ed Bouponnet, *President*
Terry Lynch, *CFO*
Les Tottino, *Bd of Directors*
Art Barrientos, *Vice Pres*
EMP: 250
SQ FT: 2,000
SALES (est): 43.2MM **Privately Held**
SIC: 0161 Lettuce & leaf vegetable farms; artichoke farm

(P-68)
OCEANVIEW PRODUCE COMPANY
5713 W Gonzales Rd, Oxnard (93036-2739)
PHONE....................805 488-6401
David H Murdock, *President*
EMP: 60
SALES (est): 4.3MM **Privately Held**
SIC: 0161 5148 Celery farm; lettuce farm; fresh fruits & vegetables

(P-69)
OPAL FRY AND SON
Also Called: Fry, Opal W & Son Farming
Maricopa Hwy, Bakersfield (93307)
PHONE....................661 858-2523
Jack Fry, *Partner*
George Fry, *Partner*
EMP: 50
SQ FT: 400

SALES (est): 2.4MM **Privately Held**
SIC: 0161 0131 Vegetables & melons; cotton

(P-70)
PAYNE BROTHERS RANCHES
13330 County Road 102, Woodland (95776-9119)
PHONE....................530 662-2354
William A Payne, *Partner*
Robert B Payne, *Partner*
EMP: 100
SALES (est): 4.7MM **Privately Held**
WEB: www.paynefarms.com
SIC: 0161 0191 Tomato farm; general farms, primarily crop

(P-71)
PFYFFER ASSOCIATES INC
2611 Mission St, Santa Cruz (95060-5702)
P.O. Box 879 (95061-0879)
PHONE....................831 423-8572
Ernie Bontadelli, *President*
Steve Bontadelli, *Vice Pres*
Charlie Bontadelli, *Principal*
EMP: 50
SALES (est): 3.2MM **Privately Held**
SIC: 0161 Brussels sprout farm

(P-72)
ROBERT CECCHINI INC
Also Called: Cecchini & Cecchini
5301 Orwood Rd, Brentwood (94513-5245)
P.O. Box 1150, Discovery Bay (94505-7150)
PHONE....................925 634-4400
Robert L Cecchini, *President*
EMP: 100 **EST:** 1933
SALES (est): 8.5MM **Privately Held**
SIC: 0161 0115 0111 0139 Asparagus farm; corn; wheat; alfalfa farm

(P-73)
ROYAL PACKING DCF
Also Called: Doll Fresh Vegetable
32839 S Lassen Ave, Huron (93234)
PHONE....................559 945-2537
Jack Shiyomura, *Manager*
EMP: 60
SALES (est): 2.2MM **Privately Held**
SIC: 0161 Lettuce farm

(P-74)
SAN MIGUEL PRODUCE INC
Also Called: Cut N Clean Greens
4444 Navalair Rd, Oxnard (93033-8298)
PHONE....................805 488-0981
Roy I Nishimori, *CEO*
Jan Berk, *COO*
John Killeen, *Vice Pres*
Angee Lau, *Info Tech Mgr*
Christopher Luu, *Purchasing*
▲ **EMP:** 500
SQ FT: 25,000
SALES: 52MM **Privately Held**
WEB: www.cutnclean.com
SIC: 0161 0723 4212 Vegetables & melons; vegetable packing services; farm to market haulage, local

(P-75)
SANTA BARBARA FARMS LLC (PA)
1200 Union Sugar Ave, Lompoc (93436-9740)
PHONE....................805 736-9776
Robert M Witt, *CEO*
Charles Witt, *COO*
RC Gerber, *CFO*
▲ **EMP:** 60
SQ FT: 2,800
SALES (est): 39.5MM **Privately Held**
WEB: www.oceanviewflowers.com
SIC: 0161 0181 Vegetables & melons; florists' greens & flowers

(P-76)
SCARBOROUGH FARMS INC
731 Pacific Ave, Oxnard (93030-7322)
P.O. Box 1267 (93032-1267)
PHONE....................805 483-9113
Ann Stein, *President*
Wayne G Jansen, *President*
Jeff Stein, *Sales Mgr*
Christina Gonzalez, *Sales Staff*
Clay Barbosa, *Manager*

EMP: 150
SALES (est): 21.6MM **Privately Held**
SIC: 0161 Vegetables & melons

(P-77)
SEASHOLTZ JOHN
1355 M St, Firebaugh (93622-2338)
PHONE....................559 659-3805
EMP: 196
SALES (corp-wide): 32.9MM **Privately Held**
SIC: 0161 Vegetables & melons
PA: Seasholtz, John
    4965 N Crystal Ave Ste A
    Fresno CA 93705
    559 229-0453

(P-78)
SILVA FARMS LLC (PA)
111 Alpine Dr, Gonzales (93926)
PHONE....................831 675-2327
Ed Silva, *Owner*
▼ **EMP:** 280
SQ FT: 30,000
SALES (est): 13.1MM **Privately Held**
WEB: www.edsilva.com
SIC: 0161 Broccoli farm; cabbage farm; lettuce farm

(P-79)
SUN AND SANDS ENTERPRISES LLC (PA)
Also Called: Prime Time International
86705 Avenue 54 Ste A, Coachella (92236-3814)
PHONE....................760 399-4278
Carl Sam Maggio,
Kathy Jones, *Administration*
Carl Maggio, *Data Proc Staff*
Stacy Macmillan, *Asst Controller*
Patricia McManus, *Controller*
▲ **EMP:** 100
SQ FT: 7,500
SALES: 123.9MM **Privately Held**
WEB: www.primetimeproduce.com
SIC: 0161 Lettuce farm; snap bean farm (bush & pole); cantaloupe farm; watermelon farm

(P-80)
TANIMURA ANTLE FRESH FOODS INC (PA)
1 Harris Rd, Salinas (93908-8608)
P.O. Box 4070 (93912-4070)
PHONE....................831 455-2950
Rick Antle, *President*
Ken Silveira, *COO*
Vic Feuerstein, *CFO*
Gary Tanimura, *Exec VP*
Mike Antle, *Vice Pres*
▲ **EMP:** 100
SQ FT: 135,000
SALES (est): 750.7MM **Privately Held**
WEB: www.taproduce.com
SIC: 0161 0182 0723 2099 Lettuce farm; celery farm; cauliflower farm; food crops grown under cover; vegetable packing services; food preparations

(P-81)
TEIXEIRA FARMS INC
2600 Bonita Lateral Rd, Santa Maria (93458-9798)
PHONE....................805 928-3801
Allan Teixeira, *President*
Chris Wong, *CFO*
Glenn Teixeira, *Treasurer*
Marvin Teixeira, *Vice Pres*
Pam Lind, *Office Mgr*
EMP: 188
SALES (est): 14.2MM **Privately Held**
WEB: www.teixeirafarms.com
SIC: 0161 Broccoli farm; cabbage farm; cauliflower farm; celery farm

(P-82)
TELESIS ONION CO (PA)
3265 W Figarden Dr, Fresno (93711-3912)
P.O. Box 9050 (93790-9050)
PHONE....................559 884-2441
Martin Britz, *Partner*
EMP: 121
SALES (est): 6.8MM **Privately Held**
SIC: 0161 0723 5148 Onion farm; vegetable packing services; fruits, fresh

(P-83)
TERRA FIRMA FARM CORP
Also Called: Terra Firma Farms
4713 Baker Rd, Winters (95694-9613)
P.O. Box 836 (95694-0836)
PHONE....................530 795-2473
Paul Underhill, *CEO*
Paul Holmes, *Treasurer*
Hector Melendes, *Admin Sec*
EMP: 50
SQ FT: 800
SALES: 1.4MM **Privately Held**
WEB: www.terrafirmafarm.com
SIC: 0161 0174 0173 0175 Rooted vegetable farms; citrus fruits; tree nuts; deciduous tree fruits

(P-84)
VAQUERO FARMS INC (PA)
24591 Silver Cloud Ct # 100, Monterey (93940-6551)
PHONE....................209 476-0002
Louis Souza, *President*
Ann Costa, *Corp Secy*
Tony F Costa, *Vice Pres*
EMP: 65
SALES (est): 7.1MM **Privately Held**
SIC: 0161 0131 Tomato farm; cotton

(P-85)
WM BOLTHOUSE FARMS INC (HQ)
7200 E Brundage Ln, Bakersfield (93307-3016)
PHONE....................661 366-7209
Jeffrey Dunn, *CEO*
Mike Fleming, *Vice Pres*
Ajay Komireddy, *Programmer Anys*
Cristina Navarro, *Personnel Assit*
◆ **EMP:** 871 **EST:** 1970
SQ FT: 700,000
SALES (est): 1.1B **Privately Held**
SIC: 0161 2037 2033 2099 Carrot farm; onion farm; fruit juices; vegetable juices; packaged in cans, jars, etc.; sauces: gravy, dressing & dip mixes
PA: Generis Holdings, Lp
    7200 E Brundage Ln
    Bakersfield CA 93307
    661 366-7209

0171 Berry Crops

(P-86)
APTOS BERRY FARMS INC
730 S A St, Oxnard (93030-7138)
PHONE....................831 726-3256
Garland Reiter, *CEO*
Joseph M Reiter Jr, *President*
EMP: 70
SQ FT: 5,000
SALES (est): 4MM **Privately Held**
SIC: 0171 Strawberry farm; raspberry farm

(P-87)
B & E FARMS INC
Also Called: Ito Farms
9112 Mcfadden Ave, Westminster (92683-6533)
PHONE....................714 893-8166
Bill Ito, *President*
Ed Ito, *Vice Pres*
EMP: 50
SQ FT: 2,000
SALES (est): 3.4MM **Privately Held**
SIC: 0171 Strawberry farm

(P-88)
CARDENAS BROS FARMING COMPANY
1141 Tama Ln, Santa Maria (93455-1127)
PHONE....................805 928-1559
Alberto Cardenas, *President*
Delfina Cardenas, *Vice Pres*
EMP: 100
SALES (est): 5.7MM **Privately Held**
SIC: 0171 Strawberry farm

(P-89)
CBS FARMS LLC
80 Sakata Ln, Watsonville (95076-5132)
P.O. Box 1825 (95077-1825)
PHONE....................831 724-0700
Ed Kelly, *Mng Member*

Carl Hamona,
Brad Peterson,
Bob Rigor,
EMP: 50
SALES: 1MM **Privately Held**
SIC: 0171 Strawberry farm

(P-90)
CJJ FARMING INC
125 W Mill St, Santa Maria (93458-4325)
PHONE............................805 739-1723
Juan Cisneros, *President*
Jesus Cisneros, *Admin Sec*
EMP: 50
SALES (est): 2.8MM **Privately Held**
SIC: 0171 0161 Strawberry farm; squash farm; broccoli farm; lettuce farm; romaine farm

(P-91)
CONROY FARMS INC
520 Maulhardt Ave, Oxnard (93030-8914)
P.O. Box 1467, Camarillo (93011-1467)
PHONE............................805 981-0537
Michael P Conroy, *President*
Willaine Conroy, *Chairman*
Alice Menchaca, *Manager*
EMP: 325
SQ FT: 700
SALES: 3MM **Privately Held**
SIC: 0171 Strawberry farm

(P-92)
DARENSBERRIES LLC
Also Called: D B Specialty Farms
714 S Blosser Rd, Santa Maria (93458-4914)
P.O. Box 549 (93456-0549)
PHONE............................805 937-8000
Daren Gee,
EMP: 250
SQ FT: 1,500
SALES (est): 14.4MM **Privately Held**
SIC: 0171 Strawberry farm

(P-93)
ECLIPSE BERRY FARMS LLC
11812 San Vicente Blvd # 250, Los Angeles (90049-6632)
PHONE............................310 207-7879
Norman Gilfenbain, *Bd of Directors*
Robert Wiviott, *General Mgr*
Precy Estanislao, *Controller*
Ventura Strawberry,
Rudy Garza, *Mng Member*
▼ **EMP:** 100
SQ FT: 2,500
SALES (est): 42.8MM **Privately Held**
SIC: 0171 5148 Berry crops; fresh fruits & vegetables

(P-94)
ETCHANDY FARMS LLC
4324 E Vineyard Ave, Oxnard (93036-1056)
P.O. Box 5770 (93031-5770)
PHONE............................805 983-4700
Michael Etchandy,
EMP: 99 EST: 2014
SQ FT: 400
SALES (est): 1.6MM **Privately Held**
SIC: 0171 Strawberry farm

(P-95)
FRESHWAY FARMS LLC
2165 W Main St, Santa Maria (93458-9739)
P.O. Box 5369 (93456-5369)
PHONE............................805 349-7170
Paul M Allen, *Mng Member*
EMP: 150 EST: 2014
SALES (est): 22MM **Privately Held**
SIC: 0171 0161 Strawberry farm; broccoli farm

(P-96)
GAMA BERRY FARMS LLC
730 S A St, Oxnard (93030-7138)
PHONE............................805 483-1000
Garland Reider, *CEO*
EMP: 60
SALES (est): 1.1MM **Privately Held**
SIC: 0171 Strawberry farm

(P-97)
GUY GEORGE
Also Called: King George Cabbage
315 2nd St Ste A, Watsonville (95076-5112)
P.O. Box 40 (95077-0040)
PHONE............................831 728-2410
Guy George, *Partner*
EMP: 50
SALES (est): 794.8K **Privately Held**
WEB: www.guygeorge.com
SIC: 0171 0161 Strawberry farm; cabbage farm; lettuce farm

(P-98)
J&G BERRY FARMS LLC
720 Rosemary Rd, Santa Maria (93454-8007)
PHONE............................831 750-9408
Jose Luis Rocha, *Mng Member*
Guadalupe Rocha,
EMP: 220
SALES (est): 1.1MM **Privately Held**
SIC: 0171 7389 Strawberry farm;

(P-99)
JAL BERRY FARMS LLC
1767 San Juan Rd, Aromas (95004-9028)
PHONE............................831 763-7200
Jose Lopez,
Robert F Dunaven Jr,
Hernando Ramirez,
EMP: 99
SALES (est): 2.5MM **Privately Held**
SIC: 0171 Strawberry farm

(P-100)
LASSEN CANYON NURSERY INC
14735 Big Springs Rd, Weed (96094-9665)
PHONE............................530 938-4720
Kenneth Elwood, *President*
EMP: 100
SALES (corp-wide): 93.1MM **Privately Held**
WEB: www.lassencanyonnursery.com
SIC: 0171 Strawberry farm
PA: Lassen Canyon Nursery, Inc.
1300 Salmon Creek Rd
Redding CA 96003
530 223-1075

(P-101)
LASSEN CANYON NURSERY INC
11651 Palm Ln, Ripon (95366)
PHONE............................209 599-7777
Kenneth Elwood, *President*
EMP: 100
SALES (corp-wide): 93.1MM **Privately Held**
WEB: www.lassencanyonnursery.com
SIC: 0171 Strawberry farm
PA: Lassen Canyon Nursery, Inc.
1300 Salmon Creek Rd
Redding CA 96003
530 223-1075

(P-102)
MARIZ BERRY FARMS
1650 E Gonzales Rd, Oxnard (93036-3700)
PHONE............................805 981-9908
Victor Lopez, *Partner*
Donald Driscoll, *Partner*
Keith Ford, *Partner*
EMP: 105
SALES (est): 3.5MM **Privately Held**
SIC: 0171 Strawberry farm

(P-103)
MORGAN FARM LLC
201 Vista Dr, Watsonville (95076-1754)
P.O. Box 758 (95077-0758)
PHONE............................831 726-5120
Jason Morgan, *President*
EMP: 70
SALES: 3MM **Privately Held**
SIC: 0171 7389 Strawberry farm;

(P-104)
NORTH RIVER RANCH LLC
3601 W Pendleton Ave, Santa Ana (92704-3814)
PHONE............................714 556-6244

George Murai,
Mark Murai, *Partner*
Triple M Packing, *Partner*
EMP: 50
SQ FT: 25,000
SALES: 7MM **Privately Held**
SIC: 0171 Strawberry farm; raspberry farm

(P-105)
ORANGE COUNTY PRODUCE LLC
11405 Jeffrey Rd, Irvine (92602-0503)
PHONE............................949 451-0880
Matthew K Kawamura, *Mng Member*
Blanca Lozoya, *MIS Mgr*
Blanca Bermudez, *Human Resources*
Ana Lozoya, *Personnel*
John Kubo, *Marketing Staff*
EMP: 100
SQ FT: 1,000
SALES (est): 42.4MM **Privately Held**
SIC: 0171 Strawberry farm

(P-106)
RED BLOSSOM SALES INC
865 Black Rd, Santa Maria (93458-9701)
PHONE............................805 349-9404
Ruben Trevino, *Manager*
Delia Galvan, *Sales Staff*
Chaz Yamamoto, *Sales Staff*
Carole Patterson, *Director*
EMP: 500 **Privately Held**
SIC: 0171 Strawberry farm
PA: Red Blossom Sales, Inc.
400 W Ventura Blvd # 140
Camarillo CA 93010

(P-107)
RINCON PACIFIC LLC
1312 Del Norte Rd, Camarillo (93010-8502)
PHONE............................805 986-8806
Kenneth Hasegawa,
EMP: 100
SALES (est): 10.4MM **Privately Held**
SIC: 0171 Strawberry farm

(P-108)
RIO MESA FARMS LLC
75 Sakata Ln, Watsonville (95076-5132)
P.O. Box 1359 (95077-1359)
PHONE............................831 728-1965
Mary Gregg, *Administration*
EMP: 99
SALES (est): 3.6MM **Privately Held**
SIC: 0171 Strawberry farm

(P-109)
SANTA ROSA BERRY FARMS LLC
3500 Camino Ave Ste 250, Oxnard (93030-7999)
PHONE............................805 981-3060
Bryan D Fiscalini,
EMP: 300
SQ FT: 3,500
SALES: 10MM **Privately Held**
SIC: 0171 Berry crops

(P-110)
SIERRA CASCADE BLUEBERRIES
12753 Doe Mill Rd, Forest Ranch (95942)
PHONE............................530 894-8728
John Carlon, *Owner*
John Carlo, *Owner*
EMP: 50
SALES: 300K **Privately Held**
SIC: 0171 Blueberry farm

(P-111)
SOLIMAR FARMS INC
1312 Del Norte Rd, Camarillo (93010-8502)
PHONE............................805 986-8806
Glen Hasegawa, *President*
Ken Hasegawa, *Vice Pres*
Susan Josue, *Office Mgr*
EMP: 80
SQ FT: 2,000
SALES (est): 14.4MM **Privately Held**
SIC: 0171 Strawberry farm

(P-112)
SUPERIOR FRUIT LLC
4324 E Vineyard Ave, Oxnard (93036-1056)
PHONE............................805 485-2519
Robert Jones,
Richard Jones,
EMP: 200 EST: 2017
SQ FT: 6,000
SALES: 200MM **Privately Held**
SIC: 0171 Strawberry farm

(P-113)
T T MIYASAKA INC
209 Riverside Rd, Watsonville (95076-3656)
PHONE............................831 722-3871
Tim Miyasaka, *President*
EMP: 400
SQ FT: 500
SALES (est): 10.8MM **Privately Held**
SIC: 0171 Strawberry farm

(P-114)
UYEMATSU INC
1004 E Lake Ave, Watsonville (95076-3406)
PHONE............................831 724-2200
Richard Uyematsu, *President*
Alan Uyematsu, *Vice Pres*
EMP: 65
SQ FT: 1,650
SALES (est): 2.1MM **Privately Held**
SIC: 0171 Strawberry farm

0172 Grapes

(P-115)
7TH STANDARD RANCH COMPANY
Also Called: Sun Pacific Farming
33374 Lerdo Hwy, Bakersfield (93308-9782)
PHONE............................661 399-0416
Berne Evans, *Partner*
Robert Reniers, *Partner*
Emily Ybarra, *VP Human Res*
EMP: 500
SQ FT: 140,000
SALES (est): 13.6MM **Privately Held**
SIC: 0172 4222 Grapes; refrigerated warehousing & storage

(P-116)
ALEXANDER DELU
15175 N Devries Rd, Lodi (95242-9217)
PHONE............................209 334-6660
EMP: 80
SALES (est): 2.8MM **Privately Held**
SIC: 0172 0722

(P-117)
ANTHONY VINEYARDS INC (PA)
5512 Valpredo Ave, Bakersfield (93307-9178)
P.O. Box 9578 (93389-9578)
PHONE............................661 858-6211
Domenick T Bianco, *President*
Paul A Loeffel, *CFO*
Domenick Bianco, *Treasurer*
Robert O Bianco, *Senior VP*
Justin McGowan, *Administration*
◆ **EMP:** 50
SQ FT: 125,000
SALES: 37.8MM **Privately Held**
WEB: www.anthonyvineyards.com
SIC: 0172 0174 Grapes; grapefruit grove; tangerine grove

(P-118)
BAZAN MARIO AG SERVICES & VINE
Also Called: Bazan Mrio Vinyrd Mgmt AG Svcs
1984 Yountville Cross Rd, Yountville (94599-1291)
P.O. Box 864, NAPA (94559-0864)
PHONE............................707 945-0718
Mario Bazan, *Owner*
Lori Valdivia, *Controller*
▲ **EMP:** 62 **EST:** 1997
SALES: 1.3MM **Privately Held**
SIC: 0172 Grapes

P
R
O
D
U
C
T
S

&

S
V
C
S

(P-119)
BEDROSIAN FARMS INC
8333 S Sunnyside Ave, Fowler
(93625-9659)
P.O. Box 219 (93625-0219)
PHONE..............................559 834-5981
Ernest Bedrosian, *President*
Kenneth Bedrosian, *Vice Pres*
Krikor Bedrosian, *Vice Pres*
EMP: 50
SALES (est): 3.2MM **Privately Held**
SIC: 0172 Grapes

(P-120)
BROCCHINI FARMS INC
27011 S Austin Rd, Ripon (95366-9627)
PHONE..............................209 599-4229
Robert Brocchini, *President*
Steve Brocchini, *Principal*
EMP: 50 EST: 1948
SALES (est): 4.3MM **Privately Held**
WEB: www.brocchinifarms.com
SIC: 0172 0173 0139 Grapes; almond
grove; alfalfa farm

(P-121)
CEDERLIND FARMS LP
2514 Kenney Ave, Winton (95388-9745)
PHONE..............................209 606-8586
Jeff Cederlind, *Partner*
EMP: 99
SALES (est): 759.4K **Privately Held**
SIC: 0172 Grapes

(P-122)
CIRCLE K RANCH
8640 E Manning Ave, Selma (93662-9763)
PHONE..............................559 834-1571
Melvin Kazarian, *General Ptnr*
Ronald Kazarian, *Partner*
EMP: 60 EST: 1971
SQ FT: 25,000
SALES (est): 3.8MM **Privately Held**
WEB: www.circlekranch.com
SIC: 0172 Grapes

(P-123)
CLARBEC INC
Also Called: Madrone Vineyard Management
19368 Orange Ave, Sonoma (95476-6249)
PHONE..............................707 996-4012
Rebecca Jenkins, *CFO*
Clarence A Jenkins Jr, *President*
EMP: 50
SQ FT: 1,600
SALES (est): 3.6MM **Privately Held**
SIC: 0172 Grapes

(P-124)
CLENDENEN VINEYARD MGT LLC
9235 W Dry Creek Rd, Healdsburg
(95448-9134)
P.O. Box 69 (95448-0069)
PHONE..............................707 473-0881
John Clendenen,
Catherine Clendenen,
EMP: 60 EST: 1993
SALES (est): 3.6MM **Privately Held**
SIC: 0172 Grapes

(P-125)
DELMART FARMS INC
30988 Riverside Cntrl Vly, Shafter (93263)
PHONE..............................661 746-2148
EMP: 100
SQ FT: 1,000
SALES (est): 2.5MM **Privately Held**
SIC: 0172 0131 0134 0724

(P-126)
DIRT FARMER & CO INC
9725 Los Guilicos Ave, Kenwood (95452)
P.O. Box 638 (95452-0638)
PHONE..............................707 833-2054
Keith Kunde, *President*
EMP: 53
SALES (est): 500K **Privately Held**
SIC: 0172 0761 Grapes; farm labor con-
tractors

(P-127)
DOMAINE CARNEROS LTD
1240 Duhig Rd, NAPA (94559-9713)
P.O. Box 5420 (94581-0420)
PHONE..............................707 257-0101
Eileen Crane, *Principal*
Sue Friedell, *Accountant*
Kristen Guiducci, *Controller*
Fernanda Castro, *Hum Res Coord*
Nicole Hamill, *Buyer*
▲ EMP: 80
SQ FT: 50,000
SALES (est): 7.5MM **Privately Held**
WEB: www.domainecarneros.com
SIC: 0172 2084 Grapes; wines

(P-128)
DRAKE LARSON RANCHS
Also Called: Larson, Drake Sales
89780 Ave 60, Thermal (92274)
P.O. Box 355 (92274-0355)
PHONE..............................760 399-5494
Drake Larson, *Partner*
Pamela Larson, *Partner*
EMP: 200
SQ FT: 3,000
SALES (est): 3.9MM **Privately Held**
SIC: 0172 0161 4222 Grapes; vegetables
& melons; refrigerated warehousing &
storage

(P-129)
E & J GALLO WINERY
Also Called: J Vineyards & Winery
11447 Old Redwood Hwy, Healdsburg
(95448-9523)
PHONE..............................707 431-5400
Joseph Gallo, *CEO*
Nicole Mitchell, *Admin Asst*
Eva Toy, *Technician*
Bill Richards, *Maint Spvr*
Jennifer Lukens, *Manager*
EMP: 52
SALES (corp-wide): 2.3B **Privately Held**
SIC: 0172 2084 Grapes; wines
PA: E. & J. Gallo Winery
600 Yosemite Blvd
Modesto CA 95354
209 341-3111

(P-130)
ENTERPRISE VINEYARDS
16600 Norrbom Rd, Sonoma (95476-4780)
P.O. Box 233, Vineburg (95487-0233)
PHONE..............................707 996-6513
Philip Coturri, *President*
EMP: 50
SALES (est): 5MM **Privately Held**
SIC: 0172 Grapes

(P-131)
GIUMARRA VINEYARDS CORPORATION
Giumarra Winery
11220 Edison Hwy, Bakersfield
(93307-8431)
P.O. Box 1969 (93303-1969)
PHONE..............................661 395-7071
Barry Douglas, *Manager*
David Aquino, *Human Res Dir*
EMP: 55
SALES (corp-wide): 162.4MM **Privately
Held**
SIC: 0172 Grapes
PA: Giumarra Vineyards Corporation
11220 Edison Hwy
Edison CA 93220
661 395-7000

(P-132)
GIUMARRA VINEYARDS CORPORATION (PA)
11220 Edison Hwy, Edison (93220)
P.O. Box 1969, Bakersfield (93303-1969)
PHONE..............................661 395-7000
Wayne Childress, *CEO*
Jeffrey Giumarra, *CFO*
Johnathan Giumarra, *Treasurer*
Mimi Corsaro-Dorsey, *Admin Sec*
Randy Giumarra, *VP Sales*
▲ EMP: 500 EST: 1946
SQ FT: 10,000

SALES: 162.4MM **Privately Held**
SIC: 0172 2084 2086 Grapes; wines; fruit
drinks (less than 100% juice): packaged
in cans, etc.; tea, iced: packaged in cans,
bottles, etc.

(P-133)
H & R GUNLUND RANCHES INC
3510 W Saginaw Ave, Caruthers
(93609-9568)
PHONE..............................559 864-8186
EMP: 220
SALES: 5.4MM **Privately Held**
SIC: 0172

(P-134)
J & L VINEYARDS
16492 Summit Crest Ln, Clovis
(93619-9345)
PHONE..............................559 268-1627
Donald Laub, *Partner*
Raymond Jacobson, *Partner*
EMP: 100
SALES (est): 2.8MM **Privately Held**
SIC: 0172 Grapes

(P-135)
JACK NEAL & SON INC
360 Lafata St, Saint Helena (94574-1410)
PHONE..............................707 963-7303
Mark J Neal, *President*
Tina Galambos, *Vice Pres*
EMP: 200
SQ FT: 20,000
SALES (est): 16.4MM **Privately Held**
SIC: 0172 Grapes

(P-136)
JAKOV P DULCICH & SONS
31956 Peterson Rd, Mc Farland
(93250-9606)
PHONE..............................661 792-6360
Jakov Dulchin, *Owner*
Jon Thomas, *CFO*
Delia Armstrong, *Executive*
Mayra Contreas, *Executive*
Mary Bisogno, *Accounting Mgr*
▲ EMP: 250
SALES: 12.7MM **Privately Held**
SIC: 0172 Grapes

(P-137)
JANE MCCLURG
4584 E Floral Ave, Selma (93662-9624)
PHONE..............................559 834-3080
Jane McClurg, *Owner*
EMP: 75
SALES (est): 1.2MM **Privately Held**
SIC: 0172 Grapes

(P-138)
KANDARIAN AGRI ENTERPRISES
Also Called: Agrichem
116 W Adams Ave, Fowler (93625-9614)
P.O. Box 278 (93625-0278)
PHONE..............................559 834-1501
Eugene Kandarian, *President*
Yvonne Kandarian, *Vice Pres*
EMP: 180
SQ FT: 6,500
SALES (est): 11.2MM **Privately Held**
SIC: 0172 4213 5191 Grapes; contract
haulers; chemicals, agricultural; fertilizer
& fertilizer materials; pesticides

(P-139)
KARAM BATH
1673 W Kamm Ave, Caruthers
(93609-9797)
PHONE..............................559 864-3868
Karam Bath, *Owner*
EMP: 50 EST: 1983
SALES (est): 1MM **Privately Held**
SIC: 0172 Grapes

(P-140)
KAUTZ VINEYARDS INC (PA)
Also Called: Kautz Ironstone Vineyards
1894 6 Mile Rd, Murphys (95247-9543)
PHONE..............................209 728-1251
John K Kautz, *CEO*
Stephen Kautz, *President*
Kurt Kautz, *Treasurer*
Gail Kautz, *Vice Pres*
Carolyn McVarish, *Executive Asst*

◆ EMP: 100
SQ FT: 75,000
SALES (est): 13.2MM **Privately Held**
WEB: www.ironstonevineyards.com
SIC: 0172 5812 Grapes; eating places

(P-141)
KLEIN FOODS INC
Also Called: Rodney Strong Vineyards
11455 Old Redwood Hwy, Healdsburg
(95448-9523)
P.O. Box 6010 (95448-6010)
PHONE..............................707 431-1533
Thomas B Klein, *President*
◆ EMP: 100
SQ FT: 20,000
SALES (est): 21.5MM **Privately Held**
WEB: www.rodneystrong.com
SIC: 0172 2084 5182 Grapes; wines;
wine & distilled beverages

(P-142)
KVL HOLDINGS INC (PA)
Also Called: Saint Nicolas Vineyard
37700 Foothill Rd, Soledad (93960-9620)
P.O. Box C (93960-0167)
PHONE..............................831 678-2132
Nicholaus Hahn, *CEO*
EMP: 50
SQ FT: 30,000
SALES (est): 19.7MM **Privately Held**
SIC: 0172 2084 6719 Grapes; wines; in-
vestment holding companies, except
banks

(P-143)
LAMANUZZI & PANTALEO LLC (PA)
11767 Road 27 1/2, Madera (93637-9108)
PHONE..............................559 432-3170
Frank P Pantaleo, *Owner*
Karol Ryals, *Accountant*
Tina Baer,
Patricia Benneyan,
Elaine Kalajian,
▲ EMP: 64
SQ FT: 1,000
SALES: 30.8MM **Privately Held**
SIC: 0172 4222 Grapes; warehousing,
cold storage or refrigerated

(P-144)
LANGETWINS INC
1298 E Jahant Rd, Acampo (95220)
PHONE..............................209 339-4055
Randy Lange, *President*
Brad Lange, *CFO*
Charlene Lange, *Vice Pres*
Susan Lange, *Admin Sec*
EMP: 75
SALES (est): 7.3MM **Privately Held**
WEB: www.langetwins.com
SIC: 0172 Grapes

(P-145)
LANZA VINEYARDS INC
Also Called: Wooden Valley Farms
4756 Suisun Valley Rd, Fairfield
(94534-3114)
PHONE..............................707 864-0730
Richard Lanza, *President*
Adrienne Lanza, *Treasurer*
Kenneth Lee Lanza, *Vice Pres*
Lawrence Dean Lanza, *Vice Pres*
Mario Richard Lanza Jr, *Vice Pres*
EMP: 50
SQ FT: 1,300
SALES (est): 4.7MM **Privately Held**
WEB: www.woodenvalley.com
SIC: 0172 2084 Grapes; wines

(P-146)
M CARATAN INC
Also Called: Caliente Farms
33787 Cecil Ave, Delano (93215-9597)
PHONE..............................661 725-2566
Martin Caratin, *CEO*
Keith Andrew, *COO*
John Carter, *Facilities Mgr*
▼ EMP: 150
SQ FT: 6,000
SALES (est): 16.7MM **Privately Held**
WEB: www.mcaratan.com
SIC: 0172 0174 0723 Grapes; orange
grove; almond hulling & shelling services

▲ = Import ▼=Export
◆ =Import/Export

(P-147)
MCCUTCHEON ENTERPRISES INC
604 W Nebraska Ave, Fresno
(93706-9280)
P.O. Box 188, Caruthers (93609-0188)
PHONE..............................559 864-3200
Mike D Mc Cutcheon, *President*
EMP: 100 **EST:** 1940
SQ FT: 4,200
SALES: 550K **Privately Held**
SIC: 0172 0173 Grapes; pistachio grove

(P-148)
MIRABELLA FARMS INC
5551 S Orange Ave, Fresno (93725-9505)
PHONE..............................559 237-4495
Paquerette Markarian, *President*
Philip Markarian, *Treasurer*
Joseph Markarian, *Vice Pres*
EMP: 75
SALES (est): 2.2MM **Privately Held**
WEB: www.mirabellafarms.com
SIC: 0172 Grapes

(P-149)
NESTOR ENTERPRISES LLC
13852 E Peltier Rd, Acampo (95220-9342)
PHONE..............................209 727-5711
Fransico Ilayala,
EMP: 50
SALES (est): 2.8MM **Privately Held**
WEB: www.nestorenterprises.com
SIC: 0172 Grapes

(P-150)
ONEILL BEVERAGES CO LLC
Also Called: O'Neill Vintners & Distillers
8418 S Lac Jac Ave, Parlier (93648-9708)
PHONE..............................559 638-3544
EMP: 200
SALES (est): 212.2K
SALES (corp-wide): 102.5MM **Privately Held**
SIC: 0172 2084 Grapes; wines; brandy
PA: O'neill Beverages Co. Llc
101 Larkspur Landing Cir
Larkspur CA 94939
844 825-6600

(P-151)
ONEILL BEVERAGES CO LLC (PA)
Also Called: O'Neill Vintners & Distillers
101 Larkspur Landing Cir, Larkspur
(94939-1746)
PHONE..............................844 825-6600
Jeffrey B O'Neill, *CEO*
Mark Federighi, *Senior VP*
Ryan Davis, *Vice Pres*
Marty Spate, *Vice Pres*
Donald Heer, *General Mgr*
◆ **EMP:** 63
SQ FT: 5,000
SALES (est): 102.5MM **Privately Held**
SIC: 0172 2084 Grapes; wines

(P-152)
PANDOL & SONS
401 Road 192, Delano (93215-9598)
PHONE..............................661 725-3755
Cheri Diebel, *CEO*
Jack Breech, *Partner*
Jack V Pandol, *Partner*
Lucy Pandol, *Partner*
Steve Pandol III, *Partner*
EMP: 50 **EST:** 1930
SQ FT: 10,000
SALES: 13.9MM **Privately Held**
SIC: 0172 0723 Grapes; fruit (fresh) packing services

(P-153)
R H PHILLIPS INC (HQ)
Also Called: R H Phillips Vineyard
26836 County Road 12a, Esparto
(95627-2139)
PHONE..............................530 757-5557
John Giguiere, *Ch of Bd*
EMP: 245
SQ FT: 4,500
SALES (est): 11.9MM
SALES (corp-wide): 8.1B **Publicly Held**
SIC: 0172 2084 5182 Grapes; wines;
wine & distilled beverages

PA: Constellation Brands, Inc.
207 High Point Dr # 100
Victor NY 14564
585 678-7100

(P-154)
RICHARD BAGDASARIAN INC
65500 Lincoln St, Mecca (92254-6500)
P.O. Box 698 (92254-0698)
PHONE..............................760 396-2168
Nicholas L Bozick, *CEO*
Michael Bozick, *President*
Darrell Billings, *CFO*
Bobbie Bozick, *Exec VP*
Stephanie Bozick, *Technology*
▲ **EMP:** 60
SQ FT: 40,000
SALES (est): 14MM **Privately Held**
WEB: www.bagdasarianinc.com
SIC: 0172 0174 Grapes; citrus fruits

(P-155)
RICHARDS GROVE SARALEES VINYRD
1998 Jones Rd, Windsor (95492-7758)
PHONE..............................707 837-9200
Saralee McClelland Kunde, *President*
EMP: 65
SQ FT: 10,333
SALES (est): 1.2MM **Privately Held**
WEB: www.saraleesvineyards.com
SIC: 0172 Grapes

(P-156)
RIOS FARMING COMPANY LLC
3851 Chiles Pope Vly Rd, Saint Helena
(94574-9588)
PHONE..............................707 965-2587
Manuel Rios, *Executive*
EMP: 140
SQ FT: 1,500
SALES (est): 6.7MM **Privately Held**
SIC: 0172 0762 Grapes; vineyard management & maintenance services

(P-157)
ROBERT ALVES FARMS INC
Also Called: Alves, Robert L
10642 E Dinuba Ave, Selma (93662-9783)
PHONE..............................559 896-3309
EMP: 70
SALES (est): 2.1MM **Privately Held**
SIC: 0172

(P-158)
RON D & SHELLEY N HORN
30912 Moonflower Ln, Murrieta
(92563-7937)
PHONE..............................559 834-2118
Ronald Horn, *Owner*
EMP: 50
SALES (est): 964.8K **Privately Held**
SIC: 0172 Grapes

(P-159)
SAN BERNABE VINEYARDS
53001 Oasis Rd, King City (93930-9667)
PHONE..............................831 385-4897
Claude Hoover, *President*
Dorothy Indelicato, *Treasurer*
Frank Indelicato, *Admin Sec*
EMP: 65
SQ FT: 15,000
SALES (est): 4.5MM
SALES (corp-wide): 56.2MM **Privately Held**
WEB: www.winequest.com
SIC: 0172 2084 Grapes; wines, brandy & brandy spirits
PA: Delicato Vineyards
12001 S Highway 99
Manteca CA 95336
209 824-3600

(P-160)
SANDRINI FARMS
6111 De La Guerra Ter, Bakersfield
(93306-9757)
PHONE..............................661 792-3192
Mae Sandrini, *Owner*
EMP: 60
SALES (est): 1.1MM **Privately Held**
SIC: 0172 Grapes

(P-161)
SCHEID VINEYARDS INC (PA)
305 Hilltown Rd, Salinas (93908-8902)
PHONE..............................831 455-9990
Scott D Scheid, *President*
Alfred G Scheid, *Ch of Bd*
Kurt J Gollnick, *COO*
Michael S Thomsen, *CFO*
Heidi M Scheid, *Treasurer*
EMP: 88
SQ FT: 6,700
SALES (est): 58.9MM **Publicly Held**
SIC: 0172 2084 Grapes; wines

(P-162)
SCHEID VINEYARDS INC
373 Healdsburg Ave, Healdsburg
(95448-4137)
PHONE..............................707 433-1858
EMP: 107
SALES (corp-wide): 56.4MM **Publicly Held**
SIC: 0172
PA: Scheid Vineyards Inc.
305 Hilltown Rd
Salinas CA 93908
310 301-1555

(P-163)
SCHRAMSBERG VINEYARDS COMPANY
1400 Schramsberg Rd, Calistoga
(94515-9624)
PHONE..............................707 942-4558
Hugh Davies, *President*
Jenn North, *Admin Asst*
Felipe Martinez, *Production*
Laurent Sarazin, *VP Sales*
Jessica Koga, *Manager*
◆ **EMP:** 50
SQ FT: 20,000
SALES (est): 5.3MM **Privately Held**
WEB: www.schramsberg.com
SIC: 0172 2084 Grapes; wines

(P-164)
STAGECOACH VINEYARDS
1345 Hestia Way, NAPA (94558-2105)
PHONE..............................707 255-5459
Jan Krupp, *Partner*
Gabrielle Shaffer, *Manager*
▲ **EMP:** 100
SALES (est): 7.4MM **Privately Held**
WEB: www.stagecoachvineyard.com
SIC: 0172 Grapes

(P-165)
SUN-MAID GROWERS CALIFORNIA
Also Called: Valley Fig Growers
4683 Chabot Dr Ste 100, Pleasanton
(94588-3863)
P.O. Box 9106 (94566-9105)
PHONE..............................800 752-9277
John Slinkard, *Vice Pres*
Frank Ferraris, *Vice Pres*
David Joseph, *Vice Pres*
Doug Nesbit, *Vice Pres*
Joe Ponder, *Vice Pres*
EMP: 50
SALES (corp-wide): 362.1MM **Privately Held**
SIC: 0172 5149 5148 Grapes; groceries & related products; fresh fruits & vegetables
PA: Sun-Maid Growers Of California
13525 S Bethel Ave
Kingsburg CA 93631
559 897-6235

(P-166)
TREASURY WINE ESTATES AMERICAS
Also Called: Meridian Vineyards
7000 E Highway 46, Paso Robles
(93446-7390)
P.O. Box 3289 (93447-3289)
PHONE..............................805 237-6000
Jim Schaefer, *Manager*
EMP: 120 **Privately Held**
WEB: www.stclement.com
SIC: 0172 2084 Grapes; wines, brandy & brandy spirits

HQ: Treasury Wine Estates Americas Company
555 Gateway Dr
Napa CA 94558
707 259-4500

(P-167)
V SANGIACOMO & SONS
Also Called: Sangiacomo Vineyards
21543 Broadway, Sonoma (95476-8205)
PHONE..............................707 938-5503
Victor F Sangiacomo, *Partner*
Angelo C Sangiacomo, *Partner*
Lorraine J Sangiacomo, *Partner*
EMP: 180
SQ FT: 1,200
SALES (est): 14.3MM **Privately Held**
WEB: www.sangiacomo-vineyards.com
SIC: 0172 Grapes

(P-168)
VINCENT B ZANINOVICH SONS INC
Also Called: V B Z
20715 Ave 8, Richgrove (93261)
P.O. Box 1000 (93261-1000)
PHONE..............................661 720-9031
John V Zaninovich, *CEO*
Vincent Zaninovich, *President*
Andrew Zaninovich, *Vice Pres*
◆ **EMP:** 1000
SQ FT: 15,450
SALES (est): 24.1MM **Privately Held**
SIC: 0172 Grapes

(P-169)
VINCENT V ZANINOVICH & SONS
2480 E Washington St, Earlimart
(93219-9694)
PHONE..............................661 849-2613
INA Zaninovich, *Partner*
Estate of Vincent V Zaninovich, *Partner*
EMP: 99
SALES (est): 3.2MM **Privately Held**
SIC: 0172 0139 0131 Grapes; alfalfa farm; cotton

0173 Tree Nuts

(P-170)
AGRESERVES INC
Also Called: Deseret Farms of California
6100 Wilson Landing Rd, Chico
(95973-8902)
PHONE..............................530 343-5365
Travis Reid, *Branch Mgr*
Sherry Andersen, *Controller*
EMP: 75
SALES (corp-wide): 247.6MM **Privately Held**
WEB: www.dlandl.com
SIC: 0173 0175 Almond grove; walnut grove; prune orchard
HQ: Agreserves, Inc.
79 S Main St Ste 1100
Salt Lake City UT 84111

(P-171)
CHARANJIT SINGH BATTH
Also Called: Batth Farms
5434 W Kamm Ave, Caruthers
(93609-9400)
PHONE..............................559 864-9421
Charanjit Singh Batth, *Owner*
EMP: 90
SQ FT: 1,200
SALES (est): 7.3MM **Privately Held**
SIC: 0173 0175 0172 2034 Almond grove; prune orchard; grapes; raisins

(P-172)
DE BENEDETTO FARMS INC
Also Called: D'Best Produce
1547 N Marks Ave, Fresno (93722-5723)
P.O. Box 9760 (93794-9760)
PHONE..............................559 276-2400
Maurice De Benedetto, *President*
Mark De Benedetto, *Shareholder*
Mathew De Benedetto, *Shareholder*
Maury De Benedetto, *Shareholder*
EMP: 80
SQ FT: 2,000

PRODUCTS & SVCS

SALES (est): 2.4MM **Privately Held**
SIC: 0173 Pecan grove; almond grove

(P-173)
ED THOMING & SONS INC
33600 S Koster Rd, Tracy (95304-8996)
PHONE..............................209 835-2792
John Thoming, *President*
James L Thoming, *Vice Pres*
EMP: 100
SQ FT: 800
SALES (est): 4.8MM **Privately Held**
SIC: 0173 0175 Almond grove; deciduous
tree fruits

(P-174)
FARMERS INTERNATIONAL INC
1260 Muir Ave, Chico (95973-8644)
PHONE..............................530 566-1405
Don Wada, *CEO*
Mohnish Seth, *Principal*
◆ **EMP:** 50
SALES (est): 10.2MM **Privately Held**
WEB: www.farmersinternational.com
SIC: 0173 Almond grove

(P-175)
FRAZIER NUT FARMS INC
10830 Yosemite Blvd, Waterford
(95386-9637)
PHONE..............................209 522-1406
Jim Frazier Jr, *President*
Heidi Frazier-Slacks, *Corp Secy*
Steve Slacks, *Vice Pres*
▼ **EMP:** 50
SALES (est): 4.7MM **Privately Held**
SIC: 0173 Walnut grove

(P-176)
INTERNATIONAL ALMOND EXCHANGE
144 W Lake Ave, Watsonville (95076-4573)
PHONE..............................831 728-4534
Jagjit Tut, *CEO*
Rajveer Tut, *Vice Pres*
▼ **EMP:** 50
SQ FT: 653,400
SALES: 1MM **Privately Held**
SIC: 0173 Almond grove

(P-177)
KEENAN FARMS INC
31510 Plymouth Ave, Kettleman City
(93239-9721)
P.O. Box 99, Avenal (93204-0099)
PHONE..............................559 945-1400
Robert M Keenan, *CEO*
Charles J Keenan III, *Vice Pres*
Bob Keenan, *Info Tech Mgr*
Peter Theodore, *Plant Mgr*
Teresa L Keenan, *Marketing Mgr*
◆ **EMP:** 100
SALES (est): 23.2MM **Privately Held**
SIC: 0173 2068 Pistachio grove; nuts:
dried, dehydrated, salted or roasted

(P-178)
MARIANI NUT COMPANY INC
12 Baker St, Winters (95694-1704)
P.O. Box 808 (95694-0808)
PHONE..............................530 795-2225
Jef McDowell, *Manager*
EMP: 70
SALES (corp-wide): 32.8MM **Privately
Held**
WEB: www.marianinut.com
SIC: 0173 Walnut grove
PA: Mariani Nut Company, Inc.
709 Dutton St
Winters CA 95694
530 795-3311

(P-179)
RICHARD SWANSON INC
17659 Swanson Rd, Delhi (95315-9636)
P.O. Box 244 (95315-0244)
PHONE..............................209 632-3883
Timothy Swanson, *President*
Erline Swanson, *Treasurer*
Richard Swanson, *Vice Pres*
EMP: 60
SALES (est): 1.5MM **Privately Held**
SIC: 0173 0175 0252 Almond grove;
peach orchard; chicken eggs

(P-180)
TEJON RANCH CO (PA)
4436 Lebec Rd, Lebec (93243-9705)
P.O. Box 1000 (93243-1000)
PHONE..............................661 248-3000
Gregory S Bielli, *President*
Richard Daley, *Records Dir*
Norman J Metcalfe, *Ch of Bd*
Allen E Lyda, *CFO*
Robert Velasquez, *CFO*
▼ **EMP:** 75 **EST:** 1936
SALES: 45.6MM **Publicly Held**
WEB: www.tejonfilm.com
SIC: 0173 0172 6531 Almond grove; pis-
tachio grove; walnut grove; grapes; real
estate brokers & agents

(P-181)
WONDERFUL ORCHARDS LLC (HQ)
Also Called: Paramount Farming
6801 E Lerdo Hwy, Shafter (93263-9610)
PHONE..............................661 399-4456
Craig Cooper,
Julie Nord, *Business Anlyst*
Joseph Mac Ilvaine,
William Phillimore,
▲ **EMP:** 150
SQ FT: 10,000
SALES (est): 171.6MM
SALES (corp-wide): 1.5B **Privately Held**
SIC: 0173 0179 Almond grove; olive grove
PA: The Wonderful Company Llc
11444 W Olympic Blvd # 210
Los Angeles CA 90064
310 966-5700

(P-182)
WONDERFUL ORCHARDS LLC
Also Called: Wonderfulpistachiosandalmonds
13646 Highway 33, Lost Hills (93249-9719)
P.O. Box 400 (93249-0400)
PHONE..............................661 797-6400
Dennis Elam, *Branch Mgr*
Juan Torres, *Sales Mgr*
Tom Hazelof, *Sales Staff*
EMP: 150
SALES (corp-wide): 1.5B **Privately Held**
SIC: 0173 0191 Almond grove; general
farms, primarily crop
HQ: Wonderful Orchards Llc
6801 E Lerdo Hwy
Shafter CA 93263
661 399-4456

0174 Citrus Fruits

(P-183)
ACEMI NURSERY INC
3626 N Howard Ave, Kerman (93630)
PHONE..............................559 842-7766
Alvaro Garcia, *President*
Carmen Garcia, *Vice Pres*
EMP: 80
SALES (est): 5MM **Privately Held**
SIC: 0174 Citrus fruits

(P-184)
ACMPC CALIFORNIA 3 LLC
Also Called: Suntreat Packing & Shipping Co
38773 Rd 48, Lindsay (93247)
PHONE..............................559 591-6140
Darren Silkins, *CEO*
Tracy Saiki, *Exec VP*
Rick Johnston, *VP Sales*
EMP: 200 **EST:** 2015
SALES (est): 3MM **Privately Held**
SIC: 0174 Citrus fruits

(P-185)
AIRDROME ORCHARDS INC (PA)
111 E Alma Ave, San Jose (95112-2792)
PHONE..............................408 297-6461
Charles Fumia, *CEO*
John Fumia Jr, *CFO*
Anthony Buldo, *Vice Pres*
Paul Buldo, *Vice Pres*
Tony Buldo, *Vice Pres*
▼ **EMP:** 50
SQ FT: 30,000
SALES (est): 8.5MM **Privately Held**
SIC: 0174 0175 Orange grove; pear or-
chard

(P-186)
BADGER FARMING COMPANY INC
150 W Pine St, Exeter (93221-1613)
PHONE..............................559 592-5520
Oleah Wilson, *President*
James Wilson, *President*
Charles Duby, *Marketing Mgr*
EMP: 60
SALES (est): 2.8MM **Privately Held**
SIC: 0174 Citrus fruits

(P-187)
BERESFORD CORP
582 Market St Ste 912, San Francisco
(94104-5310)
PHONE..............................415 981-7386
Christopher D Lange, *President*
EMP: 145
SALES (est): 8.3MM **Privately Held**
SIC: 0174 Citrus fruits

(P-188)
CALIFORNIA CITRUS COOPERATIVE
859 Center St, Riverside (92507-1408)
PHONE..............................951 683-4045
Larry Topham, *Manager*
EMP: 65
SQ FT: 2,000
SALES (est): 5.5MM **Privately Held**
SIC: 0174 Grapefruit grove; orange grove

(P-189)
HAMILTON FAMILY RANCH
2562 Doville Ranch Rd, Fallbrook
(92028-9138)
PHONE..............................760 728-1358
EMP: 70
SALES (est): 1MM **Privately Held**
SIC: 0174

(P-190)
HRONIS INC A CALIFORNIA CORP (PA)
10443 Hronis Rd, Delano (93215-9556)
PHONE..............................661 725-2503
Kosta Hronis, *President*
Pete Hronis, *Vice Pres*
Chris Fierros, *Manager*
▼ **EMP:** 54
SQ FT: 150,000
SALES (est): 50.3MM **Privately Held**
WEB: www.hronis.net
SIC: 0174 0172 Citrus fruits; grapes

(P-191)
JOHNSTON FARMS FMLY LTD PARTNR
13031 E Packinghouse Rd, Edison (93220)
PHONE..............................661 366-3201
Tari Johnston, *Principal*
Terry Henderson, *Principal*
Dennis B Johnston, *Principal*
Gerald Johnston, *Principal*
Kevin Johnston, *Principal*
◆ **EMP:** 65 **EST:** 1953
SQ FT: 100,000
SALES (est): 8MM **Privately Held**
WEB: www.johnstonfarms.com
SIC: 0174 0134 0161 Orange grove; Irish
potatoes; pepper farm, sweet & hot (veg-
etables)

(P-192)
MARLAND CO LP
444 S Flower St 1200, Los Angeles
(90071-2977)
PHONE..............................213 614-6171
Chirstopher Martin, *Partner*
Oliver Santos, *Admin Sec*
EMP: 50
SQ FT: 200
SALES (est): 888.7K **Privately Held**
SIC: 0174 Orange grove

(P-193)
PADILLA FARM LABOR INC
20486 Road 196, Lindsay (93247-9426)
PHONE..............................559 562-1166
David Padilla, *President*
Rosie Padilla, *Corp Secy*
EMP: 200
SALES (est): 5.8MM **Privately Held**
SIC: 0174 Orange grove

(P-194)
PELTZER GROVES
34286 Road 188, Woodlake (93286-9615)
PHONE..............................559 804-0661
Richard L Peltzer, *President*
Geneva Guill, *Vice Pres*
Barbara Peltzer, *Admin Sec*
EMP: 50 **EST:** 1958
SALES (est): 164.3K **Privately Held**
SIC: 0174 Citrus fruits

(P-195)
SATICOY LEMON ASSOCIATION
Also Called: Saticoy Fruit Exchange
7560 Bristol Rd, Ventura (93003-7027)
P.O. Box 46, Santa Paula (93061-0046)
PHONE..............................805 654-6500
John Elliott, *Branch Mgr*
EMP: 100
SALES (corp-wide): 171MM **Privately
Held**
SIC: 0174 Lemon grove
PA: Saticoy Lemon Association
103 N Peck Rd
Santa Paula CA 93060
805 654-6500

(P-196)
WONDERFUL COMPANY LLC
Also Called: Paramount Citrus
1901 S Lexington St, Delano (93215-9207)
PHONE..............................661 720-2400
Freddie Hernandez, *Manager*
Jennifer Allen, *Office Mgr*
Thomas Taylor, *Technology*
Barbara Mock, *Director*
EMP: 273
SALES (corp-wide): 1.5B **Privately Held**
SIC: 0174 3911 Citrus fruits; jewelry, pre-
cious metal
PA: The Wonderful Company Llc
11444 W Olympic Blvd # 210
Los Angeles CA 90064
310 966-5700

(P-197)
YOUNG DOWLIN L
Also Called: Young's Nursery
101 Clay St, San Francisco (94111-2033)
PHONE..............................760 397-4104
Dowlin L Young, *Owner*
Daisy Young, *Co-Owner*
EMP: 50
SQ FT: 1,000
SALES: 2.5MM **Privately Held**
SIC: 0174 Citrus fruits

0175 Deciduous Tree Fruits

(P-198)
ABBEY OF NEW CLAIRVAUX (PA)
Also Called: Abbey Ranch
26240 7th St, Vina (96092)
P.O. Box 80 (96092-0080)
PHONE..............................530 839-2161
Paul Mark Swan, *President*
Anthony Bellesorte, *Corp Secy*
Harold Meyer, *General Mgr*
EMP: 61
SALES (est): 3.4MM **Privately Held**
SIC: 0175 8661 Plum orchard; religious
organizations

(P-199)
ANTHONY BOTELHO
382 Olympia Ave, San Juan Bautista
(95045-9501)
PHONE..............................831 623-4228
Anthony Botelho, *Owner*
EMP: 60 **EST:** 1998
SALES (est): 1.3MM **Privately Held**
WEB: www.botelhoforsupervisor.com
SIC: 0175 Apple orchard

(P-200)
ASHLEY LANE CHERRY ORCHARDS LP
500 N Jack Tone Rd, Stockton
(95215-9725)
P.O. Box 659, Linden (95236-0659)
PHONE..............................209 546-0426
Henry J Foppiano, *Partner*
Diane Lechich, *Administration*

▲ = Import ▼=Export
◆ =Import/Export

EMP: 50
SALES (est): 1.6MM **Privately Held**
SIC: 0175 Cherry orchard

(P-201)
BT HOLDINGS INC
Also Called: Quercus Ranch
4150 Soda Bay Rd, Kelseyville (95451)
P.O. Box 548 (95451-0548)
PHONE..................707 279-4317
EMP: 50 EST: 1979
SQ FT: 120,000
SALES (est): 500K **Privately Held**
SIC: 0175 0172

(P-202)
ENNS PACKING COMPANY INC
Also Called: Enns Farms
1911 Bergren Ct, Kingsburg (93631-2705)
PHONE..................559 897-7700
Melvin Enns, *President*
Kenneth Enns, *Treasurer*
Eugene Enns, *Principal*
Mike Enns, *Admin Sec*
EMP: 50
SQ FT: 4,200
SALES: 36.9K **Privately Held**
SIC: 0175 4222 0723 Deciduous tree fruits; storage, frozen or refrigerated goods; fruit (fresh) packing services

(P-203)
HAMLOW RANCHES INC
4018 Swanson Rd, Denair (95316-9733)
P.O. Box 898 (95316-0898)
PHONE..................209 632-2873
Karen Hamlow, *CEO*
EMP: 50 EST: 1951
SALES (est): 2MM **Privately Held**
SIC: 0175 0173 Peach orchard; almond grove

(P-204)
HILDRETH FARM INCORPORATED
1520 Rddick Cunningham Rd, Ukiah (95482-9638)
PHONE..................707 462-0648
Michael L Hildreth, *President*
Susan Hildreth, *Vice Pres*
EMP: 56
SALES (est): 2.3MM **Privately Held**
SIC: 0175 0172 Pear orchard; grapes

(P-205)
J & P SOLARI
6302 Foppiano Ln, Stockton (95212-9407)
PHONE..................209 931-1765
Joe S Solari, *Partner*
Joseph Solari I I I, *Partner*
Phillip Solari, *Partner*
Raymond Solari, *Partner*
EMP: 100
SALES (est): 1.4MM **Privately Held**
SIC: 0175 0173 0811 Cherry orchard; walnut grove; almond grove; timber tracts

(P-206)
JEFF W BOLDT FARMS
Also Called: Jeff Boldt Farms
12725 S Smith Ave, Kingsburg (93631-9719)
PHONE..................559 318-6690
Jeff Boldt, *President*
Brenda Boldt, *CEO*
Tamara Boldt, *Director*
Taylor Boldt, *Director*
EMP: 74
SALES (est): 1.2MM **Privately Held**
SIC: 0175 Deciduous tree fruits

(P-207)
KAY DIX INC
14400 Andrus Island Rd, Isleton (95641-9804)
P.O. Box 248, Walnut Grove (95690-0248)
PHONE..................916 776-1701
Daniel M Wilson, *President*
Darrell Wilson, *Treasurer*
Daniel Wilson, *General Mgr*
Angela Gonzalez, *Office Mgr*
Chiles Wilson, *Admin Sec*
EMP: 50
SQ FT: 1,000

SALES (est): 1MM **Privately Held**
SIC: 0175 0115 0111 Pear orchard; corn; wheat

(P-208)
KINGSBURG APPLE PARTNERS LP
10363 Davis Ave, Kingsburg (93631-9539)
P.O. Box 456 (93631-0456)
PHONE..................559 897-5132
Colleen Jackson, *Managing Prtnr*
Susan Jackson Diepersloot, *Ltd Ptnr*
Brent Jackson, *Managing Prtnr*
▼ EMP: 100
SQ FT: 140,000
SALES (est): 5.8MM **Privately Held**
WEB: www.kingsburgorchards.com
SIC: 0175 Apple orchard; pear orchard

(P-209)
KOZUKI FARMING INC
16518 E Adams Ave, Parlier (93648-9718)
PHONE..................559 646-2652
EMP: 60
SALES: 2.2MM **Privately Held**
SIC: 0175 0172

(P-210)
MALLOY ORCHARDS INC
925 Koch Ln, Live Oak (95953-9602)
PHONE..................530 695-1861
William A Filter Jr, *President*
EMP: 200
SALES (est): 4.1MM **Privately Held**
SIC: 0175 0173 0761 Peach orchard; prune orchard; walnut grove; farm labor contractors

(P-211)
MICHELI FARMS INC
6005 Highway 99, Live Oak (95953-9749)
PHONE..................530 695-9022
John Micheli, *President*
Colleen Cecil, *Exec Dir*
Justin Micheli, *Admin Sec*
EMP: 50
SQ FT: 108,000
SALES (est): 2.6MM **Privately Held**
WEB: www.lomocold.com
SIC: 0175 0173 Peach orchard; prune orchard; walnut grove

(P-212)
MIKE JENSEN FARMS
13138 S Bethel Ave, Kingsburg (93631-9216)
PHONE..................559 897-4192
Mike Jensen, *Owner*
EMP: 200
SQ FT: 14,000
SALES (est): 6.3MM **Privately Held**
SIC: 0175 2033 2099 Apricot orchard; nectarine orchard; peach orchard; plum orchard; fruits: packaged in cans, jars, etc.; food preparations

(P-213)
PETERSON FAMILY INC
38694 Road 16, Kingsburg (93631-9106)
PHONE..................559 897-5064
Vernon E Peterson, *Owner*
EMP: 100
SALES (est): 5.4MM **Privately Held**
WEB: www.peterson.org
SIC: 0175 0174 Deciduous tree fruits; citrus fruits

(P-214)
PHILLIPS FARMS
33771 Road 156, Visalia (93292-9153)
PHONE..................559 798-1871
Douglas Phillips, *Owner*
Bobby Chavez, *Finance Mgr*
◆ EMP: 50
SALES (est): 3.3MM **Privately Held**
SIC: 0175 0723 Deciduous tree fruits; fruit (fresh) packing services

(P-215)
SACRAMENTO PACKING INC
833 Tudor Rd, Yuba City (95991-9532)
P.O. Box 3540 (95992-3540)
PHONE..................530 671-4488
Jaswant S Bains, *President*
Satwant Bains, *General Mgr*
◆ EMP: 300

SQ FT: 80,000
SALES (est): 24.9MM **Privately Held**
WEB: www.sacramentopacking.com
SIC: 0175 Deciduous tree fruits

(P-216)
SMITH RANCH
1671 Campbell Rd, Live Oak (95953-9707)
PHONE..................530 695-2521
Dale Smith, *Partner*
Dean Smith, *Partner*
Gail Hebert, *Principal*
EMP: 50 EST: 1909
SALES (est): 3.2MM **Privately Held**
SIC: 0175 0173 Peach orchard; prune orchard; walnut grove

(P-217)
VIRGINIA SARABIAN
Also Called: Sarabian Farms
2816 S Leonard Ave, Sanger (93657-9754)
PHONE..................559 493-2900
Michael Sarabian, *Owner*
Sarkis Sarabian, *Owner*
Virginia Sarabian, *Owner*
David Sarabian, *COO*
Maribel Rios, *Administration*
EMP: 50
SQ FT: 1,200
SALES: 15MM **Privately Held**
SIC: 0175 0172 4222 2033 Nectarine orchard; peach orchard; plum orchard; grapes; warehousing, cold storage or refrigerated; fruits: packaged in cans, jars, etc.

0179 Fruits & Tree Nuts, NEC

(P-218)
AGRILAND HOLDING INC
23400 Road 24, Chowchilla (93610-9558)
PHONE..................559 665-2100
James Maxwell, *President*
Sandra Bain, *Admin Sec*
EMP: 85
SQ FT: 7,500
SALES (est): 2.9MM **Privately Held**
SIC: 0179 0173 Fig orchard; tree nuts

(P-219)
CHIQUITA FRESH NORTH AMER LLC
1440 E 3rd St, Oxnard (93030-6106)
PHONE..................954 924-5642
Junior Cutrale, *Mng Member*
EMP: 300
SQ FT: 1,500
SALES: 50MM **Privately Held**
SIC: 0179 Banana grove

(P-220)
DOLE FOOD COMPANY INC (PA)
1 Dole Dr, Westlake Village (91362-7300)
PHONE..................818 874-4000
David H Murdock, *Ch of Bd*
Johan Linden, *President*
Johan Malmqvist, *CFO*
Roberta Wieman, *Exec VP*
Yoon J Hugh, *Senior VP*
◆ EMP: 188
SALES (est): 1.1B **Privately Held**
WEB: www.dole.com
SIC: 0179 0174 0175 0161 Pineapple farm; banana grove; citrus fruits; deciduous tree fruits; lettuce farm; celery farm; cauliflower farm; broccoli farm; fruits; vegetables; fruit juices: fresh; fruit juices: packaged in cans, jars, etc.

(P-221)
DOLE HOLDING COMPANY LLC
1 Dole Dr, Westlake Village (91362-7300)
PHONE..................818 879-6600
David H Murdock, *Ch of Bd*
EMP: 49207
SALES: 57.6MM **Privately Held**
SIC: 0179 0174 0175 0161 Pineapple farm; banana grove; citrus fruits; deciduous tree fruits; lettuce farm; celery farm; cauliflower farm; broccoli farm; fruits; vegetables; fruit juices: fresh; fruit juices: packaged in cans, jars, etc.

PA: Dhm Holding Company, Inc
1 Dole Dr
Westlake Village CA 91362

(P-222)
HENRY AVOCADO CORPORATION (PA)
2208 Harmony Grove Rd, Escondido (92029-2054)
P.O. Box 300867 (92030-0867)
PHONE..................760 745-6632
Philip Henry, *President*
Richard Opel, *Shareholder*
Jerry Miller, *CFO*
Vic Varvel, *Vice Pres*
Lori Deaver, *Office Mgr*
◆ EMP: 70
SQ FT: 35,000
SALES: 269.7MM **Privately Held**
SIC: 0179 4213 Avocado orchard; trucking, except local

(P-223)
IRVINE VALENCIA GROWERS
11501 Jeffrey Rd, Irvine (92602-0503)
PHONE..................949 936-8000
Peter Changala, *President*
Brian Thompson, *Treasurer*
Karen Verghese, *Executive*
EMP: 75
SQ FT: 10,000
SALES (est): 2.9MM **Privately Held**
SIC: 0179 0723 Avocado orchard; fruit (fresh) packing services

(P-224)
MUNGER BROS LLC
Also Called: Munger Farm
786 Road 188, Delano (93215-9508)
PHONE..................661 721-0390
Baldev K Munger,
Kewel K Munger,
▲ EMP: 600
SQ FT: 50,000
SALES: 10MM **Privately Held**
SIC: 0179 Avocado orchard

(P-225)
SUNDANCE NATURAL FOODS COMPANY
2231 Willowbrook Dr, Oceanside (92056-2506)
P.O. Box 5358 (92052-5358)
PHONE..................760 945-9898
K Jacob Hoffnagle, *CEO*
Mary Hahlbohm, *Treasurer*
EMP: 50
SQ FT: 40,000
SALES (est): 6.6MM **Privately Held**
WEB: www.sundancenaturalfoodscompany.com
SIC: 0179 0723 Avocado orchard; fruit (fresh) packing services

(P-226)
WILLIAM C ARTERBERRY
40147 Calle Roxanne, Fallbrook (92028-9701)
PHONE..................760 728-9096
William Arterberry, *Owner*
EMP: 62
SALES (est): 999.7K **Privately Held**
SIC: 0179 Avocado orchard

0181 Ornamental Floriculture & Nursery Prdts

(P-227)
3-WAY FARMS (PA)
428 Browns Valley Rd, Watsonville (95076-0330)
PHONE..................831 722-0748
Delbert Herschbach, *President*
Lorraine Stern, *Treasurer*
Rosemarie Herschbach, *Admin Sec*
EMP: 50
SALES (est): 3.8MM **Privately Held**
SIC: 0181 3999 Ornamental nursery products; flowers, artificial & preserved

(P-228)
AZALEA & ROSE CO
1420 N Campus Ave, Upland (91786-2317)
PHONE..................................909 949-2442
Mike Tolle, *President*
EMP: 50
SALES (est): 676.7K **Privately Held**
SIC: 0181 Roses, growing of

(P-229)
BARCELO ENTERPRISES INC
4400 Macarthur Blvd # 980, Newport Beach
(92660-2054)
PHONE..................................760 728-3444
Antonio C Barcelo Sr, *President*
Antonio Barcelo Jr, *Vice Pres*
Rosa H Barcelo, *Vice Pres*
▲ EMP: 100 EST: 1997
SALES (est): 7.9MM **Privately Held**
WEB: www.alivingfossil.com
SIC: 0181 Nursery stock, growing of

(P-230)
BAY CITY FLOWER CO
1450 Cabrillo Hwy S, Half Moon Bay
(94019-2243)
PHONE..................................650 712-8147
Harrison Higaki, *Principal*
EMP: 224
SALES (corp-wide): 79.2MM **Privately
Held**
SIC: 0181 Plants, potted: growing of
PA: Bay City Flower Co.
   2265 Cabrillo Hwy S
   Half Moon Bay CA 94019
   650 726-5535

(P-231)
BLX GROUP INC
71534 Sahara Rd, Rancho Mirage
(92270-4340)
PHONE..................................760 776-6622
EMP: 95
SALES (est): 2MM **Privately Held**
SIC: 0181

(P-232)
BROKAW NURSERY LLC
5501 Elizabeth Rd, Ventura (93004-1002)
P.O. Box 4818 (93007-0818)
PHONE..................................805 647-2262
Ellen Brokaw, *President*
Kay Mendel, *CFO*
Robert C Brokaw, *Vice Pres*
Marge Apodaca, *Principal*
Consuelo Fernandez, *Research*
EMP: 52
SQ FT: 5,000
SALES (est): 6.5MM **Privately Held**
WEB: www.brokawnursery.com
SIC: 0181 0179 Nursery stock, growing of;
avocado orchard

(P-233)
CALIFORNIA PAJAROSA
133 Hughes Rd, Watsonville (95076-9458)
PHONE..................................831 722-6374
John Furman, *President*
Albert Furman, *Shareholder*
Betty Mitchell, *Shareholder*
Alan Mitchell, *Vice Pres*
EMP: 52
SQ FT: 17,000
SALES (est): 1.7MM **Privately Held**
SIC: 0181 Roses, growing of; flowers
grown in field nurseries

(P-234)
**CALIFORNIA PAJAROSA
FLORAL**
133 Hughes Rd, Watsonville (95076-9458)
P.O. Box 684 (95077-0684)
PHONE..................................831 722-6374
John Furman, *President*
Alan Mitchell, *Vice Pres*
▲ EMP: 50
SQ FT: 10,000
SALES (est): 3.1MM **Privately Held**
WEB: www.pajarosa.com
SIC: 0181 Ornamental nursery products

(P-235)
COAST NURSERIES INC (PA)
5870 E Los Angeles Ave, Somis
(93066-9752)
PHONE..................................805 386-4253
Samuel F Fujimoto, *CEO*
Steven Fujimoto, *President*
Iyako Fujimoto, *Corp Secy*
EMP: 140
SALES (est): 5.9MM **Privately Held**
WEB: www.coastnurseries.com
SIC: 0181 5083 0191 Nursery stock,
growing of; landscaping equipment; gen-
eral farms, primarily crop

(P-236)
**DAVE WILSON NURSERY INC
(PA)**
Also Called: Dwn
19701 Lake Rd, Hickman (95323-9706)
P.O. Box 429 (95323-0429)
PHONE..................................209 874-1821
Robert B Woolley, *CEO*
Dennis Tarry, *President*
Dave Wilson, *Principal*
EMP: 50
SQ FT: 8,000
SALES (est): 17.7MM **Privately Held**
SIC: 0181 Nursery stock, growing of

(P-237)
DLT GROWERS INC
13131 S Bon View Ave, Ontario
(91761-8226)
PHONE..................................909 947-8198
Jaime Delatorre, *President*
Ricardo Delatorre, *Vice Pres*
EMP: 50
SQ FT: 400
SALES (est): 4MM **Privately Held**
SIC: 0181 5193 Nursery stock, growing of;
flowers & nursery stock

(P-238)
DUARTE NURSERY INC
23456 E Flood Rd, Linden (95236-9429)
PHONE..................................209 887-3409
Jim Duarte, *Manager*
Stephen Krauss, *Human Res Dir*
EMP: 350
SQ FT: 1,558
SALES (corp-wide): 57.6MM **Privately
Held**
WEB: www.duartenursery.com
SIC: 0181 Nursery stock, growing of
PA: Duarte Nursery, Inc.
   1555 Baldwin Rd
   Hughson CA 95326
   209 531-0351

(P-239)
DUARTE NURSERY INC (PA)
Also Called: Duarte Properties
1555 Baldwin Rd, Hughson (95326-9522)
PHONE..................................209 531-0351
John Duarte, *President*
Anita Duarte, *Treasurer*
Jeff Duarte, *Vice Pres*
Shirley Brooks, *Administration*
Michael Vietti, *Research*
EMP: 400
SALES (est): 57.6MM **Privately Held**
WEB: www.duartenursery.com
SIC: 0181 Nursery stock, growing of

(P-240)
**FRANTZ WHOLESALE NURSERY
LLC**
12161 Delaware Rd, Hickman
(95323-9602)
PHONE..................................209 874-1459
Michael Frantz,
Veronica Gonzalez, *Human Res Mgr*
Saul Vega, *Prdtn Mgr*
Mitzi Frantz,
Damion Boyd, *Manager*
▲ EMP: 150
SALES (est): 8.7MM **Privately Held**
WEB: www.frantznursery.com
SIC: 0181 Nursery stock, growing of

(P-241)
**GALLUP & STRIBLING ORCHIDS
LLC**
Also Called: Gallup and Stribling Holdings
3450 Via Real, Carpinteria (93013-3047)
PHONE..................................805 684-1998
Alexander L Stribling, *CEO*
Michael E Pfau, *Admin Sec*
Veronica Torres, *Sales Staff*
▲ EMP: 50
SQ FT: 1,400,000
SALES: 3MM **Privately Held**
SIC: 0181 Flowers grown in field nurseries

(P-242)
GLAD-A-WAY GARDENS INC
2669 E Clark Ave, Santa Maria
(93455-5815)
P.O. Box 2550 (93457-2550)
PHONE..................................805 938-0569
Brian Caird, *President*
Lance Runels, *Vice Pres*
Erin Caird, *Admin Sec*
▲ EMP: 172 EST: 1964
SQ FT: 15,000
SALES (est): 18.1MM **Privately Held**
WEB: www.gladaway.net
SIC: 0181 Flowers grown in field nurseries

(P-243)
GOLD COAST FARMS LLC
32701 Road 204, Woodlake (93286-9625)
PHONE..................................559 564-6316
Jim Means,
EMP: 50
SALES (est): 1.8MM **Privately Held**
SIC: 0181 Nursery stock, growing of

(P-244)
GOLDEN STATE HERBS (PA)
60125 Polk St, Thermal (92274-8944)
P.O. Box 756 (92274-0756)
PHONE..................................760 342-7117
Sam Vince, *President*
Jack Vince, *Corp Secy*
Curtis Vince, *Vice Pres*
Sylvia Garza, *Sales Mgr*
Grant Bouwer, *Sales Staff*
▲ EMP: 50
SQ FT: 50,000
SALES (est): 6.7MM **Privately Held**
WEB: www.goldenstateherbs.com
SIC: 0181 Ornamental nursery products

(P-245)
**GRAND VIEW GERANIUM
GRDNS INC**
18307 Central Ave, Carson (90746-4017)
PHONE..................................310 217-0490
Fax: 310 217-0536
EMP: 60
SQ FT: 2,500
SALES (est): 3.2MM **Privately Held**
WEB: www.gvgeranium.com
SIC: 0181

(P-246)
**GROVER LANDSCAPE
SERVICES INC**
6224 Stoddard Rd, Modesto (95356-9198)
PHONE..................................209 545-4401
Mark Grover, *President*
Lorraine Grover, *Treasurer*
Ruth Jupe, *Accounting Mgr*
Cathy Welch, *Purchasing*
EMP: 100 EST: 1970
SQ FT: 10,850
SALES: 16.5MM **Privately Held**
SIC: 0181 0782 0783 0781 Ornamental
nursery products; landscape contractors;
tree trimming services for public utility
lines; landscape planning services

(P-247)
HERITAGE LAND COMPANY INC
Also Called: Delta Growers
111 N Zuckerman Rd, Stockton (95206)
P.O. Box 487 (95201-0487)
PHONE..................................209 444-1700
Dennis Gardenmeyer, *CEO*
EMP: 50
SALES (est): 4.4MM **Privately Held**
SIC: 0181 Sod farms

(P-248)
HMCLAUSE INC (DH)
260 Cousteau Pl Ste 210, Davis
(95618-5490)
PHONE..................................800 320-4672
Remi Bastien, *CEO*
Matthew M Johnston, *President*
Marc Rottiers, *CFO*
Anne Azam, *Vice Pres*
S B Benon, *Vice Pres*
◆ EMP: 133 EST: 1856
SQ FT: 200,000
SALES (est): 133.2MM
SALES (corp-wide): 194.4MM **Privately
Held**
WEB: www.harrismoran.com
SIC: 0181 Seeds, vegetable: growing of
HQ: Groupe Limagrain Holding
   Clermont Limagne Rue Henri Moudor
   Saint-Beauzire 63360
   475 828-101

(P-249)
HMCLAUSE INC
42 Glenshire Ln, Chico (95973-1093)
PHONE..................................530 713-5838
EMP: 70
SALES (corp-wide): 194.4MM **Privately
Held**
SIC: 0181 Seeds, vegetable: growing of
HQ: Hm.Clause, Inc.
   260 Cousteau Pl Ste 210
   Davis CA 95618
   800 320-4672

(P-250)
J ROBERT ECHTER
Also Called: Robert J Echter Foxpoint Farms
1150 Quail Gardens Dr, Encinitas
(92024-2365)
PHONE..................................760 436-0188
Robert J Echter, *Owner*
Robert Echter, *Owner*
Eva Espinoza, *Human Res Mgr*
EMP: 50
SALES (est): 868.9K **Privately Held**
SIC: 0181 Ornamental nursery products

(P-251)
JIMENEZ NURSERY INC
Also Called: Jimenez Nursery and Land-
scapes
3800 Via Real, Carpinteria (93013-3051)
P.O. Box 2460, Santa Barbara (93120-
2460)
PHONE..................................805 684-7955
Manuel Jimenez, *CEO*
Alicia Jimenez, *Treasurer*
EMP: 100
SALES (est): 80.8K **Privately Held**
SIC: 0181 Nursery stock, growing of

(P-252)
JOHANNES FLOWERS INC
4990 Foothill Rd, Carpinteria (93013-3085)
PHONE..................................805 684-5686
Johannes A P Persoon, *President*
Madelenne Leanoard, *Vice Pres*
Jan Persoon, *Vice Pres*
Wilbert Q J Persoon, *Vice Pres*
▲ EMP: 60 EST: 1970
SALES (est): 5.3MM **Privately Held**
WEB: www.johannesflowers.com
SIC: 0181 5992 Flowers grown in field
nurseries; florists

(P-253)
KAWAHARA NURSERY INC
698 Burnett Ave, Morgan Hill (95037-9022)
P.O. Box 1358 (95038-1358)
PHONE..................................408 779-2400
David Kawahara, *President*
John Kawahara, *CFO*
Michael Willson, *CIO*
Jack Chestnut, *Info Tech Mgr*
Trevor Austin, *Technology*
▲ EMP: 240 EST: 1947
SALES (est): 15.8MM **Privately Held**
WEB: www.kawaharanursery.com
SIC: 0181 5193 Nursery stock, growing of;
flowers & florists' supplies

(P-254)
KENDALL FARMS LP
4230 White Lilac Rd, Fallbrook
(92028-8802)
PHONE.....................760 731-0681
Jason Kendall, *Managing Prtnr*
Tony Mungo, *Admin Asst*
Katalina Parga, *Purch Mgr*
Jonathan Kendall, *Opers-Prdtn-Mfg*
Katia McLaughlin, *Production*
EMP: 50
SALES (est): 4.2MM **Privately Held**
WEB: www.kendall-farms.com
SIC: 0181 Flowers grown in field nurseries

(P-255)
KITAYAMA BROTHERS INC
Also Called: Kitayama Flowers
481 San Andreas Rd, Watsonville
(95076-9524)
PHONE.....................831 722-8118
Winston Moore, *Branch Mgr*
EMP: 73
SALES (corp-wide): 5MM **Privately Held**
SIC: 0181 5261 5193 Flowers grown in field nurseries; roses, growing of; nurseries & garden centers; flowers & florists' supplies
PA: Kitayama Bros., Inc.
540 E Bridge St Ste A
Brighton CO 80601
303 659-8000

(P-256)
KOBATA GROWERS INC (PA)
17622 Van Ness Ave, Torrance
(90504-3530)
PHONE.....................310 323-0662
Jack Mayesh, *President*
Sol Mayesh, *Shareholder*
Harry Mayesh, *Corp Secy*
EMP: 53
SALES (est): 4.5MM **Privately Held**
WEB: www.kobatagrowers.com
SIC: 0181 Nursery stock, growing of

(P-257)
L E COOKE CO
26333 Road 140, Visalia (93292-9452)
PHONE.....................559 732-9146
David Henry Cox, *CEO*
Ron Ludekens, *President*
David Cox, *General Mgr*
Phillip Cox, *Admin Sec*
Rosie Frias, *Sales Mgr*
▲ **EMP:** 200
SQ FT: 6,000
SALES (est): 9.6MM **Privately Held**
WEB: www.lecooke.com
SIC: 0181 Nursery stock, growing of

(P-258)
L J T FLOWERS INC
2425 Bonita School Rd, Nipomo
(93444-9728)
PHONE.....................805 310-6036
Grace Cruz, *Principal*
EMP: 93
SALES (corp-wide): 32.6MM **Privately Held**
SIC: 0181 5191 Flowers grown in field nurseries; flower & field bulbs
PA: L J T Flowers Inc.
2425 Bonita School Rd
Nipomo CA 93444
877 929-2476

(P-259)
LA VERNE NURSERY INC
3653 Center St, Piru (93040-8051)
P.O. Box 410 (93040-0410)
PHONE.....................805 521-0111
Richard Wilson, *CEO*
EMP: 90
SQ FT: 16,000
SALES (est): 5.4MM **Privately Held**
SIC: 0181 Nursery stock, growing of; fruit stocks, growing of

(P-260)
MARATHON LAND INC (PA)
2599 E Hueneme Rd, Oxnard
(93033-8112)
P.O. Box 579, Port Hueneme (93044-0579)
PHONE.....................805 488-3585
Jurgen Gramckow, *President*

EMP: 125
SQ FT: 3,000
SALES (est): 7.4MM **Privately Held**
WEB: www.sod.com
SIC: 0181 Sod farms

(P-261)
MARTINEZ FARMS INC
2433 Cactus Rd, San Diego (92154-8008)
PHONE.....................619 661-6571
Richard Martinez, *President*
Jose Martinez, *Ch of Bd*
EMP: 400
SALES (est): 16MM **Privately Held**
WEB: www.certseedpotato.com
SIC: 0181 Nursery stock, growing of

(P-262)
MATSUI NURSERY INC (PA)
1645 Old Stage Rd, Salinas (93908-9737)
PHONE.....................831 422-6433
Toshikiyo Matsui, *President*
Jovanna Raya, *Admin Asst*
Brenda Muaoz, *Administration*
▲ **EMP:** 58 **EST:** 1967
SQ FT: 3,000,000
SALES (est): 22.8MM **Privately Held**
SIC: 0181 Nursery stock, growing of

(P-263)
MONROVIA NURSERY COMPANY (PA)
Also Called: Monrovia Growes
817 E Monrovia Pl, Azusa (91702-6297)
P.O. Box 1385 (91702-1385)
PHONE.....................626 334-9321
Miles R Rosedale, *CEO*
William B Usrey, *President*
Richard Van Landinghan, *President*
Dennis Conner, *Vice Pres*
Todd Noe, *Info Tech Mgr*
▲ **EMP:** 567
SQ FT: 50,000
SALES (est): 438.7MM **Privately Held**
WEB: www.monrovia.com
SIC: 0181 5193 5261 Nursery stock, growing of; flowers & florists' supplies; nurseries & garden centers

(P-264)
MULROSES USA INC
741 S San Pedro St, Los Angeles
(90014-2417)
PHONE.....................213 489-1761
Patricio Nasser, *Manager*
EMP: 100
SALES (est): 2MM **Privately Held**
SIC: 0181 Roses, growing of

(P-265)
NAUMES INC
3792 Feather River Blvd, Olivehurst
(95961-9688)
PHONE.....................530 743-2055
Bob Cosey, *General Mgr*
John Callis, *General Mgr*
EMP: 50
SQ FT: 66,646
SALES (corp-wide): 176.8MM **Privately Held**
WEB: www.naumes.com
SIC: 0181 0723 4731 Fruit stocks, growing of; fruit (farm-dried) packing services; agents, shipping
PA: Naumes, Inc.
2 W Barnett St
Medford OR 97501
541 772-6268

(P-266)
OCEAN BREEZE INTERNATIONAL
Also Called: Mobis Wholesale
3910 Via Real, Carpinteria (93013-1266)
PHONE.....................805 684-1747
Rene Van Wingerden, *President*
June Van Wingerden, *Vice Pres*
▲ **EMP:** 60
SQ FT: 900,000
SALES (est): 9.1MM **Privately Held**
WEB: www.oceanbreezeintl.com
SIC: 0181 Flowers: grown under cover (e.g. greenhouse production)

(P-267)
OCEAN VIEW FLOWERS LLC
1105 Union Sugar Ave, Lompoc
(93436-9737)
PHONE.....................800 736-5608
Robert M Witt,
Jana Wilcox, *Executive*
Yvette Hilario, *Sales Staff*
John Donati,
EMP: 175
SALES (est): 322.5K **Privately Held**
SIC: 0181 Florists' greens & flowers; florists' greens cultivated: growing of

(P-268)
OLIVE HILL GREENHOUSES
3508 Olive Hill Rd, Fallbrook (92028-8296)
P.O. Box 1510 (92088-1510)
PHONE.....................760 728-4596
George A Godfrey, *Owner*
Alice Hernandez, *Executive*
William McGregor, *Technology*
Denise Godfrey, *Sales Executive*
▲ **EMP:** 100
SQ FT: 2,000
SALES (est): 7MM **Privately Held**
WEB: www.olivehill.net
SIC: 0181 Nursery stock, growing of

(P-269)
PACIFIC EARTH RESOURCES (PA)
Also Called: Pacific Sd/Pcfic Arbor Nrsries
305 Hueneme Rd, Camarillo (93012-8522)
PHONE.....................805 986-8277
Richard Rogers, *Owner*
Elizabeth Rogers, *Partner*
EMP: 80 **EST:** 1958
SQ FT: 8,000
SALES (est): 21.9MM **Privately Held**
SIC: 0181 Sod farms; nursery stock, growing of

(P-270)
PLANT SOURCE INC
2029 Sycamore Dr, San Marcos
(92069-9753)
PHONE.....................760 743-7743
Steve Pyle, *CEO*
▲ **EMP:** 50 **EST:** 2003
SALES (est): 19.9MM **Privately Held**
SIC: 0181 Ornamental nursery products

(P-271)
PLUG CONNECTION INC
2627 Ramona Dr, Vista (92084-1634)
PHONE.....................760 631-0992
Tim Wada, *President*
Don Macintyre, *CFO*
Bradley Rhoads, *CFO*
Bruce Gibson, *General Mgr*
Memo Contreras, *Purchasing*
▲ **EMP:** 80
SQ FT: 350,000
SALES (est): 7.5MM **Privately Held**
WEB: www.plugconnection.com
SIC: 0181 Ornamental nursery products

(P-272)
PYRAMID FLOWERS INC
3813 Doris Ave, Oxnard (93030-4706)
PHONE.....................805 382-8070
Fred Van Wingerden, *President*
Edith Van Wingerden, *Vice Pres*
Marcos Van Wingerden, *Prdtn Mgr*
▲ **EMP:** 120
SQ FT: 900,000
SALES (est): 17.8MM **Privately Held**
WEB: www.pyramidflowers.com
SIC: 0181 Flowers grown in field nurseries

(P-273)
RICHARD WILSON WELLINGTON
Also Called: Colorama Wholesale Nursery
1025 N Todd Ave, Azusa (91702-1602)
P.O. Box 1328, Glendora (91740-1328)
PHONE.....................626 812-7881
Richard Wilson, *Owner*
Terry Wilson, *Financial Exec*
Jim Fitzpatrick, *Manager*
Phillip Sanchez, *Manager*
▲ **EMP:** 100
SQ FT: 70,000

SALES (est): 9.6MM **Privately Held**
SIC: 0181 5193 Nursery stock, growing of; nursery stock

(P-274)
RIVER RIDGE FARMS INC
3135 Los Angeles Ave, Oxnard
(93036-1010)
PHONE.....................805 647-6880
Rieuwert Jan Vis, *President*
▲ **EMP:** 95
SQ FT: 440
SALES: 13.8MM **Privately Held**
SIC: 0181 5193 Flowers grown in field nurseries; flowers: grown under cover (e.g. greenhouse production); plants, potted

(P-275)
ROCKET FARMS INC (PA)
2651 Cabrillo Hwy N, Half Moon Bay
(94019-1357)
P.O. Box 3756, Salinas (93912-3756)
PHONE.....................800 227-5229
Charles Kosmont, *CEO*
Gerald Cheng, *Vice Pres*
Mark Clark, *Vice Pres*
Jason Kamimoto, *Vice Pres*
Peter Lim, *Planning Mgr*
▲ **EMP:** 113
SQ FT: 1,500,000
SALES (est): 49.8MM **Privately Held**
SIC: 0181 Flowers: grown under cover (e.g. greenhouse production)

(P-276)
ROSE THOMPSON COMPANY
949 Cassou Rd, San Marcos (92069-9715)
PHONE.....................760 736-6020
David Thompson, *President*
Scott Thompson, *Corp Secy*
Karen Thompson, *Vice Pres*
EMP: 54
SQ FT: 1,704
SALES (est): 2.2MM **Privately Held**
WEB: www.thomprose.com
SIC: 0181 Nursery stock, growing of

(P-277)
SAN GABRIEL NURSERY AND FLOR (PA)
632 S San Gabriel Blvd, San Gabriel
(91776-2798)
PHONE.....................626 286-0787
Margie Yoshihashi, *President*
Mary Swanton, *Treasurer*
Saburo Ishihara, *Vice Pres*
Dianne Yoshimura, *Admin Sec*
EMP: 73
SQ FT: 5,000
SALES (est): 6.3MM **Privately Held**
WEB: www.sgnursery.com
SIC: 0181 Nursery stock, growing of

(P-278)
SG PERSONNEL LLC
420 Espinosa Rd, Salinas (93907-8894)
PHONE.....................831 444-0523
Michael F Vukelich, *Manager*
Patty Blackburn, *Receptionist*
EMP: 270
SALES (corp-wide): 529.6MM **Privately Held**
WEB: www.colorspot.com
SIC: 0181 Plants, potted: growing of
HQ: Csn Winddown, Inc.
27368 Via Industria # 201
Temecula CA 92590

(P-279)
SG PERSONNEL LLC
Also Called: Color Spot Lodi
5400 E Harney Ln, Lodi (95240-6903)
PHONE.....................209 369-3018
David Barrett, *President*
EMP: 60
SALES (corp-wide): 529.6MM **Privately Held**
WEB: www.colorspot.com
SIC: 0181 5193 Plants, potted: growing of; flowers & florists' supplies
HQ: Csn Winddown, Inc.
27368 Via Industria # 201
Temecula CA 92590

(P-280)
SIERRA GOLD NURSERIES INC
5320 Garden Hwy, Yuba City (95991-9499)
PHONE................530 674-1145
Jack Poukish, *CEO*
Brian Berg, *Vice Pres*
Ellen Berg, *Vice Pres*
Matthew Haddon, *Sales Staff*
▲ **EMP:** 86
SQ FT: 2,500
SALES (est): 10.6MM **Privately Held**
WEB: www.sierragoldtrees.com
SIC: 0181 Nursery stock, growing of

(P-281)
SIERRA-CASCADE NURSERY INC (PA)
472-715 Johnson Rd, Susanville (96130-8727)
PHONE................530 254-6867
Steve Fortin, *President*
Randy Jertberg, *COO*
Robert Akeson, *Vice Pres*
Beth Jertberg, *Vice Pres*
Robert Murie, *Vice Pres*
▼ **EMP:** 400
SQ FT: 2,600
SALES (est): 108.3MM **Privately Held**
SIC: 0181 Nursery stock, growing of

(P-282)
SMITH GARDENS INC
Also Called: Pacific Plug and Liner
750 Casserly Rd, Watsonville (95076-9723)
PHONE................831 768-6300
Liz Dunlop, *Manager*
Marlon Carrera, *General Mgr*
Jennifer Miner, *Sales Staff*
EMP: 50
SALES (corp-wide): 88.9MM **Privately Held**
SIC: 0181 Nursery stock, growing of
PA: Smith Gardens, Inc.
   4164 Meridian St Ste 400
   Bellingham WA 98226
   800 755-6256

(P-283)
SUN VALLEY GROUP INC (PA)
3160 Upper Bay Rd, Arcata (95521-9690)
PHONE................707 822-2885
Leendert De Vries, *President*
Casey Razma, *CFO*
Todd Walker, *CFO*
David Aronovici, *Executive*
Debbie Hartman, *Regional Mgr*
◆ **EMP:** 350
SQ FT: 8,700
SALES (est): 149.3MM **Privately Held**
WEB: www.thesunvalleygroup.com
SIC: 0181 Flowers: grown under cover
   (e.g. greenhouse production); flowers
   grown in field nurseries; bulbs, growing of

(P-284)
SUNRISE RANCH
3623 Etting Rd, Oxnard (93033-5813)
PHONE................805 488-0813
George Mimaki, *Partner*
Lori Kamei, *Partner*
Bryan Mimaki, *Partner*
Robert Robbins, *Info Tech Mgr*
Ana Knowlton, *Graphic Designe*
EMP: 90
SQ FT: 750
SALES (est): 5.2MM **Privately Held**
SIC: 0181 Flowers grown in field nurseries

(P-285)
SUPERIOR SOD I LP
17821 17th St Ste 165, Tustin (92780-2172)
P.O. Box 1911, Tehachapi (93581-5911)
PHONE................909 923-5068
Michael Considine, *Partner*
Richard H Considine, *Partner*
Trudy Considine, *Partner*
Peter Moore, *Partner*
EMP: 125
SQ FT: 1,400
SALES (est): 6.4MM **Privately Held**
WEB: www.superiorsod.com
SIC: 0181 0782 Sod farms; lawn & garden
   services

(P-286)
TOPSTAR FLORAL INC
4255 W Gonzales Rd, Oxnard (93036-7786)
PHONE................805 984-7972
Steve Van Wingerden, *President*
EMP: 50
SQ FT: 6,500
SALES (est): 5.6MM **Privately Held**
WEB: www.topstarfloral.com
SIC: 0181 Flowers grown in field nurseries

(P-287)
WEST COAST TURF (PA)
42540 Melanie Pl, Palm Desert (92211-5127)
P.O. Box 4563 (92261-4563)
PHONE................760 340-7300
John M Foster, *President*
Joe Foster, *Vice Pres*
EMP: 50
SQ FT: 2,000
SALES (est): 38MM **Privately Held**
WEB: www.westernsod.com
SIC: 0181 Sod farms

(P-288)
WEST FLOWER GROWERS
3623 Etting Rd, Oxnard (93033-5813)
PHONE................805 488-0814
Bryan H Mimaki, *President*
EMP: 70
SALES (est): 2.1MM **Privately Held**
SIC: 0181 Ornamental nursery products

0182 Food Crops Grown Under Cover

(P-289)
CHANNEL ISLNDS VEGETABLE FARMS (PA)
595 Victoria Ave, Oxnard (93030-4710)
PHONE................805 984-1910
Steve Nishimori, *President*
Karen Nishimori, *Vice Pres*
EMP: 60
SQ FT: 2,000
SALES (est): 6.4MM **Privately Held**
SIC: 0182 Vegetable crops grown under
   cover

(P-290)
COUNTRYSIDE MUSHROOMS INC
11300 Center Ave, Gilroy (95020-9257)
PHONE................408 683-2748
Donald W Hordness, *President*
Lewis Di Cecco, *Vice Pres*
EMP: 70
SALES (est): 7MM **Privately Held**
SIC: 0182 Mushrooms grown under cover

(P-291)
FITZ FRESH INC
211 Lee Rd, Watsonville (95076-9447)
P.O. Box 1450, Freedom (95019-1450)
PHONE................831 763-4440
Patrick J Fitz, *President*
▲ **EMP:** 50
SQ FT: 2,000
SALES: 5MM **Privately Held**
WEB: www.fitzfresh.com
SIC: 0182 Mushrooms grown under cover

(P-292)
GROWERS TRANSPLANTING INC (HQ)
360 Espinosa Rd, Salinas (93907-8895)
P.O. Box 3756 (93912-3756)
PHONE................831 449-3440
Charles I Kosmont, *CEO*
Leslie Surber, *CFO*
Kevin Doyle, *Vice Pres*
Bill Rover, *Vice Pres*
▲ **EMP:** 83 **EST:** 1981
SQ FT: 4,000,000
SALES (est): 37.4MM **Privately Held**
WEB: www.growerstrans.com
SIC: 0182 Vegetable crops grown under
   cover

(P-293)
MONTEREY MUSHROOMS INC (PA)
260 Westgate Dr, Watsonville (95076-2452)
PHONE................831 763-5300
Shah Kazemi, *President*
Robert V Jenkins, *CFO*
Michael O'Brien, *Vice Pres*
Kevin Morenzi, *Business Anlyst*
Robert Klinger, *Controller*
▲ **EMP:** 50
SALES (est): 706.7MM **Privately Held**
WEB: www.montereymushrooms.com
SIC: 0182 Mushrooms grown under cover

(P-294)
MONTEREY MUSHROOMS INC
Also Called: Monterey Mushrooms-Morgan Hill
642 Hale Ave, Morgan Hill (95037-9221)
P.O. Box 818 (95038-0818)
PHONE................408 779-4191
Clark Smith, *Branch Mgr*
EMP: 350
SQ FT: 5,000
SALES (corp-wide): 706.7MM **Privately Held**
WEB: www.montereymushrooms.com
SIC: 0182 2034 Mushrooms grown under
   cover; dehydrated fruits, vegetables,
   soups
PA: Monterey Mushrooms, Inc.
   260 Westgate Dr
   Watsonville CA 95076
   831 763-5300

(P-295)
MONTEREY MUSHROOMS INC
777 Maher Ct, Royal Oaks (95076-9014)
PHONE................831 728-8300
Wayne Batista, *Branch Mgr*
EMP: 501
SALES (corp-wide): 706.7MM **Privately Held**
WEB: www.montereymushrooms.com
SIC: 0182 Mushrooms grown under cover
PA: Monterey Mushrooms, Inc.
   260 Westgate Dr
   Watsonville CA 95076
   831 763-5300

(P-296)
MOUNTAIN MEADOW MUSHROOMS INC
26948 N Broadway, Escondido (92026-8315)
PHONE................760 749-1201
Bob Crouch, *President*
Elizabeth Crouch, *Vice Pres*
Roberto Ramirez, *Vice Pres*
Manuel Zuniga, *Vice Pres*
EMP: 72
SQ FT: 110,000
SALES (est): 9MM **Privately Held**
SIC: 0182 Mushrooms grown under cover

(P-297)
NORTH SHORE GREENHOUSES INC
Also Called: North Shore Living Herbs
82900 Johnson St, Thermal (92274-9319)
PHONE................760 397-0400
Leonardus Overgaag, *President*
Suzette Overgaag, *Vice Pres*
▲ **EMP:** 110
SALES (est): 11MM **Privately Held**
WEB: www.northshoregreenhouses.com
SIC: 0182 Food crops grown under cover

(P-298)
PLEASANT VALLEY FLOWERS INC
3132 E Pleasant Valley Rd, Oxnard (93033-4112)
PHONE................805 986-2776
Lane Devries, *President*
▲ **EMP:** 335
SQ FT: 7,500
SALES (est): 8.1MM **Privately Held**
WEB: www.pleasantvalleyflowers.com
SIC: 0182 Food crops grown under cover

PA: The Sun Valley Group Inc
   3160 Upper Bay Rd
   Arcata CA 95521

(P-299)
PREMIER MUSHROOMS LP
2847 Niagara Ave, Colusa (95932)
PHONE................530 458-2700
Jose Flores, *Plant Mgr*
EMP: 165 **Privately Held**
SIC: 0182 Mushrooms grown under cover
PA: Premier Mushrooms, L.P.
   2880 Niagara Ave
   Colusa CA 95932

(P-300)
ROYAL OAKS ENTERPRISES INC
Also Called: Royal Oaks Mushroom
15480 Watsonville Rd, Morgan Hill (95037-5921)
P.O. Box 447 (95038-0447)
PHONE................408 779-2362
Don Hordness, *President*
Deanne Arellano, *President*
Linda Abdella, *Treasurer*
Joseph Andrighetto, *Vice Pres*
Don Hordeness, *Vice Pres*
EMP: 50
SQ FT: 1,600
SALES (est): 3.9MM **Privately Held**
SIC: 0182 Mushrooms grown under cover

0191 Crop Farming, Misc

(P-301)
ARNAUDO BROS TRANSPORT INC (PA)
Also Called: Arnaudo Bros Trucking
16505 S Tracy Blvd, Tracy (95304-9436)
PHONE................209 835-0406
Steve Arnaudo, *President*
Leo Arnaudo, *Vice Pres*
Ed Arnaudo, *Admin Sec*
EMP: 100 **EST:** 1947
SQ FT: 1,200
SALES (est): 17.7MM **Privately Held**
SIC: 0191 4212 General farms, primarily
   crop; local trucking, without storage

(P-302)
BLACKJACK FARMS DE LA COSTA CN
Also Called: Black Jack Farms
2385 A St, Santa Maria (93455-1073)
PHONE................805 347-1333
Jose Garcia, *CEO*
Pat Iniguez, *Administration*
EMP: 140
SALES (est): 52.8K **Privately Held**
SIC: 0191 General farms, primarily crop

(P-303)
BOWLES FARMING CO INC
11609 Hereford Rd, Los Banos (93635-9514)
PHONE................209 827-3000
Phillip Bowles, *President*
Helen Bohr, *Office Mgr*
EMP: 50
SALES (corp-wide): 25MM **Privately Held**
WEB: www.bfarm.com
SIC: 0191 General farms, primarily crop
PA: Bowles Farming Company, Inc.
   545 Sansome St Ste 825
   San Francisco CA 94111
   415 421-4800

(P-304)
BURFORD FAMILY FARMING CO LP (PA)
Also Called: Burford Ranch
1443 W Sample Ave, Fresno (93711-1948)
PHONE................559 431-0902
Jill Burford, *Managing Prtnr*
EMP: 130
SQ FT: 2,000

SALES (est): 20.7MM **Privately Held**
SIC: **0191** 0131 0173 0111 General
farms, primarily crop; cotton; almond
grove; wheat; tomato farm; alfalfa farm

(P-305)
BUTTON & TURKOVICH
24604 Buckeye Rd, Winters (95694-9001)
PHONE...................530 795-2090
Tony Turkovich, *Partner*
Estate of Robert L Button, *Partner*
EMP: 100
SQ FT: 1,500
SALES (est): 7.1MM **Privately Held**
SIC: **0191** General farms, primarily crop

(P-306)
CALIFIA FARMS LLC
33502 Lerdo Hwy, Bakersfield
(93308-9438)
PHONE...................661 679-1000
Evans Berne, *Branch Mgr*
Keymi Ordenana, *CEO*
Scott McCurry, *Vice Pres*
Sonia Hendriks, *Sales Staff*
Mari Salazar, *Sales Staff*
EMP: 64
SALES (corp-wide): 100MM **Privately
Held**
SIC: **0191** General farms, primarily crop
PA: Califia Farms, Llc
1321 Palmetto St
Los Angeles CA 90013
213 694-4667

(P-307)
CAMPOS FAMILY FARMS LLC
4726 W Jacquelyn Ave, Fresno
(93722-6406)
PHONE...................559 275-3000
Fermin Campos,
EMP: 60 EST: 2011
SALES (est): 2.4MM **Privately Held**
SIC: **0191** General farms, primarily crop

(P-308)
CB NORTH LLC
480 W Beach St, Watsonville (95076-4555)
PHONE...................831 786-1642
Richard Dahl,
Jeffrey Conner,
Beth Potillo,
Bob Ritts,
EMP: 1000
SALES (est): 10.4MM **Privately Held**
SIC: **0191** General farms, primarily crop

(P-309)
**COELHO WEST CUSTOM
FARMING**
26979 S Butte Ave, Five Points (93624)
P.O. Box 434 (93624-0434)
PHONE...................559 884-2566
Anthony P Coelho Jr, *President*
EMP: 58
SALES (est): 4.7MM **Privately Held**
SIC: **0191** General farms, primarily crop

(P-310)
**CRYSTAL ORGANIC FARMS
LLC**
6900 Mountain View Rd, Bakersfield
(93307-9627)
PHONE...................661 845-5200
Jeff Meger, *President*
Mike Mooney, *Sales Staff*
Theodore Beardsley, *Manager*
EMP: 424
SALES (est): 13.9MM
SALES (corp-wide): 1.8B **Privately Held**
SIC: **0191** General farms, primarily crop
PA: Grimmway Enterprises, Inc.
14141 Di Giorgio Rd
Arvin CA 93203
800 301-3101

(P-311)
DAN R COSTA INC
17239 Louise Ave, Escalon (95320-8732)
PHONE...................209 234-2004
Dan R Costa, *President*
Shirley Costa, *Corp Secy*
EMP: 250

SALES (est): 3.5MM **Privately Held**
WEB: www.dannysfalldecor.com
SIC: **0191** 0115 0723 General farms, primarily crop; corn; vegetable packing services; fruit (fresh) packing services

(P-312)
DELTA BREEZE FARMING INC
Also Called: Courtland Farming
11566 State Highway 160, Courtland
(95615-9732)
PHONE...................916 775-2055
Mahinder S Shaliwal, *President*
Mahinder S Dhaliwal, *President*
Tawnya Dhaliwal, *Corp Secy*
EMP: 210
SQ FT: 4,000
SALES (est): 2MM **Privately Held**
SIC: **0191** General farms, primarily crop

(P-313)
**DICK ANDERSON & SONS
FARMING**
Also Called: Vasto Valle Farms
15900 W Dorris Ave, Huron (93234)
P.O. Box 10 (93234-0010)
PHONE...................559 945-2511
Richard Anderson, *President*
Robert Anderson, *Corp Secy*
Craig Anderson, *Vice Pres*
EMP: 135
SQ FT: 1,000
SALES (est): 10.8MM **Privately Held**
SIC: **0191** General farms, primarily crop

(P-314)
DON GRAGNANI FARMS
Also Called: Universal Custom Farming Co
12910 S Napa Ave, Tranquillity (93668)
P.O. Box 128 (93668-0128)
PHONE...................559 693-4352
Donald Gragnani, *Partner*
Irene Gragnani, *Partner*
Jerry Gragnani, *Partner*
Jeanne Gragnani-Lloyd, *Partner*
Martha Alejo, *Manager*
EMP: 80
SQ FT: 3,000
SALES (est): 8.9MM **Privately Held**
WEB: www.gragnanifarms.com
SIC: **0191** General farms, primarily crop

(P-315)
DV CUSTOM FARMING LLC
2101 Mettler Frontage E, Bakersfield
(93307-9649)
PHONE...................661 858-2888
Donald J Valpredo,
EMP: 80
SALES (est): 76.3K **Privately Held**
SIC: **0191** General farms, primarily crop

(P-316)
DW BERRY FARMS LLC
3960 N Rose Ave, Oxnard (93036-1820)
P.O. Box 1029 (93032-1029)
PHONE...................805 795-8403
Dean Walsh, *Mng Member*
EMP: 300 EST: 2010
SALES (est): 12.4MM **Privately Held**
SIC: **0191** General farms, primarily crop

(P-317)
E W MERRITT FARMS (PA)
11188 Road 192, Porterville (93257-9302)
PHONE...................559 784-8916
Earl Merritt, *Partner*
Eric Merritt, *Partner*
Mark Merritt, *Partner*
Monica Amarelo, *Comms Dir*
Robert Coleman, *Admin Asst*
EMP: 70
SALES (est): 8.5MM **Privately Held**
SIC: **0191** 0131 0111 0119 General
farms, primarily crop; cotton; wheat; milo
farm; corn; vegetables & melons

(P-318)
EDWARD J KELLY
Also Called: E K T Farms
959 Riverside Rd, Watsonville
(95076-9412)
P.O. Box 794 (95077-0794)
PHONE...................831 724-0832
Edward J Kelly, *Owner*
Jean Kelly, *Co-Owner*

EMP: 220
SALES (est): 11.5MM **Privately Held**
SIC: **0191** General farms, primarily crop

(P-319)
ELKHORN BERRY FARMS LLC
262 E Lake Ave, Watsonville (95076-4718)
PHONE...................831 722-2472
Thomas Amrhein, *General Mgr*
▲ EMP: 95
SALES (est): 5.6MM **Privately Held**
SIC: **0191** 0171 General farms, primarily
crop; strawberry farm

(P-320)
EMPRESAS DEL BOSQUE INC
51481 W Shields Ave, Firebaugh
(93622-9579)
P.O. Box 2455, Los Banos (93635-2455)
PHONE...................209 364-6428
Joe L Del Bosque Jr, *President*
EMP: 325
SQ FT: 1,600
SALES (est): 11MM **Privately Held**
SIC: **0191** General farms, primarily crop

(P-321)
FARM FRESH TO YOU (PA)
Also Called: Capay Organic
3880 Seaport Blvd, West Sacramento
(95691-3449)
PHONE...................916 303-7145
Freeman Barsotti, *CEO*
James Hubbard, *Principal*
EMP: 180 EST: 1976
SALES (est): 37.7MM **Privately Held**
SIC: **0191** General farms, primarily crop

(P-322)
GENE WHEELER FARMS INC
444 W Avenue H6, Lancaster
(93534-1634)
P.O. Box 10029 (93584-2029)
PHONE...................661 951-2100
Gene Wheeler, *President*
Antonio Aguilar, *Sales Staff*
▼ EMP: 250
SALES: 12.8MM **Privately Held**
WEB: www.GeneWheelerfarms.com
SIC: **0191** General farms, primarily crop

(P-323)
GOLDEN ACRES FARMS
87770 62nd Ave, Thermal (92274-9263)
P.O. Box 371 (92274-0371)
PHONE...................760 399-1923
Joe Kitagawa, *President*
Kiyoko Kitagawa, *Corp Secy*
Eugene Kitagawa, *Controller*
EMP: 50
SQ FT: 500
SALES (est): 2MM **Privately Held**
SIC: **0191** General farms, primarily crop

(P-324)
GREENHEART FARMS INC (PA)
902 Zenon Way, Arroyo Grande
(93420-5807)
P.O. Box 1510 (93421-1510)
PHONE...................805 481-2234
Hoy Buell, *CEO*
Grace Duran, *CFO*
Leo Wolf, *Treasurer*
Henry Katzenstein, *Vice Pres*
Melody Fair, *Info Tech Mgr*
▲ EMP: 87
SQ FT: 225,000
SALES (est): 27.7MM **Privately Held**
WEB: www.greenheartfarms.com
SIC: **0191** General farms, primarily crop

(P-325)
GRIMMWAY ENTERPRISES INC
Also Called: Premiere Packing
6301 S Zerker Rd, Shafter (93263)
P.O. Box 81498, Bakersfield (93380-1498)
PHONE...................661 399-0844
Randy Mower, *Vice Pres*
EMP: 400
SALES (corp-wide): 1.8B **Privately Held**
SIC: **0191** 0174 General farms, primarily
crop; citrus fruits
PA: Grimmway Enterprises, Inc.
14141 Di Giorgio Rd
Arvin CA 93203
800 301-3101

(P-326)
GRIMMWAY FARMS
2105 Anderholt Rd, Holtville (92250)
PHONE...................760 356-2513
Rancho Riddle, *Owner*
Darrin Domingos, *Manager*
EMP: 70
SALES (est): 1.4MM **Privately Held**
SIC: **0191** General farms, primarily crop

(P-327)
HALL COMPANY
44328 W Nees Ave, Firebaugh
(93622-9647)
PHONE...................209 364-0070
Tim Hall, *Partner*
Laurie Hall, *Partner*
EMP: 70
SALES (est): 7.7MM **Privately Held**
WEB: www.orolomaranch.com
SIC: **0191** General farms, primarily crop

(P-328)
HAMMONDS RANCH INC
47375 W Dakota Ave, Firebaugh
(93622-9516)
PHONE...................209 364-6185
James M Hammonds, *President*
William E Hammond, *Chairman*
Mary Hicks, *Corp Secy*
EMP: 100 EST: 1929
SQ FT: 3,500
SALES (est): 12.4MM **Privately Held**
SIC: **0191** General farms, primarily crop

(P-329)
HANSEN RANCHES
7124 Whitley Ave, Corcoran (93212-9669)
P.O. Box 398 (93212-0398)
PHONE...................559 992-3111
James Hansen, *Partner*
EMP: 60
SQ FT: 4,000
SALES (est): 20.6MM **Privately Held**
SIC: **0191** General farms, primarily crop

(P-330)
HARRIS FARMS INC
Also Called: Harris Farm Horse Division
27366 W Oakland Ave, Coalinga
(93210-9627)
PHONE...................559 884-2203
Dave McGlothlin, *Sales/Mktg Mgr*
EMP: 50
SALES (corp-wide): 3.7B **Privately Held**
WEB: www.harrisfarms.com
SIC: **0191** 0752 General farms, primarily
crop; boarding services, horses: racing &
non-racing
PA: Harris Farms, Inc.
29475 Fresno Coalinga Rd
Coalinga CA 93210
559 884-2435

(P-331)
HARRIS FARMS INC
Harris Ranch Inn & Restaurant
24505 W Dorris Ave, Coalinga
(93210-9667)
PHONE...................559 935-0717
Jonathan Farrington, *General Mgr*
John Obermire, *Manager*
EMP: 340
SALES (corp-wide): 3.7B **Privately Held**
WEB: www.harrisfarms.com
SIC: **0191** 7011 5813 5812 General
farms, primarily crop; hotels & motels;
drinking places; eating places
PA: Harris Farms, Inc.
29475 Fresno Coalinga Rd
Coalinga CA 93210
559 884-2435

(P-332)
HARRIS FARMS INC
23300 W Oakland Ave, Coalinga
(93210-9804)
PHONE...................559 884-2477
John Harris, *President*
EMP: 300
SALES (corp-wide): 3.7B **Privately Held**
WEB: www.harrisfarms.com
SIC: **0191** 0182 0161 General farms, pri-
marily crop; food crops grown under
cover; vegetables & melons

PA: Harris Farms, Inc.
29475 Fresno Coalinga Rd
Coalinga CA 93210
559 884-2435

(P-333)
HIGARD FARMS LLC
6 Quail Run Cir, Salinas (93907-2345)
PHONE...................................831 753-5982
Gary Higl,
EMP: 96
SALES (est): 1.6MM **Privately Held**
SIC: 0191 General farms, primarily crop

(P-334)
J & J FARMS
36245 W Ashlan Ave, Firebaugh (93622)
P.O. Box 155 (93622-0155)
PHONE...................................559 659-1457
Bill Jones, *Owner*
Darcy Villere, *General Mgr*
Linda Dudley, *Manager*
EMP: 50
SALES (est): 3.8MM **Privately Held**
SIC: 0191 General farms, primarily crop

(P-335)
J & S FARM
803 W Kimball Ave, Visalia (93277-6567)
PHONE...................................559 308-0294
Sasha Gonzales, *Principal*
James B Reese, *Principal*
EMP: 60
SALES (est): 650.6K **Privately Held**
SIC: 0191 General farms, primarily crop

(P-336)
J CRECELIUS INC
Also Called: Montetisea Framing
5043 N Montpelier Rd, Denair
(95316-9608)
P.O. Box 579 (95316-0579)
PHONE...................................209 883-4826
EMP: 100
SALES (est): 2.4MM **Privately Held**
SIC: 0191 0173

(P-337)
J H MEEK & SONS INC
22075 County Road 99, Woodland
(95695-9313)
P.O. Box 299 (95776-0299)
PHONE...................................530 662-1106
Steve Meek, *President*
John J Meek Jr, *President*
EMP: 50
SALES (est): 2.5MM **Privately Held**
SIC: 0191 General farms, primarily crop

(P-338)
J MARCHINI & SON INC
12000 Le Grand Rd, Le Grand
(95333-9708)
PHONE...................................559 665-2944
EMP: 93
SALES (corp-wide): 33.6MM **Privately Held**
SIC: 0191 General farms, primarily crop
PA: J. Marchini & Son, Inc.
8736 Minturn Rd
Le Grand CA 95333
559 665-2944

(P-339)
JACOBS FARM/DEL CABO INC
390 Swift Ave Ste 8, South San Francisco
(94080-6221)
PHONE...................................650 827-1133
Ted Witt, *Manager*
EMP: 75
SALES (corp-wide): 68.2MM **Privately Held**
SIC: 0191 General farms, primarily crop
PA: Jacobs Farm/Del Cabo, Inc.
2450 Stage Rd
Pescadero CA 94060
650 879-0580

(P-340)
JOHN GRIZZLE FARMING
1395 Bonds Corner Rd, Holtville
(92250-9736)
PHONE...................................760 356-4381
John Grizzle, *Owner*
Imala Rodriguez, *Owner*
EMP: 50

SALES (est): 3.7MM **Privately Held**
SIC: 0191 0212 General farms, primarily
crop; beef cattle except feedlots

(P-341)
JOSE VRAMONTES
Also Called: V and V Farms
14345 N Highway 88, Lodi (95240-9312)
PHONE...................................209 810-5384
EMP: 50
SALES: 700K **Privately Held**
SIC: 0191

(P-342)
KG BERRY FARMS LLC
1660 Philbric Rd, Santa Maria
(93454-8027)
P.O. Box 1087 (93456-1087)
PHONE...................................805 680-6751
Kevin John Guggia, *Mng Member*
Nicole Lea Guggia,
EMP: 115
SQ FT: 1,000
SALES (est): 5.4MM **Privately Held**
SIC: 0191 General farms, primarily crop

(P-343)
KIRSCHENMAN ENTERPRISES INC
10100 Digiorgio Rd, Bakersfield (93307)
PHONE...................................661 366-5736
Wayne Kirschenman, *CEO*
Norma Rapp, *Admin Sec*
▼ EMP: 60
SQ FT: 25,000
SALES (est): 10.7MM **Privately Held**
SIC: 0191 General farms, primarily crop

(P-344)
L & J FARMS CARACCIOLI LLC
27905 Corda Rd, Gonzales (93926)
P.O. Box H (93926-0239)
PHONE...................................831 675-7901
Phil Caraccioli,
Gary Caraccioli,
EMP: 50
SALES (est): 4.5MM **Privately Held**
SIC: 0191 General farms, primarily crop

(P-345)
LION RAISINS INC
Also Called: Lion Brothers Farms-Newstone
12555 Road 9, Madera (93637-9089)
P.O. Box 1350, Selma (93662-1350)
PHONE...................................559 662-8686
Jeff Bergeron, *Manager*
EMP: 200
SALES (corp-wide): 106.1MM **Privately Held**
WEB: www.lionraisins.com
SIC: 0191 General farms, primarily crop
PA: Lion Raisins, Inc.
9500 S De Wolf Ave
Selma CA 93662
559 834-6677

(P-346)
LS FARMS LLC
6111 De La Guerra Ter, Bakersfield
(93306-9757)
PHONE...................................661 792-3192
Antonette Anich, *Mng Member*
EMP: 500
SALES (est): 10.8MM **Privately Held**
SIC: 0191 General farms, primarily crop

(P-347)
LUCICH SANTOS FARMS
12631 Rogers Rd, Patterson (95363-8511)
P.O. Box 637 (95363-0637)
PHONE...................................209 892-6500
Peter Lucich, *Partner*
David Santos, *Partner*
EMP: 120
SQ FT: 20,000
SALES (est): 8.4MM **Privately Held**
SIC: 0191 General farms, primarily crop

(P-348)
MADDOX FARMS
12840 W Kamm Ave, Riverdale
(93656-9761)
PHONE...................................559 866-5308
Stephen Maddox Jr,
Brenda Maddox,
EMP: 95

SALES (est): 16.1MM **Privately Held**
SIC: 0191 General farms, primarily crop

(P-349)
MARCHINI INC
12006 Le Grand Rd, Le Grand
(95333-9708)
PHONE...................................209 389-4566
Richard Marchini, *President*
Judy Marchini, *Vice Pres*
EMP: 50
SQ FT: 1,200
SALES (est): 2.8MM **Privately Held**
SIC: 0191 0173 General farms, primarily
crop; almond grove

(P-350)
MOON MOUNTAIN FARMS LLC
3846 E Telegraph Rd, Fillmore
(93015-9779)
PHONE...................................805 521-1742
Les Blake, *Mng Member*
EMP: 50
SALES (est): 1.8MM **Privately Held**
SIC: 0191 General farms, primarily crop

(P-351)
MURANAKA FARM
11018 W Los Angeles Ave, Moorpark
(93021-9744)
P.O. Box 189 (93020-0189)
PHONE...................................805 529-0201
Greg EMI, *President*
EMP: 230
SALES (corp-wide): 44MM **Privately Held**
WEB: www.muranakafarm.com
SIC: 0191 General farms, primarily crop
PA: Muranaka Farm
11018 E Los Angeles Ave
Moorpark CA 93021
805 529-0201

(P-352)
OSCAR VALERO
Also Called: Valero Labor
1685 Jones St, Woodland (95776-6380)
PHONE...................................530 668-4342
Oscar Valero, *Owner*
EMP: 50
SALES: 100K **Privately Held**
SIC: 0191 General farms, primarily crop

(P-353)
RAINBOW RANCHES INC
13650 Copus Rd, Bakersfield
(93313-9676)
PHONE...................................661 858-2266
Michael Andrews, *CEO*
Marina Quintana, *Admin Sec*
EMP: 210
SALES (est): 6.9MM **Privately Held**
SIC: 0191 General farms, primarily crop

(P-354)
RANCHO LAGUNA FARMS LLC
2410 W Main St, Santa Maria
(93458-9712)
P.O. Box 6617 (93456-6617)
PHONE...................................805 925-7805
Larry Ferini, *Mng Member*
Tracy Ferini,
EMP: 100
SALES (est): 3.5MM **Privately Held**
WEB: www.lagunaproduce.com
SIC: 0191 General farms, primarily crop

(P-355)
RED BLOSSOM SALES INC
Also Called: Red Blossom Farms
9 Harris Pl, Salinas (93901-4563)
PHONE...................................831 751-9169
Michelle Huber, *Manager*
Velasco Adrian, *District Mgr*
EMP: 503 **Privately Held**
SIC: 0191 General farms, primarily crop
PA: Red Blossom Sales, Inc.
400 W Ventura Blvd # 140
Camarillo CA 93010

(P-356)
ROCKET FARMS HERBS INC
370 Espinosa Rd, Salinas (93907-8895)
P.O. Box 398104, San Francisco (94139-8104)
PHONE...................................562 340-5108
Don Barnett, *CEO*
EMP: 493
SALES (est): 26.8MM **Privately Held**
SIC: 0191 General farms, primarily crop

(P-357)
SAFARI HARVSTG & FARMING LLC
313 Plaza Dr Ste B12, Santa Maria
(93454-6931)
PHONE...................................805 925-2600
Robert T Sheehy,
EMP: 300
SALES (est): 9.3MM **Privately Held**
SIC: 0191 0722 General farms, primarily
crop; crop harvesting

(P-358)
SCHULTE RANCHES
Also Called: Dos Pueblos Ranch
Rr 1 Box 228, Goleta (93117)
PHONE...................................805 563-0821
Rudolph Schulte, *Owner*
EMP: 70
SQ FT: 600
SALES (est): 1.8MM **Privately Held**
SIC: 0191 0179 General farms, primarily
crop; avocado orchard

(P-359)
SERIMIAN M S D L RANCH
Also Called: D & L Produce
10463 S Del Rey Ave, Selma (93662-9706)
PHONE...................................559 896-1517
Donald Serimian, *Partner*
Lionel Serimian, *Partner*
EMP: 50 EST: 1961
SALES (est): 1.1MM **Privately Held**
SIC: 0191 General farms, primarily crop

(P-360)
SHELDON RANCHES
25140 Burr Dr, Lindsay (93247-9786)
P.O. Box 668 (93247-0668)
PHONE...................................559 562-3978
Charles H Sheldon, *President*
EMP: 60
SALES (est): 2.5MM **Privately Held**
SIC: 0191 General farms, primarily crop

(P-361)
SUN WORLD INTERNATIONAL LLC
5701 Truxtun Ave Ste 200, Bakersfield
(93309-0651)
P.O. Box 80298 (93380-0298)
PHONE...................................661 392-5000
David Marguleas, *CEO*
David Hostetter, *CFO*
Michael J Aiton, *Senior VP*
Reed E Fullmer, *Vice Pres*
Kyle Sweeney, *Vice Pres*
▲ EMP: 450
SALES (est): 57.6MM **Privately Held**
WEB: www.sun-world.com
SIC: 0191 General farms, primarily crop
PA: Sun World International, Inc.
16351 Driver Rd
Bakersfield CA 93308

(P-362)
SWANTON BERRY FARMS INC
25 Swanton Rd, Davenport (95017-9742)
P.O. Box 308 (95017-0308)
PHONE...................................831 425-8919
James Cochran, *President*
EMP: 50
SALES (est): 3.3MM **Privately Held**
SIC: 0191 General farms, primarily crop

(P-363)
TERRA LINDA FARMS 1
17625 S Marks Ave, Riverdale
(93656-9559)
P.O. Box 758 (93656-0758)
PHONE...................................559 867-3400
Joe Coelho, *Partner*
EMP: 50

▲ = Import ▼ = Export
◆ = Import/Export

SALES (est): 1.6MM **Privately Held**
SIC: 0191 General farms, primarily crop

(P-364)
TERRANOVA RANCH INC
16729 W Floral Ave, Helm (93627)
P.O. Box 130 (93627-0130)
PHONE................................559 866-5644
Diego Lissi, *President*
Don Cameron, *Vice Pres*
Annette Bauer, *Info Tech Mgr*
EMP: 50
SQ FT: 5,000
SALES (est): 5.2MM **Privately Held**
SIC: 0191 0172 General farms, primarily
crop; grapes

(P-365)
THOMPSON FAMILY FARMS LLC
16478 Beach Blvd Ste 391, Westminster
(92683-7860)
PHONE................................714 848-7536
Robert Thompson, *Mng Member*
EMP: 50
SALES (est): 665.5K **Privately Held**
SIC: 0191 General farms, primarily crop

(P-366)
TRAVIS JAMES WATTS
9631 Harvey Rd, Galt (95632-8861)
PHONE................................209 810-6159
Travis James Watts, *Owner*
EMP: 200
SALES (est): 150K **Privately Held**
SIC: 0191 General farms, primarily crop

(P-367)
V&V FARM LABOR CONTRACTOR
18396 S Wagner Ave, Ripon (95366-9720)
PHONE................................209 599-4834
Jose Villanueva, *President*
EMP: 50
SALES (est): 2MM **Privately Held**
SIC: 0191 General farms, primarily crop

(P-368)
VAN GRONINGEN & SONS INC
15100 Jack Tone Rd, Manteca
(95336-9729)
PHONE................................209 982-5248
Robert Van Groningen, *President*
Monica Cisneros, *CFO*
Monica Kuil, *CFO*
Dan Van Groningen, *Vice Pres*
Dan Vangroningen, *Vice Pres*
▼ **EMP:** 360
SQ FT: 3,000
SALES (est): 57.6MM **Privately Held**
WEB: www.vgandsons.com
SIC: 0191 0762 General farms, primarily
crop; farm management services

(P-369)
VAQUERO FARMS INC
43405 W Panoche Rd, Firebaugh
(93622-9720)
PHONE................................559 659-2790
Havier Rodriquez, *Manager*
EMP: 60
SQ FT: 150
SALES (est): 1.7MM
SALES (corp-wide): 7.1MM **Privately Held**
SIC: 0191 General farms, primarily crop
PA: Vaquero Farms, Inc.
24591 Silver Cloud Ct # 100
Monterey CA 93940
209 476-0002

(P-370)
VICTORIA ISLAND FARMS
16021 E Hwy 4, Holt (95234)
P.O. Box 87 (95234-0087)
PHONE................................209 465-5609
Eileen Nichols, *Owner*
▲ **EMP:** 70 **EST:** 1998
SQ FT: 1,484
SALES (est): 7.6MM **Privately Held**
SIC: 0191 General farms, primarily crop

(P-371)
VINO FARMS INC
51375 S Netherlands Rd, Clarksburg
(95612-5019)
PHONE................................916 775-4095
John Ledbetter, *Owner*
EMP: 116
SALES (corp-wide): 59.3MM **Privately Held**
SIC: 0191 General farms, primarily crop
PA: Vino Farms, Inc.
1377 E Lodi Ave
Lodi CA 95240
209 334-6975

(P-372)
WILLOW FARMS LLC
9452 Telephone Rd Pmb 142, Ventura
(93004-2600)
PHONE................................805 647-0720
George Ito,
EMP: 60
SALES (est): 2.1MM **Privately Held**
WEB: www.willowfarms.com
SIC: 0191 General farms, primarily crop

(P-373)
WOODSPUR FARMING LLC
Also Called: Oasis Date Gardens
59111 Grapefruit Blvd, Thermal
(92274-8813)
P.O. Box 757 (92274-0757)
PHONE................................760 398-9480
EMP: 98
SALES (corp-wide): 30.3MM **Privately Held**
SIC: 0191 General farms, primarily crop
PA: Woodspur Farming Llc
52200 Industrial Way
Coachella CA 92236
323 936-9303

(P-374)
WOOLF FARMING CO CAL INC
Also Called: Lansing Farming Co
7041 N Van Ness Blvd, Fresno
(93711-7169)
PHONE................................559 945-9292
Stuart P Woolf, *President*
John L Woolf III, *Chairman*
Michael T Woolf, *Treasurer*
Bernice Woolf, *Vice Pres*
Anne A Delaware, *Admin Sec*
EMP: 624 **EST:** 1974
SQ FT: 4,500
SALES (est): 32.2MM **Privately Held**
WEB: www.woolffarming.com
SIC: 0191 General farms, primarily crop

0211 Beef Cattle Feedlots

(P-375)
BRANDT CO INC (PA)
Also Called: Brandt Cattle
299 W Main St, Brawley (92227-2240)
P.O. Box 118 (92227-0118)
PHONE................................760 344-3430
William L Brandt, *CEO*
Susan L Brandt, *Corp Secy*
Leon R Brandt, *Vice Pres*
EMP: 60
SQ FT: 800
SALES (est): 13.1MM **Privately Held**
WEB: www.brandtco.com
SIC: 0211 0139 Beef cattle feedlots; al-
falfa farm

(P-376)
BRANDT CO INC
Also Called: Brandt Cattle
7015 Brandt Rd, Calipatria (92233-9761)
PHONE................................760 348-2295
William Brent, *Manager*
EMP: 53
SALES (corp-wide): 13.1MM **Privately Held**
WEB: www.brandtco.com
SIC: 0211 0139 Beef cattle feedlots; al-
falfa farm; grass seed farm
PA: Brandt Co., Inc.
299 W Main St
Brawley CA 92227
760 344-3430

(P-377)
MENDES CALF RANCH
13356 Avenue 168, Tipton (93272-9749)
PHONE................................559 688-4708
Victor Mendes, *Owner*
EMP: 90
SALES (est): 3MM **Privately Held**
SIC: 0211 Beef cattle feedlots

(P-378)
SUPERIOR CATTLE FEEDERS LLC (PA)
551 S Industrial Ave, Calipatria (92233)
P.O. Box 1828 (92233-1828)
PHONE................................760 348-2218
Dmingue Antchagno,
Robert A Lofton,
EMP: 55 **EST:** 1996
SALES (est): 7.5MM **Privately Held**
SIC: 0211 Beef cattle feedlots

0212 Beef Cattle, Except Feedlots

(P-379)
M & T CALF RANCH
Also Called: Tuls Cattle
14998 Avenue 192, Tulare (93274-9074)
PHONE................................559 686-7663
Sid Tuls, *Partner*
Mike Frings, *Partner*
Jason Tuls, *Partner*
EMP: 60
SQ FT: 1,800
SALES (est): 2MM **Privately Held**
SIC: 0212 Beef cattle except feedlots

(P-380)
ROBINSON & SONS
Also Called: Robinson and Enterprises
293 Lower Grass Valley Rd # 201, Nevada
City (95959-3120)
PHONE................................530 265-5844
Lowell Robinson, *Partner*
Neil Robinson, *Partner*
EMP: 70
SQ FT: 2,000
SALES (est): 1.3MM **Privately Held**
WEB: www.timrobinson.com
SIC: 0212 Beef cattle except feedlots

(P-381)
WESTERN MEAT PROCESSORS INC
Also Called: Agri-Feed Industries
502 E Barioni Blvd, Imperial (92251-1776)
P.O. Box 728 (92251-0728)
PHONE................................760 355-1175
Philip E Bauer, *Principal*
EMP: 50
SALES (est): 1.8MM **Privately Held**
SIC: 0212 0723 Beef cattle except feed-
lots; grain milling, custom services

0213 Hogs

(P-382)
LINDA TERRA FARMS (PA)
5494 W Mount Whitney Ave, Riverdale
(93656-9329)
P.O. Box 758 (93656-0758)
PHONE................................559 867-3473
John Coelho, *CEO*
EMP: 170
SQ FT: 1,014
SALES (est): 18.6MM **Privately Held**
SIC: 0213 0182 0172 Hogs; fruits grown
under cover; grapes

(P-383)
SEABOARD CORPORATION
Also Called: Texas Farm
10350 Hrītg Pk Dr Ste 111, Santa Fe
Springs (90670)
PHONE................................806 435-5935
Steven J Bresky, *CEO*
EMP: 300
SALES (corp-wide): 6.5B **Publicly Held**
SIC: 0213 Hogs

PA: Seaboard Corporation
9000 W 67th St
Merriam KS 66202
913 676-8800

0214 Sheep & Goats

(P-384)
ETCHEGARAY FARMS LLC
32324 Famoso Rd, Mc Farland (93250)
P.O. Box 964, Visalia (93279-0964)
PHONE................................661 393-0920
Sam Etchegaray,
Sam Etcegaray, *General Mgr*
EMP: 50 **EST:** 1985
SQ FT: 8,000
SALES (est): 845.1K **Privately Held**
SIC: 0214 0172 0179 0174 Lamb feedlot;
grapes; avocado orchard; grapefruit grove

0241 Dairy Farms

(P-385)
BOSMAN DAIRY LLC
6802 Avenue 120 A, Tipton (93272-9525)
PHONE................................559 752-7018
Clarence Bosman, *Partner*
Frank Bosman, *Partner*
EMP: 130 **EST:** 1959
SALES (est): 17.3MM **Privately Held**
SIC: 0241 Dairy farms

(P-386)
CASE VLOTT CATTLE
Also Called: Vlot Brothers
20330 Road 4, Chowchilla (93610-9489)
P.O. Box 309 (93610-0309)
PHONE................................559 665-7399
EMP: 50
SALES (est): 2MM **Privately Held**
SIC: 0241

(P-387)
COSTA VIEW FARMS
Also Called: Costa View Farms Shop
16800 Road 15, Madera (93637-9445)
PHONE................................559 675-3131
Darryl Azevedo, *Partner*
Linda Azevedo, *Partner*
Teresa Carr, *Partner*
William Carr, *Partner*
▲ **EMP:** 50 **EST:** 1999
SALES (est): 11.8MM **Privately Held**
SIC: 0241 0115 0211 Milk production;
corn; beef cattle feedlots

(P-388)
CURTI FAMILY INC
3235 Avenue 199, Tulare (93274-8909)
PHONE................................559 688-8323
Phillip A Curti, *President*
Preston Nicholas Curti, *Shareholder*
Phillip Curti, *Treasurer*
Phillip Justin Curti, *Corp Secy*
EMP: 54
SALES (est): 6.3MM **Privately Held**
SIC: 0241 Dairy farms

(P-389)
FERN OAKS FRMS A CAL GEN PRTNR
17001 Avenue 160, Porterville
(93257-9258)
PHONE................................559 684-8220
Greg Fernandes, *Partner*
Gregory Fernandes, *Partner*
EMP: 50 **EST:** 2017
SQ FT: 3,000
SALES (est): 972.1K **Privately Held**
SIC: 0241 Milk production

(P-390)
FOSTER DAIRY FARMS (PA)
Also Called: Crystal Creamery
529 Kansas Ave, Modesto (95351-1515)
PHONE................................209 576-3400
Frank Otis, *CEO*
Mark Shaw, *CFO*
Dennis Roberts, *Vice Pres*
Steve Brownfield, *Foreman/Supr*
Brian Carden, *Director*
▼ **EMP:** 800 **EST:** 1958

SALES (est): 397.9MM **Privately Held**
SIC: 0241 Milk production

(P-391)
FRANK J GOMES DAIRY A
CALIFO
Also Called: F and A Farms
5301 Deangelis Rd, Stevinson
(95374-9726)
PHONE..................209 669-7978
Frank J Gomes, *Partner*
Albert Xavier, *Partner*
EMP: 58
SALES (est): 8.5MM **Privately Held**
SIC: 0241 Dairy farms

(P-392)
GALLO CATTLE CO A LTD
PARTNR
Also Called: Joseph Farms Cheese
10561 State Highway 140, Atwater
(95301-9309)
P.O. Box 775 (95301-0775)
PHONE..................209 394-7984
Michael Gallo, *CEO*
Micah Gallo, *Partner*
Tiffanie Gallo, *Partner*
Linda Jelacich, *Partner*
EMP: 500
SQ FT: 6,000
SALES (est): 57.6MM **Privately Held**
SIC: 0241 2022 Milk production; cheese,
natural & processed

(P-393)
HIGH PLAINS RANCH LLC (PA)
2911 Hanford Armona Rd, Hanford
(93230-9379)
PHONE..................559 583-1277
Bernard Te Velde, *Mng Member*
EMP: 120
SQ FT: 2,000
SALES (est): 17.4MM **Privately Held**
SIC: 0241 Dairy farms

(P-394)
HOLLANDIA DAIRY INC (PA)
622 E Mission Rd, San Marcos
(92069-1999)
PHONE..................760 744-3222
Arie H Dejong, *President*
Peter De Jong, *Vice Pres*
Rudy De Jong, *Vice Pres*
Ken May, *Sales Staff*
EMP: 200
SQ FT: 20,000
SALES (est): 57.6MM **Privately Held**
WEB: www.hollandiadairy.com
SIC: 0241 Milk production

(P-395)
IEST FAMILY FARMS
Also Called: Richard Iest Dairy
14576 Avenue 14, Madera (93637-8922)
PHONE..................559 674-9417
Richard Iest, *Partner*
Danny Iest, *Partner*
Gerrlyn Iest, *Partner*
Richard C Iest, *Partner*
EMP: 70
SALES (est): 11.3MM **Privately Held**
SIC: 0241 Dairy farms

(P-396)
JAMES J STEVINSON A CORP
(PA)
Also Called: Anchor J Dairy
25079 River Rd, Stevinson (95374-9724)
P.O. Box 818, Newman (95360-0818)
PHONE..................209 632-1681
Robert Kelley, *President*
Kevin F Kelley, *Treasurer*
George Kelley, *Vice Pres*
EMP: 50
SQ FT: 1,500
SALES: 5MM **Privately Held**
SIC: 0241 0191 Dairy farms; general
farms, primarily crop

(P-397)
MADDOX DAIRY LLC
12863 W Kamm Ave Spc 2, Riverdale
(93656-9200)
PHONE..................559 866-5308
Stephen Maddox,

Julia Maddox Chow, *CFO*
EMP: 65
SALES (est): 8MM **Privately Held**
SIC: 0241 Milk production

(P-398)
MADDOX DAIRY A LTD
PARTNERSHIP (PA)
12863 W Kamm Ave Spc 2, Riverdale
(93656-9200)
PHONE..................559 867-3545
Steven Maddox, *Partner*
Douglas Maddox, *Partner*
Patrick Maddox, *Partner*
EMP: 60
SALES (est): 11.2MM **Privately Held**
SIC: 0241 Milk production

(P-399)
MADDOX DAIRY A LTD
PARTNERSHIP
Also Called: Ruann Dairy
7285 W Davis Ave, Riverdale (93656-9735)
PHONE..................559 867-4457
Patrick Maddox, *Manager*
EMP: 50
SALES (corp-wide): 11.2MM **Privately**
Held
SIC: 0241 Milk production
PA: Maddox Dairy, A Limited Partnership
12863 W Kamm Ave Spc 2
Riverdale CA 93656
559 867-3545

(P-400)
MAPLE DAIRY LP
15857 Bear Mountain Blvd, Bakersfield
(93311-9413)
PHONE..................661 396-9600
John Bos, *Partner*
A J Bos, *Partner*
EMP: 75
SALES (est): 9.9MM **Privately Held**
SIC: 0241 Dairy farms

(P-401)
NIELSENS CREAMERY (PA)
Also Called: Hoffman Farms
21346 Road 140, Tulare (93274-9363)
P.O. Box 579 (93275-0579)
PHONE..................559 686-4744
Chase Hoffman, *Partner*
Marion N Hoffman, *Partner*
EMP: 57
SQ FT: 11,000
SALES (est): 4.6MM **Privately Held**
SIC: 0241 Milk production

(P-402)
ORGANIC PASTURES DAIRY CO
LLC
7221 S Jameson Ave, Fresno
(93706-9386)
PHONE..................559 846-9732
Mark L McAfee, *Mng Member*
ADM McAfee,
Eric McAfee,
EMP: 50
SALES (est): 25.4MM **Privately Held**
SIC: 0241 Dairy farms

(P-403)
P H RANCH INC
Also Called: Veldhuis Dairy
6335 Oakdale Rd, Winton (95388-9648)
PHONE..................209 358-5111
Ray Veldhuis, *President*
Jeanette Veldhuis, *Corp Secy*
Ray Veldhuis Jr, *Vice Pres*
EMP: 50
SALES (est): 7MM **Privately Held**
WEB: www.phranch.com
SIC: 0241 Milk production

(P-404)
VALLEY MILK LLC
400 N Washington Rd, Turlock
(95380-9550)
PHONE..................209 410-6701
Donald A Machado, *Mng Member*
Kristen McCarthy, *Officer*
Kevin F Kelley,
▼ EMP: 54
SALES (est): 81.9K **Privately Held**
SIC: 0241 Milk production

(P-405)
VLOT BROTHERS TRUCKING
CO INC
Also Called: Vlot Brothers Dairy
3197 Avenue 21, Chowchilla (93610-9294)
P.O. Box 309 (93610-0309)
PHONE..................559 665-7399
Dirk J Vlot, *Partner*
Case Vlot, *Partner*
Valerie Vlot, *Partner*
EMP: 80
SALES (est): 8.8MM **Privately Held**
SIC: 0241 Dairy farms

(P-406)
WITHROW CATTLE
Also Called: Withrow Dairy
5301 Pleasant Grove Rd, Pleasant Grove
(95668-9752)
PHONE..................916 780-0364
Shane Johnson, *Manager*
EMP: 65
SALES (corp-wide): 2.6MM **Privately**
Held
WEB: www.withrowdairy.com
SIC: 0241 Dairy farms
PA: Withrow Cattle
5301 Pleasant Grove Rd
Pleasant Grove CA 95668
916 780-0364

(P-407)
ZONNEVELD DAIRIES INC
1560 Cerini Ave, Laton (93242-9700)
PHONE..................559 923-4546
John Zonneveld Jr, *President*
Frank Zonneveld, *Corp Secy*
EMP: 60
SALES (est): 10.9MM **Privately Held**
WEB: www.cainhibbard.com
SIC: 0241 Dairy farms

(P-408)
ZONNEVELD FARMS
1560 Cerini Ave, Laton (93242-9700)
PHONE..................559 923-4546
Andrew Zonneveld, *Partner*
Craig Wierenga, *Project Mgr*
EMP: 99
SALES (est): 3.5MM **Privately Held**
SIC: 0241 0191 Dairy farms; general
farms, primarily crop

0252 Chicken Egg Farms

(P-409)
DEMLER EGG RANCH
28198 Gromer Ave, Wasco (93280-9558)
P.O. Box 207 (93280-0207)
PHONE..................661 758-4577
David Demler, *Partner*
Sharman Demler, *Partner*
EMP: 50
SALES (est): 1.4MM **Privately Held**
SIC: 0252 Chicken eggs

(P-410)
FOSTER FARMS LLC
770 N Plano St, Porterville (93257-6329)
PHONE..................559 793-5501
Paul Bravinder, *Manager*
Rene Aguilar, *Controller*
David Downs, *Plant Mgr*
Tom Farrell, *Plant Mgr*
Darren Taylor, *Facilities Mgr*
EMP: 300
SQ FT: 81,000
SALES (corp-wide): 1.4B **Privately Held**
SIC: 0252 2015 Chicken eggs; poultry
slaughtering & processing
PA: Foster Farms, Llc
1000 Davis St
Livingston CA 95334
209 394-7901

(P-411)
GEMPERLE ENTERPRISES
Also Called: Gemperle Farms
10218 Lander Ave, Turlock (95380-9627)
PHONE..................209 667-2651
Steve Gemperle, *Mng Member*
▲ EMP: 90 EST: 1952
SQ FT: 8,000

SALES (est): 6.8MM **Privately Held**
SIC: 0252 5144 Chicken eggs; eggs

(P-412)
S K S ENTERPRISES INC (PA)
11830 French Camp Rd, Manteca
(95336-9732)
PHONE..................209 599-4095
Wen Chang Su, *President*
EMP: 60
SALES (est): 3.6MM **Privately Held**
SIC: 0252 2015 Chicken eggs; poultry
slaughtering & processing

(P-413)
VALLEY FRESH FOODS INC
Nest Best Egg Company
3600 E Linwood Ave, Turlock (95380-9109)
P.O. Box 370, Rochester WA (98579-0370)
PHONE..................209 669-5600
Duane Olsen, *Branch Mgr*
EMP: 61
SALES (corp-wide): 1.2B **Privately Held**
SIC: 0252 2048 Chicken eggs; prepared
feeds
PA: Valley Fresh Foods, Inc.
3600 E Linwood Ave
Turlock CA 95380
209 669-5600

(P-414)
VALLEY FRESH FOODS INC
Also Called: Rainbow Farms
1220 Hall Rd, Denair (95316-9617)
P.O. Box 910, Turlock (95381-0910)
PHONE..................209 669-5510
Danny O'Day, *Manager*
Raquel Bettencourt, *CFO*
EMP: 100
SQ FT: 1,216
SALES (corp-wide): 1.2B **Privately Held**
SIC: 0252 2015 Started pullet farm; poul-
try slaughtering & processing
PA: Valley Fresh Foods, Inc.
3600 E Linwood Ave
Turlock CA 95380
209 669-5600

0253 Turkey & Turkey Egg
Farms

(P-415)
DIESTEL TURKEY RANCH
14111 High Tech Dr C, Jamestown (95327)
P.O. Box 4314, Sonora (95370-1314)
PHONE..................209 984-0826
Tim Diestel, *Owner*
Joan Diestel, *Co-Owner*
EMP: 150
SALES (est): 5.9MM **Privately Held**
SIC: 0253 2015 Turkey farm; poultry
slaughtering & processing

(P-416)
DIESTEL TURKEY RANCH (PA)
Also Called: Distel Family Ranch
22200 Lyons Bald Mtn Rd, Sonora
(95370-8772)
P.O. Box 4314 (95370-1314)
PHONE..................209 532-4950
Timothy Diestel, *CEO*
David Harmer, *CFO*
Jared Orrock, *CFO*
Joan Diestel, *Vice Pres*
Heidi Diestel, *Principal*
EMP: 130
SQ FT: 5,000
SALES (est): 25.7MM **Privately Held**
SIC: 0253 Turkey farm

(P-417)
SWANSON FARMS
5213 W Main St, Turlock (95380-9413)
P.O. Box 2367 (95381-2367)
PHONE..................209 667-2002
Richard E Swanson, *President*
Larry Pickering, *Vice Pres*
EMP: 65 EST: 1942
SQ FT: 5,000
SALES (est): 4.5MM **Privately Held**
WEB: www.associatedfeed.com
SIC: 0253 0173 Turkey farm; almond
grove

▲ = Import ▼=Export
◆ =Import/Export

0254 Poultry Hatcheries

(P-418)
FOSTER POULTRY FARMS
843 Davis St, Livingston (95334-1525)
P.O. Box 457 (95334-0457)
PHONE....................................209 394-7901
Richie King, *Branch Mgr*
EMP: 3000
SALES (corp-wide): 3B **Privately Held**
WEB: www.fosterfarms.com
SIC: 0254 2015 Poultry hatcheries; poultry, processed
PA: Foster Poultry Farms
    1000 Davis St
    Livingston CA 95334
    209 394-6914

(P-419)
FOSTER POULTRY FARMS
Also Called: Foster Farms
2960 S Cherry Ave, Fresno (93706-5445)
PHONE....................................559 442-3771
Bob Hansen, *Manager*
Steve Yarmowich, *Vice Pres*
Tom Hendrickson, *General Mgr*
Tracy Bianchi, *Controller*
Rebeca Reyes, *Human Res Mgr*
EMP: 700
SALES (corp-wide): 3B **Privately Held**
WEB: www.fosterfarms.com
SIC: 0254 Poultry hatcheries
PA: Foster Poultry Farms
    1000 Davis St
    Livingston CA 95334
    209 394-6914

0259 Poultry & Eggs Farms, NEC

(P-420)
REICHARDT DUCK FARM INC
3770 Middle Two Rock Rd, Petaluma (94952-4625)
PHONE....................................707 762-6314
John T Reichardt, *President*
Kathy Shaw, *CFO*
▼ **EMP:** 95
SQ FT: 1,296
SALES (est): 3.6MM **Privately Held**
WEB: www.reichardtduckfarm.com
SIC: 0259 Duck farm

0279 Animal Specialties, NEC

(P-421)
BELCAMPO GROUP INC (PA)
65 Webster St, Oakland (94607-3720)
PHONE....................................510 250-7810
Anya Fernald, *CEO*
John Prescott, *Principal*
Talia Dillman, *Project Mgr*
Jeremy Fisher, *Project Mgr*
Danielle Dahlin, *Opers Mgr*
◆ **EMP:** 70 **EST:** 2011
SALES (est): 16.5MM **Privately Held**
SIC: 0279 2011 2015 5812 Domestic animal farms; beef products from beef slaughtered on site; poultry slaughtering & processing; family restaurants; office management

(P-422)
HONEY OLIVAREZ BEES INC
6398 County Road 20, Orland (95963-9475)
P.O. Box 847 (95963-0847)
PHONE....................................530 865-0298
Ray A Olivarez Jr, *CEO*
EMP: 97
SALES (est): 8.9MM **Privately Held**
SIC: 0279 Apiary (bee & honey farm)

(P-423)
SAN BERNARDINO MTNS WILDLIFE
Also Called: WILDHAVEN RANCH
29450 Pine Ridge Dr, Cedar Glen (92321)
P.O. Box 1782, Lake Arrowhead (92352-1782)
PHONE....................................909 226-6189
Diane Dragotto Williams, *CEO*
EMP: 50 **EST:** 1995
SALES: 550.4K **Privately Held**
SIC: 0279 Bird sanctuaries

0291 Animal Production, NEC

(P-424)
BOOTH RANCHES LLC
440 Anchor Ave, Orange Cove (93646-2200)
PHONE....................................559 626-4472
Otis Booth Jr, *Branch Mgr*
EMP: 76
SALES (corp-wide): 16.2MM **Privately Held**
SIC: 0291 General farms, primarily animals
PA: Booth Ranches Llc
    12201 Avenue 480
    Orange Cove CA 93646
    559 626-4732

(P-425)
DOUGLAS RANCH LLC
33200 E Carmel Valley Rd, Carmel Valley (93924-9396)
PHONE....................................949 500-7009
Joy Berry, *Principal*
EMP: 50
SALES (est): 639.9K **Privately Held**
SIC: 0291 General farms, primarily animals

(P-426)
E & T FOODS INC
Also Called: Monrovia Ranch Market
14827 Seventh St, Victorville (92395-4023)
P.O. Box 661912, Arcadia (91066-1912)
PHONE....................................760 843-7730
Franco Duenas, *Branch Mgr*
EMP: 330
SALES (corp-wide): 66.5MM **Privately Held**
SIC: 0291 General farms, primarily animals
PA: E & T Foods, Inc.
    328 W Huntington Dr
    Monrovia CA 91016
    626 357-5051

(P-427)
LAGUNA BCH GOLF BNGLOW VLG LLC
Also Called: Ranch At Laguna Beach, The
31106 Coast Hwy, Laguna Beach (92651-8130)
PHONE....................................949 499-2271
Mark Christy, *Principal*
Kurt Bjorkman, *General Mgr*
Johnny Sanabria, *Asst Controller*
Ryan Sheffer, *Instructor*
Sean Laurino, *Manager*
EMP: 50
SALES (est): 1.3MM **Privately Held**
SIC: 0291 General farms, primarily animals

(P-428)
NORCO RANCH INC (DH)
12005 Cabernet Dr, Fontana (92337-7703)
P.O. Box 910, Norco (92860-0917)
PHONE....................................951 737-6735
Ric Sundal, *CEO*
EMP: 350
SQ FT: 120,000
SALES (est): 47.9MM
SALES (corp-wide): 6.8B **Privately Held**
WEB: www.norcoeggs.com
SIC: 0291 General farms, primarily animals
HQ: Moark, Llc
    28 Under The Mountain Rd
    North Franklin CT 06254
    951 332-3300

(P-429)
R RANCH MARKET
1112 Walnut Ave, Tustin (92780-5607)
PHONE....................................714 573-1182
Jubira Martinez, *Owner*
EMP: 709
SALES: 4MM
SALES (corp-wide): 128.4MM **Privately Held**
SIC: 0291 General farms, primarily animals
PA: R-Ranch Market, Incorporated
    13985 Live Oak Ave
    Irwindale CA 91706
    626 814-2900

(P-430)
RAVA RANCHES INC
700 Airport Rd, King City (93930-2501)
P.O. Box 1600 (93930-1600)
PHONE....................................831 385-3285
Jerry J Rava Sr, *President*
EMP: 50 **EST:** 1987
SALES (est): 4.8MM **Privately Held**
SIC: 0291 General farms, primarily animals

(P-431)
RIO BRAVO RANCH SHOP
15701 Highway 178, Bakersfield (93306-9500)
PHONE....................................661 872-5050
Jim Nickel, *Partner*
EMP: 50
SALES (est): 845.6K **Privately Held**
SIC: 0291 General farms, primarily animals

0711 Soil Preparation Svcs

(P-432)
BIO INDUSTRIES INC
2060 Montgomery Rd, Red Bluff (96080-4613)
P.O. Box 732 (96080-0732)
PHONE....................................530 529-3290
Ben Sale, *President*
EMP: 50
SQ FT: 400
SALES (est): 100K **Privately Held**
SIC: 0711 Soil preparation services

0721 Soil Preparation, Planting & Cultivating Svc

(P-433)
BZ - BEE POLLINATION INC
24204 Rd 23, Esparto (95627)
P.O. Box 699 (95627-0699)
PHONE....................................530 787-3044
John Foster, *CEO*
EMP: 50
SALES (est): 511.6K **Privately Held**
WEB: www.bz-bee.com
SIC: 0721 7389 Pollinating services;

(P-434)
CALIFORNIA VALLEY LAND CO INC (PA)
Also Called: Woolf Enterprises
18036 Gale, Huron (93234)
P.O. Box 219 (93234-0219)
PHONE....................................559 945-9292
Stuart P Woolf, *President*
Michael T Woolf, *Treasurer*
Michael Woolf, *Treasurer*
John L Woolf, *Vice Ch Bd*
Susan Hornor, *Asst Controller*
EMP: 93
SQ FT: 4,500
SALES (est): 43.2MM **Privately Held**
SIC: 0721 Planting services; crop cultivating services; crop protecting services

(P-435)
CHUCK JONES FLYING SERVICE (PA)
Also Called: Aerial Applicators
216 W Hamilton Rd, Biggs (95917-9793)
P.O. Box 497 (95917-0497)
PHONE....................................530 868-5798
Dale Jones, *President*
Lori A Jones, *Treasurer*
Alan Jones, *Vice Pres*
EMP: 50
SQ FT: 25,000
SALES: 3.2MM **Privately Held**
SIC: 0721 Crop dusting services

(P-436)
GERAWAN FARMING PARTNERS INC
15749 E Ventura Ave, Sanger (93657-9657)
P.O. Box 67 (93657-0067)
PHONE....................................559 787-8780
Dan Gerawan, *President*
EMP: 300
SALES (est): 10.4MM **Privately Held**
SIC: 0721 0172 Tree orchards, cultivation of; grapes

(P-437)
JOHN H KAUTZ FARMS
5490 Bear Creek Rd, Lodi (95240-7213)
PHONE....................................209 334-4786
John H Kautz, *Co-Owner*
Gail Kautz, *Owner*
Corina Vasquez, *Manager*
EMP: 50
SQ FT: 3,000
SALES (est): 5.7MM **Privately Held**
SIC: 0721 Orchard tree & vine services

(P-438)
OAKRIDGE LANDSCAPE INC (PA)
28064 Avenue Stanford K, Valencia (91355-1158)
PHONE....................................661 295-7228
Jeffrey E Myers, *CEO*
Susie Maza, *CFO*
Mike Roberts, *Branch Mgr*
Andrea Fisher, *Administration*
Mary Grosswendt-Perd, *Business Mgr*
EMP: 52
SALES (est): 31MM **Privately Held**
WEB: www.oakridgelandscape.com
SIC: 0721 0781 Irrigation system operation, not providing water; landscape services

(P-439)
PLANT TAPE USA INC (HQ)
Also Called: Tanimura & Antle
1 Harris Rd Fl 1 # 1, Salinas (93908-8608)
P.O. Box 4070 (93912-4070)
PHONE....................................831 455-2255
Brian Antle, *President*
▼ **EMP:** 50
SALES: 3.1MM
SALES (corp-wide): 2.8MM **Privately Held**
SIC: 0721 Planting services
PA: Plant Tape Altea Sl
    Calle Llobatona (Cr), 6 - Nave D
    Viladecans 08840
    936 379-892

(P-440)
S & S RANCH INC
Also Called: Stamoules Produce Company
904 S Lyon Ave, Mendota (93640-9735)
PHONE....................................559 655-3491
Pagona Stefanopoulos, *CEO*
Athanasios Stefanopoulos, *Vice Pres*
▼ **EMP:** 85
SQ FT: 500
SALES (est): 10.6MM **Privately Held**
SIC: 0721 Planting services; crop cultivating services; crop protecting services

(P-441)
SEAMAN NURSERIES INC
336 Robertson Blvd Ste A, Chowchilla (93610-2867)
PHONE....................................559 665-1860
William Seaman, *President*
EMP: 70
SALES (est): 5.7MM **Privately Held**
SIC: 0721 0762 5261 Orchard tree & vine services; farm management services; nurseries

(P-442)
SUNRIDGE NURSERIES INC
441 Vineland Rd, Bakersfield (93307-9556)
PHONE....................................661 363-8463

Craig Stoller, *CEO*
Glen Stoller, *President*
Terrie Stoller, *Corp Secy*
EMP: 70
SQ FT: 60,000
SALES (est): 14MM **Privately Held**
WEB: www.sunridgenurseries.com
SIC: 0721 Vines, cultivation of

(P-443)
THIARA SUKHWANT
Also Called: Thiara Orchards
1537 Atkinson Ct, Yuba City (95993-9679)
PHONE......................530 673-1581
Sukhwant Thiara, *Owner*
Ravi Thiara, *Principal*
EMP: 50
SALES (est): 3.3MM **Privately Held**
SIC: 0721 Tree orchards, cultivation of

(P-444)
VISTA VERDE FARMS INC
7124 Whitley Ave, Corcoran (93212-9669)
P.O. Box 398 (93212-0398)
PHONE......................559 992-3111
Jim Hansen, *President*
Kendell W Gardner, *Corp Secy*
Jess Hansen, *Vice Pres*
EMP: 70 **EST:** 1974
SQ FT: 3,000
SALES (est): 3.1MM **Privately Held**
SIC: 0721 0173 Crop planting & protection; almond grove

0722 Crop Harvesting By Machine

(P-445)
A & G GROVE SERVICE
32731 Mesa Lilac Rd, Escondido (92026-4402)
P.O. Box 1752, Fallbrook (92088-1752)
PHONE......................760 728-5447
Angel Huerta, *Owner*
EMP: 100
SALES (est): 6.1MM **Privately Held**
SIC: 0722 Crop harvesting

(P-446)
ANTHONY HARVESTING INC
401 S Vanderhurst Ave, King City (93930-2934)
P.O. Box 608 (93930-0608)
PHONE......................831 385-6460
Scott Anthony, *President*
EMP: 110
SALES (est): 7.1MM **Privately Held**
SIC: 0722 Crop harvesting

(P-447)
AZCONA HARVESTING LLC
44 El Camino Real Unit A, Greenfield (93927-5637)
P.O. Box 3310 (93927-3310)
PHONE......................831 674-2526
Nick Azcona,
Pier Azcona,
EMP: 200
SQ FT: 1,000
SALES (est): 17.2MM **Privately Held**
SIC: 0722 Crop harvesting

(P-448)
BARNES AND BERGER
1091 S Intake Blvd, Blythe (92225-8209)
PHONE......................760 922-6136
Euell Barnes, *Partner*
Duane Berger, *Partner*
EMP: 50
SQ FT: 8,900
SALES: 3MM **Privately Held**
WEB: www.barnesandberger.com
SIC: 0722 Cotton, machine harvesting services

(P-449)
BYRD HARVEST INC
Also Called: Byrd Produce
192 Guadalupe St, Guadalupe (93434-1514)
P.O. Box 60 (93434-0060)
PHONE......................805 343-1608
Joe George, *President*
Barbara Stanley, *Treasurer*

EMP: 300
SQ FT: 5,000
SALES (est): 20.3MM **Privately Held**
SIC: 0722 Field crops, except cash grains, machine harvesting services

(P-450)
DANELL BROS INC
Also Called: Hanford Truck Repair & Parts
8265 Hanford Armona Rd, Hanford (93230-9344)
PHONE......................559 582-1251
Danny Danell, *President*
Marigail Danell, *Corp Secy*
Mike Danell, *Vice Pres*
Mary Kiely, *Finance*
▲ **EMP:** 80 **EST:** 1970
SQ FT: 3,000
SALES (est): 5.8MM **Privately Held**
SIC: 0722 0241 Crop harvesting; dairy heifer replacement farm

(P-451)
DANELL CUSTOM HARVESTING LLC
8265 Hanford Armona Rd, Hanford (93230-9344)
PHONE......................559 582-1251
Rance Danell,
EMP: 150
SALES (est): 12.4MM **Privately Held**
SIC: 0722 Crop harvesting

(P-452)
I S A CONTRACTING SVCS INC
958 O St, Firebaugh (93622-2221)
PHONE......................559 659-1080
Ileana Arvizu, *President*
EMP: 600
SQ FT: 5,000
SALES (est): 10MM **Privately Held**
SIC: 0722 Crop harvesting

(P-453)
LOPEZ HARVESTING
24079 Avenue 196, Strathmore (93267-9633)
PHONE......................559 568-2553
Danny Lopez, *Owner*
EMP: 80
SALES (est): 2.1MM **Privately Held**
SIC: 0722 Crop harvesting

(P-454)
LOS DOS VALLES HARVSTG & PKG
2365 Westgate Rd, Santa Maria (93455-1045)
P.O. Box 1942 (93456-1942)
PHONE......................805 739-1688
Felipe C Zepeda, *President*
EMP: 150
SQ FT: 4,500
SALES (est): 11.4MM **Privately Held**
SIC: 0722 0723 Vegetables & melons, machine harvesting services; vegetable packing services

(P-455)
NEW HOPE HARVESTING LLC
918 Nita Ct, Santa Maria (93454-3122)
PHONE......................805 478-4469
Guadalupe Gaspar, *Principal*
Eugenia Martinez, *Principal*
EMP: 60
SALES: 4MM **Privately Held**
SIC: 0722 Crop harvesting

(P-456)
NOBLESSE OBLIGE INC
Also Called: Eight Star Equipment
2015 Silsbee Rd, El Centro (92243-9671)
PHONE......................760 353-3336
Alex Abatti Jr, *President*
Tim Castelli, *CFO*
David Wells, *CFO*
Sid Swarthout, *Admin Sec*
EMP: 250
SALES (est): 19.1MM **Privately Held**
WEB: www.noblesseoblige.com
SIC: 0722 Combining services; cotton, machine harvesting services; hay, machine harvesting services; vegetables & melons, machine harvesting services

(P-457)
PREMIUM PACKING INC
Also Called: Premium Harvesting
449 Harrison Rd, Salinas (93907-1617)
P.O. Box 4500 (93912-4500)
PHONE......................831 443-6855
Jesus Alderete Jr, *President*
Marlene Alderete, *Corp Secy*
Ronnie Alderete, *General Mgr*
EMP: 130
SALES (est): 14.8MM **Privately Held**
WEB: www.premiumpacking.com
SIC: 0722 7361 Crop harvesting; labor contractors (employment agency)

(P-458)
R & G ENTERPRISES
627 N Main St, Porterville (93257-2358)
P.O. Box 230 (93258-0230)
PHONE......................559 781-1351
Val B Guzman, *Partner*
Jose M Rios, *Partner*
EMP: 200
SQ FT: 1,500
SALES: 3MM **Privately Held**
SIC: 0722 0761 Crop harvesting; farm labor contractors

(P-459)
RC PACKING LLC
26769 El Camino Real, Gonzales (93926-9405)
PHONE......................831 675-0308
Dennis Caprara, *Mng Member*
EMP: 300
SALES (est): 27.2MM **Privately Held**
WEB: www.rcpacking.com
SIC: 0722 Crop harvesting

(P-460)
TRI VALLEY VEGETABLE HARVSTG
123 N Depot St, Santa Maria (93458-3907)
P.O. Box 1969 (93456-1969)
PHONE......................805 928-2727
Robert Espinola, *President*
Ronald Burke, *Treasurer*
EMP: 80
SQ FT: 600
SALES (est): 5.1MM **Privately Held**
SIC: 0722 Vegetables & melons, machine harvesting services

(P-461)
VALLEY PRIDE INC
86120 Tyler Ln, Coachella (92236-3123)
PHONE......................760 398-1353
Tom Spulding, *Manager*
Mercedes Zepeda, *Office Mgr*
EMP: 60
SALES (corp-wide): 2.2MM **Privately Held**
WEB: www.valleyprideinc.com
SIC: 0722 Crop harvesting
PA: Valley Pride, Inc.
10855 Ocean Mist Pkwy D
Castroville CA 95012
831 633-5883

0723 Crop Preparation, Except Cotton Ginning

(P-462)
ADOBE PACKING COMPANY (PA)
367 W Market St, Salinas (93901-1423)
P.O. Box 4026 (93912-4026)
PHONE......................831 753-6195
Jose G Esquivel, *President*
Basil Mills, *Shareholder*
Roger Mills, *Shareholder*
Mary Esquivel, *Treasurer*
Susan Mills, *Vice Pres*
EMP: 225
SQ FT: 2,500
SALES (est): 11.1MM **Privately Held**
WEB: www.millsfamilyfarms.com
SIC: 0723 4783 Vegetable packing services; packing & crating

(P-463)
AGRO-JAL FARMS INC
257 Kathleen Ct, Santa Maria (93458-4953)
P.O. Box 1862 (93456-1862)
PHONE......................805 928-2682
Abel O Maldonado Jr, *President*
Frank Maldonado, *Vice Pres*
EMP: 100
SALES (est): 7.7MM **Privately Held**
SIC: 0723 Vegetable crops market preparation services; vegetable precooling services

(P-464)
ALL STAR SEED (PA)
Also Called: Eight Star Commodities
2015 Silsbee Rd, El Centro (92243-9671)
PHONE......................760 482-9400
Alex Abatti Jr, *President*
Tim Castelli, *CFO*
Sid Swarthout, *Vice Pres*
◆ **EMP:** 55
SALES (est): 59.4MM **Privately Held**
WEB: www.abatti.com
SIC: 0723 Seed cleaning

(P-465)
ALLDRIN BROTHERS INC
Also Called: Alldrin Brothers Almonds
584 Hi Tech Pkwy, Oakdale (95361-9371)
PHONE......................855 667-4231
Gary Alldrin, *President*
Grant Neil Alldrin, *Mktg Dir*
◆ **EMP:** 50
SQ FT: 5,000
SALES (est): 9.5MM **Privately Held**
WEB: www.alldrinbros.com
SIC: 0723 Almond hulling & shelling services

(P-466)
ALLIED AVOCADOS & CITRUS INC
1203 S Sespe St, Fillmore (93015-9767)
PHONE......................805 625-7155
Brayen Guzman, *President*
Lupe Guzman, *COO*
EMP: 60
SALES: 28MM **Privately Held**
SIC: 0723 Fruit (farm-dried) packing services

(P-467)
ANDERSEN & SONS SHELLING INC
4530 Rowles Rd, Vina (96092)
P.O. Box 100 (96092-0100)
PHONE......................530 839-2236
Patrick Knudt Andersen, *President*
Franklin Andersen, *Vice Pres*
Michael Andersen, *Vice Pres*
Ralph Andersen, *Vice Pres*
Greg Gorang, *General Mgr*
◆ **EMP:** 100
SALES (est): 38.4MM **Privately Held**
SIC: 0723 0762 Walnut hulling & shelling services; farm management services

(P-468)
ANDERSEN NUT COMPANY
Also Called: Gustine Mini Storage
3050 S Hunt Rd, Gustine (95322)
P.O. Box 445 (95322-0445)
PHONE......................209 854-6820
Brian Anderson, *Partner*
Dan Anderson, *Partner*
◆ **EMP:** 50
SQ FT: 26,500
SALES: 5MM **Privately Held**
SIC: 0723 Walnut hulling & shelling services

(P-469)
BAIRD-NEECE PACKING CORP
60 S E St, Porterville (93257-4721)
PHONE......................559 784-3393
Dick Neece, *President*
EMP: 180
SQ FT: 37,249
SALES (est): 14.8MM **Privately Held**
WEB: www.bairdneece.com
SIC: 0723 Fruit (fresh) packing services

(P-470)
BLUE DIAMOND GROWERS
4800 Sisk Rd, Modesto (95356-8730)
PHONE..........................209 545-6221
Bruce Mickelson, *Manager*
Brian Barczak, *Senior VP*
Laura Lutz, *Executive Asst*
Anthony Funaro, *Office Spvr*
Joe Mendoza, *Plant Mgr*
EMP: 200
SALES (corp-wide): 1.6B **Privately Held**
WEB: www.bluediamond.com
SIC: 0723 2068 Almond hulling & shelling
services; nuts: dried, dehydrated, salted
or roasted
PA: Diamond Blue Growers
1802 C St
Sacramento CA 95811
916 442-0771

(P-471)
BOSKOVICH FARMS INC (PA)
711 Diaz Ave, Oxnard (93030-7247)
P.O. Box 1352 (93032-1352)
PHONE..........................805 487-2299
George S Boskovich Jr, *CEO*
Philip J Boskovich Jr, *President*
Russ Weiderburg, *Officer*
Andrew Costales, *Info Tech Mgr*
Manuel Villafana, *Technology*
▲ EMP: 205
SQ FT: 7,000
SALES (est): 76.9MM **Privately Held**
WEB: www.boskovichfarms.com
SIC: 0723 5812 0161 Crop preparation
services for market; eating places; rooted
vegetable farms; lettuce & leaf vegetable
farms

(P-472)
CAL CITRUS PACKING CO
111 N Mount Vernon Ave, Lindsay
(93247-2438)
P.O. Box 637 (93247-0637)
PHONE..........................559 562-2536
Jerry Luallen, *President*
▼ EMP: 68
SQ FT: 30,000
SALES (est): 5.3MM **Privately Held**
WEB: www.calcitruspacking.com
SIC: 0723 Fruit (fresh) packing services

(P-473)
**CAL TREEHOUSE ALMONDS
LLC**
2115 Road 144, Delano (93215-9524)
P.O. Box 286 (93216-0286)
PHONE..........................661 725-6334
Robert Houston, *President*
EMP: 120
SQ FT: 68,803
SALES (corp-wide): 10.8MM **Privately
Held**
SIC: 0723 Crop preparation services for
market
PA: Treehouse California Almonds Llc
6914 Road 160
Earlimart CA 93219
559 757-5020

(P-474)
**CALIFORNIA ARTICHOKE &
VEGETAB**
Also Called: Ocean Mist Farms
10855 Ocean Mist Pkwy, Castroville
(95012-3232)
PHONE..........................831 633-2144
Edward Boutonnet, *President*
Albert Pieri, *Shareholder*
Phillip Taluban, *CFO*
Don Reasons, *Treasurer*
Dale Huss, *Vice Pres*
EMP: 60
SALES (est): 15.4MM **Privately Held**
WEB: www.oceanmist.com
SIC: 0723 Vegetable packing services

(P-475)
CARMEL VALLEY PACKING INC
26965 Encinal Rd, Salinas (93908-9539)
P.O. Box 3723 (93912-3723)
PHONE..........................831 771-8860
Oscar Gardea, *President*
EMP: 150

SALES (est): 3MM **Privately Held**
SIC: 0723 Vegetable packing services

(P-476)
**CENTRAL VALLEY AG TRNSPT
INC**
Also Called: Central Valley AG Transload
5509 Langworth Rd, Oakdale
(95361-7909)
PHONE..........................209 544-9246
Michael Barry, *President*
Ryan Hogan, *CFO*
Paul Konzen, *Admin Sec*
EMP: 93
SALES (est): 8.3MM
SALES (corp-wide): 24.5MM **Privately
Held**
SIC: 0723 1629 Field crops, except cash
grains, market preparation services; rail-
road & railway roadbed construction
PA: Central Valley Ag Grinding, Inc.
5509 Langworth Rd
Oakdale CA 95361
209 869-1721

(P-477)
CHOOLJIAN & SONS INC (PA)
Also Called: Del Rey Packing Co
5287 S Del Rey Ave, Del Rey (93616)
P.O. Box 160 (93616-0160)
PHONE..........................559 888-2031
Gerald Chooljian, *CEO*
Courtney Chooljian, *Corp Secy*
▼ EMP: 70
SQ FT: 14,400
SALES (est): 29.1MM **Privately Held**
SIC: 0723 2034 Fruit (farm-dried) packing
services; raisins

(P-478)
CIBUS GLOBAL LTD
6455 Nancy Ridge Dr, San Diego
(92121-2249)
PHONE..........................858 450-0008
Peter Beetham, *President*
Rory Riggs, *Ch of Bd*
Jim Hinrichs, *CFO*
Gerhard Prante, *Vice Ch Bd*
Greg Gocal, *Exec VP*
EMP: 134
SQ FT: 53,000
SALES: 2.6MM **Privately Held**
SIC: 0723 Crop preparation services for
market

(P-479)
**CORONA - COLLEGE HEIGHTS
ORA**
8000 Lincoln Ave, Riverside (92504-4343)
PHONE..........................951 359-6451
John Demshki, *President*
Jennie Sistos, *Controller*
Keith French, *Export Mgr*
Lupe Barajas, *Sales Staff*
Betty Arreola, *Manager*
▼ EMP: 300 EST: 1905
SQ FT: 180,000
SALES (est): 42.4MM **Privately Held**
WEB: www.cchcitrus.com
SIC: 0723 Fruit (fresh) packing services

(P-480)
CRISP WAREHOUSE INC
Also Called: Crisp California Walnuts
20500 Main St, Stratford (93266-9758)
P.O. Box 490, Lemoore (93245-0490)
PHONE..........................559 947-9221
James R Crisp, *President*
Stacie Annon, *CFO*
◆ EMP: 67
SQ FT: 50,000
SALES (est): 5.5MM **Privately Held**
SIC: 0723 Walnut hulling & shelling serv-
ices

(P-481)
DESERT VALLEY DATE INC
86740 Industrial Way, Coachella
(92236-2718)
PHONE..........................760 398-0999
George Kirkjan, *President*
Tamara Kirkjan, *Vice Pres*
◆ EMP: 50
SQ FT: 42,000

SALES (est): 9.7MM **Privately Held**
WEB: www.desertvalleydate.com
SIC: 0723 Crop preparation services for
market

(P-482)
DOLE FRESH VEGETABLES INC
16199 9th St, Huron (93234)
PHONE..........................559 945-2591
Luis Perez, *Principal*
EMP: 118
SALES (corp-wide): 1.1B **Privately Held**
SIC: 0723 Crop preparation services for
market
HQ: Dole Fresh Vegetables, Inc.
2959 Salinas Hwy
Monterey CA 93940
831 422-8871

(P-483)
EARTHBOUND FARM LLC (DH)
Also Called: Taylor Farms
1721 San Juan Hwy, San Juan Bautista
(95045-9780)
PHONE..........................831 623-7880
Cristina Eisenhard,
Marlene Culberson, *Executive Asst*
Veronica Sanchez, *Human Resources*
Katie Seldomridge, *Purch Mgr*
Sonia Manzo, *Opers Staff*
◆ EMP: 995
SQ FT: 15,000
SALES (est): 348.7MM **Privately Held**
SIC: 0723 2037 2099 Vegetable packing
services; fruit crops market preparation
services; frozen fruits & vegetables; food
preparations
HQ: Taylor Farms California, Inc.
150 Main St Ste 500
Salinas CA 93901
831 754-0471

(P-484)
EXETER ENGINEERING INC
Also Called: TTI Technologies
109 W Pine St, Exeter (93221-1612)
P.O. Box 457 (93221-0457)
PHONE..........................559 592-3161
Jeffrey Batchman, *CEO*
Boomer Batchman, *General Mgr*
Jack Bedwell, *General Mgr*
Stephanie Reynoso, *Purchasing*
Carlotta Spurger, *Purchasing*
▲ EMP: 70
SQ FT: 20,000
SALES (est): 17.5MM **Privately Held**
SIC: 0723 Vegetable sorting services; fruit
sorting services

(P-485)
EXETER PACKERS INC (PA)
Also Called: Sun Pacific Packers
1250 E Myer Ave, Exeter (93221-9345)
P.O. Box 217 (93221-0217)
PHONE..........................559 592-5168
Berne H Evans III, *CEO*
Robert Reniers, *President*
Ernie Larsen, *CFO*
Jeanne Wilkinson, *Controller*
Heidi Hill, *Clerk*
◆ EMP: 585
SQ FT: 70,000
SALES (est): 57.6MM **Privately Held**
SIC: 0723 Fruit (fresh) packing services

(P-486)
EXETER PACKERS INC
Also Called: Euclid Parking
23744 Avenue 181, Porterville
(93257-9579)
PHONE..........................559 784-8820
Lenard Shelton, *General Mgr*
EMP: 150
SALES (corp-wide): 57.6MM **Privately
Held**
SIC: 0723 Fruit (fresh) packing services
PA: Exeter Packers, Inc.
1250 E Myer Ave
Exeter CA 93221
559 592-5168

(P-487)
EXETER-IVANHOE CITRUS ASSN
901 Rocky Hill Dr, Exeter (93221-1322)
PHONE..........................559 592-3141
Kevin Riddle, *President*

Terry Orr, *General Mgr*
Joey Martinez, *Supervisor*
EMP: 75
SQ FT: 30,000
SALES (est): 12.1MM **Privately Held**
WEB: www.exetercitrus.com
SIC: 0723 Fruit (fresh) packing services

(P-488)
FAIR TRADE CORNER INC
11591 Meridian Rd, Chico (95973-9601)
PHONE..........................530 566-1405
D N Wadhwa, *President*
Mohnish Seth, *CFO*
▼ EMP: 50
SALES (est): 3.4MM **Privately Held**
SIC: 0723 0173 5145 Almond hulling &
shelling services; almond grove; nuts,
salted or roasted

(P-489)
FIENO INC
11583 Big Canyon Ln, San Diego
(92131-4308)
PHONE..........................760 352-2996
EMP: 55
SALES (est): 3.4MM **Privately Held**
SIC: 0723

(P-490)
FISHER RANCH LLC
10610 Ice Plant Rd, Blythe (92225-2757)
PHONE..........................760 922-4151
Dana B Fisher,
Meloni Carnes, *Manager*
Mike George, *Manager*
EMP: 99
SALES: 17.1MM **Privately Held**
SIC: 0723 Field crops, except cash grains,
market preparation services

(P-491)
**FOWLER PACKING COMPANY
INC**
Also Called: Telemarketing
8570 S Cedar Ave, Fresno (93725-8905)
PHONE..........................559 834-5911
Dennis Parnagian, *CEO*
Randy Parnagian, *Treasurer*
Kenneth Parnagian, *Vice Pres*
Philip Parnagian, *Admin Sec*
◆ EMP: 125
SQ FT: 6,300
SALES (est): 57.6MM **Privately Held**
WEB: www.fowlerpacking.com
SIC: 0723 4783 5148 Fruit (fresh) pack-
ing services; packing & crating; fresh
fruits & vegetables

(P-492)
GILLETTE CITRUS COMPANY
10175 S Anchor Ave, Dinuba (93618-9204)
PHONE..........................559 626-4236
Jay Gillette, *Partner*
Dean Gillette, *Partner*
Mark Gillette, *Partner*
EMP: 60
SQ FT: 14,000
SALES (est): 5.8MM **Privately Held**
SIC: 0723 Fruit (fresh) packing services

(P-493)
GOLDEN VALLEY CITRUS INC
19875 Meredith Dr, Strathmore
(93267-9691)
P.O. Box L (93267-4012)
PHONE..........................559 568-1768
Martine Mittman, *President*
Gerald Denni, *Vice Pres*
EMP: 75
SQ FT: 25,000
SALES (est): 13.2MM **Privately Held**
SIC: 0723 Fruit (fresh) packing services

(P-494)
GRIDLEY PACKING INC
1366 Larkin Rd, Gridley (95948-9708)
PHONE..........................530 846-3753
James D Sanderson, *President*
Becky Sanderson, *Vice Pres*
▲ EMP: 150
SQ FT: 25,800
SALES (est): 2.6MM **Privately Held**
SIC: 0723 Fruit (fresh) packing services

PRODUCTS & SVCS

(P-495)
GRIMMWAY ENTERPRISES INC
6101 S Zerker Rd, Shafter (93263-9611)
P.O. Box 81498, Bakersfield (93380-1498)
PHONE..................................661 393-3320
Bob Grimm, *Principal*
EMP: 233
SALES (corp-wide): 1.8B **Privately Held**
SIC: 0723 Vegetable packing services
PA: Grimmway Enterprises, Inc.
　　14141 Di Giorgio Rd
　　Arvin CA 93203
　　800 301-3101

(P-496)
GRIMMWAY ENTERPRISES INC
Also Called: Grimmway Frozen Foods
830 Sycamore Rd, Arvin (93203-2132)
P.O. Box 81498, Bakersfield (93380-1498)
PHONE..................................661 854-6250
Brandon Grimm, *Manager*
EMP: 400
SALES (corp-wide): 1.8B **Privately Held**
SIC: 0723 Vegetable packing services
PA: Grimmway Enterprises, Inc.
　　14141 Di Giorgio Rd
　　Arvin CA 93203
　　800 301-3101

(P-497)
GRIMMWAY ENTERPRISES INC
Also Called: Grimmway Farms
11412 Malaga Rd, Arvin (93203-9641)
P.O. Box 81498, Bakersfield (93380-1498)
PHONE..................................661 854-6200
Brian Manson, *Programmer Anys*
Dulce Fernandez, *Personnel*
Gerado Raya, *Purch Mgr*
Matthew Hammons, *Buyer*
Hector Pacheco, *Opers Mgr*
EMP: 100
SALES (corp-wide): 1.8B **Privately Held**
SIC: 0723 4783 Vegetable packing services; containerization of goods for shipping
PA: Grimmway Enterprises, Inc.
　　14141 Di Giorgio Rd
　　Arvin CA 93203
　　800 301-3101

(P-498)
GRIMMWAY ENTERPRISES INC
Also Called: Grimmway Farms
6900 Mountain View Rd, Bakersfield
(93307-9627)
P.O. Box 81498 (93380-1498)
PHONE..................................661 845-5200
Bob Grimm, *Owner*
Mike Anspach, *Vice Pres*
Jeff Meger, *Vice Pres*
Margaret Palmerin, *Admin Asst*
Gary Bumgarner, *Info Tech Dir*
EMP: 200
SALES (corp-wide): 1.8B **Privately Held**
SIC: 0723 Vegetable packing services
PA: Grimmway Enterprises, Inc.
　　14141 Di Giorgio Rd
　　Arvin CA 93203
　　800 301-3101

(P-499)
GROWER DIRECT NUT COMPANY INC
2288 Geer Rd, Hughson (95326-9614)
PHONE..................................209 883-4890
Aaron Martella, *President*
Kevin Chiesa, *COO*
Danny Jenkins, *Vice Pres*
Lucio Salazar, *Vice Pres*
Jennifer Martella, *Admin Sec*
▼ EMP: 50
SALES (est): 47.8MM **Privately Held**
WEB: www.grower-direct.com
SIC: 0723 Walnut hulling & shelling services

(P-500)
GROWERS STREET COOLING LLC
1080 Growers St, Salinas (93901-4445)
P.O. Box 2162 (93902-2162)
PHONE..................................831 424-2929
Ronald Mondo, *Mng Member*
EMP: 53
SQ FT: 20,000
SALES (est): 7.2MM **Privately Held**
SIC: 0723 Vegetable precooling services

(P-501)
GUERRA NUT SHELLING COMPANY
190 Hillcrest Rd, Hollister (95023-4944)
P.O. Box 1117 (95024-1117)
PHONE..................................831 637-4471
Frank Guerra, *President*
Jeff Guerra, *CFO*
▼ EMP: 55
SQ FT: 20,000
SALES (est): 8.1MM **Privately Held**
WEB: www.guerranut.com
SIC: 0723 Walnut hulling & shelling services

(P-502)
HARRIS WOOLF CAL ALMONDS LLC
26060 Colusa Ave, Coalinga (93210-9245)
P.O. Box 49, Ballico (95303-0049)
PHONE..................................559 884-2147
Joel Perkins, *CEO*
Stuart Woolf, *Managing Prtnr*
Brian Staggs, *CFO*
◆ EMP: 150
SQ FT: 110,000
SALES (est): 54.5MM **Privately Held**
WEB: www.harriswoolfalmonds.com
SIC: 0723 Tree nut crops market preparation services; almond hulling & shelling services

(P-503)
HILLTOP RANCH INC
Also Called: Hilltop Trading
13890 Looney Rd, Ballico (95303-9710)
PHONE..................................209 874-1875
David Harrison Long, *CEO*
Brad Filbrun, *CFO*
Christine Long, *Vice Pres*
Dave Long Jr, *Vice Pres*
Dexter Long, *Vice Pres*
◆ EMP: 175
SQ FT: 134,800
SALES (est): 45MM **Privately Held**
WEB: www.hilltopranch.com
SIC: 0723 5441 Almond hulling & shelling services; candy, nut & confectionery stores

(P-504)
HILLTOWN PACKING CO INC
9 Harris Pl A, Salinas (93901-4586)
PHONE..................................831 784-1931
Chris Huntington, *President*
Louis Huntington Sr, *Shareholder*
Louis Huntington Jr, *Treasurer*
▼ EMP: 300
SALES (est): 30.3MM **Privately Held**
SIC: 0723 Vegetable packing services

(P-505)
INDEX FRESH INC (PA)
3880 Lemon St Ste 210, Riverside
(92501-3355)
PHONE..................................909 877-0999
Dana L Thomas, *President*
Giovanni Cavaletto, *COO*
Merrill Causey, *CFO*
Todd Elder, *Chief Mktg Ofcr*
Lorena Dominguez, *Vice Pres*
◆ EMP: 52
SQ FT: 40,000
SALES (est): 199.9MM **Privately Held**
WEB: www.indexfresh.com
SIC: 0723 Crop preparation services for market

(P-506)
J G BOSWELL COMPANY
Also Called: Processing Office
710 Bainum Ave, Corcoran (93212-9603)
P.O. Box 457 (93212-0457)
PHONE..................................559 992-2141
John Colborn, *COO*
Neal R Hegarty, *Vice Pres*
Darren Osterland, *General Mgr*
Janice Salgado, *Info Tech Mgr*
Dominick Impemba, *Controller*
EMP: 100
SALES (corp-wide): 594.5MM **Privately Held**
SIC: 0723 Crop preparation services for market
PA: J. G. Boswell Company
　　101 W Walnut St
　　Pasadena CA 91103
　　626 583-3000

(P-507)
JLG HARVESTING INC
27 Zabala Rd, Salinas (93908-7702)
P.O. Box 5205, Yuma AZ (85366-2461)
PHONE..................................831 422-7871
Jose Luis Garcia, *President*
EMP: 400 **Privately Held**
SIC: 0723 Crop preparation services for market
PA: Jlg Harvesting, Inc.
　　1450 S Atlantic Ave
　　Yuma AZ 85365

(P-508)
KERN RIDGE GROWERS LLC
25429 Barbara St, Arvin (93203-9748)
P.O. Box 455 (93203-0455)
PHONE..................................661 854-3141
Robert Giragosian,
▼ EMP: 500
SQ FT: 53,000
SALES: 43.2MM **Privately Held**
WEB: www.kernridge.com
SIC: 0723 5148 Vegetable packing services; vegetables, fresh

(P-509)
KIRSCHENMAN PACKING INC
12826 Edison Hwy, Edison (93220)
PHONE..................................661 366-5736
Wayne Kirschenman, *President*
Paul Sandoval, *Shareholder*
Herb Spitzer, *Vice Pres*
EMP: 120 EST: 1982
SQ FT: 25,000
SALES (est): 4.4MM **Privately Held**
SIC: 0723 Vegetable packing services

(P-510)
KLINK CITRUS ASSOCIATION
Also Called: Klink Citrus Exchange
32921 Road 159, Ivanhoe (93235-1455)
P.O. Box 188 (93235-0188)
PHONE..................................559 798-1881
Eric Meling, *CEO*
EMP: 170 EST: 1917
SQ FT: 50,000
SALES (est): 17MM **Privately Held**
SIC: 0723 Fruit (fresh) packing services

(P-511)
LIMONEIRA COMPANY (PA)
1141 Cummings Rd Ofc, Santa Paula
(93060-9783)
PHONE..................................805 525-5541
Harold S Edwards, *President*
Gordon E Kimball, *Ch of Bd*
Mark Palamountain, *CFO*
Robert M Sawyer, *Vice Ch Bd*
Ramon Cardenas, *Officer*
◆ EMP: 177
SALES: 129.3MM **Publicly Held**
WEB: www.limoneira.com
SIC: 0723 0174 0179 6531 Fruit (fresh) packing services; citrus fruits; lemon grove; orange grove; avocado orchard; real estate agents & managers; real estate leasing & rentals; commodity investors

(P-512)
LO BUE BROS INC
Also Called: Lo Bue Bros East
713 E Hermosa St, Lindsay (93247-2204)
PHONE..................................559 562-6367
EMP: 200
SALES (corp-wide): 40.7MM **Privately Held**
SIC: 0723 5148 0174
PA: Lo Bue Bros., Inc.
　　201 S Sweetbriar Ave
　　Lindsay CA 93247
　　559 562-2548

(P-513)
MAGARRO FARMS
23322 Peralta Dr Ste 3, Laguna Hills
(92653-1713)
PHONE..................................949 859-6506
John Magarro, *Owner*
EMP: 80
SQ FT: 30,000
SALES (est): 3.4MM **Privately Held**
SIC: 0723 0171 Fruit precooling services; strawberry farm

(P-514)
MANN PACKING CO INC (DH)
1333 Schilling Pl, Salinas (93901-4535)
P.O. Box 690 (93902-0690)
PHONE..................................831 422-7405
Lorri Koster, *CEO*
Michael Jarrod, *President*
William Beaton, *CFO*
Richard Ramsey, *Chairman*
EMP: 450
SQ FT: 90,000
SALES (est): 212MM **Privately Held**
WEB: www.broccoli.com
SIC: 0723 4783 0722 Vegetable packing services; packing & crating; crop harvesting
HQ: Del Monte Fresh Produce N.A., Inc.
　　241 Sevilla Ave
　　Coral Gables FL 33134
　　305 520-8400

(P-515)
MARIANI PACKING CO INC (PA)
500 Crocker Dr, Vacaville (95688-8706)
PHONE..................................707 452-2800
Mark A Mariani, *CEO*
George Sousa Jr, *Vice Chairman*
Marian Ciabattari, *Corp Secy*
Craig Mackley, *Exec VP*
Paul Mariani, *Exec VP*
◆ EMP: 275 EST: 1982
SALES (est): 120.1MM **Privately Held**
WEB: www.marianifruit.com
SIC: 0723 2034 5148 Fruit (farm-dried) packing services; fruit drying services; dried & dehydrated fruits; fresh fruits & vegetables

(P-516)
MONARCH NUT COMPANY LLC
Also Called: Munger Farms
786 Road 188, Delano (93215-9508)
PHONE..................................661 725-6458
Kamie Munger, *Mng Member*
David Munger,
◆ EMP: 250 EST: 1986
SQ FT: 20,000
SALES (est): 51.8MM **Privately Held**
WEB: www.mungerfarms.com
SIC: 0723 Tree nuts (general) hulling & shelling services

(P-517)
MONTPELIER ORCHARDS MGT CO INC
Montpelier Nut Company
4931 S Montpelier Rd, Denair
(95316-9663)
PHONE..................................209 883-4079
Lupe Dalvinos, *Manager*
EMP: 50
SALES (corp-wide): 7.3MM **Privately Held**
SIC: 0723 Crop preparation services for market
PA: Montpelier Orchards Management Company, Inc.
　　1131 12th St
　　Modesto CA 95354
　　209 577-2804

(P-518)
MOONEY FARMS
1220 Fortress St, Chico (95973-9029)
PHONE..................................530 899-2661
Mary Mooney, *President*
Steve Mooney, *Vice Pres*
Steve Lansdown, *QC Mgr*
▲ EMP: 50
SQ FT: 100,000

▲ = Import ▼=Export
◆ =Import/Export

SALES (est): 30.8MM **Privately Held**
WEB: www.mooneyfarms.com
SIC: 0723 2034 2033 Fruit crops market preparation services; dried & dehydrated fruits; canned fruits & specialties

(P-519)
MORADA PRODUCE COMPANY LP
500 N Jack Tone Rd, Stockton (95215-9725)
P.O. Box 659, Linden (95236-0659)
PHONE..........................209 546-0426
Henry Foppiano, *Partner*
Sandy Haswell, *CFO*
Wendy Day, *Opers Staff*
Ana Garibay, *Director*
Linda Jenkins, *Manager*
◆ EMP: 1500
SQ FT: 98,000
SALES (est): 57.6MM **Privately Held**
SIC: 0723 Fruit (fresh) packing services; vegetable packing services

(P-520)
NATIONAL CUSTOM PACKING INC
13526 Blackie Rd, Castroville (95012-3212)
PHONE..........................831 724-2026
Jonathon Thornton, *President*
Fred J Haas, *Ch of Bd*
Ron Marker, *CFO*
Louise McNary, *Corp Secy*
Nenita Victory, *QC Mgr*
EMP: 50
SQ FT: 12,000
SALES (est): 5.6MM
SALES (corp-wide): 384MM **Privately Held**
WEB: www.nationalpacking.com
SIC: 0723 Fruit (fresh) packing services
PA: The Vps Companies Inc
310 Walker St
Watsonville CA 95076
831 724-7551

(P-521)
NEWSTAR FRESH FOODS LLC
126 Sun St, Salinas (93901-3751)
PHONE..........................831 758-7800
Brian McLaughlin, *Controller*
EMP: 100
SALES (corp-wide): 75MM **Privately Held**
WEB: www.newstarfreshfoods.com
SIC: 0723 Vegetable crops market preparation services
PA: Newstar Fresh Foods, Llc
850 Work St Ste 101
Salinas CA 93901
888 782-7220

(P-522)
NORALCO INC
Also Called: H Naraghi Farms
20001 Mchenry Ave, Escalon (95320-9614)
P.O. Box 602, Denair (95316-0602)
PHONE..........................209 551-4545
Haslem Naraghi, *President*
◆ EMP: 125
SQ FT: 120,000
SALES (est): 3.1MM **Privately Held**
SIC: 0723 5145 Almond hulling & shelling services; walnut hulling & shelling services; nuts, salted or roasted

(P-523)
NUNES COOLING INC
925 Johnson Ave, Salinas (93901-4327)
P.O. Box 1585 (93902-1585)
PHONE..........................831 751-7510
Frank R Nunes Jr, *President*
Mike Scarr, *CFO*
EMP: 50
SALES (est): 4.5MM **Privately Held**
SIC: 0723 Vacuum cooling

(P-524)
OLAM AMERICAS INC (DH)
25 Union Pl Ste 3, Fresno (93720)
PHONE..........................559 447-1390
Gregory C Estep, *CEO*
Amanda Lakin, *Executive Asst*
Jim Hastings, *Research*
Mihir Vasavada, *Research*

Narinder Palsingh, *Engineer*
◆ EMP: 1000
SALES (est): 1.4B
SALES (corp-wide): 22.2B **Privately Held**
SIC: 0723 Crop preparation services for market
HQ: Olam Us Holdings Inc
2077 Convention Ctr 150
College Park GA 30337
404 209-2676

(P-525)
OLAM WEST COAST INC (DH)
Also Called: Olam Spces Vgtable Ingredients
205 E Rver Pk Pl Ste 3, Fresno (93720)
PHONE..........................559 447-1390
John Gibbons, *President*
James Fenn, *Vice Pres*
Kazuo Ito, *Exec Dir*
Yutaka Kyoya, *Exec Dir*
Sanjiv Misra, *Exec Dir*
◆ EMP: 188
SALES (est): 476.2MM
SALES (corp-wide): 22.2B **Privately Held**
SIC: 0723 Crop preparation services for market

(P-526)
OMEGA WALNUT INC
7233 County Road 24, Orland (95963-9777)
PHONE..........................530 865-0136
Todd J Southam, *CEO*
Marsha Squier, *Office Mgr*
◆ EMP: 50
SALES (est): 7MM **Privately Held**
SIC: 0723 Walnut hulling & shelling services

(P-527)
PEARL CROP INC (PA)
Also Called: Linden Nut
1550 Industrial Dr, Stockton (95206-3929)
PHONE..........................209 808-7575
Halil Ulas Turkhan, *President*
Hulya Dayac, *Shareholder*
Negaar Turkhan, *Vice Pres*
Marcelino Martinez, *Manager*
Jared Britschgi, *Representative*
◆ EMP: 75 EST: 2007
SQ FT: 126,000
SALES: 140MM **Privately Held**
SIC: 0723 Crop preparation services for market

(P-528)
PHELAN & TAYLOR PRODUCE CO
1860 Pacific Coast Hwy, Oceano (93445)
P.O. Box 458 (93475-0458)
PHONE..........................805 489-2413
John Taylor, *President*
EMP: 150
SQ FT: 20,000
SALES (est): 5.9MM **Privately Held**
SIC: 0723 0161 4213 Crop preparation services for market; vegetables & melons; trucking, except local

(P-529)
R & N PACKING CO
47920 W Nees Ave, Firebaugh (93622-9593)
P.O. Box 130, Turlock (95381-0130)
PHONE..........................209 364-6101
Leo Rolandelli, *President*
EMP: 250
SALES (est): 7.5MM **Privately Held**
SIC: 0723 Vegetable packing services

(P-530)
RAMCO ENTERPRISES LP
Also Called: Ramco Employment Services
520 E 3rd St Ste B, Oxnard (93030-0182)
PHONE..........................805 486-9328
Jesse Espinoza, *Branch Mgr*
EMP: 743
SALES (corp-wide): 85MM **Privately Held**
SIC: 0723 Crop preparation services for market
PA: Ramco Enterprises, L.P.
710 La Guardia St
Salinas CA 93905
831 758-5272

(P-531)
READY ROAST NUT COMPANY LLC (PA)
Also Called: Madera Quality Nut
2805 Falcon Dr, Madera (93637-9287)
PHONE..........................559 661-1696
Thomas Finn, *Mng Member*
Silvanna Camacho, *Admin Asst*
Vern Simmons, *Controller*
David Wissing, *Opers Staff*
Tyler Angle,
◆ EMP: 75
SQ FT: 144,000
SALES (est): 16.2MM **Privately Held**
SIC: 0723 Tree nut crops market preparation services

(P-532)
RED TOP RICE GROWERS
3200 8th St, Biggs (95917-9623)
P.O. Box 477 (95917-0477)
PHONE..........................530 868-5975
John Adams, *President*
Doug Rudd, *Corp Secy*
Mike Caliendo, *Vice Pres*
Steve Cribari, *Vice Pres*
Sam Furno, *Vice Pres*
EMP: 50
SALES (est): 5.2MM **Privately Held**
SIC: 0723 Rice drying services

(P-533)
REDLANDS FOOTHILL GROVES
304 9th St, Redlands (92374-3404)
PHONE..........................909 793-2164
Robert Knight, *Plant Mgr*
EMP: 50
SQ FT: 48,000
SALES (est): 7.1MM **Privately Held**
SIC: 0723 Fruit (fresh) packing services

(P-534)
REDWOOD EMPIRE PACKING INC
8801 Old River Rd, Ukiah (95482-9659)
PHONE..........................707 462-5521
Randall Ruddick, *President*
EMP: 150
SALES (est): 6.9MM **Privately Held**
SIC: 0723 Fruit (fresh) packing services

(P-535)
RIVER MAID LAND CO A CAL LI (PA)
6011 E Pine St, Lodi (95240-0815)
P.O. Box 350 (95241-0350)
PHONE..........................209 369-3586
Chiles Wilson, *President*
Brian Machado, *Marketing Staff*
EMP: 340
SALES (est): 10.6MM **Privately Held**
SIC: 0723 Fruit (fresh) packing services; vegetable packing services

(P-536)
S & J RANCHES LLC
39639 Avenue 10, Madera (93636-8845)
PHONE..........................559 437-2600
James M Burkhart,
Jim Burkhart,
Kevin Olsen,
EMP: 60 EST: 1950
SQ FT: 5,133
SALES (est): 2.3MM
SALES (corp-wide): 1.5B **Privately Held**
WEB: www.paramountcitrus.com
SIC: 0723 0762 Fruit (fresh) packing services; citrus grove management & maintenance services
HQ: Wonderful Citrus Packing Llc
1901 S Lexington St
Delano CA 93215
661 720-2400

(P-537)
S STAMOULES INC
Also Called: Stamoules Produce Co
904 S Lyon Ave, Mendota (93640-9735)
PHONE..........................559 655-9777
Peggy Stefanopoulos, *President*
Chrisopher S Stefanopoulos, *Treasurer*
Danny Stefanopoulos, *Vice Pres*
Tom Stefanopoulos, *Vice Pres*
Elena Stefanopoulos, *Admin Sec*
▼ EMP: 1000

SQ FT: 40,000
SALES (est): 100MM **Privately Held**
WEB: www.stamoules.com
SIC: 0723 Fruit (fresh) packing services; vegetable packing services

(P-538)
SAN JOAQUIN FIGS INC
Also Called: Nutra-Figs
3564 N Hazel Ave, Fresno (93722-4912)
P.O. Box 9547 (93793-9547)
PHONE..........................559 224-4492
Keith Jura, *President*
Mary Jura, *Corp Secy*
Roy Jura,
◆ EMP: 50
SQ FT: 18,000
SALES (est): 9.3MM **Privately Held**
WEB: www.nutrafig.com
SIC: 0723 Fruit (fresh) packing services

(P-539)
SATICOY LEMON ASSOCIATION (PA)
Also Called: Saticoy Fruit Exchange
103 N Peck Rd, Santa Paula (93060-3099)
P.O. Box 46 (93061-0046)
PHONE..........................805 654-6500
Glenn A Miller, *President*
Jerry Pogorzelski, *CFO*
Jima Garrett, *Admin Sec*
Marty Coert, *Opers Mgr*
Raul Arias, *Plant Mgr*
▲ EMP: 100 EST: 1933
SALES: 171MM **Privately Held**
SIC: 0723 Fruit (fresh) packing services

(P-540)
SEED DYNAMICS INC
1081b Harkins Rd, Salinas (93901-4406)
P.O. Box 6069 (93912-6069)
PHONE..........................831 424-1177
David Holly, *CEO*
Curtis J Vaughan, *COO*
Mel Bachman, *Risk Mgmt Dir*
Henry Rede, *Prdtn Mgr*
EMP: 53
SQ FT: 34,000
SALES (est): 6.4MM **Privately Held**
WEB: www.seeddynamics.com
SIC: 0723 3999 Crop preparation services for market; seeds, coated or treated, from purchased seeds

(P-541)
SEQUOIA ORANGE CO INC (PA)
150 W Pine St, Exeter (93221-1699)
PHONE..........................559 592-9455
Marvin Wilson, *President*
Oleah Wilson, *Treasurer*
Linda Pescosolido, *Vice Pres*
EMP: 100
SQ FT: 5,100
SALES (est): 9.2MM **Privately Held**
WEB: www.sequoiaorange.com
SIC: 0723 5148 Fruit (fresh) packing services; fresh fruits & vegetables

(P-542)
SIMONIAN BROTHERS INC (PA)
Also Called: Simonian Fruit
511 N 7th St, Fowler (93625-2331)
P.O. Box 340 (93625-0340)
PHONE..........................559 834-5921
David Simonian, *Ch of Bd*
Harold J Simonian, *President*
James P Simonian, *Treasurer*
Jeffery Simoninan, *Admin Sec*
▼ EMP: 54 EST: 1960
SQ FT: 70,000
SALES (est): 20.6MM **Privately Held**
WEB: www.simonianfruit.com
SIC: 0723 Fruit (fresh) packing services

(P-543)
SUMA FRUIT INTL USA INC
1810 Academy Ave, Sanger (93657-3739)
PHONE..........................559 875-5000
Ralph Hackett, *CEO*
▼ EMP: 50
SQ FT: 60,000
SALES (est): 3.8MM **Privately Held**
SIC: 0723 Fruit (fresh) packing services

HQ: Del Monte Fresh Produce N.A., Inc.
　241 Sevilla Ave
　Coral Gables FL 33134
　305 520-8400

(P-544)
SUN PACIFIC MARICOPA
Also Called: Maricopa Packers
31452 Old River Rd, Bakersfield
(93311-9621)
PHONE.............................661 847-1015
Bern Evans, *Managing Prtnr*
EMP: 400
SQ FT: 450,000
SALES (est): 23.2MM **Privately Held**
SIC: 0723 Fruit (fresh) packing services

(P-545)
SUN RICH FRESH FOODS USA INC (HQ)
515 E Rincon St, Corona (92879-1391)
PHONE.............................951 735-3800
Brian Tieszen, *President*
Carl Svangtun, *President*
Neville Israel, *CFO*
▲ EMP: 65
SQ FT: 33,000
SALES (est): 30.9MM
SALES (corp-wide): 584.8MM **Privately Held**
SIC: 0723 Fruit (fresh) packing services
PA: Sun Rich Fresh Foods Inc
　22151 Fraserwood Way
　Richmond BC V6W 1
　604 244-8800

(P-546)
SUN WORLD INTERNATIONAL INC (PA)
16351 Driver Rd, Bakersfield (93308-9733)
P.O. Box 80298 (93380-0298)
PHONE.............................661 392-5000
Keith Brackpool, *Ch of Bd*
Timothy J Shaheen, *CEO*
Nicole Palmer, *Executive Asst*
Ron Schuh, *CTO*
Sharon Moore, *Info Tech Mgr*
◆ EMP: 1500
SQ FT: 160,000
SALES (est): 375.6MM **Privately Held**
SIC: 0723 0172 0174 0175 Vegetable crops market preparation services; vegetable packing services; grapes; citrus fruits; deciduous tree fruits; date orchard; mango grove; melon farms; pepper farm, sweet & hot (vegetables)

(P-547)
SUN WORLD INTERNATIONAL INC
52200 Industrial Way, Coachella
(92236-2705)
P.O. Box 1028 (92236-1028)
PHONE.............................760 398-9300
Dave Margulas, *General Mgr*
EMP: 500 **Privately Held**
SIC: 0723 Fruit (fresh) packing services
PA: Sun World International, Inc.
　16351 Driver Rd
　Bakersfield CA 93308

(P-548)
SUNKIST GROWERS INC
531 W Poplar Ave, Tipton (93272-9646)
P.O. Box 3720, Ontario (91761-0993)
PHONE.............................909 983-9811
Owen Belletto, *Branch Mgr*
Bob C Atchley, *Vice Pres*
David Robinson, *Engineer*
James Hanlon, *Manager*
EMP: 221
SALES (corp-wide): 1.3B **Privately Held**
WEB: www.sunkist.com
SIC: 0723 5149 2099 Fruit crops market preparation services; juices; food preparations
PA: Sunkist Growers, Inc.
　27770 Entertainment Dr
　Valencia CA 91355
　661 290-8900

(P-549)
SUNKIST GROWERS INC
531 W Poplar Ave, Tipton (93272-9646)
P.O. Box 3720, Ontario (91761-0993)
PHONE.............................559 752-4256
Owen Belletto, *Vice Pres*
EMP: 221
SQ FT: 25,000
SALES (corp-wide): 1.3B **Privately Held**
WEB: www.sunkist.com
SIC: 0723 Fruit crops market preparation services
PA: Sunkist Growers, Inc.
　27770 Entertainment Dr
　Valencia CA 91355
　661 290-8900

(P-550)
TALLEY FARMS
2900 Lopez Dr, Arroyo Grande
(93420-4999)
P.O. Box 360 (93421-0360)
PHONE.............................805 489-2508
Brian Talley, *President*
Todd Talley, *Treasurer*
Rayn Talley, *Vice Pres*
Rosemary Talley, *Admin Sec*
Anibal Escobar, *Director*
EMP: 175
SQ FT: 2,000
SALES (est): 28.4MM **Privately Held**
SIC: 0723 0161 Vegetable packing services; vegetables & melons

(P-551)
TANIMURA & ANTLE INC
Also Called: Salad Time Farms
4401 Foxdale St, Baldwin Park
(91706-2161)
P.O. Box 4070, Salinas (93912-4070)
PHONE.............................831 424-6100
Randy Sipled, *Manager*
EMP: 400
SALES (corp-wide): 750.7MM **Privately Held**
WEB: www.taproduce.com
SIC: 0723 Vegetable packing services
PA: Tanimura & Antle Fresh Foods, Inc.
　1 Harris Rd
　Salinas CA 93908
　831 455-2950

(P-552)
TAYLOR FARMS CALIFORNIA INC (HQ)
150 Main St Ste 500, Salinas (93901-3462)
P.O. Box 1649 (93902-1649)
PHONE.............................831 754-0471
Bruce Taylor, *Owner*
Alec Leach, *President*
Thomas Bryan, *CFO*
Phil Bradway, *Vice Pres*
Mark Campion, *Vice Pres*
◆ EMP: 1500
SALES (est): 505MM **Privately Held**
SIC: 0723 Vegetable crops market preparation services

(P-553)
TAYLOR FRESH FOODS INC (PA)
150 Main St Ste 400, Salinas (93901-3442)
P.O. Box 1649 (93902-1649)
PHONE.............................831 676-9023
Bruce Taylor, *CEO*
Nicole Devincenzo, *Officer*
Ron Guzman, *Vice Pres*
Priscilla Ritchie, *Admin Asst*
Ross Bava, *Research*
◆ EMP: 150
SQ FT: 2,500
SALES: 3B **Privately Held**
SIC: 0723 Vegetable crops market preparation services

(P-554)
TELESIS ONION CO
21484 S Colusa, Five Points (93624)
P.O. Box 690 (93624-0690)
PHONE.............................559 884-2441
Dan Garcia, *Manager*
EMP: 50

SALES (est): 1.6MM
SALES (corp-wide): 6.8MM **Privately Held**
SIC: 0723 Vegetable packing services
PA: Telesis Onion Co
　3265 W Figarden Dr
　Fresno CA 93711
　559 884-2441

(P-555)
TRINITY FRUIT PACKING COMPANY
18700 E South Ave, Reedley (93654-9711)
PHONE.............................559 743-3913
David E White, *President*
▲ EMP: 250
SQ FT: 300,000
SALES: 12MM **Privately Held**
SIC: 0723 Fruit (fresh) packing services

(P-556)
VALLEY FIG GROWERS
2028 S 3rd St, Fresno (93702-4156)
PHONE.............................559 237-3893
Gary Jue, *President*
Paul Mesple, *Chairman*
Linda Cain, *Vice Pres*
Michael N Emigh, *Principal*
Cleo Rodriguez, *Administration*
◆ EMP: 50 EST: 1959
SQ FT: 100,000
SALES (est): 24.8MM **Privately Held**
WEB: www.valleyfig.com
SIC: 0723 2033 Fruit (fresh) packing services; fruits & fruit products in cans, jars, etc.

(P-557)
VASQUEZ BROTHERS INC
Also Called: Central Coast Packing
157 Kidder St, Soledad (93960-3080)
P.O. Box 625 (93960-0625)
PHONE.............................831 678-8894
Carlos Vasquez, *President*
Arturo Vasquez, *Vice Pres*
EMP: 100
SQ FT: 10,000
SALES (est): 8.9MM **Privately Held**
WEB: www.centralcoastpacking.com
SIC: 0723 Vegetable packing services

(P-558)
VENTURA COUNTY LEMON COOPS
Also Called: Ventura Pacific Co
P.O. Box 6986, Oxnard (93031-6986)
PHONE.............................805 385-3345
Donald Dames, *President*
Milton Daily, *Ch of Bd*
Mark Jacobs, *CFO*
Jim Waters, *Treasurer*
James H Gill, *Admin Sec*
EMP: 80 EST: 1943
SQ FT: 87,000
SALES (est): 12.5MM **Privately Held**
WEB: www.venturapacific.net
SIC: 0723 Fruit crops market preparation services

(P-559)
VILLA PARK ORCHARDS ASSN (PA)
Also Called: Villa Park Trucking
960 3rd St, Fillmore (93015-1120)
P.O. Box 307 (93016-0307)
PHONE.............................805 524-0411
Brad Leichtfuss, *President*
Dyan Davis, *Manager*
Frank Rodriguez, *Manager*
EMP: 350
SQ FT: 40,000
SALES (est): 37.9MM **Privately Held**
SIC: 0723 0174 Fruit crops market preparation services; citrus fruits

(P-560)
WAWONA PACKING CO LLC (PA)
12133 Avenue 408, Cutler (93615-2056)
PHONE.............................559 528-4000
Brent Smittcamp, *Mng Member*
Justin Birch, *President*
Georgia Griffin, *Office Mgr*
Stacy Thompson, *Info Tech Dir*
Tara Sondergaard, *Controller*
▼ EMP: 95

SQ FT: 16,000
SALES (est): 206.6MM **Privately Held**
WEB: www.wawonapacking.com
SIC: 0723 Fruit (fresh) packing services

(P-561)
WILBUR PACKING COMPANY INC
1500 Eager Rd, Live Oak (95953)
P.O. Box 3730, Yuba City (95992-3730)
PHONE.............................530 671-4911
Richard G Wilbur, *President*
Randy Baucom, *Vice Pres*
Emily L Friend, *Admin Sec*
◆ EMP: 350
SQ FT: 60,650
SALES (est): 46.1MM **Privately Held**
WEB: www.wilburpacking.com
SIC: 0723 2034 Crop preparation services for market; dehydrated fruits, vegetables, soups

(P-562)
WONDERFUL CITRUS PACKING LLC
36445 Road 172, Visalia (93292-9193)
PHONE.............................559 798-3100
David Smith, *Manager*
EMP: 89
SALES (corp-wide): 1.5B **Privately Held**
WEB: www.paramountcitrus.com
SIC: 0723 0174 Fruit (fresh) packing services; orange grove
HQ: Wonderful Citrus Packing Llc
　1901 S Lexington St
　Delano CA 93215
　661 720-2400

(P-563)
WONDERFUL CITRUS PACKING LLC (HQ)
Also Called: Paramount Citrus Packing Co
1901 S Lexington St, Delano (93215-9207)
PHONE.............................661 720-2400
Craig B Cooper, *Mng Member*
◆ EMP: 273
SQ FT: 400,000
SALES (est): 259.6MM
SALES (corp-wide): 1.5B **Privately Held**
WEB: www.paramountcitrus.com
SIC: 0723 0174 2033 Fruit (fresh) packing services; orange grove; fruit juices: fresh
PA: The Wonderful Company Llc
　11444 W Olympic Blvd # 210
　Los Angeles CA 90064
　310 966-5700

(P-564)
WONDERFUL CITRUS PACKING LLC
710 Del Norte Blvd, Oxnard (93030-8963)
PHONE.............................805 988-1456
Tom Hooten, *Manager*
EMP: 60
SALES (corp-wide): 1.5B **Privately Held**
WEB: www.paramountcitrus.com
SIC: 0723 0174 Fruit (fresh) packing services; citrus fruits
HQ: Wonderful Citrus Packing Llc
　1901 S Lexington St
　Delano CA 93215
　661 720-2400

(P-565)
WONDERFUL COMPANY LLC
5001 California Ave, Bakersfield
(93309-1671)
PHONE.............................559 781-7438
EMP: 806
SALES (corp-wide): 1.5B **Privately Held**
SIC: 0723 Fruit crops market preparation services
PA: The Wonderful Company Llc
　11444 W Olympic Blvd # 210
　Los Angeles CA 90064
　310 966-5700

(P-566)
WONDERFUL COMPANY LLC
11444 W Olympic Blvd # 210, Los Angeles
(90064-1559)
PHONE.............................661 720-2609
Craig B Cooper, *Manager*
EMP: 1613

▲ = Import ▼=Export
◆ =Import/Export

SALES (corp-wide): 1.5B **Privately Held**
SIC: 0723 Fruit (fresh) packing services
PA: The Wonderful Company Llc
   11444 W Olympic Blvd # 210
   Los Angeles CA 90064
   310 966-5700

(P-567)
WONDERFUL COMPANY LLC
6801 E Lerdo Hwy, Shafter (93263-9610)
PHONE.................................661 399-4456
EMP: 806
SALES (corp-wide): 1.5B **Privately Held**
SIC: 0723 Fruit crops market preparation
   services
PA: The Wonderful Company Llc
   11444 W Olympic Blvd # 210
   Los Angeles CA 90064
   310 966-5700

0742 Veterinary Animal Specialties

(P-568)
ACCESS SPCLTY ANIMAL HOSPITALS
9599 Jefferson Blvd, Culver City
(90232-2917)
PHONE.................................310 558-6100
Amy Gram, *Administration*
Shannon Brown, *Mktg Coord*
EMP: 84
SALES (est): 3.4MM **Privately Held**
SIC: 0742 Animal hospital services, pets &
   other animal specialties

(P-569)
ADOBE ANIMAL HOSPITAL INC
4470 El Camino Real, Los Altos
(94022-1003)
PHONE.................................650 948-9661
Dave M Ross, *President*
Jerry Berg, *Vice Pres*
Summer Holmstrand, *Manager*
EMP: 100
SQ FT: 6,577
SALES (est): 9.4MM **Privately Held**
SIC: 0742 Animal hospital services, pets &
   other animal specialties

(P-570)
ADVANCED CRITICAL CARE EMERGE
18601 Hatteras St Apt 326, Tarzana
(91356-1860)
PHONE.................................818 887-2262
Howard Liberson, *CEO*
Richard J Mills, *President*
EMP: 100 EST: 2012
SALES (est): 3.6MM **Privately Held**
SIC: 0742 Animal hospital services, pets &
   other animal specialties

(P-571)
ADVANCED VETERINARY CARE CTR
15926 Hawthorne Blvd, Lawndale
(90260-2644)
PHONE.................................310 542-8018
Bonnie Mc Garr, *Principal*
EMP: 56
SALES (est): 1.7MM **Privately Held**
WEB: www.advancedveterinarycarecen-
   ter.com
SIC: 0742 Animal hospital services, pets &
   other animal specialties

(P-572)
ANIMAL CARE CENTER
Also Called: Constance Dehaan Dvm
6470 Redwood Dr, Rohnert Park
(94928-2326)
PHONE.................................707 584-4343
Constance Dehaan, *Partner*
EMP: 60
SALES (est): 1.1MM **Privately Held**
SIC: 0742 Veterinarian, animal specialties

(P-573)
BISHOP RANCH VETERINARY CENTER (PA)
2000 Bishop Dr, San Ramon (94583-2344)
PHONE.................................925 743-9300

James Delano, *Partner*
Jay Kerr, *Partner*
James Pogrel, *Partner*
Frank Utchen, *Partner*
Dennis Dizon, *Manager*
EMP: 85
SALES (est): 5MM **Privately Held**
SIC: 0742 Animal hospital services, pets &
   other animal specialties

(P-574)
BRADSHAW VETERINARY CLINIC
Also Called: Allison, Amanda Dvm
9609 Bradshaw Rd, Elk Grove
(95624-9490)
PHONE.................................916 685-2494
Michael Johnson, *Ch of Bd*
Thomas Zehnder, *President*
Becky Vanriper, *Manager*
EMP: 75
SQ FT: 8,000
SALES: 3MM **Privately Held**
SIC: 0742 0741 Veterinarian, animal spe-
   cialties; veterinarian, livestock

(P-575)
CAMP BOW WOW FRANCHISING INC
12401 W Olympic Blvd, Los Angeles
(90064-1022)
PHONE.................................310 571-6500
Robert Antin, *President*
EMP: 75
SALES (est): 155.8K
SALES (corp-wide): 37.6B **Privately Held**
SIC: 0742 Veterinary services, specialties
HQ: Vicar Operating, Inc.
   12401 W Olympic Blvd
   Los Angeles CA 90064
   310 571-6500

(P-576)
CONTRA COSTA VET MED EMRGCY CL
1145 Turtle Rock Ln, Concord
(94521-3526)
PHONE.................................925 798-5830
Peter Mangold, *President*
EMP: 50
SQ FT: 3,500
SALES (est): 1.1MM **Privately Held**
SIC: 0742 Animal hospital services, pets &
   other animal specialties

(P-577)
CRUZ VETERINARY HOSPITAL
2585 Soquel Dr, Santa Cruz (95065-1937)
PHONE.................................831 475-5400
Macy Nichols, *Owner*
Terry Cullison, *Manager*
EMP: 80
SALES (est): 1.2MM **Privately Held**
SIC: 0742 Animal hospital services, pets &
   other animal specialties

(P-578)
HAPPY PET CO
Also Called: Very Important Pet Vaccine Svc
5813 Skylane Blvd, Windsor (95492-6836)
PHONE.................................707 586-8660
Will Santana, *CEO*
Ken Pecoraro, *CFO*
EMP: 50
SQ FT: 1,700
SALES (est): 1.2MM **Privately Held**
WEB: www.vipvaccine.com
SIC: 0742 Veterinarian, animal specialties

(P-579)
JAMES I MILLER
Also Called: J I Miller
17659 Chatsworth St, Granada Hills
(91344-5602)
PHONE.................................818 363-7444
James I Miller, *Owner*
EMP: 50 EST: 2001
SALES (est): 463.6K **Privately Held**
SIC: 0742 Veterinarian, animal specialties

(P-580)
MARINE MAMMAL CENTER (PA)
2000 Bunker Rd, Sausalito (94965-2697)
PHONE.................................415 339-0430
Jeffrey Roger Boehm, *CEO*

Marci Davis, *CFO*
Jeff Boehm, *Officer*
Karen Takamoto, *Database Admin*
Hanne Larsen, *Opers Staff*
EMP: 50
SQ FT: 25,000
SALES: 12.4MM **Privately Held**
SIC: 0742 8299 8733 Animal hospital
   services, pets & other animal specialties;
   arts & crafts schools; noncommercial re-
   search organizations

(P-581)
MUELLER PET MEDICAL CENTER
Also Called: Mueller Grooming & Pet Sups
7625 Freeport Blvd, Sacramento
(95832-1084)
PHONE.................................916 428-9202
Ken Schenck, *President*
EMP: 50 EST: 1955
SQ FT: 4,000
SALES (est): 1.9MM **Privately Held**
WEB: www.muellerpmc.com
SIC: 0742 5999 Animal hospital services,
   pets & other animal specialties; pets & pet
   supplies

(P-582)
NATIONAL VETERINARY ASSOC INC
2300 N State St, Ukiah (95482-3128)
PHONE.................................707 462-8625
EMP: 51
SALES (corp-wide): 876MM **Privately Held**
SIC: 0742 Veterinarian, animal specialties;
   animal hospital services, pets & other ani-
   mal specialties
PA: National Veterinary Associates, Inc.
   29229 Canwood St Ste 100
   Agoura Hills CA 91301
   805 777-7722

(P-583)
NATIONAL VETERINARY ASSOC INC (PA)
29229 Canwood St Ste 100, Agoura Hills
(91301-1503)
PHONE.................................805 777-7722
Greg Hartmann, *CEO*
Thomas Sawicki, *COO*
R James Woloshyn, *CFO*
Kevin Schneider, *Vice Pres*
Melissa Saito, *Executive Asst*
EMP: 188
SQ FT: 5,000
SALES (est): 876MM **Privately Held**
SIC: 0742 Animal hospital services, pets &
   other animal specialties

(P-584)
NICHOLAS B MACY DVM
2585 Soquel Dr, Santa Cruz (95065-1937)
PHONE.................................831 475-5400
Nicholas Macy, *Owner*
Jay Stone, *Co-Owner*
EMP: 70 EST: 1950
SALES (est): 950.5K **Privately Held**
SIC: 0742 Veterinarian, animal specialties

(P-585)
SUNSET PET HOSPITAL INC (PA)
Also Called: AMC
7751 Sunset Ave, Fair Oaks (95628-4899)
PHONE.................................916 967-7768
Jay Griffiths, *President*
Kathy Griffiths, *Vice Pres*
EMP: 100
SQ FT: 2,400
SALES (est): 4.7MM **Privately Held**
WEB: www.sunsetpethospital.com
SIC: 0742 Animal hospital services, pets &
   other animal specialties

(P-586)
TONY LA RUSSAS ANIMAL RES FND
2890 Mitchell Dr, Walnut Creek
(94598-1635)
PHONE.................................925 256-1273
Elena Bicker, *Exec Dir*
Elaine Durkin, *Finance Dir*
Stephanie Erickson, *Opers Staff*
Tracy Gimbel, *Director*

Erin Jones, *Director*
EMP: 70
SQ FT: 37,000
SALES: 10.1MM **Privately Held**
WEB: www.arf.net
SIC: 0742 8699 Veterinary services, spe-
   cialties; animal humane society

(P-587)
VCA ANIMAL HOSPITALS INC
Also Called: VCA Holly Street
501 Laurel St, San Carlos (94070-2415)
PHONE.................................650 631-7400
Barbara Beebe, *Office Mgr*
Jenny Bour, *Technical Staff*
EMP: 50
SALES (corp-wide): 37.6B **Privately Held**
SIC: 0742 Animal hospital services, pets &
   other animal specialties
HQ: Vca Animal Hospitals, Inc.
   12401 W Olympic Blvd
   Los Angeles CA 90064

(P-588)
VCA ANIMAL HOSPITALS INC
Also Called: VCA Clfmia Vtrnary Spcialists
2310 Faraday Ave, Carlsbad (92008-7216)
PHONE.................................760 431-2273
Stephen Speredelozzi, *President*
Robert Antin, *President*
Neil Tauber, *President*
Tomas Fuller, *Vice Pres*
EMP: 75
SALES (est): 583.8K **Privately Held**
SIC: 0742 Veterinary services, specialties

(P-589)
VCA ANIMAL HOSPITALS INC (DH)
Also Called: VCA TLC Animal Hospital
12401 W Olympic Blvd, Los Angeles
(90064-1022)
PHONE.................................310 571-6500
Robert Antin, *President*
Tomas Fuller, *Treasurer*
Kim Dudder, *Technical Mgr*
Alana Jennings, *Technician*
Eisanne Tanimoto, *Project Mgr*
EMP: 188
SQ FT: 3,200
SALES (est): 101.6MM
SALES (corp-wide): 37.6B **Privately Held**
SIC: 0742 Animal hospital services, pets &
   other animal specialties
HQ: Vca Inc.
   12401 W Olympic Blvd
   Los Angeles CA 90064
   310 571-6500

(P-590)
VCA ANTECH INC
12401 W Olympic Blvd, Los Angeles
(90064-1022)
PHONE.................................310 207-0781
Bob Antin, *President*
Juli Hanson, *Advt Staff*
Kathy Olmos, *Advt Staff*
EMP: 406
SALES (est): 484.5K
SALES (corp-wide): 37.6B **Privately Held**
SIC: 0742 Animal hospital services, pets &
   other animal specialties
HQ: Vicar Operating, Inc.
   12401 W Olympic Blvd
   Los Angeles CA 90064
   310 571-6500

(P-591)
VCA DESERT ANIMAL HOSPITALS
4299 E Ramon Rd, Palm Springs
(92264-1422)
PHONE.................................760 778-9999
Raymond Mestas, *Principal*
EMP: 54
SALES (est): 1.2MM **Privately Held**
SIC: 0742 Animal hospital services, pets &
   other animal specialties

(P-592)
VCA INC
1818 S Sepulveda Blvd, Los Angeles
(90025-4314)
PHONE.................................310 473-2951
Todd Tams, *Administration*

(PA)=Parent Co (HQ)=Headquarters (DH)=Div Headquarters
♣ = New Business established in last 2 years

EMP: 80
SALES (corp-wide): 37.6B Privately Held
WEB: www.vcawoodlands.com
SIC: 0742 Veterinarian, animal specialties
HQ: Vca Inc.
12401 W Olympic Blvd
Los Angeles CA 90064
310 571-6500

(P-593)
VCA INC
Also Called: VCA-Asher Animal Hospital
2505 Hilltop Dr, Redding (96002-0505)
PHONE..................................530 224-2200
Annette Hixenbau, *Director*
EMP: 55
SALES (corp-wide): 37.6B Privately Held
WEB: www.vcawoodlands.com
SIC: 0742 Animal hospital services, pets &
other animal specialties
HQ: Vca Inc.
12401 W Olympic Blvd
Los Angeles CA 90064
310 571-6500

(P-594)
VETERINARY SURGICAL ASSOCIATES (PA)
1410 Monu Blvd Ste 100, Concord (94520)
PHONE..................................925 827-1777
Julie Smith, *Partner*
Elisabeth Richardson, *Partner*
Sharon Ullman, *Partner*
Charles Walls, *Partner*
Chuck Walls, *Partner*
EMP: 187
SALES (est): 6.1MM Privately Held
WEB: www.vsasurgery.com
SIC: 0742 Veterinary services, specialties

(P-595)
VETERNARY MED SRGCAL GROUP INC
Also Called: Vmsg
2199 Sperry Ave, Ventura (93003-7426)
PHONE..................................805 339-2290
Kenneth A Bruecker, *CEO*
Leah Basinas, *Administration*
Diane Lara, *Manager*
EMP: 80
SQ FT: 6,500
SALES (est): 2.8MM Privately Held
WEB: www.vmsg.com
SIC: 0742 Animal hospital services, pets &
other animal specialties

(P-596)
VICAR OPERATING INC (DH)
Also Called: Veterinary Centers America VCA
12401 W Olympic Blvd, Los Angeles
(90064-1022)
PHONE..................................310 571-6500
Robert Antin, *President*
Todd Lavender, *President*
Michael Everett, *Officer*
Elizabeth Ho, *Officer*
Bob Doak, *Vice Pres*
EMP: 146 EST: 1985
SALES (est): 102.9MM
SALES (corp-wide): 37.6B Privately Held
WEB: www.vcaantech.com
SIC: 0742 Veterinarian, animal specialties
HQ: Vca Inc.
12401 W Olympic Blvd
Los Angeles CA 90064
310 571-6500

(P-597)
WEST RIVERSIDE VETERINARY HOSP
5488 Mission Blvd, Riverside (92509-4514)
PHONE..................................951 686-2242
Michael Butchko, *President*
Ruby Butchko, *Vice Pres*
Steven Butchko,
EMP: 50
SALES (est): 1.8MM Privately Held
WEB: www.drbutchko.org
SIC: 0742 Animal hospital services, pets &
other animal specialties

(P-598)
WILSHIRE ANIMAL HOSPITAL
2421 Wilshire Blvd, Santa Monica
(90403-5876)
PHONE..................................310 828-4587
Natoional Pet Care Center, *Owner*
Pernilla Edstrom, *Med Doctor*
Frank Labuc, *Manager*
EMP: 50
SQ FT: 2,000
SALES (est): 1.8MM Privately Held
SIC: 0742 Animal hospital services, pets &
other animal specialties

0751 Livestock Svcs, Except Veterinary

(P-599)
AMERICAN BEEF PACKERS INC
13677 Yorba Ave, Chino (91710-5059)
PHONE..................................909 628-4888
Lawrence Miller, *President*
Rafael Santamaria, *CFO*
Cinthia Hernandez, *Human Resources*
Henry Wong, *Sales Mgr*
EMP: 250
SALES: 200MM Privately Held
SIC: 0751 2011 5147 Slaughtering: cus-
tom livestock services; beef products from
beef slaughtered on site; meats & meat
products

(P-600)
STANDARD CATTLE LLC
8105a S Lassen Ave, San Joaquin
(93660-9728)
PHONE..................................559 693-1977
Michael Vanderdussen, *Mng Member*
▲ EMP: 75 EST: 2005
SALES (est): 1.3MM Privately Held
SIC: 0751 Cattle services

0752 Animal Specialty Svcs, Exc Veterinary

(P-601)
CANINE CMPNONS FOR INDPENDENCE (PA)
2965 Dutton Ave, Santa Rosa
(95407-5711)
P.O. Box 446 (95402-0446)
PHONE..................................707 577-1700
Paul Mundell, *CEO*
John D Miller, *Ch of Bd*
Alan Feinne, *CFO*
Jack Peirce, *CFO*
Megan Koester, *Exec Dir*
EMP: 71
SQ FT: 40,000
SALES: 31.9MM Privately Held
SIC: 0752 Training services, pet & animal
specialties (not horses)

(P-602)
DEDICATION & EVERLASTING LOVE
Also Called: D E L T A Rescue
6021 Shannon Valley Rd, Acton
(93510-1190)
P.O. Box 9, Glendale (91209-0009)
PHONE..................................661 269-4010
Leo Grillo, *President*
EMP: 60
SALES: 5.9MM Privately Held
SIC: 0752 Shelters, animal

(P-603)
GUIDE DOGS FOR BLIND INC (PA)
Also Called: G D B
350 Los Ranchitos Rd, San Rafael
(94903-3606)
P.O. Box 151200 (94915-1200)
PHONE..................................415 499-4000
Chris Benninger, *CEO*
Therese Jacobson, *COO*
Cathy Martin, *CFO*
Kenneth Stupi, *CFO*
Susan Armstrong, *Vice Pres*
EMP: 170

SALES: 22.4MM Privately Held
WEB: www.guidedogs.com
SIC: 0752 8299 Animal training services;
educational service, nondegree granting;
continuing educ.

(P-604)
HANGTOWN KNNEL CLB PLCRVLLE CA
100 Placerville Dr, Placerville (95667-3910)
P.O. Box 2176 (95667-2176)
PHONE..................................530 622-4867
Pam Bectel, *President*
Joe Barnes, *Corp Secy*
EMP: 75
SALES: 110K Privately Held
SIC: 0752 Training services, pet & animal
specialties (not horses)

(P-605)
HUMBOLDT DOG OBEDIENCE GROUP
Also Called: Humdog
P.O. Box 6733 (95502-6733)
PHONE..................................707 444-3862
Marilyn Backman, *President*
Mark Nichols, *Treasurer*
EMP: 50
SALES (est): 104.8K Privately Held
SIC: 0752 Training services, pet & animal
specialties (not horses)

(P-606)
LOS ANGELES EQUESTRIAN CENTER
480 W Riverside Dr, Burbank (91506-3209)
PHONE..................................818 840-9063
Tim Behunin, *President*
Kenneth Mowry, *Admin Sec*
EMP: 75
SALES (est): 2.6MM Privately Held
WEB: www.la-equestriancenter.com
SIC: 0752 7999 Boarding services,
horses: racing & non-racing; horse shows

(P-607)
SONOMA COUNTY HUMANE SOCIETY
Also Called: Hssc
5345 Highway 12, Santa Rosa
(95407-6401)
P.O. Box 1296 (95402-1296)
PHONE..................................707 542-0882
Scott Anderson, *Director*
Don Malone, *Director*
David Kerwin, *Supervisor*
EMP: 50
SALES (est): 743.9K Privately Held
SIC: 0752 Shelters, animal

(P-608)
TOWN CATS MORGAN HILL RESCUE
195 San Pedro Ave Ste B, Morgan Hill
(95037-5141)
P.O. Box 1828 (95038-1828)
PHONE..................................408 779-5761
Rosi Mirko, *Director*
Petrica Aberu, *Director*
Petrica Guthrie, *Director*
Albert Mirko, *Director*
EMP: 50
SALES: 339.8K Privately Held
WEB: www.towncats.org
SIC: 0752 Shelters, animal

(P-609)
WAGS & WIGGLES DOG DAYCARE LLC (PA)
23171 Arroyo Vis, Rcho STA Marg
(92688-2616)
PHONE..................................949 635-9655
Laurie Zurborg,
David Zurborg, *Managing Prtnr*
Ranaye Kahn, *Manager*
Romi Tustin, *Manager*
EMP: 56
SALES (est): 1.1MM Privately Held
SIC: 0752 Boarding services, kennels

0761 Farm Labor Contractors & Crew Leaders

(P-610)
AGSOURCE SERVICES LLC
222 N Garden St Ste 400, Visalia
(93291-6328)
PHONE..................................559 735-9700
Fred Lagomarsino,
EMP: 50 EST: 1998
SALES (est): 2.4MM Privately Held
SIC: 0761 Farm labor contractors

(P-611)
ALICIA ARROYO INC
Also Called: Arroyo Labor Contracting Svc
800 Johnson Cyn Rd 4, Gonzales (93926)
P.O. Box 846 (93926-0846)
PHONE..................................831 675-2850
Alicia Arroyo, *President*
Debra Arroyo, *Treasurer*
Michael Arroyo, *Vice Pres*
EMP: 250
SQ FT: 500
SALES (est): 7MM Privately Held
SIC: 0761 Farm labor contractors

(P-612)
ARMANDO GONZALEZ CONTRACTING
32380 Elmo Hwy, Mc Farland
(93250-9616)
P.O. Box 1540 (93250-0140)
PHONE..................................661 792-3785
Armando Gonzalez, *Owner*
EMP: 300
SALES (est): 3.6MM Privately Held
SIC: 0761 Crew leaders, farm labor: con-
tracting services

(P-613)
AZTEC HARVESTING
1075 N Broadway, Blythe (92225-1664)
P.O. Box 1080 (92226-1080)
PHONE..................................760 922-7348
Charles Garcia, *President*
Marilyn Garcia, *Vice Pres*
Steve Garcia, *Vice Pres*
Tina Garcia, *Admin Sec*
EMP: 800
SALES: 5MM Privately Held
SIC: 0761 4212 0722 Farm labor contrac-
tors; local trucking, without storage; crop
harvesting

(P-614)
BORJON ISCANDER
Also Called: Bvls
18586 Highway 49, Plymouth (95669)
P.O. Box 252 (95669-0252)
PHONE..................................209 245-6289
Iscandor Borjon, *Owner*
Elana Borjon, *Co-Owner*
EMP: 250
SALES (est): 164.4K Privately Held
SIC: 0761 Farm labor contractors

(P-615)
COASTAL HARVESTING INC
503 S Palm Ave, Santa Paula
(93060-3364)
PHONE..................................805 525-6250
EMP: 300
SALES (est): 10.2MM Privately Held
SIC: 0761

(P-616)
EDWARDO Z GARCIA
Also Called: Z Garcia Farm Labor
380 Tucker St, Arvin (93203-1527)
PHONE..................................661 854-5414
Edwardo Z Garcia, *Owner*
EMP: 250
SALES (est): 4.3MM Privately Held
SIC: 0761 Crew leaders, farm labor: con-
tracting services

(P-617)
EL CAMINO LABOR LLC
815 Broadway St, King City (93930-3304)
PHONE..................................831 809-9537
Armando Zavala Chavez,
EMP: 60

▲ = Import ▼=Export
◆ =Import/Export

SALES (est): 508.9K **Privately Held**
SIC: 0761 Farm labor contractors

(P-618)
ELIOCO PRODUCE INC
Also Called: Preferred Produce
367 W Market St Ste A, Salinas
(93901-1423)
P.O. Box 5700 (93915-5700)
PHONE...............................831 424-5450
Robert Elliott, *President*
EMP: 105
SQ FT: 1,400
SALES (est): 6.5MM **Privately Held**
SIC: 0761 Farm labor contractors

(P-619)
ELISEO ESPARZA DELGADILLO
88 Wildflower Dr, Galt (95632-2329)
P.O. Box 431 (95632-0431)
PHONE...............................209 745-3937
Eliseo E Delgadillo, *President*
EMP: 50
SALES (est): 2.8MM **Privately Held**
SIC: 0761 Farm labor contractors

(P-620)
F & F CONTRACTING INC
4145 W Alamos Ave, Fresno (93722-3939)
PHONE...............................559 276-2418
Frank Echeverrie, *President*
EMP: 200
SQ FT: 500
SALES (est): 10.2MM **Privately Held**
SIC: 0761 Farm labor contractors

(P-621)
FIVE STAR PACKING LLC
437 W 5th St, Holtville (92250-1167)
P.O. Box 838 (92250-0838)
PHONE...............................760 356-4103
Marc Heraz,
John A Heraz, *Manager*
EMP: 737
SQ FT: 900
SALES (est): 13.8MM **Privately Held**
SIC: 0761 Farm labor contractors

(P-622)
FLORES LABOR CONTRACTING
501 6th St, Mc Farland (93250-1103)
PHONE...............................661 792-3061
Dora Flores, *Owner*
EMP: 300
SALES (est): 5.4MM **Privately Held**
SIC: 0761 Crew leaders, farm labor: con-
tracting services

(P-623)
**GOMEZ FARM LABOR CONTG
INC**
62610 Monroe St, Thermal (92274-9059)
PHONE...............................760 399-1994
Jose J Gomez, *President*
George Gomez, *Admin Sec*
EMP: 100
SQ FT: 900
SALES (est): 5.3MM **Privately Held**
SIC: 0761 Farm labor contractors

(P-624)
**GONZALES SALVADOR LABOR
CONTRS**
217 4th St, Galt (95632-1955)
PHONE...............................209 745-2223
Salvador Gonzalez, *President*
Theresa Gonzalez, *Treasurer*
EMP: 100
SALES (est): 3.9MM **Privately Held**
SIC: 0761 Crew leaders, farm labor: con-
tracting services

(P-625)
HALL AG ENTERPRISES INC
Also Called: Hall AG Services
759 S Madera Ave, Kerman (93630-1744)
PHONE...............................559 846-7360
Brad Hall, *President*
Loraine Garcia, *Corp Secy*
Mike Van Hooser, *Vice Pres*
EMP: 200
SALES (est): 5.6MM **Privately Held**
SIC: 0761 7361 Farm labor contractors;
labor contractors (employment agency)

(P-626)
J A CONTRACTING INC
2209 W Tulare Ave, Visalia (93277-2137)
P.O. Box 2109, Tulare (93275-2109)
PHONE...............................559 733-4865
EMP: 300
SQ FT: 1,500
SALES (est): 9MM **Privately Held**
WEB: www.jacontracting.net
SIC: 0761

(P-627)
JACOBS TREE SPECIALIST INC
2209 W Tulare Ave, Visalia (93277-2137)
P.O. Box 684, Lemoore (93245-0684)
PHONE...............................559 639-7138
Gregorio Jacobo, *President*
EMP: 50
SALES (est): 900K **Privately Held**
SIC: 0761 Farm labor contractors

(P-628)
JJ RIOS FARM SERVICES INC
4890 E Acampo Rd, Acampo (95220-9601)
P.O. Box 550 (95220-0550)
PHONE...............................209 333-7467
Fax: 209 333-3715
EMP: 80
SQ FT: 4,800
SALES (est): 2MM **Privately Held**
WEB: www.jjrios.com
SIC: 0761

(P-629)
JORGE PIMENTAL DIAZ
348 Manzanita Dr, Delano (93215-4675)
PHONE...............................661 344-5139
Jorge Pimental Diaz, *Owner*
EMP: 120
SALES (est): 5.7MM **Privately Held**
SIC: 0761 Farm labor contractors

(P-630)
L&D FARM LABOR
53762 Sapphire Ln, Coachella
(92236-7335)
PHONE...............................760 408-6311
Tania Alonzo, *President*
EMP: 50 **Privately Held**
SIC: 0761 Farm labor contractors

(P-631)
LABOR ONE INC
575 Minnewawa Ave Ste 3, Clovis
(93612-6300)
PHONE...............................559 430-4202
Cheat Nuon, *President*
EMP: 70
SALES (est): 625.3K **Privately Held**
SIC: 0761 Farm labor contractors

(P-632)
MARIN LABOR SERVICES
277 Country View Ct, Santa Paula
(93060-3015)
PHONE...............................805 525-7730
Juan Llamas, *Owner*
EMP: 200
SALES (est): 3.9MM **Privately Held**
SIC: 0761 Crew leaders, farm labor: con-
tracting services

(P-633)
MAYORAL BROS
420 Hillcrest Cir, Dixon (95620-3722)
PHONE...............................707 693-9111
Rosendo Mayoral, *Owner*
Ricardo Mayoral, *President*
Hector Mayoral, *CFO*
EMP: 400
SALES (est): 297.2K **Privately Held**
SIC: 0761 Farm labor contractors

(P-634)
**MOUNTAIN VIEW AG SERVICES
INC**
13281 Avenue 416, Orosi (93647)
PHONE...............................559 528-6004
Leonard E Hutchinson, *President*
Leonard Hutchinson, *President*
Sonya Hutchinson, *Corp Secy*
EMP: 1200
SQ FT: 800
SALES (est): 6.2MM **Privately Held**
SIC: 0761 Farm labor contractors

(P-635)
**MOYA JUAN FARM LABOR
SERVICES**
Also Called: Moya Farm Labor Services
7919 S Alta Ave, Reedley (93654-9538)
PHONE...............................559 638-9498
Rosa Moya, *President*
Juan Moya, *Vice Pres*
EMP: 150
SALES (est): 9.1MM **Privately Held**
SIC: 0761 Farm labor contractors

(P-636)
OMAR OROZCO
Also Called: Omar Orozco's Contracting
816 Gibson Rd, Woodland (95695-4935)
PHONE...............................530 723-0849
Omar Orozco, *Principal*
EMP: 55
SALES (est): 478.1K **Privately Held**
SIC: 0761 Farm labor contractors

(P-637)
PACIFIC SUN LABOR
350 G St, Brawley (92227-2413)
PHONE...............................760 556-5085
Alejandro Palacios, *President*
EMP: 52 EST: 2018
SALES (est): 459.3K **Privately Held**
SIC: 0761 Crew leaders, farm labor: con-
tracting services

(P-638)
PALO ALTO VINEYARD MGT LLC
50 Adobe Canyon Rd, Kenwood
(95452-9044)
P.O. Box 1399 (95452-1399)
PHONE...............................707 996-7725
Beverly Ordaz,
Jesus Ordaz,
EMP: 90 EST: 1997
SQ FT: 1,000
SALES (est): 7MM **Privately Held**
SIC: 0761 Farm labor contractors

(P-639)
PETE SANTELLAN
Also Called: Santellan Farm Labor Contr
176 S Valencia Blvd Ste C, Woodlake
(93286-1723)
PHONE...............................559 564-3748
Pete Santellan, *Partner*
Ruben Santellan, *Partner*
EMP: 150
SALES (est): 2.5MM **Privately Held**
SIC: 0761 Crew leaders, farm labor: con-
tracting services

(P-640)
PYRAMID PRODUCE INC
12826 Edison Hwy, Bakersfield (93307)
P.O. Box 27 (93302-0027)
PHONE...............................661 366-5736
Wayde Kirschenman, *CEO*
Norma Rapp, *Treasurer*
EMP: 250
SALES (est): 3.8MM **Privately Held**
SIC: 0761 Crew leaders, farm labor: con-
tracting services

(P-641)
R AND R LABOR INC
710 Kirkpatric Ct Ste A, Hollister
(95023-2808)
PHONE...............................831 638-0290
Ramiro Rodriguez Jr, *President*
Jose Rodriguez, *Vice Pres*
Elda Garcia, *Executive*
EMP: 300
SALES (est): 9.7MM **Privately Held**
SIC: 0761 Farm labor contractors

(P-642)
R MORA FARM LABOR
930 5th St, Wasco (93280-1348)
PHONE...............................661 746-2858
Roberto Mora, *Owner*
EMP: 50
SALES (est): 300K **Privately Held**
SIC: 0761 Farm labor contractors

(P-643)
**RANCHO SALINAS PACKING
INC**
2376 Alisal Rd, Salinas (93908-9718)
P.O. Box 5307 (93915-5307)
PHONE...............................831 758-3624
Gilberto Jimenez, *President*
EMP: 150
SQ FT: 500,000
SALES (est): 2MM **Privately Held**
SIC: 0761 Crew leaders, farm labor: con-
tracting services

(P-644)
**RODGZ FARM LABOR CONTG
LLC**
4422 College Way, Olivehurst
(95961-4622)
PHONE...............................530 329-8403
Fidel Rodriguez,
EMP: 80
SALES (est): 625.5K **Privately Held**
SIC: 0761 Crew leaders, farm labor: con-
tracting services

(P-645)
**SALAZAR LABOR
CONTRACTING**
957 Sugarloaf Dr, Escondido (92026-2364)
PHONE...............................760 746-0805
Joe Salazar, *Owner*
EMP: 60
SALES (est): 892.2K **Privately Held**
SIC: 0761 Farm labor contractors

(P-646)
SALVADOR MARTINEZ
2049 N Newcomb St, Porterville
(93257-9284)
PHONE...............................559 781-5150
Salvador Martinez, *Owner*
EMP: 120
SALES (est): 1.3MM **Privately Held**
SIC: 0761 Farm labor contractors

(P-647)
**SOUTHERN MNTRREY CNTY
LBOR SUP**
Also Called: Southern Mntrey Cnty Labor Sup
44 El Camino Real Unit A, Greenfield
(93927-5637)
P.O. Box G (93927-0105)
PHONE...............................831 674-2727
Nick Azcona, *President*
Pier Azcona, *Vice Pres*
EMP: 100
SQ FT: 1,000
SALES (est): 3.2MM **Privately Held**
SIC: 0761 Crew leaders, farm labor: con-
tracting services

(P-648)
VALLEY PRIDE INC (PA)
10855 Ocean Mist Pkwy D, Castroville
(95012-3232)
PHONE...............................831 633-5883
Joseph T Pezzini, *President*
Troy Boutonnet, *Vice Pres*
Danny Gomez, *Opers Staff*
EMP: 399
SQ FT: 1,500
SALES (est): 2.2MM **Privately Held**
WEB: www.valleyprideinc.com
SIC: 0761 Crew leaders, farm labor: con-
tracting services

(P-649)
VELAZQUEZ PACKING INC
124 N I St, Lompoc (93436-6721)
P.O. Box 488 (93438-0488)
PHONE...............................805 735-6477
Raul Velasquez Jr, *President*
EMP: 100
SALES (est): 3MM **Privately Held**
SIC: 0761 Farm labor contractors

(P-650)
VENEGAS FARMING LLC
8002 Balcom Canyon Rd, Somis
(93066-2107)
PHONE...............................805 529-5038
Guillermo Venegas,
EMP: 50
SALES (est): 446.5K **Privately Held**
SIC: 0761 Farm labor contractors

PRODUCTS & SVCS

0762 Farm Management

(P-651)
AG-WISE ENTERPRISES INC (PA)
5100 California Ave # 209, Bakersfield (93309-0716)
P.O. Box 9729 (93389-9729)
PHONE..................................661 325-1567
Bruce Berreta, *President*
Ed Ray, *CFO*
EMP: 150
SQ FT: 4,400
SALES (est): 32.3MM **Privately Held**
SIC: 0762 Farm management services

(P-652)
AGRI-WORLD COOPERATIVE
31545 Donald Ave, Madera (93636-1475)
PHONE..................................559 673-1306
Devin Aviles, *General Mgr*
EMP: 50
SQ FT: 1,500
SALES (est): 4MM **Privately Held**
SIC: 0762 Farm management services

(P-653)
ARTHUR KUNDE & SONS INC
Also Called: Kunde Estate Winery
9825 Sonoma Hwy, Kenwood (95452)
P.O. Box 638 (95452-0638)
PHONE..................................707 833-5501
Jim Mickelson, *President*
Arthur Kunde Jr, *President*
William Kunde, *Corp Secy*
▲ **EMP:** 50
SQ FT: 2,000
SALES (est): 3.5MM **Privately Held**
WEB: www.kunde.com
SIC: 0762 2084 Vineyard management & maintenance services; wines, brandy & brandy spirits

(P-654)
BIANCHI AG SERVICES INC
3056 Colusa Hwy, Yuba City (95993-8931)
PHONE..................................530 923-7675
Jim Bianchi, *Branch Mgr*
EMP: 92
SALES (corp-wide): 20.3MM **Privately Held**
SIC: 0762 Farm management services
PA: Bianchi Ag. Services, Inc.
1210 Richvale Hwy
Richvale CA 95974
530 882-4575

(P-655)
CLIMATE CORPORATION (DH)
201 3rd St Ste 1100, San Francisco (94103-3149)
PHONE..................................415 363-0500
Mike Stern, *CEO*
Erik Andrejko, *Vice Pres*
Nick Koshnick, *Vice Pres*
Daniel McCaffrey, *Vice Pres*
John Raines, *Vice Pres*
EMP: 79
SALES (est): 44.9MM
SALES (corp-wide): 45.3B **Privately Held**
SIC: 0762 Farm management services
HQ: Monsanto Company
800 N Lindbergh Blvd
Saint Louis MO 63167
314 694-1000

(P-656)
CUMMINGS-VIOLICH INC
Also Called: Cummings-Vlich Inc-Orchard MGT
1750 Dayton Rd, Chico (95928-6968)
PHONE..................................530 894-5494
Dan Cummings, *President*
Paul Violich, *CFO*
EMP: 80
SQ FT: 3,400
SALES (est): 7.3MM **Privately Held**
WEB: www.cvinc.ws
SIC: 0762 Farm management services

(P-657)
D J FARM MANAGEMENT
11298 Magnolia Ave, Wasco (93280-9647)
P.O. Box 82395, Bakersfield (93380-2395)
PHONE..................................661 792-6222
Jeff Fabry, *Owner*
EMP: 50 **EST:** 2010
SALES (est): 742K **Privately Held**
SIC: 0762 Farm management services

(P-658)
E & J GALLO WINERY
Also Called: Livingston Ranch
5953 Weir Ave, Livingston (95334-9509)
PHONE..................................209 394-6271
Alan Reynolds, *Manager*
EMP: 100
SALES (corp-wide): 2.3B **Privately Held**
WEB: www.gallo.com
SIC: 0762 2084 Vineyard management & maintenance services; wines
PA: E. & J. Gallo Winery
600 Yosemite Blvd
Modesto CA 95354
209 341-3111

(P-659)
E & M AG SVC INC A CAL CORP
1118 N Chinowth St, Visalia (93291-7896)
P.O. Box 7208 (93290-7208)
PHONE..................................559 627-2724
Matt Bakke, *President*
Evett Bakke, *Vice Pres*
EMP: 50
SALES (est): 6.1MM **Privately Held**
SIC: 0762 Farm management services

(P-660)
EASTSIDE MANAGEMENT CO INC
1131 12th St Ste C, Modesto (95354-0813)
PHONE..................................209 578-9852
Steven Zeff, *President*
EMP: 148 **Privately Held**
SIC: 0762 Farm management services
PA: Eastside Management Company, Inc.
1518 K St
Modesto CA 95354

(P-661)
ECO FARM FIELD INC
28790 Las Haciendas St, Temecula (92590-2614)
PHONE..................................951 676-4047
Steven Taft, *President*
Norman Traner, *Treasurer*
▲ **EMP:** 75
SQ FT: 20,000
SALES (est): 2.8MM **Privately Held**
SIC: 0762 6519 0722 4212 Farm management services; real property lessors; crop harvesting; local trucking, without storage

(P-662)
ESPARZA ENTERPRISES INC
251 W Main St Ste G&F, Brawley (92227-2201)
PHONE..................................760 344-2031
Luis Esparza, *Branch Mgr*
EMP: 453
SALES (corp-wide): 90.9MM **Privately Held**
SIC: 0762 Farm management services
PA: Esparza Enterprises, Inc.
3851 Fruitvale Ave
Bakersfield CA 93308
661 831-0002

(P-663)
FBN INPUTS LLC
Also Called: Farmers Business Network
388 El Camino Real, San Carlos (94070-2408)
PHONE..................................844 200-3276
Amol Deshpande, *Mng Member*
EMP: 57
SALES (est): 645.4K
SALES (corp-wide): 33.4MM **Privately Held**
SIC: 0762 Farm management services
PA: Farmer's Business Network, Inc.
388 El Camino Real
San Carlos CA 94070
650 226-3888

(P-664)
FREY FARMING & TPSRY VINEYARDS
2203 Fallen Leaf Dr, Santa Maria (93455-5736)
PHONE..................................805 937-1542
Jeff Frey, *Owner*
EMP: 90
SALES (est): 1.4MM **Privately Held**
SIC: 0762 Vineyard management & maintenance services

(P-665)
GLESS RANCH INC (PA)
18541 Van Buren Blvd, Riverside (92508-9261)
PHONE..................................951 780-8458
John J Gless, *CEO*
EMP: 50 **EST:** 1961
SALES (est): 14.2MM **Privately Held**
WEB: www.glessranch.com
SIC: 0762 Orchard management & maintenance services

(P-666)
HANSEN EQUIPMENT COMPANY LLC
7124 Whitley Ave, Corcoran (93212-9669)
P.O. Box 398 (93212-0398)
PHONE..................................559 992-3111
James B Hansen,
Betsy Hansen,
EMP: 50
SALES: 12MM **Privately Held**
SIC: 0762 Farm management services

(P-667)
J & R DEBENEDETTO ORCHARDS INC
Also Called: De Benedetto AG
26393 Road 22 1/2, Chowchilla (93610-9624)
PHONE..................................559 665-1712
Richard De Benedetto, *Owner*
Janelle Eggert, *Office Spvr*
EMP: 75
SALES (est): 3.3MM **Privately Held**
SIC: 0762 Farm management services

(P-668)
LARRY JACINTO FARMING INC
9555 N Wabash Ave, Redlands (92374-2714)
P.O. Box 275, Mentone (92359-0275)
PHONE..................................909 794-2276
Larry Jacinto, *President*
Dennis Drexler, *Corp Secy*
EMP: 100
SQ FT: 3,000
SALES (est): 1.6MM **Privately Held**
SIC: 0762 Farm management services

(P-669)
LASSEN LAND CO
320 E South St, Orland (95963-9111)
P.O. Box 607 (95963-0607)
PHONE..................................530 865-7676
Roderick Minkler, *President*
Betty Minkler, *Admin Sec*
Bill Minkler, *Director*
EMP: 50 **EST:** 1969
SQ FT: 6,000
SALES (est): 5.3MM **Privately Held**
WEB: www.lassenland.com
SIC: 0762 Farm management services

(P-670)
MESA VINEYARD MANAGEMENT INC
2570 Prell Rd, Santa Maria (93454-9110)
P.O. Box 6565 (93456-6565)
PHONE..................................805 925-7200
Callado Rodolfo, *Manager*
EMP: 75
SALES (corp-wide): 16.5MM **Privately Held**
SIC: 0762 Vineyard management & maintenance services
PA: Mesa Vineyard Management Inc
110 Gibson Rd
Templeton CA 93465
805 434-4100

(P-671)
MESA VINEYARD MANAGEMENT INC (PA)
110 Gibson Rd, Templeton (93465-9510)
P.O. Box 789 (93465-0789)
PHONE..................................805 434-4100
Dana Merrill, *President*
EMP: 75
SQ FT: 3,200
SALES (est): 16.5MM **Privately Held**
SIC: 0762 Vineyard management & maintenance services

(P-672)
MITCHELL VINEYARDS LLC
Also Called: Mitchell Vineyard Management
1831 Sarahs Way, Saint Helena (94574-9506)
PHONE..................................707 963-7050
Anthony B Mitchell,
EMP: 90
SALES (est): 5MM **Privately Held**
SIC: 0762 Vineyard management & maintenance services

(P-673)
MONTEREY PACIFIC INC (PA)
Also Called: McIntyre Vineyards
169 The Crossroads Blvd, Carmel (93923-8645)
PHONE..................................831 678-4845
Steven McIntyre, *CEO*
Kimberly McIntyre, *Corp Secy*
Jackie Skinner, *Manager*
▲ **EMP:** 50
SQ FT: 3,000
SALES (est): 9.4MM **Privately Held**
WEB: www.montereypacific.com
SIC: 0762 Vineyard management & maintenance services

(P-674)
NISSEN VINEYARD SERVICES INC
1226 Spring St, Saint Helena (94574-2024)
PHONE..................................707 963-3480
Peter G Nissen, *President*
Anne Nissen, *Vice Pres*
EMP: 60
SQ FT: 1,760
SALES (est): 6.1MM **Privately Held**
SIC: 0762 Vineyard management & maintenance services

(P-675)
OXFORD FARMS INC
Also Called: Meyers Farming
901 N St Ste 103, Firebaugh (93622-2241)
P.O. Box 457 (93622-0457)
PHONE..................................559 659-3033
Marvin Meyers, *President*
Gregory Meyers, *Vice Pres*
EMP: 50
SQ FT: 250
SALES (est): 2.1MM **Privately Held**
SIC: 0762 Farm management services

(P-676)
P C A FARM MANAGEMENT LLC
1901 S Lexington St, Delano (93215-9207)
PHONE..................................661 720-2400
David Krause,
EMP: 700
SQ FT: 10,000
SALES (est): 5.7MM **Privately Held**
SIC: 0762 Farm management services

(P-677)
PEREZ CONTRACTING LLC
12620 Snow Rd, Bakersfield (93314-8021)
PHONE..................................661 399-2700
Fax: 805 239-8076
EMP: 150
SALES (est): 4.6MM **Privately Held**
SIC: 0762

(P-678)
PINA VINEYARD MANAGEMENT LLC
7960 Silverado Trl, NAPA (94558-9433)
P.O. Box 373, Oakville (94562-0373)
PHONE..................................707 944-2229
Davie Pina, *Owner*
Omar Cruz, *Human Resources*
EMP: 50

SQ FT: 290
SALES (est): 6.4MM **Privately Held**
WEB: www.pinavineyards.com
SIC: 0762 0723 2084 Vineyard management & maintenance services; crop preparation services for market; wines, brandy & brandy spirits

(P-679)
REDWOOD EMPIRE VINEYARD MGT
22000 Geyserville Ave, Geyserville (95441)
P.O. Box 729 (95441-0729)
PHONE..................................707 857-3401
Kevin W Barr, *President*
Nancy Barr, *Treasurer*
Linda Barr, *Corp Secy*
EMP: 100
SALES (est): 12.3MM **Privately Held**
WEB: www.revm.net
SIC: 0762 0172 Vineyard management & maintenance services; grapes

(P-680)
ROBERT YOUNG FAMILY LTD PARTNR
Also Called: Robert Young Vineyards
4950 Red Winery Rd, Geyserville (95441-9573)
PHONE..................................707 433-3228
Robert Young, *Partner*
Susan Sheehy, *Partner*
Fred Young, *Partner*
James Young, *Partner*
Joann Young, *Partner*
EMP: 60
SQ FT: 5,078
SALES (est): 3.3MM **Privately Held**
WEB: www.ryew.com
SIC: 0762 Vineyard management & maintenance services

(P-681)
ROTHFLEISCH RANCHES INC
129 S El Cerrito Dr, Brawley (92227-2203)
PHONE..................................760 344-1819
Joseph Rothfleisch, *President*
Kacie Cox, *Manager*
Allison Mainas, *Manager*
EMP: 60
SALES (est): 2.7MM **Privately Held**
SIC: 0762 Farm management services

(P-682)
SIERRA PACIFIC FARMS INC (PA)
Also Called: Somis Pacific AG Management
43406 Business Park Dr, Temecula (92590-5526)
P.O. Box 1537 (92593-1537)
PHONE..................................951 699-9980
Scott A McIntyre, *CEO*
Keri Calonder, *CFO*
Debbie McIntyre, *CFO*
Ryan Rochefort, *Vice Pres*
Hector Sanchez, *General Mgr*
EMP: 68
SQ FT: 3,000
SALES (est): 16.9MM **Privately Held**
SIC: 0762 Farm management services

(P-683)
SUN PACIFIC FARMING COOP INC (PA)
Also Called: Allied Farming Company
1250 E Myer Ave, Exeter (93221-9345)
P.O. Box 1125 (93221-7125)
PHONE..................................559 592-7121
Berne H Evans III, *President*
Bob Reniers, *Corp Secy*
Oscar Leal, *Human Res Dir*
Mireya Zepeda, *Hum Res Coord*
Dave Medders, *VP Sales*
EMP: 500
SQ FT: 70,000
SALES (est): 116.8MM **Privately Held**
SIC: 0762 Citrus grove management & maintenance services

(P-684)
T AND M AGRICULTURAL SVCS LLC
493 Dowdell Ln, Saint Helena (94574-1441)
P.O. Box 122 (94574-0122)
PHONE..................................707 963-3330
Samuel Turner,
Dianne Martinez,
Mark Oberschulte, *Director*
EMP: 120
SALES (est): 4.9MM **Privately Held**
SIC: 0762 Vineyard management & maintenance services

(P-685)
UNITED BIOSOURCE LLC
303 2nd St Ste S700, San Francisco (94107-3627)
PHONE..................................415 293-1340
Mike Borkowski, *Branch Mgr*
EMP: 80
SALES (corp-wide): 106.9MM **Privately Held**
SIC: 0762 Farm management services
PA: United Biosource Llc
920 Harvest Dr Ste 200
Blue Bell PA 19422
215 591-2880

(P-686)
VALLEY FARM MANAGEMENT INC
37500 Foothill Rd, Soledad (93960-9507)
PHONE..................................831 678-1592
Richard R Smith, *President*
Alice Smith, *Treasurer*
James E Smith, *Vice Pres*
Jason Smith, *Admin Sec*
Jodi Jetton, *Bookkeeper*
EMP: 100
SQ FT: 2,880
SALES (est): 10.8MM **Privately Held**
SIC: 0762 Vineyard management & maintenance services

(P-687)
VIMARK INC
Also Called: Vimark Vineyards
19500 Geyserville Ave, Geyserville (95441-9310)
P.O. Box 576 (95441-0576)
PHONE..................................707 857-3588
Krishik Hicks, *Manager*
EMP: 60
SALES (corp-wide): 58.6MM **Privately Held**
SIC: 0762 Vineyard management & maintenance services
PA: Vimark, Inc.
101 D St Fl 2nd
Santa Rosa CA
707 542-3134

(P-688)
VINO FARMS INC (PA)
1377 E Lodi Ave, Lodi (95240-0840)
PHONE..................................209 334-6975
James D Ledbetter, *President*
John K Ledbetter, *Officer*
Kimberly Bronson, *Exec VP*
Kimberly L Bronson, *Exec VP*
Craig Ledbetter, *Vice Pres*
EMP: 50
SQ FT: 6,000
SALES (est): 59.3MM **Privately Held**
SIC: 0762 8748 Vineyard management & maintenance services; agricultural consultant

(P-689)
VINO FARMS INC
10651 Eastside Rd, Healdsburg (95448-9490)
PHONE..................................707 433-8241
Roy Davis, *Manager*
EMP: 100
SALES (corp-wide): 59.3MM **Privately Held**
SIC: 0762 Vineyard management & maintenance services
PA: Vino Farms, Inc.
1377 E Lodi Ave
Lodi CA 95240
209 334-6975

(P-690)
VYBORNY VINEYARD MANAGEMENT
7327 Silverado Trl, Rutherford (94573)
P.O. Box 367 (94573-0367)
PHONE..................................707 944-9135
J Alex Vyborny, *President*
Thomas Gore, *Vice Pres*
James M Decker, *Admin Sec*
▲ EMP: 99
SQ FT: 16,000
SALES (est): 4.4MM **Privately Held**
WEB: www.vyborny.com
SIC: 0762 Vineyard management & maintenance services

(P-691)
WEST COAST GRAPE FARMING INC
800 E Keyes Rd, Ceres (95307-7539)
P.O. Box 488 (95307-0488)
PHONE..................................209 538-3131
Fred Franzia, *President*
John Franzia, *Vice Pres*
Joseph Franzia, *Admin Sec*
EMP: 2500
SQ FT: 2,093
SALES (est): 57.6MM **Privately Held**
SIC: 0762 Farm management services

(P-692)
WEST COTTON AG MANAGEMENT INC
15900 W Dorris, Huron (93234)
P.O. Box 10 (93234-0010)
PHONE..................................559 945-2511
Bob Anderson, *President*
Richard Anderson, *Ch of Bd*
Craig Anderson, *Admin Sec*
EMP: 200
SQ FT: 1,000
SALES (est): 4.4MM **Privately Held**
SIC: 0762 Farm management services

(P-693)
WHITE HILLS VINEYARD RANC
8385 Graciosa Rd, Santa Maria (93455-6105)
PHONE..................................805 934-1986
Dale Hampton, *President*
EMP: 58
SALES (est): 1.5MM **Privately Held**
SIC: 0762 Vineyard management & maintenance services

0781 Landscape Counseling & Planning

(P-694)
A GROWING CONCERN LANDSCAPES
17382 Gothard St, Huntington Beach (92647-6203)
PHONE..................................714 843-5137
Douglas Neal, *Owner*
EMP: 82
SALES (est): 5.5MM **Privately Held**
WEB: www.growingconcern.com
SIC: 0781 Landscape services

(P-695)
ABSHEAR LANDSCAPE DEVELOPMENT
3171b Rippey Rd, Loomis (95650-9504)
P.O. Box 1817 (95650-1817)
PHONE..................................916 660-1617
Barry Abshear, *Owner*
EMP: 50
SALES (est): 1.7MM **Privately Held**
WEB: www.abshearlandscapes.com
SIC: 0781 Landscape services

(P-696)
ALLIED LANDSCAPE SVCS S INC
5542 Monterey Hwy Ste 277, San Jose (95138-1529)
PHONE..................................408 310-8476
Filiberto Fonseca, *President*
Gino Borello, *Vice Pres*
EMP: 65

SALES (est): 1.1MM **Privately Held**
WEB: www.allied-1.com
SIC: 0781 Landscape services

(P-697)
AMERICAN LANDSCAPE INC
Also Called: American Golf Construction
7013 Owensmouth Ave, Canoga Park (91303-2006)
PHONE..................................818 999-2041
Gary Peterson, *President*
Jamie Tsui, *Admin Sec*
Jim Maddox, *Human Res Dir*
Victor Silva, *Materials Mgr*
▲ EMP: 250
SQ FT: 14,000
SALES (est): 29.1MM **Privately Held**
SIC: 0781 Landscape services

(P-698)
AMERICAN LANDSCAPE MANAGEMENT (PA)
Also Called: Custom Lawn Services
7013 Owensmouth Ave, Canoga Park (91303-2006)
PHONE..................................818 999-2041
Mickey Strauss, *President*
Gary Peterson, *Vice Pres*
EMP: 400
SQ FT: 14,000
SALES (est): 14.1MM **Privately Held**
SIC: 0781 Landscape services

(P-699)
AMERINE SYSTEMS INCORPORATED
10866 Cleveland Ave, Oakdale (95361-9709)
PHONE..................................209 847-5968
Gary Amerine, *President*
Ronald Amerine, *Admin Sec*
EMP: 50
SQ FT: 20,000
SALES (est): 6.1MM **Privately Held**
WEB: www.amerinesys.com
SIC: 0781 5084 5083 Landscape services; pumps & pumping equipment; irrigation equipment

(P-700)
BARAZANI OUTDOORS INC
14101 Valleyheart Dr # 104, Sherman Oaks (91423-2885)
PHONE..................................818 701-6977
Aviva Barazani, *CEO*
Al Guadagno, *Principal*
EMP: 75
SALES (est): 2.4MM **Privately Held**
SIC: 0781 Landscape counseling & planning

(P-701)
BAYSCAPE MANAGEMENT INC
Also Called: Coast Landscape Management
1350 Pacific Ave, Alviso (95002)
P.O. Box 880 (95002-0880)
PHONE..................................408 288-2940
Thomas Ellington, *President*
Barry Cohen, *Technician*
EMP: 70
SALES (est): 10MM **Privately Held**
SIC: 0781 Landscape services

(P-702)
BENNETT ENTERPRISES A CA
Also Called: Bennett Landscape
25889 Belle Porte Ave, Harbor City (90710-3393)
PHONE..................................310 534-3543
Sean Bennett, *President*
EMP: 90
SQ FT: 10,500
SALES (est): 6.1MM **Privately Held**
SIC: 0781 Landscape services

(P-703)
BRIGHTVIEW COMPANIES LLC
2447 Stagecoach Rd, Stockton (95215-7929)
PHONE..................................209 993-9277
EMP: 105
SALES (corp-wide): 2.3B **Publicly Held**
SIC: 0781 Landscape services

PRODUCTS & SVCS

HQ: Brightview Companies, Llc
27001 Agoura Rd Ste 350
Calabasas CA 91301
818 223-8500

(P-704)
BRIGHTVIEW COMPANIES LLC
201 Longden Ave, Irwindale (91706-1329)
PHONE...........................626 574-3940
Richard Perder, *President*
EMP: 105
SALES (corp-wide): 2.3B **Publicly Held**
SIC: 0781 Landscape services
HQ: Brightview Companies, Llc
27001 Agoura Rd Ste 350
Calabasas CA 91301
818 223-8500

(P-705)
BRIGHTVIEW LANDSCAPE DEV INC (DH)
24151 Ventura Blvd, Calabasas (91302-1449)
PHONE...........................818 223-8500
Thomas Donnelly, *CEO*
Thomas C Donelly, *President*
Kenneth L Hutcheson, *President*
Andrew J Brennan, *COO*
Pamela L Stark, *Vice Pres*
◆ EMP: 50 EST: 1949
SQ FT: 25,000
SALES (est): 777.5MM
SIC: 0781 Landscape counseling & planning
HQ: Brightview Companies, Llc
27001 Agoura Rd Ste 350
Calabasas CA 91301
818 223-8500

(P-706)
BRIGHTVIEW LANDSCAPE DEV INC
1960 S Yale St, Santa Ana (92704-3929)
PHONE...........................714 546-7843
EMP: 54
SALES (corp-wide): 2.3B **Publicly Held**
SIC: 0781 Landscape services
HQ: Brightview Landscape Development, Inc.
24151 Ventura Blvd
Calabasas CA 91302
818 223-8500

(P-707)
BRIGHTVIEW LANDSCAPE SVCS INC
20551b Corsair Blvd, Hayward (94545-1005)
PHONE...........................510 487-4826
Tom Stoutt, *Branch Mgr*
Tony Fargnoli, *Manager*
EMP: 50
SALES (corp-wide): 2.3B **Publicly Held**
SIC: 0781 Landscape services
HQ: Brightview Landscape Services, Inc.
24151 Ventura Blvd
Calabasas CA 91302
818 223-8500

(P-708)
BRIGHTVIEW LANDSCAPE SVCS INC
8500 Miramar Pl, San Diego (92121-2530)
PHONE...........................858 458-1900
Patrick Ceatter, *Manager*
EMP: 200
SALES (corp-wide): 2.3B **Publicly Held**
SIC: 0781 Landscape services
HQ: Brightview Landscape Services, Inc.
24151 Ventura Blvd
Calabasas CA 91302
818 223-8500

(P-709)
BRIGHTVIEW LANDSCAPE SVCS INC
4677 Pacheco Blvd, Martinez (94553-3625)
PHONE...........................925 957-8831
Martin Becker, *Manager*
EMP: 80
SALES (corp-wide): 2.3B **Publicly Held**
SIC: 0781 Landscape services

HQ: Brightview Landscape Services, Inc.
24151 Ventura Blvd
Calabasas CA 91302
818 223-8500

(P-710)
BRIGHTVIEW LANDSCAPE SVCS INC
1960 S Yale St, Santa Ana (92704-3929)
PHONE...........................714 546-7843
Dave Hanson, *Manager*
EMP: 100
SALES (corp-wide): 2.3B **Publicly Held**
SIC: 0781 0782 Landscape services; lawn & garden services
HQ: Brightview Landscape Services, Inc.
24151 Ventura Blvd
Calabasas CA 91302
818 223-8500

(P-711)
BRIGHTVIEW LANDSCAPE SVCS INC
5745 Alder Ave, Sacramento (95828-1107)
PHONE...........................916 381-2800
John Bianco, *Manager*
Lisa Stinhilver, *Office Mgr*
EMP: 100
SALES (corp-wide): 2.3B **Publicly Held**
SIC: 0781 Landscape services
HQ: Brightview Landscape Services, Inc.
24151 Ventura Blvd
Calabasas CA 91302
818 223-8500

(P-712)
BRIGHTVIEW LANDSCAPE SVCS INC
7039 Commerce Cir Ste B, Pleasanton (94588-8006)
PHONE...........................925 924-8900
Doug Lape, *Manager*
EMP: 80
SALES (corp-wide): 2.3B **Publicly Held**
SIC: 0781 0782 Landscape services; lawn & garden services
HQ: Brightview Landscape Services, Inc.
24151 Ventura Blvd
Calabasas CA 91302
818 223-8500

(P-713)
BRIGHTVIEW LANDSCAPE SVCS INC
17813 S Main St Ste 105, Gardena (90248-3542)
PHONE...........................310 327-8700
Andrea Musick, *Manager*
Tom Cutrono, *Contractor*
EMP: 110
SQ FT: 1,530
SALES (corp-wide): 2.3B **Publicly Held**
SIC: 0781 0782 Landscape services; landscape contractors
HQ: Brightview Landscape Services, Inc.
24151 Ventura Blvd
Calabasas CA 91302
818 223-8500

(P-714)
BRIGHTVIEW LANDSCAPES LLC
2420 Cougar Dr, Carlsbad (92010-8804)
PHONE...........................760 438-3551
Trey Dupont, *Manager*
EMP: 100
SALES (corp-wide): 2.3B **Publicly Held**
SIC: 0781 Landscape services
HQ: Brightview Landscapes, Llc
980 Jolly Rd Ste 300
Blue Bell PA 19422
484 567-7204

(P-715)
BRIGHTVIEW LANDSCAPES LLC
9090 Birch St, Spring Valley (91977-4107)
PHONE...........................619 644-8584
Larry Neuhoff, *Manager*
EMP: 80
SALES (corp-wide): 2.3B **Publicly Held**
SIC: 0781 Landscape services

HQ: Brightview Landscapes, Llc
980 Jolly Rd Ste 300
Blue Bell PA 19422
484 567-7204

(P-716)
BRIGHTVIEW TREE COMPANY
28915 E Funck Rd, Farmington (95230-9567)
PHONE...........................209 886-5511
Gina Mortenson, *Executive*
EMP: 85
SQ FT: 784
SALES (corp-wide): 2.3B **Publicly Held**
WEB: www.vctree.com
SIC: 0781 Landscape services
HQ: Brightview Tree Company
24151 Ventura Blvd
Calabasas CA 91302
818 223-8500

(P-717)
CICILEO LANDSCAPES
4565 Hollister Ave, Santa Barbara (93110-1709)
P.O. Box 60912 (93160-0912)
PHONE...........................805 967-3939
Michael J Cicileo, *President*
EMP: 50
SALES (est): 4.4MM **Privately Held**
WEB: www.cicileolandscapes.com
SIC: 0781 0782 Landscape planning services; garden maintenance services

(P-718)
COMET BUILDING MAINTENANCE INC
21 Commercial Blvd Ste 12, Novato (94949-6109)
P.O. Box 2163, San Rafael (94912-2163)
PHONE...........................415 383-1035
Richard J Brasile, *CEO*
EMP: 70
SQ FT: 1,800
SALES (est): 4.9MM **Privately Held**
SIC: 0781 7349 Landscape services; janitorial service, contract basis

(P-719)
COMMERCIAL LANDSCAPE SVC
1821 Reynolds Ave, Irvine (92614-5713)
PHONE...........................949 660-8655
Mark Fitt, *President*
Joann Fitt, *Corp Secy*
Tim Skeen, *Vice Pres*
EMP: 91
SQ FT: 8,400
SALES (est): 2.1MM **Privately Held**
SIC: 0781 Landscape services

(P-720)
DESERT CNCPTS LDSCPG MAINT INC
79469 Country Club Dr I, Bermuda Dunes (92203-1206)
PHONE...........................760 200-9007
Julio Castro, *President*
Frank Castro, *Vice Pres*
Luz Mendez, *Manager*
Cecilia Puente, *Manager*
EMP: 120
SQ FT: 1,100
SALES (est): 3.4MM **Privately Held**
WEB: www.desertconcepts.net
SIC: 0781 Landscape services

(P-721)
DIRT CHEAP INC (PA)
Also Called: Dcg Fulfillment
1060 Wineville Ave, Ontario (91764-5300)
PHONE...........................909 230-6330
Jim Jennison, *CEO*
John Jennison, *Vice Pres*
Juan Sandoval, *Info Tech Dir*
Parisi Oscar, *Opers Mgr*
Margaret Rodriguez,
▲ EMP: 50
SQ FT: 50,000
SALES (est): 20.7MM **Privately Held**
WEB: www.dcgfulfillment.com
SIC: 0781 5083 Landscape services; landscaping equipment

(P-722)
DL LONG LANDSCAPING INC
5475 G St, Chino (91710-5233)
PHONE...........................909 628-5531
David L Long, *President*
EMP: 100
SQ FT: 1,550
SALES: 6.9MM **Privately Held**
WEB: www.dllong.com
SIC: 0781 Landscape architects

(P-723)
DREAMSCAPE LDSCP & MAINT INC
7192 Mission Gorge Rd, San Diego (92120-1131)
PHONE...........................619 583-4439
Thomas Bjorstrom, *President*
Douglas Leal, *VP Opers*
EMP: 50
SQ FT: 1,200
SALES (est): 3.9MM **Privately Held**
SIC: 0781 0782 Landscape planning services; landscape contractors

(P-724)
EDAW INC
401 W A St Ste 1200, San Diego (92101-7905)
PHONE...........................619 233-1454
Michael Downs, *Branch Mgr*
Teri Fenner, *Sr Project Mgr*
EMP: 80
SALES (corp-wide): 20.1B **Publicly Held**
WEB: www.edaw.com
SIC: 0781 8748 8712 Landscape counseling & planning; business consulting; architectural services
HQ: Edaw, Inc.
300 California St Fl 5
San Francisco CA 94104
415 955-2800

(P-725)
EDAW INC
2020 L St Ste 400, Sacramento (95811-4267)
PHONE...........................916 414-5800
Curtis Alling, *Manager*
EMP: 100
SALES (corp-wide): 20.1B **Publicly Held**
WEB: www.edaw.com
SIC: 0781 8711 8712 8748 Landscape architects; engineering services; architectural services; business consulting
HQ: Edaw, Inc.
300 California St Fl 5
San Francisco CA 94104
415 955-2800

(P-726)
ELS INVESTMENTS
Also Called: Environmental Ldscp Solutions
9980 Horn Rd, Sacramento (95827-1905)
PHONE...........................916 388-0308
Darryl Alan Thompson Jr, *President*
Shawna Thompson, *Vice Pres*
EMP: 110 EST: 2008
SQ FT: 7,200
SALES (est): 16.3MM **Privately Held**
SIC: 0781 1771 Landscape services; concrete work

(P-727)
EXECUTIVE LANDSCAPE INC
2131 Huffstatler St, Fallbrook (92028-8861)
P.O. Box 1075 (92088-1075)
PHONE...........................760 731-9036
Edwin Earle, *CEO*
Walter Earle, *Treasurer*
Dave Batey, *Vice Pres*
Kathleen D Earle, *Vice Pres*
Mike Lindmark, *Controller*
EMP: 230
SQ FT: 1,800
SALES (est): 19.6MM **Privately Held**
WEB: www.executivelandscapeinc.com
SIC: 0781 Landscape services

(P-728)
FC LANDSCAPE INC
43216 Madison St, Indio (92201-1944)
PHONE...........................760 347-6600
Francisco Corona, *President*
EMP: 75

SALES (est): 2.7MM **Privately Held**
SIC: 0781 Landscape services

(P-729)
GARDEN VIEW INC
417 E Huntington Dr, Monrovia
(91016-3632)
PHONE...................................626 303-4043
Mark Meahl, *President*
EMP: 50
SQ FT: 1,500
SALES: 4MM **Privately Held**
SIC: 0781 0782 Landscape architects;
garden services; landscape contractors

(P-730)
GOTHIC LANDSCAPING INC
Also Called: Gothic Grounds Mgmt
27413 Tourney Rd Ste 200, Valencia
(91355-5606)
PHONE...................................661 257-5085
Ron Georgio, *President*
Karen Klein, *Business Dir*
Autumn Conover, *Maintence Staff*
EMP: 500
SALES (corp-wide): 173.5MM **Privately**
Held
WEB: www.gothiclandscape.com
SIC: 0781 0782 Landscape services; lawn
& garden services
PA: Gothic Landscaping, Inc.
27502 Avenue Scott
Valencia CA 91355
661 257-1266

(P-731)
HAROLD JONES LANDSCAPE
INC
530 New Los Angeles Ave, Moorpark
(93021-2081)
PHONE...................................805 582-7443
Constance Wilson, *President*
EMP: 50
SALES (est): 3.9MM **Privately Held**
SIC: 0781 Landscape counseling & plan-
ning

(P-732)
HART HOWERTON LTD (PA)
1 Union St Fl 3, San Francisco
(94111-1223)
PHONE...................................415 439-2200
Dave Howerton, *CEO*
EMP: 90
SQ FT: 20,000
SALES (est): 9.5MM **Privately Held**
SIC: 0781 8712 Landscape architects; ar-
chitectural services

(P-733)
HERITAGE LANDSCAPE INC
7949 Deering Ave, Canoga Park
(91304-5009)
PHONE...................................818 999-2041
William Leighton Knell, *President*
EMP: 130
SALES (est): 3.1MM **Privately Held**
SIC: 0781 0782 Landscape architects;
landscape contractors

(P-734)
HUPPE LANDSCAPE COMPANY
INC (HQ)
9350 Viking Pl, Roseville (95747-9713)
PHONE...................................916 784-7666
Chris Huppe, *President*
Gina Huppe, *Admin Sec*
EMP: 68
SQ FT: 215,000
SALES (est): 6.7MM
SALES (corp-wide): 115.4MM **Privately**
Held
SIC: 0781 0782 Horticulture services;
lawn & garden services
PA: Jensen Corporate Holdings, Inc.
1983 Concourse Dr
San Jose CA 95131
408 446-1118

(P-735)
I PWLC INC
408 Olive Ave, Vista (92083-3438)
P.O. Box 3557 (92085-3557)
PHONE...................................760 630-0231
Richard Ruiz, *CEO*
Maribel Torres, *Manager*

EMP: 90
SQ FT: 1,000
SALES (est): 4.6MM **Privately Held**
SIC: 0781 Landscape services

(P-736)
KEVIN PERSONS INC
Also Called: Ground Maintenance Services
2977 Los Feliz Dr, Thousand Oaks
(91362-3411)
P.O. Box 879, Newbury Park (91319-0879)
PHONE...................................805 371-8746
Kevin Persons, *President*
EMP: 50
SALES (est): 5MM **Privately Held**
SIC: 0781 Landscape services

(P-737)
LAZAR LANDSCAPE DESIGN &
CNSTR
2884 Ettie St, Oakland (94608-4009)
PHONE...................................510 444-5195
Pam Cosce, *President*
Asa Sanchez, *CFO*
EMP: 55
SALES (est): 2.6MM **Privately Held**
WEB: www.lazarlandscape.com
SIC: 0781 7389 Landscape services; de-
sign services

(P-738)
MALIBU CANYON LDSCP &
MAINT
2046 Tierra Rejada Rd, Moorpark
(93021-9769)
PHONE...................................805 523-2676
David S Bateman, *President*
D Brooke Bateman, *CFO*
Lee A Tarbet, *Admin Sec*
EMP: 55
SQ FT: 1,500
SALES (est): 1.9MM **Privately Held**
WEB: www.malibulandscape.com
SIC: 0781 Landscape services

(P-739)
MARINA LANDSCAPE MAINT
INC
1900 S Lewis St, Anaheim (92805-6718)
PHONE...................................714 939-6600
Robert B Cowan, *CEO*
EMP: 450
SALES (est): 74.9K
SALES (corp-wide): 2.3B **Publicly Held**
SIC: 0781 Landscape services
HQ: Brightview Landscapes, Llc
980 Jolly Rd Ste 300
Blue Bell PA 19422
484 567-7204

(P-740)
MASUDAS LANDSCAPE
SERVICES
423 Salmar Ave, Campbell (95008-1413)
PHONE...................................408 379-7100
Ken Masuda, *Owner*
EMP: 100
SALES (est): 7.2MM **Privately Held**
SIC: 0781 Landscape architects

(P-741)
MEDALLION LANDSCAPE MGT
INC (PA)
10 San Bruno Ave, Morgan Hill
(95037-9214)
P.O. Box 1768 (95038-1768)
PHONE...................................408 782-7500
John Gates, *CEO*
Joyce Dawson, *President*
Ildefonso Fonsie Bettencourt, *COO*
Robert Rosenberg, *CFO*
Fonsie Bettencourt, *Officer*
EMP: 65
SALES (est): 25.2MM **Privately Held**
WEB: www.mlmi.com
SIC: 0781 Landscape counseling services;
landscape planning services

(P-742)
MISSION LDSCP COMPANIES
INC
536 E Dyer Rd, Santa Ana (92707-3737)
P.O. Box 15026 (92735-0026)
PHONE...................................714 545-9962

David Dubois, *CEO*
Kristen Parkins, *President*
Beth Du Boise, *Treasurer*
Cindy Clark, *Admin Sec*
Tim Abbott, *VP Opers*
EMP: 200
SQ FT: 11,000
SALES (est): 16.4MM **Privately Held**
WEB: www.missionlandscape.com
SIC: 0781 Landscape services

(P-743)
NATURES IMAGE INC
20361 Hermana Cir, Lake Forest
(92630-8701)
PHONE...................................949 680-4400
Michelle M Caruana, *CEO*
John Caruana, *Vice Pres*
Shadi Lari, *Project Mgr*
EMP: 95
SQ FT: 13,800
SALES (est): 9.4MM **Privately Held**
WEB: www.naturesimage.net
SIC: 0781 0782 Landscape services; land-
scape contractors

(P-744)
NEW EARTH ENTERPRISES INC
3790 Manchester Ave, Encinitas
(92024-4935)
PHONE...................................760 942-1298
James R Williams, *President*
Carlos Delval, *Vice Pres*
Jessie Wilhoite, *Vice Pres*
EMP: 60
SQ FT: 192
SALES (est): 1.8MM **Privately Held**
SIC: 0781 Landscape services

(P-745)
OUTSIDE LINES INC
2150 S Towne Cntre Pl 1, Anaheim (92806)
PHONE...................................714 637-4747
John Wickham Zimmerman, *CEO*
Hugh F Hughes, *President*
EMP: 50
SALES (est): 12.2MM **Privately Held**
WEB: www.otl-inc.com
SIC: 0781 Landscape counseling & plan-
ning

(P-746)
PACHECO BROTHERS
GARDENING INC (PA)
20973 Cabot Blvd, Hayward (94545-1155)
PHONE...................................510 732-6330
George A Pacheco Jr, *CEO*
Lynn Pacheco, *Corp Secy*
Gary Pacheco, *Vice Pres*
EMP: 90
SQ FT: 12,000
SALES (est): 13.8MM **Privately Held**
WEB: www.pachecobrothers.com
SIC: 0781 0782 Landscape services; land-
scape contractors

(P-747)
PACIFIC COAST LDSCP MGT INC
3960 Holway Dr, Byron (94514-1001)
P.O. Box 757 (94514-0757)
PHONE...................................925 513-2310
Alvaro Beltran, *President*
Robin Rowley, *Office Mgr*
EMP: 60
SALES (est): 6.8MM **Privately Held**
WEB: www.pacificcoastlandscape.net
SIC: 0781 0782 Landscape services; lawn
& garden services; garden services; land-
scape contractors

(P-748)
PACIFIC RESTORATION GROUP
INC
325 E Ellis Ave, Perris (92570-8413)
P.O. Box 429 (92572-0429)
PHONE...................................951 940-6069
John Richards, *President*
Daniel Richards, *CFO*
Patricia Richards, *Admin Sec*
EMP: 50
SQ FT: 10,000
SALES (est): 4.7MM **Privately Held**
SIC: 0781 Landscape services

(P-749)
PARKER LANDSCAPE DEV INC
6011 Franklin Blvd, Sacramento
(95824-2517)
PHONE...................................916 383-4071
Timothy J Parker, *President*
Conney Parker, *Admin Sec*
EMP: 50
SALES (est): 5.1MM **Privately Held**
SIC: 0781 Landscape services

(P-750)
PIERRE LANDSCAPE INC
5455 2nd St, Irwindale (91706-2072)
PHONE...................................626 587-2121
Harold Young, *CEO*
Joseph Lowden, *President*
Monty Khouri, *CFO*
Seana Smith, *Vice Pres*
Scott Horner, *Project Mgr*
EMP: 200
SQ FT: 9,425
SALES (est): 29.3MM **Privately Held**
SIC: 0781 Landscape architects; land-
scape services

(P-751)
PLATINUM LANDSCAPE INC
42575 Melanie Pl Ste C, Palm Desert
(92211-5162)
PHONE...................................760 200-3673
Christopher Johnson, *President*
Cherie Johnson, *Vice Pres*
EMP: 150
SQ FT: 3,000
SALES: 18MM **Privately Held**
WEB: www.platinumlandscape.com
SIC: 0781 Landscape services

(P-752)
PRO PONDS WEST INC
Also Called: Pacific Outdoor Living
8309 Tujunga Ave Unit 201, Sun Valley
(91352-3216)
PHONE...................................818 244-4000
Terry Morrill, *CEO*
Jerry McMahon, *Principal*
EMP: 100
SALES (est): 3.2MM **Privately Held**
SIC: 0781 Landscape services

(P-753)
PROFESSNAL LDSCP
SOLUTIONS INC
6108 27th St Ste C, Sacramento
(95822-3711)
PHONE...................................916 424-3815
Michael E Parker, *President*
Chad Bush, *Vice Pres*
Penny Parker, *Admin Sec*
EMP: 50
SQ FT: 11,000
SALES (est): 3.2MM **Privately Held**
SIC: 0781 Landscape services

(P-754)
RANCHO DEL ORO LDSCP
MAINT INC
4167 Avenida De La Plata, Oceanside
(92056-6032)
P.O. Box 4608 (92052-4608)
PHONE...................................760 726-0215
Uriel Espinoza, *President*
Richard Kirk, *CFO*
Albertano Cardenas, *Vice Pres*
EMP: 73
SQ FT: 1,400
SALES (est): 4.2MM **Privately Held**
WEB: www.rancho.sdcoxmail.com
SIC: 0781 Landscape services

(P-755)
RICH MEIERS LANDSCAPING
INC (PA)
652 W Avenue L14, Lancaster
(93534-7135)
P.O. Box 3327 (93586-0327)
PHONE...................................661 723-2220
Richard A Meier, *President*
Annamarie Meier, *Vice Pres*
EMP: 80
SALES: 3.9MM **Privately Held**
SIC: 0781 Landscape services

(P-756)
ROCKEY MURATA LANDSCAPING
15417 Cornet St, Santa Fe Springs (90670-5533)
PHONE.....................562 921-3210
Rockey Murata, *President*
Andie Murata, *Corp Secy*
EMP: 60 EST: 1951
SQ FT: 10,000
SALES (est): 3.3MM **Privately Held**
SIC: 0781 Landscape services

(P-757)
SAN DIEGO LAND SYSTEMS
8720 Miramar Pl, San Diego (92121-2551)
PHONE.....................858 558-0542
Stewart C Frederick, *President*
Yevette Deboer, *Executive*
Kim Degraw, *Sales Mgr*
EMP: 50
SQ FT: 11,700
SALES (est): 5.3MM **Privately Held**
WEB: www.landsystems.biz
SIC: 0781 Landscape services

(P-758)
SAN VAL CORP (PA)
Also Called: San Val Alarm System
72203 Adelaid St, Thousand Palms (92276-2321)
P.O. Box 12860, Palm Desert (92255-2860)
PHONE.....................760 346-3999
Robert L Sandifer, *President*
Alex Enriquez, *Vice Pres*
Carolina Felix, *Office Mgr*
Sharon L Sandifer, *Admin Sec*
EMP: 425
SALES (est): 32.8MM **Privately Held**
WEB: www.cvwebs.com
SIC: 0781 7381 Landscape services; burglary protection service

(P-759)
SEQUOIA ENVIRONMENTAL SVCS INC
1 University Dr, Aliso Viejo (92656-8081)
PHONE.....................949 480-4742
Danny McNamara, *CEO*
Scott Collins, *Treasurer*
Wendy Chen, *Office Mgr*
Malcolm Thomas, *Admin Sec*
EMP: 64
SALES (est): 2.5MM **Privately Held**
SIC: 0781 7349 Landscape services; janitorial service, contract basis

(P-760)
SERPICO LANDSCAPING INC
1764 National Ave, Hayward (94545-1722)
PHONE.....................510 293-0341
Sharon Serpico Hanson, *CEO*
Richard Hanson, *Admin Sec*
EMP: 50
SQ FT: 1,000
SALES (est): 6MM **Privately Held**
WEB: www.serpicolandscaping.com
SIC: 0781 Landscape services

(P-761)
SHOOTER & BUTTS INC
3768 Old Santa Rita Rd, Pleasanton (94588-3457)
PHONE.....................925 460-5155
James E Butts, *President*
Richard Kusaba, *Project Mgr*
Keith Hollon, *Manager*
Jamie Matthews, *Manager*
EMP: 50 EST: 1977
SQ FT: 1,800
SALES (est): 5.1MM **Privately Held**
WEB: www.shooterandbutts.com
SIC: 0781 Landscape services

(P-762)
SHORELINE LAND CARE INC
Also Called: Landcare Logic
7348 Trade St Ste B, San Diego (92121-3434)
P.O. Box 23125 (92193-3125)
PHONE.....................858 560-8555
Craig Gerber, *CEO*
EMP: 64 EST: 2007

SALES (est): 3.6MM **Privately Held**
SIC: 0781 Landscape services

(P-763)
SIERRA LANDSCAPE & MAINTENANCE
546 Hickory St, Chico (95928-4811)
PHONE.....................530 895-0263
Catherine S Gurney, *Principal*
Maria Gomez, *Office Mgr*
Syndi Winter, *Administration*
EMP: 52
SQ FT: 8,000
SALES (est): 4.7MM **Privately Held**
WEB: www.sierralandscapeinc.com
SIC: 0781 Landscape services

(P-764)
SITEWORKS LANDSCAPE INC
5327 Jacuzzi St Ste 1b, Richmond (94804-5827)
PHONE.....................510 843-0409
Thomas Brumfield, *Branch Mgr*
Tracy Yuan, *Finance Mgr*
Melissa Wong, *Manager*
EMP: 107 **Privately Held**
SIC: 0781 Landscape services
PA: Siteworks Landscape, Inc.
2319 4th St
Berkeley CA

(P-765)
SLADE INDUSTRIAL LANDSCAPE INC
8838 Zelzah Ave, Sherwood Forest (91325-3139)
P.O. Box 571960, Tarzana (91357-1960)
PHONE.....................818 885-1916
David Slade, *President*
Sylvia Slade, *Corp Secy*
Jesse Slade, *Vice Pres*
EMP: 55
SALES (est): 4.4MM **Privately Held**
SIC: 0781 0782 Landscape planning services; landscape contractors; garden maintenance services; lawn services

(P-766)
SWA GROUP (PA)
2200 Bridgeway, Sausalito (94965-1750)
P.O. Box 5904 (94966-5904)
PHONE.....................415 332-5100
Gerdo Aquino, *CEO*
Kevin Shanley, *President*
John Reynolds, *Info Tech Dir*
Andrew Watkins, *Network Enginr*
Bill Hynes, *Project Mgr*
EMP: 200
SQ FT: 12,000
SALES (est): 21.6MM **Privately Held**
SIC: 0781 Landscape architects

(P-767)
TERRA PACIFIC LANDSCAPE (HQ)
1627 E Wilshire Ave, Santa Ana (92705-4504)
PHONE.....................714 567-0177
Rich Wingard, *President*
EMP: 89
SQ FT: 6,000
SALES (est): 26.7MM
SALES (corp-wide): 173.5MM **Privately Held**
WEB: www.terrapac.com
SIC: 0781 Landscape services
PA: Gothic Landscaping, Inc.
27502 Avenue Scott
Valencia CA 91355
661 257-1266

(P-768)
VALENCIA TREE LANDSCAPE
321 N Quarantina St, Santa Barbara (93103-3228)
P.O. Box 4554 (93140-4554)
PHONE.....................805 965-4244
Rossendo Valencia, *Owner*
EMP: 50
SALES (est): 1.7MM **Privately Held**
SIC: 0781 Landscape services

(P-769)
VALLEYCREST LDSCP MAINT VCC
24121 Ventura Blvd, Calabasas (91302-1449)
PHONE.....................800 466-8510
Jon Pinkus, *President*
Aaron Pinkus, *Vice Pres*
Lillian Pinkus, *Vice Pres*
Patricia White, *Vice Pres*
Steven Brackin, *Branch Mgr*
EMP: 50 EST: 1951
SQ FT: 6,000
SALES (est): 5MM
SALES (corp-wide): 9MM **Privately Held**
SIC: 0781 Landscape services
PA: Nortex Wholesale Nursery, Inc.
7700 Northaven Rd
Dallas TX 75230
214 363-6715

0782 Lawn & Garden Svcs

(P-770)
ALL COMMERCIAL LANDSCAPE SVC
5213 E Pine Ave, Fresno (93727-2110)
PHONE.....................559 453-1670
Jack Murray, *President*
Carol Osborn, *Corp Secy*
Tom Delny, *Vice Pres*
EMP: 50
SQ FT: 22,500
SALES (est): 4.7MM **Privately Held**
WEB: www.acls.bz
SIC: 0782 Landscape contractors; lawn services

(P-771)
ALVIZIA LANDSCAPE CO LLC
2520 Cactus Rd, San Diego (92154-8009)
PHONE.....................619 661-6557
Jose Alexander Jr, *President*
Velda Pacheco, *Vice Pres*
EMP: 160
SQ FT: 1,151
SALES (est): 6.6MM **Privately Held**
SIC: 0782 Landscape contractors

(P-772)
AMERICAN LANDSCAPE MANAGEMENT
Also Called: Custom Lawn Services
1607 Los Angeles Ave I, Ventura (93004-3237)
PHONE.....................805 647-5077
Armondo Bello, *Manager*
EMP: 50
SALES (est): 747.7K **Privately Held**
SIC: 0782 0783 0781 Landscape contractors; ornamental shrub & tree services; landscape planning services
PA: American Landscape Management Inc
7013 Owensmouth Ave
Canoga Park CA 91303

(P-773)
ARAGON COMMERCIAL LDSCPG INC
2305 S Vasco Rd, Livermore (94550-9681)
PHONE.....................408 998-0600
Scott Tabler, *President*
Sophie Martinez, *Controller*
Julie Tabler, *Manager*
EMP: 135
SQ FT: 7,000
SALES (est): 8.5MM **Privately Held**
SIC: 0782 0781 Landscape contractors; landscape services

(P-774)
ARREOLAS COMPLETE LDSCP SVC
Also Called: Arreolas Complete Ldscp Svc
8671 Morrison Creek Dr # 100, Sacramento (95828-1862)
PHONE.....................916 387-6777
Humberto Arreola, *Owner*
EMP: 50
SQ FT: 10,000
SALES (est): 2.7MM **Privately Held**
SIC: 0782 Landscape contractors

(P-775)
ARTISTIC MAINTENANCE INC
603 S Milliken Ave Ste A, Ontario (91761-8102)
PHONE.....................909 390-5156
Monica Sanchez, *Manager*
EMP: 65
SALES (corp-wide): 26.3MM **Privately Held**
SIC: 0782 Garden maintenance services; lawn care services
HQ: Artistic Maintenance, Inc.
15510 Rockfield Blvd C200
Irvine CA 92618
949 581-9817

(P-776)
ARTISTIC MAINTENANCE INC
16092 Construction Cir E, Irvine (92606-4401)
PHONE.....................949 733-8690
Rudy Moracco, *Manager*
EMP: 150
SALES (corp-wide): 26.3MM **Privately Held**
SIC: 0782 Landscape contractors; garden maintenance services
HQ: Artistic Maintenance, Inc.
15510 Rockfield Blvd C200
Irvine CA 92618
949 581-9817

(P-777)
AZTEC LANDSCAPING INC (PA)
7980 Lemon Grove Way, Lemon Grove (91945-1820)
PHONE.....................619 464-3303
Genaro Garcia, *President*
Rafael Aguilar, *Treasurer*
Ramon Aguilar, *Vice Pres*
Marcy Grismer, *Director*
EMP: 180
SQ FT: 30,000
SALES (est): 32.7MM **Privately Held**
WEB: www.azteclandscaping.com
SIC: 0782 0783 7349 Landscape contractors; ornamental shrub & tree services; janitorial service, contract basis

(P-778)
BENCHMARK LANDSCAPE INC
12575 Stowe Dr, Poway (92064-6805)
PHONE.....................858 513-7190
John A Mohns, *President*
Sharon R Mohns, *Admin Sec*
Ethan Hagen, *Production*
Ross White, *Accounts Mgr*
EMP: 220
SQ FT: 18,000
SALES (est): 24.1MM **Privately Held**
WEB: www.benchmarklandscape.com
SIC: 0782 Landscape contractors

(P-779)
BLOSSOM VALLEY CNSTR INC
1125 Mabury Rd, San Jose (95133-1029)
P.O. Box 611537 (95161-1537)
PHONE.....................408 993-0766
Mark Collishaw, *President*
Robert Jimenez, *CEO*
EMP: 60
SQ FT: 5,000
SALES (est): 5MM **Privately Held**
SIC: 0782 Landscape contractors

(P-780)
C J VANDERGEEST LDSCP CARE INC
2476 Palma Dr Ste G, Ventura (93003-5760)
PHONE.....................805 650-0726
Joanne Smith, *President*
Dusty Smith, *Vice Pres*
EMP: 84
SQ FT: 2,000
SALES (est): 3.8MM **Privately Held**
SIC: 0782 Landscape contractors

(P-781)
CACHO LANDSCAPE MAINTENANCE CO
711 Truman St, San Fernando (91340-3314)
P.O. Box 922764, Sylmar (91392-2764)
PHONE.....................818 365-0773

Eddie Cacho, *President*
Diana Cacho, *CFO*
Genaro Gutierrez, *Vice Pres*
EMP: 50
SQ FT: 3,184
SALES (est): 3MM **Privately Held**
SIC: 0782 Landscape contractors

(P-782)
CAL-WEST NURSERIES INC
138 North Dr, Norco (92860-1637)
PHONE..................................951 270-0667
Michael Whiting, *President*
Matt Whiting, *Purch Agent*
Jerry Gonzalez, *Maint Spvr*
Harvey Garcia, *Supervisor*
EMP: 150
SQ FT: 1,700
SALES (est): 14.9MM **Privately Held**
WEB: www.calwestlandscape.com
SIC: 0782 0181 Landscape contractors;
nursery stock, growing of

(P-783)
CALIFORNIA LDSCP & DESIGN INC
Also Called: CA Landscape and Design
273 N Benson Ave, Upland (91786-5614)
PHONE..................................909 949-1601
Joseph Ciaglia Jr, *CEO*
Margaret Mingura, *CFO*
Andres Olguin, *Technology*
EMP: 120
SQ FT: 1,500
SALES (est): 17MM **Privately Held**
WEB: www.callandscape.com
SIC: 0782 Landscape contractors

(P-784)
CENTRESCAPES INC
165 Gentry St, Pomona (91767-2184)
PHONE..................................909 392-3303
Mark Marcus, *President*
Grace Loya, *Corp Secy*
EMP: 88
SQ FT: 7,000
SALES (est): 6.9MM **Privately Held**
WEB: www.centrescapes.com
SIC: 0782 Landscape contractors

(P-785)
CHAMPAGNE LANDSCAPE NURS INC
3233 N Cornelia Ave, Fresno (93722-4606)
P.O. Box 9755 (93794-9755)
PHONE..................................559 277-8188
Robert Champagne, *President*
Gail Champagne, *Treasurer*
Robert N Champagne, *Vice Pres*
Courtney Woody, *Admin Sec*
EMP: 87
SALES (est): 5.3MM **Privately Held**
SIC: 0782 0781 Garden maintenance
services; landscape architects

(P-786)
CIELO AZUL INC
Also Called: Blue Skies Landscape Maint
1545 Lake Dr, Encinitas (92024-5224)
P.O. Box 17026, San Diego (92177-7026)
PHONE..................................855 863-8503
Pedro Navarro Jr, *President*
Natali Navarro, *Treasurer*
Julie Navarro, *Admin Sec*
EMP: 75 **EST:** 1976
SALES (est): 3.8MM **Privately Held**
WEB: www.blueskieslandscape.com
SIC: 0782 Landscape contractors

(P-787)
CITY II ENTERPRISES INC
Also Called: Flora Terra Landscape MGT
845 Earle Ave, San Jose (95126-3404)
PHONE..................................408 275-1200
Gene E Ebertowski, *President*
Kimberly Garcia, *Admin Sec*
EMP: 50
SQ FT: 40,000
SALES (est): 3MM **Privately Held**
WEB: www.floraterra.com
SIC: 0782 Landscape contractors

(P-788)
COHEN RICHARD LDSCP & CNSTR
20795 Canada Rd, El Toro (92630-7702)
PHONE..................................949 768-0599
Richard Cohen, *President*
Linda Cohen, *Treasurer*
EMP: 50 **EST:** 1976
SQ FT: 1,000
SALES (est): 2.2MM **Privately Held**
WEB: www.richardcohenlandscape.com
SIC: 0782 Landscape contractors

(P-789)
COMMON GROUND LDSCP MGT INC
1127 Mockingbird Ct, San Jose (95120-3435)
PHONE..................................408 278-9807
William Jauch, *President*
Tris Jauch, *Treasurer*
EMP: 50
SALES (est): 2MM **Privately Held**
SIC: 0782 Landscape contractors

(P-790)
COMPLETE LANDSCAPE CARE INC
13316 Leffingwell Rd, Whittier (90605-4136)
PHONE..................................562 946-4441
Tom Murray, *President*
EMP: 57
SQ FT: 26,000
SALES (est): 5MM **Privately Held**
WEB: www.completelandscapecareinc.com
SIC: 0782 1711 Landscape contractors; ir-
rigation sprinkler system installation

(P-791)
D & H LANDSCAPING INC
4221 Appian Way, El Sobrante (94803-2203)
P.O. Box 57, Pinole (94564-0057)
PHONE..................................510 223-6597
David Treas, *President*
EMP: 60
SALES (est): 4.7MM **Privately Held**
WEB: www.dandhlandscaping.com
SIC: 0782 0781 Lawn care services; land-
scape planning services

(P-792)
DAVID OLLIS LANDSCAPE DEV INC
450 Kansas St Ste 104, Redlands (92373-1481)
PHONE..................................909 307-1911
David Ollis, *President*
EMP: 50
SALES (est): 3.8MM **Privately Held**
WEB: www.davidollis.com
SIC: 0782 Landscape contractors

(P-793)
DE LA TORRE LANDSCAPE & MAINT
656 Paseo Grande, Corona (92882-2837)
P.O. Box 3018 (92878-3018)
PHONE..................................951 549-3525
Robert De La Torre, *President*
Socorro De La Torre, *Vice Pres*
Veronica De La Torre, *Admin Sec*
Veronica Dela Torre, *Controller*
EMP: 230
SQ FT: 1,108
SALES (est): 10.2MM **Privately Held**
SIC: 0782 Landscape contractors

(P-794)
DECKER LANDSCAPING INC
13265 Bill Francis Dr, Auburn (95603-9022)
PHONE..................................916 652-1780
Christopher Decker, *President*
Dan McElvin, *CFO*
Tom Decker, *Vice Pres*
EMP: 75
SQ FT: 2,500
SALES (est): 7.9MM **Privately Held**
SIC: 0782 0781 Landscape contractors;
landscape architects

(P-795)
DEL CONTES LANDSCAPING INC
41900 Boscell Rd, Fremont (94538-3196)
PHONE..................................510 353-6030
Tom Del Conte, *CEO*
Mario Camacho, *Division Mgr*
Maria Ramirez, *Executive Asst*
John Soriano, *Facilities Mgr*
Ricardo Magana, *Manager*
EMP: 100
SQ FT: 960
SALES (est): 11.4MM **Privately Held**
WEB: www.dclandscaping.com
SIC: 0782 Landscape contractors

(P-796)
DEMARIA LANDTECH
5631 Palmer Way Ste C, Carlsbad (92010-7243)
PHONE..................................858 481-5500
John Demaria, *CEO*
EMP: 50 **EST:** 2016
SALES (est): 925K **Privately Held**
SIC: 0782 Landscape contractors

(P-797)
DEMARIA LANDTECH INC
2789 High Mead Cir, Vista (92084-1830)
PHONE..................................858 481-5500
John Demaria, *Owner*
EMP: 50
SALES (est): 1.2MM **Privately Held**
WEB: www.demarialandtech.com
SIC: 0782 Landscape contractors

(P-798)
DESERT HAVEN ENTERPRISES INC
43437 Copeland Cir, Lancaster (93535-4672)
P.O. Box 2110 (93539-2110)
PHONE..................................661 948-8402
Jenni C Moran, *CEO*
Roberta Terry, *CFO*
Ramona Aloyo, *Human Res Dir*
Jeff Whiteford, *Manager*
EMP: 536
SQ FT: 15,000
SALES (est): 8MM **Privately Held**
WEB: www.deserthaven.org
SIC: 0782 8331 Lawn & garden services;
work experience center

(P-799)
DIABLO LANDSCAPE INC
1655 Berryessa Rd, San Jose (95133-1082)
PHONE..................................408 487-9620
Fax: 408 487-9621
EMP: 80
SQ FT: 38,000
SALES (est): 6.9MM
SALES (corp-wide): 32.2MM **Privately Held**
WEB: www.diablolandscape.com
SIC: 0782
PA: The Celtis Group Inc
1655 Berryessa Rd Ste A
San Jose CA
408 487-9620

(P-800)
DIVERSCAPE INC
Also Called: Diversified Landscape Co
21730 Bundy Canyon Rd, Wildomar (92595-8780)
PHONE..................................951 245-1686
Vicki Moralez, *President*
Paul Moralez, *Vice Pres*
Anthony Rodriguez, *Area Mgr*
Juan Martinez, *Project Mgr*
EMP: 90
SQ FT: 4,000
SALES (est): 12.5MM **Privately Held**
WEB: www.diversifiedlandscape.com
SIC: 0782 1611 Garden maintenance
services; landscape contractors; general
contractor, highway & street construction

(P-801)
DMA GREENCARE CONTRACTING INC
3000 E Coronado St, Anaheim (92806-2602)
PHONE..................................714 630-9470
Dennis Aldridge, *CEO*
Darin Doucette, *Vice Pres*
EMP: 50
SQ FT: 5,000
SALES (est): 9MM **Privately Held**
SIC: 0782 Landscape contractors

(P-802)
DOMINGUEZ LANDSCAPE SVCS INC
8376 Rovana Cir, Sacramento (95828-2527)
P.O. Box 292727 (95829-2727)
PHONE..................................916 381-8855
Robert Dominguez, *President*
Bonnie J Dominguez, *Vice Pres*
EMP: 78
SQ FT: 7,200
SALES (est): 5.1MM **Privately Held**
SIC: 0782 Landscape contractors

(P-803)
DOOSE LANDSCAPE INCORPORATED
785 E Mission Rd, San Marcos (92069-1903)
PHONE..................................760 591-4500
Robert J Doose, *President*
Shelley Nolet, *Treasurer*
Tom Doose, *Vice Pres*
Susan Daugherty, *Admin Sec*
Shelly Nolet, *Purchasing*
EMP: 85
SQ FT: 11,300
SALES (est): 6.8MM **Privately Held**
WEB: www.dooselandscape.com
SIC: 0782 Landscape contractors

(P-804)
DWIW INC
Also Called: Land Scapes
700 W 16th St, Costa Mesa (92627-4303)
PHONE..................................949 574-7147
John Duley, *President*
Pam Duley, *Vice Pres*
EMP: 50
SQ FT: 5,000
SALES (est): 2.3MM **Privately Held**
WEB: www.dwiw.com
SIC: 0782 Landscape contractors

(P-805)
ECHO LANDSCAPE
2401 Grant Ave, San Lorenzo (94580-1807)
P.O. Box 20926, Castro Valley (94546-8926)
PHONE..................................510 481-8614
Troy Deherrera, *President*
EMP: 60
SQ FT: 1,600
SALES (est): 2.5MM **Privately Held**
WEB: www.scyence.com
SIC: 0782 Landscape contractors

(P-806)
ELITE LANDSCAPING INC
2972 Larkin Ave, Clovis (93612-3986)
PHONE..................................559 292-7760
Guy Stockbridge, *President*
Jill Stockbridge, *CFO*
EMP: 150
SQ FT: 20,000
SALES (est): 7.6MM **Privately Held**
WEB: www.elitelandscapinginc.com
SIC: 0782 Landscape contractors

(P-807)
EMERALD LANDSCAPE SERVICES
1041 N Kemp St, Anaheim (92801-2518)
PHONE..................................714 844-2200
John C Croul, *President*
Pam Mc Entire, *Consultant*
EMP: 70
SALES (est): 4.1MM **Privately Held**
SIC: 0782 0781 Landscape contractors;
landscape planning services

(P-808)

ENHANCED LANDSCAPE MGT INC

1938 E Thousand Oaks Blvd, Thousand
Oaks (91362-2913)
PHONE..............................805 557-2737
Gregory Epstein, *President*
EMP: 65
SALES (est): 3MM **Privately Held**
SIC: 0782 0721 Landscape contractors;
crop related entomological services (in-
sect control)

(P-809)

ESQUIRE LANDSCAPE INC

8380 Miralani Dr Ste B, San Diego
(92126-4304)
PHONE..............................858 530-2949
William A Behl, *President*
EMP: 50
SQ FT: 1,500
SALES (est): 2.2MM **Privately Held**
SIC: 0782 Landscape contractors

(P-810)

EXCEL LANDSCAPE INC

710 Rimpau Ave Ste 108, Corona
(92879-5724)
P.O. Box 77995 (92877-0133)
PHONE..............................951 735-9650
Jose Alfaro, *President*
Jason Alfaro, *Project Mgr*
Hector Lopez, *Project Mgr*
▲ EMP: 120
SQ FT: 1,200
SALES (est): 7.5MM **Privately Held**
WEB: www.excellandscape.com
SIC: 0782 Lawn care services; garden
maintenance services

(P-811)

FENDERSCAPE INC

Also Called: Proscape Landscape
1446 E Hill St, Signal Hill (90755-3527)
PHONE..............................562 988-2228
David Fender, *President*
Linda Fender, *Treasurer*
Joe Rocha, *Supervisor*
EMP: 127
SQ FT: 1,893
SALES: 1MM **Privately Held**
SIC: 0782 Landscape contractors

(P-812)

FRANK CARSON LDSCP & MAINT INC

Also Called: Carson Landscape Industries
9530 Elder Creek Rd, Sacramento
(95829-9306)
PHONE..............................916 856-5400
Frank M Carson, *CEO*
Kathy Pipis, *Admin Sec*
EMP: 200
SQ FT: 36,000
SALES: 15.2MM **Privately Held**
SIC: 0782 Landscape contractors

(P-813)

FS COMMERCIAL LANDSCAPE INC (PA)

5151 Pedley Rd, Riverside (92509-3937)
PHONE..............................951 360-7070
G John Wood, *President*
Juan Vargas, *Accounts Mgr*
EMP: 75
SQ FT: 1,500
SALES (est): 7.6MM **Privately Held**
WEB: www.fslandscapes.com
SIC: 0782 Landscape contractors

(P-814)

GACHINA LANDSCAPE MGT INC

1130 Obrien Dr, Menlo Park (94025-1411)
PHONE..............................650 853-0400
John P Gachina, *CEO*
Sharon Chao, *General Mgr*
Sylvia Espinoza, *Administration*
Scott Harris, *Project Mgr*
Dustin Stefanick, *Project Mgr*
EMP: 269
SQ FT: 12,000
SALES (est): 26.2MM **Privately Held**
WEB: www.gachina.com
SIC: 0782 Landscape contractors

(P-815)

GARDENERS GUILD INC

2780 Goodrick Ave, Richmond
(94801-1110)
PHONE..............................415 457-0400
Kevin Davis, *President*
Mike Davidson, *Vice Pres*
Donna Petralia, *Administration*
Ginny Kuhel, *Director*
Paul Swanson, *Director*
EMP: 140
SQ FT: 25,000
SALES (est): 14.8MM **Privately Held**
WEB: www.gardenersguild.com
SIC: 0782 Landscape contractors; lawn
services; garden services

(P-816)

GATEWAY LANDSCAPE CNSTR INC

6735 Sierra Ct Ste A, Dublin (94568-2656)
PHONE..............................925 875-0000
Corey Pontrelli, *President*
David J Garcia, *Vice Pres*
Hali Pontrelli, *Purchasing*
EMP: 75
SQ FT: 3,000
SALES (est): 5.9MM **Privately Held**
WEB: www.gatewaylci.com
SIC: 0782 1711 Landscape contractors; ir-
rigation sprinkler system installation

(P-817)

GOTHIC LANDSCAPING INC (PA)

Also Called: Gothic Ground Management
27502 Avenue Scott, Valencia
(91355-3911)
PHONE..............................661 257-1266
Jon S Georgio, *President*
Ronald Georgio, *Vice Pres*
Mike Georgio, *Principal*
Victor Manuel Cruz, *Area Mgr*
Ricardo Hurtado, *Opers Mgr*
EMP: 200
SQ FT: 5,000
SALES (est): 173.5MM **Privately Held**
WEB: www.gothiclandscape.com
SIC: 0782 Landscape contractors; lawn
services

(P-818)

GRANTS LANDSCAPE SERVICES INC

3046 Orange Ave, Santa Ana (92707-4248)
PHONE..............................714 444-1903
Kenneth Grant, *President*
Harold Grant, *Vice Pres*
EMP: 75
SQ FT: 4,000
SALES (est): 1.6MM **Privately Held**
SIC: 0782 Landscape contractors

(P-819)

GREEN AGAIN LDSCPG & CON INC

851 Charter St, Redwood City
(94063-3004)
PHONE..............................650 368-9304
Frederick C Nurisso, *President*
EMP: 55
SQ FT: 1,400
SALES (est): 1.4MM **Privately Held**
WEB: www.greenagain.com
SIC: 0782 Landscape contractors

(P-820)

GREEN SCENE LANDSCAPE INC

21220 Devonshire St # 102, Chatsworth
(91311-2300)
PHONE..............................818 280-0420
Scott Cohen, *CEO*
Lisa Cohen, *Vice Pres*
Jose Hernandez, *Assistant*
EMP: 58
SQ FT: 1,100
SALES (est): 1.9MM **Privately Held**
WEB: www.greenscenelandscape.com
SIC: 0782 Landscape contractors; lawn
care services

(P-821)

GREENBRIER LAWN TREE EXPRT CO

3616 Bancroft Dr, Spring Valley
(91977-2116)
PHONE..............................619 469-8720
Bill Gibson, *President*
EMP: 60
SQ FT: 6,000
SALES (est): 2.7MM **Privately Held**
SIC: 0782 Landscape contractors

(P-822)

GROWING COMPANY INC

4 Wayne Ct Ste 3, Sacramento
(95829-1305)
PHONE..............................916 379-9088
Bruno Sandoval, *President*
Anne Sandoval, *Vice Pres*
Gualberto Cardenas, *Area Spvr*
Modesto Gonzalez, *Area Spvr*
Dionisio Corona, *Production*
EMP: 100
SQ FT: 10,000
SALES (est): 10.5MM **Privately Held**
WEB: www.thegrowingcompany.net
SIC: 0782 Landscape contractors; garden
maintenance services

(P-823)

GS BROTHERS INC (PA)

2215 N Gaffey St, San Pedro (90731-1238)
PHONE..............................310 833-1369
Alan M Gaudenti, *President*
Robert M Gaudenti, *Corp Secy*
Marge Gonzalez, *Manager*
EMP: 190
SQ FT: 7,000
SALES (est): 19.7MM **Privately Held**
SIC: 0782 Landscape contractors

(P-824)

HABITAT RSTRATION SCIENCES INC (PA)

1217 Distribution Way, Vista (92081-8817)
PHONE..............................760 479-4210
Mark Girard, *President*
June Collins, *President*
Robert Mackie, *Division Mgr*
EMP: 65
SALES (est): 11MM **Privately Held**
SIC: 0782 Landscape contractors

(P-825)

HARVEST LANDSCAPE ENTPS INC

Also Called: Harvest Landscape Maintenance
2339 N Batavia St, Orange (92865-2001)
P.O. Box 3877 (92857-0877)
PHONE..............................714 693-8100
Stephen G Schinhofen, *CEO*
Mariana Salgado, *Administration*
Victoria Vasquez, *Human Res Dir*
Sierra Schinhofen, *Marketing Staff*
Cody Harkins, *Accounts Mgr*
EMP: 160
SALES (est): 16.5MM **Privately Held**
SIC: 0782 Landscape contractors

(P-826)

HE JULIEN & ASSOCIATES INC

Also Called: C&R Maintance
2275 E Hueneme Rd, Oxnard
(93033-8112)
P.O. Box 817, Port Hueneme (93044-0817)
PHONE..............................805 488-8342
EMP: 50
SQ FT: 3,568
SALES (est): 1.4MM **Privately Held**
SIC: 0782

(P-827)

HEAVILAND ENTERPRISES INC (PA)

2180 La Mirada Dr, Vista (92081-8815)
PHONE..............................760 598-7065
Thomas J Heaviland, *CEO*
Rajan Brown, *Director*
EMP: 154
SQ FT: 2,500
SALES (est): 11.4MM **Privately Held**
WEB: www.heaviland.net
SIC: 0782 1542 Landscape contractors;
commercial & office buildings, renovation
& repair

(P-828)

HEMINGTON LANDSCAPE SVCS INC

4170 Business Dr, Cameron Park
(95682-7230)
P.O. Box 1999, Shingle Springs (95682-
1999)
PHONE..............................530 677-9290
Mark E Hemington, *President*
Jill Hemington, *Corp Secy*
EMP: 100
SALES (est): 8.4MM **Privately Held**
WEB: www.hemington.com
SIC: 0782 Landscape contractors

(P-829)

HORT TECH INC

78355 Darby Rd, Bermuda Dunes
(92203-9661)
P.O. Box 3284, Palm Desert (92261-3284)
PHONE..............................760 360-9000
Bryan Jensen, *President*
Linda Gurrola, *Admin Sec*
EMP: 160
SQ FT: 8,000
SALES (est): 7MM **Privately Held**
SIC: 0782 Landscape contractors

(P-830)

IKES LANDSCAPING & MAINTENANCE

2700 Tiber Ave, Davis (95616-2958)
PHONE..............................530 758-1698
Eric Aichwalder, *President*
Don Kearney, *Vice Pres*
Aletha Aichwalder, *Admin Sec*
EMP: 80
SQ FT: 2,000
SALES (est): 3MM **Privately Held**
SIC: 0782 5992 Landscape contractors;
lawn care services; plants, potted

(P-831)

IRRI-SCAPE CONSTRUCTION INC

20182 Carancho Rd, Temecula
(92590-4348)
PHONE..............................951 694-6936
Robert Smith, *President*
EMP: 100
SQ FT: 1,500
SALES (est): 7MM **Privately Held**
SIC: 0782 Landscape contractors

(P-832)

J REDFERN INC

Also Called: Golden State Landscaping
164 N L St, Livermore (94550-2118)
P.O. Box 2091 (94551-2091)
PHONE..............................925 371-3300
John E Redfern, *President*
Rashelle Redfern, *Controller*
Michael Walker, *Director*
EMP: 108
SALES (est): 7.7MM **Privately Held**
WEB: www.jredfern.com
SIC: 0782 Landscape contractors

(P-833)

J VITALE LANDSCAPE & MAINT

8801 Cottonwood Ave, Santee
(92071-4460)
PHONE..............................619 938-2435
Jim Vitale, *President*
EMP: 90
SALES (est): 7MM **Privately Held**
SIC: 0782 Landscape contractors

(P-834)

JAMES H COWAN & ASSOCIATES INC

5126 Clareton Dr Ste 200, Agoura Hills
(91301-4529)
PHONE..............................310 457-2574
Clark J Cowan, *President*
Kendall Whitney, *Admin Sec*
EMP: 95
SQ FT: 3,500
SALES (est): 8.6MM **Privately Held**
WEB: www.jhcowan.com
SIC: 0782 Landscape contractors

▲ = Import ▼=Export
◆ =Import/Export

(P-835)
JENSEN CORP LANDSCAPE CONTR
1983 Concourse Dr, San Jose (95131-1708)
PHONE.............................408 446-4881
John Vlay, *CEO*
Shamina Edwards, *Admin Sec*
EMP: 150 EST: 2008
SALES: 10MM **Privately Held**
SIC: 0782 1521 Landscape contractors; single-family housing construction

(P-836)
JENSEN CORPORATE HOLDINGS INC (PA)
1983 Concourse Dr, San Jose (95131-1708)
PHONE.............................408 446-1118
John Vlay, *CEO*
Quang Trinh, *CFO*
Donald Defever, *Division Pres*
Glenn Berry, *Vice Pres*
Kirk Brown, *Vice Pres*
EMP: 117
SQ FT: 13,000
SALES (est): 115.4MM **Privately Held**
WEB: www.jensencorp.com
SIC: 0782 Landscape contractors

(P-837)
JENSEN LANDSCAPE SERVICES INC
Also Called: Jensen Corp Landscape Contrs
1983 Concourse Dr, San Jose (95131-1708)
PHONE.............................408 446-1118
John Vlay, *CEO*
Anthony Whalls, *President*
Paul Johnson, *CFO*
Glenn Berry, *Vice Pres*
Clint Christman, *Branch Mgr*
EMP: 163
SALES (est): 8.8MM
SALES (corp-wide): 115.4MM **Privately Held**
WEB: www.jensencorp.com
SIC: 0782 Landscape contractors
PA: Jensen Corporate Holdings, Inc.
1983 Concourse Dr
San Jose CA 95131
408 446-1118

(P-838)
JLP LANDSCAPE CONTRACTING
901 7th St, Santa Rosa (95404-4255)
PHONE.............................707 526-6285
John Prior, *President*
Alicia Lene Ruppell Prior, *Treasurer*
Joe Verdn, *Project Mgr*
EMP: 50
SQ FT: 2,000
SALES: 3.1MM **Privately Held**
SIC: 0782 0781 Landscape contractors; landscape planning services

(P-839)
JMA INVESTMENTS LTD
Also Called: Ahrens Landscape & Maintenance
9265 Beatty Dr, Sacramento (95826-9702)
P.O. Box 279199 (95827-9199)
PHONE.............................916 685-1355
Jeff Ahrens, *President*
Michele Ahrens, *Vice Pres*
EMP: 99
SQ FT: 2,000
SALES: 14MM **Privately Held**
SIC: 0782 Lawn care services

(P-840)
JPA LANDSCAPE & CNSTR INC
256 Boeing Ct, Livermore (94551-9258)
P.O. Box 1292, Pleasanton (94566-0129)
PHONE.............................925 960-9602
Ed Morrissey, *President*
Jody Morrissey, *Treasurer*
John Morrissey, *Opers Mgr*
EMP: 75 EST: 1995
SQ FT: 9,000
SALES: 3.9MM **Privately Held**
WEB: www.jpalandscape.com
SIC: 0782 Landscape contractors

(P-841)
KIRKPATRICK LDSCPG SVCS INC
43752 Jackson St, Indio (92201-2540)
P.O. Box 10430 (92202-2542)
PHONE.............................760 347-6926
Steven Kirkpatrick, *President*
EMP: 200
SQ FT: 5,000
SALES (est): 10.9MM **Privately Held**
SIC: 0782 Lawn care services; garden maintenance services

(P-842)
KITSON LANDSCAPE MGT INC
5787 Thornwood Dr, Goleta (93117-3801)
PHONE.............................805 681-9460
Sarah Kitson, *President*
Dave Fudurich, *CFO*
David Fudurich, *Treasurer*
Brent Kitson, *Vice Pres*
Sally Kitson, *Admin Sec*
EMP: 80
SQ FT: 52,272
SALES (est): 5.4MM **Privately Held**
WEB: www.kitsonlandscape.com
SIC: 0782 Landscape contractors

(P-843)
L A SWIKARD INC
Also Called: Terra Firma Landscape Company
9520 Candida St, San Diego (92126-4540)
PHONE.............................858 408-3700
Larry A Swikard, *President*
Cindy A Swikard, *CFO*
Mike Swikard, *Vice Pres*
John Savallo, *Sales Staff*
EMP: 225 EST: 1981
SQ FT: 20,000
SALES (est): 15.8MM **Privately Held**
SIC: 0782 Landscape contractors

(P-844)
L BARRIOS AND ASSOCIATES INC
302 E Fthill Blvd Ste 101, San Dimas (91773)
P.O. Box 3948 (91773-7948)
PHONE.............................909 592-5893
John Barrios, *President*
Jennifer Stock, *Admin Sec*
EMP: 50 EST: 1955
SALES (est): 3.3MM **Privately Held**
SIC: 0782 1711 Landscape contractors; lawn services; irrigation sprinkler system installation

(P-845)
LANDCARE USA LLC
Also Called: Trugreen
216 N Clara St, Santa Ana (92703-3518)
PHONE.............................949 559-7771
Kenny Stites, *Branch Mgr*
EMP: 80
SALES (corp-wide): 165MM **Privately Held**
SIC: 0782 Lawn care services
PA: Landcare Usa L.L.C.
5295 Westview Dr Ste 100
Frederick MD 21703
301 874-3300

(P-846)
LANDCARE USA LLC
Also Called: Trugreen
770 Metcalf St, Escondido (92025-1667)
PHONE.............................760 747-1174
Brett Horan, *Branch Mgr*
EMP: 80
SALES (corp-wide): 165MM **Privately Held**
SIC: 0782 Lawn care services
PA: Landcare Usa L.L.C.
5295 Westview Dr Ste 100
Frederick MD 21703
301 874-3300

(P-847)
LANDCARE USA LLC
Also Called: Trugreen
1196 Patricia Ave, Simi Valley (93065-2809)
PHONE.............................805 520-9394
Noe Alcaraz, *Branch Mgr*
EMP: 125
SALES (corp-wide): 165MM **Privately Held**
SIC: 0782 Lawn care services
PA: Landcare Usa L.L.C.
5295 Westview Dr Ste 100
Frederick MD 21703
301 874-3300

(P-848)
LANDCARE USA LLC
930 Shiloh Rd Bldg 44-B, Windsor (95492-9664)
PHONE.............................707 836-1460
Scott Hall, *Branch Mgr*
EMP: 60
SALES (corp-wide): 165MM **Privately Held**
SIC: 0782 Lawn care services
PA: Landcare Usa L.L.C.
5295 Westview Dr Ste 100
Frederick MD 21703
301 874-3300

(P-849)
LANDCARE USA LLC
Also Called: Trugreen Lndcare Michael Bogan
15606 Cornet St, Santa Fe Springs (90670-5514)
PHONE.............................714 936-9512
EMP: 82
SALES (corp-wide): 165MM **Privately Held**
SIC: 0782 Landscape contractors
PA: Landcare Usa L.L.C.
5295 Westview Dr Ste 100
Frederick MD 21703
301 874-3300

(P-850)
LANDCARE USA LLC
1315 W 130th St, Gardena (90247-1503)
PHONE.............................310 719-1008
Don Cully, *Branch Mgr*
EMP: 56
SALES (corp-wide): 165MM **Privately Held**
SIC: 0782 Landscape contractors; lawn services
PA: Landcare Usa L.L.C.
5295 Westview Dr Ste 100
Frederick MD 21703
301 874-3300

(P-851)
LANDCARE USA LLC
4134 Temple City Blvd, Rosemead (91770-1550)
PHONE.............................310 354-1520
Joe Espinoza, *Branch Mgr*
EMP: 56
SALES (corp-wide): 165MM **Privately Held**
SIC: 0782 Landscape contractors; lawn services
PA: Landcare Usa L.L.C.
5295 Westview Dr Ste 100
Frederick MD 21703
301 874-3300

(P-852)
LANDCARE USA LLC
Also Called: Trugreen
1323 W 130th St, Gardena (90247-1503)
PHONE.............................310 354-1520
Dave Evans, *Branch Mgr*
EMP: 170
SALES (corp-wide): 165MM **Privately Held**
SIC: 0782 7342 Lawn care services; disinfecting & pest control services
PA: Landcare Usa L.L.C.
5295 Westview Dr Ste 100
Frederick MD 21703
301 874-3300

(P-853)
LANDCARE USA LLC
Also Called: Trugreen
3213 Fitzgerald Rd, Rancho Cordova (95742-6813)
PHONE.............................916 635-0936
Kevin Arnett, *Branch Mgr*
EMP: 100
SALES (corp-wide): 165MM **Privately Held**
SIC: 0782 Lawn care services
PA: Landcare Usa L.L.C.
5295 Westview Dr Ste 100
Frederick MD 21703
301 874-3300

(P-854)
LANDCARE USA LLC
5248 Governor Dr, San Diego (92122-2800)
PHONE.............................858 453-1755
Craig Gerber, *VP Finance*
Jasmine Sutherland, *Administration*
Jim Clifford, *Manager*
Krista Jimenez, *Manager*
EMP: 112
SALES (corp-wide): 165MM **Privately Held**
SIC: 0782 Lawn care services
PA: Landcare Usa L.L.C.
5295 Westview Dr Ste 100
Frederick MD 21703
301 874-3300

(P-855)
LANDCARE USA LLC
Also Called: Trugreen
7755 Deering Ave, Canoga Park (91304-5653)
PHONE.............................818 346-7552
Raul Sanchez, *Branch Mgr*
EMP: 150
SALES (corp-wide): 165MM **Privately Held**
SIC: 0782 Lawn care services; landscape contractors
PA: Landcare Usa L.L.C.
5295 Westview Dr Ste 100
Frederick MD 21703
301 874-3300

(P-856)
LANDCARE USA LLC
Also Called: Trugreen
85 Old Tully Rd, San Jose (95111-1910)
PHONE.............................408 727-4099
Jeff Kunkel, *Branch Mgr*
EMP: 75
SALES (corp-wide): 165MM **Privately Held**
SIC: 0782 Lawn care services
PA: Landcare Usa L.L.C.
5295 Westview Dr Ste 100
Frederick MD 21703
301 874-3300

(P-857)
LANDCO
7333 Clybourn Ave, Sun Valley (91352-5143)
PHONE.............................818 612-0118
Martin Stowell, *Owner*
▲ EMP: 100
SALES (est): 1.7MM **Privately Held**
SIC: 0782 Landscape contractors

(P-858)
LANDESIGN CNSTR & MAINT INC
1328 Airport Blvd, Santa Rosa (95403-1009)
P.O. Box 2326 (95405-0326)
PHONE.............................707 578-2657
John Fitzgerald, *Owner*
Denise Fitzgerald, *Co-Owner*
EMP: 90
SQ FT: 1,000
SALES: 5MM **Privately Held**
SIC: 0782 Landscape contractors

(P-859)
LANDSCAPE DEVELOPMENT INC (PA)
28447 Witherspoon Pkwy, Valencia (91355-4174)
PHONE.............................661 295-1970
Gary Horton, *CEO*
Tim Myers, *CFO*
Casper Correll, *Vice Pres*
Bruce Pedersen, *Info Tech Mgr*
Patrick Kolakian, *Project Mgr*
▲ EMP: 350

SALES (est): 95.5MM **Privately Held**
WEB: www.landscapedevelopment.com
SIC: 0782 5039 Landscape contractors;
soil erosion control fabrics

(P-860)
LANDSCAPE SUPPORT SERVICES
12610 Saticoy St S, North Hollywood (91605-4313)
P.O. Box 55307, Sherman Oaks (91413-0307)
PHONE..................818 475-0680
Soheila Sturm, *President*
EMP: 52 **EST:** 2011
SQ FT: 2,500
SALES (est): 2.8MM **Privately Held**
SIC: 0782 0781 1611 1629 Landscape contractors; landscape counseling & planning; grading; irrigation system construction

(P-861)
LAWNMAN II INC
4300 82nd St Ste C, Sacramento (95826-4730)
PHONE..................916 739-1420
Burnie Lenau, *President*
▲ **EMP:** 60
SQ FT: 3,000
SALES (est): 3MM **Privately Held**
WEB: www.lawnmansac.com
SIC: 0782 Landscape contractors

(P-862)
LEONARD ANTHONY VALENTI INC
9110 Marcella Ave, Gilroy (95020-9716)
P.O. Box 1179 (95021-1179)
PHONE..................408 848-9688
Leonard A Valenti, *President*
EMP: 60
SALES (est): 2.1MM **Privately Held**
SIC: 0782 7349 1742 Landscape contractors; building maintenance, except repairs; plastering, drywall & insulation

(P-863)
LIBERTY LANDSCAPING INC (PA)
5212 El Rivino Rd, Riverside (92509-1807)
PHONE..................951 683-2999
Alejandro Casillas, *President*
EMP: 200 **EST:** 1997
SQ FT: 43,560
SALES: 11.5MM **Privately Held**
SIC: 0782 0783 Landscape contractors; tree trimming services for public utility lines

(P-864)
MACKENZIE LANDSCAPE A CAL CORP
33380 Bailey Park Blvd, Menifee (92584-9585)
PHONE..................951 679-5477
Michael Mackenzie, *President*
Judy Mackenzie, *CFO*
EMP: 100
SQ FT: 1,500
SALES (est): 2.9MM **Privately Held**
SIC: 0782 Landscape contractors; highway lawn & garden maintenance services

(P-865)
MARIPOSA LANDSCAPES INC (PA)
Also Called: Mariposa Horticultural Entps
6232 Santos Diaz St, Irwindale (91702-3267)
PHONE..................626 960-0196
Terry Noriega, *President*
Antonio Valenzuela, *Vice Pres*
Jesus Ramirez, *Accounts Mgr*
EMP: 65
SQ FT: 2,000
SALES (est): 48.6MM **Privately Held**
WEB: www.mariposahorticultural.com
SIC: 0782 Garden maintenance services; lawn care services; landscape contractors

(P-866)
MARTINA LANDSCAPE INC
811 Camden Ave, Campbell (95008-4103)
PHONE..................408 871-8800

Joe Martina, *President*
EMP: 80
SQ FT: 2,000
SALES (est): 5.2MM **Privately Held**
SIC: 0782 Landscape contractors

(P-867)
MEDLIN DEVELOPMENT
320 Tropicana Ranch Rd, Colton (92324-3605)
PHONE..................909 825-5296
EMP: 50
SQ FT: 1,800
SALES (est): 1.5MM **Privately Held**
SIC: 0782

(P-868)
MIDORI LANDSCAPE INC
Also Called: Midori Landscaping
3231 S Main St, Santa Ana (92707-4405)
PHONE..................714 751-8792
Naga Hamamoto, *President*
EMP: 80
SQ FT: 8,200
SALES (est): 5.2MM **Privately Held**
SIC: 0782 Landscape contractors

(P-869)
MIKE MCCALL LANDSCAPE INC
4749 Clayton Rd, Concord (94521-2936)
PHONE..................925 363-8100
Mike McCall, *President*
Mark Tate, *COO*
Garrett McCall, *Purch Dir*
Eloy Sanabria, *Manager*
Rob Scott, *Manager*
EMP: 140
SQ FT: 1,000
SALES (est): 13.5MM **Privately Held**
WEB: www.mikemccalllandscape.com
SIC: 0782 Landscape contractors

(P-870)
MISSION LANDSCAPE SERVICE
952 E Francis St, Ontario (91761-5630)
PHONE..................909 947-7290
David Dubois, *Owner*
Stephen Natalo, *Sr Project Mgr*
Jose Irias, *Accounts Mgr*
EMP: 80
SALES (est): 3.4MM **Privately Held**
SIC: 0782 Landscape contractors

(P-871)
MONARCH LANDSCAPE HOLDINGS LLC (PA)
550 S Hope St Ste 1675, Los Angeles (90071-2692)
PHONE..................213 816-1750
Tony W Lee, *Mng Member*
Michael Hope, *Manager*
EMP: 150 **EST:** 2015
SALES (est): 7.9MM **Privately Held**
SIC: 0782 Garden services

(P-872)
MONUMENT CONSTRUCTION INC
Also Called: Techcon
16200 Vineyard Blvd # 100, Morgan Hill (95037-7164)
PHONE..................408 778-1350
Paul Maxwell Swing, *President*
Diane Swing, *CFO*
EMP: 90
SQ FT: 6,000
SALES (est): 8.7MM **Privately Held**
SIC: 0782 Landscape contractors

(P-873)
MPL ENTERPRISES INC
Also Called: Mike Parker Landscape
2302 S Susan St, Santa Ana (92704-4421)
PHONE..................714 545-1717
Michael Parker, *President*
EMP: 90
SQ FT: 2,000
SALES (est): 5MM **Privately Held**
WEB: www.mikeparkerlandscape.com
SIC: 0782 Landscape contractors

(P-874)
N V LANDSCAPE INC
24400 Walnut St Ste D, Newhall (91321-2855)
P.O. Box 4082, Sequim WA (98382-4353)
PHONE..................661 286-8888
Jeff Brown, *President*
Holly Brown, *Corp Secy*
EMP: 60
SALES (est): 1.6MM **Privately Held**
WEB: www.nvlandscape.com
SIC: 0782 Landscape contractors

(P-875)
NATIVE SONS LANDSCAPING INC
25 Beta Ct Ste L, San Ramon (94583-1245)
PHONE..................925 837-8175
Mike Hertel, *President*
Louise Hertel, *Vice Pres*
EMP: 50
SQ FT: 1,800
SALES (est): 4.5MM **Privately Held**
WEB: www.nativesons.net
SIC: 0782 0781 Landscape contractors; landscape counseling & planning

(P-876)
NEW IMAGE LANDSCAPE COMPANY
3250 Darby Cmn, Fremont (94539-5601)
PHONE..................510 226-9191
Brian Takehara, *President*
Irene Briggs, *Controller*
Elodia Criado, *Human Res Mgr*
Carlos Barajas, *Manager*
Segi Cabral, *Accounts Mgr*
EMP: 55
SQ FT: 4,000
SALES (est): 3.8MM **Privately Held**
WEB: www.newimagelandscape.com
SIC: 0782 Landscape contractors

(P-877)
NEW VIEW LANDSCAPE INC
24860 Calabasas Rd, Calabasas (91302-1429)
PHONE..................818 222-8972
Lance Lortscher, *President*
Mike Stell, *Treasurer*
EMP: 60
SQ FT: 1,200
SALES (est): 2.8MM **Privately Held**
WEB: www.newviewlandscape.com
SIC: 0782 Garden maintenance services; turf installation services, except artificial

(P-878)
NEW WAY LANDSCAPE & TREE SVCS
7485 Ronson Rd, San Diego (92111-1507)
PHONE..................858 505-8300
Randy Newhard, *CEO*
Kathryn Dejong, *President*
Monty Bell, *COO*
Dan Suhovecky, *CFO*
Mike Atkinson, *Regional Mgr*
EMP: 175
SQ FT: 6,400
SALES (est): 20.3MM **Privately Held**
WEB: www.newwaypro.com
SIC: 0782 Landscape contractors

(P-879)
NIEVES LANDSCAPE INC
1629 E Edinger Ave, Santa Ana (92705-5001)
PHONE..................714 835-7332
Gregorio Nieves, *President*
Patricia White, *Admin Sec*
EMP: 150
SALES (est): 13.4MM **Privately Held**
SIC: 0782 Landscape contractors

(P-880)
NITTANY LION LANDSCAPING INC
Also Called: NI Services
14770 Firestone Blvd # 203, La Mirada (90638-5917)
PHONE..................714 635-1788
Sam Aldrich, *President*
Don G Abbey, *Ch of Bd*
EMP: 63 **EST:** 1994

SQ FT: 7,300
SALES: 6.5MM **Privately Held**
SIC: 0782 Landscape contractors

(P-881)
NORTHWEST LANDSCAPE MAINT CO
283 Kinney Dr, San Jose (95112-4433)
PHONE..................408 298-6489
Warren Nakamura, *President*
Douglas Nakamura, *Corp Secy*
Paul Nakamura, *Vice Pres*
EMP: 50
SQ FT: 4,808
SALES (est): 3.3MM **Privately Held**
WEB: www.northwestlandscapemc.com
SIC: 0782 Landscape contractors

(P-882)
OCONNELL LANDSCAPE MAINT INC
4600 Leisure Village Way, Oceanside (92056-5147)
PHONE..................760 630-4963
EMP: 50
SALES (corp-wide): 147.9MM **Privately Held**
SIC: 0782 Landscape contractors
PA: O'connell Landscape Maintenance Inc.
23091 Arroyo Vis
Rcho Sta Marg CA 92688
949 589-2007

(P-883)
PAC WEST LAND CARE INC
Also Called: Pacific West Tree Service
408 Olive Ave, Vista (92083-3438)
P.O. Box 99 (92085-0099)
PHONE..................760 630-0231
Barry Blue, *President*
EMP: 130
SQ FT: 3,000
SALES (est): 4.4MM **Privately Held**
SIC: 0782 Landscape contractors

(P-884)
PACIFIC GREEN LANDSCAPE INC (PA)
8834 Winter Gardens Blvd, Lakeside (92040-5419)
PHONE..................619 390-1546
Michael C Regan, *President*
Mark Mazalewski, *Branch Mgr*
Melanie Krogman, *Marketing Staff*
EMP: 110
SQ FT: 1,450
SALES (est): 8.4MM **Privately Held**
WEB: www.pacificgreenlandscape.com
SIC: 0782 Landscape contractors; lawn services

(P-885)
PARK LANDSCAPE MAINTENANCE (PA)
Also Called: Park Landscape Maint 1-2-3-4
22421 Gilberto Ste A, Rcho STA Marg (92688-2104)
PHONE..................949 546-8300
Robert Morrison, *President*
Tom Tracy, *Shareholder*
Mike Tracy, *CEO*
Tom England, *CFO*
EMP: 300
SQ FT: 10,000
SALES (est): 12.9MM **Privately Held**
SIC: 0782 Lawn care services; lawn services; landscape contractors

(P-886)
PARK WEST RESCOM INC
22421 Gilberto, Rcho STA Marg (92688-2104)
PHONE..................949 546-8300
Michael S Tracy, *CEO*
Bart Ryder, *President*
EMP: 101
SQ FT: 10,000
SALES (est): 4.8MM **Privately Held**
SIC: 0782 Landscape contractors

(P-887)
PARKWOOD LANDSCAPE MAINT INC
16443 Hart St, Van Nuys (91406-4608)
PHONE..................818 988-9677

David Melito, *President*
EMP: 95 **EST:** 1988
SQ FT: 1,500
SALES (est): 6MM **Privately Held**
WEB: www.parkwoodlandscape.com
SIC: 0782 Landscape contractors

(P-888)
PENNEY LAWN SERVICE INC
Also Called: Penny Lawn Service
4000 Allen Rd, Bakersfield (93314-9091)
PHONE..................................661 587-4788
Dan Penny, *Owner*
Sandy Penny, *Owner*
EMP: 100
SQ FT: 1,275
SALES (est): 8.7MM **Privately Held**
SIC: 0782 Landscape contractors

(P-889)
PETALON LANDSCAPE MGT INC
1766 Rogers Ave, San Jose (95112-1109)
PHONE..................................408 453-3998
Rudy Sotelo, *CEO*
John Linn, *President*
Noreen Prado, *Office Mgr*
Chris Hunger, *Accounts Mgr*
EMP: 65
SQ FT: 5,000
SALES (est): 5.1MM **Privately Held**
SIC: 0782 Landscape contractors

(P-890)
PINELANDS PRESERVATION INC
4501 Auburn Blvd Ste 201, Sacramento (95841-4213)
PHONE..................................609 703-0359
Christopher Carlino, *CEO*
Will Wheelehan, *Manager*
EMP: 60
SALES (est): 1.9MM **Privately Held**
SIC: 0782 8741 Landscape contractors; management services

(P-891)
PLANTASIA INC
Also Called: Plantasia Landscaping
2550 Via Tejon Ste 3f, Palos Verdes Estates (90274-6809)
PHONE..................................310 375-0387
Alex Colovic, *President*
EMP: 75 **EST:** 1973
SALES (est): 5.3MM **Privately Held**
SIC: 0782 1629 Landscape contractors; irrigation system construction

(P-892)
PLOWBOY LANDSCAPES INC
2190 N Ventura Ave, Ventura (93001-1343)
P.O. Box 1802 (93002-1802)
PHONE..................................805 643-4966
Douglas Wasson, *President*
Greg Dygert, *Project Mgr*
Debbie Vega, *Bookkeeper*
EMP: 55
SQ FT: 3,500
SALES (est): 4.9MM **Privately Held**
WEB: www.plowboyinc.com
SIC: 0782 Landscape contractors

(P-893)
PROCIDA LANDSCAPE INC
8465 Specialty Cir, Sacramento (95828-2523)
PHONE..................................916 387-5296
John Procida Jr, *President*
Juan Garcia, *Opers Mgr*
EMP: 160
SQ FT: 15,000
SALES (est): 10.3MM **Privately Held**
SIC: 0782 Lawn care services; lawn services; garden planting services

(P-894)
R NAVARRO LANDSCAPE SERVICES
359 West Rd, La Habra Heights (90631-8048)
PHONE..................................562 690-6414
Raul Navarro, *President*
Dana Navarro, *Vice Pres*
EMP: 60
SALES (est): 1.5MM **Privately Held**
SIC: 0782 Landscape contractors

(P-895)
RANCHO CALIFORNIA LANDSCAPING
13801 S Western Ave, Gardena (90249-2517)
PHONE..................................310 768-1680
Sal Mora, *President*
Ramon Sandoval, *Opers Staff*
EMP: 50
SQ FT: 33,610
SALES (est): 3.5MM **Privately Held**
WEB: www.ranchocalifornia.biz
SIC: 0782 Landscape contractors

(P-896)
RANCHO WEST LANDSCAPE
39140 Pala Vista Dr, Temecula (92591-7213)
PHONE..................................951 301-3979
Greg Duncan, *Owner*
Osvaldo Abarca, *Project Mgr*
Robert Calzada, *Maintnce Staff*
EMP: 50
SALES (est): 4.9MM **Privately Held**
SIC: 0782 Landscape contractors

(P-897)
RELIABLE GARDENS INC
7837 Burnet Ave, Van Nuys (91405-1046)
PHONE..................................818 904-9801
Steven Selden, *CEO*
Debra Selden, *CFO*
Laurie Levavi, *Vice Pres*
EMP: 60 **EST:** 1959
SALES (est): 3.1MM **Privately Held**
SIC: 0782 Garden planting services; garden maintenance services; landscape contractors; lawn services

(P-898)
RESCOM SERVICES INC
1637 Kings Way, Vista (92084-3641)
PHONE..................................760 930-3900
Mark Sutton, *President*
EMP: 92
SALES (est): 6.9MM **Privately Held**
WEB: www.rescomservices.com
SIC: 0782 Lawn & garden services

(P-899)
RESIDENT GROUP SERVICES INC (PA)
Also Called: Rgs Services
1156 N Grove St, Anaheim (92806-2109)
PHONE..................................714 630-5300
James M Gilly, *President*
Michael K Hayde, *CEO*
EMP: 149
SQ FT: 15,000
SALES (est): 19.8MM **Privately Held**
WEB: www.rgsservices.com
SIC: 0782 Landscape contractors

(P-900)
RICHMOND ENGINEERING CO INC
Also Called: Lewis Lifetime Tools
15472 Markar Rd, Poway (92064-2313)
PHONE..................................800 589-7058
Daniel Wright, *President*
◆ **EMP:** 120
SQ FT: 120,000
SALES (est): 9.7MM **Privately Held**
SIC: 0782 Lawn & garden services

(P-901)
RMT LANDSCAPE CONTRACTORS INC
421 Pendleton Way, Oakland (94621-2122)
PHONE..................................510 568-3208
Rick Deherrera, *President*
Julie Briggs, *Vice Pres*
Sally Lipska, *Admin Sec*
Patrick Laake, *Accounting Mgr*
David Deherrera, *Opers Staff*
EMP: 50
SQ FT: 12,000
SALES (est): 5.4MM **Privately Held**
WEB: www.rmtlandscape.com
SIC: 0782 Landscape contractors

(P-902)
S G D ENTERPRISES
Also Called: Four Seasons Landscaping
14937 Delano St, Van Nuys (91411-2123)
PHONE..................................323 658-1047
Stephen G Darrison, *President*
EMP: 50
SQ FT: 1,800
SALES (est): 5.2MM **Privately Held**
SIC: 0782 6512 6513 Landscape contractors; nonresidential building operators; apartment building operators

(P-903)
SANSEI GARDENS INC
3250 Darby Cmn, Fremont (94539-5601)
PHONE..................................510 226-9191
Brian Takehara, *President*
Allison Miner, *Assistant*
EMP: 110
SQ FT: 3,000
SALES (est): 10.6MM **Privately Held**
WEB: www.sanseigardens.com
SIC: 0782 Landscape contractors

(P-904)
SCOTTS PLANT SERVICE CO
6206 Carver Rd, Modesto (95356-9177)
P.O. Box 3723 (95352-3723)
PHONE..................................209 545-0903
Scott Reis, *President*
EMP: 67
SALES: 350K **Privately Held**
SIC: 0782 Landscape contractors

(P-905)
SHASTA LANDSCAPING INC
1340 Descanso Ave, San Marcos (92069-1306)
PHONE..................................760 744-6551
Leonard R Hogan, *CEO*
Daniel Hogan, *President*
Susan Hogan, *CFO*
Debara Prescott, *Corp Secy*
EMP: 75
SQ FT: 6,000
SALES (est): 3.9MM **Privately Held**
WEB: www.shastalandscaping.com
SIC: 0782 Landscape contractors

(P-906)
SHINSUKE CLIFFORD YAMAMOTO
Also Called: S C Yamamoto
2031 Emery Ave, La Habra (90631-5777)
PHONE..................................714 992-5783
Shinsuke C Yamamoto, *President*
EMP: 100
SQ FT: 7,660
SALES (est): 8MM **Privately Held**
WEB: www.scyamamoto.com
SIC: 0782 Garden maintenance services; landscape contractors

(P-907)
SIERRA VIEW LANDSCAPE INC
Also Called: Restoration Resources
3888 Cincinnati Ave, Rocklin (95765-1312)
PHONE..................................916 408-2990
Fax: 916 408-2999
EMP: 50
SALES (est): 7MM **Privately Held**
SIC: 0782

(P-908)
SILVERWOOD LANDSCAPE CNSTR INC
2209 S Lyon St, Santa Ana (92705-5305)
PHONE..................................714 427-6134
Steven Paul Lancaster, *President*
Marsha Lancaster, *CFO*
EMP: 50
SALES (est): 5.3MM **Privately Held**
SIC: 0782 Landscape contractors

(P-909)
SOTO COMPANY INC
34275 Camino Capistrano A, Capistrano Beach (92624-1917)
PHONE..................................949 493-9403
Joe Soto, *President*
Carol Soto, *Corp Secy*
EMP: 75
SQ FT: 4,000

SALES (est): 3.7MM **Privately Held**
WEB: www.sotocompany.com
SIC: 0782 Landscape contractors

(P-910)
SOUTHWEST LANDSCAPE INC
2205 S Standard Ave, Santa Ana (92707-3036)
P.O. Box 15611 (92735-0611)
PHONE..................................714 545-1084
Dan Hansen, *President*
Robert Hansen, *Vice Pres*
Fabiola Covarrubias, *Production*
EMP: 80
SQ FT: 7,800
SALES (est): 5.7MM **Privately Held**
WEB: www.southwestlandscapeinc.com
SIC: 0782 Landscape contractors

(P-911)
SPECIALIZED LANDSCAPE MGT SVCS
Also Called: SLM Services
4212 Peast Los Angeles, Simi Valley (93063)
PHONE..................................805 520-7590
Rene Emeterio, *President*
Wendy Emeterio, *Corp Secy*
EMP: 77
SALES (est): 3.4MM **Privately Held**
SIC: 0782 Landscape contractors

(P-912)
SUNSET LANDSCAPE MAINTENANCE
27201 Burbank, El Toro (92610-2500)
PHONE..................................949 455-4636
James Roughan, *President*
Claudia Roughan, *Corp Secy*
Laurie Savolainen, *Office Mgr*
Sarah Roughan, *Business Mgr*
EMP: 100
SQ FT: 6,300
SALES (est): 5.9MM **Privately Held**
SIC: 0782 Lawn & garden services

(P-913)
TED COOPER/COOPER INDUSTRIES
P.O. Box 36007 (95158-6007)
PHONE..................................408 358-3060
Ted Cooper, *Owner*
EMP: 50
SALES (est): 1.6MM **Privately Held**
WEB: www.coopindustries.com
SIC: 0782 1799 Landscape contractors; parking facility equipment & maintenance

(P-914)
TREE SCULPTURE GROUP
Also Called: Tarra Landscape
463 Roland Way, Oakland (94621-2014)
PHONE..................................510 562-4000
Craig Lundin, *President*
Cassidy Lundin, *Vice Pres*
Paulette Roddy, *Executive*
Dan Dachauer, *Division Mgr*
EMP: 60
SALES (est): 4MM **Privately Held**
WEB: www.treesculpture.com
SIC: 0782 Landscape contractors

(P-915)
TREEBEARD LANDSCAPE INC
9917 Campo Rd, Spring Valley (91977-1609)
P.O. Box 2777 (91979-2777)
PHONE..................................619 697-8302
Tim Hillman, *President*
Craig Des Lauriers, *Vice Pres*
EMP: 100
SQ FT: 2,500
SALES (est): 5.8MM **Privately Held**
SIC: 0782 Garden maintenance services; lawn services

(P-916)
TROPICAL PLAZA NURSERY INC
9642 Santiago Blvd, Villa Park (92867-2521)
PHONE..................................714 998-4100
Leslie T Fields, *President*
Mike Feilds, *Vice Pres*
Lucas Fields, *Marketing Staff*

P
R
O
D
U
C
T
S

&

S
V
C
S

EMP: 100
SQ FT: 5,000
SALES: 2.6MM **Privately Held**
SIC: 0782 Landscape contractors

(P-917)
TRU GREEN LANDCARE INC
5248 Governor Dr, San Diego
(92122-2800)
PHONE..............................602 276-4311
David M Flott, *President*
Joseph Hanks, *Vice Pres*
EMP: 450
SQ FT: 3,000
SALES (est): 9.2MM
SALES (corp-wide): 1.9B **Publicly Held**
WEB: www.landcareusa.com
SIC: 0782 Landscape contractors
HQ: Landcare Usa, Inc
　　2603 Augusta Dr Ste 1300
　　Houston TX 77057
　　713 692-6371

(P-918)
TRUGREEN LIMITED PARTNERSHIP
Also Called: Tru Green-Chemlawn
1130 Palmyrita Ave # 300, Riverside
(92507-1714)
P.O. Box 1359, Rancho Cucamonga
(91729-1359)
PHONE..............................951 231-2760
Jeff Martinau, *Manager*
EMP: 50
SALES (corp-wide): 3.2B **Privately Held**
SIC: 0782 Lawn care services
HQ: Trugreen Limited Partnership
　　1790 Kirby Pkwy
　　Memphis TN 38138
　　866 417-7866

(P-919)
ULTIMATE LANDSCAPING MGT
700 E Sycamore St, Anaheim
(92805-2831)
PHONE..............................714 502-9711
James Berne, *President*
Angelica Herrera, *Accounts Mgr*
EMP: 80
SALES (est): 4.6MM **Privately Held**
SIC: 0782 Landscape contractors

(P-920)
UNITED LANDSCAPE RESOURCE INC
Also Called: Botanica Landscapes
5411 Colusa Hwy, Yuba City (95993-9311)
P.O. Box 569 (95992-0569)
PHONE..............................530 671-1029
Bill Lucich, *President*
Tim Corey, *COO*
Candice Lucich, *Corp Secy*
EMP: 65
SQ FT: 2,000
SALES: 3.7MM **Privately Held**
WEB: www.botanica.net
SIC: 0782 Landscape contractors; lawn
care services

(P-921)
VALLEY LANDSCAPING & MAINT INC
12900 N Lwer Scramento Rd, Lodi (95242)
PHONE..............................209 334-3659
Don Oliver, *President*
Lori Peck, *Treasurer*
Jed Phelps, *Vice Pres*
EMP: 120
SQ FT: 5,000
SALES (est): 7.4MM **Privately Held**
SIC: 0782 Landscape contractors

(P-922)
VAUGHN WEEDMAN INC (PA)
Also Called: Northwest Landscape Services
550 S Hope St Ste 1675, Los Angeles
(90071-2692)
PHONE..............................425 481-0919
Vaughn Weedman, *President*
Joel Olivares, *Branch Mgr*
Rick Sartori, *Branch Mgr*
Monarch Tree, *Branch Mgr*
Marcelino Alvarez, *Foreman/Supr*
EMP: 125

SALES (est): 15.4MM **Privately Held**
WEB: www.nlswa.com
SIC: 0782 Landscape contractors

(P-923)
VENCO WESTERN INC (PA)
2400 Eastman Ave, Oxnard (93030-5187)
PHONE..............................805 981-2400
Linda Del Nagro Burr, *President*
Craig Owen, *Accounts Mgr*
EMP: 150
SQ FT: 15,000
SALES (est): 12.7MM **Privately Held**
WEB: www.vencowestern.com
SIC: 0782 Landscape contractors

(P-924)
VINTAGE ASSOCIATES INC
Also Called: Vintage Nursery
78755 Darby Rd, Bermuda Dunes
(92203-9621)
P.O. Box 5250, La Quinta (92248-5250)
PHONE..............................760 772-3673
Gregory Gritters, *President*
Greg Gritters, *Partner*
Alan Hollinger, *Opers Mgr*
Gary Conner, *Manager*
Joe Elkins, *Manager*
EMP: 160
SQ FT: 1,000
SALES (est): 14MM **Privately Held**
SIC: 0782 5193 5261 Landscape contractors; nursery stock; nurseries

(P-925)
W B STARR INC
20602 Canada Rd, Lake Forest
(92630-8100)
PHONE..............................949 770-8835
William B Starr, *President*
Martha L Starr, *Vice Pres*
EMP: 65
SQ FT: 10,000
SALES (est): 3.6MM **Privately Held**
WEB: www.wbstarr.com
SIC: 0782 Garden maintenance services

(P-926)
WATKIN & BORTOLUSSI INC
726 Alfred Nobel Dr, Hercules
(94547-1805)
PHONE..............................415 453-4675
Phillip Bortolussi, *President*
Peggy Bortolussi, *Vice Pres*
EMP: 60
SQ FT: 1,000
SALES (est): 3.2MM **Privately Held**
SIC: 0782 Landscape contractors

(P-927)
WENDT LANDSCAPE SERVICES INC
Also Called: Pacific Coast Sweeping
29714 Avenida De Las, Rancho Santa Margari (92688)
PHONE..............................949 589-8680
Richard Wendt, *President*
EMP: 70
SQ FT: 6,600
SALES (est): 2.7MM **Privately Held**
SIC: 0782 Landscape contractors

(P-928)
WM VANDERGEEST LANDSCAPE CARE
3342 W Castor St, Santa Ana
(92704-3908)
PHONE..............................714 545-8432
Allan M Curr, *President*
Sherry Curr, *Treasurer*
Chris Curr, *Vice Pres*
EMP: 100 EST: 1974
SQ FT: 10,000
SALES (est): 3.4MM **Privately Held**
SIC: 0782 Landscape contractors

(P-929)
WURZEL LANDSCAPE MAINTENANCE
Also Called: Canyon Way Nursery
3214 Oakdell Rd, Studio City (91604-4221)
PHONE..............................818 762-8653
Marc W Wurzel, *Partner*
Doris Wurzel, *Partner*
EMP: 50

SALES (est): 1.3MM **Privately Held**
SIC: 0782 Garden maintenance services;
landscape contractors

(P-930)
YEAR ROUND LANDSCAPE MAINT INC
15189 Sierra Bonita Ln, Chino
(91710-8904)
PHONE..............................909 597-7734
Larry M Sweeden, *President*
EMP: 50
SQ FT: 5,700
SALES (est): 1.8MM **Privately Held**
SIC: 0782 Garden maintenance services

0783 Ornamental Shrub & Tree Svc

(P-931)
ARBORWELL INC (PA)
2337 American Ave, Hayward
(94545-1807)
PHONE..............................510 881-4260
Alvin Foye Sortwell, *President*
Brad Carson, *CFO*
Dennis Shanagher, *Corp Secy*
Andy Lavelle, *Vice Pres*
Ann B Sortwell, *Vice Pres*
▲ EMP: 75
SQ FT: 5,000
SALES (est): 30.6MM **Privately Held**
WEB: www.arborwell.com
SIC: 0783 Planting, pruning & trimming
services

(P-932)
ASPLUNDH TREE EXPERT CO
Also Called: Utility Tree Services
6100 Francis Botello Rd C, Goleta
(93117-3259)
PHONE..............................805 964-9216
Alex Ramos, *Business Mgr*
EMP: 99
SALES (corp-wide): 4.5B **Privately Held**
WEB: www.asplundh.com
SIC: 0783 Tree trimming services for public
utility lines
PA: Asplundh Tree Expert, Llc
　　708 Blair Mill Rd
　　Willow Grove PA 19090
　　215 784-4200

(P-933)
ASPLUNDH TREE EXPERT LLC
2055 N Ventura Ave, Ventura (93001-1308)
PHONE..............................805 641-0528
Tony Ortiz, *Branch Mgr*
EMP: 94
SALES (corp-wide): 4.5B **Privately Held**
SIC: 0783 Tree trimming services for public
utility lines
PA: Asplundh Tree Expert, Llc
　　708 Blair Mill Rd
　　Willow Grove PA 19090
　　215 784-4200

(P-934)
ASPLUNDH TREE EXPERT LLC
6101 Gateway Dr, Cypress (90630-4841)
PHONE..............................714 893-2405
Joseph Guerrero, *Branch Mgr*
Thomas Craver, *Engineer*
EMP: 150
SALES (corp-wide): 4.5B **Privately Held**
WEB: www.asplundh.com
SIC: 0783 Tree trimming services for public
utility lines
PA: Asplundh Tree Expert, Llc
　　708 Blair Mill Rd
　　Willow Grove PA 19090
　　215 784-4200

(P-935)
BROOKER ASSOCIATES
16372 Cnstr Cir E 5, Irvine (92618)
PHONE..............................949 559-4877
EMP: 52
SALES (corp-wide): 5.4MM **Privately Held**
SIC: 0783 1721 1542

PA: Brooker Associates
　　2331 E Lambert Rd
　　La Habra CA 90631
　　714 773-9490

(P-936)
CLS LANDSCAPE MANAGEMENT INC
4329 State St Ste A, Montclair
(91763-6082)
PHONE..............................909 628-3005
Kevin L Davis, *President*
Gloria Gonzalez, *Office Mgr*
Kimberly Davis, *Admin Sec*
EMP: 325
SQ FT: 2,500
SALES (est): 16.3MM **Privately Held**
WEB: www.clslandscape.com
SIC: 0783 0782 Ornamental shrub & tree
services; lawn & garden services

(P-937)
DAVEY TREE SURGERY COMPANY
6915 Eastside Rd Ste 94, Anderson
(96007-9401)
PHONE..............................530 378-2674
Dennis Dodson, *Manager*
EMP: 60
SALES (corp-wide): 1B **Privately Held**
SIC: 0783 Surgery services, ornamental
tree
HQ: Davey Tree Surgery Company
　　2617 S Vasco Rd
　　Livermore CA 94550
　　925 443-1723

(P-938)
DAVEY TREE SURGERY COMPANY (HQ)
2617 S Vasco Rd, Livermore (94550)
P.O. Box 5015 (94551-5015)
PHONE..............................925 443-1723
Karl J Warnke, *CEO*
R Douglas Cowan, *President*
David Adante, *CFO*
Howard Bowles, *Senior VP*
Rick Edson, *Admin Sec*
EMP: 873
SQ FT: 5,000
SALES: 12.4MM
SALES (corp-wide): 1B **Privately Held**
SIC: 0783 Tree trimming services for public
utility lines
PA: The Davey Tree Expert Company
　　1500 N Mantua St
　　Kent OH 44240
　　330 673-9511

(P-939)
DAVEY TREE SURGERY COMPANY
1914 Mission Rd Ste N, Escondido
(92029-1116)
PHONE..............................760 975-0225
Brian Friedrich, *Branch Mgr*
EMP: 100
SALES (corp-wide): 1B **Privately Held**
SIC: 0783 Surgery services, ornamental
tree
HQ: Davey Tree Surgery Company
　　2617 S Vasco Rd
　　Livermore CA 94550
　　925 443-1723

(P-940)
GREAT SCOTT TREE SERVICE INC (PA)
10761 Court Ave, Stanton (90680-2435)
PHONE..............................714 826-1750
Scott Griffiths, *President*
Jacob Griffiths, *Vice Pres*
Steve Guzonski, *Administration*
EMP: 120
SQ FT: 28,675
SALES (est): 13.4MM **Privately Held**
WEB: www.gstsinc.com
SIC: 0783 Pruning services, ornamental
tree

(P-941)
LEONARD CHAIDEZ INC
Also Called: Leonard Chaidez Tree Service
2298 N Batavia St, Orange (92865-3106)
P.O. Box 29, Anaheim (92815-0029)
PHONE..................................714 279-8173
Leonard Chaidez, *President*
Deborah Foushee, *Admin Sec*
Jamie Lance, *Manager*
EMP: 60
SQ FT: 2,000
SALES (est): 3.5MM **Privately Held**
SIC: 0783 0781 8748 0782 Ornamental
shrub & tree services; landscape serv-
ices; environmental consultant; lawn &
garden services

(P-942)
ORIGINAL MOWBRAYS TREE SVC INC (PA)
1845 Bus Ctr Dr Ste 215, San Bernardino
(92408)
PHONE..................................909 383-7009
Dwight Anderson, *Principal*
EMP: 200
SQ FT: 1,000
SALES: 12MM **Privately Held**
WEB: www.mowbrays.org
SIC: 0783 Tree trimming services for public
utility lines

(P-943)
PACIFIC SLOPE TREE COOP INC
11201 State Rte One 201, Point Reyes Sta-
tion (94956)
P.O. Box 400 (94956-0400)
PHONE..................................415 663-1300
Thomas Kent, *President*
Elan Whitney, *Corp Secy*
EMP: 50
SALES: 4MM **Privately Held**
WEB: www.pacificslopetree.com
SIC: 0783 Planting, pruning & trimming
services

(P-944)
RAUL V ACEVEDO
Also Called: Ace Heating and AC
1638 W Castle Ave, Porterville
(93257-9277)
PHONE..................................559 791-1304
Raul Acevedo, *Owner*
EMP: 50
SALES: 500K **Privately Held**
SIC: 0783 0782 Ornamental shrub & tree
services; lawn & garden services

(P-945)
SP MCCLENAHAN CO
Also Called: McClenahan S P Co Tree Serv-
ice
1 Arastradero Rd, Portola Valley
(94028-8012)
PHONE..................................650 326-8781
James M Mc Clenahan, *President*
Juan Larios, *Supervisor*
EMP: 56
SQ FT: 5,000
SALES (est): 4.8MM **Privately Held**
SIC: 0783 Planting, pruning & trimming
services

(P-946)
TONY GOMEZ TREE SERVICE
700 N Johnson Ave Ste H, El Cajon
(92020-2521)
PHONE..................................619 593-1552
Antonio Gomez, *Owner*
EMP: 60
SALES (est): 2.7MM **Privately Held**
SIC: 0783 Ornamental shrub & tree serv-
ices

(P-947)
TRAVERS TREE SERVICE INC
1811 Lomita Blvd, Lomita (90717-1905)
P.O. Box 411 (90717-0411)
PHONE..................................310 545-5816
Richard Travers, *President*
Don Lorenzen, *Vice Pres*
Susan Travers, *Admin Sec*
Mary Keyse, *Manager*
EMP: 50
SQ FT: 2,000

SALES (est): 5.1MM **Privately Held**
SIC: 0783 Planting, pruning & trimming
services

(P-948)
TREEPEOPLE INC
12601 Mulholland Dr, Beverly Hills
(90210-1332)
PHONE..................................818 753-4600
Walt Burkley, *Ch of Bd*
Andy Lipkis, *President*
Tom Hansen, *COO*
Gwyn Quillen, *Treasurer*
Paul Bergman, *Admin Sec*
EMP: 50
SQ FT: 21,000
SALES: 4.4MM **Privately Held**
WEB: www.treepeople.org
SIC: 0783 8641 Planting, pruning & trim-
ming services; environmental protection
organization

(P-949)
UTILITY TREE SERVICE LLC (DH)
Also Called: Utility Tree Service, Inc.
1884 Keystone Ct Ste A, Redding
(96003-4870)
PHONE..................................530 226-0330
Scott Asplundh, *President*
Joseph P Dwyer, *Corp Secy*
Brent D Asplundh, *Vice Pres*
Carl Asplundh III, *Vice Pres*
Gregg Asplundh, *Vice Pres*
EMP: 50
SALES (est): 11.8MM
SALES (corp-wide): 4.5B **Privately Held**
SIC: 0783 Tree trimming services for public
utility lines

(P-950)
WEST COAST ARBORISTS INC
11405 Nardo St, Ventura (93004-3201)
PHONE..................................805 671-5092
Lorenzo Perez, *Owner*
Andy Trotter, *Vice Pres*
EMP: 144
SALES (corp-wide): 102.7MM **Privately
Held**
SIC: 0783 Planting, pruning & trimming
services
PA: West Coast Arborists, Inc.
2200 E Via Burton
Anaheim CA 92806
714 991-1900

(P-951)
WEST COAST ARBORISTS INC
21718 Walnut Ave, Grand Terrace
(92313-4437)
PHONE..................................909 783-6544
Patrick Mahoney, *President*
EMP: 50
SALES (corp-wide): 102.7MM **Privately
Held**
SIC: 0783 Planting, pruning & trimming
services
PA: West Coast Arborists, Inc.
2200 E Via Burton
Anaheim CA 92806
714 991-1900

0811 Timber Tracts

(P-952)
BOETHING TREELAND FARMS INC
2923 Alpine Rd, Portola Valley
(94028-7546)
PHONE..................................650 851-4770
Richard Hanley, *Branch Mgr*
EMP: 700
SALES (corp-wide): 75.8MM **Privately
Held**
WEB: www.boethingtreeland.com
SIC: 0811 5193 0181 Tree farm; nursery
stock; nursery stock, growing of
PA: Boething Treeland Farms, Inc.
23475 Long Valley Rd
Woodland Hills CA 91367
818 883-1222

(P-953)
BOETHING TREELAND FARMS INC (PA)
23475 Long Valley Rd, Woodland Hills
(91367-6006)
PHONE..................................818 883-1222
Bruce Edgar Pherson, *CEO*
Sally Boething Hilton, *Shareholder*
Cathy Boething Pherson, *Shareholder*
Marji Boething, *CFO*
Haydi Boething Danielson, *Admin Sec*
EMP: 60
SQ FT: 1,500
SALES (est): 75.8MM **Privately Held**
WEB: www.boethingtreeland.com
SIC: 0811 5261 Tree farm; nurseries

(P-954)
BOETHING TREELAND FARMS INC
Also Called: Boething Treeland Nursery
20601 E Kettleman Ln, Lodi (95240-9756)
PHONE..................................209 727-3741
Seilpe Gomez, *Branch Mgr*
Desiree Archuleta, *Sales Staff*
EMP: 175
SALES (est): 3.3MM
SALES (corp-wide): 75.8MM **Privately
Held**
WEB: www.boethingtreeland.com
SIC: 0811 Tree farm
PA: Boething Treeland Farms, Inc.
23475 Long Valley Rd
Woodland Hills CA 91367
818 883-1222

(P-955)
BRIGHTVIEW TREE COMPANY
Also Called: Specimen Contracting
9500 Foothill Blvd, Sunland (91040-1857)
PHONE..................................818 951-5500
Tadd Russikoff, *Manager*
EMP: 115
SALES (corp-wide): 2.3B **Publicly Held**
WEB: www.vctree.com
SIC: 0811 Tree farm
HQ: Brightview Tree Company
24151 Ventura Blvd
Calabasas CA 91302
818 223-8500

(P-956)
BRIGHTVIEW TREE COMPANY
Also Called: Environmental Industries
3200 W Telegraph Rd, Fillmore
(93015-9623)
PHONE..................................714 546-7975
Susan Flores, *Branch Mgr*
EMP: 160
SALES (corp-wide): 2.3B **Publicly Held**
WEB: www.vctree.com
SIC: 0811 0782 Tree farm; lawn services
HQ: Brightview Tree Company
24151 Ventura Blvd
Calabasas CA 91302
818 223-8500

(P-957)
BRIGHTVIEW TREE COMPANY
8501 Calaveras Rd, Sunol (94586-9434)
P.O. Box 289, Farmington (95230-0289)
PHONE..................................925 862-2485
John Serviss, *Branch Mgr*
Nancy Kennedy, *Office Mgr*
EMP: 100
SALES (corp-wide): 2.3B **Publicly Held**
WEB: www.vctree.com
SIC: 0811 Tree farm
HQ: Brightview Tree Company
24151 Ventura Blvd
Calabasas CA 91302
818 223-8500

(P-958)
GREEN DIAMOND RESOURCE COMPANY
900 Riverside Rd, Korbel (95550)
P.O. Box 68 (95550-0068)
PHONE..................................707 668-4400
Neal Ewald, *Manager*
EMP: 100
SALES (corp-wide): 242.9MM **Privately
Held**
SIC: 0811 0851 Timber tracts; forestry
services

HQ: Diamond Green Resource Company
1301 5th Ave Ste 2700
Seattle WA 98101
206 224-5800

(P-959)
PINERY LLC
13701 Highland Valley Rd, Escondido
(92025-2300)
P.O. Box 2484, Rancho Cucamonga
(91729-2484)
PHONE..................................858 675-3575
Philip C Guardia, *President*
Dennis Anderson, *COO*
Brad Blaes, *Sales Staff*
Lisa Bryant, *Sales Staff*
Kelsey Guardia, *Sales Staff*
▲ **EMP:** 60
SQ FT: 2,800
SALES (est): 5.4MM **Privately Held**
SIC: 0811 Christmas tree farm

(P-960)
WEYERHAEUSER COMPANY
800 Pier T Ave, Long Beach (90802-6236)
PHONE..................................562 983-6589
EMP: 77
SALES (corp-wide): 7.4B **Publicly Held**
SIC: 0811 Timber tracts
PA: Weyerhaeuser Company
220 Occidental Ave S
Seattle WA 98104
206 539-3000

(P-961)
YEW BIO-PHARM GROUP INC
9460 Telstar Ave Ste 6, El Monte
(91731-2904)
PHONE..................................626 401-9588
Zhiguo Wang, *Ch of Bd*
Guifang Qi, *Admin Sec*
EMP: 86 EST: 1996
SALES: 37.6MM **Privately Held**
SIC: 0811 Tree farm

0851 Forestry Svcs

(P-962)
ADVANCED IPM
205 Kenroy Ln, Roseville (95678-4201)
PHONE..................................916 759-1570
Adrienne Sederquist, *CEO*
EMP: 50
SALES (est): 1MM **Privately Held**
SIC: 0851 Pest control services, forest

(P-963)
CALIFORNIA SILVER-AGRICULTURE
831 Ash Ave, Lindsay (93247-1449)
PHONE..................................559 562-3795
Raul L Acevedo, *Owner*
EMP: 50
SALES: 50K **Privately Held**
SIC: 0851 Forestry services

(P-964)
FORESTRY AND FIRE PROTECTION
Also Called: Shasta-Trinity Ranger Unit
875 Cypress Ave, Redding (96001-2719)
PHONE..................................530 225-2418
Mike Chuchel, *Manager*
EMP: 150 **Privately Held**
WEB: www.calopps.org
SIC: 0851 Fire prevention services, forest
HQ: Forestry And Fire Protection California
Department Of
1416 9th St Ste 1535
Sacramento CA 95814

(P-965)
RCO REFORESTING INC
Also Called: R C O Reforesting
1332 Fairlane Rd Ste A, Yreka
(96097-8504)
P.O. Box 1370 (96097-1370)
PHONE..................................530 842-7647
Roberto C Ochoa, *President*
EMP: 50
SALES (est): 1.2MM **Privately Held**
SIC: 0851 Reforestation services; fire pre-
vention services, forest

P R O D U C T S & S V C S

(P-966)
REDDING TREE GROWERS CORP
18985 Avenue 256 Apt A, Exeter (93221-9558)
PHONE..................559 594-9299
Francisco Acevedo, *President*
Amelia Acevedo, *Vice Pres*
EMP: 100
SALES: 2MM **Privately Held**
SIC: 0851 Reforestation services

(P-967)
USDA FOREST SERVICE
100 Forni Rd, Placerville (95667-5310)
PHONE..................530 626-1546
Lawrence Crabtree, *Principal*
EMP: 53 **Publicly Held**
SIC: 0851 Forestry services
HQ: Us Dept Of Agriculture Forest Service
201 14th St Sw
Washington DC 20024

1041 Gold Ores

(P-968)
BARRICK GOLD CORPORATION
Also Called: Mc Laughlin Mine
26775 Morgan Valley Rd, Lower Lake (95457-9411)
PHONE..................707 995-6070
Pat Purtell, *Branch Mgr*
EMP: 100
SALES (est): 11.8MM
SALES (corp-wide): 7.2B **Privately Held**
WEB: www.barrick.com
SIC: 1041 Gold ores
PA: Barrick Gold Corporation
161 Bay St Suite 3700
Toronto ON M5J 2
416 861-9911

(P-969)
GOLDEN QUEEN MINING CO LLC
2818 Silver Queen Rd, Mojave (93501-7021)
P.O. Box 1030 (93502-1030)
PHONE..................661 824-4300
Thomas Clay, *Ch of Bd*
Andree St-Germain, *CFO*
Joe Balas, *Opers Staff*
EMP: 180
SQ FT: 2,500
SALES (est): 63MM **Privately Held**
SIC: 1041 Gold ores mining

(P-970)
MERIDIAN GOLD INC
Also Called: Royal Mountain King
4461 Rock Creek Rd, Copperopolis (95228)
PHONE..................209 785-3222
Edgar Smith, *Branch Mgr*
EMP: 160
SALES (corp-wide): 1.8B **Privately Held**
SIC: 1041 Gold ores
HQ: Meridian Gold Inc.
4635 Longley Ln Ste 110
Reno NV 89502

(P-971)
STAVATTI INDUSTRIES LTD
1443 S Gage St, San Bernardino (92408-2835)
P.O. Box 211258, Eagan MN (55121-2658)
PHONE..................651 238-5369
Christopher R Beskar, *Branch Mgr*
Christopher Beskar, *CEO*
EMP: 60
SALES (corp-wide): 2MM **Privately Held**
SIC: 1041 1081 3511 3533 Gold ores mining; metal mining exploration & development services; turbines & turbine generator set units, complete; oil & gas field machinery; truck trailers
PA: Stavatti Industries Ltd
1061 Tiffany Dr
Eagan MN 55123
651 238-5369

1221 Bituminous Coal & Lignite: Surface Mining

(P-972)
CHEVRON MINING INC
Moly
67750 Bailey Rd, Mountain Pass (92366)
PHONE..................760 856-7625
Allen Randle, *Branch Mgr*
EMP: 400
SALES (corp-wide): 166.3B **Publicly Held**
SIC: 1221 Surface mining, bituminous
HQ: Chevron Mining Inc.
116 Invrneco Dr E Ste 207
Englewood CO 80112
303 930-3600

1241 Coal Mining Svcs

(P-973)
GREKA INC
1791 Sinton Rd, Santa Maria (93458-9708)
P.O. Box 5489 (93456-5489)
PHONE..................805 347-8700
Andy Devegvar, *President*
Randeep Grewal, *CEO*
EMP: 150
SQ FT: 3,000
SALES: 40MM **Privately Held**
SIC: 1241 1081 Coal mining services; metal mining services

(P-974)
RIO TINTO MINERALS INC
Also Called: Reno Tenco
14486 Borax Rd, Boron (93516-2017)
PHONE..................760 762-7121
Xiaoling Liu, *CEO*
Preston Chiaro, *President*
Hugo Bague, *Principal*
Trevor Plote, *Engineer*
Shalaine Fink, *Analyst*
▼ EMP: 150
SALES (est): 17.1MM
SALES (corp-wide): 40.5B **Privately Held**
SIC: 1241 Coal mining services
HQ: U.S. Borax Inc.
8051 E Maplewood Ave # 100
Greenwood Village CO 80111
303 713-5000

(P-975)
TAFT PRODUCTION COMPANY
950 Petroleum Club Rd, Taft (93268-9748)
P.O. Box 1277 (93268-1277)
PHONE..................661 765-7194
Daniel S Jaffee, *President*
EMP: 95
SALES (est): 8.3MM
SALES (corp-wide): 277MM **Publicly Held**
WEB: www.oildri.com
SIC: 1241 1081 Coal mining services; metal mining services
PA: Oil-Dri Corporation Of America
410 N Michigan Ave Fl 4
Chicago IL 60611
312 321-1515

1311 Crude Petroleum & Natural Gas

(P-976)
BENTLEY-SIMONSON INC
1746 S Victoria Ave Ste F, Ventura (93003-6190)
PHONE..................805 650-2794
James Bentley, *Ch of Bd*
Theodore Bentley, *Ch of Bd*
Clifton O Simonson, *President*
Petter Romming, *Vice Pres*
EMP: 100
SQ FT: 1,000
SALES (est): 4.1MM **Privately Held**
SIC: 1311 Crude petroleum & natural gas production

(P-977)
BERRY PETROLEUM COMPANY LLC (HQ)
5201 Truxtun Ave Ste 100, Bakersfield (93309-0422)
PHONE..................661 616-3900
Trem Smith, *President*
Stephen Burke, *Director*
Stephen Cropper, *Director*
Michael Reddin, *Director*
EMP: 65
SALES (est): 506.4MM
SALES (corp-wide): 586.5MM **Publicly Held**
WEB: www.bry.com
SIC: 1311 Crude petroleum production; natural gas production
PA: Berry Petroleum Corporation
16000 Dallas Pkwy Ste 500
Dallas TX 75248
661 616-3900

(P-978)
BP WEST COAST PRODUCTS LLC
22600 Wilmington Ave, Carson (90745-4307)
PHONE..................310 816-8787
EMP: 310
SALES (corp-wide): 298.7B **Privately Held**
SIC: 1311 Crude petroleum & natural gas
HQ: Bp West Coast Products Llc
4519 Grandview Rd
Blaine WA 98230
310 549-6204

(P-979)
BP WEST COAST PRODUCTS LLC
1306 Canal Blvd, Richmond (94804-3556)
PHONE..................510 231-4724
Fred Glueck, *Vice Pres*
EMP: 310
SQ FT: 4,550
SALES (corp-wide): 298.7B **Privately Held**
SIC: 1311 Crude petroleum production
HQ: Bp West Coast Products Llc
4519 Grandview Rd
Blaine WA 98230
310 549-6204

(P-980)
BREITBURN GP LLC
707 Wilshire Blvd # 4600, Los Angeles (90017-3501)
PHONE..................213 225-5900
Halbert S Washburn, *CEO*
EMP: 833
SALES (est): 21.5MM **Privately Held**
SIC: 1311 Crude petroleum & natural gas

(P-981)
CALIFORNIA RESOURCES CORP (PA)
27200 Tourney Rd Ste 200, Santa Clarita (91355-4910)
PHONE..................888 848-4754
Todd A Stevens, *President*
William E Albrecht, *Ch of Bd*
Marshall D Smith, *CFO*
Justin Gannon, *Bd of Directors*
Harold Korell, *Bd of Directors*
EMP: 123
SALES: 3B **Publicly Held**
SIC: 1311 Crude petroleum & natural gas

(P-982)
CALIFORNIA RESOURCES CORP
111 W Ocean Blvd Ste 800, Long Beach (90802-7930)
PHONE..................562 624-3400
EMP: 98
SALES (corp-wide): 3B **Publicly Held**
SIC: 1311 Crude petroleum production
PA: California Resources Corporation
27200 Tourney Rd Ste 200
Santa Clarita CA 91355
888 848-4754

(P-983)
CALIFORNIA RESOURCES PROD CORP
3450 E 5th St, Oxnard (93033-2100)
PHONE..................805 483-8017
EMP: 83
SALES (corp-wide): 2.4B **Publicly Held**
SIC: 1311 1382
HQ: California Resources Production Corporation
11109 River Run Blvd
Bakersfield CA 93311
661 869-8000

(P-984)
CALIFORNIA RESOURCES PROD CORP (HQ)
Also Called: Vintage Production California
900 Old River Rd, Bakersfield (93311-9501)
PHONE..................661 869-8000
Todd A Stevens, *Principal*
Richard Oringderff, *President*
Todd Stevens, *CEO*
EMP: 125
SALES (est): 96.3MM
SALES (corp-wide): 3B **Publicly Held**
WEB: www.oxy.com
SIC: 1311 1382 Crude petroleum production; oil & gas exploration services
PA: California Resources Corporation
27200 Tourney Rd Ste 200
Santa Clarita CA 91355
888 848-4754

(P-985)
E & B NTRAL RESOURCES MGT CORP (PA)
1600 Norris Rd, Bakersfield (93308-2234)
PHONE..................661 679-1714
Steve Layton, *President*
Ronkese Frank, *CFO*
Frank J Ronkese, *CFO*
Jeff Blesener, *Senior VP*
Jeff Jones, *Vice Pres*
EMP: 65
SALES: 326.3MM **Privately Held**
WEB: www.ebresources.com
SIC: 1311 Crude petroleum & natural gas

(P-986)
FREEPORT-MCMORAN OIL & GAS LLC
1200 Discovery Dr Ste 500, Bakersfield (93309-7038)
PHONE..................661 322-7600
Kiran Leal, *Manager*
EMP: 60
SALES (corp-wide): 18.6B **Publicly Held**
SIC: 1311 Crude petroleum & natural gas
HQ: Freeport-Mcmoran Oil & Gas Llc
700 Milam St Ste 3100
Houston TX 77002
713 579-6000

(P-987)
LINNCO LLC
5201 Truxtun Ave, Bakersfield (93309-0421)
PHONE..................661 616-3900
Gordon Beagley, *Technician*
EMP: 1432
SALES (corp-wide): 40.7MM **Publicly Held**
SIC: 1311 Crude petroleum & natural gas
PA: Linnco, Llc
600 Travis St Ste 5100
Houston TX 77002
281 840-4000

(P-988)
OXY USA INC
9600 Ming Ave Ste 300, Bakersfield (93311-1365)
PHONE..................661 869-8000
Gary O Lee Jr, *Credit Mgr*
EMP: 125
SALES (corp-wide): 18.9B **Publicly Held**
SIC: 1311 Crude petroleum & natural gas
HQ: Oxy Usa Inc.
1001 S County Rd W
Odessa TX 79763
432 335-0995

(P-989)
PETROLEUM SALES INC
2066 Redwood Hwy, Greenbrae
(94904-2467)
PHONE...........................415 256-1600
Stephanie Shimk, *Branch Mgr*
EMP: 70
SALES (corp-wide): 15.5MM **Privately Held**
SIC: **1311** Crude petroleum & natural gas
PA: Petroleum Sales Inc
1475 2nd St
San Rafael CA 94901
415 256-1600

(P-990)
QUANTUM TECHNOLOGIES INC
25242 Arctic Ocean Dr, Lake Forest
(92630-8821)
PHONE...........................949 399-4500
Dean K Aoki, *CEO*
Alan Niedzwiecki, *President*
Bradley J Timon, *CFO*
Mark Arold, *Vice Pres*
Neel Sirosh, *Principal*
EMP: 140
SALES (est): 38.2MM **Privately Held**
SIC: **1311** Crude petroleum & natural gas

(P-991)
SAMEDAN OIL CORPORATION
Also Called: Noble Energy
1360 Landing Ave, Seal Beach
(90740-6525)
PHONE...........................661 319-5038
EMP: 336
SALES (corp-wide): 34.8MM **Privately Held**
SIC: **1311** Crude petroleum production
PA: Samedan Oil Corporation
1001 Noble Energy Way
Houston TX 77070
580 223-4110

(P-992)
VAQUERO ENERGY INCORPORATED
15545 Hermosa Rd, Bakersfield
(93307-9477)
PHONE...........................661 363-7240
Ken Hunter, *President*
EMP: 50
SALES (est): 953.9K **Privately Held**
SIC: **1311** Crude petroleum production

1381 Drilling Oil & Gas Wells

(P-993)
AERA ENERGY LLC (HQ)
10000 Ming Ave, Bakersfield (93311-1301)
P.O. Box 11164 (93389-1164)
PHONE...........................661 665-5000
Christina S Sistrunk, *President*
Andrew Hoyer, *Chief Mktg Ofcr*
Bill Hanson, *Exec VP*
Robert C Alberstadt, *Senior VP*
Brent D Carnahan, *Senior VP*
EMP: 800
SALES (est): 2.1B
SALES (corp-wide): 388.3B **Privately Held**
WEB: www.aeraenergy.com
SIC: **1381** Directional drilling oil & gas wells
PA: Royal Dutch Shell Plc
Shell Centre
London SE1 7
207 934-1234

(P-994)
AERA ENERGY LLC
Also Called: Aera Energy South Midway
29235 Highway 33, Maricopa
(93252-9793)
PHONE...........................661 665-3200
Andy Anderson, *Manager*
Bob Alberstadt, *Vice Pres*
Sandeep Brar, *Administration*
Jay Licata, *Production*
EMP: 60

SALES (corp-wide): 388.3B **Privately Held**
WEB: www.aeraenergy.com
SIC: **1381** Directional drilling oil & gas wells
HQ: Aera Energy Llc
10000 Ming Ave
Bakersfield CA 93311
661 665-5000

(P-995)
ALUMATEC INC
18411 Sherman Way, Reseda
(91335-4319)
PHONE...........................818 609-7460
Francesco Chinaglia, *President*
Yazmin Ibarlucea, *Treasurer*
Laura Chinaglia, *Admin Sec*
EMP: 80
SALES (est): 2.8MM **Privately Held**
WEB: www.alumatec.com
SIC: **1381** Drilling oil & gas wells

(P-996)
ELYSIUM JENNINGS LLC
1600 Norris Rd, Bakersfield (93308-2234)
PHONE...........................661 679-1700
Steve Layton,
EMP: 200
SALES (est): 8.7MM **Privately Held**
SIC: **1381** Drilling oil & gas wells
PA: E & B Natural Resources Management Corporation
1600 Norris Rd
Bakersfield CA 93308

(P-997)
EXCALIBUR WELL SERVICES CORP (PA)
22034 Rosedale Hwy, Bakersfield
(93314-9704)
PHONE...........................661 589-5338
Stephen Layton, *President*
Frachsco Galesi, *President*
Gordon Isbel, *Vice Pres*
Mary Telupessy, *Business Mgr*
EMP: 78
SALES (est): 40.3MM **Privately Held**
SIC: **1381 1389** Drilling oil & gas wells; fishing for tools, oil & gas field

(P-998)
GOLDEN STATE DRILLING INC
3500 Fruitvale Ave, Bakersfield
(93308-5106)
PHONE...........................661 589-0730
Philip F Phelps, *President*
James Phelps, *Treasurer*
Velma Phelps, *Vice Pres*
Mike McCutcheon, *Manager*
EMP: 75
SALES (est): 14.1MM **Privately Held**
WEB: www.gsdrilling.com
SIC: **1381** Directional drilling oil & gas wells

(P-999)
PAUL GRAHAM DRILLING & SVC CO
2500 Airport Rd, Rio Vista (94571-1034)
P.O. Box 669 (94571-0669)
PHONE...........................707 374-5123
Kevin P Graham, *President*
Jill Graham, *CFO*
Clarence Santos, *Vice Pres*
Eddie Woodruff, *General Mgr*
Ted Coffey, *Sales Mgr*
EMP: 170
SQ FT: 30,000
SALES (est): 30MM **Privately Held**
SIC: **1381 7389 7359** Drilling oil & gas wells; crane & aerial lift service; industrial truck rental

1382 Oil & Gas Field Exploration Svcs

(P-1000)
CALIFRNIA RSRCES ELK HILLS LLC
900 Old River Rd, Bakersfield
(93311-9501)
P.O. Box 1001, Tupman (93276-1001)
PHONE...........................661 412-5000
Karen Plotts,
Michael L Preston,
Marshall D Smith,
EMP: 400 EST: 1997
SALES (est): 35.7MM
SALES (corp-wide): 3B **Publicly Held**
WEB: www.oxy.com
SIC: **1382** Oil & gas exploration services
PA: California Resources Corporation
27200 Tourney Rd Ste 200
Santa Clarita CA 91355
888 848-4754

(P-1001)
DCOR LLC (PA)
290 Maple Ct Ste 290 # 290, Ventura
(93003-9144)
P.O. Box 3401 (93006-3401)
PHONE...........................805 535-2000
Bill Templeton,
Alan C Templeton, *CFO*
Greg Cavette, *Vice Pres*
Dennis Conley, *Vice Pres*
Bob Garcia, *Vice Pres*
EMP: 76
SALES (est): 154.1MM **Privately Held**
WEB: www.dcor.com
SIC: **1382** Oil & gas exploration services

(P-1002)
DEMENNO KERDOON
2000 N Alameda St, Compton
(90222-2799)
PHONE...........................310 537-7100
Shane Bamelin, *Principal*
Jim Tice, *Principal*
Jim Ennis, *Director*
EMP: 125
SQ FT: 11,614
SALES (est): 25.6MM **Privately Held**
WEB: www.demennokerdoon.com
SIC: **1382** Oil & gas exploration services

(P-1003)
E AND B NATURAL RESOURCES
1600 Norris Rd, Bakersfield (93308-2234)
PHONE...........................661 679-1700
Francesco Galesi, *CEO*
Melissa Ysaguirre, *Supervisor*
EMP: 52
SALES (est): 9.4MM **Privately Held**
SIC: **1382** Oil & gas exploration services

(P-1004)
GREKA INTEGRATED INC (PA)
1700 Sinton Rd, Santa Maria (93458-9708)
P.O. Box 5489 (93456-5489)
PHONE...........................805 347-8700
Randeep S Grewal, *CEO*
Ken Miller, *CFO*
Susan Whalen, *Vice Pres*
▲ EMP: 145
SALES (est): 32MM **Privately Held**
WEB: www.grekaenergy.com
SIC: **1382** Oil & gas exploration services

(P-1005)
NATIONS PETROLEUM CAL LLC
9600 Ming Ave Ste 300, Bakersfield
(93311-1365)
PHONE...........................661 387-6402
Phil Sorvet,
EMP: 60
SALES (est): 4MM
SALES (corp-wide): 2.1MM **Privately Held**
SIC: **1382** Oil & gas exploration services
PA: Nations Petroleum Company Ltd
255 5 Ave Sw Suite 750
Calgary AB T2P 3
403 206-1420

(P-1006)
QRE OPERATING LLC
707 Wilshire Blvd # 4600, Los Angeles
(90017-3501)
PHONE...........................213 225-5900
Alan L Smith, *Mng Member*
EMP: 208
SALES (est): 708K **Privately Held**
SIC: **1382** Oil & gas exploration services
PA: Qr Energy, Lp
707 Wilshire Blvd # 4600
Los Angeles CA 90017

(P-1007)
R W LYALL & COMPANY INC (DH)
2665 Research Dr, Corona (92882-6918)
P.O. Box 2259 (92878-2259)
PHONE...........................951 270-1500
Jeffrey W Lyall, *President*
Jennifer Fritchle, *COO*
Bruce Lange, *COO*
Tony Mauer, *CFO*
Andrew Babcock, *Opers Mgr*
▲ EMP: 168
SQ FT: 70,000
SALES (est): 152.4MM
SALES (corp-wide): 4.4B **Publicly Held**
WEB: www.rwlyall.com
SIC: **1382** Oil & gas exploration services

1389 Oil & Gas Field Svcs, NEC

(P-1008)
BAKER HGHES OLFLD OPRTIONS LLC
5421 Argosy Ave, Huntington Beach
(92649-1038)
PHONE...........................714 893-8511
EMP: 55
SALES (corp-wide): 22.8B **Privately Held**
WEB: www.bot.bhi-net.com
SIC: **1389** Oil field services
HQ: Baker Hughes Oilfield Operations Llc
17021 Aldine Westfield Rd
Houston TX 77073
713 879-1000

(P-1009)
BAKER HGHES OLFLD OPRTIONS LLC
5700 Doolittle Ave, Shafter (93263-4035)
PHONE...........................661 834-9654
Bob Ledet, *Manager*
EMP: 50
SALES (corp-wide): 22.8B **Privately Held**
WEB: www.bot.bhi-net.com
SIC: **1389 7353 5084** Oil field services; oil field equipment, rental or leasing; drilling bits
HQ: Baker Hughes Oilfield Operations Llc
17021 Aldine Westfield Rd
Houston TX 77073
713 879-1000

(P-1010)
BAKER HUGHES A GE COMPANY LLC
5421 Argosy Ave, Huntington Beach
(92649-1038)
PHONE...........................714 893-8511
David A Patti, *Manager*
Robert Dempsey, *District Mgr*
EMP: 84
SALES (corp-wide): 22.8B **Privately Held**
SIC: **1389** Oil field services
PA: Baker Hughes, A Ge Company Llc
17021 Aldine Westfield Rd
Houston TX 77073
713 439-8600

(P-1011)
BAKER HUGHES A GE COMPANY LLC
1127 Carrier Parkway Ave, Bakersfield
(93308-9666)
PHONE...........................661 387-1010
Charles Laymance, *Branch Mgr*
Chris Long, *Opers Mgr*
EMP: 87

SALES (corp-wide): 22.8B Privately Held
SIC: 1389 Oil field services
PA: Baker Hughes, A Ge Company Llc
  17021 Aldine Westfield Rd
  Houston TX 77073
  713 439-8600

(P-1012)
BAKER HUGHES A GE COMPANY LLC
5145 Boylan St, Bakersfield (93308-4511)
PHONE..................................800 229-7447
Lori Robinson, *Manager*
EMP: 87
SALES (corp-wide): 22.8B Privately Held
WEB: www.bakerhughes.com
SIC: 1389 Oil field services
PA: Baker Hughes, A Ge Company Llc
  17021 Aldine Westfield Rd
  Houston TX 77073
  713 439-8600

(P-1013)
BAKER PETROLITE LLC
5125 Boylan St, Bakersfield (93308-4511)
PHONE..................................661 325-4138
Doug Thomas, *Manager*
EMP: 60
SALES (corp-wide): 22.8B Privately Held
WEB: www.bakerpetrolite.com
SIC: 1389 Oil field services
HQ: Baker Petrolite Llc
  12645 W Airport Blvd
  Sugar Land TX 77478
  281 276-5400

(P-1014)
CALIFRNIA RSURCES LONG BCH INC
111 W Ocean Blvd Ste 800, Long Beach (90802-7930)
PHONE..................................562 624-3204
Frank Komin, *CEO*
EMP: 116
SALES (est): 1.6MM
SALES (corp-wide): 3B Publicly Held
SIC: 1389 Oil field services
PA: California Resources Corporation
  27200 Tourney Rd Ste 200
  Santa Clarita CA 91355
  888 848-4754

(P-1015)
CAMERON INTERNATIONAL CORP
Also Called: Camserv
1282 Bayview Farm Rd, Pinole (94564)
PHONE..................................510 928-1480
EMP: 56 Publicly Held
SIC: 1389 Oil field services
HQ: Cameron International Corporation
  4646 W Sam Houston Pkwy N
  Houston TX 77041
  -

(P-1016)
CL KNOX INC
Also Called: Advanced Industrial Services
34933 Imperial St, Bakersfield (93308)
PHONE..................................661 837-0477
Leslie Knox, *President*
Chris Knox, *Corp Secy*
Stephanie Smith, *Manager*
Will Taylor, *Manager*
EMP: 80
SALES (est): 10.6MM Privately Held
SIC: 1389 8742 Oil field services; industrial consultant

(P-1017)
CUMMINGS VACUUM SERVICE INC
Also Called: Cummings Transportation
19605 Broken Ct, Shafter (93263-9583)
PHONE..................................661 746-1786
Pam Cummings, *President*
Ted Cummings, *Vice Pres*
Dave Stitt, *Maint Spvr*
EMP: 60
SQ FT: 3,000
SALES (est): 7.6MM Privately Held
SIC: 1389 Oil field services

(P-1018)
DWAYNES ENGINEERING & CNSTR
3655 Addie Ave, Mc Kittrick (93251)
P.O. Box 116 (93251-0116)
PHONE..................................661 762-7261
Dwayne Emfinger, *President*
EMP: 78
SALES (est): 7.8MM Privately Held
WEB: www.dwayneseng.com
SIC: 1389 Construction, repair & dismantling services

(P-1019)
ENGINEERED WELL SVC INTL INC
3120 Standard St, Bakersfield (93308-6241)
PHONE..................................866 913-6283
Paul Sturgeon, *CEO*
John E Powell Jr, *Principal*
EMP: 125 **EST:** 2009
SALES (est): 44MM Privately Held
SIC: 1389 Oil field services

(P-1020)
ETHOSENERGY FIELD SERVICES LLC (DH)
Also Called: Wg
10455 Slusher Dr Bldg 12, Santa Fe Springs (90670-3750)
PHONE..................................310 639-3523
Rob Duby, *President*
Patricia Lelito, *CFO*
Mike Fieldhouse, *Vice Pres*
Mary Ros, *General Mgr*
EMP: 75
SALES (est): 29.9MM
SALES (corp-wide): 10B Privately Held
WEB: www.woodgroupgts.com
SIC: 1389 8711 3462 Oil consultants; industrial engineers; pump, compressor & turbine forgings

(P-1021)
FIELD FOUNDATION
15306 Carmenita Rd, Santa Fe Springs (90670-5606)
P.O. Box 4236, Cerritos (90703-4236)
PHONE..................................562 921-3567
Irwin Field, *Owner*
EMP: 50
SALES (est): 24.3K Privately Held
SIC: 1389 Oil sampling service for oil companies

(P-1022)
GENE WATSON CONSTRUCTION A CA
801 Kern St, Taft (93268-2734)
PHONE..................................661 763-5254
Gene Watson, *Ltd Ptnr*
Patricia Watson, *Ltd Ptnr*
EMP: 530
SALES (est): 11.2MM Privately Held
WEB: www.gwc-ltd.com
SIC: 1389 1382 Oil field services; oil & gas exploration services

(P-1023)
GRAYSON SERVICE INC
1845 Greeley Rd, Bakersfield (93314-9547)
PHONE..................................661 589-5444
Carol A Grayson, *President*
Cheryl Grayson, *Vice Pres*
EMP: 150
SALES (est): 5.7MM Privately Held
SIC: 1389 Servicing oil & gas wells

(P-1024)
HALLIBURTON COMPANY
34722 7th Standard Rd, Bakersfield (93314-9435)
PHONE..................................661 393-8111
Dennis Lovett, *Branch Mgr*
Mark Hansen, *Technical Staff*
Richard Noffke, *Engineer*
David Self, *Manager*
EMP: 87 Publicly Held
SIC: 1389 Oil field services
PA: Halliburton Company
  3000 N Sam Houston Pkwy E
  Houston TX 77032
  -

(P-1025)
HILLS WLDG & ENGRG CONTR INC
Also Called: Hwe Mechanical
22038 Stockdale Hwy, Bakersfield (93314-8889)
PHONE..................................661 746-5400
Debora M Hill, *Vice Pres*
Robert Hill, *Shareholder*
EMP: 92
SALES (est): 7.1MM Privately Held
SIC: 1389 Testing, measuring, surveying & analysis services

(P-1026)
HIRSH INC
Also Called: Better Mens Clothes
860 S Los Angeles St # 900, Los Angeles (90014-3311)
PHONE..................................213 622-9441
Mistie Banks, *General Mgr*
Stanley Hirsh, *President*
EMP: 50
SALES (est): 1MM Privately Held
SIC: 1389 Lease tanks, oil: erecting, cleaning & repairing

(P-1027)
HUNTING ENERGY SERVICES INC
Also Called: Hunting-Vinson
4900 California Ave 100a, Bakersfield (93309-7024)
PHONE..................................661 633-4272
Bobby Ford, *Branch Mgr*
EMP: 76
SALES (corp-wide): 911.4MM Privately Held
WEB: www.hunting-inc.com
SIC: 1389 Oil field services
HQ: Hunting Energy Services, Inc.
  16825 Northchase Dr # 600
  Houston TX 77060

(P-1028)
HVI CAT CANYON INC
Also Called: Greka Oil & Gas
2617 E Clark Ave, Santa Maria (93455-5815)
P.O. Box 5489 (93456-5489)
PHONE..................................805 621-5800
Alex G Dimitrijevic, *President*
Randeep S Grewal, *President*
Ken Miller, *CFO*
Susan Whalen, *Vice Pres*
EMP: 125
SALES (est): 11MM Privately Held
SIC: 1389 Oil field services

(P-1029)
JERRY MELTON & SONS CNSTR
Also Called: Jerry Melton & Sons Cnstr
100 Jamison Ln, Taft (93268-4329)
PHONE..................................661 765-5546
Jerry W Melton, *President*
Karen Melton, *Treasurer*
Judy Melton, *Vice Pres*
Steven Melton, *Admin Sec*
EMP: 85
SALES (est): 11.6MM Privately Held
WEB: www.jerrymelton.com
SIC: 1389 Oil & gas wells: building, repairing & dismantling; grading oil & gas well foundations

(P-1030)
KATERRA INC (PA)
2494 Sand Hill Rd Ste 100, Menlo Park (94025-6981)
PHONE..................................650 422-3572
Michael Marks, *CEO*
Paal Kibsgaard, *COO*
Matthew Marsh, *CFO*
Joanne Solomon, *CFO*
Winnie Geng, *Vice Pres*
EMP: 100 **EST:** 2015
SALES (est): 151.2MM Privately Held
SIC: 1389 8741 8711 Construction, repair & dismantling services; construction management; construction & civil engineering

(P-1031)
MMI SERVICES INC
4042 Patton Way, Bakersfield (93308-5030)
PHONE..................................661 589-9366
Steve McGowan, *President*
Mel McGowan, *CEO*
Eric Olson, *Vice Pres*
Roxanne Campbell, *Info Tech Dir*
Erick Olson, *Human Res Dir*
EMP: 250
SQ FT: 4,500
SALES (est): 51.3MM Privately Held
WEB: www.mmi-services.com
SIC: 1389 Oil field services

(P-1032)
NABORS WELL SERVICES CO
2567 N Ventura Ave C, Ventura (93001-1201)
PHONE..................................805 648-2731
Paul Smith, *Manager*
Charles Marshall, *Vice Pres*
James Bentley, *Branch Mgr*
Jim Brady, *Branch Mgr*
Dean Sherrill, *General Mgr*
EMP: 90 Privately Held
SIC: 1389 Oil field services
HQ: Nabors Well Services Co.
  515 W Greens Rd Ste 1000
  Houston TX 77067
  281 874-0035

(P-1033)
NABORS WELL SERVICES CO
1025 Earthmover Ct, Bakersfield (93314-9529)
PHONE..................................661 588-6140
Tom Jaquez, *Manager*
EMP: 160 Privately Held
SIC: 1389 Oil field services
HQ: Nabors Well Services Co.
  515 W Greens Rd Ste 1000
  Houston TX 77067
  281 874-0035

(P-1034)
NABORS WELL SERVICES CO
7515 Rosedale Hwy, Bakersfield (93308-5727)
PHONE..................................661 589-3970
Alan Pounds, *Sales Executive*
Jerry Fernandez, *Area Mgr*
Melanie Mendoza, *Maintence Staff*
Ron C Cleveland, *Manager*
Joe Deford, *Manager*
EMP: 270 Privately Held
SIC: 1389 1382 Servicing oil & gas wells; oil & gas exploration services
HQ: Nabors Well Services Co.
  515 W Greens Rd Ste 1000
  Houston TX 77067
  281 874-0035

(P-1035)
NABORS WELL SERVICES CO
19431 S Santa Fe Ave, Compton (90221-5912)
PHONE..................................310 639-7074
Bernie Fish, *Manager*
Juan Landron, *Technology*
Gary Kaufman, *Human Res Mgr*
EMP: 230 Privately Held
SIC: 1389 Gas field services; oil field services
HQ: Nabors Well Services Co.
  515 W Greens Rd Ste 1000
  Houston TX 77067
  281 874-0035

(P-1036)
NABORS WELL SERVICES CO
1954 James Rd, Bakersfield (93308-9749)
PHONE..................................661 392-7668
Dave Warner, *District Mgr*
EMP: 76 Privately Held
SIC: 1389 Oil field services
HQ: Nabors Well Services Co.
  515 W Greens Rd Ste 1000
  Houston TX 77067
  281 874-0035

(P-1037)
OIL WELL SERVICE COMPANY (PA)
10840 Norwalk Blvd, Santa Fe Springs (90670-3826)
PHONE..................................562 612-0600
Jack Frost, *President*
Connie Laws, *Treasurer*
Matthew Hensley, *Exec VP*
Richard Laws, *Vice Pres*
Matt Hensley, *Admin Sec*
EMP: 105
SQ FT: 9,000
SALES (est): 54.4MM **Privately Held**
WEB: www.ows1.com
SIC: 1389 Oil field services

(P-1038)
PACIFIC PROCESS SYSTEMS INC (PA)
7401 Rosedale Hwy, Bakersfield (93308-5736)
PHONE..................................661 321-9681
Jerry Wise, *CEO*
Robert Peterson, *CFO*
Alan George, *Corp Secy*
Curt Avis, *Opers Mgr*
Anthony Munoz, *Supervisor*
▼ EMP: 90
SQ FT: 7,000
SALES (est): 262.1MM **Privately Held**
WEB: www.pps-equipment.com
SIC: 1389 7353 5082 Testing, measuring, surveying & analysis services; oil field equipment, rental or leasing; oil field equipment

(P-1039)
PC MECHANICAL INC
2803 Industrial Pkwy, Santa Maria (93455-1811)
PHONE..................................805 925-2888
Lew Parker, *President*
Brandon Burginger, *COO*
Mary Parker, *Exec VP*
Mitch Caron, *Vice Pres*
EMP: 50
SQ FT: 67,000
SALES (est): 11.3MM **Privately Held**
WEB: www.pcmechanical.com
SIC: 1389 Oil field services

(P-1040)
PROS INCORPORATED
3400 Patton Way, Bakersfield (93308-5722)
P.O. Box 20996 (93390-0996)
PHONE..................................661 589-5400
Robert Lewis, *President*
Randy Dubois, *Exploration*
Jack Turner, *Sales Staff*
EMP: 58
SALES (est): 19.7MM **Privately Held**
SIC: 1389 Oil field services

(P-1041)
ROBERT HEELY CONSTRUCTION LP (PA)
Also Called: Robert Heely Construction
5401 Woodmere Dr, Bakersfield (93313-2777)
PHONE..................................661 617-1400
Robert Heely, *Chairman*
Craig Bonna, *President*
Robert Hopkins, *Engineer*
Hopkins Robert, *Engineer*
Chrystal Abbott, *Human Res Mgr*
EMP: 350
SQ FT: 7,000
SALES (est): 57.6MM **Privately Held**
WEB: www.robertheely.com
SIC: 1389 Oil field services

(P-1042)
SCHLUMBERGER TECHNOLOGY CORP
Also Called: Schlumberger Well Services
2841 Pegasus Dr, Bakersfield (93308-6896)
PHONE..................................661 864-4750
Fax: 661 642-2065
EMP: 70 **Privately Held**
SIC: 1389 1382

HQ: Schlumberger Technology Corp
100 Gillingham Ln
Sugar Land TX 77478
281 285-8500

(P-1043)
SCHLUMBERGER TECHNOLOGY CORP
Schlumberger, Well Completions
12131 Industry St, Garden Grove (92841-2813)
PHONE..................................714 379-7332
Gene Barnett, *Systems Mgr*
EMP: 51 **Publicly Held**
SIC: 1389 3561 Oil & gas wells: building, repairing & dismantling; pumps & pumping equipment
HQ: Schlumberger Technology Corp
300 Schlumberger Dr
Sugar Land TX 77478
281 285-8500

(P-1044)
SMITH INTERNATIONAL INC
Also Called: Omni Seals, Inc.
11031 Jersey Blvd Ste A, Rancho Cucamonga (91730-5150)
PHONE..................................909 906-7900
Monte Russell, *Managing Dir*
EMP: 130 **Publicly Held**
SIC: 1389 Oil field services
HQ: Smith International, Inc.
1310 Rankin Rd
Houston TX 77073
281 443-3370

(P-1045)
SOLI-BOND INC
4230 Foster Ave, Bakersfield (93308-4559)
PHONE..................................661 631-1633
Dwight Hartley, *President*
EMP: 50
SALES (corp-wide): 34.8MM **Privately Held**
SIC: 1389 Oil field services
PA: Soli-Bond, Inc.
2377 2 Mile Rd
Bay City MI 48706
989 684-9611

(P-1046)
TOTAL-WESTERN INC (HQ)
8049 Somerset Blvd, Paramount (90723-4396)
PHONE..................................562 220-1450
Paul F Conrad, *CEO*
Mary A Pool, *CFO*
Earl Grebing, *Vice Pres*
Dora Maldonado, *Personnel*
Jerry Balos, *Director*
EMP: 50
SQ FT: 13,000
SALES (est): 166.5MM
SALES (corp-wide): 381.4MM **Privately Held**
WEB: www.total-western.com
SIC: 1389 Oil field services; construction, repair & dismantling services; excavating slush pits & cellars; grading oil & gas well foundations
PA: Bragg Investment Company, Inc.
6251 N Paramount Blvd
Long Beach CA 90805
562 984-2400

(P-1047)
TRYAD SERVICE CORPORATION
5900 E Lerdo Hwy, Shafter (93263-4023)
PHONE..................................661 391-1524
James Varner, *President*
Estate of Burl G Varner, *Shareholder*
Danny Seely, *Vice Pres*
▲ EMP: 90
SALES (est): 9.7MM **Privately Held**
SIC: 1389 Oil & gas wells: building, repairing & dismantling

(P-1048)
U S WEATHERFORD L P
2815 Fruitvale Ave, Bakersfield (93308-5907)
PHONE..................................661 589-9483
Rick Benton, *Branch Mgr*
EMP: 100 **Privately Held**
WEB: www.gaslift.com
SIC: 1389 Oil field services

HQ: U S Weatherford L P
179 Weatherford Dr
Schriever LA 70395
985 493-6100

(P-1049)
WEATHERFORD INTERNATIONAL LLC
1880 Santa Barbara Ave # 220, San Luis Obispo (93401-4481)
PHONE..................................805 781-3580
Chris Smith, *Branch Mgr*
Kevin Rowley, *Manager*
EMP: 73 **Privately Held**
SIC: 1389 Oil field services
HQ: Weatherford International, Llc
2000 Saint James Pl
Houston TX 77056
713 693-4000

(P-1050)
WEATHERFORD INTERNATIONAL LLC
Also Called: Coroc
21728 Rosedale Hwy, Bakersfield (93314-9787)
PHONE..................................661 587-9753
Mark Sarcen, *Branch Mgr*
Michael Winterberg, *Sr Software Eng*
Gregg Hurst, *Sales Staff*
Jason Truitt, *Advisor*
Daniel Adame, *Supervisor*
EMP: 60 **Privately Held**
WEB: www.weatherford.com
SIC: 1389 Oil field services
HQ: Weatherford International, Llc
2000 Saint James Pl
Houston TX 77056
713 693-4000

1422 Crushed & Broken Limestone

(P-1051)
SPECIALTY MINERALS INC
Minerals Technology
6565 Meridian Rd, Lucerne Valley (92356-8602)
P.O. Box 558 (92356-0558)
PHONE..................................760 248-5300
Doug Mayger, *Branch Mgr*
EMP: 150 **Publicly Held**
WEB: www.specialtyminerals.com
SIC: 1422 Crushed & broken limestone
HQ: Specialty Minerals Inc.
622 3rd Ave Fl 38
New York NY 10017
212 878-1800

(P-1052)
SYAR INDUSTRIES INC
885 Lake Herman Rd, Vallejo (94591-8324)
P.O. Box 2540, NAPA (94558-0524)
PHONE..................................707 643-3261
Mike Burneson, *Manager*
EMP: 100
SALES (corp-wide): 100.2MM **Privately Held**
WEB: www.syar.com
SIC: 1422 5211 Crushed & broken limestone; cement
PA: Syar Industries, Inc.
2301 Napa Vallejo Hwy
Napa CA 94558
707 252-8711

1429 Crushed & Broken Stone, NEC

(P-1053)
SAN RAFAEL ROCK QUARRY INC (HQ)
Also Called: Dutra Materials
2350 Kerner Blvd Ste 200, San Rafael (94901-5595)
PHONE..................................415 459-7740
Bill Toney Dutra, *CEO*
EMP: 70

SALES (est): 65.2MM
SALES (corp-wide): 145.1MM **Privately Held**
SIC: 1429 1629 Basalt, crushed & broken-quarrying; marine construction
PA: The Dutra Group
2350 Kerner Blvd Ste 200
San Rafael CA 94901
415 258-6876

1442 Construction Sand & Gravel

(P-1054)
GRANITE ROCK CO (PA)
350 Technology Dr, Watsonville (95076-2488)
P.O. Box 50001 (95077-5001)
PHONE..................................831 768-2000
Thomas H Squeri, *CEO*
Bruce G Woolpert, *Vice Chairman*
Mary E Woolpert, *Chairman*
Todd Barreras, *Officer*
Greg Diehl, *Vice Pres*
EMP: 100
SQ FT: 10,000
SALES (est): 992MM **Privately Held**
WEB: www.graniterock.com
SIC: 1442 3273 5032 2951 Gravel mining; construction sand mining; ready-mixed concrete; sand, construction; stone, crushed or broken; asphalt & asphaltic paving mixtures (not from refineries); highway & street paving contractor; concrete block & brick

(P-1055)
GRANITE ROCK CO
Also Called: AR Wilson Quarry
Quarry Rd, Aromas (95004)
P.O. Box 699 (95004-0699)
PHONE..................................831 768-2300
Bruce Wollepert, *President*
EMP: 100
SALES (corp-wide): 992MM **Privately Held**
WEB: www.graniterock.com
SIC: 1442 2951 Gravel mining; asphalt paving mixtures & blocks
PA: Granite Rock Co.
350 Technology Dr
Watsonville CA 95076
831 768-2000

(P-1056)
HANSEN BROS ENTERPRISES (PA)
Also Called: Hbe Rental
11727 La Barr Meadows Rd, Grass Valley (95949-7722)
P.O. Box 1599 (95945-1599)
PHONE..................................530 273-3100
Orson Hansen, *President*
Frank Bennallack, *Treasurer*
Craig Arthur, *Vice Pres*
Helen Hansen, *Vice Pres*
Sue Peterson, *Vice Pres*
EMP: 90
SQ FT: 20,000
SALES (est): 36.2MM **Privately Held**
WEB: www.gohbe.com
SIC: 1442 3273 1794 7359 Gravel mining; ready-mixed concrete; excavation work; equipment rental & leasing

(P-1057)
LEGACY VULCAN LLC
San Bernardino Division
2400 W Highland Ave, San Bernardino (92407-6408)
PHONE..................................909 875-1150
Darryl Charleson, *Sales/Mktg Dir*
Allyson Noah, *Manager*
EMP: 50 **Publicly Held**
WEB: www.vulcanmaterials.com
SIC: 1442 3273 Sand mining; ready-mixed concrete
HQ: Legacy Vulcan, Llc
1200 Urban Center Dr
Vestavia AL 35242
205 298-3000

PRODUCTS & SVCS

(P-1058)
NEVOCAL ENTERPRISES INC
Also Called: Kh Construction
5320 N Barcus Ave, Fresno (93722-5050)
PHONE.................................559 277-0700
Frank Cornell, *President*
EMP: 75
SQ FT: 4,575
SALES (est): 4.2MM **Privately Held**
SIC: 1442 Construction sand & gravel

(P-1059)
WEST COAST AGGREGATE SUPPLY
Also Called: Aggregate West Coast
92500 Airport Blvd, Thermal (92274)
P.O. Box 790 (92274-0790)
PHONE.................................760 342-7598
Marvin Struiksma, *President*
EMP: 50
SALES (est): 5.4MM **Privately Held**
SIC: 1442 Common sand mining

1446 Industrial Sand

(P-1060)
PIONEER SANDS LLC
31302 Ortega Hwy, San Juan Capistrano
(92675)
PHONE.................................949 728-0171
Mike Miclette, *Branch Mgr*
EMP: 53
SALES (corp-wide): 9.4B **Publicly Held**
SIC: 1446 Silica sand mining
HQ: Pioneer Sands Llc
5205 N O Connor Blvd # 200
Irving TX 75039
972 444-9001

(P-1061)
PW GILLIBRAND CO INC (PA)
4537 Ish Dr, Simi Valley (93063-7667)
P.O. Box 1019 (93062-1019)
PHONE.................................805 526-2195
Celine Gillibrand, *CEO*
Richard Valencia, *President*
Jim Costello, *Corp Secy*
EMP: 72
SQ FT: 11,000
SALES (est): 30.9MM **Privately Held**
WEB: www.pwgcoinc.com
SIC: 1446 Grinding sand mining

1479 Chemical & Fertilizer Mining

(P-1062)
SEARLES VALLEY MINERALS INC
80201 Trona Rd, Trona (93562)
PHONE.................................760 372-2259
Burnell Blanchard, *Vice Pres*
EMP: 600
SALES (corp-wide): 873MM **Privately Held**
SIC: 1479 Salt & sulfur mining
HQ: Searles Valley Minerals Inc.
9401 Indn Crk Pkwy # 1000
Overland Park KS 66210
913 344-9500

1481 Nonmetallic Minerals Svcs, Except Fuels

(P-1063)
IMERYS MINERALS CALIFORNIA INC
Also Called: Imerys Filtration Minerals
2500 Miguelito Canyon Rd, Lompoc
(93436)
PHONE.................................805 736-1221
Kenneth Schweibert, *Manager*
Jeff Taniguchi, *Manager*
EMP: 346
SALES (corp-wide): 3MM **Privately Held**
SIC: 1481 3295 Nonmetallic mineral services; minerals, ground or treated

HQ: Imerys Minerals California, Inc.
2500 San Miguelito Rd
Lompoc CA 93436

(P-1064)
MP MINE OPERATIONS LLC
67750 Bailey Rd, Mountain Pass (92366)
PHONE.................................702 277-0848
Michael Rosethal, *Mng Member*
James H Litinsky,
EMP: 108
SALES (est): 220.2K **Privately Held**
SIC: 1481 Mine exploration, nonmetallic minerals

1499 Miscellaneous Nonmetallic Mining

(P-1065)
DICAPERL CORPORATION (DH)
Also Called: Grefco Dicaperl
23705 Crenshaw Blvd, Torrance
(90505-5236)
PHONE.................................610 667-6640
Ray Perelman, *CEO*
Glenn Jones, *President*
Mike Cull, *Treasurer*
Barry Katz, *Senior VP*
▼ EMP: 90
SQ FT: 5,000
SALES (est): 9.5MM **Privately Held**
SIC: 1499 3677 Perlite mining; filtration devices, electronic
HQ: Grefco Minerals Inc.
1 Bala Ave Ste 310
Bala Cynwyd PA 19004
610 660-8820

(P-1066)
IMERYS FILTRATION MINERALS INC (DH)
1732 N 1st St Ste 450, San Jose
(95112-4579)
PHONE.................................805 562-0200
Douglas A Smith, *CEO*
Leslie Zimmer, *CFO*
Fred Weber, *Treasurer*
Paul Woodberry, *Vice Ch Bd*
Daniel Moncino, *Vice Pres*
◆ EMP: 50
SQ FT: 11,600
SALES (est): 1.2B
SALES (corp-wide): 3MM **Privately Held**
SIC: 1499 Diatomaceous earth mining
HQ: Imerys Usa, Inc.
100 Mansell Ct E Ste 300
Roswell GA 30076
770 645-3300

(P-1067)
IMERYS MINERALS CALIFORNIA INC (DH)
2500 San Miguelito Rd, Lompoc
(93436-9743)
P.O. Box 519 (93438-0519)
PHONE.................................805 736-1221
Douglas A Smith, *President*
John Oskam, *CEO*
John Leichty, *CFO*
Bruno Van Herpen, *Vice Pres*
Ken Rasmussen, *General Mgr*
▼ EMP: 70
SQ FT: 11,600
SALES (est): 1B
SALES (corp-wide): 3MM **Privately Held**
SIC: 1499 3295 Diatomaceous earth mining; minerals, ground or treated

(P-1068)
MONARCHY DIAMOND INC
550 S Hill St Ste 1088, Los Angeles
(90013-2417)
PHONE.................................213 924-1161
Rajnikumar Patel, *President*
EMP: 425
SALES (est): 12.3MM **Privately Held**
SIC: 1499 Gem stones (natural) mining

1521 General Contractors, Single Family Houses

(P-1069)
A & W MAINTENANCE
7573 Cibola Trl, Yucca Valley (92284-3255)
P.O. Box 755 (92286-0755)
PHONE.................................310 619-8694
Alesia Ellis, *Owner*
EMP: 54
SQ FT: 3,400
SALES (est): 1.4MM **Privately Held**
SIC: 1521 7349 Townhouse construction; building maintenance, except repairs

(P-1070)
A I T DEVELOPMENT CORP
Also Called: Mega Builders
21021 Devonshire St # 205, Chatsworth
(91311-8240)
PHONE.................................818 407-5533
Alon A Toker, *President*
Isabell Toker, *Corp Secy*
EMP: 66
SQ FT: 3,300
SALES (est): 4MM **Privately Held**
SIC: 1521 General remodeling, single-family houses

(P-1071)
A M ORTEGA CONSTRUCTION INC
58 Kellogg St, Ventura (93001-1732)
PHONE.................................951 360-1352
Archie Maurice Ortega, *Branch Mgr*
EMP: 52
SALES (corp-wide): 47.7MM **Privately Held**
SIC: 1521 Single-family housing construction
PA: A. M. Ortega Construction, Inc.
10125 Channel Rd
Lakeside CA 92040
619 390-1988

(P-1072)
A W PROPERTIES WEST LLC
16236 San Dieguito Rd # 310, Rancho
Santa Fe (92091-9802)
P.O. Box 9296 (92067-4296)
PHONE.................................858 832-1462
Danny Hampel,
EMP: 68
SALES (est): 3.3MM **Privately Held**
SIC: 1521 New construction, single-family houses

(P-1073)
ACE INDUSTRIAL SUPPLY INC (PA)
7535 N San Fernando Rd, Burbank
(91505-1044)
PHONE.................................818 252-1981
Tim Stearns, *Principal*
Holden Stearns, *Executive Asst*
Richard Benton, *CIO*
Larry Lawrence, *Data Proc Dir*
Adam Raskind, *Sales Mgr*
◆ EMP: 53
SQ FT: 25,000
SALES (est): 36.1MM **Privately Held**
SIC: 1521 Single-family housing construction

(P-1074)
ALL-PRO REMODELING
706 N Tustin St, Orange (92867-7149)
PHONE.................................714 288-1314
Dale Terry, *President*
John Johnston, *General Mgr*
▲ EMP: 56
SQ FT: 5,000
SALES (est): 6.6MM **Privately Held**
WEB: www.allproremodeling.com
SIC: 1521 General remodeling, single-family houses

(P-1075)
ALLSTATE CONSTRUCTION CO
1364 Londonderry Pl, Los Angeles
(90069-1335)
PHONE.................................310 652-6942
Morris Bardoff, *President*

EMP: 50
SALES: 4.5MM **Privately Held**
SIC: 1521 General remodeling, single-family houses

(P-1076)
ALPHA-WINFIELD CONTRACTORS INC
Also Called: Winfield Construction
1096 Yerba Buena Ave, Emeryville
(94608-3836)
PHONE.................................510 652-4712
Kenneth J Winfield, *President*
EMP: 100
SQ FT: 1,200
SALES (est): 7.4MM **Privately Held**
SIC: 1521 1542 New construction, single-family houses; general remodeling, single-family houses; commercial & office buildings, renovation & repair

(P-1077)
ALTEN CONSTRUCTION INC
1141 Marina Way S, Richmond
(94804-3742)
PHONE.................................510 234-4200
Robert Andrew Alten, *CEO*
Shannon M Alten, *Vice Pres*
EMP: 80
SQ FT: 14,000
SALES: 40.8MM **Privately Held**
WEB: www.altenconstruction.com
SIC: 1521 Single-family housing construction

(P-1078)
AMERICAN SOLAR SOLUTION INC
14701 Albers St, Sherman Oaks
(91411-3713)
PHONE.................................877 946-8855
Nicki Zvik, *President*
Shay Yavor, *COO*
Jerry Goldman, *Principal*
Julihta Gershomov-Rivas, *General Mgr*
EMP: 70 EST: 2011
SALES (est): 3.6MM **Privately Held**
SIC: 1521 1711 1522 General remodeling, single-family houses; solar energy contractor; residential construction

(P-1079)
ANDREW CHEKENE ENTERPRISES INC
Also Called: AC Enterprises
21965 Meekland Ave, Hayward
(94541-3862)
PHONE.................................650 588-1001
Andrew Chekene, *President*
Rafael Munoz, *Admin Sec*
Kim Lovell, *Administration*
Helen Troosh, *Manager*
Alex Halaj, *Superintendent*
EMP: 215 EST: 2007
SQ FT: 3,000
SALES (est): 8.3MM **Privately Held**
SIC: 1521 Single-family housing construction

(P-1080)
ARYA GROUP INC
Also Called: Arya Design Group
10490 Santa Monica Blvd, Los Angeles
(90025-5033)
PHONE.................................310 446-7000
Ardie Tavangarian, *President*
EMP: 50
SQ FT: 3,000
SALES (est): 8.2MM **Privately Held**
SIC: 1521 1542 New construction, single-family houses; commercial & office building, new construction

(P-1081)
AWT CONSTRUCTION GROUP INC
4740 E 2nd St Ste 22, Benicia
(94510-1024)
PHONE.................................707 746-7500
James Kint, *President*
Gregory W Smith, *Vice Pres*
Julie Duggin, *Manager*
EMP: 65
SQ FT: 3,000

SALES: 4MM **Privately Held**
SIC: 1521 1542 Single-family housing construction; single-family home remodeling, additions & repairs; commercial & office building contractors

(P-1082)
BAILEY & DUTTON (PA)
3200 Dnville Blvd Ste 200, Alamo (94507)
PHONE..........................925 838-1460
Sue Wingard, *Controller*
EMP: 75
SQ FT: 5,000
SALES (est): 3.1MM **Privately Held**
WEB: www.baileydutton.com
SIC: 1521 Single-family housing construction

(P-1083)
BEAZER HOMES HOLDINGS CORP
1800 E Imperial Hwy # 140, Brea (92821-6072)
PHONE..........................714 285-2900
Jerry Gates, *Principal*
EMP: 69
SALES (est): 4.2MM
SALES (corp-wide): 2B **Publicly Held**
SIC: 1521 General remodeling, single-family houses; new construction, single-family houses
PA: Beazer Homes Usa, Inc.
     1000 Abernathy Rd Ste 260
     Atlanta GA 30328
     770 829-3700

(P-1084)
BERRY & BERRY INC (PA)
Also Called: Berry Construction
413 W Yosemite Ave # 106, Madera (93637-4574)
P.O. Box 278 (93639-0278)
PHONE..........................559 674-2491
David Berry, *Owner*
Gwen Cain, *Shareholder*
Pablo Aleman, *CFO*
Michael Pistoresi, *Vice Pres*
Rudy Zuniga, *Manager*
EMP: 52
SQ FT: 20,000
SALES (est): 8.3MM **Privately Held**
SIC: 1521 6552 1531 6513 New construction, single-family houses; land subdividers & developers, commercial; land subdividers & developers, residential; speculative builder, single-family houses; apartment building operators

(P-1085)
BILL BROWN CONSTRUCTION CO
242 Phelan Ave, San Jose (95112-6109)
PHONE..........................408 297-3738
William E Brown, *President*
EMP: 70
SQ FT: 1,650
SALES (est): 4.3MM **Privately Held**
WEB: www.bbrownconstruction.com
SIC: 1521 1794 1791 Single-family housing construction; excavation work; structural steel erection

(P-1086)
BOLIN BUILDERS INC
3848 Berkesey Ln, Valley Springs (95252-9506)
P.O. Box 1437 (95252-1437)
PHONE..........................209 772-9721
Benton Bolin, *President*
Thelma Bolin, *Corp Secy*
William Bolin, *Vice Pres*
EMP: 50 **EST:** 1998
SALES (est): 5MM **Privately Held**
SIC: 1521 New construction, single-family houses

(P-1087)
BREHM COMMUNITIES (PA)
1935 Camino Vida Roble # 200, Carlsbad (92008-5568)
PHONE..........................760 448-2420
Forrest W Brehm, *President*
EMP: 80 **EST:** 1963
SQ FT: 5,984

SALES (est): 4.7MM **Privately Held**
SIC: 1521 New construction, single-family houses

(P-1088)
BREHM COMMUNITIES (PA)
1825 Aston Ave Ste B, Carlsbad (92008-7341)
PHONE..........................760 448-2420
Forrest Brehm, *Managing Prtnr*
EMP: 60
SALES (est): 4.8MM **Privately Held**
SIC: 1521 New construction, single-family houses

(P-1089)
BRIECK RESTORATION INC
13750 Danielson St, Poway (92064-8889)
PHONE..........................858 679-9928
Dorothy Ledesma, *CEO*
Leanne Ledesma, *Controller*
EMP: 50
SALES (est): 3MM **Privately Held**
SIC: 1521 Single-family home remodeling, additions & repairs

(P-1090)
BROOKFELD STHLAND HOLDINGS LLC
Also Called: Brookfield Residential
3200 Park Center Dr # 1000, Costa Mesa (92626-7163)
PHONE..........................714 427-6868
Edrian Soley,
Gouliquer Matt, *Analyst*
Lui Thomas, *Controller*
Armstrong Dana, *Payroll Mgr*
Gonzalez Ileana, *Personnel Assit*
EMP: 160
SALES (est): 21.8MM
SALES (corp-wide): 43B **Publicly Held**
SIC: 1521 Single-family housing construction
HQ: Brookfield Homes Corporation
     3201 Jermantown Rd # 150
     Fairfax VA 22030
     703 270-1400

(P-1091)
BROOKFIELD HOMES OF CALIFORNIA
Also Called: Brookfield 1996 California
12865 Pointe Del Mar Way # 200, Del Mar (92014-3860)
PHONE..........................858 481-8500
EMP: 50 **EST:** 1996
SALES (est): 2.1MM **Privately Held**
SIC: 1521

(P-1092)
BX CONSTRUCTION LLC
11671 Sterling Ave Ste K, Riverside (92503-4971)
PHONE..........................951 509-9412
Aofan Wang,
Annie Naguillan,
EMP: 60
SQ FT: 1,100
SALES: 795K **Privately Held**
SIC: 1521 6552 6799 New construction, single-family houses; land subdividers & developers, residential; real estate investors, except property operators

(P-1093)
CALATLANTIC GROUP INC
Also Called: Standard Pacific Homes
5750 Fleet St Ste 200, Carlsbad (92008-4709)
PHONE..........................760 602-6824
Brian L Utsler, *Regional Mgr*
EMP: 140
SALES (corp-wide): 20.5B **Publicly Held**
WEB: www.standardpacifichomes.com
SIC: 1521 New construction, single-family houses
HQ: Calatlantic Group, Inc.
     1100 Wilson Blvd Ste 2100
     Arlington VA 22209
     240 532-3806

(P-1094)
CALATLANTIC GROUP INC
Southern Cal Inland Empire Div
355 E Rincon St Ste 300, Corona (92879-1372)
PHONE..........................951 898-5500
Douglas Krah, *Manager*
EMP: 53
SALES (corp-wide): 20.5B **Publicly Held**
SIC: 1521 New construction, single-family houses
HQ: Calatlantic Group, Inc.
     1100 Wilson Blvd Ste 2100
     Arlington VA 22209
     240 532-3806

(P-1095)
CALATLANTIC GROUP INC
Also Called: Calatlantic Homes
15131 Alton Pkwy Ste 300, Irvine (92618-2386)
PHONE..........................949 789-1600
David Desplinter, *Vice Pres*
Gary Jones, *Vice Pres*
Laurie Massas, *Vice Pres*
John Cross, *Administration*
David Stiles, *Analyst*
EMP: 60
SALES (corp-wide): 20.5B **Publicly Held**
WEB: www.standardpacifichomes.com
SIC: 1521 New construction, single-family houses
HQ: Calatlantic Group, Inc.
     1100 Wilson Blvd Ste 2100
     Arlington VA 22209
     240 532-3806

(P-1096)
CALATLANTIC GROUP INC
13200 Fiji Way, Marina Del Rey (90292)
PHONE..........................310 821-9843
EMP: 59
SALES (corp-wide): 2.4B **Publicly Held**
SIC: 1521
PA: Calatlantic Group, Inc.
     15360 Barranca Pkwy
     Irvine CA 92209
     949 789-1600

(P-1097)
CALATLANTIC GROUP INC
26 Technology Dr, Irvine (92618-2380)
PHONE..........................949 789-1600
EMP: 59
SALES (corp-wide): 20.5B **Publicly Held**
WEB: www.standardpacifichomes.com
SIC: 1521 New construction, single-family houses
HQ: Calatlantic Group, Inc.
     1100 Wilson Blvd Ste 2100
     Arlington VA 22209
     240 532-3806

(P-1098)
CALHOUN CONSTRUCTION INC
110 Gateway Dr Ste 260, Lincoln (95648-3307)
PHONE..........................916 434-8356
Robert F Calhoun, *CEO*
Thomas Calhoun, *President*
EMP: 175 **EST:** 2001
SALES (est): 12.3MM **Privately Held**
WEB: www.calhounconstruction.org
SIC: 1521 New construction, single-family houses

(P-1099)
CALIBUILDER CONSTRUCTION INC
441 N Central Ave Ste 8, Campbell (95008-1428)
PHONE..........................408 832-2337
Ramin Parsa, *President*
Ramin Masoumi, *Associate*
EMP: 50
SALES (est): 90.9K **Privately Held**
SIC: 1521 1522 1542 Single-family housing construction; residential construction; commercial & office building contractors

(P-1100)
CALIFORNIA PREFERRED BLDRS INC
20335 Ventura Blvd # 422, Woodland Hills (91364-2444)
PHONE..........................818 402-3345
Jacob Sherf, *President*
EMP: 50 **EST:** 2010
SALES (est): 2.7MM **Privately Held**
SIC: 1521 New construction, single-family houses

(P-1101)
CARROLLCO INC
3104 N Miami Ave, Fresno (93727-8069)
P.O. Box 13039 (93794-3039)
PHONE..........................559 396-3939
Benjamin Carroll, *CEO*
EMP: 50 **EST:** 2010
SQ FT: 5,000
SALES (est): 6.3MM **Privately Held**
SIC: 1521 0782 1711 Single-family home remodeling, additions & repairs; landscape contractors; warm air heating & air conditioning contractor

(P-1102)
CENTEX HOMES INC
27401 Los Altos Ste 400, Mission Viejo (92691-8550)
PHONE..........................949 453-0113
Bryan Swindell, *Branch Mgr*
EMP: 200
SALES (corp-wide): 10.1B **Publicly Held**
WEB: www.centexhomes.com
SIC: 1521 New construction, single-family houses
HQ: Centex Homes, Inc.
     9111 Cypress Waters Blvd # 200
     Coppell TX 75019
     800 777-8583

(P-1103)
CENTEX HOMES INC
Also Called: Centex Homes Central Valley
1840 S Central St, Visalia (93277-4418)
PHONE..........................559 733-2717
Laura Armas, *Manager*
EMP: 108
SALES (corp-wide): 10.1B **Publicly Held**
WEB: www.centexhomes.com
SIC: 1521 New construction, single-family houses
HQ: Centex Homes, Inc.
     9111 Cypress Waters Blvd # 200
     Coppell TX 75019
     800 777-8583

(P-1104)
CENTEX HOMES INC
250 Commerce Ste 100, Irvine (92602-1341)
PHONE..........................949 453-0113
Richard Douglass, *Branch Mgr*
EMP: 108
SALES (corp-wide): 10.1B **Publicly Held**
WEB: www.centexhomes.com
SIC: 1521 New construction, single-family houses
HQ: Centex Homes, Inc.
     9111 Cypress Waters Blvd # 200
     Coppell TX 75019
     800 777-8583

(P-1105)
CLYDE MILES CNSTR CO INC
1110 Burnett Ave Ste C, Concord (94520-5611)
PHONE..........................925 427-4473
Clyde E Miles, *President*
EMP: 100
SALES (est): 8.9MM **Privately Held**
SIC: 1521 New construction, single-family houses

(P-1106)
COASTLINE CNSTR & AWNG CO INC
5742 Research Dr, Huntington Beach (92649-1617)
PHONE..........................714 891-9798
John W Almquist, *President*
EMP: 100
SQ FT: 1,600

SALES (est): 9.2MM **Privately Held**
SIC: 1521 Mobile home repair, on site

(P-1107)
CONSTRUCTION CUSTOMER SERVICE
1320 N Hancock St Ste A, Anaheim (92807-1991)
PHONE..........................714 701-1858
Jackie Roth, *President*
EMP: 50
SQ FT: 3,600
SALES (est): 3.1MM **Privately Held**
WEB: www.constructionserviceinc.com
SIC: 1521 8711 7361 Single-family housing construction; building construction consultant; labor contractors (employment agency)

(P-1108)
CORONEL CONSTRUCTION INC
2328 Venice Dr, Delano (93215-9241)
PHONE..........................661 725-4400
Samuel Coronel, *President*
Ramona Coronel, *Treasurer*
EMP: 85
SALES (est): 6.4MM **Privately Held**
SIC: 1521 Single-family housing construction

(P-1109)
COUNTY OF RIVERSIDE
Facilities Mgmt
3133 Mission Inn Ave, Riverside (92507-4199)
PHONE..........................951 955-4800
Michael Sylvester, *Director*
EMP: 325 **Privately Held**
SIC: 1521 9532 7349 Single-family housing construction; urban & community development; ; building maintenance services
PA: County Of Riverside
4080 Lemon St Fl 11
Riverside CA 92501
951 955-1110

(P-1110)
CRAFTMAN CONCRETE
755 N Peach Ave Ste F11, Clovis (93611-7259)
PHONE..........................559 298-8864
Clyde E Been, *Partner*
David Been, *Partner*
EMP: 75
SALES (est): 3.6MM **Privately Held**
SIC: 1521 0782 New construction, single-family houses; landscape contractors

(P-1111)
DAIWA HOUSE CALIFORNIA INC
1901 Avenue Of The Stars # 264, Los Angeles (90067-6001)
PHONE..........................310 228-5675
Keiichi Yoshi, *President*
EMP: 297
SALES: 107.6MM **Privately Held**
SIC: 1521 General remodeling, single-family houses

(P-1112)
DE MATTEI CONSTRUCTION INC
1794 The Alameda, San Jose (95126-1729)
PHONE..........................408 295-7516
Mark De Mattei, *President*
John Hinton, *CFO*
Travis Cotti, *Project Mgr*
▲ **EMP:** 60
SQ FT: 5,000
SALES (est): 9.4MM **Privately Held**
WEB: www.demattei.com
SIC: 1521 1542 New construction, single-family houses; commercial & office building contractors

(P-1113)
DENNIS ALLEN ASSOCIATES (PA)
201 N Milpas St, Santa Barbara (93103-3201)
PHONE..........................805 884-8777
Dennis W Allen, *President*
Ian Cronshaw, *Vice Pres*

Steve Nelson, *Area Mgr*
Colleen Davis-Heining, *Office Admin*
Jessica Dias, *Executive Asst*
EMP: 95
SALES (est): 35.3MM **Privately Held**
WEB: www.dennisallenassociates.com
SIC: 1521 1542 General remodeling, single-family houses; new construction, single-family houses; commercial & office buildings, renovation & repair; commercial & office building, new construction

(P-1114)
DENNIS HYDE CONSTRUCTION INC
7112 Darrin Ave, Bakersfield (93308-3775)
PHONE..........................661 393-1077
Dennis Hyde, *President*
Julie Hyde, *Vice Pres*
EMP: 60
SALES (est): 5MM **Privately Held**
SIC: 1521 Single-family housing construction

(P-1115)
DEWHURST & ASSOCIATES
7533 Girard Ave, La Jolla (92037-5102)
P.O. Box 574 (92038-0574)
PHONE..........................858 456-5345
Donald Dewhurst, *Chairman*
Doug Dewhurst, *President*
Dave Dewhurst, *CEO*
Dan Sehlhorst, *Architect*
EMP: 70
SQ FT: 1,200
SALES: 6.5MM **Privately Held**
WEB: www.dewhurst.com
SIC: 1521 New construction, single-family houses

(P-1116)
DISASTER RSTRTION PRFSSNALS IN
1517 W 130th St, Gardena (90249-2103)
PHONE..........................310 301-8030
Ahmad Elzarou, *CEO*
EMP: 80
SALES (est): 4.4MM **Privately Held**
SIC: 1521 7299 1542 Repairing fire damage, single-family houses; home improvement & renovation contractor agency; commercial & office building contractors

(P-1117)
DOMUS CONSTRUCTION & DESIGN
Also Called: Statewide
8864 Fruitridge Rd, Sacramento (95826-9708)
PHONE..........................916 381-7500
Maksim R Yurtsan, *CEO*
EMP: 50 **EST:** 2008
SALES (est): 7MM **Privately Held**
SIC: 1521 Repairing fire damage, single-family houses

(P-1118)
E & E CO LTD
Also Called: Jla Home
2222 E Beamer St, Woodland (95776-6226)
PHONE..........................530 669-5991
Carys Lin, *Accountant*
EMP: 550 **Privately Held**
SIC: 1521 Single-family housing construction
PA: E & E Co., Ltd.
45875 Northport Loop E
Fremont CA 94538

(P-1119)
EBC INC (PA)
Also Called: Ellis Building Contractors
219 Manhattan Beach Blvd, Manhattan Beach (90266-5324)
PHONE..........................310 753-6407
Brad Ellis, *President*
Patricia Ellis, *Admin Sec*
EMP: 97
SALES: 922K **Privately Held**
SIC: 1521 1542 New construction, single-family houses; commercial & office building, new construction

(P-1120)
EMERCON CONSTRUCTION INC (PA)
2906 E Coronado St, Anaheim (92806-2501)
PHONE..........................714 630-9615
Richard Anderson, *President*
Joan E Anderson, *Exec VP*
Frank Brady, *Exec VP*
Ron Chavez, *Branch Mgr*
Michael Barlow, *Project Mgr*
EMP: 60
SQ FT: 30,000
SALES (est): 12.6MM **Privately Held**
WEB: www.emercon.com
SIC: 1521 Repairing fire damage, single-family houses

(P-1121)
EXCEL CONTRACTORS INC
Also Called: PROGRESSIN DRYWALL
348 E Avenue K8 Ste B, Lancaster (93535-4514)
PHONE..........................661 942-6944
John Rockey, *President*
Rose Rockey, *Vice Pres*
Jarrett Lemmon, *Project Mgr*
EMP: 100
SALES (est): 17.9MM **Privately Held**
SIC: 1521 1742 1542 Single-family home remodeling, additions & repairs; new construction, single-family houses; drywall; commercial & office building, new construction; commercial & office buildings, renovation & repair

(P-1122)
F R GHIANNI ENTERPRISES INC
Also Called: F R Ghianni Drywall Cnstr Co
1937 Friendship Dr Ste A, El Cajon (92020-1137)
PHONE..........................619 279-1073
Frank R Ghianni, *President*
Debby Weklem, *Admin Sec*
EMP: 100
SQ FT: 1,600
SALES (est): 5.6MM **Privately Held**
SIC: 1521 1771 1742 Single-family housing construction; concrete work; drywall

(P-1123)
FIELDSTONE COMMUNITIES INC
Also Called: Fieldstone Co, The
5465 Morehouse Dr Ste 250, San Diego (92121-3778)
PHONE..........................858 546-8226
Andrew Murphy, *Manager*
EMP: 50
SALES (corp-wide): 23.3MM **Privately Held**
WEB: www.fieldstone-homes.com
SIC: 1521 New construction, single-family houses
PA: Fieldstone Communities, Inc.
16 Technology Dr Ste 125
Irvine CA 92618
949 790-5400

(P-1124)
FORT HILL CONSTRUCTION (PA)
12711 Ventura Blvd # 390, Studio City (91604-2491)
PHONE..........................323 656-7425
George Peper, *President*
Gordon Foote, *CFO*
James Kweskin, *Vice Pres*
Mike Mc Grail, *Vice Pres*
Joseph Goldfarb, *Admin Sec*
▲ **EMP:** 70
SQ FT: 4,000
SALES (est): 14.3MM **Privately Held**
WEB: www.forthill.com
SIC: 1521 New construction, single-family houses

(P-1125)
FROMER INC
22225 Acorn St, Chatsworth (91311-4724)
PHONE..........................818 341-3896
Kim Fromer, *President*
Guy Zimmerman, *Vice Pres*
EMP: 70
SQ FT: 1,200

SALES (est): 6MM **Privately Held**
SIC: 1521 1522 Single-family housing construction; multi-family dwelling construction

(P-1126)
FRONTIER LAND COMPANIES
Also Called: Frontrs-Frnters Land Companies
10100 Trinity Pkwy # 420, Stockton (95219-7238)
PHONE..........................209 957-8112
Thomas Doucette, *President*
Phillip Russell, *CFO*
George K Gibson, *Vice Pres*
EMP: 50
SQ FT: 3,000
SALES (est): 6MM **Privately Held**
SIC: 1521 8742 6552 Single-family housing construction; real estate consultant; subdividers & developers

(P-1127)
G I L C INC
585 W Beach St, Watsonville (95076-5123)
P.O. Box 50085 (95077-5085)
PHONE..........................831 724-1011
David Wats, *President*
EMP: 50
SALES (est): 4.6MM **Privately Held**
SIC: 1521 Single-family housing construction

(P-1128)
GALLAHER CONSTRUCTION INC
220 Concourse Blvd, Santa Rosa (95403-8210)
PHONE..........................707 535-3200
William P Gallaher, *President*
Cynthia J Gallaher, *Admin Sec*
EMP: 50
SQ FT: 11,000
SALES: 30MM **Privately Held**
WEB: www.dflow.com
SIC: 1521 6552 New construction, single-family houses; land subdividers & developers, residential; land subdividers & developers, commercial

(P-1129)
GENE A GARCIA CONSTRUCTION
1663 E Poppy Hills Dr, Fresno (93730-4510)
PHONE..........................559 352-6173
Gene Aaron Garcia, *Principal*
EMP: 50
SALES (est): 495K **Privately Held**
SIC: 1521 New construction, single-family houses

(P-1130)
GENERATION CONTRACTING & EMERG
13685 Stowe Dr Ste B, Poway (92064-8824)
PHONE..........................858 679-9928
Dorothy Ledesma, *President*
Scott Ledesma, *General Mgr*
Paul Brieck, *Admin Sec*
EMP: 50
SQ FT: 9,940
SALES (est): 4.6MM **Privately Held**
WEB: www.contractorforlife.com
SIC: 1521 1542 Single-family home remodeling, additions & repairs; nonresidential construction

(P-1131)
GOODFELLOW BROS CALIFORNIA LLC
50 Contractors St, Livermore (94551-4863)
PHONE..........................925 245-2111
Brian Gates,
Jeff Ramirez, *Project Mgr*
Andy Jenson, *Project Engr*
Frank Williams,
EMP: 387
SALES (est): 4MM **Privately Held**
SIC: 1521 Single-family housing construction

(P-1132)
GRANITE CONSTRUCTION INC
999 Mission Rock Rd, Santa Paula
(93060-9730)
PHONE..................805 879-0033
Scott McArthur, *Branch Mgr*
EMP: 67
SALES (corp-wide): 3.3B **Publicly Held**
WEB: www.graniteconstruction.com
SIC: 1521 Single-family housing construction
PA: Granite Construction Incorporated
 585 W Beach St
 Watsonville CA 95076
 831 724-1011

(P-1133)
GRANTS CUSTOM CABINETS
7310 Kingsbury Rd, Templeton
(93465-8304)
PHONE..................805 466-9680
EMP: 185
SALES (est): 4.5MM **Privately Held**
SIC: 1521

(P-1134)
GRANVILLE HOMES INC
1396 W Herndon Ave # 101, Fresno
(93711-7126)
PHONE..................559 268-2000
Darius Assemi, *CEO*
Farid Assemi, *President*
Jesse Buglione, *Creative Dir*
Sarah Boren, *Executive Asst*
Steve Rau, *Admin Sec*
EMP: 60
SQ FT: 5,000
SALES (est): 15.9MM **Privately Held**
WEB: www.sommervilleestates.com
SIC: 1521 New construction, single-family houses

(P-1135)
GREYSTONE HOMES INC
6121 Bollinger Canyon Rd # 500, San Ramon (94583-5287)
PHONE..................925 242-0811
Dale Billy, *President*
EMP: 250
SALES (corp-wide): 20.5B **Publicly Held**
SIC: 1521 Single-family housing construction
HQ: Greystone Homes, Inc
 25 Enterprise
 Aliso Viejo CA 92656
 -

(P-1136)
HAMBURGER HOME
3701 Wilshire Blvd # 900, Los Angeles
(90010-2804)
PHONE..................213 637-5000
Sandra Cohen, *Principal*
EMP: 52
SALES (corp-wide): 18.8MM **Privately Held**
SIC: 1521 Single-family housing construction
PA: Hamburger Home
 7120 Franklin Ave
 Los Angeles CA 90046
 323 876-0550

(P-1137)
HANOVER BUILDERS INC
141 Duesenberg Dr Ste 6, Westlake Village
(91362-3471)
PHONE..................818 706-2279
Donald Hanover, *President*
EMP: 50
SALES (est): 2.4MM **Privately Held**
WEB: www.hanoverbuildersinc.com
SIC: 1521 New construction, single-family houses

(P-1138)
HINERFELD-WARD INC
8931 Ellis Ave Ste B1, Los Angeles
(90034-3336)
PHONE..................310 842-7929
Tom Hinerfeld, *President*
Peter Borrego, *Vice Pres*
EMP: 70

SALES (est): 5.7MM **Privately Held**
WEB: www.hinerfeld-ward.com
SIC: 1521 Single-family housing construction

(P-1139)
HOWARD CDM
Also Called: Howard Construction
3750 Long Beach Blvd, Long Beach
(90807-3310)
PHONE..................562 427-4124
Martin D Howard, *President*
William G Burkett, *CFO*
Steven C Phillips, *Exec VP*
Scott Peterson, *Project Mgr*
Parker Cole, *Project Engr*
◆ EMP: 50
SQ FT: 7,000
SALES (est): 11.5MM **Privately Held**
WEB: www.howardcdm.net
SIC: 1521 Single-family housing construction

(P-1140)
JDF CONSTRUCTION INC
201 Gemini Ave, Brea (92821-3704)
PHONE..................714 526-1120
John Fitzmaurice, *President*
▲ EMP: 50
SALES (est): 3.5MM **Privately Held**
SIC: 1521 Single-family housing construction

(P-1141)
JF SHEA CONSTRUCTION INC
17400 Clear Creek Rd, Redding
(96001-5113)
P.O. Box 494519 (96049-4519)
PHONE..................530 246-4292
Ed Kernaghan, *Vice Pres*
EMP: 60
SALES (corp-wide): 2.2B **Privately Held**
WEB: www.jfshea.com
SIC: 1521 New construction, single-family houses
HQ: J.F. Shea Construction, Inc.
 655 Brea Canyon Rd
 Walnut CA 91789
 909 595-4397

(P-1142)
JF SHEA CONSTRUCTION INC
Also Called: Shea Homes
2 Ada Ste 200, Irvine (92618-5325)
PHONE..................949 526-8792
Bob Yoder, *President*
EMP: 75
SALES (corp-wide): 2.2B **Privately Held**
WEB: www.jfshea.com
SIC: 1521 Single-family housing construction
HQ: J.F. Shea Construction, Inc.
 655 Brea Canyon Rd
 Walnut CA 91789
 909 595-4397

(P-1143)
JF SHEA CONSTRUCTION INC
Shea Business Properties
675 Brea Canyon Rd Ste 8, Walnut
(91789-3065)
PHONE..................909 594-0998
Bill Gaboury, *President*
EMP: 50
SQ FT: 1,500
SALES (corp-wide): 2.2B **Privately Held**
WEB: www.jfshea.com
SIC: 1521 New construction, single-family houses
HQ: J.F. Shea Construction, Inc.
 655 Brea Canyon Rd
 Walnut CA 91789
 909 595-4397

(P-1144)
JF SHEA CONSTRUCTION INC
Also Called: Shea Homes
6130 Monterey Hwy Ofc, San Jose
(95138-1797)
PHONE..................408 225-1475
Alfonso Garcia, *Manager*
EMP: 344
SQ FT: 3,500

SALES (corp-wide): 2.2B **Privately Held**
WEB: www.jfshea.com
SIC: 1521 New construction, single-family houses
HQ: J.F. Shea Construction, Inc.
 655 Brea Canyon Rd
 Walnut CA 91789
 909 595-4397

(P-1145)
JF SHEA CONSTRUCTION INC
Also Called: Shea Homes
2580 Shea Center Dr, Livermore
(94551-7547)
PHONE..................925 245-3660
Layne Marceau, *President*
EMP: 150
SALES (corp-wide): 2.2B **Privately Held**
WEB: www.jfshea.com
SIC: 1521 New construction, single-family houses
HQ: J.F. Shea Construction, Inc.
 655 Brea Canyon Rd
 Walnut CA 91789
 909 595-4397

(P-1146)
JUAN LOPEZ
Also Called: All Types of Baseboard
3065 Beyer Blvd Ste B106, San Diego
(92154-3499)
PHONE..................619 428-3138
Juan Lopez, *Owner*
EMP: 100
SALES (est): 4.6MM **Privately Held**
SIC: 1521 1542 Single-family housing construction; commercial & office building contractors

(P-1147)
K HOVNANIAN COMPANIES CAL INC (HQ)
Also Called: K Hovnanian
400 Exchange Ste 200, Irvine
(92602-1340)
PHONE..................714 368-4500
Nicholas Pappas, *President*
EMP: 65
SALES (corp-wide): 1.9B **Publicly Held**
SIC: 1521 Single-family housing construction
PA: Hovnanian Enterprises, Inc.
 90 Matawan Rd Ste 105
 Matawan NJ 07747
 732 747-7800

(P-1148)
KB HOME GRATER LOS ANGELES INC (HQ)
10990 Wilshire Blvd # 700, Los Angeles
(90024-3913)
PHONE..................310 231-4000
Bruce Karatz, *CEO*
Carolyn A Harrington, *Office Mgr*
EMP: 90
SQ FT: 40,000
SALES (est): 71.5MM
SALES (corp-wide): 4.5B **Publicly Held**
SIC: 1521 1522 Single-family home remodeling, additions & repairs; multi-family dwelling construction
PA: Kb Home
 10990 Wilshire Blvd Fl 5
 Los Angeles CA 90024
 310 231-4000

(P-1149)
KITCHEN MART INC
4381 Granite Dr Ste C, Rocklin
(95677-2173)
PHONE..................916 315-3535
Dave Hollars, *President*
EMP: 65
SALES (corp-wide): 12.5MM **Privately Held**
SIC: 1521 General remodeling, single-family houses
PA: Kitchen Mart, Inc.
 3742 Bradview Dr
 Sacramento CA
 916 362-7080

(P-1150)
LACONSTRUCTORA CO INC
2030 Broadway, Oceanside (92054-6516)
PHONE..................760 439-7686
Fabio Marchi, *President*
EMP: 50 EST: 1997
SALES (est): 2.1MM **Privately Held**
SIC: 1521 Single-family housing construction

(P-1151)
LARGO CONCRETE INC
1650 Hotel Cir N, San Diego (92108-2816)
PHONE..................619 356-2142
EMP: 219
SALES (corp-wide): 150.8MM **Privately Held**
SIC: 1521 Single-family housing construction
PA: Largo Concrete, Inc.
 2741 Walnut Ave Ste 110
 Tustin CA 92780
 714 731-3600

(P-1152)
LENNAR HOMES CALIFORNIA INC (DH)
Also Called: Lennar Builders
15131 Alton Pkwy Ste 190, Irvine
(92618-2386)
PHONE..................949 349-8000
Brent Reed, *Planning*
Kathy Dale, *Asst Controller*
EMP: 124
SALES (est): 139.7MM
SALES (corp-wide): 20.5B **Publicly Held**
SIC: 1521 6552 New construction, single-family houses; subdividers & developers
HQ: Lennar Homes, Inc.
 700 Nw 107th Ave Ste 115
 Miami FL 33172
 305 559-4000

(P-1153)
M K S CONSTRUCTION INC
Also Called: Schetter Electric
471 Bannon St, Sacramento (95811-0203)
P.O. Box 1377 (95812-1377)
PHONE..................916 446-2521
Frank Schetter, *President*
EMP: 152
SQ FT: 7,800
SALES (est): 6.3MM **Privately Held**
SIC: 1521 Single-family housing construction

(P-1154)
MACARTHUR TRANSIT COMMUNITY
345 Spear St Ste 700, San Francisco
(94105-6136)
P.O. Box 190220 (94119-0220)
PHONE..................415 989-1111
Susan Johnson, *Vice Pres*
EMP: 200
SALES (est): 1.1MM **Privately Held**
SIC: 1521 Single-family housing construction
PA: Bridge Economic Development Corporation
 345 Spear St Ste 700
 San Francisco CA 94105

(P-1155)
MACHADO & SONS CNSTR INC
1000 S Kilroy Rd, Turlock (95380-9589)
PHONE..................209 632-5260
Manuel B Machado, *President*
Mike Machado, *CFO*
Jason Machado, *Vice Pres*
Mary Machado, *Office Admin*
EMP: 50
SALES (est): 10.7MM **Privately Held**
WEB: www.machadoandsons.com
SIC: 1521 1542 1771 1541 New construction, single-family houses; commercial & office building, new construction; patio construction, concrete; industrial buildings & warehouses

(P-1156)
MARK R EGGEN
CONSTRUCTION INC
34145 Pacific Coast Hwy # 325, Dana Point
(92629-2808)
PHONE.................................949 661-2674
Mark Eggen, *President*
EMP: 50
SALES: 7.5MM Privately Held
SIC: 1521 New construction, single-family
houses

(P-1157)
MATRIX GROUP
INTERNATIONAL INC
1520 W Cameron Ave, West Covina
(91790-2713)
PHONE.................................626 960-6205
EMP: 70
SALES (est): 2.7MM Privately Held
SIC: 1521

(P-1158)
MCCLONE CONSTRUCTION
COMPANY
4340 Product Dr, Cameron Park
(95682-8492)
P.O. Box 939, Shingle Springs (95682-
0939)
PHONE.................................559 431-9411
Scott McClone, *Branch Mgr*
Travis Ferguson, *Vice Pres*
Chris Foster, *Vice Pres*
John Salluce, *Vice Pres*
Kim Wagner, *Office Mgr*
EMP: 216 Privately Held
SIC: 1521 Single-family housing construc-
tion
PA: Mcclone Construction Company
  5170 Hillsdale Cir Ste B
  El Dorado Hills CA 95762

(P-1159)
MCMILLIN CONSTRUCTION
SVCS LP
2750 Womble Rd, San Diego (92106-6114)
PHONE.................................619 477-4170
EMP: 50
SQ FT: 29,000
SALES (est): 2.3MM Privately Held
SIC: 1521

(P-1160)
MICHAEL BRUINGTON
9 Soledad Dr Ste E, Monterey
(93940-6036)
PHONE.................................831 663-1772
Michael Bruington, *Exec VP*
EMP: 50
SALES (est): 1.8MM Privately Held
SIC: 1521 Single-family housing construc-
tion

(P-1161)
MIDSTATE CONSTRUCTION
CORP
1180 Holm Rd Ste A, Petaluma
(94954-7120)
PHONE.................................707 762-3200
Roger Nelson, *President*
Richard Oberdorfer, *Vice Pres*
Linda Goldberg, *Admin Asst*
Eric Bostrom, *Administration*
Monica Nelson, *VP Mktg*
EMP: 80
SQ FT: 18,928
SALES (est): 29.5MM Privately Held
SIC: 1521 1541 1542 New construction,
single-family houses; general remodeling,
single-family houses; industrial buildings,
new construction; renovation, remodeling
& repairs: industrial buildings; commercial
& office building, new construction; com-
mercial & office buildings, renovation &
repair

(P-1162)
MIKE ROVNER CONSTRUCTION
INC
1758 Junction Ave Ste C, San Jose
(95112-1022)
PHONE.................................408 453-6070
Mike Rovner, *President*

EMP: 121 Privately Held
SIC: 1521 Single-family housing construc-
tion
PA: Mike Rovner Construction, Inc.
  5400 Tech Cir
  Moorpark CA 93021

(P-1163)
MILES CONSTRUCTION GROUP
INC
42020 Winchester Rd, Temecula
(92590-4804)
PHONE.................................951 260-2504
Adam Miles, *President*
S Parkinson, *Corp Secy*
G King, *Vice Pres*
Marty Giuliani, *Project Mgr*
EMP: 50
SQ FT: 8,000
SALES: 3.7MM Privately Held
SIC: 1521 Single-family housing construc-
tion

(P-1164)
MILLENIA DEVELOPMENT
929 Bettina Way, San Jacinto
(92582-2507)
PHONE.................................951 660-5691
Brett Stucker, *Owner*
EMP: 50
SALES: 2MM Privately Held
SIC: 1521 Single-family housing construc-
tion

(P-1165)
MJD CONSTRUCTION CORP
Also Called: M J D Concrete Works
28244 Dorothy Dr, Agoura Hills
(91301-2605)
PHONE.................................818 575-9864
Mathias Di Cecco, *President*
EMP: 60
SQ FT: 1,500
SALES (est): 7.4MM Privately Held
SIC: 1521 Single-family housing construc-
tion

(P-1166)
NICHOLAS LANE
CONTRACTORS INC
1157 N Red Gum St, Anaheim
(92806-2515)
PHONE.................................714 630-7630
Scott N Shaddix, *President*
Jo Ann Shaddix, *Corp Secy*
EMP: 400
SQ FT: 5,000
SALES: 26MM Privately Held
WEB: www.nicholaslane.com
SIC: 1521 1542 New construction, single-
family houses; commercial & office build-
ings, renovation & repair

(P-1167)
NORTH WIND CNSTR SVCS LLC
730 Howe Ave Ste 700, Sacramento
(95825-4641)
PHONE.................................916 333-3015
Brent Brooks,
EMP: 69 EST: 2011
SALES (est): 1.7MM Privately Held
SIC: 1521 Single-family housing construc-
tion

(P-1168)
OLSON COMPANY LLC (PA)
Also Called: Olson Homes
3010 Old Ranch Pkwy # 100, Seal Beach
(90740-2750)
PHONE.................................562 596-4770
Steve Olson,
Karen Hoover, *President*
Brenda Olson, *Vice Pres*
Campbell Chris, *Project Mgr*
Gabriel Chang, *Engineer*
EMP: 99
SALES: 46.9MM Privately Held
SIC: 1521 Single-family housing construc-
tion

(P-1169)
PACIFIC BAY PROPERTIES (PA)
4041 Macarthur Blvd # 500, Newport Beach
(92660-2512)
PHONE.................................949 440-7200

Malcolm S McDonald, *President*
EMP: 50
SALES (est): 9.5MM Privately Held
SIC: 1521 Single-family housing construc-
tion

(P-1170)
PACIFIC DESIGN DIRECTIONS
INC
Also Called: Pacific Interior Design
8171 E Kaiser Blvd, Anaheim
(92808-2214)
PHONE.................................714 685-7766
Susan S Stoneburner, *President*
Kristen S Stolle, *Division Mgr*
Reed Stoneburner, *Division Mgr*
EMP: 50 EST: 1979
SQ FT: 8,600
SALES: 15MM Privately Held
WEB: www.pacdesign.com
SIC: 1521 1731 7389 8712 Single-family
housing construction; general electrical
contractor; interior designer; architectural
services

(P-1171)
PAGLIA & ASSOCIATES CNSTR
Also Called: Protech Construction
2790 E Regal Park Dr, Anaheim
(92806-2417)
PHONE.................................714 982-5151
Vince Paglia, *President*
Kimm Paglia, *CFO*
▲ EMP: 65
SQ FT: 6,500
SALES: 13.1MM Privately Held
WEB: www.protechconst.com
SIC: 1521 1542 New construction, single-
family houses; commercial & office build-
ing, new construction

(P-1172)
PENINSULA CUSTOM HOMES
INC
1401 Old County Rd, San Carlos
(94070-5202)
PHONE.................................650 574-0241
Richard L Breaux, *CEO*
Bryan Murphy, *President*
EMP: 60 EST: 1979
SALES (est): 9.9MM Privately Held
WEB: www.pchi.com
SIC: 1521 New construction, single-family
houses

(P-1173)
PETERSEN BUILDERS INC
7706 Bell Rd Ste A, Windsor (95492-8546)
PHONE.................................707 838-3035
Talbert Petersen, *President*
Rex Petersen, *Treasurer*
Dwight Petersen, *Admin Sec*
▲ EMP: 50
SQ FT: 1,300
SALES (est): 7.5MM Privately Held
SIC: 1521 1522 1542 1541 New con-
struction, single-family houses; multi-fam-
ily dwellings, new construction;
commercial & office building, new con-
struction; school building construction;
food products manufacturing or packing
plant construction

(P-1174)
PINNACLE BUILDERS INC
1911 Douglas Blvd Ste 85, Roseville
(95661-3811)
PHONE.................................916 372-5000
EMP: 300
SQ FT: 3,000
SALES (est): 11.5MM Privately Held
WEB: www.pinnaclebuildersinc.com
SIC: 1521 1542 1751 1522

(P-1175)
PORTER CONSTRUCTION CO
INC
18931 Portola Dr Ste A, Salinas
(93908-1295)
PHONE.................................831 455-3020
Daniel Porter, *President*
Debra Porter, *Corp Secy*
EMP: 240

SALES (est): 11.2MM Privately Held
SIC: 1521 1542 New construction, single-
family houses; commercial & office building, new construction

(P-1176)
PRIMECARE QUALITY HM CARE
INC
2372 Morse Ave, Irvine (92614-6234)
PHONE.................................949 681-3515
EMP: 99
SALES (est): 3.6MM Privately Held
SIC: 1521

(P-1177)
PULTE HOME COMPANY LLC
6210 Stoneridge Mall Rd, Pleasanton
(94588-3268)
PHONE.................................925 249-3200
Can Carrol, *Manager*
Francisco Celis, *Engineer*
EMP: 65
SQ FT: 12,000
SALES (corp-wide): 10.1B Publicly Held
SIC: 1521 New construction, single-family
houses
HQ: Pulte Home Company, Llc
  3350 Peachtree Rd Ne # 150
  Atlanta GA 30326
  248 647-2750

(P-1178)
QUALITY GROUP HOMES INC
Also Called: Consortium For Community Svcs
250 Dos Rios St Ste A1, Sacramento
(95811-0442)
PHONE.................................916 930-0066
Sarah Thomas, *Director*
EMP: 184
SALES (corp-wide): 7.7MM Privately
Held
SIC: 1521 New construction, single-family
houses
PA: Quality Group Homes, Inc.
  4928 E Clinton Way # 108
  Fresno CA 93727
  559 255-8519

(P-1179)
R J DAILEY CONSTRUCTION CO
401 1st St, Los Altos (94022-3607)
PHONE.................................650 948-5196
Robert J Dailey, *President*
Christine Dailey, *Corp Secy*
Mike Craig, *Vice Pres*
Carol Lopez, *Administration*
Dennis Davis, *Project Mgr*
▲ EMP: 70
SQ FT: 2,000
SALES (est): 12.5MM Privately Held
SIC: 1521 New construction, single-family
houses; general remodeling, single-family
houses

(P-1180)
REDHORSE CONSTRUCTORS
INC
36 Professional Ctr Pkwy, San Rafael
(94903-2703)
PHONE.................................415 492-2020
David J Warner, *President*
Jay Blumenfeld, *General Mgr*
Thomas Bates, *Project Mgr*
Trystan Christ, *Project Mgr*
Michael Houts, *Project Mgr*
▲ EMP: 75
SQ FT: 3,500
SALES: 37.8MM Privately Held
WEB: www.redhorseconstructors.com
SIC: 1521 General remodeling, single-fam-
ily houses; new construction, single-family
houses

(P-1181)
REGIONAL CONNECTOR
CONSTRS
1995 Agua Mansa Rd, Riverside
(92509-2405)
PHONE.................................951 368-6400
Patty Macias, *Office Mgr*
EMP: 50
SALES (est): 3MM Privately Held
SIC: 1521 New construction, single-family
houses

(P-1182)
REYNEN & BARDIS CONSTRUCTION (PA)
10630 Mather Blvd, Mather (95655-4125)
PHONE....................916 366-3665
Chris Bardis, *President*
John Reynen, *Admin Sec*
EMP: 120
SALES (est): 43.5MM **Privately Held**
WEB: www.rbhome.us
SIC: 1521 6552 New construction, single-family houses; land subdividers & developers, residential

(P-1183)
RICHMOND AMERICAN HOMES
16600 Sherman Way Ste 180, Van Nuys (91406-3725)
PHONE....................818 908-3267
Bob Shiota, *Exec VP*
EMP: 50
SALES (corp-wide): 3B **Publicly Held**
SIC: 1521 Single-family housing construction
HQ: Richmond American Homes
5171 California Ave # 120
Irvine CA 92617
949 467-2600

(P-1184)
RIDGESIDE CONSTRUCTION INC
Also Called: Ridgeside Finishing
4345 E Lowell St Ste A, Ontario (91761-2223)
P.O. Box 1237 (91762-0237)
PHONE....................909 218-7593
Dan Zita, *President*
Kevin Hammond, *Vice Pres*
EMP: 65
SALES: 125.2MM **Privately Held**
SIC: 1521 Single-family housing construction

(P-1185)
ROBERT MORKEN CONSTRUCTION
1300 Regency Way Ste 59, Kings Beach (96143)
P.O. Box 415, Tahoe Vista (96148-0415)
PHONE....................530 386-1512
Robert Morken, *President*
EMP: 50
SALES: 10MM **Privately Held**
SIC: 1521 1542 New construction, single-family houses; commercial & office building, new construction

(P-1186)
RYLAND HMES INLND EMPIRE CSTMR
Also Called: Home Building
1250 Corona Pointe Ct # 100, Corona (92879-2099)
PHONE....................951 273-3473
Linda Edwards, *President*
EMP: 80
SALES (est): 6.2MM **Privately Held**
SIC: 1521 New construction, single-family houses

(P-1187)
S TAYLOR CONSTRUCTION INC
23905 Clinton Keith Rd, Wildomar (92595-7897)
PHONE....................310 291-4505
Steve Taylor, *President*
EMP: 103
SALES: 1MM **Privately Held**
SIC: 1521 Single-family housing construction

(P-1188)
SANTOS LEGACY BUILDERS LLC
2829 Watt Ave 101, Sacramento (95821-6200)
PHONE....................916 439-2777
Ernesto David Santos, *Principal*
EMP: 99
SALES (est): 3.4MM **Privately Held**
SIC: 1521 New construction, single-family houses

(P-1189)
SAVOY CONTRACTORS GROUP INC
Also Called: Ritz Companies
8905 Research Dr, Irvine (92618-4237)
PHONE....................949 753-1919
Robert Ritz Sadeghi, *Ch of Bd*
Shadi Sepehrband, *Controller*
EMP: 175
SQ FT: 2,000
SALES (est): 12.8MM **Privately Held**
WEB: www.theritzcompanies.com
SIC: 1521 7349 Single-family housing construction; building maintenance services

(P-1190)
SEARS HOME IMPRV PDTS INC
9586 Dist Ave Ste F, San Diego (92121)
PHONE....................858 790-7721
Jerry Hanosh, *Branch Mgr*
EMP: 52
SALES (corp-wide): 22.2B **Publicly Held**
SIC: 1521 General remodeling, single-family houses
HQ: Sears Home Improvement Products, Inc.
1024 Florida Central Pkwy
Longwood FL 32750
407 767-0990

(P-1191)
SELIG CONSTRUCTION CORP
337 Huss Dr, Chico (95928-8209)
PHONE....................530 893-5898
M Scott Selig, *President*
Erik Palo, *Vice Pres*
William Brereton, *Mktg Dir*
▲ EMP: 50
SALES (est): 5.8MM **Privately Held**
WEB: www.seligconstruction.com
SIC: 1521 General remodeling, single-family houses

(P-1192)
SHAPELL INDUSTRIES LLC
Also Called: Shapell's Home Center
11280 Corbin Ave, Northridge (91326-4120)
PHONE....................818 366-1132
Nathan Shapell, *Ch of Bd*
EMP: 50
SALES (corp-wide): 7.1B **Publicly Held**
WEB: www.shapell.com
SIC: 1521 New construction, single-family houses
HQ: Shapell Industries, Llc
8383 Wilshire Blvd # 700
Beverly Hills CA 90211
323 655-7330

(P-1193)
SHEA HOMES AT MONTAGE LLC
655 Brea Canyon Rd, Walnut (91789-3078)
PHONE....................909 594-9500
John C Morrissey, *Principal*
EMP: 51 EST: 2013
SALES (est): 2.9MM
SALES (corp-wide): 2.2B **Privately Held**
SIC: 1521 Single-family housing construction
HQ: Shea Homes Limited Partnership, A California Limited Partnership
655 Brea Canyon Rd
Walnut CA 91789

(P-1194)
SHEA HOMES LMTD PARTNERSHIP A (HQ)
655 Brea Canyon Rd, Walnut (91789-3078)
PHONE....................909 594-9500
Jim Shontere, *Partner*
John F Shea LP, *Partner*
EMP: 50
SQ FT: 29,000
SALES: 1.1B
SALES (corp-wide): 2.2B **Privately Held**
WEB: www.highlandsranch.com
SIC: 1521 New construction, single-family houses

PA: J. F. Shea Co., Inc.
655 Brea Canyon Rd
Walnut CA 91789
909 594-9500

(P-1195)
SHEEHAN CONSTRUCTION INC
477 Devlin Rd Ste 108, NAPA (94558-7511)
PHONE....................707 603-2610
Steve Mosiman, *President*
Tom Sheehan, *Vice Pres*
EMP: 500
SALES (est): 42.2MM **Privately Held**
WEB: www.sheehanconstruction.com
SIC: 1521 Single-family housing construction

(P-1196)
SILVERADO FRAMING & CNSTR
3091 E La Cadena Dr, Riverside (92507-2630)
PHONE....................951 352-1100
Ed Solis, *President*
EMP: 100
SQ FT: 2,500
SALES (est): 216.2K **Privately Held**
SIC: 1521 Single-family housing construction

(P-1197)
SILVERLINE CONSTRUCTION INC
1752 Junction Ave Ste E, San Jose (95112-1020)
PHONE....................408 437-8810
EMP: 172 **Privately Held**
SIC: 1521 Single-family housing construction
PA: Silverline Construction, Inc.
1421 W 132nd St
Gardena CA 90249

(P-1198)
SKYVA CONSTRUCTION INC
5781 Old Antelope N Rd, Antelope (95843-3962)
P.O. Box 8094, Citrus Heights (95621-8094)
PHONE....................916 726-4999
Vladimir Andrichuk, *President*
EMP: 50
SALES (est): 4.9MM **Privately Held**
WEB: www.skyvaconstruction.com
SIC: 1521 General remodeling, single-family houses

(P-1199)
SMA BUILDERS INC
16134 Leadwell St, Van Nuys (91406-3424)
PHONE....................818 994-8306
Shawn Antin, *President*
Diana Antin, *Vice Pres*
EMP: 50
SALES (est): 8.9MM **Privately Held**
SIC: 1521 New construction, single-family houses

(P-1200)
STEVEN N LEDSON
Also Called: Ledson Winery & Vineyards
7335 Sonoma Hwy, Santa Rosa (95409-6269)
P.O. Box 653, Kenwood (95452-0653)
PHONE....................707 537-3810
Steven N Ledson, *Owner*
Steven Ledson, *General Mgr*
EMP: 60
SALES (est): 5MM **Privately Held**
SIC: 1521 2084 Single-family housing construction; wines

(P-1201)
STOCKER & ALLAIRE INC
21 Mandeville Ct, Monterey (93940-5745)
PHONE....................831 375-1890
David Stocker, *President*
David Allaire, *CFO*
Will Gaccione, *Project Mgr*
EMP: 50
SQ FT: 3,200

SALES (est): 9.2MM **Privately Held**
WEB: www.stockerallaire.com
SIC: 1521 General remodeling, single-family houses

(P-1202)
SUMMERHILL CONSTRUCTION CO
Also Called: Summerhill Homes
3000 Executive Pkwy # 450, San Ramon (94583-4255)
PHONE....................925 244-7520
Roger Menard, *President*
EMP: 50
SQ FT: 45,000
SALES (est): 3.8MM
SALES (corp-wide): 70.9MM **Privately Held**
WEB: www.summerhillhomes.com
SIC: 1521 New construction, single-family houses
HQ: Summerhill Homes Llc
3000 Executive Pkwy # 450
San Ramon CA 94583
925 244-7500

(P-1203)
SUPERIOR CONSTRUCTION INC
265 N Joy St, Corona (92879-0600)
P.O. Box 1148 (92878-1148)
PHONE....................951 808-8780
Kenneth Day, *President*
Don Mc Lellan, *Sls & Mktg Exec*
Darren Smith, *Accounts Mgr*
EMP: 100
SQ FT: 3,000
SALES (est): 8.7MM **Privately Held**
SIC: 1521 1542 New construction, single-family houses; commercial & office building, new construction

(P-1204)
SUPPORT FOR HOME INC
1333 Howe Ave Ste 206, Sacramento (95825-3362)
PHONE....................530 792-8484
Bert Cave, *Principal*
Carlotta Sanchez, *Principal*
EMP: 50
SALES (est): 3.2MM **Privately Held**
SIC: 1521 Single-family housing construction

(P-1205)
SWINERTON BUILDERS INC
2300 Clayton Rd Ste 800, Concord (94520-2166)
PHONE....................925 602-6400
Jeffrey Hoopes, *CEO*
Gary Rafferty, *President*
Linda Schowalter, *CFO*
Charlene Atkinson, *Principal*
EMP: 79
SALES (est): 24.4MM **Privately Held**
SIC: 1521 New construction, single-family houses

(P-1206)
T B PENICK & SONS INC
41892 Enterprise Cir S, Temecula (92590-4822)
PHONE....................951 719-1492
EMP: 122
SALES (corp-wide): 139.2MM **Privately Held**
SIC: 1521 General remodeling, single-family houses
PA: T. B. Penick & Sons, Inc.
15435 Innovation Dr # 100
San Diego CA 92128
858 558-1800

(P-1207)
TIM MELLO CONSTRUCTION
464 Lamarque Ct, Grass Valley (95945-7061)
PHONE....................530 205-8588
Timothy Mello, *Principal*
EMP: 50 EST: 2011
SALES (est): 231.9K **Privately Held**
SIC: 1521 Single-family housing construction

P
R
O
D
U
C
T
S

&

S
V
C
S

(P-1208)
TIMBER WORKS CONSTRUCTION INC
7031 Roseville Rd Ste A, Sacramento (95842-1670)
PHONE..................916 786-6666
Scott D Robbins, *President*
EMP: 125 EST: 2008
SALES (est): 13.5MM **Privately Held**
SIC: 1521 1542 Single-family housing construction; nonresidential construction

(P-1209)
TOLL BROTHERS INC
Also Called: Toll Brothers Division Office
6800 Koll Center Pkwy # 320, Pleasanton (94566-7045)
PHONE..................925 855-0260
Rick Nelson, *Branch Mgr*
EMP: 60
SALES (corp-wide): 7.1B **Publicly Held**
WEB: www.tollbros.com
SIC: 1521 New construction, single-family houses; townhouse construction
PA: Toll Brothers, Inc.
   250 Gibraltar Rd
   Horsham PA 19044
   215 938-8000

(P-1210)
TORRES GENERAL INC
9484 Mission Park Pl, Santee (92071-5610)
PHONE..................619 448-8900
Carlos Torres Jr, *President*
Maria Morfin, *Technology*
EMP: 100
SALES: 7.5MM **Privately Held**
SIC: 1521 New construction, single-family houses

(P-1211)
TUPAZ HOMES LLC
2038 Biarritz Pl, San Jose (95138-2259)
PHONE..................408 377-1622
Rosario Tupaz, *Mng Member*
Beebe Tupaz, *CFO*
EMP: 100
SALES (est): 357K **Privately Held**
SIC: 1521 Single-family housing construction

(P-1212)
TURNER CONSTRUCTION COMPANY
555 S Flower St Ste 4220, Los Angeles (90071-2438)
PHONE..................213 891-3000
Michael O'Brien, *Senior VP*
Kevin Barb, *Engineer*
Stephen Caldwell, *Engineer*
EMP: 70
SALES (corp-wide): 475MM **Privately Held**
SIC: 1521 Single-family housing construction
HQ: Turner Construction Company Inc
   375 Hudson St Fl 6
   New York NY 10014
   212 229-6000

(P-1213)
US BEST REPAIR SERVICE INC
Also Called: US Best Repairs
2004 Mcgaw Ave, Irvine (92614-0911)
PHONE..................888 750-2378
Mark Zaverl, *CEO*
Kyle Keller, *COO*
Brian Craycraft, *CFO*
Jeff Bougher, *Vice Pres*
Bianca Tobias, *Finance*
EMP: 101
SALES (est): 14.2MM **Privately Held**
WEB: www.usbestrepairs.com
SIC: 1521 1522 1542 Single-family home remodeling, additions & repairs; remodeling, multi-family dwellings; commercial & office buildings, renovation & repair

(P-1214)
VALLEYWIDE CONSTRUCTION INC
284 W Lester Ave, Clovis (93619-3788)
PHONE..................559 834-6212
Christina Birdsell, *President*

John Birdsell, *Treasurer*
EMP: 150
SQ FT: 5,000
SALES: 6.8MM **Privately Held**
SIC: 1521 1751 New construction, single-family houses; framing contractor

(P-1215)
VAN ACKER CNSTR ASSOC INC
1060 Redwood Hwy Frntg Rd, Mill Valley (94941-1613)
PHONE..................415 383-5589
Gary Van Acker, *President*
Pamela Blier, *Vice Pres*
Eaton Heide, *Administration*
Heide Vasquez, *Administration*
Pederson John, *Info Tech Mgr*
▲ EMP: 134
SQ FT: 15,000
SALES (est): 29.8MM **Privately Held**
WEB: www.vanacker.com
SIC: 1521 New construction, single-family houses

(P-1216)
VASONA MANAGEMENT INC
Also Called: Vasonic Construction
37390 Central Mont Pl, Fremont (94538)
PHONE..................510 413-0091
Dan Scharnow, *Vice Pres*
EMP: 80
SALES (corp-wide): 37.3MM **Privately Held**
WEB: www.vasonamanagement.com
SIC: 1521 Single-family housing construction
PA: Vasona Management, Inc.
   18 E Main St
   Los Gatos CA 95030
   408 354-4200

(P-1217)
VENTURA STREETS DEPT
Also Called: City Hall
336 San Jon Rd, Ventura (93001-3233)
PHONE..................805 652-4515
Ron Calkins, *Director*
EMP: 100 EST: 1998
SALES (est): 2.7MM **Privately Held**
SIC: 1521 1611 General remodeling, single-family houses; highway & street construction

(P-1218)
VORWALLER & BROOKS INC
72182 Corporate Way, Thousand Palms (92276-3324)
PHONE..................760 262-6300
Eugene Sheldon Vorwaller, *President*
Jason Brooks, *Vice Pres*
EMP: 55
SALES (est): 7.9MM **Privately Held**
SIC: 1521 New construction, single-family houses

(P-1219)
WARMINGTON RESIDENTIAL CAL INC
3090 Pullman St, Costa Mesa (92626-5901)
PHONE..................714 557-5511
James Warmington Jr, *President*
Mike Riddlesberger, *CFO*
Matt Tingler, *Vice Pres*
Mario Santos, *Information Mgr*
EMP: 150
SALES (est): 24.4MM **Privately Held**
SIC: 1521 Single-family housing construction

(P-1220)
WEST COAST ARBORISTS INC
8163 Commercial St, La Mesa (91942-2928)
PHONE..................858 566-4204
Marcos Martinez, *Foreman/Supr*
Marisa Dunn, *Manager*
EMP: 217
SALES (corp-wide): 102.7MM **Privately Held**
SIC: 1521 0783 Single-family home remodeling, additions & repairs; ornamental shrub & tree services

PA: West Coast Arborists, Inc.
   2200 E Via Burton
   Anaheim CA 92806
   714 991-1900

(P-1221)
WESTCOR CONSTRUCTION OF CAL
2351 W Lugonia Ave Ste D, Redlands (92374-5014)
PHONE..................909 796-8900
Michael A Coronado, *President*
Kevin R Booth, *CFO*
James D Hammer, *Treasurer*
EMP: 120
SQ FT: 4,600
SALES: 13.9MM
SALES (corp-wide): 31MM **Privately Held**
SIC: 1521 New construction, single-family houses
PA: Westcor Construction
   5620 Stephanie St
   Las Vegas NV 89122
   702 433-1414

(P-1222)
WOOD CASTLE CONSTRUCTION INC
770 W Golden Grove Way, Covina (91722-3255)
PHONE..................626 966-8600
Daniel Toro, *President*
Victor Quintana, *Treasurer*
Julio Toro, *Vice Pres*
EMP: 50
SALES (est): 5.9MM **Privately Held**
SIC: 1521 Single-family housing construction

(P-1223)
XIN XIN CONSTRUCTION INC
6701 Koll Center Pkwy, Pleasanton (94569-8061)
PHONE..................945 560-9511
LI Hung, *President*
EMP: 54
SALES: 7MM **Privately Held**
SIC: 1521 Single-family housing construction

(P-1224)
XL CONSTRUCTION CORPORATION
1810 13th St Ste 110, Sacramento (95811-7149)
PHONE..................916 282-2900
Eric Raff, *Branch Mgr*
Marcus Staniford, *Vice Pres*
Natalia Sanchez, *Executive Asst*
Adam Akins, *Project Engr*
David Duff, *Engineer*
EMP: 75 **Privately Held**
SIC: 1521 Single-family housing construction
PA: Xl Construction Corporation
   851 Buckeye Ct
   Milpitas CA 95035

(P-1225)
ZOHAR CONSTRUCTION INC
Also Called: Quality Construction
4272 Pasadero Pl, Tarzana (91356-5218)
P.O. Box 4522, Valley Village (91617-0522)
PHONE..................818 609-7473
Zohar Haykeen, *President*
EMP: 100 EST: 2011
SALES (est): 5.6MM **Privately Held**
SIC: 1521 Single-family housing construction

1522 General Contractors, Residential Other Than Single Family

---

(P-1226)
ARNEL DEVELOPMENT COMPANY
3146 Tiger Run Ct Ste 108, Carlsbad (92010-6696)
PHONE..................760 599-6111

Carol Cole, *Principal*
EMP: 62
SALES (corp-wide): 16.6MM **Privately Held**
SIC: 1522 Residential construction
PA: Arnel Development Company
   949 S Coast Dr Ste 600
   Costa Mesa CA 92626
   714 481-5000

(P-1227)
ASHWOOD CONSTRUCTION INC
5755 E Kings Canyon Rd # 110, Fresno (93727-4744)
PHONE..................559 253-7240
Michael J Conway Jr, *President*
EMP: 50
SQ FT: 1,200
SALES (est): 11.1MM **Privately Held**
WEB: www.ashwoodco.com
SIC: 1522 Multi-family dwellings, new construction

(P-1228)
AXIS SERVICES INC
Also Called: Axis Construction
2544 Barrington Ct, Hayward (94545-1133)
PHONE..................510 732-6111
Bizhan Mahallati, *CEO*
Parisa Mahallati, *Vice Pres*
Conor Meyers, *Vice Pres*
Mario Flores, *Project Mgr*
Ren Anderson, *Controller*
EMP: 110
SALES (est): 17.9MM **Privately Held**
WEB: www.axisconstruction.com
SIC: 1522 Residential construction

(P-1229)
BERNARDS BUILDERS INC
555 1st St, San Fernando (91340-3051)
PHONE..................818 898-1521
Doug Bernards, *Chairman*
Greg Simons, *President*
Jeffrey G Bernards, *CEO*
Ken Menager, *CFO*
EMP: 270
SALES (est): 488.8K
SALES (corp-wide): 158.8MM **Privately Held**
SIC: 1522 Residential construction
PA: Bernards Bros. Inc.
   555 1st St
   San Fernando CA 91340
   818 898-1521

(P-1230)
BILL BROWN CONSTRUCTION CO
242 Phelan Ave, San Jose (95112-6109)
PHONE..................408 297-3738
Bill Brown, *Principal*
William Brown, *President*
EMP: 100
SALES (est): 15.1MM **Privately Held**
SIC: 1522 1771 Hotel/motel & multi-family home construction; concrete work

(P-1231)
BLH CONSTRUCTION COMPANY
21031 Ventura Blvd # 200, Woodland Hills (91364-6517)
PHONE..................818 905-3837
Charles Brumbaugh, *CEO*
Brian Holland, *COO*
EMP: 150
SALES (est): 26.5MM **Privately Held**
WEB: www.blhconstruction.com
SIC: 1522 Apartment building construction

(P-1232)
BRUCE OLSON CONSTRUCTION INC
7320 River Rd, Tahoe City (96145)
PHONE..................530 581-1087
Bruce Olson, *President*
EMP: 90
SQ FT: 3,050
SALES (est): 5.9MM **Privately Held**
WEB: www.bruceolsonconstruction.com
SIC: 1522 Residential construction

(P-1233)
CJ CONSTRUCTION & DEV INC
78206 Varner Rd Ste D, Palm Desert
(92211-4136)
PHONE..................................760 247-6868
Lloyd James, *President*
EMP: 52 **EST:** 2009
SQ FT: 2,200
SALES: 5MM **Privately Held**
SIC: 1522 Apartment building construction

(P-1234)
CKL CONSTRUCTION INC
967 W Hedding St, San Jose (95126-1257)
PHONE..................................408 244-7042
Cortland C Lanning Jr, *President*
EMP: 300
SQ FT: 3,133
SALES (est): 16.9MM **Privately Held**
SIC: 1522 1611 Condominium construction; general contractor, highway & street construction

(P-1235)
COBALT CONSTRUCTION COMPANY
2259 Ward Ave Ste 200, Simi Valley
(93065-1880)
PHONE..................................805 577-6222
Darin Kruse, *CEO*
David Strong, *Info Tech Mgr*
Carolyn Kruse, *Manager*
▲ **EMP:** 70
SQ FT: 43,000
SALES (est): 29.6MM **Privately Held**
SIC: 1522 8711 1542 Multi-family dwellings, new construction; construction & civil engineering; commercial & office building, new construction; specialized public building contractors

(P-1236)
COUNTRY BUILDERS INC
Also Called: Country Builders Construction
5915 Graham Ct, Livermore (94550-9710)
PHONE..................................925 373-1020
Weldon Offill, *President*
Keith Offill, *CFO*
EMP: 150
SQ FT: 5,000
SALES (est): 14.7MM **Privately Held**
WEB: www.countrybuilders.com
SIC: 1522 Apartment building construction; remodeling, multi-family dwellings

(P-1237)
COVE BUILDERS INC
2264 Arroyo Dr, Riverside (92506-1507)
PHONE..................................714 436-2973
Ed Holmes II, *President*
EMP: 120
SALES (est): 7.4MM **Privately Held**
SIC: 1522 1542 1521 Residential construction; nonresidential construction; single-family housing construction

(P-1238)
DANCO BUILDERS
5251 Ericson Way Ste A, Arcata
(95521-9274)
PHONE..................................707 822-9000
Daniel J Johnson, *President*
Kendra Johnson, *Shareholder*
Kirk Heberly, *Vice Pres*
Kira Sandoval, *Administration*
Chuck Barnhart, *Technology*
EMP: 100
SQ FT: 15,000
SALES (est): 16.8MM **Privately Held**
WEB: www.dancobuilders.com
SIC: 1522 1542 Apartment building construction; nonresidential construction; commercial & office building contractors

(P-1239)
DINYARI CONSTRUCTION INC
500 Phelan Ave, San Jose (95112-2506)
PHONE..................................408 549-5400
Toll Free:.................................888 -
Farbod Buck Dinyari, *President*
Katayoon Dinyari, *Vice Pres*
EMP: 50
SQ FT: 12,000

SALES (est): 5.5MM **Privately Held**
WEB: www.dinyari.com
SIC: 1522 1542 Residential construction; commercial & office building contractors

(P-1240)
DOUGLAS ROSS CONSTRUCTION INC
900 E Hamilton Ave # 140, Campbell
(95008-0665)
PHONE..................................408 429-7700
J Douglas Ross, *President*
Andrew Maurer, *CFO*
Jeff Jelniker, *Vice Pres*
Jeffrey Jelniker, *Vice Pres*
Mike Brophy, *Project Mgr*
EMP: 55
SQ FT: 7,158
SALES: 71.9K **Privately Held**
SIC: 1522 Hotel/motel & multi-family home renovation & remodeling

(P-1241)
EDEN HOUSING INC (PA)
22645 Grand St, Hayward (94541-5031)
PHONE..................................510 582-1460
John Gaffney, *CEO*
Linda Mandolini, *President*
Jan Peters, *COO*
Jane Barr, *Associate Dir*
Leanne Butterfield, *Associate Dir*
EMP: 68
SQ FT: 10,000
SALES: 32.9MM **Privately Held**
SIC: 1522 Multi-family dwellings, new construction

(P-1242)
FAIRFIELD DEVELOPMENT INC (PA)
Also Called: Ffd II
5510 Morehouse Dr Ste 200, San Diego
(92121-3722)
PHONE..................................858 457-2123
Christopher E Hashioka, *Principal*
Greg Pinkalla, *COO*
James A Hribar, *CFO*
James L Bosler, *Chairman*
Ted Bradford, *Senior VP*
▲ **EMP:** 225
SALES (est): 364.1MM **Privately Held**
WEB: www.westbrook-apts.com
SIC: 1522 Multi-family dwelling construction

(P-1243)
FRAMING ASSOCIATES INC
1320 Coolidge Ave, National City
(91950-4334)
PHONE..................................619 336-9991
Bruce Mc Dowell, *CEO*
Ruth Jaffe, *Administration*
EMP: 150
SALES (est): 11.6MM **Privately Held**
SIC: 1522 Residential construction

(P-1244)
G B GROUP INC (PA)
8921 Murray Ave, Gilroy (95020-3633)
PHONE..................................408 848-8118
Gregory D Brown, *CEO*
Mark Greening, *President*
Jeffery Dame, *CFO*
Regan L Brown, *Corp Secy*
Pat Falconio, *Exec VP*
EMP: 79
SQ FT: 4,300
SALES (est): 56.1MM **Privately Held**
WEB: www.gbgroupinc.com
SIC: 1522 1542 8322 1541 Hotel/motel & multi-family home renovation & remodeling; condominium construction; nonresidential construction; rehabilitation services; renovation, remodeling & repairs: industrial buildings; construction management

(P-1245)
HAMMER DOWN DAVILA CNSTR
Also Called: Hdd Construction
2338 W Erie St, Caruthers (93609-9529)
P.O. Box 642 (93609-0642)
PHONE..................................559 864-2001
David Davila, *Owner*
EMP: 85 **EST:** 1998
SQ FT: 2,400

SALES (est): 4.7MM **Privately Held**
SIC: 1522 Residential construction

(P-1246)
HEIDI CORPORATION
Also Called: Donald J Schefflers Cnstr
727 N Vernon Ave, Azusa (91702-2232)
PHONE..................................626 333-6317
Donald J Scheffler, *President*
▲ **EMP:** 75
SQ FT: 15,000
SALES (est): 11.6MM **Privately Held**
SIC: 1522 Residential construction

(P-1247)
HILLCREST SENIOR HOUSING CORP
35 Hillcrest Dr, Daly City (94014-1098)
PHONE..................................650 757-1737
Susan Ruan, *Principal*
David A Grant, *Principal*
EMP: 132 **EST:** 2005
SALES: 515.5K
SALES (corp-wide): 21.8MM **Privately Held**
SIC: 1522 Apartment building construction
HQ: Humangood Affordable Housing
6120 Stoneridge Mall Rd # 100
Pleasanton CA 94588
925 924-7163

(P-1248)
HURLEY CONSTRUCTION INC
1801 I St Ste 200, Sacramento
(95811-3000)
PHONE..................................916 446-7599
Peter H Geremia, *CEO*
Steven Eggert, *Vice Pres*
EMP: 80
SQ FT: 2,500
SALES (est): 11.6MM **Privately Held**
WEB: www.antonllc.com
SIC: 1522 Multi-family dwellings, new construction

(P-1249)
JAMES E ROBERTS-OBAYASHI CORP
20 Oak Ct, Danville (94526-4006)
PHONE..................................925 820-0600
Larry R Smith, *CEO*
Obayashi Corporation, *Principal*
Jeanine Kaufman, *Project Mgr*
Brendan Radich, *Technology*
Tracy Cheffer, *Project Engr*
EMP: 110
SQ FT: 4,000
SALES (est): 30.7MM **Privately Held**
WEB: www.jerocorp.com
SIC: 1522 1542 Multi-family dwellings, new construction; commercial & office building, new construction

(P-1250)
JAMES MCCUTCHEON
17521 Walker Basin Rd, Caliente
(93518-1407)
PHONE..................................661 867-1810
Mg Taylor, *President*
EMP: 50
SALES (est): 2.6MM **Privately Held**
SIC: 1522 Residential construction

(P-1251)
JUDSON ENTERPRISES INC (PA)
Also Called: K-Designers
2440 Gold River Rd # 100, Rancho Cordova (95670-6390)
PHONE..................................916 596-6721
Larry D Judson, *President*
Tony Tobia, *CFO*
Ryan Letz, *Sr Corp Ofcr*
Michael Burgess, *Vice Pres*
Brian Vidlock, *Vice Pres*
▲ **EMP:** 265
SQ FT: 28,000
SALES (est): 83.3MM **Privately Held**
WEB: www.k-designers.com
SIC: 1522 Residential construction

(P-1252)
JWC CONSTRUCTION INC (PA)
Also Called: Jon Wayne Construction
2580 Fortune Way, Vista (92081-8441)
PHONE..................................760 727-2494
Jon Wayne, *CEO*
Mario Alesi, *Project Mgr*
Tomasa Collazo, *Accountant*
Matt Friedman, *Director*
David Dillon, *Manager*
EMP: 50
SQ FT: 7,000
SALES (est): 27.1MM **Privately Held**
SIC: 1522 1521 Residential construction; new construction, single-family houses

(P-1253)
JWC CONSTRUCTION INC
4570 Campus Dr, Newport Beach
(92660-8809)
PHONE..................................949 252-2107
William V Gennusa, *Principal*
EMP: 50
SALES (corp-wide): 27.1MM **Privately Held**
SIC: 1522 1521 Residential construction; new construction, single-family houses
PA: Jwc Construction, Inc.
2580 Fortune Way
Vista CA 92081
760 727-2494

(P-1254)
K&M CONSTRUCTION
642 Pine Ave, Pacific Grove (93950-3347)
PHONE..................................831 643-2819
Kevin Ralph, *Partner*
EMP: 70
SALES (est): 3.3MM **Privately Held**
SIC: 1522 Residential construction

(P-1255)
KB HOME SOUTH BAY INC
5000 Executive Pkwy # 125, San Ramon
(94583-4210)
PHONE..................................925 983-2500
Chris Apostolopoulos, *CEO*
Robert Freed, *President*
Joe Gregorich, *Vice Pres*
Andrew Kusnick, *Vice Pres*
Tony Dority, *Opers Staff*
EMP: 140
SQ FT: 5,500
SALES (est): 16MM
SALES (corp-wide): 4.5B **Publicly Held**
SIC: 1522 1521 Residential construction; single-family housing construction
HQ: Kb Home Greater Los Angeles Inc.
10990 Wilshire Blvd # 700
Los Angeles CA 90024
310 231-4000

(P-1256)
KENNARD DEVELOPMENT GROUP
Also Called: Kdg Construction Consulting
1025 N Brand Blvd Ste 300, Glendale
(91202-3633)
PHONE..................................818 241-0800
Lydia Kennard, *CEO*
EMP: 98
SQ FT: 2,500
SALES (est): 3.4MM **Privately Held**
SIC: 1522 1541 1623 1611 Residential construction; industrial buildings & warehouses; water, sewer & utility lines; highway & street construction; bridge, tunnel & elevated highway

(P-1257)
KERN 2008 CMNTY PARTNERS LP
Also Called: Desert Oaks Apartments
1219 N Plaza Dr, Visalia (93291-8837)
PHONE..................................559 651-3559
Terry Coyne, *General Ptnr*
EMP: 85
SALES: 950K **Privately Held**
SIC: 1522 Residential construction

(P-1258)
LAKE MERRITT HOTEL ASSOCIATES
1800 Madison St, Oakland (94612-4638)
PHONE..................................510 832-2300

Randall C Berger, *Partner*
Cheryl Berger, *Partner*
Richard Carter, *Maintence Staff*
EMP: 50 **EST:** 1990
SQ FT: 44,155
SALES (est): 3.4MM **Privately Held**
WEB: www.lakemerritthotel.com
SIC: 1522 7011 Apartment building construction; hotels & motels

(P-1259)
MARK SCOTT CONSTRUCTION INC
241 Frank West Cir # 200, Stockton (95206-4012)
PHONE.................................209 982-0502
Mark Scott, *Principal*
EMP: 74 **Privately Held**
SIC: 1522 1521 Residential construction; single-family housing construction
PA: Mark Scott Construction, Inc.
2835 Contra Costa Blvd
Pleasant Hill CA 94523

(P-1260)
NANCY SMITH CONSTRUCTION INC
47 Yorkshire Dr, Oakland (94618-2021)
PHONE.................................510 923-1671
Ronald Smith, *President*
Christy Smith, *Treasurer*
Kristie Smith, *Treasurer*
Randal Smith, *Vice Pres*
Randall Smith, *Vice Pres*
EMP: 50
SALES: 15.3MM **Privately Held**
SIC: 1522 Apartment building construction

(P-1261)
NIBBI BROS ASSOCIATES INC
Also Called: Nibbi Bros Concrete
1000 Brannan St Ste 102, San Francisco (94103-4888)
PHONE.................................415 863-1820
Robert L Nibbi, *President*
Larry Nibbi, *CEO*
Richard Fedick, *CFO*
Mike Nibbi, *Vice Pres*
Jeff Hartman, *Division Mgr*
EMP: 150
SALES (est): 12.7MM **Privately Held**
SIC: 1522 1542 Residential construction; custom builders, non-residential

(P-1262)
OLEN RESIDENTIAL REALTY CORP (HQ)
Also Called: Olen Companies, The
7 Corporate Plaza Dr, Newport Beach (92660-7904)
PHONE.................................949 644-6536
Igor M Olenicoff, *President*
Jan Bullington, *Manager*
EMP: 70
SALES (est): 63.4MM **Privately Held**
SIC: 1522 Multi-family dwellings, new construction

(P-1263)
PARKHURST TERRACE
100 Parkhurst Cir, Aptos (95003-9657)
PHONE.................................831 685-0800
Cheryl Digrazia, *Principal*
EMP: 93
SALES (est): 3.6MM
SALES (corp-wide): 41.9K **Privately Held**
SIC: 1522 Apartment building construction
HQ: Midpen Property Management Corporation
303 Vintage Park Dr # 250
Foster City CA 94404
650 356-2900

(P-1264)
PRC BUILDERS INC
1820 E Garry Ave Ste 211, Santa Ana (92705-5807)
PHONE.................................949 529-7011
David P Fitts, *President*
Jason Pammer, *Vice Pres*
EMP: 90 **EST:** 1997
SALES: 12MM **Privately Held**
SIC: 1522 Residential construction

(P-1265)
PRIDE INDUSTRIES
Cbc Base Bldg 19 43rd St, Port Hueneme (93041)
PHONE.................................805 985-8481
Dennis Carter, *Branch Mgr*
EMP: 140
SALES (corp-wide): 290.6MM **Privately Held**
SIC: 1522 Residential construction
PA: Pride Industries
10030 Foothills Blvd
Roseville CA 95747
916 788-2100

(P-1266)
PSLQ INC
28910 Rancho California R, Temecula (92590-1870)
PHONE.................................951 795-4260
John P Swensen, *President*
Lee Quigley, *Vice Pres*
EMP: 75
SQ FT: 800
SALES (est): 11.8MM **Privately Held**
SIC: 1522 0781 Residential construction; landscape services

(P-1267)
RDR BUILDERS LP
Also Called: Rdr Production Builders
1806 W Kettleman Ln Ste F, Lodi (95242-4316)
PHONE.................................209 368-7561
Ron Dos Reis, *Partner*
Mark Barbieri, *Partner*
Ed Dos Reis, *Partner*
Ron Dos-Reis, *President*
Ed Reis, *HR Admin*
EMP: 85
SQ FT: 1,400
SALES: 18MM **Privately Held**
SIC: 1522 1542 Multi-family dwellings, new construction; hotel/motel & multi-family home renovation & remodeling; commercial & office building, new construction; commercial & office buildings, renovation & repair

(P-1268)
REEGS INC
Also Called: Monterey Construction Company
88 Monterey Salinas Hwy A, Salinas (93908-8976)
PHONE.................................831 455-7931
Richard Benjamin Rega, *President*
EMP: 65
SALES (est): 2.7MM **Privately Held**
SIC: 1522 Residential construction

(P-1269)
REGIONAL INVESTMENT & MGT LLC
4640 Admiralty Way # 1050, Marina Del Rey (90292-6642)
PHONE.................................310 821-1945
Alicia Miller,
EMP: 50
SALES (est): 3.3MM **Privately Held**
SIC: 1522 6798 Multi-family dwellings, new construction; real estate investment trusts

(P-1270)
RRM CONSTRUCTION INC
9135 Cord Ave, Downey (90240-2433)
PHONE.................................562 440-3539
Cesar Montano, *CEO*
EMP: 50
SALES (est): 702.9K **Privately Held**
SIC: 1522 Residential construction

(P-1271)
SAARMAN CONSTRUCTION LTD
683 Mcallister St, San Francisco (94102-3111)
PHONE.................................415 749-2700
Jeffrey M Saarman, *President*
Steven P Saarman, *President*
Paul Saarman, *General Mgr*
Irma Saarman, *Admin Sec*
Karl Tahir, *Info Tech Dir*
EMP: 250
SQ FT: 4,500

SALES (est): 38MM **Privately Held**
WEB: www.saarman.com
SIC: 1522 1521 Condominium construction; apartment building construction; general remodeling, single-family houses; new construction, single-family houses

(P-1272)
SHEA HOMES VANTIS LLC
655 Brea Canyon Rd, Walnut (91789-3078)
PHONE.................................909 594-9500
EMP: 55
SALES (est): 3.1MM
SALES (corp-wide): 2.2B **Privately Held**
SIC: 1522 Apartment building construction
HQ: Shea Homes Limited Partnership, A California Limited Partnership
655 Brea Canyon Rd
Walnut CA 91789

(P-1273)
SILICONSAGE CONSTRUCTION INC
560 S Mathilda Ave, Sunnyvale (94086-7607)
PHONE.................................408 916-3205
Sanjeev Acharya, *CEO*
Hassan Naboulsi, *Info Tech Mgr*
EMP: 200 **EST:** 2014
SALES: 50MM **Privately Held**
SIC: 1522 Multi-family dwellings, new construction

(P-1274)
STRATHAM HOMES INC
2201 Dupont Dr Ste 300, Irvine (92612-7509)
PHONE.................................949 833-1554
Ali Razi, *President*
David Lamb, *Shareholder*
Mehrdad Rassekh, *Shareholder*
Pat Potts, *Project Mgr*
Brandon Roth, *Project Mgr*
EMP: 100
SQ FT: 7,000
SALES: 30MM **Privately Held**
SIC: 1522 Residential construction

(P-1275)
SWINERTON INCORPORATED
2300 Clayton Rd Ste 800, Concord (94520-2166)
PHONE.................................925 689-2336
Lawrence Mathews, *Branch Mgr*
EMP: 97 **Privately Held**
SIC: 1522 8741 Residential construction; construction management
PA: Swinerton Incorporated
260 Townsend St
San Francisco CA 94107

(P-1276)
THOMPSON BUILDERS CORPORATION
250 Bel Marin Keys Blvd A, Novato (94949-5727)
PHONE.................................415 456-8972
Paul Thompson, *President*
F Joseph Hass, *Vice Pres*
Peter Hopkins, *Project Mgr*
Conor Thompson, *Project Mgr*
Pat Chavez, *Project Engr*
▲ **EMP:** 170
SQ FT: 6,000
SALES: 72.7MM **Privately Held**
WEB: www.westbaybuilders.com
SIC: 1522 1542 8711 7389 Multi-family dwelling construction; commercial & office building, new construction; construction & civil engineering; design services; general contractor, highway & street construction

(P-1277)
TONNER HILLS HSING PARTNERS LP
17701 Cowan Ste 200, Irvine (92614-6840)
PHONE.................................949 263-8676
Laura Archuleta, *Partner*
EMP: 50
SALES (est): 4.6MM **Privately Held**
SIC: 1522 Apartment building construction

(P-1278)
TOSCANA HOMES LP
Also Called: Toscana Country Club
300 Eagle Dance Cir, Palm Desert (92211-7440)
PHONE.................................760 772-7227
William Bone, *Partner*
EMP: 50
SQ FT: 6,000
SALES (est): 3.5MM **Privately Held**
WEB: www.sunrisemis.com
SIC: 1522 Residential construction

(P-1279)
TOTAL-WESTERN INC
2811 Fruitvale Ave Ste A, Bakersfield (93308-5947)
PHONE.................................661 589-5200
Jeff Jordan, *Manager*
Chad Norton, *Division Mgr*
John Hovsepian, *Maintence Staff*
EMP: 80
SALES (corp-wide): 381.4MM **Privately Held**
WEB: www.total-western.com
SIC: 1522 1542 Residential construction; nonresidential construction
HQ: Total-Western, Inc.
8049 Somerset Blvd
Paramount CA 90723
562 220-1450

(P-1280)
TRI POINTE HOMES INC (HQ)
19520 Jamboree Rd Ste 300, Irvine (92612-2429)
P.O. Box 57088 (92619-7088)
PHONE.................................949 438-1400
Barry S Sternlicht, *Ch of Bd*
Darren Dupree, *President*
Thomas J Mitchell, *President*
Douglas F Bauer, *CEO*
Michael D Grubbs, *CFO*
EMP: 146
SALES: 1.7B
SALES (corp-wide): 3.2B **Publicly Held**
SIC: 1522 Residential construction
PA: Tri Pointe Group, Inc.
19540 Jamboree Rd Ste 300
Irvine CA 92612
949 438-1400

(P-1281)
V DEVELOPMENT INC
Also Called: Capital Builders
550 Harvest Park Dr Ste A, Brentwood (94513-4058)
PHONE.................................925 634-8890
Manuel Vierra, *President*
EMP: 75
SQ FT: 2,300
SALES: 5MM **Privately Held**
SIC: 1522 Residential construction

(P-1282)
WALTON CONSTRUCTION INC
Also Called: Walton Construction Services
358 E Foothill Blvd # 100, San Dimas (91773-1264)
PHONE.................................909 267-7777
Thomas W Gibson, *President*
Tom Gibson, *Partner*
E Lee Jackson, *CEO*
Rick Walker, *CFO*
David Jackson, *Admin Sec*
EMP: 80
SQ FT: 8,000
SALES: 57MM **Privately Held**
SIC: 1522 1542 Apartment building construction; commercial & office building contractors

(P-1283)
WERMERS MULTI-FAMILY CORP
5120 Shoreham Pl Ste 150, San Diego (92122-5959)
PHONE.................................858 535-1475
Thomas W Wermers, *President*
Jeff Bunker, *President*
Tom Wermers, *CEO*
Richard Lemmel, *CFO*
Barry Weber, *Vice Pres*
EMP: 130
SQ FT: 7,000

▲ = Import ▼ = Export
◆ = Import/Export

SALES (est): 28.6MM **Privately Held**
WEB: www.wermerscontractors.com
SIC: **1522** Hotel/motel & multi-family home construction

(P-1284)
WESTERN NATIONAL PROPERTIES (PA)
Also Called: Arkebauer Properties
8 Executive Cir, Irvine (92614-6746)
P.O. Box 19528 (92623-9528)
PHONE..............................949 862-6200
David Stone, *Ch of Bd*
Rex Delong, *President*
Michael K Hayde, *CEO*
Jeffrey R Scott, *CFO*
Debra Meute, *Vice Pres*
▲ EMP: 129 EST: 1981
SQ FT: 37,000
SALES (est): 64.3MM **Privately Held**
WEB: www.wng.com
SIC: **1522** 6513 6512 6531 Apartment building construction; apartment building operators; nonresidential building operators; real estate agents & managers

(P-1285)
WL BUTLER INC
1629 Main St, Redwood City (94063-2121)
PHONE..............................650 361-1270
William Butler, *CEO*
Frank York, *President*
Dave Nevens, *COO*
David A Nevens Jr, *COO*
Gina Henson, *CFO*
EMP: 250
SALES (est): 32.2MM **Privately Held**
SIC: **1522** Residential construction

(P-1286)
ZASTROW CONSTRUCTION INC
Also Called: Reliance Company
3267 Verdugo Rd, Los Angeles (90065-2035)
PHONE..............................323 478-1956
Mark Zastrow, *President*
Patti Eldridge, *Treasurer*
Kai Wilson, *Vice Pres*
EMP: 115 EST: 1976
SQ FT: 2,000
SALES (est): 13MM **Privately Held**
SIC: **1522** Multi-family dwelling construction; multi-family dwellings, new construction

---
1531 Operative Builders

(P-1287)
ALBERT D SEENO CNSTR CO INC
4021 Port Chicago Hwy, Concord (94520-1122)
PHONE..............................925 671-7711
Albert D Seeno Jr, *CEO*
Michael Romero, *Vice Pres*
Richard B Seeno, *Principal*
Thomas A Seeno, *Principal*
Steve Lichti, *Finance Dir*
EMP: 80
SQ FT: 30,000
SALES (est): 24.2MM **Privately Held**
WEB: www.seenohomes.com
SIC: **1531** Speculative builder, single-family houses

(P-1288)
BENJAMIN KURZBAN SON CTRL INC
24533 Stagg St, West Hills (91304-6124)
PHONE..............................347 227-3425
Mitchell Kurzban, *President*
Sharlene Vadal, *Manager*
EMP: 50
SQ FT: 9,000
SALES (est): 6.7MM **Privately Held**
WEB: www.kurzban.com
SIC: **1531** Operative builders

(P-1289)
CALATLANTIC GROUP INC
3825 Hopyard Rd Ste 195, Pleasanton (94588-8529)
PHONE..............................925 847-8700
Glen Martin, *Manager*

EMP: 50
SQ FT: 5,000
SALES (corp-wide): 20.5B **Publicly Held**
WEB: www.standardpacifichomes.com
SIC: **1531** 1521 Operative builders; single-family housing construction
HQ: Calatlantic Group, Inc.
1100 Wilson Blvd Ste 2100
Arlington VA 22209
240 532-3806

(P-1290)
CALATLANTIC GROUP INC
Also Called: Ryland Homes
5740 Fleet St Ste 200, Carlsbad (92008-4704)
PHONE..............................760 931-4414
Karen Carter, *Manager*
EMP: 55
SALES (corp-wide): 20.5B **Publicly Held**
WEB: www.ryland.com
SIC: **1531** Speculative builder, single-family houses
HQ: Calatlantic Group, Inc.
1100 Wilson Blvd Ste 2100
Arlington VA 22209
240 532-3806

(P-1291)
CALIFORNIA PACIFIC HOMES INC (PA)
16530 Bake Pkwy Ste 200, Irvine (92618-4685)
PHONE..............................949 833-6000
Cary Bren, *CEO*
Richard Lyle McColloch, *CFO*
Brian Blain, *Vice Pres*
Lyle McColloch, *Vice Pres*
Janet Loyd, *Office Mgr*
▲ EMP: 93
SQ FT: 6,000
SALES (est): 25.8MM **Privately Held**
WEB: www.californiapacifichomes.com
SIC: **1531** Speculative builder, multi-family dwellings; speculative builder, single-family houses

(P-1292)
DE ANZA SQUARE SHOPPING CENTER
1306 S Mary Ave 1370, Sunnyvale (94087-3130)
PHONE..............................408 738-4444
Rosanna Callegari, *Principal*
EMP: 99
SALES (est): 950K **Privately Held**
SIC: **1531** Operative builders

(P-1293)
DONALD LAWRENCE FULBRIGHT CO
Also Called: Donald Lawrence Company
32557 Road 138, Visalia (93292-9381)
P.O. Box 2622 (93279-2622)
PHONE..............................559 625-0762
Donald Fulbright, *President*
Jeffrey Englund, *Treasurer*
Mary Fulbright, *Vice Pres*
EMP: 62
SQ FT: 1,700
SALES (est): 4.8MM **Privately Held**
SIC: **1531** Speculative builder, single-family houses

(P-1294)
DR HORTON INC
2280 Wardlow Cir Ste 100, Corona (92880-2879)
PHONE..............................951 272-9000
Steve Fitzpatrick, *Branch Mgr*
Tim Collity, *Vice Pres*
Nathan Simmons, *Info Tech Mgr*
Joe Nartea, *Technology*
Reed Ames, *Superintendent*
EMP: 50
SALES (corp-wide): 13.7B **Publicly Held**
WEB: www.drhorton.com
SIC: **1531** Speculative builder, single-family houses
PA: D.R. Horton, Inc.
1341 Horton Cir
Arlington TX 76011
817 390-8200

(P-1295)
EJM KYRENE LLC (PA)
Also Called: Ejm Property Management
9061 Santa Monica Blvd, Los Angeles (90069-5520)
PHONE..............................310 278-1830
Eugene Monkarsh,
Jerrold Monkarsh,
Leanna Carter, *Manager*
EMP: 50 EST: 1999
SQ FT: 5,500
SALES (est): 9.2MM **Privately Held**
SIC: **1531** 6531 Condominium developers; real estate managers

(P-1296)
FIELDSTONE COMMUNITIES INC (PA)
16 Technology Dr Ste 125, Irvine (92618-2325)
PHONE..............................949 790-5400
William H McFarland, *CEO*
Peter Ochs, *Ch of Bd*
Frank Foster, *President*
David Langlois, *Exec VP*
Jim Hanson, *Senior VP*
EMP: 130
SQ FT: 15,000
SALES (est): 23.3MM **Privately Held**
WEB: www.fieldstone-homes.com
SIC: **1531** Speculative builder, single-family houses

(P-1297)
GREENBRIAR HOMES COMMUNITIES
4340 Stevens Creek Blvd # 240, San Jose (95129-1102)
PHONE..............................510 497-8200
Carol M Meyer, *Ch of Bd*
Gilbert M Meyer, *President*
EMP: 100
SQ FT: 12,000
SALES (est): 8.3MM **Privately Held**
SIC: **1531** Operative builders

(P-1298)
GREENLAND US CONSULTING INC
515 S Figueroa St # 1703, Los Angeles (90071-3301)
PHONE..............................213 362-9300
Ifei Chang, *CEO*
EMP: 99 EST: 2013
SALES (est): 4MM **Privately Held**
SIC: **1531**

(P-1299)
GRUPE DEV COMPANYNORTHERN CAL
3255 W March Ln Ste 400, Stockton (95219-2352)
P.O. Box 7576 (95267-0576)
PHONE..............................209 473-6000
Fritz Unruh, *CEO*
EMP: 79
SQ FT: 7,000
SALES (est): 6.2MM
SALES (corp-wide): 86.7MM **Privately Held**
WEB: www.grupe.com
SIC: **1531** Speculative builder, single-family houses; speculative builder, multi-family dwellings; condominium developers
PA: The Grupe Company
3255 W March Ln Ste 400
Stockton CA 95219
209 473-6000

(P-1300)
HWN MARIPOSA ASSOCIATES LLC
11150 Santa Monica Blvd # 760, Los Angeles (90025-3380)
PHONE..............................310 478-8757
Thomas B Wilson,
Thomas Wilson,
EMP: 99
SALES (est): 3.3MM **Privately Held**
SIC: **1531** Operative builders

(P-1301)
INLAND VALLEY CNSTR CO INC
18382 Slover Ave, Bloomington (92316-2363)
PHONE..............................909 875-2112
Kenneth Caruso, *President*
Kelly Bird, *Treasurer*
Stacy Veggin, *Treasurer*
Tim Gaines, *Vice Pres*
Justen Baldwin, *Project Mgr*
EMP: 75
SQ FT: 4,000
SALES (est): 19.1MM **Privately Held**
WEB: www.inlandvalleyconst.com
SIC: **1531** Operative builders

(P-1302)
KAUFMAN AND BROAD LIMITED
Also Called: Kaufman & Broad
10990 Wilshire Blvd Fl 7, Los Angeles (90024-3907)
PHONE..............................310 231-4000
EMP: 151
SALES (est): 7.6MM
SALES (corp-wide): 3.5B **Publicly Held**
WEB: www.kbhomesutah.com
SIC: **1531**
PA: Kb Home
10990 Wilshire Blvd Fl 5
Los Angeles CA 90024
310 231-4000

(P-1303)
KB HOME (PA)
10990 Wilshire Blvd Fl 5, Los Angeles (90024-3902)
PHONE..............................310 231-4000
Jeffrey T Mezger, *Ch of Bd*
Jeff J Kaminski, *CFO*
Amit Desai, *Chief Mktg Ofcr*
Albert Z Praw, *Exec VP*
Brian J Woram, *Exec VP*
EMP: 100
SALES (est): 4.5B **Publicly Held**
WEB: www.kbhome.com
SIC: **1531** Speculative builder, single-family houses

(P-1304)
KB HOME COASTAL INC
10990 Wilshire Blvd Fl 7, Los Angeles (90024-3907)
PHONE..............................310 231-4000
Jeff Nezger, *President*
Domenico Cecere, *CFO*
William Hollinger, *CFO*
Kelly Allred, *Vice Pres*
Cory Cohen, *Vice Pres*
▲ EMP: 90
SQ FT: 13,346
SALES (est): 10.3MM
SALES (corp-wide): 4.5B **Publicly Held**
WEB: www.kbhome.com
SIC: **1531** Operative builders
PA: Kb Home
10990 Wilshire Blvd Fl 5
Los Angeles CA 90024
310 231-4000

(P-1305)
KBSA INC
Also Called: Kaufman & Broad
10990 Wilshire Blvd 7th, Los Angeles (90024-3913)
PHONE..............................310 231-4000
Roger Menard, *President*
Jeff Mezger, *Exec VP*
EMP: 60
SQ FT: 40,000
SALES (est): 3.1MM
SALES (corp-wide): 4.5B **Publicly Held**
WEB: www.kbhome.com
SIC: **1531** Operative builders
PA: Kb Home
10990 Wilshire Blvd Fl 5
Los Angeles CA 90024
310 231-4000

(P-1306)
LENNAR CORPORATION
15131 Alton Pkwy Ste 190, Irvine (92618-2386)
PHONE..............................949 349-8000
Jonathan Jaffe, *COO*
David James, *Vice Pres*
Max Boedder, *Info Tech Dir*

Beth Beecher, *Accounting Dir*
Adrian Vizcarra, *Accountant*
EMP: 100
SALES (corp-wide): 20.5B **Publicly Held**
WEB: www.lennar.com
SIC: 1531 Speculative builder, single-family houses
PA: Lennar Corporation
  700 Nw 107th Ave Ste 400
  Miami FL 33172
  305 559-4000

(P-1307)
LENNAR HOMES INC
3788 Edington Dr, Rancho Cordova (95742-7829)
PHONE..................916 517-4950
Brenda Coementson, *Principal*
EMP: 101
SALES (corp-wide): 20.5B **Publicly Held**
SIC: 1531 Condominium developers
HQ: Lennar Homes, Inc.
  700 Nw 107th Ave Ste 115
  Miami FL 33172
  305 559-4000

(P-1308)
LENNAR HOMES INC
980 Montecito Dr Ste 300, Corona (92879-1796)
PHONE..................951 739-0267
Maureen Johnson, *Manager*
Gary Glazer, *Vice Pres*
Monica Smith, *Controller*
Angela Wagner, *Marketing Staff*
EMP: 200
SALES (corp-wide): 20.5B **Publicly Held**
SIC: 1531 Speculative builder, single-family houses
HQ: Lennar Homes, Inc.
  700 Nw 107th Ave Ste 115
  Miami FL 33172
  305 559-4000

(P-1309)
LENNAR HOMES CALIFORNIA INC
18495 Seven Bridges Rd, Santa Clara (95050)
PHONE..................858 759-7200
Tim Walker, *General Mgr*
EMP: 56
SALES (corp-wide): 20.5B **Publicly Held**
SIC: 1531 Operative builders
HQ: Lennar Homes Of California, Inc.
  15131 Alton Pkwy Ste 190
  Irvine CA 92618

(P-1310)
LEWIS COMPANIES (PA)
1156 N Mountain Ave, Upland (91786-3633)
PHONE..................909 985-0971
Richard A Lewis, *President*
Goldy S Lewis, *Principal*
Randall W Lewis, *Principal*
Robert E Lewis, *Principal*
Roger G Lewis, *Principal*
EMP: 380 EST: 1973
SALES (est): 25.7MM **Privately Held**
WEB: www.lewishomes.com
SIC: 1531 Operative builders

(P-1311)
LYON PROMENADE LLC
4901 Birch St, Newport Beach (92660-2114)
PHONE..................949 252-9101
William Lyon,
Frank T Suryan,
EMP: 50
SALES (est): 2.7MM **Privately Held**
SIC: 1531 Operative builders

(P-1312)
MANOR BELL L P
790 Sonoma Ave, Santa Rosa (95404-4713)
PHONE..................707 526-9782
Jose Luis Caballero,
Charles A Cornell,
EMP: 99
SALES (est): 5MM **Privately Held**
SIC: 1531 Condominium developers

(P-1313)
NEW HOME COMPANY INC (PA)
85 Enterprise Ste 450, Aliso Viejo (92656-2680)
PHONE..................949 382-7800
H Lawrence Webb, *Ch of Bd*
Christopher Cady, *President*
Leonard S Miller, *President*
John M Stephens, *CFO*
John Stephens, *CFO*
EMP: 79
SQ FT: 18,700
SALES: 667.5MM **Publicly Held**
SIC: 1531 Operative builders

(P-1314)
PACIFICA REFLECTIONS
Also Called: Pacifica Crossroads
405 Reflections Cir, San Ramon (94583-5203)
PHONE..................925 275-9800
Tracy Dalton, *Principal*
EMP: 50
SALES (est): 1.9MM **Privately Held**
SIC: 1531 Condominium developers

(P-1315)
PORTER RANCH DEVELOPMENT CO
8383 Wilshire Blvd # 700, Beverly Hills (90211-2407)
PHONE..................323 655-7330
Nathan Shapell, *Partner*
I N S Corporation, *Partner*
EMP: 85 EST: 1976
SALES (est): 4.4MM
SALES (corp-wide): 7.1B **Publicly Held**
SIC: 1531 Speculative builder, single-family houses
PA: Toll Brothers, Inc.
  250 Gibralter Rd
  Horsham PA 19044
  215 938-8000

(P-1316)
RYLAND HOMES OF TEXAS INC
15360 Barranca Pkwy, Irvine (92618-2215)
PHONE..................805 367-3800
Rene L Mentch, *President*
EMP: 132
SALES (est): 13.9MM **Privately Held**
SIC: 1531 Operative builders

(P-1317)
STRAUB - BRUTOCO A JOINT VENTR
202 W College St Ste 201, Fallbrook (92028-2970)
PHONE..................760 414-9000
Richard Straub, *Partner*
Robert Mhyre, *Partner*
Michael J Murphy, *Partner*
EMP: 150
SQ FT: 17,000
SALES (est): 4.8MM **Privately Held**
SIC: 1531 1541 ; ; industrial buildings & warehouses; industrial buildings, new construction; prefabricated building erection, industrial

(P-1318)
TRI POINTE GROUP INC (PA)
19540 Jamboree Rd Ste 300, Irvine (92612-8452)
PHONE..................949 438-1400
Douglas F Bauer, *CEO*
Steven J Gilbert, *Ch of Bd*
Phil Bodem, *President*
Thomas J Mitchell, *President*
Thomas Mitchell, *COO*
EMP: 70 EST: 2009
SALES: 3.2B **Publicly Held**
SIC: 1531 Speculative builder, single-family houses

(P-1319)
US HOME CORPORATION
Also Called: US Home
980 Montecito Dr 302, Corona (92879-1792)
PHONE..................951 817-3500
Mike Lutz, *Branch Mgr*
EMP: 50

SALES (corp-wide): 20.5B **Publicly Held**
WEB: www.ushome.com
SIC: 1531 Speculative builder, single-family houses
HQ: U.S. Home Corporation
  10707 Clay Rd
  Houston TX 77041
  305 559-4000

(P-1320)
VAN DAELE DEVELOPMENT CORP
Also Called: Van Daele Homes
2900 Adams St Ste C25, Riverside (92504-8312)
PHONE..................951 354-6800
Michael B Van Daele, *CEO*
Jeff Hack, *President*
EMP: 110
SQ FT: 6,000
SALES: 3.3MM **Privately Held**
WEB: www.vandaele.com
SIC: 1531 Speculative builder, single-family houses

(P-1321)
VILLA LA ESPERANZA LP
3533 Empleo St, San Luis Obispo (93401-7334)
PHONE..................805 781-3088
John Fowler, *Managing Prtnr*
Robin Bush, *Accounting Mgr*
EMP: 99
SALES (est): 3MM **Privately Held**
SIC: 1531 Cooperative apartment developers

(P-1322)
WARMINGTON HOMES (PA)
3090 Pullman St, Costa Mesa (92626-7936)
PHONE..................714 434-4435
Timothy P Hogan, *President*
James P Warmington, *Ch of Bd*
Michael McClellan, *President*
Greg Oberling, *President*
Jack Schwellenbach, *President*
▲ **EMP:** 120 EST: 1972
SQ FT: 40,000
SALES (est): 94.3MM **Privately Held**
SIC: 1531 Speculative builder, single-family houses

(P-1323)
WARMINGTON HOMES
15615 Alton Pkwy Ste 150, Irvine (92618-7302)
PHONE..................949 679-3100
EMP: 96
SALES (corp-wide): 94.3MM **Privately Held**
SIC: 1531 Speculative builder, single-family houses
PA: Warmington Homes
  3090 Pullman St
  Costa Mesa CA 92626
  714 434-4435

(P-1324)
WARMINGTON HOMES
Also Called: Warmington Residental
2400 Camino Ramon Ste 234, San Ramon (94583-4350)
PHONE..................925 866-6700
Larry Riggs, *Exec VP*
EMP: 159
SALES (corp-wide): 94.3MM **Privately Held**
SIC: 1531 Speculative builder, single-family houses
PA: Warmington Homes
  3090 Pullman St
  Costa Mesa CA 92626
  714 434-4435

(P-1325)
WILLIAM LYON HOMES (PA)
4695 Macarthur Ct Ste 800, Newport Beach (92660-1863)
PHONE..................949 833-3600
Matthew R Zaist, *President*
EMP: 151
SALES: 2B **Publicly Held**
WEB: www.lyonhomes.com
SIC: 1531 Speculative builder, single-family houses

(P-1326)
WILLIAM LYON HOMES INC (HQ)
4695 Macarthur Ct Ste 800, Newport Beach (92660-1863)
P.O. Box 7520 (92658-7520)
PHONE..................949 833-3600
William H Lyon, *Ch of Bd*
Colin Severn, *CFO*
Doug Harris, *Senior VP*
Danny George, *Vice Pres*
Susan Menard, *Executive Asst*
EMP: 74
SQ FT: 30,000
SALES (est): 102.4MM **Publicly Held**
SIC: 1531 Operative builders

1541 General Contractors, Indl Bldgs & Warehouses

(P-1327)
ADIR INTERNATIONAL LLC
Also Called: La Curacao
4444 Ayers Ave, Vernon (90058-4317)
PHONE..................213 639-7716
Russell Yeager, *Branch Mgr*
EMP: 206
SALES (corp-wide): 500.7MM **Privately Held**
SIC: 1541 Industrial buildings & warehouses
PA: Adir International, Llc
  1605 W Olympic Blvd # 405
  Los Angeles CA 90015
  213 639-2100

(P-1328)
AHTNA-CDM JV
3200 El Camino Real, Irvine (92602-1378)
PHONE..................714 824-3470
Craig O'Rourke, *Principal*
EMP: 50
SQ FT: 5,000
SALES (est): 1.5MM **Privately Held**
SIC: 1541 Industrial buildings, new construction

(P-1329)
ARNTZ BUILDERS INC
431 Payran St Ste A, Petaluma (94952-5935)
PHONE..................415 382-1188
Donald M Arntz, *CEO*
Brian Proteau, *President*
Thomas Artz, *Corp Secy*
Arntz Julie, *Associate Dir*
Lisa Kentzell, *Controller*
EMP: 50
SALES (est): 14.7MM **Privately Held**
SIC: 1541 1542 Industrial buildings, new construction; renovation, remodeling & repairs: industrial buildings; commercial & office building, new construction; commercial & office buildings, renovation & repair

(P-1330)
BCM CONSTRUCTION COMPANY INC
2990 California 32, Chico (95973)
PHONE..................530 342-1722
Kurtis Carman, *President*
Nancy Chinn, *Treasurer*
Matt Bowman, *Vice Pres*
Matthew Bowman, *Vice Pres*
Scott January, *Vice Pres*
EMP: 50
SQ FT: 1,700
SALES (est): 17.5MM **Privately Held**
WEB: www.bcmconstruction.com
SIC: 1541 Industrial buildings, new construction

(P-1331)
BEAR VLY FBRCATORS STL SUP INC
10700 Civic Center Dr 100c, Rancho Cucamonga (91730-3897)
PHONE..................760 247-5381
Judy Carlos, *President*
Tony Carlos, *Vice Pres*

EMP: 60
SQ FT: 25,000
SALES (est): 10.6MM **Privately Held**
SIC: 1541 1791 5051 Renovation, remodeling & repairs: industrial buildings; structural steel erection; steel

(P-1332)
BECK INTERNATIONAL INC
Also Called: Beck Group, The
9641 Sunset Blvd, Beverly Hills
(90210-2938)
PHONE.................................310 281-2980
EMP: 300
SALES (corp-wide): 422.4MM **Privately Held**
WEB: www.beckarchitecture.com
SIC: 1541 1542 Industrial buildings & warehouses; nonresidential construction
PA: Beck International, Llc
1807 Ross Ave Ste 500
Dallas TX 75201
214 303-6200

(P-1333)
BLACH CONSTRUCTION COMPANY (PA)
2244 Blach Pl Ste 100, San Jose
(95131-2041)
PHONE.................................408 244-7100
Mike Blach, *President*
Juan Barroso, *Vice Pres*
Gaye Landau, *Vice Pres*
Daniel Rogers, *Vice Pres*
Ken Treadwell, *Vice Pres*
EMP: 80
SQ FT: 24,000
SALES (est): 50.3MM **Privately Held**
WEB: www.blach.com
SIC: 1541 1542 Industrial buildings & warehouses; commercial & office building, new construction

(P-1334)
BOMEL CONSTRUCTION CO INC
Also Called: Unknown
701 Palomar Airport Rd # 270, Carlsbad
(92011-1047)
PHONE.................................760 431-6360
Mike Lucio, *Branch Mgr*
EMP: 139
SALES (corp-wide): 109.4MM **Privately Held**
SIC: 1541 Industrial buildings & warehouses
PA: Bomel Construction Co., Inc.
96 Corporate Park Ste 100
Irvine CA 92606
714 921-1660

(P-1335)
BRANNON INC
Also Called: Smith Electric Service
1340 W Betteravia Rd, Santa Maria
(93455-1030)
PHONE.................................805 621-5000
Michael Brannon, *President*
Sara Dalton, *Officer*
Larry Brannon, *Vice Pres*
Joyce Gardner, *General Mgr*
Donna Michaud, *Administration*
EMP: 150
SQ FT: 10,000
SALES (est): 65.6MM **Privately Held**
WEB: www.smith-electric.com
SIC: 1541 1711 1731 1542 Industrial buildings, new construction; plumbing, heating, air-conditioning contractors; fire sprinkler system installation; fire detection & burglar alarm systems specialization; general electrical contractor; nonresidential construction

(P-1336)
C OVERAA & CO (PA)
Also Called: Overaa Construction
200 Parr Blvd, Richmond (94801-1191)
PHONE.................................510 234-0926
Jerry Overaa, *CEO*
Christopher Manning, *President*
Ellen Hoffman, *CFO*
Roy Samuelsz, *Officer*
Carl Overaa, *Business Dir*
EMP: 151 EST: 1907
SQ FT: 20,000

SALES (est): 167.8MM **Privately Held**
WEB: www.overaa.com
SIC: 1541 Industrial buildings, new construction

(P-1337)
C OVERAA & CO
Also Called: Overaa Construction
2555 El Portal Dr, San Pablo (94806-3303)
PHONE.................................510 235-0540
EMP: 198
SALES (corp-wide): 167.8MM **Privately Held**
SIC: 1541 Industrial buildings & warehouses
PA: C. Overaa & Co.
200 Parr Blvd
Richmond CA 94801
510 234-0926

(P-1338)
CALIFORNIA SHTMTL WORKS INC
1020 N Marshall Ave, El Cajon
(92020-1829)
PHONE.................................619 562-7010
Robin Hoffos, *President*
Joe Isom, *Vice Pres*
▲ EMP: 90
SQ FT: 15,000
SALES (est): 32.2MM **Privately Held**
WEB: www.califsheetmetal.com
SIC: 1541 3444 Renovation, remodeling & repairs: industrial buildings; sheet metalwork

(P-1339)
CHALMERS CORPORATION
Also Called: C.E.G. Construction
7901 Crossway Dr, Pico Rivera
(90660-4449)
PHONE.................................562 948-4850
Tracy John Chalmers, *CEO*
EMP: 55
SQ FT: 45,000
SALES (est): 17.6MM **Privately Held**
WEB: www.cegconstruction.com
SIC: 1541 8742 Industrial buildings & warehouses; management consulting services

(P-1340)
CLARION CONSTRUCTION INC
21067 Commerce Point Dr, Walnut
(91789-3052)
PHONE.................................909 598-4060
Bradley Owen, *President*
Dennis Proctor, *Exec VP*
Bruce Kidd, *Vice Pres*
Karen Snider, *Vice Pres*
Dana Spann, *Vice Pres*
EMP: 50
SQ FT: 10,000
SALES (est): 14.7MM **Privately Held**
SIC: 1541 Industrial buildings & warehouses

(P-1341)
CLARK CNSTR GROUP-CALIFORNIA
18201 Von Karman Ave # 800, Irvine
(92612-1000)
PHONE.................................714 754-0764
Richard M Heim, *President*
EMP: 450
SALES (est): 40.2MM
SALES (corp-wide): 2B **Privately Held**
SIC: 1541 1542 Industrial buildings & warehouses; nonresidential construction
HQ: Clark Construction Group, Llc
7500 Old Georgetown Rd # 3
Bethesda MD 20814
301 272-8100

(P-1342)
CMC STEEL FABRICATORS INC (DH)
Also Called: CMC Rebar West
3880 Murphy Canyon Rd # 100, San Diego
(92123-4410)
PHONE.................................858 737-7700
Christopher Ervin, *Principal*
Yuan Wang, *Vice Pres*
▲ EMP: 50

SALES (est): 503.7MM **Privately Held**
WEB: www.pcsgp.com
SIC: 1541 Steel building construction
HQ: Gerdau Ameristeel Us Inc.
4221 W Boy Scout Blvd # 600
Tampa FL 33607
813 286-8383

(P-1343)
CONEJO PACIFIC TECHNOLOGIES
1560 Newbury Rd Ste 1, Newbury Park
(91320-3448)
PHONE.................................805 498-5315
EMP: 65
SQ FT: 100
SALES (est): 4.3MM **Privately Held**
SIC: 1541 0782

(P-1344)
CUBIX CONSTRUCTION COMPANY (PA)
Also Called: Allsafe Selfstorage
5 Meadowbrook Ln, Danville (94526-1707)
PHONE.................................925 314-0770
Stanley Boersma, *President*
Geurtje Boersma, *Corp Secy*
EMP: 200
SALES (est): 27.5MM **Privately Held**
WEB: www.cubixcc.com
SIC: 1541 Warehouse construction

(P-1345)
DENVER D DARLING INC
Also Called: Darco Construction
8402 Katella Ave, Stanton (90680-3215)
PHONE.................................714 761-8299
Denver D Darling, *President*
Wayne Darling, *Vice Pres*
Kale Darling, *Project Mgr*
Ron Neilsen, *Project Mgr*
EMP: 75
SQ FT: 10,000
SALES (est): 11MM **Privately Held**
WEB: www.darcoconstruction.com
SIC: 1541 1771 Industrial buildings, new construction; concrete work

(P-1346)
EXCEL CONSTRUCTION SVCS INC (PA)
1950 Raymer Ave, Fullerton (92833-2513)
PHONE.................................714 680-9200
Karen Latzlaff, *CEO*
Dan Jurado, *President*
Todd London, *Vice Pres*
EMP: 60
SQ FT: 12,000
SALES (est): 19.5MM **Privately Held**
SIC: 1541 Industrial buildings & warehouses

(P-1347)
FRIZE CORPORATION
16605 Gale Ave, City of Industry
(91745-1802)
PHONE.................................800 834-2127
James N Frize, *President*
Brad Daugherty, *Project Mgr*
Jon Oleinick, *Project Mgr*
Paul Nevarez, *Safety Mgr*
Jeff Barber, *Foreman/Supr*
EMP: 80
SQ FT: 25,000
SALES (est): 24.7MM **Privately Held**
WEB: www.frizecorp.com
SIC: 1541 1542 Industrial buildings & warehouses; commercial & office building contractors

(P-1348)
FULLMER CONSTRUCTION
1725 S Grove Ave, Ontario (91761-4530)
PHONE.................................909 947-9467
Robert A Fullmer, *President*
Gered Yetter, *CFO*
James Fullmer, *Corp Secy*
Brad Anderson, *Vice Pres*
Bradley J Anderson, *Vice Pres*
◆ EMP: 120
SQ FT: 20,000
SALES (est): 65.4MM **Privately Held**
SIC: 1541 Industrial buildings, new construction

(P-1349)
GEORGE RICHARD
P.O. Box 712002, Santee (92072-2002)
PHONE.................................619 805-6751
George Richards, *President*
EMP: 60
SALES (est): 2.5MM **Privately Held**
SIC: 1541 Renovation, remodeling & repairs: industrial buildings

(P-1350)
GRIMMWAY ENTERPRISES INC
Grimmway Farm
12020 Malaga Rd, Arvin (93203-9527)
PHONE.................................661 854-6240
Mike Blakley, *Supervisor*
EMP: 100
SALES (corp-wide): 1.8B **Privately Held**
SIC: 1541 1542 Industrial buildings & warehouses; nonresidential construction
PA: Grimmway Enterprises, Inc.
14141 Di Giorgio Rd
Arvin CA 93203
800 301-3101

(P-1351)
H C OLSEN CNSTR CO INC
710 Los Angeles Ave, Monrovia
(91016-4250)
PHONE.................................626 359-8900
Linda Jacqueline Pearson, *CEO*
Karl Pearson, *Corp Secy*
Paul Hudson, *Sr Project Mgr*
Chris Leblanc, *Director*
Bill Hammer, *Superintendent*
EMP: 75 EST: 1946
SQ FT: 12,800
SALES (est): 27.8MM **Privately Held**
WEB: www.hcolsen.com
SIC: 1541 Industrial buildings, new construction

(P-1352)
HAL HAYS CONSTRUCTION INC (PA)
4181 Latham St, Riverside (92501-1729)
PHONE.................................951 788-0703
Hal Hays, *President*
E Denise Hays, *CFO*
Antonia Duarte, *Manager*
EMP: 113
SQ FT: 28,400
SALES (est): 76.6MM **Privately Held**
WEB: www.halhays.com
SIC: 1541 1542 1623 1629 Industrial buildings & warehouses; commercial & office buildings, renovation & repair; water, sewer & utility lines; dams, waterways, docks & other marine construction; highway & street paving contractor; concrete work

(P-1353)
HAMANN CONSTRUCTION
1000 Pioneer Way, El Cajon (92020-1923)
PHONE.................................619 440-7424
Jeffrey C Hamann, *CEO*
Gregg Hamann, *Treasurer*
EMP: 75 EST: 1954
SQ FT: 15,000
SALES (est): 17.7MM **Privately Held**
WEB: www.hamannco.com
SIC: 1541 Industrial buildings, new construction

(P-1354)
HASKELL COMPANY (INC)
478 Lindbergh Ave, Livermore
(94551-9553)
PHONE.................................925 960-1815
EMP: 185
SALES (corp-wide): 896.6MM **Privately Held**
SIC: 1541 Industrial buildings, new construction
HQ: The Haskell Company Inc
111 Riverside Ave
Jacksonville FL 32202
904 791-4500

(P-1355)
HERRERO BUILDERS INCORPORATED (PA)
2100 Oakdale Ave, San Francisco (94124-1516)
PHONE..................................415 824-7675
Mark D Herrero, *Ch of Bd*
Rick Herrero, *President*
James Totoritis, *CFO*
Craig Braccia, *Vice Pres*
Saptarshi Desai, *Executive*
▲ **EMP:** 128
SQ FT: 10,000
SALES (est): 75.6MM **Privately Held**
WEB: www.herrero.com
SIC: 1541 Industrial buildings, new construction

(P-1356)
JACKSON CONSTRUCTION (PA)
155 Cadillac Dr, Sacramento (95825-5499)
PHONE..................................916 381-8113
John Jackson Jr, *President*
Don Hanson, *CFO*
Lynda Jackson, *Treasurer*
Eric J Edelmayer, *Vice Pres*
Eric Edelmayer, *Vice Pres*
EMP: 50 **EST:** 1974
SQ FT: 10,000
SALES (est): 20.1MM **Privately Held**
WEB: www.jacksonprop.com
SIC: 1541 1542 6552 6531 Industrial buildings & warehouses; nonresidential construction; land subdividers & developers, residential; real estate agents & managers

(P-1357)
JH BRYANT JR INC (PA)
17217 S Broadway, Gardena (90248-3117)
PHONE..................................310 532-1840
Barbara Bryant, *CEO*
John Bryant III, *President*
David Bryant, *COO*
Joseph Perez, *Vice Pres*
Lillian Welch, *Office Mgr*
EMP: 50
SQ FT: 6,500
SALES: 13MM **Privately Held**
WEB: www.jhbryant.com
SIC: 1541 Industrial buildings & warehouses

(P-1358)
JULIUS STEVE CONSTRUCTION INC
Also Called: S R J
230 Calle Pintoresco, San Clemente (92672-7503)
PHONE..................................949 369-7820
Leigh Thornburg Julius, *CEO*
Pete Ferrarini, *President*
Shane Hankins, *General Mgr*
Donald Westad, *Project Mgr*
EMP: 50
SQ FT: 6,700
SALES: 12.9MM **Privately Held**
WEB: www.stevejuliusconstruction.com
SIC: 1541 Industrial buildings, new construction

(P-1359)
KAJIMA CONSTRUCTION SVCS INC
Also Called: Kajima International
250 E 1st St Ste 400, Los Angeles (90012-3820)
PHONE..................................323 269-0020
Nori Ohashi, *Branch Mgr*
Larry Atwater, *Vice Pres*
Daniel Smith, *Project Mgr*
Anthony Colla, *Project Engr*
William Kobayashi, *Business Mgr*
EMP: 50 **Privately Held**
SIC: 1541 1542 8712 Industrial buildings, new construction; commercial & office building, new construction; house designer
HQ: Kajima Construction Services, Inc.
3550 Lenox Rd Ne Ste 1850
Atlanta GA 30326

(P-1360)
KAZARIAN/JEWETT INC
Also Called: Kcb Builders
6621 Pcf Cast Hwy Ste 120, Long Beach (90803)
PHONE..................................562 594-5927
K C Kazarian, *President*
Bill Jewett, *Treasurer*
EMP: 50
SALES: 2MM **Privately Held**
SIC: 1541 1542 Industrial buildings & warehouses; commercial & office building contractors

(P-1361)
KEMP BROS CONSTRUCTION INC
10135 Geary Ave, Santa Fe Springs (90670-3253)
PHONE..................................562 236-5000
Greg S Solaas, *President*
Steve Rosenfield, *Vice Pres*
Chris Miller, *Executive*
Judy Anderson, *Office Mgr*
Chad Nelson, *Project Leader*
EMP: 50
SQ FT: 15,500
SALES (est): 15.5MM **Privately Held**
SIC: 1541 1542 Industrial buildings, new construction; hospital construction

(P-1362)
KENDRICK CONSTRUCTION SERVICES
Also Called: Kendrick Co The
3010 Old Ranch Pkwy # 470, Seal Beach (90740-2789)
PHONE..................................562 546-0200
Gregory T Hook, *President*
Randy Kendrick, *Shareholder*
Jud Leibee, *CFO*
Sandra Combee, *Admin Sec*
EMP: 55
SQ FT: 3,500
SALES (est): 6MM **Privately Held**
WEB: www.kendrickconstruction.com
SIC: 1541 1542 Industrial buildings, new construction; nonresidential construction

(P-1363)
KERNEN CONSTRUCTION
2350 Glendale Dr, McKinleyville (95519-9205)
P.O. Box 1340, Blue Lake (95525-1340)
PHONE..................................707 826-8686
Kurt Kernen, *Partner*
Scott Farley, *Partner*
EMP: 60
SQ FT: 120
SALES (est): 17.8MM **Privately Held**
WEB: www.kernenconstruction.com
SIC: 1541 1542 Industrial buildings, new construction; commercial & office building, new construction

(P-1364)
LEDCOR CMI INC
6405 Mira Mesa Blvd # 100, San Diego (92121-4120)
PHONE..................................602 595-3017
David W Lede, *CEO*
EMP: 82
SALES (est): 104MM **Privately Held**
SIC: 1541 1611 1629 1623 Industrial buildings & warehouses; highway & street construction; mine loading & discharging station construction; industrial plant construction; pipeline construction; condominium construction; communication services

(P-1365)
LEVY PRMIUM FDSRVICE LTD PRTNR
Also Called: Levy Cncessions At Staples Ctr
1111 S Figueroa St, Los Angeles (90015-1300)
PHONE..................................213 742-7867
Jeffrey Rosenbaugh, *Manager*
EMP: 70
SALES (corp-wide): 29.6B **Privately Held**
WEB: www.cafespiaggia.com
SIC: 1541 Industrial buildings & warehouses

HQ: Levy Premium Foodservice Limited Partnership
980 N Michigan Ave # 400
Chicago IL 60611
312 664-8200

(P-1366)
MA STEINER CONSTRUCTION INC
8854 Greenback Ln Ste 1, Orangevale (95662-4084)
PHONE..................................916 988-6300
Martin Steiner, *President*
EMP: 64
SALES (est): 13.4MM **Privately Held**
SIC: 1541 1794 1542 1611 Industrial buildings, new construction; excavation & grading, building construction; commercial & office building, new construction; highway & street construction; general contractor, highway & street construction

(P-1367)
MILLIE AND SEVERSON INC
3601 Serpentine Dr, Los Alamitos (90720-2440)
PHONE..................................562 493-3611
Scott Feest, *President*
Robert E Wissmann, *Senior VP*
Robert Cavecche, *Vice Pres*
John Grossman, *Vice Pres*
Mark Huber, *Vice Pres*
EMP: 75 **EST:** 1945
SQ FT: 15,000
SALES: 288.6MM **Privately Held**
WEB: www.mandsinc.com
SIC: 1541 Industrial buildings, new construction; renovation, remodeling & repairs: industrial buildings; steel building construction; warehouse construction
PA: Severson Group Incorporated
3601 Serpentine Dr
Los Alamitos CA 90720

(P-1368)
MINSHEW BROTHERS STL CNSTR INC
12578 Vigilante Rd, Lakeside (92040-1112)
P.O. Box 1000 (92040-0902)
PHONE..................................619 561-5700
James Minshew, *President*
Daniel P Minshew, *Treasurer*
John M Minshew, *Vice Pres*
EMP: 105
SQ FT: 22,000
SALES (est): 28.3MM **Privately Held**
SIC: 1541 1791 Steel building construction; structural steel erection

(P-1369)
MODERN BUILDING INC
3083 Southgate Ln, Chico (95928-7427)
P.O. Box 772 (95927-0772)
PHONE..................................530 891-4533
L Gage Chrysler, *CEO*
Gary Fowler, *Corp Secy*
James Seegert, *Vice Pres*
Terry Wolkoff, *Admin Asst*
Debbie Barnett, *Administration*
EMP: 50
SQ FT: 5,000
SALES (est): 19.5MM **Privately Held**
WEB: www.modernbuildinginc.com
SIC: 1541 1542 Industrial buildings, new construction; commercial & office building, new construction

(P-1370)
NORTH COAST FABRICATORS INC
4801 West End Rd, Arcata (95521-9242)
PHONE..................................707 822-4629
Paula E Crowley, *President*
Tim Crowley, *COO*
EMP: 50 **EST:** 1979
SQ FT: 12,000
SALES (est): 13.5MM **Privately Held**
SIC: 1541 1542 7699 Prefabricated building erection, industrial; commercial & office buildings, prefabricated erection; industrial machinery & equipment repair

(P-1371)
OLTMANS CONSTRUCTION CO (PA)
10005 Mission Mill Rd, Whittier (90601-1739)
P.O. Box 985 (90608-0985)
PHONE..................................562 948-4242
Joseph O Oltmans II, *Ch of Bd*
John Gormly, *President*
Dan Schlothan, *CFO*
Tom Augustine, *Vice Pres*
Robert Larson, *Vice Pres*
▼ **EMP:** 85
SQ FT: 33,000
SALES (est): 259.2MM **Privately Held**
WEB: www.oltmans.com
SIC: 1541 1542 Industrial buildings, new construction; renovation, remodeling & repairs: industrial buildings; commercial & office building, new construction; commercial & office buildings, renovation & repair

(P-1372)
ORANGE COAST BUILDING SERVICES
2191 S Dupont Dr, Anaheim (92806-6102)
PHONE..................................714 453-6300
Kevin W Franklin, *President*
EMP: 115
SQ FT: 6,000
SALES (est): 26.9MM **Privately Held**
WEB: www.ocbsonline.com
SIC: 1541 1542 Industrial buildings, new construction; commercial & office building contractors

(P-1373)
OUT OF SHELL LLC
Also Called: Ling's
9658 Remer St, South El Monte (91733-3033)
PHONE..................................626 401-1923
Alice Liu,
Bing Yang,
Thomas Lee, *Manager*
EMP: 200
SALES (est): 24.2MM **Privately Held**
SIC: 1541 Food products manufacturing or packing plant construction

(P-1374)
PARSONS PROJECT SERVICES INC
100 W Walnut St, Pasadena (91124-0001)
PHONE..................................626 440-4000
Charles Harrington, *CEO*
Todd K Wager, *President*
EMP: 131
SALES (est): 5.2MM **Privately Held**
SIC: 1541 Industrial buildings & warehouses

(P-1375)
PERFORMANCE CONTRACTING INC
1943 Rutan Dr, Livermore (94551-7646)
PHONE..................................925 273-3800
Mike Ligon, *Manager*
EMP: 50
SALES (corp-wide): 1.1B **Privately Held**
SIC: 1541 Industrial buildings, new construction
HQ: Performance Contracting, Inc.
11145 Thompson Ave
Lenexa KS 66219
913 888-8600

(P-1376)
RQ CONSTRUCTION LLC
3194 Lionshead Ave, Carlsbad (92010-4701)
PHONE..................................760 631-7707
George H Rogers III, *CEO*
Craig Shadle, *CFO*
Mary Baker, *Admin Sec*
EMP: 170
SALES (est): 79.4MM **Privately Held**
SIC: 1541 Industrial buildings, new construction

(P-1377)
SHIMS BARGAIN INC
Also Called: JC Sales
7030 E Slauson Ave, Commerce
(90040-3621)
PHONE..................................323 726-8800
Andy Kim, *Manager*
EMP: 210
SALES (corp-wide): 177.5MM **Privately Held**
SIC: 1541 Industrial buildings & warehouses
PA: Shims Bargain, Inc.
      2600 S Soto St
      Vernon CA 90058
      323 881-0099

(P-1378)
SIERRA BAY CONTRACTORS INC
4021 Port Chicago Hwy # 150, Concord
(94520-1122)
PHONE..................................925 671-7711
Albert D Seeno Jr, *President*
Robert Coburn, *Vice Pres*
Thomas A Seeno, *Vice Pres*
EMP: 50
SQ FT: 2,000
SALES (est): 5.4MM **Privately Held**
WEB: www.sierrabayinc.com
SIC: 1541 6221 Industrial buildings & warehouses; commodity contracts brokers, dealers

(P-1379)
SILMAN VENTURE CORPORATION (PA)
Also Called: Silman Construction
1600 Factor Ave, San Leandro
(94577-5618)
PHONE..................................510 347-4800
Tom Mangin, *CEO*
Rick Silva, *COO*
John Voris, *COO*
Mikal Brevig, *Department Mgr*
Lindsey Donaldson, *Administration*
EMP: 125 **EST:** 2007
SQ FT: 17,000
SALES: 40MM **Privately Held**
SIC: 1541 Industrial buildings, new construction

(P-1380)
STANTRU RESOURCES INC
Also Called: Stantru Reinforcing Steel
11175 Redwood Ave, Fontana
(92337-7137)
P.O. Box 310189 (92331-0189)
PHONE..................................909 587-1441
Ida Ichen, *President*
William M Klorman, *Manager*
EMP: 83
SALES (est): 6.3MM **Privately Held**
SIC: 1541 1542 Industrial buildings, new construction; pharmaceutical manufacturing plant construction; commercial & office building, new construction; school building construction; institutional building construction

(P-1381)
STEELTECH CONSTRUCTION SVCS
4081 E La Palma Ave Ste G, Anaheim
(92807-1701)
PHONE..................................714 630-2890
Edward Campbell, *President*
Alex Endress, *Manager*
EMP: 100
SQ FT: 2,200
SALES: 5MM **Privately Held**
SIC: 1541 Industrial buildings & warehouses

(P-1382)
SWINERTON BUILDERS (HQ)
Also Called: SWINERTON MANAGEMENT & CONSULTING
260 Townsend St Fl 3, San Francisco
(94107-1941)
PHONE..................................415 421-2980
Jeffrey C Hoopes, *Ch of Bd*
John T Capener, *President*
Gary J Rafferty, *President*
Linda G Schowalter, *CFO*

Frank Foellmer, *Exec VP*
▲ **EMP:** 200
SQ FT: 300,353
SALES: 3.5B **Privately Held**
SIC: 1541 1522 1542 Industrial buildings, new construction; steel building construction; hotel/motel, new construction; commercial & office building, new construction; commercial & office buildings, renovation & repair; specialized public building contractors

(P-1383)
SWINERTON BUILDERS
Swinerton Renewable Energy
16798 W Bernardo Dr, San Diego
(92127-1904)
PHONE..................................858 622-4040
Don Adair, *Manager*
Terri Schmid, *Project Mgr*
Richard Carpentier, *Asst Supt*
EMP: 65 **Privately Held**
SIC: 1541 Industrial buildings, new construction
HQ: Swinerton Builders
      260 Townsend St Fl 3
      San Francisco CA 94107
      415 421-2980

(P-1384)
T B PENICK & SONS INC (PA)
15435 Innovation Dr # 100, San Diego
(92128-3443)
PHONE..................................858 558-1800
Marc E Penick, *CEO*
Timothy Penick, *President*
John Boyd, *CFO*
Shane Willis, *Officer*
Melissa Holmes, *Executive*
EMP: 151 **EST:** 1905
SQ FT: 30,000
SALES: 139.2MM **Privately Held**
WEB: www.tbpenick.com
SIC: 1541 1542 Industrial buildings & warehouses; nonresidential construction

(P-1385)
TCB INDUSTRIAL INC (PA)
2955 Farrar Ave, Modesto (95354-4118)
PHONE..................................209 571-0569
Dave Raybourn, *CEO*
Bruce Elliott, *CFO*
EMP: 160
SALES (est): 40.1MM **Privately Held**
WEB: www.Tcbindustrial.net
SIC: 1541 Industrial buildings, new construction

(P-1386)
TEKTETCO
Also Called: Tribal Tektet
5251 Ericson Way, Arcata (95521-9273)
PHONE..................................707 822-9000
Daniel Johnson,
Terry Wilson,
EMP: 65
SALES (est): 3MM **Privately Held**
SIC: 1541 1542 1522 Industrial buildings, new construction; commercial & office building, new construction; hotel/motel, new construction; multi-family dwellings, new construction

(P-1387)
TORRES CONSTRUCTION CORP (PA)
1370 N El Molino Ave, Pasadena
(91104-5026)
PHONE..................................323 257-7460
Martha McGowin, *President*
Mael Torres, *Treasurer*
Esteban Torres, *Vice Pres*
Nick Porter, *Project Mgr*
Ismael Torres, *Opers Staff*
EMP: 59
SQ FT: 7,500
SALES (est): 24.9MM **Privately Held**
WEB: www.torresconstruction.com
SIC: 1541 Industrial buildings & warehouses

(P-1388)
TRI-TECH RESTORATION CO INC
3301 N San Fernando Blvd, Burbank
(91504-2531)
PHONE..................................818 565-3900
Armine Bakmazian, *President*
Michael Boyd, *Admin Sec*
Ed Gonzalez, *Project Mgr*
EMP: 70
SQ FT: 35,000
SALES: 8MM **Privately Held**
WEB: www.tritechrestoration.com
SIC: 1541 Industrial buildings & warehouses

(P-1389)
TRILOGY RIO VISTA
Also Called: SHEA HOMES
1200 Clubhouse Dr, Rio Vista
(94571-9801)
PHONE..................................707 374-1100
Steve Hextell, *Vice Pres*
EMP: 60
SALES: 62.2MM **Privately Held**
SIC: 1541 Industrial buildings, new construction

(P-1390)
UNIVERSAL DUST COLLECTOR (PA)
Also Called: UDC
1041 N Kraemer Pl, Anaheim (92806-2611)
PHONE..................................714 630-8588
Theresa A Shaffer, *CEO*
Curt Schendel, *President*
Deborah Huerta, *CFO*
Curtis Schendel, *Vice Pres*
Shawn E Shaffer, *Vice Pres*
EMP: 59
SQ FT: 30,000
SALES: 28MM **Privately Held**
WEB: www.udccorporation.com
SIC: 1541 Industrial buildings, new construction

(P-1391)
WATSON CONTRACTORS INC
3185 Longview Dr, Sacramento
(95821-7214)
PHONE..................................916 481-6293
Greg Watson, *President*
EMP: 65
SALES (est): 4.1MM **Privately Held**
WEB: www.watsonroofing.com
SIC: 1541 Renovation, remodeling & repairs: industrial buildings

(P-1392)
WEST HILLS CONSTRUCTION INC
423 Jenks Cir Ste 101, Corona
(92880-2540)
PHONE..................................800 515-5270
Ross L Wood, *President*
Rusty Wood, *Vice Pres*
Stephanie Wood, *Director*
EMP: 50
SQ FT: 7,500
SALES (est): 7.1MM **Privately Held**
SIC: 1541 Industrial buildings, new construction

1542 General Contractors, Nonresidential & Non-indl Bldgs

(P-1393)
2H CONSTRUCTION INC
2653 Walnut Ave, Signal Hill (90755-1830)
PHONE..................................562 424-5567
Sean Hitchcock, *President*
Ericka Hitchcock, *CFO*
Ronald Compton, *Vice Pres*
EMP: 70
SQ FT: 8,000
SALES: 50MM **Privately Held**
WEB: www.2hconstruction.com
SIC: 1542 Commercial & office building, new construction

(P-1394)
A RUIZ CNSTR CO & ASSOC INC
1601 Cortland Ave, San Francisco
(94110-5716)
PHONE..................................415 647-4010
Antonio Ruiz, *President*
Thomas Cotter, *Executive*
Henrietta Ruiz, *General Mgr*
Victor Alvarez, *Project Mgr*
Juan Gomez, *Project Mgr*
EMP: 50
SQ FT: 10,000
SALES (est): 14.9MM **Privately Held**
WEB: www.aruizconstruction.com
SIC: 1542 Commercial & office building, new construction; commercial & office building contractors

(P-1395)
AARDEX INC
1550 E Main St, Santa Maria (93454-4819)
PHONE..................................805 928-7600
Shane Fowleror, *President*
EMP: 60
SALES (est): 3.4MM **Privately Held**
SIC: 1542 Commercial & office building, new construction

(P-1396)
ABHE & SVOBODA INC
880 Tavern Rd, Alpine (91901-3810)
PHONE..................................619 659-1320
David Grant, *Manager*
Jim Ness, *Sr Project Mgr*
Daniel Markwell, *Manager*
Rex Huffman, *Superintendent*
EMP: 58
SALES (corp-wide): 1.7MM **Privately Held**
SIC: 1542 Commercial & office building, new construction
PA: Abhe & Svoboda, Inc.
      18100 Dairy Ln
      Jordan MN 55352
      952 447-6025

(P-1397)
ACCESS PACIFIC INC
2835 Sierra Grande St, Pasadena
(91107-3448)
PHONE..................................626 792-0616
Tomas Torres, *President*
EMP: 50 **EST:** 2009
SALES (est): 15.2MM **Privately Held**
SIC: 1542 Nonresidential construction

(P-1398)
ADVANTAGE FRAMING SOLUTIONS
1965 N Beale Rd, Marysville (95901-6914)
PHONE..................................530 742-7660
Joel Bueno, *CFO*
EMP: 50
SALES (est): 1.7MM **Privately Held**
SIC: 1542 Nonresidential construction

(P-1399)
AFA CONSTRCTN GRP/CAL INC JV
2040 Peabody Rd Ste 400, Vacaville
(95687-6694)
PHONE..................................707 446-7996
Ralph Hodges, *President*
Olivia Trudell, *Vice Pres*
EMP: 80
SALES (est): 4.3MM **Privately Held**
SIC: 1542 Nonresidential construction

(P-1400)
AHTNA GOVERNMENT SERVICES CORP
3100 Beacon Blvd, West Sacramento
(95691-3483)
PHONE..................................916 372-2000
Chris Smith, *President*
EMP: 60
SALES (corp-wide): 322.2MM **Privately Held**
WEB: www.ahtnagov.com
SIC: 1542 Nonresidential construction
HQ: Ahtna Government Services Corporation
      3100 Beacon Blvd
      West Sacramento CA 95691
      916 372-2000

P R O D U C T S & S V C S

(P-1401)
AIS CONSTRUCTION COMPANY
713 Rincon Hill Rd, Santa Maria (93455)
P.O. Box 4209, San Luis Obispo (93403-4209)
PHONE..............................805 928-9467
Andy Sheaffer, *President*
EMP: 85
SQ FT: 4,000
SALES (est): 12.5MM **Privately Held**
WEB: www.aisconstruction.com
SIC: 1542 Commercial & office building contractors

(P-1402)
AJW RESTORATION SERVICES LLC
7445 Raytheon Rd, San Diego (92111-1505)
PHONE..............................858 429-5641
Arthur Candland, *CEO*
Warren Thompson, *President*
Edward Chavez, *Business Mgr*
EMP: 50
SALES: 3MM **Privately Held**
SIC: 1542 Commercial & office building, new construction

(P-1403)
AK CONSTRUCTORS INC
Also Called: AK Electrical Services
1751 Jenks Dr, Corona (92880-2516)
PHONE..............................951 280-0269
Kenneth G Dougher, *President*
Kenneth Dougher, *Senior Partner*
Micheal Harrington, *Corp Secy*
Robert Griffin, *Principal*
Kurt Meyers, *Principal*
EMP: 65
SALES (est): 17.4MM **Privately Held**
WEB: www.akconstructors.com
SIC: 1542 Commercial & office building, new construction

(P-1404)
ALLEN L BENDER INC
6625 Quail Crossing Ln, Granite Bay (95746-7360)
PHONE..............................916 372-2190
Blake Bender, *President*
Brian Bender, *CFO*
EMP: 120 **EST:** 1956
SQ FT: 22,000
SALES (est): 14.1MM **Privately Held**
WEB: www.allenlbender.com
SIC: 1542 8711 Commercial & office buildings, renovation & repair; engineering services

(P-1405)
ALSTON CONSTRUCTION CO INC (PA)
8775 Folsom Blvd Ste 201, Sacramento (95826-3725)
PHONE..............................916 340-2400
Paul David Little, *CEO*
Adam Nickerson, *CFO*
Chad Bouck, *Senior VP*
Evan Hamilton, *Vice Pres*
William Hancock, *Vice Pres*
EMP: 100 **EST:** 1998
SQ FT: 36,000
SALES: 909.9MM **Privately Held**
WEB: www.panconinc.com
SIC: 1542 1541 Commercial & office building, new construction; industrial buildings & warehouses

(P-1406)
ANDREW L YOUNGQUIST CNSTR INC
3187 Red Hill Ave Ste 200, Costa Mesa (92626-3454)
PHONE..............................949 862-5611
Andrew L Youngquist, *Ch of Bd*
James Lefler, *President*
Richard Lee Youngquist, *Vice Pres*
EMP: 90
SQ FT: 10,319
SALES (est): 9.7MM **Privately Held**
WEB: www.alyconstruction.com
SIC: 1542 1522 8741 Commercial & office building contractors; residential construction; construction management

(P-1407)
ARAGON CONSTRUCTION INC
5440 Arrow Hwy, Montclair (91763-1604)
PHONE..............................909 621-2200
Joseph E Aragon, *President*
Regina Aragon, *General Mgr*
Lisa Lachowicz, *General Mgr*
Gina Aragon, *Office Mgr*
Joey Aragon, *Project Mgr*
EMP: 55
SALES (est): 24MM **Privately Held**
SIC: 1542 Institutional building construction; commercial & office buildings, renovation & repair; shopping center construction; specialized public building contractors

(P-1408)
ARB INC
50 Quint St, San Francisco (94124-1424)
PHONE..............................415 206-1015
Chris Slack, *Branch Mgr*
EMP: 50
SALES (corp-wide): 2.9B **Publicly Held**
SIC: 1542 1623 Nonresidential construction; garage construction; oil & gas line & compressor station construction
HQ: Arb, Inc.
26000 Commercentre Dr
Lake Forest CA 92630
949 598-9242

(P-1409)
ARCHER WESTERN CONTRACTORS LLC
9915 Mira Mesa Blvd # 230, San Diego (92131-7003)
PHONE..............................858 715-7200
Tim Gerken, *CFO*
EMP: 52
SALES (corp-wide): 3.2B **Privately Held**
WEB: www.walshgroup.com
SIC: 1542 Nonresidential construction
HQ: Archer Western Contractors, Llc
2410 Paces Ferry Rd Se # 600
Atlanta GA 30339
404 495-8700

(P-1410)
ASR CONSTRUCTORS INC
Also Called: Contractors Complete Surety
33891 Mission Trl, Wildomar (92595-8431)
PHONE..............................951 779-6580
Alan Lee Rigotti, *President*
Stacey Rigotti, *Corp Secy*
EMP: 270 **EST:** 1999
SQ FT: 3,000
SALES (est): 47.5MM **Privately Held**
SIC: 1542 Nonresidential construction

(P-1411)
AT YOUR SVC HTG & COOLG LLC
333 H St Ste 5000, Chula Vista (91910-5561)
PHONE..............................602 550-6946
Joe Lizarraga, *Manager*
EMP: 66
SALES: 950K **Privately Held**
SIC: 1542 Nonresidential construction

(P-1412)
B C C S INC (PA)
Also Called: South Bay Construction Company
1711 Dell Ave, Campbell (95008-6904)
PHONE..............................408 379-5500
Richard Furtado, *Partner*
Marc Morgan, *Project Mgr*
Ric Propersi, *Project Mgr*
Brett Scolari, *Project Mgr*
Ginger Creagh, *Project Engr*
EMP: 76
SQ FT: 10,100
SALES (est): 74.4MM **Privately Held**
WEB: www.sbci.com
SIC: 1542 Commercial & office buildings, prefabricated erection

(P-1413)
BALFOUR BEATTY CNSTR LLC
2335 Broadway Ste 300, Oakland (94612-2495)
PHONE..............................510 903-2060
EMP: 186

SALES (corp-wide): 8.5B **Privately Held**
SIC: 1542 Commercial & office building, new construction
HQ: Balfour Beatty Construction, Llc
3100 Mckinnon St Fl 10
Dallas TX 75201
214 451-1000

(P-1414)
BALFOUR BEATTY CNSTR LLC
10620 Treena St Ste 300, San Diego (92131-1141)
PHONE..............................858 635-7400
Britani Harris, *Project Engr*
Wendy Anderson, *Accountant*
Shari Caton, *Accountant*
Kate Wade, *Human Res Dir*
Nicole Hurley, *Marketing Mgr*
EMP: 100
SALES (corp-wide): 8.5B **Privately Held**
SIC: 1542 Commercial & office building, new construction; specialized public building contractors
HQ: Balfour Beatty Construction, Llc
3100 Mckinnon St Fl 10
Dallas TX 75201
214 451-1000

(P-1415)
BALLIET BROS CONSTRUCTION CORP
390 Swift Ave Ste 14, South San Francisco (94080-6221)
PHONE..............................650 871-9000
Robert F Balliet, *President*
Michael Warren, *Vice Pres*
Mike Warren, *Vice Pres*
Mareth Vedder, *Office Mgr*
Blanca Garache, *Bookkeeper*
EMP: 50
SQ FT: 9,000
SALES (est): 2.8MM **Privately Held**
WEB: www.ballietbros.com
SIC: 1542 1522 2434 2431 Commercial & office buildings, renovation & repair; remodeling, multi-family dwellings; wood kitchen cabinets; trim, wood

(P-1416)
BAYSIDE INSULATION & CNSTR
1635 Challenge Dr, Concord (94520-5206)
PHONE..............................925 288-8960
Shahram Ameli, *CEO*
Al Badakhshan, *Vice Pres*
EMP: 62
SQ FT: 10,000
SALES: 18.8MM **Privately Held**
WEB: www.baysideinsulation.com
SIC: 1542 Commercial & office building, new construction

(P-1417)
BCCI CONSTRUCTION COMPANY (DH)
Also Called: Bcci Builders
1160 Battery St Ste 250, San Francisco (94111-1216)
PHONE..............................415 817-5100
Michael Scribner, *President*
Dominic Sarica, *Vice Pres*
Todd Swartz, *Vice Pres*
EMP: 140
SQ FT: 15,121
SALES (est): 75.6MM
SALES (corp-wide): 4.3B **Privately Held**
WEB: www.bcciconst.com
SIC: 1542 Commercial & office buildings, renovation & repair
HQ: Sto Building Group Inc.
330 W 34th St
New York NY 10001
732 362-3472

(P-1418)
BEL ESPRIT BUILDERS INC
23112 Alcalde Dr Ste A, Laguna Hills (92653-1458)
PHONE..............................949 709-3500
David K Jackson, *President*
Debra Jackson, *Admin Sec*
EMP: 50
SALES (est): 7.6MM **Privately Held**
SIC: 1542 Nonresidential construction

(P-1419)
BELMONT BRUNS CONSTRUCTION INC
1125 Mabury Rd, San Jose (95133-1029)
P.O. Box 1369, Lathrop (95330-1369)
PHONE..............................408 977-1708
Mark A Collishaw, *CEO*
Paul J Helvik, *Vice Pres*
Jack Collishaw, *Admin Sec*
EMP: 55
SALES (est): 14MM **Privately Held**
SIC: 1542 1541 Commercial & office building, new construction; commercial & office buildings, renovation & repair; industrial buildings & warehouses

(P-1420)
BENNATHON CORP (PA)
Also Called: Tudor Cnstr & Restoration
10278 Iron Rock Way, Elk Grove (95624-1355)
P.O. Box 5426, Stockton (95205-0426)
PHONE..............................916 405-2100
David Urman, *President*
Tony Huynh, *CFO*
Peter Jones, *Vice Pres*
EMP: 60
SQ FT: 30,000
SALES (est): 12.6MM **Privately Held**
SIC: 1542 1541 1521 Commercial & office buildings, renovation & repair; renovation, remodeling & repairs; industrial buildings; repairing fire damage, single-family houses

(P-1421)
BERGMAN KPRS LLC (PA)
2850 Saturn St Ste 100, Brea (92821-1701)
PHONE..............................714 924-7000
Mark C Bergman,
Carlos Cornejo, *Project Mgr*
Aaron Messmer, *Project Mgr*
Christina Edwards, *Sales Mgr*
Paul Kristedja,
EMP: 125
SQ FT: 7,500
SALES (est): 63.5MM **Privately Held**
WEB: www.thebergman.com
SIC: 1542 Restaurant construction; shopping center construction

(P-1422)
BLAZONA CONCRETE CNSTR INC
525 Harbor Blvd Ste 10, West Sacramento (95691-2246)
PHONE..............................916 375-8337
J Dennis Blazona, *CEO*
Karen Blazona, *Vice Pres*
Rhett Havner, *Vice Pres*
Randy Thayer, *General Mgr*
Terry Blazona, *Project Mgr*
EMP: 100
SALES (est): 23.9MM **Privately Held**
WEB: www.blazona.com
SIC: 1542 Commercial & office building contractors

(P-1423)
BOGART CONSTRUCTION INC
9980 Irvine Center Dr # 200, Irvine (92618-4365)
PHONE..............................949 453-1400
Brad K Bogart, *President*
Amanda Gadde, *Administration*
Jason Flores, *Project Mgr*
Dan Miller, *Project Mgr*
Daniel Stone, *Project Mgr*
EMP: 55
SQ FT: 10,000
SALES: 38.7MM **Privately Held**
WEB: www.bogartconstruction.com
SIC: 1542 Commercial & office building, new construction

(P-1424)
BOMEL CONSTRUCTION CO INC (PA)
96 Corporate Park Ste 100, Irvine (92606-3136)
PHONE..............................714 921-1660
Kent Matranga, *CEO*
Lisa McGinnis, *CFO*
Shawn Devine, *Vice Pres*

▲ = Import ▼=Export
◆ =Import/Export

James Ure, *Vice Pres*
Jim Ure, *Vice Pres*
EMP: 51 **EST:** 1970
SQ FT: 8,000
SALES (est): 109.4MM **Privately Held**
WEB: www.bomelconstruction.com
SIC: 1542 Commercial & office building,
new construction

(P-1425)
**BRADDOCK & LOGAN
SERVICES INC**
4155 Blackhawk Plaza Cir # 201, Danville
(94506-4613)
P.O. Box 5300 (94526-1076)
PHONE....................925 736-4000
Joseph E Raphel, *CEO*
Kari Cartner, *Administration*
Jim Demartini, *Finance*
Nancy Johannessen, *Controller*
Jeff Lawrence, *Manager*
EMP: 200
SALES (est): 40.5MM **Privately Held**
SIC: 1542 1522 Nonresidential construc-
tion; residential construction

(P-1426)
BROWARD BUILDERS INC
1200 E Kentucky Ave, Woodland
(95776-5906)
PHONE....................530 666-5635
Dennis Broward, *President*
Randy Cantrell, *Vice Pres*
EMP: 100
SQ FT: 7,000
SALES: 50.3MM **Privately Held**
WEB: www.browardbros.com
SIC: 1542 1531 School building construc-
tion; cooperative apartment developers

(P-1427)
BROWN CONSTRUCTION INC
1465 Entp Blvd Ste 100, West Sacramento
(95691)
P.O. Box 980700 (95798-0700)
PHONE....................916 374-8616
Ron Brown, *President*
Ken Brown, *CFO*
Diana Houston, *CFO*
Kathryn Mc Guire, *Treasurer*
Matt Defazio, *Vice Pres*
EMP: 71
SQ FT: 11,000
SALES: 151.1MM **Privately Held**
WEB: www.brown-construction.com
SIC: 1542 1522 Commercial & office build-
ing, new construction; apartment building
construction

(P-1428)
**BROWNCO CONSTRUCTION CO
INC**
1000 E Katella Ave, Anaheim (92805-6617)
PHONE....................714 935-9600
Scot Alan Brown, *President*
Zoe Kelso, *COO*
Jeff Radtke, *Vice Pres*
Michael Campbell, *Project Mgr*
Carla Marquez, *Persnl Mgr*
EMP: 87
SQ FT: 15,000
SALES (est): 23.9MM **Privately Held**
WEB: www.browncoinc.com
SIC: 1542 Commercial & office building
contractors

(P-1429)
BUILD GROUP INC (PA)
457 Minna St Ste 100, San Francisco
(94103-2914)
PHONE....................415 367-9399
Ross Edwards, *President*
Eric Horn, *Ch of Bd*
Todd C Pennington, *President*
Ron Marano, *CFO*
Kenneth Jones, *Exec VP*
▲ **EMP:** 131 **EST:** 2006
SQ FT: 8,000
SALES: 808MM **Privately Held**
SIC: 1542 Commercial & office building,
new construction

(P-1430)
BUILD GROUP INC
Also Called: Build Sjc
1210 Coleman Ave, Santa Clara
(95050-4338)
PHONE....................408 986-8711
EMP: 65
SALES (corp-wide): 808MM **Privately
Held**
SIC: 1542 Commercial & office building,
new construction
PA: Build Group, Inc.
457 Minna St Ste 100
San Francisco CA 94103
415 367-9399

(P-1431)
**BURCH CONSTRUCTION
COMPANY INC**
405 Maple St Ste C-101, Ramona
(92065-1890)
P.O. Box 395 (92065-0395)
PHONE....................760 788-9370
Nancy Burch, *CEO*
Mitchell Burch, *President*
EMP: 50
SQ FT: 4,000
SALES (est): 12.5MM **Privately Held**
SIC: 1542 Commercial & office building,
new construction

(P-1432)
**BURNER SHEET METAL LLC
(HQ)**
9749 Cactus St Ste A, Lakeside
(92040-4117)
PHONE....................619 938-9727
Scott McClure, *President*
Mark Finch, *Admin Sec*
EMP: 50
SALES (est): 473.9K
SALES (corp-wide): 25MM **Privately
Held**
SIC: 1542 Service station construction;
custom builders, non-residential
PA: Johnson, Finch & Mcclure Construc-
tion, Inc.
9749 Cactus St
Lakeside CA 92040
619 938-9727

(P-1433)
**BYCOR GENERAL
CONTRACTORS INC**
6490 Marindustry Dr Ste A, San Diego
(92121-5297)
PHONE....................858 587-1901
Scott Kaats, *CEO*
Richard A Byer, *President*
Scott Hodges, *Vice Pres*
Brian Stanton, *Project Mgr*
Christian Santiesteban, *Foreman/Supr*
EMP: 90
SQ FT: 10,041
SALES: 134.4MM **Privately Held**
WEB: www.bycor.com
SIC: 1542 Commercial & office building,
new construction; commercial & office
buildings, renovation & repair

(P-1434)
C & C CONSTRUCTION INC
7941 E Hidden Lakes Dr, Granite Bay
(95746-9539)
PHONE....................916 434-5280
Paul Cavaghan, *CEO*
EMP: 50
SQ FT: 12,800
SALES (est): 10.1MM **Privately Held**
SIC: 1542 Commercial & office building
contractors

(P-1435)
**C W DRIVER INCORPORATED
(PA)**
468 N Rosemead Blvd, Pasadena
(91107-3010)
PHONE....................626 351-8800
Dana Roberts, *President*
Bessie Kouvara, *CFO*
Carl Lowman, *CFO*
Robert Maxwell, *Senior VP*
Robb Good, *Vice Pres*
EMP: 60 **EST:** 1919
SQ FT: 14,000

SALES (est): 186.9MM **Privately Held**
WEB: www.cwdriver.com
SIC: 1542 Commercial & office building,
new construction

(P-1436)
**CAHILL CONTRACTORS INC
(PA)**
425 California St # 2200, San Francisco
(94104-2207)
PHONE....................415 986-0600
John E Cahill Jr, *CEO*
Chuck Palley, *President*
Darrell Diamond, *Corp Secy*
Arash Baradaran, *Vice Pres*
Matt Irwin, *Vice Pres*
▲ **EMP:** 86 **EST:** 1974
SALES: 233MM **Privately Held**
WEB: www.cahill-sf.com
SIC: 1542 Commercial & office building,
new construction

(P-1437)
CAHILL CONTRACTORS LLC
425 California St # 2200, San Francisco
(94104-2207)
PHONE....................415 986-0600
Michael Grant, *CFO*
Trilce Farrugia, *Exec Sec*
EMP: 99
SALES (est): 5.3MM **Privately Held**
SIC: 1542 1522 Commercial & office build-
ing, new construction; residential con-
struction

(P-1438)
**CAL-PACIFIC CONSTRUCTION
INC**
1009 Terra Nova Blvd, Pacifica
(94044-4308)
PHONE....................650 557-1238
John Wah Chan, *President*
Kennedy Chan, *CEO*
EMP: 50
SQ FT: 4,500
SALES: 5.1MM **Privately Held**
SIC: 1542 1521 Commercial & office build-
ing contractors; general remodeling, sin-
gle-family houses

(P-1439)
**CALIFORNIA STRL CONCEPTS
INC**
28358 Constellation Rd # 660, Valencia
(91355-5040)
PHONE....................661 257-6903
Jeffrey Horne, *CEO*
Penny Horne, *Vice Pres*
EMP: 85 **EST:** 2006
SALES: 20.1MM **Privately Held**
SIC: 1542 Commercial & office building,
new construction

(P-1440)
CAPTURED SEA INC
5901 Warner Ave, Huntington Beach
(92649-4659)
P.O. Box 407, Sunset Beach (90742-0407)
PHONE....................714 856-3358
Dave Wooten, *President*
EMP: 60
SQ FT: 24,000
SALES (est): 6.5MM **Privately Held**
WEB: www.capturedsea.com
SIC: 1542 Nonresidential construction

(P-1441)
**CELLO & MAUDRU CNSTR CO
INC**
2505 Oak St, NAPA (94559-2226)
P.O. Box 10106 (94581-2106)
PHONE....................707 257-0454
William F Maudru, *CEO*
Michael Zatorski, *Partner*
Chela Ramos, *Admin Sec*
Sherry Rochester, *Admin Asst*
Fred Duarte, *CTO*
EMP: 50
SQ FT: 2,000
SALES (est): 26.1MM **Privately Held**
WEB: www.cello-maudru.com
SIC: 1542 Commercial & office build-
ing, new construction; new construction,
single-family houses

(P-1442)
**CENTURY VISION DEVELOPERS
INC**
3000 Oak Rd Ste 360, Walnut Creek
(94597-7782)
P.O. Box 907, Concord (94522-0907)
PHONE....................925 588-7390
John E Amaral, *CEO*
EMP: 50
SALES (est): 9.6MM **Privately Held**
SIC: 1542 6512 Commercial & office build-
ing, new construction; commercial & in-
dustrial building operation

(P-1443)
**CHARLES E THOMAS COMPANY
INC (PA)**
Also Called: C E T
13701 Alma Ave, Gardena (90249-2523)
PHONE....................310 323-6730
Jerry Thomas, *President*
Brian Hurley, *Vice Pres*
Ann Thomas, *Vice Pres*
Greg Thomas, *Vice Pres*
Bari Thomas, *Human Resources*
▼ **EMP:** 60
SQ FT: 15,000
SALES (est): 61MM **Privately Held**
WEB: www.cethomas.net
SIC: 1542 7699 Design & erection, com-
bined; non-residential; service station
equipment repair

(P-1444)
**CHARLES PANKOW BLDRS LTD
A CAL (PA)**
199 S Los Robles Ave # 300, Pasadena
(91101-2452)
PHONE....................626 304-1190
Rik Kunnath, *Ch of Bd*
Kim Lum, *Partner*
Dick Walterhouse, *COO*
Kim Petersen, *CFO*
Rick Schutter, *Executive*
EMP: 50
SQ FT: 40,000
SALES (est): 163.9MM **Privately Held**
WEB: www.pankow.com
SIC: 1542 Commercial & office building,
new construction

(P-1445)
**CHARLES PANKOW BLDRS LTD
A CAL**
1111 Broadway Ste 200, Oakland
(94607-4171)
PHONE....................510 893-5170
Scott Anderson, *Manager*
Brent Conrado, *Engineer*
EMP: 450
SALES (corp-wide): 163.9MM **Privately
Held**
SIC: 1542 Commercial & office building
contractors
PA: Charles Pankow Builders, Ltd., A Cali-
fornia Limited Partnership
199 S Los Robles Ave # 300
Pasadena CA 91101
626 304-1190

(P-1446)
CIRKS CONSTRUCTION INC
Also Called: Kdc Construction
3300 Industrial Blvd, West Sacramento
(95691-5028)
PHONE....................916 362-5460
Ryan Ferris, *Branch Mgr*
Dale Nelson, *Superintendent*
EMP: 152
SALES (corp-wide): 141.8MM **Privately
Held**
SIC: 1542 Commercial & office building,
new construction
PA: Cirks Construction Inc.
2570 E Cerritos Ave
Anaheim CA 92806
714 632-6717

(P-1447)
**CLARK & SULLIVAN BUILDERS
INC**
2024 Opportunity Dr # 150, Roseville
(95678-3026)
P.O. Box 7100, Reno NV (89510-7100)
PHONE....................916 338-7707

P
R
O
D
U
C
T
S

&

S
V
C
S

B J Sullivan, *President*
Kevin Stroupe, *CFO*
EMP: 150
SQ FT: 5,000
SALES (est): 17.4MM
SALES (corp-wide): 74.8MM **Privately Held**
SIC: 1542 1541 Commercial & office building, new construction; industrial buildings, new construction
PA: C.S. General, Inc.
905 Industrial Way
Sparks NV 89431
775 355-8500

(P-1448)
CLARK CNSTR GRUP-CALIFORNIA LP
18201 Von Karman Ave, Irvine (92612-1000)
PHONE..................................714 429-9779
Richard M Heim, *CEO*
EMP: 393
SQ FT: 5,000
SALES (est): 2.6MM
SALES (corp-wide): 2B **Privately Held**
WEB: www.clarkus.com
SIC: 1542 Commercial & office building, new construction
HQ: Clark Construction Group, Llc
7500 Old Georgetown Rd # 3
Bethesda MD 20814
301 272-8100

(P-1449)
CODDING CONSTRUCTION CO
1400 Valley House Dr # 100, Rohnert Park (94928-4935)
P.O. Box 5800, Santa Rosa (95406-5800)
PHONE..................................707 795-3550
John Gordon, *CEO*
Reginald E Bayley, *Corp Secy*
Rick Freeman, *Vice Pres*
EMP: 50 **EST:** 1986
SQ FT: 5,000
SALES: 6.9MM
SALES (corp-wide): 21.6MM **Privately Held**
WEB: www.codding.com
SIC: 1542 Commercial & office building contractors
PA: Codding Enterprises Lp
1400 Valley House Dr # 100
Rohnert Park CA 94928
707 795-3550

(P-1450)
CONNECT YOUR HOME LLC
Also Called: Dish Systems
1 Park Plz Ste 600, Irvine (92614-5987)
PHONE..................................949 777-0100
Brookhollow Marketing, *Principal*
Andy Salisbury, *Bd of Directors*
EMP: 90 **EST:** 2010
SQ FT: 14,000
SALES (est): 9.3MM **Privately Held**
SIC: 1542 Commercial & office building contractors

(P-1451)
CONTRACTOR WAREHOUSE
5950 N Paramount Blvd, Lakewood (90805-3710)
PHONE..................................562 633-1428
Greg Inshinsha, *Manager*
EMP: 52
SALES (est): 2.7MM **Privately Held**
SIC: 1542 Commercial & office building contractors

(P-1452)
CUSTOM DESIGN CO INC
20969 Ventura Blvd # 217, Woodland Hills (91364-6617)
PHONE..................................818 507-5959
Mina Hamedani, *President*
Jalil Hamedani, *Vice Pres*
EMP: 50
SQ FT: 5,000
SALES (est): 4.2MM **Privately Held**
SIC: 1542 1751 1521 Nonresidential construction; cabinet & finish carpentry; general remodeling, single-family houses

(P-1453)
DAL CAIS INC
5101 Florin Perkins Rd, Sacramento (95826-4817)
PHONE..................................916 381-8080
Tim Obrian, *President*
Phyllis O'Brien, *Corp Secy*
EMP: 80
SQ FT: 24,000
SALES (est): 5.5MM **Privately Held**
WEB: www.dalcais.com
SIC: 1542 6552 Commercial & office building, new construction; subdividers & developers

(P-1454)
DAVLOR COMPANY
Also Called: Davlor Constructio Corp
12 Oakbrook, Trabuco Canyon (92679-4722)
P.O. Box 892799, Temecula (92589-2799)
PHONE..................................949 244-9748
Dave Fenton, *Owner*
EMP: 94
SALES (est): 5.6MM **Privately Held**
SIC: 1542 Commercial & office building contractors

(P-1455)
DEACON CONSTRUCTION - CAL
7745 Greenback Ln Ste 250, Citrus Heights (95610-5865)
PHONE..................................916 969-0900
Richard Smith, *President*
Steven D Deacon, *CEO*
Julie Rodrigues, *Controller*
EMP: 70
SQ FT: 5,000
SALES (est): 397.8K
SALES (corp-wide): 391.5MM **Privately Held**
SIC: 1542 Commercial & office building, new construction
PA: Deacon Holdings, Inc.
7745 Greenback Ln Ste 250
Citrus Heights CA 95610
916 969-0900

(P-1456)
DEACON CORP
17880 Fitch, Irvine (92614-6002)
PHONE..................................949 222-9060
John Steffens, *Manager*
EMP: 60
SALES (corp-wide): 391.5MM **Privately Held**
WEB: www.deacon.com
SIC: 1542 Commercial & office building, new construction
PA: Deacon Holdings, Inc.
7745 Greenback Ln Ste 250
Citrus Heights CA 95610
916 969-0900

(P-1457)
DEACON HOLDINGS INC (PA)
7745 Greenback Ln Ste 250, Citrus Heights (95610-5865)
PHONE..................................916 969-0900
Steven D Deacon, *CEO*
Bob Miller, *Partner*
Richard Smith, *President*
Paul Cunha, *Vice Pres*
Pete Snook, *Principal*
EMP: 100
SQ FT: 5,000
SALES: 391.5MM **Privately Held**
WEB: www.deacon.com
SIC: 1542 Commercial & office building, new construction

(P-1458)
DEL AMO CONSTRUCTION
23840 Madison St, Torrance (90505-6009)
PHONE..................................310 378-6203
Steve Donahue, *CEO*
Ed Hong, *CFO*
Susan Donahue, *Corp Secy*
Jason Cave, *Vice Pres*
Harry Donahue, *Vice Pres*
EMP: 55
SQ FT: 4,000
SALES (est): 33.9MM **Privately Held**
SIC: 1542 1771 Commercial & office building, new construction; concrete work

(P-1459)
DESIGNED MBL SYSTEMS INDS INC
800 S State Highway 33, Patterson (95363-9148)
P.O. Box 367 (95363-0367)
PHONE..................................209 892-6298
David W Smith, *President*
Edward Smith, *Vice Pres*
EMP: 130
SQ FT: 100,000
SALES (est): 17MM **Privately Held**
WEB: www.dmsi-inc.com
SIC: 1542 2451 3448 2452 Design & erection, combined: non-residential; mobile classrooms; mobile buildings: for commercial use; prefabricated metal buildings; prefabricated wood buildings

(P-1460)
DEVCON CONSTRUCTION INC (PA)
690 Gibraltar Dr, Milpitas (95035-6317)
PHONE..................................408 942-8200
Gary Filizetti, *President*
Justine Pereira, *CFO*
Brett Sisney, *CFO*
Ken Sullivan, *Officer*
Jonathan Harvey, *Vice Pres*
EMP: 320
SQ FT: 45,000
SALES: 1.2B **Privately Held**
WEB: www.devcon-const.com
SIC: 1542 Commercial & office building, new construction

(P-1461)
DIANI BUILDING CORP (PA)
351 N Blosser Rd, Santa Maria (93458-4219)
P.O. Box 5757 (93456-5757)
PHONE..................................805 925-9533
Michael J Diani, *President*
Lowell Ledgerwood, *Treasurer*
Jeffrey Neal, *Senior VP*
Peter Hemesath, *Vice Pres*
Jason Diani, *Admin Sec*
EMP: 100
SQ FT: 11,000
SALES (est): 29.1MM **Privately Held**
SIC: 1542 Commercial & office building, new construction

(P-1462)
DIEDE CONSTRUCTION INC
12393 N Hwy 99, Lodi (95240-7269)
P.O. Box 1007, Woodbridge (95258-1007)
PHONE..................................209 369-8255
Steven L Diede, *President*
Lillian Diede, *Corp Secy*
Bruce J Diede, *Vice Pres*
Wayne J Diede, *Vice Pres*
Alyson Origone, *Accounting Mgr*
EMP: 100
SQ FT: 23,000
SALES (est): 68.8MM **Privately Held**
SIC: 1542 1771 1761 Commercial & office buildings, renovation & repair; foundation & footing contractor; roof repair

(P-1463)
DIVISION THREE CNSTR SVCS
30620 Plumas St, Lake Elsinore (92530-6915)
PHONE..................................951 609-3043
Steve Fisher, *President*
Randy Kendrick, *Shareholder*
EMP: 80
SALES (est): 5.7MM **Privately Held**
SIC: 1542 Commercial & office building contractors

(P-1464)
DMC CONSTRUCTION INCORPORATED
2110 Del Monte Ave, Monterey (93940-3712)
PHONE..................................831 656-1600
Dan McAweeney, *President*
Dan Mc Aweeney, *President*
EMP: 80
SQ FT: 3,500

SALES: 41MM **Privately Held**
SIC: 1542 1541 School building construction; hospital construction; commercial & office building, new construction; renovation, remodeling & repairs: industrial buildings; industrial buildings, new construction

(P-1465)
DPR CONSTRUCTION INC (PA)
1450 Veterans Blvd, Redwood City (94063-2617)
PHONE..................................650 474-1450
George Pfeffer, *President*
Brandon Liming, *Project Mgr*
Bala Purushothaman, *Project Engr*
Kenny Starling, *Project Engr*
Lucy Bailey, *Accountant*
▲ **EMP:** 1200
SQ FT: 36,300
SALES (est): 4.2B **Privately Held**
WEB: www.dprconstruction.com
SIC: 1542 Commercial & office building contractors

(P-1466)
DPR CONSTRUCTION A GEN PARTNR
1510 S Winchester Blvd, San Jose (95128-4334)
PHONE..................................408 370-2322
Jim Carter, *Manager*
George Achica, *Safety Mgr*
EMP: 50
SALES (corp-wide): 4.2B **Privately Held**
WEB: www.dprconstruction.com
SIC: 1542 Nonresidential construction
HQ: Dpr Construction, A General Partnership
1450 Veterans Blvd
Redwood City CA 94063

(P-1467)
DPR CONSTRUCTION A GEN PARTNR
2480 Natomas Park Dr # 100, Sacramento (95833-2979)
PHONE..................................916 568-3434
Trish Timothy, *Manager*
EMP: 300
SALES (corp-wide): 4.2B **Privately Held**
WEB: www.dprconstruction.com
SIC: 1542 Commercial & office building contractors
HQ: Dpr Construction, A General Partnership
1450 Veterans Blvd
Redwood City CA 94063

(P-1468)
DPR CONSTRUCTION A GEN PARTNR
5010 Shoreham Pl Ste 100, San Diego (92122-6900)
PHONE..................................858 646-0757
Peter Salvati, *Director*
EMP: 300
SALES (corp-wide): 4.2B **Privately Held**
WEB: www.dprconstruction.com
SIC: 1542 Commercial & office building contractors
HQ: Dpr Construction, A General Partnership
1450 Veterans Blvd
Redwood City CA 94063

(P-1469)
DPR CONSTRUCTION A GEN PARTNR
4665 Macarthur Ct Ste 100, Newport Beach (92660-1825)
PHONE..................................949 955-3771
Jim Washburn, *Regional Mgr*
EMP: 50
SALES (corp-wide): 4.2B **Privately Held**
WEB: www.dprconstruction.com
SIC: 1542 Commercial & office building contractors

HQ: Dpr Construction, A General Partnership
1450 Veterans Blvd
Redwood City CA 94063

(P-1470)
DPR CONSTRUCTION A GEN PARTNR (HQ)
1450 Veterans Blvd, Redwood City (94063-2617)
PHONE..................650 474-1450
George Pfeffer, *President*
Michele Leiva, *CFO*
Ron J Davidowski, *Corp Secy*
James F Dolen, *Exec VP*
Michael Ford, *Exec VP*
EMP: 6500
SQ FT: 36,300
SALES (est): 2.3B
SALES (corp-wide): 4.2B **Privately Held**
SIC: 1542 Nonresidential construction
PA: Dpr Construction, Inc.
1450 Veterans Blvd
Redwood City CA 94063
650 474-1450

(P-1471)
DRAGADOS/FLATIRON JOINT VENTR
14555 S Peach Ave, Selma (93662-9657)
PHONE..................559 847-5388
EMP: 93
SALES (corp-wide): 19.1MM **Privately Held**
SIC: 1542 Nonresidential construction
PA: Dragados/Flatiron Joint Venture
1775 Park St Ste 75
Selma CA 93662
559 558-5213

(P-1472)
EAGLE LATH & PLASTER INC
4350 Warehouse Ct, North Highlands (95660-5809)
PHONE..................916 925-1435
Robert P Milani, *President*
EMP: 100 EST: 2010
SQ FT: 10,000
SALES: 10MM **Privately Held**
SIC: 1542 Commercial & office building contractors

(P-1473)
ELEVEN WESTERN BUILDERS INC (PA)
2862 Executive Pl, Escondido (92029-1524)
PHONE..................760 796-6346
Rick W Backus, *CEO*
Richard Huey, *CFO*
Vern Alderton, *Vice Pres*
Tamara J Backus, *Admin Sec*
Erik Bracone, *Info Tech Mgr*
EMP: 110
SQ FT: 20,000
SALES (est): 56.3MM **Privately Held**
SIC: 1542 Commercial & office building, new construction

(P-1474)
EMS CONSTRUCTION INC
3276 Highland Dr, Carlsbad (92008-1918)
PHONE..................858 679-8292
Charles S Speck, *President*
Sean Speck, *President*
Marybeth Edwards, *Vice Pres*
EMP: 75
SALES (est): 12.9MM **Privately Held**
SIC: 1542 Nonresidential construction

(P-1475)
ENVIRONMENTAL CONSTRUCTION INC
21550 Oxnard St Ste 1060, Woodland Hills (91367-7123)
PHONE..................818 449-8920
Farid Soroudi, *CEO*
Zia Abhari, *President*
EMP: 90
SQ FT: 2,500
SALES (est): 37.3MM **Privately Held**
SIC: 1542 Commercial & office building contractors

(P-1476)
ERICKSON-HALL CONSTRUCTION CO (PA)
500 Corporate Dr, Escondido (92029-1517)
PHONE..................760 796-7700
Dave Erickson, *CEO*
Mike Hall, *COO*
Mike Conroy, *CFO*
Chris Bartok, *Admin Sec*
Evelyn Zaragoza, *Administration*
EMP: 88
SALES (est): 45.5MM **Privately Held**
WEB: www.ericksonhall.com
SIC: 1542 Commercial & office building, new construction

(P-1477)
F & H CONSTRUCTION (PA)
1115 E Lockeford St, Lodi (95240-0878)
P.O. Box 2329 (95241-2329)
PHONE..................209 931-3738
Charles Allen Ferrell, *President*
Dan Blackburn, *Partner*
Stephen Seibly, *Corp Secy*
Harold Erwin Jones, *Vice Pres*
Dana Leatherwood, *Project Mgr*
EMP: 75 EST: 1972
SQ FT: 8,000
SALES: 81MM **Privately Held**
SIC: 1542 1541 Commercial & office building, new construction; industrial buildings, new construction

(P-1478)
FINE LINE GROUP INC
457 Minna St, San Francisco (94103-2914)
PHONE..................415 777-4070
John S Santori, *Ch of Bd*
Robert M Helmers, *Exec VP*
EMP: 50
SQ FT: 7,000
SALES (est): 7.1MM **Privately Held**
WEB: www.finelinegroup.com
SIC: 1542 Commercial & office buildings, renovation & repair

(P-1479)
FRANK SCHIPPER CONSTRUCTION CO
Also Called: Fscc
610 E Cota St, Santa Barbara (93103-3166)
P.O. Box 246 (93102-0246)
PHONE..................805 963-4359
Frank Schipper, *President*
Arlan Schipper, *Vice Pres*
Paul Wieckowski, *Vice Pres*
Marc Cunningham, *Project Mgr*
Matt Scranton, *Project Mgr*
EMP: 50
SQ FT: 2,200
SALES (est): 13.1MM **Privately Held**
SIC: 1542 8742 1611 Commercial & office buildings, renovation & repair; commercial & office building, new construction; business consultant; general contractor, highway & street construction

(P-1480)
GENERATION CONSTRUCTION INC
15650 El Prado Rd, Chino (91710-9108)
P.O. Box 991 (91708-0991)
PHONE..................909 923-2077
Antwan De Paul, *President*
Tony Dakwar, *General Mgr*
Alicia Nash, *Financial Exec*
EMP: 150
SALES (est): 33.3MM **Privately Held**
SIC: 1542 Commercial & office buildings, renovation & repair

(P-1481)
GILBANE BUILDING COMPANY
2033 Gateway Pl Ste 450, San Jose (95110-3726)
PHONE..................408 660-4400
Matthew Tierney, *Branch Mgr*
EMP: 100
SALES (corp-wide): 5.4B **Privately Held**
SIC: 1542 Nonresidential construction
HQ: Gilbane Building Company
7 Jackson Walkway Ste 2
Providence RI 02903
401 456-5800

(P-1482)
GILBANE SMCC LLC
1655 Grant St 12f, Concord (94520-2600)
PHONE..................925 946-3100
Lenoard Garner, *Admin Sec*
EMP: 99
SQ FT: 24,408
SALES (est): 3MM **Privately Held**
SIC: 1542 Nonresidential construction

(P-1483)
GOLDCOAST LIQUIDATING LLC
Also Called: Cwn Management
27845 Snta Margarita Pkwy, Mission Viejo (92691-6701)
PHONE..................949 461-7170
Robert Ott, *Branch Mgr*
EMP: 110
SALES (corp-wide): 126.6MM **Privately Held**
SIC: 1542 Restaurant construction
PA: Goldcoast Liquidating, Llc
1510 West Loop S
Houston TX 77027

(P-1484)
GOLDEN COAST CNSTR RESTORATION
4811 Chippendale Dr # 301, Sacramento (95841-2552)
PHONE..................916 955-7461
Alex Kotyakov, *President*
EMP: 68
SALES: 10MM **Privately Held**
SIC: 1542 1521 Commercial & office buildings, renovation & repair; new construction, single-family houses

(P-1485)
GRANI INSTALLATION INC (PA)
5411 Commercial Dr, Huntington Beach (92649-1231)
PHONE..................714 898-0441
Gregory A Grani, *CEO*
Manisha Phanasgaonkar, *Officer*
Garrett Price, *Project Mgr*
Henry Uranga, *Project Mgr*
Kristy Pletyak, *Controller*
EMP: 100
SQ FT: 6,000
SALES (est): 41.2MM **Privately Held**
SIC: 1542 1742 Commercial & office buildings, renovation & repair; acoustical & ceiling work

(P-1486)
GREEN VALLEY CORPORATION (PA)
Also Called: Swenson, Barry Builder
777 N 1st St Fl 5, San Jose (95112-6350)
PHONE..................408 287-0246
C Barron Swenson, *Chairman*
Case Swenson, *President*
Lee Ann Woodard, *CFO*
Steven W Andrews, *Senior VP*
Ronald L Cot, *Senior VP*
▲ EMP: 50 EST: 1961
SQ FT: 12,000
SALES (est): 68.9MM **Privately Held**
WEB: www.barryswensonbuilder.com
SIC: 1542 1522 6512 Commercial & office building, new construction; multi-family dwelling construction; commercial & industrial building operation

(P-1487)
H2C2 & ASSOCIATES INC (PA)
6925 San Leandro St, Oakland (94621-3320)
PHONE..................510 562-6181
Mike Christie, *President*
Richard Cleveland, *Corp Secy*
Marvin Henderson, *Vice Pres*
EMP: 50
SALES (est): 42.4MM **Privately Held**
SIC: 1542 1795 Commercial & office building contractors; demolition, buildings & other structures

(P-1488)
HARDISTY CONSTRUCTION ADMINIST
410 W 30th St Ste A, National City (91950-7269)
PHONE..................619 245-6828
John T Hardisty, *President*
Wade Lindsay, *Vice Pres*
EMP: 70
SALES (est): 9MM **Privately Held**
SIC: 1542 1521 1522 Nonresidential construction; single-family housing construction; residential construction

(P-1489)
HAREL GENERAL CONTRACTORS INC
6015 Washington Blvd, Culver City (90232-7425)
PHONE..................310 558-8304
Gill Harel, *President*
Ron Harel, *Vice Pres*
EMP: 50
SALES (est): 6.8MM **Privately Held**
WEB: www.harelgc.com
SIC: 1542 Commercial & office building, new construction

(P-1490)
HARPER CONSTRUCTION CO INC (PA)
2241 Kettner Blvd Ste 300, San Diego (92101-1769)
PHONE..................619 233-7900
Jeffrey A Harper, *CEO*
Jeff Harper, *CEO*
Ron Harper, *Chairman*
Stephen Marble, *Vice Pres*
Peter Wheeler, *Project Mgr*
EMP: 55
SQ FT: 17,000
SALES (est): 87.6MM **Privately Held**
SIC: 1542 1521 Commercial & office building, new construction; single-family housing construction

(P-1491)
HARRIS CONSTRUCTION CO INC
5286 E Home Ave, Fresno (93727-2103)
PHONE..................559 251-0301
Mike Spencer, *President*
Timothy Thornton, *CFO*
Richard F Spencer, *Chairman*
Courtney Miller, *Project Mgr*
Tim Thornton, *Director*
▲ EMP: 150 EST: 1914
SQ FT: 6,000
SALES (est): 59.2MM **Privately Held**
SIC: 1542 1541 Hospital construction; commercial & office building, new construction; food products manufacturing or packing plant construction

(P-1492)
HARVEY INC
Also Called: Harvey General Contracting
9455 Ridgehaven Ct # 200, San Diego (92123-1649)
PHONE..................858 769-4000
Stephen Harvey, *CEO*
Paul J Pietsch, *Vice Pres*
EMP: 125
SALES: 30.9MM **Privately Held**
SIC: 1542 Commercial & office building, new construction

(P-1493)
HATHAWAY DINWIDDIE CNSTR CO
565 Laurelwood Rd, Santa Clara (95054-2419)
PHONE..................415 986-2718
Greg Cosko, *President*
David A Lee, *Senior VP*
EMP: 100
SQ FT: 7,000
SALES (est): 18.6MM **Privately Held**
SIC: 1542 Commercial & office building, new construction

PRODUCTS & SVCS

(P-1494)
HATHAWAY DINWIDDIE CNSTR CO
275 Battery St Ste 300, San Francisco (94111-3378)
PHONE..................415 986-2718
Greg Cosko, *CEO*
Gordon D Smith, *Senior VP*
Ed Conlon, *Vice Pres*
Kelly Owens, *Office Admin*
Gayle Angulo, *Admin Sec*
▲ **EMP:** 400
SQ FT: 21,000
SALES (est): 158.5MM **Privately Held**
WEB: www.hdcco.com
SIC: 1542 Commercial & office building, new construction
PA: Hathaway Dinwiddie Construction Group
275 Battery St Ste 300
San Francisco CA 94111

(P-1495)
HATHAWAY DINWIDDIE CNSTR GROUP (PA)
275 Battery St Ste 300, San Francisco (94111-3378)
PHONE..................415 986-2718
Greg Cosko, *CEO*
David Miller, *CFO*
Stephen E Smith, *Senior VP*
Stephen W McCoid, *Vice Pres*
Amy Maclear, *Executive*
EMP: 60
SQ FT: 18,000
SALES (est): 158.5MM **Privately Held**
SIC: 1542 Commercial & office building, new construction

(P-1496)
HENSEL PHELPS CONSTRUCTION CO
5271 Viewridge Ct Frnt, San Diego (92123-1604)
PHONE..................858 266-7979
Scott Schilling, *Manager*
EMP: 60
SALES (corp-wide): 4.6B **Privately Held**
SIC: 1542 Commercial & office building, new construction
PA: Hensel Phelps Construction Co.
420 6th Ave
Greeley CO 80631
970 352-6565

(P-1497)
HENSEL PHELPS CONSTRUCTION CO
226 Airport Pkwy Ste 150, San Jose (95110-1024)
PHONE..................408 452-1800
Jon W Ball, *Vice Pres*
Crystal Camarena, *Assistant*
EMP: 200
SALES (corp-wide): 4.6B **Privately Held**
WEB: www.henselphelps.com
SIC: 1542 1541 Commercial & office building contractors; industrial buildings & warehouses
PA: Hensel Phelps Construction Co.
420 6th Ave
Greeley CO 80631
970 352-6565

(P-1498)
HENSEL PHELPS CONSTRUCTION CO
9404 Genesee Ave Ste 140, La Jolla (92037-1353)
PHONE..................619 544-6828
Thom Diersbock, *Branch Mgr*
EMP: 70
SALES (corp-wide): 4.6B **Privately Held**
SIC: 1542 Commercial & office building contractors
PA: Hensel Phelps Construction Co.
420 6th Ave
Greeley CO 80631
970 352-6565

(P-1499)
HENSEL PHELPS CONSTRUCTION CO
18850 Von Karman 100, Irvine (92612)
PHONE..................949 852-0111
Cuyler R McGinley, *Branch Mgr*
EMP: 200
SALES (corp-wide): 4.6B **Privately Held**
SIC: 1542 Nonresidential construction
PA: Hensel Phelps Construction Co.
420 6th Ave
Greeley CO 80631
970 352-6565

(P-1500)
HILBERS INC
Also Called: Hilbers Contractors & Engrg
770 N Walton Ave Ste 100, Yuba City (95993-9469)
PHONE..................530 673-2947
Kurt G Hilbers, *President*
Doug Heacock, *COO*
Glenn Hilbers, *Treasurer*
Larry E Hilbers, *Vice Pres*
Tom Jones, *Vice Pres*
EMP: 75
SQ FT: 6,790
SALES: 121.7MM **Privately Held**
WEB: www.hilbersinc.com
SIC: 1542 1541 Commercial & office building, new construction; industrial buildings, new construction

(P-1501)
HOLBROOK CONSTRUCTION INC
9814 Norwalk Blvd Ste 200, Santa Fe Springs (90670-2992)
PHONE..................714 523-1150
Laurence A Holbrook, *President*
Richard Holbrook, *CFO*
Lisa Garcia, *Controller*
EMP: 75
SQ FT: 3,000
SALES (est): 4.4MM **Privately Held**
WEB: www.holbrookconstruction.net
SIC: 1542 Commercial & office building, new construction

(P-1502)
HOUALLA ENTERPRISES LTD
Also Called: Metro Bldrs & Engineers Group
2610 Avon St, Newport Beach (92663-4706)
PHONE..................949 515-4350
Fouad Houalla, *President*
Shelly Irvine, *Admin Asst*
▲ **EMP:** 85
SQ FT: 1,200
SALES (est): 26MM **Privately Held**
SIC: 1542 Commercial & office building, new construction; specialized public building contractors

(P-1503)
HOWARD BUILDING CORPORATION (PA)
707 Wilshire Blvd # 3750, Los Angeles (90017-3535)
PHONE..................213 683-1850
Paul McGunnigle, *CEO*
Michael Howard, *President*
Don Fraser, *Exec VP*
Matt Loorya, *Vice Pres*
Craig Roalf, *Vice Pres*
EMP: 152
SQ FT: 11,325
SALES: 364.3MM **Privately Held**
WEB: www.howardbuilding.com
SIC: 1542 Commercial & office building, new construction

(P-1504)
HPM CONSTRUCTION LLC
17911 Mitchell S, Irvine (92614-6015)
PHONE..................949 474-9170
Karen Price, *President*
Cuyler McGinley, *Corp Secy*
Cindy McMackin, *Vice Pres*
Hensel Phelps Construction,
Morrow-Meadows Corporation,
EMP: 100 **EST:** 2012
SALES: 300MM
SALES (corp-wide): 4.6B **Privately Held**
SIC: 1542 Nonresidential construction

(P-1505)
I WMI
17100 Pioneer Blvd # 230, Artesia (90701-2776)
PHONE..................562 977-4906
David T Gajdzik, *President*
Chris Gajdzik, *CFO*
EMP: 280
SALES: 40MM **Privately Held**
SIC: 1542 Commercial & office building contractors

(P-1506)
J B COMPANY
1825 Bell St Ste 100, Sacramento (95825-1020)
PHONE..................916 929-3003
EMP: 70
SQ FT: 24,000
SALES (est): 5.8MM **Privately Held**
SIC: 1542 1541

(P-1507)
J M C INTERNATIONAL LLC
1470 W Herndon Ave # 100, Fresno (93711-0552)
PHONE..................559 256-1300
Paul Owhadi,
EMP: 50
SQ FT: 14,000
SALES: 22MM **Privately Held**
SIC: 1542 1522 Commercial & office building contractors; residential construction

(P-1508)
J R ROBERTS CORP (HQ)
7745 Greenback Ln Ste 300, Citrus Heights (95610-5866)
PHONE..................916 729-5600
Robert Olsen, *CEO*
Robert C Hall Jr, *President*
Maura Moylan, *CFO*
Mike Vinks, *Vice Pres*
EMP: 100
SQ FT: 9,000
SALES (est): 20.8MM
SALES (corp-wide): 391.5MM **Privately Held**
SIC: 1542 Commercial & office building, new construction
PA: Deacon Holdings, Inc.
7745 Greenback Ln Ste 250
Citrus Heights CA 95610
916 969-0900

(P-1509)
J R ROBERTS ENTERPRISES INC
7745 Greenback Ln Ste 300, Citrus Heights (95610-5866)
PHONE..................916 729-5600
Robert F Olsen, *Ch of Bd*
Robert C Hall Jr, *President*
James F Reilly, *Corp Secy*
EMP: 110
SALES (est): 11.6MM **Privately Held**
WEB: www.jrroberts.com
SIC: 1542 1522 Commercial & office building contractors; multi-family dwellings, new construction; remodeling, multi-family dwellings

(P-1510)
JACOBS ENGINEERING GROUP INC
4435 First St, Livermore (94551-4915)
PHONE..................925 423-7564
Arlene Emmert, *Branch Mgr*
Mark Zygutis, *Project Mgr*
EMP: 90
SALES (corp-wide): 14.9B **Publicly Held**
SIC: 1542 Commercial & office building, new construction
PA: Jacobs Engineering Group Inc.
1999 Bryan St Ste 1200
Dallas TX 75201
214 583-8500

(P-1511)
JAYNES CORPORATION CALIFORNIA
111 Elm St Fl 4, San Diego (92101-2649)
P.O. Box 26841, Albuquerque NM (87125-6841)
PHONE..................619 233-4080
Donald Power, *CEO*
Wayne Davenport, *Corp Secy*
Rick Marquardt, *Exec VP*
Richard Cohen, *Senior VP*
EMP: 105
SALES (est): 12.8MM
SALES (corp-wide): 12.3MM **Privately Held**
WEB: www.janescorp.com
SIC: 1542 Commercial & office building contractors
HQ: Jaynes Corporation
2906 Broadway Blvd Ne
Albuquerque NM 87107
505 345-8591

(P-1512)
JM STREAMLINE INC
Also Called: Streamline Construction
154 Scandling Ave, Grass Valley (95945-5816)
PHONE..................530 272-6806
Jesse McKenna, *President*
EMP: 55
SALES: 10.3MM **Privately Held**
SIC: 1542 Commercial & office building contractors

(P-1513)
JOHN F OTTO INC
Also Called: OTTO CONSTRUCTION
1717 2nd St, Sacramento (95811-6214)
PHONE..................916 441-6870
Carl Barrett, *President*
Carol Otto, *Corp Secy*
Allison Otto, *Vice Pres*
Elease Terry, *Vice Pres*
EMP: 120 **EST:** 1958
SQ FT: 10,000
SALES: 107.8MM **Privately Held**
WEB: www.ottoconstruction.com
SIC: 1542 1541 Commercial & office building, new construction; industrial buildings, new construction

(P-1514)
JOHN M FRANK CONSTRUCTION INC
Also Called: John M Frank Service Group
913 E 4th St, Santa Ana (92701-4748)
PHONE..................714 210-3600
John M Frank, *CEO*
Myra Mageo, *Officer*
Laurie Dawson, *Admin Sec*
Shaun Bell, *Safety Dir*
EMP: 80
SALES (est): 22.1MM **Privately Held**
WEB: www.cscconcreteservices.com
SIC: 1542 5411 Commercial & office building, new construction; commercial & office buildings, renovation & repair; supermarkets; family restaurants; restaurant, lunch counter

(P-1515)
JOHN PLANE CONSTRUCTION INC
661 Hayne Rd, Hillsborough (94010-7006)
PHONE..................415 468-0555
John Plane, *President*
Paul Grech, *Vice Pres*
Betty Sullivan, *Receptionist*
EMP: 120
SQ FT: 4,500
SALES: 8.7MM **Privately Held**
WEB: www.johnplane.com
SIC: 1542 Commercial & office building, new construction

(P-1516)
JR CONSTRUCTION INC
8123 Engineer Rd, San Diego (92111-1907)
PHONE..................858 505-4760
Ramon B Camacho, *President*
EMP: 70

SALES (est): 14.8MM **Privately Held**
WEB: www.jrconstruction.net
SIC: 1542 Nonresidential construction

(P-1517)
JUNE A GROTHE CONSTRUCTION INC
Also Called: J G Construction
15632 El Prado Rd, Chino (91710-9108)
PHONE..............................909 993-9393
Jack Grothe, *Principal*
June A Grothe, *CEO*
Wally Clark, *Vice Pres*
EMP: 65
SQ FT: 15,500
SALES: 32.9MM **Privately Held**
SIC: 1542 Shopping center construction

(P-1518)
KADENA PACIFIC INC
3421 Gato Ct Ste A, Riverside (92507-6819)
PHONE..............................951 990-7865
Fred Neff, *President*
Scott Bailey, *Treasurer*
Beverly Bailey, *Admin Sec*
EMP: 50
SALES (est): 4.9MM **Privately Held**
WEB: www.kadenapacific.com
SIC: 1542 Nonresidential construction

(P-1519)
KARSYN CONSTRUCTION INC
4697 W Jacquelyn Ave, Fresno (93722-6413)
PHONE..............................559 271-2900
Joseph C Parker, *President*
Judith Parnell, *CFO*
Kristin Parker, *Corp Secy*
EMP: 60
SALES (est): 15.5MM **Privately Held**
WEB: www.karsyn.com
SIC: 1542 Commercial & office building, new construction

(P-1520)
KEENAN HOPKINS SUDER & STOWELL
Also Called: Khss Contractors
5109 E La Palma Ave Ste A, Anaheim (92807-2066)
PHONE..............................714 695-3670
Doug Downing, *Manager*
Kim Guzman, *Administration*
Nichole Schwarz, *Engineer*
Joseph Mello, *Sr Project Mgr*
Andrea Peltier, *Assistant*
EMP: 100
SALES (corp-wide): 253MM **Privately Held**
SIC: 1542 1742 Nonresidential construction; drywall
PA: Keenan, Hopkins, Suder & Stowell Contractors, Inc.
   5109 E La Palma Ave Ste A
   Anaheim CA 92807
   714 695-3670

(P-1521)
KIE-CON INC
3551 Wilbur Ave, Antioch (94509-8530)
PHONE..............................925 754-9494
Allen Kung, *President*
Mike Porter, *Plant Supt*
EMP: 90
SALES (est): 13.6MM
SALES (corp-wide): 16.1B **Privately Held**
SIC: 1542 Commercial & office building contractors
HQ: Kiewit Corporation
   3555 Farnam St Ste 1000
   Omaha NE 68131
   402 342-2052

(P-1522)
KIEWIT CORPORATION
Also Called: Keiwit Infrastructure West Co
4650 Business Center Dr, Fairfield (94534-6890)
PHONE..............................707 439-7300
Jeff Petersen, *Branch Mgr*
John Nsey, *General Mgr*
John Hassard, *Administration*
Dave Hazen, *Project Mgr*
Brian Gardner, *Manager*
EMP: 80

SALES (corp-wide): 16.1B **Privately Held**
SIC: 1542 Nonresidential construction
HQ: Kiewit Corporation
   3555 Farnam St Ste 1000
   Omaha NE 68131
   402 342-2052

(P-1523)
KIEWIT CORPORATION
10704 Shoemaker Ave, Santa Fe Springs (90670-4040)
PHONE..............................907 222-9350
EMP: 80
SALES (corp-wide): 16.1B **Privately Held**
SIC: 1542 Nonresidential construction
HQ: Kiewit Corporation
   3555 Farnam St Ste 1000
   Omaha NE 68131
   402 342-2052

(P-1524)
KLASSEN CORPORATION (PA)
2021 Westwind Dr, Bakersfield (93301-3015)
PHONE..............................661 327-0875
Jerry D Klassen, *President*
Bob Klassen, *COO*
Troy Fringer, *CFO*
Ed Childres, *Vice Pres*
Mark Delmarter, *Vice Pres*
EMP: 70
SQ FT: 7,981
SALES (est): 27.3MM **Privately Held**
WEB: www.klassencorp.com
SIC: 1542 Commercial & office building, new construction

(P-1525)
KPRS CONSTRUCTION SERVICES INC (PA)
2850 Saturn St Ste 110, Brea (92821-1701)
PHONE..............................714 672-0800
Joel H Stensby, *President*
Lev Rabinovich, *Treasurer*
Paul Kristedja, *Vice Pres*
Keith Taylor, *Executive*
Lela Bernal, *Office Mgr*
EMP: 95 **EST:** 1995
SQ FT: 31,000
SALES: 546.9MM **Privately Held**
WEB: www.kprsinc.com
SIC: 1542 8711 Commercial & office building, new construction; building construction consultant

(P-1526)
LAMON CONSTRUCTION COMPANY INC
871 Von Geldern Way, Yuba City (95991-4215)
P.O. Box 632 (95992-0632)
PHONE..............................530 671-1370
Henry S Lamon, *President*
Steve Ithurum, *Vice Pres*
Ken Northon, *Vice Pres*
EMP: 50 **EST:** 1952
SQ FT: 3,200
SALES: 7.8MM **Privately Held**
WEB: www.lamonconstruction.com
SIC: 1542 Commercial & office building, new construction

(P-1527)
LEDESMA & MEYER CNSTR CO INC
9441 Haven Ave, Rancho Cucamonga (91730-5845)
PHONE..............................909 297-1100
Joseph M Ledesma, *CEO*
Kris Meyer, *President*
Tom Smith, *Opers Staff*
Jeff Jaso, *Superintendent*
EMP: 55
SALES (est): 8.1MM **Privately Held**
SIC: 1542 School building construction

(P-1528)
LEVEL 10 CONSTRUCTION LP
1050 Entp Way Ste 250, Sunnyvale (94089)
PHONE..............................408 747-5000
Dennis Giles, *President*
Jim Evans, *CFO*
Kevin Englund, *Vice Pres*

Kevin Fettig, *Vice Pres*
Mike Castillo, *Executive*
EMP: 220 **EST:** 2011
SQ FT: 12,000
SALES: 200MM **Privately Held**
SIC: 1542 Commercial & office buildings, renovation & repair

(P-1529)
LEVEL-IT INSTALLATIONS LTD
2443 Fillmore St, San Francisco (94115-1814)
PHONE..............................604 942-2022
Colin Rimes, *CEO*
Todd Isackson, *Admin Sec*
Angie Marston, *Manager*
EMP: 50 **EST:** 2014
SQ FT: 15,000
SALES: 12MM
SALES (corp-wide): 10.2MM **Privately Held**
SIC: 1542 Commercial & office building contractors
PA: Level It Installations Ltd
   1515 Broadway St Unit 804
   Port Coquitlam BC V3C 6
   604 942-2022

(P-1530)
LMC HOLLYWOOD HIGHLAND
Also Called: Lennar Multi Family Community
95 Enterprise Ste 200, Aliso Viejo (92656-2611)
PHONE..............................949 448-1600
Todd Farrell, *CEO*
EMP: 500 **EST:** 2013
SALES (est): 24.3MM **Privately Held**
SIC: 1542 Commercial & office building contractors

(P-1531)
LUSARDI CONSTRUCTION CO
6376 Clark Ave, Dublin (94568-3036)
PHONE..............................925 829-1114
Kurt Evans, *Manager*
EMP: 200
SALES (corp-wide): 129.1MM **Privately Held**
SIC: 1542 Commercial & office building, new construction
PA: Lusardi Construction Co.
   1570 Linda Vista Dr
   San Marcos CA 92078
   760 744-3133

(P-1532)
M P M & ASSOCIATES INC
7011 Hayvenhurst Ave F, Van Nuys (91406-3822)
PHONE..............................818 708-9676
Parviz Danesh, *General Mgr*
EMP: 100
SQ FT: 9,000
SALES: 2MM **Privately Held**
WEB: www.mpmassociates.com
SIC: 1542 Commercial & office building, new construction; shopping center construction

(P-1533)
MALLCRAFT INC
2225 Windsor Ave, Altadena (91001-5306)
P.O. Box 91983, Pasadena (91109-1983)
PHONE..............................626 765-9100
Gerald L Fishbein, *Ch of Bd*
Leslie E Hansen, *President*
Sheena E Pappas, *Vice Pres*
Sheena Pappas, *Vice Pres*
Jill Garber, *Admin Sec*
EMP: 50
SQ FT: 5,000
SALES (est): 11.2MM **Privately Held**
WEB: www.mallcraft.com
SIC: 1542 Commercial & office building, new construction

(P-1534)
MARK DIVERSIFIED INC
650 Howe Ave Ste 1045, Sacramento (95825-4700)
PHONE..............................916 923-6275
David Mark, *President*
Cecil J Mark, *Officer*
EMP: 50
SQ FT: 16,000

SALES: 30MM **Privately Held**
SIC: 1542 1541 Commercial & office building, new construction; industrial buildings, new construction

(P-1535)
MARK SCOTT CONSTRUCTION INC (PA)
Also Called: M S
2835 Contra Costa Blvd, Pleasant Hill (94523-4221)
P.O. Box 4658, Walnut Creek (94596-0658)
PHONE..............................925 944-0502
Mark A Scott, *CEO*
Vince Curtis, *Project Mgr*
Frank Gagliardi, *Project Mgr*
Ralph Huddleston, *Project Mgr*
Sandra Madani, *Project Mgr*
EMP: 50
SQ FT: 16,000
SALES (est): 65.2MM **Privately Held**
WEB: www.msconstruction.com
SIC: 1542 Commercial & office building, new construction

(P-1536)
MATT-COLOMBO A JOINT VENTURE
9814 Norwalk Blvd Ste 100, Santa Fe Springs (90670-2997)
PHONE..............................562 903-2277
Paul Matt, *Partner*
Faron Vandissel, *Manager*
EMP: 99
SALES: 950K **Privately Held**
SIC: 1542 Commercial & office building, new construction

(P-1537)
MATTHEW BURNS
Also Called: Act Associates
617 Flower Dr, Folsom (95630-4816)
PHONE..............................209 676-4940
EMP: 60
SALES (est): 6.2MM **Privately Held**
SIC: 1542 0851

(P-1538)
MCCARTHY BLDG COMPANIES INC
20401 Sw Birch St Ste 200, Newport Beach (92660-1796)
PHONE..............................949 851-8383
Tony Church, *Vice Pres*
Eric Israel, *Project Engr*
Amit Kale, *Manager*
EMP: 347
SALES (corp-wide): 3.9B **Privately Held**
SIC: 1542 1541 Institutional building construction; commercial & office building, new construction; industrial buildings, new construction
HQ: Mccarthy Building Companies, Inc.
   1341 N Rock Hill Rd
   Saint Louis MO 63124
   314 968-3300

(P-1539)
MCCARTHY BLDG COMPANIES INC
Southern California Division
20401 Sw Birch St Ste 300, Newport Beach (92660-1798)
PHONE..............................949 851-8383
Randy Highland, *Branch Mgr*
EMP: 75
SALES (corp-wide): 3.9B **Privately Held**
WEB: www.mccarthy.com
SIC: 1542 Commercial & office building contractors
HQ: Mccarthy Building Companies, Inc.
   1341 N Rock Hill Rd
   Saint Louis MO 63124
   314 968-3300

(P-1540)
MCCUEN CONSTRUCTION INC (PA)
3269 Swetzer Rd, Loomis (95650-7607)
PHONE..............................916 652-7824
Trenton B McCuen, *President*
EMP: 50
SQ FT: 1,300

SALES (est): 10.7MM **Privately Held**
WEB: www.mccueco.com
SIC: 1542 Commercial & office building
contractors

(P-1541)
MENEMSHA DEVELOPMENT GROUP INC (PA)
Also Called: Menemsha Solutions
20521 Earl St, Torrance (90503-3006)
PHONE..........................310 343-3430
John V Daigle, *CEO*
Robert Baldassari, *Project Mgr*
EMP: 130
SQ FT: 10,000
SALES: 50.6MM **Privately Held**
SIC: 1542 8741 8712 7373 Commercial & office building contractors; construction management; architectural services; computer-aided design (CAD) systems service

(P-1542)
MERUELO ENTERPRISES INC (PA)
9550 Firestone Blvd # 105, Downey (90241-5560)
PHONE..........................562 745-2300
Alex Meruelo, *CEO*
David Fehrenbach, *CFO*
Al Stoller, *CFO*
Joe Marchica, *Vice Pres*
EMP: 501
SALES (est): 377.5MM **Privately Held**
SIC: 1542 Nonresidential construction

(P-1543)
MICHAEL REYES
Also Called: Bender Miles Construction
577 N D St Ste 111a14, San Bernardino (92401-1324)
PHONE..........................909 444-0120
Michael Reyes, *Owner*
EMP: 125
SQ FT: 1,600
SALES: 300K **Privately Held**
SIC: 1542 Nonresidential construction

(P-1544)
MICON CONSTRUCTION CAL INC
1616 Sierra Madre Cir, Placentia (92870-6626)
PHONE..........................714 666-0203
Gene F Holle, *Principal*
Rashmi Shah, *Bookkeeper*
EMP: 54
SQ FT: 9,000
SALES (est): 9.8MM **Privately Held**
WEB: www.miconconstruction.com
SIC: 1542 1771 0782 Nonresidential construction; concrete work; landscape contractors

(P-1545)
MOOREFIELD CONSTRUCTION INC (PA)
600 N Tustin Ave Ste 210, Santa Ana (92705-3781)
PHONE..........................714 972-0700
Ann Moorefield, *CEO*
Mike Moorefield, *President*
Hal Moorefield, *Vice Pres*
Larry Moorefield, *Vice Pres*
Noel Campos, *Project Engr*
EMP: 60
SQ FT: 8,490
SALES: 222.9MM **Privately Held**
WEB: www.moorefieldconst.com
SIC: 1542 Shopping center construction; commercial & office building, new construction

(P-1546)
MTM & THOMASVILLE CO
16035 Phoenix Dr, City of Industry (91745-1624)
PHONE..........................626 934-1112
Howard Lee, *Owner*
EMP: 51
SALES (est): 2.6MM **Privately Held**
SIC: 1542 Nonresidential construction

(P-1547)
MURPHY-TRUE INC
Also Called: Jim Murphy & Associates
464 Kenwood Ct Ste B, Santa Rosa (95407-5709)
PHONE..........................707 576-7337
Jim M Murphy, *CEO*
Leighton J True III, *Vice Pres*
Danny Arrow, *Project Mgr*
Tom Fruiht, *Project Mgr*
Andrew Supinger, *Project Mgr*
EMP: 60
SQ FT: 5,000
SALES: 35.1MM **Privately Held**
SIC: 1542 1521 Commercial & office building, new construction; new construction, single-family houses

(P-1548)
NATIONAL CONSTRUCTION & MAINT
Also Called: NCM
23846 Sunnymead Blvd # 10, Moreno Valley (92553-7737)
PHONE..........................909 888-7042
John Omar Blanco, *CEO*
EMP: 50
SQ FT: 600
SALES (est): 16.4MM **Privately Held**
SIC: 1542 Commercial & office building contractors

(P-1549)
NEAR-CAL CORP
512 Chaney St, Lake Elsinore (92530-2747)
PHONE..........................951 245-5400
Carl J Johnson, *Ch of Bd*
John Jacobs, *Vice Pres*
Mary Saenz, *Admin Sec*
Dwight Johnson, *Project Mgr*
Steven Lewis, *Project Mgr*
EMP: 50
SQ FT: 10,000
SALES (est): 19.1MM **Privately Held**
WEB: www.nearcal.com
SIC: 1542 1541 Commercial & office building, new construction; factory construction

(P-1550)
NEVELL GROUP INC (PA)
Also Called: N G I
3001 Enterprise St # 200, Brea (92821-6210)
PHONE..........................714 579-7501
Michael J Nevell, *President*
Bryan Bodine, *CFO*
Bruce Pasqua, *Senior VP*
Troy Chavez, *Project Mgr*
Amber Cortes, *Purchasing*
EMP: 125
SQ FT: 35,000
SALES: 120.5MM **Privately Held**
SIC: 1542 Commercial & office building, new construction

(P-1551)
NEXT VENTURE INC
Also Called: Sierra Group
560 Rverdale Drv Glendale, Glendale (91204)
PHONE..........................818 637-2888
Carl Frommer, *President*
Scott Martin, *CFO*
Richard Freeman, *Exec VP*
Jose Chavez, *Technician*
Jorge Corrales, *Project Mgr*
EMP: 55
SQ FT: 7,000
SALES: 14MM **Privately Held**
SIC: 1542 Commercial & office buildings, renovation & repair

(P-1552)
NORDBY CONSTRUCTION CO
Also Called: Nordby Wine Caves
1550 Airport Blvd Ste 101, Santa Rosa (95403-1095)
PHONE..........................707 526-4500
Wendell F Nordby Jr, *Ch of Bd*
Rick Shone, *President*
Nancy C Nordby, *Admin Sec*
EMP: 50 EST: 1977
SQ FT: 8,000

SALES (est): 10.6MM **Privately Held**
WEB: www.nordby.net
SIC: 1542 School building construction; commercial & office building, new construction; restaurant construction; shopping center construction

(P-1553)
NOVO CONSTRUCTION INC (PA)
1460 Obrien Dr, Menlo Park (94025-1432)
PHONE..........................650 701-1500
James C Fowler, *CEO*
Jim Fowler, *President*
Doug Ballou, *Executive*
Robert Williamson, *Admin Sec*
Abigail Hernandez, *Administration*
EMP: 155 EST: 2000
SQ FT: 10,000
SALES: 684.9MM **Privately Held**
WEB: www.novoconstruction.com
SIC: 1542 Commercial & office buildings, renovation & repair

(P-1554)
OLIVER & COMPANY INC
1300 S 51st St, Richmond (94804-4628)
PHONE..........................510 412-9090
Steven Henri Oliver, *CEO*
Steve Cetrone, *Vice Pres*
Josh Oliver, *Vice Pres*
Jeff Shields, *Vice Pres*
Brendan Glueck, *Project Leader*
▲ EMP: 90
SQ FT: 6,302
SALES (est): 45.8MM **Privately Held**
WEB: www.oliverandco.net
SIC: 1542 Commercial & office building, new construction

(P-1555)
PAAT & KIMMEL DEVELOPMENT INC
600 N Mountain Ave, Upland (91786-4359)
PHONE..........................909 315-8074
Victor Paat, *CEO*
EMP: 60 EST: 2014
SALES (est): 12MM **Privately Held**
SIC: 1542 Commercial & office building, new construction

(P-1556)
PACIFIC BUILDING GROUP (PA)
9752 Aspen Creek Ct # 100, San Diego (92126-1082)
PHONE..........................858 552-0600
Gregory A Rogers, *CEO*
Jim Roherty, *President*
Lisa Hitt, *CFO*
William Hansen, *Vice Pres*
Ron Maize, *Vice Pres*
▲ EMP: 190
SQ FT: 17,880
SALES: 52MM **Privately Held**
WEB: www.pacificbuildinggroup.com
SIC: 1542 Commercial & office building, new construction

(P-1557)
PACIFIC ENGINEERING BUILDERS
1009 Terra Nova Blvd, Pacifica (94044-4308)
PHONE..........................650 557-1238
John Chan, *President*
Kennedy Chan, *Treasurer*
Ada Lee, *Admin Sec*
EMP: 85
SALES (est): 7.3MM **Privately Held**
SIC: 1542 Commercial & office buildings, renovation & repair

(P-1558)
PACIFIC STTES ENVMTL CNTRS INC
11555 Dublin Blvd, Dublin (94568-2854)
P.O. Box 11357, Pleasanton (94588-1357)
PHONE..........................925 803-4333
Robert E McCarrick, *CEO*
Ernie Lampkin, *Treasurer*
Robert Ludden, *Foreman/Supr*
Robin Gomes, *Manager*
EMP: 50
SQ FT: 2,000

SALES (est): 16.1MM **Privately Held**
WEB: www.pacificstates.net
SIC: 1542 1791 1794 8744 Nonresidential construction; storage tanks, metal; erection; excavation & grading, building construction;

(P-1559)
PARKCO BUILDING COMPANY
3190 Airport Loop Dr F, Costa Mesa (92626-3408)
PHONE..........................714 444-1441
W Adrian Hoyle, *President*
Joel Templeton, *Project Mgr*
Zach Brewster, *Business Mgr*
EMP: 99
SALES: 10.1MM **Privately Held**
SIC: 1542 1771 1799 Commercial & office building, new construction; garage construction; foundation & footing contractor; erection & dismantling of forms for poured concrete

(P-1560)
PARSONS GVRNMENT SVCS INTL INC
100 W Walnut St, Pasadena (91124-0001)
PHONE..........................626 440-6000
Thomas L Roell, *President*
Curtis A Bower, *Exec VP*
Gary L Stone, *Senior VP*
EMP: 268 EST: 1969
SALES: 408.1MM
SALES (corp-wide): 3.5B **Publicly Held**
SIC: 1542 Commercial & office building, new construction
PA: The Parsons Corporation
5875 Trinity Pkwy Ste 300
Centreville VA 20120
703 988-8500

(P-1561)
PCL CONSTRUCTION SERVICES INC
500 N Brand Blvd Ste 1500, Glendale (91203-3938)
PHONE..........................818 246-3481
Dale Kain, *Manager*
Stamp Paula, *Business Mgr*
Dan Sliter, *Business Mgr*
Jeff Lee, *Purch Mgr*
EMP: 191
SQ FT: 17,619
SALES (corp-wide): 5.9B **Privately Held**
SIC: 1542 Commercial & office building, new construction
HQ: Pcl Construction Services, Inc.
2000 S Colo Blvd Ste 2-50
Denver CO 80222
303 365-6500

(P-1562)
PCL CONSTRUCTION SERVICES INC
100 Universal City Plz, North Hollywood (91608-1002)
PHONE..........................818 509-7816
EMP: 111
SALES (corp-wide): 5.9B **Privately Held**
SIC: 1542 Commercial & office building, new construction
HQ: Pcl Construction Services, Inc.
2000 S Colo Blvd Ste 2-50
Denver CO 80222
303 365-6500

(P-1563)
PCL INDUSTRIAL SERVICES INC
1500 S Union Ave, Bakersfield (93307-4144)
PHONE..........................661 832-3995
Joe W Carrieri, *CEO*
Gary L Basher, *Corp Secy*
Randy Simmons, *Project Mgr*
Hayden Bishop, *Project Engr*
Mark Schneider, *Project Engr*
EMP: 300
SALES (est): 92.1MM **Privately Held**
SIC: 1542 Nonresidential construction

▲ = Import ▼=Export
◆ =Import/Export

(P-1564)
PENWAL INDUSTRIES INC
10611 Acacia St, Rancho Cucamonga
(91730-5410)
PHONE...................................909 466-1555
Chris A Pennington, *Principal*
Rusty Lamberson, *Manager*
▲ EMP: 100 EST: 1981
SQ FT: 65,000
SALES (est): 21.8MM **Privately Held**
WEB: www.penwal.com
SIC: 1542 3999 8742 3993 Shopping
center construction; advertising display
products; management consulting serv-
ices; signs & advertising specialties

(P-1565)
**PERRY COAST CONSTRUCTION
INC**
Also Called: West Coast Construction
14130 Meridian Pkwy, Riverside
(92518-3043)
PHONE...................................951 774-0677
Robert Perry, *President*
Erin Perry, *Treasurer*
Britney Perry, *Admin Sec*
EMP: 105
SALES: 21.3MM **Privately Held**
SIC: 1542 Restaurant construction

(P-1566)
PHILMONT MANAGEMENT INC
3450 Wilshire Blvd # 850, Los Angeles
(90010-2211)
PHONE...................................213 380-0159
Monica Nam, *President*
EMP: 99 EST: 1997
SQ FT: 6,000
SALES: 5MM **Privately Held**
SIC: 1542 Commercial & office building,
new construction

(P-1567)
**PINNACLE CONTRACTING
CORP**
21800 Burbank Blvd # 210, Woodland Hills
(91367-6470)
PHONE...................................818 888-6548
Mark Tieman, *CEO*
Mark A Tieman, *President*
Michael Grossman, *Chairman*
Susan Berson, *Vice Pres*
Denise Grossman, *Admin Sec*
EMP: 50
SQ FT: 3,500
SALES (est): 12.1MM **Privately Held**
WEB: www.pincon.com
SIC: 1542 Commercial & office building,
new construction

(P-1568)
**PINNER CONSTRUCTION CO
INC (PA)**
1255 S Lewis St, Anaheim (92805-6424)
PHONE...................................714 490-4000
John Pinner, *President*
Dirk Griffin, *CFO*
Johnny R Pinner, *Vice Pres*
Stephanie Burdo, *Administration*
Roxanne Udave, *Administration*
▲ EMP: 75
SQ FT: 6,700
SALES: 137.2MM **Privately Held**
WEB: www.pinnerconstruction.com
SIC: 1542 Commercial & office building,
new construction; hospital construction;
stadium construction

(P-1569)
**PREFERRED CONSTRUCTION
CO INC**
3926 E Broadway, Long Beach
(90803-6109)
PHONE...................................714 630-3004
Thomas Cordova, *President*
▲ EMP: 60
SQ FT: 2,500
SALES (est): 8.2MM **Privately Held**
SIC: 1542 Commercial & office buildings,
renovation & repair

(P-1570)
PRS/ROEBBELEN JV
4811 Tunis Rd, Sacramento (95835-1007)
PHONE...................................916 641-0324

EMP: 50
SALES (est): 5.2MM **Privately Held**
SIC: 1542

(P-1571)
QUIRING CORPORATION
5118 E Clinton Way # 201, Fresno
(93727-2094)
PHONE...................................559 432-2800
Paul K Quiring, *President*
Greg Quiring, *Treasurer*
Esther Cuevas, *Business Dir*
Kirk Miyake, *Controller*
Tiffany Spencer, *Human Res Dir*
EMP: 62
SQ FT: 4,000
SALES (est): 16.6MM **Privately Held**
WEB: www.quiring.com
SIC: 1542 Commercial & office building,
new construction

(P-1572)
QUIRING GENERAL LLC
Also Called: Construction
5118 E Clinton Way # 201, Fresno
(93727-2088)
PHONE...................................559 432-2800
Greg A Quiring, *Mng Member*
Paul Quiring, *CEO*
John Wood, *CFO*
Kit Bedell, *Project Engr*
Brian Reitz, *Asst Controller*
EMP: 80
SQ FT: 6,200
SALES: 46MM **Privately Held**
SIC: 1542 Commercial & office building,
new construction

(P-1573)
**R J DAUM CONSTRUCTION CO
(PA)**
11581 Monarch St, Garden Grove
(92841-1814)
PHONE...................................714 894-4300
Harold I Perong, *President*
Mark Perong, *CFO*
Christina M Perong, *Admin Sec*
Michelle A Perong, *Admin Sec*
Jeff Manning, *Superintendent*
EMP: 120 EST: 1936
SQ FT: 10,000
SALES: 23.4MM **Privately Held**
SIC: 1542 Hospital construction; school
building construction

(P-1574)
R J M CONSTRUCTION INC
224 Donna Dr, Redlands (92374-5526)
PHONE...................................909 794-8853
Belinda Marin, *Corp Secy*
Roger Marin, *President*
EMP: 50
SALES (est): 3.5MM **Privately Held**
SIC: 1542 Commercial & office building,
new construction

(P-1575)
R Q CONSTRUCTION INC
3194 Lionshead Ave, Carlsbad
(92010-4701)
PHONE...................................760 631-7707
George H Rogers III, *CEO*
Michael D Patterson, *President*
Craig Shadle, *CFO*
Donald M Rogers, *Vice Pres*
EMP: 140
SQ FT: 8,000
SALES (est): 22MM **Privately Held**
SIC: 1542 Nonresidential construction

(P-1576)
**RANCHWOOD CONTRACTORS
INC**
923 E Pacheco Blvd, Los Banos
(93635-4327)
PHONE...................................209 826-6200
Greg Hostetler, *President*
Catherine Hostetler, *Corp Secy*
EMP: 80
SQ FT: 3,500
SALES (est): 14.6MM **Privately Held**
SIC: 1542 1521 Commercial & office build-
ing, new construction; new construction,
single-family houses

(P-1577)
RANSOME COMPANY
1933 Williams St, San Leandro
(94577-2303)
P.O. Box 2177 (94577-0217)
PHONE...................................510 686-9900
Myles Oberto, *Ch of Bd*
Geoff Raaka, *President*
Peter Scott, *Vice Pres*
EMP: 50
SALES: 8MM **Privately Held**
WEB: www.ransomeco.com
SIC: 1542 Nonresidential construction

(P-1578)
**RED ONE - PSI JOINT VENTR
LLC**
310 W Murray Ave, Visalia (93291-4937)
PHONE...................................559 772-8264
Reynaldo Ruiz, *Partner*
Angelina Derossett, *Manager*
EMP: 50
SALES (est): 2.4MM **Privately Held**
SIC: 1542 1541 Commercial & office build-
ings, renovation & repair; hospital con-
struction; school building construction;
renovation, remodeling & repairs: indus-
trial buildings

(P-1579)
**REEVE-KNIGHT
CONSTRUCTION INC**
128 Ascot Dr, Roseville (95661-3422)
PHONE...................................916 786-5112
Robert H Reeve, *CEO*
Joe E Knight, *President*
Cynthia Knight, *Treasurer*
M Kathy Reeve, *Admin Sec*
Christine Tadlock, *Admin Asst*
EMP: 75
SQ FT: 9,200
SALES (est): 45.7MM **Privately Held**
WEB: www.reeve-knight.com
SIC: 1542 Commercial & office building,
new construction

(P-1580)
**RESOURCE ENVIRONMENTAL
INC**
6634 Schilling Ave, Long Beach
(90805-1745)
PHONE...................................562 468-7000
Jared Sloan Cooper, *President*
EMP: 75
SQ FT: 4,400
SALES: 10MM **Privately Held**
SIC: 1542 Nonresidential construction

(P-1581)
RHC EQUIPMENT LLC
5237 Mallard Estates Rd, Chico
(95973-9524)
PHONE...................................530 892-1918
Randy Hill, *Manager*
EMP: 50
SALES: 85K **Privately Held**
SIC: 1542 Nonresidential construction

(P-1582)
**RMR CONSTRUCTION
COMPANY**
2424 Oakdale Ave, San Francisco
(94124-1581)
PHONE...................................415 647-0884
Ray Reinertson Jr, *President*
Robert Reinertson, *Vice Pres*
Marie Reinertson, *Admin Sec*
EMP: 140
SQ FT: 12,000
SALES (est): 33.2MM **Privately Held**
SIC: 1542 Commercial & office buildings,
renovation & repair

(P-1583)
**ROBERT CLAPPER CNSTR
SVCS INC**
Also Called: RC Construction Services
2223 N Locust Ave, Rialto (92377-4113)
PHONE...................................909 829-3688
Robert W Clapper, *Principal*
Rebecca Clapper, *Treasurer*
Howard Brissette, *Project Mgr*
Rich Negley, *Project Mgr*
Gabriel Urioste, *Project Engr*

EMP: 100
SALES: 35MM **Privately Held**
WEB: www.rcconstructionservices.com
SIC: 1542 Commercial & office building,
new construction

(P-1584)
**ROCKLAND BUILDERS
SERVICES INC**
3261 1/2 Main St, Chula Vista
(91911-5824)
P.O. Box 121356 (91912-4956)
PHONE...................................619 592-9582
Frank De La Rosa, *President*
Robert Graham, *Vice Pres*
EMP: 55
SALES (est): 123K **Privately Held**
SIC: 1542 1771 Nonresidential construc-
tion; concrete work

(P-1585)
**ROEBBELEN CONSTRUCTION
INC**
1241 Hawks Flight Ct, El Dorado Hills
(95762-9648)
PHONE...................................916 939-4000
Hans J Roebbelen, *CEO*
Kenneth Roebbelen, *President*
Dennis Daniell, *CFO*
David Thuleen, *Exec VP*
Kenneth Debruhl, *Vice Pres*
EMP: 80
SQ FT: 25,000
SALES (est): 17.7MM **Privately Held**
SIC: 1542 1541 Commercial & office build-
ing, new construction; industrial buildings
& warehouses

(P-1586)
**ROEBBELEN CONTRACTING
INC**
1241 Hawks Flight Ct, El Dorado Hills
(95762-9648)
PHONE...................................916 939-4000
Kenneth Wenham, *President*
Robert McLean, *COO*
Bruce Stimson, *CFO*
Kenneth Debruhl, *Officer*
Bob Kjome, *Exec VP*
EMP: 350
SQ FT: 28,000
SALES: 248MM **Privately Held**
SIC: 1542 1541 8741 Commercial & of-
fice building, new construction; industrial
buildings & warehouses; construction
management

(P-1587)
RORE INC (PA)
5151 Shoreham Pl Ste 260, San Diego
(92122-5962)
PHONE...................................858 404-7393
Gita Murthy, *CEO*
Christa Flores, *Office Mgr*
Jennifer Masterson, *Administration*
Jonathan Stratton, *Project Mgr*
Nandita Murthy, *Contract Mgr*
EMP: 64
SQ FT: 3,500
SALES: 16MM **Privately Held**
WEB: www.roreinc.com
SIC: 1542 1541 4959 Commercial & of-
fice building, new construction; commer-
cial & office buildings, renovation & repair;
renovation, remodeling & repairs: indus-
trial buildings; toxic or hazardous waste
cleanup

(P-1588)
**RUDOLPH AND SLETTEN INC
(HQ)**
2 Circle Star Way Fl 4, San Carlos
(94070-6200)
PHONE...................................650 216-3600
Martin B Sisemore, *President*
Terry Huie, *CFO*
Daniel J Dolinar, *Exec VP*
Jon Foad, *Senior VP*
Rene Olivo, *Senior VP*
EMP: 100 EST: 1960
SQ FT: 27,000

P R O D U C T S & S V C S

SALES (est): 1.3B
SALES (corp-wide): 4.4B **Publicly Held**
WEB: www.rsconstruction.com
SIC: 1542 1541 Commercial & office building, new construction; industrial buildings & warehouses
PA: Tutor Perini Corporation
15901 Olden St
Sylmar CA 91342
818 362-8391

(P-1589)
S J AMOROSO CNSTR CO INC (PA)
390 Bridge Pkwy, Redwood City (94065-1061)
PHONE..................650 654-1900
Dana McManus, *Ch of Bd*
Robert Erskine, *Vice Pres*
Mike Cleveland, *Executive*
Valerie L Frahm, *Executive Asst*
Sangmin Chung, *Project Mgr*
EMP: 400
SQ FT: 22,500
SALES (est): 158.5MM **Privately Held**
SIC: 1542 Commercial & office building, new construction

(P-1590)
SAFEWAY STORES INCORPORATED
750 Walsh Ave, Santa Clara (95050-2613)
PHONE..................408 719-9460
Marc Wilson, *Owner*
EMP: 73
SALES (corp-wide): 60.5B **Privately Held**
SIC: 1542 1522 Commercial & office building, new construction; residential construction
HQ: Safeway Stores, Incorporated
5918 Stoneridge Mall Rd
Pleasanton CA 94588
925 467-3000

(P-1591)
SAVANT CONSTRUCTION INC
13830 Mountain Ave, Chino (91710-9014)
P.O. Box 636 (91708-0636)
PHONE..................909 614-4300
John L Aldridge, *President*
Brad Hastings, *Corp Secy*
Darren Nowicki, *Vice Pres*
EMP: 52
SQ FT: 36,000
SALES (est): 22.8MM **Privately Held**
WEB: www.savantconst.com
SIC: 1542 Commercial & office building, new construction

(P-1592)
SC BUILDERS INC (PA)
910 Thompson Pl, Sunnyvale (94085-4517)
PHONE..................408 328-0688
Samuel B Abbey, *CEO*
Chris Smither, *Vice Pres*
Liz Bandalan, *Administration*
Tara Dickson, *Administration*
Greg Burda, *Project Mgr*
EMP: 55
SALES (est): 35.9MM **Privately Held**
WEB: www.scbuilders.com
SIC: 1542 1611 8711 Custom builders, non-residential; general contractor, highway & street construction; building construction consultant

(P-1593)
SD DEACON CORP CALIFORNIA
7745 Greenback Ln Ste 250, Citrus Heights (95610-5865)
PHONE..................916 969-0900
Richard G Smith, *President*
Robert K Aroyan, *Vice Pres*
Paul B Cunha, *Vice Pres*
Brett Mykrantz, *Vice Pres*
EMP: 70
SALES (est): 5.9MM
SALES (corp-wide): 391.5MM **Privately Held**
SIC: 1542 Commercial & office building contractors
PA: Deacon Holdings, Inc.
7745 Greenback Ln Ste 250
Citrus Heights CA 95610
916 969-0900

(P-1594)
SERVICE FIRST CONTRACTORS
2510 N Grand Ave Ste 110, Santa Ana (92705-8754)
PHONE..................714 573-2200
Mark Bucher, *CEO*
Frank Vanderberg, *President*
Stan Hatch, *Treasurer*
Gary Bucher, *Admin Sec*
EMP: 50
SQ FT: 6,500
SALES (est): 15.5MM **Privately Held**
SIC: 1542 1522 6512 Commercial & office building contractors; residential construction; nonresidential building operators

(P-1595)
SEVERSON GROUP INCORPORATED (PA)
3601 Serpentine Dr, Los Alamitos (90720-2440)
PHONE..................562 493-3611
Jonathan Edward Severson, *President*
Brian Cresap, *Treasurer*
Scott Feest, *Vice Pres*
Ben Severson, *Vice Pres*
Robert Severson, *Vice Pres*
EMP: 76
SQ FT: 15,000
SALES (est): 10MM **Privately Held**
WEB: www.millieseverson.com
SIC: 1542 1541 Commercial & office building, new construction; hospital construction; institutional building construction; industrial buildings, new construction

(P-1596)
SHAWMUT WOODWORKING & SUP INC
Also Called: Shawmut Design and Cnstr
11390 W Olympic Blvd Fl 2, Los Angeles (90064-1607)
PHONE..................323 602-1000
Leonard Porzio, *Principal*
Reza Amirkhalili, *COO*
Marianne Monte, *Officer*
Dave Benson, *Vice Pres*
Sharon Cadman, *Vice Pres*
EMP: 145
SALES (corp-wide): 1.1B **Privately Held**
SIC: 1542 Commercial & office building contractors; commercial & office building, new construction
PA: Shawmut Woodworking & Supply, Inc.
560 Harrison Ave Ste 200
Boston MA 02118
617 622-7000

(P-1597)
SIERRA PACIFIC WEST INC
2125 La Mirada Dr, Vista (92081-8830)
P.O. Box 231640, Encinitas (92023-1640)
PHONE..................760 599-0755
Sandra L Brown, *CEO*
Chad Sheridan, *Project Mgr*
Luis Hernandez, *Project Engr*
Kay McCain, *Human Res Mgr*
Karen Gohringer, *Receptionist*
EMP: 56
SALES (est): 16.3MM **Privately Held**
WEB: www.sierrapacificwest.com
SIC: 1542 1611 Nonresidential construction; highway & street construction

(P-1598)
SIGMA SERVICES INC (PA)
2140 Eastman Ave Ste 110, Ventura (93003-7786)
P.O. Box 368, Goleta (93116-0368)
PHONE..................805 642-8377
Vivian Solodkin, *President*
Louie Valenzuala, *CFO*
Louie Valenzuala, *CFO*
Benjamin Valenzuela Jr, *Vice Pres*
EMP: 60
SQ FT: 4,200
SALES (est): 12.8MM **Privately Held**
WEB: www.sigmaconstruction.net
SIC: 1542 6531 7349 1731 Commercial & office building contractors; real estate managers; janitorial service, contract basis; electrical work; facilities support services

(P-1599)
SILVER CREEK INDUSTRIES INC
2830 Barrett Ave, Perris (92571-3258)
PHONE..................951 943-5393
Brett D Bashaw, *CEO*
Micheal Rhodes, *Corp Secy*
EMP: 175
SQ FT: 25,000
SALES (est): 89.1MM **Privately Held**
WEB: www.silver-creek.net
SIC: 1542 2452 Commercial & office building contractors; prefabricated wood buildings

(P-1600)
SIMMONS CONSTRUCTION INC
19252 Flypath Way, Bakersfield (93308)
PHONE..................661 636-1321
Charles J Simmons, *President*
Evalee Simmons, *Vice Pres*
EMP: 50 EST: 1988
SALES (est): 17.8MM **Privately Held**
SIC: 1542 Commercial & office building, new construction

(P-1601)
SINANIAN DEVELOPMENT INC
18980 Ventura Blvd # 200, Tarzana (91356-3228)
PHONE..................818 996-9666
Antranik Sinanian, *CEO*
Harry Sinanian, *Shareholder*
Sinan Sinanian, *President*
Andy Sinanian, *Co-President*
EMP: 70
SQ FT: 4,000
SALES (est): 27.1MM **Privately Held**
SIC: 1542 1522 6552 Commercial & office building, new construction; residential construction; subdividers & developers

(P-1602)
SKYLINE COMMERCIAL INTERIORS (PA)
Also Called: Skyline Construction
505 Sansome St Fl 7, San Francisco (94111-3108)
PHONE..................415 908-1020
David Hayes, *CEO*
Rick Militello, *President*
Craig Jones, *Officer*
Randy Scott, *Senior VP*
Dan Duncan, *Project Mgr*
EMP: 80
SQ FT: 9,000
SALES (est): 136MM **Privately Held**
WEB: www.skylineconst.com
SIC: 1542 Commercial & office buildings, renovation & repair

(P-1603)
SMP CONSTRUCTION & MAINT INC (PA)
Also Called: Foundation Repair of CA
1813 Rutan Dr Ste A, Livermore (94551-7620)
PHONE..................925 961-9012
Mark Phelps, *CEO*
Matthew Phelps, *President*
Brett Parise, *Accountant*
EMP: 65
SALES (est): 9.1MM **Privately Held**
SIC: 1542 1521 Commercial & office building contractors; single-family housing construction

(P-1604)
SNYDER LANGSTON L P
Also Called: Snyder Langston
17962 Cowan, Irvine (92614-6026)
PHONE..................949 863-9200
Stephen Jones, *Chairman*
Jason Rich, *President*
John F Rochford, *CEO*
Gary Campanaro, *CFO*
Chip McCorkle, *VP Bus Dvlpt*
EMP: 70
SQ FT: 16,000
SALES: 413MM **Privately Held**
WEB: www.snyderlangston.com
SIC: 1542 8742 1522 Commercial & office building, new construction; real estate consultant; residential construction

(P-1605)
SO CALIFORNIA VENTURES LTD
1101 Richfield Rd, Placentia (92870-6790)
PHONE..................714 524-0021
John T Palazzo, *President*
EMP: 80
SALES (est): 8.9MM **Privately Held**
SIC: 1542 Commercial & office building contractors

(P-1606)
SOLPAC INC
Also Called: Soltek Pacific
2424 Congress St, San Diego (92110-2819)
PHONE..................619 296-6247
Stephen W Thompson, *CEO*
Dave Carlin, *President*
Heather Wiley, *COO*
John Myers, *Senior VP*
Kevin Cammall, *Vice Pres*
EMP: 112
SQ FT: 7,386
SALES (est): 59.7MM **Privately Held**
SIC: 1542 Commercial & office building, new construction; commercial & office buildings, renovation & repair

(P-1607)
SOUTH COAST PIERING INC
Also Called: Saber
41357 Date St, Murrieta (92562-7030)
PHONE..................800 922-2488
Franz M Froehlich, *CEO*
EMP: 70
SALES (est): 8.5MM **Privately Held**
SIC: 1542 Commercial & office buildings, renovation & repair

(P-1608)
SPAN CONSTRUCTION & ENGRG INC (PA)
1841 Howard Rd, Madera (93637-5122)
PHONE..................559 661-1111
King F Husein, *CEO*
George Goddard, *President*
Firoz Mohamed Husein, *CEO*
Douglas M Standing, *Admin Sec*
Laura Flores, *Admin Asst*
▼ EMP: 100 EST: 1979
SQ FT: 120,000
SALES (est): 95.8MM **Privately Held**
WEB: www.spanconstruction.com
SIC: 1542 1541 1791 Commercial & office buildings, prefabricated erection; agricultural building contractors; industrial buildings, new construction; structural steel erection

(P-1609)
STREAMLINE FINISHES INC
26429 Rancho Pkwy S # 140, Lake Forest (92630-8330)
PHONE..................949 600-8964
William Seidel, *President*
Austin Seidel, *Director*
EMP: 80 EST: 2004
SQ FT: 6,000
SALES (est): 13.9MM **Privately Held**
SIC: 1542 Commercial & office building contractors

(P-1610)
STRONGHOLD ENGINEERING INC (PA)
2000 Market St, Riverside (92501-1769)
PHONE..................951 684-9303
Beverly A Bailey, *President*
Oliver Baptiste, *Officer*
Cory Vaughan, *Exec VP*
Scott Bailey, *Vice Pres*
Patricia McNicholas, *Risk Mgmt Dir*
EMP: 250
SQ FT: 21,000
SALES (est): 152.9MM **Privately Held**
SIC: 1542 Specialized public building contractors

(P-1611)
SUMMER SYSTEMS INC
28942 Hancock Pkwy, Valencia (91355-1069)
PHONE..................661 257-4419
Don London, *President*
Connie London, *Admin Sec*

EMP: 80
SQ FT: 20,000
SALES (est): 22.8MM **Privately Held**
WEB: www.summersystemsinc.com
SIC: 1542 Nonresidential construction

(P-1612)
SWINERTON BLDRS PACIFIC R
16798 W Bernardo Dr, San Diego
(92127-1904)
PHONE..........................619 954-8011
Mark Payne, *Principal*
George Ehara, *Division Mgr*
EMP: 65
SALES (est): 8.6MM **Privately Held**
SIC: 1542 Nonresidential construction

(P-1613)
SWINERTON BUILDERS
865 S Figueroa St # 3000, Los Angeles
(90017-3009)
PHONE..........................213 896-3400
Gust Soteropulos, *Branch Mgr*
Mikan Szeto, *Project Mgr*
Debra Leyden, *Assistant*
Nick Thomas, *Superintendent*
EMP: 100 **Privately Held**
SIC: 1542 1541 Commercial & office build-
ing, new construction; industrial buildings
& warehouses
HQ: Swinerton Builders
260 Townsend St Fl 3
San Francisco CA 94107
415 421-2980

(P-1614)
SWINERTON BUILDERS HC
Also Called: HMH BUILDERS
15 Business Park Way # 101, Sacramento
(95828-0959)
PHONE..........................916 383-4825
Gary J Rafferty, *Ch of Bd*
Eric M Foster, *President*
Leonard J Bischel, *CFO*
Frank Foellmer, *Exec VP*
Linda J Schowalter, *Senior VP*
EMP: 150
SQ FT: 25,000
SALES: 33MM **Privately Held**
WEB: www.hmh.com
SIC: 1542 Commercial & office building,
new construction; hospital construction;
institutional building construction
PA: Swinerton Incorporated
260 Townsend St
San Francisco CA 94107

(P-1615)
SWINERTON INCORPORATED (PA)
260 Townsend St, San Francisco
(94107-1761)
PHONE..........................415 421-2980
Jeffrey C Hoopes, *CEO*
Brenda A Reimche, *Vice Pres*
Sue E Twitchel, *Vice Pres*
Scott Tomhave, *Opers Staff*
Lisa M Telles, *Asst Sec*
▲ **EMP:** 200
SQ FT: 66,943
SALES: 3.6B **Privately Held**
SIC: 1542 1541 6531 1522 Commercial
& office building, new construction; indus-
trial buildings & warehouses; real estate
managers; residential construction

(P-1616)
TASLIMI CONSTRUCTION CO INC
1805 Colorado Ave, Santa Monica
(90404-3411)
PHONE..........................310 447-3000
Shidan Taslimi, *Principal*
Mehran Taslimi, *Vice Pres*
Susanne Taslimi, *Admin Sec*
Niki Afsharian, *Project Engr*
Usman Azam, *Project Engr*
EMP: 66
SQ FT: 8,500
SALES (est): 24.4MM **Privately Held**
SIC: 1542 Commercial & office building,
new construction; commercial & office
buildings, renovation & repair

(P-1617)
TAYLOR BAILEY INC
355 Lafata St Ste E, Saint Helena
(94574-1413)
PHONE..........................707 967-8090
Mike Digiulio, *President*
Robert Covey, *Vice Pres*
Gerald Eastman, *Vice Pres*
EMP: 60
SQ FT: 2,000
SALES (est): 10.5MM **Privately Held**
WEB: www.baileyandtaylor.com
SIC: 1542 Agricultural building contractors

(P-1618)
TAYLOR STRUCTURES INC
905 Cotting Ln Ste 100, Vacaville
(95688-8777)
PHONE..........................707 499-6870
Ridley Taylor, *President*
Scott Taylor, *Vice Pres*
EMP: 75
SQ FT: 3,000
SALES (est): 8.9MM **Privately Held**
SIC: 1542 Commercial & office building,
new construction

(P-1619)
TCG BUILDERS INC
Also Called: Core Group, The
890 N Mccarthy Blvd # 100, Milpitas
(95035-5127)
PHONE..........................408 321-6450
Andrew W Meade, *CEO*
Timothy Tempel, *President*
Jillian Dressel, *Corp Secy*
Robert Wagle, *Vice Pres*
Dolores Manriquez, *Controller*
EMP: 50
SQ FT: 6,000
SALES (est): 14.1MM **Privately Held**
SIC: 1542 Commercial & office building
contractors; commercial & office building,
new construction; commercial & office
buildings, renovation & repair

(P-1620)
TECHNO COATINGS INC
795 Debra St, Anaheim (92805)
PHONE..........................714 774-4671
Michael Birney, *President*
EMP: 150
SALES (corp-wide): 98.3MM **Privately Held**
WEB: www.technocoatings.com
SIC: 1542 1629 1721 1799 Commercial
& office buildings, renovation & repair;
blasting contractor, except building demolition; painting & paper hanging; wallcovering contractors; coating of concrete
structures with plastic; coating of metal
structures at construction site; waterproofing
PA: Techno Coatings, Inc.
1391 S Allec St
Anaheim CA 92805
714 635-1130

(P-1621)
TEMALPAKH INC
Also Called: Works Floor & Wall, The
979 S Gene Autry Trl, Palm Springs
(92264-3464)
PHONE..........................760 770-5778
Gerald A Flowers, *CEO*
Michael Collins, *Vice Pres*
Rusty Harling, *Admin Sec*
EMP: 65
SQ FT: 13,000
SALES (est): 14.5MM **Privately Held**
SIC: 1542 5713 5211 Commercial & office
buildings, renovation & repair; floor cover-
ing stores; tile, ceramic

(P-1622)
TILLER CONSTRUCTORS PARTNR INC
306 W Katella Ave Ste A, Orange
(92867-4755)
PHONE..........................714 771-5600
Lin Lindstedt, *President*
Kerry Evert, *Vice Pres*
Patty Baker, *Administration*
Amanda Stern, *Accountant*
Bob Surmon, *Superintendent*
EMP: 64

SQ FT: 4,000
SALES (est): 26.8MM **Privately Held**
WEB: www.tillerconstructors.com
SIC: 1542 Institutional building construc-
tion; commercial & office building contrac-
tors

(P-1623)
TOTAL BUILDING CARE INC
21228 Norwalk Blvd, Hawaiian Gardens
(90716-1021)
PHONE..........................562 467-8333
Yong A Kim, *CEO*
Yong Kim, *CEO*
Colin Oconnell, *Vice Pres*
EMP: 70
SALES (est): 10.1MM **Privately Held**
WEB: www.totalbuildingcare.com
SIC: 1542 Commercial & office buildings,
renovation & repair

(P-1624)
TRENDEX CORPORATION
9353 Eton Ave, Chatsworth (91311-5810)
PHONE..........................818 407-9600
William Vincent, *President*
Janet Ayers, *Corp Secy*
April Helvig, *Office Mgr*
EMP: 60
SQ FT: 3,500
SALES: 11MM **Privately Held**
SIC: 1542 1742 Commercial & office build-
ing contractors; drywall

(P-1625)
TRICORP CONSTRUCTION INC (PA)
Also Called: Tricorp Hearn Construction
1030 G St, Sacramento (95814-0823)
PHONE..........................916 779-8010
Steve Hunter, *President*
Tony Moayed, *Vice Pres*
Ken Cohen, *Principal*
EMP: 60
SQ FT: 10,000
SALES (est): 26.8MM **Privately Held**
WEB: www.tricorpconstruction.com
SIC: 1542 1521 Commercial & office build-
ing, new construction; single-family hous-
ing construction

(P-1626)
TRITON STRUCTURAL CONCRETE INC
15435 Innovation Dr # 100, San Diego
(92128-3443)
PHONE..........................858 866-2450
Tim Penick, *President*
Ted Kluska, *Project Mgr*
Eugene Namyotov, *Project Mgr*
Mike Porvaznik, *Project Mgr*
Khanna Tsymuk, *Project Mgr*
EMP: 250
SALES: 57.5MM **Privately Held**
SIC: 1542 Commercial & office building,
new construction

(P-1627)
TRUEBECK CONSTRUCTION INC (PA)
951 Mariners, San Mateo (94404)
PHONE..........................650 227-1957
David C Becker, *President*
Brad Bastian, *Shareholder*
Jeff Nielson, *Shareholder*
Kathy Reiner, *CFO*
Sean Truedale, *Vice Pres*
EMP: 55
SQ FT: 6,000
SALES (est): 23.2MM **Privately Held**
SIC: 1542 Commercial & office building,
new construction; custom builders, non-
residential

(P-1628)
TURELK INC
Also Called: Turelk San Diego
11622 El Camino Real # 100, San Diego
(92130-2049)
PHONE..........................858 633-8085
Michael Turi, *Branch Mgr*
EMP: 85

SALES (corp-wide): 110MM **Privately
Held**
SIC: 1542 Commercial & office buildings,
renovation & repair
PA: Turelk, Inc.
3700 Santa Fe Ave Ste 200
Long Beach CA 90810
310 835-3736

(P-1629)
TURELK INC (PA)
3700 Santa Fe Ave Ste 200, Long Beach
(90810-2169)
P.O. Box 93101 (90809-3101)
PHONE..........................310 835-3736
Michael G Turi, *CEO*
Michael R Paselk, *President*
Fred Capper, *Vice Pres*
Darwin Arayata, *Project Engr*
Karen Farias, *Project Engr*
EMP: 110
SQ FT: 14,000
SALES: 110MM **Privately Held**
WEB: www.turelk.com
SIC: 1542 Commercial & office building,
new construction

(P-1630)
TURNER CONSTRUCTION COMPANY
1900 S State College Blvd # 200, Anaheim
(92806-6197)
PHONE..........................714 940-9000
Bernie Morrissey, *Vice Pres*
John Lockareff, *Project Mgr*
Hugo Recinos, *Project Engr*
EMP: 300
SALES (corp-wide): 475MM **Privately
Held**
WEB: www.tcco.com
SIC: 1542 Commercial & office building,
new construction
HQ: Turner Construction Company Inc
375 Hudson St Fl 6
New York NY 10014
212 229-6000

(P-1631)
TURNER CONSTRUCTION COMPANY
2500 Venture Oaks Way # 200, Sacra-
mento (95833-4222)
PHONE..........................916 444-4421
Donna Afflerdach, *Branch Mgr*
Hayley Hintz, *Project Mgr*
EMP: 75
SALES (corp-wide): 475MM **Privately
Held**
WEB: www.tcco.com
SIC: 1542 Commercial & office building,
new construction
HQ: Turner Construction Company Inc
375 Hudson St Fl 6
New York NY 10014
212 229-6000

(P-1632)
TURNER CONSTRUCTION COMPANY
300 Frank H Ogawa Plz # 510, Oakland
(94612-2040)
PHONE..........................510 267-8100
Danny Cooke, *Branch Mgr*
EMP: 50
SALES (corp-wide): 475MM **Privately
Held**
WEB: www.tcco.com
SIC: 1542 8742 6531 Commercial & of-
fice building, new construction; manage-
ment consulting services; real estate
agents & managers
HQ: Turner Construction Company Inc
375 Hudson St Fl 6
New York NY 10014
212 229-6000

(P-1633)
TURNER CONSTRUCTION COMPANY
311 California St Ste 450, San Francisco
(94104-2616)
PHONE..........................415 705-8900
Dan Wheeler, *Branch Mgr*
Zita Oxford, *Manager*
EMP: 60

SALES (corp-wide): 475MM Privately Held
WEB: www.tcco.com
SIC: **1542** Commercial & office building, new construction
HQ: Turner Construction Company Inc
375 Hudson St Fl 6
New York NY 10014
212 229-6000

(P-1634)
TURNER CONSTRUCTION COMPANY
15378 Ave Of Science # 100, San Diego (92128-3451)
PHONE..................................858 320-4040
Richard C Bach, *Senior VP*
Tim Carter, *Project Engr*
Lisa Wuller, *Marketing Staff*
EMP: 61
SALES (corp-wide): 475MM Privately Held
WEB: www.tcco.com
SIC: **1542** Commercial & office building, new construction
HQ: Turner Construction Company Inc
375 Hudson St Fl 6
New York NY 10014
212 229-6000

(P-1635)
TUTOR PERINI CORPORATION (PA)
15901 Olden St, Sylmar (91342-1051)
PHONE..................................818 362-8391
Ronald N Tutor, *Ch of Bd*
James A Frost, *President*
Leonard J Rejcek, *President*
Gary G Smalley, *CFO*
Michael R Klein, *Vice Ch Bd*
▲ EMP: 160 EST: 1894
SALES: 4.4B Publicly Held
WEB: www.perini.com
SIC: **1542** 8741 1611 1791 Commercial & office building contractors; construction management; concrete construction: roads, highways, sidewalks, etc.; structural steel erection; concrete reinforcement, placing of; construction & civil engineering

(P-1636)
TUTOR-SALIBA CORPORATION (HQ)
15901 Olden St, Sylmar (91342-1051)
PHONE..................................818 362-8391
Ronald N Tutor, *CEO*
Jack Frost, *COO*
John D Barrett, *Senior VP*
David L Randall, *Senior VP*
William B Sparks, *Senior VP*
▲ EMP: 100
SQ FT: 20,000
SALES: 30MM
SALES (corp-wide): 4.4B Publicly Held
WEB: www.tutorsaliba.com
SIC: **1542** 1629 7353 1799 Commercial & office building, new construction; subway construction; cranes & aerial lift equipment, rental or leasing; rigging & scaffolding; subdividers & developers
PA: Tutor Perini Corporation
15901 Olden St
Sylmar CA 91342
818 362-8391

(P-1637)
UNITED SEAL COATING SLURRYSEAL
3463 State St Ste 522, Santa Barbara (93105-2662)
PHONE..................................805 563-4922
Luis Rodriguez, *President*
Justin Rodriguez, *Treasurer*
Al Rodriguez, *Vice Pres*
Michelle Rodriguez, *Admin Sec*
EMP: 57
SQ FT: 2,500
SALES: 12.2MM Privately Held
WEB: www.unitedpavinginc.com
SIC: **1542** 1522 7363 2951 Commercial & office building, new construction; residential construction; truck driver services; asphalt paving mixtures & blocks

(P-1638)
USS CAL BUILDERS INC
8051 Main St, Stanton (90680-2452)
PHONE..................................714 828-4882
Allen Othman, *CEO*
Jennifer Hotrum, *President*
Arlene Bautista, *Office Mgr*
Eric Othman, *Admin Sec*
Omar Abotalib, *Project Mgr*
EMP: 135
SQ FT: 15,000
SALES (est): 93.3MM Privately Held
SIC: **1542** Specialized public building contractors

(P-1639)
VANCREST CONSTRUCTION CORP
7171 N Figueroa St, Los Angeles (90042-1279)
PHONE..................................323 256-0011
John T Van Dyke, *President*
Jim Van Dyke, *Vice Pres*
EMP: 50
SQ FT: 2,000
SALES (est): 10MM Privately Held
SIC: **1542** Commercial & office buildings, renovation & repair

(P-1640)
VILA CONSTRUCTION CO
Also Called: Richard H Vila
590 S 33rd St, Richmond (94804-4108)
PHONE..................................510 236-9111
Richard H Vila, *President*
Maria Elena Vila, *Office Mgr*
Bert Brendlinger, *Project Mgr*
Henry Vila, *Sr Project Mgr*
EMP: 75 EST: 1946
SQ FT: 8,000
SALES: 30MM Privately Held
WEB: www.vilaconstruction.com
SIC: **1542** 1751 1541 Commercial & office buildings, renovation & repair; carpentry work; industrial buildings & warehouses

(P-1641)
W L BUTLER CONSTRUCTION INC (PA)
735 Shasta St, Redwood City (94063-2124)
PHONE..................................650 361-1270
William L Butler, *CEO*
Gina Tankersley, *Vice Pres*
Emily McBain, *Executive Asst*
Morgan Prior, *Executive Asst*
Lori Schlegel, *Executive Asst*
EMP: 50
SQ FT: 13,500
SALES: 272.4MM Privately Held
SIC: **1542** Commercial & office building, new construction

(P-1642)
W M KLORMAN CONSTRUCTION CORP
23047 Ventura Blvd Fl 2, Woodland Hills (91364-1146)
PHONE..................................818 591-5969
William M Klorman, *President*
Doug Fowler, *Vice Pres*
Rick Bottrell, *Project Mgr*
Alla Sandler, *Accountant*
Ida Chen, *Controller*
EMP: 65
SQ FT: 4,000
SALES: 50MM Privately Held
WEB: www.klorman.com
SIC: **1542** 1521 Commercial & office building, new construction; new construction; single-family houses

(P-1643)
WEBCOR CONSTRUCTION LP (DH)
Also Called: Webcor Builders
1751 Harbor Bay Pkwy # 200, Alameda (94502-3001)
PHONE..................................415 978-1000
Jes Pedersen, *Partner*
Vince Sarubbi, *Officer*
Kim Bates, *Vice Pres*
Shelly Doran, *Vice Pres*
Leonard Hayden, *Vice Pres*
EMP: 71
SALES: 2.2B Privately Held
WEB: www.webcor.com
SIC: **1542** Commercial & office building, new construction
HQ: Obayashi Usa, Llc
577 Airport Blvd Ste 600
Burlingame CA 94010
650 952-4910

(P-1644)
WEINSTEIN CONSTRUCTION CORP
15102 Raymer St, Van Nuys (91405-1143)
PHONE..................................818 782-4000
Itzcik Weinstein, *President*
Johnathan Weinstein, *Vice Pres*
Ilana Nisnevich, *Human Res Mgr*
EMP: 50
SALES (est): 8.4MM Privately Held
WEB: www.weinsteinconstruction.com
SIC: **1542** 1521 Commercial & office building, new construction; new construction; single-family houses

(P-1645)
WEST COAST CONTRACTORS INC
2320 Courage Dr Ste 111, Fairfield (94533-6743)
PHONE..................................541 267-7689
Alan Bond, *President*
Sharon Newcomer, *CFO*
Mark Dietlin, *Vice Pres*
James Latner, *Vice Pres*
EMP: 130
SQ FT: 15,000
SALES (est): 16.4MM Privately Held
WEB: www.westcoastcontractors.com
SIC: **1542** Specialized public building contractors; school building construction; commercial & office buildings, renovation & repair

(P-1646)
WESTGATE CNSTR & MAINT INC
5045 Fulton Dr Ste D, Fairfield (94534-1635)
PHONE..................................707 208-5763
Hilton Ham, *President*
EMP: 86
SALES: 1.8MM Privately Held
SIC: **1542** Commercial & office building, new construction; commercial & office buildings, renovation & repair; restaurant construction; shopping center construction

(P-1647)
WHITING-TURNER CONTRACTING CO
250 Commerce Ste 150, Irvine (92602-1345)
PHONE..................................949 863-0800
Len Cannatelli Jr, *Exec VP*
Chang Jeffrey, *Project Mgr*
Billy Gibbons, *Project Engr*
Shantel Higgs, *Project Engr*
Sean Kaford, *Project Engr*
EMP: 50
SALES (corp-wide): 8.6B Privately Held
WEB: www.whiting-turner.com
SIC: **1542** 1541 Commercial & office building, new construction; industrial buildings & warehouses
PA: The Whiting-Turner Contracting Company
300 E Joppa Rd Ste 800
Baltimore MD 21286
410 821-1100

(P-1648)
WIER CONSTRUCTION CORPORATION
16884 Old Survey Rd, Escondido (92025-3601)
PHONE..................................760 743-6776
Cathy Wier, *President*
Brian Wier, *Vice Pres*
EMP: 50
SQ FT: 10,000
SALES (est): 9.8MM Privately Held
WEB: www.wierconstruction.com
SIC: **1542** Specialized public building contractors

(P-1649)
WIMER CONSTRUCTION
10855 Wimer Country Rd, Sunland (91040-1348)
PHONE..................................818 848-0400
Rick Wimer, *Owner*
EMP: 50
SALES (est): 3.8MM Privately Held
WEB: www.wimerconstruction.com
SIC: **1542** Commercial & office building contractors

(P-1650)
WR CHAVEZ CONSTRUCTION INC
Also Called: Wr Chavez Company
12125 Kear Pl Ste A, Poway (92064-7131)
PHONE..................................858 375-2100
Wilfred R Chavez, *President*
Debbie L Chavez, *Treasurer*
EMP: 80
SQ FT: 15,000
SALES: 21.5MM Privately Held
SIC: **1542** 1721 Commercial & office building, new construction; commercial painting

(P-1651)
WRIGHT CONTRACTING LLC
Also Called: Wright Contracting EPA
3020 Dutton Ave, Santa Rosa (95407-7886)
P.O. Box 1270 (95402-1270)
PHONE..................................707 528-1172
Mark Davis, *President*
Stephen M Wright, *COO*
Bryan Wright, *Vice Pres*
Shane Magee, *Project Mgr*
Douglas Marshall, *Project Mgr*
EMP: 60
SALES: 22MM Privately Held
SIC: **1542** Nonresidential construction

(P-1652)
XL CONSTRUCTION CORPORATION (PA)
851 Buckeye Ct, Milpitas (95035-7408)
PHONE..................................408 240-6000
Eric Raff, *President*
Richard Walker, *COO*
Tom Humbert, *CFO*
Dave Beck, *Exec VP*
Steve Winslow, *Exec VP*
EMP: 122
SALES (est): 171.3MM Privately Held
WEB: www.xlconst.com
SIC: **1542** Commercial & office building, new construction; commercial & office buildings, renovation & repair

(P-1653)
ZUMWALT CONSTRUCTION INC
5520 E Lamona Ave, Fresno (93727-2276)
PHONE..................................559 252-1000
Kurt E Zumwalt, *President*
Teri Zumwalt, *Admin Sec*
Pamela Lacone, *Admin Asst*
Tyson Peters, *Project Mgr*
Richard Rathbone, *Project Mgr*
EMP: 100
SQ FT: 2,000
SALES: 22.8MM Privately Held
WEB: www.zumwaltconst.com
SIC: **1542** 1522 Commercial & office building, new construction; residential construction

---
1611 Highway & Street Construction

(P-1654)
A CSG-NOVA JOINT VENTURE
3960 Industrial Blvd # 500, West Sacramento (95691-3496)
P.O. Box 1505 (95691-1505)
PHONE..................................916 371-7303
Shelli Moreda, *Manager*
Scott Victor, *Co-Venturer*
EMP: 99

▲ = Import ▼=Export
◆ =Import/Export

SALES (est): 3MM **Privately Held**
SIC: **1611** 1623 1629 Airport runway construction; concrete construction: roads, highways, sidewalks, etc.; oil & gas pipeline construction; levee construction

(P-1655)
ADOPT-A-HIGHWAY MAINTENANCE
Also Called: Adopt-A-Beach
3158 Red Hill Ave Ste 200, Costa Mesa (92626-3416)
PHONE..................800 200-0003
Peter Morin, *CEO*
Patricia Nelson, *President*
Dan Day, *CFO*
Dennis Day, *Admin Sec*
EMP: 104
SQ FT: 6,000
SALES (est): 17.5MM **Privately Held**
WEB: www.adoptabeach.com
SIC: **1611** 4959 Highway & street maintenance; sanitary services

(P-1656)
AECOM ENERGY & CNSTR INC
Also Called: Washington Group
2850 Carmel Valley Rd, Del Mar (92014-3800)
PHONE..................858 481-9502
EMP: 359
SALES (corp-wide): 20.1B **Publicly Held**
WEB: www.wgint.com
SIC: **1611** Highway & street construction
HQ: Aecom Energy & Construction, Inc.
1999 Avenue Of The Stars
Los Angeles CA 90067
213 593-8100

(P-1657)
ALL AMERICAN ASPHALT (PA)
Also Called: All American Agrigate
400 E 6th St, Corona (92879-1521)
P.O. Box 2229 (92878-2229)
PHONE..................951 736-7600
Mark Albert Luer, *President*
Mark Luer, *President*
Eric Lohrenz, *Program Mgr*
Gordon Kline, *Project Mgr*
Jim McGee, *Project Mgr*
EMP: 60
SALES (est): 170.5MM **Privately Held**
WEB: www.allamericanasphalt.net
SIC: **1611** 5032 Highway & street paving contractor; brick, stone & related material

(P-1658)
ALL AMERICAN ASPHALT
All American Service and Sup
1776 All American Way, Corona (92879-2070)
P.O. Box 2229 (92878-2229)
PHONE..................951 736-7617
Kim McGuire, *Manager*
EMP: 150
SALES (corp-wide): 170.5MM **Privately Held**
WEB: www.allamericanasphalt.net
SIC: **1611** Highway & street paving contractor
PA: All American Asphalt
400 E 6th St
Corona CA 92879
951 736-7600

(P-1659)
ALL AMERICAN ASPHALT
Camco Construction Supply
1776 All American Way, Corona (92879-2070)
PHONE..................951 736-7617
Kim McGuire, *Branch Mgr*
EMP: 150
SALES (corp-wide): 170.5MM **Privately Held**
WEB: www.allamericanasphalt.net
SIC: **1611** Highway & street paving contractor
PA: All American Asphalt
400 E 6th St
Corona CA 92879
951 736-7600

(P-1660)
AMERICAN ASPHALT SOUTH INC
14436 Santa Ana Ave, Fontana (92337-7141)
P.O. Box 310036 (92331-0036)
PHONE..................909 427-8276
Alan Henderson, *President*
Kim Henschel, *Vice Pres*
Jeff Petty, *Vice Pres*
Lyle Stone, *Admin Sec*
EMP: 65
SALES (est): 12.3MM **Privately Held**
WEB: www.americanasphaltsouth.com
SIC: **1611** Highway & street maintenance; surfacing & paving

(P-1661)
AMERICAN CIVIL CONST
Also Called: ACC West Coast
2990 Bay Vista Ct Ste D, Benicia (94510-1195)
PHONE..................707 746-8028
Jeffrey Foerste, *President*
Clifford Barber, *Vice Pres*
David Wilkerson, *Vice Pres*
EMP: 75
SQ FT: 19,000
SALES (est): 13.5MM **Privately Held**
WEB: www.wcbridge.com
SIC: **1611** 1622 Surfacing & paving; bridge construction
PA: American Civil Constructors Holdings, Inc.
4901 S Windermere St
Littleton CO 80120

(P-1662)
AMERICAN PAVING CO
Also Called: WM LYLES CO
315 N Thorne Ave, Fresno (93706-1444)
P.O. Box 4348 (93744-4348)
PHONE..................559 268-9886
Steve Poindexter, *President*
Ross Jenkins, *COO*
John Leonardo, *CFO*
Jimmy Brager, *Manager*
EMP: 50
SQ FT: 9,000
SALES: 17.2MM
SALES (corp-wide): 28.6MM **Privately Held**
WEB: www.americanpavingco.com
SIC: **1611** 1771 Highway & street paving contractor; curb construction; sidewalk contractor
PA: Lyles Diversified, Inc.
1210 W Olive Ave
Fresno CA 93728
559 441-1900

(P-1663)
AMG CONSTRUCTION GROUP
1103 W Gardena Blvd # 201, Gardena (90248-5239)
PHONE..................800 310-2609
Calvin Jackson, *CEO*
EMP: 69
SQ FT: 1,600
SALES (est): 2.8MM **Privately Held**
SIC: **1611** General contractor, highway & street construction

(P-1664)
AMS PAVING INC (PA)
11060 Rose Ave, Fontana (92337-7051)
PHONE..................909 357-0711
William E Hawkins, *Principal*
EMP: 50
SQ FT: 4,000
SALES (est): 15.9MM **Privately Held**
WEB: www.amspaving.com
SIC: **1611** Highway & street paving contractor; surfacing & paving

(P-1665)
ANVIL BUILDERS INC
1475 Donner Ave, San Francisco (94124-3614)
PHONE..................415 285-5000
Alan Guy, *COO*
Ann Hauer, *Vice Pres*
Richard Leider, *Admin Sec*
EMP: 125
SQ FT: 4,000

SALES: 28MM **Privately Held**
SIC: **1611** 1623 General contractor, highway & street construction; water, sewer & utility lines

(P-1666)
ARGONAUT CONSTRUCTORS
360 Sutton Pl, Santa Rosa (95407-8121)
P.O. Box 639 (95402-0639)
PHONE..................707 542-4862
Michael D Smith, *CEO*
Michael A Smith, *Vice Pres*
EMP: 175 EST: 1957
SQ FT: 10,000
SALES: 28.1MM **Privately Held**
WEB: www.argonautconstructors.com
SIC: **1611** 1623 Highway & street paving contractor; oil & gas pipeline construction

(P-1667)
ATKINSON CONSTRUCTION INC
18201 Von Karman Ave # 800, Irvine (92612-1092)
PHONE..................303 410-2540
John O'Keefe, *President*
EMP: 450
SALES (est): 44.7MM
SALES (corp-wide): 2B **Privately Held**
SIC: **1611** 1622 Highway & street construction; bridge, tunnel & elevated highway
HQ: Clark Construction Group, Llc
7500 Old Georgetown Rd # 3
Bethesda MD 20814
301 272-8100

(P-1668)
AVAR CONSTRUCTION INC
GMI
47375 Fremont Blvd, Fremont (94538-6521)
PHONE..................510 354-2000
EMP: 79
SALES (corp-wide): 25MM **Privately Held**
SIC: **1611** Highway & street construction
PA: Avar Construction, Inc
47375 Fremont Blvd
Fremont CA 94538
510 354-2000

(P-1669)
BASIC RESOURCES INC (PA)
928 12th St Ste 700, Modesto (95354-2330)
P.O. Box 3191 (95353-3191)
PHONE..................209 521-9771
Jeffrey Reed, *CEO*
Wendell Reed, *President*
Leatha Wilson, *Admin Sec*
John Birchall, *Sales Mgr*
▲ EMP: 50
SALES (est): 214.4MM **Privately Held**
SIC: **1611** 3273 2951 3532 Highway & street paving contractor; ready-mixed concrete; asphalt & asphaltic paving mixtures (not from refineries); mining machinery; construction machinery

(P-1670)
BEADOR CONSTRUCTION CO INC
26320 Lester Cir, Corona (92883-6399)
PHONE..................951 674-7352
David A Beador, *President*
EMP: 80
SQ FT: 1,415
SALES (est): 20.4MM **Privately Held**
SIC: **1611** General contractor, highway & street construction

(P-1671)
BECHO INC
15901 Olden St, Sylmar (91342-1051)
PHONE..................818 362-8391
Tim Smith, *President*
Louis Lucido, *President*
William B Sparks, *Treasurer*
Steve Pavoggi, *Vice Pres*
Jim Tripp, *Vice Pres*
▲ EMP: 60 EST: 1979
SQ FT: 8,000

SALES: 9.4MM
SALES (corp-wide): 4.4B **Publicly Held**
WEB: www.bechoinc.com
SIC: **1611** 1622 1799 Highway & street paving contractor; bridge construction; shoring & underpinning work
PA: Tutor Perini Corporation
15901 Olden St
Sylmar CA 91342
818 362-8391

(P-1672)
BENS ASPHALT & MAINT CO INC
Also Called: Medina Construction
2537 Rubidoux Blvd, Riverside (92509-2142)
PHONE..................951 248-1103
EMP: 50
SALES (corp-wide): 21.6MM **Privately Held**
WEB: www.bensasphalt.com
SIC: **1611** Surfacing & paving
PA: Ben's Asphalt & Maintenance Company, Inc.
2200 S Yale St Ste A
Santa Ana CA 92704
714 540-1700

(P-1673)
BRODERICK GEN ENGINNEERING INC
21750 8th St E Ste B, Sonoma (95476-9803)
PHONE..................707 996-7809
John Benward, *President*
Earl G Broderick, *Vice Pres*
EMP: 50
SQ FT: 6,400
SALES (est): 13.8MM **Privately Held**
WEB: www.benwardco.com
SIC: **1611** Surfacing & paving

(P-1674)
BURTCH TRUCKING INC
Also Called: Burtch Construction
18815 Highway 65, Bakersfield (93308-9794)
P.O. Box 80546 (93380-0546)
PHONE..................661 399-1736
Brenn Burtch McGowan, *President*
Linda Kay Burtch, *Principal*
Josh Rhoden, *Superintendent*
Marian Arandel, *Clerk*
EMP: 53
SQ FT: 4,000
SALES (est): 12.1MM **Privately Held**
WEB: www.burtchconstruction.com
SIC: **1611** Highway & street paving contractor

(P-1675)
CALIFORNIA PAV GRADING CO INC
3253 Verdugo Rd, Los Angeles (90065-2035)
P.O. Box 65966 (90065-0966)
PHONE..................323 372-5920
Foster Dennis, *President*
Lee Sepielli, *Corp Secy*
EMP: 58
SQ FT: 1,600
SALES (est): 17.9MM **Privately Held**
WEB: www.calpave.com
SIC: **1611** Surfacing & paving

(P-1676)
CALIFORNIA PAVEMENT MAINT INC
Also Called: RAYNER EQUIPMENT SYSTEMS
9390 Elder Creek Rd, Sacramento (95829-9326)
PHONE..................916 381-8033
Gordon L Rayner, *CEO*
Richard Rayner, *President*
Mick Marchini, *Vice Pres*
Bruce Taylor, *Vice Pres*
Kristofer Hendren, *Info Tech Mgr*
EMP: 107 EST: 1979
SQ FT: 24,300
SALES: 15.2MM **Privately Held**
WEB: www.cpmamerica.com
SIC: **1611** Highway & street paving contractor; surfacing & paving

PRODUCTS & SVCS

(P-1677)
CHIEF TRNSP & ENGRG CONTRS INC
Also Called: Chief Engineering Co
4056 Tamarind Rdg, Lake Elsinore
(92530-2041)
P.O. Box 677 (92531-0677)
PHONE..................951 258-6607
Jose Aceituno Jr, *CEO*
EMP: 78
SALES (est): 1.6MM **Privately Held**
SIC: 1611 Highway & street construction

(P-1678)
CHRISP COMPANY (PA)
43650 Osgood Rd, Fremont (94539-5631)
P.O. Box 1368 (94538-0136)
PHONE..................510 656-2840
Robert P Chrisp, *CEO*
Rob Bilotti, *CFO*
David Morris, *Vice Pres*
Roger Weisbrod, *Vice Pres*
Jake Chrisp, *Branch Mgr*
EMP: 140
SQ FT: 8,000
SALES (est): 69.3MM **Privately Held**
WEB: www.chrispco.com
SIC: 1611 Highway signs & guardrails

(P-1679)
CITY OF BURLINGAME
Also Called: Public Works and Highway Dept
1361 N Carolan Ave, Burlingame
(94010-2401)
PHONE..................650 558-7670
Rob Mallick, *Branch Mgr*
EMP: 50 **Privately Held**
SIC: 1611 Surfacing & paving
PA: City Of Burlingame
501 Primrose Rd
Burlingame CA 94010
650 558-7203

(P-1680)
CITY OF EL CENTRO
307 W Brighton Ave, El Centro
(92243-3004)
PHONE..................760 337-4505
Terry Heagan, *Principal*
Sergio Hernandez, *Deacon*
EMP: 200 **Privately Held**
SIC: 1611 Highway & street construction
PA: City Of El Centro
1275 W Main St
El Centro CA 92243
760 337-4510

(P-1681)
CITY OF ENCINITAS
Also Called: Street Maintenance Department
160 Calle Magdalena, Encinitas
(92024-3721)
PHONE..................760 633-2850
Larry Watt, *Branch Mgr*
EMP: 50 **Privately Held**
WEB: www.cityofencinitas.org
SIC: 1611 Highway & street maintenance
PA: City Of Encinitas
505 S Vulcan Ave
Encinitas CA 92024

(P-1682)
CITY OF LA MESA
Also Called: Lamesa City Public Works
8152 Commercial St, La Mesa
(91942-2926)
PHONE..................619 667-1450
Eric Johnson, *Superintendent*
EMP: 50 **Privately Held**
SIC: 1611 Highway & street maintenance
PA: La Mesa, City Of (Inc)
8130 Allison Ave
La Mesa CA 91942
619 463-6611

(P-1683)
CITY OF LONG BEACH
Public Works Department
411 W Ocean Blvd, Long Beach
(90802-4664)
PHONE..................562 570-6383
Raymond T Holland, *Director*
EMP: 500 **Privately Held**
SIC: 1611 Highway & street construction

PA: City Of Long Beach
411 W Ocean Blvd
Long Beach CA 90802
562 570-6450

(P-1684)
CITY OF MILL VALLEY
Also Called: Department of Public Works
26 Corte Madera Ave, Mill Valley
(94941-1830)
PHONE..................415 388-4033
Don Hunter, *Manager*
EMP: 120 **Privately Held**
WEB: www.donnadacuti.com
SIC: 1611 Highway & street maintenance
PA: City Of Mill Valley
26 Corte Madera Ave
Mill Valley CA 94941
415 388-4033

(P-1685)
CITY SERVICE CONTRACTING INC (PA)
Also Called: City Service Paving
920 Lawrence St, Placentia (92870-7031)
PHONE..................714 632-6610
Mike Garvin, *CEO*
Jon Beach, *CFO*
George Puente, *Vice Pres*
Brian Cunningham, *Project Mgr*
EMP: 74
SALES: 23MM **Privately Held**
WEB: www.citypaving.com
SIC: 1611 Surfacing & paving

(P-1686)
COMMERCIAL COATING COMPANY INC
Also Called: Commercial Paving
2809 W Avenue 37, Los Angeles
(90065-3620)
P.O. Box 65557 (90065-0557)
PHONE..................323 256-1331
Andrian Loera, *President*
William Emerson, *Treasurer*
EMP: 52
SQ FT: 10,000
SALES (est): 14.7MM **Privately Held**
SIC: 1611 Resurfacing contractor

(P-1687)
COUNTY OF ALAMEDA
Also Called: Public Works Dept
399 Elmhurst St, Hayward (94544-1307)
PHONE..................510 670-5455
Daniel Woldesenbet, *Director*
James Chu, *Engineer*
Arthur Valderrama, *Engineer*
Denise Fetty, *Human Res Mgr*
Cheri Harraway, *Personnel*
EMP: 300 **Privately Held**
WEB: www.co.alameda.ca.us
SIC: 1611 9199 Highway & street paving contractor; general government administration;
PA: County Of Alameda
1221 Oak St Ste 555
Oakland CA 94612
510 272-6691

(P-1688)
COUNTY OF CONTRA COSTA
Also Called: Administration of Public Works
255 Glacier Dr, Martinez (94553-4825)
PHONE..................925 313-2000
Julia Bueren, *Director*
EMP: 250
SQ FT: 29,865 **Privately Held**
SIC: 1611 Highway & street maintenance
PA: County Of Contra Costa
625 Court St Ste 100
Martinez CA 94553
925 957-5280

(P-1689)
COUNTY OF GLENN
Also Called: Planning and Public Works Agcy
777 N Colusa St, Willows (95988-2211)
P.O. Box 1070 (95988-1070)
PHONE..................530 934-6530
Dan Obermyer, *Manager*
EMP: 125 **Privately Held**
WEB: www.countyofglen.net
SIC: 1611 Highway & street maintenance

PA: County Of Glenn
516 W Sycamore St Fl 2
Willows CA 95988
530 934-6410

(P-1690)
COUNTY OF IMPERIAL
Also Called: Public Works
304 E 4th St, Imperial (92251-1725)
PHONE..................760 355-1748
Willy Riven, *Manager*
EMP: 60 **Privately Held**
WEB: www.imperialcounty.net
SIC: 1611 Concrete construction: roads, highways, sidewalks, etc.
PA: County Of Imperial
940 W Main St Ste 208
El Centro CA 92243
760 482-4556

(P-1691)
COUNTY OF LOS ANGELES
Also Called: Public Works, Dept of
38126 Sierra Hwy, Palmdale (93550-4607)
PHONE..................661 947-7173
Mark Caddick, *Manager*
EMP: 130 **Privately Held**
WEB: www.co.la.ca.us
SIC: 1611 9621 Highway & street maintenance; regulation, administration of transportation;
PA: County Of Los Angeles
500 W Temple St Ste 437
Los Angeles CA 90012
213 974-1101

(P-1692)
COUNTY OF LOS ANGELES
Also Called: Public Works, Dept of
1525 Alcazar St Bldg 1, Los Angeles
(90033-1001)
PHONE..................626 458-1700
Robert Scharf, *Director*
EMP: 250 **Privately Held**
WEB: www.co.la.ca.us
SIC: 1611 9511 Highway & street maintenance; sanitary engineering agency, government;
PA: County Of Los Angeles
500 W Temple St Ste 437
Los Angeles CA 90012
213 974-1101

(P-1693)
COUNTY OF MENDOCINO
Also Called: Transportation Dept
340 Lake Mendocino Dr, Ukiah
(95482-9432)
PHONE..................707 463-4363
Howard Dashiell, *Director*
EMP: 104 **Privately Held**
WEB: www.mcdss.org
SIC: 1611 8741 Highway & street construction; management services
PA: County Of Mendocino
501 Low Gap Rd Rm 1010
Ukiah CA 95482
707 463-4441

(P-1694)
COUNTY OF MONTEREY
Also Called: Monterey County Public Works
168 W Alisal St Fl 3, Salinas (93901-2487)
PHONE..................831 755-4800
Yaz Emrani, *Director*
EMP: 300 **Privately Held**
WEB: www.montereycountyfarmbureau.org
SIC: 1611 Highway & street construction
PA: County Of Monterey
168 W Alisal St Fl 2
Salinas CA 93901
831 755-5040

(P-1695)
D A MCCOSKER CONSTRUCTION CO
Also Called: Independent Construction Co
3911 Laura Alice Way, Concord
(94520-8544)
PHONE..................925 686-1780
Brian Clay McCosker, *President*
David A McCosker, *Ch of Bd*
Mike Morris, *Treasurer*
Brian Cartmell, *Admin Sec*
James Huff, *Foreman/Supr*
EMP: 50 EST: 1910

SALES (est): 26.3MM **Privately Held**
SIC: 1611 Surfacing & paving; grading; highway & street paving contractor

(P-1696)
D W POWELL CONSTRUCTION INC
8555 Banana Ave, Fontana (92335-3019)
PHONE..................909 356-8880
Doyle W Powell, *President*
Suzanne Powell, *Admin Sec*
Richard Wiley, *Manager*
EMP: 50
SQ FT: 2,000
SALES (est): 7MM **Privately Held**
SIC: 1611 General contractor, highway & street construction

(P-1697)
DENNIS M MCCOY & SONS INC
32107 Lindero Canyon Rd # 212, Westlake Village (91361-4255)
PHONE..................818 874-3872
Dennis McCoy, *CEO*
Morgan McCoy, *President*
Greg Abercrombie, *Controller*
Sean Ada, *Hum Res Coord*
EMP: 75
SQ FT: 3,000
SALES (est): 14.2MM **Privately Held**
WEB: www.mccoyandsons.com
SIC: 1611 Grading

(P-1698)
DESILVA GATES CONSTRUCTION LP
7700 College Town Dr # 230, Sacramento
(95826-2303)
PHONE..................916 386-9708
Edwin O Desilva, *Branch Mgr*
EMP: 124 **Privately Held**
SIC: 1611 General contractor, highway & street construction
PA: Desilva Gates Construction L.P.
11555 Dublin Blvd
Dublin CA 94568

(P-1699)
DESILVA GATES CONSTRUCTION LP (PA)
11555 Dublin Blvd, Dublin (94568-2854)
P.O. Box 2909 (94568-0909)
PHONE..................925 361-1380
Edwin O Desilva, *President*
David Desilva, *Exec VP*
Richard B Gates, *Exec VP*
J Scott Archibald, *Vice Pres*
Pete Davos, *Vice Pres*
EMP: 100
SALES (est): 117.8MM **Privately Held**
WEB: www.desilvagates.com
SIC: 1611 1794 1542 General contractor, highway & street construction; excavation & grading, building construction; nonresidential construction

(P-1700)
DISNEY CONSTRUCTION INC
533 Airport Blvd Ste 120, Burlingame
(94010-2007)
PHONE..................650 689-5149
Richard L Disney, *President*
Paul Kvam, *Project Engr*
Sean Lennan, *Project Engr*
Omid Miri, *Engineer*
EMP: 60
SALES: 30MM **Privately Held**
SIC: 1611 Highway & street construction

(P-1701)
DOUMIT COMMUNICATION INC
25 Cadillac Dr Ste 134, Sacramento
(95825-8358)
PHONE..................916 362-3519
Samir Doumit, *President*
Geralee Doumit, *Corp Secy*
EMP: 58 EST: 1996
SALES (est): 6.5MM **Privately Held**
SIC: 1611 7389 General contractor, highway & street construction;

▲ = Import ▼=Export
◆ =Import/Export

(P-1702)
DRYCO CONSTRUCTION INC
(PA)
42745 Boscell Rd, Fremont (94538-3106)
PHONE..................................510 438-6500
Daren R Young, *President*
Kevin Mitchell, *Vice Pres*
Rafael Torres, *Vice Pres*
Sandra Young, *Admin Sec*
Brian Robertson, *Info Tech Dir*
EMP: 180
SQ FT: 3,700
SALES (est): 78.9MM **Privately Held**
WEB: www.dryco.com
SIC: **1611** 1721 5211 Highway & street paving contractor; pavement marking contractor; lumber & other building materials

(P-1703)
DUSTIN HOKE
999 Corporate Dr, Ladera Ranch (92694-2146)
PHONE..................................949 347-8670
Dustin Hoke, *Owner*
EMP: 65
SQ FT: 11,000
SALES (est): 361K **Privately Held**
SIC: **1611** General contractor, highway & street construction

(P-1704)
EBS GENERAL ENGINEERING INC
1320 E 6th St Ste 100, Corona (92879-1700)
PHONE..................................951 279-6869
Joe Nanci, *President*
Tom Nanci, *Controller*
EMP: 80
SQ FT: 4,000
SALES (est): 13.2MM **Privately Held**
SIC: **1611** Highway & street construction

(P-1705)
ED SAFETY SERVICES INC
1040 W Kettleman Ln # 388, Lodi (95240-6056)
PHONE..................................209 333-0807
Nicole Beadles, *President*
Robert Beadles, *Director*
EMP: 112
SALES (est): 11.5MM **Privately Held**
SIC: **1611** Highway & street construction

(P-1706)
FOOTH THE / EASTE TRANS CORRI
125 Pacifica Ste 100, Irvine (92618-3324)
PHONE..................................949 754-3400
Michael Kraman, *CEO*
Amy Potter, *CFO*
EMP: 70
SQ FT: 10,000
SALES: 214.4MM **Privately Held**
SIC: **1611** General contractor, highway & street construction

(P-1707)
GCI CONSTRUCTION INC
1031 Calle Recodo Ste D, San Clemente (92673-6269)
PHONE..................................714 957-0233
Terry Gillespie, *President*
Floyd Bennett, *Treasurer*
Richard Tirrell, *Vice Pres*
EMP: 50
SQ FT: 3,000
SALES (est): 8.3MM **Privately Held**
SIC: **1611** Highway & street construction

(P-1708)
GHILOTTI BROS INC
525 Jacoby St, San Rafael (94901-5370)
PHONE..................................415 454-7011
Dante W Ghilotti, *CEO*
Michael M Ghilotti, *President*
Daniel Y Chin, *CFO*
Thomas G Barr, *Vice Pres*
Tom Barr, *Vice Pres*
▲ EMP: 290 EST: 1914
SQ FT: 86,249
SALES (est): 103MM **Privately Held**
WEB: www.ghilottibros.com
SIC: **1611** 1794 1623 Surfacing & paving; grading; highway & street paving contractor; excavation work; water, sewer & utility lines

(P-1709)
GHILOTTI CONSTRUCTION CO INC
600 S Napa Junction Rd, American Canyon (94503-1277)
PHONE..................................707 556-9145
Mark Bower, *Branch Mgr*
EMP: 119 **Privately Held**
WEB: www.ghilotti.com
SIC: **1611** 1623 General contractor, highway & street construction; underground utilities contractor
PA: Ghilotti Construction Company, Inc.
246 Ghillotti Ave
Santa Rosa CA 95407
-

(P-1710)
GLENN CNTY PLG PUB WORKS AGCY
777 N Colusa St, Willows (95988-2211)
P.O. Box 1070 (95988-1070)
PHONE..................................530 934-6541
David Shoemaker, *Director*
EMP: 75
SALES (est): 6.1MM **Privately Held**
SIC: **1611** Highway & street construction

(P-1711)
GRAHAM CONTRACTORS INC
860 Lonus St, San Jose (95126-3713)
P.O. Box 26770 (95159-6770)
PHONE..................................408 293-9516
Gerald Graham Jr, *President*
Reed Graham, *Vice Pres*
John Waiters, *General Mgr*
Damen Bertola, *Controller*
EMP: 50
SQ FT: 1,200
SALES (est): 10.4MM **Privately Held**
WEB: www.grahamcontractors.com
SIC: **1611** Highway & street paving contractor

(P-1712)
GRANIT-BAYASHI 3 A JOINT VENTR
585 W Beach St, Watsonville (95076-5123)
P.O. Box 50085 (95077-5085)
PHONE..................................831 724-1011
Tobi Stonich, *Administration*
Rinkou Aki,
Jigisha Desai,
Mathew Tyler,
EMP: 50
SALES (est): 1.3MM **Privately Held**
SIC: **1611** 1542 Highway & street construction; nonresidential construction

(P-1713)
GRANITE CONSTRUCTION COMPANY (HQ)
585 W Beach St, Watsonville (95076-5123)
P.O. Box 50085 (95077-5085)
PHONE..................................831 724-1011
James H Roberts, *President*
Laurel Krzeminski, *Exec VP*
Christopher S Miller, *Exec VP*
Richard A Watts, *Vice Pres*
Mike Barker, *Controller*
▼ EMP: 200 EST: 1922
SQ FT: 39,000
SALES (est): 868.9MM
SALES (corp-wide): 3.3B **Publicly Held**
WEB:
www.graniteconstructioncompany.com
SIC: **1611** 1622 Highway & street construction; general contractor, highway & street construction; bridge construction; tunnel construction
PA: Granite Construction Incorporated
585 W Beach St
Watsonville CA 95076
831 724-1011

(P-1714)
GRANITE CONSTRUCTION COMPANY
3005 James Rd, Bakersfield (93308-9179)
P.O. Box 5127 (93388-5127)
PHONE..................................661 399-3361
Bruce McGowan, *Branch Mgr*
Tina Bird, *Principal*
Timothy Findley, *Project Mgr*
EMP: 200
SALES (corp-wide): 3.3B **Publicly Held**
WEB: www.graniteconstruction.com
SIC: **1611** Highway & street construction
HQ: Granite Construction Company
585 W Beach St
Watsonville CA 95076
831 724-1011

(P-1715)
GRANITE CONSTRUCTION COMPANY
Also Called: Southern California Regional
38000 Monroe St, Indio (92203-9500)
PHONE..................................760 775-7500
Jay McQuillen, *Manager*
EMP: 393
SALES (corp-wide): 3.3B **Publicly Held**
WEB:
www.graniteconstructioncompany.com
SIC: **1611** 1771 Highway & street construction; concrete work
HQ: Granite Construction Company
585 W Beach St
Watsonville CA 95076
831 724-1011

(P-1716)
GRANITE CONSTRUCTION COMPANY
5335 Debbie Rd, Santa Barbara (93111-2001)
P.O. Box 6744 (93160-6744)
PHONE..................................805 964-9951
Bruce McGowan, *Manager*
Quan-Handley Patty, *Manager*
EMP: 169
SQ FT: 65,396
SALES (corp-wide): 3.3B **Publicly Held**
WEB: www.graniteconstruction.com
SIC: **1611** Highway & street construction
HQ: Granite Construction Company
585 W Beach St
Watsonville CA 95076
831 724-1011

(P-1717)
GRANITE CONSTRUCTION COMPANY
21541 E Bear Mtn Blvd, Arvin (93203)
PHONE..................................661 854-3051
Mike Hosley, *Branch Mgr*
EMP: 67
SALES (corp-wide): 3.3B **Publicly Held**
WEB: www.graniteconstruction.com
SIC: **1611** Highway & street construction
HQ: Granite Construction Company
585 W Beach St
Watsonville CA 95076
831 724-1011

(P-1718)
GRANITE CONSTRUCTION COMPANY
Also Called: Palmdale Area
213 E Avenue M, Lancaster (93535-5335)
PHONE..................................661 726-4447
Steve Bridge, *Branch Mgr*
EMP: 150
SQ FT: 12,716
SALES (corp-wide): 3.3B **Publicly Held**
WEB: www.graniteconstruction.com
SIC: **1611** Highway & street paving contractor
HQ: Granite Construction Company
585 W Beach St
Watsonville CA 95076
831 724-1011

(P-1719)
GRANITE CONSTRUCTION COMPANY
715 Comstock St, Santa Clara (95054-3403)
PHONE..................................408 327-7000

Pat Traberso, *Manager*
EMP: 182
SQ FT: 22,902
SALES (corp-wide): 3.3B **Publicly Held**
WEB: www.corpconstruction.com
SIC: **1611** 1622 1629 General contractor, highway & street construction; bridge construction; dams, waterways, docks & other marine construction
HQ: Granite Construction Company
585 W Beach St
Watsonville CA 95076
831 724-1011

(P-1720)
GRANITE CONSTRUCTION COMPANY
2716 S Granite Ct, Fresno (93706-5455)
PHONE..................................559 441-5700
Todd Hill, *Manager*
EMP: 225
SALES (corp-wide): 3.3B **Publicly Held**
SIC: **1611** General contractor, highway & street construction
HQ: Granite Construction Company
585 W Beach St
Watsonville CA 95076
831 724-1011

(P-1721)
GRANITE CONSTRUCTION INC
2095 Us Highway 111, El Centro (92243-9731)
PHONE..................................760 337-3030
Jeff Mercer, *Manager*
EMP: 120
SALES (corp-wide): 3.3B **Publicly Held**
WEB: www.graniteconstruction.com
SIC: **1611** General contractor, highway & street construction
PA: Granite Construction Incorporated
585 W Beach St
Watsonville CA 95076
831 724-1011

(P-1722)
GRANITE CONSTRUCTION INC
5 Justin Ct, Monterey (93940-5733)
P.O. Box 720, Watsonville (95077-0720)
PHONE..................................831 657-1700
Kurt Kniffin, *Principal*
EMP: 67
SALES (corp-wide): 3.3B **Publicly Held**
WEB: www.graniteconstruction.com
SIC: **1611** General contractor, highway & street construction
PA: Granite Construction Incorporated
585 W Beach St
Watsonville CA 95076
831 724-1011

(P-1723)
GRANITE CONSTRUCTION INC
4291 Bradshaw Rd, Sacramento (95827-3805)
PHONE..................................916 855-4495
Ryan Bingle, *Manager*
Sandy Smithers, *Executive Asst*
Amy Tobia, *Administration*
Brian Kotaska, *MIS Mgr*
Kelly Mitchell, *Business Mgr*
EMP: 67
SALES (corp-wide): 3.3B **Publicly Held**
WEB: www.graniteconstruction.com
SIC: **1611** General contractor, highway & street construction
PA: Granite Construction Incorporated
585 W Beach St
Watsonville CA 95076
831 724-1011

(P-1724)
GRANITE CONSTRUCTION INC
1324 S State St, Ukiah (95482-6414)
PHONE..................................707 467-4100
Dan Schuster, *Manager*
EMP: 67
SALES (corp-wide): 3.3B **Publicly Held**
WEB: www.graniteconstruction.com
SIC: **1611** General contractor, highway & street construction
PA: Granite Construction Incorporated
585 W Beach St
Watsonville CA 95076
831 724-1011

(P-1725)
GRANITE CONSTRUCTION INC
25485 Iverson Rd, Gonzales (93926-9403)
PHONE..................831 763-5595
Eric Gaboury, *Manager*
EMP: 67
SALES (corp-wide): 3.3B **Publicly Held**
WEB: www.graniteconstruction.com
SIC: 1611 General contractor, highway &
street construction
PA: Granite Construction Incorporated
585 W Beach St
Watsonville CA 95076
831 724-1011

(P-1726)
GRANITE CONSTRUCTION INC
1800 Felton Quarry Rd, Felton
(95018-9153)
PHONE..................831 335-3445
Eric Gaboury, *Manager*
EMP: 67
SALES (corp-wide): 3.3B **Publicly Held**
WEB: www.graniteconstruction.com
SIC: 1611 General contractor, highway &
street construction
PA: Granite Construction Incorporated
585 W Beach St
Watsonville CA 95076
831 724-1011

(P-1727)
GRANITE ROCK CO
1900 Quarry Rd, Aromas (95004)
P.O. Box 699 (95004-0699)
PHONE..................831 768-2330
Carey Wong, *Branch Mgr*
EMP: 151
SALES (corp-wide): 992MM **Privately
Held**
SIC: 1611 Surfacing & paving
PA: Granite Rock Co.
350 Technology Dr
Watsonville CA 95076
831 768-2000

(P-1728)
GRANITE ROCK CO
Also Called: Pavex Construction Company
355 Blomquist St, Redwood City
(94063-2701)
PHONE..................650 869-3370
John Franich, *Manager*
Wayne Holman, *Vice Pres*
Jason Alger, *Financial Analy*
EMP: 300
SALES (corp-wide): 992MM **Privately
Held**
WEB: www.graniterock.com
SIC: 1611 Highway & street paving con-
tractor
PA: Granite Rock Co.
350 Technology Dr
Watsonville CA 95076
831 768-2000

(P-1729)
GRIFFITH COMPANY (PA)
3050 E Birch St, Brea (92821-6248)
PHONE..................714 984-5500
Thomas L Foss, *CEO*
Jim Waltze, *Ch of Bd*
Jaimie Angus, *COO*
Dan McGrew, *VP Bus Dvlpt*
Mike Fenley, *Division Mgr*
EMP: 60 **EST:** 1922
SQ FT: 100,000
SALES (est): 117.9MM **Privately Held**
SIC: 1611 General contractor, highway &
street construction

(P-1730)
GRIFFITH COMPANY
12200 Bloomfield Ave, Santa Fe Springs
(90670-4742)
PHONE..................562 929-1128
Dan Magrew, *Manager*
Walt Weishaar, *Regional Mgr*
Tracey Novak, *Administration*
Dan Leeper, *Project Mgr*
Scott McLure, *Project Mgr*
EMP: 60
SQ FT: 4,036

SALES (corp-wide): 117.9MM **Privately
Held**
SIC: 1611 1622 General contractor, highway & street construction; bridge construction; tunnel construction
PA: Griffith Company
3050 E Birch St
Brea CA 92821
714 984-5500

(P-1731)
HARDY & HARPER INC
32 Rancho Cir, Lake Forest (92630-8325)
PHONE..................714 444-1851
Daniel Thomas Maas, *CEO*
Fred T Maas Sr, *Director*
EMP: 50 **EST:** 1946
SALES (est): 13.1MM **Privately Held**
WEB: www.hardyandharper.com
SIC: 1611 2951 Surfacing & paving; as-
phalt paving mixtures & blocks

(P-1732)
HILLCREST CONTRACTING INC
1467 Circle City Dr, Corona (92879-1668)
P.O. Box 1898 (92878-1898)
PHONE..................951 273-9600
Glenn J Salsbury, *President*
E G Lindholm, *Vice Pres*
Amanda Gutierrez, *Administration*
Jason Jones, *Project Mgr*
Darcy Searle, *Project Mgr*
EMP: 75
SQ FT: 11,600
SALES (est): 20.5MM **Privately Held**
SIC: 1611 General contractor, highway &
street construction

(P-1733)
**INTERNATIONAL PAVING SVCS
INC**
Also Called: I P S
1199 Opal Ave, Mentone (92359-1284)
P.O. Box 10458, San Bernardino (92423-
0458)
PHONE..................909 794-2101
Brent Rieger, *President*
EMP: 80 **EST:** 2007
SALES (est): 11.5MM **Privately Held**
SIC: 1611 Surfacing & paving

(P-1734)
**J B BOSTICK COMPANY INC
(PA)**
2870 E La Cresta Ave, Anaheim
(92806-1816)
PHONE..................714 238-2121
James B Bostick, *President*
Jerry Hamlin, *Vice Pres*
EMP: 75
SQ FT: 2,870
SALES (est): 31.4MM **Privately Held**
WEB: www.jbbostick.net
SIC: 1611 1771 Grading; highway & street
paving contractor; concrete work

(P-1735)
J HARRIS SIM INC (PA)
9685 Via Excelencia # 200, San Diego
(92126-7500)
PHONE..................858 437-0190
James Coffman, *President*
John Palmer, *Vice Pres*
EMP: 85 **EST:** 2005
SQ FT: 10,000
SALES (est): 4.5MM **Privately Held**
SIC: 1611 General contractor, highway &
street construction

(P-1736)
**JACOBSSON ENGRG CNSTR
INC**
72310 Varner Rd, Thousand Palms
(92276-3362)
P.O. Box 14430, Palm Desert (92255-
4430)
PHONE..................760 345-8700
Dan Jacobsson, *President*
Ingeborg Jacobsson, *Treasurer*
EMP: 75
SQ FT: 9,000
SALES (est): 11.3MM **Privately Held**
WEB: www.jacobssoninc.com
SIC: 1611 Highway & street construction

(P-1737)
JAMES MCMINN INC
21834 Cactus Ave, Riverside (92518-3005)
PHONE..................909 514-1231
Jim McMinn, *President*
Rick Monge, *Vice Pres*
EMP: 50
SALES: 12MM **Privately Held**
SIC: 1611 Grading

(P-1738)
JJ FISHER CONSTRUCTION INC
261 W Dana St Ste 100, Nipomo
(93444-9151)
P.O. Box 2219 (93444-2219)
PHONE..................805 723-5220
Jayson Fisher, *CEO*
Mark Sczbecki, *CFO*
EMP: 65
SALES: 12MM **Privately Held**
SIC: 1611 1771 1794 1761 Gravel or dirt
road construction; concrete work; curb
construction; blacktop (asphalt) work; ex-
cavation work; gutter & downspout con-
tractor

(P-1739)
**JOHN BRINK GENERAL
CONTRACTOR**
1760 W Lake Blvd Ste 3, Tahoe City
(96145-1868)
P.O. Box 1902 (96145-1902)
PHONE..................530 583-2005
John Brink, *Owner*
Garrett Shick, *Project Mgr*
EMP: 50 **EST:** 1974
SALES (est): 4MM **Privately Held**
SIC: 1611 General contractor, highway &
street construction

(P-1740)
KEC ENGINEERING
200 N Sherman Ave, Corona (92882-7162)
P.O. Box 909 (92878-0909)
PHONE..................951 734-3010
James Elfring, *President*
Les Card, *Vice Pres*
EMP: 110
SQ FT: 9,600
SALES (est): 23.8MM **Privately Held**
WEB: www.kecengineering.com
SIC: 1611 General contractor, highway &
street construction

(P-1741)
**KIEWIT INFRASTRUCTURE
WEST CO**
12700 Stowe Dr Ste 180, Poway
(92064-8883)
PHONE..................360 693-1478
R Michael Phelps, *President*
Jack Goldberg, *Info Tech Mgr*
James Nolan, *Director*
EMP: 60
SALES (corp-wide): 16.1B **Privately Held**
SIC: 1611 Highway & street construction
HQ: Kiewit Infrastructure West Co.
3555 Farnam St
Omaha NE 68131
402 342-2052

(P-1742)
**KIEWIT INFRASTRUCTURE
WEST CO**
1111 Broadway, Oakland (94607-4139)
PHONE..................510 452-1400
William Silver, *Branch Mgr*
EMP: 54
SALES (corp-wide): 16.1B **Privately Held**
SIC: 1611 General contractor, highway &
street construction
HQ: Kiewit Infrastructure West Co.
3555 Farnam St
Omaha NE 68131
402 342-2052

(P-1743)
**KIEWIT INFRASTRUCTURE
WEST CO**
3200 Busch Rd, Pleasanton (94566)
PHONE..................925 462-1088
Allan Kung, *General Mgr*
EMP: 80

SALES (corp-wide): 16.1B **Privately Held**
WEB: www.kiecon.com
SIC: 1611 General contractor, highway &
street construction
HQ: Kiewit Infrastructure West Co.
3555 Farnam St
Omaha NE 68131
402 342-2052

(P-1744)
**KIEWIT INFRASTRUCTURE
WEST CO**
10704 Shoemaker Ave, Santa Fe Springs
(90670-4040)
PHONE..................562 946-1816
Ken Riley, *Manager*
David Linderman, *Project Mgr*
EMP: 125
SQ FT: 12,514
SALES (corp-wide): 16.1B **Privately Held**
WEB: www.kiecon.com
SIC: 1611 1542 1541 General contractor,
highway & street construction; nonresi-
dential construction; industrial buildings &
warehouses
HQ: Kiewit Infrastructure West Co.
3555 Farnam St
Omaha NE 68131
402 342-2052

(P-1745)
**KIEWIT INFRASTRUCTURE
WEST CO**
Also Called: Kie Con
3551 Wilbur Ave, Antioch (94509-8530)
PHONE..................925 754-9494
John Burke, *Manager*
EMP: 50
SQ FT: 4,320
SALES (corp-wide): 16.1B **Privately Held**
WEB: www.kiecon.com
SIC: 1611 General contractor, highway &
street construction
HQ: Kiewit Infrastructure West Co.
3555 Farnam St
Omaha NE 68131
402 342-2052

(P-1746)
**LARRY JACINTO
CONSTRUCTION INC**
9555 N Wabash Ave, Redlands
(92374-2714)
P.O. Box 615, Mentone (92359-0615)
PHONE..................909 794-2151
Larry Frankland Jacinto, *President*
Dennis Drexler, *Vice Pres*
Scott Dickerson, *Sales Staff*
Alyssa Mobley, *Receptionist*
Scott Smith, *Superintendent*
EMP: 80
SQ FT: 8,500
SALES (est): 23.6MM **Privately Held**
SIC: 1611 Grading; highway & street
paving contractor; sidewalk construction

(P-1747)
**LEGACY PARTNERS LIMITED
INC**
Also Called: Legacy Paving
738 W Washington Ave A, Escondido
(92025-1692)
PHONE..................760 747-2711
EMP: 53
SALES (est): 4.4MM **Privately Held**
WEB: www.legacypaving.com
SIC: 1611

(P-1748)
LUND EQUIPMENT LP
5302 Roseville Rd, North Highlands
(95660-5036)
PHONE..................916 344-5800
Walter Martinez, *Principal*
EMP: 50
SALES (est): 6.5MM **Privately Held**
SIC: 1611 General contractor, highway &
street construction

(P-1749)
M F MAHER INC
Also Called: Maher M F Concrete Cnstr
490 Ryder St, Vallejo (94590-7217)
PHONE..................707 552-2774
Malcolm F Maher, *President*

Janice K Maher, *Corp Secy*
Ronald Maher, *Vice Pres*
Steve Maher, *Executive*
Mike Maher, *Office Mgr*
EMP: 70
SQ FT: 4,000
SALES (est): 11.8MM **Privately Held**
WEB: www.mfmaher.com
SIC: 1611 General contractor, highway & street construction

(P-1750)
MACRO-Z-TECHNOLOGY COMPANY (PA)
Also Called: M Z T
841 E Washington Ave, Santa Ana (92701-3878)
PHONE....................714 564-1130
Bryan J Zatica, *CEO*
Julie Moore, *Manager*
EMP: 97
SQ FT: 3,000
SALES (est): 45.8MM **Privately Held**
SIC: 1611 1542 8711 Concrete construction: roads, highways, sidewalks, etc.; commercial & office building contractors; engineering services

(P-1751)
MAMCO INC (PA)
Also Called: Alabbasi
764 Ramona Expy Ste C, Perris (92571-9716)
PHONE....................951 776-9300
Marwan Alabbasi, *CEO*
Elizabeth Alabbasi, *President*
Rumzi Alabbasi, *Vice Pres*
EMP: 120
SQ FT: 2,200
SALES (est): 34.6MM **Privately Held**
SIC: 1611 General contractor, highway & street construction

(P-1752)
MANHOLE ADJUSTING CONTRS INC
9500 Beverly Rd, Pico Rivera (90660-2135)
PHONE....................323 725-1387
John Corcoran, *President*
Maria E Corcoran, *Vice Pres*
Aung Win, *Controller*
EMP: 50
SALES (est): 10.8MM **Privately Held**
SIC: 1611 General contractor, highway & street construction; highway & street paving contractor

(P-1753)
MARATHON GENERAL INC
1728 Mission Rd, Escondido (92029-1111)
PHONE....................760 738-9714
Mark Miller, *President*
Steven Gallant, *CFO*
Donald Tolen, *Vice Pres*
EMP: 80
SQ FT: 3,000
SALES (est): 18.5MM **Privately Held**
WEB: www.maragen.com
SIC: 1611 Grading; highway & street paving contractor

(P-1754)
MARTIN BROTHERS CONSTRUCTION (PA)
8801 Folsom Blvd Ste 260, Sacramento (95826-3250)
PHONE....................916 386-1600
Felipe Martin, *President*
EMP: 75
SQ FT: 9,300
SALES (est): 26MM **Privately Held**
SIC: 1611 1794 1541 1795 General contractor, highway & street construction; surfacing & paving; highway & street paving contractor; excavation work; excavation & grading, building construction; industrial buildings, new construction; demolition, buildings & other structures

(P-1755)
MATICH CORPORATION (PA)
1596 E Harry Shepard Blvd, San Bernardino (92408-0197)
P.O. Box 10, Highland (92346-1010)
PHONE....................909 382-7400
Stephen A Matich, *CEO*
Martin A Matich, *Chairman*
Randall Valadez, *Treasurer*
Patrick A Matich, *Exec VP*
Robert M Matich, *Exec VP*
EMP: 60 **EST:** 1918
SQ FT: 10,000
SALES (est): 58.7MM **Privately Held**
WEB: www.matichcm.com
SIC: 1611 2951 General contractor, highway & street construction; asphalt paving mixtures & blocks

(P-1756)
MATICH CORPORATION
13984 Apache Trl, Cabazon (92230-2143)
PHONE....................951 849-8280
Nikolas Matich, *Branch Mgr*
EMP: 50
SALES (corp-wide): 58.7MM **Privately Held**
SIC: 1611 General contractor, highway & street construction
PA: Matich Corporation
1596 E Harry Shepard Blvd
San Bernardino CA 92408
909 382-7400

(P-1757)
MCCULLOUGH CONSTRUCTION INC
57 Aldergrove Rd, Arcata (95521-9276)
PHONE....................707 825-1014
Jens Karlshoej, *Partner*
Dena McCullough, *Partner*
Hugh McCullough, *Partner*
Dan Schultz, *Partner*
EMP: 80
SALES (est): 2.1MM **Privately Held**
SIC: 1611 1622 Highway & street construction; tunnel construction

(P-1758)
MCE CORPORATION (PA)
4000 Industrial Way, Concord (94520-1289)
P.O. Box 508 (94522-0508)
PHONE....................925 803-4111
Jeff Core, *President*
Justin Bray, *Vice Pres*
Dan Furtado, *Vice Pres*
Steve Loweree, *Vice Pres*
Bill Macedo, *General Mgr*
EMP: 65
SQ FT: 12,000
SALES (est): 53.6MM **Privately Held**
WEB: www.mce-corp.com
SIC: 1611 0782 General contractor, highway & street construction; lawn & garden services

(P-1759)
MGB CONSTRUCTION INC
91 Commercial Ave, Riverside (92507-1111)
PHONE....................951 342-0303
Emily Beach, *President*
Emilly Beach, *President*
EMP: 150
SALES (est): 17MM **Privately Held**
SIC: 1611 Highway & street paving contractor

(P-1760)
MIDSTATE BARRIER INC
Also Called: MBI
3291 S Highway 99, Stockton (95215-8032)
P.O. Box 30550 (95213-0550)
PHONE....................209 944-9565
Dale Breen, *CEO*
Clark Ebinger, *President*
EMP: 75
SQ FT: 20,000
SALES (est): 20MM **Privately Held**
WEB: www.hwysfty.com
SIC: 1611 Highway signs & guardrails

(P-1761)
MORRO BAY PUBLIC WORKS
Also Called: City of Morro Bay
955 Shasta Ave, Morro Bay (93442-1934)
PHONE....................805 772-6261
Janice Peters, *Mayor*
EMP: 100
SALES (est): 8.2MM **Privately Held**
SIC: 1611 Highway & street construction

(P-1762)
MUSE CONCRETE CONTRACTORS INC
8599 Commercial Way, Redding (96002-3902)
PHONE....................530 226-5151
Boyce Muse, *President*
Joan Muse, *CFO*
EMP: 94
SALES (est): 19.6MM **Privately Held**
WEB: www.museconcrete.com
SIC: 1611 1771 Concrete construction: roads, highways, sidewalks, etc.; concrete work; curb construction

(P-1763)
MYERS & SONS CONSTRUCTION LP
5200 W Century Blvd, Los Angeles (90045-5928)
PHONE....................424 227-3285
EMP: 99 **Privately Held**
SIC: 1611 Highway & street construction
PA: Myers & Sons Construction, L.P.
4600 Northgate Blvd # 100
Sacramento CA 95834

(P-1764)
MYERS & SONS CONSTRUCTION LP (PA)
4600 Northgate Blvd # 100, Sacramento (95834-1103)
PHONE....................916 283-9950
Clinton C Myers, *Partner*
Felipe Olivar, *Deputy Dir*
Sonia Rodriguez, *Receptionist*
EMP: 151
SALES: 181.5MM **Privately Held**
SIC: 1611 Highway & street construction

(P-1765)
NATIONAL PAVING COMPANY INC
4361 Fort Dr, Riverside (92509-6784)
P.O. Box 3649 (92519-3649)
PHONE....................951 369-1332
Richard J Lindholm, *President*
Lawrence Spicher, *CFO*
EMP: 78
SQ FT: 4,000
SALES (est): 15.1MM **Privately Held**
WEB: www.nationalpaving.com
SIC: 1611 Highway & street paving contractor; surfacing & paving

(P-1766)
NEHEMIAH CONSTRUCTION INC
12150 Tributary Ln P, Rancho Cordova (95670)
PHONE....................707 746-6815
EMP: 50
SQ FT: 2,500
SALES: 98.4K **Privately Held**
WEB: www.nehemiahconst.com
SIC: 1611

(P-1767)
NICHOLAS GRANT CORPORATION
Also Called: Daley
12570 Highway 67, Lakeside (92040-1159)
PHONE....................619 390-3900
John Daley Jr, *President*
Mark Thunder, *Exec VP*
▲ **EMP:** 100
SALES (est): 18.3MM **Privately Held**
SIC: 1611 Highway & street construction

(P-1768)
NORTH BAY CONSTRUCTION INC
431 Payran St, Petaluma (94952-5908)
P.O. Box 751389 (94975-1389)
PHONE....................707 283-0093
John E Barella, *President*
Steve Geney, *Vice Pres*
EMP: 80
SQ FT: 7,000
SALES (est): 8.2MM **Privately Held**
WEB: www.nbcinc.net
SIC: 1611 1623 Highway & street paving contractor; grading; sewer line construction

(P-1769)
O C JONES & SONS INC (PA)
1520 4th St, Berkeley (94710-1748)
PHONE....................510 526-3424
Kelly Kolander, *President*
Robert Pelascini, *Ch of Bd*
Rob Layne, *CEO*
Beth Yoshida, *CFO*
Kim Freese, *Administration*
EMP: 250 **EST:** 1924
SQ FT: 80,000
SALES (est): 78.5MM **Privately Held**
WEB: www.ocjones.com
SIC: 1611 Grading; highway & street paving contractor

(P-1770)
OGRADY PAVING INC
2513 Wyandotte St, Mountain View (94043-2311)
PHONE....................650 966-1926
Thomas M O'Grady Jr, *President*
Celine Duran, *Corp Secy*
Craig Young, *Vice Pres*
Erica Lopez, *Administration*
Bob Taylor, *Manager*
EMP: 110
SQ FT: 3,200
SALES (est): 23.8MM **Privately Held**
WEB: www.ogradypaving.com
SIC: 1611 Highway & street paving contractor; grading

(P-1771)
ORTIZ ASPHALT PAVING INC
16588 Farmington St, Hesperia (92345-8825)
P.O. Box 401370 (92340-1370)
PHONE....................951 966-7060
Bruce Kevin Ortiz, *President*
EMP: 50
SQ FT: 1,000
SALES: 17MM **Privately Held**
SIC: 1611 Highway & street paving contractor

(P-1772)
ORTIZ ENTERPRISES INCORPORATED (PA)
6 Cushing Ste 200, Irvine (92618-4230)
PHONE....................949 753-1414
Patrick Ortiz, *President*
Cary B Purves, *Vice Pres*
Doug Dawson, *Project Mgr*
EMP: 80
SQ FT: 12,000
SALES: 31.5MM **Privately Held**
SIC: 1611 General contractor, highway & street construction

(P-1773)
PALP INC
Also Called: Excel Paving Co
2230 Lemon Ave, Long Beach (90806-5124)
P.O. Box 16405 (90806-0995)
PHONE....................562 599-5841
Curtis P Brown, *CEO*
George McRae, *Senior VP*
Bruce Flatt, *Vice Pres*
Darryl Rutledge, *General Mgr*
Michelle Drakulich, *Admin Sec*
EMP: 225 **EST:** 1976
SQ FT: 11,000
SALES (est): 59.9MM **Privately Held**
WEB: www.palp.com
SIC: 1611 8711 Highway & street paving contractor; grading; engineering services

PRODUCTS & SVCS

(P-1774)
PARSONS CORPORATION
44 Montgomery St Ste 880, San Francisco
(94104-4620)
PHONE..........................415 490-2400
Brad Braddock, *Manager*
Elizabeth Hughes, *Manager*
EMP: 63
SALES (corp-wide): 3.5B **Publicly Held**
SIC: 1611 Highway & street construction
PA: The Parsons Corporation
5875 Trinity Pkwy Ste 300
Centreville VA 20120
703 988-8500

(P-1775)
PAVE-TECH INC
2231 La Mirada Dr, Vista (92081-8828)
PHONE..........................760 727-8700
Rudy Zavalani, *CEO*
Larry Keepers, *Shareholder*
EMP: 50
SALES (est): 14.6MM **Privately Held**
SIC: 1611 Highway & street paving contractor

(P-1776)
PENA GRADING & DEMOLITION INC
Also Called: Pena Trucking
11253 Vinedale St, Sun Valley
(91352-3217)
PHONE..........................818 768-5202
Orestes Pena, *President*
Irma Pena, *Vice Pres*
Michael Hernandez, *Opers Mgr*
EMP: 50
SQ FT: 8,000
SALES (est): 9.4MM **Privately Held**
SIC: 1611 4953 1795 1794 Grading; recycling, waste materials; wrecking & demolition work; demolition, buildings & other structures; excavation work; excavation & grading, building construction

(P-1777)
PETER KIEWIT SONS INC
1925 Wright Ave Ste C, La Verne
(91750-5847)
PHONE..........................909 962-6001
Rohit Shard, *Branch Mgr*
EMP: 177
SALES (corp-wide): 16.1B **Privately Held**
SIC: 1611 General contractor, highway & street construction
PA: Peter Kiewit Sons', Inc.
3555 Farnam St Ste 1000
Omaha NE 68131
402 342-2052

(P-1778)
QUAIL ENGINEERING INC
Also Called: Pacific Exteriors
2230 E Lambert Rd, La Habra
(90631-5746)
PHONE..........................714 636-0612
Mark Kabarsky, *President*
▲ EMP: 50
SALES (est): 4.9MM **Privately Held**
SIC: 1611 Grading

(P-1779)
REEVES TRACTOR SERVICE INC
5455 Blue Ridge Dr, Yorba Linda
(92887-4234)
P.O. Box 702 (92885-0702)
PHONE..........................714 692-4020
Jeffrey G Reeves, *President*
Laurie Reeves, *Manager*
EMP: 60
SALES (est): 4.4MM **Privately Held**
SIC: 1611 Grading

(P-1780)
RICK HAMM CONSTRUCTION INC
201 W Carleton Ave, Orange (92867-3607)
PHONE..........................714 532-0815
Rick Hamm, *President*
Llana Hamm, *Corp Secy*
EMP: 90
SQ FT: 25,000

SALES (est): 19.6MM **Privately Held**
WEB: www.rickhamm.com
SIC: 1611 1771 1791 1741 General contractor, highway & street construction; patio construction, concrete; precast concrete structural framing or panels, placing of; masonry & other stonework; stone masonry; concrete block masonry laying; erection & dismantling of forms for poured concrete

(P-1781)
RJ NOBLE COMPANY (PA)
15505 E Lincoln Ave, Orange
(92865-1015)
P.O. Box 620 (92856-9020)
PHONE..........................714 637-1550
Michael J Carver, *President*
James N Ducote, *CFO*
Brenda Carver, *Vice Pres*
Craig Porter, *Vice Pres*
Terry McGill, *General Mgr*
EMP: 145 EST: 1950
SQ FT: 5,500
SALES (est): 60.5MM **Privately Held**
WEB: www.rjnoblecompany.com
SIC: 1611 Highway & street paving contractor

(P-1782)
ROMERO GENERAL CNSTR CORP
Also Called: Romero Construction
2150 N Centre City Pkwy, Escondido
(92026-1347)
PHONE..........................760 489-8412
Keith Reilly, *President*
EMP: 175
SQ FT: 3,500
SALES: 17MM **Privately Held**
WEB: www.romerogc.com
SIC: 1611 Highway & street paving contractor

(P-1783)
ROY E LADD INC
Also Called: Ladd Construction Co
3724 Sunlight Ct, Redding (96001-0173)
PHONE..........................530 241-6102
Craig Wiseman, *President*
Tom Capener, *Treasurer*
Mark Christopher, *Vice Pres*
Eric Ladd, *Vice Pres*
Bill Schoonmaker, *Vice Pres*
EMP: 50
SQ FT: 3,000
SALES: 20MM **Privately Held**
SIC: 1611 1622 Grading; bridge construction

(P-1784)
SAN JOAQUIN HILLS TRANSPORTTN (PA)
Also Called: Transprttion Corridor Agencies
125 Pacifica Ste 100, Irvine (92618-3324)
P.O. Box 53770 (92619-3770)
PHONE..........................949 754-3400
Michael Kraman, *CEO*
EMP: 56
SQ FT: 17,000
SALES: 198MM **Privately Held**
SIC: 1611 General contractor, highway & street construction

(P-1785)
SECURITY PAVING COMPANY INC (PA)
Also Called: Valley Base Materials
3075 Townsgate Rd Ste 210, Westlake Village (91361-3223)
PHONE..........................818 362-9200
Mike Mattivi, *CEO*
Albert Mattivi, *President*
Brian Algren, *Vice Pres*
Thomas J Mattivi, *Vice Pres*
EMP: 100 EST: 1947
SALES (est): 54.9MM **Privately Held**
SIC: 1611 Surfacing & paving

(P-1786)
SEQUEL CONTRACTORS INC
13546 Imperial Hwy, Santa Fe Springs
(90670-4821)
PHONE..........................562 802-7227
Thomas S Pack, *CEO*

Abel Magellanes, *Vice Pres*
EMP: 50
SQ FT: 80,000
SALES (est): 8.6MM **Privately Held**
SIC: 1611 Highway & street construction

(P-1787)
SHELTON CONSTRUCTION COMPANY
5628 Spinnaker Bay Dr, Long Beach
(90803-6806)
PHONE..........................714 903-7853
William Shelton, *President*
EMP: 60
SQ FT: 3,200
SALES: 6MM **Privately Held**
WEB: www.sheltonconst.com
SIC: 1611 Grading

(P-1788)
SIALIC CONTRACTORS CORPORATION
Also Called: Shawnan
12240 Woodruff Ave, Downey
(90241-5608)
PHONE..........................562 803-9977
Shawn Smith, *President*
John Smith, *Admin Sec*
EMP: 68
SQ FT: 24,000
SALES (est): 6.1MM **Privately Held**
SIC: 1611 General contractor, highway & street construction

(P-1789)
SKANSKA USA CVIL W CAL DST INC (DH)
1995 Agua Mansa Rd, Riverside
(92509-2405)
PHONE..........................951 684-5360
Richard Cavallero, *CEO*
Michael Cobelli, *COO*
Joseph Nogues, *CFO*
Michael Aparicio, *Exec VP*
Chris Toher, *Exec VP*
EMP: 700 EST: 1919
SQ FT: 15,000
SALES (est): 289.1MM
SALES (corp-wide): 19B **Privately Held**
SIC: 1611 1622 1629 8711 General contractor, highway & street construction; bridge construction; highway construction, elevated; dam construction; engineering services; asphalt paving mixtures & blocks
HQ: Skanska Usa Civil Inc.
7520 Astoria Blvd Ste 200
East Elmhurst NY 11370
718 340-0777

(P-1790)
SKANSKA-RADOS A JOINT VENTURE
11390 W Olympic Blvd, Los Angeles
(90064-1619)
PHONE..........................213 978-0600
Kent Percy, *Partner*
Michael Witz, *Partner*
EMP: 70
SALES (est): 1.2MM **Privately Held**
SIC: 1611 Highway & street construction

(P-1791)
SOUTH COAST STONE PAVING
Also Called: Hillside Contractor
2618 N Baker St, Santa Ana (92706-1511)
PHONE..........................714 835-0258
David Lopez, *Principal*
EMP: 65
SALES (est): 6MM **Privately Held**
SIC: 1611 Highway & street construction

(P-1792)
STEVE MANNING CONSTRUCTION INC
5211 Churn Creek Rd, Redding
(96002-3914)
P.O. Box 491660 (96049-1660)
PHONE..........................530 222-0810
Steve Manning, *President*
Arlene T Litsey, *Treasurer*
Arlene Litsey, *Controller*
Jennie Davis, *Payroll Mgr*
EMP: 54
SQ FT: 2,200

SALES (est): 17.3MM **Privately Held**
SIC: 1611 Highway & street construction

(P-1793)
STEVENS CREEK QUARRY INC (PA)
12100 Stevens Canyon Rd, Cupertino
(95014-5443)
PHONE..........................408 253-2512
Richard A Voss, *President*
Richard Voss, *President*
Bob Romano, *Principal*
Diana Voss, *Admin Sec*
EMP: 60 EST: 1954
SALES (est): 20.3MM **Privately Held**
WEB: www.scqinc.com
SIC: 1611 7353 1442 General contractor, highway & street construction; highway & street maintenance; heavy construction equipment rental; construction sand mining

(P-1794)
SUDHAKAR COMPANY INTERNATIONAL
1450 N Fitzgerald Ave, Rialto (92376-8621)
PHONE..........................909 879-2933
Ashok Sudhakar, *President*
Betty Bogle, *Vice Pres*
EMP: 100 EST: 1998
SQ FT: 16,000
SALES: 21MM **Privately Held**
WEB: www.sudhakarco.com
SIC: 1611 Highway & street sign installation; highway reflector installation

(P-1795)
SULLY-MILLER CONTRACTING CO (DH)
Also Called: Blue Diamond Materials
135 S State College Blvd # 400, Brea
(92821-5819)
PHONE..........................714 578-9600
John Harrington, *President*
Christian Ransinangue, *CFO*
Jon Layne, *Chief Mktg Ofcr*
Scott Bottomley, *Vice Pres*
William Boyd, *Vice Pres*
EMP: 248
SALES: 210.3MM
SALES (corp-wide): 83.5MM **Privately Held**
WEB: www.thebluediamond.com
SIC: 1611 Highway & street construction
HQ: Colas Inc.
73 Headquarters Plz 10t
Morristown NJ 07960
973 290-9082

(P-1796)
SUPERIOR PAVING COMPANY INC
Also Called: United Paving Company
1880 N Delilah St, Corona (92879-1892)
PHONE..........................951 739-9200
Sabas Trujillo, *CEO*
EMP: 85
SQ FT: 3,000
SALES (est): 22.7MM **Privately Held**
WEB: www.united-paving.com
SIC: 1611 Highway & street paving contractor

(P-1797)
SYSTEMS PAVING INC (PA)
1570 Brookhollow Dr, Santa Ana
(92705-5438)
PHONE..........................949 263-8301
Larry Green, *CEO*
Douglas Lueck, *President*
Steven Leuck, *Vice Pres*
Niels Jungersen, *Sales Mgr*
EMP: 61
SQ FT: 13,000
SALES (est): 42.5MM **Privately Held**
SIC: 1611 Surfacing & paving

(P-1798)
TEAM GHILOTTI INC
2531 Petaluma Blvd S, Petaluma
(94952-5523)
PHONE..........................707 763-8700
Glen Ghilotti, *President*
Glen C Ghilotti, *President*
Monica Bourdens, *Office Mgr*

EMP: 50
SQ FT: 5,900
SALES (est): 10MM **Privately Held**
WEB: www.teamghilotti.com
SIC: 1611 General contractor, highway & street construction

(P-1799)
TELFER OIL COMPANY (PA)
Also Called: Western Oil & Spreading
211 Foster St, Martinez (94553-1029)
P.O. Box 709 (94553-0151)
PHONE..............................925 228-1515
Michael S Telfer, *Owner*
John Telfer, *Owner*
EMP: 55
SQ FT: 5,000
SALES (est): 63.6MM **Privately Held**
WEB: www.telfercompanies.com
SIC: 1611 2951 4213 4212 Highway & street paving contractor; resurfacing contractor; paving mixtures; liquid petroleum transport, non-local; local trucking, without storage

(P-1800)
TNT GRADING INC
Also Called: T-N-T Grading
529 W 4th Ave B, Escondido (92025-4037)
PHONE..............................760 736-4054
EMP: 95
SQ FT: 2,500
SALES (est): 5.5MM **Privately Held**
WEB: www.tntgrading.com
SIC: 1611

(P-1801)
TORO ENTERPRISES INC
2101 Ventura Blvd, Oxnard (93036-8951)
P.O. Box 6285 (93031-6285)
PHONE..............................805 483-4515
Sean Castillo, *President*
Buffy Castillo, *Shareholder*
Teresa Ortega, *Shareholder*
Reuben Ortega, *Vice Pres*
Monica Ramirez, *Accountant*
EMP: 67
SALES (est): 21.5MM **Privately Held**
WEB: www.toroenterprises.com
SIC: 1611 Concrete construction: roads, highways, sidewalks, etc.

(P-1802)
TRANSPORTATION CALIFORNIA DEPT
Also Called: Maintenance Department
611 Payran St, Petaluma (94952-5910)
PHONE..............................707 762-6641
John Peterson, *Manager*
EMP: 110 **Privately Held**
WEB: www.caltip.org
SIC: 1611 9621 Highway & street maintenance; regulation, administration of transportation;
HQ: California Dept Of Transportation
1120 N St
Sacramento CA 95814

(P-1803)
TRANSPORTATION CALIFORNIA DEPT
Also Called: Caltrans
2019 W Texas St, Fairfield (94533-4461)
P.O. Box 8 (94533-0084)
PHONE..............................707 428-2031
E L Poplin, *Branch Mgr*
EMP: 150 **Privately Held**
WEB: www.caltip.org
SIC: 1611 9621 Highway & street maintenance; regulation, administration of transportation;
HQ: California Dept Of Transportation
1120 N St
Sacramento CA 95814

(P-1804)
TRANSPORTATION CALIFORNIA DEPT
Also Called: Caltrans Eastern Reg Rd Maint
1940 Workman Mill Rd, Whittier (90601-1414)
PHONE..............................562 692-0823
Edward Toledo, *Manager*

Art Duffy, *Engineer*
Alfonso Sanchez, *Manager*
EMP: 200 **Privately Held**
WEB: www.caltip.org
SIC: 1611 9621 Highway & street maintenance; regulation, administration of transportation;
HQ: California Dept Of Transportation
1120 N St
Sacramento CA 95814

(P-1805)
UNITED ROCK PRODUCTS CORP
Also Called: Sully Miller Contracting
135 S State College Blvd # 400, Brea (92821-5819)
PHONE..............................714 578-9600
John Harrington, *President*
Scott Bottomley, *Vice Pres*
▲ **EMP:** 62
SQ FT: 2,000
SALES (est): 6.9MM
SALES (corp-wide): 83.5MM **Privately Held**
SIC: 1611 Highway & street construction
HQ: Sully-Miller Contracting Company Inc
135 S State College Blvd # 400
Brea CA 92821
714 578-9600

(P-1806)
UNIVERSAL ASPHALT CO INC
10610 Painter Ave, Santa Fe Springs (90670-4091)
P.O. Box 2548 (90670-0548)
PHONE..............................562 941-0201
Daniel M Houck, *President*
EMP: 50
SQ FT: 22,000
SALES (est): 7.1MM **Privately Held**
SIC: 1611 Highway & street paving contractor

(P-1807)
VANCE CORPORATION
17761 Slover Ave, Bloomington (92316-2330)
PHONE..............................909 355-4333
Verner E Thomas, *CEO*
Darrel L Lohman, *CFO*
EMP: 50
SQ FT: 10,000
SALES (est): 10.3MM **Privately Held**
SIC: 1611 General contractor, highway & street construction

(P-1808)
VSS INTERNATIONAL INC (HQ)
Also Called: V S S
3785 Channel Dr, West Sacramento (95691-3421)
P.O. Box 981330 (95798-1330)
PHONE..............................916 373-1500
Jeffrey Reed, *President*
Ron Bolles, *Treasurer*
John Shoden, *Treasurer*
Alan Berger, *Vice Pres*
Gary Houston, *General Mgr*
▲ **EMP:** 62
SQ FT: 5,000
SALES (est): 45MM
SALES (corp-wide): 214.4MM **Privately Held**
SIC: 1611 3531 2951 Highway & street paving contractor; construction machinery; asphalt paving mixtures & blocks
PA: Basic Resources Inc
928 12th St Ste 700
Modesto CA 95354
209 521-9771

(P-1809)
WESTERN PAVING CONTRACTORS INC
15533 Arrow Hwy, Irwindale (91706-2002)
PHONE..............................626 338-7889
Enrique Castillo, *CEO*
Henry Castillo, *President*
EMP: 65
SQ FT: 3,200
SALES: 20.4MM **Privately Held**
SIC: 1611 Highway & street paving contractor; grading

(P-1810)
WESTERN RIM CONSTRUCTORS INC
621 S Andreasen Dr Ste B, Escondido (92029-1904)
PHONE..............................760 489-4328
Ray C Samuelson, *President*
EMP: 50
SALES (est): 10.5MM **Privately Held**
WEB: www.westernrim.net
SIC: 1611 General contractor, highway & street construction

(P-1811)
WR FORDE ASSOCIATES INC
984 Hensley St, Richmond (94801-2117)
PHONE..............................510 215-9338
Donald Russell, *CEO*
EMP: 55
SQ FT: 4,500
SALES: 17.6MM **Privately Held**
SIC: 1611 1622 1794 Grading; bridge construction; excavation & grading, building construction

---

1622 Bridge, Tunnel & Elevated Hwy Construction

(P-1812)
AECOM ENERGY & CNSTR INC (DH)
1999 Avenue Of The Stars, Los Angeles (90067-6022)
PHONE..............................213 593-8100
Thomas H Zarges, *CEO*
Robert Zaist, *President*
Judy L Rodgers, *Treasurer*
Randolph J Hill, *Senior VP*
H Thomas Hicks, *Principal*
◆ **EMP:** 151
SQ FT: 214,000
SALES (est): 4.6B
SALES (corp-wide): 20.1B **Publicly Held**
WEB: www.wgint.com
SIC: 1622 1629 1081 4953 Bridge, tunnel & elevated highway; oil refinery construction; metal mining services; refuse systems; engineering services

(P-1813)
AMERICAN BRDGE/FLUOR ENTPS INC
1390 Willow Pass Rd, Concord (94520-5200)
PHONE..............................510 808-4623
Robert Luffy, *President*
David Degney, *Exec VP*
Douglas Fuller, *Vice Pres*
Donald Jones, *Vice Pres*
▲ **EMP:** 80
SALES (est): 14MM **Privately Held**
SIC: 1622 Bridge construction

(P-1814)
APW CONSTRUCTION INC (PA)
Also Called: Ace Fence Company
727 Glendora Ave, La Puente (91744-4014)
PHONE..............................626 820-0812
Amy Tsui, *President*
Wayne Wong, *Treasurer*
Jose Ramirez, *Vice Pres*
America Tang, *Vice Pres*
Jorge Zarate, *Project Mgr*
▲ **EMP:** 95
SQ FT: 8,000
SALES: 20MM **Privately Held**
WEB: www.acefencecompany.com
SIC: 1622 1799 Bridge, tunnel & elevated highway; fence construction

(P-1815)
AVAR CONSTRUCTION SYSTEMS INC (PA)
47375 Fremont Blvd, Fremont (94538-6521)
PHONE..............................510 354-2000
Michael Anthony Pagano, *CEO*
Amy Winford, *Vice Pres*
▲ **EMP:** 50
SQ FT: 41,700

SALES (est): 11.5MM **Privately Held**
SIC: 1622 Bridge, tunnel & elevated highway

(P-1816)
COUNTY OF SACRAMENTO
Also Called: Municipal Svcs Agency
9700 Goethe Rd Ste D, Sacramento (95827-3558)
PHONE..............................916 875-2711
Thor Lude, *Chief*
EMP: 100 **Privately Held**
WEB: www.sna.com
SIC: 1622 9199 Bridge, tunnel & elevated highway; general government administration;
PA: County Of Sacramento
700 H St Ste 7650
Sacramento CA 95814
916 874-5544

(P-1817)
FLATIRON WEST INC
2100 Goodyear Rd, Benicia (94510-1216)
PHONE..............................707 742-6000
Richard Tradinski, *Manager*
EMP: 150
SALES (corp-wide): 475MM **Privately Held**
SIC: 1622 1629 Bridge construction; industrial plant construction
HQ: Flatiron West, Inc.
16470 W Bernardo Dr 120
San Diego CA 92127

(P-1818)
FLATIRON WEST INC
16341 Chino Corona Rd, Chino (91708)
PHONE..............................909 597-8413
Thomas J Rademacher, *Ch of Bd*
EMP: 95
SALES (corp-wide): 475MM **Privately Held**
SIC: 1622 1611 Bridge construction; highway & street construction
HQ: Flatiron West, Inc.
16470 W Bernardo Dr 120
San Diego CA 92127

(P-1819)
FLUOR DANIEL CONSTRUCTION CO (DH)
3 Polaris Way, Aliso Viejo (92656-5338)
PHONE..............................949 349-2000
Paul Buckham, *President*
EMP: 500
SALES: 3.3MM
SALES (corp-wide): 19.1B **Publicly Held**
SIC: 1622 Bridge, tunnel & elevated highway
HQ: Fluor Enterprises, Inc.
6700 Las Colinas Blvd
Irving TX 75039
469 398-7000

(P-1820)
GRANITE CONSTRUCTION INC (PA)
585 W Beach St, Watsonville (95076-5123)
P.O. Box 50085 (95077-5085)
PHONE..............................831 724-1011
James H Roberts, *President*
EMP: 250
SALES: 3.3B **Publicly Held**
WEB: www.graniteconstruction.com
SIC: 1622 1629 1442 1611 Bridge construction; tunnel construction; dam construction; canal construction; land leveling; construction sand & gravel; general contractor, highway & street construction

(P-1821)
HAZARD CONSTRUCTION COMPANY
6465 Marindustry Dr, San Diego (92121-2536)
P.O. Box 229000 (92192-9000)
PHONE..............................858 587-3600
Jason Mordhorst, *President*
Noli Gavino, *Treasurer*
Klaus Guttau, *Vice Pres*
Mark Thunder, *Vice Pres*

Charles White, *Vice Pres*
EMP: 100
SQ FT: 37,000
SALES (est): 37.3MM **Privately Held**
WEB: www.hazardconstruction.com
SIC: 1622 1611 Bridge construction; highway & street construction; grading; surfacing & paving; highway & street paving contractor

(P-1822)
MCM CONSTRUCTION INC (PA)
6413 32nd St, North Highlands (95660-3001)
P.O. Box 620 (95660-0620)
PHONE................916 334-1221
James A Carter, *President*
Harry D McGovern, *Vice Pres*
Harry McGovern, *Vice Pres*
Connie Chiddister, *Administration*
EMP: 70
SQ FT: 5,000
SALES: 150MM **Privately Held**
WEB: www.mcmconstructioninc.com
SIC: 1622 Bridge construction

(P-1823)
MCM CONSTRUCTION INC
19010 Slover Ave, Bloomington (92316-2459)
PHONE................909 875-0533
Nella Flores, *Branch Mgr*
EMP: 180
SALES (corp-wide): 150MM **Privately Held**
WEB: www.mcmconstructioninc.com
SIC: 1622 Bridge construction
PA: M.C.M. Construction, Inc.
6413 32nd St
North Highlands CA 95660
916 334-1221

(P-1824)
OC 405 PARTNERS JOINT VENTURE
3100 W Lake Center Dr # 200, Santa Ana (92704-6917)
PHONE................858 251-2200
Ashok Patel,
EMP: 75
SQ FT: 69,000
SALES: 61MM
SALES (corp-wide): 696.8MM **Privately Held**
SIC: 1622 Bridge construction
HQ: Ohl Usa, Inc.
2615 Ulmer St
Flushing NY 11354

(P-1825)
R M HARRIS COMPANY INC
1000 Howe Rd Ste 200, Martinez (94553-3446)
PHONE................925 335-3000
David R Harris, *CEO*
Mark Snapp, *Admin Sec*
John Tymo, *Technology*
John Hoover, *Purch Mgr*
EMP: 100
SQ FT: 4,500
SALES (est): 18.4MM **Privately Held**
SIC: 1622 1611 Bridge, tunnel & elevated highway; highway & street construction

(P-1826)
SEMA CONSTRUCTION INC
6 Orchard Ste 150, Irvine (92618-4534)
PHONE................949 330-4300
Steve Mills, *Manager*
EMP: 90
SALES (corp-wide): 293.3MM **Privately Held**
SIC: 1622 Bridge, tunnel & elevated highway
PA: Sema Construction, Inc.
7353 S Eagle St
Centennial CO 80112
303 627-2600

1623 Water, Sewer & Utility Line Construction

(P-1827)
A & H COMMUNICATIONS INC
1791 Reynolds Ave, Irvine (92614-5711)
PHONE................949 250-4555
Brian Elliott, *President*
Brett Howard, *COO*
Tom Howard, *Director*
EMP: 250 **EST:** 2000
SQ FT: 4,500
SALES (est): 20.8MM **Privately Held**
SIC: 1623 Cable laying construction

(P-1828)
ADVANCED CABLE TECHNOLOGIES
13400 Saticoy St Ste 30, North Hollywood (91605-7615)
PHONE................818 262-6484
Yader V Gomez, *President*
Josh Neaf, *Vice Pres*
EMP: 50
SALES: 5.5MM **Privately Held**
SIC: 1623 Cable laying construction

(P-1829)
AIRX UTILITY SURVEYORS INC (PA)
2534 E El Nrte Pkwy Ste C, Escondido (92027)
PHONE................760 480-2347
Gail McMorran, *President*
Steve Tueting, *Vice Pres*
EMP: 55
SALES (est): 9.1MM **Privately Held**
SIC: 1623 1389 3272 1611 Underground utilities contractor; testing, measuring, surveying & analysis services; monuments, concrete; highway & street construction; sidewalk construction; highway & street maintenance; flagging service (traffic control)

(P-1830)
ARIZONA PIPELINE COMPANY (PA)
17372 Lilac St, Hesperia (92345-5162)
P.O. Box 401865 (92340-1865)
PHONE................760 244-8212
Lowell Duane Moyers, *Chairman*
Nina Moyers, *CEO*
Steven Lords, *CFO*
Tom Seals, *Corp Secy*
John W Gulzow, *Officer*
EMP: 400 **EST:** 1979
SQ FT: 5,000
SALES: 224.4MM **Privately Held**
SIC: 1623 Pipeline construction

(P-1831)
ARIZONA PIPELINE COMPANY
1745 Sampson Ave, Corona (92879-1864)
PHONE................951 270-3100
John Guzlow, *Vice Pres*
Steve Dilday, *Manager*
EMP: 200
SALES (corp-wide): 224.4MM **Privately Held**
SIC: 1623 8711 Underground utilities contractor; engineering services
PA: Arizona Pipeline Company
17372 Lilac St
Hesperia CA 92345
760 244-8212

(P-1832)
BALI CONSTRUCTION INC
9852 Joe Vargas Way, South El Monte (91733-3108)
PHONE................626 442-8003
Ted Polich III, *President*
Michael E Brooks, *CEO*
Trina Samba, *Office Mgr*
Steven Tam, *Administration*
Kevin Delate, *Project Mgr*
EMP: 100
SQ FT: 7,000
SALES: 58MM **Privately Held**
WEB: www.baliconstruction.com
SIC: 1623 Underground utilities contractor

(P-1833)
BESS TESTLAB INC
2461 Tripaldi Way, Hayward (94545-5018)
PHONE................408 988-0101
Juan Jose Bohorquez, *President*
Brandy Molina, *Manager*
EMP: 50
SALES (est): 9.2MM **Privately Held**
WEB: www.besstestlab.com
SIC: 1623 Water, sewer & utility lines

(P-1834)
BILL NLSON GEN ENGRG CNSTR INC
Also Called: Bill Nelson GEC
7600 N Ingram Ave Ste 126, Fresno (93711-5852)
PHONE................559 439-1756
Bill Nelson, *President*
Kristin Nelson, *Admin Sec*
EMP: 60
SQ FT: 1,200
SALES (est): 14.4MM **Privately Held**
SIC: 1623 Water, sewer & utility lines

(P-1835)
BLOIS CONSTRUCTION INC
3201 Sturgis Rd, Oxnard (93030-8931)
P.O. Box 672 (93032-0672)
PHONE................805 485-0011
James B Blois, *President*
Steve Woodworth, *CFO*
Dan Schultz, *Vice Pres*
Palmer Douglas, *Info Tech Dir*
Susan Segebartt, *Accounting Mgr*
EMP: 150 **EST:** 1965
SQ FT: 10,000
SALES: 22MM **Privately Held**
WEB: www.bloisconstruction.com
SIC: 1623 Underground utilities contractor

(P-1836)
BURTECH PIPELINE INCORPORATED
102 2nd St, Encinitas (92024-3203)
PHONE................760 634-2822
Dominic J Burtech, *President*
Julie Burtech, *Vice Pres*
EMP: 70
SQ FT: 3,000
SALES (est): 23.6MM **Privately Held**
WEB: www.burtechpipeline.com
SIC: 1623 Water main construction; sewer line construction; pipe laying construction

(P-1837)
C P CONSTRUCTION CO INC
105 N Loma Pl, Upland (91786-5620)
P.O. Box 1206, Ontario (91762-0206)
PHONE................909 981-1091
Charles Pfister Jr, *President*
Charles Michael Pfister, *Corp Secy*
Mark E Pfister, *Vice Pres*
Russel Pfister, *Vice Pres*
EMP: 50
SQ FT: 4,000
SALES: 13MM **Privately Held**
SIC: 1623 Sewer line construction; pipeline construction

(P-1838)
CA STATION MANAGEMENT INC
3200 E Guasti Rd Ste 100, Ontario (91761-8661)
PHONE................909 245-6251
Taqi Chaudry, *CEO*
EMP: 250 **EST:** 2016
SALES (est): 8.3MM **Privately Held**
SIC: 1623 7389 8082 Underground utilities contractor; telephone answering service; home health care services

(P-1839)
CAL SIERRA CONSTRUCTION INC
5904 Van Alstine Ave 1, Carmichael (95608-5327)
PHONE................916 416-7901
Joel Lucich, *President*
Greg Lucich, *Corp Secy*
Marco Lucich, *Vice Pres*
EMP: 80
SQ FT: 3,800

SALES (est): 12.9MM **Privately Held**
WEB: www.calsierra.net
SIC: 1623 8711 Underground utilities contractor; pipeline construction; sewer line construction; engineering services

(P-1840)
CAMERON INTRSTATE PIPELINE LLC
488 8th Ave, San Diego (92101-7123)
PHONE................619 696-3110
Ryan O'Neal, *President*
EMP: 200
SALES: 20MM **Privately Held**
SIC: 1623 Oil & gas pipeline construction

(P-1841)
CASS CONSTRUCTION INC (PA)
1100 Wagner Dr, El Cajon (92020-3047)
P.O. Box 309 (92022-0309)
PHONE................619 590-0929
Jimmie Nelson, *Ch of Bd*
Kyle P Nelson, *President*
Jerry Gaeir, *Vice Pres*
Laura Nelson, *Vice Pres*
Breyon Maasch, *Administration*
EMP: 111
SQ FT: 5,700
SALES (est): 103.5MM **Privately Held**
WEB: www.casssconstruction.com
SIC: 1623 1611 Underground utilities contractor; grading

(P-1842)
CDM CONSTRUCTORS INC
9220 Cleveland Ave # 100, Rancho Cucamonga (91730-8560)
PHONE................909 579-3500
Joyce Jackson, *Branch Mgr*
Mario J Marcaccio, *Legal Staff*
Gae Walters, *Director*
EMP: 90
SALES (corp-wide): 1.1B **Privately Held**
SIC: 1623 Water, sewer & utility lines
HQ: Cdm Constructors Inc.
75 State St Ste 701
Boston MA 02109

(P-1843)
CH2M HILL CONSTRUCTORS INC
2485 Natomas Park Dr # 600, Sacramento (95833-2975)
PHONE................916 920-0212
Craig Eldrich, *Branch Mgr*
EMP: 270
SALES (corp-wide): 14.9B **Publicly Held**
SIC: 1623 8711 Water, sewer & utility lines; engineering services
HQ: Ch2m Hill Constructors, Inc.
9189 S Jamaica St
Englewood CO 80112

(P-1844)
CITY HANFORD PUBLIC IMPRV CORP
900 S 10th Ave, Hanford (93230-5234)
PHONE................559 585-2550
Gary Misenhimer, *Branch Mgr*
EMP: 54 **Privately Held**
SIC: 1623 9199 Water, sewer & utility lines;
PA: City Of Hanford
315 N Douty St 321
Hanford CA 93230
559 585-2515

(P-1845)
CMAC CONSTRUCTION COMPANY
Also Called: Cmac Cnstr Refinery & Pipeline
1450 Santa Fe Ave, Long Beach (90813-1248)
PHONE................562 435-5611
Michael L Mc Fadden, *CEO*
Debra Loveall, *General Mgr*
John Day, *Safety Dir*
Bart Bartolome, *Supervisor*
EMP: 55
SQ FT: 3,000
SALES: 9.3MM **Privately Held**
WEB: www.cmac.us
SIC: 1623 Pipeline construction

(P-1846)
COLICH SONS
Also Called: Colich & Sons
547 W 140th St, Gardena (90248-1589)
PHONE..........................323 770-2920
Tom Colich, *Partner*
John Colich, *Partner*
EMP: 160
SQ FT: 4,500
SALES (est): 9.9MM **Privately Held**
SIC: 1623 8711 Sewer line construction;
engineering services

(P-1847)
CONSTRUCTION SPECIALTY SVC INC
Also Called: C S S
4550 Buck Owens Blvd, Bakersfield
(93308-4948)
P.O. Box 9429 (93389-9429)
PHONE..........................661 864-7573
Daniel I George, *President*
Denise George, *CFO*
EMP: 53
SQ FT: 1,000
SALES (est): 13.5MM **Privately Held**
WEB: www.CSSIncorp.biz
SIC: 1623 3271 Pipeline construction;
concrete block & brick

(P-1848)
COVENTINA-GSE JV LLC
6950 Preston Ave, Livermore (94551-9545)
PHONE..........................813 509-0669
John Coccaro, *Mng Member*
Dennis Gutierrez,
EMP: 50
SALES (est): 1.3MM **Privately Held**
SIC: 1623 Water, sewer & utility lines

(P-1849)
D S S COMPANY
655 W Clay St, Stockton (95206-1722)
P.O. Box 6099 (95206-0099)
PHONE..........................209 948-0302
David C Barney, *CEO*
Phillip R Dunn, *President*
EMP: 50
SQ FT: 5,000
SALES (est): 8.7MM
SALES (corp-wide): 4.5B **Publicly Held**
WEB: www.dsscompany.com
SIC: 1623 1611 Sewer line construction;
general contractor, highway & street con-
struction
HQ: Knife River Corporation
1150 W Century Ave
Bismarck ND 58503
701 530-1400

(P-1850)
DALEO INC
550 E Luchessa Ave, Gilroy (95020-7068)
PHONE..........................408 846-9621
David A Levisay, *Principal*
Susan Levisay, *Corp Secy*
EMP: 54
SALES (est): 11.1MM **Privately Held**
WEB: www.daleoinc.com
SIC: 1623 Cable television line construc-
tion

(P-1851)
DBI SERVICES INC
2775 Hollister St, Simi Valley (93065-4737)
PHONE..........................805 523-7114
Derek Crombie, *President*
Bruce Sakamogo, *Shareholder*
EMP: 70
SALES (est): 7.2MM **Privately Held**
SIC: 1623 Telephone & communication line
construction

(P-1852)
DIVERSIFIED UTILITY SVCS INC
3105 Unicorn Rd, Bakersfield
(93308-6858)
P.O. Box 80417 (93380-0417)
PHONE..........................661 325-3212
Leigh Ann Anderson, *CEO*
Cody Anderson, *Shareholder*
William Mitchell, *Shareholder*
Steven S Anderson, *CFO*
Matthew Derosa, *Project Mgr*
EMP: 272

SALES (est): 74.4MM **Privately Held**
SIC: 1623 Underground utilities contractor

(P-1853)
ELECTRIC TECH CONSTRUCTION INC
1910 Mark Ct Ste 130, Concord
(94520-1280)
PHONE..........................925 849-5324
Tim Pessin, *Principal*
Dean Balough, *CFO*
Kathryn Balough, *Admin Sec*
EMP: 80
SQ FT: 5,000
SALES: 14.5MM **Privately Held**
SIC: 1623 1731 Telephone & communica-
tion line construction; electrical work

(P-1854)
FISHEL COMPANY
647 Young St, Santa Ana (92705-5633)
PHONE..........................714 668-9268
Jeong Jeon, *Branch Mgr*
EMP: 86
SALES (corp-wide): 434.8MM **Privately Held**
SIC: 1623 Underground utilities contractor
PA: The Fishel Company
1366 Dublin Rd
Columbus OH 43215
614 274-8100

(P-1855)
FLOYD JOHNSTON CNSTR CO INC
2301 Herndon Ave, Clovis (93611-8911)
PHONE..........................559 299-7373
Evelyn Johnston, *Principal*
Steve Little, *Executive*
EMP: 75
SQ FT: 6,000
SALES (est): 14.9MM **Privately Held**
SIC: 1623 Water main construction; sewer
line construction; pipeline construction

(P-1856)
GD NIELSON CONSTRUCTION INC
147 Camino Oruga, NAPA (94558-6215)
PHONE..........................707 253-8774
Diann Nielson, *President*
George S Nielson, *Corp Secy*
George Nielson, *Vice Pres*
Sue Branson, *Controller*
EMP: 60
SALES (est): 16.5MM **Privately Held**
WEB: www.nielsoninc.com
SIC: 1623 1629 1799 Sewer line con-
struction; drainage system construction;
boring for building construction

(P-1857)
GENERAL PRODUCTION SVC CAL INC
Also Called: G P S
1333 Kern St, Taft (93268-9700)
P.O. Box 344 (93268-0344)
PHONE..........................661 765-5330
Charles Beard, *CEO*
Oreste Risi, *President*
Ryan Abbott, *Office Mgr*
George Harmer, *Safety Mgr*
Scott Brocaille, *Foreman/Supr*
EMP: 180
SALES (est): 54.6MM **Privately Held**
SIC: 1623 Oil & gas pipeline construction

(P-1858)
GEO TELECOM
252 Woodcrest Ln, Aliso Viejo
(92656-2134)
PHONE..........................949 362-0921
Peter Skerlos, *Owner*
EMP: 50
SALES (est): 1.7MM **Privately Held**
SIC: 1623 Transmitting tower (telecommu-
nication) construction

(P-1859)
GRANIT-BAYASHI 2 A JOINT VENTR
585 W Beach St, Watsonville (95076-5123)
PHONE..........................831 724-1011
Jigisha Desai, *Partner*
Mathew Tyler, *Partner*

EMP: 60 EST: 2016
SALES (est): 1.5MM **Privately Held**
SIC: 1623 Water & sewer line construction

(P-1860)
GSE CONSTRUCTION COMPANY INC (PA)
6950 Preston Ave, Livermore (94551-9545)
PHONE..........................925 447-0292
Orlando Gutierrez, *CEO*
Sue Gutierrez, *Admin Sec*
Jj Macarandan, *Project Engr*
Iris Sosa, *Accounts Mgr*
EMP: 140
SQ FT: 23,400
SALES (est): 63.6MM **Privately Held**
SIC: 1623 1542 Water & sewer line con-
struction; pipe laying construction;
pipeline construction; nonresidential con-
struction

(P-1861)
HCI INC (HQ)
Also Called: H C I
3166 Hrseless Carriage Rd, Norco
(92860-3612)
P.O. Box 5389 (92860-8097)
PHONE..........................951 520-4200
Steven G Silagi, *President*
◆ **EMP:** 300 **EST:** 1981
SQ FT: 100,000
SALES (est): 85MM **Privately Held**
SIC: 1623 Telephone & communication line
construction
PA: Lombardy Holdings, Inc.
151 Kalmus Dr Ste F6
Costa Mesa CA 92626
951 808-4550

(P-1862)
HENKELS & MCCOY INC
2840 Ficus St, Pomona (91766-6501)
PHONE..........................909 517-3011
Michael Giarratano, *Senior VP*
Pamela Aquino, *Administration*
Dan Feeney, *Project Mgr*
John Bean, *Controller*
Darryl Witmer, *QC Mgr*
EMP: 300
SALES (corp-wide): 1.5B **Privately Held**
SIC: 1623 Electric power line construction;
transmitting tower (telecommunication)
construction; oil & gas pipeline construc-
tion
HQ: Henkels & Mccoy, Inc
985 Jolly Rd
Blue Bell PA 19422
215 283-7600

(P-1863)
HENKELS & MCCOY INC
2840 Ficus St, Pomona (91766-6501)
PHONE..........................909 590-8419
Ed Campbell, *Manager*
EMP: 60
SALES (corp-wide): 1.5B **Privately Held**
WEB: www.henkels.com
SIC: 1623 Water, sewer & utility lines
HQ: Henkels & Mccoy, Inc
985 Jolly Rd
Blue Bell PA 19422
215 283-7600

(P-1864)
HERMAN WEISSKER INC (HQ)
1645 Brown Ave, Riverside (92509-1859)
PHONE..........................951 826-8800
Luis Alberto Armona, *CEO*
Ron Politte, *President*
Marty Mayeda, *CFO*
Brandi Green, *Admin Asst*
Katrina Suman, *Admin Asst*
EMP: 134 **EST:** 1959
SQ FT: 12,000
SALES (est): 118.2MM
SALES (corp-wide): 377.5MM **Privately Held**
WEB: www.hermanweissker.com
SIC: 1623 1731 Underground utilities con-
tractor; electrical work
PA: Meruelo Enterprises, Inc.
9550 Firestone Blvd # 105
Downey CA 90241
562 745-2300

(P-1865)
HP COMMUNICATIONS INC
13341 Temescal Canyon Rd, Corona
(92883-4980)
PHONE..........................951 572-1200
Nicholas Goldman, *President*
Ahmad Olomi, *Exec VP*
Chris Price, *Vice Pres*
Dale Barnhart, *Area Mgr*
Dustin Walters, *Area Mgr*
EMP: 240 **EST:** 1998
SQ FT: 130,680
SALES: 195.4MM **Privately Held**
SIC: 1623 Communication line & transmis-
sion tower construction

(P-1866)
HPS PLUMBING SERVICE INC
3100 E Belle Ter, Bakersfield (93307-6830)
P.O. Box 6386 (93386-6386)
PHONE..........................661 324-2121
Leslie Denherder, *President*
Jay Buenviaje, *Project Mgr*
EMP: 300
SALES (est): 21.8MM **Privately Held**
WEB: www.hpsmechanical.com
SIC: 1623 1711 Water, sewer & utility
lines; plumbing contractors

(P-1867)
INSITUFORM TECHNOLOGIES LLC
19000 Macarthur Blvd # 800, Irvine
(92612-1461)
PHONE..........................714 724-2324
Elva Alatorre, *Branch Mgr*
EMP: 50
SALES (corp-wide): 1.3B **Publicly Held**
SIC: 1623 Pipeline construction
HQ: Insituform Technologies, Llc
17988 Edison Ave
Chesterfield MO 63005
636 530-8000

(P-1868)
IRBY CONSTRUCTION COMPANY
100 W Keystone Rd, Brawley
(92227-9741)
PHONE..........................760 344-4478
Pat Shouse, *Manager*
Howard Oleson, *Office Mgr*
EMP: 66
SALES (corp-wide): 11.1B **Publicly Held**
WEB: www.irbyconst.com
SIC: 1623 Electric power line construction
HQ: Irby Construction Company
318 Old Highway 49 S
Richland MS 39218
601 709-4729

(P-1869)
IRISH COMMUNICATION COMPANY (DH)
2649 Stingle Ave, Rosemead (91770-3326)
P.O. Box 457 (91770-0457)
PHONE..........................626 288-6170
Gregory C Warde, *CEO*
Dan Mitchell, *President*
Pat D Furnare, *Chairman*
Dennis Brackney, *Vice Pres*
Larry Manke, *Vice Pres*
EMP: 100
SQ FT: 9,000
SALES (est): 62.5MM
SALES (corp-wide): 72.4MM **Privately Held**
WEB: www.irishteam.com
SIC: 1623 8748 1731 Telephone & com-
munication line construction; telecommu-
nications consultant; communications
specialization
HQ: Irish Construction
2641 River Ave
Rosemead CA 91770
626 288-8530

(P-1870)
IRISH CONSTRUCTION (HQ)
2641 River Ave, Rosemead (91770-3392)
P.O. Box 579 (91770-0579)
PHONE..........................626 288-8530
Gregory C Warde, *Ch of Bd*
Ken West, *President*
William E Wilbanks, *President*

P R O D U C T S & S V C S

Randall W Dale, *Corp Secy*
Lonnie Gentry, *Vice Pres*
EMP: 150 **EST:** 1947
SQ FT: 15,000
SALES (est): 90.1MM **Privately Held**
WEB: www.irishconstruction.com
SIC: 1623 Communication line & transmission tower construction; telephone & communication line construction
PA: Manhattan Capital Corporation
2641 River Ave
Rosemead CA 91770
626 288-8530

(P-1871)
IRISH CONSTRUCTION
19490 Monterey St, Morgan Hill
(95037-2606)
PHONE.........................408 612-8440
Sue Nakagawa, *Manager*
EMP: 100
SQ FT: 18,004
SALES (est): 8.3MM
SALES (corp-wide): 72.4MM **Privately Held**
WEB: www.irishconstruction.com
SIC: 1623 1799 Telephone & communication line construction; athletic & recreation facilities construction
HQ: Irish Construction
2641 River Ave
Rosemead CA 91770
626 288-8530

(P-1872)
IRISH CONSTRUCTION
1329 Sweetwater Ln, Spring Valley
(91977-4147)
P.O. Box 580, San Marcos (92079-0580)
PHONE.........................619 713-1991
Dave Watson, *Manager*
EMP: 60
SALES (est): 5.3MM
SALES (corp-wide): 72.4MM **Privately Held**
WEB: www.irishconstruction.com
SIC: 1623 1622 Telephone & communication line construction; bridge, tunnel & elevated highway
HQ: Irish Construction
2641 River Ave
Rosemead CA 91770
626 288-8530

(P-1873)
IRISH CONSTRUCTION
1028 Marchy Ln, Ceres (95307-6649)
PHONE.........................209 576-8766
Ron McMillan, *President*
EMP: 63
SALES (est): 4.1MM
SALES (corp-wide): 72.4MM **Privately Held**
SIC: 1623 Telephone & communication line construction
HQ: Irish Construction
2641 River Ave
Rosemead CA 91770
626 288-8530

(P-1874)
J & M INC
6700 National Dr, Livermore (94550-8804)
PHONE.........................925 724-0300
Manuel Marques III, *CEO*
EMP: 50
SQ FT: 2,000
SALES (est): 15.2MM **Privately Held**
SIC: 1623 1629 Underground utilities contractor; drainage system construction

(P-1875)
JMB CONSTRUCTION INC
132 S Maple Ave, South San Francisco
(94080-6302)
PHONE.........................650 267-5300
Margaret P Burke, *President*
Cormac Hehir, *Project Mgr*
Sean Quinn, *Project Mgr*
Stephen Campbell, *Project Engr*
Ciaran Crossan, *Project Engr*
▲ **EMP:** 100
SALES (est): 36.5MM **Privately Held**
SIC: 1623 Water & sewer line construction

(P-1876)
JR FILANC CNSTR CO INC (PA)
740 N Andreasen Dr, Escondido
(92029-1414)
PHONE.........................760 941-7130
Mark E Filanc, *CEO*
Harry S Cosmos, *President*
Kevin Elliotts, *CFO*
Vincent L Diaz, *Vice Pres*
Chuck Mead, *Admin Asst*
EMP: 100
SQ FT: 13,200
SALES (est): 123.5MM **Privately Held**
WEB: www.filanc.com
SIC: 1623 1629 Pumping station construction; waste water & sewage treatment plant construction

(P-1877)
K S FABRICATION & MACHINE INC
Also Called: KS Fabrication & Machine
6205 District Blvd, Bakersfield
(93313-2141)
P.O. Box 41630 (93384-1630)
PHONE.........................661 617-1700
Kevin S Small, *CEO*
Becky Scott, *CFO*
EMP: 150
SALES (est): 39.6MM **Privately Held**
SIC: 1623 Water, sewer & utility lines

(P-1878)
K T A CONSTRUCTION INC
1920 Cordell Ct Ste 105, El Cajon
(92020-0900)
PHONE.........................619 562-9464
Paul Michael Henderson, *CEO*
Mike Henderson, *President*
Marilyn L Henderson, *Vice Pres*
EMP: 62
SQ FT: 5,200
SALES (est): 18.1MM **Privately Held**
SIC: 1623 Sewer line construction; water main construction

(P-1879)
KANA PIPELINE INC
12620 Magnolia Ave, Riverside
(92503-4636)
PHONE.........................714 986-1400
Dan Locke, *President*
EMP: 100
SQ FT: 55,000
SALES (est): 33.7MM **Privately Held**
WEB: www.kanapipeline.com
SIC: 1623 1629 Water main construction; sewer line construction; drainage system construction

(P-1880)
KENNEDY PIPELINE COMPANY
61 Argonaut, Laguna Hills (92656-1423)
PHONE.........................949 380-8363
Stuart P Trumble, *Owner*
Michael Trumble, *President*
Mark Trumble, *Vice Pres*
Matthew Trumble, *Purch Agent*
John Shoffeitt, *Superintendent*
EMP: 80 **EST:** 1969
SQ FT: 20,000
SALES (est): 15.4MM **Privately Held**
WEB: www.kennedypipeline.com
SIC: 1623 Oil & gas pipeline construction

(P-1881)
KS INDUSTRIES LP (PA)
Also Called: K S I
6205 District Blvd, Bakersfield
(93313-2141)
P.O. Box 41630 (93384-1630)
PHONE.........................661 617-1700
Kevin Small, *CEO*
Doug Erickson, *Vice Pres*
Becky Nelson, *Human Res Mgr*
Allan Faughn, *VP Opers*
Mark Bledsoe, *Mfg Staff*
EMP: 2000
SQ FT: 20,000
SALES (est): 367.2MM **Privately Held**
WEB: www.ksilp.com
SIC: 1623 Water, sewer & utility lines

(P-1882)
LARKIN LEASING INC
674 N Batavia St, Orange (92868-1221)
PHONE.........................714 528-3232
William Larkin, *President*
EMP: 80
SQ FT: 15,000
SALES (est): 6.3MM **Privately Held**
SIC: 1623 Underground utilities contractor

(P-1883)
LIGHTBEAM POWER COMPANY GRIDLE
100 Century Center Ct # 100, San Jose
(95112-4535)
PHONE.........................800 696-7114
John Fong,
Brendan Beasley,
John Gann,
EMP: 51
SALES (est): 1.6MM **Privately Held**
SIC: 1623 Electric power line construction

(P-1884)
LIGHTBEAM PWR GRIDLEY MAIN LLC
100 Century Center Ct # 100, San Jose
(95112-4535)
PHONE.........................800 696-7114
John Fong,
Brendan Beasley,
John Gann,
EMP: 51
SALES (est): 1.7MM **Privately Held**
SIC: 1623 Electric power line construction

(P-1885)
LINKUS ENTERPRISES LLC
Also Called: Honeywell Authorized Dealer
5595 W San Madele Ave, Fresno
(93722-5068)
PHONE.........................559 256-6600
Horacio Guzman, *CEO*
EMP: 302 **Privately Held**
SIC: 1623 Telephone & communication line construction
PA: Linkus Enterprises, Llc
18631 Lloyd Ln
Anderson CA 96007

(P-1886)
LINKUS ENTERPRISES LLC (PA)
18631 Lloyd Ln, Anderson (96007-8459)
PHONE.........................530 229-9197
Horacio Guzman, *CEO*
John Daily, *COO*
Dant Morris, *Vice Pres*
Jon Warren, *VP Finance*
EMP: 133
SQ FT: 3,200
SALES (est): 133.5MM **Privately Held**
SIC: 1623 5731 4813 Telephone & communication line construction; antennas, satellite dish;

(P-1887)
LOMBARDY HOLDINGS INC (PA)
151 Kalmus Dr Ste F6, Costa Mesa
(92626-5965)
P.O. Box 6019, Norco (92860-8034)
PHONE.........................951 808-4550
Marc Laulhere, *CEO*
Mary K Jones, *Vice Pres*
Pam Laulhere, *Admin Sec*
EMP: 200
SQ FT: 80,000
SALES (est): 85MM **Privately Held**
SIC: 1623 5211 Telephone & communication line construction; cable television line construction; electrical construction materials

(P-1888)
MARGATE CONSTRUCTION INC
25007 Figueroa St, Carson (90745-6316)
P.O. Box 4507 (90749-4507)
PHONE.........................310 830-8610
Charles T Riegelhuth, *President*
EMP: 150 **EST:** 1965
SQ FT: 3,000
SALES (est): 9.9MM **Privately Held**
SIC: 1623 1541 Pumping station construction; industrial buildings & warehouses

(P-1889)
MCELVANY INC
13343 Johnson Rd, Los Banos
(93635-9704)
PHONE.........................209 826-1102
Charles McElvany, *President*
Holli McElvany, *Treasurer*
Isaac McElvany, *Vice Pres*
Helen McElvany, *Principal*
EMP: 52
SQ FT: 1,200
SALES (est): 10.8MM **Privately Held**
WEB: www.mcelvany.com
SIC: 1623 1629 Sewer line construction; land preparation construction

(P-1890)
MCGUIRE AND HESTER (PA)
2810 Harbor Bay Pkwy, Alameda
(94502-3040)
PHONE.........................510 632-7676
Michael R Hester, *President*
Bruce Daseking, *Treasurer*
Robert Doud, *Exec VP*
Brock Grunt, *Area Mgr*
Kevin Hester, *Area Mgr*
EMP: 300
SQ FT: 22,000
SALES (est): 140.4MM **Privately Held**
WEB: www.mcguireandhester.com
SIC: 1623 7353 1611 0782 Underground utilities contractor; heavy construction equipment rental; general contractor, highway & street construction; garden planting services

(P-1891)
MGE UNDERGROUND INC
816 26th St, Paso Robles (93446-1243)
P.O. Box 4189 (93447-4189)
PHONE.........................805 238-3510
Michael Joe Goldstein, *President*
Summer Goldstein, *CFO*
Matt Cruzat, *Division Mgr*
Summer Golstein, *Admin Sec*
Jedd Ingraham, *Project Mgr*
EMP: 85
SQ FT: 780
SALES: 18MM **Privately Held**
WEB: www.mgeunderground.com
SIC: 1623 Underground utilities contractor

(P-1892)
MLADEN BUNTICH CNSTR CO INC
1500 W 9th St, Upland (91786-5636)
PHONE.........................909 920-9977
Mladen Buntich Jr, *Ch of Bd*
Lee Roesner, *Vice Pres*
Scott Peterson, *Admin Sec*
▲ **EMP:** 60 **EST:** 1975
SQ FT: 4,000
SALES (est): 20MM **Privately Held**
WEB: www.buntich.com
SIC: 1623 8711 8322 Sewer line construction; engineering services; individual & family services

(P-1893)
NOR-CAL PIPELINE SERVICES
1875 S River Rd, West Sacramento
(95691-2896)
PHONE.........................530 673-3886
David Jaeger, *President*
David L Jaeger, *Vice Pres*
William Jaeger, *Admin Sec*
Manny Badyal, *Project Mgr*
Aaron Clark, *Technology*
EMP: 70
SALES (est): 28.9MM **Privately Held**
SIC: 1623 Pipeline construction

(P-1894)
NOVA GROUP INC (HQ)
185 Devlin Rd, NAPA (94558-6255)
P.O. Box 4050 (94558-0450)
PHONE.........................707 265-1100
Ronald M Fedrick, *Ch of Bd*
Scott R Victor, *President*
Scott Victor, *COO*
Carole Bionda, *Vice Pres*
Walter Birdsall, *Vice Pres*
◆ **EMP:** 200 **EST:** 1957
SQ FT: 15,000

SALES: 2.9MM
SALES (corp-wide): 11.1B **Publicly Held**
SIC: **1623** Underground utilities contractor
PA: Quanta Services, Inc.
2800 Post Oak Blvd # 2600
Houston TX 77056
713 629-7600

(P-1895)
NOVA-CPF INC
7411 Napa Vallejo Hwy, NAPA
(94558-7501)
P.O. Box 4050 (94558-0450)
PHONE.................................707 257-3200
Charles Fedrick, *President*
Elbert C Lewey, *Treasurer*
Carole Bionda, *Vice Pres*
David W Fedrick, *Vice Pres*
EMP: 200
SQ FT: 11,000
SALES (est): 9.3MM **Privately Held**
SIC: **1623** Underground utilities contractor

(P-1896)
NOVA/TIC GOV PROJ JV
185 Devlin Rd, NAPA (94558-6255)
P.O. Box 4050 (94558-0450)
PHONE.................................707 257-3200
Ronald M Fedrick, *President*
Scott R Victor, *President*
Carole L Bionda, *Vice Pres*
Walter M Birdsall, *Vice Pres*
Chris Mathies, *Vice Pres*
▲ EMP: 150
SQ FT: 15,000
SALES (est): 1.8MM **Privately Held**
SIC: **1623** Water, sewer & utility lines

(P-1897)
ORION CONSTRUCTION CORPORATION
2185 La Mirada Dr, Vista (92081-8830)
PHONE.................................760 597-9660
Richard Dowsing, *CEO*
Mark Dowsing, *Vice Pres*
EMP: 80
SQ FT: 7,000
SALES (est): 29.5MM **Privately Held**
WEB: www.orionconstruction.com
SIC: **1623** 1629 1542 Water, sewer & utility lines; industrial plant construction; non-residential construction

(P-1898)
PACIFIC BORING INCORPORATED
1985 W Mountain View Ave, Caruthers (93609)
P.O. Box 727 (93609-0727)
PHONE.................................559 864-9444
David Cline, *President*
James Gardner, *Vice Pres*
Calastro Terrasas, *Admin Sec*
EMP: 50
SQ FT: 750
SALES (est): 9.4MM **Privately Held**
WEB: www.pacificboring.com
SIC: **1623** Water, sewer & utility lines

(P-1899)
PACIFIC SOUTHWEST CNSTR & EQP
2308 Shaylene Way, Alpine (91901-3174)
PHONE.................................619 445-5190
Thomas L Scanlan, *President*
Kristina Scanlan, *Vice Pres*
EMP: 65
SALES (est): 5.4MM **Privately Held**
SIC: **1623** Underground utilities contractor

(P-1900)
PACIFIC W SPACE CMMNCTIONS INC
Also Called: P W C
900 W Gladstone St, San Dimas (91773-1734)
PHONE.................................909 592-4321
Sheryl F Patton, *CEO*
Joanna Patton, *CFO*
John Tarango, *Treasurer*
Betty Fonteno, *Corp Secy*
Rich Patton, *Vice Pres*
EMP: 69 EST: 1981
SQ FT: 2,000

SALES (est): 21.5MM **Privately Held**
SIC: **1623** Communication line & transmission tower construction

(P-1901)
PAULUS ENGINEERING INC
2871 E Coronado St, Anaheim (92806-2504)
PHONE.................................714 632-3322
Ronald Paulus, *President*
Jason Paulus, *Vice Pres*
Roger Betten, *Project Mgr*
Mike Whipple, *Project Mgr*
Michelle Obermeier, *Asst Controller*
EMP: 60
SQ FT: 40,000
SALES (est): 10.3MM **Privately Held**
WEB: www.paulusengineering.com
SIC: **1623** Sewer line construction; pipeline construction

(P-1902)
PEARCE SERVICES LLC (HQ)
Also Called: Cross Rock
3720 La Cruz Way, Paso Robles (93446-5907)
P.O. Box 1708 (93447-1708)
PHONE.................................805 237-7480
Brett Forester, *CEO*
Kristen Osborne, *CFO*
Kullen Burk, *VP Opers*
EMP: 50 EST: 1998
SQ FT: 2,800
SALES (est): 31.6MM **Privately Held**
WEB: www.psixbox.com
SIC: **1623** Communication line & transmission tower construction; telephone & communication line construction
PA: Willcrest Partners, Llc
100 Spear St
San Francisco CA 94105
415 816-0086

(P-1903)
PRESTON PIPELINES INC (PA)
133 Botehlo Ave, Milpitas (95035-5325)
PHONE.................................408 262-1418
Michael D Preston, *President*
Ron Bianchini, *COO*
Dave Heslop, *Vice Pres*
Rich Lewis, *Vice Pres*
Gary Menges, *Vice Pres*
EMP: 150
SQ FT: 12,000
SALES (est): 100.3MM **Privately Held**
WEB: www.prestonpipelines.com
SIC: **1623** Pipeline construction

(P-1904)
QUALITY TELECOM CONSULTANTS (PA)
Also Called: Quality Techniques Engrg Cnstr
3740 Cincinnati Ave, Rocklin (95765-1204)
P.O. Box 807, Loomis (95650-0807)
PHONE.................................916 315-0500
Scott Duncan, *President*
Candice Northam, *Treasurer*
Jacob Duncan, *Vice Pres*
Osh Duncan, *Admin Sec*
Adam Lieb, *Project Mgr*
EMP: 89
SALES (est): 23.6MM **Privately Held**
WEB:
www.qualitytelecomconsultantsinc.com
SIC: **1623** 1731 4899 8748 Communication line & transmission tower construction; communications specialization; communication signal enhancement network system; telecommunications consultant

(P-1905)
RANGER PIPELINES INCORPORATED
1790 Yosemite Ave, San Francisco (94124-2622)
P.O. Box 24109 (94124-0109)
PHONE.................................415 822-3700
Thomas Hunt, *President*
Mary Shea-Hunt, *Corp Secy*
Peter Cuddihy, *Vice Pres*
EMP: 101
SQ FT: 20,000
SALES (est): 37.9MM **Privately Held**
SIC: **1623** Pipeline construction

(P-1906)
S E C C CORPORATION
16224 Koala Rd, Adelanto (92301-3915)
PHONE.................................760 246-6218
Manuel Armenta, *Manager*
EMP: 56 **Privately Held**
SIC: **1623** Transmitting tower (telecommunication) construction
PA: S E C C Corporation
14945 La Palma Dr
Chino CA 91710

(P-1907)
S E PIPE LINE CONSTRUCTION CO
11832 Bloomfield Ave, Santa Fe Springs (90670-4693)
PHONE.................................562 868-9771
Charles Rikel, *President*
James Doulames, *Vice Pres*
Thomas Tustin, *Admin Sec*
Daniel Ibarra, *Manager*
EMP: 100
SQ FT: 5,000
SALES (est): 39.6MM **Privately Held**
SIC: **1623** Gas main construction; electric power line construction; oil & gas pipeline construction

(P-1908)
SAM HILL & SONS INC
Also Called: WMS Transportation
2627 Beene Rd, Ventura (93003-7203)
P.O. Box 5670 (93005-0670)
PHONE.................................805 620-0828
Ronald Hill, *President*
Brett Franklin, *Foreman/Supr*
EMP: 50
SQ FT: 1,000
SALES (est): 8.4MM **Privately Held**
WEB: www.samhillandsons.com
SIC: **1623** Underground utilities contractor

(P-1909)
SANCO PIPELINES INCORPORATED
727 University Ave, Los Gatos (95032-7610)
PHONE.................................408 377-2793
David R Schrader, *Principal*
EMP: 50 EST: 1956
SQ FT: 3,000
SALES (est): 23MM **Privately Held**
WEB: www.sancopipelines.com
SIC: **1623** Pipeline construction

(P-1910)
SCHILLING PARADISE CORP
697 Greenfield Dr, El Cajon (92021-2983)
PHONE.................................619 449-4141
Jeff Platt, *President*
Michael Manos, *Principal*
Jackie Corbin, *Human Res Mgr*
John Meyers, *Purch Agent*
Daniel J Shay, *Opers Staff*
EMP: 175
SALES (est): 17.9MM **Privately Held**
SIC: **1623** 1731 Underground utilities contractor; general electrical contractor

(P-1911)
SHOFFEITT PIPELINE INC
15801 Rockfield Blvd L, Irvine (92618-2869)
PHONE.................................949 581-1600
Kathy Shoffeitt, *President*
John Shoffeitt, *Vice Pres*
Laura Hudson, *Manager*
EMP: 80
SQ FT: 3,200
SALES (est): 1.2MM **Privately Held**
SIC: **1623** Underground utilities contractor

(P-1912)
SOLCOM INC
Also Called: Solcom Communications Inc
24801 Huntwood Ave, Hayward (94544-1813)
PHONE.................................510 940-2490
Tony McMenamin, *President*
EMP: 500
SALES: 50MM **Privately Held**
SIC: **1623** Telephone & communication line construction

(P-1913)
SOLEX CONTRACTING INC
42146 Remington Ave, Temecula (92590-2547)
PHONE.................................951 308-1706
Jerry Allen, *President*
EMP: 70
SQ FT: 12,000
SALES: 40.3MM **Privately Held**
SIC: **1623** 1542 1541 Communication line & transmission tower construction; commercial & office building, new construction; renovation, remodeling & repairs: industrial buildings

(P-1914)
SOUTHWEST CONTRACTORS (PA)
Also Called: Bowman Pipeline Contractors
3235 Unicorn Rd, Bakersfield (93308-6850)
PHONE.................................661 588-0484
Floyd E Bowman Jr, *CEO*
Kathy Bowman, *Vice Pres*
Marilyn Buys, *Executive*
Donald Swank, *Project Mgr*
Amanda Diaz, *Accountant*
EMP: 150
SQ FT: 10,000
SALES (est): 57MM **Privately Held**
SIC: **1623** 3443 Oil & gas pipeline construction; industrial vessels, tanks & containers

(P-1915)
SPIESS CONSTRUCTION CO INC
Also Called: Scci
201 S Broadway St Ste 140, Orcutt (93455-4611)
P.O. Box 2849, Santa Maria (93457-2849)
PHONE.................................805 937-5859
Scott A Coleman, *President*
Barry L Matchett, *Vice Pres*
Frank L Forthun, *Assistant VP*
EMP: 60
SALES (est): 27.2MM **Privately Held**
WEB: www.sccitanks.com
SIC: **1623** Sewer line construction; water main construction

(P-1916)
SPINIELLO COMPANIES
2650 Pomona Blvd, Pomona (91768-3220)
PHONE.................................909 629-1000
Priscilla Moyer, *Manager*
Kent Meier, *Project Mgr*
Abby Cruz, *Project Engr*
EMP: 100
SALES (corp-wide): 90MM **Privately Held**
SIC: **1623** Water, sewer & utility lines
PA: Spiniello Companies
354 Eisenhower Pkwy # 1200
Livingston NJ 07039
973 808-8383

(P-1917)
SRD ENGINEERING INC
3578 E Enterprise Dr, Anaheim (92807-1627)
PHONE.................................714 630-2480
Deborah Denton, *CEO*
Jason Kenney, *Deputy Dir*
Jim Calton, *Manager*
EMP: 65
SQ FT: 5,000
SALES (est): 8.8MM **Privately Held**
SIC: **1623** Water & sewer line construction

(P-1918)
SUKUT CONSTRUCTION LLC
4010 W Chandler Ave, Santa Ana (92704-5202)
PHONE.................................714 540-5351
Michael Crawford, *Principal*
Paul Kuliev, *CFO*
Joe Philbin, *Principal*
Mike Zanaboni, *Principal*
EMP: 99 EST: 2014
SALES (est): 6.7MM **Privately Held**
SIC: **1623** 1629 1611 Water, sewer & utility lines; earthmoving contractor; grading

(P-1919)
T C CONSTRUCTION COMPANY INC
10540 Prospect Ave, Santee (92071-4591)
PHONE..........................619 448-4560
Terry W Cameron, *CEO*
Austin Cameron, *President*
Jack Gieffels, *CFO*
Derek Franken, *Vice Pres*
Darren Tharp, *Vice Pres*
EMP: 150
SQ FT: 16,000
SALES: 62.2MM **Privately Held**
SIC: 1623 1611 Underground utilities contractor; highway & street paving contractor

(P-1920)
TRITON TOWER INC (PA)
3200 Jefferson Blvd, West Sacramento (95691-5418)
PHONE..........................916 375-8546
Kevin Wingard, *President*
Mike Monroe, *Treasurer*
Rex Avakian, *Admin Sec*
EMP: 54
SALES: 2.5MM **Privately Held**
SIC: 1623 Transmitting tower (telecommunication) construction

(P-1921)
TURN AROUND COMMUNICATIONS INC
4400 Temple City Blvd A, El Monte (91731-1090)
P.O. Box 6121 (91734-2121)
PHONE..........................626 443-2400
Sayeid Kouhkan, *President*
EMP: 170
SQ FT: 23,683
SALES: 7.6MM **Privately Held**
SIC: 1623 Telephone & communication line construction

(P-1922)
UNITED POWER CONTRACTORS INC
405 Maple St Ste A-103, Ramona (92065-1890)
PHONE..........................760 735-8028
Andres A Canales, *President*
Jerome Reuben Rodriguez, *CEO*
Mark Walken, *Senior VP*
Reuben Rodriguez, *Vice Pres*
EMP: 117 EST: 2007
SALES (est): 15.3MM **Privately Held**
SIC: 1623 Electric power line construction

(P-1923)
UTAH PACIFIC CONSTRUCTION CO
40940 Eleanora Way, Murrieta (92562-5946)
PHONE..........................951 677-9876
Craig R Young, *President*
Brian Keeline, *Vice Pres*
Jason Bent, *Safety Mgr*
Chris Medellin, *Manager*
Ann Young, *Manager*
EMP: 50
SQ FT: 5,000
SALES (est): 8.3MM **Privately Held**
SIC: 1623 Sewer line construction; water main construction; pipeline construction

(P-1924)
UTI LEAK SEEKERS
Also Called: Uti Underground Technology
1398 Monterey Pass Rd, Monterey Park (91754-3619)
PHONE..........................323 724-0081
Lisa Pickareela, *Manager*
EMP: 70
SALES (est): 2.5MM **Privately Held**
SIC: 1623 Underground utilities contractor

(P-1925)
VADNAIS TRENCHLESS SVCS INC
2130 La Mirada Dr, Vista (92081-8815)
PHONE..........................858 550-1460
Paul Vadnais, *CEO*
Jesse Mangan, *CFO*
Jeff Anderson, *Vice Pres*

▲ EMP: 100
SALES (est): 21.8MM **Privately Held**
WEB: www.vadnaiscorp.com
SIC: 1623 Sewer line construction

(P-1926)
VALVERDE CONSTRUCTION INC
10936 Shoemaker Ave, Santa Fe Springs (90670-4533)
P.O. Box 3223 (90670-0223)
PHONE..........................562 906-1826
Joe A Valverde, *President*
Rose Valverde, *Treasurer*
Edward Valverde, *Vice Pres*
Christopher Valverde, *Admin Sec*
EMP: 75
SQ FT: 9,000
SALES (est): 32.6MM **Privately Held**
SIC: 1623 Water main construction; sewer line construction; telephone & communication line construction; cable laying construction

(P-1927)
VCI CONSTRUCTION LLC (HQ)
1921 W 11th St Ste A, Upland (91786-3508)
PHONE..........................909 946-0905
John Xanthos, *President*
Vic Marovish, *CFO*
Edgar Escobar, *Vice Pres*
Logan Teal, *Vice Pres*
Patrick Davies, *Division Mgr*
EMP: 100 EST: 1998
SQ FT: 29,500
SALES: 68MM
SALES (corp-wide): 3.1B **Publicly Held**
WEB: www.vcicom.com
SIC: 1623 Underground utilities contractor; transmitting tower (telecommunication) construction
PA: Dycom Industries, Inc.
11780 Us Highway 1 # 600
Palm Beach Gardens FL 33408
561 627-7171

(P-1928)
W A RASIC CNSTR CO INC (PA)
4150 Long Beach Blvd, Long Beach (90807-2650)
PHONE..........................562 928-6111
Peter L Rasic, *CEO*
Shane Sato, *Division Mgr*
Randall Yoo, *CTO*
Wes Brodeur, *Project Mgr*
Howard Frausto, *Project Mgr*
EMP: 151
SQ FT: 8,500
SALES (est): 150MM **Privately Held**
WEB: www.warasic.com
SIC: 1623 Sewer line construction; water main construction

(P-1929)
W M LYLES CO (HQ)
Also Called: WM LYLES CO
1210 W Olive Ave, Fresno (93728-2816)
P.O. Box 4348 (93744-4348)
PHONE..........................559 441-1900
David Dawson, *President*
Andrea Oliver, *President*
Dave Dawson, *Vice Pres*
Pat Saleen, *Vice Pres*
Ken Strosnider, *Vice Pres*
EMP: 151
SQ FT: 6,200
SALES: 211.6MM
SALES (corp-wide): 28.6MM **Privately Held**
WEB: www.wmlyles.com
SIC: 1623 Pipeline construction; underground utilities contractor
PA: Lyles Diversified, Inc.
1210 W Olive Ave
Fresno CA 93728
559 441-1900

(P-1930)
WATER & SEWER SERVICE
7051 Dublin Blvd, Dublin (94568-3018)
PHONE..........................925 828-8524
Berrt Michalzzyk, *General Mgr*
EMP: 80
SALES (est): 2.7MM **Privately Held**
SIC: 1623 Water, sewer & utility lines

(P-1931)
WATKINS CONSTRUCTION CO INC
Also Called: Johnston Vacuum Tank Service
112 E Cedar St, Taft (93268-9708)
P.O. Box 243 (93268-0243)
PHONE..........................661 763-5395
Eddie Watkins Sr, *President*
Mary King, *Manager*
EMP: 60 EST: 1967
SQ FT: 4,800
SALES (est): 9.9MM **Privately Held**
WEB: www.watkinsconstructionco.com
SIC: 1623 Oil & gas pipeline construction

(P-1932)
WDC EXPLRTION WELLS HOLDG CORP
1300 National Dr Ste 140, Sacramento (95834-1981)
PHONE..........................916 419-6043
Robert L Ruck, *CEO*
Ray Imbsen, *CFO*
EMP: 203
SQ FT: 8,788
SALES (est): 18.1MM **Privately Held**
SIC: 1623 1629 Pumping station construction; waste water & sewage treatment plant construction

(P-1933)
WEST STATES SKANSKA INC
1995 Agua Mansa Rd, Riverside (92509-2405)
PHONE..........................970 565-4903
Curtis Brotten, *President*
Matt Johnson, *Sr Project Mgr*
EMP: 150
SQ FT: 800
SALES (est): 8.2MM
SALES (corp-wide): 19B **Privately Held**
SIC: 1623 1541 Water, sewer & utility lines; industrial buildings & warehouses
HQ: Skanska Usa Civil West Rocky Mountain District Inc.
1995 Agua Mansa Rd
Riverside CA 92509
970 565-8000

(P-1934)
WEST VALLEY CNSTR CO INC (PA)
580 E Mcglincy Ln, Campbell (95008-4999)
PHONE..........................408 371-5510
Kevin Kelly, *CEO*
David Barnes, *CFO*
Jeff Azevedo, *Vice Pres*
Jeff Boss, *Vice Pres*
James Vosburgh, *Vice Pres*
EMP: 150 EST: 1958
SQ FT: 9,000
SALES (est): 136MM **Privately Held**
WEB: www.westvalleyconstruction.com
SIC: 1623 Water main construction; telephone & communication line construction

(P-1935)
WEST VALLEY CNSTR CO INC
Also Called: West Valley Cnstr - Stockton
2655 E Miner Ave Ste A, Stockton (95205-4762)
PHONE..........................209 943-6812
EMP: 95
SALES (corp-wide): 136MM **Privately Held**
SIC: 1623 Telephone & communication line construction; water main construction
PA: West Valley Construction Company, Inc.
580 E Mcglincy Ln
Campbell CA 95008
408 371-5510

(P-1936)
WHITTIER EQUIPMENT RENTALS
11832 Bloomfield Ave, Santa Fe Springs (90670-4610)
PHONE..........................562 863-0641
Charles Rikel, *President*
T C Tustin, *Treasurer*
James Doulames, *Vice Pres*
EMP: 85
SQ FT: 5,000

SALES (est): 4.3MM **Privately Held**
SIC: 1623 Pipeline construction

```
1629 Heavy Construction,
NEC
```

(P-1937)
ALLOY CONSTRUCTION INC
701 Gardner Field Rd, Taft (93268)
P.O. Box 661 (93268-0661)
PHONE..........................661 203-2592
James Folkner, *President*
EMP: 60 EST: 1991
SQ FT: 300
SALES: 4.5MM **Privately Held**
WEB: www.alloyconstruction.com
SIC: 1629 Oil refinery construction

(P-1938)
AMERICAN CIVIL CONSTRS LLC
3701 Mallard Dr, Benicia (94510-1246)
PHONE..........................707 746-8028
Pete Wells, *Manager*
EMP: 150 **Privately Held**
WEB: www.americancivilconstructors.com
SIC: 1629 0783 0181 Land preparation construction; earthmoving contractor; golf course construction; dam construction; spraying services, ornamental bush; removal services, bush & tree; sod farms
HQ: American Civil Constructors Llc
4901 S Windermere St
Littleton CO 80120
303 795-2582

(P-1939)
ANDERSON PCF ENGRG CNSTR INC
1390 Norman Ave, Santa Clara (95054-2056)
PHONE..........................408 970-9900
Peter E Anderson, *CEO*
Matthew Mirenda, *Vice Pres*
Ann Anderson, *Admin Sec*
Bob Colah, *Project Mgr*
Michael Gossett, *Project Mgr*
EMP: 100
SQ FT: 3,000
SALES (est): 44.2MM **Privately Held**
WEB: www.andpac.com
SIC: 1629 1623 Dams, waterways, docks & other marine construction; pumping station construction; underground utilities contractor

(P-1940)
ARB INC (HQ)
26000 Commercentre Dr, Lake Forest (92630-8816)
PHONE..........................949 598-9242
Brian Pratt, *President*
John P Schauerman, *Corp Secy*
Timothy Healy, *Vice Pres*
Scott Summers, *Vice Pres*
John M Perisich, *Admin Sec*
▲ EMP: 140
SALES (est): 525.8MM
SALES (corp-wide): 2.9B **Publicly Held**
WEB: www.arbinc.com
SIC: 1629 1623 Industrial plant construction; waste disposal plant construction; waste water & sewage treatment plant construction; oil & gas line & compressor station construction
PA: Primoris Services Corporation
2300 N Field St Ste 1900
Dallas TX 75201
214 740-5600

(P-1941)
AUBURN CONSTRUCTORS LLC
730 W Stadium Ln, Sacramento (95834-1130)
PHONE..........................916 924-0344
Dean Bailey, *President*
Bill Franceschini, *Corp Secy*
Kevin Couper, *Vice Pres*
EMP: 80
SQ FT: 5,500
SALES: 48.8MM **Privately Held**
WEB: www.auburnconstructors.com
SIC: 1629 Industrial plant construction

▲ = Import ▼=Export
◆ =Import/Export

(P-1942)
BARNARD BESSAC JOINT VENTURE
395 Shoreway Rd, Redwood City
(94065-1601)
PHONE.................650 212-8957
EMP: 100
SALES (est): 1.9MM Privately Held
SIC: 1629 Industrial plant construction

(P-1943)
BEMUS LANDSCAPE INC
1225 Puerta Del Sol # 500, San Clemente
(92673-6312)
P.O. Box 74268 (92673-0143)
PHONE.................714 557-7910
William Howard Bemus, President
Jonathon Parry, Corp Secy
Martine Bemus, Vice Pres
Spencer Bemus, Branch Mgr
Felix Montano, Branch Mgr
EMP: 300 EST: 1973
SQ FT: 7,000
SALES (est): 44.8MM Privately Held
WEB: www.bemuslandscape.com
SIC: 1629 0782 Drainage system construction; landscape contractors

(P-1944)
BILL PAPICH CONSTRUCTION INC
398 Sunrise Ter, Arroyo Grande
(93420-4419)
PHONE.................805 489-9420
Jason Papich, President
Marcia Papich, Corp Secy
EMP: 50
SALES (est): 787.8K Privately Held
SIC: 1629 Blasting contractor, except building demolition

(P-1945)
BRIGHTVIEW COMPANIES LLC (DH)
27001 Agoura Rd Ste 350, Calabasas
(91301-5112)
PHONE.................818 223-8500
John Feenan, CEO
Eric Johnson, Partner
Thomas C Donnelly, President
Jeff Herold, President
Greg Pieschala, Exec VP
◆ EMP: 175
SALES (est): 2.4B
SALES (corp-wide): 2.3B Publicly Held
WEB: www.valleycrest.com
SIC: 1629 0782 0781 Golf course construction; lawn & garden services; landscape services; landscape planning services
HQ: Brightview Landscapes, Llc
980 Jolly Rd Ste 300
Blue Bell PA 19422
484 567-7204

(P-1946)
BRIGHTVIEW GOLF MAINT INC
405 Glen Annie Rd, Santa Barbara
(93117-1427)
PHONE.................805 968-6400
Richard Hasah, Manager
EMP: 50
SALES (corp-wide): 2.3B Publicly Held
SIC: 1629 Golf course construction
HQ: Brightview Golf Maintenance, Inc.
24151 Ventura Blvd
Calabasas CA 91302
818 223-8500

(P-1947)
BRIGHTVIEW GOLF MAINT INC (DH)
24151 Ventura Blvd, Calabasas
(91302-1449)
PHONE.................818 223-8500
Burton Sperber, Ch of Bd
Richard A Sperber, Ch of Bd
Gregory Pieschala, President
Andrew Mandell, CFO
Michael L Dingman, Chairman
EMP: 100
SQ FT: 80,000
SALES (est): 158.7MM
SALES (corp-wide): 2.3B Publicly Held
SIC: 1629 Golf course construction

HQ: Brightview Companies, Llc
27001 Agoura Rd Ste 350
Calabasas CA 91301
818 223-8500

(P-1948)
BRIGHTVIEW LANDSCAPE DEV INC
8450 Miramar Pl, San Diego (92121-2528)
PHONE.................858 458-9900
Vince Germann, Manager
EMP: 300
SQ FT: 16,050
SALES (corp-wide): 2.3B Publicly Held
SIC: 1629 Irrigation system construction; land preparation construction
HQ: Brightview Landscape Development, Inc.
24151 Ventura Blvd
Calabasas CA 91302
818 223-8500

(P-1949)
BYROM-DAVEY INC
13220 Evnng Crk Dr S # 103, San Diego
(92128-4103)
PHONE.................858 513-7199
Steve V Davey, Owner
Joanne Caspersen, Treasurer
Christine Butler, Vice Pres
Raul Gilbert, Vice Pres
Eric Jennings Sr, Vice Pres
EMP: 50
SQ FT: 2,200
SALES (est): 12.3MM Privately Held
WEB: www.byromdavey.com
SIC: 1629 1611 Land preparation construction; athletic field construction; highway & street construction

(P-1950)
C A RASMUSSEN INC (PA)
28548 Livingston Ave, Valencia
(91355-4171)
PHONE.................661 367-9040
Charles A Rasmussen, President
D I C K Greenburg, CFO
Tim Macdonald, Vice Pres
Mike Medema, Vice Pres
Doug Misley, Vice Pres
EMP: 50
SQ FT: 20,000
SALES (est): 82.2MM Privately Held
WEB: www.carasmussen.com
SIC: 1629 1611 Earthmoving contractor; grading

(P-1951)
CAL WEST UNDERGROUND INC
951 6th St, Norco (92860-1442)
PHONE.................951 371-6775
Jeffrey M Abernathy, President
Wendy Davidson, Office Mgr
EMP: 63
SQ FT: 1,200
SALES (est): 9.2MM Privately Held
SIC: 1629 Trenching contractor

(P-1952)
CATTRAC CONSTRUCTION INC
15030 Slover Ave, Fontana (92337-7237)
PHONE.................909 355-1146
Stephanie A Jacinto, CEO
Greg Dineen, Vice Pres
Rita Stark, Controller
Michael Storms, Manager
EMP: 60
SQ FT: 5,000
SALES (est): 14.6MM Privately Held
WEB: www.cattrac.com
SIC: 1629 7353 4213 Earthmoving contractor; earth moving equipment, rental or leasing; trucking, except local

(P-1953)
CE ALLENCOMPANY INC
2109 Gundry Ave, Long Beach
(90755-3517)
PHONE.................562 989-6100
C E Peter Allen, President
EMP: 50
SQ FT: 1,277
SALES (est): 8.2MM Privately Held
SIC: 1629 7353 Industrial plant construction; oil equipment rental services

(P-1954)
CITY OF LIVERMORE
Also Called: Water Resources Division
101 W Jack London Blvd, Livermore
(94551-7632)
PHONE.................925 960-8100
Darren Greenwood, Manager
EMP: 50 Privately Held
SIC: 1629 Waste water & sewage treatment plant construction
PA: City Of Livermore
1052 S Livermore Ave
Livermore CA 94550
925 960-4020

(P-1955)
DOD CONSTRUCTORS A JV
185 Devlin Rd, NAPA (94558-6255)
PHONE.................707 265-1100
Ronald Fedrick, CEO
Scott Victor, President
Walter Birdsall, CFO
Carole Bionda, Vice Pres
EMP: 99 EST: 2013
SALES (est): 2.6MM Privately Held
SIC: 1629 Dams, waterways, docks & other marine construction

(P-1956)
DOD FUELING CONSTRUCTORS A JV
185 Devlin Rd, NAPA (94558-6255)
PHONE.................707 265-1100
Ronald Fedrick, Principal
Walter Birdsall, CFO
Carole Bionda, Principal
Chris Mathies, Principal
Scott Victor, Principal
EMP: 99 EST: 2013
SALES (est): 2.4MM Privately Held
SIC: 1629 Dams, waterways, docks & other marine construction

(P-1957)
DOD MARINE CONSTRUCTORS A JV
185 Devlin Rd, NAPA (94558-6255)
PHONE.................707 265-1100
Ronald Fedrick, Partner
Carole Bionda, Partner
Walter Birdsall, Partner
Chris Mathies, Partner
Scott Victor, Partner
EMP: 99 EST: 2013
SALES (est): 2.4MM Privately Held
SIC: 1629 Dams, waterways, docks & other marine construction

(P-1958)
DUTRA DREDGING COMPANY (HQ)
2350 Kerner Blvd Ste 200, San Rafael
(94901-5595)
PHONE.................415 721-2131
Bill T Dutra, CEO
EMP: 60
SQ FT: 2,000
SALES (est): 14MM
SALES (corp-wide): 145.1MM Privately Held
WEB: www.dutragroup.com
SIC: 1629 Dredging contractor
PA: The Dutra Group
2350 Kerner Blvd Ste 200
San Rafael CA 94901
415 258-6876

(P-1959)
DUTRA GROUP (PA)
Also Called: Dutra Dredging
2350 Kerner Blvd Ste 200, San Rafael
(94901-5595)
PHONE.................415 258-6876
Bill T Dutra, CEO
Harry Stewart, COO
James Hagood, CFO
Jim Davidson, Division Mgr
Sharon Gardiner, Office Mgr
▲ EMP: 100
SQ FT: 22,000

SALES (est): 145.1MM Privately Held
SIC: 1629 8711 1429 Marine construction; dredging contractor; earthmoving contractor; civil engineering; igneous rock, crushed & broken-quarrying

(P-1960)
DUTRA MANSON JV
1000 Point San Pedro Rd, San Rafael
(94901-8312)
PHONE.................415 258-6876
Harry K Stewart, Director
Cliff Hunt, Manager
EMP: 60
SALES (est): 2.3MM Privately Held
SIC: 1629 Marine construction

(P-1961)
ESOLAR INC (DH)
900 Glenneyre St, Laguna Beach
(92651-2707)
PHONE.................818 303-9500
John Van Scoter, CEO
Bill Gross, President
Rayan Kassis, President
Linda Heller, CFO
Dale Rogers, Exec VP
▲ EMP: 78
SALES (est): 12.5MM
SALES (corp-wide): 152.9MM Privately Held
SIC: 1629 Power plant construction

(P-1962)
FORD CONSTRUCTION COMPANY INC
300 W Pine St, Lodi (95240-2022)
PHONE.................209 333-1116
Richard Piombo, Treasurer
Nicholas B Jones, President
Nick Jones, Executive
Amy Moore, Manager
Donna Goff, Clerk
EMP: 100
SQ FT: 8,500
SALES (est): 18.4MM Privately Held
WEB: www.ford-construction.com
SIC: 1629 1623 Dam construction; earthmoving contractor; water & sewer line construction

(P-1963)
FOUNDATION CONSTRUCTORS INC (PA)
81 Big Break Rd, Oakley (94561)
P.O. Box 97 (94561-0097)
PHONE.................925 754-6633
Derek Halecky, President
Pete Brandl, President
Nikki Sjoblom, Corp Secy
Don Hilton, Vice Pres
Gary Prlichek, Vice Pres
▲ EMP: 100
SQ FT: 6,000
SALES (est): 68.3MM Privately Held
SIC: 1629 Pile driving contractor

(P-1964)
FOUNDATION PILE INC
8375 Almeria Ave, Fontana (92335-3283)
PHONE.................909 350-1584
Derek Halecky, CEO
Peter Brandl, President
Nikki Sjoblom, CFO
Dermot Fallon, Vice Pres
Mike Lindsay, Vice Pres
EMP: 97 EST: 1978
SALES (est): 7.8MM
SALES (corp-wide): 68.3MM Privately Held
SIC: 1629 1794 Pile driving contractor; excavation & grading, building construction
PA: Foundation Constructors, Inc.
81 Big Break Rd
Oakley CA 94561
925 754-6633

(P-1965)
GHILOTTI CONSTRUCTION CO INC (PA)
Also Called: Gcc
246 Ghillotti Ave, Santa Rosa
(95407-8152)
PHONE.................707 585-1221
Richard W Ghilotti, CEO

EMP: 151
SQ FT: 9,000
SALES (est): 135.2MM **Privately Held**
WEB: www.ghilotti.com
SIC: 1629 Land preparation construction

(P-1966)
GRANITE CONSTRUCTION COMPANY
Also Called: Northern California Regional
4001 Bradshaw Rd, Sacramento
(95827-3800)
PHONE...............................916 855-4400
Wayne Cornelius, *Manager*
EMP: 61
SQ FT: 1,364
SALES (corp-wide): 3.3B **Publicly Held**
WEB:
www.graniteconstructioncompany.com
SIC: 1629 1611 Land preparation construction; highway & street construction
HQ: Granite Construction Company
585 W Beach St
Watsonville CA 95076
831 724-1011

(P-1967)
GREAT LAKES E & I/ INQUIP JV
6558 Lonetree Blvd, Rocklin (95765-5874)
P.O. Box 6277, Mc Lean VA (22106-6277)
PHONE...............................805 687-2007
Dominique Namy, *Principal*
Oscar Hensgen, *Principal*
Louay Owaidat, *Principal*
EMP: 99
SQ FT: 30,000
SALES (est): 1.9MM **Privately Held**
SIC: 1629 Dams, waterways, docks & other marine construction; dam construction; levee construction

(P-1968)
HANS TECHNOLOGIES INC
1300 Clay St Ste 600, Oakland
(94612-1427)
PHONE...............................510 464-8018
Jerry Moseley, *President*
Craig Johns, *Vice Pres*
Kenneth Norcross III, *Vice Pres*
Weiping Xia, *Vice Pres*
James LI, *Admin Sec*
▼ **EMP:** 58
SQ FT: 6,500
SALES: 13.5MM **Privately Held**
SIC: 1629 Waste water & sewage treatment plant construction

(P-1969)
HAT CREEK CNSTR & MTLS INC (PA)
24339 State Highway 89, Burney
(96013-9615)
PHONE...............................530 335-5501
Robert Thompson, *President*
Perry Thompson, *Corp Secy*
Howard A Lakey Jr, *Vice Pres*
EMP: 50
SALES (est): 19.3MM **Privately Held**
WEB: www.hatcreekconstruction.com
SIC: 1629 1771 1521 5032 Earthmoving contractor; concrete work; single-family housing construction; sand, construction; gravel; highway & street construction

(P-1970)
JAMES-TIMEC INTERNATIONAL
155 Corporate Pl, Vallejo (94590-6968)
PHONE...............................707 642-2222
Anthony Marquez, *Manager*
EMP: 50
SALES (corp-wide): 571K **Privately Held**
SIC: 1629 Industrial plant construction
HQ: James-Timec International, Inc
2315 W Main St
Baytown TX 77520
281 471-3209

(P-1971)
JILK HEAVY CONSTRUCTION INC
14732 S Maple Ave, Gardena
(90248-1934)
PHONE...............................310 830-6323
John S Meek, *President*
Dan Lewis, *Mktg Dir*

Lisa Paila, *Manager*
EMP: 60
SQ FT: 5,000
SALES (est): 19MM **Privately Held**
WEB: www.johnsmeek.com
SIC: 1629 Marine construction

(P-1972)
K G WALTERS CNSTR CO INC
195 Concourse Blvd Ste A, Santa Rosa
(95403-8217)
P.O. Box 4359 (95402-4359)
PHONE...............................707 527-9968
Walt Johnson, *President*
David A Backman, *Senior VP*
Thomas Crotty, *Vice Pres*
Valerie Carmichael, *Admin Sec*
EMP: 55 **EST:** 1974
SQ FT: 4,000
SALES: 17.2MM **Privately Held**
WEB: www.kgwalters.com
SIC: 1629 Waste water & sewage treatment plant construction

(P-1973)
MARATHON CONSTRUCTION CORP
10108 Riverford Rd, Lakeside
(92040-2740)
PHONE...............................619 276-4401
Michael V Furby, *President*
Charles Cunningham, *Vice Pres*
Robert A Wheelington, *Vice Pres*
R B Zinser, *Vice Pres*
Joe Ellis, *Superintendent*
◆ **EMP:** 60
SQ FT: 2,500
SALES (est): 12.2MM **Privately Held**
SIC: 1629 Marine construction

(P-1974)
MARCH INTERNATIONAL INC
Also Called: Wall Tech
1249 S Dmnd Bar Blvd 20, Diamond Bar
(91765-4122)
PHONE...............................909 821-5128
Frank Tilton, *CFO*
EMP: 50
SALES (est): 1.6MM **Privately Held**
SIC: 1629 Canal construction

(P-1975)
MILCO CONSTRUCTORS INC
3930b Cherry Ave, Long Beach
(90807-3727)
P.O. Box 2150 (90801-2150)
PHONE...............................562 595-1977
Charles Miller, *President*
Duane C Miller, *Corp Secy*
EMP: 50 **EST:** 1973
SQ FT: 17,000
SALES (est): 9.3MM **Privately Held**
WEB: www.milcoconstructors.com
SIC: 1629 Industrial plant construction

(P-1976)
MITCH BROWN CONSTRUCTION INC
14200 Road 284, Porterville (93257-9374)
PHONE...............................559 781-6389
Mitchell F Brown, *President*
Elizabeth Brown, *Treasurer*
EMP: 60
SALES (est): 5MM **Privately Held**
SIC: 1629 Earthmoving contractor

(P-1977)
MONTEREY MECHANICAL CO (PA)
Also Called: Contra Costa Metal Fabricators
8275 San Leandro St, Oakland
(94621-1972)
PHONE...............................510 632-3173
Milton C Burleson, *CEO*
Jim Troup, *President*
Paul Moreira, *CFO*
Vy Nguyen, *Executive*
Karl Hoiser, *Project Mgr*
▲ **EMP:** 50
SQ FT: 40,000

SALES (est): 75MM **Privately Held**
WEB: www.montmech.com
SIC: 1629 1711 1761 3444 Waste disposal plant construction; waste water & sewage treatment plant construction; mechanical contractor; boiler setting contractor; boiler maintenance contractor; sheet metalwork; sheet metalwork; fabricated structural metal; nonresidential construction

(P-1978)
NORDIC INDUSTRIES INC
1437 Furneaux Rd, Olivehurst
(95961-7404)
PHONE...............................530 742-7124
Jens Karlshoej, *President*
John Hicks, *Project Mgr*
Brian Bushnell, *Superintendent*
Poul Karlshoej, *Superintendent*
EMP: 60
SQ FT: 5,000
SALES (est): 18.6MM **Privately Held**
WEB: www.nordicind.com
SIC: 1629 4212 4213 Dam construction; levee construction; local trucking, without storage; trucking, except local

(P-1979)
NORDIC/GREAT LAKES E&I JV
1437 Furneaux Rd, Olivehurst
(95961-7404)
PHONE...............................530 742-7124
Louay Owaidat, *Partner*
Jens Karlshoej, *Partner*
EMP: 99
SQ FT: 30,000
SALES (est): 2.2MM **Privately Held**
SIC: 1629 Dams, waterways, docks & other marine construction; dam construction; levee construction

(P-1980)
NOVA ATL ELC A JOINT VENTR
185 Devlin Rd, NAPA (94558-6255)
PHONE...............................707 265-1100
Scott Victor, *Principal*
Carole Bionda, *Principal*
Dee Fedrick, *Principal*
Ronald Fedrick, *Principal*
Legrand Richardson, *Principal*
EMP: 99
SQ FT: 18,000
SALES (est): 1.9MM **Privately Held**
SIC: 1629 Pier construction

(P-1981)
NOVA BRINK A JOINT VENTURE
185 Devlin Rd, NAPA (94558-6255)
PHONE...............................707 265-1100
Ronld Fedrick, *Partner*
Brent Albrecht, *Partner*
Carole Bionda, *Partner*
Scott Victor, *Partner*
EMP: 99
SQ FT: 18,000
SALES (est): 2.1MM **Privately Held**
SIC: 1629 1623 1622 Dams, waterways, docks & other marine construction; water, sewer & utility lines; tunnel construction

(P-1982)
NOVA LANE CONSTRUCTORS A JV
185 Devlin Rd, NAPA (94558-6255)
PHONE...............................707 265-1100
Ronald Fedrick, *CEO*
Carole Bionda, *Principal*
Walter Birdsall, *Principal*
Chris Mathies, *Principal*
Scott Victor, *Principal*
EMP: 99 **EST:** 2013
SALES (est): 2.4MM **Privately Held**
SIC: 1629 Dams, waterways, docks & other marine construction

(P-1983)
PARSONS CORPORATION
1 Centerpointe Dr Ste 210, La Palma
(90623-2524)
PHONE...............................714 562-5725
EMP: 175
SALES (corp-wide): 3.5B **Publicly Held**
SIC: 1629 Dams, waterways, docks & other marine construction

PA: The Parsons Corporation
5875 Trinity Pkwy Ste 300
Centreville VA 20120
703 988-8500

(P-1984)
PATRICKS CONSTRUCTION CLEAN-UP
7851 14th Ave, Sacramento (95826-4301)
PHONE...............................916 452-5495
Patricio Mercado, *Owner*
EMP: 100
SALES (est): 8.2MM **Privately Held**
SIC: 1629 Land clearing contractor

(P-1985)
POWERPLANT MINT SPCIALISTS INC
2900 Bristol St Ste H202, Costa Mesa
(92626-7917)
PHONE...............................714 427-6900
Jim McEachern, *CEO*
Richard G Engel, *President*
J Alexandra Barretto, *Vice Pres*
Dave Gatti, *Vice Pres*
Michael Medock, *Vice Pres*
EMP: 200
SQ FT: 3,300
SALES (est): 18.5MM **Privately Held**
WEB: www.pmsipower.com
SIC: 1629 Dams, waterways, docks & other marine construction

(P-1986)
RAIN BIRD DISTRIBUTION CORP
1000 W Sierra Madre Ave, Azusa
(91702-1700)
P.O. Box 37 (91702-0037)
PHONE...............................626 963-9311
Anthony Lafetra, *CEO*
Anthony W Lafetra, *CEO*
Nick Kaleyias, *CFO*
Arthur Ludwick, *Corp Secy*
Matt Prucinsky, *Info Tech Mgr*
EMP: 52
SQ FT: 20,000
SALES (est): 2MM **Privately Held**
SIC: 1629 3523 Irrigation system construction; fertilizing, spraying, dusting & irrigation machinery

(P-1987)
RE LA MESA LLC
300 California St Fl 8, San Francisco
(94104-1416)
PHONE...............................415 675-1500
Arno Harris,
Greg Wilson,
EMP: 100
SALES (est): 2.7MM **Privately Held**
SIC: 1629 Land leveling

(P-1988)
SAN DIEGO HBR EXCURSIONS INC
1050 N Harbor Dr, San Diego
(92101-3316)
P.O. Box 120751 (92112-0751)
PHONE...............................619 234-4111
Arthur E Engel, *President*
EMP: 100
SALES: 15MM
SALES (corp-wide): 17.4MM **Privately Held**
SIC: 1629 Harbor construction
PA: Star & Crescent Boat Company
1311 1st St
Coronado CA 92118
619 234-4111

(P-1989)
SCHWAGER DAVIS INC
198 Hillsdale Ave, San Jose (95136-1398)
PHONE...............................408 281-9300
Guido A Schwager, *President*
Robert Parkhurst, *CFO*
Michael Williams, *QA Dir*
Josh McBride, *Project Mgr*
Keith McKenna, *Project Mgr*
▲ **EMP:** 112
SQ FT: 12,000
SALES (est): 41.6MM **Privately Held**
SIC: 1629 1622 Railroad & railway roadbed construction; bridge construction

(P-1990)
SHIMMICK CONSTRUCTION CO INC (HQ)
8201 Edgewater Dr Ste 202, Oakland (94621-2023)
PHONE...................510 777-5000
Paul Cocotis, *Ch of Bd*
Scott Fairgrieve, *CFO*
Christian Fassari, *Exec VP*
Jeffrey Lessman, *Exec VP*
Fernando Deleon, *Area Mgr*
EMP: 151
SQ FT: 30,000
SALES (est): 351.5MM
SALES (corp-wide): 20.1B **Publicly Held**
SIC: 1629 1623 Earthmoving contractor; sewer line construction
PA: Aecom
1999 Avenue Of The Stars # 2600
Los Angeles CA 90067
213 593-8000

(P-1991)
SIGMA INVESTMENT HOLDINGS LLC
2288 Villa Heights Rd, Pasadena (91107-1141)
PHONE...................626 398-3098
Geoffrey G Ren, *Mng Member*
Asong Fu,
Chauan Ren,
Guang Ren,
▼ **EMP:** 50
SQ FT: 3,178
SALES: 50MM **Privately Held**
SIC: 1629 Industrial plant construction

(P-1992)
SKANSKA USA CIVIL WEST ROCKY M (DH)
Also Called: Skanska Rocky Mountain Dst
1995 Agua Mansa Rd, Riverside (92509-2405)
PHONE...................970 565-8000
Curtis Broughton, *Senior VP*
David Sitton, *Vice Pres*
Gary Moss, *Project Mgr*
Dylan Thompson, *Project Mgr*
Sally Smith, *Human Res Mgr*
EMP: 70
SQ FT: 22,500
SALES (est): 11.6MM
SALES (corp-wide): 19B **Privately Held**
SIC: 1629 1611 1711 Dam construction; general contractor, highway & street construction; mechanical contractor
HQ: Skanska Usa Civil Inc.
7520 Astoria Blvd Ste 200
East Elmhurst NY 11370
718 340-0777

(P-1993)
SLATER INC
11045 Rose Ave, Fontana (92337-7051)
P.O. Box 759 (92334-0759)
PHONE...................909 822-6800
Phillip S Slater, *CEO*
Edward Johnson, *CFO*
Steve David, *Vice Pres*
EMP: 97
SQ FT: 6,000
SALES (est): 13.4MM **Privately Held**
WEB: www.slaterinc.com
SIC: 1629 8711 Drainage system construction; engineering services

(P-1994)
SOLTIS GOLF INCORPORATED
869 W 9th St, Upland (91786-4541)
P.O. Box 1309 (91785-1309)
PHONE...................909 822-7000
Christopher Soltis, *President*
EMP: 75
SALES (est): 6.3MM **Privately Held**
WEB: www.soltisgolf.com
SIC: 1629 Golf course construction

(P-1995)
TEAM WEST CONTRACTING CORP
2733 S Vista Ave, Bloomington (92316-3269)
PHONE...................951 340-3426
Jerry R Pacheco, *President*
Steve Knehans, *CFO*

Stephen Knehans, *Treasurer*
Michael Ellefson, *Officer*
Bryan Girard, *Officer*
EMP: 92
SQ FT: 7,200
SALES (est): 7.2MM **Privately Held**
SIC: 1629 1799 Railroad & railway roadbed construction; fence construction

(P-1996)
TEICHERT/GREAT LAKES E&I JV
3500 American River Dr, Sacramento (95864-5802)
P.O. Box 15002 (95851-0002)
PHONE...................916 484-3011
Louay Owaidat, *Partner*
Judson Riggs, *Partner*
EMP: 99
SQ FT: 30,000
SALES (est): 1.9MM **Privately Held**
SIC: 1629 Dams, waterways, docks & other marine construction; dam construction; levee construction

(P-1997)
THOMAS CRANE AND TRCKG CO INC
18851 Stewart Ln, Huntington Beach (92648-1520)
P.O. Box 640 (92648-0640)
PHONE...................562 592-2837
Michael Thomas, *CEO*
John Thomas, *Principal*
Mike Thomas, *Principal*
Linda Thomas, *Admin Sec*
Steve Dutt, *Opers Mgr*
EMP: 50
SQ FT: 800
SALES (est): 8.4MM **Privately Held**
SIC: 1629 4212 Oil refinery construction; light haulage & cartage, local

(P-1998)
TIMEC ACQUISITIONS INC (DH)
155 Corporate Pl, Vallejo (94590-6968)
PHONE...................707 642-2222
Pat McMahon, *President*
Gary Green, *COO*
Dennis Turnipseed, *CFO*
EMP: 850 **EST:** 1998
SQ FT: 25,000
SALES (est): 142.2MM
SALES (corp-wide): 571K **Privately Held**
SIC: 1629 Industrial plant construction; chemical plant & refinery construction

(P-1999)
TIMEC COMPANIES INC (DH)
155 Corporate Pl, Vallejo (94590-6968)
PHONE...................707 642-2222
Denis Turnipseed, *President*
EMP: 350
SQ FT: 80,000
SALES (est): 142.2MM
SALES (corp-wide): 571K **Privately Held**
SIC: 1629 1799 Industrial plant construction; chemical plant & refinery construction; oil refinery construction; welding on site
HQ: Timec Acquisitions Inc
155 Corporate Pl
Vallejo CA 94590
707 642-2222

(P-2000)
TUTOR PERINI/ZACHRY/PARSONS
1401 Fulton St Ste 400, Fresno (93721-1645)
PHONE...................559 385-7025
James Frost, *Partner*
Carol Einfalt, *Partner*
EMP: 99
SQ FT: 15,000
SALES (est): 7.2MM **Privately Held**
SIC: 1629 Railroad & railway roadbed construction

(P-2001)
VISTA STEEL CO INC
331 W Lewis St, Ventura (93001-1394)
PHONE...................805 653-1189
John Swaffar, *Branch Mgr*
EMP: 50

SALES (corp-wide): 7.9MM **Privately Held**
SIC: 1629 3449 Dams, waterways, docks & other marine construction; miscellaneous metalwork
PA: Vista Steel Co Inc
6100 Francis Botello Rd C
Goleta CA 93117
805 964-4732

(P-2002)
WINDROW EARTH TRANSPORT INC
14032 Santa Ana Ave, Fontana (92337-7035)
PHONE...................909 355-5531
Bruce Degler, *President*
Kim Pugmire, *Vice Pres*
EMP: 50
SQ FT: 1,100
SALES: 40MM
SALES (corp-wide): 28MM **Privately Held**
SIC: 1629 Earthmoving contractor
PA: Pro Loaders, Inc.
14032 Santa Ana Ave
Fontana CA 92337
909 355-5531

(P-2003)
WOOD BROS INC
14147 18th Ave, Lemoore (93245-9741)
P.O. Box 216 (93245-0216)
PHONE...................559 924-7715
William S Wood, *CEO*
Donald T Wood, *Corp Secy*
Brianna Hill, *Administration*
Don Wood, *Marketing Staff*
EMP: 100
SQ FT: 30,000
SALES (est): 32MM **Privately Held**
SIC: 1629 Dredging contractor

(P-2004)
WORLEY FIELD SERVICES INC
2600 Michelson Dr Ste 500, Irvine (92612-6506)
P.O. Box 6025, Cypress (90630-0025)
PHONE...................949 224-7585
Brandy Marquez, *Branch Mgr*
EMP: 250 **Privately Held**
WEB: www.jemcidecatur.com
SIC: 1629 Earthmoving contractor
HQ: Worley Field Services, Inc.
5995 Rogerdale Rd
Houston TX 77072
832 351-6000

1711 Plumbing, Heating & Air Conditioning Contractors

(P-2005)
20/20 PLUMBING & HEATING INC (PA)
Also Called: Honeywell Authorized Dealer
7343 Orangewood Dr Ste B, Riverside (92504-1053)
PHONE...................951 396-2020
Thomas Lew Baker, *CEO*
EMP: 62
SALES (est): 35.7MM **Privately Held**
SIC: 1711 Plumbing contractors

(P-2006)
20/20 PLUMBING & HEATING INC
325 Market Pl, Escondido (92029-1302)
PHONE...................760 535-3101
EMP: 138
SALES (corp-wide): 35.7MM **Privately Held**
SIC: 1711 Plumbing contractors
PA: 20/20 Plumbing & Heating, Inc.
7343 Orangewood Dr Ste B
Riverside CA 92504
951 396-2020

(P-2007)
A & A MECHANICAL CONTRACTORS
2943 Daylight Way, San Jose (95111-3194)
PHONE...................408 225-1321
George A Reppas, *President*
Arthur G Reppas, *Ch of Bd*
Michael Reppas, *CFO*
EMP: 85 **EST:** 1955
SQ FT: 32,000
SALES (est): 4.5MM **Privately Held**
SIC: 1711 Warm air heating & air conditioning contractor

(P-2008)
A & D FIRE PROTECTION INC
7130 Convoy Ct, San Diego (92111-1019)
PHONE...................619 258-7697
Andrew R Otero, *President*
Rose Pullaro, *Administration*
Jeff Jukes, *Info Tech Mgr*
Debbie Robinson, *Accounting Mgr*
Sara Hewitt, *Marketing Mgr*
EMP: 80
SQ FT: 10,000
SALES (est): 11.2MM **Privately Held**
WEB: www.adcompaniesinc.com
SIC: 1711 1542 Fire sprinkler system installation; nonresidential construction

(P-2009)
A A A FURNACE AC CO
1712 Stone Ave Ste 1, San Jose (95125-1387)
PHONE...................408 293-4717
Jim Rendo, *President*
EMP: 60
SALES (est): 2MM **Privately Held**
SIC: 1711 Warm air heating & air conditioning contractor

(P-2010)
A C RENTALS LLC
8540 Production Ave Ste A, San Diego (92121-2263)
PHONE...................858 271-8571
EMP: 50
SALES (est): 1.8MM **Privately Held**
SIC: 1711

(P-2011)
A O REED & CO
4777 Ruffner St, San Diego (92111-1578)
P.O. Box 85226 (92186-5226)
PHONE...................858 565-4131
Steve Andrade, *Ch of Bd*
David Clarkin, *President*
Craig Koehler, *CFO*
Robin Callaway, *Exec VP*
Martin Naranjo, *Vice Pres*
EMP: 400
SQ FT: 55,000
SALES (est): 158.5MM **Privately Held**
WEB: www.aoreed.com
SIC: 1711 Plumbing contractors

(P-2012)
AAA DRAIN PATROL
Also Called: Preferred Plumbing and Drain
3437 Myrtle Ave Ste 440, North Highlands (95660-5147)
PHONE...................916 348-3098
Kathleen Graves, *Owner*
EMP: 50
SALES (est): 2.2MM **Privately Held**
SIC: 1711 Plumbing contractors

(P-2013)
ACCO ENGINEERED SYSTEMS INC
1133 Aladdin Ave, San Leandro (94577-4311)
PHONE...................510 346-4300
Ron Krassensky, *Manager*
Ricardo Norm, *Area Spvr*
Don Staben, *Info Tech Mgr*
Stefan Colvey, *Design Engr*
Sean Cua, *Design Engr*
EMP: 200

SALES (corp-wide): 777.3MM **Privately Held**
WEB: www.accoair.com
SIC: **1711** 7623 Process piping contractor; solar energy contractor; ventilation & duct work contractor; warm air heating & air conditioning contractor; air conditioning repair
PA: Acco Engineered Systems, Inc.
888 E Walnut St
Pasadena CA 91101
818 244-6571

(P-2014)
ACCUTHERM REFRIGERATON INC
Also Called: Accutherm Air Heating & Coolg
11264 Monarch St Ste A, Garden Grove (92841-1449)
PHONE..................................714 766-7800
Jeff Recker, *President*
EMP: 53
SQ FT: 6,800
SALES: 6.9MM **Privately Held**
WEB: www.accuthermrefrigeration.com
SIC: **1711** Refrigeration contractor

(P-2015)
ACETLD SOLAR
425 National Ave Ste 199, Mountain View (94043-2219)
PHONE..................................800 241-6030
John Morris, *Principal*
EMP: 120
SQ FT: 150
SALES: 1.2MM **Privately Held**
SIC: **1711** Solar energy contractor

(P-2016)
ACH MECHANICAL CONTRACTORS INC
411 Business Center Ct, Redlands (92373-8084)
PHONE..................................909 307-2850
Hector Vargas, *President*
EMP: 80
SQ FT: 14,450
SALES: 35MM **Privately Held**
SIC: **1711** Mechanical contractor

(P-2017)
ADEE PLUMBING AND HEATING INC (PA)
5457 Crenshaw Blvd, Los Angeles (90043-2496)
P.O. Box 431490 (90043-9490)
PHONE..................................323 296-8787
Jack Stephan Sr, *President*
Jack Stephan Jr, *Vice Pres*
Russell Stephan, *Admin Sec*
EMP: 64
SQ FT: 18,000
SALES (est): 11.3MM **Privately Held**
SIC: **1711** Plumbing contractors; warm air heating & air conditioning contractor

(P-2018)
ADVANTAGE PLUMBING GROUP INC
3331 Orangewood Ave, Los Alamitos (90720-3813)
P.O. Box 733 (90720-0733)
PHONE..................................714 898-6020
EMP: 67
SALES (est): 4.6MM **Privately Held**
SIC: **1711** 5074

(P-2019)
AEGIS ENTERPRISES INC
Also Called: Aegis Fire Systems
500 Boulder Ct Ste A, Pleasanton (94566-8311)
PHONE..................................925 417-5550
Thomas J McKinnon, *President*
Timothy Higgins, *Vice Pres*
Kelly Sleek, *Accounting Mgr*
Kristen Quintana, *Payroll Mgr*
John Moreno, *Purch Mgr*
EMP: 100
SALES (est): 17.6MM **Privately Held**
SIC: **1711** Fire sprinkler system installation

(P-2020)
AG AIR CONDITIONING & HTG INC
Also Called: AG Heating and AC
14620 Keswick St, Van Nuys (91405-1203)
PHONE..................................818 988-5388
Yuval Giron, *CEO*
Yitchak Giron, *President*
EMP: 50
SALES: 3.6MM **Privately Held**
SIC: **1711** Warm air heating & air conditioning contractor

(P-2021)
AIR CONTROL SYSTEMS INC
1940 S Grove Ave, Ontario (91761-5615)
PHONE..................................909 786-4230
Robert Leotaud, *President*
EMP: 50
SQ FT: 17,995
SALES: 15MM **Privately Held**
SIC: **1711** Warm air heating & air conditioning contractor; ventilation & duct work contractor

(P-2022)
AIR MECHANICAL INC
608 S Vicki Ln, Anaheim (92804-3207)
PHONE..................................714 995-3947
Wallace Fox, *Principal*
EMP: 62
SALES (corp-wide): 23.1MM **Privately Held**
SIC: **1711** Warm air heating & air conditioning contractor
PA: Air Mechanical, Inc.
16411 Aberdeen St Ne
Anoka MN 55304
763 434-7747

(P-2023)
AIR SYSTEMS INC
940 Remillard Ct Frnt, San Jose (95122-2684)
PHONE..................................408 280-1666
John W Davis, *President*
William J Wayker, *CFO*
Don Billups, *Vice Pres*
Eric Ensenat, *Vice Pres*
Jon Gundersen, *Vice Pres*
EMP: 750
SALES (est): 337.7K
SALES (corp-wide): 8.1B **Publicly Held**
SIC: **1711** 7623 Mechanical contractor; warm air heating & air conditioning contractor; ventilation & duct work contractor; plumbing contractors; refrigeration service & repair
PA: Emcor Group, Inc.
301 Merritt 7 Fl 6
Norwalk CT 06851
203 849-7800

(P-2024)
AIR SYSTEMS SERVICE & CNSTR
10381 Old Placerville Rd # 100, Sacramento (95827-2558)
PHONE..................................916 368-0336
Garry Westover, *CEO*
Jim Meurer, *Vice Pres*
Carlos Quinones, *Sr Project Mgr*
EMP: 130
SQ FT: 10,000
SALES: 39.1MM **Privately Held**
WEB: www.airsystems1.com
SIC: **1711** 7623 Mechanical contractor; warm air heating & air conditioning contractor; ventilation & duct work contractor; plumbing contractors; refrigeration service & repair

(P-2025)
AIRCO MECHANICAL INC (PA)
Also Called: AMI Manufacturing
8210 Demetre Ave, Sacramento (95828-0919)
PHONE..................................916 381-4523
Wyatt Jones, *CEO*
Joann Hillendrand, *CFO*
Frank Provost, *Sales Executive*
EMP: 122
SQ FT: 105,000

SALES: 40MM **Privately Held**
WEB: www.aircomech.com
SIC: **1711** 8711 Mechanical contractor; engineering services

(P-2026)
AIRCO MECHANICAL INC
401 13th St, San Francisco (94130-2003)
PHONE..................................415 982-4726
EMP: 128
SALES (corp-wide): 40MM **Privately Held**
SIC: **1711** Mechanical contractor
PA: Airco Mechanical, Inc.
8210 Demetre Ave
Sacramento CA 95828
916 381-4523

(P-2027)
AIRE-RITE AC & RFRGN INC
15122 Bolsa Chica St, Huntington Beach (92649-1025)
P.O. Box 3419 (92605-3419)
PHONE..................................714 895-2338
Donald Langston, *Principal*
Carol Langston, *Corp Secy*
David Langston, *Vice Pres*
Thaer Mustafa, *Technician*
Aaron Jonas, *Supervisor*
EMP: 97
SQ FT: 22,000
SALES: 16.6MM **Privately Held**
WEB: www.airerite.com
SIC: **1711** Warm air heating & air conditioning contractor

(P-2028)
ALDOC INC
910 E Orangefair Ln, Anaheim (92801-1103)
PHONE..................................714 836-8477
P S Meckley, *President*
Philip Shurman Meckley, *President*
EMP: 60
SALES (est): 5.2MM **Privately Held**
SIC: **1711** Plumbing contractors

(P-2029)
ALISO MECHANICAL INCORPORATED
29736 A De Las Bandera, Rancho Santa Margari (92688)
PHONE..................................949 544-1601
Christopher H Loftus, *CEO*
Jeffrey T Loftus, *President*
Debbie Covarrubias, *Administration*
EMP: 150
SQ FT: 8,000
SALES (est): 9.7MM **Privately Held**
WEB: www.alisoair.com
SIC: **1711** Warm air heating & air conditioning contractor

(P-2030)
ALL AREA PLUMBING INC
5742 Venice Blvd, Los Angeles (90019-5016)
PHONE..................................323 939-9990
Robert Felix, *President*
Beni Monaco, *CFO*
EMP: 235
SQ FT: 3,000
SALES: 1.1MM **Privately Held**
WEB: www.allareaco.com
SIC: **1711** Plumbing, heating, air-conditioning contractors

(P-2031)
ALL TMPERATURES CONTROLLED INC
Also Called: Honeywell Authorized Dealer
9720 Topanga Canyon Pl, Chatsworth (91311-4134)
PHONE..................................818 882-1478
George Mego, *President*
Kathy Gomes, *Executive*
Brent Brubaker, *Project Mgr*
Cheryl Piper, *Technology*
Nancy Miller, *Financial Exec*
EMP: 72 EST: 1978
SQ FT: 13,481
SALES (est): 13.7MM **Privately Held**
SIC: **1711** Warm air heating & air conditioning contractor; heating & air conditioning contractors

(P-2032)
ALLAN AUTOMATIC SPRINKLER CORP
3233 Enterprise St, Brea (92821-6239)
PHONE..................................714 993-9500
Jim Charrette, *Vice Pres*
EMP: 80
SQ FT: 40,000
SALES (est): 9.2MM
SALES (corp-wide): 8.1B **Publicly Held**
WEB: www.allansocal.com
SIC: **1711** 5084 Fire sprinkler system installation; industrial machinery & equipment
HQ: Shambaugh & Son, L.P.
7614 Opportunity Dr
Fort Wayne IN 46825
260 487-7777

(P-2033)
ALLIED FIRE PROTECTION
555 High St, Oakland (94601-3989)
PHONE..................................510 533-5516
Ted Vinther, *President*
Dwayne Atkinson, *Design Engr*
EMP: 150
SQ FT: 29,000
SALES (est): 28.9MM **Privately Held**
WEB: www.alliedfire.com
SIC: **1711** Fire sprinkler system installation

(P-2034)
ALPHA MECHANICAL INC
4990 Greencraig Ln Ste A, San Diego (92123-1673)
PHONE..................................858 278-3500
Boris Barshak, *Branch Mgr*
Cort Clifford, *Business Mgr*
EMP: 88 **Privately Held**
SIC: **1711** Fire sprinkler system installation
PA: Alpha Mechanical, Inc.
4885 Greencraig Ln
San Diego CA 92123

(P-2035)
ALPHA MECHANICAL INC (PA)
4885 Greencraig Ln, San Diego (92123-1664)
PHONE..................................858 278-3500
Boris Barshak, *Principal*
Stacy Camacho, *Project Engr*
David Luhm, *Sr Project Mgr*
Cameron Dickinson, *Manager*
Leonard Hayward, *Manager*
EMP: 97
SQ FT: 8,000
SALES (est): 42.6MM **Privately Held**
SIC: **1711** Fire sprinkler system installation

(P-2036)
ALTERNATIVE ENERGY SYSTEMS INC
Also Called: AES
13620 State Highway 99 N, Chico (95973-9481)
P.O. Box 9231 (95927-9231)
PHONE..................................530 345-6980
Lance McClung, *President*
Jason Grant, *Business Dir*
Tim Hamor, *Principal*
Debbie Nixon, *Office Admin*
Jenny Zimmerman, *Marketing Staff*
EMP: 70
SALES (est): 11.9MM **Privately Held**
SIC: **1711** Solar energy contractor

(P-2037)
AMERICAN AC DISTRS LLC
Also Called: Florida Conditioning
16900 Chestnut St, City of Industry (91748-1012)
PHONE..................................407 850-0147
John Staples,
Kevin Lentz, *General Mgr*
John Scarsi,
Lori Thomas, *Mng Member*
▲ EMP: 92
SALES (est): 4.7MM **Privately Held**
SIC: **1711** Heating & air conditioning contractors

(P-2038)
AMERICAN CONTRACTORS INC
404 W Blueridge Ave, Orange
(92865-4204)
PHONE..................714 282-5700
Gilbert L Wiggam, *CEO*
Christopher Wiggam, *Vice Pres*
EMP: 65 **EST:** 1974
SQ FT: 11,000
SALES: 18.3MM **Privately Held**
SIC: 1711 1623 Plumbing contractors; sewer line construction

(P-2039)
AMERICAN INCORPORATED
Also Called: American Air
1345 N American St, Visalia (93291-9334)
PHONE..................559 651-1776
Corwyn Oldfield, *CEO*
Frank Saucedo, *CFO*
Lois Oldfield, *Vice Pres*
Deanna Menezes, *Executive*
Nate Strable, *General Mgr*
EMP: 425
SQ FT: 115,000
SALES: 75MM **Privately Held**
SIC: 1711 1542 1541 1731 Warm air heating & air conditioning contractor; refrigeration contractor; plumbing contractors; commercial & office building contractors; industrial buildings & warehouses; electrical work

(P-2040)
AMERICAN LEAK DETECTION INC
910 E Orangefair Ln, Anaheim
(92801-1103)
PHONE..................714 836-8477
Steve Lee, *Manager*
EMP: 50
SALES (corp-wide): 21.7MM **Privately Held**
SIC: 1711 Plumbing contractors
PA: American Leak Detection, Inc.
888 E Research Dr Ste 100
Palm Springs CA 92262
203 433-2510

(P-2041)
AMERICAN RESIDENTIAL SVCS LLC
9895 Olson Dr Ste A, San Diego
(92121-2841)
PHONE..................858 457-5547
Bonnie Bakken, *General Mgr*
EMP: 80
SALES (corp-wide): 2.3B **Privately Held**
WEB: www.ars.com
SIC: 1711 Plumbing contractors
PA: American Residential Services Llc
965 Ridge Lake Blvd # 201
Memphis TN 38120
901 271-9700

(P-2042)
AMERICAN RESIDENTIAL SVCS LLC
15707 S Main St, Gardena (90248-2506)
PHONE..................310 808-0279
Daniel Dunduenabad, *Manager*
EMP: 50
SALES (corp-wide): 2.3B **Privately Held**
WEB: www.ars.com
SIC: 1711 Plumbing contractors
PA: American Residential Services Llc
965 Ridge Lake Blvd # 201
Memphis TN 38120
901 271-9700

(P-2043)
AMERICAN RESIDENTIAL SVCS LLC
P.O. Box 1592 (92022-1592)
PHONE..................858 292-4452
Ray Olsen, *Branch Mgr*
EMP: 59
SALES (corp-wide): 2.3B **Privately Held**
SIC: 1711 Plumbing contractors
PA: American Residential Services Llc
965 Ridge Lake Blvd # 201
Memphis TN 38120
901 271-9700

(P-2044)
AMERICAN RESIDENTIAL SVCS LLC
Also Called: Atlas Heating
1965 Kyle Park Ct, San Jose (95125-1029)
P.O. Box 610490 (95161-0490)
PHONE..................650 856-1612
EMP: 60
SALES (corp-wide): 2.3B **Privately Held**
SIC: 1711 Plumbing contractors
PA: American Residential Services Llc
965 Ridge Lake Blvd # 201
Memphis TN 38120
901 271-9700

(P-2045)
AMERICAN RESIDENTIAL SVCS LLC
Also Called: Rescue Rotter
1520 W Linden St, Riverside (92507-6808)
PHONE..................951 341-9371
Dave Slott, *COO*
EMP: 55
SALES (corp-wide): 2.3B **Privately Held**
WEB: www.ars.com
SIC: 1711 Plumbing contractors
PA: American Residential Services Llc
965 Ridge Lake Blvd # 201
Memphis TN 38120
901 271-9700

(P-2046)
AMERICAN RESIDENTIAL SVCS LLC
Also Called: Rescue Rooter Bay Area North
1618 Doolittle Dr, San Leandro
(94577-2230)
PHONE..................510 729-6227
Larry Dehart, *General Mgr*
EMP: 59
SALES (corp-wide): 2.3B **Privately Held**
WEB: www.ars.com
SIC: 1711 Plumbing contractors
PA: American Residential Services Llc
965 Ridge Lake Blvd # 201
Memphis TN 38120
901 271-9700

(P-2047)
AMERICAN RESIDENTIAL SVCS LLC
Also Called: Rescue Rooter
29196 Simms Ct, Hayward (94544-6911)
P.O. Box 3098 (94540-3098)
PHONE..................510 657-7601
Chris Peterson, *Manager*
EMP: 70
SALES (corp-wide): 2.3B **Privately Held**
WEB: www.ars.com
SIC: 1711 Plumbing contractors
PA: American Residential Services Llc
965 Ridge Lake Blvd # 201
Memphis TN 38120
901 271-9700

(P-2048)
AMERICAN RESIDENTIAL SVCS LLC
Also Called: Rescue Rooter
740 N Hariton St, Orange (92868-1314)
PHONE..................714 634-1826
Dave Krol, *Manager*
EMP: 100
SALES (corp-wide): 2.3B **Privately Held**
WEB: www.ars.com
SIC: 1711 Plumbing contractors
PA: American Residential Services Llc
965 Ridge Lake Blvd # 201
Memphis TN 38120
901 271-9700

(P-2049)
AMERICAN RESIDENTIAL SVCS LLC
Also Called: Rescue Rooter
12507 San Fernando Rd, Sylmar
(91342-5023)
PHONE..................818 833-6677
Darl Coopper, *General Mgr*
EMP: 60
SALES (corp-wide): 2.3B **Privately Held**
WEB: www.ars.com
SIC: 1711 Warm air heating & air conditioning contractor

PA: American Residential Services Llc
965 Ridge Lake Blvd # 201
Memphis TN 38120
901 271-9700

(P-2050)
AMGREEN SOLAR & ELECTRIC INC
1367 Venice Blvd, Los Angeles
(90006-5519)
PHONE..................213 388-5647
Minseon Ko, *CEO*
Eunice Ko, *Principal*
▲ **EMP:** 50
SALES (est): 2.7MM **Privately Held**
SIC: 1711 1731 Solar energy contractor; lighting contractor

(P-2051)
AMPAM PARKS MECHANICAL INC
17036 Avalon Blvd, Carson (90746-1206)
PHONE..................310 835-1532
Charles E Parks III, *CEO*
James C Wright, *CFO*
John D Parks, *Vice Pres*
Drew Defalle, *VP Bus Dvlpt*
Jeff Addington, *Project Mgr*
▲ **EMP:** 800
SQ FT: 16,000
SALES (est): 158.5MM **Privately Held**
WEB: www.parksmechanical.com
SIC: 1711 Plumbing contractors

(P-2052)
AMS AMERICAN MECH SVCS MD INC
2116 E Walnut Ave, Fullerton (92831-4845)
PHONE..................714 888-6820
Charles S Knight, *General Mgr*
Mitch Haynam, *General Mgr*
EMP: 54
SALES (corp-wide): 2.3B **Privately Held**
SIC: 1711 Mechanical contractor
HQ: Ams American Mechanical Services Of Maryland, Inc.
13300 Mid Atlantic Blvd
Laurel MD 20708
301 206-5070

(P-2053)
ANDERSON ROWE & BUCKLEY INC
2833 3rd St, San Francisco (94107-3532)
PHONE..................415 282-1625
Robert E Buckley III, *President*
Rosy Zucchiatti, *Corp Secy*
Richard I Buckley Jr, *Vice Pres*
Hratch Krikorian, *Technology*
Rod Blackmon, *Foreman/Supr*
EMP: 170
SQ FT: 40,000
SALES (est): 55MM **Privately Held**
SIC: 1711 Mechanical contractor

(P-2054)
ANDERSON AIR CONDITIONING LP
2100 E Walnut Ave, Fullerton (92831-4845)
PHONE..................714 998-6850
Edward Dunn, *General Ptnr*
Mitchell J Haynam, *Partner*
EMP: 60
SALES (est): 10.3MM **Privately Held**
SIC: 1711 Warm air heating & air conditioning contractor; heating & air conditioning contractors
PA: American Mechanical Services Of Maryland, L.L.C.
13300 Mid Atlantic Blvd
Laurel MD 20708

(P-2055)
APEX MECHANICAL SYSTEMS INC
7440 Trade St Ste A, San Diego
(92121-3412)
PHONE..................858 536-8700
Randall E Melhouse, *CEO*
Edward Draper, *Shareholder*
Blaine Stratton, *Shareholder*
David R Draper, *CFO*
Kathy Draper, *Admin Sec*
EMP: 79

(P-2056)
APPRENTICE & JOURNEYMEN TRAINI
7850 Haskell Ave, Van Nuys (91406-1907)
PHONE..................818 464-4579
Leroy Riffel, *Director*
EMP: 99
SALES: 950K **Privately Held**
SIC: 1711 Plumbing contractors

(P-2057)
AQUALINE PIPING INC
Also Called: Residential Plumbing
2108 Bering Dr Ste C, San Jose
(95131-2029)
PHONE..................408 745-7100
Joshua B Moores, *CEO*
Chrystal L Steele, *Vice Pres*
EMP: 75
SALES (est): 14.4MM **Privately Held**
SIC: 1711 7389 Plumbing contractors;

(P-2058)
ARISE CONSTRUCTION INC
Also Called: Arise Solar
5390 E Pine Ave, Fresno (93727-2113)
P.O. Box 8456 (93747-8456)
PHONE..................559 449-8989
Paul Rutkowski, *CEO*
Glenn Siemens, *CEO*
Michael Perez, *Opers Staff*
EMP: 52
SALES (est): 6MM **Privately Held**
SIC: 1711 Solar energy contractor

(P-2059)
ARRAYCON LLC (PA)
1143 Blumenfeld Dr # 200, Sacramento
(95815-3921)
PHONE..................916 925-0201
Rick Lavezzo, *Mng Member*
Donald Miller, *CFO*
Jeff Calabro, *Exec VP*
Mathew Ricci, *Exec VP*
Dan Hubiak, *Principal*
EMP: 50 **EST:** 2010
SQ FT: 50,000
SALES: 31.1MM **Privately Held**
SIC: 1711 8748 Solar energy contractor; business consulting

(P-2060)
ARTIC MECHANICAL INC (PA)
10440 Trademark St, Rancho Cucamonga
(91730-5826)
PHONE..................909 980-2539
Daniel Hallisey, *President*
John Hadley, *CFO*
Ray Freeman, *Technician*
Devin Smith, *Technician*
Ashley Smith, *Accounting Mgr*
EMP: 80
SQ FT: 15,500
SALES (est): 27.3MM **Privately Held**
WEB: www.arcticmechanical.com
SIC: 1711 Warm air heating & air conditioning contractor; refrigeration contractor

(P-2061)
ASI HASTINGS INC
Also Called: Asi Heating, Air and Solar
4870 Vewridge Ave Ste 200, San Diego
(92123)
PHONE..................619 590-9300
Philip Justo, *President*
Kenneth Justo, *Vice Pres*
Phil Justo, *Administration*
EMP: 120
SQ FT: 2,000
SALES: 23MM **Privately Held**
WEB: www.asihastings.com
SIC: 1711 Heating systems repair & maintenance; solar energy contractor

(P-2062)
ASSOCIATE MECHANICAL CONTRS
622 S Vinewood St, Escondido
(92029-1925)
PHONE..................760 294-3517
Richard Reinholz, *President*
Laura Reinholz, *Admin Sec*
Christina Payne, *Accounting Mgr*

PA: American Residential Services Llc
965 Ridge Lake Blvd # 201
Memphis TN 38120
901 271-9700

SALES (est): 16.5MM **Privately Held**
SIC: 1711 Mechanical contractor

Scott Swearingen, *Opers Staff*
Alex Ryan, *Superintendent*
EMP: 70
SALES: 30MM **Privately Held**
SIC: 1711 Mechanical contractor

(P-2063)
AYOOB & PEERY PLUMBING CO INC
975 Indiana St, San Francisco (94107-3007)
PHONE................................415 550-0975
Peter Vincent McHugh, *CEO*
Mylene Pabilona, *Admin Asst*
Elliott McHugh, *Manager*
EMP: 80
SQ FT: 20,000
SALES (est): 17.1MM **Privately Held**
WEB: www.ayoobpeery.com
SIC: 1711 Mechanical contractor

(P-2064)
B Z PLUMBING COMPANY INC
1901 Aviation Blvd, Lincoln (95648-9557)
PHONE................................916 645-1600
William J Zmrzel, *President*
Diane Zmrzel, *Corp Secy*
Ingrid Zmrzel, *Vice Pres*
Sara Ladeas, *General Mgr*
Chuck Robertson, *Controller*
EMP: 120
SQ FT: 12,000
SALES (est): 7.5MM **Privately Held**
WEB: www.bzplumbing.com
SIC: 1711 Plumbing contractors

(P-2065)
BAKERSFIELD KITCHEN & BATH
3529 Pegasus Dr, Bakersfield (93308-6856)
PHONE................................661 836-2284
Don Chminowski, *President*
EMP: 80
SALES (est): 3MM **Privately Held**
SIC: 1711 Plumbing contractors

(P-2066)
BARR ENGINEERING INC
12612 Clark St, Santa Fe Springs (90670-3950)
PHONE................................562 944-1722
Peter Buongiorno, *President*
Ken Rogers, *COO*
Pamela Price-Recchia, *Corp Secy*
Mike Buongiorno, *Vice Pres*
Frank Pengal, *Vice Pres*
EMP: 82 **EST:** 1958
SQ FT: 12,200
SALES (est): 14.7MM **Privately Held**
WEB: www.barrengineering.com
SIC: 1711 Warm air heating & air conditioning contractor

(P-2067)
BAY CITY MECHANICAL INC
4124 Lakeside Dr, Richmond (94806-1941)
PHONE................................510 233-7000
Helge Theiss-Nyland, *President*
Chris Cochrane, *Corp Secy*
Jason Yano, *Project Mgr*
Dan Denofrio, *Foreman/Supr*
EMP: 150
SQ FT: 6,000
SALES (est): 40.6MM **Privately Held**
WEB: www.baycitymech.com
SIC: 1711 Mechanical contractor

(P-2068)
BAYVIEW ENGRG & CNSTR CO INC
5040 Rbert J Mathews Pkwy, El Dorado Hills (95762-5702)
PHONE................................916 939-8986
Robert Ellery, *CEO*
Pete Ellery, *Vice Pres*
Bart Wood, *Vice Pres*
EMP: 80
SQ FT: 6,000
SALES (est): 9MM **Privately Held**
SIC: 1711 8711 Boiler setting contractor; engineering services

(P-2069)
BCM CUSTOMER SERVICE
12155 Kirkham Rd, Poway (92064-6870)
PHONE................................858 679-5757

Brian R Cox, *CEO*
Levi Moses, *Purchasing*
EMP: 90 **EST:** 1996
SQ FT: 30,000
SALES (est): 3MM **Privately Held**
SIC: 1711 1796 Plumbing, heating, air-conditioning contractors; installing building equipment

(P-2070)
BDS PLUMBING INC
2125 Youngs Ct, Walnut Creek (94596-6319)
PHONE................................925 939-1004
Brett M Stom, *President*
Dawn L Stom, *Treasurer*
EMP: 100
SQ FT: 400
SALES (est): 11.4MM **Privately Held**
SIC: 1711 Plumbing contractors

(P-2071)
BELL PRODUCTS INC
722 Soscol Ave, NAPA (94559-3014)
P.O. Box 396 (94559-0396)
PHONE................................707 255-1811
Paul D Irwin, *President*
Stan Foltz, *Corp Secy*
Josh Gayski, *Project Mgr*
Eric Martin, *Project Mgr*
Mitch Vavricka, *Project Mgr*
EMP: 74
SQ FT: 24,400
SALES (est): 21.3MM **Privately Held**
WEB: www.bellproducts.com
SIC: 1711 Ventilation & duct work contractor; warm air heating & air conditioning contractor; mechanical contractor

(P-2072)
BENICIA PLUMBING INC
265 W Channel Rd, Benicia (94510-1146)
P.O. Box 1095 (94510-4095)
PHONE................................707 745-2930
William J Cawley Jr, *CEO*
Doug Kuznik, *President*
Karen Ramey, *Corp Secy*
William J Cawley III, *Vice Pres*
EMP: 55
SQ FT: 10,000
SALES (est): 13MM **Privately Held**
WEB: www.beniciaplumbing.com
SIC: 1711 Plumbing contractors

(P-2073)
BERNEL INC
Also Called: Vfs Fire Protection Services
501 W Southern Ave, Orange (92865-3217)
PHONE................................714 778-6070
Randy Roland Nelson, *CEO*
Kevin Berthoud, *Vice Pres*
Mario Lopez, *Vice Pres*
EMP: 105
SQ FT: 7,800
SALES (est): 21.4MM **Privately Held**
SIC: 1711 7382 Fire sprinkler system installation; security systems services; fire alarm maintenance & monitoring

(P-2074)
BFP FIRE PROTECTION INC
17 Janis Way, Scotts Valley (95066-3537)
PHONE................................831 461-1100
Chris Amos, *President*
EMP: 60
SQ FT: 6,400
SALES (est): 12.8MM **Privately Held**
SIC: 1711 8711 Fire sprinkler system installation; engineering services

(P-2075)
BILL HOWE PLUMBING INC
Also Called: Am-PM Sewer & Drain Cleaning
9085 Aero Dr Ste B, San Diego (92123-2378)
PHONE................................800 245-5469
William Howe, *President*
Tina Howe, *Vice Pres*
Jason Bolas, *Technician*
Sarah Bolas, *Technician*
Dana Parks, *Technician*
EMP: 85
SQ FT: 21,000

SALES (est): 24.5MM **Privately Held**
WEB: www.billhowe.com
SIC: 1711 Plumbing contractors; septic system construction

(P-2076)
BLOCKA CONSTRUCTION INC
4455 Enterprise St, Fremont (94538-6306)
PHONE................................510 657-3686
Bob Blocka, *President*
Jean Blocka, *CFO*
Mike Doerger, *Admin Dir*
Chad Blocka, *Project Mgr*
Danny Dang, *Project Mgr*
EMP: 70
SQ FT: 7,300
SALES: 39.3MM **Privately Held**
WEB: www.blockainc.com
SIC: 1711 1731 Mechanical contractor; general electrical contractor

(P-2077)
BLUE MOUNTAIN CNSTR SVCS INC
Also Called: Blue Mountain Air
707 Aldridge Rd Ste B, Vacaville (95688-9561)
PHONE................................800 889-2085
Gregory S Owen, *President*
Doug Morse, *Vice Pres*
Michael Spier, *Vice Pres*
Jeff Farnsworth, *Project Mgr*
Miguel Martinez, *Project Mgr*
▲ **EMP:** 200
SQ FT: 37,000
SALES (est): 90.3MM **Privately Held**
WEB: www.bluemountainair.net
SIC: 1711 Heating & air conditioning contractors

(P-2078)
BONANZA PLUMBING INC (PA)
2259 Hamner Ave, Norco (92860-2608)
PHONE................................951 360-8262
James Dean Potts, *President*
EMP: 80
SALES (est): 10.1MM **Privately Held**
SIC: 1711 Plumbing contractors

(P-2079)
BONESO BROTHERS CNSTR INC
2758 Concrete Ct, Paso Robles (93446-5936)
PHONE................................805 227-4450
Steve Boneso, *President*
Rob Boneso, *Vice Pres*
Amber Harms, *Info Tech Mgr*
EMP: 80
SQ FT: 4,000
SALES: 40MM **Privately Held**
SIC: 1711 1542 Mechanical contractor; nonresidential construction

(P-2080)
BRIGHTVIEW LANDSCAPE DEV INC
13691 Vaughn St, San Fernando (91340-3072)
PHONE................................818 838-4700
Greg Motschenbacher, *Branch Mgr*
EMP: 60
SALES (corp-wide): 2.3B **Publicly Held**
SIC: 1711 0781 Irrigation sprinkler system installation; landscape services
HQ: Brightview Landscape Development, Inc.
24151 Ventura Blvd
Calabasas CA 91302
818 223-8500

(P-2081)
BRIGHTVIEW LANDSCAPE DEV INC
11555 Cley Rver Cir Ste A, Fountain Valley (92708)
PHONE................................714 546-7975
Gins Garmann, *Manager*
Greg Barker, *VP Opers*
Jeff Mutch, *Sales Staff*
Jeff Waltz, *Manager*
EMP: 450

SALES (corp-wide): 2.3B **Publicly Held**
SIC: 1711 0781 Irrigation sprinkler system installation; heating & air conditioning contractors; landscape services
HQ: Brightview Landscape Development, Inc.
24151 Ventura Blvd
Calabasas CA 91302
818 223-8500

(P-2082)
BROADSTREET SOLAR INC
Also Called: Broadstreet Power
16112 Hart St, Van Nuys (91406-3903)
PHONE................................818 206-1464
Ahmad M Yakub, *CEO*
EMP: 50
SQ FT: 2,400
SALES: 6.9MM **Privately Held**
SIC: 1711 Solar energy contractor

(P-2083)
BROADWAY MECH - CONTRS INC
873 81st Ave, Oakland (94621-2509)
PHONE................................510 746-4000
Fred Nurisso, *President*
Jill Demar, *Executive Asst*
Frank Yankey, *Info Tech Dir*
Jacky Tran, *Accountant*
Brett Shiraishi, *Purch Agent*
EMP: 150
SALES (est): 33.7MM **Privately Held**
WEB: www.broadwaymechanical.com
SIC: 1711 Mechanical contractor

(P-2084)
C & L REFRIGERATION CORP
Also Called: HONEYWELL AUTHORIZED DEALER
4111 N Palm St, Fullerton (92835-1025)
P.O. Box 2319, Brea (92822-2319)
PHONE................................800 901-4822
Ronald J Cassell Jr, *CEO*
Larry Jaslove, *Vice Pres*
Joe Knotts, *Info Tech Mgr*
Daniel Alvidrez, *Technician*
Cory Gillman, *Technology*
EMP: 150 **EST:** 1978
SQ FT: 18,000
SALES: 48MM **Privately Held**
SIC: 1711 Refrigeration contractor; warm air heating & air conditioning contractor

(P-2085)
CALIFORNIA COMFORT SYSTEMS USA
7740 Kenamar Ct, San Diego (92121-2425)
PHONE................................858 564-1100
Kenneth Hoving, *CEO*
Roger Well, *President*
William George, *Vice Pres*
Trent McKenna, *Vice Pres*
Bo Macaraeg, *General Mgr*
EMP: 399
SALES (est): 18.9MM
SALES (corp-wide): 2.1B **Publicly Held**
SIC: 1711 Warm air heating & air conditioning contractor; heating & air conditioning contractors
PA: Comfort Systems Usa, Inc.
675 Bering Dr Ste 400
Houston TX 77057
713 830-9600

(P-2086)
CALIFORNIA COML SOLAR INC
Also Called: Calcom Energy
9479 N Fort Washington Rd # 105, Fresno (93730-5939)
PHONE................................559 667-9200
Dylan Dupre, *CEO*
Rob Burkholder, *CFO*
John Doyle, *Managing Dir*
Alison Baird, *Admin Sec*
Anamaree Martinez, *Administration*
EMP: 56 **EST:** 2012
SALES (est): 16.4MM **Privately Held**
SIC: 1711 Solar energy contractor

▲ = Import ▼=Export
◆ =Import/Export

(P-2087)
CALIFORNIA UNITED MECH INC (PA)
2185 Oakland Rd, San Jose (95131-1574)
PHONE..................408 232-9000
Tom Sosine, *CEO*
Jon Gundersen, *President*
Blaine Flickner, *Vice Pres*
Neal Fox, *Vice Pres*
Marian Medrano, *Administration*
EMP: 350
SQ FT: 40,000
SALES (est): 158.5MM **Privately Held**
WEB: www.umi1.com
SIC: 1711 Mechanical contractor

(P-2088)
CAN-AM PLUMBING INC
151 Wyoming St, Pleasanton (94566-6277)
PHONE..................925 846-1833
Ronald Capilla, *President*
Karl Kyriss, *CFO*
Martin Ogara, *CFO*
Michael Capilla, *Vice Pres*
Rebecca Jose, *Supervisor*
EMP: 250
SQ FT: 16,000
SALES (est): 17.6MM **Privately Held**
WEB: www.canamplumbing.com
SIC: 1711 Plumbing contractors

(P-2089)
CARRIER CORPORATION
600 Mccormick St Ste B, San Leandro (94577-1128)
PHONE..................510 347-2000
Craig Sweeney, *General Mgr*
Chris Burns, *Sales Staff*
EMP: 280
SALES (corp-wide): 66.5B **Publicly Held**
SIC: 1711 Heating & air conditioning contractors
HQ: Carrier Corporation
13995 Pasteur Blvd
Palm Beach Gardens FL 33418
800 379-6484

(P-2090)
CASPIAN COMMERCIAL PLBG INC
711 Ivy St, Glendale (91204-1003)
PHONE..................818 649-2500
Anahit Alexandrian, *President*
Unice Liu,
EMP: 65
SALES (est): 7.2MM **Privately Held**
SIC: 1711 Plumbing contractors

(P-2091)
CERTIFIED AIR CONDITIONING INC
12520 High Bluff Dr # 312, San Diego (92130-2063)
PHONE..................858 292-5740
Brian Lynch, *President*
Terry Erickson, *Vice Pres*
▲ **EMP:** 150 **EST:** 1964
SALES (est): 13.6MM **Privately Held**
WEB: www.certifiedair.net
SIC: 1711 Warm air heating & air conditioning contractor

(P-2092)
CFP DESIGNS INC
Also Called: Dlb Fire Protection
3121 N Sillect Ave # 300, Bakersfield (93308-6364)
PHONE..................661 903-8940
EMP: 51
SALES (est): 3.6MM **Privately Held**
SIC: 1711 Fire sprinkler system installation

(P-2093)
CFP FIRE PROTECTION INC
153 Technology Dr Ste 200, Irvine (92618-2461)
PHONE..................949 727-3277
Matt Krofcheck, *President*
Josh Hobgood, *Corp Secy*
Richard Hellewell, *Controller*
EMP: 100
SQ FT: 21,960
SALES (est): 5.3MM **Privately Held**
SIC: 1711 Fire sprinkler system installation

PA: Mx Holdings Us, Inc.
153 Technology Dr Ste 200
Irvine CA 92618

(P-2094)
CINTAS CORPORATION
Also Called: Cintas Fire
4320 E Miraloma Ave, Anaheim (92807-1886)
P.O. Box 636525, Cincinnati OH (45263-6525)
PHONE..................714 646-2550
Winter Barry, *General Mgr*
Jason Dupuis, *General Mgr*
EMP: 80
SALES (corp-wide): 6.8B **Publicly Held**
SIC: 1711 7389 8711 Fire sprinkler system installation; fire protection service other than forestry or public; fire protection engineering
PA: Cintas Corporation
6800 Cintas Blvd
Cincinnati OH 45262
513 459-1200

(P-2095)
CIRCULATING AIR INC (PA)
Also Called: Honeywell Authorized Dealer
7337 Varna Ave, North Hollywood (91605-4009)
PHONE..................818 764-0530
Joseph Gallagher, *CEO*
Susan Gallagher, *President*
Marcy Ahlstrom, *CFO*
Tom Kuper, *Info Tech Dir*
David Sandvig, *Technical Mgr*
EMP: 100
SQ FT: 13,000
SALES (est): 39MM **Privately Held**
WEB: www.circulatingair.com
SIC: 1711 Mechanical contractor; warm air heating & air conditioning contractor

(P-2096)
CITYWIDE PLUMBING HEATING
9825 Carroll Centre Rd, San Diego (92126-6508)
PHONE..................619 231-2022
John Taylor, *Principal*
EMP: 50
SALES (est): 5.6MM **Privately Held**
SIC: 1711 Plumbing, heating, air-conditioning contractors

(P-2097)
CLAY DUNN ENTERPRISES INC
Also Called: Air-TEC
1606 E Carson St, Carson (90745-2504)
P.O. Box 5444 (90749-5444)
PHONE..................310 549-1698
Clayton N Dunn, *President*
Kurt Kredel, *Project Mgr*
Osvaldo Orozco, *Project Mgr*
Jorge Viveros, *Project Engr*
Mike Conkey, *Controller*
EMP: 120
SALES (est): 32.4MM **Privately Held**
WEB: www.airtecperforms.com
SIC: 1711 Warm air heating & air conditioning contractor

(P-2098)
CMA FIRE PROTECTION (PA)
Also Called: Rlh Fire Protection
4300 Stine Rd Ste 800, Bakersfield (93313-2354)
P.O. Box 42470 (93384-2470)
PHONE..................661 322-9344
Terrence J Olson, *CEO*
Gary Stites, *Partner*
Michael Hardcastle, *Ch of Bd*
Jason Norton, *President*
Margaret McCarty, *Treasurer*
EMP: 75
SQ FT: 8,000
SALES (est): 30.4MM **Privately Held**
WEB: www.rlhfp.com
SIC: 1711 1542 Fire sprinkler system installation; nonresidential construction

(P-2099)
COMFORT AIR INC
1607 French Camp Tpke, Stockton (95206-1960)
P.O. Box 1969 (95201-1969)
PHONE..................209 466-4601
Steven J Evans, *President*
Gregory A Gaut, *Vice Pres*
Paulette Gaut, *Admin Sec*
EMP: 75 **EST:** 1946
SQ FT: 7,000
SALES: 11MM **Privately Held**
WEB: www.comfortairinc.com
SIC: 1711 Warm air heating & air conditioning contractor

(P-2100)
COMFORT SYSTEMS USA INC
4189 Santa Ana St Ste D, Ontario (91761-1557)
PHONE..................909 390-6677
Joe Nichter, *Branch Mgr*
EMP: 83
SALES (corp-wide): 2.1B **Publicly Held**
SIC: 1711 Mechanical contractor
PA: Comfort Systems Usa, Inc.
675 Bering Dr Ste 400
Houston TX 77057
713 830-9600

(P-2101)
COMMERCIAL RFRGN SPCALISTS LLC (HQ)
Also Called: CRS
3480 Arden Rd, Hayward (94545-3906)
PHONE..................510 784-8990
Todd Ernest, *CEO*
EMP: 102
SQ FT: 7,500
SALES (est): 24.7MM
SALES (corp-wide): 53.6MM **Privately Held**
WEB: www.crsref.com
SIC: 1711 5078 Heating & air conditioning contractors; refrigerators, commercial (reach-in & walk-in)
PA: Climate Pros, Llc
55 N Brandon Dr
Glendale Heights IL 60139
630 893-8511

(P-2102)
CONFORTI PLUMBING INC
6080 Pleasant Valley Rd C, El Dorado (95623-4257)
P.O. Box 1090 (95623-1090)
PHONE..................530 622-0202
Marvin Collins, *President*
Jan Zygalinski, *CFO*
EMP: 1020
SQ FT: 1,000
SALES (est): 65.8MM **Privately Held**
WEB: www.confortiplumbing.com
SIC: 1711 Plumbing contractors

(P-2103)
CONTROL AC SVC CORP
5200 E La Palma Ave, Anaheim (92807-2019)
PHONE..................714 777-8600
Kendrick Ellis, *President*
Greg Rummler, *CFO*
Stanley Ellis, *Vice Pres*
Jay McEntire, *VP Bus Dvlpt*
Antony Assaf, *Project Mgr*
EMP: 51 **EST:** 1990
SALES (est): 4.4MM **Privately Held**
SIC: 1711 Plumbing, heating, air-conditioning contractors

(P-2104)
CONTROL AIR NORTH INC
30655 San Clemente St, Hayward (94544-7133)
PHONE..................510 441-1800
Greg Ellis, *President*
Darrell Griffith, *Vice Pres*
Mike Pence, *Vice Pres*
Ken Ellis, *Principal*
Stan Ellis, *Principal*
EMP: 100
SALES: 46.9MM **Privately Held**
WEB: www.cmihvac.com
SIC: 1711 Plumbing, heating, air-conditioning contractors

(P-2105)
COSCO FIRE PROTECTION INC
Also Called: 76
4990 Greencraig Ln, San Diego (92123-1673)
PHONE..................858 444-2000
Alexander Hernandez, *Manager*
Rory Low, *Branch Mgr*
EMP: 75 **Privately Held**
WEB: www.coscofireprotection.com
SIC: 1711 Fire sprinkler system installation
HQ: Cosco Fire Protection, Inc.
29222 Rancho Viejo Rd # 205
San Juan Capistrano CA 92675
714 974-8770

(P-2106)
COSCO FIRE PROTECTION INC
Also Called: Cosco Garvin Fire Protection
1075 W Lambert Rd Ste D, Brea (92821-2944)
PHONE..................714 989-1800
Barry Fielding, *Branch Mgr*
EMP: 193 **Privately Held**
SIC: 1711 Fire sprinkler system installation
HQ: Cosco Fire Protection, Inc.
29222 Rancho Viejo Rd # 205
San Juan Capistrano CA 92675
714 974-8770

(P-2107)
COUNTYWIDE MECH SYSTEMS INC
1400 N Johnson Ave # 114, El Cajon (92020-1651)
PHONE..................619 449-9900
Paul Duke, *President*
David Cimpl, *CFO*
Mike McDowell, *Vice Pres*
Connie Valencia, *Executive Asst*
Marc Monoy, *Admin Asst*
EMP: 230
SQ FT: 5,000
SALES (est): 51.2MM
SALES (corp-wide): 459.6MM **Privately Held**
SIC: 1711 Mechanical contractor
PA: Mmc Corp
10955 Lowell Ave Ste 350
Overland Park KS 66210
913 469-0101

(P-2108)
CRITCHFIELD MECH INC STHERN CAL
15391 Springdale St, Huntington Beach (92649-1100)
PHONE..................949 390-2900
Mike Pearlman, *CEO*
EMP: 100
SALES: 51.2MM **Privately Held**
SIC: 1711 Warm air heating & air conditioning contractor

(P-2109)
CRITCHFIELD MECHANICAL INC
4085 Campbell Ave, Menlo Park (94025-1939)
PHONE..................650 321-7801
Joe Critchfield, *Chairman*
Tim Spooner, *Project Mgr*
Euft Kruithof, *Engineer*
EMP: 394
SALES (corp-wide): 162.2MM **Privately Held**
SIC: 1711 Mechanical contractor
PA: Critchfield Mechanical, Inc.
1901 Junction Ave
San Jose CA 95131
408 437-7000

(P-2110)
D & J PLUMBING INC
4341 Winters St, Sacramento (95838-3031)
PHONE..................916 922-4888
Steve Waldron, *President*
Geri Richards, *Shareholder*
John Richards, *Shareholder*
Randy Golden, *Vice Pres*
EMP: 100
SQ FT: 5,000
SALES (est): 12.3MM **Privately Held**
SIC: 1711 Plumbing contractors

P R O D U C T S & S V C S

(P-2111)
D W NICHOLSON
CORPORATION (PA)
24747 Clawiter Rd, Hayward (94545-2225)
P.O. Box 4197 (94540-4197)
PHONE...............................510 887-0900
John L Nicholson, *Principal*
Melinda Silva, *COO*
Herb Mehner, *Project Mgr*
Mari Duncan, *Accountant*
Tom Reed Jr, *Safety Mgr*
EMP: 250 **EST:** 1935
SQ FT: 12,000
SALES: 32MM **Privately Held**
WEB: www.dwnicholson.com
SIC: 1711 1731 8711 1796 Mechanical
contractor; general electrical contractor;
engineering services; millwright; residen-
tial construction; industrial buildings &
warehouses

(P-2112)
D/K MECHANICAL
CONTRACTORS INC
3870 E Eagle Dr, Anaheim (92807-1706)
PHONE...............................714 970-0180
Gary Brubaker, *President*
Don Giarratano, *Vice Pres*
EMP: 200
SALES (est): 13.6MM **Privately Held**
WEB: www.dkmechanical.com
SIC: 1711 Plumbing contractors; warm air
heating & air conditioning contractor

(P-2113)
DAART ENGINEERING
COMPANY INC
1598 N H St, San Bernardino
(92405-4318)
PHONE...............................909 888-8696
Timothy C Cantwell, *President*
James D Dunn, *Corp Secy*
Robert Pfeifer, *Admin Sec*
EMP: 70
SQ FT: 8,000
SALES: 9MM **Privately Held**
WEB: www.daarteng.com
SIC: 1711 Fire sprinkler system installation

(P-2114)
DAVE WILLIAMS PLBG & ELEC
INC
75140 Saint Charles Pl C, Palm Desert
(92211-9044)
PHONE...............................760 296-1397
Daniel Williams, *President*
Dave Williams, *Vice Pres*
Mike Perezchica, *Purch Agent*
EMP: 110 **EST:** 2008
SALES: 10MM **Privately Held**
SIC: 1711 Plumbing contractors; fire sprin-
kler system installation

(P-2115)
DESERT MECHANICAL INC
Also Called: Dmi
15870 Olden St, Sylmar (91342-1241)
PHONE...............................702 873-7333
Casey M Condron, *President*
Joseph Guglielmo, *Senior VP*
Andre Burnthon, *Vice Pres*
Alex L Hodson, *Vice Pres*
Dan Naylor, *Vice Pres*
EMP: 1100
SQ FT: 25,000
SALES: 43.4MM
SALES (corp-wide): 4.4B **Publicly Held**
WEB: www.lvdph.com
SIC: 1711 Plumbing contractors
PA: Tutor Perini Corporation
15901 Olden St
Sylmar CA 91342
818 362-8391

(P-2116)
DON BRANDEL PLUMBING INC
15100 Texaco Ave, Paramount
(90723-3916)
PHONE...............................562 408-0400
Greg Brandel, *President*
Dennis Castaldo, *Exec VP*
Jim Brandel, *Vice Pres*
Charron Castaldo, *Admin Sec*
EMP: 50
SQ FT: 20,000

SALES (est): 10MM **Privately Held**
WEB: www.brandelplumbing.com
SIC: 1711 Plumbing contractors

(P-2117)
DONALD P DICK AC INC (PA)
Also Called: Mr Cool
1444 N Whitney Ave, Fresno (93703-4513)
PHONE...............................559 255-1644
James B Dick, *President*
David B Dick, *Vice Pres*
David Dick, *Vice Pres*
Jeffrey Dick, *Admin Sec*
Ramon Rendon, *Consultant*
EMP: 100 **EST:** 1970
SQ FT: 30,000
SALES (est): 14.7MM **Privately Held**
WEB: www.mrcool4ac.com
SIC: 1711 Warm air heating & air condi-
tioning contractor

(P-2118)
DRAIN PATROL
7764 Arjons Dr, San Diego (92126-4391)
P.O. Box 503053 (92150-3053)
PHONE...............................858 560-1137
Scot Buck, *Manager*
EMP: 64
SALES (est): 4.9MM **Privately Held**
SIC: 1711 1623 Plumbing contractors;
sewer line construction

(P-2119)
DYNAMIC PLUMBING
COMMERCIAL
5920 Winterhaven Ave, Riverside
(92504-1048)
PHONE...............................951 343-1200
Thomas L Baker, *President*
EMP: 84
SALES (est): 6.7MM **Privately Held**
SIC: 1711 Plumbing, heating, air-condition-
ing contractors

(P-2120)
E L PAYNE HEATING COMPANY
Also Called: Payne, E L Company
226 S Lucerne Blvd, Los Angeles
(90004-3727)
PHONE...............................310 275-5331
Gordon Payne Jr, *President*
Gordon Payne Sr, *Ch of Bd*
EMP: 50
SQ FT: 1,200
SALES (est): 4.9MM **Privately Held**
SIC: 1711 Warm air heating & air condi-
tioning contractor; heating & air condition-
ing contractors

(P-2121)
EAGLE SYSTEMS INTL INC
Also Called: Synergy Companies
28436 Satellite St, Hayward (94545-4863)
PHONE...............................510 259-1700
Steven R Shallenberger, *President*
Russell Jacobsen, *CFO*
EMP: 375
SQ FT: 6,962
SALES (est): 27.8MM **Privately Held**
SIC: 1711 1731 1742 1793 Warm air
heating & air conditioning contractor; gen-
eral electrical contractor; plastering; dry-
wall & insulation; glass & glazing work

(P-2122)
ECB CORP (PA)
Also Called: Omniduct
6400 Artesia Blvd, Buena Park
(90620-1006)
PHONE...............................714 385-8900
Robert Brumleu, *President*
Steven G Philp, *CFO*
Kyle Brumleu, *Vice Pres*
Ian Castellanos, *Info Tech Mgr*
George Austin, *Manager*
▲ **EMP:** 150
SQ FT: 56,000
SALES (est): 48.8MM **Privately Held**
WEB: www.omniduct.com
SIC: 1711 3444 Ventilation & duct work
contractor; ducts; sheet metal

(P-2123)
ECONO AIR CONDITIONING INC
3366 E La Palma Ave, Anaheim
(92806-2814)
PHONE...............................714 630-3090
Mike Richard, *CEO*
EMP: 50
SALES (est): 2MM **Privately Held**
SIC: 1711 Warm air heating & air condi-
tioning contractor

(P-2124)
ECOTECH RFRGN & HVAC INC
630 S Sunkist St Ste R, Anaheim (92806)
PHONE...............................888 833-8100
Erich Christopher Munzner, *CEO*
EMP: 60
SALES (est): 759.7K **Privately Held**
SIC: 1711 Refrigeration contractor

(P-2125)
EDGEWATER PLUMBING OF
BENICIA
576 Hastings Dr, Benicia (94510-1375)
PHONE...............................707 747-9204
Richard M Klauber, *Ch of Bd*
Steve Wilkerson, *President*
Lisa Wilkerson, *Corp Secy*
EMP: 50
SALES (est): 5.2MM **Privately Held**
SIC: 1711 6531 Plumbing contractors; real
estate leasing & rentals

(P-2126)
EMCOR FCLITIES SVCS N AMER
INC
9505 Chesapeake Dr, San Diego
(92123-1304)
PHONE...............................858 712-4700
David Rastolich, *Vice Pres*
EMP: 230
SALES (corp-wide): 8.1B **Publicly Held**
SIC: 1711 Heating & air conditioning con-
tractors
HQ: Emcor Facilities Services Of North
America, Inc.
306 Northern Ave Ste 5
Boston MA

(P-2127)
ENERGY ENTERPRISES USA
INC (PA)
Also Called: Canopy Energy
6842 Van Nuys Blvd # 800, Van Nuys
(91405-4660)
PHONE...............................424 339-0005
Lior Agam, *CEO*
Zariel Kogan, *Project Mgr*
Heather Pollock, *Project Mgr*
Frank Schwartz, *Controller*
Jennifer Martin, *Sales Mgr*
EMP: 100 **EST:** 2011
SQ FT: 11,000
SALES (est): 50MM **Privately Held**
SIC: 1711 Solar energy contractor

(P-2128)
ENERGY STORE OF
CALIFORNIA INC
Also Called: Qc Wall Systems
14958 Venado Dr, Rancho Murieta
(95683-9322)
PHONE...............................916 825-8751
Dennis M Barsam, *President*
W Joe Mitchell, *Vice Pres*
EMP: 100
SALES: 3.5MM **Privately Held**
SIC: 1711 1742 Heating & air conditioning
contractors; drywall

(P-2129)
ENVIRONMENTAL SYSTEMS
INC (PA)
Also Called: HONEYWELL AUTHORIZED
DEALER
3353 De La Cruz Blvd, Santa Clara
(95054-2633)
PHONE...............................408 980-1711
V C Enfantino, *President*
Tracey Enfantino, *General Mgr*
Lisa Enfantino, *Office Mgr*
Eugene L Enfantino, *Admin Sec*
Tammy Heimgartner, *Administration*

EMP: 85
SQ FT: 13,800
SALES: 40.6MM **Privately Held**
SIC: 1711 7623 3444 Mechanical contractor; ventilation & duct work contractor;
plumbing contractors; refrigeration service
& repair; sheet metalwork

(P-2130)
ENVISE
12131 Western Ave, Garden Grove
(92841-2914)
PHONE...............................714 901-5800
Travis Feltcher, *Branch Mgr*
Karena Salch, *Accounts Mgr*
Jeremy Crowley, *Associate*
EMP: 63
SALES (corp-wide): 1B **Privately Held**
SIC: 1711 Plumbing, heating, air-condition-
ing contractors
HQ: Envise
12131 Western Ave
Garden Grove CA 92841
800 613-6240

(P-2131)
ESS
Also Called: Evergreen Solar Services
5227 Dantes View Dr, Agoura Hills
(91301-2313)
PHONE...............................888 303-6424
Jacob Stephens, *President*
EMP: 100
SALES: 30.8MM **Privately Held**
SIC: 1711 Solar energy contractor

(P-2132)
F J HOOVER PLUMBING INC
Also Called: Pipeline Plumbing
2259 Hamner Ave, Norco (92860-2608)
PHONE...............................951 360-8262
Pamela Reno-Kemp, *President*
Hank Kemp, *Vice Pres*
James Dean Potts, *Principal*
EMP: 53
SQ FT: 1,500
SALES (est): 4.9MM **Privately Held**
SIC: 1711 Plumbing contractors

(P-2133)
F W SPENCER & SON INC
Also Called: Brisbane Mechanical
99 S Hill Dr, Brisbane (94005-1274)
PHONE...............................415 468-5000
William D Spencer, *President*
Dan Everett, *Vice Pres*
John Hohman, *Project Mgr*
Tom Mariano, *Manager*
EMP: 200 **EST:** 1903
SQ FT: 140,000
SALES (est): 42.5MM **Privately Held**
SIC: 1711 Plumbing contractors; warm air
heating & air conditioning contractor

(P-2134)
FAMAND INC
1604 Airport Blvd, Santa Rosa
(95403-8204)
PHONE...............................707 255-9295
Charlie Butts, *Branch Mgr*
Stan Butts, *President*
Rus Andrews, *Vice Pres*
Mike Ferguson, *Engineer*
EMP: 106
SALES (corp-wide): 37.7MM **Privately
Held**
SIC: 1711 Plumbing, heating, air-condition-
ing contractors
PA: Famand, Inc.
1512 Silica Ave
Sacramento CA 95815
916 988-8808

(P-2135)
FAULT LINE PLUMBING
7640 National Dr, Livermore (94550-8809)
PHONE...............................925 443-6450
Sean Collins, *President*
Karrie Collins, *Treasurer*
Milani Lindgren, *Office Mgr*
Josh Elsbernd, *Manager*
EMP: 50 **EST:** 1997
SALES (est): 7.8MM **Privately Held**
SIC: 1711 Plumbing contractors

▲ = Import ▼=Export
◆ =Import/Export

(P-2136)
FERREIRA SERVICE INC (PA)
3150 Crow Canyon Pl # 230, San Ramon
(94583-1778)
PHONE..................925 831-9330
Susan Ferreira, *CEO*
Albert Ferreira, *President*
Susan Town, *Data Proc Exec*
Mitzi Smith, *Mktg Dir*
Al Ferreira, *Director*
EMP: 70 **EST:** 1978
SQ FT: 10,000
SALES (est): 10.3MM **Privately Held**
WEB: www.ferreira.com
SIC: 1711 Mechanical contractor

(P-2137)
**FIDELITY HOME ENERGY INC
(PA)**
2235 Polvorosa Ave # 230, San Leandro
(94577-2249)
PHONE..................858 220-7784
Brad Smith, *Principal*
Kris Baker, *Human Resources*
EMP: 73
SQ FT: 12,000
SALES (est): 20.7MM **Privately Held**
WEB: www.thesungate.com
SIC: 1711 1522 Solar energy contractor;
remodeling, multi-family dwellings

(P-2138)
FIRE SAFE SYSTEMS INC
1312 Kingsdale Ave, Redondo Beach
(90278-3926)
PHONE..................310 542-0585
Michael Moller, *CEO*
Joyce Moller, *President*
Sandra Marquez, *Office Mgr*
Nora Llamas, *Admin Asst*
Oscar Castro, *Manager*
EMP: 60
SQ FT: 3,000
SALES (est): 9MM **Privately Held**
WEB: www.firesafesystems.com
SIC: 1711 Fire sprinkler system installation

(P-2139)
**FIRE SPRINKLER SYSTEMS INC
(PA)**
705 E Harrison St Ste 200, Corona
(92879-1398)
P.O. Box 2378 (92878-2378)
PHONE..................800 915-3473
Harold Roger, *President*
Michael Kerby, *CFO*
Lilia Castro, *Human Res Mgr*
Juan Nieto, *Opers Mgr*
EMP: 86
SALES (est): 25.3MM **Privately Held**
WEB: www.fireinc.net
SIC: 1711 Fire sprinkler system installation

(P-2140)
FISCHER INC
1372 W 26th St, San Bernardino
(92405-3029)
PHONE..................909 881-2910
Michael G Fischer, *President*
EMP: 70
SQ FT: 1,600
SALES (est): 8.7MM **Privately Held**
SIC: 1711 Plumbing contractors

(P-2141)
FRESCHI AIR SYSTEMS INC
Also Called: Freschi Service Experts
715 Fulton Shipyard Rd, Antioch
(94509-7557)
PHONE..................925 827-9761
John R Freschi Jr, *President*
EMP: 55
SQ FT: 5,000
SALES (est): 5.9MM
SALES (corp-wide): 985.7MM **Privately
Held**
WEB: www.lennoxinternational.com
SIC: 1711 3444 Warm air heating & air
conditioning contractor; sheet metalwork
HQ: Service Experts Llc
3820 American Dr Ste 200
Plano TX 75075

(P-2142)
**FRESNO PLUMBING & HEATING
INC (PA)**
Also Called: Ace Hardware
2585 N Larkin Ave, Fresno (93727-1357)
PHONE..................559 294-0200
Larry Kumpe, *CEO*
Dean Kumpe, *Corp Secy*
Gary Kumpe, *Vice Pres*
Dave Holman, *Project Mgr*
Shayne Smith, *Technology*
EMP: 202
SQ FT: 20,000
SALES (est): 43.4MM **Privately Held**
WEB: www.fphinc.com
SIC: 1711 5251 Plumbing contractors;
hardware; door locks & lock sets; tools,
hand; tools, power

(P-2143)
FRONTIER MECHANICAL INC
Also Called: Frontier Plumbing
6309 Seven Seas Ave, Bakersfield
(93308-5133)
PHONE..................661 589-6203
Rick Palmer, *President*
Brenda Palmer, *Shareholder*
EMP: 93
SQ FT: 120,000
SALES (est): 14.6MM **Privately Held**
WEB: www.frontier-plumbing.com
SIC: 1711 1521 Plumbing contractors;
new construction, single-family houses

(P-2144)
**GENERAL ENGINEERING WSTN
INC (PA)**
Also Called: Thermal Air
1140 N Red Gum St, Anaheim
(92806-2516)
PHONE..................714 630-3200
Stephen Weiss, *CEO*
Joseph Urban, *President*
EMP: 80
SQ FT: 10,000
SALES (est): 12.1MM **Privately Held**
SIC: 1711 Mechanical contractor; ventila-
tion & duct work contractor

(P-2145)
GENERAL UNDERGROUND
701 W Grove Ave, Orange (92865-3213)
P.O. Box 29830, Anaheim (92809-0194)
PHONE..................714 632-8646
Robert Anderson, *President*
Terry Householder, *President*
Karla Distrola, *Vice Pres*
Jason Stout, *Project Mgr*
Keith Kroeger, *Manager*
EMP: 110
SQ FT: 8,000
SALES (est): 22.2MM **Privately Held**
WEB: www.gufpinc.com
SIC: 1711 Fire sprinkler system installation

(P-2146)
**GEORGE M ROBINSON & CO
(PA)**
1461 Atteberry Ln, San Jose (95131-1409)
PHONE..................510 632-7017
John P Joyce, *President*
Ned Raudsep, *Treasurer*
EMP: 100
SQ FT: 20,000
SALES (est): 5.6MM **Privately Held**
WEB: www.geomrobinson.com
SIC: 1711 3498 Fire sprinkler system in-
stallation; fabricated pipe & fittings

(P-2147)
GRAYCON INC
232 S 8th Ave, City of Industry
(91746-3200)
PHONE..................626 961-9640
Joseph F Klein, *CEO*
Jim Smith, *Regional Mgr*
Mike Yackee, *Project Mgr*
Roger Vargas, *Controller*
EMP: 50
SQ FT: 12,000
SALES (est): 9.9MM **Privately Held**
WEB: www.graycon.net
SIC: 1711 Ventilation & duct work contrac-
tor; warm air heating & air conditioning
contractor

(P-2148)
**GREATER SAN DIEGO AC CO
INC**
Also Called: Honeywell Authorized Dealer
3883 Ruffin Rd Ste C, San Diego
(92123-4813)
PHONE..................619 469-7818
Randy Baillargeon, *President*
Ryan Baillargeon, *Vice Pres*
Danielle Zuniga, *Accounts Mgr*
EMP: 115
SQ FT: 8,500
SALES (est): 12.3MM **Privately Held**
WEB: www.gsdac.com
SIC: 1711 Heating & air conditioning con-
tractors; ventilation & duct work contractor

(P-2149)
H L MOE CO INC (PA)
Also Called: Keefe Plumbing Services
526 Commercial St, Glendale
(91203-2861)
PHONE..................818 572-2100
Martha Tennyson, *CEO*
Michael C Davis, *President*
Bob Francis, *Vice Pres*
Robert Francis, *Vice Pres*
Jeff Hachey, *Vice Pres*
EMP: 130 **EST:** 1927
SALES (est): 34.8MM **Privately Held**
WEB: www.hlmoeco.com
SIC: 1711 Plumbing contractors

(P-2150)
HALDEMAN INC
2937 Tanager Ave, Commerce
(90040-2761)
PHONE..................323 726-7011
Tom Haldeman, *Ch of Bd*
Mark O Donnell, *President*
Jeff Dandridge, *CFO*
Sue Haldeman, *Treasurer*
Holt Dandridge, *Vice Pres*
EMP: 50
SQ FT: 45,000
SALES (est): 3.6MM **Privately Held**
WEB: www.haldeman.com
SIC: 1711 Mechanical contractor

(P-2151)
HPS MECHANICAL INC (PA)
3100 E Belle Ter, Bakersfield (93307-6830)
PHONE..................661 397-2121
Les Denherder, *President*
Scott Denherder, *Vice Pres*
Jamie Ramos, *Executive Asst*
Renee Denesha, *Administration*
Roger Lane, *Project Mgr*
EMP: 130
SALES (est): 46.4MM **Privately Held**
SIC: 1711 Plumbing contractors

(P-2152)
HUMPHREY PLUMBING INC
880 S Kilroy Rd, Turlock (95380-9570)
PHONE..................209 634-4626
Justin Humphrey, *President*
Robin Humphrey, *Treasurer*
EMP: 75
SQ FT: 7,500
SALES (est): 9.5MM **Privately Held**
SIC: 1711 Plumbing contractors

(P-2153)
INCOM MECHANICAL INC
975 Transport Way Ste 5, Petaluma
(94954-6860)
PHONE..................707 586-0511
Charles J Lacoti, *President*
Gabrielle Candrian, *Treasurer*
Jeff Lacoti, *Vice Pres*
Phil Lacoti, *Vice Pres*
Leavell Jennifer, *Administration*
EMP: 65
SQ FT: 7,000
SALES (est): 10.3MM **Privately Held**
WEB: www.incommechanical.com
SIC: 1711 Plumbing contractors; mechani-
cal contractor

(P-2154)
**INDUSTRIAL COML SYSTEMS
INC**
Also Called: SAN MARCOS MECHANICAL
1165 Joshua Way, Vista (92081-7840)
PHONE..................760 300-4094
Robin Sides, *President*
Matt Harbin, *Vice Pres*
Cindy Sides, *Admin Sec*
EMP: 160
SQ FT: 15,000
SALES (est): 29.8MM **Privately Held**
SIC: 1711 Ventilation & duct work contrac-
tor

(P-2155)
INFINITY ENERGY INC
3855 Atherton Rd, Rocklin (95765-3700)
PHONE..................916 474-4723
Mark Stacy, *CEO*
Bryson Solomon, *COO*
Cory Gilbert, *CFO*
Cameron Kelly, *Security Dir*
John Lapray, *CTO*
EMP: 150
SALES (est): 347.7K **Privately Held**
SIC: 1711 Solar energy contractor

(P-2156)
**INFINITY PLUMBING DESIGNS
INC**
9182 Stellar Ct, Corona (92883-4923)
PHONE..................951 737-4436
Andrew D Carlson, *President*
Tomas Llamas Sr, *Exec VP*
John M Raya, *Exec VP*
Joe Beckworth, *Vice Pres*
Zujeiy Jimenez, *Admin Asst*
EMP: 300
SQ FT: 5,925
SALES (est): 2.2MM **Privately Held**
SIC: 1711 Plumbing contractors

(P-2157)
**INFINITY SVC GROUP INC A CAL
C**
Also Called: Allstar Home Services
9155 Archibald Ave # 302, Rancho Cuca-
monga (91730-5238)
P.O. Box 4229 (91729-4229)
PHONE..................909 466-6237
Justin Speelman, *President*
Leighton Jenner, *Vice Pres*
James McNeeley, *Admin Sec*
EMP: 54
SQ FT: 3,200
SALES: 7.1MM **Privately Held**
SIC: 1711 Plumbing contractors

(P-2158)
**INTECH MECHANICAL
COMPANY LLC**
7501 Galilee Rd, Roseville (95678-6905)
PHONE..................916 797-4900
Richard B Chowdry,
Dena Randall, *CFO*
Julie Chowdry, *Corp Secy*
Mike Friesen, *Vice Pres*
Nicole Billings, *Project Mgr*
EMP: 150
SQ FT: 39,775
SALES: 32.3MM **Privately Held**
SIC: 1711 8711 Plumbing contractors;
heating & air conditioning contractors;
mechanical contractor; process piping
contractor; heating & ventilation engineer-
ing

(P-2159)
J & J AIR CONDITIONING INC
Also Called: Honeywell Authorized Dealer
1086 N 11th St, San Jose (95112-2927)
PHONE..................408 920-0662
Jerry Hurwitz, *Owner*
Susan Borkin, *Treasurer*
Pam York, *Admin Asst*
Alex Alas, *Project Mgr*
Dave Kester, *Project Mgr*
EMP: 60
SQ FT: 10,000
SALES (est): 13.8MM **Privately Held**
WEB: www.jjair.com
SIC: 1711 Warm air heating & air condi-
tioning contractor; ventilation & duct work
contractor

(P-2160)
J M CARDEN SPRINKLER CO INC
2909 Fletcher Dr, Los Angeles (90065-1479)
PHONE.................................323 258-8300
Michael Carden, *President*
Carroll B Carden, *Corp Secy*
Richard Wallace, *Vice Pres*
Mark Berru, *Controller*
Curt Dowling, *Opers Mgr*
EMP: 60
SQ FT: 48,000
SALES (est): 9.7MM **Privately Held**
WEB: www.jmcfire.com
SIC: 1711 Fire sprinkler system installation

(P-2161)
J R PIERCE PLUMBING COMPANY
14481 Wicks Blvd, San Leandro (94577-6711)
PHONE.................................510 483-5473
Richard Pierce, *President*
Dave Barich, *General Mgr*
Rob Brown, *Purchasing*
Mike McGuffin, *Assistant*
EMP: 100
SQ FT: 4,000
SALES (est): 14MM **Privately Held**
SIC: 1711 Plumbing contractors

(P-2162)
JACKSON & BLANC
7929 Arjons Dr, San Diego (92126-4301)
PHONE.................................858 831-7900
Kirk Jackson, *CEO*
John Fusca, *President*
Debbie Rives, *Office Mgr*
Mark Dudley, *Project Mgr*
Chris McGill, *Foreman/Supr*
▲ EMP: 110 EST: 1931
SQ FT: 36,000
SALES: 65.4MM **Privately Held**
WEB: www.jacksonandblanc.com
SIC: 1711 Mechanical contractor

(P-2163)
JASON MECHANICAL INC
1379 Fitzgerald Rd, Rancho Cordova (95742)
PHONE.................................916 638-8763
Jason Gerald Voll, *CEO*
EMP: 50
SALES (est): 298.9K **Privately Held**
SIC: 1711 Mechanical contractor

(P-2164)
JCT COMPANY LLC
Also Called: Aliso Air Conditioning & Htg
29736 Avenida&Bandera, Rancho Santa Margari (92688)
PHONE.................................949 589-2021
Jeffrey Loftus,
Monika Hall, *Department Mgr*
Lauren Barbarino, *Administration*
Shawn Cooney, *Sales Staff*
Kc Fowler, *Manager*
EMP: 50
SALES (est): 5.9MM **Privately Held**
SIC: 1711 Heating & air conditioning contractors

(P-2165)
JEFF TRACY INC
Also Called: Land Forms Landscape Cnstr
15375 Barranca Pkwy A110, Irvine (92618-2217)
PHONE.................................949 582-0877
Jeff Thomas Tracy, *CEO*
Jon Gilmer, *President*
Brian Olsen, *President*
Sandy Wallace, *CFO*
Luke Alvarado, *Manager*
EMP: 50
SQ FT: 1,608
SALES (est): 6.7MM **Privately Held**
SIC: 1711 0782 Irrigation sprinkler system installation; landscape contractors

(P-2166)
JOHNSON CONTROLS
1868 Palma Dr, Ventura (93003-6300)
PHONE.................................805 642-0366
EMP: 64 **Privately Held**

SIC: 1711 Fire sprinkler system installation
HQ: Johnson Controls Fire Protection Lp
6600 Congress Ave
Boca Raton FL 33487
561 988-7200

(P-2167)
JOHNSON CONTROLS
3077 Wiljan Ct Ste B, Santa Rosa (95407-5764)
PHONE.................................707 578-3212
John Becker, *Branch Mgr*
Laura Burkman, *Director*
EMP: 61 **Privately Held**
WEB: www.simplexgrinnell.com
SIC: 1711 Fire sprinkler system installation
HQ: Johnson Controls Fire Protection Lp
6600 Congress Ave
Boca Raton FL 33487
561 988-7200

(P-2168)
JPI DEVELOPMENT GROUP INC
41205 Golden Gate Cir, Murrieta (92562-6991)
PHONE.................................951 973-7680
Brad Janikowski, *President*
Dan Janikowski, *Vice Pres*
EMP: 60
SQ FT: 6,000
SALES (est): 8.3MM **Privately Held**
SIC: 1711 Plumbing contractors

(P-2169)
JR PERCE PLBG INC SACRAMENTO
3610 Cincinnati Ave, Rocklin (95765-1203)
PHONE.................................916 434-9554
Dennis Pierce, *President*
EMP: 150 EST: 1927
SQ FT: 11,000
SALES (est): 38.3MM **Privately Held**
SIC: 1711 Plumbing contractors

(P-2170)
K & S AIR CONDITIONING INC
Also Called: K&S
143 E Meats Ave, Orange (92865-3309)
PHONE.................................714 685-0077
Steven Patz, *President*
Renee Patz, *Vice Pres*
Dave Guido, *General Mgr*
Andy Garcia, *Sales Engr*
Paul N Cameron, *Director*
EMP: 140
SQ FT: 18,000
SALES (est): 27.5MM **Privately Held**
SIC: 1711 Warm air heating & air conditioning contractor

(P-2171)
KEN STARR INC
Also Called: Home Comfort USA
1120 N Tustin Ave, Anaheim (92807-1712)
PHONE.................................714 632-8789
Ken Starr, *President*
Paul Buono, *Vice Pres*
EMP: 80
SQ FT: 9,000
SALES (est): 14MM **Privately Held**
SIC: 1711 Warm air heating & air conditioning contractor

(P-2172)
KEY AIR CNDITIONING CONTRS INC
10905 Laurel Ave, Santa Fe Springs (90670-4513)
PHONE.................................562 941-2233
Richard Rivera, *President*
Robert Donat, *Vice Pres*
Larry Stikeleather, *Vice Pres*
Matt Walters, *Manager*
EMP: 53
SQ FT: 35,000
SALES (est): 11.3MM **Privately Held**
SIC: 1711 Heating & air conditioning contractors

(P-2173)
KINCAID INDUSTRIES INC
31065 Plantation Dr, Thousand Palms (92276-6623)
PHONE.................................760 343-5457
Scott Kincaid, *CEO*
Dave Seipel, *Project Mgr*

EMP: 116
SQ FT: 7,000
SALES (est): 18.2MM **Privately Held**
WEB: www.kincaidplumbing.com
SIC: 1711 Plumbing contractors

(P-2174)
KINETIC SYSTEMS INC
1620 S Sunkist St, Anaheim (92806-5811)
PHONE.................................949 502-4856
Dan Naylor, *Opers Mgr*
EMP: 50
SALES (corp-wide): 342.4K **Privately Held**
SIC: 1711 Mechanical contractor
HQ: Kinetic Systems, Inc.
3083 Independence Dr
Livermore CA 94551
510 683-6000

(P-2175)
KINETICS MECHANICAL SVC INC
6336 Patterson Pass Rd H, Livermore (94550-9577)
PHONE.................................925 245-6200
Ralph E Dorotinsky, *President*
Craig Kirk, *Vice Pres*
EMP: 100 EST: 1997
SQ FT: 10,000
SALES (est): 16.2MM **Privately Held**
SIC: 1711 Mechanical contractor

(P-2176)
L A SERVICES INC
Also Called: George Brazil Plbg Htg & AC
9405 Jefferson Blvd, Culver City (90232-2915)
PHONE.................................310 838-0408
Michael N Diamond, *President*
Goldyne Diamond, *Corp Secy*
Kenneth E Barbura, *Vice Pres*
EMP: 50
SQ FT: 4,000
SALES (est): 2.4MM **Privately Held**
SIC: 1711 Plumbing contractors

(P-2177)
L J KRUSE CO
Also Called: Honeywell Authorized Dealer
920 Pardee St, Berkeley (94710-2626)
P.O. Box 2900 (94702-0900)
PHONE.................................510 644-0260
David J Kruse, *President*
Karen Lown, *CFO*
Andrew S Kruse, *Exec VP*
Nathan Kruse, *Vice Pres*
Janell Yates, *Vice Pres*
EMP: 60
SQ FT: 14,000
SALES (est): 12.3MM **Privately Held**
WEB: www.ljkruse.com
SIC: 1711 Plumbing contractors

(P-2178)
L&H AIRCO LLC
2530 Warren Dr, Rocklin (95677-2167)
PHONE.................................916 677-1000
Eric Crise, *President*
Jake Garcis, *Vice Pres*
John Harris, *Vice Pres*
Richard Racette, *Finance*
EMP: 80
SALES (est): 1.6MM **Privately Held**
SIC: 1711 5084 Mechanical contractor; instruments & control equipment

(P-2179)
LADELL INC
Also Called: Johnson Air
605 N Halifax Ave, Clovis (93611-7270)
PHONE.................................559 650-2000
Steve Johnson, *President*
EMP: 50
SQ FT: 38,000
SALES (est): 6.4MM **Privately Held**
WEB: www.ladell.com
SIC: 1711 Warm air heating & air conditioning contractor

(P-2180)
LAWSON MECHANICAL CONTRACTORS (PA)
6090 S Watt Ave, Sacramento (95829-1302)
P.O. Box 15224 (95851-0224)
PHONE.................................916 381-5000
Rodney Lawson, *President*
David Lawson, *Corp Secy*
Rod Barbour, *Vice Pres*
Rodney Barbour, *Vice Pres*
Nick Davis, *Project Mgr*
EMP: 100 EST: 1947
SQ FT: 31,000
SALES (est): 26.1MM **Privately Held**
WEB: www.lawsonmechanical.com
SIC: 1711 Plumbing contractors; heating & air conditioning contractors; mechanical contractor

(P-2181)
LDI MECHANICAL INC
3760 Happy Ln, Sacramento (95827-9731)
PHONE.................................916 361-3925
Shane Moser, *Manager*
Mike Smith, *Vice Pres*
Patrick Nunes, *General Mgr*
EMP: 50
SALES (corp-wide): 87.5MM **Privately Held**
SIC: 1711 Mechanical contractor
PA: Ldi Mechanical, Inc.
1587 E Bentley Dr
Corona CA 92879
951 340-9685

(P-2182)
LDI MECHANICAL INC (PA)
Also Called: Honeywell Authorized Dealer
1587 E Bentley Dr, Corona (92879-1738)
PHONE.................................951 340-9685
Lloyd Smith, *President*
Mike Smith, *Senior VP*
Robert Smith, *Senior VP*
Steve Buren, *Vice Pres*
Jeff Minarik, *Vice Pres*
EMP: 151
SQ FT: 38,000
SALES (est): 87.5MM **Privately Held**
WEB: www.ldimechanical.com
SIC: 1711 Mechanical contractor

(P-2183)
LED GLOBAL LLC
1010 Wilshire Blvd, Los Angeles (90017-5662)
PHONE.................................917 921-4315
Saila Smith,
EMP: 100
SALES: 10MM **Privately Held**
SIC: 1711 Solar energy contractor

(P-2184)
LEGACY MECH & ENRGY SVCS INC
3130 Crow Canyon Pl # 410, San Ramon (94583-1346)
PHONE.................................925 820-6938
Bill Longbotham, *Vice Pres*
Chip Eskildsen, *Vice Pres*
Jack Larkin, *Vice Pres*
Bill Call, *Project Mgr*
David Zapf, *Engineer*
EMP: 100
SQ FT: 4,000
SALES (est): 26.2MM **Privately Held**
WEB: www.legacymechanical.com
SIC: 1711 Mechanical contractor

(P-2185)
LESCURE COMPANY INC
2301 Arnold Industrial Wa, Concord (94520-5376)
P.O. Box 968, Lafayette (94549-0968)
PHONE.................................925 283-2528
Michael Lescure, *President*
Allen Lescure, *Vice Pres*
Conrad Chin, *Sales Mgr*
Heath Schmalzried, *Manager*
EMP: 70 EST: 1947
SQ FT: 10,000

SALES (est): 11.3MM **Privately Held**
WEB: www.lescurecompany.com
SIC: 1711 Plumbing contractors; mechanical contractor; warm air heating & air conditioning contractor

(P-2186)
LIMBACH COMPANY LP
Also Called: Western Air & Refrigeration
1709 Apollo Ct, Seal Beach (90740-5617)
PHONE...............................714 653-7000
Charlie Bacon, CEO
John T Jordan Jr, CFO
Robert C Morgan, Vice Pres
Virginia Baumgardner, Asst Sec
EMP: 167
SALES (est): 36.6MM **Privately Held**
SIC: 1711 Mechanical contractor
HQ: Limbach Company Llc
1251 Waterfront Pl # 201
Pittsburgh PA 15222
412 359-2173

(P-2187)
LINDLEY FIRE PROTECTION CO
2220 E Via Burton, Anaheim (92806-1221)
PHONE...............................714 535-5761
Leslie Lee Lindley II, President
Ann Lindley-Biship, Office Mgr
Linda Kocher, Controller
Jefe F Rodriguez, Purchasing
EMP: 50
SQ FT: 5,000
SALES: 9MM **Privately Held**
SIC: 1711 Fire sprinkler system installation

(P-2188)
LITE SOLAR CORP
3553 Atlantic Ave, Long Beach (90807-5606)
PHONE...............................562 256-1249
Ranbir Sahni, CEO
EMP: 150
SALES (est): 11.5MM **Privately Held**
SIC: 1711 Solar energy contractor

(P-2189)
LOUIS LUSKIN & SONS INC
6004 Venice Blvd, Los Angeles (90034)
PHONE...............................323 938-5142
Martin Luskin, President
Robert Luskin, Treasurer
Vivian Rupert, Admin Asst
Roberto Peccei, Research
Gene Block, Chancellor
EMP: 53
SQ FT: 7,000
SALES (est): 3.2MM **Privately Held**
SIC: 1711 Plumbing contractors

(P-2190)
LOVAZZANO MECHANICAL INC
189 Constitution Dr, Menlo Park (94025-1106)
PHONE...............................650 367-6216
Bruce Lovazzano Sr, CEO
Ed Mariano, Purch Mgr
EMP: 70
SQ FT: 3,100
SALES (est): 11.5MM **Privately Held**
SIC: 1711 Plumbing contractors

(P-2191)
LOZANO PLUMBING SERVICES INC
Also Called: Plumbing Master
3615 Presley Ave, Riverside (92507-4448)
P.O. Box 53137 (92517-4137)
PHONE...............................951 683-4840
EMP: 130 EST: 2004
SALES (est): 13.2MM **Privately Held**
SIC: 1711

(P-2192)
LPSH HOLDINGS INC
Also Called: Horizon Solar Power
3570 W Florida Ave # 168, Hemet (92545-3518)
PHONE...............................951 926-1176
Zachary Allman, Accounts Mgr
EMP: 504
SALES (corp-wide): 16.5MM **Privately Held**
SIC: 1711 Solar energy contractor

PA: Lpsh Holdings, Inc.
27368 Via Industria
Temecula CA 92590
855 647-5061

(P-2193)
LUPPEN AND HAWLEY INC
6330 N Point Way, Sacramento (95831-1067)
PHONE...............................916 456-7831
John O'Connor, President
Terrence O'Connor, Vice Pres
Greg O'Connor, Admin Sec
Todd Lewis, Controller
EMP: 110 EST: 1920
SQ FT: 30,000
SALES (est): 14.3MM **Privately Held**
WEB: www.luppenandhawleyinc.com
SIC: 1711 1731 Plumbing contractors; warm air heating & air conditioning contractor; electrical work

(P-2194)
M & L PLUMBING CO INC
3540 N Duke Ave, Fresno (93727-7896)
PHONE...............................559 291-5525
Fred C Ede III, President
Fred C Ede, President
EMP: 50 EST: 1961
SQ FT: 6,000
SALES (est): 5MM **Privately Held**
SIC: 1711 Plumbing contractors

(P-2195)
M & M PLUMBING INC
6782 Columbus St, Riverside (92504-1118)
PHONE...............................951 354-5388
Robert Malcom, President
Glenn Malcolm, Principal
EMP: 80
SALES (est): 5.9MM **Privately Held**
SIC: 1711 Plumbing contractors

(P-2196)
MARELICH MECHANICAL CO INC (HQ)
24041 Amador St, Hayward (94544-1201)
PHONE...............................510 785-5500
Keith R Atteberry, President
Chad Johnston, Vice Pres
Terry J Kvochak, Vice Pres
Andrew Ostrowski, Vice Pres
John Powell, Vice Pres
EMP: 65
SQ FT: 40,000
SALES (est): 33.9MM
SALES (corp-wide): 8.1B **Publicly Held**
WEB: www.marelich.com
SIC: 1711 1623 3822 Mechanical contractor; pipeline construction; auto controls regulating residntl & coml environmt & applncs
PA: Emcor Group, Inc.
301 Merritt 7 Fl 6
Norwalk CT 06851
203 849-7800

(P-2197)
MARQUEE FIRE PROTECTION (PA)
710 W Stadium Ln, Sacramento (95834-1130)
PHONE...............................916 641-7997
Donna Awtrey, Principal
Jeff Awtrey, Vice Pres
Rick Awtrey, Vice Pres
Kimberly Reed, Vice Pres
EMP: 56
SQ FT: 5,400
SALES: 14MM **Privately Held**
WEB: www.marqueefire.com
SIC: 1711 Fire sprinkler system installation

(P-2198)
MDDR INC
Also Called: Econo Air
555 Vanguard Way, Brea (92821-3933)
PHONE...............................714 792-1993
Michael Richards, President
Rhonda Richards, Vice Pres
EMP: 110
SALES (est): 29.1MM **Privately Held**
WEB: www.e-conoair.com
SIC: 1711 1731 Warm air heating & air conditioning contractor; electrical work

(P-2199)
MEMEGED TEVUOT SHEMESH (PA)
Also Called: Titan Solar
5550 Topanga Canyon Blvd # 280, Woodland Hills (91367-7471)
PHONE...............................866 575-1211
Ofir Haimoff, Owner
EMP: 152 EST: 2011
SQ FT: 20,000
SALES (est): 27.8MM **Privately Held**
SIC: 1711 5074 Solar energy contractor; heating equipment & panels, solar

(P-2200)
MESA ENERGY SYSTEMS INC (HQ)
Also Called: Emcor Services
2 Cromwell, Irvine (92618-1816)
PHONE...............................949 460-0460
Robert A Lake, President
Steve Hunt, CFO
Kip Bagley, Vice Pres
Michael Ecshner, Vice Pres
Charles G Fletcher Jr, Vice Pres
EMP: 210
SQ FT: 55,000
SALES (est): 140.7MM
SALES (corp-wide): 8.1B **Publicly Held**
SIC: 1711 7623 Warm air heating & air conditioning contractor; refrigeration service & repair
PA: Emcor Group, Inc.
301 Merritt 7 Fl 6
Norwalk CT 06851
203 849-7800

(P-2201)
MESA ENERGY SYSTEMS INC
3980 N Chestnut Ave, Fresno (93726-4730)
PHONE...............................559 277-7900
Michael Echsner, Branch Mgr
EMP: 60
SALES (corp-wide): 8.1B **Publicly Held**
SIC: 1711 Warm air heating & air conditioning contractor
HQ: Mesa Energy Systems, Inc.
2 Cromwell
Irvine CA 92618
949 460-0460

(P-2202)
MESA ENERGY SYSTEMS INC
16130 Sherman Way, Van Nuys (91406-3907)
PHONE...............................818 756-0500
Craig Lacko, Manager
EMP: 104
SALES (corp-wide): 8.1B **Publicly Held**
SIC: 1711 Warm air heating & air conditioning contractor
HQ: Mesa Energy Systems, Inc.
2 Cromwell
Irvine CA 92618
949 460-0460

(P-2203)
MONSTER MECHANICAL INC
1521 Terminal Ave, San Jose (95112-4316)
P.O. Box 6, Los Gatos (95031-0006)
PHONE...............................408 727-8362
Jeffery Miller, President
EMP: 60
SQ FT: 10,000
SALES (est): 5.7MM **Privately Held**
WEB: www.monstermechanical.com
SIC: 1711 Mechanical contractor

(P-2204)
MOUNTING SYSTEMS INC
180 Promenade Cir Ste 300, Sacramento (95834-2952)
PHONE...............................916 374-8872
Kasim Ersoy, President
▲ EMP: 51
SALES (est): 8.4MM
SALES (corp-wide): 453.4MM **Privately Held**
SIC: 1711 Mechanical contractor
HQ: Mounting Systems Gmbh
Mittenwalder Str. 9a
Rangsdorf 15834
337 085-2910

(P-2205)
MUIR-CHASE PLUMBING CO INC
Also Called: M C
4530 Brazil St Ste 1, Los Angeles (90039-1000)
PHONE...............................818 500-1940
Don Chase, President
Jay Chase, Vice Pres
Grant Muir, Vice Pres
James M Muir, Vice Pres
Gail Comstock, Admin Sec
EMP: 90
SQ FT: 5,000
SALES (est): 26.9MM **Privately Held**
WEB: www.muirchase.com
SIC: 1711 7699 Plumbing contractors; sewer cleaning & rodding

(P-2206)
MULTI MECHANICAL INC
Also Called: Honeywell Authorized Dealer
469 Blaine St, Corona (92879-1304)
PHONE...............................714 632-7404
Brandon Abblitt, CEO
Thomas Alvey, Purch Mgr
Jeremy Towers, Superintendent
EMP: 75
SALES (est): 13.1MM **Privately Held**
WEB: www.multimechanical.com
SIC: 1711 Mechanical contractor; warm air heating & air conditioning contractor

(P-2207)
MUNI-FED ENERGY INC
192 N Marina Dr, Long Beach (90803-4601)
PHONE...............................714 321-3346
Phil Bowman, President
Clay Sandidge, Treasurer
Vince Scarfo, Exec VP
Abbey Lam, Principal
Rick Greenwood, Director
EMP: 50 EST: 2011
SALES (est): 2.7MM **Privately Held**
SIC: 1711 8748 Solar energy contractor; systems analysis & engineering consulting services

(P-2208)
MURRAY PLUMBING AND HTG CORP (PA)
Also Called: Murray Company
18414 S Santa Fe Ave, E Rncho Dmngz (90221-5612)
PHONE...............................310 637-1500
Kevan Steffey, Chairman
Jim Deflavio, CEO
Alvin Aeschlimann, CFO
Don Odom, Vice Pres
James Patton, Vice Pres
EMP: 1000 EST: 1913
SQ FT: 26,000
SALES: 310.6MM **Privately Held**
SIC: 1711 Plumbing contractors; warm air heating & air conditioning contractor

(P-2209)
N V HEATHORN INC
Also Called: N V H
1155 Beecher St, San Leandro (94577-1251)
PHONE...............................510 569-9100
Edward W Heathorn, President
David A Heathorn, CFO
David Heathorn, CFO
Norman T R Heathorn, Principal
Jon Hill, Project Mgr
EMP: 59 EST: 1932
SQ FT: 57,500
SALES (est): 13.9MM **Privately Held**
WEB: www.nvheathorn.com
SIC: 1711 1629 Warm air heating & air conditioning contractor; plumbing contractors; ventilation & duct work contractor; waste water & sewage treatment plant construction

(P-2210)
NATIONAL AIR INC
Also Called: National Air and Energy
2053 Kurtz St, San Diego (92110-2014)
PHONE...............................619 299-2500
Jared M Wells, CEO
Anthony Brunelle, Engineer

EMP: 110
SQ FT: 10,500
SALES (est): 20MM **Privately Held**
SIC: 1711 Warm air heating & air conditioning contractor

(P-2211)
NP MECHANICAL INC
9225 Stellar Ct Ste A, Corona
(92883-4919)
P.O. Box 309 (92878-0309)
PHONE..................951 667-4220
Cecil J Hallinan, *CEO*
Richard Hallinan, *COO*
EMP: 400
SQ FT: 102,231
SALES: 60.3MM **Privately Held**
SIC: 1711 Mechanical contractor; fire sprinkler system installation

(P-2212)
NU FLOW AMERICA INC (PA)
7710 Kenamar Ct, San Diego
(92121-2425)
PHONE..................619 275-9130
Cameron Sean Manners, *President*
Steven Howe, *President*
Dennis Persaud, *General Mgr*
Josh Victorino, *Sr Project Mgr*
Tom Bowman, *Director*
EMP: 53
SQ FT: 15,488
SALES (est): 24.2MM **Privately Held**
WEB: www.nuflowtech.com
SIC: 1711 3317 Plumbing contractors; steel pipe & tubes

(P-2213)
O C MCDONALD CO INC
1150 W San Carlos St, San Jose
(95126-3440)
P.O. Box 26560 (95159-6560)
PHONE..................408 295-2182
James Mc Donald, *President*
Melissa Allison, *General Mgr*
Letty Yee, *Project Mgr*
Matthew McDonald, *Engineer*
J Brennan, *Controller*
EMP: 150 **EST:** 1906
SQ FT: 10,500
SALES (est): 53.9MM **Privately Held**
WEB: www.ocmcdonald.com
SIC: 1711 3585 3541 3444 Mechanical contractor; refrigeration & heating equipment; machine tools, metal cutting type; sheet metalwork; plumbing fixture fittings & trim

(P-2214)
OHAGIN MANUFACTURING LLC
210 Classic Ct Ste 100, Rohnert Park
(94928-1660)
PHONE..................707 872-3620
Greg Daniels, *President*
Mark Marquez, *COO*
Jake Carlson, *Sales Staff*
Carl Forman, *Sales Staff*
Danielle Kinney, *Mktg Coord*
EMP: 50
SALES (est): 4.2MM **Privately Held**
SIC: 1711 Ventilation & duct work contractor

(P-2215)
OHAGINS INC
210 Classic Ct Ste 100, Rohnert Park
(94928-1660)
PHONE..................707 303-3660
Carolina O'Hagin, *CEO*
Greg Daniels, *CEO*
Mark Marquez, *COO*
Mike Fulton, *Technical Staff*
▲ **EMP:** 60
SQ FT: 57,000
SALES (est): 7.8MM **Privately Held**
WEB: www.ohaginvent.com
SIC: 1711 Ventilation & duct work contractor

(P-2216)
ON-TIME AC & HTG INC (PA)
Also Called: Service Champions
7020 Commerce Dr, Pleasanton
(94588-8021)
PHONE..................925 598-1911
Keviin J Comerford, *CEO*

Mark Stewart, *General Mgr*
Ray Dias, *VP Opers*
Lyndy Rose, *Prdtn Mgr*
David Sturgeon, *Manager*
EMP: 115
SALES (est): 23.4MM
SALES (corp-wide): 21.3MM **Privately Held**
SIC: 1711 Warm air heating & air conditioning contractor

(P-2217)
ONE CALL PLUMBER SANTA BARBARA
1016 Cliff Dr Apt 309, Santa Barbara
(93109-1784)
PHONE..................805 364-6337
EMP: 100
SALES (est): 2.1MM **Privately Held**
SIC: 1711 Plumbing contractors

(P-2218)
ONTARIO REFRIGERATION SVC INC (PA)
635 S Mountain Ave, Ontario (91762-4114)
PHONE..................909 984-2771
Phillip C Talleur, *President*
Julie Carrington, *President*
Phil Talleur, *General Mgr*
Tammy Aragon, *Admin Sec*
Koko Toprakjian, *Technician*
EMP: 54 **EST:** 1971
SQ FT: 5,300
SALES (est): 46.9MM **Privately Held**
SIC: 1711 Warm air heating & air conditioning contractor; heating & air conditioning contractors

(P-2219)
ORANGE COUNTY SERVICES INC
Also Called: George Brazil Plbg Htg & AC
3022 N Hesperian St, Santa Ana
(92706-1151)
PHONE..................714 541-9753
Mike Jones, *General Mgr*
EMP: 50
SALES (corp-wide): 1.9MM **Privately Held**
SIC: 1711 1731 Plumbing contractors; electrical work
PA: Orange County Services Inc
9405 Jefferson Blvd
Culver City CA 90232
310 515-1001

(P-2220)
ORANGE PACIFIC PLUMBING INC
801 Panorama Rd, Fullerton (92831-1029)
PHONE..................714 992-4547
Steven Hartshorn, *President*
Bonnie Hartshorn, *Treasurer*
EMP: 66
SQ FT: 5,000
SALES (est): 3.9MM **Privately Held**
WEB: www.orangepacific.com
SIC: 1711 Plumbing contractors

(P-2221)
ORIGINAL SID BLACKMAN PLBG INC
1160 S 2nd St, El Centro (92243-3446)
PHONE..................760 352-3632
Thomas Blackman, *President*
Monique Caldera, *Office Mgr*
Michael Wickline, *Admin Sec*
EMP: 68
SALES: 8.2MM **Privately Held**
WEB: www.blackmanplumbing.net
SIC: 1711 Plumbing contractors

(P-2222)
PACIFIC PRODUCTION PLUMBING (PA)
1584 Pioneer Way, El Cajon (92020-1638)
PHONE..................951 509-3100
Daniel Whitt, *President*
Kim Whitt, *Treasurer*
Bruce Magellan, *Vice Pres*
Tobin Whitt, *Vice Pres*
Karen Whitt, *Admin Sec*
EMP: 50
SQ FT: 3,000

SALES (est): 48.4MM **Privately Held**
SIC: 1711 Plumbing contractors

(P-2223)
PACIFIC RIM MECH CONTRS INC
1701 E Edinger Ave Ste F2, Santa Ana
(92705-5028)
PHONE..................714 285-2600
John Heusner, *Manager*
EMP: 61
SALES (corp-wide): 131.9MM **Privately Held**
WEB: www.prmech.com
SIC: 1711 Mechanical contractor
PA: Pacific Rim Mechanical Contractors, Inc.
7655 Convoy Ct
San Diego CA 92111
858 974-6500

(P-2224)
PACIFIC RIM MECH CONTRS INC (PA)
Also Called: HONEYWELL AUTHORIZED DEALER
7655 Convoy Ct, San Diego (92111-1103)
PHONE..................858 974-6500
Joseph Mucher, *CEO*
Eric Bader, *CFO*
Craig Condon, *Vice Pres*
Colin Cook, *Vice Pres*
John Heusner, *Vice Pres*
EMP: 400
SQ FT: 50,000
SALES: 131.9MM **Privately Held**
WEB: www.prmech.com
SIC: 1711 Mechanical contractor

(P-2225)
PAN-PACIFIC MECHANICAL LLC (PA)
18250 Euclid St, Fountain Valley
(92708-6112)
PHONE..................949 474-9170
Cindy Lanette McMackin, *President*
Ronald G McMackin, *CEO*
Steve Sylvester, *CFO*
Ryan Cavanaugh, *Vice Pres*
Pat George, *Vice Pres*
▲ **EMP:** 150
SQ FT: 60,000
SALES: 237MM **Privately Held**
WEB: www.panpacplumbing.com
SIC: 1711 Plumbing contractors

(P-2226)
PAN-PACIFIC MECHANICAL LLC
1205 Chrysler Dr, Menlo Park
(94025-1134)
PHONE..................650 561-8810
Tom Sakurai, *Manager*
Henry Hillebrecht, *Foreman/Supr*
EMP: 661
SALES (corp-wide): 237MM **Privately Held**
SIC: 1711 Plumbing contractors
PA: Pan-Pacific Mechanical Llc
18250 Euclid St
Fountain Valley CA 92708
949 474-9170

(P-2227)
PAN-PACIFIC MECHANICAL LLC
Also Called: Pan-Pacific Plumbing & Mech
11622 El Camino Real, San Diego
(92130-2049)
PHONE..................858 764-2464
EMP: 189
SALES (corp-wide): 290MM **Privately Held**
SIC: 1711 Mechanical contractor
PA: Pan-Pacific Mechanical Llc
18250 Euclid St
Fountain Valley CA 92708
949 474-9170

(P-2228)
PAR ENGINEERING INC
Also Called: Commercial Cooling
17855 Arenth Ave, City of Industry
(91748-1129)
PHONE..................626 964-8700
Hassan John Milani, *President*
Jacky Vong, *Accountant*
Jeannine Lugo, *Supervisor*
EMP: 50 **EST:** 1965

SQ FT: 70,000
SALES (est): 13MM **Privately Held**
SIC: 1711 Refrigeration contractor

(P-2229)
PATTERN RENEWABLES 2 LP (HQ)
1088 Sansome St, San Francisco
(94111-1308)
PHONE..................415 283-4000
EMP: 150 **EST:** 2016
SALES: 2MM
SALES (corp-wide): 483MM **Publicly Held**
SIC: 1711 Solar energy contractor
PA: Pattern Energy Group Inc.
1088 Sansome St
San Francisco CA 94111
415 283-4000

(P-2230)
PINASCO PLUMBING & HEATING INC
Also Called: Pinasco Mechinical
2145 E Taylor St, Stockton (95205-6337)
P.O. Box 55287 (95205-8787)
PHONE..................209 463-7793
Tom Pinasco, *President*
John Pinasco, *Treasurer*
Joseph Pinasco, *Admin Sec*
EMP: 50
SQ FT: 1,000
SALES (est): 8.3MM **Privately Held**
SIC: 1711 Plumbing contractors

(P-2231)
PIPE RESTORATION INC
Also Called: Ace Duraflo Pipe Restoration
3122 W Alpine St, Santa Ana (92704-6912)
PHONE..................714 564-7600
Larry Gillanders, *CEO*
Mike Carper, *Exec VP*
Ray Munguia, *VP Opers*
EMP: 50 **EST:** 2001
SQ FT: 6,000
SALES (est): 8.3MM **Privately Held**
WEB: www.restoremypipes.com
SIC: 1711 Plumbing contractors

(P-2232)
PIPELINE RESTORATION PLUMBING
2700 S Main St Ste E, Santa Ana
(92707-3431)
PHONE..................714 957-5836
EMP: 50
SALES (est): 83.4K **Privately Held**
SIC: 1711 Plumbing contractors

(P-2233)
PLUMB TECH INC
1242 E Maple Ave, El Segundo
(90245-3258)
PHONE..................310 322-4925
Greg Misic, *President*
Jim Gonzales, *Vice Pres*
EMP: 57
SALES (est): 2.6MM **Privately Held**
SIC: 1711 Plumbing contractors

(P-2234)
PLUMBING PIPING & CNSTR INC
5950 Lakeshore Dr, Cypress (90630-3371)
PHONE..................714 821-0490
Bruce Cook Jr, *President*
Craig Zimmerman, *Vice Pres*
Sheryl Spark, *Instructor*
EMP: 100 **EST:** 1960
SQ FT: 12,600
SALES (est): 29.9MM **Privately Held**
WEB: www.1ppc.com
SIC: 1711 Plumbing, heating, air-conditioning contractors

(P-2235)
PLUMBING SYSTEMS WEST INC
31491 Outer Highway 10, Redlands
(92373-7568)
PHONE..................909 794-3823
Bob Grable, *President*
EMP: 68
SALES (est): 1.4MM **Privately Held**
SIC: 1711 Plumbing contractors

(P-2236)
PPC ENTERPRISES INC
Also Called: Premier Plumbing Company
5920 Rickenbacker Ave, Riverside
(92504-1042)
PHONE..................951 354-5402
Jeffrey Geiger, *President*
Dawn Geiger, *CFO*
EMP: 125
SQ FT: 10,000
SALES (est): 15.3MM **Privately Held**
SIC: 1711 Plumbing contractors

(P-2237)
PRIBUSS ENGINEERING INC
523 Mayfair Ave, South San Francisco
(94080-4509)
PHONE..................650 588-0447
Bayardo Chamorro, *President*
John Pribuss, *CFO*
Augustin Chamorro, *Vice Pres*
Rick Bergamaschi, *Project Mgr*
Erik Dohemann, *Project Mgr*
EMP: 70
SQ FT: 16,000
SALES (est): 19.9MM **Privately Held**
WEB: www.pribuss.com
SIC: 1711 7623 Warm air heating & air
conditioning contractor; fire sprinkler sys-
tem installation; refrigeration service & re-
pair

(P-2238)
PRO-CRAFT CONSTRUCTION INC
500 Iowa St Ste 100, Redlands
(92373-8070)
PHONE..................909 790-5222
Timothy McFayden, *President*
Susan Mc Fayden, *CFO*
Susan McFayden, *CFO*
Chris McFayden, *Vice Pres*
Anthony Avila, *Project Mgr*
EMP: 142
SALES (est): 17.3MM **Privately Held**
SIC: 1711 Plumbing contractors

(P-2239)
PRODUCTION PLUS PLUMBING INC
2472 Grand Ave, Vista (92081-7804)
PHONE..................760 597-0235
Robert Labaron, *President*
McIntosh Cindy, *Manager*
EMP: 126
SALES (corp-wide): 12.4MM **Privately Held**
WEB: www.productionplusplumbing.com
SIC: 1711 Plumbing contractors
PA: Production Plus Plumbing, Inc.
312 Dawson Dr
Camarillo CA
760 597-0235

(P-2240)
PROGRESSIVE POWER GROUP INC
12552 Western Ave, Garden Grove
(92841-4013)
PHONE..................714 899-2300
Ross A Butcher, *CEO*
Scott Kessinger, *Vice Pres*
Chris Hammerstone, *Principal*
Chris Staskewicz, *Principal*
Travis Mashin, *General Mgr*
EMP: 50
SQ FT: 12,000
SALES (est): 12.2MM **Privately Held**
SIC: 1711 5211 Solar energy contractor;
solar heating equipment

(P-2241)
PURONICS RETAIL SERVICES INC
5775 Las Positas Rd, Livermore
(94551-7819)
PHONE..................925 456-7000
Scott A Batiste, *CEO*
Mark H Cosmez II, *CFO*
EMP: 60
SQ FT: 25,000
SALES (est): 4.6MM **Privately Held**
SIC: 1711 Plumbing contractors

(P-2242)
QUICK SYSTEMS INC
5042 Wilshire Blvd # 28533, Los Angeles
(90036-4305)
PHONE..................702 335-3574
Alma Roundy, *CEO*
Stewart Knudson, *CEO*
EMP: 50 EST: 2011
SQ FT: 6,000
SALES: 6.4MM **Privately Held**
SIC: 1711 Solar energy contractor

(P-2243)
R A SCHREIBER PLUMBING
2358 Tavern Rd, Alpine (91901-3107)
P.O. Box 1315 (91903-1315)
PHONE..................619 659-3101
R A Schreiber, *Owner*
EMP: 50 EST: 1986
SALES: 8MM **Privately Held**
SIC: 1711 Plumbing contractors

(P-2244)
R B SPENCER INC
Also Called: Honeywell Authorized Dealer
1188 Hassett Ave, Yuba City (95991-7212)
PHONE..................530 674-8307
Robert B Spencer, *President*
Brigit Spencer, *CFO*
EMP: 52
SQ FT: 8,000
SALES (est): 10.2MM **Privately Held**
WEB: www.rbspencerinc.com
SIC: 1711 Warm air heating & air condi-
tioning contractor

(P-2245)
RA HUGHES ENTERPRISES IN
9316 Abraham Way, Santee (92071-2861)
PHONE..................619 390-4880
Ra Hughes, *Owner*
EMP: 50
SALES (est): 1.5MM **Privately Held**
SIC: 1711 Septic system construction

(P-2246)
RAM MECHANICAL INC
3506 Moore Rd, Ceres (95307-9402)
PHONE..................209 531-9155
Neil Hodgson, *Principal*
Tom Bawdon, *Project Mgr*
Greg Peden, *Project Mgr*
Gary Broadwell, *Electrical Engi*
Rob Stevenson, *Controller*
EMP: 60
SQ FT: 22,500
SALES: 15MM **Privately Held**
WEB: www.ram-mechanical.com
SIC: 1711 8711 3599 3535 Mechanical
contractor; engineering services; custom
machinery; conveyors & conveying equip-
ment

(P-2247)
RANDO AAA HVAC INC
Also Called: A A A Furnace Company
1712 Stone Ave Ste 1, San Jose
(95125-1309)
PHONE..................408 293-4717
Jim Rando, *President*
Marrissa Rando, *Principal*
EMP: 50
SQ FT: 5,000
SALES (est): 8.7MM **Privately Held**
SIC: 1711 3444 3433 Warm air heating &
air conditioning contractor; ventilation &
duct work contractor; sheet metalwork;
heating equipment, except electric

(P-2248)
RAWLINGS MECHANICAL CORP (PA)
11615 Pendleton St, Sun Valley
(91352-2502)
P.O. Box 703 (91353-0703)
PHONE..................323 875-2040
Robert S Bratton, *President*
Rex Horney, *Vice Pres*
Patricia Wood, *Admin Sec*
Ken Burton, *Project Mgr*
Brian Foster, *Project Mgr*
EMP: 69 EST: 1953
SQ FT: 22,000
SALES: 29.8MM **Privately Held**
SIC: 1711 Mechanical contractor

(P-2249)
RE MILANO PLUMBING CORP
4881 Sunrise Dr Ste B, Martinez
(94553-4304)
P.O. Box 1383 (94553-7383)
PHONE..................925 500-1372
Leigha M Ramirez, *CEO*
Robert Romeo, *President*
EMP: 50
SQ FT: 7,000
SALES: 4MM **Privately Held**
SIC: 1711 Plumbing contractors

(P-2250)
REAL GOODS SOLAR INC
41567 Cherry St, Murrieta (92562-9193)
PHONE..................951 304-3301
John Shaeffer, *Branch Mgr*
EMP: 125 **Publicly Held**
SIC: 1711 Solar energy contractor
PA: Real Goods Solar, Inc.
110 16th St Ste 300
Denver CO 80202

(P-2251)
REFRIGERATION SOLUTIONS LLC
1166 National Dr Ste 10, Sacramento
(95834-1978)
PHONE..................916 281-2000
Thomas A Ryan, *Mng Member*
EMP: 135
SALES (est): 83.4K
SALES (corp-wide): 958.4MM **Publicly Held**
SIC: 1711 Refrigeration contractor
HQ: Source Refrigeration & Hvac, Inc.
800 E Orangethorpe Ave
Anaheim CA 92801

(P-2252)
REGENCY FIRE PROTECTION INC
7651 Densmore Ave, Van Nuys
(91406-2043)
PHONE..................818 982-0126
Jay Zohar Rapaport, *President*
Tal Dagan, *Executive*
Ron Parsay, *Manager*
EMP: 60
SQ FT: 7,500
SALES (est): 11.4MM **Privately Held**
WEB: www.regencyfire.com
SIC: 1711 7382 Fire sprinkler system in-
stallation; burglar alarm maintenance &
monitoring; fire alarm maintenance &
monitoring; protective devices, security

(P-2253)
RELIABLE ENERGY MANAGEMENT INC
Also Called: Honeywell Authorized Dealer
7201 Rosecrans Ave, Paramount
(90723-2501)
PHONE..................562 984-5511
George R Garcia, *President*
Judy Garcia, *Exec VP*
David Reyes, *Vice Pres*
Sal Salazar, *Program Mgr*
Isabel Garibay, *Office Mgr*
EMP: 80
SQ FT: 6,000
SALES (est): 19.1MM **Privately Held**
WEB: www.relenergy.com
SIC: 1711 Heating & air conditioning con-
tractors

(P-2254)
RENOVA ENERGY CORP
75181 Mediterranean, Palm Desert
(92211-9094)
PHONE..................760 568-3413
Vincent Battaglia, *Ch of Bd*
Marvin Roman, *President*
Lea Goodsell, *Exec VP*
Patrick Sheehan, *Vice Pres*
Aaron Gamez, *Human Res Mgr*
EMP: 50
SQ FT: 5,200
SALES (est): 14.1MM **Privately Held**
WEB: www.renovasolar.com
SIC: 1711 Solar energy contractor

(P-2255)
RESIDENTIAL FIRE SYSTEMS INC
8085 E Crystal Dr, Anaheim (92807-2523)
PHONE..................714 666-8450
Ty Maley, *President*
Ruben Hernandez, *Treasurer*
Cesar Anchondo, *Vice Pres*
Jack Maley, *Vice Pres*
Danny Camorlinga, *General Mgr*
EMP: 75 EST: 2000
SQ FT: 6,200
SALES: 19.5MM **Privately Held**
WEB: www.residentialfiresys.com
SIC: 1711 5063 Fire sprinkler system in-
stallation; signaling equipment, electrical

(P-2256)
RITCHIE PLUMBING INC
11320 Lombardy Ln, Moreno Valley
(92557-5739)
PHONE..................949 709-7575
Lance Ritchie, *President*
EMP: 120
SQ FT: 7,500
SALES (est): 6.7MM **Privately Held**
WEB: www.ritchieplumbing.com
SIC: 1711 Plumbing contractors

(P-2257)
ROBINSON COMPANY CONTRS INC
Also Called: Robinson Electric
8871 Troy St, Spring Valley (91977-2638)
PHONE..................619 697-6040
Thomas Petree, *CEO*
Donna Garrett, *Office Mgr*
Spencer Tilton, *Director*
EMP: 52
SQ FT: 1,200
SALES (est): 10MM **Privately Held**
WEB: www.robinsonelectric.com
SIC: 1711 6513 Warm air heating & air
conditioning contractor; apartment build-
ing operators

(P-2258)
RODDA ELECTRIC INC (PA)
380 Carrol Ct Ste L, Brentwood
(94513-7353)
PHONE..................925 240-6024
Raymond Rodda, *CEO*
EMP: 60
SQ FT: 21,000
SALES (est): 26.5MM **Privately Held**
SIC: 1711 1731 Solar energy contractor;
general electrical contractor

(P-2259)
ROUNTREE PLUMBING AND HTG INC
1624 Santa Clara Dr 130, Roseville
(95661-3554)
PHONE..................650 298-0300
Stephen Singewald, *President*
Pat Singewald, *Corp Secy*
EMP: 60
SQ FT: 10,000
SALES (est): 11.7MM **Privately Held**
WEB: www.rountreeinc.com
SIC: 1711 Plumbing contractors; warm air
heating & air conditioning contractor

(P-2260)
RPM MECHANICAL - A JOINT VENTR
2919 E Victoria St, Compton (90221-5614)
PHONE..................858 565-4131
Kevan Steffey, *President*
EMP: 100
SALES (est): 7.2MM **Privately Held**
SIC: 1711 Plumbing contractors

(P-2261)
RUSSELL MECHANICAL INC
3251 Monier Cir Ste A, Rancho Cordova
(95742-6812)
PHONE..................916 635-2522
Danny L Russell, *President*
Steve Russell, *Vice Pres*
Karen Russell, *Principal*
Will Wakamiya, *Engrg Dir*
Jeremy Hodges, *Purchasing*
EMP: 90
SQ FT: 22,000

SALES (est): 18.9MM **Privately Held**
SIC: 1711 1799 7389 3441 Mechanical contractor; welding on site; design services; fabricated structural metal

(P-2262)
S S W MECHANICAL CNSTR INC
Also Called: Ssw
670 S Oleander Rd, Palm Springs (92264-1502)
P.O. Box 3160 (92263-3160)
PHONE..................760 327-1481
Sean Wood, *President*
W T Hayes, *Vice Pres*
EMP: 140
SQ FT: 7,000
SALES (est): 24.1MM **Privately Held**
WEB: www.sswmechanical.com
SIC: 1711 Plumbing contractors

(P-2263)
SABER PLUMBING INC
325 Market Pl, Escondido (92029-1302)
P.O. Box 1779, San Marcos (92079-1779)
PHONE..................760 480-5716
Glenn Phil Napierskie II, *President*
Annette Mott, *Admin Mgr*
Leo Kambara, *Assistant*
EMP: 60 EST: 1980
SQ FT: 12,500
SALES (est): 10MM **Privately Held**
WEB: www.saberplumbing.com
SIC: 1711 Plumbing contractors

(P-2264)
SAN BENITO HTG & SHTMTL INC
Also Called: Honeywell Authorized Dealer
1771 San Felipe Rd, Hollister (95023-2543)
P.O. Box 321 (95024-0321)
PHONE..................831 637-1112
Robert Rodriguez, *President*
Enrique T Rodriguez, *Treasurer*
Araceli Rodriguez, *Vice Pres*
Priscilla Rodriguez, *Vice Pres*
EMP: 85
SQ FT: 12,000
SALES (est): 10.4MM **Privately Held**
SIC: 1711 1761 Warm air heating & air conditioning contractor; sheet metalwork; roofing contractor

(P-2265)
SAWYERS HEATING & AC
5272 Jerusalem Ct Ste D, Modesto (95356-9278)
PHONE..................209 416-7700
Derek Sawyer, *President*
Weston Sawyer, *Admin Sec*
EMP: 75
SQ FT: 10,000
SALES (est): 8MM **Privately Held**
SIC: 1711 Warm air heating & air conditioning contractor

(P-2266)
SCHMIDT FIRE PROTECTION CO INC
4760 Murphy Canyon Rd # 100, San Diego (92123-4334)
PHONE..................858 279-6122
John J Durso, *President*
Greg Konold, *Vice Pres*
Leonard Moore, *Project Mgr*
Michael Davis, *Purch Agent*
EMP: 72
SQ FT: 13,800
SALES (est): 13.1MM **Privately Held**
WEB: www.schmidtfireprotection.com
SIC: 1711 Fire sprinkler system installation

(P-2267)
SCORPIO ENTERPRISES
Also Called: Airemasters Air Conditioning
12556 Mccann Dr, Santa Fe Springs (90670-3337)
PHONE..................562 946-9464
Charles Everett Thompson, *CEO*
Linda Thompson, *Vice Pres*
Ness Melham, *Project Mgr*
Glenn Gracie, *Manager*
▼ EMP: 55
SQ FT: 14,800

SALES (est): 11.6MM **Privately Held**
WEB: www.airemasters-ac.com
SIC: 1711 Warm air heating & air conditioning contractor; heating & air conditioning contractors

(P-2268)
SDG ENTERPRISES
Also Called: Century West Plumbing
822 Hampshire Rd Ste H, Westlake Village (91361-2850)
PHONE..................805 777-7978
Nick Simili, *President*
Vincent Simili, *CFO*
Vincent Dipinto, *Vice Pres*
Robert Garcia, *Vice Pres*
EMP: 100
SQ FT: 3,000
SALES (est): 14.8MM **Privately Held**
SIC: 1711 Plumbing, heating, air-conditioning contractors

(P-2269)
SEEMS PLUMBING CO INC
5400 W Rosecrans Ave Lowr, Hawthorne (90250-6686)
PHONE..................310 297-4969
Ed Hutcherson, *President*
Jonathan Sevel, *Administration*
EMP: 50
SALES (est): 7.4MM **Privately Held**
SIC: 1711 Plumbing contractors

(P-2270)
SERVI-TECH CONTROLS INC (PA)
470 W Warwick Ave, Clovis (93619-0405)
PHONE..................559 264-6679
Glenn L Johnson, *President*
Janelle R Silva, *Treasurer*
Nicholas Johnson, *Project Mgr*
Clint Petty, *Project Mgr*
Esther Gregory, *Controller*
EMP: 53
SALES (est): 11.3MM **Privately Held**
WEB: www.servi-techcontrols.com
SIC: 1711 Warm air heating & air conditioning contractor; ventilation & duct work contractor

(P-2271)
SERVICE GENIUS LOS ANGELES INC
9761 Variel Ave, Chatsworth (91311-4315)
PHONE..................818 200-3379
William Monk, *President*
EMP: 100
SALES (est): 10MM **Privately Held**
SIC: 1711 Heating & air conditioning contractors

(P-2272)
SHELDON MECHANICAL CORPORATION
26015 Avenue Hall, Santa Clarita (91355-1241)
PHONE..................661 286-1361
Dan Boute, *President*
Beverly Nisenson, *Treasurer*
Stanley Nisenson, *Vice Pres*
Chrystal Bout'e, *Admin Sec*
Shaun Ostrowsky, *Accountant*
EMP: 80
SQ FT: 45,000
SALES (est): 18.9MM **Privately Held**
SIC: 1711 Mechanical contractor; warm air heating & air conditioning contractor

(P-2273)
SHERWOOD MECHANICAL INC
6630 Top Gun St, San Diego (92121-4112)
PHONE..................858 679-3000
Mitch Roberts, *President*
James Robert, *COO*
James Roberts, *COO*
Bill Smyth, *CFO*
Art Ojeda, *Risk Mgmt Dir*
EMP: 100
SALES (est): 17.8MM **Privately Held**
WEB: www.sherwoodmechanical.com
SIC: 1711 Mechanical contractor

(P-2274)
SILICON VALLEY MECHANICAL INC
2115 Ringwood Ave, San Jose (95131-1725)
P.O. Box 10415, Southport NC (28461-0415)
PHONE..................408 943-0380
Blaine Flickner, *CEO*
Dania Amireh-Baker, *CFO*
Donavon Winters, *Officer*
Hannah Monteiro, *Office Mgr*
Daniel Neumeister, *IT Specialist*
EMP: 89
SALES (est): 35MM **Privately Held**
SIC: 1711 Mechanical contractor; heating & air conditioning contractors

(P-2275)
SKYPOWER HOLDINGS LLC
4700 Wilshire Blvd, Los Angeles (90010-3853)
PHONE..................323 860-4900
Kerry Adler, *CEO*
AVI Shemesh, *President*
EMP: 101
SALES (est): 27MM **Privately Held**
SIC: 1711 Solar energy contractor

(P-2276)
SMART ENERGY SOLAR INC
Also Called: Smart Energy USA
1641 Comm St, Corona (92880)
PHONE..................800 405-1978
Leo Joaquin Bautista, *Principal*
EMP: 120
SALES (est): 16.9MM **Privately Held**
SIC: 1711 Solar energy contractor

(P-2277)
SOLAR COMPANY INC
20861 Wilbeam Ave Ste 1, Castro Valley (94546-5832)
PHONE..................510 888-9488
Mark Danenhower, *President*
Duane Redman, *CFO*
Adrian Hirt, *Web Dvlpr*
Rachelle Houle, *Human Res Mgr*
George Koliavas, *Sales Staff*
EMP: 90
SQ FT: 4,000
SALES: 28MM **Privately Held**
SIC: 1711 Solar energy contractor

(P-2278)
SOLAR ENERGY LLC
21600 Oxnard St Ste 1200, Woodland Hills (91367-4949)
PHONE..................818 449-5816
EMP: 80 EST: 2009
SALES (est): 7.2MM **Privately Held**
SIC: 1711

(P-2279)
SOLAR SPECTRUM LLC
Also Called: Sungevity
150 Linden St, Oakland (94607-2538)
PHONE..................844 777-6527
Patrick McGivern, *CEO*
William Nettles, *President*
David White, *CFO*
Sloane Morgan, *Officer*
Chris Murphy, *Vice Pres*
EMP: 266
SALES (est): 6.5MM **Privately Held**
SIC: 1711 8713 Solar energy contractor; surveying services

(P-2280)
SOLCIUS LLC
12155 Magnolia Ave 12b, Riverside (92503-4967)
PHONE..................951 772-0030
Bryan Jackson, *Branch Mgr*
Wayne Tomlinson, *Vice Pres*
Jason Harman, *Surgery Dir*
Neil Merkling, *Financial Analy*
Savanna Meyers, *Opers Staff*
EMP: 324
SALES (corp-wide): 45MM **Privately Held**
SIC: 1711 Solar energy contractor
PA: Solcius, Llc
1555 N Freedom Blvd
Provo UT 84604
800 960-4150

(P-2281)
SOLECON INDUSTRIAL CONTRS INC
1401 Mcwilliams Way, Modesto (95351-1125)
PHONE..................209 572-7390
Jeffrey Grover, *President*
Allen Layman, *Treasurer*
Elaine Grover, *Vice Pres*
Will Grover, *Vice Pres*
Dave Hedrick, *Vice Pres*
EMP: 70
SQ FT: 15,000
SALES: 16.3MM **Privately Held**
WEB: www.soleconindustrial.com
SIC: 1711 Plumbing contractors

(P-2282)
SOLEEVA ENERGY INC
1938 Junction Ave, San Jose (95131-2102)
PHONE..................408 396-4954
Ahmad Qazi, *CEO*
CJ Jocson, *Partner*
Ralph Ahlgren, *President*
Klaus Petry, *CTO*
Michele Miranda, *Project Mgr*
▲ EMP: 55
SQ FT: 17,000
SALES (est): 4.4MM **Privately Held**
SIC: 1711 Solar energy contractor

(P-2283)
SOURCE RFRGN & HVAC INC (DH)
800 E Orangethorpe Ave, Anaheim (92801-1123)
PHONE..................714 578-2300
Adam Coffey, *President*
Rick Kwiatkowski, *Vice Pres*
Scott Smith, *Principal*
Phil Norman, *Business Anlyst*
Mike Ellis, *Technical Staff*
EMP: 183
SALES (est): 356.7MM
SALES (corp-wide): 958.4MM **Publicly Held**
WEB: www.sourcerefrigeration.com
SIC: 1711 1731 Refrigeration contractor; electrical work
HQ: Coolsys, Inc.
145 S State College Blvd
Brea CA 92821
714 510-9577

(P-2284)
SOUTH CHINA SHEET METAL INC
Also Called: General Restaurant Equipment
1740 Albion St, Los Angeles (90031-2520)
PHONE..................323 225-1522
Kam C Law, *CEO*
T K Yeung, *Vice Pres*
▲ EMP: 65
SQ FT: 24,000
SALES (est): 7.3MM **Privately Held**
WEB: www.generalrestaurant.com
SIC: 1711 3589 3444 Ventilation & duct work contractor; refrigeration contractor; commercial cooking & foodwarming equipment; sheet metalwork

(P-2285)
SOUTH COAST MECHANICAL INC
800 E Orangethorpe Ave, Anaheim (92801-1123)
PHONE..................714 738-6644
James Reynolds, *CEO*
Zoltan Bulgozdi, *President*
Joe Wisdom, *Project Mgr*
Sergio Corona, *Project Engr*
John Shirley, *Foreman/Supr*
EMP: 75
SALES (est): 22MM **Privately Held**
WEB: www.southcoastmechanical.com
SIC: 1711 Mechanical contractor

(P-2286)
SOUTH VALLEY PLUMBING INC
3750 Charter Park Dr F, San Jose (95136-1394)
PHONE..................408 265-5566
Robert Walker III, *President*
EMP: 150 EST: 1960
SQ FT: 19,000

▲ = Import ▼=Export
◆ =Import/Export

SALES (est): 10.2MM **Privately Held**
SIC: 1711 Plumbing contractors; fire sprinkler system installation

(P-2287)
SOUTHLAND INDUSTRIES (PA)
12131 Western Ave, Garden Grove (92841-2914)
PHONE..........................800 613-6240
Theodore D Lynch, *Ch of Bd*
Charles M Allen, *COO*
Kevin J Coghlan, *CFO*
Kevin Coghlan, *CFO*
Tony SF Wang, *Treasurer*
EMP: 50 EST: 1949
SALES: 1B **Privately Held**
WEB: www.southlandind.com
SIC: 1711 Plumbing, heating, air-conditioning contractors

(P-2288)
STERLING PLUMBING INC
3111 W Central Ave, Santa Ana (92704-5302)
PHONE..........................714 641-5480
Rodney Robbins, *President*
Leslie Schaefer, *CFO*
Lesley Levinson, *Human Resources*
EMP: 100
SALES (est): 13.5MM **Privately Held**
WEB: www.sterlingplumbinginc.com
SIC: 1711 Plumbing contractors

(P-2289)
STRATEGIC MECHANICAL INC
4661 E Commerce Ave, Fresno (93725-2204)
PHONE..........................559 291-1952
Lonnie F Petty, *President*
Donn Petty, *Treasurer*
Chad Petty, *Admin Sec*
Katherine Aldrich, *Controller*
EMP: 120
SQ FT: 60,000
SALES (est): 26MM **Privately Held**
SIC: 1711 3444 3441 Mechanical contractor; awnings & canopies; fabricated structural metal

(P-2290)
SUNBELT CONTROLS INC
735 N Todd Ave, Azusa (91702-2244)
PHONE..........................626 610-2340
Jim Boyd, *Branch Mgr*
Bob Hamill, *Vice Pres*
Scott Conley, *General Mgr*
Francis-Paul Dela Cruz, *Design Engr*
Jerry Le, *Design Engr*
EMP: 60
SALES (corp-wide): 777.3MM **Privately Held**
SIC: 1711 Heating & air conditioning contractors
HQ: Sunbelt Controls, Inc.
    4511 Willow Rd Ste 4
    Pleasanton CA 94588

(P-2291)
SUNPOWER CORPORATION SYSTEMS (DH)
Also Called: Powerlight
1414 Hrbour Way S Ste 190, Richmond (94804)
P.O. Box 3821, Sunnyvale (94088-3821)
PHONE..........................510 260-8200
Thomas L Dinwoodie, *CEO*
Daniel S Shugar, *President*
Peter Aschenbrenner, *Exec VP*
Lisa Bodensteiner, *Exec VP*
Charles D Boynton, *Exec VP*
◆ EMP: 100
SQ FT: 5,000
SALES (est): 55.2MM
SALES (corp-wide): 8.4B **Publicly Held**
WEB: www.powerlight.com
SIC: 1711 Solar energy contractor
HQ: Sunpower Corporation
    51 Rio Robles
    San Jose CA 95134
    408 240-5500

(P-2292)
SUNPRO SOLAR INC
34859 Frederick St # 101, Wildomar (92595-7007)
PHONE..........................951 678-7733
Adam Evans, *President*
Adam Joshua Evans, *President*
Bob Kornmann, *Engineer*
Kari Daum, *Consultant*
Lawrence Goda, *Consultant*
EMP: 64
SQ FT: 2,300
SALES (est): 4.7MM **Privately Held**
WEB: www.sunpro-solar.com
SIC: 1711 Solar energy contractor

(P-2293)
SUNRISE PLUMBING & MECH INC
7581 Hazard Ave Ste C, Westminster (92683-5351)
PHONE..........................562 424-0332
Richard Hubbel, *CEO*
Garnet Hubbel, *Principal*
EMP: 50
SALES (est): 6.5MM **Privately Held**
SIC: 1711 Plumbing contractors

(P-2294)
SUNRUN INSTALLATION SVCS INC
575 Dado St, San Jose (95131-1207)
PHONE..........................408 746-3062
EMP: 2000 **Publicly Held**
SIC: 1711 Solar energy contractor
HQ: Sunrun Installation Services Inc.
    775 Fiero Ln Ste 200
    San Luis Obispo CA 93401
    415 580-6900

(P-2295)
SUNRUN INSTALLATION SVCS INC (HQ)
775 Fiero Ln Ste 200, San Luis Obispo (93401-7904)
PHONE..........................415 580-6900
Lynn Jurich, *CEO*
Ryan Stepp, *Partner*
Robert Komin Jr, *CFO*
Lou Anatrella, *Vice Pres*
Mina Kim, *Admin Sec*
▲ EMP: 151
SQ FT: 26,000
SALES (est): 162.8MM **Publicly Held**
WEB: www.recsolar.com
SIC: 1711 Solar energy contractor

(P-2296)
SUPERIOR AUTOMATIC SPRNKLR CO
4378 Enterprise St, Fremont (94538-6305)
PHONE..........................408 946-7272
Bob Lawson, *President*
Peter Hulin, *President*
Marci Kearney, *Vice Pres*
EMP: 100 EST: 1973
SQ FT: 15,000
SALES (est): 24.5MM **Privately Held**
WEB: www.superior-fire.com
SIC: 1711 Fire sprinkler system installation

(P-2297)
SUTTLES PLUMBING & MECH CORP
2267 Agate Ct, Simi Valley (93065-1843)
PHONE..........................818 718-9779
Stephanie Aguilar, *President*
Bryan Suttles, *Vice Pres*
Stephen Suttles, *Vice Pres*
Sheralyn Suttles, *Admin Sec*
Todd Aguilar, *Safety Mgr*
EMP: 75 EST: 1970
SQ FT: 6,000
SALES: 12MM **Privately Held**
SIC: 1711 Plumbing contractors; warm air heating & air conditioning contractor

(P-2298)
TAO MECHANICAL LTD
136 Wright Brothers Ave, Livermore (94551-9240)
PHONE..........................925 447-5220
Mitchell Ibsen, *President*
EMP: 50

SQ FT: 16,250
SALES (est): 8.7MM **Privately Held**
SIC: 1711 Plumbing contractors

(P-2299)
TARPY HEATING & AIR
Also Called: Tarpy Plumbing Heating and Air
9723 Roe Dr, Santee (92071-1451)
PHONE..........................619 485-3311
Paul Tarpy, *President*
Jenee Tarpy, *Treasurer*
EMP: 50 EST: 2007
SQ FT: 2,100
SALES: 3MM **Privately Held**
SIC: 1711 Warm air heating & air conditioning contractor; heating & air conditioning contractors

(P-2300)
THERMA HOLDINGS LLC
2390 Bateman Ave, Duarte (91010-3312)
PHONE..........................626 446-1854
EMP: 50
SALES (corp-wide): 325.9MM **Privately Held**
SIC: 1711 Mechanical contractor
PA: Therma Holdings Llc
    1601 Las Plumas Ave
    San Jose CA 95133
    408 347-3400

(P-2301)
THERMAL MECHANICAL
425 Aldo Ave, Santa Clara (95054-2322)
P.O. Box 4730 (95056-4730)
PHONE..........................408 988-8744
Richard Rood, *CEO*
David Rood, *President*
Noel Pascual, *Officer*
Martin Burke, *Department Mgr*
Jennifer Mosher, *Administration*
EMP: 77
SQ FT: 30,000
SALES: 20.7MM **Privately Held**
WEB: www.thermalmech.com
SIC: 1711 Mechanical contractor

(P-2302)
THERMALAIR INC (HQ)
1140 N Red Gum St, Anaheim (92806-2516)
PHONE..........................714 630-3200
Stephen C Weiss, *CEO*
William Reece, *President*
Rich Perez, *Exec VP*
Theresa Bransky, *Admin Asst*
Delena Leanza, *Admin Asst*
EMP: 70 EST: 1948
SQ FT: 8,500
SALES (est): 16.7MM
SALES (corp-wide): 12.1MM **Privately Held**
WEB: www.thermalair.com
SIC: 1711 Mechanical contractor; ventilation & duct work contractor; refrigeration contractor
PA: General Engineering Western, Inc.
    1140 N Red Gum St
    Anaheim CA 92806
    714 630-3200

(P-2303)
THORPE DESIGN INC
410 Beatrice St Ct Ste A, Brentwood (94513)
P.O. Box 1149 (94513-3149)
PHONE..........................925 634-0787
James Thorpe, *President*
Renee Thorpe, *Treasurer*
Kim Jones, *Executive*
Scott Burke, *Department Mgr*
Eric Gonzales, *Department Mgr*
EMP: 60
SQ FT: 500
SALES (est): 13.3MM **Privately Held**
WEB: www.thorpedesign.com
SIC: 1711 Fire sprinkler system installation

(P-2304)
TONOPAH SOLAR ENERGY LLC
520 Broadway Fl 6, Santa Monica (90401-2420)
PHONE..........................310 315-2200
Kevin Smith,
Rosie Sandoval, *General Mgr*
▲ EMP: 60

SALES (est): 5.8MM **Privately Held**
SIC: 1711 Solar energy contractor

(P-2305)
TRILOGY PLUMBING INC
1525 S Sinclair St, Anaheim (92806-5934)
PHONE..........................714 441-2952
Dennis Burk, *President*
Linda Burk, *Vice Pres*
Mike McManus, *Director*
EMP: 250
SQ FT: 18,000
SALES (est): 32.6MM **Privately Held**
WEB: www.trilogyplumbing.com
SIC: 1711 Septic system construction

(P-2306)
TRUE AIR MECHANICAL INC
Also Called: True Home Heating and AC
4 Faraday, Irvine (92618-2714)
PHONE..........................888 316-0642
Scott Flora, *CEO*
Jeff Flora, *Principal*
Kaycee Stack, *Principal*
Steve Sippola, *Sales Staff*
EMP: 180
SALES (est): 18MM **Privately Held**
SIC: 1711 Heating & air conditioning contractors

(P-2307)
UNIVERSITY MARELICH MECH INC
1000 N Kraemer Pl, Anaheim (92806-2610)
PHONE..........................714 632-2600
Scott Baker, *Senior VP*
Walter S Baker, *CEO*
John R Wycoff, *CFO*
John Ellis, *Vice Pres*
EMP: 150
SQ FT: 24,384
SALES (est): 15.3MM
SALES (corp-wide): 8.1B **Publicly Held**
WEB: www.umm-inc.com
SIC: 1711 Mechanical contractor
PA: Emcor Group, Inc.
    301 Merritt 7 Fl 6
    Norwalk CT 06851
    203 849-7800

(P-2308)
UNIVERSITY MECHANICAL & (DH)
Also Called: Spira-Loc
1168 Fesler St, El Cajon (92020-1812)
PHONE..........................619 956-2500
Steve Shirley, *President*
Peter Novak, *CFO*
John Modjeski, *Senior VP*
Steve Thompson, *Vice Pres*
Jennifer Reilly, *Executive Asst*
EMP: 151
SQ FT: 47,000
SALES (est): 94.8MM
SALES (corp-wide): 8.1B **Publicly Held**
WEB: www.umec-ca.com
SIC: 1711 1623 8741 Mechanical contractor; plumbing contractors; warm air heating & air conditioning contractor; pipeline construction; construction management

(P-2309)
VALLEY CLARK PLBG & HTG CO INC (PA)
Also Called: Clark Plumbing Co
7640 Gloria Ave Ste L, Van Nuys (91406-1800)
PHONE..........................818 782-1047
Robert J Brunald, *President*
Traci Brunald, *Vice Pres*
EMP: 100
SQ FT: 8,000
SALES (est): 15MM **Privately Held**
WEB: www.clarkplumbing.com
SIC: 1711 Plumbing contractors

(P-2310)
VALLEY PROCESS SYSTEMS INC
3567 Benton St Ste 341, Santa Clara (95051-4404)
PHONE..........................408 261-1277
Kenneth D Salazar, *CEO*

P R O D U C T S & S V C S

EMP: 66
SQ FT: 3,200
SALES (est): 7.6MM **Privately Held**
WEB: www.valleyprocessinc.com
SIC: 1711 Process piping contractor

(P-2311)
VALS PLUMBING AND HEATING INC
413 Front St, Salinas (93901-3690)
PHONE.....................................831 424-1633
Ray Spears, *President*
Valerio L Roberti, *Chairman*
Laura Roberti, *Vice Pres*
EMP: 60
SQ FT: 12,500
SALES (est): 12.5MM **Privately Held**
SIC: 1711 5999 Warm air heating & air conditioning contractor; plumbing contractors; plumbing & heating supplies

(P-2312)
VILLARA CORPORATION (PA)
Also Called: Walk Through Video
4700 Lang Ave, McClellan (95652-2023)
PHONE.....................................916 646-2700
Calvin Rick Wylie, *Principal*
Gary Beutler, *CEO*
Tom Beutler, *Vice Pres*
Jeffrey Starsky, *Vice Pres*
Ali Cakus, *Executive*
▲ **EMP:** 482
SALES (est): 152MM **Privately Held**
WEB: www.beutlerhvac.com
SIC: 1711 Warm air heating & air conditioning contractor

(P-2313)
VILLARA CORPORATION
Also Called: Beutler Heating & AC
332 E Wetmore St, Manteca (95337-5741)
PHONE.....................................209 824-1082
Glen Hartsough, *General Mgr*
Scott Eagle, *Opers Staff*
Justin Sahota, *Sales Staff*
EMP: 65
SALES (corp-wide): 152MM **Privately Held**
WEB: www.beutlerhvac.com
SIC: 1711 Mechanical contractor
PA: Villara Corporation
   4700 Lang Ave
   Mcclellan CA 95652
   916 646-2700

(P-2314)
W L HICKEY SONS INC
930 E California Ave, Sunnyvale (94085-4502)
P.O. Box 61209 (94088-1209)
PHONE.....................................408 736-4938
Adam Hickey, *President*
Edward Hickey, *CFO*
Deborah Lopez, *General Mgr*
Enis Tursic, *Foreman/Supr*
Jody Ruiz, *Assistant*
EMP: 150 **EST:** 1904
SQ FT: 10,000
SALES (est): 24.5MM **Privately Held**
WEB: www.wlhs.com
SIC: 1711 Plumbing contractors

(P-2315)
WALTER ANDERSON PLUMBING INC
Also Called: Anderson Plbg Htg A Condition
1830 John Towers Ave, El Cajon (92020-1134)
PHONE.....................................619 449-7646
Mary Jean Anderson, *CEO*
Kyle Anderson, *Vice Pres*
Dick Crandall, *General Mgr*
Kelly Anderson, *Office Mgr*
EMP: 125 **EST:** 1978
SQ FT: 10,000
SALES (est): 27.9MM **Privately Held**
WEB: www.walterandersonplumbing.com
SIC: 1711 Plumbing contractors

(P-2316)
WAYNE MAPLES PLUMBING & HTG
317 W Cedar St, Eureka (95501-1698)
PHONE.....................................707 445-2500
Rodney Maples, *Partner*

Dale Maples, *Partner*
Mike Maples, *Partner*
Roger Maples, *Partner*
EMP: 55 **EST:** 1960
SQ FT: 7,000
SALES (est): 6.8MM **Privately Held**
WEB: www.maplesplumb.com
SIC: 1711 1623 Plumbing contractors; warm air heating & air conditioning contractor; underground utilities contractor

(P-2317)
WEEKS DRILLING AND PUMP CO (PA)
6100 Highway 12, Sebastopol (95472)
PHONE.....................................707 823-3184
Chris A Thompson, *CEO*
Charles Judson, *President*
EMP: 50
SQ FT: 13,000
SALES (est): 8MM **Privately Held**
SIC: 1711 5251 5084 3589 Plumbing, heating, air-conditioning contractors; pumps & pumping equipment; pumps & pumping equipment; water treatment equipment, industrial; water well servicing

(P-2318)
WEST COAST AC CO INC
1155 Pioneer Way Ste 101, El Cajon (92020-1964)
PHONE.....................................619 561-8000
David Dudley, *CEO*
James Clower, *Vice Pres*
Colin Fisher, *Vice Pres*
Katy Junk, *Admin Asst*
Christin Fisher, *Project Engr*
EMP: 150 **EST:** 1960
SQ FT: 24,000
SALES (est): 35.5MM **Privately Held**
WEB: www.wcac.com
SIC: 1711 Warm air heating & air conditioning contractor

(P-2319)
WESTATES MECHANICAL CORP INC
2566 Barrington Ct, Hayward (94545-1133)
PHONE.....................................510 635-9830
Nigel Cowan, *CEO*
Daniel Loeffler, *Senior VP*
William Bird, *Director*
EMP: 60
SALES (est): 12.7MM **Privately Held**
WEB: www.westatesmechanical.com
SIC: 1711 Fire sprinkler system installation

(P-2320)
WESTERN ALLIED MECHANICAL INC
1180 Obrien Dr, Menlo Park (94025-1411)
PHONE.....................................650 326-8290
Angela Simon, *CEO*
Robert Dills, *Shareholder*
Peter Kelly, *Shareholder*
Richard Taipale, *Shareholder*
James A Muscarella, *President*
EMP: 175
SALES (est): 63MM **Privately Held**
SIC: 1711 3444 Mechanical contractor; sheet metalwork

(P-2321)
WESTERN STATES FIRE PROTECTION
3720 Industry Ave Ste 107, Lakewood (90712-4135)
PHONE.....................................562 279-0770
Wesley Sue, *Manager*
EMP: 59
SALES (corp-wide): 3.7B **Privately Held**
SIC: 1711 Fire sprinkler system installation
HQ: Western States Fire Protection Company Inc
   7026 S Tucson Way
   Centennial CO 80112
   303 792-0022

(P-2322)
WESTERN STATES FIRE PROTECTION
4740 Northgate Blvd # 150, Sacramento (95834-1150)
PHONE.....................................916 924-1631
Jack White, *Manager*

Robert Soehner, *Manager*
EMP: 80
SALES (corp-wide): 3.7B **Privately Held**
SIC: 1711 Fire sprinkler system installation
HQ: Western States Fire Protection Company Inc
   7026 S Tucson Way
   Centennial CO 80112
   303 792-0022

(P-2323)
WHOLESALE SOLAR INC
412 N Mount Shasta Blvd, Mount Shasta (96067-2232)
P.O. Box 124 (96067-0124)
PHONE.....................................800 472-1142
Wil J Vandewiel, *CEO*
Jeremy Allen, *COO*
Charles Hirsh, *COO*
Michael Murray, *CFO*
Judith Roda, *Officer*
▼ **EMP:** 52
SQ FT: 5,000
SALES (est): 26.7MM **Privately Held**
WEB: www.wholesalesolar.com
SIC: 1711 Solar energy contractor

(P-2324)
WILMOR & SONS PLUMBING & CNSTR
8510 Thys Ct, Sacramento (95828-1007)
PHONE.....................................916 381-9114
Terry Wilson, *President*
Gary Morrissette, *CEO*
EMP: 80
SQ FT: 6,000
SALES (est): 11.1MM **Privately Held**
WEB: www.wilmorplumbing.com
SIC: 1711 Plumbing contractors

(P-2325)
XCEL MECHANICAL SYSTEMS INC
1710 W 130th St, Gardena (90249-2004)
PHONE.....................................310 660-0090
Kevin Michel, *President*
Phil Bonney, *Comms Mgr*
Bill Balch, *Project Mgr*
Jason Gordon, *Project Mgr*
Jesse Gaytan, *Foreman/Supr*
EMP: 175
SQ FT: 10,000
SALES (est): 49.5MM **Privately Held**
WEB: www.xcelmech.com
SIC: 1711 Mechanical contractor

(P-2326)
XL FIRE PROTECTION CO (PA)
3022 N Hesperian St, Santa Ana (92706-1151)
PHONE.....................................714 554-6132
Gregory J Caniglia, *President*
Laura Himmelberg, *Vice Pres*
Angel George, *Accountant*
Ron Dickson, *VP Sales*
Carlos Nunez, *Superintendent*
EMP: 65
SQ FT: 17,000
SALES (est): 23.5MM **Privately Held**
SIC: 1711 Fire sprinkler system installation

(P-2327)
ZERO ENERGY CONTRACTING LLC
13850 Cerritos Corporate, Cerritos (90703-2467)
PHONE.....................................626 701-3180
Michael Murphy,
EMP: 93
SALES (est): 6.8MM **Privately Held**
SIC: 1711 Solar energy contractor

1721 Painting & Paper Hanging Contractors

(P-2328)
A-1 ELITE PAINTING INC
56409 Yuma Trl, Yucca Valley (92284-3614)
PHONE.....................................760 365-6702
Charles Soffel, *President*
Ted Decicco, *Partner*
Glen Soffel, *Partner*

John Wright, *Partner*
Sharon Soffel, *Corp Secy*
EMP: 50
SALES: 2MM **Privately Held**
SIC: 1721 Painting & paper hanging

(P-2329)
ADVANCED INDUSTRIAL SVCS INC
Also Called: Advanced Industrial Svcs Cal
7831 Alondra Blvd, Paramount (90723-5005)
PHONE.....................................562 940-8305
Rex Johnston Jr, *President*
EMP: 85
SALES (est): 13.3MM **Privately Held**
SIC: 1721 Industrial painting

(P-2330)
ADVANTAGE PNTG SOLUTIONS INC
14734 Yorba Ct, Chino (91710-9210)
PHONE.....................................951 739-9204
Anthony Trujillo, *CEO*
Shevon Gonzales, *CFO*
EMP: 60
SALES: 3MM **Privately Held**
SIC: 1721 Commercial painting

(P-2331)
ANNA CORPORATION
Also Called: Jfp Company
2078 2nd St, Norco (92860-2804)
PHONE.....................................951 736-6037
Anna L Degiacomo, *President*
Jaime Flores, *Vice Pres*
Luis Tull, *Project Mgr*
EMP: 50
SQ FT: 6,500
SALES (est): 2.9MM **Privately Held**
SIC: 1721 Commercial painting

(P-2332)
ARCHITECTURAL COATINGS INC
1565 E Edinger Ave, Santa Ana (92705-4907)
PHONE.....................................714 701-1360
Sally K Rimmer, *President*
EMP: 50
SALES (est): 4.5MM **Privately Held**
SIC: 1721 Residential painting; commercial painting

(P-2333)
ARENA PAINTING CONTRACTORS INC
525 E Alondra Blvd, Gardena (90248-2903)
PHONE.....................................310 316-2446
Wilson Grant, *CEO*
Guy Grant II, *President*
EMP: 100
SQ FT: 10,000
SALES (est): 12.7MM **Privately Held**
SIC: 1721 Commercial painting

(P-2334)
ARMSTRONG INSTALLATION SERVICE
Also Called: Armstrong Construction Co
4575 San Pablo Ave, Emeryville (94608-3325)
PHONE.....................................408 777-1234
Mitchell Fine, *CEO*
Arthur Levine, *CFO*
EMP: 75
SQ FT: 8,000
SALES (est): 7.8MM **Privately Held**
WEB: www.armstrong1234.com
SIC: 1721 1761 1793 Exterior residential painting contractor; interior residential painting contractor; exterior commercial painting contractor; interior commercial painting contractor; roofing, siding & sheet metal work; glass & glazing work

(P-2335)
BORBON INCORPORATED
2560 W Woodland Dr, Anaheim (92801-2636)
PHONE.....................................714 994-0170
David Morales, *President*
Nicole Fiorentino, *Manager*
Tom Kim, *Manager*

EMP: 120 **EST:** 1974
SALES (est): 12.5MM **Privately Held**
WEB: www.borbon.net
SIC: 1721 Exterior residential painting contractor; wallcovering contractors

(P-2336)
C & O PAINTING INC
1500 N 4th St, San Jose (95112-4606)
PHONE..................................408 279-8011
Rick Ohlund, *President*
EMP: 50
SQ FT: 6,000
SALES (est): 4.3MM **Privately Held**
WEB: www.candopainting.com
SIC: 1721 Exterior commercial painting contractor; commercial wallcovering contractor

(P-2337)
C B B Z S INC
Also Called: Shapiro Ben Basat Painting
7015 Valjean Ave, Van Nuys (91406-3915)
PHONE..................................818 908-1900
Zvi Shapiro, *President*
Chaim B Basat, *Vice Pres*
EMP: 55
SQ FT: 5,500
SALES (est): 3.7MM **Privately Held**
SIC: 1721 Interior commercial painting contractor

(P-2338)
CAL/PAC PAINTINGS & COATINGS
608 N Eckhoff St, Orange (92868-1004)
PHONE..................................714 628-1514
Dave Bedillion, *President*
Mike Stevenson, *CFO*
Lee Ann Green, *Controller*
EMP: 60
SQ FT: 2,000
SALES (est): 5.5MM **Privately Held**
WEB: www.calpacpainting.com
SIC: 1721 Residential painting

(P-2339)
CERTIFIED COATINGS COMPANY
2320 Cordelia Rd, Fairfield (94534-1600)
PHONE..................................707 639-4414
David Joseph Brockman, *CEO*
Pamela Langan, *Admin Sec*
EMP: 100
SQ FT: 8,000
SALES (est): 24.7MM
SALES (corp-wide): 306.5MM **Privately Held**
SIC: 1721 Industrial painting
PA: Muehlhan Ag
Schlinckstr. 3
Hamburg 21107
407 527-10

(P-2340)
CRAMER PAINTING INC
4080 Mission Blvd, Montclair (91763-6011)
PHONE..................................909 397-5770
Steven L Cramer, *President*
Anne McWeeney, *Admin Sec*
EMP: 50
SQ FT: 6,800
SALES (est): 3.6MM **Privately Held**
WEB: www.cramerpainting.com
SIC: 1721 Commercial painting

(P-2341)
D C VIENT INC (PA)
1556 Cummins Dr, Modesto (95358-6412)
P.O. Box D (95352-3668)
PHONE..................................209 578-1224
Darlene Vient, *President*
Danielle Bell, *Shareholder*
Douglas J Vient Jr, *Corp Secy*
Douglas C Vient, *Vice Pres*
Alex Rowell, *Manager*
EMP: 300
SQ FT: 12,000
SALES (est): 21.7MM **Privately Held**
WEB: www.dcvient.com
SIC: 1721 Commercial painting

(P-2342)
D P S INC
Also Called: Empire Community Painting
1682 Langley Ave, Irvine (92614-5620)
PHONE..................................714 564-7900
Jason Reid, *President*
Tracy Meneses, *CFO*
Jeff Gunhus, *Vice Pres*
Matt Stewart, *Vice Pres*
Spencer Pepe, *Admin Sec*
EMP: 91
SQ FT: 1,000
SALES: 2.8MM **Privately Held**
WEB: www.nsgmail.com
SIC: 1721 Painting & paper hanging
PA: National Services Group, Inc.
1682 Langley Ave
Irvine CA 92614

(P-2343)
DAPCON INC
877 Commercial St, San Jose (95112-1411)
PHONE..................................408 573-7200
Fernando Silva, *President*
Albert Gomes, *Vice Pres*
Lucia Silva, *Vice Pres*
EMP: 80
SQ FT: 6,000
SALES (est): 3.4MM **Privately Held**
WEB: www.dapconinc.com
SIC: 1721 1742 Residential painting; commercial painting; drywall

(P-2344)
DUGGAN & ASSOCIATES INC
1442 W 135th St, Gardena (90249-2218)
PHONE..................................323 965-1502
Chris M Duggan, *President*
◆ **EMP:** 65
SQ FT: 10,000
SALES (est): 7.9MM **Privately Held**
SIC: 1721 Interior commercial painting contractor; commercial wallcovering contractor

(P-2345)
EMPCC INC
Also Called: Empire Community Painting
1682 Langley Ave Fl 2, Irvine (92614-5620)
PHONE..................................714 564-7900
Jason Reid, *President*
Tracy Meneses, *CFO*
Jeff Gunhus, *Vice Pres*
Matt Stewart, *Vice Pres*
Spencer Pepe, *Admin Sec*
EMP: 59
SQ FT: 1,000
SALES: 1.1MM **Privately Held**
SIC: 1721 Painting & paper hanging
PA: Mip Empire, Inc.
1682 Langley Ave Fl 2
Irvine CA 92614

(P-2346)
EUROPEAN PAVING DESIGNS INC
1474 Berger Dr, San Jose (95112-2701)
PHONE..................................408 283-5230
Randy Hays, *CEO*
Robyn Cerutti, *COO*
Javier Licea, *Project Engr*
Fabian Gomez, *Project Mgr*
John Lohman, *Director*
EMP: 55
SQ FT: 3,000
SALES (est): 6.3MM **Privately Held**
SIC: 1721 Pavement marking contractor

(P-2347)
FREEDOM PAINTING INC
8822 Calmada Ave, Whittier (90605-2006)
PHONE..................................562 696-0785
Gerald Lundgren, *President*
Roselina Lundgren, *Treasurer*
Beverly Lundgren, *Vice Pres*
Darren Lundgren, *Supervisor*
EMP: 50
SQ FT: 8,000
SALES: 4MM **Privately Held**
SIC: 1721 Residential painting

(P-2348)
GENERAL COATINGS CORPORATION
9349 Feron Blvd, Rancho Cucamonga (91730-4516)
PHONE..................................909 204-4150
Craig Kinsman, *Owner*
EMP: 250
SALES (corp-wide): 86.2MM **Privately Held**
SIC: 1721 Painting & paper hanging
PA: General Coatings Corporation
6711 Nancy Ridge Dr
San Diego CA 92121
858 587-1277

(P-2349)
GENERAL COATINGS CORPORATION
600 W Freedom Ave, Orange (92865-2537)
PHONE..................................858 587-1277
Craig Kinsman, *Branch Mgr*
EMP: 250
SQ FT: 7,047
SALES (corp-wide): 86.2MM **Privately Held**
WEB: www.gencoat.com
SIC: 1721 Painting & paper hanging
PA: General Coatings Corporation
6711 Nancy Ridge Dr
San Diego CA 92121
858 587-1277

(P-2350)
GENERAL COATINGS CORPORATION (PA)
6711 Nancy Ridge Dr, San Diego (92121-2231)
PHONE..................................858 587-1277
Craig A Kinsman, *CEO*
Andrew Fluken, *Vice Pres*
Todd Seaboch, *Division Mgr*
Hector Cueva, *Project Mgr*
Kathy Farrington, *Accountant*
EMP: 250
SQ FT: 14,000
SALES (est): 86.2MM **Privately Held**
WEB: www.gencoat.com
SIC: 1721 1799 Painting & paper hanging; waterproofing

(P-2351)
GENERAL COATINGS CORPORATION
1220 E North Ave, Fresno (93725-1930)
PHONE..................................559 495-4004
Lee Morrison, *Principal*
EMP: 250
SALES (est): 2.8MM
SALES (corp-wide): 86.2MM **Privately Held**
SIC: 1721 1799 Painting & paper hanging; coating of concrete structures with plastic
PA: General Coatings Corporation
6711 Nancy Ridge Dr
San Diego CA 92121
858 587-1277

(P-2352)
GEORGE E MASKER INC
Also Called: Masker Painting
7699 Edgewater Dr, Oakland (94621-3028)
PHONE..................................510 568-1206
Alan Bjerke, *President*
Claudia Ornelas, *Administration*
Newt Millward, *Project Mgr*
Alan Murdoch, *Project Mgr*
Juan Bonilla, *Foreman/Supr*
EMP: 100
SQ FT: 18,000
SALES (est): 9.1MM **Privately Held**
WEB: www.maskerpainting.com
SIC: 1721 Exterior commercial painting contractor; interior commercial painting contractor

(P-2353)
GIAMPOLINI & CO
Also Called: Giampolini/Courtney
1482 67th St, Emeryville (94608-1016)
PHONE..................................415 673-1236
Greg Quilici, *President*
Patrick Roland, *CFO*
Tom Quilici, *Exec VP*
James Patrick Roland, *Principal*
Diane Smith, *Administration*
EMP: 225
SQ FT: 9,720
SALES (est): 20MM **Privately Held**
WEB: www.giampolini.com
SIC: 1721 1542 1742 Exterior commercial painting contractor; interior commercial painting contractor; commercial & office buildings, renovation & repair; plastering, drywall & insulation

(P-2354)
GOLD COAST DESIGN INC
7667 Vickers St, San Diego (92111-1525)
PHONE..................................619 574-0111
David L Gash, *CEO*
Kathleen Gash, *Vice Pres*
EMP: 80
SQ FT: 7,331
SALES (est): 6.7MM **Privately Held**
SIC: 1721 Residential painting

(P-2355)
GONZALES PAINTING CORP
14437 Meridian Pkwy, Riverside (92518-3007)
PHONE..................................951 214-6400
John J Gonzales, *President*
EMP: 90
SALES (est): 3.1MM **Privately Held**
SIC: 1721 Interior residential painting contractor; exterior residential painting contractor; interior commercial painting contractor; exterior commercial painting contractor

(P-2356)
GPS PAINTING WALLCOVERING INC
1307 E Saint Gertrude Pl C, Santa Ana (92705-5228)
PHONE..................................714 730-8904
Eliot Schneider, *President*
David Cuevas, *Project Mgr*
Ed Lares, *Project Mgr*
Sergio Gutierrez, *Manager*
Alonso Estrada, *Superintendent*
EMP: 110
SALES (est): 9.6MM **Privately Held**
WEB: www.gpspainting.com
SIC: 1721 Painting & paper hanging

(P-2357)
HARRIS & RUTH PAINTING CONTG (PA)
28408 Lorna Ave, West Covina (91790)
PHONE..................................626 960-4004
Terry Cairy, *President*
Mark Heydorff, *COO*
Kathleen Boyer, *Office Admin*
Bruce Boyer, *VP Sales*
Chanel Salazar-Perez, *Assistant*
EMP: 70 **EST:** 1970
SQ FT: 1,000
SALES: 10.4MM **Privately Held**
WEB: www.harris-ruthpainting.com
SIC: 1721 Exterior commercial painting contractor; industrial painting

(P-2358)
INTERNTNAL AROSPC COATINGS INC
13640 Phantom St, Victorville (92394-7900)
PHONE..................................760 246-1651
Niall Cunningham, *Branch Mgr*
EMP: 209 **Privately Held**
SIC: 1721 4581 Aircraft painting; aircraft maintenance & repair services
PA: International Aerospace Coatings, Inc.
5709 W Sunset Hwy Ste 205
Spokane WA 99224

(P-2359)
J C FRENCH & COMPANY
2984 1st St Ste L, La Verne (91750-5675)
PHONE..................................909 596-1423
Sandra Perry, *President*
John C French, *CFO*
Robert French, *Corp Secy*
August Jacobson, *Senior VP*
EMP: 60 **EST:** 1977
SQ FT: 12,000

P
R
O
D
U
C
T
S

&

S
V
C
S

SALES (est): 4.8MM **Privately Held**
WEB: www.jcfrench.com
SIC: 1721 Residential painting

(P-2360)
J M V B INC
Also Called: Spc Building Services
12118 Severn Way, Riverside
(92503-4804)
P.O. Box 614, Orange (92856-6614)
PHONE...............................714 288-9797
Benjamin J Rodriguez, *President*
EMP: 80 **EST:** 1993
SALES (est): 4.6MM **Privately Held**
SIC: 1721 Painting & paper hanging

(P-2361)
J P CARROLL CO INC
5707 Milton Ave, Whittier (90601-2420)
PHONE...............................323 660-9230
H B Fitzpatrick, *Ch of Bd*
Kevin Fitzpatrick, *President*
Rebecca Derry, *Vice Pres*
Barbara Fitzpatrick, *Admin Sec*
EMP: 60
SQ FT: 25,000
SALES (est): 2.6MM **Privately Held**
WEB: www.jpcarrollco.com
SIC: 1721 Residential painting; commercial
painting; wallcovering contractors

(P-2362)
JD MILLER CONSTRUCTION INC
506 W Graham Ave Ste 202, Lake Elsinore
(92530-3600)
PHONE...............................951 471-3513
Jeff Mosher, *CEO*
Jeffery D Miller, *President*
EMP: 50
SALES (est): 7.2MM **Privately Held**
SIC: 1721 Painting & paper hanging

(P-2363)
JEFFCO PAINTING & COATING INC
1260 Railroad Ave, Vallejo (94592-1012)
P.O. Box 1888 (94590-0655)
PHONE...............................707 562-1900
Steve Jeffress, *President*
Gene Glockner, *CFO*
Aaron West, *Project Mgr*
Jacki Matejka, *Human Res Dir*
Mike Maldonado, *Manager*
EMP: 100
SALES (est): 11.5MM **Privately Held**
WEB: www.jeffcoptg.com
SIC: 1721 3471 Industrial painting; sand
blasting of metal parts

(P-2364)
JERRY THOMPSON & SONS PNTG INC
3 Simms St, San Rafael (94901-5414)
PHONE...............................415 454-1500
Stephen G Thompson, *President*
Dennis J Thompson, *Corp Secy*
Sharon Baxter, *Officer*
Amaya Ben, *Project Mgr*
Tim Sasan, *Project Mgr*
EMP: 140
SALES (est): 13.8MM **Privately Held**
SIC: 1721 Residential painting

(P-2365)
JOHNSON & TURNER PAINTING CO
8241 Electric Ave, Stanton (90680-2640)
PHONE...............................714 828-8282
Dale Bodwell, *President*
Michelle Bodwell, *Office Mgr*
▲ **EMP:** 50 **EST:** 1955
SQ FT: 6,000
SALES: 4.1MM **Privately Held**
SIC: 1721 Residential painting

(P-2366)
LAWRENCE B BONAS COMPANY
3197 Arprt Loop Dr Ste C, Costa Mesa
(92626)
PHONE...............................714 668-5250
Guy A Bonas, *President*
Doris A Bonas, *Treasurer*
EMP: 75

SQ FT: 7,200
SALES (est): 4.9MM **Privately Held**
SIC: 1721 Wallcovering contractors

(P-2367)
LIVING COLORS INC
16026 Rayen St, North Hills (91343-4814)
PHONE...............................818 893-5068
Raymond Sponsler, *President*
Paula Sponsler, *Treasurer*
Daniel Barton, *Sales Executive*
EMP: 60
SALES (est): 3.9MM **Privately Held**
WEB: www.livingcolorsinc.com
SIC: 1721 Residential painting

(P-2368)
M C BUILDER CORP
3500 E Tachevah Dr Ste C, Palm Springs
(92262-5491)
PHONE...............................760 323-8010
Ernest Castro, *Owner*
EMP: 50
SALES (est): 3.6MM **Privately Held**
SIC: 1721 Commercial painting; residential
painting

(P-2369)
MEYER COATINGS INC
1927 N Glassell St, Orange (92865-4313)
PHONE...............................714 467-4600
Diana Meyer, *CEO*
Scott Meyer, *President*
Kylie Suica, *Admin Asst*
Lennon Leblanc, *Project Mgr*
Ricky Martinez, *Project Engr*
EMP: 50
SQ FT: 4,800
SALES (est): 7.2MM **Privately Held**
WEB: www.meyercoatings.com
SIC: 1721 Commercial painting

(P-2370)
MICKEY WALL PAINTING INC
250 East Ave, Turlock (95380-4941)
P.O. Box 3302 (95381-3302)
PHONE...............................209 669-0557
Mickey Wall, *President*
Kathy Wall, *CFO*
EMP: 50
SQ FT: 6,000
SALES (est): 3.7MM **Privately Held**
WEB: www.mickeywallpainting.com
SIC: 1721 Residential painting; exterior
residential painting contractor; interior
residential painting contractor

(P-2371)
MIKE CHAMPLIN
Also Called: Mike Champlin Painting
4374 Contractors Cmn, Livermore
(94551-7544)
PHONE...............................925 961-1004
Mike Champlin, *Owner*
EMP: 100
SALES (est): 6MM **Privately Held**
SIC: 1721 Painting & paper hanging

(P-2372)
MJP EMPIRE INC (PA)
1682 Langley Ave Fl 2, Irvine (92614-5620)
PHONE...............................714 564-7900
Jason Reid, *President*
Tracy Meneses, *CFO*
Jeff Gunhus, *Vice Pres*
Matt Stewart, *Vice Pres*
Spencer Pepe, *Admin Sec*
EMP: 300
SALES (est): 5.8MM **Privately Held**
SIC: 1721 Painting & paper hanging

(P-2373)
MOLINAS PNTG WALLCOVERING INC
4285 Pacheco Blvd, Martinez
(94553-2227)
PHONE...............................925 228-7487
Oscar Molina, *CEO*
Oscar M Molina, *CFO*
Vanessa Molina, *Admin Sec*
Marissa Molina, *Bookkeeper*
EMP: 75
SQ FT: 3,750
SALES: 4.8MM **Privately Held**
SIC: 1721 Wallcovering contractors

(P-2374)
NORCAL PAINTERS INC
Also Called: Certapro Painters
60 29th St 241, San Francisco
(94110-4929)
PHONE...............................415 566-6800
Terrance Ladd, *President*
George Irving, *General Mgr*
EMP: 53
SALES (est): 3.1MM **Privately Held**
SIC: 1721 Painting & paper hanging

(P-2375)
NORTH ORANGE COAST PNTG INC
3969 Sierra Ave, Norco (92860-1390)
P.O. Box 520 (92860-0520)
PHONE...............................951 279-2694
Fax: 951 279-9510
EMP: 100
SALES (est): 5MM **Privately Held**
SIC: 1721

(P-2376)
P B C PAVERS INC
Also Called: Peterson Bros Construction
1560 W Lambert Rd, Brea (92821-2826)
PHONE...............................714 278-0488
Robert Peterson, *President*
Valerie Payne, *CFO*
Eldin Peterson, *Vice Pres*
Gabriela Guidero, *Technology*
Dirk Moore, *Purchasing*
▲ **EMP:** 80
SALES (est): 7.4MM **Privately Held**
SIC: 1721 Pavement marking contractor

(P-2377)
PETERSON PAINTING INC
5750 La Ribera St, Livermore
(94590-9204)
PHONE...............................925 455-5864
Raymond Peterson, *President*
John Peterson, *Vice Pres*
Kyle Peterson, *Opers Mgr*
EMP: 350
SQ FT: 10,000
SALES (est): 17.4MM **Privately Held**
WEB: www.petersonpainting.com
SIC: 1721 Residential painting

(P-2378)
POWER MAINTENANCE SERVICES INC
Also Called: Pilot Painting & Construction
5555 Corporate Ave, Cypress
(90630-4708)
P.O. Box 6377, Anaheim (92816-0377)
PHONE...............................714 229-5900
Steve Gilkey, *President*
EMP: 60
SQ FT: 7,856
SALES (est): 3.2MM **Privately Held**
SIC: 1721 Residential painting

(P-2379)
PRIMECO PAINTING & CNSTR
220 Oceanside Blvd, Oceanside
(92054-4903)
PHONE...............................760 967-8278
Brett Musgrove, *President*
Stacey Musgrove, *Admin Sec*
Kathy Hancock, *Human Res Dir*
Kristopher Jones, *Manager*
EMP: 90
SQ FT: 2,100
SALES (est): 8.4MM **Privately Held**
WEB: www.primecopainting.com
SIC: 1721 1542 Residential painting; commercial & office building contractors

(P-2380)
PS2 (PA)
17903 S Hobart Blvd, Gardena
(90248-3613)
PHONE...............................310 243-2980
Peter Schmit, *President*
Peter Short, *Admin Sec*
Jahaziel Delgado, *Project Mgr*
EMP: 68
SQ FT: 2,000
SALES (est): 10.3MM **Privately Held**
SIC: 1721 Residential painting

(P-2381)
PYRAMID PAINTING INC
2925 Bayview Dr, Fremont (94538-6520)
PHONE...............................650 903-9791
Craig Ruybalid, *President*
EMP: 50
SQ FT: 6,240
SALES (est): 4.2MM **Privately Held**
WEB: www.pyramidpainting.com
SIC: 1721 Exterior commercial painting
contractor; interior commercial painting
contractor

(P-2382)
QUALITY WALL SYSTEMS INC
Also Called: Residential Wall Systems
104 S Maple St, Corona (92880-1704)
P.O. Box 2649 (92878-2649)
PHONE...............................951 739-4409
Glenn L Crowther, *President*
EMP: 99
SALES (est): 5.8MM **Privately Held**
SIC: 1721 1742 Painting & paper hanging;
drywall

(P-2383)
R & A PAINTING INC
11730 Sheldon Lake Dr, Elk Grove
(95624-9649)
P.O. Box 292730, Sacramento (95829-
2730)
PHONE...............................916 688-3955
Antonio Rodrigues, *President*
Cidalia Rodrigues, *Corp Secy*
EMP: 60
SALES (est): 2.5MM **Privately Held**
SIC: 1721 Commercial painting; residential
painting

(P-2384)
R-BROS PAINTING INC
707 W Hedding St, San Jose (95110-1533)
PHONE...............................408 291-6820
Rod Rodriquez, *President*
▲ **EMP:** 50
SQ FT: 3,000
SALES (est): 5.2MM **Privately Held**
WEB: www.rbrothers.com
SIC: 1721 Commercial painting

(P-2385)
RANDALL MC-ANANY COMPANY
1528 W 178th St, Gardena (90248-3204)
PHONE...............................310 822-3344
Timothy Mc Anany, *President*
Nancy Mc Anany, *Corp Secy*
Karl Keeney, *Exec VP*
Priscilla Dipierro, *Admin Asst*
Don Murray, *Project Mgr*
EMP: 60
SALES: 5.5MM **Privately Held**
WEB: www.rmcompany.com
SIC: 1721 Commercial painting; commercial wallcovering contractor

(P-2386)
RC WENDT PAINTING INC
21612 Surveyor Cir, Huntington Beach
(92646-7068)
PHONE...............................714 960-2700
Robert C Wendt, *President*
Jeri Wendt, *Corp Secy*
Scott Wendt, *Vice Pres*
EMP: 110
SALES (est): 7.7MM **Privately Held**
WEB: www.wendtcompanies.com
SIC: 1721 Residential painting; commercial
painting

(P-2387)
REDWOOD PAINTING CO INC
620 W 10th St, Pittsburg (94565-1806)
P.O. Box 1269 (94565-0126)
PHONE...............................925 432-4500
Charles Duke Del Monte, *CEO*
George Del Monte, *Exec VP*
Ross Buchanon, *CIO*
EMP: 110
SQ FT: 19,000
SALES: 31.7MM **Privately Held**
WEB: www.redwoodptg.com
SIC: 1721 Commercial painting; industrial
painting

(P-2388)

ROBERT MEUSCHKE COMPANY INC

Also Called: RMC Painting & Restoration
1039 Edwards Rd, Burlingame
(94010-2318)
PHONE..................650 342-3993
Bob Meuschke, *President*
Andy Smith, *Admin Sec*
EMP: 50
SQ FT: 1,200
SALES (est): 2.4MM **Privately Held**
WEB: www.rmcpainting.com
SIC: 1721 Exterior commercial painting
contractor; interior commercial painting
contractor

(P-2389)

RODIN & CO INC

7411 Laurel Canyon Blvd # 10, North Hollywood (91605-3160)
PHONE..................818 358-3427
Fred Rodin, *President*
Rowena Rodin, *Admin Sec*
EMP: 60
SQ FT: 4,400
SALES (est): 2.7MM **Privately Held**
WEB: www.rodincompany.com
SIC: 1721 Wallcovering contractors

(P-2390)

RTE ENTERPRISES INC

Also Called: Color Concepts
21530 Roscoe Blvd, Canoga Park
(91304-4144)
PHONE..................818 999-5300
Ron Evenhaim, *President*
EMP: 100
SQ FT: 2,000
SALES (est): 5.3MM **Privately Held**
WEB: www.colorconcepts.net
SIC: 1721 1742 Painting & paper hanging;
plastering, drywall & insulation

(P-2391)

S W P T X INC

Also Called: Student Works Painting
1682 Langley Ave, Irvine (92614-5620)
PHONE..................714 564-7900
Matthew Stewart, *President*
EMP: 120
SALES (est): 2.8MM **Privately Held**
WEB: www.nsgmail.com
SIC: 1721 Painting & paper hanging
PA: National Services Group, Inc.
1682 Langley Ave
Irvine CA 92614

(P-2392)

SANDERS & WOHRMAN CORPORATION

709 N Poplar St, Orange (92868-1013)
PHONE..................714 919-0446
John Thomas Wohrman, *Principal*
Todd Wohrman, *Treasurer*
Jack Murphy, *Manager*
Ron Edmonds, *Superintendent*
EMP: 150
SQ FT: 12,000
SALES (est): 18.1MM **Privately Held**
WEB: www.swpainting.com
SIC: 1721 Residential painting; industrial
painting

(P-2393)

SCHAPER CONSTRUCTION INC (PA)

1177 N 15th St, San Jose (95112-1422)
PHONE..................408 437-0337
Leon Schaper, *CEO*
Greg Sipe, *General Mgr*
Jina Duncan, *Executive Asst*
Paul Schaper, *Project Mgr*
Mara Frey, *Project Engr*
EMP: 90
SQ FT: 8,400
SALES (est): 31.1MM **Privately Held**
WEB: www.schaperco.com
SIC: 1721 1611 1542 Exterior residential
painting contractor; interior residential
painting contractor; general contractor,
highway & street construction; nonresidential construction

(P-2394)

SIGNATURE PAINTING & CNSTR INC

1559 3rd Ave, Walnut Creek (94597-2604)
PHONE..................925 287-0444
Brian Mitchell, *President*
Erik Oller, *Vice Pres*
Christian Cupolo, *Project Mgr*
Charlie Johnson, *Superintendent*
Yama Sekander, *Superintendent*
EMP: 50
SALES (est): 5.7MM **Privately Held**
SIC: 1721 Painting & paper hanging

(P-2395)

SOCAL COATINGS INC

2820 Via Orange Way Ste J, Spring Valley
(91978-1742)
PHONE..................619 660-5395
Norma Alicia Alonso, *CEO*
John Thomas Fox, *Vice Pres*
EMP: 50
SALES (est): 2.7MM **Privately Held**
SIC: 1721 Residential painting

(P-2396)

STEGER INC

1938 N Batavia St Ste L, Orange
(92865-4140)
PHONE..................714 974-4383
Michael Steger, *President*
EMP: 50
SALES (est): 3.8MM **Privately Held**
WEB: www.steger.com
SIC: 1721 Residential painting; commercial
painting

(P-2397)

STEVE BEATTIE INC

Also Called: Steve Beattie Painting
1766 Westridge Rd, Los Angeles
(90049-2516)
PHONE..................310 454-1786
Steve Beattie, *President*
Patricia H McGuire, *CEO*
EMP: 60 **EST:** 1986
SALES (est): 2.5MM **Privately Held**
SIC: 1721 Residential painting

(P-2398)

STUCCO WORKS INC

5451 Whse Way Ste 105, Sacramento
(95826)
PHONE..................916 383-6699
Kevin Nelson, *President*
Anselmo Padilla, *Vice Pres*
Xavier Valdez, *Admin Sec*
EMP: 300
SQ FT: 26,000
SALES (est): 10MM **Privately Held**
SIC: 1721 Painting & paper hanging

(P-2399)

STUDENT WORKS PAINTING INC

1682 Langley Ave, Irvine (92614-5620)
PHONE..................714 564-7900
Spencer Pepe, *President*
Mathew Stewart, *Treasurer*
Matthew Stewart, *Treasurer*
Mathew Landauer, *Vice Pres*
Matthew Landauer, *Vice Pres*
EMP: 300
SALES (est): 6.7MM **Privately Held**
WEB: www.nsgmail.com
SIC: 1721 Residential painting
PA: National Services Group, Inc.
1682 Langley Ave
Irvine CA 92614

(P-2400)

T & R PAINTING CONSTRUCTION

7116 Valjean Ave, Van Nuys (91406-3901)
PHONE..................818 779-3800
Robin Rapaport, *President*
EMP: 110
SALES (est): 4.6MM **Privately Held**
WEB: www.tandrweb.com
SIC: 1721 Residential painting; commercial
painting

(P-2401)

TRANS WORLD MAINTENANCE INC

Also Called: S A S
1590 Rollins Rd, Millbrae (94030)
PHONE..................650 455-2450
Theodore Siotos, *President*
Ted Siotos, *Vice Pres*
Costandinos Siotos, *Principal*
Alexandra Siotos, *Admin Sec*
EMP: 71
SQ FT: 5,700
SALES: 772.7K **Privately Held**
SIC: 1721 8742 1542 Residential painting; construction project management
consultant; commercial & office buildings,
renovation & repair

(P-2402)

TWI- TECHNO WEST INC

1391 S Allec St, Anaheim (92805-6304)
PHONE..................714 635-4070
Marcia Birney, *President*
EMP: 85
SQ FT: 30,000
SALES (est): 3.7MM **Privately Held**
WEB: www.multipleplantservices.com
SIC: 1721 Commercial painting

(P-2403)

URBAN PAINTING INC

40 Lisbon St, San Rafael (94901-4709)
PHONE..................415 485-1130
Michael James Urban, *President*
Robert S Urban, *Shareholder*
James De Martini, *Vice Pres*
Chris Urban, *Vice Pres*
Marshall Johnson, *Technology*
EMP: 60
SQ FT: 6,000
SALES (est): 4.9MM **Privately Held**
WEB: www.urbanco.com
SIC: 1721 Commercial painting; residential
painting

(P-2404)

VERTEX COATINGS INC

1291 W State St, Ontario (91762-4015)
PHONE..................909 923-5795
Russ Phillips, *President*
Stacy Phillips, *Executive*
Veronica Ibarra, *Office Mgr*
Gerald Aguilar, *Superintendent*
EMP: 70
SQ FT: 11,000
SALES (est): 9.3MM **Privately Held**
WEB: www.vertexcoatings.com
SIC: 1721 Commercial painting

(P-2405)

WEST COAST INTERIORS INC

Also Called: West Coast Painting
1610 W Linden St, Riverside (92507-6810)
PHONE..................951 778-3592
Mark Herbert, *CEO*
Dan Slavin, *President*
Santos Garcia, *COO*
Keith Caneva, *Controller*
Colleen Butler, *Human Resources*
EMP: 600
SQ FT: 8,000
SALES (est): 39.6MM **Privately Held**
SIC: 1721 Wallcovering contractors

(P-2406)

WILSON HAMPTON PNTG CONTRS INC

1524 W Mable St, Anaheim (92802-1097)
P.O. Box 9949 (92812-7949)
PHONE..................714 772-5091
Doug Hampton, *President*
Douglas J Hampton, *President*
Clifford C Hampton, *Vice Pres*
Robert D Hampton III, *Admin Sec*
EMP: 60 **EST:** 1923
SQ FT: 44,000
SALES (est): 6.9MM **Privately Held**
WEB: www.wilsonhampton.com
SIC: 1721 7641 Residential painting; furniture repair & maintenance; office furniture
repair & maintenance

(P-2407)

WM B SALEH CO

1364 N Jackson Ave, Fresno (93703-4624)
PHONE..................559 255-2046
Mark Saleh, *President*
Katherine Brusellas, *Corp Secy*
William B Saleh, *Vice Pres*
EMP: 75 **EST:** 1959
SQ FT: 6,800
SALES (est): 3.8MM **Privately Held**
SIC: 1721 Commercial painting; industrial
painting; commercial wallcovering contractor

1731 Electrical Work

(P-2408)

A M ORTEGA CONSTRUCTION INC (PA)

Also Called: Western Rim Pipeline
10125 Channel Rd, Lakeside (92040-1703)
PHONE..................619 390-1988
Archie Maurice Ortega, *President*
Randy Michael, *Division Mgr*
Linda Ortega, *Admin Sec*
EMP: 110 **EST:** 1974
SQ FT: 10,000
SALES (est): 47.7MM **Privately Held**
WEB: www.amortega.com
SIC: 1731 Electrical work

(P-2409)

A-1 ELECTRIC SERVICE CO INC

4204 Sepulveda Blvd, Culver City
(90230-4709)
P.O. Box 6453, Malibu (90264-6453)
PHONE..................310 204-1077
Linda Pieper, *CEO*
Scott Pieper, *Vice Pres*
Eric Cashman, *Technology*
EMP: 50
SQ FT: 5,000
SALES (est): 13.1MM **Privately Held**
WEB: www.a-1electric.com
SIC: 1731 Electrical work

(P-2410)

A-C ELECTRIC COMPANY (PA)

Also Called: Automted Cntrls Technical Svcs
2921 Hanger Way, Bakersfield
(93308-1643)
P.O. Box 81977 (93380-1977)
PHONE..................661 410-0000
Thomas J Alexander, *Ch of Bd*
Daren T Alexander, *President*
Thomas P Zauder, *CFO*
David M Morton, *Exec VP*
Rusty Stone, *Division Mgr*
EMP: 50 **EST:** 1945
SQ FT: 10,000
SALES: 66.6MM **Privately Held**
SIC: 1731 General electrical contractor

(P-2411)

AA/ACME LOCKSMITHS INC

1660 Factor Ave, San Leandro
(94577-5618)
PHONE..................510 483-6584
Timothy J Whall, *CEO*
Jim Devries, *President*
Donald Young, *COO*
Jeff Likosar, *CFO*
P Gray Finney, *Senior VP*
EMP: 95
SQ FT: 20,000
SALES (est): 15.4MM
SALES (corp-wide): 4.5B **Publicly Held**
SIC: 1731 5999 Fire detection & burglar
alarm systems specialization; alarm signal systems
PA: Adt Inc.
1501 W Yamato Rd
Boca Raton FL 33431
561 988-3600

(P-2412)

AAA ELCTRCAL CMMUNICATIONS INC (PA)

Also Called: AAA Property Services
25007 Anza Dr, Valencia (91355-3414)
PHONE..................800 892-4784
Joann Katinos, *CEO*
Brian Higgins, *President*
Michael Scalzo, *Project Mgr*

PRODUCTS & SVCS

Hubert Hodgin, *Sales Executive*
Josh King, *Manager*
EMP: 133
SQ FT: 6,000
SALES: 17MM **Privately Held**
SIC: 1731 1711 7349 1721 General electrical contractor; plumbing, heating, air-conditioning contractors; building maintenance services; commercial painting; commercial & office buildings, renovation & repair

(P-2413)
AAA NETWORK SOLUTIONS INC
8401 Page St, Buena Park (90621-3821)
PHONE.............................714 484-2711
Hoai-Phuong Huynh Ngo, *CEO*
Keith Hippard, *Senior VP*
EMP: 60
SALES: 7MM **Privately Held**
SIC: 1731 Electrical work

(P-2414)
ACS COMMUNICATIONS INC
Also Called: Fiber Optic Technologies
680 Knox St Ste 150, Torrance (90502-1325)
PHONE.............................310 767-2145
Robby Sawyer, *President*
EMP: 50 **Privately Held**
WEB: www.acsdataline.com
SIC: 1731 Communications specialization
HQ: Acs Communications, Inc.
2535 Brockton Dr Ste 400
Austin TX 78758
512 837-4400

(P-2415)
AJ KIRKWOOD & ASSOCIATES INC
4300 N Harbor Blvd, Fullerton (92835-1091)
PHONE.............................714 505-1977
Arch Kirkwood, *Chairman*
James Klassen, *President*
Michael Hewson, *CFO*
Aidan Culligan, *Senior VP*
Sam Sandoval, *Vice Pres*
EMP: 115
SALES: 110MM **Privately Held**
WEB: www.ajk-a.com
SIC: 1731 8748 7389 General electrical contractor; communications consulting; design services

(P-2416)
ALBD ELECTRIC AND CABLE
Also Called: A Lighting By Design
995 E Discovery Ln, Anaheim (92801-1147)
PHONE.............................949 440-1216
Chad Lambert, *CEO*
EMP: 100
SQ FT: 12,000
SALES: 15MM **Privately Held**
SIC: 1731 3651 General electrical contractor; household audio & video equipment

(P-2417)
ALL-GUARD ALARM SYSTEMS INC (PA)
Also Called: Grand Central Station
1306 Stealth St, Livermore (94551-9356)
PHONE.............................800 255-4273
Denis Cooke, *President*
Michael Cooke, *Corp Secy*
Patricia Cooke, *Vice Pres*
Jodie L Osborne, *Controller*
EMP: 68
SQ FT: 12,600
SALES: 12.5MM **Privately Held**
SIC: 1731 7382 Fire detection & burglar alarm systems specialization; burglar alarm maintenance & monitoring

(P-2418)
AMERICAN ELECTRICAL SVCS INC
501 San Benito St Fl 3, Hollister (95023-3903)
PHONE.............................831 638-1737
Ignacio Velazquez, *CEO*
Richard Champion, *President*

▲ **EMP:** 110
SQ FT: 1,700
SALES (est): 8.4MM **Privately Held**
SIC: 1731 General electrical contractor

(P-2419)
AMERICAN ENGRG CONTRS INC
Also Called: Budget Electric
25445 S Schulte Rd, Tracy (95377-9709)
PHONE.............................209 229-1591
Larry Walling, *President*
Patricia Walling, *Corp Secy*
EMP: 180
SQ FT: 4,000
SALES (est): 19MM **Privately Held**
WEB: www.budgete.com
SIC: 1731 General electrical contractor

(P-2420)
AMERICAN HOME ALARMS INC
128 E Huntington Dr Ste B, Arcadia (91006-7054)
P.O. Box 5394, El Monte (91734-1394)
PHONE.............................888 531-5065
Jean Nguyen, *President*
Anthony Nguyen, *Vice Pres*
EMP: 120
SALES (est): 13.5MM **Privately Held**
SIC: 1731 7382 Fire detection & burglar alarm systems specialization; burglar alarm maintenance & monitoring; fire alarm maintenance & monitoring

(P-2421)
AMS ELECTRIC INC
6905 Sierra Ct Ste A, Dublin (94568-2708)
PHONE.............................925 961-1600
William Breyton, *Principal*
Craig Ayers, *Treasurer*
John Modica, *Vice Pres*
Don Dixon, *Project Mgr*
Kevin Kincaid, *Project Mgr*
EMP: 75
SQ FT: 25,000
SALES (est): 18.2MM **Privately Held**
WEB: www.amselectric.com
SIC: 1731 General electrical contractor

(P-2422)
ANDERSON & HOWARD ELECTRIC INC
Also Called: Anderson Howard
1791 Reynolds Ave, Irvine (92614-5711)
PHONE.............................949 250-4555
Brian E Elliott, *President*
Charles B Howard, *Vice Pres*
Tom Howard, *Admin Sec*
Tess Joncich, *Accountant*
Brian Busch, *Sr Project Mgr*
EMP: 210 **EST:** 1967
SQ FT: 10,500
SALES (est): 63.9MM **Privately Held**
WEB: www.aandh.com
SIC: 1731 General electrical contractor

(P-2423)
APOLLO ELECTRIC
330 N Basse Ln, Brea (92821-3906)
PHONE.............................714 256-8414
Leroy H Holt, *CEO*
Gregg L Holt, *Corp Secy*
Brent Holt, *Vice Pres*
Kelly Shay, *Vice Pres*
Whitney Hunter, *Administration*
EMP: 60
SQ FT: 18,000
SALES (est): 13.6MM **Privately Held**
WEB: www.apolloelect.com
SIC: 1731 General electrical contractor

(P-2424)
ASSI SECURITY (PA)
1370 Reynolds Ave Ste 201, Irvine (92614-5547)
PHONE.............................949 955-0244
William Dominic Vuono, *President*
Michael Willey, *Vice Pres*
Laura Petras, *Administration*
Daniel Gonzalez, *Project Mgr*
Ismael Mercado, *Project Mgr*
EMP: 67
SQ FT: 10,000

SALES (est): 17.5MM **Privately Held**
WEB: www.assisecurity.com
SIC: 1731 7382 Voice, data & video wiring contractor; fire detection & burglar alarm systems specialization; security systems services; protective devices, security; burglar alarm maintenance & monitoring; confinement surveillance systems maintenance & monitoring

(P-2425)
ATK AUDIOTEK
Also Called: Atk Services
28238 Avenue Crocker, Valencia (91355-1248)
PHONE.............................661 705-3700
Michael Murray Macdonald, *President*
James Harmala, *CFO*
J Scott Harmala, *Vice Pres*
Brett Valasek, *General Mgr*
John M Stewart, *Admin Sec*
EMP: 85
SQ FT: 25,000
SALES (est): 23.6MM **Privately Held**
WEB: www.atkcorp.com
SIC: 1731 7359 Voice, data & video wiring contractor; sound & lighting equipment rental

(P-2426)
ATMC INCORPORATED (PA)
Also Called: Atm Consultants
725 W Baseline Rd, Claremont (91711-1615)
PHONE.............................909 390-0470
Toshio Hashioka, *President*
EMP: 66
SQ FT: 12,000
SALES (est): 4.4MM **Privately Held**
WEB: www.atmc.com
SIC: 1731 5044 Banking machine installation & service; bank automatic teller machines

(P-2427)
B F C INC
675 Davis St, San Francisco (94111-1903)
PHONE.............................415 495-3085
John M Walsh, *President*
Novelynn Tejada, *CFO*
Miles Luquingan, *Admin Asst*
Lindsay Rosecrans, *Admin Asst*
JP Sassenberg, *Project Mgr*
EMP: 110 **EST:** 1951
SQ FT: 6,300
SALES: 91MM **Privately Held**
WEB: www.cbfelectric.com
SIC: 1731 General electrical contractor

(P-2428)
BANISTER ELECTRICAL INC
2532 Verne Roberts Cir, Antioch (94509-7904)
PHONE.............................925 778-7801
Daniel T Pauline, *President*
Shovawn Barrera, *Controller*
EMP: 70
SALES (est): 2.3MM **Privately Held**
SIC: 1731 General electrical contractor

(P-2429)
BARNUM & CELILLO ELECTRIC INC (PA)
135 Main Ave Ste A, Sacramento (95838-2090)
PHONE.............................916 646-4661
Fred Troy Barnum, *CEO*
Lee Sanders, *Trustee*
Paul Celillo, *Vice Pres*
John Aspling, *Project Mgr*
Matthew Evans, *Project Mgr*
EMP: 95
SQ FT: 3,000
SALES: 50.5MM **Privately Held**
WEB: www.barnumcelillo.com
SIC: 1731 General electrical contractor

(P-2430)
BAY ALARM COMPANY (PA)
Also Called: S A S
5130 Commercial Cir, Concord (94520-8522)
P.O. Box 8140, Walnut Creek (94596-8140)
PHONE.............................925 935-1100
Bruce A Westphal, *Ch of Bd*

Roger L Westphal, *CEO*
Graham Westphal, *Co-President*
Matt Westphal, *Co-President*
Shane Clary, *Vice Pres*
◆ **EMP:** 70
SQ FT: 12,000
SALES (est): 160.9MM **Privately Held**
WEB: www.bayalarm.com
SIC: 1731 7382 5063 Fire detection & burglar alarm systems specialization; burglar alarm maintenance & monitoring; fire alarm maintenance & monitoring; electrical apparatus & equipment

(P-2431)
BEAM VACUUMS CALIFORNIA INC
Also Called: Beam "easy Living" Center
422 Henderson St, Grass Valley (95945-7311)
P.O. Box 1803 (95945-1803)
PHONE.............................916 564-3279
Robert Medlyn, *President*
Julie Medlyn, *Planning*
Brian O''brien, *Sales Executive*
EMP: 50
SQ FT: 13,000
SALES (est): 7.8MM **Privately Held**
WEB: www.beameasy.com
SIC: 1731 1799 5722 5731 Environmental system control installation; sound equipment specialization; voice, data & video wiring contractor; closet organizers, installation & design; vacuum cleaners; high fidelity stereo equipment; communication equipment; closet organizers & shelving units

(P-2432)
BERGELECTRIC CORP (PA)
3182 Lionshead Ave, Carlsbad (92010-4701)
PHONE.............................760 638-2374
Thomas R Anderson, *Ch of Bd*
Alan Mashburn, *President*
William Wingrning, *CEO*
William M Wingerning, *Exec VP*
Edward P Billig, *Senior VP*
▲ **EMP:** 250
SALES: 483.1MM **Privately Held**
WEB: www.bergelectric.com
SIC: 1731 General electrical contractor

(P-2433)
BERGELECTRIC CORP
650 Opper St, Escondido (92029-1020)
PHONE.............................760 746-1003
Tom Anderson, *Branch Mgr*
Eileen Cedano, *Admin Asst*
Lupe Zacarias, *Administration*
Stephen Smith, *Technical Mgr*
Bill Peot, *Project Mgr*
EMP: 760
SALES (corp-wide): 483.1MM **Privately Held**
WEB: www.bergelectric.com
SIC: 1731 General electrical contractor
PA: Bergelectric Corp.
3182 Lionshead Ave
Carlsbad CA 92010
760 638-2374

(P-2434)
BERGELECTRIC CORP
11333 Sunrise Park Dr, Rancho Cordova (95742-6532)
PHONE.............................916 636-1880
Matt Ordway, *Branch Mgr*
EMP: 100
SALES (corp-wide): 483.1MM **Privately Held**
WEB: www.bergelectric.com
SIC: 1731 General electrical contractor
PA: Bergelectric Corp.
3182 Lionshead Ave
Carlsbad CA 92010
760 638-2374

(P-2435)
BERGELECTRIC CORP
1935 Deere Ave, Irvine (92606-4818)
PHONE.............................949 250-7005
Mark Bauer, *Manager*
Wilson Toro, *Project Mgr*
EMP: 95

▲ = Import ▼=Export
◆ =Import/Export

SALES (corp-wide): 483.1MM **Privately Held**
WEB: www.bergelectric.com
SIC: 1731 General electrical contractor
PA: Bergelectric Corp.
3182 Lionshead Ave
Carlsbad CA 92010
760 638-2374

(P-2436)
BLACK DIAMOND ELECTRIC INC
2595 W 10th St, Antioch (94509-1374)
PHONE..............................925 777-3440
Jason C Pauline, *CEO*
Carey Neely, *Officer*
Mike Pauline, *General Mgr*
Greg Lloyd, *Administration*
Naila Viveros, *Administration*
EMP: 100
SQ FT: 9,000
SALES (est): 21.1MM **Privately Held**
SIC: 1731 General electrical contractor

(P-2437)
BOCKMON & WOODY ELC CO INC
1528 El Pinal Dr, Stockton (95205-2643)
P.O. Box 1018 (95201-1018)
PHONE..............................209 464-4878
Gary E Woody, *President*
Jeff Bockmon, *Vice Pres*
Gary M Woody, *Vice Pres*
Matt Sappington, *Project Mgr*
Daniel Schoennauer, *Project Mgr*
EMP: 190
SQ FT: 36,000
SALES: 40MM **Privately Held**
WEB: www.bockmonwoody.com
SIC: 1731 General electrical contractor

(P-2438)
BRAUN ELECTRIC COMPANY INC (HQ)
3000 E Belle Ter, Bakersfield (93307-7093)
PHONE..............................661 633-1451
John A Braun, *President*
Kevin B Coghlin, *Vice Pres*
Jeff Coghlin, *IT/INT Sup*
Butch Bradford, *Manager*
EMP: 50 **EST:** 1945
SQ FT: 11,000
SALES (est): 34.3MM
SALES (corp-wide): 38.6MM **Privately Held**
WEB: www.braunelec.com
SIC: 1731 General electrical contractor
PA: C&B Holding Co., Inc.
3000 Belle Terrace
Bakersfield CA 93304
661 633-1451

(P-2439)
BRAUN ELECTRIC COMPANY INC
111 Main St, Taft (93268-3519)
P.O. Box 335 (93268-0335)
PHONE..............................661 763-1531
John Braun, *Manager*
EMP: 140
SALES (corp-wide): 38.6MM **Privately Held**
WEB: www.braunelec.com
SIC: 1731 General electrical contractor
HQ: Braun Electric Company, Inc.
3000 E Belle Ter
Bakersfield CA 93307
661 633-1451

(P-2440)
BRENNAN ELECTRIC INC
460 S Stoddard Ave Ste 3, San Bernardino (92401-2039)
P.O. Box 1028, Rancho Cucamonga (91729-1028)
PHONE..............................909 772-2263
Robert Brennan, *President*
Jeff Deputy, *Vice Pres*
EMP: 180
SQ FT: 2,000
SALES (est): 13.7MM **Privately Held**
SIC: 1731 General electrical contractor

(P-2441)
BRIGGS ELECTRIC INC (PA)
14381 Franklin Ave, Tustin (92780-7010)
PHONE..............................714 544-2500
Jeff Perry, *President*
Thomas J Perry, *President*
Todd Perry, *CFO*
▲ **EMP:** 100
SQ FT: 5,500
SALES: 83.5MM **Privately Held**
WEB: www.briggselectric.com
SIC: 1731 General electrical contractor

(P-2442)
BRUDVIK INC (PA)
Also Called: BRUDVIK RENTAL DIVISION
600 S Eugene Rd, Palm Springs (92264-1514)
PHONE..............................760 320-4429
John Brudvik, *President*
Veneita Brudvik, *Corp Secy*
Bo Ford, *Vice Pres*
EMP: 70
SQ FT: 1,000
SALES: 3.9MM **Privately Held**
WEB: www.brudvikelectric.com
SIC: 1731 8711 7359 5063 General electrical contractor; electrical or electronic engineering; stores & yards equipment rental; lighting fixtures

(P-2443)
BUDGET ELECTRICAL CONTRS INC
25051 5th St, San Bernardino (92410-5119)
PHONE..............................909 381-2646
Danny E Guy, *CEO*
William Morris Diesel, *President*
EMP: 150
SQ FT: 5,000
SALES (est): 18MM **Privately Held**
WEB: www.becelectric.com
SIC: 1731 General electrical contractor

(P-2444)
BUILDING ELCTRONIC CONTRLS INC (PA)
2246 Lindsay Way, Glendora (91740-5398)
PHONE..............................909 305-1600
Richard Taylor, *President*
Shelley Taylor, *Vice Pres*
EMP: 50
SQ FT: 13,000
SALES: 17.2MM **Privately Held**
WEB: www.becinc.net
SIC: 1731 3699 General electrical contractor; security control equipment & systems; security devices

(P-2445)
BUTTERFIELD ELECTRIC INC (PA)
2101 Freeway Dr Ste A, Woodland (95776-9510)
P.O. Box 25 (95776-0025)
PHONE..............................530 666-2116
Rick Butterfield, *President*
Rorie Butterfield, *Vice Pres*
EMP: 165
SQ FT: 14,000
SALES (est): 29MM **Privately Held**
WEB: www.butterfieldelectric.com
SIC: 1731 General electrical contractor

(P-2446)
C & R SYSTEMS INC (PA)
1835 Capital St, Corona (92880-1727)
PHONE..............................951 270-0255
Pam Mosbaugh, *President*
Robert V Cross, *Principal*
Timothy Potts, *Senior Engr*
Linda Van Meter, *Sales Staff*
Robbie Sorensen, *Warehouse Mgr*
EMP: 50
SQ FT: 8,000
SALES (est): 14.3MM **Privately Held**
WEB: www.crsys.net
SIC: 1731 Telephone & telephone equipment installation

(P-2447)
C H REYNOLDS ELECTRIC INC
Also Called: Ch Reynolds
1281 Wayne Ave, San Jose (95131-3599)
PHONE..............................408 436-9280
Charles Reynolds, *President*
EMP: 500
SQ FT: 25,000
SALES (est): 51MM **Privately Held**
WEB: www.chreynolds.com
SIC: 1731 General electrical contractor

(P-2448)
CALENERGY LLC
7030 Gentry Rd, Calipatria (92233-9720)
PHONE..............................402 231-1527
Bill Fehrman, *President*
Mary Jo Ayala, *Manager*
EMP: 350 **EST:** 2013
SALES (est): 30.3MM **Privately Held**
SIC: 1731 Electric power systems contractors

(P-2449)
CALIFORNIA AND NEVADA IBEW/NEC
Also Called: California Lmcc/Ibew-Neca
7041 Koll Center Pkwy # 100, Pleasanton (94566-3175)
PHONE..............................925 828-6322
Bernie Kotlier, *Principal*
EMP: 99
SALES: 923.9K **Privately Held**
SIC: 1731 Electrical work

(P-2450)
CAROL ELECTRIC COMPANY INC
3822 Cerritos Ave, Los Alamitos (90720-2420)
PHONE..............................562 431-1870
John R Fuqua, *Ch of Bd*
Allen Moffitt, *President*
Brian Moffitt, *Vice Pres*
Erik Anderson, *Project Mgr*
Jeff Fetters, *Project Mgr*
EMP: 90
SQ FT: 10,000
SALES (est): 17.4MM **Privately Held**
WEB: www.carolelectric.com
SIC: 1731 General electrical contractor

(P-2451)
CHAMPION ELECTRIC INC
3950 Garner Rd, Riverside (92501-1005)
PHONE..............................951 276-9619
Glenn Rowden, *President*
Tom Rowden, *Vice Pres*
Roger Hernandez, *Project Engr*
Liset Galv N, *Accountant*
Salina Corral, *Personnel Assit*
EMP: 65
SQ FT: 12,000
SALES (est): 8MM **Privately Held**
WEB: www.championelec.com
SIC: 1731 General electrical contractor

(P-2452)
CHICO ELECTRIC INC
36 W Eaton Rd, Chico (95973-0160)
PHONE..............................530 891-1933
Norman Nielsen, *CEO*
Debora Robison, *Analyst*
EMP: 60
SQ FT: 8,500
SALES: 12MM **Privately Held**
SIC: 1731 General electrical contractor

(P-2453)
CLIMATEC LLC
13715 Stowe Dr, Poway (92064-6836)
PHONE..............................858 391-7000
Eince Scalise, *Branch Mgr*
EMP: 50
SALES (corp-wide): 294.8MM **Privately Held**
SIC: 1731 Environmental system control installation; energy management controls
HQ: Climatec, Llc
2851 W Kathleen Rd
Phoenix AZ 85053
602 944-3330

(P-2454)
COCKRELL ELECTRIC INC
79553 Country Club Dr B, Bermuda Dunes (92203-1283)
PHONE..............................760 864-6233
John Cockrell, *President*
Michele Cockrell, *Vice Pres*
EMP: 85
SQ FT: 5,000
SALES (est): 9.1MM **Privately Held**
WEB: www.cockrellelectric.com
SIC: 1731 General electrical contractor

(P-2455)
COGAR INTERNATIONAL ENRGY CORP (PA)
5286 Industrial Dr, Huntington Beach (92649-1515)
P.O. Box 93967, Pasadena (91109-3967)
PHONE..............................626 494-8157
Gabriel Obadan, *President*
Karen Harris, *Vice Pres*
Connie ISA, *Vice Pres*
EMP: 50
SQ FT: 5,000
SALES (est): 2.4MM **Privately Held**
SIC: 1731 Electric power systems contractors

(P-2456)
COLLINS ELECTRICAL COMPANY INC (PA)
3412 Metro Dr, Stockton (95215-9440)
PHONE..............................209 466-3691
Eugene C Gini, *President*
Phil Asborno, *COO*
Brian Gini, *Vice Pres*
Craig Gini, *Vice Pres*
Dianne R Gini, *Vice Pres*
EMP: 200 **EST:** 1928
SQ FT: 80,000
SALES (est): 64.8MM **Privately Held**
WEB: www.collinselectric.com
SIC: 1731 General electrical contractor

(P-2457)
COLLINS ELECTRICAL COMPANY INC
1902 Channel Dr, West Sacramento (95691-3441)
PHONE..............................209 466-3691
Kevin Gini, *Branch Mgr*
Joe Moreno, *Executive*
Adam Wasche, *Foreman/Supr*
EMP: 108
SALES (corp-wide): 64.8MM **Privately Held**
WEB: www.collinselectric.com
SIC: 1731 General electrical contractor
PA: Collins Electrical Company, Inc.
3412 Metro Dr
Stockton CA 95215
209 466-3691

(P-2458)
COLLINS ELECTRICAL COMPANY INC
385 Reservation Rd, Marina (93933-3229)
PHONE..............................831 384-0114
Eric Tonnesen, *Branch Mgr*
EMP: 77
SALES (corp-wide): 64.8MM **Privately Held**
WEB: www.collinselectric.com
SIC: 1731 General electrical contractor
PA: Collins Electrical Company, Inc.
3412 Metro Dr
Stockton CA 95215
209 466-3691

(P-2459)
COMET ELECTRIC INC
21625 Prairie St, Chatsworth (91311-5833)
PHONE..............................818 340-0965
Adam Saitman, *Principal*
Keith Berson, *COO*
Jason Pennington, *CFO*
Steve Goad, *Vice Pres*
Amy Padilla, *Administration*
EMP: 150
SQ FT: 12,000
SALES (est): 41.1MM **Privately Held**
WEB: www.cometelectric.com
SIC: 1731 General electrical contractor

PRODUCTS & SVCS

(P-2460)
COMMUNCTION WIRG SPCALISTS INC
Also Called: C W S
8909 Complex Dr Ste F, San Diego
(92123-1418)
PHONE..............................858 278-4545
Eric Templin, *Owner*
Donna Templin, *Shareholder*
Richard Templin, *Vice Pres*
Barbara Gerardi, *Admin Asst*
Darren Waitley, *Admin Asst*
EMP: 80
SQ FT: 5,500
SALES: 8MM **Privately Held**
WEB: www.cwssandiego.com
SIC: 1731 Telephone & telephone equipment installation; voice, data & video wiring contractor

(P-2461)
COMTEL SYSTEMS TECHNOLOGY
1292 Hammerwood Ave, Sunnyvale
(94089-2232)
PHONE..............................408 543-5600
Richard Nielsen, *President*
Andrea Nielsen, *Vice Pres*
Bryan Herrin, *Engineer*
Haig Kambourian, *Engineer*
Mark Realina, *Engineer*
EMP: 70
SQ FT: 10,760
SALES (est): 14MM **Privately Held**
WEB: www.comtelsys.com
SIC: 1731 Communications specialization; access control systems specialization; fire detection & burglar alarm systems specialization

(P-2462)
CONTRA COSTA ELECTRIC INC (DH)
825 Howe Rd, Martinez (94553-3441)
P.O. Box 2523 (94553-0317)
PHONE..............................925 229-4250
Michael Dias, *President*
Dave Galli, *CFO*
Charlie Hadsell, *Vice Pres*
Joey Ramirez, *Vice Pres*
Tom Tatro, *Vice Pres*
EMP: 300
SALES (est): 84.1MM
SALES (corp-wide): 8.1B **Publicly Held**
WEB: www.ccelectric.com
SIC: 1731 General electrical contractor

(P-2463)
CONTRA COSTA ELECTRIC INC
3208 Landco Dr, Bakersfield (93308-6156)
PHONE..............................661 322-4036
Richard Trainer, *Manager*
Andy Zepeda, *Project Mgr*
Morris Coleman, *Manager*
EMP: 104
SALES (corp-wide): 8.1B **Publicly Held**
WEB: www.ccelectric.com
SIC: 1731 General electrical contractor
HQ: Contra Costa Electric, Inc.
825 Howe Rd
Martinez CA 94553
925 229-4250

(P-2464)
COSCO FIRE PROTECTION INC
7455 Longard Rd, Livermore (94551-8238)
PHONE..............................925 455-2751
Phil Raya, *Manager*
Jamie Duncan, *Administration*
EMP: 96 **Privately Held**
SIC: 1731 3494 8711 7382 General electrical contractor; sprinkler systems, field; engineering services; security systems services; plumbing, heating, air-conditioning contractors
HQ: Cosco Fire Protection, Inc.
29222 Rancho Viejo Rd # 205
San Juan Capistrano CA 92675
714 974-8770

(P-2465)
COVE ELECTRIC INC
77971 Wildcat Dr Ste F, Palm Desert
(92211-4133)
PHONE..............................760 568-9924

Charles Bojkovsky, *President*
Michele Bojkovsky, *Shareholder*
Jeannie Stewart, *CFO*
Steve Tavares, *Vice Pres*
EMP: 70 **EST:** 1976
SQ FT: 4,500
SALES: 8.7MM **Privately Held**
WEB: www.coveelectric.com
SIC: 1731 General electrical contractor

(P-2466)
CSI ELECTRICAL CONTRACTORS INC
41769 11th St W Ste B, Palmdale
(93551-1418)
PHONE..............................661 723-0869
Roland Tamayo, *General Mgr*
EMP: 90
SALES (corp-wide): 1.5B **Publicly Held**
SIC: 1731 General electrical contractor
HQ: Csi Electrical Contractors, Inc.
10623 Fulton Wells Ave
Santa Fe Springs CA 90670
562 946-0700

(P-2467)
CSI ELECTRICAL CONTRACTORS INC (HQ)
Also Called: C S I
10623 Fulton Wells Ave, Santa Fe Springs
(90670-3741)
P.O. Box 2887 (90670-0887)
PHONE..............................562 946-0700
Steven M Watts, *CEO*
Andy Klein, *President*
EMP: 150
SALES (est): 101.5MM
SALES (corp-wide): 1.5B **Publicly Held**
WEB: www.csielectric.com
SIC: 1731 General electrical contractor
PA: Myr Group Inc.
1701 Golf Rd Ste 3-1012
Rolling Meadows IL 60008
847 290-1891

(P-2468)
CUPERTINO ELECTRIC INC
350 Lenore Way, Felton (95018-8973)
P.O. Box 1517 (95018-1517)
PHONE..............................408 808-8260
EMP: 1019
SALES (corp-wide): 400MM **Privately Held**
SIC: 1731 General electrical contractor
PA: Cupertino Electric, Inc.
1132 N 7th St
San Jose CA 95112
408 808-8000

(P-2469)
CUPERTINO ELECTRIC INC (PA)
Also Called: Cei
1132 N 7th St, San Jose (95112-4438)
PHONE..............................408 808-8000
Tom Schott, *President*
Gene Ryley, *COO*
Bill Slakey, *CFO*
Bruce Baxter, *Vice Pres*
James Medefesser, *Vice Pres*
▲ **EMP:** 400
SQ FT: 90,000
SALES: 400MM **Privately Held**
WEB: www.cei.com
SIC: 1731 General electrical contractor

(P-2470)
CUPERTINO ELECTRIC INC
1740 Cesar Chavez Fl 2, San Francisco
(94124-1134)
PHONE..............................415 970-3400
Adam Spillane, *Branch Mgr*
BJ Johnson, *Administration*
Melanie Avery, *Project Mgr*
Michael Burnaugh, *Project Mgr*
Michele Heppler, *Credit Staff*
EMP: 55
SALES (corp-wide): 400MM **Privately Held**
WEB: www.cei.com
SIC: 1731 General electrical contractor
PA: Cupertino Electric, Inc.
1132 N 7th St
San Jose CA 95112
408 808-8000

(P-2471)
D M ELECTRIC INC
336 S Waterman Ave Ste K, San
Bernardino (92408-1533)
PHONE..............................909 888-8639
Danny Moore, *President*
Michelle Moore, *Corp Secy*
EMP: 80
SQ FT: 1,000
SALES (est): 6.2MM **Privately Held**
SIC: 1731 Electrical work

(P-2472)
DAMON ELECTRICAL
7800 Bobbyboyar Ave, West Hills
(91304-4418)
PHONE..............................818 426-3450
Zekrollah Ali, *Principal*
EMP: 65 **EST:** 2011
SALES (est): 3.1MM **Privately Held**
SIC: 1731 General electrical contractor

(P-2473)
DAN FREITAS ELECTRIC
983 E Levin Ave, Tulare (93274-6525)
PHONE..............................559 686-9572
Daniel Freitas, *President*
Jeanette Freitas, *Vice Pres*
EMP: 60
SQ FT: 14,460
SALES (est): 11.2MM **Privately Held**
WEB: www.danfreitaselectric.com
SIC: 1731 General electrical contractor

(P-2474)
DECKER ELC CO INC ELEC CONTRS
147 Beacon St, South San Francisco
(94080-6921)
PHONE..............................650 635-1390
David Chad, *Vice Pres*
EMP: 100
SALES (corp-wide): 112.3MM **Privately Held**
WEB: www.deckerelectric.com
SIC: 1731 General electrical contractor
PA: Decker Electric Co., Inc., Electrical Contractors
1282 Folsom St
San Francisco CA 94103
415 552-1622

(P-2475)
DEPLOYMENT SOLUTIONS LLC
332 Bandini Pl, Vista (92083-5903)
PHONE..............................317 281-9682
Jennifer Shaffer, *Partner*
Martin Keith, *Partner*
EMP: 50
SALES (est): 5.4MM **Privately Held**
WEB: www.deploymentsolutions.com
SIC: 1731 Electronic controls installation; communications specialization

(P-2476)
DYNALECTRIC COMPANY
668 Flinn Ave, Moorpark (93021-2077)
PHONE..............................805 517-1253
Frank Miller, *Vice Pres*
EMP: 127
SALES (corp-wide): 8.1B **Publicly Held**
SIC: 1731 General electrical contractor
HQ: Dynalectric Company
22930 Shaw Rd Ste 100
Dulles VA 20166
703 288-2866

(P-2477)
DYNALECTRIC COMPANY
9505 Chesapeake Dr, San Diego
(92123-6393)
PHONE..............................858 712-4700
Daivd Rispolrch, *Manager*
Will Coyle, *Planning Mgr*
Eric Clevenger, *Project Mgr*
Jim Medland, *Engineer*
Philip Cafaro, *Associate*
EMP: 300
SALES (corp-wide): 8.1B **Publicly Held**
WEB: www.dyna-fl.com
SIC: 1731 General electrical contractor
HQ: Dynalectric Company
22930 Shaw Rd Ste 100
Dulles VA 20166
703 288-2866

(P-2478)
DYNALECTRIC COMPANY
4462 Corporate Center Dr, Los Alamitos
(90720-2539)
PHONE..............................714 236-2242
Christopher Pesavento, *Branch Mgr*
EMP: 127
SALES (corp-wide): 8.1B **Publicly Held**
WEB: www.dyna-fl.com
SIC: 1731 General electrical contractor
HQ: Dynalectric Company
22930 Shaw Rd Ste 100
Dulles VA 20166
703 288-2866

(P-2479)
DYNALECTRIC COMPANY
825 Howe Rd, Martinez (94553-3441)
PHONE..............................415 487-4700
David Raspolich, *Manager*
EMP: 150
SALES (corp-wide): 8.1B **Publicly Held**
SIC: 1731 General electrical contractor
HQ: Dynalectric Company
22930 Shaw Rd Ste 100
Dulles VA 20166
703 288-2866

(P-2480)
EDWARD STRALING
Also Called: Quality Electrical Services
2940 Grace Ln Ste C, Costa Mesa
(92626-4133)
PHONE..............................760 887-3673
Edward Sterling, *Owner*
EMP: 50
SQ FT: 7,500
SALES (est): 4.1MM **Privately Held**
SIC: 1731 General electrical contractor

(P-2481)
EDWARDS TECHNOLOGIES INC
139 Maryland St, El Segundo (90245-4116)
PHONE..............................310 536-7070
Brian Edwards, *President*
▲ **EMP:** 51
SQ FT: 10,000
SALES (est): 17.3MM **Privately Held**
WEB: www.edwardstechnologies.com
SIC: 1731 Sound equipment specialization

(P-2482)
ELCOR ELECTRIC INC
3310 Bassett St, Santa Clara (95054-2702)
PHONE..............................408 986-1320
George Woodley, *General Mgr*
Clint Woodley, *Vice Pres*
EMP: 120
SQ FT: 5,000
SALES (est): 17.4MM **Privately Held**
SIC: 1731 General electrical contractor

(P-2483)
ELECTRIC SVC & SUP CO PASADENA
Also Called: Essco
2668 E Foothill Blvd, Pasadena
(91107-3409)
PHONE..............................626 795-8641
Stanley R Lazarian, *President*
Nancy Rose, *Treasurer*
Iris Lazarian, *Vice Pres*
EMP: 70 **EST:** 1946
SALES (est): 7.1MM **Privately Held**
WEB: www.esscoelectric.com
SIC: 1731 General electrical contractor

(P-2484)
ELECTRIC USA
480 Aldo Ave, Santa Clara (95054-2304)
PHONE..............................800 921-1151
John Lim, *Owner*
EMP: 50
SALES (est): 1.4MM **Privately Held**
SIC: 1731 1711 General electrical contractor; plumbing contractors

(P-2485)
ELECTRONIC CONTROL SYSTEMS LLC
Also Called: Albireo Energy
12575 Kirkham Ct Ste 1, Poway
(92064-8844)
PHONE..............................858 513-1911
Dan Coler, *Mng Member*

EMP: 145
SQ FT: 17,000
SALES: 27MM
SALES (corp-wide): 55MM **Privately Held**
WEB: www.ecscontrols.com
SIC: 1731 7382 Energy management controls; security systems services
PA: Albireo Energy, Llc
3 Ethel Rd Ste 300
Edison NJ 08817
732 512-9100

(P-2486)
ELITE ELECTRIC
9415 Bellegrave Ave, Riverside (92509-2741)
PHONE...................................951 681-5811
Carl Eric Dawson, *President*
Krista Olson, *Division Mgr*
Marshall Hockersmith, *Project Mgr*
Tara Fogliasso, *Controller*
EMP: 80
SQ FT: 1,720
SALES (est): 8.8MM **Privately Held**
SIC: 1731 General electrical contractor

(P-2487)
ELITE POWER INC
6530 Asher Ln, Sacramento (95828-1832)
PHONE...................................916 739-1580
Walt Zacharias, *President*
Shannon Allen, *Accounting Mgr*
Todd May, *Director*
EMP: 54
SQ FT: 15,000
SALES: 9.7MM **Privately Held**
WEB: www.elitepower.com
SIC: 1731 General electrical contractor

(P-2488)
ENERPATH SERVICES INC
1758 Orange Tree Ln, Redlands (92374-2856)
PHONE...................................909 335-1699
Stephen Guthrie, *President*
Janina Guthrie, *Treasurer*
Jonathan Baty, *Admin Sec*
EMP: 100
SQ FT: 4,500
SALES (est): 16.9MM **Privately Held**
WEB: www.expertlighting.com
SIC: 1731 8748 Lighting contractor; lighting consultant

(P-2489)
EQUAL ACCESS INTERNATIONAL
1212 Market St Ste 200, San Francisco (94102-4817)
PHONE...................................415 561-4884
Ronni Goldfarb, *President*
Lisa Ellis, *COO*
Jennifer Koliba, *Vice Pres*
Michael Bowman, *Executive*
Gordon Shettle, *Program Mgr*
EMP: 52
SQ FT: 2,459
SALES: 12.2MM **Privately Held**
WEB: www.equalaccess.org
SIC: 1731 Communications specialization

(P-2490)
ESYS ENERGY CONTROL COMPANY
4520 Stine Rd Ste 7, Bakersfield (93313-2372)
PHONE...................................661 833-1902
Fabio Russoniello, *President*
Brian Frasnelly, *Engineer*
Cody Willis, *Engineer*
Andrea Prise, *Auditor*
EMP: 60
SQ FT: 12,000
SALES (est): 12.9MM **Privately Held**
WEB: www.esys-tecc.com
SIC: 1731 5084 Electronic controls installation; controlling instruments & accessories

(P-2491)
FAITH ELECTRIC LLC
12350 Hesperia Rd Ste 215, Victorville (92395)
PHONE...................................909 767-2682
Elijah Adams, *CEO*

EMP: 135
SQ FT: 5,000
SALES (est): 2.3MM **Privately Held**
SIC: 1731 Electrical work

(P-2492)
FAR WEST ELECTRIC INC
6094 Keswick Ave, Riverside (92506-3747)
PHONE...................................909 684-8661
Joe Ruzzamenti, *President*
Rick Ruzzamanti, *Vice Pres*
Judy Ruzzamanti, *Admin Sec*
EMP: 60
SQ FT: 2,100
SALES: 10MM **Privately Held**
SIC: 1731 General electrical contractor

(P-2493)
FEI ENTERPRISES INC
633 S La Brea Ave, Los Angeles (90036-3521)
PHONE...................................323 937-0856
Gabriel Fedida, *CEO*
▲ EMP: 50
SALES (est): 6.8MM **Privately Held**
WEB: www.feienterprises.com
SIC: 1731 5063 General electrical contractor; burglar alarm systems

(P-2494)
FIRST ALARM
1 Lower Ragsdale Dr # 3700, Monterey (93940-5769)
PHONE...................................831 649-1111
David Hood, *Manager*
John L Fala, *Sales Executive*
EMP: 869
SALES (corp-wide): 45.8MM **Privately Held**
SIC: 1731 Fire detection & burglar alarm systems specialization
PA: First Alarm
1111 Estates Dr
Aptos CA 95003
831 476-1111

(P-2495)
FISK ELECTRIC COMPANY
15870 Olden St, Sylmar (91342-1241)
PHONE...................................818 884-1166
Orvil Anthony, *Senior VP*
EMP: 165
SALES (corp-wide): 4.4B **Publicly Held**
SIC: 1731 General electrical contractor
HQ: Fisk Electric Company
10855 Westview Dr
Houston TX 77043
713 868-6111

(P-2496)
FLATIRON ELECTRIC GROUP INC
15335 Fairfield Ranch Rd # 200, Chino Hills (91709-8833)
PHONE...................................714 228-9631
Kurt Welter, *President*
John Diciurcio, *CEO*
Javier Sevilla, *COO*
Lars Leitner, *CFO*
EMP: 50
SALES (est): 5.3MM
SALES (corp-wide): 475MM **Privately Held**
SIC: 1731 General electrical contractor
HQ: Flatiron West, Inc.
16470 W Bernardo Dr 120
San Diego CA 92127

(P-2497)
FODDRILL CONSTRUCTION CORP
13831 Roswell Ave Ste H, Chino (91710-5470)
P.O. Box 826 (91708-0826)
PHONE...................................909 591-4095
Leonora Foddrill, *President*
Abel Munoz, *Vice Pres*
EMP: 59
SQ FT: 2,500
SALES: 7.5MM **Privately Held**
SIC: 1731 Lighting contractor

(P-2498)
FOSHAY ELECTRIC COINC
1555 Laurel Bay Ln, San Diego (92154-7715)
PHONE...................................858 277-7676
Theresa M Faucher, *President*
Michael Beringhaus, *Vice Pres*
Mark Faucher, *Vice Pres*
EMP: 100
SQ FT: 8,000
SALES (est): 15.8MM **Privately Held**
WEB: www.foshayelectric.com
SIC: 1731 General electrical contractor

(P-2499)
FRANKE CON J ELECTRIC INC
317 N Grant St, Stockton (95202-2633)
PHONE...................................209 462-0717
Barry Frain, *President*
Diana Frain, *Corp Secy*
James A Ratner, *Exec VP*
Lewis Frain, *Vice Pres*
Lori Cass, *Office Mgr*
EMP: 100 EST: 1925
SQ FT: 7,000
SALES (est): 24.2MM **Privately Held**
WEB: www.cjfranke.com
SIC: 1731 General electrical contractor

(P-2500)
FRANKLIN ELECTRIC CO INC
1129 Brussels St, San Francisco (94134-2105)
PHONE...................................415 467-2693
EMP: 563
SALES (corp-wide): 1.3B **Publicly Held**
SIC: 1731 Electrical work
PA: Franklin Electric Co., Inc.
9255 Coverdale Rd
Fort Wayne IN 46809
260 824-2900

(P-2501)
GLOBAL POWER GROUP INC (PA)
12060 Woodside Ave, Lakeside (92040-2949)
PHONE...................................619 579-1221
Terry Mammen, *CEO*
Salvatore Martorana, *President*
Salvador Ceballos, *CFO*
William Havrilla, *Director*
EMP: 61
SQ FT: 10,000
SALES: 13.4MM **Privately Held**
SIC: 1731 Electric power systems contractors

(P-2502)
GRC ELECTRIC INC
Also Called: Wired Rite Electric
675 S Glenwood Pl, Burbank (91506-2819)
PHONE...................................818 242-9891
Glen Christensen, *Principal*
EMP: 80
SALES (est): 2.9MM **Privately Held**
SIC: 1731 Electrical work

(P-2503)
GREGG ELECTRIC INC
608 W Emporia St, Ontario (91762-3709)
PHONE...................................909 983-1794
Randall F Fehlman, *President*
Victoria Mensen, *CFO*
James Fehlman, *Vice Pres*
Michelle Fehlman, *Manager*
EMP: 150 EST: 1961
SQ FT: 15,000
SALES (est): 22.9MM **Privately Held**
WEB: www.greggelectric.com
SIC: 1731 General electrical contractor

(P-2504)
GUILLEN ELECTRIC COMPANY INC
1485 Andrew Dr Ste D, Claremont (91711-5766)
PHONE...................................909 480-3915
Julio Raymond Guillen, *CEO*
EMP: 50
SALES (est): 74.5K **Privately Held**
SIC: 1731 Electrical work

(P-2505)
H & D ELECTRIC
5237 Walnut Ave Ste 100, Sacramento (95841-2694)
P.O. Box 41360 (95841-0360)
PHONE...................................916 332-0794
Mark E Cooper, *President*
EMP: 360
SQ FT: 14,400
SALES (est): 36.5MM **Privately Held**
WEB: www.hdelectric.com
SIC: 1731 General electrical contractor

(P-2506)
H A BOWEN ELECTRIC INC
2055 Williams St, San Leandro (94577-2305)
P.O. Box 2153 (94577-0329)
PHONE...................................510 483-0500
Herbert A Bowen, *President*
EMP: 60 EST: 1979
SQ FT: 9,000
SALES (est): 33.7MM **Privately Held**
WEB: www.bowenelectric.com
SIC: 1731 General electrical contractor

(P-2507)
HACKNEY ELECTRIC INC (PA)
23286 Arroyo Vis, Rcho STA Marg (92688-2610)
PHONE...................................949 264-4000
David J Hackney, *President*
Rebecca Hackney, *Vice Pres*
EMP: 65
SQ FT: 6,200
SALES: 16.1MM **Privately Held**
WEB: www.hackneyelectric.com
SIC: 1731 Electrical work

(P-2508)
HAMILTON AND DILLON ELC INC
1128 Reno Ave, Modesto (95351-1128)
P.O. Box 581890 (95358-0033)
PHONE...................................209 529-6292
Bobby Hamilton, *President*
John Dillon, *Vice Pres*
EMP: 60
SQ FT: 5,000
SALES (est): 7.7MM **Privately Held**
SIC: 1731 General electrical contractor

(P-2509)
HAROLD E NUTTER INC (PA)
Also Called: Harold E Nutter & Son
5930 Rosebud Ln, Sacramento (95841-2989)
PHONE...................................916 334-4343
Norman Nutter, *President*
EMP: 70 EST: 1970
SQ FT: 16,000
SALES (est): 14.9MM **Privately Held**
WEB: www.henutter.com
SIC: 1731 General electrical contractor

(P-2510)
HARRIS L WOODS ELEC CONTR
Also Called: Woods Electric Company
9214 Norwalk Blvd, Santa Fe Springs (90670-2924)
P.O. Box 2367 (90670-0367)
PHONE...................................562 945-8751
Sandra Woods, *President*
Ralph L Woods, *Admin Sec*
EMP: 55 EST: 1975
SQ FT: 5,000
SALES (est): 9.2MM **Privately Held**
SIC: 1731 General electrical contractor

(P-2511)
HCI SYSTEMS INC (PA)
1354 S Parkside Pl, Ontario (91761-4555)
PHONE...................................909 628-7773
Hany Dimitry, *President*
Michael Peters, *President*
Andrew Fahrenhorst, *Senior VP*
Don Harrison, *Vice Pres*
Drew Turner, *Vice Pres*
EMP: 50 EST: 2008
SQ FT: 12,000
SALES (est): 18.4MM **Privately Held**
SIC: 1731 General electrical contractor

(P-2512)
HHS COMMUNICATIONS INC
2042 S Grove Ave, Ontario (91761-5617)
PHONE..................909 230-5170
Royce S Jaime, *President*
EMP: 60 EST: 2007
SALES (est): 7.5MM
SALES (corp-wide): 63.1MM **Privately Held**
SIC: 1731 Fiber optic cable installation
PA: Congruex Llc
2615 13th St
Boulder CO 80304
720 749-2318

(P-2513)
HIGH-LIGHT ELECTRIC INC
6942 Ed Perkic St, Riverside (92504-1005)
P.O. Box 7339 (92513-7339)
PHONE..................951 352-9646
Erwin Mendoza, *President*
Alfredo Limon, *Foreman/Supr*
EMP: 60
SALES: 19.2MM **Privately Held**
WEB: www.mbe-hlj.com
SIC: 1731 General electrical contractor

(P-2514)
HMT ELECTRIC INC
2340 Meyers Ave, Escondido (92029-1008)
PHONE..................858 458-9771
Brian Hudak, *CEO*
Howard Powell, *Division Mgr*
David Holm, *Foreman/Supr*
Craig Landry, *Sr Project Mgr*
Halston Rowe, *Sr Project Mgr*
EMP: 85
SQ FT: 2,000
SALES: 53.8MM **Privately Held**
SIC: 1731 General electrical contractor

(P-2515)
HODGES ELECTRIC INC
1239 Hoblitt Ave, Clovis (93612-2807)
PHONE..................559 298-5533
Roger L Hidy, *President*
Janel M Hidy, *CFO*
EMP: 50
SQ FT: 5,000
SALES (est): 5.8MM **Privately Held**
SIC: 1731 General electrical contractor

(P-2516)
HOT LINE CONSTRUCTION INC
9020 Brentwood Blvd Ste H, Brentwood (94513-4049)
PHONE..................925 634-9333
Carol Bade, *President*
Kelly G Kutchera, *CFO*
Troy Myers, *Vice Pres*
EMP: 425
SQ FT: 4,000
SALES (est): 164.7MM **Privately Held**
WEB: www.hotlineconstructioninc.com
SIC: 1731 1799 Electric power systems contractors; cable splicing service

(P-2517)
HOTLINE TELECOMMUNICATIONS (PA)
528 Bethany Cir, Claremont (91711-2231)
PHONE..................909 593-6575
Harold Hung Kim, *Co-Owner*
Helen Hehja Kim, *Co-Owner*
EMP: 100
SALES (est): 6.2MM **Privately Held**
WEB: www.hotlinetelecom.com
SIC: 1731 Telephone & telephone equipment installation

(P-2518)
HOWE ELECTRIC CONSTRUCTION INC
4682 E Olive Ave, Fresno (93702-1689)
PHONE..................559 255-8992
Todd Howe, *President*
Marjorie Montes, *Treasurer*
Ty Howe, *Vice Pres*
EMP: 140
SALES (est): 18.6MM **Privately Held**
SIC: 1731 General electrical contractor

(P-2519)
ICKLER ELECTRIC CORPORATION
13250 Kirkham Way, Poway (92064)
PHONE..................858 486-1585
Kurt Ickler, *CEO*
Laurie Ickler, *Vice Pres*
EMP: 50
SQ FT: 5,435
SALES (est): 13.5MM **Privately Held**
WEB: www.icklerelectric.com
SIC: 1731 General electrical contractor

(P-2520)
ICS INTEGRATED COMM SYSTEMS
6680 Via Del Oro, San Jose (95119-1392)
PHONE..................408 491-6000
Aaron Colton, *CEO*
Tammy Bailey, *Administration*
Tim Silva, *Administration*
Vince Lacorte, *Project Mgr*
Jim Schmidt, *Project Mgr*
▲ EMP: 65
SQ FT: 18,000
SALES (est): 27.2MM **Privately Held**
WEB: www.ceitronics.com
SIC: 1731 Fire detection & burglar alarm systems specialization; access control systems specialization; cable television installation; voice, data & video wiring contractor

(P-2521)
INTERIOR ELECTRIC INCORPORATED
747 N Main St, Orange (92868-1105)
PHONE..................714 771-9098
Mark Beverly, *President*
Gus Baquerizo, *Vice Pres*
Mark Maskevich, *Vice Pres*
Glen Nielsen, *Vice Pres*
Chad Stewart, *Vice Pres*
EMP: 75
SQ FT: 10,000
SALES (est): 13.3MM **Privately Held**
WEB: www.interiorelectric.com
SIC: 1731 General electrical contractor

(P-2522)
IPITEK INC
2461 Impala Dr, Carlsbad (92010-7227)
P.O. Box 130878 (92013-0878)
PHONE..................760 438-1010
Michael M Salour, *Ch of Bd*
EMP: 170
SQ FT: 40,000
SALES (est): 16.1MM **Privately Held**
WEB: www.ipitek.com
SIC: 1731 Fiber optic cable installation

(P-2523)
ITRON INC
1111 Broadway Ste 1800, Oakland (94607-4091)
PHONE..................510 844-2800
Derek Hall, *Manager*
Kenneth Ambory, *Surgery Dir*
Robin Hill, *Administration*
David Yee, *Director*
Christina Haslund, *Manager*
EMP: 2000
SALES (corp-wide): 2.3B **Publicly Held**
WEB: www.siliconenergy.com
SIC: 1731 3571 Energy management controls; electronic computers
PA: Itron, Inc.
2111 N Molter Rd
Liberty Lake WA 99019
509 924-9900

(P-2524)
JAROTH INC
Also Called: Pacific Telemanagement Svcs
2001 Crow Canyon Rd # 200, San Ramon (94583-5368)
PHONE..................925 553-3650
Thomas R Keane, *CEO*
Michael R Zumbo, *President*
Nancy Rossi, *CFO*
EMP: 130

SALES (est): 33.6MM **Privately Held**
WEB: www.pts-telecom.com
SIC: 1731 7349 Telephone & telephone equipment installation; telephone booth cleaning & maintenance

(P-2525)
JEEVA CORP
Also Called: Satellite Pros
750 E E St Unit B, Ontario (91764-3821)
PHONE..................909 238-4073
Orlando Uranga, *CEO*
Rita Uranga, *CFO*
EMP: 70 EST: 2011
SQ FT: 1,800
SALES: 2.5MM **Privately Held**
SIC: 1731 Cable television installation

(P-2526)
JENSCO INC
Also Called: J M Electric
400 Griffin St, Salinas (93901-4344)
PHONE..................831 422-7819
Frederick A Jensen, *President*
Chris Jensen, *CFO*
Linda Taylan, *Manager*
EMP: 50
SQ FT: 8,400
SALES (est): 8.2MM **Privately Held**
SIC: 1731 General electrical contractor

(P-2527)
JMG SECURITY SYSTEMS INC
17150 Newhope St Ste 109, Fountain Valley (92708-4273)
PHONE..................714 545-8882
Ken Jacobs, *CEO*
Michael Christensen, *Exec VP*
Gil Ledesma, *Exec VP*
Sue Tjelmeland, *Vice Pres*
Chris Ponchak, *Administration*
EMP: 70
SQ FT: 14,000
SALES (est): 14.2MM **Privately Held**
SIC: 1731 5063 Safety & security specialization; burglar alarm systems

(P-2528)
JOE LUNARDI ELECTRIC INC
5334 Sebastopol Rd, Santa Rosa (95407-6423)
P.O. Box 120, Sebastopol (95473-0120)
PHONE..................707 545-4755
Joseph I Lunardi, *Ch of Bd*
Jolene A Corcoran, *President*
Ronald J Lunardi, *Corp Secy*
Raymond J Lunardi, *Vice Pres*
EMP: 52
SQ FT: 12,000
SALES: 10.5MM **Privately Held**
WEB: www.lunardielectric.com
SIC: 1731 General electrical contractor

(P-2529)
JOIE DE VIVRE HOSPITALITY LLC
210 E Main St, Los Gatos (95030-6107)
PHONE..................408 335-1700
EMP: 618
SALES (corp-wide): 231.8MM **Privately Held**
SIC: 1731 Electrical work
PA: Joie De Vivre Hospitality, Llc
1750 Geary Blvd
San Francisco CA 94115
415 835-0300

(P-2530)
KCS ELECTRIC INC
1585 N Harmony Cir, Anaheim (92807-6003)
P.O. Box 1478, Big Bear Lake (92315-1478)
PHONE..................623 551-1500
Kenneth C Simonds, *President*
EMP: 60
SALES (est): 4.1MM **Privately Held**
WEB: www.kcselectric.com
SIC: 1731 Electrical work

(P-2531)
KDC INC (HQ)
Also Called: Kdc Systems
4462 Corporate Center Dr, Los Alamitos (90720-2539)
PHONE..................714 828-7000

Johnny Menninga, *President*
William B Davenport, *CFO*
Jim Bratton, *Engineer*
Charlene Ewell, *Controller*
Dusty Lord, *Human Res Dir*
EMP: 151
SQ FT: 57,000
SALES (est): 64MM
SALES (corp-wide): 8.1B **Publicly Held**
WEB: www.dyna-la.com
SIC: 1731 1611 3823 General electrical contractor; general contractor, highway & street construction; industrial instrmnts msrmnt display/control process variable
PA: Emcor Group, Inc.
301 Merritt 7 Fl 6
Norwalk CT 06851
203 849-7800

(P-2532)
KERTEL COMMUNICATIONS INC (HQ)
Also Called: Sebastian
7600 N Palm Ave Ste 101, Fresno (93711-5520)
PHONE..................559 432-5800
William S Barcus, *CEO*
Jim Sidoti, *Division Mgr*
Sarah Gonzales, *Office Mgr*
Joe Figueroa, *Admin Sec*
Susan Moran, *Admin Sec*
EMP: 92
SQ FT: 9,436
SALES (est): 23.3MM
SALES (corp-wide): 51.4MM **Privately Held**
SIC: 1731 Telephone & telephone equipment installation
PA: Sebastian Enterprises, Inc.
811 S Madera Ave
Kerman CA 93630
559 946-4954

(P-2533)
KITE ELECTRIC INC
Also Called: K E
2 Thomas, Irvine (92618-2512)
PHONE..................949 380-7471
Tracy Adams, *President*
EMP: 120
SALES (est): 14.6MM **Privately Held**
SIC: 1731 Electrical work

(P-2534)
KOSITCH ENTERPRISES INC
Also Called: MISSION ELECTRIC COMPANY
5700 Boscell Cmn, Fremont (94538-5111)
PHONE..................510 657-4460
Jeffrey Kositch, *CEO*
Jeffrey A Kositch, *Treasurer*
Simon Rincon, *Foreman/Supr*
Patrick Macones, *Manager*
Loren Olk, *Manager*
EMP: 80
SQ FT: 9,000
SALES: 29.7MM **Privately Held**
WEB: www.mission-elec.com
SIC: 1731 General electrical contractor

(P-2535)
L TECH NETWORK SERVICES INC
9926 Pioneer Blvd Ste 101, Santa Fe Springs (90670-6248)
PHONE..................562 222-1121
Robert O Lopez, *President*
EMP: 65
SQ FT: 4,060
SALES: 5MM **Privately Held**
WEB: www.ltechnet.com
SIC: 1731 Communications specialization

(P-2536)
LASER ELECTRIC INC (PA)
2250 Micro Pl Ste 200, Escondido (92029-1011)
PHONE..................760 658-6626
Denise Hartnett, *CEO*
Kevin Hartnett, *Vice Pres*
EMP: 50
SQ FT: 11,000
SALES: 18.3MM **Privately Held**
SIC: 1731 General electrical contractor

▲ = Import ▼=Export
◆ =Import/Export

(P-2537)
LEED ELECTRIC INC
13138 Arctic Cir, Santa Fe Springs
(90670-5508)
PHONE..........................562 270-9500
Seth Jamali, *President*
Ali Pakzad, *Vice Pres*
EMP: 51
SQ FT: 7,000
SALES: 14.5MM **Privately Held**
WEB: www.leedelect.com
SIC: 1731 General electrical contractor

(P-2538)
LELAND STANFORD JUNIOR UNIV
Also Called: Department of Public Safety
711 Serra St, Stanford (94305-7203)
PHONE..........................650 723-9633
Laura Wilson, *Director*
EMP: 58
SQ FT: 10,000
SALES (corp-wide): 11.3B **Privately Held**
SIC: 1731 8221 Safety & security specialization; university
PA: Leland Stanford Junior University
450 Jane Stanford Way
Stanford CA 94305
650 723-2300

(P-2539)
M & R JOINT VENTURE ELECTRICAL
Also Called: Marrow Meadows
231 Benton Ct, Walnut (91789-5213)
PHONE..........................909 598-7700
Robert E Meadows, *Vice Pres*
Morrow-Meadows Corporation, *Co-Venturer*
Ray Ellis, *Vice Pres*
David Hill, *Vice Pres*
Chris Salorio, *Planning*
EMP: 60
SALES (est): 6.5MM **Privately Held**
SIC: 1731 General electrical contractor

(P-2540)
MARK III CONSTRUCTION INC (PA)
Also Called: Mark III Dvlpers Dsgn/Builders
5101 Florin Perkins Rd, Sacramento
(95826-4817)
PHONE..........................916 381-8080
Daniel Carlton, *CEO*
Jennifer O'Brien Cooley, *President*
John Cassidy, *CFO*
Michael Brien, *Treasurer*
Michael O'Brien, *Treasurer*
EMP: 75
SQ FT: 11,000
SALES (est): 26.7MM **Privately Held**
SIC: 1731 1542 1711 General electrical contractor; electronic controls installation; commercial & office building, new construction; plumbing contractors; fire sprinkler system installation

(P-2541)
MARK LAND ELECTRIC INC
7876 Deering Ave, Canoga Park
(91304-5005)
PHONE..........................818 883-5110
Lloyd Saitman, *CEO*
John Bennet, *CFO*
Don Dewhurst, *Vice Pres*
Stewart Franklin, *Vice Pres*
John Higham, *Vice Pres*
EMP: 68
SQ FT: 10,000
SALES (est): 25MM **Privately Held**
WEB: www.landmarkelec.com
SIC: 1731 General electrical contractor

(P-2542)
MARTICUS ELECTRIC INC
9266 Beatty Dr Ste D, Sacramento
(95826-9732)
PHONE..........................916 368-2186
Art Munoz, *President*
Susan Munoz, *Corp Secy*
David Munoz, *Vice Pres*
Tim Collins, *Opers Spvr*
EMP: 80
SQ FT: 14,000

SALES (est): 7.3MM **Privately Held**
WEB: www.marticus.com
SIC: 1731 General electrical contractor

(P-2543)
MASS ELECTRIC CONSTRUCTION CO
1925 Wright Ave Ste D, La Verne
(91750-5847)
PHONE..........................800 933-6322
Rohit Shard, *Branch Mgr*
H Richard Case, *Manager*
EMP: 100
SALES (corp-wide): 16.1B **Privately Held**
WEB: www.masselec.com
SIC: 1731 General electrical contractor
HQ: Mass. Electric Construction Co.
400 Totten Pond Rd # 400
Waltham MA 02451
781 290-1000

(P-2544)
MATSON ALARM CO INC (PA)
581 W Fallbrook Ave # 100, Fresno
(93711-5519)
PHONE..........................559 438-8000
Larry E Matson, *President*
Mike Matson, *Vice Pres*
EMP: 50
SQ FT: 1,000
SALES (est): 13.9MM **Privately Held**
WEB: www.matsonalarm.com
SIC: 1731 Fire detection & burglar alarm systems specialization

(P-2545)
MAY-HAN ELECTRIC INC
Also Called: M & M Electric
1600 Auburn Blvd, Sacramento
(95815-1906)
PHONE..........................916 929-0150
Cecilia J Hanson, *CEO*
Audrey Daugherty, *President*
Connie Gisler, *Corp Secy*
EMP: 65
SQ FT: 16,000
SALES (est): 12.7MM **Privately Held**
WEB: www.sacmmelectric.com
SIC: 1731 Lighting contractor

(P-2546)
MB HERZOG ELECTRIC INC
15709 Illinois Ave, Paramount
(90723-4112)
PHONE..........................562 531-2002
Ryan M Herzog, *CEO*
Kevin Ryan, *Vice Pres*
Gail Acosta, *Executive*
Paul Perrizo, *Manager*
EMP: 200
SQ FT: 6,200
SALES (est): 45.1MM **Privately Held**
WEB: www.herzogelectric.com
SIC: 1731 General electrical contractor

(P-2547)
MCMILLAN DATA CMMNICATIONS INC
1950 Cesar Chavez, San Francisco
(94124-1132)
PHONE..........................415 826-5100
Patrick J McMillan, *CEO*
Mark Mahoney, *Managing Prtnr*
Jim Murray, *Managing Prtnr*
Patrick McMillan, *CEO*
EMP: 55
SALES (est): 1.9MM **Privately Held**
SIC: 1731 Electrical work

(P-2548)
MCMILLAN ELECTRIC
1950 Cesar Chavez, San Francisco
(94124-1132)
PHONE..........................415 826-5100
William Musgrave, *President*
Russell Schmittou, *CFO*
David Auch, *Vice Pres*
Ryan Mahoney, *Vice Pres*
Michael McAlister, *Vice Pres*
EMP: 280 EST: 1965
SQ FT: 30,000
SALES (est): 76.5MM **Privately Held**
SIC: 1731 General electrical contractor

(P-2549)
MDE ELECTRIC COMPANY INC
Also Called: MDE Electric
152 Commercial St, Sunnyvale
(94086-5201)
PHONE..........................408 738-8600
Marshall Goldman, *CEO*
Harry Goldman, *Corp Secy*
Ranfis Villatoro, *Purch Agent*
Rudy Cervantes, *Foreman/Supr*
Josh Cipolla, *Foreman/Supr*
EMP: 50
SQ FT: 5,000
SALES (est): 9.2MM **Privately Held**
WEB: www.mde-electric.com
SIC: 1731 General electrical contractor

(P-2550)
MEDLEY COMMUNICATIONS INC
255 N Ash St, Escondido (92027-3068)
PHONE..........................760 294-4579
EMP: 82 **Privately Held**
WEB: www.medleycom.com
SIC: 1731 8748 Cable television installation; communications consulting
PA: Medley Communications, Inc
43015 Black Deer Loop # 103
Temecula CA 92590

(P-2551)
MEDLEY COMMUNICATIONS INC (PA)
43015 Black Deer Loop # 203, Temecula
(92590-3575)
PHONE..........................951 245-5200
Darrin Medley, *President*
EMP: 175
SALES (est): 20.2MM **Privately Held**
WEB: www.medleycom.com
SIC: 1731 8748 Cable television installation; communications consulting

(P-2552)
METROPOLITAN ELEC CNSTR INC
2400 3rd St, San Francisco (94107-3111)
PHONE..........................415 642-3000
Nick Dutto, *Principal*
Mark Friedeberg, *CFO*
Maddie Dong, *Technology*
Tiersa Aldridge, *Human Res Dir*
Jason Griffin, *Manager*
EMP: 210 EST: 1981
SQ FT: 23,000
SALES: 63MM **Privately Held**
WEB: www.metroelectric.com
SIC: 1731 General electrical contractor

(P-2553)
METROPOWER INC
941 Grand Ave, Long Beach (90804-5214)
PHONE..........................562 305-9617
Gary Evan Freenleaf, *Branch Mgr*
EMP: 85
SALES (corp-wide): 149.9MM **Privately Held**
SIC: 1731 Electrical work
HQ: Metropower, Inc.
798 21st Ave
Albany GA 31701
229 432-7345

(P-2554)
MIKE BROWN ELECTRIC CO
561a Mercantile Dr, Cotati (94931-3040)
PHONE..........................707 792-8100
James G Brown, *President*
Tiffany Howe, *Vice Pres*
Susan Allred, *Administration*
Arnold Gonzales, *Project Mgr*
Gregg Mills, *Project Mgr*
EMP: 65
SQ FT: 14,000
SALES (est): 22.3MM **Privately Held**
WEB: www.mbelectric.com
SIC: 1731 General electrical contractor

(P-2555)
MJ STAR-LITE INC
Also Called: Star - Lite Electric
9232 Independence Ave, Chatsworth
(91311-5931)
PHONE..........................818 717-0834

Michael Rios, *President*
EMP: 50
SALES (est): 3MM **Privately Held**
SIC: 1731 Electrical work

(P-2556)
ML ELECTRICWORKS INC
11325 Magnolia Ave, Riverside
(92505-3609)
P.O. Box 70962 (92513-0962)
PHONE..........................951 687-5078
Mark S Lowen, *President*
EMP: 67
SQ FT: 2,000
SALES (est): 5.5MM **Privately Held**
WEB: www.mlelectricworks.com
SIC: 1731 Electrical work

(P-2557)
MODESTO INDUSTRIAL ELEC CO INC (PA)
Also Called: Industrial Electrical Company
1417 Coldwell Ave, Modesto (95350-5703)
PHONE..........................209 527-2800
David Howell, *President*
Michelle Howell, *Admin Sec*
Harold Dawson, *Project Mgr*
Joel Salinas, *Technology*
Tammy Dolberry, *Accounting Mgr*
EMP: 151
SQ FT: 21,000
SALES: 51MM **Privately Held**
WEB: www.i-e-c.net
SIC: 1731 5063 7694 General electrical contractor; motors, electric; electric motor repair

(P-2558)
MORROW-MEADOWS CORPORATION (PA)
Also Called: Cherry City Electric
231 Benton Ct, City of Industry
(91789-5213)
PHONE..........................858 974-3650
Robert E Meadows, *Vice Pres*
Tim Langley, *CFO*
Bob Atkinson, *Vice Pres*
Rick Jarvis, *Vice Pres*
Ed Slingluff, *Vice Pres*
EMP: 2000 EST: 1964
SQ FT: 55,000
SALES (est): 158.5MM **Privately Held**
WEB: www.morrow-meadows.com
SIC: 1731 General electrical contractor

(P-2559)
MSL ELECTRIC INC
2918 E La Jolla St, Anaheim (92806-1305)
PHONE..........................714 693-4837
Warren L Moore, *President*
Sally Moore, *Admin Sec*
EMP: 60
SALES (est): 12.1MM **Privately Held**
SIC: 1731 General electrical contractor

(P-2560)
MURRIETTA CIRCUITS
5000 E Landon Dr, Anaheim (92807-1978)
PHONE..........................714 970-2430
Andrew Murrietta, *CEO*
Albert G Murrietta, *President*
Albert A Murrieta, *COO*
Helen Murrietta, *Treasurer*
Josh Murrietta, *Vice Pres*
EMP: 75
SQ FT: 48,500
SALES: 8.2MM **Privately Held**
WEB: www.murrietta.com
SIC: 1731 3672 8711 Closed circuit television installation; printed circuit boards; engineering services

(P-2561)
NATIONAL FAIL SAFE INC
Also Called: National Fail-Safe SEC Systems
6442 Industry Way, Westminster
(92683-3600)
PHONE..........................562 493-5447
Al Puskas, *President*
Kathy Puskas, *Vice Pres*
Ricardo Rivas, *Engineer*
Bill Bennett, *Sales Associate*
Cristyn Van Fossen, *Sales Staff*
EMP: 50 EST: 1972
SQ FT: 10,000

SALES (est): 8.3MM **Privately Held**
WEB: www.nf-s.com
SIC: 1731 7382 Fire detection & burglar alarm systems specialization; fire alarm maintenance & monitoring

(P-2562)
NAZZARENO ELECTRIC CO INC
1250 E Gene Autry Way, Anaheim (92805-6716)
PHONE...................714 712-4744
Paul Rick Nazzareno, *President*
Leissa Nazzareno, *CFO*
Mindy Sheets, *Admin Asst*
Andrew Mead, *Foreman/Supr*
Jessica Nazzareno, *Manager*
EMP: 75
SQ FT: 10,000
SALES (est): 9.6MM **Privately Held**
SIC: 1731 General electrical contractor

(P-2563)
NEAL ELECTRIC CORP (HQ)
2790 Business Park Dr, Vista (92081-7860)
P.O. Box 1655, Poway (92074-1655)
PHONE...................858 513-2525
Daniel Zupp, *President*
Alex Meruelo, *Treasurer*
Luis Armona, *Vice Pres*
Lance Neal, *Vice Pres*
Dennis Ramsey, *Vice Pres*
EMP: 75
SQ FT: 30,000
SALES (est): 54.4MM
SALES (corp-wide): 377.5MM **Privately Held**
WEB: www.whitney.com
SIC: 1731 General electrical contractor
PA: Meruelo Enterprises, Inc.
　9550 Firestone Blvd # 105
　Downey CA 90241
　562 745-2300

(P-2564)
NELSON & SONS ELECTRIC INC
401 N Walnut Rd, Turlock (95380-9426)
PHONE...................209 667-4343
Keith Nelson, *President*
Shelly Nelson, *Treasurer*
David Nelson, *Vice Pres*
Travis Nelson, *Vice Pres*
EMP: 50
SALES (est): 8.7MM **Privately Held**
SIC: 1731 General electrical contractor

(P-2565)
NETRONIX INTEGRATION INC (PA)
2170 Paragon Dr, San Jose (95131-1305)
PHONE...................408 573-1444
Craig E Jarrett, *President*
Rigoberto Gomez, *Technician*
Charles Haze, *Technician*
David Beale, *Project Mgr*
Eric Jones, *Project Mgr*
EMP: 92
SQ FT: 13,500
SALES (est): 26.7MM **Privately Held**
SIC: 1731 General electrical contractor

(P-2566)
NETVERSANT - SILICON VLY INC (PA)
Also Called: Apex Communications
47811 Warm Springs Blvd, Fremont (94539-7400)
PHONE...................510 771-1200
John Chelstowski, *President*
EMP: 125
SQ FT: 14,000
SALES (est): 13.5MM **Privately Held**
WEB: www.apexcommunications.com
SIC: 1731 7376 Communications specialization; telephone & telephone equipment installation; computer facilities management

(P-2567)
NEVADA REPUBLIC ELECTRIC N INC
11855 White Rock Rd, Rancho Cordova (95742-6603)
PHONE...................916 294-0140
Eric Stafford, *President*
Jeff Stafford, *Treasurer*

Jerry Stafford, *Director*
Linda Stafford, *Director*
EMP: 140
SQ FT: 14,000
SALES (est): 16MM **Privately Held**
WEB: www.republicelectricwest.com
SIC: 1731 General electrical contractor

(P-2568)
NEW AGE ELECTRIC INC
1085 N 11th St, San Jose (95112-2928)
PHONE...................408 279-8787
Kurt Rocklage, *President*
Rachel Pimentel, *Admin Asst*
Chloe Brubaker, *Administration*
Sean Nuesmeyer, *Project Mgr*
Dave Targett, *Purch Mgr*
EMP: 60
SQ FT: 8,500
SALES (est): 13.1MM **Privately Held**
SIC: 1731 General electrical contractor

(P-2569)
NORTH STATE ELEC CONTRS INC
11101 White Rock Rd, Rancho Cordova (95670-6996)
PHONE...................916 572-0571
Rodney Bingaman, *President*
Lori Kirk, *CFO*
Larry Logue, *Project Mgr*
EMP: 80
SQ FT: 24,000
SALES (est): 26.8MM **Privately Held**
SIC: 1731 General electrical contractor

(P-2570)
NORTHLAND CONTROL SYSTEMS INC (PA)
1533 California Cir, Milpitas (95035-3023)
PHONE...................510 226-1015
Pierre Trapanese, *CEO*
Jim Conley, *CFO*
Terrence Graham, *Program Mgr*
Brendan McFall, *Executive Asst*
Henry Hoyne, *CTO*
EMP: 102
SALES (est): 34.2MM **Privately Held**
WEB: www.northlandcontrols.com
SIC: 1731 7389 Fire detection & burglar alarm systems specialization; automobile recovery service

(P-2571)
NRG POWER INC
3011 S Shannon St, Santa Ana (92704-6320)
PHONE...................714 424-6484
Than V Nguyen, *President*
John Toan Nguyen, *Vice Pres*
Daniel MAI, *General Mgr*
Elaine Diep, *Office Mgr*
EMP: 57
SQ FT: 5,700
SALES (est): 6.3MM **Privately Held**
SIC: 1731 General electrical contractor

(P-2572)
OBRYANT ELECTRIC INC
9314 Eton Ave, Chatsworth (91311-5809)
PHONE...................818 407-1986
Cathy O'Bryant, *President*
Steve O'Bryant, *Admin Sec*
EMP: 200 **EST:** 1978
SQ FT: 25,000
SALES (est): 51.4MM **Privately Held**
WEB: www.obryantelectric.com
SIC: 1731 General electrical contractor

(P-2573)
OILFIELD ELECTRIC COMPANY
Also Called: Oilfield Electric & Motor
1801 N Ventura Ave, Ventura (93001-1597)
PHONE...................805 648-3131
Alan Dale Fletcher, *CEO*
Jana Fletcher, *President*
EMP: 60
SQ FT: 10,000
SALES (est): 14.7MM **Privately Held**
SIC: 1731 7629 General electrical contractor; electrical repair shops

(P-2574)
ONLINE COMMUNICATIONS INC
3291 Swetzer Rd, Loomis (95650-7607)
PHONE...................916 652-7253

Martin P Green, *President*
Christopher Green, *Vice Pres*
EMP: 110
SALES (est): 6.9MM **Privately Held**
SIC: 1731 4813 8748 Fiber optic cable installation; telephone & telephone equipment installation; telephone communication, except radio; telecommunications consultant

(P-2575)
PACIFIC METRO ELECTRIC INC
3150 E Fremont St, Stockton (95205-3918)
P.O. Box 127 (95201-0127)
PHONE...................209 939-3222
Glen Rigsbee, *President*
Jim Bohacek, *Project Mgr*
Krista Rigsbee, *Project Mgr*
EMP: 60
SALES (est): 10.3MM **Privately Held**
WEB: www.pacificmetroelectric.com
SIC: 1731 General electrical contractor

(P-2576)
PACIFIC UTLITY INSTLLATION INC
1585 N Harmony Cir, Anaheim (92807-6003)
PHONE...................714 970-6430
William B Pfeifer, *CEO*
Daniel Mole, *President*
Rosi Patino, *Accountant*
▲ **EMP:** 65
SALES (est): 14.8MM **Privately Held**
SIC: 1731 1623 General electrical contractor; water, sewer & utility lines

(P-2577)
PAGANINI ELECTRIC CORPORATION
Also Called: Paganini Companies
190 Hubbell St Ste 200, San Francisco (94107-2240)
PHONE...................415 575-3900
Kenneth A Paganini, *CEO*
Michael K Paganini, *President*
Kristi Dougherty, *Info Tech Dir*
Shane Brown, *Project Mgr*
Jason Deryckx, *Project Mgr*
EMP: 115
SQ FT: 20,000
SALES (est): 28.4MM **Privately Held**
WEB: www.pagcos.com
SIC: 1731 General electrical contractor

(P-2578)
PAR ELECTRICAL CONTRACTORS INC
525 Corporate Dr, Escondido (92029-1500)
PHONE...................760 291-1192
Jay Taylor, *Vice Pres*
Lon Peterson, *Vice Pres*
James Skinner, *Director*
Dan Avalle, *Manager*
Judy Bubash, *Assistant*
EMP: 58
SALES (corp-wide): 11.1B **Publicly Held**
SIC: 1731 General electrical contractor
HQ: Par Electrical Contractors, Inc.
　4770 N Belleview Ave # 109
　Kansas City MO 64116
　816 474-9340

(P-2579)
PAR ELECTRICAL CONTRACTORS INC
11276 5th St Ste 100, Rancho Cucamonga (91730-0922)
PHONE...................909 854-2880
Jim Stapp, *Manager*
Shenna Tabbutt, *Assistant*
Welshons Steve, *Superintendent*
EMP: 100
SALES (corp-wide): 11.1B **Publicly Held**
WEB: www.parelectric.com
SIC: 1731 General electrical contractor
HQ: Par Electrical Contractors, Inc.
　4770 N Belleview Ave # 109
　Kansas City MO 64116
　816 474-9340

(P-2580)
PAR ELECTRICAL CONTRACTORS INC
1416 Midway Rd, Vacaville (95688-9437)
PHONE...................707 693-1237
Kenny Bruce, *Vice Pres*
Shelby Mitchell, *Project Mgr*
EMP: 80
SALES (corp-wide): 11.1B **Publicly Held**
WEB: www.parelectric.com
SIC: 1731 General electrical contractor
HQ: Par Electrical Contractors, Inc.
　4770 N Belleview Ave # 109
　Kansas City MO 64116
　816 474-9340

(P-2581)
PARADISE ELECTRIC INC
697 Greenfield Dr, El Cajon (92021-2983)
PHONE...................619 449-4141
Mike Manos, *President*
Jeff Platt, *CFO*
EMP: 70
SQ FT: 7,000
SALES: 6MM
SALES (corp-wide): 99.5MM **Privately Held**
WEB: www.paradise-electric.com
SIC: 1731 General electrical contractor
HQ: Builders Tradesource Corp
　697 Greenfield Dr
　El Cajon CA 92021
　619 792-1795

(P-2582)
PATRIC COMMUNICATIONS INC (PA)
Also Called: Advanced Electronic Solutions
15215 Alton Pkwy Ste 200, Irvine (92618-2613)
PHONE...................619 579-2898
Sean P McDermott, *President*
Colleen Emick, *CFO*
Richard P Apgar, *Vice Pres*
Katherine Alford, *Admin Sec*
Kathy Alford, *Admin Sec*
EMP: 105
SALES (est): 10.8MM **Privately Held**
WEB: www.aes2.net
SIC: 1731 1731 3699 Fire detection & burglar alarm systems specialization; carpentry work; security devices

(P-2583)
PAVLETICH ELC CMMNICATIONS INC (PA)
6308 Seven Seas Ave, Bakersfield (93308-5132)
PHONE...................661 589-9473
John Pavletich, *CEO*
Andy Sweaney, *Manager*
Melissa Arceo, *Receptionist*
EMP: 90
SQ FT: 15,000
SALES (est): 18MM **Privately Held**
WEB: www.pavelectric.com
SIC: 1731 General electrical contractor; fiber optic cable installation

(P-2584)
PETRELLI ELECTRIC INC
11615 Davenport Rd, Agua Dulce (91390-4690)
P.O. Box 801148, Santa Clarita (91380-1148)
PHONE...................661 268-7312
Cindy Petrelli, *CEO*
Bill Murray, *Vice Pres*
Salvatore Petrelli, *Vice Pres*
Linda Pellico, *Office Mgr*
Katelyn Petrelli, *Admin Asst*
EMP: 66
SALES (est): 14.5MM **Privately Held**
SIC: 1731 7629 General electrical contractor; electrical equipment repair, high voltage

(P-2585)
PHASE 3 COMMUNICATIONS INC
3091 Monterey Hwy, San Jose (95111-3204)
PHONE...................408 946-9011
Nicolas Dezubiria, *President*
Ruben N Yusi, *CFO*

Kenneth Harris, *Office Mgr*
Walid Azizi, *Engineer*
Bosuet Dezubiria, *Manager*
EMP: 98
SALES: 14.3MM **Privately Held**
WEB: www.p3com.net
SIC: 1731 1799 Fiber optic cable installation; cable splicing service

(P-2586)
PINNACLE NETWORKING SVCS INC
Also Called: Pinnacle Communication Svcs
730 Fairmont Ave, Glendale (91203-1078)
PHONE.........................818 241-6009
Avo Amirian, *CEO*
Joe Licursi, *President*
Andy Hernandez, *Vice Pres*
Carlos Barajas, *Admin Asst*
Roupen Dilan, *Administration*
EMP: 75
SQ FT: 10,000
SALES (est): 19.9MM **Privately Held**
SIC: 1731 Communications specialization

(P-2587)
PIVOT INTERIORS INC
Pivot Interiors-Receiving Only
3200 Park Center Dr # 100, Costa Mesa
(92626-7104)
PHONE.........................949 988-5400
Ken Baugh, *CEO*
EMP: 60
SALES (corp-wide): 88.7MM **Privately Held**
WEB: www.pivotinteriors.com
SIC: 1731 Electrical work
PA: Pivot Interiors, Inc.
3355 Scott Blvd Ste 110
Santa Clara CA 95054
408 432-5600

(P-2588)
PMD INDUSTRIES INC
Also Called: Eie Electric
703 Randolph Ave, Costa Mesa
(92626-5917)
PHONE.........................949 222-0999
Phillip M Davis, *President*
Howard C Waters, *CFO*
EMP: 50
SQ FT: 2,500
SALES (est): 7.7MM **Privately Held**
WEB: www.eieelectric.com
SIC: 1731 7373 Electrical work; computer integrated systems design

(P-2589)
POINT ONE ELEC SYSTEMS INC
6751 Southfront Rd, Livermore
(94551-8218)
PHONE.........................925 667-2935
Michael G Curran, *President*
Thomas F Curran, *Vice Pres*
Ken Miller, *Vice Pres*
EMP: 60
SQ FT: 30,000
SALES (est): 15MM **Privately Held**
SIC: 1731 Electrical work

(P-2590)
PONDEROSA ELECTRIC INC
3911 E La Palma Ave Ste D, Anaheim
(92807-1719)
PHONE.........................949 253-3100
Dale Arnold, *President*
EMP: 60
SALES (est): 4.8MM **Privately Held**
SIC: 1731 General electrical contractor

(P-2591)
PORTERMATT ELECTRIC INC
5431 Production Dr, Huntington Beach
(92649-1524)
PHONE.........................714 596-8788
Tim Matthews, *President*
John F Porter III, *Vice Pres*
EMP: 90
SQ FT: 5,300
SALES (est): 19.5MM **Privately Held**
SIC: 1731 1799 General electrical contractor; athletic & recreation facilities construction

(P-2592)
POWER PLUS SOLUTIONS CORP
1210 N Red Gum St, Anaheim
(92806-1820)
PHONE.........................714 507-1881
Steven Bray, *President*
EMP: 50
SALES (est): 1.8MM **Privately Held**
SIC: 1731 Electric power systems contractors
PA: Power Plus International, Inc.
1210 N Red Gum St
Anaheim CA 92806

(P-2593)
PROFESSNL ELEC CNSTR SVCS INC
Also Called: Pecs
9112 Santa Anita Ave, Rancho Cucamonga
(91730-6143)
PHONE.........................909 373-4100
Diane Casey, *CEO*
Robert W Casey, *CFO*
Jose Ramirez, *Project Mgr*
EMP: 102
SQ FT: 15,000
SALES (est): 17.8MM **Privately Held**
SIC: 1731 General electrical contractor

(P-2594)
PS DEVELOPMENT CORPORATION
21625 Prairie St, Chatsworth (91311-5833)
PHONE.........................818 340-0965
Adam Saitman, *President*
EMP: 100
SQ FT: 5,000
SALES (est): 4.9MM **Privately Held**
SIC: 1731 General electrical contractor

(P-2595)
PYRO-COMM SYSTEMS INC (PA)
15531 Container Ln, Huntington Beach
(92649-1530)
PHONE.........................714 902-8000
Michael Donahue, *President*
Nanci Donahue, *Vice Pres*
Lisa Ayala, *Administration*
Melissa Tadlock, *Administration*
Greg Shewman, *Project Mgr*
EMP: 150
SQ FT: 10,000
SALES (est): 42.7MM **Privately Held**
WEB: www.pyrocomm.com
SIC: 1731 5063 Fire detection & burglar alarm systems specialization; fire alarm systems

(P-2596)
R & R ELECTRIC
2029 Century Park E A4, Los Angeles
(90067-1915)
PHONE.........................310 785-0288
Ricardo Ramos, *Owner*
Brenda Mitchell, *Office Admin*
Omar Ramos, *Controller*
Miguel Navarrete, *Purch Agent*
Mario Mata, *Superintendent*
EMP: 50
SQ FT: 5,000
SALES (est): 4.2MM **Privately Held**
SIC: 1731 General electrical contractor

(P-2597)
RADONICH CORP
Also Called: Cal Coast Telecom
886 Faulstich Ct, San Jose (95112-1361)
PHONE.........................408 275-8888
Rick M Radonich, *CEO*
David S Miguel, *Corp Secy*
William L Radonich Jr, *Vice Pres*
EMP: 50
SQ FT: 5,000
SALES (est): 18MM **Privately Held**
WEB: www.calcoasttelecom.com
SIC: 1731 Fiber optic cable installation; voice, data & video wiring contractor

(P-2598)
RANCHO PACIFIC ELECTRIC INC
9063 Santa Anita Ave, Rancho Cucamonga
(91730-6142)
PHONE.........................909 476-1022
Steve Robinson, *President*
Dave Robinson, *Corp Secy*
EMP: 50
SQ FT: 4,500
SALES (est): 2.8MM **Privately Held**
SIC: 1731 General electrical contractor

(P-2599)
RAYLEE ELECTRIC
1202 Tarapin Ln, Lincoln (95648-8138)
PHONE.........................916 408-7556
R George Alvarado, *President*
Raymond George Alvarado, *President*
Cindy Alvarado, *Vice Pres*
EMP: 50
SALES (est): 206K **Privately Held**
SIC: 1731 Electrical work

(P-2600)
RCI ELECTRIC INC
Also Called: Rayco Electric
3144 Fitzgerald Rd, Rancho Cordova
(95742-6802)
PHONE.........................916 858-8000
Raymond Alvarado, *President*
Chuck Knoble, *Vice Pres*
Mike Tedder, *Vice Pres*
Kim Shuman, *Office Mgr*
Jimmy Green, *Purch Mgr*
EMP: 99
SALES (est): 14.7MM **Privately Held**
WEB: www.raycoelectric.com
SIC: 1731 General electrical contractor

(P-2601)
RDM ELECTRIC CO INC (PA)
4260 E Brickell St, Ontario (91761-1511)
PHONE.........................909 591-0990
Robert McDonnell, *President*
Diane McDonnell, *Officer*
Anthony Gerdes, *Vice Pres*
Robert D McDonnell Jr, *Vice Pres*
Maria Bernabe, *Administration*
EMP: 63
SALES: 19MM **Privately Held**
SIC: 1731 General electrical contractor

(P-2602)
RED HAWK FIRE & SEC CA INC
4384 Enterprise Pl, Fremont (94538-6365)
PHONE.........................510 438-1300
Mack Katal, *President*
EMP: 90
SALES (corp-wide): 4.5B **Publicly Held**
SIC: 1731 Fire detection & burglar alarm systems specialization
HQ: Red Hawk Fire & Security (Ca), Inc.
7605 N San Fernando Rd
Los Angeles CA 90065

(P-2603)
RED HAWK FIRE & SEC CA INC
1640 N Batavia St, Orange (92867-3509)
PHONE.........................714 685-8100
Bob Berkery, *Manager*
EMP: 105
SALES (corp-wide): 4.5B **Publicly Held**
WEB: www.detectionlogic.com
SIC: 1731 Fire detection & burglar alarm systems specialization
HQ: Red Hawk Fire & Security (Ca), Inc.
7605 N San Fernando Rd
Los Angeles CA 90065

(P-2604)
RED HAWK FIRE & SEC CA INC (DH)
7605 N San Fernando Rd, Los Angeles
(90065)
PHONE.........................818 683-1500
Sean Flint, *CEO*
EMP: 77
SQ FT: 15,500

SALES (est): 26.3MM
SALES (corp-wide): 4.5B **Publicly Held**
WEB: www.chubbfs.com
SIC: 1731 Fire detection & burglar alarm systems specialization
HQ: Red Hawk Fire & Security, Llc
5100 Town Center Cir # 350
Boca Raton FL 33486
877 387-0188

(P-2605)
RED HAWK FIRE & SEC CA INC
920 S Andreasen Dr # 102, Escondido
(92029-1936)
PHONE.........................760 233-9787
Brad Mattonen, *Branch Mgr*
EMP: 68
SALES (corp-wide): 4.5B **Publicly Held**
SIC: 1731 Fire detection & burglar alarm systems specialization
HQ: Red Hawk Fire & Security (Ca), Inc.
7605 N San Fernando Rd
Los Angeles CA 90065

(P-2606)
REDWOOD ELECTRIC GROUP INC (PA)
2775 Northwestern Pkwy, Santa Clara
(95051-0947)
PHONE.........................707 451-7348
Victor Castello, *President*
Jeff Tarzwell, *CFO*
Gordon Armstrong, *Vice Pres*
Bruce Kelly, *Vice Pres*
Allan Ford, *Executive*
EMP: 680 **EST:** 1974
SQ FT: 35,000
SALES (est): 190.2MM
SALES (corp-wide): 171.2MM **Privately Held**
SIC: 1731 General electrical contractor

(P-2607)
REPUBLIC ELECTRIC INC
3820 Happy Ln, Sacramento (95827-9721)
PHONE.........................916 294-0140
Eric Stafford, *Manager*
EMP: 100
SALES (corp-wide): 24.8MM **Privately Held**
SIC: 1731 Electrical work
PA: Republic Electric, Inc.
3985 N Pecos Rd
Las Vegas NV 89115
702 643-2688

(P-2608)
REPUBLIC ELECTRIC WEST INC
3820 Happy Ln, Sacramento (95827-9721)
PHONE.........................916 294-0140
Eric J Stafford, *President*
Gerald Stafford, *CFO*
Rachel Staples, *Chief Mktg Ofcr*
Hope Weber, *Executive*
Michael Bloom, *Division Mgr*
EMP: 70
SALES (est): 10.3MM **Privately Held**
SIC: 1731 General electrical contractor

(P-2609)
REX MOORE GROUP INC
6001 Outfall Cir, Sacramento (95828-1020)
PHONE.........................916 372-1300
David Rex Moore, *President*
Doug Cuthbert, *President*
J Brock Littlejohn, *CFO*
James Brock Littlejohn, *CFO*
Bill Hubbard, *Exec VP*
EMP: 450
SQ FT: 36,000
SALES (est): 121.2MM **Privately Held**
WEB: www.rmi-systems.com
SIC: 1731 8711 General electrical contractor; engineering services

(P-2610)
REX MORE ELEC CONTRS ENGINEERS (PA)
6001 Outfall Cir, Sacramento (95828-1066)
PHONE.........................916 372-1300
David R Moore, *CEO*
William C Hubbard, *Partner*
James B Littlejohn, *Partner*
Steven R Moore, *Partner*
Nathan Gosink, *Area Mgr*

PRODUCTS & SVCS

EMP: 550
SQ FT: 36,000
SALES (est): 74.1MM **Privately Held**
WEB: www.rexmoore.com
SIC: 1731 General electrical contractor

(P-2611)
REX MORE ELEC CONTRS ENGINEERS
5803 E Harvard Ave, Fresno (93727-1366)
P.O. Box 7677 (93747-7677)
PHONE.................................559 294-1300
John Abele, *Manager*
Abram Bowman, *Project Engr*
Daniel Costilla, *Project Engr*
Jamison Rease, *Engineer*
EMP: 70
SALES (est): 4.1MM
SALES (corp-wide): 74.1MM **Privately Held**
SIC: 1731 General electrical contractor
PA: Rex Moore Electrical Contractors & Engineers, Inc
　　6001 Outfall Cir
　　Sacramento CA 95828
　　916 372-1300

(P-2612)
REX MORE ELEC CONTRS ENGINEERS
6001 Outfall Cir, Sacramento (95828-1066)
PHONE.................................510 785-1300
Brent Iseman, *Manager*
EMP: 100
SALES (est): 4.6MM
SALES (corp-wide): 74.1MM **Privately Held**
SIC: 1731 General electrical contractor
PA: Rex Moore Electrical Contractors & Engineers, Inc
　　6001 Outfall Cir
　　Sacramento CA 95828
　　916 372-1300

(P-2613)
RFI ENTERPRISES INC (PA)
Also Called: RFI Communications SEC Systems
360 Turtle Creek Ct, San Jose (95125-1389)
PHONE.................................408 298-5400
Dee Ann Harn, *President*
Brian Lund, *Senior VP*
Michelle Brooks, *Vice Pres*
Dale Mac McComb, *Vice Pres*
Dale Mc Comb, *Vice Pres*
EMP: 54
SQ FT: 30,000
SALES (est): 60.9MM **Privately Held**
SIC: 1731 7382 Safety & security specialization; communications specialization; security systems services

(P-2614)
RIIVOS INC
101 California St # 1500, San Francisco (94111-5888)
PHONE.................................415 813-1840
Michele Wardell McGovern, *CEO*
EMP: 60
SALES (est): 105.1K **Privately Held**
SIC: 1731 Electrical work

(P-2615)
RIS ELECTRICAL CONTRS INC
7330 Sycamore Canyon Blvd # 1, Riverside (92508-2317)
PHONE.................................951 688-8049
Bob Hayes, *President*
Donna Blankenship, *Office Mgr*
EMP: 50
SQ FT: 1,600
SALES (est): 7MM **Privately Held**
SIC: 1731 General electrical contractor

(P-2616)
RJB ENTERPRISES INC
Also Called: Ultimate Communication Systems
2579 W Woodland Dr, Anaheim (92801-2608)
PHONE.................................714 484-3101
Robert Bohan, *President*
EMP: 50
SQ FT: 3,500

SALES (est): 6.7MM **Privately Held**
WEB: www.ucomsys.com
SIC: 1731 Voice, data & video wiring contractor

(P-2617)
RK ELECTRIC INC
42021 Osgood Rd, Fremont (94539-5028)
PHONE.................................510 580-2850
Lonnie Robinson, *President*
Raul Real, *Vice Pres*
Dale Swanson, *Vice Pres*
Dan Yeggy, *Vice Pres*
Alexis Zankich, *Administration*
EMP: 130
SQ FT: 11,500
SALES: 27.5MM **Privately Held**
SIC: 1731 General electrical contractor

(P-2618)
ROSENDIN ELECTRIC INC (PA)
880 Mabury Rd, San Jose (95133-1021)
P.O. Box 49070 (95161-9070)
PHONE.................................408 286-2800
Tom Sorley, *Ch of Bd*
Larry Beltramo, *President*
Lorne Rundquist, *CFO*
Joe Neumayer, *Vice Pres*
Sam Lamonica, *CIO*
EMP: 3000 EST: 1919
SQ FT: 45,000
SALES (est): 1.6B **Privately Held**
WEB: www.rosendin.com
SIC: 1731 General electrical contractor

(P-2619)
ROSENDIN ELECTRIC INC
1730 S Anaheim Way, Anaheim (92805-6537)
PHONE.................................714 739-1334
Cliff Thompson, *Branch Mgr*
Rick Gonzales, *Sr Project Mgr*
EMP: 668
SALES (corp-wide): 1.6B **Privately Held**
SIC: 1731 General electrical contractor
PA: Rosendin Electric, Inc.
　　880 Mabury Rd
　　San Jose CA 95133
　　408 286-2800

(P-2620)
ROSENDIN ELECTRIC INC
2698 Orchard Pkwy, San Jose (95134-2020)
PHONE.................................408 321-2200
Mary Marshall, *Principal*
EMP: 668
SALES (corp-wide): 1.6B **Privately Held**
SIC: 1731 General electrical contractor
PA: Rosendin Electric, Inc.
　　880 Mabury Rd
　　San Jose CA 95133
　　408 286-2800

(P-2621)
ROSENDIN ELECTRIC INC
2121 Oakdale Ave, San Francisco (94124-1530)
PHONE.................................415 495-9300
Rick Shandrew, *Manager*
EMP: 213
SALES (corp-wide): 1.6B **Privately Held**
WEB: www.rosendin.com
SIC: 1731 General electrical contractor
PA: Rosendin Electric, Inc.
　　880 Mabury Rd
　　San Jose CA 95133
　　408 286-2800

(P-2622)
ROSENDIN ELECTRIC INC
1001 Potrero Ave, San Francisco (94110-3518)
PHONE.................................415 495-9300
EMP: 668
SALES (corp-wide): 1.6B **Privately Held**
SIC: 1731 General electrical contractor
PA: Rosendin Electric, Inc.
　　880 Mabury Rd
　　San Jose CA 95133
　　408 286-2800

(P-2623)
ROWAN INCORPORATED
Also Called: Rowan Electric
2778 Loker Ave W, Carlsbad (92010-6611)
PHONE.................................760 692-0700
Paul J Rowan, *CEO*
Mark B Rowan, *Vice Pres*
Mark Rowan, *Vice Pres*
Brad Parkinson, *Project Mgr*
Mathew Steinbacher, *Project Mgr*
EMP: 67
SQ FT: 6,000
SALES (est): 14.4MM **Privately Held**
WEB: www.rowanelectric.com
SIC: 1731 General electrical contractor

(P-2624)
RYE ELECTRIC INC
3940 Electric Ave, Laguna Hills (92653)
PHONE.................................949 441-0545
Christopher Dale Golden, *CEO*
EMP: 50
SALES (est): 284.8K **Privately Held**
SIC: 1731 Electrical work

(P-2625)
SABAH INTERNATIONAL INC (HQ)
5925 Stoneridge Dr, Pleasanton (94588-2705)
PHONE.................................925 463-0431
Michele Sabah, *CEO*
Jason Hughes, *Project Mgr*
Stan Kain, *Project Mgr*
Jay Keenan, *Project Mgr*
Tim Olson, *Project Mgr*
EMP: 51
SQ FT: 13,000
SALES (est): 15.2MM
SALES (corp-wide): 77.7MM **Privately Held**
WEB: www.sabah-intl.com
SIC: 1731 7382 Safety & security specialization; protective devices, security
PA: Sciens Building Solutions, Llc
　　541 29th St
　　San Francisco CA 94131
　　925 249-7700

(P-2626)
SAGE ELECTRIC COMPANY
9144 Owensmouth Ave, Chatsworth (91311-5851)
P.O. Box 1266, Agoura Hills (91376-1266)
PHONE.................................818 718-9080
Greg Stevens, *President*
Ilya Sitnitsky, *President*
Mark Custodero, *Treasurer*
Donald Huff, *Vice Pres*
Brad Pennington, *Admin Sec*
EMP: 75
SQ FT: 3,500
SALES (est): 11.7MM **Privately Held**
SIC: 1731 General electrical contractor

(P-2627)
SAN DIEGO BAY AREA ELC INC
13100 Kirkham Way Ste 205, Poway (92064-7128)
PHONE.................................858 748-2060
Dennis P Phillips, *President*
EMP: 60
SQ FT: 3,500
SALES (est): 6.2MM **Privately Held**
SIC: 1731 General electrical contractor

(P-2628)
SANTA CRUZ WESTSIDE ELC INC
Also Called: Sandbar Solar and Electric
2656 Mission St, Santa Cruz (95060-5703)
PHONE.................................831 469-8888
Scott Laskey, *President*
Denny Mosher, *Vice Pres*
Dave Brill, *Opers Staff*
Sean Thiel, *Consultant*
EMP: 55 EST: 2004
SALES (est): 2.1MM **Privately Held**
SIC: 1731 Electrical work

(P-2629)
SATURN ELECTRIC INC
7552 Trade St Ste A, San Diego (92121-2412)
PHONE.................................858 271-4100

Ron Dudek, *President*
Tim A Dudek, *President*
Thomas J Dudek, *Vice Pres*
EMP: 50
SQ FT: 7,000
SALES (est): 6.4MM **Privately Held**
WEB: www.saturnelectric.com
SIC: 1731 General electrical contractor

(P-2630)
SB PRODUCT GROUP LLC
1 Circle Star Way Fl 3, San Carlos (94070-6288)
PHONE.................................650 562-8221
R Marcelo Claure, *Mng Member*
Kahori Matsui,
EMP: 200
SALES (est): 7MM **Privately Held**
SIC: 1731 Communications specialization

(P-2631)
SBE CONTRACTING
17256 Red Hill Ave, Irvine (92614-5628)
PHONE.................................714 544-5066
Jeff Wilson, *President*
EMP: 50
SALES: 10.4MM **Privately Held**
SIC: 1731 General electrical contractor

(P-2632)
SBE ELECTRICAL CONTRACTING INC
2961 W Macarthur Blvd # 128, Santa Ana (92704-6931)
PHONE.................................714 544-5066
Jeffery S Wilson, *CEO*
EMP: 105
SALES: 9.4MM **Privately Held**
SIC: 1731 Electrical work

(P-2633)
SCHETTER ELECTRIC INC (PA)
471 Bannon St, Sacramento (95811-0296)
P.O. Box 1377 (95812-1377)
PHONE.................................916 446-2521
Frank E Schetter, *President*
Linda Schetter, *Shareholder*
Roger Ghilain, *CFO*
Vince Bernacchi, *Vice Pres*
Brett Nogleberg, *Vice Pres*
EMP: 90
SQ FT: 7,800
SALES (est): 25.3MM **Privately Held**
WEB: www.schetter.com
SIC: 1731 General electrical contractor

(P-2634)
SCHETTER ELECTRIC INC
737 Arnold Dr Ste D, Martinez (94553-6859)
PHONE.................................925 228-2424
Tom Stucker, *Branch Mgr*
EMP: 120
SALES (corp-wide): 25.3MM **Privately Held**
SIC: 1731 General electrical contractor
PA: Schetter Electric, Inc.
　　471 Bannon St
　　Sacramento CA 95811
　　916 446-2521

(P-2635)
SCHETTER ELECTRIC LLC
471 Bannon St, Sacramento (95811-0296)
P.O. Box 1377 (95812-1377)
PHONE.................................916 446-2521
Frank Schetter, *CEO*
Vince Bernacchi, *President*
Marlin Cole, *Vice Pres*
Brett Nogleberg, *Vice Pres*
Christy Johnston, *Administration*
EMP: 90
SALES (est): 1.7MM
SALES (corp-wide): 25.3MM **Privately Held**
SIC: 1731 Electrical work
PA: Schetter Electric, Inc.
　　471 Bannon St
　　Sacramento CA 95811
　　916 446-2521

(P-2636)
SEAL ELECTRIC INC
1162 Greenfield Dr, El Cajon (92021-3314)
PHONE.................................619 449-7323
Frank Bongiovanni, *President*

Joe Bongiovanni, *Vice Pres*
Kathy Bongiovanni, *Network Mgr*
Kevin Putrus, *Project Mgr*
Roy Wheeler, *Technology*
EMP: 145
SQ FT: 5,000
SALES (est): 26MM **Privately Held**
WEB: www.sealelectric.com
SIC: 1731 General electrical contractor

(P-2637)
SECURECOM INC
4822 Golden Foothill Pkwy, El Dorado Hills
(95762-9829)
PHONE..................................916 638-2855
Kevin McElwee, *President*
EMP: 50
SALES (est): 2.2MM **Privately Held**
WEB: www.securecom.net
SIC: 1731 Fire detection & burglar alarm
  systems specialization
PA: Securecom, Inc.
  1940 Don St Ste 100
  Springfield OR 97477
-

(P-2638)
SEMANS COMMUNICATIONS (PA)
112 Stonegate Rd, Portola Vally
(94028-7649)
PHONE..................................650 529-9984
Greg Semans, *President*
Roland Valtierra, *Vice Pres*
Bonnie Semans, *Admin Sec*
EMP: 80
SQ FT: 10,000
SALES (est): 6.6MM **Privately Held**
SIC: 1731 Telephone & telephone equip-
  ment installation

(P-2639)
SERRANO ELECTRIC INC
1705 Russell Ave, Santa Clara
(95054-2032)
PHONE..................................408 986-1570
Daniel Serrano, *President*
Leslie Nakamura, *Admin Sec*
Bob Vangelder, *Purch Mgr*
Joe Copado, *Warehouse Mgr*
David Haney, *Manager*
EMP: 50
SQ FT: 8,000
SALES (est): 10.4MM **Privately Held**
WEB: www.serranoelectric.com
SIC: 1731 General electrical contractor

(P-2640)
SERVICE 1ST ELECTRICAL SVCS
1092 N Armando St, Anaheim
(92806-2605)
PHONE..................................714 630-9699
James Graham, *President*
EMP: 50
SALES (est): 4.8MM **Privately Held**
SIC: 1731 Electrical work

(P-2641)
SFADIA INC
Also Called: Green Energy Innovations
12505 Florence Ave, Santa Fe Springs
(90670-3919)
PHONE..................................323 622-1930
Pilje Park, *President*
Pil Soon Um, *Vice Pres*
Jay Lee, *Research*
▲ **EMP:** 86
SALES (est): 10.3MM **Privately Held**
SIC: 1731 Energy management controls

(P-2642)
SIMPLEX TIME RECORDER LLC
Also Called: Simplex Time Recorder 480
9855 Carroll Canyon Rd, San Diego
(92131-1103)
PHONE..................................858 740-0100
Ross Larson, *Branch Mgr*
EMP: 100 **Privately Held**
WEB: www.comtec-alaska.com
SIC: 1731 5063 7382 Fire detection &
  burglar alarm systems specialization;
  electrical apparatus & equipment; security
  systems services

HQ: Simplex Time Recorder Llc
  50 Technology Dr
  Westminster MA 01441
-

(P-2643)
SOUTHERN CONTRACTING COMPANY
559 N Twin Oaks Valley Rd, San Marcos
(92069-1798)
P.O. Box 445 (92079-0445)
PHONE..................................760 744-0760
Timothy R McBride, *CEO*
Richard W Mc Bride, *President*
David Eveland, *CFO*
Tim Mc Bride, *Vice Pres*
James Filanc, *Business Dir*
▲ **EMP:** 125
SQ FT: 8,400
SALES (est): 40.6MM **Privately Held**
WEB: www.southerncontracting.com
SIC: 1731 General electrical contractor

(P-2644)
SOUTHLAND ELECTRIC INC
4950 Greencraig Ln, San Diego
(92123-1673)
PHONE..................................858 634-5050
Leanne M Peterson, *President*
Dan Vickery, *Project Mgr*
Harold Ryden, *Foreman/Supr*
Glidden Robert, *Manager*
EMP: 54
SQ FT: 18,000
SALES (est): 25.3MM **Privately Held**
SIC: 1731 General electrical contractor

(P-2645)
SPECIALTY CONSTRUCTION INC
645 Clarion Ct, San Luis Obispo
(93401-8177)
PHONE..................................805 543-1706
Rudolph Bachmann, *President*
Chris Teaford, *CFO*
Jeffrey Martin, *Senior VP*
Doug Clay, *Vice Pres*
Steve Haymaker, *Vice Pres*
EMP: 80
SQ FT: 8,000
SALES (est): 33.7MM **Privately Held**
WEB: www.specialtyconstruction.com
SIC: 1731 Telephone & telephone equip-
  ment installation

(P-2646)
SPECTRA I CALIFORNIA
Also Called: Spectra Industrial Electric
21818 S Wilmington Ave # 402, Carson
(90810-1642)
PHONE..................................310 835-0808
Michael J Merrill, *President*
Cliff Krueger, *CFO*
Richard Mangan, *Vice Pres*
Ray Nearey, *Division Mgr*
Patricia Sanchez, *Finance Mgr*
EMP: 70
SQ FT: 20,000
SALES (est): 7.1MM **Privately Held**
WEB: www.spectrainc.com
SIC: 1731 Access control systems special-
  ization

(P-2647)
SPRIG ELECTRIC CO
65 Oak Grove St, San Francisco
(94107-1018)
PHONE..................................408 298-3134
Michael McAlister, *Branch Mgr*
EMP: 66
SALES (corp-wide): 69.8MM **Privately Held**
SIC: 1731 General electrical contractor
PA: Sprig Electric Co.
  1860 S 10th St
  San Jose CA 95112
  408 298-3134

(P-2648)
SPRIG ELECTRIC CO (PA)
1860 S 10th St, San Jose (95112-4108)
PHONE..................................408 298-3134
Medford Snyder, *CEO*
Mark Mandarelli, *President*
Laura Lacomble, *Officer*
Hossein Tofangsazan, *Officer*

Michael Glogovac, *Vice Pres*
EMP: 151 **EST:** 1970
SQ FT: 24,100
SALES (est): 69.8MM **Privately Held**
WEB: www.sprigelectric.com
SIC: 1731 General electrical contractor

(P-2649)
SR BRAY LLC (PA)
Also Called: Power Plus
1210 N Red Gum St, Anaheim
(92806-1820)
PHONE..................................714 765-7551
Steven R Bray, *President*
Brian Schultz, *Vice Pres*
Philip Mayer, *Executive*
Doug Harvey, *General Mgr*
Alysha Gerst, *Administration*
EMP: 50
SQ FT: 60,000
SALES (est): 120.9MM **Privately Held**
SIC: 1731 7359 Standby or emergency
  power specialization; equipment rental &
  leasing

(P-2650)
ST DENIS ELECTRIC INC
734 Ralcoa Way, Arroyo Grande
(93420-9620)
PHONE..................................805 343-9999
Jeffery S St Denis, *President*
EMP: 50
SALES (est): 729.6K **Privately Held**
SIC: 1731 Electrical work

(P-2651)
ST FRANCIS ELECTRIC INC
975 Carden St, San Leandro (94577-1102)
P.O. Box 2057 (94577-0317)
PHONE..................................510 639-0639
Robert Spinardi, *President*
Joseph Medeiros, *Vice Pres*
Guy Smith, *Vice Pres*
Ivana Gery, *Manager*
EMP: 250 **EST:** 1947
SQ FT: 32,500
SALES (est): 60MM **Privately Held**
SIC: 1731 General electrical contractor

(P-2652)
ST FRANCIS ELECTRIC LLC
975 Carden St, San Leandro (94577-1102)
P.O. Box 2057 (94577-0317)
PHONE..................................510 639-0639
Guy Smith, *CEO*
EMP: 250
SALES (est): 70MM **Privately Held**
SIC: 1731 Electrical work

(P-2653)
STADTNER CO INC
Also Called: Sierra Electric Co
3112 Geary Blvd, San Francisco
(94118-3317)
PHONE..................................415 752-2850
Rose Stadtner, *President*
David Stadtner, *Vice Pres*
Larry Stadtner, *Vice Pres*
Josephine Brennan, *Administration*
Bianca Gogna, *Administration*
EMP: 50 **EST:** 1953
SQ FT: 2,500
SALES (est): 9.3MM **Privately Held**
SIC: 1731 General electrical contractor

(P-2654)
STC NETCOM INC (PA)
11611 Industry Ave, Fontana (92337-6931)
PHONE..................................951 685-8181
Giuseppe Floro, *President*
Shawnda Letourneau, *Treasurer*
Jeffry Kinne, *Admin Sec*
Ramon Estrada, *Project Mgr*
Aaron Semenoff, *Manager*
EMP: 70
SQ FT: 6,000
SALES (est): 13.6MM **Privately Held**
WEB: www.stcnetcom.com
SIC: 1731 Fiber optic cable installation;
  telephone & telephone equipment instal-
  lation

(P-2655)
STEINY AND COMPANY INC (PA)
221 N Ardmore Ave, Los Angeles
(90004-4503)
PHONE..................................213 382-2331
Susan Steiny, *CEO*
John O Steiny, *Ch of Bd*
Vincent Mauch, *CFO*
Gayle Kappelman, *Admin Sec*
Brian Kanamoto, *Project Mgr*
EMP: 65 **EST:** 1956
SQ FT: 13,000
SALES (est): 47.5MM **Privately Held**
WEB: www.steinyco.com
SIC: 1731 General electrical contractor;
  safety & security specialization

(P-2656)
STOMMEL INC (PA)
Also Called: Lehr
4707 Northgate Blvd, Sacramento
(95834-1120)
PHONE..................................916 646-6626
Jim Stommel, *President*
Linda Stommel, *Vice Pres*
Mark Matthews, *Sales Staff*
Tia Niles, *Sales Staff*
EMP: 50
SQ FT: 20,000
SALES (est): 16.2MM **Privately Held**
WEB: www.lehrauto.com
SIC: 1731 7539 5531 Safety & security
  specialization; electrical services; auto-
  motive parts

(P-2657)
SUMMIT TECHNOLOGY GROUP INC
Also Called: Summit Electric
2450c Bluebell Dr Ste C, Santa Rosa
(95403-2509)
PHONE..................................707 542-4773
Laurence W Dashiell, *President*
EMP: 50
SALES (est): 2.1MM **Privately Held**
SIC: 1731 Voice, data & video wiring con-
  tractor

(P-2658)
SUN ELECTRIC LP
2101 S Yale St Ste B, Santa Ana
(92704-4424)
PHONE..................................714 210-3744
Jeffery J Bernardino, *Ltd Ptnr*
Duncan Frederick, *Partner*
Another Lighting Service, *Principal*
EMP: 100 **EST:** 2003
SALES (est): 3.9MM **Privately Held**
SIC: 1731 General electrical contractor

(P-2659)
SUNSHINE COMMUNICATIONS INC
350 Cypress Ln Ste D, El Cajon
(92020-1664)
P.O. Box 3509, Apollo Beach FL (33572-
1005)
PHONE..................................619 448-7600
Robert Straub, *CEO*
EMP: 235
SALES (est): 19.8MM **Privately Held**
WEB: www.sunshinecom.com
SIC: 1731 Cable television installation

(P-2660)
SUNWEST ELECTRIC INC
3064 E Miraloma Ave, Anaheim
(92806-1810)
PHONE..................................714 630-8700
Brien Pariseau, *President*
Doug Lyvers, *CFO*
Jim Aaron, *Project Mgr*
Lonnie White, *Safety Mgr*
Nadal Habash, *Opers Mgr*
EMP: 175
SQ FT: 20,000
SALES (est): 32.7MM **Privately Held**
SIC: 1731 Electrical work

(P-2661)
SUPERIOR ELEC MECH & PLBG INC
8613 Helms Ave, Rancho Cucamonga
(91730-4521)
PHONE..................................909 357-9400

David A Stone Jr, *CEO*
Walt Schobel, *President*
Pam Metzer, *CFO*
Tammy Stone, *Executive*
EMP: 291
SQ FT: 50,000
SALES (est): 81.4MM **Privately Held**
SIC: 1731 1711 General electrical contractor; mechanical contractor

(P-2662)
SURGENER ELECTRIC INC
Also Called: McKee Electric
1406 N Chester Ave, Bakersfield (93308-3525)
PHONE..................................661 399-3321
Lester C Surgener II, *CEO*
R L Surgener, *President*
Diane Dansby, *Corp Secy*
Anthony Felix, *Project Mgr*
Brent Reno, *Project Mgr*
EMP: 85 EST: 1947
SQ FT: 5,000
SALES (est): 17.5MM **Privately Held**
SIC: 1731 General electrical contractor

(P-2663)
SWINFORD ELECTRIC INC
Also Called: A & R Electric
1150 E Elm Ave, Fullerton (92831-5024)
PHONE..................................714 578-8888
Sharon Swinford, *President*
Michael Swinford, *Treasurer*
Jayzell Johnson, *Admin Asst*
EMP: 50
SQ FT: 5,400
SALES (est): 9.9MM **Privately Held**
SIC: 1731 General electrical contractor

(P-2664)
SYNCHRONOSS TECHNOLOGIES INC
60 S Market St Ste 700, San Jose (95113-2370)
PHONE..................................800 575-7606
EMP: 316
SALES (corp-wide): 325.8MM **Publicly Held**
SIC: 1731 7379 7371 Computerized controls installation; access control systems specialization; cogeneration specialization; electronic controls installation; ; computer software development & applications
PA: Synchronoss Technologies, Inc.
200 Crossing Blvd Fl 8
Bridgewater NJ 08807
866 620-3940

(P-2665)
T BOYER COMPANY
1656 Babcock St, Costa Mesa (92627-4330)
PHONE..................................949 642-2431
Thomas Boyer, *President*
EMP: 50
SQ FT: 1,600
SALES (est): 6.9MM **Privately Held**
SIC: 1731 General electrical contractor

(P-2666)
T MCGEE ELECTRIC INC
2390 S Reservoir St, Pomona (91766-6410)
P.O. Box 1111, Chino (91708-1111)
PHONE..................................909 591-6461
Trent L Mc Gee, *President*
EMP: 100
SALES (est): 10.2MM **Privately Held**
SIC: 1731 General electrical contractor

(P-2667)
TAFT ELECTRIC COMPANY (PA)
1694 Eastman Ave, Ventura (93003-5782)
P.O. Box 3416 (93006-3416)
PHONE..................................805 642-0121
Walter E Hartman, *Chairman*
James Marsh, *President*
Carol A Smith, *Admin Sec*
Brian Eberhard, *Project Mgr*
EMP: 127 EST: 1942
SQ FT: 40,000

SALES (est): 54.9MM **Privately Held**
WEB: www.tecelect.com
SIC: 1731 1629 General electrical contractor; waste water & sewage treatment plant construction

(P-2668)
TEL TECH PLUS INC
Also Called: Ttp-US
393 Enterprise St, San Marcos (92078-4374)
PHONE..................................760 510-1323
Gregory A Stearns, *President*
Cindy Stearns, *Admin Sec*
EMP: 50
SQ FT: 10,268
SALES (est): 7.9MM **Privately Held**
SIC: 1731 1623 7382 Voice, data & video wiring contractor; telephone & communication line construction; security systems services

(P-2669)
TELECMMNCTONS MGT SLUTIONS INC
Also Called: T M S
570 Division St, Campbell (95008-6906)
PHONE..................................408 866-5495
Bruce Jaftok, *President*
Michael Finn, *Vice Pres*
Jay Wiles, *Project Mgr*
EMP: 57
SALES (est): 11.5MM **Privately Held**
WEB: www.yru.com
SIC: 1731 Voice, data & video wiring contractor

(P-2670)
TELSTAR INSTRUMENTS (PA)
1717 Solano Way Ste 34, Concord (94520-5478)
PHONE..................................925 671-2888
Robert S Marston Jr, *CEO*
John Gardiner, *Vice Pres*
Alan D Strong, *Branch Mgr*
Paul Berson, *Engineer*
Kathy Katsuleres, *Finance Mgr*
EMP: 53 EST: 1981
SQ FT: 4,000
SALES (est): 23.9MM **Privately Held**
SIC: 1731 7629 General electrical contractor; electrical repair shops

(P-2671)
TENNYSON ELECTRIC INC
7275 National Dr, Livermore (94550-8869)
PHONE..................................925 606-1038
Michael A Tennyson, *CEO*
Cathleen Tennyson, *Treasurer*
EMP: 50
SQ FT: 26,000
SALES (est): 20.6MM **Privately Held**
SIC: 1731 General electrical contractor

(P-2672)
THOMA ELECTRIC INC
Also Called: Thoma Electric Co
3562 Empleo St Ste C, San Luis Obispo (93401-7367)
P.O. Box 1167 (93406-1167)
PHONE..................................805 543-3850
William A Thoma, *President*
Ed Thoma, *Vice Pres*
Edward C Thoma, *Vice Pres*
Bill Thoma, *Admin Sec*
Sheri Budrow, *Administration*
EMP: 55
SQ FT: 7,500
SALES (est): 9.9MM **Privately Held**
WEB: www.thomaelec.com
SIC: 1731 8711 General electrical contractor; electrical or electronic engineering

(P-2673)
TIGER ELECTRIC INC (PA)
650 N Berry St, Brea (92821-3011)
PHONE..................................714 529-8061
Stanley Longenecker, *President*
Carol Capon, *Office Mgr*
Mary D Longenecker, *Admin Sec*
Timica Lowe, *Admin Asst*
Don Capon, *Project Mgr*
▲ EMP: 82
SQ FT: 12,500

SALES (est): 13.9MM **Privately Held**
WEB: www.tigerelectric.com
SIC: 1731 General electrical contractor

(P-2674)
TIME AND ALARM SYSTEMS (PA)
3828 Wacker Dr, Jurupa Valley (91752-1147)
PHONE..................................951 685-1761
Keith A Senn, *CEO*
EMP: 53
SQ FT: 12,000
SALES (est): 12.4MM **Privately Held**
WEB: www.timeandalarm.com
SIC: 1731 Fire detection & burglar alarm systems specialization; communications specialization; telephone & telephone equipment installation

(P-2675)
TRI-SIGNAL INTEGRATION INC (PA)
Also Called: Honeywell Authorized Dealer
15853 Monte St Ste 101, Sylmar (91342-7671)
PHONE..................................818 566-8558
Robert McKibben, *President*
Michael Swisher, *COO*
Mike Swisher, *COO*
Dennis Furden, *CFO*
Tom Kommer, *Senior VP*
EMP: 100 EST: 1998
SQ FT: 16,000
SALES (est): 87.5MM **Privately Held**
WEB: www.tri-signal.com
SIC: 1731 Fire detection & burglar alarm systems specialization

(P-2676)
TRL SYSTEMS INCORPORATED
Also Called: T R L
9531 Milliken Ave, Rancho Cucamonga (91730-6006)
PHONE..................................909 390-8392
Lynn Purdy, *Chairman*
Mark L Purdy, *President*
John Janosik, *CFO*
Steve Adams, *Vice Pres*
Patrick Lewis, *Vice Pres*
EMP: 100
SQ FT: 14,000
SALES (est): 51.2MM **Privately Held**
SIC: 1731 General electrical contractor

(P-2677)
TUCKER ELECTRIC CORPORATION
Also Called: Tucker Electrical
3365 Chestnut Ln, Santa Rosa Valley (93012-8225)
PHONE..................................818 426-7645
Dean Tucker, *CEO*
Ray Marino, *Vice Pres*
EMP: 50
SQ FT: 1,500
SALES (est): 5.8MM **Privately Held**
SIC: 1731 General electrical contractor

(P-2678)
TUCKER TECHNOLOGY INC
300 Frnk H Ogw Plz 208, Oakland (94612)
PHONE..................................510 836-0422
Frank Tucker, *President*
Conchita Tucker, *Senior VP*
Rodney Stanley, *Vice Pres*
Hernan Camacho, *General Mgr*
Tony Fletcher, *Project Mgr*
EMP: 55
SQ FT: 5,000
SALES (est): 6.7MM **Privately Held**
WEB: www.tuckertech.com
SIC: 1731 Communications specialization

(P-2679)
TURNUPSEED ELECTRIC SERVICE
1580 S K St, Tulare (93274-6400)
P.O. Box 26 (93275-0026)
PHONE..................................559 686-1541
Wallace J Nelson, *President*
Terri Grant, *Corp Secy*
David Turnupseed, *Vice Pres*
Stephen Powell, *Manager*
EMP: 55

SQ FT: 8,000
SALES (est): 9.3MM **Privately Held**
WEB: www.turnupseed.com
SIC: 1731 7694 5063 General electrical contractor; rewinding stators; electric motor repair; motors, electric

(P-2680)
UNISON ELECTRIC
16652 Gemini Ln, Huntington Beach (92647-4429)
PHONE..................................714 375-5915
Lance E Charlesworth, *President*
Kristi Kirkenslager, *Corp Secy*
Gary Charlesworth, *Exec VP*
EMP: 58
SQ FT: 6,000
SALES (est): 9.4MM **Privately Held**
WEB: www.unisonltd.com
SIC: 1731 General electrical contractor

(P-2681)
UNITED STATES INFO SYSTEMS INC
7621 Galilee Rd, Roseville (95678-6972)
PHONE..................................845 353-9224
EMP: 152
SALES (corp-wide): 123.5MM **Privately Held**
SIC: 1731 Communications specialization
PA: United States Information Systems Inc.
35 W Jefferson Ave
Pearl River NY 10965
845 358-7755

(P-2682)
VALLEY COMMUNICATIONS INC (PA)
6921 Roseville Rd, Sacramento (95842-1660)
PHONE..................................916 349-7300
Ken Hurst, *President*
Mike Cordisco, *COO*
Kate Dewitt, *Vice Pres*
Jeff Frydenlund, *Vice Pres*
Katie Chunn, *Admin Asst*
EMP: 60
SQ FT: 12,000
SALES: 11.8MM **Privately Held**
SIC: 1731 3699 Voice, data & video wiring contractor; closed circuit television installation; security control equipment & systems

(P-2683)
VALLEY UNIQUE ELECTRIC INC
75 Park Creek Dr Ste 101, Clovis (93611-4432)
PHONE..................................559 237-4795
Mark Worthington, *Director*
Hogi Selling III, *CFO*
Colleen Golden, *Office Mgr*
Walt Worthington, *Admin Sec*
Tom Moore, *Project Mgr*
EMP: 100
SALES (est): 7.8MM **Privately Held**
WEB: www.valleyunique.com
SIC: 1731 5719 5063 General electrical contractor; lighting fixtures; lamps & lamp shades; lighting fixtures, residential

(P-2684)
VASKO ELECTRIC INC
4300 Astoria St, Sacramento (95838-3004)
PHONE..................................916 568-7700
Darryl A Vasko, *President*
Ron Gracik, *Vice Pres*
EMP: 80
SQ FT: 8,500
SALES: 20.9MM **Privately Held**
WEB: www.vasko.com
SIC: 1731 General electrical contractor

(P-2685)
VECTOR RESOURCES INC (PA)
Also Called: Vectorusa
20917 Higgins Ct, Torrance (90501-1723)
PHONE..................................310 436-1000
David Zukerman, *President*
Bethany Drogula, *Admin Asst*
Briana Fernandes, *Admin Asst*
Will Smith, *Info Tech Mgr*
Brian Hepworth, *Network Enginr*
EMP: 151

SALES (est): 71MM Privately Held
SIC: 1731 3651 7373 Communications
specialization; clock radio & telephone
combinations; systems engineering, computer related

(P-2686)
VECTOR SECURITY INC
5411 Valley Blvd, Los Angeles
(90032-3518)
PHONE....................................323 224-6700
John Murphy, *Manager*
David Levine, *Branch Mgr*
Steve Anderson, *Director*
EMP: 59
SALES (corp-wide): 444.1MM Privately
Held
SIC: 1731 7382 Fire detection & burglar
alarm systems specialization; burglar
alarm maintenance & monitoring
HQ: Vector Security Inc.
2000 Ericsson Dr Ste 250
Warrendale PA 15086
724 741-2200

(P-2687)
W BRADLEY ELECTRIC INC
501 Seaport Ct Ste 103a, Redwood City
(94063-2776)
PHONE....................................650 701-1502
EMP: 125
SALES (corp-wide): 61.4MM Privately
Held
SIC: 1731
PA: W. Bradley Electric, Inc.
90 Hill Rd
Novato CA 94945
415 898-1400

(P-2688)
W BRADLEY ELECTRIC INC (PA)
90 Hill Rd, Novato (94945-4506)
PHONE....................................415 898-1400
Leslie Murphy, *CEO*
Mike Murphy, *COO*
Ralph Greenwood, *CFO*
Bob Bourdet, *Vice Pres*
▲ EMP: 50 EST: 1977
SQ FT: 24,000
SALES (est): 54.7MM Privately Held
SIC: 1731 General electrical contractor

(P-2689)
WALKER COMMUNICATIONS INC
521 Railroad Ave, Suisun City
(94585-4244)
PHONE....................................707 421-1300
Gary Walker, *President*
EMP: 100
SQ FT: 2,200
SALES (est): 5.8MM Privately Held
SIC: 1731 3669 4812 Communications
specialization; emergency alarms; radio
telephone communication

(P-2690)
WALTON ELECTRIC CORPORATION
755 N Central Ave, Upland (91786-9474)
P.O. Box 1599, Claremont (91711-8599)
PHONE....................................909 981-5051
Tanyon D Dunkley, *CEO*
Don R Davis, *Exec VP*
Ron C Stickel, *Vice Pres*
Michael Brady, *Project Mgr*
EMP: 60
SQ FT: 10,150
SALES: 7MM Privately Held
SIC: 1731 3669 General electrical contractor; fire alarm apparatus, electric

(P-2691)
WB ELECTRIC INC
30611 Road 400, Coarsegold
(93614-9437)
P.O. Box 319 (93614-0319)
PHONE....................................408 842-7911
Randy Walker, *CEO*
Susan Walker, *CFO*
Arnold Monaco, *Project Mgr*
EMP: 60
SALES: 11.7MM Privately Held
WEB: www.wbelectric.com
SIC: 1731 General electrical contractor

(P-2692)
WECKWORTH CONSTRUCTION CO INC
Also Called: Weckworth Electric Company
3941 Park Dr Ste 20-373, El Dorado Hills
(95762-4549)
PHONE....................................916 939-6636
Kristen Weckworth, *President*
EMP: 65
SALES (est): 6MM Privately Held
SIC: 1731 Switchgear & related devices installation

(P-2693)
WEST COAST LTG & ENRGY INC
18550 Minthorn St, Lake Elsinore
(92530-2784)
PHONE....................................951 296-0680
Johnny Odell Leach, *President*
Tammy Leach, *Corp Secy*
EMP: 90
SQ FT: 2,646
SALES (est): 13.1MM Privately Held
WEB: www.es-corp.com
SIC: 1731 General electrical contractor

(P-2694)
WESTECH SYSTEMS INC
827 Jefferson Ave, Clovis (93612-2260)
PHONE....................................559 298-5237
Larry Troglin, *President*
Helder Domingos, *Vice Pres*
Darin Culbertson, *Project Mgr*
Santiago Rendon, *Engineer*
Matt James, *Purch Mgr*
EMP: 60 EST: 1997
SQ FT: 10,000
SALES (est): 16.9MM Privately Held
SIC: 1731 Computer installation

(P-2695)
WESTERN SUN ENTERPRISES INC
Also Called: Three D Electric
4690 E 2nd St Ste 4, Benicia (94510-1008)
PHONE....................................707 748-2542
David Alan Whitt, *President*
Laura Whitt, *Treasurer*
EMP: 150
SQ FT: 4,700
SALES (est): 16.5MM Privately Held
WEB: www.threedelectric.com
SIC: 1731 General electrical contractor

(P-2696)
WILD ELECTRIC INCORPORATED
4626 E Olive Ave, Fresno (93702-1660)
PHONE....................................559 251-7770
Fred Merlo, *President*
Jan Merlo, *Vice Pres*
Craig Mull, *Project Mgr*
Evan Santos, *Project Mgr*
Jacqueline Bacorn, *Controller*
EMP: 55 EST: 1973
SQ FT: 3,750
SALES: 8MM Privately Held
WEB: www.wildelectric.net
SIC: 1731 General electrical contractor

(P-2697)
WOLTCOM INC
Also Called: W C I
2300 Tech Pkwy Ste 8, Hollister (95023)
PHONE....................................831 638-4900
Mona K Wolters, *President*
Lisa Scheufler, *Shareholder*
Pat Scheufler, *CFO*
Kimberly A Morgan, *Vice Pres*
EMP: 150
SQ FT: 2,250
SALES (est): 10.3MM Privately Held
SIC: 1731 Communications specialization

(P-2698)
WORLDWIND SERVICES LLC
915 Tehachapi Wllw Spgs, Tehachapi
(93561-8178)
PHONE....................................661 822-4877
Edward Cummings,
Suzannah Cummings,
EMP: 51

SALES (est): 10.6MM Privately Held
SIC: 1731 1389 8742 Electrical work;
construction, repair & dismantling services; maintenance management consultant

(P-2699)
WP ELECTRIC COMMUNICATIONS INC
14198 Albers Way, Chino (91710-6938)
PHONE....................................909 606-3510
Debra Rooney, *President*
Jim Roche, *Vice Pres*
Roseann Briggs, *Office Mgr*
Greg Sanchez, *Opers Mgr*
Ryan Marshall, *Manager*
EMP: 50
SQ FT: 8,100
SALES: 6MM Privately Held
SIC: 1731 General electrical contractor

(P-2700)
WPCS INTRNTIONAL-SUISUN CY INC
2208 Srra Madows Dr Ste B, Rocklin
(95677)
PHONE....................................916 624-1300
EMP: 60
SALES (corp-wide): 24.4MM Publicly
Held
SIC: 1731
HQ: Wpcs International-Suisun City, Inc.
521 Railroad Ave
Suisun City CA 94585
707 398-3421

(P-2701)
WSD ENGINEERING INC
9245 Sky Park Ct Ste 105, San Diego
(92123-4311)
PHONE....................................619 954-7850
Denis Morgan, *CEO*
EMP: 50
SQ FT: 3,800
SALES: 4MM Privately Held
SIC: 1731 Telephone & telephone equipment installation

(P-2702)
YOUNG ELECTRIC CO
Also Called: Young Communications
195 Erie St, San Francisco (94103-2416)
PHONE....................................415 648-3355
James P Young, *President*
Wayne Huie, *President*
James Young, *Treasurer*
Richard Green, *Corp Secy*
Tina Young, *Controller*
EMP: 120 EST: 1977
SQ FT: 5,000
SALES: 28MM Privately Held
WEB: www.youngelec.com
SIC: 1731 General electrical contractor

1741 Masonry & Other Stonework

(P-2703)
B&B INDUSTRIAL SERVICES INC (PA)
14549 Manzanita Dr, Fontana
(92335-5378)
PHONE....................................909 428-3167
Lyndon Brewer, *President*
Ted Brewer, *Vice Pres*
Tim Brewer, *Admin Sec*
EMP: 67
SQ FT: 12,000
SALES (est): 27.3MM Privately Held
WEB: www.bb-industrial.com
SIC: 1741 Refractory or acid brick masonry

(P-2704)
BARAZANI PAVE STONE INC
14546 Hamlin St Ste 201, Van Nuys
(91411-4194)
PHONE....................................818 701-6977
Yuval Barazani, *President*
Aviva Barazani, *Vice Pres*
EMP: 185
SQ FT: 20,000

SALES (est): 9.8MM Privately Held
WEB: www.barazani.com
SIC: 1741 1771 1611 Masonry & other
stonework; driveway, parking lot & blacktop contractors; surfacing & paving

(P-2705)
BLEDSOE MASONRY INC
Also Called: RMC Transport
4680 Felspar St Ste A, Riverside
(92509-3086)
PHONE....................................951 360-6140
Dyana Bledsoe, *President*
Robert Bledsoe, *Corp Secy*
EMP: 60
SQ FT: 1,300
SALES: 1MM Privately Held
SIC: 1741 Masonry & other stonework

(P-2706)
BOSTON BRICK & STONE INC
2005 Lincoln Ave, Pasadena (91103-1322)
PHONE....................................626 269-2622
David Laverdiere, *President*
Karen Laverdiere, *CEO*
Dan Shay, *CEO*
Mark Peters, *Vice Pres*
EMP: 50
SALES (est): 5MM Privately Held
WEB: www.bostonbrick.com
SIC: 1741 Chimney construction & maintenance

(P-2707)
BRAD WATKINS MASONRY INC
10315 Woodley Ave Ste 130, Granada Hills
(91344-6953)
P.O. Box 8466, Mission Hills (91346-8466)
PHONE....................................818 360-3796
Brad Watkins, *President*
EMP: 70
SALES: 15MM Privately Held
SIC: 1741 Masonry & other stonework

(P-2708)
CLEVELAND MARBLE LP
219 E Bristol Ln, Orange (92865-2715)
PHONE....................................714 998-3280
Elias N Ghattas, *Partner*
Gale Chrostowski, *Controller*
▲ EMP: 50
SALES (est): 950K Privately Held
SIC: 1741 Masonry & other stonework

(P-2709)
DESIGN MASONRY INC
20703 Santa Clara St, Canyon Country
(91351-2424)
PHONE....................................661 252-2784
Scott Floyd, *President*
EMP: 70
SALES (est): 7.8MM Privately Held
SIC: 1741 Stone masonry

(P-2710)
DJ SCHEFFLER INC (PA)
2500 Pomona Blvd, Pomona (91768-3218)
PHONE....................................909 595-2924
Dale J Scheffler, *President*
Mark Nye, *Vice Pres*
Cindy Scheffler, *Manager*
▲ EMP: 50
SALES (est): 10.8MM Privately Held
WEB: www.djscheffler.com
SIC: 1741 Foundation building

(P-2711)
ENGINEERED SOIL REPAIRS INC (PA)
1267 Springbrook Rd, Walnut Creek
(94597-3916)
PHONE....................................408 297-2150
Steve O'Connor, *President*
Mark Wilhite, *Treasurer*
Morgan Anderson, *Vice Pres*
Bill Gibson, *Vice Pres*
Donna Byrne, *Office Mgr*
EMP: 55
SQ FT: 3,000
SALES (est): 7.9MM Privately Held
SIC: 1741 1771 Foundation building; foundation & footing contractor

---

(PA)=Parent Co (HQ)=Headquarters (DH)=Div Headquarters
✪ = New Business established in last 2 years

(P-2712)
FRANK S SMITH MASONRY INC
2830 Pomona Blvd, Pomona (91768-3224)
PHONE.................................909 468-0525
Frank E Smith, *President*
Kevin J Smith, *CFO*
Brian E Smith, *Vice Pres*
EMP: 100
SQ FT: 54,000
SALES (est): 10.4MM **Privately Held**
WEB: www.fssmi.com
SIC: 1741 Bricklaying

(P-2713)
GBC CONCRETE MASNRY CNSTR INC
561 Birch St, Lake Elsinore (92530-2732)
PHONE.................................951 245-2355
Tom Daniel, *President*
EMP: 170
SQ FT: 8,000
SALES (est): 18.7MM **Privately Held**
WEB: www.gbcconstruction.com
SIC: 1741 1771 Foundation building; concrete work

(P-2714)
HARDROCK TILE & MARBLE INC
23151 Verdugo Dr Ste 111, Laguna Hills (92653-1340)
PHONE.................................714 282-1766
Fax: 714 282-0501
EMP: 52
SQ FT: 1,400
SALES (est): 4.9MM **Privately Held**
WEB: www.hardrocktilemarble.com
SIC: 1741

(P-2715)
HBA INCORPORATED
512 E Vermont Ave, Anaheim (92805-5603)
P.O. Box 25861 (92825-5861)
PHONE.................................714 635-8602
Gerald G Pyle, *President*
Joe Alessandrini, *CFO*
EMP: 100
SALES (est): 11MM **Privately Held**
SIC: 1741 Masonry & other stonework

(P-2716)
INDUSTRIAL MASONRY INC
3299 Horse Carri Rd Ste H, Norco (92860)
PHONE.................................951 284-0251
Greg E Wilson, *President*
Guy W Yocom, *CFO*
EMP: 100
SALES (est): 5.3MM **Privately Held**
SIC: 1741 Bricklaying

(P-2717)
J GINGER MASONRY LP (PA)
8188 Lincoln Ave Ste 100, Riverside (92504-4329)
PHONE.................................951 688-5050
John L Ginger, *Partner*
Brad Fogg, *President*
EMP: 265
SALES (est): 47.6MM **Privately Held**
SIC: 1741 Masonry & other stonework

(P-2718)
JAMES FEDOR MASONRY INC
54859 Bodine Dr, Thermal (92274-8911)
P.O. Box 1397, La Quinta (92247-1397)
PHONE.................................760 772-3036
EMP: 70
SALES (est): 2MM **Privately Held**
WEB: www.jamesfedormasonryinc.com
SIC: 1741

(P-2719)
JOHN JACKSON MASONRY
5691 Power Inn Rd Ste B, Sacramento (95824-2361)
PHONE.................................916 381-8021
Jeffrey Barber, *President*
Cheryl Lincoln, *Corp Secy*
Donald C Ekstrom, *Vice Pres*
Jim Loehr,
John Jackson, *Commercial*
EMP: 60
SQ FT: 6,200

SALES: 12.5MM **Privately Held**
WEB: www.johnjacksonmasonry.com
SIC: 1741 Bricklaying

(P-2720)
JOHN L GINGER MASONRY INC
8188 Lincoln Ave Ste 100, Riverside (92504-4329)
PHONE.................................951 688-5050
John L Ginger, *President*
EMP: 100
SQ FT: 8,000
SALES (est): 6.1MM **Privately Held**
WEB: www.gingermasonry.com
SIC: 1741 Masonry & other stonework

(P-2721)
MASONRY CONCEPTS INC
15408 Cornet St, Santa Fe Springs (90670-5534)
PHONE.................................562 802-3700
Ronald O Udall, *President*
Peter Sturdivant, *Corp Secy*
Russell Knight, *Vice Pres*
EMP: 100
SQ FT: 10,000
SALES (est): 9.9MM **Privately Held**
WEB: www.masonry-concepts.com
SIC: 1741 Masonry & other stonework

(P-2722)
MONTEREY BAY MASONRY INC
333 Phelan Ave, San Jose (95112-4104)
PHONE.................................408 289-8295
Casey Ricks, *President*
EMP: 50
SQ FT: 11,000
SALES (est): 1.3MM **Privately Held**
SIC: 1741 Concrete block masonry laying

(P-2723)
NIBBELINK MASONRY CNSTR CORP
2010 W Avenue K, Lancaster (93536-5229)
PHONE.................................661 948-7859
Troy Nibbelink, *President*
Gerald J Nibbelink, *Vice Pres*
EMP: 60 EST: 1976
SQ FT: 2,000
SALES (est): 11.4MM **Privately Held**
SIC: 1741 1771 Masonry & other stonework; exterior concrete stucco contractor

(P-2724)
ORANGE COAST MASONRY ACQUISIT
601 N Batavia St, Orange (92868-1220)
P.O. Box 608 (92856-6608)
PHONE.................................714 538-4386
Todd Essenmacher, *President*
EMP: 100
SQ FT: 10,000
SALES: 16MM **Privately Held**
SIC: 1741 Masonry & other stonework

(P-2725)
PACIFIC SHORES MASONRY
1369 Walker Ln, Corona (92879-1775)
PHONE.................................951 371-8550
Jeff McAninch, *President*
EMP: 50
SALES (est): 5.2MM **Privately Held**
SIC: 1741 Stone masonry

(P-2726)
PRO STRUCTURAL INC
26105 Sherman Rd, Menifee (92585-9249)
PHONE.................................951 526-2010
Robert A Yowell, *President*
Holly Yowell, *CFO*
Russell T Frazier, *Vice Pres*
EMP: 60
SALES (est): 1.9MM **Privately Held**
SIC: 1741 Masonry & other stonework

(P-2727)
RAYCON CONSTRUCTION INC
1795 E Lemonwood Dr, Santa Paula (93060-9651)
P.O. Box 910 (93061-0910)
PHONE.................................805 525-5256
Paul Reyes, *President*
Robert Reyes, *Treasurer*
Augie Reyes, *Vice Pres*

Chris Urrea, *Admin Sec*
EMP: 50
SQ FT: 6,000
SALES: 8MM **Privately Held**
SIC: 1741 Masonry & other stonework

(P-2728)
SMG STONE COMPANY INC
8460 San Fernando Rd, Sun Valley (91352-3227)
PHONE.................................818 767-0000
Solomon Aryeh, *President*
▲ EMP: 80
SQ FT: 12,000
SALES (est): 11.2MM **Privately Held**
WEB: www.smgstone.com
SIC: 1741 8711 5032 Masonry & other stonework; engineering services; marble building stone

(P-2729)
SPECTRA COMPANY
2510 Supply St, Pomona (91767-2113)
PHONE.................................909 599-0760
Ray Adamyk, *CEO*
Tim Harris, *COO*
Ann Dresselhaus, *Admin Sec*
▲ EMP: 125
SQ FT: 7,000
SALES: 21.6MM **Privately Held**
WEB: www.spectracompany.com
SIC: 1741 1771 1743 1721 Masonry & other stonework; concrete work; terrazzo, tile, marble, mosaic work; painting & paper hanging; carpentry work

(P-2730)
SUPERIOR MASONRY WALLS LTD
300 W Olive St Ste A, Colton (92324-1765)
PHONE.................................909 370-1800
Daniel Lee, *President*
Jeremiah Curtis, *CFO*
Mike Patchen, *Vice Pres*
Mike Chester, *Project Mgr*
EMP: 75
SALES: 950K **Privately Held**
SIC: 1741 Masonry & other stonework

(P-2731)
VARIATIONS IN STONE INC
360 La Perle Pl, Costa Mesa (92627-3758)
PHONE.................................949 438-8337
Joseph Dorando, *CFO*
James Joseph Dorando, *President*
EMP: 75
SALES (est): 198.4K **Privately Held**
SIC: 1741 Masonry & other stonework

(P-2732)
VILLA PACIFIC CONTRACTORS INC
3303 Harbor Blvd Ste D6, Costa Mesa (92626-1519)
PHONE.................................714 850-1640
Brad Gilbert, *President*
EMP: 50
SALES (est): 3MM **Privately Held**
SIC: 1741 Masonry & other stonework

(P-2733)
VINCENT CONTRACTORS INC
4501 E La Palma Ave # 200, Anaheim (92807-1904)
PHONE.................................714 693-1726
Justin Erdtsieck, *President*
Kenny Vo, *Accounts Mgr*
EMP: 430
SQ FT: 5,538
SALES (est): 4.5MM **Privately Held**
SIC: 1741 1742 Masonry & other stonework; plastering, drywall & insulation

(P-2734)
WILKIE MASONRY INC
4016 Hunter Oaks Ln, Loomis (95650-9280)
P.O. Box 387 (95650-0387)
PHONE.................................916 652-0118
Brian Wilkie, *President*
EMP: 50
SQ FT: 700
SALES: 750K **Privately Held**
SIC: 1741 5082 Masonry & other stonework; masonry equipment & supplies

(P-2735)
WILLIAMS & SONS MASONRY INC
8531 Winter Gardens Blvd A, Lakeside (92040-5475)
PHONE.................................619 443-1751
Darwin Todd Williams, *President*
Derrick Williams, *Admin Sec*
EMP: 70
SQ FT: 1,200
SALES (est): 4.5MM **Privately Held**
WEB: www.sons.sdcoxmail.com
SIC: 1741 Masonry & other stonework

(P-2736)
WINEGARDNER MASONRY INC
32147 Dunlap Blvd Ste A, Yucaipa (92399-1757)
PHONE.................................909 795-9711
Carolyn Winegardner, *CEO*
Julie Salazar, *President*
Dean Saavedra, *Project Mgr*
Susie Sheppard, *Accounting Mgr*
EMP: 50
SQ FT: 7,500
SALES (est): 7.5MM **Privately Held**
SIC: 1741 Bricklaying; concrete block masonry laying

(P-2737)
WIRTZ QULTY INSTALLATIONS INC
7932 Armour St, San Diego (92111-3718)
PHONE.................................858 569-3816
Amber Fox, *President*
Ida Wirtz, *Vice Pres*
John Wirtz, *Vice Pres*
EMP: 65
SALES (est): 6MM **Privately Held**
SIC: 1741 1752 1743 1799 Masonry & other stonework; floor laying & floor work; wood floor installation & refinishing; terrazzo, tile, marble, mosaic work; cleaning building exteriors

---

1742 Plastering, Drywall, Acoustical & Insulation Work

(P-2738)
A A GONZALEZ INC
13264 Ralston Ave, Sylmar (91342-7607)
P.O. Box 408, San Fernando (91341-0408)
PHONE.................................818 367-2242
Albert Gonzales, *President*
Aida Lepe, *Treasurer*
EMP: 100
SALES (est): 8MM **Privately Held**
SIC: 1742 Plastering, drywall & insulation

(P-2739)
A COLMENERO PLASTERING INC
1710 W San Madele Ave, Fresno (93711-2929)
PHONE.................................559 435-3606
Augie Colmenero, *President*
EMP: 55
SALES (est): 3.8MM **Privately Held**
SIC: 1742 Plastering, plain or ornamental

(P-2740)
ADERHOLT SPECIALTY COMPANY INC
1020 15th St Ste 9, Modesto (95354-1132)
PHONE.................................209 526-2000
Herbert Aderholt, *Ch of Bd*
Sherry Lynette Aderholt, *CEO*
Helen Aderholt, *Treasurer*
EMP: 100
SALES (est): 8.5MM **Privately Held**
WEB: www.aderholt.com
SIC: 1742 1799 Drywall; plastering, plain or ornamental; fireproofing buildings

(P-2741)
ADVANCED ACOUSTICS
3430 Golden Gate Way, Lafayette (94549-4518)
PHONE.................................925 299-0515
Steve Bossert, *Partner*

Ron Bossert, *Partner*
EMP: 50
SQ FT: 850
SALES (est): 1.8MM **Privately Held**
WEB: www.advancedacoustics.net
SIC: 1742 Acoustical & ceiling work

(P-2742)
ALAN SMITH POOL PLASTERING INC
227 W Carleton Ave, Orange (92867-3607)
PHONE..............................714 628-9494
Stephen Scherer, *President*
Teresa Smith, *CFO*
Alan Smith, *Executive*
Chris Smith, *Project Mgr*
▲ **EMP:** 78
SQ FT: 5,000
SALES (est): 9MM **Privately Held**
WEB: www.alansmithpools.com
SIC: 1742 Plastering, plain or ornamental

(P-2743)
ALERT INSULATION COMPANY INC
15913 Old Valley Blvd A, La Puente (91744-5439)
PHONE..............................626 961-9113
Donald W Kent, *President*
Charles Klinakis, *Vice Pres*
Joe Rodriguez, *General Mgr*
Bruce Abott, *Project Mgr*
Odalys Segovia, *Bookkeeper*
EMP: 66
SQ FT: 4,500
SALES (est): 8.8MM **Privately Held**
WEB: www.alertinsulation.net
SIC: 1742 Insulation, buildings

(P-2744)
ALL PRO DRYWALL
22148 Buckeye Pl, Cottonwood (96022-7701)
PHONE..............................530 722-5182
EMP: 50
SALES: 3MM **Privately Held**
SIC: 1742

(P-2745)
ALLEN DRYWALL & ASSOCIATES
380 Lang Rd, Burlingame (94010-2003)
PHONE..............................650 579-0664
Richard Allen, *President*
Julie Allen, *Corp Secy*
Katie Lawton, *Office Mgr*
Bill Lorenzini, *Project Mgr*
Nick Allen, *Manager*
EMP: 60
SALES (est): 6.1MM **Privately Held**
SIC: 1742 Drywall

(P-2746)
ALLIANCE WALL SYSTEMS INC
4638 Skyway Dr, Marysville (95901)
PHONE..............................530 740-7800
Gregory L Bolin, *President*
Shawn Shingler, *Vice Pres*
EMP: 50
SALES (est): 1.8MM **Privately Held**
SIC: 1742 Plastering, drywall & insulation

(P-2747)
ANCCA CORPORATION
Also Called: N-U Enterprise
7 Goddard, Irvine (92618-4600)
PHONE..............................949 553-0084
Nicole Hunt, *Treasurer*
EMP: 99
SALES: 950K **Privately Held**
SIC: 1742 Plastering, drywall & insulation

(P-2748)
ANNING-JOHNSON COMPANY
22955 Kidder St, Hayward (94545-1670)
PHONE..............................510 670-0100
R Todd Fearon, *Vice Pres*
Marilou Marcelo, *Administration*
Rafael Luna, *Project Mgr*
Ray Smith, *Sr Project Mgr*
EMP: 140
SQ FT: 16,000

SALES (corp-wide): 461.9MM **Privately Held**
SIC: 1742 Drywall; acoustical & ceiling work
HQ: Anning-Johnson Company
1959 Anson Dr
Melrose Park IL 60160
708 681-1300

(P-2749)
ANNING-JOHNSON COMPANY
13250 Temple Ave, City of Industry (91746-1583)
PHONE..............................626 369-7131
Larry Domino, *Vice Pres*
Jennifer Garcia, *Administration*
Joe Brosseau, *Purch Mgr*
Frank Valencia, *Superintendent*
EMP: 50
SALES (corp-wide): 461.9MM **Privately Held**
SIC: 1742 1761 1799 Acoustical & ceiling work; roofing, siding & sheet metal work; building site preparation
HQ: Anning-Johnson Company
1959 Anson Dr
Melrose Park IL 60160
708 681-1300

(P-2750)
ANSCHUTZ FILM GROUP
1888 Century Park E # 1400, Los Angeles (90067-1718)
PHONE..............................310 887-1000
EMP: 5002
SALES (est): 4.9MM
SALES (corp-wide): 110.5MM **Privately Held**
SIC: 1742
PA: The Anschutz Corporation
555 17th St Ste 2400
Denver CO 80202
303 298-1000

(P-2751)
AYALA DRYWALL
2600 Alexander St, Oxnard (93033-4728)
PHONE..............................805 487-3392
Abel Ayala, *Owner*
Abe Ayala, *Owner*
EMP: 50
SALES (est): 1.1MM **Privately Held**
SIC: 1742 Drywall

(P-2752)
B S I HOLDINGS INC
100 Clock Tower Pl # 200, Carmel (93923-8774)
PHONE..............................831 622-1840
EMP: 2000
SQ FT: 1,400
SALES (est): 44.4MM
SALES (corp-wide): 7.1B **Publicly Held**
WEB: www.bsiholdings.com
SIC: 1742
PA: Masco Corporation
21001 Van Born Rd
Taylor MI 48152
313 274-7400

(P-2753)
BAYSIDE INTERIORS INC (PA)
3220 Darby Cmn, Fremont (94539-5601)
PHONE..............................510 438-9171
Steven A Rivera, *CEO*
Tim Hogan, *President*
Michael Nicholson, *COO*
Jon Braden, *CFO*
Norma Nicholson, *Treasurer*
▲ **EMP:** 145
SQ FT: 20,000
SALES (est): 25.1MM **Privately Held**
WEB: www.baysideinteriors.com
SIC: 1742 Drywall

(P-2754)
BEST INTERIORS INC (PA)
2100 E Via Burton, Anaheim (92806-1219)
PHONE..............................714 490-7999
Dennis Ayres, *President*
Michael Herrig, *CFO*
Elise Wright, *Administration*
Ruben Aceves, *Purch Mgr*
Pete Villanueva, *Foreman/Supr*
EMP: 150
SQ FT: 20,000

SALES: 26.3MM **Privately Held**
WEB: www.bestinteriors.net
SIC: 1742 Drywall

(P-2755)
BOYETT CONSTRUCTION INC (PA)
2404 Tripaldi Way, Hayward (94545-5017)
PHONE..............................510 264-9100
Vernon H Boyett, *President*
Julie Mah, *Accountant*
Steve Baccei, *Manager*
Gary Coakley, *Manager*
Mark Sylva, *Superintendent*
EMP: 78
SQ FT: 2,600
SALES (est): 24MM **Privately Held**
SIC: 1742 1751 Drywall; acoustical & ceiling work; window & door installation & erection

(P-2756)
BRADY COMPANY/CENTRAL CAL
13540 Blackie Rd, Castroville (95012-3212)
PHONE..............................831 633-3315
Allen D Larson, *President*
Keith Eshelman, *CFO*
Gregg Brady, *Admin Sec*
EMP: 200
SALES (est): 12.7MM **Privately Held**
SIC: 1742 Plastering, plain or ornamental; insulation, buildings; acoustical & ceiling work; drywall

(P-2757)
BRADY COMPANY/LOS ANGELES INC
1010 N Olive St, Anaheim (92801-2539)
P.O. Box 470 (92815-0470)
PHONE..............................714 533-9850
William Saddler, *CEO*
Ron Brady, *Admin Sec*
EMP: 100
SALES (est): 6.9MM **Privately Held**
SIC: 1742 1791 Drywall; metal lath & furring

(P-2758)
BRADY COMPANY/SAN DIEGO INC
8100 Center St, La Mesa (91942-2925)
P.O. Box 968 (91944-0968)
PHONE..............................619 462-2600
Scott Brady, *CEO*
Gerry Geron, *Director*
EMP: 300
SQ FT: 4,000
SALES (est): 21.6MM **Privately Held**
SIC: 1742 1542 Plastering, plain or ornamental; insulation, buildings; acoustical & ceiling work; drywall; commercial & office buildings, renovation & repair

(P-2759)
BRADY SOCAL INCORPORATED
8100 Center St, La Mesa (91942-2925)
PHONE..............................619 462-2600
Ricky Marshall, *President*
Scott Brady, *Senior VP*
Kelly Galeazzi, *Vice Pres*
Troy Horn, *Purchasing*
Derek Miller, *Buyer*
EMP: 99
SALES: 8.8MM **Privately Held**
SIC: 1742 1751 Drywall; window & door installation & erection

(P-2760)
C A HOFMANN CONSTRUCTION INC
8923 Laramie Dr, Rancho Cucamonga (91737-1466)
P.O. Box 8463 (91701-0463)
PHONE..............................909 484-5888
Clarence A Hofmann, *CEO*
EMP: 50
SALES (est): 3.8MM **Privately Held**
SIC: 1742 1751 7389 Drywall; framing contractor;

(P-2761)
C D R ENTERPRISES INC
42302 8th St E, Lancaster (93535-5440)
P.O. Box 507, Friant (93626-0507)
PHONE..............................661 940-0344
EMP: 70
SALES (est): 2.6MM **Privately Held**
SIC: 1742

(P-2762)
C R S DRYWALL INC
Also Called: Cr Drywall
135 San Jose Ave, San Jose (95125-1018)
PHONE..............................408 998-4360
Carlos Silveria, *President*
EMP: 80
SQ FT: 4,000
SALES (est): 5.4MM **Privately Held**
SIC: 1742 Drywall

(P-2763)
CALIFORNIA DRYWALL CO (PA)
2290 S 10th St, San Jose (95112-4114)
PHONE..............................408 292-7500
Greg Eckstrom, *Vice Pres*
Kent Bowles, *President*
David Garrett, *COO*
Stephen Eckstrom, *Vice Pres*
Michael Gutierrez, *Vice Pres*
EMP: 250
SQ FT: 15,000
SALES (est): 54.7MM **Privately Held**
WEB: www.caldrywall.com
SIC: 1742 Drywall

(P-2764)
CANYON INSULATION INC
645 E Harrison St Ste 100, Corona (92879-1376)
PHONE..............................951 278-9200
Gerald Volas, *CEO*
Mick McGuire, *Vice Pres*
Christine Weigel, *Administration*
EMP: 70
SALES: 16.5MM
SALES (corp-wide): 2.3B **Publicly Held**
SIC: 1742 Insulation, buildings
PA: Topbuild Corp.
475 N Williamson Blvd
Daytona Beach FL 32114
386 304-2200

(P-2765)
CAPITAL CITY DRYWALL INC
6525 32nd St Ste B1, North Highlands (95660-3028)
PHONE..............................916 331-9200
John Beers, *President*
Andrew Sellers, *Vice Pres*
EMP: 100 **EST:** 2000
SQ FT: 2,500
SALES (est): 9MM **Privately Held**
WEB: www.capitalcitydrywall.com
SIC: 1742 Drywall

(P-2766)
CAPITAL DRYWALL LP
333 S Grand Ave Ste 4070, Los Angeles (90071-1544)
PHONE..............................909 599-6818
Frank Scardino, *President*
Art Toscano, *Vice Pres*
Angela Gates, *Admin Sec*
EMP: 150
SQ FT: 8,000
SALES (est): 7.9MM
SALES (corp-wide): 280MM **Privately Held**
SIC: 1742 Drywall
PA: U.S. Builder Services, Llc
272 E Deerpath Ste 308
Lake Forest IL 60045
847 735-2066

(P-2767)
CASTON INC
354 S Allen St, San Bernardino (92408-1508)
PHONE..............................909 381-1619
James I Malachowski Jr, *President*
EMP: 100
SALES (est): 12MM **Privately Held**
SIC: 1742 Drywall

(P-2768)
CEN CAL PLASTERING INC
15300 E Wyman Rd, Lathrop (95330)
PHONE..................................209 981-5265
EMP: 437
SALES (corp-wide): 17MM **Privately Held**
SIC: 1742 Plastering, plain or ornamental
PA: Cen Cal Plastering, Inc.
    1256 W Lathrop Rd
    Manteca CA 95336
    209 858-1045

(P-2769)
CHARLES CULBERSON INC
Also Called: Culberson Drywall
1084 Allen Way, Campbell (95008-4509)
P.O. Box 1954, Chester (96020-1954)
PHONE..................................650 335-4730
Fax: 650 335-4736
EMP: 150
SQ FT: 8,000
SALES (est): 7.3MM **Privately Held**
SIC: 1742

(P-2770)
CHURCH & LARSEN INC
16103 Avenida Padilla, Irwindale
(91702-3223)
PHONE..................................626 303-8741
Raymond W Larsen, *President*
Kenneth R Larsen, *Vice Pres*
EMP: 250
SQ FT: 10,800
SALES (est): 18.6MM **Privately Held**
SIC: 1742 Plaster & drywall work

(P-2771)
CLOVIS CUSTOM DRYWALL INC
Also Called: Custom Drywall Service
141 Sunnyside Ave Ste 108, Clovis
(93611-0570)
PHONE..................................559 297-7073
Dan Ploy, *Owner*
D Ployangunsri, *President*
Khatiya Hanvongse, *Vice Pres*
EMP: 50
SQ FT: 5,000
SALES (est): 2.8MM **Privately Held**
SIC: 1742 Drywall

(P-2772)
COAST INSULATION CONTRS INC (DH)
Also Called: Coast Building Products
1341 Old Oakland Rd, San Jose
(95112-1317)
PHONE..................................386 304-2222
Michael Raridon, *President*
EMP: 65
SQ FT: 10,000
SALES (est): 12.6MM
SALES (corp-wide): 2.3B **Publicly Held**
SIC: 1742 Insulation, buildings
HQ: American National Services, Inc.
    475 N Williamson Blvd
    Daytona Beach FL 32114
    386 304-2200

(P-2773)
CUSTOM DRYWALL INC
1570 Gladding Ct, Milpitas (95035-6814)
PHONE..................................408 263-1616
Gene Cox, *President*
Christine Cox, *Manager*
Craig Lammers, *Manager*
EMP: 90
SQ FT: 10,000
SALES (est): 7.5MM **Privately Held**
WEB: www.custom-drywall-inc.com
SIC: 1742 Drywall

(P-2774)
CUTTING EDGE DRYWALL INC
7046 Convoy Ct, San Diego (92111-1017)
PHONE..................................858 408-0870
Robert Pearn, *President*
EMP: 50
SQ FT: 4,800
SALES (est): 4MM **Privately Held**
WEB: www.cuttingedgedrywall.net
SIC: 1742 Drywall

(P-2775)
DALEYS DRYWALL AND TAPING INC
960 Camden Ave, Campbell (95008-4104)
PHONE..................................408 378-9500
Craig Spencer Daley, *President*
Brittni Bailey, *CFO*
Brittni Daley, *CFO*
Chris Daley, *Vice Pres*
Steve Spangenberg, *Division Mgr*
EMP: 550
SQ FT: 20,000
SALES (est): 84MM **Privately Held**
WEB: www.daleysdrywall.com
SIC: 1742 Drywall

(P-2776)
DEL MAR PLASTERING INC
7085 Jurupa Ave Ste 2, Riverside
(92504-1044)
PHONE..................................951 343-5955
Dale Pratte, *President*
EMP: 100
SQ FT: 2,000
SALES: 12MM **Privately Held**
SIC: 1742 Plastering, plain or ornamental

(P-2777)
DEMKO DRYWALL & DEMOLITION CO
419 S Marshall Ave, El Cajon (92020-4210)
PHONE..................................619 590-0025
Nicholas Demko, *President*
Debra Demko, *Corp Secy*
Alexis Demko, *Opers Mgr*
James Woodford, *Opers Staff*
EMP: 50 EST: 1971
SALES (est): 5.8MM **Privately Held**
WEB: www.demkodemolition.com
SIC: 1742 1751 1795 Drywall; framing
    contractor; wrecking & demolition work

(P-2778)
DH SMITH COMPANY INC
6000 Hellyer Ave Ste 150, San Jose
(95138-1031)
P.O. Box 730189 (95173-0189)
PHONE..................................408 532-7617
Daniel Smith III, *President*
Cheryl Smith, *Corp Secy*
Steven Smith, *Vice Pres*
EMP: 85
SQ FT: 20,000
SALES (est): 9.1MM **Privately Held**
SIC: 1742 Plastering, plain or ornamental

(P-2779)
DIAZ PLASTERING INC
4900 California Ave 210b, Bakersfield
(93309-7024)
P.O. Box 11014 (93389-1014)
PHONE..................................661 244-8228
Jovani Diaz, *President*
EMP: 60
SALES: 8MM **Privately Held**
SIC: 1742 Plaster & drywall work

(P-2780)
DOVE CEILINGS INC (PA)
22991 Belquest Dr, Lake Forest
(92630-4007)
PHONE..................................949 597-1794
David W Cowan, *CEO*
David Cowan, *President*
Carolyn Hacking, *CFO*
Mark Hacking, *Vice Pres*
EMP: 50 EST: 1981
SQ FT: 1,500
SALES (est): 3.9MM **Privately Held**
WEB: www.doveceilings.com
SIC: 1742 Drywall

(P-2781)
DRY CREEK LATH & PLASTER INC
27940 Kennefick Rd, Galt (95632-8290)
P.O. Box 1051 (95632-1051)
PHONE..................................209 367-8607
Ron Bohlender, *President*
EMP: 70
SQ FT: 6,000
SALES: 4MM **Privately Held**
SIC: 1742 Plaster & drywall work

(P-2782)
DRYWALL WORKS INC
5451 Whse Way Ste 105, Sacramento
(95826)
PHONE..................................916 383-6667
Xavier Valdez, *President*
Michael A Rizo, *Treasurer*
EMP: 80
SQ FT: 26,000
SALES: 9MM **Privately Held**
SIC: 1742 Drywall

(P-2783)
EDCO DRYWALL INC
Also Called: Edco Drywall Company
7200 Hazard Ave, Westminster
(92683-5027)
PHONE..................................714 799-9886
Dave Blunk, *President*
EMP: 50
SQ FT: 4,257
SALES (est): 2.4MM **Privately Held**
SIC: 1742 Drywall; acoustical & ceiling
    work

(P-2784)
ELLJAY ACOUSTICS INC
511 Cameron St, Placentia (92870-6425)
PHONE..................................714 961-1173
Ronald B Bishop, *President*
Tim Coggins, *Vice Pres*
Matt Paul, *Project Mgr*
Narda Reyes, *Assistant*
EMP: 70
SQ FT: 6,900
SALES (est): 8.2MM **Privately Held**
WEB: www.elljay.com
SIC: 1742 Acoustical & ceiling work

(P-2785)
ENERGETIC PNTG & DRYWALL INC (PA)
Also Called: Energetic Lath & Plaster
2929 Orange Grove Ave, North Highlands
(95660-5703)
PHONE..................................916 488-8455
EMP: 210
SQ FT: 10,000
SALES: 12MM **Privately Held**
SIC: 1742 Drywall

(P-2786)
ERIC STARK INTERIORS INC
2284 Paragon Dr, San Jose (95131-1306)
PHONE..................................408 441-6136
Eric Stark, *President*
EMP: 100
SQ FT: 10,000
SALES (est): 9.5MM **Privately Held**
WEB: www.ericstarkinteriors.com
SIC: 1742 Drywall

(P-2787)
FARWEST INSULATION CONTRACTING
Also Called: Pacific Insulation
2741 Yates Ave, Commerce (90040-2623)
PHONE..................................310 634-2800
Linda Chadarria, *Manager*
EMP: 50
SALES (corp-wide): 46.5MM **Privately Held**
SIC: 1742 Insulation, buildings
PA: Farwest Insulation Contracting, Inc
    1220 S Sherman St
    Anaheim CA 92805
    714 520-5600

(P-2788)
FUTURE ENERGY CORPORATION
4120 Avenida De La Plata, Oceanside
(92056-6001)
PHONE..................................760 477-9700
Jeffrey Adkins, *Branch Mgr*
EMP: 73
SALES (corp-wide): 28.4MM **Privately Held**
SIC: 1742 1521 Acoustical & insulation
    work; single-family home remodeling, ad-
    ditions & repairs
PA: Future Energy Corporation
    8980 Grant Line Rd
    Elk Grove CA 95624
    800 985-0733

(P-2789)
FUTURE ENERGY CORPORATION (PA)
Also Called: Future Energy Savers
8980 Grant Line Rd, Elk Grove
(95624-1415)
P.O. Box 87, Wilton (95693-0087)
PHONE..................................800 985-0733
Jeffrey Adkins, *CEO*
Trevor Fisher, *Controller*
EMP: 50
SQ FT: 6,800
SALES (est): 28.4MM **Privately Held**
WEB: www.energysavers.com
SIC: 1742 Insulation, buildings

(P-2790)
G BROTHERS CONSTRUCTION INC
7070 Patterson Dr, Garden Grove
(92841-1438)
PHONE..................................714 590-3070
Rick Gutierrez, *President*
Mike Gutierrez, *Vice Pres*
EMP: 50
SQ FT: 6,500
SALES (est): 6.6MM **Privately Held**
WEB: www.gbrothers.net
SIC: 1742 Drywall

(P-2791)
GIERAHN DRY WALL INC
28490 Westinghouse Pl # 150, Santa
Clarita (91355-0955)
PHONE..................................661 257-7900
Henry Carl Gierahn, *President*
Jim House, *Manager*
EMP: 50
SQ FT: 1,200
SALES (est): 3.8MM **Privately Held**
WEB: www.gierahn.com
SIC: 1742 Drywall

(P-2792)
GREYSTONE PLASTERING INC
1716 Stone Ave Ste B, San Jose
(95125-1308)
P.O. Box 41457 (95160-1457)
PHONE..................................408 298-5934
Michael Stonehocker, *President*
EMP: 80
SQ FT: 1,500
SALES (est): 7.2MM **Privately Held**
SIC: 1742 Plaster & drywall work

(P-2793)
GYPSUM CONTRACTORS INC
23785 El Toro Rd Ste 135, Lake Forest
(92630-4762)
PHONE..................................949 340-9100
Aram Fatourehchian, *CEO*
Aram Fatoure, *President*
EMP: 50 EST: 2012
SQ FT: 1,000
SALES (est): 2.8MM **Privately Held**
SIC: 1742 Insulation, buildings

(P-2794)
H B J CORPORATION
Also Called: Superior Pntg Drywall Fnshings
5806 Frontier Way, Carmichael
(95608-5137)
PHONE..................................707 333-7066
Harry Boyajian Jr, *President*
EMP: 80
SQ FT: 2,000
SALES: 1.5MM **Privately Held**
SIC: 1742 Drywall

(P-2795)
HARRISON DRYWALL INC
447 10th St, San Francisco (94103-4303)
P.O. Box 508, Cotati (94931-0508)
PHONE..................................415 821-9584
Jeff Harrison, *President*
Dan Harrison, *Project Mgr*
David Larson, *Project Mgr*
Erik Kristensen, *Project Engr*
Sasha Brady, *Controller*
EMP: 50
SQ FT: 5,000
SALES (est): 6.7MM **Privately Held**
WEB: www.harrisondrywallinc.com
SIC: 1742 Plastering, plain or ornamental;
    drywall

(P-2796)
HUTCHISON CORPORATION
Also Called: Inner Space Constructors Div
6107 Obispo Ave, Long Beach
(90805-3799)
PHONE......................310 763-7991
Robert J Hutchison, *Ch of Bd*
Linda Mc Dannold, *Corp Secy*
Stephen Mc Dannold, *Vice Pres*
EMP: 80
SQ FT: 50,000
SALES (est): 20MM **Privately Held**
SIC: 1742 1521 1542 Acoustical & ceiling
work; single-family housing construction;
commercial & office building, new con-
struction

(P-2797)
INFINITY DRYWALL CONTG INC
225 S Loara St, Anaheim (92802-1019)
PHONE......................714 634-2255
Dennis Lafreniere, *President*
James Darling, *Vice Pres*
Liza Lafreniere, *Vice Pres*
EMP: 60
SALES (est): 6.5MM **Privately Held**
SIC: 1742 1751 Drywall; framing contrac-
tor

(P-2798)
**INNOVATIVE DRYWALL
SYSTEMS INC**
Also Called: Alta Drywall
19192 Via Cuesta, Ramona (92065-5815)
PHONE......................760 743-0331
Doug Bellamy, *President*
Larry Johnson, *Director*
EMP: 80
SALES (est): 4.5MM **Privately Held**
SIC: 1742 Drywall

(P-2799)
INSUL ACOUSTICS INC
1432 Chico Ave, El Monte (91733-2995)
PHONE......................323 686-2670
Roy W Tonks, *President*
Don C Tonks, *Vice Pres*
EMP: 200
SQ FT: 10,000
SALES (est): 9.1MM **Privately Held**
WEB: www.insulacoustics.com
SIC: 1742 Drywall; plastering, plain or or-
namental; acoustical & ceiling work

(P-2800)
**INTERIOR EXPERTS GENERAL
BLDRS**
4534 Carter Ct, Chino (91710-5060)
PHONE......................909 203-4922
Adam Lopez, *President*
Ed Ortega, *Project Mgr*
EMP: 80
SQ FT: 9,000
SALES (est): 7.7MM **Privately Held**
WEB: www.expert-email.com
SIC: 1742 Drywall

(P-2801)
INTERWALL DEV SYSTEMS INC
17401 Armstrong Ave, Irvine (92614-5723)
PHONE......................949 553-9102
William Hunt, *President*
Cynthia Hunt, *Vice Pres*
EMP: 75
SQ FT: 2,100
SALES (est): 3.8MM **Privately Held**
WEB: www.wchuntco.com
SIC: 1742 Drywall

(P-2802)
IVO WALL EXPERTS INC
5359 Sheila St, Commerce (90040-2101)
PHONE......................323 246-4026
Ildefonso V Osorio, *President*
Frank Osorio, *Vice Pres*
Jose A Osorio, *Vice Pres*
Valentin Osorio, *Admin Sec*
EMP: 98
SQ FT: 7,200
SALES (est): 6.9MM **Privately Held**
SIC: 1742 Drywall

(P-2803)
J & J ACOUSTICS INC
2260 De La Cruz Blvd, Santa Clara
(95050-3008)
PHONE......................408 275-9255
James Jean, *President*
Joseph Jean, *Vice Pres*
Marge Meide, *Admin Sec*
Kim Herrmann, *Manager*
Sam McCroskey, *Superintendent*
EMP: 140 **EST:** 1975
SALES (est): 20.1MM **Privately Held**
WEB: www.jjacoustics.com
SIC: 1742 Drywall; acoustical & ceiling
work

(P-2804)
JADE INC
11126 Sepulveda Blvd B, Mission Hills
(91345-1130)
PHONE......................818 365-7137
Steven Arteaga, *CEO*
Jay Arteaga, *President*
Cheryl Taylor, *Treasurer*
Michelle Vojtech, *Vice Pres*
Gail De Ande, *Admin Sec*
EMP: 75
SQ FT: 5,000
SALES (est): 7.7MM **Privately Held**
WEB: www.jade.net
SIC: 1742 Drywall

(P-2805)
JCV INC
1118 W Orangethorpe Ave, Fullerton
(92833-4743)
P.O. Box 856 (92836-0856)
PHONE......................714 871-2007
Mario Valadez, *CFO*
Juan Valadez, *CEO*
EMP: 50
SQ FT: 1,900
SALES (est): 3.6MM **Privately Held**
SIC: 1742 Drywall

(P-2806)
JOHN JORY CORPORATION (PA)
2180 N Glassell St, Orange (92865-3308)
PHONE......................714 279-7901
Kenneth Johnson, *CEO*
Jack Jory, *Admin Sec*
Chuck Carroll, *Superintendent*
Bob Price, *Superintendent*
EMP: 385
SALES (est): 53.6MM **Privately Held**
WEB: www.johnjorycorp.com
SIC: 1742 Drywall

(P-2807)
**KEENAN HOPKINS SUDER &
STOWELL (PA)**
Also Called: Khs & S Contractors
5109 E La Palma Ave Ste A, Anaheim
(92807-2066)
PHONE......................714 695-3670
David Suder, *President*
Philip Cherne, *COO*
Christopher Spendley, *CFO*
Dennis Norman, *Corp Secy*
James Stafford, *Exec VP*
▲ **EMP:** 65
SALES (est): 253MM **Privately Held**
SIC: 1742 1751 1743 1741 Plastering,
plain or ornamental; carpentry work; ter-
razzo, tile, marble, mosaic work; masonry
& other stonework; painting & paper
hanging

(P-2808)
KENYON CONSTRUCTION INC
4667 N Blythe Ave, Fresno (93722-3908)
PHONE......................559 277-5645
Jose Valenzuela, *Manager*
EMP: 56
SQ FT: 9,182
SALES (corp-wide): 134.6MM **Privately
Held**
SIC: 1742 Plastering, drywall & insulation
PA: Kenyon Construction, Inc.
    4001 W Indian School Rd
    Phoenix AZ 85019
    602 484-0080

(P-2809)
KENYON CONSTRUCTION INC
Also Called: Kenyon Plastering
3223 E St, North Highlands (95660-4606)
P.O. Box 2077 (95660-8077)
PHONE......................916 514-9502
Carl Schmidt, *Principal*
EMP: 200
SALES (corp-wide): 134.6MM **Privately
Held**
WEB: www.kenyonconstruction.com
SIC: 1742 Plastering, drywall & insulation
PA: Kenyon Construction, Inc.
    4001 W Indian School Rd
    Phoenix AZ 85019
    602 484-0080

(P-2810)
KENYON CONSTRUCTION INC
Also Called: Kenyon Plastering
1286 N Broadway Ave, Stockton
(95205-3039)
PHONE......................209 462-4060
Don Bee, *General Mgr*
EMP: 250
SALES (corp-wide): 134.6MM **Privately
Held**
WEB: www.kenyonconstruction.com
SIC: 1742 Stucco work, interior
PA: Kenyon Construction, Inc.
    4001 W Indian School Rd
    Phoenix AZ 85019
    602 484-0080

(P-2811)
KERDUS PLASTERING INC
575 6th St, Norco (92860-1540)
PHONE......................951 272-6720
Craig L Kerdus, *President*
Laura T Kerdus, *Corp Secy*
EMP: 165
SQ FT: 2,000
SALES (est): 16.4MM **Privately Held**
SIC: 1742 Stucco work, interior

(P-2812)
KURT MEISWINKEL INC
1407 E 3rd Ave, San Mateo (94401-2109)
PHONE......................650 344-7200
Kurt Meiswinkel, *President*
EMP: 50
SQ FT: 25,000
SALES (est): 3.3MM **Privately Held**
WEB: www.km.net
SIC: 1742 Drywall

(P-2813)
LANCASTER BURNS CNSTR INC
Also Called: L B Construction
8655 Washington Blvd, Roseville
(95678-5945)
PHONE......................916 624-8404
Jordan Edward Burns, *President*
Christine Lancaster, *CFO*
Vance Lancaster, *Vice Pres*
EMP: 150
SQ FT: 43,000
SALES (est): 33.4MM **Privately Held**
SIC: 1742 1751 1791 3449 Drywall;
framing contractor; building front installa-
tion metal; bars, concrete reinforcing: fab-
ricated steel

(P-2814)
**LEAVY BROTHERS
INCORPORATED**
Also Called: Solid Drywall
4117 Elverta Rd Ste 102, Antelope
(95843-4734)
PHONE......................916 773-5636
Joseph W Leavy, *CEO*
Masami Yoshieda, *Corp Secy*
Kevin Leavy, *Vice Pres*
EMP: 54
SALES: 500K **Privately Held**
SIC: 1742 Plastering, drywall & insulation

(P-2815)
MAGNUM DRYWALL INC
42027 Boscell Rd, Fremont (94538-3106)
PHONE......................510 979-0420
Gary Robinson, *President*
EMP: 72
SQ FT: 3,200

SALES (est): 17.8MM **Privately Held**
WEB: www.magnumdrywall.com
SIC: 1742 Drywall

(P-2816)
**MARTIN BROS/MARCOWALL
INC (PA)**
17104 S Figueroa St, Gardena
(90248-3097)
P.O. Box 2089 (90247-0089)
PHONE......................310 532-5335
Mohammad Chahine, *CEO*
Damon Hoover, *Vice Pres*
Raffi Ounanian, *Vice Pres*
Ana Tinajero, *Office Mgr*
Sarah Peru, *Project Mgr*
EMP: 150
SQ FT: 6,000
SALES (est): 25.7MM **Privately Held**
WEB: www.martinbros-marcowall.com
SIC: 1742 Plastering, drywall & insulation

(P-2817)
MARTIN INTEGRATED SYSTEMS
2330 N Pacific St, Orange (92865-2618)
PHONE......................714 998-9100
Marshall Hovivian, *President*
Anne Reizer, *Corp Secy*
Jeff Anderson, *Project Mgr*
EMP: 55
SQ FT: 5,540
SALES (est): 7MM **Privately Held**
SIC: 1742 Acoustical & ceiling work

(P-2818)
MASTER DESIGN DRYWALL INC
Also Called: Pacific Lath & Plaster
360 S Spruce St, Escondido (92025-4052)
P.O. Box 3058 (92033-3058)
PHONE......................760 480-9001
Mary Kathawa, *President*
EMP: 140
SALES (est): 7.9MM **Privately Held**
WEB: www.pacificlathandplaster.com
SIC: 1742 Drywall

(P-2819)
MASTER DRYWALL INC
6727 Bucktown Ln, Vacaville (95688-9719)
PHONE......................707 448-8659
Joseph R Mendonca, *President*
Manuela Mendonc, *Vice Pres*
EMP: 125
SALES (est): 7.8MM **Privately Held**
WEB: www.masterdrywall.com
SIC: 1742 Drywall

(P-2820)
MELOS PLST LTHG & DRYWALL
2038 E Jensen Ave, Fresno (93706-5054)
PHONE......................559 237-0028
Carlos Melo, *President*
Maria Melo, *Vice Pres*
EMP: 100
SQ FT: 5,820
SALES (est): 5.5MM **Privately Held**
SIC: 1742 Plastering, plain or ornamental;
plaster & drywall work; drywall

(P-2821)
MGM DRYWALL INC
1050 Coml St Ste 102, San Jose (95112)
PHONE......................408 292-4085
Miguel Guillen, *President*
Martina Guillen, *CFO*
Gonzalo Guillen, *Vice Pres*
William Guillen, *Project Engr*
Thomas Engel, *Manager*
EMP: 100
SALES (est): 5.1MM **Privately Held**
WEB: www.mgmdrywall.com
SIC: 1742 1721 3446 Drywall; acoustical
& insulation work; acoustical & ceiling
work; residential painting; commercial
painting; acoustical suspension systems,
metal

(P-2822)
MICHAEL B MAYOCK INC
Also Called: A Complete Drywall Co
1945 Francisco Blvd E # 31, San Rafael
(94901-5525)
PHONE......................415 456-9306
Michael B Mayock, *President*
Lisa Mayock, *Corp Secy*
EMP: 60 **EST:** 1977

SALES (est): 3.9MM **Privately Held**
SIC: 1742 1751 Drywall; lightweight steel framing (metal stud) installation

(P-2823)
MID VALLEY PLASTERING INC
15300 Mckinley Ave, Lathrop (95330-8782)
PHONE..................................209 858-9766
Jeff Gann, *President*
Kevin Gann, *Treasurer*
Jeremy Gann, *Vice Pres*
EMP: 400
SQ FT: 5,000
SALES (est): 32.7MM **Privately Held**
WEB: www.midvalleyplastering.com
SIC: 1742 Plastering, plain or ornamental

(P-2824)
MOWERY THOMASON INC
1225 N Red Gum St, Anaheim (92806-1821)
PHONE..................................714 666-1717
Robert J Heimerl, *President*
Toni Heimerl, *Corp Secy*
Todd Heimerl, *Vice Pres*
EMP: 175 **EST:** 1957
SQ FT: 8,000
SALES (est): 17.7MM **Privately Held**
WEB: www.mowerythomason.com
SIC: 1742 Drywall; plastering, plain or ornamental

(P-2825)
NEW WEST PARTITIONS
2550 Sutterville Rd, Sacramento (95820-1020)
PHONE..................................916 456-8365
Kem P Modellas, *CEO*
Mark Modellas, *Admin Sec*
EMP: 120
SQ FT: 3,000
SALES (est): 9.8MM **Privately Held**
SIC: 1742 Drywall

(P-2826)
NOROGACHI CONSTRUCTION INC/CA
600 Industrial Dr Ste 100, Galt (95632-8164)
PHONE..................................916 236-4201
Anival Guerrero, *CEO*
Laura Guerrero, *Vice Pres*
EMP: 100
SALES (est): 9.1MM **Privately Held**
SIC: 1742 1542 Drywall; acoustical & insulation work; acoustical & ceiling work; institutional building construction

(P-2827)
NORTH COUNTIES DRYWALL INC
20563 Broadway, Sonoma (95476-7590)
P.O. Box 260 (95476-0260)
PHONE..................................707 996-0198
Diane Merlo, *President*
Dennis Thomas, *Project Mgr*
Olivia Acevedo, *HR Admin*
EMP: 50
SQ FT: 2,000
SALES (est): 7.1MM **Privately Held**
WEB: www.ncdinc.net
SIC: 1742 1542 1521 Drywall; commercial & office building, new construction; new construction, single-family houses

(P-2828)
OJ INSULATION LP
5820 Obata Way Ste B, Gilroy (95020-7093)
PHONE..................................408 842-6315
Griff Jenkins, *Branch Mgr*
EMP: 73
SALES (corp-wide): 32.8MM **Privately Held**
SIC: 1742 1751 1741 Insulation, buildings; carpentry work; masonry & other stonework
PA: Oj Insulation, L.P.
600 S Vincent Ave
Azusa CA 91702
626 812-6070

(P-2829)
OJ INSULATION LP
Also Called: Oj Insulation & Fireplaces
2061 Albergrov Ave, Escondido (92029)
PHONE..................................760 839-3200
Tom Berry, *Manager*
EMP: 50
SALES (corp-wide): 32.8MM **Privately Held**
WEB: www.ojinc.com
SIC: 1742 Insulation, buildings
PA: Oj Insulation, L.P.
600 S Vincent Ave
Azusa CA 91702
626 812-6070

(P-2830)
OJ INSULATION LP
78 015 Wildcat Dr, Palm Desert (92211)
PHONE..................................760 200-4343
Griff Jenkins, *Branch Mgr*
EMP: 73
SALES (corp-wide): 32.8MM **Privately Held**
SIC: 1742 1751 1741 Insulation, buildings; carpentry work; masonry & other stonework
PA: Oj Insulation, L.P.
600 S Vincent Ave
Azusa CA 91702
626 812-6070

(P-2831)
OJ INSULATION LP (PA)
Also Called: Abco Insulation
600 S Vincent Ave, Azusa (91702-5145)
PHONE..................................626 812-6070
Pamela A Henson, *Partner*
Mark Newman, *Division Mgr*
Yahoska Montenegro, *Administration*
Charlene Smith, *Human Res Dir*
Rocco Tannascoli, *Director*
EMP: 148
SQ FT: 12,000
SALES (est): 32.8MM **Privately Held**
WEB: www.ojinc.com
SIC: 1742 1751 1741 Insulation, buildings; carpentry work; masonry & other stonework

(P-2832)
ORANGE COUNTY PLST CO INC
3191 Arprt Loop Dr Ste B1, Costa Mesa (92626)
PHONE..................................714 957-1971
Robert G Smith, *President*
EMP: 128
SALES (est): 11.8MM **Privately Held**
WEB: www.ocplastering.com
SIC: 1742 Plastering, plain or ornamental

(P-2833)
P H B CONTRACTING INC
43180 Sunburst St, Indio (92201-2083)
PHONE..................................760 347-7290
Dave Boggs, *President*
Nicholas Panzarini, *Vice Pres*
EMP: 225
SALES (est): 7.9MM **Privately Held**
SIC: 1742 Plaster & drywall work

(P-2834)
PACE INC
Also Called: Pace Drywall
2301 Arnold Industrial Wa, Concord (94520-5375)
P.O. Box 573 (94522-0573)
PHONE..................................925 602-0900
Alan D Mauldin, *President*
Patricia Mauldin, *Corp Secy*
Elizabeth Snedeker, *Office Mgr*
EMP: 80
SQ FT: 17,000
SALES (est): 8.4MM **Privately Held**
WEB: www.pacedrywall.com
SIC: 1742 Drywall

(P-2835)
PACIFIC BUILDING GROUP
13541 Stoney Creek Rd, San Diego (92129-2050)
PHONE..................................858 552-0600
Jim Roherty, *Branch Mgr*
EMP: 100

SALES (corp-wide): 52MM **Privately Held**
SIC: 1742 Acoustical & ceiling work
PA: Pacific Building Group
9752 Aspen Creek Ct # 100
San Diego CA 92126
858 552-0600

(P-2836)
PACIFIC EXTERIORS INC
13911 Enterprise Dr Ste B, Garden Grove (92843-4042)
PHONE..................................714 265-1998
Frank Blasetti, *President*
Christine Blasetti, *CFO*
Mark Blasetti, *Treasurer*
EMP: 75
SALES (est): 6.1MM **Privately Held**
WEB: www.pacificexteriors.com
SIC: 1742 Plastering, plain or ornamental

(P-2837)
PACIFIC RIM CONTRACTORS INC
1315 E Saint Andrew Pl B, Santa Ana (92705-4919)
PHONE..................................714 641-7380
Jerry Tyner, *President*
Aaron Tyner, *Vice Pres*
Tina Feraco, *Manager*
EMP: 65
SQ FT: 3,000
SALES (est): 5.3MM **Privately Held**
WEB: www.pacificrimcontractors.com
SIC: 1742 1721 Drywall; painting & paper hanging

(P-2838)
PACIFIC SYSTEMS INTERIORS INC
190 E Arrow Hwy Ste D, San Dimas (91773-3314)
PHONE..................................310 436-6820
Jonathan Miasnik, *President*
EMP: 150
SQ FT: 30,000
SALES: 39.7MM **Privately Held**
SIC: 1742 1542 Drywall; nonresidential construction

(P-2839)
PACIFIC WEST LATH & PLASTER
6853 Mccomber St, Sacramento (95828-2515)
PHONE..................................916 387-5773
Paul Maples, *President*
EMP: 50
SALES (est): 5.1MM **Privately Held**
SIC: 1742 Drywall

(P-2840)
PADILLA CONSTRUCTION COMPANY
Also Called: Garris Plastering
205 W Bristol Ln, Orange (92865-2605)
P.O. Box 2847 (92859-0847)
PHONE..................................714 685-8500
Ralph Padilla, *Principal*
Tom Mattera, *Vice Pres*
Harold Norton, *Executive*
Dennis Davies, *VP Opers*
Mark Murrow, *VP Opers*
EMP: 250
SQ FT: 5,000
SALES (est): 25.5MM **Privately Held**
WEB: www.padillaconstruction.com
SIC: 1742 Plastering, drywall & insulation

(P-2841)
PAUL PIETRZYK
Also Called: Pauls Drywall
1142 Acapulco Ct, Merced (95348-1859)
PHONE..................................209 726-5034
Paul Pietrzyk, *President*
Loree Pietryk, *CFO*
EMP: 50
SALES: 2.5MM **Privately Held**
SIC: 1742 Drywall

(P-2842)
PETROCHEM INSULATION INC
19010 S Alameda St, Compton (90221-6201)
PHONE..................................310 638-6663

Erich Freudenthaler, *Manager*
Eric Freudenthaler, *Marketing Mgr*
Dianna Ghorley, *Manager*
EMP: 200
SALES (corp-wide): 2.9B **Privately Held**
WEB: www.petrocheminc.com
SIC: 1742 3531 Insulation, buildings; construction machinery
HQ: Petrochem Insulation, Inc.
2300 Clayton Rd Ste 1050
Concord CA 94520
707 644-7455

(P-2843)
PREMIER DRYWALL
725 Oak St, Santa Maria (93454-6215)
P.O. Box 57 (93456-0057)
PHONE..................................805 928-3397
John Amburgey, *CEO*
Danny Amburgery, *Principal*
EMP: 99 **EST:** 1990
SALES (est): 5.3MM **Privately Held**
SIC: 1742 Drywall

(P-2844)
PREMIUM ROCK DRYWALL INC
31348 Via Colinas Ste 103, Westlake Village (91362-6805)
PHONE..................................818 676-3350
Rick Cook, *President*
Stacy Cook, *Corp Secy*
EMP: 80
SQ FT: 800
SALES: 3MM **Privately Held**
SIC: 1742 Drywall

(P-2845)
PROWALL LATH AND PLASTER
360 S Spruce St, Escondido (92025-4052)
P.O. Box 3058 (92033-3058)
PHONE..................................760 480-9001
Mary Kathawa, *President*
EMP: 99
SALES (est): 6.5MM **Privately Held**
SIC: 1742 Plastering, plain or ornamental

(P-2846)
QUALITY PRODUCTION SVCS INC
18711 S Broadwick St, Compton (90220-6427)
PHONE..................................310 406-3350
Arshak George Kotoyantz, *President*
Jesus Garcia, *Manager*
EMP: 100
SALES (est): 11.4MM **Privately Held**
SIC: 1742 Drywall

(P-2847)
REDDING DRYWALL SYSTEMS INC
Also Called: High Performance Wall Systems
3092 Crossroads Dr, Redding (96003-8058)
P.O. Box 494156 (96049-4156)
PHONE..................................530 222-8767
Marvin O'Dell, *President*
EMP: 50
SQ FT: 3,800
SALES (est): 4.3MM **Privately Held**
WEB: www.drywallsystems.com
SIC: 1742 Drywall

(P-2848)
RFJ CORPORATION
Also Called: Rfj Meiswinkel
930 Innes Ave, San Francisco (94124-2905)
PHONE..................................415 824-6890
Joseph Meiswinkel, *President*
EMP: 60
SQ FT: 15,000
SALES (est): 8.8MM **Privately Held**
WEB: www.rfjmeiswinkel.com
SIC: 1742 Plastering, plain or ornamental; drywall

(P-2849)
RICE DRYWALL INC
919 E 6th St, Santa Ana (92701-4725)
PHONE..................................714 543-5400
John H Laing, *President*
Keith Barakat, *Vice Pres*
Kim Riker, *Admin Sec*
EMP: 90 **EST:** 1973
SQ FT: 8,000

SALES: 2.3MM **Privately Held**
SIC: **1742** Drywall

(P-2850)
RICHMOND PLASTERING INC
12102 Centralia Rd Ste B, Hawaiian Gardens (90716-1003)
PHONE.....................562 924-4202
Tim Richmond, *President*
Debbie Richmond, *Treasurer*
Mark Nevin, *Vice Pres*
Sue Bredesen, *Office Mgr*
Claude Curtis, *Opers Staff*
▲ EMP: 50 EST: 1979
SQ FT: 1,375
SALES (est): 5.6MM **Privately Held**
WEB: www.richmondplastering.com
SIC: **1742** Plastering, plain or ornamental

(P-2851)
RICK H HITCH PLASTERING INC
Also Called: Venture Lath and Plaster
3306 Orange Grove Ave, North Highlands (95660-5808)
P.O. Box 1391 (95660-1391)
PHONE.....................916 334-3591
Jason Wu, *President*
Loretta Hitch, *Vice Pres*
EMP: 125
SALES (est): 4.3MM **Privately Held**
WEB: www.venturelp.com
SIC: **1742** Plastering, plain or ornamental

(P-2852)
ROYAL WEST DRYWALL INC
2008 2nd St, Norco (92860-2804)
PHONE.....................951 271-4600
Paul Diguiseppe, *CEO*
EMP: 100 EST: 1988
SQ FT: 20,473
SALES (est): 8.1MM **Privately Held**
WEB: www.westcoastdrywallinc.com
SIC: **1742** Drywall

(P-2853)
RUDY CARRILLO DRYWALL INC
1913 W Magnolia Blvd, Burbank (91506-1727)
PHONE.....................818 841-2011
Rudy Carrillo, *CEO*
Darcy Carrillo, *Vice Pres*
EMP: 80
SQ FT: 2,399
SALES (est): 5.3MM **Privately Held**
SIC: **1742** Drywall

(P-2854)
RUTHERFORD CO INC (PA)
2107 Crystal St, Los Angeles (90039-2901)
PHONE.....................323 666-5284
Paul Rutherford, *President*
James Rutherford, *Treasurer*
Brad Rutherford, *Vice Pres*
Sheila Rutherford, *Admin Sec*
EMP: 100
SQ FT: 15,000
SALES: 19MM **Privately Held**
SIC: **1742** Plastering, plain or ornamental

(P-2855)
S A CALI-U ACOUSTICS INC
Also Called: Acoustical Contractor
1111 Rnch Conejo Blvd # 501, Thousand Oaks (91320-1412)
PHONE.....................805 376-9300
Diego Velasquez, *President*
Anna Velasquez, *Vice Pres*
Federico Velasquez, *Project Mgr*
Tim Velasquez, *Technology*
EMP: 60
SQ FT: 3,000
SALES: 1.5MM **Privately Held**
WEB: www.caliusa.net
SIC: **1742** Acoustical & ceiling work; insulation, buildings

(P-2856)
SAN MARINO PLASTERING INC
4501 E La Palma Ave # 200, Anaheim (92807-1950)
PHONE.....................714 693-7840
Fred Erdtsieck, *President*
Edward Birn, *CFO*
EMP: 820

SALES (est): 30.7MM **Privately Held**
WEB: www.smcompanies.com
SIC: **1742** Plastering, plain or ornamental

(P-2857)
SERVICE LATHING COMPANY
1090 139th Ave, San Leandro (94578-2615)
PHONE.....................510 483-9732
Robert G Brown, *President*
Ernest Schorno, *Treasurer*
EMP: 50
SQ FT: 4,500
SALES (est): 4.5MM **Privately Held**
SIC: **1742** **1751** Plastering, plain or ornamental; framing contractor

(P-2858)
SIERRA LATHING COMPANY INC
1189 Leiske Dr, Rialto (92376-8633)
PHONE.....................909 421-0211
Gary K Waldron, *CEO*
Connie Waldron, *Treasurer*
EMP: 200
SQ FT: 10,000
SALES (est): 14MM **Privately Held**
SIC: **1742** **1751** Drywall; framing contractor

(P-2859)
SNEARY CONSTRUCTION INC
1182 Monte Vista Ave # 2, Upland (91786-8204)
PHONE.....................909 982-1833
Montie Sneary, *President*
Nicole Van Gundy, *CFO*
Shawna Sneary, *Vice Pres*
Deborah Herring, *Manager*
EMP: 50
SALES (est): 3.5MM **Privately Held**
SIC: **1742** Drywall

(P-2860)
SPACETONE ACOUSTICS INC
1051 Serpentine Ln # 300, Pleasanton (94566-8451)
PHONE.....................925 931-0749
Robert A Libby, *President*
Joan Libby, *Vice Pres*
Robert Libby, *Vice Pres*
Dominic Sanchez, *Manager*
EMP: 50
SQ FT: 3,500
SALES (est): 6.8MM **Privately Held**
WEB: www.spacetoneacoustics.com
SIC: **1742** Drywall

(P-2861)
SPECIALTY TEAM PLASTERING INC
4652 Vintage Ranch Ln, Santa Barbara (93110-2079)
PHONE.....................805 966-3858
Jaime Melgosa, *President*
Robin Melgosa, *Vice Pres*
EMP: 130
SQ FT: 1,000
SALES: 8.2MM **Privately Held**
SIC: **1742** Plastering, drywall & insulation

(P-2862)
STANDARD DRYWALL INC (HQ)
Also Called: S D I
9902 Channel Rd, Lakeside (92040-3042)
PHONE.....................619 443-7034
Robert E Caya, *Principal*
Ed Capparelli, *Vice Pres*
Blaine Caya, *Vice Pres*
Greg Marusich, *Project Mgr*
Randy Washburn, *Project Mgr*
EMP: 300
SQ FT: 4,500
SALES (est): 123.9MM **Privately Held**
WEB: www.standarddrywall.net
SIC: **1742** Drywall; acoustical & ceiling work

(P-2863)
SUNSHINE METAL CLAD INC
7201 Edison Hwy, Bakersfield (93307-9011)
PHONE.....................661 366-0575
James R Eudy, *President*
Linda Payne, *CFO*
Sandy Eudy, *Vice Pres*

▲ EMP: 100
SQ FT: 50,000
SALES (est): 11.5MM **Privately Held**
WEB: www.smc3000.com
SIC: **1742** Insulation, buildings

(P-2864)
SUPERIOR CONTRACTING CORP
Also Called: Coast Building Products
45 N Main St, Salinas (93901-2892)
PHONE.....................831 757-1089
EMP: 50
SALES (corp-wide): 2.3B **Publicly Held**
SIC: **1742** Insulation, buildings
HQ: Superior Contracting Corporation
475 N Williamson Blvd
Daytona Beach FL 32114
386 304-2200

(P-2865)
SUPERIOR WALL SYSTEMS INC
Also Called: Sws
1232 E Orangethorpe Ave, Fullerton (92831-5224)
PHONE.....................714 278-0000
Ronald Lee Hudson, *CEO*
EMP: 500
SQ FT: 40,000
SALES: 48.9MM **Privately Held**
SIC: **1742** Drywall

(P-2866)
TEMECULA VALLEY DRYWALL INC
Also Called: Timberlake Painting
41228 Raintree Ct, Murrieta (92562-7089)
PHONE.....................951 600-1742
Doug A Misemer, *CEO*
Sandy Villella, *Corp Secy*
Lorry Hales, *Vice Pres*
Jim Morton, *Manager*
EMP: 75
SQ FT: 8,000
SALES (est): 10.8MM **Privately Held**
SIC: **1742** **1721** Drywall; painting & paper hanging

(P-2867)
THERMO POWER INDUSTRIES
10570 Humbolt St, Los Alamitos (90720-2439)
PHONE.....................562 799-0087
Edward Lydic, *CEO*
John G Carroll, *CFO*
EMP: 50
SQ FT: 5,500
SALES (est): 8.4MM **Privately Held**
WEB: www.thermopowerindustries.com
SIC: **1742** **1721** **3479** Insulation, buildings; commercial painting; coating, rust preventive

(P-2868)
TOMMY GUN PLASTERING INC
944 4th St, Calimesa (92320-1205)
PHONE.....................909 795-9966
Tommy Lucero, *CEO*
EMP: 60
SQ FT: 1,800
SALES (est): 4.7MM **Privately Held**
SIC: **1742** Plastering, plain or ornamental

(P-2869)
TONY MARQUEZ POOL PLST INC
14960 Foothill Blvd, Sylmar (91342-1301)
PHONE.....................818 833-5872
Antonio R Marquez, *President*
Tony Marquez, *President*
Georgette Marquez, *CFO*
EMP: 63
SALES (est): 3.8MM **Privately Held**
SIC: **1742** **1799** Plastering, plain or ornamental; swimming pool construction

(P-2870)
TOUCH-UP INC
Also Called: T & R Painting & Drywall
7116 Valjean Ave, Van Nuys (91406-3901)
PHONE.....................818 994-6166
Hagai Rapaport, *President*
Aviv Ilan, *Sales Staff*
EMP: 120
SQ FT: 2,500

SALES (est): 6.5MM **Privately Held**
SIC: **1742** **1721** Drywall; painting & paper hanging

(P-2871)
TOWNE CONSTRUCTION INC
12115 Lakeside Ave, Lakeside (92040-1712)
PHONE.....................619 390-4557
Tom Towne, *President*
EMP: 60
SQ FT: 1,700
SALES (est): 6.8MM **Privately Held**
SIC: **1742** Drywall

(P-2872)
TRI-STAR DRYWALL LP
2479 Burgan Ave, Clovis (93611-4107)
P.O. Box 1081 (93613-1081)
PHONE.....................559 299-9858
Raymond William McGuire, *Partner*
EMP: 80
SALES (est): 3.2MM **Privately Held**
SIC: **1742** Drywall

(P-2873)
VANTAGE PLASTER & DRYWALL
79607 Country Club Dr, Bermuda Dunes (92203-1207)
PHONE.....................760 345-3622
Jim Morales, *President*
EMP: 85
SALES (est): 2.7MM **Privately Held**
SIC: **1742** Plastering, plain or ornamental

(P-2874)
W F HAYWARD CO
629 Main St Ste 101, Placerville (95667-5752)
PHONE.....................530 303-3030
Daryll Hayward, *Vice Pres*
EMP: 64
SALES (corp-wide): 4.8MM **Privately Held**
SIC: **1742** Drywall
PA: W. F. Hayward Co.
1264 W 130th St
Gardena CA 90247
310 532-9501

(P-2875)
WALL SYSTEMS INC
11975 Discovery Ct, Moorpark (93021-7120)
PHONE.....................805 523-9091
Kenyon Lee, *President*
Frank Bass, *Vice Pres*
Darrell Talavera, *Vice Pres*
EMP: 90
SQ FT: 6,200
SALES: 10MM **Privately Held**
SIC: **1742** Drywall; stucco work, interior

(P-2876)
WEST COAST DRYWALL & CO INC
1610 W Linden St, Riverside (92507-6810)
PHONE.....................951 778-3592
Mark Herbert, *CEO*
Dan Slavin, *President*
Santos Garcia, *Vice Pres*
Colleen Butler, *Human Resources*
EMP: 400
SQ FT: 18,962
SALES (est): 30.7MM **Privately Held**
WEB: www.westcoastpainting.com
SIC: **1742** Drywall

(P-2877)
WESTERN BUILDING MATERIALS CO (PA)
4620 E Olive Ave, Fresno (93702-1660)
PHONE.....................559 454-8500
Peter Hastrup, *President*
EMP: 60
SQ FT: 32,000
SALES: 17MM **Privately Held**
WEB: www.western-building.com
SIC: **1742** **5211** Acoustical & ceiling work; millwork & lumber

P R O D U C T S & S V C S

(P-2878)
WGG ENTERPRISES INC
Also Called: Pierce Enterprises
11340 Stewart St, El Monte (91731-2747)
PHONE..........................626 442-5493
Weldon G Gainer, *President*
EMP: 150
SQ FT: 25,000
SALES (est): 10.2MM **Privately Held**
SIC: 1742 Plastering, plain or ornamental

(P-2879)
WINEGARD ENERGY INC
2885 S Chestnut Ave, Fresno
(93725-2211)
PHONE..........................559 441-0243
Wallas Winegard, *Owner*
EMP: 100 **Privately Held**
WEB: www.winegardenergy.com
SIC: 1742 Insulation, buildings
PA: Winegard Energy, Inc.
　　5354 Irwindale Ave Ste B
　　Irwindale CA 91706

(P-2880)
WINEGARD ENERGY INC
2159 Zeus Ct, Bakersfield (93308-6866)
PHONE..........................661 393-9467
Jessica Landrum, *Manager*
Bryce Larson, *Manager*
EMP: 72
SALES (est): 2.1MM **Privately Held**
WEB: www.winegardenergy.com
SIC: 1742 Insulation, buildings
PA: Winegard Energy, Inc.
　　5354 Irwindale Ave Ste B
　　Irwindale CA 91706

(P-2881)
**WM ONEILL LATH AND PLST
CORP**
1261 Birchwood Dr, Sunnyvale
(94089-2206)
P.O. Box 60352 (94088-0352)
PHONE..........................408 329-1413
William O'Neill, *President*
Sandra O'Neill, *Admin Sec*
EMP: 50 EST: 2009
SALES (est): 5.2MM **Privately Held**
SIC: 1742 Plastering, plain or ornamental

**1743 Terrazzo, Tile, Marble &
Mosaic Work**

(P-2882)
**AMERICAN TILE BRICK VENEER
INC**
1389 E 28th St, Signal Hill (90755-1841)
PHONE..........................562 595-9293
Albert Weinstein, *President*
Taghi Nahidi, *CFO*
Andrew Nahidi, *Vice Pres*
Bardia Nahidi, *Vice Pres*
EMP: 50
SQ FT: 3,000
SALES: 6MM **Privately Held**
SIC: 1743 1741 Tile installation, ceramic;
bricklaying

(P-2883)
ARRIAGA USA INC
11831 Vose St, North Hollywood
(91605-5748)
PHONE..........................818 982-9559
EMP: 75
SALES (corp-wide): 31.9MM **Privately
Held**
SIC: 1743 Tile installation, ceramic
PA: Arriaga Usa, Inc.
　　12000 Sherman Way
　　North Hollywood CA 91605
　　818 982-9559

(P-2884)
BREWSTER MARBLE CO INC
20801 Dearborn St, Chatsworth
(91311-5916)
PHONE..........................818 834-2195
Teo Zeolla, *President*
▲ **EMP:** 50
SQ FT: 11,000

SALES (est): 3.9MM **Privately Held**
WEB: www.brewstermarble.net
SIC: 1743 Marble installation, interior

(P-2885)
CAL CUSTOM TILE
1300 Commerce Way, Sanger
(93657-8731)
PHONE..........................559 875-1460
Rick Berry, *President*
Michele Berry, *Vice Pres*
EMP: 95
SQ FT: 10,000
SALES (est): 10.2MM **Privately Held**
SIC: 1743 Tile installation, ceramic

(P-2886)
CERAMIC TILE ART INC
11601 Pendleton St, Sun Valley
(91352-2502)
PHONE..........................818 767-9088
Itamar Levy, *President*
Bobbie Kmet, *Office Mgr*
▲ **EMP:** 75
SALES (est): 6MM **Privately Held**
WEB: www.ceramictileart.us
SIC: 1743 Tile installation, ceramic

(P-2887)
COASTAL TILE INC
Also Called: Coastal The
7403 Greenbush Ave, North Hollywood
(91605-4006)
PHONE..........................818 988-6134
Ronig Yemini, *President*
Eyal Reguev, *Vice Pres*
▲ **EMP:** 100
SALES (est): 8.8MM **Privately Held**
SIC: 1743 Tile installation, ceramic

(P-2888)
D & J TILE COMPANY INC
1045 Terminal Way, San Carlos
(94070-3226)
PHONE..........................650 632-4000
David Newman, *Principal*
Michael Brady, *Treasurer*
John Reich, *Admin Sec*
Jaleh Dale, *Project Mgr*
Victor Zamora, *Project Mgr*
◆ **EMP:** 100
SQ FT: 145
SALES (est): 12.3MM **Privately Held**
WEB: www.djtile.com
SIC: 1743 Tile installation, ceramic

(P-2889)
DAL-TILE CORPORATION
7484 Raytheon Rd Ste A, San Diego
(92111-1551)
PHONE..........................858 571-0283
Gregg Hudson, *Office Mgr*
Kelsy Bergeson, *Consultant*
EMP: 68
SALES (corp-wide): 9.9B **Publicly Held**
SIC: 1743 Tile installation, ceramic
HQ: Dal-Tile Corporation
　　7834 C F Hawn Fwy
　　Dallas TX 75217
　　214 398-1411

(P-2890)
DAL-TILE CORPORATION
2303 Merced St, San Leandro
(94577-4208)
PHONE..........................510 357-6197
Kevin Murphy, *Principal*
EMP: 68
SALES (corp-wide): 9.9B **Publicly Held**
SIC: 1743 Tile installation, ceramic
HQ: Dal-Tile Corporation
　　7834 C F Hawn Fwy
　　Dallas TX 75217
　　214 398-1411

(P-2891)
DAL-TILE CORPORATION
3625 Jurupa St, Ontario (91761-2905)
PHONE..........................909 390-7000
Liz Haendiges, *President*
EMP: 68
SALES (corp-wide): 9.9B **Publicly Held**
WEB: www.mohawk.com
SIC: 1743 Tile installation, ceramic

HQ: Dal-Tile Corporation
　　7834 C F Hawn Fwy
　　Dallas TX 75217
　　214 398-1411

(P-2892)
DELLA MAGGIORE TILE INC
87 N 30th St, San Jose (95116-1124)
PHONE..........................408 286-3991
Nick D Maggiore, *President*
Julie D Maggiore, *Admin Sec*
Rich D Maggiore, *Manager*
▲ **EMP:** 80
SQ FT: 20,000
SALES (est): 7.3MM **Privately Held**
WEB: www.slabshop.com
SIC: 1743 Tile installation, ceramic

(P-2893)
DENNETT TILE & STONE INC
4536 Bennett View Dr, Santa Rosa
(95404-6204)
PHONE..........................707 541-3700
Rick Dennett, *President*
Bambi Dennett, *Admin Sec*
EMP: 50
SQ FT: 5,500
SALES (est): 6.2MM **Privately Held**
WEB: www.dennett-tile.com
SIC: 1743 Tile installation, ceramic

(P-2894)
ELEGANZA TILES INC (PA)
3125 E Coronado St, Anaheim
(92806-1915)
PHONE..........................714 224-1700
Mike Darmawan, *CEO*
Vonny Purnama, *Vice Pres*
Kevin Kuhner, *Branch Mgr*
Mark Nielsen, *Branch Mgr*
Robert Cordero, *Info Tech Mgr*
◆ **EMP:** 70
SQ FT: 145
SALES (est): 22.8MM **Privately Held**
WEB: www.eleganzatiles.com
SIC: 1743 Tile installation, ceramic

(P-2895)
EMSER TILE LLC
5300 Shea Center Dr, Ontario
(91761-7883)
PHONE..........................909 974-1600
Gabriel Castro, *Branch Mgr*
Scott Charlesworth, *Manager*
EMP: 60
SALES (corp-wide): 285.4MM **Privately
Held**
SIC: 1743 Tile installation, ceramic
PA: Emser Tile, Llc
　　8431 Santa Monica Blvd
　　Los Angeles CA 90069
　　323 650-2000

(P-2896)
**FISCHER TILE AND MARBLE
INC**
1800 23rd St, Sacramento (95816-7112)
PHONE..........................916 452-1426
Jay H Fischer, *President*
Larry Olson, *Info Tech Dir*
Matthew Beauchamp, *Opers Mgr*
Marty Lim, *Assistant*
▲ **EMP:** 150 EST: 1906
SQ FT: 22,000
SALES (est): 19.1MM **Privately Held**
WEB: www.fischertile.com
SIC: 1743 Tile installation, ceramic; marble
installation, interior

(P-2897)
GINO RINALDI INC
Also Called: Rinaldi Tile & Marble
51 Fremont St, Royal Oaks (95076-5213)
PHONE..........................831 761-0195
Gino Rinaldi, *President*
Yvonne Rinaldi, *Corp Secy*
Rogelio Barranco, *Controller*
Paul Rosewall, *Opers Mgr*
Lee Vega, *Manager*
▲ **EMP:** 80
SQ FT: 10,000
SALES (est): 10.7MM **Privately Held**
WEB: www.rinalditileandmarble.com
SIC: 1743 Tile installation, ceramic

(P-2898)
KDI ELEMENTS
79431 Country Club Dr, Bermuda Dunes
(92203-1200)
P.O. Box 14150, Palm Desert (92255-
4150)
PHONE..........................760 345-9933
Paul Klein, *CEO*
Lauri Nichols, *Senior VP*
EMP: 250
SALES (est): 25.7MM **Privately Held**
WEB: www.kdistoneworks.com
SIC: 1743 5999 1741 Tile installation, ce-
ramic; monuments & tombstones; ma-
sonry & other stonework

(P-2899)
KELLY MOSES FLOORS
27430 Bostik Ct Ste 101, Temecula
(92590-5511)
PHONE..........................951 296-5147
Moses Kelly, *Principal*
EMP: 50
SALES (est): 1.7MM **Privately Held**
SIC: 1743 Tile installation, ceramic

(P-2900)
LEGACY TILE AND STONE INC
26825 Jefferson Ave Ste D, Murrieta
(92562-8964)
PHONE..........................951 296-1096
Robert Blackmore Jr, *President*
EMP: 50 EST: 2014
SALES (est): 3.7MM **Privately Held**
SIC: 1743 Tile installation, ceramic

(P-2901)
MARBLEWEST INC
Also Called: Marbleworks
7421 Vincent Cir, Huntington Beach
(92648-1246)
PHONE..........................714 847-6472
Gordon Bair, *President*
Suzanne Bair, *Vice Pres*
▲ **EMP:** 50
SQ FT: 6,800
SALES (est): 3.5MM **Privately Held**
WEB: www.marbleworks.org
SIC: 1743 Marble installation, interior

(P-2902)
MATRIX SURFACES INC
5449 E La Palma Ave, Anaheim
(92807-2022)
PHONE..........................714 696-5449
Jerry Eugene Jones, *CEO*
Laura J Jones, *Vice Pres*
▲ **EMP:** 60
SQ FT: 5,000
SALES (est): 8.8MM **Privately Held**
WEB: www.matrixtile.com
SIC: 1743 Tile installation, ceramic

(P-2903)
MTHURON INC
Also Called: Elite Tile
1903 Rutan Dr, Livermore (94551-7646)
PHONE..........................925 932-4101
Dennis Hourany, *President*
EMP: 115 EST: 1976
SQ FT: 7,474
SALES (est): 7.8MM **Privately Held**
WEB: www.elitetileusa.com
SIC: 1743 Marble installation, interior; tile
installation, ceramic

(P-2904)
PAUL WILLIAMS TILE CO INC
77570 Springfield Ln K, Palm Desert
(92211-0473)
PHONE..........................760 772-7440
Randy Coulter, *President*
▲ **EMP:** 60
SQ FT: 10,000
SALES (est): 4.5MM **Privately Held**
WEB: www.paulwilliamstile.com
SIC: 1743 Tile installation, ceramic

(P-2905)
PENNACCHIO TILE INC
655 Carlson Ct, Rohnert Park
(94928-2038)
PHONE..........................707 586-8858
Leo Pennacchio, *President*
Leo Pennacchio, *President*
Wendy Pennacchio, *Vice Pres*

▲ = Import ▼=Export
◆ =Import/Export

EMP: 57
SQ FT: 4,000
SALES (est): 6.6MM **Privately Held**
WEB: www.pennacchiotile.com
SIC: **1743** Tile installation, ceramic

(P-2906)
PREMIER TILE & MARBLE
15000 S Main St, Gardena (90248-1945)
PHONE..................................310 516-1712
Greg Games, *President*
Lilian Games, *Admin Sec*
EMP: 55
SALES: 15MM **Privately Held**
SIC: **1743** 5032 Tile installation, ceramic;
ceramic wall & floor tile

(P-2907)
S C TILE COMPANY INC
Also Called: S C Tile and Surfaces
606 S Marshall Ave, El Cajon (92020-4215)
PHONE..................................619 669-1575
Scott Cowles, *President*
Scott H Cowles, *President*
▲ EMP: 50
SALES (est): 1.6MM **Privately Held**
SIC: **1743** Tile installation, ceramic

(P-2908)
SAMPLE TILE AND STONE INC
1410 Richardson St, San Bernardino
(92408-2962)
PHONE..................................951 776-8562
Curtis Sample, *CEO*
Bob Glaser, *Manager*
EMP: 65
SQ FT: 13,500
SALES (est): 458.8K **Privately Held**
SIC: **1743** 2493 3281 5032 Terrazzo, tile,
marble, mosaic work; marbleboard (stone
face hard board); cut stone & stone prod-
ucts; limestone; stone masonry; limestone
& marble dimension stone

(P-2909)
SHERMN-LEHR CSTM TILE WRKS INC
5691 Power Inn Rd Ste A, Sacramento
(95824-2361)
PHONE..................................916 386-0417
James P Loehr, *President*
Jane Sherman, *Treasurer*
Eber T Sherman, *Vice Pres*
Joyce Loehr, *Admin Sec*
EMP: 100
SQ FT: 3,400
SALES (est): 11.6MM **Privately Held**
SIC: **1743** Tile installation, ceramic

(P-2910)
SOSA GRANITE & MARBLE INC
Also Called: Sosa Tile Co
7701 Marathon Dr, Livermore
(94550-9550)
PHONE..................................925 373-7675
Mario Sosa, *President*
Tracy Ruiz, *Accountant*
▲ EMP: 50
SQ FT: 16,000
SALES (est): 5.8MM **Privately Held**
WEB: www.sosagranite.com
SIC: **1743** Tile installation, ceramic

(P-2911)
TILE WEST INC (PA)
11 Hamilton Dr, Novato (94949-5602)
P.O. Box 5789 (94948-5789)
PHONE..................................415 382-7550
Carl E Jacobson, *President*
Julia M Ratto, *Corp Secy*
Cliff E Jacobson, *Vice Pres*
Wayne Jackson, *Project Mgr*
▲ EMP: 82
SQ FT: 5,000
SALES (est): 9.3MM **Privately Held**
WEB: www.tilewestinc.com
SIC: **1743** Tile installation, ceramic

(P-2912)
TRM CORPORATION (PA)
Also Called: Superior Tile Co
2378 Polvorosa Ave, San Leandro
(94577-2218)
P.O. Box 2106, Oakland (94621-0006)
PHONE..................................510 895-2700
Tommy Conner, *CEO*

Robert Herman, *President*
Jerry T Sue, *CFO*
Bob Herman, *Vice Pres*
Patty Moore, *Vice Pres*
▲ EMP: 65 EST: 1975
SQ FT: 12,000
SALES (est): 37.2MM **Privately Held**
SIC: **1743** Tile installation, ceramic; marble
installation, interior

(P-2913)
U S PERMA INC
Also Called: California Tile Installers
1696 Rogers Ave, San Jose (95112-1105)
PHONE..................................408 436-0600
Jack O'Brien, *President*
Randall Sundberg, *Vice Pres*
Donald K O'Brien, *Admin Sec*
Summer Martinez, *Administration*
▲ EMP: 50
SQ FT: 9,000
SALES (est): 7MM **Privately Held**
WEB: www.usperma.com
SIC: **1743** Tile installation, ceramic

1751 Carpentry Work

(P-2914)
ALL SEASONS FRAMING CORP
644 N Eckhoff St, Orange (92868-1004)
PHONE..................................714 634-2324
Dave Karos, *President*
Gerado Rodarte, *Admin Sec*
EMP: 50
SQ FT: 3,600
SALES: 4MM **Privately Held**
WEB: www.allseasonspressed.com
SIC: **1751** Framing contractor

(P-2915)
ALLEN CONSTRUCTION INC
31356 Via Colinas Ste 107, Westlake Vil-
lage (91362-6799)
PHONE..................................818 879-5334
Darrel Allen, *President*
Karen Scheneman, *Vice Pres*
EMP: 50
SALES (est): 3.5MM **Privately Held**
SIC: **1751** Framing contractor

(P-2916)
ALLIED FRAMERS INC
4990 Allison Pkwy, Vacaville (95688-9346)
PHONE..................................707 452-7050
Jakki Kutz, *President*
Dave Burrell, *Vice Pres*
Mark Johnson, *Vice Pres*
Mike Thomason, *Vice Pres*
Dawn Richardson, *Administration*
EMP: 130
SQ FT: 6,000
SALES (est): 12.5MM **Privately Held**
WEB: www.alliedframers.com
SIC: **1751** Framing contractor

(P-2917)
BAY AREA CNSTR FRAMERS INC
1150 W Center St Ste 105, Manteca
(95337-4313)
PHONE..................................925 454-8514
Fax: 925 454-0507
EMP: 175
SQ FT: 6,700
SALES (est): 14MM **Privately Held**
SIC: **1751** 1521

(P-2918)
BOB DILLON CONSTRUCTION INC
856 Calle Margarita, Thousand Oaks
(91360-4852)
PHONE..................................805 495-2607
Bob Dillon, *President*
Tracy Dillon, *Admin Sec*
EMP: 150
SALES (est): 6.7MM **Privately Held**
SIC: **1751** Framing contractor

(P-2919)
CLOSET WORLD INC
14438 Don Julian Rd, City of Industry
(91746-3101)
PHONE..................................626 855-0846

EMP: 251 **Privately Held**
WEB: www.closetworld.net
SIC: **1751** 5211 Cabinet building & instal-
lation; closets, interiors & accessories
PA: Closet World, Inc.
3860 Capitol Ave
City Of Industry CA 90601

(P-2920)
COMMERCIAL DOOR COMPANY INC
1374 E 9th St, Pomona (91766-3831)
PHONE..................................714 529-2179
David O Holmes, *CEO*
Carol Holmes, *Treasurer*
Sandra Garcia, *Admin Asst*
Karla Norman, *Administration*
Steven Holmes, *Manager*
EMP: 60
SQ FT: 10,000
SALES (est): 9.9MM **Privately Held**
WEB: www.commercialdoorcompany.com
SIC: **1751** Garage door, installation or
erection

(P-2921)
COOK CABINETS INC
6428 Capitol Ave, Diamond Springs
(95619-9521)
PHONE..................................530 621-0851
Richard Gularte, *President*
Steve Gularte, *Vice Pres*
EMP: 65
SQ FT: 35,000
SALES (est): 3.5MM **Privately Held**
SIC: **1751** 5712 5031 2434 Cabinet
building & installation; cabinet work, cus-
tom; lumber, plywood & millwork; wood
kitchen cabinets

(P-2922)
CRAFTSMAN LATH AND PLASTER INC
8325 63rd St, Riverside (92509-6004)
PHONE..................................951 685-9922
Kevin Tunstill, *President*
EMP: 350 EST: 2015
SALES (est): 11.1MM **Privately Held**
SIC: **1751** Carpentry work

(P-2923)
CWP CABINETS INC
10007 Yucca Rd, Adelanto (92301-2242)
PHONE..................................760 246-4530
Michael Rodriguez, *CEO*
EMP: 115 EST: 2011
SALES (est): 6.2MM **Privately Held**
SIC: **1751** 2434 2541 5712 Cabinet
building & installation; wood kitchen cabi-
nets; wood partitions & fixtures; cabinet
work, custom

(P-2924)
D F RIOS CONSTRUCTION INC
45847 Warm Springs Blvd, Fremont
(94539-6779)
PHONE..................................510 226-7467
David F Rios, *President*
EMP: 75
SQ FT: 4,000
SALES (est): 4.1MM **Privately Held**
SIC: **1751** Framing contractor

(P-2925)
DAVIS BROTHERS FRAMING INC
8780 Prestige Ct, Rancho Cucamonga
(91730-5138)
PHONE..................................909 944-4899
Randy Davis, *President*
George E Davis, *CEO*
EMP: 200
SALES (est): 10.1MM **Privately Held**
SIC: **1751** Framing contractor

(P-2926)
DAVIS FRAMING INC
8103 Commercial St, La Mesa
(91942-2927)
PHONE..................................619 463-2394
Steve Davis, *President*
EMP: 50
SQ FT: 1,200

SALES (est): 4.1MM **Privately Held**
SIC: **1751** Framing contractor

(P-2927)
DAY STAR FIXTURES
1802 Riverford Rd, Tustin (92780-3950)
P.O. Box 238 (92781-0238)
PHONE..................................714 838-4613
Dan Prigmore, *Owner*
EMP: 50
SALES (est): 1.9MM **Privately Held**
SIC: **1751** Cabinet building & installation

(P-2928)
DON KINZEL CONSTRUCTION INC
4300 Easton Dr Ste 2, Bakersfield
(93309-9420)
PHONE..................................661 322-9105
Donald Kinzel, *President*
▲ EMP: 93
SQ FT: 2,700
SALES (est): 4.6MM **Privately Held**
SIC: **1751** 1542 Carpentry work; commer-
cial & office building contractors

(P-2929)
ELLISON FRAMING INC
Also Called: Ellison Construction-Framing
160 Guthrie Ln Ste 13, Brentwood
(94513-4060)
P.O. Box 580 (94513-0580)
PHONE..................................925 516-9269
Matthew M Ellison, *President*
Ron Kapphahn, *Treasurer*
EMP: 125
SQ FT: 15,000
SALES (est): 9.1MM **Privately Held**
WEB: www.ellisonframing.com
SIC: **1751** Framing contractor

(P-2930)
EMPIRE LEASING INC
Also Called: Alliance Construction
2045 Placentia Ave Ste A, Costa Mesa
(92627-6239)
PHONE..................................949 646-7400
Fax: 949 645-3461
EMP: 75
SALES (est): 3.1MM **Privately Held**
WEB: www.empireleasinginc.com
SIC: **1751** 1795

(P-2931)
EPPINK OF CALIFORNIA INC
11900 Center St, South Gate (90280-7834)
PHONE..................................562 633-1275
Erik Eppink, *CEO*
Michael Hunter, *Vice Pres*
▲ EMP: 50
SQ FT: 20,000
SALES (est): 6.2MM **Privately Held**
WEB: www.davisandwells.com
SIC: **1751** Carpentry work

(P-2932)
ERICKSON CONSTRUCTION LP
8350 Industrial Ave, Roseville
(95678-6239)
PHONE..................................916 774-1100
Randall Folts, *President*
Anthony D'Attomo, *CFO*
EMP: 200
SALES (est): 7.9MM
SALES (corp-wide): 8.3B **Publicly Held**
SIC: **1751** Carpentry work
PA: Masco Corporation
17450 College Pkwy
Livonia MI 48152
313 274-7400

(P-2933)
FENNEL INC
Also Called: Thompson Cnstr Sup Door
Frame
1169 Sherborn St, Corona (92879-5005)
P.O. Box 78300 (92877-0143)
PHONE..................................951 284-2020
Kenneth R Thompson, *CEO*
Robert Leos, *Vice Pres*
EMP: 65
SALES (est): 1.3MM **Privately Held**
SIC: **1751** 5251 5999 Garage door, instal-
lation or erection; door locks & lock sets;
art, picture frames & decorations

(P-2934)
FORCE FRAMING INC
21520 Yorba Linda Blvd G, Yorba Linda
(92887-3764)
PHONE..............................714 970-3888
Donald Briscoe, *President*
Christina Matlack, *Controller*
EMP: 50
SQ FT: 2,400
SALES (est): 1.2MM **Privately Held**
SIC: 1751 Framing contractor

(P-2935)
GATEHOUSE MSI LLC
Also Called: McMurray Stern
15511 Carmenita Rd, Santa Fe Springs
(90670-5609)
PHONE..............................562 623-3000
Kenneth De Angelis, *Principal*
Donise Jackson, *CFO*
Collin Straus, *Vice Pres*
Timothy Hill, *Principal*
Hank Miller, *Principal*
EMP: 50
SQ FT: 30,000
SALES: 15MM **Privately Held**
SIC: 1751 1771 Cabinet & finish carpen-
try; stucco, gunite & grouting contractors

(P-2936)
GRANT CONSTRUCTION INC
7702 Meany Ave Ste 103, Bakersfield
(93308-5199)
PHONE..............................661 588-4586
Grant Fraysier, *President*
EMP: 230 EST: 1994
SQ FT: 1,000
SALES: 31MM **Privately Held**
WEB: www.gciframing.com
SIC: 1751 1771 Framing contractor; con-
crete work

(P-2937)
HAKES SASH & DOOR INC
31945 Corydon St, Lake Elsinore
(92530-8524)
PHONE..............................951 674-2414
Allen J Hakes, *President*
Bill Wunderlich, *Department Mgr*
Christopher Lockwood, *Accountant*
Charles Pumphrey, *Accountant*
Joe Torregano, *Production*
EMP: 190
SQ FT: 2,000
SALES (est): 25.5MM **Privately Held**
SIC: 1751 3442 5211 Window & door in-
stallation & erection; window & door
frames; sash, wood or metal

(P-2938)
HARDWOOD CREATIONS (PA)
Also Called: H C I
1560 N Maple St, Corona (92880-1783)
PHONE..............................714 674-0527
Thomas Steele, *President*
Melvin Grimes, *CEO*
EMP: 80
SQ FT: 8,000
SALES (est): 9.6MM **Privately Held**
WEB: www.hardwoodcreations.com
SIC: 1751 Cabinet building & installation

(P-2939)
HERITAGE INTERESTS LLC (PA)
4300 Jetway Ct, North Highlands
(95660-5702)
P.O. Box 214609, Sacramento (95821-
0609)
PHONE..............................916 481-5030
Edward Zuckerman, *President*
Dennis Gardemeyer, *CFO*
Charlie Gardemeyer, *Vice Pres*
EMP: 90
SQ FT: 80,000
SALES (est): 89.5MM **Privately Held**
SIC: 1751 5031 2431 Cabinet & finish
carpentry; finish & trim carpentry; lumber,
plywood & millwork; windows & window
parts & trim, wood; louver windows, glass,
wood frame

(P-2940)
**HEWITT AND CANFIELD CNSTR
INC**
495 E Easy St Ste A, Simi Valley
(93065-1845)
PHONE..............................805 522-4426
Ron Hewitt, *President*
Liz Weigand, *Office Mgr*
Dale Canfield, *Admin Sec*
EMP: 80
SQ FT: 10,000
SALES: 13MM **Privately Held**
WEB: www.rondaleconstruction.com
SIC: 1751 Framing contractor

(P-2941)
HOME ORGANIZERS INC
Also Called: Closet World, The
3860 Capitol Ave, City of Industry
(90601-1733)
PHONE..............................562 699-9945
Frank Melkonian, *President*
EMP: 660
SALES (est): 32MM **Privately Held**
WEB: www.closetworld.com
SIC: 1751 2541 Cabinet building & instal-
lation; cabinets, lockers & shelving

(P-2942)
JAG FRAMING INC
16741 Los Alimos St, Granada Hills
(91344-5052)
PHONE..............................818 822-7110
Jose Antoio Guerra, *President*
EMP: 50
SALES: 3.9MM **Privately Held**
SIC: 1751 Framing contractor

(P-2943)
JB FINISH INC
82750 Atlantic St, Indio (92203-9626)
P.O. Box 3093 (92202-3093)
PHONE..............................760 342-6300
John Broyles, *President*
EMP: 56
SQ FT: 12,500
SALES (est): 3.8MM **Privately Held**
WEB: www.johnbroyles.com
SIC: 1751 5211 Finish & trim carpentry;
lumber & other building materials

(P-2944)
JENCOR DOOR AND TRIM INC
26845 Oak Ave Ste 12, Canyon Country
(91351-6645)
PHONE..............................661 251-8161
Jeno Horvath, *President*
EMP: 50
SQ FT: 10,000
SALES (est): 2.8MM **Privately Held**
SIC: 1751 Finish & trim carpentry

(P-2945)
**JONCE THOMAS
CONSTRUCTION CO**
3390 Seldon Ct, Fremont (94539-5625)
P.O. Box 1856 (94538-0034)
PHONE..............................510 657-7171
Donna Jean Thomas, *President*
Jonce Thomas, *Vice Pres*
EMP: 50
SQ FT: 10,000
SALES (est): 3.5MM **Privately Held**
SIC: 1751 Framing contractor

(P-2946)
**KRC BUILDERS
INCORPORATED**
6141 W 4th St, Rio Linda (95673-4011)
PHONE..............................916 417-1200
Gene M Kindy, *CEO*
Jack E Ross, *Admin Sec*
EMP: 80
SALES (est): 3.6MM **Privately Held**
SIC: 1751 1521 Framing contractor; new
construction, single-family houses

(P-2947)
LAURENCE-HOVENIER INC
179 N Maple St, Corona (92880-1760)
PHONE..............................951 736-2990
Ronald Laurence, *President*
Fred Hovenier, *Vice Pres*
Karen Diercksmeier, *Administration*
EMP: 190

SQ FT: 6,000
SALES (est): 23.9MM **Privately Held**
WEB: www.framingcontractor.com
SIC: 1751 Framing contractor

(P-2948)
**LEXINGTON SCENERY & PROPS
INC**
12800 Rangoon St, Arleta (91331-4321)
PHONE..............................818 768-5768
EMP: 120
SALES (est): 4.9MM **Privately Held**
SIC: 1751 2542 3993

(P-2949)
**MCCARTHY FRAMING
CONSTRUCTION**
Also Called: McCarthy Construction
15133 Grevillea Ave, Lawndale
(90260-2017)
PHONE..............................310 219-3038
Patrick McCarthy, *Owner*
▲ EMP: 100
SALES (est): 7.2MM **Privately Held**
SIC: 1751 Framing contractor

(P-2950)
NORCAL INC
Also Called: Seeley Brothers
1400 Moonstone, Brea (92821-2801)
PHONE..............................714 224-3949
Michael Seeley, *Partner*
Joe Calvillo, *Partner*
Phil Norys, *Partner*
EMP: 175
SQ FT: 62,000
SALES (est): 25.2MM **Privately Held**
SIC: 1751 Finish & trim carpentry

(P-2951)
NORCAL INC
Also Called: Seeley Brothers
1400 Moonstone, Brea (92821-2801)
PHONE..............................714 224-3949
EMP: 105
SQ FT: 60,000
SALES (est): 4.5MM **Privately Held**
WEB: www.seeleybros.com
SIC: 1751

(P-2952)
OLIVIERI ENTERPRISES LP
Also Called: Olympic Construction
210 Estates Dr Ste 200, Roseville
(95678-2300)
P.O. Box 2490, Granite Bay (95746-2490)
PHONE..............................916 791-7857
John Olivieri, *Partner*
Teresa Olivieri, *Partner*
EMP: 200
SQ FT: 2,300
SALES (est): 6.1MM **Privately Held**
SIC: 1751 Framing contractor

(P-2953)
**ON TRAC OVERHEAD DOOR CO
INC**
1430 Richardson St, San Bernardino
(92408-2962)
PHONE..............................909 799-8555
Charles L Colton, *CEO*
Chuck Colton, *President*
Terri Colton, *Vice Pres*
EMP: 50
SQ FT: 16,600
SALES (est): 5MM **Privately Held**
WEB: www.ontracdoor.com
SIC: 1751 Garage door, installation or
erection

(P-2954)
**OVERHEAD DOOR
CORPORATION**
1617 N Orangethorpe Way, Anaheim
(92801-1228)
PHONE..............................714 680-0600
Dave Fowler, *Vice Pres*
EMP: 93 **Privately Held**
SIC: 1751 Garage door, installation or
erection
HQ: Overhead Door Corporation
2501 S State Hwy 121 Ste
Lewisville TX 75067
469 549-7100

(P-2955)
PANORAMIC DOORS LLC
3265 Production Ave Ste A, Oceanside
(92058-1361)
PHONE..............................760 722-1300
Raffy Timonian, *Vice Pres*
EMP: 63
SALES (corp-wide): 25MM **Privately
Held**
SIC: 1751 Window & door installation &
erection
PA: Panoramic Doors, Llc
2515 Industry St
Oceanside CA 92054
760 722-1300

(P-2956)
PRE CON INDUSTRIES INC
950 Riata Ln, Nipomo (93444-9484)
P.O. Box 5728, Santa Maria (93456-5728)
PHONE..............................805 481-7305
John Amburgey, *President*
EMP: 50 **Privately Held**
SIC: 1751 1742 1542 Carpentry work;
drywall; commercial & office building con-
tractors
PA: Pre Con Industries, Inc.
725 Oak St
Santa Maria CA 93454

(P-2957)
PRECISION FRAMING INC
1504 Eureka Rd Ste 160, Roseville
(95661-3084)
PHONE..............................916 791-7464
William Peterson, *President*
EMP: 260
SQ FT: 1,100
SALES (est): 7.4MM **Privately Held**
SIC: 1751 Framing contractor

(P-2958)
PRIME TECH CABINETS INC
2215 S Standard Ave, Santa Ana
(92707-3036)
PHONE..............................949 757-4900
Hassan Farjamrad, *President*
David Bondy, *Purch Agent*
Nina Vazin, *Sales Staff*
EMP: 110
SALES (est): 10.4MM **Privately Held**
WEB: www.ptcabinets.com
SIC: 1751 Cabinet building & installation

(P-2959)
PRODUCTION FRAMING INC
2000 Opportunity Dr # 140, Roseville
(95678-3020)
PHONE..............................916 978-2843
Doyle Headrick, *President*
EMP: 99
SALES (est): 3.1MM **Privately Held**
SIC: 1751 Framing contractor

(P-2960)
**PRODUCTION FRAMING
SYSTEMS INC (PA)**
2000 Opportunity Dr # 140, Roseville
(95678-3020)
PHONE..............................916 978-2888
Steve J Benjamin, *President*
Kerry Palmer, *Vice Pres*
Christie Robinson, *Controller*
EMP: 150
SALES (est): 11.9MM **Privately Held**
WEB: www.productionframing.com
SIC: 1751 Framing contractor

(P-2961)
**PROFESSIONAL CABINET
SOLUTIONS**
Also Called: RSI Professional Cab Solutions
11350 Riverside Dr Frnt, Jurupa Valley
(91752-3703)
PHONE..............................909 614-2900
S Cary Dunston, *CEO*
Rosalind J Manning, *Executive Asst*
Audra Greenberg, *Credit Mgr*
Jose Delgado, *Production*
Ed Marquez, *Manager*
EMP: 250
SALES (est): 21.8MM
SALES (corp-wide): 1.6B **Publicly Held**
SIC: 1751 Cabinet & finish carpentry

HQ: Rsi Home Products, Inc.
400 E Orangethorpe Ave
Anaheim CA 92801
714 449-2200

(P-2962)
PROTEGE BUILDERS INC
4306 Pinell St, Sacramento (95838-2928)
PHONE....................916 825-8478
Leah Rivera, *President*
Shelly Hinkle, *Admin Sec*
EMP: 50
SALES (est): 2.5MM **Privately Held**
WEB: www.protegebuilders.com
SIC: 1751 Framing contractor

(P-2963)
**R & S ERECTION
INCORPORATED (PA)**
2057 W Avenue 140th, San Leandro
(94577-5623)
PHONE....................510 483-3710
Ray Ellias Zarodney, *CEO*
Dennis Hansen, *Project Mgr*
EMP: 62
SALES (est): 6MM **Privately Held**
SIC: 1751 Garage door, installation or
erection; window & door installation &
erection

(P-2964)
R D S UNLIMITED INC
14372 Olde Highway 80 E, El Cajon
(92021-2865)
P.O. Box 21066 (92021-0982)
PHONE....................619 443-0221
Ronnie Swaim, *President*
EMP: 50
SQ FT: 3,000
SALES: 3.5MM **Privately Held**
SIC: 1751 Framing contractor

(P-2965)
R T FRAMING CORPORATION
299 W Hillcrest Dr # 212, Thousand Oaks
(91360-7838)
PHONE....................805 496-3985
Lorene Fuess, *President*
Raymond Fuess, *Vice Pres*
EMP: 100
SQ FT: 1,000
SALES (est): 5.7MM **Privately Held**
SIC: 1751 Framing contractor

(P-2966)
RANCH HOUSE DOORS INC
Also Called: R H D
1527 Pomona Rd, Corona (92880-6959)
PHONE....................951 278-2884
Michael James Neal, *CEO*
Sandra Neal, *President*
Cristian Neal, *CFO*
Roy Dickinson, *Business Mgr*
Lise Diego, *Sales Staff*
EMP: 70
SQ FT: 33,000
SALES (est): 7MM **Privately Held**
WEB: www.ranchhousedoors.com
SIC: 1751 Garage door, installation or
erection

(P-2967)
RH FRAMING INC
815 Quail Ridge Ln, Salinas (93908-8966)
PHONE....................831 759-8860
Ryan Harrod, *President*
EMP: 150
SALES (est): 5.9MM **Privately Held**
SIC: 1751 Framing contractor

(P-2968)
RICHARD HANCOCK INC
Also Called: Rhi
1029 3rd St, Santa Rosa (95404-6635)
PHONE....................707 528-4900
Bruce Lamar, *President*
EMP: 50
SQ FT: 1,600
SALES: 10MM **Privately Held**
SIC: 1751 Carpentry work

(P-2969)
RJP FRAMING INC
1139 Sibley St Ste 100, Folsom
(95630-3572)
P.O. Box 5057, El Dorado Hills (95762-
0001)
PHONE....................916 941-3934
Laurie Payne, *President*
Robert Payne, *Vice Pres*
Mary Jackson, *Office Mgr*
EMP: 180
SALES (est): 13.6MM **Privately Held**
SIC: 1751 Framing contractor

(P-2970)
ROCKY COAST BUILDERS INC
135 Market Pl, Escondido (92029-1353)
PHONE....................760 489-7770
Douglas J Ladderbush, *CEO*
Cris Madsen, *Treasurer*
Amanda Kerins, *Admin Sec*
Heather Rice, *Administration*
EMP: 60
SQ FT: 6,200
SALES: 8.7MM **Privately Held**
SIC: 1751 Framing contractor

(P-2971)
ROY E WHITEHEAD INC
Also Called: Rew Inc
2245 Via Cerro, Riverside (92509-2412)
PHONE....................951 682-1490
David Whitehead, *CEO*
Chris Bagley, *President*
Dennis Whitehead, *Treasurer*
Dan Gilley, *Vice Pres*
Byron Mitchell, *Vice Pres*
EMP: 75
SQ FT: 36,000
SALES (est): 11.1MM **Privately Held**
WEB: www.royewhitehead.com
SIC: 1751 Cabinet building & installation

(P-2972)
S I J INC
26035 Jefferson Ave, Murrieta
(92562-6983)
PHONE....................951 304-9444
Briana Sather-Layfield, *President*
Joseph Sather, *Treasurer*
Patricia Sather, *Admin Sec*
EMP: 50
SALES: 5.5MM **Privately Held**
WEB: www.sicorp.us
SIC: 1751 Carpentry work

(P-2973)
S W CONSTRUCTION INC
Also Called: Wilson Stephen Construction Co
1145 E Stanford Ct, Anaheim (92805-6822)
PHONE....................714 978-7871
Stephen L Wilson, *President*
EMP: 120
SQ FT: 7,500
SALES (est): 8.7MM **Privately Held**
SIC: 1751 Framing contractor

(P-2974)
**SAN-MAR CONSTRUCTION CO
INC**
4875 E La Palma Ave # 601, Anaheim
(92807-1955)
PHONE....................714 693-5400
Sandra Drew, *CEO*
Darren Drew, *Project Mgr*
EMP: 200
SQ FT: 3,000
SALES (est): 20.8MM **Privately Held**
SIC: 1751 Carpentry work

(P-2975)
**SANTA CLARITA VALLEY BLDRS
INC**
Also Called: Main Frame Construction
24307 Magic Mountain Pkwy # 122, Santa
Clarita (91355-3402)
PHONE....................661 295-6722
Mike Spigno, *President*
Cheryl A Spigno, *Shareholder*
Frank Oviedo, *Manager*
EMP: 225
SALES (est): 7.9MM **Privately Held**
SIC: 1751 7389 Framing contractor; inte-
rior design services

(P-2976)
SHOOK & WALLER CNSTR INC
7677 Bell Rd Ste 101, Windsor
(95492-7432)
PHONE....................707 578-3933
Eddie Waller, *President*
Shawn Dolan, *CFO*
Steven Shook, *Corp Secy*
EMP: 64
SQ FT: 8,000
SALES (est): 26.5MM **Privately Held**
WEB: www.shookandwaller.com
SIC: 1751 1521 1542 Framing contractor;
new construction, single-family houses;
nonresidential construction

(P-2977)
SI INC
Also Called: Sather Installation
26035 Jefferson Ave, Murrieta
(92562-6983)
PHONE....................951 304-9444
EMP: 50
SQ FT: 8,000
SALES (est): 4.7MM **Privately Held**
WEB: www.sicorp.us
SIC: 1751

(P-2978)
SIERRA LUMBER CO
Also Called: Sierra Lumber & Decking
1711 Senter Rd, San Jose (95112-2598)
PHONE....................408 286-7071
Roger Burch, *President*
James Moblad, *Vice Pres*
EMP: 125
SQ FT: 22,000
SALES: 7MM
SALES (corp-wide): 161.8MM **Privately
Held**
WEB: www.sierrafence.com
SIC: 1751 5211 Carpentry work; lumber
products
PA: Pacific States Industries, Incorporated
10 Madrone Ave
Morgan Hill CA 95037
408 779-7354

(P-2979)
**SIERRA WEST CONSTRUCTION
INC**
24744 Connie Ct, Auburn (95602-8525)
PHONE....................530 268-7614
Richard T Ahrens, *President*
Melinda Ahrens, *Corp Secy*
EMP: 50
SALES (est): 4.5MM **Privately Held**
SIC: 1751 Framing contractor

(P-2980)
SILVER STRAND
8945 Fullbright Ave, Chatsworth
(91311-6124)
PHONE....................818 701-9707
David Meador, *Principal*
EMP: 50
SQ FT: 7,500
SALES (est): 5.8MM **Privately Held**
WEB: www.silverstrandinc.com
SIC: 1751 Cabinet & finish carpentry

(P-2981)
SMITH BROS INC (PA)
Also Called: Smith Bros Finished Carpentry
2301 Townsgate Rd Ste A, Westlake Village
(91361-2502)
PHONE....................805 449-2841
Dan Smith, *President*
Shirley Letizia, *Admin Asst*
Marc Dean, *Project Mgr*
EMP: 60
SQ FT: 9,000
SALES (est): 4.3MM **Privately Held**
SIC: 1751 Finish & trim carpentry

(P-2982)
**SOUTHWEST RGNAL CNCIL
CRPNTERS (PA)**
533 S Fremont Ave Fl 10, Los Angeles
(90071-1712)
PHONE....................213 385-1457
Jacky Barnett, *President*
Mike McCarron, *President*
Hal Jensen, *Vice Pres*
Jim Bernsen, *Admin Sec*

EMP: 50
SQ FT: 4,000
SALES (est): 44.1MM **Privately Held**
SIC: 1751 Carpentry work

(P-2983)
SR FREEMAN INC
2380 S Bascom Ave Ste 200, Campbell
(95008-4389)
PHONE....................408 364-2200
Shone Freeman, *President*
Josie Freeman, *Admin Sec*
Shayne Freeman, *Manager*
EMP: 60 EST: 1992
SALES: 12.3MM **Privately Held**
WEB: www.srfreemaninc.com
SIC: 1751 Framing contractor

(P-2984)
**STOCKHAM CONSTRUCTION
INC**
475 Portal St, Cotati (94931-3006)
PHONE....................707 664-0945
Boyd L Stockham, *President*
Dani Stockham, *Treasurer*
Shani Cavazos, *Controller*
EMP: 450
SQ FT: 15,301
SALES: 65.3MM **Privately Held**
WEB: www.stockhamconstruction.com
SIC: 1751 1742 Lightweight steel framing
(metal stud) installation; drywall; acousti-
cal & ceiling work

(P-2985)
**SUNDANCE CONSTRUCTION
INC**
3500 W Lake Center Dr B, Santa Ana
(92704-6900)
PHONE....................714 437-0802
Tim Boggess, *President*
Ernie Castro Sr, *CEO*
Mario Munoz, *Vice Pres*
EMP: 200
SALES (est): 6.8MM **Privately Held**
WEB: www.woodsgrouparch.com
SIC: 1751 Framing contractor

(P-2986)
TONE FRAMING INC
1821 Winterwarm Dr, Fallbrook
(92028-8255)
PHONE....................951 304-0303
Janet E Campbell, *CEO*
Neil Campbell, *Shareholder*
Aaron Parcell, *Officer*
Mike Campbell, *Vice Pres*
Barbara Weaver, *Accountant*
EMP: 50
SQ FT: 10,000
SALES (est): 6MM **Privately Held**
SIC: 1751 Framing contractor

(P-2987)
**TRUFORM CONSTRUCTION
CORP**
1041 N Shepard St, Anaheim
(92806-2817)
PHONE....................714 630-7447
Dan Ruppe, *President*
EMP: 50
SQ FT: 1,400
SALES (est): 3.5MM **Privately Held**
SIC: 1751 1742 Lightweight steel framing
(metal stud) installation; drywall

(P-2988)
TWR ENTERPRISES INC
1661 Railroad St, Corona (92880-2503)
PHONE....................951 279-2000
Thomas W Rhodes, *President*
Deborah Dieter, *Finance*
Debbie Diter, *Controller*
Amy Strommer, *Human Res Dir*
Yesenia Salazar, *Human Res Mgr*
EMP: 200
SQ FT: 20,000
SALES (est): 18.3MM **Privately Held**
SIC: 1751 Framing contractor

(P-2989)
ULTIMATE CONSTRUCTION INC
8811 Alonzo Blvd, Long Beach (90805)
P.O. Box 571117, Tarzana (91357-1117)
PHONE....................562 633-3389

Enrique Vera, *President*
Gloria Vera, *CFO*
EMP: 112
SQ FT: 10,000
SALES (est): 7MM **Privately Held**
SIC: 1751 1522 1541 1521 Carpentry
work; residential construction; industrial
buildings; new construction; new con-
struction, single-family houses

(P-2990)
WALTERS & WOLF INTERIORS (PA)
41450 Boscell Rd, Fremont (94538-3103)
PHONE....................415 243-9400
Randall Alan Wolf, *CEO*
Michael Wolf, *President*
Nick Koselj, *COO*
Jeff Belzer, *CFO*
▲ **EMP:** 80
SQ FT: 30,000
SALES (est): 13MM **Privately Held**
SIC: 1751 Carpentry work

(P-2991)
WESLAR INC
28310 Constellation Rd, Valencia
(91355-5078)
PHONE....................661 702-1362
Larry Kern, *President*
Wes Toy, *Vice Pres*
EMP: 100
SQ FT: 5,500
SALES (est): 9.1MM **Privately Held**
WEB: www.weslarinc.com
SIC: 1751 Framing contractor

(P-2992)
X-ACT FINISH & TRIM INC
248 Glider Cir, Corona (92880-2533)
PHONE....................951 582-9229
Jessie A Moreno, *President*
EMP: 60
SALES (est): 9.2MM **Privately Held**
SIC: 1751 Finish & trim carpentry

1752 Floor Laying & Other Floor Work, NEC

(P-2993)
ACE FLOOR CO INC
Also Called: Naturally Aged Flooring
5155 Goldman Ave, Moorpark
(93021-1759)
PHONE....................866 522-4500
Jack Schoen, *President*
Angela Schoen, *Vice Pres*
Hugh Hamasaki, *Purch Agent*
▲ **EMP:** 55
SQ FT: 20,000
SALES (est): 11.7MM **Privately Held**
SIC: 1752 Wood floor installation & refin-
ishing

(P-2994)
ANTHONY TREVINO
Also Called: A&S Floors
938 Adams St Ste A, Benicia (94510-2948)
PHONE....................707 747-4776
Anthony Trevino, *Owner*
Shelley Hunter, *Principal*
EMP: 52 **EST:** 1993
SALES (est): 3.8MM **Privately Held**
SIC: 1752 Carpet laying

(P-2995)
B T MANCINI CO INC (PA)
Also Called: B.T. Mancini Company
876 S Milpitas Blvd, Milpitas (95035-6311)
P.O. Box 361930 (95036-1930)
PHONE....................408 942-7900
Brooks T Mancini Jr, *President*
Jim Evans, *Vice Pres*
Greg Hartwick, *Vice Pres*
Brooks T Mancini Sr, *Vice Pres*
Tom McGovern, *Vice Pres*
▲ **EMP:** 300
SQ FT: 36,000
SALES (est): 99.2MM **Privately Held**
WEB: www.btmancini.com
SIC: 1752 1761 Wood floor installation &
refinishing; roofing; siding & sheet metal
work; siding contractor

(P-2996)
CAPITAL COMMERCIAL FLRG INC
3709 Bradview Dr Ste 100, Sacramento
(95827-9737)
PHONE....................916 569-1960
Douglas Vincent Lawson, *CEO*
Scott Fairley, *CFO*
Jenasis Fullmer, *Executive*
Diana Lawson, *Admin Sec*
Carlos Cabera, *Data Proc Exec*
EMP: 50
SQ FT: 14,000
SALES (est): 6.9MM **Privately Held**
WEB: www.ccfinc.net
SIC: 1752 Carpet laying

(P-2997)
CREATIVE DESIGN INTERIORS INC (PA)
Also Called: C D I
737 Del Paso Rd, Sacramento
(95834-1106)
PHONE....................916 641-1121
Ronald Lapp, *President*
Kathy Lapp, *Vice Pres*
EMP: 100
SQ FT: 10,000
SALES (est): 29MM **Privately Held**
SIC: 1752 Ceramic floor tile installation

(P-2998)
DAVENPORT DEVELOPMENT CORP
Also Called: Classic Hardwood Floors
8360 Clairemont Mesa Blvd # 111, San
Diego (92111-1321)
PHONE....................858 300-3333
Marc Davenport, *President*
Lisa Davenport, *Admin Sec*
▲ **EMP:** 50
SALES (est): 5.4MM **Privately Held**
SIC: 1752 Wood floor installation & refin-
ishing

(P-2999)
DFS FLOORING INC (PA)
15651 Saticoy St, Van Nuys (91406-3234)
PHONE....................818 374-5200
Richard Friedman, *CEO*
Greg Keyes, *Vice Pres*
Scott Sidlow, *Vice Pres*
Bel Bitok, *Administration*
Marc Mooshagian, *Administration*
EMP: 65
SQ FT: 19,865
SALES (est): 30.3MM **Privately Held**
WEB: www.dfsflooring.com
SIC: 1752 Wood floor installation & refin-
ishing

(P-3000)
DT FLOORMASTERS INC
Also Called: Floormasters, The
31164 Huntwood Ave, Hayward
(94544-7817)
PHONE....................510 476-1000
Teresa Lau, *CEO*
Brian Higgins, *Vice Pres*
Garrett Gollnick, *Executive*
Nidia Ramirez, *Administration*
Guy Vernikovsky, *Opers Staff*
EMP: 70
SQ FT: 1,000
SALES (est): 14.6MM **Privately Held**
SIC: 1752 Wood floor installation & refin-
ishing

(P-3001)
FASHIONCRAFT FLOORS INC (PA)
1630 Faraday Ave, Carlsbad (92008-7313)
PHONE....................714 255-8400
Thomas R Roberts, *President*
Ken Hoffman, *Vice Pres*
EMP: 50
SQ FT: 10,000
SALES (est): 4.2MM **Privately Held**
WEB: www.fashioncraftfloors.com
SIC: 1752 Resilient floor laying; carpet lay-
ing; vinyl floor tile & sheet installation;
wood floor installation & refinishing

(P-3002)
FLOORGATE INC
3350 N San Fernando Rd, Los Angeles
(90065-1417)
PHONE....................323 478-2000
Al Hembarsoonian, *President*
EMP: 55
SQ FT: 27,400
SALES: 3.2MM **Privately Held**
SIC: 1752 5713 Carpet laying; floor cover-
ing stores

(P-3003)
H V WELKER CO INC
Also Called: Welker Bros
970 S Milpitas Blvd, Milpitas (95035-6323)
PHONE....................408 263-4400
Stuart Welker, *President*
Chuck Gulan, *Shareholder*
Stuart H Welker, *President*
Jack Sanguinitti, *Exec VP*
Vincent A Grana, *Vice Pres*
EMP: 65
SQ FT: 18,375
SALES: 33.8MM **Privately Held**
WEB: www.welkers.com
SIC: 1752 Floor laying & floor work

(P-3004)
HOEM & ASSOCIATES INC
951 Linden Ave, South San Francisco
(94080-1753)
PHONE....................650 871-5194
Russell William Hoem, *CEO*
Sean Hogan, *President*
Russ Hoem, *CFO*
Mike Valerio, *Vice Pres*
Jeannine Denardi, *Admin Asst*
EMP: 85
SQ FT: 24,000
SALES: 38MM **Privately Held**
WEB: www.hoemschurba.com
SIC: 1752 Carpet laying; vinyl floor tile &
sheet installation; wood floor installation &
refinishing

(P-3005)
HOME CARPET INVESTMENT INC (PA)
Also Called: Americas Finest Carpet Com-
pany
730 Design Ct Ste 401, Chula Vista
(91911-6160)
PHONE....................619 262-8040
Carlos Ledesma, *CEO*
Jonathan Escobedo, *Sales Staff*
EMP: 81
SQ FT: 2,500
SALES (est): 22.3MM **Privately Held**
WEB: www.americasfinestcarpet.com
SIC: 1752 7217 Carpet laying; carpet &
upholstery cleaning; carpet & upholstery
cleaning on customer premises; carpet &
upholstery cleaning plants

(P-3006)
HY-TECH TILE INC
1355 Palmyrita Ave, Riverside
(92507-1601)
PHONE....................951 788-0550
Tom Shoemaker, *President*
Narcis Postolache, *CEO*
Cristina Olteanu, *CFO*
Mario Factor, *Vice Pres*
Danelle Hill, *Department Mgr*
EMP: 110
SQ FT: 12,000
SALES (est): 15.1MM **Privately Held**
WEB: www.hytechtile.com
SIC: 1752 1743 Ceramic floor tile installa-
tion; terrazzo, tile, marble, mosaic work

(P-3007)
ICS PROFESSIONAL SERVICES INC
7755 Center Ave Fl 11, Huntington Beach
(92647-3007)
PHONE....................714 868-3900
Jessie Croteau, *CEO*
Vance Cook, *Vice Pres*
▲ **EMP:** 123
SALES: 7.7MM **Privately Held**
SIC: 1752 Floor laying & floor work

(P-3008)
INTERIOR SPECIALISTS INC (HQ)
1630 Faraday Ave, Carlsbad (92008-7313)
P.O. Box 61929, Irvine (92602-6064)
PHONE....................760 929-6700
Alan Davenport, *President*
Jeff Fenton, *Vice Chairman*
Brian Reed, *President*
Lee Singer, *President*
Joe Terrana, *President*
▲ **EMP:** 75
SALES (est): 767.6MM **Privately Held**
SALES (corp-wide): 458.3MM **Privately
Held**
WEB: www.isidc.com
SIC: 1752 1799 Carpet laying; drapery
track installation
PA: Faraday Holdings, Llc
1630 Faraday Ave
Carlsbad CA 92008
760 929-6700

(P-3009)
INTERIOR SPECIALISTS INC
9300 Hubbard Rd, Auburn (95602-7819)
PHONE....................530 885-0632
Doug Ederer, *Owner*
EMP: 70
SALES (corp-wide): 458.3MM **Privately
Held**
SIC: 1752 Floor laying & floor work
HQ: Interior Specialists, Inc.
1630 Faraday Ave
Carlsbad CA 92008
760 929-6700

(P-3010)
J W FLOOR COVERING INC (PA)
9881 Carroll Centre Rd, San Diego
(92126-4554)
PHONE....................858 536-8565
John Wallace, *Owner*
John S Wallace, *President*
Christopher Tiffany, *COO*
Sally Watson, *Payroll Mgr*
Steve Carroll, *Opers Mgr*
EMP: 140
SQ FT: 20,500
SALES (est): 43.6MM **Privately Held**
WEB: www.jwfloors.com
SIC: 1752 Floor laying & floor work

(P-3011)
JJJ FLOOR COVERING INC (PA)
4831 Passons Blvd Ste A, Pico Rivera
(90660-2173)
PHONE....................562 692-9008
Rick Barba, *President*
Maria Gutierrez, *CEO*
Joseph P Miano, *COO*
Yolanda Escovar, *Officer*
Kevin Copeland, *Vice Pres*
▲ **EMP:** 52
SQ FT: 13,000
SALES (est): 9MM **Privately Held**
WEB: www.jjjfloorcovering.com
SIC: 1752 5023 Carpet laying; resilient
floor laying; carpets; resilient floor cover-
ings: tile or sheet

(P-3012)
KYA SERVICES LLC
1800 E Mcfadden Ave, Santa Ana
(92705-4708)
PHONE....................714 659-6476
John Leyds, *Mng Member*
Richard Contreras, *Regional Mgr*
Ramiesha Randle, *Administration*
Ed Perez, *Project Mgr*
Terri Bell, *Controller*
EMP: 50
SALES (est): 793.7K **Privately Held**
SIC: 1752 Carpet laying

(P-3013)
MAGNESITE SPECIALTIES INC
Also Called: American Deck Systems
8686 Production Ave Ste A, San Diego
(92121-2207)
PHONE....................858 578-4186
Curtis Tyree, *President*
Dwain Stratton, *Shareholder*
Vikki J Tyree, *Corp Secy*
Gary E English, *General Mgr*
EMP: 50

SQ FT: 2,500
SALES (est): 7.5MM **Privately Held**
WEB: www.magnesitespecialties.com
SIC: **1752** 1521 1799 1743 Floor laying
& floor work; patio & deck construction &
repair; waterproofing; terrazzo, tile, marble, mosaic work

(P-3014)
NATIONAL APARTMENT FLRG LLC
3205 Ocean Park Blvd # 180, Santa Monica
(90405-3233)
PHONE.....................800 773-6904
Richard Berle, *President*
Brent Matteson, *VP Finance*
Jackie Lemus, *Opers Staff*
Forrest Clark, *Manager*
Robert Hernandez, *Manager*
EMP: 75
SALES (est): 10.1MM **Privately Held**
SIC: **1752** Access flooring system installa-
tion

(P-3015)
PROGRESSIVE FLOOR COVERING INC
924 S Highland Ave, Fullerton
(92832-2903)
PHONE.....................714 213-8805
Rita Spinella, *President*
Oanh Pham, *CFO*
Kevin Deehan, *Vice Pres*
EMP: 50
SQ FT: 17,500
SALES: 9.2MM **Privately Held**
WEB: www.progressivefloorcovering.com
SIC: **1752** Floor laying & floor work

(P-3016)
R E CUDDIE CO
1751 Junction Ave, San Jose (95112-1029)
PHONE.....................408 998-1250
Thomas Cuddie, *CEO*
Robert Cuddie, *Vice Pres*
Tish Allen, *Admin Sec*
Sandra Kaiser, *Accounting Mgr*
EMP: 50
SQ FT: 30,000
SALES (est): 9.5MM **Privately Held**
WEB: www.recuddie.com
SIC: **1752** Floor laying & floor work

(P-3017)
SIGNATURE FLOORING INC
Also Called: SIGNATURE FLOORS
701 N Hariton St, Orange (92868-1313)
PHONE.....................714 558-9200
Jeffery Grimsley, *President*
Margaret Anderson, *COO*
Michael Gray, *Vice Pres*
Dave Garrett, *Project Mgr*
Blake Grimsley, *Sales Staff*
EMP: 65
SALES: 11.8MM **Privately Held**
WEB: www.floorsbysignature.com
SIC: **1752** Floor laying & floor work

(P-3018)
SIMAS FLOOR CO INC (PA)
Also Called: Simas Floor Co Design Center
3550 Power Inn Rd, Sacramento
(95826-3892)
PHONE.....................916 452-4933
Ken Simas, *President*
David G Simas, *Vice Pres*
John U Simas, *Vice Pres*
EMP: 180
SQ FT: 10,000
SALES (est): 35.2MM **Privately Held**
SIC: **1752** 5713 Floor laying & floor work;
floor covering stores

(P-3019)
VINTAGE DESIGN LLC (HQ)
25200 Commercentre Dr, Lake Forest
(92630-8810)
PHONE.....................949 900-5400
Timothy Patrick Buckley, *CEO*
Jason Weiner, *Vice Pres*
Megan Bolton, *Admin Asst*
Connor Mawson, *Purch Agent*
Stacey Donnelly, *Consultant*
EMP: 60
SQ FT: 16,000

SALES (est): 27.8MM
SALES (corp-wide): 48.5MM **Privately
Held**
WEB: www.vintagedesigninc.com
SIC: **1752** Carpet laying; vinyl floor tile &
sheet installation; asphalt tile installation

(P-3020)
WIRTZ TILE & STONE INC
7932 Armour St, San Diego (92111-3718)
PHONE.....................858 569-3816
John David Wirtz, *President*
Ida F Wirtz, *Vice Pres*
EMP: 86 EST: 1974
SQ FT: 4,600
SALES (est): 6.4MM **Privately Held**
WEB: www.wirtztile.com
SIC: **1752** Ceramic floor tile installation

1761 Roofing, Siding & Sheet Metal Work

(P-3021)
ABSOLUTE URETHANE
Also Called: Absolute Roofing CA
6614 S Elm Ave, Fresno (93706-9213)
PHONE.....................877 471-3626
Eric Plaza, *CEO*
Carolyn Plaza, *CFO*
EMP: 50
SALES: 5MM **Privately Held**
SIC: **1761** 1721 1742 7389 Roofing con-
tractor; painting & paper hanging; insula-
tion, buildings;

(P-3022)
ACETECK ROOFING CO INC
5830 Woodlawn Ave, Los Angeles
(90003-1226)
PHONE.....................323 231-6060
Jay Kim, *President*
Song Kim, *Treasurer*
Tim Park, *Project Mgr*
Tiffany Ho, *Assistant*
EMP: 50
SALES (est): 5MM **Privately Held**
WEB: www.acetekroofing.com
SIC: **1761** Roofing contractor

(P-3023)
AEP SPAN INC
2110 Enterprise Blvd, West Sacramento
(95691-3428)
PHONE.....................916 372-0933
Al Price, *Manager*
EMP: 85
SQ FT: 16,000
SALES (est): 2.9MM **Privately Held**
WEB: www.ascpacific.com
SIC: **1761** 3448 3444 3443 Roofing con-
tractor; prefabricated metal buildings;
sheet metalwork; fabricated plate work
(boiler shop)
HQ: Asc Profiles Llc
2110 Enterprise Blvd
West Sacramento CA 95691
916 376-2800

(P-3024)
ALCAL SPECIALTY CONTG INC (DH)
946 N Market Blvd, Sacramento
(95834-1268)
PHONE.....................916 929-3100
Darren C Morris, *President*
Sonny Kooner, *CFO*
Arthur R Gardner, *Exec VP*
Richard Bledsoe, *Vice Pres*
Robert Colla, *Vice Pres*
EMP: 94
SALES (est): 31MM
SALES (corp-wide): 1.5B **Privately Held**
WEB: www.paccoast.com
SIC: **1761** 1793 1742 1799 Roofing con-
tractor; glass & glazing work; plastering,
drywall & insulation; coating, caulking &
weather, water & fireproofing; garage
door, installation or erection

(P-3025)
ALL FAB PRCSION SHEETMETAL INC
1015 Timothy Dr, San Jose (95133-1050)
PHONE.....................408 279-1099

Son P Ho, *CEO*
Kelly T Ho, *CFO*
▲ EMP: 100
SQ FT: 58,000
SALES (est): 19.4MM **Privately Held**
SIC: **1761** 3444 Sheet metalwork; sheet
metalwork

(P-3026)
AZTEC SHEET METAL INC
11222 Woodside Ave N, Santee
(92071-4716)
PHONE.....................619 937-0005
Dick Buxton, *President*
Tom Buxton, *CFO*
Larry Hendry, *Admin Sec*
EMP: 60
SALES (est): 4.1MM **Privately Held**
WEB: www.ltdsheetmetal.com
SIC: **1761** Architectural sheet metal work

(P-3027)
BEST CONTRACTING SERVICES INC
4301 Bettencourt Way, Union City
(94587-1519)
PHONE.....................510 886-7240
Mohmmad Beigi, *Branch Mgr*
Mohammad Beigi, *General Mgr*
EMP: 75
SALES (corp-wide): 108.4MM **Privately
Held**
SIC: **1761** Roofing contractor
PA: Best Contracting Services, Inc.
19027 S Hamilton Ave
Gardena CA 90248

(P-3028)
BIGHAM TAYLOR ROOFING CORP
22721 Alice St, Hayward (94541-6401)
PHONE.....................510 886-0197
Stephen E Bigham, *CEO*
Laura Jo Bigham, *Corp Secy*
Don Taylor, *Vice Pres*
Steve Galli, *General Mgr*
Rod Freitas, *Opers Mgr*
EMP: 70 EST: 1977
SQ FT: 10,000
SALES (est): 12.4MM **Privately Held**
WEB: www.btroof.com
SIC: **1761** Roofing contractor

(P-3029)
BORAL ROOFING LLC
Also Called: Boral Industries
3093 Industry St Ste A, Oceanside
(92054-4895)
PHONE.....................760 967-0827
Jose Davila, *Manager*
EMP: 122 **Privately Held**
SIC: **1761** Roofing, siding & sheet metal
work
HQ: Boral Roofing Llc
7575 Irvine Center Dr # 100
Irvine CA 92618
949 756-1605

(P-3030)
BYERS ENTERPRISES INC
Also Called: Byers Leafguard Gutter Systems
11773 Slow Poke Ln, Grass Valley
(95945-8417)
PHONE.....................530 272-7777
Raymond W Byers Sr, *CEO*
Jeff Fierstein, *General Mgr*
Patty Moore, *General Mgr*
Patty Sarkisian, *Bookkeeper*
Mandy Gallardo, *Human Res Dir*
EMP: 69
SQ FT: 2,400
SALES: 8MM **Privately Held**
WEB: www.byersleafguard.com
SIC: **1761** Sheet metalwork

(P-3031)
CANNON FABRICATION INC
Also Called: Canfab
182 Granite St Ste 101, Corona
(92879-1288)
PHONE.....................951 278-1830
Donald J Prosser, *CEO*
Mary D Prosser, *President*
William Prosser Jr, *Vice Pres*
EMP: 61

SQ FT: 43,000
SALES (est): 9.6MM **Privately Held**
WEB: www.canfab.com
SIC: **1761** Sheet metalwork

(P-3032)
CARMEL ARCHITECTURAL SALES
2300 E Katella Ave # 370, Anaheim
(92806-6046)
PHONE.....................714 630-7221
David Traino, *CEO*
James M Henry, *Vice Pres*
Patricia Dalton, *Admin Sec*
▲ EMP: 60
SQ FT: 10,500
SALES (est): 6.1MM **Privately Held**
WEB: www.carmelsales.com
SIC: **1761** Skylight installation; architec-
tural sheet metal work

(P-3033)
CENTIMARK CORPORATION
Also Called: Questmark
1420 S Archibald Ave, Ontario
(91761-7626)
PHONE.....................909 652-9280
Jong S Lee, *Manager*
Jeff Johnson, *Manager*
EMP: 50
SALES (corp-wide): 723.7MM **Privately
Held**
WEB: www.centimark.com
SIC: **1761** Roofing contractor
PA: Centimark Corporation
12 Grandview Cir
Canonsburg PA 15317
724 514-8700

(P-3034)
CENTIMARK CORPORATION
Also Called: Centimark Roofing Systems
2380 W Winton Ave, Hayward
(94545-1102)
PHONE.....................510 921-5500
Anthony Zahteila, *President*
Rob Dennis, *Opers Mgr*
EMP: 108
SALES (corp-wide): 723.7MM **Privately
Held**
WEB: www.centimark.com
SIC: **1761** 1752 6331 Roofing contractor;
floor laying & floor work; resilient floor lay-
ing; fire, marine & casualty insurance; au-
tomobile insurance; workers'
compensation insurance
PA: Centimark Corporation
12 Grandview Cir
Canonsburg PA 15317
724 514-8700

(P-3035)
CHALLENGER SHEET METAL INC
9353 Abraham Way Ste A, Santee
(92071-5641)
PHONE.....................619 596-8040
Joel Quinonez, *CEO*
Robert Basso, *CFO*
▲ EMP: 80
SQ FT: 18,000
SALES: 17MM **Privately Held**
WEB: www.challengersm.com
SIC: **1761** Sheet metalwork

(P-3036)
CITADEL ROOFING & SOLAR
4980 Allison Pkwy, Vacaville (95688-9346)
PHONE.....................707 446-5500
Dieter Folk, *CEO*
Aaron Nitzkin, *Exec VP*
EMP: 150
SALES (est): 91.1K **Privately Held**
SIC: **1761** Roofing contractor

(P-3037)
CLAUD TOWNSLEY INC
Also Called: Central Roofing Company
555 W 182nd St, Gardena (90248-3400)
PHONE.....................310 527-6770
William E Knapp, *President*
Jonathan Townsley, *CEO*
Janet Townsley, *Exec VP*
EMP: 60
SQ FT: 12,000

PRODUCTS & SVCS

SALES (est): 7.6MM **Privately Held**
WEB: www.centralroof.com
SIC: 1761 Roofing contractor

(P-3038)
CMF INC
Also Called: Custom Metal Fabricators
1317 W Grove Ave, Orange (92865-4137)
PHONE................714 637-2409
David Duclett, *CEO*
Vic Maynez, *President*
Chris Demott, *CFO*
Darren Sagert, *CFO*
Mark Allen, *Vice Pres*
EMP: 100
SQ FT: 11,000
SALES (est): 21.4MM **Privately Held**
SIC: 1761 Siding contractor

(P-3039)
COMMERCIAL INDUS ROOFG CO INC
Also Called: C & I
9239 Olive Dr, Spring Valley (91977-2306)
PHONE................619 465-3737
Barry Turnour, *President*
Ron Albrecht, *Project Mgr*
EMP: 60
SQ FT: 4,500
SALES (est): 9.9MM **Privately Held**
SIC: 1761 Roofing contractor

(P-3040)
COMMERCIAL ROOFING SYSTEMS INC
11735 Goldring Rd, Arcadia (91006-5894)
PHONE................626 359-5354
Glenn Hiller, *President*
Allan Londo, *Superintendent*
EMP: 55
SQ FT: 9,800
SALES (est): 7.7MM **Privately Held**
WEB: www.comroofsys.com
SIC: 1761 Roofing contractor

(P-3041)
COOL ROOFING SYSTEMS INC (PA)
1286 Dupont Ct, Manteca (95336-6003)
PHONE................209 825-0818
Jamie Billman, *President*
Jesus Oliva, *Officer*
Daniel Edge, *Vice Pres*
Misty Beslanowitch, *Office Mgr*
Thurston Kiang, *Technology*
EMP: 55
SQ FT: 3,000
SALES (est): 25MM **Privately Held**
WEB: www.coolroofingsystems.net
SIC: 1761 Roofing contractor

(P-3042)
CROWNER SHEET METAL PDTS INC
14346 Arrow Hwy, Baldwin Park (91706-1335)
PHONE................626 960-4971
Kim M Baier, *CEO*
Dennis Curran, *Vice Pres*
Russell Dunegan, *Admin Sec*
EMP: 50 **EST:** 1945
SQ FT: 9,000
SALES (est): 9.7MM **Privately Held**
WEB: www.crowner.net
SIC: 1761 Sheet metalwork

(P-3043)
CUSTOM PRODUCT DEV CORP
4603 Las Positas Rd Ste A, Livermore (94551-8845)
PHONE................925 960-0577
Gerald John Ammirato, *President*
Nancy Ammirato, *Admin Sec*
Ed Tahvilian, *Info Tech Mgr*
Judy Fenta, *Purchasing*
▲ **EMP:** 55
SQ FT: 33,500
SALES (est): 14.7MM **Privately Held**
WEB: www.cpd-corp.com
SIC: 1761 Sheet metalwork

(P-3044)
D C TAYLOR CO
5060 Forni Dr Ste B, Concord (94520-8579)
PHONE................925 603-1100
James Meyersieck, *Branch Mgr*
Jana Madsen, *Comms Dir*
EMP: 50
SALES (corp-wide): 96.9MM **Privately Held**
WEB: www.dctaylorco.com
SIC: 1761 Roofing contractor
PA: D. C. Taylor Co.
312 29th St Ne
Cedar Rapids IA 52402
319 363-2073

(P-3045)
D7 ROOFING SERVICES INC
2851 Gold Tailings Ct, Rancho Cordova (95670-6189)
PHONE................916 447-2175
Jeffrey Lyn Williamson, *CEO*
James J English Jr, *Vice Pres*
Elazabath Roses, *Director*
EMP: 70
SQ FT: 15,000
SALES (est): 11.1MM **Privately Held**
WEB: www.d7roofing.com
SIC: 1761 Roofing contractor

(P-3046)
DE MELLO ROOFING INC
45 Jordan St, San Rafael (94901-3918)
PHONE................415 456-0741
Richard H Garzoli Jr, *President*
EMP: 55
SQ FT: 500
SALES (est): 5.2MM **Privately Held**
WEB: www.demelloroofing.com
SIC: 1761 Roofing contractor

(P-3047)
DESERT AIR CONDITIONING INC
Also Called: Honeywell Authorized Dealer
590 S Williams Rd, Palm Springs (92264-1551)
PHONE................760 323-3383
Jeffrey Shaw, *CEO*
Todd Shaw, *Vice Pres*
Michael Trefun, *Office Mgr*
Valerie Botts, *Admin Sec*
Steve Gortz, *Sales Mgr*
EMP: 50 **EST:** 1954
SQ FT: 1,500
SALES (est): 9.6MM **Privately Held**
WEB: www.desertairconditioning.com
SIC: 1761 1711 Sheet metalwork; warm air heating & air conditioning contractor

(P-3048)
DUKE PACIFIC INC
13950 Monte Vista Ave, Chino (91710-5535)
P.O. Box 1800 (91708-1800)
PHONE................909 591-0191
Gregory C Severson, *President*
Judith E Braaten, *Corp Secy*
James J Enright IV, *Vice Pres*
Stan Little, *Sales Staff*
Brian Lamarca, *Manager*
EMP: 100 **EST:** 1958
SQ FT: 10,000
SALES (est): 18.1MM **Privately Held**
WEB: www.dukepacific.com
SIC: 1761 Roofing contractor

(P-3049)
DWAYNE NASH INDUSTRIES INC
Also Called: Kodiak Roofing & Waterproofing
8825 Washington Blvd # 100, Roseville (95678-6213)
PHONE................916 253-1900
Dwayne Nash, *CEO*
Erin Anderson, *CFO*
David Pope, *Vice Pres*
Kay Brannen, *Director*
▲ **EMP:** 250
SQ FT: 23,617
SALES (est): 64.5MM **Privately Held**
WEB: www.kodiakroofing.com
SIC: 1761 Roofing contractor

(P-3050)
EDJE-ENTERPRISES
520 Crane St Ste B, Lake Elsinore (92530-2777)
PHONE................951 245-7070
Edward Joseph Jennen, *CEO*
Maryjane Jennen, *Admin Sec*
EMP: 82
SQ FT: 8,000
SALES: 7.9MM **Privately Held**
SIC: 1761 Architectural sheet metal work

(P-3051)
EHMCKE SHEET METAL CORP
840 W 19th St, National City (91950-5406)
P.O. Box 13010, San Diego (92170-3010)
PHONE................619 477-6484
John F Cornell, *CEO*
Dennis Isaacs, *Treasurer*
Dennis Stainbrook, *Admin Sec*
Richard Parra, *Director*
Vi Tang, *Supervisor*
▲ **EMP:** 55
SQ FT: 25,000
SALES (est): 13.7MM **Privately Held**
WEB: www.ehmckesheetmetal.com
SIC: 1761 8712 3446 Sheet metalwork; architectural services; architectural metalwork

(P-3052)
ENTERPRISE ROOFING SERVICE INC
2400 Bates Ave, Concord (94520-1217)
P.O. Box 5130 (94524-0130)
PHONE................925 689-8100
Lawrence T Reardon, *President*
Steven L Reardon, *Vice Pres*
Aubrey Shehorn, *Treasurer*
Lynda She Horn, *Admin Sec*
Mike Reardon, *Admin Sec*
EMP: 80
SQ FT: 1,200
SALES (est): 17MM **Privately Held**
WEB: www.enterpriseroofing.com
SIC: 1761 Roofing contractor

(P-3053)
FIDELITY ROOF COMPANY (PA)
1075 40th St, Oakland (94608-3691)
PHONE................510 547-6330
Montague M Upshaw Sr, *Ch of Bd*
Stephen H Cadet, *President*
Kenneth White, *COO*
Montague M Upshaw Jr, *Vice Pres*
Weston Faison, *Manager*
EMP: 60
SQ FT: 8,000
SALES: 13.8MM **Privately Held**
WEB: www.fidelityroof.com
SIC: 1761 Roofing contractor

(P-3054)
FIRST AVENUE INC
5105 Heintz St, Baldwin Park (91706-1820)
PHONE................626 856-2076
Brett Maurer, *President*
EMP: 60
SALES (est): 4.1MM **Privately Held**
SIC: 1761 Roofing, siding & sheet metal work

(P-3055)
FOREVER FIREWOOD INC (PA)
Also Called: Warren Knox Roofing
46 El Pueblo Rd Ste A, Santa Cruz (95066-3544)
PHONE................831 461-0634
Warren Knox, *President*
Mark Thenhaus, *Vice Pres*
EMP: 50
SALES (est): 5.6MM **Privately Held**
SIC: 1761 Roofing contractor

(P-3056)
FOUR CS SERVICE INC
1560 H St, Fresno (93721-1616)
PHONE................559 237-3990
Preston Cross, *CEO*
Graydon Cross, *Vice Pres*
Joanne Berryhill, *Controller*
EMP: 80
SQ FT: 22,500

SALES (est): 12.4MM **Privately Held**
WEB: www.sheetmetalco.com
SIC: 1761 Sheet metalwork

(P-3057)
FRESNO ROOFING CO INC
5950 E Olive Ave, Fresno (93727-2710)
P.O. Box 7676 (93747-7676)
PHONE................559 255-8377
Scott Logan Raypholtz, *CEO*
Michael Raypholtz, *Corp Secy*
Michael C Raypholtz, *General Mgr*
EMP: 60
SQ FT: 23,746
SALES (est): 8MM **Privately Held**
SIC: 1761 Roofing contractor; roof repair

(P-3058)
GARCIA ROOFING INC
201 Mount Vernon Ave, Bakersfield (93307-2741)
P.O. Box 70250 (93387-0250)
PHONE................661 325-5736
Mike Garcia, *President*
Denise Roberts, *Corp Secy*
▲ **EMP:** 50 **EST:** 1975
SQ FT: 5,000
SALES (est): 7.7MM **Privately Held**
WEB: www.garciaroofinginc.com
SIC: 1761 Roofing contractor

(P-3059)
GRAHAM-PREWETT INC
2773 N Bus Park Ave # 101, Fresno (93727-8662)
PHONE................559 291-3741
Sean Prewett, *President*
Gary Graham, *Vice Pres*
EMP: 50
SQ FT: 2,000
SALES (est): 13.1MM **Privately Held**
WEB: www.grahamprewett.com
SIC: 1761 Roofing contractor

(P-3060)
GUDGEL ROOFING INC
Also Called: Yancey Roofing
5321 84th St, Sacramento (95826-4803)
PHONE................916 387-6900
Janet M Gudgel, *President*
Jason Gudgel, *Vice Ch Bd*
Stephen Reiland, *Exec VP*
Jason W Gudgel, *Vice Pres*
Catherine Youngblood, *Admin Sec*
EMP: 50
SQ FT: 6,000
SALES (est): 12.2MM **Privately Held**
WEB: www.yanceyroofing.com
SIC: 1761 Roofing contractor

(P-3061)
HERBERT MALARKEY ROOFING CO
9301 Garfield Ave, South Gate (90280-3804)
PHONE................562 806-8000
John Stromme, *Manager*
EMP: 77
SALES (est): 5.2MM
SALES (corp-wide): 158.5MM **Privately Held**
SIC: 1761 Roofing contractor
PA: Herbert Malarkey Roofing Company
3131 N Columbia Blvd
Portland OR 97217
503 283-1191

(P-3062)
HILLCREST SHEET METAL INC
Also Called: Hillcrest AC & Shtmtl
2324 Perseus Ct, Bakersfield (93308-6943)
PHONE................661 335-1500
Jim Barker, *President*
EMP: 67 **EST:** 1952
SQ FT: 14,010
SALES (est): 7.7MM
SALES (corp-wide): 8.1B **Publicly Held**
WEB: www.emcorgroup.com
SIC: 1761 1711 Sheet metalwork; heating & air conditioning contractors; ventilation & duct work contractor
HQ: Mesa Energy Systems, Inc.
2 Cromwell
Irvine CA 92618
949 460-0460

(P-3063)
HOWARD ROOFING COMPANY INC
245 N Mountain View Ave, Pomona (91767-5629)
PHONE...........................909 622-5598
Larry K Malekow, *President*
Mitch T Caldwell, *Vice Pres*
Ron A Malekow, *Vice Pres*
Ron Malekow, *Vice Pres*
Rick Marion, *Project Mgr*
EMP: 70
SQ FT: 27,000
SALES (est): 12.3MM **Privately Held**
SIC: 1761 Roofing contractor

(P-3064)
IRC TECHNOLOGIES INC (PA)
Also Called: Independent Roofing Cons
2901 Pullman St, Santa Ana (92705-5818)
PHONE...........................949 476-8626
Phillip L Penney, *President*
Jeff Starr, *CFO*
Michael A Wilsey, *Principal*
Darlene Boggini, *Administration*
Tony Cancio, *Consultant*
▲ **EMP:** 70
SQ FT: 5,000
SALES (est): 6.7MM **Privately Held**
WEB: www.irctech.com
SIC: 1761 Roofing contractor

(P-3065)
J P WITHEROW ROOFING COMPANY
1083 N Cuyamaca St, El Cajon (92020-1803)
PHONE...........................619 297-4701
Richard S Witherow, *President*
Doug Barry, *General Mgr*
Charlie Walters, *General Mgr*
Linda Witherow, *Admin Sec*
EMP: 53 **EST:** 1935
SQ FT: 42,000
SALES (est): 13.8MM **Privately Held**
SIC: 1761 Roofing contractor

(P-3066)
JM ROOFING COMPANY INC
Also Called: Action Roofing
534 E Ortega St, Santa Barbara (93103-3016)
PHONE...........................805 966-3696
John J Martin Jr, *President*
Sharon Fritz, *Corp Secy*
Peggy Martin, *Vice Pres*
Steve Martin, *Vice Pres*
Action Roofing, *General Mgr*
EMP: 70
SQ FT: 5,000
SALES (est): 10.2MM **Privately Held**
SIC: 1761 Roofing contractor

(P-3067)
KINGSPAN LIGHT & AIR LLC
401 Goetz Ave, Santa Ana (92707-3709)
PHONE...........................714 540-8950
Gene Murtagh,
Adam Toogood, *Technician*
EMP: 150 **EST:** 2016
SALES: 36.7MM **Privately Held**
SIC: 1761 Skylight installation

(P-3068)
KPU ROOFING
1497 Freesia Way, Beaumont (92223-7806)
PHONE...........................909 586-2531
Juan Gomez, *President*
EMP: 50
SALES (est): 1MM **Privately Held**
SIC: 1761 Roofing contractor

(P-3069)
L I METAL SYSTEMS
9041 Bermudez St, Pico Rivera (90660-4505)
PHONE...........................562 948-5950
Anthony Chiovare, *President*
Peter Bueckert, *Treasurer*
Frank Lemmo, *Vice Pres*
▲ **EMP:** 50
SQ FT: 12,600
SALES (est): 5.1MM **Privately Held**
SIC: 1761 Gutter & downspout contractor

(P-3070)
LAWSON ROOFING CO INC
1495 Tennessee St, San Francisco (94107-3420)
PHONE...........................415 285-1661
Frank E Lawson Sr, *Ch of Bd*
Frank E Lawson Jr, *President*
Richard J Lawson, *Vice Pres*
Richard Lawson, *Vice Pres*
Manny Cotla, *Warehouse Mgr*
EMP: 70
SQ FT: 10,000
SALES (est): 12.6MM **Privately Held**
WEB: www.lawsonroofing.com
SIC: 1761 1799 Roofing contractor; water-proofing

(P-3071)
LBC INC
1881 Duncan St, Simi Valley (93065-3411)
PHONE...........................805 581-1068
Luke Richard Bancroft, *Principal*
EMP: 60
SALES (est): 3MM **Privately Held**
SIC: 1761 Roofing, siding & sheet metal work

(P-3072)
LJC CONSTRUCTION INC
712 W Harding Rd, Turlock (95380-9743)
PHONE...........................209 668-2700
Lon Jones, *President*
EMP: 55 **EST:** 2000
SQ FT: 2,719
SALES (est): 3.5MM **Privately Held**
SIC: 1761 Roofing, siding & sheet metal work

(P-3073)
LUCKY INSTALLATIONS
9041 Bermudez St, Pico Rivera (90660-4505)
PHONE...........................562 948-5950
Frank Lemmo, *Owner*
EMP: 50
SALES (est): 1.6MM **Privately Held**
SIC: 1761 Gutter & downspout contractor

(P-3074)
MASTER ROOFING SYSTEMS INC
52 S Linden Ave Ste 5, South San Francisco (94080-6432)
PHONE...........................415 407-4450
Angela Sohn-Lee, *CEO*
Stephen Lee, *Director*
EMP: 60
SALES (est): 439.3K **Privately Held**
SIC: 1761 Roofing, siding & sheet metal work

(P-3075)
MCCORMACK ROOFNG CONSTRCTN & E
1260 N Hancock St Ste 108, Anaheim (92807-1951)
PHONE...........................714 777-4040
James McCormack, *Owner*
Jana Almazan, *Office Mgr*
Tanya Cook, *Office Mgr*
EMP: 60
SALES (est): 5.1MM **Privately Held**
SIC: 1761 Roofing contractor

(P-3076)
MCMURRAY & SONS INC (PA)
Also Called: M & S SUPPLY CO
1818 Allard Ave, Eureka (95503-5704)
P.O. Box 1111 (95502-1111)
PHONE...........................707 443-3088
David W McMurray, *CEO*
Heidi Bersin, *Shareholder*
Kim Brookshire, *Office Admin*
Cathy Minkema, *Admin Sec*
EMP: 80
SQ FT: 14,500
SALES: 5.5MM **Privately Held**
SIC: 1761 1742 Roofing contractor; insulation, buildings

(P-3077)
MID-PENINSULA ROOFING INC
1326 Marsten Rd, Burlingame (94010-2406)
PHONE...........................650 375-7850

Matthew Greening, *President*
Ronald Stahl, *Vice Pres*
EMP: 55
SQ FT: 10,000
SALES (est): 9.4MM **Privately Held**
SIC: 1761 Roofing contractor

(P-3078)
MILAN CORPORATION
Also Called: Marco Roofing
43230 Osgood Rd, Fremont (94539-5607)
P.O. Box 1691 (94538-0169)
PHONE...........................510 656-6400
Michael Edward Creeden, *President*
EMP: 50
SQ FT: 20,000
SALES (est): 6.3MM **Privately Held**
SIC: 1761 Roofing contractor

(P-3079)
MS INDUSTRIAL SHTMTL INC
Also Called: Baghouse and Indus Shtmtl Svcs
1731 Pomona Rd, Corona (92880-6963)
PHONE...........................951 272-6610
Nancy Nicola, *Ch of Bd*
Dan Suffel, *Vice Pres*
Warren Lampkin, *Principal*
Jessica Salas, *Office Mgr*
Mary Serna, *Info Tech Mgr*
EMP: 130
SQ FT: 35,000
SALES (est): 49.7MM **Privately Held**
SIC: 1761 Sheet metalwork

(P-3080)
NUSHAKE INC
Also Called: Nushake Roofing
319 S Parallel Ave, Ripon (95366-2910)
PHONE...........................209 239-8616
Douglas Heath, *President*
Elizabeth Heath, *Vice Pres*
EMP: 60
SQ FT: 2,800
SALES (est): 7.2MM **Privately Held**
WEB: www.nushake.com
SIC: 1761 Roofing contractor

(P-3081)
OSSCIM INC
Also Called: Royal Roofing Construction Co
172 E Orangethorpe Ave, Placentia (92870-6410)
PHONE...........................714 680-0015
Ronald Ossenberg, *President*
Janine Ossenberg, *Vice Pres*
Curtis Ide, *General Mgr*
EMP: 50
SQ FT: 3,000
SALES (est): 3.7MM **Privately Held**
SIC: 1761 Roofing contractor

(P-3082)
PACIFIC STRUCFRAME LLC
1600 Chicago Ave Ste R11, Riverside (92507-2040)
PHONE...........................951 405-8536
John B Hanna, *President*
EMP: 91
SQ FT: 2,000
SALES (est): 4.5MM **Privately Held**
SIC: 1761 Roofing, siding & sheet metal work

(P-3083)
PATTON SHEET METAL WORKS INC
Also Called: Patton Air Conditioning
272 N Palm Ave, Fresno (93701-1436)
PHONE...........................559 486-5222
Robert M Patton, *President*
Ellen D Patton, *Corp Secy*
Steve Gejeian, *Controller*
Dan Reyes, *Manager*
▲ **EMP:** 50
SQ FT: 14,500
SALES (est): 10.8MM **Privately Held**
WEB: www.pattonac.com
SIC: 1761 1711 Sheet metalwork; warm air heating & air conditioning contractor

(P-3084)
PENNY ROOFING COMPANY
2501 Exposition Blvd, Los Angeles (90018-4299)
P.O. Box 18737 (90018-0737)
PHONE...........................323 731-5424

Lance Mahler, *President*
EMP: 50
SQ FT: 3,000
SALES (est): 4MM **Privately Held**
SIC: 1761 Roofing contractor

(P-3085)
PERFORMANCE SHEETS LLC
440 Baldwin Park Blvd, City of Industry (91746-1407)
PHONE...........................626 333-0195
Mike Crosson, *President*
Forest Felvey,
Michael Feterik, *Mng Member*
Greg Hall, *Mng Member*
▲ **EMP:** 125
SALES (est): 10.6MM **Privately Held**
SIC: 1761 Sheet metalwork
HQ: Smurfit Kappa North America Llc
125 E John Carpenter Fwy # 150
Irving TX 75062
800 306-8326

(P-3086)
PETERSEN-DEAN INC
Also Called: Petersendean
21616 Golden Triangle Rd # 101, Santa Clarita (91350-3993)
PHONE...........................661 254-3322
EMP: 100
SALES (corp-wide): 335.8MM **Privately Held**
WEB: www.needaroof.com
SIC: 1761
PA: Petersen-Dean, Inc.
39300 Civic Center Dr # 300
Fremont CA 94538
707 469-7470

(P-3087)
PETERSEN-DEAN INC
Petersendean
1705 Enterprise Dr, Fairfield (94533-5801)
PHONE...........................707 469-7470
Dieter Folk, *Senior VP*
Jim Petersen, *CEO*
EMP: 50
SALES (corp-wide): 369.9MM **Privately Held**
WEB: www.needaroof.com
SIC: 1761 Roofing contractor
PA: Petersen-Dean, Inc.
39300 Civic Center Dr # 300
Fremont CA 94538
707 469-7470

(P-3088)
PETERSEN-DEAN INC
Also Called: Petersendean
2210 S Dupont Dr, Anaheim (92806-6104)
PHONE...........................714 629-9670
Greg O'Donnell, *Manager*
EMP: 202
SALES (corp-wide): 369.9MM **Privately Held**
WEB: www.needaroof.com
SIC: 1761 Roofing contractor
PA: Petersen-Dean, Inc.
39300 Civic Center Dr # 300
Fremont CA 94538
707 469-7470

(P-3089)
PETERSEN-DEAN COMMERCIAL INC
Also Called: Petersendean
1705 Enterprise Dr, Fairfield (94533-5801)
PHONE...........................707 469-7470
James Petersen, *President*
Gary Phillips, *Sales Staff*
Paul Beckman, *Accounts Mgr*
EMP: 170
SALES (est): 8.1MM
SALES (corp-wide): 369.9MM **Privately Held**
WEB: www.needaroof.com
SIC: 1761 1711 Roofing contractor; solar energy contractor
PA: Petersen-Dean, Inc.
39300 Civic Center Dr # 300
Fremont CA 94538
707 469-7470

(P-3090)
PLATINUM ROOFING INC
800 Charcot Ave Ste 107, San Jose
(95131-2211)
PHONE.....................408 280-5028
Bill Shevlin, *CEO*
Sean Marzola, *COO*
Rafael Lapizco, *Vice Pres*
Juan Orosco, *Opers Mgr*
EMP: 80
SALES (est): 13.1MM **Privately Held**
SIC: 1761 Roofing contractor

(P-3091)
PROGRESSIVE SERVICES INC
Also Called: Progressive Roofing
3832 S Highway 99 Ste A, Stockton
(95215-8000)
PHONE.....................209 824-2837
John William, *Branch Mgr*
EMP: 95
SALES (corp-wide): 153.3MM **Privately Held**
SIC: 1761 Roof repair
PA: Progressive Services, Inc.
　23 N 35th Ave
　Phoenix AZ 85009
　602 278-4900

(P-3092)
R HAUPT ROOFING CONSTRUCTION
1305 W 132nd St Fl 2, Gardena
(90247-1507)
PHONE.....................310 515-9709
Robert Haupt, *President*
Donna Haupt, *Principal*
EMP: 50
SALES (est): 5.2MM **Privately Held**
SIC: 1761 Roofing contractor

(P-3093)
R2G ENTERPRISES INC
Also Called: Advanced Fabrication Tech
31154 San Benito St, Hayward
(94544-7912)
PHONE.....................510 489-6218
Stephen Green, *President*
Todd Morey, *Vice Pres*
EMP: 65
SALES (est): 5.5MM **Privately Held**
SIC: 1761 Sheet metalwork

(P-3094)
RED POINTE ROOFING LP (PA)
1814 N Neville St, Orange (92865-4216)
PHONE.....................714 685-0010
Aaron Martin, *Partner*
Sean Brophy, *Partner*
John Patterson, *Partner*
Felipe Coronel, *Director*
EMP: 85
SALES (est): 21.6MM **Privately Held**
SIC: 1761 Roofing contractor

(P-3095)
REINHARDT ROOFING INC
19258 Donna Ct, Morgan Hill (95037-9319)
PHONE.....................510 713-7014
Carole Lowrance, *President*
Ray Lowrance, *Vice Pres*
EMP: 60
SQ FT: 17,000
SALES (est): 3.8MM **Privately Held**
WEB: www.reinhardtroofing.net
SIC: 1761 Roofing contractor

(P-3096)
ROOFING CONSTRUCTORS INC
Also Called: Western Roofing Service
15002 Wicks Blvd, San Leandro
(94577-6600)
PHONE.....................415 648-6472
Mark F Santacrose, *Principal*
Robert Ferrando, *CFO*
George O'Neill, *Senior VP*
John Nolan, *Vice Pres*
Erica Mapp, *Admin Sec*
▼ **EMP:** 150
SQ FT: 3,000
SALES (est): 20.6MM
SALES (corp-wide): 876MM **Privately Held**
WEB: www.westroof.com
SIC: 1761 Roofing contractor

PA: Tecta America Corp.
　9450 Bryn Mawr Ave
　Rosemont IL 60018
　847 581-3888

(P-3097)
SBB ROOFING INC (PA)
Also Called: Bilt-Well Roofing & Mtl Co
3310 Verdugo Rd, Los Angeles
(90065-2845)
P.O. Box 65827 (90065-0827)
PHONE.....................323 254-2888
Bruce Radenbaugh, *President*
Steven Radenbaugh, *Vice Pres*
Lupe Diaz, *Executive*
EMP: 180
SQ FT: 5,000
SALES (est): 9.8MM **Privately Held**
SIC: 1761 Roofing contractor

(P-3098)
SONORAN ROOFING INC
4161 Citrus Ave, Rocklin (95677-4008)
PHONE.....................916 624-1080
John Daly, *CEO*
Jim Pelton, *Corp Secy*
EMP: 160
SQ FT: 5,000
SALES (est): 18.4MM **Privately Held**
SIC: 1761 Roofing contractor

(P-3099)
STATE ROOFING SYSTEMS INC
15444 Hesperian Blvd, San Leandro
(94578-3959)
PHONE.....................510 317-1477
Keith Symons, *President*
Jack White, *Corp Secy*
James Ellis, *General Mgr*
Stephen Tong, *Project Mgr*
Ed Walters, *Purch Mgr*
EMP: 100 **EST:** 1981
SQ FT: 6,000
SALES (est): 22MM **Privately Held**
WEB: www.stateroofingsystems.com
SIC: 1761 Roofing contractor

(P-3100)
STRAIGHT LINE ROOFING & CNSTR
3811 Dividend Dr Ste A, Shingle Springs
(95682-8592)
PHONE.....................530 672-9995
John Borba, *President*
EMP: 50
SALES (est): 7.7MM **Privately Held**
WEB: www.straightlineroofing.com
SIC: 1761 Roofing contractor

(P-3101)
SYLVESTER ROOFING COMPANY INC (PA)
2593 Auto Park Way, Escondido
(92029-2088)
PHONE.....................760 743-0048
Anthony Zaffuto, *CEO*
Wesley Sylvester, *CFO*
Carla Beveridge, *Administration*
Ivan Graham, *Project Mgr*
Kurt King, *Project Mgr*
EMP: 50
SQ FT: 1,000
SALES (est): 32.6MM **Privately Held**
WEB: www.sylvesterroofing.com
SIC: 1761 Roofing contractor

(P-3102)
T&C ROOFING INC
Also Called: Town & Country Roofing
2155 Elkins Way Ste H, Brentwood
(94513-7365)
PHONE.....................925 513-8463
Jeff Tamayo, *President*
Sara Tamayo, *Corp Secy*
Sophie Tamayo, *VP Bus Dvlpt*
EMP: 75
SQ FT: 5,000
SALES (est): 12.7MM **Privately Held**
WEB: www.canawine.com
SIC: 1761 Roofing contractor

(P-3103)
TECTA AMERICA SOUTHERN CAL INC
1217 E Wakeham Ave, Santa Ana
(92705-4145)
PHONE.....................714 973-6233
Daniel L Klein, *CEO*
Wendy Wetzel, *Asst Controller*
EMP: 60 **EST:** 2002
SALES (est): 8.2MM
SALES (corp-wide): 876MM **Privately Held**
WEB: www.laveyroofingservices.com
SIC: 1761 Roofing contractor
PA: Tecta America Corp.
　9450 Bryn Mawr Ave
　Rosemont IL 60018
　847 581-3888

(P-3104)
THORSENS INC
Also Called: Thorsens Plumbing & AC
2310 N Walnut Rd, Turlock (95382-8910)
PHONE.....................209 524-5296
Craig Vernon Pitau, *CEO*
Esther Thorsen, *Corp Secy*
EMP: 55
SQ FT: 19,500
SALES (est): 8.8MM **Privately Held**
WEB: www.thorsensinc.com
SIC: 1761 1711 5722 5075 Sheet metal-
　work; plumbing contractors; heating & air
　conditioning contractors; household appli-
　ance stores; warm air heating equipment
　& supplies; sheet metalwork

(P-3105)
TINCO SHEET METAL INC
958 N Eastern Ave, Los Angeles
(90063-1308)
PHONE.....................323 263-0511
Brian Powell, *President*
John Millan, *CFO*
Michael Nevarez, *Chairman*
Laura Nevarez, *Admin Sec*
▲ **EMP:** 250
SQ FT: 18,000
SALES: 38MM **Privately Held**
SIC: 1761 Roofing contractor

(P-3106)
VILLARA CORPORATION
Also Called: Beutler Heating & AC
5005 Fulton Dr Ste F, Fairfield
(94534-1645)
PHONE.....................707 863-8222
Rod Schoppe, *General Mgr*
EMP: 50
SALES (corp-wide): 152MM **Privately Held**
WEB: www.beutlerhvac.com
SIC: 1761 1711 Sheet metalwork; heating
　& air conditioning contractors; warm air
　heating & air conditioning contractor
PA: Villara Corporation
　4700 Lang Ave
　Mcclellan CA 95652
　916 646-2700

(P-3107)
WESTERN TEAR-OFF & DISPOSAL
Also Called: Western Waste Services
10920 Grand Ave, Temple City
(91780-3551)
P.O. Box 1794, Glendora (91740-1794)
PHONE.....................626 443-9984
Michael D Debarry, *President*
EMP: 70 **EST:** 1994
SALES (est): 5.7MM **Privately Held**
SIC: 1761 Roofing contractor

(P-3108)
ZIMMERMAN ROOFING INC
3675 R St, Sacramento (95816-6624)
P.O. Box 19056 (95819-0056)
PHONE.....................916 454-3667
David Zimmerman, *President*
EMP: 65
SQ FT: 5,500
SALES: 12MM **Privately Held**
SIC: 1761 Roofing contractor; siding con-
　tractor; sheet metalwork

1771 Concrete Work

(P-3109)
ADORNO CONSTRUCTION INC
520 Westchester Dr Ste A, Campbell
(95008-5070)
PHONE.....................408 369-8675
Frank Adorno III, *President*
Frank Adorno Jr, *CFO*
Victor M Perez Jr, *Vice Pres*
Sherry Jackson, *Executive*
Janet Sanchez, *Admin Sec*
EMP: 52
SQ FT: 1,300
SALES (est): 6MM **Privately Held**
SIC: 1771 Concrete work

(P-3110)
AMERICAN ASP REPR RSRFCING INC (PA)
24200 Clawiter Rd, Hayward (94545-2216)
P.O. Box 3367 (94540-3367)
PHONE.....................510 723-0280
Allan A Henderson, *CEO*
Steve Aguirre, *COO*
Kim Henschel, *Vice Pres*
Alex Christianson, *Manager*
Sean Kunz, *Manager*
EMP: 100
SALES (est): 21.2MM **Privately Held**
SIC: 1771 Blacktop (asphalt) work

(P-3111)
AMERICAN CONCRETE
1125 Linda Vista Dr Ste 1, San Marcos
(92078-3819)
PHONE.....................760 471-9907
Anthony Cannariato, *President*
EMP: 90
SQ FT: 1,500
SALES (est): 5.1MM **Privately Held**
SIC: 1771 Concrete work

(P-3112)
ASPHALT MANAGEMENT INC
7243 Somerset Blvd, Paramount
(90723-3998)
PHONE.....................562 630-6811
Fax: 562 529-5899
EMP: 50
SQ FT: 5,000
SALES (est): 2.7MM **Privately Held**
SIC: 1771

(P-3113)
AUS DECKING INC
2999 Promenade St Ste 100, West Sacra-
mento (95691-6418)
P.O. Box 698 (95691-0698)
PHONE.....................916 373-5320
Eric Meissner, *President*
Patty Rawstron, *Accounting Mgr*
EMP: 57
SQ FT: 56,628
SALES (est): 6.5MM **Privately Held**
SIC: 1771 Concrete work

(P-3114)
B & M CONTRACTORS INC
4473 Cochran St, Simi Valley (93063-3065)
PHONE.....................805 581-5480
Dave C Moore, *CEO*
Randall Bilsland, *Vice Pres*
EMP: 68
SALES (est): 7.8MM **Privately Held**
WEB: www.bandmcontractors.com
SIC: 1771 Concrete work

(P-3115)
B S HAND & SONS INC
4450 Shopping Ln, Simi Valley
(93063-3451)
PHONE.....................818 983-1155
Gary B Hand, *President*
Todd Hand, *Vice Pres*
EMP: 50 **EST:** 1964
SQ FT: 4,300
SALES (est): 5.4MM **Privately Held**
WEB: www.bshand.com
SIC: 1771 1522 Concrete work; residential
　construction

▲ = Import ▼=Export
◆ =Import/Export

(P-3116)
BALTAZAR CONSTRUCTION INC
236 E Arrow Hwy, Covina (91722-1817)
PHONE......................626 339-8620
Baltazar Jimenez Siqueiros, *CEO*
EMP: 50
SALES: 12MM **Privately Held**
SIC: 1771 Blacktop (asphalt) work

(P-3117)
BAYMARR CONSTRUCTORS INC
6950 Mcdivitt Dr, Bakersfield (93313-2046)
PHONE......................661 395-1676
Eric Recktenwald, *CEO*
Jack Whitney, *President*
Pat Howes, *Corp Secy*
EMP: 100
SQ FT: 10,000
SALES (est): 20.4MM **Privately Held**
WEB: www.baymarr.com
SIC: 1771 Concrete work

(P-3118)
BEDROCK COMPANY
2970 Myers St, Riverside (92503-5524)
PHONE......................951 273-1931
Glenn E Jackson Jr, *CEO*
Jackie O Connell, *Office Mgr*
Carlene Jackson, *Admin Sec*
Michelle Herrera, *Admin Asst*
Steve Mesner, *Project Mgr*
EMP: 70 **EST:** 1993
SQ FT: 5,000
SALES: 8MM **Privately Held**
SIC: 1771 Concrete work

(P-3119)
BEN F SMITH INC
Also Called: Concrete Construction
8655 Miramar Pl Ste B, San Diego
(92121-2567)
PHONE......................858 271-4320
Stuart Shelton, *Manager*
Stuart Schouten, *Vice Pres*
EMP: 120
SALES (corp-wide): 21.9MM **Privately Held**
WEB: www.benfsmithinc.com
SIC: 1771 Concrete work
PA: Ben F. Smith, Inc.
       4420 Baldwin Ave
       El Monte CA 91731
       626 444-2543

(P-3120)
BERKELEY CEMENT INC
1200 6th St, Berkeley (94710-1402)
PHONE......................510 525-8175
Ron Fadelli, *CEO*
Andy A Fadelli, *President*
Ronald M Fadelli, *Vice Pres*
Scott Fadelli, *Admin Sec*
EMP: 140 **EST:** 1947
SQ FT: 10,000
SALES (est): 29.9MM **Privately Held**
WEB: www.bciconcrete.com
SIC: 1771 Concrete pumping

(P-3121)
BITECH-ACE A JOINT VENTURE
7371 Walnut Ave, Buena Park
(90620-1759)
PHONE......................714 521-1477
Benjamin Kim, *CEO*
Simon Jeon, *Vice Pres*
EMP: 75
SALES (est): 1.9MM **Privately Held**
SIC: 1771 1522 1611 1623 Concrete work; remodeling, multi-family dwellings; general contractor, highway & street construction; water, sewer & utility lines; renovation, remodeling & repairs: industrial buildings

(P-3122)
C TEAM CONSTRUCTION INC
1272 Greenfield Dr, El Cajon (92021-3316)
PHONE......................619 579-6572
David Clarke, *President*
Alan Salherst, *Manager*
EMP: 70 **EST:** 1995
SQ FT: 2,000

SALES (est): 8.8MM **Privately Held**
WEB: www.teamcconstruction.com
SIC: 1771 Concrete work

(P-3123)
CAL-WEST CONCRETE CUTTING INC (PA)
3000 Tara Ct, Union City (94587-1508)
PHONE......................510 656-0253
Marvin Weldon Birch, *CEO*
Weldon Birch, *President*
Barbara Birch, *Treasurer*
Jan Jeffreys, *Admin Sec*
EMP: 250
SQ FT: 100,000
SALES (est): 13.8MM **Privately Held**
WEB: www.calwestconcretecutting.com
SIC: 1771 Concrete repair

(P-3124)
CALMEX ENGINEERING INC
2764 S Vista Ave, Bloomington
(92316-3270)
PHONE......................909 546-1311
Robert Stone, *President*
Rosie Lopez, *Director*
EMP: 51
SQ FT: 11,000
SALES (est): 8.5MM **Privately Held**
SIC: 1771 Blacktop (asphalt) work

(P-3125)
CASPER COMPANY
3825 Bancroft Dr, Spring Valley
(91977-2122)
PHONE......................619 589-6001
Roger Casper, *CEO*
William R Haithcock, *President*
Greg T Casper, *Vice Pres*
Steven Casper, *Vice Pres*
Isabel Ortiz Marocco, *Vice Pres*
EMP: 143
SQ FT: 6,000
SALES (est): 35.9MM **Privately Held**
SIC: 1771 Concrete work

(P-3126)
CELL-CRETE CORPORATION
995 Zephyr Ave, Hayward (94544-7917)
PHONE......................510 471-7257
Joe Barclay, *Branch Mgr*
EMP: 55
SALES (corp-wide): 37.1MM **Privately Held**
SIC: 1771 1761 Flooring contractor; roofing contractor
PA: Cell-Crete Corporation
       135 Railroad Ave
       Monrovia CA 91016
       626 357-3500

(P-3127)
CEMENT CUTTING INC
3610 Hancock St Frnt Frnt, San Diego
(92110-4335)
PHONE......................619 296-9592
Harold O Grafton, *CEO*
Steve Quinn, *Treasurer*
John Gregory Becker, *Vice Pres*
Donald Valadao, *Executive*
Steven Morgan, *Admin Sec*
EMP: 80
SQ FT: 7,000
SALES (est): 16.8MM **Privately Held**
WEB: www.cementcutting.com
SIC: 1771 Concrete work

(P-3128)
COAN CONSTRUCTION CO INC
1481 E Grand Ave, Pomona (91766-3806)
PHONE......................909 868-6812
Perry Coan, *President*
Sharon Coan, *Admin Sec*
Ryan Granger, *Project Mgr*
John Rich, *Project Mgr*
EMP: 100
SQ FT: 4,300
SALES: 8.7MM **Privately Held**
WEB: www.coanconstruction.com
SIC: 1771 Foundation & footing contractor

(P-3129)
COASTAL PAVING INCORPORATED
1295 Norman Ave, Santa Clara
(95054-2027)
PHONE......................408 988-5559
Anna Jarvis, *CEO*
Clifford Heaps, *Treasurer*
Ray Jarvis, *Vice Pres*
Clifford J Heaps, *General Mgr*
EMP: 52
SQ FT: 1,000
SALES (est): 10.1MM **Privately Held**
WEB: www.coastalpaving.com
SIC: 1771 1611 Blacktop (asphalt) work; surfacing & paving; concrete construction: roads, highways, sidewalks, etc.; sidewalk construction

(P-3130)
COFFMAN SPECIALTIES INC (PA)
9685 Via Excelencia # 200, San Diego
(92126-7500)
PHONE......................858 536-3100
Colleen Coffman, *President*
Kevin Coffman, *Vice Pres*
Mel Nutter, *Sr Software Eng*
Pablo Aranalde, *Project Mgr*
Greg Brown, *Project Mgr*
EMP: 151
SQ FT: 6,000
SALES (est): 73.8MM **Privately Held**
WEB: www.coffmanspecialties.com
SIC: 1771 Concrete work

(P-3131)
CONCO PUMPING
13052 Dahlia St, Fontana (92337-6926)
PHONE......................909 350-0503
Doug Marquis, *Manager*
EMP: 60
SALES (est): 3.1MM **Privately Held**
SIC: 1771 Concrete pumping

(P-3132)
CONCRETE CONCEPTS INC
2317 Auto Park Way, Escondido
(92029-1218)
PHONE......................760 737-5470
Chuck Clary, *President*
Christopher Bramwell, *Vice Pres*
EMP: 60
SQ FT: 8,000
SALES (est): 4MM **Privately Held**
SIC: 1771 Concrete work

(P-3133)
CONCRETE IMAGES INTERNATIONAL
17237 Saint Andrews Dr, Poway
(92064-1228)
PHONE......................858 676-1253
Ernest Hoffman, *CEO*
Edward Stafford, *President*
EMP: 75
SALES (est): 6MM **Privately Held**
SIC: 1771 Concrete work

(P-3134)
CONCRETE NORTH INC
10274 Iron Rock Way, Elk Grove
(95624-1355)
PHONE......................209 745-7400
James Grimes, *Owner*
Kim Grimes, *Principal*
Jenny Quigel, *Office Mgr*
Lisa Rodriguez, *Manager*
EMP: 75
SALES: 11MM **Privately Held**
SIC: 1771 Foundation & footing contractor

(P-3135)
CONDON-JOHNSON & ASSOC INC (PA)
480 Roland Way Ste 200, Oakland
(94621-2053)
PHONE......................510 636-2100
Gerard Jerry Condon, *President*
Jeremy Condon, *Vice Pres*
Douglas Watt, *District Mgr*
Marilyn Cooper, *Admin Asst*
Tony Tincher, *CTO*
▲ **EMP:** 50
SQ FT: 12,400

SALES (est): 71.4MM **Privately Held**
SIC: 1771 1799 Concrete work; shoring & underpinning work

(P-3136)
CS CONCRETE SOLUTIONS INC
Also Called: Concrete Contractor
47 Goldbriar Way, Mission Viejo
(92692-5986)
PHONE......................949 285-3122
Curt Stidham, *President*
EMP: 99
SALES (est): 4.1MM **Privately Held**
SIC: 1771 Concrete work

(P-3137)
D AND D CONCRETE CNSTR INC
13795 Blaisdell Pl # 201, Poway
(92064-8896)
PHONE......................619 518-9737
Dereck Leffler, *President*
Diane Leffler, *Admin Sec*
EMP: 60 **EST:** 1989
SQ FT: 2,500
SALES (est): 7.9MM **Privately Held**
SIC: 1771 Foundation & footing contractor

(P-3138)
DAVID L AMADOR INC
Also Called: Amador Development
762 N Loren Ave, Azusa (91702-2255)
P.O. Box 907 (91702-0907)
PHONE......................626 334-2011
David Amador, *President*
Debra Amador, *Treasurer*
EMP: 55
SQ FT: 2,500
SALES (est): 6.7MM **Privately Held**
SIC: 1771 Curb construction

(P-3139)
DE OLIVIERA CONCRETE INC
14111 Soledad Canyon Rd, Santa Clarita
(91387-2224)
PHONE......................661 252-7522
Fred De Oliviera, *President*
Alfred Samora, *Vice Pres*
EMP: 50
SQ FT: 1,000
SALES (est): 3.7MM **Privately Held**
SIC: 1771 Concrete work

(P-3140)
DEMCON CONCRETE CONTRS INC
13795 Blaisdell Pl # 202, Poway
(92064-8896)
PHONE......................858 748-5090
Derek Leffler, *President*
Mike Wildley, *Corp Secy*
Edwin Stougton, *Vice Pres*
Ed Stoughton, *General Mgr*
Diane Leffler, *Admin Sec*
EMP: 75
SALES (est): 7.7MM **Privately Held**
SIC: 1771 Concrete work

(P-3141)
DENNIS BLAZONA CONSTRUCTION
525 Harbor Blvd Ste 10, West Sacramento
(95691-2246)
PHONE......................916 375-8337
J Dennis Balzona, *President*
Karin Blazona, *Admin Sec*
EMP: 65
SALES (est): 4.5MM **Privately Held**
SIC: 1771 Concrete work

(P-3142)
DEVINCENZI CONCRETE CNSTR
3276 Dutton Ave, Santa Rosa
(95407-7866)
P.O. Box 508 (95402-0508)
PHONE......................707 568-4370
Gary Dahl, *President*
Gina Dahl, *Vice Pres*
Jean Dahl, *Vice Pres*
EMP: 50
SQ FT: 3,500
SALES (est): 11.6MM **Privately Held**
SIC: 1771 Curb construction; sidewalk contractor; driveway contractor; parking lot construction

(P-3143)
DISTINCTIVE CONCRETE INC
9320 Chesapeake Dr # 214, San Diego
(92123-1021)
PHONE..................858 277-9707
Steven G Zoumaras, *President*
EMP: 50
SALES (est): 3.6MM Privately Held
SIC: 1771 Concrete work

(P-3144)
DOLAN CONCRETE CONSTRUCTION
3045 Alfred St, Santa Clara (95054-3303)
PHONE..................408 869-3250
Leo A Gutierrez, *President*
Benjamin C Newsom, *Corp Secy*
Robert F Dumesnil Jr, *Vice Pres*
EMP: 90
SQ FT: 8,500
SALES (est): 11MM Privately Held
WEB: www.dolanconcrete.com
SIC: 1771 Curb construction

(P-3145)
E & M CONCRETE CONSTRUCTION
2842 Sherwin Ave Ste A, Ventura
(93003-7272)
P.O. Box 5600 (93005-0600)
PHONE..................805 658-2888
Edmundo Mendez, *President*
Mariel Mendez, *Admin Sec*
EMP: 80
SQ FT: 3,478
SALES (est): 8.6MM Privately Held
WEB: www.emconcrete.com
SIC: 1771 Concrete work

(P-3146)
EBS CONCRETE INC
1320 E 6th St Ste 100, Corona
(92879-1700)
PHONE..................951 279-6869
Thomas Nanci, *President*
EMP: 50 EST: 2000
SQ FT: 3,000
SALES (est): 3.9MM Privately Held
SIC: 1771 Concrete work

(P-3147)
EMPIRE DEMOLITION INC
1623 Leeson Ln, Corona (92879-2061)
PHONE..................909 393-8300
Kris Huff, *CEO*
Collin Cumbee, *CFO*
EMP: 100 EST: 1997
SQ FT: 8,000
SALES (est): 11.9MM Privately Held
WEB: www.empiredemolition.com
SIC: 1771 Concrete work

(P-3148)
EPIDENDIO CONSTRUCTION INC
11325 Highway 29, Lower Lake (95457)
P.O. Box 452 (95457-0452)
PHONE..................707 994-5100
Mike Epidendio, *President*
Joan Epidendio, *Corp Secy*
Anthony Epidendio, *Vice Pres*
Donald Epidendio, *Vice Pres*
EMP: 50 EST: 1973
SQ FT: 14,000
SALES (est): 6.8MM Privately Held
SIC: 1771 Blacktop (asphalt) work

(P-3149)
FORD PLASTERING INC
732 W Grove Ave, Orange (92865-3214)
PHONE..................714 921-0624
Gary L Ford, *President*
Darrell Ford, *Vice Pres*
EMP: 300
SQ FT: 1,200
SALES (est): 9.5MM Privately Held
WEB: www.fordplastering.com
SIC: 1771 1742 Stucco, gunite & grouting
contractors; plastering, drywall & insula-
tion

(P-3150)
GINO/GIUSEPPE INC
Also Called: G & G Construction Co
700 Enterprise Ct Ste A, Atwater
(95301-9512)
PHONE..................209 358-0556
Giusppe Castiglione, *CEO*
Giuseppe Castiglione, *CEO*
Gino Graziano, *CFO*
EMP: 250
SQ FT: 7,600
SALES (est): 30MM Privately Held
WEB: www.ggconcrete.com
SIC: 1771 Foundation & footing contractor

(P-3151)
GOLDEN EMPIRE CONCRETE PDTS
Also Called: Structure Cast
8261 Mccutchen Rd, Bakersfield
(93311-9407)
PHONE..................661 833-4490
Brent Dezember, *CEO*
Anna Dezember, *Admin Sec*
EMP: 60 EST: 2011
SALES (est): 10MM Privately Held
SIC: 1771 Concrete work

(P-3152)
GOLDSMITH CONSTRUCTION CO INC
2683 Lime Ave, Signal Hill (90755-2709)
PHONE..................562 595-5975
William Goldsmith, *President*
Susan Goldsmith, *Corp Secy*
Kelly Goldsmith, *Vice Pres*
Kelly Mogg, *Office Mgr*
EMP: 50
SQ FT: 6,000
SALES (est): 10.7MM Privately Held
SIC: 1771 1629 5082 Concrete work; oil
refinery construction; construction & min-
ing machinery

(P-3153)
GONSALVES & SANTUCCI INC (PA)
Also Called: Conco Cement Company
5141 Commercial Cir, Concord
(94520-8523)
PHONE..................925 685-6799
Mathew Gonsalves, *Ch of Bd*
Steven Gonsalves, *President*
Barry Silberman, *CFO*
Holly Bertuccelli, *Vice Pres*
Gary Brandt, *Vice Pres*
EMP: 50
SQ FT: 35,000
SALES (est): 164.7MM Privately Held
WEB: www.theconcocompanies.com
SIC: 1771 Concrete work

(P-3154)
GRAHAM CONCRETE CNSTR INC
1323 Dayton Ave Ste 103, Clovis
(93612-5869)
PHONE..................559 292-6571
James Graham, *President*
Jason Graham, *Admin Sec*
Tom Shields, *Project Mgr*
EMP: 75
SQ FT: 10,000
SALES (est): 8.7MM Privately Held
WEB: www.grahamconcrete.com
SIC: 1771 Concrete work

(P-3155)
GREG H CARPENTER CONCRETE INC
955 N Guild Ave, Lodi (95240-0877)
PHONE..................209 367-4224
Greg Carpenter, *President*
EMP: 50
SALES (est): 7.1MM Privately Held
SIC: 1771 Concrete work

(P-3156)
GROUNDWORKS INC
2145 Elkins Way Ste C, Brentwood
(94513-7363)
PHONE..................925 513-0300
Bryan Lucay, *President*
Lalo Sanchez, *Opers Mgr*

EMP: 80
SQ FT: 2,500
SALES (est): 5.8MM Privately Held
SIC: 1771 1611 1629 Concrete work;
grading; drainage system construction

(P-3157)
GUY YOCOM CONSTRUCTION INC
10712 E Mariposa Rd, Stockton
(95215-9595)
PHONE..................951 284-3456
EMP: 244
SALES (corp-wide): 33.6MM Privately
Held
SIC: 1771 Concrete work
PA: Guy Yocom Construction, Inc.
3299 Horseless Carriage R
Norco CA 92860
951 284-3456

(P-3158)
GUY YOCOM CONSTRUCTION INC (PA)
3299 Horseless Carriage R, Norco
(92860-3604)
PHONE..................951 284-3456
Guy W Yocom, *Principal*
Greg Wilson, *CFO*
Richard Majestic, *Exec VP*
Dave Kent, *Vice Pres*
Jimmy West, *Vice Pres*
EMP: 113
SQ FT: 41,000
SALES (est): 33.6MM Privately Held
WEB: www.yocominc.com
SIC: 1771 Concrete work

(P-3159)
HB PARKCO CONSTRUCTION INC (PA)
3190 Arprt Loop Dr Ste F, Costa Mesa
(92626)
PHONE..................714 444-1441
Brett D Behrns, *CEO*
W Adrian Hoyle, *President*
Micheal Barry, *CFO*
EMP: 394
SQ FT: 4,000
SALES (est): 40.4MM Privately Held
WEB: www.hbparkco.com
SIC: 1771 Parking lot construction

(P-3160)
HOFFMAN CONCRETE COMPANY INC
2621 Green Rver Rd Ste 10, Corona
(92882)
PHONE..................951 372-8333
Dean Hoffman Jr, *President*
EMP: 50
SALES (est): 15MM Privately Held
SIC: 1771 Concrete work

(P-3161)
HOME FRANCHISE CONCEPTS LLC (PA)
Also Called: All American Decorative Con
19000 Macarthur Blvd # 100, Irvine
(92612-1416)
PHONE..................949 404-1100
Chad Hallock, *President*
Todd Jackson, *COO*
Shirin Behzadi, *CFO*
Tom Hillebrandt, *CFO*
Tony Forbes, *Exec VP*
EMP: 90
SALES (est): 35.2MM Privately Held
SIC: 1771 6794 Concrete work; fran-
chises, selling or licensing

(P-3162)
INLAND CC INC
Also Called: ICC
13820 Slover Ave, Fontana (92337-7037)
PHONE..................909 355-1318
Marvin Hawkins, *CEO*
Karen Hawkins, *President*
Dave Galban, *Manager*
EMP: 150
SALES (est): 16.7MM Privately Held
SIC: 1771 Foundation & footing contractor

(P-3163)
INTERNTNAL PVMENT SLUTIONS INC
1209 Van Buren St Ste 3, Thermal
(92274-8800)
P.O. Box 10458, San Bernardino (92423-
0458)
PHONE..................909 794-2101
Brent Rieger, *President*
Dennis Rieger, *Treasurer*
EMP: 80
SQ FT: 3,000
SALES (est): 5.7MM Privately Held
WEB: www.pavement-solutions.com
SIC: 1771 Blacktop (asphalt) work

(P-3164)
INTERSTATE CON PMPG CO INC
11180 Vallejo Ct, French Camp
(95231-9783)
PHONE..................209 983-3092
Andy Paulazzo, *CEO*
Shawn Slate, *Treasurer*
Mark Bobbitt, *Maintence Staff*
Judy Paulazzo, *Manager*
EMP: 52
SALES (est): 10.8MM Privately Held
WEB: www.icpumps.com
SIC: 1771 Concrete pumping

(P-3165)
J L S CONCRETE PUMPING INC
2055 N Ventura Ave, Ventura (93001-1308)
PHONE..................805 643-0766
▲ EMP: 75
SQ FT: 10,000
SALES (est): 5.4MM Privately Held
WEB: www.jlspumping.com
SIC: 1771 Concrete pumping

(P-3166)
JEZOWSKI & MARKEL CONTRS INC
749 N Poplar St, Orange (92868-1013)
PHONE..................714 978-2222
Leonard Michael Barth, *Principal*
Joseph Dean, *Vice Pres*
Dorothy Destefano, *Admin Sec*
Sean Gallagher, *Manager*
EMP: 145
SQ FT: 4,500
SALES (est): 26.3MM Privately Held
SIC: 1771 Foundation & footing contractor

(P-3167)
JKB CORPORATION
561 S Walnut St, La Habra (90631-6035)
PHONE..................562 905-3477
John D Brown, *President*
Kathy Brown, *Vice Pres*
John Brown, *Sales Executive*
EMP: 50
SQ FT: 4,000
SALES (est): 5.8MM Privately Held
SIC: 1771 Concrete work

(P-3168)
JOHN KENNEY CONSTRUCTION INC
619 E Montecito St, Santa Barbara
(93103-3217)
P.O. Box 40929 (93140-0929)
PHONE..................805 884-1579
Jonathan Kenney, *President*
Jordan Kenney, *Vice Pres*
Ashley Lopez, *Project Mgr*
Tricia Ford, *Bookkeeper*
EMP: 52
SQ FT: 5,000
SALES (est): 8.1MM Privately Held
SIC: 1771 Concrete work

(P-3169)
JOHNSEN CONSTRUCTION INC
6448 Capitol Ave, Diamond Springs
(95619-9393)
PHONE..................530 642-2123
David W Johnsen, *President*
David W Johnson, *President*
EMP: 70
SQ FT: 300
SALES (est): 5.6MM Privately Held
WEB: www.johnsenconstruction.com
SIC: 1771 Concrete work

(P-3170)
JOSEPH J ALBANESE INC
851 Martin Ave, Santa Clara (95050-2903)
P.O. Box 667 (95052-0667)
PHONE..............................408 727-5700
Joseph J Albanese, *Principal*
Phil Roby, *Vice Pres*
Stephanie Nguyen, *Executive*
Dave Alaimo, *Admin Sec*
John Formoso, *Info Tech Mgr*
EMP: 700
SALES (est): 158.5MM **Privately Held**
WEB: www.jjalbanese.com
SIC: 1771 Foundation & footing contractor

(P-3171)
JT WIMSATT CONTG CO INC
(PA)
28064 Avenue Stanford B, Valencia
(91355-1159)
PHONE..............................661 775-8090
John E Wimsatt III, *President*
Tricia Wimsatt, *Vice Pres*
Maria Dela Cruz, *Director*
EMP: 68
SALES (est): 40.5MM **Privately Held**
WEB: www.jtwimsatt.com
SIC: 1771 Concrete work

(P-3172)
JYG CONCRETE
CONSTRUCTION INC
24841 Avenue Tibbitts, Valencia
(91355-3405)
PHONE..............................661 607-0337
John Stich, *President*
EMP: 110
SALES (est): 6.3MM **Privately Held**
WEB: www.jygconstruction.com
SIC: 1771 Concrete work

(P-3173)
KENYON CONSTRUCTION INC
Also Called: Kenyon Plastream
63 Trevarno Rd D, Livermore (94551-4931)
PHONE..............................925 371-8102
Laura Neil, *Manager*
EMP: 300
SALES (corp-wide): 134.6MM **Privately Held**
WEB: www.kenyonconstruction.com
SIC: 1771 1742 Stucco, gunite & grouting contractors; plastering, plain or ornamental
PA: Kenyon Construction, Inc.
4001 W Indian School Rd
Phoenix AZ 85019
602 484-0080

(P-3174)
LARGO CONCRETE INC
1690 W Foothill Blvd B, Upland
(91786-8433)
PHONE..............................909 981-7844
Paul Burkel, *Principal*
Milton Stout, *Superintendent*
EMP: 548
SALES (corp-wide): 150.8MM **Privately Held**
SIC: 1771 Concrete work
PA: Largo Concrete, Inc.
2741 Walnut Ave Ste 110
Tustin CA 92780
714 731-3600

(P-3175)
LARGO CONCRETE INC
891 W Hamilton Ave, Campbell
(95008-0402)
PHONE..............................408 874-2500
Ken Long, *Manager*
EMP: 658
SALES (corp-wide): 150.8MM **Privately Held**
SIC: 1771 Concrete work
PA: Largo Concrete, Inc.
2741 Walnut Ave Ste 110
Tustin CA 92780
714 731-3600

(P-3176)
LEONARDS CARPET SERVICE
INC
6767 Nancy Ridge Dr, San Diego
(92121-2225)
PHONE..............................858 453-9525
Daniel Nagel, *Manager*
EMP: 50
SQ FT: 12,000
SALES (corp-wide): 33.3MM **Privately Held**
WEB: www.lcsdesign.com
SIC: 1771 Flooring contractor
PA: Leonard's Carpet Service, Inc.
1121 N Red Gum St
Anaheim CA 92806
714 630-1930

(P-3177)
LOMBARDO DIAMND CORE
DRLG INC
2225 De La Cruz Blvd, Santa Clara
(95050-3007)
PHONE..............................408 727-7922
Richard D Long, *President*
Dorothy Long, *Admin Sec*
EMP: 58 **EST:** 1961
SQ FT: 1,300
SALES (est): 11MM **Privately Held**
WEB: www.lombardodrilling.com
SIC: 1771 1795 Concrete work; demolition, buildings & other structures

(P-3178)
MARNE CONSTRUCTION INC
Also Called: Newval Chemical
749 N Poplar St, Orange (92868-1013)
PHONE..............................714 935-0995
Charles Randolph, *President*
Gustavo Vega, *Project Mgr*
Tony Naranjo, *VP Sales*
Steven McKeon, *Director*
EMP: 80
SQ FT: 10,000
SALES (est): 12.3MM **Privately Held**
WEB: www.marneconstruction.com
SIC: 1771 Concrete work

(P-3179)
MCGUIRE CONTRACTING INC
16579 Slover Ave, Fontana (92337-7508)
PHONE..............................909 357-1200
David McGuire, *President*
Kathie Vilas, *CEO*
Sandy McGuire, *Admin Sec*
Manny Wilson, *Project Mgr*
EMP: 51
SQ FT: 1,800
SALES (est): 6.4MM **Privately Held**
WEB: www.mcguirecontracting.com
SIC: 1771 Concrete work

(P-3180)
MCM CONSTRUCTION INC
708 Pier A St, Wilmington (90744-6433)
PHONE..............................310 549-9207
EMP: 60
SALES (corp-wide): 150MM **Privately Held**
SIC: 1771 1521 Concrete work; single-family housing construction
PA: M.C.M. Construction, Inc.
6413 32nd St
North Highlands CA 95660
916 334-1221

(P-3181)
MEDINA CONCRETE
CONSTRUCTION
Also Called: Alejandro Medina
2368 W 1st Ave, San Bernardino
(92407-6134)
P.O. Box 1341, Azusa (91702-1341)
PHONE..............................909 474-9640
Alex Medina, *Owner*
EMP: 50
SALES (est): 3.8MM **Privately Held**
WEB: www.alejandromedina.com
SIC: 1771 Concrete work

(P-3182)
MELO CONCRETE
CONSTRUCTION
5820 Obata Way, Gilroy (95020-7093)
PHONE..............................408 842-3484

Manuel Melo, *President*
Maria Melo, *Vice Pres*
EMP: 80
SALES (est): 9MM **Privately Held**
WEB: www.meloconcrete.com
SIC: 1771 Concrete work

(P-3183)
MINEGAR CONTRACTING INC
925 Poinsettia Ave Ste 10, Vista
(92081-8452)
PHONE..............................760 598-5001
Michael Dahlquist, *President*
EMP: 50
SALES (est): 5.9MM **Privately Held**
SIC: 1771 Concrete work

(P-3184)
MITCHELL JONES CONCRETE
INC
Also Called: Mitchell Concrete
3185 Fitzgerald Rd, Rancho Cordova
(95742-6801)
PHONE..............................916 638-6870
Mitchell L Jones, *President*
Peggy Jones, *Vice Pres*
Bob Miller, *Manager*
EMP: 175
SQ FT: 7,200
SALES (est): 17.6MM **Privately Held**
WEB: www.mitchellconcrete.com
SIC: 1771 Concrete work

(P-3185)
MORLEY CONSTRUCTION
COMPANY (HQ)
3330 Ocean Park Blvd # 101, Santa Monica
(90405-3202)
PHONE..............................310 399-1600
Mark Benjamin, *Ch of Bd*
Tod Paris, *CFO*
Bert Lewitt, *Exec VP*
Arun Asher, *Vice Pres*
Reginald Jackson, *Vice Pres*
▲ **EMP:** 80
SQ FT: 20,000
SALES (est): 30.2MM
SALES (corp-wide): 168.7MM **Privately Held**
WEB: www.morleybuilders.com
SIC: 1771 1522 1542 Concrete work; condominium construction; commercial & office building, new construction
PA: Morley Builders, Inc.
3330 Ocean Park Blvd # 101
Santa Monica CA 90405
310 399-1600

(P-3186)
MORRISON CONCRETE INC
14114 Rosecrans Ave Ste C, Santa Fe
Springs (90670-5214)
PHONE..............................562 802-1450
Bradley Morrison, *President*
Karen Allison, *Manager*
EMP: 50
SALES (est): 8MM **Privately Held**
SIC: 1771 Concrete work

(P-3187)
NED L WEBSTER CONCRETE
CNSTR
8800 Grimes Canyon Rd, Moorpark
(93021-9768)
PHONE..............................805 529-4900
Ned Webster, *Principal*
EMP: 75
SALES (est): 7.2MM **Privately Held**
SIC: 1771 Concrete work

(P-3188)
NMN CONSTRUCTION INC
1077 Lakeville St, Petaluma (94952-3331)
P.O. Box 110244, Campbell (95011-0244)
PHONE..............................707 763-6981
Fax: 408 874-2574
EMP: 100
SALES (est): 4.5MM **Privately Held**
SIC: 1771

(P-3189)
NOAH CONCRETE
CORPORATION
5900 Rossi Ln, Gilroy (95020-7013)
PHONE..............................408 842-7211

Don Alvarez, *CEO*
Christine Morales, *Office Mgr*
▲ **EMP:** 60
SALES (est): 8.6MM **Privately Held**
SIC: 1771 Concrete work

(P-3190)
NORTH BAY CONSTRUCTION
INC
930 Shiloh Rd Bldg 46, Windsor
(95492-9679)
P.O. Box 1635 (95492-1635)
PHONE..............................707 836-8500
Lohrie Pardue, *President*
Robert Pardue, *Vice Pres*
EMP: 50
SQ FT: 10,000
SALES (est): 6.9MM **Privately Held**
SIC: 1771 Foundation & footing contractor

(P-3191)
NORTHSTATE PLASTERING INC
2210 Cordelia Rd, Fairfield (94534-1912)
PHONE..............................707 207-0950
Buck W Kimbriel Jr, *President*
Francisco Tolento, *Vice Pres*
EMP: 80
SALES (est): 6MM **Privately Held**
WEB: www.northstateplastering.com
SIC: 1771 Stucco, gunite & grouting contractors

(P-3192)
ODYSSEY LANDSCAPING CO
INC
Also Called: Odyssey Environmental Services
5400 W Highway 12, Lodi (95242-9170)
PHONE..............................209 369-6197
Martin Gates, *President*
Brian Zanni, *Division Mgr*
EMP: 80
SQ FT: 2,400
SALES (est): 11.5MM **Privately Held**
WEB: www.odysseylandscape.com
SIC: 1771 0781 Concrete work; landscape architects

(P-3193)
OPTIMUM CON FUNDATIONS
USA INC
6258 Rustic Ln, Jurupa Valley
(92509-7228)
PHONE..............................877 212-7994
Mario Garcia, *CEO*
Scott Cable, *President*
EMP: 55
SALES: 20MM **Privately Held**
SIC: 1771 Concrete work

(P-3194)
PACIFIC PAVINGSTONE INC
Also Called: Pacific Outdoor Living
8309 Tujunga Ave Unit 201, Sun Valley
(91352-3216)
PHONE..............................818 244-4000
Terry Morrill, *President*
Trent Morrill, *Vice Pres*
Chad Morrill, *Admin Sec*
EMP: 115
SALES (est): 13MM **Privately Held**
WEB: www.pacificpavingstone.com
SIC: 1771 Driveway contractor

(P-3195)
PACIFIC STHWEST
STRUCTURES INC
7845 Lemon Grove Way A, Lemon Grove
(91945-1880)
PHONE..............................619 469-2323
Daniel Fitzgerald, *President*
EMP: 150
SQ FT: 7,500
SALES (est): 14MM **Privately Held**
WEB: www.pswsi.com
SIC: 1771 Concrete work

(P-3196)
PACIFIC STRUCTURES INC (PA)
457 Minna St, San Francisco (94103-2914)
PHONE..............................415 970-5434
Ross Edwards, *Ch of Bd*
David E Williams, *President*
Ron Marano, *CFO*
Eric Horn, *Treasurer*
Kris Fahrion, *Vice Pres*

EMP: 249
SALES: 275.7MM **Privately Held**
SIC: **1771** Concrete work

(P-3197)
**PACIFIC STRUCTURES CNSTR
INC**
101 State Pl Ste E, Escondido
(92029-1365)
P.O. Box 502648, San Diego (92150-2648)
PHONE....................740 480-4133
Michael Meier, *President*
L Chris Meier, *CFO*
Andrew Meier III, *Vice Pres*
EMP: 50
SQ FT: 2,500
SALES (est): 5.8MM **Privately Held**
SIC: **1771** Concrete work

(P-3198)
PECK & HILLER COMPANY
870 Napa Valley Corp Way, NAPA (94558)
PHONE....................707 258-8800
Russell B Peck, *Principal*
Ben Kerr, *Vice Pres*
Tom H O'Connor, *Vice Pres*
Cindy Joy Westerberg, *Controller*
Axel Heredia, *Superintendent*
EMP: 100
SQ FT: 8,680
SALES (est): 22.4MM **Privately Held**
WEB: www.peckandhiller.com
SIC: **1771** Foundation & footing contractor

(P-3199)
PENHALL COMPANY
Also Called: Penhall San Leandro 153
13750 Catalina St, San Leandro
(94577-5502)
PHONE....................510 357-8810
Scott Hustad, *Manager*
EMP: 60
SALES (corp-wide): 1.6B **Privately Held**
SIC: **1771** Concrete work
HQ: Penhall Company
7501 Esters Blvd Ste 150
Irving TX 75063

(P-3200)
PERRY FLOOR SYSTEMS INC
963 Seaboard Ct, Upland (91786-4572)
PHONE....................909 949-1211
Brian Perry, *President*
Angela Perry, *Vice Pres*
EMP: 65
SQ FT: 6,000
SALES (est): 6.8MM **Privately Held**
SIC: **1771** Flooring contractor

(P-3201)
**PETERSON BROS
CONTRUCTION INC**
Also Called: Pbc Companies
1560 W Lambert Rd, Brea (92821-2826)
PHONE....................714 278-0488
Elden Peterson, *CEO*
Robert K Peterson, *Ch of Bd*
Patrick Burns, *CFO*
Mike Hoefnagels, *Vice Pres*
Jack Saldate, *Vice Pres*
▲ EMP: 600
SQ FT: 24,000
SALES (est): 50.5MM **Privately Held**
SIC: **1771** 3531 1741 Concrete work;
pavers; concrete block masonry laying

(P-3202)
POWERHOUSE BUILDING INC
4320 Redwood Hwy Ste 200, San Rafael
(94903-2151)
PHONE....................415 446-0188
David Hynes, *President*
Philip Hynes, *Vice Pres*
EMP: 60
SQ FT: 1,200
SALES (est): 5.3MM **Privately Held**
SIC: **1771** 1522 Concrete work; residential
construction

(P-3203)
PRESTIGE CONCRETE
13507 Midland Rd, Poway (92064-4711)
PHONE....................858 679-2772
Jerry Green, *President*
EMP: 60

SALES (est): 7.2MM **Privately Held**
SIC: **1771** Concrete work

(P-3204)
**R & R MAHER CONSTRUCTION
CO**
1324 Lemon St, Vallejo (94590-7250)
PHONE....................707 552-0330
Brad Maher, *President*
Bradley V Maher, *Vice Pres*
Bradley Maher, *Vice Pres*
Doug Maher, *Vice Pres*
Richard D Maher, *Vice Pres*
EMP: 50 EST: 1970
SQ FT: 1,600
SALES (est): 6.7MM **Privately Held**
SIC: **1771** Concrete work

(P-3205)
R E MAHER INC
4545 Hess Rd, American Canyon
(94503-9727)
PHONE....................707 642-3907
Rod E Maher, *CEO*
Rod Maher, *Executive*
Linda Green, *Controller*
EMP: 95
SQ FT: 1,000
SALES: 22MM **Privately Held**
SIC: **1771** Foundation & footing contractor

(P-3206)
RESCUE CONCRETE INC
9275 Beatty Dr, Sacramento (95826-9702)
P.O. Box 276812 (95827-6812)
PHONE....................916 852-2400
David Winn, *President*
EMP: 60 EST: 1995
SALES (est): 4MM **Privately Held**
WEB: www.rescueconcrete.com
SIC: **1771** Concrete work

(P-3207)
REY CON CONSTRUCTION INC
1795 E Lemonwood Dr, Santa Paula
(93060-9651)
P.O. Box 910 (93061-0910)
PHONE....................805 525-8134
Paul Reyes, *President*
Robert Reyes, *Treasurer*
Augie Reyes, *Vice Pres*
Chris Urrea, *Admin Sec*
EMP: 150
SQ FT: 5,000
SALES (est): 16.4MM **Privately Held**
SIC: **1771** 1741 1751 Sidewalk contrac-
tor; masonry & other stonework; framing
contractor

(P-3208)
RJS & ASSOCIATES INC
1675 Sabre St, Hayward (94545-1013)
PHONE....................510 670-9111
Robert J Simmons, *President*
EMP: 225
SQ FT: 10,000
SALES (est): 29.5MM **Privately Held**
SIC: **1771** 1521 Foundation & footing con-
tractor; single-family housing construction

(P-3209)
ROBERT A BOTHMAN INC (PA)
Also Called: B & B Concrete
2690 Scott Blvd, Santa Clara (95050-2511)
PHONE....................408 279-2277
Robert A Bothman, *CEO*
Saeed Yousuf, *COO*
Andy Bothman, *Vice Pres*
Brian Bothman, *Vice Pres*
Jim Brogoitti, *Vice Pres*
EMP: 118 EST: 1978
SQ FT: 20,000
SALES (est): 38.8MM **Privately Held**
WEB: www.bothman.com
SIC: **1771** 0782 Concrete work; landscape
contractors

(P-3210)
RON NURSS INC
Also Called: Blueline Construction
11290 Sunrise Park Dr B, Rancho Cordova
(95742-6895)
PHONE....................916 631-9761
Ron Nurss, *President*
Darcy Nurss, *Admin Sec*
EMP: 65

SQ FT: 6,400
SALES (est): 5.3MM **Privately Held**
WEB: www.blueline-construction.com
SIC: **1771** Concrete work

(P-3211)
**SACRAMENTO PRESTIGE
GUNITE INC**
8634 Antelope North Rd, Antelope
(95843-3930)
PHONE....................916 723-0404
George Wagner, *President*
EMP: 50
SQ FT: 1,100
SALES (est): 3.7MM **Privately Held**
WEB: www.sacgunite.com
SIC: **1771** Gunite contractor
HQ: Vcna Prestige Gunite Inc
8529 Suthpark Cir Ste 320
Orlando FL 32819
407 802-3540

(P-3212)
SANTA CLARITA CONCRETE
16164 Sierra Hwy, Santa Clarita
(91390-4733)
PHONE....................661 252-2012
Wayne Crawford, *President*
Keith Crawford, *Vice Pres*
Eric Stoh, *Vice Pres*
Curtis Marzinzik, *Project Mgr*
EMP: 50
SQ FT: 5,000
SALES (est): 7.7MM **Privately Held**
SIC: **1771** Foundation & footing contractor

(P-3213)
SANTANA CONCRETE
4253 Fairgrounds St, Riverside
(92501-1771)
PHONE....................909 421-2218
Jesse Santana, *Owner*
EMP: 60
SALES (est): 4.6MM **Privately Held**
SIC: **1771** Concrete work

(P-3214)
SCI INC
18501 Collier Ave B106, Lake Elsinore
(92530-2764)
PHONE....................951 245-7511
Mark A Dix, *President*
Mark Dix, *Manager*
EMP: 65
SQ FT: 3,000
SALES: 13MM **Privately Held**
WEB: www.tiltupsbysci.com
SIC: **1771** Concrete work

(P-3215)
SCOTT SILVA CONCRETE INC
11374 Gold Dredge Way, Rancho Cordova
(95742)
PHONE....................916 859-0593
Scott Silva, *President*
EMP: 100
SALES (est): 3.6MM **Privately Held**
SIC: **1771** Concrete work

(P-3216)
SERVICON SYSTEMS INC
3329 Jack Northrop Ave, Hawthorne
(90250-4426)
PHONE....................310 970-0700
Julio E Ramirez, *Branch Mgr*
Tate Rick, *Vice Pres*
Stephanie Mejia, *Human Resources*
EMP: 1472
SALES (corp-wide): 98.4MM **Privately
Held**
SIC: **1771** Flooring contractor
PA: Servicon Systems, Inc.
3965 Landmark St
Culver City CA 90232
310 204-5040

(P-3217)
SIMPLE LUXURIES LLC
1560 N Sycamore Ave, Rialto
(92376-3666)
PHONE....................310 627-6514
Heather Tiger,
EMP: 50

SALES (est): 1.7MM **Privately Held**
SIC: **1771** 7389 8712 Exterior concrete
stucco contractor; interior design services; house designer

(P-3218)
SINCLAIR CONCRETE
7205 Church St, Penryn (95663-9411)
PHONE....................916 663-0303
Keith Sinclair, *Admin Sec*
Karin Sinclair, *CFO*
EMP: 85
SALES (est): 7.6MM **Privately Held**
SIC: **1771** Foundation & footing contractor

(P-3219)
**SOUTH COAST CONCRETE
CNSTR**
6770 Central Ave Ste B, Riverside
(92504-1443)
PHONE....................951 351-7777
Monica Perry, *President*
Bob Perry, *CFO*
Pedro Rico, *Vice Pres*
EMP: 50
SQ FT: 14,000
SALES (est): 8.7MM **Privately Held**
SIC: **1771** Concrete work

(P-3220)
SOUTHLAND PAVING INC
361 N Hale Ave, Escondido (92029-1798)
PHONE....................760 747-6895
Richard Fleck, *CEO*
Anne Fleck, *Treasurer*
Daniel Devlin, *Vice Pres*
Bob Kennedy, *Vice Pres*
Robert Kennedy, *Vice Pres*
EMP: 75
SQ FT: 35,000
SALES (est): 15.9MM **Privately Held**
WEB: www.southlandpaving.com
SIC: **1771** 2951 Blacktop (asphalt) work;
asphalt paving mixtures & blocks; asphalt
paving blocks (not from refineries)

(P-3221)
**SOUTHWEST CONSTRUCTION
CO INC**
2909 Rainbow Valley Blvd, Fallbrook
(92028-8859)
PHONE....................760 728-4460
David Simon, *President*
Lorie Simon, *Vice Pres*
Paul Simon, *Admin Sec*
EMP: 60
SQ FT: 5,000
SALES (est): 8.5MM **Privately Held**
SIC: **1771** Concrete work

(P-3222)
**STEFAN MERLI PLASTERING CO
INC (PA)**
Also Called: Merli Concrete Pumping
1230 W 130th St, Gardena (90247-1502)
PHONE....................310 323-0404
Stefan R Merli, *President*
Adele Merli, *Treasurer*
Gunther Merli, *Admin Sec*
EMP: 63
SQ FT: 5,000
SALES (est): 19.7MM **Privately Held**
SIC: **1771** Concrete pumping

(P-3223)
STEVE DUICH INC
Also Called: H & D Construction
1369 N Magnolia Ave, El Cajon
(92020-1619)
P.O. Box 12859 (92022-2859)
PHONE....................619 444-6118
Steve Duich, *President*
Joyce Duich, *Vice Pres*
Ginger Poutous, *Administration*
EMP: 50
SQ FT: 3,700
SALES (est): 6.3MM **Privately Held**
SIC: **1771** Sidewalk contractor

(P-3224)
STRUCTURES WEST INC
300 W Grand Ave Ste 201, Escondido
(92025-2617)
PHONE....................760 737-2349
Jeff Steele, *President*

Robert Davidson, *CFO*
EMP: 100
SALES (est): 6.9MM **Privately Held**
SIC: 1771 Concrete work

(P-3225)
SUPERIOR GUNITE (PA)
12306 Van Nuys Blvd, Sylmar
(91342-6086)
PHONE..........................818 896-9199
Anthony L Federico, *President*
Steve Crawford, *Vice Pres*
David Bowers, *Admin Sec*
Gene McKay, *Info Tech Mgr*
Michael Ricci, *Project Engr*
EMP: 145
SQ FT: 5,000
SALES (est): 37.3MM **Privately Held**
WEB: www.shotcrete.com
SIC: 1771 Gunite contractor

(P-3226)
SURE FORMING SYSTEMS INC
10602 Humbolt St, Los Alamitos
(90720-2448)
PHONE..........................562 598-6348
Samuel F Shon, *President*
Wanda L Shon, *Corp Secy*
EMP: 50
SQ FT: 6,200
SALES (est): 5.8MM **Privately Held**
SIC: 1771 Concrete work

(P-3227)
TEAM FINISH INC
155 Arovista Cir Ste A, Brea (92821-3842)
PHONE..........................714 671-9190
Thomas M Stangl, *President*
Mary Stangl, *CFO*
EMP: 80
SQ FT: 1,200
SALES (est): 12.6MM **Privately Held**
WEB: www.teamvelocity.org
SIC: 1771 Concrete work

(P-3228)
TERRY TUELL CONCRETE INC
287 W Fallbrook Ave # 105, Fresno
(93711-5805)
P.O. Box 3933 (93650-3933)
PHONE..........................559 431-0812
Terry Tuell, *President*
Matthew Tuell, *Treasurer*
EMP: 90
SQ FT: 3,000
SALES (est): 9MM **Privately Held**
SIC: 1771 Concrete work

(P-3229)
TRADEMARK CONCRETE SYSTEMS (PA)
4015 Via Pescador, Camarillo
(93012-5050)
PHONE..........................714 970-8200
Lance A Boyer, *President*
Carlos Rodriguez, *Shareholder*
Arthur Rodriguez, *Admin Sec*
EMP: 50
SQ FT: 6,000
SALES (est): 10.2MM **Privately Held**
SIC: 1771 Concrete pumping

(P-3230)
UNITED BROTHERS CONCRETE INC
41905 Boardwalk Ste K, Palm Desert
(92211-9091)
PHONE..........................760 346-1013
Lauro Barcenas, *President*
Oscar Barcenas, *Treasurer*
Luis Barcenas, *Vice Pres*
EMP: 150 EST: 1999
SQ FT: 2,000
SALES (est): 16.6MM **Privately Held**
SIC: 1771 Concrete work

(P-3231)
URATA & SONS CONCRETE INC
3430 Luyung Dr, Rancho Cordova
(95742-6871)
PHONE..........................916 638-5364
Charles Urata, *President*
Darrell Dwyer, *CFO*
Kelly Urata, *Corp Secy*
John Bell, *Vice Pres*
John Enriquez, *Superintendent*

EMP: 125
SQ FT: 10,000
SALES: 71MM **Privately Held**
WEB: www.urataconcrete.com
SIC: 1771 Foundation & footing contractor

(P-3232)
URATA & SONS CONCRETE LLC
3430 Luyung Dr, Rancho Cordova
(95742-6871)
PHONE..........................916 638-5364
Charles A Urata, *Mng Member*
EMP: 99
SALES (est): 4.2MM **Privately Held**
SIC: 1771 Concrete work

(P-3233)
VALENCIA BROS INC
Also Called: Valencia Brothers Concrete
257 Maple Ave, El Centro (92243-3311)
PHONE..........................760 353-2168
EMP: 80 EST: 2000
SQ FT: 1,700
SALES (est): 4.4MM **Privately Held**
SIC: 1771

(P-3234)
VALENTE CONCRETE
255 Benjamin Dr, Corona (92879-6509)
PHONE..........................951 279-2221
Matthew R Valente, *President*
EMP: 70
SQ FT: 3,600
SALES (est): 5.2MM **Privately Held**
WEB: www.valenteconcrete.com
SIC: 1771 Foundation & footing contractor

(P-3235)
VALLEY PACIFIC CONCRETE INC
27580 Tabb Ln, Menifee (92584-9521)
PHONE..........................951 672-6151
Chris Russo, *President*
Kristi Russo, *Vice Pres*
EMP: 110
SQ FT: 1,500
SALES (est): 11MM **Privately Held**
WEB: www.vpconcrete.com
SIC: 1771 Concrete work

(P-3236)
WAGNER CONSTRUCTION CO (PA)
12512 Ca 67, Lakeside (92040)
PHONE..........................619 873-2160
Lee James Wagner, *President*
Ed Brelling, *Vice Pres*
Suzanne Wagner, *Buyer*
EMP: 125 EST: 1974
SQ FT: 5,000
SALES (est): 7.3MM **Privately Held**
SIC: 1771 Foundation & footing contractor

(P-3237)
WAYNE E SWISHER CEM CONTR INC
2620 E 18th St, Antioch (94509-7229)
PHONE..........................925 757-3660
Wayne Swisher, *President*
Elma Swisher, *Vice Pres*
EMP: 75
SQ FT: 4,000
SALES (est): 12.5MM **Privately Held**
SIC: 1771 Foundation & footing contractor

(P-3238)
WESTERN CONCRETE PUMPING INC (PA)
2181 La Mirada Dr, Vista (92081-8830)
PHONE..........................760 598-7855
Charles D Reed, *President*
Brett Reid, *CFO*
Judy Reid, *Vice Pres*
EMP: 55
SQ FT: 5,000
SALES (est): 39.9MM **Privately Held**
SIC: 1771 Concrete pumping

(P-3239)
WHITING CONSTRUCTION INC
Also Called: Whiting Concrete Construction
7281 Lone Pine Dr, Rancho Murieta
(95683-9715)
P.O. Box 887, Sloughhouse (95683-0887)
PHONE..........................916 354-2756

Tim Whiting, *President*
Sarah Hallam, *Manager*
EMP: 55
SALES (est): 5.2MM **Privately Held**
WEB: www.whitingcc.com
SIC: 1771 Concrete work

(P-3240)
Z-BEST CONCRETE INC
2575 Main St, Riverside (92501-2238)
PHONE..........................951 774-1870
Roger Crott, *President*
Jerry Faust, *Vice Pres*
EMP: 80
SQ FT: 2,400
SALES (est): 13.7MM **Privately Held**
SIC: 1771 1741 Concrete work; masonry & other stonework

1781 Water Well Drilling

(P-3241)
BEKS ACQUISITION INC
Also Called: Bc2 Environmental
1150 W Trenton Ave, Orange (92867-3536)
PHONE..........................714 744-2990
Kurt Samuelson, *President*
EMP: 50
SALES (est): 3.8MM **Privately Held**
SIC: 1781 Water well drilling

(P-3242)
GREGG DRILLING LLC (PA)
2726 Walnut Ave, Signal Hill (90755-1832)
PHONE..........................562 427-6899
John Gregg, *President*
Chris Christensen, *Vice Pres*
Patrick Keating, *Vice Pres*
Sonja De Keyser-Meurs, *Admin Sec*
Stacey Fuller, *Admin Asst*
EMP: 77
SQ FT: 17,000
SALES: 8MM **Privately Held**
SIC: 1781 Water well drilling

(P-3243)
GREGG DRILLING LLC
950 Howe Rd, Martinez (94553-3444)
PHONE..........................925 313-5800
EMP: 83
SALES (corp-wide): 8MM **Privately Held**
SIC: 1781 Water well drilling
PA: Gregg Drilling, Llc
2726 Walnut Ave
Signal Hill CA 90755
562 427-6899

(P-3244)
GREGG DRILLING & TESTING INC
Also Called: Gregg Dilling and Testing
950 Howe Rd, Martinez (94553-3444)
PHONE..........................925 313-5800
Chris Christensen, *Branch Mgr*
EMP: 61
SALES (corp-wide): 43.1MM **Privately Held**
WEB: www.greggdrilling.com
SIC: 1781 Water well drilling
PA: Gregg Drilling & Testing, Inc.
2726 Walnut Ave
Signal Hill CA 90755
562 427-6899

(P-3245)
MAGGIORA BROS DRILLING INC (PA)
595 Airport Blvd, Watsonville (95076-2094)
PHONE..........................831 724-1338
David T Maggiora, *CEO*
Mark Maggiora, *Treasurer*
Joanne Maggiora, *Vice Pres*
Michael Maggiora, *Admin Sec*
EMP: 70
SQ FT: 5,000
SALES (est): 13.4MM **Privately Held**
SIC: 1781 1711 Water well drilling; plumbing contractors

(P-3246)
YELLOW JACKET DRLG SVCS LLC
9460 Lucas Ranch Rd, Rancho Cucamonga (91730-5743)
PHONE..........................909 989-8563
Richard Leblenc,
EMP: 51
SALES (corp-wide): 21.4MM **Privately Held**
SIC: 1781 Water well drilling
PA: Yellow Jacket Drilling Services, Llc
3445 E Illini St
Phoenix AZ 85040
602 453-3252

(P-3247)
ZIM INDUSTRIES INC
Bakersfield Well & Pump Co
7212 Fruitvale Ave, Bakersfield
(93308-9529)
PHONE..........................661 393-9661
John Zimmerer, *Manager*
EMP: 90
SALES (corp-wide): 63.8MM **Privately Held**
SIC: 1781 7699 Water well servicing; pumps & pumping equipment repair
PA: Zim Industries, Inc.
4532 E Jefferson Ave
Fresno CA 93725
559 834-1551

1791 Structural Steel Erection

(P-3248)
A&M RINFORCING SPECIALISTS INC
10520 Kenney St Ste A, Santee
(92071-4507)
PHONE..........................619 334-6608
Chad Minshew, *President*
Kevin Ardent, *Vice Pres*
Mary Ardent, *Manager*
EMP: 50
SQ FT: 1,200
SALES: 8MM **Privately Held**
SIC: 1791 Concrete reinforcement, placing of

(P-3249)
ALLIED STEEL CO INC
1027 Palmyrita Ave, Riverside
(92507-1701)
PHONE..........................951 241-7000
Brian P Chapman, *President*
Nicky Chapman, *Treasurer*
Perry K Chapman, *Vice Pres*
Gary Chapman, *General Mgr*
Jeanette Chapman, *Admin Sec*
EMP: 60
SQ FT: 48,000
SALES (est): 15.9MM **Privately Held**
WEB: www.alliedsteelco.com
SIC: 1791 3441 Structural steel erection; fabricated structural metal

(P-3250)
ANDERSON CHRNESKY STRL STL INC
Also Called: Acss
353 Risco Cir, Beaumont (92223-2676)
PHONE..........................951 769-5700
Kevin Charneskey, *President*
Kevin Charnesky, *President*
EMP: 72
SQ FT: 6,600
SALES (est): 21.6MM **Privately Held**
SIC: 1791 Structural steel erection

(P-3251)
ANVIL STEEL CORPORATION
Also Called: Anvil Iron
134 W 168th St, Gardena (90248-2729)
PHONE..........................310 329-5811
Gerry Bustrum, *CEO*
Paul Schifino, *President*
Mike Norton, *Vice Pres*
Flores Jazmin, *Administration*
Chilito Ramirez, *Project Mgr*
▲ **EMP:** 90
SQ FT: 4,000

SALES (est): 25.1MM **Privately Held**
WEB: www.anvilsteel.com
SIC: 1791 Iron work, structural

(P-3252)
ARTIMEX IRON COMPANY INC
315 Cypress Ln, El Cajon (92020-1695)
PHONE..................................619 444-3155
EMP: 116
SQ FT: 4,000
SALES (est): 14.3MM **Privately Held**
WEB: www.artimexiron.com
SIC: 1791 Iron work, structural

(P-3253)
BAJA CONSTRUCTION CO INC (PA)
223 Foster St, Martinez (94553-1029)
P.O. Box 3080 (94553-8080)
PHONE..................................925 229-0732
Robert Hayworth, *Chairman*
Laura Daum, *President*
Brandon Morford, *CEO*
Robert J Hayworth, *Chairman*
Luis Fabian, *Vice Pres*
EMP: 90
SQ FT: 7,200
SALES (est): 26MM **Privately Held**
SIC: 1791 Structural steel erection

(P-3254)
BAPKO METAL INC
180 S Anita Dr, Orange (92868-3306)
PHONE..................................714 639-9380
Fred Bagatourian, *President*
Clint Rieber, *CFO*
Heather Wiliams, *Admin Sec*
EMP: 80
SQ FT: 4,000
SALES (est): 28.9MM **Privately Held**
WEB: www.bapko.com
SIC: 1791 3441 Structural steel erection;
fabricated structural metal

(P-3255)
BELLIS STEEL COMPANY INC (PA)
8740 Vanalden Ave, Northridge
(91324-3691)
PHONE..................................818 886-5601
Theron Arthur Ghrist, *CEO*
Gail R Ghrist, *Vice Pres*
Alan Miley, *General Mgr*
Veronica Salazar, *Controller*
Andrea Cervantes, *HR Admin*
EMP: 52 **EST:** 1961
SQ FT: 2,500
SALES (est): 16MM **Privately Held**
WEB: www.bellissteel.com
SIC: 1791 5051 Concrete reinforcement,
placing of; iron & steel (ferrous) products

(P-3256)
C M C STEEL FABRICATORS INC
Also Called: Fontana Steel
12451 Arrow Rte, Etiwanda (91739-9601)
P.O. Box 2219, Rancho Cucamonga
(91729-2219)
PHONE..................................909 899-9993
Deborah Marshall, *Manager*
EMP: 200
SQ FT: 70,348
SALES (corp-wide): 5.8B **Publicly Held**
WEB: www.cmcsg.com
SIC: 1791 3441 3496 Concrete reinforce-
ment, placing of; fabricated structural
metal; miscellaneous fabricated wire
products
HQ: C M C Steel Fabricators, Inc.
1 Steel Mill Dr
Seguin TX 78155
830 372-8200

(P-3257)
C M C STEEL FABRICATORS INC
Also Called: CMC Rebar Fabricators
2755 S Willow Ave, Bloomington
(92316-3260)
PHONE..................................909 873-3060
Keith Dixon, *Branch Mgr*
EMP: 75
SQ FT: 45,032

SALES (corp-wide): 5.8B **Publicly Held**
WEB: www.cmcsg.com
SIC: 1791 Iron work, structural
HQ: C M C Steel Fabricators, Inc.
1 Steel Mill Dr
Seguin TX 78155
830 372-8200

(P-3258)
CAL-STATE STEEL CORPORATION
1801 W Compton Blvd, Compton
(90220-2758)
P.O. Box 572034, Tarzana (91357-2034)
PHONE..................................310 632-2772
Salvador Valenzuelam, *CEO*
Dave Olson, *COO*
Les Furdek, *CFO*
David Olson, *Corp Secy*
Jack Furdek, *Project Dir*
▲ **EMP:** 150 **EST:** 1963
SQ FT: 10,000
SALES (est): 20.1MM **Privately Held**
WEB: www.calstatesteel.com
SIC: 1791 Iron work, structural

(P-3259)
CALIFRNIA ERCTORS BAY AREA INC
4500 California Ct, Benicia (94510-1021)
PHONE..................................707 746-1990
David W McEuen, *CEO*
Dennis Mc Euen, *Ch of Bd*
Galen Jaeger, *Vice Pres*
Robert McEuen, *Foreman/Supr*
EMP: 150
SQ FT: 16,000
SALES (est): 19.5MM **Privately Held**
WEB: www.calerectors.com
SIC: 1791 Iron work, structural; concrete
reinforcement, placing of

(P-3260)
CENTRAL REINFORCING CORP
14166 Slover Ave, Fontana (92337-7162)
P.O. Box 4967, San Dimas (91773-8967)
PHONE..................................909 773-0840
Eugene E Gutierrez, *President*
Patricia Cipriano, *CFO*
EMP: 60
SQ FT: 8,000
SALES: 6MM **Privately Held**
SIC: 1791 Concrete reinforcement, placing

(P-3261)
COAST IRON & STEEL CO
12300 Lakeland Rd, Santa Fe Springs
(90670-3869)
P.O. Box 2846 (90670-0846)
PHONE..................................562 946-4421
Greg White, *President*
Cyndi White Cramer, *Shareholder*
Carrie White, *Shareholder*
Jared White, *Shareholder*
Ronald G White, *CEO*
▲ **EMP:** 50 **EST:** 1953
SQ FT: 360,000
SALES (est): 11.4MM **Privately Held**
WEB: www.indiainfoline.com
SIC: 1791 3441 Structural steel erection;
fabricated structural metal

(P-3262)
COMMERCIAL METALS COMPANY
12451 Arrow Rte, Rancho Cucamonga
(91739-9601)
PHONE..................................909 899-9993
Paul D Ware, *Branch Mgr*
Kevin Soli, *Superintendent*
▲ **EMP:** 300
SALES (corp-wide): 5.8B **Publicly Held**
SIC: 1791 Concrete reinforcement, placing
of
PA: Commercial Metals Company
6565 N Macarthur Blvd # 800
Irving TX 75039
214 689-4300

(P-3263)
HARRIS REBAR NORTHERN CAL INC
355 S Vasco Rd, Livermore (94550-5300)
PHONE..................................925 373-0733

Tyler Keith, *President*
Connie Caisse, *CFO*
Brady Buckley, *Vice Pres*
Ed Mize, *Vice Pres*
Lyle Sieg, *Vice Pres*
▲ **EMP:** 250
SQ FT: 4,000
SALES (est): 41.8MM **Privately Held**
SIC: 1791 Structural steel erection

(P-3264)
INTEGRITY REBAR PLACERS
1345 Nandina Ave, Perris (92571-9402)
PHONE..................................951 696-6843
Kenneth Negrete, *President*
Richard Rabay, *Vice Pres*
Jay Ferguson, *Technology*
▲ **EMP:** 200
SALES (est): 29.5MM **Privately Held**
SIC: 1791 Structural steel erection

(P-3265)
IWORKS US INC
2501 S Malt Ave, Commerce (90040-3203)
PHONE..................................323 278-8363
Eric Dortch, *CEO*
▲ **EMP:** 53
SQ FT: 35,000
SALES (est): 10.1MM **Privately Held**
WEB: www.interironworks.com
SIC: 1791 Iron work, structural

(P-3266)
JS REAL ESTATE PRPTS INC
134 W 168th St, Gardena (90248-2729)
PHONE..................................310 856-6868
Gerry A Bustrum, *CEO*
Paul Schisino, *President*
EMP: 85
SQ FT: 4,000
SALES (est): 7.9MM **Privately Held**
WEB: www.juniorsteel.com
SIC: 1791 Structural steel erection

(P-3267)
KCB TOWERS INC
27260 Meines St, Highland (92346-4223)
P.O. Box 100 (92346-0100)
PHONE..................................909 862-0322
S Lynn Bogh, *CEO*
Sharon Bogh, *Corp Secy*
Miles Bogh, *Vice Pres*
EMP: 100
SQ FT: 12,000
SALES (est): 18.2MM **Privately Held**
WEB: www.kcbtowers.com
SIC: 1791 3441 Concrete reinforcement,
placing of; fabricated structural metal

(P-3268)
KWAN WO IRONWORKS INC
31628 Hayman St, Hayward (94544-7122)
PHONE..................................415 822-9628
Florence Kong, *President*
Ada Tang, *Office Mgr*
Fay Chu, *Admin Asst*
▲ **EMP:** 120
SQ FT: 32,000
SALES (est): 37.1MM **Privately Held**
SIC: 1791 Iron work, structural

(P-3269)
LA STEEL SERVICES INC
1760 California Ave # 201, Corona
(92881-3396)
PHONE..................................951 393-2013
Pamela L Albright, *CEO*
Lee Albright, *President*
Richard Rabay, *Vice Pres*
Pamela Albright, *General Mgr*
EMP: 50
SALES (est): 1.7MM **Privately Held**
SIC: 1791 Structural steel erection

(P-3270)
LONG SWIMMING POOL STEEL INC
3920 E Coronado St # 205, Anaheim
(92807-1623)
PHONE..................................714 524-8172
Larry E Long, *President*
EMP: 50 **EST:** 1971
SQ FT: 15,000

SALES (est): 6.3MM **Privately Held**
WEB: www.lspsinc.com
SIC: 1791 Concrete reinforcement, placing

(P-3271)
M BAR C CONSTRUCTION INC
1770 La Costa Meadows Dr, San Marcos
(92078-5106)
PHONE..................................760 744-4131
Jason Ianni, *CEO*
EMP: 85
SALES (est): 45.3MM **Privately Held**
WEB: www.mbarcconstruction.com
SIC: 1791 1623 Structural steel erection;
electric power line construction

(P-3272)
MCINTYRE COMPANY (PA)
2817 E Cedar St Ste 200, Ontario
(91761-8568)
PHONE..................................909 962-6322
Roger Mc Intyre, *President*
Scott Mc Intyre, *Vice Pres*
EMP: 60
SQ FT: 10,000
SALES (est): 9.3MM **Privately Held**
WEB: www.justdeckit.com
SIC: 1791 Structural steel erection

(P-3273)
MECHANICAL INDUSTRIES INC
Also Called: M I I
314 Yampa St, Bakersfield (93307-2722)
PHONE..................................661 634-9477
Jerry L Nordine, *President*
Jerry Miranda, *Vice Pres*
Nicole Hernandez, *Administration*
Rick Martin, *Production*
EMP: 50
SQ FT: 43,000
SALES (est): 13MM **Privately Held**
SIC: 1791 Structural steel erection

(P-3274)
MID STATE STEEL ERECTION (PA)
1916 Cherokee Rd, Stockton (95205-2721)
PHONE..................................209 464-9497
Jerry Shipman, *President*
Patty Shipman, *Corp Secy*
Glenda Roe, *Technology*
EMP: 70 **EST:** 1978
SALES (est): 14.3MM **Privately Held**
SIC: 1791 Structural steel erection

(P-3275)
PACIFIC REBAR INC
501 S Oaks Ave, Ontario (91762-4020)
PHONE..................................909 984-7199
Tim Herwehe, *President*
EMP: 60
SQ FT: 3,000
SALES (est): 7.8MM **Privately Held**
SIC: 1791 Concrete reinforcement, placing
of

(P-3276)
PARCELL STEEL CORP (PA)
26365 Earthmover Cir, Corona
(92883-5270)
PHONE..................................951 471-3200
Terry L Parcell, *President*
Ron J Parcell Sr, *Vice Pres*
Kristen Parcell, *Admin Sec*
EMP: 140
SQ FT: 3,500
SALES (est): 17.9MM **Privately Held**
WEB: www.parcellsteel.com
SIC: 1791 Structural steel erection

(P-3277)
PASO ROBLES TANK INC (PA)
825 26th St, Paso Robles (93446-1242)
P.O. Box 3229 (93447-3229)
PHONE..................................805 227-1641
Shawn P Owens, *CEO*
Robert Caldwell, *Vice Pres*
Waldon Davis, *Vice Pres*
Renee Cook, *Principal*
▲ **EMP:** 63
SALES: 39.1MM **Privately Held**
WEB: www.pasaroblestank.com
SIC: 1791 3795 Storage tanks, metal:
erection; amphibian tanks, military

▲ = Import ▼=Export
◆ =Import/Export

(P-3278)
PJS LUMBER INC
Also Called: P.J.'s Rebar
250 D St, Turlock (95380-5431)
PHONE..........................209 850-9444
Shane McMillan, *Principal*
EMP: 60
SALES (est): 159.3K **Privately Held**
SIC: **1791** Structural steel erection

(P-3279)
QUALITY REINFORCING INC
13275 Gregg St, Poway (92064-7120)
PHONE..........................858 748-8400
Bryan Miller, *President*
▲ EMP: 85
SQ FT: 5,000
SALES (est): 11.2MM **Privately Held**
WEB: www.qualityreinforcing.com
SIC: **1791** Concrete reinforcement, placing of

(P-3280)
R & B REINFORCING STEEL CORP
13581 5th St, Chino (91710-5166)
PHONE..........................909 591-1726
David McDaniel, *CEO*
Robert Bessette, *President*
Dave McDaniel, *CFO*
Nancy Bessette, *Admin Sec*
EMP: 80
SQ FT: 30,000
SALES: 24MM **Privately Held**
SIC: **1791** Iron work, structural

(P-3281)
REBAR ENGINEERING INC
10706 Painter Ave, Santa Fe Springs (90670-4581)
P.O. Box 3986 (90670-1986)
PHONE..........................562 946-2461
Charles L Krebs, *President*
Jack Garroutte, *Exec VP*
EMP: 250
SQ FT: 6,500
SALES: 45MM **Privately Held**
WEB: www.rebareng.com
SIC: **1791** Concrete reinforcement, placing of

(P-3282)
RIKA CORPORATION
Also Called: Diversified Metal Works
332 W Brenna Ln, Orange (92867-5637)
PHONE..........................949 830-9050
John E Ferguson, *CEO*
Justin Ferguson, *Vice Pres*
Rick Ferguson, *Manager*
▲ EMP: 100 EST: 1977
SQ FT: 8,000
SALES: 15MM **Privately Held**
SIC: **1791** Structural steel erection

(P-3283)
SANTA CLARITA INTERIORS INC
25682 Springbrook Ave # 130, Santa Clarita (91350-2432)
PHONE..........................661 253-0861
Brian Schienle, *President*
Patty Schienle, *Treasurer*
EMP: 75
SQ FT: 10,000
SALES (est): 5.7MM **Privately Held**
SIC: **1791** 1742 Iron work, structural; drywall

(P-3284)
SCHUFF STEEL COMPANY
10100 Trinity Pkwy # 400, Stockton (95219-7240)
PHONE..........................209 938-0869
Chase Abbott, *Branch Mgr*
Rob McGregor, *Sales Staff*
EMP: 149 **Publicly Held**
SIC: **1791** 3441 Structural steel erection; fabricated structural metal
HQ: Schuff Steel Company
3003 N Central Ave # 700
Phoenix AZ 85012
602 252-7787

(P-3285)
SO-CAL STRL STL FBRICATION INC
130 S Spruce Ave, Rialto (92376-9005)
PHONE..........................909 877-1299
Craig B Yates, *CEO*
Kim Yates, *Vice Pres*
EMP: 50
SQ FT: 40,000
SALES (est): 9.3MM **Privately Held**
SIC: **1791** Structural steel erection

(P-3286)
T L FABRICATIONS LP
2921 E Coronado St, Anaheim (92806-2502)
PHONE..........................562 802-3980
Ryan Kerrigan, *President*
Vic O'Mara, *Exec VP*
Michael Hsu, *Vice Pres*
Jorge Hernandez, *Manager*
▲ EMP: 60
SQ FT: 30,000
SALES (est): 8.8MM **Privately Held**
WEB: www.tlfab.com
SIC: **1791** Structural steel erection

(P-3287)
TAP RAM REINFORCING INC
11658 Excelsior Dr, Norwalk (90650-5826)
PHONE..........................562 484-0859
Maria G Tapia, *President*
EMP: 80
SALES (est): 810.1K **Privately Held**
SIC: **1791** Smoke stacks, steel: installation & maintenance

(P-3288)
TEXTURE SPECIALTIES INC
295 Mccreary Ave, Hanford (93230-2032)
PHONE..........................559 904-6047
Robert Tarlton, *President*
Mollie Pusich, *Principal*
EMP: 50
SALES: 950K **Privately Held**
SIC: **1791** 1742 Metal lath & furring; plaster & drywall work

1793 Glass & Glazing Work

(P-3289)
ALCAL GLASS SYSTEMS INC
946 N Market Blvd, Sacramento (95834-1268)
PHONE..........................916 929-3100
Richard Bledsoe, *President*
EMP: 55 EST: 2017
SALES (est): 2.8MM
SALES (corp-wide): 1.5B **Privately Held**
SIC: **1793** Glass & glazing work
HQ: Pacific Coast Building Services, Inc.
946 N Market Blvd
Sacramento CA 95834

(P-3290)
BAGATELOS GLASS SYSTEMS INC (PA)
Also Called: Bagatlos Archtctral GL Systems
2750 Redding Ave, Sacramento (95820-2156)
PHONE..........................916 364-3600
Nick Bagatelos, *CEO*
Chris Bagatelos, *Admin Sec*
▲ EMP: 72 EST: 1999
SQ FT: 50,000
SALES (est): 21.6MM **Privately Held**
WEB: www.bagatelos.com
SIC: **1793** Glass & glazing work

(P-3291)
CENTER GLASS CO NO 3
7853 El Cajon Blvd, La Mesa (91942-0621)
P.O. Box 1088 (91944-1088)
PHONE..........................619 469-6181
Jackson R Witte, *Ch of Bd*
Donald Witte, *Shareholder*
Ronald A Leaverton, *President*
David C Lawrenz, *Vice Pres*
Paul Bailey, *Project Mgr*
EMP: 55 EST: 1963
SQ FT: 20,000
SALES: 13.7MM **Privately Held**
WEB: www.centerglass.com
SIC: **1793** Glass & glazing work

(P-3292)
DIVISION 8 INC
1920 Cordell Ct Ste 105, El Cajon (92020-0900)
PHONE..........................619 741-7552
Robert Hoyt, *President*
David W Vincent, *CFO*
Debra Hoyt, *Corp Secy*
Miguel Rodriguez, *Vice Pres*
Dawn K Vincent, *Director*
EMP: 50
SQ FT: 5,000
SALES: 4MM **Privately Held**
WEB: www.division8inc.com
SIC: **1793** Glass & glazing work

(P-3293)
GIROUX GLASS INC (PA)
850 W Wash Blvd Ste 200, Los Angeles (90015-3359)
PHONE..........................213 747-7406
Anne M Murrell, *Ch of Bd*
Blane Midkiff, *Partner*
Anne-Merelie Murrell, *Ch of Bd*
Nataline Lomedico, *CEO*
Stephanie Lamb, *COO*
▲ EMP: 120 EST: 1946
SALES: 25.2MM **Privately Held**
WEB: www.girouxglass.com
SIC: **1793** Glass & glazing work

(P-3294)
HABENICHT & HOWLETT A CORP
25 Patterson St, San Francisco (94124-1328)
PHONE..........................415 824-7040
Tom Bukard, *CEO*
EMP: 75
SALES (est): 2.4MM **Privately Held**
SIC: **1793** 5231 Glass & glazing work; glass

(P-3295)
PERFECTION GLASS INC
554 3rd St, Lake Elsinore (92530-2729)
PHONE..........................951 674-0240
Richard L Warren, *President*
Dane Warren, *Treasurer*
Chris Bonnet, *Admin Sec*
EMP: 50
SQ FT: 4,200
SALES (est): 7.7MM **Privately Held**
SIC: **1793** Glass & glazing work

(P-3296)
PROGRESS GLASS CO INC (PA)
25 Patterson St, San Francisco (94124-1377)
PHONE..........................415 824-7040
Tom Burkard, *CEO*
Chuck Burkard, *President*
Thomas C Burkard III, *President*
Shirley Wallace, *Treasurer*
Jim Holmberg, *Senior VP*
▲ EMP: 105 EST: 1956
SQ FT: 16,250
SALES (est): 25.3MM **Privately Held**
WEB: www.progressglass.com
SIC: **1793** Glass & glazing work

(P-3297)
ROYAL GLASS COMPANY INC
3200 De La Cruz Blvd, Santa Clara (95054-2602)
PHONE..........................408 969-0444
John Maggiore, *CEO*
James Maggiore, *Vice Pres*
▲ EMP: 80
SALES (est): 22.6MM **Privately Held**
SIC: **1793** Glass & glazing work

(P-3298)
SAFECO DOOR & HARDWARE INC
Also Called: Safeco Glass
31054 San Antonio St, Hayward (94544-7904)
PHONE..........................510 429-4768
Mahboubeh Ahmadi, *President*
Milagors Missaghi, *Treasurer*
Ali Missaghi Akoub, *Vice Pres*
Hamid Ahmadi, *Admin Sec*
Sina Ahmadi, *Controller*
EMP: 65
SQ FT: 13,000
SALES (est): 11.9MM **Privately Held**
SIC: **1793** Glass & glazing work

(P-3299)
TOWER GLASS INC
9570 Pathway St Ste A, Santee (92071-4100)
PHONE..........................619 596-6199
Evelyn Dee Swaim, *CEO*
Susan Johnson, *Office Mgr*
Julie McConnaughy, *Admin Asst*
Greg Gates, *Project Mgr*
Jeff Swaim, *VP Opers*
EMP: 100
SQ FT: 15,000
SALES (est): 22MM **Privately Held**
WEB: www.towerglass.com
SIC: **1793** Glass & glazing work

(P-3300)
WALTERS & WOLF GLASS COMPANY (PA)
Also Called: Walter & Wolf
41450 Boscell Rd, Fremont (94538-3103)
PHONE..........................510 490-1115
Randall A Wolf, *President*
Jeff Belzer, *CFO*
Nick Kocelj, *Vice Pres*
Tina Fugit, *Software Dev*
Tina Wade, *Software Dev*
▲ EMP: 135 EST: 1977
SALES (est): 104.1MM **Privately Held**
WEB: www.waltersandwolf.com
SIC: **1793** Glass & glazing work

(P-3301)
WOODBRIDGE GLASS INC
14321 Myford Rd, Tustin (92780-7022)
PHONE..........................714 838-4444
Virginia Siciliani, *President*
Jim Siciliani, *Corp Secy*
Jeff Siciliani, *Vice Pres*
John Siciliani, *Vice Pres*
Trent Zinn, *Info Tech Mgr*
▲ EMP: 205
SQ FT: 8,500
SALES (est): 90MM **Privately Held**
WEB: www.woodbridgeglass.com
SIC: **1793** 5231 Glass & glazing work; glass, leaded or stained

1794 Excavating & Grading Work

(P-3302)
A J EXCAVATION INC
Also Called: American Fencing
514 N Brawley Ave, Fresno (93706-1014)
PHONE..........................559 408-5908
Alisa Emmett, *President*
EMP: 150
SALES (est): 220K **Privately Held**
SIC: **1794** Excavation work

(P-3303)
ANDREW M JORDAN INC
Also Called: A & B Construction
1350 4th St, Berkeley (94710)
PHONE..........................510 999-6000
Andrew M Jordan, *President*
Antonio Mencarini, *Project Mgr*
EMP: 90
SQ FT: 1,000
SALES: 30MM **Privately Held**
WEB: www.a-bconstruction.net
SIC: **1794** Excavation & grading, building construction

(P-3304)
BAY CITIES PAV & GRADING INC
1450 Civic Ct Bldg B, Concord (94520-5295)
PHONE..........................925 687-6666
Ben L Rodriguez, *CEO*
Marlo Manqueros, *Vice Pres*
Kim Rodriguez, *Admin Sec*
Saul Gonzaga, *Project Engr*
Drake Roach, *Assistant*
EMP: 250
SQ FT: 4,000

SALES (est): 63.3MM **Privately Held**
SIC: **1794** 1611 7353 Excavation work; highway & street construction; earth moving equipment, rental or leasing

(P-3305)
CALEX ENGINEERING INC
23651 Pine St, Newhall (91321-3106)
PHONE..................661 254-1866
Kenny Seitz, *President*
Mike Neilson, *CEO*
EMP: 70
SQ FT: 1,800
SALES (est): 12.8MM **Privately Held**
SIC: **1794** Excavation work

(P-3306)
CARONE & COMPANY INC
Also Called: Diablo Valley Rock
5009 Forni Dr Ste A, Concord (94520-8525)
PHONE..................925 602-8800
Richard Lloyd Carone, *President*
EMP: 60
SQ FT: 48,000
SALES (est): 13.1MM **Privately Held**
SIC: **1794** Excavation work

(P-3307)
CHINO GRADING INC
3613 Philadelphia St, Chino (91710-2068)
PHONE..................909 364-8667
Norm Gorgone, *President*
EMP: 60
SALES (est): 4.9MM **Privately Held**
SIC: **1794** Excavation & grading, building construction

(P-3308)
COASTAL GRADING AND EXCAVATING
756 Calle Plano, Camarillo (93012-8555)
P.O. Box 2459, Moorpark (93020-2459)
PHONE..................805 445-6433
Thomas Staben Jr, *President*
EMP: 50
SALES (est): 4.7MM **Privately Held**
SIC: **1794** Excavation work

(P-3309)
COMMERCIAL SITE IMPRVS INC
192 Poker Flat Rd, Copperopolis (95228-9601)
PHONE..................209 785-1920
Kimberly Batch, *President*
Ron Batch, *Vice Pres*
EMP: 50
SALES (est): 1.4MM **Privately Held**
SIC: **1794** Excavation & grading, building construction

(P-3310)
CREW INC
19618 S Susana Rd, Compton (90221-5716)
PHONE..................310 608-6860
David M Lalonde, *President*
Darrin Lalonde, *Vice Pres*
Elisa Ra, *Asst Controller*
EMP: 60
SQ FT: 5,000
SALES (est): 14MM **Privately Held**
WEB: www.crew.net
SIC: **1794** Excavation & grading, building construction

(P-3311)
DAVE SPURR EXCAVATING INC
Also Called: Spurr Co.
935 Riverside Ave Ste 18, Paso Robles (93446-2649)
P.O. Box 1920 (93447-1920)
PHONE..................805 238-0834
David Spurr, *President*
EMP: 50
SQ FT: 1,000
SALES (est): 8MM **Privately Held**
SIC: **1794** Excavation & grading, building construction

(P-3312)
EMERALD SITE SERVICES INC
9883 Kent St, Elk Grove (95624-4009)
PHONE..................916 685-7211
Kaycie Edwards, *President*
Mark Edwards, *Treasurer*

Gordon Peters, *General Mgr*
Austin Edwards, *Admin Sec*
Dustin Lamantain, *Project Mgr*
EMP: 55
SALES: 9.5MM **Privately Held**
SIC: **1794** 1796 0782 Excavation & grading, building construction; pollution control equipment installation; garden maintenance services; turf installation services, except artificial; highway lawn & garden maintenance services

(P-3313)
FJ WILLERT CONTRACTING CO
1869 Nirvana Ave, Chula Vista (91911-6117)
PHONE..................619 421-1980
Fred M Willert, *President*
Nancy Walker, *Controller*
EMP: 110 EST: 1972
SQ FT: 11,748
SALES (est): 37.9MM **Privately Held**
WEB: www.fjwillert.com
SIC: **1794** Excavation & grading, building construction

(P-3314)
G AND L BROCK CNSTR CO INC
4145 Calloway Ct, Stockton (95215-2400)
PHONE..................209 931-3626
Lynne Brock, *President*
Gary Brock, *Vice Pres*
EMP: 50
SQ FT: 5,800
SALES (est): 9.6MM **Privately Held**
SIC: **1794** Excavation work

(P-3315)
GALLAGHER PROPERTIES INC (PA)
344 High St, Oakland (94601-3902)
P.O. Box 779, Lafayette (94549-0779)
PHONE..................510 261-0466
Allen McKeen, *Vice Pres*
Denise Barger, *Admin Sec*
EMP: 75
SQ FT: 20,000
SALES (est): 9.5MM **Privately Held**
SIC: **1794** 1611 2951 1771 Excavation & grading, building construction; highway & street construction; asphalt paving mixtures & blocks; concrete work

(P-3316)
GILLIAM & SONS INC
Also Called: Valco Construction
9831 Rosedale Hwy, Bakersfield (93312-2604)
P.O. Box 9955 (93389-1955)
PHONE..................661 589-0913
Bill W Gilliam, *CEO*
Scott Gilliam, *Vice Pres*
Ken Spiker, *Human Res Dir*
EMP: 50
SQ FT: 2,500
SALES (est): 10.2MM **Privately Held**
WEB: www.gilliamandsons.com
SIC: **1794** Excavation & grading, building construction

(P-3317)
GUINN CORPORATION
6533 Rosedale Hwy, Bakersfield (93308-5903)
P.O. Box 1339 (93302-1339)
PHONE..................661 325-6109
Gary Guinn, *CEO*
Jeff Affonso, *Corp Secy*
Tim Guinn, *Vice Pres*
EMP: 75
SQ FT: 3,600
SALES (est): 18MM **Privately Held**
WEB: www.guinnconstruction.com
SIC: **1794** Excavation & grading, building construction

(P-3318)
HOWARD CONTRACTING INC
12354 Carson St, Hawaiian Gardens (90716-1604)
PHONE..................562 596-2969
Frederick Stanley Howard, *CEO*
Viki R Howard, *Corp Secy*
Stanley L Howard, *Vice Pres*
Stanley Howard, *Vice Pres*
Denise Pontius, *Controller*

EMP: 50
SQ FT: 3,500
SALES (est): 9.2MM **Privately Held**
SIC: **1794** Excavation work

(P-3319)
INLAND EROSION CONTROL SVCS
42181 Avenida Alvarado A, Temecula (92590-3429)
P.O. Box 728, Murrieta (92564-0728)
PHONE..................951 301-8334
Todd Close, *President*
Carlos Garcia, *Vice Pres*
EMP: 59
SQ FT: 1,000
SALES (est): 7.4MM **Privately Held**
SIC: **1794** Excavation & grading, building construction

(P-3320)
JEFF CARPENTER INC
1380 W Oleander Ave, Perris (92571-7863)
PHONE..................951 657-5115
Jeff Carpenter, *President*
EMP: 60
SQ FT: 1,300
SALES (est): 10.1MM **Privately Held**
SIC: **1794** Excavation work

(P-3321)
LOVCO CONSTRUCTION INC
1300 E Burnett St, Signal Hill (90755-3512)
P.O. Box 90335, Long Beach (90809-0335)
PHONE..................562 595-1601
Terry C Lovingier, *President*
Katie Lovingier, *Treasurer*
Steve Barnett, *Vice Pres*
Matt Lovinger, *Vice Pres*
Terry Lovingier, *Vice Pres*
EMP: 125
SQ FT: 2,500
SALES (est): 33.5MM **Privately Held**
WEB: www.lovco.com
SIC: **1794** 1771 1611 Excavation & grading, building construction; concrete work; highway & street construction; general contractor, highway & street construction

(P-3322)
LUPTON EXCAVATION INC
8467 Florin Rd, Sacramento (95828-2512)
PHONE..................916 387-1104
Kenneth Lupton Jr, *President*
EMP: 75
SQ FT: 4,000
SALES (est): 9.9MM **Privately Held**
SIC: **1794** Excavation & grading, building construction

(P-3323)
MEYERS EARTHWORK INC
4150 Fig Tree Ln, Redding (96002-9315)
P.O. Box 493730 (96049-3730)
PHONE..................530 365-8858
Jacob Meyers, *President*
Charleen Meyers, *Vice Pres*
Charlene Meyers, *General Mgr*
▼ EMP: 55
SQ FT: 2,000
SALES (est): 10.2MM **Privately Held**
SIC: **1794** Excavation & grading, building construction

(P-3324)
MITCHELL ENGINEERING
1395 Evans Ave, San Francisco (94124-1703)
P.O. Box 880308 (94188-0308)
PHONE..................415 227-1040
Michael A Silva, *President*
Curtis F Mitchell, *Vice Pres*
Don Hart, *Project Mgr*
Thelma Welch, *Manager*
▲ EMP: 50
SQ FT: 2,000
SALES (est): 12MM **Privately Held**
WEB: www.mitchell-engineering.com
SIC: **1794** 1623 1622 1629 Excavation & grading, building construction; water main construction; pipeline construction; bridge, tunnel & elevated highway; railroad & subway construction

(P-3325)
MOZINGO CONSTRUCTION INC
751 Wakefield Ct, Oakdale (95361-7761)
PHONE..................209 848-0160
Kurtis Mozingo, *CEO*
Doni Mozingo, *President*
Michael Freeman, *Vice Pres*
Philip Gianfortone, *Vice Pres*
Nicole Davis, *Project Engr*
EMP: 50
SALES (est): 11.2MM **Privately Held**
SIC: **1794** Excavation work

(P-3326)
PACIFIC EXCAVATION INC
9796 Kent St, Elk Grove (95624-4823)
PHONE..................916 686-2800
Tim Paxin, *President*
Jim Paxin, *Vice Pres*
EMP: 75 EST: 2003
SQ FT: 30,000
SALES (est): 10.5MM **Privately Held**
WEB: www.pacexcavation.com
SIC: **1794** Excavation & grading, building construction

(P-3327)
PAPICH CONSTRUCTION CO INC (PA)
398 Sunrise Ter, Arroyo Grande (93420-4419)
P.O. Box 2210, Pismo Beach (93448-2210)
PHONE..................805 473-3016
Jason William Papich, *President*
April Papich, *Admin Sec*
Craig Caballero, *Project Mgr*
Nickie Zepeda, *Analyst*
EMP: 151
SQ FT: 6,000
SALES (est): 64.3MM **Privately Held**
WEB: www.papichconstruction.com
SIC: **1794** Excavation work

(P-3328)
REED THOMAS COMPANY INC
1025 N Santiago St, Santa Ana (92701-3800)
PHONE..................714 558-7691
Harvey T Biegle, *President*
Sam Matthews, *Info Tech Dir*
EMP: 90
SQ FT: 8,800
SALES (est): 13.2MM **Privately Held**
WEB: www.reedthomas.com
SIC: **1794** Excavation & grading, building construction

(P-3329)
STURGEON SON GRADING & PAV INC (PA)
3511 Gilmore Ave, Bakersfield (93308-6205)
P.O. Box 2840 (93303-2840)
PHONE..................661 322-4408
John E Powell, *CEO*
Paul Sturgeon, *President*
Jack Janszen, *Vice Pres*
Oliver Sturgeon, *Principal*
EMP: 180
SQ FT: 3,500
SALES (est): 51.5MM **Privately Held**
WEB: www.sturgeonandson.com
SIC: **1794** 8711 Excavation work; engineering services

(P-3330)
SUKUT CONSTRUCTION INC
4010 W Chandler Ave, Santa Ana (92704-5202)
PHONE..................714 540-5351
Michael H Crawford, *President*
Myron C Sukut, *Chairman*
Greg Leblanc, *Vice Pres*
Jerry Pabbruwee, *Vice Pres*
Robbie Zwick, *Vice Pres*
▲ EMP: 60
SQ FT: 12,000
SALES (est): 44.2MM **Privately Held**
WEB: www.sukut.com
SIC: **1794** 1611 1623 1629 Excavation & grading, building construction; general contractor, highway & street construction; water & sewer line construction; dams, waterways, docks & other marine construction

▲ = Import ▼=Export
◆ =Import/Export

(P-3331)
SWAN ENGINEERING INC
4470 Yankee Hill Rd # 200, Rocklin
(95677-1631)
PHONE...................916 474-5299
Justin Swanson, *President*
Brendin Swanson, *Superintendent*
EMP: 54 **EST:** 2010
SALES (est): 4MM **Privately Held**
WEB: www.swaneinc.com
SIC: 1794 1623 1611 Excavation & grading, building construction; water & sewer line construction; telephone & communication line construction; gravel or dirt road construction

(P-3332)
TIDWELL EXCAV ACQUISITION INC
1691 Los Angeles Ave, Ventura
(93004-3213)
PHONE...................805 647-4707
Alex Miruello, *President*
Louis Armona, *Treasurer*
Timothy Wayne Goodwin, *Vice Pres*
EMP: 90 **EST:** 1956
SALES (est): 12.4MM
SALES (corp-wide): 377.5MM **Privately Held**
SIC: 1794 Excavation & grading, building construction
PA: Meruelo Enterprises, Inc.
9550 Firestone Blvd # 105
Downey CA 90241
562 745-2300

(P-3333)
TIM PAXINS PACIFIC EXCAVATION
9796 Kent St, Elk Grove (95624-4823)
PHONE...................916 686-2800
Tim Paxin, *President*
EMP: 50
SQ FT: 2,500
SALES (est): 4.7MM **Privately Held**
SIC: 1794 Excavation & grading, building construction

(P-3334)
VANDER WEERD GENERAL CNSTR
837 Commercial Ave, Tulare (93274-7101)
PHONE...................559 688-1099
Ron A Vander Weerd, *President*
Rosalinda Vander Weerd, *Corp Secy*
EMP: 65
SQ FT: 10,000
SALES (est): 4MM **Privately Held**
SIC: 1794 Excavation & grading, building construction

1795 Wrecking & Demolition Work

(P-3335)
AMERICAN CONCRETE CUTTING INC
Also Called: American Dmlton/Concrete Cutng
620 N Poinsettia St, Santa Ana
(92701-3999)
PHONE...................714 547-7181
F Richard Stewart, *President*
John Moore, *Vice Pres*
EMP: 100
SALES (est): 8.8MM **Privately Held**
WEB: www.americandemo.com
SIC: 1795 Concrete breaking for streets & highways

(P-3336)
AMERICAN WRECKING INC
2459 Lee Ave, South El Monte
(91733-1407)
PHONE...................626 350-8303
Jose Luis Galaviz, *President*
Warne Galaviz, *Vice Pres*
Robert Hall, *Vice Pres*
EMP: 100
SQ FT: 1,000

SALES (est): 25.9MM **Privately Held**
WEB: www.americanwreckinginc.com
SIC: 1795 Demolition, buildings & other structures

(P-3337)
CAL EMPIRE ENGINEERING INC
628 E Edna Pl, Covina (91723-1312)
PHONE...................626 915-8030
Greg Miller, *President*
Sheree Kaplan, *Administration*
Dan Gallet, *Master*
EMP: 50 **EST:** 2016
SALES (est): 8.4MM **Privately Held**
SIC: 1795 1794 1623 Concrete breaking for streets & highways; demolition, buildings & other structures; excavation work; underground utilities contractor

(P-3338)
CLAUSS CONSTRUCTION
9911 Maine Ave, Lakeside (92040-3107)
PHONE...................619 390-4940
Patrick Michael Clauss, *CEO*
Briana Munoz, *Admin Asst*
Aaron Vincent, *Project Mgr*
Benny Garcia, *Purchasing*
Jim Clauss, *Warehouse Mgr*
EMP: 80
SALES (est): 18.1MM **Privately Held**
WEB: www.claussconstruction.com
SIC: 1795 1629 4959 Wrecking & demolition work; earthmoving contractor; toxic or hazardous waste cleanup

(P-3339)
DANNY RYAN PRECISION CONTG INC
1818 N Orangethorpe Park, Anaheim
(92801-1140)
PHONE...................949 642-6664
Danny Ryan, *President*
EMP: 90
SQ FT: 10,000
SALES (est): 19MM **Privately Held**
SIC: 1795 1799 Demolition, buildings & other structures; asbestos removal & encapsulation

(P-3340)
DIRT CHEAP DEMOLITION INC
171 Mace St Ste A4, Chula Vista
(91911-5861)
P.O. Box 1186, Bonita (91908-1186)
PHONE...................619 426-9598
Dan Cannon, *President*
EMP: 50
SALES (est): 3.4MM **Privately Held**
SIC: 1795 Demolition, buildings & other structures

(P-3341)
EVANS BROTHERS INC (PA)
Also Called: Ebi Aggregates
7589 National Dr, Livermore (94550-8803)
PHONE...................925 443-0225
Dan L Evans, *CEO*
Wayne E Evans, *Treasurer*
Wayne Evans, *Vice Pres*
Kathy Evans, *Executive*
Kathy M Evans, *Admin Sec*
EMP: 85
SQ FT: 1,271
SALES (est): 18.4MM **Privately Held**
WEB: www.evansbrothers.com
SIC: 1795 1794 Demolition, buildings & other structures; excavation work

(P-3342)
GD HEIL INC
1031 Segovia Cir, Placentia (92870-7137)
PHONE...................714 687-9100
James A Langford, *CEO*
Gary Heil, *President*
Steve Mc Clain, *Vice Pres*
Laura Heil, *Admin Sec*
EMP: 160
SQ FT: 20,770
SALES (est): 27.3MM **Privately Held**
WEB: www.gdheil.com
SIC: 1795 Demolition, buildings & other structures

(P-3343)
HULK CONSTRUCTION
4352 Lakeview Ave, Yorba Linda
(92886-2422)
PHONE...................714 701-9458
Ronald Short, *President*
EMP: 80
SALES (est): 3.2MM **Privately Held**
SIC: 1795 Dismantling steel oil tanks

(P-3344)
INTERIOR RMOVAL SPECIALIST INC
8990 Atlantic Ave, South Gate
(90280-3505)
PHONE...................323 357-6900
Carlos Herrera, *CEO*
Isabel Herrera, *Vice Pres*
EMP: 150
SALES (est): 24.2MM **Privately Held**
WEB: www.irsdemo.com
SIC: 1795 Demolition, buildings & other structures

(P-3345)
KROEKER INC
4627 S Chestnut Ave, Fresno
(93725-9238)
PHONE...................559 237-3764
Joyce Kroeker, *President*
Jeff Kroeker, *Treasurer*
Ed Kroeker, *Vice Pres*
Rodney Ainsworth, *General Mgr*
John Ramirez, *Office Mgr*
EMP: 120
SQ FT: 9,000
SALES: 25MM **Privately Held**
SIC: 1795 1629 4953 Wrecking & demolition work; land reclamation; earthmoving contractor; recycling, waste materials

(P-3346)
MILLER ENVIRONMENTAL INC
1130 W Trenton Ave, Orange (92867-3536)
PHONE...................714 385-0099
Gregg Miller, *President*
Deborah Holland, *Vice Pres*
Rob Schaefer, *Vice Pres*
Rosie Lizarraga, *Controller*
George Rios, *Superintendent*
EMP: 150
SQ FT: 3,000
SALES (est): 34.5MM **Privately Held**
WEB: www.millerenvironmental.com
SIC: 1795 4953 Demolition, buildings & other structures; hazardous waste collection & disposal

(P-3347)
NORTHSTAR CONTG GROUP INC
13320 Cambridge St, Santa Fe Springs
(90670-4904)
PHONE...................714 639-7600
John Leonard, *Vice Pres*
EMP: 60
SALES (corp-wide): 503.7MM **Privately Held**
SIC: 1795 1799 Wrecking & demolition work; asbestos removal & encapsulation
HQ: Northstar Contracting Group, Inc.
2614-20 Barrington Ct
Hayward CA 94545
510 491-1330

(P-3348)
NORTHSTAR DEM & REMEDIATION LP (DH)
404 N Berry St, Brea (92821-3104)
PHONE...................714 672-3500
Jose Alonso, *Vice Pres*
Jeffrey P Adix, *Treasurer*
Andrew Munro, *Officer*
Gregory G Dicarlo, *Vice Pres*
Andy Hixson, *Vice Pres*
EMP: 174
SQ FT: 19,000
SALES (est): 88.8MM
SALES (corp-wide): 503.7MM **Privately Held**
SIC: 1795 1799 8744 Demolition, buildings & other structures; decontamination services;

HQ: Northstar Group Services, Inc.
370 7th Ave Ste 1803
New York NY 10001
212 951-3660

(P-3349)
RANDAZZO ENTERPRISES INC
13550 Blackie Rd, Castroville
(95012-3200)
PHONE...................831 633-4420
John Randazzo, *President*
Alice Randazzo, *CFO*
Mark Randazzo, *Vice Pres*
BJ Betiong, *Manager*
EMP: 55
SQ FT: 13,000
SALES (est): 11.2MM **Privately Held**
WEB: www.randazzoenterprises.com
SIC: 1795 Demolition, buildings & other structures

(P-3350)
SECA EQP REMOVAL & DISMANTLE
Also Called: Seca Eqp Removal & Dismantling
684 Bitritto Ct, Modesto (95356-9272)
PHONE...................209 543-1600
Maria Carbenas, *President*
EMP: 50
SQ FT: 2,300
SALES (est): 3.1MM **Privately Held**
SIC: 1795 Demolition, buildings & other structures

(P-3351)
SIERRA RECYCLING & DEM INC
1620 E Brundage Ln Frnt, Bakersfield
(93307-2756)
PHONE...................661 327-7073
Philip Sacco, *President*
EMP: 71
SQ FT: 20,000
SALES (est): 8.8MM **Privately Held**
SIC: 1795 Demolition, buildings & other structures

(P-3352)
SILVERADO CONTRACTORS INC (PA)
2855 Mandela Pkwy Fl 2, Oakland
(94608-4050)
PHONE...................510 658-9960
Joseph M Capriola, *President*
Sue Capriola, *Treasurer*
Peter Knutch, *Vice Pres*
Richard Riggs, *Vice Pres*
Nancy Meesai, *Accountant*
EMP: 65
SALES (est): 17.7MM **Privately Held**
WEB: www.silveradocontractors.com
SIC: 1795 Demolition, buildings & other structures

(P-3353)
STOMPER CO INC
3135 Diablo Ave, Hayward (94545-2701)
PHONE...................510 574-0570
Donna R Rehrmann, *President*
George Rehrmann, *Vice Pres*
EMP: 60
SQ FT: 15,000
SALES (est): 9.6MM **Privately Held**
WEB: www.stomper.org
SIC: 1795 Concrete breaking for streets & highways

(P-3354)
TWO RIVERS DEMOLITION INC
2620 Mercantile Dr 100, Rancho Cordova
(95742-6519)
PHONE...................916 638-6775
W Roderick Palon, *President*
EMP: 55
SALES (est): 11.7MM **Privately Held**
WEB: www.2riversdemo.com
SIC: 1795 Demolition, buildings & other structures; concrete breaking for streets & highways

(P-3355)
ULTIMATE REMOVAL INC
Also Called: ULTIMATE DEMO
2168 Pomona Blvd, Pomona (91768-3332)
P.O. Box 1220 (91769-1220)
PHONE...................909 524-0800

John W Welch, *President*
Patrick Coleman, *CFO*
EMP: 124
SQ FT: 9,900
SALES: 9.4MM **Privately Held**
WEB: www.ultimateremoval.com
SIC: 1795 Demolition, buildings & other structures

(P-3356)
VIKING EQUIPMENT CORP
Also Called: Viking Demolition
540 W Windsor Rd, Glendale
(91204-1812)
P.O. Box 251257 (91225-1257)
PHONE.................................818 500-9447
Berger Jostad, *President*
John Mike Tredick, *CFO*
Scott Tredick, *Corp Secy*
EMP: 65
SALES (est): 6.5MM **Privately Held**
WEB: www.vikingdemo.com
SIC: 1795 1799 5932 Demolition, buildings & other structures; building mover, including houses; building materials, secondhand

1796 Installation Or Erection Of Bldg Eqpt & Machinery, NEC

(P-3357)
ANDERSON & MARTELLA INC
1200 Mt Diablo Blvd # 400, Walnut Creek
(94596-4890)
PHONE.................................925 934-3831
Marc Anderson, *President*
EMP: 50
SQ FT: 1,000
SALES (est): 5.4MM **Privately Held**
SIC: 1796 Installing building equipment

(P-3358)
CLASSIC INSTALLS INC
22475 Baxter Rd, Wildomar (92595-9040)
PHONE.................................951 678-9906
Dirk Steffen, *CEO*
Stephen Burris, *Admin Sec*
Brian Machay, *Administration*
EMP: 70
SALES: 75.5K **Privately Held**
SIC: 1796 Installing building equipment

(P-3359)
FOSTER WHEELER ENERGY SVCS INC
9645 Scranton Rd Ste 230, San Diego
(92121-1790)
PHONE.................................800 500-1993
Ed Linck, *President*
EMP: 50
SALES (est): 3.1MM
SALES (corp-wide): 10B **Privately Held**
SIC: 1796 1629 1731 4911 Power generating equipment installation; power plant construction; electric power systems contractors; cogeneration specialization; generation, electric power
HQ: Amec Foster Wheeler North America Corp.
53 Frontage Rd
Hampton NJ 08827
936 448-6323

(P-3360)
HARELSON MECHANICAL INC
Also Called: Hmi Industrial Contractors Inc
3899 Security Park Dr, Rancho Cordova
(95742-6920)
PHONE.................................916 386-2586
Ruth Gilman, *CEO*
Don Gilman, *Vice Pres*
Jonathan Reimer, *Foreman/Supr*
EMP: 62
SQ FT: 37,000
SALES: 15MM **Privately Held**
SIC: 1796 Millwright

(P-3361)
MITSUBISHI ELECTRIC US INC (DH)
Also Called: Meus
5900 Katella Ave Ste A, Cypress
(90630-5019)
P.O. Box 6007 (90630-0007)
PHONE.................................714 220-2500
Hora Keijiro, *CEO*
Mike Corbo, *COO*
Makoto Kono, *Treasurer*
Perry Pappous, *Exec VP*
Jared Baker, *Senior VP*
◆ **EMP:** 200
SQ FT: 10,400
SALES: 1.1B **Privately Held**
WEB: www.diamond-vision.com
SIC: 1796 3534 5065 3669 Elevator installation & conversion; escalators, passenger & freight; electronic parts; semiconductor devices; visual communication systems
HQ: Mitsubishi Electric Us Holdings, Inc.
5900 Katella Ave Ste A
Cypress CA 90630
714 220-2500

(P-3362)
OTIS ELEVATOR INTL INC
1358 14th St, Oakland (94607-2209)
PHONE.................................510 874-5129
Dennis Fuller, *Branch Mgr*
EMP: 58
SALES (corp-wide): 66.5B **Publicly Held**
WEB: www.otis.com
SIC: 1796 7699 Elevator installation & conversion; elevators: inspection, service & repair
HQ: Otis Elevator Company
1 Carrier Pl
Farmington CT 06032
860 674-3000

(P-3363)
PACIFIC COAST EQUIPMENT CO INC (PA)
3839 E Coronado St, Anaheim
(92807-1606)
PHONE.................................714 630-5957
David E Walker, *CEO*
Curtis Walker, *Vice Pres*
Todd Kilian, *Warehouse Mgr*
EMP: 50
SQ FT: 67,500
SALES (est): 14.7MM **Privately Held**
WEB: www.walkerbro.com
SIC: 1796 Machine moving & rigging

(P-3364)
PERFORMANCE CONTRACTING INC
4955 E Landon Dr, Anaheim (92807-1972)
PHONE.................................913 310-7120
William Massey, *Manager*
EMP: 99
SALES (corp-wide): 1.1B **Privately Held**
SIC: 1796 Installing building equipment
HQ: Performance Contracting, Inc.
11145 Thompson Ave
Lenexa KS 66219
913 888-8600

(P-3365)
TRANSBAY FIRE PROTECTION INC (PA)
2182 Rheem Dr, Pleasanton (94588-2796)
PHONE.................................925 846-9484
Charlie Marlin, *President*
Julie Schmidt, *CFO*
Nicholas Balaban, *Design Engr*
Christian Gerbich, *Design Engr*
John Canright, *Project Mgr*
▲ **EMP:** 50
SQ FT: 17,000
SALES (est): 10.4MM **Privately Held**
WEB: www.transbayfire.com
SIC: 1796 7389 Installing building equipment; safety inspection service

(P-3366)
UNITED RIGGERS & ERECTORS INC (PA)
4188 Valley Blvd, Walnut (91789-1446)
P.O. Box 728 (91788-0728)
PHONE.................................909 978-0400

Brian D Kelley, *CEO*
Thomas J Kruss, *COO*
Merary Argueta, *Administration*
Tom Larsen, *Project Mgr*
Frank Cangey, *Engineer*
EMP: 120 **EST:** 1966
SQ FT: 58,000
SALES: 21.4MM **Privately Held**
SIC: 1796 Machinery installation

1799 Special Trade Contractors, NEC

(P-3367)
1ST LIGHT ENERGY INC (PA)
1869 Moffat Blvd, Manteca (95336-8944)
PHONE.................................209 824-5500
Justin Krum, *CEO*
Gregory Smith, *CFO*
John McIntosh, *Director*
EMP: 50
SQ FT: 6,300
SALES (est): 51.6MM **Privately Held**
SIC: 1799 1711 Hydraulic equipment, installation & service; solar energy contractor

(P-3368)
AAA RESTORATION INC
29850 2nd St, Lake Elsinore (92532-2420)
PHONE.................................951 471-5828
Kirk Munio, *President*
EMP: 50
SQ FT: 1,400
SALES (est): 3.8MM **Privately Held**
SIC: 1799 Home/office interiors finishing, furnishing & remodeling

(P-3369)
AJC SANDBLASTING INC
932 Schley Ave, Wilmington (90744-4060)
PHONE.................................562 436-3606
Lisa Charleston, *President*
Larry Dowling, *Corp Secy*
EMP: 90
SQ FT: 10,000
SALES (est): 8MM **Privately Held**
SIC: 1799 Sandblasting of building exteriors; epoxy application

(P-3370)
ALCORN FENCE COMPANY (PA)
9901 Glenoaks Blvd, Sun Valley
(91352-1089)
P.O. Box 1249 (91353-1249)
PHONE.................................818 983-0650
Thomas Joseph Stack, *CEO*
Greg Erickson, *President*
Oscar Mancialla, *CFO*
Bob Gibson, *Vice Pres*
Rick Sohns, *Project Mgr*
EMP: 150 **EST:** 1942
SQ FT: 18,000
SALES (est): 23MM **Privately Held**
SIC: 1799 Fence construction

(P-3371)
ALL STAR MAINTENANCE INC
12250 El Camino Real # 300, San Diego
(92130-3076)
PHONE.................................858 259-0900
John Junge, *President*
EMP: 100
SALES (est): 5.3MM **Privately Held**
SIC: 1799 Building site preparation

(P-3372)
AMERICAN SYNERGY ASBESTOS REMO
Also Called: Synergy Environmental
28436 Satellite St, Hayward (94545-4863)
PHONE.................................510 444-2333
David C Clark, *President*
Douglas Price, *Manager*
EMP: 100
SQ FT: 6,000
SALES (est): 10MM **Privately Held**
WEB: www.synergyenvironmental.com
SIC: 1799 Asbestos removal & encapsulation

(P-3373)
AMERICAN TECHNOLOGIES INC
Also Called: American Restoration Services
25000 Industrial Blvd, Hayward
(94545-2349)
PHONE.................................510 429-5000
Toll Free:.................................888 -
Kyle Picket, *Manager*
Dan Ward, *Branch Mgr*
Shannon Bowen, *Admin Asst*
EMP: 60
SALES (corp-wide): 287.1MM **Privately Held**
WEB: www.amer-tech.com
SIC: 1799 Antenna installation
PA: American Technologies Inc.
3360 E La Palma Ave
Anaheim CA 92806
714 283-9990

(P-3374)
AMERICAN TECHNOLOGIES INC (PA)
Also Called: ATI
3360 E La Palma Ave, Anaheim
(92806-2814)
PHONE.................................714 283-9990
Gary Moore, *CEO*
Kelly Kambs, *COO*
Jeff Moore, *Co-President*
Ryan Moore, *Co-President*
Doug Fairless, *Exec VP*
▲ **EMP:** 128
SQ FT: 57,000
SALES: 287.1MM **Privately Held**
WEB: www.amer-tech.com
SIC: 1799 1541 1742 1731 Antenna installation; industrial buildings & warehouses; plastering, drywall & insulation; electrical work; painting & paper hanging; plumbing, heating, air-conditioning contractors

(P-3375)
AMERICAN TECHNOLOGIES INC
Also Called: American Restoration Services
2688 Westhills Ct, Simi Valley
(93065-6234)
PHONE.................................818 700-5060
Doug Waters, *Branch Mgr*
Joanne Kelley, *Admin Asst*
Matt Kittleson, *Project Mgr*
Daniel Drabant, *Superintendent*
Anto Kocar, *Superintendent*
EMP: 50
SALES (corp-wide): 287.1MM **Privately Held**
WEB: www.amer-tech.com
SIC: 1799 Antenna installation
PA: American Technologies Inc.
3360 E La Palma Ave
Anaheim CA 92806
714 283-9990

(P-3376)
ANDRIAN INC
Also Called: Stations
1935 Lundy Ave, San Jose (95131-1848)
PHONE.................................408 434-0730
Andrew Lanier, *President*
Brian Fajardo, *CEO*
Joel Lira, *Opers Mgr*
EMP: 50
SQ FT: 11,000
SALES (est): 6.6MM **Privately Held**
SIC: 1799 Office furniture installation

(P-3377)
ANDRIGHETTO PRODUCE INC
Also Called: Shasta Produce Co
155 Terminal Ct Stalls 15 Stalls, South San
Francisco (94083)
P.O. Box 2328 (94083-2328)
PHONE.................................650 588-0930
Steven Andrighetto, *CEO*
David Andrighetto, *Owner*
Peter Carcione, *President*
Steven Hurwitz, *Treasurer*
Domenic Andrighetto, *Vice Pres*
EMP: 55
SQ FT: 10,000
SALES (est): 10.8MM **Privately Held**
SIC: 1799 5411 Bowling alley installation; supermarkets, chain

(P-3378)
APW CONSTRUCTION INC
15135 Salt Lake Ave, City of Industry
(91746-3316)
PHONE..........................626 855-1720
America Tang, *Branch Mgr*
EMP: 65
SALES (corp-wide): 20MM **Privately Held**
SIC: 1799 Fence construction
PA: Apw Construction, Inc.
727 Glendora Ave
La Puente CA 91744
626 820-0812

(P-3379)
AQUA GUNITE INC
5830 S Naylor Rd, Livermore (94551-8308)
PHONE..........................408 271-2782
Jose G Aguayo, *CEO*
Fargio Garcia, *Vice Pres*
EMP: 50
SQ FT: 2,120
SALES (est): 5.2MM **Privately Held**
SIC: 1799 Swimming pool construction

(P-3380)
ASBESTOS INSTANT RESPONSE INC
3517 W Washington Blvd, Los Angeles
(90018-1122)
PHONE..........................323 733-0508
Eric Chevasson, *President*
Steven Liedernan, *COO*
Roberto Urbina, *Manager*
EMP: 65
SQ FT: 1,500
SALES (est): 7.8MM **Privately Held**
WEB: www.airinc.ws
SIC: 1799 Asbestos removal & encapsulation

(P-3381)
AZ COUNTERTOPS INC
1445 S Hudson Ave, Ontario (91761)
PHONE..........................909 983-5386
Jay Shah, *President*
Ray Shah, *Vice Pres*
▲ EMP: 50
SALES (est): 4.6MM **Privately Held**
SIC: 1799 Counter top installation

(P-3382)
BARON POOL PLSTR STHERN CAL INC
495 Industrial Rd, San Bernardino
(92408-3715)
PHONE..........................909 792-8891
Craig Bennion, *President*
EMP: 55
SQ FT: 5,000
SALES (est): 5.1MM **Privately Held**
WEB: www.baronpool.com
SIC: 1799 Swimming pool construction

(P-3383)
BAY AREA INSTALLATIONS INC (PA)
2481 Verna Ct, San Leandro (94577-4222)
PHONE..........................510 895-8196
Thomas Clark Mohamed, *President*
Herman B Chibnick, *Vice Pres*
Alta Clark, *Admin Sec*
Taj Chibnik, *Accounting Mgr*
▲ EMP: 53
SQ FT: 25,000
SALES (est): 8.8MM **Privately Held**
WEB: www.baiinc.com
SIC: 1799 4212 Demountable partition installation; office furniture installation; delivery service, vehicular

(P-3384)
BLUEWATER ENVMTL SVCS INC
2075 Williams St, San Leandro
(94577-2305)
PHONE..........................510 346-8800
Chris J Kirschenheuter, *CEO*
Humberto Navarro, *Project Mgr*
Ron Drummond, *Purchasing*
EMP: 100
SQ FT: 15,000

SALES (est): 15MM **Privately Held**
WEB: www.bwserv.com
SIC: 1799 Asbestos removal & encapsulation

(P-3385)
BRAND SERVICES LLC
Also Called: Brand Scaffold Service
940 Hensley St, Richmond (94801-2106)
PHONE..........................510 231-9640
EMP: 52
SALES (corp-wide): 2.1B **Privately Held**
WEB: www.brandscaffold.com
SIC: 1799 Scaffolding construction
HQ: Brand Shared Services Llc
1325 Cobb Intl Dr Nw
Kennesaw GA 30152
678 285-1400

(P-3386)
BRICKLEY CONSTRUCTION CO INC
Also Called: Brickley Environmental
957 Reece St, San Bernardino
(92411-2356)
PHONE..........................909 888-2010
James L Brickley, *CEO*
Thomas Brickley, *President*
Annorr Gowdy, *CFO*
Shane Brickley, *Vice Pres*
Kathleen Herrera, *Admin Asst*
EMP: 50
SQ FT: 10,000
SALES (est): 7MM **Privately Held**
WEB: www.brickleyenv.com
SIC: 1799 4959 Asbestos removal & encapsulation; environmental cleanup services

(P-3387)
BURDICK PAINTING
705 Nuttman St, Santa Clara (95054-2623)
PHONE..........................408 567-1330
John C Cintas, *CEO*
Rory Bauer, *Controller*
Penny Francis, *Controller*
EMP: 67
SQ FT: 8,000
SALES (est): 7.7MM **Privately Held**
SIC: 1799 1721 Paint & wallpaper stripping; coating, caulking & weather, water & fireproofing; coating of concrete structures with plastic; coating of metal structures at construction site; commercial painting

(P-3388)
C E TOLAND & SON
5300 Industrial Way, Benicia (94510-1025)
PHONE..........................707 747-1000
Clyde E Toland Jr, *Ch of Bd*
Blake Toland, *President*
Rey Trias, *Vice Pres*
Jeanette Vaiana, *Executive*
Lisa Castro, *Human Res Mgr*
▲ EMP: 120
SQ FT: 90,000
SALES (est): 20.4MM **Privately Held**
WEB: www.cetoland.com
SIC: 1799 Ornamental metal work

(P-3389)
CALIFORNIA ACCESS SCAFFOLD LLC
331 Vineland Ave, City of Industry
(91746-2321)
PHONE..........................310 324-3388
Daniel Johnson, *CEO*
Daniel Styles, *CFO*
James Johnson, *Vice Pres*
Kevin Johnson, *Info Tech Mgr*
Travis Crowell, *Project Mgr*
EMP: 56 EST: 2012
SALES: 5.6MM **Privately Held**
SIC: 1799 Scaffolding construction

(P-3390)
CALIFORNIA CLOSET CO O
42210 Cook St Ste E, Palm Desert
(92211-5199)
PHONE..........................760 773-4784
Steve Coughlin, *Manager*
EMP: 83

SALES (corp-wide): 16MM **Privately Held**
SIC: 1799 Closet organizers, installation & design
PA: California Closet Co. Of Orange County/Long Beach, Inc.
5921 Skylab Rd
Huntington Beach CA 92647
714 899-4905

(P-3391)
CALIFRNIAS GNITE POOL PLSTR INC
510 Greenville Rd, Livermore
(94550-9297)
PHONE..........................925 960-9500
Manuel Rodriguez, *President*
Jose Arellano, *Vice Pres*
Alvaro Lando, *Vice Pres*
Monroe Rodriguez, *Vice Pres*
EMP: 60
SQ FT: 15,625
SALES (est): 7.6MM **Privately Held**
SIC: 1799 Swimming pool construction

(P-3392)
CALSPEC ENTERPRISES INC (PA)
Also Called: California Bath Restoration
1920 E Warner Ave Ste 3p, Santa Ana
(92705-5547)
PHONE..........................949 263-0779
Scott Davis, *President*
Daniel Liechty, *Vice Pres*
EMP: 62
SQ FT: 12,000
SALES: 6MM **Privately Held**
SIC: 1799 Kitchen & bathroom remodeling

(P-3393)
CITY OF SANTA CLARA
Also Called: City of Santa Clra Parks Svc
2600 Benton St, Santa Clara (95051-4802)
PHONE..........................408 615-3770
George Friedenbach, *Manager*
EMP: 55 **Privately Held**
SIC: 1799 Parking facility equipment & maintenance
PA: City Of Santa Clara
1500 Warburton Ave
Santa Clara CA 95050
408 615-2200

(P-3394)
CLARO POOL SERVICES INC
42161 Beacon Hl, Palm Desert
(92211-5108)
PHONE..........................760 341-3377
Stephen Little, *CEO*
EMP: 53
SQ FT: 8,000
SALES (est): 296.5K **Privately Held**
SIC: 1799 Swimming pool construction

(P-3395)
COURTNEY INC (PA)
16781 Millikan Ave, Irvine (92606-5009)
PHONE..........................949 222-2050
George Courtney, *CEO*
Mildred Courtney, *Admin Sec*
EMP: 80
SALES (est): 32.6MM **Privately Held**
SIC: 1799 Waterproofing

(P-3396)
CROWN FENCE CO
12118 Bloomfield Ave, Santa Fe Springs
(90670-4703)
PHONE..........................562 864-5177
Eric Fiedler, *Principal*
Eric W Fiedler, *Vice Pres*
Hillary Nelson, *Office Mgr*
Murat Ortun, *Project Mgr*
Carlos Punzalan, *Project Mgr*
▲ EMP: 96
SQ FT: 36,000
SALES (est): 34.6MM **Privately Held**
SIC: 1799 5039 Fence construction; wire fence, gates & accessories

(P-3397)
DAVE GROSS ENTERPRISES INC
Also Called: Adams Pool Specialties
7 Wayne Ct, Sacramento (95829-1300)
PHONE..........................916 388-2000
David William Gross, *CEO*
Michel McDonnell, *Vice Pres*
Barbara Hall, *Controller*
EMP: 65
SQ FT: 25,000
SALES: 7MM **Privately Held**
SIC: 1799 Swimming pool construction

(P-3398)
DEHART INC
Also Called: California Closet Co
7550 Miramar Rd Ste 300, San Diego
(92126-4217)
PHONE..........................858 695-0882
Mike Cayheart, *President*
Pauline Wesley, *Administration*
Regan Hebert, *Consultant*
Ben Weiss, *Consultant*
EMP: 72
SQ FT: 5,700
SALES (est): 5.3MM **Privately Held**
WEB: www.dehart.com
SIC: 1799 2541 2521 1751 Closet organizers, installation & design; wood partitions & fixtures; wood office furniture; carpentry work; wood television & radio cabinets

(P-3399)
EASYTURF INC (DH)
2750 La Mirada Dr, Vista (92081-8401)
PHONE..........................760 745-7026
David Hartman, *CEO*
Charles Colletti, *Director*
Lou Fagula, *Manager*
Steve Bowles, *Consultant*
Chris Buono, *Consultant*
◆ EMP: 79
SQ FT: 30,000
SALES (est): 10.4MM
SALES (corp-wide): 589.6K **Privately Held**
SIC: 1799 Artificial turf installation

(P-3400)
ENCORE AEROSPACE LLC
1729 Apollo Ct, Seal Beach (90740-5617)
PHONE..........................562 344-1700
Tom McFarland,
EMP: 100
SALES (est): 3.9MM **Privately Held**
SIC: 1799 Renovation of aircraft interiors

(P-3401)
ENVIRONMENTS PLUS (PA)
1700 1st St, San Fernando (91340-2711)
PHONE..........................866 865-8120
Regina Gomez, *Ch of Bd*
Mark Cordell, *President*
Brian Pang, *Software Engr*
William Donahoe, *Opers Staff*
EMP: 60
SQ FT: 9,000
SALES (est): 9.6MM **Privately Held**
WEB: www.epi-usa.com
SIC: 1799 Office furniture installation

(P-3402)
ERNIE & SONS SCAFFOLDING
Also Called: Unique Scaffold
1960 Olivera Rd, Concord (94520-5425)
PHONE..........................925 446-4442
Ernesto Negrete Jr, *CEO*
Joe Garcia, *CFO*
John Soto, *Vice Pres*
Gilbert Soto, *Project Mgr*
▲ EMP: 180 EST: 2010
SQ FT: 47,000
SALES: 21MM **Privately Held**
SIC: 1799 Scaffolding construction

(P-3403)
EXCEL MDULAR SCAFFOLD LSG CORP
2555 Birch St, Vista (92081-8433)
PHONE..........................760 598-0050
Benjamin Bartlett, *Branch Mgr*
Richard Williams, *Senior Mgr*
EMP: 1851 **Privately Held**

PRODUCTS & SVCS

SIC: 1799 Rigging & scaffolding
PA: Excel Modular Scaffold And Leasing Corporation
720 Washington St Unit 5
Hanover MA 02339
-

(P-3404)
FARWEST CORROSION CONTROL CO (PA)
12029 Regentview Ave, Downey (90241-5517)
PHONE..........................310 532-9524
Troy G Rankin, *CEO*
Roy Rankin Jr, *President*
Marnie Rankin, *COO*
Marian Rankin, *Treasurer*
Steve Sosa, *Principal*
◆ **EMP:** 173
SQ FT: 42,000
SALES (est): 100.6MM **Privately Held**
WEB: www.farwst.com
SIC: 1799 Corrosion control installation

(P-3405)
FENCECORP INC (HQ)
18440 Van Buren Blvd, Riverside (92508-9258)
PHONE..........................951 686-3170
T Perrry Massie, *CEO*
Dale Marriott, *President*
Gary Hansen, *Vice Pres*
Rhonda Marks, *Office Mgr*
Floyd Nixon, *Admin Sec*
EMP: 340
SQ FT: 5,000
SALES (est): 18.4MM
SALES (corp-wide): 121MM **Privately Held**
SIC: 1799 Fence construction
PA: Fenceworks, Inc.
870 Main St
Riverside CA 92501
951 788-5620

(P-3406)
FENCEWORKS INC
Also Called: Golden State Fence
2861 E La Cresta Ave, Anaheim (92806-1817)
PHONE..........................714 238-0091
Steve Anderson, *Principal*
EMP: 75
SALES (corp-wide): 121MM **Privately Held**
WEB: www.goldenstatefence.com
SIC: 1799 Fence construction
PA: Fenceworks, Inc.
870 Main St
Riverside CA 92501
951 788-5620

(P-3407)
FENCEWORKS INC (PA)
Also Called: Golden State Fence Co.
870 Main St, Riverside (92501-1016)
PHONE..........................951 788-5620
Jason Ostrander, *CEO*
Mel Kay, *President*
Rene Tavares, *CFO*
John Wilmore, *Exec VP*
Elizabeth Olive, *Branch Mgr*
▲ **EMP:** 250
SQ FT: 20,000
SALES (est): 121MM **Privately Held**
WEB: www.goldenstatefence.com
SIC: 1799 Fence construction

(P-3408)
FENCEWORKS INC
Also Called: Golden State Fence
891 Corporation St, Santa Paula (93060-3005)
PHONE..........................661 265-0082
Pete Schank, *Manager*
EMP: 100
SALES (corp-wide): 121MM **Privately Held**
WEB: www.goldenstatefence.com
SIC: 1799 Fence construction
PA: Fenceworks, Inc.
870 Main St
Riverside CA 92501
951 788-5620

(P-3409)
FRESH AIR ENVIRONMENTAL SVCS
10675 Rush St, South El Monte (91733-3439)
PHONE..........................323 913-1965
Kevan Stark, *President*
Michael Davis, *Project Mgr*
David Delgado, *Project Mgr*
EMP: 60
SQ FT: 7,000
SALES (est): 4.4MM **Privately Held**
WEB: www.4freshair.biz
SIC: 1799 Asbestos removal & encapsulation

(P-3410)
G W SURFACES (PA)
Also Called: Showershapes
2432 Palma Dr, Ventura (93003-5732)
PHONE..........................805 642-5004
James A Garver, *President*
Georgann Garver, *Treasurer*
Tidus Gutierrez, *Vice Pres*
EMP: 170
SQ FT: 30,000
SALES (est): 18.8MM **Privately Held**
WEB: www.gwsurfaces.com
SIC: 1799 Counter top installation

(P-3411)
GARDNER POOL COMPANY INC (PA)
Also Called: Gardner Pool Plastering
801 Gable Way, El Cajon (92020-1910)
PHONE..........................619 593-8880
Scott McKenna, *President*
Josh Owsley, *General Mgr*
EMP: 51 **EST:** 1967
SQ FT: 6,000
SALES (est): 17.5MM **Privately Held**
WEB: www.gardnerpoolplastering.com
SIC: 1799 Swimming pool construction

(P-3412)
GETTLER-RYAN INC (PA)
6805 Sierra Ct Ste G, Dublin (94568-2694)
PHONE..........................925 551-7555
Jeffrey M Ryan, *CEO*
Dave Byron, *Vice Pres*
Janice Grant, *Admin Sec*
Desiree Walton, *Admin Asst*
Liddy McKenzie, *Design Engr*
EMP: 65
SQ FT: 20,000
SALES (est): 19.1MM **Privately Held**
WEB: www.grinc.com
SIC: 1799 Petroleum storage tanks, pumping & draining; service station equipment installation, maintenance & repair

(P-3413)
GLOBAL ENTERTAINMENT INDS INC
2948 N Ontario St, Burbank (91504-2016)
PHONE..........................818 567-0000
Christopher Hyde, *President*
Teresa Harris, *Manager*
▲ **EMP:** 55
SQ FT: 65,000
SALES (est): 6.3MM **Privately Held**
WEB: www.globalentind.com
SIC: 1799 Prop, set or scenery construction, theatrical

(P-3414)
GREGG DRILLING & TESTING INC (PA)
2726 Walnut Ave, Signal Hill (90755-1832)
PHONE..........................562 427-6899
John M Gregg, *President*
Chris Christensen, *Vice Pres*
Patrick Keating, *Vice Pres*
▲ **EMP:** 71
SQ FT: 17,000
SALES (est): 43.1MM **Privately Held**
WEB: www.greggdrilling.com
SIC: 1799 1781 Core drilling & cutting; water well drilling

(P-3415)
HAYWARD BAKER INC
1780 E Lemonwood Dr, Santa Paula (93060-9510)
PHONE..........................805 933-1331

Alan Ringen, *Branch Mgr*
Gary Taylor, *Vice Pres*
Lisheng Shao, *Chief Engr*
Robert Mendez, *Purch Agent*
EMP: 75
SALES (corp-wide): 2.8B **Privately Held**
WEB: www.haywardbaker.com
SIC: 1799 Building site preparation
HQ: Hayward Baker Inc
7550 Teague Rd Ste 300
Hanover MD 21076
410 551-8200

(P-3416)
HEAVENLY CONSTRUCTION INC
Also Called: Heavenly Greens
370 Umbarger Rd Ste A, San Jose (95111-2070)
PHONE..........................408 723-4954
Daniel Theis, *President*
EMP: 73
SQ FT: 75,000
SALES (est): 7.7MM **Privately Held**
WEB: www.heavenlygreens.com
SIC: 1799 Artificial turf installation

(P-3417)
HEINAMAN CONTRACT GLAZING INC (PA)
26981 Vista Ter Ste E, Lake Forest (92630-8127)
PHONE..........................949 587-0266
John L Heinaman, *President*
Gaye Howhannesian, *Treasurer*
Angela Heinaman, *Exec VP*
Mark Heinaman, *Vice Pres*
◆ **EMP:** 50
SQ FT: 4,950
SALES (est): 21.1MM **Privately Held**
SIC: 1799 1793 Window treatment installation; glass & glazing work

(P-3418)
HERZOG CONTRACTING CORP
2155 Hancock St, San Diego (92110-2012)
PHONE..........................619 849-6990
EMP: 374
SALES (corp-wide): 269MM **Privately Held**
SIC: 1799 Antenna installation
PA: Herzog Contracting Corp.
600 S Riverside Rd
Saint Joseph MO 64507
816 233-9001

(P-3419)
HIGH END DEVELOPMENT INC
665 Stone Rd, Benicia (94510-1141)
PHONE..........................925 687-2540
Jim Metzger, *President*
Larry V Harmen, *CFO*
Anthony Froyd, *Admin Sec*
EMP: 60
SALES (est): 26.5MM **Privately Held**
SIC: 1799 Waterproofing

(P-3420)
HOME IMPROVEMENT COMPANY INC
1585 Creek St, San Marcos (92078-2442)
PHONE..........................760 744-4840
Chet Johnston, *President*
Ron Helmes, *CFO*
EMP: 50
SALES (est): 4.5MM **Privately Held**
SIC: 1799 1521 1541 Post-disaster renovations; general remodeling, single-family houses; renovation, remodeling & repairs; industrial buildings

(P-3421)
J PEREZ ASSOCIATES INC (PA)
Also Called: J. Perez & Associates
10833 Valley View St # 200, Cypress (90630-5046)
PHONE..........................562 801-5397
Joe Perez, *CEO*
Craig Hammond, *CFO*
Peter Beath, *Vice Pres*
Tony Perez, *Vice Pres*
Crystal Vigil, *Accounting Mgr*
EMP: 55
SQ FT: 15,000

SALES (est): 16.5MM **Privately Held**
WEB: www.jperez.com
SIC: 1799 Sign installation & maintenance

(P-3422)
JANUS CORPORATION (PA)
1081 Shary Cir, Concord (94518-2407)
PHONE..........................925 969-9200
Mike Ely, *CEO*
Sean Tavernier, *President*
Craig M Uhle, *Vice Pres*
Barb Eaves, *Admin Sec*
EMP: 100
SQ FT: 15,000
SALES (est): 30.1MM **Privately Held**
WEB: www.januscorp.com
SIC: 1799 Asbestos removal & encapsulation; decontamination services

(P-3423)
JANUS CORPORATION
2025 Tandem, Norco (92860-3610)
PHONE..........................951 479-0700
Chad Chandler, *Manager*
EMP: 50
SQ FT: 21,780
SALES (corp-wide): 30.1MM **Privately Held**
WEB: www.januscorp.com
SIC: 1799 Asbestos removal & encapsulation
PA: Janus Corporation
1081 Shary Cir
Concord CA 94518
925 969-9200

(P-3424)
JARKA ENTERPRISES INC
1059 Vine St Ste 108, Sacramento (95811-0339)
PHONE..........................916 491-6180
Ken Binsmore, *Branch Mgr*
EMP: 61
SALES (corp-wide): 14.7MM **Privately Held**
SIC: 1799 Office furniture installation
PA: Jarka Enterprises, Inc.
675 Brennan St
San Jose CA 95131
408 325-5700

(P-3425)
JEFF KERBER POOL PLST INC
166 San Lorenzo St, Pomona (91766-2334)
PHONE..........................909 465-0677
Jeff Kerber, *President*
▲ **EMP:** 260
SQ FT: 77,100
SALES (est): 22.1MM **Privately Held**
WEB: www.jeffkerber.com
SIC: 1799 Swimming pool construction

(P-3426)
JONES/COVEY GROUP INCORPORATED
Also Called: Jones Covey Group
9595 Lucas Ranch Rd # 100, Rancho Cucamonga (91730-5725)
PHONE..........................888 972-7581
Bret Christopher Covey, *CEO*
James Chamberlain, *CFO*
Robert Christie, *Principal*
Jim Gonzales, *Project Mgr*
Jason Hermosillo, *Project Mgr*
EMP: 63
SQ FT: 2,400
SALES (est): 21.6MM **Privately Held**
SIC: 1799 Service station equipment installation & maintenance

(P-3427)
KARCHER ENVIRONMENTAL INC (PA)
2300 E Orangewood Ave, Anaheim (92806-6112)
P.O. Box 7385, Orange (92863-7385)
PHONE..........................714 385-1490
Benjamin R Karcher, *President*
Mark Kavanaugh, *Sales Staff*
EMP: 120
SQ FT: 26,400
SALES (est): 9.7MM **Privately Held**
WEB: www.karcherenv.com
SIC: 1799 1742 Asbestos removal & encapsulation; insulation, buildings

(P-3428)
L&G CABLE CONSTRUCTION
2776 E Miraloma Ave, Anaheim
(92806-1701)
PHONE...................................714 630-6174
Lou Gentile, *President*
Joe Winek, *Supervisor*
EMP: 60
SALES (est): 5.5MM **Privately Held**
SIC: 1799 Cable splicing service

(P-3429)
LATHAM POOL PRODUCTS INC
121 Crawford Rd, Williams (95987)
PHONE...................................530 473-5319
Alan K Stahl, *Manager*
EMP: 50 **Privately Held**
WEB: www.cpcpools.com
SIC: 1799 Swimming pool construction
HQ: Latham Pool Products, Inc.
787 Watervliet Shaker Rd
Latham NY 12110

(P-3430)
LAYFIELD USA CORPORATION
(DH)
2500 Sweetwater Springs B, Spring Valley
(91978-2007)
PHONE...................................619 562-1200
Thomas Rose, *CEO*
Steve Palubiski, *CFO*
Rob Rempel, *Vice Pres*
Laura Quillen, *Executive*
▲ EMP: 100
SQ FT: 1,000
SALES (est): 25.4MM
SALES (corp-wide): 3.7MM **Privately Held**
SIC: 1799 Building board-up contractor
HQ: Layfield Group Limited
11131 Hammersmith Gate
Richmond BC V7A 5
604 275-5588

(P-3431)
M GAW INC
Also Called: Jet Sets
6910 Farmdale Ave, North Hollywood
(91605-6210)
PHONE...................................818 503-7997
Michael Gaw, *President*
EMP: 90
SQ FT: 15,000
SALES (est): 9.2MM **Privately Held**
SIC: 1799 Prop, set or scenery construction, theatrical

(P-3432)
MALCO MAINTENANCE INC
Also Called: Malco Services
3703 E Melville Way, Anaheim
(92806-2122)
PHONE...................................714 630-0194
Duane Malone, *President*
Katie Goldsberry, *Manager*
EMP: 66
SQ FT: 15,000
SALES (est): 6.2MM **Privately Held**
SIC: 1799 Exterior cleaning, including sandblasting; cleaning building exteriors; cleaning new buildings after construction; steam cleaning of building exteriors

(P-3433)
MALCOLM DRILLING COMPANY INC (PA)
92 Natoma St Ste 400, San Francisco
(94105-2685)
PHONE...................................415 901-4400
John M Malcolm, *CEO*
Jerry Riggs, *President*
Terry Tucker, *President*
Heinrich Majewski, *Vice Pres*
John Roe, *Vice Pres*
▲ EMP: 151
SQ FT: 7,500
SALES (est): 657.6MM **Privately Held**
WEB: www.malcolmdrilling.com
SIC: 1799 Building site preparation; boring for building construction

(P-3434)
MATRIX ENVIRONMENTAL INC
2330 Cherry Indus Cir, Long Beach
(90805-4417)
PHONE...................................562 236-2704
Jason McKeever, *President*
Chris Dickinson, *Project Mgr*
James Petri, *Supervisor*
EMP: 60
SQ FT: 9,000
SALES: 21.9MM **Privately Held**
SIC: 1799 Athletic & recreation facilities construction

(P-3435)
MATRIX INDUSTRIES INC
2330 E Cherry Indus Cir, Long Beach
(90805-4417)
PHONE...................................562 236-2700
EMP: 260
SQ FT: 10,000
SALES (est): 15.5MM **Privately Held**
SIC: 1799

(P-3436)
MEMO SCAFFOLDING INC
12722 Carmenita Rd, Santa Fe Springs
(90670-4804)
PHONE...................................562 404-8600
Jose G Santos, *President*
Lynn Hollister, *CFO*
EMP: 100
SQ FT: 9,000
SALES (est): 7.8MM **Privately Held**
WEB: www.memoscaffolding.com
SIC: 1799 Scaffolding construction

(P-3437)
MOVER SERVICES INC
Also Called: Atlas Mover Services
721 E Compton Blvd, Rancho Dominguez
(90220-1153)
PHONE...................................310 868-5143
John Moses, *President*
Michelle Moses, *Vice Pres*
EMP: 50
SQ FT: 33,000
SALES: 6.6MM **Privately Held**
WEB: www.msiatlas.com
SIC: 1799 4214 5712 Office furniture installation; household goods moving & storage, local; office furniture

(P-3438)
MP AERO LLC
7701 Woodley Ave, Van Nuys
(91406-1732)
PHONE...................................818 901-9828
Christine Paschal, *CFO*
EMP: 85 EST: 2013
SQ FT: 165,000
SALES (est): 12.5MM **Privately Held**
SIC: 1799 Renovation of aircraft interiors

(P-3439)
MUEHLHAN CERTIFED COATINGS INC
2320 Cordelia Rd, Fairfield (94534-1600)
PHONE...................................707 639-4414
David Brockman, *President*
EMP: 150
SQ FT: 18,000
SALES (est): 5.6MM
SALES (corp-wide): 306.5MM **Privately Held**
SIC: 1799 Coating, caulking & weather, water & fireproofing; coating of metal structures at construction site; coating of concrete structures with plastic
HQ: Muehlhan Surface Protection Inc
2320 Cordelia Rd
Fairfield CA 94534
707 639-4421

(P-3440)
MY OFFICE INC
6060 Nncy Rdge Dr Ste 100, San Diego
(92121)
PHONE...................................858 549-6700
Ronald D Harrell, *CEO*
▲ EMP: 65
SQ FT: 40,000
SALES (est): 18.7MM **Privately Held**
WEB: www.4myoffice.com
SIC: 1799 Office furniture installation

(P-3441)
NAVAL COATING INC
3475 E St, San Diego (92102-3335)
PHONE...................................619 234-8366
Alan Lerchbacker, *President*
Gabriela Flores, *Officer*
Oscar Mondaca, *Controller*
Adam Johnson, *Manager*
EMP: 149
SQ FT: 50,000
SALES (est): 22.6MM **Privately Held**
WEB: www.navalcoating.com
SIC: 1799 1721 2851 Sandblasting of building exteriors; industrial painting; paints & allied products

(P-3442)
NORTH VALLEY CONSTRUCTION INC
4010 Raymond Rd, Livermore
(94551-9776)
P.O. Box 2511 (94551-2511)
PHONE...................................925 373-1246
Charles E Inderbitzen, *President*
Sandra Inderbitzen, *Treasurer*
EMP: 70
SQ FT: 1,000
SALES (est): 4.7MM **Privately Held**
SIC: 1799 Construction site cleanup

(P-3443)
NORTHSTAR CONTG GROUP INC (DH)
2614-20 Barrington Ct, Hayward (94545)
PHONE...................................510 491-1330
John Leonard, *President*
Jeffrey P Adix, *Treasurer*
Bryan Diloreto, *Co-President*
Gregory G Dicarlo, *Vice Pres*
Ramon Rivera, *Vice Pres*
EMP: 59
SALES (est): 44MM
SALES (corp-wide): 503.7MM **Privately Held**
SIC: 1799 1795 Asbestos removal & encapsulation; wrecking & demolition work
HQ: Northstar Group Services, Inc.
370 7th Ave Ste 1803
New York NY 10001
212 951-3660

(P-3444)
PACIFIC AQUASCAPE INC
17520 Newhope St Ste 120, Fountain Valley (92708-8203)
PHONE...................................714 843-5734
Johan Perslow, *Chairman*
Kevin Curran, *Vice Pres*
Michael Krebs, *Vice Pres*
Bob Lobo, *Vice Pres*
Candace Hough, *Admin Asst*
EMP: 75
SQ FT: 21,000
SALES (est): 16.7MM **Privately Held**
SIC: 1799 Swimming pool construction

(P-3445)
PACIFIC HOME WORKS INC
20725 S Wstn Ave Ste 100, Torrance
(90501)
PHONE...................................310 781-3012
Marcus Mac, *President*
Adam Konrad, *Vice Pres*
EMP: 195
SQ FT: 7,000
SALES (est): 18.8MM **Privately Held**
SIC: 1799 1751 Kitchen & bathroom remodeling; window & door installation & erection; window & door (prefabricated) installation

(P-3446)
PACIFIC LINE CLEAN-UP INC
27601 Forbes Rd Ste 29, Laguna Niguel
(92677-1240)
P.O. Box 7765 (92607-7765)
PHONE...................................949 348-0245
Raul Rios, *President*
Fermina Rios, *Vice Pres*
EMP: 120
SQ FT: 1,000
SALES (est): 8.2MM **Privately Held**
SIC: 1799 Cleaning new buildings after construction

(P-3447)
PARC SPECIALTY CONTRACTORS
1400 Vinci Ave, Sacramento (95838-1716)
PHONE...................................916 992-5405
Greg Johnson, *President*
John Kimmel, *Vice Pres*
Paul Lane, *Admin Sec*
Stuart Webb, *Project Mgr*
Mike Kidd,
EMP: 85
SQ FT: 10,000
SALES (est): 6.7MM **Privately Held**
SIC: 1799 Asbestos removal & encapsulation

(P-3448)
PARKING NETWORK INC
255 S Grand Ave Apt 314, Los Angeles
(90012-3024)
PHONE...................................213 613-1500
Frank Zelaya, *CEO*
Rose Zelaya, *President*
Ron Parto, *Vice Pres*
Todd Wensley, *Vice Pres*
EMP: 120
SALES: 4MM **Privately Held**
WEB: www.parkingnetwork.net
SIC: 1799 8748 Parking lot maintenance; business consulting

(P-3449)
PARTITIONS INSTALLATION INC
Also Called: Showcase Installations
13021 Leffingwell Ave, Santa Fe Springs
(90670-6341)
PHONE...................................562 207-9868
Rick A Faist Jr, *President*
▲ EMP: 60
SQ FT: 60,000
SALES: 4MM **Privately Held**
WEB: www.showcaseinstall.com
SIC: 1799 Demountable partition installation

(P-3450)
PATRICK DEAN BRYAN
Also Called: Affordable Installations
12481 Lttle Deer Creek Ln, Nevada City
(95959-8919)
PHONE...................................530 273-5484
Patrick Dean Bryan, *Owner*
Patricia Bryan, *Principal*
EMP: 60
SALES (est): 2.9MM **Privately Held**
SIC: 1799 Office furniture installation

(P-3451)
PREFERRED INSULATION CONTRS (PA)
1691 Jenks Dr, Corona (92880-2514)
PHONE...................................951 735-3725
Charles Steinhaus, *President*
EMP: 52
SALES (est): 6.9MM **Privately Held**
SIC: 1799 Insulation of pipes & boilers

(P-3452)
PREMIER POOLS AND SPAS LP (PA)
11250 Pyrites Way, Gold River
(95670-4481)
PHONE...................................916 852-0223
Keith H Harbeck, *General Ptnr*
Paul Porter, *General Ptnr*
Karen Querido, *Technology*
Noona Synhorst, *Manager*
EMP: 90
SQ FT: 3,500
SALES (est): 28.3MM **Privately Held**
SIC: 1799 Spa or hot tub installation or construction

(P-3453)
PROFORM INTERIOR CNSTR INC
663 33rd St Ste C, San Diego
(92102-3300)
PHONE...................................619 881-0041
James Pettit, *President*
Reid Schneider, *Vice Pres*
EMP: 73
SQ FT: 5,000

P R O D U C T S & S V C S

SALES (est): 6MM **Privately Held**
SIC: **1799** Home/office interiors finishing, furnishing & remodeling

(P-3454)
PROJECT GO INCORPORATED
801 Vernon St, Roseville (95678-3149)
PHONE..................................916 782-3443
Linda Timbers, *Exec Dir*
Lillian Durbin, *Opers Staff*
EMP: 50
SQ FT: 3,000
SALES: 3.7MM **Privately Held**
SIC: **1799** Waterproofing

(P-3455)
PW STEPHENS ENVMTL INC (PA)
15201 Pipeline Ln Ste B, Huntington Beach (92649-5704)
PHONE..................................714 892-2028
Scott Johnson, *President*
Paco Mendez, *Purchasing*
EMP: 52 EST: 2008
SALES (est): 27.6MM **Privately Held**
WEB: www.pwsei.com
SIC: **1799** Athletic & recreation facilities construction; asbestos removal & encapsulation

(P-3456)
PW STEPHENS ENVMTL INC
4047 Clipper Ct, Fremont (94538-6540)
PHONE..................................510 651-9506
Steve Macfarlane, *Principal*
EMP: 55
SALES (corp-wide): 27.6MM **Privately Held**
SIC: **1799** Athletic & recreation facilities construction
PA: P.W. Stephens Environmental, Inc.
15201 Pipeline Ln Ste B
Huntington Beach CA 92649
714 892-2028

(P-3457)
QUALITY SYSTEMS INSTALLATIONS
Also Called: Q S I
212 Shaw Rd Ste 3, South San Francisco (94080-6613)
PHONE..................................650 875-9000
Jon Chase, *President*
Daniel Castillo, *Vice Pres*
Robert W Lindstrom, *Vice Pres*
EMP: 60
SQ FT: 40,000
SALES (est): 4.3MM **Privately Held**
WEB: www.qsiltd.com
SIC: **1799** Office furniture installation

(P-3458)
RAINBOW WTRPROFING RESTORATION
600 Treat Ave, San Francisco (94110-2016)
PHONE..................................415 641-1578
Christopher Abel, *President*
Rob Browne, *Corp Secy*
Leticia Ramirez, *Admin Asst*
EMP: 124
SALES: 18MM **Privately Held**
WEB: www.rainbow415.com
SIC: **1799** Waterproofing

(P-3459)
REGENT AEROSPACE CORPORATION (PA)
28110 Harrison Pkwy, Valencia (91355-4109)
PHONE..................................661 257-3000
Reza Soltanianzadeh, *CEO*
Reza Soltanian, *President*
Everardo Guereca, *COO*
Louie David, *CFO*
Tim Garvin, *Vice Pres*
▲ EMP: 200
SQ FT: 90,000
SALES (est): 45MM **Privately Held**
WEB: www.regentaerospace.com
SIC: **1799 5088** Athletic & recreation facilities construction; aircraft & parts

(P-3460)
RESTEC CONTRACTORS INC
22955 Kidder St, Hayward (94545-1670)
PHONE..................................510 670-0100
John Andrzejewski, *President*
Freeman Boyett, *Treasurer*
R Todd Fearon, *Vice Pres*
David Brueggen, *Asst Sec*
EMP: 100
SALES (est): 9.9MM
SALES (corp-wide): 461.9MM **Privately Held**
WEB: www.resteccontractors.com
SIC: **1799** Asbestos removal & encapsulation
HQ: Vertecs Corporation
14700 Ne 95th St Ste 201
Redmond WA
425 885-1990

(P-3461)
REY-CREST ROOFG WATERPROOFING
Also Called: Rey-Crest Roofg Waterproofing
3065 Verdugo Rd, Los Angeles (90065-2014)
PHONE..................................323 257-9329
George Reyes, *President*
Georgia Reyes, *Corp Secy*
Harold Lim, *Project Mgr*
Michael Reyes, *Project Mgr*
EMP: 80
SQ FT: 10,000
SALES (est): 8.8MM **Privately Held**
WEB: www.reycrest.com
SIC: **1799 1761** Waterproofing; roofing contractor

(P-3462)
SADDLE CORP (PA)
Also Called: Saddleback Waterproofing
23531 Ridge Route Dr C, Laguna Hills (92653-1504)
PHONE..................................949 589-3422
Larry Goldenberg, *President*
Susan Goldenberg, *Vice Pres*
Ann Pellegrino, *Controller*
EMP: 60
SQ FT: 4,800
SALES (est): 7.7MM **Privately Held**
SIC: **1799** Waterproofing

(P-3463)
SCENIC ROUTE INC
13516 Desmond St, Pacoima (91331-2315)
PHONE..................................818 896-6006
Ulf Henriksson, *President*
Sean Culhane, *Vice Pres*
Micheal Goglia, *Vice Pres*
John Giordano, *Info Tech Mgr*
Jordan Woods-Wahl, *Technical Staff*
▲ EMP: 50 EST: 1987
SQ FT: 25,000
SALES (est): 6.4MM **Privately Held**
WEB: www.the-scenic-route.com
SIC: **1799** Prop, set or scenery construction, theatrical

(P-3464)
SCHAEFER MARY-JUDITH
Also Called: Schaefer Parking Lot Service
7202 Petterson Ln, Paramount (90723-2022)
PHONE..................................562 634-3164
Mary-Judith Schaefer, *Owner*
EMP: 55
SALES (est): 1.3MM **Privately Held**
SIC: **1799** Parking lot maintenance

(P-3465)
SELEX INC (PA)
Also Called: Borg Redwood Fences
442 Longfellow St, Livermore (94550-7122)
P.O. Box 5430, Pleasanton (94566-1430)
PHONE..................................707 836-8836
Julie Borg, *CEO*
Reuben Borg, *President*
Dave Lamarre, *Vice Pres*
EMP: 100 EST: 1995
SALES (est): 12.3MM **Privately Held**
WEB: www.borgfence.com
SIC: **1799** Fence construction

(P-3466)
SELEX INC
930 Shiloh Rd, Windsor (95492-9659)
PHONE..................................707 836-8836
Dave Boettger, *Branch Mgr*
EMP: 51
SALES (corp-wide): 12.3MM **Privately Held**
SIC: **1799** Fence construction
PA: Selex, Inc.
442 Longfellow St
Livermore CA 94550
707 836-8836

(P-3467)
SHORING ENGINEERS
Also Called: Shoring & Excavating
12645 Clark St, Santa Fe Springs (90670-3951)
PHONE..................................562 944-9331
George A Woodley Sr, *Vice Pres*
George A Woodleysr, *President*
Ren Contreras, *Vice Pres*
Rene Contreras, *Vice Pres*
Jason E Weinstein, *Vice Pres*
▲ EMP: 60
SALES (est): 14.1MM **Privately Held**
WEB: www.shoringengineers.com
SIC: **1799 8711** Shore cleaning & maintenance; engineering services

(P-3468)
SOUTH COAST FENCING CENTER
3518 W Lake Center Dr C, Santa Ana (92704-6979)
PHONE..................................714 549-2946
Brenden Richard, *President*
EMP: 60
SALES (est): 135.8K **Privately Held**
WEB: www.southcoastfencing.com
SIC: **1799** Fence construction

(P-3469)
SPECIAL SERVICE CONTRS INC
3580 Airport Rd, Paso Robles (93446-9554)
P.O. Box 3121 (93447-3121)
PHONE..................................805 227-1081
Russell Wilson, *President*
EMP: 51
SQ FT: 1,600
SALES (est): 7.1MM **Privately Held**
WEB: www.sscinfo.com
SIC: **1799** Cable splicing service

(P-3470)
STUMBAUGH & ASSOCIATES INC (PA)
3303 N San Fernando Blvd, Burbank (91504-2531)
PHONE..................................818 240-1627
Jeff Stumbaugh, *President*
Richard Stumbaugh, *Ch of Bd*
Steve Archer, *Vice Pres*
Tim Reardon, *Vice Pres*
Chris Zimmerman, *Administration*
EMP: 54 EST: 1965
SALES (est): 12.9MM **Privately Held**
WEB: www.stumbaugh.net
SIC: **1799 5046** Demountable partition installation; partitions

(P-3471)
SUNLAND SCAFFOLD
24885 Whitewood Rd # 106, Murrieta (92563-2014)
PHONE..................................951 595-9402
Arnulfo Wiedensohler, *President*
EMP: 60
SALES (est): 1.1MM **Privately Held**
SIC: **1799** Scaffolding construction

(P-3472)
SUNRIZE STAGING INC
1326 Mission Rd, Escondido (92029-1101)
P.O. Box 300067 (92030-0067)
PHONE..................................760 743-2043
Lucian Luly, *President*
EMP: 51
SQ FT: 600
SALES (est): 2.5MM **Privately Held**
WEB: www.sunrizestaging.com
SIC: **1799** Scaffolding construction

(P-3473)
TAILORED LIVING CHOICES LLC
1957 Sierra Ave, NAPA (94558-2840)
PHONE..................................707 259-0526
Vicki Robinson, *Mng Member*
Glenda Thomas, *Office Mgr*
Stacy Perez,
EMP: 112
SALES (est): 7.3MM **Privately Held**
SIC: **1799** Home/office interiors finishing, furnishing & remodeling

(P-3474)
TAIT ENVIRONMENTAL SVCS INC (PA)
701 Parkcenter Dr, Santa Ana (92705-3541)
P.O. Box 11118 (92711-1118)
PHONE..................................714 560-8200
Thomas F Tait, *CEO*
Richard Tait, *President*
Jason Morris, *Design Engr*
Laurie Clark, *Project Mgr*
Nick Nyugen, *Project Mgr*
▲ EMP: 55
SQ FT: 8,900
SALES (est): 13.6MM **Privately Held**
SIC: **1799 8748** Gas leakage detection; environmental consultant

(P-3475)
TBC - BORING COMPANY
12200 Crenshaw Blvd, Hawthorne (90250-3332)
PHONE..................................425 495-4215
Steve Davis, *Exec Dir*
Elisa Suarez, *Principal*
EMP: 100
SALES (est): 75.5K **Privately Held**
SIC: **1799** Boring for building construction

(P-3476)
TESERRA (PA)
Also Called: California Pools
86100 Avenue 54, Coachella (92236-3813)
P.O. Box 1280 (92236-1280)
PHONE..................................760 340-9000
Bob Smith, *President*
James Harebottle, *CFO*
EMP: 400
SQ FT: 10,000
SALES (est): 43.1MM **Privately Held**
SIC: **1799** Swimming pool construction

(P-3477)
THE TEECOR GROUP INC
Also Called: Key Environmental Services
1450 S Burlington Ave, Los Angeles (90006-5409)
PHONE..................................213 632-2350
Kalani Childs, *President*
Eric Youssef, *Vice Pres*
EMP: 60
SQ FT: 5,000
SALES (est): 5.5MM **Privately Held**
WEB: www.teecor.com
SIC: **1799** Asbestos removal & encapsulation

(P-3478)
THUNDER MOUNTAIN ENTERPRISES (PA)
9335 Elder Creek Rd, Sacramento (95829-9339)
P.O. Box 292821 (95829-2821)
PHONE..................................916 381-3400
Dave Smiley, *President*
Beth Smiley, *Corp Secy*
Carrie Young, *Manager*
EMP: 61
SQ FT: 5,000
SALES: 7MM **Privately Held**
WEB: www.tme1.com
SIC: **1799** Corrosion control installation

(P-3479)
TOPBUILD SERVICES GROUP CORP
Also Called: Masco
1341 Old Oakland Rd, San Jose (95112-1317)
PHONE..................................408 882-0411
Bob Colla, *Branch Mgr*
EMP: 75

▲ = Import ▼=Export
◆ =Import/Export

SALES (corp-wide): 2.3B **Publicly Held**
WEB: www.galeind.com
SIC: 1799 Prefabricated fireplace installation
HQ: Topbuild Services Group Corp.
475 N Williamson Blvd
Daytona Beach FL 32114
386 304-2200

(P-3480)

TORRES FENCE CO INC

2357 S Orange Ave, Fresno (93725-1021)
P.O. Box 10137 (93745-0137)
PHONE.................................559 237-4141
Ralph Torres, *President*
Rebecca Torres, *Corp Secy*
Ralph Torres Jr, *Vice Pres*
Rene J Torres, *Vice Pres*
Mari Salas, *Admin Sec*
▲ **EMP:** 50
SQ FT: 6,000
SALES (est): 6.3MM **Privately Held**
WEB: www.torresfence.com
SIC: 1799 3315 3496 Fence construction; chain link fencing; barbed wire, made from purchased wire

(P-3481)

TOURNESOL SITEWORKS LLC (PA)

2930 Faber St, Union City (94587-1214)
PHONE.................................800 542-2282
Christopher J Lyon, *Mng Member*
Tony Rizzo, *Engineer*
Corina Ornelas, *Human Resources*
Kerry Townson, *Prdtn Mgr*
John Denman, *Sales Mgr*
▲ **EMP:** 55
SQ FT: 10,000
SALES: 18.7MM **Privately Held**
WEB: www.plantertechnology.com
SIC: 1799 5023 3444 1521 Fiberglass work; home furnishings, wicker, rattan or reed; metal roofing & roof drainage equipment; patio & deck construction & repair; retaining wall construction; fountain repair

(P-3482)

TROYER CONTRACTING COMPANY INC

10122 Freeman Ave, Santa Fe Springs (90670-3408)
PHONE.................................562 944-6452
Mark Troyer, *CEO*
▲ **EMP:** 55 **EST:** 1995
SQ FT: 15,208
SALES (est): 9.5MM **Privately Held**
SIC: 1799 1761 Waterproofing; roofing contractor

(P-3483)

UNITED SPECTRUM INC

Also Called: Spectrum Abatement
1910 N Lime St, Orange (92865-4123)
P.O. Box 5747 (92863-5747)
PHONE.................................714 283-1010
David Fischer, *President*
EMP: 50
SQ FT: 20,000
SALES (est): 5.3MM **Privately Held**
WEB: www.asbestos-removal.com
SIC: 1799 1795 Asbestos removal & encapsulation; demolition, buildings & other structures

(P-3484)

VALENTINE CORPORATION

111 Pelican Way, San Rafael (94901-5519)
P.O. Box 9337 (94912-9337)
PHONE.................................415 453-3732
Toll Free:.................................877 -
Robert O Valentine, *CEO*
Robert Valentine Jr, *President*
Alan Hanley, *CFO*
Madeline Valentine, *Corp Secy*
David Levine, *Vice Pres*
EMP: 50
SQ FT: 3,000
SALES (est): 11.9MM **Privately Held**
SIC: 1799 8711 1622 Waterproofing; building construction consultant; bridge construction

(P-3485)

VALLEY SUN MECHANICAL CNSTR

4205 Atlas Ct, Bakersfield (93308-4510)
P.O. Box 515, Oxford IN (47971-0515)
PHONE.................................661 321-9070
Charles J Richmond, *President*
EMP: 64
SQ FT: 5,200
SALES (est): 4.6MM **Privately Held**
WEB: www.vsmc.com
SIC: 1799 Food service equipment installation; welding on site

(P-3486)

VALLEY WATER PROOFING INC

825 Civic Center Dr Ste 6, Santa Clara (95050-3961)
P.O. Box 20003, San Jose (95160-0003)
PHONE.................................408 985-7701
Donna O'Brien, *President*
Michael O'Brien, *Vice Pres*
Kevin Ruffoni, *General Mgr*
Jay Perez, *Project Mgr*
Mark Furtado, *Opers Mgr*
EMP: 80
SQ FT: 1,000
SALES (est): 9.2MM **Privately Held**
WEB: www.valleyh2o.com
SIC: 1799 Waterproofing

(P-3487)

WALTON ENGINEERING INC

3900 Commerce Dr, West Sacramento (95691-2157)
P.O. Box 1025 (95691-1025)
PHONE.................................916 372-1888
Michael Walton, *President*
Richard Walton, *Vice Pres*
EMP: 65
SQ FT: 13,000
SALES (est): 13.4MM **Privately Held**
SIC: 1799 1542 7389 Service station equipment installation, maintenance & repair; service station construction; drafting service, except temporary help

(P-3488)

WASHINGTON ORNA IR WORKS INC (PA)

Also Called: Washington Iron Works
17926 S Broadway, Gardena (90248-3540)
P.O. Box 460 (90247-0846)
PHONE.................................310 327-8660
Daniel Welsh, *CEO*
Chris Powell, *CFO*
Tom Pederson, *Treasurer*
Steve Simester, *Project Mgr*
Brooke Walton, *Project Mgr*
EMP: 90
SQ FT: 141,240
SALES (est): 24.6MM **Privately Held**
WEB: www.washingtoniron.com
SIC: 1799 3446 Ornamental metal work; architectural metalwork

(P-3489)

WAYNE PERRY INC (PA)

8281 Commonwealth Ave, Buena Park (90621-2537)
PHONE.................................714 826-0352
Wayne Perry, *President*
Adam Leiter, *Treasurer*
Ed Smith, *Assoc VP*
Daniel McGill, *Vice Pres*
Greg Nicholson, *Vice Pres*
EMP: 185
SQ FT: 4,000
SALES (est): 45.7MM **Privately Held**
WEB: www.wpinc.com
SIC: 1799 8711 Decontamination services; petroleum storage tank installation, underground; engineering services

(P-3490)

WELL WITHIN SPA

417 Cedar St, Santa Cruz (95060-4304)
PHONE.................................831 458-9355
David Levan, *Owner*
Eric Heckert, *Co-Owner*
EMP: 60

SALES: 360K **Privately Held**
WEB: www.wellwithinspa.com
SIC: 1799 7299 Spa or hot tub installation or construction; massage parlor & steam bath services

(P-3491)

WEST COAST FIRESTOPPING INC

1130 W Trenton Ave, Orange (92867-3536)
PHONE.................................714 935-1104
Karl Stoll, *President*
Lisa Stoll, *Executive Asst*
EMP: 80
SALES (est): 6.9MM **Privately Held**
SIC: 1799 Fireproofing buildings

(P-3492)

WESTAR MANUFACTURING INC

Also Called: Quik-Shor
13217 Laureldale Ave, Downey (90242-5140)
PHONE.................................562 633-0581
Bill Fick, *Vice Pres*
Becky Antinone, *Executive*
Chris Russell, *General Mgr*
EMP: 60
SALES (est): 1.9MM
SALES (corp-wide): 56.5MM **Privately Held**
SIC: 1799 3531 Shoring & underpinning work; construction machinery
PA: Trench Plate Rental Co.
13217 Laureldale Ave
Downey CA 90242
562 602-1642

(P-3493)

WESTERN MAGNESITE INC

11927 Sherman Rd Unit 1, North Hollywood (91605-3717)
PHONE.................................818 255-1150
Bernard Fainstein, *Owner*
EMP: 50 **EST:** 2000
SALES (est): 1.9MM **Privately Held**
WEB: www.westernmagnesite.com
SIC: 1799 Waterproofing

(P-3494)

WLMD

Also Called: Wellmade Products
1715 Kibby Rd, Merced (95341-9301)
PHONE.................................209 723-9120
Mark R Riley, *CEO*
Doug Bartman, *CFO*
Steve Squires, *General Mgr*
Jerry Yon, *Controller*
▲ **EMP:** 130
SQ FT: 120,000
SALES (est): 15.8MM **Privately Held**
WEB: www.wlmd.com
SIC: 1799 1761 Lightning conductor erection; roofing, siding & sheet metal work

(P-3495)

WOODS MAINTENANCE SERVICES INC

Also Called: Hydro-Pressure Systems
7250 Coldwater Canyon Ave, North Hollywood (91605-4203)
PHONE.................................818 764-2515
Barry Woods, *President*
Diane Woods, *Principal*
Jeff Woods, *General Mgr*
Doris Lemaire, *Office Mgr*
Enrique Lopez, *Project Mgr*
EMP: 135
SALES (est): 17.1MM **Privately Held**
WEB: www.graffiticontrol.com
SIC: 1799 Cleaning building exteriors

4011 Railroads, Line-Hauling Operations

(P-3496)

BNSF RAILWAY COMPANY

Also Called: Burlington Northern
740 Carnegie Dr, San Bernardino (92408-3571)
PHONE.................................909 386-4148
Michael Shirelif, *General Mgr*
David Ayers, *Manager*
EMP: 120

SALES (corp-wide): 225.3B **Publicly Held**
WEB: www.billpurdy.com
SIC: 4011 Railroads, line-haul operating
HQ: Bnsf Railway Company
2650 Lou Menk Dr
Fort Worth TX 76131
800 795-2673

(P-3497)

BNSF RAILWAY COMPANY

200 N Avenue H, Barstow (92311-2553)
PHONE.................................760 255-7803
Brandon Mabry, *Superintendent*
EMP: 110
SALES (corp-wide): 225.3B **Publicly Held**
WEB: www.billpurdy.com
SIC: 4011 4111 4213 4225 Interurban railways; commuter rail passenger operation; trucking, except local; general warehousing; railroad freight agency; railroad property lessors
HQ: Bnsf Railway Company
2650 Lou Menk Dr
Fort Worth TX 76131
800 795-2673

(P-3498)

BNSF RAILWAY COMPANY

Also Called: Burlington Northern
6300 Sheila St, Commerce (90040-2411)
PHONE.................................323 869-3002
Julian Sanchez, *Superintendent*
EMP: 180
SALES (corp-wide): 225.3B **Publicly Held**
WEB: www.billpurdy.com
SIC: 4011 Railroads, line-haul operating
HQ: Bnsf Railway Company
2650 Lou Menk Dr
Fort Worth TX 76131
800 795-2673

(P-3499)

BNSF RAILWAY COMPANY

Also Called: Burlington Northern
3770 E Washington Blvd, Vernon (90058-8125)
PHONE.................................323 267-4133
John Hynes, *Principal*
EMP: 200
SALES (corp-wide): 225.3B **Publicly Held**
WEB: www.billpurdy.com
SIC: 4011 Railroads, line-haul operating
HQ: Bnsf Railway Company
2650 Lou Menk Dr
Fort Worth TX 76131
800 795-2673

(P-3500)

CALIFRNIA HIGH SPEED RAIL AUTH

770 L St Ste 620, Sacramento (95814-3385)
PHONE.................................916 324-1541
Dan Richard, *Ch of Bd*
EMP: 100
SALES (est): 8.8MM **Privately Held**
SIC: 4011 Railroads, line-haul operating
PA: State Of California
State Capital
Sacramento CA 95814
916 445-2864

(P-3501)

CSX CORPORATION

14863 Clark Ave, Hacienda Heights (91745-1308)
PHONE.................................626 336-1377
EMP: 149
SALES (corp-wide): 12.6B **Publicly Held**
SIC: 4011
PA: Csx Corporation
500 Water St Fl 15
Jacksonville FL 32202
904 359-3200

(P-3502)

MODESTO & EMPIRE TRACTION CO (HQ)

530 11th St, Modesto (95354-3518)
P.O. Box 3106 (95353-3106)
PHONE.................................209 524-4631

Ronald Jackson, *CEO*
James L Beard, *President*
Tom L Nielsen, *President*
William R Beard, *Treasurer*
Kennan Beard Jr, *Vice Pres*
EMP: 69 EST: 1911
SQ FT: 7,500
SALES (est): 9.6MM
SALES (corp-wide): 9MM **Privately Held**
SIC: 4011 Interurban railways
PA: Beard Land & Investment Co
    530 11th St
    Modesto CA 95354
    209 524-4631

(P-3503)
NATIONAL RAILROAD PASS CORP
Also Called: Amtrak
1050 Kettner Blvd Ste 1, San Diego
(92101-3339)
PHONE.................................619 239-9989
Debbi Dewfwood, *Branch Mgr*
EMP: 138 Publicly Held
WEB: www.amtrak.com
SIC: 4011 9621 Interurban railways; regulation, administration of transportation;
HQ: National Railroad Passenger Corporation
    1 Massachusetts Ave Nw
    Washington DC 20001
    202 906-3000

(P-3504)
PACIFIC HARBOR LINE INC (HQ)
705 N Henry Ford Ave, Wilmington
(90744-6716)
PHONE.................................310 834-4594
Peter Gilbertson, *Ch of Bd*
Otis L Cliatt, *President*
Bruce A Lieberman, *CFO*
Justin Moon, *Officer*
R Scott Morgan, *Controller*
EMP: 150
SALES (est): 15.2MM
SALES (corp-wide): 49.5MM **Privately Held**
SIC: 4011 Railroads, line-haul operating
PA: Anacostia Rail Holdings Company
    224 S Michigan Ave # 330
    Chicago IL 60604
    312 362-1888

(P-3505)
R R DONNELLEY & SONS COMPANY
Also Called: Moore Business Forms
1646 N Calif Blvd Ste 510, Walnut Creek
(94596-4171)
PHONE.................................925 951-1320
Wes McCracken, *Branch Mgr*
EMP: 50
SQ FT: 9,000
SALES (corp-wide): 6.8B **Publicly Held**
WEB: www.moore.com
SIC: 4011 5943 Railroads, line-haul operating; office forms & supplies
PA: R. R. Donnelley & Sons Company
    35 W Wacker Dr
    Chicago IL 60601
    312 326-8000

(P-3506)
SAN JOAQUIN VALLEY RAILROAD CO
221 N F St, Exeter (93221-1119)
P.O. Box 937 (93221-0937)
PHONE.................................559 592-1857
Randy Perry, *CEO*
Rex Bergholm, *President*
Steve Coomes, *Vice Pres*
Joe Evans, *General Mgr*
EMP: 200
SQ FT: 1,100
SALES (est): 14.8MM
SALES (corp-wide): 2.3B **Publicly Held**
WEB: www.statesrail.com
SIC: 4011 Railroads, line-haul operating
HQ: Railamerica, Inc.
    20 West Ave
    Darien CT 06820

(P-3507)
SIERRA ENTERTAINMENT
341 Industrial Way, Woodland
(95776-6012)
PHONE.................................530 666-9646
David Magew, *President*
Robert Pinoli, *Vice Pres*
Torgny Nilsson, *Admin Sec*
EMP: 50
SALES (est): 83.7K **Privately Held**
SIC: 4011 Railroads, line-haul operating
PA: Sierra Railroad Company
    341 Industrial Way
    Woodland CA 95776

(P-3508)
SIERRA RAILROAD COMPANY
1222 Research Park Dr, Davis
(95618-4849)
PHONE.................................530 554-2522
Christopher Hart, *Principal*
EMP: 55 **Privately Held**
SIC: 4011 Railroads, line-haul operating
PA: Sierra Railroad Company
    341 Industrial Way
    Woodland CA 95776

(P-3509)
UNION PACIFIC CORPORATION
9451 Atkinson St Ste 100, Roseville
(95747-9301)
P.O. Box 42 (95747)
PHONE.................................916 789-5311
Mike Evans, *President*
EMP: 503
SALES (corp-wide): 22.8B **Publicly Held**
SIC: 4011 Railroads, line-haul operating
PA: Union Pacific Corporation
    1400 Douglas St
    Omaha NE 68179
    402 544-5000

(P-3510)
UNION PACIFIC RAILROAD COMPANY
999 Paso Robles St, Paso Robles
(93446-2628)
PHONE.................................805 286-5851
Athey Roy, *Branch Mgr*
EMP: 80
SALES (corp-wide): 22.8B **Publicly Held**
SIC: 4011 Railroads, line-haul operating
HQ: Union Pacific Railroad Company Inc
    1400 Douglas St
    Omaha NE 68179
    402 544-5000

(P-3511)
UNION PACIFIC RAILROAD COMPANY
3135 N Weber Ave, Fresno (93705-3655)
PHONE.................................559 443-2244
Randy Esquiza, *Manager*
EMP: 125
SALES (corp-wide): 22.8B **Publicly Held**
WEB: www.uprr.com
SIC: 4011 Railroads, line-haul operating
HQ: Union Pacific Railroad Company Inc
    1400 Douglas St
    Omaha NE 68179
    402 544-5000

(P-3512)
UNION PACIFIC RAILROAD COMPANY
2000 S Sycamore Ave, Bloomington
(92316-2463)
PHONE.................................909 685-2710
EMP: 80
SALES (corp-wide): 22.8B **Publicly Held**
SIC: 4011 Railroads, line-haul operating
HQ: Union Pacific Railroad Company Inc
    1400 Douglas St
    Omaha NE 68179
    402 544-5000

(P-3513)
UNION PACIFIC RAILROAD COMPANY
9391 Atkinson St Ste 100, Roseville
(95747-9605)
PHONE.................................916 789-5930
Jack Huddleston, *Branch Mgr*

EMP: 80
SALES (corp-wide): 22.8B **Publicly Held**
SIC: 4011 Railroads, line-haul operating
HQ: Union Pacific Railroad Company Inc
    1400 Douglas St
    Omaha NE 68179
    402 544-5000

(P-3514)
UNION PACIFIC RAILROAD COMPANY
4341 E Washington Blvd, Commerce
(90023-4470)
PHONE.................................213 446-1900
Ramiro Barba, *Manager*
EMP: 80
SALES (corp-wide): 22.8B **Publicly Held**
SIC: 4011 Railroads, line-haul operating
HQ: Union Pacific Railroad Company Inc
    1400 Douglas St
    Omaha NE 68179
    402 544-5000

(P-3515)
UNION PACIFIC RAILROAD COMPANY
10031 Fthlls Blvd Ste 200, Roseville
(95747)
PHONE.................................916 789-6055
Karen Calli, *Manager*
Robert N Belt,
Michael L Johnson,
James C Spaulding,
Jeffrey Mancuso, *Director*
EMP: 120
SALES (corp-wide): 22.8B **Publicly Held**
WEB: www.uprr.com
SIC: 4011 Railroads, line-haul operating
HQ: Union Pacific Railroad Company Inc
    1400 Douglas St
    Omaha NE 68179
    402 544-5000

(P-3516)
UNION PACIFIC RAILROAD COMPANY
Also Called: Southern Pacific Railroad
730 Sumner St, Bakersfield (93305)
PHONE.................................661 321-4604
Bill Gafford, *President*
EMP: 80
SALES (corp-wide): 22.8B **Publicly Held**
WEB: www.uprr.com
SIC: 4011 Railroads, line-haul operating
HQ: Union Pacific Railroad Company Inc
    1400 Douglas St
    Omaha NE 68179
    402 544-5000

(P-3517)
UNION PACIFIC RAILROAD COMPANY
Also Called: Union Pacific Lines
2401 E Sepulveda Blvd, Long Beach
(90810-1945)
PHONE.................................562 490-7000
Herman Madden, *Superintendent*
EMP: 300
SALES (corp-wide): 22.8B **Publicly Held**
WEB: www.uprr.com
SIC: 4011 Railroads, line-haul operating
HQ: Union Pacific Railroad Company Inc
    1400 Douglas St
    Omaha NE 68179
    402 544-5000

4111 Local & Suburban Transit

(P-3518)
A-PARA TRANSIT CORP
Also Called: Yefllow Shttle Vtrans Sdan Svc
1400 Doolittle Dr, San Leandro
(94577-2226)
PHONE.................................510 562-5500
Shiv D Kumar, *President*
EMP: 110
SQ FT: 2,200
SALES (est): 7.4MM **Privately Held**
SIC: 4111 Local & suburban transit

(P-3519)
ACCESS SERVICES
Also Called: Access Paratransit
3449 Santa Anita Ave, El Monte
(91731-2424)
P.O. Box 5728 (91734-1728)
PHONE.................................213 270-6000
Doran J Barnes, *CEO*
Shelly Verrinder, *Exec Dir*
EMP: 80
SALES: 144.1MM **Privately Held**
SIC: 4111 Local & suburban transit

(P-3520)
AERO TECHNOLOGIES INC
555 Mission St, San Francisco
(94105-0920)
PHONE.................................415 314-7479
Garrett Camp, *CEO*
EMP: 50
SALES (est): 483.1K **Privately Held**
SIC: 4111 Airport transportation

(P-3521)
AIRLINE COACH SERVICE INC (PA)
863 Malcolm Rd, Burlingame (94010-1406)
P.O. Box 282998, San Francisco (94128-2998)
PHONE.................................650 697-7733
Gregory Choo, *Ch of Bd*
Kyung C Lee, *President*
Alex Morrison, *Vice Pres*
EMP: 90
SQ FT: 7,000
SALES (est): 6.6MM **Privately Held**
SIC: 4111 Airport transportation services, regular route

(P-3522)
AIRPORT CONNECTION INC
Also Called: Roadrunner Shuttle
95 Dawson Dr, Camarillo (93012-8001)
PHONE.................................805 389-8196
Sumaia Sandlin, *CEO*
Desmond P Sandlin, *Admin Sec*
Charles Sandlin, *Technology*
Sue Sandlin, *Train & Dev Mgr*
EMP: 180
SQ FT: 3,500
SALES (est): 23.7MM **Privately Held**
WEB: www.rrshuttle.com
SIC: 4111 4119 Airport transportation; airport transportation services, regular route; limousine rental, with driver

(P-3523)
ALAMEDA-CONTRA COSTA TRNST DST (PA)
Also Called: AC TRANSIT
1600 Franklin St, Oakland (94612-2806)
P.O. Box 28507 (94604-8507)
PHONE.................................510 891-4777
David J Armijo, *General Mgr*
Salvador Llamas, *COO*
Lewis Clinton, *CFO*
Chris Peeples, *Bd of Directors*
Kathleen Kelly, *Officer*
▲ **EMP:** 2210
SQ FT: 100,000
SALES: 70.5MM **Privately Held**
WEB: www.actransit.org
SIC: 4111 Bus line operations

(P-3524)
ARCADIA TRANSIT INC
Also Called: Super Shuttle
7955 San Fernando Rd, Sun Valley
(91352-4614)
PHONE.................................818 252-0630
Tim Mardirossian, *President*
Patrick Voskian, *CFO*
Sedik Mardirossian, *Treasurer*
Rozan Mardosian, *Accounting Mgr*
EMP: 50
SQ FT: 25,000
SALES (est): 2.5MM **Privately Held**
SIC: 4111 Airport transportation services, regular route

(P-3525)
CALIFORNIA TRANSIT INC
1900 S Alameda St, Vernon (90058-1014)
PHONE.................................323 234-8750
Timmy Mardirossian, *President*

▲ = Import ▼=Export
◆ =Import/Export

Eda Aghajanian, *Treasurer*
Carol Story, *Treasurer*
Christina Pineda, *General Mgr*
Sedik Mardirossian, *Admin Sec*
EMP: 99 **EST:** 2008
SALES (est): 2.7MM
SALES (corp-wide): 21.5MM **Privately Held**
SIC: 4111 Bus line operations
PA: San Gabriel Transit, Inc.
   3650 Rockwell Ave
   El Monte CA 91731
   626 258-1310

(P-3526)
CITY OF ARCADIA
240 W Huntington Dr, Arcadia
(91007-3401)
PHONE..................626 574-5435
EMP: 300 **Privately Held**
SIC: 4111 Local & suburban transit
PA: City Of Arcadia
   240 W Huntington Dr
   Arcadia CA 91007
   626 574-5400

(P-3527)
CITY OF FRESNO
Fresno Area Express
2223 G St, Fresno (93706-1631)
PHONE..................559 621-7433
Bruce Red, *General Mgr*
Bruce Robinson, *Supervisor*
EMP: 460 **Privately Held**
WEB: www.fresnocitizencorps.org
SIC: 4111 Bus transportation
PA: City Of Fresno
   2600 Fresno St
   Fresno CA 93721
   559 621-7001

(P-3528)
CITY OF GARDENA
Also Called: Gardena Municipal Bus Lines
13999 S Western Ave, Gardena
(90249-3005)
PHONE..................310 324-1475
Whitman Ballenger, *Director*
Joseph Collins, *Maintence Staff*
Frazier Watts, *Supervisor*
EMP: 97 **Privately Held**
WEB: www.gardenapd.org
SIC: 4111 9621 Bus line operations; regulation, administration of transportation;
PA: City Of Gardena
   1700 W 162nd St
   Gardena CA 90247
   310 217-9500

(P-3529)
CUSA AWC LLC
Also Called: All West Coachlines
7701 Wilbur Way, Sacramento
(95828-4929)
PHONE..................916 423-4000
Linda King,
Craig Lentzch,
EMP: 50
SALES (est): 2.1MM **Privately Held**
SIC: 4111 Bus transportation

(P-3530)
DESTINATION SHUTTLE SVCS LLC
6150 W 96th St, Los Angeles (90045-5218)
PHONE..................310 338-9466
Brian Clark,
Jose Amaya, *General Mgr*
Brian Lott,
Jack Lott,
EMP: 130
SALES (est): 4.1MM **Privately Held**
SIC: 4111 Airport transportation

(P-3531)
DIVERSIFIED TRANSPORTATION LLC
6053 W Century Blvd # 900, Los Angeles
(90045-6400)
PHONE..................310 981-9500
Lisa Jasper, *Manager*
EMP: 58
SALES (corp-wide): 4.2MM **Privately Held**
SIC: 4111 4121 Airport transportation; taxicabs

HQ: Diversified Transportation Llc
   1400 E Mission Blvd
   Pomona CA
   909 622-1313

(P-3532)
EAST BAY CONNECTION INC
Also Called: East Bay Airport Shuttle
140 Mayhew Way Ste 1002, Pleasant Hill
(94523-4370)
PHONE..................925 609-1920
Amid Alefi, *Manager*
EMP: 50
SQ FT: 11,600
SALES: 2MM **Privately Held**
WEB: www.eastbayconnection.net
SIC: 4111 Airport transportation

(P-3533)
FIRST STUDENT INC
Also Called: Community Transit Services
4337 Rowland Ave, El Monte (91731-1119)
PHONE..................626 448-9446
John Desmond, *Branch Mgr*
EMP: 100
SALES (corp-wide): 9.1B **Privately Held**
WEB: www.leag.com
SIC: 4111 4119 Bus line operations; local passenger transportation
HQ: First Student, Inc.
   600 Vine St Ste 1400
   Cincinnati OH 45202

(P-3534)
FIRST TRANSIT
Also Called: First Group of America
1303 Fairway Dr, Santa Maria
(93455-1407)
PHONE..................805 925-5254
EMP: 71
SALES (est): 3.4MM **Privately Held**
SIC: 4111

(P-3535)
FIRST TRANSIT INC
2400 E Dominguez St, Long Beach
(90810-1012)
PHONE..................310 515-8270
EMP: 54
SALES (corp-wide): 9.2B **Privately Held**
SIC: 4111
HQ: First Transit, Inc.
   600 Vine St Ste 1400
   Cincinnati OH 45202
   513 241-2200

(P-3536)
FIRST TRANSIT INC
411 High St, Oakland (94601-3903)
PHONE..................510 535-9192
Brian Nieman, *Branch Mgr*
EMP: 100
SALES (corp-wide): 9.1B **Privately Held**
WEB: www.firsttransit.com
SIC: 4111 Local & suburban transit
HQ: First Transit, Inc.
   600 Vine St Ste 1400
   Cincinnati OH 45202
   513 241-2200

(P-3537)
FIRST TRANSIT INC
Also Called: Dispatch Office
407 High St, Oakland (94601-3903)
PHONE..................510 437-8990
Harris, *Branch Mgr*
EMP: 54
SALES (corp-wide): 9.1B **Privately Held**
WEB: www.firsttransit.com
SIC: 4111 Bus transportation
HQ: First Transit, Inc.
   600 Vine St Ste 1400
   Cincinnati OH 45202
   513 241-2200

(P-3538)
FOOTHILL TRANSIT SERVICE CORP (PA)
100 S Vincent Ave Ste 200, West Covina
(91790-2944)
PHONE..................626 967-3147
Julie Austin, *CEO*
Toran Barns, *Exec Dir*
John Xie, *Manager*
EMP: 55

SQ FT: 9,626
SALES (est): 7.9MM **Privately Held**
SIC: 4111 Bus line operations

(P-3539)
FRESNO COUNTY RURAL TRNST AGCY (PA)
Also Called: Fcrta
2035 Tulare St, Fresno (93721-2004)
PHONE..................559 233-6789
Barbara Goodwin, *Director*
EMP: 53
SALES (est): 1.5MM **Privately Held**
SIC: 4111 Bus transportation

(P-3540)
GOLDEN EMPIRE TRANSIT DISTRICT (PA)
Also Called: Get-A-Lift Handicap Bus Trnsp
1830 Golden State Ave, Bakersfield
(93301-1012)
PHONE..................661 869-2438
Steven Woods, *CEO*
Karen King, *President*
Jill Smith, *Administration*
Jeanie Hill, *Human Res Mgr*
Toddasha Kim, *Opers Spvr*
EMP: 232
SALES: 30.3MM **Privately Held**
WEB: www.getbus.org
SIC: 4111 Bus line operations

(P-3541)
IDEAL TRANSIT INC
13404 Waco St, Baldwin Park
(91706-4734)
PHONE..................626 448-2690
Baldo M Paseta, *President*
Alicia Chavira, *Supervisor*
EMP: 50
SALES (est): 3.7MM **Privately Held**
SIC: 4111 Local & suburban transit

(P-3542)
KEOLIS TRANSIT AMERICA INC
14663 Keswick St, Van Nuys (91405-1204)
PHONE..................818 616-5254
Steve Shaw, *President*
EMP: 175
SALES (corp-wide): 4.2MM **Privately Held**
SIC: 4111 Local & suburban transit
HQ: Keolis Transit America, Inc.
   6053 W Century Blvd # 900
   Los Angeles CA 90045

(P-3543)
KEOLIS TRANSIT AMERICA INC
4488 N Blackstone Ave, Fresno
(93726-1903)
PHONE..................559 621-5783
Steve Shaw, *President*
Kim Jamron, *Accounting Mgr*
EMP: 100
SALES (corp-wide): 4.2MM **Privately Held**
SIC: 4111 Local & suburban transit
HQ: Keolis Transit America, Inc.
   6053 W Century Blvd # 900
   Los Angeles CA 90045

(P-3544)
KEOLIS TRANSIT AMERICA INC
660 W Avenue L, Lancaster (93534-7117)
PHONE..................661 341-3910
Steve Shaw, *President*
Kim Jamron, *Accounting Mgr*
EMP: 90
SALES (corp-wide): 4.2MM **Privately Held**
SIC: 4111 Local & suburban transit
HQ: Keolis Transit America, Inc.
   6053 W Century Blvd # 900
   Los Angeles CA 90045

(P-3545)
KOTOBUKI-YA INC
Also Called: CPS
314 Lang Rd, Burlingame (94010-2003)
PHONE..................650 344-7955
Koichi Suyama, *President*
EMP: 70
SQ FT: 1,000,000

SALES: 2MM **Privately Held**
WEB: www.kotobukiyausa.com
SIC: 4111 Airport transportation

(P-3546)
LONG BEACH PUBLIC TRNSP CO
1300 Gardenia Ave, Long Beach
(90813-2599)
PHONE..................562 591-2301
Laurence Jackson, *Branch Mgr*
Sanchez Oscar, *QA Dir*
EMP: 325
SALES (est): 3.6MM
SALES (corp-wide): 66.5MM **Privately Held**
SIC: 4111 Bus line operations
PA: Long Beach Public Transportation Co Inc
   1963 E Anaheim St
   Long Beach CA 90813
   562 591-8753

(P-3547)
LONG BEACH PUBLIC TRNSP CO
1963 E Anaheim St, Long Beach
(90813-3907)
P.O. Box 731 (90801-0731)
PHONE..................562 591-8753
Larry Jackson, *Manager*
EMP: 80
SALES (corp-wide): 66.5MM **Privately Held**
SIC: 4111 Bus line operations
PA: Long Beach Public Transportation Co Inc
   1963 E Anaheim St
   Long Beach CA 90813
   562 591-8753

(P-3548)
LOS ANGELES COUNTY MTA
9201 Canoga Ave, Chatsworth
(91311-5839)
PHONE..................213 922-6308
Pat Orr, *Manager*
EMP: 217
SALES (corp-wide): 682.5MM **Privately Held**
WEB: www.mta.net
SIC: 4111 Bus line operations
PA: Los Angeles County Metropolitan Transportation Authority
   1 Gateway Plz Fl 25
   Los Angeles CA 90012
   323 466-3876

(P-3549)
LOS ANGELES COUNTY MTA
900 Lyon St, Los Angeles (90012-2913)
PHONE..................213 922-5887
John Drayton, *Manager*
EMP: 217
SALES (corp-wide): 682.5MM **Privately Held**
WEB: www.mta.net
SIC: 4111 Bus line operations
PA: Los Angeles County Metropolitan Transportation Authority
   1 Gateway Plz Fl 25
   Los Angeles CA 90012
   323 466-3876

(P-3550)
LOS ANGELES COUNTY MTA
Also Called: Division 1
1130 E 6th St, Los Angeles (90021-1108)
PHONE..................213 922-6301
Ron Reedy, *Branch Mgr*
Aida Asuncion, *Officer*
EMP: 150
SALES (corp-wide): 682.5MM **Privately Held**
WEB: www.mta.net
SIC: 4111 Bus line operations
PA: Los Angeles County Metropolitan Transportation Authority
   1 Gateway Plz Fl 25
   Los Angeles CA 90012
   323 466-3876

PRODUCTS & SVCS

(P-3551)
LOS ANGELES COUNTY MTA
630 W Avenue 28, Los Angeles
(90065-1502)
PHONE..................213 922-6203
Cheryl Brown, *Manager*
EMP: 400
SALES (corp-wide): 682.5MM **Privately Held**
WEB: www.mta.net
SIC: 4111 Bus line operations
PA: Los Angeles County Metropolitan
　Transportation Authority
　1 Gateway Plz Fl 25
　Los Angeles CA 90012
　323 466-3876

(P-3552)
LOS ANGELES COUNTY MTA
Also Called: Los Angeles Cnty Mtro Trnspt
1 Gateway Plz, Los Angeles (90012-3745)
PHONE..................213 922-6202
Maria Japardi, *Branch Mgr*
EMP: 217
SALES (corp-wide): 682.5MM **Privately Held**
WEB: www.mta.net
SIC: 4111 Bus line operations
PA: Los Angeles County Metropolitan
　Transportation Authority
　1 Gateway Plz Fl 25
　Los Angeles CA 90012
　323 466-3876

(P-3553)
LOS ANGELES COUNTY MTA (PA)
1 Gateway Plz Fl 25, Los Angeles
(90012-3745)
P.O. Box 512296 (90051-0296)
PHONE..................323 466-3876
Philip Washington, *CEO*
Rick Thorpe, *CEO*
Nalini Ahuja, *CFO*
Bronwen Trice, *Officer*
Mario Del Rosario, *Project Engr*
EMP: 900
SALES (est): 682.5MM **Privately Held**
WEB: www.mta.net
SIC: 4111 Bus line operations; subway operation

(P-3554)
LOS ANGELES COUNTY MTA
8800 Santa Monica Blvd, Los Angeles
(90069-4536)
PHONE..................213 922-6207
Grant Myers, *Manager*
EMP: 700
SALES (corp-wide): 682.5MM **Privately Held**
WEB: www.mta.net
SIC: 4111 Bus line operations; local railway
passenger operation
PA: Los Angeles County Metropolitan
　Transportation Authority
　1 Gateway Plz Fl 25
　Los Angeles CA 90012
　323 466-3876

(P-3555)
LOS ANGELES COUNTY MTA
11900 Branford St, Sun Valley
(91352-1003)
PHONE..................213 922-6215
Gary Stivack, *Manager*
EMP: 500
SALES (corp-wide): 682.5MM **Privately Held**
WEB: www.mta.net
SIC: 4111 Bus line operations
PA: Los Angeles County Metropolitan
　Transportation Authority
　1 Gateway Plz Fl 25
　Los Angeles CA 90012
　323 466-3876

(P-3556)
LOS ANGELES COUNTY MTA
720 E 15th St, Los Angeles (90021-2122)
PHONE..................213 533-1506
Carla Aleman, *Branch Mgr*
EMP: 360
SALES (corp-wide): 682.5MM **Privately Held**
SIC: 4111 Bus line operations

PA: Los Angeles County Metropolitan
　Transportation Authority
　1 Gateway Plz Fl 25
　Los Angeles CA 90012
　323 466-3876

(P-3557)
LOS ANGELES COUNTY MTA
Also Called: Lacmta
470 Bauchet St, Los Angeles (90012-2907)
PHONE..................213 922-5012
Jim Montoya, *Branch Mgr*
EMP: 217
SALES (corp-wide): 682.5MM **Privately Held**
WEB: www.mta.net
SIC: 4111 Bus transportation
PA: Los Angeles County Metropolitan
　Transportation Authority
　1 Gateway Plz Fl 25
　Los Angeles CA 90012
　323 466-3876

(P-3558)
LOS ANGELES COUNTY MTA
Also Called: Division 7
100 Sunset Ave, Venice (90291-2517)
PHONE..................310 392-8636
John Adams, *Manager*
EMP: 120
SALES (corp-wide): 682.5MM **Privately Held**
WEB: www.mta.net
SIC: 4111 Bus transportation
PA: Los Angeles County Metropolitan
　Transportation Authority
　1 Gateway Plz Fl 25
　Los Angeles CA 90012
　323 466-3876

(P-3559)
LOS ANGELES COUNTY MTA
Also Called: Office of Inspector General
818 W 7th St Ste 500, Los Angeles
(90017-3463)
PHONE..................213 244-6783
Arthur Sinai, *Manager*
EMP: 217
SALES (corp-wide): 682.5MM **Privately Held**
WEB: www.mta.net
SIC: 4111 Bus line operations
PA: Los Angeles County Metropolitan
　Transportation Authority
　1 Gateway Plz Fl 25
　Los Angeles CA 90012
　323 466-3876

(P-3560)
LOS ANGELES COUNTY MTA
320 S Santa Fe Ave, Los Angeles
(90013-1812)
P.O. Box 194 (90078-0194)
PHONE..................213 626-4455
Julian Burke, *CEO*
EMP: 217
SALES (corp-wide): 682.5MM **Privately Held**
WEB: www.mta.net
SIC: 4111 Bus line operations
PA: Los Angeles County Metropolitan
　Transportation Authority
　1 Gateway Plz Fl 25
　Los Angeles CA 90012
　323 466-3876

(P-3561)
MARIN AIRPORTER INC (PA)
Also Called: Marin Airporter Chrtr & Tours
8 Lovell Ave, San Rafael (94901-3921)
PHONE..................415 256-8833
Randy J Kokke, *President*
Grace Hughes, *Vice Pres*
David Hughes, *General Mgr*
Thelma Espino, *Technology*
Margie Franklin, *Bookkeeper*
EMP: 70 EST: 1972
SQ FT: 2,160
SALES (est): 4MM **Privately Held**
SIC: 4111 4141 Airport transportation
services, regular route; local bus charter
service

(P-3562)
MENDOCINO TRANSIT AUTHORITY
111 Boatyard Dr, Fort Bragg (95437-5709)
P.O. Box 556, Gualala (95445-0556)
PHONE..................707 462-1422
Sam Kingsley, *Principal*
EMP: 60
SALES (corp-wide): 6.4MM **Privately Held**
WEB: www.4mta.org
SIC: 4111 4131 Bus line operations; intercity & rural bus transportation
PA: Mendocino Transit Authority
　241 Plant Rd
　Ukiah CA 95482
　707 462-3881

(P-3563)
METROPOLITAN TRNSP COMM (PA)
Also Called: M T C
375 Beale St Ste 800, San Francisco
(94105-2179)
PHONE..................415 778-6700
Steve Hieminger, *Exec Dir*
Brian Mayhew, *CFO*
Jake Mackenzie, *Vice Ch Bd*
Brenda Kahn, *Officer*
Therese McMillan, *Exec Dir*
EMP: 115 EST: 1970
SQ FT: 21,000
SALES: 313.1MM **Privately Held**
SIC: 4111 Bus line operations

(P-3564)
MONTEBELLO TRANSIT
400 S Taylor Ave, Montebello (90640-5057)
PHONE..................323 887-4600
Allan Pollock, *Director*
EMP: 250
SALES (est): 3.6MM **Privately Held**
SIC: 4111 Local & suburban transit

(P-3565)
MV TRANSPORTATION INC
13690 Vaughn St, San Fernando
(91340-3017)
PHONE..................323 666-0856
EMP: 78
SALES (corp-wide): 1B **Privately Held**
SIC: 4111 Local & suburban transit
PA: Mv Transportation, Inc.
　2711 N Haskell Ave # 1500
　Dallas TX 75204
　214 265-3400

(P-3566)
MV TRANSPORTATION INC
1242 Los Angeles St, Glendale
(91204-2404)
PHONE..................818 409-3387
Jesse Saavedra, *Branch Mgr*
EMP: 78
SALES (corp-wide): 1B **Privately Held**
SIC: 4111 Local & suburban transit
PA: Mv Transportation, Inc.
　2711 N Haskell Ave # 1500
　Dallas TX 75204
　214 265-3400

(P-3567)
MV TRANSPORTATION INC
1250 S Wilson Way Ste A1, Stockton
(95205-7026)
PHONE..................209 547-7879
Nick Harbut, *Branch Mgr*
Harold Allan, *Maintence Staff*
EMP: 78
SALES (corp-wide): 1B **Privately Held**
SIC: 4111 Local & suburban transit
PA: Mv Transportation, Inc.
　2711 N Haskell Ave # 1500
　Dallas TX 75204
　214 265-3400

(P-3568)
MV TRANSPORTATION INC
24 S Sacramento St, Lodi (95240-2150)
PHONE..................209 339-1972
Elizabeth Davidiaz, *Manager*
EMP: 78
SALES (corp-wide): 1B **Privately Held**
SIC: 4111 Local & suburban transit

PA: Mv Transportation, Inc.
　2711 N Haskell Ave # 1500
　Dallas TX 75204
　214 265-3400

(P-3569)
MV TRANSPORTATION INC
479 Mason St Ste 221, Vacaville
(95688-4548)
PHONE..................707 446-5573
Nigel Browne, *Manager*
Shawn Gilbert, *Foreman/Supr*
Sharon Cox, *Manager*
Michele Kapphahn, *Manager*
Ernesto Sanchez, *Manager*
EMP: 60
SALES (corp-wide): 1B **Privately Held**
WEB: www.mvtransit.com
SIC: 4111 Local & suburban transit
PA: Mv Transportation, Inc.
　2711 N Haskell Ave # 1500
　Dallas TX 75204
　214 265-3400

(P-3570)
MV TRANSPORTATION INC
3550 3rd St, San Francisco (94124-1404)
PHONE..................415 206-7386
Tim Dumandan, *Manager*
Cristina Russell, *VP Bus Dvlpt*
Carol Ckson, *Maintence Staff*
EMP: 120
SALES (corp-wide): 1B **Privately Held**
WEB: www.mvtransit.com
SIC: 4111 Local & suburban transit
PA: Mv Transportation, Inc.
　2711 N Haskell Ave # 1500
　Dallas TX 75204
　214 265-3400

(P-3571)
NORTH COUNTY TRANSIT DISTRICT (PA)
Also Called: NCTD
810 Mission Ave, Oceanside (92054-2825)
PHONE..................760 966-6500
Matt Tucker, *Exec Dir*
Jason Dixon, *Officer*
Bryan Killian, *Officer*
Matthew Tucker, *Exec Dir*
Imelda Kubota, *Admin Asst*
EMP: 103
SQ FT: 7,000
SALES: 28.6MM **Privately Held**
SIC: 4111 Bus transportation

(P-3572)
NORWALK TRANSIT SYSTEM
Also Called: City of Norwalk
12650 Imperial Hwy, Norwalk (90650-3137)
PHONE..................562 929-5550
James C Parker, *Director*
Barbara Esparza, *Admin Sec*
Nancy Jalomo, *Admin Asst*
Theresa Clark, *Planning*
Vickie Yoshikawa, *Analyst*
EMP: 99
SALES (est): 4.4MM **Privately Held**
SIC: 4111 Local & suburban transit

(P-3573)
OMNITRANS INC
4748 Arrow Hwy, Montclair (91763-1208)
PHONE..................909 379-7100
John Steffon, *Branch Mgr*
EMP: 150
SALES (corp-wide): 13.3MM **Privately Held**
SIC: 4111 Bus line operations
PA: Omnitrans, Inc.
　1700 W 5th St
　San Bernardino CA 92411
　909 379-7100

(P-3574)
ORANGE COUNTY TRNSP AUTH
11790 Cardinal Cir, Garden Grove
(92843-3839)
P.O. Box 14184, Orange (92863-1584)
PHONE..................714 560-6282
Arthur Leahy, *CEO*
EMP: 1000
SALES (corp-wide): 634.7MM **Privately Held**
WEB: www.octa.net
SIC: 4111 Bus line operations

▲ = Import ▼=Export
◆ =Import/Export

PA: Orange County Transportation Authority
550 S Main St
Orange CA 92868
714 636-7433

(P-3575)
ORANGE COUNTY TRNSP AUTH (PA)
Also Called: Orange County Trnsp Auth
550 S Main St, Orange (92868-4506)
P.O. Box 14184 (92863-1584)
PHONE.........................714 636-7433
Darrell Johnson, *CEO*
EMP: 350
SQ FT: 77,000
SALES: 634.7MM **Privately Held**
WEB: www.octa.net
SIC: 4111 8711 Bus line operations; construction & civil engineering

(P-3576)
ORANGE COUNTY TRNSP AUTH
Also Called: Octa
600 S Main St Ste 910, Orange (92868-4689)
PHONE.........................714 999-1726
Oscar Moreno, *Branch Mgr*
EMP: 600
SALES (corp-wide): 634.7MM **Privately Held**
WEB: www.octa.net
SIC: 4111 Bus line operations
PA: Orange County Transportation Authority
550 S Main St
Orange CA 92868
714 636-7433

(P-3577)
PENINSULA CRRDOR JINT PWERS BD
Also Called: Caltrain
1250 San Carlos Ave, San Carlos (94070-2468)
P.O. Box 3006 (94070-1306)
PHONE.........................650 508-6200
Michael J Scanlon, *Exec Dir*
Virginia Harrington, *CEO*
Chuck Harvey, *CEO*
John Ficarra, *COO*
Jeremy Lipps, *Officer*
EMP: 105
SALES: 107MM **Privately Held**
SIC: 4111 Local railway passenger operation

(P-3578)
REDDING AERO ENTERPRISES INC
Also Called: Redding Jet Center
3775 Flight Ave Ste 100, Redding (96002-9376)
PHONE.........................530 224-2300
Jack Kilpatrick, *President*
Steve Hoppes, *Corp Secy*
Victor Clarke, *Vice Pres*
EMP: 60
SQ FT: 31,000
SALES (est): 5.8MM **Privately Held**
WEB: www.reddingjet.com
SIC: 4111 4581 Airport transportation services, regular route; aircraft servicing & repairing

(P-3579)
RIVERSIDE TRANSIT AGENCY (PA)
Also Called: R T A
1825 3rd St, Riverside (92507-3484)
P.O. Box 59968 (92517-1968)
PHONE.........................951 565-5000
Larry Rubio, *CEO*
Darlees Brogdon, *Administration*
Laura Camacho, *Technology*
Tim Porterfield, *Technology*
Melissa Blankenship, *Contract Mgr*
EMP: 350
SQ FT: 10,400
SALES: 10.7MM **Privately Held**
WEB: www.riversidetransit.com
SIC: 4111 Bus transportation

(P-3580)
SACRAMENTO REGIONAL TRNST DIST (PA)
1400 29th St, Sacramento (95816-6406)
P.O. Box 2110 (95812-2110)
PHONE.........................916 726-2877
Mike Wiley, *CEO*
Neil Nance, *Vice Pres*
Edward Diolazo, *Technician*
Boris Rozenberg, *Engineer*
Wendy Williams, *Director*
EMP: 700
SQ FT: 10,000
SALES: 28MM **Privately Held**
WEB: www.sacrt.com
SIC: 4111 Bus line operations; commuter rail passenger operation

(P-3581)
SACRAMENTO REGIONAL TRNST DIST
Transit System Development
1400 29th St, Sacramento (95816-6406)
P.O. Box 2110 (95812-2110)
PHONE.........................916 321-2800
Beverly Scott, *Manager*
Neil Nance, *Vice Pres*
Maria Whitworth, *Admin Asst*
Robin Haswell, *Technology*
Craig Norman, *Engineer*
EMP: 118
SALES (corp-wide): 28MM **Privately Held**
SIC: 4111 Bus line operations
PA: Sacramento Regional Transit Dist.
1400 29th St
Sacramento CA 95816
916 726-2877

(P-3582)
SAN DIEGO METRO TRNST SYS
1255 Imperial Ave # 1000, San Diego (92101-7490)
PHONE.........................619 231-1466
Paul Jadlonski, *CEO*
Stan Abrams, *CEO*
Sergio Iniguez, *Officer*
Jeff Stumbo, *Executive*
Julia Tuer, *Executive Asst*
EMP: 1600
SQ FT: 40,000
SALES: 113.5MM **Privately Held**
WEB: www.sdtc.sdmts.com
SIC: 4111 Bus line operations

(P-3583)
SAN DIEGO TRANSIT CORPORATION (PA)
100 16th St, San Diego (92101-7694)
PHONE.........................619 238-0100
Langley Powell, *President*
Bill Spraul, *COO*
Wayne Terry, *Officer*
Tom Lee, *Executive Asst*
Thomas Frantz, *Admin Sec*
EMP: 650
SQ FT: 20,000
SALES (est): 52.4MM **Privately Held**
WEB: www.sdcommute.com
SIC: 4111 Commuter bus operation; bus line operations

(P-3584)
SAN DIEGO TROLLEY INC
1341 Commercial St, San Diego (92113-1021)
PHONE.........................619 595-4933
Bill Brown, *Branch Mgr*
EMP: 370
SALES (corp-wide): 28.6MM **Privately Held**
WEB: www.sdrotary.org
SIC: 4111 Trolley operation
PA: San Diego Trolley Inc
1255 Imperial Ave Ste 900
San Diego CA 92101
619 595-4949

(P-3585)
SAN FRANCISCO BAY AREA RAPID
Also Called: 1st Interstate Bank Building
1330 Broadway, Oakland (94612-2503)
PHONE.........................510 464-6000
Thomas Margro, *Branch Mgr*

EMP: 50
SALES (corp-wide): 605.6MM **Privately Held**
SIC: 4111 Local railway passenger operation
PA: San Francisco Bay Area Rapid Transit District
300 Lakeside Dr
Oakland CA 94604
510 464-6000

(P-3586)
SAN FRANCISCO BAY AREA RAPID
Also Called: Operations Control Center
800 Madison St, Oakland (94607-4730)
PHONE.........................510 834-1297
Rudy Crespo, *Manager*
Paula Eubanks-Major, *Buyer*
EMP: 100
SALES (corp-wide): 605.6MM **Privately Held**
SIC: 4111 Local railway passenger operation
PA: San Francisco Bay Area Rapid Transit District
300 Lakeside Dr
Oakland CA 94604
510 464-6000

(P-3587)
SAN FRANCISCO BAY AREA RAPID
Also Called: Records Center/Storage
300 Lakeside Dr 23, Oakland (94612-3534)
PHONE.........................510 464-6126
Tom Margaro, *Branch Mgr*
EMP: 103
SALES (corp-wide): 605.6MM **Privately Held**
SIC: 4111 Local railway passenger operation
PA: San Francisco Bay Area Rapid Transit District
300 Lakeside Dr
Oakland CA 94604
510 464-6000

(P-3588)
SAN FRANCISCO BAY AREA RAPID
Also Called: Richmond Repair Shop
1101 13th St, Richmond (94801-2302)
PHONE.........................510 233-6848
Sean Steel, *Branch Mgr*
EMP: 150
SALES (corp-wide): 605.6MM **Privately Held**
SIC: 4111 Local railway passenger operation
PA: San Francisco Bay Area Rapid Transit District
300 Lakeside Dr
Oakland CA 94604
510 464-6000

(P-3589)
SAN FRANCISCO BAY AREA RAPID
Also Called: Richmond Yard Tower
1101 13th St, Richmond (94801-2302)
PHONE.........................510 233-7444
Steve Brigham, *Branch Mgr*
EMP: 100
SALES (corp-wide): 605.6MM **Privately Held**
SIC: 4111 Local & suburban transit
PA: San Francisco Bay Area Rapid Transit District
300 Lakeside Dr
Oakland CA 94604
510 464-6000

(P-3590)
SAN FRANCISCO BAY AREA RAPID
Also Called: Oakland Shops/Annex
601 E 8th St, Oakland (94606-3606)
PHONE.........................510 286-2893
Tom Delaney, *Superintendent*
EMP: 2000

SALES (corp-wide): 605.6MM **Privately Held**
SIC: 4111 Local railway passenger operation
PA: San Francisco Bay Area Rapid Transit District
300 Lakeside Dr
Oakland CA 94604
510 464-6000

(P-3591)
SAN FRANCISCO BAY AREA RAPID
Also Called: Police Department
800 Madison St, Oakland (94607-4730)
P.O. Box 12668 (94604)
PHONE.........................510 464-7000
Kenton Rainey, *Chief*
EMP: 99
SALES (corp-wide): 605.6MM **Privately Held**
SIC: 4111 Local railway passenger operation
PA: San Francisco Bay Area Rapid Transit District
300 Lakeside Dr
Oakland CA 94604
510 464-6000

(P-3592)
SAN FRANCISCO BAY AREA RAPID
Also Called: Madison Square Building
300 Lakeside Dr Fl 17, Oakland (94612-3534)
PHONE.........................510 464-6000
Thomas Margro, *Manager*
EMP: 103
SALES (corp-wide): 605.6MM **Privately Held**
SIC: 4111 Local railway passenger operation
PA: San Francisco Bay Area Rapid Transit District
300 Lakeside Dr
Oakland CA 94604
510 464-6000

(P-3593)
SAN FRNCSCO BAY AREA RPID TRNS (PA)
Also Called: Bart
300 Lakeside Dr, Oakland (94604)
P.O. Box 12688 (94604-2688)
PHONE.........................510 464-6000
Grace Crunican, *General Mgr*
Louise Holsten, *CFO*
Scott Schroeder, *Treasurer*
Jim Allison, *Officer*
Gary Anderson, *Officer*
▲ **EMP:** 400
SQ FT: 150,000
SALES: 605.6MM **Privately Held**
SIC: 4111 Local railway passenger operation

(P-3594)
SAN GABRIEL TRANSIT INC (PA)
Also Called: San Gabriel Valley Cab Co
3650 Rockwell Ave, El Monte (91731-2322)
PHONE.........................626 258-1310
Timmy Mardirossian, *President*
Eda Aghajanian, *Treasurer*
Sedik Mardirossian, *Admin Sec*
Mike Hakopyan, *Info Tech Mgr*
Luisa Sun, *Info Tech Mgr*
EMP: 220
SQ FT: 8,000
SALES (est): 21.5MM **Privately Held**
WEB: www.sgtransit.com
SIC: 4111 Local & suburban transit

(P-3595)
SAN JOAQUIN REGIONAL TRNST DST
Also Called: Sjrtd
421 E Weber Ave, Stockton (95202-3024)
P.O. Box 201010 (95201-9010)
PHONE.........................209 948-5566
Donna Demartino, *CEO*
Gloria Salazar, *CFO*
Max Vargas, *Officer*
Donna Kelsay, *General Mgr*
Sean Messick, *Technology*

P R O D U C T S & S V C S

EMP: 201
SQ FT: 29,100
SALES (est): 13.4MM **Privately Held**
WEB: www.sanjoaquinrtd.com
SIC: 4111 Bus line operations

(P-3596)
SAN LUIS OBISPO REGIONAL
Also Called: Slorta
179 Cross St Ste A, San Luis Obispo
(93401-7597)
PHONE..................................805 781-4465
Omar McPherson, *Principal*
Tania Arnold, *CFO*
Geoff Straw, *Director*
EMP: 90
SALES (est): 5MM **Privately Held**
WEB: www.caltip.org
SIC: 4111 Local & suburban transit

(P-3597)
SAN MATEO COUNTY TRANSIT DST (PA)
1250 San Carlos Ave, San Carlos
(94070-2468)
P.O. Box 3006 (94070-1306)
PHONE..................................650 508-6200
Mike Scanlon, *CEO*
Bill Likens, *President*
Ch Harvey, *COO*
Virginia Harrington, *CFO*
Rita Haskin, *Ch Credit Ofcr*
EMP: 250
SQ FT: 20,000
SALES: 15.7MM **Privately Held**
WEB: www.samtrans.com
SIC: 4111 Bus line operations

(P-3598)
SAN MATEO COUNTY TRANSIT DST
Also Called: Sam Trans
301 N Access Rd, South San Francisco
(94080-6901)
PHONE..................................650 588-4860
John Gerbo, *Branch Mgr*
Elliot Rivas, *Maint Spvr*
EMP: 300
SQ FT: 2,000
SALES (corp-wide): 15.7MM **Privately Held**
SIC: 4111 Bus line operations
PA: San Mateo County Transit District
1250 San Carlos Ave
San Carlos CA 94070
650 508-6200

(P-3599)
SANTA BARBARA METRO TRNST DST (PA)
Also Called: M T D
550 Olive St, Santa Barbara (93101-1610)
PHONE..................................805 963-3364
David Davis, *Chairman*
John Britton, *Ch of Bd*
Chuck McQuary, *Vice Chairman*
Gary Gleason, *General Mgr*
Bill Shelor, *Admin Sec*
EMP: 66
SQ FT: 8,500
SALES (est): 16.4MM **Privately Held**
WEB: www.sbmtd.gov
SIC: 4111 Bus line operations

(P-3600)
SANTA CLARA VALLEY TRNSP AUTH (PA)
3331 N 1st St, San Jose (95134-1906)
PHONE..................................408 321-2300
Nuria Fernandez, *CEO*
David Ledwitz, *Analyst*
Mary AP, *Accountant*
Grace Salandanan, *Auditor*
Sylvester Barnes, *Human Res Dir*
▲ **EMP:** 2053
SQ FT: 217,000
SALES (est): 18.2MM **Privately Held**
SIC: 4111 Local & suburban transit

(P-3601)
SANTA CLARA VALLEY TRNSP AUTH
Document Control-Central File
3331 N 1st St Bldg B, San Jose
(95134-1906)
PHONE..................................408 321-5559
Michael Burns, *Manager*
EMP: 120
SALES (est): 2.1MM
SALES (corp-wide): 18.2MM **Privately Held**
SIC: 4111 9621 Local & suburban transit;
PA: Santa Clara Valley Transportation Authority
3331 N 1st St
San Jose CA 95134
408 321-2300

(P-3602)
SANTA CRUZ METRO TRNST DST
135 Aviation Way Ste 2, Watsonville
(95076-2046)
PHONE..................................831 426-6080
Lesley White, *Branch Mgr*
EMP: 300
SALES (corp-wide): 10.2MM **Privately Held**
SIC: 4111 Local & suburban transit
PA: Santa Cruz Metropolitan Transit District
110 Vernon St
Santa Cruz CA 95060
831 426-6143

(P-3603)
SFO AIRPORTER INC (PA)
Also Called: Compass Transportation Charter
160 S Linden Ave Ste 300, South Francisco (94080-6436)
PHONE..................................650 246-2734
Nicholas C Leonoudakis, *Ch of Bd*
Jeffrey G Leonoudakis, *President*
Stephan C Leonoudakis, *Exec VP*
Timothy K Leonoudakis, *Vice Pres*
EMP: 100
SALES (est): 26.3MM **Privately Held**
SIC: 4111 4141 4131 Airport transportation; local bus charter service; intercity bus line

(P-3604)
SFO AIRPORTER INC
325 5th St, San Francisco (94107-1040)
PHONE..................................415 495-3909
Gordis Esposto, *Branch Mgr*
EMP: 100
SALES (corp-wide): 26.3MM **Privately Held**
SIC: 4111 4141 4131 Airport transportation; local bus charter service; intercity bus line
PA: Sfo Airporter, Inc.
160 S Linden Ave Ste 300
South San Francisco CA 94080
650 246-2734

(P-3605)
SFO SHUTTLE BUS INC
San Francisco Intl Arprt, San Francisco
(94128)
PHONE..................................650 877-0430
Jeffrey Leonoudakis, *President*
Tim Leonoudakis, *Vice Pres*
EMP: 197
SQ FT: 20,000
SALES: 7.2MM **Privately Held**
SIC: 4111 Airport transportation services, regular route

(P-3606)
SMS TRANSPORTATION SVCS INC
865 S Figueroa St # 2750, Los Angeles
(90017-2627)
PHONE..................................213 489-5367
John Harris, *CEO*
Delilah Lanoix, *President*
Jennifer Wiltz, *COO*
Danielle Wiltz, *CFO*
EMP: 150
SQ FT: 3,000
SALES: 10MM **Privately Held**
SIC: 4111 Airport transportation

(P-3607)
SONOMA COUNTY AIRPORT EX INC
5807 Old Redwood Hwy, Santa Rosa
(95403-1167)
PHONE..................................707 837-8700
Howard Emigh, *President*
Tony Geraldi, *Corp Secy*
EMP: 80
SQ FT: 5,500
SALES: 5.5MM
SALES (corp-wide): 40.9MM **Privately Held**
WEB: www.airportexpressinc.com
SIC: 4111 4141 Airport transportation services, regular route; local bus charter service
PA: Groome Transportation, Incorporated
2289 Dabney Rd
Richmond VA 23230
804 222-7226

(P-3608)
SOUTH BAY AIRPORT SHUTTLE
Also Called: East Bay Airport Shuttle
14420 Union Ave, San Jose (95124-2815)
P.O. Box 219, Campbell (95009-0219)
PHONE..................................408 225-4444
Behzad Fatemi, *President*
Donia Fatemi, *Treasurer*
EMP: 95
SQ FT: 2,000
SALES: 15MM **Privately Held**
WEB: www.southbayairportshuttle.com
SIC: 4111 Airport transportation services, regular route

(P-3609)
STARLIGHT CORPORATION (PA)
2100 Palomar Airpt Rd # 2, Carlsbad
(92011-4402)
PHONE..................................858 509-9006
Leslie Hall, *President*
Casey Bennett, *Exec VP*
EMP: 120
SALES: 3.8MM **Privately Held**
SIC: 4111 4581 7349 8742 Airport transportation; aircraft cleaning & janitorial service; building & office cleaning services; materials mgmt. (purchasing, handling, inventory) consultant

(P-3610)
SUPERSHUTTLE INTERNATIONAL INC
9559 Center Ave Ste F, Rancho Cucamonga (91730-5815)
PHONE..................................909 944-2606
Margaret Nathan, *Principal*
Jennifer Streeter, *Director*
EMP: 150
SALES (corp-wide): 1.3B **Privately Held**
SIC: 4111 Airport transportation
HQ: Supershuttle International, Inc.
14500 N Northsight Blvd # 329
Scottsdale AZ 85260
480 609-3000

(P-3611)
SUPERSHUTTLE INTERNATIONAL INC
Also Called: Supershuttle Sacramento
3100 Northgate Blvd, Sacramento
(95833-1349)
PHONE..................................916 648-2500
Igor Avanto, *General Mgr*
EMP: 65
SQ FT: 1,600
SALES (corp-wide): 1.3B **Privately Held**
WEB: www.execucar.com
SIC: 4111 Airport transportation services, regular route
HQ: Supershuttle International, Inc.
14500 N Northsight Blvd # 329
Scottsdale AZ 85260
480 609-3000

(P-3612)
SUPERSHUTTLE LOS ANGELES INC
531 Van Ness Ave, Torrance (90501-6233)
PHONE..................................310 222-5500
Gene Hauk, *President*
R Brian Wier, *CEO*
Thomas C Lavoy, *CFO*

EMP: 165
SQ FT: 15,000
SALES (est): 4.8MM
SALES (corp-wide): 1.3B **Privately Held**
WEB: www.execucar.com
SIC: 4111 Local & suburban transit
HQ: Supershuttle International, Inc.
14500 N Northsight Blvd # 329
Scottsdale AZ 85260
480 609-3000

(P-3613)
SUPERSHUTTLE ORANGE COUNTY INC
531 Van Ness Ave, Torrance (90501-6233)
PHONE..................................310 222-5500
Steven Allan, *President*
EMP: 300
SQ FT: 12,000
SALES (est): 5.6MM
SALES (corp-wide): 1.3B **Privately Held**
WEB: www.execucar.com
SIC: 4111 Airport transportation
HQ: Supershuttle International, Inc.
14500 N Northsight Blvd # 329
Scottsdale AZ 85260
480 609-3000

(P-3614)
TRANSPORTATION CONCEPT INC
Also Called: T C I
1521 Kingsdale Ave, Redondo Beach
(90278-3939)
PHONE..................................323 268-2202
Brian Connell, *Manager*
Brett Baum, *General Mgr*
EMP: 70
SALES (est): 2.2MM **Privately Held**
SIC: 4111 Bus transportation

(P-3615)
TWO HARBORS ENTERPRISES INC
150 Metropole Ave, Avalon (90704)
P.O. Box 5086 (90704-5086)
PHONE..................................310 510-2000
Kathy Thompson, *Vice Pres*
EMP: 75
SALES (est): 4.7MM **Privately Held**
SIC: 4111 Bus transportation

(P-3616)
WEST COUNTY TRNSP AGCY
367 W Robles Ave, Santa Rosa
(95407-8126)
PHONE..................................707 206-9988
Chad Barksdale, *Exec Dir*
Michael REA, *Principal*
Dee Khaleck, *Tech/Comp Coord*
EMP: 177
SQ FT: 125,017
SALES: 16.7MM **Privately Held**
SIC: 4111 Local & suburban transit

4119 Local Passenger Transportation: NEC

(P-3617)
ADVANTAGE GROUND TRNSP CORP
Also Called: Advantage Ground Trnsp
2960 Airway Ave Ste B102, Costa Mesa
(92626-6001)
PHONE..................................714 557-2465
Vo Van Vu, *President*
Joseph Dullulo, *Vice Pres*
EMP: 80
SQ FT: 3,200
SALES (est): 4MM **Privately Held**
WEB: www.agtcorp.com
SIC: 4119 Limousine rental, with driver

(P-3618)
AEGIS AMBULANCE SERVICE INC (PA)
1151 S Boyle Ave, Los Angeles
(90023-2109)
PHONE..................................626 685-9410
Paul Richart, *President*
Jimmy Tripodi, *Opers Mgr*
EMP: 62

SALES (est): 1.7MM **Privately Held**
WEB: www.aegisambulance.com
SIC: **4119** Ambulance service

(P-3619)
ALLIED MEDICAL SERVICE OF CAL
2570 Bush St, San Francisco (94115-3002)
PHONE..................................415 931-1400
Josette Mani, *President*
Leif Engman, *President*
Glen Millar, *CFO*
EMP: 50
SQ FT: 6,000
SALES (est): 1.9MM **Privately Held**
WEB: www.kingamerican.com
SIC: **4119** 6411 Ambulance service; insurance agents, brokers & service

(P-3620)
AMATO INDUSTRIES INCORPORATED
Also Called: Gateway Limousine
1550 Gilbreth Rd, Burlingame (94010-1605)
PHONE..................................650 697-5548
Sam Amato, *CEO*
Joel Amato, *Vice Pres*
Karen Amato, *Vice Pres*
Gina Bonelli, *Administration*
Tom Amato, *Finance*
EMP: 75
SQ FT: 9,500
SALES (est): 5.8MM **Privately Held**
WEB: www.gatewaylimousine.com
SIC: **4119** Limousine rental, with driver

(P-3621)
AMBULNZ HEALTH LLC
12531 Vanowen St, North Hollywood (91605-5321)
PHONE..................................877 311-5555
EMP: 293
SALES (corp-wide): 17MM **Privately Held**
SIC: **4119** Ambulance service
PA: Ambulnz Health, Llc
    1151 S Boyle Ave
    Los Angeles CA 90023
    877 311-5555

(P-3622)
AMERICAN MED
Also Called: Redlands Division
600 Iowa St, Redlands (92373-8047)
PHONE..................................909 793-7676
James Price, *Director*
EMP: 250 **Privately Held**
WEB: www.amr-inc.com
SIC: **4119** Ambulance service
HQ: American Medical Response, Inc.
    6363 S Fiddlers Green Cir # 1400
    Greenwood Village CO 80111

(P-3623)
AMERICAN MED
Also Called: A M R
5257 Vincent Ave, Irwindale (91706-2042)
PHONE..................................626 633-4600
Art McKierman, *Branch Mgr*
EMP: 260 **Privately Held**
SIC: **4119** Ambulance service
HQ: American Medical Response, Inc.
    6363 S Fiddlers Green Cir # 1400
    Greenwood Village CO 80111

(P-3624)
AMERICAN MED
1510 Rollins Rd, Burlingame (94010-2306)
PHONE..................................650 235-1333
John Odle, *Principal*
EMP: 106 **Privately Held**
WEB: www.amr-inc.com
SIC: **4119** Ambulance service
HQ: American Medical Response, Inc.
    6363 S Fiddlers Green Cir # 1400
    Greenwood Village CO 80111

(P-3625)
AMERICAN MED
7575 Southfront Rd, Livermore (94551-8226)
PHONE..................................510 895-7600

Brad Cooper, *CFO*
EMP: 106 **Privately Held**
SIC: **4119** Ambulance service
HQ: American Medical Response, Inc.
    6363 S Fiddlers Green Cir # 1400
    Greenwood Village CO 80111

(P-3626)
AMERICAN MED
7925 Center Ave, Rancho Cucamonga (91730-3007)
PHONE..................................909 948-1714
Rene Polarossa, *General Mgr*
EMP: 106 **Privately Held**
WEB: www.amr-inc.com
SIC: **4119** Ambulance service
HQ: American Medical Response, Inc.
    6363 S Fiddlers Green Cir # 1400
    Greenwood Village CO 80111

(P-3627)
AMERICAN MED RESP AMBLNC SVC
Also Called: Sonoma Life Support
930 S A St, Santa Rosa (95404-5439)
PHONE..................................707 536-0400
Lori Price, *Director*
EMP: 70 **Privately Held**
WEB: www.amr-inc.com
SIC: **4119** Ambulance service
HQ: American Medical Response, Inc.
    6363 S Fiddlers Green Cir # 1400
    Greenwood Village CO 80111

(P-3628)
AMERICAN MED RSPNSE STHERN CAL
1055 W Avenue J, Lancaster (93534-3328)
PHONE..................................661 945-9310
Louis Meyer, *President*
Don Harvey, *COO*
Randel Owen, *CFO*
Todd Zimmerman, *Exec VP*
Tim Dorn, *Vice Pres*
EMP: 2806 EST: 2000
SALES (est): 20.8MM **Privately Held**
SIC: **4119** Ambulance service
HQ: American Medical Response, Inc.
    6363 S Fiddlers Green Cir # 1400
    Greenwood Village CO 80111
-

(P-3629)
AMERICAN MEDICAL RESPONSE
2400 Bisso Ln, Concord (94520-4832)
PHONE..................................925 454-6000
EMP: 180 **Privately Held**
SIC: **4119** Ambulance service
HQ: American Medical Response
    879 Marlborough Ave
    Riverside CA 92507

(P-3630)
AMERICAN MEDICAL RESPONSE
1041 Fee Dr, Sacramento (95815-3908)
PHONE..................................916 563-0600
Doug Petric, *Director*
EMP: 400 **Privately Held**
SIC: **4119** Ambulance service
HQ: American Medical Response
    879 Marlborough Ave
    Riverside CA 92507

(P-3631)
AMERICAN MEDICAL RESPONSE
1300 Illinois St, San Francisco (94107-3107)
PHONE..................................415 922-9400
James Salvante, *Manager*
EMP: 75 **Privately Held**
SIC: **4119** Ambulance service
HQ: American Medical Response
    879 Marlborough Ave
    Riverside CA 92507

(P-3632)
AMERICAN MEDICAL RESPONSE
116 Hubbard St, Santa Cruz (95060-2938)
PHONE..................................831 423-7030
David Zenker, *Manager*
EMP: 57 **Privately Held**
SIC: **4119** Ambulance service
HQ: American Medical Response
    879 Marlborough Ave
    Riverside CA 92507

(P-3633)
AMERICAN MEDICAL RESPONSE (DH)
879 Marlborough Ave, Riverside (92507-2133)
PHONE..................................951 782-5200
Bill Fanger, *President*
EMP: 80
SQ FT: 24,000
SALES (est): 38MM **Privately Held**
SIC: **4119** Ambulance service

(P-3634)
AMERICAN MEDICAL RESPONSE
1510 Rollins Rd, Burlingame (94010-2306)
PHONE..................................650 235-1333
EMP: 100 **Privately Held**
SIC: **4119** Ambulance service
HQ: American Medical Response
    879 Marlborough Ave
    Riverside CA 92507

(P-3635)
AMERICAN MEDICAL RESPONSE INC
2400 Bisso Ln, Concord (94520-4832)
PHONE..................................925 602-1300
EMP: 106 **Privately Held**
SIC: **4119** Ambulance service
HQ: American Medical Response, Inc.
    6363 S Fiddlers Green Cir # 1400
    Greenwood Village CO 80111

(P-3636)
AMERICAN MEDICAL RESPONSE INC
1420 Lander Ave, Turlock (95380-6202)
PHONE..................................209 567-4030
Cindy Woolston, *Manager*
EMP: 106 **Privately Held**
SIC: **4119** Ambulance service
HQ: American Medical Response, Inc.
    6363 S Fiddlers Green Cir # 1400
    Greenwood Village CO 80111

(P-3637)
AMERICAN MEDICAL RESPONSE INC
3465 Camino Del Rio S # 410, San Diego (92108-3909)
PHONE..................................858 492-3500
Rich Ahrendt, *Vice Pres*
EMP: 250 **Privately Held**
WEB: www.amr-inc.com
SIC: **4119** Ambulance service
HQ: American Medical Response, Inc.
    6363 S Fiddlers Green Cir # 1400
    Greenwood Village CO 80111

(P-3638)
AMERICAN MEDICAL RESPONSE INC
Mobile Life Support
240 E Highway 246 Ste 300, Buellton (93427-9648)
PHONE..................................805 688-6550
John H Eaglesham, *Branch Mgr*
EMP: 125
SQ FT: 2,000 **Privately Held**
WEB: www.amr-inc.com
SIC: **4119** Ambulance service
HQ: American Medical Response, Inc.
    6363 S Fiddlers Green Cir # 1400
    Greenwood Village CO 80111

(P-3639)
AMERICAN MEDICAL RESPONSE INC
1111 Montalvo Way, Palm Springs (92262-5440)
PHONE..................................760 883-5000
Wayne Dennis, *Principal*
EMP: 160 **Privately Held**
SIC: **4119** 8099 Ambulance service; medical rescue squad
HQ: American Medical Response, Inc.
    6363 S Fiddlers Green Cir # 1400
    Greenwood Village CO 80111

(P-3640)
AMERICAN MEDICAL RESPONSE INC
4548 A St, Marina (93933)
PHONE..................................831 718-9555
Chris Weinress, *Manager*
EMP: 175 **Privately Held**
WEB: www.amr-inc.com
SIC: **4119** Ambulance service
HQ: American Medical Response, Inc.
    6363 S Fiddlers Green Cir # 1400
    Greenwood Village CO 80111

(P-3641)
AMERICAN MEDICAL RESPONSE INC
Also Called: Hemet Valley Ambulance
208 E Devonshire Ave A, Hemet (92543-2985)
PHONE..................................951 765-3900
Jack Hansen, *Branch Mgr*
EMP: 106 **Privately Held**
SIC: **4119** Ambulance service
HQ: American Medical Response, Inc.
    6363 S Fiddlers Green Cir # 1400
    Greenwood Village CO 80111
-

(P-3642)
AMERICAN MEDICAL RESPONSE INC
1870 Hillcrest Rd, Hollister (95023-5204)
PHONE..................................831 636-9391
Edward Van Horne, *Branch Mgr*
EMP: 107 **Privately Held**
SIC: **4119** Ambulance service
HQ: American Medical Response, Inc.
    6363 S Fiddlers Green Cir # 1400
    Greenwood Village CO 80111
-

(P-3643)
AMERICAN MEDICAL RESPONSE INC
13146 Lincoln Way, Auburn (95603-4114)
PHONE..................................530 887-9440
Michael Mendenhall, *Manager*
EMP: 50 **Privately Held**
WEB: www.amr-inc.com
SIC: **4119** Ambulance service
HQ: American Medical Response, Inc.
    6363 S Fiddlers Green Cir # 1400
    Greenwood Village CO 80111

(P-3644)
AMERICAN MEDICAL RESPONSE INC
13992 Catalina St, San Leandro (94577-5506)
PHONE..................................415 794-9204
Thomas Wagner, *CEO*
EMP: 250 EST: 1992
SALES (est): 1.8MM
SALES (corp-wide): 643.1MM **Privately Held**
SIC: **4119** 7372 Ambulance service; application computer software
HQ: Envision Healthcare Corporation
    1a Burton Hills Blvd
    Nashville TN 37215
    615 665-1283

PRODUCTS & SVCS

(P-3645)
AMERICAN MEDICAL RESPONSE WEST
Also Called: San Joaquin County Operations
3755 West Ln, Stockton (95204-2431)
PHONE..................................209 948-5136
Barry Elzig, *Regional Dir*
EMP: 320　**Privately Held**
SIC: 4119 Ambulance service
HQ: American Medical Response West
6363 S Fiddlers Green Cir # 1400
Greenwood Village CO 80111

(P-3646)
AMERICAN PROF AMBULANCE CORP
16945 Sherman Way, Van Nuys
(91406-3614)
P.O. Box 7263 (91409-7263)
PHONE..................................818 996-2200
Lyubov Popok, *President*
EMP: 175
SALES (est): 5.5MM　**Privately Held**
SIC: 4119 Ambulance service

(P-3647)
AMERICARE MEDSERVICES INC
Also Called: Americare Ambulance Service
6524 Fremont Cir, Huntington Beach
(92648-6637)
PHONE..................................310 632-1141
Michael Summers, *President*
EMP: 155
SQ FT: 10,000
SALES (est): 6.1MM　**Privately Held**
WEB: www.americare.org
SIC: 4119 Ambulance service

(P-3648)
ATLANTIC EXPRESS TRNSP
Also Called: Atlantic Express of California
2450 Long Beach Blvd, Long Beach
(90806-3125)
PHONE..................................562 997-6868
Darinda Garnett, *Manager*
EMP: 120
SALES (corp-wide): 334.6MM　**Privately Held**
SIC: 4119 8748 4151 Local passenger transportation; traffic consultant; school buses
HQ: Atlantic Express Transportation Corp
7 North St
Staten Island NY 10302
718 442-7000

(P-3649)
BAUERS INTELLIGENT TRNSP INC (PA)
50 Pier, San Francisco (94158-2193)
PHONE..................................415 522-1212
Gary Bauer, *CEO*
Dennis Jackson, *COO*
Gary Schwartz, *CFO*
Mike Harshfield MBA, *Senior VP*
Erik Verboonen, *Executive*
EMP: 250
SQ FT: 125,000
SALES: 38.5MM　**Privately Held**
WEB: www.bauersIT.com
SIC: 4119 Limousine rental, with driver

(P-3650)
BAY MEDIC TRANSPORTATION INC
959 Detroit Ave, Concord (94518-2501)
PHONE..................................800 689-9511
Nesar Abdiani, *CEO*
Ali Abdani, *President*
EMP: 56
SQ FT: 1,600
SALES (est): 2.1MM　**Privately Held**
WEB: www.baymedic.com
SIC: 4119 Ambulance service

(P-3651)
BAYSHORE AMBULANCE INC (PA)
370 Hatch Dr, Foster City (94404-1106)
P.O. Box 4622 (94404-0622)
PHONE..................................650 525-9700
William Bockholt, *President*
David Bockholt, *Treasurer*

EMP: 51
SQ FT: 5,000
SALES (est): 5.9MM　**Privately Held**
WEB: www.bayshoreambulance.com
SIC: 4119 Ambulance service

(P-3652)
BI-COUNTY AMBULANCE SERVICE
1700 Poole Blvd, Yuba City (95993-2610)
P.O. Box 3130 (95992-3130)
PHONE..................................530 674-2780
Kelly W Bumpus, *President*
EMP: 50
SQ FT: 1,600
SALES (est): 1.9MM　**Privately Held**
WEB: www.bicountyambulance.com
SIC: 4119 Ambulance service

(P-3653)
BLACK TIE TRANSPORTATION LLC
7080 Commerce Dr, Pleasanton
(94588-8021)
PHONE..................................925 847-0747
Bill Wheeler, *Mng Member*
Debbie Moore,
Jennifer Wheeler,
EMP: 130
SQ FT: 18,000
SALES (est): 6.7MM　**Privately Held**
WEB: www.blacktietrans.com
SIC: 4119 4724 Limousine rental, with driver; travel agencies

(P-3654)
BLS LMSINE SVC LOS ANGELES INC
Also Called: B L S Limousine Service
2860 Fletcher Dr, Los Angeles
(90039-2452)
PHONE..................................323 644-7166
Jay D Okon, *President*
William Kain, *Manager*
EMP: 350
SQ FT: 20,000
SALES (est): 10.1MM　**Privately Held**
SIC: 4119 Limousine rental, with driver

(P-3655)
C O T S INC (PA)
Also Called: Continental Trnsp Svcs
6242 Cherry Ave, Long Beach
(90805-3205)
P.O. Box 4742, Irvine (92616-4742)
PHONE..................................714 751-5466
Anne Stachel Garkani, *President*
MO Garkani, *Controller*
EMP: 53
SALES (est): 1.6MM　**Privately Held**
SIC: 4119 Limousine rental, with driver

(P-3656)
CALIFORNIA LIMOUSINES
9851 Irvine Center Dr, Irvine (92618-4307)
PHONE..................................949 581-7531
Joseph Magnano, *President*
Frank J Duvall, *Senior VP*
EMP: 55
SQ FT: 5,600
SALES (est): 3.1MM　**Privately Held**
SIC: 4119 Limousine rental, with driver

(P-3657)
CALIFORNIA MED RESPONSE INC
Also Called: Cal-Med Ambulance
1557 Santa Anita Ave, South El Monte
(91733-3313)
PHONE..................................562 968-1818
Ronald A Marks, *President*
Linda Marks, *Treasurer*
Tyler Marks, *Officer*
EMP: 70
SALES (est): 2.5MM　**Privately Held**
SIC: 4119 Ambulance service

(P-3658)
CALIFRNIA SHOCK TRUMA A RESCUE (PA)
Also Called: Calstar
4933 Bailey Loop, McClellan (95652-2516)
PHONE..................................916 921-4000
Lynn Malmstrom, *President*
Sonja Vargas, *Admin Asst*

EMP: 63
SQ FT: 44,000
SALES: 52.9MM　**Privately Held**
WEB: www.calstar.org
SIC: 4119 Ambulance service

(P-3659)
CARE AMBULANCE SERVICE INC
8932 Katella Ave Ste 201, Anaheim
(92804-6299)
PHONE..................................714 828-7750
Dan Richardson, *Principal*
EMP: 636
SALES (corp-wide): 91.3MM　**Privately Held**
SIC: 4119 Ambulance service
PA: Care Ambulance Service, Inc.
1517 W Braden Ct
Orange CA 92868
714 288-3800

(P-3660)
CARE AMBULANCE SERVICE INC
515 W Beverly Blvd, Montebello
(90640-3665)
PHONE..................................323 838-0542
EMP: 318
SALES (corp-wide): 91.3MM　**Privately Held**
SIC: 4119 Ambulance service
PA: Care Ambulance Service, Inc.
1517 W Braden Ct
Orange CA 92868
714 288-3800

(P-3661)
CAV INC
Also Called: Care A Van Transport
5411 Avenida Encinas # 210, Carlsbad
(92008-4409)
PHONE..................................760 729-5199
Richard Dripps, *President*
Robert Newkirk, *Opers Staff*
Bob Newkirk, *Director*
Robert Sneedon, *Director*
Deana Mason, *Manager*
EMP: 75
SQ FT: 1,200
SALES (est): 4.4MM　**Privately Held**
SIC: 4119 Ambulance service

(P-3662)
CLS TRNSPRTTION LOS ANGLES LLC (HQ)
Also Called: Empire Cls Worldwide
600 S Allied Way, El Segundo
(90245-4727)
PHONE..................................310 414-8189
David Singler, *Mng Member*
Jamie Thompson, *Human Res Mgr*
Joel Stein, *Opers Staff*
EMP: 150
SALES (est): 17MM　**Privately Held**
WEB: www.clslimo.com
SIC: 4119 Limousine rental, with driver

(P-3663)
COLS INC
1611 S Melrose Dr 253&278, Vista
(92081-5407)
PHONE..................................714 720-6100
MO Garkani, *President*
EMP: 150 EST: 2008
SALES: 12MM　**Privately Held**
SIC: 4119 Limousine rental, with driver

(P-3664)
CROWN TRANSPORTATION INC
Also Called: Crown Limousine L.A.
12300 W Washington Blvd, Los Angeles
(90066-5510)
PHONE..................................310 737-0888
David Navon, *President*
Memphis Jasper, *Admin Asst*
EMP: 51
SQ FT: 1,000
SALES (est): 3.5MM　**Privately Held**
WEB: www.crownlimola.com
SIC: 4119 Limousine rental, with driver

(P-3665)
EAST SAN GBRIEL VLY CONSORTIUM
Also Called: La Works
5200 Irwindale Ave # 210, Irwindale
(91706-2097)
PHONE..................................626 960-3964
Salvador Velasquez, *President*
Kevin Stapleston, *Chairman*
EMP: 60
SQ FT: 28,000
SALES (est): 2.6MM　**Privately Held**
SIC: 4119 8331 Local passenger transportation; job training services

(P-3666)
EASTWESTPROTO INC
Also Called: Lifeline Ambulance
1120 S Maple Ave Ste 200, Montebello
(90640-6043)
PHONE..................................888 535-5728
Genady Gorin, *CEO*
Genia Gorin, *President*
Larry Cruz, *Vice Pres*
Jordan Weiss, *Vice Pres*
Santillan Daniel, *Opers Staff*
EMP: 120
SQ FT: 10,000
SALES (est): 6MM　**Privately Held**
SIC: 4119 Ambulance service

(P-3667)
EMERGENCY AMBULANCE SERVICE
3200 E Birch St Ste A, Brea (92821-6287)
PHONE..................................714 990-1331
Phillip E Davis, *President*
Scott Pipkin, *CFO*
Randy Wolmart, *Exec Dir*
Max Liphart, *Controller*
Cory Osburn, *Controller*
EMP: 80
SALES (est): 4.1MM　**Privately Held**
WEB: www.emergencyambulance.com
SIC: 4119 Ambulance service

(P-3668)
EMPIRE ENTERPRISES INC
Also Called: Empire Parking
8800 Park St, Bellflower (90706-5529)
PHONE..................................562 529-2676
Mike Oliver, *President*
EMP: 145
SQ FT: 1,700
SALES (est): 3.7MM　**Privately Held**
SIC: 4119 7521 4725 4142 Local rental transportation; automobile parking; tour operators; bus charter service, except local; local bus charter service

(P-3669)
EXECUTIVE NETWORK ENTPS INC
1224 21st St Apt E, Santa Monica
(90404-1390)
PHONE..................................310 457-8822
Patricia Stephenson, *Manager*
EMP: 60　**Privately Held**
WEB: www.ezeclimo.com
SIC: 4119 Limousine rental, with driver
PA: Executive Network Enterprises, Inc.
13440 Beach Ave
Marina Del Rey CA 90292

(P-3670)
EXECUTIVE NETWORK ENTPS INC (PA)
Also Called: Malibu Limousine Service
13440 Beach Ave, Marina Del Rey
(90292-5624)
PHONE..................................310 447-2759
Patricia Stephenson, *President*
Trish Rudd, *CFO*
Stori Stephenson, *Vice Pres*
EMP: 80
SQ FT: 5,000
SALES (est): 22.8MM　**Privately Held**
WEB: www.ezeclimo.com
SIC: 4119 Limousine rental, with driver

▲ = Import ▼=Export
◆ =Import/Export

(P-3671)
FILYN CORPORATION
Also Called: Lynch Ambulance Service
2950 E La Jolla St, Anaheim (92806-1307)
PHONE......................714 632-0225
Walter John Lynch, *CEO*
Nancy Lynch, *CEO*
Tina Heinemann, *Director*
Eric Somers, *Director*
Kathy Shoemake, *Manager*
EMP: 200
SALES (est): 9.7MM **Privately Held**
WEB: www.lynchambulance.com
SIC: 4119 Ambulance service

(P-3672)
FIRST RESPONDER EMS
333 Huss Dr Ste 100, Chico (95928-8242)
P.O. Box 24 (95927-0024)
PHONE......................530 897-6345
Byron Parsons, *CEO*
EMP: 114
SALES (est): 3MM **Privately Held**
SIC: 4119 Ambulance service

(P-3673)
FIRST RESPONDER EMS INC
Also Called: Paradise Ambulance Service
333 Huss Dr Ste 100, Chico (95928-8242)
PHONE......................530 897-6345
Byron Parsons, *President*
Bob Hall, *Manager*
EMP: 80
SALES (est): 1.3MM **Privately Held**
SIC: 4119 Ambulance service

(P-3674)
**FIRST RSPONDER EMRGNCY
MED SVC**
Also Called: Chico Paramedic Rescue
333 Huss Dr Ste 300, Chico (95928-8242)
PHONE......................530 891-4357
Byron Parsons, *President*
Louwayne Parsons, *Admin Sec*
EMP: 106
SALES (est): 3.8MM **Privately Held**
SIC: 4119 4522 Ambulance service; air
transportation, nonscheduled

(P-3675)
FRANCISCAN LINES INC
Also Called: San Francisco Sightseeing
41 Pier, San Francisco (94133-1009)
PHONE......................415 642-9400
Michael Waters, *Vice Pres*
Jim Casey, *General Mgr*
EMP: 130
SQ FT: 50,000
SALES (est): 3.5MM **Privately Held**
WEB: www.graylinesanfrancisco.com
SIC: 4119 Sightseeing bus

(P-3676)
**GARY CARDIFF ENTERPRISES
INC**
Also Called: Cardiff Transportation
75255 Sheryl Ave, Palm Desert
(92211-5129)
PHONE......................760 568-1403
Gary Cardiff, *CEO*
Sharon Cardiff, *Admin Sec*
Cathy Smith, *Human Res Dir*
EMP: 89
SQ FT: 10,000
SALES (est): 5.7MM **Privately Held**
WEB: www.cardifflimo.com
SIC: 4119 Limousine rental, with driver

(P-3677)
GENTLECARE TRANSPORT INC
Also Called: Gcti
3539 Casitas Ave, Los Angeles
(90039-1903)
PHONE......................323 662-8777
Mike Panassian, *CEO*
Eddie Avakian, *CFO*
EMP: 75
SQ FT: 8,000
SALES (est): 3MM **Privately Held**
SIC: 4119 Ambulance service

(P-3678)
**GERBER AMBULANCE
COMPANY INC**
Also Called: Gerber Ambulance Service
19801 Mariner Ave, Torrance (90503-1651)
P.O. Box 3487 (90510-3487)
PHONE......................310 542-6464
Robert Gerber, *President*
Rebecca Gerber, *Vice Pres*
EMP: 110
SQ FT: 2,400
SALES (est): 3.8MM **Privately Held**
SIC: 4119 Ambulance service

(P-3679)
**GLOBAL EMERGENCY ROAD
SVC LLC**
9908 San Fernando Rd, Pacoima
(91331-2605)
PHONE......................818 518-1166
Max Krumer, *Mng Member*
EMP: 50
SQ FT: 1,000
SALES (est): 2MM **Privately Held**
SIC: 4119 Local passenger transportation

(P-3680)
GLOBAL PARATRANSIT INC
400 W Compton Blvd, Gardena
(90248-1700)
PHONE......................310 715-7550
Reza Nasrollahy, *President*
Luis Garcia, *General Mgr*
Lee Habibi, *General Mgr*
Karina Abrica, *Project Mgr*
Victor Garate, *Cust Mgr*
EMP: 300 **EST:** 2000
SQ FT: 17,000
SALES (est): 13.7MM **Privately Held**
SIC: 4119 Ambulance service

(P-3681)
GM CRUISE LLC (HQ)
1201 Bryant St, San Francisco
(94103-4306)
PHONE......................415 335-4097
Kyle Vogt, *Mng Member*
Caitlin Hayes, *Executive Asst*
Jien Cao, *Software Engr*
Christophe Philippona, *Technical Staff*
Rick Fulton, *Engineer*
EMP: 75
SALES (est): 52.8MM **Publicly Held**
SIC: 4119 Automobile rental, with driver

(P-3682)
**GREYBOR MEDICAL
TRANSPORTATION**
119 Belmont Ave Ste 107, Los Angeles
(90026-5708)
P.O. Box 17239, Beverly Hills (90209-
3239)
PHONE......................213 250-4444
Gregory Plotkin, *Ch of Bd*
Boris Shpirt, *President*
EMP: 50
SQ FT: 1,000
SALES (est): 1MM **Privately Held**
SIC: 4119 5999 Ambulance service; tech-
nical aids for the handicapped

(P-3683)
**HALL AMBULANCE SERVICE
INC**
2001 O St O, Bakersfield (93301-4724)
PHONE......................661 322-8741
Harvy Hall, *President*
Johnathon Surface, *COO*
Rick Davis,
Robin Slater, *Manager*
EMP: 55
SALES (corp-wide): 25.1MM **Privately
Held**
WEB: www.hallamb.com
SIC: 4119 Ambulance service
PA: Hall Ambulance Service, Inc.
1001 21st St
Bakersfield CA 93301
661 322-8741

(P-3684)
**HALL AMBULANCE SERVICE
INC (PA)**
1001 21st St, Bakersfield (93301-4792)
PHONE......................661 322-8741
Harvey L Hall, *President*
Mary Kenny, *CFO*
Mark Moyes, *Technology*
Esther Silva, *Accountant*
Jackie ATT, *Controller*
EMP: 60
SQ FT: 4,000
SALES (est): 25.1MM **Privately Held**
WEB: www.hallamb.com
SIC: 4119 4729 4789 Ambulance service;
transportation ticket offices; cargo loading
& unloading services

(P-3685)
HERREN ENTERPRISES INC
Also Called: Doctors Ambulance Services
23091 Terra Dr, Laguna Hills (92653-1320)
PHONE......................949.951-1666
Bruce W Herren, *President*
Michael Herren, *Vice Pres*
EMP: 56
SQ FT: 4,000
SALES (est): 1.9MM
SALES (corp-wide): 643.1MM **Privately
Held**
WEB: www.doctorsambulance.com
SIC: 4119 Ambulance service
HQ: Envision Healthcare Corporation
1a Burton Hills Blvd
Nashville TN 37215
615 665-1283

(P-3686)
HYRECAR INC
355 S Grand Ave Ste 1650, Los Angeles
(90071-3172)
PHONE......................888 688-6769
Joseph Furnari, *CEO*
Grace Mellis, *Ch of Bd*
Henry Park, *COO*
Scott Brogi, *CFO*
Kit Tran, *Chief Mktg Ofcr*
EMP: 87 **EST:** 2014
SALES (est): 9.7MM **Privately Held**
SIC: 4119 Local rental transportation

(P-3687)
INTEGRATED TRNSP SVCS INC
9740 W Pico Blvd, Los Angeles
(90035-4711)
P.O. Box 6960, Beverly Hills (90212-6960)
PHONE......................310 553-6060
Albert E Sabroff, *President*
Jonna Sabroff, *Vice Pres*
EMP: 75
SQ FT: 3,000
SALES (est): 5.5MM **Privately Held**
WEB: www.itslimo.com
SIC: 4119 Limousine rental, with driver

(P-3688)
JASON PROCTOR TRNSP CO
2375 Dairy Ave, Corcoran (93212-3503)
P.O. Box 623 (93212-0623)
PHONE......................559 992-1767
Jason Proctor, *Owner*
EMP: 50
SALES (est): 1.1MM **Privately Held**
SIC: 4119 Automobile rental, with driver

(P-3689)
JP MOTORSPORTS INC
11582 Sheldon St, Sun Valley
(91352-1501)
PHONE......................818 381-8313
George Sukunyan, *President*
Ovsep Sukunyan, *CEO*
EMP: 54 **EST:** 2009
SQ FT: 18,000
SALES (est): 2.9MM **Privately Held**
SIC: 4119 Automobile rental, with driver

(P-3690)
K W P H ENTERPRISES
Also Called: American Ambulance
2911 E Tulare St, Fresno (93721-1502)
PHONE......................559 443-5900
Todd Valeri, *President*
Todd R Valeri, *President*
Markus Kantarci, *Software Engr*
Hal Fielding, *Supervisor*

EMP: 700
SQ FT: 22,000
SALES (est): 24.7MM **Privately Held**
WEB: www.americanambulance.com
SIC: 4119 Ambulance service

(P-3691)
**KEOLIS TRANSIT AMERICA INC
(DH)**
6053 W Century Blvd # 900, Los Angeles
(90045-6400)
PHONE......................310 981-9500
Steve Shaw, *President*
Joseph Cardoso, *CFO*
Kevin Adams, *Exec VP*
Michael Ake, *Senior VP*
Christina Bird, *Vice Pres*
EMP: 50
SQ FT: 17,194
SALES (est): 221.1MM
SALES (corp-wide): 4.2MM **Privately
Held**
WEB: www.tectransinc.com
SIC: 4119 Local passenger transportation
HQ: Keolis America Inc.
3003 Washington Blvd
Arlington VA 22201
301 251-5612

(P-3692)
**KMA EMERGENCY SERVICES
INC**
Also Called: West Medions
14275 Wicks Blvd, San Leandro
(94577-5613)
PHONE......................510 614-1420
Erik Mandler, *President*
EMP: 100
SALES (est): 2.9MM **Privately Held**
SIC: 4119 Ambulance service

(P-3693)
LA COSTA LIMOUSINE (PA)
2770 Loker Ave W, Carlsbad (92010-6610)
PHONE......................760 438-4455
Rick Brown, *Partner*
Dale Theriot, *Partner*
Merry Geurin, *Sales Executive*
EMP: 95
SQ FT: 11,000
SALES (est): 4.9MM **Privately Held**
WEB: www.lacostalimo.com
SIC: 4119 Limousine rental, with driver

(P-3694)
LEADER INDUSTRIES INC
Also Called: Leader Emergency Vehicles
10941 Weaver Ave, South El Monte
(91733-2752)
PHONE......................626 575-0880
Gary Hunter, *Principal*
EMP: 160
SALES (est): 9MM **Privately Held**
WEB: www.leader-ambulance.com
SIC: 4119 5046 3711 Ambulance service;
commercial equipment; motor vehicles &
car bodies

(P-3695)
LEGRANDE AFFAIRE INC
651 Aldo Ave, Santa Clara (95054-2208)
PHONE......................408 988-4884
James Brown, *CEO*
Phil Restivo, *President*
EMP: 120
SQ FT: 25,000
SALES (est): 3.6MM **Privately Held**
WEB: www.lagrandeaffaire.com
SIC: 4119 4724 Limousine rental, with
driver; travel agencies

(P-3696)
LIBERTY AMBULANCE LLC
9441 Washburn Rd, Downey (90242-2912)
PHONE......................562 741-6230
Kelvin Carlisle,
EMP: 68
SALES (est): 2.9MM **Privately Held**
SIC: 4119 Ambulance service

(P-3697)
LYFT INC (PA)
185 Berry St Ste 5000, San Francisco
(94107-2503)
PHONE......................844 250-2773
Logan Green, *CEO*

P R O D U C T S & S V C S

Jon McNeill, *COO*
Brian Roberts, *CFO*
Ran Makavy,
Ron Storn, *Vice Pres*
EMP: 273
SALES: 2.1B **Publicly Held**
SIC: 4119 Local rental transportation; automobile rental, with driver

(P-3698)
MED-LIFE AMBULANCE SERVICES
4304 Alger St, Los Angeles (90039-1206)
P.O. Box 4525, Glendale (91222-0525)
PHONE..................................818 242-1785
EMP: 94
SQ FT: 3,000
SALES (est): 2.5MM **Privately Held**
SIC: 4119

(P-3699)
MEDIC AMBULANCE SERVICE INC (PA)
506 Couch St, Vallejo (94590-2408)
P.O. Box 4467 (94590-0459)
PHONE..................................707 644-1761
Rodolfo Manfredi, *President*
Helen Pierson, *CFO*
Marissa Luchini, *Vice Pres*
Jimmy Pierson, *Vice Pres*
Kristi Kendall, *Finance*
EMP: 130
SQ FT: 7,000
SALES (est): 15.3MM **Privately Held**
SIC: 4119 Ambulance service

(P-3700)
MEDSTAR LLC
20 Busneca Pk Way Ste 100, Sacramento (95828)
P.O. Box 292007 (95829-2007)
PHONE..................................916 669-0550
Adam C Ruggles,
Alison Lugo, *General Mgr*
Todd J Ruggles,
Todd Ruggles,
EMP: 65
SQ FT: 2,000
SALES: 2.9MM **Privately Held**
SIC: 4119 Ambulance service

(P-3701)
MISSION AMBULANCE INC
1055 E 3rd St, Corona (92879-1606)
P.O. Box 3111 (92878-3111)
PHONE..................................951 272-2300
Daniel Gold, *President*
EMP: 81
SALES (est): 4.7MM **Privately Held**
WEB: www.missionambulance.com
SIC: 4119 Ambulance service

(P-3702)
NIPOMO DIAL A RIDE
179 Cross St, San Luis Obispo (93401-7597)
PHONE..................................805 929-2881
Catherine Wynn, *Manager*
EMP: 80
SALES (est): 977.6K **Privately Held**
SIC: 4119 Local passenger transportation

(P-3703)
NORTH STAR EMERGENCY SVCS INC
Also Called: Norcal Ambulance Services
2537 Willow St, Oakland (94607-1723)
P.O. Box 12347, Pleasanton (94588-2347)
PHONE..................................510 452-3400
David Plaza, *COO*
Barry Sutherland, *CEO*
Makenzie Kelly, *CFO*
Karla Nazareno, *Administration*
EMP: 52
SALES: 2.1MM **Privately Held**
WEB: www.norcalambulance.com
SIC: 4119 Ambulance service

(P-3704)
OJAI AMBULANCE INC
Also Called: Lifeline Medical Transport
632 E Thompson Blvd, Ventura (93001-2829)
P.O. Box 1089 (93002-1089)
PHONE..................................805 653-9111

Stephen Frank, *President*
Karen Frank, *Vice Pres*
Wynne Schumacher, *Director*
EMP: 50
SALES: 7MM **Privately Held**
WEB: www.lifelineems.net
SIC: 4119 Ambulance service

(P-3705)
PARATRANSIT INCORPORATED (PA)
2501 Florin Rd, Sacramento (95822-4467)
P.O. Box 231100 (95823-0401)
PHONE..................................916 429-2009
Linda Jean Deavens, *CEO*
Ninh Dao-Dickinson, *COO*
Steve Robinson-Burmester, *CFO*
Patricia Williams, *Rector*
EMP: 220
SQ FT: 250,000
SALES: 31.5MM **Privately Held**
SIC: 4119 7539 Ambulance service; automotive repair shops

(P-3706)
PARATRANSIT INCORPORATED
3300 Tully Rd, Modesto (95350-0836)
PHONE..................................209 522-2300
Andrea Anderson, *Branch Mgr*
EMP: 146
SALES (corp-wide): 31.5MM **Privately Held**
SIC: 4119 Ambulance service
PA: Paratransit, Incorporated
2501 Florin Rd
Sacramento CA 95822
916 429-2009

(P-3707)
PREMIER MEDICAL TRNSP INC
575 Maple Ct Ste A, Colton (92324-3209)
P.O. Box 690 (92324-0690)
PHONE..................................909 433-3939
Antonio Myrell, *CEO*
Bo Myrell, *COO*
Rick Card, *Vice Pres*
Richmond Taylor, *Vice Pres*
Susana Garcia, *Human Resources*
EMP: 65
SALES (est): 4.8MM **Privately Held**
WEB:
www.premiermedicaltransportation.com
SIC: 4119 Ambulance service

(P-3708)
PRIORITY ONE MED TRNSPT INC (PA)
9327 Fairway View Pl # 300, Rancho Cucamonga (91730-0968)
PHONE..................................909 948-4400
Michael Parker, *President*
EMP: 70
SQ FT: 7,000
SALES (est): 9.8MM **Privately Held**
WEB: www.prioritylink.com
SIC: 4119 Ambulance service

(P-3709)
PRN AMBULANCE LLC
8928 Sepulveda Blvd, North Hills (91343-4306)
PHONE..................................818 810-3600
Mike Sechrist, *CEO*
Avo Avetisyan, *President*
Elena Whorton, *President*
Michael Gorman, *COO*
Kevin Gorman, *CFO*
EMP: 300
SQ FT: 3,000
SALES (est): 12.8MM
SALES (corp-wide): 70MM **Privately Held**
WEB: www.prnambulance.com
SIC: 4119 Ambulance service
PA: Pt-1 Holdings, Llc
720 Portal St
Cotati CA 94931
707 665-4295

(P-3710)
PROTRANSPORT-1 LLC (HQ)
720 Portal St, Cotati (94931-3060)
PHONE..................................707 975-2386
Michael Sechrist,
Kelley Sechrist,
Elena Whorton,

Kurt Whorton,
EMP: 555
SQ FT: 2,600
SALES (est): 20.7MM
SALES (corp-wide): 70MM **Privately Held**
WEB: www.protransport-1.com
SIC: 4119 Ambulance service
PA: Pt-1 Holdings, Llc
720 Portal St
Cotati CA 94931
707 665-4295

(P-3711)
PURE LUXURY LIMOUSINE SERVICE
Also Called: Pure Luxury Worldwide Trnsp
4246 Petaluma Blvd N, Petaluma (94952-1240)
P.O. Box 910, Penngrove (94951-0910)
PHONE..................................800 626-5466
Gary L Buffo Jr, *CEO*
Antoinette Allison, *Business Mgr*
Linda Reinecke, *Business Mgr*
Debbie Hawkins, *Human Resources*
John Byers, *Opers Staff*
EMP: 111
SQ FT: 35,000
SALES (est): 7.1MM **Privately Held**
WEB: www.pureluxury.com
SIC: 4119 Limousine rental, with driver

(P-3712)
QUICKSILVER DELIVERY INC
Also Called: Quicksilver Delivery Service
129 Kissling St, San Francisco (94103-3726)
PHONE..................................415 431-1600
Phil Mc Cafee, *President*
Ronak Dattani, *Finance*
EMP: 65
SQ FT: 5,000
SALES (est): 1.4MM **Privately Held**
SIC: 4119 Limousine rental, with driver

(P-3713)
RENTY LLC
8025 Clairemont Mesa Blvd, San Diego (92111-1634)
PHONE..................................858 560-0066
Shariar Delalat, *Mng Member*
EMP: 50
SQ FT: 45,000
SALES: 5MM **Privately Held**
SIC: 4119 Limousine rental, with driver

(P-3714)
RESTIVO ENTERPRISES
Also Called: Legrande Affaire
2590 Lafayette St, Santa Clara (95050-2602)
PHONE..................................408 988-4884
Phil Restivo, *General Mgr*
EMP: 100
SQ FT: 22,120
SALES (est): 2.3MM **Privately Held**
SIC: 4119 Limousine rental, with driver

(P-3715)
ROYAL AMBULANCE INC
14472 Wicks Blvd, San Leandro (94577-6712)
PHONE..................................510 568-6161
Steve Grau, *President*
Leon Botoshansky, *CFO*
EMP: 120
SQ FT: 5,000
SALES (est): 9.1MM **Privately Held**
WEB: www.royalambulance.com
SIC: 4119 Ambulance service

(P-3716)
RURAL/METRO CORPORATION
2364 W Winton Ave, Hayward (94545-1102)
PHONE..................................510 266-0885
EMP: 111
SALES (corp-wide): 3.7B **Publicly Held**
SIC: 4119
HQ: Rural/Metro Corporation
8465 N Pima Rd
Scottsdale AZ 85258
480 606-3886

(P-3717)
RURAL/METRO CORPORATION
1345 Vander Way, San Jose (95112-2809)
PHONE..................................888 876-0740
Scott Bartos, *Branch Mgr*
EMP: 111 **Privately Held**
SIC: 4119 Ambulance service
HQ: Rural/Metro Corporation
8465 N Pima Rd Ste 100
Scottsdale AZ 85258
480 606-3886

(P-3718)
RURAL/METRO SAN DIEGO INC
10405 San Diego Mission R, San Diego (92108-2174)
PHONE..................................619 280-6060
EMP: 99
SALES (est): 3.4MM
SALES (corp-wide): 643.1MM **Privately Held**
SIC: 4119
HQ: Rural/Metro Of California, Inc.
1345 Vander Way
San Jose CA 95112

(P-3719)
SAN DIEGO MED SVCS ENTP LLC
10405 Sn Diego Mn Rd 20, San Diego (92108)
PHONE..................................619 280-6060
Michael P Dimino,
Rural Metro Corporation,
EMP: 375
SALES (est): 5.9MM
SALES (corp-wide): 643.1MM **Privately Held**
SIC: 4119 Ambulance service
HQ: Envision Healthcare Corporation
1a Burton Hills Blvd
Nashville TN 37215
615 665-1283

(P-3720)
SAN LUIS AMBULANCE SERVICE INC
3546 S Higuera St, San Luis Obispo (93401-7352)
P.O. Box 954 (93406-0954)
PHONE..................................805 543-2626
Frank I Kelton, *President*
Betsy Kelton, *Corp Secy*
EMP: 124 **EST:** 1967
SQ FT: 7,500
SALES: 14.3MM **Privately Held**
WEB: www.sanluisambulance.com
SIC: 4119 Ambulance service

(P-3721)
SANTA BARBARA AIRBUS
750 Technology Dr, Goleta (93117-3839)
PHONE..................................805 964-7759
Eric Onnen, *President*
Kelly Onnen, *Corp Secy*
Mark Klopstein, *Vice Pres*
EMP: 60
SQ FT: 10,000
SALES: 5MM **Privately Held**
WEB: www.sbairbus.com
SIC: 4119 4724 Limousine rental, with driver; travel agencies

(P-3722)
SCHAEFER AMBULANCE SERVICE INC
Also Called: Gold Cross Ambulance
4627 Beverly Blvd, Los Angeles (90004-3101)
P.O. Box 74609 (90004-0609)
PHONE..................................323 468-1642
Louella M McNeal, *CEO*
Louella McNeal, *President*
James McNeal II, *CEO*
Leslie McNeal, *Treasurer*
Samir Yanni, *Vice Pres*
EMP: 463
SQ FT: 45,000
SALES (est): 23.7MM **Privately Held**
WEB: www.schaeferamb.com
SIC: 4119 Ambulance service

(P-3723)
SECURE TRANSPORTATION COMPANY
12785 Magnolia Ave # 102, Riverside
(92503-4686)
PHONE..................................951 737-7300
EMP: 71
SALES (corp-wide): 48.2MM Privately Held
SIC: 4119
PA: Secure Transportation Company, Inc.
  13111 Meyer Rd
  Whittier CA 90605
  562 941-0107

(P-3724)
SOL TRANSPORTATION INC
2525 Ramona Dr, Vista (92084-1632)
PHONE..................................760 720-4327
Arturo Ayala, President
Marco Cardoso, Principal
EMP: 50
SALES: 426K Privately Held
SIC: 4119 Ambulance service

(P-3725)
SOUTHLAND TRANSIT INC (PA)
3650 Rockwell Ave, El Monte (91731-2322)
PHONE..................................626 258-1310
Timmy Mardirossian, CEO
Dave Daley, President
Scott Transue, Vice Pres
Jaime Lopez, General Mgr
EMP: 200
SALES (est): 8.4MM Privately Held
WEB: www.southlandtransit.com
SIC: 4119 Local rental transportation

(P-3726)
SPRINGS AMBULANCE SERVICE INC
Also Called: American Medical Response
1111 Montalvo Way, Palm Springs
(92262-5440)
PHONE..................................760 883-5000
Edward Vanhorne, President
Timothy Dorn, CFO
EMP: 99
SALES: 923.2K
SALES (corp-wide): 643.1MM Privately Held
SIC: 4119 Ambulance service
HQ: Envision Healthcare Corporation
  1a Burton Hills Blvd
  Nashville TN 37215
  615 665-1283

(P-3727)
STUDENT TRNSP AMER INC
Also Called: Student Transportation America
1540 S 7th St, San Jose (95112-5929)
PHONE..................................408 998-8275
Evie Galdraith, Manager
EMP: 100
SALES (corp-wide): 2B Privately Held
SIC: 4119 4151 Local passenger transportation; school buses
PA: Student Transportation Of America, Inc.
  3349 Hwy 138
  Wall Township NJ 07719
  732 280-4200

(P-3728)
SUNLINE TRANSIT AGENCY
790 Vine Ave, Coachella (92236-1736)
PHONE..................................760 972-4059
EMP: 119
SALES (corp-wide): 20.7MM Privately Held
SIC: 4119 Local passenger transportation
PA: Sunline Transit Agency
  32505 Harry Oliver Trl
  Thousand Palms CA 92276
  760 343-3456

(P-3729)
TRANSDEV SERVICES INC
5640 Peck Rd, Arcadia (91006-5850)
PHONE..................................626 357-7912
EMP: 251
SALES (corp-wide): 1.3B Privately Held
SIC: 4119 4121 Local passenger transportation; taxicabs

HQ: Transdev Services, Inc.
  720 E Bttrfeld Rd Ste 300
  Lombard IL 60148
  630 571-7070

(P-3730)
TRIPLE R TRANSPORTATION INC
978 Rd 192, Delano (93215)
P.O. Box 38 (93216-0038)
PHONE..................................661 725-6494
Joe Rodriguez, President
EMP: 80
SALES (est): 3.2MM Privately Held
SIC: 4119 Local rental transportation

(P-3731)
UBER TECHNOLOGIES INC (PA)
1455 Market St Fl 4, San Francisco
(94103-1355)
PHONE..................................415 612-8582
Dara Khosrowshahi, CEO
Ronald Sugar, Ch of Bd
Barney Harford, COO
Nelson Chai, CFO
Rebecca Messina, Chief Mktg Ofcr
EMP: 9000
SQ FT: 2,200,000
SALES: 11.2B Publicly Held
SIC: 4119 7371 Local passenger transportation; software programming applications

(P-3732)
UNITED CEREBRAL PALSY ASSOC OF
Also Called: Ride On Transportation
3620 Sacramento Dr # 201, San Luis Obispo (93401-7215)
PHONE..................................805 543-2039
Mark Shaffer, Exec Dir
EMP: 100
SQ FT: 1,600
SALES: 6MM Privately Held
WEB: www.ucp-oc.org
SIC: 4119 Local passenger transportation

(P-3733)
UNIVERSAL LIMOUSINE & TRNSP CO
9944 Mills Station Rd C, Sacramento
(95827-2202)
PHONE..................................916 361-5466
Marc Sievers, CEO
EMP: 70
SQ FT: 10,000
SALES (est): 2.2MM Privately Held
SIC: 4119 Limousine rental, with driver

(P-3734)
VALLEY MEDICAL TRNSP LLC
43612 Jackson St Ste 4, Indio
(92201-2567)
P.O. Box 1327 (92202-1327)
PHONE..................................760 501-8929
Jose Efren Padilla,
EMP: 60
SALES (est): 1.3MM Privately Held
SIC: 4119 Ambulance service

(P-3735)
VIRGIN FISH INC (PA)
Also Called: Avalon Transportation Co
1000 Corporate Pointe # 150, Culver City
(90230-7690)
PHONE..................................310 391-6161
Jeff Brush, Principal
David Dinwiddie, Vice Pres
Margot Cooperman-Ford, General Mgr
EMP: 150
SQ FT: 3,000
SALES (est): 30.5MM Privately Held
WEB: www.avalontrans.com
SIC: 4119 Limousine rental, with driver

(P-3736)
VOYAGE AUTO INC
844 E Charleston Rd, Palo Alto
(94303-4611)
PHONE..................................917 588-1249
Oliver Cameron, CEO
EMP: 75
SALES (est): 2.1MM Privately Held
SIC: 4119 Local passenger transportation

(P-3737)
WEST COAST AMBULANCE CORP
Also Called: Wca
6739 S Victoria Ave, Los Angeles
(90043-4617)
P.O. Box 8721 (90008-0721)
PHONE..................................310 435-1862
Olga Binman, President
EMP: 135
SALES (est): 3.9MM Privately Held
SIC: 4119 Ambulance service

(P-3738)
WESTMED AMBULANCE
14275 Wicks Blvd, San Leandro
(94577-5613)
PHONE..................................510 401-5420
Alan Cress, Director
Andrew Thomas, Admin Mgr
Joe Chiedley, Director
EMP: 88
SALES (est): 3.2MM Privately Held
WEB: www.westmedambulance.com
SIC: 4119 Ambulance service

(P-3739)
WESTMED AMBULANCE INC
3872 Las Flores Canyon Rd, Malibu
(90265-5264)
PHONE..................................310 456-3830
EMP: 165
SALES (corp-wide): 37MM Privately Held
SIC: 4119 Ambulance service
PA: Westmed Ambulance, Inc
  13933 Crenshaw Blvd
  Hawthorne CA 90250
  510 614-1420

(P-3740)
WESTMED AMBULANCE INC
2537 Old San Pasqual Rd, Escondido
(92027-4753)
PHONE..................................310 219-1779
Allen Cress, Principal
EMP: 254
SALES (corp-wide): 37MM Privately Held
SIC: 4119 Ambulance service
PA: Westmed Ambulance, Inc
  13933 Crenshaw Blvd
  Hawthorne CA 90250
  510 614-1420

(P-3741)
WORLDWIDE GROUND TRANSPORTATIO
Also Called: El Paseo Limousine
651 Aldo Ave, Santa Clara (95054-2208)
PHONE..................................408 727-0000
James Brown, President
EMP: 75
SQ FT: 8,900
SALES (est): 3.3MM Privately Held
SIC: 4119 4131 Limousine rental, with driver; intercity bus line

---

4121 Taxi Cabs

(P-3742)
A WHITE AND YELLOW CAB INC
Also Called: A Taxi Cab
2082 Se Bristol St # 212, Newport Beach
(92660-1740)
PHONE..................................714 258-1000
Hossein Nabati, President
EMP: 180
SALES (est): 9.8MM Privately Held
SIC: 4121 Taxicabs

(P-3743)
ADMINISTRATIVE SERVICES SD
Also Called: Yellow Radio Service
3473 Kurtz St, San Diego (92110-4430)
PHONE..................................619 398-2314
Anthony Palmeri, Principal
Charlene Ewell, Controller
EMP: 50
SALES: 950K Privately Held
SIC: 4121 Taxicabs

(P-3744)
ADMINISTRATIVE SVCS COOP INC
2129 W Rosecrans Ave, Gardena
(90249-2933)
PHONE..................................310 715-1968
Martiros Manukyan, CEO
Raymond McGreevy, President
William J Rouse, General Mgr
EMP: 200
SALES (est): 10.2MM Privately Held
SIC: 4121 Taxicabs

(P-3745)
CHECKER CAB CO
Also Called: La Checker Cab Co
14943 Califa St, Van Nuys (91411-3002)
PHONE..................................818 488-5088
Eugene Smolyar, President
EMP: 52
SALES (est): 3.2MM Privately Held
SIC: 4121 Taxicabs

(P-3746)
LUXOR CABS INC
531 Bay Shore Blvd, San Francisco
(94124-1511)
PHONE..................................415 282-4141
John Lazar, CEO
William Falcon, Corp Secy
Dolores Parlomenko, Vice Pres
Rick Larsen, Manager
EMP: 51 EST: 1946
SALES (est): 3.2MM Privately Held
WEB: www.luxorcab.com
SIC: 4121 7521 Taxicabs; parking lots

(P-3747)
NEESE INC
Also Called: Georges Yellow Taxi Cab Co
588 Roseland Ave, Santa Rosa
(95407-6837)
PHONE..................................707 544-4444
Ray Neese, President
EMP: 50
SQ FT: 1,500
SALES: 1.6MM Privately Held
SIC: 4121 Taxicabs

(P-3748)
SAN GABRIEL TRANSIT INC
Also Called: Southland Transit Co
14913 Ramona Blvd, Baldwin Park
(91706-3421)
PHONE..................................626 430-3650
EMP: 78
SALES (corp-wide): 20.3MM Privately Held
SIC: 4121
PA: San Gabriel Transit, Inc.
  3650 Rockwell Ave
  El Monte CA 91731
  626 258-1310

(P-3749)
SAN GABRIEL TRANSIT INC
7955 San Fernando Rd, Sun Valley
(91352-4614)
PHONE..................................818 771-0374
Debbie Waters, Manager
EMP: 75
SALES (est): 1.9MM
SALES (corp-wide): 21.6MM Privately Held
WEB: www.sgtransit.com
SIC: 4121 4119 Taxicabs; local passenger transportation
PA: San Gabriel Transit, Inc.
  3650 Rockwell Ave
  El Monte CA 91731
  626 258-1310

(P-3750)
SITOA
6900 Airport Blvd, Sacramento (95837)
PHONE..................................916 444-0008
Kuldip Dosanjh, Owner
EMP: 98 EST: 2015
SALES (est): 1.1MM Privately Held
SIC: 4121 Taxicabs

P
R
O
D
U
C
T
S

&

S
V
C
S

(P-3751)
UBER TECHNOLOGIES INC
900 Arastradero Rd Bldg B, Palo Alto
(94304-1332)
PHONE..............................832 610-0359
Chad Burton, *Manager*
EMP: 150
SQ FT: 140,000
SALES (corp-wide): 11.2B **Publicly Held**
SIC: 4121 Taxicabs
PA: Uber Technologies, Inc.
    1455 Market St Fl 4
    San Francisco CA 94103
    415 612-8582

(P-3752)
UNITED IND TAXI DRIVERS (PA)
Also Called: United Taxi San Fernando Vly
900 N Alvarado St, Los Angeles
(90026-3105)
PHONE..............................323 462-1088
Andrey Primushko, *CEO*
Martin Shatakhyan, *President*
Jacob Eskin, *Treasurer*
Mohammed Pourrastegar, *Vice Pres*
EMP: 60
SQ FT: 3,500
SALES (est): 3.6MM **Privately Held**
SIC: 4121 Taxicabs

(P-3753)
UNITED INDEPENDENT TAXI CO
900 N Alvarado St, Los Angeles
(90026-3105)
PHONE..............................213 385-2227
Andrey Primushko, *President*
Mohammad Pourrsegar, *Vice Pres*
EMP: 50 **EST:** 1977
SALES (est): 1.5MM **Privately Held**
SIC: 4121 Taxicabs

(P-3754)
WESTERN TRANSIT SYSTEMS INC
13591 Harbor Blvd, Garden Grove
(92843-3818)
PHONE..............................949 515-0188
Michael Griffus, *President*
Francis G Homan, *CFO*
EMP: 65
SQ FT: 6,000
SALES (est): 2.2MM
SALES (corp-wide): 4.2MM **Privately Held**
WEB: www.tectransinc.com
SIC: 4121 Taxicabs
HQ: Keolis Transit America, Inc.
    6053 W Century Blvd # 900
    Los Angeles CA 90045

(P-3755)
YELLOW CAB COMPANY PENNINSULA
Also Called: Yellow Cabs
7013 Realm Dr Ste A, San Jose
(95119-1354)
PHONE..............................408 739-1234
Vikramjeet Singh, *President*
EMP: 150 **EST:** 1948
SQ FT: 5,000
SALES: 1.2MM **Privately Held**
WEB: www.yellowcabpeninsula.com
SIC: 4121 Taxicabs

(P-3756)
YELLOW CAB COOPERATIVE INC
Also Called: All Taxi Electronics
55 New Montgomery St # 208, San Francisco (94105-3421)
PHONE..............................415 333-3333
Richard Wiener, *CEO*
Harlan Mellegard, *Exec VP*
Sheldon Miller, *Admin Sec*
Pam Martinez, *Controller*
EMP: 90
SQ FT: 150,000
SALES (est): 10MM **Privately Held**
SIC: 4121 Taxicabs

| 4131 Intercity & Rural Bus Transportation |

(P-3757)
CITY OF NAPA
Also Called: Vine Transit
1151 Pearl St, NAPA (94559-2528)
PHONE..............................707 255-7631
Rick Levitt, *General Mgr*
EMP: 50 **Privately Held**
WEB: www.naparcd.org
SIC: 4131 9111 Intercity & rural bus transportation; mayors' offices
PA: City Of Napa
    955 School St
    Napa CA 94559
    707 257-9516

(P-3758)
EASTERN SIERRA TRANSIT AUTH
703 Airport Rd, Bishop (93514-3603)
P.O. Box 1357 (93515-1357)
PHONE..............................760 872-1901
Brad Koehn, *Principal*
John Helm, *Principal*
EMP: 50
SALES (est): 2.2MM **Privately Held**
SIC: 4131 Intercity & rural bus transportation

(P-3759)
GREYHOUND LINES INC
1033 Broadway St, Fresno (93721-2535)
PHONE..............................559 268-1829
Tom Fries, *Manager*
EMP: 118
SALES (corp-wide): 9.1B **Privately Held**
WEB: www.greyhound.com
SIC: 4131 Intercity & rural bus transportation
HQ: Greyhound Lines, Inc.
    350 N Saint Paul St # 300
    Dallas TX 75201
    214 849-8000

(P-3760)
LINCOLN SCHOOL BUS TRNSP
6749 Harrisburg Pl, Stockton (95207)
PHONE..............................209 953-8596
George Anzo, *Director*
Tanisha Sykes, *Bd of Directors*
Saragon Yousef, *Principal*
Dwight Fanning, *Director*
EMP: 65
SALES (est): 1.3MM **Privately Held**
WEB: www.lusd.net
SIC: 4131 Intercity & rural bus transportation

(P-3761)
LONG BEACH PUBLIC TRNSP CO (PA)
Also Called: Long Beach Public Transit
1963 E Anaheim St, Long Beach
(90813-3907)
PHONE..............................562 591-8753
Laurence W Jackson, *President*
Kenneth A McDonald, *CEO*
Robyn Peterson, *COO*
Aida Douglas, *Officer*
Christopher Sapien, *Officer*
EMP: 650
SQ FT: 10,000
SALES (est): 66.5MM **Privately Held**
SIC: 4131 Intercity & rural bus transportation

(P-3762)
MONTEREY-SALINAS TRANSIT CORP
1375 Burton Ave, Salinas (93901-4403)
PHONE..............................831 754-2804
Carl Sedoryk, *Branch Mgr*
EMP: 140
SALES (corp-wide): 17.9MM **Privately Held**
SIC: 4131 Intercity & rural bus transportation
PA: Monterey-Salinas Transit Corporation
    19 Upper Ragsdale Dr # 200
    Monterey CA 93940
    888 678-2871

(P-3763)
SANTA CLARA VALLEY TRNSP AUTH
3331 N 1st St, San Jose (95134-1906)
PHONE..............................408 321-5555
Michael Burns, *Manager*
EMP: 500
SALES (est): 8.1MM **Privately Held**
SIC: 4131 9111 Intercity bus line; county supervisors' & executives' offices
PA: Santa Clara Valley Transportation Authority
    3331 N 1st St
    San Jose CA 95134
    408 321-2300

(P-3764)
SANTA CLARITA CITY OF
Also Called: Bus Company
28250 Constellation Rd, Santa Clarita
(91355-5000)
PHONE..............................661 294-1287
Mike Hynes, *Director*
EMP: 300 **Privately Held**
WEB: www.golfsantaclarita.com
SIC: 4131 9111 Intercity & rural bus transportation; mayors' offices
PA: Santa Clarita, City Of
    23920 Valencia Blvd # 300
    Santa Clarita CA 91355
    661 259-2489

(P-3765)
SANTA CRUZ METRO TRNST DST
Also Called: Fleet Maintenance Dept
110 Vernon St Ste B, Santa Cruz
(95060-2130)
PHONE..............................831 469-1954
Tom Stickel, *Manager*
EMP: 54
SALES (corp-wide): 10.2MM **Privately Held**
WEB: www.scmtd.com
SIC: 4131 Intercity bus line
PA: Santa Cruz Metropolitan Transit District
    110 Vernon St
    Santa Cruz CA 95060
    831 426-6143

(P-3766)
SANTA MONICA CITY OF
Santa Monica Big Blue Bus
1334 5th St, Santa Monica (90401)
PHONE..............................310 451-5444
Edward King, *Manager*
John Catoe, *Director*
EMP: 325 **Privately Held**
SIC: 4131 Intercity & rural bus transportation
PA: City Of Santa Monica
    1685 Main St
    Santa Monica CA 90401
    310 458-8411

(P-3767)
SUNLINE TRANSIT AGENCY (PA)
Also Called: STA
32505 Harry Oliver Trl, Thousand Palms
(92276-3501)
PHONE..............................760 343-3456
Glenn Miller, *Chairman*
Greg Pettis, *Principal*
Caroline Rude, *Admin Sec*
Anita Petke, *Planning*
Rob Gustafson, *CIO*
EMP: 160 **EST:** 1977
SQ FT: 19,006
SALES (est): 20.7MM **Privately Held**
WEB: www.sunline.org
SIC: 4131 Intercity bus line

| 4141 Local Bus Charter Svc |

(P-3768)
AMADOR STAGE LINES INC
Also Called: Allen Transportation Co
1331 C St, Sacramento (95814-0913)
P.O. Box 15707 (95852-0707)
PHONE..............................916 444-7880
W R Allen, *CEO*
Alex B Allen, *President*

William R Allen, *Treasurer*
R E Allen, *Vice Pres*
EMP: 80
SQ FT: 2,000
SALES (est): 6.1MM **Privately Held**
SIC: 4141 Local bus charter service

(P-3769)
EMPIRE TRANSPORTATION
8800 Park St, Bellflower (90706-5529)
PHONE..............................562 529-2676
Miguel Oliver, *CEO*
Bertha Aguirre, *President*
EMP: 425
SQ FT: 25,000
SALES (est): 30.2MM **Privately Held**
SIC: 4141 7521 4111 Local bus charter service; indoor parking services; bus transportation

(P-3770)
MICHAELS TRNSP SVC INC
140 Yolano Dr, Vallejo (94589-2251)
PHONE..............................707 674-6013
Michael Brown, *President*
Carl Mosebach, *General Mgr*
Corby Harvey, *Human Res Dir*
Keith Judkins, *Recruiter*
Geneva Thornton, *Director*
EMP: 95
SQ FT: 26,000
SALES (est): 9.3MM **Privately Held**
WEB: www.bustransportation.com
SIC: 4141 7363 8331 4111 Local bus charter service; employee leasing service; job training services; bus transportation; school buses

(P-3771)
STORER TRANSPORTATION SERVICE (PA)
Also Called: Storer Travel Service
3519 Mcdonald Ave, Modesto
(95358-9771)
PHONE..............................209 521-8250
Donald Storer, *CEO*
Warren Storer, *CEO*
Erica Gonzales, *Executive*
Sarah Storer, *Executive*
Alberta Deanda, *Business Mgr*
EMP: 275
SQ FT: 6,000
SALES (est): 43.4MM **Privately Held**
WEB: www.storercoachways.com
SIC: 4141 4725 4724 4151 Local bus charter service; tours, conducted; travel agencies; school buses; bus charter service, except local

---

| 4142 Bus Charter Service, Except Local |

(P-3772)
COACH USA INC
Also Called: Pacific Cast Sightseeing Tours
2001 S Manchester Ave, Anaheim
(92802-3803)
PHONE..............................714 978-8855
Darlene Cochran, *Branch Mgr*
EMP: 200 **Privately Held**
SIC: 4142 Bus charter service, except local
HQ: Coach Usa, Inc.
    160 S Route 17 N
    Paramus NJ 07652

(P-3773)
CUSA FL LLC
Also Called: Coach Bus Lines
41 Pier, San Francisco (94133-1009)
PHONE..............................415 642-9400
Michael Waters,
Craig Lentzch,
EMP: 150
SALES (est): 3.6MM **Privately Held**
WEB: www.cusa.org
SIC: 4142 Bus charter service, except local

(P-3774)
EL PAS-LOS ANGLES LMSNE EX INC
Also Called: Los Angeles Terminal
260 E 6th St, Los Angeles (90014-2117)
PHONE..............................213 623-2323

▲ = Import ▼=Export
◆ =Import/Export

Marisela Gonzalez, *Branch Mgr*
EMP: 50
SQ FT: 5,680
SALES (corp-wide): 23.4MM **Privately Held**
SIC: 4142 Bus charter service, except local
PA: El Paso-Los Angeles Limousine Express, Inc.
720 S Oregon St
El Paso TX 79901

(P-3775)
FAST DEER BUS CHRTR INCRPRTION
8105 Slauson Ave, Montebello (90640-6621)
PHONE...........................323 201-8988
Eddie Wong, *President*
Carmina Delacruz, *General Mgr*
EMP: 57
SQ FT: 65,000
SALES (est): 2.3MM **Privately Held**
WEB: www.fastdeerbus.com
SIC: 4142 Bus charter service, except local

(P-3776)
GREEN TORTOISE ADVENTURE TRVL
494 Broadway, San Francisco (94133-4515)
PHONE...........................415 834-1000
Gardner L Kent, *President*
James Barbush, *Vice Pres*
EMP: 65 **EST:** 1975
SALES (est): 2.8MM **Privately Held**
WEB: www.greyrabbit.com
SIC: 4142 Bus charter service, except local

(P-3777)
HOT DOGGER TOURS INC
Also Called: Gold Coast Tours
223 Imperial Hwy Ste 165, Fullerton (92835-1060)
PHONE...........................714 988-4088
John Hartley, *President*
Mark Wilkerson, *Vice Pres*
EMP: 120
SQ FT: 955
SALES (est): 11.7MM **Privately Held**
WEB: www.goldcoasttours.com
SIC: 4142 4725 4141 Bus charter service, except local; tours, conducted; local bus charter service

(P-3778)
MCCLINTOCK ENTERPRISES INC
Also Called: Goldfield Stage Company
777 Gable Way, El Cajon (92020-1908)
PHONE...........................619 579-5300
Kevin McClintock, *President*
Dalyce McClintock, *Admin Sec*
EMP: 60
SQ FT: 1,000
SALES: 6.7MM **Privately Held**
WEB: www.goldfieldstage.com
SIC: 4142 Bus charter service, except local

(P-3779)
ORANGE BELT STAGES (PA)
Also Called: Orange Belt Adventures
2134 E Mineral King Ave, Visalia (93292-6905)
P.O. Box 949 (93279-0949)
PHONE...........................559 733-4408
Michael Haworth, *President*
Bryan A Haworth Trust, *Shareholder*
Margaret V Haworth Trust, *Shareholder*
Bruce Lynn, *President*
EMP: 65
SQ FT: 10,000
SALES (est): 14.9MM **Privately Held**
WEB: www.orangebelt.com
SIC: 4142 4141 Bus charter service, except local; local bus charter service

(P-3780)
ROYAL COACH TOURS (PA)
630 Stockton Ave, San Jose (95126-2433)
PHONE...........................408 279-4801
Sandra Allen, *CEO*
Joanne Smith Christian, *Shareholder*
Daniel Smith, *Vice Pres*
Diana Yuan, *Finance*

Veronica Paganelli, *Human Res Dir*
EMP: 110 **EST:** 1960
SQ FT: 2,500
SALES: 13MM **Privately Held**
WEB: www.royal-coach.com
SIC: 4142 Bus charter service, except local

(P-3781)
RYANS EXPRESS TRNSP SVCS INC (PA)
19500 Mariner Ave, Torrance (90503-1644)
PHONE...........................310 219-2960
John Busskohl, *CEO*
George Cohen, *CFO*
Alexander E Hansen, *CFO*
Chris Sanchez, *Vice Pres*
Jessie Alcocer, *General Mgr*
EMP: 80
SQ FT: 20,000
SALES (est): 16.6MM **Privately Held**
SIC: 4142 Bus charter service, except local

(P-3782)
SURERIDE CHARTER INC
Also Called: Sun Diego Charter
522 W 8th St, National City (91950-1004)
PHONE...........................619 336-9200
Richard Illes, *President*
Brian Webber, *Business Mgr*
Lisa Alton, *Controller*
Sherri Gonzalez, *Human Res Mgr*
Carolina Urista, *Human Res Mgr*
EMP: 120
SQ FT: 60,000
SALES (est): 8.3MM **Privately Held**
WEB: www.sundiegocharter.com
SIC: 4142 Bus charter service, except local

(P-3783)
TRANSPORTATION CHRTR SVCS INC
1931 N Batavia St, Orange (92865-4107)
PHONE...........................714 396-0346
Terry Fischer, *President*
Kevin Fischer, *Vice Pres*
Kathryn Mayer, *Vice Pres*
Dave Jeffers, *Principal*
Candice Martinez, *Controller*
EMP: 50
SALES: 9.7MM **Privately Held**
WEB: www.tcsbus.com
SIC: 4142 Bus charter service, except local

(P-3784)
VIA ADVENTURES INC (PA)
Also Called: Via Charter Lines
300 Grogan Ave, Merced (95341-6446)
PHONE...........................209 384-1315
Curtis A Riggs, *President*
Gaye Riggs, *Corp Secy*
Denise Demery, *Opers Mgr*
EMP: 50
SALES (est): 8.6MM **Privately Held**
WEB: www.via-adventures.com
SIC: 4142 4724 4725 Bus charter service, except local; travel agencies; sightseeing tour companies

4151 School Buses

(P-3785)
ANTELOPE VLY SCHL TRNSP AGCY
670 W Avenue L8, Lancaster (93534-7100)
PHONE...........................661 945-3621
Jene Jansen, *CEO*
Jeff Foster, *Executive*
Kathy Phillips, *Info Tech Mgr*
Joanne Downen, *Accountant*
Tony Inglima, *Director*
EMP: 190
SALES: 12.5MM **Privately Held**
WEB: www.avsta.com
SIC: 4151 School buses

(P-3786)
BEAUMONT UNIFIED SCHOOL DST
1001 Cougar Way, Beaumont (92223-5124)
P.O. Box 187 (92223-0187)
PHONE...........................951 845-3010
Robin Dailey, *Director*

EMP: 2755
SALES (corp-wide): 124.7MM **Privately Held**
SIC: 4151 School buses
PA: Beaumont Unified School District Public Facilities Corporation
350 W Brookside Ave
Cherry Valley CA 92223
951 845-1631

(P-3787)
BERKELEY UNIFIED SCHOOL DST
Also Called: Transportation Department
1314 7th St, Berkeley (94710-1465)
PHONE...........................510 644-6182
Bernadette Cormier, *Manager*
Marlee Blasenheim, *Instructor*
Josh Church, *Athletic Dir*
Pauline Follansbee, *Director*
EMP: 50
SALES (corp-wide): 194.6MM **Privately Held**
WEB: www.latms.berkeley.k12.ca.us
SIC: 4151 School buses
PA: Berkeley Unified School District
2020 Bonar St Rm 202
Berkeley CA 94702
510 644-4500

(P-3788)
CATHOLIC CHRTS CYO ARCHDIOCS
Also Called: CATHOLIC YOUTH ORGANIZATION
699 Serramonte Blvd 210, Daly City (94015-4132)
PHONE...........................650 757-2110
Bill Avalos, *Manager*
EMP: 50
SALES (corp-wide): 39.6MM **Privately Held**
SIC: 4151 8322 School buses; individual & family services
PA: Catholic Charities Cyo Of The Archdiocese Of San Francisco
990 Eddy St
San Francisco CA 94109
415 972-1200

(P-3789)
CERTIFIED TRNSP SVCS INC
1038 N Custer St, Santa Ana (92701-3915)
PHONE...........................714 835-8676
David Gregory, *CEO*
EMP: 70
SQ FT: 3,000
SALES (est): 5.6MM **Privately Held**
WEB: www.ctsbus.com
SIC: 4151 School buses

(P-3790)
COUNTY OF LOS ANGELES
Also Called: Pupil Transportation
9402 Greenleaf Ave, Whittier (90605)
PHONE...........................562 945-2581
Dan Ibarra, *Director*
Dan Gonzales, *Training Super*
Monica Rodrigues, *Opers Staff*
EMP: 110 **Privately Held**
WEB: www.co.la.ca.us
SIC: 4151 9621 School buses; regulation, administration of transportation;
PA: County Of Los Angeles
500 W Temple St Ste 437
Los Angeles CA 90012
213 974-1101

(P-3791)
DURHAM SCHOOL SERVICES
Also Called: Perterman
3001 Ross Ave Ste 11, San Jose (95124-2358)
PHONE...........................408 448-0740
Ron Mahler, *Branch Mgr*
EMP: 80 **Privately Held**
SIC: 4151 School buses
HQ: Durham School Services
2601 Navistar Dr
Lisle IL 60532
816 690-3813

(P-3792)
DURHAM SCHOOL SERVICES L P
16627 Avalon Blvd Ste B, Carson (90746-1051)
PHONE...........................310 767-5820
Raphael Balonos, *Manager*
Alma Lawrence, *Human Res Dir*
EMP: 250 **Privately Held**
SIC: 4151 School buses
HQ: Durham School Services, L. P.
2601 Navistar Dr
Lisle IL 60532
630 836-0292

(P-3793)
DURHAM SCHOOL SERVICES L P
1506 White Oaks Rd, Campbell (95008-6724)
PHONE...........................408 377-6655
Lance Sloan, *Regional Mgr*
EMP: 105 **Privately Held**
SIC: 4151 School buses
HQ: Durham School Services, L. P.
2601 Navistar Dr
Lisle IL 60532
630 836-0292

(P-3794)
DURHAM SCHOOL SERVICES L P
365 E Avnda De Los Alvare, Thousand Oaks (91360)
PHONE...........................805 495-8338
Terry Walker, *Branch Mgr*
Terry L Walker, *Manager*
EMP: 55 **Privately Held**
SIC: 4151 4142 4141 School buses; bus charter service, except local; local bus charter service
HQ: Durham School Services, L. P.
2601 Navistar Dr
Lisle IL 60532
630 836-0292

(P-3795)
DURHAM SCHOOL SERVICES L P
27577 Industrial Blvd A, Hayward (94545-4044)
PHONE...........................510 887-6005
EMP: 190
SQ FT: 1,200 **Privately Held**
SIC: 4151
HQ: Durham School Services, L. P.
2601 Navistar Dr
Lisle IL 60532
630 836-0292

(P-3796)
DURHAM SCHOOL SERVICES L P
10701 E Bennett Rd, Grass Valley (95945-9361)
PHONE...........................530 273-7282
Paula Davidson, *General Mgr*
EMP: 70 **Privately Held**
SIC: 4151 4119 4111 School buses; local passenger transportation; local & suburban transit
HQ: Durham School Services, L. P.
2601 Navistar Dr
Lisle IL 60532
630 836-0292

(P-3797)
DURHAM SCHOOL SERVICES L P
2121 Piedmont Way, Pittsburg (94565-5017)
PHONE...........................925 686-3391
Joe Cobillas, *Branch Mgr*
EMP: 120 **Privately Held**
SIC: 4151 School buses
HQ: Durham School Services, L. P.
2601 Navistar Dr
Lisle IL 60532
630 836-0292

P R O D U C T S & S V C S

(P-3798)

DURHAM SCHOOL SERVICES L P

2713 River Ave, Rosemead (91770-3303)
PHONE..........................626 573-3769
David Gonzales, *General Mgr*
EMP: 150 **Privately Held**
SIC: 4151 School buses
HQ: Durham School Services, L. P.
2601 Navistar Dr
Lisle IL 60532
630 836-0292

(P-3799)

ELK GROVE UNIFIED SCHOOL DST

Also Called: Transportation Department
8421 Gerber Rd, Sacramento
(95828-3711)
PHONE..........................916 686-7733
Jill Gayaldo, *Branch Mgr*
Gary Dodson, *Maintence Staff*
EMP: 200
SALES (corp-wide): 741.9MM **Privately Held**
SIC: 4151 School buses
PA: Grove Elk Unified School District
9510 Elk Grove Florin Rd
Elk Grove CA 95624
916 686-5085

(P-3800)

FACILITIES OPERATION AND TRNSP

Also Called: Los Banos School District
2657 E Pacheco Blvd, Los Banos
(93635-9417)
PHONE..........................209 826-1936
Tom Worthy, *Director*
Laurie Sadler, *Admin Sec*
EMP: 100
SALES (est): 2.3MM **Privately Held**
SIC: 4151 School buses

(P-3801)

FIRST STUDENT INC

436 Parr Blvd, Richmond (94801-1123)
PHONE..........................510 237-6677
Brian Rutford, *Principal*
EMP: 79
SALES (corp-wide): 9.1B **Privately Held**
SIC: 4151 School buses
HQ: First Student, Inc.
600 Vine St Ste 1400
Cincinnati OH 45202

(P-3802)

FIRST STUDENT INC

2477 Arnold Indus Way, Concord
(94520-5327)
PHONE..........................925 676-1976
Mary Walker, *Manager*
EMP: 90
SALES (corp-wide): 9.1B **Privately Held**
WEB: www.leag.com
SIC: 4151 School buses
HQ: First Student, Inc.
600 Vine St Ste 1400
Cincinnati OH 45202

(P-3803)

FIRST STUDENT INC

991 E Poplar Ave, San Mateo
(94401-1479)
PHONE..........................650 685-8245
EMP: 83
SALES (corp-wide): 9.1B **Privately Held**
SIC: 4151 School buses
HQ: First Student, Inc.
600 Vine St Ste 1400
Cincinnati OH 45202

(P-3804)

FIRST STUDENT INC

234 S I St, San Bernardino (92410-2408)
PHONE..........................909 383-1640
Cheryl Seifert, *Manager*
EMP: 100
SALES (corp-wide): 9.1B **Privately Held**
WEB: www.leag.com
SIC: 4151 School buses

HQ: First Student, Inc.
600 Vine St Ste 1400
Cincinnati OH 45202

(P-3805)

FIRST STUDENT INC

Also Called: Laidlaw Educational Services
5006 E Calle San Raphael, Palm Springs
(92264-3452)
PHONE..........................760 320-4659
Mike Robertson, *Manager*
EMP: 75
SALES (corp-wide): 9.1B **Privately Held**
WEB: www.leag.com
SIC: 4151 School buses
HQ: First Student, Inc.
600 Vine St Ste 1400
Cincinnati OH 45202

(P-3806)

FIRST STUDENT INC

2005 Navy Dr, Stockton (95206-1142)
PHONE..........................209 466-7737
Drigden Summers, *Manager*
EMP: 200
SALES (corp-wide): 9.1B **Privately Held**
WEB: www.leag.com
SIC: 4151 School buses
HQ: First Student, Inc.
600 Vine St Ste 1400
Cincinnati OH 45202

(P-3807)

FIRST STUDENT INC

Also Called: Laidlaw Education Services
844 E 9th St, San Bernardino
(92410-4012)
PHONE..........................909 383-7104
Norm Foisy, *Manager*
EMP: 65
SQ FT: 2,500
SALES (corp-wide): 9.1B **Privately Held**
WEB: www.leag.com
SIC: 4151 School buses
HQ: First Student, Inc.
600 Vine St Ste 1400
Cincinnati OH 45202

(P-3808)

FIRST STUDENT INC

2270 Jerrold Ave, San Francisco
(94124-1012)
PHONE..........................415 647-9012
Bob Gonzales, *Manager*
EMP: 285
SALES (corp-wide): 9.1B **Privately Held**
WEB: www.leag.com
SIC: 4151 School buses
HQ: First Student, Inc.
600 Vine St Ste 1400
Cincinnati OH 45202

(P-3809)

FIRST STUDENT INC

5320 Derry Ave Ste O, Agoura Hills
(91301-5029)
PHONE..........................818 707-2082
EMP: 79
SALES (corp-wide): 9.2B **Privately Held**
SIC: 4151
HQ: First Student, Inc.
600 Vine St Ste 1400
Cincinnati OH 45202
513 241-2200

(P-3810)

FIRST STUDENT INC

Also Called: Laidlaw Education Services
3401 W Castor St, Santa Ana
(92704-3909)
PHONE..........................714 850-7578
Debi Manley, *Manager*
EMP: 100
SALES (corp-wide): 9.1B **Privately Held**
WEB: www.leag.com
SIC: 4151 School buses
HQ: First Student, Inc.
600 Vine St Ste 1400
Cincinnati OH 45202

(P-3811)

FIRST STUDENT INC

801 Wilbur Ave, Antioch (94509-7500)
PHONE..........................925 754-4878
Susan Hinson, *Branch Mgr*
EMP: 160
SALES (corp-wide): 9.1B **Privately Held**
WEB: www.leag.com
SIC: 4151 School buses
HQ: First Student, Inc.
600 Vine St Ste 1400
Cincinnati OH 45202

(P-3812)

FIRST STUDENT INC

11233 San Fernando Rd, San Fernando
(91340-3409)
PHONE..........................818 896-0333
Sue Wagnon, *Branch Mgr*
EMP: 135
SALES (corp-wide): 9.1B **Privately Held**
WEB: www.leag.com
SIC: 4151 School buses
HQ: First Student, Inc.
600 Vine St Ste 1400
Cincinnati OH 45202

(P-3813)

FIRST STUDENT INC

Also Called: Laidlaw Transit Services
123 N E St Ste 102, Madera (93638-3286)
PHONE..........................559 661-7433
Roberta Collins, *Branch Mgr*
EMP: 126
SALES (corp-wide): 9.1B **Privately Held**
WEB: www.leag.com
SIC: 4151 School buses
HQ: First Student, Inc.
600 Vine St Ste 1400
Cincinnati OH 45202

(P-3814)

FIRST STUDENT INC

Also Called: Cardinal Transportation
14800 S Avalon Blvd, Gardena
(90248-2012)
PHONE..........................310 769-2400
Ray Borales, *President*
Roy J Weber, *President*
▲ **EMP:** 220
SQ FT: 18,000
SALES (est): 5.8MM
SALES (corp-wide): 9.1B **Privately Held**
WEB: www.cardinaltransportationltd.com
SIC: 4151 School buses
HQ: Firstgroup America, Inc.
600 Vine St Ste 1400
Cincinnati OH 45202
513 241-2200

(P-3815)

FRESNO CNTY SPRNTNDENT SCHOOLS

Also Called: Southwest Transportation Agcy
16644 S Elm Ave, Caruthers (93609-9757)
P.O. Box 785, Riverdale (93656-0785)
PHONE..........................559 644-1000
Tony Mendes, *Branch Mgr*
Dennis Wells, *IT/INT Sup*
Greg Durrenberger, *Technology*
Maricela Ordonez, *Finance*
Kathy Devries, *Training Super*
EMP: 75
SALES (corp-wide): 85.4MM **Privately Held**
WEB: www.southwestjpa.org
SIC: 4151 School buses
PA: Fresno County Superintendent Of
Schools
1111 Van Ness Ave
Fresno CA 93721
559 265-3000

(P-3816)

IRVINE UNIFIED SCHOOL DISTICT

Also Called: Maintenance & Trnsp Fcilty
100 Nightmist, Irvine (92618-1710)
PHONE..........................949 936-5300
Rose Clegg, *Director*
EMP: 100

SALES (corp-wide): 497.1MM **Privately Held**
WEB: www.gvarvas.com
SIC: 4151 7349 School buses; building maintenance services
PA: Irvine Unified School Distict
5050 Barranca Pkwy
Irvine CA 92604
949 936-5000

(P-3817)

LAKE ELSINORE UNIFIED SCHL DST

Also Called: Lake Elsn SC Trans
21641 Bundy Canyon Rd, Wildomar
(92595-8778)
PHONE..........................951 253-7830
Silvia Schwing, *Director*
EMP: 100
SALES (corp-wide): 283.5MM **Privately Held**
WEB: www.leusd.k12.ca.us
SIC: 4151 School buses
PA: Lake Elsinore Unified School District
545 Chaney St
Lake Elsinore CA 92530
951 253-7000

(P-3818)

LODI UNIFIED SCHOOL DISTRICT

Also Called: Transportation
820 S Cuff Ave, Lodi (95240)
PHONE..........................209 331-7169
Carlos Garcia, *Director*
EMP: 120
SALES (corp-wide): 360.5MM **Privately Held**
WEB: www.lodiusd.net
SIC: 4151 School buses
PA: Lodi Unified School District
1305 E Vine St
Lodi CA 95240
209 331-7000

(P-3819)

LONG BEACH UNIFIED SCHOOL DST

Also Called: Transportation Department
2700 Pine Ave, Long Beach (90806-2617)
PHONE..........................562 426-6176
Paul Bailey, *Director*
Sara Slater, *Accountant*
David Lawson, *Facilities Mgr*
Darrell Oshita, *Maintence Staff*
Krisie Babcock, *Teacher*
EMP: 100
SALES (corp-wide): 865.3MM **Privately Held**
WEB: www.lbusd.k12.ca.us
SIC: 4151 School buses
PA: Long Beach Unified School District
1515 Hughes Way
Long Beach CA 90810
562 997-8000

(P-3820)

MERCED TRANSPORTATION COMPANY

300 Grogan Ave, Merced (95341-6446)
PHONE..........................209 384-2575
Curtis Riggs, *President*
Gaye Riggs, *CFO*
EMP: 100
SQ FT: 8,000
SALES (est): 7.2MM **Privately Held**
SIC: 4151 School buses

(P-3821)

MONTEBELLO SCHOOL TRANSPORTION

505 S Greenwood Ave, Montebello
(90640-5109)
PHONE..........................323 887-7900
Kennedy E Benedetta, *Principal*
Lea Yeng, *Admin Sec*
Daniel Ibarra, *Director*
EMP: 55
SALES (est): 1.2MM **Privately Held**
SIC: 4151 School buses

(P-3822)
SANTA BARBARA TRNSP CORP (HQ)
6414 Hollister Ave, Goleta (93117-3145)
PHONE.................................805 681-8355
Denis J Hallagher, *CEO*
Patrick Walker, *CFO*
EMP: 90
SQ FT: 15,000
SALES (est): 48.2MM
SALES (corp-wide): 2B Privately Held
WEB: www.sta-ips.com
SIC: 4151 4141 School buses; local bus charter service
PA: Student Transportation Of America, Inc.
   3349 Hwy 138
   Wall Township NJ 07719
   732 280-4200

(P-3823)
SANTA BARBARA TRNSP CORP
Also Called: Student Transportation America
1331 Jason Way, Santa Maria (93455-1000)
PHONE.................................805 928-0402
Paula Sauvadon, *Vice Pres*
EMP: 75
SALES (corp-wide): 2B Privately Held
WEB: www.sta-ips.com
SIC: 4151 4121 School buses; taxicabs
HQ: Santa Barbara Transportation Corporation
   6414 Hollister Ave
   Goleta CA 93117
   805 681-8355

(P-3824)
TEMECULA VALLEY UNIFIED SCHOOL
40516 Roripaugh Rd, Temecula (92591-4563)
PHONE.................................951 695-7110
Thomas Forrest, *Branch Mgr*
Jason Osborn, *Director*
Irene Correa, *Clerk*
EMP: 429
SALES (corp-wide): 325MM Privately Held
SIC: 4151 School buses
PA: Temecula Valley Unified School District
   School Facilities Corporation
   31350 Rancho Vista Rd
   Temecula CA 92592
   951 676-2661

(P-3825)
WOODLAND JINT UNIFIED SCHL DST
25 Matmor Rd, Woodland (95776-6008)
PHONE.................................530 662-0201
John Houston, *Manager*
EMP: 50
SALES (corp-wide): 125.5MM Privately Held
WEB: www.leejhs.wjusd.k12.ca.us
SIC: 4151 School buses
PA: Woodland Joint Unified School District
   435 6th St
   Woodland CA 95695
   530 662-0201

4173 Bus Terminal & Svc Facilities

(P-3826)
ALAMEDA-CONTRA COSTA TRNST DST
A C Transit
10626 International Blvd, Oakland (94603-3806)
PHONE.................................510 577-8816
Glen Andrade, *Manager*
EMP: 130
SALES (corp-wide): 70.5MM Privately Held
WEB: www.actransit.org
SIC: 4173 Maintenance facilities for motor vehicle passenger transport
PA: Alameda-Contra Costa Transit District
   1600 Franklin St
   Oakland CA 94612
   510 891-4777

(P-3827)
CITY OF LOS ANGELES
Also Called: Port of Los Angeles
500 Pier A Pl, Wilmington (90744-6210)
PHONE.................................310 732-3550
Joannie Mukai, *Branch Mgr*
Tricia Cary, *Director*
EMP: 500 Privately Held
WEB: www.lacity.org
SIC: 4173 9621 Maintenance facilities for motor vehicle passenger transport; regulation, administration of transportation;
PA: City Of Los Angeles
   200 N Spring St Ste 303
   Los Angeles CA 90012
   213 978-0600

(P-3828)
CITY OF LOS ANGELES
Also Called: General Services
2513 E 24th St, Vernon (90058-1205)
PHONE.................................213 485-4981
John Ferris, *Superintendent*
EMP: 100 Privately Held
WEB: www.lacity.org
SIC: 4173 9621 Maintenance facilities for motor vehicle passenger transport; regulation, administration of transportation;
PA: City Of Los Angeles
   200 N Spring St Ste 303
   Los Angeles CA 90012
   213 978-0600

(P-3829)
DURHAM SCHOOL SERVICES L P
2818 W 5th St, Santa Ana (92703-1824)
PHONE.................................714 542-8989
Debbie Williams, *Manager*
EMP: 200
SQ FT: 4,843 Privately Held
SIC: 4173 4151 Maintenance facilities for motor vehicle passenger transport; school buses
HQ: Durham School Services, L. P.
   2601 Navistar Dr
   Lisle IL 60532
   630 836-0292

(P-3830)
FIRST STUDENT INC
300 S Buena Vista Ave, Corona (92882-1937)
PHONE.................................951 736-3234
Jackie Mansperger, *Manager*
Payne Eric, *Opers Mgr*
EMP: 101
SALES (corp-wide): 9.1B Privately Held
WEB: www.leag.com
SIC: 4173 4151 Maintenance facilities, buses; school buses
HQ: First Student, Inc.
   600 Vine St Ste 1400
   Cincinnati OH 45202

(P-3831)
GREYHOUND LINES INC
1716 E 7th St, Los Angeles (90021-1202)
PHONE.................................213 629-8400
Mark Jacobson, *Principal*
EMP: 400
SQ FT: 100,000
SALES (corp-wide): 9.1B Privately Held
WEB: www.greyhound.com
SIC: 4173 Bus terminal operation
HQ: Greyhound Lines, Inc.
   350 N Saint Paul St # 300
   Dallas TX 75201
   214 849-8000

(P-3832)
SACRAMENTO REGIONAL TRNST DIST
Also Called: Light Rail
2700 Academy Way, Sacramento (95815-2362)
PHONE.................................916 869-8611
Gabriel Avila, *Director*
EMP: 200

SALES (corp-wide): 28MM Privately Held
WEB: www.sacrt.com
SIC: 4173 4111 Maintenance facilities for motor vehicle passenger transport; local & suburban transit
PA: Sacramento Regional Transit Dist.
   1400 29th St
   Sacramento CA 95816
   916 726-2877

(P-3833)
SAN MATEO COUNTY TRANSIT DST
Also Called: Sam Trans
501 Pico Blvd, San Carlos (94070-2706)
PHONE.................................650 508-6412
Ed Proctor, *Manager*
Ronald Stuart, *Supervisor*
EMP: 175
SALES (corp-wide): 15.7MM Privately Held
SIC: 4173 4111 Maintenance facilities, buses; local & suburban transit
PA: San Mateo County Transit District
   1250 San Carlos Ave
   San Carlos CA 94070
   650 508-6200

4212 Local Trucking Without Storage

(P-3834)
365 DELIVERY INC
440 E Huntington Dr # 300, Arcadia (91006-3775)
PHONE.................................818 815-5005
Bernardo Anders, *President*
Ariana Barrera, *Office Mgr*
EMP: 100
SALES (est): 122.5K Privately Held
SIC: 4212 Delivery service, vehicular

(P-3835)
4AS TRUCKING
20604 Belshaw Ave, Carson (90746-3508)
PHONE.................................424 308-9563
Alnair Tanaleon, *CEO*
EMP: 50
SALES (est): 63.6K Privately Held
SIC: 4212 4491 Local trucking, without storage; marine cargo handling

(P-3836)
A & D HAULING SERVICES INC
13337 South St, Cerritos (90703-7308)
PHONE.................................310 514-8969
Lillian Wang, *Exec Dir*
Andrew Wang, *General Mgr*
Grace Wang, *General Mgr*
EMP: 60
SQ FT: 75,000
SALES (est): 5.2MM Privately Held
WEB: www.adhls.net
SIC: 4212 Light haulage & cartage, local

(P-3837)
A & I TRUCKING INC (PA)
Also Called: A & I Transportation
123 Lee Rd Ste E, Watsonville (95076-9422)
P.O. Box 1270 (95077-1270)
PHONE.................................831 763-7805
Albert Tadevosyan, *CEO*
EMP: 50
SQ FT: 1,000
SALES (est): 11.6MM Privately Held
SIC: 4212 Local trucking, without storage

(P-3838)
A A A PACKING AND SHIPPING INC
2000 E 49th St, Vernon (90058-2802)
PHONE.................................626 310-7787
Bruce Nebens, *President*
Frank Hallberg, *COO*
EMP: 50 EST: 1978
SQ FT: 80,000
SALES (est): 5.3MM Privately Held
WEB: www.aaapack.com
SIC: 4212 4213 4783 Local trucking, without storage; trucking, except local; packing goods for shipping

(P-3839)
A G HACIENDA INCORPORATED
32794 Sherwood Ave, Mc Farland (93250-9626)
P.O. Box 367 (93250-0367)
PHONE.................................661 792-2418
Xochilht Gonzalez, *President*
EMP: 400
SALES (est): 28.4MM Privately Held
SIC: 4212 0761 4214 Local trucking, without storage; farm labor contractors; local trucking with storage

(P-3840)
A J R TRUCKING INC
915 Monterey Rd, Glendale (91206-2518)
PHONE.................................562 989-9555
Khachatur Khudikyan, *President*
Jehan Reyes, *Shareholder*
Hakop Khudikyan, *CFO*
Angel Reyes, *Director*
EMP: 84
SQ FT: 12,000
SALES (est): 9.9MM Privately Held
SIC: 4212 Mail carriers, contract

(P-3841)
A-1 DELIVERY CO
1777 S Vintage Ave, Ontario (91761-3659)
PHONE.................................909 444-1220
Joe Romine, *President*
William Turner, *Corp Secy*
Johnny Romine, *Vice Pres*
EMP: 75
SQ FT: 10,000
SALES (est): 8.5MM Privately Held
WEB: www.jromine.com
SIC: 4212 Delivery service, vehicular

(P-3842)
ACCURATE COURIER SERVICES INC
11022 Santa Monica Blvd # 360, Los Angeles (90025-7513)
P.O. Box 252061 (90025-8977)
PHONE.................................310 481-3937
Joseph Yemini, *President*
EMP: 92
SALES (est): 7.7MM Privately Held
SIC: 4212 Delivery service, vehicular

(P-3843)
ACCURATE DELIVERY SYSTEMS INC
Also Called: ADS
173 Resource Dr, Bloomington (92316-3540)
P.O. Box 1620, Chino (91708-1620)
PHONE.................................951 823-8870
Mahmoud Maraach, *President*
EMP: 55
SQ FT: 10,000
SALES (est): 8.5MM Privately Held
SIC: 4212 Delivery service, vehicular

(P-3844)
ACE RELOCATION SYSTEMS INC (PA)
5608 Eastgate Dr, San Diego (92121-2816)
PHONE.................................858 677-5500
Lawrence R Lammers, *President*
Daniel J Lammers, *Vice Pres*
▲ EMP: 69
SQ FT: 48,000
SALES: 82.1MM Privately Held
WEB: www.acerelocation.com
SIC: 4212 Moving services

(P-3845)
ACE RELOCATION SYSTEMS INC
189 W Victoria St, Long Beach (90805-2162)
PHONE.................................310 632-2800
Kevin Casey, *Branch Mgr*
EMP: 50
SALES (corp-wide): 82.1MM Privately Held
WEB: www.acerelocation.com
SIC: 4212 4213 Moving services; trucking, except local

P
R
O
D
U
C
T
S

&

S
V
C
S

PA: Ace Relocation Systems, Inc.
5608 Eastgate Dr
San Diego CA 92121
858 677-5500

(P-3846)
ADVANCED ENVIRONMENTAL INC
Also Called: Advanced Resources
13579 Whittram Ave, Fontana
(92335-2950)
PHONE..................909 356-9025
Bruce De Menno, *President*
EMP: 50
SALES (est): 3.5MM
SALES (corp-wide): 119.4MM **Privately Held**
SIC: 4212 8742 Hazardous waste transport; management consulting services
HQ: De Menno-Kerdoon Trading Company
2000 N Alameda St
Compton CA 90222

(P-3847)
AGRI-MIX TRANSPORT INC
1400 S Union Ave Ste 110, Bakersfield
(93307-4179)
P.O. Box 327, Lamont (93241-0327)
PHONE..................661 833-6280
Cesar Juarez, *President*
Gonzalo Juarez, *Treasurer*
Walter Juarez, *Vice Pres*
Ramon Juarez, *Admin Sec*
EMP: 150
SQ FT: 435,600
SALES: 30MM **Privately Held**
SIC: 4212 Local trucking, without storage

(P-3848)
AJR TRUCKING INC
435 E Weber Ave, Compton (90222-1424)
P.O. Box 10129, Glendale (91209-3129)
PHONE..................562 989-9555
Jack Khudikyan, *Vice Pres*
EMP: 140
SALES (est): 10.2MM **Privately Held**
SIC: 4212 Delivery service, vehicular

(P-3849)
ANDERSNCTTONWOOD DISPOSAL SVCS
Also Called: Waste Managment
3281 State Highway 99w S, Corning
(96021-9736)
P.O. Box 496 (96021-0496)
PHONE..................530 824-4700
Bill Manneo, *Manager*
EMP: 51
SALES (corp-wide): 4.9MM **Privately Held**
SIC: 4212 Garbage collection & transport, no disposal
PA: Andersoncottonwood Disposal Services Inc
8592 Commercial Way
Redding CA 96002
530 221-6510

(P-3850)
ARMADA TRUCKING GROUP INC
225 Hermosa Ave Unit 202, Long Beach
(90802-3970)
PHONE..................800 620-8592
Zoran Maric, *President*
Boris Stricevic, *Vice Pres*
Rene Jimenez, *Human Resources*
EMP: 74 **EST:** 2014
SQ FT: 972
SALES: 2.9MM **Privately Held**
SIC: 4212 Delivery service, vehicular

(P-3851)
ASBURY ENVIRONMENTAL SERVICES (PA)
1300 S Santa Fe Ave, Compton
(90221-4916)
PHONE..................310 886-3400
Steve Kerdoon, *CEO*
Chris Mahoney, *CFO*
Anne Asbury, *Treasurer*
Bruce De Menno, *Vice Pres*
Ken Jenkins, *Engineer*
EMP: 75

SQ FT: 22,000
SALES (est): 68.2MM **Privately Held**
WEB: www.asburyenv.com
SIC: 4212 Local trucking, without storage

(P-3852)
ATCHESONS EXPRESS INC
1590 S Archibald Ave, Ontario
(91761-7629)
PHONE..................714 808-9199
Brad Atcheson, *President*
Gail Atcheson, *CFO*
Mark Atcheson, *Vice Pres*
Evelyn Abel, *Accounts Exec*
EMP: 50
SQ FT: 10,000
SALES (est): 6.5MM **Privately Held**
WEB: www.atchesonexpress.com
SIC: 4212 4731 Local trucking, without storage; freight transportation arrangement

(P-3853)
BLUE EAGLE CONTRACTING INC
113 Presley Way Ste 8, Grass Valley
(95945-5847)
PHONE..................530 272-0287
Daniel L Rackley, *President*
Marvin L Rackley, *Ch of Bd*
Ray Rackley, *Vice Pres*
EMP: 53
SALES (est): 6.2MM **Privately Held**
SIC: 4212 Mail carriers, contract

(P-3854)
BOB HUBBARD HORSE TRNSP INC (PA)
3730 S Riverside Ave, Colton
(92324-3329)
PHONE..................951 369-3770
Bob Hubbard, *CEO*
Tom Hubbard, *President*
Pat Hubbard, *Vice Pres*
Patricia Hubbard, *Vice Pres*
Kathy Copeland, *CIO*
EMP: 50
SQ FT: 9,375
SALES (est): 12.6MM **Privately Held**
WEB: www.bobhubbardhorsetrans.com
SIC: 4212 4213 4789 Animal transport; trucking, except local; cargo loading & unloading services

(P-3855)
BUDS & SON TRUCKING INC
12570 Highway 67, Lakeside (92040-1159)
P.O. Box 1521 (92040-0912)
PHONE..................619 443-4200
Marvin J Struiksma, *President*
Robert Struiksma, *Corp Secy*
John Struiksma, *Vice Pres*
EMP: 85 **EST:** 1942
SQ FT: 10,800
SALES (est): 5MM **Privately Held**
SIC: 4212 4213 Local trucking, without storage; trucking, except local

(P-3856)
BURNS AND SONS TRUCKING INC
Also Called: Dependable Disposal and Recycl
9210 Olive Dr, Spring Valley (91977-2305)
P.O. Box 1640 (91979-1640)
PHONE..................619 460-5394
Eva N Burns, *CEO*
Jack Burns Sr, *President*
Tom McFarlane, *CFO*
Jim Burns, *Vice Pres*
Sonia Serrano, *Accounts Mgr*
EMP: 85
SQ FT: 6,000
SALES (est): 16.7MM **Privately Held**
WEB: www.burnsandsonstrucking.com
SIC: 4212 4214 Local trucking, without storage; local trucking with storage

(P-3857)
BURRTEC WASTE GROUP INC
2340 W Main St, Barstow (92311-3612)
PHONE..................760 256-2730
EMP: 73

SALES (corp-wide): 309.8MM **Privately Held**
SIC: 4212 Garbage collection & transport, no disposal
PA: Burrtec Waste Group, Inc.
9890 Cherry Ave
Fontana CA 92335
909 429-4200

(P-3858)
C P S EXPRESS (HQ)
3401 Etiwanda Ave B, Jurupa Valley
(91752-1128)
P.O. Box 248, Mira Loma (91752-0248)
PHONE..................951 685-1041
William Smerber, *CEO*
Kirt Allen, *Corp Secy*
James E Ford, *Vice Pres*
EMP: 100
SQ FT: 7,000
SALES (est): 13.3MM
SALES (corp-wide): 10.5MM **Privately Held**
SIC: 4212 4213 4214 Local trucking, without storage; trucking, except local; local trucking with storage
PA: Haddy, J G Sales Co, Inc
3401 Etiwanda Ave
Jurupa Valley CA 91752
951 685-4100

(P-3859)
C S TRANSPORT INC
Also Called: Southern California Carriers
425 E Heber Rd Ste 200, Heber
(92249-9660)
PHONE..................760 666-5661
Samuel Colin, *President*
EMP: 64
SQ FT: 700
SALES: 9MM **Privately Held**
SIC: 4212 4731 Local trucking, without storage; transportation agents & brokers

(P-3860)
CALIFORNIA MATERIALS INC
Also Called: Cmat
3736 S Highway 99, Stockton
(95215-8028)
P.O. Box 32314 (95213-2314)
PHONE..................209 472-7422
Earl Rogers, *President*
EMP: 50 **EST:** 2008
SALES (est): 7MM **Privately Held**
SIC: 4212 Dump truck haulage

(P-3861)
CAROLINA TRUCKING INC (PA)
Also Called: Infinite Global Logistics
552 Alta Rd Ste 8, San Diego
(92154-5716)
PHONE..................619 661-1554
Tom Lee, *President*
Mina Park, *General Mgr*
Gris Sanchez, *General Mgr*
Carolina Favela, *Opers Mgr*
EMP: 50
SALES (est): 5.6MM **Privately Held**
SIC: 4212 Local trucking, without storage

(P-3862)
CEMAK TRUCKING INC (PA)
4621 Teller Ave Ste 130, Newport Beach
(92660-2165)
PHONE..................949 253-2800
Kurt Callier, *President*
Randy Callier, *Vice Pres*
EMP: 70
SQ FT: 8,000
SALES (est): 7MM **Privately Held**
SIC: 4212 Local trucking, without storage

(P-3863)
CENTRAL COURIER LLC
758 Calle Plano, Camarillo (93012-8555)
PHONE..................805 654-1145
Nkosi Khumalo, *President*
EMP: 55
SALES (est): 3.3MM **Privately Held**
SIC: 4212 Light haulage & cartage, local; delivery service, vehicular

(P-3864)
CENTRAL FREIGHT LINES INC
4575 S Chestnut Ave, Fresno
(93725-9211)
PHONE..................559 233-5559
Robert Ibarra, *Manager*
EMP: 53
SQ FT: 5,790
SALES (corp-wide): 1.6B **Privately Held**
WEB: www.centralfreight.com
SIC: 4212 4213 Local trucking, without storage; trucking, except local
HQ: Central Freight Lines, Inc.
5601 W Waco Dr
Waco TX 76710
254 772-2120

(P-3865)
CENTRAL VALLEY CONCRETE INC (PA)
Also Called: Central Valley Trucking
3823 N State Highway 59, Merced
(95348-9370)
PHONE..................209 723-8846
Scott Neal, *CEO*
Brandon Williams, *General Mgr*
Pete Cambianica, *Manager*
EMP: 150
SQ FT: 2,000
SALES (est): 33.3MM **Privately Held**
WEB: www.centralvalleyconcrete.com
SIC: 4212 3273 Local trucking, without storage; ready-mixed concrete

(P-3866)
CLAY MIRANDA TRUCKING INC
3220 W Belmont Ave, Fresno
(93722-5905)
P.O. Box 11983 (93776-1983)
PHONE..................559 275-6250
Debbie Cooper, *Vice Pres*
Mike Miranda, *President*
EMP: 53
SQ FT: 9,600
SALES (est): 6.1MM **Privately Held**
SIC: 4212 5032 Dump truck haulage; asphalt mixture; gravel; sand, construction; stone, crushed or broken

(P-3867)
CNET EXPRESS
15134 Indiana Ave Apt 38, Paramount
(90723-3582)
PHONE..................949 357-5475
Diana Diaz Vargas, *CEO*
EMP: 102
SALES: 5.6MM **Privately Held**
SIC: 4212 Delivery service, vehicular

(P-3868)
COASTAL TRANSPORT CO INC
9950 San Diego Mission Rd F, San Diego
(92108-1705)
PHONE..................619 584-1055
Brian Martin, *Manager*
EMP: 52
SALES (corp-wide): 95.3MM **Privately Held**
SIC: 4212 4213 Liquid haulage, local; liquid petroleum transport, non-local
PA: Coastal Transport Co., Inc.
1603 Ackerman Rd
San Antonio TX 78219
210 661-4287

(P-3869)
COMMAND DELIVERY SYSTEMS INC (PA)
20935 Currier Rd, Walnut (91789-3020)
P.O. Box 190, Los Alamitos (90720-0190)
PHONE..................909 444-1475
Gregory Selmanson, *President*
EMP: 65
SQ FT: 14,000
SALES (est): 8.8MM **Privately Held**
SIC: 4212 4213 Delivery service, vehicular; trucking, except local

(P-3870)
COMPLETE LOGISTICS COMPANY
13831 Slover Ave, Fontana (92337-7037)
PHONE..................909 427-9800
Tim Telbsio, *Manager*
EMP: 150

SALES (corp-wide): 70.7MM **Privately Held**
SIC: 4212 Local trucking, without storage
PA: The Complete Logistics Company
1670 Etiwanda Ave Ste A
Ontario CA 91761
909 544-5040

(P-3871)
COORDNTED DLVRY INSTLLTION INC
905 E Katella Ave, Anaheim (92805-6616)
PHONE................714 501-4040
Flynn A Olsen, *CEO*
Jimmie D Mc Gee, *President*
EMP: 60
SQ FT: 35,000
SALES (est): 3.8MM **Privately Held**
WEB: www.coordinateddelivery.com
SIC: 4212 Delivery service, vehicular

(P-3872)
DAVID W GOLEN
Also Called: Dw Logistix
20253 Gifford St, Winnetka (91306-3210)
PHONE................213 716-0706
David W Golen, *Owner*
EMP: 80
SALES (est): 1.1MM **Privately Held**
SIC: 4212 7389 Local trucking, without storage;

(P-3873)
DAVIS TRUCKING LLC (PA)
7345 Mission Gorge Rd H, San Diego (92120-1268)
PHONE................619 229-9997
Gary Davis, *President*
Maria Da, *CFO*
Brandon Davis, *Vice Pres*
EMP: 50
SQ FT: 40,000
SALES (est): 7.6MM **Privately Held**
WEB: www.davistrucking.com
SIC: 4212 4213 Local trucking, without storage; less-than-truckload (LTL) transport

(P-3874)
DEDICATED FLEET SYSTEMS INC (PA)
1350 Philadelphia St, Pomona (91766-5563)
P.O. Box 2829 (91769-2829)
PHONE................909 590-8209
Anthony Osterkamp Jr, *Ch of Bd*
Gene Segrist, *Vice Pres*
Shelley Fajardo, *Admin Sec*
Susan Badgett, *Administration*
EMP: 59 **EST:** 1970
SALES (est): 4.9MM **Privately Held**
WEB: www.dedicatedfleetsystems.com
SIC: 4212 Local trucking, without storage

(P-3875)
DELUXE AUTO CARRIERS INC
Also Called: Excel Auto Transporting Towing
4788 Brookhollow Cir, Jurupa Valley (92509-3072)
PHONE................909 746-0900
Jesus Holguin, *President*
Jason Evans, *Vice Pres*
EMP: 60
SALES (est): 12.6MM **Privately Held**
SIC: 4212 Local trucking, without storage

(P-3876)
DEMENNO-KERDOON
1300 S Santa Fe Ave, Compton (90221-4916)
PHONE................310 898-3848
Steve Kerdoon, *President*
EMP: 500
SALES (est): 19.9MM **Privately Held**
SIC: 4212 Hazardous waste transport

(P-3877)
DEPENDABLE HIGHWAY EXPRESS INC
830 E St, West Sacramento (95605-2309)
PHONE................916 374-0782
Tim Wallmark, *Branch Mgr*
Mike La Porte, *Manager*
EMP: 50

SALES (corp-wide): 229.2MM **Privately Held**
WEB: www.godependable.com
SIC: 4212 4213 Local trucking, without storage; trucking, except local
PA: Dependable Highway Express, Inc.
2555 E Olympic Blvd
Los Angeles CA 90023
323 526-2200

(P-3878)
DESMOND MAIL DELIVERY SERVICE
4600 Worth St, Los Angeles (90063-1623)
P.O. Box 4836, Anaheim (92803-4836)
PHONE................323 262-1085
Fax: 323 262-6440
EMP: 75
SQ FT: 3,000
SALES (est): 2.6MM
SALES (corp-wide): 33.1MM **Privately Held**
SIC: 4212
PA: Norco Delivery Service, Inc.
1560 N Missile Way
Anaheim CA 92801
714 520-8600

(P-3879)
DOUGLAS L MYOVICH TRUCKING INC
1895 W Jefferson Ave, Fresno (93706-9732)
PHONE................559 233-8242
Douglas Myovich, *President*
Cynthia Myovich, *Admin Sec*
EMP: 60
SALES (est): 4.6MM **Privately Held**
SIC: 4212 Liquid haulage, local

(P-3880)
DSC LOGISTICS LLC
12350 Philadelphia Ave, Eastvale (91752-3228)
PHONE................909 605-7233
Adrian Potgieter, *Manager*
Mark Diaz, *General Mgr*
Chris Boughey, *Opers Mgr*
Rigo Mendoza, *Manager*
EMP: 56
SALES (corp-wide): 355MM **Privately Held**
SIC: 4212 4213 4225 4731 Local trucking, without storage; trucking, except local; general warehousing & storage; freight consolidation
PA: Dsc Logistics, Llc
1750 S Wolf Rd
Des Plaines IL 60018
847 390-6800

(P-3881)
EDCO DISPOSAL CORPORATION INC (PA)
Also Called: La Mesa Disposal
2755 California Ave, Signal Hill (90755-3304)
PHONE................619 287-7555
Steve South, *CEO*
Edward Burr, *President*
Sandra Burr, *Vice Pres*
Yvette Snyder, *Comms Dir*
Elmer Heap, *Division Mgr*
EMP: 250 **EST:** 1967
SQ FT: 8,000
SALES (est): 145.2MM **Privately Held**
SIC: 4212 Garbage collection & transport, no disposal

(P-3882)
EDS WEST LLC
6666 E Washington Blvd, Commerce (90040-1814)
PHONE................323 887-7367
Ronnie Moyal, *Opers Staff*
EMP: 75
SALES (est): 5.2MM **Privately Held**
SIC: 4212 Local trucking, without storage

(P-3883)
EMERALD TRANS LOS ANGELES LLC
5756 Alba St, Los Angeles (90058-3808)
PHONE................323 277-2500
Al Harrell, *Manager*

Eric Zimmer, *Senior VP*
Mark Zimmerman, *Senior VP*
Clyde Phillips, *Vice Pres*
Alex Richard, *Vice Pres*
EMP: 50
SQ FT: 23,350
SALES (corp-wide): 247.7MM **Privately Held**
SIC: 4212 Hazardous waste transport
HQ: Emerald Transformer Los Angeles Llc
9820 Westpoint Dr Ste 300
Indianapolis IN 46256
972 841-7690

(P-3884)
EMPIRE CHAUFFEUR SERVICE LTD
Also Called: Empire International
600 S Allied Way, El Segundo (90245-4727)
PHONE................310 414-8189
David Seelinger, *President*
EMP: 80
SALES (est): 5.4MM **Privately Held**
SIC: 4212 Local trucking, without storage

(P-3885)
FEDERAL EXPRESS CORPORATION
Also Called: Fedex
1600 63rd St, Emeryville (94608-2033)
PHONE................800 463-3339
EMP: 120
SALES (corp-wide): 69.6B **Publicly Held**
WEB: www.federalexpress.com
SIC: 4212 4513 Local trucking, without storage; air courier services
HQ: Federal Express Corporation
3610 Hacks Cross Rd
Memphis TN 38125
901 369-3600

(P-3886)
FEDEX FREIGHT CORPORATION
3255 Victor St, Santa Clara (95054-2318)
PHONE................408 988-2111
EMP: 50
SQ FT: 18,200
SALES (corp-wide): 69.6B **Publicly Held**
SIC: 4212 4213 Local trucking, without storage; trucking, except local
HQ: Fedex Freight Corporation
1715 Aaron Brenner Dr
Memphis TN 38120

(P-3887)
FOOD EXPRESS INC
5127 Maywood Ave, Maywood (90270-2009)
PHONE................323 589-1417
Mike Hess, *Manager*
Radhbier Ghoman, *Mktg Dir*
EMP: 50
SALES (corp-wide): 36.2MM **Privately Held**
WEB: www.foodexp.com
SIC: 4212 5411 4214 Local trucking, without storage; grocery stores; local trucking with storage
PA: Food Express Inc.
521 N 1st Ave
Arcadia CA 91006
626 574-9094

(P-3888)
FRANK GHIGLIONE INC (PA)
Also Called: Rodgers Trucking Co
14327 Washington Ave, San Leandro (94578-3418)
P.O. Box 923 (94577-0445)
PHONE................510 483-7000
Frank Ghiglione, *President*
Alan Osofsky, *Vice Pres*
Winifred Ghiglione, *Admin Sec*
Steve Strom, *Personnel*
John Ghiglione, *Opers Staff*
EMP: 160
SQ FT: 8,000
SALES (est): 17.6MM **Privately Held**
WEB: www.rodgerstrucking.com
SIC: 4212 Delivery service, vehicular

(P-3889)
FRANK GHIGLIONE INC
Also Called: Rogers Trucking
2972 Alvarado St Ste H, San Leandro (94577-5732)
PHONE................510 483-2063
Frank Ghiglione, *Manager*
EMP: 100
SALES (est): 2.3MM
SALES (corp-wide): 17.6MM **Privately Held**
WEB: www.rodgerstrucking.com
SIC: 4212 4214 Delivery service, vehicular; local trucking with storage
PA: Frank Ghiglione, Inc.
14327 Washington Ave
San Leandro CA 94578
510 483-7000

(P-3890)
HANKS INC
Also Called: Sun Express
13866 Slover Ave, Fontana (92337-7037)
PHONE................909 350-8365
Brian Bachar, *President*
Shirley Bachar, *Vice Pres*
EMP: 68
SQ FT: 24,000
SALES (est): 11.5MM **Privately Held**
WEB: www.shipsun.com
SIC: 4212 4213 Local trucking, without storage; trucking, except local

(P-3891)
HARTWICK & HAND INC (PA)
Also Called: H & H Truck Terminal
16953 N D St, Victorville (92394-1417)
P.O. Box 1595 (92393-1595)
PHONE................760 245-1666
Stacy L Hand, *CEO*
Edward Perreria, *President*
EMP: 73
SQ FT: 8,800
SALES (est): 14MM **Privately Held**
SIC: 4212 Local trucking, without storage

(P-3892)
HD SUPPLY INC
101 Rverview Pkwy Ste 100, Santee (92071)
P.O. Box 2273, Orlando FL (32802-2273)
PHONE................800 431-3000
Tarang Dave, *Branch Mgr*
Mark Wilson, *Branch Mgr*
Joe Kim, *General Mgr*
Leslie Taylor, *Sr Ntwrk Engine*
Jesse Campos, *Network Enginr*
EMP: 51 **Publicly Held**
SIC: 4212 Delivery service, vehicular
HQ: Hd Supply, Inc.
3100 Cumberland Blvd Se # 1700
Atlanta GA 30339
770 852-9000

(P-3893)
HEAVY LOAD TRANSFER LLC
18735 S Ferris Pl, Rancho Dominguez (90220-6405)
PHONE................310 816-0260
Victor Larosa,
EMP: 75 **EST:** 2016
SALES (est): 2.5MM **Privately Held**
SIC: 4212 Local trucking, without storage

(P-3894)
HUB GROUP TRUCKING INC
13867 Valley Blvd, Fontana (92335-5230)
PHONE................909 770-8950
Roy Sheredon, *Branch Mgr*
EMP: 500
SALES (corp-wide): 3.6B **Publicly Held**
SIC: 4212 Local trucking, without storage
HQ: Hub Group Trucking, Inc.
2000 Clearwater Dr
Oak Brook IL 60523
630 271-3600

(P-3895)
HUB GROUP TRUCKING INC
Also Called: Hgt
3801 E Guasti Rd, Ontario (91761-1575)
PHONE................951 693-9813
EMP: 174
SALES (corp-wide): 4B **Publicly Held**
SIC: 4212

P
R
O
D
U
C
T
S

&

S
V
C
S

HQ: Hub Group Trucking, Inc.
2000 Clearwater Dr
Oak Brook IL 60523
630 271-3600

(P-3896)
ICE DELIVERY SYSTEMS INC
Also Called: Inner-City Express
6920 Santa Teresa Blvd # 206, San Jose
(95119-1344)
PHONE................................408 640-4625
Michael S Hubert, *President*
Lizette P Hubert, *Principal*
EMP: 130
SQ FT: 30,000
SALES (est): 11.7MM **Privately Held**
SIC: 4212 7389 4215 Delivery service,
vehicular; courier or messenger service;
courier services, except by air

(P-3897)
J D L MOTOR EXPRESS
1250 Delevan Dr, San Diego (92102-2437)
PHONE................................619 232-6136
John Lenore, *President*
Dorothy Lenore, *Treasurer*
Harold Gursky, *Vice Pres*
Bob Goods, *Sales Mgr*
EMP: 75
SALES (est): 3.3MM
SALES (corp-wide): 173.8MM **Privately
Held**
WEB: www.johnlenore.com
SIC: 4212 4213 Local trucking, without
storage; automobiles, transport & delivery
PA: Lenore John & Co
1250 Delevan Dr
San Diego CA 92102
619 232-6136

(P-3898)
JACOBS FARM/DEL CABO INC
144 Holm Rd Spc 42, Watsonville
(95076-2428)
PHONE................................831 460-3500
Paul Rabadan, *Branch Mgr*
EMP: 178
SALES (corp-wide): 68.2MM **Privately
Held**
WEB: www.delcabo.com
SIC: 4212 5148 Farm to market haulage,
local; fresh fruits & vegetables
PA: Jacobs Farm/Del Cabo, Inc.
2450 Stage Rd
Pescadero CA 94060
650 879-0580

(P-3899)
JEREMIAH PHILLIPS LLC
Also Called: Airline Coach Service
863 Malcolm Rd, Burlingame (94010-1406)
P.O. Box 4427 (94011-4427)
PHONE................................650 697-7733
Alex Morrison,
Charles Morrison,
EMP: 105
SQ FT: 10,000
SALES: 6.3MM **Privately Held**
SIC: 4212 Local trucking, without storage

(P-3900)
**JOHN AGUILAR & COMPANY
INC**
Also Called: Vernon Transportation Company
1505 Navy Dr, Stockton (95206-4104)
P.O. Box 31450 (95213-1450)
PHONE................................209 546-0171
Gregg Wilson, *President*
Joe Lacey, *CFO*
Dennis Carey, *General Mgr*
Dave Wilson, *Admin Sec*
Donna Acosta, *Technology*
EMP: 85
SQ FT: 5,600
SALES (est): 20.3MM **Privately Held**
WEB: www.sugartrux.com
SIC: 4212 Liquid haulage, local

(P-3901)
JS HOMEN TRUCKING INC
4224 Turlock Rd, Snelling (95369-9729)
P.O. Box 382 (95369-0382)
PHONE................................209 723-9559
Joe Homen, *President*
Margaret Homen, *Corp Secy*
EMP: 65

SQ FT: 2,484
SALES (est): 1.8MM **Privately Held**
SIC: 4212 Local trucking, without storage

(P-3902)
K W K TRUCKING INC
6131 Manorfield Dr, Huntington Beach
(92648-1066)
PHONE................................714 791-7928
Kirt W Keller, *President*
Gina Keller, *Corp Secy*
EMP: 137
SALES (est): 6MM **Privately Held**
SIC: 4212 Local trucking, without storage

(P-3903)
KEENEY TRUCK LINES INC
3500 Fruitland Ave, Maywood
(90270-2008)
PHONE................................323 589-3231
Dan Hubbard, *President*
Carol Alsip, *Corp Secy*
Lindsay Derryberry, *Director*
EMP: 50
SALES (est): 8MM **Privately Held**
WEB: www.keeneytruck.com
SIC: 4212 4731 Local trucking, without
storage; freight transportation arrange-
ment

(P-3904)
KELVIN HILDEBRAND INC
6 Lewis Rd, Royal Oaks (95076-5303)
PHONE................................831 768-9104
Kelvin Hildebrand, *President*
EMP: 50 EST: 1983
SALES (est): 1.2MM **Privately Held**
SIC: 4212 Local trucking, without storage

(P-3905)
KFCO INC
Also Called: Labite
12100 W Washington Blvd, Los Angeles
(90066-5502)
PHONE................................310 441-2483
Kenneth Fischer, *President*
Quinton Creapeau, *Supervisor*
EMP: 117 EST: 2014
SQ FT: 300
SALES (est): 3.5MM **Privately Held**
SIC: 4212 5812 Delivery service, vehicu-
lar; carry-out only (except pizza) restau-
rant

(P-3906)
LAZTRANS INC
5200 District Blvd, Bakersfield
(93313-2330)
P.O. Box 9517 (93389-9517)
PHONE................................661 833-3783
Bill Lazzerini Jr, *President*
Mary Huser, *Shareholder*
Maria Pisar, *Shareholder*
Anthony Lazzerini, *Vice Pres*
EMP: 50
SQ FT: 52,000
SALES (est): 4.8MM **Privately Held**
WEB: www.laztrans.com
SIC: 4212 Local trucking, without storage

(P-3907)
**LEE JENNINGS TARGET EX INC
(PA)**
1465 E Franklin Ave, Pomona
(91766-5453)
PHONE................................909 868-1040
L Lee Jennings, *CEO*
Brent Campbell, *Director*
EMP: 123
SALES (est): 19.4MM **Privately Held**
SIC: 4212 4213 Delivery service, vehicu-
lar; trucking, except local

(P-3908)
MAD DOG EXPRESS INC (PA)
299 Lawrence Ave, South San Francisco
(94080-6818)
P.O. Box 281585, San Francisco (94128-
1585)
PHONE................................650 588-1900
Steve Harth, *President*
John Coleman, *Vice Pres*
EMP: 70
SQ FT: 18,500

SALES (est): 3.7MM **Privately Held**
WEB: www.maddogexpress.com
SIC: 4212 Local trucking, without storage

(P-3909)
MAPLEBEAR INC (PA)
Also Called: Instacart
50 Beale St Ste 600, San Francisco
(94105-1871)
PHONE................................888 246-7822
Apoorva Mehta, *CEO*
Eric Sadkin, *Partner*
Ravi Gupta, *CFO*
Mathew Caldwell, *Vice Pres*
Juanjo Feijoo, *Vice Pres*
EMP: 67
SALES (est): 41.2MM **Privately Held**
SIC: 4212 4215 Delivery service, vehicu-
lar; package delivery, vehicular

(P-3910)
MASSOLO TRUCKING LLC (PA)
18765 Gould Rd, Salinas (93908-9703)
PHONE................................831 424-7205
Joseph Massolo, *President*
Steve Massolo, *Vice Pres*
EMP: 50
SQ FT: 5,997
SALES (est): 5.2MM **Privately Held**
SIC: 4212 Local trucking, without storage

(P-3911)
**MAT PARCEL EXPRESS INC
(PA)**
Also Called: Mat Express
2719 Kurtz St Ste C, San Diego
(92110-3117)
PHONE................................619 849-9600
Thomas A Eggert, *President*
Diane Eggert, *Vice Pres*
EMP: 100
SQ FT: 28,000
SALES (est): 25.6MM **Privately Held**
SIC: 4212 Delivery service, vehicular

(P-3912)
MEDICAL COURIERS INC
176 Otto Cir, Sacramento (95822-3817)
PHONE................................916 452-5700
Steve Reiff, *Vice Pres*
EMP: 85
SALES (est): 1.5MM **Privately Held**
SIC: 4212 Delivery service, vehicular

(P-3913)
**MISSION TRAIL WSTE SYSTEMS
INC**
Also Called: Recycle Waste
1060 Richard Ave, Santa Clara
(95050-2816)
PHONE................................408 727-5365
Louie Pellegrini, *President*
William Dobert, *CFO*
Robert Molinaro, *Vice Pres*
Douglas Button, *Admin Sec*
EMP: 75 EST: 1960
SALES (est): 17.2MM **Privately Held**
SIC: 4212 4953 Garbage collection &
transport, no disposal; recycling, waste
materials

(P-3914)
MORE TRUCK LINES INC
1776 All American Way, Corona
(92879-2070)
P.O. Box 2229 (92878-2229)
PHONE................................951 371-6673
Daniel D Sisemore, *President*
Thomas Toscas, *Corp Secy*
EMP: 80 EST: 1952
SQ FT: 800
SALES (est): 5.2MM **Privately Held**
WEB: www.moretrucklines.com
SIC: 4212 Local trucking, without storage

(P-3915)
MORGAN TRUCK BODY LLC
Morgan Truck Body Div
7888 Lincoln Ave, Riverside (92504-4443)
PHONE................................951 689-0800
Barry Price, *Manager*
EMP: 90
SALES (corp-wide): 1.2B **Privately Held**
WEB: www.morgancorp.com
SIC: 4212 Local trucking, without storage

HQ: Morgan Truck Body, Llc
111 Morgan Way
Morgantown PA 19543
610 286-5025

(P-3916)
**MT DBLO RESOURCE
RECOVERY LLC**
4080 Mallard Dr, Concord (94520-1245)
PHONE................................925 682-9113
Gregory Brumfield,
EMP: 300
SALES (est): 3.5MM **Privately Held**
SIC: 4212 4953 Garbage collection &
transport, no disposal; liquid waste, col-
lection & disposal

(P-3917)
MULECHAIN INC
2901 W Coast Hwy Ste 200, Newport
Beach (92663-4045)
PHONE................................888 456-8881
Ralph Liu, *CEO*
EMP: 56
SALES: 1MM **Privately Held**
SIC: 4212 7372 Delivery service, vehicu-
lar; application computer software

(P-3918)
NEAL TRUCKING INC
9749 Bellegrave Ave, Riverside
(92509-2642)
PHONE................................951 685-5048
Dianne Neal, *CEO*
Randy Neal, *Principal*
EMP: 65
SQ FT: 1,500
SALES (est): 7.9MM **Privately Held**
SIC: 4212 Dump truck haulage

(P-3919)
NING TRUCKING INC
1160 Battery St, San Francisco
(94111-1213)
PHONE................................415 544-2531
King Zhang, *President*
EMP: 71
SQ FT: 11,000
SALES: 7MM **Privately Held**
SIC: 4212 Local trucking, without storage

(P-3920)
**NIPPON EX NEC LGSTICS AMER
INC**
18615 S Ferris Pl, Rancho Dominguez
(90220-6452)
PHONE................................310 604-6100
Kazuhiko Takahashi, *CEO*
Hidehito Tachikawa, *CEO*
Gerald Sabino, *Director*
▲ EMP: 75
SQ FT: 353,000
SALES (est): 17.3MM **Privately Held**
WEB: www.necam.com
SIC: 4212 4213 4225 Local trucking, with-
out storage; trucking, except local; gen-
eral warehousing & storage
HQ: Nec Corporation Of America
3929 W John Carpenter Fwy
Irving TX 75063
214 262-6000

(P-3921)
NR 2 GROUP INC
1561 Chapin Unit C, Baldwin Park (91706)
PHONE................................626 251-6681
CHI On Wong, *CEO*
EMP: 50
SQ FT: 100,000
SALES: 2.5MM **Privately Held**
SIC: 4212 Local trucking, without storage

(P-3922)
**OCEAN BLUE ENVMTL SVCS
INC (PA)**
925 W Esther St, Long Beach
(90813-1423)
PHONE................................562 624-4120
Maria C Lee, *CEO*
Ron Dare, *President*
Moonho C Lee, *CFO*
Cherisse Patterson, *Admin Asst*
Wendy Mejia, *Administration*
EMP: 63
SQ FT: 5,000

SALES (est): 11.9MM **Privately Held**
WEB: www.ocean-blue.com
SIC: **4212 8734** Hazardous waste transport; hazardous waste testing

(P-3923)
OLDENKAMP TRUCKING INC (PA)
13535 S Union Ave, Bakersfield (93307-9124)
PHONE..................................661 833-3400
Harold Oldenkamp, *CEO*
Dana Oldenkamp, *CFO*
Dana L Oldenkamp, *Vice Pres*
EMP: 62
SALES (est): 7.7MM **Privately Held**
SIC: **4212** Light haulage & cartage, local

(P-3924)
PACIFIC WINE DISTRIBUTORS INC
15751 Tapia St, Irwindale (91706-2177)
PHONE..................................626 471-9997
Gino Pacella, *President*
Eyvonne Nong, *Human Res Mgr*
EMP: 85
SQ FT: 46,546
SALES: 6MM **Privately Held**
SIC: **4212 4225 4213** Local trucking, without storage; general warehousing & storage; trucking, except local

(P-3925)
PROPANE TRANSPORT SERVICE INC
903 W Center St Ste 7, Manteca (95337-7315)
PHONE..................................209 823-8005
John Paul, *President*
Jan Peterson, *CFO*
Jack Penzes, *Vice Pres*
EMP: 170
SALES (est): 8.2MM **Privately Held**
WEB: www.economytransport.com
SIC: **4212** Petroleum haulage, local
PA: Kamps Propane, Inc.
1262 Dupont Ct
Manteca CA 95336

(P-3926)
PSC INDUSTRIAL OUTSOURCING LP
Also Called: Hydrochempsc
62117 Railroad St, San Ardo (93450-8033)
P.O. Box 431 (93450-0431)
PHONE..................................831 627-2595
Paul Dewitt, *Principal*
Joe Hamby, *General Mgr*
Elaine Talerico, *Human Res Mgr*
EMP: 55
SALES (corp-wide): 607.5MM **Privately Held**
WEB: www.tscnow.com
SIC: **4212** Hazardous waste transport
PA: Psc Industrial Outsourcing, Lp
900 Georgia Ave
Deer Park TX 77536
713 393-5600

(P-3927)
PT LOGISTICS INC
144 W Lake Ave Ste B, Watsonville (95076-4554)
PHONE..................................831 728-4535
Rainderpau S Tut, *President*
EMP: 50
SALES (est): 1.8MM **Privately Held**
SIC: **4212** Light haulage & cartage, local

(P-3928)
QUIK PICK EXPRESS LLC
Also Called: Quik Pick Express Delivery Svc
1021 E 233rd St, Carson (90745-6206)
PHONE..................................310 763-3000
Thomas Javor, *President*
EMP: 85
SALES (est): 111.3K **Privately Held**
SIC: **4212** Delivery service, vehicular

(P-3929)
RADFORD ALEXANDER CORPORATION
Also Called: Chemtrans
14700 S Avalon Blvd, Gardena (90248-2010)
PHONE..................................310 523-2555
Reginald Lathan, *CEO*
Nancy Lathan, *Vice Pres*
EMP: 55
SQ FT: 4,000
SALES (est): 7.7MM **Privately Held**
WEB: www.chemtrans.com
SIC: **4212** Light haulage & cartage, local

(P-3930)
RHINO READY MIX TRUCKING INC (PA)
3701 Pegasus Dr Ste 126, Bakersfield (93308-6843)
P.O. Box 80297 (93380-0297)
PHONE..................................661 679-3643
EMP: 50
SALES: 8MM **Privately Held**
SIC: **4212**

(P-3931)
ROY MILLER FREIGHT LINES LLC (PA)
3165 E Coronado St, Anaheim (92806-1915)
P.O. Box 18419 (92817-8419)
PHONE..................................714 632-5511
Danny Miller, *CEO*
Wiley R Miller Jr, *Mng Member*
EMP: 100 EST: 1942
SALES (est): 29.5MM **Privately Held**
WEB: www.roymiller.com
SIC: **4212** Local trucking, without storage

(P-3932)
RUAN
830 W Glenwood Ave, Turlock (95380-5751)
PHONE..................................209 634-4928
Bill Hagney, *Manager*
EMP: 85
SALES (corp-wide): 5.4MM **Privately Held**
SIC: **4212** Local trucking, without storage
PA: Ruan
1354 S Blackstone St
Tulare CA 93274
559 688-0591

(P-3933)
SANTA MONICA EXPRESS INC
11150 W Olympic Blvd # 150, Los Angeles (90064-1831)
P.O. Box 7457, Santa Monica (90406-7457)
PHONE..................................310 458-6000
Muhammed Mahmodi, *President*
EMP: 65
SQ FT: 3,500
SALES: 3MM **Privately Held**
WEB: www.smexpress.com
SIC: **4212 7389** Delivery service, vehicular; mailing & messenger services

(P-3934)
SHIPBYCOM LLC
218 Machlin Ct, Walnut (91789-3048)
PHONE..................................626 271-9800
Jeff Wu, *Branch Mgr*
EMP: 74
SALES (corp-wide): 8.3MM **Privately Held**
SIC: **4212** Local trucking, without storage
PA: Shipby.Com, Llc
900 Turnbull Canyon Rd
City Of Industry CA 91745
626 271-9800

(P-3935)
SHUSTERS TRANSPORTATION INC
750 E Valley St, Willits (95490-9749)
PHONE..................................707 459-4131
Phillip L Shuster, *President*
Marvin Lawrence, *Corp Secy*
Steve Shuster, *Vice Pres*
EMP: 100
SQ FT: 3,000

SALES (est): 5.7MM **Privately Held**
SIC: **4212** Local trucking, without storage

(P-3936)
SIERRA TRANSPORT INC
12856 Old River Rd, Bakersfield (93311-9707)
PHONE..................................661 399-0246
Roy Lutrel, *President*
Mark Lutrel, *Vice Pres*
Gayle Lutrel, *Admin Sec*
EMP: 53
SALES (est): 6MM **Privately Held**
WEB: www.sierratransport.com
SIC: **4212** Local trucking, without storage

(P-3937)
SILVA TRUCKING INC
36 W Mathews Rd, French Camp (95231-9684)
P.O. Box 1449 (95231-1449)
PHONE..................................209 982-1114
David Silva, *President*
EMP: 50 EST: 1943
SQ FT: 4,000
SALES (est): 8.1MM **Privately Held**
SIC: **4212** Dump truck haulage

(P-3938)
SOUTHWEST EXPRESS LLC
1720 E Garry Ave Ste 107, Santa Ana (92705-5831)
PHONE..................................949 474-5038
Bill Ruxby,
William Roxby, *Financial Exec*
Ron Lind,
Charles McDonald,
Michael O'Brien,
EMP: 60
SQ FT: 1,000
SALES: 1.2MM **Privately Held**
WEB: www.southwestexpress.net
SIC: **4212 4731** Delivery service, vehicular; freight transportation arrangement

(P-3939)
STANFORD TRANSPORTATION INC
10201 Alondra Dr, Bakersfield (93311-4550)
PHONE..................................661 302-3288
Gurjeet Singh, *President*
Charnhjit Badhesha, *CFO*
Navjot Singh, *Vice Pres*
EMP: 60
SALES: 7MM **Privately Held**
SIC: **4212** Local trucking, without storage

(P-3940)
TALLEY TRANSPORTATION
12325 Road 29, Madera (93638-8401)
P.O. Box 568 (93639-0568)
PHONE..................................559 673-9013
Martin Talley, *CEO*
Kenneth Talley, *Vice Pres*
EMP: 57 EST: 1946
SQ FT: 5,500
SALES (est): 6.8MM **Privately Held**
WEB: www.talleytrans.com
SIC: **4212** Local trucking, without storage

(P-3941)
TRAIL LINES INC
9415 Sorensen Ave, Santa Fe Springs (90670-2648)
P.O. Box 3567 (90670-1567)
PHONE..................................562 758-6980
Ofer Shitrit, *CEO*
Reuven Spivak, *Vice Pres*
EMP: 75
SALES (est): 16.4MM **Privately Held**
SIC: **4212 4789** Local trucking, without storage; pipeline terminal facilities, independently operated

(P-3942)
TRANSPORTATION MANAGEMENT LLC
880 Apollo St Ste 235, El Segundo (90245-4752)
PHONE..................................310 524-1555
Eric Reese,
Chris Carey,
EMP: 50
SQ FT: 14,000

SALES (est): 5.4MM **Privately Held**
SIC: **4212 4513** Delivery service, vehicular; air courier services

(P-3943)
TRIPLE E TRUCKING
1215 E White Ln, Bakersfield (93307-5061)
PHONE..................................661 834-0071
Mike Ehoff, *Partner*
Jim Ehoff, *Partner*
Loretta Ehoff, *Partner*
EMP: 50
SALES (est): 5.7MM **Privately Held**
SIC: **4212** Local trucking, without storage

(P-3944)
TST INC
Also Called: Timco
11601 Etiwanda Ave, Fontana (92337-6929)
P.O. Box 1563, Wildomar (92595-1563)
PHONE..................................310 835-0115
Andrew G Stein, *CEO*
EMP: 100
SALES (corp-wide): 64.6MM **Privately Held**
SIC: **4212** Local trucking, without storage
PA: Tst, Inc.
13428 Benson Ave
Chino CA 91710
951 737-3169

(P-3945)
UNION ASPHALT INC
1625 E Donovan Rd, Santa Maria (93454-2500)
PHONE..................................805 922-3551
George Hamill, *President*
Andy Hermreck, *Admin Sec*
EMP: 60
SQ FT: 4,000
SALES (est): 2.6MM **Privately Held**
SIC: **4212** Dump truck haulage

(P-3946)
UNITED PUMPING SERVICE INC
14000 Valley Blvd, City of Industry (91746-2801)
PHONE..................................626 961-9326
Eduardo T Perry Sr, *President*
Eduardo Perry Jr, *Corp Secy*
Daniel C Perry, *Vice Pres*
Margaret Perry, *Vice Pres*
Daniel Perry, *Project Mgr*
EMP: 95
SQ FT: 25,000
SALES (est): 27.6MM **Privately Held**
WEB: www.unitedpumping.com
SIC: **4212** Hazardous waste transport

(P-3947)
USA WASTE OF CALIFORNIA INC
Also Called: Sac Val Waste Disposal
8761 Younger Creek Dr, Sacramento (95828-1023)
PHONE..................................916 379-2611
Alex Oseguerra, *General Mgr*
EMP: 115
SALES (corp-wide): 14.9B **Publicly Held**
SIC: **4212 4953** Garbage collection & transport, no disposal; refuse systems
HQ: Usa Waste Of California, Inc.
11931 Foundation Pl # 200
Gold River CA 95670
916 387-1400

(P-3948)
USA WASTE OF CALIFORNIA INC
Also Called: Carmel Marina
11240 Commercial Pkwy, Castroville (95012-3206)
P.O. Box 1306 (95012-1306)
PHONE..................................831 384-4860
George Reddom, *President*
EMP: 120
SALES (est): 5.6MM **Privately Held**
SIC: **4212** Local trucking, without storage

P
R
O
D
U
C
T
S

&

S
V
C
S

(P-3949)
USA WASTE OF CALIFORNIA INC
Also Called: Stockton Scavengers Assn
1240 Navy Dr, Stockton (95206-1167)
PHONE..............................209 946-5721
Frank Jarvis, *Branch Mgr*
EMP: 50
SALES (corp-wide): 14.9B **Publicly Held**
SIC: 4212 Garbage collection & transport, no disposal
HQ: Usa Waste Of California, Inc.
　11931 Foundation Pl # 200
　Gold River CA 95670
　916 387-1400

(P-3950)
USA WASTE OF CALIFORNIA INC
Also Called: Waste Management Nevada County
13083 Grass Valley Ave, Grass Valley (95945-9325)
PHONE..............................530 274-3090
Art Rassmussen, *Principal*
EMP: 50
SQ FT: 8,000
SALES (corp-wide): 14.9B **Publicly Held**
SIC: 4212 8748 4953 Garbage collection & transport, no disposal; business consulting; refuse systems
HQ: Usa Waste Of California, Inc.
　11931 Foundation Pl # 200
　Gold River CA 95670
　916 387-1400

(P-3951)
VALLEY AGGREGATE TRANSPORT INC
753 N George Wash Blvd, Yuba City (95993-9065)
PHONE..............................530 821-2600
Kevin Cotter, *CEO*
EMP: 65
SALES (est): 4.2MM **Privately Held**
WEB: www.valleyaggregate.com
SIC: 4212 4213 Local trucking, without storage; trucking, except local

(P-3952)
VAN DYK TANK LINES INC
Also Called: Cool Transport
1800 S Riverside Ave, Colton (92324-3349)
P.O. Box 341, Bloomington (92316-0341)
PHONE..............................951 682-5000
Ronald Nuckles, *President*
EMP: 50
SALES (est): 4.7MM **Privately Held**
SIC: 4212 4213 Local trucking, without storage; trucking, except local

(P-3953)
WASTE MANAGEMENT RECYCLING
9227 Tujunga Ave, Sun Valley (91352-1542)
P.O. Box 7400, Pasadena (91109-7400)
PHONE..............................818 767-6180
EMP: 52
SALES (est): 17.6MM
SALES (corp-wide): 14.9B **Publicly Held**
WEB: www.wm.com
SIC: 4212 4953 Garbage collection & transport, no disposal; sanitary landfill operation
PA: Waste Management, Inc.
　1001 Fannin St Ste 4000
　Houston TX 77002
　713 512-6200

(P-3954)
WASTE MGT COLLECTN & RECYCL
2658 N Main St, Walnut Creek (94597-2729)
PHONE..............................925 935-8900
Ronald J Proto, *Manager*
EMP: 170
SALES (corp-wide): 14.9B **Publicly Held**
SIC: 4212 4953 Garbage collection & transport, no disposal; refuse systems

HQ: Waste Management Collection And Recycling, Inc.
　1001 Fannin St Ste 4000
　Houston TX 77002

(P-3955)
WESTERN MESSENGER SERVICE INC
75 Columbia Sq, San Francisco (94103-4099)
PHONE..............................415 487-4229
Dennis Golladay, *President*
Joe McManus, *President*
Patty Sokolecki, *Admin Sec*
Raymond Crosetti, *Assistant VP*
EMP: 115
SQ FT: 11,000
SALES (est): 10.2MM **Privately Held**
WEB: www.westernmessenger.com
SIC: 4212 Delivery service, vehicular

4213 Trucking, Except Local

(P-3956)
ABF FREIGHT SYSTEM INC
2135 Otoole Ave, San Jose (95131-1314)
PHONE..............................408 435-8550
Penny Podio, *Manager*
Tom Hale, *Opers Mgr*
Ron Silva, *Opers Mgr*
Aaron Gold, *Manager*
EMP: 50
SALES (corp-wide): 3B **Publicly Held**
WEB: www.abfs.com
SIC: 4213 Contract haulers
HQ: Abf Freight System, Inc.
　3801 Old Greenwood Rd
　Fort Smith AR 72903
　479 785-8700

(P-3957)
ABF FREIGHT SYSTEM INC
8001 Telegraph Rd, Pico Rivera (90660-4822)
PHONE..............................323 773-2580
Kelly Underwood, *Manager*
Matt Turrieta, *Branch Mgr*
EMP: 50
SALES (corp-wide): 3B **Publicly Held**
WEB: www.abfs.com
SIC: 4213 Contract haulers
HQ: Abf Freight System, Inc.
　3801 Old Greenwood Rd
　Fort Smith AR 72903
　479 785-8700

(P-3958)
ABF FREIGHT SYSTEM INC
4575 Tidewater Ave, Oakland (94601-3917)
PHONE..............................510 533-8575
Josh Eversville, *Manager*
Doug Thiel, *Branch Mgr*
EMP: 70
SQ FT: 10,000
SALES (corp-wide): 3B **Publicly Held**
WEB: www.abfs.com
SIC: 4213 Contract haulers
HQ: Abf Freight System, Inc.
　3801 Old Greenwood Rd
　Fort Smith AR 72903
　479 785-8700

(P-3959)
ABF FREIGHT SYSTEM INC
1601 N Batavia St, Orange (92867-3508)
PHONE..............................714 974-2485
Jerry Wright, *Manager*
EMP: 50
SQ FT: 13,326
SALES (corp-wide): 3B **Publicly Held**
WEB: www.abfs.com
SIC: 4213 Contract haulers
HQ: Abf Freight System, Inc.
　3801 Old Greenwood Rd
　Fort Smith AR 72903
　479 785-8700

(P-3960)
ABF FREIGHT SYSTEM INC
3250 47th Ave, Sacramento (95824-2441)
PHONE..............................916 428-3531

David Fox, *General Mgr*
Jeremy Sands, *General Mgr*
EMP: 65
SALES (corp-wide): 3B **Publicly Held**
WEB: www.abfs.com
SIC: 4213 Contract haulers
HQ: Abf Freight System, Inc.
　3801 Old Greenwood Rd
　Fort Smith AR 72903
　479 785-8700

(P-3961)
ABF FREIGHT SYSTEM INC
10744 Almond Ave, Fontana (92337-7153)
PHONE..............................909 355-9805
Matt Trirta, *Manager*
Todd Foster, *Branch Mgr*
EMP: 200
SQ FT: 30,248
SALES (corp-wide): 3B **Publicly Held**
WEB: www.abfs.com
SIC: 4213 Contract haulers
HQ: Abf Freight System, Inc.
　3801 Old Greenwood Rd
　Fort Smith AR 72903
　479 785-8700

(P-3962)
ADVANCED LOGISTICS MGT INC
Also Called: Advanced Trans Grp
19067 S Reyes Ave, Compton (90221-5813)
PHONE..............................310 638-0715
Rene Edmunds, *President*
Gerald R Edmunds, *Vice Pres*
EMP: 50
SQ FT: 100,000
SALES (est): 8.2MM **Privately Held**
SIC: 4213 Trucking, except local

(P-3963)
AMAR TRANSPORTATION INC (PA)
Also Called: Paul Trucking
144 W Lake Ave Ste C, Watsonville (95076-4554)
P.O. Box 39 (95077-0039)
PHONE..............................831 728-8209
Amarjit S Tut, *President*
Surjit S Tut, *Treasurer*
Paritan S Tut, *Vice Pres*
Ranjit S Tut, *Vice Pres*
EMP: 130
SQ FT: 4,872
SALES (est): 9.9MM **Privately Held**
SIC: 4213 4212 Trucking, except local; local trucking, without storage

(P-3964)
AMERICAN FREIGHTWAYS LP
10845 Rancho Bernardo Rd # 100, San Diego (92127-2107)
PHONE..............................866 326-5902
Kirk Carmichael, *General Ptnr*
Mark Goodacre, *General Ptnr*
Renee Goodacre, *Accountant*
Cole Gretler, *Opers Mgr*
Michael West, *Opers Mgr*
EMP: 62
SQ FT: 10,000
SALES (est): 19.5MM **Privately Held**
SIC: 4213 Trucking, except local

(P-3965)
AMERICAN WEST WORLDWIDE EX INC
511 Zaca Ln Ste 120, San Luis Obispo (93401)
PHONE..............................805 926-2800
Josh Brown, *Branch Mgr*
EMP: 50 **Privately Held**
SIC: 4213 Heavy hauling
PA: American West Worldwide Express, Inc.
　51 Zaca Ln Ste 120
　San Luis Obispo CA 93401

(P-3966)
AMGEN DISTRIBUTION INC
1244 Valley View Rd # 119, Glendale (91202-1752)
PHONE..............................760 989-4424
EMP: 73
SQ FT: 3,900

SALES (est): 4.8MM **Privately Held**
SIC: 4213

(P-3967)
ARDWIN INC
Also Called: Ardwin Freight
2940 N Hollywood Way, Burbank (91505-1024)
P.O. Box 1609 (91507-1609)
PHONE..............................818 767-7777
Edwin Sahakian, *President*
Bruce Roberts, *Vice Pres*
Richard Breault, *Info Tech Mgr*
Cesar Quijano, *Opers Mgr*
David Holland, *Cust Mgr*
EMP: 130
SQ FT: 10,000
SALES (est): 28.9MM **Privately Held**
WEB: www.ardwin.com
SIC: 4213 Contract haulers

(P-3968)
ASBURY TRANSPORTATION CO
2144 Mohawk St, Bakersfield (93308-6001)
PHONE..............................661 327-2271
Richard Boyer, *CEO*
EMP: 52
SQ FT: 2,100
SALES (est): 10.9MM **Privately Held**
WEB: www.asburytrans.com
SIC: 4213 Contract haulers

(P-3969)
ATECH WAREHOUSING & DIST INC (PA)
7 College Ave, Santa Rosa (95401-4702)
P.O. Box 6836 (95406-0836)
PHONE..............................707 526-1910
Jesse E Amaral, *President*
Geri Amaral, *Vice Pres*
Isaias Santos, *Opers Mgr*
Jeremy Thayne, *Opers Mgr*
Travis Amaral, *Manager*
EMP: 60
SQ FT: 35,000
SALES (est): 14.4MM **Privately Held**
WEB: www.atechdist.com
SIC: 4213 Less-than-truckload (LTL) transport

(P-3970)
BERT E JESSUP TRANSPORTATION
641 Old Gilroy St, Gilroy (95020-6233)
PHONE..............................408 848-3390
Leonard Milanowski, *CEO*
Len Milanowski, *CFO*
Robin Jessup, *Admin Sec*
EMP: 85
SQ FT: 10,000
SALES (est): 15.8MM **Privately Held**
WEB: www.jessup.net
SIC: 4213 Trucking, except local

(P-3971)
BEST OVERNITE EXPRESS INC (PA)
Also Called: Best Overnight Express
406 Live Oak Ave, Irwindale (91706-1314)
P.O. Box 90816, City of Industry (91715-0816)
PHONE..............................626 256-6340
William K Applebee, *President*
Mike Salcedo, *COO*
Mike White, *CFO*
John Polisatuk, *Executive*
Jeff Siri, *Branch Mgr*
EMP: 160
SQ FT: 25,000
SALES (est): 32MM **Privately Held**
SIC: 4213 Trucking, except local

(P-3972)
BETTENDORF ENTERPRISES INC
Also Called: Bettendorf Trucking
20943 Bettendorf Way, Anderson (96007-8721)
PHONE..............................530 365-1937
Mike Tully, *Branch Mgr*
EMP: 60

SALES (corp-wide): 35.1MM **Privately Held**
WEB: www.bettendorftrucking.com
SIC: 4213 Contract haulers
PA: Bettendorf Enterprises, Inc.
4545 West End Rd
Arcata CA 95521
707 822-0173

(P-3973)
BHANDAL BROS INC
2490 San Juan Rd, Hollister (95023-9107)
P.O. Box 190 (95024-0190)
PHONE..........................831 728-2691
Maninder Singh, *President*
EMP: 50 EST: 2012
SALES (est): 8MM **Privately Held**
SIC: 4213 Trucking, except local

(P-3974)
BHANDAL BROS TRUCKING INC
2490 San Juan Rd, Hollister (95023-9107)
P.O. Box 1900 (95024-1900)
PHONE..........................831 728-2691
Mangal S Bhandal, *President*
EMP: 55
SQ FT: 4,000
SALES (est): 12.6MM **Privately Held**
WEB: www.bhandalbrotherstrucking.com
SIC: 4213 Refrigerated products transport

(P-3975)
BIAGI BROS INC
Also Called: F & G Biagi Transportation
3655 E Airport Dr, Ontario (91761-1562)
PHONE..........................909 390-6910
John Boggus, *Branch Mgr*
EMP: 200
SALES (corp-wide): 116.3MM **Privately Held**
WEB: www.biagibros.com
SIC: 4213 Trucking, except local
PA: Biagi Bros., Inc.
787 Airpark Rd
Napa CA 94558
707 745-8115

(P-3976)
BIAGI BROS INC
Also Called: Biagi Brothers Bezzerides Co
650 Stone Rd, Benicia (94510-1140)
PHONE..........................707 745-8115
Tom Tunt, *Branch Mgr*
EMP: 80
SALES (corp-wide): 116.3MM **Privately Held**
WEB: www.biagibros.com
SIC: 4213 Trucking, except local
PA: Biagi Bros., Inc.
787 Airpark Rd
Napa CA 94558
707 745-8115

(P-3977)
BJJ COMPANY LLC (PA)
Also Called: Westland Trailer Mfg
1040 W Kettleman Ln, Lodi (95240-6056)
PHONE..........................209 941-8361
Fax: 209 941-0476
EMP: 70
SQ FT: 4,000
SALES: 12.1MM **Privately Held**
SIC: 4213

(P-3978)
BLUE CHIP MOVING AND STOR INC
Also Called: Blue Chip Mayflower
13525 Crenshaw Blvd, Hawthorne (90250-7811)
PHONE..........................323 463-6888
Dennis Doody, *CEO*
Jack Doody, *Vice Pres*
EMP: 55 EST: 1963
SQ FT: 30,000
SALES (est): 8.7MM **Privately Held**
SIC: 4213 4214 Household goods transport; contract haulers; local trucking with storage

(P-3979)
BUDWAY ENTERPRISES INC (PA)
Also Called: Budway Trucking & Warehousing
13600 Napa St, Fontana (92335-2944)
PHONE..........................909 463-0500
Vincent McLeod, *CEO*
Jim Barbour, *CFO*
Daniel Heykoop, *Exec VP*
Marcy McKenzie, *Vice Pres*
Alex Nicholas, *Vice Pres*
EMP: 55 EST: 1974
SQ FT: 120,000
SALES (est): 20.9MM **Privately Held**
SIC: 4213 Contract haulers

(P-3980)
BULK TRANSPORTATION (PA)
415 S Lemon Ave, Walnut (91789-2911)
P.O. Box 390 (91788-0390)
PHONE..........................909 594-2855
Brett Richardson, *President*
Gary K Cross, *President*
George G Cross, *CEO*
Susan Duffield, *Admin Sec*
Karen Finley, *Controller*
EMP: 60
SQ FT: 3,500
SALES: 38.4MM **Privately Held**
WEB: www.bulk-dti.com
SIC: 4213 4789 Contract haulers; cargo loading & unloading services

(P-3981)
BUTTON TRANSPORTATION INC
7000 Button Ln, Dixon (95620-9116)
PHONE..........................707 678-7434
Robert Button, *President*
Anthony Iten, *President*
Bob Button, *Manager*
EMP: 175
SQ FT: 5,000
SALES (est): 37.5MM **Privately Held**
SIC: 4213 Contract haulers; liquid petroleum transport, non-local

(P-3982)
CALIFRNIA INTERMODAL ASSOC INC (PA)
6666 E Washington Blvd, Commerce (90040-1814)
PHONE..........................323 562-7788
Gabriel Chaul, *CEO*
Ron Mejia, *Manager*
EMP: 60
SALES (est): 7.2MM **Privately Held**
WEB: www.ciatrucking.com
SIC: 4213 Trucking, except local

(P-3983)
CENTRAL FREIGHT LINES INC
1621 Main Ave, Sacramento (95838-2427)
PHONE..........................800 782-5036
Jack Buckley, *Manager*
EMP: 100
SALES (corp-wide): 1.6B **Privately Held**
WEB: www.centralfreight.com
SIC: 4213 Trucking, except local
HQ: Central Freight Lines, Inc.
5601 W Waco Dr
Waco TX 76710
254 772-2120

(P-3984)
CERTIFIED FRT LOGISTICS INC (PA)
1344 White Ct, Santa Maria (93458-3732)
P.O. Box 5668 (93456-5668)
PHONE..........................800 592-5906
James O Nelson, *President*
Scott Cramer, *CFO*
Jon Cramer, *Vice Pres*
Edwin F Nelson Jr, *Vice Pres*
Chuck Alloway, *Info Tech Mgr*
EMP: 120
SQ FT: 40,000
SALES: 42MM **Privately Held**
WEB: www.cfl-usa.com
SIC: 4213 Refrigerated products transport

(P-3985)
CHIPMAN CORPORATION (PA)
Also Called: Caton Moving & Storage
1040 Marina Village Pkwy # 100, Alameda (94501-6478)
PHONE..........................510 748-8700
Tom Chipman, *CEO*
Justin Chipman, *President*
John H Chipman Sr, *Chairman*
Gregg Brenner, *Vice Pres*
Rick Carreon, *Vice Pres*
▲ EMP: 50
SQ FT: 400,000
SALES (est): 30MM **Privately Held**
WEB: www.chipmancorp.com
SIC: 4213 4731 Trucking, except local; foreign freight forwarding

(P-3986)
CHIPMAN CORPORATION
Also Called: Unitd Van Lines Agnt
1555 Zephyr Ave, Hayward (94544-7835)
PHONE..........................510 748-8787
John Chipman Jr, *Branch Mgr*
EMP: 60
SALES (corp-wide): 30MM **Privately Held**
WEB: www.chipmancorp.com
SIC: 4213 4212 Trucking, except local; moving services
PA: Chipman Corporation
1040 Marina Village Pkwy # 100
Alameda CA 94501
510 748-8700

(P-3987)
CONTRACTORS CARGO COMPANY (PA)
Also Called: Contractors Rigging & Erectors
500 S Alameda St, Compton (90221-3801)
P.O. Box 5290 (90224-5290)
PHONE..........................310 609-1957
Carla Ann Wheeler, *CEO*
Gerald D Wheeler, *President*
Kimberly Dorio, *Corp Secy*
Steve Cummins, *Natl Sales Mgr*
Andy Mello, *Natl Sales Mgr*
◆ EMP: 120
SQ FT: 25,000
SALES (est): 49.2MM **Privately Held**
WEB: www.contractorscargo.com
SIC: 4213 4731 1623 4741 Contract haulers; freight transportation arrangement; water, sewer & utility lines; rental of railroad cars; cargo loading & unloading services; boiler maintenance contractor

(P-3988)
COROVAN CORPORATION (PA)
12302 Kerran St, Poway (92064-6884)
PHONE..........................858 762-8100
Richard R Schmitz, *CEO*
Harrison Beall, *IT/INT Sup*
Lawrence Soriano, *IT/INT Sup*
Jim Goff, *Technician*
John Schmitthenner, *Controller*
EMP: 175
SQ FT: 80,000
SALES (est): 72.2MM **Privately Held**
SIC: 4213 Trucking, except local

(P-3989)
CRST INTERNATIONAL INC
10641 Calabash Ave, Fontana (92337-7011)
PHONE..........................909 829-1313
EMP: 149
SALES (corp-wide): 2B **Privately Held**
SIC: 4213
PA: Crst International, Inc.
3930 16th Ave Sw
Cedar Rapids IA 52401
319 396-4400

(P-3990)
CUNHA DRAYING INC
1500 Madruga Rd, Lathrop (95330-9779)
PHONE..........................209 858-1400
Paul Buttini, *President*
Peggy Deforest, *Vice Pres*
EMP: 65
SQ FT: 10,000
SALES (est): 9.9MM **Privately Held**
WEB: www.cunhadraying.com
SIC: 4213 Contract haulers

(P-3991)
DART INTERNATIONAL A CORP (HQ)
Also Called: Dart Entities
1430 S Eastman Ave, Commerce (90023-4006)
P.O. Box 23944, Los Angeles (90023-0944)
PHONE..........................323 264-8746
Terence Dedeaux, *CEO*
Paul Martin, *President*
William J Smollen, *Corp Secy*
Larry Nelson, *President*
Lorena Paredes, *Administration*
EMP: 110
SQ FT: 50,000
SALES (est): 26.5MM
SALES (corp-wide): 107.1MM **Privately Held**
SIC: 4213 Trucking, except local
PA: Dart Transportation Service, A Corporation
1430 S Eastman Ave Ste 1
Commerce CA 90023
323 981-8205

(P-3992)
DAYLIGHT TRANSPORT LLC (PA)
1501 Hughes Way Ste 200, Long Beach (90810-1879)
P.O. Box 93155 (90809-3155)
PHONE..........................310 507-8200
Richard S Breen, *CEO*
Jim Mc Carthy, *CFO*
Jim McCarthy, *CFO*
Edward Marsh, *Vice Pres*
Barbara Elliott, *Executive*
EMP: 100 EST: 1997
SQ FT: 3,000
SALES (est): 47.3MM **Privately Held**
WEB: www.dylt.com
SIC: 4213 Contract haulers

(P-3993)
DC TRANSPORT INC
5411 Raley Blvd, Sacramento (95838-1726)
PHONE..........................916 438-0888
Andrew Romanov, *President*
Sergey Romanov, *Vice Pres*
Evelina R Popovich, *Admin Sec*
Evelina Popovich, *Admin Sec*
Slava Chmel, *Opers Mgr*
EMP: 55
SQ FT: 21,000
SALES (est): 18.9MM **Privately Held**
WEB: www.dctransport.com
SIC: 4213 Trucking, except local

(P-3994)
DEPENDABLE HIGHWAY EXPRESS INC
Also Called: Dhe
1351 S Campus Ave, Ontario (91761-4352)
PHONE..........................909 923-0065
Bob Bianchi, *Branch Mgr*
EMP: 60
SALES (corp-wide): 229.2MM **Privately Held**
WEB: www.godependable.com
SIC: 4213 Contract haulers
PA: Dependable Highway Express, Inc.
2555 E Olympic Blvd
Los Angeles CA 90023
323 526-2200

(P-3995)
DEPENDABLE HIGHWAY EXPRESS INC
800 E 230th St, Carson (90745-5002)
PHONE..........................310 522-4111
Keith Norris, *Manager*
EMP: 216
SALES (corp-wide): 229.2MM **Privately Held**
SIC: 4213 4225 Contract haulers; general warehousing & storage
PA: Dependable Highway Express, Inc.
2555 E Olympic Blvd
Los Angeles CA 90023
323 526-2200

PRODUCTS & SVCS

(P-3996)
DEPENDABLE HIGHWAY EXPRESS INC
1343 Lone Palm Ave, Modesto (95351-1536)
PHONE..............................209 342-0184
Don Hillman, *President*
EMP: 100
SALES (corp-wide): 229.2MM **Privately Held**
SIC: 4213 Trucking, except local
PA: Dependable Highway Express, Inc.
2555 E Olympic Blvd
Los Angeles CA 90023
323 526-2200

(P-3997)
DEPENDABLE HIGHWAY EXPRESS INC
3012 Alvarado St, San Leandro (94577-5735)
PHONE..............................510 357-2223
Trevor Schirmer, *Manager*
EMP: 50
SALES (corp-wide): 229.2MM **Privately Held**
SIC: 4213 Trucking, except local
PA: Dependable Highway Express, Inc.
2555 E Olympic Blvd
Los Angeles CA 90023
323 526-2200

(P-3998)
DEPENDABLE HIGHWAY EXPRESS INC (PA)
Also Called: Dependable Logistics Services
2555 E Olympic Blvd, Los Angeles (90023-2605)
P.O. Box 58047 (90058-0047)
PHONE..............................323 526-2200
Ronald Massman, *President*
Nicole Felix, *Partner*
Nancy Ordaz, *Partner*
Blanca Reyes, *Partner*
Karen Shaw, *Partner*
◆ **EMP:** 300
SQ FT: 1,680,000
SALES (est): 229.2MM **Privately Held**
WEB: www.godependable.com
SIC: 4213 4225 Contract haulers; general warehousing & storage

(P-3999)
DEPENDABLE HIGHWAY EXPRESS INC
Also Called: Dhe
3199 Alvarado St, San Leandro (94577-5709)
PHONE..............................510 357-2223
Georgia Briggs, *Branch Mgr*
EMP: 82
SALES (corp-wide): 229.2MM **Privately Held**
WEB: www.godependable.com
SIC: 4213 4225 Trucking, except local; general warehousing & storage
PA: Dependable Highway Express, Inc.
2555 E Olympic Blvd
Los Angeles CA 90023
323 526-2200

(P-4000)
DESERT COASTAL TRANSPORT INC (PA)
Also Called: Dct
10686 Banana Ave, Fontana (92337-7002)
PHONE..............................909 357-3395
Tim Wyant, *President*
Timothy A Wyant, *CEO*
Chuck Wyant, *Admin Sec*
EMP: 55
SQ FT: 6,000
SALES: 29.2MM **Privately Held**
WEB: www.desertcoastal.com
SIC: 4213 Trucking, except local

(P-4001)
DOT-LINE TRANSPORTATION INC
4366 E 26th St, Vernon (90058-4301)
P.O. Box 8739, Fountain Valley (92728-8739)
PHONE..............................877 900-7768
Dennis Watson, *President*

Dottie Watson, *Corp Secy*
EMP: 55
SALES (est): 4.8MM **Privately Held**
SIC: 4213 Trucking, except local

(P-4002)
DOUBLE EAGLE TRNSP CORP
12135 Scarbrough Ct, Oak Hills (92344-9200)
PHONE..............................760 956-3770
Gerald E Butcher, *President*
EMP: 140
SQ FT: 10,125
SALES: 16MM **Privately Held**
SIC: 4213 4212 Contract haulers; local trucking, without storage

(P-4003)
DOUDELL TRUCKING COMPANY (PA)
1505 N 4th St, San Jose (95112-4607)
P.O. Box 5879 (95150-5879)
PHONE..............................408 263-7300
Armand Kunde, *President*
EMP: 180
SQ FT: 20,000
SALES (est): 12.9MM **Privately Held**
SIC: 4213 4214 4212 Contract haulers; local trucking with storage; local trucking, without storage

(P-4004)
DSC LOGISTICS INC
1895 Marigold Ave, Redlands (92374-5028)
PHONE..............................909 363-4354
Greg Hart, *General Ptnr*
EMP: 68
SALES (corp-wide): 355MM **Privately Held**
SIC: 4213 4212 Trucking, except local; local trucking, without storage
PA: Dsc Logistics, Llc
1750 S Wolf Rd
Des Plaines IL 60018
847 390-6800

(P-4005)
DTI INC
1628 S Sportsman Dr, Compton (90221-4714)
P.O. Box 390, Walnut (91788-0390)
PHONE..............................310 635-9002
Gary Cross, *Partner*
Geoff Cross, *Partner*
▲ **EMP:** 57 EST: 1975
SQ FT: 90,000
SALES (est): 4.5MM **Privately Held**
SIC: 4213 Trucking, except local

(P-4006)
EAGLE SYSTEMS INC
Also Called: Eagle Intermodel Services
1535 W 4th St, San Bernardino (92411-2674)
P.O. Box 617, Wenatchee WA (98807-0617)
PHONE..............................909 386-4343
EMP: 250 **Privately Held**
WEB: www.eagleis.com
SIC: 4213 Contract haulers
HQ: Eagle Systems, Inc.
230 Grant Rd Ste A1
East Wenatchee WA 98802
509 884-7575

(P-4007)
EARLY TRANSPORTATION SERVICES
Also Called: Bay Area Garment
30796 San Clemente St, Hayward (94544-7131)
PHONE..............................510 324-1119
Earl I Ramer Sr, *President*
EMP: 100
SALES (est): 5.7MM **Privately Held**
SIC: 4213 Trucking, except local

(P-4008)
ED ROCHA LIVESTOCK TRNSP INC
Also Called: Rocha Transportation
2400 Nickerson Dr, Modesto (95358-9409)
P.O. Box 40, Ceres (95307-0040)
PHONE..............................209 538-1302

Henry Dirksen, *President*
Zachary Dirksen, *Treasurer*
Corrie M Toste, *Admin Sec*
Grant Hannink, *Opers Mgr*
Faina Senderzon, *Manager*
EMP: 70
SQ FT: 5,500
SALES (est): 11.3MM **Privately Held**
WEB: www.rochatrans.com
SIC: 4213 Contract haulers

(P-4009)
ERRAMA TRUCKING COMPANY INC
Also Called: Tough2beat Auto Sales
11336 Montgomery Ave, Granada Hills (91344-3841)
PHONE..............................818 381-3341
Souhayl Errama, *President*
Alejandro Pacheco, *Vice Pres*
Taha Aerrama, *Director*
EMP: 50
SQ FT: 15,000
SALES (est): 3MM **Privately Held**
SIC: 4213 5511 Household goods transport; automobiles, new & used

(P-4010)
ESPARZA ENTERPRISES INC
500 Workman St, Bakersfield (93307-6871)
PHONE..............................661 631-0347
EMP: 1360
SALES (corp-wide): 90.9MM **Privately Held**
SIC: 4213 Trucking, except local
PA: Esparza Enterprises, Inc.
3851 Fruitvale Ave
Bakersfield CA 93308
661 831-0002

(P-4011)
ESTES EXPRESS LINES INC
14727 Alondra Blvd, La Mirada (90638-5617)
PHONE..............................714 994-3770
Benjamin J Torman, *Branch Mgr*
Patrick Lynch, *Manager*
EMP: 121
SALES (corp-wide): 3.1B **Privately Held**
SIC: 4213 Trucking, except local
PA: Estes Express Lines
3901 W Broad St
Richmond VA 23230
804 353-1900

(P-4012)
ESTES EXPRESS LINES INC
10736 Cherry Ave, Fontana (92337-7196)
PHONE..............................909 427-9850
Mark Brown, *Manager*
EMP: 58
SALES (corp-wide): 3.1B **Privately Held**
WEB: www.estes-express.com
SIC: 4213 4212 Less-than-truckload (LTL) transport; local trucking, without storage
PA: Estes Express Lines
3901 W Broad St
Richmond VA 23230
804 353-1900

(P-4013)
ESTES EXPRESS LINES INC
13327 Temple Ave, City of Industry (91746-1513)
PHONE..............................626 333-9090
Kieran O'Carroll, *Manager*
EMP: 67
SQ FT: 6,156
SALES (corp-wide): 3.1B **Privately Held**
WEB: www.estes-express.com
SIC: 4213 4212 Less-than-truckload (LTL) transport; local trucking, without storage
PA: Estes Express Lines
3901 W Broad St
Richmond VA 23230
804 353-1900

(P-4014)
ESTES EXPRESS LINES INC
1634 S 7th St, San Jose (95112-5931)
PHONE..............................408 286-3894
John Martin, *Branch Mgr*
EMP: 50
SALES (corp-wide): 3.1B **Privately Held**
WEB: www.estes-express.com
SIC: 4213 Contract haulers

PA: Estes Express Lines
3901 W Broad St
Richmond VA 23230
804 353-1900

(P-4015)
ESTES EXPRESS LINES INC
1750 Adams Ave, San Leandro (94577-1002)
PHONE..............................510 635-0165
Bill Wardell, *Manager*
EMP: 58
SALES (corp-wide): 3.1B **Privately Held**
WEB: www.estes-express.com
SIC: 4213 Contract haulers
PA: Estes Express Lines
3901 W Broad St
Richmond VA 23230
804 353-1900

(P-4016)
ESTES EXPRESS LINES INC
9120 San Fernando Rd, Sun Valley (91352-1413)
PHONE..............................818 504-4155
Eric Reyes, *Manager*
EMP: 58
SALES (corp-wide): 3.1B **Privately Held**
WEB: www.estes-express.com
SIC: 4213 Contract haulers
PA: Estes Express Lines
3901 W Broad St
Richmond VA 23230
804 353-1900

(P-4017)
ESTES EXPRESS LINES INC
7611 S Airport Way, Stockton (95206-3918)
PHONE..............................209 982-1841
Mark Hancock, *Branch Mgr*
EMP: 58
SALES (corp-wide): 3.1B **Privately Held**
WEB: www.estes-express.com
SIC: 4213 Trucking, except local
PA: Estes Express Lines
3901 W Broad St
Richmond VA 23230
804 353-1900

(P-4018)
ESTES EXPRESS LINES INC
1531 Blinn Ave, Wilmington (90744-1601)
PHONE..............................310 549-7306
Rob Clagg, *Manager*
EMP: 58
SALES (corp-wide): 3.1B **Privately Held**
WEB: www.estes-express.com
SIC: 4213 Contract haulers
PA: Estes Express Lines
3901 W Broad St
Richmond VA 23230
804 353-1900

(P-4019)
FAST LANE TRANSPORTATION INC (PA)
Also Called: Fast Lane Container Services
2400 E Pacific Coast Hwy, Wilmington (90744-2921)
PHONE..............................562 435-3000
Patrick L Wilson, *President*
Christine Henry, *Corp Secy*
James Henry, *Exec VP*
Chris Henry, *Info Tech Mgr*
Les Peter's, *Facilities Mgr*
EMP: 70 EST: 1979
SQ FT: 36,000
SALES (est): 9.9MM **Privately Held**
WEB: www.fastlanetrans.com
SIC: 4213 4214 Trailer or container on flat car (TOFC/COFC); local trucking with storage

(P-4020)
FEDERAL EXPRESS CORPORATION
Also Called: Fedex
3333 S Grand Ave, Los Angeles (90007-4116)
PHONE..............................800 463-3339
EMP: 100
SALES (corp-wide): 69.6B **Publicly Held**
WEB: www.federalexpress.com
SIC: 4213 Contract haulers

▲ = Import ▼=Export
◆ =Import/Export

HQ: Federal Express Corporation
3610 Hacks Cross Rd
Memphis TN 38125
901 369-3600

(P-4021)
FEDEX FREIGHT CORPORATION
4500 Bandini Blvd, Vernon (90058-5409)
PHONE..................................323 269-9800
Matt Lowe, *Manager*
EMP: 200
SQ FT: 20,000
SALES (corp-wide): 69.6B **Publicly Held**
WEB: www.watkins.com
SIC: **4213** 4231 Contract haulers; trucking terminal facilities
HQ: Fedex Freight Corporation
1715 Aaron Brenner Dr
Memphis TN 38120

(P-4022)
FEDEX FREIGHT CORPORATION
1379 N Miller St, Anaheim (92806-1412)
PHONE..................................714 996-8720
Patricia Janas, *Admin Asst*
Mark Aparicio, *Analyst*
Deanna Josselyn, *Sales Staff*
Cruz Mendoza, *Warehouse Mgr*
Lanny Ball, *Maintence Staff*
EMP: 160
SQ FT: 20,802
SALES (corp-wide): 69.6B **Publicly Held**
SIC: **4213** 4212 7538 Trucking, except local; delivery service, vehicular; general automotive repair shops
HQ: Fedex Freight Corporation
1715 Aaron Brenner Dr
Memphis TN 38120

(P-4023)
FEDEX FREIGHT CORPORATION
7250 Cajon Blvd, San Bernardino (92407-1887)
PHONE..................................909 887-3970
EMP: 185
SALES (corp-wide): 69.6B **Publicly Held**
SIC: **4213** 7513 Less-than-truckload (LTL) transport; truck leasing, without drivers
HQ: Fedex Freight Corporation
1715 Aaron Brenner Dr
Memphis TN 38120

(P-4024)
FEDEX FREIGHT CORPORATION
193 Willow St, Bishop (93514-2750)
PHONE..................................760 873-8655
EMP: 53
SALES (corp-wide): 69.6B **Publicly Held**
SIC: **4213** Less-than-truckload (LTL) transport
HQ: Fedex Freight Corporation
1715 Aaron Brenner Dr
Memphis TN 38120

(P-4025)
FEDEX FREIGHT CORPORATION
2250 Airway Ln, San Diego (92154-6205)
PHONE..................................619 710-0268
Ivan Walker, *Accounts Exec*
EMP: 76
SALES (corp-wide): 69.6B **Publicly Held**
SIC: **4213** Trucking, except local
HQ: Fedex Freight Corporation
1715 Aaron Brenner Dr
Memphis TN 38120

(P-4026)
FEDEX FREIGHT CORPORATION
15200 S Main St, Gardena (90248-1957)
PHONE..................................310 323-5230
Robert Painter, *Opers Mgr*
EMP: 280
SALES (corp-wide): 69.6B **Publicly Held**
SIC: **4213** 4215 4731 Trucking, except local; courier services, except by air; freight forwarding
HQ: Fedex Freight Corporation
1715 Aaron Brenner Dr
Memphis TN 38120

(P-4027)
FEDEX FREIGHT CORPORATION
29001 Hopkins St, Hayward (94545-5003)
PHONE..................................510 895-0440
EMP: 350
SALES (corp-wide): 69.6B **Publicly Held**
SIC: **4213** 4231 4212 4731 Trucking, except local; trucking terminal facilities; local trucking, without storage; freight forwarding; airports, flying fields & services
HQ: Fedex Freight Corporation
1715 Aaron Brenner Dr
Memphis TN 38120

(P-4028)
FEDEX FREIGHT CORPORATION
11911 Branford St, Sun Valley (91352-1026)
PHONE..................................818 899-1141
EMP: 75
SALES (corp-wide): 69.6B **Publicly Held**
SIC: **4213** Less-than-truckload (LTL) transport
HQ: Fedex Freight Corporation
1715 Aaron Brenner Dr
Memphis TN 38120

(P-4029)
FEDEX FREIGHT CORPORATION
4520 S Highway 99, Stockton (95215-8235)
PHONE..................................209 466-7726
EMP: 200
SALES (corp-wide): 69.6B **Publicly Held**
SIC: **4213** Trucking, except local
HQ: Fedex Freight Corporation
1715 Aaron Brenner Dr
Memphis TN 38120

(P-4030)
FEDEX FREIGHT CORPORATION
56 Fairbanks, Irvine (92618-1602)
PHONE..................................800 706-1687
EMP: 76
SALES (corp-wide): 69.6B **Publicly Held**
SIC: **4213** 4731 Trucking, except local; freight forwarding
HQ: Fedex Freight Corporation
1715 Aaron Brenner Dr
Memphis TN 38120

(P-4031)
FEDEX FREIGHT WEST INC
3050 Teagarden St, San Leandro (94577-5721)
PHONE..................................650 244-9522
EMP: 89
SALES (corp-wide): 47.4B **Publicly Held**
SIC: **4213**
HQ: Fedex Freight West, Inc.
6411 Guadalupe Mines Rd
San Jose CA 95120
775 356-7600

(P-4032)
FEDEX FREIGHT WEST INC
4570 S Maple Ave, Fresno (93725-9358)
PHONE..................................559 266-0732
EMP: 125
SALES (corp-wide): 47.4B **Publicly Held**
SIC: **4213** 4231 4214
HQ: Fedex Freight West, Inc.
6411 Guadalupe Mines Rd
San Jose CA 95120
775 356-7600

(P-4033)
FEDEX FREIGHT WEST INC
11153 Mulberry Ave, Fontana (92337-7030)
PHONE..................................909 357-3555
EMP: 355
SQ FT: 79,735
SALES (corp-wide): 47.4B **Publicly Held**
SIC: **4213** 4731 4212
HQ: Fedex Freight West, Inc.
6411 Guadalupe Mines Rd
San Jose CA 95120
775 356-7600

(P-4034)
FEDEX FREIGHT WEST INC
1230 N Mcdowell Blvd, Petaluma (94954-1113)
PHONE..................................707 778-3191
EMP: 50
SQ FT: 13,920
SALES (corp-wide): 47.4B **Publicly Held**
SIC: **4213**
HQ: Fedex Freight West, Inc.
6411 Guadalupe Mines Rd
San Jose CA 95120
775 356-7600

(P-4035)
FEDEX GROUND PACKAGE SYS INC
1497 George Dr Ste G, Redding (96003-1472)
PHONE..................................800 463-3339
EMP: 50
SALES (corp-wide): 69.6B **Publicly Held**
SIC: **4213** Contract haulers
HQ: Fedex Ground Package System, Inc.
1000 Fed Ex Dr
Coraopolis PA 15108
800 463-3339

(P-4036)
FEDEX GROUND PACKAGE SYS INC
590 E Orangethorpe Ave, Anaheim (92801-1021)
PHONE..................................800 463-3339
Sean Davis, *Manager*
Martin Daza, *Manager*
EMP: 250
SALES (corp-wide): 69.6B **Publicly Held**
SIC: **4213** 4215 Contract haulers; courier services, except by air
HQ: Fedex Ground Package System, Inc.
1000 Fed Ex Dr
Coraopolis PA 15108
800 463-3339

(P-4037)
FEDEX GROUND PACKAGE SYS INC
1844 S Haster St, Anaheim (92802-3737)
PHONE..................................800 463-3339
EMP: 88
SALES (corp-wide): 69.6B **Publicly Held**
SIC: **4213** Contract haulers
HQ: Fedex Ground Package System, Inc.
1000 Fed Ex Dr
Coraopolis PA 15108
800 463-3339

(P-4038)
FEDEX GROUND PACKAGE SYS INC
1 Carousel Ln Unit B, Ukiah (95482-9509)
PHONE..................................800 463-3339
EMP: 87
SALES (corp-wide): 69.6B **Publicly Held**
SIC: **4213** Contract haulers
HQ: Fedex Ground Package System, Inc.
1000 Fed Ex Dr
Coraopolis PA 15108
800 463-3339

(P-4039)
FEDEX GROUND PACKAGE SYS INC
101 Book Farm Rd, Durham (95938-9521)
PHONE..................................800 463-3339
EMP: 146
SALES (corp-wide): 69.6B **Publicly Held**
SIC: **4213** Contract haulers
HQ: Fedex Ground Package System, Inc.
1000 Fed Ex Dr
Coraopolis PA 15108
800 463-3339

(P-4040)
FEDEX GROUND PACKAGE SYS INC
1725 Charles Willard St, Carson (90746-4031)
PHONE..................................800 463-3339
EMP: 146
SALES (corp-wide): 69.6B **Publicly Held**
SIC: **4213** Contract haulers

HQ: Fedex Ground Package System, Inc.
1000 Fed Ex Dr
Coraopolis PA 15108
800 463-3339

(P-4041)
FEDEX GROUND PACKAGE SYS INC
311 Otterson Dr, Chico (95928-8236)
PHONE..................................800 463-3339
EMP: 146
SALES (corp-wide): 69.6B **Publicly Held**
SIC: **4213** Contract haulers
HQ: Fedex Ground Package System, Inc.
1000 Fed Ex Dr
Coraopolis PA 15108
800 463-3339

(P-4042)
FEDEX GROUND PACKAGE SYS INC
375 Airport Rd, Bishop (93514-3614)
PHONE..................................800 463-3339
EMP: 146
SALES (corp-wide): 69.6B **Publicly Held**
SIC: **4213** Contract haulers
HQ: Fedex Ground Package System, Inc.
1000 Fed Ex Dr
Coraopolis PA 15108
800 463-3339

(P-4043)
FEDEX GROUND PACKAGE SYS INC
500 Caletti Ave, Windsor (95492-6822)
PHONE..................................800 463-3339
EMP: 146
SALES (corp-wide): 69.6B **Publicly Held**
SIC: **4213** Contract haulers
HQ: Fedex Ground Package System, Inc.
1000 Fed Ex Dr
Coraopolis PA 15108
800 463-3339

(P-4044)
FEDEX GROUND PACKAGE SYS INC
1500 E Wooley Rd Ste B, Oxnard (93030-7381)
PHONE..................................800 463-3339
EMP: 88
SALES (corp-wide): 69.6B **Publicly Held**
SIC: **4213** Contract haulers
HQ: Fedex Ground Package System, Inc.
1000 Fed Ex Dr
Coraopolis PA 15108
800 463-3339

(P-4045)
FEDEX GROUND PACKAGE SYS INC
696 E Trimble Rd Ste 10, San Jose (95131-1236)
PHONE..................................800 463-3339
EMP: 300
SALES (corp-wide): 69.6B **Publicly Held**
SIC: **4213** Contract haulers
HQ: Fedex Ground Package System, Inc.
1000 Fed Ex Dr
Coraopolis PA 15108
800 463-3339

(P-4046)
FEDEX GROUND PACKAGE SYS INC
300 Manabe Ow Rd, Watsonville (95076-7200)
PHONE..................................800 463-3339
EMP: 88
SALES (corp-wide): 69.6B **Publicly Held**
SIC: **4213** Contract haulers
HQ: Fedex Ground Package System, Inc.
1000 Fed Ex Dr
Coraopolis PA 15108
800 463-3339

(P-4047)
FEDEX GROUND PACKAGE SYS INC
9175 San Fernando Rd, Sun Valley (91352-1414)
PHONE..................................800 463-3339
Andrew Drossel, *Manager*
EMP: 90

P R O D U C T S & S V C S

SALES (corp-wide): 69.6B **Publicly Held**
SIC: 4213 Contract haulers
HQ: Fedex Ground Package System, Inc.
1000 Fed Ex Dr
Coraopolis PA 15108
800 463-3339

(P-4048)
FRANK C ALEGRE TRUCKING INC (PA)
5100 W Highway 12, Lodi (95242-9529)
P.O. Box 1508 (95241-1508)
PHONE...................................209 334-2112
Anthony J Alegre, *President*
Michelle Schultz, *General Mgr*
EMP: 230
SQ FT: 34,200
SALES (est): 44.5MM **Privately Held**
SIC: 4213 4212 Contract haulers; dump truck haulage

(P-4049)
FREDERICKSEN TANK LINES INC (PA)
Also Called: Nevada Truck & Trailer Repair
840 Delta Ln, West Sacramento (95691-2801)
PHONE...................................916 371-4960
Leonard D Robinson, *CEO*
Jeanne Haskell, *President*
Larry Kenobbie, *Vice Pres*
EMP: 93
SQ FT: 8,000
SALES (est): 6.8MM **Privately Held**
SIC: 4213 4212 Liquid petroleum transport, non-local; petroleum haulage, local

(P-4050)
FRIENDS GROUP EXPRESS INC
14520 Village Dr Apt 1013, Fontana (92337-2501)
P.O. Box 310488 (92331-0488)
PHONE...................................909 346-6814
Parmjit Singh Grewal, *Principal*
EMP: 78 EST: 2014
SQ FT: 700
SALES: 194K **Privately Held**
SIC: 4213 4212 Trucking, except local; local trucking, without storage

(P-4051)
FUEL DELIVERY SERVICES INC
4895 S Airport Way, Stockton (95206-3915)
P.O. Box 1369 (95201-1369)
PHONE...................................209 751-2185
Ronald M Vandepol, *CEO*
David Atwater, *Shareholder*
Mike Boswart, *Shareholder*
Tom V Depol, *Shareholder*
EMP: 94
SQ FT: 2,000
SALES (est): 15.2MM **Privately Held**
SIC: 4213 Liquid petroleum transport, non-local

(P-4052)
GARDNER TRUCKING INC (HQ)
1219 E Elm St, Ontario (91761-4585)
P.O. Box 747, Chino (91708-0747)
PHONE...................................909 563-5606
Thomas J Lanting, *President*
Sohn Tippetts, *Admin Asst*
Mariela Diaz, *Administration*
Richard Galvan, *Software Dev*
Kim Apodaca, *Accountant*
EMP: 490
SQ FT: 3,000
SALES (est): 87.2MM
SALES (corp-wide): 2.1B **Privately Held**
SIC: 4213 4212 Trucking, except local; local trucking, without storage
PA: Crst International, Inc.
201 1st St Se
Cedar Rapids IA 52401
319 396-4400

(P-4053)
GCU TRUCKING INC
7819 Crane Rd, Oakdale (95361-8114)
P.O. Box 1423 (95361-1423)
PHONE...................................209 845-2117
Leo Arcos, *CEO*
EMP: 52
SQ FT: 7,000

SALES (est): 9.1MM **Privately Held**
SIC: 4213 5032 Contract haulers; brick, stone & related material

(P-4054)
GILL TRANSPORT LLC
1051 Pacific Ave, Oxnard (93030-7254)
PHONE...................................805 240-1979
Steven H Gill, *Mng Member*
David L Gill, *Mng Member*
EMP: 400
SALES (est): 22.2MM **Privately Held**
SIC: 4213 Trucking, except local

(P-4055)
GREEN VALLEY TRNSP CORP
30131 Highway 33, Tracy (95304-9319)
PHONE...................................209 836-5192
Mike Taylor, *CEO*
Nancy J Houghton, *President*
Kevin West, *COO*
Cathy Gilbert, *Admin Sec*
EMP: 50
SQ FT: 3,800
SALES (est): 9.7MM **Privately Held**
SIC: 4213 4212 Contract haulers; local trucking, without storage

(P-4056)
H & H TRANSPORTATION LLC
300 El Sobrante Rd, Corona (92879-5757)
P.O. Box 77697 (92877-0123)
PHONE...................................951 817-2300
Tim Hyde,
EMP: 60
SALES (est): 6.6MM **Privately Held**
SIC: 4213 4212 Trucking, except local; local trucking, without storage

(P-4057)
H F COX INC (PA)
Also Called: Cox Petroleum Transport
118 Cox Transport Way, Bakersfield (93307)
PHONE...................................661 366-3236
Dainiel L Mairs, *President*
Gwen Mairs, *Treasurer*
Teri Gonzalez, *Vice Pres*
Bruce McKinnon, *Vice Pres*
Travis Uhles, *Manager*
EMP: 60
SQ FT: 5,000
SALES: 683.2K **Privately Held**
WEB: www.coxpetroleum.com
SIC: 4213 4212 Trucking, except local; petroleum haulage, local

(P-4058)
HAWK TRANSPORTATION INC
15238 Arrow Blvd, Fontana (92335-3250)
PHONE...................................800 709-4295
Manprit K Sandhu, *CEO*
Jagtar Sandhu, *President*
Harry Bhangu, *Manager*
EMP: 60
SQ FT: 1,300
SALES (est): 13.1MM **Privately Held**
WEB: www.hawktrans.com
SIC: 4213 Trucking, except local

(P-4059)
HEARTLAND EXPRESS INC IOWA
10131 Redwood Ave, Fontana (92335-6236)
PHONE...................................319 626-3600
Matthew Gonzalez, *Supervisor*
EMP: 50
SALES (corp-wide): 610.8MM **Publicly Held**
WEB: www.intd.com
SIC: 4213 Trucking, except local
HQ: Heartland Express, Inc. Of Iowa
901 N Kansas Ave
North Liberty IA 52317
319 626-3600

(P-4060)
HENDRICKSON TRUCK LINES INC
7080 Florin Perkins Rd, Sacramento (95828-2609)
P.O. Box 277806 (95827-7806)
PHONE...................................916 387-9614
William Hendrickson, *Chairman*
Ward Hendrickson, *CEO*

Alban Lang, *CFO*
EMP: 148
SALES: 23MM **Privately Held**
SIC: 4213 Trucking, except local

(P-4061)
HENDRICKSON TRUCKING INC
7080 Florin Perkins Rd, Sacramento (95828-2609)
P.O. Box 292219 (95829-2219)
PHONE...................................916 387-9614
William Hendrickson, *CEO*
Ward Hendrickson, *President*
EMP: 280
SQ FT: 5,480
SALES (est): 70.2MM **Privately Held**
WEB: www.hendricksontrucking.com
SIC: 4213 Trucking, except local

(P-4062)
INDIAN RIVER TRANSPORT CO
8444 W Doe Ave, Visalia (93291-9261)
PHONE...................................209 664-0456
John J Harned Jr, *Branch Mgr*
Mark Gressett, *Safety Dir*
EMP: 290
SALES (corp-wide): 104.5MM **Privately Held**
SIC: 4213 Contract haulers
PA: Indian River Transport Co.
2580 Executive Rd
Winter Haven FL 33884
863 324-2430

(P-4063)
INLAND STAR DIST CTRS INC (PA)
3146 S Chestnut Ave, Fresno (93725-2606)
P.O. Box 2396 (93745-2396)
PHONE...................................559 237-2052
Michael K Kelton, *CEO*
Kim Shirkey, *Vice Pres*
John Neale, *Comms Dir*
Daniel Alvarado, *General Mgr*
Richard Smith, *General Mgr*
◆ EMP: 60 EST: 1985
SQ FT: 550,000
SALES (est): 35.2MM **Privately Held**
WEB: www.inlandstar.com
SIC: 4213 4225 Trucking, except local; general warehousing

(P-4064)
J B HUNT TRANSPORT INC
11559 Jersey Blvd, Rancho Cucamonga (91730-4924)
PHONE...................................909 466-5361
EMP: 167
SALES (corp-wide): 6.1B **Publicly Held**
SIC: 4213
HQ: J. B. Hunt Transport, Inc.
615 J B Hunt Corporate Dr
Lowell AR 72745
479 820-0000

(P-4065)
J B HUNT TRANSPORT SVCS INC
Also Called: J.B. Hunt Transport Services
3124 E Manning Ave, Fowler (93625-9785)
PHONE...................................559 834-3852
Briana Richards, *Sales Staff*
EMP: 673
SALES (corp-wide): 8.6B **Publicly Held**
SIC: 4213 Trucking, except local
PA: J. B. Hunt Transport Services, Inc.
615 J B Hunt Corporate Dr
Lowell AR 72745
479 820-0000

(P-4066)
JACK JONES TRUCKING INC
1090 E Belmont St, Ontario (91761-4501)
PHONE...................................909 456-2500
Valerie Liese, *President*
Erin Craig, *Exec VP*
Mike Brooks, *Vice Pres*
Robert Liese, *Vice Pres*
Bob Liese, *General Mgr*
EMP: 100
SQ FT: 3,000
SALES (est): 13.2MM **Privately Held**
WEB: www.jjtinc.com
SIC: 4213 Trucking, except local

(P-4067)
JAMES B BRANCH INC (PA)
Also Called: Gemini Moving Specialists
4367 Clybourn Ave, Toluca Lake (91602-2906)
PHONE...................................818 765-3521
Eugene W Luni, *President*
Mark A Luni, *Corp Secy*
Louise W Luni, *Vice Pres*
EMP: 50
SQ FT: 35,000
SALES (est): 6.5MM **Privately Held**
SIC: 4213 Trucking, except local

(P-4068)
JE WILLIAMS TRUCKING INC
1875 Century Park E # 600, Los Angeles (90067-2507)
PHONE...................................406 248-7397
Bobby L Williams, *President*
EMP: 50 EST: 1969
SALES (est): 7.9MM **Privately Held**
WEB: www.jewilliamstrucking.com
SIC: 4213 Contract haulers

(P-4069)
JOE L COELHO INC
18637 E Bradbury Rd, Turlock (95380)
P.O. Box 3640 (95381-3640)
PHONE...................................209 667-2676
Dominic Coelho, *President*
Mary Kelly, *Admin Sec*
EMP: 50
SQ FT: 3,100
SALES: 5.4MM **Privately Held**
SIC: 4213 5191 Trucking, except local; hay

(P-4070)
KENAN ADVANTAGE GROUP INC
2709 E 37th St, Vernon (90058-1706)
PHONE...................................323 582-3778
Tom Franz, *Manager*
EMP: 70
SALES (corp-wide): 2.3B **Privately Held**
SIC: 4213 Trucking, except local
PA: The Kenan Advantage Group Inc
4366 Mount Pleasant St Nw
North Canton OH 44720
800 969-5419

(P-4071)
KINGDOM EXPRESS INC
18640 Crenshaw Blvd, Torrance (90504-5032)
P.O. Box 622, Newbury Park (91319-0622)
PHONE...................................310 258-0900
Larry King, *President*
Brenda King, *Shareholder*
Greg King, *Vice Pres*
EMP: 65
SQ FT: 40,000
SALES (est): 6.4MM **Privately Held**
WEB: www.kingdomexpress.com
SIC: 4213 Trucking, except local

(P-4072)
KINGS COUNTY TRUCK LINES (HQ)
754 S Blackstone St, Tulare (93274-5757)
P.O. Box 1016 (93275-1016)
PHONE...................................559 686-2857
Mark Tisdale, *Vice Pres*
EMP: 162 EST: 1940
SQ FT: 45,000
SALES (est): 13.4MM
SALES (corp-wide): 1.7B **Privately Held**
WEB: www.kctl.com
SIC: 4213 Refrigerated products transport
PA: Ruan Transportation Management Systems, Inc.
666 Grand Ave Ste 3100
Des Moines IA 50309
515 245-2500

(P-4073)
KLX INC
3645 S K St, Tulare (93274-7178)
P.O. Box 4438, Visalia (93278-4438)
PHONE...................................559 684-1037
Ron Greenberg, *President*
Jeff Peterson, *Corp Secy*
Christina Scites, *IT/INT Sup*
Pamela Titus, *Benefits Mgr*

Jim Fowler, *Opers Staff*
EMP: 65
SQ FT: 12,000
SALES (est): 9MM **Privately Held**
WEB: www.klx.net
SIC: 4213 Trucking, except local

(P-4074)
KNIGHT TRANSPORTATION INC
Also Called: Knight Port Services
2960 E Victoria St, Compton (90221-5615)
PHONE..................888 549-7802
EMP: 130
SALES (corp-wide): 5.3B **Publicly Held**
SIC: 4213 Trucking, except local
HQ: Knight Transportation, Inc.
20002 N 19th Ave
Phoenix AZ 85027
602 269-2000

(P-4075)
KNIGHT-SWIFT TRNSP HLDINGS INC
901 Darcy Pkwy, Lathrop (95330-8764)
PHONE..................209 858-1630
Kevin Vadnal, *Branch Mgr*
Vivian Navarro, *Executive*
EMP: 100
SALES (corp-wide): 5.3B **Publicly Held**
SIC: 4213 Contract haulers
PA: Knight-Swift Transportation Holdings Inc.
20002 N 19th Ave
Phoenix AZ 85027
602 269-2000

(P-4076)
KNIGHT-SWIFT TRNSP HLDINGS INC
2797 S Orange Ave, Fresno (93725-1919)
PHONE..................559 441-0340
Mark Peed, *Manager*
EMP: 56
SALES (corp-wide): 5.3B **Publicly Held**
SIC: 4213 Trucking, except local
PA: Knight-Swift Transportation Holdings Inc.
20002 N 19th Ave
Phoenix AZ 85027
602 269-2000

(P-4077)
KNIGHT-SWIFT TRNSP HLDINGS INC
11888 Mission Blvd, Jurupa Valley (91752-1003)
PHONE..................951 360-0130
Renaldo Gonzales, *Manager*
EMP: 56
SALES (corp-wide): 5.3B **Publicly Held**
SIC: 4213 Contract haulers
PA: Knight-Swift Transportation Holdings Inc.
20002 N 19th Ave
Phoenix AZ 85027
602 269-2000

(P-4078)
KNIGHT-SWIFT TRNSP HLDINGS INC
6933 Calle De Linea, Chula Vista (91911)
PHONE..................619 671-0588
Dennis Brown, *Branch Mgr*
EMP: 56
SALES (corp-wide): 5.3B **Publicly Held**
SIC: 4213 Trucking, except local
PA: Knight-Swift Transportation Holdings Inc.
20002 N 19th Ave
Phoenix AZ 85027
602 269-2000

(P-4079)
L A S TRANSPORTATION INC
Also Called: Produces Dairy
250 E Belmont Ave, Fresno (93701-1405)
P.O. Box 1231 (93715-1231)
PHONE..................559 264-6583
Richard Shehady, *President*
Lawrence Shehady, *Chairman*
Paul Garoogian, *Controller*
Marc Antonetti, *Sales Staff*
EMP: 300
SQ FT: 30,000

SALES (est): 27.7MM **Privately Held**
SIC: 4213 Refrigerated products transport

(P-4080)
L J TRUCKING USA
120 S Anderson St, Los Angeles (90033-3220)
PHONE..................323 469-9663
John Stewart, *President*
Carlin Ferro, *Vice Pres*
EMP: 80
SALES (est): 7.5MM **Privately Held**
SIC: 4213 Trucking, except local

(P-4081)
LANDFORCE EXPRESS CORPORATION
17201 N D St, Victorville (92394-1401)
PHONE..................760 843-7839
Rajinder Bhangu, *CEO*
EMP: 120
SALES (est): 30.8MM **Privately Held**
SIC: 4213 Trucking, except local

(P-4082)
LAS VEGAS / LA EXPRESS INC (PA)
1000 S Cucamonga Ave, Ontario (91761-3461)
PHONE..................909 972-3100
Ronald Cain Jr, *CEO*
Beverly A Adley, *Vice Pres*
Michael P Adley, *Admin Sec*
EMP: 170
SQ FT: 163,000
SALES (est): 53.1MM **Privately Held**
WEB: www.lvla.com
SIC: 4213 Trucking, except local

(P-4083)
LEMORE TRANSPORTATION INC (PA)
Also Called: Royal Trucking
1420 Royal Industrial Way, Concord (94520-4914)
P.O. Box 6085 (94524-1085)
PHONE..................925 689-6444
Barbara Querio, *CEO*
Roy Querio, *President*
Heidi Becker, *Vice Pres*
Jeremy Hunt, *Administration*
Charlene Boston, *Credit Staff*
EMP: 73
SQ FT: 6,000
SALES (est): 8.9MM **Privately Held**
WEB: www.royaltruckingco.com
SIC: 4213 Contract haulers

(P-4084)
LEXMAR DISTRIBUTION INC
200 Erie St, Pomona (91768-3327)
PHONE..................909 620-7001
Alex Kole, *President*
Antoinette Magpily, *Officer*
Alex Kolesnikov, *Vice Pres*
Apollo Reyes, *Information Mgr*
Clint Dotson, *Opers Mgr*
EMP: 170
SQ FT: 10,000
SALES (est): 24.7MM **Privately Held**
WEB: www.lexmardistribution.com
SIC: 4213 Trucking, except local

(P-4085)
MAJOR TRANSPORTATION SVCS INC
3342 N Weber Ave, Fresno (93722-4909)
PHONE..................559 485-5949
Gill Baljinder, *President*
Bhupinde Gill, *Vice Pres*
Joe Garcia, *Principal*
EMP: 50
SALES (est): 7.3MM **Privately Held**
SIC: 4213 Trucking, except local

(P-4086)
MARK CLEMONS
Also Called: Mtc Transportation
4584 Adobe Rd, Twentynine Palms (92277-1671)
P.O. Box 148 (92277-0148)
PHONE..................760 361-1531
Mark Clemons, *Owner*
Rebecca Hewson Hubbard, *Office Mgr*
Genevieve Clemons, *Manager*

EMP: 200
SALES: 21MM **Privately Held**
SIC: 4213 4212 4513 4522 Heavy machinery transport; local trucking, without storage; mail carriers, contract; air courier services; air transportation, nonscheduled

(P-4087)
MASHBURN TRNSP SVCS INC
1423 Kern St, Taft (93268-4607)
P.O. Box 66 (93268-8066)
PHONE..................661 763-5724
Denise Mashburn, *President*
Michael Mashburn, *Vice Pres*
EMP: 120
SQ FT: 2,000
SALES: 15.1MM **Privately Held**
SIC: 4213 4212 Contract haulers; local trucking, without storage

(P-4088)
MATHESON FAST FREIGHT INC
9785 Goethe Rd, Sacramento (95827-3559)
PHONE..................209 342-0184
Mark Matheson, *Branch Mgr*
EMP: 70
SALES (corp-wide): 390MM **Privately Held**
SIC: 4213 Less-than-truckload (LTL) transport
HQ: Matheson Fast Freight, Inc.
9780 Dino Dr
Elk Grove CA 95624
916 686-4600

(P-4089)
MATHESON FAST FREIGHT INC (HQ)
9780 Dino Dr, Elk Grove (95624-9477)
PHONE..................916 686-4600
Robert B Matheson, *Ch of Bd*
Mark B Matheson, *President*
Laurie Johnson, *Corp Secy*
Carole L Matheson, *Exec VP*
Donald G Brocca, *Vice Pres*
EMP: 70
SQ FT: 7,200
SALES (est): 24.9MM
SALES (corp-wide): 390MM **Privately Held**
SIC: 4213 Less-than-truckload (LTL) transport
PA: Matheson Trucking, Inc.
9785 Goethe Rd
Sacramento CA 95827
916 685-2330

(P-4090)
MATHESON TRUCKING INC (PA)
9785 Goethe Rd, Sacramento (95827-3559)
PHONE..................916 685-2330
Mark Matheson, *President*
Patricia Kepner, *CEO*
Tamrya Ford, *CFO*
Charles J Mellor, *Officer*
Carole L Matheson, *Exec VP*
EMP: 50
SQ FT: 3,000
SALES (corp-wide): 390MM **Privately Held**
SIC: 4213 4731 Contract haulers; less-than-truckload (LTL) transport; freight transportation arrangement

(P-4091)
MCCOLLISTERS TRNSP GROUP INC
Also Called: United Van Lines
10672 Jasmine St, Fontana (92337-8242)
PHONE..................909 428-5700
Chris Ciofreddi, *Branch Mgr*
EMP: 54
SALES (corp-wide): 194.4MM **Privately Held**
SIC: 4213 Trucking, except local
PA: Mccollister's Transportation Group, Inc.
1800 N Route 130
Burlington NJ 08016
609 386-0600

(P-4092)
MEATHEAD MOVERS
101 W Canon Perdido St, Santa Maria (93454)
PHONE..................805 349-8000

Aaron Steed, *Branch Mgr*
EMP: 70
SALES (corp-wide): 13.7MM **Privately Held**
SIC: 4213 4789 Household goods transport; cargo loading & unloading services
PA: Meathead Movers, Inc.
3600 S Higuera St
San Luis Obispo CA 93401
805 544-6328

(P-4093)
MEATHEAD MOVERS INC
300 Rolling Oaks Dr, Thousand Oaks (91361-1269)
PHONE..................805 496-1416
EMP: 70
SALES (corp-wide): 13.7MM **Privately Held**
SIC: 4213 4212 Household goods transport; moving services
PA: Meathead Movers, Inc.
3600 S Higuera St
San Luis Obispo CA 93401
805 544-6328

(P-4094)
MEATHEAD MOVERS INC (PA)
3600 S Higuera St, San Luis Obispo (93401-7306)
PHONE..................805 544-6328
Evan Steed, *COO*
Aaron Steed, *Sales Executive*
Ali Coleman, *Sales Staff*
EMP: 68
SQ FT: 1,700
SALES (est): 13.7MM **Privately Held**
WEB: www.meatheadmovers.com
SIC: 4213 Household goods transport

(P-4095)
MEATHEAD MOVERS INC
412 Calle San Pablo, Camarillo (93012-8502)
PHONE..................805 437-5100
Aaron Steed, *Branch Mgr*
EMP: 70
SALES (corp-wide): 13.7MM **Privately Held**
SIC: 4213 4212 Household goods transport; moving services
PA: Meathead Movers, Inc.
3600 S Higuera St
San Luis Obispo CA 93401
805 544-6328

(P-4096)
MEATHEAD MOVERS INC
1524 State St, Santa Barbara (93101-2514)
PHONE..................805 966-6328
EMP: 70
SALES (corp-wide): 13.7MM **Privately Held**
SIC: 4213 4212 Household goods transport; moving services
PA: Meathead Movers, Inc.
3600 S Higuera St
San Luis Obispo CA 93401
805 544-6328

(P-4097)
MICHAEL DUSI TRUCKING INC
4305 Second Wind Way, Paso Robles (93446-6304)
P.O. Box 2339 (93447-2339)
PHONE..................805 237-9499
Michael Dusi, *President*
Matt Dusi, *CFO*
Sharon Lawson, *Manager*
EMP: 68
SALES (est): 21.3MM **Privately Held**
WEB: www.michaeldusitrucking.com
SIC: 4213 Trucking, except local

(P-4098)
MOUNTAIN VALLEY EXPRESS CO INC (PA)
6750 Longe St Ste 100, Stockton (95206-4938)
P.O. Box 2569, Manteca (95336-1167)
PHONE..................209 823-2168
James Scott Blevins, *President*
Penny Regelman, *Office Mgr*
Ryan V Veen, *Info Tech Mgr*
Marlinda Ayala-Harris, *Recruiter*

Ken Brandon, *VP Sales*
EMP: 100
SALES (est): 52.6MM **Privately Held**
WEB: www.mountainvalleyexpress.com
SIC: 4213 Contract haulers

(P-4099)
MULTIMODAL ESQUER INC
8856 Siempre Viva Rd, San Diego
(92154-6272)
PHONE....................619 710-0477
Alfonsa Esquer, *CEO*
Federico Esquer, *Treasurer*
Jose Esquer, *Admin Sec*
Pablo Gomez, *Manager*
EMP: 56
SQ FT: 2,100
SALES (est): 8.2MM **Privately Held**
WEB: www.fletesesquer.com
SIC: 4213 Trucking, except local

(P-4100)
NATIONAL RETAIL TRNSP INC
355 W Carob St, Compton (90220-5212)
PHONE....................310 605-3777
Manuel Villasenor, *Branch Mgr*
EMP: 100
SALES (corp-wide): 245MM **Privately
Held**
WEB: www.nrsonline.com
SIC: 4213 Trucking, except local
HQ: National Retail Transportation, Inc.
2820 16th St
North Bergen NJ 07047
201 866-0462

(P-4101)
NEW LEGEND INC
Also Called: Legend Transpotation
1235 Oswald Rd, Yuba City (95991-9719)
PHONE....................530 674-3100
Baveljit Singh Samara, *Branch Mgr*
EMP: 292 **Privately Held**
SIC: 4213 4212 Trucking, except local;
local trucking, without storage
PA: New Legend, Inc.
3617 W Cmbridge Ave Ste B
Phoenix AZ 85009

(P-4102)
NEW LEGEND INC
8613 Etiwanda Ave, Rancho Cucamonga
(91739-9611)
PHONE....................855 210-2300
EMP: 219 **Privately Held**
SIC: 4213 4212 Trucking, except local;
local trucking, without storage
PA: New Legend, Inc.
3617 W Cmbridge Ave Ste B
Phoenix AZ 85009

(P-4103)
NORTHERN RFRIGERATED TRNSP INC (PA)
2700 W Main St, Turlock (95380-9537)
PHONE....................209 664-3800
Richard Mello, *CEO*
Judi Mello, *Treasurer*
John Doidge, *Vice Pres*
EMP: 120
SQ FT: 25,000
SALES (est): 40.6MM **Privately Held**
WEB: www.northernrefrigerated.com
SIC: 4213 Refrigerated products transport

(P-4104)
NY TRANSPORT INC
10191 Redwood Ave, Fontana
(92335-6236)
PHONE....................909 355-9832
Nazario Yanez, *CEO*
Nazario Y Perez, *President*
EMP: 65
SALES: 16MM **Privately Held**
SIC: 4213 Trucking, except local

(P-4105)
OAK HARBOR FREIGHT LINES INC
6700 Smith Ave, Newark (94560-4222)
PHONE....................510 608-8841
Toll Free:....................888 -
Dennis Weishaar, *Manager*
Andrew Jonsson, *Opers Mgr*

EMP: 75
SALES (corp-wide): 201.6MM **Privately
Held**
WEB: www.oakh.com
SIC: 4213 Contract haulers
PA: Oak Harbor Freight Lines, Inc
1339 W Valley Hwy N
Auburn WA 98001
206 246-2600

(P-4106)
OAK HARBOR FREIGHT LINES INC
832 F St, West Sacramento (95605-2314)
PHONE....................916 371-3960
Greg Gommenginger, *Manager*
EMP: 80
SALES (corp-wide): 201.6MM **Privately
Held**
WEB: www.oakh.com
SIC: 4213 4212 Contract haulers; local
trucking, without storage
PA: Oak Harbor Freight Lines, Inc
1339 W Valley Hwy N
Auburn WA 98001
206 246-2600

(P-4107)
OLD DOMINION FREIGHT LINE INC
1225 Washington Blvd, Montebello
(90640-6013)
PHONE....................323 725-3400
Marc Meskin, *CFO*
EMP: 200
SQ FT: 4,000
SALES (corp-wide): 4B **Publicly Held**
WEB: www.odfl.com
SIC: 4213 4212 Contract haulers; local
trucking, without storage
PA: Old Dominion Freight Line Inc
500 Old Dominion Way
Thomasville NC 27360
336 889-5000

(P-4108)
PAN PACIFIC PETROLEUM CO INC (PA)
9302 Garfield Ave, South Gate
(90280-3805)
P.O. Box 1966 (90280-1966)
PHONE....................562 928-0100
Robert Roth, *CEO*
Dale Snyder, *Exec VP*
Steven Roth, *Vice Pres*
EMP: 300
SQ FT: 600
SALES (est): 664.6K **Privately Held**
SIC: 4213 5172 Liquid petroleum trans-
port, non-local; petroleum brokers

(P-4109)
PAN PACIFIC PETROLEUM CO INC
Also Called: Truck Terminal
1850 Coffee Rd, Bakersfield (93308-5746)
PHONE....................661 589-3200
Dave Palmer, *Manager*
EMP: 100
SALES (corp-wide): 664.6K **Privately
Held**
SIC: 4213 Liquid petroleum transport, non-
local
PA: Pan Pacific Petroleum Company, Inc.
9302 Garfield Ave
South Gate CA 90280
562 928-0100

(P-4110)
PEETERS TRANSPORTATION CO
Also Called: Peeters/Mayflower
451 Eccles Ave, South San Francisco
(94080-1902)
P.O. Box 2724 (94083-2724)
PHONE....................800 356-5877
Robert Peeters, *President*
Frederick D Peeters, *CEO*
Shirley Peeters, *Corp Secy*
De Loss Wood, *Vice Pres*
◆ EMP: 50 EST: 1915
SALES (est): 3.6MM **Privately Held**
SIC: 4213 Trucking, except local

(P-4111)
PENSKE LOGISTICS LLC
2090 Etiwanda Ave, Ontario (91761-2803)
PHONE....................800 529-6531
EMP: 60
SALES (corp-wide): 2.4B **Privately Held**
WEB: www.penskelogistics.com
SIC: 4213 4212 Trucking, except local;
furniture moving, local: without storage
HQ: Penske Logistics Llc
2675 Morgantown Rd
Reading PA 19607
610 775-6000

(P-4112)
PIEDMONT TRANSFER & STORAGE
1555 S 7th St Ste A, San Jose
(95112-5926)
PHONE....................408 288-5600
David R Bartels, *President*
EMP: 50
SQ FT: 100,000
SALES (est): 4.7MM **Privately Held**
WEB: www.piedmontmoving.com
SIC: 4213 4214 Household goods trans-
port; local trucking with storage

(P-4113)
POPPY STATE EXPRESS INC
2700 W Main St, Turlock (95380-9537)
PHONE....................209 664-3950
Richard D Mello, *President*
Daniel N Watson, *CFO*
Judy Mello, *Treasurer*
John Doidge, *Vice Pres*
Claudia Doidge, *Admin Sec*
EMP: 80
SQ FT: 30,000
SALES (est): 5.9MM **Privately Held**
WEB: www.poppystate.com
SIC: 4213 Refrigerated products transport

(P-4114)
PRODUCTION DELIVERY SVCS INC
Also Called: Production Transport
12133 Greenstone Ave, Santa Fe Springs
(90670-4728)
PHONE....................562 777-0060
James Harkins, *President*
Michelle Harkins, *Corp Secy*
EMP: 55
SALES (est): 7MM **Privately Held**
SIC: 4213 Trucking, except local

(P-4115)
QUALITY CARRIERS INC
Also Called: Montgomery Tank Lines
5042 Cecelia St, South Gate (90280-3511)
PHONE....................800 282-2031
George Heinze, *Manager*
EMP: 70 **Privately Held**
WEB: www.qualitycarriers.com
SIC: 4213 Contract haulers
HQ: Quality Carriers, Inc.
1208 E Kennedy Blvd
Tampa FL 33602
800 282-2031

(P-4116)
REEVE TRUCKING COMPANY INC (PA)
5050 Carpenter Rd, Stockton
(95215-8105)
P.O. Box 5126 (95205-0126)
PHONE....................209 948-4061
Lori J Reeve, *President*
Don Reeve, *Vice Pres*
Donald E Reeve, *Vice Pres*
Donald J Reeve Aka Spike, *Vice Pres*
Robert Protz, *Principal*
EMP: 70
SQ FT: 100,000
SALES (est): 35.6MM **Privately Held**
WEB: www.reevetrucking.com
SIC: 4213 Contract haulers; heavy machin-
ery transport

(P-4117)
RELIABLE CARRIERS INC
Also Called: Relibale Carries
9122 Glenoaks Blvd, Sun Valley
(91352-2611)
PHONE....................818 252-6400

Tom Abraham, *Branch Mgr*
EMP: 50
SALES (corp-wide): 30.3MM **Privately
Held**
SIC: 4213 Automobiles, transport & deliv-
ery
PA: Reliable Carriers, Inc.
41555 Koppernick Rd
Canton MI 48187
734 453-6677

(P-4118)
RENN TRANSPORTATION INC
8845 Forest St, Gilroy (95020-3651)
PHONE....................408 842-3545
Brad E Renn, *President*
Robert Renn, *Vice Pres*
Patricia Renn, *Admin Sec*
EMP: 100
SQ FT: 9,609
SALES (est): 19.1MM **Privately Held**
WEB: www.renntransportation.com
SIC: 4213 Trucking, except local

(P-4119)
RICK STUDER
Also Called: Nordstrom
2610 Wisconsin Ave, South Gate
(90280-5598)
P.O. Box 471 (90280-0471)
PHONE....................323 357-1720
Rick Studer, *Owner*
EMP: 50
SALES (est): 5.4MM **Privately Held**
SIC: 4213 Trucking, except local

(P-4120)
RPM TRANSPORTATION INC (HQ)
11660 Arroyo Ave, Santa Ana
(92705-3057)
PHONE....................714 388-3500
Shawn Duke, *President*
Andrew Lewes, *CFO*
Robert Ogdon, *Manager*
EMP: 110
SQ FT: 175,000
SALES (est): 22.7MM
SALES (corp-wide): 63.5MM **Privately
Held**
SIC: 4213 4225 4214 Trailer or container
on flat car (TOFC/COFC); general ware-
housing; local trucking with storage
PA: Rpm Consolidated Services, Inc.
1901 Raymer Ave
Fullerton CA 92833
714 388-3500

(P-4121)
S & M MOVING SYSTEMS
Also Called: SM International
48551 Warm Springs Blvd, Fremont
(94539-7765)
PHONE....................510 497-2300
Gerald P Stadler, *Principal*
John Stadler, *Vice Pres*
▲ EMP: 60
SQ FT: 38,000
SALES (est): 12.9MM
SALES (corp-wide): 99.5MM **Privately
Held**
WEB: www.sandmoving.com
SIC: 4213 4214 Trucking, except local;
local trucking with storage
PA: Torrance Van & Storage Company
12128 Burke St
Santa Fe Springs CA 90670
562 567-2100

(P-4122)
SAIA INC
Also Called: Saia S Reno Barbara K
1508 Wyant Way, Sacramento
(95864-2642)
PHONE....................916 483-8331
EMP: 115
SALES (corp-wide): 1.6B **Publicly Held**
SIC: 4213 Trucking, except local
PA: Saia, Inc.
11465 Johns Creek Pkwy # 400
Johns Creek GA 30097
770 232-5067

(P-4123)
SAIA MOTOR FREIGHT LINE LLC
9119 Elkmont Dr, Elk Grove (95624-9706)
PHONE..............................916 690-8417
Joe Meyer, *Branch Mgr*
EMP: 50
SALES (corp-wide): 1.6B **Publicly Held**
WEB: www.saia.com
SIC: 4213 Contract haulers
HQ: Saia Motor Freight Line, Llc
11465 Johns Creek Pkwy # 400
Duluth GA 30097
770 232-5067

(P-4124)
SAIA MOTOR FREIGHT LINE LLC
2550 E 28th St, Vernon (90058-1430)
PHONE..............................323 277-2880
Gerard Francois, *Branch Mgr*
EMP: 100
SALES (corp-wide): 1.6B **Publicly Held**
WEB: www.saia.com
SIC: 4213 Contract haulers
HQ: Saia Motor Freight Line, Llc
11465 Johns Creek Pkwy # 400
Duluth GA 30097
770 232-5067

(P-4125)
SAIA MOTOR FREIGHT LINE LLC
1755 Aurora Dr, San Leandro (94577-3103)
PHONE..............................510 347-6890
John Dentony, *Manager*
EMP: 51
SALES (corp-wide): 1.6B **Publicly Held**
WEB: www.saia.com
SIC: 4213 4212 Contract haulers; local trucking, without storage
HQ: Saia Motor Freight Line, Llc
11465 Johns Creek Pkwy # 400
Duluth GA 30097
770 232-5067

(P-4126)
SCAN-VINO LLC (PA)
Also Called: Cherokee Freight Lines
5463 Cherokee Rd, Stockton (95215-1128)
PHONE..............................209 931-3570
Leanne Scannavino, *Principal*
James Fisher, *Controller*
John Ott, *Safety Mgr*
EMP: 100 EST: 1965
SQ FT: 1,000
SALES (est): 23MM **Privately Held**
WEB: www.gocfl.com
SIC: 4213 Contract haulers

(P-4127)
SCHNEIDER NATIONAL INC
4193 Industrial Pkwy Dr, Lebec (93243-9719)
PHONE..............................661 858-1031
Mark Griffin, *Branch Mgr*
Stephen Bruffett, *CFO*
Van Shared, *Director*
EMP: 205
SALES (corp-wide): 4.9B **Publicly Held**
SIC: 4213 Trucking, except local
PA: Schneider National, Inc.
3101 Packerland Dr
Green Bay WI 54313
920 592-2000

(P-4128)
SCHNEIDER NATIONAL INC
14392 Valley Blvd, Fontana (92335-5240)
PHONE..............................909 574-2165
Ray Eastwood, *Manager*
Jason Potts, *Marketing Staff*
Alex Khan, *Director*
Mark Nightingale, *Director*
Patrick Wartgow, *Director*
EMP: 140
SALES (corp-wide): 4.9B **Publicly Held**
SIC: 4213 Trucking, except local
PA: Schneider National, Inc.
3101 Packerland Dr
Green Bay WI 54313
920 592-2000

(P-4129)
SEA-LOGIX LLC
1425 Maritime St, Oakland (94607-1022)
PHONE..............................510 271-1400
Mary Brown, *Superintendent*
EMP: 60
SALES (corp-wide): 359.1MM **Privately Held**
SIC: 4213 Trucking, except local
HQ: Sea-Logix, Llc
4040 Civic Center Dr # 350
San Rafael CA 94903
415 927-6400

(P-4130)
SEASIDE RFRIGERATED TRNSPT INC (PA)
7041 Las Positas Rd Ste H, Livermore (94551-5124)
PHONE..............................510 732-0472
Lynn Johnson, *President*
Beverly Johnson, *Treasurer*
EMP: 50
SQ FT: 9,000
SALES (est): 6.5MM **Privately Held**
WEB: www.seasidetransport.com
SIC: 4213 Trucking, except local

(P-4131)
SIRVA INC
2010 Crow Canyon Pl, San Ramon (94583-4634)
PHONE..............................925 824-3109
EMP: 130
SALES (corp-wide): 1.7B **Privately Held**
SIC: 4213 Household goods transport
PA: Sirva, Inc.
1 Parkview Plz
Oakbrook Terrace IL 60181
630 570-3047

(P-4132)
SNOOZIE SHAVINGS INC (PA)
525 Elk Valley Rd, Crescent City (95531-9460)
PHONE..............................707 464-6186
Dwayne C Reichlin, *President*
Robert Matthess, *Treasurer*
Jay M Freeman, *Vice Pres*
Charlie F Compton, *Admin Sec*
EMP: 51 EST: 1967
SQ FT: 18,000
SALES (est): 2.5MM **Privately Held**
WEB: www.ssitrucking.com
SIC: 4213 5099 Trucking, except local; shavings, wood; wood & wood by-products

(P-4133)
SPECIAL DISPATCH CAL INC
8328 Central Ave, Newark (94560-3432)
PHONE..............................510 713-0300
Keith Donahue, *Manager*
Martin Mantilla, *President*
EMP: 60
SALES (corp-wide): 24.9MM **Privately Held**
SIC: 4213 Trucking, except local
PA: Special Dispatch Of California, Inc.
16330 Phoebe Ave
La Mirada CA 90638
714 521-8200

(P-4134)
SS HERT TRUCKING INC (PA)
33924 Old Woman Sprng Rd, Lucerne Valley (92356-8869)
P.O. Box 590 (92356-0590)
PHONE..............................760 248-9327
Scott Hert, *President*
Katherine Hert, *Corp Secy*
EMP: 50
SQ FT: 726
SALES: 9.8MM **Privately Held**
SIC: 4213 Trucking, except local

(P-4135)
SUDDATH RELO SYS OF NO CA
2055 S 7th St, San Jose (95112-6141)
PHONE..............................408 288-3030
Gene Kopecky, *President*
EMP: 51

SALES (est): 7.9MM
SALES (corp-wide): 456.3MM **Privately Held**
SIC: 4213 4731 4214 Household goods transport; freight forwarding; household goods moving & storage, local
HQ: Suddath Van Lines Inc
815 S Main St Ste 400
Jacksonville FL 32207
904 390-7100

(P-4136)
SUDDATH RELOCATION SYSTEMS OF
2020 S 10th St, San Jose (95112-4112)
PHONE..............................904 858-1273
Jacob Moreno, *President*
EMP: 50
SALES (est): 1MM **Privately Held**
SIC: 4213 Household goods transport

(P-4137)
SUGAR TRANSPORT OF THE NW
5463 Cherokee Rd, Stockton (95215-1128)
PHONE..............................209 931-3587
Gary Scannavino, *President*
Leanne Scannavino, *Corp Secy*
Jack Riella, *Vice Pres*
EMP: 100
SQ FT: 1,000
SALES (est): 6MM **Privately Held**
SIC: 4213 Trucking, except local

(P-4138)
SULLIVAN MOVING & STORAGE (HQ)
Also Called: United Van Lines
5704 Copley Dr, San Diego (92111-7905)
PHONE..............................858 874-2600
Rick Smith, *CEO*
Mark Fischer, *President*
Pat Reid, *CFO*
Mark Keiper, *Vice Pres*
▲ EMP: 50 EST: 1988
SQ FT: 60,000
SALES: 16MM **Privately Held**
WEB: www.sullivanunited.com
SIC: 4213 4214 Trucking, except local; local trucking with storage
PA: Corporate Moving Systems, Inc.
21620 88th Pl S
Kent WA 98031
253 395-5432

(P-4139)
SUPERIOR TRUCK LINES INC
527 F St, Lemoore (93245-2601)
PHONE..............................559 924-6418
Calvin Fagundes, *Manager*
EMP: 50
SALES (corp-wide): 12.4MM **Privately Held**
WEB: www.stlinc.com
SIC: 4213 Contract haulers
PA: Superior Truck Lines, Inc.
1457 Main St Ste A
Newman CA 95360
209 862-9430

(P-4140)
SUPERIOR TRUCK LINES INC (PA)
1457 Main St Ste A, Newman (95360-1342)
P.O. Box 307, Gustine (95322-0307)
PHONE..............................209 862-9430
Frank R Amaral III, *President*
Deanie Azevedo, *Corp Secy*
Frank R Amaral Jr, *Vice Pres*
EMP: 75
SQ FT: 1,238
SALES (est): 12.4MM **Privately Held**
WEB: www.stlinc.org
SIC: 4213 Contract haulers

(P-4141)
T & T TRUCKING INC (PA)
11396 N Hwy 99, Lodi (95240-6899)
PHONE..............................800 692-3457
Terry M Tarditi, *President*
John King, *Treasurer*
Mary Lou Tarditi, *Admin Sec*
Dan Badger, *Traffic Mgr*
Lisa Garcia, *Manager*

EMP: 107
SQ FT: 25,000
SALES (est): 23MM **Privately Held**
WEB: www.tttrucking.com
SIC: 4213 Contract haulers

(P-4142)
TIGER LINES LLC (HQ)
927 Black Diamond Way, Lodi (95240-0738)
P.O. Box 1120 (95241-1120)
PHONE..............................209 334-4100
Dennis Altnow, *CEO*
David Hembree, *Vice Pres*
Emil Canlas, *Human Res Dir*
Jason Henry, *Purch Agent*
Gray Greg, *Opers Staff*
EMP: 75 EST: 1935
SQ FT: 20,000
SALES: 35.5MM
SALES (corp-wide): 2.2MM **Privately Held**
SIC: 4213 4214 4212 Contract haulers; local trucking with storage; local trucking, without storage
PA: Lts Rentals, Llc
927 Black Diamond Way
Lodi CA 95240
209 334-4100

(P-4143)
TIMMERMAN STARLITE TRCKG INC
3955 Starlite Dr, Ceres (95307-9733)
P.O. Box 2710 (95307-7710)
PHONE..............................209 538-1706
Colby Bell, *CEO*
Agnes Timmerman, *Corp Secy*
Geneveve Timmerman, *Vice Pres*
EMP: 65 EST: 1976
SALES: 9.7MM **Privately Held**
SIC: 4213 4212 Trucking, except local; farm to market haulage, local

(P-4144)
TMT INDUSTRIES INC
14774 Jurupa Ave, Fontana (92337-7263)
PHONE..............................909 493-3441
Antonio Y Martinez, *CEO*
Tony Martinez Sr, *President*
Evelyn Martinez, *Corp Secy*
Tony Martinez Jr, *Vice Pres*
Debbie Rush, *Office Mgr*
EMP: 63
SALES (est): 22.4MM **Privately Held**
SIC: 4213 4212 Trucking, except local; local trucking, without storage

(P-4145)
TOTAL TRNSP LOGISTICS INC
4325 Etiwanda Ave Ste A, Jurupa Valley (91752-3720)
PHONE..............................951 360-9521
Robert E Hicks, *President*
Michael Oliveira, *CFO*
Mike Stadler, *CFO*
Steve Todare, *Vice Pres*
Kai Scharnweber, *Executive*
EMP: 75
SQ FT: 125,000
SALES (est): 24.1MM **Privately Held**
WEB: www.ttlogistics.com
SIC: 4213 Contract haulers

(P-4146)
TRIPLE-E MACHINERY MOVING INC
3301 Gilman Rd, El Monte (91732-3225)
PHONE..............................626 444-1137
Steve Englebrecht, *CEO*
Joe Englbrecht, *Vice Pres*
Ben Englebrecht, *General Mgr*
Ed Langan, *Foreman/Supr*
EMP: 60
SQ FT: 12,000
SALES (est): 7.7MM **Privately Held**
WEB: www.tripleemachinery.com
SIC: 4213 Heavy machinery transport

(P-4147)
TRIUS TRUCKING INC
4692 E Lincoln Ave, Fowler (93625-9685)
P.O. Box 2700, Fresno (93745-2700)
PHONE..............................559 834-4000
Tehal Singh Thandi, *CEO*
EMP: 87

PRODUCTS & SVCS

SQ FT: 3,900
SALES (est): 30.5MM **Privately Held**
SIC: 4213 Trucking, except local

(P-4148)
TRIWAYS INC
Also Called: Warehouse and Distribution
11201 Iberia St Ste B, Jurupa Valley
(91752-3280)
P.O. Box 9342, Ontario (91762-9342)
PHONE..................................951 361-4840
Juan M Jauregui, *President*
Fredy R Jimenez, *CFO*
Bob Schwenig, *Vice Pres*
▲ EMP: 65
SQ FT: 228,000
SALES (est): 15.3MM **Privately Held**
WEB: www.triways.net
SIC: 4213 Trucking, except local

(P-4149)
U S XPRESS INC
363 Nina Lee Rd, Calexico (92231-9527)
PHONE..................................760 768-6707
EMP: 124 **Publicly Held**
SIC: 4213 Trucking, except local
HQ: U. S. Xpress, Inc.
4080 Jenkins Rd
Chattanooga TN 37421
866 266-7270

(P-4150)
UPS FREIGHT SERVICES INC
2650 S Willow Ave, Bloomington
(92316-3257)
PHONE..................................909 879-7400
Criss Sowers, *Manager*
EMP: 73
SALES (corp-wide): 71.8B **Publicly Held**
SIC: 4213 Contract haulers
HQ: Ups Freight Services, Inc.
1000 Semmes Ave
Richmond VA 23224
804 231-8000

(P-4151)
UPS GROUND FREIGHT INC
Also Called: Martrac
4587 S Chestnut Ave, Fresno
(93725-9211)
PHONE..................................559 445-9010
Steve Sutton, *Manager*
EMP: 56
SALES (corp-wide): 71.8B **Publicly Held**
SIC: 4213 Contract haulers
HQ: Ups Ground Freight, Inc.
1000 Semmes Ave
Richmond VA 23224
866 372-5619

(P-4152)
UPS GROUND FREIGHT INC
600 Williams St, Bakersfield (93305-5438)
PHONE..................................661 395-9500
Fax: 661 395-9510
EMP: 95
SALES (corp-wide): 58.2B **Publicly Held**
SIC: 4213
HQ: Ups Ground Freight, Inc.
1000 Semmes Ave
Richmond VA 23224
804 231-8000

(P-4153)
UPS GROUND FREIGHT INC
1444 Lathrop Rd, Lathrop (95330-9771)
PHONE..................................209 858-5095
Bill Rose, *Branch Mgr*
EMP: 98
SALES (corp-wide): 71.8B **Publicly Held**
SIC: 4213 Contract haulers
HQ: Ups Ground Freight, Inc.
1000 Semmes Ave
Richmond VA 23224
866 372-5619

(P-4154)
UPS GROUND FREIGHT INC
7 College Ave, Santa Rosa (95401-4702)
P.O. Box 6836 (95406-0836)
PHONE..................................707 526-1910
Jesse Amarel, *Manager*
EMP: 95
SALES (corp-wide): 71.8B **Publicly Held**
WEB: www.overnite.com
SIC: 4213 Contract haulers

HQ: Ups Ground Freight, Inc.
1000 Semmes Ave
Richmond VA 23224
866 372-5619

(P-4155)
UPS GROUND FREIGHT INC
925 Morse Ave, Sunnyvale (94089-1601)
PHONE..................................408 400-0595
EMP: 95
SALES (corp-wide): 58.2B **Publicly Held**
SIC: 4213
HQ: Ups Ground Freight, Inc.
1000 Semmes Ave
Richmond VA 23224
804 231-8000

(P-4156)
UPS GROUND FREIGHT INC
Also Called: UPS Freight
7754 Paramount Blvd, Pico Rivera
(90660-4309)
PHONE..................................562 801-1300
Cliff Sowers, *Branch Mgr*
EMP: 95
SALES (corp-wide): 71.8B **Publicly Held**
WEB: www.overnite.com
SIC: 4213 Contract haulers
HQ: Ups Ground Freight, Inc.
1000 Semmes Ave
Richmond VA 23224
866 372-5619

(P-4157)
UPS GROUND FREIGHT INC
900 E St, West Sacramento (95605-2310)
PHONE..................................916 371-9101
EMP: 60
SALES (corp-wide): 58.2B **Publicly Held**
SIC: 4213
HQ: Ups Ground Freight, Inc.
1000 Semmes Ave
Richmond VA 23224
804 231-8000

(P-4158)
UPS GROUND FREIGHT INC
650 S Acacia Ave, Fullerton (92831-5107)
PHONE..................................866 372-5619
Arthur Morales, *General Mgr*
EMP: 80
SALES (corp-wide): 71.8B **Publicly Held**
WEB: www.overnite.com
SIC: 4213 Automobiles, transport & delivery
HQ: Ups Ground Freight, Inc.
1000 Semmes Ave
Richmond VA 23224
866 372-5619

(P-4159)
USA TRUCK INC
5861 Pine Ave Ste A-2, Chino Hills
(91709-6540)
PHONE..................................909 334-1406
EMP: 67
SALES (corp-wide): 534MM **Publicly Held**
SIC: 4213 Trucking, except local
PA: Usa Truck, Inc.
3200 Industrial Park Rd
Van Buren AR 72956
479 471-2500

(P-4160)
USF REDDAWAY INC
11937 Regentview Ave, Downey
(90241-5515)
PHONE..................................562 923-0648
Sal Leal, *Manager*
EMP: 150
SQ FT: 28,300
SALES (corp-wide): 5B **Publicly Held**
SIC: 4213 Less-than-truckload (LTL) transport
HQ: Usf Reddaway Inc.
7720 Sw Mohawk St Bldg H
Tualatin OR 97062
503 650-1286

(P-4161)
VALLEY BULK INC
17649 Turner Rd, Victorville (92394-8716)
P.O. Box 1100 (92393-1100)
PHONE..................................760 843-0574
Jeff W Golson, *President*

EMP: 85
SALES (est): 14.2MM **Privately Held**
WEB: www.valleybulk.com
SIC: 4213 Contract haulers

(P-4162)
VAN KING & STORAGE INC
Also Called: King Relocation Services
13535 Larwin Cir, Santa Fe Springs
(90670-5032)
PHONE..................................562 921-0555
Steve Komorous, *President*
Edwin Nabal, *CFO*
Keith Hindsley, *Senior VP*
Martin Delaney, *Vice Pres*
Jj Krukenkamp, *Vice Pres*
EMP: 74 EST: 1955
SQ FT: 60,000
SALES (est): 16.5MM **Privately Held**
WEB: www.kingrelocation.com
SIC: 4213 4225 Trucking, except local;
general warehousing & storage

(P-4163)
**VENTURA TRANSFER COMPANY
(PA)**
2418 E 223rd St, Long Beach
(90810-1697)
PHONE..................................310 549-1660
Randall J Clifford, *CEO*
Ian Hart, *CFO*
Galen Clifford, *Vice Pres*
Greg Clifford, *Vice Pres*
Steven F Clifford, *Vice Pres*
EMP: 75 EST: 1927
SQ FT: 10,000
SALES (est): 18.5MM **Privately Held**
WEB: www.venturatransfercompany.com
SIC: 4213 4212 4214 Contract haulers;
local trucking, without storage; local trucking with storage

(P-4164)
VIP TRANSPORT INC
2703 Wardlow Rd, Corona (92882-2869)
PHONE..................................951 272-3700
Brittany Johnson, *President*
Laurie Griffiths, *Treasurer*
Laurie L Griffiths, *Treasurer*
Brittany Griffiths, *Admin Sec*
Josh Toth, *Opers Mgr*
EMP: 50 EST: 1982
SQ FT: 127,000
SALES (est): 10.4MM **Privately Held**
WEB: www.viptransport.com
SIC: 4213 4214 4731 Trucking, except
local; local trucking with storage; foreign
freight forwarding

(P-4165)
WAGGONERS TRUCKING
801 Mcwane Blvd, Port Hueneme
(93043-0001)
PHONE..................................800 999-9097
Rick Salazar, *Manager*
EMP: 60
SALES (corp-wide): 234.4MM **Privately
Held**
SIC: 4213 Contract haulers
PA: The Waggoners Trucking
5220 Midland Rd
Billings MT 59101
406 248-1919

(P-4166)
WERNER ENTERPRISES INC
10251 Calabash Ave, Fontana
(92335-5275)
PHONE..................................909 823-5803
John Bidaurri, *Branch Mgr*
EMP: 50
SQ FT: 1,316
SALES (corp-wide): 2.4B **Publicly Held**
WEB: www.werner.com
SIC: 4213 4731 Contract haulers; freight
consolidation
PA: Werner Enterprises, Inc
14507 Frontier Rd
Omaha NE 68138
402 895-6640

(P-4167)
WESTERN STAR TRNSP LLC
1065 E Walnut St, Carson (90746-1346)
PHONE..................................310 605-1300
Lee Cadwallader,

Kelly Cadwallader, *VP Sales*
Warren Cadwallader,
Norm Fritz,
Gail Werner,
EMP: 240
SQ FT: 80,000
SALES (est): 720.5K **Privately Held**
WEB: www.westernstartransportation.com
SIC: 4213 Less-than-truckload (LTL) transport

(P-4168)
WILDWOOD EXPRESS
12416 Swanson Ave, Kingsburg
(93631-9516)
P.O. Box 397 (93631-0397)
PHONE..................................559 805-3237
Mark Anthony Woods, *President*
Matthew Woods, *Treasurer*
Sue Woods, *Vice Pres*
EMP: 50
SQ FT: 3,500
SALES (est): 11.9MM **Privately Held**
SIC: 4213 Contract haulers

(P-4169)
WILLIAMS TANK LINES (PA)
1477 Tillie Lewis Dr, Stockton
(95206-1130)
PHONE..................................209 944-5613
Michael I Williams, *CEO*
Marlys A Williams, *Admin Sec*
Garth Williams, *Maintence Staff*
EMP: 90 EST: 1978
SQ FT: 15,000
SALES (est): 62.9MM **Privately Held**
SIC: 4213 Liquid petroleum transport, non-local

(P-4170)
WOLFE TRUCKING INC
7131 Valjean Ave, Van Nuys (91406-3917)
PHONE..................................818 376-6960
Jack Wolfe, *President*
Helen Wolfe, *CFO*
EMP: 107
SQ FT: 7,200
SALES (est): 10.7MM **Privately Held**
SIC: 4213 Trucking, except local

(P-4171)
**XPO ENTERPRISE SERVICES
INC**
Also Called: Con-Way
3810 Hill Rd, Lakeport (95453-7015)
PHONE..................................916 399-8291
EMP: 120
SALES (corp-wide): 7.6B **Publicly Held**
SIC: 4213
HQ: Xpo Enterprise Services, Inc.
2211 Old Earhart Rd # 100
Ann Arbor MI 48105
734 998-4200

(P-4172)
XPO LOGISTICS FREIGHT INC
5475 S Airport Way, Stockton
(95206-3918)
PHONE..................................209 983-8285
Rudy Romo, *Manager*
EMP: 60
SQ FT: 1,000
SALES (corp-wide): 17.2B **Publicly Held**
WEB: www.con-way.com
SIC: 4213 Contract haulers
HQ: Xpo Logistics Freight, Inc.
2211 Old Earhart Rd # 100
Ann Arbor MI 48105
800 755-2728

(P-4173)
XPO LOGISTICS FREIGHT INC
2171 Otoole Ave, San Jose (95131-1314)
PHONE..................................408 435-3876
Jon Sullivan, *Branch Mgr*
EMP: 60
SQ FT: 8,834
SALES (corp-wide): 17.2B **Publicly Held**
WEB: www.con-way.com
SIC: 4213 Contract haulers
HQ: Xpo Logistics Freight, Inc.
2211 Old Earhart Rd # 100
Ann Arbor MI 48105
800 755-2728

(P-4174)
XPO LOGISTICS FREIGHT INC
4965 Convoy St, San Diego (92111-1600)
PHONE 858 569-8921
Tim Tuerk, *Manager*
EMP: 50
SQ FT: 20,344
SALES (corp-wide): 17.2B **Publicly Held**
WEB: www.con-way.com
SIC: 4213 Contract haulers
HQ: Xpo Logistics Freight, Inc.
2211 Old Earhart Rd # 100
Ann Arbor MI 48105
800 755-2728

(P-4175)
XPO LOGISTICS FREIGHT INC
4195 E Central Ave, Fresno (93725-9026)
PHONE 559 485-1164
Bud Whitney, *Principal*
Larry Wells, *Human Res Mgr*
EMP: 62
SQ FT: 39,620
SALES (corp-wide): 17.2B **Publicly Held**
WEB: www.con-way.com
SIC: 4213 Contract haulers
HQ: Xpo Logistics Freight, Inc.
2211 Old Earhart Rd # 100
Ann Arbor MI 48105
800 755-2728

(P-4176)
XPO LOGISTICS FREIGHT INC
787 Airport Blvd, Salinas (93901-4509)
PHONE 831 758-8874
Nick Fletcher, *Sales/Mktg Mgr*
EMP: 62
SALES (corp-wide): 17.2B **Publicly Held**
WEB: www.con-way.com
SIC: 4213 Contract haulers
HQ: Xpo Logistics Freight, Inc.
2211 Old Earhart Rd # 100
Ann Arbor MI 48105
800 755-2728

(P-4177)
XPO LOGISTICS FREIGHT INC
12466 Montague St, Pacoima
(91331-2121)
PHONE 818 890-2095
Paul Styers, *Manager*
Todd Williams, *General Mgr*
EMP: 200
SQ FT: 20,187
SALES (corp-wide): 17.2B **Publicly Held**
WEB: www.con-way.com
SIC: 4213 4214 Contract haulers; local
trucking with storage
HQ: Xpo Logistics Freight, Inc.
2211 Old Earhart Rd # 100
Ann Arbor MI 48105
800 755-2728

(P-4178)
XPO LOGISTICS FREIGHT INC
2102 N Batavia St, Orange (92865-3104)
PHONE 714 282-7717
Tim Worner, *Manager*
EMP: 100
SALES (corp-wide): 17.2B **Publicly Held**
WEB: www.con-way.com
SIC: 4213 Contract haulers
HQ: Xpo Logistics Freight, Inc.
2211 Old Earhart Rd # 100
Ann Arbor MI 48105
800 755-2728

(P-4179)
XPO LOGISTICS FREIGHT INC
3516 Kiessig Ave, Sacramento
(95823-1036)
PHONE 916 399-8291
John Sullivan, *Branch Mgr*
Andrea Fong, *Office Mgr*
EMP: 120
SALES (corp-wide): 17.2B **Publicly Held**
WEB: www.con-way.com
SIC: 4213 Contract haulers
HQ: Xpo Logistics Freight, Inc.
2211 Old Earhart Rd # 100
Ann Arbor MI 48105
800 755-2728

(P-4180)
XPO LOGISTICS FREIGHT INC
20697 Prism Pl, Lake Forest (92630-7803)
PHONE 949 581-9030
Joseph Tickford, *Branch Mgr*
EMP: 60
SQ FT: 13,890
SALES (corp-wide): 17.2B **Publicly Held**
WEB: www.con-way.com
SIC: 4213 Less-than-truckload (LTL) trans-
port
HQ: Xpo Logistics Freight, Inc.
2211 Old Earhart Rd # 100
Ann Arbor MI 48105
800 755-2728

(P-4181)
XPO LOGISTICS FREIGHT INC
1955 E Washington Blvd, Los Angeles
(90021-3206)
PHONE 213 744-0664
Todd Liverman, *Branch Mgr*
EMP: 120
SQ FT: 39,842
SALES (corp-wide): 17.2B **Publicly Held**
WEB: www.con-way.com
SIC: 4213 4212 4731 Contract haulers;
local trucking, without storage; freight for-
warding
HQ: Xpo Logistics Freight, Inc.
2211 Old Earhart Rd # 100
Ann Arbor MI 48105
800 755-2728

(P-4182)
XPO LOGISTICS FREIGHT INC
Also Called: Con-Way
12555 Mesa Dr, Blythe (92225-3363)
PHONE 760 922-8538
Butch Russell, *Manager*
EMP: 62
SALES (corp-wide): 17.2B **Publicly Held**
WEB: www.con-way.com
SIC: 4213 Contract haulers
HQ: Xpo Logistics Freight, Inc.
2211 Old Earhart Rd # 100
Ann Arbor MI 48105
800 755-2728

(P-4183)
XPO LOGISTICS FREIGHT INC
Also Called: Con-Way
4095 S Moorland Ave, Santa Rosa
(95407-8110)
PHONE 707 584-0211
Rich Gonzales, *Manager*
EMP: 62
SALES (corp-wide): 17.2B **Publicly Held**
WEB: www.con-way.com
SIC: 4213 Contract haulers
HQ: Xpo Logistics Freight, Inc.
2211 Old Earhart Rd # 100
Ann Arbor MI 48105
800 755-2728

(P-4184)
XPO LOGISTICS FREIGHT INC
2200 Claremont Ct, Hayward (94545-5002)
PHONE 510 785-6920
Terry Smith, *Manager*
EMP: 200
SQ FT: 28,704
SALES (corp-wide): 17.2B **Publicly Held**
WEB: www.con-way.com
SIC: 4213 4212 4731 Contract haulers;
local trucking, without storage; freight
transportation arrangement
HQ: Xpo Logistics Freight, Inc.
2211 Old Earhart Rd # 100
Ann Arbor MI 48105
800 755-2728

(P-4185)
XPO LOGISTICS FREIGHT INC
13364 Marlay Ave, Fontana (92337-6919)
PHONE 951 685-1244
Mark Logan, *General Mgr*
John Sheriff, *Opers Mgr*
EMP: 200
SALES (corp-wide): 17.2B **Publicly Held**
SIC: 4213 Contract haulers
HQ: Xpo Logistics Freight, Inc.
2211 Old Earhart Rd # 100
Ann Arbor MI 48105
800 755-2728

(P-4186)
XPO LOGISTICS FREIGHT INC
12903 Lakeland Rd, Santa Fe Springs
(90670-4516)
PHONE 562 946-8331
Jim Lutze, *Manager*
EMP: 200
SALES (corp-wide): 17.2B **Publicly Held**
WEB: www.con-way.com
SIC: 4213 Contract haulers
HQ: Xpo Logistics Freight, Inc.
2211 Old Earhart Rd # 100
Ann Arbor MI 48105
800 755-2728

(P-4187)
YRC INC
Also Called: Yellow Transportation
25555 Clawiter Rd, Hayward (94545-2740)
PHONE 510 783-7010
Pete Kell, *Manager*
EMP: 100
SQ FT: 33,872
SALES (corp-wide): 5B **Publicly Held**
WEB: www.roadway.com
SIC: 4213 4231 Contract haulers; trucking
terminal facilities
HQ: Yrc Inc.
10990 Roe Ave
Overland Park KS 66211
913 696-6100

(P-4188)
YRC INC
Also Called: Yellow Transportation
15400 S Main St, Gardena (90248-2215)
PHONE 310 404-2221
Tony Edmondson, *Manager*
EMP: 200
SQ FT: 56,821
SALES (corp-wide): 5B **Publicly Held**
WEB: www.roadway.com
SIC: 4213 Trucking, except local
HQ: Yrc Inc.
10990 Roe Ave
Overland Park KS 66211
913 696-6100

(P-4189)
YRC INC
Also Called: Yrc Freight
17401 Adelanto Rd, Adelanto
(92301-2701)
PHONE 760 246-0031
Randy Perez, *Branch Mgr*
EMP: 54
SALES (corp-wide): 5B **Publicly Held**
SIC: 4213 Trucking, except local
HQ: Yrc Inc.
10990 Roe Ave
Overland Park KS 66211
913 696-6100

(P-4190)
YRC INC
3210 52nd Ave, Sacramento (95823-1024)
PHONE 916 371-4555
Scott Kamman, *Owner*
Denise Hummer, *Admin Sec*
EMP: 99
SALES (corp-wide): 5B **Publicly Held**
SIC: 4213 Contract haulers
HQ: Yrc Inc.
10990 Roe Ave
Overland Park KS 66211
913 696-6100

(P-4191)
YRC INC
Also Called: Yellow Transportation
1535 E Pescadero Ave, Tracy
(95304-8501)
PHONE 209 833-1300
Maynard Skarka, *Manager*
Kevin Anderson, *Manager*
Kevin Shoemaker, *Manager*
EMP: 217
SALES (corp-wide): 5B **Publicly Held**
WEB: www.roadway.com
SIC: 4213 Trucking, except local
HQ: Yrc Inc.
10990 Roe Ave
Overland Park KS 66211
913 696-6100

(P-4192)
YRC WORLDWIDE INC
201 Haskins Way, South San Francisco
(94080-6215)
PHONE 650 952-1112
Mike Sighn, *Principal*
EMP: 100
SALES (corp-wide): 5B **Publicly Held**
SIC: 4213 Contract haulers
PA: Yrc Worldwide Inc.
10990 Roe Ave
Overland Park KS 66211
913 696-6100

4214 Local Trucking With Storage

(P-4193)
AMERICAN WEST WORLDWIDE EX INC (PA)
51 Zaca Ln Ste 120, San Luis Obispo
(93401-7353)
PHONE 800 788-4534
Josh Brown, *CEO*
Cathie Brown, *President*
EMP: 68
SALES (est): 38MM **Privately Held**
SIC: 4214 4213 4225 Local trucking with
storage; trucking, except local; general
warehousing

(P-4194)
AMS RELOCATION INCORPORATED
Also Called: AMS Bekins Van Lines
1873 Rollins Rd, Burlingame (94010-2209)
PHONE 650 697-3530
Mike Foster, *General Mgr*
Gary P Wolfe, *President*
EMP: 55
SQ FT: 45,000
SALES (est): 6.2MM **Privately Held**
SIC: 4214 Household goods moving &
storage, local

(P-4195)
BEAR TRUCKING INC
Also Called: Gate City Beverage Bear Trckg
19768 Kendall Dr, San Bernardino
(92407-1633)
P.O. Box 9158 (92427-0158)
PHONE 909 799-1616
Leona Aronoff, *President*
Sharon Campion,
EMP: 100
SQ FT: 10,000
SALES (est): 18.9MM **Privately Held**
SIC: 4214 Local trucking with storage

(P-4196)
BEKINS MOVING SOLUTIONS INC (PA)
Also Called: Bekins Moving & Storage
12610 Shoemaker Ave, Santa Fe Springs
(90670-6344)
PHONE 562 356-9460
David Caruso, *President*
EMP: 71
SALES (est): 18.5MM **Privately Held**
SIC: 4214 4213 Local trucking with stor-
age; trucking, except local

(P-4197)
C & M TRANSFER SAN DIEGO INC
Also Called: C&M Relocation Systems
8787 Olive Ln, Santee (92071-4137)
P.O. Box 2184, Ramona (92065-0937)
PHONE 619 562-6111
Mick Mahaffey, *President*
EMP: 60
SALES (est): 6.4MM **Privately Held**
WEB: www.cmtransfer.com
SIC: 4214 Local trucking with storage

(P-4198)
CALKO TRANSPORT COMPANY INC
Also Called: Redman Container
720 E Watson Center Rd, Carson
(90745-4108)
PHONE 310 816-0602

Chong Suh, *President*
Simon Chung, *Vice Pres*
Tim Suh, *Manager*
Sophia Song, *Supervisor*
▲ EMP: 58
SQ FT: 24,000
SALES (est): 6MM **Privately Held**
WEB: www.calko.com
SIC: 4214 4225 Local trucking with storage; general warehousing

(P-4199)
CITY MOVING INC
6319 Colfax Ave, North Hollywood (91606-3409)
PHONE..................888 794-8808
Lior Oren, *President*
EMP: 50
SALES (est): 839.3K **Privately Held**
SIC: 4214 Local trucking with storage

(P-4200)
COMPLETE RELOCATION SVCS INC
7361 Doig Dr, Garden Grove (92841-1806)
PHONE..................714 901-7411
Marc Kranz, *President*
Pat Garvey, *Manager*
EMP: 99 EST: 2007
SALES (est): 4.6MM **Privately Held**
SIC: 4214 Local trucking with storage

(P-4201)
COROVAN MOVING & STORAGE CO (HQ)
12302 Kerran St, Poway (92064-6884)
PHONE..................858 748-1100
Richard R Schmitz, *President*
Jerry P Brothers, *CFO*
Robert J Schmitz, *Co-President*
Thomas A Schmitz, *Admin Sec*
Owen Shoopman, *Project Mgr*
EMP: 100
SQ FT: 600,000
SALES (est): 34.2MM **Privately Held**
SIC: 4214 4213 Household goods moving & storage, local; household goods transport

(P-4202)
CRUZ MODULAR INC (PA)
Also Called: Systechs
249 W Baywood Ave Ste B, Orange (92865-2604)
PHONE..................714 283-2890
Linda Galleran, *CEO*
Vince Schlachter, *President*
Malcolm Craycroft, *Vice Pres*
EMP: 56
SALES (est): 11.6MM **Privately Held**
WEB: www.systechs.com
SIC: 4214 7641 4226 1799 Furniture moving & storage, local; reupholstery & furniture repair; special warehousing & storage; office furniture installation

(P-4203)
DARRELL L GREEN INC
Also Called: Green Trucking
12652 Avenue 240, Tulare (93274-9531)
PHONE..................559 688-0686
Phyllis Green, *President*
Darrell L Green, *Corp Secy*
EMP: 67 EST: 1973
SQ FT: 4,000
SALES: 12MM **Privately Held**
WEB: www.greentrucking.com
SIC: 4214 Local trucking with storage

(P-4204)
DGA SERVICES INC (PA)
Also Called: J I T Transportation
1075 Montague Expy, Milpitas (95035-6828)
P.O. Box 41372, San Jose (95160-1372)
PHONE..................408 232-4800
Deborah S Ashley, *CEO*
David Butcher, *Executive*
Russ Watkins, *Opers Mgr*
Jose Crespo, *Opers Staff*
John Bonasera, *Manager*
EMP: 54
SQ FT: 125,000

SALES (est): 14.1MM **Privately Held**
WEB: www.jittransportation.com
SIC: 4214 4213 Local trucking with storage; trucking, except local

(P-4205)
DOUBLE DAY OFFICE SERVICES INC
340 Shaw Rd, South San Francisco (94080-6606)
P.O. Box 591405, San Francisco (94159-1405)
PHONE..................650 872-6600
Cheryl Ringelmann, *President*
EMP: 50
SQ FT: 45,000
SALES (est): 4.5MM **Privately Held**
WEB: www.doubleday-corprelo.com
SIC: 4214 7389 Local trucking with storage; relocation service

(P-4206)
DURKEE DRAYAGE COMPANY
539 Stone Rd, Benicia (94510-1113)
PHONE..................510 970-7550
Jeffrey J Fenton, *President*
Cathy Lashin, *Vice Pres*
EMP: 80 EST: 1933
SQ FT: 80,000
SALES (est): 7.3MM **Privately Held**
WEB: www.durkeedrayage.com
SIC: 4214 Local trucking with storage

(P-4207)
EXCEL MOVING SERVICES
30047 Ahern Ave, Union City (94587-1234)
PHONE..................800 392-3596
Bruce D Owashi, *President*
Vyvyanne S Owashi, *Shareholder*
Robert Friederang, *Vice Pres*
EMP: 60
SQ FT: 23,400
SALES (est): 3.9MM **Privately Held**
SIC: 4214 Household goods moving & storage, local

(P-4208)
GILBERT SERVICE CORP
Also Called: Gilbert West
6725 Kimball Ave, Chino (91708-9177)
PHONE..................909 393-7575
Ken Gross, *President*
Richard Gilbert, *Vice Pres*
EMP: 125
SALES (est): 13.2MM **Privately Held**
SIC: 4214 4225 Local trucking with storage; general warehousing

(P-4209)
GREAT AMRCN LOGISTICS DIST INC
13565 Larwin Cir, Santa Fe Springs (90670-5032)
PHONE..................800 381-4527
Lawrence D Whittet, *CEO*
James Hooper, *President*
Robert Lechich, *CFO*
Bill Doherty,
EMP: 86
SQ FT: 120,000
SALES (est): 12.7MM **Privately Held**
WEB: www.american-logistics.com
SIC: 4214 4213 6719 Household goods moving & storage, local; moving services; trucking, except local; investment holding companies, except banks

(P-4210)
GSC LOGISTICS INC (PA)
530 Water St Fl 5, Oakland (94607-3532)
PHONE..................510 844-3700
Scott E Taylor, *CEO*
Marc Jensen, *CFO*
Joel Lesser, *CFO*
Garcia Andres, *Vice Pres*
Jeff Tanner, *Info Tech Dir*
EMP: 120
SQ FT: 8,000
SALES (est): 17.9MM **Privately Held**
SIC: 4214 4225 4213 Local trucking with storage; general warehousing; trucking, except local

(P-4211)
HALBERT BROTHERS INC
17400 Chestnut St, City of Industry (91748-1013)
PHONE..................626 913-1800
John W Miller, *CEO*
James R Miller, *Treasurer*
John Miller, *Admin Sec*
EMP: 60
SQ FT: 110,000
SALES: 7.2MM **Privately Held**
WEB: www.halbertbrothersinc.com
SIC: 4214 1796 Local trucking with storage; machine moving & rigging

(P-4212)
HARRISON NICHOLS CO LTD
14080 Slover Ave, Fontana (92337-7039)
PHONE..................626 337-5020
Kenneth Harrison, *CEO*
Randall P Harrison, *President*
EMP: 133
SALES (est): 14MM **Privately Held**
SIC: 4214 4212 Local trucking with storage; local trucking, without storage

(P-4213)
HIDDEN VALLEY MVG & STOR INC (PA)
1218 Pacific Oaks Pl, Escondido (92029-2900)
PHONE..................602 252-7800
Robert L Berti, *CEO*
David Boeller, *CFO*
EMP: 100 EST: 1964
SQ FT: 55,000
SALES (est): 11.7MM **Privately Held**
SIC: 4214 4213 Household goods moving & storage, local; contract haulers

(P-4214)
JAVELIN LOGISTICS CORPORATION (PA)
7025 Central Ave, Newark (94560-4201)
PHONE..................510 795-7287
Malcolm George Winspear, *CEO*
Jeff Hoover, *Vice Pres*
Mary White, *Admin Mgr*
Mike Sacrey, *General Mgr*
Veronica Castillo, *Administration*
EMP: 50
SALES (est): 39.6MM **Privately Held**
SIC: 4214 4731 4225 Local trucking with storage; freight transportation arrangement; general warehousing & storage

(P-4215)
LDI TRANSPORTATION INC
200 Erie St, Pomona (91768-3327)
PHONE..................909 620-7001
Alex Kolesnikov, *President*
EMP: 100
SQ FT: 2,500
SALES: 3.5MM **Privately Held**
SIC: 4214 Local trucking with storage

(P-4216)
LEGACY TRANSPORTATION SVCS INC (PA)
Also Called: Legacy Global Logistics Svcs
935 Mclaughlin Ave, San Jose (95122-2612)
PHONE..................408 294-9800
John Migliozzi, *President*
Kerry Carlson, *President*
Michael Quinn, *Exec VP*
Shelly Gipson, *Senior VP*
Shelly J McAllister, *Vice Pres*
EMP: 140
SQ FT: 200,000
SALES (est): 48.9MM **Privately Held**
SIC: 4214 4213 Local trucking with storage; trucking, except local

(P-4217)
LINEAGE LOGISTICS HOLDINGS LLC
Also Called: Inland Cold Storage
2551 S Lilac Ave, Bloomington (92316-3209)
PHONE..................909 874-1200
Bill Hendricksen, *CEO*
Mandar Prabhu Gaunker, *Manager*
EMP: 800

SALES (corp-wide): 1.1B **Privately Held**
SIC: 4214 4222 Household goods moving & storage, local; warehousing, cold storage or refrigerated
PA: Lineage Logistics Holdings, Llc
1 Park Plz Ste 550
Irvine CA 92614
800 678-7271

(P-4218)
MOVING SOLUTIONS INC
Also Called: North American Van Lines
7093 Central Ave, Newark (94560-4201)
PHONE..................408 920-0110
Rick S Philpott, *CEO*
Janet Philpott, *Vice Pres*
EMP: 150
SQ FT: 200,000
SALES (est): 14.4MM **Privately Held**
WEB: www.movingsolutionsinc.com
SIC: 4214 8742 7376 1799 Local trucking with storage; construction project management consultant; computer facilities management; office furniture installation

(P-4219)
NELSON MOVING & STORAGE INC
Also Called: Nelson North American
25742 Atlantic Ocean Dr, Lake Forest (92630-8854)
PHONE..................949 582-0380
Gust Nelson, *President*
Rosean Maricondo, *Office Mgr*
EMP: 50
SQ FT: 24,000
SALES (est): 5.9MM **Privately Held**
WEB: www.nelsonmoving.com
SIC: 4214 4731 Local trucking with storage; freight transportation arrangement

(P-4220)
NOR-CAL MOVING SERVICES (PA)
Also Called: Allied Intl San Franisco
3129 Corporate Pl, Hayward (94545-3915)
PHONE..................510 371-4942
Peter Mazzetti Jr, *CEO*
Dennis D Goza, *President*
John Mizera, *CFO*
Dave Konecny, *Exec VP*
Louis Marchiorlatti, *Admin Sec*
EMP: 125
SQ FT: 200,000
SALES (est): 20MM **Privately Held**
WEB: www.nor-calmoving.com
SIC: 4214 4213 Household goods moving & storage, local; furniture moving & storage, local; household goods transport

(P-4221)
NOR-CAL MOVING SERVICES
560 E Trimble Rd, San Jose (95131-1221)
PHONE..................408 954-1175
Karen Aparton, *Branch Mgr*
EMP: 100
SALES (corp-wide): 20MM **Privately Held**
WEB: www.nor-calmoving.com
SIC: 4214 4213 Household goods moving & storage, local; trucking, except local
PA: Nor-Cal Moving Services
3129 Corporate Pl
Hayward CA 94545
510 371-4942

(P-4222)
OFFICE MOVERS INC
4020 Nelson Ave Ste 200, Concord (94520-8526)
PHONE..................408 254-5010
James Robinson, *President*
EMP: 50
SALES (est): 2.2MM **Privately Held**
SIC: 4214 Household goods moving & storage, local

(P-4223)
PACK & CRATE SERVICES INC
238 N Quince St, Escondido (92025-2518)
P.O. Box 2964 (92033-2964)
PHONE..................760 737-6893
EMP: 50
SQ FT: 35,000

SALES (est): 4.8MM **Privately Held**
SIC: 4214

(P-4224)
PORT LOGISTICS GROUP INC
14210 Telephone Ave, Chino (91710-5734)
PHONE....................909 539-0478
EMP: 61 **Privately Held**
SIC: 4214 Local trucking with storage
PA: Port Logistics Group, Inc.
288 S Mayo Ave
City Of Industry CA 91789

(P-4225)
PORT LOGISTICS GROUP INC
19801 S Santa Fe Ave, Compton (90221-5915)
PHONE....................310 669-2551
Timothy Page, *Principal*
EMP: 87 **Privately Held**
SIC: 4214 Local trucking with storage
PA: Port Logistics Group, Inc.
288 S Mayo Ave
City Of Industry CA 91789

(P-4226)
PORT LOGISTICS GROUP INC
5026 Chino Hills Pkwy, Chino (91710-5643)
PHONE....................909 539-9773
EMP: 50 **Privately Held**
SIC: 4214 Local trucking with storage
PA: Port Logistics Group, Inc.
288 S Mayo Ave
City Of Industry CA 91789

(P-4227)
PRECISION RELOCATION INC
16055 Heron Ave Ste B, La Mirada (90638-5514)
PHONE....................714 690-9344
Kirk O O'Gilvy, *CEO*
Douglas Piersant, *President*
Patsy Ogilvy, *Controller*
Jose Navarro, *Manager*
EMP: 120
SQ FT: 60,000
SALES (est): 7.8MM **Privately Held**
WEB: www.precisionrelocation.com
SIC: 4214 Local trucking with storage

(P-4228)
ROYAL EXPRESS INC (PA)
3545 E Date Ave, Fresno (93725-1933)
PHONE....................559 272-3500
Kirpal S Shiota, *CEO*
EMP: 111
SQ FT: 435,600
SALES (est): 29.3MM **Privately Held**
WEB: www.royalexp.com
SIC: 4214 Local trucking with storage

(P-4229)
SAMUEL J PIAZZA & SON INC (PA)
Also Called: Piazza Trucking
9001 Rayo Ave, South Gate (90280-3606)
PHONE....................323 357-1999
Michael Piazza, *CEO*
Robert Piazza, *Vice Pres*
William Piazza, *Vice Pres*
Beth Elkins, *Regional Mgr*
Bob Piazza, *Regl Sales Mgr*
EMP: 70
SQ FT: 20,000
SALES (est): 21.7MM **Privately Held**
WEB: www.piazzatrucking.com
SIC: 4214 4213 Local trucking with storage; trucking, except local

(P-4230)
SCHICK MOVING & STORAGE CO (PA)
2721 Michelle Dr, Tustin (92780-7018)
P.O. Box 3627 (92781-3627)
PHONE....................714 731-5500
Gordon C Schick, *President*
Lynn Larson, *CFO*
Lynne M Larson, *Treasurer*
Arthur C Schick Jr, *Vice Pres*
Beverly C Schick, *Vice Pres*
EMP: 100 **EST:** 1956
SQ FT: 113,000

SALES: 6.9MM **Privately Held**
WEB: www.schickusa.com
SIC: 4214 Household goods moving & storage, local

(P-4231)
SERVICE TRANSPORT INC
29991 Cyn Hls Rd Ste 137, Lake Elsinore (92532-2578)
PHONE....................951 403-3464
Robert Kausman, *CEO*
EMP: 65
SQ FT: 2,500
SALES: 4MM **Privately Held**
SIC: 4214 Local trucking with storage

(P-4232)
SOUTH COAST LOGISTICS
Also Called: North American Van Lines
4160 Temescal Canyon Rd # 311, Corona (92883-4629)
PHONE....................714 894-4744
Craig Schueller, *President*
EMP: 50
SALES (est): 5.4MM **Privately Held**
WEB: www.southcoastlogistics.com
SIC: 4214 Local trucking with storage

(P-4233)
SPECIAL DISPATCH CAL INC (PA)
16330 Phoebe Ave, La Mirada (90638-5612)
P.O. Box 3838, Cerritos (90703-3838)
PHONE....................714 521-8200
John Edward Dearing, *CEO*
Ty Clarno, *Opers Mgr*
John Dearing, *Opers Staff*
John Munoz, *Opers Staff*
EMP: 60
SQ FT: 120,000
SALES (est): 24.6MM **Privately Held**
SIC: 4214 4212 Local trucking with storage; delivery service, vehicular

(P-4234)
SPIREON INC (PA)
Also Called: Goldstar
16802 Aston, Irvine (92606-4835)
PHONE....................800 557-1449
Kevin Weiss, *CEO*
Brian Skutta, *President*
Tim Welch, *COO*
Rita Parvaneh, *CFO*
Carla Fitzgerald, *Chief Mktg Ofcr*
EMP: 175
SALES (est): 111MM **Privately Held**
WEB: www.procon.net
SIC: 4214 8741 Local trucking with storage; business management

(P-4235)
SS SKIKOS INCORPORATED
1289 Sebastopol Rd, Santa Rosa (95407-6834)
PHONE....................707 575-3000
Shad Skikos, *CEO*
Pete Skikos, *President*
EMP: 80
SALES (est): 8.5MM **Privately Held**
SIC: 4214 Local trucking with storage

(P-4236)
TRANSPORT EXPRESS INC
19801 S Santa Fe Ave, Compton (90221-5915)
PHONE....................310 898-2000
Robert L Stull, *CEO*
Steven Senecal, *President*
William Meroth, *Vice Pres*
Patricia Senecal, *Admin Sec*
EMP: 55
SQ FT: 230,000
SALES (est): 8.6MM **Privately Held**
SIC: 4214 4225 4731 Local trucking with storage; general warehousing; brokers, shipping

(P-4237)
TRANSWEST SAN DIEGO LLC
Also Called: Miramar Truck Center
6066 Miramar Rd, San Diego (92121-2542)
PHONE....................858 450-0707
Brad Fauvre, *President*
EMP: 500

SALES (est): 21.1MM **Privately Held**
SIC: 4214 Local trucking with storage

(P-4238)
URIBE TRUCKING INC
Also Called: Alex Moving & Storage
542 Flynn Rd, Camarillo (93012-8027)
PHONE....................805 483-1125
Alejandro Uribe, *President*
Christine Uribe, *Corp Secy*
EMP: 130
SQ FT: 60,000
SALES (est): 9.4MM **Privately Held**
SIC: 4214 4731 4225 Local trucking with storage; freight forwarding; warehousing, self-storage

(P-4239)
USA TRANSPORT INC
12191 Violet Rd, Adelanto (92301-2713)
PHONE....................559 783-3563
Gary Leslie, *President*
EMP: 50
SQ FT: 5,000
SALES (est): 3MM **Privately Held**
SIC: 4214 4213 Local trucking with storage; trucking, except local

(P-4240)
VALLEY RELOCATION AND STORAGE (PA)
Also Called: Valley Northamerican
5000 Marsh Dr, Concord (94520-5322)
PHONE....................925 230-2025
James Robson, *President*
John A Burks, *CEO*
EMP: 200
SQ FT: 58,000
SALES (est): 27.9MM **Privately Held**
SIC: 4214 Local trucking with storage

(P-4241)
VAN TORRANCE & STORAGE COMPANY (PA)
Also Called: S & M Moving Systems
12128 Burke St, Santa Fe Springs (90670-2678)
PHONE....................562 567-2100
Steven Todare, *President*
Martin Stadler, *Vice Pres*
Kathy Siatuu, *Opers Mgr*
◆ **EMP:** 100
SQ FT: 95,000
SALES (est): 99.5MM **Privately Held**
WEB: www.sandmoving.com
SIC: 4214 4213 Local trucking with storage; trucking, except local

(P-4242)
VERNON CENTRAL WAREHOUSE INC
Also Called: Vernon Warehouse Co
2050 E 38th St, Vernon (90058-1615)
P.O. Box 58426 (90058-0426)
PHONE....................323 234-2200
Joseph E Tack, *CEO*
Joe Tack, *President*
Jim Boltinghouse, *Corp Secy*
Tom Rodd, *Vice Pres*
Steve Shanklin, *Vice Pres*
EMP: 125
SQ FT: 100,000
SALES (est): 26.8MM **Privately Held**
WEB: www.vernonwarehouse.com
SIC: 4214 5149 Local trucking with storage; natural & organic foods

(P-4243)
W WHY W ENTERPRISES INC
Also Called: Atlas/Eastern Van Lines
2671 Pomona Blvd, Pomona (91768-3221)
PHONE....................626 969-4292
William Coffman, *President*
Yvonne Coffman, *Vice Pres*
Noel Fernandez, *Accountant*
EMP: 60
SALES (est): 6.4MM **Privately Held**
SIC: 4214 4213 Local trucking with storage; household goods transport

(P-4244)
WATERS MOVING & STORAGE INC
37 Bridgehead Rd, Martinez (94553-1300)
P.O. Box 1029 (94553-0102)
PHONE....................925 372-0914
Ken Waters, *CEO*
Paulette Waters, *CFO*
EMP: 75
SQ FT: 50,000
SALES (est): 6.5MM **Privately Held**
SIC: 4214 Furniture moving & storage, local

(P-4245)
WETZEL & SONS MOVING AND STOR
Also Called: Wetzel Trucking
12400 Osborne St, Pacoima (91331-2002)
PHONE....................818 890-0992
Donald C Wetzel, *President*
Daniel S Wetzel, *Vice Pres*
Debbe Wetzel, *Executive*
Stacie Vereuck, *Associate*
EMP: 70 **EST:** 1976
SQ FT: 146,000
SALES (est): 5.4MM **Privately Held**
WEB: www.wetzelmovingandstorage.com
SIC: 4214 Furniture moving & storage, local; household goods moving & storage, local

4215 Courier Svcs, Except Air

(P-4246)
ALL COUNTIES COURIER INC
1642 Kaiser Ave, Irvine (92614-5700)
PHONE....................714 599-9300
Patricia Cochran, *President*
Dean Steward, *Senior VP*
Jack Lipczynski, *General Mgr*
EMP: 200
SALES (est): 18.4MM **Privately Held**
SIC: 4215 Package delivery, vehicular

(P-4247)
APOLLO COURIERS INC (PA)
1039 W Hillcrest Blvd, Inglewood (90301-2023)
PHONE....................310 337-0377
Frank Ghamari, *President*
Fred Ghamarifard, *President*
Payman Khosravi, *CFO*
EMP: 70
SQ FT: 2,200
SALES (est): 9.3MM **Privately Held**
WEB: www.apollocouriers.com
SIC: 4215 Package delivery, vehicular

(P-4248)
CEA-PACK SERVICES INC
Also Called: Cea-Pack Logistics
12607 Hiddencreek Way, Cerritos (90703-2146)
P.O. Box 3777 (90703-3777)
PHONE....................562 407-0660
Robert Ceja-Simpson, *President*
EMP: 235
SQ FT: 2,730
SALES (est): 16.6MM **Privately Held**
SIC: 4215 Parcel delivery, vehicular

(P-4249)
DYNAMEX INC
4790 Frontier Way Ste A, Stockton (95215-9424)
PHONE....................209 464-7008
EMP: 60
SALES (corp-wide): 3.2B **Privately Held**
SIC: 4215
HQ: Dynamex Inc.
5429 L B Johnson Fwy 90 Ste 900
Dallas TX 75254
214 560-9000

(P-4250)
DYNAMEX OPERATIONS WEST INC
16900 Valley View Ave, La Mirada (90638-5825)
PHONE....................714 994-1615
Scott Levrage, *Manager*

PRODUCTS & SVCS

EMP: 50
SALES (corp-wide): 3.8B **Privately Held**
SIC: 4215 Courier services, except by air
HQ: Dynamex Operations West, Inc
　　1870 Crown Dr
　　Dallas TX 75234

(P-4251)
EXPRESS GROUP INC (PA)
Also Called: Westwood Express Messenger
Svc
10801 National Blvd # 104, Los Angeles
(90064-4140)
PHONE..............................310 474-5999
David F Davoodian, *President*
Malek Neman, *Vice Pres*
Joanna Young, *Managing Dir*
EMP: 75
SQ FT: 4,000
SALES (est): 7.4MM **Privately Held**
WEB: www.expressgroup.net
SIC: 4215 Courier services, except by air

(P-4252)
**EXPRESS MESSENGER
SYSTEMS INC**
5829 Smithway St, Commerce
(90040-1605)
PHONE..............................323 725-2100
Kim Kugel, *Branch Mgr*
Mikel Mobley, *Sales Staff*
EMP: 68 **Privately Held**
SIC: 4215 Courier services, except by air
PA: Express Messenger Systems, Inc.
　　2501 S Price Rd Ste 201
　　Chandler AZ 85286

(P-4253)
**EXPRESS MESSENGER
SYSTEMS INC**
1627 Industrial Dr, Stockton (95206-4984)
PHONE..............................209 234-8255
EMP: 68 **Privately Held**
SIC: 4215 Courier services, except by air
PA: Express Messenger Systems, Inc.
　　2501 S Price Rd Ste 201
　　Chandler AZ 85286

(P-4254)
**EXPRESS MESSENGER
SYSTEMS INC**
Also Called: California Overnight
555 Zephyr St, Stockton (95206-4209)
PHONE..............................209 234-8255
EMP: 55 **Privately Held**
SIC: 4215 Package delivery, vehicular
PA: Express Messenger Systems, Inc.
　　2501 S Price Rd Ste 201
　　Chandler AZ 85286

(P-4255)
**EXPRESS MESSENGER
SYSTEMS INC**
Also Called: California Overnight
1240 S Allec St, Anaheim (92805-6301)
PHONE..............................949 235-1400
Dave Denholm, *Manager*
EMP: 70 **Privately Held**
WEB: www.calover.com
SIC: 4215 7389 Courier services, except
　　by air; courier or messenger service
PA: Express Messenger Systems, Inc.
　　2501 S Price Rd Ste 201
　　Chandler AZ 85286

(P-4256)
**EXPRESS MESSENGER
SYSTEMS INC**
Also Called: Ontrac
914 W Boone St, Santa Maria
(93458-5450)
PHONE..............................800 488-2829
Polo Cabello, *Branch Mgr*
EMP: 70 **Privately Held**
SIC: 4215 Courier services, except by air
PA: Express Messenger Systems, Inc.
　　2501 S Price Rd Ste 201
　　Chandler AZ 85286

(P-4257)
**EXPRESS MESSENGER
SYSTEMS INC**
Ontrac
11085 Olinda St, Sun Valley (91352-3302)
PHONE..............................818 504-9043
Larry Hardie, *Manager*
EMP: 107 **Privately Held**
SIC: 4215 Courier services, except by air
PA: Express Messenger Systems, Inc.
　　2501 S Price Rd Ste 201
　　Chandler AZ 85286

(P-4258)
**EXPRESS MESSENGER
SYSTEMS INC**
Also Called: Ontrac
375 W Apra St, Compton (90220-5528)
PHONE..............................800 359-2959
Michael Kerper, *Principal*
EMP: 54 **Privately Held**
SIC: 4215 Package delivery, vehicular
PA: Express Messenger Systems, Inc.
　　2501 S Price Rd Ste 201
　　Chandler AZ 85286

(P-4259)
**EXPRESS MESSENGER
SYSTEMS INC**
Ontrac
9974 Calabash Ave, Fontana (92335-5204)
PHONE..............................804 334-5000
EMP: 71 **Privately Held**
SIC: 4215 Package delivery, vehicular
PA: Express Messenger Systems, Inc.
　　2501 S Price Rd Ste 201
　　Chandler AZ 85286

(P-4260)
**EXPRESS MESSENGER
SYSTEMS INC**
Also Called: California Overnight
1635 Main Ave Ste 3, Sacramento
(95838-2452)
PHONE..............................916 921-6016
Ian Burton, *Manager*
EMP: 60 **Privately Held**
WEB: www.calover.com
SIC: 4215 Package delivery, vehicular
PA: Express Messenger Systems, Inc.
　　2501 S Price Rd Ste 201
　　Chandler AZ 85286

(P-4261)
**EXPRESS MESSENGER
SYSTEMS INC**
Also Called: Ontrac
4603 N Brawley Ave # 103, Fresno
(93722-3960)
PHONE..............................559 277-4910
EMP: 56 **Privately Held**
SIC: 4215
PA: Express Messenger Systems, Inc.
　　2501 S Price Rd Ste 201
　　Chandler AZ 85286

(P-4262)
**EXPRESS MESSENGER
SYSTEMS INC**
Also Called: California Overnight
101 Spear St Ste A1, San Francisco
(94105-1557)
PHONE..............................415 495-7300
Fax: 415 495-7420
EMP: 63 **Privately Held**
SIC: 4215
PA: Express Messenger Systems, Inc.
　　2501 S Price Rd Ste 201
　　Chandler AZ 85286

(P-4263)
**FEDERAL EXPRESS
CORPORATION**
Also Called: Fedex
2660 Research Park Dr, Soquel
(95073-2087)
PHONE..............................800 463-3339
EMP: 56

SALES (corp-wide): 69.6B **Publicly Held**
SIC: 4215 Package delivery, vehicular
HQ: Federal Express Corporation
　　3610 Hacks Cross Rd
　　Memphis TN 38125
　　901 369-3600

(P-4264)
**FEDERAL EXPRESS
CORPORATION**
Also Called: Fedex
1081 Fullerton Rd, City of Industry
(91748-1234)
PHONE..............................800 463-3339
Rick Sanqui, *Project Engr*
EMP: 200
SALES (corp-wide): 69.6B **Publicly Held**
WEB: www.federalexpress.com
SIC: 4215 4513 Package delivery, vehicu-
　　lar; package delivery, private air
HQ: Federal Express Corporation
　　3610 Hacks Cross Rd
　　Memphis TN 38125
　　901 369-3600

(P-4265)
**FEDERAL EXPRESS
CORPORATION**
Also Called: Fedex
710 Dado St, San Jose (95131-1225)
PHONE..............................800 463-3339
EMP: 150
SALES (corp-wide): 69.6B **Publicly Held**
WEB: www.federalexpress.com
SIC: 4215 4512 Package delivery, vehicu-
　　lar; air cargo carrier, scheduled
HQ: Federal Express Corporation
　　3610 Hacks Cross Rd
　　Memphis TN 38125
　　901 369-3600

(P-4266)
**FEDERAL EXPRESS
CORPORATION**
Also Called: Fedex
9190 Edes Ave, Oakland (94603-1116)
PHONE..............................510 382-2344
EMP: 300
SALES (corp-wide): 47.4B **Publicly Held**
SIC: 4215 4513
HQ: Federal Express Corporation
　　3610 Hacks Cross Rd
　　Memphis TN 38125
　　901 369-3600

(P-4267)
**FEDEX GROUND PACKAGE SYS
INC**
10132 Airway Rd, San Diego (92154-7901)
PHONE..............................800 463-3339
Richard Rodriguez, *Associate*
EMP: 104
SALES (corp-wide): 69.6B **Publicly Held**
SIC: 4215 Parcel delivery, vehicular
HQ: Fedex Ground Package System, Inc.
　　1000 Fed Ex Dr
　　Coraopolis PA 15108
　　800 463-3339

(P-4268)
**FEDEX GROUND PACKAGE SYS
INC**
1070 San Mateo Ave, South San Francisco
(94080-6601)
PHONE..............................800 463-3339
EMP: 50
SALES (corp-wide): 69.6B **Publicly Held**
SIC: 4215 Package delivery, vehicular
HQ: Fedex Ground Package System, Inc.
　　1000 Fed Ex Dr
　　Coraopolis PA 15108
　　800 463-3339

(P-4269)
**FEDEX GROUND PACKAGE SYS
INC**
601 Stone Rd, Benicia (94510-1141)
PHONE..............................800 463-3339
EMP: 89
SALES (corp-wide): 69.6B **Publicly Held**
SIC: 4215 Parcel delivery, vehicular
HQ: Fedex Ground Package System, Inc.
　　1000 Fed Ex Dr
　　Coraopolis PA 15108
　　800 463-3339

(P-4270)
**FEDEX OFFICE & PRINT SVCS
INC**
8642 Whittier Blvd, Pico Rivera
(90660-2655)
PHONE..............................562 942-1953
EMP: 100
SALES (corp-wide): 47.4B **Publicly Held**
SIC: 4215 5999 7221 7389
HQ: Fedex Office And Print Services, Inc.
　　7900 Legacy Dr
　　Dallas TX 75024
　　214 550-7000

(P-4271)
FEDEX SMARTPOST INC
5560 Ferguson Dr, Commerce
(90022-5140)
PHONE..............................323 888-8879
EMP: 85
SALES (corp-wide): 47.4B **Publicly Held**
SIC: 4215
HQ: Fedex Smartpost, Inc.
　　16555 W Rogers Dr
　　New Berlin WI 53151
　　262 796-6800

(P-4272)
**INTEGRATED PARCEL
NETWORK**
Also Called: Pacific Couriers
4373 Santa Anita Ave, El Monte
(91731-1690)
PHONE..............................714 278-6100
Nadia Youssef, *CEO*
EMP: 275
SALES (est): 17MM **Privately Held**
WEB: www.pacific-couriers.com
SIC: 4215 4214 7389 Package delivery,
　　vehicular; local trucking with storage;
　　courier or messenger service

(P-4273)
JET DELIVERY INC (PA)
2169 Wright Ave, La Verne (91750-5835)
PHONE..............................800 716-7177
Michael Barbata, *President*
Mark Sur, *Vice Pres*
Jason Barbata, *CIO*
Susie Alvarez, *Accounting Mgr*
Shannon Cermak, *Controller*
EMP: 90
SQ FT: 34,000
SALES (est): 22.6MM **Privately Held**
WEB: www.jetdelivery.com
SIC: 4215 4231 4212 4213 Package de-
　　livery, vehicular; trucking terminal facili-
　　ties; local trucking, without storage;
　　trucking, except local

(P-4274)
MEDICAL COURIERS INC
1611 Neptune Dr, San Leandro
(94577-3162)
PHONE..............................650 872-1144
Stephen Reiff, *President*
Richard Reiff, *Vice Pres*
EMP: 60
SQ FT: 5,000
SALES (est): 4.4MM **Privately Held**
SIC: 4215 Courier services, except by air

(P-4275)
MESSENGER EXPRESS (PA)
5435 Cahuenga Blvd Ste C, North Holly-
wood (91601-2948)
PHONE..............................213 614-0475
Gilbert Kort, *President*
EMP: 143
SALES (est): 5.4MM **Privately Held**
WEB: www.messengerexpress.net
SIC: 4215 7389 4212 Package delivery,
　　vehicular; courier or messenger service;
　　delivery service, vehicular

(P-4276)
MESSENGER EXPRESS
10671 Roselle St Ste 200, San Diego
(92121-1525)
P.O. Box 12424 (92112-3424)
PHONE..............................858 550-1400
Greg King, *Manager*
EMP: 85

SALES (corp-wide): 5.4MM **Privately Held**
WEB: www.messengerexpress.net
SIC: 4215 Package delivery, vehicular
PA: Messenger Express
5435 Cahuenga Blvd Ste C
North Hollywood CA 91601
213 614-0475

(P-4277)
PEACH INC
Also Called: Action Messenger Service
1311 N Highland Ave, Los Angeles
(90028-7608)
P.O. Box 69673 (90069-0673)
PHONE....................323 654-2333
Arthur P Ruben, *President*
Brian Nealy, *Opers Mgr*
EMP: 125
SQ FT: 3,500
SALES: 5MM **Privately Held**
WEB: www.actionmessenger.com
SIC: 4215 7389 Courier services, except
by air; courier or messenger service

(P-4278)
PRIORITY DISPATCH SERVICE INC
309 Laurelwood Rd Ste 10, Santa Clara
(95054-2313)
PHONE....................408 400-3860
Walter Strobel, *CEO*
EMP: 60 EST: 2009
SALES: 950K **Privately Held**
SIC: 4215 Courier services, except by air

(P-4279)
SAN DIEGO MESSENGER INC
Also Called: The Messenger Company
4848 Ronson Ct Ste G, San Diego
(92111-1809)
PHONE....................858 514-8866
Richard Villalodos, *President*
Rick Smith, *Vice Pres*
EMP: 50 EST: 2000
SQ FT: 3,000
SALES: 1.3MM **Privately Held**
SIC: 4215 Courier services, except by air

(P-4280)
SUNRISE DELIVERY SERVICE INC
13351 Riverside Dr 672d, Sherman Oaks
(91423-2542)
PHONE....................323 464-5121
Charles R Audia, *President*
EMP: 60
SQ FT: 3,000
SALES (est): 4.5MM **Privately Held**
SIC: 4215 Courier services, except by air

(P-4281)
SYNCTRUCK LLC
415 Darrell Rd, Hillsborough (94010-6709)
PHONE....................415 425-0447
Luis Toledo, *Principal*
EMP: 116
SALES (corp-wide): 4.2MM **Privately Held**
SIC: 4215 Package delivery, vehicular
PA: Synctruck Llc
510 Eccles Ave
South San Francisco CA 94080
650 239-6231

(P-4282)
TELE-CAR COURIERS INC
Also Called: Tele-Car Courier Service
4035 Eagle Rock Blvd, Los Angeles
(90065-3607)
PHONE....................877 910-1313
Shagen Galstanyan, *Principal*
EMP: 75
SALES: 2.8MM **Privately Held**
SIC: 4215 Courier services, except by air

(P-4283)
TF COURIER INC
8331 Demetre Ave, Sacramento
(95828-0920)
PHONE....................916 379-0708
Ed Feliciano, *Manager*
Ruiz Eduardo, *Opers Mgr*
Brooks David, *Transportation*
Terrence Johnson, *Supervisor*
EMP: 60

SALES (corp-wide): 3.8B **Privately Held**
SIC: 4215 Courier services, except by air
HQ: Tf Courier, Inc.
14881 Quorum Dr Ste 700
Dallas TX 75254

(P-4284)
TF COURIER INC
7130 Miramar Rd Ste 400, San Diego
(92121-2340)
PHONE....................888 541-2965
John Mc Loughlin, *Manager*
Steve Merriweather, *Opers Mgr*
EMP: 60
SALES (corp-wide): 3.8B **Privately Held**
SIC: 4215 Courier services, except by air
HQ: Tf Courier, Inc.
14881 Quorum Dr Ste 700
Dallas TX 75254

(P-4285)
TF COURIER INC
2051 Raymer Ave Ste A, Fullerton
(92833-2678)
PHONE....................714 888-1452
Scott Leveridge, *Manager*
EMP: 70
SALES (corp-wide): 3.8B **Privately Held**
SIC: 4215 Courier services, except by air
HQ: Tf Courier, Inc.
14881 Quorum Dr Ste 700
Dallas TX 75254

(P-4286)
TF COURIER INC
21760 Garcia Ln, City of Industry
(91789-0940)
PHONE....................214 560-9000
EMP: 60
SALES (corp-wide): 3.8B **Privately Held**
SIC: 4215 Courier services, except by air
HQ: Tf Courier, Inc.
14881 Quorum Dr Ste 700
Dallas TX 75254

(P-4287)
TOP PRIORITY COURIERS INC (PA)
1257 Columbia Ave Ste D1, Riverside
(92507-2124)
P.O. Box 20376 (92516-0376)
PHONE....................951 781-1000
Siroos Zakikhani, *President*
Rick Johnson, *Exec VP*
EMP: 60
SQ FT: 6,000
SALES (est): 10.8MM **Privately Held**
WEB: www.topprioritycouriers.com
SIC: 4215 Package delivery, vehicular

(P-4288)
TRICOR AMERICA INC
Also Called: Tricor California
1690 Cebrian St, West Sacramento
(95691-3802)
PHONE....................916 371-1704
Fred Kamper, *Branch Mgr*
EMP: 125
SALES (corp-wide): 92.6MM **Privately Held**
WEB: www.tricor.com
SIC: 4215 4212 Courier services, except
by air; delivery service, vehicular
PA: Tricor America, Inc.
717 Airport Blvd
South San Francisco CA 94080
650 877-3650

(P-4289)
ULTRAEX LLC
2633 Barrington Ct, Hayward (94545-1100)
PHONE....................510 723-3760
William Carlson,
Alfredo Flores,
Ernesto Holbrook,
EMP: 75 EST: 2014
SALES (est): 3.1MM **Privately Held**
SIC: 4215 4513 4225 Courier services,
except by air; air courier services; general
warehousing & storage

(P-4290)
UNITED PARCEL SERVICE INC
Also Called: UPS
12745 Arroyo St, Sylmar (91342-5332)
PHONE....................800 742-5877
EMP: 86
SALES (corp-wide): 71.8B **Publicly Held**
SIC: 4215 4513 Package delivery,
vehicular; parcel delivery, vehicular; letter
delivery, private air; package delivery, private air; parcel delivery, private air; flying
charter service
PA: United Parcel Service, Inc.
55 Glenlake Pkwy
Atlanta GA 30328
404 828-6000

(P-4291)
UNITED PARCEL SERVICE INC
Also Called: UPS
657 Forbes Blvd, South San Francisco
(94080-2059)
PHONE....................650 737-3737
Timothy Huxtable, *Branch Mgr*
EMP: 159
SALES (corp-wide): 71.8B **Publicly Held**
WEB: www.martrac.com
SIC: 4215 Parcel delivery, vehicular
PA: United Parcel Service, Inc.
55 Glenlake Pkwy
Atlanta GA 30328
404 828-6000

(P-4292)
UNITED PARCEL SERVICE INC OH
Also Called: UPS
160 W Main St, El Centro (92243-2513)
PHONE....................858 541-2336
Edgar Zaragoza, *Manager*
EMP: 85
SALES (corp-wide): 71.8B **Publicly Held**
WEB: www.upsscs.com
SIC: 4215 4513 Parcel delivery, vehicular;
parcel delivery, private air
HQ: United Parcel Service, Inc.
55 Glenlake Pkwy
Atlanta GA 30328
404 828-6000

(P-4293)
UNITED PARCEL SERVICE INC OH
Also Called: UPS
650 N Commercial Rd, Palm Springs
(92262-6299)
PHONE....................760 325-1762
Doug Nelson, *Manager*
Rick Vanden Bossche, *Business Mgr*
Richard Day, *Manager*
Rick Vandenbossche, *Manager*
EMP: 500
SALES (corp-wide): 71.8B **Publicly Held**
WEB: www.upsscs.com
SIC: 4215 4513 Parcel delivery, vehicular;
air courier services
HQ: United Parcel Service, Inc.
55 Glenlake Pkwy
Atlanta GA 30328
404 828-6000

(P-4294)
UNITED PARCEL SERVICE INC OH
Also Called: UPS
1601 Atlas Rd, Richmond (94806-1101)
PHONE....................510 262-2338
Jim Kelly, *President*
EMP: 152
SALES (corp-wide): 71.8B **Publicly Held**
WEB: www.upsscs.com
SIC: 4215 4513 Parcel delivery, vehicular;
air courier services
HQ: United Parcel Service, Inc.
55 Glenlake Pkwy
Atlanta GA 30328
404 828-6000

(P-4295)
UNITED PARCEL SERVICE INC OH
Also Called: UPS
1139 Madison Ln, Salinas (93907-1817)
PHONE....................831 758-9112
EMP: 158

SQ FT: 3,000
SALES (corp-wide): 71.8B **Publicly Held**
SIC: 4215 Parcel delivery, vehicular
HQ: United Parcel Service, Inc.
55 Glenlake Pkwy
Atlanta GA 30328
404 828-6000

(P-4296)
UNITED PARCEL SERVICE INC OH
Also Called: UPS
2800 W 227th St, Torrance (90505-2912)
PHONE....................800 742-5877
EMP: 80
SALES (corp-wide): 71.8B **Publicly Held**
WEB: www.upsscs.com
SIC: 4215 Package delivery, vehicular
HQ: United Parcel Service, Inc.
55 Glenlake Pkwy
Atlanta GA 30328
404 828-6000

(P-4297)
UNITED PARCEL SERVICE INC OH
Also Called: UPS
6845 Eastside Rd, Anderson (96007-9406)
PHONE....................530 365-7850
Lauren Lnd, *Manager*
EMP: 100
SALES (corp-wide): 71.8B **Publicly Held**
WEB: www.upsscs.com
SIC: 4215 4213 Parcel delivery, vehicular;
trucking, except local
HQ: United Parcel Service, Inc.
55 Glenlake Pkwy
Atlanta GA 30328
404 828-6000

(P-4298)
UNITED PARCEL SERVICE INC OH
Also Called: UPS
2915 N Sierra Hwy, Bishop (93514-7633)
PHONE....................760 872-7661
EMP: 158
SALES (corp-wide): 71.8B **Publicly Held**
WEB: www.upsscs.com
SIC: 4215 Parcel delivery, vehicular
HQ: United Parcel Service, Inc.
55 Glenlake Pkwy
Atlanta GA 30328
404 828-6000

(P-4299)
UNITED PARCEL SERVICE INC OH
Also Called: UPS
5000 W Cordelia Rd, Fairfield
(94534-1628)
PHONE....................707 864-8200
EMP: 158
SALES (corp-wide): 71.8B **Publicly Held**
SIC: 4215 Parcel delivery, vehicular
HQ: United Parcel Service, Inc.
55 Glenlake Pkwy
Atlanta GA 30328
404 828-6000

(P-4300)
UNITED PARCEL SERVICE INC OH
Also Called: UPS
1400 Hil Mor Dr, Ceres (95307-9292)
PHONE....................800 742-5877
Dave Walker, *Principal*
EMP: 200
SALES (corp-wide): 71.8B **Publicly Held**
WEB: www.upsscs.com
SIC: 4215 Parcel delivery, vehicular
HQ: United Parcel Service, Inc.
55 Glenlake Pkwy
Atlanta GA 30328
404 828-6000

(P-4301)
UNITED PARCEL SERVICE INC OH
Also Called: UPS
1380 Shore St, West Sacramento
(95691-3522)
PHONE....................916 373-4076
Tom Karls, *Manager*
Lance Cole, *Accounts Exec*

P
R
O
D
U
C
T
S

&

S
V
C
S

Tim Francis, *Superintendent*
EMP: 200
SALES (corp-wide): 71.8B **Publicly Held**
WEB: www.upsscs.com
SIC: 4215 Parcel delivery, vehicular
HQ: United Parcel Service, Inc.
55 Glenlake Pkwy
Atlanta GA 30328
404 828-6000

(P-4302)
UNITED PARCEL SERVICE INC
OH
Also Called: UPS
2531 Napa Valley Corp Dr, NAPA (94558)
PHONE...............................707 224-1205
Josh Young, *Principal*
EMP: 158
SALES (corp-wide): 71.8B **Publicly Held**
SIC: 4215 Package delivery, vehicular
HQ: United Parcel Service, Inc.
55 Glenlake Pkwy
Atlanta GA 30328
404 828-6000

(P-4303)
UNITED PARCEL SERVICE INC
OH
Also Called: UPS
128 Shore St, Sacramento (95829)
PHONE...............................916 373-4089
Chris Wagner, *Manager*
EMP: 70
SALES (corp-wide): 71.8B **Publicly Held**
WEB: www.upsscs.com
SIC: 4215 Parcel delivery, vehicular
HQ: United Parcel Service, Inc.
55 Glenlake Pkwy
Atlanta GA 30328
404 828-6000

(P-4304)
UNITED PARCEL SERVICE INC
OH
Also Called: UPS
17115 S Western Ave, Gardena
(90247-5299)
PHONE...............................310 217-2646
Randy Hulhellt, *Manager*
Roger Flores, *Opers Mgr*
EMP: 500
SALES (corp-wide): 71.8B **Publicly Held**
WEB: www.upsscs.com
SIC: 4215 4513 Parcel delivery, vehicular;
air courier services
HQ: United Parcel Service, Inc.
55 Glenlake Pkwy
Atlanta GA 30328
404 828-6000

(P-4305)
UNITED PARCEL SERVICE INC
OH
Also Called: UPS
1999 S 7th St, San Jose (95112-6009)
PHONE...............................408 291-2942
Frank Cademarti, *Manager*
Peter Kolotouros, *Director*
EMP: 300
SALES (corp-wide): 71.8B **Publicly Held**
WEB: www.upsscs.com
SIC: 4215 Parcel delivery, vehicular
HQ: United Parcel Service, Inc.
55 Glenlake Pkwy
Atlanta GA 30328
404 828-6000

(P-4306)
UNITED PARCEL SERVICE INC
OH
UPS
2222 17th St, San Francisco (94103-5015)
PHONE...............................415 252-4564
Tom Dalto, *Manager*
Ly Ngow, *Clerk*
EMP: 152
SALES (corp-wide): 71.8B **Publicly Held**
WEB: www.upsscs.com
SIC: 4215 4513 Parcel delivery, vehicular;
air courier services
HQ: United Parcel Service, Inc.
55 Glenlake Pkwy
Atlanta GA 30328
404 828-6000

(P-4307)
UNITED PARCEL SERVICE INC
OH
Also Called: UPS
1012 Sterling St, Vallejo (94591-8686)
PHONE...............................707 252-4560
EMP: 165
SALES (corp-wide): 71.8B **Publicly Held**
WEB: www.upsscs.com
SIC: 4215 Parcel delivery, vehicular
HQ: United Parcel Service, Inc.
55 Glenlake Pkwy
Atlanta GA 30328
404 828-6000

(P-4308)
UNITED PARCEL SERVICE INC
OH
Also Called: UPS
10690 Santa Monica Blvd, Los Angeles
(90025-4838)
PHONE...............................310 474-0019
EMP: 158
SALES (corp-wide): 71.8B **Publicly Held**
SIC: 4215 Parcel delivery, vehicular
HQ: United Parcel Service, Inc.
55 Glenlake Pkwy
Atlanta GA 30328
404 828-6000

(P-4309)
UNITED PARCEL SERVICE INC
OH
Also Called: UPS
22 Brookline, Aliso Viejo (92656-1461)
PHONE...............................949 643-6595
Carolyn Macneil, *Branch Mgr*
EMP: 152
SALES (corp-wide): 71.8B **Publicly Held**
SIC: 4215 Parcel delivery, vehicular
HQ: United Parcel Service, Inc.
55 Glenlake Pkwy
Atlanta GA 30328
404 828-6000

(P-4310)
UNITED PARCEL SERVICE INC
OH
Also Called: UPS
290 W Avenue L, Lancaster (93534-7109)
PHONE...............................800 828-8264
James Adams, *Principal*
EMP: 150
SALES (corp-wide): 71.8B **Publicly Held**
WEB: www.upsscs.com
SIC: 4215 Parcel delivery, vehicular
HQ: United Parcel Service, Inc.
55 Glenlake Pkwy
Atlanta GA 30328
404 828-6000

(P-4311)
UNITED PARCEL SERVICE INC
OH
Also Called: UPS
16000 Arminta St, Van Nuys (91406-1895)
PHONE...............................404 828-6000
Klotonya Hamilton, *Engineer*
EMP: 158
SALES (corp-wide): 71.8B **Publicly Held**
SIC: 4215 Parcel delivery, vehicular
HQ: United Parcel Service, Inc.
55 Glenlake Pkwy
Atlanta GA 30328
404 828-6000

(P-4312)
UNITED PARCEL SERVICE INC
OH
Also Called: UPS
7925 Ronson Rd, San Diego (92111-1997)
PHONE...............................909 279-5111
Jeff Walsingham, *Marketing Mgr*
EMP: 158
SALES (corp-wide): 71.8B **Publicly Held**
SIC: 4215 Parcel delivery, vehicular
HQ: United Parcel Service, Inc.
55 Glenlake Pkwy
Atlanta GA 30328
404 828-6000

(P-4313)
UNITED PARCEL SERVICE INC
OH
Also Called: UPS
8400 Pardee Dr, Oakland (94621-1456)
PHONE...............................510 813-5662
Shurn Rick, *Technician*
EMP: 158
SALES (corp-wide): 71.8B **Publicly Held**
SIC: 4215 Parcel delivery, vehicular
HQ: United Parcel Service, Inc.
55 Glenlake Pkwy
Atlanta GA 30328
404 828-6000

(P-4314)
UNITED PARCEL SERVICE INC
OH
Also Called: UPS
13233 Moore St, Cerritos (90703-2276)
PHONE...............................562 404-3236
Gary Mieredos, *Manager*
EMP: 152
SALES (corp-wide): 71.8B **Publicly Held**
WEB: www.upsscs.com
SIC: 4215 Parcel delivery, vehicular
HQ: United Parcel Service, Inc.
55 Glenlake Pkwy
Atlanta GA 30328
404 828-6000

(P-4315)
UNITED PARCEL SERVICE INC
OH
Also Called: UPS
259 Cherry St, Ukiah (95482-5804)
PHONE...............................707 468-5481
EMP: 158
SALES (corp-wide): 71.8B **Publicly Held**
WEB: www.upsscs.com
SIC: 4215 Parcel delivery, vehicular
HQ: United Parcel Service, Inc.
55 Glenlake Pkwy
Atlanta GA 30328
404 828-6000

(P-4316)
UNITED PARCEL SERVICE INC
OH
Also Called: UPS
6 Upper Ragsdale Dr, Monterey
(93940-5730)
PHONE...............................831 757-6294
EMP: 158
SALES (corp-wide): 71.8B **Publicly Held**
SIC: 4215 Parcel delivery, vehicular
HQ: United Parcel Service, Inc.
55 Glenlake Pkwy
Atlanta GA 30328
404 828-6000

(P-4317)
UNITED PARCEL SERVICE INC
OH
Also Called: UPS
3601 Sacramento Dr, San Luis Obispo
(93401-7115)
PHONE...............................801 973-3400
EMP: 158
SALES (corp-wide): 71.8B **Publicly Held**
SIC: 4215 Parcel delivery, vehicular
HQ: United Parcel Service, Inc.
55 Glenlake Pkwy
Atlanta GA 30328
404 828-6000

(P-4318)
UNITED PARCEL SERVICE INC
OH
Also Called: UPS
1970 Olivera Rd, Concord (94520-5425)
PHONE...............................925 689-6584
EMP: 158
SALES (corp-wide): 71.8B **Publicly Held**
SIC: 4215 Parcel delivery, vehicular
HQ: United Parcel Service, Inc.
55 Glenlake Pkwy
Atlanta GA 30328
404 828-6000

(P-4319)
UNITED PARCEL SERVICE INC
OH
Also Called: UPS
505 Pine Ave, Goleta (93117-3707)
PHONE...............................805 964-7848
Jason Chang, *Manager*
EMP: 112
SALES (corp-wide): 71.8B **Publicly Held**
WEB: www.upsscs.com
SIC: 4215 Parcel delivery, vehicular
HQ: United Parcel Service, Inc.
55 Glenlake Pkwy
Atlanta GA 30328
404 828-6000

(P-4320)
UNITED PARCEL SERVICE INC
OH
Also Called: UPS
309 Cooley Ln, Santa Maria (93455-1218)
PHONE...............................805 922-7851
Michael King, *Manager*
EMP: 140
SALES (corp-wide): 71.8B **Publicly Held**
WEB: www.upsscs.com
SIC: 4215 Parcel delivery, vehicular
HQ: United Parcel Service, Inc.
55 Glenlake Pkwy
Atlanta GA 30328
404 828-6000

(P-4321)
UNITED PARCEL SERVICE INC
OH
Also Called: UPS
2342 Gun Club Rd, Angels Camp (95222)
PHONE...............................209 736-0878
EMP: 158
SALES (corp-wide): 71.8B **Publicly Held**
SIC: 4215 Parcel delivery, vehicular
HQ: United Parcel Service, Inc.
55 Glenlake Pkwy
Atlanta GA 30328
404 828-6000

(P-4322)
UNITED PARCEL SERVICE INC
OH
Also Called: UPS
1501 Rancho Conejo Blvd, Newbury Park
(91320-1410)
PHONE...............................805 375-1832
Grant Nissan, *Branch Mgr*
EMP: 200
SALES (corp-wide): 71.8B **Publicly Held**
WEB: www.upsscs.com
SIC: 4215 Parcel delivery, vehicular
HQ: United Parcel Service, Inc.
55 Glenlake Pkwy
Atlanta GA 30328
404 828-6000

(P-4323)
UNITED PARCEL SERVICE INC
OH
Also Called: UPS
3000 E Washington Blvd, Los Angeles
(90023-4220)
PHONE...............................323 729-6762
Art Nakamoto, *Branch Mgr*
EMP: 800
SALES (corp-wide): 71.8B **Publicly Held**
WEB: www.upsscs.com
SIC: 4215 Parcel delivery, vehicular
HQ: United Parcel Service, Inc.
55 Glenlake Pkwy
Atlanta GA 30328
404 828-6000

(P-4324)
UNITED PARCEL SERVICE INC
OH
Also Called: UPS
2300 Boswell Ct, Chula Vista (91914-3520)
PHONE...............................619 482-8119
Erik Archambault, *Director*
EMP: 158
SALES (corp-wide): 71.8B **Publicly Held**
SIC: 4215 Parcel delivery, vehicular
HQ: United Parcel Service, Inc.
55 Glenlake Pkwy
Atlanta GA 30328
404 828-6000

▲ = Import ▼=Export
◆ =Import/Export

(P-4325)
UNITED PARCEL SERVICE INC OH
Also Called: UPS
251 Sylvania Ave, Santa Cruz
(95060-2161)
PHONE..................................831 425-1054
EMP: 158
SALES (corp-wide): 71.8B **Publicly Held**
WEB: www.upsscs.com
SIC: 4215 Parcel delivery, vehicular
HQ: United Parcel Service, Inc.
55 Glenlake Pkwy
Atlanta GA 30328
404 828-6000

(P-4326)
UNITED PARCEL SERVICE INC OH
Also Called: UPS
3140 Jurupa St, Ontario (91761-2902)
PHONE..................................909 974-7000
Brenda Hiza, *Branch Mgr*
EMP: 80
SALES (corp-wide): 71.8B **Publicly Held**
WEB: www.upsscs.com
SIC: 4215 Package delivery, vehicular; parcel delivery, vehicular
HQ: United Parcel Service, Inc.
55 Glenlake Pkwy
Atlanta GA 30328
404 828-6000

(P-4327)
UNITED PARCEL SERVICE INC OH
Also Called: UPS
4500 Norris Canyon Rd, San Ramon
(94583-1369)
PHONE..................................800 833-9943
EMP: 164
SALES (corp-wide): 71.8B **Publicly Held**
WEB: www.upsscs.com
SIC: 4215 Parcel delivery, vehicular
HQ: United Parcel Service, Inc.
55 Glenlake Pkwy
Atlanta GA 30328
404 828-6000

(P-4328)
UNITED PARCEL SERVICE INC OH
Also Called: UPS
2559 Palma Dr, Ventura (93003-5733)
PHONE..................................805 642-6784
EMP: 158
SALES (corp-wide): 71.8B **Publicly Held**
WEB: www.upsscs.com
SIC: 4215 Parcel delivery, vehicular
HQ: United Parcel Service, Inc.
55 Glenlake Pkwy
Atlanta GA 30328
404 828-6000

(P-4329)
UNITED PARCEL SERVICE INC OH
Also Called: UPS
1100 Baldwin Park Blvd, Baldwin Park
(91706-5895)
PHONE..................................626 814-6216
Lero Stamply, *Manager*
EMP: 200
SALES (corp-wide): 71.8B **Publicly Held**
WEB: www.upsscs.com
SIC: 4215 4513 Parcel delivery, vehicular; air courier services
HQ: United Parcel Service, Inc.
55 Glenlake Pkwy
Atlanta GA 30328
404 828-6000

(P-4330)
UNITED PARCEL SERVICE INC OH
Also Called: UPS
3930 Kristi Ct, Sacramento (95827-9716)
PHONE..................................916 857-0311
Stan Kamimura, *Supervisor*
EMP: 152
SALES (corp-wide): 71.8B **Publicly Held**
SIC: 4215 Parcel delivery, vehicular

HQ: United Parcel Service, Inc.
55 Glenlake Pkwy
Atlanta GA 30328
404 828-6000

(P-4331)
UNITY COURIER SERVICE INC (PA)
3231 Fletcher Dr, Los Angeles
(90065-2919)
PHONE..................................323 255-9800
Ali Sharifi, *President*
Larry Lum, *CEO*
Manmohan Bhamra, *Info Tech Mgr*
Eric Cook, *IT/INT Sup*
Corina Martinez, *Human Res Mgr*
EMP: 200
SQ FT: 11,000
SALES (est): 45.8MM **Privately Held**
WEB: www.unitycourier.com
SIC: 4215 Package delivery, vehicular

4221 Farm Product Warehousing & Storage

(P-4332)
BUTTE-YB-STTER WTR QLTY CLTION
625 Cooper Ave, Yuba City (95991-3864)
P.O. Box 729 (95992-0729)
PHONE..................................530 673-5131
Stephen F Danna, *Chairman*
EMP: 75
SALES: 428.7K **Privately Held**
SIC: 4221 Farm product warehousing & storage

(P-4333)
HONEYVILLE INC
11600 Dayton Dr, Rancho Cucamonga
(91730-5525)
PHONE..................................909 980-9500
Johnny Ferry, *President*
Enrique Erazo, *Manager*
Joshua Fischer, *Accounts Mgr*
EMP: 85
SALES (corp-wide): 179.6MM **Privately Held**
WEB: www.honeyvillegrain.com
SIC: 4221 5153 2045 2041 Grain elevator, storage only; grains; prepared flour mixes & doughs; flour & other grain mill products
PA: Honeyville, Inc.
1040 W 600 N
Ogden UT 84404
435 494-4193

(P-4334)
PURATOS CORPORATION
Also Called: Puratos Bakery Supply
11167 White Birch Dr, Rancho Cucamonga
(91730-3820)
PHONE..................................909 484-1312
Ron Bouter, *General Mgr*
EMP: 100
SALES (corp-wide): 30.1MM **Privately Held**
WEB: www.puratos.com
SIC: 4221 2041 Farm product warehousing & storage; flour
HQ: Puratos Corporation
1660 Suckle Hwy
Pennsauken NJ 08110

(P-4335)
VEG-LAND INC
Also Called: J B J Distributing
1518 E Valencia Dr, Fullerton (92831-4734)
P.O. Box 1287 (92836-8287)
PHONE..................................714 871-6712
James E Matiasevich, *President*
John P Matiasevich, *Corp Secy*
EMP: 50 EST: 1976
SQ FT: 70,000
SALES (est): 7MM
SALES (corp-wide): 29.4MM **Privately Held**
SIC: 4221 Farm product warehousing & storage

PA: Veg Land Sales Inc
1518 E Valencia Dr
Fullerton CA 92831
714 871-6712

4222 Refrigerated Warehousing & Storage

(P-4336)
AMERICOLD LOGISTICS LLC
Also Called: (P&O COLD LOGISTICS, LLC)
2750 Orbiter St, Brea (92821-6256)
PHONE..................................714 993-3533
Brent Sugden,
Randy Benish, *Regional VP*
Rich Kappmeier, *Regional VP*
Hal Leddy, *Regional VP*
Richard Bastianelli, *Senior VP*
EMP: 1230 EST: 1952
SQ FT: 194,000
SALES (est): 899.2K
SALES (corp-wide): 1.6B **Publicly Held**
SIC: 4222 Warehousing, cold storage or refrigerated
HQ: Versacold U.S. Inc
19840 S Rancho Way
Compton CA 90220
310 632-6265

(P-4337)
AMERICOLD LOGISTICS LLC
1415 N Raymond Ave, Anaheim
(92801-1111)
PHONE..................................678 441-1468
Tony Esquivel, *Branch Mgr*
Montes Armondo, *Manager*
EMP: 60
SALES (corp-wide): 1.6B **Publicly Held**
SIC: 4222 4213 Warehousing, cold storage or refrigerated; refrigerated products transport
HQ: Americold Logistics, Llc
10 Glenlake Pkwy Ste 324
Atlanta GA 30328
678 441-1400

(P-4338)
AMERICOLD LOGISTICS LLC
950 S Sanborn Rd, Salinas (93901-4530)
P.O. Box 1548 (93902-1548)
PHONE..................................831 424-1537
Pat Zimmerman, *General Mgr*
Patrick Zimmerman, *General Mgr*
EMP: 50
SALES (corp-wide): 1.6B **Publicly Held**
SIC: 4222 Warehousing, cold storage or refrigerated
HQ: Americold Logistics, Llc
10 Glenlake Pkwy Ste 324
Atlanta GA 30328
678 441-1400

(P-4339)
AMERICOLD LOGISTICS LLC
Also Called: Americold Realty
700 Malaga St, Ontario (91761-8627)
PHONE..................................909 390-4950
Jeff Canfield, *Manager*
Bonne Martin, *Admin Asst*
EMP: 50
SALES (corp-wide): 1.6B **Publicly Held**
WEB: www.americoldlogistics.com
SIC: 4222 Warehousing, cold storage or refrigerated
HQ: Americold Logistics, Llc
10 Glenlake Pkwy Ste 324
Atlanta GA 30328
678 441-1400

(P-4340)
AMERICOLD LOGISTICS LLC
3420 E Vernon Ave, Vernon (90058-1812)
PHONE..................................323 581-0025
Ian McGagh, *Branch Mgr*
EMP: 78
SALES (corp-wide): 1.6B **Publicly Held**
SIC: 4222 Warehousing, cold storage or refrigerated
HQ: Americold Logistics, Llc
10 Glenlake Pkwy Ste 324
Atlanta GA 30328
678 441-1400

(P-4341)
CAL PACKING & STORAGE LP
Also Called: Bravante Produce
1356 S Buttonwillow Ave, Reedley
(93654-9333)
PHONE..................................559 638-2929
George Bravante, *Managing Prtnr*
Adriana Plascencia, *Sales Staff*
Steve Shearer, *Manager*
EMP: 70
SQ FT: 100,000
SALES (est): 12.1MM **Privately Held**
SIC: 4222 7389 5148 Warehousing, cold storage or refrigerated; packaging & labeling services; fresh fruits & vegetables

(P-4342)
CENTRAL COAST COOLING LLC
1107 Merrill St, Salinas (93901-4430)
P.O. Box 1527 (93902-1527)
PHONE..................................831 422-7265
Mike Storm, *President*
Denny Bertlesman, *Vice Pres*
EMP: 90
SQ FT: 30,000
SALES (est): 15MM **Privately Held**
WEB: www.centralcoastcooling.com
SIC: 4222 Warehousing, cold storage or refrigerated

(P-4343)
E STREET COLD LOGISTICS LLC (PA)
901 E E St, Wilmington (90744-6144)
PHONE..................................310 233-7300
Richard Burke, *Mng Member*
G Brent Larson, *Exec VP*
EMP: 50
SQ FT: 150,000
SALES (est): 4.9MM **Privately Held**
SIC: 4222 Warehousing, cold storage or refrigerated

(P-4344)
EXEL N AMERCN LOGISTICS INC
Freeze Point Cold Storage Div
3735 Imperial Way, Stockton (95215-9691)
PHONE..................................209 942-0102
Mike Hernandez, *Manager*
Chris Lares, *Opers Mgr*
EMP: 100
SALES (corp-wide): 70.4B **Privately Held**
SIC: 4222 Storage, frozen or refrigerated goods
HQ: Exel North American Logistics, Inc.
570 Players Pkwy
Westerville OH 43081
800 272-1052

(P-4345)
EXEL N AMERCN LOGISTICS INC
Also Called: Power Logistics
4512 Frontier Way, Stockton (95215-9676)
PHONE..................................209 932-2400
Charles McElwain, *Manager*
EMP: 100
SALES (corp-wide): 70.4B **Privately Held**
SIC: 4222 5149 Storage, frozen or refrigerated goods; groceries & related products
HQ: Exel North American Logistics, Inc.
570 Players Pkwy
Westerville OH 43081
800 272-1052

(P-4346)
EXETER PACKERS INC
Also Called: Sun Pacific Cold Storage
33374 Lerdo Hwy, Bakersfield
(93308-9782)
PHONE..................................661 399-0416
Richard Peters, *Manager*
EMP: 220
SALES (est): 5.8MM
SALES (corp-wide): 57.6MM **Privately Held**
SIC: 4222 0172 Warehousing, cold storage or refrigerated; grapes
PA: Exeter Packers, Inc.
1250 E Myer Ave
Exeter CA 93221
559 592-5168

P R O D U C T S & S V C S

(P-4347)
LINEAGE LOGISTICS LLC
3141 E 44th St, Vernon (90058-2405)
PHONE..............................323 583-3163
Ralph Newton, *Manager*
EMP: 150
SALES (corp-wide): 1.1B **Privately Held**
WEB: www.usgrowers.com
SIC: 4222 Warehousing, cold storage or refrigerated
HQ: Lineage Logistics, Llc
46500 Humboldt Dr
Novi MI 48377
248 863-4400

(P-4348)
LINEAGE LOGISTICS LLC
3251 De Forest Cir Ste C, Jurupa Valley (91752-3277)
PHONE..............................951 360-7970
Reginald Burke, *General Mgr*
EMP: 50
SALES (corp-wide): 1.1B **Privately Held**
SIC: 4222 Warehousing, cold storage or refrigerated
HQ: Lineage Logistics, Llc
46500 Humboldt Dr
Novi MI 48377
248 863-4400

(P-4349)
LINEAGE LOGISTICS HOLDINGS LLC (PA)
1 Park Plz Ste 550, Irvine (92614-2594)
PHONE..............................800 678-7271
Greg Lehmkuhl, *President*
Timothy Dayton, *President*
Paul Hendricksen, *President*
Mike McClendon, *President*
Bill Hendricksen, *CEO*
EMP: 180
SALES (est): 1.1B **Privately Held**
SIC: 4222 Warehousing, cold storage or refrigerated

(P-4350)
MIKE CAMPBELL & ASSOCIATES LTD
Also Called: Mike Campbell Assoc Logistics
10907 Downey Ave Ste 203, Downey (90241-3737)
PHONE..............................626 369-3981
Vickie J Campbell, *CEO*
James Heermans, *President*
Paul Trump, *President*
EMP: 1000
SALES (est): 91.1MM **Privately Held**
SIC: 4222 4225 4214 4213 Storage, frozen or refrigerated goods; general warehousing & storage; local trucking with storage; trucking, except local

(P-4351)
PREFERRED FRZR SVCS - LBF LLC
4901 Bandini Blvd, Vernon (90058-5400)
PHONE..............................323 263-8811
Brian Beattie, *CEO*
Ivette Quezadas, *Administration*
▲ **EMP:** 100 **EST:** 2013
SALES (est): 1.8MM **Privately Held**
SIC: 4222 Warehousing, cold storage or refrigerated

(P-4352)
STANDARD-SOUTHERN CORPORATION
Also Called: Los Angeles Cold Storage Co
400 S Central Ave, Los Angeles (90013-1712)
P.O. Box 54244 (90054-0244)
PHONE..............................213 624-1831
Larry Rauch, *Manager*
EMP: 80
SALES (corp-wide): 36.5MM **Privately Held**
WEB: www.lacold.com
SIC: 4222 Warehousing, cold storage or refrigerated
PA: Standard-Southern Corporation
4635 Suthwest Fwy Ste 910
Houston TX 77027
713 627-1700

(P-4353)
STANDARD-SOUTHERN CORPORATION
Also Called: L.A. Cold Storage
440 S Central Ave, Los Angeles (90013-1712)
PHONE..............................213 624-1831
Larry Rauch, *President*
Harris Smith, *General Mgr*
John Scherer, *Engineer*
Chuck Gunther, *Chief Engr*
Terry Miller Sr, *Warehouse Mgr*
EMP: 130
SALES (corp-wide): 36.5MM **Privately Held**
SIC: 4222 Warehousing, cold storage or refrigerated
PA: Standard-Southern Corporation
4635 Suthwest Fwy Ste 910
Houston TX 77027
713 627-1700

(P-4354)
STANDARD-SOUTHERN CORPORATION
Also Called: Los Angeles Cold Storage
715 E 4th St, Los Angeles (90013-1727)
PHONE..............................213 624-1831
Thom Thomas, *Branch Mgr*
EMP: 90
SALES (corp-wide): 36.5MM **Privately Held**
WEB: www.lacold.com
SIC: 4222 Warehousing, cold storage or refrigerated
PA: Standard-Southern Corporation
4635 Suthwest Fwy Ste 910
Houston TX 77027
713 627-1700

(P-4355)
UNITED STATES COLD STORAGE INC
Also Called: United States Cold Storage Cal
6501 District Blvd, Bakersfield (93313-2000)
P.O. Box 45001 (93384-5001)
PHONE..............................661 832-2653
Randall Dorrell, *Manager*
Riad Sweilem, *Warehouse Mgr*
Patricia Washington, *Clerk*
EMP: 75
SALES (corp-wide): 13.5B **Privately Held**
WEB: www.uscold.com
SIC: 4222 Warehousing, cold storage or refrigerated
HQ: United States Cold Storage, Inc.
2 Aquarium Dr Ste 400
Camden NJ 08103
856 354-8181

(P-4356)
UNITED STATES COLD STORAGE INC
810 E Continental Ave, Tulare (93274-6816)
PHONE..............................559 686-1110
Brian Ford, *Opers-Prdtn-Mfg*
EMP: 50
SALES (corp-wide): 13.5B **Privately Held**
WEB: www.uscold.com
SIC: 4222 Warehousing, cold storage or refrigerated
HQ: United States Cold Storage, Inc.
2 Aquarium Dr Ste 400
Camden NJ 08103
856 354-8181

(P-4357)
UNITED STATES COLD STORAGE INC
2003 S Cherry Ave, Fresno (93721-3300)
PHONE..............................559 237-6145
John Bodden, *Manager*
Jeremy Gearhart, *Supervisor*
Miguel Machado, *Supervisor*
EMP: 50
SQ FT: 87,184
SALES (corp-wide): 13.5B **Privately Held**
WEB: www.uscold.com
SIC: 4222 Warehousing, cold storage or refrigerated

HQ: United States Cold Storage, Inc.
2 Aquarium Dr Ste 400
Camden NJ 08103
856 354-8181

(P-4358)
UNITED STATES COLD STORAGE INC
1400 N Macarthur Dr Ste A, Tracy (95376-2829)
PHONE..............................209 835-2653
Stanley Moya, *Manager*
EMP: 50
SALES (corp-wide): 13.5B **Privately Held**
WEB: www.uscold.com
SIC: 4222 Warehousing, cold storage or refrigerated
HQ: United States Cold Storage, Inc.
2 Aquarium Dr Ste 400
Camden NJ 08103
856 354-8181

(P-4359)
VALLEY SWEET LLC
222 N Garden St Ste 400, Visalia (93291-6328)
PHONE..............................559 686-3381
F C Farming,
Steven Blizzard, *General Mgr*
EMP: 100
SQ FT: 163,000
SALES (est): 5.1MM **Privately Held**
SIC: 4222 0723 Warehousing, cold storage or refrigerated; fruit (fresh) packing services

(P-4360)
WEBER DISTRIBUTION LLC (PA)
Also Called: Weber Logistics
13530 Rosecrans Ave, Santa Fe Springs (90670-5087)
PHONE..............................855 469-3237
Harry Drajpuch, *President*
Connie Anderson, *Senior VP*
Jim Emmerling, *Senior VP*
Marc Levin, *Senior VP*
Michael Accomando, *Vice Pres*
EMP: 382
SALES (est): 52.7MM **Privately Held**
SIC: 4222 4225 4213 4212 Refrigerated warehousing & storage; general warehousing & storage; trucking, except local; local trucking, without storage; local trucking with storage

---

4225 General Warehousing & Storage

(P-4361)
3M COMPANY
5151 E Philadelphia St, Ontario (91761-2801)
P.O. Box 51459 (91761-1049)
PHONE..............................909 974-3004
Richard Campbell, *Manager*
Mark Howlett, *Marketing Mgr*
EMP: 150
SALES (corp-wide): 32.7B **Publicly Held**
WEB: www.mmm.com
SIC: 4225 General warehousing
PA: 3m Company
3m Center
Saint Paul MN 55144
651 733-1110

(P-4362)
99 CENTS ONLY STORES LLC (HQ)
Also Called: Bargain Wholesale
4000 Union Pacific Ave, Commerce (90023-3202)
PHONE..............................323 980-8145
Jack Sinclair, *CEO*
Travis Hill, *President*
Steven Thagard, *President*
Jason Kidd, *COO*
Ashok Walia, *CFO*
◆ **EMP:** 500 **EST:** 1982
SALES (est): 5.7B **Privately Held**
WEB: www.99only.com
SIC: 4225 5331 5199 General warehousing & storage; variety stores; general merchandise, non-durable

PA: Number Holdings, Inc.
4000 Union Pacific Ave
Commerce CA 90023
323 980-8145

(P-4363)
ACE HARDWARE CORPORATION
3305 Industrial Ave, Rocklin (95765-1211)
PHONE..............................916 435-4567
James Worley, *Manager*
EMP: 360
SQ FT: 10,000
SALES (corp-wide): 5.7B **Privately Held**
SIC: 4225 General warehousing & storage
PA: Ace Hardware Corporation
2200 Kensington Ct
Oak Brook IL 60523
630 368-3393

(P-4364)
ACT FULFILLMENT INC
3155 Universe Dr, Mira Loma (91752-3252)
PHONE..............................909 930-9083
Randolph Cox, *President*
Lydiann Cox, *CFO*
Brennan Haines, *Info Tech Mgr*
EMP: 220
SALES (est): 25.2MM **Privately Held**
WEB: www.allcartage.com
SIC: 4225 General warehousing

(P-4365)
ACTIVISION BLIZZARD INC
653 W Fallbrook Ave # 104, Fresno (93711-5503)
PHONE..............................310 431-4000
Tony Suarez, *Branch Mgr*
EMP: 200
SALES (corp-wide): 7.5B **Publicly Held**
WEB: www.blizzard.com
SIC: 4225 General warehousing & storage
PA: Activision Blizzard, Inc.
3100 Ocean Park Blvd
Santa Monica CA 90405
310 255-2000

(P-4366)
ADIR INTERNATIONAL LLC
4444-46 Ayers Ave, Los Angeles (90023)
PHONE..............................213 386-4412
Russell Yeager, *Manager*
EMP: 77
SALES (corp-wide): 500.7MM **Privately Held**
WEB: www.lacuracao.com
SIC: 4225 Warehousing, self-storage
PA: Adir International, Llc
1605 W Olympic Blvd # 405
Los Angeles CA 90015
213 639-2100

(P-4367)
ADVANCED STERLIZATION
13135 Napa St, Fontana (92335-2961)
PHONE..............................909 350-6987
Ted Snavely, *Manager*
EMP: 100
SALES (corp-wide): 6.4B **Publicly Held**
SIC: 4225 General warehousing & storage
HQ: Advanced Sterlization Products Services Inc.
33 Technology Dr
Irvine CA 92618

(P-4368)
ADVANTAGE MEDIA SERVICES INC
Also Called: AMS Fulfillment
28220 Industry Dr, Valencia (91355-4105)
PHONE..............................661 705-7588
John Bevacqua, *Vice Pres*
EMP: 245
SALES (corp-wide): 62.3MM **Privately Held**
SIC: 4225 General warehousing
PA: Advantage Media Services, Inc.
29010 Commerce Center Dr
Valencia CA 91355
661 775-0611

(P-4369)
ALBERTSONS LLC
Also Called: Albertsons Dist Ctr 8760
777 S Harbor Blvd, La Habra (90631-6800)
PHONE..................................714 578-4670
Tony Vasquez, *Manager*
EMP: 100
SALES (corp-wide): 60.5B **Privately Held**
SIC: 4225 General warehousing & storage
HQ: Albertson's Llc
250 E Parkcenter Blvd
Boise ID 83706
208 395-6200

(P-4370)
ALBERTSONS LLC
Also Called: Albertsons Brea Dist Ctr
200 N Puente St, Brea (92821-3841)
PHONE..................................714 990-8200
Mike Ketcham, *Branch Mgr*
EMP: 1000
SALES (corp-wide): 60.5B **Privately Held**
SIC: 4225 General warehousing & storage
HQ: Albertson's Llc
250 E Parkcenter Blvd
Boise ID 83706
208 395-6200

(P-4371)
ALBERTSONS LLC
Also Called: Albertson's Distribution Ctr
9300 Toledo Way, Irvine (92618-1802)
PHONE..................................949 855-2465
Jim Rollins, *General Mgr*
EMP: 400
SALES (corp-wide): 60.5B **Privately Held**
SIC: 4225 General warehousing & storage
HQ: Albertson's Llc
250 E Parkcenter Blvd
Boise ID 83706
208 395-6200

(P-4372)
AMERIFREIGHT INC
Also Called: Logistics Team
218 Machlin Ct, Walnut (91789-3048)
PHONE..................................909 839-2600
Alan Mao Yang, *President*
Joe Dabbs, *Vice Pres*
EMP: 675
SALES (est): 55.6MM **Privately Held**
SIC: 4225 4731 General warehousing;
freight transportation arrangement

(P-4373)
ARB INC
Also Called: Northern Division
1875 Loveridge Rd, Pittsburg (94565-4110)
P.O. Box 8189 (94565-8189)
PHONE..................................925 432-3649
Donnie Brown, *Branch Mgr*
EMP: 50
SALES (corp-wide): 2.9B **Publicly Held**
WEB: www.arbinc.com
SIC: 4225 1623 3444 General warehous-
ing & storage; pipeline construction; sheet
metalwork
HQ: Arb, Inc.
26000 Commercentre Dr
Lake Forest CA 92630
949 598-9242

(P-4374)
ARDEN-MAYFAIR INC
Arden Group
6191 Peachtree St, Commerce
(90040-4064)
PHONE..................................310 638-2842
Jim Baron, *Manager*
Jim Lowe, *Receiver*
Aldo Malesci, *Business Mgr*
Robert Langley, *Opers Staff*
EMP: 50
SALES (corp-wide): 317MM **Privately
Held**
SIC: 4225 General warehousing
HQ: Arden-Mayfair, Inc.
13833 Freeway Dr
Santa Fe Springs CA 90670
310 638-2842

(P-4375)
BACO REALTY CORPORATION
2071 Camino Ramon, San Ramon
(94583-1378)
PHONE..................................925 275-0100

George Bamburg, *Principal*
EMP: 86
SQ FT: 48,000
SALES (corp-wide): 37.1MM **Privately
Held**
SIC: 4225 Warehousing, self-storage
PA: Baco Realty Corporation
51 Federal St Ste 202
San Francisco CA 94107
415 281-3700

(P-4376)
BIG 5 CORP
Also Called: Big 5 Sporting Goods
6125 Sycamore Canyon Blvd, Riverside
(92507-0712)
PHONE..................................951 774-1600
William Liechty, *Branch Mgr*
EMP: 300 **Publicly Held**
WEB: www.big5sportinggoods.com
SIC: 4225 General warehousing & storage
HQ: Big 5 Corp.
2525 E El Segundo Blvd
El Segundo CA 90245
310 536-0611

(P-4377)
C & B DELIVERY SERVICES
Also Called: Temco
230 Diamond St, Laguna Beach
(92651-3610)
PHONE..................................909 623-4708
Virginia Templeton, *President*
EMP: 85
SQ FT: 91,000
SALES (est): 9.2MM **Privately Held**
SIC: 4225 General warehousing & storage

(P-4378)
C & S WHOLESALE GROCERS INC
8301 Fruitridge Rd, Sacramento
(95826-4806)
PHONE..................................916 383-5275
Ric Clark, *General Mgr*
Frank Currier, *Buyer*
Verseman Roger, *Merchandising*
John Petersen, *Manager*
Kelly Weaver, *Manager*
EMP: 285
SALES (corp-wide): 3.9B **Privately Held**
SIC: 4225 General warehousing
PA: C&S Wholesale Grocers, Inc.
7 Corporate Dr
Keene NH 03431
603 354-7000

(P-4379)
CALIFORNIA SUPER MARKET
Also Called: California Mayoreo-Y-Menudeo
363 W 2nd St, Calexico (92231-2114)
PHONE..................................760 357-3065
Alex Loo Jr, *Manager*
Rita Guzman, *Bookkeeper*
Carlos Cuevas, *Opers-Prdtn-Mfg*
EMP: 61
SALES (corp-wide): 19.9MM **Privately
Held**
SIC: 4225 General warehousing & storage
PA: California Super Market
601 S Imperial Ave
Calexico CA 92231
760 357-6888

(P-4380)
CASAS INTERNATIONAL BRKG INC (PA)
9355 Airway Rd Ste 4, San Diego
(92154-7931)
PHONE..................................619 661-6162
Sylvia Casas, *President*
John Jolliffe, *Vice Pres*
EMP: 100
SQ FT: 120,000
SALES (est): 15.7MM **Privately Held**
WEB: www.casasinternational.com
SIC: 4225 4731 General warehousing;
customhouse brokers; freight forwarding

(P-4381)
CASCADE LOGISTICS LLC
857 Stonebridge Dr, Tracy (95376-2852)
P.O. Box 1157, Brattleboro VT (05302-
1157)
PHONE..................................209 832-4205
James Bringham,

Brian Shaver, *Software Engr*
EMP: 51
SALES (est): 2.2MM
SALES (corp-wide): 3.9B **Privately Held**
WEB: www.es3.com
SIC: 4225 General warehousing & storage
HQ: Es3, Llc
6 Optical Ave
Keene NH 03431
603 354-6100

(P-4382)
CASESTACK LLC (HQ)
Also Called: Casestack, Inc.
3000 Ocean Park Blvd, Santa Monica
(90405-3020)
PHONE..................................310 473-8885
Daniel A Sanker, *President*
Steve Sezna, *COO*
David Isaksen, *CFO*
Colby Beland, *Vice Pres*
Pei-Ching Ling, *Vice Pres*
▲ EMP: 65
SQ FT: 10,000
SALES (est): 52.7MM
SALES (corp-wide): 3.6B **Publicly Held**
WEB: www.casestack.com
SIC: 4225 4731 General warehousing &
storage; freight transportation arrange-
ment
PA: Hub Group, Inc.
2000 Clearwater Dr
Oak Brook IL 60523
630 271-3600

(P-4383)
CAT LOGISTICS INC
Also Called: Caterpillar
5491 E Francis St, Ontario (91761-3604)
PHONE..................................909 390-1920
James Ralston, *Manager*
EMP: 69
SALES (corp-wide): 54.7B **Publicly Held**
SIC: 4225 General warehousing
HQ: C.A.T. Logistics Inc.
500 N Morton Ave
Morton IL 61550
309 675-1000

(P-4384)
CHARLES KOMAR & SONS INC
Also Called: Komar Distribution Services
11850 Riverside Dr, Jurupa Valley
(91752-1001)
PHONE..................................951 934-1377
Lisa Casillas, *Branch Mgr*
EMP: 307
SALES (corp-wide): 260MM **Privately
Held**
WEB: www.komar-ny.com
SIC: 4225 General warehousing & storage
PA: Charles Komar & Sons, Inc.
90 Hudson St Fl 9
Jersey City NJ 07302
212 725-1500

(P-4385)
CHARLIES ENTERPRISES
Also Called: OK Produce
1888 S East Ave, Fresno (93721-3231)
P.O. Box 12838 (93779-2838)
PHONE..................................559 445-8600
Matty Matoian, *President*
Angel Burnett, *Partner*
Kyle Ogan, *Buyer*
Dan Millican, *Sales Mgr*
Richard Ovalle, *Maint Spvr*
EMP: 200
SQ FT: 70,000
SALES (est): 31.1MM **Privately Held**
WEB: www.okproduce.com
SIC: 4225 General warehousing; miniware-
house, warehousing

(P-4386)
CHINO-PACIFIC WAREHOUSE CORP (PA)
Also Called: Pcwc
3601 Jurupa St, Ontario (91761-2905)
PHONE..................................909 545-8100
Jim Marcoly, *President*
David Boras, *CFO*
George Ramirez, *Vice Pres*
David Strawn, *Vice Pres*
Marty Jones, *Programmer Anys*
▲ EMP: 66

SQ FT: 975,000
SALES (est): 17.9MM **Privately Held**
WEB: www.pcwc.com
SIC: 4225 General warehousing

(P-4387)
CITY FIBERS INC
2525 E 25th St, Vernon (90058)
PHONE..................................323 583-1013
David Jones, *Manager*
EMP: 60
SALES (corp-wide): 27.2MM **Privately
Held**
SIC: 4225 General warehousing & storage
PA: City Fibers, Inc.
2500 S Santa Fe Ave
Vernon CA 90058
323 583-1013

(P-4388)
COASTAL PACIFIC FD DISTRS INC (PA)
1015 Performance Dr, Stockton
(95206-4925)
P.O. Box 30910 (95213-0910)
PHONE..................................909 947-2066
Terrence Wood, *CEO*
Jeff King, *COO*
Matthew Payne, *CFO*
John Payne, *Treasurer*
Edmond Jared, *Vice Pres*
◆ EMP: 220
SQ FT: 500,000
SALES: 1.2B **Privately Held**
WEB: www.cpfd.com
SIC: 4225 7519 General warehousing;
trailer rental

(P-4389)
COASTAL PACIFIC FD DISTRS INC
Also Called: Coastal Pacific Foods
1520 E Mission Blvd Ste B, Ontario
(91761-2124)
PHONE..................................909 947-2066
David Jared, *President*
EMP: 150
SALES (corp-wide): 1.2B **Privately Held**
WEB: www.cpfd.com
SIC: 4225 General warehousing & storage
PA: Coastal Pacific Food Distributors, Inc.
1015 Performance Dr
Stockton CA 95206
909 947-2066

(P-4390)
CONCORDE BATTERY CORP
1125 N Azusa Canyon Rd, West Covina
(91790-1002)
PHONE..................................626 813-1234
Donald Godberg, *Principal*
EMP: 115
SALES (corp-wide): 23.3MM **Privately
Held**
WEB: www.concordebattery.com
SIC: 4225 General warehousing & storage
PA: Concorde Battery Corp
2009 W San Bernardino Rd
West Covina CA 91790
626 813-1234

(P-4391)
COSTCO WHOLESALE CORPORATION
Also Called: Costco 179
25382 Schulte Ct, Tracy (95377-8643)
PHONE..................................209 835-5222
EMP: 300
SALES (corp-wide): 152.7B **Publicly
Held**
WEB: www.costco.com
SIC: 4225 General warehousing
PA: Costco Wholesale Corporation
999 Lake Dr Ste 200
Issaquah WA 98027
425 313-8100

(P-4392)
COSTCO WHOLESALE CORPORATION
Also Called: Costco Wholesale Depot
11600 Riverside Dr Ste A, Jurupa Valley
(91752-3700)
PHONE..................................951 361-3606
Stu Bell, *Branch Mgr*

Felix Carrera, *Manager*
EMP: 450
SALES (corp-wide): 152.7B **Publicly Held**
WEB: www.costco.com
SIC: 4225 General warehousing & storage
PA: Costco Wholesale Corporation
999 Lake Dr Ste 200
Issaquah WA 98027
425 313-8100

(P-4393)
CUSTOM GOODS LLC (PA)
1035 E Watson Center Rd, Carson
(90745-4203)
PHONE..................................310 241-6700
Tony Gregory,
Jerry Delamora, *Warehouse Mgr*
Anita Valles, *Warehouse Mgr*
Billy Cathcart,
Alan Oto, *Director*
EMP: 50
SQ FT: 240,000
SALES: 62MM **Privately Held**
WEB: www.custom-goods.com
SIC: 4225 General warehousing

(P-4394)
DALTON TRUCKING INC (PA)
13560 Whittram Ave, Fontana
(92335-2951)
P.O. Box 5025 (92334-5025)
PHONE..................................909 823-0663
Terry Klenske, *CEO*
Mathew Klenske, *Vice Pres*
Matt Kunkel, *Executive*
Eleanor Klenske, *Admin Sec*
EMP: 215
SQ FT: 11,000
SALES: 23.9MM **Privately Held**
SIC: 4225 General warehousing & storage

(P-4395)
DART WAREHOUSE CORPORATION (HQ)
1430 S Eastman Ave Ste 1, Commerce
(90023-4091)
P.O. Box 23931, Los Angeles (90023-0931)
PHONE..................................323 264-1011
Robert Anthony Santich, *CEO*
Raoul Dedeaux, *President*
Ashok Agarwal, *Treasurer*
Steve Roskelley, *Exec VP*
Don Brown, *Vice Pres*
▲ **EMP:** 255 **EST:** 1938
SQ FT: 1,200,000
SALES (est): 70.5MM
SALES (corp-wide): 107.1MM **Privately Held**
WEB: www.dartentities.com
SIC: 4225 General warehousing & storage
PA: Dart Transportation Service, A Corporation
1430 S Eastman Ave Ste 1
Commerce CA 90023
323 981-8205

(P-4396)
DHL SUPPLY CHAIN (USA)
9211 Kaiser Way, Fontana (92335-2600)
PHONE..................................909 350-6976
John Haley, *Branch Mgr*
EMP: 50
SALES (corp-wide): 70.4B **Privately Held**
SIC: 4225 General warehousing
HQ: Exel Inc.
570 Polaris Pkwy
Westerville OH 43082
614 865-8500

(P-4397)
DHL SUPPLY CHAIN (USA)
2391 W Winton Ave, Hayward
(94545-1101)
PHONE..................................510 784-7360
Mario Lombardi, *Branch Mgr*
EMP: 55
SALES (corp-wide): 70.4B **Privately Held**
WEB: www.exel-logistics.com
SIC: 4225 General warehousing
HQ: Exel Inc.
570 Polaris Pkwy
Westerville OH 43082
614 865-8500

(P-4398)
DIGNITY HEALTH
Regional Distribution Center
3400 Data Dr, Rancho Cordova
(95670-7956)
PHONE..................................916 851-3800
Bob Rodda, *Dir Ops-Prd-Mfg*
EMP: 50 **Privately Held**
WEB: www.mercycare.net
SIC: 4225 General warehousing & storage
HQ: Dignity Health
185 Berry St Ste 300
San Francisco CA 94107
415 438-5500

(P-4399)
DISTRIBUTION ALTERNATIVES INC
Also Called: Scholls
1990 S Cucamonga Ave, Ontario
(91761-5605)
PHONE..................................909 673-1000
Mark Chase, *Manager*
EMP: 92
SALES (corp-wide): 89.3MM **Privately Held**
SIC: 4225 7319 General warehousing; distribution of advertising material or sample services
PA: Distribution Alternatives, Inc.
435 Park Ct
Lino Lakes MN 55014
651 636-9167

(P-4400)
DIVERSIFIED TRANSPORT SYSTEMS
3150 S Willow Ave, Fresno (93725-9349)
P.O. Box 2879 (93745-2879)
PHONE..................................559 268-2760
Michael Gambos, *Owner*
EMP: 50
SALES (est): 2.1MM **Privately Held**
SIC: 4225 General warehousing & storage

(P-4401)
DOT PRINTER INC
Also Called: DOT Printer Warehouse
1801 S Standard Ave, Santa Ana
(92707-2465)
PHONE..................................949 752-7730
Jeff Shattuck, *General Mgr*
Roy Vij, *IT/INT Sup*
EMP: 50
SALES (corp-wide): 51.4MM **Privately Held**
WEB: www.dotprinter.com
SIC: 4225 General warehousing
PA: The Dot Printer Inc
2424 Mcgaw Ave
Irvine CA 92614
949 474-1100

(P-4402)
DSC LOGISTICS INC
Also Called: DSC LOGISTICS, INC.
1565 N Macarthur Dr, Tracy (95376-2846)
PHONE..................................209 362-2232
Bob Justice, *Manager*
Kent Sparks, *Opers Mgr*
Laila Belmonte, *Director*
Mitch Furr, *Manager*
EMP: 60
SALES (corp-wide): 355MM **Privately Held**
SIC: 4225 General warehousing & storage
PA: Dsc Logistics, Llc
1750 S Wolf Rd
Des Plaines IL 60018
847 390-6800

(P-4403)
EPSON AMERICA INC
Also Called: Epson West
1650 Glenn Curtiss St, Carson
(90746-4013)
PHONE..................................562 290-5855
Dan Wolsey, *Branch Mgr*
Alan Rupert, *Engineer*
Victor Gomez, *Business Mgr*
Rick Brookshire, *Senior Mgr*
Jason Meyer, *Manager*
EMP: 140 **Privately Held**
WEB: www.presentersonline.com

SIC: 4225 5045 5044 General warehousing & storage; computers, peripherals & software; office equipment
HQ: Epson America Inc
3840 Kilroy Airport Way
Long Beach CA 90806
800 463-7766

(P-4404)
ERLANGER DISTRIBUTION CTR INC
Also Called: Erlanger Sales
797 Palmyrita Ave, Riverside (92507-1811)
PHONE..................................951 784-5147
David Erlanger, *CEO*
Claude M Erlanger, *President*
Doris Erlanger, *Vice Pres*
Steve Erlanger, *Vice Pres*
Maria Calvillo, *Sales Mgr*
▲ **EMP:** 50 **EST:** 1946
SQ FT: 160,000
SALES (est): 8.7MM **Privately Held**
WEB: www.erlangerdc.com
SIC: 4225 5192 5099 5137 General warehousing; books; luggage; handbags

(P-4405)
ES3 LLC
Also Called: Cascade Logistics
857 Stonebridge Dr, Tracy (95376-2852)
PHONE..................................209 832-4205
James Bringham, *Manager*
EMP: 50
SALES (corp-wide): 3.9B **Privately Held**
WEB: www.es3.com
SIC: 4225 General warehousing & storage
HQ: Es3, Llc
6 Optical Ave
Keene NH 03431
603 354-6100

(P-4406)
EXEL INC
Also Called: Exel Reporters & Interpreters
788 W 9th St, San Pedro (90731-3602)
P.O. Box 6160 (90734-6160)
PHONE..................................310 832-3376
EMP: 64
SALES (corp-wide): 70.4B **Privately Held**
SIC: 4225 General warehousing
HQ: Exel Inc.
570 Polaris Pkwy
Westerville OH 43082
614 865-8500

(P-4407)
F R T INTERNATIONAL INC (PA)
Also Called: Frontier Logistics Services
1700 N Alameda St, Compton
(90222-4128)
PHONE..................................310 604-8208
Brian Chung, *CEO*
Joyce Chung, *Admin Sec*
◆ **EMP:** 227
SQ FT: 200,000
SALES (est): 27.6MM **Privately Held**
WEB: www.frontier-logistics.com
SIC: 4225 4731 4412 4214 General warehousing; customhouse brokers; deep sea foreign transportation of freight; local trucking with storage

(P-4408)
FARO SERVICES INC
Also Called: Faro Logistics
15625 Shoemaker Ave, Norwalk
(90650-6862)
PHONE..................................562 483-7799
Tim Thomas, *Branch Mgr*
EMP: 102
SALES (est): 5MM **Privately Held**
SIC: 4225 General warehousing & storage
PA: Faro Services, Inc.
7070 Pontius Rd
Groveport OH 43125

(P-4409)
FEDEX SUP CHAIN DIST SYS INC
Also Called: Genco
1670 Champagne Ave, Ontario
(91761-3612)
PHONE..................................909 605-9210
EMP: 50

SALES (corp-wide): 69.6B **Publicly Held**
SIC: 4225 General warehousing & storage
HQ: Fedex Supply Chain Distribution System, Inc.
700 Cranberry Woods Dr
Cranberry Township PA 16066

(P-4410)
FORD MOTOR COMPANY
812 Union St, Montebello (90640-6523)
PHONE..................................323 267-6121
Helmut Nittman, *Manager*
EMP: 225
SALES (corp-wide): 160.3B **Publicly Held**
WEB: www.ford.com
SIC: 4225 General warehousing & storage
PA: Ford Motor Company
1 American Rd
Dearborn MI 48126
313 322-3000

(P-4411)
FTDI WEST INC
3375 Enterprise Dr, Bloomington
(92316-3539)
PHONE..................................909 473-1111
Alan Baum, *President*
Steve Rocha, *Vice Pres*
EMP: 80
SALES: 11MM **Privately Held**
SIC: 4225 Warehousing, self-storage

(P-4412)
G3 ENTERPRISES INC (PA)
502 E Whitmore Ave, Modesto
(95358-9411)
P.O. Box 624 (95353-0624)
PHONE..................................209 341-7515
Robert Lubeck, *President*
Stephanie Hardy, *Partner*
Michael Ellis, *CFO*
Steven Anderson, *Vice Pres*
Thomas Gallo, *Vice Pres*
▲ **EMP:** 160 **EST:** 1961
SQ FT: 10,000
SALES (est): 106.8MM **Privately Held**
SIC: 4225 General warehousing & storage

(P-4413)
GENERAL MOTORS LLC
9150 Hermosa Ave, Rancho Cucamonga
(91730-5304)
PHONE..................................800 521-7300
Mark Smith, *Branch Mgr*
Patrick Yau, *Sr Software Eng*
EMP: 141 **Publicly Held**
SIC: 4225 General warehousing & storage
HQ: General Motors Llc
300 Renaissance Ctr L1
Detroit MI 48243

(P-4414)
GENERAL MOTORS LLC
11900 Cabernet Dr Dr1, Fontana
(92337-7707)
PHONE..................................951 361-6302
EMP: 80 **Publicly Held**
SIC: 4225
HQ: General Motors Llc
300 Renaissance Ctr L1
Detroit MI 48243

(P-4415)
GENERATIONAL PROPERTIES INC
3141 E 44th St, Vernon (90058-2405)
PHONE..................................323 583-3163
Angelo V Antoci, *Principal*
Sam Perricone, *Admin Sec*
EMP: 291 **EST:** 1950
SQ FT: 4,000
SALES (est): 26.9MM **Privately Held**
WEB: www.usgrowers.com
SIC: 4225 General warehousing & storage

(P-4416)
GENESIS LOGISTICS INC
4013 Whipple Rd, Union City (94587-1521)
PHONE..................................510 476-0790
Scott Mullins, *General Mgr*
Aran Kahn, *Executive*
EMP: 70

SQ FT: 37,000
SALES (est): 6.7MM
SALES (corp-wide): 70.4B **Privately Held**
WEB: www.genesislogistics.net
SIC: **4225** General warehousing & storage
HQ: Exel Inc.
570 Polaris Pkwy
Westerville OH 43082
614 865-8500

(P-4417)
GEODIS LOGISTICS LLC
301 W Walnut St, Compton (90220-5219)
PHONE..................................310 604-8185
Robert Sanders, *Branch Mgr*
EMP: 88
SALES (corp-wide): 4.2MM **Privately Held**
SIC: **4225** General warehousing & storage
HQ: Geodis Logistics Llc
7101 Executive Center Dr # 333
Brentwood TN 37027
615 401-6400

(P-4418)
GEODIS LOGISTICS LLC
Also Called: Ohl
2301 W San Bernardino Ave, Redlands (92374-5007)
PHONE..................................909 801-3145
Jim Moynihan, *Branch Mgr*
EMP: 83
SALES (corp-wide): 4.2MM **Privately Held**
SIC: **4225** General warehousing
HQ: Geodis Logistics Llc
7101 Executive Center Dr # 333
Brentwood TN 37027
615 401-6400

(P-4419)
GEODIS LOGISTICS LLC
1710 W Base Line Rd, Rialto (92376-3015)
PHONE..................................909 240-6298
EMP: 90
SALES (corp-wide): 4.2MM **Privately Held**
SIC: **4225** General warehousing & storage
HQ: Geodis Logistics Llc
7101 Executive Center Dr # 333
Brentwood TN 37027
615 401-6400

(P-4420)
GEODIS LOGISTICS LLC
Also Called: Stila Styles
3285 De Forest Cir, Jurupa Valley (91752-3239)
PHONE..................................951 571-2481
Ozburn Hholdin, *Branch Mgr*
Jane Jones, *General Mgr*
EMP: 60
SALES (corp-wide): 4.2MM **Privately Held**
SIC: **4225** General warehousing & storage
HQ: Geodis Logistics Llc
7101 Executive Center Dr # 333
Brentwood TN 37027
615 401-6400

(P-4421)
GOLDEN EAGLE MOVING SVCS INC
1450 N Benson Ave Unit B, Upland (91786-2127)
PHONE..................................909 946-7655
Robert Johnson, *President*
Thomas Johnson Jr, *CFO*
Constance Johnson, *Vice Pres*
EMP: 55
SQ FT: 50,000
SALES: 6.2MM **Privately Held**
WEB: www.goldeneaglemoving.com
SIC: **4225** 4214 General warehousing & storage; household goods moving & storage, local

(P-4422)
GOODWIN AMMONIA COMPANY
Also Called: The Goodwin Company
12361 Monarch St, Garden Grove (92841-2908)
PHONE..................................714 894-0531
Tom Goodwin, *President*
EMP: 100

SALES (corp-wide): 31.9MM **Privately Held**
SIC: **4225** General warehousing & storage
PA: The Goodwin Ammonia Company
12102 Industry St
Garden Grove CA 92841
714 894-0531

(P-4423)
GRIFOLS BIOLOGICALS LLC
2410 Lillyvale Ave, Los Angeles (90032-3514)
PHONE..................................323 255-2221
Edward Colton, *CEO*
EMP: 350
SALES (corp-wide): 741MM **Privately Held**
WEB: www.alphather.com
SIC: **4225** 8731 3085 2836 General warehousing & storage; commercial physical research; plastics bottles; biological products, except diagnostic
HQ: Grifols Biologicals Llc
2410 Lillyvale Ave
Los Angeles CA 90032
323 225-2221

(P-4424)
GRUPE PROPERTIES CO
Also Called: Executive Living Apartments
2944 W Swain Rd, Stockton (95219-3917)
P.O. Box 7576 (95267-0576)
PHONE..................................209 956-7885
Michael V Clark, *President*
EMP: 50
SQ FT: 1,000
SALES (est): 2.2MM
SALES (corp-wide): 86.7MM **Privately Held**
WEB: www.grupe.com
SIC: **4225** Warehousing, self-storage
PA: The Grupe Company
3255 W March Ln Ste 400
Stockton CA 95219
209 473-6000

(P-4425)
GUITAR CENTER HOLDINGS INC
Also Called: Guitar Center Store Wcdc
1508 W Casmalia St, Rialto (92377-4300)
PHONE..................................818 735-8800
Ohn Van Steenwyk, *Branch Mgr*
EMP: 50
SQ FT: 220,000 **Privately Held**
SIC: **4225** General warehousing & storage
PA: Guitar Center Holdings, Inc.
5795 Lindero Canyon Rd
Westlake Village CA 91362

(P-4426)
H RAUVEL INC (PA)
Also Called: Nova Container Freight Station
1710 E Sepulveda Blvd, Carson (90745-6142)
PHONE..................................310 604-0060
Hector R Velasco, *President*
Mike Lee, *Info Tech Mgr*
Vicky Ruste, *Manager*
Lori Jennings, *Supervisor*
EMP: 70
SQ FT: 258,000
SALES (est): 33.8MM **Privately Held**
WEB: www.novafreight.net
SIC: **4225** 4731 General warehousing; agents, shipping; brokers, shipping; freight consolidation; railroad freight agency

(P-4427)
HARTE HANKS INC
2337 W Commonwealth Ave, Fullerton (92833-2997)
PHONE..................................210 829-9000
Maria Koebel, *Manager*
EMP: 100
SALES (corp-wide): 284.6MM **Publicly Held**
SIC: **4225** 7389 7374 General warehousing; telemarketing services; calculating service (computer)
PA: Harte Hanks, Inc.
9601 Mcallister Fwy # 610
San Antonio TX 78216
210 829-9000

(P-4428)
HAULAWAY STORAGE CNTRS INC
11292 Western Ave, Stanton (90680-2912)
P.O. Box 125 (90680-0125)
PHONE..................................800 826-9040
Clifford Robert Ronnenberg, *CEO*
Daniel Letto, *President*
Joyce Amato, *CFO*
Dwayne Bartel, *General Mgr*
John Boyle, *Manager*
EMP: 922
SALES (est): 8.7MM
SALES (corp-wide): 133.1MM **Privately Held**
SIC: **4225** General warehousing & storage
PA: Cr&R Incorporated
11292 Western Ave
Stanton CA 90680
714 826-9049

(P-4429)
HAYWARD AREA RECREATION PKDIST
Also Called: Corporate Yard
1099 E St Rear, Hayward (94541-5210)
PHONE..................................510 881-6750
Eric Willyerd, *Superintendent*
EMP: 65
SALES (corp-wide): 46.9MM **Privately Held**
SIC: **4225** General warehousing & storage
PA: Hayward Area Recreation & Pk.Dist
1099 E St
Hayward CA 94541
510 670-1665

(P-4430)
HOME DEPOT USA INC
Also Called: Home Depot, The
11650 Venture Dr, Jurupa Valley (91752-3209)
PHONE..................................951 361-1235
John Lawson, *Branch Mgr*
EMP: 190
SALES (corp-wide): 108.2B **Publicly Held**
WEB: www.homerentalsdepot.com
SIC: **4225** General warehousing & storage
HQ: Home Depot U.S.A., Inc.
2455 Paces Ferry Ave
Atlanta GA 30339

(P-4431)
HOME DEPOT USA INC
Also Called: Home Depot, The
18300 S Harlan Rd, Lathrop (95330-8765)
PHONE..................................209 858-9243
EMP: 72
SALES (corp-wide): 108.2B **Publicly Held**
WEB: www.homerentalsdepot.com
SIC: **4225** General warehousing & storage
HQ: Home Depot U.S.A., Inc.
2455 Paces Ferry Ave
Atlanta GA 30339

(P-4432)
HOUDINI INC
6311 Knott Ave, Buena Park (90620-1021)
PHONE..................................714 228-4406
EMP: 125
SALES (corp-wide): 71.8MM **Privately Held**
SIC: **4225**
PA: Houdini, Inc.
4225 N Palm St
Fullerton CA 92835
714 525-0325

(P-4433)
HOWARDS APPLIANCES INC
Also Called: Howards Warehouse & Svc Ctr
5102 Industry Ave, Pico Rivera (90660-2504)
PHONE..................................626 288-4010
Rudy Rodriquez, *Branch Mgr*
EMP: 69
SQ FT: 173,100
SALES (corp-wide): 39.8MM **Privately Held**
SIC: **4225** 5722 General warehousing; electric household appliances, major

PA: Howard's Appliances, Inc.
901 E Imperial Hwy
La Habra CA 90631
714 871-2700

(P-4434)
J C PENNEY PURCHASING CORP
700 Darcy Pkwy, Lathrop (95330-8755)
PHONE..................................209 858-9463
EMP: 115
SALES (corp-wide): 12B **Publicly Held**
SIC: **4225** General warehousing & storage
HQ: J. C. Penney Purchasing Corporation
6501 Legacy Dr
Plano TX 75024
972 431-1000

(P-4435)
J G HADDY SALES CO INC (PA)
3401 Etiwanda Ave, Jurupa Valley (91752-1128)
P.O. Box 248, Mira Loma (91752-0248)
PHONE..................................951 685-4100
Joseph G Haddy, *President*
William J Smerber, *Corp Secy*
James E Ford, *Vice Pres*
▲ **EMP:** 121 **EST:** 1971
SALES (est): 10.5MM **Privately Held**
SIC: **4225** 4213 4212 General warehousing & storage; trucking, except local; local trucking, without storage

(P-4436)
J T R COMPANY INC
Also Called: Area Distributing Company
1102 S 3rd St, San Jose (95112-5918)
P.O. Box 8589 (95155-8589)
PHONE..................................408 293-3272
Josephine Ryan, *Manager*
EMP: 50
SALES (corp-wide): 41.9MM **Privately Held**
WEB: www.jtrsport.com
SIC: **4225** General warehousing & storage
PA: J. T. R. Company, Inc.
1102 S 3rd St
San Jose CA 95112
408 975-7733

(P-4437)
JAM INDUSTRIES INC
Also Called: Jam Warehouse
2101 E Via Arado, Compton (90220-6113)
PHONE..................................310 254-0300
Mautiscio Enriques, *Manager*
EMP: 80
SALES (corp-wide): 17.8MM **Privately Held**
WEB: www.jamwarehouse.com
SIC: **4225** General warehousing & storage
PA: J.A.M. Industries, Inc.
13605 Cimarron Ave
Gardena CA
310 532-4526

(P-4438)
JAVELIN LOGISTICS COMPANY INC
7025 Central Ave, Newark (94560-4201)
PHONE..................................800 577-1060
Malcolm Winspear, *President*
Michael Sacrey, *General Mgr*
EMP: 225
SALES (est): 2.7MM **Privately Held**
SIC: **4225** General warehousing & storage

(P-4439)
K K W TRUCKING INC (PA)
3100 Pomona Blvd, Pomona (91768-3230)
P.O. Box 2960 (91769-2960)
PHONE..................................909 869-1200
Dennis W Firestone, *CEO*
Lynnette Brown, *CFO*
Susan Dancel, *Office Mgr*
Heather Hess, *Asst Controller*
Natalya Lacy, *Accountant*
EMP: 350
SQ FT: 150,000
SALES (est): 88.7MM **Privately Held**
SIC: **4225** 4231 4226 4214 General warehousing & storage; trucking terminal facilities; special warehousing & storage; local trucking with storage

PRODUCTS & SVCS

(P-4440)
KOHLS CORPORATION
890 E Mill St, San Bernardino
(92408-1614)
PHONE...................................909 382-4300
Richard Jones, *Vice Pres*
EMP: 308 **Publicly Held**
SIC: 4225 General warehousing
PA: Kohl's Corporation
    N56w17000 Ridgewood Dr
    Menomonee Falls WI 53051

(P-4441)
KONOIKE-PACIFIC CALIFORNIA INC (HQ)
Also Called: Kpac
1420 Coil Ave, Wilmington (90744-2205)
PHONE...................................310 518-1000
Bob Smola, *President*
Ulises Sam, *CFO*
Wayne Lamb, *Vice Pres*
Tamio Nanase, *Vice Pres*
Yutaka Kane Urabe, *Vice Pres*
◆ EMP: 65
SQ FT: 784,080
SALES (est): 26.7MM **Privately Held**
SIC: 4225 General warehousing & storage

(P-4442)
LINDA PLACENTIA-YORBA
Also Called: District Warehouse
1301 E Orangethorpe Ave, Placentia
(92870-5302)
PHONE...................................714 985-8775
EMP: 69
SALES (corp-wide): 323.9MM **Privately Held**
SIC: 4225 General warehousing
PA: Placentia-Yorba Linda Unified School District
    1301 E Orangethorpe Ave
    Placentia CA 92870
    714 986-7000

(P-4443)
LOCKHEED MARTIN CORPORATION
Also Called: Rotary and Miission Systems
South Loop Bldg 821, Fort Irwin (92310)
PHONE...................................760 386-2572
Kurt Pinkerton, *Manager*
EMP: 142 **Publicly Held**
SIC: 4225 General warehousing & storage
PA: Lockheed Martin Corporation
    6801 Rockledge Dr
    Bethesda MD 20817

(P-4444)
LONG BEACH CMNTY COLLEGE DST
Also Called: Long Beach City College Whse
1855 Walnut Ave, Long Beach
(90806-5724)
PHONE...................................562 938-4291
John Peterson, *Branch Mgr*
EMP: 1093
SALES (corp-wide): 100.9MM **Privately Held**
SIC: 4225 8222 General warehousing & storage; community college
PA: Long Beach Community College District
    4901 E Carson St
    Long Beach CA 90808
    562 938-5020

(P-4445)
M BLOCK & SONS INC
26875 Pioneer Ave, Redlands
(92374-2026)
PHONE...................................909 335-6684
Ken Oliveira, *Branch Mgr*
EMP: 200
SALES (corp-wide): 286.6MM **Privately Held**
SIC: 4225 General warehousing
PA: M. Block & Sons, Inc.
    5020 W 73rd St
    Bedford Park IL 60638
    708 728-8400

(P-4446)
MAGNELL ASSOCIATE INC
Also Called: ABS Computer Technologies
9997 Rose Hills Rd, Whittier (90601-1701)
PHONE...................................626 271-1420
Brian Cheng, *Branch Mgr*
EMP: 200
SALES (corp-wide): 2B **Privately Held**
SIC: 4225 General warehousing
HQ: Magnell Associate, Inc.
    17560 Rowland St
    City Of Industry CA 91748
    626 271-9700

(P-4447)
MARUCHAN INC
15800 Laguna Canyon Rd, Irvine
(92618-3103)
PHONE...................................949 789-2300
Tom Yoshimora, *General Mgr*
EMP: 100
SQ FT: 90,200 **Privately Held**
WEB: www.maruchaninc.com
SIC: 4225 General warehousing & storage
HQ: Maruchan, Inc.
    15800 Laguna Canyon Rd
    Irvine CA 92618
    949 789-2300

(P-4448)
MCR PRINTING AND PACKG CORP
8830 Siempre Viva Rd, San Diego
(92154-6278)
PHONE...................................619 488-3012
Edgar Perez, *Human Resources*
EMP: 170
SALES (corp-wide): 26.7MM **Privately Held**
SIC: 4225 General warehousing
PA: Mcr Printing And Packaging, Corp.
    15630 Timberidge Ln
    Chino Hills CA 91709
    619 488-3169

(P-4449)
MEIKO AMERICA INC
Also Called: American Honda
12300 Riverside Dr, Eastvale (91752-1006)
PHONE...................................951 360-0281
Mike Sole, *Branch Mgr*
EMP: 63 **Privately Held**
WEB: www.meikoamerica.com
SIC: 4225 General warehousing
HQ: Meiko America, Inc.
    19600 Magellan Dr
    Torrance CA 90502
    310 483-7400

(P-4450)
MICHAELS STORES INC
Also Called: Warehouse
3501 W Avenue H, Lancaster
(93536-8341)
PHONE...................................661 951-3500
John Vilotta, *General Mgr*
EMP: 200
SALES (corp-wide): 5.2B **Publicly Held**
WEB: www.michaels.com
SIC: 4225 General warehousing & storage
HQ: Michaels Stores, Inc.
    8000 Bent Branch Dr
    Irving TX 75063
    972 409-1300

(P-4451)
MIDAS EXPRESS LOS ANGELES INC
11854 Alameda St, Lynwood (90262-4019)
PHONE...................................310 609-0366
Jack Wu, *President*
Jacky Strong, *Shareholder*
▲ EMP: 200
SQ FT: 90,000
SALES (est): 18.4MM **Privately Held**
WEB: www.midasexpress.com
SIC: 4225 4731 4226 General warehousing & storage; freight forwarding; textile warehousing

(P-4452)
MITSUBISHI WAREHOUSE CAL CORP
3040 E Victoria St, Compton (90221-5617)
PHONE...................................310 886-5500

Soichiro Sam Orihara, *President*
EMP: 100
SQ FT: 750,000
SALES (est): 10.4MM **Privately Held**
WEB: www.mwc-corp.com
SIC: 4225 General warehousing
PA: Mitsubishi Logistics Corporation
    1-19-1, Nihombashi
    Chuo-Ku TKY 103-0

(P-4453)
MOTIVATIONAL MARKETING INC
Also Called: Motivational Fulfillmen
15785 Mountain Ave, Chino (91708-9131)
PHONE...................................909 517-2200
Hal Altman, *President*
Anthony Altman, *Principal*
Melanie Altman, *Principal*
Andrea Stuhley, *Principal*
EMP: 234
SQ FT: 50,500 **Privately Held**
SIC: 4225 General warehousing & storage
PA: Motivational Marketing, Inc.
    15820 Euclid Ave
    Chino CA 91708

(P-4454)
MOULTON LOGISTICS MANAGEMENT (PA)
7855 Hayvenhurst Ave, Van Nuys
(91406-1712)
P.O. Box 8191 (91409-8191)
PHONE...................................818 997-1800
Aj Khubani, *CEO*
Lawrence Moulton, *President*
Patrick Moulton, *Vice Pres*
Tom Moulton, *Vice Pres*
Elaine Sanders, *Telecom Exec*
◆ EMP: 100 EST: 1968
SALES (est): 21.6MM **Privately Held**
WEB: www.moultonlogistics.com
SIC: 4225 4822 General warehousing & storage; electronic mail

(P-4455)
MRS GOCHS NATURAL FD MKTS INC
711 University Ave, San Diego
(92103-3202)
PHONE...................................619 294-2800
Dave Sanders, *Manager*
Connie Powers, *Purch Agent*
EMP: 140 **Publicly Held**
SIC: 4225 General warehousing & storage
HQ: Mrs. Gooch's Natural Food Markets, Inc.
    207 N Goode Ave Fl 7
    Glendale CA 91203
    858 642-6700

(P-4456)
MSBLOUS LLC
11671 Dayton Dr, Rancho Cucamonga
(91730-5526)
PHONE...................................909 929-9689
Jiayi CU, *Manager*
EMP: 96
SALES (corp-wide): 400K **Privately Held**
SIC: 4225 General warehousing & storage
PA: Msblous Llc
    8 The Grn Ste 7360
    Dover DE 19901
    909 908-1889

(P-4457)
NAVY EXCHANGE SERVICE COMMAND
4250 Eucalyptus Ave, Chino (91710-9704)
PHONE...................................909 517-2640
Ron Patel, *Manager*
EMP: 155 **Publicly Held**
WEB: www.navy-nex.com
SIC: 4225 9711 General warehousing & storage; Navy;
HQ: Navy Exchange Service Command
    3280 Virginia Beach Blvd
    Virginia Beach VA 23452
    757 631-3696

(P-4458)
NETWORK GLOBAL LOGISTICS LLC
Also Called: NGL
13479 Valley Blvd, Fontana (92335-5245)
PHONE...................................888 285-7447
EMP: 139
SALES (corp-wide): 200.1MM **Privately Held**
SIC: 4225 4214 General warehousing & storage; local trucking with storage
PA: Network Global Logistics, Llc
    320 Interlocken Pkwy # 100
    Broomfield CO 80021
    866 938-1870

(P-4459)
NISSAN NORTH AMERICA INC
3939 N Freeway Blvd, Sacramento
(95834-1217)
PHONE...................................916 920-4712
Mariano Loria, *General Mgr*
EMP: 51 **Privately Held**
WEB: www.nissan-na.com
SIC: 4225 General warehousing
HQ: Nissan North America Inc
    1 Nissan Way
    Franklin TN 37067
    615 725-1000

(P-4460)
NOR-CAL PRODUCE INC
2995 Oates St, West Sacramento
(95691-5902)
P.O. Box 980188 (95798-0188)
PHONE...................................916 373-0830
Todd Achondo, *CEO*
▼ EMP: 130
SQ FT: 85,000
SALES (est): 18.4MM **Publicly Held**
WEB: www.nor-calproduce.com
SIC: 4225 General warehousing & storage
PA: United Natural Foods, Inc.
    313 Iron Horse Way
    Providence RI 02908

(P-4461)
NORDSTROM INC
1600 S Milliken Ave, Ontario (91761-2301)
PHONE...................................909 390-1040
Pat Smith, *Manager*
EMP: 300
SALES (corp-wide): 15.8B **Publicly Held**
WEB: www.nordstrom.com
SIC: 4225 4226 General warehousing & storage; special warehousing & storage
PA: Nordstrom, Inc.
    1617 6th Ave
    Seattle WA 98101
    206 628-2111

(P-4462)
NORTH BAY DISTRIBUTION INC (PA)
2050 Cessna Dr, Vacaville (95688-8712)
PHONE...................................707 452-9984
Lee Perry, *President*
Riza Suma, *Vice Pres*
Phoebe Nguyen, *Controller*
Greg Cioffi, *VP Opers*
Diane Ruud, *Director*
EMP: 100
SQ FT: 220,000
SALES: 40MM **Privately Held**
WEB: www.northbaydistribution.net
SIC: 4225 General warehousing

(P-4463)
NUGGET MARKET INC
Also Called: Nugget Mkts Pharmacy
157 Main St, Woodland (95695-3163)
PHONE...................................530 662-5479
Ray Munoz, *Manager*
EMP: 120
SALES (corp-wide): 311.5MM **Privately Held**
WEB: www.nuggetmarket.com
SIC: 4225 5411 5912 5461 General warehousing; grocery stores; drug stores & proprietary stores; bakeries
PA: Nugget Market Inc.
    168 Court St
    Woodland CA 95695
    530 669-3300

▲ = Import ▼=Export
◆ =Import/Export

(P-4464)
OAKLEY INC
Also Called: Luxottica
11296 Harrell, Ontario (91761)
PHONE..............................951 685-0038
Jim Genard, *Branch Mgr*
Erik Searles, *Vice Pres*
David Sferrella, *Software Dev*
Duane Lee, *Design Engr*
Eric Strobel, *Project Mgr*
EMP: 65
SALES (corp-wide): 1.4MM Privately
Held
WEB: www.oakley.com
SIC: 4225 General warehousing
HQ: Oakley, Inc.
1 Icon
Foothill Ranch CA 92610
949 951-0991

(P-4465)
OFFICEMAX INCORPORATED
7300 Chapman Ave, Garden Grove
(92841-2105)
PHONE..............................951 485-9353
Harry Goodman, *Admin Sec*
Nicole Rasic, *Business Dir*
Ted Walter, *Opers Mgr*
Julie Cade, *Manager*
Jane Neubert, *Manager*
EMP: 82
SALES (corp-wide): 11B Publicly Held
SIC: 4225 5112 5021 General warehous-
ing & storage; stationery & office supplies;
furniture
HQ: Officemax Incorporated
6600 N Military Trl
Boca Raton FL 33496
630 438-7800

(P-4466)
PACIFIC CYCLE INC
Also Called: Pacific Cycle P Finished Goods
9282 Pittsburgh Ave, Rancho Cucamonga
(91730-5516)
PHONE..............................909 481-5613
EMP: 50
SALES (corp-wide): 2.6B Privately Held
WEB: www.pacific-cycle.com
SIC: 4225 General warehousing & storage
HQ: Pacific Cycle Inc.
4902 Hammersley Rd
Madison WI 53711
608 268-2468

(P-4467)
PANAMA-BUENA VISTA UN SCHL DST
Also Called: Purchasing & Warehouse
4200 Ashe Rd, Bakersfield (93313-2029)
PHONE..............................661 831-7879
Kip Hearron, *Manager*
EMP: 89
SALES (corp-wide): 214.5MM Privately
Held
SIC: 4225 7389 General warehousing;
purchasing service
PA: Panama-Buena Vista Union School
District
4200 Ashe Rd
Bakersfield CA 93313
661 831-8331

(P-4468)
PATINA FREIGHT INC
Also Called: Dura Freight Lines
525 S Lemon Ave, Walnut (91789-2912)
PHONE..............................909 444-1025
Clint Schaffer, *Manager*
EMP: 110
SALES (corp-wide): 32.8MM Privately
Held
SIC: 4225 General warehousing
PA: Patina Freight, Inc.
20405 Business Pkwy
Walnut CA 91789
909 595-8100

(P-4469)
PERFORMANCE TEAM FRT SYS INC
Also Called: PERFORMANCE TEAM
FREIGHT SYSTEM, INC.
12816 Shoemaker Ave, Santa Fe Springs
(90670-6346)
PHONE..............................562 741-1300
Bob Kaplan, *Branch Mgr*
Tom Wilkinson, *Vice Pres*
Brian Briggs, *Opers Dir*
Art Chavarin, *Opers Dir*
Sonya Medlin, *Opers Dir*
EMP: 55
SALES (corp-wide): 382.2MM Privately
Held
SIC: 4225 4731 4213 General warehous-
ing; freight transportation arrangement;
trucking, except local
PA: Performance Team Llc
2240 E Maple Ave
El Segundo CA 90245
562 345-2200

(P-4470)
PERFORMANCE TEAM FRT SYS INC
Also Called: Gale/Triangle
401 Westmont Dr, San Pedro (90731-1011)
PHONE..............................310 241-4100
Scott Pearigan, *Manager*
Susan McHugh, *Admin Asst*
EMP: 120
SALES (corp-wide): 382.2MM Privately
Held
WEB: www.ptgt.net
SIC: 4225 General warehousing
PA: Performance Team Llc
2240 E Maple Ave
El Segundo CA 90245
562 345-2200

(P-4471)
PHYSICAL DISTRIBUTION SVC INC (PA)
16000 Heron Ave, La Mirada (90638-5513)
P.O. Box 60622, Los Angeles (90060-0622)
PHONE..............................323 881-0886
Trygve W Lodrup Jr, *President*
Steven Wheeldon, *Warehouse Mgr*
EMP: 65 EST: 1969
SQ FT: 120,000
SALES (est): 9.4MM Privately Held
SIC: 4225 4214 General warehousing;
local trucking with storage

(P-4472)
PILOT INC (PA)
Also Called: Pilot Automotive
13000 Temple Ave, City of Industry
(91746-1416)
PHONE..............................626 937-6988
Scott Webb, *President*
Martha Gonzalez, *Human Res Mgr*
Aaron Lyle, *Manager*
▼ EMP: 100 EST: 1994
SQ FT: 407,000
SALES (est): 24.6MM Privately Held
WEB: www.pilotautomotive.com
SIC: 4225 5015 General warehousing &
storage; automotive accessories, used

(P-4473)
PRECISE DISTRIBUTION INC
12215 Holly St, Riverside (92509-2315)
PHONE..............................951 367-1037
Debra Catherine Martinez, *CEO*
Levone Myro, *Vice Pres*
Ricardo Cazessus, *Admin Sec*
EMP: 50
SQ FT: 350,000
SALES (est): 9.3MM Privately Held
SIC: 4225 General warehousing & storage

(P-4474)
PREMIUM TRNSP SVCS INC (PA)
Also Called: Ttsi
18735 S Ferris Pl, Rancho Dominguez
(90220-6405)
PHONE..............................310 816-0260
Victor Larosa, *CEO*
Tom Franklin, *CFO*
Bill Allen, *Exec VP*
Pam Reinoehl, *Vice Pres*
Tony Williamson, *Director*

EMP: 58
SQ FT: 10,000
SALES: 53MM Privately Held
SIC: 4225 5399 4212 General warehous-
ing & storage; warehouse club stores;
local trucking, without storage

(P-4475)
PRIORITY 1 WAREHOUSING INC (PA)
2577 W Yosemite Ave, Manteca
(95337-9641)
PHONE..............................209 824-8876
Ron Lanting, *Owner*
James D Van Otterloo, *CFO*
Emma Dirksen, *Admin Sec*
EMP: 65 EST: 1997
SQ FT: 350,000
SALES (est): 5MM Privately Held
SIC: 4225 General warehousing

(P-4476)
PS PARTNERS III LTD
701 Western Ave Ste 200, Glendale
(91201-2349)
PHONE..............................818 244-8080
B Wayne Hughes, *General Ptnr*
EMP: 114
SALES (est): 4.8MM Privately Held
SIC: 4225 Miniwarehouse, warehousing

(P-4477)
PUBLIC STORAGE (PA)
701 Western Ave, Glendale (91201-2349)
PHONE..............................818 244-8080
Ronald L Havner Jr, *Ch of Bd*
Joseph D Russell, *President*
John Reyes, *CFO*
Nathaniel A Vitan, *President*
Vicky Coleman, *Vice Pres*
EMP: 200
SALES: 2.7B Publicly Held
WEB: www.publicstorage.com
SIC: 4225 Miniwarehouse, warehousing;
warehousing, self-storage

(P-4478)
PUBLIC STORAGE PRPTS IV LTD
701 Western Ave, Glendale (91201-2349)
PHONE..............................818 244-8080
Ronald L Havner Jr, *President*
Mark C Good, *COO*
John Reyes, *CFO*
Candace N Krol, *Senior VP*
EMP: 54
SALES: 12.9MM Privately Held
SIC: 4225 Warehousing, self-storage

(P-4479)
PUBLIC STORAGE PRPTS XVIII INC
701 Western Ave Ste 200, Glendale
(91201-2349)
PHONE..............................818 244-8080
B Wayne Hughes, *Ch of Bd*
Harvey Lenkin, *President*
Orben B Gerich, *CFO*
Ronald L Havner Jr, *Vice Pres*
Hugh W Horne, *Vice Pres*
EMP: 100
SALES (est): 3.3MM Privately Held
SIC: 4225 Warehousing, self-storage

(P-4480)
PYRAMID LOGISTICS SERVICES INC (PA)
14650 Hoover St, Westminster
(92683-5346)
PHONE..............................714 903-2600
Timothy J Winningham, *CEO*
Mark Rinehart, *COO*
Tj Winningham, *Treasurer*
Jeannie Rivera, *Executive*
Michael Connolly, *Principal*
▲ EMP: 57
SQ FT: 59,000
SALES (est): 13.4MM Privately Held
SIC: 4225 4731 General warehousing &
storage; foreign freight forwarding

(P-4481)
QUAKER OATS COMPANY
2501 E Orangethorpe Ave, Fullerton
(92831-5333)
PHONE..............................714 526-8800
EMP: 50
SALES (corp-wide): 66.4B Publicly Held
SIC: 4225 5149
HQ: The Quaker Oats Company
555 W Monroe St Fl 1
Chicago IL 60661
312 821-1000

(P-4482)
RALEYS
Also Called: Raleys Distribution Ctr 836
4061 Gateway Park Blvd, Sacramento
(95834-1951)
PHONE..............................916 928-0575
Bob Abel, *Branch Mgr*
EMP: 500
SALES (corp-wide): 2.3B Privately Held
WEB: www.raleys.com
SIC: 4225 General warehousing & storage
PA: Raley's
500 W Capitol Ave
West Sacramento CA 95605
916 373-3333

(P-4483)
RALPHS GROCERY COMPANY
Also Called: Ralphs 00134
211 N Glendale Ave, Glendale
(91206-4455)
PHONE..............................818 549-0035
Peggy Lizarraga, *Branch Mgr*
EMP: 164
SALES (corp-wide): 121.1B Publicly
Held
WEB: www.ralphs.com
SIC: 4225 General warehousing & storage
HQ: Ralphs Grocery Company
1100 W Artesia Blvd
Compton CA 90220

(P-4484)
RALPHS GROCERY COMPANY
4841-45 San Fernando W, Los Angeles
(90039)
PHONE..............................310 637-1101
Larry Cooper, *Vice Pres*
EMP: 700
SQ FT: 275,000
SALES (corp-wide): 121.1B Publicly
Held
SIC: 4225 General warehousing & storage
HQ: Ralphs Grocery Company
1100 W Artesia Blvd
Compton CA 90220

(P-4485)
RALPHS GROCERY COMPANY
Also Called: Food 4 Less
13525 Lakewood Blvd, Downey
(90242-5229)
PHONE..............................562 633-0830
Dave Dopson, *Director*
EMP: 75
SALES (corp-wide): 121.1B Publicly
Held
WEB: www.ralphs.com
SIC: 4225 4212 General warehousing &
storage; local trucking, without storage
HQ: Ralphs Grocery Company
1100 W Artesia Blvd
Compton CA 90220

(P-4486)
RALPHS GROCERY COMPANY
Also Called: Ralphs 6
17840 Ventura Blvd, Encino (91316-3615)
PHONE..............................818 345-6882
Jim Sanders, *Manager*
EMP: 135
SQ FT: 37,059
SALES (corp-wide): 121.1B Publicly
Held
WEB: www.ralphs.com
SIC: 4225 General warehousing & storage
HQ: Ralphs Grocery Company
1100 W Artesia Blvd
Compton CA 90220

(P-4487)
RALPHS GROCERY COMPANY
Also Called: Ralphs 00173
9200 Lakewood Blvd, Downey
(90240-2909)
PHONE..................562 869-2042
Fernando Ortiz, *Manager*
EMP: 62
SALES (corp-wide): 121.1B **Publicly
Held**
WEB: www.ralphs.com
SIC: 4225 General warehousing & storage
HQ: Ralphs Grocery Company
1100 W Artesia Blvd
Compton CA 90220

(P-4488)
RALPHS GROCERY COMPANY
Also Called: Ralphs 96
160 N Lake Ave, Pasadena (91101-1836)
PHONE..................626 793-7480
Chuck Hamman, *Manager*
EMP: 100
SALES (corp-wide): 121.1B **Publicly
Held**
WEB: www.ralphs.com
SIC: 4225 General warehousing & storage
HQ: Ralphs Grocery Company
1100 W Artesia Blvd
Compton CA 90220

(P-4489)
RAS MANAGEMENT INC (PA)
Also Called: Aaaaa Rent-A-Space
4545 Crow Canyon Pl, Castro Valley
(94552-4803)
P.O. Box 20385 (94546-8385)
PHONE..................510 727-1800
H James Knuppe, *President*
Barbara Knuppe, *Corp Secy*
David O' Brien, *Manager*
EMP: 50
SQ FT: 6,000
SALES (est): 14.5MM **Privately Held**
SIC: 4225 Warehousing, self-storage

(P-4490)
**REDWOOD VALLEY INDUSTRIAL
PARK**
8800 West Rd, Redwood Valley
(95470-6199)
PHONE..................707 485-8766
Orin Burgess, *President*
EMP: 65
SALES (est): 1.8MM **Privately Held**
SIC: 4225 General warehousing

(P-4491)
RITE AID DRUG PALACE INC
1755 E Beamer St, Woodland
(95776-6204)
PHONE..................530 661-1800
Don Holmes, *Branch Mgr*
Rory Kaiser, *Maintence Staff*
EMP: 50
SALES (corp-wide): 21.6B **Publicly Held**
SIC: 4225 5122 General warehousing &
storage; drugs, proprietaries & sundries
HQ: Rite Aid Drug Palace, Inc.
30 Hunter Ln
Camp Hill PA 17011

(P-4492)
RK LOGISTICS GROUP INC (PA)
41707 Christy St, Fremont (94538-4195)
P.O. Box 610670, San Jose (95161-0670)
PHONE..................408 942-8107
Rodney F Kalune, *President*
Rock Magnan, *Officer*
Kip Shepard, *Vice Pres*
Tennisha Traver, *Vice Pres*
Victoria Jones, *Finance*
EMP: 79 EST: 1983
SQ FT: 180,000
SALES (est): 29MM **Privately Held**
WEB: www.rkgllc.com
SIC: 4225 8742 4214 General warehous-
ing & storage; transportation consultant;
local trucking with storage

(P-4493)
ROADEX AMERICA INC
1515 W 178th St, Gardena (90248-3203)
PHONE..................310 878-9800
Nicholas Sim, *President*
Rob Chan, *CFO*
Russle Loh, *Vice Pres*
Johnny Kwan, *Principal*
Derek Wong, *Project Mgr*
▲ EMP: 100
SALES (est): 23MM **Privately Held**
WEB: www.roadexamerica.com
SIC: 4225 5113 4789 General warehous-
ing & storage; industrial & personal serv-
ice paper; cargo loading & unloading
services

(P-4494)
**ROMARK LOGISTICS OF
CALIFORNIA**
13521 Santa Ana Ave Ste A, Fontana
(92337-8243)
PHONE..................909 356-5600
Michael O Conner, *President*
EMP: 75
SQ FT: 320,000
SALES (est): 4.7MM **Privately Held**
SIC: 4225 General warehousing & storage

(P-4495)
**RPM CONSOLIDATED SERVICES
INC (PA)**
1901 Raymer Ave, Fullerton (92833-2512)
PHONE..................714 388-3500
Shawn K Duke, *CEO*
Dan Laporte, *Vice Pres*
Ian Smith, *Admin Asst*
Daniel Powell, *Opers Mgr*
Kevin Jackson, *Manager*
EMP: 100
SQ FT: 15,000
SALES: 63.5MM **Privately Held**
WEB: www.rpmcsi.com
SIC: 4225 4214 General warehousing &
storage; local trucking with storage

(P-4496)
RUSH ORDER INC (PA)
6600 Silacci Way, Gilroy (95020-7019)
PHONE..................408 848-3525
James Chapman, *President*
Doris Kanemura, *Vice Pres*
Ariel Maciel, *Sr Project Mgr*
▲ EMP: 50
SQ FT: 50,000
SALES (est): 10.5MM **Privately Held**
WEB: www.rushorder.com
SIC: 4225 General warehousing & storage

(P-4497)
**SAFEWAY STORES
INCORPORATED**
16900 W Schulte Rd, Tracy (95377-8985)
PHONE..................209 833-4700
Mike Kindy, *Branch Mgr*
Connie Thirionet, *Maintence Staff*
EMP: 315
SALES (corp-wide): 60.5B **Privately Held**
WEB: www.safeway.com
SIC: 4225 General warehousing & storage
HQ: Safeway Stores, Incorporated
5918 Stoneridge Mall Rd
Pleasanton CA 94588
925 467-3000

(P-4498)
**SAN BERNARDINO CITY UNF
SCHOOL**
Also Called: Warehouse
871 N J St, San Bernardino (92411-2831)
PHONE..................909 388-6137
Robert L Foster, *Branch Mgr*
EMP: 76
SALES (corp-wide): 712MM **Privately
Held**
WEB: www.sbcusd.k12.ca.us
SIC: 4225 General warehousing
PA: San Bernardino City Unified School
District
777 N F St
San Bernardino CA 92410
909 381-1100

(P-4499)
**SCHAFER BROS TRNSF PANO
MOVERS (PA)**
Also Called: Schafer Logistics
1981 E 213th St, Carson (90810-1202)
PHONE..................310 835-7231
Gary A Schafer, *President*
Richard W Schafer, *Vice Pres*
Cynthia Villa, *Human Res Mgr*
EMP: 55 EST: 1951
SQ FT: 402,000
SALES: 10.4MM **Privately Held**
WEB: www.schaferbros.com
SIC: 4225 4214 4213 General warehous-
ing; local trucking with storage; heavy
hauling

(P-4500)
SCHNEIDER ELECTRIC USA INC
Also Called: Pelco By Schneider Electric
14725 Monte Vista Ave, Chino
(91710-5732)
PHONE..................909 438-2295
Jessie Ortega, *Director*
EMP: 100
SALES (corp-wide): 177.9K **Privately
Held**
SIC: 4225 General warehousing & storage
HQ: Schneider Electric Usa, Inc.
201 Wshington St Ste 2700
Boston MA 02108
978 975-9600

(P-4501)
**SEABOARD PRODUCE DISTRS
INC**
Also Called: Del Norte Distribution
710 Del Norte Blvd, Oxnard (93030-8963)
PHONE..................805 981-8001
J Woodford Hansen, *President*
Heather Wise, *Controller*
EMP: 64
SALES (corp-wide): 25.2MM **Privately
Held**
SIC: 4225 General warehousing & storage
PA: Seaboard Produce Distributors, Inc.
601 Mountain View Ave
Oxnard CA 93030

(P-4502)
**SIERRA PACIFIC DIST SVCS INC
(PA)**
Also Called: Sierra Pacific Warehouse Group
3731 Finch Rd, Modesto (95357-4143)
PHONE..................209 572-2882
Christopher Murphy, *President*
Michelle Van Artsdalen, *CFO*
Michael J McNulty, *Admin Sec*
Matt Burke, *Engineer*
▲ EMP: 76
SQ FT: 750,000
SALES: 10.9MM **Privately Held**
SIC: 4225 General warehousing

(P-4503)
SKY CHEFS INC
1845 Rollins Rd, Burlingame (94010-2209)
PHONE..................650 652-7886
Dan Joseph, *Branch Mgr*
EMP: 106
SALES (corp-wide): 41B **Privately Held**
SIC: 4225 General warehousing
HQ: Sky Chefs, Inc.
6191 N State Highway 161 # 100
Irving TX 75038
972 793-9000

(P-4504)
**SOUTH COAST TRNSP & DIST
INC (PA)**
Also Called: Western Regional Delivery Svc
1424 S Raymond Ave, Fullerton
(92831-5235)
PHONE..................714 683-2300
Elias Youkhehpaz, *President*
▲ EMP: 100
SALES (est): 13.2MM **Privately Held**
SIC: 4225 General warehousing & storage

(P-4505)
SPACE SYSTEMS/LORAL LLC
1140 Hamilton Ct, Menlo Park
(94025-1425)
PHONE..................650 852-4000

Pat Downey, *Branch Mgr*
EMP: 200
SALES (corp-wide): 2.1B **Publicly Held**
SIC: 4225 General warehousing
HQ: Space Systems/Loral, Llc
3825 Fabian Way
Palo Alto CA 94303
650 852-7320

(P-4506)
**SPROUTS FARMERS MARKET
INC**
280 De Berry St, Colton (92324-4404)
PHONE..................888 577-7688
EMP: 190
SALES (corp-wide): 5.2B **Publicly Held**
SIC: 4225 5411 General warehousing &
storage; grocery stores
PA: Sprouts Farmers Market, Inc.
5455 E High St Ste 111
Phoenix AZ 85054
480 814-8016

(P-4507)
**STATES LOGISTICS SERVICES
INC**
7151 Cate Dr, Buena Park (90621-1881)
PHONE..................714 523-1276
EMP: 133
SALES (corp-wide): 60.6MM **Privately
Held**
SIC: 4225 General warehousing & storage
PA: States Logistics Services, Inc.
5650 Dolly Ave
Buena Park CA 90621
714 521-6520

(P-4508)
**STATES LOGISTICS SERVICES
INC (PA)**
5650 Dolly Ave, Buena Park (90621-1872)
PHONE..................714 521-6520
Daniel Monson, *CEO*
▲ EMP: 140
SQ FT: 900,000
SALES (est): 60.6MM **Privately Held**
WEB: www.stateslogistics.com
SIC: 4225 General warehousing & storage

(P-4509)
**STORQUEST SELF STORAGE
(HQ)**
201 Wilshire Blvd Ste 102, Santa Monica
(90401-1220)
P.O. Box 2034 (90406-2034)
PHONE..................310 451-2130
William Hobin, *Principal*
Tracey Powell, *Store Mgr*
Maria Valverde, *Property Mgr*
Johnnie Greene, *Manager*
EMP: 69
SALES (est): 27.7MM
SALES (corp-wide): 33.9MM **Privately
Held**
SIC: 4225 Warehousing, self-storage
PA: The William Warren Group Inc
201 Wilshire Blvd Ste 102
Santa Monica CA 90401
310 451-2130

(P-4510)
SYNNEX CORPORATION
Also Called: Ontario-Don
3655 E Philadelphia St, Ontario
(91761-2959)
PHONE..................909 923-8900
Edgar Mendez, *Branch Mgr*
Kirk Nesbit, *Vice Pres*
Carlie Eastman, *Sales Staff*
Brandon Lipchek, *Director*
Joni Algary, *Manager*
EMP: 52
SALES (corp-wide): 20B **Publicly Held**
SIC: 4225 General warehousing
PA: Synnex Corporation
44201 Nobel Dr
Fremont CA 94538
510 656-3333

(P-4511)
**TACTICAL LGISTIC SOLUTIONS
INC**
13799 Monte Vista Ave, Chino
(91710-5562)
PHONE..................909 464-2813

▲ = Import ▼=Export
◆ =Import/Export

Abraham Ausch, *Branch Mgr*
Keith Parks, *Opers Staff*
EMP: 65
SALES (corp-wide): 9.7MM **Privately Held**
SIC: 4225 General warehousing
PA: Tactical Logistic Solutions Inc.
1000 Jefferson Ave
Elizabeth NJ 07201
201 809-1222

(P-4512)
TANIMURA & ANTLE INC
761 Commercial Ave, Oxnard
(93030-7233)
PHONE.................805 483-2358
Sergio Romero, *Manager*
EMP: 100
SALES (corp-wide): 750.7MM **Privately Held**
WEB: www.taproduce.com
SIC: 4225 Warehousing, self-storage
PA: Tanimura & Antle Fresh Foods, Inc.
1 Harris Rd
Salinas CA 93908
831 455-2950

(P-4513)
TARGET CORPORATION
Also Called: T.com Ontario Fc T-9479
1505 S Haven Ave, Ontario (91761-2928)
PHONE.................909 937-5500
Jacqueline Yee, *Branch Mgr*
EMP: 177
SALES (corp-wide): 75.3B **Publicly Held**
SIC: 4225 General warehousing & storage
PA: Target Corporation
1000 Nicollet Mall
Minneapolis MN 55403
612 304-6073

(P-4514)
TARGET CORPORATION
14750 Miller Ave, Fontana (92336-1685)
PHONE.................909 355-6000
George Spreiser, *General Mgr*
Peter Donlan, *Sr Project Mgr*
EMP: 446
SALES (corp-wide): 75.3B **Publicly Held**
SIC: 4225 General warehousing & storage
PA: Target Corporation
1000 Nicollet Mall
Minneapolis MN 55403
612 304-6073

(P-4515)
TARGET CORPORATION
2050 E Beamer St, Woodland
(95776-6213)
PHONE.................530 666-3705
Dave Sartin, *Manager*
EMP: 400
SALES (corp-wide): 75.3B **Publicly Held**
WEB: www.target.com
SIC: 4225 General warehousing & storage
PA: Target Corporation
1000 Nicollet Mall
Minneapolis MN 55403
612 304-6073

(P-4516)
TAYLORED SERVICES LLC (DH)
1495 E Locust St, Ontario (91761-4570)
PHONE.................909 510-4800
Jim Deveau, *CEO*
Mark Chamberlain, *Controller*
Steven Aceves, *Opers Spvr*
EMP: 80
SQ FT: 330,000
SALES (est): 27MM
SALES (corp-wide): 30MM **Privately Held**
WEB: www.tpservices.com
SIC: 4225 4731 General warehousing & storage; agents, shipping
HQ: Taylored Services Holdings, Llc
1495 E Locust St
Ontario CA 91761
909 510-4800

(P-4517)
TAYLORED SERVICES HOLDINGS LLC (HQ)
1495 E Locust St, Ontario (91761-4570)
PHONE.................909 510-4800
Bill Butler, *CEO*

Michael Yusko, *CFO*
Chris Kearns, *Exec VP*
Jesse Fernandez, *Opers Staff*
EMP: 80
SQ FT: 330,000
SALES (est): 27MM
SALES (corp-wide): 30MM **Privately Held**
SIC: 4225 General warehousing & storage
PA: Taylored Services Parent Co. Inc.
1495 E Locust St
Ontario CA 91761
909 510-4800

(P-4518)
TONYS EXPRESS INC (PA)
10613 Jasmine St, Fontana (92337-8241)
PHONE.................909 427-8700
George Raluy, *President*
Lorraine Khair, *Corp Secy*
Tony Raluy, *Exec VP*
Ken Fasola, *Vice Pres*
Anthony Raluy, *Vice Pres*
▲ **EMP:** 127
SQ FT: 180,000
SALES (est): 20.5MM **Privately Held**
SIC: 4225 4214 4212 General warehousing & storage; local trucking with storage; local trucking, without storage

(P-4519)
TONYS FINE FOODS (HQ)
3575 Reed Ave, West Sacramento
(95605-1628)
P.O. Box 1501, Broderick (95605-0698)
PHONE.................916 374-4000
Karl Berger, *President*
Steve Dietz, *Vice Pres*
David Nasater, *Technology*
Miranda Voinar, *Buyer*
Tom Robbins, *Sales Staff*
▲ **EMP:** 390
SQ FT: 143,000
SALES (est): 77.5MM **Publicly Held**
WEB: www.tonysfinefoods.com
SIC: 4225 5143 5149 General warehousing & storage; cheese; groceries & related products

(P-4520)
UNIFIED GROCERS INC (DH)
Also Called: Supervalu
5200 Sheila St, Commerce (90040-3906)
P.O. Box 513396, Los Angeles (90051-1396)
PHONE.................323 264-5200
Karla C Robertson, *President*
Bruce H Besanko, *CFO*
Leon Bergmann, *Exec VP*
Greg Vick, *Exec Dir*
John Leonard, *General Mgr*
◆ **EMP:** 550
SQ FT: 344,203
SALES (est): 3.7B **Publicly Held**
SIC: 4225 6331 General warehousing & storage; fire, marine & casualty insurance; workers' compensation insurance
HQ: Supervalu Inc.
11840 Valley View Rd
Eden Prairie MN 55344
952 828-4000

(P-4521)
UNIFIED GROCERS INC
Also Called: U W G Southern California Div
457 E Martin Luther King, Los Angeles
(90011-5650)
PHONE.................323 232-6124
Maurice Ochua, *Branch Mgr*
Julio Ceasar Ramirez, *Transportation*
EMP: 74 **Publicly Held**
SIC: 4225 8742 2051 General warehousing & storage; marketing consulting services; bread, cake & related products
HQ: Unified Grocers, Inc.
5200 Sheila St
Commerce CA 90040
323 264-5200

(P-4522)
UNIFIED GROCERS INC
Also Called: U W G Northern California Div
1990 Piccoli Rd, Stockton (95215-2324)
PHONE.................209 931-1990
Glenn King, *Administration*
EMP: 238 **Publicly Held**

SIC: 4225 5149 4222 General warehousing & storage; groceries & related products; refrigerated warehousing & storage
HQ: Unified Grocers, Inc.
5200 Sheila St
Commerce CA 90040
323 264-5200

(P-4523)
UNIS LLC
19914 S Via Baron, Rancho Dominguez
(90220-6104)
PHONE.................310 747-7388
Omar Garcia, *Branch Mgr*
EMP: 90
SALES (corp-wide): 63.8MM **Privately Held**
SIC: 4225 General warehousing & storage
PA: Unis, Llc
218 Machlin Ct Ste A
Walnut CA 91789
909 839-2600

(P-4524)
UNITED FACILITIES INC
11618 Mulberry Ave, Fontana
(92337-7618)
P.O. Box 559, Peoria IL (61651-0559)
PHONE.................951 685-7030
Kevin Alderson, *Manager*
EMP: 50
SALES (corp-wide): 67.2MM **Privately Held**
WEB: www.unifac.com
SIC: 4225 General warehousing
PA: United Facilities, Inc.
603 N Main St
East Peoria IL 61611
309 699-7271

(P-4525)
UNITED NATURAL FOODS WEST INC (HQ)
Also Called: Unfi
1101 Sunset Blvd, Rocklin (95765-3786)
PHONE.................916 625-4100
Kurt M Luttecke, *CEO*
Michael S Funk, *Ch of Bd*
Steven L Spinner, *President*
Eric A Dorne, *Senior VP*
Sean F Griffin, *Vice Pres*
▲ **EMP:** 385 **EST:** 1976
SQ FT: 150,000
SALES (est): 76.6MM **Publicly Held**
WEB: www.mpwnw.com
SIC: 4225 5141 General warehousing & storage; groceries, general line

(P-4526)
UNIVERSAL PACKG SYSTEMS INC
Also Called: Paklab
14570 Monte Vista Ave, Chino
(91710-5743)
PHONE.................909 517-2442
Rheana Harrison, *Purch Agent*
EMP: 125
SALES (corp-wide): 359.7MM **Privately Held**
SIC: 4225 General warehousing
PA: Universal Packaging Systems, Inc.
380 Townline Rd Ste 130
Hauppauge NY 11788
631 543-2277

(P-4527)
UNIVERSAL SELF STORAGE
25980 Barton Rd, Loma Linda
(92354-3869)
P.O. Box 8008, Newport Beach (92658-8008)
PHONE.................951 206-5263
Rene Jacober, *Managing Prtnr*
EMP: 50
SALES (est): 2.4MM **Privately Held**
SIC: 4225 Warehousing, self-storage

(P-4528)
UNIVERSAL WILKES CO INC (PA)
2899 Agoura Rd Ste 114, City of Industry
(91715)
P.O. Box 90215 (91715-0215)
PHONE.................626 839-2022

Gary Wilkes, *President*
▲ **EMP:** 60 **EST:** 1948
SALES (est): 3.9MM **Privately Held**
WEB: www.universalwarehouses.com
SIC: 4225 General warehousing

(P-4529)
UNIVERSITY CAL SAN FRANCISCO
Materiel Management
616 Forbes Blvd, South San Francisco
(94080-2009)
PHONE.................510 987-0700
Diana Hopper, *Principal*
EMP: 100 **Privately Held**
SIC: 4225 8221 9411 General warehousing & storage; university; administration of educational programs;
HQ: University Cal San Francisco
513 Parnassus Ave 115f
San Francisco CA 94143

(P-4530)
US ELOGISTICS SERVICE CORP
1521 E Francis St, Ontario (91761-8326)
PHONE.................732 357-6665
Hang Feng Wu, *CEO*
EMP: 60
SALES (corp-wide): 14MM **Privately Held**
SIC: 4225 General warehousing & storage
PA: Us Elogistics Service Corp
1100 Cranbury S River Rd
Monroe NJ 08831
732 881-6606

(P-4531)
US ELOGISTICS SERVICE CORP
13725 Pipeline Ave, Chino (91710-5417)
PHONE.................732 881-6606
EMP: 60
SALES (corp-wide): 14MM **Privately Held**
SIC: 4225 General warehousing & storage
PA: Us Elogistics Service Corp
1100 Cranbury S River Rd
Monroe NJ 08831
732 881-6606

(P-4532)
VANGUARD LGISTICS SVCS USA INC (DH)
2665 E Del Amo Blvd, E Rncho Dmngz
(90221-6003)
PHONE.................310 637-3700
Jeff Alinsangan, *Treasurer*
Graham Cousins, *Officer*
Derek Moore, *Vice Pres*
Jenny Koh, *Executive*
Tina Fung, *Controller*
◆ **EMP:** 52
SALES (est): 13.4MM
SALES (corp-wide): 232.2MM **Privately Held**
SIC: 4225 General warehousing & storage
HQ: Vanguard Logistics Services (Usa), Inc.
5000 Arprt Plz Dr Ste 200
Long Beach CA 90815
310 847-3000

(P-4533)
VANGUARD LGISTICS SVCS USA INC
2665 E Del Amo Blvd, Compton
(90221-6003)
PHONE.................310 637-3700
Owen Glenn, *Manager*
EMP: 100
SALES (corp-wide): 232.2MM **Privately Held**
SIC: 4225 4731 General warehousing & storage; freight transportation arrangement
HQ: Vanguard Logistics Services (Usa), Inc.
5000 Arprt Plz Dr Ste 200
Long Beach CA 90815
310 847-3000

(P-4534)
VERIFONE INC
1401 Aviation Blvd, Lincoln (95648-9312)
PHONE.................916 408-4900

P R O D U C T S & S V C S

Darrin Richards, *Manager*
EMP: 100
SALES (corp-wide): 183MM **Privately Held**
SIC: 4225 Warehousing, self-storage
HQ: Verifone, Inc.
88 W Plumeria Dr
San Jose CA 95134
408 232-7800

(P-4535)
VITRAN LOGISTICS INC
1000 S Cucamonga Ave, Ontario (91761-3461)
PHONE..............................909 972-3100
Rick Gaetz, *CEO*
Mike Glodziak, *President*
Joanna Pencak, *Admin Sec*
EMP: 78 **EST:** 2009
SALES (est): 6.5MM **Privately Held**
SIC: 4225 General warehousing

(P-4536)
WALMART INC
13550 Valley Blvd, Fontana (92335-5243)
PHONE..............................909 349-3600
Marcus Lester, *Branch Mgr*
EMP: 477
SALES (corp-wide): 514.4B **Publicly Held**
SIC: 4225 General warehousing & storage
PA: Walmart Inc.
702 Sw 8th St
Bentonville AR 72716
479 273-4000

(P-4537)
WALMART INC
21101 Johnson Rd, Apple Valley (92307-9357)
PHONE..............................760 961-6300
Scott Kubicek, *Manager*
Christopher Santana, *Manager*
EMP: 484
SALES (corp-wide): 514.4B **Publicly Held**
SIC: 4225 General warehousing & storage
PA: Walmart Inc.
702 Sw 8th St
Bentonville AR 72716
479 273-4000

(P-4538)
WALMART INC
10815 Highway 99w, Red Bluff (96080-7747)
PHONE..............................530 529-0916
Darwyn Jones, *Manager*
Debbie Miller, *Executive*
Jamie Rowley, *Department Mgr*
Darla Sweeney, *General Mgr*
EMP: 670
SALES (corp-wide): 514.4B **Publicly Held**
WEB: www.walmartstores.com
SIC: 4225 General warehousing & storage
PA: Walmart Inc.
702 Sw 8th St
Bentonville AR 72716
479 273-4000

(P-4539)
WALMART INC
4250 Hamner Ave, Eastvale (91752-1019)
PHONE..............................951 681-7256
EMP: 450
SALES (corp-wide): 514.4B **Publicly Held**
WEB: www.walmartstores.com
SIC: 4225 General warehousing & storage
PA: Walmart Inc.
702 Sw 8th St
Bentonville AR 72716
479 273-4000

(P-4540)
WALMART INC
1300 S F St, Porterville (93257-5968)
PHONE..............................559 783-1109
Kent Delperdang, *Manager*
EMP: 477
SALES (corp-wide): 514.4B **Publicly Held**
WEB: www.walmartstores.com
SIC: 4225 General warehousing & storage

PA: Walmart Inc.
702 Sw 8th St
Bentonville AR 72716
479 273-4000

(P-4541)
WEBER DISTRIBUTION LLC
1651 California St Ste A, Redlands (92374-2904)
PHONE..............................909 335-8800
Ron Wilson, *Manager*
EMP: 345 **Privately Held**
SIC: 4225 General warehousing & storage
PA: Weber Distribution, Llc
13530 Rosecrans Ave
Santa Fe Springs CA 90670

(P-4542)
WEBER DISTRIBUTION WAREHOUSES
Also Called: Weber Distribution Cwo
9345 Santa Anita Ave B, Rancho Cucamonga (91730-6126)
PHONE..............................909 481-1600
John Nutt, *Vice Pres*
EMP: 50
SALES (corp-wide): 94.5MM **Privately Held**
WEB: www.weberdist.com
SIC: 4225 4214 General warehousing; local trucking with storage
PA: Weber Distribution Warehouses
13530 Rosecrans Ave
Santa Fe Springs CA 90670
562 356-6300

(P-4543)
WEBER DISTRIBUTION WAREHOUSES
15301 Shoemaker Ave, Norwalk (90650-6859)
PHONE..............................562 404-9996
John Nutt, *Vice Pres*
EMP: 50
SALES (corp-wide): 94.5MM **Privately Held**
WEB: www.weberdist.com
SIC: 4225 4214 General warehousing; local trucking with storage
PA: Weber Distribution Warehouses
13530 Rosecrans Ave
Santa Fe Springs CA 90670
562 356-6300

(P-4544)
WESTERN WINE SERVICES INC (PA)
880 Hanna Dr, American Canyon (94503-9605)
PHONE..............................800 999-8463
Michael W Hodes, *President*
Bruce Cohen, *Senior VP*
Marc Cohen, *Vice Pres*
Tad Franzman, *Vice Pres*
▲ **EMP:** 100
SALES (est): 14.7MM **Privately Held**
SIC: 4225 General warehousing & storage

(P-4545)
WHOLE FOODS MARKET CAL INC
4315 Arden Way, Sacramento (95864-3102)
PHONE..............................916 488-2800
Andy Wergedal, *Branch Mgr*
EMP: 132 **Publicly Held**
SIC: 4225 General warehousing & storage
HQ: Whole Foods Market California, Inc.
5980 Horton St Ste 200
Emeryville CA 94608

(P-4546)
WHOLE FOODS MARKET CAL INC
650 W Shaw Ave, Fresno (93704-2424)
PHONE..............................559 241-0300
David Cosper, *Manager*
EMP: 135 **Publicly Held**
SIC: 4225 General warehousing & storage
HQ: Whole Foods Market California, Inc.
5980 Horton St Ste 200
Emeryville CA 94608

(P-4547)
WINCO FOODS LLC
4400 Crows Landing Rd, Modesto (95358-9304)
P.O. Box 581770 (95358-0031)
PHONE..............................209 556-6040
Branden Frank, *Branch Mgr*
EMP: 90
SALES (corp-wide): 2.1B **Privately Held**
WEB: www.wincofoods.com
SIC: 4225 1541 General warehousing; industrial buildings & warehouses
HQ: Winco Foods, Llc
650 N Armstrong Pl
Boise ID 83704
208 377-0110

(P-4548)
WORLD CLASS DISTRIBUTION INC
2121 Boeing Way, Stockton (95206-4934)
PHONE..............................909 574-4140
Michael Campbell, *Principal*
EMP: 130 **Privately Held**
SIC: 4225 General warehousing & storage
PA: World Class Distribution Inc.
10288 Calabash Ave
Fontana CA 92335

(P-4549)
WORLD CLASS DISTRIBUTION INC
800 S Shamrock Ave, Monrovia (91016-6346)
PHONE..............................909 574-4140
Charles Pilliter, *Branch Mgr*
EMP: 157 **Privately Held**
SIC: 4225 General warehousing & storage
PA: World Class Distribution Inc.
10288 Calabash Ave
Fontana CA 92335

(P-4550)
WORLD CLASS DISTRIBUTION INC
343 S Lena Rd, San Bernardino (92408-1601)
PHONE..............................909 574-4140
EMP: 78 **Privately Held**
SIC: 4225 General warehousing & storage
PA: World Class Distribution Inc.
10288 Calabash Ave
Fontana CA 92335

(P-4551)
WORLD CLASS DISTRIBUTION INC (PA)
Also Called: Trader Joe Fontana Warehouse
10288 Calabash Ave, Fontana (92335-5272)
PHONE..............................909 574-4140
Danny Bane, *CEO*
Robert Camarena, *President*
Sharon A Drabeck, *Corp Secy*
Barry Sutliff, *Info Tech Mgr*
Angus Armstrong, *Director*
EMP: 52
SALES (est): 74MM **Privately Held**
SIC: 4225 General warehousing & storage

(P-4552)
WWL VEHICLE SVCS AMERICAS INC
500 E Water St, Wilmington (90744-6517)
PHONE..............................310 835-8806
Martin Richards, *Branch Mgr*
Carlos Gomez, *Vice Pres*
Len Mazzella, *Vice Pres*
Jens Norgaard, *Vice Pres*
Benjamin Browning, *General Mgr*
EMP: 163 **Privately Held**
SIC: 4225 5531 7549 General warehousing & storage; automotive accessories; automotive maintenance services
HQ: Wwl Vehicle Services Americas, Inc.
300 Interpace Pkwy Ste A
Parsippany NJ 07054
201 505-5100

4226 Special Warehousing & Storage, NEC

(P-4553)
ACCESS INFO MGT SHRED SVCS LLC
6818 Patterson Pass Rd A, Livermore (94550-4230)
PHONE..............................925 461-5352
EMP: 144 **Privately Held**
SIC: 4226 Document & office records storage
PA: Access Information Management Shared Services, Llc
500 Unicorn Park Dr # 503
Woburn MA 01801

(P-4554)
ACCESS INFO MGT SHRED SVCS LLC
4501 Pell Dr, Sacramento (95838-2172)
PHONE..............................925 461-5352
Susan Gee, *Branch Mgr*
EMP: 66 **Privately Held**
SIC: 4226 Document & office records storage
PA: Access Information Management Shared Services, Llc
500 Unicorn Park Dr # 503
Woburn MA 01801

(P-4555)
AZ/CFS WEST INC
Also Called: AZ West
250 W Manville St, Compton (90220-5600)
PHONE..............................310 898-2090
Richard Lombardi, *President*
EMP: 60
SQ FT: 175,000
SALES (est): 14.3MM
SALES (corp-wide): 1.4B **Privately Held**
SIC: 4226 Storage of goods at foreign trade zones
HQ: Az Container Freight Station, Inc.
4 Commerce Dr Ste 1
Cranford NJ 07016
908 374-2250

(P-4556)
CAPACITY LLC
19852 Business Pkwy, Walnut (91789-2838)
PHONE..............................732 745-7770
Anthony P Ruiz, *Branch Mgr*
EMP: 171 **Privately Held**
SIC: 4226 Special warehousing & storage
PA: Capacity Llc
1112 Corporate Rd
North Brunswick NJ 08902

(P-4557)
CCC2931 LLC
2401 E Pacific Coast Hwy, Wilmington (90744-2920)
PHONE..............................562 590-8591
Pete Jacpin, *General Mgr*
David Garcia, *General Mgr*
Martin Verma, *General Mgr*
Diana West, *Facilities Mgr*
EMP: 70
SALES (corp-wide): 3B **Privately Held**
SIC: 4226 4225 Storage of goods at foreign trade zones; general warehousing & storage
HQ: Ccc2931, Llc
2931 Redondo Ave
Long Beach CA 90806
888 537-1432

(P-4558)
CONGLOBAL INDUSTRIES LLC
1711 Alameda St, Wilmington (90744-1700)
P.O. Box 1617 (90748-1617)
PHONE..............................310 518-2850
Tom Dielman, *Branch Mgr*
EMP: 73

SALES (corp-wide): 165.3MM **Privately Held**
WEB: www.cgini.com
SIC: 4226 Special warehousing & storage
HQ: Conglobal Industries, Llc
8200 185th St Ste A
Tinley Park IL 60487

(P-4559)
CORODATA CORPORATION (PA)
12375 Kerran St, Poway (92064-6801)
PHONE....................858 748-1100
Robert J Schmitz, *President*
Jerry Brothers, *CFO*
Richard R Schmitz, *Principal*
Thomas A Schmitz, *Admin Sec*
Andrew Cook, *Manager*
EMP: 59 **EST:** 1974
SQ FT: 600,000
SALES (est): 33.8MM **Privately Held**
SIC: 4226 Document & office records storage

(P-4560)
DATASAFE INC (PA)
574 Eccles Ave, South San Francisco (94080-1905)
P.O. Box 7794, San Francisco (94120-7794)
PHONE....................650 875-3800
Robert S Reis, *Ch of Bd*
Thomas S Reis, *CEO*
Rob Reis, *COO*
Ronald P Reis, *Vice Pres*
Jose Moreno, *Info Tech Dir*
EMP: 50 **EST:** 1898
SQ FT: 375,000
SALES (est): 10.8MM **Privately Held**
WEB: www.datasafe.com
SIC: 4226 Document & office records storage

(P-4561)
DATASAFE INC
3160 W Bayshore Rd, Palo Alto (94303-4042)
P.O. Box 7794, San Francisco (94120-7794)
PHONE....................650 875-3800
Tom Reis, *CEO*
Andrea Barnes, *Opers Staff*
Kristina Santos, *Client Mgr*
EMP: 50
SALES (corp-wide): 10.8MM **Privately Held**
WEB: www.datasafe.com
SIC: 4226 4225 Document & office records storage; general warehousing & storage
PA: Datasafe, Inc.
574 Eccles Ave
South San Francisco CA 94080
650 875-3800

(P-4562)
DNOW LP
Also Called: Wilson Supply
1111 W Artesia Blvd, Compton (90220-5107)
PHONE....................310 900-3900
Nick Leute, *Branch Mgr*
EMP: 53
SALES (corp-wide): 3.1B **Publicly Held**
WEB: www.iwilson.com
SIC: 4226 Special warehousing & storage
HQ: Dnow L.P.
7402 N Eldridge Pkwy
Houston TX 77041
281 823-4700

(P-4563)
DOMINOS PIZZA LLC
301 S Rockefeller Ave, Ontario (91761-7865)
PHONE....................909 390-1990
Sal Melgoza, *General Mgr*
EMP: 120
SALES (corp-wide): 3.4B **Publicly Held**
SIC: 4226 4222 Special warehousing & storage; refrigerated warehousing & storage
HQ: Domino's Pizza Llc
30 Frank Lloyd Wright Dr
Ann Arbor MI 48105
734 930-3030

(P-4564)
EXPRESS IMAGING SERVICES INC
1805 W 208th St Ste 202, Torrance (90501-1808)
PHONE....................888 846-8804
Paul Terry, *President*
Kenny Ly, *Vice Pres*
Tan Ly, *CIO*
Anh Le, *Opers Mgr*
Anni Ly, *Manager*
EMP: 100
SQ FT: 10,000
SALES: 13MM **Privately Held**
SIC: 4226 Document & office records storage

(P-4565)
GRIFOLS WORLDWIDE OPERATIONS
13111 Temple Ave, City of Industry (91746-1500)
PHONE....................626 435-2600
Red Fredericksen, *General Mgr*
EMP: 70
SALES (corp-wide): 741MM **Privately Held**
SIC: 4226 Special warehousing & storage
HQ: Grifols Worldwide Operations Usa, Inc.
5555 Valley Blvd
Los Angeles CA 90032
323 225-2221

(P-4566)
IMPERIAL CFS INC
1000 Francisco St, Torrance (90502-1216)
PHONE....................310 768-8188
Tong Hsing Hsu, *CEO*
Kathy Hsu, *CFO*
Rene Lopez, *Vice Pres*
Penny Hsing, *General Mgr*
I-Hsin Chen, *Admin Sec*
EMP: 50
SQ FT: 200,000
SALES (est): 14.9MM **Privately Held**
WEB: www.imperialcfs.com
SIC: 4226 Document & office records storage

(P-4567)
IRON MOUNTAIN INCORPORATED
28751 Witherspoon Pkwy, Valencia (91355-5415)
PHONE....................661 775-9008
EMP: 51
SALES (corp-wide): 4.2B **Publicly Held**
SIC: 4226 Document & office records storage
PA: Iron Mountain Incorporated
1 Federal St Fl 7
Boston MA 02110
617 535-4766

(P-4568)
IRON MOUNTAIN INCORPORATED
P.O. Box 7877 (92658-7877)
PHONE....................562 345-6900
EMP: 51
SALES (corp-wide): 4.2B **Publicly Held**
SIC: 4226 Document & office records storage
PA: Iron Mountain Incorporated
1 Federal St Fl 7
Boston MA 02110
617 535-4766

(P-4569)
IRON MOUNTAIN INFO MGT LLC
12958 Midway Pl, Cerritos (90703-2119)
PHONE....................714 526-0916
Richard Melrose, *Manager*
EMP: 60
SALES (corp-wide): 4.2B **Publicly Held**
SIC: 4226 Document & office records storage
HQ: Iron Mountain Information Management, Llc
1 Federal St
Boston MA 02110
800 899-4766

(P-4570)
KINDER MRGAN ENRGY PARTNERS LP
2000 E Sepulveda Blvd, Carson (90810-1937)
P.O. Box 9007, Long Beach (90810-0007)
PHONE....................310 518-7700
Randy Hartle, *Branch Mgr*
EMP: 50 **Publicly Held**
SIC: 4226 Oil & gasoline storage caverns for hire
HQ: Kinder Morgan Energy Partners, L.P.
1001 La St Ste 1000
Houston TX 77002
713 369-9000

(P-4571)
KINDER MRGAN LQDS TRMINALS LLC
950 Tunnel Ave, Brisbane (94005-1100)
PHONE....................415 467-8107
Mike Rounds, *Branch Mgr*
EMP: 62 **Publicly Held**
SIC: 4226 Special warehousing & storage
HQ: Kinder Morgan Liquids Terminals Llc
1001 La St Ste 1000
Houston TX 77002
713 369-9000

(P-4572)
KINDER MRGAN LQDS TRMINALS LLC
2150 Kruse Dr, San Jose (95131-1213)
PHONE....................408 435-7399
Kelly Johnson, *Manager*
EMP: 62 **Publicly Held**
SIC: 4226 Special warehousing & storage
HQ: Kinder Morgan Liquids Terminals Llc
1001 La St Ste 1000
Houston TX 77002
713 369-9000

(P-4573)
KW INTERNATIONAL INC
18724 S Broadwick St, Rancho Dominguez (90220-6426)
PHONE....................213 703-6914
Allen Lee, *Branch Mgr*
EMP: 336 **Privately Held**
SIC: 4226 8744 4731 Special warehousing & storage; facilities support services; freight forwarding
PA: Kw International, Inc.
18655 Bishop Ave
Carson CA 90746

(P-4574)
MACYS INC
6200 Franklin Blvd, Sacramento (95824-3400)
PHONE....................916 373-0333
EMP: 80
SALES (corp-wide): 25.7B **Publicly Held**
SIC: 4226 4225 Special warehousing & storage; general warehousing & storage
PA: Macy's, Inc.
7 W 7th St
Cincinnati OH 45202
513 579-7000

(P-4575)
PACIFIC CHEMICAL DIST CORP (HQ)
6250 Caballero Blvd, Buena Park (90620-1124)
PHONE....................714 521-7161
James N Tausz, *President*
Rhonda Tausz, *Corp Secy*
James Banister, *Vice Pres*
EMP: 100 **EST:** 1978
SQ FT: 144,000
SALES (est): 9.2MM
SALES (corp-wide): 294.5MM **Privately Held**
SIC: 4226 Special warehousing & storage
PA: A&R Logistics, Inc.
600 N Hurstbourne Pkwy # 110
Louisville KY 40222
800 542-8058

(P-4576)
PRIDE INDUSTRIES (PA)
10030 Foothills Blvd, Roseville (95747-7102)
P.O. Box 1200, Rocklin (95677-7200)
PHONE....................916 788-2100
Michael Ziegler, *CEO*
Everett Crane, *President*
Peter Berghuis, *COO*
Casey Blake, *COO*
Leslie King, *COO*
▲ **EMP:** 250 **EST:** 1966
SQ FT: 177,000
SALES: 326.5MM **Privately Held**
WEB: www.prideindustries.com/
SIC: 4226 7349 3679 Special warehousing & storage; building maintenance services; electronic circuits

(P-4577)
TAYLOR COMMUNICATIONS INC
5775 Brisa St, Livermore (94550-2513)
PHONE....................925 245-6420
Randy Dehart, *Branch Mgr*
EMP: 62
SALES (corp-wide): 2.8B **Privately Held**
SIC: 4226 Document & office records storage
HQ: Taylor Communications, Inc.
1725 Roe Crest Dr
North Mankato MN 56003
507 625-2828

(P-4578)
VINTRUST INC
38 Keyes Ave Ste 200, San Francisco (94129-1769)
PHONE....................877 846-8787
Barry Waitte, *CEO*
Ozzie Ayscue, *CFO*
Andr De Baubigny, *Chairman*
EMP: 50
SALES (est): 3.7MM **Privately Held**
WEB: www.vintrust.com
SIC: 4226 Whiskey warehousing

4231 Terminal & Joint Terminal Maint Facilities

(P-4579)
FEDEX FREIGHT CORPORATION
310 W Grove Ave, Orange (92865-3206)
PHONE....................714 637-9346
EMP: 50
SQ FT: 18,195
SALES (corp-wide): 69.6B **Publicly Held**
WEB: www.watkins.com
SIC: 4231 Trucking terminal facilities
HQ: Fedex Freight Corporation
1715 Aaron Brenner Dr
Memphis TN 38120

(P-4580)
FEDEX FREIGHT CORPORATION
3200 Workman Mill Rd, Whittier (90601-1550)
PHONE....................800 288-0743
EMP: 500
SQ FT: 38,090
SALES (corp-wide): 69.6B **Publicly Held**
SIC: 4231 4785 4213 Trucking terminal facilities; inspection & fixed facilities; trucking, except local
HQ: Fedex Freight Corporation
1715 Aaron Brenner Dr
Memphis TN 38120

(P-4581)
INTRADE INDUSTRIES INC (PA)
2559 S East Ave, Fresno (93706-5104)
PHONE....................559 274-9877
Tejinder S Mehta, *CEO*
Baljinder Kaur, *Vice Pres*
Sandi Azua, *Marketing Staff*
EMP: 84
SALES (est): 18.4MM **Privately Held**
SIC: 4231 Trucking terminal facilities

4412 Deep Sea Foreign Transportation Of Freight

(P-4582)
APL LOGISTICS LTD
180 E Ocean Blvd Ste 800, Long Beach
(90802-4720)
PHONE..................310 548-8700
Gale Bull, *Branch Mgr*
EMP: 200 Privately Held
WEB: www.apl.com
SIC: 4412 Deep sea foreign transportation
of freight
HQ: Apl Logistics, Ltd.
17600 N Perimeter Dr # 150
Scottsdale AZ 85255
602 357-9100

(P-4583)
FOSS MARITIME COMPANY
1316 Canal Blvd, Richmond (94804-3556)
PHONE..................510 307-4271
Bob Gregory, *Manager*
EMP: 100
SALES (corp-wide): 1.9B **Privately Held**
WEB: www.foss-maritime.com
SIC: 4412 4492 Deep sea foreign trans-
portation of freight; tugboat service
HQ: Foss Maritime Company, Llc.
450 Alaskan Way S Ste 706
Seattle WA 98104
206 281-3800

(P-4584)
FOSS MARITIME COMPANY LLC
Also Called: Pacific Southwest
Berth 35 Pier D, Long Beach (90801)
P.O. Box 1940 (90801-1940)
PHONE..................562 435-0171
Bob Gregory, *Manager*
EMP: 200
SALES (corp-wide): 1.9B **Privately Held**
WEB: www.foss-maritime.com
SIC: 4412 4492 Deep sea foreign trans-
portation of freight; towing & tugboat serv-
ice
HQ: Foss Maritime Company, Llc.
450 Alaskan Way S Ste 706
Seattle WA 98104
206 281-3800

(P-4585)
K LINE AMERICA INC
950 S Coast Dr Ste 178, Costa Mesa
(92626-7731)
PHONE..................714 861-5000
Michelle Boden, *Manager*
Michelle Savage, *Human Resources*
EMP: 50 Privately Held
SIC: 4412 4212 Deep sea foreign trans-
portation of freight; local trucking, without
storage
HQ: K Line America, Inc.
4860 Cox Rd Ste 300
Glen Allen VA 23060
804 762-6600

(P-4586)
PATRIOT CONTRACT SERVICES LLC
Also Called: P C S
1320 Willow Pass Rd # 485, Concord
(94520-5232)
PHONE..................925 296-2000
Jordan Truchan, *CEO*
Judy Collins, *CFO*
Frank Angelacci, *Vice Pres*
Timothy M Gill,
EMP: 400
SQ FT: 7,800
SALES (est): 28.5MM **Privately Held**
SIC: 4412 4424 4449 4481 Deep sea for-
eign transportation of freight; deep sea
domestic transportation of freight; canal &
intracoastal freight transportation; deep
sea passenger transportation, except
ferry; ferries; marine surveyors

4424 Deep Sea Domestic Transportation Of Freight

(P-4587)
MATSON NAVIGATION COMPANY INC (HQ)
555 12th St Fl 7, Oakland (94607-4046)
PHONE..................510 628-4000
Matthew J Cox, *President*
Ronald J Forest, *President*
Joel M Wine, *CFO*
Ben Bowler, *Treasurer*
Benedict J Bowler, *Treasurer*
◆ **EMP: 200 EST:** 1882
SQ FT: 105,000
SALES (est): 592.3MM
SALES (corp-wide): 2.2B **Publicly Held**
WEB: www.matson.com
SIC: 4424 4491 4492 Deep sea domestic
transportation of freight; marine cargo
handling; stevedoring; marine terminals;
tugboat service
PA: Matson, Inc.
1411 Sand Island Pkwy
Honolulu HI 96819
808 848-1211

(P-4588)
PASHA HAWAII TRNSPT LINES LLC
1425 Maritime St, Oakland (94607-1022)
PHONE..................510 271-1400
Mary Brown, *Office Mgr*
EMP: 100
SALES (est): 2.2MM
SALES (corp-wide): 13.8MM **Privately Held**
WEB: www.horizonlines.net
SIC: 4424 4783 Deep sea domestic trans-
portation of freight; containerization of
goods for shipping
PA: Pasha Hawaii Transport Lines Llc
4040 Civic Center Dr # 350
San Rafael CA 94903
415 927-6400

(P-4589)
PASHA STEVEDORING TERMINALS LP
802 S Fries Ave, Wilmington (90744-6415)
PHONE..................415 927-6353
Jeff Burgin, *Senior VP*
Jackie Bailey, *Treasurer*
Braxton Craghill, *Controller*
▲ **EMP:** 50
SALES (est): 6.8MM
SALES (corp-wide): 359.1MM **Privately Held**
WEB: www.psterminals.com
SIC: 4424 4412 Deep sea domestic trans-
portation of freight; deep sea foreign
transportation of freight
PA: The Pasha Group
4040 Civic Center Dr # 350
San Rafael CA 94903
415 927-6400

(P-4590)
POLAR TANKERS INC (DH)
300 Oceangate, Long Beach (90802-6801)
PHONE..................562 388-1400
John R Hennon, *President*
George McShea, *Vice Pres*
John L Sullivan, *Vice Pres*
EMP: 75
SALES (est): 22MM
SALES (corp-wide): 38.7B **Publicly Held**
WEB: www.polartankers.com
SIC: 4424 4412 Deep sea domestic trans-
portation of freight; deep sea foreign
transportation of freight
HQ: Conocophillips Company
925 N Eldridge Pkwy
Houston TX 77079
281 293-1000

4449 Water Transportation Of Freight, NEC

(P-4591)
CHEEMA LOGISTICS
968 Sierra St Ste 130, Kingsburg
(93631-1554)
PHONE..................559 702-1444
Parminder Singh, *President*
EMP: 65 EST: 2014
SALES (est): 1MM **Privately Held**
SIC: 4449 Intracoastal (freight) transporta-
tion

(P-4592)
DEVINE & SON TRUCKING CO INC (PA)
Also Called: Devine Intermodal
3870 Channel Dr, West Sacramento
(95691-3466)
P.O. Box 980160 (95798-0160)
PHONE..................559 486-7440
John Frederick Drewes, *CEO*
Richard Coyle, *President*
Adam Gallagher, *Safety Mgr*
Amanda Nichols, *Cust Mgr*
EMP: 200
SQ FT: 6,000
SALES (est): 31.4MM **Privately Held**
WEB: www.devineintermodal.com
SIC: 4449 4213 Canal & intracoastal
freight transportation; trucking, except
local

(P-4593)
FINN HOLDING CORPORATION (PA)
Also Called: Platinum Equity
360 N Crescent Dr, Beverly Hills
(90210-4874)
PHONE..................310 712-1850
Tom Gores, *Ch of Bd*
Mary Ann Sigler, *CFO*
Eva M Kalawski, *Vice Pres*
EMP: 2575
SALES (est): 1B **Privately Held**
SIC: 4449 3731 4491 Canal barge opera-
tions; barges, building & repairing; marine
terminals

(P-4594)
PASHA HAWAII TRNSPT LINES LLC (PA)
Also Called: Phtl
4040 Civic Center Dr # 350, San Rafael
(94903-4187)
PHONE..................415 927-6400
Steve Hunter,
EMP: 102
SALES (est): 13.8MM **Privately Held**
WEB: www.pashahawaii.com
SIC: 4449 Transportation (freight) on bays
& sounds of the ocean

4481 Deep Sea Transportation Of

(P-4595)
CRYSTAL CRUISES LLC (DH)
11755 Wilshire Blvd # 900, Los Angeles
(90025-1506)
PHONE..................310 785-9300
Tom Wolber, *President*
Helen Beck, *Vice Pres*
Angela Composto, *Vice Pres*
Bertha Espinosa, *Vice Pres*
Carmen Roig, *Vice Pres*
◆ **EMP:** 150
SQ FT: 50,000
SALES (est): 56MM **Privately Held**
WEB: www.crystalcruises.com
SIC: 4481 4724 Deep sea passenger
transportation, except ferry; travel agen-
cies

(P-4596)
PRINCESS CRUISE LINES LTD (HQ)
Also Called: Princess Cruises
24305 Town Center Dr, Santa Clarita
(91355-1307)
PHONE..................661 753-0000
Jan Swartz, *CEO*
Nina Kass, *President*
Mary Horwath, *Exec VP*
Mark Barnes, *Vice Pres*
Paul Debnam, *Vice Pres*
◆ **EMP: 2000 EST:** 1965
SALES (est): 2.4B
SALES (corp-wide): 8.3B **Privately Held**
WEB: www.princess.com
SIC: 4481 4725 7011 Deep sea passen-
ger transportation, except ferry; tour oper-
ators; hotels
PA: Carnival Plc
Carnival House
Southampton HANTS SO15
843 374-0111

4489 Water Transport Of Passengers, NEC

(P-4597)
BAHIA STERNWHEELERS INC
998 W Mission Bay Dr, San Diego
(92109-7803)
PHONE..................858 539-7720
William L Evans, *Ch of Bd*
Grace Chershore, *President*
Nancy Evans-Kyzer, *Treasurer*
Anne Evans-Quinn, *Vice Pres*
Margaret Evans, *Admin Sec*
EMP: 50
SQ FT: 5,000
SALES (est): 3.4MM **Privately Held**
WEB: www.bahiahotel.com
SIC: 4489 7299 4499 Excursion boat op-
erators; banquet hall facilities; chartering
of commercial boats

(P-4598)
BLUE AND GOLD FLEET
Also Called: Pier Restaurant
Marine Terminal Pier 41 St Pier, San Fran-
cisco (94133)
PHONE..................415 705-8200
Ron Duckhorn, *Owner*
Molly South, *Treasurer*
Robert Moore, *Admin Sec*
Peter Belden, *Opers Mgr*
Rachel Rodriguez, *Opers Staff*
EMP: 70 EST: 1979
SALES (est): 13.3MM
SALES (corp-wide): 40MM **Privately Held**
WEB: www.blueandgoldfleet.com
SIC: 4489 4724 Excursion boat operators;
travel agencies
PA: Pier 39 Limited Partnership
Beach Embarcadero Level 3
San Francisco CA 94133
415 705-5500

(P-4599)
CATALINA CHANNEL EXPRESS INC (HQ)
Also Called: Catalina Express Cruises
385 E Swinford St, San Pedro
(90731-1002)
PHONE..................310 519-7971
Greg Bombard, *President*
Douglas Bombard, *Ch of Bd*
EMP: 375
SQ FT: 20,000
SALES (est): 55.6MM
SALES (corp-wide): 26.3MM **Privately Held**
WEB: www.catalinaexpress.com
SIC: 4489 Excursion boat operators
PA: Bombard Marine And Resort Manage-
ment Services Inc
95 Berth
San Pedro CA 90731
310 519-7971

(P-4600)
CATALINA CHANNEL EXPRESS INC
Also Called: Catalina Express
385 E Swinford St, San Pedro (90731-1002)
PHONE..................................562 495-3565
Greg Bombard, *Manager*
EMP: 200
SALES (corp-wide): 26.3MM **Privately Held**
WEB: www.catalinaexpress.com
SIC: 4489 4481 Excursion boat operators; deep sea passenger transportation, except ferry
HQ: Catalina Channel Express, Inc.
385 E Swinford St
San Pedro CA 90731
310 519-7971

(P-4601)
CATALINA GLASSBOTTOM BOAT INC
1 Cabrillo Mole, Avalon (90704)
PHONE..................................310 510-2888
Jeff Stickler, *CEO*
Steve Smith, *Vice Pres*
EMP: 65
SALES: 6MM **Privately Held**
SIC: 4489 Sightseeing boats

(P-4602)
COMMODORE DINING CRUISES INC (PA)
Also Called: Commodore Events
2394 Mariner Square Dr A, Alameda (94501-1023)
PHONE..................................510 337-9000
Morgan Proescher, *CEO*
Susan Proescher, *President*
Amber Klein, *Sales Staff*
Hannah Miller, *Sales Staff*
EMP: 100
SQ FT: 1,000
SALES (est): 6.1MM **Privately Held**
WEB: www.commodoreevents.com
SIC: 4489 Excursion boat operators

(P-4603)
GOLDEN GATE SCNIC STMSHIP CORP
Also Called: Red and White Fleet
Shed C Pier 45 St Pier, San Francisco (94133)
PHONE..................................415 901-5249
Thomas E Escher, *President*
EMP: 50
SALES: 10MM **Privately Held**
SIC: 4489 4482 Sightseeing boats; ferries

(P-4604)
HORNBLOWER GROUP INC
The Embarcadero Pier 3 St Pier, San Francisco (94111)
PHONE..................................415 635-2210
Terry A Macrae, *CEO*
EMP: 500
SALES: 360MM **Privately Held**
SIC: 4489 Airboats

(P-4605)
HORNBLOWER YACHTS INC
Also Called: Hornblower Cruises & Events
2825 5th Ave, San Diego (92103-6326)
PHONE..................................619 686-8700
Jim Unger, *Branch Mgr*
Michael Burke, *COO*
Scott Thornton, *General Mgr*
John Vissat, *Business Mgr*
Raima McDaniel, *Human Res Mgr*
EMP: 160
SALES (corp-wide): 125.4MM **Privately Held**
WEB: www.hornbloweryachts.com
SIC: 4489 7299 4499 Excursion boat operators; banquet hall facilities; chartering of commercial boats
PA: Hornblower Yachts, Llc
On The Embarcadero Pier 3 St Pier
San Francisco CA 94111
415 788-8866

(P-4606)
HORNBLOWER YACHTS LLC
200 Marina Blvd, Berkeley (94710-1608)
PHONE..................................916 446-1185
Daniel Montoya, *Manager*
Shay Rosner, *Marketing Staff*
Denise Erfe, *Sales Staff*
Erin Frye, *Sales Staff*
Junior Volpe, *Director*
EMP: 87
SALES (corp-wide): 125.4MM **Privately Held**
SIC: 4489 Excursion boat operators
PA: Hornblower Yachts, Llc
On The Embarcadero Pier 3 St Pier
San Francisco CA 94111
415 788-8866

(P-4607)
SO CAL SHIP SERVICES
971 S Seaside Ave, San Pedro (90731-7331)
PHONE..................................310 519-8411
Michael A Lanham, *President*
Mark Wrobel, *General Mgr*
Freddy Saenz, *Opers Mgr*
Doug Malin, *Manager*
Larry Smith, *Manager*
EMP: 85
SQ FT: 10,000
SALES (est): 13.6MM **Privately Held**
WEB: www.ship-services.com
SIC: 4489 Water taxis

(P-4608)
STAR & CRESCENT BOAT COMPANY (PA)
Also Called: San Diego Harbor Excursion
1311 1st St, Coronado (92118-1502)
P.O. Box 120751, San Diego (92112-0751)
PHONE..................................619 234-4111
Arthur E Engel, *CEO*
George Palermo, *President*
David Engel, *Vice Pres*
Herbert Engel, *Vice Pres*
William Johnston, *Vice Pres*
EMP: 50
SALES (est): 17.4MM **Privately Held**
WEB: www.sdhe.com
SIC: 4489 4482 5812 5947 Excursion boat operators; sightseeing boats; ferries operating across rivers or within harbors; cafe; gift shop

4491 Marine Cargo Handling

(P-4609)
APM TERMINALS PACIFIC LLC (DH)
2500 Navy Way, San Pedro (90731-7554)
PHONE..................................704 571-2768
Steven Trombley, *CEO*
EMP: 104
SQ FT: 33,000
SALES (est): 56.1MM
SALES (corp-wide): 1.9MM **Privately Held**
SIC: 4491 Stevedoring
HQ: Apm Terminals North America, Inc.
9300 Arrowpoint Blvd
Charlotte NC 28273
704 571-2768

(P-4610)
CATALINA CHANNEL EXPRESS INC
Also Called: Catalina Express
320 Golden Shore Lbby, Long Beach (90802-4200)
PHONE..................................562 435-8686
Rachel Lane, *Branch Mgr*
EMP: 125
SALES (corp-wide): 26.3MM **Privately Held**
WEB: www.catalinaexpress.com
SIC: 4491 Docks, piers & terminals
HQ: Catalina Channel Express, Inc.
385 E Swinford St
San Pedro CA 90731
310 519-7971

(P-4611)
CITY OF LOS ANGELES
Also Called: Harbor Department
425 S Palos Verdes St, San Pedro (90731-3309)
PHONE..................................310 732-7681
Geraldine Knatz, *Branch Mgr*
EMP: 250 **Privately Held**
WEB: www.lacity.org
SIC: 4491 9199 Marine cargo handling; general government administration;
PA: City Of Los Angeles
200 N Spring St Ste 303
Los Angeles CA 90012
213 978-0600

(P-4612)
INTERNATIONAL TRNSP SVC (HQ)
Also Called: I T S
1281 Pier G Way, Long Beach (90802-6353)
P.O. Box 22704 (90801-5704)
PHONE..................................562 435-7781
Sho Ishitobi, *President*
Yuji Yamamoto, *Corp Secy*
John Miller, *Exec VP*
Michael Shanks, *Vice Pres*
EMP: 220
SQ FT: 10,000
SALES (est): 69.1MM **Privately Held**
WEB: www.itsasafety.org
SIC: 4491 Marine loading & unloading services

(P-4613)
LEVIN-RICHMOND TERMINAL CORP
402 Wright Ave, Richmond (94804-3532)
PHONE..................................510 232-4422
Gary Levin, *President*
Sylvia San Andres, *Admin Asst*
Pat O'Driscoll, *Opers Mgr*
EMP: 60
SALES (est): 7.7MM
SALES (corp-wide): 9.7MM **Privately Held**
WEB: www.levinterminal.com
SIC: 4491 Marine cargo handling
PA: Levin Enterprises Inc
112 Wshington Ave Ste 250
Richmond CA 94801
510 215-1515

(P-4614)
M T C HOLDINGS (DH)
3 Embarcadero Ctr Ste 550, San Francisco (94111-4048)
PHONE..................................912 651-4000
Michael Hassing, *President*
Gail Parris, *CFO*
Christopher Redlich Jr, *Chairman*
EMP: 50
SALES (est): 43.8MM
SALES (corp-wide): 43B **Publicly Held**
SIC: 4491 Stevedoring; marine terminals; loading vessels; unloading vessels
HQ: Ports America, Inc.
525 Washington Blvd
Jersey City NJ 07310
732 635-3899

(P-4615)
PASHA STEVEDORING TERMINALS LP
802 S Fries Ave, Wilmington (90744-6415)
PHONE..................................310 233-2006
EMP: 50
SALES (est): 1.6MM **Privately Held**
SIC: 4491

(P-4616)
PORT DEPT CITY OF OAKLAND (PA)
Also Called: Port of Oakland
530 Water St Fl 3, Oakland (94607-3525)
P.O. Box 2064 (94604-2064)
PHONE..................................510 627-1100
Veteran Chris Lytle, *Exec Dir*
Laurice Henry-Ross, *President*
Sara Lee, *CFO*
Donna Cason, *Officer*
Rebecca Haggerty, *Officer*
EMP: 350
SQ FT: 285,600

SALES (est): 65.3MM **Privately Held**
WEB: www.portofoakland.com
SIC: 4491 4581 Marine cargo handling; airport leasing, if operating airport

(P-4617)
PORT OF LOS ANGELES
425 S Palos Verdes St, San Pedro (90731-3309)
PHONE..................................310 732-3508
Gene Seroka, *Exec Dir*
William Yocham, *Officer*
Lisa Cloud Ochsner, *Manager*
EMP: 51
SALES: 490.7MM **Privately Held**
SIC: 4491 Waterfront terminal operation

(P-4618)
PORTS AMERICA INC
1601 Harbor Bay Pkwy # 150, Alameda (94502-3028)
PHONE..................................510 749-7400
Michael Hassing, *President*
Irina Sheykh-Zade, *Manager*
EMP: 80
SALES (corp-wide): 43B **Publicly Held**
SIC: 4491 Stevedoring; marine terminals
HQ: Ports America, Inc.
525 Washington Blvd
Jersey City NJ 07310
732 635-3899

(P-4619)
SACRAMENTO-YOLO PORT DISTRICT
Also Called: Port of Sacramento
1110 W Capitol Ave, West Sacramento (95691-2717)
PHONE..................................916 371-8000
Mike Luken, *Principal*
Polly Harris, *Admin Sec*
EMP: 125 EST: 1963
SALES (est): 8.6MM **Privately Held**
WEB: www.portofsacramento.com
SIC: 4491 Marine terminals

(P-4620)
SAN DIEGO UNIFIED PORT DST
1400 Tidelands Ave, National City (91950-4224)
PHONE..................................619 686-6200
Wendy Ong, *Program Mgr*
Jason Giffen, *Assistant VP*
EMP: 106
SALES (corp-wide): 172.8MM **Privately Held**
SIC: 4491 Marine cargo handling
PA: San Diego Unified Port District
3165 Pacific Hwy
San Diego CA 92101
619 686-6200

(P-4621)
SAN DIEGO UNIFIED PORT DST
Also Called: San Diego Unified Hbr Police
3380 N Harbor Dr, San Diego (92101-1023)
PHONE..................................619 686-6585
Betty Kelepecz, *Branch Mgr*
Aldo Gutierrez, *Officer*
Sheila Abrenica, *Info Tech Mgr*
Shirley Hirai, *Manager*
EMP: 120
SALES (corp-wide): 172.8MM **Privately Held**
WEB: www.thebigbay.com
SIC: 4491 Marine cargo handling
PA: San Diego Unified Port District
3165 Pacific Hwy
San Diego CA 92101
619 686-6200

(P-4622)
SAN DIEGO UNIFIED PORT DST (PA)
Also Called: PORT OF SAN DIEGO
3165 Pacific Hwy, San Diego (92101-1128)
P.O. Box 120488 (92112-0488)
PHONE..................................619 686-6200
John Bolduc, *CEO*
Denise Buth, *President*
Robert Deangelis, *CFO*
Mike Bishop, *Officer*
James Jordan, *Officer*
EMP: 240 EST: 1962
SQ FT: 120,000

SALES: 172.8MM **Privately Held**
WEB: www.thebigbay.com
SIC: 4491 Marine cargo handling

(P-4623)
SSA CONTAINERS INC
1521 Pier J Ave, Long Beach (90802-6327)
P.O. Box 24868, Seattle WA (98124-0868)
PHONE..........................206 623-0304
Knud Stubkjaer, *CEO*
John Aldaya, *CFO*
Jaime Neal, *Senior VP*
Theresa Bicknell, *Vice Pres*
Kyle Lukins, *Admin Sec*
EMP: 99
SALES (est): 5MM
SALES (corp-wide): 1.9B **Privately Held**
SIC: 4491 Stevedoring
HQ: Ssa Marine, Inc.
      1131 Sw Klickitat Way
      Seattle WA 98134
      206 623-0304

(P-4624)
SSA MARINE INC
1521 Pier J Ave, Long Beach (90802-6327)
PHONE..........................562 983-1001
Sal Ferrigno, *Manager*
Cesar Salas, *Prgrmr*
EMP: 50
SALES (corp-wide): 1.9B **Privately Held**
WEB: www.ssamarine.com
SIC: 4491 Stevedoring
HQ: Ssa Marine, Inc.
      1131 Sw Klickitat Way
      Seattle WA 98134
      206 623-0304

(P-4625)
STOCKTON PORT DISTRICT
Also Called: PORT OF STOCKTON
2201 W Washington St # 13, Stockton
(95203-2991)
P.O. Box 2089 (95201-2089)
PHONE..........................209 946-0246
Richard Aschieris, *Director*
Jim Cooper, *Info Tech Mgr*
Tricia Rosenow, *Technology*
Timothy Deerinck, *Engineer*
Dianna L Baker, *Finance*
EMP: 100
SQ FT: 18,000
SALES: 56MM **Privately Held**
WEB: www.stocktonport.com
SIC: 4491 4225 Waterfront terminal opera-
tion; warehousing, self-storage

(P-4626)
TOTAL INTERMODAL SERVICES INC (PA)
2396 E Sepulveda Blvd, Long Beach
(90810-1943)
PHONE..........................562 427-6300
Amador Sanchez Jr, *President*
EMP: 50
SALES (est): 6.1MM **Privately Held**
WEB: www.totalintermodal.com
SIC: 4491 4213 7534 4731 Marine cargo
handling; trucking, except local; tire re-
treading & repair shops; freight forwarding

(P-4627)
TRAPAC LLC (HQ)
630 W Harry Bridges Blvd, Wilmington
(90744-5733)
P.O. Box 1178 (90748-1178)
PHONE..........................310 513-1572
Yoshiharu Hirakawa, *CEO*
K Kurahara, *CFO*
Robert Owens, *Vice Pres*
Jerome Marshall, *Info Tech Mgr*
Bryon Young, *Info Tech Mgr*
EMP: 50
SQ FT: 50,000
SALES (est): 21.2MM **Privately Held**
WEB: www.trapac.com
SIC: 4491 Waterfront terminal operation

(P-4628)
YUSEN TERMINALS LLC (DH)
Also Called: Yti
701 New Dock St, San Pedro
(90731-7535)
PHONE..........................310 548-8000
Patrick Burgoyne, *CEO*
Betsy Christie, *CFO*

Eric Martinez, *General Mgr*
KY Hiu, *Planning Mgr*
Ken Hunter, *Planning Mgr*
EMP: 63
SALES (est): 13.5MM **Privately Held**
WEB: www.yti.com
SIC: 4491 Marine terminals

4492 Towing & Tugboat

(P-4629)
CROSS LINK INC
Also Called: Westar Marine Services
Bldg C Pier 50, San Francisco (94158)
P.O. Box 78100 (94107-8100)
PHONE..........................415 495-3191
Mary C McMillan, *CEO*
Wendy Heffron-Morrow, *Vice Pres*
Sarah Morrow, *Personnel Assit*
Dennis Oconnor, *Manager*
▲ **EMP:** 65
SQ FT: 16,000
SALES (est): 8.9MM **Privately Held**
SIC: 4492 Marine towing services

(P-4630)
FOSS MARITIME CO INC
Also Called: Pacific Towboat & Salvage Co
Berth 35 Pier D, Long Beach (90802)
PHONE..........................562 435-0171
Steve Scalzo, *President*
EMP: 85
SQ FT: 50,000
SALES (est): 4.5MM
SALES (corp-wide): 1.9B **Privately Held**
WEB: www.foss-maritime.com
SIC: 4492 Marine towing services
HQ: Foss Maritime Company, Llc.
      450 Alaskan Way S Ste 706
      Seattle WA 98104
      206 281-3800

(P-4631)
OFFICIAL POLICE GARAGE ASSN OF
67 W Boulder Creek Rd, Simi Valley
(93065-7362)
PHONE..........................805 624-0572
Eric Rose, *Exec Dir*
EMP: 800
SALES (est): 20MM **Privately Held**
SIC: 4492 Towing & tugboat service

(P-4632)
PACIFIC MARITIME GROUP INC (PA)
Also Called: Pacific Tugboat Service
1444 Cesar E Chavez Pkwy, San Diego
(92113-2132)
P.O. Box 12787 (92112-3787)
PHONE..........................619 533-7932
Grant Westmorland, *CEO*
Theodore Griffith Sr, *President*
Jason Hope, *CFO*
Ralph Botticelli, *Vice Pres*
Stephen P Frailey, *Vice Pres*
EMP: 125
SQ FT: 2,200
SALES (est): 20.7MM **Privately Held**
WEB: www.pacifictugboats.com
SIC: 4492 Tugboat service

4493 Marinas

(P-4633)
CALIFORNIA YACHT MARINA INC (PA)
Also Called: Port Royal Marina
22905 Lockness Ave, Torrance
(90501-5118)
PHONE..........................310 534-8436
Gerald Thomas, *Vice Pres*
Kathie Sitton, *CFO*
William Thomas, *Treasurer*
Kellie Foster, *HR Admin*
EMP: 50
SQ FT: 3,000
SALES (est): 5.1MM **Privately Held**
SIC: 4493 4225 5551 Marine basins;
miniwarehouse, warehousing; marine
supplies

(P-4634)
HARBOR FUEL DOCK
1 Johnson Pier, Half Moon Bay
(94019-4000)
P.O. Box 158 (94019-0158)
PHONE..........................650 726-4419
Keith Nerhan, *Owner*
EMP: 100
SALES (est): 2.6MM **Privately Held**
SIC: 4493 Marinas

(P-4635)
OAKLAND MRTIME SPPORT SVCS INC
11 Burma Rd, Oakland (94607)
PHONE..........................510 868-1005
William Aboudi, *President*
Nishant Sharma, *CFO*
EMP: 50
SALES (est): 2.1MM **Privately Held**
SIC: 4493 Marinas

(P-4636)
SHELTER POINTE LLC
Also Called: Shelter Pointe Hotel & Marina
1551 Shelter Island Dr, San Diego
(92106-3102)
PHONE..........................619 221-8000
Jeff Foster, *Mng Member*
EMP: 200
SALES (est): 14.4MM
SALES (corp-wide): 59.1MM **Privately Held**
WEB: www.shelterpointe.com
SIC: 4493 7011 7997 5812 Marinas; re-
sort hotel; country club, membership;
American restaurant; drinking places
HQ: Pacifica Hotel Company
      39 Argonaut
      Aliso Viejo CA 92656
      805 957-0095

(P-4637)
WESTREC MARINA MANAGEMENT INC
Also Called: Tower Park Marina
14900 W Highway 12 Frnt, Lodi
(95242-9514)
PHONE..........................209 369-1041
Jeff Lewis, *Manager*
EMP: 60
SALES (corp-wide): 30MM **Privately Held**
WEB: www.martinez-marina.com
SIC: 4493 7299 Marine basins; banquet
hall facilities
HQ: Westrec Marina Management Inc
      16633 Ventura Blvd Fl 6
      Encino CA 91436

4499 Water Transportation Svcs, NEC

(P-4638)
C & C BOATS INC
1861 Baja Vista Way, Camarillo
(93010-9273)
P.O. Box 2359 (93011-2359)
PHONE..........................805 445-9456
Tom Croft, *President*
EMP: 50
SALES (est): 2.3MM **Privately Held**
SIC: 4499 Chartering of commercial boats

(P-4639)
HANJIN SHIPPING CO LTD
301 Hanjin Rd, Long Beach (90802)
PHONE..........................201 291-4600
Taisoo Suk, *Exec Dir*
◆ **EMP:** 691
SALES (est): 73.8MM **Privately Held**
WEB: www.cyberlogitec.com
SIC: 4499 Steamship leasing

(P-4640)
WESTSTAR MARINE SERVICES INC
50 Pier, San Francisco (94158-2193)
PHONE..........................415 495-3191
Mary McMillan, *President*
Janis Smith, *Mktg Coord*
Ken Friman, *Director*

EMP: 160
SALES (est): 9.1MM **Privately Held**
SIC: 4499 7359 Boat & ship rental & leasing, except pleasure; equipment rental &
leasing

4512 Air Transportation, Scheduled

(P-4641)
AEROFLOT RUSSIAN AIRLINES
Also Called: Aeroflot Rssina Internatl Arln
8383 Wilshire Blvd # 648, Beverly Hills
(90211-2444)
PHONE..........................323 272-4861
Olga Alexeva, *Manager*
Yuriy Gregorev, *Manager*
EMP: 75
SALES (corp-wide): 50.3MM **Privately
Held**
WEB: www.aeroflot.ru
SIC: 4512 Air passenger carrier, scheduled
HQ: Aeroflot, Pao
      1 Ul. Arbat
      Moscow 11901
      499 500-6868

(P-4642)
AEROTRANSPORTE DE CARGE UNION
Also Called: Aerounion
5625 W Imperial Hwy, Los Angeles
(90045-6323)
PHONE..........................310 649-0069
Luis Ramo, *Partner*
Steven Connolly, *Partner*
EMP: 400
SALES (est): 21.9MM **Privately Held**
SIC: 4512 Air cargo carrier, scheduled

(P-4643)
AIR FRANCE (AIR NATIONALE)
San Francisco Intl A, San Francisco
(94125)
PHONE..........................415 877-0179
Percy Bouloux, *Branch Mgr*
EMP: 51
SALES (corp-wide): 56.1MM **Privately
Held**
WEB: www.airfrance.com
SIC: 4512 Air transportation, scheduled
PA: Air France - Klm
      Air France Klm Group
      Paris 7e Arrondissement 75007

(P-4644)
AIR NEW ZEALAND LIMITED
222 N Pacific Coast Hwy # 900, El Se-
gundo (90245-5648)
PHONE..........................310 648-7000
Roger Poulton, *Vice Pres*
Janet Eden, *Executive Asst*
Kelly White, *Technology*
Chrystal Peters, *Human Res Mgr*
Casey Goodman, *Marketing Staff*
EMP: 100 **Privately Held**
SIC: 4512 Air transportation, scheduled
PA: Air New Zealand Limited
      185 Fanshawe Street
      Auckland 1010

(P-4645)
ALASKA AIRLINES INC
1800 W Airport Dr Han Hangar, Ontario
(91761)
PHONE..........................800 426-0333
John Kelly, *President*
Flores Joe, *QA Dir*
Chan Derek, *Manager*
EMP: 75
SALES (corp-wide): 8.2B **Publicly Held**
WEB: www.alaskaair.com
SIC: 4512 Air passenger carrier, scheduled
HQ: Alaska Airlines, Inc
      19300 International Blvd
      Seatac WA 98188
      206 433-3200

(P-4646)
ALASKA AIRLINES INC
600 World Way, Los Angeles (90045-5897)
PHONE..........................310 925-2409

▲ = Import ▼=Export
◆ =Import/Export

Linn Sloper, *Manager*
EMP: 150
SALES (corp-wide): 8.2B **Publicly Held**
WEB: www.alaskaair.com
SIC: 4512 Air cargo carrier, scheduled; air passenger carrier, scheduled
HQ: Alaska Airlines, Inc
19300 International Blvd
Seatac WA 98188
206 433-3200

(P-4647)
ALASKA AIRLINES INC
1 Alan Shepard Way, Oakland (94621)
PHONE..................510 577-5813
Kathy Denkar, *General Mgr*
EMP: 64
SALES (corp-wide): 8.2B **Publicly Held**
WEB: www.alaskaair.com
SIC: 4512 4729 Air cargo carrier, scheduled; air passenger carrier, scheduled; airline ticket offices
HQ: Alaska Airlines, Inc
19300 International Blvd
Seatac WA 98188
206 433-3200

(P-4648)
AMERICA WEST AIRLINES INC
3835 N Harbor Dr Ste 128, San Diego (92101-1081)
PHONE..................619 231-7340
Murray Bauer, *Manager*
EMP: 150
SALES (corp-wide): 44.5B **Publicly Held**
WEB: www.americawest.com
SIC: 4512 Air passenger carrier, scheduled
HQ: America West Airlines, Inc.
4000 E Sky Harbor Blvd
Phoenix AZ 85034
480 693-0800

(P-4649)
AMERICA WEST AIRLINES INC
18601 Airport Way Ste 238, Santa Ana (92707-5204)
PHONE..................949 852-5471
EMP: 80
SALES (corp-wide): 42.2B **Publicly Held**
SIC: 4512
HQ: America West Airlines, Inc.
4000 E Sky Harbor Blvd
Phoenix AZ 85034
480 693-0800

(P-4650)
AMERICAN AIRLINES INC
2077 Airport Blvd Ste 103, San Jose (95110-1219)
PHONE..................408 291-3800
Lee Sims, *General Mgr*
EMP: 80
SALES (corp-wide): 44.5B **Publicly Held**
WEB: www.aa.com
SIC: 4512 Air passenger carrier, scheduled
HQ: American Airlines, Inc.
1 Skyview Dr
Fort Worth TX 76155
817 963-1234

(P-4651)
AMERICAN AIRLINES INC
International Airport, San Francisco (94128)
P.O. Box 8277 (94128-8277)
PHONE..................650 877-6000
Phillip Bock, *Manager*
EMP: 450
SQ FT: 4,000
SALES (corp-wide): 44.5B **Publicly Held**
WEB: www.aa.com
SIC: 4512 Air passenger carrier, scheduled
HQ: American Airlines, Inc.
1 Skyview Dr
Fort Worth TX 76155
817 963-1234

(P-4652)
AMERICAN AIRLINES INC
Also Called: AMR
5950 Avion Dr, Los Angeles (90045-5682)
PHONE..................310 215-7054
Gerard Arpey, *CEO*
EMP: 228

SALES (corp-wide): 44.5B **Publicly Held**
WEB: www.aa.com
SIC: 4512 Air cargo carrier, scheduled; air passenger carrier, scheduled
HQ: American Airlines, Inc.
1 Skyview Dr
Fort Worth TX 76155
817 963-1234

(P-4653)
AMERICAN AIRLINES INC
18601 Airport Way Ste 213, Santa Ana (92707-5219)
PHONE..................949 852-5470
Catherine Connolly, *Branch Mgr*
EMP: 250
SALES (corp-wide): 44.5B **Publicly Held**
WEB: www.aa.com
SIC: 4512 4729 Air cargo carrier, scheduled; air passenger carrier, scheduled
HQ: American Airlines, Inc.
1 Skyview Dr
Fort Worth TX 76155
817 963-1234

(P-4654)
AMERICAN AIRLINES INC
7000 World Way W, Los Angeles (90045-7503)
PHONE..................213 935-6045
EMP: 150
SALES (corp-wide): 42.2B **Publicly Held**
SIC: 4512
HQ: American Airlines, Inc.
4333 Amon Carter Blvd
Fort Worth TX 76155
817 963-1234

(P-4655)
AMERICAN AIRLINES INC
Also Called: US Airways
3707 N Harbor Dr Ste 103, San Diego (92101-1068)
PHONE..................619 574-0615
Lynn Silva, *Manager*
Letty Villamarin, *Human Resources*
EMP: 50
SALES (corp-wide): 44.5B **Publicly Held**
WEB: www.usair.com
SIC: 4512 Air passenger carrier, scheduled
HQ: American Airlines, Inc.
1 Skyview Dr
Fort Worth TX 76155
817 963-1234

(P-4656)
AMERICAN AIRLINES INC
Also Called: US Airways
7183 World Way W, Los Angeles (90045-5824)
PHONE..................310 646-3013
George Knoblock, *Branch Mgr*
EMP: 175
SALES (corp-wide): 44.5B **Publicly Held**
WEB: www.usair.com
SIC: 4512 Air passenger carrier, scheduled
HQ: American Airlines, Inc.
1 Skyview Dr
Fort Worth TX 76155
817 963-1234

(P-4657)
AMERICAN AIRLINES INC
3100 Wright Rd, Camarillo (93010-8307)
PHONE..................805 988-0407
Wilma Barkley, *Branch Mgr*
EMP: 75
SALES (corp-wide): 44.5B **Publicly Held**
WEB: www.aa.com
SIC: 4512 Air passenger carrier, scheduled
HQ: American Airlines, Inc.
1 Skyview Dr
Fort Worth TX 76155
817 963-1234

(P-4658)
AMERICAN AIRLINES GROUP INC
3543 Carlisle St, Perris (92571-7303)
PHONE..................310 251-9184
Susie Kimball, *Principal*
EMP: 658
SALES (corp-wide): 44.5B **Publicly Held**
SIC: 4512 Air passenger carrier, scheduled

PA: American Airlines Group Inc.
4333 Amon Carter Blvd
Fort Worth TX 76155
817 963-1234

(P-4659)
AMERIFLIGHT LLC
21889 Skywest Dr, Hayward (94541-7021)
PHONE..................510 569-6000
EMP: 57
SALES (corp-wide): 183.1MM **Privately Held**
SIC: 4512
PA: Ameriflight, Llc
4700 W Empire Ave
Burbank CA 75261
818 847-0000

(P-4660)
CALIFORNIA AIR CARTAGE INC (PA)
Also Called: Shaker Express
2357 Airlane Rd Ste B, San Diego (92101-1060)
P.O. Box 122430 (92112-2430)
PHONE..................619 291-8544
Ralph A Wilson, *President*
EMP: 96 EST: 1959
SQ FT: 11,000
SALES (est): 6.9MM **Privately Held**
SIC: 4512 4513 Air cargo carrier, scheduled; parcel delivery, private air

(P-4661)
CHINA AIRLINES LTD (HQ)
11201 Aviation Blvd, Los Angeles (90045-6100)
PHONE..................310 646-4233
Huang Hsiang Sun, *President*
Yu-Kuang Yu, *Human Res Mgr*
David Tang, *Opers Mgr*
Allen Lee, *Marketing Staff*
Jenny Lee, *Marketing Staff*
EMP: 95
SALES (est): 28.3MM **Privately Held**
SIC: 4512 Air transportation, scheduled

(P-4662)
DELTA AIR LINES INC
Also Called: Delta Airlines
500 World Way, Los Angeles (90045-5891)
P.O. Box 90676 (90009-0676)
PHONE..................323 417-7374
Dick Cassella, *Manager*
EMP: 64
SALES (corp-wide): 44.4B **Publicly Held**
WEB: www.delta.com
SIC: 4512 Air passenger carrier, scheduled
PA: Delta Air Lines, Inc.
1030 Delta Blvd
Atlanta GA 30354
404 715-2600

(P-4663)
ENVOY AIR INC
Also Called: AMR Eagle
3707 N Harbor Dr Ste 124, San Diego (92101-1080)
PHONE..................619 260-9069
Steve Terry, *Branch Mgr*
EMP: 50
SALES (corp-wide): 44.5B **Publicly Held**
WEB: www.americanair.com
SIC: 4512 Air passenger carrier, scheduled
HQ: Envoy Air Inc.
4301 Regent Blvd
Irving TX 75063
972 374-5200

(P-4664)
FEDERAL EXPRESS CORPORATION
Also Called: Fedex
11340 Sherman Way, Sun Valley (91352-4944)
PHONE..................800 463-3339
EMP: 135
SALES (corp-wide): 69.6B **Publicly Held**
WEB: www.federalexpress.com
SIC: 4512 4513 4215 Air transportation, scheduled; air courier services; courier services, except by air
HQ: Federal Express Corporation
3610 Hacks Cross Rd
Memphis TN 38125
901 369-3600

(P-4665)
FEDERAL EXPRESS CORPORATION
Also Called: Fedex
1500 Nichols Dr, Rocklin (95765-1310)
PHONE..................800 463-3339
EMP: 122
SALES (corp-wide): 69.6B **Publicly Held**
WEB: www.federalexpress.com
SIC: 4512 Air cargo carrier, scheduled
HQ: Federal Express Corporation
3610 Hacks Cross Rd
Memphis TN 38125
901 369-3600

(P-4666)
FEDERAL EXPRESS CORPORATION
Also Called: Fedex
1111 Bird Center Dr, Palm Springs (92262-8000)
PHONE..................800 463-3339
EMP: 122
SALES (corp-wide): 69.6B **Publicly Held**
WEB: www.federalexpress.com
SIC: 4512 Air cargo carrier, scheduled
HQ: Federal Express Corporation
3610 Hacks Cross Rd
Memphis TN 38125
901 369-3600

(P-4667)
FEDERAL EXPRESS CORPORATION
Also Called: Fedex
2601 Main St Ste 1000, Irvine (92614-4233)
PHONE..................949 862-4500
EMP: 120
SALES (corp-wide): 47.4B **Publicly Held**
SIC: 4512 4513
HQ: Federal Express Corporation
3610 Hacks Cross Rd
Memphis TN 38125
901 369-3600

(P-4668)
HAWAIIAN AIRLINES INC
200 World Way Ste 9, Los Angeles (90045-5844)
PHONE..................310 417-1677
Lisa Jones, *General Mgr*
EMP: 55
SALES (corp-wide): 2.8B **Publicly Held**
WEB: www.hawaiianair.com
SIC: 4512 Air passenger carrier, scheduled
HQ: Hawaiian Airlines, Inc.
3375 Koapaka St Ste G350
Honolulu HI 96819
808 835-3700

(P-4669)
JETBLUE AIRWAYS CORPORATION
Also Called: Burbank Bob Hope Airport
2627 N Hollywood Way, Burbank (91505-1062)
PHONE..................718 286-7900
Tom Greer, *Branch Mgr*
Jillian Barra, *Analyst*
Laurie Allen, *Supervisor*
Julie Brakey, *Supervisor*
EMP: 77
SALES (corp-wide): 7.6B **Publicly Held**
SIC: 4512 Air passenger carrier, scheduled
PA: Jetblue Airways Corporation
2701 Queens Plz N
Long Island City NY 11101
718 286-7900

(P-4670)
JETBLUE AIRWAYS CORPORATION
130 Alan Shepard Way M, Oakland (94621-4501)
PHONE..................510 381-1369
EMP: 81
SALES (corp-wide): 7.6B **Publicly Held**
SIC: 4512 Air passenger carrier, scheduled
PA: Jetblue Airways Corporation
2701 Queens Plz N
Long Island City NY 11101
718 286-7900

PRODUCTS & SVCS

(P-4671)
JETBLUE AIRWAYS CORPORATION
3707 N Harbor Dr 1, San Diego
(92101-1096)
PHONE...............................619 725-0807
EMP: 81
SALES (corp-wide): 7.6B **Publicly Held**
SIC: 4512 Air passenger carrier, scheduled
PA: Jetblue Airways Corporation
2701 Queens Plz N
Long Island City NY 11101
718 286-7900

(P-4672)
KOREAN AIR LINES CO LTD
380 World Way Ste S4, Los Angeles
(90045-5847)
PHONE...............................310 646-4866
EMP: 175 **Privately Held**
WEB: www.laxda.koreanair.com
SIC: 4512 Air transportation, scheduled
PA: Korean Air Lines Co., Ltd.
260 Haneul-Gil, Gangseo-Gu
Seoul 07505

(P-4673)
KOREAN AIRLINES
380 World Way, Los Angeles (90045-5800)
PHONE...............................310 417-5294
Tom Bradley, *Manager*
EMP: 175 **Privately Held**
WEB: www.laxda.koreanair.com
SIC: 4512 Air transportation, scheduled
PA: Korean Air Lines Co., Ltd.
260 Haneul-Gil, Gangseo-Gu
Seoul 07505

(P-4674)
KOREAN AIRLINES CO LTD
Also Called: Korean Arln Crgo Reservations
6101 W Imperial Hwy, Los Angeles
(90045-6305)
PHONE...............................310 410-2000
Jinkul Lee, *President*
Jong Myung Park, *Treasurer*
Sung Kim, *General Mgr*
Steven Kang, *Technology*
Yoonsun Park, *Analyst*
EMP: 250 **Privately Held**
WEB: www.laxda.koreanair.com
SIC: 4512 4513 Air transportation, sched-
uled; package delivery, private air
PA: Korean Air Lines Co., Ltd.
260 Haneul-Gil, Gangseo-Gu
Seoul 07505

(P-4675)
KOREAN AIRLINES CO LTD
1813 Wilshire Blvd # 400, Los Angeles
(90057-3600)
PHONE...............................213 484-1900
Kyung Kim, *Branch Mgr*
Jungsik Kim, *General Mgr*
Luke Kim, *General Mgr*
Jusil Lee, *General Mgr*
Dante Dionne, *Technology*
EMP: 100 **Privately Held**
WEB: www.laxda.koreanair.com
SIC: 4512 4729 Air passenger carrier,
scheduled; airline ticket offices
PA: Korean Air Lines Co., Ltd.
260 Haneul-Gil, Gangseo-Gu
Seoul 07505

(P-4676)
LUKENBILL ENTERPRISES
Also Called: Sky King
3600 Power Inn Rd Ste H, Sacramento
(95826-3826)
PHONE...............................916 454-2400
Greg Lukenbill, *Partner*
EMP: 100
SQ FT: 12,000
SALES (est): 7.6MM **Privately Held**
SIC: 4512 6531 Air transportation, sched-
uled; real estate agents & managers

(P-4677)
PHILIPPINE AIRLINES
11001 Aviation Blvd, Los Angeles
(90045-6123)
PHONE...............................310 646-1981
CHI Marquec, *Branch Mgr*
EMP: 65 **Privately Held**
WEB: www.pal.com
SIC: 4512 Air passenger carrier, scheduled
HQ: Philippine Airlines, Inc.
8th Floor Pnb Financial Center
Pasay 1307
-

(P-4678)
PHILIPPINE AIRLINES INC
447 Sutter St Ste 200, San Francisco
(94108-4636)
PHONE...............................415 217-3100
Rodolfo Llora, *Branch Mgr*
EMP: 150 **Privately Held**
WEB: www.pal.com
SIC: 4512 8741 4513 Air passenger car-
rier, scheduled; management services;
package delivery, private air
HQ: Philippine Airlines, Inc.
8th Floor Pnb Financial Center
Pasay 1307

(P-4679)
SINGAPORE AIRLINES LIMITED
222 N Pacific Coast Hwy # 1600, El Se-
gundo (90245-5615)
PHONE...............................310 647-1922
Tee Hooi Teoh, *Manager*
Loh Meng See Meng See, *Senior VP*
Yau Seng Chin, *Vice Pres*
Kok Wah Chow, *Vice Pres*
Kah Kheng Goh, *Vice Pres*
EMP: 135
SALES (corp-wide): 13MM **Privately Held**
WEB: www.singaporeair.com
SIC: 4512 Air passenger carrier, scheduled
HQ: Singapore Airlines Limited
25 Airline Road
Singapore 81982
678 981-88

(P-4680)
SKYWEST AIRLINES INC
32128 Chagall Ct, Winchester
(92596-9024)
PHONE...............................951 926-9511
EMP: 75
SALES (corp-wide): 3.5B **Publicly Held**
SIC: 4512
HQ: Skywest Airlines, Inc.
444 S River Rd
St George UT 84790
435 634-3000

(P-4681)
SKYWEST AIRLINES INC
26818 Bahama Way, Murrieta
(92563-2553)
PHONE...............................951 600-9181
EMP: 75
SALES (corp-wide): 3.2B **Publicly Held**
SIC: 4512 7389 Air passenger carrier,
scheduled;
HQ: Skywest Airlines, Inc.
444 S River Rd
St George UT 84790
435 634-3000

(P-4682)
SOUTHWEST AIRLINES CO
1 Airport Dr Ste 25, Oakland (94621-1432)
PHONE...............................510 563-1000
Teddy Rowell, *Manager*
EMP: 75
SALES (corp-wide): 21.9B **Publicly Held**
WEB: www.southwest.com
SIC: 4512 Air passenger carrier, scheduled
PA: Southwest Airlines Co.
2702 Love Field Dr
Dallas TX 75235
214 792-4000

(P-4683)
SOUTHWEST AIRLINES CO
100 World Way Ste 328, Los Angeles
(90045-5854)
PHONE...............................310 665-5700

Fax: 310 670-0723
EMP: 70
SALES (corp-wide): 21.1B **Publicly Held**
SIC: 4512 4581
PA: Southwest Airlines Co.
2702 Love Field Dr
Dallas TX 75235
214 792-4000

(P-4684)
SOUTHWEST AIRLINES CO
10 Alan Shepard Way, Oakland
(94621-4501)
PHONE...............................510 563-1234
John Mactherson, *Manager*
EMP: 105
SALES (corp-wide): 21.9B **Publicly Held**
WEB: www.southwest.com
SIC: 4512 Air passenger carrier, scheduled
PA: Southwest Airlines Co.
2702 Love Field Dr
Dallas TX 75235
214 792-4000

(P-4685)
UNITED AIRLINES INC
United Airlines Mnt Optnb, San Francisco
(94128)
PHONE...............................650 634-4209
Bill Norman, *Vice Pres*
Karen Morrison, *Sales Mgr*
EMP: 102
SALES (corp-wide): 41.3B **Publicly Held**
WEB: www.united.com
SIC: 4512 Air passenger carrier, scheduled
HQ: United Airlines, Inc.
233 S Wacker Dr Ste 710
Chicago IL 60606
872 825-4000

(P-4686)
UNITED AIRLINES INC
2435 Whitman Way, San Bruno
(94066-3852)
PHONE...............................650 634-2468
Lon Wildurin, *Manager*
EMP: 101
SALES (corp-wide): 41.3B **Publicly Held**
WEB: www.united.com
SIC: 4512 Air passenger carrier, scheduled
HQ: United Airlines, Inc.
233 S Wacker Dr Ste 710
Chicago IL 60606
872 825-4000

(P-4687)
UNITED AIRLINES INC
6018 Avion Dr, Los Angeles (90045-5679)
PHONE...............................310 342-8086
Don Nelson, *Office Mgr*
Darcy Banks, *Vice Pres*
EMP: 102
SALES (corp-wide): 41.3B **Publicly Held**
SIC: 4512 Air passenger carrier, scheduled
HQ: United Airlines, Inc.
233 S Wacker Dr Ste 710
Chicago IL 60606
872 825-4000

(P-4688)
UNITED AIRLINES INC
Maintenance Operation Ctr, San Francisco
(94128)
PHONE...............................650 634-7800
D K Loo, *Director*
EMP: 60
SALES (corp-wide): 41.3B **Publicly Held**
WEB: www.united.com
SIC: 4512 Air passenger carrier, scheduled
HQ: United Airlines, Inc.
233 S Wacker Dr Ste 710
Chicago IL 60606
872 825-4000

(P-4689)
UNITED AIRLINES INC
3835 N Harbor Dr Ste 115, San Diego
(92101-1081)
PHONE...............................619 692-3310
Al Turner, *Manager*
EMP: 140
SQ FT: 80,705
SALES (corp-wide): 41.3B **Publicly Held**
WEB: www.united.com
SIC: 4512 Air passenger carrier, scheduled

HQ: United Airlines, Inc.
233 S Wacker Dr Ste 710
Chicago IL 60606
872 825-4000

(P-4690)
UNITED AIRLINES INC
Also Called: Continental Airlines
7300 World Way W Rm 144, Los Angeles
(90045-5829)
PHONE...............................310 258-3319
Ken Jaminson, *Manager*
EMP: 275
SALES (corp-wide): 41.3B **Publicly Held**
WEB: www.continental.com
SIC: 4512 Air passenger carrier, scheduled
HQ: United Airlines, Inc.
233 S Wacker Dr Ste 710
Chicago IL 60606
872 825-4000

(P-4691)
UNITED AIRLINES INC
San Francisco Intl Arprt, San Francisco
(94128)
PHONE...............................650 634-4469
Daniel Cummins, *Manager*
EMP: 102
SALES (corp-wide): 41.3B **Publicly Held**
WEB: www.united.com
SIC: 4512 Air passenger carrier, scheduled
HQ: United Airlines, Inc.
233 S Wacker Dr Ste 710
Chicago IL 60606
872 825-4000

(P-4692)
UNITED AIRLINES INC
3400 E Tahquitz Cyn 17, Palm Springs
(92262-6920)
PHONE...............................760 778-5690
Peg James, *Manager*
EMP: 57
SALES (corp-wide): 41.3B **Publicly Held**
WEB: www.united.com
SIC: 4512 Air passenger carrier, scheduled
HQ: United Airlines, Inc.
233 S Wacker Dr Ste 710
Chicago IL 60606
872 825-4000

(P-4693)
UNITED AIRLINES INC
545 Mcdonald Rd 68305, San Francisco
(94128)
PHONE...............................650 634-2772
DK Loo, *Branch Mgr*
EMP: 101
SALES (corp-wide): 41.3B **Publicly Held**
SIC: 4512 Air passenger carrier, scheduled
HQ: United Airlines, Inc.
233 S Wacker Dr Ste 710
Chicago IL 60606
872 825-4000

(P-4694)
UNITED AIRLINES INC
800 S Arprt Blvd Bldg 84, San Francisco
(94128)
PHONE...............................650 634-2085
Edward De Bono, *Opers Mgr*
EMP: 51
SALES (corp-wide): 41.3B **Publicly Held**
SIC: 4512 Air passenger carrier, scheduled
HQ: United Airlines, Inc.
233 S Wacker Dr Ste 710
Chicago IL 60606
872 825-4000

(P-4695)
UNITED COURIERS INC (DH)
Also Called: U C I Distribution Plus
3280 E Foothill Blvd, Pasadena
(91107-3103)
PHONE...............................213 383-3611
Stephan Cretier, *CEO*
Richard R Irvin, *President*
Robert G Irvin, *Treasurer*
EMP: 200
SQ FT: 25,000

SALES (est): 31.2MM
SALES (corp-wide): 1.5MM **Privately Held**
WEB: www.unitedcouriers.net
SIC: 4512 4215 4212 7381 Air cargo carrier, scheduled; courier services, except by air; local trucking, without storage; armored car services; freight forwarding
HQ: Ati Systems International, Inc.
2000 Nw Corp Blvd Ste 101
Boca Raton FL 33431
561 939-7000

(P-4696)
VIRGIN AMERICA INC (HQ)
555 Airport Blvd, Burlingame (94010-2000)
PHONE..........................877 359-8474
Benito Minicucci, *CEO*
Christina Brunn, *Technical Staff*
EMP: 198
SQ FT: 85,674
SALES: 1.5B
SALES (corp-wide): 8.2B **Publicly Held**
WEB: www.virginamerica.com
SIC: 4512 Air passenger carrier, scheduled
PA: Alaska Air Group, Inc
19300 International Blvd
Seatac WA 98188
206 392-5040

4513 Air Courier Svcs

(P-4697)
DHL EXPRESS (USA) INC
401 23rd St, San Francisco (94107-3102)
PHONE..........................415 826-7338
Jeffrey Funk, *Manager*
Warfield Thornton, *General Mgr*
EMP: 70
SALES (corp-wide): 70.4B **Privately Held**
SIC: 4513 Air courier services
HQ: Dhl Express (Usa), Inc.
1210 S Pine Island Rd
Plantation FL 33324
954 888-7000

(P-4698)
FEDERAL EXPRESS CORPORATION
Also Called: Fedex
3541 Regional Pkwy, Petaluma (94954)
PHONE..........................800 463-3339
EMP: 80
SALES (corp-wide): 47.4B **Publicly Held**
SIC: 4513
HQ: Federal Express Corporation
3610 Hacks Cross Rd
Memphis TN 38125
901 369-3600

(P-4699)
FEDERAL EXPRESS CORPORATION
Also Called: Fedex
1650 47th St, San Diego (92102-2508)
PHONE..........................800 463-3339
EMP: 225
SALES (corp-wide): 69.6B **Publicly Held**
WEB: www.federalexpress.com
SIC: 4513 Air courier services
HQ: Federal Express Corporation
3610 Hacks Cross Rd
Memphis TN 38125
901 369-3600

(P-4700)
FEDERAL EXPRESS CORPORATION
Also Called: Fedex
1330 Fortress St, Chico (95973-9031)
PHONE..........................800 463-3339
EMP: 109
SALES (corp-wide): 69.6B **Publicly Held**
SIC: 4513 Air courier services
HQ: Federal Express Corporation
3610 Hacks Cross Rd
Memphis TN 38125
901 369-3600

(P-4701)
FEDERAL EXPRESS CORPORATION
Also Called: Fedex
1286 Lawrence Station Rd, Sunnyvale (94089-2220)
PHONE..........................800 463-3339
EMP: 100
SALES (corp-wide): 69.6B **Publicly Held**
WEB: www.federalexpress.com
SIC: 4513 4215 Letter delivery, private air; package delivery, private air; parcel delivery, private air; courier services, except by air
HQ: Federal Express Corporation
3610 Hacks Cross Rd
Memphis TN 38125
901 369-3600

(P-4702)
FEDERAL EXPRESS CORPORATION
Also Called: Fedex
12600 Prairie Ave, Hawthorne (90250-4685)
PHONE..........................800 463-3339
EMP: 200
SALES (corp-wide): 69.6B **Publicly Held**
WEB: www.federalexpress.com
SIC: 4513 4215 Air courier services; courier services, except by air
HQ: Federal Express Corporation
3610 Hacks Cross Rd
Memphis TN 38125
901 369-3600

(P-4703)
FEDERAL EXPRESS CORPORATION
Also Called: Fedex
1601 Aurora Dr, San Leandro (94577-3101)
PHONE..........................510 347-2430
EMP: 130
SALES (corp-wide): 47.4B **Publicly Held**
SIC: 4513 4215
HQ: Federal Express Corporation
3610 Hacks Cross Rd
Memphis TN 38125
901 369-3600

(P-4704)
FEDERAL EXPRESS CORPORATION
Also Called: Fedex
1650 Sunflower Ave, Costa Mesa (92626-1513)
PHONE..........................800 463-3339
EMP: 53
SQ FT: 75,000
SALES (corp-wide): 69.6B **Publicly Held**
WEB: www.federalexpress.com
SIC: 4513 Air courier services
HQ: Federal Express Corporation
3610 Hacks Cross Rd
Memphis TN 38125
901 369-3600

(P-4705)
FEDERAL EXPRESS CORPORATION
Also Called: Fedex
1 Lower Ragsdale Dr # 4, Monterey (93940-5757)
PHONE..........................800 463-3339
Dave Cox, *General Mgr*
EMP: 60
SALES (corp-wide): 69.6B **Publicly Held**
WEB: www.federalexpress.com
SIC: 4513 Package delivery, private air
HQ: Federal Express Corporation
3610 Hacks Cross Rd
Memphis TN 38125
901 369-3600

(P-4706)
FEDERAL EXPRESS CORPORATION
Also Called: Fedex
500 12th St Ste 139, Oakland (94607-4010)
PHONE..........................510 465-5209
EMP: 107

(P-4707)
FEDERAL EXPRESS CORPORATION
Also Called: Fedex
8455 Pardee Dr, Oakland (94621-1411)
PHONE..........................800 463-3339
EMP: 100
SALES (corp-wide): 69.6B **Publicly Held**
WEB: www.federalexpress.com
SIC: 4513 4215 Letter delivery, private air; package delivery, private air; parcel delivery, private air; courier services, except by air
HQ: Federal Express Corporation
3610 Hacks Cross Rd
Memphis TN 38125
901 369-3600

(P-4708)
FEDERAL EXPRESS CORPORATION
Also Called: Fedex
6775 Woodrum Cir, Redding (96002-9386)
PHONE..........................800 463-3339
EMP: 150
SALES (corp-wide): 69.6B **Publicly Held**
WEB: www.federalexpress.com
SIC: 4513 4215 Letter delivery, private air; package delivery, private air; parcel delivery, private air; package delivery, vehicular
HQ: Federal Express Corporation
3610 Hacks Cross Rd
Memphis TN 38125
901 369-3600

(P-4709)
FEDERAL EXPRESS CORPORATION
Also Called: Fedex
935 Performance Dr, Stockton (95206-4930)
PHONE..........................800 463-3339
EMP: 50
SALES (corp-wide): 69.6B **Publicly Held**
SIC: 4513 Package delivery, private air; letter delivery, private air
HQ: Federal Express Corporation
3610 Hacks Cross Rd
Memphis TN 38125
901 369-3600

(P-4710)
FEDERAL EXPRESS CORPORATION
Also Called: Fedex
9339 Ann St, Santa Fe Springs (90670-2655)
PHONE..........................800 463-3339
EMP: 100
SALES (corp-wide): 69.6B **Publicly Held**
WEB: www.federalexpress.com
SIC: 4513 Package delivery, private air; letter delivery, private air
HQ: Federal Express Corporation
3610 Hacks Cross Rd
Memphis TN 38125
901 369-3600

(P-4711)
FEDERAL EXPRESS CORPORATION
Also Called: Fedex
9510 W Airport Dr, Visalia (93277-9501)
PHONE..........................800 463-3339
EMP: 150
SALES (corp-wide): 69.6B **Publicly Held**
WEB: www.federalexpress.com
SIC: 4513 Package delivery, private air; letter delivery, private air
HQ: Federal Express Corporation
3610 Hacks Cross Rd
Memphis TN 38125
901 369-3600

(P-4712)
FEDERAL EXPRESS CORPORATION
Also Called: Fedex
2060 S Wineville Ave B, Ontario (91761-3633)
PHONE..........................909 390-3237
EMP: 60
SALES (corp-wide): 47.4B **Publicly Held**
SIC: 4513
HQ: Federal Express Corporation
3610 Hacks Cross Rd
Memphis TN 38125
901 369-3600

(P-4713)
FEDERAL EXPRESS CORPORATION
Also Called: Fedex
2500 Kimberly Ave, Fullerton (92831-5142)
PHONE..........................800 463-3339
EMP: 130
SALES (corp-wide): 69.6B **Publicly Held**
WEB: www.federalexpress.com
SIC: 4513 Letter delivery, private air; package delivery, private air; parcel delivery, private air
HQ: Federal Express Corporation
3610 Hacks Cross Rd
Memphis TN 38125
901 369-3600

(P-4714)
FEDERAL EXPRESS CORPORATION
Also Called: Fedex
3150 Paseo Mercado, Oxnard (93036-8918)
PHONE..........................800 463-3339
David Teems, *Manager*
EMP: 70
SALES (corp-wide): 69.6B **Publicly Held**
WEB: www.federalexpress.com
SIC: 4513 Letter delivery, private air; package delivery, private air; parcel delivery, private air
HQ: Federal Express Corporation
3610 Hacks Cross Rd
Memphis TN 38125
901 369-3600

(P-4715)
FEDERAL EXPRESS CORPORATION
Also Called: Fedex
8950 Cal Center Dr # 370, Sacramento (95826-3262)
PHONE..........................916 361-5500
EMP: 100
SALES (corp-wide): 47.4B **Publicly Held**
SIC: 4513 4512 4212 4213
HQ: Federal Express Corporation
3610 Hacks Cross Rd
Memphis TN 38125
901 369-3600

(P-4716)
FEDERAL EXPRESS CORPORATION
Also Called: Fedex
1875 Marin St, San Francisco (94124-1139)
PHONE..........................800 463-3339
EMP: 109
SALES (corp-wide): 69.6B **Publicly Held**
WEB: www.federalexpress.com
SIC: 4513 4512 4522 4213 Letter delivery, private air; air transportation, scheduled; air transportation, nonscheduled; trucking, except local
HQ: Federal Express Corporation
3610 Hacks Cross Rd
Memphis TN 38125
901 369-3600

(P-4717)
FEDERAL EXPRESS CORPORATION
Also Called: Fedex
2451 N Palm Dr, Long Beach (90755-4006)
PHONE..........................800 463-3339
EMP: 150

P
R
O
D
U
C
T
S

&

S
V
C
S

SALES (corp-wide): 47.4B **Publicly Held**
SIC: 4513
HQ: Federal Express Corporation
3610 Hacks Cross Rd
Memphis TN 38125
901 369-3600

(P-4718)
FEDERAL EXPRESS CORPORATION
Also Called: Fedex
1 World Trade Ctr Ste 191, Long Beach
(90831-0191)
PHONE...................562 522-4014
EMP: 150
SALES (corp-wide): 45.5B **Publicly Held**
SIC: 4513
HQ: Federal Express Corporation
3610 Hacks Cross Rd
Memphis TN 38125
901 369-3600

(P-4719)
FEDEX GROUND PACKAGE SYS INC
9999 Olson Dr Ste 100, San Diego
(92121-2837)
PHONE...................800 463-3339
Teresa Lyda, *Executive*
Steve Morgan, *Administration*
EMP: 107
SALES (corp-wide): 69.6B **Publicly Held**
SIC: 4513 Package delivery, private air
HQ: Fedex Ground Package System, Inc.
1000 Fed Ex Dr
Coraopolis PA 15108
800 463-3339

(P-4720)
FEDEX GROUND PACKAGE SYS INC
330 Resource Dr, Bloomington
(92316-3528)
PHONE...................800 463-3339
David Kodek, *Manager*
EMP: 800
SALES (corp-wide): 69.6B **Publicly Held**
SIC: 4513 Air courier services
HQ: Fedex Ground Package System, Inc.
1000 Fed Ex Dr
Coraopolis PA 15108
800 463-3339

(P-4721)
GREYHOUND LINES INC
121 S Center St, Stockton (95202-2817)
PHONE...................209 466-3568
Jackie Wilson, *Manager*
EMP: 50
SALES (corp-wide): 9.1B **Privately Held**
WEB: www.greyhound.com
SIC: 4513 Package delivery, private air
HQ: Greyhound Lines, Inc.
350 N Saint Paul St # 300
Dallas TX 75201
214 849-8000

(P-4722)
LBC MUNDIAL CORPORATION (DH)
Also Called: LBC North America
3563 Inv Blvd Ste 3, Hayward (94545)
PHONE...................650 873-0750
Miguel Angel Camahort, *President*
EMP: 60
SQ FT: 25,000
SALES (est): 54.9MM **Privately Held**
SIC: 4513 4215 6099 6221 Air courier services; courier services, except by air; foreign currency exchange; commodity contracts brokers, dealers

(P-4723)
MEJICO EXPRESS INC (PA)
Also Called: Grupoex
14849 Firestone Blvd Fl 1, La Mirada
(90638)
PHONE...................714 690-8300
Jose Leon, *President*
EMP: 150
SALES (est): 23.3MM **Privately Held**
SIC: 4513 Letter delivery, private air

(P-4724)
MIDNITE AIR CORP
8801 Bellanca Ave, Los Angeles
(90045-4705)
PHONE...................310 330-2300
Tom Belmont, *Branch Mgr*
Wendy Alfredsen, *Director*
Benjamin Gatt, *Manager*
EMP: 50
SALES (corp-wide): 1.1B **Privately Held**
SIC: 4513 Air courier services
HQ: Midnite Air Corp.
5001 Arprt Plz Dr Ste 250
Long Beach CA 90815
310 910-9199

(P-4725)
MIDNITE AIR CORP (HQ)
Also Called: MNX
5001 Arprt Plz Dr Ste 250, Long Beach
(90815)
PHONE...................310 910-9199
Paul J Martins, *President*
Thomas Belmont, *COO*
Fred Deleeuw, *CFO*
Nathan Gesse, *Exec VP*
Paul Hickey, *Exec VP*
EMP: 55
SQ FT: 10,000
SALES (est): 104.7MM
SALES (corp-wide): 1.1B **Privately Held**
WEB: www.mnx.com
SIC: 4513 Air courier services
PA: Audax Private Equity Fund Ii, L.P.
101 Huntington Ave
Boston MA 02199
617 859-1500

(P-4726)
RLCS INC (PA)
Also Called: Redline Courier Service
10550 Sepulveda Blvd # 203, Mission Hills
(91345-1965)
PHONE...................818 898-1164
Steven Sundling, *CEO*
Jason Sundling, *CFO*
Alex Vucurevic, *Admin Sec*
EMP: 89
SQ FT: 700
SALES (est): 11.8MM **Privately Held**
WEB: www.redlinecourier.com
SIC: 4513 7389 Air courier services; courier or messenger service

(P-4727)
TNT USA INC
Also Called: TNT Express Worldwide
8500 Osage Ave, Los Angeles
(90045-4421)
PHONE...................310 242-9700
EMP: 70
SALES (corp-wide): 69.6B **Publicly Held**
WEB: www.tnt.com
SIC: 4513 Air courier services
HQ: Tnt Usa Inc.
510 Stewart Ave
Garden City NY 11530
631 712-6700

(P-4728)
TRICOR AMERICA INC
3149 Diablo Ave, Hayward (94545-2701)
PHONE...................510 293-3960
Mike Chung, *Branch Mgr*
EMP: 150
SALES (corp-wide): 92.6MM **Privately Held**
WEB: www.tricor.com
SIC: 4513 4215 Package delivery, private air; courier services, except by air
PA: Tricor America, Inc.
717 Airport Blvd
South San Francisco CA 94080
650 877-3650

(P-4729)
ULTRAEX INC
2633 Barrington Ct, Hayward (94545-1100)
PHONE...................800 882-1000
Ernest Holbrook, *President*
Patrick Larouche, *Technology*
Shirley Sun, *Technology*
EMP: 100
SQ FT: 10,000

SALES (est): 10.1MM **Privately Held**
WEB: www.ultraex.com
SIC: 4513 4214 4215 Air courier services; local trucking with storage; package delivery, vehicular

(P-4730)
UNITED PARCEL SERVICE INC OH
Also Called: UPS
3333 S Downey Rd, Vernon (90058-4116)
PHONE...................323 260-8957
Tony Peralta, *Sales Staff*
EMP: 350
SALES (corp-wide): 71.8B **Publicly Held**
WEB: www.upsscs.com
SIC: 4513 4215 Air courier services; courier services, except by air
HQ: United Parcel Service, Inc.
55 Glenlake Pkwy
Atlanta GA 30328
404 828-6000

(P-4731)
UNITED PARCEL SERVICE INC OH
Also Called: UPS
25283 Sherman Rd, Sun City
(92585-9352)
PHONE...................951 928-5221
Sean Nichols, *Branch Mgr*
EMP: 208
SALES (corp-wide): 71.8B **Publicly Held**
SIC: 4513 Parcel delivery, private air
HQ: United Parcel Service, Inc.
55 Glenlake Pkwy
Atlanta GA 30328
404 828-6000

(P-4732)
UNITED PARCEL SERVICE INC OH
Also Called: UPS
1724 Wawona St, Manteca (95337-9437)
PHONE...................209 944-5932
EMP: 208
SALES (corp-wide): 71.8B **Publicly Held**
WEB: www.upsscs.com
SIC: 4513 Parcel delivery, private air
HQ: United Parcel Service, Inc.
55 Glenlake Pkwy
Atlanta GA 30328
404 828-6000

(P-4733)
UNITED PARCEL SERVICE INC OH
Also Called: UPS
Ontario Airport, Ontario (91758)
PHONE...................909 974-7190
Steve Welsh, *Manager*
EMP: 208
SALES (corp-wide): 71.8B **Publicly Held**
WEB: www.upsscs.com
SIC: 4513 Parcel delivery, private air
HQ: United Parcel Service, Inc.
55 Glenlake Pkwy
Atlanta GA 30328
404 828-6000

(P-4734)
WEST AIR INC
5005 E Andersen Ave, Fresno
(93727-1502)
PHONE...................559 454-7843
Lawrence W Olson, *Ch of Bd*
Timothy Flynn, *Shareholder*
Maurice Gallagher, *Shareholder*
Beth Wood, *President*
Sherry Mahan, *Manager*
EMP: 70 **EST:** 1940
SQ FT: 10,000
SALES: 7.5MM **Privately Held**
WEB: www.westair.net
SIC: 4513 Package delivery, private air

(P-4735)
WING AVIATION LLC
3400 Hillview Ave Bldg 4, Palo Alto
(94304-1346)
PHONE...................650 224-1198
James Burgess, *CEO*
EMP: 120
SALES (est): 2.2MM **Privately Held**
SIC: 4513 Package delivery, private air

(P-4736)
WING AVIATION LLC
100 Mayfield Ave, Mountain View
(94043-4122)
PHONE...................650 260-8170
James Burgess, *CEO*
Adam Woodworth, *CTO*
Divya Chandra, *Controller*
EMP: 100
SALES (est): 2.2MM
SALES (corp-wide): 136.8B **Publicly Held**
SIC: 4513 Package delivery, private air
PA: Alphabet Inc.
1600 Amphitheatre Pkwy
Mountain View CA 94043
650 253-0000

4522 Air Transportation, Nonscheduled

(P-4737)
AIR RUTTER INTERNATIONAL LLC
Also Called: Alerion Aviation
3501 N Lakewood Blvd, Long Beach
(90808-1736)
PHONE...................855 359-2576
Ernest Bill Cripe, *Mng Member*
Robert A Seidel,
EMP: 50
SQ FT: 2,500
SALES (est): 6.6MM **Privately Held**
WEB: www.arijets.com
SIC: 4522 Air passenger carriers, non-scheduled

(P-4738)
BOUTIQUE AIR INC (PA)
5 3rd St Ste 925, San Francisco
(94103-3220)
PHONE...................415 449-0505
Shawn Simpson, *President*
Brian Murphy, *COO*
Roman Tatiana, *Project Mgr*
Cornelius Owens, *Maintence Staff*
Jared Carlstrom, *Asst Director*
EMP: 63
SALES (est): 38MM **Privately Held**
SIC: 4522 4512 Flying charter service; air passenger carrier, scheduled

(P-4739)
ELITE AVIATION LLC
7501 Hayvenhurst Pl, Van Nuys
(91406-2851)
PHONE...................818 988-5387
Kacani Shina, *Mng Member*
EMP: 100
SQ FT: 54,000
SALES (est): 16.4MM **Privately Held**
WEB: www.eliteaviation.com
SIC: 4522 4581 Flying charter service; aircraft maintenance & repair services

(P-4740)
FAYAKA AIRWAYS LLC
659 Macarthur Blvd, San Leandro
(94577-2115)
PHONE...................800 771-5489
Yannick Kamate, *CEO*
EMP: 200
SALES: 1MM **Privately Held**
SIC: 4522 Air transportation, nonscheduled

(P-4741)
JET EDGE INTERNATIONAL LLC
16700 Roscoe Blvd Hngr C, Van Nuys
(91406-1102)
PHONE...................818 442-0096
William Papariella, *CEO*
Kevin White, *Partner*
Mike Sanders, *CFO*
Robert Schiller, *CFO*
Clayton Smith, *Vice Pres*
EMP: 100 **EST:** 2011
SALES (est): 13.3MM **Privately Held**
SIC: 4522 Air transportation, nonscheduled

(P-4742)
JETSUITE INC (PA)
18952 Macarthur Blvd # 200, Irvine
(92612-1401)
PHONE...................949 892-4300

Alex Wilcox, *CEO*
Stephanie Chung, *President*
Keith Rabin, *CFO*
Austin Alexander, *Officer*
Gerardo Labrador, *Officer*
EMP: 58
SQ FT: 7,641
SALES (est): 42.3MM **Privately Held**
SIC: 4522 Flying charter service

(P-4743)
KAISERAIR INC (PA)
8735 Earhart Rd, Oakland (94621-4547)
P.O. Box 2626 (94614-0626)
PHONE..................................510 569-9622
Ronald J Guerra, *President*
Rob Guerra, *Senior VP*
Glenn Barrett, *Vice Pres*
David A Mancebo, *Vice Pres*
Gregg Rorabaugh, *Vice Pres*
EMP: 185 **EST:** 1979
SQ FT: 970,000
SALES (est): 48.8MM **Privately Held**
WEB: www.kaiserair.com
SIC: 4522 Flying charter service

(P-4744)
MAGUIRE AVIATION GROUP LLC
7155 Valjean Ave, Van Nuys (91406-3917)
PHONE..................................818 989-2300
Alec Maguire, *President*
Mark Nawrocki, *VP Mktg*
EMP: 50
SALES (est): 5.8MM **Privately Held**
SIC: 4522 Flying charter service

(P-4745)
MERCY AIR TRI-COUNTY LLC
1670 Miro Way, Rialto (92376-8629)
P.O. Box 2532, Fontana (92334-2532)
PHONE..................................909 829-1051
David Dolstein, *Mng Member*
Aaron Todd,
EMP: 250
SQ FT: 11,288
SALES (est): 9.2MM
SALES (corp-wide): 1.6B **Privately Held**
SIC: 4522 4119 7623 7359 Ambulance services, air; local passenger transportation; air conditioning repair; aircraft & industrial truck rental services; helicopters
HQ: Air Methods Corporation
5500 S Quebec St Ste 300
Greenwood Village CO 80111
303 792-7400

(P-4746)
MERLIN GLOBAL SERVICES LLC
Also Called: Aevex Flight Operations
440 Stevens Ave Ste 150, Solana Beach (92075-2058)
PHONE..................................904 305-9559
Conner Searcy, *President*
Brian Raduenz, *CEO*
David Scott, *COO*
J Wayne Miller, *Vice Pres*
David Stinnett, *Admin Sec*
EMP: 110
SALES (est): 13.2MM **Privately Held**
WEB: www.merlinramco.com
SIC: 4522 8711 8731 8748 Air transportation, nonscheduled; engineering services; commercial physical research; test development & evaluation service; educational services

(P-4747)
SUTTER CENTRAL VLY HOSPITALS
Also Called: Medi-Flight Northern Cal
1700 Coffee Rd, Modesto (95355-2803)
PHONE..................................209 526-4500
Terry Sweeney, *Director*
EMP: 50
SALES (corp-wide): 12.7B **Privately Held**
WEB: www.memorialmedicalcenter.org
SIC: 4522 Air transportation, nonscheduled
HQ: Sutter Central Valley Hospitals
1700 Coffee Rd
Modesto CA 95355
209 526-4500

4581 Airports, Flying Fields & Terminal Svcs

(P-4748)
ABM AVIATION INC
601 Gateway Blvd Ste 1145, South San Francisco (94080-7413)
PHONE..................................650 872-5400
Doug Kreuckamp, *Vice Pres*
EMP: 400
SALES (corp-wide): 6.4B **Publicly Held**
SIC: 4581 Airport
HQ: Abm Aviation, Inc.
3399 Peachtree Rd Ne
Atlanta GA 30326
404 926-4200

(P-4749)
AIRPORT COMMISIONS
Also Called: Business of Finance
San Francisco Intl Arprt, San Francisco (94128)
PHONE..................................650 821-5000
John L Martin, *Director*
EMP: 1121
SALES (est): 30MM **Privately Held**
SIC: 4581 Airports, flying fields & services
PA: City & County Of San Francisco
1 Dr Carlton B Goodlett P
San Francisco CA 94102
415 554-7500

(P-4750)
ALLIANCE GROUND INTL LLC
6181 W Imperial Hwy, Los Angeles (90045-6305)
PHONE..................................310 646-2446
EMP: 73
SALES (corp-wide): 114.7MM **Privately Held**
SIC: 4581 Airfreight loading & unloading services
PA: Alliance Ground International, Llc
2 Datran Ctr
Miami FL 33156
305 740-3252

(P-4751)
ALLIANCE GROUND INTL LLC
648 Rest Field Rd, San Francisco (94128)
PHONE..................................650 821-0855
EMP: 73
SALES (corp-wide): 114.7MM **Privately Held**
SIC: 4581 Airfreight loading & unloading services
PA: Alliance Ground International, Llc
2 Datran Ctr
Miami FL 33156
305 740-3252

(P-4752)
ARINWINE ARCFT MAINT SVCS LLC
Also Called: F&E Aircraft Maintenance
6201 W Imperial Hwy, Los Angeles (90045-6306)
PHONE..................................310 338-0063
Lisa Arinwine, *COO*
EMP: 63
SQ FT: 10,000
SALES (est): 2.1MM **Privately Held**
SIC: 4581 Aircraft maintenance & repair services; aircraft servicing & repairing

(P-4753)
ATLANTIC AVIATION SVC
1250 Aviation Ave Hngr E2, San Jose (95110-1142)
PHONE..................................408 297-7552
Dan Ryan, *President*
Harold Deguzman, *CFO*
Jim Blair, *Treasurer*
Jim Rutherford, *Exec VP*
Barry Fernald, *Admin Sec*
EMP: 50
SQ FT: 196,000
SALES (est): 4.8MM **Privately Held**
WEB: www.sjjc.com
SIC: 4581 Aircraft maintenance & repair services; hangars & other aircraft storage facilities

(P-4754)
AVIATION & DEFENSE INC
Also Called: ADI
255 S Leland Norton Way, San Bernardino (92408-0103)
PHONE..................................909 382-3487
Daniel M Scanlon, *CEO*
Hector Guerrero, *Ch of Bd*
Mike Scanlon, *President*
Ben Flores, *CFO*
Dan Scanlon, *Vice Pres*
EMP: 180
SQ FT: 180,000
SALES (est): 24.4MM **Privately Held**
SIC: 4581 Aircraft maintenance & repair services

(P-4755)
AVIATION MAINTENANCE GROUP INC
8352 Kimball Ave Hngr 3, Chino (91708-9267)
PHONE..................................714 469-0515
Jeremy G Schuster, *President*
Doug Crowther, *Vice Pres*
Douglas Crowther, *Sales Staff*
Jerry Perez, *Director*
Nicole Dilullo, *Manager*
EMP: 85
SALES (est): 2.2MM **Privately Held**
SIC: 4581 Aircraft maintenance & repair services

(P-4756)
BOEING COMPANY
Slc 2 Bldg 1628, San Luis Obispo (93401)
P.O. Box 5219, Lompoc (93437-0219)
PHONE..................................805 606-6340
Rich Niederhauser, *Manager*
EMP: 80
SALES (corp-wide): 101.1B **Publicly Held**
SIC: 4581 3761 3721 Airports & flying fields; guided missiles & space vehicles; aircraft
PA: The Boeing Company
100 N Riverside Plz
Chicago IL 60606
312 544-2000

(P-4757)
CERTIFIED AVIATION SVCS LLC
5720 Avion Dr, Los Angeles (90045-5662)
PHONE..................................310 338-1224
Henry Havash, *Manager*
EMP: 66
SALES (corp-wide): 52.1MM **Privately Held**
SIC: 4581 Aircraft maintenance & repair services
PA: Certified Aviation Services Llc
1150 S Vineyard Ave
Ontario CA 91761
909 605-0380

(P-4758)
CITY OF LONG BEACH
Also Called: Long Beach Airport
4100 E Don Douglas Dr Fl Flr 2, Long Beach (90808)
PHONE..................................562 570-2600
Chris Kunze, *Manager*
EMP: 65 **Privately Held**
WEB: www.polb.com
SIC: 4581 9111 Airport; mayors' offices
PA: City Of Long Beach
411 W Ocean Blvd
Long Beach CA 90802
562 570-6450

(P-4759)
CITY OF LOS ANGELES
Also Called: Van Nuys Airport
16461 Sherman Way Ste 210, Van Nuys (91406-3841)
PHONE..................................818 908-5950
Selena Birk, *Manager*
Danielle Stewart, *Sales Executive*
EMP: 100 **Privately Held**
WEB: www.lacity.org
SIC: 4581 9621 6531 Airport; regulation, administration of transportation; ; real estate managers

PA: City Of Los Angeles
200 N Spring St Ste 303
Los Angeles CA 90012
213 978-0600

(P-4760)
CITY OF PALM SPRINGS
3400 E Tahquitz Canyon Wa, Palm Springs (92262-6966)
P.O. Box 2743 (92263-2743)
PHONE..................................760 318-3800
Thomas Nolan, *Director*
EMP: 58 **Privately Held**
WEB: www.psfire.com
SIC: 4581 Airport
PA: City Of Palm Springs
3200 E Tahquitz Cyn Way
Palm Springs CA 92262
760 322-8362

(P-4761)
CITY OF SAN JOSE
Also Called: Mineta San Jose Intl Arprt
1701 Arprt Blvd Ste B1130, San Jose (95110)
PHONE..................................408 392-3600
William Sherry, *Director*
EMP: 310
SQ FT: 30,000 **Privately Held**
WEB: www.csjfinance.org
SIC: 4581 9199 Airport;
PA: City Of San Jose
200 E Santa Clara St
San Jose CA 95113
408 535-3500

(P-4762)
CLAY LACY AVIATION INC (PA)
Also Called: C L A
7435 Valjean Ave, Van Nuys (91406-2977)
PHONE..................................818 989-2900
Brian Kirkdoffer, *President*
Jimmy Dailey, *COO*
Bradford Wright, *CFO*
Hershel Clay Lacy, *Founder*
Joe Barber, *Vice Pres*
EMP: 350
SQ FT: 18,000
SALES (est): 69.4MM **Privately Held**
WEB: www.claylacy.com
SIC: 4581 Airport terminal services

(P-4763)
COMAV TECHNICAL SERVICES LLC
Also Called: S C A
18438 Readiness St, Victorville (92394-7945)
PHONE..................................760 530-2400
Craig Garrick, *CEO*
Jon Day, *CFO*
▲ **EMP:** 155
SQ FT: 47,625
SALES (est): 26.7MM
SALES (corp-wide): 154.8MM **Privately Held**
WEB: www.scaviation.com
SIC: 4581 Aircraft servicing & repairing
PA: Comav, Llc
18499 Phantom St Ste 17
Victorville CA 92394
760 523-5100

(P-4764)
COUNTY OF MENDOCINO
Also Called: Department of Transportation
340 Lake Mendocino Dr, Ukiah (95482-9432)
PHONE..................................707 463-4363
Howard Dashiell, *Branch Mgr*
EMP: 96 **Privately Held**
WEB: www.mcdss.org
SIC: 4581 Airport
PA: County Of Mendocino
501 Low Gap Rd Rm 1010
Ukiah CA 95482
707 463-4441

(P-4765)
COUNTY OF ORANGE
Also Called: John Wayne Airport
3160 Airway Ave, Costa Mesa (92626-4608)
PHONE..................................949 252-5006
Loan Leblow, *Branch Mgr*
Martin Ness, *Maintence Staff*

P R O D U C T S & S V C S

Rick Cathey, *Sr Project Mgr*
Steve Siemion, *Director*
Lea Choum, *Manager*
EMP: 135 **Privately Held**
SIC: 4581 9621 Airport; aircraft regulating
agencies;
PA: County Of Orange
333 W Santa Ana Blvd 3f
Santa Ana CA 92701
714 834-6200

(P-4766)
COUNTY OF SACRAMENTO
Also Called: Airports Dept
6900 Airport Blvd, Sacramento (95837)
PHONE.................................916 874-0912
Hardy Acree, *Director*
Joe Luna, *Technology*
EMP: 275 **Privately Held**
WEB: www.sna.com
SIC: 4581 9621 Airport; aircraft regulating
agencies;
PA: County Of Sacramento
700 H St Ste 7650
Sacramento CA 95814
916 874-5544

(P-4767)
DSD TRUCKING INC (PA)
2411 Santa Fe Ave, Redondo Beach
(90278-1125)
PHONE.................................310 338-3395
Dan Cuevas, *President*
Jovita Reyes, *Office Mgr*
Kalonde Gilbert, *CTO*
Danielle Martinez, *Hum Res Coord*
EMP: 100
SQ FT: 300,000
SALES (est): 17.2MM **Privately Held**
SIC: 4581 Air freight handling at airports

(P-4768)
DYNAMO AVIATION INC
16760 Schoenborn St, North Hills
(91343-6108)
P.O. Box 14040, Van Nuys (91409-4040)
PHONE.................................818 785-9561
Masoud S Rabadi, *CEO*
Robin C Scott, *CFO*
Lary Hockens, *Officer*
George Qatto, *General Mgr*
Young Lee, *Info Tech Mgr*
EMP: 75
SALES (est): 41.3MM **Privately Held**
WEB: www.dynamoaviation.com
SIC: 4581 3444 3679 5063 Aircraft serv-
icing & repairing; sheet metalwork; har-
ness assemblies for electronic use: wire
or cable; storage batteries, industrial

(P-4769)
DYNCORP INTERNATIONAL LLC
Also Called: Logcap IV - Task Order 7
896 Langford Lake Rd, Fort Irwin (92310)
P.O. Box 105033 (92310-5033)
PHONE.................................817 224-8200
Steve Gassney, *Branch Mgr*
EMP: 53
SALES (corp-wide): 28B **Privately Held**
SIC: 4581 Aircraft maintenance & repair
services
HQ: Dyncorp International Llc
1700 Old Meadow Rd
Mc Lean VA 22102
571 722-0210

(P-4770)
F KORBEL & BROS
Korbel Flight Department
4384 Becker Blvd, Santa Rosa
(95403-8283)
PHONE.................................707 525-1875
Gary Krambs, *Branch Mgr*
EMP: 129
SALES (corp-wide): 98.2MM **Privately
Held**
SIC: 4581 Airport
PA: F. Korbel & Bros.
13250 River Rd
Guerneville CA 95446
707 824-7000

(P-4771)
F&E AIRCRAFT MAINTENANCE (PA)
531 Main St, El Segundo (90245-3060)
PHONE.................................310 338-0063
Everett R Arinwine,
Keiney Mosley, *Manager*
EMP: 350
SALES (est): 23.7MM **Privately Held**
SIC: 4581 7699 Aircraft servicing & repair-
ing; aircraft & heavy equipment repair
services

(P-4772)
GAT - ARLN GROUND SUPPORT INC
6701 Lindbergh Dr, Sacramento
(95837-1138)
PHONE.................................916 923-2349
Tina Stupa, *Admin Asst*
EMP: 304
SALES (corp-wide): 116MM **Privately
Held**
SIC: 4581 Aircraft maintenance & repair
services; airfreight loading & unloading
services
PA: Gat - Airline Ground Support, Inc.
246 City Cir
Peachtree City GA 30269
251 633-3888

(P-4773)
GE AVIATION SYSTEMS LLC
295 N Wolfe Ave Bldg 3810, Edwards Afb
(93524-6003)
PHONE.................................661 277-7308
EMP: 193
SALES (corp-wide): 121.6B **Publicly
Held**
SIC: 4581 Airports, flying fields & services
HQ: Ge Aviation Systems Llc
1 Neumann Way
Cincinnati OH 45215
937 898-9600

(P-4774)
HUNTLEIGH USA CORPORATION
3707 N Harbor Dr A-110, San Diego
(92101-1096)
PHONE.................................619 231-8111
Richard Madison, *Branch Mgr*
EMP: 75
SALES (corp-wide): 298.2MM **Privately
Held**
SIC: 4581 Airports, flying fields & services
HQ: Huntleigh Usa Corporation
545 E John Carpenter Fwy
Irving TX

(P-4775)
ICARUS FUEL SERVICES US CORP
7251 World Way W, Los Angeles
(90045-5826)
PHONE.................................310 417-0124
David C Matthew, *CEO*
EMP: 65
SALES (est): 5.5MM **Privately Held**
SIC: 4581 Aircraft servicing & repairing

(P-4776)
JET SOURCE INC
2056 Palomar Airport Rd, Carlsbad
(92011-4463)
PHONE.................................760 438-0877
Vivianne B McWilliam, *CEO*
Jay Brentzel, *President*
Ian Ewing, *Vice Pres*
Joey Crawford, *CTO*
EMP: 80
SALES (est): 11.5MM **Privately Held**
SIC: 4581 Airports, flying fields & services

(P-4777)
JETT PRO LINE MAINTENANCE INC (PA)
8225 White Oak Ave, Rancho Cucamonga
(91730-7671)
P.O. Box 3190, Ontario (91761-0919)
PHONE.................................909 980-0552
Sam Nugud, *CEO*
Willie Nugud, *President*

Al Nugud, *CFO*
Miguel Itriago, *Technology*
Grant Moore, *Director*
EMP: 59
SALES (est): 11.1MM **Privately Held**
SIC: 4581 Aircraft maintenance & repair
services

(P-4778)
LOS ANGELES WORLD AIRPORTS (PA)
6320 W 96th St, Los Angeles (90045-5233)
P.O. Box 92216 (90009-2216)
PHONE.................................310 646-7911
Arif Alikhan, *Director*
Robert L Gilbert, *Officer*
Michael Cummings, *Principal*
Roger Johnson, *Exec Dir*
Carol Moody, *Admin Sec*
EMP: 158 **EST:** 2010
SALES (est): 78.6MM **Privately Held**
SIC: 4581 Airport

(P-4779)
LOS ANGELES WORLD AIRPORTS
1230 Tower St, Ontario (91761-2400)
PHONE.................................909 544-5490
Dan Meier, *President*
EMP: 54
SALES (est): 2.4MM **Privately Held**
SIC: 4581 Airport

(P-4780)
MATHER AVIATION LLC (PA)
10360 Macready Ave, Mather
(95655-4109)
PHONE.................................916 364-4711
Victor Cushing, *President*
Anita Cushing, *Vice Pres*
Frank Shaver, *Technician*
Brenda Pena, *Technology*
Candice Cushing, *Human Resources*
EMP: 63
SQ FT: 95,000
SALES (est): 13.5MM **Privately Held**
WEB: www.matheraviationllc.com
SIC: 4581 7699 Aircraft hangar rental; air-
craft maintenance & repair services; air-
craft & heavy equipment repair services

(P-4781)
MENZIES AVIATION (TEXAS) INC
Also Called: Asig
1049 S Vineyard Ave, Ontario
(91761-8029)
P.O. Box 4178 (91761-1011)
PHONE.................................909 937-3998
Debbie Martin, *Manager*
EMP: 63
SALES (corp-wide): 1.6B **Privately Held**
WEB: www.asig.com
SIC: 4581 Airport
HQ: Menzies Aviation (Texas), Inc.
4900 Diplomacy Rd
Fort Worth TX 76155
469 281-8200

(P-4782)
MERCURY AIR CARGO INC (HQ)
Also Called: Mercury World Cargo
6040 Avion Dr Ste 200, Los Angeles
(90045-5654)
PHONE.................................310 258-6100
Joseph A Czyzyk, *CEO*
John Peery, *President*
Lawrence Samuels, *CFO*
Dan K Barnard, *Treasurer*
Clive Langeveldt, *Exec VP*
▲ **EMP:** 180
SQ FT: 206,000
SALES (est): 57.9MM
SALES (corp-wide): 444.5MM **Privately
Held**
WEB: www.mercuryaircargo.com
SIC: 4581 4512 4522 Airports, flying
fields & services; air cargo carrier, sched-
uled; air cargo carriers, nonscheduled
PA: Mercury Air Group, Inc.
2780 Skypark Dr Ste 300
Torrance CA 90505
310 602-3770

(P-4783)
PACIFIC AVIATION CORPORATION
P.O. Box 250758 (94125-0758)
PHONE.................................650 821-1190
Addie E Castillo, *Branch Mgr*
EMP: 193 **Privately Held**
WEB: www.pacificaviation.com
SIC: 4581 Airport
PA: Pacific Aviation Corporation
201 Continental Blvd # 220
El Segundo CA 90245

(P-4784)
PACIFIC AVIATION CORPORATION (PA)
201 Continental Blvd # 220, El Segundo
(90245-4507)
PHONE.................................310 646-4015
Phil Shah, *President*
Victor Mena, *Corp Secy*
Preethi Cheriyan, *Human Res Mgr*
Nileshni Devi, *Manager*
Sofiyan Mamsa, *Manager*
EMP: 200
SALES: 13.8MM **Privately Held**
WEB: www.pacificaviation.com
SIC: 4581 Airport terminal services

(P-4785)
PHS / MWA (HQ)
Also Called: Phs/Mwa Aviation Services
42355 Rio Nedo, Temecula (92590-3701)
PHONE.................................950 695-1008
Mary Bale, *CEO*
Craig Bale, *Marketing Staff*
EMP: 50
SQ FT: 30,000
SALES (est): 38.2MM
SALES (corp-wide): 441.5MM **Privately
Held**
WEB: www.phsmwa.com
SIC: 4581 3492 7629 Aircraft servicing &
repairing; control valves, aircraft: hy-
draulic & pneumatic; electrical repair
shops
PA: Wencor Group, Llc
416 Dividend Dr
Peachtree City GA 30269
678 490-0140

(P-4786)
PLH AVIATION SERVICES INC
7251 World Way W, Los Angeles
(90045-5826)
PHONE.................................310 417-0124
Charles Arford, *Branch Mgr*
EMP: 50
SALES (corp-wide): 709.3MM **Privately
Held**
SIC: 4581 Aircraft servicing & repairing
PA: Menzies Aviation Fueling Canada Lim-
ited
10 Carlson Ct Unit 301
Etobicoke ON M9W 6
647 798-3890

(P-4787)
PORT DEPT CITY OF OAKLAND
Also Called: Metroplitan Oakland Intl Arprt
1 Airport Dr Ste 45, Oakland (94621-1476)
PHONE.................................510 563-3300
Bill Wade, *Manager*
EMP: 250
SALES (corp-wide): 65.3MM **Privately
Held**
WEB: www.portofoakland.com
SIC: 4581 Airport
PA: Port Department Of The City Of Oak-
land
530 Water St Fl 3
Oakland CA 94607
510 627-1100

(P-4788)
ROTORCRAFT SUPPORT INC
67 D St, Fillmore (93015-1668)
PHONE.................................818 997-7667
Phillip G Difiore, *President*
Teri Neville, *Vice Pres*
Jeffrey Teubner, *Vice Pres*
▲ **EMP:** 63
SQ FT: 10,000

SALES: 24MM **Privately Held**
SIC: **4581** 5088 5599 Aircraft maintenance & repair services; helicopter parts;
aircraft instruments, equipment or parts

(P-4789)
SAN DEGO CNTY RGNAL ARPRT AUTH (PA)
Also Called: Sdcraa
3225 N Harbor Dr Fl 3, San Diego
(92101-1045)
P.O. Box 82776 (92138-2776)
PHONE..............................619 400-2400
Thella F Bowens, *CEO*
Maria Quiroz, *Vice Pres*
Ajay Babla, *Program Mgr*
Cynthia Hawthorne, *Executive Asst*
Naty Santos, *Executive Asst*
EMP: 90
SALES (est): 56.7MM **Privately Held**
SIC: **4581** Airport; air freight handling at
airports

(P-4790)
SAN DEGO CNTY RGNAL ARPRT AUTH
2320 Stillwater Rd, San Diego
(92101-1016)
PHONE..............................619 400-2404
Michael Ross, *Manager*
EMP: 143
SALES (corp-wide): 56.7MM **Privately
Held**
SIC: **4581** Airport
PA: San Diego County Regional Airport Au-
thority
3225 N Harbor Dr Fl 3
San Diego CA 92101
619 400-2400

(P-4791)
SIGNATURE FLIGHT SUPPORT CORP
3050 N Winery Ave, Fresno (93703-1616)
PHONE..............................559 981-2490
Justin Zaklan, *Manager*
EMP: 74
SALES (corp-wide): 2.3B **Privately Held**
SIC: **4581** Aircraft maintenance & repair
services
HQ: Signature Flight Support Corporation
13485 Veterans Way # 600
Orlando FL 32827

(P-4792)
SIGNATURE FLIGHT SUPPORT CORP
1052 N Access Rd, San Francisco
(94128-3120)
PHONE..............................650 877-6800
Ken Setser, *Manager*
EMP: 76
SALES (corp-wide): 2.3B **Privately Held**
SIC: **4581** Airports, flying fields & services
HQ: Signature Flight Support Corporation
13485 Veterans Way # 600
Orlando FL 32827

(P-4793)
SIGNATURE FLIGHT SUPPORT CORP
7240 Hayvenhurst Ave, Van Nuys (91406)
PHONE..............................818 464-9500
Stephen W Lee, *Vice Pres*
EMP: 74
SALES (corp-wide): 2.3B **Privately Held**
SIC: **4581** Airports, flying fields & services
HQ: Signature Flight Support Corporation
13485 Veterans Way # 600
Orlando FL 32827

(P-4794)
SIGNATURE FLIGHT SUPPORT CORP
3333 E Spring St Ste 205, Long Beach
(90806-2446)
PHONE..............................562 997-0700
Eric Hill, *Branch Mgr*
EMP: 74
SALES (corp-wide): 2.3B **Privately Held**
SIC: **4581** Aircraft servicing & repairing

HQ: Signature Flight Support Corporation
13485 Veterans Way # 600
Orlando FL 32827
-

(P-4795)
SUNSET AVIATION LLC (PA)
Also Called: Solairus Aviation
201 1st St Ste 307, Petaluma
(94952-4290)
PHONE..............................707 775-2786
Daniel Drohan, *CEO*
John King, *President*
Greg Petersen, *COO*
Mark Dennen, *CFO*
Bob Marinace, *Exec VP*
EMP: 50
SALES (est): 80.7MM **Privately Held**
SIC: **4581** Airports, flying fields & services

(P-4796)
SWISSPORT CARGO SERVICES LP
Also Called: Cargo Service Center
11001 Aviation Blvd, Los Angeles
(90045-6123)
PHONE..............................310 910-9541
Mark Wood, *General Mgr*
EMP: 562
SALES (corp-wide): 1.1MM **Privately
Held**
SIC: **4581** Air freight handling at airports
HQ: Swissport Cargo Services, L.P.
23723 Air Frt Ln Bldg 5
Dulles VA 20166
703 742-4300

(P-4797)
SWISSPORT USA INC
San Francisco Intl Arprt, San Francisco
(94128)
PHONE..............................650 821-6220
Cecilia Guillen, *Station Mgr*
EMP: 220
SALES (corp-wide): 1.1MM **Privately
Held**
WEB: www.swissport-sfo.com
SIC: **4581** Airport terminal services
HQ: Swissport Usa, Inc.
45025 Aviation Dr Ste 350
Dulles VA 20166

(P-4798)
SWISSPORT USA INC
Also Called: Employment Intake Training Ctr
7025 W Imperial Hwy, Los Angeles
(90045-6313)
PHONE..............................310 345-1986
Jerry Harris, *General Mgr*
EMP: 400
SALES (corp-wide): 1.1MM **Privately
Held**
SIC: **4581** Air freight handling at airports
HQ: Swissport Usa, Inc.
45025 Aviation Dr Ste 350
Dulles VA 20166

(P-4799)
SWISSPORT USA INC
Delta Cargo Bldg 612, San Francisco
(94128)
PHONE..............................571 214-7068
Joe Phelan, *Exec VP*
EMP: 216
SALES (corp-wide): 1.1MM **Privately
Held**
SIC: **4581** Airports, flying fields & services
HQ: Swissport Usa, Inc.
45025 Aviation Dr Ste 350
Dulles VA 20166

(P-4800)
SWISSPORT USA INC
11001 Aviation Blvd, Los Angeles
(90045-6123)
PHONE..............................310 910-9560
Dion Fatafehi, *Manager*
EMP: 453
SALES (corp-wide): 1.1MM **Privately
Held**
WEB: www.swissport-sfo.com
SIC: **4581** Airport terminal services

HQ: Signature Flight Support Corporation
13485 Veterans Way # 600
Orlando FL 32827
-

HQ: Swissport Usa, Inc.
45025 Aviation Dr Ste 350
Dulles VA 20166
-

(P-4801)
TEXTRON AVIATION INC
Also Called: Cessna Scrmnto Ctation Svc Ctr
5850 Citation Way, Sacramento
(95837-1105)
PHONE..............................916 929-5656
Thomas Defoe, *Sales/Mktg Mgr*
Gwen Rieschick, *Maintence Staff*
Ken Kantola, *Manager*
EMP: 85
SALES (est): 13.9B **Publicly Held**
WEB: www.cessna.com
SIC: **4581** Aircraft maintenance & repair
services
HQ: Textron Aviation Inc.
1 Cessna Blvd
Wichita KS 67215
316 517-6000

(P-4802)
THRESHOLD TECHNOLOGIES INC
8352 Kimball Ave Bldg F35, Chino
(91708-9267)
PHONE..............................909 606-1666
Mark Dilullo, *CEO*
Lisa Dilullo, *President*
EMP: 55
SQ FT: 10,000
SALES (est): 8MM **Privately Held**
WEB: www.flytti.com
SIC: **4581** Aircraft storage at airports; air-
port hangar rental; aircraft cleaning & jani-
torial service; aircraft servicing & repairing

(P-4803)
TOTAL AIRPORT SERVICES LLC
3537 Branson Dr, San Mateo (94403-2901)
PHONE..............................650 358-0144
Ralph Eichenbaum, *Branch Mgr*
EMP: 65
SALES (corp-wide): 168.2MM **Privately
Held**
SIC: **4581** Aircraft maintenance & repair
services
PA: Total Airport Services, Llc
28420 Hardy Toll Rd # 220
Spring TX 77373
832 592-0048

(P-4804)
UNICAL AVIATION INC (PA)
680 S Lemon Ave, City of Industry
(91789-2934)
PHONE..............................909 348-1700
Han Tan, *President*
Sera Bong, *Executive*
Belinda Hernandez, *Executive*
David Hoang, *Executive*
Andy Lu, *Executive*
◆ EMP: 190
SQ FT: 480,000
SALES (est): 68.8MM **Privately Held**
WEB: www.unical.com
SIC: **4581** Airports, flying fields & services

(P-4805)
WORLD SERVICE WEST
Also Called: L A Inflight Service Company
1812 W 135th St, Gardena (90249-2520)
PHONE..............................310 538-7000
Byung Yoon, *Owner*
Mall Yoon,
◆ EMP: 170
SQ FT: 13,572
SALES (est): 9.6MM **Privately Held**
SIC: **4581** Aircraft cleaning & janitorial
service

(P-4806)
WORLDWIDE FLIGHT SERVICES INC
5908 Avion Dr, Los Angeles (90045-5622)
P.O. Box 90220 (90009-0220)
PHONE..............................310 646-7510
Dennis Hudson, *Manager*
EMP: 250
SALES (corp-wide): 2.1B **Privately Held**
SIC: **4581** Aircraft upholstery repair

PA: Worldwide Flight Services, Inc.
B151 E Hngar Rd Cir Rm 36
Jamaica NY 11430
718 244-0900

(P-4807)
WORLDWIDE FLIGHT SERVICES INC
Also Called: Wfs
5758 W Century Blvd, Los Angeles
(90045-5613)
P.O. Box 90220 (90009-0220)
PHONE..............................310 342-7830
John OH, *Branch Mgr*
EMP: 120
SALES (corp-wide): 2.1B **Privately Held**
SIC: **4581** Airports, flying fields & services
PA: Worldwide Flight Services, Inc.
B151 E Hngar Rd Cir Rm 36
Jamaica NY 11430
718 244-0900

(P-4808)
XOJET INC (PA)
2000 Sierra Point Pkwy # 200, Brisbane
(94005-1846)
PHONE..............................650 594-6300
Bradley Stewart, *CEO*
Shari Jones, *Chief Mktg Ofcr*
Adam Komack, *Chief Mktg Ofcr*
James Henderson, *Officer*
Jerry Joondeph, *Exec VP*
EMP: 54
SALES (est): 53MM **Privately Held**
WEB: www.xojet.com
SIC: **4581** Aircraft servicing & repairing

4613 Refined Petroleum Pipelines

(P-4809)
SFPP LP (DH)
1100 W Town And Country R, Orange
(92868-4647)
PHONE..............................714 560-4400
Park Shaper, *General Ptnr*
Richard D Kinder, *General Ptnr*
EMP: 150
SQ FT: 75,000
SALES: 302.3MM **Publicly Held**
SIC: **4613** Gasoline pipelines (common
carriers)
HQ: Kinder Morgan Energy Partners, L.P.
1001 La St Ste 1000
Houston TX 77002
713 369-9000

4619 Pipelines, NEC

(P-4810)
KINDER MRGAN ENRGY PARTNERS LP
Also Called: Santa Fe Pacific Pipeline
2319 S Riverside Ave, Bloomington
(92316-2931)
PHONE..............................909 873-5100
Ron Moranes, *Manager*
EMP: 50 **Publicly Held**
WEB: www.kindermorgan.com
SIC: **4619** 1623 Coal pipeline operation;
pipeline construction
HQ: Kinder Morgan Energy Partners, L.P.
1001 La St Ste 1000
Houston TX 77002
713 369-9000

(P-4811)
UNITED STATES PIPE FNDRY LLC
1295 Whipple Rd, Union City (94587-2036)
P.O. Box 707 (94587-0707)
PHONE..............................510 441-5810
Jim Kelly, *General Mgr*
EMP: 115
SALES (corp-wide): 1.4B **Publicly Held**
SIC: **4619** Coal pipeline operation
HQ: United States Pipe And Foundry Com-
pany Llc
2 Chase Corporate Dr # 200
Hoover AL 35244
205 263-8540

4724 Travel Agencies

(P-4812)
ALTOUR INTERNATIONAL INC
Also Called: Altour Travel Master
12100 W Olympic Blvd # 300, Los Angeles
(90064-1051)
PHONE...........................310 571-6000
Julie Valentine, *Branch Mgr*
EMP: 130
SALES (corp-wide): 80.9MM **Privately Held**
WEB: www.altourtravelmaster.com
SIC: 4724 Travel agencies
PA: Altour International, Inc.
1270 Avenue Of The Flr 15
New York NY 10020
212 897-5000

(P-4813)
ALTOUR INTERNATIONAL INC (PA)
12100 W Olympic Blvd # 300, Los Angeles
(90064-1051)
PHONE...........................310 571-6000
Alexander Chemla, *President*
David Sefton, *Senior VP*
Omar Ondoy, *Info Tech Dir*
Cindy McGee, *Info Tech Mgr*
Patrick Tapley, *Technology*
EMP: 80
SQ FT: 8,000
SALES: 1.6MM **Privately Held**
SIC: 4724 Travel agencies

(P-4814)
AMERICAN EXPRESS TRAVEL
15353 Barranca Pkwy, Irvine (92618-2216)
PHONE...........................949 453-7123
Linda Duffy, *Director*
EMP: 100
SALES (corp-wide): 43.2B **Publicly Held**
WEB: www.astoriasoftware.com
SIC: 4724 Travel agencies
HQ: American Express Travel Related
Services Company, Inc.,
200 Vesey St
New York NY 10285
212 640-2000

(P-4815)
AMERICAN TRAVEL SOLUTIONS LLC
Also Called: Amtrav
26707 Agoura Rd Ste 204, Calabasas
(91302-3831)
PHONE...........................818 359-6514
Jeff Klee, *CEO*
Eric Fichtelberg, *Exec VP*
Gregory Samson, *Vice Pres*
Bulent Keskin, *Sr Software Eng*
Wayne Hustis, *CIO*
EMP: 65
SQ FT: 4,000
SALES (est): 12.3MM **Privately Held**
SIC: 4724 4729 Tourist agency arranging
transport, lodging & car rental; airline
ticket offices

(P-4816)
AMERICANTOURS INTL LLC (HQ)
6053 W Century Blvd, Los Angeles
(90045-6430)
PHONE...........................310 641-9953
Noel Irwin-Hentschel,
Michael Fitzpatrick,
EMP: 105
SQ FT: 20,000
SALES (est): 30.2MM
SALES (corp-wide): 30.3MM **Privately Held**
SIC: 4724 4725 Travel agencies; tour operators
PA: Americantours International Inc
6053 W Century Blvd # 70
Los Angeles CA 90045
310 641-9953

(P-4817)
B T & T TRAVEL INC
Also Called: Best Tours & Travel
2609 E Mckinley Ave Ste N, Fresno
(93703-3028)
PHONE...........................559 237-9410
Nick W Sayah, *President*
Margaret Sayah, *Treasurer*
Jasmine Sayah, *Opers Mgr*
EMP: 56 EST: 1980
SQ FT: 4,200
SALES (est): 14.1MM **Privately Held**
WEB: www.besttoursandtravel.com
SIC: 4724 4725 Travel agencies; tours,
conducted

(P-4818)
BRENDAN TOURS (PA)
Also Called: Brendan Worldwide Vacations
5551 Katella Ave, Cypress (90630-5002)
PHONE...........................818 428-6000
James J Murphy, *CEO*
Gary J Murphy, *President*
Carl Laury, *CIO*
Stephannie Beets, *Human Res Mgr*
Robbe Pollack, *Sales Mgr*
EMP: 146
SALES (est): 15.5MM **Privately Held**
SIC: 4724 Travel agencies

(P-4819)
CARIBBEAN SOUTH AMERCN COUNCIL
Also Called: Internationl TV Media Wireless
12 Ambrose Ave, Bay Point (94565-3106)
PHONE...........................925 709-3433
Dalchand Singhbhairo, *President*
EMP: 50 EST: 1984
SALES (est): 4MM **Privately Held**
SIC: 4724 8748 Travel agencies; telecommunications consultant

(P-4820)
GEOGRAPHIC EXPEDITIONS INC
Also Called: Innerasia Travel Group
1008 General Kennedy Ave # 3, San Francisco (94129-1731)
P.O. Box 29902 (94129-0902)
PHONE...........................415 922-0448
George Doubleday, *Ch of Bd*
Lisa Parker, *Admin Sec*
EMP: 54
SALES (est): 21.8MM **Privately Held**
WEB: www.geoex.com
SIC: 4724 Travel agencies

(P-4821)
GOWAY TRAVEL INC
Also Called: Global Network Travel
505 N Brand Blvd Ste 810, Glendale
(91203-4723)
PHONE...........................800 810-3687
Bruce Hodge, *CEO*
Peter Lacy, *CFO*
Craig Canvin, *Vice Pres*
Nadya Phelan, *Manager*
Samantha Buckley, *Consultant*
EMP: 95
SQ FT: 1,200
SALES (est): 11.9MM **Privately Held**
WEB: www.goway.com
SIC: 4724 Tourist agency arranging transport, lodging & car rental

(P-4822)
HELLOWORLD TRAVEL SVCS USA INC
Also Called: Qantas Vctons Nwmans Vacations
6171 W Century Blvd # 160, Los Angeles
(90045-5300)
PHONE...........................310 535-1000
Ross Webster, *President*
Mark Punshon, *President*
Gary Goeldner, *CEO*
Justine Liddelow, *Vice Pres*
Brittany Alvarez, *Marketing Mgr*
EMP: 100
SQ FT: 18,000
SALES (est): 19.5MM **Privately Held**
WEB: www.jetaboutfijivacations.com
SIC: 4724 Tourist agency arranging transport, lodging & car rental

PA: Helloworld Travel Limited
L 10 338 Pitt St
Sydney NSW 2000

(P-4823)
HORNBLOWER YACHTS LLC (PA)
Also Called: Hornblower Cruises & Event
On The Embarcadero Pier 3 St Pier, San
Francisco (94111)
PHONE...........................415 788-8866
Terry Macrae, *CEO*
Annabella Stagner, *Vice Pres*
Lisa Medulun, *Human Res Dir*
Jacquelyn Wilcox, *Sales Mgr*
Tyler Fields, *Marketing Staff*
EMP: 250
SALES (est): 125.4MM **Privately Held**
WEB: www.hornbloweryachts.com
SIC: 4724 Travel agencies

(P-4824)
IDEA TRAVEL COMPANY
13145 Byrd Ln Ste 101, Los Altos Hills
(94022-3211)
PHONE...........................650 948-0207
Michael Schoendorf, *CEO*
Ram Bodapati, *CTO*
Beverly Hoh, *Software Dev*
EMP: 1100
SALES: 453.4MM **Privately Held**
WEB: www.ideatravel.com
SIC: 4724 Tourist agency arranging transport, lodging & car rental

(P-4825)
IDS INC
Also Called: IDS Technology
20300 Ventura Blvd # 200, Woodland Hills
(91364-2448)
PHONE...........................866 297-5757
Nathan Morad, *CEO*
Alberto Gamez, *Chief Mktg Ofcr*
ARI Daniels, *Vice Pres*
John Ledo, *CTO*
Gary Kurtz, *Legal Staff*
EMP: 52
SQ FT: 9,000
SALES: 65MM **Privately Held**
SIC: 4724 7372 Travel agencies; business
oriented computer software

(P-4826)
JAPAN AIRLINES CO LTD
300 Continental Blvd # 620, El Segundo
(90245-5047)
PHONE...........................310 607-2305
Hiroyuki Hioka, *CEO*
Paul Moore, *Officer*
Yusuke Araki, *Vice Pres*
Akira Mitsumasu, *Vice Pres*
Steve Smith, *Vice Pres*
EMP: 90 **Privately Held**
WEB: www.jal.co.jp
SIC: 4724 8741 4581 4512 Tourist
agency arranging transport, lodging & car
rental; management services; airports, flying fields & services; air transportation,
scheduled
PA: Japan Airlines Co.,Ltd.
2-4-11, Higashishinagawa
Shinagawa-Ku TKY 140-0

(P-4827)
JTB AMERICAS LTD (HQ)
19700 Mariner Ave, Torrance (90503-1648)
PHONE...........................310 303-3750
Tsuneo Irita, *President*
EMP: 100
SALES (est): 245.3MM **Privately Held**
SIC: 4724 Travel agencies

(P-4828)
L B C HOLDINGS U S A CORP (PA)
362 E Grand Ave, South San Francisco
(94080-6210)
PHONE...........................650 873-0750
Carlos Araneta, *Ch of Bd*
EMP: 164
SQ FT: 25,000

SALES (est): 20.5MM **Privately Held**
SIC: 4724 4513 4412 Travel agencies; air
courier services; deep sea foreign transportation of freight

(P-4829)
NIPPON TRAVEL AGENCY AMER INC
Also Called: Nta America
1411 W 190th St Ste 650, Gardena
(90248-4369)
PHONE...........................310 768-1817
Tadashi Wakayama, *President*
Julie Kawaguchi, *Purchasing*
Tsutomu Ochiai, *Senior Mgr*
Yoshiko Bustillos, *Manager*
Romeo Dublin, *Asst Mgr*
EMP: 70 EST: 1999
SQ FT: 8,000
SALES (est): 14.1MM **Privately Held**
WEB: www.ntasfb.com
SIC: 4724 Tourist agency arranging transport, lodging & car rental
HQ: Nippon Travel Agency Pacific, Inc.
1025 W 190th St Ste 300
Gardena CA 90248
310 768-0017

(P-4830)
NIPPON TRAVEL AGENCY PCF INC (DH)
Also Called: Nta Pacific
1025 W 190th St Ste 300, Gardena
(90248-4332)
PHONE...........................310 768-0017
Tadashi Wakayama, *President*
Akio Tsuna, *CFO*
Yoshikazu Morizuka, *Info Tech Mgr*
EMP: 80
SQ FT: 20,000
SALES (est): 34.5MM **Privately Held**
SIC: 4724 Tourist agency arranging transport, lodging & car rental

(P-4831)
PENINSULA WORLD TRAVEL LLC (PA)
Also Called: Meridian World Travel
825 Santa Cruz Ave, Menlo Park
(94025-4609)
PHONE...........................650 328-2030
Don Freeman,
Barbara Freeman,
EMP: 50
SALES (est): 5.6MM **Privately Held**
WEB: www.summittravelgroup.com
SIC: 4724 Travel agencies

(P-4832)
PINNACLE TRAVEL SERVICES LLC
390 N Pacific Coast Hwy, El Segundo
(90245-4475)
PHONE...........................310 414-1787
Robert G Singh, *CEO*
Chris Winchell, *Exec VP*
Kathy Underwood, *Human Res Dir*
Lora Mayfield, *Supervisor*
EMP: 151
SQ FT: 15,000
SALES: 10MM **Privately Held**
WEB: www.ptsla.com
SIC: 4724 Tourist agency arranging transport, lodging & car rental

(P-4833)
PRINCESS CRUISE LINES LTD
Also Called: Princess Cruises
24833 Anza Dr, Santa Clarita (91355-1259)
P.O. Box 966 (91380-9066)
PHONE...........................661 753-2197
Princess Cruise, *Principal*
EMP: 1114
SALES (corp-wide): 8.3B **Privately Held**
SIC: 4724 Travel agencies
HQ: Princess Cruise Lines, Ltd.
24305 Town Center Dr
Santa Clarita CA 91355
661 753-0000

(P-4834)

PRINCESS CRUISES AND TOURS INC (HQ)
24305 Town Center Dr # 200, Valencia (91355-4999)
PHONE..............................206 336-6000
Will Wenholz, *Principal*
EMP: 5027
SALES (est): 91.1MM
SALES (corp-wide): 18.8B **Publicly Held**
SIC: 4724 Travel agencies
PA: Carnival Corporation
3655 Nw 87th Ave
Doral FL 33178
305 599-2600

(P-4835)

PROTRAVEL INTERNATIONAL LLC
9171 Wilshire Blvd # 428, Beverly Hills (90210-5516)
PHONE..............................310 271-9566
Sara Sessa, *Branch Mgr*
EMP: 100
SALES (corp-wide): 88.8MM **Privately Held**
WEB: www.protravelinternational.com
SIC: 4724 Travel agencies
PA: Protravel International Llc
1633 Broadway Fl 35
New York NY 10019
212 755-4550

(P-4836)

REVEL TRAVEL SERVICE INC
Also Called: Revel Travel At Altour
449 S Beverly Dr Ste 101, Beverly Hills (90212-4463)
PHONE..............................310 553-5555
Jack Revel, *President*
EMP: 65 **EST:** 1933
SALES (est): 1MM **Privately Held**
SIC: 4724 Travel agencies
PA: Altour International Inc.
12100 W Olympic Blvd # 300
Los Angeles CA 90064

(P-4837)

STUDENT GOVERNMENT ASSOCIAT
Also Called: Associated Students Uc Irvine
D200 Student Center, Irvine (92697-0001)
PHONE..............................949 824-5547
Dennis Hampton, *Exec Dir*
EMP: 155
SQ FT: 6,000
SALES: 4.2MM **Privately Held**
SIC: 4724 5813 5947 4481 Travel agencies; drinking places; gifts & novelties; deep sea passenger transportation, except ferry; women's accessory & specialty stores

(P-4838)

TRAVEL STORE
633 S Brea Blvd, Brea (92821-5308)
PHONE..............................714 529-1947
Eva Bailon, *Manager*
Jerri Williams, *Master*
EMP: 71
SALES (est): 5.1MM
SALES (corp-wide): 40.2MM **Privately Held**
SIC: 4724 Tourist agency arranging transport, lodging & car rental
PA: Travel Store
11601 Wilshire Blvd
Los Angeles CA 90025
310 575-5540

(P-4839)

TRAVEL STORE (PA)
Also Called: Travelstore
11601 Wilshire Blvd, Los Angeles (90025-0509)
PHONE..............................310 575-5540
Wido Schaefer, *President*
EMP: 70
SQ FT: 7,000

SALES (est): 37.5MM
SALES (corp-wide): 40.2MM **Privately Held**
WEB: www.travel-store.com
SIC: 4724 Tourist agency arranging transport, lodging & car rental

(P-4840)

TRAVEL SYNDICATE
350 S Beverly Dr Ste 170, Beverly Hills (90212-4818)
PHONE..............................818 297-9979
Arline Fiorto, *Partner*
Roger Lipkis, *Partner*
EMP: 60
SQ FT: 9,800
SALES (est): 6.8MM **Privately Held**
WEB: www.travelsyndicate.com
SIC: 4724 Travel agencies

(P-4841)

TRAVELMASTERS INC
Also Called: Goldrush Getaways
8350 Auburn Blvd Ste 200, Citrus Heights (95610-0396)
PHONE..............................916 722-1648
Brian A Carr, *President*
Karen Chavez, *Training Spec*
Beatriz De La Torre, *Director*
Maria Cardenas, *Agent*
EMP: 50
SALES (est): 8MM **Privately Held**
WEB: www.goldrushgetaways.com
SIC: 4724 Tourist agency arranging transport, lodging & car rental

(P-4842)

UNIGLOBE TRAVEL WEST INC (PA)
Also Called: Uniglobe Travel Planner
18662 Macarthur Blvd # 100, Irvine (92612-1200)
PHONE..............................949 623-9000
Gary Charlewood, *President*
Raymond Townsend, *Ch of Bd*
EMP: 60
SQ FT: 5,920
SALES (est): 7.7MM **Privately Held**
SIC: 4724 Travel agencies

(P-4843)

UNIWORLD RIVER CRUISES INC
Also Called: Uniworld Boutique River Cruise
17323 Ventura Blvd # 300, Encino (91316-3964)
PHONE..............................818 382-2322
Guy A Young, *President*
Silva Reyes, *Office Mgr*
Jennifer Corona, *Executive Asst*
Wesley Bosnic, *Info Tech Dir*
Jonathan Melendez, *Webmaster*
EMP: 110
SALES (est): 19.1MM
SALES (corp-wide): 355.8K **Privately Held**
SIC: 4724 Travel agencies
PA: Uniworld River Cruises Sa
Rue Guillaume J. Kroll 5
Luxembourg

(P-4844)

VIKING RIVER CRUISES INC (HQ)
Also Called: Viking Ocean Cruises
5700 Canoga Ave Ste 200, Woodland Hills (91367-6569)
PHONE..............................818 227-1234
Torstein Hagen, *CEO*
Cheri Allen, *Vice Pres*
Nielsen Anders, *Vice Pres*
Jeffrey Dash, *Vice Pres*
Tony Hofmann, *Vice Pres*
EMP: 84
SALES (est): 42.9MM
SALES (corp-wide): 5.7MM **Privately Held**
WEB: www.vikingrivercruises.com
SIC: 4724 Tourist agency arranging transport, lodging & car rental
PA: Viking River Cruises Ag
Schaferweg 18
Basel BS 4057
616 386-011

4725 Tour Operators

(P-4845)

AAT KINGS TOURS USA INC
801 E Katella Ave Fl 3, Anaheim (92805-6614)
PHONE..............................714 456-0505
Richard Launder, *President*
Don Angus, *General Mgr*
Jeff Adam, *VP Sales*
EMP: 75
SALES (est): 6.9MM **Privately Held**
SIC: 4725 Tours, conducted

(P-4846)

ALCATRAZ CRUISES LLC
Hornb Alcat Landi Pier 33 St Pier, San Francisco (94111)
PHONE..............................415 981-7625
Terry A Macrae,
Yuki Watanabe, *Controller*
Bobby Martinez, *Purch Mgr*
Elizabeth Vonesh, *Marketing Staff*
EMP: 120
SALES (est): 14.5MM **Privately Held**
SIC: 4725 Arrangement of travel tour packages, wholesale

(P-4847)

APPELLATION TOURS INC
Also Called: Beau Wine Tours
21707 8th St E, Sonoma (95476-9781)
PHONE..............................707 938-9390
Thomas Buck, *President*
EMP: 50
SQ FT: 21,000
SALES (est): 8.4MM **Privately Held**
WEB: www.appellationtours.com
SIC: 4725 4111 4141 Tours, conducted; airport limousine, scheduled service; local bus charter service

(P-4848)

BACKROADS (PA)
801 Cedar St, Berkeley (94710-1800)
PHONE..............................510 527-1555
Tom Hale, *CEO*
Robert Greeneisen, *Principal*
Mark Selcon, *Regional Mgr*
Stacy Loucks, *General Mgr*
Chris Glenn, *Info Tech Mgr*
EMP: 100
SQ FT: 10,000
SALES (est): 46.7MM **Privately Held**
WEB: www.walkingvacation.com
SIC: 4725 4724 Sightseeing tour companies; travel agencies

(P-4849)

CLASSIC CUSTOM VACATIONS INC
5893 Rue Ferrari, San Jose (95138-1857)
PHONE..............................800 221-3949
Timothy Scott Macdonald, *CEO*
Gregge Brockway, *President*
Thomas Van Dorn, *Business Mgr*
EMP: 250
SQ FT: 31,000
SALES (est): 2.1MM
SALES (corp-wide): 11.2B **Publicly Held**
WEB: www.classicvacations.com
SIC: 4725 Arrangement of travel tour packages, wholesale
PA: Expedia Group, Inc.
333 108th Ave Ne
Bellevue WA 98004
425 679-7200

(P-4850)

CLASSIC VACATIONS LLC
Also Called: Classic Custom Vacations
5893 Rue Ferrari, San Jose (95138-1857)
PHONE..............................800 221-3949
David Hu, *President*
Ronald M Letterman, *Vice Chairman*
EMP: 149
SALES (est): 16.1MM
SALES (corp-wide): 11.2B **Publicly Held**
WEB: www.expedia.com
SIC: 4725 Arrangement of travel tour packages, wholesale

PA: Expedia Group, Inc.
333 108th Ave Ne
Bellevue WA 98004
425 679-7200

(P-4851)

CONTIKI US HOLDINGS INC
Also Called: Contiki Holidays
801 E Katella Ave Frnt, Anaheim (92805-6614)
PHONE..............................714 935-0808
Frank Marini, *President*
Michael Kidd, *CFO*
Josh Hepp, *Sales Mgr*
EMP: 60
SALES (est): 10.9MM **Privately Held**
SIC: 4725 4724 Tours, conducted; tourist agency arranging transport, lodging & car rental

(P-4852)

CUSA GCBS LLC
Also Called: Goodall's Charter Bus Company
3888 Beech St, San Diego (92105-5905)
PHONE..............................619 266-7365
Craig Lentzsch, *Mng Member*
John Busskohl, *Mng Member*
EMP: 100
SALES (est): 7.4MM **Privately Held**
SIC: 4725 Arrangement of travel tour packages, wholesale; sightseeing tour companies

(P-4853)

GO WEST TOURS INC (PA)
790 Eddy St, San Francisco (94109-7806)
PHONE..............................415 837-0154
Stephan Forget, *President*
Julia Matheson, *Vice Pres*
Florence Solal, *Vice Pres*
David Nicoletti, *Executive*
Benoit Demonsant, *General Mgr*
EMP: 50
SQ FT: 2,858
SALES: 61.2MM **Privately Held**
WEB: www.gowesttours.com
SIC: 4725 Tours, conducted

(P-4854)

JOGURU INC
2600 El Camino Real Ste 4, Palo Alto (94306-1705)
PHONE..............................855 526-4332
Praveen Kumar, *CEO*
Saket Newaskar, *Director*
EMP: 75
SQ FT: 2,500
SALES: 500K **Privately Held**
SIC: 4725 Arrangement of travel tour packages, wholesale

(P-4855)

LAS VEGAS INTRNTNL TOURS
Also Called: La City Tours.com
18147 Coastline Dr Apt 1, Malibu (90265-5748)
PHONE..............................323 960-0300
Monique Chu, *President*
Jan Sherwood, *Principal*
Lindsay Lefler, *Marketing Staff*
EMP: 81
SQ FT: 129,800
SALES: 750K **Privately Held**
SIC: 4725 Tours, conducted

(P-4856)

MARITZCX RESEARCH LLC
20285 S Wstn Ave Ste 101, Torrance (90501)
PHONE..............................310 783-4300
Joe Sarquiz, *Principal*
Ron Steinkamp, *President*
Mark Schrum, *Data Proc Staff*
EMP: 61
SALES (corp-wide): 1.3B **Privately Held**
SIC: 4725 8748 8732 4899 Arrangement of travel tour packages, wholesale; employee programs administration; market analysis or research; data communication services; advertising consultant
HQ: Maritzcx Research Llc
1355 N Highway Dr
Fenton MO 63026
636 827-4000

(P-4857)
OKABE INTERNATIONAL INC (PA)
Also Called: Pacific Leisure Management
1739 Buchanan St Ste B, San Francisco
(94115-3208)
PHONE..................................415 921-0808
Mitsufumi Okabe, *President*
Rumi Okabe, *Corp Secy*
EMP: 50 **EST:** 1973
SQ FT: 3,600
SALES (est): 2.7MM **Privately Held**
SIC: 4725 4833 5941 Tours, conducted;
television broadcasting stations; sporting
goods & bicycle shops; tennis goods &
equipment; golf goods & equipment

(P-4858)
OLD TOWN TRLLEY TURS SAN DIEGO
Also Called: Historic Tours of America
2115 Kurtz St, San Diego (92110-2016)
PHONE..................................619 298-8687
Chris Belland, *CEO*
Edwin O Swift, *President*
Gerald Mosher, *Vice Pres*
Carmen Thulin, *Human Res Mgr*
EMP: 60
SQ FT: 22,000
SALES (est): 8.4MM
SALES (corp-wide): 135MM **Privately Held**
WEB: www.conchtourtrain.com
SIC: 4725 Tours, conducted
HQ: Conch Tour Trains Inc
   1805 Staples Ave Ste 101
   Key West FL 33040
   305 294-5161

(P-4859)
PACIFIC COAST SIGHTSEEING TOUR
2001 S Manchester Ave, Anaheim
(92802-3803)
PHONE..................................714 507-1157
Kristin Martinez, *Vice Pres*
Luis Silva, *Controller*
EMP: 230
SALES: 23MM **Privately Held**
SIC: 4725 4173 Arrangement of travel tour
packages, wholesale; sightseeing tour
companies; bus terminal operation
HQ: Coach Usa, Inc.
   160 S Route 17 N
   Paramus NJ 07652

(P-4860)
PLEASANT HOLIDAYS LLC (HQ)
Also Called: Pleasant Hawaiian Holiday
2404 Townsgate Rd, Westlake Village
(91361-2505)
PHONE..................................818 991-3390
Jack E Richards, *CEO*
Dal Dewolf, *Vice Pres*
Mark Klaschka, *Vice Pres*
Duke Ah Moo, *Vice Pres*
Delmar Steurmer, *Vice Pres*
EMP: 300
SQ FT: 55,000
SALES (est): 104.7MM
SALES (corp-wide): 7.2B **Privately Held**
WEB: www.pleasantactivities.com
SIC: 4725 Tour operators
PA: Automobile Club Of Southern California
   2601 S Figueroa St
   Los Angeles CA 90007
   213 741-3686

(P-4861)
ROYALTY TOURS
630 Stockton Ave, San Jose (95126-2433)
PHONE..................................408 279-4801
Sandra S Allen, *President*
EMP: 50
SQ FT: 3,000
SALES (est): 4.2MM
SALES (corp-wide): 13MM **Privately Held**
WEB: www.royal-coach.com
SIC: 4725 Arrangement of travel tour pack-
ages, wholesale; sightseeing tour compa-
nies

PA: Royal Coach Tours
   630 Stockton Ave
   San Jose CA 95126
   408 279-4801

(P-4862)
SAN FRNCISCO INCOMING SVCS LLC (PA)
Also Called: Gray Line of San Francisco
50 Quint St, San Francisco (94124-1424)
PHONE..................................415 777-2288
Ray Sargoni, *President*
Anna Sargonia, *President*
Ferris O Suer, *CFO*
Chris Crompton, *General Mgr*
EMP: 65
SQ FT: 20,000
SALES (est): 7.1MM **Privately Held**
WEB: www.supersightseeing.com
SIC: 4725 Tours, conducted

(P-4863)
SANTA BARBARA CITY OF
Also Called: Courthuse Tours-Docent Council
1100 Anacapa St Dept 3, Santa Barbara
(93101-6013)
PHONE..................................805 962-6464
Lori Bevon, *President*
EMP: 60 **Privately Held**
SIC: 4725 Tour operators
PA: City Of Santa Barbara
   735 Anacapa St
   Santa Barbara CA 93101
   805 564-5334

(P-4864)
SANTA CATALINA ISLAND COMPANY (PA)
Also Called: Scico
150 Metropole Ave, Avalon (90704)
P.O. Box 737 (90704-0737)
PHONE..................................310 510-2000
Randall Herrel Sr, *CEO*
Paxson H Offield, *Ch of Bd*
John T Dravinski, *COO*
Ronald C Doutt, *Treasurer*
Roberto Perico, *Vice Pres*
EMP: 71 **EST:** 1959
SALES (est): 36.5MM **Privately Held**
WEB: www.scico.com
SIC: 4725 Sightseeing tour companies

(P-4865)
SCREAMLINE INVESTMENT CORP (PA)
Also Called: Tourcoach Transportation
2130 S Tubeway Ave, Commerce
(90040-1614)
PHONE..................................323 201-0114
Kamrouz Farhadi, *CEO*
Vahid Sapir, *President*
Shoeleh Sapir, *Treasurer*
Serge Ermakov, *Info Tech Mgr*
Farima Akopians, *VP Sales*
EMP: 120
SQ FT: 8,000
SALES (est): 22.6MM **Privately Held**
WEB: www.tourcoach.com
SIC: 4725 Sightseeing tour companies;
tours, conducted

(P-4866)
STARLINE TOURS HOLLYWOOD INC
2130 S Tubeway Ave, Commerce
(90040-1614)
PHONE..................................323 262-1114
Tony Cordon, *Manager*
EMP: 60 **Privately Held**
WEB: www.starlinetours.com
SIC: 4725 Tours, conducted
PA: Starline Tours Of Hollywood, Inc.
   6801 Hollywood Blvd # 221
   Los Angeles CA 90028

(P-4867)
STARLINE TOURS HOLLYWOOD INC (PA)
6801 Hollywood Blvd # 221, Los Angeles
(90028-6142)
PHONE..................................323 463-3333
Kamrouz Farhadi, *CEO*
Noonoosh Farhadi, *Vice Pres*
Galina Kirkilevich, *Controller*

EMP: 71
SALES (est): 15.9MM **Privately Held**
WEB: www.starlinetours.com
SIC: 4725 Tours, conducted

(P-4868)
THE GRAY-LINE TOURS COMPANY
6541 Hollywood Blvd, Los Angeles
(90028-6256)
PHONE..................................323 463-3333
Vahid Sapir, *President*
EMP: 200
SQ FT: 10,000
SALES (est): 6.6MM **Privately Held**
SIC: 4725 Tours, conducted

(P-4869)
VIP TOURS OF CALIFORNIA INC
1419 E Maple Ave, El Segundo
(90245-3302)
PHONE..................................310 216-7507
Marco Khorasani, *President*
Nicole J Khorasani, *Vice Pres*
Fred Vardeh, *Mktg Dir*
EMP: 70
SALES (est): 10.1MM **Privately Held**
WEB: www.viptoursandcharters.com
SIC: 4725 Tours, conducted

(P-4870)
YOUR MAN TOURS MERGER INC (DH)
Also Called: Your Man Tours, Inc.
100 N Pacific Coast Hwy # 1700, El Se-
gundo (90245-5662)
PHONE..................................310 649-3820
William Price, *President*
Frank Chanell, *Vice Pres*
James Gallas, *Vice Pres*
EMP: 80
SQ FT: 20,000
SALES (est): 16.7MM
SALES (corp-wide): 22.3B **Privately Held**
WEB: www.ymtvacations.com
SIC: 4725 Tour operators

4729 Passenger Transportation

(P-4871)
CATHAY PACIFIC AIRWAYS LIMITED
1960 E Grand Ave Ste 540, El Segundo
(90245-5092)
PHONE..................................310 615-1113
Jake Olver, *Branch Mgr*
James Barrington, *Marketing Staff*
EMP: 100 **Privately Held**
WEB: www.cathaypacific.com
SIC: 4729 4512 Airline ticket offices; air
transportation, scheduled
PA: Cathay Pacific Airways Limited
   33/F One Pacific Place
   Admiralty HK

(P-4872)
CUSTOM TOURS INC
Also Called: Kushner & Associates
24003 Ventura Blvd Ste A, Calabasas
(91302-3926)
PHONE..................................310 274-8819
Susan Kushner, *CEO*
Cristina Arroyo, *Senior Mgr*
Leanne Anell, *Director*
Val Hamann, *Director*
Jae Owh, *Director*
EMP: 85
SQ FT: 3,000
SALES (est): 9.1MM **Privately Held**
WEB: www.kushnerdmc.com
SIC: 4729 Carpool/vanpool arrangement

(P-4873)
EL AL ISRAEL AIRLINES LTD
6404 Wilshire Blvd # 1250, Los Angeles
(90048-5501)
PHONE..................................323 852-1252
Michael Escalante, *Sales Staff*
EMP: 150

SALES (corp-wide): 578.2MM **Privately Held**
WEB: www.elal.co.il
SIC: 4729 4512 Ticket offices, transporta-
tion; air transportation, scheduled
PA: El Al Israel Airlines Ltd
   Lod Airport
   Lod Airport 70100
   397 162-02

(P-4874)
ELITE AIRWAYS LLC
4607 Lakeview Canyon Rd, Westlake Vil-
lage (91361-4028)
PHONE..................................805 496-3334
Robert Lyle, *Exec VP*
Jackie Smock, *Accountant*
EMP: 145
SQ FT: 5,000
SALES (est): 13.6MM **Privately Held**
SIC: 4729 Airline ticket offices

(P-4875)
FIVE STAR TRANSPORTATION INC
8703 La Tijera Blvd # 102, Los Angeles
(90045-3900)
PHONE..................................310 348-0820
George Reyes, *President*
Linda Reyes, *Vice Pres*
Demetri Ross, *Exec Dir*
EMP: 50
SALES (est): 6MM **Privately Held**
SIC: 4729 Airline ticket offices

(P-4876)
GAT - ARLN GROUND SUPPORT INC
2627 N Hollywood Way, Burbank
(91505-1062)
PHONE..................................818 847-9127
Lenore Lahti, *Finance*
Mary Marietta, *Director*
EMP: 243
SALES (corp-wide): 116MM **Privately Held**
SIC: 4729 Airline ticket offices
PA: Gat - Airline Ground Support, Inc.
   246 City Cir
   Peachtree City GA 30269
   251 633-3888

(P-4877)
MATRIX AVIATION SERVICES INC
6171 W Century Blvd Ste 1, Los Angeles
(90045-5300)
PHONE..................................310 337-3037
Ramez Reno, *CEO*
Borseen Oushana, *CFO*
EMP: 175 **EST:** 2008
SQ FT: 3,000
SALES (est): 15.4MM **Privately Held**
SIC: 4729 Airline ticket offices

(P-4878)
UNITED AIRLINES INC
6850 Airport Blvd Ste 34, Sacramento
(95837-1126)
PHONE..................................916 877-3002
Ken Brown, *Manager*
EMP: 150
SALES (corp-wide): 41.3B **Publicly Held**
WEB: www.united.com
SIC: 4729 4512 Airline ticket offices; air
transportation, scheduled
HQ: United Airlines, Inc.
   233 S Wacker Dr Ste 710
   Chicago IL 60606
   872 825-4000

4731 Freight Forwarding & Arrangement

(P-4879)
AGILITY HOLDINGS INC (DH)
Also Called: Agility Logistics
310 Commerce Ste 250, Irvine
(92602-1399)
PHONE..................................714 617-6300
Essa Al-Saleh, *President*
John Iacouzzi, *President*
Jamie Robertson, *President*

Mark Soubry, *CEO*
James Fredholm, *CFO*
EMP: 80
SALES (est): 394.6MM
SALES (corp-wide): 5B **Privately Held**
WEB: www.agilitylogistics.com
SIC: 4731 4213 4214 Domestic freight forwarding; foreign freight forwarding; transportation agents & brokers; household goods transport; heavy machinery transport; household goods moving & storage, local
HQ: Agility Logistics International B.V.
Fokkerweg 300 Gebouw 2a
Oude Meer 1438
884 360-105

(P-4880)
AGILITY LOGISTICS CORP
21906 Arnold Center Rd, Carson
(90810-1646)
PHONE..................................310 507-6700
Kia Kittscher, *Manager*
EMP: 65
SALES (corp-wide): 5B **Privately Held**
SIC: 4731 Freight forwarding
HQ: Agility Logistics Corp.
310 Commerce Ste 250
Irvine CA 92602
714 617-6300

(P-4881)
AGRIHOLDING INC (PA)
Also Called: Fts Global
3330 S Fairway St, Visalia (93277-8109)
P.O. Box 334, Pebble Beach (93953-0334)
PHONE..................................559 738-5880
Charles Schimmel, *President*
Robert Igleheart, *Ch of Bd*
EMP: 70
SALES (est): 9.6MM **Privately Held**
SIC: 4731 Truck transportation brokers

(P-4882)
AIR EXPRESS INTL USA INC
Also Called: Dhl Global Forwarding
6800 Gateway Park Dr, San Diego
(92154-7536)
PHONE..................................858 578-9602
Fernando Alba, *General Mgr*
Juanita Martinez, *Manager*
EMP: 50
SALES (corp-wide): 70.4B **Privately Held**
SIC: 4731 Freight forwarding
HQ: Air Express International Usa, Inc.
1801 Nw 82nd Ave
Doral FL 33126
786 264-3500

(P-4883)
AIR TIGER EXPRESS (USA) INC
17000 Gale Ave, City of Industry
(91745-1807)
PHONE..................................626 965-8647
Sean Lee, *Manager*
EMP: 50 **Privately Held**
WEB: www.airtiger.com
SIC: 4731 Freight forwarding
PA: Air Tiger Express (Usa), Inc.
14909 183rd St Ste 2
Springfield Gardens NY 11413

(P-4884)
AIR-SEA FORWARDERS INC (PA)
9009 S La Cienega Blvd, Inglewood
(90301-4459)
P.O. Box 90637, Los Angeles (90009-0637)
PHONE..................................310 216-1616
Todd Hinkley, *CEO*
Paul Talley, *COO*
Monica Villavicencio, *CFO*
Luisa Nakamura, *Vice Pres*
Mark Kolber, *District Mgr*
EMP: 60
SQ FT: 42,000
SALES (est): 18.3MM **Privately Held**
WEB: www.airseainc.com
SIC: 4731 Foreign freight forwarding; customhouse brokers

(P-4885)
AIT WORLDWIDE LOGISTICS INC
19901 Hamilton Ave Ste D, Torrance
(90502-1364)
PHONE..................................310 538-4383
Ty Bradford, *Manager*
Sam Cortez, *Manager*
EMP: 100
SALES (corp-wide): 449.3MM **Privately Held**
WEB: www.aitworldwide.com
SIC: 4731 Domestic freight forwarding
PA: Ait Worldwide Logistics, Inc.
701 N Rohlwing Rd
Itasca IL 60143
630 766-8300

(P-4886)
ALLEN LUND COMPANY LLC (HQ)
4529 Angeles Crest Hwy # 300, La Canada Flintridge (91011-3247)
P.O. Box 1369, La Canada (91012-5369)
PHONE..................................818 790-8412
Allen Lund, *Mng Member*
Steve Doerfler, *CFO*
David F Lund, *Vice Pres*
David Lund, *Vice Pres*
Edward V Lund, *Vice Pres*
EMP: 70 **EST:** 1976
SQ FT: 16,000
SALES (est): 661.7MM **Privately Held**
WEB: www.allenlund.com
SIC: 4731 Truck transportation brokers

(P-4887)
ALLEN LUND COMPANY LLC
1875 S Grant St Ste 110, San Mateo
(94402-2667)
PHONE..................................650 358-9454
Bob Rose, *Branch Mgr*
EMP: 60 **Privately Held**
SIC: 4731 Truck transportation brokers
HQ: Allen Lund Company, Llc
4529 Angeles Crest Hwy # 300
La Canada Flintridge CA 91011
818 790-8412

(P-4888)
ALLEN LUND CORPORATION (PA)
4529 Angeles Crest Hwy, La Canada Flintridge (91011-3247)
P.O. Box 1369, La Canada (91012-5369)
PHONE..................................818 790-8412
David Allen Lund, *President*
Steve Doerfler, *CFO*
Tracey Lewin, *Vice Pres*
David F Lund, *Vice Pres*
Edward V Lund, *Vice Pres*
EMP: 50
SQ FT: 18,000
SALES (est): 661.7MM **Privately Held**
SIC: 4731 Truck transportation brokers

(P-4889)
ALLPRO INDUSTRY SOLUTIONS LLC
7850 White Ln, Bakersfield (93309-7698)
PHONE..................................661 854-3613
Joshua R Kimball,
Josh Kimball, *President*
EMP: 50
SALES (est): 4.2MM **Privately Held**
SIC: 4731 4212 3537 3523 Freight transportation arrangement; local trucking, without storage; platforms, stands, tables, pallets & similar equipment; crop storage bins; grain storage bins

(P-4890)
AMERICAN PRESIDENT LINES LLC
1579 Middle Harbor Rd, Oakland
(94607-1808)
PHONE..................................510 272-3990
Paul Clouse, *Manager*
EMP: 80
SALES (corp-wide): 20.8MM **Privately Held**
SIC: 4731 Foreign freight forwarding

HQ: American President Lines, Llc
1667 K St Nw Ste 400
Washington DC 20006
602 586-4894

(P-4891)
AO FREIGHT CORPORATION (PA)
419 N Oak St, Inglewood (90302-3314)
PHONE..................................310 419-8833
Alex Chan, *President*
Cherry Chan, *Partner*
Margaret LI, *Partner*
Spencer Ho, *Vice Pres*
EMP: 50
SQ FT: 3,000
SALES (est): 13.5MM **Privately Held**
SIC: 4731 4412 Foreign freight forwarding; domestic freight forwarding; deep sea foreign transportation of freight

(P-4892)
AP EXPRESS LLC
Also Called: A P Express Worldwide
5301a Rivergrade Rd, Irwindale
(91706-1347)
PHONE..................................562 236-2250
Jeffery D Pont, *Mng Member*
Keith Davis, *Exec VP*
EMP: 75
SQ FT: 170,000
SALES (est): 24.2MM **Privately Held**
WEB: www.apexpress.com
SIC: 4731 Freight forwarding

(P-4893)
APEX LOGISTICS INTL INC (PA)
Also Called: Apex USA
18554 S Susana Rd, Compton
(90221-5620)
PHONE..................................310 665-0288
Elsie Qian, *CEO*
Hui Qian, *Exec VP*
▲ **EMP:** 80
SALES (est): 51.6MM **Privately Held**
SIC: 4731 Freight forwarding

(P-4894)
APM TERMINALS PACIFIC LLC
Also Called: Mearsk
2500 Navy Way Pier 400, San Pedro
(90731-7554)
PHONE..................................310 221-4000
Milan Do, *Branch Mgr*
EMP: 50
SALES (corp-wide): 1.9MM **Privately Held**
SIC: 4731 Agents, shipping
HQ: Apm Terminals Pacific Llc
2500 Navy Way
San Pedro CA 90731
704 571-2768

(P-4895)
APM TERMINALS PACIFIC LTD
5801 Christie Ave, Emeryville
(94608-1964)
PHONE..................................510 992-6430
EMP: 350
SALES (corp-wide): 38.6B **Privately Held**
SIC: 4731
HQ: Apm Terminals Pacific Ltd.
9300 Arrowpoint Blvd
Charlotte NC 90731
704 571-2768

(P-4896)
ATECH LOGISTICS INC
7 College Ave, Santa Rosa (95401-4702)
P.O. Box 6836 (95406-0836)
PHONE..................................707 526-1910
Jesse E Amaral, *President*
Geri Amaral, *Vice Pres*
Yvonne Motherwell, *Accounting Mgr*
Brian Rhoden, *Opers Mgr*
Travis Amaral, *Manager*
EMP: 130
SQ FT: 35,000
SALES (est): 42.3MM **Privately Held**
WEB: www.atechlogistics.com
SIC: 4731 Freight forwarding

(P-4897)
BAJA FREIGHT FORWARDERS INC (PA)
8662 Siempre Viva Rd, San Diego
(92154-6211)
PHONE..................................619 671-3100
Miguel Perez, *CEO*
Ana Diaz, *CFO*
Sergio Rodriguez, *General Mgr*
EMP: 55
SQ FT: 50,000
SALES (est): 14.5MM **Privately Held**
WEB: www.bajafreight.com
SIC: 4731 Foreign freight forwarding; freight forwarding

(P-4898)
BINEX LINE CORP (PA)
19515 S Vermont Ave, Torrance
(90502-1121)
PHONE..................................310 416-8600
David Paek, *President*
Hyun K Cho, *CFO*
Tim Park, *Vice Pres*
◆ **EMP:** 70
SQ FT: 32,000
SALES: 99.8MM **Privately Held**
SIC: 4731 4513 Freight forwarding; air courier services

(P-4899)
BLACKROCK LOGISTICS INC
14601 Slover Ave, Fontana (92337-7163)
PHONE..................................909 259-5357
Larry T James, *President*
EMP: 150
SALES (corp-wide): 211.9MM **Privately Held**
SIC: 4731 Freight forwarding
PA: Blackrock Logistics Inc.
7031 Koll Center Pkwy # 250
Pleasanton CA 94566
925 523-3878

(P-4900)
BLUE SKY SERVICES INC
Also Called: Blue Freight
5530 Corbin Ave Ste 220, Tarzana
(91356-6020)
P.O. Box 571085 (91357-1085)
PHONE..................................818 609-8779
Barry Keller, *President*
Brian Friedman, *Regl Sales Mgr*
EMP: 100
SQ FT: 1,500
SALES: 2.8MM **Privately Held**
SIC: 4731 Freight forwarding

(P-4901)
BROCK LLC (PA)
Also Called: Brock Transportation
333 N Canyons Pkwy # 221, Livermore
(94551-7700)
PHONE..................................925 371-2184
Christopher R Obrien, *Mng Member*
Patty Paolini, *Mktg Dir*
William T Obrien, *Mng Member*
Patton Gabriel, *Manager*
Steve Hill, *Agent*
EMP: 65
SQ FT: 3,000
SALES (est): 40.1MM **Privately Held**
WEB: www.brockweb.com
SIC: 4731 4789 4212 Brokers, shipping; pipeline terminal facilities, independently operated; local trucking, without storage

(P-4902)
BROKERAGE LGSTICS SLUTIONS INC
Also Called: JD Group
1659 Gailes Blvd Ste 101, San Diego
(92154-8230)
PHONE..................................619 671-0276
Jorge Diaz Jr, *President*
Ricardo Rebeil, *Vice Pres*
Laura Diego, *Executive*
Alexandra Ramos, *Financial Exec*
Bertha Carrera, *Sales Dir*
EMP: 55
SQ FT: 50,000
SALES (est): 14.8MM **Privately Held**
WEB: www.agenciajorgediaz.com
SIC: 4731 Domestic freight forwarding

PRODUCTS & SVCS

(P-4903)
C H ROBINSON INTL INC
Also Called: Robinson Fresh
680 Knox St Ste 210, Torrance
(90502-1325)
PHONE............................310 763-6080
John Vestal, *Manager*
EMP: 100
SALES (corp-wide): 16.6B **Publicly Held**
SIC: 4731 Foreign freight forwarding
HQ: C. H. Robinson International, Inc.
    14701 Charlson Rd
    Eden Prairie MN 55347

(P-4904)
C-AIR INTERNATIONAL INC
9841 Arprt Blvd Ste 1400, Los Angeles
(90045)
PHONE............................310 695-3400
Guss Antico, *President*
Eric Jones, *Executive*
EMP: 55
SQ FT: 7,000
SALES (est): 15.5MM **Privately Held**
WEB: www.cairla.com
SIC: 4731 Customhouse brokers; domestic
    freight forwarding

(P-4905)
**CALIFORNIA SIERRA EXPRESS
INC**
2975 Oates St Ste 30, West Sacramento
(95691-6401)
PHONE............................916 375-7070
Jeff Phillips, *Manager*
Kandra Ebster, *Finance Mgr*
Matt Gaines, *Opers Mgr*
EMP: 144
SALES (corp-wide): 20MM **Privately
Held**
WEB: www.calsierraexpress.com
SIC: 4731 4212 Agents, shipping; delivery
    service, vehicular
PA: California Sierra Express, Inc.
    4965 Joule St
    Reno NV 89502
    775 856-8008

(P-4906)
**CARMICHAEL INTERNATIONAL
SVC (DH)**
Also Called: C I Container Line
533 Glendale Blvd Ste 102, Los Angeles
(90026-5097)
PHONE............................213 353-0800
John Salvo, *President*
Vince Salvo, *President*
Jim Ryan, *CFO*
EMP: 100
SQ FT: 19,000
SALES: 24MM **Privately Held**
WEB: www.carmnet.com
SIC: 4731 Customhouse brokers
HQ: Apl Logistics Americas, Ltd
    17600 N Perimeter Dr # 150
    Scottsdale AZ 85255
    602 586-4800

(P-4907)
CEVA FREIGHT LLC
Also Called: Ceva Ocean Line
19600 S Western Ave, Torrance
(90501-1117)
PHONE............................310 972-5500
Randy Mondello, *Vice Pres*
EMP: 80
SALES (corp-wide): 20.8MM **Privately
Held**
WEB: www.tntlogistics.com
SIC: 4731 Foreign freight forwarding
HQ: Ceva Freight, Llc
    15350 Vickery Dr
    Houston TX 77032

(P-4908)
CEVA FREIGHT LLC
Also Called: Ceva Ocean Line
8670 Younger Creek Dr, Sacramento
(95828-1043)
PHONE............................916 379-6000
Scott Mann, *Branch Mgr*
EMP: 150

SALES (corp-wide): 20.8MM **Privately
Held**
WEB: www.tntlogistics.com
SIC: 4731 Domestic freight forwarding
HQ: Ceva Freight, Llc
    15350 Vickery Dr
    Houston TX 77032

(P-4909)
CEVA LOGISTICS LLC
19600 S Western Ave, Torrance
(90501-1117)
PHONE............................310 223-6500
Marvin O Schlanger, *Manager*
Randy Mondello, *Vice Pres*
Camille Utter, *Director*
EMP: 300
SALES (corp-wide): 20.8MM **Privately
Held**
SIC: 4731 Domestic freight forwarding; for-
    eign freight forwarding
HQ: Ceva Logistics, Llc
    15350 Vickery Dr
    Houston TX 77032
    281 618-3100

(P-4910)
CEVA LOGISTICS US INC
11290 Cntu Gllano Rnch Rd, Jurupa Valley
(91752-1448)
PHONE............................951 332-3202
Greg Hart, *Branch Mgr*
EMP: 50
SQ FT: 400,000
SALES (corp-wide): 20.8MM **Privately
Held**
SIC: 4731 Freight transportation arrange-
    ment
HQ: Ceva Logistics U.S., Inc.
    15350 Vickery Dr
    Houston TX 77032
    281 618-3100

(P-4911)
CFR RINKENS LLC (PA)
15501 Texaco Ave, Paramount
(90723-3921)
PHONE............................310 639-7725
Maximiliaan Hoes, *Mng Member*
Ivo Lindner, *Info Tech Mgr*
Mayra Sanchez, *Human Res Mgr*
Gino Bermeo, *Export Mgr*
Sharon Graffia, *Export Mgr*
▼ **EMP:** 93
SALES (est): 18.7MM **Privately Held**
SIC: 4731 Freight forwarding

(P-4912)
**CH ROBINSON FREIGHT SVCS
LTD**
Also Called: Phoenix International
680 Knox St Ste 210, Torrance
(90502-1325)
PHONE............................310 515-7755
Pat Nelms, *Branch Mgr*
Amy K Elliott, *Marketing Staff*
Craig S Carter, *Warehouse Mgr*
John Bestal, *Manager*
Viet Nguyen, *Supervisor*
EMP: 50
SALES (corp-wide): 16.6B **Publicly Held**
SIC: 4731 4225 Freight forwarding; cus-
    tomhouse brokers; general warehousing
HQ: C.H. Robinson Freight Services, Ltd.
    1501 N Mittel Blvd Ste A
    Wood Dale IL 60191
    630 766-4445

(P-4913)
CHEEMA FREIGHTLINES LLC
Also Called: Cheema Logistics
223 W 5th St, Ripon (95366-2771)
P.O. Box 2234, Sumner WA (98390-0490)
PHONE............................209 599-0777
Harman Cheema, *Mng Member*
Jessica Henry, *Manager*
EMP: 53
SQ FT: 1,900
SALES: 28.8MM **Privately Held**
SIC: 4731 Transportation agents & brokers
PA: Cheema Freightlines, Llc
    2720 E Vly Hwy E Sumner
    Sumner WA 98390
    253 733-5718

(P-4914)
CITY FASHION EXPRESS INC
Also Called: C F X
2888 E El Presidio St, Carson
(90810-1119)
PHONE............................310 223-1010
Walter John Malishka, *CEO*
Cammie Leroy, *Technology*
EMP: 58
SALES (est): 14.3MM **Privately Held**
WEB: www.cityx.com
SIC: 4731 Freight forwarding

(P-4915)
CNS LOGISTICS INC
108 W Walnut St Ste 270, Gardena
(90248-3102)
PHONE............................562 229-1133
Kevin Kim, *COO*
Jae Lee, *CFO*
EMP: 84 EST: 2008
SALES (est): 13.7MM **Privately Held**
SIC: 4731 Foreign freight forwarding

(P-4916)
**COMMODITY FORWARDERS
INC (DH)**
Also Called: C F I
11101 S La Cienega Blvd, Los Angeles
(90045-6111)
P.O. Box 894925 (90189-4925)
PHONE............................310 348-8855
Alfred P Kuehlewind, *CEO*
Christopher A Connell, *President*
Ron Reuter, *Vice Pres*
Jennifer Martin, *Admin Sec*
Jenny Mendez, *Accounting Mgr*
◆ **EMP:** 150
SQ FT: 30,000
SALES (est): 85.1MM
SALES (corp-wide): 20.9B **Privately Held**
WEB: www.cfi-lax.com
SIC: 4731 Foreign freight forwarding;
    freight forwarding
HQ: Kuhne + Nagel International Ag
    Dorfstrasse 50
    Schindellegi SZ
    447 869-511

(P-4917)
CONNER LOGISTICS INC
4057 W Shaw Ave Ste 110, Fresno
(93722-6212)
PHONE............................888 939-4637
Dave Conner, *President*
Mike Conner, *Opers Spvr*
Sean Conner, *Opers Mgr*
Susan Rockey, *Opers Staff*
Tim Robinson, *Transptn Dir*
EMP: 90
SQ FT: 1,200
SALES (est): 2.5MM **Privately Held**
SIC: 4731 Freight forwarding

(P-4918)
**CONTINENTAL AGENCY INC
(PA)**
1768 W 2nd St, Pomona (91766-1206)
PHONE............................909 595-8884
Jimmy Jaing, *CEO*
Beverly Jiang, *President*
Josephine Chien, *Manager*
Wilson Hu, *Supervisor*
Wen Yen, *Supervisor*
EMP: 64
SQ FT: 105,000
SALES (est): 150.6MM **Privately Held**
WEB: www.continentalagency.com
SIC: 4731 Customhouse brokers

(P-4919)
**COSCO AGENCIES (LOS
ANGELES) (DH)**
588 Harbor Scenic Way, Long Beach
(90802-6317)
PHONE............................213 689-6700
Jin Guoqiang, *President*
Tom Somma, *Exec VP*
Arthur Mathis, *Assistant VP*
▲ **EMP:** 56
SQ FT: 11,000
SALES (est): 7MM
SALES (corp-wide): 18.9B **Privately Held**
SIC: 4731 Agents, shipping

HQ: Cosco Shipping Lines (North America)
    Inc.
    100 Lighting Way Fl 3
    Secaucus NJ 07094
    201 422-0500

(P-4920)
**CSC AUTO SALV DISMANTLING
INC**
12207 Branford St, Sun Valley
(91352-1010)
PHONE............................818 532-4624
Scott Sakajian, *President*
Garrett Brady, *Admin Sec*
EMP: 54
SALES: 8MM **Privately Held**
SIC: 4731 4953 Freight transportation
    arrangement; refuse systems

(P-4921)
CUSTOM COMPANIES INC
13012 Molette St, Santa Fe Springs
(90670-5522)
PHONE............................310 672-8800
Mark Inman, *Manager*
EMP: 70
SALES (corp-wide): 122.6MM **Privately
Held**
SIC: 4731 4214 Transportation agents &
    brokers; freight forwarding; local trucking
    with storage
PA: The Custom Companies Inc
    317 W Lake St
    Northlake IL 60164
    708 344-5555

(P-4922)
DELTA AIR LINES INC
Also Called: Delta Airlines
5625 W Imperial Hwy, Los Angeles
(90045-6323)
PHONE............................310 646-9614
Kelvin Wimbish, *Branch Mgr*
Kathryn Pope, *Sales Staff*
Rebecca Dematos,
Paul Volcheff, *Manager*
EMP: 72
SALES (corp-wide): 44.4B **Publicly Held**
WEB: www.delta.com
SIC: 4731 4581 4512 Freight forwarding;
    airports, flying fields & services; air trans-
    portation, scheduled
PA: Delta Air Lines, Inc.
    1030 Delta Blvd
    Atlanta GA 30354
    404 715-2600

(P-4923)
**DEPENDABLE AIRCARGO EX
INC**
19201 S Susana Rd, Compton
(90221-5710)
PHONE............................310 537-2000
Bradley Dechter, *President*
EMP: 150
SALES (est): 13MM **Privately Held**
SIC: 4731 Freight forwarding

(P-4924)
**DFDS INTERNATIONAL
CORPORATION**
Also Called: Dfds Transport US
898 N Pacific Coast Hwy # 6, El Segundo
(90245-2705)
PHONE............................310 414-1516
Tina Larsen, *General Mgr*
EMP: 80
SALES (corp-wide): 2.4B **Privately Held**
WEB: www.us.dsv.com
SIC: 4731 Foreign freight forwarding
HQ: Dfds International Corporation
    100 Walnut Ave Ste 405
    Clark NJ 07066

(P-4925)
DHL SUPPLY CHAIN (USA)
Also Called: Msas Cargo International
485 Valley Dr, Brisbane (94005-1209)
PHONE............................415 531-0596
Kevin Duson, *General Mgr*
Octavio Madera, *Opers Spvr*
EMP: 125
SALES (corp-wide): 70.4B **Privately Held**
SIC: 4731 Freight forwarding

HQ: Exel Inc.
570 Polaris Pkwy
Westerville OH 43082
614 865-8500

(P-4926)
DHX-DEPENDABLE HAWAIIAN EX INC
2375 Davis St, San Leandro (94577-2205)
PHONE...................................510 686-2600
Wilfred Robello, *General Mgr*
Georgia Briggs, *Office Mgr*
Richard Holtgrew, *Opers Mgr*
EMP: 127
SALES (corp-wide): 81.8MM **Privately Held**
SIC: 4731 Freight forwarding
PA: Dhx-Dependable Hawaiian Express, Inc.
19201 S Susana Rd
Compton CA 90221
310 537-2000

(P-4927)
DHX-DEPENDABLE HAWAIIAN EX INC (PA)
19201 S Susana Rd, Compton (90221-5710)
PHONE...................................310 537-2000
Ronald Massman, *Chairman*
Cammie Laster, *President*
Tim Rice, *CFO*
Denise Jackson, *Officer*
Kane McEwen, *General Mgr*
EMP: 150
SQ FT: 106,000
SALES (est): 81.8MM **Privately Held**
SIC: 4731 Foreign freight forwarding; freight forwarding

(P-4928)
DIRECTED LLC
1 Viper Way Ste 1 # 1, Vista (92081-7811)
PHONE...................................800 876-0800
Robert Struble, *CEO*
Kevin Duffy, *COO*
James Wiesen, *CFO*
Joseph Tristani, *Treasurer*
David Meisels, *Admin Sec*
EMP: 164
SQ FT: 83,057
SALES: 80MM **Privately Held**
SIC: 4731 Domestic freight forwarding

(P-4929)
DISPATCH TRUCKING LLC (PA)
14032 Santa Ana Ave, Fontana (92337-7035)
PHONE...................................909 355-5531
Bruce L Degler, *CEO*
Jalayne Pugmire, *Vice Pres*
EMP: 70 EST: 1991
SQ FT: 600
SALES (est): 9.2MM **Privately Held**
WEB: www.dispatchtrans.com
SIC: 4731 Truck transportation brokers

(P-4930)
DSC LOGISTICS LLC
5690 Industrial Pkwy, San Bernardino (92407-1885)
PHONE...................................540 377-2302
Enrique Tirado, *Manager*
EMP: 451
SALES (corp-wide): 355MM **Privately Held**
SIC: 4731 Freight transportation arrangement
PA: Dsc Logistics, Llc
1750 S Wolf Rd
Des Plaines IL 60018
847 390-6800

(P-4931)
DSV SOLUTIONS LLC
Also Called: Corp., R.g Barry
13230 San Bernardino Ave, Fontana (92335-5229)
PHONE...................................909 349-6100
EMP: 152
SALES (corp-wide): 12.1B **Privately Held**
SIC: 4731 Freight forwarding
HQ: Dsv Solutions, Llc
100 Walnut Ave Ste 405
Clark NJ 07066
732 850-8000

(P-4932)
DSV SOLUTIONS LLC
3454 E Miraloma Ave, Anaheim (92806-2101)
PHONE...................................714 630-0110
EMP: 74
SALES (corp-wide): 12.1B **Privately Held**
SIC: 4731 Freight forwarding
HQ: Dsv Solutions, Llc
100 Walnut Ave Ste 405
Clark NJ 07066
732 850-8000

(P-4933)
DTM SERVICES INC (PA)
Also Called: Diversified Trnsp Svcs
19829 Hamilton Ave, Torrance (90502-1341)
PHONE...................................310 521-1200
Marc Meskin, *CEO*
Robbie Thone, *Senior VP*
Michael Doyle, *Vice Pres*
Richard W Greenbaum, *Director*
Carl Koski, *Accounts Mgr*
EMP: 54
SQ FT: 7,000
SALES (est): 10.1MM **Privately Held**
WEB: www.dtsone.com
SIC: 4731 Truck transportation brokers

(P-4934)
DW MORGAN LLC
4185 Blackhawk, Danville (94506)
PHONE...................................925 460-2700
David W Morgan, *CEO*
EMP: 63 EST: 2013
SALES (est): 4.5MM **Privately Held**
SIC: 4731 4212 4789 Domestic freight forwarding; local trucking, without storage; cargo loading & unloading services

(P-4935)
DYNAMIC WORLDWIDE WEST INC (PA)
14141 Alondra Blvd, Santa Fe Springs (90670-5804)
PHONE...................................562 407-1000
John J Belsito, *CEO*
Andrew D Rotondi, *COO*
Richard Morabito, *CFO*
▲ EMP: 150
SQ FT: 395,000
SALES (est): 40.5MM **Privately Held**
WEB: www.pdsidistribution.com
SIC: 4731 Freight consolidation

(P-4936)
ECO FLOW TRANSPORTATION LLC
18735 S Ferris Pl, Rancho Dominguez (90220-6405)
PHONE...................................310 816-0260
Bill Allen, *President*
EMP: 60
SALES (est): 2.3MM **Privately Held**
SIC: 4731 Freight transportation arrangement

(P-4937)
ERIC JONES CUSTOMS BROKERAGE
9841 Arprt Blvd Ste 1400, Los Angeles (90045)
PHONE...................................310 348-3777
Eric Jones, *Vice Pres*
EMP: 50
SALES (est): 3.3MM **Privately Held**
SIC: 4731 Customhouse brokers

(P-4938)
EXPEDITORS INTL WASH INC
Also Called: Sfo-3 - San Francisco Full Svc
425 Valley Dr, Brisbane (94005-1209)
PHONE...................................415 657-3600
Kevin Niduaza, *General Mgr*
Judith Ross, *Accounts Mgr*
EMP: 50
SALES (corp-wide): 8.1B **Publicly Held**
WEB: www.expd.com
SIC: 4731 Freight forwarding
PA: Expeditors International Of Washington, Inc.
1015 3rd Ave Fl 12
Seattle WA 98104
206 674-3400

(P-4939)
EXPEDITORS INTL WASH INC
578 Eccles Ave, South San Francisco (94080-1905)
PHONE...................................919 489-7431
Brandi Altamirano, *Manager*
EMP: 131
SALES (corp-wide): 8.1B **Publicly Held**
WEB: www.expd.com
SIC: 4731 Freight forwarding; foreign freight forwarding; domestic freight forwarding
PA: Expeditors International Of Washington, Inc.
1015 3rd Ave Fl 12
Seattle WA 98104
206 674-3400

(P-4940)
EXPEDITORS INTL WASH INC
12200 Wilkie Ave 100, Hawthorne (90250-1838)
PHONE...................................310 343-6200
Nicole Gamret, *Analyst*
EMP: 64
SALES (corp-wide): 8.1B **Publicly Held**
SIC: 4731 Foreign freight forwarding
PA: Expeditors International Of Washington, Inc.
1015 3rd Ave Fl 12
Seattle WA 98104
206 674-3400

(P-4941)
EXPEDITORS INTL WASH INC
1470 Expo Way Ste 110, San Diego (92154)
PHONE...................................619 710-1900
Trevor Moulton, *Manager*
EMP: 60
SALES (corp-wide): 8.1B **Publicly Held**
WEB: www.expd.com
SIC: 4731 Freight forwarding
PA: Expeditors International Of Washington, Inc.
1015 3rd Ave Fl 12
Seattle WA 98104
206 674-3400

(P-4942)
EXPRESS SYSTEM INTERMODAL INC
2633 Camino Ramon Ste 400, San Ramon (94583-2176)
PHONE...................................801 302-6625
Peter Leng, *President*
EMP: 150
SALES (est): 16.5MM **Privately Held**
WEB: www.esi-intermodal.com
SIC: 4731 Freight transportation arrangement
HQ: Oocl (Usa) Inc.
10913 S River Front Pkwy # 200
South Jordan UT 84095
801 302-6625

(P-4943)
EXTRA EXPRESS (CERRITOS) INC
20405 Business Pkwy, Walnut (91789-2939)
P.O. Box 5100, Cerritos (90703-5100)
PHONE...................................714 985-6000
Kirk Baerwaldt, *President*
Robert Bell, *Vice Pres*
Tom Webb, *Director*
EMP: 50
SALES (est): 9.5MM
SALES (corp-wide): 21MM **Privately Held**
WEB: www.extraexpress.com
SIC: 4731 Freight transportation arrangement
HQ: Dicom West Llc
676 N Michigan Ave # 3700
Chicago IL 60611
312 255-4800

(P-4944)
F R T INTERNATIONAL INC
Also Called: Frontier Logistics Services
2825 Jurupa St, Ontario (91761-2903)
PHONE...................................909 390-4892
Steven Hall, *Branch Mgr*
EMP: 123

SALES (corp-wide): 27.6MM **Privately Held**
SIC: 4731 Customhouse brokers
PA: F. R. T. International, Inc.
1700 N Alameda St
Compton CA 90222
310 604-8208

(P-4945)
FEDERAL EXPRESS CORPORATION
Also Called: Fedex
2221 W Washington St, San Diego (92110-2037)
PHONE...................................800 463-3339
EMP: 140
SALES (corp-wide): 69.6B **Publicly Held**
WEB: www.federalexpress.com
SIC: 4731 Agents, shipping
HQ: Federal Express Corporation
3610 Hacks Cross Rd
Memphis TN 38125
901 369-3600

(P-4946)
FNS INC (PA)
1545 Francisco St, Torrance (90501-1330)
PHONE...................................661 615-2300
Bennett B Koo, *CEO*
Wook Jin Choi, *Admin Sec*
Jae Kim, *Planning*
Soyoun Han, *Hum Res Coord*
Paul Mosher, *Purch Mgr*
EMP: 100
SQ FT: 100,000
SALES (est): 94.2MM **Privately Held**
WEB: www.fnsusa.com
SIC: 4731 Freight forwarding

(P-4947)
FNS CUSTOMS BROKERS INC
18301 S Broadwick St, Compton (90220-6442)
PHONE...................................310 667-4880
Bennett Koo, *CEO*
Wookjin Choi, *CFO*
EMP: 50
SQ FT: 2,000
SALES (est): 7.7MM **Privately Held**
SIC: 4731 Customhouse brokers

(P-4948)
FORWARD AIR INC
30108 Eigenbrodt Way # 100, Union City (94587-1225)
PHONE...................................415 570-6040
Fax: 650 794-9923
EMP: 50
SALES (corp-wide): 1.1B **Publicly Held**
SIC: 4731
HQ: Forward Air, Inc.
430 Airport Rd
Greeneville TN 37745
423 639-7196

(P-4949)
FURNITURE TRNSP SYSTEMS
3100 Pomona Blvd, Pomona (91768-3230)
P.O. Box 2960 (91769-2960)
PHONE...................................909 869-1200
Dennis Firestone, *President*
Lynnette Genereux, *Corp Secy*
John Naughton, *Vice Pres*
EMP: 65
SQ FT: 100,000
SALES (est): 12.5MM
SALES (corp-wide): 88.7MM **Privately Held**
SIC: 4731 4212 Freight consolidation; local trucking, without storage
PA: K. K. W. Trucking, Inc.
3100 Pomona Blvd
Pomona CA 91768
909 869-1200

(P-4950)
G KATEN PARTNERS LTD LBLTY CO
Also Called: My Express Freight
9903 Santa Monica Blvd, Beverly Hills (90212-1671)
PHONE...................................424 354-3241
Gerald Katen,
EMP: 550
SALES (est): 41.6MM **Privately Held**
SIC: 4731 Freight forwarding

PRODUCTS & SVCS

(P-4951)
G3 ENTERPRISES INC
G3 Enterprises Mineral Div
1300 Camino Diablo Rd, Byron (94514)
P.O. Box 216 (94514-0216)
PHONE..................................209 341-3441
EMP: 82
SALES (corp-wide): 106.8MM **Privately Held**
SIC: **4731** Truck transportation brokers
PA: G3 Enterprises, Inc.
502 E Whitmore Ave
Modesto CA 95358
209 341-7515

(P-4952)
G3 ENTERPRISES INC
G3 Enterprises Closure Div
500 S Santa Rosa Ave, Modesto
(95354-3717)
PHONE..................................209 341-4045
EMP: 55
SALES (corp-wide): 106.8MM **Privately Held**
SIC: **4731** Truck transportation brokers
PA: G3 Enterprises, Inc.
502 E Whitmore Ave
Modesto CA 95358
209 341-7515

(P-4953)
GEBRUDER WEISS INC
19701 Hamilton Ave # 200, Torrance
(90502-1352)
PHONE..................................310 414-9300
Andrei Jansen, Branch Mgr
EMP: 56
SALES (corp-wide): 21.7MM **Privately Held**
SIC: **4731** Freight forwarding
PA: Gebruder Weiss, Inc.
251 Wille Rd Ste C
Des Plaines IL 60018
847 795-4300

(P-4954)
GELS LOGISTICS INC
20275 Business Pkwy, City of Industry
(91789-2950)
PHONE..................................909 610-2277
Xindi Hu, CEO
Ling Wang, CFO
Liangna Zhong, General Mgr
EMP: 60
SALES (est): 1MM **Privately Held**
SIC: **4731** Transportation agents & brokers

(P-4955)
GEODIS WILSON USA INC
229 Littlefield Ave Ste 1, South San Francisco (94080-6926)
PHONE..................................650 692-9850
Jimmy Huang, Branch Mgr
EMP: 125
SALES (corp-wide): 4.2MM **Privately Held**
SIC: **4731** Freight forwarding
HQ: Geodis Wilson Usa, Inc.
75a Northfield Ave
Edison NJ 08837
732 362-0600

(P-4956)
GLOBAL MAIL INC
921 W Artesia Blvd, Compton
(90220-5105)
PHONE..................................310 735-0800
Eric Ricardo, Branch Mgr
EMP: 200
SALES (corp-wide): 70.4B **Privately Held**
SIC: **4731** Freight transportation arrangement
HQ: Global Mail, Inc.
2700 S Commerce Pkwy Ste 300
Weston FL 33331
800 805-9306

(P-4957)
GLOVIS AMERICA INC (HQ)
17305 Von Karman Ave # 200, Irvine
(92614-6674)
PHONE..................................714 435-2960
Kyung B Kim, President
Glenn Clift, COO
Sandra V BSN, Bd of Directors
Sonia V Aprn, Vice Pres

Mark Sur, Executive
◆ EMP: 80
SQ FT: 34,700
SALES (est): 57.9MM **Privately Held**
WEB: www.glovisusa.com
SIC: **4731** Freight forwarding

(P-4958)
GOLDEN BRIDGE INTL GROUP
727 9th Ave, City of Industry (91745-1416)
PHONE..................................626 968-8229
EMP: 87
SALES (est): 17.4MM **Privately Held**
SIC: **4731** Freight forwarding

(P-4959)
GOLDEN HOUR DATA SYSTEMS INC
10052 Mesa Ridge Ct # 200, San Diego
(92121-2971)
PHONE..................................858 768-2500
Kevin Hutton, President
Charles Haczewski, President
Bill Dow, CFO
Eric Fleming, Security Dir
Peter Goutmann, CTO
EMP: 120 EST: 1997
SQ FT: 14,000
SALES (est): 31.2MM **Privately Held**
WEB: www.goldenhour.com
SIC: **4731** Transportation agents & brokers
HQ: Zoll Medical Corporation
269 Mill Rd
Chelmsford MA 01824
978 421-9655

(P-4960)
GONZALEZ BARBA ENTERPRISES
1575 E 46th St, Los Angeles (90011-4315)
PHONE..................................323 233-7995
Elizabeth Gonzalez, Principal
EMP: 50
SALES (est): 3.8MM **Privately Held**
SIC: **4731** Transportation agents & brokers

(P-4961)
GREATWIDE LOGISTICS SVCS LLC
Also Called: Greatwide Dedicated Transport
4310 Bandini Blvd, Vernon (90058-4308)
PHONE..................................323 268-7100
Angela Remling, Branch Mgr
Jose Morataya, Supervisor
EMP: 75 **Privately Held**
SIC: **4731** Truck transportation brokers
HQ: Greatwide Logistics Services, Llc.
12404 Park Central Dr # 300
Dallas TX 75251

(P-4962)
HANJIN TRANSPORTATION CO LTD
Also Called: Hanjin Global Logistics
1111 E Watson Center Rd A, Carson
(90745-4217)
PHONE..................................310 522-5030
Bryce Dalziel, President
J B Park, Admin Sec
EMP: 90
SQ FT: 28,000
SALES (est): 36.4MM **Privately Held**
SIC: **4731** Transportation agents & brokers
PA: Hanjin Corporation Co., Ltd
137 Hongdo-Dong, Tong-Gu
Daejeon

(P-4963)
HANSOL GOLDPOINT LLC
12792 Valley View St # 211, Garden Grove
(92845-2510)
PHONE..................................714 594-5073
Min Ho Inn, Branch Mgr
EMP: 84
SALES (corp-wide): 4.5MM **Privately Held**
SIC: **4731** Freight forwarding
PA: Hansol Goldpoint Llc
2396 E Pacifica Pl # 290
Rancho Dominguez CA
619 710-1728

(P-4964)
HELLMANN WRLDWIDE LGISTICS INC
2270 E 220th St, Long Beach
(90810-1638)
PHONE..................................310 847-4600
Jonas Welch, Branch Mgr
Jacqueline Flores, Executive
Maureen Lapiz, Executive
Steve Kim, Manager
EMP: 60
SALES (corp-wide): 2.9B **Privately Held**
SIC: **4731** Freight forwarding
HQ: Hellmann Worldwide Logistics Inc.
10450 Doral Blvd
Doral FL 33178
305 406-4500

(P-4965)
HELLMANN WRLDWIDE LGISTICS INC
2270 E 220th St, Carson (90810-1638)
PHONE..................................310 847-4600
Roger Haeussler, President
EMP: 50
SALES (corp-wide): 2.9B **Privately Held**
WEB: www.hellmann.net
SIC: **4731** Freight forwarding
HQ: Hellmann Worldwide Logistics Inc.
10450 Doral Blvd
Doral FL 33178
305 406-4500

(P-4966)
HES TRANSPORTATION SVCS INC
3623 Munster St, Hayward (94545-1646)
P.O. Box 57136 (94545-7136)
PHONE..................................510 783-6100
Jeff Graham, President
Joyce C Schaul, Vice Pres
Kathy Manus, Manager
EMP: 50
SQ FT: 38,000
SALES (est): 5.9MM **Privately Held**
SIC: **4731** Freight forwarding

(P-4967)
HOME EXPRESS DELIVERY SVC LLC
Also Called: Temco Logistics
230 Diamond St, Laguna Beach
(92651-3610)
PHONE..................................949 715-9844
Lance Templeton,
Charlie Sunberg, Controller
Virginia Templeton,
EMP: 1000
SQ FT: 900
SALES: 35MM **Privately Held**
SIC: **4731** Freight transportation arrangement

(P-4968)
HONOLULU FREIGHT SERVICE (PA)
1400 Date St, Montebello (90640-6323)
PHONE..................................323 887-6777
Michael Biedleman, President
Dorene Beidleman, CFO
Thomas Biedleman, Vice Pres
Patrick Toves, General Mgr
Christopher Toye, Administration
EMP: 50 EST: 1945
SQ FT: 1,500
SALES (est): 20.9MM **Privately Held**
WEB: www.hfsnet.com
SIC: **4731** Foreign freight forwarding; domestic freight forwarding

(P-4969)
ICAT LOGISTICS INC
11 Wandering Rill, Irvine (92603-3430)
PHONE..................................310 884-5923
EMP: 93 **Privately Held**
SIC: **4731** Freight transportation arrangement
PA: Icat Logistics, Inc.
6805 Douglas Legum Dr # 3
Elkridge MD 21075

(P-4970)
INLOG INC
6765 Westminster Blvd # 424, Westminster
(92683-3769)
PHONE..................................949 212-3867
EMP: 85
SALES (corp-wide): 6.8MM **Privately Held**
SIC: **4731** Freight transportation arrangement
PA: Inlog, Inc.
4760 Preston Rd
Frisco TX 75034
949 212-5241

(P-4971)
INNOVEL SOLUTIONS INC
Also Called: Sears
521 Stone Rd, Benicia (94510-1113)
PHONE..................................707 748-1940
Dixie Shaw, Manager
EMP: 99
SALES (corp-wide): 22.2B **Publicly Held**
WEB: www.slslogistics.com+%22sears+logistics+servi
SIC: **4731** Agents, shipping
HQ: Innovel Solutions, Inc.
3333 Beverly Rd
Hoffman Estates IL 60179
847 286-2500

(P-4972)
INNOVEL SOLUTIONS INC
Also Called: Sears
1700 Schuster Rd, Delano (93215-9572)
PHONE..................................661 721-5910
Mike Velton, General Mgr
EMP: 600
SALES (corp-wide): 22.2B **Publicly Held**
WEB: www.slslogistics.com+%22sears+logistics+servi
SIC: **4731** Agents, shipping
HQ: Innovel Solutions, Inc.
3333 Beverly Rd
Hoffman Estates IL 60179
847 286-2500

(P-4973)
INNOVEL SOLUTIONS INC
Also Called: Sears
5691 E Philadelphia St # 200, Ontario
(91761-2805)
PHONE..................................909 605-1446
Derrick Daniel, Manager
EMP: 100
SALES (corp-wide): 22.2B **Publicly Held**
WEB: www.slslogistics.com+%22sears+logistics+servi
SIC: **4731** Agents, shipping
HQ: Innovel Solutions, Inc.
3333 Beverly Rd
Hoffman Estates IL 60179
847 286-2500

(P-4974)
JS INTERNATIONAL SHIPG CORP (PA)
Also Called: Jsi Shipping
33215 Dowe Ave, Union City (94587-2000)
P.O. Box 4267, Burlingame (94011-4267)
PHONE..................................650 697-3963
James G Cullen, CEO
Richard Bryant, Vice Pres
Vicky Los Santos, Sr Software Eng
Will Waller, IT/INT Sup
Dan Cha, Technology
◆ EMP: 70
SQ FT: 50,000
SALES (est): 229.9MM **Privately Held**
WEB: www.jsishipping.com
SIC: **4731** Freight forwarding; custom-house brokers

(P-4975)
KOJENOV ARKADI NILOVICH
5335 Hackberry Ln, Sacramento
(95841-3268)
PHONE..................................916 718-1790
Arkadi Kojenov, Owner
EMP: 50 EST: 1997
SQ FT: 2,000
SALES: 5MM **Privately Held**
SIC: **4731** Freight transportation arrangement

(P-4976)
KSI CORP (PA)
839 Mitten Rd, San Bruno (94066)
P.O. Box 2182, South San Francisco
(94083-2182)
PHONE..................................650 952-0815
Carl Bellante, *CEO*
Dennis Siu, *CFO*
Michael Ford, *Senior VP*
Chris Ramos, *Vice Pres*
Albert Foong, *Manager*
EMP: 64
SQ FT: 13,000
SALES (est): 8.1MM **Privately Held**
WEB: www.ksicorp.com
SIC: 4731 8741 Customhouse brokers;
management services

(P-4977)
KSI CORP
839 Mitten Rd Ste 200, Burlingame
(94010-1331)
PHONE..................................650 952-0815
Carl Bellante, *CEO*
Dennis Siu, *CFO*
Michael Ford, *Senior VP*
Chris Ramos, *Vice Pres*
EMP: 60
SALES (est): 6MM **Privately Held**
SIC: 4731 Freight transportation arrange-
ment

(P-4978)
KUEHNE + NAGEL INC
150 W Hill Pl, Brisbane (94005-1216)
PHONE..................................415 656-4100
Christian Herwig, *Branch Mgr*
Rick Delapaz, *Vice Pres*
Len Sokaloski, *General Mgr*
Manuel Ramirez, *Broker*
Maria Mallari, *Export Mgr*
EMP: 50
SALES (corp-wide): 20.9B **Privately Held**
WEB: www.kuehnenagel.com
SIC: 4731 Freight forwarding
HQ: Kuehne + Nagel Inc.
10 Exchange Pl Fl 19
Jersey City NJ 07302
201 413-5500

(P-4979)
KUEHNE + NAGEL INC
2660 W Winton Ave, Hayward
(94545-1108)
PHONE..................................510 785-0555
Arlene Van Meter, *Manager*
EMP: 57
SALES (corp-wide): 20.9B **Privately Held**
WEB: www.kuehnenagel.com
SIC: 4731 Freight transportation arrange-
ment
HQ: Kuehne + Nagel Inc.
10 Exchange Pl Fl 19
Jersey City NJ 07302
201 413-5500

(P-4980)
KUEHNE + NAGEL INC
9425 Nevada St, Redlands (92374-5106)
PHONE..................................909 574-2300
Paul Schmidt, *Branch Mgr*
Paul Schmitt, *Opers Mgr*
EMP: 52
SALES (corp-wide): 20.9B **Privately Held**
WEB: www.kuehnenagel.com
SIC: 4731 Freight transportation arrange-
ment
HQ: Kuehne + Nagel Inc.
10 Exchange Pl Fl 19
Jersey City NJ 07302
201 413-5500

(P-4981)
KW INTERNATIONAL INC
18511 S Broadwick St, Rancho Dominguez
(90220-6440)
PHONE..................................310 747-1380
Dj Kim, *Manager*
EMP: 70 **Privately Held**
SIC: 4731 Freight forwarding
PA: Kw International, Inc.
18655 Bishop Ave
Carson CA 90746

(P-4982)
**KXP ADVANTAGE SERVICES
LLC (PA)**
Also Called: Expak Logistics
11777 San Vicente Blvd # 747, Los Angeles
(90049-5052)
PHONE..................................424 320-5300
Michael Kraus, *CEO*
EMP: 148
SQ FT: 1,200
SALES (est): 21.2MM **Privately Held**
SIC: 4731 4215 Freight transportation
arrangement; courier services, except by
air

(P-4983)
L E COPPERSMITH INC (PA)
Also Called: Coppersmith Global Logistics
525 S Douglas St Ste 100, El Segundo
(90245-4828)
PHONE..................................310 607-8000
Jeffrey Craig Coppersmith, *President*
Douglas S Walkley, *CFO*
Lew Coppersmith Jr, *Vice Pres*
L E Coppersmith, *Admin Sec*
Lew E Coppersmith II, *Admin Sec*
EMP: 80
SQ FT: 40,000
SALES: 20MM **Privately Held**
SIC: 4731 4789 Customhouse brokers;
cargo loading & unloading services

(P-4984)
L E COPPERSMITH INC
525 S Douglas St, El Segundo
(90245-4826)
PHONE..................................310 607-8000
D Walkley, *Branch Mgr*
EMP: 80
SALES (corp-wide): 20MM **Privately
Held**
SIC: 4731 Freight forwarding
PA: L. E. Coppersmith, Inc.
525 S Douglas St Ste 100
El Segundo CA 90245
310 607-8000

(P-4985)
LOUP LOGISTICS COMPANY
Also Called: Union Pacific
2121 S Browning Rd, Delano (93215-9298)
PHONE..................................661 370-4341
Kim Sakata, *Branch Mgr*
EMP: 135
SALES (corp-wide): 22.8B **Publicly Held**
WEB: www.railex.net
SIC: 4731 Railroad freight agency
HQ: Loup Logistics Company
1400 Douglas St Stop 1230
Omaha NE 68179
402 544-7094

(P-4986)
**LUFTHNSA CRGO
AKTNGESELLSCHAFT**
5721 W Imperial Hwy, Los Angeles
(90045-6301)
PHONE..................................310 242-2590
Veli Polat, *President*
EMP: 150
SALES (corp-wide): 41B **Privately Held**
SIC: 4731 Freight forwarding
HQ: Lufthansa Cargo Ag
Flughafen Frankfurt Am Main
Frankfurt Am Main 60549
696 960-

(P-4987)
LUTREL TRUCKING INC
12856 Old River Rd, Bakersfield
(93311-9707)
PHONE..................................661 397-9756
Roy G Lutrel, *President*
Gail Lutrel, *Treasurer*
Mark Lutrel, *Vice Pres*
EMP: 65 EST: 1973
SALES (est): 12.2MM **Privately Held**
WEB: www.lutreltrucking.com
SIC: 4731 Customs clearance of freight;
freight forwarding

(P-4988)
MAERSK INC
Also Called: Maersk Line
555 Anton Blvd Ste 300, Costa Mesa
(92626-7667)
PHONE..................................714 428-5500
Celia Miller, *Branch Mgr*
EMP: 80
SALES (corp-wide): 1.9MM **Privately
Held**
WEB: www.maersksealand.com
SIC: 4731 Agents, shipping
HQ: Maersk Inc.
180 Park Ave Ste 105
Florham Park NJ 07932
973 514-5000

(P-4989)
MAINFREIGHT INC (HQ)
1400 Glenn Curtiss St, Carson
(90746-4030)
PHONE..................................310 900-1974
John Hepworth, *President*
Matt Gustafson, *Branch Mgr*
Mark Overmyer, *Branch Mgr*
Eduardo Rivera, *Branch Mgr*
Ron Frady, *Admin Sec*
◆ EMP: 90
SQ FT: 100,000
SALES: 493.9MM
WEB: www.mainfreightusa.com
SIC: 4731 Transportation agents & brokers
PA: Mainfreight Limited
2 Railway Lane
Auckland 1062
925 955-00

(P-4990)
**MAP CARGO GLOBAL
LOGISTICS (PA)**
2501 Santa Fe Ave, Redondo Beach
(90278-1117)
PHONE..................................310 297-8300
Marek Adam Panasewicz, *President*
John Climaco, *Manager*
EMP: 74
SQ FT: 20,000
SALES (est): 26.9MM **Privately Held**
WEB: www.mapcargo.com
SIC: 4731 2448 Domestic freight forward-
ing; cargo containers, wood & wood with
metal

(P-4991)
MATUS INTERNATIONAL INC
1120 De Forest Ave, Long Beach
(90813-2824)
PHONE..................................562 435-5200
Luis Matus, *Principal*
EMP: 155 EST: 2014
SALES (est): 30.8MM **Privately Held**
SIC: 4731 Freight forwarding

(P-4992)
MHX LLC
22707 Wilmington Ave, Carson
(90745-4321)
PHONE..................................800 234-2098
Rick McLeod, *President*
Conrad Hardin,
Vincent McLeod,
EMP: 75 EST: 2016
SALES (est): 6.7MM **Privately Held**
SIC: 4731 Domestic freight forwarding

(P-4993)
**MILLENNIUM TRANSPORTATION
INC**
3164 E La Palma Ave Ste D, Anaheim
(92806-2811)
PHONE..................................714 956-7882
Reuban Bedi, *President*
EMP: 99
SALES (est): 11.6MM **Privately Held**
SIC: 4731 Truck transportation brokers

(P-4994)
**MIRAMAR TRANSPORTATION
INC**
Also Called: Pilot Freight Services
9340 Cabot Dr Ste I, San Diego
(92126-4397)
P.O. Box 502850 (92150-2850)
PHONE..................................858 693-0071

Richard Evan Fore, *President*
Bob Mirinda, *Vice Pres*
Liz Beck, *District Mgr*
Fred Mackay, *District Mgr*
Pam Fore, *Human Resources*
EMP: 100
SALES (est): 28.4MM **Privately Held**
SIC: 4731 Freight forwarding

(P-4995)
**MOTIVATIONAL MARKETING
INC**
Also Called: Motivational Fulfillment
16133 Fern Ave, Chino (91708-9001)
PHONE..................................909 517-2200
EMP: 78 **Privately Held**
SIC: 4731 Freight transportation arrange-
ment
PA: Motivational Marketing, Inc.
15820 Euclid Ave
Chino CA 91708

(P-4996)
**MOUNTAIN VALLEY EXPRESS
CO INC**
7701 Rosecrans Ave, Paramount
(90723-2534)
P.O. Box 2569, Manteca (95336-1167)
PHONE..................................562 630-5500
Robert Baker, *Branch Mgr*
EMP: 130
SALES (corp-wide): 52.6MM **Privately
Held**
WEB: www.mountainvalleyexpress.com
SIC: 4731 4212 Freight transportation
arrangement; local trucking, without stor-
age
PA: Mountain Valley Express Co. , Inc.
6750 Longe St Ste 100
Stockton CA 95206
209 823-2168

(P-4997)
NATIONAL AIR CARGO INC
222 N Sepulveda Blvd # 2000, El Segundo
(90245-5648)
PHONE..................................310 662-4766
Ray Macchlowski, *Manager*
EMP: 80 **Privately Held**
SIC: 4731 Freight forwarding
HQ: National Air Cargo Inc
350 Windward Dr
Orchard Park NY 14127

(P-4998)
NATIONWIDE TRANS INC (PA)
1633 S Campus Ave, Ontario (91761-4335)
P.O. Box 4207 (91761-8907)
PHONE..................................909 355-3211
Kong Lee, *President*
EMP: 100 EST: 2006
SALES (est): 17.8MM **Privately Held**
SIC: 4731 Freight transportation arrange-
ment

(P-4999)
NEOVIA LOGISTICS DIST LP
600 Live Oak Ave, Irwindale (91706-1344)
PHONE..................................626 359-4500
Hector Legaspi, *Branch Mgr*
EMP: 106
SALES (corp-wide): 69.9MM **Privately
Held**
SIC: 4731 Truck transportation brokers
HQ: Neovia Logistics Distribution, Lp
6363 N State Highway # 700
Irving TX 75038

(P-5000)
NEXT TRUCKING INC
2383 Utah Ave Ste 108, El Segundo
(90245-4845)
PHONE..................................855 688-6398
Lidia Yan, *CEO*
EMP: 200
SALES (est): 4.2MM **Privately Held**
SIC: 4731 4225 Freight forwarding; gen-
eral warehousing & storage

(P-5001)
NIPPON EXPRESS USA INC
970 Francisco St, Torrance (90502-1201)
PHONE..................................310 532-6300

PRODUCTS & SVCS

Yozo Komiya, *Vice Pres*
EMP: 50 **Privately Held**
SIC: 4731 4412 4491 Freight forwarding;
deep sea foreign transportation of freight;
marine cargo handling
HQ: Nippon Express U.S.A., Inc.
2401 44th Rd Fl 14
Long Island City NY 11101
212 758-6100

(P-5002)
NIPPON EXPRESS USA INC
300 Westmont Dr, San Pedro
(90731-1000)
PHONE..................310 532-6300
Y Totani, *Manager*
EMP: 62 **Privately Held**
SIC: 4731 4424 Freight forwarding; deep
sea domestic transportation of freight
HQ: Nippon Express U.S.A., Inc.
2401 44th Rd Fl 14
Long Island City NY 11101
212 758-6100

(P-5003)
NIPPON EXPRESS USA INC
2233 E Grand Ave, El Segundo
(90245-2837)
PHONE..................310 535-7200
Yozo Komiya, *Manager*
EMP: 56 **Privately Held**
SIC: 4731 Foreign freight forwarding; domestic freight forwarding; customhouse
brokers
HQ: Nippon Express U.S.A., Inc.
2401 44th Rd Fl 14
Long Island City NY 11101
212 758-6100

(P-5004)
NISSIN INTL TRNSPT USA INC (HQ)
1540 W 190th St, Torrance (90501-1121)
PHONE..................310 222-8500
Yasushi Ihara, *CEO*
Mitsugu Matsusaka, *CFO*
Hirokazu Ikuta, *Vice Pres*
Mark Sclafani, *Vice Pres*
Francisco Marquez, *Branch Mgr*
EMP: 50
SQ FT: 98,000
SALES (est): 181.9MM **Privately Held**
WEB: www.nitusa.com
SIC: 4731 Domestic freight forwarding;
customhouse brokers

(P-5005)
NNR GLOBAL LOGISTICS USA INC
Also Called: N N R
21023 Main St Ste D, Carson
(90745-1246)
PHONE..................310 357-2100
Natomi Yamata, *Branch Mgr*
William Chancy, *Supervisor*
EMP: 110
SQ FT: 23,650 **Privately Held**
WEB: www.northportlandwellness.com
SIC: 4731 Foreign freight forwarding
HQ: Nnr Global Logistics Usa Inc.
2 Pierce Pl Ste 1800
Itasca IL 60143
630 773-1490

(P-5006)
NRI USA LLC (PA)
Also Called: Nri Distribution
13200 S Broadway, Los Angeles
(90061-1124)
PHONE..................323 345-6456
Chris Maydaniuk,
EMP: 100
SQ FT: 65,000
SALES (est): 29.9MM **Privately Held**
SIC: 4731 Freight forwarding

(P-5007)
NRI USA LLC
227 E Compton Blvd, Gardena
(90248-1909)
PHONE..................323 345-6456
EMP: 55
SALES (corp-wide): 29.9MM **Privately Held**
SIC: 4731 Freight transportation arrange-
ment

PA: Nri Usa, Llc
13200 S Broadway
Los Angeles CA 90061
323 345-6456

(P-5008)
O E C SHIPG LOS ANGELES INC
Also Called: Oec Group
13100 Alondra Blvd # 100, Cerritos
(90703-2278)
PHONE..................562 926-7186
Robert Han, *President*
John Su, *President*
◆ **EMP:** 50 **EST:** 1998
SALES (est): 30.5MM **Privately Held**
SIC: 4731 Foreign freight forwarding
PA: Oec Freight Worldwide Co., Ltd.
7f, No. 131, Nanjing E. Rd., Sec. 3
Taipei City TAP 10410

(P-5009)
OCEAN KNIGHT SHIPPING INC
19516 S Susana Rd # 101, Compton
(90221-5714)
PHONE..................310 885-3388
Henry Chu, *President*
EMP: 200
SALES: 3.1MM **Privately Held**
WEB: www.okshipping.com
SIC: 4731 Freight forwarding

(P-5010)
OCEANLAND SERVICE INC (PA)
Also Called: Oceanland Customhouse Broker
15241 Don Julian Rd, City of Industry
(91745-1002)
PHONE..................626 573-8429
Shirley Wu, *President*
Shirley Wong, *Manager*
◆ **EMP:** 55
SQ FT: 19,000
SALES (est): 12.4MM **Privately Held**
WEB: www.oceanlandchb.com
SIC: 4731 Customhouse brokers; foreign
freight forwarding

(P-5011)
OOCL (USA) INC
2700 Zanker Rd Ste 200, San Jose
(95134-2140)
PHONE..................408 576-6543
Karen Heller, *Branch Mgr*
Elisabeth Erickson, *General Mgr*
Scott Dille, *Marketing Staff*
Ray Mesgarzadeh, *Manager*
Scott Stogner, *Manager*
EMP: 64 **Privately Held**
SIC: 4731 Freight forwarding
HQ: Oocl (Usa) Inc.
10913 S River Front Pkwy # 200
South Jordan UT 84095
801 302-6625

(P-5012)
OOCL (USA) INC
111 W Ocean Blvd Ste 1800, Long Beach
(90802-7936)
PHONE..................562 499-2600
Chris Favro, *Human Res Mgr*
Richard Yuen, *Network Mgr*
EMP: 56 **Privately Held**
WEB: www.esi-intermodal.com
SIC: 4731 4729 Agents, shipping;
steamship ticket offices
HQ: Oocl (Usa) Inc.
10913 S River Front Pkwy # 200
South Jordan UT 84095
801 302-6625

(P-5013)
OOCL (USA) INC
17777 Center Court Dr N # 500, Cerritos
(90703-9320)
PHONE..................562 499-2600
Paul Conolly, *Principal*
Jeffrey Bermant, *Info Tech Mgr*
James Lester, *Manager*
EMP: 65 **Privately Held**
WEB: www.esi-intermodal.com
SIC: 4731 Freight forwarding
HQ: Oocl (Usa) Inc.
10913 S River Front Pkwy # 200
South Jordan UT 84095
801 302-6625

(P-5014)
P& JP BROKERAGE LLC
15301 Ventura Blvd Ste P2, Sherman Oaks
(91403-5882)
PHONE..................310 801-9707
Paul Mantea,
EMP: 50
SQ FT: 15,000
SALES (est): 3.9MM **Privately Held**
SIC: 4731 Brokers, shipping

(P-5015)
PACIFIC LOGISTICS CORP (PA)
Also Called: Paclo
7255 Rosemead Blvd, Pico Rivera
(90660-4047)
PHONE..................562 478-4700
Douglas E Hockersmith, *President*
Timothy K Hewey, *COO*
Mark Nakamura, *CFO*
Cherise Sorbello, *Executive*
Diane J Hockersmith, *Admin Sec*
EMP: 208
SQ FT: 206,000
SALES (est): 115.5MM **Privately Held**
WEB: www.pacific-logistics.com
SIC: 4731 Freight forwarding

(P-5016)
PACIFICA TRUCKS LLC
1450 Dominguez St, Carson (90810-1463)
PHONE..................310 549-1351
Aris Lazo, *President*
EMP: 55
SQ FT: 2,500 **Privately Held**
SIC: 4731 4213 4212 4214 Freight trans-
portation arrangement; trucking, except
local; local trucking, without storage; local
trucking with storage
PA: Pacifica Trucks, Llc
340 Golden Shore Ste 240
Long Beach CA 90802

(P-5017)
PANALPINA INC
400 Oyster Point Blvd # 30, South San
Francisco (94080-1904)
P.O. Box 1850 (94083)
PHONE..................650 825-3036
Tommy Lau, *Branch Mgr*
EMP: 50
SALES (corp-wide): 12.1B **Privately Held**
WEB: www.panalpina.com
SIC: 4731 Freight forwarding
HQ: Panalpina, Inc.
703 Waterford Way Ste 890
Miami FL 33126
305 894-1300

(P-5018)
PANALPINA INC
19900 S Vermont Ave Ste A, Torrance
(90502-1147)
PHONE..................310 819-4060
Maurice Joseph, *Branch Mgr*
Audrey Lim, *Export Mgr*
Cynthia Underwood, *Sales Staff*
EMP: 60
SALES (corp-wide): 12.1B **Privately Held**
WEB: www.panalpina.com
SIC: 4731 Freight forwarding
HQ: Panalpina, Inc.
703 Waterford Way Ste 890
Miami FL 33126
305 894-1300

(P-5019)
PARAMOUNT TRNSP SYSTEMS INC (PA)
1350 Grand Ave, San Marcos
(92078-2404)
PHONE..................760 510-7979
Mike Keller, *CEO*
Grace Bishar, *CFO*
Kanahele Keenan, *Executive*
Robin Schrader, *General Mgr*
Isabelle Cruciere, *Office Mgr*
◆ **EMP:** 50
SQ FT: 32,000
SALES (est): 83.8MM **Privately Held**
WEB: www.pts-ca.com
SIC: 4731 Transportation agents & brokers

(P-5020)
PASHA DISTRIBUTION SVCS LLC
3010 Old Ranch Pkwy # 220, Seal Beach
(90740-2750)
PHONE..................714 889-2460
George W Pasha IV, *Branch Mgr*
EMP: 60 **Privately Held**
SIC: 4731 Freight transportation arrange-
ment
PA: Pasha Distribution Services Llc
500 W Elm St
Lebanon MO 65536

(P-5021)
PASHA GROUP (PA)
Also Called: Pasha Freight
4040 Civic Center Dr # 350, San Rafael
(94903-4150)
PHONE..................415 927-6400
George W Pasha III, *Ch of Bd*
James Britton, *CFO*
Joseph Doherty, *Treasurer*
Steve Hunter, *Treasurer*
Jeff Burgin, *Senior VP*
◆ **EMP:** 400
SQ FT: 18,000
SALES (est): 359.1MM **Privately Held**
WEB: www.pashagroup.com
SIC: 4731 Freight forwarding

(P-5022)
PASHA GROUP
19020 S Dminguez Hills Dr, Compton
(90220-6404)
PHONE..................310 735-0952
EMP: 103
SALES (corp-wide): 359.1MM **Privately Held**
SIC: 4731 Freight forwarding
PA: The Pasha Group
4040 Civic Center Dr # 350
San Rafael CA 94903
415 927-6400

(P-5023)
PATINA FREIGHT INC
Also Called: St George Logistics
1650 S Central Ave, Compton
(90220-5317)
PHONE..................310 764-4395
Elva Perea, *Finance Mgr*
EMP: 55
SALES (corp-wide): 32.8MM **Privately Held**
SIC: 4731 Shipping documents preparation
PA: Patina Freight, Inc.
20405 Business Pkwy
Walnut CA 91789
909 595-8100

(P-5024)
PATRIOT BROKERAGE INC
7840 Foothill Blvd Ste H, Sunland
(91040-2907)
PHONE..................910 227-4142
Ross Tsarukyan, *Mng Member*
Liyan Tsarukyan,
EMP: 84
SQ FT: 13,000
SALES: 13MM **Privately Held**
SIC: 4731 Freight forwarding

(P-5025)
PEGASUS MARITIME INC
535 N Brand Blvd Ste 400, Glendale
(91203-3907)
PHONE..................714 728-8565
Khurram Mahmood, *President*
Moazam Mahmood, *CEO*
Mookie Mahmood, *Exec VP*
Syed M Ali, *Vice Pres*
Imran Ahmed, *Opers Staff*
EMP: 75
SQ FT: 10,000
SALES (est): 15.3MM **Privately Held**
SIC: 4731 Freight forwarding

(P-5026)
PERFORMANCE TEAM FRT SYS INC
1331 Torrance Blvd, Torrance
(90501-2351)
PHONE..................562 345-2200

Craig Kaplan, *CEO*
EMP: 77
SALES (corp-wide): 382.2MM **Privately Held**
SIC: 4731 Customs clearance of freight
PA: Performance Team Llc
2240 E Maple Ave
El Segundo CA 90245
562 345-2200

(P-5027)
PERFORMANCE TEAM FRT SYS INC
1651 California St, Redlands (92374-2904)
PHONE.................................424 358-6943
EMP: 108
SALES (corp-wide): 382.2MM **Privately Held**
SIC: 4731 Freight forwarding
PA: Performance Team Llc
2240 E Maple Ave
El Segundo CA 90245
562 345-2200

(P-5028)
PERFORMANCE TEAM LLC
1651 California St Ste A, Redlands (92374-2904)
PHONE.................................801 301-1732
EMP: 251
SALES (corp-wide): 382.2MM **Privately Held**
SIC: 4731 Freight transportation arrangement
PA: Performance Team Llc
2240 E Maple Ave
El Segundo CA 90245
562 345-2200

(P-5029)
PERFORMANCE TEAM LLC (PA)
2240 E Maple Ave, El Segundo (90245-6507)
PHONE.................................562 345-2200
Craig Kaplan,
Jim Snodgrass, *President*
Mark Norris, *CFO*
James Snodgrass, *VP Bus Dvlpt*
Linda Kaplan, *Admin Sec*
EMP: 200
SQ FT: 80,000
SALES (est): 382.2MM **Privately Held**
WEB: www.ptgt.net
SIC: 4731 4225 4213 Freight forwarding; general warehousing & storage; trucking, except local

(P-5030)
POINTDIRECT TRANSPORT INC
10858 Almond Ave, Fontana (92337-7103)
PHONE.................................909 371-0837
Adolfo De La Herran, *President*
Adolfo D La Herran, *President*
EMP: 100
SQ FT: 2,500
SALES: 500K **Privately Held**
SIC: 4731 Freight forwarding

(P-5031)
PREMIER MEDICAL TRANSPORT INC
260 N Palm St 200, Brea (92821-2870)
PHONE.................................888 353-9556
David Johnson, *President*
Greg Valenzuela, *Opers Mgr*
Elizabeth Arevalo, *Chief*
EMP: 90
SALES (est): 15MM **Privately Held**
SIC: 4731 Freight transportation arrangement

(P-5032)
PRIMARY FREIGHT SERVICES INC (PA)
6545 Caballero Blvd, Buena Park (90620-1133)
PHONE.................................310 635-3000
John Brown, *CEO*
Ernie Donner, *CFO*
Bob Gordon, *Vice Pres*
Karen Liu, *Vice Pres*
Renee Yepez, *Vice Pres*
EMP: 65 **EST:** 1998
SQ FT: 87,900

SALES: 32.3MM **Privately Held**
SIC: 4731 4212 4789 Customs clearance of freight; baggage transfer; pipeline terminal facilities, independently operated

(P-5033)
PRIME GLOBAL SOLUTIONS INC (PA)
Also Called: PGS 360
15801 E Valley Blvd, City of Industry (91744-3929)
P.O. Box 1669, Walnut (91788-1669)
PHONE.................................800 424-7746
Michael Katyal, *CEO*
Garrett Fisher, *CFO*
Jess Khorana, *Vice Pres*
Gomez Ron, *Human Res Mgr*
EMP: 60
SQ FT: 125,000
SALES: 9.2MM **Privately Held**
WEB: www.primeamerica.biz
SIC: 4731 4225 Domestic freight forwarding; general warehousing & storage

(P-5034)
PRO LOADERS INC (PA)
14032 Santa Ana Ave, Fontana (92337-7035)
PHONE.................................909 355-5531
Bruce Degler, *President*
Christopher Ebert, *CFO*
Kim Pugmire, *Vice Pres*
Bob Titular, *Info Tech Dir*
Michael Ramos, *Maintence Staff*
EMP: 200
SQ FT: 600
SALES (est): 28MM **Privately Held**
SIC: 4731 1629 7359 7519 Truck transportation brokers; earthmoving contractor; equipment rental & leasing; trailer rental

(P-5035)
PUROLATOR INTERNATIONAL INC
2310 E Gladwick St, Compton (90220-6208)
PHONE.................................888 511-4811
John T Costanzo, *Branch Mgr*
EMP: 59
SALES (corp-wide): 223.4B **Privately Held**
SIC: 4731 Customhouse brokers
HQ: Purolator International, Inc.
2 Jericho Plz Ste 204
Jericho NY 11753
888 511-4811

(P-5036)
QUARTZ LOGISTICS INC
780 Nogales St Ste D, City of Industry (91748-1306)
PHONE.................................626 606-2001
Tai Ruenn Wang, *CEO*
Sandy Chen, *Admin Sec*
George Chiu, *Info Tech Mgr*
EMP: 60 **EST:** 2010
SQ FT: 12,000
SALES: 5.9MM **Privately Held**
SIC: 4731 Freight forwarding

(P-5037)
QUIK PICK EXPRESS LLC
1021 E 233rd St, Carson (90745-6206)
P.O. Box 1129, Lakewood (90714-1129)
PHONE.................................310 763-3000
George Boyle, *CEO*
Mirian Zuniga, *Admin Asst*
Patricia Andrade, *Technology*
Chinedu Okonkwo, *Manager*
EMP: 150
SQ FT: 500,000
SALES (est): 29.9MM **Privately Held**
WEB: www.quikpickexpress.com
SIC: 4731 4214 Freight transportation arrangement; local trucking with storage

(P-5038)
R L JONES-SAN DIEGO INC (PA)
1778 Zinetta Rd Ste A, Calexico (92231-9511)
P.O. Box 472 (92232-0472)
PHONE.................................760 357-3177
Russell L Jones, *President*
Earl Roberts, *Vice Pres*
Gustavo Acosta, *General Mgr*
Lucy Topete, *Info Tech Dir*

Baltazar Espinoza, *Info Tech Mgr*
EMP: 100
SALES (est): 35.1MM **Privately Held**
WEB: www.rljones.com
SIC: 4731 4225 Customhouse brokers; freight forwarding; general warehousing & storage

(P-5039)
R L JONES-SAN DIEGO INC
1778 Zinetta Rd Ste A1, Calexico (92231-9510)
PHONE.................................760 357-0140
Russell L Jones, *Branch Mgr*
EMP: 63
SALES (corp-wide): 35.1MM **Privately Held**
SIC: 4731 4225 Customhouse brokers; general warehousing & storage
PA: R. L. Jones-San Diego, Inc.
1778 Zinetta Rd Ste A
Calexico CA 92231
760 357-3177

(P-5040)
RESOURCE MANAGEMENT GROUP INC (PA)
Also Called: Rmg Recycling
4686 Mercury St, San Diego (92111-2428)
PHONE.................................858 677-0884
Armen Derderian, *President*
Robert Garcia, *COO*
Josie Pantangco, *CFO*
John Lentz, *Vice Pres*
Steve Joseph, *Managing Dir*
▲ **EMP:** 70
SQ FT: 3,000
SALES (est): 18.3MM **Privately Held**
WEB: www.rmgrecycling.com
SIC: 4731 Freight transportation arrangement

(P-5041)
RITE WAY ENTERPRISES
7131 Valjean Ave, Van Nuys (91406-3917)
PHONE.................................818 376-6960
Helen Wolfe, *President*
EMP: 50
SQ FT: 18,000
SALES (est): 8.1MM **Privately Held**
SIC: 4731 Truck transportation brokers

(P-5042)
RK LOGISTICS GROUP INC
44951 Industrial Dr, Fremont (94538-6486)
PHONE.................................510 298-5128
EMP: 107
SALES (corp-wide): 29MM **Privately Held**
SIC: 4731 Freight transportation arrangement
PA: The Rk Logistics Group Inc
41707 Christy St
Fremont CA 94538
408 942-8107

(P-5043)
ROCK-IT CARGO USA LLC
120 N Topanga Canyon Blvd # 215, Topanga (90290-3851)
PHONE.................................310 455-1900
Sasha Goodman, *Branch Mgr*
EMP: 60 **Privately Held**
SIC: 4731 Freight forwarding
PA: Rock-It Cargo Usa Llc
201 Rock Lititz Blvd # 90
Lititz PA 17543

(P-5044)
ROCK-IT CARGO USA LLC
5343 W Imperial Hwy # 900, Los Angeles (90045-6262)
PHONE.................................310 410-0935
Raimar Schmitt, *COO*
Jordan Lenhoff, *Administration*
Erin Cutri, *Accountant*
Michelle Hayflich, *Opers Mgr*
Cassie McCarter, *Manager*
EMP: 184 **Privately Held**
SIC: 4731 Freight forwarding
PA: Rock-It Cargo Usa Llc
201 Rock Lititz Blvd # 90
Lititz PA 17543

(P-5045)
SCHENKER INC
380 Littlefield Ave, South San Francisco (94080-6103)
PHONE.................................650 745-3000
Tammy Breen, *Manager*
EMP: 61
SQ FT: 60,000
SALES (corp-wide): 10.1MM **Privately Held**
SIC: 4731 Foreign freight forwarding
HQ: Schenker, Inc.
1305 Executive Blvd # 200
Chesapeake VA 23320
757 821-3400

(P-5046)
SCHUMACHER CARGO LOGISTICS INC (PA)
Also Called: S C L
550 W 135th St, Gardena (90248-1506)
PHONE.................................562 408-6677
Martin D Baker, *CEO*
EMP: 59
SQ FT: 200,000
SALES (est): 14.4MM **Privately Held**
WEB: www.schumachercargo.com
SIC: 4731 Foreign freight forwarding; freight forwarding

(P-5047)
SEA-AIR INTERNATIONAL INC
11222 S La Cienega Blvd # 100, Inglewood (90304-1109)
PHONE.................................310 338-0778
Milton Heid, *President*
Eric Jones, *Vice Pres*
EMP: 52
SALES (est): 4.1MM **Privately Held**
SIC: 4731 Customhouse brokers

(P-5048)
SEAWORLD GLOBAL LOGISTICS
1421 Barry Ave Apt 5, Los Angeles (90025-2309)
PHONE.................................310 208-9488
Dhakshitha Gabriel, *President*
EMP: 385 **EST:** 2017
SALES (est): 6.3MM **Privately Held**
SIC: 4731 Foreign freight forwarding

(P-5049)
SHIPCO TRANSPORT INC
100 W Victoria St, Long Beach (90805-2147)
PHONE.................................562 295-2900
Gary Osterbach, *Principal*
Jacob Niemiec, *Accounts Exec*
EMP: 65
SALES (corp-wide): 62.8K **Privately Held**
SIC: 4731 Freight forwarding
HQ: Shipco Transport Inc.
127 Main St
Chatham NJ 07928
973 457-3300

(P-5050)
SHO-AIR INTERNATIONAL INC (PA)
5401 Argosy Ave Ste 102, Huntington Beach (92649-1038)
PHONE.................................949 476-9111
James Nicoll, *Ch of Bd*
R Scott Tedro, *President*
Eric Monroe, *COO*
Jessica Elende, *CFO*
Kendi Britton, *Vice Pres*
EMP: 50
SQ FT: 18,000
SALES (est): 17.1MM **Privately Held**
WEB: www.shoair.com
SIC: 4731 Domestic freight forwarding

(P-5051)
SIMPLER POSTAGE INC (PA)
Also Called: Easypost
1 Montgomery St Ste 400, San Francisco (94104-4533)
PHONE.................................408 915-0063
Jarrett Lee Streebin, *CEO*
Paul Wagner, *CFO*
Julian Thomas, *Vice Pres*
Kathryn Berry, *Office Mgr*
April Rosenberg, *IT/INT Sup*

EMP: 100
SALES (est): 22.9MM **Privately Held**
SIC: 4731 Brokers, shipping

(P-5052)
SMARTWAY EXPRESS INC
2660 S Railroad Ave, Fresno (93725-1925)
PHONE...................................559 272-3500
Kirpal S Sihota, *CEO*
Tarlochan Singh, *President*
EMP: 120
SALES (est): 14.5MM **Privately Held**
SIC: 4731 Freight transportation arrangement

(P-5053)
SMD LOGISTICS INC
26710 Encinal Rd, Salinas (93908-9763)
PHONE...................................831 758-5300
Steve Scaroni, *President*
EMP: 155
SALES (corp-wide): 20.2MM **Privately Held**
SIC: 4731 Freight transportation arrangement
PA: Smd Logistics, Inc.
101 E Main St
Heber CA 92249
760 352-3194

(P-5054)
SOURCE LOGISTICS CENTER CORP
812 Union St, Montebello (90640-6523)
PHONE...................................323 887-3884
Marcelo Sada, *President*
Wendy Escobedo, *Vice Pres*
Raul Villarrael, *Vice Pres*
Fernando Ramirez, *Admin Sec*
EMP: 75
SQ FT: 300,000
SALES (est): 501.9K **Privately Held**
SIC: 4731 Freight transportation arrangement

(P-5055)
SOUTH BAY FREIGHT SYSTEM LLC (PA)
Also Called: South Bay Group
900 Turnbull Canyon Rd, City of Industry (91745-1404)
PHONE...................................626 271-9800
James Lin, *Mng Member*
EMP: 100
SALES (est): 28.7MM **Privately Held**
SIC: 4731 Freight forwarding

(P-5056)
STATES LOGISTICS SERVICES INC
7221 Cate Dr, Buena Park (90621-1883)
PHONE...................................714 523-1276
Cathy J Monson, *Branch Mgr*
EMP: 67
SALES (corp-wide): 60.6MM **Privately Held**
SIC: 4731 Truck transportation brokers
PA: States Logistics Services, Inc.
5650 Dolly Ave
Buena Park CA 90621
714 521-6520

(P-5057)
STEVENS GLOBAL LOGISTICS INC (PA)
Also Called: Steven Global Freight Services
3700 Redondo Beach Ave, Redondo Beach (90278-1108)
P.O. Box 729, Lawndale (90260-0729)
PHONE...................................310 216-5645
Thomas J Petrizzio, *CEO*
Gary Hooper, *CFO*
Karl Chambers, *Vice Pres*
Tim O'Neill, *Regional Mgr*
Jesus Salabarria, *Warehouse Mgr*
◆ EMP: 95
SQ FT: 48,000
SALES (est): 37.5MM **Privately Held**
WEB: www.stevensglobal.com
SIC: 4731 Freight forwarding

(P-5058)
SUPRA NATIONAL EXPRESS INC
1411 E Watson Center Rd, Carson (90745-4305)
PHONE...................................310 549-7105
Daniel Linares, *CEO*
EMP: 65
SALES (est): 755.3K **Privately Held**
SIC: 4731 Truck transportation brokers

(P-5059)
SURETY WEST LOGISTICS INC
Also Called: Surety West Transportation
980 9th St Fl 16, Sacramento (95814-2736)
PHONE...................................800 761-2551
Barry Henning, *President*
EMP: 77
SALES (est): 3.2MM **Privately Held**
SIC: 4731 Truck transportation brokers

(P-5060)
TAYLORED SVCS PARENT CO INC (PA)
1495 E Locust St, Ontario (91761-4570)
PHONE...................................909 510-4800
Bill Butler, *CEO*
Michael Yusko, *CFO*
EMP: 80 EST: 2012
SQ FT: 330,000
SALES (est): 30MM **Privately Held**
SIC: 4731 Agents, shipping

(P-5061)
THREE WAY LOGISTICS INC (PA)
42505 Christy St, Fremont (94538-3993)
P.O. Box 1806 (94538-0032)
PHONE...................................408 748-3929
Anthony J Bonino, *CEO*
Kevin Scherer, *President*
Philipp Scherer, *CFO*
Stan Aikman, *Vice Pres*
Michael Bonino, *Vice Pres*
▲ EMP: 60
SQ FT: 135,000
SALES (est): 38.2MM **Privately Held**
WEB: www.threeway.com
SIC: 4731 Freight transportation arrangement

(P-5062)
TOLL GLOBAL FWDG SCS USA INC
3355 Dulles Dr, Jurupa Valley (91752-3244)
PHONE...................................951 360-8310
Bryan Howber, *Senior VP*
EMP: 100 **Privately Held**
SIC: 4731 Freight forwarding
HQ: Toll Global Forwarding Scs (Usa) Inc.
800 Federal Blvd Ste 2
Carteret NJ 07008
732 750-9000

(P-5063)
TOPOCEAN CONSOLIDATION SERVICE (PA)
2727 Workman Mill Rd, City of Industry (90601-1452)
PHONE...................................562 908-1688
Robert Wang, *President*
Andy Wang, *Vice Pres*
◆ EMP: 145
SQ FT: 350,000
SALES (est): 41.5MM **Privately Held**
WEB: www.topocean.com
SIC: 4731 Foreign freight forwarding; freight forwarding

(P-5064)
TRAFFIC TECH INC
910 Hale Pl Ste 100, Chula Vista (91914-3598)
PHONE...................................800 396-2531
Paul Johnson, *President*
Peter Goldberg, *Vice Pres*
Joe Tully, *Vice Pres*
Bill Mellecker, *Executive*
Brian Hunt, *Broker*
EMP: 155

SALES (corp-wide): 214MM **Privately Held**
SIC: 4731 Brokers, shipping
HQ: Traffic Tech, Inc.
180 N Michigan Ave # 700
Chicago IL 60601
877 383-1167

(P-5065)
TRANSIT AIR CARGO INC
2204 E 4th St, Santa Ana (92705-3868)
PHONE...................................714 571-0393
Gulnawaz Khodayar, *CEO*
Christy Colton, *Vice Pres*
Michelle Nguyen, *Vice Pres*
Angela Kee, *Business Mgr*
Rick Caldira, *Sales Mgr*
EMP: 75
SQ FT: 10,000
SALES (est): 30.7MM **Privately Held**
WEB: www.transitair.com
SIC: 4731 Foreign freight forwarding

(P-5066)
TRI-TECH LOGISTICS LLC
3230 E Imperial Hwy # 140, Brea (92821-6721)
PHONE...................................855 373-7049
Kuldip S Dhaliwal,
Gurdeep Singh Dhaliwal,
Jeremy Engstrom, *Manager*
EMP: 210
SALES (est): 261.9K
SALES (corp-wide): 6.5MM **Privately Held**
SIC: 4731 Freight transportation arrangement
PA: Tri-Tech Logistics Ltd
17660 65a Ave Unit 208
Surrey BC V3S 5
604 415-9898

(P-5067)
TRICOR AMERICA INC
12441 Eucalyptus Ave 7, Hawthorne (90250-4208)
PHONE...................................310 676-0800
Fax: 310 973-1565
EMP: 100
SALES (corp-wide): 102.7MM **Privately Held**
SIC: 4731
PA: Tricor America, Inc.
717 Airport Blvd
South San Francisco CA 94080
650 877-3650

(P-5068)
TRICOR INTERNATIONAL
717 Airport Blvd, South San Francisco (94080-1815)
P.O. Box 8100, San Francisco (94128-8100)
PHONE...................................650 877-3678
Chee B Louie, *President*
John Hoard, *Controller*
Peter Shue, *Opers Staff*
EMP: 100
SQ FT: 20,000
SALES (est): 10.8MM **Privately Held**
SIC: 4731 4581 4424 Freight forwarding; airports, flying fields & services; deep sea domestic transportation of freight

(P-5069)
TRIPLE B FORWARDERS INC (PA)
Also Called: Triple B Forwarders
1511 Glenn Curtiss St, Carson (90746-4035)
PHONE...................................310 604-5840
Richard Beliveau, *CEO*
Connie Ladin, *Treasurer*
Sal Lacagnina, *Business Mgr*
Heidi O'Neill, *Opers Mgr*
Joleen Fejeran, *Sales Staff*
◆ EMP: 103 EST: 1976
SQ FT: 37,800
SALES (est): 22MM **Privately Held**
WEB: www.pmlfreight.com
SIC: 4731 4783 Domestic freight forwarding; foreign freight forwarding; packing goods for shipping

(P-5070)
TRITON LOGISTICS CORPORATION
706 Steffy Rd, Ramona (92065-3533)
PHONE...................................619 822-8832
Jason Lawrence Foyer, *Principal*
Jason Foyer, *Principal*
EMP: 72
SALES (corp-wide): 4.4MM **Privately Held**
SIC: 4731 Foreign freight forwarding
PA: Triton Logistics, Corporation
6780 Miramar Rd Ste 200b
San Diego CA 92121
619 822-8832

(P-5071)
UNIS LLC (PA)
Also Called: United Network Info Svcs
218 Machlin Ct Ste A, Walnut (91789-3057)
PHONE...................................909 839-2600
James Lin, *President*
Gracie Leung, *CFO*
Robert Chung, *Vice Pres*
Joe Dabbs, *Vice Pres*
EMP: 200
SALES (est): 63.8MM **Privately Held**
SIC: 4731 Freight forwarding

(P-5072)
UNITED FACILITIES INC
25451 Mountain House Pkwy, Tracy (95377-8903)
PHONE...................................209 839-8051
Rich Turner, *Branch Mgr*
EMP: 50
SALES (corp-wide): 67.2MM **Privately Held**
WEB: www.unifac.com
SIC: 4731 Freight transportation arrangement
PA: United Facilities, Inc.
603 N Main St
East Peoria IL 61611
309 699-7271

(P-5073)
UNITED STTES INTRMDAL SVCS LLC
Also Called: G3 Enterprises
502 E Whitmore Ave, Modesto (95358-9411)
PHONE...................................209 341-4045
John R Gallo,
Gregory J Coleman,
EMP: 75
SQ FT: 10,000
SALES (est): 16.8MM **Privately Held**
SIC: 4731 5182 Truck transportation brokers; bottling wines & liquors

(P-5074)
UPS SUPPLY CHAIN SOLUTIONS INC
550-3 Eccles Ave, San Francisco (94101)
PHONE...................................650 635-2693
EMP: 9000
SALES (corp-wide): 71.8B **Publicly Held**
SIC: 4731 Freight transportation arrangement
HQ: Ups Supply Chain Solutions, Inc.
12380 Morris Rd
Alpharetta GA 30005
800 742-5727

(P-5075)
UPS SUPPLY CHAIN SOLUTIONS INC
U P S
19701 Hamilton Ave # 250, Torrance (90502-1316)
PHONE...................................310 404-2719
Homayoun Kandari, *Branch Mgr*
Olga Garcia, *Manager*
EMP: 200
SALES (corp-wide): 71.8B **Publicly Held**
SIC: 4731 Freight forwarding
HQ: Ups Supply Chain Solutions, Inc.
12380 Morris Rd
Alpharetta GA 30005
800 742-5727

(P-5076)
UPS SUPPLY CHAIN SOLUTIONS INC
455 Forbes Blvd, South San Francisco (94080-2017)
PHONE..................................650 875-8300
Randy Nelson, *Manager*
Randy Nelsen, *Manager*
EMP: 50
SQ FT: 14,000
SALES (corp-wide): 71.8B **Publicly Held**
SIC: 4731 Freight transportation arrangement
HQ: Ups Supply Chain Solutions, Inc.
12380 Morris Rd
Alpharetta GA 30005
800 742-5727

(P-5077)
UPS SUPPLY CHAIN SOLUTIONS INC
601 Van Neca Ave Ste E, San Francisco (94102)
PHONE..................................415 775-6644
Debbie Wong, *Manager*
EMP: 50
SALES (corp-wide): 71.8B **Publicly Held**
SIC: 4731 Freight transportation arrangement
HQ: Ups Supply Chain Solutions, Inc.
12380 Morris Rd
Alpharetta GA 30005
800 742-5727

(P-5078)
UPS WORLDWIDE LOGISTICS INC
3600 W Century Blvd, Inglewood (90303-1139)
PHONE..................................310 673-7661
Tom Bliss, *Branch Mgr*
Pietro Barone, *Manager*
EMP: 200
SALES (corp-wide): 71.8B **Publicly Held**
SIC: 4731 Freight forwarding
HQ: Ups Worldwide Logistics Inc
12380 Morris Rd
Alpharetta GA 30005

(P-5079)
USAS EXPRESS INTERNATIONAL
420 Hindry Ave Ste G, Inglewood (90301-2062)
PHONE..................................310 645-2313
Young I Choi, *President*
EMP: 56
SALES (est): 7.6MM **Privately Held**
WEB: www.usasexpress.com
SIC: 4731 Freight forwarding

(P-5080)
USKO EXPEDITE INC
11290 Point East Dr # 110, Rancho Cordova (95742-6243)
PHONE..................................916 233-4455
Vlad Skots, *CEO*
EMP: 50
SALES (est): 1.3MM **Privately Held**
SIC: 4731 Transportation agents & brokers

(P-5081)
VANGUARD LGISTICS SVCS USA INC (HQ)
5000 Arprt Plz Dr Ste 200, Long Beach (90815)
PHONE..................................310 847-3000
Charles Brennan, *Chairman*
James Julian, *President*
J Thurso Barendse, *CFO*
Scott Shellow, *Treasurer*
Rob Sutton, *Officer*
EMP: 100
SALES (est): 171.1MM
SALES (corp-wide): 232.2MM **Privately Held**
SIC: 4731 Freight consolidation
PA: Naca Holdings, Inc.
5000 Arprt Plz Dr Ste 200
Long Beach CA 90815
310 847-3000

(P-5082)
WATCHPOINT LOGISTICS INC
Also Called: Main Freight Sfo
50 Tanforan Ave, South San Francisco (94080-6608)
PHONE..................................650 871-4747
Jay Bellin, *CEO*
◆ **EMP:** 110
SQ FT: 35,000
SALES (est): 13.8MM **Privately Held**
SIC: 4731 Freight forwarding

(P-5083)
WESTERN FREIGHT CARRIER INC
13819 Slover Ave, Fontana (92337-7037)
PHONE..................................909 357-1011
Tony Kim, *Owner*
EMP: 52
SALES (corp-wide): 15MM **Privately Held**
SIC: 4731 Transportation agents & brokers
PA: Western Freight Carrier, Inc.
321 E Gardena Blvd
Gardena CA 90248
310 767-1042

(P-5084)
WESTERN OVERSEAS CORPORATION (PA)
10731 Walker St Ste B, Cypress (90630-4757)
P.O. Box 90099, Long Beach (90809-0099)
PHONE..................................562 985-0616
Michael F Dugan, *President*
Carlo Deatougia, *Vice Pres*
Fred Bebee, *Admin Sec*
Diana Martinez, *Manager*
Lorraine McClary, *Manager*
◆ **EMP:** 50
SQ FT: 40,000
SALES: 11MM **Privately Held**
SIC: 4731 Customhouse brokers; foreign freight forwarding

(P-5085)
WESTRUX INTERNATIONAL INC
2200 E Steel Rd, Colton (92324-4509)
PHONE..................................909 825-5121
Don Kenney, *CFO*
EMP: 60
SALES (corp-wide): 118.4MM **Privately Held**
SIC: 4731 Truck transportation brokers
PA: Westrux International, Inc.
15555 Valley View Ave
Santa Fe Springs CA 90670
562 404-1020

(P-5086)
XPO LOGISTICS SUPPLY CHAIN INC
3825 S Willow Ave, Fresno (93725-9025)
PHONE..................................559 408-7951
EMP: 109
SALES (corp-wide): 17.2B **Publicly Held**
SIC: 4731 Freight forwarding
HQ: Xpo Logistics Supply Chain, Inc.
4035 Piedmont Pkwy
High Point NC 27265
336 232-4100

(P-5087)
XPO LOGISTICS SUPPLY CHAIN INC
26525 Pioneer Ave, Redlands (92374-2052)
PHONE..................................909 518-2095
Sonja Lawson, *General Mgr*
EMP: 90
SALES (corp-wide): 17.2B **Publicly Held**
SIC: 4731 Freight transportation arrangement
HQ: Xpo Logistics Supply Chain, Inc.
4035 Piedmont Pkwy
High Point NC 27265
336 232-4100

(P-5088)
XPO LOGISTICS SUPPLY CHAIN INC
5200a E Airport Dr, Ontario (91761-8601)
PHONE..................................909 975-6300
Steve Mackintosh, *Branch Mgr*

EMP: 124
SALES (corp-wide): 17.2B **Publicly Held**
SIC: 4731 Freight forwarding
HQ: Xpo Logistics Supply Chain, Inc.
4035 Piedmont Pkwy
High Point NC 27265
336 232-4100

(P-5089)
YUSEN LOGISTICS AMERICAS INC
2417 E Carson St Ste 100, Carson (90810-1252)
PHONE..................................310 518-3008
P Smith, *Branch Mgr*
Steve Frasco, *Opers Staff*
EMP: 200 **Privately Held**
SIC: 4731 Freight forwarding
HQ: Yusen Logistics (Americas) Inc.
300 Lighting Way Ste 600
Secaucus NJ 07094
201 553-3800

4783 Packing & Crating Svcs

(P-5090)
AMAWATERWAYS LLC (PA)
26010 Mureau Rd, Calabasas (91302-3130)
PHONE..................................800 626-0126
Rudi Schreiner, *Mng Member*
Ron Santangelo, *President*
Michelle Liechty, *CFO*
Janet Bava, *Chief Mktg Ofcr*
Brandon Oscarson, *Admin Sec*
EMP: 250
SALES: 6.2MM **Privately Held**
SIC: 4783 Packing goods for shipping

(P-5091)
CALAVO GROWERS INC
Also Called: Calavo Foods
15765 W Telegraph Rd, Santa Paula (93060-3041)
P.O. Box 751 (93061-0751)
PHONE..................................805 525-5511
EMP: 80
SALES (corp-wide): 1B **Publicly Held**
SIC: 4783
PA: Calavo Growers, Inc.
1141 Cummings Rd Ste A
Santa Paula CA 93060
805 525-1245

(P-5092)
CENTRA FREIGHT SERVICES INC (PA)
279 Lawrence Ave, South San Francisco (94080-6818)
PHONE..................................650 873-8147
Jonathan Wang, *CEO*
Stanley Wang, *President*
Goldine Wang, *Vice Pres*
Winnie Lo, *General Mgr*
Julie Wang, *Admin Sec*
EMP: 53 **EST:** 1980
SQ FT: 11,500
SALES (est): 18MM **Privately Held**
SIC: 4783 4731 Containerization of goods for shipping; domestic freight forwarding

(P-5093)
GLASS PAK INC
5825 Old School Rd, Pleasanton (94588-9407)
PHONE..................................707 207-0400
Marc Silvani, *President*
Rick Silvani, *Vice Pres*
Dallas Nelson, *General Mgr*
▲ **EMP:** 70
SQ FT: 90,000
SALES (est): 7MM **Privately Held**
WEB: www.glasspak.com
SIC: 4783 Packing goods for shipping

(P-5094)
INTEGRATED PKG & CRATING SVCS
Also Called: Inovative Packaging
38505 Cherry St, Newark (94560-4700)
PHONE..................................510 745-8180
Ben F Polando, *CEO*

Donna Fernandez, *HR Admin*
EMP: 50
SQ FT: 90,000
SALES (est): 7.2MM **Privately Held**
SIC: 4783 Packing & crating

(P-5095)
MANN PACKING CO INC
Also Called: Mann Packing Pea Plant
1347 Harkins Rd, Salinas (93901)
PHONE..................................831 796-2670
EMP: 70 **Privately Held**
SIC: 4783 Packing & crating
HQ: Mann Packing Co., Inc.
1333 Schilling Pl
Salinas CA 93901
831 422-7405

(P-5096)
MANN PACKING CO INC
49 Katherine St, Gonzales (93926)
PHONE..................................831 245-0814
EMP: 60 **Privately Held**
SIC: 4783 Packing & crating
HQ: Mann Packing Co., Inc.
1333 Schilling Pl
Salinas CA 93901
831 422-7405

(P-5097)
MOONLIGHT PACKING CORPORATION
Also Called: Plant 04
17770 E Huntsman Ave, Reedley (93654-9205)
PHONE..................................559 638-7799
EMP: 1800 **Privately Held**
SIC: 4783 5148 Packing & crating; fruits, fresh
PA: Moonlight Packing Corporation
17719 E Huntsman Ave
Reedley CA 93654

(P-5098)
PETCO ANIMAL SUPPLIES INC (DH)
10850 Via Frontera, San Diego (92127-1705)
PHONE..................................858 453-7845
Ron Coughlin, *CEO*
James M Myers, *Ch of Bd*
Brad Weston, *President*
James Lampassi, *CEO*
Michael M Nuzzo, *CFO*
◆ **EMP:** 500
SQ FT: 164,000
SALES (est): 11.5B
SALES (corp-wide): 264.1K **Privately Held**
WEB: www.petco.com
SIC: 4783 Crating goods for shipping
HQ: Petco Holdings, Inc. Llc
10850 Via Frontera
San Diego CA 92127
858 453-7845

(P-5099)
SUNTREAT PKG SHIPG A LTD PRTNR
391 Oxford Ave, Lindsay (93247-2208)
P.O. Box 850 (93247-0850)
PHONE..................................559 562-4991
Dennis A Griffith, *Managing Prtnr*
Dwight J Griffith, *Partner*
Tom Clark, *Vice Pres*
Dan Kass, *Vice Pres*
Kevin Watson, *Opers Staff*
EMP: 200
SQ FT: 75,000
SALES (est): 28.2MM **Privately Held**
WEB: www.suntreat.net
SIC: 4783 8742 Packing goods for shipping; management consulting services

(P-5100)
TRANSPAK INC
8710 Avenida De La Fuente # 1, San Diego (92154-6243)
PHONE..................................858 292-9094
Jennifer Kay, *Branch Mgr*
Arlene Inch, *CEO*
EMP: 51

P
R
O
D
U
C
T
S

&

S
V
C
S

SALES (corp-wide): 187.9MM **Privately Held**
SIC: 4783 2449 3081 3086 Packing & crating; wood containers; packing materials, plastic sheet; packaging & shipping materials, foamed plastic; corrugated & solid fiber boxes; nailed wood boxes & shook
PA: Transpak, Inc.
520 Marburg Way
San Jose CA 95133
408 254-0500

(P-5101)
UNIFIED AIRCRAFT SERVICES INC (PA)
1571 S Lilac Ave, Bloomington (92316-2141)
P.O. Box 401060, Las Vegas NV (89140-1060)
PHONE..........................909 877-0535
Ben C Warren, *President*
Venida L Warren, *Corp Secy*
Benjamin T Warren, *Vice Pres*
EMP: 65
SQ FT: 14,500
SALES (est): 15.4MM **Privately Held**
WEB: www.uasnet.com
SIC: 4783 Packing goods for shipping; containerization of goods for shipping

(P-5102)
VENIDA PACKING COMPANY
19823 Avenue 300, Exeter (93221-9771)
P.O. Box 212 (93221-0212)
PHONE..........................559 592-2816
Verne Crookshanks, *CEO*
Michael Murray, *Treasurer*
George Tantua, *Admin Sec*
EMP: 125
SQ FT: 50,000
SALES (est): 17.5MM **Privately Held**
SIC: 4783 Packing goods for shipping

4785 Fixed Facilities, Inspection, Weighing Svcs Transptn

(P-5103)
CALIFORNIA PRIVATE TRNSP CO LP
Also Called: C P T C
180 N Rverview Dr Ste 200, Anaheim (92808)
PHONE..........................714 637-9191
Greg Hulsizer, *General Mgr*
EMP: 75
SQ FT: 5,000
SALES (est): 3MM **Privately Held**
SIC: 4785 Toll road operation

(P-5104)
COFIROUTE USA LLC
200 Spectrum Center Dr # 1650, Irvine (92618-5012)
PHONE..........................949 754-0198
Gary Hausdorfer, *CEO*
Darla Casby, *VP Finance*
EMP: 112
SQ FT: 9,000
SALES: 18MM
SALES (corp-wide): 18.3MM **Privately Held**
WEB: www.cofiroutegm.com
SIC: 4785 Toll road operation
HQ: Vinci Concessions
12 14
Rueil-Malmaison 92500
147 164-477

(P-5105)
GOLDEN GATE
Also Called: Golden Gate Ferry
101 E Sir Francis Drake, Larkspur (94939-1803)
PHONE..........................415 455-2000
David Clark, *Manager*
EMP: 84

SALES (corp-wide): 19.3MM **Privately Held**
WEB: www.goldengatetransit.org
SIC: 4785 4482 Toll bridge operation; ferries operating across rivers or within harbors
PA: Golden Gate Bridge Highway & Transportation District
Toll Plz
San Francisco CA 94129
415 921-5858

(P-5106)
GOLDEN GATE BRDG HWY & TRANSPO (PA)
Toll Plz, San Francisco (94129)
PHONE..........................415 921-5858
James C Eddie, *President*
Kellee Hopper, *Chief Mktg Ofcr*
Denis J Mulligan, *General Mgr*
Dennis Mulligan, *General Mgr*
James Swindler, *General Mgr*
EMP: 250
SQ FT: 20,000
SALES (est): 19.3MM **Privately Held**
WEB: www.goldengatetransit.org
SIC: 4785 4131 4482 4111 Toll bridge operation; interstate bus line; ferries operating across rivers or within harbors; bus transportation

(P-5107)
GOLDEN GATE BRIDGE HIGH
Also Called: Golden Gate Transit
1011 Andersen Dr, San Rafael (94901-5318)
PHONE..........................415 457-3110
Susan Chiaroni, *Manager*
Aida Caputo, *Officer*
Marcus Lo, *Admin Asst*
Sonia Pedlar, *Technology*
Jose Velazquez, *Traffic Dir*
EMP: 535
SQ FT: 50,000
SALES (corp-wide): 19.3MM **Privately Held**
WEB: www.goldengatetransit.org
SIC: 4785 4111 Toll bridge operation; air transportation services, regular route
PA: Golden Gate Bridge Highway & Transportation District
Toll Plz
San Francisco CA 94129
415 921-5858

4789 Transportation Svcs, NEC

(P-5108)
AMBIANCE TRANSPORTATION LLC
13782 Foothill Blvd D, Sylmar (91342-3374)
PHONE..........................818 955-5757
Ryan Ferreira,
EMP: 90
SALES (est): 2.9MM **Privately Held**
SIC: 4789 Transportation services

(P-5109)
ANS WORLD SERVICE INC
2751 E Chapman Ave # 204, Fullerton (92831-3752)
P.O. Box 784, Placentia (92871-0784)
PHONE..........................714 441-2400
Charles S An, *President*
EMP: 100
SQ FT: 600
SALES (est): 3.2MM **Privately Held**
SIC: 4789 4212 Cargo loading & unloading services; local trucking, without storage

(P-5110)
AP EXPRESS INTERNATIONAL LLC
Also Called: Champion Transportation Svcs
8500 Rex Rd, Pico Rivera (90660-3779)
PHONE..........................562 236-2250
Jeff Pont, *President*
EMP: 75
SQ FT: 50,000

SALES: 14.5MM **Privately Held**
WEB: www.championtransportation.com
SIC: 4789 Freight car loading & unloading

(P-5111)
COMPREHENSIVE DIST SVCS INC
18726 S Wstn Ave Ste 300, Gardena (90248)
PHONE..........................310 523-1546
Sam Lee, *President*
EMP: 150
SALES (est): 1.9MM **Privately Held**
SIC: 4789 Freight car loading & unloading

(P-5112)
COUNTY OF LOS ANGELES
Also Called: Transportation Bureau
441 Bauchet St, Los Angeles (90012-2906)
PHONE..........................213 974-4561
EMP: 250 **Privately Held**
SIC: 4789 9621
PA: County Of Los Angeles
500 W Temple St Ste 375
Los Angeles CA 90012
213 974-1101

(P-5113)
EASY RIDE TRANSPORTATION
1820 W Carson St Ste 202, Torrance (90501-2885)
PHONE..........................424 999-8830
Said Dabas, *President*
EMP: 100 EST: 2014
SALES (est): 2.1MM **Privately Held**
SIC: 4789 Transportation services

(P-5114)
EDGE LOGISTICS SERVICES CORP
Also Called: Expak Logistics
11777 San Vicente Blvd, Los Angeles (90049-5011)
PHONE..........................424 320-5300
Steve Schmidt, *President*
EMP: 504
SALES (est): 10.1MM **Privately Held**
SIC: 4789 Cargo loading & unloading services

(P-5115)
FLEXPORT INC (PA)
760 Market St Fl 8, San Francisco (94102-2300)
PHONE..........................415 231-5252
Ryan Petersen, *CEO*
Sandy Manders, *CFO*
Sudhanshu Priyadarshi, *CFO*
Jeff Thomas, *Chief Mktg Ofcr*
Paige Delacey,
EMP: 71
SALES (est): 188.6MM **Privately Held**
SIC: 4789 4731 Pipeline terminal facilities, independently operated; freight transportation arrangement

(P-5116)
GATX CORPORATION
Also Called: G A T X Rail
20878 Slover St, Colton (92324-7300)
PHONE..........................909 825-3043
James Allen, *Manager*
EMP: 60
SALES (corp-wide): 1.3B **Publicly Held**
WEB: www.gatx.com
SIC: 4789 Railroad car repair
PA: Gatx Corporation
233 S Wacker Dr
Chicago IL 60606
312 621-6200

(P-5117)
HEALTH LINK MEDI VAN
Also Called: Medi-Van Ambulette
6053 W Century Blvd # 900, Los Angeles (90045-6430)
PHONE..........................310 981-9500
Greg Linsmeier, *General Mgr*
EMP: 100
SALES (est): 6.5MM **Privately Held**
SIC: 4789 Freight car loading & unloading

(P-5118)
HYPERLOOP TECHNOLOGIES INC (PA)
Also Called: Hyperloop One
2159 Bay St, Los Angeles (90021-1707)
PHONE..........................213 800-3270
Jay Walder, *CEO*
Sultan Ahmed Bin Sulayem, *Ch of Bd*
Brent Callinicos, *COO*
William Mulholland, *Exec VP*
Rob Ferber, *Vice Pres*
EMP: 71
SALES (est): 59.9MM **Privately Held**
SIC: 4789 Pipeline terminal facilities, independently operated

(P-5119)
INTER-RAIL TRNSPT NSHVILLE LLC
861 Wharf St, Richmond (94804-3557)
PHONE..........................510 231-2744
Francisco Oliver, *Manager*
EMP: 52
SALES (corp-wide): 31.1MM **Privately Held**
WEB: www.interrail-transport.com
SIC: 4789 Freight car loading & unloading
PA: Inter-Rail Transport, Inc
115 Lawyers Row Ste 3
Centreville MD 21617
410 758-2893

(P-5120)
INTER-RAIL TRNSPT NSHVILLE LLC
3800 Industrial Way, Benicia (94510-1200)
PHONE..........................707 746-1695
Luis Michel, *Manager*
EMP: 60
SALES (corp-wide): 31.1MM **Privately Held**
WEB: www.interrail-transport.com
SIC: 4789 4213 Freight car loading & unloading; automobiles, transport & delivery
PA: Inter-Rail Transport, Inc
115 Lawyers Row Ste 3
Centreville MD 21617
410 758-2893

(P-5121)
ITS TECHNOLOGIES LOGISTICS LLC
6540 Austin Rd, Stockton (95215-9662)
PHONE..........................209 460-6023
Dave Carlock, *Branch Mgr*
EMP: 60
SALES (corp-wide): 165.3MM **Privately Held**
SIC: 4789 Cargo loading & unloading services
HQ: Its Technologies & Logistics, Llc
8205 Cass Ave Ste 115
Darien IL 60561
708 225-2400

(P-5122)
J B HUNT TRANSPORT SVCS INC
Also Called: Jbhunt Transport
1620 5th Ave, San Diego (92101-2703)
PHONE..........................619 230-0054
Steve Trish, *Marketing Staff*
EMP: 673
SALES (corp-wide): 8.6B **Publicly Held**
SIC: 4789 Cargo loading & unloading services
PA: J. B. Hunt Transport Services, Inc.
615 J B Hunt Corporate Dr
Lowell AR 72745
479 820-0000

(P-5123)
JESSE ALEXANDER TRANSPORT
9338 Azurite Ave, Hesperia (92344-4611)
PHONE..........................760 669-0379
Jesus Gomez, *Mng Member*
EMP: 60 EST: 2014
SALES (est): 164.7K **Privately Held**
SIC: 4789 Transportation services

(P-5124)
LOCATION SERVICES LLC (PA)
Also Called: Pathfinder Services
2365 Iron Point Rd # 160, Folsom
(95630-8711)
PHONE..................................800 588-0097
Lee McCarty, *CEO*
Karen Gordon, *CFO*
Randy Robinson, *Vice Pres*
EMP: 90 **EST:** 2014
SQ FT: 15,000
SALES (est): 23.6MM **Privately Held**
SIC: 4789 Car loading

(P-5125)
MERIT LOGISTICS LLC
Also Called: Drop Lot Services
33332 Valle Rd Ste 100, San Juan Capistrano (92675-4856)
PHONE..................................949 481-0685
Cesar Raul Scolari, *Mng Member*
Brian Richmond, *Senior VP*
Vern Malpass, *Vice Pres*
Bob Shade, *Vice Pres*
EMP: 1100 **EST:** 2012
SALES (est): 60MM **Privately Held**
SIC: 4789 4225 Cargo loading & unloading services; general warehousing & storage

(P-5126)
MV TRANSPORTATION INC
1944 Williams St, San Leandro
(94577-2304)
PHONE..................................510 351-1603
Jay Jeter, *Branch Mgr*
EMP: 180
SALES (corp-wide): 1B **Privately Held**
WEB: www.mvtransit.com
SIC: 4789 Cargo loading & unloading services
PA: Mv Transportation, Inc.
2711 N Haskell Ave # 1500
Dallas TX 75204
214 265-3400

(P-5127)
MV TRANSPORTATION INC
1375 Burton Ave, Salinas (93901-4403)
PHONE..................................831 373-1395
Don Parslow, *Branch Mgr*
EMP: 124
SALES (corp-wide): 1B **Privately Held**
SIC: 4789 Pipeline terminal facilities, independently operated
PA: Mv Transportation, Inc.
2711 N Haskell Ave # 1500
Dallas TX 75204
214 265-3400

(P-5128)
MV TRANSPORTATION INC
265 S Rancho Rd, Thousand Oaks
(91361-5222)
PHONE..................................805 557-7372
Cheryl Seafert, *Branch Mgr*
EMP: 76
SALES (corp-wide): 1B **Privately Held**
SIC: 4789 Cargo loading & unloading services
PA: Mv Transportation, Inc.
2711 N Haskell Ave # 1500
Dallas TX 75204
214 265-3400

(P-5129)
MV TRANSPORTATION INC
7231 Rosecrans Ave, Paramount
(90723-2501)
PHONE..................................562 790-8642
EMP: 78
SALES (corp-wide): 1B **Privately Held**
SIC: 4789 Pipeline terminal facilities, independently operated
PA: Mv Transportation, Inc.
2711 N Haskell Ave # 1500
Dallas TX 75204
214 265-3400

(P-5130)
NERYS LOGISTICS INC
9925 Airway Rd, San Diego (92154-7932)
PHONE..................................619 616-2124
EMP: 139

SALES (corp-wide): 12.2MM **Privately Held**
SIC: 4789 Cargo loading & unloading services
PA: Nery's Logistics, Inc.
774 Mays Blvd
Incline Village NV 89451
775 338-7060

(P-5131)
PACIFIC COAST CONTAINER INC (PA)
Also Called: PCC Northwest
432 Estudillo Ave Ste 1, San Leandro
(94577-4908)
PHONE..................................510 346-6100
Michael Mc Donnell, *CEO*
Abdel Zaharan, *Officer*
◆ **EMP:** 112
SQ FT: 12,000
SALES (est): 65.3MM **Privately Held**
WEB: www.pccfs.com
SIC: 4789 4225 4222 Cargo loading & unloading services; general warehousing; warehousing, cold storage or refrigerated

(P-5132)
PACIFIC COAST TRNSP SVCS INC
Also Called: Material Transport
7500 San Joaquin St, Sacramento
(95820-2141)
PHONE..................................916 266-5300
Tom Allgaier, *Manager*
EMP: 50
SALES (corp-wide): 1.5B **Privately Held**
SIC: 4789 Cargo loading & unloading services
HQ: Pacific Coast Transportation Services, Inc.
10600 White Rock Rd Ste 1
Rancho Cordova CA 95670
916 631-6500

(P-5133)
PARSEC INC
4940 Sheila St, Commerce (90040-1112)
PHONE..................................323 268-5011
Jose Huerta, *Manager*
EMP: 600
SALES (corp-wide): 170MM **Privately Held**
WEB: www.parsecinc.com
SIC: 4789 1629 Cargo loading & unloading services; railroad & subway construction
PA: Parsec Inc.
1100 Gest St
Cincinnati OH 45203
513 621-6111

(P-5134)
PARSEC INC
750 Lamar St, Los Angeles (90031-2515)
PHONE..................................323 276-3116
Tony Madrigar, *Manager*
Hildur Vera, *Clerk*
EMP: 54
SALES (corp-wide): 170MM **Privately Held**
WEB: www.parsecinc.com
SIC: 4789 Cargo loading & unloading services
PA: Parsec Inc.
1100 Gest St
Cincinnati OH 45203
513 621-6111

(P-5135)
POSTMATES INC (PA)
201 3rd St Fl 2, San Francisco
(94103-3153)
PHONE..................................800 882-6106
Bastian Lehmann, *CEO*
Sean Plaice, *Chief Engr*
EMP: 207
SQ FT: 2,400
SALES (est): 15MM **Privately Held**
SIC: 4789 Cargo loading & unloading services

(P-5136)
RIOLO TRANSPORTATION INC
2725 Jefferson St Ste 2d, Carlsbad
(92008-1705)
PHONE..................................760 729-4405

Gail Phipps, *Branch Mgr*
EMP: 216
SALES (corp-wide): 64.3MM **Privately Held**
SIC: 4789 Pipeline terminal facilities, independently operated
PA: Riolo Transportation, Inc.
759 N Vulcan Ave
Encinitas CA 92024
760 635-8500

(P-5137)
ROCK-IT CARGO USA LLC
5343 W Imperial Hwy # 900, Los Angeles
(90045-6262)
PHONE..................................215 947-5400
Diarmuid Egan, *Opers Staff*
EMP: 67 **Privately Held**
SIC: 4789 Cargo loading & unloading services
PA: Rock-It Cargo Usa Llc
201 Rock Lititz Blvd # 90
Lititz PA 17543

(P-5138)
SALSON LOGISTICS INC
1331 Torrance Blvd, Torrance
(90501-2351)
PHONE..................................310 328-6800
Fax: 310 328-6897
EMP: 145
SALES (corp-wide): 237.1MM **Privately Held**
SIC: 4789
PA: Salson Logistics, Inc.
888 Doremus Ave
Newark NJ 07114
973 986-0200

(P-5139)
SECURE TRANSPORTATION CO INC
8304 Clairemont Mesa Blvd # 202, San Diego (92111-1315)
PHONE..................................858 790-3958
Shawana Walters, *Manager*
EMP: 111
SALES (corp-wide): 34MM **Privately Held**
SIC: 4789 Pipeline terminal facilities, independently operated
PA: Secure Transportation Company, Inc.
13111 Meyer Rd
Whittier CA 90605
562 941-0107

(P-5140)
SIERRA WASTE TRANSPORT INC
8191 Elder Creek Rd, Sacramento
(95824-2307)
PHONE..................................916 386-9937
Sunil Dutt, *CEO*
EMP: 50
SALES (est): 3.5MM **Privately Held**
SIC: 4789 Cargo loading & unloading services

(P-5141)
SOUTHERN CALIFORNIA CAR TRANSF
11139 Roxboro Rd, San Diego
(92131-3655)
PHONE..................................858 586-0006
Mike Magnett, *President*
EMP: 100 **EST:** 1994
SALES (est): 3.6MM **Privately Held**
SIC: 4789 Cargo loading & unloading services

(P-5142)
TRANSMONTAIGNE PDT SVCS LLC
Also Called: Morgan Stanley
555 California St # 2100, San Francisco
(94104-1503)
PHONE..................................415 576-2000
Susan Clampsey, *Branch Mgr*
John Marren, *Principal*
EMP: 300
SALES (corp-wide): 135.2MM **Privately Held**
SIC: 4789 Pipeline terminal facilities, independently operated

PA: Transmontaigne Product Services Llc
1670 Broadway Ste 3100
Denver CO 80202

(P-5143)
TTX COMPANY
Calpro Division
10800 San Sevaine Way, Jurupa Valley
(91752-1116)
PHONE..................................951 685-0158
Tom Peterson, *Principal*
EMP: 290
SALES (corp-wide): 542.4MM **Privately Held**
WEB: www.ttx.com
SIC: 4789 Railroad car repair
PA: Ttx Company
101 N Wacker Dr
Chicago IL 60606
312 853-3223

(P-5144)
TW SERVICES INC
2751 E Chapman Ave # 204, Fullerton
(92831-3758)
PHONE..................................714 441-2400
Charles An, *President*
EMP: 300
SALES (est): 20MM **Privately Held**
SIC: 4789 Freight car loading & unloading

(P-5145)
VIRGIN GALACTIC LLC (DH)
16555 Spcship Landing Way, Mojave
(93501-1534)
PHONE..................................562 384-4400
George Whitesides, *CEO*
Jonathan Firth, *Exec VP*
Michael P Moses Sr, *Senior VP*
Mike Cosenza, *Info Tech Dir*
Kenneth Dawson, *Engineer*
EMP: 99
SALES (est): 211.4MM **Privately Held**
WEB: www.virgingalactic.com/overview/
SIC: 4789 3761 Space flight operations, except government; space vehicles, complete
HQ: Virgin Management Limited
The Battleship Building
London
207 313-2000

(P-5146)
VITAL EXPRESS INC
4000 Macarthur Blvd Ste 6, Newport Beach
(92660-2558)
PHONE..................................330 777-5450
Steve Janssen, *President*
Dan Boaz, *President*
Lisa Boaz, *CEO*
EMP: 50
SQ FT: 10,000
SALES (est): 5.5MM **Privately Held**
SIC: 4789 4212 Pipeline terminal facilities, independently operated; delivery service, vehicular

(P-5147)
WHO DAT NATION TRNSP LLC
13186 Rincon Rd, Apple Valley
(92308-6214)
PHONE..................................760 403-7237
Ricky D Jones, *Mng Member*
EMP: 73 **EST:** 2017
SALES (est): 1.1MM **Privately Held**
SIC: 4789 Cargo loading & unloading services

4812 Radiotelephone Communications

(P-5148)
4G WIRELESS INC (PA)
Also Called: Verizon Wireless
8871 Research Dr, Irvine (92618-4236)
PHONE..................................949 748-6100
Mohammad Honarkar, *President*
Bill Carter, *Officer*
Eric Harkins, *Officer*
Octavis Poe, *Vice Pres*
Stephen Stanton, *Vice Pres*
EMP: 163
SQ FT: 5,000

PRODUCTS & SVCS

SALES (est): 353.1MM **Privately Held**
SIC: **4812** Cellular telephone services

(P-5149)
ABC PHONES NORTH CAROLINA INC
Also Called: A Wireless
1029 11th St, Lakeport (95453-4105)
PHONE..................707 263-3959
EMP: 71
SALES (corp-wide): 149.7MM **Privately Held**
SIC: **4812** Cellular telephone services
PA: Abc Phones Of North Carolina, Inc.
8510 Colonnade Center Dr
Raleigh NC 27615
252 317-0388

(P-5150)
AERONAUTICAL RADIO INC
6011 Industrial Way, Livermore (94551-9755)
PHONE..................925 294-8400
Mike Ostapiej, Manager
EMP: 80
SQ FT: 27,781
SALES (corp-wide): 66.5B **Publicly Held**
SIC: **4812** Radio telephone communication
HQ: Aeronautical Radio, Inc.
2551 Riva Rd
Annapolis MD 21401
410 266-4000

(P-5151)
AMERICAN VOICE MAIL INC (PA)
11150 W Olympic Blvd # 975, Los Angeles (90064-1850)
PHONE..................310 478-4949
Mark Gordon, President
Sam Gordon, Treasurer
Robert Gordon, Admin Sec
EMP: 50
SQ FT: 7,800
SALES (est): 2.7MM **Privately Held**
WEB: www.americanvoicemail.com
SIC: **4812** **7389** Radio pager (beeper) communication services; telephone services

(P-5152)
ARCH TELECOM INC (PA)
Also Called: Sprint
1940 W Corporate Way, Anaheim (92801-5373)
PHONE..................714 312-2724
Vijayant Ghai, CEO
Suresh Sachdeva, President
Tonika Burns, Executive Asst
EMP: 51 EST: 2010
SALES (est): 84.5MM **Privately Held**
SIC: **4812** Cellular telephone services

(P-5153)
AT&T CORP
10035 Adams Ave, Huntington Beach (92646-4940)
PHONE..................714 965-4685
Nora Facenda, Branch Mgr
Anthony McGlade, Sales Staff
EMP: 69
SALES (corp-wide): 170.7B **Publicly Held**
WEB: www.att.com
SIC: **4812** Cellular telephone services
HQ: At&T Corp.
1 At&T Way
Bedminster NJ 07921
800 403-3302

(P-5154)
AT&T CORP
2390 Monument Blvd, Pleasant Hill (94523-3983)
PHONE..................925 603-9476
Nichol McCroy, Branch Mgr
EMP: 69
SALES (corp-wide): 170.7B **Publicly Held**
SIC: **4812** Cellular telephone services
HQ: At&T Corp.
1 At&T Way
Bedminster NJ 07921
800 403-3302

(P-5155)
AT&T CORP
2410 Mission St, San Francisco (94110-2415)
PHONE..................415 970-8520
Neil Dana P, Planning
Susana Corona, Technology
Pavani Manthana, Technical Staff
EMP: 69
SALES (corp-wide): 170.7B **Publicly Held**
SIC: **4812** Cellular telephone services
HQ: At&T Corp.
1 At&T Way
Bedminster NJ 07921
800 403-3302

(P-5156)
AT&T CORP
50 Town Center Pkwy, Santee (92071-5806)
PHONE..................619 448-1798
Zac Ordene, Technician
EMP: 69
SALES (corp-wide): 170.7B **Publicly Held**
WEB: www.sbc.com
SIC: **4812** Cellular telephone services
HQ: At&T Corp.
1 At&T Way
Bedminster NJ 07921
800 403-3302

(P-5157)
AT&T CORP
2219 Park Ave Ste 8a, Tustin (92782-2701)
PHONE..................714 258-8290
Russel Martinez, Branch Mgr
Mark Hardy, Technician
EMP: 69
SALES (corp-wide): 170.7B **Publicly Held**
WEB: www.sbc.com
SIC: **4812** Cellular telephone services
HQ: At&T Corp.
1 At&T Way
Bedminster NJ 07921
800 403-3302

(P-5158)
AT&T CORP
12379 S Mainstreet, Rancho Cucamonga (91739-8810)
PHONE..................909 646-9644
EMP: 69
SALES (corp-wide): 170.7B **Publicly Held**
WEB: www.sbc.com
SIC: **4812** Cellular telephone services
HQ: At&T Corp.
1 At&T Way
Bedminster NJ 07921
800 403-3302

(P-5159)
AT&T CORP
2508 S Grove Ave, Ontario (91761-6253)
PHONE..................909 930-6508
Lorenzo Mejia, Branch Mgr
EMP: 97
SALES (corp-wide): 170.7B **Publicly Held**
SIC: **4812** Cellular telephone services
HQ: At&T Corp.
1 At&T Way
Bedminster NJ 07921
800 403-3302

(P-5160)
AT&T CORP
830 W Arrow Hwy, San Dimas (91773-2498)
PHONE..................626 912-0600
Carolyn Wilder, Manager
EMP: 97
SALES (corp-wide): 170.7B **Publicly Held**
WEB: www.cingular.com
SIC: **4812** Cellular telephone services
HQ: At&T Corp.
1 At&T Way
Bedminster NJ 07921
800 403-3302

(P-5161)
AT&T CORP
20810 Avalon Blvd, Carson (90746-3316)
PHONE..................310 225-3028
Carolyn Wilder, Manager
EMP: 69
SALES (corp-wide): 170.7B **Publicly Held**
SIC: **4812** Cellular telephone services
HQ: At&T Corp.
1 At&T Way
Bedminster NJ 07921
800 403-3302

(P-5162)
AT&T CORP
27762 Antonio Pkwy Ste L3, Ladera Ranch (92694-1141)
PHONE..................949 364-4052
Denny Tsai, Branch Mgr
EMP: 69
SALES (corp-wide): 170.7B **Publicly Held**
WEB: www.att.com
SIC: **4812** Cellular telephone services
HQ: At&T Corp.
1 At&T Way
Bedminster NJ 07921
800 403-3302

(P-5163)
AT&T CORP
1100 Pacific Coast Hwy # 5, Hermosa Beach (90254-3951)
PHONE..................310 303-3888
Dennis Graber, Branch Mgr
EMP: 97
SALES (corp-wide): 170.7B **Publicly Held**
WEB: www.cingular.com
SIC: **4812** Cellular telephone services
HQ: At&T Corp.
1 At&T Way
Bedminster NJ 07921
800 403-3302

(P-5164)
AT&T CORP
6833 Pacific Blvd, Huntington Park (90255-4111)
PHONE..................323 589-7045
Frankie Valenzuela, Manager
EMP: 97
SALES (corp-wide): 170.7B **Publicly Held**
WEB: www.cingular.com
SIC: **4812** Cellular telephone services
HQ: At&T Corp.
1 At&T Way
Bedminster NJ 07921
800 403-3302

(P-5165)
AT&T CORP
6328 Irvine Blvd, Irvine (92620-2102)
PHONE..................949 559-1457
Linda Fisher, Owner
EMP: 97
SALES (corp-wide): 170.7B **Publicly Held**
WEB: www.att.com
SIC: **4812** Cellular telephone services
HQ: At&T Corp.
1 At&T Way
Bedminster NJ 07921
800 403-3302

(P-5166)
AT&T CORP
2333 S Sepulveda Blvd, Los Angeles (90064-1910)
PHONE..................310 473-3649
Carolyn Wilder, Manager
Julie Nguyen, Vice Pres
Chris Mayotte, Analyst
EMP: 97
SALES (corp-wide): 170.7B **Publicly Held**
WEB: www.att.com
SIC: **4812** Cellular telephone services
HQ: At&T Corp.
1 At&T Way
Bedminster NJ 07921
800 403-3302

(P-5167)
AT&T CORP
83 E Colorado Blvd, Pasadena (91105-1916)
PHONE..................626 396-0100
Martin Choe, Branch Mgr
EMP: 69
SALES (corp-wide): 170.7B **Publicly Held**
WEB: www.att.com
SIC: **4812** Cellular telephone services
HQ: At&T Corp.
1 At&T Way
Bedminster NJ 07921
800 403-3302

(P-5168)
AT&T CORP
7060 Market Place Dr, Goleta (93117-5902)
PHONE..................805 562-0121
Nicole Jurzenski, Manager
EMP: 97
SALES (corp-wide): 170.7B **Publicly Held**
WEB: www.cingular.com
SIC: **4812** Cellular telephone services
HQ: At&T Corp.
1 At&T Way
Bedminster NJ 07921
800 403-3302

(P-5169)
AT&T CORP
980 N Western Ave Ste H, San Pedro (90732-2451)
PHONE..................310 547-0400
Jack Aiello, Manager
EMP: 69
SALES (corp-wide): 170.7B **Publicly Held**
WEB: www.att.com
SIC: **4812** Cellular telephone services
HQ: At&T Corp.
1 At&T Way
Bedminster NJ 07921
800 403-3302

(P-5170)
AT&T CORP
26453 Bouquet Canyon Rd, Santa Clarita (91350-2396)
PHONE..................661 297-1720
Carolyn Wilder, Owner
Edgar Dubon, Manager
EMP: 69
SALES (corp-wide): 170.7B **Publicly Held**
WEB: www.att.com
SIC: **4812** Cellular telephone services
HQ: At&T Corp.
1 At&T Way
Bedminster NJ 07921
800 403-3302

(P-5171)
AT&T CORP
217 N Lemon St Rm 205, Anaheim (92805-2943)
PHONE..................714 284-3818
EMP: 95
SALES (corp-wide): 170.7B **Publicly Held**
SIC: **4812** Cellular telephone services
HQ: At&T Corp.
1 At&T Way
Bedminster NJ 07921
800 403-3302

(P-5172)
AT&T CORP
24935 Pico Canyon Rd, Stevenson Ranch (91381-1708)
PHONE..................661 799-0800
Chris Lopez, Branch Mgr
EMP: 69
SALES (corp-wide): 170.7B **Publicly Held**
WEB: www.att.com
SIC: **4812** Cellular telephone services
HQ: At&T Corp.
1 At&T Way
Bedminster NJ 07921
800 403-3302

(P-5173)
AT&T CORP
3977 Chicago Ave, Riverside (92507-5338)
PHONE.....................................951 275-8801
Gil Leon, *Branch Mgr*
EMP: 69
SALES (corp-wide): 170.7B **Publicly Held**
SIC: **4812** Cellular telephone services
HQ: At&T Corp.
1 At&T Way
Bedminster NJ 07921
800 403-3302

(P-5174)
AT&T CORP
4332 Tweedy Blvd, South Gate
(90280-6220)
PHONE.....................................323 568-2006
Carolyn Wilder, *Branch Mgr*
EMP: 69
SALES (corp-wide): 170.7B **Publicly Held**
WEB: www.att.com
SIC: **4812** Cellular telephone services
HQ: At&T Corp.
1 At&T Way
Bedminster NJ 07921
800 403-3302

(P-5175)
AT&T CORP
3750 Morrow Ln, Chico (95928-8865)
PHONE.....................................530 891-2025
Bill Rose, *Branch Mgr*
EMP: 96
SALES (corp-wide): 170.7B **Publicly Held**
SIC: **4812** Cellular telephone services
HQ: At&T Corp.
1 At&T Way
Bedminster NJ 07921
800 403-3302

(P-5176)
AT&T CORP
1955 E Daily Dr, Camarillo (93010-6300)
PHONE.....................................805 445-6562
EMP: 82
SALES (corp-wide): 170.7B **Publicly Held**
SIC: **4812** Cellular telephone services
HQ: At&T Corp.
1 At&T Way
Bedminster NJ 07921
800 403-3302

(P-5177)
AT&T CORP
1054 Harter Pkwy Ste 9, Yuba City
(95993-2653)
PHONE.....................................530 822-2700
Raj Sharma, *Branch Mgr*
EMP: 69
SALES (corp-wide): 170.7B **Publicly Held**
SIC: **4812** Cellular telephone services
HQ: At&T Corp.
1 At&T Way
Bedminster NJ 07921
800 403-3302

(P-5178)
AT&T CORP
133 S Las Posas Rd # 141, San Marcos
(92078-2468)
PHONE.....................................760 752-3273
Ron Manley, *Branch Mgr*
EMP: 69
SALES (corp-wide): 170.7B **Publicly Held**
WEB: www.att.com
SIC: **4812** Cellular telephone services
HQ: At&T Corp.
1 At&T Way
Bedminster NJ 07921
800 403-3302

(P-5179)
AT&T CORP
835 4th St, San Rafael (94901-3260)
PHONE.....................................415 721-1470
Don Klein, *Branch Mgr*
EMP: 97

SALES (corp-wide): 170.7B **Publicly Held**
SIC: **4812** Cellular telephone services
HQ: At&T Corp.
1 At&T Way
Bedminster NJ 07921
800 403-3302

(P-5180)
AT&T CORP
1855 41st Ave, Capitola (95010-2511)
PHONE.....................................831 465-6771
Amel Dunanes, *Principal*
EMP: 97
SALES (corp-wide): 170.7B **Publicly Held**
SIC: **4812** Cellular telephone services
HQ: At&T Corp.
1 At&T Way
Bedminster NJ 07921
800 403-3302

(P-5181)
AT&T CORP
1263 Simi Town Center Way, Simi Valley
(93065-8406)
PHONE.....................................805 583-9483
Kim Erwin, *Branch Mgr*
EMP: 97
SALES (corp-wide): 170.7B **Publicly Held**
SIC: **4812** Cellular telephone services
HQ: At&T Corp.
1 At&T Way
Bedminster NJ 07921
800 403-3302

(P-5182)
AT&T CORP
8225 Mira Mesa Blvd, San Diego
(92126-2603)
PHONE.....................................858 693-0815
Matt Holderness, *Branch Mgr*
EMP: 69
SALES (corp-wide): 170.7B **Publicly Held**
WEB: www.att.com
SIC: **4812** Cellular telephone services
HQ: At&T Corp.
1 At&T Way
Bedminster NJ 07921
800 403-3302

(P-5183)
AT&T CORP
1810 E Main St, Woodland (95776-6234)
PHONE.....................................530 661-7724
EMP: 97
SALES (corp-wide): 170.7B **Publicly Held**
SIC: **4812** Cellular telephone services
HQ: At&T Corp.
1 At&T Way
Bedminster NJ 07921
800 403-3302

(P-5184)
AT&T CORP
7100 Santa Monica Blvd # 125, West Holly-
wood (90046-5896)
PHONE.....................................323 874-7000
EMP: 95
SALES (corp-wide): 170.7B **Publicly Held**
SIC: **4812** Cellular telephone services
HQ: At&T Corp.
1 At&T Way
Bedminster NJ 07921
800 403-3302

(P-5185)
AT&T CORP
134 Sunset Dr, San Ramon (94583-2340)
PHONE.....................................925 327-7100
Carolyn Wilder, *Owner*
EMP: 95
SALES (corp-wide): 170.7B **Publicly Held**
SIC: **4812** Cellular telephone services
HQ: At&T Corp.
1 At&T Way
Bedminster NJ 07921
800 403-3302

(P-5186)
AT&T CORP
1705 Story Rd, San Jose (95122-1935)
PHONE.....................................408 729-8400
EMP: 68
SALES (corp-wide): 170.7B **Publicly Held**
SIC: **4812** Cellular telephone services
HQ: At&T Corp.
1 At&T Way
Bedminster NJ 07921
800 403-3302

(P-5187)
AT&T CORP
17675 Harvard Ave Ste B, Irvine
(92614-3527)
PHONE.....................................949 622-8240
Travis Stanford, *Branch Mgr*
EMP: 69
SALES (corp-wide): 170.7B **Publicly Held**
SIC: **4812** Cellular telephone services
HQ: At&T Corp.
1 At&T Way
Bedminster NJ 07921
800 403-3302

(P-5188)
AT&T CORP
998 S Robertson Blvd # 103, Los Angeles
(90035-1637)
PHONE.....................................310 659-7600
EMP: 94
SALES (corp-wide): 160.5B **Publicly Held**
SIC: **4812**
HQ: At&T Corp.
1 At&T Way
Bedminster NJ 07921
800 403-3302

(P-5189)
AT&T CORP
2105 Macdonald Ave, Richmond
(94801-3310)
PHONE.....................................510 965-9714
EMP: 69
SALES (corp-wide): 170.7B **Publicly Held**
WEB: www.att.com
SIC: **4812** Cellular telephone services
HQ: At&T Corp.
1 At&T Way
Bedminster NJ 07921
800 403-3302

(P-5190)
AT&T CORP
400 Del Monte Ctr, Monterey (93940-6159)
PHONE.....................................831 642-0100
Mike Godina, *Branch Mgr*
EMP: 97
SALES (corp-wide): 170.7B **Publicly Held**
WEB: www.att.com
SIC: **4812** Cellular telephone services
HQ: At&T Corp.
1 At&T Way
Bedminster NJ 07921
800 403-3302

(P-5191)
AT&T CORP
8420 Firestone Blvd, Downey
(90241-3844)
PHONE.....................................562 923-3032
Carolyn Wilder, *Branch Mgr*
EMP: 69
SALES (corp-wide): 170.7B **Publicly Held**
WEB: www.att.com
SIC: **4812** Cellular telephone services
HQ: At&T Corp.
1 At&T Way
Bedminster NJ 07921
800 403-3302

(P-5192)
AT&T CORP
2701 Verne Roberts Cir, Antioch
(94509-7913)
PHONE.....................................925 776-1200
Chris Wiggin, *President*
EMP: 70

SALES (corp-wide): 170.7B **Publicly Held**
SIC: **4812** Cellular telephone services
HQ: At&T Corp.
1 At&T Way
Bedminster NJ 07921
800 403-3302

(P-5193)
AT&T SERVICES INC
Also Called: SBC
2 Circle E Ranch Pl, San Ramon
(94583-9134)
PHONE.....................................925 901-9318
William Dyer, *Branch Mgr*
EMP: 87
SALES (corp-wide): 170.7B **Publicly Held**
WEB: www.dsdllc.com
SIC: **4812** Cellular telephone services
HQ: At&T Services, Inc.
208 S Akard St Ste 110
Dallas TX 75202
210 821-4105

(P-5194)
AT&T SERVICES INC
Also Called: SBC
161 Calle Del Oaks, Monterey
(93940-5701)
PHONE.....................................831 394-2690
Rodney Graves, *Manager*
EMP: 57
SALES (corp-wide): 170.7B **Publicly Held**
WEB: www.dsdllc.com
SIC: **4812** Cellular telephone services
HQ: At&T Services, Inc.
208 S Akard St Ste 110
Dallas TX 75202
210 821-4105

(P-5195)
AT&T SERVICES INC
Also Called: S B C
5555 E Olive Ave Ste A315, Fresno
(93727-2559)
PHONE.....................................559 454-3579
Greg Toeman, *Manager*
EMP: 243
SALES (corp-wide): 170.7B **Publicly Held**
WEB: www.dsdllc.com
SIC: **4812** Cellular telephone services
HQ: At&T Services, Inc.
208 S Akard St Ste 110
Dallas TX 75202
210 821-4105

(P-5196)
AT&T SERVICES INC
3900 Channel Dr, West Sacramento
(95691-3432)
PHONE.....................................916 376-2006
Richard Cronan, *Branch Mgr*
Mike Kolar, *IT/INT Sup*
Will Venlos, *Business Mgr*
EMP: 151
SALES (corp-wide): 170.7B **Publicly Held**
WEB: www.dsdllc.com
SIC: **4812** Cellular telephone services
HQ: At&T Services, Inc.
208 S Akard St Ste 110
Dallas TX 75202
210 821-4105

(P-5197)
B-PER ELECTRONIC INC
Also Called: My Wireless
1600 N Brwy, Santa Ana (92706)
PHONE.....................................626 912-0600
Shawn Yeh, *CEO*
Jeffrey Guerrero, *Engineer*
EMP: 100
SALES (est): 10.4MM **Privately Held**
SIC: **4812** Cellular telephone services

(P-5198)
BLACK DOT WIRELESS LLC
27271 Las Ramblas Ste 300, Mission Viejo
(92691-8042)
PHONE.....................................949 502-3800
Marc Anthony, *Mng Member*
Howard Forgey, *Vice Pres*
Joseph Winkler, *Vice Pres*

P
R
O
D
U
C
T
S

&

S
V
C
S

Sergey Varlitskiy, *Software Dev*
Doug Getty, *Marketing Staff*
EMP: 85
SQ FT: 22,000
SALES (est): 11MM **Privately Held**
SIC: 4812 Cellular telephone services

(P-5199)
BRAVO TECH INC
Also Called: Bti Wireless
14600 Industry Cir, La Mirada
(90638-5815)
PHONE..............................714 230-8333
Bailey Zheng, *CEO*
Trevor Phillips, *Technical Staff*
Tammy Metzger, *Marketing Mgr*
Dadrian Carrington, *Director*
Gilbert Pang, *Director*
▲ **EMP:** 50
SALES (est): 5.3MM **Privately Held**
WEB: www.bravotechinc.com
SIC: 4812 Cellular telephone services

(P-5200)
CELLCO PARTNERSHIP
Also Called: Verizon Wireless
1484 E Second St, Beaumont
(92223-3161)
PHONE..............................951 769-0985
EMP: 71
SALES (corp-wide): 130.8B **Publicly Held**
SIC: 4812 4813 Cellular telephone services; telephone communication, except radio
HQ: Cellco Partnership
1 Verizon Way
Basking Ridge NJ 07920

(P-5201)
CELLCO PARTNERSHIP
Also Called: Verizon Wireless
1680 Del Monte Ctr, Monterey
(93940-6169)
PHONE..............................831 644-0858
EMP: 71
SALES (corp-wide): 130.8B **Publicly Held**
SIC: 4812 Cellular telephone services
HQ: Cellco Partnership
1 Verizon Way
Basking Ridge NJ 07920

(P-5202)
CELLCO PARTNERSHIP
Also Called: Verizon Wireless
1500 E Village Way # 2205, Orange
(92865-3616)
PHONE..............................714 921-5130
EMP: 76
SALES (corp-wide): 130.8B **Publicly Held**
SIC: 4812 Cellular telephone services
HQ: Cellco Partnership
1 Verizon Way
Basking Ridge NJ 07920

(P-5203)
CELLCO PARTNERSHIP
Also Called: Verizon Wireless
6471 Lone Tree Way, Brentwood
(94513-5265)
PHONE..............................925 626-3480
EMP: 71
SALES (corp-wide): 130.8B **Publicly Held**
SIC: 4812 Cellular telephone services
HQ: Cellco Partnership
1 Verizon Way
Basking Ridge NJ 07920

(P-5204)
CELLCO PARTNERSHIP
Also Called: Verizon Wireless
2851 Canyon Springs Pkwy, Riverside
(92507-0935)
PHONE..............................951 697-3035
EMP: 76
SALES (corp-wide): 130.8B **Publicly Held**
SIC: 4812 Cellular telephone services

HQ: Cellco Partnership
1 Verizon Way
Basking Ridge NJ 07920

(P-5205)
CELLCO PARTNERSHIP
255 Parkshore Dr, Folsom (95630-4716)
P.O. Box 2167 (95763-2167)
PHONE..............................212 395-1000
EMP: 71
SALES (corp-wide): 130.8B **Publicly Held**
SIC: 4812 Cellular telephone services
HQ: Cellco Partnership
1 Verizon Way
Basking Ridge NJ 07920

(P-5206)
CELLCO PARTNERSHIP
Also Called: Verizon Wireless
550 S Clovis Ave Ste 105, Fresno
(93727-4513)
PHONE..............................559 454-0803
Joe Gomez, *Branch Mgr*
EMP: 71
SALES (corp-wide): 130.8B **Publicly Held**
SIC: 4812 Cellular telephone services
HQ: Cellco Partnership
1 Verizon Way
Basking Ridge NJ 07920

(P-5207)
CELLCO PARTNERSHIP
Also Called: Verizon
901 S Coast Dr Ste K120, Costa Mesa
(92626-7710)
PHONE..............................714 427-0733
David Mendoza, *Manager*
EMP: 71
SALES (corp-wide): 130.8B **Publicly Held**
SIC: 4812 5999 Cellular telephone services; telephone equipment & systems
HQ: Cellco Partnership
1 Verizon Way
Basking Ridge NJ 07920

(P-5208)
CELLCO PARTNERSHIP
Also Called: Verizon Wireless
12459 Limonite Ave C-2, Eastvale
(91752-2458)
PHONE..............................951 361-1850
EMP: 71
SALES (corp-wide): 130.8B **Publicly Held**
SIC: 4812 Cellular telephone services
HQ: Cellco Partnership
1 Verizon Way
Basking Ridge NJ 07920

(P-5209)
CELLCO PARTNERSHIP
Also Called: Verizon
1900 Douglas Blvd Ste D, Roseville
(95661-3823)
PHONE..............................916 786-6151
Rapheal Jones, *Branch Mgr*
EMP: 71
SALES (corp-wide): 130.8B **Publicly Held**
SIC: 4812 Cellular telephone services
HQ: Cellco Partnership
1 Verizon Way
Basking Ridge NJ 07920

(P-5210)
CELLCO PARTNERSHIP
Also Called: Verizon
15505 Sand Canyon Ave, Irvine
(92618-3114)
PHONE..............................949 286-7000
Margaret Holzmann, *Administration*
Sheena Joseph, *Technology*
Joe Ito, *Engineer*
Heury Covarrubias, *Manager*
Lasni Gunawardena, *Manager*
EMP: 2000

SALES (corp-wide): 130.8B **Publicly Held**
SIC: 4812 Cellular telephone services
HQ: Cellco Partnership
1 Verizon Way
Basking Ridge NJ 07920

(P-5211)
CELLCO PARTNERSHIP
Also Called: Verizon
2701 Ming Ave Spc 100a, Bakersfield
(93304-4451)
PHONE..............................661 827-8728
Tricia Brown, *Branch Mgr*
EMP: 71
SALES (corp-wide): 130.8B **Publicly Held**
SIC: 4812 5999 Cellular telephone services; mobile telephones & equipment
HQ: Cellco Partnership
1 Verizon Way
Basking Ridge NJ 07920

(P-5212)
CELLCO PARTNERSHIP
Also Called: Verizon
1846 Marron Rd, Carlsbad (92008-1172)
PHONE..............................760 720-8400
Arlene Strametz, *Principal*
Jeff Cummins, *Executive*
EMP: 71
SALES (corp-wide): 130.8B **Publicly Held**
SIC: 4812 5999 Cellular telephone services; telephone equipment & systems
HQ: Cellco Partnership
1 Verizon Way
Basking Ridge NJ 07920

(P-5213)
CELLCO PARTNERSHIP
Also Called: Verizon
12607 Artesia Blvd, Cerritos (90703-8501)
PHONE..............................562 809-5650
Bill Seager, *Manager*
Farrah Wynne, *Sales Staff*
EMP: 71
SALES (corp-wide): 130.8B **Publicly Held**
SIC: 4812 5999 Cellular telephone services; mobile telephones & equipment
HQ: Cellco Partnership
1 Verizon Way
Basking Ridge NJ 07920

(P-5214)
CELLCO PARTNERSHIP
Also Called: Verizon
2210 Griffin Way Ste 101, Corona
(92879-6532)
PHONE..............................951 549-6400
Kyung OH, *Manager*
EMP: 71
SALES (corp-wide): 130.8B **Publicly Held**
SIC: 4812 5999 Cellular telephone services; mobile telephones & equipment
HQ: Cellco Partnership
1 Verizon Way
Basking Ridge NJ 07920

(P-5215)
CELLCO PARTNERSHIP
Also Called: Verizon Wireless
39050 Argonaut Way, Fremont
(94538-1302)
PHONE..............................510 490-3800
Dolores Joy, *Manager*
EMP: 71
SALES (corp-wide): 130.8B **Publicly Held**
SIC: 4812 Cellular telephone services
HQ: Cellco Partnership
1 Verizon Way
Basking Ridge NJ 07920

(P-5216)
CELLCO PARTNERSHIP
1023 E Colorado St, Glendale
(91205-4542)
PHONE..............................818 500-7779
EMP: 71
SALES (corp-wide): 126B **Publicly Held**
SIC: 4812
HQ: Cellco Partnership
1 Verizon Way
Basking Ridge NJ 07920

(P-5217)
CELLCO PARTNERSHIP
10525 Vista Sorrento Pkwy # 150, San Diego (92121-2745)
PHONE..............................858 625-7751
Michael Bohrer, *Admin Sec*
Stan Parker, *Opers Staff*
EMP: 71
SALES (corp-wide): 130.8B **Publicly Held**
SIC: 4812 Cellular telephone services
HQ: Cellco Partnership
1 Verizon Way
Basking Ridge NJ 07920

(P-5218)
CELLCO PARTNERSHIP
205 Oak Hill Rd, Paso Robles
(93446-5438)
PHONE..............................805 237-8200
Maria Navarro, *Manager*
EMP: 71
SALES (corp-wide): 130.8B **Publicly Held**
SIC: 4812 Cellular telephone services
HQ: Cellco Partnership
1 Verizon Way
Basking Ridge NJ 07920

(P-5219)
CELLCO PARTNERSHIP
Also Called: Verizon Wireless
1729 N Victory Pl, Burbank (91502-1646)
PHONE..............................818 842-2722
Abe Osman, *Principal*
EMP: 71
SALES (corp-wide): 130.8B **Publicly Held**
SIC: 4812 Cellular telephone services
HQ: Cellco Partnership
1 Verizon Way
Basking Ridge NJ 07920

(P-5220)
CELLCO PARTNERSHIP
Also Called: Verizon Wireless
172 Ranch Dr, Milpitas (95035-5101)
PHONE..............................408 263-1960
Paul Gutierrez, *Principal*
Michael Rojas, *Asst Mgr*
EMP: 71
SALES (corp-wide): 130.8B **Publicly Held**
SIC: 4812 Cellular telephone services
HQ: Cellco Partnership
1 Verizon Way
Basking Ridge NJ 07920

(P-5221)
CELLCO PARTNERSHIP
Also Called: Verizon Wireless
768 Market St, San Francisco
(94102-2514)
PHONE..............................415 402-0640
Bob Wall, *Principal*
Daniel Estelita, *Sales Staff*
EMP: 71
SALES (corp-wide): 130.8B **Publicly Held**
SIC: 4812 Cellular telephone services
HQ: Cellco Partnership
1 Verizon Way
Basking Ridge NJ 07920

(P-5222)
CELLCO PARTNERSHIP
18012 Bollinger Canyon Rd, San Ramon
(94583-1502)
PHONE...............................925 743-9327
EMP: 74
SALES (corp-wide): 127B **Publicly Held**
SIC: 4812
HQ: Cellco Partnership
   1 Verizon Way
   Basking Ridge NJ 07920

(P-5223)
CELLCO PARTNERSHIP
Also Called: Verizon Wireless
3264 Lakeshore Ave, Oakland
(94610-2720)
PHONE...............................510 267-0731
EMP: 71
SALES (corp-wide): 130.8B **Publicly Held**
SIC: 4812 Cellular telephone services
HQ: Cellco Partnership
   1 Verizon Way
   Basking Ridge NJ 07920

(P-5224)
CELLCO PARTNERSHIP
Also Called: Verizon Wireless
3458 Wilshire Blvd, Los Angeles
(90010-2204)
PHONE...............................213 380-2299
Jay Trujillo, *Principal*
EMP: 71
SALES (corp-wide): 130.8B **Publicly Held**
SIC: 4812 Cellular telephone services
HQ: Cellco Partnership
   1 Verizon Way
   Basking Ridge NJ 07920

(P-5225)
CELLCO PARTNERSHIP
Also Called: Verizon Wireless
12006 Lakewood Blvd, Downey
(90242-2661)
PHONE...............................562 401-1045
Ronnie Mendoza, *Branch Mgr*
EMP: 71
SALES (corp-wide): 130.8B **Publicly Held**
SIC: 4812 Cellular telephone services
HQ: Cellco Partnership
   1 Verizon Way
   Basking Ridge NJ 07920

(P-5226)
CELLCO PARTNERSHIP
Also Called: Verizon Wireless
1398 Shaw Ave, Clovis (93612-3977)
PHONE...............................559 325-1420
EMP: 71
SALES (corp-wide): 130.8B **Publicly Held**
SIC: 4812 Cellular telephone services
HQ: Cellco Partnership
   1 Verizon Way
   Basking Ridge NJ 07920

(P-5227)
CELLCO PARTNERSHIP
Also Called: Verizon Wireless
39575 Trade Center Dr, Palmdale
(93551-3783)
PHONE...............................661 274-2112
Andy Taylor, *Principal*
EMP: 71
SALES (corp-wide): 130.8B **Publicly Held**
SIC: 4812 Cellular telephone services
HQ: Cellco Partnership
   1 Verizon Way
   Basking Ridge NJ 07920

(P-5228)
CELLCO PARTNERSHIP
Also Called: Verizon Wireless
16120 Beach Blvd, Huntington Beach
(92647-3805)
PHONE...............................714 847-8799

Thomas Johnson, *Branch Mgr*
EMP: 71
SALES (corp-wide): 130.8B **Publicly Held**
SIC: 4812 Cellular telephone services
HQ: Cellco Partnership
   1 Verizon Way
   Basking Ridge NJ 07920
-

(P-5229)
CELLCO PARTNERSHIP
Also Called: Verizon Wireless
100 N La Cienega Blvd # 233, Los Angeles
(90048-1938)
PHONE...............................310 659-0775
Tony Chu, *Principal*
EMP: 71
SALES (corp-wide): 130.8B **Publicly Held**
SIC: 4812 Cellular telephone services
HQ: Cellco Partnership
   1 Verizon Way
   Basking Ridge NJ 07920

(P-5230)
CELLCO PARTNERSHIP
Also Called: Verizon Wireless
3801 Pelandale Ave Ste B3, Modesto
(95356-8308)
PHONE...............................209 543-6500
EMP: 76
SALES (corp-wide): 130.8B **Publicly Held**
SIC: 4812 Cellular telephone services
HQ: Cellco Partnership
   1 Verizon Way
   Basking Ridge NJ 07920

(P-5231)
CELLCO PARTNERSHIP
Also Called: Verizon Wireless
3785 Wilshire Blvd, Los Angeles
(90010-2889)
PHONE...............................213 738-9771
EMP: 76
SALES (corp-wide): 130.8B **Publicly Held**
SIC: 4812 Cellular telephone services
HQ: Cellco Partnership
   1 Verizon Way
   Basking Ridge NJ 07920
-

(P-5232)
CELLCO PARTNERSHIP
Also Called: Verizon Wireless
20820 Avalon Blvd, Carson (90746-3300)
PHONE...............................310 329-9325
EMP: 76
SALES (corp-wide): 130.8B **Publicly Held**
SIC: 4812 Cellular telephone services
HQ: Cellco Partnership
   1 Verizon Way
   Basking Ridge NJ 07920
-

(P-5233)
CELLCO PARTNERSHIP
Also Called: Verizon Wireless
1503 Vine St, Hollywood (90028-7304)
PHONE...............................323 465-0640
EMP: 76
SALES (corp-wide): 130.8B **Publicly Held**
SIC: 4812 Cellular telephone services
HQ: Cellco Partnership
   1 Verizon Way
   Basking Ridge NJ 07920
-

(P-5234)
CELLCO PARTNERSHIP
Also Called: Verizon Wireless
2654 Mission St, San Francisco
(94110-3102)
PHONE...............................415 695-8400
EMP: 76
SALES (corp-wide): 130.8B **Publicly Held**
SIC: 4812 Cellular telephone services

HQ: Cellco Partnership
   1 Verizon Way
   Basking Ridge NJ 07920

(P-5235)
CELLCO PARTNERSHIP
Also Called: Verizon Wireless
30935 Courthouse Dr Spc 1, Union City
(94587-1716)
PHONE...............................510 324-5740
EMP: 76
SALES (corp-wide): 130.8B **Publicly Held**
SIC: 4812 Cellular telephone services
HQ: Cellco Partnership
   1 Verizon Way
   Basking Ridge NJ 07920

(P-5236)
CELLCO PARTNERSHIP
Also Called: Verizon Wireless
24201 Valencia Blvd, Valencia
(91355-1861)
PHONE...............................661 286-2399
EMP: 76
SALES (corp-wide): 130.8B **Publicly Held**
SIC: 4812 Cellular telephone services
HQ: Cellco Partnership
   1 Verizon Way
   Basking Ridge NJ 07920

(P-5237)
CELLCO PARTNERSHIP
Also Called: Verizon Wireless
6856 Katella Ave, Cypress (90630-5108)
PHONE...............................714 899-4690
EMP: 76
SALES (corp-wide): 130.8B **Publicly Held**
SIC: 4812 Cellular telephone services
HQ: Cellco Partnership
   1 Verizon Way
   Basking Ridge NJ 07920

(P-5238)
CELLCO PARTNERSHIP
Also Called: Verizon Wireless
880 N Imperial Ave, El Centro
(92243-1916)
PHONE...............................760 337-5508
EMP: 76
SALES (corp-wide): 130.8B **Publicly Held**
SIC: 4812 Cellular telephone services
HQ: Cellco Partnership
   1 Verizon Way
   Basking Ridge NJ 07920

(P-5239)
CELLCO PARTNERSHIP
Also Called: Verizon Wireless
1555 Simi Town Center Way, Simi Valley
(93065-0518)
PHONE...............................805 955-9035
EMP: 76
SALES (corp-wide): 130.8B **Publicly Held**
SIC: 4812 Cellular telephone services
HQ: Cellco Partnership
   1 Verizon Way
   Basking Ridge NJ 07920

(P-5240)
CELLCO PARTNERSHIP
Also Called: Verizon Wireless
110 Cooper St Ste A, Santa Cruz
(95060-4566)
PHONE...............................831 421-0753
EMP: 76
SALES (corp-wide): 130.8B **Publicly Held**
SIC: 4812 Cellular telephone services
HQ: Cellco Partnership
   1 Verizon Way
   Basking Ridge NJ 07920

(P-5241)
CELLCO PARTNERSHIP
Also Called: Verizon Wireless
500 Inland Center Dr # 459, San
Bernardino (92408-1912)
PHONE...............................909 381-0576
EMP: 76
SALES (corp-wide): 130.8B **Publicly Held**
SIC: 4812 Cellular telephone services
HQ: Cellco Partnership
   1 Verizon Way
   Basking Ridge NJ 07920

(P-5242)
CELLCO PARTNERSHIP
Also Called: Verizon Wireless
6065 Sunrise Blvd, Citrus Heights
(95610-6833)
PHONE...............................916 536-0440
EMP: 76
SALES (corp-wide): 130.8B **Publicly Held**
SIC: 4812 Cellular telephone services
HQ: Cellco Partnership
   1 Verizon Way
   Basking Ridge NJ 07920

(P-5243)
CELLCO PARTNERSHIP
Also Called: Verizon
1 Daniel Burnham Ct Bsmt, San Francisco
(94109-5474)
PHONE...............................415 351-1700
Minh Luong, *Manager*
EMP: 71
SALES (corp-wide): 130.8B **Publicly Held**
SIC: 4812 5999 Cellular telephone services; mobile telephones & equipment
HQ: Cellco Partnership
   1 Verizon Way
   Basking Ridge NJ 07920

(P-5244)
CELLCO PARTNERSHIP
Also Called: Verizon Wireless
2980 State St, Santa Barbara
(93105-3445)
PHONE...............................805 569-2525
Kevin Warren, *Principal*
EMP: 71
SALES (corp-wide): 130.8B **Publicly Held**
SIC: 4812 Cellular telephone services
HQ: Cellco Partnership
   1 Verizon Way
   Basking Ridge NJ 07920

(P-5245)
CELLCO PARTNERSHIP
Also Called: Verizon Wireless
844 4th St, Santa Rosa (95404-4505)
PHONE...............................707 525-5010
EMP: 71
SALES (corp-wide): 130.8B **Publicly Held**
SIC: 4812 Cellular telephone services
HQ: Cellco Partnership
   1 Verizon Way
   Basking Ridge NJ 07920

(P-5246)
CELLCO PARTNERSHIP
Also Called: Verizon Wireless
503 N State College Blvd, Fullerton
(92831-3545)
PHONE...............................714 449-0715
EMP: 71
SALES (corp-wide): 130.8B **Publicly Held**
SIC: 4812 Cellular telephone services
HQ: Cellco Partnership
   1 Verizon Way
   Basking Ridge NJ 07920

(P-5247)
CELLCO PARTNERSHIP
Also Called: Verizon Wireless
219 University Ave, Palo Alto (94301-1712)
PHONE...............................650 323-6127

PRODUCTS & SVCS

Ian Yahya, *Manager*
EMP: 71
SALES (corp-wide): 130.8B **Publicly Held**
SIC: 4812 5065 5999 Cellular telephone services; telephone & telegraphic equipment; mobile telephones & equipment
HQ: Cellco Partnership
1 Verizon Way
Basking Ridge NJ 07920

(P-5248)
CELLCO PARTNERSHIP
Also Called: Verizon
994 Mill St Ste 100, San Luis Obispo (93401-2777)
PHONE.....................................805 549-6260
Robin Okoneski, *Branch Mgr*
EMP: 71
SALES (corp-wide): 130.8B **Publicly Held**
SIC: 4812 Cellular telephone services
HQ: Cellco Partnership
1 Verizon Way
Basking Ridge NJ 07920

(P-5249)
CELLCO PARTNERSHIP
Also Called: Verizon Wireless
3770 W Mcfadden Ave Ste H, Santa Ana (92704-1395)
PHONE.....................................714 775-0600
EMP: 76
SALES (corp-wide): 130.8B **Publicly Held**
SIC: 4812 Cellular telephone services
HQ: Cellco Partnership
1 Verizon Way
Basking Ridge NJ 07920

(P-5250)
CELLCO PARTNERSHIP
Also Called: Verizon Wireless
5438 Whittier Blvd, Commerce (90022-4113)
PHONE.....................................323 725-9750
Kristina King, *Branch Mgr*
EMP: 71
SALES (corp-wide): 130.8B **Publicly Held**
SIC: 4812 Cellular telephone services
HQ: Cellco Partnership
1 Verizon Way
Basking Ridge NJ 07920

(P-5251)
COMCAST OF CALIFORNIA/COLO
3055 Comcast Pl, Livermore (94551-7594)
PHONE.....................................925 424-0273
Stephen B Burke, *President*
Loni Morgan, *Project Mgr*
David Higginbotham, *Analyst*
Glenna Lee, *Analyst*
Elaine Barden, *VP Mktg*
EMP: 69
SALES (est): 654.2K
SALES (corp-wide): 94.5B **Publicly Held**
SIC: 4812 4841 Radio telephone communication; cable television services
PA: Comcast Corporation
1701 Jfk Blvd
Philadelphia PA 19103
215 286-1700

(P-5252)
CORTEL INC
14621 Arroyo Hondo, San Diego (92127-3641)
PHONE.....................................650 703-7217
Michael Jackson, *President*
John Barker, *CFO*
Michael Miller, *Admin Sec*
EMP: 52
SALES (est): 3.6MM **Privately Held**
SIC: 4812 Cellular telephone services

(P-5253)
CRICKET COMMUNICATIONS LLC (DH)
Also Called: Cricket Wireless
7337 Trade St, San Diego (92121-2423)
PHONE.....................................858 882-6000
S Douglas Hutcheson, *CEO*
Nitu Arora, *President*
David Davis, *President*
Glen Flowers, *President*
Annette Jacobs, *President*
EMP: 65
SALES (est): 623.1MM
SALES (corp-wide): 170.7B **Publicly Held**
WEB: www.cricketcommunications.com
SIC: 4812 Cellular telephone services
HQ: Leap Wireless International, Inc.
7337 Trade St
San Diego CA 92121
858 882-6000

(P-5254)
CRICKET INDIANA PROPERTY CO
10307 Pacific Center Ct, San Diego (92121-4340)
PHONE.....................................858 587-2648
EMP: 86
SALES (est): 1.8MM
SALES (corp-wide): 170.7B **Publicly Held**
WEB: www.leapwireless.com
SIC: 4812 Radio telephone communication
HQ: Leap Wireless International, Inc.
7337 Trade St
San Diego CA 92121
858 882-6000

(P-5255)
DIGITAL COMMUNICATIONS NETWORK (PA)
Also Called: D C N Wireless
6300 Canoga Ave Ste 1625, Woodland Hills (91367-8045)
PHONE.....................................818 227-3333
Robert H Mogadam, *President*
Margrit Dorgelo, *Vice Pres*
EMP: 54
SALES (est): 6.3MM **Privately Held**
WEB: www.digitalcomnet.com
SIC: 4812 5999 Cellular telephone services; telephone & communication equipment

(P-5256)
DOWNTOWN METRO
1030 6th St Ste 16, Coachella (92236-1710)
PHONE.....................................760 398-3310
H Yun, *Owner*
EMP: 50 **EST:** 2012
SALES (est): 717.9K **Privately Held**
SIC: 4812 Cellular telephone services

(P-5257)
DUST NETWORKS INC
32990 Alvrdo Niles Rd # 910, Union City (94587-8106)
PHONE.....................................510 400-2900
Joy Weiss, *President*
Eva Chen, *Vice Pres*
Brenda Glaze, *Vice Pres*
Dave Lynch, *Vice Pres*
EMP: 51
SQ FT: 15,000
SALES (est): 3.8MM
SALES (corp-wide): 6.2B **Publicly Held**
WEB: www.dust-inc.com
SIC: 4812 Cellular telephone services
HQ: Linear Technology Llc
1630 Mccarthy Blvd
Milpitas CA 95035
408 432-1900

(P-5258)
EA MOBILE INC
5510 Lincoln Blvd, Los Angeles (90094-2034)
PHONE.....................................310 754-7125
Mitch Lasky, *Ch of Bd*
Scott Lahman, *President*
Craig Gatarz, *COO*
Michael Marchetti, *CFO*
Minard Hamilton, *Exec VP*

EMP: 400
SQ FT: 23,000
SALES (est): 14.3MM
SALES (corp-wide): 4.9B **Publicly Held**
SIC: 4812 Cellular telephone services
PA: Electronic Arts Inc.
209 Redwood Shores Pkwy
Redwood City CA 94065
650 628-1500

(P-5259)
FRONTIER CALIFORNIA INC
Also Called: Verizon
5195 N Blackstone Ave, Fresno (93710-6701)
PHONE.....................................559 224-9222
Randall Petty-John, *Manager*
EMP: 60
SALES (corp-wide): 8.6B **Publicly Held**
SIC: 4812 Cellular telephone services
HQ: Frontier California Inc.
140 West St
New York NY 10007
212 395-1000

(P-5260)
IMOBILE LLC
2613 Naglee Rd, Tracy (95304-7317)
PHONE.....................................209 833-6757
Armando Baltazar, *President*
EMP: 263 **Privately Held**
SIC: 4812 Cellular telephone services
PA: Imobile Llc
206 Terminal Dr
Plainview NY 11803

(P-5261)
IMOBILE LLC
875 W Arrow Hwy, San Dimas (91773-2406)
PHONE.....................................909 599-8822
Nahrain Simonov, *Branch Mgr*
EMP: 368 **Privately Held**
SIC: 4812 Cellular telephone services
PA: Imobile Llc
206 Terminal Dr
Plainview NY 11803

(P-5262)
J5 INFRASTRUCTURE PARTNERS LLC
2030 Main St Ste 200, Irvine (92614-8223)
PHONE.....................................949 299-5258
Jerry Elliott, *CEO*
Brian Kennell, *Exec VP*
Briana Jolicoeur, *VP Human Res*
EMP: 58
SALES (est): 1.8MM **Privately Held**
SIC: 4812 Cellular telephone services

(P-5263)
MOBILITIE INVESTMENTS III LLC
2955 Red Hill Ave Ste 200, Costa Mesa (92626-1205)
PHONE.....................................877 999-7070
Gary Jabara, *Chairman*
Christos Karmis, *CEO*
Dana Tardelli, *COO*
Dissy Saraboing, *CFO*
EMP: 125
SALES: 50MM
SALES (corp-wide): 407.6MM **Privately Held**
SIC: 4812 Radio telephone communication
PA: Mobilitie Management, Llc
660 Nwport Ctr Dr Ste 200
Newport Beach CA 92660
877 999-7070

(P-5264)
NEW CINGULAR WIRELESS SVCS INC
Also Called: AT&T
P.O. Box 68055
PHONE.....................................562 924-0000
Hank Bonde, *Branch Mgr*
EMP: 89
SALES (corp-wide): 170.7B **Publicly Held**
WEB: www.attws.com
SIC: 4812 Cellular telephone services

HQ: New Cingular Wireless Services, Inc.
7277 164th Ave Ne
Redmond WA 98052

(P-5265)
NEXTEL COMMUNICATIONS INC
1810 W Slauson Ave Ste G, Los Angeles (90047-1133)
PHONE.....................................323 290-2400
Ivan Arvizu, *Principal*
EMP: 60 **Publicly Held**
SIC: 4812 Cellular telephone services
HQ: Nextel Communications, Inc.
12502 Sunrise Valley Dr
Reston VA 20191
703 433-4000

(P-5266)
NEXTEL COMMUNICATIONS INC
272 Sun Valley Mall, Concord (94520-5808)
PHONE.....................................925 682-2355
Sean Fanopulous, *Manager*
EMP: 60 **Publicly Held**
WEB: www.nextel.com
SIC: 4812 5999 Cellular telephone services; mobile telephones & equipment
HQ: Nextel Communications, Inc.
12502 Sunrise Valley Dr
Reston VA 20191
703 433-4000

(P-5267)
OFFICE OF THE LEGISLATIVE COUN
Also Called: Legislative Data Center
1100 J St Fl 7, Sacramento (95814-2826)
PHONE.....................................916 341-8708
Nancy Pabst, *IT/INT Sup*
EMP: 330 **Privately Held**
SIC: 4812 Radio telephone communication
HQ: Office Of The Legislative Counsel
State Cpitol Bldg Rm 3021
Sacramento CA 95814

(P-5268)
PRIME COMMUNICATIONS LP
29273 Central Ave, Lake Elsinore (92532-2254)
PHONE.....................................951 253-3304
EMP: 69
SALES (corp-wide): 280MM **Privately Held**
SIC: 4812 Cellular telephone services
PA: Prime Communications, L.P.
12550 Reed Rd Ste 100
Sugar Land TX 77478
281 240-7800

(P-5269)
SIERRA WIRELESS AMERICA INC (HQ)
2738 Loker Ave W Ste A, Carlsbad (92010-6629)
PHONE.....................................760 444-5650
Jason W Cohenour, *CEO*
Dave Overend, *Technical Staff*
Gondava Hilz, *Manager*
EMP: 82
SALES (est): 10.2MM
SALES (corp-wide): 193.6MM **Privately Held**
SIC: 4812 Cellular telephone services
PA: Sierra Wireless, Inc
13811 Wireless Way
Richmond BC V6V 3
604 231-1100

(P-5270)
SONIM TECHNOLOGIES INC (PA)
1875 S Grant St Ste 750, San Mateo (94402-2670)
PHONE.....................................650 378-8100
Robert Plaschke, *CEO*
Maurice Hochschild, *Ch of Bd*
James Walker, *CFO*
Charles Becher, *Officer*
Bengt Jonassen, *Senior VP*
▲ **EMP:** 53
SALES: 135.6MM **Publicly Held**
WEB: www.sonimtech.com
SIC: 4812 Cellular telephone services

▲ = Import ▼=Export
◆ =Import/Export

(P-5271)
SPRINT CORPORATION
6591 Irvine Center Dr # 100, Irvine
(92618-2130)
PHONE.....................949 748-3353
Mohammed Nasser, *Exec Dir*
EMP: 400 Publicly Held
SIC: 4812 Cellular telephone services
HQ: Sprint Corporation
6200 Sprint Pkwy
Overland Park KS 66251
877 564-3166

(P-5272)
STX WIRELESS OPERATIONS LLC
Also Called: Cricket Stx
5887 Copley Dr, San Diego (92111-7906)
PHONE.....................858 882-6000
Douglas Hutcheson, *President*
Raymond Roman, *COO*
Jerry Elliot, *CFO*
Al Moschner, *Exec VP*
Aaron Maddox, *Vice Pres*
EMP: 4000
SALES (est): 410.7MM Privately Held
SIC: 4812 Cellular telephone services

(P-5273)
T-MOBILE USA INC
Also Called: Metropcs-Fremont
4095 Mowry Ave, Fremont (94538-1339)
PHONE.....................510 797-8290
EMP: 170
SALES (corp-wide): 86.6B Publicly Held
SIC: 4812 4813 Cellular telephone services; telephone communication, except radio; wire telephone
HQ: T-Mobile Usa, Inc.
12920 Se 38th St
Bellevue WA 98006
425 378-4000

(P-5274)
T-MOBILE USA INC
Also Called: Metropcs-Modesto
2225 Plaza Pkwy Ste I1b, Modesto
(95350-6220)
PHONE.....................209 529-0539
EMP: 170
SALES (corp-wide): 88.3B Publicly Held
SIC: 4812 4813
HQ: T-Mobile Usa, Inc.
12920 Se 38th St
Bellevue WA 98006
425 378-4000

(P-5275)
T-MOBILE USA INC
Also Called: Metropcs-Van Ness
900 Van Ness Ave Ste 1, San Francisco
(94109-6970)
PHONE.....................415 440-5370
EMP: 153
SALES (corp-wide): 86.6B Publicly Held
SIC: 4812 4813 Cellular telephone services; telephone communication, except radio; wire telephone
HQ: T-Mobile Usa, Inc.
12920 Se 38th St
Bellevue WA 98006
425 378-4000

(P-5276)
TARANA WIRELESS INC
2105 Martin Luther King, Berkeley
(94704-1108)
PHONE.....................510 868-3359
Gisli Hermannsson, *Controller*
Marcus Weber, *Director*
EMP: 185 Privately Held
SIC: 4812 Cellular telephone services
PA: Tarana Wireless, Inc.
590 Alder Dr
Milpitas CA 95035

(P-5277)
TEXTPLUS INC
Also Called: Gogii
13160 Mindanao Way # 200, Marina Del
Rey (90292-7907)
PHONE.....................424 272-0296
Nanea Reeves, *President*
Zachary Norman, *President*
Chandra Hill, *Vice Pres*

Cory Radcliff, *Vice Pres*
Alex Scissors, *Project Mgr*
EMP: 65
SALES (est): 8.2MM Privately Held
SIC: 4812 Cellular telephone services

(P-5278)
TRELLISWARE TECHNOLOGIES INC
10641 Scripps Summit Ct # 100, San Diego
(92131-3939)
PHONE.....................858 753-1600
Thomas Carter, *CEO*
Michael Smith, *Officer*
Metin Bayram, *Vice Pres*
Jonathan Cromwell, *Vice Pres*
Jim Morse, *Vice Pres*
EMP: 90
SQ FT: 46,000
SALES (est): 22.2MM Privately Held
WEB: www.trellisware.com
SIC: 4812 4813 3663 Radio telephone communication; local & long distance telephone communications; airborne radio communications equipment

(P-5279)
TWILIO INC (PA)
375 Beale St Ste 300, San Francisco
(94105-2177)
PHONE.....................415 390-2337
Jeffrey Lawson, *Ch of Bd*
George Hu, *COO*
Khozema Shipchandler, *CFO*
Byron Deeter, *Bd of Directors*
Scott Raney, *Bd of Directors*
EMP: 154
SQ FT: 90,000
SALES: 650MM Publicly Held
SIC: 4812 7372 Cellular telephone services; business oriented computer software

(P-5280)
U S MBILE WRLESS CMMUNICATIONS (PA)
Also Called: Day Wireless Systems
8300 Juniper Creek Ln # 100, San Diego
(92126-1072)
PHONE.....................858 537-0709
Stanley A Decosmo, *Ch of Bd*
Gordon Day, *President*
Edward Carey, *Vice Pres*
Julio Chavez, *Opers Mgr*
EMP: 75
SQ FT: 18,000
SALES: 5.5MM Privately Held
SIC: 4812 Cellular telephone services

(P-5281)
VERIZON WIRELESS (PA)
15505 Sand Canyon Ave, Irvine
(92618-3114)
PHONE.....................949 286-7000
Dana Z Keefer, *Exec Dir*
Stephanie Munerlyn, *Technology*
Chris Nguyen, *Engineer*
Tyeeluh Hughes, *Training Spec*
Sarah Bohannon, *Sales Staff*
EMP: 50
SALES (est): 78.3MM Privately Held
SIC: 4812 Cellular telephone services

(P-5282)
WM WIRELESS INC
6723 N Paramount Blvd, Long Beach
(90805-1901)
PHONE.....................562 633-9288
Ferdinand L Aguinaldo, *President*
EMP: 50
SALES (est): 6.9MM Privately Held
SIC: 4812 Cellular telephone services

**4813 Telephone
Communications, Except**

(P-5283)
11 MAIN INC
527 Flume St, Chico (95928-5608)
PHONE.....................530 892-9191
Jeff Schlicht, *CEO*
Mike Effle, *President*
Ray Kaminski, *Vice Pres*
Christina Liu, *Vice Pres*

Amber Minson, *Vice Pres*
EMP: 105
SALES (est): 18.7MM Privately Held
SIC: 4813
HQ: Alibaba.Com Inc
400 S El Camino Real # 400
San Mateo CA 94402
408 785-5580

(P-5284)
2WIRE INC (DH)
2450 Walsh Ave, Santa Clara
(95051-1303)
PHONE.....................408 235-5500
Tim O'Loughlin, *CEO*
Pasquale Romano, *President*
Tom Bohan, *Admin Sec*
Matt Spears, *Technical Staff*
David Atkins, *Manager*
▲ EMP: 138
SQ FT: 82,000
SALES (est): 92.1MM Privately Held
SALES (corp-wide): 6.7B Privately Held
WEB: www.2wire.com
SIC: 4813
HQ: Ruckus Wireless, Inc.
350 W Java Dr
Sunnyvale CA 94089
650 265-4200

(P-5285)
4G WIRELESS INC
Also Called: Verizon Wireless Authorized Ret
7220 Eastern Ave, Bell (90201-4505)
PHONE.....................562 928-2972
EMP: 55 Privately Held
SIC: 4813 4812 Telephone communication, except radio; cellular telephone services
PA: 4g Wireless, Inc.
8871 Research Dr
Irvine CA 92618

(P-5286)
4G WIRELESS INC
Also Called: Verizon Wireless Authorized Ret
4620 Tassajara Rd, Dublin (94568-4607)
PHONE.....................925 307-8990
EMP: 55 Privately Held
SIC: 4813 4812 Telephone communication, except radio; cellular telephone services
PA: 4g Wireless, Inc.
8871 Research Dr
Irvine CA 92618

(P-5287)
4G WIRELESS INC
Also Called: Verizon Wireless Authorized Ret
8342 Lincoln Blvd, Los Angeles
(90045-2414)
PHONE.....................310 429-9048
EMP: 55 Privately Held
SIC: 4813 4812 Telephone communication, except radio; cellular telephone services
PA: 4g Wireless, Inc.
8871 Research Dr
Irvine CA 92618

(P-5288)
4G WIRELESS INC
Also Called: Verizon Wireless Authorized Ret
4925 Eagle Rock Blvd, Los Angeles
(90041-1906)
PHONE.....................323 679-9991
EMP: 55 Privately Held
SIC: 4813 4812 Telephone communication, except radio; cellular telephone services
PA: 4g Wireless, Inc.
8871 Research Dr
Irvine CA 92618

(P-5289)
4G WIRELESS INC
Also Called: Verizon Wireless Authorized Ret
501 W Felicita Ave # 104, Escondido
(92025-5638)
PHONE.....................760 705-7133
EMP: 55 Privately Held

SIC: 4813 4812 Telephone communication, except radio; cellular telephone services
PA: 4g Wireless, Inc.
8871 Research Dr
Irvine CA 92618

(P-5290)
4G WIRELESS INC
Also Called: Verizon Wireless Premium Ret
2635 Gateway Rd Ste 103, Carlsbad
(92009-1753)
PHONE.....................760 828-2543
Ameen Elashqar, *Branch Mgr*
EMP: 55 Privately Held
SIC: 4813 4812 4833 Telephone communication, except radio; cellular telephone services; television broadcasting stations
PA: 4g Wireless, Inc.
8871 Research Dr
Irvine CA 92618

(P-5291)
4G WIRELESS INC
Also Called: Verizon Wireless Authorized Ret
2560 N Perris Blvd Ste G8, Perris
(92571-3253)
PHONE.....................951 210-7980
EMP: 55 Privately Held
SIC: 4813 4812 Telephone communication, except radio; cellular telephone services
PA: 4g Wireless, Inc.
8871 Research Dr
Irvine CA 92618

(P-5292)
4G WIRELESS INC
Also Called: Verizon Wireless Authorized Ret
407 N Pacific Coast Hwy # 101, Redondo
Beach (90277-2872)
PHONE.....................310 376-2299
EMP: 55 Privately Held
SIC: 4813 4812 Telephone communication, except radio; cellular telephone services
PA: 4g Wireless, Inc.
8871 Research Dr
Irvine CA 92618

(P-5293)
4G WIRELESS INC
Also Called: Verizon Wireless Authorized Ret
285 E 5th St, Long Beach (90802-2484)
PHONE.....................562 432-7744
EMP: 55 Privately Held
SIC: 4813 4812 Telephone communication, except radio; cellular telephone services
PA: 4g Wireless, Inc.
8871 Research Dr
Irvine CA 92618

(P-5294)
8X8 INC (PA)
2125 Onel Dr, San Jose (95131-2032)
PHONE.....................408 727-1885
Vikram Verma, *CEO*
Bryan R Martin, *Ch of Bd*
Steven Gatoff, *CFO*
Rani Hublou, *Chief Mktg Ofcr*
Dejan Deklich,
EMP: 145
SQ FT: 140,831
SALES: 352.5MM Publicly Held
WEB: www.bryanandlisa.com
SIC: 4813 7372 ; ; prepackaged software

(P-5295)
AAMCOM LLC
800 N Pacific Coast Hwy, Redondo Beach
(90277-2148)
PHONE.....................310 318-8100
Steve Diels, *Treasurer*
Jose Carrera, *Info Tech Dir*
Norma Soto, *Business Mgr*
Elisabeth Diels,
Carlton Bonner, *Director*
EMP: 50 EST: 2009
SQ FT: 4,000

PRODUCTS & SVCS

SALES: 2.6MM **Privately Held**
SIC: 4813 Telephone communication, except radio

(P-5296)
AB CELLULAR HOLDING LLC
Also Called: At & T Wireless Service
1452 Edinger Ave, Tustin (92780-6246)
PHONE..............................562 468-6846
Glen Lurie,
EMP: 2100
SALES (est): 229.3MM
SALES (corp-wide): 170.7B **Publicly Held**
WEB: www.cingular.com
SIC: 4813 Local & long distance telephone communications; local telephone communications; long distance telephone communications
HQ: At&T Mobility Llc
1025 Lenox Park Blvd Ne
Brookhaven GA 30319
800 331-0500

(P-5297)
ADAPTIVE SPECTRUM AND SIGNAL A
333 Twin Dolphin Dr # 300, Redwood City (94065-1449)
PHONE..............................650 264-2667
John M Cioffi, *CEO*
Barry Gray, *Senior VP*
David Stevenson, *Risk Mgmt Dir*
David Fligor, *Admin Sec*
Amit Kathuria, *Technology*
EMP: 60
SALES (est): 3.1MM
SALES (corp-wide): 4.6MM **Privately Held**
SIC: 4813
PA: Assia Eal Sl.
Calle Claudio Coello, 24 - Piso 4 A 2
Madrid 28001
917 815-130

(P-5298)
ADICIO INC
5857 Owens Ave Ste 300, Carlsbad (92008-5507)
PHONE..............................760 602-9502
Richard Miller, *President*
Richette Lock, *COO*
Bob Miller, *Officer*
Mike Cavallo, *Exec VP*
Ryan Casebier, *Info Tech Mgr*
EMP: 90
SALES: 15MM **Privately Held**
WEB: www.adicio.com
SIC: 4813

(P-5299)
AERIS COMMUNICATIONS INC (PA)
2099 Gateway Pl Ste 600, San Jose (95110-1048)
PHONE..............................408 557-1900
Marc Jones, *CEO*
John Molise, *CFO*
Mark Cratsenburg, *Vice Pres*
Michael Doran, *Vice Pres*
Andy Greig, *Vice Pres*
EMP: 57
SQ FT: 30,000
SALES (est): 19.3MM **Privately Held**
WEB: www.aeris.net
SIC: 4813 4812 Local & long distance telephone communications; cellular telephone services

(P-5300)
AIRESPRING INC
Also Called: Global Fibernet
7800 Woodley Ave, Van Nuys (91406-1722)
PHONE..............................818 786-8990
AVI Lonstein, *CEO*
Daniel Lonstein, *COO*
Arno Vigen, *CFO*
Tony Lonstein, *Exec VP*
Ron McNab, *Senior VP*
▲ EMP: 100 EST: 2001
SQ FT: 12,500
SALES (est): 35.8MM **Privately Held**
SIC: 4813

(P-5301)
ALLSTATE TECHNOLOGIES INC (PA)
Also Called: Allstate Communications
5699 Kanan Rd Ste 455, Agoura Hills (91301-3358)
P.O. Box 332 (91376-0332)
PHONE..............................818 889-7600
Gail S Ramas, *President*
Jodie L Gardener, *Vice Pres*
Milton Ramas, *General Mgr*
EMP: 60
SQ FT: 2,400
SALES (est): 4.1MM **Privately Held**
SIC: 4813 Telephone communication, except radio

(P-5302)
ALTABA INC
Also Called: Geocities
3420 Central Expy, Santa Clara (95051-0703)
PHONE..............................408 349-5080
Terry Semel, *Principal*
Patrick Bennett, *President*
Chuck Haas, *President*
P Hanley, *President*
EMP: 200 **Privately Held**
WEB: www.yahoo.com
SIC: 4813 7375 ; information retrieval services
PA: Altaba Inc.
140 E 45th St Ste 15a
New York NY 10017

(P-5303)
ASIAINFO-LINKAGE INC
5201 Great America Pkwy # 356, Santa Clara (95054-1122)
PHONE..............................408 970-9788
Steve Zhang, *CEO*
Ying Han, *CFO*
Yadong Jin, *Exec VP*
Jie LI, *Vice Pres*
EMP: 1500
SALES: 481MM **Privately Held**
SIC: 4813
HQ: Asiainfo Technologies (China), Inc.
Asiainfo Headquarters, No. 10, Northwest Wangdong Road, Zhonggua
Beijing 10019
108 216-6066

(P-5304)
AT&T CORP
795 Folsom St, San Francisco (94107-1243)
PHONE..............................415 442-2600
K McNeely, *Principal*
Bailey Hartmeyer, *Sales Dir*
Padraic Kelly, *Sales Staff*
Walter Hagge, *Manager*
Jenny Leipziger, *Manager*
EMP: 575
SALES (corp-wide): 170.7B **Publicly Held**
WEB: www.att.com
SIC: 4813 4812 Long distance telephone communications; radio telephone communication
HQ: At&T Corp.
1 At&T Way
Bedminster NJ 07921
800 403-3302

(P-5305)
AT&T CORP
2745 Cloverdale Ave, Concord (94518-2402)
PHONE..............................925 356-6204
Hugh Johnston, *Branch Mgr*
EMP: 69
SALES (corp-wide): 170.7B **Publicly Held**
SIC: 4813 Telephone communication, except radio
HQ: At&T Corp.
1 At&T Way
Bedminster NJ 07921
800 403-3302

(P-5306)
AT&T CORP
624 S Grand Ave Ste 2940, Los Angeles (90017-3872)
PHONE..............................213 787-0055
Arnold Larson, *Branch Mgr*
EMP: 69
SALES (corp-wide): 170.7B **Publicly Held**
WEB: www.att.com
SIC: 4813 Telephone communication, except radio
HQ: At&T Corp.
1 At&T Way
Bedminster NJ 07921
800 403-3302

(P-5307)
AT&T CORP
6920 Van Nuys Blvd Rm 100, Van Nuys (91405-3986)
PHONE..............................818 374-6458
Randy Paquette, *Manager*
EMP: 100
SALES (corp-wide): 170.7B **Publicly Held**
WEB: www.swbell.com
SIC: 4813 Local & long distance telephone communications
HQ: At&T Corp.
1 At&T Way
Bedminster NJ 07921
800 403-3302

(P-5308)
AT&T CORP
14709 Vanoan St, Van Nuys (91405)
PHONE..............................818 373-6896
EMP: 69
SALES (corp-wide): 170.7B **Publicly Held**
SIC: 4813 Telephone communication, except radio
HQ: At&T Corp.
1 At&T Way
Bedminster NJ 07921
800 403-3302

(P-5309)
AT&T CORP
1121 Jefferson Ave Rm 222, Redwood City (94063-1814)
PHONE..............................650 780-1005
EMP: 69
SALES (corp-wide): 170.7B **Publicly Held**
SIC: 4813 Telephone communication, except radio
HQ: At&T Corp.
1 At&T Way
Bedminster NJ 07921
800 403-3302

(P-5310)
AT&T CORP
2600 Camino Ramon, San Ramon (94583-5000)
PHONE..............................415 394-3000
EMP: 200
SALES (corp-wide): 170.7B **Publicly Held**
WEB: www.swbell.com
SIC: 4813 7375 Local telephone communications; information retrieval services
HQ: At&T Corp.
1 At&T Way
Bedminster NJ 07921
800 403-3302

(P-5311)
AT&T CORP
1546 Saratoga Ave, San Jose (95129-4961)
PHONE..............................408 871-3870
Ben Hosseini, *Manager*
EMP: 69
SALES (corp-wide): 170.7B **Publicly Held**
SIC: 4813 Telephone communication, except radio
HQ: At&T Corp.
1 At&T Way
Bedminster NJ 07921
800 403-3302

(P-5312)
AT&T CORP
6000 Lankershim Blvd, North Hollywood (91606-4806)
PHONE..............................818 506-9118
EMP: 69
SALES (corp-wide): 170.7B **Publicly Held**
SIC: 4813 Telephone communication, except radio
HQ: At&T Corp.
1 At&T Way
Bedminster NJ 07921
800 403-3302

(P-5313)
AT&T CORP
2600 Camino Ramon 2w856, San Ramon (94583-5000)
PHONE..............................925 823-5388
Debbie Johnson, *Manager*
EMP: 7650
SALES (corp-wide): 170.7B **Publicly Held**
WEB: www.att.com
SIC: 4813 Telephone communication, except radio
HQ: At&T Corp.
1 At&T Way
Bedminster NJ 07921
800 403-3302

(P-5314)
AT&T CORP
3925 E Coronado St, Anaheim (92807-1608)
PHONE..............................714 666-5504
EMP: 69
SALES (corp-wide): 170.7B **Publicly Held**
WEB: www.swbell.com
SIC: 4813 Local & long distance telephone communications
HQ: At&T Corp.
1 At&T Way
Bedminster NJ 07921
800 403-3302

(P-5315)
AT&T CORP
4130 S Market Ct, Sacramento (95834-1222)
PHONE..............................916 830-5000
Welty P Espine, *Manager*
Malachi Elledge, *Technician*
EMP: 400
SALES (corp-wide): 170.7B **Publicly Held**
WEB: www.att.com
SIC: 4813 Local telephone communications
HQ: At&T Corp.
1 At&T Way
Bedminster NJ 07921
800 403-3302

(P-5316)
AT&T CORP
3375 Peach Ave, Clovis (93612-5617)
PHONE..............................559 294-5431
EMP: 69
SALES (corp-wide): 170.7B **Publicly Held**
SIC: 4813 Telephone communication, except radio
HQ: At&T Corp.
1 At&T Way
Bedminster NJ 07921
800 403-3302

(P-5317)
AT&T CORP
455 W 2nd St, San Bernardino (92401-1525)
PHONE..............................909 381-7729
Ken Fenton, *Manager*
John Bradley, *Manager*
EMP: 69
SALES (corp-wide): 170.7B **Publicly Held**
WEB: www.att.com
SIC: 4813 Telephone communication, except radio

HQ: At&T Corp.
 1 At&T Way
 Bedminster NJ 07921
 800 403-3302

(P-5318)
AT&T CORP
3025 Raymond St, Santa Clara
(95054-3431)
PHONE..................408 980-2004
EMP: 69
SALES (corp-wide): 170.7B Publicly Held
SIC: 4813 Telephone communication, except radio
HQ: At&T Corp.
 1 At&T Way
 Bedminster NJ 07921
 800 403-3302

(P-5319)
AT&T CORP
625 Ellis St Ste 205, Mountain View
(94043-2223)
PHONE..................415 276-0039
Ed Trumbull, *Branch Mgr*
EMP: 69
SALES (corp-wide): 170.7B Publicly Held
WEB: www.att.com
SIC: 4813 Telephone communication, except radio
HQ: At&T Corp.
 1 At&T Way
 Bedminster NJ 07921
 800 403-3302

(P-5320)
AT&T CORP
700 S Flower St Ste 810, Los Angeles
(90017-4101)
PHONE..................213 787-0055
Robert Annunziata, *President*
Edgar Castaneda, *Executive*
Yuvette Eaton, *Manager*
EMP: 80
SALES (corp-wide): 170.7B Publicly Held
WEB: www.att.com
SIC: 4813 Telephone communication, except radio
HQ: At&T Corp.
 1 At&T Way
 Bedminster NJ 07921
 800 403-3302

(P-5321)
AT&T DATACOMM LLC
16755 Von Karman Ave # 120, Irvine
(92606-4930)
PHONE..................714 675-9752
Kent Kofai, *Manager*
EMP: 50
SALES (corp-wide): 170.7B Publicly Held
SIC: 4813 Telephone communication, except radio
HQ: At&T Datacomm, Llc
 175 E Houston St Ste 100
 San Antonio TX 78205
 210 821-4105

(P-5322)
AT&T SERVICES INC
Also Called: SBC
101 Broadway, San Diego (92101-5001)
PHONE..................619 515-5100
Daena Mason, *Principal*
EMP: 168
SALES (corp-wide): 170.7B Publicly Held
WEB: www.dsdllc.com
SIC: 4813 Telephone communication, except radio
HQ: At&T Services, Inc.
 208 S Akard St Ste 110
 Dallas TX 75202
 210 821-4105

(P-5323)
AT&T SERVICES INC
4300 Ming Ave, Bakersfield (93309-4802)
PHONE..................661 398-2000
Charles Moe, *Branch Mgr*
Harlan Alpert, *Technician*
EMP: 168

SALES (corp-wide): 170.7B Publicly Held
WEB: www.dsdllc.com
SIC: 4813 Local & long distance telephone communications
HQ: At&T Services, Inc.
 208 S Akard St Ste 110
 Dallas TX 75202
 210 821-4105

(P-5324)
AT&T SERVICES INC
610 Brannan St, San Francisco
(94107-1512)
PHONE..................415 545-9051
EMP: 187
SALES (corp-wide): 146.8B Publicly Held
SIC: 4813
HQ: At&T Services, Inc.
 208 S Akard St Ste 110
 Dallas TX 75202
 210 821-4105

(P-5325)
AT&T SERVICES INC
Also Called: SBC
303 Church St, Jackson (95642-2103)
PHONE..................209 223-0012
Dan Adam, *Manager*
EMP: 168
SALES (corp-wide): 170.7B Publicly Held
WEB: www.dsdllc.com
SIC: 4813 Local telephone communications
HQ: At&T Services, Inc.
 208 S Akard St Ste 110
 Dallas TX 75202
 210 821-4105

(P-5326)
AT&T SERVICES INC
50101 Office Park Dr, Bakersfield (93304)
PHONE..................661 327-6030
Janice Bernette, *Manager*
EMP: 270
SALES (corp-wide): 170.7B Publicly Held
WEB: www.dsdllc.com
SIC: 4813 4812 Local telephone communications; radio telephone communication
HQ: At&T Services, Inc.
 208 S Akard St Ste 110
 Dallas TX 75202
 210 821-4105

(P-5327)
AT&T SERVICES INC
Also Called: SBC
200 W Center Street Prome, Anaheim
(92805-3960)
PHONE..................210 886-4922
Heewon Lee, *Exec Dir*
Aleck Galuska, *Technical Staff*
George Warf, *Sr Project Mgr*
EMP: 168
SALES (corp-wide): 170.7B Publicly Held
WEB: www.dsdllc.com
SIC: 4813 Telephone communication, except radio
HQ: At&T Services, Inc.
 208 S Akard St Ste 110
 Dallas TX 75202
 210 821-4105

(P-5328)
AT&T SERVICES INC
Also Called: SBC
7337 Trade St Rm 3600, San Diego
(92121-2423)
PHONE..................858 886-2762
John Nelson, *Manager*
Kellie Scroggins, *Info Tech Mgr*
Chuck Ault, *Technical Mgr*
Fred Kaelber, *Technical Staff*
Doug Shimansky, *Director*
EMP: 168
SALES (corp-wide): 170.7B Publicly Held
WEB: www.dsdllc.com
SIC: 4813 Telephone communication, except radio

HQ: At&T Services, Inc.
 208 S Akard St Ste 110
 Dallas TX 75202
 210 821-4105

(P-5329)
AT&T SERVICES INC
1834 W Victoria Ave, Anaheim
(92804-2537)
P.O. Box 3644, Tustin (92781-3644)
PHONE..................714 259-4441
Glyns Falls, *Manager*
EMP: 168
SALES (corp-wide): 170.7B Publicly Held
WEB: www.dsdllc.com
SIC: 4813 Telephone communication, except radio
HQ: At&T Services, Inc.
 208 S Akard St Ste 110
 Dallas TX 75202
 210 821-4105

(P-5330)
AT&T SERVICES INC
Also Called: SBC
3580 Warm St, Riverside (92501)
PHONE..................951 369-2282
EMP: 168
SALES (corp-wide): 170.7B Publicly Held
WEB: www.dsdllc.com
SIC: 4813 Telephone communication, except radio
HQ: At&T Services, Inc.
 208 S Akard St Ste 110
 Dallas TX 75202
 210 821-4105

(P-5331)
AT&T SERVICES INC
Also Called: SBC
908 28th St, Paso Robles (93446-1250)
PHONE..................805 237-9503
EMP: 168
SALES (corp-wide): 170.7B Publicly Held
WEB: www.dsdllc.com
SIC: 4813 Telephone communication, except radio
HQ: At&T Services, Inc.
 208 S Akard St Ste 110
 Dallas TX 75202
 210 821-4105

(P-5332)
AT&T SERVICES INC
Also Called: S B C
787 Munras Ave, Monterey (93940-3128)
PHONE..................831 649-2029
Carlime Plummer, *General Mgr*
Klyde Aipoalani, *Manager*
EMP: 66
SALES (corp-wide): 170.7B Publicly Held
WEB: www.dsdllc.com
SIC: 4813 Local telephone communications
HQ: At&T Services, Inc.
 208 S Akard St Ste 110
 Dallas TX 75202
 210 821-4105

(P-5333)
AT&T SERVICES INC
Also Called: SBC
360 Pioneer Way, Mountain View
(94041-1506)
PHONE..................650 960-2255
Nancy Cruz, *Manager*
EMP: 153
SALES (corp-wide): 170.7B Publicly Held
WEB: www.dsdllc.com
SIC: 4813 Telephone communication, except radio
HQ: At&T Services, Inc.
 208 S Akard St Ste 110
 Dallas TX 75202
 210 821-4105

(P-5334)
AT&T SERVICES INC
3464 El Camino Ave, Sacramento
(95821-6310)
P.O. Box 15038 (95851-0038)
PHONE..................916 972-2248
Ed Widker, *Manager*
EMP: 168
SALES (corp-wide): 170.7B Publicly Held
WEB: www.dsdllc.com
SIC: 4813 Telephone communication, except radio
HQ: At&T Services, Inc.
 208 S Akard St Ste 110
 Dallas TX 75202
 210 821-4105

(P-5335)
AT&T SERVICES INC
Also Called: SBC
1010 Wilshire Blvd, Los Angeles
(90017-5662)
PHONE..................213 975-4089
Cathy Bazieto, *Branch Mgr*
EMP: 720
SALES (corp-wide): 170.7B Publicly Held
WEB: www.dsdllc.com
SIC: 4813 2741 7331 4812 Local & long distance telephone communications; local telephone communications; directories, telephone: publishing only, not printed on site; direct mail advertising services; radio telephone communication
HQ: At&T Services, Inc.
 208 S Akard St Ste 110
 Dallas TX 75202
 210 821-4105

(P-5336)
AT&T SERVICES INC
666 Folsom St Rm 1132, San Francisco
(94107-1397)
PHONE..................415 545-9058
EMP: 90
SALES (corp-wide): 160.5B Publicly Held
SIC: 4813 4812
HQ: At&T Services, Inc.
 208 S Akard St Ste 110
 Dallas TX 75202
 210 821-4105

(P-5337)
AT&T SERVICES INC
1270 Arroyo Way, Walnut Creek
(94596-4216)
PHONE..................510 836-6889
Bill Blase, *Manager*
Robert C Wiles, *Analyst*
Robert Bailey, *Consultant*
EMP: 270
SALES (corp-wide): 170.7B Publicly Held
WEB: www.dsdllc.com
SIC: 4813 7375 4812 Telephone communication, except radio; information retrieval services; radio telephone communication
HQ: At&T Services, Inc.
 208 S Akard St Ste 110
 Dallas TX 75202
 210 821-4105

(P-5338)
AT&T SERVICES INC
Also Called: SBC Communications
2615 Mercantile Dr, Rancho Cordova
(95742-6521)
PHONE..................916 638-6096
Scott Heiser, *Manager*
EMP: 180
SALES (corp-wide): 170.7B Publicly Held
WEB: www.dsdllc.com
SIC: 4813 1542 Telephone communication, except radio; nonresidential construction
HQ: At&T Services, Inc.
 208 S Akard St Ste 110
 Dallas TX 75202
 210 821-4105

PRODUCTS & SVCS

(P-5339)
AT&T SERVICES INC
Also Called: SBC
2125 Occidental Rd, Santa Rosa
(95401-9034)
PHONE.....................707 545-5000
Curtis Cavin, *Manager*
EMP: 180
SALES (corp-wide): 170.7B **Publicly Held**
WEB: www.dsdllc.com
SIC: 4813 4812 Local telephone communications; radio telephone communication
HQ: At&T Services, Inc.
208 S Akard St Ste 110
Dallas TX 75202
210 821-4105

(P-5340)
AT&T SERVICES INC
1480 Burlingame Ave, Burlingame
(94010-4111)
PHONE.....................650 579-5266
Sally Calvert, *Branch Mgr*
EMP: 168
SALES (corp-wide): 170.7B **Publicly Held**
WEB: www.dsdllc.com
SIC: 4813 Local telephone communications
HQ: At&T Services, Inc.
208 S Akard St Ste 110
Dallas TX 75202
210 821-4105

(P-5341)
AT&T SERVICES INC
1122 Western St, Fairfield (94533-2459)
PHONE.....................707 428-2512
Carl Alexander, *Branch Mgr*
EMP: 450
SALES (corp-wide): 170.7B **Publicly Held**
WEB: www.dsdllc.com
SIC: 4813 Local telephone communications
HQ: At&T Services, Inc.
208 S Akard St Ste 110
Dallas TX 75202
210 821-4105

(P-5342)
AT&T SERVICES INC
Also Called: SBC
1900 S Grand Ave Rm 100, Los Angeles
(90007-1436)
PHONE.....................213 741-3111
Al Hernandez, *Branch Mgr*
EMP: 50
SALES (corp-wide): 170.7B **Publicly Held**
WEB: www.dsdllc.com
SIC: 4813 Local telephone communications
HQ: At&T Services, Inc.
208 S Akard St Ste 110
Dallas TX 75202
210 821-4105

(P-5343)
AT&T SERVICES INC
Also Called: SBC
485 S Monroe St 13a, San Jose (95128)
PHONE.....................408 554-3335
EMP: 168
SALES (corp-wide): 160.5B **Publicly Held**
SIC: 4813
HQ: At&T Services, Inc.
208 S Akard St Ste 110
Dallas TX 75202
210 821-4105

(P-5344)
AT&T SERVICES INC
Also Called: SBC
140 New Montgomery St, San Francisco
(94105-3705)
PHONE.....................415 394-3000
Ed Mueller, *President*
Michael J Fitzpatrick, *President*
L N Causby,
Steven P Coger,
Ruth Dev,
EMP: 270

SALES (corp-wide): 170.7B **Publicly Held**
WEB: www.dsdllc.com
SIC: 4813 2741 Local & long distance telephone communications; directories, telephone: publishing only, not printed on site

(P-5345)
AT&T SERVICES INC
146 S Broadway, Escondido (92025-4239)
PHONE.....................760 489-3519
EMP: 168
SALES (corp-wide): 170.7B **Publicly Held**
WEB: www.dsdllc.com
SIC: 4813 Local telephone communications
HQ: At&T Services, Inc.
208 S Akard St Ste 110
Dallas TX 75202
210 821-4105

(P-5346)
AT&T SERVICES INC
Also Called: SBC
8925 Orangethorpe Ave, Buena Park
(90621-3716)
PHONE.....................714 992-3359
Pat Gonzalez, *Systems Analyst*
Long T Truong, *Technical Staff*
EMP: 89
SALES (corp-wide): 170.7B **Publicly Held**
WEB: www.dsdllc.com
SIC: 4813 2741 4822 7331 Local & long distance telephone communications; local telephone communications; voice telephone communications; data telephone communications; directories, telephone: publishing only, not printed on site; telegraph & other communications; electronic mail; direct mail advertising services; radio telephone communication
HQ: At&T Services, Inc.
208 S Akard St Ste 110
Dallas TX 75202
210 821-4105

(P-5347)
AT&T SERVICES INC
Also Called: SBC
1714 Colfax St Ste 300, Concord
(94520-2134)
PHONE.....................925 671-1902
Jennifer Sullivan, *Manager*
EMP: 90
SALES (corp-wide): 170.7B **Publicly Held**
WEB: www.dsdllc.com
SIC: 4813 4812 Local telephone communications; radio telephone communication
HQ: At&T Services, Inc.
208 S Akard St Ste 110
Dallas TX 75202
210 821-4105

(P-5348)
AT&T SERVICES INC
2345 Pine St, San Francisco (94115-2714)
PHONE.....................415 774-1957
Robert L Miller, *Branch Mgr*
EMP: 168
SALES (corp-wide): 170.7B **Publicly Held**
WEB: www.dsdllc.com
SIC: 4813 Local telephone communications
HQ: At&T Services, Inc.
208 S Akard St Ste 110
Dallas TX 75202
210 821-4105

(P-5349)
AT&T SERVICES INC
7701 Artesia Blvd, Buena Park
(90621-2313)
PHONE.....................510 732-0830
EMP: 168

SALES (corp-wide): 170.7B **Publicly Held**
WEB: www.dsdllc.com
SIC: 4813 Local & long distance telephone communications
HQ: At&T Services, Inc.
208 S Akard St Ste 110
Dallas TX 75202
210 821-4105

(P-5350)
AT&T SERVICES INC
Also Called: SBC
1821 24th St Rm 122, Sacramento
(95816-7208)
PHONE.....................916 453-6267
Steven Solis, *Principal*
EMP: 69
SALES (corp-wide): 170.7B **Publicly Held**
WEB: www.dsdllc.com
SIC: 4813 Local & long distance telephone communications
HQ: At&T Services, Inc.
208 S Akard St Ste 110
Dallas TX 75202
210 821-4105

(P-5351)
AT&T SERVICES INC
Also Called: SBC
2727 Oceanside Blvd, Oceanside
(92054-4542)
PHONE.....................760 722-7261
Daniel Menendez, *Manager*
EMP: 168
SALES (corp-wide): 170.7B **Publicly Held**
WEB: www.dsdllc.com
SIC: 4813 Local telephone communications
HQ: At&T Services, Inc.
208 S Akard St Ste 110
Dallas TX 75202
210 821-4105

(P-5352)
AT&T SERVICES INC
Also Called: SBC
3707 Kings Way, Sacramento
(95821-6405)
PHONE.....................916 972-2423
Hector Lenaos, *Manager*
EMP: 114
SALES (corp-wide): 170.7B **Publicly Held**
WEB: www.dsdllc.com
SIC: 4813 4812 Telephone communication, except radio; radio telephone communication
HQ: At&T Services, Inc.
208 S Akard St Ste 110
Dallas TX 75202
210 821-4105

(P-5353)
AT&T SERVICES INC
Also Called: SBC
1033 Shary Cir Ste A, Concord
(94518-2469)
PHONE.....................925 671-1059
EMP: 450
SQ FT: 15,600
SALES (corp-wide): 170.7B **Publicly Held**
WEB: www.dsdllc.com
SIC: 4813 4812 Local & long distance telephone communications; radio telephone communication
HQ: At&T Services, Inc.
208 S Akard St Ste 110
Dallas TX 75202
210 821-4105

(P-5354)
AT&T SERVICES INC
Also Called: SBC
7650 Convoy Ct Ste 106, San Diego
(92111-1104)
PHONE.....................858 495-3907
Pattie St Clair, *Branch Mgr*
EMP: 450

SALES (corp-wide): 170.7B **Publicly Held**
WEB: www.dsdllc.com
SIC: 4813 4812 Local & long distance telephone communications; local telephone communications; radio telephone communication
HQ: At&T Services, Inc.
208 S Akard St Ste 110
Dallas TX 75202
210 821-4105

(P-5355)
AT&T SERVICES INC
Also Called: SBC
950 W Washington Ave, Escondido
(92025-1637)
PHONE.....................760 489-3187
George Rivera, *Principal*
EMP: 450
SALES (corp-wide): 170.7B **Publicly Held**
WEB: www.dsdllc.com
SIC: 4813 2741 4822 7331 Local & long distance telephone communications; local telephone communications; voice telephone communications; data telephone communications; directories, telephone: publishing only, not printed on site; telegraph & other communications; electronic mail; direct mail advertising services; radio telephone communication
HQ: At&T Services, Inc.
208 S Akard St Ste 110
Dallas TX 75202
210 821-4105

(P-5356)
AT&T SERVICES INC
1755 Locust St Fl 2, Walnut Creek
(94596-4120)
PHONE.....................925 943-4383
Timothy Bayliss, *Manager*
EMP: 450
SALES (corp-wide): 170.7B **Publicly Held**
WEB: www.dsdllc.com
SIC: 4813 Telephone communication, except radio
HQ: At&T Services, Inc.
208 S Akard St Ste 110
Dallas TX 75202
210 821-4105

(P-5357)
AT&T SERVICES INC
1429 N Gower St, Los Angeles
(90028-8317)
PHONE.....................323 468-6813
Dovon Green, *Branch Mgr*
EMP: 450
SALES (corp-wide): 170.7B **Publicly Held**
WEB: www.dsdllc.com
SIC: 4813 Local telephone communications
HQ: At&T Services, Inc.
208 S Akard St Ste 110
Dallas TX 75202
210 821-4105

(P-5358)
AT&T SERVICES INC
504 C 1550, Oakland (94612)
PHONE.....................510 645-7684
Paul Burke, *Branch Mgr*
EMP: 168
SALES (corp-wide): 170.7B **Publicly Held**
WEB: www.dsdllc.com
SIC: 4813 Local telephone communications
HQ: At&T Services, Inc.
208 S Akard St Ste 110
Dallas TX 75202
210 821-4105

(P-5359)
AT&T SERVICES INC
Also Called: SBC
501 S Marengo Ave, Alhambra
(91803-1640)
PHONE.....................626 308-8582
Ed Mueller, *CEO*
EMP: 450

▲ = Import ▼=Export
◆ =Import/Export

SALES (corp-wide): 170.7B **Publicly Held**
WEB: www.dsdllc.com
SIC: **4813** 4812 Local telephone communications; radio telephone communication
HQ: At&T Services, Inc.
208 S Akard St Ste 110
Dallas TX 75202
210 821-4105

(P-5360)
AT&T SERVICES INC
2600 Camino Ramon Rm 1-E, San Ramon (94583-5000)
PHONE.....................415 823-0993
Greg Torretta, *Exec Dir*
Sophia Chang,
EMP: 168
SALES (corp-wide): 170.7B **Publicly Held**
WEB: www.dsdllc.com
SIC: **4813** Local telephone communications
HQ: At&T Services, Inc.
208 S Akard St Ste 110
Dallas TX 75202
210 821-4105

(P-5361)
AT&T SERVICES INC
Also Called: SBC
5285 Doyle Rd Rm 3, San Jose (95129-4230)
PHONE.....................408 973-7504
Art Sebantis, *Manager*
EMP: 63
SALES (corp-wide): 170.7B **Publicly Held**
WEB: www.dsdllc.com
SIC: **4813** Telephone communication, except radio
HQ: At&T Services, Inc.
208 S Akard St Ste 110
Dallas TX 75202
210 821-4105

(P-5362)
AUTOMATTIC INC
60 29th St Ste 343, San Francisco (94110-4929)
PHONE.....................877 273-3049
Mattew Mullenweg, *CEO*
Mark Davies, *CFO*
Stuart West, *CFO*
MO Carter, *Executive*
Toni Schneider, *Admin Sec*
EMP: 62
SALES (est): 27MM **Privately Held**
SIC: **4813** 7375 7371 ; information retrieval services; data base information retrieval; on-line data base information retrieval; computer software development & applications

(P-5363)
AVAYA INC
18201 Von Karman Ave # 600, Irvine (92612-1176)
PHONE.....................949 225-5678
Marci Mobely, *Principal*
EMP: 111 **Publicly Held**
WEB: www.avaya.com
SIC: **4813**
HQ: Avaya Inc.
4655 Great America Pkwy
Santa Clara CA 95054
908 953-6000

(P-5364)
AXAIO INDUSTRIES LLC
538 S Oxford Ave Apt 302, Los Angeles (90020-4288)
PHONE.....................323 504-1074
An Arafat Abir,
EMP: 50
SALES (est): 555.1K **Privately Held**
SIC: **4813**

(P-5365)
BIZRINGER INC
1221 E Dyer Rd Ste 250, Santa Ana (92705-5678)
PHONE.....................949 396-0162
Vivek Baid, *CEO*
Ratan Baid, *President*
EMP: 75 **EST: 2013**

SALES (est): 1.9MM **Privately Held**
SIC: **4813** 7389 Telephone communication, except radio;

(P-5366)
BLUE CASA COMMUNICATIONS INC
114 E Haley St Ste A, Santa Barbara (93101-2347)
PHONE.....................805 966-1669
Donald N Oas, *CEO*
Brian Plackischeng, *CFO*
Todd Eichler, *Director*
EMP: 50
SALES (est): 5.2MM **Privately Held**
WEB: www.bluecasa.com
SIC: **4813** Telephone communications broker

(P-5367)
BRAFTON INCORPORATED
220 Montgomery St Ste 917, San Francisco (94104-3440)
PHONE.....................617 206-3040
Ian Loader, *Director*
EMP: 63 **Privately Held**
SIC: **4813**
PA: Brafton, Incorporated
2 Oliver St Lbby 2 # 2
Boston MA 02109

(P-5368)
BRIGHTERTECH INCORPORATED
510 Strtford Ct Unit 204a, Del Mar (92014)
PHONE.....................310 909-4940
Thomas Gonzales, *President*
EMP: 50
SALES (est): 351K **Privately Held**
SIC: **4813**

(P-5369)
BROADSPIRE INC
19425 Soled Canyo Rd Ste, Santa Clarita (91351)
PHONE.....................213 785-8043
Suresh Srinivasan, *CEO*
Arun Srinivasan, *COO*
Muniz Isabel, *Administration*
Gonzalez Ruby, *Med Doctor*
Jones Bonnie, *Manager*
EMP: 65 **EST: 2000**
SALES (est): 3.8MM **Privately Held**
WEB: www.broadspire.com
SIC: **4813**
PA: Platinum Equity, Llc
360 N Crescent Dr Bldg S
Beverly Hills CA 90210

(P-5370)
CAL CONSOLDATED COMMUNICATIONS
211 Lincoln St, Roseville (95678-2614)
PHONE.....................916 786-6141
Bob Udell, *CEO*
David Herrick, *Vice Pres*
James Player, *Engineer*
Doreen Paige, *Human Res Mgr*
Mike Johnson, *Manager*
EMP: 78
SQ FT: 21,500
SALES (est): 7.6MM
SALES (corp-wide): 1.4B **Publicly Held**
SIC: **4813** Local telephone communications; long distance telephone communications
HQ: Surewest Communications
211 Lincoln St
Roseville CA 95678
916 786-6141

(P-5371)
CALIFRNIA RGIONAL INTRANET INC
Also Called: Carinet
8929 Complex Dr Ste A, San Diego (92123-1454)
PHONE.....................858 974-5080
Tim Caulfield, *CEO*
Michael C Robert, *CFO*
Joe McMillen, *Principal*
Esfandiar Namiranian, *IT/INT Sup*
EMP: 85

SQ FT: 40,000
SALES (est): 16.8MM **Privately Held**
WEB: www.cari.net
SIC: **4813**

(P-5372)
CBS MAXPREPS INC
4364 Town Center Blvd # 320, El Dorado Hills (95762-7127)
PHONE.....................530 676-6440
Andy Beal, *President*
Bryce Escobar, *Project Mgr*
John Stockett, *Merchandising*
Rui Ewald, *Director*
Todd Shurtleff, *Director*
EMP: 50
SQ FT: 9,000
SALES (est): 8.5MM
SALES (corp-wide): 25.9B **Publicly Held**
WEB: www.maxpreps.com
SIC: **4813**
HQ: Cbs Corporation
51 W 52nd St Bsmt 1
New York NY 10019
212 975-4321

(P-5373)
CDNETWORKS INC (DH)
1550 Valley Vista Dr # 110, Diamond Bar (91765-3929)
PHONE.....................408 228-3379
Jongchan Kim, *CEO*
John J Kang, *President*
Samuyeol Ko, *President*
EMP: 50
SALES (est): 18.2MM
SALES (corp-wide): 912.9MM **Privately Held**
SIC: **4813**

(P-5374)
CERTONA CORPORATION
10431 Wtridge Cir Ste 200, San Diego (92121)
PHONE.....................858 369-3888
David Post, *CEO*
Meyar Sheik, *Officer*
Ram Venkataraman, *Officer*
Vinesh Vis, *Officer*
Yvonne Blankenship, *Vice Pres*
EMP: 140
SALES (est): 9.2MM
SALES (corp-wide): 58.1MM **Privately Held**
SIC: **4813**
PA: Kibo Software, Inc.
717 N Harwood St Ste 1800
Dallas TX 75201
707 780-1600

(P-5375)
CLEAR WORLD COMMUNICATIONS
3100 S Harbor Blvd # 300, Santa Ana (92704-6823)
PHONE.....................714 445-3900
Mike Mancuso, *President*
James Mancuso, *Admin Sec*
EMP: 450
SQ FT: 10,000
SALES (est): 27.7MM **Privately Held**
SIC: **4813**

(P-5376)
CLEARCAPTIONS LLC
3001 Lava Ridge Ct # 100, Roseville (95661-2837)
PHONE.....................866 868-8695
Robert Rae, *President*
Corrine Perritano, *COO*
Raghu Dhulipala, *Officer*
Rita Beier Braman, *Vice Pres*
Gordon L Ellis, *Vice Pres*
EMP: 50 **EST: 2015**
SALES (est): 3.1MM
SALES (corp-wide): 288.6MM **Privately Held**
SIC: **4813** ; telephone/video communications
PA: Purple Communications, Inc.
595 Menlo Dr
Rocklin CA 95765
888 600-4780

(P-5377)
CLOVER NETWORK INC
415 N Mathilda Ave, Sunnyvale (94085-4222)
PHONE.....................650 210-7888
Leonard Speiser, *CEO*
Zan Aronowitz, *COO*
John Beatty, *Vice Pres*
Ronnie Mongon, *Vice Pres*
Walter Nirenberg, *VP Bus Dvlpt*
EMP: 65
SQ FT: 8,200
SALES (est): 9MM
SALES (corp-wide): 5.8B **Publicly Held**
WEB: www.clover.com
SIC: **4813**
HQ: First Data Corporation
225 Liberty St Fl 29
New York NY 10281
800 735-3362

(P-5378)
COFA MEDIA GROUP LLC
5650 El Camino Real, Carlsbad (92008-7124)
PHONE.....................877 293-2007
Edwin Lap, *CEO*
EMP: 84 **EST: 2009**
SALES (est): 224K
SALES (corp-wide): 58.5MM **Privately Held**
SIC: **4813**
PA: Geary Lsf Group, Inc.
332 Pine St Ste 600
San Francisco CA 94104
877 616-8226

(P-5379)
COMPUTER CONSULTING (PA)
600 Corporate Pointe # 1010, Culver City (90230-7677)
PHONE.....................310 568-5000
Brian Hardy, *President*
Shirley Franklin, *Vice Pres*
EMP: 2000
SQ FT: 20,000
SALES (est): 338.3MM **Privately Held**
WEB: www.ccops.com
SIC: **4813** 4899 5045 7378 Telephone communication, except radio; data communication services; computers, peripherals & software; computer maintenance & repair

(P-5380)
CONDUIT INC
180 Sansome St 18, San Francisco (94104-3713)
PHONE.....................650 340-1550
Ronen Shilo, *CEO*
Adam Boyden, *President*
Gaby Bilczyk, *COO*
Roy Gen, *CFO*
Dror Erez, *CTO*
EMP: 200
SALES (est): 9.3MM **Privately Held**
SIC: **4813**

(P-5381)
CONNEXITY INC (HQ)
Also Called: Shopzilla.com
2120 Colorado Ave Ste 400, Santa Monica (90404-3563)
PHONE.....................310 571-1235
William Glass, *CEO*
Blythe Holden, *Senior VP*
Lonna Bell Rimestad, *Senior VP*
Niladri Batabyal, *Vice Pres*
Bob Caputo, *Vice Pres*
EMP: 203
SALES (est): 121.2MM
SALES (corp-wide): 604.2MM **Privately Held**
WEB: www.shopzilla.com
SIC: **4813** 7383 7331 ; news syndicates; direct mail advertising services
PA: Symphony Technology Group, L.L.C.
428 University Ave
Palo Alto CA 94301
650 935-9500

(P-5382)
**COVAD COMMUNICATIONS
GROUP INC (DH)**
Also Called: Megapath
6800 Koll Center Pkwy, Pleasanton
(94566-7045)
PHONE..............................408 952-6400
D Craig Young, *CEO*
Brett Flinchum, *COO*
Jeffrey Bailey, *CFO*
Douglas A Carlen, *Senior VP*
Chris Tsichlis, *VP Human Res*
▲ EMP: 113
SQ FT: 133,310
SALES (est): 344.9MM
SALES (corp-wide): 124.6MM **Publicly
Held**
WEB: www.covad.com
SIC: **4813** Voice telephone communica-
tions; data telephone communications;
HQ: Fusion Mphc Holding Corporation
6800 Koll Center Pkwy
Pleasanton CA 94566
925 201-2500

(P-5383)
COX CALIFORNIA TELCOM LLC
43 Peninsula Ctr, Rllng HLS Est
(90274-3583)
PHONE..............................310 377-1800
Paul Fornelli, *Branch Mgr*
Katherine Paezle Harris, *Manager*
EMP: 85
SALES (corp-wide): 32.3B **Privately Held**
SIC: **4813** Telephone communication,
except radio
HQ: Cox California Telcom, L.L.C.
6205-B Pchtree Dnwoody Rd
Atlanta GA 30328

(P-5384)
COX COMMUNICATIONS INC
26181 Avenida Aeropuerto, San Juan
Capistrano (92675-4821)
PHONE..............................949 240-1212
Leo Brennan, *Branch Mgr*
EMP: 250
SALES (corp-wide): 32.3B **Privately Held**
SIC: **4813** Telephone communication, ex-
cept radio
HQ: Cox Communications, Inc.
6205 B Pchtree Dnwody Rd
Atlanta GA 30328

(P-5385)
COX COMMUNICATIONS INC
3303 State St, Santa Barbara
(93105-2603)
PHONE..............................805 681-6600
Janice Cass, *Branch Mgr*
Katherine Paezle Harris, *Manager*
Maureen Andrews, *Supervisor*
EMP: 85
SALES (corp-wide): 32.3B **Privately Held**
SIC: **4813** Telephone communication, ex-
cept radio
HQ: Cox Communications, Inc.
6205 B Pchtree Dnwody Rd
Atlanta GA 30328

(P-5386)
CREDO MOBILE INC
Also Called: Working Assets Long Distance
101 Market St Ste 700, San Francisco
(94105-1533)
P.O. Box 7015 (94120-7015)
PHONE..............................415 369-2000
Michael Hall Kieschnick, *CEO*
Janice Crump, *CFO*
Douglas Moore, *CFO*
Stephen Gunn, *Vice Pres*
Haruko Kurata, *Vice Pres*
EMP: 100
SQ FT: 21,000
SALES (est): 24.9MM **Privately Held**
WEB: www.giveforchange.com
SIC: **4813** Long distance telephone com-
munications

(P-5387)
CURATEL LLC
1605 W Olympic Blvd # 600, Los Angeles
(90015-3808)
PHONE..............................213 427-7411
Ron Sahar Azarkman,
Jerry Azarkman,
EMP: 300
SALES (est): 13.5MM **Privately Held**
WEB: www.curatel.com
SIC: **4813** Local & long distance telephone
communications

(P-5388)
DAVIS ZIFF PUBLISHING INC
235 2nd St, San Francisco (94105-3124)
PHONE..............................415 551-4800
Kenneth Evans, *Principal*
EMP: 150
SALES (corp-wide): 1.2B **Publicly Held**
WEB: www.zdnet.com
SIC: **4813**
HQ: Ziff Davis Publishing, Llc
28 E 28th St Fl 10
New York NY 10016

(P-5389)
DEVXCOM INC
Also Called: Development Exchange
310 Villa St, Mountain View (94041-1321)
PHONE..............................650 390-6553
James E Fawcette, *President*
Peter Horan, *CEO*
Jim Cook, *COO*
Greg Stern, *Vice Pres*
EMP: 50
SALES (est): 1.7MM **Privately Held**
SIC: **4813**

(P-5390)
DIGEX INC
2950 Zanker Rd, San Jose (95134-2113)
PHONE..............................408 468-5000
Benjamin Yang, *Principal*
EMP: 50
SALES (corp-wide): 130.8B **Publicly
Held**
WEB: www.digex.com
SIC: **4813**
HQ: Digex, Incorporated
14400 Sweitzer Ln
Laurel MD 20707

(P-5391)
DIGITAL PATH INC
1065 Marauder St, Chico (95973-9039)
PHONE..............................800 676-7284
James A Higgins, *President*
Erica Higgins, *CFO*
Maxwell Hinckley, *Engineer*
▲ EMP: 50
SALES (est): 20.1MM **Privately Held**
WEB: www.digitalpath.net
SIC: **4813** 5045 ; computers, peripherals
& software

(P-5392)
DIGITALMOJO INC
3111 Camino Del Rio N # 400, San Diego
(92108-5724)
PHONE..............................800 413-5916
Martin Smith, *CEO*
Martin Caverly, *CFO*
Jerry Papazian, *CFO*
Michael Hart, *Vice Pres*
Mary Khoury, *Vice Pres*
EMP: 75
SQ FT: 800
SALES (est): 4.3MM **Privately Held**
WEB: www.gobroadband.com
SIC: **4813** 8742 ; marketing consulting
services

(P-5393)
**DIVERSFIED CMMNCTIONS
SVCS INC**
Also Called: D C S
1260 Pioneer St, Brea (92821-3725)
PHONE..............................562 696-9660
Ken Doll, *President*
Steven Hurley, *Vice Pres*
Bill Shields, *Vice Pres*
Cesar Ramirez, *Project Mgr*
Elizabeth Brezden, *Payroll Mgr*

▲ EMP: 63
SQ FT: 19,000
SALES (est): 20.1MM **Privately Held**
WEB: www.diversified.net
SIC: **4813** Telephone communications bro-
ker

(P-5394)
DOCIRCLE INC
Also Called: Trumpia
2544 W Woodland Dr, Anaheim
(92801-2636)
PHONE..............................415 484-4221
Kyung Hoon Rhie, *CEO*
Grace Rhie, *CEO*
Jihoon Koo, *CTO*
Rosendo Inzunza, *Technical Staff*
Andrew Su, *Technical Staff*
EMP: 50
SALES (est): 8MM **Privately Held**
SIC: **4813**

(P-5395)
ECOMPANIES LLC
2120 Colorado Ave Fl 3, Santa Monica
(90404-5510)
PHONE..............................310 586-4000
Jake Winebaum,
Sky Dayton,
EMP: 50
SALES: 38.2K **Privately Held**
WEB: www.ecompanies.com
SIC: **4813**

(P-5396)
EDGEWATER NETWORKS INC
5225 Hellyer Ave Ste 100, San Jose
(95138-1021)
PHONE..............................408 351-7200
David G Norman, *CEO*
Steve Pattison, *COO*
John Macario, *Senior VP*
Rumus Sakya, *Senior VP*
Russell Johnson, *Vice Pres*
▲ EMP: 75
SALES (est): 16.1MM
SALES (corp-wide): 618.5MM **Publicly
Held**
WEB: www.edgewaternetworks.com
SIC: **4813** Telephone/video communica-
tions
PA: Ribbon Communications Inc.
4 Technology Park Dr
Westford MA 01886
978 614-8100

(P-5397)
ENVIVIO INC
535 Mission St Fl 27, San Francisco
(94105-3224)
PHONE..............................650 243-2700
Julien Signes, *President*
Terry D Kramer, *Ch of Bd*
Erik E Miller, *CFO*
Jean-Pierre Henot, *CTO*
EMP: 163
SALES (est): 33.6MM
SALES (corp-wide): 23.4B **Privately Held**
WEB: www.envivio.com
SIC: **4813** Telephone/video communica-
tions
HQ: Ericsson Inc.
6300 Legacy Dr
Plano TX 75024
972 583-0000

(P-5398)
ERICSSON INC
2755 Augustine Dr, Santa Clara
(95054-2919)
PHONE..............................408 750-5000
Kevin A Denuccio, *Manager*
EMP: 1100
SALES (corp-wide): 23.4B **Privately Held**
WEB: www.redbacknetworks.com
SIC: **4813** Telephone communication, ex-
cept radio
HQ: Ericsson Inc.
6300 Legacy Dr
Plano TX 75024
972 583-0000

(P-5399)
EXTREME TELECOM INC
9221 Corbin Ave Ste 260, Northridge
(91324-1625)
PHONE..............................818 902-4821
ARI Ramezani, *CEO*
James Murphy, *President*
EMP: 113 EST: 1997
SQ FT: 12,000
SALES (est): 5.4MM **Privately Held**
SIC: **4813**

(P-5400)
FLEXTRONICS INTL USA INC
Also Called: Flextronics Global Services
890 Yosemite Dr Bldg 14, Milpitas
(95035-5437)
PHONE..............................408 576-6769
Mike McNamara, *Principal*
EMP: 170
SALES (corp-wide): 26.2B **Privately Held**
SIC: **4813** Telephone communication, ex-
cept radio
HQ: Flextronics International Usa, Inc.
6201 America Center Dr
San Jose CA 95002

(P-5401)
**FREE CONFERENCING
CORPORATION**
Also Called: Freeconferencecall.com
4300 E Pacific Coast Hwy, Long Beach
(90804-2114)
P.O. Box 41069 (90853-1069)
PHONE..............................562 437-1411
David Erickson, *CEO*
Josh Lowenthal, *COO*
Scott Southron, *CFO*
Robert Wise, *Exec VP*
Jeff Erickson, *Vice Pres*
EMP: 116
SQ FT: 10,000
SALES: 65MM **Privately Held**
SIC: **4813** 7389 Voice telephone commu-
nications;

(P-5402)
FRONTIER CALIFORNIA INC
Also Called: Verizon
83793 Dr Carreon Blvd, Indio
(92201-7035)
PHONE..............................760 342-0500
EMP: 64
SALES (corp-wide): 8.6B **Publicly Held**
SIC: **4813** Local & long distance telephone
communications
HQ: Frontier California Inc.
140 West St
New York NY 10007
212 395-1000

(P-5403)
FRONTIER CALIFORNIA INC
Also Called: Verizon
200 W Church St, Santa Maria
(93458-5005)
PHONE..............................805 925-0000
Carrie Ramsey, *Manager*
EMP: 64
SALES (corp-wide): 8.6B **Publicly Held**
SIC: **4813** Long distance telephone com-
munications
HQ: Frontier California Inc.
140 West St
New York NY 10007
212 395-1000

(P-5404)
FRONTIER CALIFORNIA INC
Also Called: Verizon
510 Park Ave, San Fernando (91340-2527)
PHONE..............................818 365-0542
Gloria Caudill, *Branch Mgr*
EMP: 150
SALES (corp-wide): 8.6B **Publicly Held**
SIC: **4813** Telephone communication, ex-
cept radio
HQ: Frontier California Inc.
140 West St
New York NY 10007
212 395-1000

(P-5405)
FRONTIER CALIFORNIA INC
Also Called: Verizon
525 E Yosemite Ave, Manteca
(95336-5806)
P.O. Box 992 (95336-1139)
PHONE.....................209 239-4128
Luanne Weldon, *Branch Mgr*
EMP: 180
SALES (corp-wide): 8.6B **Publicly Held**
SIC: 4813 4812 Local telephone communications; radio telephone communication
HQ: Frontier California Inc.
140 West St
New York NY 10007
212 395-1000

(P-5406)
FRONTIER CALIFORNIA INC
Also Called: Verizon
1 Wellpoint Way, Westlake Village
(91362-3893)
PHONE.....................805 372-6000
Alex Stadler, *Principal*
John Dixon,
EMP: 64
SALES (corp-wide): 8.6B **Publicly Held**
SIC: 4813 Telephone communication, except radio
HQ: Frontier California Inc.
140 West St
New York NY 10007
212 395-1000

(P-5407)
FRONTIER CALIFORNIA INC
Also Called: Verizon
200 W Firebaugh Ave, Exeter
(93221-1653)
PHONE.....................559 592-2100
Steve Bryant, *Branch Mgr*
EMP: 64
SALES (corp-wide): 8.6B **Publicly Held**
SIC: 4813 Local telephone communications
HQ: Frontier California Inc.
140 West St
New York NY 10007
212 395-1000

(P-5408)
FRONTIIR CORPORATION
1586 Parkview Ave Apt 3, San Jose
(95130-1042)
PHONE.....................510 996-2071
Godfrey Tan, *CEO*
EMP: 250
SALES: 3MM **Privately Held**
SIC: 4813 7389 ;

(P-5409)
FUSION CLOUD COMPANY LLC (DH)
6800 Koll Center Pkwy, Pleasanton
(94566-7045)
PHONE.....................925 201-2500
Donald C Young, *Mng Member*
Derek Heins,
Paul Milley,
EMP: 55
SALES (est): 127.6MM
SALES (corp-wide): 124.6MM **Publicly Held**
SIC: 4813 Data telephone communications
HQ: Covad Communications Group, Inc.
6800 Koll Center Pkwy
Pleasanton CA 94566
408 952-6400

(P-5410)
FUSION MPHC GROUP INC
2510 Zanker Rd, San Jose (95131-1127)
PHONE.....................408 324-1353
EMP: 203
SALES (corp-wide): 124.6MM **Publicly Held**
WEB: www.covad.com
SIC: 4813 Data telephone communications
HQ: Covad Communications Group, Inc.
6800 Koll Center Pkwy
Pleasanton CA 94566
408 952-6400

(P-5411)
GAIA INTERACTIVE INC
Also Called: Gaia Online
2540 N 1st St Ste 101, San Jose
(95131-1016)
PHONE.....................408 573-8800
Gary A Schofield, *CEO*
Elaine Kitagawa, *CFO*
▲ **EMP:** 105
SALES (est): 15MM **Privately Held**
SIC: 4813

(P-5412)
GLOBAL DOMAINS INTERNATIONAL
Also Called: Worldsite.ws
701 Palomar Airport Rd # 300, Carlsbad
(92011-1027)
PHONE.....................760 602-3000
Michael S Starr, *President*
Allen Ezier, *Vice Pres*
Stas Yakovina, *Info Tech Dir*
Imad Kawar, *Controller*
Paul Apanowicz, *Director*
EMP: 50
SQ FT: 5,000
SALES: 14MM **Privately Held**
WEB: www.globaldomainsinternational.com
SIC: 4813

(P-5413)
GOOGLE FIBER INC (DH)
1600 Amphitheatre Pkwy, Mountain View
(94043-1351)
PHONE.....................650 253-0000
Milo Medin, *Vice Pres*
EMP: 74 **EST:** 2010
SALES (est): 37.9MM
SALES (corp-wide): 136.8B **Publicly Held**
SIC: 4813
HQ: Google Llc
1600 Amphitheatre Pkwy
Mountain View CA 94043
650 253-0000

(P-5414)
GOOGLE INTERNATIONAL LLC (DH)
1600 Amphitheatre Pkwy, Mountain View
(94043-1351)
PHONE.....................650 253-0000
Eric Schmidt, *Ch of Bd*
Larry Page, *CEO*
David C Drummond, *Senior VP*
Debbie Newhouse, *Marketing Mgr*
Dave Rolefson, *Director*
▼ **EMP:** 76
SALES (est): 1.7B
SALES (corp-wide): 136.8B **Publicly Held**
SIC: 4813 7375 ; ; information retrieval services
HQ: Google Llc
1600 Amphitheatre Pkwy
Mountain View CA 94043
650 253-0000

(P-5415)
GTT COMMUNICATIONS (MP) INC (DH)
Also Called: Megapath
6700 Koll Center Pkwy, Pleasanton
(94566-7060)
PHONE.....................925 201-2500
Craig Young, *CEO*
Kurt Hoffman, *Co-President*
Steve Chisholm, *Senior VP*
David Williams, *Senior VP*
EMP: 150
SQ FT: 12,000
SALES (est): 95.3MM **Publicly Held**
WEB: www.megapath.net
SIC: 4813 7375 ; information retrieval services
HQ: Gtt Americas, Llc
7900 Tysons One Pl
Mc Lean VA 22102
703 442-5500

(P-5416)
HIVE TECH GURUS INCORPORATED
510 Strtford Ct Unit 204a, Del Mar (92014)
PHONE.....................323 445-1770

Adrian Escobar, *President*
EMP: 50 **EST:** 2017
SALES (est): 351K **Privately Held**
SIC: 4813

(P-5417)
HORNITOS TELEPHONE CO
Also Called: TDS
2896 Bear Vly, Hornitos (95325)
PHONE.....................608 831-1000
David Wittwer, *President*
Mike Gasser, *Principal*
EMP: 99
SQ FT: 4,000
SALES: 950K
SALES (corp-wide): 5.1B **Publicly Held**
SIC: 4813 Telephone communication, except radio
HQ: Tds Telecommunications Corporation
525 Junction Rd Ste 1000
Madison WI 53717
608 664-4000

(P-5418)
HOTWIRE INC
114 Sansome St Ste 400, San Francisco
(94104-3810)
PHONE.....................415 343-8400
Dara Khosrowshahi, *CEO*
Clem Bason, *President*
Mahesh Jhala, *Administration*
Ash Sohi, *Administration*
Payal Mahajan, *Software Engr*
EMP: 175
SALES (est): 30.3MM
SALES (corp-wide): 11.2B **Publicly Held**
WEB: www.hotwire.com
SIC: 4813
PA: Expedia Group, Inc.
333 108th Ave Ne
Bellevue WA 98004
425 679-7200

(P-5419)
HUAWEI ENTERPRISE USA INC
20400 Stevens Creek Blvd, Cupertino
(95014-2217)
PHONE.....................408 394-4295
EMP: 80
SALES (est): 6.4MM **Privately Held**
SIC: 4813
PA: Huawei Investment & Holding Co., Ltd.
Bantian Huawei Base, Longgang District
Shenzhen 51812
-

(P-5420)
HULU LLC
12312 W Olympic Boulev, Los Angeles
(90064)
PHONE.....................888 631-4858
Mike Hopkins, *CEO*
EMP: 155
SALES (corp-wide): 90.2B **Publicly Held**
SIC: 4813 4833 ; television translator station
HQ: Hulu, Llc
2500 Broadway Ste 200
Santa Monica CA 90404

(P-5421)
HULU LLC (HQ)
2500 Broadway Ste 200, Santa Monica
(90404-3071)
PHONE.....................310 571-4700
Randy Freer, *CEO*
Alicia Coudurier, *Partner*
Jason Nellis, *Partner*
Chadwick Ho, *Senior VP*
Jim O'Donnell, *Vice Pres*
EMP: 170
SALES (est): 404MM
SALES (corp-wide): 90.2B **Publicly Held**
WEB: www.hulu.com
SIC: 4813 4833 ; television translator station
PA: The Walt Disney Company
500 S Buena Vista St
Burbank CA 91521
818 560-1000

(P-5422)
IAC PUBLISHING LLC
555 12th St Ste 300, Oakland
(94607-3698)
PHONE.....................510 985-7400
Adam Roston, *CEO*
Jeffrey Spitzer, *Vice Pres*
EMP: 100
SQ FT: 47,679
SALES (est): 1.7MM **Privately Held**
SIC: 4813

(P-5423)
IFNCOM INC (PA)
Also Called: Tollfreeforwarding.com
5901 W Century Blvd Fl 9, Los Angeles
(90045-5432)
PHONE.....................213 452-1505
Travis May, *CEO*
Jason O'Brien, *COO*
Adam Cheung, *Executive*
Josh May, *Executive*
John Carter, *Exec Dir*
▲ **EMP:** 51 **EST:** 2009
SQ FT: 3,000
SALES (est): 20.6MM **Privately Held**
SIC: 4813 Local & long distance telephone communications; voice telephone communications

(P-5424)
INGENIO INC
182 Howard St 826, San Francisco
(94105-1611)
PHONE.....................415 248-4000
Warren Heffelfinger, *CEO*
Mark Britto, *CEO*
EMP: 120
SQ FT: 25,000
SALES (est): 12.3MM
SALES (corp-wide): 170.7B **Publicly Held**
SIC: 4813
PA: At&T Inc.
208 S Akard St
Dallas TX 75202
210 821-4105

(P-5425)
INMOTION HOSTING INC
360 N Pacific Coast Hwy # 1055, El Segundo (90245-4414)
PHONE.....................888 321-4678
Dominic Napolitano, *Branch Mgr*
Mike Zyvoloski, *Marketing Staff*
EMP: 50
SALES (corp-wide): 26.6MM **Privately Held**
SIC: 4813
PA: Inmotion Hosting, Inc.
3629 Sentara Way Ste 303
Virginia Beach VA 23452
757 416-6575

(P-5426)
INREACH INTERNET LLC (HQ)
4635 Georgetown Pl, Stockton
(95207-6203)
P.O. Box 312, West Enfield ME (04493-0312)
PHONE.....................888 467-3224
EMP: 57
SQ FT: 5,075
SALES (est): 7.5MM
SALES (corp-wide): 16.4MM **Privately Held**
SIC: 4813
PA: Mobilepro Corp.
6100 Oak Tree Blvd # 200
Independence OH 44131
216 986-2745

(P-5427)
INTELPEER CLOUD CMMNCTIONS LLC
155 Bovet Rd Ste 405, San Mateo
(94402-3137)
PHONE.....................650 525-9200
Frank Fawzi, *President*
Andre Simone, *CFO*
Rob Clarke, *Ch Credit Ofcr*
Robert Galop, *Chief Mktg Ofcr*
Luis Mago, *Officer*
EMP: 106
SQ FT: 6,000

SALES (est): 23.3MM **Privately Held**
WEB: www.intelepeer.com
SIC: **4813** Data telephone communications; telephone/video communications

(P-5428)
IPASS INC (HQ)
3800 Bridge Pkwy, Redwood City
(94065-1171)
PHONE....................650 232-4100
Darin R Vickery, *CFO*
Shiva Valakunja, *Managing Dir*
Raghu Konka, *Software Engr*
Keith Waldorf, *VP Engrg*
Gilbert Rios, *Technology*
EMP: 75
SQ FT: 25,000
SALES: 54.4MM
SALES (corp-wide): 13.5MM **Publicly Held**
SIC: **4813** 7374 ; ; data processing & preparation
PA: Pareteum Corporation
1185 Ave Of The Amrcas Fl
New York NY 10036
212 984-1096

(P-5429)
JAMCRACKER INC
4677 Old Ironsides Dr # 450, Santa Clara
(95054-1845)
PHONE....................408 496-5500
K B Chandrasekhar, *Ch of Bd*
Todd Johnson, *President*
Harold Chen, *CFO*
Jim Titchen, *Vice Pres*
Jay Gokul, *Architect*
EMP: 50
SALES (est): 8.3MM **Privately Held**
WEB: www.jamcracker.com
SIC: **4813** 7375 ; information retrieval services

(P-5430)
KERMAN TELEPHONE CO
Also Called: Sebastian
811 S Madera Ave, Kerman (93630-1740)
PHONE....................559 846-4954
William S Barcus, *President*
Ruth Barcus, *Vice Pres*
Mitch Drake, *Vice Pres*
Susan Moran, *Admin Sec*
EMP: 52 EST: 1911
SQ FT: 36,000
SALES: 12.7MM
SALES (corp-wide): 51.4MM **Privately Held**
WEB: www.kermantel.net
SIC: **4813** Local telephone communications
PA: Sebastian Enterprises, Inc.
811 S Madera Ave
Kerman CA 93630
559 946-4954

(P-5431)
KERMANTELNET INTERNET SERVICE
811 S Madera Ave, Kerman (93630-1740)
PHONE....................559 842-2223
Bill Sebastian, *Owner*
EMP: 60
SALES (est): 1.2MM **Privately Held**
WEB: www.kertelweb.com
SIC: **4813**

(P-5432)
KNOT WEDDING WIRE
Also Called: Bridalink Store
1679 Insight Pl, Redding (96003-1492)
PHONE....................530 242-1621
Greg Anderson, *Principal*
EMP: 50
SALES (corp-wide): 160.5MM **Privately Held**
WEB: www.bridalink.com
SIC: **4813**
HQ: Xo Group Inc.
195 Broadway Fl 25
New York NY 10007

(P-5433)
LIVEWORLD INC (PA)
4340 Stevens Creek Blvd # 101, San Jose
(95129-1147)
PHONE....................800 301-9507
Peter H Friedman, *CEO*
David Houston, *CFO*
Chris N Christensen, *Exec VP*
Jenna Woodul, *Exec VP*
Martin Bishop, *Vice Pres*
EMP: 52
SQ FT: 2,500
SALES (est): 14.3MM **Publicly Held**
WEB: www.liveworld.com
SIC: **4813**

(P-5434)
LUXAR TECH INC
42840 Christy St Ste 231, Fremont
(94538-3194)
PHONE....................408 835-2551
Tongqing Wang, *CEO*
Richard Bergstrom, *VP Bus Dvlpt*
EMP: 130 EST: 2014
SQ FT: 4,000
SALES: 16MM **Privately Held**
SIC: **4813** Data telephone communications

(P-5435)
MCI COMMUNICATIONS SVCS INC
Also Called: Verizon Business
700 S Flower St Ste 1600, Los Angeles
(90017-4203)
PHONE....................213 625-1005
Ron Garretson, *Manager*
EMP: 200
SALES (corp-wide): 130.8B **Publicly Held**
WEB: www.mci.com
SIC: **4813** 4812 Long distance telephone communications; radio telephone communication
HQ: Mci Communications Services, Inc.
22001 Loudoun County Pkwy
Ashburn VA 20147
703 886-5600

(P-5436)
MEDIA TEMPLE INC
12130 Millennium Ste 300, Playa Vista
(90094-3156)
PHONE....................877 578-4000
Russell P Reeder, *CEO*
Marc Dumont, *Ch of Bd*
Rod Stoddard, *President*
John Carey, *COO*
Albert Lopez, *CTO*
EMP: 203
SALES (est): 41.2MM
SALES (corp-wide): 2.6B **Publicly Held**
WEB: www.mediatemple.net
SIC: **4813** 7371 ; computer software development & applications
HQ: Godaddy.Com, Llc
14455 N Hayden Rd Ste 219
Scottsdale AZ 85260

(P-5437)
MEGAPATH INC (PA)
6800 Koll Center Pkwy # 200, Pleasanton
(94566-7053)
PHONE....................877 611-6342
D Craig Young, *Ch of Bd*
Dan Foster, *President*
Mark Senda, *COO*
Paul Milley, *CFO*
Steve Chisholm, *Senior VP*
EMP: 60
SALES (est): 258.1MM **Privately Held**
WEB: www.megapath.com
SIC: **4813**

(P-5438)
MIS SCIENCES CORP
2550 N Hollywood Way, Burbank
(91505-1055)
PHONE....................818 847-0213
Lauren Ross, *President*
Jeff Willis, *CFO*
Sharon Greathouse, *Program Mgr*
Ricky Torre, *General Mgr*
Christopher Voisey, *CTO*
EMP: 125
SQ FT: 7,500

SALES (est): 16MM **Privately Held**
WEB: www.missciences.com
SIC: **4813** 8748 7376 8742 ; ; systems engineering consultant, ex. computer or professional; computer facilities management; management information systems consultant; custom computer programming services

(P-5439)
MOBILITIE SERVICES LLC
660 Newport Center Dr, Newport Beach
(92660-6401)
PHONE....................877 999-7070
Gary Jabara, *Chairman*
Christos Karmis, *CEO*
Dana Tardelli, *COO*
Dissy Sarabosing, *CFO*
EMP: 500
SALES: 350MM
SALES (corp-wide): 407.6MM **Privately Held**
SIC: **4813** Local telephone communications
PA: Mobilitie Management, Llc
660 Nwport Ctr Dr Ste 200
Newport Beach CA 92660
877 999-7070

(P-5440)
MOBITV INC
1900 Powell St Ste 900, Emeryville
(94608-1885)
PHONE....................510 981-1303
Charlie Nooney, *Ch of Bd*
Stephen Coney, *President*
Paul Scanlan, *President*
Anders Norstr M, *COO*
Anders Norstrom, *COO*
EMP: 100 EST: 2000
SQ FT: 3,200
SALES (est): 20.8MM **Privately Held**
WEB: www.mobitv.com
SIC: **4813** 4899 ; data communication services

(P-5441)
MPOWER COMMUNICATIONS CORP (DH)
515 S Flower St, Los Angeles
(90071-2201)
PHONE....................866 699-8242
Rolla P Huff, *Ch of Bd*
Joseph M Wetzel, *President*
S Gregory Clevenger, *CFO*
Michael J Tschiderer, *Treasurer*
Russell I Zuckerman, *Senior VP*
▲ EMP: 75
SQ FT: 20,000
SALES (est): 110.2MM **Privately Held**
WEB: www.mpowercom.com
SIC: **4813** Telephone communication, except radio
HQ: Mpower Holding Corporation
515 S Flower St Fl 36
Los Angeles CA 90071
866 699-8242

(P-5442)
MYINTERNETSERVICESCOM LLC
Also Called: Fairfight
1010 E Union St Ste 125, Pasadena
(91106-1793)
PHONE....................213 256-0575
Greg Howard, *CEO*
Trenton Hill, *COO*
Edmar Mendizabal, *Director*
EMP: 100
SQ FT: 2,000
SALES (est): 1.1MM **Privately Held**
WEB: www.myinternetservices.com
SIC: **4813**

(P-5443)
NAVISITE LLC
2805 Lafayette St, Santa Clara
(95050-2639)
PHONE....................408 965-9000
Lorie Tolley, *Branch Mgr*
Mike Davis, *Technology*
Richard Bueno, *Manager*
EMP: 50

SALES (corp-wide): 118.2MM **Privately Held**
WEB: www.navisite.com
SIC: **4813**
HQ: Navisite Llc
400 Minuteman Rd
Andover MA 01810

(P-5444)
NEOPETS INC
412 W Broadway Ste 303, Glendale
(91204-1297)
PHONE....................818 551-4338
Doug Dohring, *President*
Patty Lutton, *CFO*
Kyra E Reppen, *Senior VP*
Peter Green, *Vice Pres*
Debra Pierson, *Vice Pres*
EMP: 50
SALES (est): 2.1MM
SALES (corp-wide): 12.9B **Publicly Held**
WEB: www.neopets.com
SIC: **4813**
HQ: Viacom International Inc.
1515 Broadway
New York NY 10036

(P-5445)
NETNOW
41 Heritage Village Ln, Campbell
(95008-2036)
PHONE....................408 370-0425
Daniel Bryant, *Owner*
Peggy Patwardhan, *Vice Pres*
EMP: 300
SALES: 15MM **Privately Held**
WEB: www.netnow.com
SIC: **4813**

(P-5446)
NEW DREAM NETWORK LLC (PA)
Also Called: Dreamhost.com
135 S State College Blvd, Brea
(92821-5823)
PHONE....................626 644-9466
Simon Anderson, *Mng Member*
Kathy Brahm, *Vice Pres*
Brandon Simpson, *Technical Staff*
David ABO, *Sales Staff*
Dallas Bethune,
EMP: 60
SQ FT: 16,380
SALES (est): 56.6MM **Privately Held**
WEB: www.newdream.net
SIC: **4813**

(P-5447)
NEW DREAM NETWORK LLC
Also Called: Dreamhost.com
707 Wilshire Blvd # 5050, Los Angeles
(90017-3607)
PHONE....................323 375-3842
Art Elivarov, *Manager*
Art Elizarov, *VP Human Res*
EMP: 74
SALES (corp-wide): 56.6MM **Privately Held**
SIC: **4813**
PA: New Dream Network, Llc
135 S State College Blvd
Brea CA 92821
626 644-9466

(P-5448)
NEXTPOINT INC (PA)
Also Called: Break Media
8750 Wilshire Blvd 300e, Beverly Hills
(90211-2700)
PHONE....................310 360-5904
Keith Richman, *President*
Andrew Doyle, *CFO*
David Subar, *CTO*
EMP: 80
SALES (est): 30.8MM **Privately Held**
SIC: **4813**

(P-5449)
O1 COMMUNICATIONS INC
4359 Town Center Blvd # 217, El Dorado Hills (95762-7113)
PHONE....................888 444-1111
Bradley Jenkins, *CEO*
Jim Beausoleil, *CFO*

Max Seely, *Senior VP*
EMP: 89
SQ FT: 20,000
SALES (est): 29MM **Privately Held**
WEB: www.o1tel.com
SIC: 4813 Data telephone communications

(P-5450)
ODYSSEY TELECORP INC
550 Lytton Ave Fl 2, Palo Alto
(94301-1577)
PHONE..............................650 470-7550
Sean Doherty, *CEO*
Joe Stockwell, *COO*
Karl O Forsman, *Software Engr*
EMP: 131
SALES (est): 5.2MM **Privately Held**
WEB: www.odysseytel.com
SIC: 4813

(P-5451)
OPEX COMMUNICATIONS INC
3777 Long Beach Blvd # 400, Long Beach
(90807-3341)
P.O. Box 9270, Uniondale NY (11555-
9270)
PHONE..............................562 968-5420
Mark Leafstedt, *CEO*
Sean Trepeta, *President*
John Wonak, *CFO*
Lucy Sung, *Principal*
Robert Yap, *Admin Sec*
EMP: 50 **EST:** 1998
SQ FT: 14,400
SALES (est): 7.1MM **Privately Held**
WEB: www.opexld.com
SIC: 4813 Local telephone communica-
tions
PA: Premiercom Management Company
6 Jacqueline Ln
Fox River Grove IL

(P-5452)
**PACIFIC BELL TELEPHONE
COMPANY (HQ)**
Also Called: Pacbell
430 Bush St Fl 3, San Francisco
(94108-3735)
PHONE..............................415 542-9000
Kenneth P McNeely, *CEO*
Ray Wilkins Jr, *President*
Amita Gupta, *Database Admin*
Leslie Thomas, *Technician*
Sandy Young, *Technical Staff*
▲ **EMP:** 2000
SQ FT: 500,000
SALES (est): 8.3B
SALES (corp-wide): 170.7B **Publicly
Held**
WEB: www.pacbell.com
SIC: 4813 2741 4822 Local & long dis-
tance telephone communications; local
telephone communications; voice tele-
phone communications; data telephone
communications; directories, telephone:
publishing only, not printed on site; tele-
graph & other communications; electronic
mail
PA: At&T Inc.
208 S Akard St
Dallas TX 75202
210 821-4105

(P-5453)
**PACIFIC CENTREX SERVICES
INC**
Also Called: Pcs1
114 E Haley St Ste A, Santa Barbara
(93101-2347)
PHONE..............................818 623-2300
M Devin Semler, *President*
Damon Kenney, *Sales Mgr*
EMP: 52
SALES (est): 5.3MM **Privately Held**
WEB: www.pcs1.net
SIC: 4813 5999 ; telephone equipment &
systems

(P-5454)
PARETO NETWORKS INC
1183 Bordeaux Dr Ste 22, Sunnyvale
(94089-1201)
PHONE..............................877 727-8020
Daniel Ryan, *CEO*
EMP: 219

SALES (est): 4.9MM **Publicly Held**
SIC: 4813
HQ: Aerohive Networks, Inc.
1011 Mccarthy Blvd
Milpitas CA 95035
-

(P-5455)
PAYCHEX BENEFIT TECH INC
Also Called: Benetrac
2385 Northside Dr Ste 100, San Diego
(92108-2716)
PHONE..............................800 322-7292
Martin Mucci, *CEO*
John B Gibson, *Senior VP*
Jan Hawthorne, *Vice Pres*
Susan Short, *Vice Pres*
Melissa Guerrero, *Executive*
EMP: 110
SALES (est): 14.1MM
SALES (corp-wide): 3.7B **Publicly Held**
WEB: www.benetrac.com
SIC: 4813
PA: Paychex, Inc.
911 Panorama Trl S
Rochester NY 14625
585 385-6666

(P-5456)
PAYCYCLE INC
210 Portage Ave, Palo Alto (94306-2242)
P.O. Box 397850, Mountain View (94039-
7850)
PHONE..............................866 729-2925
Jim Heeger, *CEO*
John Eichhorn, *CFO*
Martin Gates, *CTO*
Susan Dunn, *General Counsel*
EMP: 75
SQ FT: 15,000
SALES (est): 4.7MM
SALES (corp-wide): 6.7B **Publicly Held**
WEB: www.paycycle.com
SIC: 4813 8721 ; accounting, auditing &
bookkeeping
PA: Intuit Inc.
2700 Coast Ave
Mountain View CA 94043
650 944-6000

(P-5457)
PAYPAL INC (HQ)
2211 N 1st St, San Jose (95131-2021)
PHONE..............................877 981-2163
Daniel H Schulman, *President*
Shannon Batson, *Partner*
Steve Jasa, *Partner*
Ken Lagman, *Partner*
Daniel Schulman, *President*
◆ **EMP:** 170
SALES (est): 3.3B
SALES (corp-wide): 15.4B **Publicly Held**
WEB: www.paypal.com
SIC: 4813 5961 8741 ; catalog & mail-
order houses; management services
PA: Paypal Holdings, Inc.
2211 N 1st St
San Jose CA 95131
408 967-1000

(P-5458)
PCS MOBILE SOLUTIONS LLC
3534 Tweedy Blvd, South Gate
(90280-6026)
PHONE..............................323 567-2490
EMP: 74
SALES (corp-wide): 129.1MM **Privately
Held**
SIC: 4813 4812 Local & long distance
telephone communications; cellular tele-
phone services
PA: Pcs Mobile Solutions, Llc
32000 Northwestern Hwy # 279
Farmington Hills MI 48334
248 539-2221

(P-5459)
**PUBLIC COMMUNICATIONS
SVCS INC**
11859 Wilshire Blvd # 600, Los Angeles
(90025-6616)
P.O. Box 2868, Mobile AL (36652-2868)
PHONE..............................310 231-1000
Paul Jennings, *CEO*
Tommie Joe, *President*
Dennis Komai, *CFO*

EMP: 150
SQ FT: 15,000
SALES (est): 15.8MM **Privately Held**
WEB: www.pcstelcom.com
SIC: 4813 Local & long distance telephone
communications

(P-5460)
QWEST CORPORATION
1350 Treat Blvd Ste 200, Walnut Creek
(94597-2150)
PHONE..............................925 974-4908
Trish Stuber, *Branch Mgr*
EMP: 59
SALES (corp-wide): 23.4B **Publicly Held**
SIC: 4813 Telephone communication, ex-
cept radio
HQ: Qwest Corporation
100 Centurylink Dr
Monroe LA 71203
318 388-9000

(P-5461)
RED POCKET INC
Also Called: Red Pocket Mobile
2060d E Avenida De Los, Thousand Oaks
(91362)
PHONE..............................888 993-3888
Joshua Gordon, *President*
Steve Bowman, *CFO*
EMP: 75 **EST:** 2005
SALES (est): 2.9MM **Privately Held**
SIC: 4813 Telephone communication, ex-
cept radio

(P-5462)
RENTJUICE CORPORATION
225 Bush St Ste 1100, San Francisco
(94104-4250)
PHONE..............................415 376-0369
David Vivero, *CEO*
Kunal Shah, *CTO*
EMP: 91
SALES (est): 5.5MM
SALES (corp-wide): 1.3B **Publicly Held**
SIC: 4813
HQ: Zillow, Inc.
1301 2nd Ave Fl 31
Seattle WA 98101
206 470-7000

(P-5463)
RHYTHMONE LLC (DH)
601 Montgomery St Fl 16, San Francisco
(94111-2620)
PHONE..............................415 655-1450
Mark Bonney, *President*
Frank Pao, *Officer*
Amy Rothstein, *Officer*
Gal Topaz, *Senior VP*
Edward Hastings, *Exec Dir*
EMP: 80
SALES (est): 83.8MM
SALES (corp-wide): 60MM **Privately
Held**
WEB: www.blinkx.com
SIC: 4813 2741 7319 ; ; display advertis-
ing service

(P-5464)
RIVIO INC
2500 Augustine Dr Ste 100, Santa Clara
(95054-3020)
PHONE..............................408 653-4400
Navin Chaddha, *President*
Pradip Madan, *COO*
James Walker, *Exec VP*
Craig Douchy, *Admin Sec*
EMP: 50
SALES (est): 1.6MM
SALES (corp-wide): 266.8MM **Privately
Held**
WEB: www.cpa2biz.com
SIC: 4813
HQ: Cpa2biz, Inc.
1345 Avenue Of The Americ
New York NY 10105
212 596-6230

(P-5465)
RUCKUS WIRELESS INC (HQ)
350 W Java Dr, Sunnyvale (94089-1026)
PHONE..............................650 265-4200
Ken Cheng, *CEO*
Bart Giordano, *Senior VP*
Larry Birnbaum, *Vice Pres*

Louis Au Kwok-Leung, *Vice Pres*
Steve Martin, *Vice Pres*
▲ **EMP:** 170
SQ FT: 95,000
SALES (est): 1.3B
SALES (corp-wide): 6.7B **Privately Held**
WEB: www.ruckuswireless.com
SIC: 4813
PA: Arris International Limited
Salts Mill, Victoria Road
Shipley BD18
127 453-2000

(P-5466)
**SEBASTIAN ENTERPRISES INC
(PA)**
811 S Madera Ave, Kerman (93630-1740)
PHONE..............................559 946-4954
Ruth Barcus, *President*
William Barcus, *Vice Pres*
Susan Moran, *Admin Sec*
Jeff McClure, *Info Tech Dir*
Al Baumgarner, *IT/INT Sup*
EMP: 65
SQ FT: 70,775
SALES (est): 51.4MM **Privately Held**
SIC: 4813 1731 Local telephone commu-
nications; telephone & telephone equip-
ment installation; general electrical
contractor

(P-5467)
SENDMAIL INC
892 Ross Dr, Sunnyvale (94089-1443)
PHONE..............................510 594-5400
Gary Steele, *CEO*
Sandy Abbott, *CFO*
Paul Auvil, *CFO*
Tracey Newell, *Exec VP*
Kimberly Getgem Bargero, *Vice Pres*
EMP: 75
SQ FT: 30,000
SALES (est): 18.1MM
SALES (corp-wide): 716.9MM **Publicly
Held**
WEB: www.sendmail.com
SIC: 4813 7371 7372 7373 ; computer
software development; prepackaged soft-
ware; computer integrated systems de-
sign
PA: Proofpoint, Inc.
892 Ross Dr
Sunnyvale CA 94089
408 517-4710

(P-5468)
**SIERRA TEL CMMUNICATIONS
GROUP**
Also Called: Sierra Tel Business Systems
40044 Highway 49 Ste C2, Oakhurst
(93644-8875)
P.O. Box 160 (93644-0160)
PHONE..............................559 683-7777
Mike Cary, *Manager*
EMP: 80
SALES (corp-wide): 111.6MM **Privately
Held**
WEB: www.sierratelephone.com
SIC: 4813 Local telephone communica-
tions
PA: Sierra Tel Communications Group
49150 Road 426
Oakhurst CA 93644
559 683-4611

(P-5469)
**SIERRA TEL CMMUNICATIONS
GROUP (PA)**
Also Called: Seirra Telephone
49150 Road 426, Oakhurst (93644-8702)
P.O. Box 219 (93644-0219)
PHONE..............................559 683-4611
John H Baker, *CEO*
Harry H Baker, *Ch of Bd*
Lynn Forleo, *General Mgr*
Linda Oldfield, *HR Admin*
EMP: 54
SQ FT: 12,000
SALES (est): 111.6MM **Privately Held**
WEB: www.sierratelephone.com
SIC: 4813 Local telephone communica-
tions; long distance telephone communi-
cations;

(P-5470)
SIERRA TELEPHONE COMPANY INC
49150 Crane Valley Rd 426, Oakhurst (93644)
P.O. Box 219 (93644-0219)
PHONE.....................559 683-4611
Harry H Held, *President*
John H Baker, *Vice Pres*
Heidi D Baker, *Admin Sec*
Judi Thomas, *Info Tech Mgr*
Eva Busto, *Business Anlyst*
EMP: 190
SALES (est): 35.4MM
SALES (corp-wide): 111.6MM **Privately Held**
WEB: www.stcg.net
SIC: 4813 Local telephone communications; long distance telephone communications
PA: Sierra Tel Communications Group
49150 Road 426
Oakhurst CA 93644
559 683-4611

(P-5471)
SIGMA NETWORKS INC
2191 Zanker Rd, San Jose (95131-2109)
PHONE.....................408 876-4002
John K Peters, *President*
Michael A Depatie, *CFO*
Robert Decker, *Vice Pres*
Lonny Orona, *Vice Pres*
Scott Young, *Vice Pres*
EMP: 120
SALES (est): 4.2MM **Privately Held**
SIC: 4813 Local telephone communications

(P-5472)
SKYPE INC
1 Microsoft Way Redmond, Palo Alto (94304)
PHONE.....................650 493-7900
Donald Albert, *President*
Tony Bates, *CEO*
Laura Shesgreen, *Vice Pres*
Shauna Kline, *Controller*
▲ **EMP:** 70
SQ FT: 90,698
SALES (est): 10.6MM
SALES (corp-wide): 125.8B **Publicly Held**
SIC: 4813 ;
PA: Microsoft Corporation
1 Microsoft Way
Redmond WA 98052
425 882-8080

(P-5473)
SOUTHERN CALIFORNIA TELE CO (PA)
Also Called: Southern Cal Tele & Enrgy
27515 Enterprise Cir W, Temecula (92590-4864)
PHONE.....................951 693-1880
Greg Michaels, *President*
Kristine Michaels, *CFO*
Bill Short, *Officer*
Kevin Reno, *Vice Pres*
Ryan McGuire, *Executive Asst*
EMP: 60
SQ FT: 10,000
SALES (est): 10.2MM **Privately Held**
SIC: 4813 Local & long distance telephone communications

(P-5474)
SPRINT COMMUNICATIONS CO LP
111 Universal Hollywood Dr, Universal City (91608-1054)
PHONE.....................818 755-7100
Bill Henry, *Manager*
EMP: 50 **Publicly Held**
SIC: 4813 4812 Long distance telephone communications; radio telephone communication
HQ: Sprint Communications Company L.P.
6391 Sprint Pkwy
Overland Park KS 66251
800 829-0965

(P-5475)
SPRINT COMMUNICATIONS CO LP
1505 E Enterprise Dr, San Bernardino (92408-0159)
PHONE.....................909 382-6030
Bill Neece, *Manager*
EMP: 100 **Publicly Held**
SIC: 4813 4812 Long distance telephone communications; radio telephone communications
HQ: Sprint Communications Company L.P.
6391 Sprint Pkwy
Overland Park KS 66251
800 829-0965

(P-5476)
SYDATA INC
6494 Weathers Pl Ste 100, San Diego (92121-2938)
PHONE.....................760 444-4368
Sindhura Thummalasetty, *CEO*
EMP: 125
SALES (est): 40.1K **Privately Held**
SIC: 4813 7371 ; custom computer programming services

(P-5477)
TACHYON INC
9339 Carroll Park Dr # 150, San Diego (92121-3247)
PHONE.....................858 882-8108
EMP: 50
SALES (est): 4.9MM **Privately Held**
SIC: 4813

(P-5478)
TACTIVOS INC
Also Called: Mural
303 2nd St Ste S200, San Francisco (94107-1328)
PHONE.....................415 687-2501
Mariano Suarez Battan, *CEO*
Pato Jutard, *CTO*
EMP: 52
SALES (est): 289.5K **Privately Held**
SIC: 4813 ;

(P-5479)
TEKWORKS INC
12742 Knott St, Garden Grove (92841-3904)
PHONE.....................877 835-9675
William E Bourgeois, *CEO*
EMP: 70
SALES (corp-wide): 13.1MM **Privately Held**
SIC: 4813 1731 Telephone communication, except radio; communications specialization
PA: Paladin Technologies Inc
3001 Wayburne Dr Suite 201
Burnaby BC V5G 4
604 677-8700

(P-5480)
TELISIMO INTERNATIONAL CORP
2330 Shelter Island Dr 210a, San Diego (92106-3126)
PHONE.....................619 325-1593
Linda G Noda Hobbs, *President*
Mark D Wooster, *CFO*
EMP: 400
SQ FT: 15,000
SALES (est): 19.6MM **Privately Held**
SIC: 4813 Telephone communication, except radio

(P-5481)
TNCI OPERATING COMPANY LLC (HQ)
114 E Haley St Ste I, Santa Barbara (93101-5323)
PHONE.....................800 800-8400
Brian McClintock, *COO*
Alan Nafziger, *Info Tech Dir*
Virginia Tam, *Accounting Mgr*
EMP: 85 **EST:** 2013
SQ FT: 5,000
SALES (est): 24.6MM **Privately Held**
SIC: 4813 Telephone communication, except radio

(P-5482)
TOPICA INC
1 Post St Ste 875, San Francisco (94104-5262)
PHONE.....................415 344-0800
Ariel Poler, *CEO*
Anna Zornosa, *President*
Roy Maynard, *CFO*
Glenn Marcus, *CTO*
EMP: 93
SALES (est): 6.3MM **Privately Held**
WEB: www.topica.com
SIC: 4813 7375 ; information retrieval services

(P-5483)
TRUCONNECT COMMUNICATIONS INC (PA)
Also Called: Telescape
1149 S Hill St Ste 400, Los Angeles (90015-2894)
PHONE.....................512 919-2641
Mathew Johnson, *CEO*
Robert A Yap, *President*
Nathan Johnson, *CEO*
Juan Carlos Davila, *Senior VP*
Melanie Warner, *Project Mgr*
EMP: 201
SALES (est): 22.9MM **Privately Held**
WEB: www.telscape.net
SIC: 4813

(P-5484)
US INTERSTATE DISTRG INC
Also Called: Allstate Communications ASC
21621 Nordhoff St, Chatsworth (91311-5828)
PHONE.....................818 678-4592
Russel Leventhal, *President*
Frank Montelione, *Vice Pres*
EMP: 150
SALES (est): 11.9MM **Privately Held**
SIC: 4813 Telephone communication, except radio

(P-5485)
US TELEPACIFIC CORP (HQ)
Also Called: Tpx Communications
515 S Flower St Ste 4500, Los Angeles (90071-2237)
PHONE.....................866 699-8242
Richard A Jalkut, *President*
Tania Powe, *Partner*
David Glickman, *Ch of Bd*
Timothy Medina, *CFO*
Ken Bisnoff, *Senior VP*
◆ **EMP:** 50
SQ FT: 75,000
SALES (est): 434MM **Privately Held**
WEB: www.telepacific.com
SIC: 4813 Local & long distance telephone communications

(P-5486)
USTREAM INC
410 Townsend St Fl 4, San Francisco (94107-1581)
PHONE.....................415 489-9400
John Ham, *CEO*
Brad Hunstable, *President*
EMP: 65
SALES (est): 10.3MM
SALES (corp-wide): 79.5B **Publicly Held**
SIC: 4813
PA: International Business Machines Corporation
1 New Orchard Rd Ste 1 # 1
Armonk NY 10504
914 499-1900

(P-5487)
UVNV INC (PA)
Also Called: Ultra Mobile
1550 Scenic Ave Ste 100, Costa Mesa (92626-1420)
PHONE.....................888 777-0446
David Glickman, *CEO*
Tyler R Leshney, *President*
Dave Schofield, *COO*
Sherrie Simmons, *COO*
Chris Furlong, *Exec VP*
EMP: 115
SQ FT: 8,600
SALES (est): 20MM **Privately Held**
SIC: 4813 Telephone communication, except radio

(P-5488)
VERIZON BUS NETWRK SVCS INC
11080 White Rock Rd # 100, Rancho Cordova (95670-6299)
PHONE.....................916 779-5600
Bert C Roberts, *Branch Mgr*
EMP: 225
SALES (corp-wide): 130.8B **Publicly Held**
WEB: www.gtl.net
SIC: 4813 Long distance telephone communications
HQ: Verizon Business Network Services Inc.
1 Verizon Way
Basking Ridge NJ 07920
908 559-2000

(P-5489)
VERIZON BUS NETWRK SVCS INC
1740 Creekside Oaks 200, Sacramento (95833)
PHONE.....................916 569-5999
Suresh Madala, *Principal*
EMP: 119
SALES (corp-wide): 130.8B **Publicly Held**
WEB: www.gtl.net
SIC: 4813 Long distance telephone communications
HQ: Verizon Business Network Services Inc.
1 Verizon Way
Basking Ridge NJ 07920
908 559-2000

(P-5490)
VERIZON COMMUNICATIONS INC
Also Called: GTE
2943 Exposition Blvd, Santa Monica (90404-5024)
PHONE.....................310 319-6148
Steve Campanion, *Manager*
EMP: 300
SALES (corp-wide): 130.8B **Publicly Held**
WEB: www.gte.com
SIC: 4813 4812 Local & long distance telephone communications; radio telephone communication
PA: Verizon Communications Inc.
1095 Ave Of The Americas
New York NY 10036
212 395-1000

(P-5491)
VERIZON NETWORK INTEGRATION
12905 Los Nietos Rd, Santa Fe Springs (90670-3011)
PHONE.....................562 903-7953
Mark Ryan, *Manager*
EMP: 250
SALES (corp-wide): 130.8B **Publicly Held**
WEB: www.ba-dsg.com
SIC: 4813 Telephone communication, except radio
HQ: Verizon Network Integration Corp
1050 Virginia Dr 3
Fort Washington PA 19034

(P-5492)
VINCENT HUANG & ASSOCIATES LLC (PA)
1550 Valley Vista Dr, Diamond Bar (91765-3957)
PHONE.....................909 861-9600
Vincent WEI Cheng Huang, *CEO*
Cyndia Lin, *CFO*
Joe Dunkle, *Administration*
Ryan Emerick, *Business Anlyst*
Steve Kim, *Opers Mgr*
▲ **EMP:** 100
SQ FT: 9,500
SALES (est): 19.4MM **Privately Held**
SIC: 4813 Telephone communications broker

(P-5493)
VOLCANO COMMUNICATIONS COMPANY (PA)
Also Called: Volcano Telephone Company
20000 State Highway 88, Pine Grove
(95665-9512)
P.O. Box 1070 (95665-1070)
PHONE...................................209 296-7502
Sharon J Lundgren, *President*
Elizabeth Lundgren, *Treasurer*
John M Lundgren, *Vice Pres*
Delia P Dede Harder, *Admin Sec*
Angela Lundgren, *Director*
EMP: 100
SQ FT: 19,600
SALES (est): 21.2MM **Privately Held**
WEB: www.volcanovti.com
SIC: 4813 4841 Local telephone communications; cable television services

(P-5494)
VSS MONITORING INC (HQ)
178 E Tasman Dr, San Jose (95134-1619)
PHONE...................................408 585-6800
Terrence M Breslin, *President*
James McNicholas, *CFO*
Andrew R Harding, *Vice Pres*
EMP: 160
SQ FT: 10,000
SALES (est): 30.5MM
SALES (corp-wide): 909.9MM **Publicly Held**
WEB: www.vssmonitoring.com
SIC: 4813
PA: Netscout Systems, Inc.
310 Littleton Rd
Westford MA 01886
978 614-4000

(P-5495)
WEBPASS INC
267 8th St, San Francisco (94103-3910)
PHONE...................................415 233-4100
Charles Barr, *President*
Blake Drager, *Vice Pres*
Jennifer Gayden, *Executive*
Nancy Jimenez, *Executive*
Melissa Pieroni, *Creative Dir*
EMP: 100
SQ FT: 8,000
SALES (est): 13.7MM **Privately Held**
SIC: 4813

(P-5496)
WHOLESALE AIR-TIME INC
27515 Enterprise Cir W, Temecula
(92590-4864)
PHONE...................................951 693-1880
Greg Michaels, *President*
Kevin Reno, *Vice Pres*
Wendy L Walker, *Admin Sec*
EMP: 50
SQ FT: 9,000
SALES (est): 6.2MM **Privately Held**
SIC: 4813 Local & long distance telephone communications

(P-5497)
XOBEE NETWORKS INC
7910 N Ingram Ave Ste 101, Fresno
(93711-5828)
PHONE...................................559 579-1300
Eric Raw, *President*
Bryan Smith, *Vice Pres*
Edie Roach, *Executive Asst*
Matt Sotomayor, *Administration*
Jason Wells, *Administration*
EMP: 53
SQ FT: 5,500
SALES: 5MM **Privately Held**
SIC: 4813 7379 8741 8748 ; computer related consulting services; management services; telecommunications consultant

(P-5498)
YTEL INC
94 Icon, Foothill Ranch (92610-3000)
PHONE...................................800 382-4913
Nick Newsom, *CEO*
Patrick Kennedy, *Comms Dir*
Taylor Sturtz, *Web Dvlpr*
Larry Caudill, *Engineer*
Ira Axner, *Controller*
EMP: 100
SALES: 4MM **Privately Held**
SIC: 4813

(P-5499)
ZADAONET
685 Scofield Ave Apt 22, East Palo Alto
(94303-2350)
PHONE...................................650 556-6377
Wenda Zhao, *President*
EMP: 60
SALES (est): 399.6K **Privately Held**
SIC: 4813

(P-5500)
ZOOSK INC (HQ)
989 Market St Fl 5, San Francisco
(94103-1741)
PHONE...................................415 728-9543
Jeronimo Folgueira, *CEO*
Justin Roberts, *Vice Pres*
Andre Wang, *Executive*
Kris Murray, *Exec Dir*
Larry Chen, *Software Engr*
EMP: 52
SALES (est): 24.1MM
SALES (corp-wide): 548.7K **Privately Held**
SIC: 4813 7299 ; dating service
PA: Spark Networks Se
Kohlfurter Str. 41/
Berlin 10999
309 919-4951

(P-5501)
ZYXEL COMMUNICATIONS INC
1130 N Miller St, Anaheim (92806-2001)
PHONE...................................714 632-0882
Howie Chu, *President*
Nikki Battista, *Manager*
Shawn Rogers, *Manager*
◆ EMP: 80
SQ FT: 32,000
SALES: 100MM **Privately Held**
WEB: www.zyxel.com.tw
SIC: 4813
HQ: Zyxel Communications Corporation
11f, No. 223, Beixin Rd., Sec. 3
New Taipei City TAP 23143

4822 Telegraph & Other Message Communications

(P-5502)
INTRADO INTERACTIVE SVCS CORP
100 Enterprise Way A-3, Scotts Valley
(95066-3248)
PHONE...................................888 527-5225
EMP: 89
SALES (corp-wide): 2.2B **Privately Held**
SIC: 4822 Nonvocal message communications
HQ: Intrado Interactive Services Corporation
11808 Miracle Hills Dr
Omaha NE 68154

(P-5503)
J2 CLOUD SERVICES LLC (HQ)
Also Called: J2 Cloud Services, Inc.
6922 Hollywood Blvd # 500, Los Angeles
(90028-6117)
PHONE...................................323 860-9200
Nehemia Zucker, *CEO*
Laura Hinson, *President*
Vince Niedzielski, *President*
Ken Truesdale, *President*
R Scott Turicchi, *President*
EMP: 52
SQ FT: 40,000
SALES (est): 828.3MM
SALES (corp-wide): 1.2B **Publicly Held**
WEB: www.efaxcorporate.com
SIC: 4822 Telegraph & other communications
PA: J2 Global, Inc.
6922 Hollywood Blvd # 500
Los Angeles CA 90028
323 860-9200

(P-5504)
J2 GLOBAL INC (PA)
6922 Hollywood Blvd # 500, Los Angeles
(90028-6125)
PHONE...................................323 860-9200

Chul Min Chun, *CEO*
Richard S Ressler, *Ch of Bd*
Nate Simmons, *President*
R Scott Turicchi, *President*
Vivek Shah, *CEO*
▲ EMP: 131
SQ FT: 43,000
SALES: 1.2B **Publicly Held**
SIC: 4822 Telegraph & other communications

4832 Radio Broadcasting Stations

(P-5505)
ABC CABLE NETWORKS GROUP (DH)
500 S Buena Vista St, Burbank
(91521-0007)
PHONE...................................818 460-7477
John F Cooke, *President*
Anne M Sweeney, *President*
Paul Friedman, *Exec VP*
Andy Kubitz, *Exec VP*
Patrick Moran, *Exec VP*
▲ EMP: 200
SALES (est): 269.3MM
SALES (corp-wide): 90.2B **Publicly Held**
WEB: www.breakbar.com
SIC: 4832 4833 Radio broadcasting stations; television broadcasting stations
HQ: Disney Enterprises, Inc.
500 S Buena Vista St
Burbank CA 91521
818 560-1000

(P-5506)
ABC CABLE NETWORKS GROUP
Also Called: Jimmy Kimmel Live
6834 Hollywood Blvd, Los Angeles
(90028-6116)
PHONE...................................323 860-5900
Jill Leiderman, *Principal*
EMP: 200
SALES (corp-wide): 90.2B **Publicly Held**
SIC: 4832 4833 Radio broadcasting stations; television broadcasting stations
HQ: Abc Cable Networks Group
500 S Buena Vista St
Burbank CA 91521
818 460-7477

(P-5507)
AMATURO SONOMA MEDIA GROUP LLC
1410 Neotomas Ave Ste 200, Santa Rosa
(95405-7533)
PHONE...................................707 543-0126
Michael Williams, *President*
Danny Wright, *Program Dir*
Cathy Slack, *Manager*
Victoria Mann, *Supervisor*
EMP: 67
SALES: 5.5MM **Privately Held**
SIC: 4832 Radio broadcasting stations

(P-5508)
BONNEVILLE INTERNATIONAL CORP
Also Called: Kswb
5900 Wilshire Blvd # 1900, Los Angeles
(90036-5020)
PHONE...................................323 634-1800
Peter Durton, *Branch Mgr*
Linda Jacobson, *Marketing Staff*
Swift Tim, *Director*
Terry Hritz, *Accounts Exec*
EMP: 50
SALES (corp-wide): 3.5B **Privately Held**
SIC: 4832 Radio broadcasting stations
HQ: Bonneville International Corporation
55 N 300 W Ste 315
Salt Lake City UT 84101
303 321-0950

(P-5509)
BONNEVILLE INTERNATIONAL CORP
Also Called: Koit
201 3rd St Fl 12, San Francisco
(94103-3133)
PHONE...................................415 777-0965

Chuck Tweedle, *General Mgr*
Lakshmi Meadows, *Accounts Exec*
EMP: 50
SALES (corp-wide): 3.5B **Privately Held**
SIC: 4832 7313 Radio broadcasting stations, music format; radio advertising representative
HQ: Bonneville International Corporation
55 N 300 W Ste 315
Salt Lake City UT 84101
303 321-0950

(P-5510)
BROADCAST CO OF AMERICAS LLC (PA)
6160 Cornerstone Ct E # 100, San Diego
(92121-3724)
P.O. Box 928333 (92192-8333)
PHONE...................................858 453-0658
Larry Patrick, *CEO*
John T Lynch, *President*
EMP: 62
SALES (est): 3.7MM **Privately Held**
SIC: 4832 Radio broadcasting stations

(P-5511)
CAPITAL PUBLIC RADIO INC
7055 Folsom Blvd, Sacramento
(95826-2625)
PHONE...................................916 278-8900
Rick Eytcheson, *President*
EMP: 50
SQ FT: 19,838
SALES: 74.4K **Privately Held**
WEB: www.capradio.net
SIC: 4832 Radio broadcasting stations

(P-5512)
CBS BROADCASTING INC
A65 Bettery St, San Francisco (94111)
PHONE...................................415 765-4097
Doug Harvill, *CEO*
EMP: 100
SALES (corp-wide): 25.9B **Publicly Held**
WEB: www.cbs4.com
SIC: 4832 Radio broadcasting stations
HQ: Cbs Broadcasting Inc.
524 W 57th St
New York NY 10019
212 975-4321

(P-5513)
CBS CORPORATION
865 Battery St Fl 2/3, San Francisco
(94111-1503)
PHONE...................................415 765-4000
Doug Harvill, *General Mgr*
Howard Silver, *Manager*
EMP: 84
SALES (corp-wide): 25.9B **Publicly Held**
SIC: 4832 Radio broadcasting stations
HQ: Cbs Corporation
51 W 52nd St Bsmt 1
New York NY 10019
212 975-4321

(P-5514)
CBS RADIO INC
1071 W Shaw Ave, Fresno (93711-3702)
PHONE...................................559 490-0106
El Smith, *Manager*
EMP: 195
SQ FT: 5,938
SALES (corp-wide): 1.4B **Publicly Held**
WEB: www.infinityradio.com
SIC: 4832 Radio broadcasting stations, music format
HQ: Cbs Radio Inc.
345 Hudson St Fl 10
New York NY 10014
212 314-9200

(P-5515)
CBS RADIO INC
865 Battery St Fl 3, San Francisco
(94111-1503)
PHONE...................................415 765-4097
Michael Martin, *Vice Pres*
EMP: 100
SALES (corp-wide): 1.4B **Publicly Held**
SIC: 4832 Radio broadcasting stations, music format
HQ: Cbs Radio Inc.
345 Hudson St Fl 10
New York NY 10014
212 314-9200

(P-5516)
CBS RADIO INC
900 E Washington St # 315, Colton
(92324-8182)
PHONE..................................909 825-9525
Kevin Murphy, *General Mgr*
EMP: 65
SALES (corp-wide): 1.4B **Publicly Held**
WEB: www.infinityradio.com
SIC: 4832 Radio broadcasting stations
HQ: Cbs Radio Inc.
345 Hudson St Fl 10
New York NY 10014
212 314-9200

(P-5517)
CBS RADIO INC
280 Commerce Cir, Sacramento
(95815-4212)
PHONE..................................916 923-6800
Micheal Hornetto, *Manager*
EMP: 100
SALES (corp-wide): 1.4B **Publicly Held**
WEB: www.infinityradio.com
SIC: 4832 Radio broadcasting stations,
music format
HQ: Cbs Radio Inc.
345 Hudson St Fl 10
New York NY 10014
212 314-9200

(P-5518)
CM WIND DOWN TOPCO INC
Also Called: Cumulus Media
750 Battery St Ste 300, San Francisco
(94111-1525)
PHONE..................................415 995-6800
Mary G Berner, *President*
EMP: 93
SALES (corp-wide): 1.6B **Publicly Held**
SIC: 4832 Radio broadcasting stations
PA: Cm Wind Down Topco Inc.
3280 Peachtree Rd Ne Ne2300
Atlanta GA 30305
404 949-0700

(P-5519)
**CUMULUS INTRMDATE
HOLDINGS INC**
Also Called: Kabc 790 Talk Radio
3321 S La Cienega Blvd, Los Angeles
(90016-3114)
PHONE..................................310 840-4900
Octavio Gallardo, *Principal*
EMP: 74
SALES (corp-wide): 1.6B **Publicly Held**
SIC: 4832 Radio broadcasting stations
HQ: Cumulus Intermediate Holdings Inc.
3280 Peachtree Rd Ne # 2300
Atlanta GA 30305

(P-5520)
**CUMULUS INTRMDATE
HOLDINGS INC**
Also Called: Khop
3136 Boeing Way 125, Stockton
(95206-4989)
PHONE..................................209 766-5103
Roy Williams, *General Mgr*
EMP: 125
SALES (corp-wide): 1.6B **Publicly Held**
WEB: www.citadelradio.com
SIC: 4832 Radio broadcasting stations
HQ: Cumulus Intermediate Holdings Inc.
3280 Peachtree Rd Ne # 2300
Atlanta GA 30305

(P-5521)
DISNEY ENTERPRISES INC (DH)
500 S Buena Vista St, Burbank
(91521-0001)
P.O. Box 3232, Anaheim (92803-3232)
PHONE..................................818 560-1000
Robert Iger, *President*
Renu Thomas, *Exec VP*
Matthew L McGinnis, *Principal*
David Ambroz, *Exec Dir*
Robert Dellosa, *Technology*
◆ EMP: 170 **EST:** 1986

SALES (est): 25.8B
SALES (corp-wide): 90.2B **Publicly Held**
SIC: 4832 6794 5331 7996 Radio broadcasting stations; copyright buying & licensing; music royalties, sheet & record;
performance rights, publishing & licensing; variety stores; theme park, amusement; ice hockey club

(P-5522)
**EDUCATIONAL MEDIA
FOUNDATION (PA)**
Also Called: K-LOVE RADIO NETWORK
5700 West Oaks Blvd, Rocklin
(95765-3719)
PHONE..................................916 251-1600
Darrell Chambliss, *Ch of Bd*
Richard Jenkins, *President*
Mike Novak, *CEO*
Jon Taylor, *CFO*
David Atkinson, *Vice Pres*
EMP: 200
SQ FT: 55,000
SALES: 188.5MM **Privately Held**
SIC: 4832 Radio broadcasting stations

(P-5523)
**EMMIS COMMUNICATIONS
CORP**
Emmis Marketting Group
2600 W Olive Ave Fl 8, Burbank
(91505-4553)
PHONE..................................818 238-6705
Val Maki, *Branch Mgr*
EMP: 175
SALES (corp-wide): 114.1MM **Publicly
Held**
WEB: www.emmis.com
SIC: 4832 Radio broadcasting stations
PA: Emmis Communications Corp
40 Monument Cir Ste 700
Indianapolis IN 46204
317 266-0100

(P-5524)
**EMMIS COMMUNICATIONS
CORP**
790 E Colorado Blvd Fl 9, Pasadena
(91101-2193)
PHONE..................................626 484-4440
EMP: 123
SALES (corp-wide): 114.1MM **Publicly
Held**
SIC: 4832 Radio broadcasting stations
PA: Emmis Communications Corp
40 Monument Cir Ste 700
Indianapolis IN 46204
317 266-0100

(P-5525)
**ENTERCOM COMMUNICATIONS
CORP**
Also Called: Kseg-FM
5345 Madison Ave, Sacramento
(95841-3141)
PHONE..................................916 766-5000
John Geary, *Manager*
Jim Fox, *Vice Pres*
Stacey Larson, *Vice Pres*
Lance Richard, *Vice Pres*
Rick Rapalee, *Engineer*
EMP: 120
SALES (corp-wide): 1.4B **Publicly Held**
WEB: www.entercom.com
SIC: 4832 7929 Radio broadcasting sta-
tions, music format; entertainers & enter-
tainment groups
PA: Entercom Communications Corp.
2400 Market St Fl 4
Philadelphia PA 19103
610 660-5610

(P-5526)
**ENTERCOM COMMUNICATIONS
CORP**
201 3rd St Fl 12, San Francisco
(94103-3133)
PHONE..................................610 660-5610
Betsy O'Connor, *Branch Mgr*
Steve Parker, *Executive*
Lynn Hooper, *Executive Asst*
EMP: 109
SALES (corp-wide): 1.4B **Publicly Held**
WEB: www.entercom.com
SIC: 4832 Radio broadcasting stations

PA: Entercom Communications Corp.
2400 Market St Fl 4
Philadelphia PA 19103
610 660-5610

(P-5527)
**ENTERCOM COMMUNICATIONS
CORP**
Also Called: K S S J Radio-101.9 FM City
5345 Madison Ave Ste 100, Sacramento
(95841-3141)
PHONE..................................916 334-7777
John Geary, *Vice Pres*
EMP: 120
SALES (corp-wide): 1.4B **Publicly Held**
WEB: www.entercom.com
SIC: 4832 7929 Radio broadcasting sta-
tions; entertainers & entertainment groups
PA: Entercom Communications Corp.
2400 Market St Fl 4
Philadelphia PA 19103
610 660-5610

(P-5528)
**ENTRAVSION
COMMUNICATIONS CORP**
Also Called: Krcx 99 9 FM Tricolor
1792 Tribute Rd Ste 450, Sacramento
(95815-4320)
PHONE..................................916 646-4000
Angie Balderas, *Manager*
EMP: 50 **Publicly Held**
SIC: 4832 Radio broadcasting stations
PA: Entravision Communications Corpora-
tion
2425 Olympic Blvd Ste 600
Santa Monica CA 90404

(P-5529)
FAMILY STATIONS INC (PA)
Also Called: Family Radio
1350 S Loop Rd, Alameda (94502-7095)
PHONE..................................510 568-6200
Harold Camping, *President*
Gary Cook, *CFO*
Bill Thornton, *Treasurer*
Jeff Zimmer, *Engineer*
EMP: 130 **EST:** 1958
SQ FT: 3,000
SALES: 5.4MM **Privately Held**
WEB: www.familyradio.com
SIC: 4832 Radio broadcasting stations

(P-5530)
**FAR EAST BROADCASTING CO
INC**
Also Called: Radio Station Kfbs
15700 Imperial Hwy, La Mirada
(90638-2598)
P.O. Box 1 (90637-0001)
PHONE..................................562 947-4651
Gregg Harris, *President*
Victor Akhterov, *COO*
Charles Blake, *CFO*
Scott Hassel, *CFO*
Wesley Wes Willmer, *Vice Pres*
▲ EMP: 52 **EST:** 1945
SQ FT: 20,000
SALES: 14.6MM **Privately Held**
SIC: 4832 Radio broadcasting stations

(P-5531)
**FOOTH-DE ANZA COMMUN
COLLEG DI**
Also Called: Kfjc FM
12345 S El Monte Rd # 6202, Los Altos
Hills (94022-4504)
PHONE..................................650 949-7260
Eric Johnson, *General Mgr*
EMP: 70
SALES (corp-wide): 128.3MM **Privately
Held**
WEB: www.fhda.edu
SIC: 4832 Radio broadcasting stations,
music format
PA: Foothill-De Anza Community College
District Financing Corporation
12345 S El Monte Rd
Los Altos Hills CA 94022
650 949-6100

(P-5532)
GOLD DERBY MEDIA LLC
Also Called: Goldderby.com
11175 Santa Monica Blvd, Los Angeles
(90025-3330)
PHONE..................................310 321-5000
Jay Penske, *CEO*
EMP: 53
SALES (est): 357.5K
SALES (corp-wide): 40.8MM **Privately
Held**
SIC: 4832 News
PA: Penske Media Corporation
11175 Santa Monica Blvd
Los Angeles CA 90025
310 321-5000

(P-5533)
HENRY BROADCASTING CO
2277 Jerrold Ave, San Francisco
(94124-1011)
PHONE..................................415 285-1133
C H Buckley, *President*
EMP: 50 **EST:** 1996
SALES (est): 1.8MM
SALES (corp-wide): 1.4B **Publicly Held**
SIC: 4832 Radio broadcasting stations
HQ: Cbs Radio Inc.
83 Leo M Birmingham Pkwy
Boston MA

(P-5534)
IHEARTCOMMUNICATIONS INC
Also Called: K Y L D
340 Townsend St Fl 4, San Francisco
(94107-1633)
PHONE..................................415 975-5555
Kim Bryant, *Manager*
Joe Bayliss, *Vice Pres*
EMP: 300 **Publicly Held**
SIC: 4832 7313 Radio broadcasting sta-
tions; radio advertising representative
HQ: Iheartcommunications, Inc.
20880 Stone Oak Pkwy
San Antonio TX 78258
210 822-2828

(P-5535)
IHEARTCOMMUNICATIONS INC
Also Called: Clear Channel Riverside
2030 Iowa Ave Ste A, Riverside
(92507-7415)
PHONE..................................951 684-1992
Bob Ridzak, *General Mgr*
EMP: 61 **Publicly Held**
SIC: 4832 Radio broadcasting stations
HQ: Iheartcommunications, Inc.
20880 Stone Oak Pkwy
San Antonio TX 78258
210 822-2828

(P-5536)
IHEARTCOMMUNICATIONS INC
Also Called: Krzr 103 7 FM
83 E Shaw Ave Ste 150, Fresno
(93710-7622)
PHONE..................................559 230-4300
Jeff Negrete, *Branch Mgr*
EMP: 75 **Publicly Held**
SIC: 4832 Radio broadcasting stations
HQ: Iheartcommunications, Inc.
20880 Stone Oak Pkwy
San Antonio TX 78258
210 822-2828

(P-5537)
IHEARTCOMMUNICATIONS INC
Also Called: Kogoam
9660 Gran Rdge Dr Ste 100, San Diego
(92123)
PHONE..................................858 522-5547
Dave Schroeder, *Manager*
Mike Glickenhaus, *Principal*
Melissa Bigay, *Technology*
EMP: 280 **Publicly Held**
SIC: 4832 Radio broadcasting stations
HQ: Iheartcommunications, Inc.
20880 Stone Oak Pkwy
San Antonio TX 78258
210 822-2828

(P-5538)
IHEARTCOMMUNICATIONS INC
9660 Gran Rdge Dr Ste 200, San Diego
(92123)
PHONE.....................858 292-2000
Dave Schroeder, *Controller*
EMP: 61 **Publicly Held**
SIC: 4832 Radio broadcasting stations
HQ: Iheartcommunications, Inc.
20880 Stone Oak Pkwy
San Antonio TX 78258
210 822-2828

(P-5539)
IHEARTCOMMUNICATIONS INC
3400 W Olive Ave Ste 550, Burbank
(91505-5544)
PHONE.....................818 846-0029
Greg Ashlock, *Executive*
Maryann Niland, *Executive Asst*
Raul Altamar, *Administration*
Katie Petito, *Technical Staff*
Eric Dunsworth, *Engineer*
EMP: 81 **Publicly Held**
WEB: www.kget.com
SIC: 4832 Radio broadcasting stations
HQ: Iheartcommunications, Inc.
20880 Stone Oak Pkwy
San Antonio TX 78258
210 822-2828

(P-5540)
IHEARTCOMMUNICATIONS INC
1545 River Park Dr # 500, Sacramento
(95815-4616)
PHONE.....................916 929-5325
Sarah McClure, *General Mgr*
EMP: 120 **Publicly Held**
SIC: 4832 Radio broadcasting stations
HQ: Iheartcommunications, Inc.
20880 Stone Oak Pkwy
San Antonio TX 78258
210 822-2828

(P-5541)
IHEARTCOMMUNICATIONS INC
352 E Avenue K4, Lancaster (93535-4505)
PHONE.....................661 942-1268
EMP: 61
SALES (corp-wide): 6.2B **Publicly Held**
SIC: 4832
HQ: Iheartcommunications, Inc.
200 E Basse Rd
San Antonio TX 78258
210 822-2828

(P-5542)
IHEARTCOMMUNICATIONS INC
1440 Ethan Way, Sacramento
(95825-2225)
PHONE.....................916 929-5325
EMP: 61 **Publicly Held**
SIC: 4832 Radio broadcasting stations
HQ: Iheartcommunications, Inc.
20880 Stone Oak Pkwy
San Antonio TX 78258
210 822-2828

(P-5543)
INFINITY BROADCASTING CORP CAL
Also Called: Krth Radio 101 FM
5670 Wilshire Blvd # 200, Los Angeles
(90036-5679)
PHONE.....................323 936-5784
John Sykes, *President*
Maureen Lesourd, *Vice Pres*
EMP: 60 **EST:** 2001
SALES (est): 2.6MM
SALES (corp-wide): 25.9B **Publicly Held**
SIC: 4832 Radio broadcasting stations
HQ: Cbs Corporation
51 W 52nd St Bsmt 1
New York NY 10019
212 975-4321

(P-5544)
K G O T V NEWS BUREAU
520 3rd St Ste 200, Oakland (94607-3505)
PHONE.....................510 451-4772
Ed Kosowski, *Principal*
EMP: 100
SALES (est): 87.4K
SALES (corp-wide): 1.6B **Publicly Held**
SIC: 4832 Radio broadcasting stations

HQ: San Francisco Radio Assets Llc
750 Battery St Fl 2
San Francisco CA 94111

(P-5545)
KCBS NEWS RADIO 74
865 Battery St, San Francisco
(94111-1554)
PHONE.....................415 765-4112
Doug Harvill, *Manager*
Douglas Sterne, *General Mgr*
Ed Cavagnaro, *Director*
EMP: 90
SALES (est): 4.3MM **Privately Held**
SIC: 4832 Radio broadcasting stations

(P-5546)
KIFM SMOOTH JAZZ 981 INC
1615 Murray Canyon Rd, San Diego
(92108-4314)
PHONE.....................619 297-3698
Mike Stafford, *President*
EMP: 110
SQ FT: 12,000
SALES (est): 1.9MM
SALES (corp-wide): 1.4B **Publicly Held**
SIC: 4832 Radio broadcasting stations
HQ: Abe Entercom Holdings Llc
401 E City Ave Ste 809
Bala Cynwyd PA 19004
404 239-7211

(P-5547)
KKZZ 1590
Also Called: Gold Coast Broadcasting
2284 S Victoria Ave 2g, Ventura
(93003-6641)
PHONE.....................805 289-1400
Chip Ehrhardt, *Partner*
John Hearne, *Partner*
EMP: 50
SALES (est): 1.3MM **Privately Held**
SIC: 4832 Radio broadcasting stations

(P-5548)
KOXR SPANISH RADIO
Also Called: K O X R
200 S A St Ste 400, Oxnard (93030-5723)
PHONE.....................805 487-0444
Alfredo Placencia, *Owner*
Vicky Orozco, *Sales Mgr*
Maria Foster, *Accounts Exec*
EMP: 50
SALES (est): 1.5MM **Privately Held**
SIC: 4832 Radio broadcasting stations

(P-5549)
KPWR INC
Also Called: Kpwr Power 106
2600 W Olive Ave Ste 850, Burbank
(91505-4568)
PHONE.....................818 953-4200
Jeffrey Smulyan, *CEO*
Doyle Rose, *President*
Candice Del Villar, *Executive*
Terri Dourian, *Human Res Dir*
Andy Lam, *Manager*
EMP: 88
SQ FT: 1,700
SALES (est): 16.2MM
SALES (corp-wide): 114.1MM **Publicly Held**
WEB: www.power106la.com
SIC: 4832 Radio broadcasting stations
PA: Emmis Communications Corp
40 Monument Cir Ste 700
Indianapolis IN 46204
317 266-0100

(P-5550)
KRTY LTD A CAL LTD PARTNR
1887 Monterey Hwy Ste 250, San Jose
(95112-6192)
PHONE.....................408 293-8030
Robert S Kieve, *Partner*
EMP: 50
SALES (est): 2.9MM **Privately Held**
WEB: www.krty.com
SIC: 4832 Radio broadcasting stations

(P-5551)
KUIC INC
Also Called: Kuic-Fm
555 Mason St Ste 245, Vacaville
(95688-4640)
PHONE.....................707 446-0200
James Levitt, *Ch of Bd*
John F Levitt, *President*
Robin Mitchell, *Executive*
Joe Scholtes, *Executive*
Barbara Hoover, *Executive*
EMP: 60
SQ FT: 4,200
SALES (est): 2.1MM
SALES (corp-wide): 27MM **Privately Held**
WEB: www.kuic.com
SIC: 4832 2711 Radio broadcasting stations; newspapers
PA: Coast Radio Company Inc
555 Mason St Ste 245
Vacaville CA 95688
707 446-0200

(P-5552)
KUSC RADIO
1149 S Hill St Ste H100, Los Angeles
(90015-4804)
PHONE.....................213 225-7400
Christopher Mendez, *Director*
Pablo Garcia, *Director*
EMP: 50
SQ FT: 12,000
SALES (est): 1.4MM **Privately Held**
SIC: 4832 Radio broadcasting stations

(P-5553)
LBI MEDIA INC
1845 W Empire Ave, Burbank
(91504-3402)
PHONE.....................818 729-5316
Peter Markham, *CEO*
Laura Fisher, *Vice Pres*
Alison Rae, *Sales Mgr*
EMP: 510
SALES (est): 385.1K
SALES (corp-wide): 283.6MM **Privately Held**
SIC: 4832 Radio broadcasting stations
HQ: Lbi Media Holdings, Inc.
1845 W Empire Ave
Burbank CA 91504

(P-5554)
LELAND STANFORD JUNIOR UNIV
Also Called: Kzsu 90.1 FM
551 Srra Mall Mem Adtrium Memorial Auditorium, Stanford (94305)
PHONE.....................650 725-4868
Mark Lawrence, *Principal*
EMP: 100
SALES (corp-wide): 11.3B **Privately Held**
SIC: 4832 Radio broadcasting stations
PA: Leland Stanford Junior University
450 Jane Stanford Way
Stanford CA 94305
650 723-2300

(P-5555)
LIBERMAN BROADCASTING INC (PA)
1845 W Empire Ave, Burbank
(91504-3402)
PHONE.....................818 729-5300
Lenard D Liberman, *CEO*
Jose Liberman, *President*
Frederic T Boyer, *CFO*
Cathy Lewis, *Senior VP*
Michael Sheron, *Senior VP*
EMP: 83
SALES (est): 283.6MM **Privately Held**
SIC: 4832 Radio broadcasting stations

(P-5556)
LIBERMAN BROADCASTING INC
Also Called: Kkhj 930 AM
1845 W Empire Ave, Burbank
(91504-3402)
PHONE.....................323 461-9300
Leonard Liberman, *President*
EMP: 50

SALES (corp-wide): 283.6MM **Privately Held**
SIC: 4832 Radio broadcasting stations
PA: Liberman Broadcasting, Inc.
1845 W Empire Ave
Burbank CA 91504
818 729-5300

(P-5557)
LOCAL MEDIA SAN DIEGO LLC
Also Called: Magic 92.5
6160 Cornerstone Ct E # 150, San Diego
(92121-3720)
PHONE.....................858 888-7000
John Lynch, *CEO*
Norman McKee, *CFO*
EMP: 100
SALES (est): 6.4MM **Privately Held**
SIC: 4832 Radio broadcasting stations, music format

(P-5558)
LOTUS COMMUNICATIONS CORP (PA)
3301 Barham Blvd Ste 200, Los Angeles
(90068-1358)
PHONE.....................323 512-2225
Howard Kalmenson, *President*
William H Shriftman, *Treasurer*
Jim Kalmenson, *Senior VP*
Jerry Roy, *Senior VP*
Jasmin Dorismond, *Vice Pres*
EMP: 60 **EST:** 1959
SQ FT: 25,848
SALES (est): 101.1MM **Privately Held**
WEB: www.lotuscorp.com
SIC: 4832 Radio broadcasting stations

(P-5559)
LOYOLA MARYMOUNT UNIVERSITY
Also Called: Radio Station
1 Lmu Dr Ste 100, Los Angeles
(90045-2677)
PHONE.....................310 338-2866
Lily O'Brien, *General Mgr*
EMP: 120
SALES (corp-wide): 393.2MM **Privately Held**
WEB: www.lmu.edu
SIC: 4832 8221 Radio broadcasting stations; university
PA: Loyola Marymount University
1 Lmu Dr Uhall Ste 4900
Los Angeles CA 90045
310 338-2700

(P-5560)
PACIFIC SPANISH NETWORK INC
296 H St Ste 300, Chula Vista
(91910-4753)
PHONE.....................619 427-6323
Jaime Bonilla Valdez, *President*
EMP: 69
SQ FT: 5,000
SALES (est): 2.7MM **Privately Held**
SIC: 4832 Radio broadcasting stations

(P-5561)
PANDORA MEDIA LLC (DH)
2100 Franklin St Ste 700, Oakland
(94612-3145)
PHONE.....................510 451-4100
Roger Lynch, *President*
David Gerbitz, *COO*
Naveen Chopra, *CFO*
Aimee Lapic, *Chief Mktg Ofcr*
Christopher Phillips, *Officer*
EMP: 162
SQ FT: 250,000
SALES (est): 1.4B
SALES (corp-wide): 8B **Publicly Held**
WEB: www.pandora.com
SIC: 4832 Radio broadcasting stations

(P-5562)
POWER 106 RADIO
2600 W Olive Ave Fl 8, Burbank
(91505-4553)
PHONE.....................818 953-4200
Pat Thomas, *Manager*
Jimmy Steal, *Vice Pres*
Val Maki, *General Mgr*
Edgar Preciado, *Production*

Aimee Bittourna, *Director*
EMP: 90
SALES (est): 3.4MM **Privately Held**
WEB: www.power106radio.com
SIC: 4832 Radio broadcasting stations

(P-5563)
SALEM MEDIA GROUP INC (PA)
4880 Santa Rosa Rd, Camarillo
(93012-5190)
PHONE..................805 987-0400
Edward G Atsinger III, *CEO*
Stuart W Epperson, *Ch of Bd*
David A R Evans, *President*
David P Santrella, *President*
Evan D Masyr, *CFO*
EMP: 141
SQ FT: 46,000
SALES: 262.7MM **Publicly Held**
WEB: www.srnradio.com
SIC: 4832 2731 4813 Radio broadcasting
stations; book publishing;

(P-5564)
SALEM MEDIA GROUP INC
Also Called: Krlh-AM 590-AM
701 N Brand Blvd Ste 550, Glendale
(91203-1235)
P.O. Box 29023 (91209-9023)
PHONE..................818 956-5254
Terry Sahy, *Manager*
Richard Blythe, *Opers-Prdtn-Mfg*
Dave Benzing, *Director*
Larry Marino, *Director*
Terry Fahy, *Manager*
EMP: 100
SALES (corp-wide): 262.7MM **Publicly
Held**
WEB: www.srnradio.com
SIC: 4832 Radio broadcasting stations
PA: Salem Media Group, Inc.
4880 Santa Rosa Rd
Camarillo CA 93012
805 987-0400

(P-5565)
**SAN FRANCISCO RADIO
ASSETS LLC (DH)**
Also Called: Kgo 810am
750 Battery St Fl 2, San Francisco
(94111-1523)
PHONE..................415 216-1300
Deidrea Lieberman,
Jack Swanson, *Administration*
EMP: 150
SQ FT: 51,000
SALES (est): 32MM
SALES (corp-wide): 1.6B **Publicly Held**
SIC: 4832 Radio broadcasting stations

(P-5566)
TOAD 1350
2030 Iowa Ave Ste A, Riverside
(92507-7415)
PHONE..................951 369-1350
Bob Ridzak, *Administration*
EMP: 50
SALES (est): 703.1K **Privately Held**
SIC: 4832 Radio broadcasting stations

(P-5567)
**TRIAD BROADCASTING
COMPANY (PA)**
2511 Garden Rd Ste A104, Monterey
(93940-5376)
P.O. Box 7539, Carmel By The Sea
(93921-7539)
PHONE..................831 655-6350
David J Benjamin, *President*
Steve Feder, *Vice Pres*
EMP: 140
SALES (est): 28.7MM **Privately Held**
SIC: 4832 Radio broadcasting stations

(P-5568)
**TRITON MEDIA GROUP LLC
(PA)**
15303 Ventura Blvd # 1500, Sherman Oaks
(91403-3137)
PHONE..................323 290-6900
Nathaniel Parker Hudnut, *CEO*
Sean Moriarty, *Ch of Bd*
EMP: 1500

SALES (est): 54.9MM **Privately Held**
SIC: 4832 Radio broadcasting stations,
music format

(P-5569)
TRITON MEDIA GROUP LLC
Also Called: Dial Global Digital
8935 Lindblade St, Culver City
(90232-2438)
PHONE..................661 294-9000
Phil Barry, *Branch Mgr*
EMP: 75 **Privately Held**
SIC: 4832 Radio broadcasting stations,
music format
PA: Triton Media Group, Llc
15303 Ventura Blvd # 1500
Sherman Oaks CA 91403

(P-5570)
TUNEIN INC
Also Called: Radio Time
210 King St Fl 3, San Francisco
(94107-1702)
PHONE..................650 319-7100
Juliette Morris, *CEO*
Holly Lim, *CFO*
Geoff Dowd, *Vice Pres*
George Kristin, *Vice Pres*
Yuanming Shan, *Vice Pres*
EMP: 200
SALES: 73.7MM **Privately Held**
SIC: 4832 Radio broadcasting stations

(P-5571)
**TURNER BROADCASTING
SYSTEM INC**
1888 Century Park E # 1200, Los Angeles
(90067-1715)
PHONE..................310 788-6767
Frank Merauto, *Principal*
Shimrit Sheetrit, *Director*
EMP: 70
SALES (corp-wide): 170.7B **Publicly
Held**
WEB: www.turner.com
SIC: 4832 Radio broadcasting stations
HQ: Turner Broadcasting System, Inc.
1 Cnn Ctr Nw 14sw
Atlanta GA 30303
404 575-7250

(P-5572)
**UNIVISION COMMUNICATIONS
INC**
655 N Central Ave # 2500, Glendale
(91203-1422)
PHONE..................818 484-7399
Thomas McSweeney, *Branch Mgr*
EMP: 140 **Privately Held**
WEB: www.univision.com
SIC: 4832 Radio broadcasting stations
HQ: Univision Communications Inc.
114 5th Ave
New York NY 10011
212 455-5200

(P-5573)
UNIVISION RADIO INC
601 W Univision Plz, Fresno (93704-1092)
PHONE..................559 430-8500
Angela Navarrete, *Branch Mgr*
EMP: 50 **Privately Held**
WEB: www.heftel.com
SIC: 4832 Radio broadcasting stations
HQ: Univision Radio, Inc.
2323 Bryan St Ste 1900
Dallas TX 75201

(P-5574)
WALT DISNEY COMPANY
Also Called: Kiid
8265 Sierra College Blvd # 21, Roseville
(95661-9403)
PHONE..................916 780-1470
EMP: 53 **Publicly Held**
SIC: 4832
PA: The Walt Disney Company
500 S Buena Vista St
Burbank CA 91521

**4833 Television
Broadcasting Stations**

(P-5575)
ABC INC
500 Circle Seven Dr, Glendale
(91201-2331)
PHONE..................818 863-7801
Arnold J Kleiner, *Director*
EMP: 500
SALES (corp-wide): 90.2B **Publicly Held**
WEB: www.abc.com
SIC: 4833 Television broadcasting stations
HQ: Abc, Inc.
77 W 66th St Rm 100
New York NY 10023
212 456-7777

(P-5576)
**ABC CABLE NETWORKS
GROUP**
900 Front St, San Francisco (94111-1427)
PHONE..................415 954-7911
Lynn Dooley, *Branch Mgr*
Rosendo Pena, *Info Tech Mgr*
Richard Tom, *Engineer*
EMP: 200
SALES (corp-wide): 90.2B **Publicly Held**
WEB: www.breakbar.com
SIC: 4833 Television broadcasting stations
HQ: Abc Cable Networks Group
500 S Buena Vista St
Burbank CA 91521
818 460-7477

(P-5577)
ABC SIGNATURE STUDIOS INC
500 S Buena Vista St, Burbank
(91521-0001)
PHONE..................818 569-7500
Linda A Bagley, *CEO*
EMP: 86
SALES (est): 504.9K **Privately Held**
SIC: 4833 Television broadcasting stations

(P-5578)
ACCESS HOLLYWOOD
Also Called: Channel 4-NBC 4 Television
3000 W Alameda Ave, Burbank
(91523-0001)
PHONE..................818 840-4444
Jeff Zaker, *CEO*
Ellen Rand, *Vice Pres*
Greg Couture, *Program Mgr*
Carole Johns, *Administration*
Terry Smith, *Technology*
EMP: 170
SALES (est): 6.1MM **Privately Held**
SIC: 4833 Television broadcasting stations

(P-5579)
AMERICAN MULTIMEDIA TV USA
Also Called: Amtv USA
530 S Lake Ave Unit 368, Pasadena
(91101-3515)
PHONE..................626 466-1038
Jason Quin, *President*
EMP: 67
SALES: 357K **Privately Held**
SIC: 4833 7372 Television broadcasting
stations; application computer software

(P-5580)
BAY CITY TELEVISION INC (PA)
8253 Ronson Rd, San Diego (92111-2004)
P.O. Box 712109 (92171-2109)
PHONE..................858 279-6666
Jose Antonio Baston Patino, *CEO*
Robert Taylor, *President*
Rodrigo Salazar, *Vice Pres*
Veronica Chavez, *Executive Asst*
Samantha Larson, *Accounts Exec*
EMP: 100 EST: 1953
SQ FT: 12,000
SALES (est): 34.6MM **Privately Held**
SIC: 4833 7311 Television broadcasting
stations; advertising agencies

(P-5581)
**BURBANK TELEVISION ENTPS
LLC**
4000 Warner Blvd, Burbank (91522-0001)
PHONE..................818 954-6000

Barry M Meyer, *CEO*
EMP: 200
SALES (est): 2.9MM
SALES (corp-wide): 170.7B **Publicly
Held**
SIC: 4833 Television broadcasting stations
HQ: Warner Bros. Entertainment Inc.
4000 Warner Blvd
Burbank CA 91522
818 954-6000

(P-5582)
BUZZTIME INC
2231 Rutherford Rd # 200, Carlsbad
(92008-8820)
PHONE..................760 476-1976
Dario Santana, *CEO*
EMP: 120
SALES (est): 5.2MM **Privately Held**
WEB: www.buzztime.com
SIC: 4833 Television broadcasting stations

(P-5583)
**CALIFORNIA OREGON
BROADCASTING (HQ)**
Also Called: Krcr TV
755 Auditorium Dr, Redding (96001-0920)
PHONE..................530 243-7777
Sarah Smith, *General Mgr*
EMP: 60 EST: 1963
SQ FT: 14,000
SALES (est): 8.2MM
SALES (corp-wide): 25.9MM **Privately
Held**
WEB: www.krcrtv.com
SIC: 4833 Television broadcasting stations
PA: Appalachian Broadcasting Corp
101 Lee St
Bristol VA
276 645-1555

(P-5584)
**CATAMOUNT BROADCASTING
OF CHIC (PA)**
Also Called: Khsl TV
3460 Silverbell Rd, Chico (95973-0388)
PHONE..................530 893-2424
Raymond Johns, *President*
EMP: 104
SQ FT: 18,000
SALES (est): 13.6MM **Privately Held**
WEB: www.knvn.com
SIC: 4833 Television broadcasting stations

(P-5585)
CBS BROADCASTING INC
855 Battery St, San Francisco
(94111-1503)
PHONE..................415 765-0928
Bruno Cohen, *Manager*
Mallory Baker, *Vice Pres*
Jerry Brandt, *Vice Pres*
Gary Silver, *Vice Pres*
Crystal Myers, *Executive*
EMP: 300
SALES (corp-wide): 25.9B **Publicly Held**
WEB: www.cbs4.com
SIC: 4833 Television broadcasting stations
HQ: Cbs Broadcasting Inc.
524 W 57th St
New York NY 10019
212 975-4321

(P-5586)
CBS BROADCASTING INC
4200 Radford Ave, Studio City
(91604-2189)
PHONE..................818 655-2000
Steve Mauldin, *General Mgr*
EMP: 500
SALES (corp-wide): 25.9B **Publicly Held**
WEB: www.cbs4.com
SIC: 4833 Television broadcasting stations
HQ: Cbs Broadcasting Inc.
524 W 57th St
New York NY 10019
212 975-4321

(P-5587)
CBS CORPORATION
7800 Beverly Blvd, Los Angeles
(90036-2112)
PHONE..................323 575-2345
Jonathan Anshell, *Branch Mgr*
Karen McLaughlin, *Vice Pres*
Brian Naguit, *Executive Asst*

Ashleigh Sigal, *Executive Asst*
Jim Ripple, *Technical Staff*
EMP: 72
SALES (corp-wide): 25.9B **Publicly Held**
SIC: 4833 Television broadcasting stations
HQ: Cbs Corporation
51 W 52nd St Bsmt 1
New York NY 10019
212 975-4321

(P-5588)
CBS CORPORATION
31276 Dunham Way, Thousand Palms
(92276-3310)
PHONE...................................760 343-5700
Mike Stutz, *Office Mgr*
EMP: 64
SALES (corp-wide): 25.9B **Publicly Held**
SIC: 4833 Television broadcasting stations
HQ: Cbs Corporation
51 W 52nd St Bsmt 1
New York NY 10019
212 975-4321

(P-5589)
CHANNEL 40 INC
Also Called: Ktxl-Fox 40
4655 Fruitridge Rd, Sacramento
(95820-5201)
PHONE...................................916 454-4422
Jerry Del Core, *Vice Pres*
Leigh White, *Vice Pres*
EMP: 105
SQ FT: 25,000
SALES (est): 8.6MM
SALES (corp-wide): 2.7B **Publicly Held**
WEB: www.tribune.com
SIC: 4833 Television translator station
HQ: Tribune Media Company
515 N State St Ste 2400
Chicago IL 60654
312 222-3394

(P-5590)
CHRONICLE BROADCASTING CO
Also Called: Kron-Tv
900 Front St, San Francisco (94111-1427)
PHONE...................................415 561-8000
Francis A Martin III, *President*
Glen E Pickell, *Treasurer*
Ronald Ingram, *Vice Pres*
Robert M Raymer, *Admin Sec*
Christina Bennett, *Producer*
EMP: 400 **EST:** 1966
SQ FT: 90,000
SALES (est): 15.8MM
SALES (corp-wide): 8.3B **Privately Held**
SIC: 4833 Television broadcasting stations
HQ: Hearst Communications, Inc.
300 W 57th St
New York NY 10019
212 649-2000

(P-5591)
COLLINS AVENUE LLC
5410 Wilshire Blvd # 800, Los Angeles
(90036-4267)
PHONE...................................323 930-6633
Jeff Collins, *President*
Michael Hammond, *Senior VP*
Melanie Moreau, *Senior VP*
John Bradley, *Vice Pres*
Sandi Johnson, *Vice Pres*
EMP: 50
SALES (est): 4.7MM **Privately Held**
SIC: 4833 Television broadcasting stations

(P-5592)
COMCA SPORT NET BAY AREA
360 3rd St Fl 2, San Francisco
(94107-2154)
PHONE...................................415 896-2557
Richard Cotton, *Mng Member*
National Broadcasting, *General Ptnr*
G C Broadc, *Director*
EMP: 150
SALES (est): 5.5MM
SALES (corp-wide): 94.5B **Publicly Held**
WEB: www.ifc.com
SIC: 4833 Television broadcasting stations
HQ: Nbcuniversal Media, Llc
30 Rockefeller Plz Fl 2
New York NY 10112
212 664-4444

(P-5593)
CW NETWORK LLC (PA)
Also Called: Cwtv
3300 W Olive Ave Fl 3, Burbank
(91505-4640)
PHONE...................................818 977-2500
John Maatta, *CEO*
Dana Abel, *CFO*
Rick Haskins, *Exec VP*
Russell Myerson, *Exec VP*
Thomas Sherman, *Exec VP*
EMP: 210
SALES (est): 26.9MM **Privately Held**
WEB: www.cwtv.com
SIC: 4833 Television broadcasting stations

(P-5594)
DESERT TELEVISION LLC
Also Called: U-Dub Productions
73185 Highway 111 Ste D, Palm Desert
(92260-3929)
P.O. Box 13917 (92255-3917)
PHONE...................................760 343-5700
Jacqueline L Houston,
James R Houston,
Coleen Call, *Accounts Exec*
EMP: 85
SQ FT: 6,500
SALES (est): 5.3MM **Privately Held**
WEB: www.deserttelevision.com
SIC: 4833 Television broadcasting stations

(P-5595)
ENTERTAINMENT & SPORTS TODAY
Also Called: Rakstar Production
2966 Wilshire Blvd Ste C, Los Angeles
(90010-1128)
PHONE...................................213 388-9050
William Sturges, *CEO*
Frank Rakovic, *Vice Pres*
Martin Altonaga, *Director*
Greg Pyatt, *Director*
EMP: 100
SALES (est): 22MM **Privately Held**
SIC: 4833 7812 Television broadcasting stations; video production

(P-5596)
ENTRAVSION COMMUNICATIONS CORP
Also Called: Univision 67
67 Garden Ct, Monterey (93940-5302)
PHONE...................................831 333-9736
Aaron Scoby, *Manager*
EMP: 50 **Publicly Held**
SIC: 4833 Television translator station
PA: Entravsion Communications Corporation
2425 Olympic Blvd Ste 600
Santa Monica CA 90404

(P-5597)
ENTRAVSION COMMUNICATIONS CORP
Also Called: K S S C - F M
5700 Wilshire Blvd # 250, Los Angeles
(90036-3659)
PHONE...................................323 900-6100
Jeff Liberman, *President*
Dawn Rice,
EMP: 100 **Publicly Held**
SIC: 4833 4832 Television broadcasting stations; radio broadcasting stations
PA: Entravsion Communications Corporation
2425 Olympic Blvd Ste 600
Santa Monica CA 90404

(P-5598)
ENTRAVSION COMMUNICATIONS CORP
Also Called: Kmir-Tv6
72920 Parkview Dr, Palm Desert
(92260-9357)
PHONE...................................760 568-3636
Craig E Marrs, *President*
Gene Steinberg, *Vice Pres*
Sandie Ware, *Natl Sales Mgr*
David Reese, *Director*
EMP: 75 **Publicly Held**
WEB: www.journalbroadcastgroup.com
SIC: 4833 Television broadcasting stations

PA: Entravsion Communications Corporation
2425 Olympic Blvd Ste 600
Santa Monica CA 90404

(P-5599)
ENTRAVSION COMMUNICATIONS CORP
Also Called: Entravsion Radio
1792 Tribute Rd Ste 450, Sacramento
(95815-4320)
PHONE...................................916 648-6029
Larry Lamansky, *Manager*
EMP: 50 **Publicly Held**
SIC: 4833 4832 Television broadcasting stations; radio broadcasting stations
PA: Entravsion Communications Corporation
2425 Olympic Blvd Ste 600
Santa Monica CA 90404

(P-5600)
ENTRAVSION COMMUNICATIONS CORP (PA)
2425 Olympic Blvd Ste 600, Santa Monica
(90404-4030)
PHONE...................................310 447-3870
Walter F Ulloa, *Ch of Bd*
Jeffery A Liberman, *COO*
Christopher T Young, *CFO*
Juan Saldivar, *Bd of Directors*
Paul Zevnik, *Bd of Directors*
EMP: 170
SQ FT: 16,000
SALES: 297.8MM **Publicly Held**
SIC: 4833 4832 Television broadcasting stations; radio broadcasting stations

(P-5601)
ESTRELLA COMMUNICATIONS INC
Also Called: Kvea-Tv-Channel 52
3000 W Alameda Ave, Burbank
(91523-0001)
PHONE...................................818 260-5700
EMP: 90
SALES (est): 3.7MM
SALES (corp-wide): 68.7B **Publicly Held**
SIC: 4833
HQ: Telemundo Communications Group, Inc.
2290 W 8th Ave
Hialeah FL 33010
305 884-8200

(P-5602)
EW SCRIPPS COMPANY
Also Called: Kgtv
4600 Air Way, San Diego (92102-2528)
PHONE...................................619 237-1010
Derek Dalton, *Vice Pres*
Ally Flahive, *Producer*
Steve Lyew, *Marketing Staff*
EMP: 150
SALES (corp-wide): 1.2B **Publicly Held**
WEB: www.rtv6radio.com
SIC: 4833 Television broadcasting stations
PA: The E W Scripps Company
312 Walnut St Ste 2800
Cincinnati OH 45202
513 977-3000

(P-5603)
FISHER COMMUNICATIONS INC
Also Called: Kbaktv
1901 Westwind Dr, Bakersfield
(93301-3016)
PHONE...................................661 327-7955
Teresa Burgess, *Manager*
EMP: 85
SALES (corp-wide): 3B **Publicly Held**
SIC: 4833 Television broadcasting stations
HQ: Fisher Communications, Inc.
140 4th Ave N Ste 500
Seattle WA 98109
206 404-7000

(P-5604)
FOX INC (DH)
Also Called: Home Entertainment Div
2121 Avenue Of The Stars, Los Angeles
(90067-5010)
P.O. Box 900, Beverly Hills (90213-0900)
PHONE...................................310 369-1000
K Rupert Murdoch, *Ch of Bd*
Mike Dunn, *President*
Robert Fusco, *President*
Jay Itzkowitz, *President*
Russell Wetanson, *Vice Pres*
▲ **EMP:** 2000
SQ FT: 25,000
SALES (est): 904.5MM
SALES (corp-wide): 90.2B **Publicly Held**
WEB: www.foxhome.com
SIC: 4833 7812 Television broadcasting stations; motion picture production & distribution; motion picture production & distribution, television
HQ: 21st Century Fox America, Inc.
1211 Ave Of The Americas
New York NY 10036
212 852-7000

(P-5605)
FOX BROADCASTING COMPANY (HQ)
10201 W Pico Blvd, Los Angeles
(90064-2606)
P.O. Box 900, Beverly Hills (90213-0900)
PHONE...................................310 369-1000
David F Devoe Jr, *CEO*
Michael Thorn, *President*
Nancy Utley, *President*
Charlie Collier, *CEO*
Joe Earley, *COO*
EMP: 200
SQ FT: 41,000
SALES (est): 158.5MM
SALES (corp-wide): 11.3B **Publicly Held**
WEB: www.wghp.com
SIC: 4833 Television broadcasting stations
PA: Fox Corporation
1211 Avenue Of The Americ
New York NY 10036
212 852-7000

(P-5606)
FOX SPORTS PRODUCTIONS INC
10201 W Pico Blvd, Los Angeles
(90064-2606)
P.O. Box 900, Beverly Hills (90213-0900)
PHONE...................................310 369-1000
David Hill, *Ch of Bd*
EMP: 2777
SALES (est): 378K
SALES (corp-wide): 11.3B **Publicly Held**
WEB: www.foxtv.com
SIC: 4833 Television broadcasting stations
PA: Fox Corporation
1211 Avenue Of The Americ
New York NY 10036
212 852-7000

(P-5607)
FOX TELEVISION STATIONS INC (HQ)
Also Called: Fox Entertainment Television
1999 S Bundy Dr, Los Angeles
(90025-5203)
PHONE...................................310 584-2000
Jim Burke, *President*
Roger Ailes, *Ch of Bd*
Tom Herwitz, *President*
Dennis Swanson, *President*
Amy Carney, *COO*
▲ **EMP:** 300
SALES (est): 502.2MM
SALES (corp-wide): 11.3B **Publicly Held**
WEB: www.foxtv.com
SIC: 4833 7313 Television broadcasting stations; radio, television, publisher representatives
PA: Fox Corporation
1211 Avenue Of The Americ
New York NY 10036
212 852-7000

(P-5608)
FUEL TV
1440 S Sepulveda Blvd, Los Angeles
(90025-3458)
PHONE.....................310 444-8564
John Stouffer, *Director*
Nick Grad, *Exec VP*
Julie Piepenkotter, *Exec VP*
Eric Schrier, *Exec VP*
Gina Balian, *Vice Pres*
EMP: 75
SALES (est): 5.5MM **Privately Held**
SIC: 4833 Television broadcasting stations

(P-5609)
**GULF- CALIFORNIA
BROADCAST CO**
Also Called: Kesq TV
31276 Dunham Way, Thousand Palms
(92276-3310)
PHONE.....................760 773-0342
John Kuenuke, *President*
Chip Shenkan, *Sales Staff*
Jerry Upham, *Sales Staff*
Kathleen Huber, *Director*
Rebecca Johnson, *Director*
EMP: 116
SALES (est): 6.4MM
SALES (corp-wide): 201.1MM **Privately
Held**
WEB: www.kesq.com
SIC: 4833 7922 Television broadcasting
stations; theatrical producers & services
PA: News-Press & Gazette Company Inc
825 Edmond St
Saint Joseph MO 64501
816 271-8500

(P-5610)
HEARST STATIONS INC
Also Called: K S B W- T V
238 John St, Salinas (93901-3339)
P.O. Box 81651 (93912)
PHONE.....................831 758-8888
Joseph W Heston, *President*
Wendy Hillan, *Sales Mgr*
EMP: 80
SQ FT: 31,681
SALES (corp-wide): 8.3B **Privately Held**
WEB: www.wbal.com
SIC: 4833 Television translator station
HQ: Hearst Stations Inc.
3 Television Cir
Sacramento CA 95814
916 446-3333

(P-5611)
**HERRING BROADCASTING
COMPANY**
Also Called: Wealthtv
4757 Morena Blvd, San Diego
(92117-3462)
PHONE.....................858 270-6900
Robert Herring Sr, *President*
Graham Ledger, *Vice Pres*
Bonnie Breuner, *Editor*
EMP: 50
SQ FT: 40,000
SALES (est): 6.3MM **Privately Held**
SIC: 4833 Television broadcasting stations

(P-5612)
HERRING NETWORKS INC
Also Called: Awe
4757 Morena Blvd, San Diego
(92117-3462)
PHONE.....................858 270-6900
Charles P Herring, *President*
Bruce Littman, *Exec VP*
Graham Ledger, *Vice Pres*
Ann Schick, *Vice Pres*
Tim Robertson, *Web Dvlpr*
EMP: 130
SALES (est): 5MM **Privately Held**
SIC: 4833 Television broadcasting stations

(P-5613)
**INTERNATIONAL MEDIA GROUP
INC**
1990 S Bundy Dr Ste 850, Los Angeles
(90025-5253)
PHONE.....................310 478-1818
Peter Mathes, *Ch of Bd*
Beverly McMillan, *Executive Asst*
EMP: 80

SQ FT: 17,000
SALES (est): 3.5MM
SALES (corp-wide): 9.2MM **Privately
Held**
SIC: 4833 Television broadcasting stations
PA: Asianmedia Group Llc
1990 S Bundy Dr Ste 850
Los Angeles CA 90025
310 478-1818

(P-5614)
ION MEDIA NETWORKS INC
Also Called: Kpxn-TV
2531 Nina St, Pasadena (91107-3708)
PHONE.....................818 953-7193
Tyra Donatto, *Branch Mgr*
EMP: 50
SALES (corp-wide): 259.5MM **Privately
Held**
SIC: 4833 Television broadcasting stations
PA: Ion Media Networks, Inc.
601 Clearwater Park Rd
West Palm Beach FL 33401
561 659-4122

(P-5615)
KAZA AZTECA AMERICA INC
3900 W Alameda Ave # 1200, Burbank
(91505-4317)
PHONE.....................818 241-5400
Eduardo Urdiola, *President*
Germon Santiago, *Manager*
Alejandra Wachler, *Manager*
EMP: 140
SALES (est): 7MM **Privately Held**
SIC: 4833 Television translator station

(P-5616)
KBAK TV CHANNEL 29 CBS
Also Called: Westwind Communications
1901 Westwind Dr, Bakersfield
(93301-3016)
PHONE.....................661 327-7955
Wayne Lansche, *Owner*
EMP: 80
SALES (est): 1.9MM **Privately Held**
SIC: 4833 Television broadcasting stations

(P-5617)
KCETLINK (PA)
2900 W Alameda Ave # 600, Burbank
(91505-4267)
PHONE.....................714 241-4100
Andrew Russell, *President*
Jamie Myers, *COO*
Paul Nelson, *CFO*
Bernie Roscetti, *Associate Dir*
EMP: 150
SQ FT: 50,000
SALES (est): 21.7MM **Privately Held**
SIC: 4833 Television broadcasting stations

(P-5618)
KFSN TELEVISION LLC
Also Called: ABC 30
1777 G St, Fresno (93706-1688)
PHONE.....................559 442-1170
Dan Adams, *President*
EMP: 117
SQ FT: 26,962
SALES (est): 9.7MM
SALES (corp-wide): 90.2B **Publicly Held**
SIC: 4833 Television broadcasting stations
HQ: Disney Enterprises, Inc.
500 S Buena Vista St
Burbank CA 91521
818 560-1000

(P-5619)
KFTV
601 W Univision Plz, Fresno (93704-1092)
PHONE.....................559 222-2121
Jose Elgorriaga, *General Mgr*
EMP: 85 EST: 2011
SALES (est): 1.1MM **Privately Held**
SIC: 4833 Television broadcasting stations

(P-5620)
KGO TELEVISION INC
Also Called: Abc7 Broadcast Center
900 Front St, San Francisco (94111-1413)
PHONE.....................415 954-7777
Bill Burton, *President*
EMP: 230
SQ FT: 153,000

SALES (est): 24MM
SALES (corp-wide): 90.2B **Publicly Held**
WEB: www.kgoam810.com
SIC: 4833 Television broadcasting stations
HQ: Abc Holding Company Inc.
77 W 66th St Rm 100
New York NY 10023
212 456-7777

(P-5621)
KMPH FOX 26
Also Called: Pappas Telecasting Company
5111 E Mckinley Ave, Fresno (93727-2033)
PHONE.....................559 255-2600
Harry Pappas, *Principal*
EMP: 170
SALES (est): 7.4MM
SALES (corp-wide): 3B **Publicly Held**
WEB: www.kmph.com
SIC: 4833 Television broadcasting stations
PA: Sinclair Broadcast Group, Inc.
10706 Beaver Dam Rd
Hunt Valley MD 21030
410 568-1500

(P-5622)
KNET TV
5757 Wilshire Blvd # 470, Los Angeles
(90036-5810)
PHONE.....................323 469-5638
Larry Rogow, *Chairman*
EMP: 50
SALES (est): 855.1K **Privately Held**
SIC: 4833 Television broadcasting stations

(P-5623)
KOCE-TV FOUNDATION
Also Called: Pbs Socal
3080 Bristol St Ste 400, Costa Mesa
(92626-7335)
P.O. Box 25113, Santa Ana (92799-5113)
PHONE.....................714 241-4100
EMP: 52
SALES (est): 15.7MM **Privately Held**
WEB: www.koce.org
SIC: 4833 Television broadcasting stations

(P-5624)
KQED INC (PA)
Also Called: KQED PUBLIC MEDIA
2601 Mariposa St, San Francisco
(94110-1426)
P.O. Box 410865 (94141-0865)
PHONE.....................415 864-2000
John Boland, *President*
Donald W Derheim, *COO*
Mitzie Kelley, *CFO*
Craig Martin, *Officer*
Jo Anne Wallace, *Vice Pres*
EMP: 258 EST: 1952
SQ FT: 75,000
SALES: 83.5MM **Privately Held**
WEB: www.kqed.net
SIC: 4833 4832 Television broadcasting
stations; radio broadcasting stations

(P-5625)
KSBY COMMUNICATIONS LLC
1772 Calle Joaquin, San Luis Obispo
(93405-7210)
PHONE.....................805 541-6666
Kathleen Choal, *President*
Steve Barth, *Director*
EMP: 80
SALES (est): 5.3MM
SALES (corp-wide): 1.2B **Publicly Held**
WEB: www.ksby.com
SIC: 4833 Television broadcasting stations
PA: The E W Scripps Company
312 Walnut St Ste 2800
Cincinnati OH 45202
513 977-3000

(P-5626)
KSWB INC
Also Called: C W 5
7191 Engineer Rd, San Diego
(92111-1406)
PHONE.....................858 492-9269
Robert J Ramsey, *President*
Scott Heath, *Vice Pres*
EMP: 56
SQ FT: 30,000

SALES (est): 5.5MM
SALES (corp-wide): 2.7B **Publicly Held**
WEB: www.tribune.com
SIC: 4833 Television broadcasting stations
HQ: Tribune Media Company
515 N State St Ste 2400
Chicago IL 60654
312 222-3394

(P-5627)
KTSF CHANNEL 26
100 Valley Dr, Brisbane (94005-1318)
PHONE.....................415 467-6397
Lincoln Howell, *CEO*
EMP: 50
SALES (est): 5MM
SALES (corp-wide): 13.6MM **Privately
Held**
WEB: www.ktsf.com
SIC: 4833 Television broadcasting stations
PA: Lincoln Broadcasting Company, A Cali-
fornia Limited Partnership
100 Valley Dr
Brisbane CA 94005
415 508-1056

(P-5628)
KTVU PARTNERSHIP INC
Also Called: Ktvu Television Fox 2
2 Jack London Sq, Oakland (94607-3727)
PHONE.....................510 834-1212
Murdock Lachlan, *CEO*
◆ EMP: 230
SALES (est): 23.9MM
SALES (corp-wide): 11.3B **Publicly Held**
SIC: 4833 Television broadcasting stations
HQ: Fox Television Stations, Inc.
1999 S Bundy Dr
Los Angeles CA 90025
310 584-2000

(P-5629)
KVIE INC (PA)
Also Called: Kvie Channel 6
2030 W El Camino Ave # 100, Sacramento
(95833-1867)
P.O. Box 6 (95812-0006)
PHONE.....................916 929-5843
David Lowe, *CEO*
David Hosley, *President*
Julie Saqueton, *CFO*
Scott Moak, *Vice Pres*
Mike Cappi, *Info Tech Dir*
EMP: 60 EST: 1955
SQ FT: 69,000
SALES: 11.2MM **Privately Held**
WEB: www.capitolweek.com
SIC: 4833 Television broadcasting stations

(P-5630)
KXTV INC
Also Called: K X T V Channel 10
400 Broadway, Sacramento (95818-2041)
PHONE.....................916 441-2345
Risa Omega, *President*
Pat Sullivan, *Editor*
EMP: 155
SQ FT: 29,000
SALES (est): 31.2MM
SALES (corp-wide): 2.2B **Publicly Held**
WEB: www.news10.net
SIC: 4833 Television broadcasting stations
PA: Tegna Inc.
8350 Broad St Ste 2000
Tysons VA 22102
703 873-6600

(P-5631)
LIFETIME ENTRMT SVCS LLC
Also Called: Lifetime TV Network
2049 Century Park E # 840, Los Angeles
(90067-3101)
PHONE.....................310 556-7500
Maryann Harris, *General Mgr*
EMP: 70
SALES (corp-wide): 699.8MM **Privately
Held**
WEB: www.lifetimepress.com
SIC: 4833 5942 Television broadcasting
stations; book stores
HQ: Lifetime Entertainment Services, Llc
235 E 45th St
New York NY 10017
212 424-7000

(P-5632)
LINCOLN TELEVISION INC
Also Called: Ktff
100 Valley Dr, Brisbane (94005-1318)
PHONE................................415 468-2626
Lillian Lincoln Howell, *President*
EMP: 60
SQ FT: 20,800
SALES (est): 2.9MM **Privately Held**
SIC: 4833 Television broadcasting stations

(P-5633)
M NETWORK TELEVISION INC
6007 Sepulveda Blvd, Van Nuys
(91411-2502)
PHONE................................818 756-5150
Jonathan Murray, *President*
EMP: 50
SALES (est): 724.7K **Privately Held**
SIC: 4833 Television broadcasting stations

(P-5634)
**MCKINNON BROADCASTING
COMPANY (HQ)**
Also Called: Kusi TV Channel 51
4575 Viewridge Ave, San Diego
(92123-1623)
P.O. Box 719051 (92171-9051)
PHONE................................858 571-5151
Michael D McKinnon, *CEO*
Tommy Sablan, *Producer*
Heather Culver, *Manager*
Jim Angel, *Accounts Exec*
Beth Pearson, *Accounts Exec*
EMP: 150
SQ FT: 30,000
SALES (est): 17.2MM
SALES (corp-wide): 12.8MM **Privately Held**
WEB: www.kusi.com
SIC: 4833 Television broadcasting stations
PA: San Diego's Fifty One, Inc.
5002 S Padre Island Dr
Corpus Christi TX 78411
361 986-8300

(P-5635)
**MCKINNON PUBLISHING
COMPANY**
4575 Viewridge Ave, San Diego
(92123-1623)
PHONE................................858 571-5151
Michael McKinnon, *President*
EMP: 600
SALES (est): 14MM
SALES (corp-wide): 12.8MM **Privately Held**
WEB: www.kusi.com
SIC: 4833 Television broadcasting stations
HQ: Mckinnon Broadcasting Company
4575 Viewridge Ave
San Diego CA 92123
858 571-5151

(P-5636)
**NBC SUBSIDIARY (KNBC-TV)
LLC**
100 Unvrsal Cy Plz Bldg 2, Universal City
(91608)
PHONE................................818 684-5746
Steve Carlston, *President*
Jose Cancela, *Vice Pres*
Phil Perry, *Vice Pres*
Alicen Schneider, *Vice Pres*
Graham Smalley, *Vice Pres*
EMP: 250
SALES (est): 5.5MM
SALES (corp-wide): 94.5B **Publicly Held**
SIC: 4833 Television broadcasting stations
PA: Comcast Corporation
1701 Jfk Blvd
Philadelphia PA 19103
215 286-1700

(P-5637)
NBC UNIVERSAL INC
3000 W Alameda Ave, Burbank
(91523-0002)
PHONE................................818 260-5746
Greg Robinson, *Manager*
Alana Worotko, *Info Tech Dir*
Katie Trainor, *Marketing Staff*
Kevin McCormick, *Editor*
EMP: 250

SALES (corp-wide): 94.5B **Publicly Held**
WEB: www.nbc.com
SIC: 4833 Television broadcasting stations
HQ: Nbcuniversal, Llc
1221 Ave Of The Amer
New York NY 10020
212 664-4444

(P-5638)
NEWPORT TELEVISION LLC
Kget-TV
2120 L St, Bakersfield (93301-2331)
PHONE................................661 283-1700
Sandy Dipasquale, *President*
EMP: 90
SALES (corp-wide): 51.2MM **Privately
Held**
SIC: 4833 Television translator station
PA: Newport Television Llc
460 Nichols Rd Ste 250
Kansas City MO 64112
816 751-0200

(P-5639)
NEXSTAR BROADCASTING INC
Also Called: Ksee
5035 E Mckinley Ave, Fresno (93727-1964)
PHONE................................559 222-2411
Elena Valles, *Manager*
Colleen Pendergrass, *Producer*
Kathleen Goble, *Natl Sales Mgr*
EMP: 125
SALES (corp-wide): 2.7B **Publicly Held**
SIC: 4833 Television broadcasting stations
HQ: Nexstar Broadcasting, Inc.
545 E John Carpenter Fwy # 700
Irving TX 75062
972 373-8800

(P-5640)
NEXSTAR BROADCASTING INC
Also Called: Kron
900 Front St Ste 300, San Francisco
(94111-1445)
P.O. Box 3412 (94109)
PHONE................................415 441-4444
Angela Fawcett, *Manager*
Amy Mc Combs, *Administration*
EMP: 300
SALES (corp-wide): 2.7B **Publicly Held**
WEB: www.telegram.com
SIC: 4833 Television broadcasting stations
HQ: Nexstar Broadcasting, Inc.
545 E John Carpenter Fwy # 700
Irving TX 75062
972 373-8800

(P-5641)
ODS TECHNOLOGIES LP
Also Called: Television Games Network
6701 Center Dr W Ste 160, Los Angeles
(90045-1558)
PHONE................................310 242-9400
David Nathanson, *General Ptnr*
Ryan Dixon, *IT/INT Sup*
Tracy Beasley, *VP Finance*
Luciana Bach, *Marketing Mgr*
Danny Kovoloff, *Marketing Mgr*
EMP: 165
SQ FT: 20,000
SALES (est): 20MM **Privately Held**
SIC: 4833 7948 Television broadcasting
stations; horses, racing
HQ: Betfair Group Limited
Waterfront
London
208 834-8000

(P-5642)
PARTICIPANT CHANNEL INC
331 Foothill Rd Fl 3, Beverly Hills
(90210-3669)
PHONE................................310 550-7715
Evan Shapiro, *President*
Janae Desire, *President*
Robert Murphy, *CFO*
Jonathan King, *Exec VP*
Bob Murphy, *Exec VP*
EMP: 63
SALES: 13.8MM **Privately Held**
SIC: 4833 Television broadcasting stations

(P-5643)
REVOLT MEDIA AND TV LLC
1800 N Highland Ave Fl 7, Los Angeles
(90028-4522)
PHONE................................323 645-3000
Keith Clinkscales,
David Duff, *Vice Pres*
Angela Turner, *Vice Pres*
Marquetta Moore, *Director*
EMP: 120
SALES (est): 12.4MM **Privately Held**
SIC: 4833 Television broadcasting stations

(P-5644)
**S F BROADCASTING OF
WISCONSIN**
2425 Olympic Blvd, Santa Monica
(90404-4030)
PHONE................................310 586-2410
EMP: 151
SALES (est): 2.9MM
SALES (corp-wide): 3.2B **Publicly Held**
SIC: 4833
PA: Iac/Interactivecorp
555 W 18th St
New York NY 10011
212 314-7300

(P-5645)
**SACRAMENTO TELEVISION
STNS INC (DH)**
Also Called: Kmax TV
2713 Kovr Dr, West Sacramento
(95605-1600)
PHONE................................916 374-1452
Peter Dunn, *CEO*
EMP: 152
SQ FT: 40,000
SALES (est): 47.9MM
SALES (corp-wide): 25.9B **Publicly Held**
SIC: 4833 Television broadcasting stations
HQ: Cbs Corporation
51 W 52nd St Bsmt 1
New York NY 10019
212 975-4321

(P-5646)
**SAN MATEO COUNTY
COMMUNITY**
Also Called: Kcsm TV & Radio
1700 W Hillsdale Blvd, San Mateo
(94402-3757)
PHONE................................650 574-6586
Marilyn Lawrence, *Manager*
Matt Montgomery, *Technical Staff*
EMP: 51
SALES (corp-wide): 83MM **Privately
Held**
WEB: www.smcccd.cc.ca.us
SIC: 4833 4832 Television broadcasting
stations; radio broadcasting stations
PA: San Mateo County Community College
District
3401 Csm Dr
San Mateo CA 94402

(P-5647)
**SMITH BROADCASTING GROUP
INC**
Also Called: Keyt Television
730 Miramonte Dr, Santa Barbara
(93109-1417)
P.O. Box 729 (93102-0729)
PHONE................................805 882-3933
Michael Granados, *General Mgr*
EMP: 85
SALES (corp-wide): 15.2MM **Privately
Held**
SIC: 4833 7313 Television broadcasting
stations; television & radio time sales
PA: Smith Broadcasting Group, Inc
2315 Red Rose Way
Santa Barbara CA 93109
805 965-0400

(P-5648)
**STATION VENTURE
OPERATIONS LP**
Also Called: NBC 7/Channel 39
9680 Granite Ridge Dr, San Diego
(92123-2673)
PHONE................................619 231-3939
Dick Kelley, *General Mgr*
Greg Dawson, *Vice Pres*

Jackie Bradford, *General Mgr*
Patricia Casillas, *Traffic Mgr*
May Tjoa, *Producer*
▲ **EMP:** 76
SQ FT: 23,000
SALES (est): 6.9MM
SALES (corp-wide): 94.5B **Publicly Held**
WEB: www.nbc.com
SIC: 4833 Television broadcasting stations
HQ: Nbcuniversal, Llc
1221 Ave Of The Amer
New York NY 10020
212 664-4444

(P-5649)
TRINITY BRDCSTG NETWRK INC
Also Called: Trinity Christn Ctr Santa Ana
2442 Michelle Dr, Tustin (92780-7015)
PHONE................................714 665-3619
Paul F Crouch, *President*
EMP: 150
SALES: 5MM
SALES (corp-wide): 141.2MM **Privately
Held**
SIC: 4833 Television broadcasting stations
PA: Trinity Christian Center Of Santa Ana,
Inc.
2442 Michelle Dr
Tustin CA 92780
714 665-3619

(P-5650)
**TRINITY CHRISTIAN CENTER OF
SA (PA)**
Also Called: Trinity Broadcasting Network
2442 Michelle Dr, Tustin (92780-7015)
P.O. Box A, Santa Ana (92711-2101)
PHONE................................714 665-3619
Janice W Crouch, *Principal*
Paul F Crouch, *President*
Jim Mittan, *CFO*
Rosa Marin, *Vice Pres*
Mike Everett, *General Mgr*
▲ **EMP:** 200
SQ FT: 20,000
SALES: 141.2MM **Privately Held**
WEB: www.paulcrouch.com
SIC: 4833 7922 Television broadcasting
stations; television program, including
commercial producers

(P-5651)
TWDC ENTERPRISES 18 CORP
P.O. Box 4410 (92803-4410)
PHONE................................818 754-6921
John Ballas, *Risk Mgmt Dir*
Roger Worden, *Info Tech Mgr*
Rita Brue, *Human Res Dir*
Joe Pittaluga, *Opers Mgr*
Scott Noble, *Manager*
EMP: 304
SALES (corp-wide): 90.2B **Publicly Held**
SIC: 4833 Television broadcasting stations
HQ: Twdc Enterprises 18 Corp.
500 S Buena Vista St
Burbank CA 91521

(P-5652)
TWDC ENTERPRISES 18 CORP
532 Paula Ave, Glendale (91201-2328)
PHONE................................818 544-5009
Sam Moody, *Analyst*
EMP: 331
SALES (corp-wide): 90.2B **Publicly Held**
SIC: 4833 Television broadcasting stations
HQ: Twdc Enterprises 18 Corp.
500 S Buena Vista St
Burbank CA 91521

(P-5653)
TWDC ENTERPRISES 18 CORP
914 N Victory Blvd, Burbank (91502-1632)
PHONE................................818 295-3134
EMP: 331
SALES (corp-wide): 90.2B **Publicly Held**
SIC: 4833 4841 7011 7996 Television
broadcasting stations; cable television
services; resort hotel; amusement parks;
motion picture & video production; books;
publishing only
HQ: Twdc Enterprises 18 Corp.
500 S Buena Vista St
Burbank CA 91521

(P-5654)
TWDC ENTERPRISES 18 CORP
Also Called: Lighting Department
121 E Buena Vista, Burbank　(91521-0001)
PHONE........................818 560-1268
Anthony Orefice, *Branch Mgr*
EMP: 100
SALES (corp-wide): 90.2B　**Publicly Held**
SIC: 4833　Television broadcasting stations
HQ: Twdc Enterprises 18 Corp.
　500 S Buena Vista St
　Burbank CA 91521

(P-5655)
TWDC ENTERPRISES 18 CORP
1133 Flower St, Glendale　(91201)
PHONE........................818 544-6500
Grant Crabtree, *Vice Pres*
EMP: 714
SALES (corp-wide): 90.2B　**Publicly Held**
SIC: 4833　Television broadcasting stations
HQ: Twdc Enterprises 18 Corp.
　500 S Buena Vista St
　Burbank CA 91521

(P-5656)
TWDC ENTERPRISES 18 CORP
500 S Buena Vista St, Burbank
(91521-0001)
PHONE........................818 460-6655
EMP: 331
SALES (corp-wide): 90.2B　**Publicly Held**
SIC: 4833　4841　7011　7996　Television
　broadcasting stations; cable television
　services; resort hotel; amusement parks;
　motion picture & video production; books;
　publishing only
HQ: Twdc Enterprises 18 Corp.
　500 S Buena Vista St
　Burbank CA 91521

(P-5657)
TWDC ENTERPRISES 18 CORP
Walt Disney Studios HM Entrmt
500 S Buena Vista St, Burbank
(91521-0001)
PHONE........................818 560-1000
EMP: 1000
SALES (corp-wide): 90.2B　**Publicly Held**
SIC: 4833　Television broadcasting stations
HQ: Twdc Enterprises 18 Corp.
　500 S Buena Vista St
　Burbank CA 91521

(P-5658)
**TWDC ENTERPRISES 18 CORP
(HQ)**
500 S Buena Vista St, Burbank
(91521-0001)
PHONE........................818 560-1000
Robert A Iger, *Ch of Bd*
Alan N Braverman, *Executive*
Kevin A Mayer, *Executive*
M Jayne Parker, *Executive*
Ted Leung, *Exec Dir*
◆ EMP: 730
SALES: 59.4B
SALES (corp-wide): 90.2B　**Publicly Held**
WEB: www.corporate.disney.go.com
SIC: 4833　4841　7011　7996　Television
　broadcasting stations; cable television
　services; resort hotel; amusement parks;
　motion picture & video production; books;
　publishing only
PA: The Walt Disney Company
　500 S Buena Vista St
　Burbank CA 91521
　818 560-1000

(P-5659)
TWDC ENTERPRISES 18 CORP
Also Called: Walt Disney Studios
350 S Buena Vista St, Burbank
(91521-0004)
PHONE........................818 560-1000
Walter Disney, *Owner*
Scott St George, *Sales Mgr*
EMP: 331
SALES (corp-wide): 90.2B　**Publicly Held**
SIC: 4833　4841　7011　7996　Television
　broadcasting stations; cable television
　services; resort hotel; amusement parks

HQ: Twdc Enterprises 18 Corp.
　500 S Buena Vista St
　Burbank CA 91521

(P-5660)
**UNIVISION TELEVISION GROUP
INC**
601 W Univision Plz, Fresno　(93704-1092)
PHONE........................559 222-2121
Maria Guttierrez, *Branch Mgr*
EMP: 65　**Privately Held**
WEB: www.univison.net
SIC: 4833　Television broadcasting stations
HQ: Univision Television Group, Inc.
　500 Frank W Burr Blvd # 20
　Teaneck NJ 07666
　201 287-4141

(P-5661)
**UNIVISION TELEVISION GROUP
INC**
Also Called: Kdtv
1940 Zanker Rd, San Jose　(95112-4216)
PHONE........................415 538-8000
Marcela Medina, *Principal*
EMP: 70　**Privately Held**
WEB: www.univison.net
SIC: 4833　Television broadcasting stations
HQ: Univision Television Group, Inc.
　500 Frank W Burr Blvd # 20
　Teaneck NJ 07666
　201 287-4141

(P-5662)
**UNIVISION TELEVISION GROUP
INC**
5770 Ruffin Rd, San Diego　(92123-1013)
PHONE........................858 576-1919
Philip Wilkinson, *Manager*
EMP: 50　**Privately Held**
WEB: www.univison.net
SIC: 4833　Television broadcasting stations
HQ: Univision Television Group, Inc.
　500 Frank W Burr Blvd # 20
　Teaneck NJ 07666
　201 287-4141

(P-5663)
**YOUNG BRDCSTG OF SAN
FRANCISCO**
Also Called: Kron-Tv
900 Front St, San Francisco　(94111-1427)
PHONE........................415 441-4444
Deb McDermot, *President*
EMP: 150
SALES (est): 9.1MM
SALES (corp-wide): 2.7B　**Publicly Held**
WEB: www.kron-tv.com
SIC: 4833　Television broadcasting stations
HQ: Young Broadcasting, Llc
　599 Lexington Ave
　New York NY 10022
　517 372-8282

**4841 Cable & Other Pay TV
Svcs**

(P-5664)
**A&E TELEVISION NETWORKS
LLC**
2049 Century Park E # 800, Los Angeles
(90067-3101)
PHONE........................310 201-6015
Jenny Barmach, *Branch Mgr*
Steven Goore, *Account Dir*
EMP: 208
SALES (corp-wide): 699.8MM　**Privately
Held**
SIC: 4841　Cable television services
PA: A&E Television Networks, Llc
　235 E 45th St Fl 9
　New York NY 10017
　212 210-1400

(P-5665)
ABS-CBN INTERNATIONAL (DH)
2001 Junipero Serra Blvd # 200, Daly City
(94014-3886)
PHONE........................800 527-2820
Eugenio Lopez III, *CEO*
Raffy Lopez, *COO*
Carlo Katigbak, *Managing Dir*

Tina Zamora, *Managing Dir*
Genemar Simpao, *CIO*
▲ EMP: 140
SQ FT: 12,000
SALES (est): 67.8MM　**Privately Held**
WEB: www.abs-cbni.com
SIC: 4841　7822　Cable & other pay televi-
　sion services; television & video tape dis-
　tribution

(P-5666)
BDR INDUSTRIES INC (PA)
Also Called: R N D Enterprises
820 E Avenue L12, Lancaster
(93535-5403)
PHONE........................661 940-8554
Scott Riddle, *President*
Edward Donovan, *Vice Pres*
▲ EMP: 95
SQ FT: 30,000
SALES (est): 21.7MM　**Privately Held**
WEB: www.rndcable.com
SIC: 4841　Cable television services

(P-5667)
**BRIGHT HOUSE NETWORKS
LLC**
4450 California Ave Ste A, Bakersfield
(93309-1196)
PHONE........................661 634-2200
Joseph Schoenstein, *Manager*
EMP: 90
SALES (corp-wide): 43.6B　**Publicly Held**
SIC: 4841　Cable television services
HQ: Bright House Networks, Llc
　5823 Widewaters Pkwy # 2
　East Syracuse NY 13057
　315 438-4100

(P-5668)
**BRITISH AMERICAN
COMMUNICATION**
7965 Foothill Blvd, Sunland　(91040-2958)
PHONE........................818 943-6111
John Cheeseman, *President*
EMP: 75
SQ FT: 7,000
SALES (est): 2.2MM　**Privately Held**
SIC: 4841　4899　Subscription television
　services; television antenna construction
　& rental

(P-5669)
**CALIFORNIA BROADCAST CTR
LLC**
3800 Via Oro Ave, Long Beach
(90810-1866)
PHONE........................310 233-2425
Bruce Churchill, *CEO*
EMP: 200
SALES (est): 7.8MM
SALES (corp-wide): 170.7B　**Publicly
Held**
SIC: 4841　Cable & other pay television
　services
HQ: Directv Latin America, Llc
　1 Rockefeller Plz
　New York NY 10020
　212 205-0500

(P-5670)
**CHARTER CMMNCTONS
OPRATING LLC**
12180 Ridgecrest Rd # 102, Victorville
(92395-7798)
PHONE........................760 452-8609
Toll Free:........................877
Robert Brown, *Branch Mgr*
EMP: 100
SALES (corp-wide): 43.6B　**Publicly Held**
WEB: www.charter.ordercableonline.com
SIC: 4841　Cable television services
HQ: Charter Communications Operating Llc
　12405 Powerscourt Dr
　Saint Louis MO 63131
　314 965-0555

(P-5671)
**CHARTER CMMNCTONS
OPRATING LLC**
4031 Via Oro Ave, Long Beach
(90810-1458)
PHONE........................310 971-4001
Eric Brown, *Vice Pres*
EMP: 300

SALES (corp-wide): 43.6B　**Publicly Held**
WEB: www.charter.ordercableonline.com
SIC: 4841　7371　Cable television services;
　custom computer programming services
HQ: Charter Communications Operating Llc
　12405 Powerscourt Dr
　Saint Louis MO 63131
　314 965-0555

(P-5672)
**CHARTER CMMNCTONS
OPRATING LLC**
5797 Eastside Rd, Redding　(96001-4548)
PHONE........................530 241-7352
Marcie Farmer, *Manager*
EMP: 50
SALES (corp-wide): 43.6B　**Publicly Held**
WEB: www.charter.ordercableonline.com
SIC: 4841　Cable television services
HQ: Charter Communications Operating Llc
　12405 Powerscourt Dr
　Saint Louis MO 63131
　314 965-0555

(P-5673)
CNN AMERICA INC
6430 W Sunset Blvd # 300, Los Angeles
(90028-7901)
PHONE........................323 993-5000
Suzanne Spurgeon, *Principal*
EMP: 80
SALES (corp-wide): 170.7B　**Publicly
Held**
SIC: 4841　Cable television services
HQ: Cnn America Inc
　190 Marietta St Nw 12s
　Atlanta GA 30303
　404 827-1700

(P-5674)
COMCAST CALIFORNIA IX INC
1111 Andersen Dr, San Rafael
(94901-5394)
PHONE........................215 286-3345
Paul Gibson, *Vice Pres*
Chris Coffman, *Technician*
EMP: 99
SALES: 950K
SALES (corp-wide): 94.5B　**Publicly Held**
SIC: 4841　Cable & other pay television
　services
HQ: Nbcuniversal Media, Llc
　30 Rockefeller Plz Fl 2
　New York NY 10112
　212 664-4444

(P-5675)
**COMCAST CBLE
CMMUNICATIONS LLC**
6320 Arizona Cir, Los Angeles
(90045-1202)
PHONE........................310 216-3500
Donna Delaney, *Manager*
EMP: 50
SALES (corp-wide): 94.5B　**Publicly Held**
WEB: www.comcastmediacenter.com
SIC: 4841　Cable television services
HQ: Comcast Cable Communications, Llc
　1701 John F Kennedy Blvd
　Philadelphia PA 19103

(P-5676)
**COMCAST CBLE
CMMUNICATIONS LLC**
Also Called: Comcast West Bay Area
1485 Bay Shore Blvd # 125, San Francisco
(94124-3002)
PHONE........................415 715-0524
Darrell Johnson, *Manager*
EMP: 101
SALES (corp-wide): 94.5B　**Publicly Held**
WEB: www.comcastmediacenter.com
SIC: 4841　Cable television services
HQ: Comcast Cable Communications, Llc
　1701 John F Kennedy Blvd
　Philadelphia PA 19103

(P-5677)
**COMCAST CBLE
CMMUNICATIONS LLC**
1031 N Plaza Dr, Visalia　(93291-9473)
PHONE........................559 253-4050
Tony Queasada, *Principal*

Demetrio Santos, *Technical Staff*
EMP: 101
SALES (corp-wide): 94.5B **Publicly Held**
SIC: 4841 Cable television services
HQ: Comcast Cable Communications, Llc
1701 John F Kennedy Blvd
Philadelphia PA 19103
-

(P-5678)
COMCAST CBLE CMMUNICATIONS LLC
6357 Arizona Cir, Los Angeles
(90045-1201)
PHONE.....................310 216-3686
Dave Scharrer, *Manager*
EMP: 101
SALES (corp-wide): 94.5B **Publicly Held**
WEB: www.comcastmediacenter.com
SIC: 4841 Cable television services
HQ: Comcast Cable Communications, Llc
1701 John F Kennedy Blvd
Philadelphia PA 19103
-

(P-5679)
COMCAST CORPORATION
2860 Gateway Oaks Dr, Sacramento
(95833-3508)
PHONE.....................916 459-2964
Bruce W Quick, *Manager*
EMP: 56
SALES (corp-wide): 94.5B **Publicly Held**
SIC: 4841 Cable television services
PA: Comcast Corporation
1701 Jfk Blvd
Philadelphia PA 19103
215 286-1700

(P-5680)
COMCAST CORPORATION
860 Stanton Rd, Burlingame (94010-1404)
PHONE.....................650 689-5392
EMP: 57
SALES (corp-wide): 94.5B **Publicly Held**
SIC: 4841 Cable television services
PA: Comcast Corporation
1701 Jfk Blvd
Philadelphia PA 19103
215 286-1700

(P-5681)
COMCAST CORPORATION
1 La Avanzada St Rm 111, San Francisco
(94131-1124)
PHONE.....................415 665-5507
Bob Dichappari, *Branch Mgr*
Riley Laws, *Technician*
Thomas Muller, *Research*
Chuck Hucks, *Supervisor*
EMP: 57
SALES (corp-wide): 94.5B **Publicly Held**
WEB: www.comcast.com
SIC: 4841 Cable television services
PA: Comcast Corporation
1701 Jfk Blvd
Philadelphia PA 19103
215 286-1700

(P-5682)
COMCAST CORPORATION
166 Watson Ln, American Canyon
(94503-9632)
PHONE.....................707 266-7584
EMP: 57
SALES (corp-wide): 94.5B **Publicly Held**
SIC: 4841 Cable television services
PA: Comcast Corporation
1701 Jfk Blvd
Philadelphia PA 19103
215 286-1700

(P-5683)
COMCAST CORPORATION
Also Called: A Comcast
3801 Pelandale Ave A11, Modesto
(95356-8303)
PHONE.....................209 222-3656
EMP: 56
SALES (corp-wide): 94.5B **Publicly Held**
SIC: 4841 Cable television services
PA: Comcast Corporation
1701 Jfk Blvd
Philadelphia PA 19103
215 286-1700

(P-5684)
COMCAST CORPORATION
221 2nd St, Sausalito (94965-2429)
PHONE.....................415 367-4153
EMP: 55
SALES (corp-wide): 94.5B **Publicly Held**
SIC: 4841 Cable television services
PA: Comcast Corporation
1701 Jfk Blvd
Philadelphia PA 19103
215 286-1700

(P-5685)
COMCAST CORPORATION
23525 Clawiter Rd, Hayward (94545-1328)
PHONE.....................510 266-3200
Neal James, *Chairman*
Rudy Babich, *Network Tech*
EMP: 57
SALES (corp-wide): 94.5B **Publicly Held**
SIC: 4841 Cable television services
PA: Comcast Corporation
1701 Jfk Blvd
Philadelphia PA 19103
215 286-1700

(P-5686)
COMCAST CORPORATION
425 Corona Mall, Corona (92879-1419)
PHONE.....................951 268-9378
Mark Hooper, *Principal*
EMP: 57
SALES (corp-wide): 94.5B **Publicly Held**
SIC: 4841 Cable television services
PA: Comcast Corporation
1701 Jfk Blvd
Philadelphia PA 19103
215 286-1700

(P-5687)
COMCAST CORPORATION
Also Called: Comcast Cable
203 N 27th St, San Jose (95116-1121)
PHONE.....................408 216-2878
James Marquez, *Supervisor*
EMP: 56
SALES (corp-wide): 94.5B **Publicly Held**
SIC: 4841 Cable television services
PA: Comcast Corporation
1701 Jfk Blvd
Philadelphia PA 19103
215 286-1700

(P-5688)
COMCAST CORPORATION
Also Called: Comcast Cable
1300 W Yosemite Ave, Madera
(93637-6320)
PHONE.....................559 474-4194
EMP: 56
SALES (corp-wide): 94.5B **Publicly Held**
SIC: 4841 Cable television services
PA: Comcast Corporation
1701 Jfk Blvd
Philadelphia PA 19103
215 286-1700

(P-5689)
COMCAST CORPORATION
Also Called: Comcast Cable
2414 E Acacia Ave, Fresno (93726-0303)
PHONE.....................559 718-9917
EMP: 56
SALES (corp-wide): 94.5B **Publicly Held**
SIC: 4841 Cable television services
PA: Comcast Corporation
1701 Jfk Blvd
Philadelphia PA 19103
215 286-1700

(P-5690)
COMCAST CORPORATION
Also Called: Comcast Cable
810 Randolph St, NAPA (94559-2911)
PHONE.....................707 266-7012
EMP: 56
SALES (corp-wide): 94.5B **Publicly Held**
SIC: 4841 Cable television services
PA: Comcast Corporation
1701 Jfk Blvd
Philadelphia PA 19103
215 286-1700

(P-5691)
COMCAST CORPORATION
Also Called: Advertising Department
5462 E Del Amo Blvd 239, Long Beach
(90808-1122)
PHONE.....................800 240-3640
EMP: 57
SALES (corp-wide): 94.5B **Publicly Held**
SIC: 4841 4813 7812 7996 Cable television services; subscription television services; telephone communication, except radio; ; ; television film production; theme park, amusement
PA: Comcast Corporation
1701 Jfk Blvd
Philadelphia PA 19103
215 286-1700

(P-5692)
COMCAST CORPORATION
550 Garcia Ave, Pittsburg (94565-4901)
PHONE.....................925 432-0500
Dee Trotta, *Principal*
Lesia Johnson, *Manager*
EMP: 81
SALES (corp-wide): 94.5B **Publicly Held**
WEB: www.comcast.com
SIC: 4841 Cable television services
PA: Comcast Corporation
1701 Jfk Blvd
Philadelphia PA 19103
215 286-1700

(P-5693)
COMCAST CORPORATION
1750 Creekside Oaks Dr # 100, Sacramento (95833-3647)
PHONE.....................916 830-6790
Marty Robinson, *Branch Mgr*
Quintan Taylor, *Engineer*
EMP: 300
SALES (corp-wide): 94.5B **Publicly Held**
WEB: www.comcast.com
SIC: 4841 Cable television services
PA: Comcast Corporation
1701 Jfk Blvd
Philadelphia PA 19103
215 286-1700

(P-5694)
COMCAST CORPORATION
6505 Tam O Shanter Dr, Stockton
(95210-3349)
PHONE.....................209 955-6521
Eileen Martin, *Manager*
Alex Arestegui, *Sales Staff*
EMP: 57
SALES (corp-wide): 94.5B **Publicly Held**
WEB: www.comcast.com
SIC: 4841 Cable television services
PA: Comcast Corporation
1701 Jfk Blvd
Philadelphia PA 19103
215 286-1700

(P-5695)
COMCAST CORPORATION
900 N Cahuenga Blvd, Los Angeles
(90038-2615)
PHONE.....................323 993-8000
Paula David, *Principal*
Bill Ferry, *Director*
EMP: 57
SALES (corp-wide): 94.5B **Publicly Held**
WEB: www.comcast.com
SIC: 4841 Cable television services
PA: Comcast Corporation
1701 Jfk Blvd
Philadelphia PA 19103
215 286-1700

(P-5696)
COMCAST CORPORATION
2001 Diamond Blvd Ste 150, Concord
(94520-5738)
PHONE.....................925 271-9794
EMP: 300
SALES (corp-wide): 94.5B **Publicly Held**
WEB: www.comcast.com
SIC: 4841 Cable television services
PA: Comcast Corporation
1701 Jfk Blvd
Philadelphia PA 19103
215 286-1700

(P-5697)
COMCAST CORPORATION
2455 Henderson Way, Monterey
(93940-5303)
P.O. Box 1711 (93942-1711)
PHONE.....................831 657-6095
Bob Haehnel, *Branch Mgr*
EMP: 57
SALES (corp-wide): 94.5B **Publicly Held**
WEB: www.comcast.com
SIC: 4841 Cable television services
PA: Comcast Corporation
1701 Jfk Blvd
Philadelphia PA 19103
215 286-1700

(P-5698)
COX COMMUNICATIONS INC
140 Columbia, Aliso Viejo (92656-1495)
PHONE.....................949 716-2020
Michael Hale, *Manager*
EMP: 76
SALES (corp-wide): 32.3B **Privately Held**
SIC: 4841 Cable television services
HQ: Cox Communications, Inc.
6205 B Pchtree Dnwody Rd
Atlanta GA 30328

(P-5699)
COX COMMUNICATIONS INC
1535 Euclid Ave, San Diego (92105-5426)
PHONE.....................858 715-4500
Deborah Lawrence, *Director*
Larry Coval, *Vice Pres*
David Loveland, *Manager*
EMP: 100
SALES (corp-wide): 32.3B **Privately Held**
SIC: 4841 4812 1731 Cable television services; radio telephone communication; electrical work
HQ: Cox Communications, Inc.
6205 B Pchtree Dnwody Rd
Atlanta GA 30328

(P-5700)
COX COMMUNICATIONS INC
6771 Quail Hill Pkwy, Irvine (92603-4233)
PHONE.....................949 546-1000
Leone Duffy, *Owner*
EMP: 76
SALES (corp-wide): 32.3B **Privately Held**
SIC: 4841 Cable television services
HQ: Cox Communications, Inc.
6205 B Pchtree Dnwody Rd
Atlanta GA 30328

(P-5701)
COX COMMUNICATIONS CAL LLC
1175 N Cuyamaca St, El Cajon
(92020-1805)
PHONE.....................619 562-9820
Randall Phillips, *Manager*
Don Eccles, *Technician*
EMP: 380
SALES (corp-wide): 32.3B **Privately Held**
SIC: 4841 Cable television services
HQ: Cox Communications California, Llc
6205 Pachtree Dunwoody Rd
Atlanta GA 30328
404 843-5000

(P-5702)
COX COMMUNICATIONS CAL LLC
5159 Federal Blvd, San Diego
(92105-5428)
PHONE.....................619 262-1122
James Robbins, *CEO*
David Zuniga, *IT/INT Sup*
Dan Willan, *Sales Engr*
Martin Jones, *Marketing Staff*
EMP: 380
SALES (corp-wide): 32.3B **Privately Held**
SIC: 4841 Cable television services
HQ: Cox Communications California, Llc
6205 Pachtree Dunwoody Rd
Atlanta GA 30328
404 843-5000

(P-5703)
COX COMMUNICATIONS CAL LLC
581 Telegraph Canyon Rd, Chula Vista (91910-6436)
PHONE..............................619 263-9251
Bill Geppert, *Branch Mgr*
EMP: 380
SQ FT: 3,025
SALES (corp-wide): 32.3B **Privately Held**
SIC: 4841 Cable television services
HQ: Cox Communications California, Llc
6205 Pachtree Dunwoody Rd
Atlanta GA 30328
404 843-5000

(P-5704)
CROWN MEDIA UNITED STATES LLC (DH)
Also Called: Hallmark Channel
12700 Ventura Blvd # 100, Studio City (91604-2469)
PHONE..............................818 755-2400
David Evans,
Susanne McAvoy, *President*
Susanne Smit McAvoy, *Exec VP*
Kristen Roberts, *Exec VP*
Charles Stanford, *Exec VP*
EMP: 95
SALES (est): 23MM
SALES (corp-wide): 3.2B **Privately Held**
SIC: 4841 Cable television services
HQ: Crown Media Holdings, Inc.
12700 Ventura Blvd # 100
Studio City CA 91604
888 390-7474

(P-5705)
DIRECTV INC
2230 E Imperial Hwy, El Segundo (90245-3504)
P.O. Box 105249, Atlanta GA (30348-5249)
PHONE..............................888 388-4249
April Ammeter, *Vice Pres*
Dennis B Fleming, *Vice Pres*
Tony Goncalves, *Vice Pres*
Frank A Palase, *Vice Pres*
Cleo Wilson, *Vice Pres*
EMP: 476
SALES: 45.3MM **Privately Held**
SIC: 4841 Cable & other pay television services

(P-5706)
DIRECTV LLC
1055 E Francis St, Ontario (91761-5633)
PHONE..............................909 509-4790
Don Gillespie, *Branch Mgr*
EMP: 80
SALES (corp-wide): 170.7B **Publicly Held**
SIC: 4841 Direct broadcast satellite services (DBS)
HQ: Directv, Llc
2260 E Imperial Hwy
El Segundo CA 90245

(P-5707)
DIRECTV ENTERPRISES LLC
2230 E Imperial Hwy, El Segundo (90245-3504)
PHONE..............................310 535-5000
Michael D White, *Site Mgr*
Odie C Donald, *President*
R L Myers, *CFO*
EMP: 1500
SQ FT: 75,000
SALES (est): 97.8MM
SALES (corp-wide): 170.7B **Publicly Held**
SIC: 4841 Direct broadcast satellite services (DBS)
HQ: Directv Holdings Llc
2230 E Imperial Hwy
El Segundo CA 90245
310 964-5000

(P-5708)
DIRECTV GROUP INC
340 Commerce Ave, Fairfield (94533)
PHONE..............................707 452-7409
EMP: 128
SALES (corp-wide): 31.7B **Publicly Held**
SIC: 4841

HQ: The Directv Group Inc
2260 E Imperial Hwy
El Segundo CA 90245
310 964-5000

(P-5709)
DIRECTV GROUP INC
1129 B St, San Lorenzo (94580)
PHONE..............................510 481-1324
EMP: 128
SALES (corp-wide): 31.7B **Publicly Held**
SIC: 4841
HQ: The Directv Group Inc
2260 E Imperial Hwy
El Segundo CA 90245
310 964-5000

(P-5710)
DIRECTV GROUP HOLDINGS LLC (HQ)
2260 E Imperial Hwy, El Segundo (90245-3501)
PHONE..............................310 964-5000
Michael White, *President*
Patrick Doyle, *CFO*
Fazal Merchant, *Treasurer*
Joseph Bosch, *Officer*
Larry Hunter, *Exec VP*
▲ EMP: 170
SALES (est): 11.3B
SALES (corp-wide): 170.7B **Publicly Held**
SIC: 4841 Direct broadcast satellite services (DBS)
PA: At&T Inc.
208 S Akard St
Dallas TX 75202
210 821-4105

(P-5711)
DIRECTV GROUP INC (DH)
2260 E Imperial Hwy, El Segundo (90245-3501)
PHONE..............................310 964-5000
Michael White, *CEO*
Patrick T Doyle, *CFO*
J William Little, *Treasurer*
Romulo Pontual, *Exec VP*
John F Murphy, *Senior VP*
▲ EMP: 128 128 EST: 1977
SALES (est): 6B
SALES (corp-wide): 170.7B **Publicly Held**
WEB: www.hughes.com
SIC: 4841 Direct broadcast satellite services (DBS)

(P-5712)
DIRECTV INTERNATIONAL INC (DH)
2230 E Imperial Hwy Fl 10, El Segundo (90245-3504)
PHONE..............................310 964-6460
Michael D White, *Site Mgr*
Kevin McGrath, *President*
Celso Azevedo, *Senior VP*
EMP: 150
SALES (est): 124.8MM
SALES (corp-wide): 170.7B **Publicly Held**
SIC: 4841 Cable & other pay television services
HQ: The Directv Group Inc
2260 E Imperial Hwy
El Segundo CA 90245
310 964-5000

(P-5713)
DISH NETWORK CORPORATION
396 Orange Show Ln, San Bernardino (92408-2012)
PHONE..............................909 381-4767
EMP: 52 **Publicly Held**
SIC: 4841 Direct broadcast satellite services (DBS)
PA: Dish Network Corporation
9601 S Meridian Blvd
Englewood CO 80112

(P-5714)
DISH NETWORK CORPORATION
1297 N Verdugo Rd, Glendale (91206-1508)
PHONE..............................818 334-8740
EMP: 50 **Publicly Held**

SIC: 4841 Direct broadcast satellite services (DBS)
PA: Dish Network Corporation
9601 S Meridian Blvd
Englewood CO 80112

(P-5715)
DISH NETWORK CORPORATION
2602 Halladay St, Santa Ana (92705-5601)
PHONE..............................714 424-0503
Raul Guidi, *General Mgr*
Laura Lewis, *Natl Sales Mgr*
EMP: 50 **Publicly Held**
SIC: 4841 Direct broadcast satellite services (DBS)
PA: Dish Network Corporation
9601 S Meridian Blvd
Englewood CO 80112

(P-5716)
DISH NETWORK SERVICE LLC
8318 Miramar Mall, San Diego (92121-2520)
PHONE..............................858 452-2239
Den Borum, *General Mgr*
EMP: 50 **Publicly Held**
WEB: www.channelchoicetv.com
SIC: 4841 Direct broadcast satellite services (DBS)
HQ: Dish Network Service L.L.C.
9601 S Meridian Blvd
Englewood CO 80112

(P-5717)
DIVA SYSTEMS CORPORATION
800 Saginaw Dr, Redwood City (94063-4740)
PHONE..............................650 779-3000
Hendrik A Hanselaar, *President*
Paul Cook, *Ch of Bd*
Robert B Snow, *COO*
William M Scharninghausen, *CFO*
Steven Brookstein, *Senior VP*
EMP: 179
SQ FT: 82,000
SALES: 18.4MM **Privately Held**
SIC: 4841 7829 7822 Cable & other pay television services; motion picture distribution services; motion picture distribution

(P-5718)
ESPN INC
800 W Olympic Blvd, Los Angeles (90015-1360)
PHONE..............................212 456-7439
Steven Bornstein, *Ch of Bd*
Hernani Lantin, *Associate Dir*
Jeffrey Abraham, *Art Dir*
EMP: 300
SALES (corp-wide): 90.2B **Publicly Held**
SIC: 4841 Cable television services
HQ: Espn, Inc.
Espn Plz
Bristol CT 06010
860 766-2000

(P-5719)
ETTV AMERICA CORP
Also Called: B N E U S A
18430 San Jose Ave Ste A, City of Industry (91748-1263)
PHONE..............................626 581-8899
May Chiang, *Exec VP*
EMP: 80
SQ FT: 300,000
SALES (est): 5.8MM **Privately Held**
SIC: 4841 Cable television services

(P-5720)
EXPRESS CABLE COMMUNICATION
350 S Maple St Ste L, Corona (92880-6948)
PHONE..............................951 272-2029
Sam Kouhkan, *President*
EMP: 60
SALES: 12.1MM **Privately Held**
SIC: 4841 Cable television services

(P-5721)
FOX LATIN AMERICAN CHANNEL LLC
10201 W Pico Blvd, Los Angeles (90064-2606)
PHONE..............................305 774-4167
Ruben Arreola, *Exec Dir*
Stephanie Gibbons, *Exec VP*
Scott Groneman, *Vice Pres*
Todd Heughens, *Vice Pres*
Kate Lambert, *Vice Pres*
EMP: 500
SALES (est): 16.3MM **Privately Held**
SIC: 4841 Cable television services

(P-5722)
FOX NETWORKS GROUP INC
Also Called: Nat Geo TV
10201 W Pico Blvd, Los Angeles (90064-2606)
PHONE..............................310 369-5104
Brian Sullivan, *President*
EMP: 122
SALES (corp-wide): 90.2B **Publicly Held**
SIC: 4841 Direct broadcast satellite services (DBS)
HQ: Fox Networks Group, Inc.
10201 W Pico Blvd 101
Los Angeles CA 90064
310 369-9369

(P-5723)
FOX NETWORKS GROUP INC (DH)
Also Called: Fox Network Center
10201 W Pico Blvd 101, Los Angeles (90064-2606)
P.O. Box 900, Beverly Hills (90213-0900)
PHONE..............................310 369-9369
Brian Sullivan, *President*
Raul De Quesada, *Info Tech Dir*
Sanchez Christine, *Technology*
Ryan Tomlin, *Senior Mgr*
Christopher Park, *Manager*
EMP: 68
SALES (est): 61.5MM
SALES (corp-wide): 90.2B **Publicly Held**
SIC: 4841 Direct broadcast satellite services (DBS)
HQ: Fox Entertainment Group, Llc
1211 Ave Of The Americas
New York NY 10036
212 852-7000

(P-5724)
FX NETWORKS LLC
10201 W Pico Blvd, Los Angeles (90064-2606)
P.O. Box 900, Beverly Hills (90213-0900)
PHONE..............................310 369-1000
John Landgraf, *President*
Gina Balian, *President*
Eric Schrier, *President*
Adrienne Gary, *Vice Pres*
Julie Graham, *Production*
EMP: 150
SALES (est): 14.3MM
SALES (corp-wide): 90.2B **Publicly Held**
WEB: www.fox.com
SIC: 4841 Cable television services
HQ: Fox Entertainment Group, Llc
1211 Ave Of The Americas
New York NY 10036
212 852-7000

(P-5725)
GAME SHOW NETWORK LLC (DH)
Also Called: G S N
2150 Colorado Ave Ste 100, Santa Monica (90404-5514)
PHONE..............................310 255-6800
Mark Seldman, *Mng Member*
Steven Brunell, *Exec VP*
Mark Feldman, *Exec VP*
Dale Hopkins, *Exec VP*
Jeffrey Anderson, *Vice Pres*
EMP: 99
SALES (est): 49.5MM **Privately Held**
WEB: www.gsn.com
SIC: 4841 Cable television services
HQ: Sony Pictures Entertainment, Inc.
10202 Washington Blvd
Culver City CA 90232
310 244-4000

▲ = Import ▼ =Export
◆ =Import/Export

(P-5726)
GLOBECAST AMERICA INCORPORATED (DH)
10525 Washington Blvd, Culver City
(90232-3311)
PHONE..................................310 845-3900
Michele Gosetti, *CEO*
Elisabeth Mazurie, *Vice Pres*
Jimmy Kim, *Managing Dir*
Eric Heckendorn, *Project Mgr*
Frederic Lefevre, *Project Mgr*
▲ EMP: 56
SALES (est): 96MM
SALES (corp-wide): 26.4B **Privately Held**
SIC: 4841 Satellite master antenna systems services (SMATV)

(P-5727)
HEARST COMMUNICATIONS INC
Also Called: Western Communications
2323 Teller Rd, Newbury Park
(91320-2219)
PHONE..................................805 375-3121
Dave Laroue, *Branch Mgr*
EMP: 500
SALES (corp-wide): 8.3B **Privately Held**
WEB: www.telegram.com
SIC: 4841 Cable television services
HQ: Hearst Communications, Inc.
300 W 57th St
New York NY 10019
212 649-2000

(P-5728)
HOME BOX OFFICE INC
2500 Broadway Ste 400, Santa Monica
(90404-3176)
PHONE..................................310 382-3000
Chris Albrecht, *Manager*
EMP: 95
SALES (corp-wide): 170.7B **Publicly Held**
WEB: www.hbo.com
SIC: 4841 7812 Cable television services; motion picture & video production
HQ: Home Box Office, Inc.
1100 Avenue Of The Americ
New York NY 10036
212 512-1000

(P-5729)
INTEL MEDIA INC
2200 Mission College Blvd, Santa Clara
(95054-1549)
PHONE..................................408 765-0063
Erik Huggers, *President*
EMP: 350
SALES: 33.2K
SALES (corp-wide): 70.8B **Publicly Held**
SIC: 4841 Subscription television services
PA: Intel Corporation
2200 Mission College Blvd
Santa Clara CA 95054
408 765-8080

(P-5730)
INTERNATIONAL FMLY ENTRMT INC (DH)
Also Called: Fox Family Channel
3800 W Alameda Ave, Burbank
(91505-4300)
PHONE..................................818 560-1000
Mel Woods, *President*
EMP: 144
SALES (est): 40MM
SALES (corp-wide): 90.2B **Publicly Held**
SIC: 4841 7812 7922 7999 Cable television services; television film production; theatrical producers; legitimate live theater producers; television program, including commercial producers; recreation services
HQ: Abc Family Worldwide, Inc.
500 S Buena Vista St
Burbank CA 91521
818 560-1000

(P-5731)
NDS AMERICAS INC (DH)
3500 Hyland Ave, Costa Mesa
(92626-1459)
PHONE..................................714 434-2100
Abe Peled, *President*
Peter Lynskey, *Vice Pres*

Dov Rubin, *Vice Pres*
Alex Gersh, *Admin Sec*
EMP: 90
SALES (est): 72.9MM
SALES (corp-wide): 51.9B **Publicly Held**
WEB: www.ndsuk.com
SIC: 4841 Cable & other pay television services
HQ: Nds Group Limited
One London Road
Staines MIDDX
178 484-8500

(P-5732)
OC COMMUNICATIONS INC (PA)
2204 Kausen Dr Ste 100, Elk Grove
(95758-7176)
PHONE..................................916 686-3700
Forrest C Freeman, *CEO*
Craig Freeman, *President*
Larry Wray, *COO*
Peter Tataryn, *CFO*
Steve Fazio, *Vice Pres*
EMP: 115
SQ FT: 7,335
SALES (est): 184MM **Privately Held**
WEB: www.occommunications.com
SIC: 4841 Cable & other pay television services

(P-5733)
OWN LLC
Also Called: Oprah Winfrey Network
1041 N Formosa Ave, West Hollywood
(90046-6703)
PHONE..................................323 602-5500
Oprah Winfrey, *CEO*
Joe Klopp, *CFO*
Erik Logan, *Co-President*
Sheri Salata, *Co-President*
Jill Dickerson, *Vice Pres*
EMP: 140
SQ FT: 50,000
SALES (est): 16.8MM
SALES (corp-wide): 6.2MM **Privately Held**
SIC: 4841 Cable television services
PA: Discovery Communications, Inc.
10100 Santa Monica Blvd
Los Angeles CA 90067
310 975-5906

(P-5734)
PETES CONNECTION INC
407 Ranger Rd, Fallbrook (92028-8482)
P.O. Box 2080 (92088-2080)
PHONE..................................760 723-1972
Peter Cavaretta, *President*
Ann Cavaretta, *Vice Pres*
EMP: 50
SALES (est): 2.4MM **Privately Held**
SIC: 4841 Direct broadcast satellite services (DBS)

(P-5735)
PHOENIX AMERICAN INCORPORATED (PA)
2401 Kerner Blvd, San Rafael
(94901-5569)
PHONE..................................415 485-4500
Gus Constantin, *Ch of Bd*
Andrew N Gregson, *CFO*
Gary W Martinez, *Exec VP*
Muna A Hobaika, *Vice Pres*
Lisa A Olsen, *Admin Sec*
EMP: 100
SQ FT: 60,000
SALES (est): 36.4MM **Privately Held**
SIC: 4841 7377 Cable television services; computer rental & leasing

(P-5736)
PHOENIX SATELLITE TV US INC
3810 Durbin St, Baldwin Park
(91706-6800)
PHONE..................................626 388-1188
Xiaoyong Wu, *CEO*
Shing Ping, *CEO*
▲ EMP: 50
SQ FT: 18,000
SALES (est): 5.1MM **Privately Held**
WEB: www.pstv-us.net
SIC: 4841 Cable television services

HQ: Phoenix Media Investment (Holdings) Limited (Formerly Known As ?phoenix Satellite Televisi
Tai Po Industrial Estate
Tai Po NT

(P-5737)
ROKU INC (PA)
150 Winchester Cir, Los Gatos
(95032-1812)
PHONE..................................408 556-9040
Anthony Wood, *Ch of Bd*
Seth Walters, *Partner*
Steve Louden, *CFO*
Alan Henricks, *Bd of Directors*
Neil Hunt, *Bd of Directors*
▲ EMP: 360
SQ FT: 156,000
SALES: 742.5MM **Publicly Held**
WEB: www.roku.com
SIC: 4841 Cable & other pay television services

(P-5738)
SKY SCAN SATELITE SYSTEMS
9994 Willowbrook Rd, Riverside
(92509-8827)
PHONE..................................909 322-1393
Mike Khan, *Owner*
EMP: 68
SALES (est): 1.5MM **Privately Held**
SIC: 4841 Satellite master antenna systems services (SMATV)

(P-5739)
SONIFI SOLUTIONS INC
1065 E Hillsdale Blvd # 228, Foster City
(94404-1614)
PHONE..................................650 752-1980
Sean Minnit, *Branch Mgr*
EMP: 109
SALES (corp-wide): 95.7MM **Privately Held**
SIC: 4841 Subscription television services
PA: Sonifi Solutions, Inc.
3900 W Innovation St
Sioux Falls SD 57107
605 988-1000

(P-5740)
SPECTRUM MGT HOLDG CO LLC
Also Called: Time Warner Media Sales
6021 Katella Ave Ste 100, Cypress
(90630-5250)
PHONE..................................714 657-1040
Rich Ambrose, *Vice Pres*
EMP: 83
SALES (corp-wide): 43.6B **Publicly Held**
SIC: 4841 Cable television services
HQ: Spectrum Management Holding Company, Llc
400 Atlantic St
Stamford CT 06901
203 905-7801

(P-5741)
SPECTRUM MGT HOLDG CO LLC
4077 W Stetson Ave, Hemet (92545-9704)
PHONE..................................951 260-3143
Andre Mora, *Manager*
EMP: 83
SALES (corp-wide): 43.6B **Publicly Held**
SIC: 4841 Cable television services
HQ: Spectrum Management Holding Company, Llc
400 Atlantic St
Stamford CT 06901
203 905-7801

(P-5742)
SPECTRUM MGT HOLDG CO LLC
1041 E Route 66, Glendora (91740-6357)
PHONE..................................626 857-1075
Erwin Tando, *Branch Mgr*
EMP: 86
SALES (corp-wide): 43.6B **Publicly Held**
SIC: 4841 Cable television services

HQ: Spectrum Management Holding Company, Llc
400 Atlantic St
Stamford CT 06901
203 905-7801

(P-5743)
SPECTRUM MGT HOLDG CO LLC
Also Called: Time Warner
27555 Ynez Rd Ste 203, Temecula
(92591-4677)
PHONE..................................951 587-8660
Doug Walker, *Branch Mgr*
EMP: 83
SALES (corp-wide): 43.6B **Publicly Held**
SIC: 4841 Cable television services
HQ: Spectrum Management Holding Company, Llc
400 Atlantic St
Stamford CT 06901
203 905-7801

(P-5744)
SPECTRUM MGT HOLDG CO LLC
Also Called: Time Warner
1078 E Hospitality Ln D, San Bernardino
(92408-2878)
PHONE..................................909 918-6972
Kathleen Ouilette, *Branch Mgr*
EMP: 83
SALES (corp-wide): 43.6B **Publicly Held**
SIC: 4841 Cable television services; subscription television services
HQ: Spectrum Management Holding Company, Llc
400 Atlantic St
Stamford CT 06901
203 905-7801

(P-5745)
SPECTRUM MGT HOLDG CO LLC
17777 Center Court Dr N, Cerritos
(90703-9320)
PHONE..................................562 677-0228
Mark Coleman, *Vice Pres*
EMP: 84
SALES (corp-wide): 43.6B **Publicly Held**
SIC: 4841 Cable television services
HQ: Spectrum Management Holding Company, Llc
400 Atlantic St
Stamford CT 06901
203 905-7801

(P-5746)
SPECTRUM MGT HOLDG CO LLC
Also Called: Adelphia
1565 S Harbor Blvd, Fullerton
(92832-3402)
PHONE..................................714 871-2643
Rick Rivas, *Branch Mgr*
EMP: 84
SALES (corp-wide): 43.6B **Publicly Held**
SIC: 4841 Cable television services
HQ: Spectrum Management Holding Company, Llc
400 Atlantic St
Stamford CT 06901
203 905-7801

(P-5747)
SPECTRUM MGT HOLDG CO LLC
350 Stonewood St, Downey (90241-3909)
PHONE..................................562 372-4008
EMP: 83
SALES (corp-wide): 43.6B **Publicly Held**
SIC: 4841 Cable television services
HQ: Spectrum Management Holding Company, Llc
400 Atlantic St
Stamford CT 06901
203 905-7801

(P-5748)
SPECTRUM MGT HOLDG CO LLC
9260 Topanga Canyon Blvd, Chatsworth
(91311-5726)
PHONE..................................818 700-6126
Michael Snider, *Branch Mgr*

PRODUCTS & SVCS

EMP: 86
SALES (corp-wide): 43.6B **Publicly Held**
SIC: 4841 Cable television services
HQ: Spectrum Management Holding Company, Llc
400 Atlantic St
Stamford CT 06901
203 905-7801

(P-5749)
SPECTRUM MGT HOLDG CO LLC
500 Lakewood Center Mall, Lakewood (90712-2407)
PHONE...................................424 529-6011
EMP: 153
SALES (corp-wide): 43.6B **Publicly Held**
SIC: 4841 Cable television services
HQ: Spectrum Management Holding Company, Llc
400 Atlantic St
Stamford CT 06901
203 905-7801

(P-5750)
SPECTRUM MGT HOLDG CO LLC
Also Called: Time Warner
6021 Katella Ave Ste 100, Cypress (90630-5250)
PHONE..................................714 657-1060
EMP: 120
SALES (corp-wide): 29B **Publicly Held**
SIC: 4841
HQ: Spectrum Management Holding Company, Llc
400 Atlantic St
Stamford CT 06901
203 905-7801

(P-5751)
SPECTRUM MGT HOLDG CO LLC
Also Called: Time Warner
12040 Western Ave, Garden Grove (92841-2913)
PHONE..................................714 903-4000
Tad Yo, *Manager*
EMP: 83
SALES (corp-wide): 43.6B **Publicly Held**
SIC: 4841 Cable television services
HQ: Spectrum Management Holding Company, Llc
400 Atlantic St
Stamford CT 06901
203 905-7801

(P-5752)
SPECTRUM MGT HOLDG CO LLC
Also Called: Time Warner
550 Continental Blvd # 250, El Segundo (90245-5049)
PHONE..................................310 647-3000
Debi Picciolo, *Branch Mgr*
Kathryn St John, *Vice Pres*
Lisa Simon, *Senior Mgr*
EMP: 83
SALES (corp-wide): 43.6B **Publicly Held**
SIC: 4841 Cable television services
HQ: Spectrum Management Holding Company, Llc
400 Atlantic St
Stamford CT 06901
203 905-7801

(P-5753)
SPECTRUM MGT HOLDG CO LLC
1500 Auto Center Dr, Ontario (91761-2243)
PHONE..................................909 821-8159
Brian Ha, *Manager*
EMP: 83
SALES (corp-wide): 43.6B **Publicly Held**
SIC: 4841 Cable television services
HQ: Spectrum Management Holding Company, Llc
400 Atlantic St
Stamford CT 06901
203 905-7801

(P-5754)
SPECTRUM MGT HOLDG CO LLC
Also Called: Time Warner
3430 E Miraloma Ave, Anaheim (92806-2101)
PHONE..................................714 414-1431
Preston Hayslette, *Branch Mgr*
EMP: 83
SALES (corp-wide): 43.6B **Publicly Held**
SIC: 4841 Cable television services
HQ: Spectrum Management Holding Company, Llc
400 Atlantic St
Stamford CT 06901
203 905-7801

(P-5755)
SPECTRUM MGT HOLDG CO LLC
12625 Frederick St F10, Moreno Valley (92553-5216)
PHONE..................................951 571-8738
Steve Naber, *Branch Mgr*
EMP: 83
SALES (corp-wide): 43.6B **Publicly Held**
SIC: 4841 Cable television services
HQ: Spectrum Management Holding Company, Llc
400 Atlantic St
Stamford CT 06901
203 905-7801

(P-5756)
TIME WARNER CABLE ENTPS LLC
3500 W Olive Ave Ste 1000, Burbank (91505-5515)
PHONE..................................818 972-0808
EMP: 75
SALES (corp-wide): 43.6B **Publicly Held**
SIC: 4841 Cable television services
HQ: Time Warner Cable Enterprises Llc
400 Atlantic St Ste 6
Stamford CT 06901

(P-5757)
TIME WARNER CABLE ENTPS LLC
1438 N Gower St, Los Angeles (90028-8383)
PHONE..................................323 993-7076
Richard Battaglia, *President*
EMP: 120
SALES (corp-wide): 43.6B **Publicly Held**
SIC: 4841 Cable television services
HQ: Time Warner Cable Enterprises Llc
400 Atlantic St Ste 6
Stamford CT 06901

(P-5758)
TIME WARNER CABLE ENTPS LLC
550 Continental Blvd # 250, El Segundo (90245-5049)
PHONE..................................469 665-7735
Debi Picciolo, *Principal*
EMP: 2500
SALES (corp-wide): 43.6B **Publicly Held**
SIC: 4841 Cable television services
HQ: Time Warner Cable Enterprises Llc
400 Atlantic St Ste 6
Stamford CT 06901

(P-5759)
TIME WARNER CABLE ENTPS LLC
3300 Warner Blvd, Burbank (91505-4632)
PHONE..................................818 953-3283
Tom Whalley, *Branch Mgr*
EMP: 200
SALES (corp-wide): 43.6B **Publicly Held**
SIC: 4841 Cable television services
HQ: Time Warner Cable Enterprises Llc
400 Atlantic St Ste 6
Stamford CT 06901

(P-5760)
TIME WARNER CABLE INC
3051 Clairemont Dr, San Diego (92117-6802)
PHONE..................................619 346-4573
Margie Herrera, *Branch Mgr*
EMP: 76
SALES (corp-wide): 43.6B **Publicly Held**
SIC: 4841 Cable television services
HQ: Spectrum Management Holding Company, Llc
400 Atlantic St
Stamford CT 06901
203 905-7801

(P-5761)
TIME WARNER CABLE INC
118 N 8th St, Santa Paula (93060-2710)
PHONE..................................888 892-2253
Warner Cable, *Owner*
EMP: 86
SALES (corp-wide): 43.6B **Publicly Held**
SIC: 4841 Cable television services
HQ: Spectrum Management Holding Company, Llc
400 Atlantic St
Stamford CT 06901
203 905-7801

(P-5762)
TIME WARNER CABLE INC
2323 Teller Rd, Newbury Park (91320-2219)
PHONE..................................805 214-1353
David Bultman, *Branch Mgr*
EMP: 83
SALES (corp-wide): 43.6B **Publicly Held**
SIC: 4841 Cable television services
HQ: Spectrum Management Holding Company, Llc
400 Atlantic St
Stamford CT 06901
203 905-7801

(P-5763)
TIME WARNER CABLE INC
10450 Pacific Center Ct, San Diego (92121-4338)
PHONE..................................858 695-3220
Jim Fellhauer, *President*
EMP: 410
SQ FT: 25,500
SALES (corp-wide): 43.6B **Publicly Held**
SIC: 4841 Cable television services
HQ: Spectrum Management Holding Company, Llc
400 Atlantic St
Stamford CT 06901
203 905-7801

(P-5764)
TIME WARNER CABLE INC
660 W Acacia Ave, Hemet (92543-4073)
PHONE..................................951 306-3117
EMP: 84
SALES (corp-wide): 43.6B **Publicly Held**
SIC: 4841 Cable television services
HQ: Spectrum Management Holding Company, Llc
400 Atlantic St
Stamford CT 06901
203 905-7801

(P-5765)
TIME WARNER CABLE INC
15255 Salt Lake Ave, City of Industry (91745-1130)
PHONE..................................626 705-7482
Kurt Taylor, *Manager*
EMP: 95
SALES (corp-wide): 43.6B **Publicly Held**
SIC: 4841 Cable television services
HQ: Spectrum Management Holding Company, Llc
400 Atlantic St
Stamford CT 06901
203 905-7801

(P-5766)
TIME WARNER CABLE INC
900 N Cahuenga Blvd, Los Angeles (90038-2615)
PHONE..................................323 993-8000
Debbie Piccolio, *Branch Mgr*
EMP: 300

SALES (corp-wide): 43.6B **Publicly Held**
SIC: 4841 Cable television services
HQ: Spectrum Management Holding Company, Llc
400 Atlantic St
Stamford CT 06901
203 905-7801

(P-5767)
TIME WARNER CABLE INC
8949 Ware Ct, San Diego (92121-2222)
PHONE..................................858 695-3110
Lisa Simon, *Branch Mgr*
EMP: 300
SALES (corp-wide): 43.6B **Publicly Held**
SIC: 4841 Cable television services; subscription television services
HQ: Spectrum Management Holding Company, Llc
400 Atlantic St
Stamford CT 06901
203 905-7801

(P-5768)
TIME WARNER CABLE INC
313 N 8th St, El Centro (92243-2303)
PHONE..................................760 335-4800
EMP: 83
SALES (corp-wide): 41.5B **Publicly Held**
SIC: 4841
HQ: Spectrum Management Holding Company, Llc
400 Atlantic St
Stamford CT 06901
203 905-7801

(P-5769)
TVB (USA) INC (DH)
15411 Blackburn Ave, Norwalk (90650-6844)
PHONE..................................562 345-9871
Philip Tam, *President*
Melissa Wang, *Vice Pres*
▲ EMP: 50
SQ FT: 25,000
SALES (est): 8.5MM **Privately Held**
SIC: 4841 Cable television services
HQ: Tvb Holdings (Usa) Inc
15411 Blackburn Ave
Norwalk CA 90650
562 802-8868

(P-5770)
VOLCANO VISION INC
Also Called: Volcano Telephone Co.
20000 State Highway 88, Pine Grove (95665-9512)
P.O. Box 1070 (95665-1070)
PHONE..................................209 296-2288
Toll Free:.................................888 -
Sharon J Lundgren, *President*
John M Lundgren, *Vice Pres*
Deilia P Harder, *Human Resources*
EMP: 115
SQ FT: 1,000
SALES (est): 2.6MM **Privately Held**
SIC: 4841 Cable television services

(P-5771)
WARNER MEDIA LLC
Also Called: Time Warner
2014 W Avenue K, Lancaster (93536-5229)
PHONE..................................661 344-1546
EMP: 76
SALES (corp-wide): 170.7B **Publicly Held**
SIC: 4841 Cable television services
HQ: Warner Media, Llc
1 Time Warner Ctr
New York NY 10019

(P-5772)
WARNER MEDIA LLC
Also Called: Time Warner
2650 Tapo Canyon Rd, Simi Valley (93063-2226)
PHONE..................................805 421-4467
EMP: 76
SALES (corp-wide): 170.7B **Publicly Held**
SIC: 4841 Cable television services
HQ: Warner Media, Llc
1 Time Warner Ctr
New York NY 10019

▲ = Import ▼=Export
◆ =Import/Export

4899 Communication Svcs, NEC

(P-5773)
1105 MEDIA INC
2121 Alton Pkwy Ste 240, Irvine (92606-4979)
PHONE..................................949 265-1520
Richard Vitale, *Owner*
Shane Lee, *Administration*
Mallory Bundy, *Director*
EMP: 194
SALES (corp-wide): 136.4MM **Privately Held**
SIC: 4899 Data communication services
PA: 1105 Media, Inc.
6300 Canoga Ave Ste 1150
Woodland Hills CA 91367
818 814-5200

(P-5774)
ALCHEMY COMMUNICATIONS INC
6171 W Century Blvd, Los Angeles (90045-5300)
PHONE..................................310 568-0700
Jamie Daquino, *Branch Mgr*
EMP: 53 **Privately Held**
SIC: 4899 Data communication services
PA: Alchemy Communications, Inc.
1200 W 7th St Ste L1 100
Chatsworth CA 91311

(P-5775)
BELLA TERRA TECHNOLOGIES INC
1600 Amphitheatre Pkwy, Mountain View (94043-1351)
PHONE..................................650 316-6660
Tom Ingersoll, *CEO*
Dan Berkenstock,
EMP: 54
SALES (est): 2.9MM
SALES (corp-wide): 136.8B **Publicly Held**
SIC: 4899 Satellite earth stations
HQ: Google Llc
1600 Amphitheatre Pkwy
Mountain View CA 94043
650 253-0000

(P-5776)
BLUE JEANS NETWORK INC (PA)
3098 Olsen Dr, San Jose (95128-2048)
PHONE..................................408 550-2828
Quentin Gallivan, *CEO*
Robert Park, *CFO*
Krish Ramakrishnan, *Chairman*
Rosanne Saccone, *Chief Mktg Ofcr*
Lori Wright, *Chief Mktg Ofcr*
EMP: 86
SALES (est): 22.6MM **Privately Held**
SIC: 4899 Data communication services

(P-5777)
BYTEMOBILE INC (DH)
Also Called: Byte Mobile
2860 De La Cruz Blvd # 200, Santa Clara (95050-2635)
PHONE..................................408 327-7700
Hatim Tyabji, *CEO*
Adrian Hall, *COO*
Thomas Hubbs, *CFO*
JD Howard, *Vice Pres*
Andy Missan, *Vice Pres*
▲ EMP: 260
SQ FT: 30,000
SALES (est): 8.7MM
SALES (corp-wide): 242.1K **Privately Held**
SIC: 4899 7361 Communication signal enhancement network system; employment agencies
HQ: Citrix Systems International Gmbh
Rheinweg 9
Schaffhausen SH 8200
526 357-700

(P-5778)
CAMBIUM NETWORKS INC
2010 N 1st St, San Jose (95131-2018)
PHONE..................................847 640-3809
EMP: 155
SALES (corp-wide): 69.3MM **Privately Held**
SIC: 4899 Data communication services
PA: Cambium Networks, Inc.
3800 Golf Rd Ste 360
Rolling Meadows IL 60008
888 863-5250

(P-5779)
CENTERFIELD MEDIA HOLDINGS LLC (PA)
12130 Millennium Ste 500, Los Angeles (90094-2946)
PHONE..................................310 341-4420
Brett Cravatt, *Co-President*
Jason Cohen, *Co-President*
Brad Green, *Vice Pres*
Alex Horton, *Accounting Mgr*
Tiffany Sayers, *Manager*
EMP: 52 EST: 2010
SALES (est): 122.1MM **Privately Held**
SIC: 4899 Data communication services

(P-5780)
COMMUNICATIONS SUPPLY CORP
6251 Knott Ave, Buena Park (90620-1010)
PHONE..................................714 670-7711
Michael Davis, *General Mgr*
Miryam Lopez, *Sales Associate*
EMP: 70 **Publicly Held**
WEB: www.gocsc.com
SIC: 4899 1731 3577 3357 Data communication services; communications specialization; computer peripheral equipment; nonferrous wiredrawing & insulating
HQ: Communications Supply Corp
200 E Lies Rd
Carol Stream IL 60188
630 221-6400

(P-5781)
CONVO COMMUNICATIONS LLC
6601 Owens Dr Ste 155, Pleasanton (94588-3356)
PHONE..................................925 227-5500
Wayne G Betts, *Principal*
Jeff Rosen, *Executive*
Isidore Niyongabo, *Human Res Mgr*
Fallon Haney, *Personnel Assit*
Manny Johnson, *Marketing Staff*
EMP: 241
SALES (est): 1.2MM **Privately Held**
SIC: 4899 Data communication services

(P-5782)
COX CALIFORNIA TELCOM LLC
1922 Avenida Del Oro, Oceanside (92056-5803)
PHONE..................................760 966-0447
Jeff Trotter, *Manager*
Jim Bulliung, *Technician*
Katherine Paezle Harris, *Manager*
EMP: 190
SALES (corp-wide): 32.3B **Privately Held**
SIC: 4899 Data communication services
HQ: Cox California Telcom, L.L.C.
6205-B Pchtree Dnwoody Rd
Atlanta GA 30328

(P-5783)
DANG QUINTEN
Also Called: T2d Media
11272 Frankmont Ct, El Monte (91732-2152)
PHONE..................................626 429-6332
Quinten Dang, *Director*
EMP: 60
SALES (est): 499.7K **Privately Held**
SIC: 4899 Communication services

(P-5784)
DIGITAL MAP PRODUCTS INC
5201 California Ave # 200, Irvine (92617-3098)
PHONE..................................949 333-5111
James Skurzynski, *President*
Colleen Ellison, *Vice Pres*

Annie Schwab, *Vice Pres*
Steve Stautzenbach, *Vice Pres*
Eade Hopkinson, *Administration*
EMP: 51
SQ FT: 8,000
SALES (est): 7MM **Privately Held**
WEB: www.digmap.com
SIC: 4899 Data communication services

(P-5785)
DISCOVERY COMMUNICATIONS INC (PA)
10100 Santa Monica Blvd, Los Angeles (90067-4003)
PHONE..................................310 975-5906
David Zazlov, *CEO*
Kathleen Penny, *Vice Pres*
Lauren Tuck, *Admin Asst*
Jorge Hernandez, *Sr Software Eng*
Jojo Jalapit, *Technician*
EMP: 400
SALES (est): 6.2MM **Privately Held**
SIC: 4899 Data communication services

(P-5786)
EQUINIX (US) ENTERPRISES INC (HQ)
1 Lagoon Dr, Redwood City (94065-1562)
PHONE..................................650 598-6363
Donald Campbell, *CFO*
EMP: 99 EST: 2005
SALES (est): 2.4MM
SALES (corp-wide): 5B **Publicly Held**
SIC: 4899 Communication signal enhancement network system
PA: Equinix, Inc.
1 Lagoon Dr Ste 400
Redwood City CA 94065
650 598-6000

(P-5787)
FOUR MEDICA INC
13160 Mindanao Way # 280, Marina Del Rey (90292-6358)
PHONE..................................310 348-4100
Oleg Bess, *Principal*
EMP: 74 EST: 2011
SALES (est): 9MM **Privately Held**
SIC: 4899 Data communication services

(P-5788)
GODIGITAL MEDIA GROUP LLC
3103 S La Cienega Blvd, Los Angeles (90016-3110)
PHONE..................................310 853-7940
Jason Peterson, *Chairman*
Jay Winship, *COO*
Hunter Paletsas, *CFO*
Manfred Van Ursel, *CTO*
Logan Mulvey,
EMP: 60
SALES (est): 129.8K **Privately Held**
SIC: 4899 8741 7389 Data communication services; business management; copyright protection service

(P-5789)
INTELSAT US LLC
Also Called: Intell Set
1600 Forbes Way, Long Beach (90810-1830)
PHONE..................................310 525-5500
Tom Nassis, *Vice Pres*
EMP: 150
SALES (corp-wide): 177.9K **Privately Held**
SIC: 4899 Satellite earth stations; data communication services
HQ: Intelsat Us Llc
7900 Tysons One Pl
Mc Lean VA 22102

(P-5790)
IPS GROUP INC (PA)
7737 Kenamar Ct, San Diego (92121-2425)
PHONE..................................858 404-0607
David W King, *CEO*
Chad Randall, *COO*
Dario Paduano, *CFO*
Amir Sedadi, *Vice Pres*
Alexander M Schwarz, *CTO*
▲ EMP: 58

SALES (est): 26.4MM **Privately Held**
WEB: www.ipsgroupinc.com
SIC: 4899 3824 Communication signal enhancement network system; parking meters

(P-5791)
ITRON NETWORKED SOLUTIONS INC (HQ)
230 W Tasman Dr, San Jose (95134-1714)
PHONE..................................669 770-4000
Thomas L Deitrich, *President*
Gary Galensky, *Vice Pres*
Craig Lawson, *Vice Pres*
Don Reeves, *Vice Pres*
Howell Leung, *Program Mgr*
▲ EMP: 400
SQ FT: 191,800
SALES: 311MM
SALES (corp-wide): 2.3B **Publicly Held**
WEB: www.silverspringnetworks.com
SIC: 4899 7372 Communication signal enhancement network system; prepackaged software
PA: Itron, Inc.
2111 N Molter Rd
Liberty Lake WA 99019
509 924-9900

(P-5792)
KBRWYLE TECH SOLUTIONS LLC
Also Called: Honeywell
Vanonbrg Air Frc Bldg 660, Lompoc (93438)
PHONE..................................805 734-2982
T A Yancey, *Manager*
EMP: 277 **Publicly Held**
WEB: www.honeywell-tsi.com
SIC: 4899 Missile tracking by telemetry & photography
HQ: Kbrwyle Technology Solutions, Llc
7000 Columbia Gateway Dr # 100
Columbia MD 21046
410 964-7000

(P-5793)
LUXN INC
580 Maude Ct, Sunnyvale (94085-2822)
PHONE..................................408 213-7437
Thomas Alexander, *President*
Lee Zipin, *Ch of Bd*
Agnes Emory, *Vice Pres*
Paul Strudwick, *Vice Pres*
EMP: 53 EST: 1998
SALES (est): 1.5MM **Publicly Held**
WEB: www.luxn.com
SIC: 4899 Data communication services
HQ: Sorrento Networks Corporation
7195 Oakport St
Oakland CA 94621
510 577-1400

(P-5794)
NPHASE LLC
6195 Lusk Blvd Ste 200, San Diego (92121-3723)
PHONE..................................312 577-1650
EMP: 75
SQ FT: 20,000
SALES (est): 4.3MM **Privately Held**
WEB: www.nphasem2m.com
SIC: 4899

(P-5795)
OPLINK COMMUNICATIONS LLC (DH)
Also Called: Oplink Communications, Inc.
46360 Fremont Blvd, Fremont (94538-6406)
PHONE..................................510 933-7200
Joseph Y Liu, *CEO*
Peter Lee, *President*
Shirley Yin, *CFO*
River Gong, *Exec VP*
Stephen M Welles, *Senior VP*
▲ EMP: 57
SQ FT: 51,000
SALES (est): 749.6MM
SALES (corp-wide): 40.6B **Privately Held**
WEB: www.oplink.com
SIC: 4899 3661 Communication signal enhancement network system; data communication services; fiber optics communications equipment

PRODUCTS & SVCS

HQ: Molex, Llc
2222 Wellington Ct
Lisle IL 60532
630 969-4550

(P-5796)
PROSOFT TECHNOLOGY INC (HQ)
9201 Camino Media Ste 200, Bakersfield (93311-1362)
PHONE..............................661 716-5100
Thomas Crone, *President*
Stephen Wojtowicz, *Business Dir*
Todd Wiese, *Software Engr*
Juliane Bone, *Graphic Designe*
Josh Machado, *Engineer*
EMP: 70
SALES (est): 49.5MM
SALES (corp-wide): 2.5B **Publicly Held**
WEB: www.psft.com
SIC: 4899 Data communication services
PA: Belden Inc.
1 N Brentwood Blvd Fl 15
Saint Louis MO 63105
314 854-8000

(P-5797)
PURPLE COMMUNICATIONS INC
1000 Broadway Ste 252, Oakland (94607-4090)
PHONE..............................510 268-0120
Dennice Madlaid, *Branch Mgr*
EMP: 151
SALES (corp-wide): 288.6MM **Privately Held**
SIC: 4899 Data communication services
PA: Purple Communications, Inc.
595 Menlo Dr
Rocklin CA 95765
888 600-4780

(P-5798)
R F METRO SERVICES INC (PA)
Also Called: Metro Rf
2320 S Archibald Ave, Ontario (91761-8520)
PHONE..............................909 230-4920
Mehrzad Sarfehnia, *CEO*
Rebecca Stalter, *Administration*
John Rogers, *Project Leader*
Jorge Castaneda, *Technician*
Jim Focht, *Opers Mgr*
EMP: 58
SQ FT: 8,142
SALES (est): 16.2MM **Privately Held**
WEB: www.metromobile.net
SIC: 4899 Communication signal enhancement network system

(P-5799)
SCHOOLWIRES INC
645 S Barranca St, West Covina (91791-2943)
PHONE..............................626 974-7600
Kris Kemp, *Principal*
EMP: 56
SALES (est): 557.9K **Privately Held**
SIC: 4899 Communication services

(P-5800)
SOUTH BAY RGONAL PUB COMM AUTH
Also Called: S B Communications
4440 W Broadway, Hawthorne (90250-3802)
PHONE..............................310 973-1802
Lena Ramos, *Corp Comm Staff*
EMP: 50
SQ FT: 1,632
SALES: 10.3MM **Privately Held**
SIC: 4899 Communication signal enhancement network system

(P-5801)
SPACE SYSTEMS/LORAL LLC (DH)
Also Called: Ssl
3825 Fabian Way, Palo Alto (94303-4604)
PHONE..............................650 852-7320
John Celli, *President*
Barbara Ellis, *President*
Ed McFarlane, *President*
Ron Haley, *CFO*
Michael Santoro, *CFO*

◆ EMP: 75
SALES (est): 445.9MM
SALES (corp-wide): 2.1B **Publicly Held**
SIC: 4899 3663 Satellite earth stations; satellites, communications
HQ: Maxar Technologies Ltd
200 Burrard St Suite 1570
Vancouver BC V6C 3
604 974-5275

(P-5802)
SS8 NETWORKS INC (PA)
Also Called: S S 8
750 Tasman Dr, Milpitas (95035-7456)
PHONE..............................408 894-8400
Dennis Haar, *CEO*
Keith Bhatia, *COO*
Kam Wong, *CFO*
Cemal Dikmen, *CTO*
EMP: 161
SQ FT: 83,000
SALES (est): 28.9MM **Privately Held**
WEB: www.ss8.com
SIC: 4899 7381 Communication signal enhancement network system; detective services

(P-5803)
TELETRAC INC (HQ)
Also Called: Fleet Mangement Solutions
7391 Lincoln Way, Garden Grove (92841-1428)
PHONE..............................714 897-0877
Tj Chung, *President*
Tim Van Cleve, *COO*
Rachel Trindade, *Vice Pres*
Gary Angelo, *Executive*
Natasha Keech, *Executive*
▲ EMP: 91
SQ FT: 40,000
SALES (est): 82.1MM
SALES (corp-wide): 6.4B **Publicly Held**
WEB: www.teletrac.net
SIC: 4899 Data communication services
PA: Fortive Corporation
6920 Seaway Blvd
Everett WA 98203
425 446-5000

(P-5804)
TERABURST NETWORKS INC
1289 Anvilwood Ave, Sunnyvale (94089-2204)
PHONE..............................408 400-4100
Ashok Jain, *CEO*
EMP: 50
SALES (est): 3.5MM **Privately Held**
WEB: www.teraburst.com
SIC: 4899 Communication signal enhancement network system

(P-5805)
THINKOM SOLUTIONS INC
4881 W 145th St, Hawthorne (90250-6701)
PHONE..............................310 371-5486
Mark Silk, *CEO*
Michael Burke, *President*
Stuart Coppedge, *CFO*
Matthew Turk, *CFO*
William W Milroy, *Principal*
EMP: 116
SQ FT: 74,000
SALES (est): 14.8MM **Privately Held**
WEB: www.thin-kom.com
SIC: 4899 Satellite earth stations; television antenna construction & rental

(P-5806)
TRI-POWER GROUP INC
617 N Mary Ave, Sunnyvale (94085-2907)
PHONE..............................925 583-8200
Seth Buechley, *CEO*
Chip Laughton, *President*
Bryan Kemper, *COO*
Barry Bruce, *CFO*
▲ EMP: 60
SQ FT: 13,000
SALES (est): 5.4MM **Privately Held**
WEB: www.tripowergroup.com
SIC: 4899 Data communication services

(P-5807)
US DEPT OF THE AIR FORCE
Also Called: 95cs/Scxc Comp
35 N Wolfe Ave, Edwards (93524-6701)
PHONE..............................661 277-3030

EMP: 250 **Publicly Held**
WEB: www.af.mil
SIC: 4899 9711 Communication signal enhancement network system; Air Force;
HQ: United States Department Of The Air Force
1000 Air Force Pentagon
Washington DC 20330

(P-5808)
VIDEO VICE DATA COMMUNICATIONS
Also Called: Vvd Comuunications
12681 Pala Dr, Garden Grove (92841-3926)
P.O. Box 91421, Long Beach (90809-1421)
PHONE..............................714 897-6300
Bantofin Montoya, *President*
Annie Yonemura, *Admin Asst*
EMP: 396 EST: 2002
SALES: 9.7MM **Privately Held**
SIC: 4899 1731 Data communication services; electrical work; cable television installation; fiber optic cable installation; voice, data & video wiring contractor

(P-5809)
WOVEXX HOLDINGS INC (DH)
Also Called: Redwood
10381 Jefferson Blvd, Culver City (90232-3511)
PHONE..............................310 424-2080
Benjamin Blank, *CEO*
Jarret Myer, *Founder*
Julie Butler, *Vice Pres*
Jenny Chen, *Vice Pres*
Jeffrey Cohen, *Vice Pres*
EMP: 90
SQ FT: 12,000
SALES (est): 22.8MM **Privately Held**
SIC: 4899 7929 Data communication services; entertainment service
HQ: Warner Music Group Corp.
1633 Broadway Fl 11
New York NY 10019
212 275-2000

4911 Electric Svcs

(P-5810)
AES ALAMITOS LLC
690 N Studebaker Rd, Long Beach (90803-2221)
PHONE..............................562 493-7891
Weikko Wirta, *Mng Member*
Sid Phan, *Plant Engr*
Jim Beach, *Maintence Staff*
EMP: 90
SALES: 200MM
SALES (corp-wide): 10.7B **Publicly Held**
SIC: 4911 Electric services
PA: The Aes Corporation
4300 Wilson Blvd Ste 1100
Arlington VA 22203
703 522-1315

(P-5811)
AES HUNTINGTON BEACH LLC
21730 Newland St, Huntington Beach (92646-7612)
PHONE..............................714 374-1476
Eric Pendergraft,
Weikko Wirta, *Plant Mgr*
Minh Hoang,
Stephen O'Kane, *Mng Member*
EMP: 50
SALES (est): 33MM
SALES (corp-wide): 10.7B **Publicly Held**
WEB: www.aescorp.com
SIC: 4911 Generation, electric power
PA: The Aes Corporation
4300 Wilson Blvd Ste 1100
Arlington VA 22203
703 522-1315

(P-5812)
AES SOUTHLAND LLC
690 N Studebaker Rd, Long Beach (90803-2221)
PHONE..............................562 430-8685
Jeff Evans, *Mng Member*
EMP: 89 EST: 1998

SALES (est): 20.2MM
SALES (corp-wide): 10.7B **Publicly Held**
WEB: www.aescorp.com
SIC: 4911 Generation, electric power
PA: The Aes Corporation
4300 Wilson Blvd Ste 1100
Arlington VA 22203
703 522-1315

(P-5813)
ALAMEDA BUREAU ELEC IMPRV CORP (HQ)
Also Called: Alameda Municipal Power
2000 Grand St, Alameda (94501-1228)
P.O. Box H (94501-0263)
PHONE..............................510 748-3902
Edwin Dankworth, *CEO*
Gregory Hamm, *President*
Laura Giuntini, *Vice Pres*
Peter Holmes, *Vice Pres*
Margie Sherratt, *Vice Pres*
▲ EMP: 85
SALES (est): 79.1MM **Privately Held**
WEB: www.alamedapt.com
SIC: 4911 Distribution, electric power; transmission, electric power
PA: City Of Alameda
2263 Santa Clara Ave
Alameda CA 94501
510 747-7400

(P-5814)
ALTAMONT INFRASTRUCTURE CO
6185 Industrial Way, Livermore (94551-9750)
PHONE..............................925 245-5500
Tom Kelly, *Principal*
Green Ridge LLC, *Mng Member*
EMP: 60
SQ FT: 8,000
SALES: 30MM **Privately Held**
SIC: 4911 Generation, electric power

(P-5815)
CALIFRNIA IND SYS OPRATOR CORP (PA)
Also Called: California ISO
250 Outcropping Way, Folsom (95630-8773)
P.O. Box 639014 (95763-9014)
PHONE..............................916 351-4400
Stephen Berberich, *President*
Karen Edson, *Vice Pres*
Charles King, *Vice Pres*
Chris McIntosh, *Vice Pres*
Jodi Ziemathis, *Vice Pres*
EMP: 530
SQ FT: 79,000
SALES: 223.8MM **Privately Held**
WEB: www.caiso.com
SIC: 4911 Distribution, electric power; transmission, electric power

(P-5816)
CALPINE CORPORATION
5029 S Township Rd, Yuba City (95993-9748)
PHONE..............................530 821-2075
Scott Reynolds, *Branch Mgr*
EMP: 50
SALES (corp-wide): 9.5B **Privately Held**
WEB: www.calpine.com
SIC: 4911 Generation, electric power;
HQ: Calpine Corporation
717 Texas St Ste 1000
Houston TX 77002
713 830-2000

(P-5817)
CATALINA SOLAR 2 LLC
15445 Innovation Dr, San Diego (92128-3432)
PHONE..............................888 903-6926
Tristan Grimbert, *President*
Ryan Pfaff, *Vice Pres*
Robert Miller, *Admin Sec*
EMP: 826
SQ FT: 70,000
SALES (est): 299.2MM **Privately Held**
SIC: 4911 Generation, electric power

▲ = Import ▼=Export
◆ =Import/Export

(P-5818)
CATALINA SOLAR LESSEE LLC
11585 Willow Springs Rd, Rosamond
(93560)
PHONE....................888 903-6926
Tristan Grimbert, *President*
Robert Miller, *Admin Sec*
EMP: 826 **EST:** 2014
SQ FT: 70,000
SALES (est): 213.4MM
SALES (corp-wide): 971.6MM **Privately Held**
SIC: 4911 Electric services
PA: Edf Renewables, Inc.
15445 Innovation Dr
San Diego CA 92128
858 521-3300

(P-5819)
CITY OF GLENDALE
Also Called: Glendale Water & Power
141 N Glendale Ave Fl 2, Glendale
(91206-4975)
PHONE....................818 548-3300
John Dolan, *Manager*
Atineh Haroutunian, *Marketing Staff*
Craig Kuennen, *Marketing Staff*
EMP: 300 **Privately Held**
WEB: www.glendaleca.com
SIC: 4911 Electric services
PA: City Of Glendale
141 N Glendale Ave Fl 2
Glendale CA 91206
818 548-2085

(P-5820)
CITY OF GLENDALE
Also Called: Power Plant
634 Bekins Way, Glendale (91201-3013)
PHONE....................818 548-3980
Larry Moorehouse, *Superintendent*
EMP: 50 **Privately Held**
WEB: www.glendaleca.com
SIC: 4911 Generation, electric power
PA: City Of Glendale
141 N Glendale Ave Fl 2
Glendale CA 91206
818 548-2085

(P-5821)
CITY OF SANTA CLARA
Also Called: Silicon Valley Power
1500 Warburton Ave, Santa Clara
(95050-3796)
PHONE....................408 615-2300
John Roukema, *Director*
Lenka Wright, *Comms Dir*
EMP: 50 **Privately Held**
SIC: 4911 Electric services
PA: City Of Santa Clara
1500 Warburton Ave
Santa Clara CA 95050
408 615-2200

(P-5822)
CITY OF SANTA CLARA
Also Called: Electric Department
1705 Martin Ave, Santa Clara
(95050-2557)
PHONE....................408 615-2046
Chris Cervelli, *Principal*
EMP: 125
SQ FT: 15,000 **Privately Held**
SIC: 4911
PA: City Of Santa Clara
1500 Warburton Ave
Santa Clara CA 95050
408 615-2200

(P-5823)
COMBUSTION ASSOCIATES INC
Also Called: Cai
555 Monica Cir, Corona (92880-5447)
PHONE....................951 272-6999
Mukund Kavia, *President*
Kusum Kavia, *Vice Pres*
Prajesh Kavia, *Admin Sec*
Bharat Kavia, *Administration*
Jorge Villegas, *Project Mgr*
▲ **EMP:** 50
SQ FT: 40,000
SALES (est): 85.3MM **Privately Held**
WEB: www.cai3.com
SIC: 4911 3443 ; boiler & boiler shop
work

(P-5824)
CONSTELLATION NEWENERGY INC
350 S Grand Ave Ste 3800, Los Angeles
(90071-3479)
PHONE....................213 576-6001
Michael Peevey, *Branch Mgr*
EMP: 70
SALES (corp-wide): 35.9B **Publicly Held**
SIC: 4911 Generation, electric power
HQ: Constellation Newenergy, Inc.
1310 Point St Fl 8
Baltimore MD 21231

(P-5825)
COSO OPERATING COMPANY LLC
2 Gill Station Coso Rd, Little Lake (93542)
P.O. Box 1690, Inyokern (93527-1690)
PHONE....................760 764-1300
Jim Pagano, *CEO*
Joseph Greco, *Senior VP*
▲ **EMP:** 90
SALES (est): 55MM **Privately Held**
SIC: 4911 Generation, electric power
PA: Terra-Gen Power, Llc
437 Madison Ave Fl 22
New York NY 10022

(P-5826)
COVANTA DELANO INC
Also Called: Delano Energy
31500 Pond Rd, Delano (93215)
P.O. Box 39, Mariposa (95338-0039)
PHONE....................661 792-3067
Stephen J Jones, *CEO*
▲ **EMP:** 50
SALES (est): 25.4MM
SALES (corp-wide): 1.8B **Publicly Held**
WEB: www.aescorp.com
SIC: 4911 Generation, electric power
HQ: Covanta Projects, Llc
445 South St
Morristown NJ 07960

(P-5827)
CPN WILD HORSE GEOTHERMAL LLC
10350 Socrates Mine Rd, Middletown
(95461-9732)
PHONE....................707 431-6229
Alison Mannwieler, *President*
EMP: 300
SQ FT: 4,000
SALES: 1.8MM
SALES (corp-wide): 9.5B **Privately Held**
SIC: 4911 Generation, electric power;
HQ: Calpine Corporation
717 Texas St Ste 1000
Houston TX 77002
713 830-2000

(P-5828)
CYPRESS CREEK HOLDINGS LLC
3250 Ocean Park Blvd # 355, Santa Monica
(90405-3206)
PHONE....................310 581-6299
Ben Van De Bunt, *Chairman*
Michael Cohen, *President*
Matthew McGovern, *CEO*
EMP: 100
SALES (est): 20.5MM **Privately Held**
SIC: 4911

(P-5829)
CYPRESS CREEK RENEWABLES LLC
445 Bush St Fl 7, San Francisco
(94108-3728)
PHONE....................415 306-5300
Matthew McGovern, *Branch Mgr*
Garrett Hollingsworth, *Project Mgr*
Geoffrey Green, *Engineer*
Jeffrey Webber, *Engineer*
Alex Cloyd, *Director*
EMP: 60
SALES (corp-wide): 5.8MM **Privately Held**
SIC: 4911

PA: Cypress Creek Renewables, Llc
3250 Ocean Park Blvd # 355
Santa Monica CA 90405
310 581-6299

(P-5830)
DUKE ENERGY CORPORATION
8001 Irvine Center Dr, Irvine (92618-2938)
PHONE....................949 727-7434
EMP: 170
SALES (corp-wide): 23.4B **Publicly Held**
SIC: 4911 4924
PA: Duke Energy Corporation
550 S Tryon St
Charlotte NC 28202
704 382-3853

(P-5831)
DYNEGY MARKETING & TRADE LLC
Hwy 1 & Dolan Rd, Moss Landing (95039)
PHONE....................831 633-6700
Janet Bowen, *Train & Dev Mgr*
EMP: 100
SALES (corp-wide): 9.1B **Publicly Held**
SIC: 4911 4923 Generation, electric
power; gas transmission & distribution
HQ: Dynegy Marketing & Trade, Llc
6555 Sierra Dr
Irving TX 75039
214 812-4600

(P-5832)
DYNEGY MOSS LANDING LLC
Also Called: Moss Landing Power Plant
7301 Highway 1, Moss Landing (95039)
P.O. Box 690 (95039-0690)
PHONE....................831 633-6618
Robert C Flexon, *CEO*
Michael Sandlin, *IT/INT Sup*
Gretchen Schott, *Asst Sec*
▲ **EMP:** 75
SALES (est): 51.8MM
SALES (corp-wide): 9.1B **Publicly Held**
WEB: www.dynegy.com
SIC: 4911 Electric services
PA: Vistra Energy Corp.
6555 Sierra Dr
Irving TX 75039
214 812-4600

(P-5833)
EDF MSSCHSTTS SPNSOR MMBER LLC
15445 Innovation Dr, San Diego
(92128-3432)
PHONE....................888 903-6926
Tristan Grimber, *President*
Kara Vongphakdy, *Treasurer*
Larry Barr, *Exec VP*
Robert Miller, *Exec VP*
Ryan Pfaff, *Exec VP*
EMP: 827 **EST:** 2014
SQ FT: 70,000
SALES (est): 248.1K
SALES (corp-wide): 971.6MM **Privately Held**
SIC: 4911 Electric services
PA: Edf Renewables, Inc.
15445 Innovation Dr
San Diego CA 92128
858 521-3300

(P-5834)
EDF RENEWABLES INC (PA)
15445 Innovation Dr, San Diego
(92128-3432)
P.O. Box 504080 (92150-4080)
PHONE....................858 521-3300
Tristan Grimbert, *President*
Ryan Pfaff, *Exec VP*
Larry Barr, *Vice Pres*
Robert F Miller, *Admin Sec*
Art Del Rio, *Director*
▲ **EMP:** 225
SALES (est): 971.6MM **Privately Held**
WEB: www.enxco.com
SIC: 4911 Electric services

(P-5835)
EDF RNWBLES ASSET HOLDINGS INC
15445 Innovation Dr, San Diego
(92128-3432)
PHONE....................888 903-6926

Tristan Grimbert, *President*
Richard Jigarjian, *Vice Pres*
Robert Miller, *Admin Sec*
EMP: 826 **EST:** 2009
SQ FT: 70,000
SALES (est): 302.5MM **Privately Held**
SIC: 4911 Generation, electric power

(P-5836)
EDISON CAPITAL
18101 Von Karman Ave, Irvine
(92612-1012)
PHONE....................909 594-3789
Thomas Mc Daniel, *President*
Oded Rhone, *President*
Phillip Dandridge, *CFO*
Steve Dandridge, *CFO*
Jim Phillipsen, *Treasurer*
EMP: 103
SQ FT: 12,000
SALES (est): 25.5MM
SALES (corp-wide): 12.6B **Publicly Held**
WEB: www.edisoncapital.com
SIC: 4911 Electric services
HQ: Edison Mission Group Inc.
2244 Walnut Grove Ave
Rosemead CA 91770
626 302-2222

(P-5837)
EDISON INTERNATIONAL (PA)
2244 Walnut Grove Ave, Rosemead
(91770-3714)
P.O. Box 976 (91770-0976)
PHONE....................626 302-2222
Pedro J Pizarro, *President*
Kevin M Payne, *CEO*
Maria Rigatti, *CFO*
Adam S Umanoff, *Exec VP*
Caroline Choi, *Senior VP*
EMP: 52
SALES: 12.6B **Publicly Held**
WEB: www.edisonx.com
SIC: 4911 Electric services; distribution,
electric power; generation, electric power;
transmission, electric power

(P-5838)
EDISON MSSION MIDWEST HOLDINGS
2244 Walnut Grove Ave, Rosemead
(91770-3714)
PHONE....................626 302-2222
Guy F Gorney, *President*
Cindy Creed, *Vice Pres*
Dena Perkin, *Business Anlyst*
Mike Chandler, *Technical Staff*
Greg Henry, *Financial Analy*
EMP: 2483
SALES (est): 3.2B
SALES (corp-wide): 12.6B **Publicly Held**
SIC: 4911 Electric services
HQ: Edison Mission Group Inc.
2244 Walnut Grove Ave
Rosemead CA 91770
626 302-2222

(P-5839)
ELK HILLS POWER LLC
101 Ash St, San Diego (92101-3017)
PHONE....................661 763-2730
EMP: 107
SALES (est): 2MM
SALES (corp-wide): 3B **Publicly Held**
SIC: 4911 Electric services
PA: California Resources Corporation
27200 Tourney Rd Ste 200
Santa Clarita CA 91355
888 848-4754

(P-5840)
ENPOWER MANAGEMENT CORP
2410 Camino Ramon Ste 360, San Ramon
(94583-4318)
PHONE....................925 244-1100
Edward Tomeo, *President*
Alex Sugaoka, *Vice Pres*
EMP: 50
SALES (est): 9.9MM
SALES (corp-wide): 53.5MM **Privately Held**
WEB: www.enpowercorp.com
SIC: 4911 Generation, electric power; dis-
tribution, electric power

PA: Enpower Corp.
2410 Camino Ramon Ste 360
San Ramon CA 94583
925 244-1100

(P-5841)
GENERAL ELECTRIC COMPANY
288 Campus Dr Bldg 14105, Stanford
(94305-4109)
PHONE..........................650 725-0516
Ron Dahlin, *Manager*
EMP: 217
SALES (corp-wide): 121.6B **Publicly Held**
SIC: 4911 Generation, electric power
PA: General Electric Company
41 Farnsworth St
Boston MA 02210
617 443-3000

(P-5842)
GOLDEN STATE WATER COMPANY
Bear Valley Electric
42020 Garstin Dr, Big Bear Lake
(92315-1580)
P.O. Box 1547 (92315-1547)
PHONE..........................909 866-4678
Roger Kropke, *Manager*
EMP: 50
SALES (corp-wide): 436.8MM **Publicly Held**
WEB: www.gswater.com
SIC: 4911 Distribution, electric power
HQ: Golden State Water Company
630 E Foothill Blvd
San Dimas CA 91773
909 394-3600

(P-5843)
GREEN RIDGE SERVICES LLC
6185 Industrial Way, Livermore
(94551-9750)
PHONE..........................925 245-5500
Tom Kelly,
EMP: 60
SQ FT: 30,000
SALES (est): 23.8MM **Privately Held**
SIC: 4911 Electric services

(P-5844)
HANERGY HOLDING AMERICA INC
1350 Bayshore Hwy Ste 825, Burlingame
(94010-1848)
PHONE..........................650 288-3722
Yi Wu, *Ch of Bd*
Jeff Zhou, *President*
Richard Gaertner, *COO*
Anny Hu, *Executive*
Abraham Liu, *Technology*
EMP: 360
SQ FT: 7,000
SALES (est): 227.3MM
SALES (corp-wide): 782.7MM **Privately Held**
SIC: 4911 6719 Generation, electric power; investment holding companies, except banks
PA: Jinjiang Hydroelectric Power Group Co., Ltd.
No.0-A, Anli Road, Chaoyang Dist.
Beijing 10010
108 391-4567

(P-5845)
HIGH RIDGE WIND LLC
15445 Innovation Dr, San Diego
(92128-3432)
PHONE..........................888 903-6926
Tristan Grimbert, *President*
Ryan Pfaff, *Vice Pres*
Robert Miller, *Admin Sec*
EMP: 826 **EST:** 2013
SQ FT: 70,000
SALES (est): 258.5MM **Privately Held**
SIC: 4911 Electric services

(P-5846)
HUDSON RANCH POWER I LLC
12250 El Camino Real # 280, San Diego
(92130-2226)
P.O. Box 67, Calipatria (92233-0067)
PHONE..........................858 509-0150
Eric L Spomer, *Mng Member*
George Donlou, *Treasurer*

Carol A Thimot, *Asst Treas*
David K Watson,
EMP: 55
SALES (est): 42.2MM **Privately Held**
SIC: 4911 Generation, electric power

(P-5847)
IMPERIAL IRRIGATION DISTRICT (PA)
Also Called: I I D
333 E Barioni Blvd, Imperial (92251-1773)
P.O. Box 937 (92251-0937)
PHONE..........................800 303-7756
Stephen Benson, *President*
Anthony Sanchez, *President*
Keven Kelly, *President*
Mike Abatti, *Vice Pres*
Norma Sierra Galindo, *Vice Pres*
▲ **EMP:** 700
SQ FT: 10,000
SALES: 615.2MM **Privately Held**
WEB: www.iidwater.com
SIC: 4911 4971 4931 ; water distribution or supply systems for irrigation; electric & other services combined

(P-5848)
INSPIRE ENERGY HOLDINGS LLC
3402 Pico Blvd Ste 215, Santa Monica
(90405-2091)
PHONE..........................866 403-2620
Patrick Maloney, *CEO*
Blake Lasuzzo, *COO*
Zac Lowder, *Vice Pres*
Shanna Hu, *Accounting Mgr*
EMP: 138 **EST:** 2013
SALES (est): 3.2MM **Privately Held**
SIC: 4911 Distribution, electric power

(P-5849)
JETMORE WIND LLC
15445 Innovation Dr, San Diego
(92128-3432)
PHONE..........................888 903-6926
Tristan Grimbert, *President*
Ryan Pfaff, *Vice Pres*
Robert Miller, *Admin Sec*
EMP: 826
SQ FT: 70,000
SALES (est): 180.6MM **Privately Held**
SIC: 4911 Electric services

(P-5850)
KERN RIVER CO GENERATION CO
Sw China Grade Loop, Bakersfield (93308)
PHONE..........................661 392-2663
Neil Bridges, *Exec Dir*
Gaylord Edward, *Treasurer*
EMP: 65
SALES (est): 26.9MM **Publicly Held**
SIC: 4911 4961 ; steam supply systems, including geothermal
HQ: Southern Sierra Energy Company
18101 Von Karman Ave
Irvine CA 92612

(P-5851)
KJC OPERATING COMPANY
41100 Us Highway 395, Boron
(93516-2109)
PHONE..........................760 762-5562
Chris Kelleher, *Chairman*
Janet Doyle, *President*
Scott Frier, *COO*
EMP: 117
SQ FT: 10,000
SALES (est): 30.8MM **Privately Held**
WEB: www.kjcsolar.com
SIC: 4911 Electric services

(P-5852)
LEEMAH ELECTRONICS INC
Also Called: (415 LOCATION)
1080 Sansome St, San Francisco (94111)
PHONE..........................415 394-1288
Jack Wang, *Manager*
EMP: 120

SALES (corp-wide): 101MM **Privately Held**
SIC: 4911 3672 3669 3571 Electric services; printed circuit boards; intercommunication systems, electric; electronic computers
HQ: Leemah Electronics, Inc.
155 S Hill Dr
Brisbane CA 94005
415 394-1288

(P-5853)
LIBERTY UTLTIES CLPECO ELC LLC
Also Called: Liberty Energy
933 Eloise Ave, South Lake Tahoe
(96150-6470)
PHONE..........................800 782-2506
Ian Robertson, *Mng Member*
Mike Smart, *President*
Chico Dafonte, *Vice Pres*
Craig Jennings, *Vice Pres*
Markus Mueller, *Sr Ntwrk Engine*
EMP: 60
SQ FT: 10,000
SALES: 80.7MM **Privately Held**
SIC: 4911 Distribution, electric power

(P-5854)
LOS ANGELES DEPT WTR & PWR
Also Called: Ladwp
111 N Hope St, Los Angeles (90012-2607)
P.O. Box 51111 (90051-5700)
PHONE..........................213 367-4211
Ronald Nichols, *Branch Mgr*
Sunil Dharmarathne, *Info Tech Mgr*
Minh Le, *Info Tech Mgr*
Alina Cummings, *Information Mgr*
Cecilia Huynh, *Prgrmr*
EMP: 99
SALES (corp-wide): 1.1B **Privately Held**
SIC: 4911 4941 Generation, electric power; water supply
PA: Los Angeles Department Of Water And Power
111 N Hope St
Los Angeles CA 90012
213 367-4211

(P-5855)
LUZ SOLAR PARTNERS IX
Also Called: L S P Ix
43880 Harper Lake Rd, Hinkley
(92347-9541)
PHONE..........................760 762-3113
Chris Allen, *Partner*
EMP: 71
SALES (est): 405.5K **Privately Held**
SIC: 4911 Generation, electric power

(P-5856)
MARIN CLEAN ENERGY
Also Called: McE
1125 Tamalpais Ave, San Rafael
(94901-3221)
PHONE..........................415 464-6028
Dawn Weisz, *CEO*
Flores Brooks, *Admin Asst*
Allen Chiu, *Business Mgr*
Chris Kubik, *Business Mgr*
David McNeil, *Finance Mgr*
EMP: 75
SQ FT: 10,000
SALES (est): 151.6MM **Privately Held**
SIC: 4911 Distribution, electric power

(P-5857)
MERCED IRRIGATION DISTRICT (PA)
744 W 20th St, Merced (95340-3601)
P.O. Box 2288 (95344-0288)
PHONE..........................209 722-5761
Tim Pellissier, *President*
Andre Urquidez, *Treasurer*
Dave Long, *Vice Pres*
Brooke Gutierrez, *Director*
EMP: 50 **EST:** 1919
SQ FT: 20,000
SALES: 95.5MM **Privately Held**
WEB: www.mercedid.org
SIC: 4911 4971 Generation, electric power; water distribution or supply systems for irrigation

(P-5858)
MILO WIND PROJECT LLC
Also Called: Edf Renewable Energy
15445 Innovation Dr, San Diego
(92128-3432)
PHONE..........................888 903-6926
Tristan Grimbert, *President*
Ryan Pfaff, *Vice Pres*
Robert Miller, *Admin Sec*
EMP: 82
SQ FT: 70,000
SALES (est): 6.1MM **Privately Held**
SIC: 4911 Electric services

(P-5859)
MODESTO IRRIGATION DISTRICT
1231 11th St, Modesto (95354-0701)
P.O. Box 4060 (95352-4060)
PHONE..........................209 526-7563
Don Durman, *Treasurer*
EMP: 400
SALES (corp-wide): 412.3MM **Privately Held**
SIC: 4911 4941 ; water supply
PA: Modesto Irrigation District (Inc)
1231 11th St
Modesto CA 95354
209 526-7337

(P-5860)
MODESTO IRRIGATION DISTRICT (PA)
1231 11th St, Modesto (95354-0701)
P.O. Box 4060 (95352-4060)
PHONE..........................209 526-7337
Allen Short, *President*
Scott Vuren, *Risk Mgmt Dir*
Scott Furgerson, *General Mgr*
Angela Cartisano, *Admin Sec*
Karri Daves, *Administration*
EMP: 175 **EST:** 1887
SQ FT: 90,000
SALES: 412.3MM **Privately Held**
SIC: 4911 4971 ; water distribution or supply systems for irrigation

(P-5861)
MODESTO IRRIGATION DISTRICT
929 Woodland Ave, Modesto (95351-1553)
P.O. Box 4060 (95352-4060)
PHONE..........................209 526-7373
Ellen Short, *General Mgr*
EMP: 400
SALES (corp-wide): 412.3MM **Privately Held**
SIC: 4911 4971 Distribution, electric power; irrigation systems
PA: Modesto Irrigation District (Inc)
1231 11th St
Modesto CA 95354
209 526-7337

(P-5862)
NORTHERN CALIFORNIA POWER AGCY (PA)
Also Called: Ncpa
651 Commerce Dr, Roseville (95678-6411)
PHONE..........................916 781-3636
Sondra Ainsworth, *Treasurer*
Vicki Cichocki, *General Mgr*
Sandy Rainey, *Technical Staff*
Ronald Yuen, *Engineer*
Miranda Shumaker, *Business Mgr*
EMP: 65 **EST:** 1968
SQ FT: 17,400
SALES (est): 113.4MM **Privately Held**
WEB: www.NCPA.com
SIC: 4911 Transmission, electric power; generation, electric power

(P-5863)
NORTHERN CALIFORNIA POWER AGCY
Also Called: Ncpa- Plant 1
12000 Ridge Rd, Middletown (95461-9585)
P.O. Box 663 (95461-0663)
PHONE..........................707 987-2381
Murry Grande, *Opers-Prdtn-Mfg*
EMP: 56
SALES (est): 9.8MM
SALES (corp-wide): 113.4MM **Privately Held**
SIC: 4911 Generation, electric power

PA: Northern California Power Agency
651 Commerce Dr
Roseville CA 95678
916 781-3636

(P-5864)
NRG CALIFORNIA SOUTH LP
Also Called: Etiwanda Power Plant
8996 Etiwanda Ave, Rancho Cucamonga
(91739-9662)
PHONE.....................909 899-7241
Lee Moore, *Branch Mgr*
Gary Ackerman, *Exec Dir*
Vince Munoz, *Analyst*
EMP: 55 **Publicly Held**
SIC: 4911 Generation, electric power
HQ: Nrg California South Lp
804 Carnegie Ctr
Princeton NJ 08540

(P-5865)
NRG CLEAN POWER INC
7012 Owensmouth Ave, Canoga Park
(91303-2005)
PHONE.....................818 444-2020
Oren Tamir, *CEO*
EMP: 50 **EST:** 2016
SALES (est): 1.2MM **Privately Held**
SIC: 4911

(P-5866)
NRG EL SEGUNDO OPERATIONS INC
301 Vista Del Mar, El Segundo
(90245-3650)
PHONE.....................310 615-6344
John Ragan, *President*
▲ **EMP:** 65
SALES (est): 77.5MM **Publicly Held**
SIC: 4911 Electric services
PA: Nrg Energy, Inc.
804 Carnegie Ctr
Princeton NJ 08540

(P-5867)
NRG ENERGY INC
3201 Wilbur Ave, Antioch (94509-8546)
PHONE.....................913 689-3904
EMP: 55 **Publicly Held**
SIC: 4911 Generation, electric power
PA: Nrg Energy, Inc.
804 Carnegie Ctr
Princeton NJ 08540

(P-5868)
OASIS REPOWER LLC
15445 Innovation Dr, San Diego
(92128-3432)
PHONE.....................888 903-6926
Tristan Grimbert, *President*
Ryan Pfaff, *Vice Pres*
Robert Miller, *Admin Sec*
EMP: 826
SQ FT: 70,000
SALES (est): 283.6MM **Privately Held**
SIC: 4911 Electric services

(P-5869)
OLYMPUS POWER LLC
34759 Lencioni Ave, Bakersfield
(93308-9797)
PHONE.....................661 393-6885
Todd Witwer, *Manager*
EMP: 147 **Privately Held**
WEB: www.deltapower.com
SIC: 4911 Generation, electric power
HQ: Olympus Power, Llc
19 Headquarters Plz
Morristown NJ 07960
973 889-9100

(P-5870)
ORMESA LLC
3300 E Evan Hewes Hwy, Holtville
(92250-9429)
P.O. Box 86 (92250-0086)
PHONE.....................760 356-3020
Lucien Brunicki,
▲ **EMP:** 55
SALES (est): 14.4MM **Publicly Held**
WEB: www.ormesa.com
SIC: 4911

PA: Ormat Technologies, Inc.
6140 Plumas St Ste 200
Reno NV 89519

(P-5871)
PACIFIC GAS AND ELECTRIC CO
Also Called: PG&e
425 Beck Ave, Fairfield (94533-6808)
PHONE.....................415 973-7000
Dana McKiddin, *Principal*
EMP: 100 **Publicly Held**
WEB: www.pge.com
SIC: 4911 Transmission, electric power
HQ: Pacific Gas And Electric Company
77 Beale St
San Francisco CA 94105
415 973-7000

(P-5872)
PACIFIC GAS AND ELECTRIC CO
Also Called: PG&e
150 Spear St Ste 1770, San Francisco
(94105-1541)
PHONE.....................415 972-5654
Chris Chung, *Manager*
John Giovannetti, *Director*
Larry Levitt, *Manager*
EMP: 65 **Publicly Held**
WEB: www.pge.com
SIC: 4911 4922 4924 Generation, electric
power; transmission, electric power; distri-
bution, electric power; pipelines, natural
gas; natural gas distribution
HQ: Pacific Gas And Electric Company
77 Beale St
San Francisco CA 94105
415 973-7000

(P-5873)
PACIFIC GAS AND ELECTRIC CO (HQ)
Also Called: PG&e
77 Beale St, San Francisco (94105-1814)
P.O. Box 770000 (94177-0001)
PHONE.....................415 973-7000
Andrew M Vesey, *President*
David S Thomason, *CFO*
Allan Smith, *Bd of Directors*
Michael A Lewis, *Senior VP*
Steven E Malnight, *Senior VP*
▲ **EMP:** 3000 **EST:** 1905
SQ FT: 160,000
SALES: 16.7B **Publicly Held**
WEB: www.pge.com
SIC: 4911 4924 Generation, electric
power; transmission, electric power; distri-
bution, electric power; natural gas distri-
bution

(P-5874)
PACIFIC GAS AND ELECTRIC CO
Also Called: PG&e
885 Embarcadero Dr, West Sacramento
(95605-1503)
PHONE.....................916 375-5005
Richard Yamacuchi, *Branch Mgr*
EMP: 130 **Publicly Held**
WEB: www.pge.com
SIC: 4911 Transmission, electric power
HQ: Pacific Gas And Electric Company
77 Beale St
San Francisco CA 94105
415 973-7000

(P-5875)
PACIFIC GAS AND ELECTRIC CO
Also Called: PG&e
2730 Gateway Oaks Dr # 220, Sacramento
(95833-3503)
PHONE.....................916 923-7007
Russ Jackson, *Manager*
EMP: 200 **Publicly Held**
WEB: www.pge.com
SIC: 4911 Transmission, electric power
HQ: Pacific Gas And Electric Company
77 Beale St
San Francisco CA 94105
415 973-7000

(P-5876)
PACIFIC GAS AND ELECTRIC CO
PG&e
4525 Hollis St, Oakland (94608-2911)
PHONE.....................510 450-5744
G L Fairbanks, *Branch Mgr*

EMP: 90 **Publicly Held**
WEB: www.pge.com
SIC: 4911 Transmission, electric power
HQ: Pacific Gas And Electric Company
77 Beale St
San Francisco CA 94105
415 973-7000

(P-5877)
PACIFIC GAS AND ELECTRIC CO
PG&e
1970 Industrial Way, Belmont (94002)
PHONE.....................650 592-9411
Michele A Silva, *Branch Mgr*
Wendy Bossier, *Supervisor*
EMP: 300 **Publicly Held**
WEB: www.pge.com
SIC: 4911 4923 Electric services; gas
transmission & distribution
HQ: Pacific Gas And Electric Company
77 Beale St
San Francisco CA 94105
415 973-7000

(P-5878)
PACIFIC GAS AND ELECTRIC CO
Also Called: PG&e
777 Railroad Ave, Pittsburg (94565-2651)
P.O. Box 590 (94565-0590)
PHONE.....................925 757-2000
Barbara Corsi, *Branch Mgr*
EMP: 270 **Publicly Held**
WEB: www.pge.com
SIC: 4911 Electric services
HQ: Pacific Gas And Electric Company
77 Beale St
San Francisco CA 94105
415 973-7000

(P-5879)
PACIFIC GAS AND ELECTRIC CO
Also Called: PG&e
650 O St, Fresno (93721-2708)
PHONE.....................559 263-7361
C R Martin, *Branch Mgr*
EMP: 450 **Publicly Held**
WEB: www.pge.com
SIC: 4911 4922 Generation, electric
power; natural gas transmission
HQ: Pacific Gas And Electric Company
77 Beale St
San Francisco CA 94105
415 973-7000

(P-5880)
PACIFIC GAS AND ELECTRIC CO
Also Called: PG&e
210 Corona Rd, Petaluma (94954-1319)
PHONE.....................707 765-5118
Tom Reimer, *Manager*
EMP: 50
SQ FT: 168,577 **Publicly Held**
WEB: www.pge.com
SIC: 4911 Transmission, electric power
HQ: Pacific Gas And Electric Company
77 Beale St
San Francisco CA 94105
415 973-7000

(P-5881)
PACIFIC GAS AND ELECTRIC CO
Also Called: PG&e
788 Taylorville Rd, Grass Valley
(95949-7713)
PHONE.....................530 477-3245
Art Bartolome, *Manager*
EMP: 200 **Publicly Held**
WEB: www.pge.com
SIC: 4911 4922 Generation, electric
power; natural gas transmission
HQ: Pacific Gas And Electric Company
77 Beale St
San Francisco CA 94105
415 973-7000

(P-5882)
PACIFIC GAS AND ELECTRIC CO
PG&e
111 Stony Cir, Santa Rosa (95401-9599)
PHONE.....................800 756-7243
Gary F Heitz, *Principal*
EMP: 240
SQ FT: 100,000 **Publicly Held**
WEB: www.pge.com
SIC: 4911 Transmission, electric power

HQ: Pacific Gas And Electric Company
77 Beale St
San Francisco CA 94105
415 973-7000

(P-5883)
PACIFIC GAS AND ELECTRIC CO
Also Called: PG&e
4690 Evora Rd, Concord (94520-1004)
PHONE.....................925 676-0948
John Glenn, *Branch Mgr*
EMP: 65 **Publicly Held**
WEB: www.pge.com
SIC: 4911 Transmission, electric power
HQ: Pacific Gas And Electric Company
77 Beale St
San Francisco CA 94105
415 973-7000

(P-5884)
PACIFIC GAS AND ELECTRIC CO
Also Called: PG&e
4636 Missouri Flat Rd, Placerville
(95667-6823)
PHONE.....................530 621-7237
Gordon Smith, *Branch Mgr*
EMP: 50 **Publicly Held**
WEB: www.pge.com
SIC: 4911 Transmission, electric power
HQ: Pacific Gas And Electric Company
77 Beale St
San Francisco CA 94105
415 973-7000

(P-5885)
PACIFIC GAS AND ELECTRIC CO
Also Called: PG&e
1567 Huntoon St, Oroville (95965-4921)
PHONE.....................530 532-4093
Gene Murray, *Branch Mgr*
EMP: 150 **Publicly Held**
WEB: www.pge.com
SIC: 4911 Electric services
HQ: Pacific Gas And Electric Company
77 Beale St
San Francisco CA 94105
415 973-7000

(P-5886)
PACIFIC GAS AND ELECTRIC CO
Also Called: PG&e
9 Mi Nw Of Avila Bch, Avila Beach (93424)
PHONE.....................805 506-5280
David Oatley, *Branch Mgr*
Olin Gillis, *Prgrmr*
Chad Sorensen, *Engineer*
Guy Vaughan, *Regl Sales Mgr*
Michael Oien, *Maintence Staff*
EMP: 1400 **Publicly Held**
WEB: www.pge.com
SIC: 4911 Generation, electric power
HQ: Pacific Gas And Electric Company
77 Beale St
San Francisco CA 94105
415 973-7000

(P-5887)
PACIFIC GAS AND ELECTRIC CO
Also Called: PG&e
33995 Alta Bonny Nook Rd, Alta (95701)
P.O. Box 688 (95701-0688)
PHONE.....................530 389-2202
Dave Barret, *Foreman/Supr*
EMP: 65 **Publicly Held**
WEB: www.pge.com
SIC: 4911 Electric services
HQ: Pacific Gas And Electric Company
77 Beale St
San Francisco CA 94105
415 973-7000

(P-5888)
PACIFIC GAS AND ELECTRIC CO
Also Called: PG&e
3600 Meadow View Dr, Redding
(96002-9701)
PHONE.....................530 365-7672
John Duncan, *Manager*
EMP: 109 **Publicly Held**
WEB: www.pge.com
SIC: 4911 Transmission, electric power
HQ: Pacific Gas And Electric Company
77 Beale St
San Francisco CA 94105
415 973-7000

P R O D U C T S & S V C S

(P-5889)
PACIFIC GAS AND ELECTRIC CO
Also Called: PG&e
12840 Bill Clark Way, Auburn (95602-9527)
PHONE..............................530 889-3102
Steve Pennett, *Manager*
EMP: 50 **Publicly Held**
SIC: 4911 Transmission, electric power
HQ: Pacific Gas And Electric Company
77 Beale St
San Francisco CA 94105
415 973-7000

(P-5890)
PACIFIC GAS AND ELECTRIC CO
Also Called: PG&e
1850 Gateway Blvd Ste 800, Concord
(94520-8473)
PHONE..............................925 674-6305
EMP: 65 **Publicly Held**
SIC: 4911
HQ: Pacific Gas And Electric Company
77 Beale St
San Francisco CA 94105
415 973-7000

(P-5891)
PACIFIC GAS AND ELECTRIC CO
810 4th St, Orland (95963-1715)
PHONE..............................530 865-4461
Gary Freeman, *Manager*
EMP: 153 **Publicly Held**
WEB: www.pge.com
SIC: 4911 Electric services
HQ: Pacific Gas And Electric Company
77 Beale St
San Francisco CA 94105
415 973-7000

(P-5892)
PACIFIC GAS AND ELECTRIC CO
Also Called: PG&e
4040 West Ln, Stockton (95204-2436)
PHONE..............................209 942-1523
Ken Wells, *Manager*
EMP: 250 **Publicly Held**
WEB: www.pge.com
SIC: 4911 Distribution, electric power
HQ: Pacific Gas And Electric Company
77 Beale St
San Francisco CA 94105
415 973-7000

(P-5893)
PACIFIC GAS AND ELECTRIC CO
Also Called: PG&e
2311 Garden Rd, Monterey (93940-5325)
PHONE..............................831 648-3231
Richard Brent, *Branch Mgr*
EMP: 50 **Publicly Held**
WEB: www.pge.com
SIC: 4911 Transmission, electric power
HQ: Pacific Gas And Electric Company
77 Beale St
San Francisco CA 94105
415 973-7000

(P-5894)
PACIFIC GAS AND ELECTRIC CO
Also Called: PG&e
42105 Boyce Rd, Fremont (94538)
PHONE..............................510 770-2025
Gary Commick, *Principal*
EMP: 150 **Publicly Held**
WEB: www.pge.com
SIC: 4911 Transmission, electric power
HQ: Pacific Gas And Electric Company
77 Beale St
San Francisco CA 94105
415 973-7000

(P-5895)
PACIFIC GAS AND ELECTRIC CO
Also Called: PG&e
1000 King Salmon Ave, Eureka
(95503-6859)
PHONE..............................707 444-0700
Roy Willis, *Manager*
EMP: 100 **Publicly Held**
WEB: www.pge.com
SIC: 4911 Generation, electric power
HQ: Pacific Gas And Electric Company
77 Beale St
San Francisco CA 94105
415 973-7000

(P-5896)
PACIFIC GAS AND ELECTRIC CO
Also Called: PG&e
33755 Old Mill Rd, Auberry (93602-9655)
P.O. Box 425 (93602-0425)
PHONE..............................559 855-6112
John Moore, *General Mgr*
EMP: 50 **Publicly Held**
WEB: www.pge.com
SIC: 4911 ; generation, electric power
HQ: Pacific Gas And Electric Company
77 Beale St
San Francisco CA 94105
415 973-7000

(P-5897)
PACIFIC GAS AND ELECTRIC CO
Also Called: PG&e
450 Eastmoor Ave, Daly City (94015-2041)
PHONE..............................650 755-1236
Len Jackson, *Branch Mgr*
EMP: 150 **Publicly Held**
WEB: www.pge.com
SIC: 4911 Transmission, electric power
HQ: Pacific Gas And Electric Company
77 Beale St
San Francisco CA 94105
415 973-7000

(P-5898)
PACIFIC GAS AND ELECTRIC CO
Also Called: PG&e
1524 N Carpenter Rd, Modesto
(95351-1110)
PHONE..............................209 576-6636
Sheila Radford, *Branch Mgr*
Kevin Chacon, *Manager*
EMP: 50 **Publicly Held**
WEB: www.pge.com
SIC: 4911 4923 4932 Transmission, electric power; gas transmission & distribution; gas & other services combined
HQ: Pacific Gas And Electric Company
77 Beale St
San Francisco CA 94105
415 973-7000

(P-5899)
PACIFIC GAS AND ELECTRIC CO
Also Called: PG&e
3136 Boeing Way 2nd, Stockton
(95206-4989)
PHONE..............................209 942-1787
Robert Eggert, *Branch Mgr*
EMP: 54
SQ FT: 138,000 **Publicly Held**
WEB: www.pge.com
SIC: 4911 4922 Generation, electric power; natural gas transmission
HQ: Pacific Gas And Electric Company
77 Beale St
San Francisco CA 94105
415 973-7000

(P-5900)
PACIFIC GAS AND ELECTRIC CO
Also Called: PG&e
5555 Florin Perkins Rd, Sacramento
(95826-4815)
P.O. Box 997300 (95899-7300)
PHONE..............................916 275-2763
Maria Jordan, *Manager*
Bob Dieterich, *Manager*
Glenn Reece, *Manager*
EMP: 200 **Publicly Held**
WEB: www.pge.com
SIC: 4911 4923 Distribution, electric power; generation, electric power; transmission, electric power; gas transmission & distribution
HQ: Pacific Gas And Electric Company
77 Beale St
San Francisco CA 94105
415 973-7000

(P-5901)
PACIFIC GAS AND ELECTRIC CO
Also Called: PG&e
3797 1st St, Livermore (94551-4905)
PHONE..............................925 373-2623
Kermit Pol, *Branch Mgr*
EMP: 120 **Publicly Held**
WEB: www.pge.com
SIC: 4911 Transmission, electric power

HQ: Pacific Gas And Electric Company
77 Beale St
San Francisco CA 94105
415 973-7000

(P-5902)
PACIFIC GAS AND ELECTRIC CO
Also Called: PG&e
316 L St, Davis (95616-4231)
PHONE..............................530 757-5803
Gail Sanchez, *Manager*
EMP: 300 **Publicly Held**
WEB: www.pge.com
SIC: 4911 Transmission, electric power
HQ: Pacific Gas And Electric Company
77 Beale St
San Francisco CA 94105
415 973-7000

(P-5903)
PACIFIC GAS AND ELECTRIC CO
Also Called: PG&e
2180 Harrison St, San Francisco
(94110-1300)
PHONE..............................415 695-3513
Dave Bradley, *Branch Mgr*
EMP: 300 **Publicly Held**
WEB: www.pge.com
SIC: 4911 4922 4924 1311 Generation, electric power; transmission, electric power; distribution, electric power; pipelines, natural gas; natural gas distribution; natural gas production; crude petroleum production; land subdividers & developers, residential; land subdividers & developers, commercial; power plant construction
HQ: Pacific Gas And Electric Company
77 Beale St
San Francisco CA 94105
415 973-7000

(P-5904)
PACIFIC GAS AND ELECTRIC CO
Also Called: PG&e
66 Ranch Dr, Milpitas (95035-5103)
PHONE..............................408 945-6215
Jeff Klotz, *Branch Mgr*
EMP: 65 **Publicly Held**
WEB: www.pge.com
SIC: 4911 Transmission, electric power
HQ: Pacific Gas And Electric Company
77 Beale St
San Francisco CA 94105
415 973-7000

(P-5905)
PACIFIC GAS AND ELECTRIC CO
Also Called: PG&e
28570 Tiger Creek Rd, Pioneer
(95666-9646)
PHONE..............................209 295-2651
EMP: 65 **Publicly Held**
WEB: www.pge.com
SIC: 4911 Transmission, electric power
HQ: Pacific Gas And Electric Company
77 Beale St
San Francisco CA 94105
415 973-7000

(P-5906)
PACIFIC GAS AND ELECTRIC CO
Also Called: PG&e
4201 Arrow St, Bakersfield (93308-4938)
PHONE..............................661 398-5918
Don Hacks, *Manager*
EMP: 65 **Publicly Held**
WEB: www.pge.com
SIC: 4911 Transmission, electric power
HQ: Pacific Gas And Electric Company
77 Beale St
San Francisco CA 94105
415 973-7000

(P-5907)
PACIFIC GAS AND ELECTRIC CO
Also Called: PG&e
160 Cow Meadow Pl, Templeton (93465)
PHONE..............................805 434-4418
Bob Burroughs, *Branch Mgr*
EMP: 60 **Publicly Held**
WEB: www.pge.com
SIC: 4911 Transmission, electric power

HQ: Pacific Gas And Electric Company
77 Beale St
San Francisco CA 94105
415 973-7000

(P-5908)
PATTERN ENERGY GROUP LP
(PA)
1088 Sansome St, San Francisco
(94111-1308)
PHONE..............................415 283-4000
Michael Garland, *CEO*
Alan Batkin, *Partner*
Brandon Inabinet, *IT/INT Sup*
EMP: 87
SALES (est): 89.6MM **Privately Held**
SIC: 4911 Transmission, electric power

(P-5909)
PLACER COUNTY WATER AGENCY (PA)
144 Ferguson Rd, Auburn (95603-3231)
P.O. Box 6570 (95604-6570)
PHONE..............................530 823-4850
David Breninger, *General Mgr*
Andy Fecko, *Planning*
Ross Branch, *Info Tech Mgr*
Sandra Hewston, *Technician*
Frank Nann, *Technician*
EMP: 90
SQ FT: 22,750
SALES: 70.7MM **Privately Held**
WEB: www.pcwa.net
SIC: 4911 4941 4971 Electric services; water supply; irrigation systems

(P-5910)
RE BARREN RIDGE 1 LLC
300 California St Fl 7, San Francisco
(94104-1415)
PHONE..............................415 675-1500
Greg Wilson,
EMP: 130
SQ FT: 10,000
SALES (est): 19.2MM **Privately Held**
SIC: 4911

(P-5911)
RIDGETOP ENERGY LLC
7021 Oak Creek Rd, Mojave (93501-7723)
PHONE..............................661 822-2400
Dale L Smith,
EMP: 50 **EST:** 1998
SALES (est): 19.7MM **Privately Held**
SIC: 4911 Generation, electric power

(P-5912)
ROCKLIN POWER INVESTORS LP
Also Called: Rio Bravo Rocklin
3100 Thunder Valley Ct, Lincoln
(95648-9579)
PHONE..............................916 645-3383
Stephen B Gross, *CFO*
EMP: 60
SALES (est): 45.2MM **Privately Held**
SIC: 4911 Generation, electric power

(P-5913)
SACRAMENTO MUNICPL UTILITY DST (PA)
Also Called: S M U D
6201 S St, Sacramento (95817-1818)
P.O. Box 15830 (95852-0830)
PHONE..............................916 452-3211
Arlen Orchard, *CEO*
Jim Tracy, *CFO*
Dale Johnson, *Treasurer*
Noreen Roche-Carter, *Treasurer*
Michael Deangelis, *Program Mgr*
▲ **EMP:** 710
SQ FT: 118,000
SALES: 1.6B **Privately Held**
WEB: www.smud.org
SIC: 4911 Generation, electric power

(P-5914)
SACRAMENTO MUNICPL UTILITY DST
6201 S St, Sacramento (95817-1818)
PHONE..............................916 452-3211
Carlos Diaz, *Branch Mgr*
EMP: 1000
SALES (corp-wide): 1.6B **Privately Held**
SIC: 4911 Generation, electric power

PA: Sacramento Municipal Utility District
6201 S St
Sacramento CA 95817
916 452-3211

(P-5915)
**SACRAMENTO MUNICPL
UTILITY DST**
Also Called: Smud Energy Services
6301 S St, Sacramento (95817)
P.O. Box 15830 (95852-0830)
PHONE..............................916 732-5155
Jan Schori, *Manager*
Gregory Hensley, *CIO*
Ann Graef, *Project Mgr*
Tom JAS, *Research*
David Bitter, *Technology*
EMP: 88
SALES (corp-wide): 1.6B **Privately Held**
SIC: 4911 Generation, electric power
PA: Sacramento Municipal Utility District
6201 S St
Sacramento CA 95817
916 452-3211

(P-5916)
**SACRAMENTO MUNICPL
UTILITY DST**
Also Called: Supply Change Services
6201 S St, Sacramento (95817-1818)
P.O. Box 15830 (95852-0830)
PHONE..............................916 732-5616
Frankie McDermott, *Manager*
EMP: 300
SALES (corp-wide): 1.6B **Privately Held**
SIC: 4911 ; generation, electric power
PA: Sacramento Municipal Utility District
6201 S St
Sacramento CA 95817
916 452-3211

(P-5917)
**SAN DIEGO GAS & ELECTRIC
CO**
Project Construction Metro
701 33rd St, San Diego (92102-3341)
PHONE..............................619 699-1018
Scott Furgerson, *Manager*
EMP: 200
SALES (corp-wide): 11.6B **Publicly Held**
SIC: 4911 Electric services
HQ: San Diego Gas & Electric Company
8326 Century Park Ct
San Diego CA 92123
619 696-2000

(P-5918)
SCE EASTERN HYDRO DIVISION
4000 Bishop Creek Rd, Bishop
(93514-7026)
PHONE..............................760 873-0767
John Bryson, *Principal*
Susie Davis, *Principal*
EMP: 99
SALES (est): 6.9MM **Privately Held**
SIC: 4911 Electric services

(P-5919)
SEMPRA ENERGY
9305 Lightwave Ave, San Diego
(92123-6463)
PHONE..............................619 696-2000
Sean Luko, *Branch Mgr*
Marissa Colburn, *Manager*
Zachary Randel, *Manager*
Carl Villarreal, *Supervisor*
EMP: 1000
SALES (corp-wide): 11.6B **Publicly Held**
SIC: 4911 4923 Distribution, electric
power; gas transmission & distribution
PA: Sempra Energy
488 8th Ave
San Diego CA 92101
619 696-2000

(P-5920)
**SEMPRA ENERGY
INTERNATIONAL (HQ)**
Also Called: Sempra Energy Utilities
101 Ash St, San Diego (92101-3017)
PHONE..............................619 696-2000
Luis Eduardo Pawluszek, *CEO*
Mark A Snell, *President*
Bret Lane, *COO*
Donald E Felsinger, *Chairman*

Javade Chaudhri, *Exec VP*
EMP: 800
SALES (est): 429.7MM
SALES (corp-wide): 11.6B **Publicly Held**
SIC: 4911 Electric services
PA: Sempra Energy
488 8th Ave
San Diego CA 92101
619 696-2000

(P-5921)
SILVERADO ENERGY COMPANY
18101 Von Karman Ave, Irvine
(92612-1012)
PHONE..............................949 752-5588
Thomas McDaniel, *Principal*
Alan Fohrer, *President*
EMP: 300
SALES (est): 63.2MM **Publicly Held**
SIC: 4911 Generation, electric power
HQ: Edison Mission Energy
2244 Walnut Grove Ave
Rosemead CA 91770
626 302-5778

(P-5922)
**SLATE CREEK WIND PROJECT
LLC**
15445 Innovation Dr, San Diego
(92128-3432)
PHONE..............................888 903-6926
Tristan Grimbert, *President*
Kara Vongphakdy, *Treasurer*
Ryan Pfaff, *Vice Pres*
Robert Miller, *Admin Sec*
EMP: 826 EST: 2013
SQ FT: 70,000
SALES (est): 339.3MM **Privately Held**
SIC: 4911 Generation, electric power

(P-5923)
**SMART SYSTEMS
TECHNOLOGIES (PA)**
9 Goodyear, Irvine (92618-2001)
PHONE..............................949 367-9375
Craig Steven Curran, *CEO*
Peter Scolara, *CFO*
Melissa Ramos, *Office Mgr*
Gregory Valdovinos, *Controller*
Jimmy Salloum, *VP Sales*
EMP: 64
SQ FT: 7,000
SALES (est): 31MM **Privately Held**
WEB: www.smartsystechnologies.com
SIC: 4911 Electric services

(P-5924)
SOLARRESERVE INC
520 Broadway Fl 6, Santa Monica
(90401-2420)
PHONE..............................310 315-2200
Kevin B Smith, *CEO*
Tim Connor, *President*
Stephen Mullennix, *CFO*
Bill Gould, *Officer*
Sumeet Bidani, *Vice Pres*
EMP: 99
SQ FT: 20,000
SALES: 18.1MM **Privately Held**
SIC: 4911 Distribution, electric power

(P-5925)
**SOUTHERN CALIFORNIA
EDISON CO (HQ)**
Also Called: SCE
2244 Walnut Grove Ave, Rosemead
(91770-3714)
P.O. Box 976 (91770-0976)
PHONE..............................626 302-1212
Kevin M Payne, *President*
William M Petmecky III, *CFO*
Caroline Choi, *Senior VP*
Janet T Clayton, *Senior VP*
Stuart R Hemphill, *Senior VP*
▲ EMP: 1200
SALES: 12.6B
SALES (corp-wide): 12.6B **Publicly Held**
WEB: www.sce.com
SIC: 4911 Generation, electric power;
transmission, electric power; distribution,
electric power
PA: Edison International
2244 Walnut Grove Ave
Rosemead CA 91770
626 302-2222

(P-5926)
**SOUTHERN CALIFORNIA
EDISON CO**
4900 Rivergrade Rd 2b1, Irwindale
(91706-1401)
PHONE..............................626 543-8081
Peter Quon, *Branch Mgr*
EMP: 155
SALES (corp-wide): 12.6B **Publicly Held**
SIC: 4911 Generation, electric power
HQ: Southern California Edison Company
2244 Walnut Grove Ave
Rosemead CA 91770
626 302-1212

(P-5927)
**SOUTHERN CALIFORNIA
EDISON CO**
Also Called: Northern Hydro
54205 Mt Poplar Ave, Big Creek (93605)
PHONE..............................559 893-3611
David Dormire, *Manager*
Bryan Troll, *Human Res Mgr*
EMP: 160
SALES (corp-wide): 12.6B **Publicly Held**
SIC: 4911 Electric services
HQ: Southern California Edison Company
2244 Walnut Grove Ave
Rosemead CA 91770
626 302-1212

(P-5928)
**SOUTHERN CALIFORNIA
EDISON CO**
Also Called: Monrovia Service Center
1440 S California Ave, Monrovia
(91016-4211)
PHONE..............................626 303-8480
Robert Robinson, *Principal*
EMP: 97
SQ FT: 31,603
SALES (corp-wide): 12.6B **Publicly Held**
WEB: www.sce.com
SIC: 4911 Electric services
HQ: Southern California Edison Company
2244 Walnut Grove Ave
Rosemead CA 91770
626 302-1212

(P-5929)
**SOUTHERN CALIFORNIA
EDISON CO**
4000 Bishop Creek Rd, Bishop
(93514-7026)
PHONE..............................760 873-0715
EMP: 155
SALES (corp-wide): 12.6B **Publicly Held**
SIC: 4911 Generation, electric power
HQ: Southern California Edison Company
2244 Walnut Grove Ave
Rosemead CA 91770
626 302-1212

(P-5930)
**SOUTHERN CALIFORNIA
EDISON CO**
14799 Chestnut St, Westminster
(92683-5240)
PHONE..............................714 934-0838
Frank Salomone, *CEO*
EMP: 176
SALES (corp-wide): 12.6B **Publicly Held**
SIC: 4911 Generation, electric power
HQ: Southern California Edison Company
2244 Walnut Grove Ave
Rosemead CA 91770
626 302-1212

(P-5931)
**SOUTHERN CALIFORNIA
EDISON CO**
55481 Mt Poplar, Big Creek (93605)
P.O. Box 130 (93605-0130)
PHONE..............................559 893-2037
Southern Edison, *Branch Mgr*
EMP: 155
SALES (corp-wide): 12.6B **Publicly Held**
SIC: 4911 Distribution, electric power;
transmission, electric power
HQ: Southern California Edison Company
2244 Walnut Grove Ave
Rosemead CA 91770
626 302-1212

(P-5932)
**SOUTHERN CALIFORNIA
EDISON CO**
8380 Klingerman St, Rosemead (91770)
PHONE..............................626 302-5101
Arthur Guerra, *Principal*
EMP: 176
SALES (corp-wide): 12.6B **Publicly Held**
SIC: 4911 Generation, electric power
HQ: Southern California Edison Company
2244 Walnut Grove Ave
Rosemead CA 91770
626 302-1212

(P-5933)
**SOUTHERN CALIFORNIA
EDISON CO**
4900 Rivergrade Rd, Baldwin Park
(91706-1401)
PHONE..............................626 543-6093
Linda Gilleland, *Principal*
EMP: 149
SALES (corp-wide): 12.6B **Publicly Held**
SIC: 4911 Generation, electric power
HQ: Southern California Edison Company
2244 Walnut Grove Ave
Rosemead CA 91770
626 302-1212

(P-5934)
**SOUTHERN CALIFORNIA
EDISON CO**
Also Called: North Orange County Svc Ctr
1851 W Valencia Dr, Fullerton
(92833-3215)
PHONE..............................714 870-3225
David Kama, *District Mgr*
James Thaxter, *Clerk*
EMP: 70
SALES (corp-wide): 12.6B **Publicly Held**
WEB: www.sce.com
SIC: 4911 Distribution, electric power
HQ: Southern California Edison Company
2244 Walnut Grove Ave
Rosemead CA 91770
626 302-1212

(P-5935)
**SOUTHERN CALIFORNIA
EDISON CO**
Also Called: San Onfre Nclear Gnerating Stn
14300 Mesa Rd, San Clemente (92672)
PHONE..............................949 368-2881
R W Kreiger, *Vice Pres*
EMP: 1998
SALES (corp-wide): 12.6B **Publicly Held**
SIC: 4911 Generation, electric power
HQ: Southern California Edison Company
2244 Walnut Grove Ave
Rosemead CA 91770
626 302-1212

(P-5936)
**SOUTHERN CALIFORNIA
EDISON CO**
Also Called: Southern Clfrn Edsn - Prvt CHR
2131 Walnut Grove Ave, Rosemead
(91770-3769)
PHONE..............................626 302-1212
Grant Thomas, *Branch Mgr*
Brenda Torres, *Executive Asst*
Albert Melikian, *Design Engr*
Anthony Chan, *Project Mgr*
John Minnicucci, *Research*
EMP: 155
SALES (corp-wide): 12.6B **Publicly Held**
SIC: 4911 Distribution, electric power; gen-
eration, electric power; transmission,
electric power
HQ: Southern California Edison Company
2244 Walnut Grove Ave
Rosemead CA 91770
626 302-1212

(P-5937)
**SOUTHERN CALIFORNIA
EDISON CO**
Also Called: Central Orange County Svc Ctr
1241 S Grand Ave, Santa Ana
(92705-4404)
PHONE..............................714 973-5481
Percy Haralson, *Principal*
Cindy Leejulien, *Engineer*
Dean Sutliff, *Opers Spvr*

P
R
O
D
U
C
T
S

&

S
V
C
S

EMP: 216
SALES (corp-wide): 12.6B **Publicly Held**
WEB: www.sce.com
SIC: 4911 Electric services
HQ: Southern California Edison Company
2244 Walnut Grove Ave
Rosemead CA 91770
626 302-1212

(P-5938)
**SOUTHERN CALIFORNIA
EDISON CO**
Also Called: Thousand Oaks Service Center
3589 Foothill Dr, Thousand Oaks
(91361-2475)
PHONE..................................818 999-1880
Jerry Willaferd, *Branch Mgr*
EMP: 122
SALES (corp-wide): 12.6B **Publicly Held**
WEB: www.sce.com
SIC: 4911 8741 Electric services; business management
HQ: Southern California Edison Company
2244 Walnut Grove Ave
Rosemead CA 91770
626 302-1212

(P-5939)
**SOUTHERN CALIFORNIA
EDISON CO**
Also Called: Irwindale 6000
6000 N Irwindale Ave A, Irwindale
(91702-3200)
PHONE..................................626 815-7296
Ray Maese, *Branch Mgr*
EMP: 50
SALES (corp-wide): 12.6B **Publicly Held**
WEB: www.sce.com
SIC: 4911 Electric services
HQ: Southern California Edison Company
2244 Walnut Grove Ave
Rosemead CA 91770
626 302-1212

(P-5940)
**SOUTHERN CALIFORNIA
EDISON CO**
265 N East End Ave, Pomona
(91767-5803)
PHONE..................................909 469-0251
John Risen, *Branch Mgr*
Juan Argueta, *Admin Mgr*
Javier Garcia, *Technical Staff*
Diego Hinojosa, *Engineer*
Edward Kellogg, *Engineer*
EMP: 65
SALES (corp-wide): 12.6B **Publicly Held**
WEB: www.sce.com
SIC: 4911 Electric services
HQ: Southern California Edison Company
2244 Walnut Grove Ave
Rosemead CA 91770
626 302-1212

(P-5941)
**SOUTHERN CALIFORNIA
EDISON CO**
Also Called: San Dimas Bushnell Building
1515 Walnut Grove Ave, Rosemead
(91770-3710)
PHONE..................................714 895-0488
Helen Ronando, *Manager*
Greg Buchler, *Project Mgr*
Venus Jenkins, *Project Mgr*
Louise Tang, *Project Mgr*
Catherine Hoang, *Analyst*
EMP: 67
SALES (corp-wide): 12.6B **Publicly Held**
WEB: www.sce.com
SIC: 4911 Electric services
HQ: Southern California Edison Company
2244 Walnut Grove Ave
Rosemead CA 91770
626 302-1212

(P-5942)
**SOUTHERN CALIFORNIA
EDISON CO**
Also Called: Compton Service Center
1924 E Cashdan St, Compton
(90220-6403)
PHONE..................................310 608-5029
Floyd Rich, *Branch Mgr*
EMP: 180

SALES (corp-wide): 12.6B **Publicly Held**
WEB: www.sce.com
SIC: 4911 Electric services
HQ: Southern California Edison Company
2244 Walnut Grove Ave
Rosemead CA 91770
626 302-1212

(P-5943)
**SOUTHERN CALIFORNIA
EDISON CO**
Also Called: Santa Barbara Service Center
103 Love Pl, Goleta (93117-3200)
PHONE..................................805 683-5291
Brian Adair, *Manager*
EMP: 60
SALES (corp-wide): 12.6B **Publicly Held**
WEB: www.sce.com
SIC: 4911 Generation, electric power
HQ: Southern California Edison Company
2244 Walnut Grove Ave
Rosemead CA 91770
626 302-1212

(P-5944)
**SOUTHERN CALIFORNIA
EDISON CO**
Also Called: Southeastern Westminster
7300 Fenwick Ln, Westminster
(92683-5238)
PHONE..................................714 895-0420
Dee Pak Nanda, *Vice Pres*
Charles Rihbany, *Technology*
Kwai Tam, *Technical Staff*
Ruben Claudio, *Engineer*
Jason Fosse, *Engineer*
EMP: 320
SALES (corp-wide): 12.6B **Publicly Held**
WEB: www.sce.com
SIC: 4911 Electric services
HQ: Southern California Edison Company
2244 Walnut Grove Ave
Rosemead CA 91770
626 302-1212

(P-5945)
**SOUTHERN CALIFORNIA
EDISON CO**
Also Called: Saddleback Valley Service Ctr
14155 Bake Pkwy, Irvine (92618-1818)
PHONE..................................949 587-5416
Robert Torres, *Manager*
Edgardo Cruz, *Supervisor*
EMP: 143
SALES (corp-wide): 12.6B **Publicly Held**
WEB: www.sce.com
SIC: 4911 Electric services
HQ: Southern California Edison Company
2244 Walnut Grove Ave
Rosemead CA 91770
626 302-1212

(P-5946)
**SOUTHERN CALIFORNIA
EDISON CO**
6042 N Irwindale Ave A, Irwindale
(91702-3250)
PHONE..................................626 633-3070
Jami McDonald, *Branch Mgr*
Maria Becca, *Executive Asst*
Genevieve Feng, *Technology*
CHI Marie, *Analyst*
Gwen Yamasaki, *Marketing Staff*
EMP: 147
SALES (corp-wide): 12.6B **Publicly Held**
WEB: www.sce.com
SIC: 4911 Generation, electric power
HQ: Southern California Edison Company
2244 Walnut Grove Ave
Rosemead CA 91770
626 302-1212

(P-5947)
**SOUTHERN CALIFORNIA
EDISON CO**
Also Called: Orange Coast Service Center
7333 Bolsa Ave, Westminster
(92683-5210)
PHONE..................................714 895-0163
Jeff Lebow, *Branch Mgr*
EMP: 133
SALES (corp-wide): 12.6B **Publicly Held**
WEB: www.sce.com
SIC: 4911 Electric services

HQ: Southern California Edison Company
2244 Walnut Grove Ave
Rosemead CA 91770
626 302-1212

(P-5948)
**SOUTHERN CALIFORNIA
EDISON CO**
13025 Los Angeles St, Irwindale
(91706-2241)
PHONE..................................626 814-4212
Ed Entillon, *Branch Mgr*
EMP: 53
SQ FT: 21,000
SALES (corp-wide): 12.6B **Publicly Held**
WEB: www.sce.com
SIC: 4911 Electric services
HQ: Southern California Edison Company
2244 Walnut Grove Ave
Rosemead CA 91770
626 302-1212

(P-5949)
**SOUTHERN CALIFORNIA
EDISON CO**
Also Called: Covina Service Center
800 W Cienega Ave, San Dimas
(91773-2490)
PHONE..................................909 592-3757
Gary Martinez, *Branch Mgr*
Kenneth Kurasz, *Opers Spvr*
EMP: 210
SALES (corp-wide): 12.6B **Publicly Held**
WEB: www.sce.com
SIC: 4911 Electric services
HQ: Southern California Edison Company
2244 Walnut Grove Ave
Rosemead CA 91770
626 302-1212

(P-5950)
**SOUTHERN CALIFORNIA
EDISON CO**
Also Called: Whittier Service Center
9901 Geary Ave, Santa Fe Springs
(90670-3251)
PHONE..................................562 903-3191
Fred Swearingen, *Principal*
EMP: 60
SALES (corp-wide): 12.6B **Publicly Held**
WEB: www.sce.com
SIC: 4911 Electric services
HQ: Southern California Edison Company
2244 Walnut Grove Ave
Rosemead CA 91770
626 302-1212

(P-5951)
**SOUTHERN CALIFORNIA
EDISON CO**
Also Called: Western Division Regional Off
125 Elm Ave, Long Beach (90802-4918)
PHONE..................................562 491-3803
Lorene Miller, *Manager*
EMP: 310
SALES (corp-wide): 12.6B **Publicly Held**
WEB: www.sce.com
SIC: 4911 Electric services
HQ: Southern California Edison Company
2244 Walnut Grove Ave
Rosemead CA 91770
626 302-1212

(P-5952)
**SOUTHERN CALIFORNIA
EDISON CO**
Also Called: High Desert
12353 Hesperia Rd, Victorville
(92395-4797)
PHONE..................................760 951-3172
Sheila Luna, *Branch Mgr*
Victor Magana, *Graphic Designe*
EMP: 200
SALES (corp-wide): 12.6B **Publicly Held**
WEB: www.sce.com
SIC: 4911 Electric services
HQ: Southern California Edison Company
2244 Walnut Grove Ave
Rosemead CA 91770
626 302-1212

(P-5953)
**SOUTHERN CALIFORNIA
EDISON CO**
Also Called: So CA Edison
1515 Walnut Grove Ave, Rosemead
(91770-3710)
PHONE..................................626 302-0530
EMP: 149
SALES (corp-wide): 12.6B **Publicly Held**
SIC: 4911 Electric services
HQ: Southern California Edison Company
2244 Walnut Grove Ave
Rosemead CA 91770
626 302-1212

(P-5954)
**SPINNING SPUR WIND THREE
LLC**
15445 Innovation Dr, San Diego
(92128-3432)
PHONE..................................858 521-3319
Tristan Grimbert, *President*
Kara Vongphakdy, *Treasurer*
Larry Barr, *Exec VP*
Robert Miller, *Exec VP*
Ryan Pfaff, *Exec VP*
EMP: 827 **EST:** 2014
SQ FT: 70,000
SALES (est): 1.5MM
SALES (corp-wide): 971.6MM **Privately
Held**
SIC: 4911 Electric services
PA: Edf Renewables, Inc.
15445 Innovation Dr
San Diego CA 92128
858 521-3300

(P-5955)
**SYCAMORE COGENERATION
CO (PA)**
1546 China Grade Loop, Bakersfield
(93308-9700)
P.O. Box 81438 (93380-1438)
PHONE..................................661 615-4630
Neal Burgess, *Exec Dir*
▲ **EMP:** 57
SQ FT: 10,000
SALES (est): 41.9MM **Privately Held**
SIC: 4911 4961 Distribution, electric power; steam supply systems, including geothermal

(P-5956)
**TRUCKEE DONNER PUB UTLY
DIST F**
Also Called: TRUCKEE DONNER PUD
11570 Donner Pass Rd, Truckee
(96161-4992)
PHONE..................................530 587-3896
Michael D Holley, *General Mgr*
Trey Griffin, *IT/INT Sup*
Roe Vernon, *Technology*
EMP: 68 **EST:** 1927
SQ FT: 48,000
SALES: 37.6MM **Privately Held**
WEB: www.tdpud.org
SIC: 4911 4941 Distribution, electric power; water supply

(P-5957)
TWIN OAKS POWER LP (HQ)
101 Ash St Hq10b, San Diego
(92101-3017)
PHONE..................................619 696-2034
Mike Niggli, *Managing Dir*
EMP: 100
SALES (est): 53.7MM
SALES (corp-wide): 11.6B **Publicly Held**
SIC: 4911 4924 Generation, electric power; transmission, electric power; distribution, electric power; natural gas distribution
PA: Sempra Energy
488 8th Ave
San Diego CA 92101
619 696-2000

(P-5958)
**TYLER BLUFF WIND PROJECT
LLC**
15445 Innovation Dr, San Diego
(92128-3432)
PHONE..................................888 903-6926
Tristan Grimbert, *President*
Kara Vongphakdy, *Treasurer*

▲ = Import ▼=Export
◆ =Import/Export

Larry Barr, *Exec VP*
Robert Miller, *Exec VP*
Ryan Pfaff, *Exec VP*
EMP: 827
SQ FT: 70,000
SALES (est): 103.4MM
SALES (corp-wide): 971.6MM **Privately Held**
SIC: 4911 Electric services
PA: Edf Renewables, Inc.
15445 Innovation Dr
San Diego CA 92128
858 521-3300

(P-5959)
V3 ELECTRIC INC
4925 Rj Mathews Pkwy 100, El Dorado Hills (95762)
PHONE................916 597-2627
Joshua D Collette, *CEO*
EMP: 184
SQ FT: 15,000
SALES: 23.8MM **Privately Held**
SIC: 4911 1731 ; electric power systems contractors

(P-5960)
VEXILLUM INC
Also Called: EZ Electric
10636 Industrial Ave, Roseville (95678-5902)
PHONE................916 218-3815
Scott Zachman, *President*
EMP: 175
SALES (corp-wide): 20.5MM **Privately Held**
WEB: www.ez-electric.com
SIC: 4911 Electric services
PA: Vexillum, Inc.
1250 Birchwood Dr
Sunnyvale CA 94089
408 541-4245

(P-5961)
WATSON COGENERATION CO INC
22850 Wilmington Ave, Carson (90745-5021)
P.O. Box 6203 (90749-6203)
PHONE................310 816-8100
Paul L Foster, *Ch of Bd*
EMP: 63
SQ FT: 1,000
SALES (est): 37.3MM **Publicly Held**
SIC: 4911 Generation, electric power
HQ: Western Refining, Inc.
212 N Clark Dr
El Paso TX 79905
915 775-3300

(P-5962)
WELLHEAD ELECTRIC COMPANY INC
650 Bercut Dr Ste C, Sacramento (95811-0100)
PHONE................916 447-5171
Harold Dittner, *President*
Paul Cummins, *Vice Pres*
Sharon Stureman, *Administration*
Josh Curtis, *Technician*
Jon Kimble, *Plant Mgr*
EMP: 50
SALES (est): 30.7MM **Privately Held**
SIC: 4911 Generation, electric power

(P-5963)
WHEATLAND WIND PROJECT LLC
15445 Innovation Dr, San Diego (92128-3432)
PHONE................888 903-6926
Tristan Grimbert, *President*
Ryan Pfaff, *Vice Pres*
Robert Miller, *Admin Sec*
EMP: 826 **EST:** 2013
SQ FT: 70,000
SALES (est): 206.6MM **Privately Held**
SIC: 4911 Generation, electric power

4922 Natural Gas Transmission

(P-5964)
KINDER MRGAN LQDS TRMINALS LLC
9950 San Diego Mission Rd, San Diego (92108-1705)
PHONE................619 283-6511
Craig Bishop, *Branch Mgr*
EMP: 62 **Publicly Held**
SIC: 4922 Natural gas transmission
HQ: Kinder Morgan Liquids Terminals Llc
1001 La St Ste 1000
Houston TX 77002
713 369-9000

(P-5965)
SAN DIEGO GAS & ELECTRIC CO
Also Called: South Bay Power Plant
990 Bay Blvd, Chula Vista (91911-1651)
PHONE................800 411-7343
Carl Creelman, *Branch Mgr*
EMP: 120
SALES (corp-wide): 11.6B **Publicly Held**
SIC: 4922 4911 Natural gas transmission; generation, electric power
HQ: San Diego Gas & Electric Company
8326 Century Park Ct
San Diego CA 92123
619 696-2000

(P-5966)
SOUTHERN CALIFORNIA GAS CO
9400 Oakdale Ave, Chatsworth (91311-6511)
P.O. Box 2300 (91313-2300)
PHONE................818 701-2592
Cathy Maguire, *Branch Mgr*
Edward Wiegman, *Info Tech Dir*
EMP: 300
SALES (corp-wide): 11.6B **Publicly Held**
WEB: www.gasselect.com
SIC: 4922 4923 Pipelines, natural gas; gas transmission & distribution
HQ: Southern California Gas Company
555 W 5th St
Los Angeles CA 90013
213 244-1200

(P-5967)
WILD GOOSE STORAGE INC
2780 W Liberty Rd, Gridley (95948-9335)
P.O. Box 8 (95948-0008)
PHONE................530 846-7350
David Pope, *President*
EMP: 70
SALES (est): 9.3MM **Privately Held**
SIC: 4922 Storage, natural gas

4923 Natural Gas Transmission & Distribution

(P-5968)
PACIFIC TANK LINES INC
5230 Wilson St Ste A, Riverside (92509-2435)
PHONE................951 680-1900
Ted Honcharik, *CEO*
Gregory Batten, *President*
Curtis Christy, *Business Mgr*
▲ **EMP:** 68
SALES (est): 19.5MM **Privately Held**
WEB: www.pacifictanklines.com
SIC: 4923 Gas transmission & distribution

4924 Natural Gas Distribution

(P-5969)
CLEAN ENERGY
4675 Macarthur Ct Ste 800, Newport Beach (92660-1895)
PHONE................949 437-1000
Andrew Littlefair, *President*
Mitchell Pratt, *COO*
Robert Vreeland, *CFO*

Nate Jensen, *Vice Pres*
Richard Remillard, *Vice Pres*
EMP: 832
SALES (est): 665.8MM
SALES (corp-wide): 346.4MM **Publicly Held**
SIC: 4924 Natural gas distribution
PA: Clean Energy Fuels Corp.
4675 Macarthur Ct Ste 800
Newport Beach CA 92660
949 437-1000

(P-5970)
PACIFIC ENERGY FUELS COMPANY
Also Called: PG&e
77 Beale St Ste 100, San Francisco (94105-1814)
PHONE................415 973-8200
Gordon Smith, *President*
EMP: 999
SALES (est): 33.3MM **Publicly Held**
WEB: www.pge.com
SIC: 4924 Natural gas distribution
HQ: Pacific Gas And Electric Company
77 Beale St
San Francisco CA 94105
415 973-7000

(P-5971)
PACIFIC GAS AND ELECTRIC CO
Also Called: PG&e
24300 Clawiter Rd, Hayward (94545-2218)
PHONE................510 784-3253
Tom Webb, *Branch Mgr*
EMP: 409 **Publicly Held**
WEB: www.pge.com
SIC: 4924 4911 Natural gas distribution; distribution, electric power
HQ: Pacific Gas And Electric Company
77 Beale St
San Francisco CA 94105
415 973-7000

(P-5972)
PACIFIC GAS AND ELECTRIC CO
Also Called: PG&e
460 Rio Lindo Ave, Chico (95926-1815)
PHONE................530 894-4739
Todd Stewart, *Manager*
EMP: 110 **Publicly Held**
WEB: www.pge.com
SIC: 4924 4911 4923 Natural gas distribution; electric services; gas transmission & distribution
HQ: Pacific Gas And Electric Company
77 Beale St
San Francisco CA 94105
415 973-7000

(P-5973)
SEMPRA ENERGY GLOBAL ENTPS
101 Ash St, San Diego (92101-3017)
PHONE................619 696-2000
Mark Snell, *President*
Michael Allman, *CFO*
Mark Fisher, *Vice Pres*
EMP: 1000
SQ FT: 10,000
SALES (est): 374.1MM
SALES (corp-wide): 11.6B **Publicly Held**
SIC: 4924 4911 Natural gas distribution; generation, electric power
PA: Sempra Energy
488 8th Ave
San Diego CA 92101
619 696-2000

(P-5974)
SOUTHERN CALIFORNIA GAS CO (DH)
Also Called: GAS COMPANY, THE
555 W 5th St, Los Angeles (90013-1010)
PHONE................213 244-1200
Bret Lane, *CEO*
Maryam Sabbaghian Brown, *President*
Jimmie I Cho, *COO*
Debra L Reed, *Chairman*
Steven D Davis, *Exec VP*
EMP: 170

SALES: 3.9B
SALES (corp-wide): 11.6B **Publicly Held**
WEB: www.gasselect.com
SIC: 4924 4922 4932 Natural gas distribution; natural gas transmission; gas & other services combined
HQ: Pacific Enterprises
101 Ash St
San Diego CA 92101
619 696-2020

(P-5975)
SOUTHERN CALIFORNIA GAS CO
1 Liberty, Aliso Viejo (92656-3830)
PHONE................714 634-7221
Bill Jameson, *Branch Mgr*
EMP: 54
SALES (corp-wide): 11.6B **Publicly Held**
SIC: 4924 Natural gas distribution
HQ: Southern California Gas Company
555 W 5th St
Los Angeles CA 90013
213 244-1200

(P-5976)
SOUTHERN CALIFORNIA GAS CO
Also Called: Northern Reg. Sub Base
1510 N Chester Ave, Bakersfield (93308-2559)
PHONE................661 399-4431
James Pina, *Manager*
EMP: 50
SALES (corp-wide): 11.6B **Publicly Held**
WEB: www.gasselect.com
SIC: 4924 Natural gas distribution
HQ: Southern California Gas Company
555 W 5th St
Los Angeles CA 90013
213 244-1200

(P-5977)
SOUTHERN CALIFORNIA GAS CO
1801 S Atlantic Blvd, Monterey Park (91754-5207)
PHONE................213 244-1200
W J Torres, *Branch Mgr*
Warren Mitchell, *President*
Anthony Orta, *Manager*
Earl A Smitley, *Manager*
EMP: 293
SALES (corp-wide): 11.6B **Publicly Held**
WEB: www.gasselect.com
SIC: 4924 Natural gas distribution
HQ: Southern California Gas Company
555 W 5th St
Los Angeles CA 90013
213 244-1200

(P-5978)
SOUTHERN CALIFORNIA GAS CO
Also Called: Regional Office
1981 W Lugonia Ave, Redlands (92374-9796)
P.O. Box 3003 (92373-0306)
PHONE................909 335-7802
James Boland, *Manager*
EMP: 383
SALES (corp-wide): 11.6B **Publicly Held**
WEB: www.gasselect.com
SIC: 4924 Natural gas distribution
HQ: Southern California Gas Company
555 W 5th St
Los Angeles CA 90013
213 244-1200

(P-5979)
SOUTHERN CALIFORNIA GAS CO
Also Called: Industry Station
920 S Stimson Ave, City of Industry (91745-1640)
PHONE................213 244-1200
EMP: 69
SALES (corp-wide): 11.6B **Publicly Held**
SIC: 4924 Natural gas distribution
HQ: Southern California Gas Company
555 W 5th St
Los Angeles CA 90013
213 244-1200

(P-5980)

SOUTHERN CALIFORNIA GAS CO

25200 Trumble Rd, Romoland
(92585-9664)
PHONE...................213 244-1200
EMP: 69
SALES (corp-wide): 11.6B **Publicly Held**
SIC: 4924 Natural gas distribution
HQ: Southern California Gas Company
555 W 5th St
Los Angeles CA 90013
213 244-1200

(P-5981)

SOUTHERN CALIFORNIA GAS CO

333 E Main St Ste J, Alhambra
(91801-3914)
PHONE...................323 881-3587
G H Chavez, *Branch Mgr*
EMP: 72
SALES (corp-wide): 11.6B **Publicly Held**
WEB: www.gasselect.com
SIC: 4924 Natural gas distribution
HQ: Southern California Gas Company
555 W 5th St
Los Angeles CA 90013
213 244-1200

(P-5982)

SOUTHERN CALIFORNIA GAS CO

6738 Bright Ave, Whittier (90601-4306)
PHONE...................562 803-3341
Richard Duran, *Branch Mgr*
EMP: 69
SALES (corp-wide): 11.6B **Publicly Held**
WEB: www.gasselect.com
SIC: 4924 Natural gas distribution
HQ: Southern California Gas Company
555 W 5th St
Los Angeles CA 90013
213 244-1200

(P-5983)

SOUTHERN CALIFORNIA GAS CO

8141 Gulana Ave, Venice (90293-7930)
PHONE...................310 823-7945
James Wine, *Manager*
Evelyn Reyes, *Clerk*
EMP: 67
SALES (corp-wide): 11.6B **Publicly Held**
WEB: www.gasselect.com
SIC: 4924 Natural gas distribution
HQ: Southern California Gas Company
555 W 5th St
Los Angeles CA 90013
213 244-1200

(P-5984)

SOUTHERN CALIFORNIA GAS CO

155 S G St, San Bernardino (92410-3317)
PHONE...................909 335-7941
Al Garcia, *Branch Mgr*
EMP: 117
SALES (corp-wide): 11.6B **Publicly Held**
WEB: www.gasselect.com
SIC: 4924 Natural gas distribution
HQ: Southern California Gas Company
555 W 5th St
Los Angeles CA 90013
213 244-1200

(P-5985)

SOUTHERN CALIFORNIA GAS CO

1600 Corporate Center Dr, Monterey Park
(91754-7626)
P.O. Box C (91756-0001)
PHONE...................213 244-1200
Joe M Rivera, *Regional Mgr*
EMP: 223
SALES (corp-wide): 11.6B **Publicly Held**
WEB: www.gasselect.com
SIC: 4924 Natural gas distribution
HQ: Southern California Gas Company
555 W 5th St
Los Angeles CA 90013
213 244-1200

(P-5986)

SOUTHERN CALIFORNIA GAS CO

Also Called: Energy Resource Center
9240 Firestone Blvd, Downey
(90241-5388)
PHONE...................562 803-7453
Carlos Ruiz, *Manager*
EMP: 50
SALES (corp-wide): 11.6B **Publicly Held**
WEB: www.gasselect.com
SIC: 4924 Natural gas distribution
HQ: Southern California Gas Company
555 W 5th St
Los Angeles CA 90013
213 244-1200

(P-5987)

SOUTHERN CALIFORNIA GAS CO

1050 Overland Ct, San Dimas
(91773-1704)
PHONE...................909 305-8297
Janet Yee, *Manager*
EMP: 600
SQ FT: 39,344
SALES (corp-wide): 11.6B **Publicly Held**
WEB: www.gasselect.com
SIC: 4924 Natural gas distribution
HQ: Southern California Gas Company
555 W 5th St
Los Angeles CA 90013
213 244-1200

(P-5988)

SOUTHERN CALIFORNIA GAS CO

Also Called: Honor Rancho Station
23130 Valencia Blvd, Valencia
(91355-1716)
PHONE...................800 427-2200
Dan Skope, *Vice Pres*
EMP: 64
SALES (corp-wide): 11.6B **Publicly Held**
WEB: www.gasselect.com
SIC: 4924 Natural gas distribution
HQ: Southern California Gas Company
555 W 5th St
Los Angeles CA 90013
213 244-1200

(P-5989)

SOUTHERN CALIFORNIA GAS TOWER

555 W 5th St, Los Angeles (90013-1010)
PHONE...................213 244-1200
Ed Guiles, *President*
EMP: 400
SALES (est): 133.1MM
SALES (corp-wide): 11.6B **Publicly Held**
SIC: 4924 Natural gas distribution
HQ: Southern California Gas Company
555 W 5th St
Los Angeles CA 90013
213 244-1200

(P-5990)

SOUTHWEST GAS CORPORATION

S W Gas Southern California
13471 Mariposa Rd, Victorville
(92395-5396)
P.O. Box 1498 (92393-1498)
PHONE...................760 951-4000
Joan Rowell, *Manager*
Jennifer Smith, *Representative*
Jason Hall, *Supervisor*
EMP: 100
SALES (corp-wide): 2.8B **Publicly Held**
SIC: 4924 Natural gas distribution;
gas transmission & distribution
HQ: Southwest Gas Corporation
5241 Spring Mountain Rd
Las Vegas NV 89150
702 876-7237

(P-5991)

STEELRIVER INFRASTRUCTURE FUND (HQ)

1 Letterman Dr Bldg C, San Francisco
(94129-2402)
PHONE...................415 291-2200
Chris Kinney, *Partner*
John Anderson, *Partner*

Dennis Mahoney, *Partner*
John Fenton, *Consultant*
EMP: 200
SALES (est): 175.4MM **Privately Held**
SIC: 4924 Natural gas distribution

4931 Electric & Other Svcs Combined

(P-5992)

CALPINE ENERGY SOLUTIONS LLC (DH)

401 W A St Ste 500, San Diego
(92101-7991)
PHONE...................877 273-6772
Jim Wood, *President*
Gayle McCutchan, *Vice Pres*
Pat Roskowski, *Portfolio Mgr*
Vicki Moore, *Sales Dir*
Jon Shore, *Sales Mgr*
EMP: 88
SALES (est): 427.5MM
SALES (corp-wide): 9.5B **Privately Held**
WEB: www.noblesolutions.com
SIC: 4931 4932 Electric & other services
combined; gas & other services combined
HQ: Calpine Corporation
717 Texas St Ste 1000
Houston TX 77002
713 830-2000

(P-5993)

CITY OF BURBANK

Also Called: Burbank Water & Power
164 W Magnolia Blvd, Burbank
(91502-1772)
PHONE...................818 238-3550
Ronald E Davis, *Branch Mgr*
Joyce Thompson, *Executive Asst*
Sherry Kristoff, *Admin Sec*
Karamjit Chahal, *Technician*
Jeanne Keeler, *Analyst*
EMP: 315 **Privately Held**
SIC: 4931 4941 4911 7389 Electric &
other services combined; water supply;
electric services; interior design services
PA: City Of Burbank
275 E Olive Ave
Burbank CA 91502
818 238-5800

(P-5994)

CITY OF CORONADO

Also Called: Public Services
101 B Ave, Coronado (92118-1510)
PHONE...................619 522-7380
Scott Huth, *Director*
Cliff Maurer, *Director*
EMP: 55 **Privately Held**
WEB: www.coronadoplayhouse.com
SIC: 4931 9111 Electric & other services
combined; mayors' offices
PA: City Of Coronado
1825 Strand Way
Coronado CA 92118
619 522-7300

(P-5995)

IMPERIAL IRRIGATION DISTRICT

2151 W Adams Ave, El Centro
(92243-9457)
P.O. Box 937, Imperial (92251-0937)
PHONE...................760 339-9800
Frank Montoya, *Branch Mgr*
Efren Garcia, *Engineer*
EMP: 75
SALES (corp-wide): 615.2MM **Privately Held**
WEB: www.iidwater.com
SIC: 4931 Electric & other services combined
PA: Imperial Irrigation District
333 E Barioni Blvd
Imperial CA 92251
800 303-7756

(P-5996)

MEKWUS SOLAR ENERGY

20283 Santa Maria Ave # 2103, Castro Valley (94546-5098)
PHONE...................510 731-4134
De Anna Mekwunye, *Partner*
Elijah Mekwunye, *Partner*
EMP: 99

SQ FT: 1,200
SALES (est): 1.2MM **Privately Held**
SIC: 4931

(P-5997)

SAN DIEGO GAS & ELECTRIC CO (DH)

Also Called: SDG&E
8326 Century Park Ct, San Diego
(92123-1530)
PHONE...................619 696-2000
J Walker Martin, *CEO*
Jessie J Knight Jr, *Ch of Bd*
Steven D Davis, *President*
Scott D Drury, *President*
Robert M Schlax, *CFO*
◆ EMP: 170
SALES: 4.5B
SALES (corp-wide): 11.6B **Publicly Held**
SIC: 4931 4911 4924 Electric & other
services combined; generation, electric
power; transmission, electric power; distri-
bution, electric power; natural gas distri-
bution

(P-5998)

SAN DIEGO GAS & ELECTRIC CO

Also Called: Orange County Service Center
662 Camino De Los Mares, San Clemente
(92673-2827)
PHONE...................949 361-8090
James Valentine, *Branch Mgr*
EMP: 50
SALES (corp-wide): 11.6B **Publicly Held**
SIC: 4931 4911 Electric & other services
combined; electric services
HQ: San Diego Gas & Electric Company
8326 Century Park Ct
San Diego CA 92123
619 696-2000

(P-5999)

UNDERGROUND CNSTR CO INC

5145 Industrial Way, Benicia (94510-1042)
PHONE...................707 746-8800
Christopher Ronco, *President*
Jeff Tinsley, *CFO*
George R Bradshaw, *Exec VP*
Loren Hudson, *Vice Pres*
Giff Ludwigsen, *Vice Pres*
EMP: 250 EST: 1936
SQ FT: 32,946
SALES (est): 95.6MM
SALES (corp-wide): 11.1B **Publicly Held**
WEB: www.undergrnd.com
SIC: 4931 5172 4923 Electric & other
services combined; aircraft fueling serv-
ices; gas transmission & distribution
PA: Quanta Services, Inc.
2800 Post Oak Blvd # 2600
Houston TX 77056
713 629-7600

4932 Gas & Other Svcs Combined

(P-6000)

CITY OF LONG BEACH

City of Long Beach Gas & Oil
2400 E Spring St, Long Beach
(90806-2203)
PHONE...................562 570-2000
Christopher J Garner, *Manager*
EMP: 204 **Privately Held**
WEB: www.polb.com
SIC: 4932 9111 4924 Gas & other serv-
ices combined; mayors' offices; natural
gas distribution
PA: City Of Long Beach
411 W Ocean Blvd
Long Beach CA 90802
562 570-6450

(P-6001)

CLEAN ENERGY FUELS CORP (PA)

4675 Macarthur Ct Ste 800, Newport Beach
(92660-1895)
PHONE...................949 437-1000
Warren I Mitchell, *Ch of Bd*
Stephen A Scully, *Ch of Bd*
Andrew J Littlefair, *President*
Mitchell W Pratt, *COO*

Robert M Vreeland, *CFO*
▲ **EMP:** 170
SQ FT: 48,000
SALES: 346.4MM **Publicly Held**
SIC: 4932 4924 4922 Gas & other services combined; natural gas distribution; natural gas transmission

(P-6002)
FIELDSERVER TECHNOLOGIES
1991 Tarob Ct, Milpitas (95035-6825)
PHONE..................408 262-2299
Loree Calderon, *President*
EMP: 50
SALES (est): 2.5MM
SALES (corp-wide): 1.3B **Publicly Held**
WEB: www.fieldserver.com
SIC: 4932 Gas & other services combined
HQ: Sierra Monitor Corporation
1991 Tarob Ct
Milpitas CA 95035
408 262-6611

(P-6003)
MAXGEN ENERGY SERVICES CORP (DH)
1690 Scenic Ave, Costa Mesa (92626-1410)
PHONE..................714 908-5266
Mark McLanahan, *CEO*
Michael Eyman, *VP Bus Dvlpt*
James Tillman, *Business Dir*
Trent Gould, *Project Mgr*
Jessica Losch, *Engineer*
EMP: 80
SALES (est): 216.7MM
SALES (corp-wide): 43B **Publicly Held**
SIC: 4932 Gas & other services combined

(P-6004)
SEMPRA ENERGY (PA)
488 8th Ave, San Diego (92101-7123)
PHONE..................619 696-2000
Jeffrey W Martin, *Ch of Bd*
Dennis V Arriola, *President*
George W Bilicic, *President*
Maryam Sabbaghian Brown, *President*
Joseph A Householder, *President*
EMP: 1000
SALES: 11.6B **Publicly Held**
WEB: www.sempra.com
SIC: 4932 4911 5172 4922 Gas & other services combined; electric services; distribution, electric power; generation, electric power; transmission, electric power; petroleum products; natural gas transmission; pipelines, natural gas; storage, natural gas

---

4939 Combination Utilities, NEC

(P-6005)
AGILE SOURCING PARTNERS INC
2385 Railroad St, Corona (92880-5411)
PHONE..................951 279-4154
Maria Thompson, *President*
Mitchell Diehl, *President*
Sherry Neu, *Program Mgr*
Kristy Othman, *Human Resources*
Ryan Swindel, *Manager*
EMP: 180
SQ FT: 2,300
SALES: 222.5MM **Privately Held**
SIC: 4939 Combination utilities

(P-6006)
CHESTER PUBLIC UTILITY DST
251 Chester Airport Rd, Chester (96020)
P.O. Box 177 (96020-0177)
PHONE..................530 258-2171
William D Turner, *Manager*
▲ **EMP:** 70
SALES (est): 3.9MM **Privately Held**
SIC: 4939 Combination utilities

(P-6007)
CITY OF CORONA
Also Called: Public Works
400 S Vicentia Ave # 210, Corona (92882-2187)
PHONE..................951 736-2266
Kip D Field, *Manager*

EMP: 99 **Privately Held**
WEB: www.coronautilities.com
SIC: 4939 Combination utilities
PA: City Of Corona
400 S Vicentia Ave
Corona CA 92882
951 736-2372

(P-6008)
IMPERIAL IRRIGATION DISTRICT
81600 58th Ave, La Quinta (92253-7663)
P.O. Box 1080 (92247-1080)
PHONE..................760 398-5811
Charles Haskin, *General Mgr*
Oscar Jauregui, *Info Tech Mgr*
Dan Devoy, *Human Res Mgr*
Luis Garcia, *Marketing Staff*
EMP: 150
SALES (corp-wide): 615.2MM **Privately Held**
WEB: www.iidwater.com
SIC: 4939 4911 Combination utilities; electric services
PA: Imperial Irrigation District
333 E Barioni Blvd
Imperial CA 92251
800 303-7756

(P-6009)
LA DEPARTMENT WATER AND POWER
17031 State Highway 14, Mojave (93501-1230)
PHONE..................661 824-7900
Mike Gratt, *Superintendent*
Robert Chaney, *Superintendent*
◆ **EMP:** 54
SALES (est): 3.1MM **Privately Held**
SIC: 4939 Combination utilities

(P-6010)
LOS ANGELES DEPT WTR & PWR
Also Called: Scattergood Generation Plant
12700 Vista Del Mar, Playa Del Rey (90293-8502)
PHONE..................310 524-8500
Nazih Batarseh, *Branch Mgr*
EMP: 100
SALES (corp-wide): 1.1B **Privately Held**
SIC: 4939 Combination utilities
PA: Los Angeles Department Of Water And Power
111 N Hope St
Los Angeles CA 90012
213 367-4211

(P-6011)
ORMAT NEVADA INC
947 Dogwood Rd, Heber (92249-9762)
PHONE..................760 353-8200
Celia Velasco, *Admin Mgr*
EMP: 50 **Publicly Held**
SIC: 4939 Combination utilities
HQ: Ormat Nevada, Inc.
6140 Plumas St Ste 200
Reno NV 89519
-

(P-6012)
SAN DIEGO GAS & ELECTRIC CO
North Coast O & M Center
5016 Carlsbad Blvd, Carlsbad (92008-4303)
PHONE..................760 438-6200
Jim Boland, *Director*
EMP: 120
SALES (corp-wide): 11.6B **Publicly Held**
SIC: 4939 4924 4911 Combination utilities; natural gas distribution; electric services
HQ: San Diego Gas & Electric Company
8326 Century Park Ct
San Diego CA 92123
619 696-2000

(P-6013)
TRIUNFO PUBLIC FACILITIES CORP
1001 Partridge Dr, Ventura (93003-5562)
PHONE..................805 658-4605
Vickie Dragan, *Principal*
EMP: 70 **EST:** 2010

SALES (est): 884.1K **Privately Held**
SIC: 4939 Combination utilities

4941 Water Sply

(P-6014)
ALAMEDA COUNTY WATER DISTRICT (PA)
Also Called: ACWD
43885 S Grimmer Blvd, Fremont (94538-6375)
P.O. Box 5110 (94537-5110)
PHONE..................510 668-4200
Walt Wadlow, *General Mgr*
Paul Piraino, *General Mgr*
Robert Shaver, *General Mgr*
Gina Markou, *Executive Asst*
Todd Christner, *Administration*
EMP: 217
SQ FT: 60,000
SALES: 115.6MM **Privately Held**
WEB: www.acwd.org
SIC: 4941 Water supply

(P-6015)
AMADOR WATER AGENCY
12800 Ridge Rd, Sutter Creek (95685-9630)
PHONE..................209 223-3018
Jim Abercrombie, *General Mgr*
Terance W Moore, *President*
David N McGee, *CFO*
John P Swift, *Vice Pres*
David Gronseth, *Principal*
EMP: 52
SQ FT: 2,000
SALES: 10.3MM **Privately Held**
WEB: www.amadorwa.org
SIC: 4941 4952 Water supply; sewerage systems

(P-6016)
AMERICAN WATER WORKS CO INC
4701 Beloit Dr, Sacramento (95838-2434)
P.O. Box 15468 (95851-0468)
PHONE..................916 568-4236
Rob Roscoe, *Engineer*
Steve Dutch, *Engineer*
EMP: 80
SALES (corp-wide): 3.4B **Publicly Held**
WEB: www.amwater.com
SIC: 4941 Water supply
PA: American Water Works Company, Inc.
1 Water St
Camden NJ 08102
856 955-4001

(P-6017)
ANDERSON PUMP COMPANY
Also Called: Dragon Engineering
24719 Robertson Blvd, Chowchilla (93610-9090)
P.O. Box 906 (93610-0906)
PHONE..................559 665-4477
Daniel Skeen, *President*
Imogene Anderson, *Treasurer*
Leon Anderson, *Vice Pres*
Jim Smith, *Vice Pres*
EMP: 55
SQ FT: 10,000
SALES (est): 20.1MM **Privately Held**
WEB: www.andersonpumpcompany.com
SIC: 4941 4971 Water supply; irrigation systems

(P-6018)
CALAVERAS COUNTY WATER DST
120 Toma Ct, San Andreas (95249)
P.O. Box 846 (95249-9002)
PHONE..................209 754-3543
Scott Ratterman, *President*
Jeff Davidson, *Vice Pres*
Deja Howarth, *Technician*
EMP: 66
SQ FT: 5,000
SALES: 12.2MM **Privately Held**
WEB: www.ccwd.org
SIC: 4941 Water supply

(P-6019)
CALIFORNIA AMERICAN WATER CO
880 Kuhn Dr, Chula Vista (91914-3514)
PHONE..................619 656-2400
Kent Turner, *Controller*
EMP: 70
SALES (corp-wide): 3.4B **Publicly Held**
SIC: 4941 Water supply
HQ: California-American Water Company
655 W Broadway Ste 1410
San Diego CA 92101
619 446-4760

(P-6020)
CALIFORNIA AMERICAN WATER CO
4787 Old Redwood Hwy, Santa Rosa (95403-1485)
PHONE..................707 542-1717
Tony Lindstrom, *Manager*
EMP: 50
SALES (corp-wide): 3.4B **Publicly Held**
SIC: 4941 4953 Water supply; refuse systems
HQ: California-American Water Company
655 W Broadway Ste 1410
San Diego CA 92101
619 446-4760

(P-6021)
CALIFORNIA AMERICAN WATER CO
4701 Beloit Dr, Sacramento (95838-2434)
PHONE..................916 568-4216
Robert Bloor, *CFO*
EMP: 50
SALES (corp-wide): 3.4B **Publicly Held**
SIC: 4941 4953 Water supply; refuse systems
HQ: California-American Water Company
655 W Broadway Ste 1410
San Diego CA 92101
619 446-4760

(P-6022)
CALIFORNIA WATER SERVICE CO (HQ)
1720 N 1st St, San Jose (95112-4598)
PHONE..................408 367-8200
Martin A Kropelnicki, *CEO*
Michael P Ireland, *President*
Helen Del Grosso, *Vice Pres*
Francis S Ferraro, *Vice Pres*
Robert R Guzzetta, *Vice Pres*
EMP: 160
SQ FT: 43,000
SALES (est): 550.2MM
SALES (corp-wide): 666.8MM **Publicly Held**
SIC: 4941 Water supply
PA: California Water Service Group
1720 N 1st St
San Jose CA 95112
408 367-8200

(P-6023)
CALIFORNIA WATER SERVICE CO
3725 S H St, Bakersfield (93304-6535)
PHONE..................661 396-2400
Tim Terloar, *Manager*
EMP: 77
SALES (corp-wide): 666.8MM **Publicly Held**
SIC: 4941 Water supply
HQ: California Water Service Company
1720 N 1st St
San Jose CA 95112
408 367-8200

(P-6024)
CALIFORNIA WATER SERVICE CO
1505 E Sonora St, Stockton (95205-6112)
PHONE..................209 547-7900
Henry Wind, *Manager*
EMP: 51
SALES (corp-wide): 666.8MM **Publicly Held**
SIC: 4941 Water supply

HQ: California Water Service Company
1720 N 1st St
San Jose CA 95112
408 367-8200

(P-6025)
CALIFORNIA-AMERICAN WATER CO (HQ)
655 W Broadway Ste 1410, San Diego
(92101-8491)
PHONE...................................619 446-4760
Kent Turner, *President*
Judith Almond, *COO*
Anthony J Cerasuolo, *Vice Pres*
Edward Simon, *Director*
EMP: 57
SQ FT: 16,500
SALES (est): 82.7MM
SALES (corp-wide): 3.4B **Publicly Held**
SIC: 4941 Water supply
PA: American Water Works Company, Inc.
1 Water St
Camden NJ 08102
856 955-4001

(P-6026)
CALLEGUAS MUNICIPAL WATER DICT
2100 E Olsen Rd, Thousand Oaks
(91360-6800)
PHONE...................................805 526-9323
Thomas Slosson, *President*
Jeff Mocalis, *Officer*
Candace Cooper, *Admin Asst*
Cesar Romero, *Project Mgr*
Kristine McCaffrey, *Engineer*
EMP: 62
SQ FT: 8,000
SALES: 120MM **Privately Held**
WEB: www.calleguas.com
SIC: 4941 Water supply

(P-6027)
CARLSBAD MUNICIPAL WATER DST
5950 El Camino Real, Carlsbad
(92008-8802)
PHONE...................................760 438-2722
Robert Greaney, *Manager*
EMP: 50
SQ FT: 12,000
SALES (est): 6.8MM **Privately Held**
SIC: 4941 Water supply
PA: City Of Carlsbad
1635 Faraday Ave
Carlsbad CA 92008
760 602-2490

(P-6028)
CASTAIC LK WTR AGCY FING CORP
27234 Bouquet Canyon Rd, Santa Clarita
(91350-2102)
PHONE...................................661 259-2737
Tom Campbell, *CEO*
Matt Stone, *Ch of Bd*
Ronald J Kelly, *President*
Dan Masnada, *Treasurer*
William Cooper, *Vice Pres*
EMP: 120
SQ FT: 1,000
SALES (est): 38.1MM **Privately Held**
WEB: www.clwa.org
SIC: 4941 Water supply

(P-6029)
CITY & COUNTY OF SAN FRANCISCO
Also Called: San Frncsco Pub Utilities Comm
525 Golden Gate Ave Fl 5, San Francisco
(94102-3220)
PHONE...................................415 551-3000
Barbara Hale, *Branch Mgr*
Sanda Thaik, *Manager*
EMP: 900 **Privately Held**
SIC: 4941 9631 Water supply;
PA: City & County Of San Francisco
1 Dr Carlton B Goodlett P
San Francisco CA 94102
415 554-7500

(P-6030)
CITY OF FRESNO
Also Called: Water Division
1910 E University Ave, Fresno
(93703-2927)
PHONE...................................559 621-5300
Lon Martin, *Manager*
EMP: 165 **Privately Held**
WEB: www.fresnocitizencorps.org
SIC: 4941 Water supply
PA: City Of Fresno
2600 Fresno St
Fresno CA 93721
559 621-7001

(P-6031)
CITY OF GLENDALE
Also Called: Public Service Yard
800 Air Way, Glendale (91201-3012)
PHONE...................................818 548-2011
Pat Reily, *Manager*
EMP: 150 **Privately Held**
WEB: www.glendaleca.com
SIC: 4941 Water supply
PA: City Of Glendale
141 N Glendale Ave Fl 2
Glendale CA 91206
818 548-2085

(P-6032)
CITY OF LOMITA
Also Called: Publis Works
24373 Walnut St, Lomita (90717-1259)
PHONE...................................310 325-9830
Vince Demasse, *Manager*
EMP: 50
SQ FT: 59,893 **Privately Held**
WEB: www.lomita.com
SIC: 4941 9111 Water supply; mayors' offices
PA: City Of Lomita
24300 Narbonne Ave
Lomita CA 90717
310 325-7110

(P-6033)
CITY OF LONG BEACH
Also Called: Water Emergency Dispatch
1800 E Wardlow Rd, Long Beach
(90807-4931)
PHONE...................................562 570-2390
Kevin Wattier, *General Mgr*
Robert Cole, *President*
EMP: 100 **Privately Held**
WEB: www.polb.com
SIC: 4941 9511 Water supply; air, water & solid waste management;
PA: City Of Long Beach
411 W Ocean Blvd
Long Beach CA 90802
562 570-6450

(P-6034)
CITY OF NORCO
Parks and Recreation Dept
2870 Clark Ave, Norco (92860-1903)
PHONE...................................951 270-5632
Brian Petree, *Director*
EMP: 75 **Privately Held**
WEB: www.ci.norco.ca.us
SIC: 4941 4953 Water supply; refuse systems
PA: City Of Norco
2870 Clark Ave
Norco CA 92860
951 270-5617

(P-6035)
CITY OF OXNARD
Also Called: Water Svcs Operations & Repr
251 S Hayes Ave, Oxnard (93030-6058)
PHONE...................................805 385-8136
Anthony Emmert, *Superintendent*
David Birch, *Manager*
EMP: 60 **Privately Held**
WEB: www.oxnardtourism.com
SIC: 4941 9111 Water supply; mayors' offices
PA: City Of Oxnard
300 W 3rd St Uppr Fl4
Oxnard CA 93030
805 385-7803

(P-6036)
COACHELLA VALLEY WATER DST (PA)
Also Called: C V WATER DISTRICT
85995 Avenue 52, Coachella (92236-2568)
P.O. Box 1058 (92236-1058)
PHONE...................................760 398-2651
Toll Free:...................................888
Steve Robbins, *General Mgr*
Jim Barrett, *General Mgr*
Robert Cheng, *General Mgr*
Isabel Luna, *Executive Asst*
Amy Ammons, *Finance Dir*
▲ EMP: 515 EST: 1918
SALES: 173.7MM **Privately Held**
SIC: 4941 4971 4952 7389 Water supply; water distribution or supply systems for irrigation; sewerage systems; water softener service

(P-6037)
COACHELLA VALLEY WATER DST
75515 Hovley Ln E, Palm Desert
(92211-5104)
PHONE...................................760 398-2651
Steve Robins, *Branch Mgr*
EMP: 226
SALES (corp-wide): 173.7MM **Privately Held**
SIC: 4941 4952 4971 Water supply; sewerage systems; water distribution or supply systems for irrigation
PA: Coachella Valley Water District
85995 Avenue 52
Coachella CA 92236
760 398-2651

(P-6038)
COACHELLA VALLEY WATER DST
75 525 Hovley Ln, Palm Desert (92260)
PHONE...................................760 398-2651
Steve Robins, *Branch Mgr*
EMP: 226
SALES (corp-wide): 173.7MM **Privately Held**
SIC: 4941 4952 4971 Water supply; sewerage systems; irrigation systems
PA: Coachella Valley Water District
85995 Avenue 52
Coachella CA 92236
760 398-2651

(P-6039)
CONTRA COSTA WATER DISTRICT (PA)
Also Called: Ccwd
1331 Concord Ave, Concord (94520-4907)
PHONE...................................925 688-8000
Lisa Borba, *President*
Chris Dundon, *Vice Pres*
Wendy Chriss, *Admin Sec*
Christine Helton, *Admin Sec*
Shelly Wise, *Admin Sec*
▲ EMP: 225
SQ FT: 22,000
SALES: 3.8MM **Privately Held**
WEB: www.ccwater.com
SIC: 4941 Water supply

(P-6040)
CONTRA COSTA WATER DISTRICT
Also Called: Randall-Bold Wtr Trtmnt Plant
3760 Neroly Rd, Oakley (94561-2084)
PHONE...................................925 383-2576
Walter Bishop, *General Mgr*
EMP: 55
SALES (corp-wide): 3.8MM **Privately Held**
WEB: www.ccwater.com
SIC: 4941 Water supply
PA: Contra Costa Water District Inc
1331 Concord Ave
Concord CA 94520
925 688-8000

(P-6041)
COUNTY OF LOS ANGELES
Also Called: Water & Power Department
6801 E 2nd St, Long Beach (90803-4324)
PHONE...................................213 367-3176
Victor Barra, *Director*
EMP: 160 **Privately Held**

WEB: www.co.la.ca.us
SIC: 4941 9511 9631 4939 Water supply; air, water & solid waste management; ; regulation, administration of utilities; combination utilities
PA: County Of Los Angeles
500 W Temple St Ste 437
Los Angeles CA 90012
213 974-1101

(P-6042)
COUNTY OF LOS ANGELES
Also Called: Department of Public Works
900 S Fremont Ave, Alhambra
(91803-1331)
P.O. Box 1460 (91802-2460)
PHONE...................................626 458-4000
Gail Farber, *Director*
Azam Popalzai, *Info Tech Mgr*
Hector Bordas, *IT/INT Sup*
Armon Derjianian, *Electrical Engi*
Steve Burger, *Engineer*
EMP: 300 **Privately Held**
WEB: www.co.la.ca.us
SIC: 4941 9511 4971 Water supply; air, water & solid waste management; irrigation systems
PA: County Of Los Angeles
500 W Temple St Ste 437
Los Angeles CA 90012
213 974-1101

(P-6043)
COUNTY OF LOS ANGELES
Also Called: Community Facilities Dst No 6
500 W Temple St Ste 525, Los Angeles
(90012-3873)
PHONE...................................213 974-8301
EMP: 172 **Privately Held**
SIC: 4941 Water supply
PA: County Of Los Angeles
500 W Temple St Ste 437
Los Angeles CA 90012
213 974-1101

(P-6044)
COUNTY OF SOLANO
Also Called: Water Supply
810 Vaca Valley Pkwy # 203, Vacaville
(95688-8835)
PHONE...................................707 451-6090
David Okita, *Manager*
Thomas Pate, *Director*
EMP: 100 **Privately Held**
SIC: 4941 8641 Water supply; civic social & fraternal associations
PA: County Of Solano
675 Texas St Ste 2600
Fairfield CA 94533
707 784-6706

(P-6045)
CUCAMONGA VALLEY WATER DST
10440 Ashford St, Rancho Cucamonga
(91730-3057)
P.O. Box 638 (91729-0638)
PHONE...................................909 987-2591
Martin Zvirbulis, *CEO*
Diane Schumacher, *Senior Partner*
Kathleen Tiegs, *President*
Chad Brantley, *Officer*
Oscar Gonzalez, *Vice Pres*
EMP: 100 EST: 1955
SQ FT: 15,000
SALES: 92.9MM **Privately Held**
WEB: www.ccwdwater.com
SIC: 4941 Water supply

(P-6046)
DESERT WATER AGENCY FING CORP
Also Called: DWA
1200 S Gene Autry Trl, Palm Springs
(92264-3533)
P.O. Box 1710 (92263-1710)
PHONE...................................760 323-4971
Patricia G Oyga, *CEO*
Joseph Stuart, *Vice Pres*
Mario Ballesteros, *Info Tech Dir*
Kristy Scaletta, *Human Res Mgr*
Kris Hopping, *Manager*
EMP: 72
SQ FT: 38,000

▲ = Import ▼=Export
◆ =Import/Export

SALES: 35.8MM **Privately Held**
WEB: www.dwa.org
SIC: **4941** Water supply

(P-6047)
DUBLIN SAN RAMON SERVICES DST (PA)
7051 Dublin Blvd, Dublin (94568-3018)
PHONE.........................925 875-2276
Bert Michalczyk, *CEO*
Lori Rose, *Treasurer*
▲ EMP: 110 EST: 1953
SQ FT: 19,400
SALES: 62.2MM **Privately Held**
WEB: www.dsrsd.com
SIC: **4941** Water supply

(P-6048)
DUBLIN SAN RAMON SERVICES DST
7399 Johnson Dr, Pleasanton (94588-3862)
PHONE.........................925 846-4565
Bert Michalczyk, *General Mgr*
EMP: 100
SALES (corp-wide): 62.2MM **Privately Held**
WEB: www.dsrsd.com
SIC: **4941** Water supply
PA: Dublin San Ramon Services District
7051 Dublin Blvd
Dublin CA 94568
925 875-2276

(P-6049)
EAST BAY MUNICIPL UTILTY DISTR
Also Called: Ebmud
3999 Lakeside Dr, Richmond (94806-1964)
PHONE.........................866 403-2683
Karl Gillson, *Branch Mgr*
EMP: 110
SALES (corp-wide): 599.1MM **Privately Held**
WEB: www.ebmud.com
SIC: **4941** Water supply
PA: East Bay Municipal Utility District, Water System
375 11th St
Oakland CA 94607
866 403-2683

(P-6050)
EAST BAY MUNICIPL UTILTY DISTR (PA)
Also Called: Ebmud
375 11th St, Oakland (94607-4246)
P.O. Box 24055 (94623-1055)
PHONE.........................866 403-2683
Alexander Coate, *General Mgr*
Jay Morgan, *Vice Pres*
Serge Terentieff, *Division Mgr*
Dawn Benson, *Executive Asst*
Gina Bellingham, *Admin Sec*
EMP: 629
SQ FT: 264,427
SALES: 599.1MM **Privately Held**
WEB: www.ebmud.com
SIC: **4941** Water supply

(P-6051)
EAST BAY MUNICIPL UTILTY DISTR
Also Called: Ebmud
375 11th St, Oakland (94607-4246)
PHONE.........................510 287-0760
Alexander Coate, *General Mgr*
Elizabeth Grassetti, *Senior VP*
Michael Nguyen, *Prgrmr*
Katherine Tate, *Technician*
David Graham, *Engineer*
EMP: 51
SALES (corp-wide): 599.1MM **Privately Held**
SIC: **4941** Water supply
PA: East Bay Municipal Utility District, Water System
375 11th St
Oakland CA 94607
866 403-2683

(P-6052)
EAST BAY MUNICIPL UTILTY DISTR
Also Called: Ebmud - Construction and Maint
2149 Union St, Oakland (94607)
PHONE.........................866 403-2683
Alexander Coate, *Branch Mgr*
EMP: 54
SALES (corp-wide): 599.1MM **Privately Held**
SIC: **4941** Water supply
PA: East Bay Municipal Utility District, Water System
375 11th St
Oakland CA 94607
866 403-2683

(P-6053)
EAST VALLEY WATER DISTRICT
31111 Greenspot Rd, Highland (92346-4427)
P.O. Box 3427, San Bernardino (92413-3427)
PHONE.........................909 889-9501
John Mura, *CEO*
Matt Levesque, *President*
Brian W Tompkins, *CFO*
Brian Tompkins, *CFO*
Kip E Sturgeon, *Vice Pres*
EMP: 61
SALES: 40.2MM **Privately Held**
WEB: www.eastvalley.org
SIC: **4941 8734** Water supply; water testing laboratory

(P-6054)
EASTERN MUNICIPAL WATER DST (PA)
2270 Trumble Rd, Perris (92572)
P.O. Box 8300 (92572-8300)
PHONE.........................951 928-3777
Paul D Jones II, *CEO*
Susan Barnes, *Officer*
Nick Kanetis, *General Mgr*
Terri Guerrero, *Executive Asst*
Sheldon Glaha, *Information Mgr*
▲ EMP: 420
SQ FT: 160,000
SALES: 240.5MM **Privately Held**
SIC: **4941 4952** Water supply; sewerage systems

(P-6055)
EASTERN MUNICIPAL WATER DST
19750 Evans Rd, Perris (92571-7469)
PHONE.........................951 657-7469
Paul D Jones II, *Branch Mgr*
EMP: 200
SALES (corp-wide): 240.5MM **Privately Held**
SIC: **4941** Water supply
PA: Eastern Municipal Water District
2270 Trumble Rd
Perris CA 92572
951 928-3777

(P-6056)
EL DORADO HILLS COUNTY WTR DST
Also Called: El Dorado Hills Fire Dept
1050 Wilson Blvd, El Dorado Hills (95762-7263)
PHONE.........................916 933-6623
John Hidahl, *President*
James O'Camb, *COO*
Jessica Braddock, *Finance*
Mike Lilienthal, *Chief*
Dan Nelson,
EMP: 51
SALES (est): 6.9MM **Privately Held**
WEB: www.edhfire.com
SIC: **4941** Water supply

(P-6057)
EL DORADO IRRIGATION DISTRICT
2890 Mosquito Rd, Placerville (95667-4700)
PHONE.........................530 622-4513
George Osborne, *President*
Darcy Millward, *Vice Pres*
Ane Deister, *General Mgr*
Elizabeth Wells, *General Mgr*
Linda King, *Admin Asst*

EMP: 300 EST: 1925
SQ FT: 27,000
SALES: 64.1MM **Privately Held**
SIC: **4941 4952 8741 4971** Water supply; sewerage systems; management services; irrigation systems

(P-6058)
EL DORADO WATER & SHOWER SVC
5821 Mother Lode Dr, Placerville (95667-8227)
P.O. Box 944 (95667-0944)
PHONE.........................530 622-8995
Robert V Williams, *President*
Mellisa Peterson, *Principal*
EMP: 50
SQ FT: 816
SALES (est): 2MM **Privately Held**
SIC: **4941** Water supply

(P-6059)
EL TORO WATER DISTR PUBLIC FAC (PA)
24251 Los Alisos Blvd, Lake Forest (92630-5246)
P.O. Box 4000, Laguna Hills (92654-4000)
PHONE.........................949 837-1662
Robert R Hill, *Admin Sec*
Michael Miazga, *COO*
Jose Vergara, *Treasurer*
Polly Welsch, *Bd of Directors*
Chau Vuong, *Technician*
EMP: 54 EST: 1960
SQ FT: 7,200
SALES: 23.1MM **Privately Held**
WEB: www.etwd.com
SIC: **4941 4959** Water supply; sanitary services

(P-6060)
ELSINORE VLY MUNICPL WTR DST (PA)
31315 Chaney St, Lake Elsinore (92530-2743)
P.O. Box 3000 (92531-3000)
PHONE.........................951 674-3146
Harvey R Ryan, *President*
Andy Morris, *Treasurer*
Phil Williams, *Vice Pres*
Ronald Young, *Vice Pres*
Tammy Ramirez, *General Mgr*
EMP: 65
SQ FT: 4,000
SALES: 74.3MM **Privately Held**
WEB: www.evmwd.com
SIC: **4941 4971 4952** Water supply; water distribution or supply systems for irrigation; sewerage systems

(P-6061)
FALLBROOK PUBLIC UTILITY DST
990 E Mission Rd, Fallbrook (92028-2232)
P.O. Box 2290 (92088-2290)
PHONE.........................760 728-1125
Nick Hoskot, *President*
Marcie Eilers, *Treasurer*
Mary McNeil, *Vice Pres*
Ruth Resch, *Admin Sec*
Soleil Develle, *Technician*
EMP: 81
SQ FT: 12,000
SALES: 25.3MM **Privately Held**
WEB: www.fpud.com
SIC: **4941** Water supply

(P-6062)
FRIANT WATER USERS ASSOCIATION
Also Called: Friant Water Users Authority
854 N Harvard Ave, Lindsay (93247-1715)
PHONE.........................559 562-6305
Marvin Huss, *Chairman*
Douglas Deflitch, *COO*
Becky Brionen, *Director*
Stephen Ottemoeller, *Manager*
Eric R Quinley, *Manager*
EMP: 53
SQ FT: 4,000
SALES (est): 6.3MM **Privately Held**
SIC: **4941** Water supply

(P-6063)
GOLDEN STATE WATER COMPANY
1920 W Corporate Way, Anaheim (92801-5373)
PHONE.........................714 535-7711
Randall Vogel, *Vice Pres*
Toby Moore, *Chief*
EMP: 70
SALES (corp-wide): 436.8MM **Publicly Held**
WEB: www.gswater.com
SIC: **4941 4911** Water supply; distribution, electric power
HQ: Golden State Water Company
630 E Foothill Blvd
San Dimas CA 91773
909 394-3600

(P-6064)
GOLDEN STATE WATER COMPANY (HQ)
Also Called: AWR
630 E Foothill Blvd, San Dimas (91773-1212)
PHONE.........................909 394-3600
Robert J Sprowls, *President*
Eva G Tang, *CFO*
Eva Tang, *Treasurer*
Richard Mathis, *General Mgr*
Paul Schubert, *General Mgr*
EMP: 170
SALES: 329.6MM
SALES (corp-wide): 436.8MM **Publicly Held**
WEB: www.gswater.com
SIC: **4941 4911** Water supply; distribution, electric power
PA: American States Water Company
630 E Foothill Blvd
San Dimas CA 91773
909 394-3600

(P-6065)
GOLDEN STATE WATER COMPANY
Also Called: American State Water Company
630 E Foothill Blvd, San Dimas (91773-1212)
PHONE.........................909 394-3600
Floydee Wibks, *CEO*
EMP: 100
SALES (corp-wide): 436.8MM **Publicly Held**
WEB: www.gswater.com
SIC: **4941** Water supply
HQ: Golden State Water Company
630 E Foothill Blvd
San Dimas CA 91773
909 394-3600

(P-6066)
GOLDEN STATE WATER COMPANY
Also Called: Sanitation
600 W Los Angeles Ave, Simi Valley (93065-1642)
PHONE.........................805 583-6400
Jim Buell, *Manager*
EMP: 50
SALES (corp-wide): 436.8MM **Publicly Held**
WEB: www.gswater.com
SIC: **4941** Water supply
HQ: Golden State Water Company
630 E Foothill Blvd
San Dimas CA 91773
909 394-3600

(P-6067)
HELIX WATER DISTRICT
Also Called: Nat L Eggert Operations Center
1233 Vernon Way, El Cajon (92020-1838)
PHONE.........................619 596-3860
Doug Emery, *Branch Mgr*
EMP: 55
SALES (corp-wide): 85.8MM **Privately Held**
WEB: www.hwd.com
SIC: **4941** Water supply
PA: Helix Water District
7811 University Ave
La Mesa CA 91942
619 466-0585

(P-6068)
INLAND EMPIRE UTILITIES AGENCY
12811 6th St, Rancho Cucamonga (91739-9222)
PHONE...................909 993-1755
Dan Foley, *Branch Mgr*
EMP: 71
SALES (corp-wide): 119.6MM **Privately Held**
SIC: 4941 Water supply
PA: Inland Empire Utilities Agency A Municipal Water District (Inc)
6075 Kimball Ave
Chino CA 91708
909 993-1600

(P-6069)
INLAND EMPIRE UTILITIES AGENCY (PA)
6075 Kimball Ave, Chino (91708-9174)
P.O. Box 9020, Chino Hills (91709-0902)
PHONE...................909 993-1600
Terry Catlin, *President*
John Anderson, *President*
Ging Cookman, *Corp Secy*
Steve Elie, *Corp Secy*
Michael Camacho, *Vice Pres*
EMP: 92
SQ FT: 60,000
SALES: 119.6MM **Privately Held**
SIC: 4941 Water supply

(P-6070)
INLAND EMPIRE UTILITIES AGENCY
9400 Cherry Ave, Fontana (92335-5359)
PHONE...................909 993-1600
Cameron Langner, *Branch Mgr*
EMP: 71
SALES (corp-wide): 119.6MM **Privately Held**
SIC: 4941 Water supply
PA: Inland Empire Utilities Agency A Municipal Water District (Inc)
6075 Kimball Ave
Chino CA 91708
909 993-1600

(P-6071)
IRVINE RANCH WATER DISTRICT (PA)
15600 Sand Canyon Ave, Irvine (92618-3102)
P.O. Box 57000 (92619-7000)
PHONE...................949 453-5300
Paul Jones, *General Mgr*
Robert Jacobson, *Treasurer*
Kristine Swan, *Admin Asst*
Sergio De La Torre, *Supervisor*
Rick Perry, *Supervisor*
EMP: 110
SQ FT: 52,000
SALES: 88.9MM **Privately Held**
SIC: 4941 4952 Water supply; sewerage systems

(P-6072)
IRVINE RANCH WATER DISTRICT
3512 Michelson Dr, Irvine (92612-1757)
P.O. Box 14128 (92623-4128)
PHONE...................949 453-5300
Carl Ballard, *Director*
EMP: 170
SALES (est): 13.5MM
SALES (corp-wide): 88.9MM **Privately Held**
SIC: 4941 4952 Water supply; sewerage systems
PA: Irvine Ranch Water District Inc
15600 Sand Canyon Ave
Irvine CA 92618
949 453-5300

(P-6073)
KERN COUNTY WATER AGENCY
811 Nadine Ln, Bakersfield (93308)
P.O. Box 58 (93302-0058)
PHONE...................661 634-1512
James M Beck, *District Mgr*
James Beck, *Manager*
EMP: 63

SALES (corp-wide): 34MM **Privately Held**
SIC: 4941 Water supply
PA: Kern County Water Agency
3200 Rio Mirada Dr
Bakersfield CA 93308
661 634-1400

(P-6074)
LAKE HEMET MUNICIPAL WTR DST (PA)
26385 Fairview Ave, Hemet (92544-6607)
P.O. Box 5039 (92544-0039)
PHONE...................951 927-1816
Tom Wagoner, *General Mgr*
Leann Markham, *Admin Mgr*
Jason Venable, *Technician*
Shirley Lipiarski, *HR Admin*
Matt Park, *Purch Mgr*
EMP: 58 **EST:** 1955
SQ FT: 4,900
SALES: 18.6MM **Privately Held**
WEB: www.lhmwd.org
SIC: 4941 4971 Water supply; water distribution or supply systems for irrigation

(P-6075)
LAS VIRGENES MUNICIPAL WTR DST
4232 Las Virgenes Rd Lbby, Calabasas (91302-3594)
PHONE...................818 251-2100
Glen Peterson, *President*
Jay Lewitt, *Treasurer*
Lee Renger, *Vice Pres*
David Pedersen, *General Mgr*
Andrew Spear, *Analyst*
EMP: 125
SQ FT: 10,000
SALES: 69MM **Privately Held**
WEB: www.lvmwd.com
SIC: 4941 Water supply

(P-6076)
LIBERTY UTILITIES PK WTR CORP (DH)
9750 Washburn Rd, Downey (90241-5625)
PHONE...................562 923-0711
Greg Sorensen, *President*
Chris Alario, *CFO*
Jeanne Marie Bruno, *Senior VP*
Larry Lee, *Executive*
Jeanne-Marie Bruno, *General Mgr*
EMP: 68
SQ FT: 15,000
SALES (est): 81.8MM
SALES (corp-wide): 1.6B **Privately Held**
SIC: 4941 Water supply
HQ: Liberty Utilities (Canada) Corp
2845 Bristol Cir
Oakville ON L6H 7
905 465-4500

(P-6077)
LINDA YORBA WATER DISTRICT (PA)
1717 E Miraloma Ave, Placentia (92870-6785)
P.O. Box 309, Yorba Linda (92885-0309)
PHONE...................714 701-3000
Ken Vecchiarelli, *General Mgr*
Al Nederhood, *Bd of Directors*
Ariel Bacani, *Technician*
Jacqueline Segura, *Technician*
Steve Conklin, *Engineer*
▲ **EMP:** 76
SQ FT: 7,900
SALES: 35.2MM **Privately Held**
WEB: www.ylwd.com
SIC: 4941 4952 Water supply; sewerage systems

(P-6078)
LOS ANGELES DEPT WTR & PWR
4030 Crenshaw Blvd, Los Angeles (90008-2533)
P.O. Box 51211 (90051-5511)
PHONE...................323 256-8079
Jeffrey McCann, *IT/INT Sup*
Martin Ningo, *Electrical Engi*
Alexander Santos, *Engineer*
Alise Asadourian, *Training Spec*
Mark Sedlacek, *Manager*
EMP: 4655

SALES (corp-wide): 1.1B **Privately Held**
SIC: 4941 4911 Water supply; electric services
PA: Los Angeles Department Of Water And Power
111 N Hope St
Los Angeles CA 90012
213 367-4211

(P-6079)
LOS ANGELES DEPT WTR & PWR
11801 Sheldon St, Sun Valley (91352-1508)
PHONE...................213 367-1342
Kirk Bergland, *Branch Mgr*
Dennis Luker, *Engineer*
Richard Willi Sims, *Supervisor*
EMP: 895
SALES (corp-wide): 1.1B **Privately Held**
SIC: 4941 Water supply
PA: Los Angeles Department Of Water And Power
111 N Hope St
Los Angeles CA 90012
213 367-4211

(P-6080)
LOS ANGELES DEPT WTR & PWR
Also Called: Ladwp
201 S Webster St, Independence (93526-1769)
PHONE...................760 878-2156
Dale Schmidt, *Fire Chief*
Steve Howe, *Supervisor*
EMP: 1969
SALES (corp-wide): 1.1B **Privately Held**
SIC: 4941 Water supply
PA: Los Angeles Department Of Water And Power
111 N Hope St
Los Angeles CA 90012
213 367-4211

(P-6081)
LOS ANGELES DEPT WTR & PWR (PA)
Also Called: Ladwp
111 N Hope St, Los Angeles (90012-2607)
P.O. Box 51111 (90051-5700)
PHONE...................213 367-4211
David H Wright, *General Mgr*
Martin L Adams, *COO*
Ann M Santilli, *CFO*
Donna I Stevener, *Officer*
Nancy Sutley, *Officer*
▲ **EMP:** 170
SALES: 1.1B **Privately Held**
WEB: www.lacity.org
SIC: 4941 4911 Water supply; electric services

(P-6082)
LOS ANGELES DEPT WTR & PWR
1141 W 2nd St Bldg D, Los Angeles (90012-2007)
PHONE...................213 367-5706
Carol Tharp, *Branch Mgr*
Rafik Alsawalhy, *Project Mgr*
Steven Ceniceros, *Engineer*
Heather Yegiazaryan, *Engineer*
John Cox, *Manager*
EMP: 895
SALES (corp-wide): 1.1B **Privately Held**
SIC: 4941 Water supply
PA: Los Angeles Department Of Water And Power
111 N Hope St
Los Angeles CA 90012
213 367-4211

(P-6083)
MARIN MUNICIPAL WATER DISTRICT (PA)
220 Nellen Ave, Corte Madera (94925-1169)
PHONE...................415 945-1455
Krishna Kumar, *General Mgr*
Van Trump, *Bd of Directors*
Libby Pischel, *Executive*
Mark Williamson, *Executive*
Merlene Fundaro, *General Mgr*
EMP: 220

SQ FT: 32,000
SALES: 78.6MM **Privately Held**
SIC: 4941 4971 Water supply; irrigation systems

(P-6084)
MESA CNSLD WTR DST IMPRV CORP (PA)
Also Called: MESA WATER DISTRICT
1965 Placentia Ave, Costa Mesa (92627-3420)
PHONE...................949 631-1200
Lee Pearl, *Director*
James R Fisler, *President*
Shawn Dewane, *Vice Pres*
Coleen L Monteleone, *Admin Sec*
Dustin Burnside, *Opers Staff*
EMP: 64
SQ FT: 26,000
SALES: 35.7MM **Privately Held**
WEB: www.mesawater.org
SIC: 4941 Water supply

(P-6085)
METROPOLITAN WATER DISTRICT
1820 Commercenter Cir, San Bernardino (92408-3430)
PHONE...................909 890-3776
Ron Gastelum, *Principal*
EMP: 50
SALES (corp-wide): 1.4B **Privately Held**
WEB: www.mwdh2o.com
SIC: 4941 Water supply
PA: The Metropolitan Water District Of Southern California
700 N Alameda St
Los Angeles CA 90012
213 217-6000

(P-6086)
METROPOLITAN WATER DISTRICT
18250 La Sierra Ave, Riverside (92503-6531)
PHONE...................951 688-5672
Al Ubrun, *Manager*
EMP: 50
SALES (corp-wide): 1.4B **Privately Held**
WEB: www.mwdh2o.com
SIC: 4941 1711 Water supply; septic system construction
PA: The Metropolitan Water District Of Southern California
700 N Alameda St
Los Angeles CA 90012
213 217-6000

(P-6087)
METROPOLITAN WATER DISTRICT
Also Called: Robert B Diemer Trtmnt Plant
3972 Valley View Ave, Yorba Linda (92886-1828)
PHONE...................714 577-5031
Trudi Loy, *Manager*
EMP: 80
SALES (corp-wide): 1.4B **Privately Held**
WEB: www.mwdh2o.com
SIC: 4941 Water supply
PA: The Metropolitan Water District Of Southern California
700 N Alameda St
Los Angeles CA 90012
213 217-6000

(P-6088)
METROPOLITAN WATER DISTRICT
Also Called: Joseph Jensen Filtration Plant
13100 Balboa Blvd, Granada Hills (91344-1199)
PHONE...................818 368-3731
Ezell Culver, *Manager*
EMP: 72
SALES (corp-wide): 1.4B **Privately Held**
WEB: www.mwdh2o.com
SIC: 4941 Water supply
PA: The Metropolitan Water District Of Southern California
700 N Alameda St
Los Angeles CA 90012
213 217-6000

(P-6089)
METROPOLITAN WATER DISTRICT
Also Called: Metropolitan Water Lavern
700 Moreno Ave, La Verne (91750-3399)
P.O. Box 54153, Los Angeles (90054-0153)
PHONE....................................909 593-7474
Wendell Williams, *Branch Mgr*
EMP: 370
SALES (corp-wide): 1.4B **Privately Held**
WEB: www.mwdh2o.com
SIC: 4941 Water supply
PA: The Metropolitan Water District Of
Southern California
700 N Alameda St
Los Angeles CA 90012
213 217-6000

(P-6090)
METROPOLITAN WATER DISTRICT
33752 Newport Rd, Winchester (92596-9475)
PHONE....................................951 926-7095
Marty Hundley, *Manager*
EMP: 66
SALES (corp-wide): 1.4B **Privately Held**
WEB: www.mwdh2o.com
SIC: 4941 Water supply
PA: The Metropolitan Water District Of
Southern California
700 N Alameda St
Los Angeles CA 90012
213 217-6000

(P-6091)
METROPOLITAN WATER DISTRICT
550 E Alessandro Blvd, Riverside (92508-2400)
PHONE....................................951 780-1511
Richard Green, *Branch Mgr*
EMP: 75
SALES (corp-wide): 1.4B **Privately Held**
WEB: www.mwdh2o.com
SIC: 4941 Water supply
PA: The Metropolitan Water District Of
Southern California
700 N Alameda St
Los Angeles CA 90012
213 217-6000

(P-6092)
METROPOLITAN WATER DISTRICT
2300 Palos Verdes Dr N, Rllng HLS Est (90274-4222)
PHONE....................................310 832-6106
Dave Rendon, *Manager*
EMP: 2000
SALES (corp-wide): 1.4B **Privately Held**
WEB: www.mwdh2o.com
SIC: 4941 Water supply
PA: The Metropolitan Water District Of
Southern California
700 N Alameda St
Los Angeles CA 90012
213 217-6000

(P-6093)
METROPOLITAN WATER DISTRICT
Also Called: Robert Sknner Filtration Plant
33740 Borel Rd, Winchester (92596-9625)
PHONE....................................951 926-1501
Fax: 951 926-3531
EMP: 80
SALES (corp-wide): 1.5B **Privately Held**
SIC: 4941
PA: The Metropolitan Water District Of
Southern California
700 N Alameda St
Los Angeles CA 90012
213 217-6000

(P-6094)
MOULTON NIGUEL WATER (PA)
27500 La Paz Rd, Laguna Niguel (92677-3402)
P.O. Box 30203 (92607-0203)
PHONE....................................949 831-2500
Richard Fiore, *President*
David Cain, *Treasurer*
Matthew Brown, *Officer*
John V Foley, *General Mgr*

Deena Malone-Collom, *Admin Asst*
EMP: 97 EST: 1960
SQ FT: 9,000
SALES: 61MM **Privately Held**
WEB: www.mnwd.com
SIC: 4941 4959 Water supply; sanitary services

(P-6095)
NORTH MARIN WATER DISTRICT (PA)
Also Called: NMWD
999 Rush Creek Pl, Novato (94945-7716)
P.O. Box 146 (94948-0146)
PHONE....................................415 897-4133
Chris Degabriele, *Principal*
Carmela Chandrasekera, *Engineer*
David Jackson, *Engineer*
Robert Clark, *Facilities Mgr*
Pete Castellucci, *Maintence Staff*
EMP: 50
SQ FT: 7,200
SALES: 22MM **Privately Held**
WEB: www.nmwd.com
SIC: 4941 Water supply

(P-6096)
OAKDALE IRRGTION DST FING CORP
1205 E F St, Oakdale (95361-4112)
PHONE....................................209 847-0341
Alfred Bairos, *President*
Kathy Cook, *CFO*
Steve Knell, *Exec Dir*
▲ EMP: 69 EST: 1909
SQ FT: 5,000
SALES: 2.7MM **Privately Held**
WEB: www.oakdaleirrigation.com
SIC: 4941 Water supply

(P-6097)
OLIVENHAIN MUNICIPAL WATER DST
1966 Olivenhain Rd, Encinitas (92024-5676)
PHONE....................................760 753-6466
Edmund Sprague, *President*
Mark A Muir, *Treasurer*
Robert F Topolavac, *Vice Pres*
Robert Topolavac, *Vice Pres*
Kimberly A Thorner, *General Mgr*
EMP: 79
SQ FT: 11,000
SALES: 60.1MM **Privately Held**
SIC: 4941 4971 Water supply; impounding reservoir, irrigation

(P-6098)
ORANGE COUNTY WATER DISTRICT
Also Called: Accounts Payable Dept
18700 Ward St, Fountain Valley (92708-6930)
P.O. Box 20845 (92728-0845)
PHONE....................................714 378-3200
Dina L Nguyen, *Branch Mgr*
EMP: 113
SALES (corp-wide): 147.8MM **Privately Held**
SIC: 4941 Water supply
PA: Orange County Water District
18700 Ward St
Fountain Valley CA 92708
714 378-3200

(P-6099)
OTAY WATER DISTRICT
2554 Swetwater Sprng Blvd, Spring Valley (91978-2096)
PHONE....................................619 670-2222
Gary Croucher, *President*
Jose Lopez, *President*
Joseph R Beachem, *CFO*
David Gonzalez, *Vice Pres*
Jenny Diaz, *Executive*
EMP: 170 EST: 1956
SQ FT: 6,000
SALES: 97.4MM **Privately Held**
WEB: www.otaywater.gov
SIC: 4941 1623 Water supply; water, sewer & utility lines

(P-6100)
PADRE DAM MUNICIPAL WATER DST (PA)
9300 Fanita Pkwy, Santee (92071-7906)
P.O. Box 719003 (92072-9003)
PHONE....................................619 258-4617
Allen Carlisle, *CEO*
William Pommering, *President*
Karen Jassoy, *CFO*
Doug Wilson, *Treasurer*
August Caires, *Vice Pres*
EMP: 63
SQ FT: 10,000
SALES: 72.9MM **Privately Held**
WEB: www.padredam.org
SIC: 4941 4952 7033 Water supply; sewerage systems; campgrounds

(P-6101)
PALMDALE WATER DISTRICT
2029 E Avenue Q, Palmdale (93550-4050)
PHONE....................................661 947-4111
Michael Williams, *CFO*
EMP: 93
SALES: 24.8MM **Privately Held**
SIC: 4941 Water supply

(P-6102)
RAINBOW MUNICIPAL WATER DST
3707 Old Highway 395, Fallbrook (92028-9372)
PHONE....................................760 728-1178
Tom Kennedy, *General Mgr*
Dave Seymour, *General Mgr*
EMP: 53
SALES: 22MM **Privately Held**
SIC: 4941 Water supply

(P-6103)
RANCHO CALIFORNIA WATER DST (PA)
Also Called: RCWD
42135 Winchester Rd, Temecula (92590-4800)
P.O. Box 9017 (92589-9017)
PHONE....................................951 296-6900
William E Plummer, *Principal*
Stephen J Corona, *President*
Ralph Daily, *President*
Bennet Drake, *President*
Jeff Armstrong, *CFO*
EMP: 145
SQ FT: 71,000
SALES: 64.6MM **Privately Held**
WEB: www.ranchowater.com
SIC: 4941 Water supply

(P-6104)
SACRAMENTO COUNTY WATER AGENCY
Also Called: Scwa
827 7th St Ste 301, Sacramento (95814-2406)
PHONE....................................916 874-6851
Susan Purdin, *Principal*
William Konigsmark, *Principal*
EMP: 99
SALES (est): 5.4MM **Privately Held**
SIC: 4941 Water supply
PA: County Of Sacramento
700 H St Ste 7650
Sacramento CA 95814
916 874-5544

(P-6105)
SACRAMENTO SUBURBAN WATER DST
3701 Marconi Ave Ste 100, Sacramento (95821-5346)
PHONE....................................916 972-7171
Robert Roscoe, *General Mgr*
Annette Oleary, *Principal*
Matthew Winans, *CIO*
Ken Gebert, *Technology*
David Espinoza, *Engineer*
EMP: 60 EST: 1958
SQ FT: 13,500
SALES: 44.1MM **Privately Held**
SIC: 4941 Water supply

(P-6106)
SACRAMENTO SUBURBAN WATER DST
3701 Marconi Ave Ste 100, Sacramento (95821-5346)
PHONE....................................916 972-7171
Robert Rosco, *General Mgr*
EMP: 52
SALES: 41.8MM **Privately Held**
WEB: www.sswd.org
SIC: 4941 Water supply

(P-6107)
SAN DIEGO COUNTY WATER AUTH (PA)
4677 Overland Ave, San Diego (92123-1233)
PHONE....................................858 522-6600
Maureen Stapleton, *General Mgr*
Eric Sandler, *CFO*
Mark Muir, *Chairman*
Lisa M Harris, *Treasurer*
Joe Aguilar, *Bd of Directors*
▲ EMP: 280
SQ FT: 26,000
SALES (est): 44.4MM **Privately Held**
SIC: 4941 Water supply

(P-6108)
SAN DIEGO COUNTY WATER AUTH
610 W 5th Ave, Escondido (92025-4093)
PHONE....................................760 480-1991
Brendan Sheehan, *President*
Al Gaza, *Manager*
EMP: 70
SALES (corp-wide): 44.4MM **Privately Held**
SIC: 4941 Water supply
PA: San Diego County Water Authority
4677 Overland Ave
San Diego CA 92123
858 522-6600

(P-6109)
SAN GABRIEL VALLEY WATER ASSN
725 N Azusa Ave, Azusa (91702-2528)
PHONE....................................626 815-1305
Carol Williams, *Principal*
EMP: 100
SALES: 181.7K **Privately Held**
SIC: 4941 Water supply

(P-6110)
SAN GABRIEL VALLEY WATER CO (PA)
Also Called: Fontana Water Company
11142 Garvey Ave, El Monte (91733-2498)
P.O. Box 6010 (91734-2010)
PHONE....................................626 448-6183
R H Nicholson Jr, *Ch of Bd*
Michael L Whitehead, *President*
David Batt, *Treasurer*
Robert Diprimio, *Senior VP*
Frank A Lo Guidice, *Vice Pres*
EMP: 125 EST: 1936
SQ FT: 30,000
SALES (est): 133.3MM **Privately Held**
WEB: www.fontanawater.com
SIC: 4941 Water supply

(P-6111)
SAN GABRIEL VALLEY WATER CO
8440 Nuevo Ave, Fontana (92335-3824)
P.O. Box 987 (92334-0987)
PHONE....................................909 822-2201
Mike McGraw, *Manager*
EMP: 76
SQ FT: 2,727
SALES (corp-wide): 133.3MM **Privately Held**
WEB: www.fontanawater.com
SIC: 4941 Water supply
PA: San Gabriel Valley Water Co.
11142 Garvey Ave
El Monte CA 91733
626 448-6183

(P-6112)
SAN JOSE WATER COMPANY (HQ)
Also Called: S J W
110 W Taylor St, San Jose (95110-2131)
PHONE.................................408 288-5314
W Richard Roth, *CEO*
Charles Toeniskoetter, *Ch of Bd*
Angela Yip, *CFO*
Richard Balocco, *Vice Pres*
Geaorge Belhumeur, *Vice Pres*
EMP: 140
SQ FT: 5,000
SALES: 374.7MM
SALES (corp-wide): 397.7MM **Publicly Held**
SIC: 4941 Water supply
PA: Sjw Group
110 W Taylor St
San Jose CA 95110
408 279-7800

(P-6113)
SAN JOSE WATER COMPANY
1221 S Bascom Ave, San Jose (95128-3514)
PHONE.................................408 298-0364
Paul Schreiber, *Manager*
EMP: 180
SALES (corp-wide): 397.7MM **Publicly Held**
SIC: 4941 Water supply
HQ: San Jose Water Company
110 W Taylor St
San Jose CA 95110
408 288-5314

(P-6114)
SAN LORENZO VALLEY WATER DST (PA)
13060 Highway 9, Boulder Creek (95006-9119)
PHONE.................................831 338-2153
James Mueller, *General Mgr*
James Furtado, *Opers Staff*
EMP: 50
SALES: 5.2MM **Privately Held**
WEB: www.slvwd.com
SIC: 4941 Water supply

(P-6115)
SANTA CLARA VALLEY WATER (PA)
5750 Almaden Expy, San Jose (95118-3614)
P.O. Box 20670 (95160-0670)
PHONE.................................408 265-2600
Beau Goldie, *CEO*
Jim Fiedler, *Officer*
Katherine Oven, *Officer*
Angelica Cruz, *Executive*
Hernan Rivero, *Risk Mgmt Dir*
▲ EMP: 850 EST: 1951
SQ FT: 40,780
SALES: 144.6MM **Privately Held**
WEB: www.valleywater.org
SIC: 4941 Water supply

(P-6116)
SANTA CLARA VALLEY WATER
400 More Ave, Los Gatos (95032-1111)
PHONE.................................408 395-8121
Greg Gibson, *Branch Mgr*
EMP: 70
SALES (corp-wide): 144.6MM **Privately Held**
WEB: www.valleywater.org
SIC: 4941 Water supply
PA: Santa Clara Valley Water District Public Facilities Financing Corporation
5750 Almaden Expy
San Jose CA 95118
408 265-2600

(P-6117)
SANTA CLARITA VALLEY WTR AGCY
Also Called: Santa Clarita Water Division
26521 Summit Cir, Santa Clarita (91350-3049)
PHONE.................................661 259-2737
Mauricio E Guardado Jr, *Principal*
Matt Stone, *General Mgr*
EMP: 160

SALES (corp-wide): 39.1MM **Privately Held**
SIC: 4941 Water supply
PA: Santa Clarita Valley Water Agency
27234 Bouquet Canyon Rd
Santa Clarita CA 91350
661 297-1600

(P-6118)
SANTA MARGARITA WATER DISTRICT (PA)
26111 Antonio Pkwy, Rcho STA Marg (92688-5596)
PHONE.................................949 459-6400
Daniel R Ferons, *Manager*
Justin McCusker, *Bd of Directors*
Laurel Haberchak, *Admin Sec*
Dustin Navarro, *Info Tech Mgr*
Nicole Stanfield, *Information Mgr*
EMP: 70
SQ FT: 5,600
SALES: 60MM **Privately Held**
WEB: www.smwd.com
SIC: 4941 4952 Water supply; sewerage systems

(P-6119)
SJW GROUP (PA)
110 W Taylor St, San Jose (95110-2131)
PHONE.................................408 279-7800
Eric W Thornburg, *Ch of Bd*
James P Lynch, *CFO*
Suzy Papazian, *Admin Sec*
Wendy Avila-Walker, *Controller*
EMP: 357
SALES: 397.7MM **Publicly Held**
WEB: www.sjwater.com
SIC: 4941 6531 Water supply; real estate agent, commercial

(P-6120)
SONOMA COUNTY WATER AGENCY
404 Aviation Blvd Ste 0, Santa Rosa (95403-9019)
PHONE.................................707 526-5370
Grant Davis, *General Mgr*
Ann Dubay, *Officer*
Ellen Simm, *Lab Dir*
Kevin Booker, *General Mgr*
Wendy Gjestland, *General Mgr*
EMP: 200 EST: 1950
SQ FT: 57,000
SALES: 43.9MM **Privately Held**
SIC: 4941 Water supply

(P-6121)
SOUTH COAST WATER DISTRICT (PA)
Also Called: SCWD
31592 West St, Laguna Beach (92651-6907)
P.O. Box 30205, Laguna Niguel (92607-0205)
PHONE.................................949 499-4555
Wayne Rayfield, *President*
Michele Collins, *Officer*
Joe McDivitt, *Officer*
Rober Moore, *Vice Pres*
Betty Burnett, *General Mgr*
EMP: 100
SQ FT: 8,400
SALES: 32.4MM **Privately Held**
WEB: www.scwd.org
SIC: 4941 1629 Water supply; waste water & sewage treatment plant construction

(P-6122)
SOUTH SAN JQUIN IRRIGATION DST
Also Called: Ssjid
11011 E Highway 120, Manteca (95336-9751)
P.O. Box 747, Ripon (95366-0747)
PHONE.................................209 249-4600
Betty Garcia, *Exec Sec*
Joe Hasten, *Division Mgr*
Collin Hodge, *Division Mgr*
Julie Jeleti, *Division Mgr*
Thomas Johnson, *Division Mgr*
EMP: 93
SQ FT: 8,500

SALES: 9.6MM **Privately Held**
WEB: www.ssjid.com
SIC: 4941 Water supply

(P-6123)
SWEETWATER AUTHORITY (PA)
505 Garrett Ave, Chula Vista (91910-5584)
P.O. Box 2328 (91912-2328)
PHONE.................................619 422-8395
Mark Rogers, *COO*
Margaret C Welsh, *President*
Andrew Reitzel, *Treasurer*
Maria Rubalcaba, *Bd of Directors*
Ron Morrison, *Vice Pres*
EMP: 112
SQ FT: 11,000
SALES: 53.4MM **Privately Held**
SIC: 4941 Water supply

(P-6124)
TUOLUMNE UTILITIES DISTRICT
Also Called: T U D
18885 Nugget Blvd, Sonora (95370-9284)
PHONE.................................209 532-5536
Pet Kampa, *General Mgr*
Edwin Pattison, *General Mgr*
Erik Johnson, *Engineer*
Glen Nunnelley, *Engineer*
Don Perkins, *Opers Staff*
EMP: 80
SQ FT: 6,000
SALES (est): 18MM **Privately Held**
WEB: www.tuolumneutilities.com
SIC: 4941 4952 Water supply; sewerage systems

(P-6125)
VALLEY CENTER MUNICIPAL
29300 Valley Center Rd, Valley Center (92082-6207)
P.O. Box 67 (92082-0067)
PHONE.................................760 735-4500
Gary Broomell, *President*
Bill Jeffrey, *CFO*
Robert A Polito, *Vice Pres*
Gary Arant, *General Mgr*
Kathy Stetson, *Admin Sec*
EMP: 69
SQ FT: 40,000
SALES (est): 19.3MM **Privately Held**
SIC: 4941 Water supply

(P-6126)
WALNUT VALLEY WATER DISTRICT
271 Brea Canyon Rd, Walnut (91789-3002)
P.O. Box 508 (91788-0508)
PHONE.................................909 595-7554
Theodore Ebenkamp, *President*
Scarlet Kwong, *Vice Pres*
Edwin Hilden, *Principal*
Michael Holmes, *General Mgr*
Sherry Shaw, *Engineer*
EMP: 55
SQ FT: 7,900
SALES: 38.2MM **Privately Held**
WEB: www.wvwd.com
SIC: 4941 Water supply

(P-6127)
YUCAIPA VALLEY WATER DISTRICT (PA)
12770 2nd St, Yucaipa (92399-5670)
P.O. Box 730 (92399-0730)
PHONE.................................909 797-5117
Bruce Granlund, *President*
Joan Cadiz, *Purch Agent*
EMP: 62
SQ FT: 2,500
SALES: 22.1MM **Privately Held**
SIC: 4941 Water supply

4952 Sewerage Systems

(P-6128)
BIG BEAR CITY CMNTY SVCS DST (PA)
Also Called: Bbccsd
139 E Big Bear Blvd, Big Bear City (92314-9130)
P.O. Box 558 (92314-0558)
PHONE.................................909 585-2565
Scott Heule, *General Mgr*

Nathan Zamorano, *Superintendent*
EMP: 63
SQ FT: 7,000
SALES (est): 9.4MM **Privately Held**
WEB: www.bbccsd.org
SIC: 4952 4941 4953 Sewerage systems; water supply; garbage: collecting, destroying & processing

(P-6129)
CENTRAL CONTRA COSTA SANIT
5019 Imhoff Pl, Martinez (94553-4316)
PHONE.................................925 228-9500
Roger Bailey, *General Mgr*
EMP: 99
SQ FT: 40,000
SALES (est): 23.9MM **Privately Held**
SIC: 4952 8699 Sewerage systems; charitable organization

(P-6130)
ENCINA WASTEWATER AUTHORITY
Also Called: Encina Water Pollution Control
6200 Avenida Encinas, Carlsbad (92011-1009)
PHONE.................................760 438-3941
Kevinmhardy, *Principal*
Donald Little, *Vice Pres*
Irek Wenske, *Vice Pres*
Kevin Hardy, *General Mgr*
Paula Clowar, *Executive Asst*
EMP: 52
SQ FT: 30,000
SALES (est): 19.3MM **Privately Held**
WEB: www.encinajpa.com
SIC: 4952 Sewerage systems

(P-6131)
MONTEREY ONE WATER (PA)
Also Called: MRWPCA
5 Harris Ct Bldg D, Monterey (93940-5756)
PHONE.................................831 372-3367
Keith Israel, *General Mgr*
Paul Sciuto, *General Mgr*
EMP: 80
SQ FT: 9,000
SALES: 31MM **Privately Held**
WEB: www.mrwpca.org
SIC: 4952 Sewerage systems

(P-6132)
NAPA SANITATION DISTRICT
1515 Soscol Ferry Rd, NAPA (94558-6247)
P.O. Box 2480 (94558-0522)
PHONE.................................707 254-9231
Tim Healy, *General Mgr*
John Cuevas, *CFO*
Elsa Seal, *Admin Asst*
Gamble Holley, *Project Mgr*
Andrew Damron, *Engineer*
EMP: 50 EST: 1945
SQ FT: 3,600
SALES: 33.5MM **Privately Held**
WEB: www.napasanitationdistrict.com
SIC: 4952 Sewerage systems

(P-6133)
OCCIDENTAL CNTY SANITATION DST
404 Aviation Blvd, Santa Rosa (95403-1069)
PHONE.................................707 547-1900
Grant Davis, *General Mgr*
Eric Wilhelm, *Info Tech Mgr*
Lynne Rosselli, *Accounts Mgr*
EMP: 99
SALES: 590.3K **Privately Held**
SIC: 4952 Sewerage systems

(P-6134)
ORANGE COUNTY SANITATION
22212 Brookhurst St, Huntington Beach (92646-8406)
PHONE.................................714 962-2411
Blake Anderson, *Manager*
EMP: 200
SALES (corp-wide): 315.4MM **Privately Held**
WEB: www.ocsd.com
SIC: 4952 Sewerage systems

PA: Orange County Sanitation District Financing Corporation
10844 Ellis Ave
Fountain Valley CA 92708
714 962-2411

(P-6135)
SACRAMENTO REG CO SANIT DIST
Sacramento Regional Waste
8521 Laguna Station Rd, Elk Grove (95758-9550)
PHONE..................916 875-9000
Ruben Robles, *Manager*
Jodie Sites, *Technician*
Chris Heikkila, *Technology*
AMI Patrick, *Engineer*
Dean Wyley, *Engineer*
EMP: 500
SALES (est): 37.5MM
SALES (corp-wide): 105.5MM **Privately Held**
SIC: 4952 Sewerage systems
PA: Sacramento Regional County Sanitation District
10060 Goethe Rd
Sacramento CA 95827
916 876-6000

(P-6136)
SILICON VALLEY CLEAN WATER
Also Called: SBSA
1400 Radio Rd, Redwood City (94065-1220)
PHONE..................650 591-7121
Ronald W Shepherd, *Principal*
Daniel T Child, *Manager*
EMP: 79 **EST:** 1975
SQ FT: 180,000
SALES: 45MM **Privately Held**
WEB: www.sbsa.org
SIC: 4952 Sewerage systems

(P-6137)
SONOMA VLY CNTY SANITATION DST
404 Aviation Blvd, Santa Rosa (95403-1069)
PHONE..................707 547-1900
Grant Davis, *General Mgr*
Lynne Rosselli, *Accounting Mgr*
David Rabbitt, *Supervisor*
EMP: 200
SALES: 14.5MM **Privately Held**
SIC: 4952 Sewerage systems

(P-6138)
SOUTH TAHOE PUBLIC UTILITY DST
1275 Meadow Crest Dr, South Lake Tahoe (96150-7401)
PHONE..................530 544-6474
Richard Solbrig, *General Mgr*
Paul Hughes, *CFO*
Paul Sciuto, *Principal*
Star Glaze, *Administration*
Delores Trebotich, *Technician*
EMP: 113
SALES: 26.2MM **Privately Held**
WEB: www.stpud.dst.ca.us
SIC: 4952 Sewerage systems; water supply

(P-6139)
STREET AND SEWER YARD CORP
Also Called: Public Work Dept
1361 N Carolan Ave, Burlingame (94010-2401)
PHONE..................650 696-7260
EMP: 50
SALES (est): 650.4K **Privately Held**
SIC: 4952 Sewerage systems

(P-6140)
TAHOE-TRUCKEE SANITATION AGCY
Also Called: TTSA
13720 Butterfield Dr, Truckee (96161-3316)
PHONE..................530 587-2525
Marcia Beals, *General Mgr*
Michael Peak, *Vice Pres*
Laura Mader, *Lab Dir*
Larue Griffin, *General Mgr*

Robert Gray, *Info Tech Mgr*
▲ **EMP:** 59 **EST:** 1972
SQ FT: 500,083
SALES: 12.5MM **Privately Held**
WEB: www.ttsa.net
SIC: 4952 Sewerage systems

(P-6141)
UNION SANITARY DISTRICT
Also Called: Usd
5072 Benson Rd, Union City (94587-2508)
PHONE..................510 477-7500
Paul Eldredge, *General Mgr*
Armando Lopez, *Opers Mgr*
Robert Simonich, *Maintence Staff*
Manny Fernandez,
Tom Handley,
▲ **EMP:** 130
SALES: 51.9MM **Privately Held**
WEB: www.unionsanitary.com
SIC: 4952 Sewerage systems

(P-6142)
VALLEY CENTER MUNICPL WTR DST
29300 Valley Center Rd, Valley Center (92082-6207)
PHONE..................760 735-4500
Gary Broomell, *President*
Gary Arant, *General Mgr*
Marlene Martinez, *Technician*
Wally Grabbe, *Engineer*
Jim Pugh, *Finance*
EMP: 64
SQ FT: 5,000
SALES (est): 492.5K **Privately Held**
SIC: 4952 4941 Sewerage systems; water supply

4953 Refuse Systems

(P-6143)
AER ELECTRONICS INC (PA)
Also Called: Aerelectronics
42744 Boscell Rd, Fremont (94538-5132)
PHONE..................510 300-0500
Andre Weiglein, *President*
William Schoening, *CFO*
John Dickenson, *Vice Pres*
Janet Rianda, *Vice Pres*
James Quintal, *Admin Sec*
▲ **EMP:** 55
SQ FT: 75,000
SALES (est): 38.4MM **Privately Held**
WEB: www.aerworldwide.com
SIC: 4953 5093 Recycling, waste materials; scrap & waste materials

(P-6144)
ALAMEDA COUNTY INDUSTRIES INC
610 Aladdin Ave, San Leandro (94577-4302)
PHONE..................510 357-7282
Louis Pellegrini, *Exec VP*
Robert Molinaro, *CEO*
Kent Kenney, *CFO*
Jason Dobert, *Sales Staff*
Carrie Dobert, *Manager*
EMP: 50
SQ FT: 39,648
SALES (est): 9.7MM **Privately Held**
WEB: www.alamedacountyindustries.com
SIC: 4953 Rubbish collection & disposal

(P-6145)
ALEMEDA COUNTY INDUSTRIES LLC
610 Aladdin Ave, San Leandro (94577-4302)
PHONE..................510 357-7282
Robert Molinaro,
Brenda Perez, *Opers Staff*
EMP: 70 **EST:** 1999
SQ FT: 5,400
SALES (est): 5.7MM **Privately Held**
SIC: 4953 Refuse systems

(P-6146)
ANTELOPE VALLEY RECYCLING
Also Called: Arklin Brothers Hauling
1200 W City Ranch Rd, Palmdale (93551-4456)
PHONE..................661 945-5944

Lee Hicks, *Principal*
EMP: 99
SALES (est): 33.6MM
SALES (corp-wide): 14.9B **Publicly Held**
SIC: 4953 Refuse systems
PA: Waste Management, Inc.
1001 Fannin St Ste 4000
Houston TX 77002
713 512-6200

(P-6147)
APPLIANCE RECYCLING CTRS AMER
Also Called: Arca Los Angeles
1920 S Acacia Ave, Compton (90220-4945)
PHONE..................310 223-2800
Edward Cameron, *President*
EMP: 64
SQ FT: 40,000
SALES (est): 7.6MM
SALES (corp-wide): 36.7MM **Publicly Held**
WEB: www.arcainc.com
SIC: 4953 Recycling, waste materials
PA: Janone Inc.
325 E Warm Springs Rd
Las Vegas NV 89119
952 930-9000

(P-6148)
ARACO ENTERPRISES LLC
Also Called: Athens Environmental Services
9189 De Garmo Ave, Sun Valley (91352-2609)
PHONE..................818 767-0675
Ronald Krall,
Michael R Arakelian,
EMP: 400 **EST:** 2017
SALES (est): 2.5MM **Privately Held**
SIC: 4953 Garbage: collecting, destroying & processing

(P-6149)
ARAKELIAN ENTERPRISES INC
Also Called: Athens Services
15045 Salt Lake Ave, City of Industry (91746-3315)
PHONE..................626 336-3636
Ron Arakelian Jr, *Owner*
Steven Estrada, *Sales Staff*
David Miramontes, *Supervisor*
EMP: 417
SALES (corp-wide): 181.5MM **Privately Held**
SIC: 4953 Rubbish collection & disposal; street refuse systems
PA: Arakelian Enterprises, Inc.
14048 Valley Blvd
City Of Industry CA 91746
626 336-3636

(P-6150)
ARAKELIAN ENTERPRISES INC
687 Iowa Ave, Riverside (92507-1610)
PHONE..................951 342-3300
Sal Orozco, *Manager*
EMP: 208
SALES (corp-wide): 181.5MM **Privately Held**
SIC: 4953 Recycling, waste materials; hazardous waste collection & disposal
PA: Arakelian Enterprises, Inc.
14048 Valley Blvd
City Of Industry CA 91746
626 336-3636

(P-6151)
ARAKELIAN ENTERPRISES INC (PA)
Also Called: Athens Services
14048 Valley Blvd, City of Industry (91746-2801)
P.O. Box 60009 (91716-0009)
PHONE..................626 336-3636
Ron Arakelian Jr, *CEO*
Michael Arakelian, *CEO*
Gary Clifford, *COO*
Kevin Hanifin, *CFO*
Harry Kazarian, *Officer*
EMP: 125
SQ FT: 10,000
SALES (est): 181.5MM **Privately Held**
WEB: www.athensservices.com
SIC: 4953 Rubbish collection & disposal; street refuse systems

(P-6152)
ARROW DISPOSAL SERVICES INC
14332 Valley Blvd, La Puente (91746-2931)
P.O. Box 2917 (91746-0917)
PHONE..................626 336-2255
Kirk Tahmizian, *President*
EMP: 50
SQ FT: 40,000
SALES: 10MM **Privately Held**
SIC: 4953 Garbage: collecting, destroying & processing

(P-6153)
ASCON RECYCLING CO
17671 Bear Valley Rd, Hesperia (92345-4902)
PHONE..................760 948-1538
John Hove, *President*
EMP: 250
SALES (est): 5.3MM **Privately Held**
SIC: 4953 Recycling, waste materials

(P-6154)
ATHENS DISPOSAL COMPANY INC (PA)
14048 Valley Blvd, La Puente (91746-2801)
P.O. Box 60009, City of Industry (91716-0009)
PHONE..................626 336-3636
Ron Arakelian Sr, *President*
Ron Arakelian Jr, *Vice Pres*
David Patterson, *CIO*
EMP: 350
SALES (est): 261.4MM **Privately Held**
SIC: 4953 Rubbish collection & disposal

(P-6155)
ATLAS DISPOSAL INDUSTRIES LLC
3000 Power Inn Rd, Sacramento (95826-3801)
PHONE..................916 455-2800
Dave Sikich, *CEO*
Nick Sikich, *COO*
Steven Bruce, *Vice Pres*
Robin Stuhr, *Controller*
Art Flores, *Sales Mgr*
EMP: 70
SALES (est): 17.7MM **Privately Held**
WEB: www.atlasdisposal.com
SIC: 4953 Garbage: collecting, destroying & processing; refuse collection & disposal services

(P-6156)
AUBURN PLACER DISPOSAL SERVICE
Also Called: Auburn-Placer Recycling Center
12305 Shale Ridge Ln, Auburn (95602-8879)
P.O. Box 6566 (95604-6566)
PHONE..................530 885-3735
Michael Sangiacomo, *President*
Mark Lomele, *Vice Pres*
EMP: 80
SQ FT: 2,200
SALES (est): 7.4MM
SALES (corp-wide): 1.4B **Privately Held**
WEB: www.auburnplacer.com
SIC: 4953 Recycling, waste materials
PA: Recology Inc.
50 California St Ste 2400
San Francisco CA 94111
415 875-1000

(P-6157)
BAY AREA CONCRETE LLC
24701 Clawiter Rd, Hayward (94545-2225)
PHONE..................510 294-0220
Preet Johal,
EMP: 100
SALES (est): 159K **Privately Held**
SIC: 4953 Recycling, waste materials

(P-6158)
BAY COUNTIES WASTE SVCS INC
Also Called: Specialty Solid Waste & Recycl
3355 Thomas Rd, Santa Clara (95054-2060)
PHONE..................408 565-9900

Robert J Molinaro, *CEO*
William Dobert, *CFO*
Douglas Button, *Treasurer*
Nick Nabhan, *General Mgr*
Jerry Nabhan, *Admin Sec*
▲ **EMP:** 80 **EST:** 1930
SQ FT: 2,000
SALES (est): 18.5MM **Privately Held**
WEB: www.sswr.com
SIC: 4953 Recycling, waste materials

(P-6159)
BERTOLOTTIS CERES DISPOSAL
231 Flamingo Rd, Ceres (95307)
P.O. Box 127 (95307-0127)
PHONE............................209 537-8000
Bert Bertolotti, *President*
Steve Holloway, *General Mgr*
EMP: 74
SALES (est): 7.3MM **Privately Held**
SIC: 4953 Garbage: collecting, destroying & processing

(P-6160)
BEST WAY DISPOSAL CO INC
Also Called: Advance Disposal Company
17105 Mesa St, Hesperia (92345-5155)
P.O. Box 400997 (92340-0997)
PHONE............................760 244-9773
Robert Bath, *Ch of Bd*
Sheila Bath, *President*
EMP: 56
SALES (est): 15.2MM **Privately Held**
WEB: www.advancedisposal.com
SIC: 4953 Rubbish collection & disposal

(P-6161)
BFI WASTE SERVICES LLC
5501 N Golden State Blvd, Fresno (93722-5021)
PHONE............................559 275-1551
Keith Hester, *General Mgr*
EMP: 70
SALES (corp-wide): 10B **Publicly Held**
WEB: www.sunsetwaste.com
SIC: 4953 Refuse systems
HQ: Bfi Waste Services, Llc
18500 N Allied Way # 100
Phoenix AZ 85054
480 627-2700

(P-6162)
BFI WASTE SYSTEMS N AMER INC
Also Called: Site 910
800 Cacique St, Santa Barbara (93103-3622)
P.O. Box 4010 (93140-4010)
PHONE............................805 965-5248
Darryl Reno, *General Mgr*
EMP: 82
SALES (corp-wide): 10B **Publicly Held**
WEB: www.mjes.com
SIC: 4953 Garbage: collecting, destroying & processing; street refuse systems
HQ: Bfi Waste Systems Of North America, Inc.
2394 E Camelback Rd
Phoenix AZ 85016

(P-6163)
BFI WASTE SYSTEMS N AMER INC
Also Called: Republic Services
271 Rianda St, Salinas (93901-3725)
PHONE............................831 775-3850
Doug Kenyon, *Manager*
EMP: 54
SALES (corp-wide): 10B **Publicly Held**
WEB: www.mjes.com
SIC: 4953 Garbage: collecting, destroying & processing
HQ: Bfi Waste Systems Of North America, Inc.
2394 E Camelback Rd
Phoenix AZ 85016

(P-6164)
BFI WASTE SYSTEMS N AMER INC
Also Called: Site 916
42600 Boyce Rd, Fremont (94538-3131)
P.O. Box 5013 (94537-5013)
PHONE............................510 657-1350
Fred Penning, *Manager*
EMP: 95
SALES (corp-wide): 10B **Publicly Held**
WEB: www.mjes.com
SIC: 4953 4212 Refuse collection & disposal services; local trucking, without storage
HQ: Bfi Waste Systems Of North America, Inc.
2394 E Camelback Rd
Phoenix AZ 85016

(P-6165)
BISHOP WASTE DISPOSAL INC
100 Snland Reservation Rd, Bishop (93514)
PHONE............................760 872-6561
George Kelley, *President*
EMP: 50
SQ FT: 7,300
SALES (est): 3.7MM **Privately Held**
SIC: 4953 4952 Garbage: collecting, destroying & processing; sewerage systems

(P-6166)
BKK CORPORATION (PA)
2210 S Azusa Ave, West Covina (91792-1510)
PHONE............................626 965-0911
Fax: 626 965-9569
EMP: 57
SALES (est): 22.2MM **Privately Held**
SIC: 4953

(P-6167)
BROWNING-FERRIS INDUSTRIES INC
Solid Waste Division
9200 Glenoaks Blvd, Sun Valley (91352-2613)
PHONE............................818 790-5410
Pat Gavin, *Manager*
EMP: 140
SALES (corp-wide): 10B **Publicly Held**
SIC: 4953 Rubbish collection & disposal
HQ: Browning-Ferris Industries, Llc
18500 N Allied Way # 100
Phoenix AZ 85054
480 627-2700

(P-6168)
BROWNING-FERRIS INDUSTRIES LLC
Also Called: Site R45
1601 Dixon Landing Rd, Milpitas (95035-8100)
PHONE............................408 262-1401
Gil Cheso, *Manager*
EMP: 65
SALES (corp-wide): 10B **Publicly Held**
WEB: www.alliedwaste.com
SIC: 4953 Refuse collection & disposal services
HQ: Browning-Ferris Industries, Llc
18500 N Allied Way # 100
Phoenix AZ 85054
480 627-2700

(P-6169)
BURRTEC WASTE INDUSTRIES INC (HQ)
9890 Cherry Ave, Fontana (92335-5298)
PHONE............................909 429-4200
Cole Burr, *President*
Trevor Scrogins, *Vice Pres*
Alfonso Arias, *Division Mgr*
Nick Burciaga, *Division Mgr*
Octavio Camacho, *Division Mgr*
▲ **EMP:** 150
SQ FT: 10,000
SALES (est): 305.6MM
SALES (corp-wide): 309.8MM **Privately Held**
WEB: www.burrtec.com
SIC: 4953 4212 Rubbish collection & disposal; recycling, waste materials; local trucking, without storage

PA: Burrtec Waste Group, Inc.
9890 Cherry Ave
Fontana CA 92335
909 429-4200

(P-6170)
CACTUS RECYCLING INC (PA)
8710 Avenida Fuente, San Diego (92154)
PHONE............................619 661-1283
Edward M Fitch III, *President*
Richard Russell, *Vice Pres*
Steve Russell, *Vice Pres*
Steven Russell, *Vice Pres*
EMP: 125
SQ FT: 4,000
SALES (est): 13.8MM **Privately Held**
WEB: www.cactusrecycling.com
SIC: 4953 Recycling, waste materials

(P-6171)
CALIFORNIA MARINE CLEANING INC (PA)
2049 Main St, San Diego (92113-2216)
P.O. Box 13653 (92170-3653)
PHONE............................619 231-8788
Matthew R Carr, *President*
Hazel Carr, *CFO*
EMP: 160
SQ FT: 10,000
SALES (est): 25.7MM **Privately Held**
WEB: www.calmarineinc.com
SIC: 4953 Hazardous waste collection & disposal

(P-6172)
CALIFORNIA WASTE SERVICES LLC
621 W 152nd St, Gardena (90247-2732)
PHONE............................310 538-5998
Eric Casper, *President*
Oscar Cruel, *Accounting Mgr*
Ricardo Vallejo, *Human Resources*
Giovanni Lopez, *Opers Mgr*
EMP: 120
SQ FT: 20,000
SALES (est): 27.5MM **Privately Held**
WEB: www.californiawasteservices.com
SIC: 4953 Refuse collection & disposal services

(P-6173)
CALIFORNIA WASTE SOLUTIONS INC
1820 10th St, Oakland (94607-1450)
PHONE............................408 292-0830
David Duong, *President*
EMP: 75 **Privately Held**
WEB: www.calwaste.com
SIC: 4953 Garbage: collecting, destroying & processing
PA: California Waste Solutions Inc.
1005 Timothy Dr
San Jose CA 95133

(P-6174)
CALIFORNIA WASTE SOLUTIONS INC (PA)
1005 Timothy Dr, San Jose (95133-1043)
PHONE............................510 832-8111
David Duong, *CEO*
Victor Duong, *Vice Pres*
Kristina Duong, *Exec Dir*
Linda Duong, *Admin Sec*
Sherri Ornelas, *Admin Asst*
◆ **EMP:** 75
SQ FT: 120,000
SALES (est): 61.7MM **Privately Held**
WEB: www.calwaste.com
SIC: 4953 Garbage: collecting, destroying & processing

(P-6175)
CALMET INC (PA)
Also Called: Metropolitan Waste Disposal
7202 Petterson Ln, Paramount (90723-2022)
PHONE............................323 721-8120
Thomas K Blackman, *President*
Gary Kazarian, *Treasurer*
William Kalpakoff, *Vice Pres*
Kris Kazarian, *Admin Sec*
EMP: 180
SQ FT: 38,000

SALES (est): 54.2MM **Privately Held**
WEB: www.calmet.com
SIC: 4953 4212 Rubbish collection & disposal; recycling, waste materials; local trucking, without storage

(P-6176)
CARAUSTAR INDUSTRIES INC
Newark Recovery & Recycling
2800 W March Ln Ste 480, Stockton (95219-8220)
PHONE............................209 476-7710
Crawford Carpenter, *Manager*
Kabrina Cabalar, *Admin Asst*
EMP: 120
SALES (corp-wide): 3.8B **Publicly Held**
SIC: 4953 Recycling, waste materials
HQ: Caraustar Industries, Inc.
5000 Austell Powder Sprin
Austell GA 30106
770 948-3101

(P-6177)
CASTLE & COOKE CALIFORNIA INC
10000 Stockdale Hwy # 300, Bakersfield (93311-3604)
P.O. Box 11165 (93389-1165)
PHONE............................661 664-6500
Bruce Freeman, *President*
Edward C Roohan, *Treasurer*
Bruce Davis, *Vice Pres*
Takashi Fujii, *Vice Pres*
Robert W Hibbs, *Vice Pres*
EMP: 50
SALES (est): 5.9MM
SALES (corp-wide): 893.5MM **Privately Held**
WEB: www.sevenoaksrealestate.com
SIC: 4953 Sanitary landfill operation
PA: Castle & Cooke, Inc.
1 Dole Dr
Westlake Village CA 91362

(P-6178)
CEDARWOOD-YOUNG COMPANY (PA)
Also Called: Allan Company
14620 Joanbridge St, Baldwin Park (91706-1750)
PHONE............................626 962-4047
Jason Young, *President*
Michael Ochniak, *CFO*
Stephen Young, *Chairman*
Francisco Del Rincon, *Vice Pres*
Yun Koo, *Vice Pres*
◆ **EMP:** 175
SQ FT: 4,350
SALES: 299.9MM **Privately Held**
WEB: www.allancompany.com
SIC: 4953 Recycling, waste materials

(P-6179)
CHEMICAL WASTE MANAGEMENT INC
35251 Old Skyline Rd, Kettleman City (93239-4534)
P.O. Box 471 (93239-0471)
PHONE............................559 386-9711
Robert Henry, *Manager*
EMP: 80
SQ FT: 5,000
SALES (corp-wide): 14.9B **Publicly Held**
WEB: www.wastemanagement.com
SIC: 4953 Non-hazardous waste disposal sites
HQ: Chemical Waste Management, Inc.
1001 Fannin St Ste 4000
Houston TX 77002
713 512-6200

(P-6180)
CHINO VALLEY SAWDUST INC
Also Called: Chino Valley Rock
13434 S Ontario Ave, Ontario (91761-7956)
PHONE............................909 947-5983
Brigiette Delaura, *President*
Mary W Hebb, *Treasurer*
EMP: 75
SALES (est): 3.5MM **Privately Held**
SIC: 4953 Recycling, waste materials

(P-6181)
CITY OF LEMOORE
Also Called: Refuse Department
711 W Cinnamon Dr, Lemoore
(93245-9142)
PHONE...................559 924-6744
David Wlaschin, *Director*
EMP: 50 **Privately Held**
SIC: 4953 Refuse systems
PA: City Of Lemoore
119 Fox St
Lemoore CA 93245
559 924-6700

(P-6182)
CITY OF POMONA
Also Called: Pomona City Refuse Collection
636 W Monterey Ave, Pomona
(91768-3527)
PHONE...................909 620-2361
Henry Pepper, *Manager*
EMP: 132 **Privately Held**
SIC: 4953 Refuse collection & disposal
services
PA: Pomona, City Of (Inc)
585 E Holt Ave
Pomona CA 91766
909 620-2051

(P-6183)
CITY OF REDLANDS
Also Called: Purchasing Department
35 Cajon St, Redlands (92373-4746)
PHONE...................909 798-7525
Gary Vendorst, *Manager*
EMP: 50
SALES (corp-wide): 79MM **Privately
Held**
WEB: www.akspl.org
SIC: 4953 Refuse collection & disposal
services
PA: City Of Redlands
35 Cajon St
Redlands CA 92373
909 798-7531

(P-6184)
CITY OF TULARE
3981 S K St, Tulare (93274-7189)
PHONE...................559 684-4200
Kevin Northcraft, *Manager*
EMP: 60 **Privately Held**
WEB: www.ci.tulare.ca.us
SIC: 4953 Refuse collection & disposal
services
PA: City Of Tulare
411 E Kern Ave
Tulare CA 93274
559 685-2300

(P-6185)
CIVICORPS
6315 San Leandro St, Oakland
(94621-3727)
PHONE...................510 992-7800
Bill Zenoni, *Branch Mgr*
Aakash Desai, *Director*
EMP: 184
SALES (corp-wide): 8.2MM **Privately
Held**
SIC: 4953 Recycling, waste materials
PA: Civicorps
101 Myrtle St
Oakland CA 94607
510 992-7800

(P-6186)
COAST WASTE MANAGEMENT
5960 El Camino Real, Carlsbad
(92008-8802)
PHONE...................760 753-9412
Arie De Jong, *Director*
Conrad B Pawelski, *President*
Margaret Bierd, *Admin Sec*
Arie D Jong, *Director*
EMP: 180
SQ FT: 3,000
SALES (est): 61.2MM
SALES (corp-wide): 14.9B **Publicly Held**
SIC: 4953 Rubbish collection & disposal
PA: Waste Management, Inc.
1001 Fannin St Ste 4000
Houston TX 77002
713 512-6200

(P-6187)
COMMODITY RESOURCE ENVMTL INC (PA)
Also Called: Cre
116 E Prospect Ave, Burbank
(91502-2035)
PHONE...................818 843-2811
Larry J Dewitt, *President*
Don Buckles, *Vice Pres*
Chuck Yohn, *VP Sales*
Jim Ferns, *Sales Staff*
Sandra Murguia, *Manager*
▲ **EMP:** 55
SQ FT: 10,000
SALES (est): 7.9MM **Privately Held**
SIC: 4953 Recycling, waste materials

(P-6188)
CORRIDOR RECYCLING INC
22500 S Alameda St, Long Beach
(90810-1905)
PHONE...................310 835-3849
Gilbert Dodson, *President*
Steve Young, *Vice Pres*
Mark Tranckino, *CPA*
▲ **EMP:** 52
SQ FT: 13,594
SALES (est): 10.1MM **Privately Held**
WEB: www.corridorrecycling.com
SIC: 4953 5941 5093 Recycling, waste
materials; sporting goods & bicycle
shops; metal scrap & waste materials

(P-6189)
COUNTY OF EL DORADO
Also Called: Waste Connections
3940 Hwy 49, Diamond Springs (95619)
PHONE...................530 626-4141
Sue Farris, *Manager*
EMP: 93 **Privately Held**
WEB: www.filmtahoe.com
SIC: 4953 Garbage: collecting, destroying
& processing
PA: County Of El Dorado
330 Fair Ln
Placerville CA 95667
530 621-5830

(P-6190)
COUNTY OF ORANGE
Also Called: Oc Waste & Recycling
300 N Sunflower Ste 400, Santa Ana
(92703)
PHONE...................714 834-4000
Mike Giancola, *Manager*
EMP: 350 **Privately Held**
SIC: 4953 Recycling, waste materials
PA: County Of Orange
333 W Santa Ana Blvd 3f
Santa Ana CA 92701
714 834-6200

(P-6191)
COUNTY SANTTN DIST 2 OF LA CO
Also Called: Puente Hills Landfill
2800 Workman Mill Rd, Whittier
(90601-1548)
P.O. Box 4998 (90607-4998)
PHONE...................562 699-5204
Grace Han, *Chief*
Howard Wolfer, *Technical Staff*
Beth Tan, *Purch Mgr*
EMP: 100
SALES (corp-wide): 1.1B **Privately Held**
SIC: 4953 9511 Sanitary landfill operation;
PA: County Sanitation District No. 2 Of Los
Angeles County
1955 Workman Mill Rd
Whittier CA 90601
562 699-7411

(P-6192)
CROWN DISPOSAL COMPANY INC
Also Called: Coastal Rubbish
9189 De Garmo Ave, Sun Valley
(91352-2609)
P.O. Box 1063 (91353-1063)
PHONE...................818 767-0675
Thomas H Fry, *CEO*
John Richardson, *Treasurer*
EMP: 200
SQ FT: 12,000

SALES (est): 42.3MM **Privately Held**
WEB: www.crowndisposal.com
SIC: 4953 Rubbish collection & disposal

(P-6193)
DESERT RECYCLING INC
17105 Mesa St, Hesperia (92345-5155)
P.O. Box 400725 (92340-0725)
PHONE...................760 948-3122
Sheila Bath, *President*
EMP: 50
SALES (est): 1.8MM **Privately Held**
SIC: 4953 5093 Recycling, waste materi-
als; metal scrap & waste materials

(P-6194)
E J HARRISON & SONS INC
Also Called: Harrison, E J & Sons Recycling
1589 Lirio Ave, Ventura (93004-3227)
PHONE...................805 647-1414
Ken Keys, *General Mgr*
David Tripp, *Data Proc Staff*
David Harrison, *Sales Mgr*
EMP: 175
SALES (corp-wide): 90.7MM **Privately
Held**
WEB: www.ejharrison.com
SIC: 4953 2611 Rubbish collection & dis-
posal; pulp mills
PA: E. J. Harrison & Sons, Inc.
5275 Colt St
Ventura CA 93003
805 647-1414

(P-6195)
EARTH TECHNOLOGY CORP USA
1999 Avenue Of, Los Angeles (90067)
PHONE...................213 593-8000
Michael S Burke, *Ch of Bd*
EMP: 4655
SALES (est): 673K
SALES (corp-wide): 20.1B **Publicly Held**
SIC: 4953 8748 8742 8711 Refuse sys-
tems; environmental consultant; manage-
ment consulting services; engineering
services
PA: Aecom
1999 Avenue Of The Stars # 2600
Los Angeles CA 90067
213 593-8000

(P-6196)
EAST BAY MUNICIPL UTILTY DISTR
Also Called: Ebmud
2020 Wake Ave, Oakland (94607-5100)
PHONE...................866 403-2683
Alexander Coate, *General Mgr*
EMP: 70
SALES (corp-wide): 599.1MM **Privately
Held**
SIC: 4953 9511 ;
PA: East Bay Municipal Utility District,
Water System
375 11th St
Oakland CA 94607
866 403-2683

(P-6197)
ECS REFINING INC
2222 S Sinclair Ave, Stockton
(95215-7551)
PHONE...................209 774-5000
Jack Rockwood, *President*
Mark Robards, *Vice Pres*
Jim Taggart, *Principal*
Ken Taggart, *Principal*
Mark Verheyden, *Principal*
EMP: 250
SQ FT: 40,000
SALES (est): 5.1MM **Privately Held**
SIC: 4953 Recycling, waste materials

(P-6198)
ECULLET INC
1 Vintage Ct, Woodside (94062-2560)
PHONE...................650 493-7300
Craig J London, *CEO*
Mark D Muenchow, *CFO*
Farook Afsari, *Chairman*
Kasra Khazeni, *Vice Pres*
Dr Yue Min Wong, *Director*
EMP: 100 **EST:** 1999
SALES (est): 3MM **Privately Held**
SIC: 4953 Recycling, waste materials

(P-6199)
EDCO DISPOSAL CORPORATION INC
Also Called: Park Disposal Service
6762 Stanton Ave, Buena Park
(90621-3611)
P.O. Box 398 (90621-0398)
PHONE...................714 522-3577
Efrain Ramirez, *Manager*
Mark Billings, *Sales Staff*
EMP: 70
SALES (corp-wide): 145.2MM **Privately
Held**
SIC: 4953 Rubbish collection & disposal
PA: Edco Disposal Corporation Inc.
2755 California Ave
Signal Hill CA 90755
619 287-7555

(P-6200)
EDCO WASTE & RECYCL SVCS INC (HQ)
Also Called: Solid Waste Services
224 S Las Posas Rd, San Marcos
(92078-2421)
PHONE...................760 744-2700
Steve South, *CEO*
Edward Burr, *President*
Sandra Burr, *Corp Secy*
Jeffrey Ritchie, *Vice Pres*
EMP: 74 **EST:** 1954
SQ FT: 37,000
SALES (est): 138.9MM
SALES (corp-wide): 145.2MM **Privately
Held**
SIC: 4953 4212 Rubbish collection & dis-
posal; garbage: collecting, destroying &
processing; local trucking, without storage
PA: Edco Disposal Corporation Inc.
2755 California Ave
Signal Hill CA 90755
619 287-7555

(P-6201)
ELECTRONIC RECYCLERS
7815 N Palm Ave Ste 140, Fresno
(93711-5531)
PHONE...................253 736-2627
John Shegerian, *President*
Tammy Shegerian, *Treasurer*
Linda Ramos, *Admin Sec*
EMP: 99
SALES (est): 5.6MM
SALES (corp-wide): 529.1MM **Privately
Held**
SIC: 4953 Non-hazardous waste disposal
sites
PA: Electronic Recyclers International Inc.
7815 N Palm Ave Ste 140
Fresno CA 93711
800 374-3473

(P-6202)
ELECTRONIC RECYCLERS INTL INC (PA)
Also Called: Electronic Recyclers America
7815 N Palm Ave Ste 140, Fresno
(93711-5531)
PHONE...................800 374-3473
John S Shegerian, *CEO*
Dann V Angeloff, *President*
Kelly Thomas, *COO*
James Kim, *CFO*
Rich Calzada, *Officer*
▲ **EMP:** 111
SQ FT: 75,000
SALES (est): 529.1MM **Privately Held**
SIC: 4953 Recycling, waste materials

(P-6203)
EMPIRE DISPOSAL LLC
Also Called: Curran's Disposal
5455 Industrial Pkwy, San Bernardino
(92407-1803)
PHONE...................909 797-9125
Cole Burr,
EMP: 50
SALES (est): 1.8MM
SALES (corp-wide): 309.8MM **Privately
Held**
SIC: 4953 4212 Garbage: collecting, de-
stroying & processing; local trucking, with-
out storage

PA: Burrtec Waste Group, Inc.
9890 Cherry Ave
Fontana CA 92335
909 429-4200

(P-6204)
FAIRFIELD-SUISUN SEWER DST
1010 Chadbourne Rd, Fairfield
(94534-9700)
PHONE..................707 429-8930
Richard F Luthy Jr, *General Mgr*
EMP: 65
SQ FT: 15,000
SALES: 24.9MM **Privately Held**
WEB: www.fssd.com
SIC: 4953 Refuse collection & disposal
services

(P-6205)
FLAT WHITE ECONOMY INV USA LLC
5151 Cal Ave Ste 100, Costa Mesa
(92626)
PHONE..................949 344-5013
Ionut Georgescu, *CEO*
EMP: 165
SALES: 1MM **Privately Held**
SIC: 4953 Recycling, waste materials

(P-6206)
FOOTHILL WASTE RECLAMATION INC
12221 Lopez Canyon Rd, Sylmar
(91342-5730)
P.O. Box 923637 (91392-3637)
PHONE..................818 897-5099
Kevork Sarkisian, *President*
Dick Sarkisian, *Vice Pres*
EMP: 55
SQ FT: 2,500
SALES (est): 3.1MM **Privately Held**
SIC: 4953 Recycling, waste materials

(P-6207)
GI INDUSTRIES
195 W Los Angeles Ave, Simi Valley
(93065-1651)
P.O. Box 940430 (93094-0430)
PHONE..................805 522-2150
Michael Smith, *Senior VP*
EMP: 100
SQ FT: 7,000
SALES (est): 34MM
SALES (corp-wide): 14.9B **Publicly Held**
WEB: www.wm.com
SIC: 4953 4212 Garbage: collecting, de-
stroying & processing; recycling, waste
materials; local trucking, without storage
PA: Waste Management, Inc.
1001 Fannin St Ste 4000
Houston TX 77002
713 512-6200

(P-6208)
GILTON RESOURCE RECOVERY
755 S Yosemite Ave, Oakdale
(95361-4039)
PHONE..................209 527-3781
Richard Gilton, *President*
Tedford Gilton, *Vice Pres*
Karen Gilton Hardister, *Vice Pres*
Donna Love, *Vice Pres*
EMP: 55
SALES (est): 5.5MM **Privately Held**
SIC: 4953 Recycling, waste materials

(P-6209)
GILTON SOLID WASTE MGT INC
755 S Yosemite Ave, Oakdale
(95361-4991)
PHONE..................209 527-3781
Richard Gilton, *President*
Tedford Gilton, *Vice Pres*
Karen Gilton Hardister, *Vice Pres*
Karen Hardister, *Vice Pres*
Donna Gilton Love, *Vice Pres*
EMP: 136
SQ FT: 3,000
SALES (est): 41.4MM **Privately Held**
WEB: www.gilton.com
SIC: 4953 Rubbish collection & disposal;
recycling, waste materials

(P-6210)
GREENWASTE RECOVERY INC
565 Charles St, San Jose (95112-1402)
PHONE..................408 283-4804
Chris Almeida, *Manager*
EMP: 50
SQ FT: 7,050 **Privately Held**
SIC: 4953 Garbage: collecting, destroying
& processing
PA: Greenwaste Recovery, Inc.
1500 Berger Dr
Watsonville CA 95077

(P-6211)
GREENWASTE RECOVERY INC (PA)
1500 Berger Dr, Watsonville (95077)
P.O. Box 2347 (95077-2347)
PHONE..................408 283-4800
Richard Christina, *President*
Don Dean, *CFO*
Dave Tilton, *CFO*
Jesse Weigel, *Corp Secy*
Murray Hall, *Vice Pres*
EMP: 88
SQ FT: 115,000
SALES (est): 100.5MM **Privately Held**
SIC: 4953 Rubbish collection & disposal;
waste materials, disposal at sea

(P-6212)
HAZMAT TSDF INC (PA)
180 W Monte Ave, Rialto (92376)
PHONE..................909 873-4141
Jon L Bennett Jr, *President*
Jim Arnold, *Treasurer*
Jim Goyich, *Vice Pres*
Dianna Vepeda, *Admin Sec*
▲ **EMP:** 63
SQ FT: 33,000
SALES (est): 59MM **Privately Held**
WEB: www.filterrecycling.com
SIC: 4953 Hazardous waste collection &
disposal

(P-6213)
IMS RECYCLING SERVICES INC (PA)
2697 Main St, San Diego (92113-3612)
P.O. Box 13666 (92170-3666)
PHONE..................619 231-2521
Robert M Davis, *CEO*
Teddy Davis, *CFO*
Theodora Davis Inman, *CFO*
Ruth Davis, *Chairman*
Deborah Odle, *Vice Pres*
▼ **EMP:** 70
SQ FT: 25,000
SALES (est): 113.6MM **Privately Held**
WEB: www.imsrecyclingservices.com
SIC: 4953 Recycling, waste materials

(P-6214)
INTERNTIONAL DISPOSAL CORP CAL
Also Called: Site L69
1601 Dixon Landing Rd, Milpitas
(95035-8100)
PHONE..................408 945-2802
Bruce Ranck, *President*
EMP: 75
SQ FT: 1,613
SALES (est): 4.3MM
SALES (corp-wide): 10B **Publicly Held**
WEB: www.alliedwaste.com
SIC: 4953 Sanitary landfill operation
HQ: Browning-Ferris Industries, Llc
18500 N Allied Way # 100
Phoenix AZ 85054
480 627-2700

(P-6215)
JOES SWEEPING INC
Also Called: Nationwide Environmental Svcs
11914 Front St, Norwalk (90650-2911)
PHONE..................562 929-4344
Never Samuelian, *President*
Joe Samuelian, *Vice Pres*
Ani Samuelian, *Admin Sec*
EMP: 65
SQ FT: 10,500
SALES (est): 18MM **Privately Held**
WEB: www.nes-sweeping.com
SIC: 4953 Street refuse systems

(P-6216)
LOONEY BINS INC (PA)
12153 Montague St, Pacoima
(91331-2210)
PHONE..................818 485-8200
Myan Spaccarelli, *President*
Jerry Lucera, *CFO*
Phyllis Shukiar, *Admin Sec*
EMP: 70
SQ FT: 1,000
SALES (est): 20.4MM **Privately Held**
WEB: www.looneybins.com
SIC: 4953 Garbage: collecting, destroying
& processing

(P-6217)
LOPEZ CANYON LANDFILL
11950 Lopez Canyon Rd, Sylmar
(91342-6036)
PHONE..................818 834-5122
James Kurz, *Superintendent*
Paul Blount, *Manager*
EMP: 110
SALES (est): 2.7MM **Privately Held**
SIC: 4953 Sanitary landfill operation

(P-6218)
MADISON MATERIALS
1035 E 4th St, Santa Ana (92701-4750)
PHONE..................714 664-0159
Judith Ware, *President*
Ben Ware, *Vice Pres*
Jay Ware, *General Mgr*
EMP: 70
SQ FT: 10,400
SALES (est): 7.7MM **Privately Held**
SIC: 4953 Recycling, waste materials

(P-6219)
MAIN STREET FIBERS INC
608 E Main St, Ontario (91761-1711)
P.O. Box 51491 (91761-0091)
PHONE..................909 986-6310
Gregory S Young, *CEO*
Wayne Young, *President*
Ernie Alvarez, *CFO*
Steve Young, *Corp Secy*
EMP: 60
SQ FT: 25,000
SALES: 46MM **Privately Held**
WEB: www.mainstreetfibers.com
SIC: 4953 Recycling, waste materials

(P-6220)
MARBORG INDUSTRIES (PA)
728 E Yanonali St, Santa Barbara
(93103-3233)
P.O. Box 4127 (93140-4127)
PHONE..................805 963-1852
Mario Borgatello Jr, *President*
David Borgatello, *CFO*
Vince Villagomez, *Officer*
Robert Caldwell, *Executive*
Peter Tierney, *Department Mgr*
EMP: 254 **EST:** 1974
SALES (est): 43.6MM **Privately Held**
WEB: www.marborg.com
SIC: 4953 7359 7699 4212 Rubbish col-
lection & disposal; portable toilet rental;
septic tank cleaning service; local truck-
ing, without storage

(P-6221)
MARIN SANITARY SERVICE (PA)
Also Called: Marin Resource Recovery Cen-
ter
1050 Andersen Dr, San Rafael
(94901-5316)
P.O. Box 10067 (94912-0067)
PHONE..................415 456-2601
Patricia Garbarino, *CEO*
Kathy Wall, *COO*
John Oranje, *Vice Pres*
Ron Piombo, *Vice Pres*
Steve Rosa, *Vice Pres*
EMP: 85
SALES (est): 82.3MM **Privately Held**
WEB: www.marinsanitary.com
SIC: 4953 5099 4212 Garbage: collect-
ing, destroying & processing; recycling,
waste materials; wood chips; local truck-
ing, without storage

(P-6222)
MASTER DISPOSAL CO
1980 S Reservoir St, Pomona
(91766-5543)
PHONE..................626 444-6789
Dave Samarin, *President*
Bill Nazaroff Sr, *Vice Pres*
Bill Nazaroff Jr, *Admin Sec*
EMP: 50
SALES (est): 3.4MM **Privately Held**
SIC: 4953 Recycling, waste materials

(P-6223)
MILL VALLEY REFUSE SERVICE INC
112 Front St, San Rafael (94901-4011)
P.O. Box 3557 (94912-3557)
PHONE..................415 457-2287
Dave Biggio, *President*
James Iavarone, *Corp Secy*
Dave Dellazoppa, *Vice Pres*
Lynda Mendoza, *Sales Mgr*
Danielle Engstrom, *Manager*
EMP: 57 **EST:** 1906
SQ FT: 52,000
SALES (est): 13MM **Privately Held**
WEB: www.millvalleyrefuse.com
SIC: 4953 Rubbish collection & disposal;
recycling, waste materials

(P-6224)
MODESTO WSTEWATER TRTMNT PLANT
1221 Sutter Ave, Modesto (95351-3603)
PHONE..................209 577-5300
Dan Wilkowsky, *Director*
EMP: 70
SALES (est): 2.6MM **Privately Held**
SIC: 4953

(P-6225)
MONTEREY RGIONAL WASTE MGT DST
14201 Del Monte Blvd, Marina (93933)
P.O. Box 1670 (93933-1670)
PHONE..................831 384-5313
William Merry, *President*
Charles Rees, *CFO*
Leo Laska, *Chairman*
Timothy Flanagan, *General Mgr*
Peter Skinner, *Finance*
EMP: 120 **EST:** 1951
SQ FT: 5,500
SALES: 29.4MM **Privately Held**
WEB: www.mrwmd.org
SIC: 4953 4911 4931 Sanitary landfill op-
eration; recycling, waste materials; gener-
ation, electric power; electric & other
services combined

(P-6226)
MP ENVIRONMENTAL SERVICES INC (PA)
Also Called: M P Vacuum Truck Service
3400 Manor St, Bakersfield (93308-1451)
P.O. Box 80358 (93380-0358)
PHONE..................800 458-3036
Dawn Calderwood, *President*
Laren Kaufman, *Project Mgr*
Jesse Soltero, *Project Mgr*
Kevin Terrio, *Safety Dir*
Todd Johnson, *Traffic Dir*
▲ **EMP:** 117
SQ FT: 8,000
SALES (est): 121.1MM **Privately Held**
WEB: www.mpenviro.com
SIC: 4953 4213 8748 7699 Hazardous
waste collection & disposal; radioactive
waste materials, disposal; trucking, ex-
cept local; environmental consultant; tank
repair & cleaning services

(P-6227)
NORTECH WASTE LLC
3033 Fiddyment Rd, Roseville
(95747-9705)
PHONE..................916 645-5230
Paul Szura, *Mng Member*
Arthur A Daniels,
Donald M Moriel,
Michael J Sangiacomo,
Jerry Jackson, *Mng Member*
EMP: 120
SQ FT: 9,000

SALES (est): 34.7MM **Privately Held**
WEB: www.nortechwaste.com
- **SIC: 4953** 3341 3312 3231 Sanitary landfill operation; secondary nonferrous metals; blast furnaces & steel mills; products of purchased glass; pulp mills

(P-6228)
NOVATO DISPOSAL SERVICE INC (PA)
Also Called: Total Waste Systems
3417 Standish Ave, Santa Rosa (95407-8135)
P.O. Box 1916 (95402-1916)
PHONE..................707 765-9995
James Ratto, *President*
Diana Ratto, *Corp Secy*
Robert M Mattos, *Vice Pres*
Raymond D Myers, *Vice Pres*
Audra Loehner, *Manager*
EMP: 67 **EST:** 1947
SQ FT: 3,000
SALES (est): 5.6MM **Privately Held**
SIC: 4953 Recycling, waste materials

(P-6229)
NRC ENVIRONMENTAL SERVICES INC
3777 Long Beach Blvd, Long Beach (90807-3325)
PHONE..................562 432-1304
Todd Roloff, *Branch Mgr*
EMP: 60
SALES (corp-wide): 360.1MM **Privately Held**
WEB: www.nrces.com
SIC: 4953 Hazardous waste collection & disposal
HQ: Nrc Environmental Services, Inc.
1605 Ferry Pt
Alameda CA 94501

(P-6230)
ORANGE COUNTY SANITATION (PA)
10844 Ellis Ave, Fountain Valley (92708-7018)
P.O. Box 8127 (92728-8127)
PHONE..................714 962-2411
James Herberg, *General Mgr*
▲ **EMP:** 300
SALES (est): 315.4MM **Privately Held**
WEB: www.ocsd.com
SIC: 4953 Waste materials, disposal at sea

(P-6231)
PALM SPRINGS DISPOSAL SERVICES
4690 E Mesquite Ave, Palm Springs (92264-3510)
P.O. Box 2711 (92263-2711)
PHONE..................760 327-1351
Frederic Wade, *CEO*
James Cunningham, *President*
Mike Jaycox, *Treasurer*
Ray Wade, *Vice Pres*
Rick Wade, *General Mgr*
EMP: 82
SQ FT: 2,000
SALES (est): 21.4MM **Privately Held**
WEB: www.palmspringsdisposal.com
SIC: 4953 Rubbish collection & disposal

(P-6232)
PENAS DISPOSAL INC
Also Called: Pena's Recycling Center
12094 Avenue 408, Cutler (93615-2055)
PHONE..................559 528-3909
Gabriel Pena, *President*
Arthur Pena, *Vice Pres*
Maria Pena, *Admin Sec*
Yvette Botello, *Manager*
EMP: 91 **EST:** 1968
SQ FT: 1,000
SALES (est): 21.9MM **Privately Held**
WEB: www.penasdisposal.com
SIC: 4953 Garbage: collecting, destroying & processing

(P-6233)
PJBS HOLDINGS INC (PA)
Also Called: Benz - One Complete Operation
1401 Goodrick Dr, Tehachapi (93561-1532)
P.O. Box 1750 (93581-1750)
PHONE..................661 822-5273
Paul Benz, *CEO*
Joan Benz, *Corp Secy*
Louis Visco, *Vice Pres*
Julie Sanchez, *Human Resources*
Alison Ledwidge, *Director*
EMP: 75
SQ FT: 4,500
SALES (est): 61.9MM **Privately Held**
SIC: 4953 4212 Refuse collection & disposal services; petroleum haulage, local

(P-6234)
PLEASANT HL BYSHORE DSPSAL INC
Also Called: Site 210
441 N Buchanan Cir, Pacheco (94553-5119)
PHONE..................925 685-4711
J Frederick Snyder, *CEO*
Tim Argenti, *General Mgr*
EMP: 200
SQ FT: 4,000
SALES (est): 12.3MM
SALES (corp-wide): 10B **Publicly Held**
WEB: www.pleasanthillbayshoredisposal.com
SIC: 4953 Refuse collection & disposal services
HQ: Allied Waste Industries, Llc
18500 N Allied Way # 100
Phoenix AZ 85054
480 627-2700

(P-6235)
POTENTIAL INDUSTRIES INC (PA)
922 E E St, Wilmington (90744-6145)
P.O. Box 293 (90748-0293)
PHONE..................310 807-4466
Anthony J Fan, *President*
Simon Chen, *President*
Tony Fan, *President*
Henry J Chen, *CEO*
Jessie Chen, *Corp Secy*
◆ **EMP:** 149
SQ FT: 45,000
SALES (est): 207.6MM **Privately Held**
SIC: 4953 5093 Recycling, waste materials; scrap & waste materials

(P-6236)
PSC INDUSTRIAL OUTSOURCING LP
Also Called: Philip West Industrial Service
1661 E 32nd St, Long Beach (90807-5233)
PHONE..................562 997-6000
Bill Hearley, *Manager*
Mark Geraghty, *Executive*
Edwin Sargenti, *Project Mgr*
EMP: 99
SALES (corp-wide): 607.5MM **Privately Held**
SIC: 4953 4959 5093 Hazardous waste collection & disposal; environmental cleanup services; ferrous metal scrap & waste
PA: Psc Industrial Outsourcing, Lp
900 Georgia Ave
Deer Park TX 77536
713 393-5600

(P-6237)
RAINBOW DISPOSAL CO INC (HQ)
Also Called: Rainbow Refuse Recycling
17121 Nichols Ln, Huntington Beach (92647-5719)
P.O. Box 1026 (92647-1026)
PHONE..................714 847-3581
Jerry Moffatt, *CEO*
Stan Tkaczyck, *President*
Cynthia Covarrubias, *Opers Staff*
Francisco Espinoza, *Opers Staff*
Octavio Camacho, *Asst Mgr*
EMP: 115 **EST:** 1956
SQ FT: 6,000

SALES (est): 98.9MM
SALES (corp-wide): 10B **Publicly Held**
WEB: www.rainbowdisposal.com
SIC: 4953 Garbage: collecting, destroying & processing; recycling, waste materials
PA: Republic Services, Inc.
18500 N Allied Way # 100
Phoenix AZ 85054
480 627-2700

(P-6238)
RAINBOW TRANSFER RECYCLING
17121 Nichols Ln, Huntington Beach (92647-5719)
P.O. Box 1026 (92647-1026)
PHONE..................714 847-5818
Jim Brownell, *Principal*
Stan Tkaczyk, *President*
Bruce Shuman, *CFO*
EMP: 165
SQ FT: 10,000
SALES (est): 7.5MM
SALES (corp-wide): 10B **Publicly Held**
WEB: www.rainbowdisposal.com
SIC: 4953 Rubbish collection & disposal
HQ: Rainbow Disposal Co. Inc.
17121 Nichols Ln
Huntington Beach CA 92647
714 847-3581

(P-6239)
RECOLOGY INC (PA)
50 California St Ste 2400, San Francisco (94111-4796)
PHONE..................415 875-1000
Michael J Sangiacomo, *President*
George P McGrath, *COO*
Mark R Lomele, *CFO*
Dennis Wu, *Chairman*
Julie Bertani-Kiser, *Vice Pres*
EMP: 60 **EST:** 1988
SQ FT: 25,000
SALES (est): 1.4B **Privately Held**
WEB: www.norcalwastesystemsofbutte-county.com
SIC: 4953 Garbage: collecting, destroying & processing; recycling, waste materials

(P-6240)
RECOLOGY INC
Tunnel Ave And Beatty Rd, San Francisco (94134)
PHONE..................415 330-1300
Mike Sangiacomo, *Branch Mgr*
Sandra Herrera, *Cust Mgr*
Daniel Negron, *Manager*
EMP: 64
SALES (corp-wide): 1.4B **Privately Held**
WEB: www.norcalwastesystemsofbutte-county.com
SIC: 4953 Recycling, waste materials
PA: Recology Inc.
50 California St Ste 2400
San Francisco CA 94111
415 875-1000

(P-6241)
RECOLOGY INC
245 N 1st St, Dixon (95620-3027)
PHONE..................916 379-3300
Jim Sullivan, *Administration*
EMP: 63
SALES (corp-wide): 1.4B **Privately Held**
SIC: 4953 Garbage: collecting, destroying & processing
PA: Recology Inc.
50 California St Ste 2400
San Francisco CA 94111
415 875-1000

(P-6242)
RECOLOGY INC
Also Called: Recology Sustainable Crushing
100 Cargo Way, San Francisco (94124-1734)
PHONE..................415 970-1582
EMP: 56
SALES (corp-wide): 1.4B **Privately Held**
SIC: 4953 Garbage: collecting, destroying & processing
PA: Recology Inc.
50 California St Ste 2400
San Francisco CA 94111
415 875-1000

(P-6243)
RECOLOGY INC
2720 S 5th Ave, Oroville (95965-5826)
P.O. Box 1512 (95965-1512)
PHONE..................530 533-5868
Joe Matz, *Manager*
Sharbel Eid, *General Mgr*
EMP: 76
SQ FT: 9,086
SALES (corp-wide): 1.4B **Privately Held**
WEB: www.norcalwastesystemsofbutte-county.com
SIC: 4953 Garbage: collecting, destroying & processing
PA: Recology Inc.
50 California St Ste 2400
San Francisco CA 94111
415 875-1000

(P-6244)
RECOLOGY INC
Also Called: Sanitary Fill
501 Tunnel Ave, San Francisco (94134-2940)
PHONE..................415 330-1400
John Legnitto, *Branch Mgr*
EMP: 150
SALES (corp-wide): 1.4B **Privately Held**
WEB: www.norcalwastesystemsofbutte-county.com
SIC: 4953 8611 Recycling, waste materials; business associations
PA: Recology Inc.
50 California St Ste 2400
San Francisco CA 94111
415 875-1000

(P-6245)
RECOLOGY LOS ALTOS
650 Martin Ave, Santa Clara (95050-2914)
PHONE..................650 961-8044
Michael Sangiacomo, *President*
EMP: 89 **EST:** 1923
SALES (est): 6.4MM
SALES (corp-wide): 1.4B **Privately Held**
WEB: www.losaltosgarbage.com
SIC: 4953 Garbage: collecting, destroying & processing; recycling, waste materials
PA: Recology Inc.
50 California St Ste 2400
San Francisco CA 94111
415 875-1000

(P-6246)
RECOLOGY SAN FRANCISCO
501 Tunnel Ave, San Francisco (94134-2940)
PHONE..................415 468-1752
Michael Sangiacomo, *President*
Robert Coyle, *COO*
EMP: 167
SQ FT: 3,800
SALES (est): 20MM
SALES (corp-wide): 1.4B **Privately Held**
WEB: www.sfrecyclinganddisposal.com
SIC: 4953 Garbage: collecting, destroying & processing
PA: Recology Inc.
50 California St Ste 2400
San Francisco CA 94111
415 875-1000

(P-6247)
RECOLOGY SAN MATEO COUNTY
225 Shoreway Rd, San Carlos (94070-2712)
PHONE..................650 595-3900
Michael J Sangiacomo, *CEO*
Paul Dougherty, *Manager*
EMP: 99
SALES: 950K **Privately Held**
SIC: 4953 Garbage: collecting, destroying & processing

(P-6248)
RECOLOGY SOUTH VALLEY (HQ)
1351 Pacheco Pass Hwy, Gilroy (95020-9579)
PHONE..................408 842-3358
Robert Coyle, *President*
Mike Sanjiacomo, *Vice Pres*
EMP: 65 **EST:** 1949
SQ FT: 6,000

P R O D U C T S & S V C S

SALES (est): 20.5MM
SALES (corp-wide): 1.4B **Privately Held**
SIC: 4953 Garbage: collecting, destroying & processing; recycling, waste materials; sanitary landfill operation
PA: Recology Inc.
50 California St Ste 2400
San Francisco CA 94111
415 875-1000

(P-6249)
RECOLOGY VACAVILLE SOLANO
1 Town Sq Ste 200, Vacaville (95688-3928)
PHONE..............707 448-2945
Michael Sangiacomo, *President*
David Soli, *Accountant*
EMP: 75
SQ FT: 10,000
SALES (est): 9.3MM
SALES (corp-wide): 1.4B **Privately Held**
WEB: www.norcalwastesystemsofbutte-county.com
SIC: 4953 Garbage: collecting, destroying & processing; recycling, waste materials
PA: Recology Inc.
50 California St Ste 2400
San Francisco CA 94111
415 875-1000

(P-6250)
RECOLOGY VALLEJO (HQ)
Also Called: Vallejo Garbage & Recycling
2021 Broadway St, Vallejo (94589-1701)
PHONE..............707 552-3110
Ed Farewell, *General Mgr*
EMP: 115
SQ FT: 40,000
SALES: 16MM
SALES (corp-wide): 1.4B **Privately Held**
WEB: www.vallejogarbage.com
SIC: 4953 Garbage: collecting, destroying & processing
PA: Recology Inc.
50 California St Ste 2400
San Francisco CA 94111
415 875-1000

(P-6251)
RECOLOGY YUBA-SUTTER
3001 N Levee Rd, Marysville (95901-3600)
P.O. Box G (95901-0062)
PHONE..............530 743-6933
Michael Sangiacomo, *President*
Robert Coyle, *COO*
EMP: 90 **EST:** 1974
SQ FT: 7,000
SALES (est): 12.7MM
SALES (corp-wide): 1.4B **Privately Held**
WEB: www.ysdi.com
SIC: 4953 4212 Garbage: collecting, destroying & processing; recycling, waste materials; hazardous waste collection & disposal; hazardous waste transport
PA: Recology Inc.
50 California St Ste 2400
San Francisco CA 94111
415 875-1000

(P-6252)
RECYCLERS I ELECTRONIC
7815 N Palm Ave Ste 140, Fresno (93711-5531)
PHONE..............317 522-1414
John S Shegerian, *President*
Tammy L Shegerian, *Treasurer*
Linda L Ramos, *Admin Sec*
▼ **EMP:** 99
SALES (est): 14.3MM
SALES (corp-wide): 529.1MM **Privately Held**
SIC: 4953 Recycling, waste materials
PA: Electronic Recyclers International Inc.
7815 N Palm Ave Ste 140
Fresno CA 93711
800 374-3473

(P-6253)
RECYCLING INDUSTRIES INC
4741 Watt Ave, North Highlands (95660-5526)
PHONE..............916 452-3961
Scott Kuhnen, *President*
David Kuhnen, *CFO*
EMP: 75
SQ FT: 155,000

SALES (est): 19.9MM **Privately Held**
WEB: www.recyclingindustries.com
SIC: 4953 Recycling, waste materials

(P-6254)
REDWOOD EMPIR
3400 Standish Ave, Santa Rosa (95407-8112)
PHONE..............707 586-5533
James Rappo, *President*
EMP: 70
SALES (est): 5MM **Privately Held**
SIC: 4953 Refuse systems

(P-6255)
REPLANET LLC
Also Called: Tomra Recycling Network
9910 6th St, Rancho Cucamonga (91730-5715)
PHONE..............951 892-3079
Ralph Alcantar, *Manager*
EMP: 55
SALES (corp-wide): 294.6MM **Privately Held**
SIC: 4953 8741 5093 Recycling, waste materials; management services; metal scrap & waste materials
HQ: Replanet, Llc
800 N Haven Ave Ste 120
Ontario CA 91764
951 520-1700

(P-6256)
REPUBLIC SERVICES INC
2059 E Steel Rd, Colton (92324-4008)
PHONE..............909 370-3377
Peter Sperenberg, *Manager*
EMP: 50
SQ FT: 3,200
SALES (corp-wide): 10B **Publicly Held**
SIC: 4953 Garbage: collecting, destroying & processing
PA: Republic Services, Inc.
18500 N Allied Way # 100
Phoenix AZ 85054
480 627-2700

(P-6257)
REPUBLIC SERVICES INC
1449 W Rosecrans Ave, Gardena (90249-2639)
PHONE..............310 527-6980
Lewis Glynn, *President*
EMP: 100
SQ FT: 39,755
SALES (corp-wide): 10B **Publicly Held**
WEB: www.republicservices.com
SIC: 4953 Medical waste disposal
PA: Republic Services, Inc.
18500 N Allied Way # 100
Phoenix AZ 85054
480 627-2700

(P-6258)
REPUBLIC SERVICES INC
111 S Del Norte Blvd, Oxnard (93030-7915)
PHONE..............805 385-8060
Anthony Bertrand, *Branch Mgr*
EMP: 58
SALES (corp-wide): 10B **Publicly Held**
WEB: www.republicservices.com
SIC: 4953 Recycling, waste materials
PA: Republic Services, Inc.
18500 N Allied Way # 100
Phoenix AZ 85054
480 627-2700

(P-6259)
RETRIEV TECHNOLOGIES INC (PA)
Also Called: Lithchem
125 E Commercial St Ste A, Anaheim (92801-1214)
PHONE..............714 738-8516
Steven Kinsbursky, *President*
Joseph A Acker, *President*
Andrew Christmas, *CFO*
Aaron Zisman, *Treasurer*
Ed Green, *Vice Pres*
▲ **EMP:** 51
SALES (est): 40.9MM **Privately Held**
SIC: 4953 3341 2819 Recycling, waste materials; recovery & refining of nonferrous metals; industrial inorganic chemicals

(P-6260)
RUUHWA DANN AND ASSOCIATES INC
Also Called: Cal Micro
1541 Brooks St, Ontario (91762-3619)
PHONE..............909 467-4800
Ruuhwa Dann, *CEO*
Harry Saliba, *President*
◆ **EMP:** 77
SQ FT: 88,000
SALES (est): 19.9MM **Privately Held**
SIC: 4953 Recycling, waste materials

(P-6261)
SA RECYCLING LLC
3055 Commercial St, San Diego (92113-1412)
PHONE..............619 238-6740
Mark Sweetman, *Manager*
EMP: 68 **Privately Held**
SIC: 4953 Recycling, waste materials
PA: Sa Recycling Llc
2411 N Glassell St
Orange CA 92865
-

(P-6262)
SA RECYCLING LLC
10313 S Alameda St, Los Angeles (90002-3838)
PHONE..............323 564-5601
Carlos Escamilla, *Manager*
EMP: 68 **Privately Held**
SIC: 4953 Recycling, waste materials
PA: Sa Recycling Llc
2411 N Glassell St
Orange CA 92865
-

(P-6263)
SA RECYCLING LLC
2006 W 5th St, Santa Ana (92703-2806)
PHONE..............714 667-7898
EMP: 68 **Privately Held**
SIC: 4953 5093 Recycling, waste materials; scrap & waste materials; ferrous metal scrap & waste; nonferrous metals scrap
PA: Sa Recycling Llc
2411 N Glassell St
Orange CA 92865
-

(P-6264)
SA RECYCLING LLC
9754 San Fernando Rd, Sun Valley (91352-1424)
PHONE..............323 875-2520
Steve Rios, *Branch Mgr*
EMP: 68 **Privately Held**
SIC: 4953 Recycling, waste materials
PA: Sa Recycling Llc
2411 N Glassell St
Orange CA 92865
-

(P-6265)
SA RECYCLING LLC
2525 S K St, Tulare (93274-6875)
PHONE..............559 688-0271
Brandon Dye, *General Mgr*
EMP: 68 **Privately Held**
SIC: 4953 Recycling, waste materials
PA: Sa Recycling Llc
2411 N Glassell St
Orange CA 92865
-

(P-6266)
SA RECYCLING LLC
521 N Rice Ave, Oxnard (93030-8924)
PHONE..............805 486-7525
Matt Essler, *Branch Mgr*
EMP: 68 **Privately Held**
SIC: 4953 5093 Recycling, waste materials; scrap & waste materials
PA: Sa Recycling Llc
2411 N Glassell St
Orange CA 92865
-

(P-6267)
SA RECYCLING LLC
2495 Buena Vista St, Duarte (91010-3330)
PHONE..............626 359-5815

Carlos Rodriguez, *Manager*
EMP: 68 **Privately Held**
SIC: 4953 5093 Recycling, waste materials; scrap & waste materials; ferrous metal scrap & waste; nonferrous metals scrap
PA: Sa Recycling Llc
2411 N Glassell St
Orange CA 92865

(P-6268)
SA RECYCLING LLC
1540 S Greenwood Ave, Montebello (90640-6536)
PHONE..............323 723-8327
James Adams, *Branch Mgr*
EMP: 68 **Privately Held**
SIC: 4953 5093 Recycling, waste materials; scrap & waste materials; ferrous metal scrap & waste; nonferrous metals scrap
PA: Sa Recycling Llc
2411 N Glassell St
Orange CA 92865

(P-6269)
SA RECYCLING LLC
3489 S Chestnut Ave, Fresno (93725-2610)
PHONE..............559 237-6677
Mark Leizer, *Branch Mgr*
Hortensia Juarez, *Manager*
EMP: 64 **Privately Held**
SIC: 4953 Recycling, waste materials
PA: Sa Recycling Llc
2411 N Glassell St
Orange CA 92865

(P-6270)
SA RECYCLING LLC
48100 Harrison St, Coachella (92236-1214)
PHONE..............760 391-5591
Ben Wilcox, *Branch Mgr*
EMP: 68 **Privately Held**
SIC: 4953 Recycling, waste materials
PA: Sa Recycling Llc
2411 N Glassell St
Orange CA 92865

(P-6271)
SA RECYCLING LLC
12301 Valley Blvd, El Monte (91732-3603)
PHONE..............626 444-9530
Carlos Escamilla, *Branch Mgr*
EMP: 64 **Privately Held**
SIC: 4953 Recycling, waste materials
PA: Sa Recycling Llc
2411 N Glassell St
Orange CA 92865

(P-6272)
SA RECYCLING LLC
2000 E Brundage Ln, Bakersfield (93307-2734)
PHONE..............661 327-3559
Brandon Dye, *Manager*
EMP: 65 **Privately Held**
SIC: 4953 Recycling, waste materials
PA: Sa Recycling Llc
2411 N Glassell St
Orange CA 92865

(P-6273)
SA RECYCLING LLC
11614 Eastend Ave, Chino (91710-1557)
PHONE..............909 622-3337
EMP: 68
SALES (corp-wide): 49.7MM **Privately Held**
SIC: 4953 5093
PA: Sa Recycling Llc
2411 N Glassell St
Orange CA 92865
714 632-2000

(P-6274)
SA RECYCLING LLC (PA)
2411 N Glassell St, Orange (92865-2717)
PHONE..............714 632-2000

▲ = Import ▼=Export
◆ =Import/Export

George Adams, *Mng Member*
Cristi Rossi, *Vice Pres*
Jess Anthony, *General Mgr*
David Garmon, *General Mgr*
Saul Haro, *General Mgr*
◆ **EMP:** 160
SQ FT: 40,000
SALES (est): 1.6B **Privately Held**
SIC: 4953 Recycling, waste materials

(P-6275)
SA RECYCLING LLC
42353 8th St E, Lancaster (93535-5439)
PHONE..................661 723-1383
EMP: 68
SALES (corp-wide): 49.7MM **Privately
Held**
SIC: 4953
PA: Sa Recycling Llc
2411 N Glassell St
Orange CA 92865
714 632-2000

(P-6276)
SA RECYCLING LLC
790 E M St, Colton (92324-3910)
PHONE..................909 825-1662
Alex Arriaga, *Branch Mgr*
EMP: 68 **Privately Held**
SIC: 4953 Recycling, waste materials
PA: Sa Recycling Llc
2411 N Glassell St
Orange CA 92865

(P-6277)
SA RECYCLING LLC
3202 Main St, San Diego (92113-3719)
PHONE..................714 632-2000
EMP: 68 **Privately Held**
SIC: 4953 Recycling, waste materials
PA: Sa Recycling Llc
2411 N Glassell St
Orange CA 92865

(P-6278)
SACRAMENTO AREA SEWER DISTRICT (PA)
10060 Goethe Rd, Sacramento
(95827-3553)
PHONE..................916 876-6000
Joseph Maestretti, *CFO*
Claudia Goss, *COO*
Joe Maestretti, *CFO*
Prabhaker Somavarapu, *Principal*
Steven Delozier, *Exec Dir*
EMP: 300
SALES (est): 270.4MM **Privately Held**
SIC: 4953 Rubbish collection & disposal

(P-6279)
SAN DIEGO RECYLING INC
6670 Federal Blvd, Lemon Grove
(91945-1312)
PHONE..................619 287-7555
Edward Burr, *President*
EMP: 300
SALES (est): 9.5MM **Privately Held**
SIC: 4953 Recycling, waste materials

(P-6280)
SANITATION DISTRICTS
1955 Workman Mill Rd, Whittier
(90601-1415)
P.O. Box 4998 (90607-4998)
PHONE..................562 908-4288
Steve McGuin, *Manager*
Sam Perdoza, *General Mgr*
Kimberly Christensen, *Admin Sec*
Gabriel Martinez, *Admin Sec*
Denise Springer, *Admin Sec*
EMP: 1698
SALES: 576MM **Privately Held**
SIC: 4953 Sanitary landfill operation; rubbish collection & disposal

(P-6281)
SELF SERVE AUTO DISMANTLERS (PA)
Also Called: Adams Steel
3200 E Frontera St, Anaheim (92806-2822)
P.O. Box 6258 (92816-0258)
PHONE..................714 630-8901
George Adams Jr, *President*
Wendy Adams, *CFO*

Mike Adams, *Vice Pres*
Thomas Knippel, *Vice Pres*
Terry Adams, *Admin Sec*
◆ **EMP:** 215
SQ FT: 41,000
SALES (est): 28.2MM **Privately Held**
WEB: www.remedyenvironmental.com
SIC: 4953 Recycling, waste materials

(P-6282)
SHUBIN SERVICES INC
Also Called: Federal Disposal Service
15031 Parkway Loop Ste A, Tustin
(92780-6527)
P.O. Box 14730, Irvine (92623-4730)
PHONE..................714 259-0908
Donald B Shubin, *CEO*
EMP: 50
SQ FT: 7,000
SALES (est): 5.4MM **Privately Held**
WEB: www.federaldisposalservice.com
SIC: 4953 Rubbish collection & disposal

(P-6283)
SIMS GROUP USA CORPORATION
Simsmtals America-Richmond Div
600 S 4th St, Richmond (94804-3504)
PHONE..................510 236-0606
Jimmie Buckland, *Vice Pres*
EMP: 75 **Privately Held**
SIC: 4953 Recycling, waste materials
HQ: Sims Group Usa Corporation
600 S 4th St
Richmond CA 94804
510 412-5300

(P-6284)
SOLAG INCORPORATED
Also Called: Solag Disposal Co
31641 Ortega Hwy, San Juan Capistrano
(92675)
PHONE..................949 728-1206
Clifford Ronnenberg, *Ch of Bd*
Patricia Leyes, *Vice Pres*
EMP: 58
SALES (est): 3.6MM
SALES (corp-wide): 133.1MM **Privately
Held**
WEB: www.crrincorporated.com
SIC: 4953 4212 Rubbish collection & disposal; local trucking, without storage
PA: Cr&R Incorporated
11292 Western Ave
Stanton CA 90680
714 826-9049

(P-6285)
SOLANO GARBAGE COMPANY INC
2901 Industrial Ct, Fairfield (94533-6500)
P.O. Box B (94533-0601)
PHONE..................707 437-8900
Richard Granzella, *President*
Dennis Varni, *CFO*
Joe Della Zoppa, *Exec VP*
Pina Barbieri, *Admin Sec*
EMP: 55 EST: 1978
SQ FT: 2,000
SALES: 11MM **Privately Held**
WEB: www.solanorecycles.com
SIC: 4953 Garbage: collecting, destroying & processing

(P-6286)
SOUTH TAHOE REFUSE CO
Also Called: Sierra Disposal Service
2140 Ruth Ave, South Lake Tahoe
(96150-4357)
PHONE..................530 541-5105
Jeffrey Tillman, *President*
Gloria Lehman, *Treasurer*
John Tillman, *Vice Pres*
Jeanette Tillman, *Office Admin*
John De Marchini, *Admin Sec*
EMP: 100
SQ FT: 5,000
SALES (est): 17.2MM **Privately Held**
WEB: www.southtahoerefuse.com
SIC: 4953 Garbage: collecting, destroying & processing

(P-6287)
STAR SCRAP METAL COMPANY INC
1509 S Bluff Rd, Montebello (90640-6601)
PHONE..................562 921-5045
Rose Starow Stein, *President*
Allen Stein, *Vice Pres*
▼ **EMP:** 70 EST: 1974
SQ FT: 600
SALES (est): 12.3MM **Privately Held**
SIC: 4953 Recycling, waste materials

(P-6288)
STRATEGIC MATERIALS INC
7000 Bandini Blvd, Commerce
(90040-3303)
PHONE..................323 887-6831
Sal Ramirez, *Manager*
EMP: 65
SALES (corp-wide): 564.7MM **Privately
Held**
SIC: 4953 Recycling, waste materials
HQ: Strategic Materials, Inc.
17220 Katy Fwy Ste 150
Houston TX 77094
281 647-2700

(P-6289)
SUNSET SCAVENGER COMPANY
Also Called: Recology Sunset Scavenger
250 Executive Park Blvd # 2100, San Francisco (94134-3306)
PHONE..................415 330-1300
Archie Humphrey, *COO*
Gary Kirk, *Administration*
John Legnitto, *Manager*
EMP: 420 EST: 1920
SQ FT: 3,800
SALES (est): 31.3MM
SALES (corp-wide): 1.4B **Privately Held**
WEB: www.norcalwastesystemsofbutte-county.com
SIC: 4953 Recycling, waste materials
PA: Recology Inc.
50 California St Ste 2400
San Francisco CA 94111
415 875-1000

(P-6290)
TALCO PLASTICS INC (PA)
1000 W Rincon St, Corona (92880-9228)
PHONE..................951 531-2000
John L Shedd Sr, *Chairman*
John L Shedd Jr, *President*
William O'Grady, *Vice Pres*
Ron Petty, *Vice Pres*
Bob Shedd, *Vice Pres*
EMP: 85
SQ FT: 110,000
SALES (est): 90.5MM **Privately Held**
WEB: www.talcoplastics.com
SIC: 4953 2821 Recycling, waste materials; plastics materials & resins

(P-6291)
TEMARRY RECYCLING INC
476 Tecate Rd, Tecate (91980)
PHONE..................619 270-9453
Matt Songer, *CEO*
Teresa Songer, *Vice Pres*
Larry Burton, *Business Dir*
EMP: 63 EST: 2004
SALES (est): 4.4MM **Privately Held**
SIC: 4953 Recycling, waste materials

(P-6292)
TRACY DLTA SOLID WASTE MGT INC
Also Called: Delta Disposal Service Co
30703 S Macarthur Dr, Tracy (95377-9170)
P.O. Box 274 (95378-0274)
PHONE..................209 835-0601
Michael Repetto, *President*
Carl Repetto, *Vice Pres*
Scott Stortroen, *Executive*
Anna Lovecchio, *CPA*
Gina Baker, *Controller*
EMP: 61
SQ FT: 1,000
SALES (est): 12MM **Privately Held**
SIC: 4953 Garbage: collecting, destroying & processing; recycling, waste materials

(P-6293)
TRI-CITY ECONOMIC DEV CORP
Also Called: Tri Ced Community Recycling
33377 Western Ave, Union City
(94587-2210)
PHONE..................510 429-8030
Richard Valle, *Principal*
Larry Cheeves, *Engineer*
Mangee Austria, *Opers Staff*
Wilson Lee, *Manager*
EMP: 59
SQ FT: 74,055
SALES: 10.2MM **Privately Held**
SIC: 4953 Recycling, waste materials

(P-6294)
UNITED PACIFIC WASTE
4334 San Gbriel Rver Pkwy, Pico Rivera
(90660-1837)
P.O. Box 908 (90660-0908)
PHONE..................562 699-7600
Michael Kandilian, *President*
Mike Kandilian, *Exec VP*
Shawna Kandilian, *Admin Sec*
EMP: 70
SQ FT: 3,500
SALES: 12MM **Privately Held**
SIC: 4953 4213 Garbage: collecting, destroying & processing; rubbish collection & disposal; contract haulers

(P-6295)
UNITED SITE SERVICES CAL INC
1 Oak Rd, Benicia (94510-2910)
PHONE..................707 747-2810
Debbi Thornton, *Manager*
EMP: 50
SALES (corp-wide): 3.9MM **Privately
Held**
WEB: www.americanclassicsanitation.com
SIC: 4953 4959 5082 7359 Refuse systems; sanitary services; construction & mining machinery; equipment rental & leasing
PA: United Site Services Of California, Inc.
242 Live Oak Ave
Irwindale CA 91706
626 462-9110

(P-6296)
USA WASTE OF CALIFORNIA INC
Also Called: Waste Management
26951 Road 140, Visalia (93292-9454)
P.O. Box 7400, Pasadena (91109-7400)
PHONE..................559 741-1766
Kurt Nielson, *Manager*
EMP: 75
SALES (corp-wide): 14.9B **Publicly Held**
WEB: www.wastebusinessjournal.com
SIC: 4953 Ashes, collection & disposal
HQ: Usa Waste Of California, Inc.
11931 Foundation Pl # 200
Gold River CA 95670
916 387-1400

(P-6297)
USA WASTE OF CALIFORNIA INC
8491 Fruitridge Rd, Sacramento
(95826-4807)
PHONE..................916 379-0500
Alex Oseguera, *Manager*
EMP: 93
SALES (corp-wide): 14.9B **Publicly Held**
SIC: 4953 Refuse collection & disposal services
HQ: Usa Waste Of California, Inc.
11931 Foundation Pl # 200
Gold River CA 95670
916 387-1400

(P-6298)
USA WASTE OF CALIFORNIA INC
Also Called: Los Angeles City Hauling
9081 Tujunga Ave, Sun Valley
(91352-1516)
P.O. Box 541, Los Angeles (90078-0541)
PHONE..................818 252-3112
Jim Fish, *CEO*
EMP: 100
SALES (corp-wide): 14.9B **Publicly Held**
SIC: 4953 Recycling, waste materials

HQ: Usa Waste Of California, Inc.
11931 Foundation Pl # 200
Gold River CA 95670
916 387-1400

(P-6299)
USA WASTE OF CALIFORNIA INC (HQ)
Also Called: Waste Management
11931 Foundation Pl # 200, Gold River
(95670-4540)
PHONE...................................916 387-1400
Barry S Skolnick, *CEO*
Mike Witt, *CEO*
Earl E Defrates, *Treasurer*
Ed Aurand, *Ch Credit Ofcr*
Alex Oseguera, *General Mgr*
EMP: 150
SQ FT: 3,200
SALES (est): 51MM
SALES (corp-wide): 14.9B **Publicly Held**
WEB: www.wm.com
SIC: 4953 Refuse collection & disposal
services
PA: Waste Management, Inc.
1001 Fannin St Ste 4000
Houston TX 77002
713 512-6200

(P-6300)
USA WASTE OF CALIFORNIA INC
Also Called: Inland Empire Hauling
800 S Temescal St, Corona (92879-2058)
PHONE...................................800 423-9986
EMP: 100
SALES (corp-wide): 14.9B **Publicly Held**
SIC: 4953 Refuse systems
HQ: Usa Waste Of California, Inc.
11931 Foundation Pl # 200
Gold River CA 95670
916 387-1400

(P-6301)
USA WASTE OF CALIFORNIA INC
Also Called: Salinas Disposal Service
29331 Pacific St, Hayward (94544-6017)
PHONE...................................831 384-5000
Paul Pistono, *Branch Mgr*
EMP: 100
SALES (corp-wide): 14.9B **Publicly Held**
SIC: 4953 Refuse systems
HQ: Usa Waste Of California, Inc.
11931 Foundation Pl # 200
Gold River CA 95670
916 387-1400

(P-6302)
USA WASTE OF CALIFORNIA INC
Also Called: San Gabriel-Pomona Valley Hlg
13970 Live Oak Ave, Baldwin Park (91706)
PHONE...................................626 856-1285
Richard Schackel, *Director*
EMP: 100
SALES (corp-wide): 14.9B **Publicly Held**
SIC: 4953 Garbage: collecting, destroying
& processing
HQ: Usa Waste Of California, Inc.
11931 Foundation Pl # 200
Gold River CA 95670
916 387-1400

(P-6303)
USA WASTE OF CALIFORNIA INC
Also Called: Waste Management
8740 Pueblo Ave Ste B, Atascadero
(93422-4605)
PHONE...................................805 466-3636
Randi Rebhan, *Branch Mgr*
EMP: 100
SALES (corp-wide): 14.9B **Publicly Held**
SIC: 4953 Refuse collection & disposal
services
HQ: Usa Waste Of California, Inc.
11931 Foundation Pl # 200
Gold River CA 95670
916 387-1400

(P-6304)
USA WASTE OF CALIFORNIA INC
Also Called: Waste Management
1001 W Bradley Ave, El Cajon
(92020-1501)
PHONE...................................619 596-5117
Paul Pistono, *Vice Pres*
EMP: 100
SALES (corp-wide): 14.9B **Publicly Held**
SIC: 4953 Refuse systems
HQ: Usa Waste Of California, Inc.
11931 Foundation Pl # 200
Gold River CA 95670
916 387-1400

(P-6305)
USA WASTE OF CALIFORNIA INC
Also Called: Waste Management
13793 Redwood St, Chino (91710-5506)
PHONE...................................909 590-1793
Steve Kanow, *Director*
EMP: 100
SALES (corp-wide): 14.9B **Publicly Held**
SIC: 4953 Refuse systems
HQ: Usa Waste Of California, Inc.
11931 Foundation Pl # 200
Gold River CA 95670
916 387-1400

(P-6306)
USA WASTE OF CALIFORNIA INC
Also Called: Fresno Hauling
4333 E Jefferson Ave, Fresno
(93725-9707)
PHONE...................................559 834-9151
Paul Pistono, *Vice Pres*
EMP: 100
SALES (corp-wide): 14.9B **Publicly Held**
SIC: 4953 Refuse collection & disposal
services
HQ: Usa Waste Of California, Inc.
11931 Foundation Pl # 200
Gold River CA 95670
916 387-1400

(P-6307)
USA WASTE OF CALIFORNIA INC
Also Called: La Metro Hauling
1970 E 213th St, Long Beach
(90810-1201)
PHONE...................................310 830-7100
Ed King, *Manager*
Maria Diaz, *Human Resources*
EMP: 100
SALES (corp-wide): 14.9B **Publicly Held**
SIC: 4953 Recycling, waste materials
HQ: Usa Waste Of California, Inc.
11931 Foundation Pl # 200
Gold River CA 95670
916 387-1400

(P-6308)
USA WASTE OF CALIFORNIA INC
Also Called: Compton Hauling
407 E El Segundo Blvd, Compton
(90222-2316)
PHONE...................................310 763-8500
Hovseb Shadarevian, *Branch Mgr*
EMP: 100
SALES (corp-wide): 14.9B **Publicly Held**
SIC: 4953 Refuse systems
HQ: Usa Waste Of California, Inc.
11931 Foundation Pl # 200
Gold River CA 95670
916 387-1400

(P-6309)
USA WASTE OF CALIFORNIA INC
Also Called: Paradise Solid Waste
951 American Way, Paradise (95969-6315)
PHONE...................................530 877-2777
Bill Mannel, *General Mgr*
Doug Speicher, *General Mgr*
Ron Law, *Controller*
Lee Hicks, *Contract Law*
EMP: 100
SALES (corp-wide): 14.9B **Publicly Held**
SIC: 4953 Refuse systems

HQ: Usa Waste Of California, Inc.
11931 Foundation Pl # 200
Gold River CA 95670
916 387-1400

(P-6310)
USA WASTE OF CALIFORNIA INC
Also Called: Salinas Disposal Service
1120 Madison Ln, Salinas (93907-1818)
PHONE...................................831 754-2500
Jan McCombs, *Branch Mgr*
EMP: 93
SALES (corp-wide): 14.9B **Publicly Held**
SIC: 4953 Refuse systems
HQ: Usa Waste Of California, Inc.
11931 Foundation Pl # 200
Gold River CA 95670
916 387-1400

(P-6311)
USA WASTE OF CALIFORNIA INC
Also Called: Fresno Hauling
10725 W Goshen Ave, Visalia
(93291-9496)
P.O. Box 541065, Los Angeles (90054-
1065)
PHONE...................................559 834-4070
Kurt Nielson, *Branch Mgr*
EMP: 100
SALES (corp-wide): 14.9B **Publicly Held**
SIC: 4953 Refuse systems
HQ: Usa Waste Of California, Inc.
11931 Foundation Pl # 200
Gold River CA 95670
916 387-1400

(P-6312)
USA WASTE OF CALIFORNIA INC
Also Called: Santa Clarita Hauling/Blue
25772 Springbrook Ave, Santa Clarita
(91350-2563)
PHONE...................................661 259-2398
EMP: 100
SALES (corp-wide): 14.9B **Publicly Held**
SIC: 4953 Refuse systems
HQ: Usa Waste Of California, Inc.
11931 Foundation Pl # 200
Gold River CA 95670
916 387-1400

(P-6313)
USA WASTE OF CALIFORNIA INC
Also Called: Waste Management Orange
County
1800 S Grand Ave, Santa Ana
(92705-4800)
PHONE...................................714 637-3010
Jeremiah Gilliam, *Accounts Mgr*
EMP: 74
SALES (corp-wide): 14.9B **Publicly Held**
SIC: 4953 Refuse systems
HQ: Usa Waste Of California, Inc.
11931 Foundation Pl # 200
Gold River CA 95670
916 387-1400

(P-6314)
VALLEY GARBAGE RUBBISH CO INC
Also Called: Heallth Sanitation Services
1850 W Betteravia Rd, Santa Maria
(93455-1065)
PHONE...................................805 614-1131
Keith Ramsey, *Principal*
EMP: 70
SQ FT: 3,000
SALES (est): 23.8MM
SALES (corp-wide): 14.9B **Publicly Held**
WEB: www.wm.com
SIC: 4953 Rubbish collection & disposal
PA: Waste Management, Inc.
1001 Fannin St Ste 4000
Houston TX 77002
713 512-6200

(P-6315)
WARE DISPOSAL INC
1451 Manhattan Ave, Fullerton
(92831-5221)
PHONE...................................714 834-0234
Judith Helaine Ware, *CEO*

Michael Shaffer, *CFO*
Ben Ware, *Vice Pres*
Jay Ware, *General Mgr*
Lucy Aguilar, *Office Mgr*
EMP: 120
SQ FT: 48,900
SALES (est): 25.7MM **Privately Held**
WEB: www.waredisposal.com
SIC: 4953 Refuse collection & disposal
services

(P-6316)
WASTE CONNECTIONS CAL INC
301 Carl Rd, Sunnyvale (94089-1012)
PHONE...................................408 752-8530
Todd Storti, *Manager*
Roxanne Gutierrez, *Sales Staff*
EMP: 110
SALES (corp-wide): 3.3B **Privately Held**
WEB: www.greenteam.com
SIC: 4953 Garbage: collecting, destroying
& processing
HQ: Waste Connections Of California, Inc.
1333 Oakland Rd
San Jose CA 95112
408 282-4400

(P-6317)
WASTE CONNECTIONS CAL INC (DH)
Also Called: Greenteam of San Jose
1333 Oakland Rd, San Jose (95112-1364)
PHONE...................................408 282-4400
Paul Nelson, *Vice Pres*
Ron Mittelstaedt, *CEO*
Pual Nelson, *Vice Pres*
EMP: 150
SQ FT: 6,000
SALES (est): 85.5MM
SALES (est): 4.6B **Privately Held**
WEB: www.greenteam.com
SIC: 4953 Garbage: collecting, destroying
& processing

(P-6318)
WASTE MANAGEMENT CAL INC (HQ)
9081 Tujunga Ave, Sun Valley
(91352-1516)
PHONE...................................877 836-6526
Larry Metter, *Vice Pres*
Pat Desimone, *Planning*
Rebecca Zayatz, *Engineer*
Scott Slighting, *Manager*
Colleen Jacobson, *Clerk*
EMP: 230 EST: 1953
SQ FT: 35,000
SALES (est): 408.9MM
SALES (corp-wide): 14.9B **Publicly Held**
SIC: 4953 Garbage: collecting, destroying
& processing; recycling, waste materials
PA: Waste Management, Inc.
1001 Fannin St Ste 4000
Houston TX 77002
713 512-6200

(P-6319)
WASTE MANAGEMENT CAL INC
1001 W Bradley Ave, El Cajon
(92020-1501)
PHONE...................................619 596-5100
Rex Buck, *Principal*
EMP: 68
SQ FT: 2,000
SALES (corp-wide): 14.9B **Publicly Held**
WEB: www.wastebusinessjournal.com
SIC: 4953 Rubbish collection & disposal
HQ: Waste Management Of California, Inc.
9081 Tujunga Ave
Sun Valley CA 91352
877 836-6526

(P-6320)
WASTE MANAGEMENT CAL INC
1200 W City Ranch Rd, Palmdale
(93551-4456)
PHONE...................................661 947-7197
Carl McCarthy, *Manager*
EMP: 54
SALES (corp-wide): 14.9B **Publicly Held**
WEB: www.wastebusinessjournal.com
SIC: 4953 Rubbish collection & disposal
HQ: Waste Management Of California, Inc.
9081 Tujunga Ave
Sun Valley CA 91352
877 836-6526

(P-6321)
WASTE MANAGEMENT CAL INC
2141 Oceanside Blvd, Oceanside
(92054-4405)
PHONE..............................760 439-2824
John Lusignan, *Manager*
EMP: 95
SQ FT: 4,500
SALES (corp-wide): 14.9B **Publicly Held**
SIC: 4953 4212 Garbage: collecting, destroying & processing; local trucking, without storage
HQ: Waste Management Of California, Inc.
9081 Tujunga Ave
Sun Valley CA 91352
877 836-6526

(P-6322)
WASTE MGT COLLECTN & RECYCL
5701 S Eastrn Ave Ste 300, Commerce
(90040)
PHONE..............................626 960-7551
Rick Decaiva, *Manager*
EMP: 245
SALES (corp-wide): 14.9B **Publicly Held**
SIC: 4953 4212 Rubbish collection & disposal; local trucking, without storage
HQ: Waste Management Collection And Recycling, Inc.
1001 Fannin St Ste 4000
Houston TX 77002

(P-6323)
WASTE MGT COLLECTN & RECYCL
1340 W Beach St, Watsonville
(95076-5122)
P.O. Box 2347 (95077-2347)
PHONE..............................831 768-9505
James Moresco, *Branch Mgr*
Rini Van Every, *Info Tech Dir*
EMP: 93
SALES (corp-wide): 14.9B **Publicly Held**
SIC: 4953 Refuse collection & disposal services
HQ: Waste Management Collection And Recycling, Inc.
1001 Fannin St Ste 4000
Houston TX 77002

(P-6324)
WASTE MGT COLLECTN & RECYCL
219 Pudding Creek Rd, Fort Bragg
(95437-8136)
PHONE..............................707 462-0210
Kaladas Ginger, *Branch Mgr*
EMP: 93
SALES (corp-wide): 14.9B **Publicly Held**
SIC: 4953 Refuse systems
HQ: Waste Management Collection And Recycling, Inc.
1001 Fannin St Ste 4000
Houston TX 77002

(P-6325)
WASTE MGT COLLECTN & RECYCL
17700 Indian St, Moreno Valley
(92551-9511)
PHONE..............................909 242-0421
EMP: 93
SALES (corp-wide): 14.9B **Publicly Held**
SIC: 4953 Refuse systems
HQ: Waste Management Collection And Recycling, Inc.
1001 Fannin St Ste 4000
Houston TX 77002

(P-6326)
WASTE MGT COLLECTN & RECYCL
450 Orr Springs Rd, Ukiah (95482-3131)
PHONE..............................707 462-0210
Lee Hicks, *Branch Mgr*
EMP: 93
SALES (corp-wide): 14.9B **Publicly Held**
SIC: 4953 Refuse systems

HQ: Waste Management Collection And Recycling, Inc.
1001 Fannin St Ste 4000
Houston TX 77002

(P-6327)
WASTE MGT COLLECTN RECYCL INC
17700 Indian St, Moreno Valley
(92551-9511)
PHONE..............................951 242-0421
Scott Jenkins, *Manager*
Carson Brown, *Manager*
EMP: 200
SALES (corp-wide): 14.9B **Publicly Held**
WEB: www.wastemanagement.com
SIC: 4953 Garbage: collecting, destroying & processing
HQ: Waste Management Collection And Recycling, Inc.
1001 Fannin St Ste 4000
Houston TX 77002

(P-6328)
WASTE MGT COLLECTN RECYCL INC
16122 Construction Cir E, Irvine
(92606-4498)
PHONE..............................949 451-2600
Fidel Gutierrez, *Branch Mgr*
David Steiner, *CEO*
Joel Robledo, *Project Mgr*
EMP: 93
SALES (corp-wide): 14.9B **Publicly Held**
SIC: 4953 4212 Recycling, waste materials; garbage collection & transport, no disposal
HQ: Waste Management Collection And Recycling, Inc.
1001 Fannin St Ste 4000
Houston TX 77002

(P-6329)
WASTE MGT OF ALAMEDA CNTY (HQ)
172 98th Ave, Oakland (94603-1004)
PHONE..............................510 613-8710
Barry S Skolnick, *CEO*
James C Fish Jr, *Exec VP*
James E Trevathan, *Exec VP*
Angel Gallardo, *Info Tech Mgr*
EMP: 550
SALES (est): 288.9MM
SALES (corp-wide): 14.9B **Publicly Held**
WEB: www.wastebusinessjournal.com
SIC: 4953 Rubbish collection & disposal
PA: Waste Management, Inc.
1001 Fannin St Ste 4000
Houston TX 77002
713 512-6200

(P-6330)
WASTE MGT OF ALAMEDA CNTY
2615 Davis St, San Leandro (94577-2211)
PHONE..............................510 638-2303
Jack Isloa, *Manager*
EMP: 100
SALES (corp-wide): 14.9B **Publicly Held**
WEB: www.wastebusinessjournal.com
SIC: 4953 5093 Dumps, operation of; scrap & waste materials
HQ: Waste Management Of Alameda County, Inc
172 98th Ave
Oakland CA 94603
510 613-8710

(P-6331)
WASTE MGT OF ALAMEDA CNTY
800 S Temescal St, Corona (92879-2058)
PHONE..............................951 280-5471
Alex Braicovich, *Manager*
EMP: 150
SALES (corp-wide): 14.9B **Publicly Held**
WEB: www.wastebusinessjournal.com
SIC: 4953 4212 Rubbish collection & disposal; local trucking, without storage

HQ: Waste Management Of Alameda County, Inc
172 98th Ave
Oakland CA 94603
510 613-8710

(P-6332)
WEST COUNTY RESOURCE RECOVERY
101 Pittsburg Ave, Richmond (94801-1201)
PHONE..............................510 231-4200
Richard Granzella, *President*
EMP: 50
SALES: 12.8MM
SALES (corp-wide): 10B **Publicly Held**
WEB: www.recyclemore.com
SIC: 4953 Non-hazardous waste disposal sites
HQ: Richmond Sanitary Service, Inc.
3260 Blume Dr Ste 100
Richmond CA 94806
510 262-7100

(P-6333)
WEST VALLEY MANUFACTURING LLC
Also Called: West Valley M R F
13373 Napa St, Fontana (92335-2930)
PHONE..............................909 899-5501
Richard Crockett, *General Mgr*
Kaiser Recycling Corporation, West Valley Recycling Transf,
EMP: 120 **EST:** 1997
SQ FT: 65,000
SALES (est): 6MM **Privately Held**
SIC: 4953 4212 Refuse collection & disposal services; recycling, waste materials; local trucking, without storage

(P-6334)
WM HEALTHCARE SOLUTIONS INC
4280 Bandini Blvd, Vernon (90058-4207)
PHONE..............................713 328-7350
David Steiner, *President*
EMP: 99
SALES (est): 4.5MM **Privately Held**
SIC: 4953 Refuse systems

(P-6335)
WM RECYCLE AMERICA LLC
Waste Management
8405 Loch Lomond Dr, Pico Rivera
(90660-2508)
PHONE..............................562 948-3888
Gary Lane, *Branch Mgr*
EMP: 90
SALES (corp-wide): 14.9B **Publicly Held**
WEB: www.wm.com
SIC: 4953 Recycling, waste materials
HQ: Wm Recycle America, L.L.C.
1001 Fannin St Ste 4000
Houston TX 77002
713 512-6200

(P-6336)
ZANKER ROAD RESOURCE MGT LTD
Also Called: Zanker Road Landfill
675 Los Esteros Rd, San Jose
(95134-1004)
PHONE..............................408 457-1189
Scott Beal, *Manager*
Kenneth Borgault, *MIS Dir*
William Lineberry, *Enginr/R&D Asst*
EMP: 90
SALES (corp-wide): 57.2MM **Privately Held**
WEB: www.greenwaste.com
SIC: 4953 Rubbish collection & disposal
PA: Zanker Road Resource Management, Ltd.
705 Los Esteros Rd
San Jose CA 95134
408 263-2385

(P-6337)
ZEREP MANAGEMENT CORPORATION
17445 Railroad St, City of Industry
(91748-1026)
PHONE..............................626 961-6291
Manuel Perez, *CEO*
Jesse Quintana, *Controller*
Andrew Palomares, *Opers Mgr*

EMP: 100
SQ FT: 4,000
SALES (est): 24.6MM **Privately Held**
SIC: 4953 4212 Refuse systems; local trucking, without storage

4959 Sanitary Svcs, NEC

(P-6338)
AMPCO CONTRACTING INC
1420 S Allec St, Anaheim (92805-6305)
PHONE..............................949 955-2255
Andrew Pennor, *President*
Matthew Suiter, *President*
Benjamin Reynolds, *CFO*
Trung Joe Q Ha, *Vice Pres*
Michael King, *Vice Pres*
EMP: 220
SALES (est): 105.5MM **Privately Held**
SIC: 4959 1795 1794 Environmental cleanup services; wrecking & demolition work; excavation & grading, building construction

(P-6339)
CITY OF ANTIOCH
Also Called: Dept of Maintenance
1201 W 4th St, Antioch (94509-1005)
P.O. Box 5007 (94531-5007)
PHONE..............................925 779-6950
Pat Scott, *Director*
EMP: 100 **Privately Held**
WEB: www.ci.antioch.ca.us
SIC: 4959 9111 Sanitary services; mayors' offices
PA: City Of Antioch
200 H St
Antioch CA 94509
925 779-7055

(P-6340)
CITY OF CHINO
Also Called: Street Sidewalks St Tree Maint
5050 Schaefer Ave, Chino (91710-5549)
PHONE..............................909 591-9843
Ed Nylund, *Principal*
EMP: 66 **Privately Held**
WEB: www.chinopd.org
SIC: 4959 Sweeping service: road, airport, parking lot, etc.
PA: City Of Chino
13220 Central Ave
Chino CA 91710
909 591-9824

(P-6341)
CITY OF LONG BEACH
Also Called: City Long Bch Prkg Enforcement
2929 E Willow St, Long Beach
(90806-2303)
PHONE..............................562 570-2890
James Kuhl, *Manager*
EMP: 250 **Privately Held**
WEB: www.polb.com
SIC: 4959 Sweeping service: road, airport, parking lot, etc.
PA: City Of Long Beach
411 W Ocean Blvd
Long Beach CA 90802
562 570-6450

(P-6342)
CLEANSTREET
1937 W 169th St, Gardena (90247-5253)
PHONE..............................310 329-3078
Jere Costello, *CEO*
Claudia Cervantes, *Executive*
Richard Anderson, *General Mgr*
Debby Garnica, *Admin Asst*
Jennifer Mejia, *Administration*
EMP: 137
SQ FT: 15,000
SALES (est): 35MM **Privately Held**
WEB: www.cleanstreet.com
SIC: 4959 Sweeping service: road, airport, parking lot, etc.

(P-6343)
COUNTY SANTTN DIST 2 OF LA CO (PA)
Also Called: L.A.cO.
1955 Workman Mill Rd, Whittier (90601-1415)
P.O. Box 4998 (90607-4998)
PHONE.....................................562 699-7411
Stephen Maguin, *General Mgr*
Rechelle Asperin, *Bd of Directors*
Dan Sanchez,
Sam Perdoza, *General Mgr*
Jodie Lanza, *Admin Sec*
EMP: 850
SALES (est): 1.1B **Privately Held**
SIC: 4959 Sanitary services

(P-6344)
COUNTY SANTTN DIST 2 OF LA CO
24501 Figueroa St, Carson (90745-6311)
PHONE.....................................310 830-2400
Ken Redemacher, *Manager*
Ramon Rivera, *Buyer*
Joe McCaffrey, *Safety Mgr*
EMP: 500
SALES (corp-wide): 1.1B **Privately Held**
SIC: 4959 Sanitary services
PA: County Sanitation District No. 2 Of Los
   Angeles County
   1955 Workman Mill Rd
   Whittier CA 90601
   562 699-7411

(P-6345)
COUNTY SANTTN DIST 2 OF LA CO
920 S Alameda St, Compton (90221-4807)
PHONE.....................................310 638-1161
Samuel Espinoza, *Manager*
EMP: 100
SALES (corp-wide): 1.1B **Privately Held**
SIC: 4959 9511 Sanitary services; sanitary
   engineering agency, government;
PA: County Sanitation District No. 2 Of Los
   Angeles County
   1955 Workman Mill Rd
   Whittier CA 90601
   562 699-7411

(P-6346)
ECOLOGY CONTROL INDUSTRIES
255 Parr Blvd, Richmond (94801-1119)
PHONE.....................................510 235-1393
Curtis Lindskog, *Manager*
EMP: 100 **Privately Held**
SIC: 4959 4953 4212 Environmental
   cleanup services; hazardous waste col-
   lection & disposal; hazardous waste
   transport
PA: Ecology Control Industries, Inc
   15707 S Main St
   Gardena CA 90248

(P-6347)
ENGINEERING/REMDTN RSRCS GRP (PA)
Also Called: Errg
4585 Pacheco Blvd Ste 200, Martinez (94553-2228)
PHONE.....................................925 839-2200
Cynthia A Liu, *CEO*
Todd Katz, *CFO*
Marilyn Plitnik, *Project Mgr*
Matthew Dwyer, *Sr Project Mgr*
Tami Tripp, *Manager*
EMP: 70 EST: 1997
SQ FT: 31,000
SALES: 42MM **Privately Held**
WEB: www.errg.com
SIC: 4959 8744 Environmental cleanup
   services;

(P-6348)
ENVIRONMENTAL PROTECTION AGCY
Also Called: E P A
1001 I St Ste 19b, Sacramento (95814-2828)
PHONE.....................................916 324-7572
Joan Denton, *Director*
EMP: 55 **Publicly Held**

WEB: www.epa.gov
SIC: 4959 Toxic or hazardous waste
   cleanup
HQ: Environmental Protection Agency
   1200 Pennsylvania Ave Nw
   Washington DC 20460
   202 564-4700

(P-6349)
GARYS CONSTRUCTION INC
2517 Dos Lomas, Fallbrook (92028-9159)
P.O. Box 189, Bonsall (92003-0189)
PHONE.....................................760 639-4456
Gary Albery, *President*
Tammy Albery, *Admin Sec*
EMP: 120
SQ FT: 1,200
SALES (est): 9.9MM **Privately Held**
SIC: 4959 1799 0782 Sweeping service:
   road, airport, parking lot, etc.; construc-
   tion site cleanup; lawn & garden services

(P-6350)
JONSET CORPORATION
Also Called: Sunset Property Services
16251 Construction Cir W, Irvine (92606-4412)
PHONE.....................................949 551-5151
John Howhannesian, *President*
Andrea Howhannesian, *General Mgr*
Carmen Howhannesian, *Admin Sec*
EMP: 96
SQ FT: 6,000
SALES (est): 16.1MM **Privately Held**
WEB: www.sunsetpropertyservices.com
SIC: 4959 7349 Sweeping service: road,
   airport, parking lot, etc.; janitorial service,
   contract basis

(P-6351)
NRC ENVIRONMENTAL SERVICES INC (DH)
1605 Ferry Pt, Alameda (94501)
PHONE.....................................510 749-1390
Steven Candito, *President*
Neil Challis, *Senior VP*
Mike Reese, *Senior VP*
Todd Roloff, *Senior VP*
Sal Sacco, *Senior VP*
▲ EMP: 80
SQ FT: 18,000
SALES (est): 231.6MM
SALES (corp-wide): 360.1MM **Privately Held**
WEB: www.nrces.com
SIC: 4959 Toxic or hazardous waste
   cleanup; oil spill cleanup; environmental
   cleanup services

(P-6352)
PACIFIC PARKING & VALET LLC
Also Called: National Parking & Valet
2555 Garden Rd, Monterey (93940-5306)
PHONE.....................................831 646-0426
Steven Summers, *President*
EMP: 130
SALES: 1.3MM **Privately Held**
SIC: 4959 1799 7521 Road, airport &
   parking lot maintenance services; parking
   facility equipment & maintenance; parking
   garage

(P-6353)
RHO CHEM LLC (DH)
425 Isis Ave, Inglewood (90301-2076)
PHONE.....................................323 776-6234
Ramon Robles, *CEO*
▲ EMP: 50
SALES (est): 17.3MM
SALES (corp-wide): 3.4B **Publicly Held**
SIC: 4959 Sanitary services
HQ: Nortru, Llc
   515 Lycaste St
   Detroit MI 48214
   313 824-5840

(P-6354)
RICHMOND SANITARY SERVICE INC (HQ)
Also Called: Crockett Garbage Service
3260 Blume Dr Ste 100, Richmond (94806-1960)
P.O. Box 4100 (94804-0100)
PHONE.....................................510 262-7100
Richard Granzella, *President*
Dennis Varni, *CFO*

Mario Acquilino, *Vice Pres*
Pina Barbiere, *Principal*
Loyd Bonfante, *Principal*
▲ EMP: 200 EST: 1924
SALES (est): 78MM
SALES (corp-wide): 10B **Publicly Held**
SIC: 4959 Sanitary services
PA: Republic Services, Inc.
   18500 N Allied Way # 100
   Phoenix AZ 85054
   480 627-2700

(P-6355)
SACRAMENTO REG CO SANIT DIST (PA)
Also Called: Srcsd
10060 Goethe Rd, Sacramento (95827-3553)
PHONE.....................................916 876-6000
Prabhakar Somavarapu, *Director*
Peter Castles, *Bd of Directors*
Phil Serna, *Principal*
Mary Weber, *Admin Sec*
Glen Iwamura, *Info Tech Mgr*
EMP: 700 EST: 1973
SQ FT: 136,000
SALES (est): 105.5MM **Privately Held**
SIC: 4959 Sanitary services

(P-6356)
SACRAMENTO YOLO CNTY MOSQUITO
8631 Bond Rd, Elk Grove (95624-1477)
PHONE.....................................916 685-1022
Raul Deanda, *President*
Vern Bruhn, *Vice Pres*
Janna McLeod, *Admin Mgr*
Marcia Reed, *Admin Mgr*
Raj Badhan, *Technology*
EMP: 51
SALES (est): 7.7MM **Privately Held**
WEB: www.sac-yolomvcd.com
SIC: 4959 Mosquito eradication

(P-6357)
STATEWIDE CNSTR SWEEPING INC
45945 Warm Springs Blvd, Fremont (94539-6746)
PHONE.....................................510 683-9584
Gina Vella, *President*
Joseph Vella, *Admin Sec*
Greg Petrosian, *Sales Executive*
Dennis Pierce, *Manager*
EMP: 50
SQ FT: 8,000
SALES (est): 6.9MM **Privately Held**
SIC: 4959 Sweeping service: road, airport,
   parking lot, etc.

(P-6358)
SULLINOVO
2750 Womble Rd Ste 100, San Diego (92106-6114)
PHONE.....................................619 260-1432
Steven Sullivan, *Partner*
Scott Blount, *Partner*
Steven Bonde, *Partner*
EMP: 206
SALES (est): 5.7MM **Privately Held**
SIC: 4959 8744 Toxic or hazardous waste
   cleanup;

4961 Steam & Air Conditioning Sply

(P-6359)
CGP HOLDINGS LLC
2 Gill Station Coastal Rd, Little Lake (93542)
PHONE.....................................760 764-1300
EMP: 82
SALES (est): 439.9K **Privately Held**
SIC: 4961

(P-6360)
TRI-STATE AG INC
Also Called: Priority Cooling
47375 W Dakota Ave, Firebaugh (93622-9516)
PHONE.....................................209 364-6185
James M Hammonds, *President*
Mary H Hicks, *Treasurer*

William E Hammond, *Vice Pres*
William E Hammonds, *Vice Pres*
EMP: 82
SALES (est): 4.5MM **Privately Held**
SIC: 4961 Cooled air supplier

4971 Irrigation Systems

(P-6361)
ARVIN-EDISON WATER STORAGE DST (PA)
20401 E Bear Mtn Blvd, Arvin (93203-9475)
P.O. Box 175 (93203-0175)
PHONE.....................................661 854-5573
Howard Frick, *President*
John C Moore, *Corp Secy*
Salvadore Giumarra, *Vice Pres*
Christy Kong, *Accountant*
EMP: 50
SQ FT: 5,000
SALES: 17.7MM **Privately Held**
SIC: 4971 Water distribution or supply sys-
   tems for irrigation

(P-6362)
FRESNO IRRIGATION DISTRICT
2907 S Maple Ave, Fresno (93725-2218)
PHONE.....................................559 233-7161
Gary R Serrato, *General Mgr*
Deann Hailey, *CFO*
Laurence Kimura, *Manager*
EMP: 83
SQ FT: 18,000
SALES: 18.4MM **Privately Held**
WEB: www.fresnoirrigation.com
SIC: 4971 Water distribution or supply sys-
   tems for irrigation

(P-6363)
GLENN-COLUSA IRRIGATION DST (PA)
344 E Laurel St, Willows (95988-3114)
P.O. Box 150 (95988-0150)
PHONE.....................................530 934-8881
Donald Bransford, *President*
Dennis Michum, *Treasurer*
EMP: 75
SQ FT: 5,000
SALES: 14MM **Privately Held**
WEB: www.gcid.net
SIC: 4971 Water distribution or supply sys-
   tems for irrigation

(P-6364)
IMPERIAL IRRIGATION DISTRICT
Also Called: Imperial Irrgtion Dst Wtr Dept
333 E Barioni Blvd, Imperial (92251-1773)
P.O. Box 937 (92251-0937)
PHONE.....................................760 339-9220
Robert McCullough, *Branch Mgr*
EMP: 400
SQ FT: 10,000
SALES (corp-wide): 615.2MM **Privately Held**
WEB: www.iidwater.com
SIC: 4971 Water distribution or supply sys-
   tems for irrigation
PA: Imperial Irrigation District
   333 E Barioni Blvd
   Imperial CA 92251
   800 303-7756

(P-6365)
MERCED IRRIGATION DISTRICT
3321 Franklin Rd, Merced (95348-9345)
PHONE.....................................209 722-2719
Jarith Krause, *Manager*
EMP: 160
SALES (corp-wide): 95.5MM **Privately Held**
WEB: www.mercedid.org
SIC: 4971 Water distribution or supply sys-
   tems for irrigation
PA: Merced Irrigation District
   744 W 20th St
   Merced CA 95340
   209 722-5761

(P-6366)
NEVADA IRRIGATION DISTRICT (PA)
Also Called: N I D
1036 W Main St, Grass Valley
(95945-5424)
PHONE....................530 273-6185
Remleh Scherzinger, *General Mgr*
John H Drew, *President*
Keane Sommers, *CEO*
Marie Owens, *Treasurer*
Monica Reyes, *Vice Pres*
▲ EMP: 160
SQ FT: 11,050
SALES: 48.7MM **Privately Held**
SIC: 4971 4911 Water distribution or supply systems for irrigation; generation, electric power

(P-6367)
OAK SPRINGS NURSERY INC
13761 Eldridge Ave, Sylmar (91342-1764)
P.O. Box 922906 (91392-2906)
PHONE....................818 367-5832
Manuel Cacho, *President*
Fred Siegler, *Contractor*
EMP: 90
SALES (est): 10.3MM **Privately Held**
SIC: 4971 0781 Irrigation systems; landscape services

(P-6368)
PALO VERDE IRRIGATION DISTRICT
180 W 14th Ave, Blythe (92225-2714)
PHONE....................760 922-3144
Ed Smith, *General Mgr*
Janice Love, *Treasurer*
EMP: 85 EST: 1923
SQ FT: 8,125
SALES (est): 14MM **Privately Held**
WEB: www.pvid.org
SIC: 4971 Water distribution or supply systems for irrigation

(P-6369)
PANOCHE WATER DISTRICT
52027 W Althea Ave, Firebaugh
(93622-9401)
PHONE....................209 364-6136
ARA Azhderian, *General Mgr*
John Bennet, *President*
Sue Redfern, *Vice Pres*
Michael Linneman, *Director*
Mike Sterns, *Director*
EMP: 50
SQ FT: 1,200
SALES (est): 4.1MM **Privately Held**
WEB: www.panochewd.org
SIC: 4971 Water distribution or supply systems for irrigation

(P-6370)
RAIN BIRD CORPORATION
2475-A Paseo De Las Ameri, San Diego
(92154-7255)
PHONE....................619 661-4493
Catherine Wade, *Branch Mgr*
EMP: 64
SALES (corp-wide): 86.7MM **Privately Held**
WEB: www.rainbird.com
SIC: 4971 Irrigation systems
PA: Rain Bird Corporation
970 W Sierra Madre Ave
Azusa CA 91702
626 812-3400

(P-6371)
SAN LUIS DLTA-MENDOTA WTR AUTH
15990 Kelso Rd, Byron (94514-1916)
PHONE....................209 835-2593
Frances Mizuno, *Principal*
EMP: 80
SALES (corp-wide): 34.4MM **Privately Held**
SIC: 4971 8611 Water distribution or supply systems for irrigation; public utility association
PA: San Luis & Delta-Mendota Water Authority
842 6th St
Los Banos CA 93635
209 826-9696

(P-6372)
SOLANO IRRIGATION DISTRICT
810 Vaca Valley Pkwy # 201, Vacaville
(95688-8835)
PHONE....................707 448-6847
Robert Hansen, *President*
Victor Fortenberry, *Officer*
Guido E Colla, *Vice Pres*
Cary Keaten, *General Mgr*
Natasha Montgomery, *General Mgr*
EMP: 99
SQ FT: 8,500
SALES: 12.9MM **Privately Held**
WEB: www.sidwater.org
SIC: 4971 Irrigation systems

(P-6373)
SOUTH FEATHER WATER & PWR AGCY (PA)
2310 Oro Quincy Hwy, Oroville
(95966-5226)
PHONE....................530 533-4578
James Edward, *Director*
Lou Lodigiani, *President*
Patricia A Sands, *Treasurer*
Dennis Moreland, *Bd of Directors*
Michael Glaze, *General Mgr*
EMP: 57 EST: 1919
SQ FT: 5,000
SALES (est): 12.2MM **Privately Held**
WEB: www.southfeather.com
SIC: 4971 Water distribution or supply systems for irrigation

(P-6374)
TURLOCK IRRIGATION DISTRICT
Also Called: T I D
901 N Broadway, Turlock (95380-3012)
P.O. Box 949 (95381-0949)
PHONE....................209 883-8300
Larry Weis, *Branch Mgr*
Casey Hashimoto, *General Mgr*
Jessica Vieths, *Technician*
Smart Grid, *Engineer*
Brian Stubbert, *Manager*
EMP: 400
SQ FT: 1,554
SALES (corp-wide): 54.8MM **Privately Held**
WEB: www.tid.com
SIC: 4971 Impounding reservoir, irrigation; water distribution or supply systems for irrigation
PA: Turlock Irrigation District
333 E Canal Dr
Turlock CA 95380
209 883-8222

(P-6375)
VISTA IRRIGATION DISTRICT
Also Called: Vid
1391 Engineer St, Vista (92081-8836)
PHONE....................760 597-3100
John Amodeo, *General Mgr*
Phil Zamora, *Executive*
Roy Coox, *General Mgr*
Ramae Ogilvie, *Admin Sec*
Brian Fisher, *Technology*
EMP: 99
SQ FT: 2,500
SALES: 43.1MM **Privately Held**
WEB: www.vid-h2o.org
SIC: 4971 Water distribution or supply systems for irrigation

---

5012 Automobiles & Other Motor Vehicles Wholesale

(P-6376)
A-Z BUS SALES INC (PA)
Also Called: John Deere Authorized Dealer
1900 S Riverside Ave, Colton
(92324-3344)
PHONE....................951 781-7188
Edwin John Landherr, *CEO*
James Reynolds, *President*
Rubi Lawson, *Admin Asst*
Jessica Smith, *Purchasing*
Cole Crockett, *Regl Sales Mgr*
▼ EMP: 90

SQ FT: 20,000
SALES: 3.9MM **Privately Held**
WEB: www.a-zbus.com
SIC: 5012 5082 Buses; construction & mining machinery

(P-6377)
ABC BUS INC
1485 Dale Way, Costa Mesa (92626-3918)
PHONE....................714 444-5888
Dane Cornell, *CEO*
EMP: 57
SALES (corp-wide): 172.7MM **Privately Held**
SIC: 5012 4173 Buses; bus terminal & service facilities
HQ: Abc Bus, Inc.
1506 30th St Nw
Faribault MN 55021
507 334-1871

(P-6378)
ABC BUS INC
3508 Haven Ave, Redwood City
(94063-4603)
PHONE....................650 368-3364
Mike Lawrence, *Manager*
EMP: 57
SALES (corp-wide): 172.7MM **Privately Held**
SIC: 5012 4173 Buses; bus terminal & service facilities
HQ: Abc Bus, Inc.
1506 30th St Nw
Faribault MN 55021
507 334-1871

(P-6379)
ADESA CORPORATION LLC
Also Called: Adesa Auction
8649 Kiefer Blvd, Sacramento
(95826-3907)
PHONE....................916 388-8899
Jim Sale, *Branch Mgr*
Raymond Klingaman, *General Mgr*
Raymond Killingaman, *Info Tech Mgr*
EMP: 115 **Publicly Held**
WEB: www.adesa.com
SIC: 5012 Automobile auction
HQ: Adesa Corporation, Llc
11299 Illinois St
Carmel IN 46032
-

(P-6380)
ADESA CORPORATION LLC
11625 Nino Way, Jurupa Valley
(91752-1437)
PHONE....................951 361-9400
Scott Spalder, *Manager*
Lora Rivera, *Human Res Dir*
EMP: 50 **Publicly Held**
WEB: www.adesa.com
SIC: 5012 7549 Automobile auction; automotive maintenance services
HQ: Adesa Corporation, Llc
11299 Illinois St
Carmel IN 46032
-

(P-6381)
ADESA CORPORATION LLC
2175 Cactus Rd, San Diego (92154-8002)
PHONE....................619 661-5565
Dale Mcllroy, *Manager*
Curt Madvig, *General Mgr*
Jose Hyoro, *Mktg Dir*
Dale Mc Ilroy, *Manager*
EMP: 120 **Publicly Held**
WEB: www.adesa.com
SIC: 5012 5521 Automobile auction; used car dealers
HQ: Adesa Corporation, Llc
11299 Illinois St
Carmel IN 46032
-

(P-6382)
AICHINGER INTERNATIONAL INC
5423 Littlebow Rd, Pls Vrds Pnsl
(90275-2364)
PHONE....................310 375-1533
Hans Aichinger, *President*
EMP: 70

SALES (est): 2.8MM **Privately Held**
SIC: 5012 Automobiles

(P-6383)
AMERICAN HONDA MOTOR CO INC (HQ)
1919 Torrance Blvd, Torrance
(90501-2722)
P.O. Box 2200 (90509-2200)
PHONE....................310 783-2000
Takuji Yamada, *CEO*
Alex Wu, *Partner*
Takanobu Ito, *President*
Hiroyuki Suganuma, *CFO*
H Okada, *Treasurer*
◆ EMP: 2375 EST: 1959
SALES (est): 8.3B **Privately Held**
WEB: www.honda.com
SIC: 5012 3732 Automobiles; jet skis

(P-6384)
AQUIRECORPS NORWALK AUTO AUCTN
12405 Rosecrans Ave, Norwalk
(90650-5056)
PHONE....................562 864-7464
Rj Romero, *Ch of Bd*
Lou Rudich, *COO*
Steve Fleurant, *CFO*
Chuck Doskow, *Admin Sec*
David Aker, *Controller*
EMP: 125 EST: 1979
SQ FT: 55,000
SALES (est): 23.8MM **Privately Held**
WEB: www.norwalkautoauction.com
SIC: 5012 Automobile auction

(P-6385)
AUTO BUYLINE SYSTEMS INC (PA)
Also Called: A B S Auto Auctions
341 Corporate Terrace Cir, Corona
(92879-6028)
P.O. Box 78086 (92877-0136)
PHONE....................951 271-8999
Thomas Harmon, *President*
Mark Frank, *Vice Pres*
Richard Stankiewicz, *Business Dir*
George Chickering, *District Mgr*
Vince Pytel, *District Mgr*
EMP: 50
SQ FT: 23,000
SALES (est): 34.2MM **Privately Held**
WEB: www.absbidsales.com
SIC: 5012 Automobile auction

(P-6386)
CALIFRNIA AUTO DALERS EXCH LLC
Also Called: Riverside Auto Auction
1320 N Tustin Ave, Anaheim (92807-1619)
PHONE....................714 996-2400
Tim Van Dam, *General Mgr*
Amanda Savage, *General Mgr*
Jay Waterman, *General Mgr*
Tom Wemhoff, *General Mgr*
Donna Bolt, *Office Mgr*
EMP: 400
SALES (est): 78.6MM
SALES (corp-wide): 32.3B **Privately Held**
WEB: www.riversideautoauction.com
SIC: 5012 Automobile auction
HQ: Manheim Investments, Inc.
6205 Peachtree Dunwoody Rd
Atlanta GA 30328
866 626-4346

(P-6387)
CARSON CAPITAL CORP (PA)
42882 Ivy St, Murrieta (92562-7218)
PHONE....................951 684-9585
Dale E Carson, *President*
Michael Hearne, *Treasurer*
Terri L Carson, *Corp Secy*
EMP: 51
SQ FT: 5,000
SALES (est): 11.8MM **Privately Held**
WEB: www.carsoncapital.com
SIC: 5012 5511 4111 Buses; new & used car dealers; commuter bus operation

P R O D U C T S & S V C S

(P-6388)
COAST COUNTIES TRUCK & EQP CO
Also Called: Coast Counties Peterbilt
260 Doolittle Dr, San Leandro
(94577-1014)
PHONE..................510 568-6933
Jon Wacker, *Branch Mgr*
EMP: 52
SALES (corp-wide): 79.9MM **Privately Held**
WEB: www.coastcounties.com
SIC: 5012 Automobiles & other motor vehicles
PA: Coast Counties Truck & Equipment Company
1740 N 4th St
San Jose CA 95112
408 453-5510

(P-6389)
COX AUTOMOTIVE INC
10700 Beech Ave, Fontana (92337-7205)
PHONE..................404 843-5000
Russ Norrish, *Manager*
Mark Roth, *Controller*
Sheri Lewis, *Opers Staff*
Cameron Byers, *Manager*
Sandra Garcia, *Supervisor*
EMP: 600
SALES (corp-wide): 32.3B **Privately Held**
WEB: www.manheim.com
SIC: 5012 5521 5531 Automobile auction; used car dealers; automotive accessories
HQ: Cox Automotive, Inc.
6205-A Pchtree Dnwoody Rd
Atlanta GA 30328
404 843-5000

(P-6390)
COX AUTOMOTIVE INC
29900 Auction Ct, Hayward (94544-6914)
PHONE..................510 786-4500
Tina Novoa, *General Mgr*
EMP: 500
SQ FT: 150,000
SALES (corp-wide): 32.3B **Privately Held**
WEB: www.manheim.com
SIC: 5012 Automobile auction
HQ: Cox Automotive, Inc.
6205-A Pchtree Dnwoody Rd
Atlanta GA 30328
404 843-5000

(P-6391)
COX AUTOMOTIVE INC
Also Called: Manheim Riverside Auto Auction
6446 Fremont St, Riverside (92504-1437)
PHONE..................951 689-6000
Scott Hurst, *Manager*
EMP: 440
SALES (corp-wide): 32.3B **Privately Held**
WEB: www.manheim.com
SIC: 5012 7389 5531 5521 Automobile auction; auctioneers, fee basis; automotive accessories; automobiles, used cars only
HQ: Cox Automotive, Inc.
6205-A Pchtree Dnwoody Rd
Atlanta GA 30328
404 843-5000

(P-6392)
COX AUTOMOTIVE INC
Also Called: Manheim San Diego
691 Calle Joven, Oceanside (92057)
PHONE..................760 754-3600
Jill Scott, *Branch Mgr*
EMP: 290
SALES (corp-wide): 32.3B **Privately Held**
WEB: www.manheim.com
SIC: 5012 Automobile auction
HQ: Cox Automotive, Inc.
6205-A Pchtree Dnwoody Rd
Atlanta GA 30328
404 843-5000

(P-6393)
E M THARP INC (PA)
Also Called: Golden Peterbilt
15243 Road 192, Porterville (93257-8967)
PHONE..................559 782-5800
Morris Tharp, *President*
Morris A Tharp, *President*
Pat Cornaggia, *Sales Staff*
Randy Ray, *Sales Staff*

Jeff Peterson, *Manager*
EMP: 97
SALES (est): 58.3MM **Privately Held**
SIC: 5012 5013 5511 5531 Trucks, commercial; truck parts & accessories; trucks, tractors & trailers: new & used; truck equipment & parts; recreational vehicle repairs

(P-6394)
FRESNO AUTO DEALERS AUCTION
278 N Marks Ave, Fresno (93706-1136)
PHONE..................559 268-8051
Darryl Ceccolil, *President*
Robert Cavazos, *Opers Staff*
▼ EMP: 107
SQ FT: 15,000
SALES (est): 10.6MM
SALES (corp-wide): 32.3B **Privately Held**
SIC: 5012 Automobile auction
HQ: Manheim Investments, Inc.
6205 Pachtree Dunwoody Rd
Atlanta GA 30328
866 626-4346

(P-6395)
FRESNO TRUCK CENTER
2727 E Central Ave, Fresno (93725-2425)
P.O. Box 12346 (93777-2346)
PHONE..................559 486-4310
Randy Moore, *Manager*
Michael Belles, *Principal*
EMP: 80
SQ FT: 40,000
SALES (corp-wide): 195.4MM **Privately Held**
WEB: www.fresnotruckcenter.com
SIC: 5012 5511 7538 5531 Truck tractors; trucks, tractors & trailers: new & used; general truck repair; truck equipment & parts; truck tires & tubes
PA: Fresno Truck Center
2727 E Central Ave
Fresno CA 93725
559 486-4310

(P-6396)
FRESNO TRUCK CENTER
Also Called: Delta Truck Center
10182 S Harlan Rd, French Camp (95231-9647)
P.O. Box 20 (95231-0020)
PHONE..................209 983-2400
John Gannon, *Manager*
EMP: 125
SALES (corp-wide): 195.4MM **Privately Held**
WEB: www.fresnotruckcenter.com
SIC: 5012 5013 7538 5531 Trucks, commercial; automotive supplies & parts; general automotive repair shops; truck equipment & parts; pickups, new & used; engines & parts, diesel
PA: Fresno Truck Center
2727 E Central Ave
Fresno CA 93725
559 486-4310

(P-6397)
GATEWAY AUTO SALES & LSG INC
Also Called: Gateway Auto Auction Group
3260 E Annadale Ave, Fresno (93725-1903)
PHONE..................800 921-4336
Larry B Champagne, *President*
EMP: 52
SQ FT: 4,000
SALES (est): 18.7MM **Privately Held**
WEB: www.champagnecars.com
SIC: 5012 Automobile auction

(P-6398)
HAAKER EQUIPMENT COMPANY (PA)
Also Called: TOTAL CLEAN
2070 N White Ave, La Verne (91750-5679)
PHONE..................909 542-0800
Edward R Blackman, *CEO*
Randy Blackman, *President*
Edward C Haaker, *CFO*
Wilson Shyu, *General Mgr*
Cindy Y Haaker, *Admin Sec*
▼ EMP: 76
SQ FT: 50,000

SALES: 56.2MM **Privately Held**
SIC: 5012 5087 5999 Ambulances; cleaning & maintenance equipment & supplies; cleaning equipment & supplies

(P-6399)
IAA INC
7245 Laurel Canyon Blvd # 5, North Hollywood (91605-3718)
PHONE..................818 487-2222
Charles Sanders, *Manager*
EMP: 59 **Publicly Held**
SIC: 5012 5531 5093 Automobile auction; automobiles; automotive accessories; automotive wrecking for scrap
HQ: Insurance Auto Auctions, Inc.
2 Westbrook Corporate Ctr # 1000
Westchester IL 60154
708 492-7000

(P-6400)
INDIEV INC
Also Called: Independent Electric Vehicles
5001 S Soto St, Vernon (90058)
PHONE..................323 703-5720
Shi Hai, *CEO*
Esther Kimm, *Principal*
Jim Tsai, *Principal*
Ying Zhou, *Principal*
EMP: 55
SALES (est): 18.6MM **Privately Held**
SIC: 5012 Automobiles & other motor vehicles

(P-6401)
INLAND KENWORTH (US) INC (HQ)
9730 Cherry Ave, Fontana (92335-5257)
PHONE..................909 823-9955
Leigh Parker, *Chairman*
Jim Beidrwieden, *President*
William Currie, *CEO*
Les Ziegler, *CFO*
▼ EMP: 105 EST: 1934
SQ FT: 60,000
SALES (est): 141.2MM
SALES (corp-wide): 1.1MM **Privately Held**
WEB: www.inland-group.com
SIC: 5012 7538 5013 7513 Trucks, commercial; diesel engine repair: automotive; truck parts & accessories; truck rental & leasing, no drivers
PA: Inland Industries Ltd
2482 Douglas Rd
Burnaby BC V5C 6
604 291-6021

(P-6402)
INTERSTATE TRUCK CENTER LLC (PA)
Also Called: Valley Peterbilt
2110 S Sinclair Ave, Stockton (95215-7556)
PHONE..................209 944-5821
David T Morganson, *Mng Member*
Don Hoffman, *Info Tech Mgr*
Radawna Hanson, *Asst Controller*
Mark Wells, *Marketing Staff*
John Barnes, *Sales Staff*
EMP: 100
SQ FT: 22,000
SALES (est): 66.8MM **Privately Held**
WEB: www.itctrucks.com
SIC: 5012 7513 Trucks, commercial; truck rental, without drivers

(P-6403)
JETWORLD INC
Also Called: Jetmore International
2656 Chico Ave, South El Monte (91733-1617)
PHONE..................626 448-0150
Leo Lea Young Lee, *President*
Chen Li-Fun Lee, *Corp Secy*
▲ EMP: 110
SQ FT: 5,000
SALES: 11.1MM **Privately Held**
WEB: www.jetworld.com
SIC: 5012 5065 5063 5999 Automobiles & other motor vehicles; security control equipment & systems; flashlights; alarm signal systems; automotive supplies & parts

(P-6404)
LOS ANGELES TRUCK CENTERS LLC
Also Called: Los Angeles Freightliner
13800 Valley Blvd, Fontana (92335-5216)
PHONE..................909 510-4000
Ricardo Flores, *Manager*
Priscilla Segala, *Technology*
Mark Sorensen, *Sales Staff*
EMP: 200
SALES (corp-wide): 115.4MM **Privately Held**
WEB: www.laflr.com
SIC: 5012 7538 5531 5511 Trucks, commercial; general automotive repair shops; automotive & home supply stores; new & used car dealers
PA: Los Angeles Truck Centers, Llc
2429 Peck Rd
Whittier CA 90601
562 447-1200

(P-6405)
MARATHON INDUSTRIES INC
Also Called: Marathon Truck Bodies
25597 Springbrook Ave, Santa Clarita (91350-2427)
P.O. Box 800279 (91380-0279)
PHONE..................661 286-1520
Chad Hess, *President*
Roger K Hess, *Chairman*
Tom Garcia, *VP Sales*
EMP: 145
SQ FT: 75,000
SALES (est): 25MM **Privately Held**
WEB: www.marathontruckbody.com
SIC: 5012 3713 Automobiles & other motor vehicles; truck & bus bodies

(P-6406)
MIRAMAR FORD TRUCK SALES INC
Also Called: NationaLease
6066 Miramar Rd, San Diego (92121-2591)
PHONE..................619 272-5340
Michael Buscher, *President*
Karrie Charest, *Treasurer*
Michael Maury, *Corp Secy*
Richard Harrigan, *Vice Pres*
Justin Brown, *Purch Mgr*
EMP: 74 EST: 1982
SQ FT: 22,000
SALES: 15.8MM **Privately Held**
WEB: www.miramartruck.com
SIC: 5012 5013 7513 Trucks, commercial; trucks, noncommercial; truck parts & accessories; truck rental & leasing, no drivers

(P-6407)
NORMANDIN AUTO BROKERS
900 Cptl Expy Aut Mall, San Jose (95136-1102)
PHONE..................408 266-2824
Louis Normandin, *Owner*
EMP: 80
SALES (est): 4.3MM **Privately Held**
SIC: 5012 Automobiles & other motor vehicles

(P-6408)
SHIFT TECHNOLOGIES INC
2525 16th St Ste 310, San Francisco (94103-4243)
PHONE..................415 800-2038
George Arison, *CEO*
I Arison Areshidze, *President*
Minnie Ingersoll, *COO*
Joel Washington, *CFO*
Katie Horne, *Principal*
EMP: 60
SALES (est): 21.8MM **Privately Held**
SIC: 5012 5511 Automotive brokers; automobiles, new & used

(P-6409)
SSMB PACIFIC HOLDING CO INC (HQ)
Also Called: Bay Area Kenworth
1755 Adams Ave, San Leandro (94577-1001)
PHONE..................510 836-6100
Harry Mamizuka, *President*
Tom Bertolino, *Vice Pres*

▼ EMP: 55 EST: 1942
SQ FT: 35,000
SALES (est): 132.3MM
SALES (corp-wide): 23.5B **Publicly Held**
WEB: www.bayareakenworth.com
SIC: 5012 7699 Trucks, commercial; industrial truck repair
PA: Paccar Inc
777 106th Ave Ne
Bellevue WA 98004
425 468-7400

(P-6410)
SSMB PACIFIC HOLDING CO INC
20769 Industry Rd, Anderson
(96007-8703)
PHONE...................................530 222-1212
Glenn Reed, *Branch Mgr*
EMP: 52
SALES (corp-wide): 23.5B **Publicly Held**
SIC: 5012 Trucks, commercial
HQ: Ssmb Pacific Holding Co Inc
1755 Adams Ave
San Leandro CA 94577
510 836-6100

(P-6411)
SSMB PACIFIC HOLDING CO INC
Also Called: Sacramento Kenworth
707 Display Way, Sacramento
(95838-3386)
PHONE...................................916 371-3372
Tom Bertilino, *Branch Mgr*
EMP: 52
SALES (corp-wide): 23.5B **Publicly Held**
WEB: www.bayareakenworth.com
SIC: 5012 7538 5531 5511 Trucks, commercial; general truck repair; truck equipment & parts; pickups, new & used
HQ: Ssmb Pacific Holding Co Inc
1755 Adams Ave
San Leandro CA 94577
510 836-6100

(P-6412)
TRUECAR INC
140 New Montgomery St # 2400, San Francisco (94105-3824)
PHONE...................................415 821-8270
Kristina Wilson, *Opers Mgr*
Derek Meyer, *Manager*
Pham Van, *Superintendent*
EMP: 281
SALES (corp-wide): 353.5MM **Publicly Held**
SIC: 5012 7299 Automotive brokers; information services, consumer
PA: Truecar, Inc.
120 Broadway Ste 200
Santa Monica CA 90401
800 200-2000

(P-6413)
UTILITY TRAILER SALES OF S CA (PA)
15567 Valley Blvd, Fontana (92335-6351)
PHONE...................................877 275-4887
Paul F Bennett,
Angelo Dugquem, *Branch Mgr*
Daniel Anchia, *Inv Control Mgr*
Bobby Garcia, *Marketing Staff*
Ralph Keaton, *Sales Staff*
EMP: 100
SALES: 88.1MM **Privately Held**
SIC: 5012 5013 5531 5561 Trailers for passenger vehicles; automotive supplies & parts; automobile & truck equipment & parts; travel trailers: automobile, new & used

(P-6414)
WAH HUNG INTL MCHY INC
800 Monterey Pass Rd, Monterey Park
(91754-3609)
PHONE...................................323 263-3513
Raymond Ng, *Manager*
EMP: 69 **Privately Held**
SIC: 5012 5521 Automobiles; automobiles, used cars only
PA: Wah Hung International Machinery, Inc.
1000 E Garvey Ave
Monterey Park CA 91755
-

(P-6415)
WIND RIVER ENTERPRISES INC
Also Called: North Bay Auto Auction
250 Dittmer Rd, Fairfield (94534-1621)
PHONE...................................707 864-1040
Don Morrow, *President*
Maureen Green, *Corp Secy*
David Aahl, *Director*
EMP: 95
SQ FT: 20,000
SALES: 14.3MM **Privately Held**
WEB: www.nbauto.com
SIC: 5012 Automobile auction

5013 Motor Vehicle Splys & New Parts Wholesale

(P-6416)
1-800 RADIATOR & A/C (PA)
Also Called: 1-800-Radiator
4401 Park Rd, Benicia (94510-1124)
PHONE...................................707 747-7400
Mike Rippey, *Ch of Bd*
Joe Rippey, *President*
David Gruner, *Officer*
Ted Rippey, *Exec VP*
Tyson Garrett, *Regional Mgr*
◆ EMP: 100
SALES (est): 42.9MM **Privately Held**
WEB: www.radiater.com
SIC: 5013 Radiators

(P-6417)
ALL STAR AUTOMOTIVE PRODUCTS
4257 Auction Ave Ste N, Baldwin Park
(91706-3497)
PHONE...................................626 960-5164
Fritz Ehlers, *President*
▲ EMP: 80
SQ FT: 28,000
SALES (est): 9.3MM **Privately Held**
WEB: www.allstarproducts.com
SIC: 5013 3714 3694 Automotive supplies & parts; clutches, motor vehicle; engine electrical equipment

(P-6418)
ANTHONY LAMBE
Also Called: Fashion Wheel
1521 W Nielsen Ave Ste 69, Fresno
(93706-1309)
PHONE...................................559 268-0709
Anthony Lambe, *Manager*
Jack Glos, *Owner*
EMP: 66
SQ FT: 25,000
SALES (est): 4.2MM **Privately Held**
WEB: www.steelband.com
SIC: 5013 Wheels, motor vehicle

(P-6419)
APU INC (PA)
14939 Oxnard St, Van Nuys (91411-2611)
PHONE...................................661 948-2880
John Christy Jr, *President*
EMP: 60
SQ FT: 20,000
SALES (est): 18.3MM **Privately Held**
WEB: www.apu.com
SIC: 5013 5531 Automotive supplies & parts; automotive parts

(P-6420)
APW INTERNATIONAL INC
1073 E Artesia Blvd, Carson (90746-1601)
PHONE...................................310 884-5003
Jae W Chang, *President*
Young Suhr, *Exec VP*
▲ EMP: 140
SALES (est): 10.7MM **Privately Held**
SIC: 5013 Automotive supplies & parts

(P-6421)
APW KNOX-SEEMAN WAREHOUSE INC (HQ)
1073 E Artesia Blvd, Carson (90746-1601)
PHONE...................................310 604-4373
Tong Y Suhr, *CEO*
Susan Suhr, *Admin Sec*
Sonia Barahona, *Sales Staff*
▲ EMP: 98 EST: 1972
SQ FT: 32,000

SALES (est): 56.9MM
SALES (corp-wide): 72.2MM **Privately Held**
WEB: www.apwks.com
SIC: 5013 5531 Automotive supplies & parts; automotive parts
PA: Auto Parts Warehouse, Inc.
16941 Keegan Ave
Carson CA 90746
800 913-6119

(P-6422)
AUTO EXPRESSIONS LLC
505 E Euclid Ave, Compton (90222-2811)
PHONE...................................310 639-0666
Lawrence McIsaac, *President*
Blake Barnett, *CFO*
John Fiumefreddo, *Senior VP*
Steve Lazzara, *Senior VP*
▲ EMP: 100 EST: 2010
SALES (est): 19.5MM **Privately Held**
SIC: 5013 Alternators

(P-6423)
AUTO PARTS WAREHOUSE INC (PA)
16941 Keegan Ave, Carson (90746-1307)
PHONE...................................800 913-6119
Tong Young Suhr, *Principal*
Jim Hastie, *President*
Sleung Ja Suhr, *Vice Pres*
Byung Joon Lee, *Admin Sec*
Benjamin Ramos, *Administration*
▼ EMP: 50
SQ FT: 40,000
SALES (est): 72.2MM **Privately Held**
SIC: 5013 Automotive supplies & parts

(P-6424)
AZIMC INVESTMENTS INC
8901 Canoga Ave, Canoga Park
(91304-1512)
PHONE...................................818 678-1200
William C Rhodes III, *CEO*
Thomas Kliman, *Vice Pres*
Perry Friedman, *Director*
◆ EMP: 250 EST: 1962
SALES (est): 149.3MM
SALES (corp-wide): 11.8B **Publicly Held**
WEB: www.imcparts.com
SIC: 5013 Automotive supplies & parts
PA: Autozone, Inc.
123 S Front St
Memphis TN 38103
901 495-6500

(P-6425)
BBK PERFORMANCE INC
Also Called: Gripp
27440 Bostik Ct, Temecula (92590-3698)
PHONE...................................951 296-1771
Brian Murphy, *President*
Ken Murphy, *Treasurer*
EMP: 75
SQ FT: 40,000
SALES (est): 12.1MM **Privately Held**
WEB: www.bbkperformance.com
SIC: 5013 5531 Automotive supplies & parts; automotive parts

(P-6426)
BI WAREHOUSING INC
Also Called: Riebes Auto Parts
1490 Bridge St, Yuba City (95993-3506)
PHONE...................................530 671-8787
Doug Duncan, *Branch Mgr*
EMP: 50
SALES (corp-wide): 137MM **Privately Held**
WEB: www.riebes.com
SIC: 5013 5531 Automotive supplies & parts; automotive parts
PA: Bi Warehousing, Inc.
5404 Pacific St
Rocklin CA 95677
916 624-0654

(P-6427)
BST ENTERPRISES INC
Also Called: Saddlemen
17801 S Susana Rd, Compton
(90221-5411)
PHONE...................................310 638-1222
David Echert, *Treasurer*
Zulema Cruz, *Administration*
▲ EMP: 65

SQ FT: 20,000
SALES (est): 15.7MM **Privately Held**
WEB: www.saddlemen.com
SIC: 5013 3751 Motorcycle parts; motorcycle accessories

(P-6428)
CAL-STATE AUTO PARTS INC (PA)
Also Called: Auto Pride
1361 N Red Gum St, Anaheim
(92806-1318)
PHONE...................................714 630-5950
Richard J Deblasi, *CEO*
John McMillin, *CFO*
Steven Brooker, *Vice Pres*
Douglas Mayes, *Prdtn Mgr*
▲ EMP: 105
SQ FT: 76,000
SALES (est): 58.8MM **Privately Held**
WEB: www.csautoparts.com
SIC: 5013 Automotive supplies & parts

(P-6429)
CLUB ASSIST NORTH AMERICA INC (DH)
888 W 6th St Ste 300, Los Angeles
(90017-2729)
PHONE...................................213 388-4333
Brett Davies, *CEO*
Scott Davies, *COO*
Alex Leombruni, *CFO*
Candace Enman, *Treasurer*
Stephane Belisle, *Vice Pres*
▲ EMP: 64
SALES (est): 100.3MM **Privately Held**
SIC: 5013 Automotive batteries

(P-6430)
CLUB ASSIST US LLC
Also Called: Battery Assist
888 W 6th St Ste 300, Los Angeles
(90017-2729)
PHONE...................................213 388-4333
John Tutt, *President*
Stephane Belisle, *Treasurer*
Stuart Davies, *Admin Sec*
Julie Robinson, *Admin Sec*
Nick Sanfilippo, *CTO*
▲ EMP: 250
SQ FT: 6,382
SALES (est): 110.3MM **Privately Held**
SIC: 5013 Automotive batteries
HQ: Club Assist North America Inc.
888 W 6th St Ste 300
Los Angeles CA 90017
213 388-4333

(P-6431)
DAE-IL USA INC
Also Called: Custom Chrome
15750 Vineyard Blvd # 100, Morgan Hill
(95037-7119)
PHONE...................................559 651-5170
Robert Russell, *Director*
EMP: 69 **Privately Held**
SIC: 5013 Motorcycle parts
HQ: Dae-Il Usa, Inc.
112 Robert Young Blvd
Murray KY 42071

(P-6432)
DENSO PDTS & SVCS AMERICAS INC (DH)
Also Called: Dsca
3900 Via Oro Ave, Long Beach
(90810-1868)
PHONE...................................310 834-6352
Yoshihiko Yamada, *CEO*
Hirokatsu Yamashita, *President*
Roy Nakaue, *Exec VP*
Peter Clotz, *Vice Pres*
Jeff Rogers, *Vice Pres*
◆ EMP: 153
SQ FT: 235,000
SALES (est): 245MM **Privately Held**
WEB: www.densorobots.com
SIC: 5013 7361 5075 3714 Automotive supplies & parts; employment agencies; warm air heating & air conditioning; motor vehicle parts & accessories
HQ: Denso International America, Inc.
24777 Denso Dr
Southfield MI 48033
248 350-7500

(P-6433)
DNA SPECIALTY INC
200 W Artesia Blvd, Compton
(90220-5500)
PHONE...............................310 767-4070
James Choi, *President*
Sun Choi, *Admin Sec*
Aileen Zhang, *Manager*
▲ **EMP:** 90
SQ FT: 80,000
SALES (est): 23.4MM **Privately Held**
SIC: 5013 3714 Wheels, motor vehicle; wheels, motor vehicle

(P-6434)
DRIVEN PERFORMANCE BRANDS INC (PA)
Also Called: B & M Racing
100 Stony Point Rd # 125, Santa Rosa
(95401-4117)
PHONE...............................707 544-4761
Brian Applegate, *President*
Steve Potter, *CFO*
Jonathan Miller, *Principal*
▲ **EMP:** 71 **EST:** 2000
SALES (est): 139.7MM
SALES (corp-wide): 113.2MM **Privately Held**
WEB: www.bmracing.com
SIC: 5013 Automotive engines & engine parts; automotive supplies & parts

(P-6435)
ELLIOTT AUTO SUPPLY CO INC
Also Called: Factory Motor Parts
448 W Katella Ave, Orange (92867-4604)
PHONE...............................800 278-6394
Mike Cote, *Manager*
EMP: 50
SALES (corp-wide): 726.1MM **Privately Held**
SIC: 5013 5015 Automotive supplies & parts; automotive parts & supplies, used
PA: Elliott Auto Supply Co., Inc.
1380 Corporate Center Cur
Eagan MN 55121
651 454-4100

(P-6436)
ELLIOTT AUTO SUPPLY CO INC
Factory Motor Parts
1600 E Orangethorpe Ave, Fullerton
(92831-5231)
PHONE...............................310 527-2500
Rich Carol, *Principal*
EMP: 65
SALES (corp-wide): 726.1MM **Privately Held**
SIC: 5013 Automotive supplies & parts
PA: Elliott Auto Supply Co., Inc.
1380 Corporate Center Cur
Eagan MN 55121
651 454-4100

(P-6437)
EMPI INC
301 E Orangethorpe Ave, Anaheim
(92801-1032)
PHONE...............................714 446-9606
Phillip Kane, *CEO*
Todd Tyler, *CFO*
Tamara Minarsch, *Manager*
EMP: 80
SQ FT: 127,000
SALES (est): 55.9K **Privately Held**
SIC: 5013 Automotive supplies & parts

(P-6438)
FAST PRO INC
Also Called: Fast Undercar
2555 Lafayette St Ste 103, Santa Clara
(95050-2644)
PHONE...............................408 566-0200
Brian Smits, *President*
Ken Luchswich, *Sales Executive*
Tom Croker, *Sales Mgr*
EMP: 60
SQ FT: 13,000
SALES (est): 12.6MM **Privately Held**
SIC: 5013 Automotive supplies; automotive supplies & parts

(P-6439)
FORD MOTOR COMPANY
1269 Phoenix Dr, Manteca (95336-6006)
P.O. Box 1666, Richmond (94802-0666)
PHONE...............................209 824-6600
William Stewart, *Manager*
Rachel Varias, *Analyst*
EMP: 220
SALES (corp-wide): 160.3B **Publicly Held**
WEB: www.ford.com
SIC: 5013 5531 Automotive supplies & parts; automotive parts
PA: Ford Motor Company
1 American Rd
Dearborn MI 48126
313 322-3000

(P-6440)
FOX FACTORY HOLDING CORP
750 Vernon Way Ste 101, El Cajon
(92020-1979)
PHONE...............................619 768-1800
John Marking, *Branch Mgr*
EMP: 558
SALES (corp-wide): 619.2MM **Publicly Held**
SIC: 5013 Springs, shock absorbers & struts
PA: Fox Factory Holding Corp.
915 Disc Dr
Scotts Valley CA 95066
831 274-6500

(P-6441)
GENUINE PARTS DISTRIBUTORS
Also Called: Tracy Industries
3200 E Guasti Rd Ste 100, Ontario
(91761-8661)
PHONE...............................562 692-9034
Tim Engball, *CEO*
Erma Tracy, *Vice Pres*
David M Rosenberger, *Admin Sec*
Lisa Schumacher, *Info Tech Dir*
EMP: 75
SALES (est): 6.2MM
SALES (corp-wide): 28.2MM **Privately Held**
SIC: 5013 Automotive engines & engine parts
PA: Fred Jones Enterprises, L.L.C.
6200 Sw 29th St
Oklahoma City OK 73179
800 927-7845

(P-6442)
GOODRIDGE USA INC (DH)
529 Van Ness Ave, Torrance (90501-1424)
PHONE...............................310 533-1924
Celso Pierre, *CEO*
Perla Alcaraz, *Administration*
Kim Tait, *Human Res Mgr*
Loretta Jaimes, *Buyer*
Brendan McGrath, *Sales Staff*
▲ **EMP:** 55
SQ FT: 15,000
SALES (est): 27.1MM **Privately Held**
WEB: www.goodridge.net
SIC: 5013 Automotive supplies
HQ: Goodridge Limited
Dart Building
Exeter EX1 3
139 236-9090

(P-6443)
HANSON DISTRIBUTING COMPANY (PA)
975 W 8th St, Azusa (91702-2246)
PHONE...............................626 224-9800
Daniel Hanson, *CEO*
Adam Holloway, *IT/INT Sup*
Laurie Hanson, *Buyer*
EMP: 115
SQ FT: 160,000
SALES (est): 77.2MM
SALES (corp-wide): 85MM **Privately Held**
WEB: www.HansonDistributing.com
SIC: 5013 Automotive supplies & parts

(P-6444)
HARRISON INVENTORY SERVICES
37051 Graphic Ave, Littlerock
(93543-1802)
PHONE...............................661 269-9220
Tony J Ferraro, *President*
EMP: 50
SALES (est): 4MM **Privately Held**
SIC: 5013 Automotive supplies & parts

(P-6445)
HINO MOTORS MFG USA INC
4550 Wineville Ave, Jurupa Valley
(91752-3723)
PHONE...............................951 727-0286
Debra Martinas, *Branch Mgr*
EMP: 159 **Privately Held**
WEB: www.hinointl.com
SIC: 5013 Truck parts & accessories
HQ: Hino Motors Manufacturing U.S.A., Inc.
45501 W 12 Mile Rd
Novi MI 48377

(P-6446)
IAP WEST INC
20036 S Via Baron, Rancho Dominguez
(90220-6105)
PHONE...............................310 667-9720
Michel Berg, *CEO*
Louis L Berg, *President*
John Kelley, *CFO*
Sharon Berg, *Admin Sec*
◆ **EMP:** 54
SQ FT: 80,000
SALES (est): 15.2MM **Privately Held**
SIC: 5013 Automotive engines & engine parts

(P-6447)
INTERSTATE BTRY SAN DIEGO INC
9345 Cabot Dr, San Diego (92126-4310)
PHONE...............................858 790-8244
Ron Cummings, *President*
EMP: 50
SQ FT: 20,000
SALES: 21MM **Privately Held**
WEB: www.battery.com
SIC: 5013 5531 Automotive batteries; batteries, automotive & truck

(P-6448)
JAMM MANAGEMENT LLC
Also Called: Fast Undercar Stockton
2447 Stanford Way, Antioch (94531-8249)
PHONE...............................510 437-5200
Jose R Montilla,
Stockton Fast, *Warehouse Mgr*
Francisco Mendoza,
EMP: 50
SQ FT: 4,100
SALES (est): 5.4MM **Privately Held**
WEB: www.jammentgraphics.net
SIC: 5013 Automotive engines & engine parts

(P-6449)
KEYSTONE AUTOMOTIVE INDS INC
2530 Lindsey Privado Dr C, Ontario
(91761-3459)
PHONE...............................909 986-4586
Jim Francis, *Branch Mgr*
EMP: 75
SALES (corp-wide): 11.8B **Publicly Held**
WEB: www.kool-vue.com
SIC: 5013 Automotive supplies & parts
HQ: Keystone Automotive Industries, Inc.
5846 Crossings Blvd
Antioch TN 37013
615 781-5200

(P-6450)
LAX WHEEL REFINISHING INC
1520 Spence St, Los Angeles
(90023-3920)
PHONE...............................323 269-1484
Jesus Sanchez, *President*
EMP: 60
SALES (est): 4.7MM **Privately Held**
SIC: 5013 Wheels, motor vehicle

(P-6451)
LEXANI WHEEL CORPORATION
2380 Railroad St Ste 101, Corona
(92880-5471)
PHONE...............................951 808-4220
Frank J Hodges, *CEO*
Carlos Parrott, *Marketing Mgr*
Jon Welti, *Sales Mgr*
◆ **EMP:** 60
SQ FT: 35,000
SALES (est): 16MM **Privately Held**
SIC: 5013 Motor vehicle supplies & new parts

(P-6452)
MAXZONE VEHICLE LIGHTING CORP (HQ)
Also Called: Depo Auto Parts
15889 Slover Ave Unit A, Fontana
(92337-7299)
PHONE...............................909 822-3288
Polo Hsu, *President*
Hojin Lee, *Executive*
Shu Sheng Hsu, *Principal*
David Sanchez, *Sales Executive*
Daniel Tsai, *Assistant*
◆ **EMP:** 50
SQ FT: 32,000
SALES (est): 40.8MM **Privately Held**
SIC: 5013 3714 Automotive supplies & parts; motor vehicle electrical equipment

(P-6453)
MERIDIAN RACK & PINION INC
6740 Cobra Way Ste 200, San Diego
(92121-4102)
PHONE...............................858 587-8777
Dara Greaney, *CEO*
Matt Glauber, *President*
Chris Struempler, *CFO*
Brad Paugh, *Marketing Mgr*
Steve Crossley, *Manager*
▲ **EMP:** 130
SQ FT: 55,000
SALES (est): 57.2MM **Privately Held**
WEB: www.meridianautoparts.com
SIC: 5013 5961 Automotive supplies & parts; mail order house, order taking office only

(P-6454)
MIKUNI AMERICAN CORPORATION (HQ)
Also Called: M A C
8910 Mikuni Ave, Northridge (91324-3403)
PHONE...............................310 676-0522
Satoshi Fujimori, *CEO*
Hirokazu Masahashi, *CFO*
Masaki Ikuta, *Chairman*
Shigeru Ikuta, *Vice Pres*
Mitch Wada, *Vice Pres*
▲ **EMP:** 64
SQ FT: 50,000
SALES (est): 99MM **Privately Held**
WEB: www.mikuni.com
SIC: 5013 5088 Automotive hardware; aircraft engines & engine parts; aircraft & parts

(P-6455)
MOBIS PARTS AMERICA LLC (HQ)
10550 Talbert Ave Fl 4, Fountain Valley
(92708-6031)
PHONE...............................786 515-1101
Yun Dong Park, *Mng Member*
Rheia Szymczyk, *Planning*
Joyce Nakamura, *Analyst*
Kristine Coine, *Buyer*
Rolando De La Rosa, *Opers Staff*
◆ **EMP:** 90
SALES (est): 212.6MM **Privately Held**
SIC: 5013 Automotive supplies & parts

(P-6456)
MYERS TIRE SUPPLY DIST INC
Also Called: Myers Tire Supply Division
107 Exchange Pl, Pomona (91768-4307)
PHONE...............................602 233-1037
Joel Schotz, *Branch Mgr*
John Orr, *CEO*
EMP: 99

▲ = Import ▼=Export
◆ =Import/Export

SALES (corp-wide): 566.7MM **Publicly Held**
WEB: www.myerstiresupply.com
SIC: 5013 Automotive supplies & parts
HQ: Myers Tire Supply Distribution, Inc.
1293 S Main St
Akron OH 44301
330 253-5592

(P-6457)
MYGRANT GLASS COMPANY INC (PA)
3271 Arden Rd, Hayward (94545-3901)
PHONE.................................510 785-4360
Michael Mygrant, *CEO*
Kathy Mygrant, *Treasurer*
Craig Schoeneshoefer, *Regional Mgr*
Domenic Badalamenti, *Area Mgr*
Scott Hughan, *Branch Mgr*
◆ **EMP:** 50
SQ FT: 128,222
SALES (est): 191.1MM **Privately Held**
SIC: 5013 Automobile glass

(P-6458)
NSV INTERNATIONAL CORP
1250 E 29th St, Signal Hill (90755-1800)
P.O. Box 14660, Long Beach (90853-4660)
PHONE.................................562 438-3836
Stephan Humphries, *CEO*
Isabel Palafox, *COO*
EMP: 100
SQ FT: 1,200
SALES: 1.1MM **Privately Held**
SIC: 5013 Automotive supplies

(P-6459)
PACIFIC COAST TRUCK AND WHSE (PA)
692 Anita St, Chula Vista (91911-4620)
P.O. Box 13400, San Diego (92170-3400)
PHONE.................................619 661-5451
Mark Secord, *President*
Jennifer Secord, *Admin Sec*
▲ **EMP:** 50
SALES (est): 7.2MM **Privately Held**
WEB: www.e-pacificcoast.com
SIC: 5013 Truck parts & accessories

(P-6460)
PARTSCHANNEL INC
8905 Rex Rd, Pico Rivera (90660-3799)
PHONE.................................562 654-3400
Alex Marquez, *Manager*
EMP: 50
SALES (corp-wide): 11.8B **Publicly Held**
SIC: 5013 Body repair or paint shop supplies, automotive
HQ: Partschannel, Inc.
4003 Grand Lakes Way # 200
Grand Prairie TX 75050
214 688-0018

(P-6461)
PERFORMANCE WAREHOUSE CO
901 Arden Way, Sacramento (95815-3201)
PHONE.................................916 920-2221
Gary Petit, *Branch Mgr*
EMP: 85
SALES (corp-wide): 85.8MM **Privately Held**
SIC: 5013 5531 Automotive supplies & parts; automotive & home supply stores
PA: Performance Warehouse Co.
9440 N Whitaker Rd
Portland OR 97217
503 417-5302

(P-6462)
QUALITY PLUS AUTO PARTS INC
1333 30th St Ste C, San Diego (92154-3486)
PHONE.................................619 424-9991
Roger Yang, *President*
Jeffrey Shong Lowe, *Admin Sec*
Fernando Torres, *Buyer*
▲ **EMP:** 50
SQ FT: 17,000
SALES (est): 8.5MM **Privately Held**
WEB: www.qualityplusauto.com
SIC: 5013 5531 Automotive supplies & parts; automotive parts

(P-6463)
RAMCAR BATTERIES INC
2700 Carrier Ave, Commerce (90040-2572)
PHONE.................................323 726-1212
Clifford J Crowe, *President*
▲ **EMP:** 50
SQ FT: 90,000
SALES (est): 17.8MM **Privately Held**
SIC: 5013 3691 Automotive batteries; lead acid batteries (storage batteries)

(P-6464)
RECYCLER CORE COMPANY INC
Also Called: Northwest Recycler Core
2727 Kansas Ave, Riverside (92507-2638)
PHONE.................................951 276-1687
Kenneth Meier, *President*
Gisela Meier, *Corp Secy*
Robert Palmer, *Executive*
Alan Hart, *General Mgr*
Simona Johnson, *Office Mgr*
▲ **EMP:** 100
SQ FT: 280,000
SALES (est): 34.9MM **Privately Held**
WEB: www.rccauto.com
SIC: 5013 Automotive supplies & parts

(P-6465)
RICHARD HUETTER INC
Also Called: Pacific Parts International
21050 Osborne St, Canoga Park (91304-1744)
PHONE.................................818 700-8001
Richard Huetter, *CEO*
Maria L Huetter, *Treasurer*
▲ **EMP:** 70
SQ FT: 30,000
SALES (est): 12.8MM **Privately Held**
SIC: 5013 Automotive supplies & parts

(P-6466)
S F AUTO PARTS WHSE INC
Also Called: Mac Kenzie Warehouse
6000 3rd St, San Francisco (94124-3106)
PHONE.................................415 255-0115
M Mackenzie Menendez, *President*
Michelle Mackenzie Menendez, *President*
Anna-Maria Mac Kenzie, *Treasurer*
Eduardo Menendez, *Exec VP*
EMP: 56 **EST:** 1951
SQ FT: 53,000
SALES (est): 17.5MM **Privately Held**
WEB: www.mackenziewarehouse.com
SIC: 5013 Automotive supplies

(P-6467)
SCAT ENTERPRISES INC
1400 Kingsdale Ave, Redondo Beach (90278-3983)
PHONE.................................310 370-5501
Philip T Lieb, *President*
Craig Schenasi, *CFO*
Travis Kennedy, *Engineer*
Toby Raine, *Analyst*
Anthony Sierra, *Human Res Mgr*
◆ **EMP:** 65
SQ FT: 42,000
SALES (est): 21MM **Privately Held**
WEB: www.scatenterprises.com
SIC: 5013 3714 Automotive supplies & parts; automotive supplies; motor vehicle parts & accessories

(P-6468)
SERRATO-MCDERMOTT INC
Also Called: Allied Auto Store
43815 S Grimmer Blvd, Fremont (94538-6348)
PHONE.................................510 656-6233
Bill Bailey, *CEO*
Anthony Barnes, *Sales Staff*
EMP: 55
SQ FT: 17,000
SALES (est): 21.7MM **Privately Held**
SIC: 5013 5531 Automotive supplies & parts; automotive parts

(P-6469)
SILLA AUTOMOTIVE LLC
1901 Mineral Ct Ste C, Bakersfield (93308-6819)
PHONE.................................661 392-8880
EMP: 52

SALES (corp-wide): 73.4MM **Privately Held**
SIC: 5013
PA: Silla Automotive, Llc
1217 W Artesia Blvd
Compton CA 90220
310 323-0001

(P-6470)
SPECTRA PREMIUM (USA) CORP
2220 Almond Ave, Redlands (92374-2073)
PHONE.................................951 653-0640
Sergio Zapata, *Branch Mgr*
EMP: 58
SALES (corp-wide): 462.1MM **Privately Held**
SIC: 5013 Automotive supplies & parts
HQ: Spectra Premium (Usa) Corp.
3052 N Distribution Way
Greenfield IN 46140
317 891-1700

(P-6471)
SSF IMPORTED AUTO PARTS LLC
21175 Main St Ste A, Carson (90745-1500)
PHONE.................................310 782-8859
Bruce Brown, *Manager*
EMP: 60
SALES (corp-wide): 1.8B **Privately Held**
WEB: www.ssfautoparts.com
SIC: 5013 4225 Automotive supplies & parts; general warehousing & storage
HQ: Ssf Imported Auto Parts Llc
466 Forbes Blvd
South San Francisco CA 94080
800 203-9287

(P-6472)
SSF IMPORTED AUTO PARTS LLC (DH)
Also Called: S S F
466 Forbes Blvd, South San Francisco (94080-2015)
PHONE.................................800 203-9287
Thomas Beer, *Mng Member*
Nerissa Wong, *Prgrmr*
Carol Cotter, *IT/INT Sup*
Roger Guedikian, *IT/INT Sup*
Mark Gunson, *Graphic Designe*
▲ **EMP:** 100
SALES (est): 111.6MM
SALES (corp-wide): 1.8B **Privately Held**
WEB: www.ssfautoparts.com
SIC: 5013 Automotive supplies & parts
HQ: Wm Se
Pagenstecherstr. 121
Osnabruck 49090
541 998-90

(P-6473)
TAP OPERATING CO LLC
400 W Artesia Blvd, Compton (90220-5501)
PHONE.................................310 900-5500
EMP: 1200
SALES (est): 87.2MM **Privately Held**
SIC: 5013 Truck parts & accessories

(P-6474)
TAP WORLDWIDE LLC (PA)
Also Called: 4 Wheel Parts Performance Ctrs
400 W Artesia Blvd, Compton (90220-5501)
PHONE.................................310 900-5500
Greg Adler, *President*
Tim Mongi, *COO*
Mark Lane, *CFO*
Shelly Manuel, *Credit Mgr*
Darren Marcus Salvin,
◆ **EMP:** 127
SALES (est): 706.2MM **Privately Held**
SIC: 5013 Motor vehicle supplies & new parts

(P-6475)
TRANSTAR INDUSTRIES INC
Also Called: Transtar Automotive
15010 Calvert St, Van Nuys (91411-2605)
PHONE.................................818 785-2000
David Pianannamore, *Manager*
EMP: 50 **Privately Held**
WEB: www.transtarindustries.com
SIC: 5013 Automotive supplies & parts

HQ: Transtar Industries Llc
7350 Young Dr
Cleveland OH 44146
440 232-5100

(P-6476)
UQUALITY AUTOMOTIVE PDTS CORP (PA)
16411 Shoemaker Ave, Cerritos (90703-2217)
PHONE.................................562 282-2888
Zhongren Meng, *CEO*
John Aniunas, *Vice Pres*
Rich Sanderson, *Vice Pres*
▲ **EMP:** 50
SQ FT: 70,000
SALES (est): 15.4MM **Privately Held**
WEB: www.uquality.com
SIC: 5013 Automotive supplies & parts

(P-6477)
VEHICLE ACCESSORY CENTER LLC
10863 Jersey Blvd # 101, Rancho Cucamonga (91730-5151)
PHONE.................................909 987-8237
Russell Hoyt, *Mng Member*
Ana McDonald, *Office Mgr*
Justin Roberts, *Opers Mgr*
Cory Mitchem, *Sales Staff*
Bryan Sawyer, *Manager*
EMP: 53
SQ FT: 100,000
SALES (est): 8MM
SALES (corp-wide): 71.8MM **Privately Held**
WEB: www.vehicleaccessorycenter.com
SIC: 5013 Automotive supplies & parts
PA: Mark Christopher Chevrolet Inc
2131 E Convention Ctr Way
Ontario CA 91764
909 321-5860

(P-6478)
VETRONIX SALES CORPORATION
Also Called: Vetronix Crpration/Bosch Group
2030 Alameda Padre Serra, Santa Barbara (93103-1716)
PHONE.................................805 966-2000
James Zaleski, *President*
EMP: 68
SQ FT: 26,000
SALES: 8.9MM
SALES (corp-wide): 294.8MM **Privately Held**
WEB: www.vetronix.com
SIC: 5013 Testing equipment, electrical: automotive
HQ: Bosch Automotive Service Solutions Inc.
2030 Alameda Padre Serra
Santa Barbara CA 93103
805 966-2000

(P-6479)
WAGAN CORPORATION
31088 San Clemente St, Hayward (94544-7811)
PHONE.................................510 471-9221
Alex Hsu, *CEO*
John Hsu, *Ch of Bd*
Po-Jung Hsu, *CEO*
Mamie Hsu, *CFO*
Bryan Kawaye, *Engineer*
◆ **EMP:** 50
SQ FT: 30,000
SALES (est): 13.4MM **Privately Held**
WEB: www.wagan.com
SIC: 5013 Automotive supplies & parts

(P-6480)
WARREN DISTRIBUTING INC (PA)
Also Called: Wdi
8737 Dice Rd, Santa Fe Springs (90670-2513)
PHONE.................................562 789-3360
Brian Weiss, *President*
Linnea Herndon, *CFO*
Jake Boggs, *Vice Pres*
Dave Erlenbach, *Vice Pres*
Gary Jacobson, *Vice Pres*
◆ **EMP:** 55
SQ FT: 68,000

SALES (est): 70.1MM **Privately Held**
WEB: www.warrendist.com
SIC: 5013 Automotive supplies

(P-6481)
WEBASTO CHARGING SYSTEMS INC (DH)
1333 S Mayflower Ave # 100, Monrovia (91016-5265)
PHONE...................................626 415-4000
John Thomas, *CEO*
Doug McElroy, *CFO*
EMP: 85 EST: 2018
SALES (est): 71.6MM
SALES (corp-wide): 411.9K **Privately Held**
SIC: 5013 Automobile service station equipment
HQ: Webasto Roof Systems Inc.
    1757 Northfield Dr
    Rochester Hills MI 48309
    248 997-5100

(P-6482)
YOSHIMURA RESEARCH & DEV AMER
5420 Daniels St Ste A, Chino (91710-9012)
PHONE...................................909 628-4722
Fujio Yoshimura, *President*
Suehiro Watanabe, *CFO*
Don Sakakura, *Senior VP*
Briseida Hultz, *Human Resources*
▲ EMP: 100
SQ FT: 12,000
SALES (est): 34.9MM **Privately Held**
WEB: www.yoshimura-rd.com
SIC: 5013 Motorcycle parts

5014 Tires & Tubes Wholesale

(P-6483)
AMERICAN TIRE DISTRIBUTORS
645 Dado St, San Jose (95131-1209)
PHONE...................................408 435-3340
Bob Goularte, *Manager*
Dave Barry, *Vice Pres*
EMP: 50
SALES (corp-wide): 5B **Privately Held**
WEB: www.heafnertire.com
SIC: 5014 Tires & tubes
HQ: American Tire Distributors Inc.
    12200 Herbert Wayne Ct # 150
    Huntersville NC 28078
    704 992-2000

(P-6484)
CARROLLS LLC
Also Called: National Tire Wholesale
2478 S Golden State Blvd, Fresno (93706-4532)
PHONE...................................800 559-4897
Al Martinez, *Manager*
EMP: 61
SALES (corp-wide): 205.4MM **Privately Held**
SIC: 5014 Automobile tires & tubes
PA: Carroll's, Llc
    4281 Old Dixie Hwy
    Atlanta GA 30354
    404 366-5476

(P-6485)
FALKEN TIRE HOLDINGS INC
Also Called: Falken Tires
8656 Haven Ave, Rancho Cucamonga (91730-9103)
PHONE...................................800 723-2553
Richard Smallwood, *President*
Hideo Honda, *President*
Monica Fuqua, *Executive Asst*
Joyce Ho, *Executive Asst*
Ken Masaoka, *Planning*
▲ EMP: 80
SALES (est): 20.5MM **Privately Held**
WEB: www.sri.dunlop.co.jp
SIC: 5014 Automobile tires & tubes
PA: Sumitomo Rubber Industries, Ltd.
    3-6-9, Wakinohamacho, Chuo-Ku
    Kobe HYO 651-0

(P-6486)
GITI TIRE (USA) LTD (DH)
10404 6th St, Rancho Cucamonga (91730-5831)
PHONE...................................909 527-8800
Enki Tan, *CEO*
Armand Allaire, *Exec VP*
Julianto Djajadi, *Exec VP*
John Aben, *Vice Pres*
Hank Eisenga, *Vice Pres*
▲ EMP: 55
SALES (est): 63.3MM **Privately Held**
SIC: 5014 Tires & tubes

(P-6487)
GREENBALL CORP (PA)
Also Called: Towmaster Tire & Wheel
222 S Harbor Blvd Ste 700, Anaheim (92805-3730)
PHONE...................................714 782-3060
Chris S H Tsai, *CEO*
Jenny Tsai, *Vice Pres*
Phil Browning, *Warehouse Mgr*
Michelle Roberts, *Accounts Mgr*
◆ EMP: 50
SQ FT: 80,000
SALES (est): 51.8MM **Privately Held**
WEB: www.greenball.com
SIC: 5014 5013 3999 Automobile tires & tubes; wheels, motor vehicle; atomizers, toiletry

(P-6488)
LAKIN TIRE WEST INCORPORATED (PA)
Also Called: Lakin Tire of Calif
15305 Spring Ave, Santa Fe Springs (90670-5645)
PHONE...................................562 802-2752
Robert Lakin, *CEO*
Cynthia Swartz, *CFO*
Marco Jimenez, *Vice Pres*
David Lakin, *Vice Pres*
Sean Lakin, *Vice Pres*
▼ EMP: 81
SQ FT: 50,000
SALES (est): 85.5MM **Privately Held**
WEB: www.lakintire.com
SIC: 5014 5531 Tires, used; automotive & home supply stores

(P-6489)
SEALANT SYSTEMS INTERNATIONAL
Also Called: Ssi
125 Venture Dr Ste 210, San Luis Obispo (93401-9105)
PHONE...................................805 489-0490
Chris Auerbach, *President*
EMP: 67
SALES (est): 6.5MM **Privately Held**
SIC: 5014 Tires & tubes

(P-6490)
SUMITOMO RUBBER NORTH AMER INC (HQ)
Also Called: Falken Tire
8656 Haven Ave, Rancho Cucamonga (91730-9103)
PHONE...................................909 466-1116
Richard Smallwood, *CEO*
Andrew Hoit, *Vice Pres*
Fumikazu Yamashita, *Vice Pres*
Rick Brennan, *Exec Dir*
Violet Marin, *Administration*
◆ EMP: 75
SQ FT: 190,000
SALES (est): 125.3MM **Privately Held**
WEB: www.falkentire.com
SIC: 5014 Automobile tires & tubes

(P-6491)
TIRE CENTERS WEST LLC
10516 Commerce Way # 875, Fontana (92337-8236)
PHONE...................................909 854-1200
J D Cassa, *General Mgr*
EMP: 135
SQ FT: 83,470
SALES (corp-wide): 1B **Privately Held**
WEB: www.tirecenters.com
SIC: 5014 5531 7534 Automobile tires & tubes; automotive tires; rebuilding & retreading tires

HQ: Tire Centers West, Llc
    1 Parkway S
    Greenville SC 29615
    864 458-5000

(P-6492)
TIRECO INC (PA)
500 W 190th St Ste 100, Gardena (90248-4270)
PHONE...................................310 767-7990
Robert W Liu, *CEO*
John Chen, *CFO*
Andrew Hoit, *Vice Pres*
Chris Holbert, *Vice Pres*
Silvia Van Dusen, *Vice Pres*
▲ EMP: 150
SALES (est): 149.2MM **Privately Held**
WEB: www.tireco.com
SIC: 5014 5013 5051 Tires, used; wheels, motor vehicle; tubing, metal

(P-6493)
TOYO TIRE USA CORP
2151 S Vintage Ave, Ontario (91761-2824)
PHONE...................................562 431-6502
Steve Morgan, *Manager*
EMP: 50 **Privately Held**
SIC: 5014 Automobile tires & tubes
HQ: Toyo Tire U.S.A. Corp.
    5665 Plaza Dr Ste 300
    Cypress CA 90630
    714 236-2080

5015 Motor Vehicle Parts, Used Wholesale

(P-6494)
AMERICAN CORPORATION
315 N Doheny Dr, Beverly Hills (90211-1621)
PHONE...................................310 274-1800
David Morad, *President*
Eli Yadegar, *Vice Pres*
EMP: 80
SQ FT: 300,000
SALES: 22.5MM **Privately Held**
SIC: 5015 Automotive supplies, used

(P-6495)
CADNCHEV INC
Also Called: Lakenor Auto Salvage
13603 Foster Rd, Santa Fe Springs (90670-4834)
PHONE...................................562 944-6422
Donald Flynn, *Ch of Bd*
Thomas Raterman, *CFO*
Frank Erlain, *Vice Pres*
EMP: 60
SQ FT: 10,000
SALES (est): 11.1MM
SALES (corp-wide): 11.8B **Publicly Held**
WEB: www.lkqcorp.com
SIC: 5015 5531 Automotive parts & supplies, used; automotive parts
PA: Lkq Corporation
    500 W Madison St Ste 2800
    Chicago IL 60661
    312 621-1950

(P-6496)
PICK PULL AUTO DISMANTLING INC (HQ)
Also Called: Auto Parts Group
10850 Gold Center Dr # 325, Rancho Cordova (95670-6045)
PHONE...................................916 689-2000
Thomas Klauer, *President*
Katherine Dunn, *Store Mgr*
Glenn Soden, *Administration*
Teresa Haagensen, *Training Spec*
Alejandra Tomasello, *Sales Staff*
EMP: 50
SQ FT: 9,000
SALES (est): 292.8MM
SALES (corp-wide): 2.1B **Publicly Held**
WEB: www.picknpull.com
SIC: 5015 Automotive parts & supplies, used
PA: Schnitzer Steel Industries, Inc.
    299 Sw Clay St Ste 350
    Portland OR 97201
    503 224-9900

(P-6497)
TEAM TRUCK DISMANTLING INC
Also Called: Hillside Auto Salvage
3760 Pyrite St, Riverside (92509-1103)
PHONE...................................951 685-6744
Ted Smith, *President*
Jerry Jaeckles, *Corp Secy*
Tom Hutton, *Vice Pres*
EMP: 70
SQ FT: 1,500
SALES (est): 9.2MM **Privately Held**
WEB: www.hillsideautosalvage.com
SIC: 5015 Automotive parts & supplies, used

5021 Furniture Wholesale

(P-6498)
ABBYSON LIVING CORP
26500 Agoura Rd Ste 102, Calabasas (91302-3571)
PHONE...................................805 465-5500
Yavar A Rafieha, *President*
Doddy Rafieha, *COO*
Dana Andrew, *Principal*
◆ EMP: 325
SQ FT: 156,000
SALES (est): 142MM **Privately Held**
WEB: www.abbysonliving.com
SIC: 5021 Household furniture

(P-6499)
ABM OFFICE SOLUTIONS INC
9550 Hermosa Ave, Rancho Cucamonga (91730-5810)
PHONE...................................909 527-8145
Jorge E Robles, *CEO*
Cecilia Varas, *CFO*
Evelyn Enriquez, *Info Tech Mgr*
▲ EMP: 62
SALES (est): 25.1MM **Privately Held**
SIC: 5021 Office furniture

(P-6500)
ACME FURNITURE INDUSTRY INC (PA)
Also Called: Acme Trading
18895 Arenth Ave, City of Industry (91748-1304)
PHONE...................................626 964-3456
George Chen, *CEO*
Tomy Chen, *Treasurer*
James Chen, *Vice Pres*
Jean Chen, *Vice Pres*
Vincent Shieh, *Vice Pres*
◆ EMP: 85
SQ FT: 330,000
SALES (est): 42.9MM **Privately Held**
SIC: 5021 Furniture

(P-6501)
ADM FURNITURE INC
11680 Wright Rd, Lynwood (90262-3945)
PHONE...................................310 762-2800
Alfonso Ayon, *President*
▲ EMP: 55
SALES (est): 8.6MM **Privately Held**
SIC: 5021 2511 Household furniture; wood household furniture

(P-6502)
ALTON IRVINE INC
Also Called: Millwork Holdings
2052 Alton Pkwy, Irvine (92606-4905)
PHONE...................................949 428-4141
Alan True, *CEO*
Dan Tacheny, *President*
Joanna Chavez, *Accountant*
▲ EMP: 53
SQ FT: 45,000
SALES (est): 20.1MM **Privately Held**
WEB: www.trueseating.com
SIC: 5021 Office furniture

(P-6503)
AMINI INNOVATION CORP
Also Called: Aico
8725 Rex Rd, Pico Rivera (90660-6703)
PHONE...................................562 222-2500
Michael Amini, *CEO*
Martin Ploy, *Exec VP*
Michael Orth, *Vice Pres*
Jeff Santanello, *Vice Pres*

Lily Yeh, *Executive*
◆ **EMP:** 110
SQ FT: 320,000
SALES (est): 58.2MM **Privately Held**
WEB: www.amini.com
SIC: 5021 Office furniture

(P-6504)
ASPECTS FURNITURE MFG INC
15830 El Prado Rd Ste A, Chino
(91708-9127)
PHONE.....................909 606-5806
Amy Sivixay, *President*
Amy A Sivixay, *Vice Pres*
▲ **EMP:** 170
SQ FT: 12,900
SALES (est): 25.3MM **Privately Held**
WEB: www.aspectsfurniture.com
SIC: 5021 Office furniture

(P-6505)
BENCHMASTER FURNITURE LLC
1481 N Hundley St, Anaheim (92806-1323)
PHONE.....................714 414-0240
Gene Trobaugh,
Eugene V Trobaugh, *President*
Emmy Chen, *Vice Pres*
◆ **EMP:** 300
SALES (est): 122MM **Privately Held**
WEB: www.benchmasterfurniture.com
SIC: 5021 Furniture

(P-6506)
BENETTIS ITALIA INC
3037 E Maria St, Compton (90221-5803)
PHONE.....................310 537-8036
Mohammad A Ahmadinia, *CEO*
Sarah Ahmadinia, *CFO*
◆ **EMP:** 56
SQ FT: 120,000
SALES (est): 11.4MM **Privately Held**
SIC: 5021 2426 Office furniture; furniture
stock & parts, hardwood

(P-6507)
BLUMENTHAL DISTRIBUTING INC (PA)
Also Called: Office Star Products
1901 S Archibald Ave, Ontario
(91761-8548)
P.O. Box 3520 (91761-0952)
PHONE.....................909 930-2000
Richard Blumenthal, *President*
Rose Blumenthal, *Shareholder*
Jennifer Blumenthal, *Corp Secy*
Lili Avimi, *Vice Pres*
Steve Harris, *Executive*
◆ **EMP:** 150
SQ FT: 200,000
SALES (est): 52.2MM **Privately Held**
WEB: www.officestar.net
SIC: 5021 2522 Office furniture; chairs, office: padded or plain, except wood

(P-6508)
BUSINESS FURN SOLUTIONS INC (PA)
Also Called: Vangard Concept Offices
2150 N 1st St Ste 100, San Jose
(95131-2045)
P.O. Box 641417 (95164-1417)
PHONE.....................408 325-3100
Jeff Tuttle, *CEO*
Dwight A Jackson, *President*
Tim Thomas, *CFO*
April Andre, *Vice Pres*
Joe Azzolina, *Vice Pres*
EMP: 60
SALES (est): 39.7MM **Privately Held**
SIC: 5021 Office furniture

(P-6509)
CAMBIUM BUSINESS GROUP INC (PA)
Also Called: Fairmont Designs
6950 Noritsu Ave, Buena Park
(90620-1311)
PHONE.....................714 670-1171
George Tsai, *Chairman*
Kevin Fitzgerald, *President*
Jason Liu, *CEO*
David Campbell, *CFO*
Mark Klingensmith, *Vice Pres*
▲ **EMP:** 120

SQ FT: 200,000
SALES (est): 53.4MM **Privately Held**
WEB: www.fairmontdesigns.com
SIC: 5021 2511 Household furniture; dining room furniture; tables, occasional;
beds; wood household furniture

(P-6510)
COMPLETE OFFICE CALIFORNIA INC
12724 Moore St, Cerritos (90703-2121)
PHONE.....................714 880-1222
Edward B Walter, *CEO*
Rick Israel, *Principal*
EMP: 62
SQ FT: 28,000
SALES (est): 15MM
SALES (corp-wide): 11B **Publicly Held**
WEB: www.completeofficeca.com
SIC: 5021 5112 Office furniture; office supplies
PA: Office Depot, Inc.
6600 N Military Trl
Boca Raton FL 33496
561 438-4800

(P-6511)
COPPEL CORPORATION
503 Scaroni Ave, Calexico (92231-9791)
PHONE.....................760 357-3707
Olegario Gomez, *CFO*
▲ **EMP:** 80
SQ FT: 70,000
SALES: 500.6MM **Privately Held**
SIC: 5021 5137 5136 Household furniture; women's & children's clothing; men's
& boys' clothing
HQ: Coppel, S.A. De C.V.
Republica Poniente No. 2855
Culiacan SIN. 80105

(P-6512)
EC GROUP INC (PA)
Also Called: Dennis & Leen
5960 Bowcroft St, Los Angeles
(90016-4302)
PHONE.....................310 815-2700
Richard Hallberg, *President*
Daniel Cuevas, *Vice Pres*
Barbara Wiseley, *Admin Sec*
▲ **EMP:** 80
SQ FT: 18,000
SALES (est): 34.1MM **Privately Held**
SIC: 5021 Furniture

(P-6513)
ERGOMOTION INC
6790 Navigator Way, Goleta (93117-3656)
P.O. Box 8330 (93118-8330)
PHONE.....................805 979-9400
Wenbiao Hou, *CEO*
Guohai Tang, *CEO*
Damien Clenet, *Creative Dir*
Emily Hanson, *Purchasing*
Blake Pettit, *QC Mgr*
▲ **EMP:** 70
SALES (est): 27.8MM **Privately Held**
SIC: 5021 Beds & bedding

(P-6514)
FURNITURE AMERICA CAL INC (PA)
Also Called: Furniture America California
19605 E Walnut Dr N, City of Industry
(91789-2815)
PHONE.....................909 718-7276
George Wells, *CEO*
Rocky Yang, *Vice Pres*
Aki Furutani, *Superintendent*
◆ **EMP:** 71
SQ FT: 200,000
SALES (est): 28.8MM **Privately Held**
WEB: www.importdirectinc.com
SIC: 5021 2512 Furniture; upholstered household furniture

(P-6515)
GOFORTH & MARTI (PA)
Also Called: G/M Business Interiors
110 W A St Ste 140, San Diego
(92101-3702)
PHONE.....................951 684-0870
Stephen L Easley, *President*
Edward Lasak, *COO*
Josie Donley, *Officer*

Mike Akin, *Vice Pres*
William F Easley, *Vice Pres*
▲ **EMP:** 90
SQ FT: 38,000
SALES (est): 92.1MM **Privately Held**
WEB: www.gmbi.net
SIC: 5021 Office furniture

(P-6516)
HAWORTH INC
931 Cadillac Ct, Milpitas (95035-3053)
PHONE.....................408 262-6400
Agnes Allen, *Branch Mgr*
EMP: 75
SALES (corp-wide): 1.8B **Privately Held**
WEB: www.haworth-furn.com
SIC: 5021 Office furniture
HQ: Haworth, Inc.
1 Haworth Ctr
Holland MI 49423
616 393-3000

(P-6517)
HOMELEGANCE INC
Also Called: A G A
48200 Fremont Blvd, Fremont
(94538-6509)
PHONE.....................510 933-6888
Puhsien C Chao, *CEO*
Rosa Chao, *President*
Hutch Chao, *Vice Pres*
Chrissy Chang, *General Mgr*
◆ **EMP:** 90
SQ FT: 800,000
SALES (est): 31.8MM **Privately Held**
SIC: 5021 Household furniture

(P-6518)
HUMAN TOUCH LLC
4600 E Conant St, Long Beach
(90808-1874)
PHONE.....................562 426-8700
Andrew Cohen, *President*
David Wood, *CEO*
Chang Han, *Principal*
Ralph Obregon, *Technical Mgr*
Bruce Maccallum,
◆ **EMP:** 80
SQ FT: 98,500
SALES (est): 38.9MM **Privately Held**
SIC: 5021 Chairs

(P-6519)
INSIDE SOURCE INC (PA)
Also Called: Inside Source/Young
985 Industrial Rd Ste 101, San Carlos
(94070-4157)
PHONE.....................650 508-9101
David Denny, *President*
Kristen Haren, *COO*
Gary Young, *Senior VP*
Tina Fong, *Vice Pres*
David Lombardi, *Vice Pres*
EMP: 75
SQ FT: 50,000
SALES (est): 120MM **Privately Held**
WEB: www.insidesource.com
SIC: 5021 Office furniture

(P-6520)
INTEX RECREATION CORP
4001 Via Oro Ave Ste 210, Long Beach
(90810-1400)
PHONE.....................310 549-1846
Tien P Zee, *CEO*
Jim Lai, *President*
Bill Smith, *Vice Pres*
Bob Howe, *Asst Treas*
◆ **EMP:** 100 **EST:** 1966
SQ FT: 330,000
SALES (est): 19.3MM
SALES (corp-wide): 171.8MM **Privately Held**
WEB: www.intexcorp.com
SIC: 5021 5092 5091 5162 Waterbeds;
toys; watersports equipment & supplies;
plastics materials & basic shapes
PA: Intex Recreation Corp
4001 Via Oro Ave Ste 210
Long Beach CA 90810
310 549-5400

(P-6521)
JANUS ET CIE (PA)
12310 Greenstone Ave, Santa Fe Springs
(90670-4737)
PHONE.....................310 601-2908
Janice K Feldman, *CEO*
Paul Warren, *COO*
Greg Buscher, *CFO*
Danya Lane, *Vice Pres*
Cindy Wolf, *VP Bus Dvlpt*
◆ **EMP:** 110
SQ FT: 154,000
SALES (est): 58.5MM **Privately Held**
WEB: www.janusetcie.com
SIC: 5021 5712 Outdoor & lawn furniture;
household furniture; furniture stores

(P-6522)
K&I INTERNATIONAL TRADE INC
3592 Rosemead Blvd # 220, Rosemead
(91770-2053)
PHONE.....................312 766-1848
Jinhong Lin, *CEO*
EMP: 50
SALES (est): 2.2MM **Privately Held**
SIC: 5021 Furniture

(P-6523)
NOBLE HOUSE HOME FURN LLC (PA)
Also Called: Heavy Metal
21325 Superior St, Chatsworth
(91311-4313)
PHONE.....................818 884-7059
Marshall Bernes,
Cynthia Vazquez, *Admin Asst*
Shenderovich Alex, *Info Tech Mgr*
Angelee Phongpiramorn, *Finance*
Rachelle Monzon, *Purch Agent*
▲ **EMP:** 74
SALES (est): 2.6MM **Privately Held**
SIC: 5021 Furniture

(P-6524)
OMNIA ITALIAN DESIGN LLC
4900 Edison Ave, Chino (91710-5713)
PHONE.....................909 393-4400
Peter Zolferino, *Mng Member*
Frank Schneider, *CFO*
Luie Nastri,
◆ **EMP:** 200
SQ FT: 110,000
SALES (est): 57.5MM **Privately Held**
SIC: 5021 Household furniture

(P-6525)
ONE WORKPLACE L FERRARI LLC
Also Called: One Workplace L Ferrari
475 Brannan St, San Francisco
(94107-5418)
PHONE.....................415 357-2200
Brian Wilson, *Mng Member*
Aaron Uyehara, *Info Tech Mgr*
Kourtney Fuller, *Project Mgr*
Maria Preciado, *Credit Staff*
Frank Stout, *Opers Staff*
EMP: 50
SALES (est): 7.7MM
SALES (corp-wide): 273MM **Privately Held**
SIC: 5021 Filing units; office furniture
PA: One Workplace L. Ferrari, Llc
2500 De La Cruz Blvd
Santa Clara CA 95050
669 800-2500

(P-6526)
PALECEK IMPORTS INC (PA)
601 Parr Blvd, Richmond (94801-1316)
PHONE.....................510 236-7730
Allan Palecek, *President*
Andrew T Palecek, *Vice Pres*
Eric Carlson, *QA Dir*
Chuck Riesbol, *MIS Staff*
Rose CHI, *Accountant*
◆ **EMP:** 74
SQ FT: 250,000
SALES (est): 37.5MM **Privately Held**
WEB: www.palecek.com
SIC: 5021 5023 Household furniture;
home furnishings

PRODUCTS & SVCS

(P-6527)
PARRON-HALL CORPORATION
Also Called: Parron Hall Office Interiors
9655 Gran Ridge Dr Ste 10, San Diego
(92123)
PHONE................................858 268-1212
James Herr, *President*
Victoria Needham, *Vice Pres*
Donna Shirley, *Vice Pres*
Lauren Wheeler, *Admin Sec*
Suzanne Ieler, *Project Mgr*
EMP: 68
SQ FT: 8,000
SALES: 27.5MM **Privately Held**
WEB: www.parronhall.com
SIC: 5021 Office furniture

(P-6528)
POUNDEX ASSOCIATES CORPORATION
21490 Baker Pkwy, City of Industry
(91789-5239)
PHONE................................909 444-5878
Lionel Chen, *President*
Lance Yin, *Opers Staff*
◆ EMP: 100
SQ FT: 55,000
SALES (est): 39.9MM **Privately Held**
SIC: 5021 Household furniture; dining room furniture; tables, occasional

(P-6529)
PRIVILEGE INTERNATIONAL INC
2323 Firestone Blvd, South Gate
(90280-2684)
PHONE................................323 585-0777
Eddy Sarraf, *President*
Mark Darwish, *Senior VP*
Richard Darwish, *Vice Pres*
Elizabeth Alvarado, *Office Mgr*
Christine Alvarado, *Cust Mgr*
▲ EMP: 75
SQ FT: 350,000
SALES (est): 22.2MM **Privately Held**
WEB: www.privilegeinc.com
SIC: 5021 Furniture

(P-6530)
SITONIT SEATING INC
6415 Katella Ave, Cypress (90630-5245)
PHONE................................714 995-4800
Paul Devries, *CEO*
EMP: 200
SALES (est): 34.1MM **Privately Held**
SIC: 5021 Office furniture
PA: Exemplis Llc
6415 Katella Ave
Cypress CA 90630

(P-6531)
STEELCASE INC
7510 Airway Rd Ste 7, San Diego
(92154-8303)
PHONE................................619 671-1040
Mark Baker, *Manager*
Angela Mullins, *Education*
Martin Alvarez, *Manager*
Heather Bishop, *Manager*
Kelly Eliscu, *Accounts Mgr*
EMP: 300
SALES (corp-wide): 3.4B **Publicly Held**
SIC: 5021 Office furniture
PA: Steelcase Inc.
901 44th St Se
Grand Rapids MI 49508
616 247-2710

(P-6532)
UNISOURCE SOLUTIONS INC (PA)
8350 Rex Rd, Pico Rivera (90660-3785)
PHONE................................562 654-3500
James Kastner, *CEO*
Marc Flax, *President*
Ken Kastner, *President*
Clem Nieto, *CFO*
Jim Kastner, *Chairman*
▲ EMP: 105
SQ FT: 186,000
SALES: 67.6MM **Privately Held**
WEB: www.unisourceit.com
SIC: 5021 Office furniture

(P-6533)
VAN SARK INC
Also Called: Dependable Furniture Mfrs
1255 Battery St Ste 200, San Francisco
(94111-1164)
PHONE................................415 362-5888
Edwin Essary, *Officer*
Doug Tong, *Engineer*
EMP: 75
SALES (corp-wide): 13.4MM **Privately Held**
SIC: 5021 Furniture
PA: Van Sark, Inc.
888 Doolittle Dr
San Leandro CA 94577
510 635-1111

(P-6534)
VANGUARD LEGATO A CAL CORP
Also Called: Vanguard Legato
2121 Williams St, San Leandro
(94577-3224)
PHONE................................510 351-3333
Darlene Patch, *Director*
EMP: 68
SQ FT: 20,000
SALES (est): 9.3MM **Privately Held**
WEB: www.brg.com
SIC: 5021 5112 5023 Furniture; office supplies; home furnishings

(P-6535)
VERSA PRODUCTS INC (PA)
Also Called: Versatables.com
14105 Avalon Blvd, Los Angeles
(90061-2637)
PHONE................................310 353-7100
Christopher Laudadio, *CEO*
Han Sun, *Engineer*
Thomas Tanaka, *Engineer*
Brad Stevens, *Senior Engr*
Frank Jamison, *Contract Mgr*
▲ EMP: 82 EST: 2000
SQ FT: 35,000
SALES: 22MM **Privately Held**
WEB: www.versatables.com
SIC: 5021 2512 Office furniture; couches, sofas & davenports: upholstered on wood frames

(P-6536)
VIRCO INC (HQ)
2027 Harpers Way, Torrance (90501-1524)
PHONE................................310 533-0474
Robert Virtue, *CEO*
Dawn Beigel, *President*
Robert Lind, *Bd of Directors*
Robert Dose, *Vice Pres*
James Johnson, *Vice Pres*
▼ EMP: 56
SQ FT: 560,000
SALES (est): 124.1MM
SALES (corp-wide): 200.7MM **Publicly Held**
WEB: www.virco.com
SIC: 5021 Furniture
PA: Virco Mfg. Corporation
2027 Harpers Way
Torrance CA 90501
310 533-0474

(P-6537)
WATERHILL LTD
140 N Orange Ave, City of Industry
(91744-3431)
PHONE................................626 369-6828
Brian Yip, *President*
Carol Yip, *Admin Sec*
▲ EMP: 50
SQ FT: 125,000
SALES (est): 6.6MM **Privately Held**
WEB: www.waterhill.com
SIC: 5021 Dining room furniture

(P-6538)
WINNERS ONLY INC
1365 Park Center Dr, Vista (92081-8338)
PHONE................................760 599-0300
Alex Shu, *Chairman*
Sheue-Wen Lee, *CEO*
Fred Dizon, *CFO*
▲ EMP: 200

SALES (est): 81.3MM **Privately Held**
WEB: www.winnersonly.com
SIC: 5021 Office furniture; dining room furniture

(P-6539)
WMK OFFICE SAN DIEGO LLC (PA)
Also Called: BKM Officeworks
4780 Estgate Mall Ste 100, San Diego
(92121)
PHONE................................858 569-4700
William Kuhnert, *CEO*
Jim Skidmore, *COO*
Nicole Hogeda, *Vice Pres*
Michelle Hanes, *Info Tech Mgr*
Dan Martinez, *Project Mgr*
EMP: 70
SQ FT: 100,000
SALES (est): 76.1MM **Privately Held**
WEB: www.bkmofficeworks.com
SIC: 5021 Office furniture

5023 Home Furnishings Wholesale

(P-6540)
ALPINE INTERIORS CORPORATION (PA)
Also Called: Alpine Carpets
3961 Sepulveda Blvd # 205, Culver City
(90230-4600)
PHONE................................310 390-7639
Johannes Van Ierland, *CEO*
Klaus Friederic, *President*
EMP: 90 EST: 1966
SQ FT: 21,000
SALES (est): 17.6MM **Privately Held**
SIC: 5023 5713 Floor coverings; carpets; carpets

(P-6541)
AMERICAN FAUCET COATINGS CORP
3280 Corporate Vw, Vista (92081-8528)
PHONE................................760 598-5895
Susan E Butler, *President*
◆ EMP: 50
SALES (est): 21.1MM **Privately Held**
WEB: www.sigmafaucet.com
SIC: 5023 3432 Home furnishings; plumbing fixture fittings & trim

(P-6542)
ARDMORE HOME DESIGN INC (PA)
Also Called: Pigeon and Poodle
768 Turnbull Canyon Rd, City of Industry
(91745-1401)
PHONE................................626 333-1177
Chris Dewitt, *CEO*
Oscar Yague, *Vice Pres*
Nancy Cusato, *Cust Svc Dir*
Elizabeth Banks, *Sales Staff*
Stephanie Makaroff, *Sales Staff*
▲ EMP: 50
SALES (est): 26MM **Privately Held**
SIC: 5023 Decorative home furnishings & supplies

(P-6543)
B R FUNSTEN & CO
Also Called: BR Funsten
105 Lndustrial Park, Manteca (95337)
PHONE................................209 825-5375
Rod Tilson, *Branch Mgr*
EMP: 60
SALES (corp-wide): 95.2MM **Privately Held**
WEB: www.brfunsten.com
SIC: 5023 5713 Resilient floor coverings: tile or sheet; floor covering stores
PA: B. R. Funsten & Co.
5200 Watt Ct Ste B
Fairfield CA 94534
209 825-5375

(P-6544)
B R FUNSTEN & CO
Tom Duffy Company Division
5200 Watt Ct Ste B, Fairfield (94534-4209)
PHONE................................707 863-8300
Don Jackson, *Manager*

EMP: 100
SALES (corp-wide): 95.2MM **Privately Held**
WEB: www.brfunsten.com
SIC: 5023 Carpets
PA: B. R. Funsten & Co.
5200 Watt Ct Ste B
Fairfield CA 94534
209 825-5375

(P-6545)
BECKER INTERIORS LTD
Also Called: Alexander Becker Carpets
5552 Hollywood Blvd, Los Angeles (90028)
PHONE................................323 469-1938
Theodore Fox, *President*
EMP: 50
SQ FT: 10,000
SALES: 5MM **Privately Held**
SIC: 5023 5713 2273 Carpets; carpets; carpets & rugs

(P-6546)
BP INDUSTRIES INCORPORATED
5300 E Concours St, Ontario (91764)
PHONE................................909 481-0227
Dong Koo Kim, *President*
Wayne Craparo, *Exec VP*
Kathy Choi, *Administration*
Maria Hon, *Controller*
Charles Wang, *Controller*
▲ EMP: 57
SQ FT: 140,000
SALES (est): 26.9MM **Privately Held**
WEB: www.bpindustries.com
SIC: 5023 Mirrors & pictures, framed & unframed

(P-6547)
BRADSHAW INTERNATIONAL INC (HQ)
Also Called: Bradshaw Home
9409 Buffalo Ave, Rancho Cucamonga
(91730-6012)
PHONE................................909 476-3884
Michael Rodrigue, *CEO*
Thomas Barber, *President*
Brett R Bradshaw, *President*
Julie Hayes, *President*
Sandip Grewald, *CFO*
◆ EMP: 280
SQ FT: 750,000
SALES: 311MM
SALES (corp-wide): 337.5MM **Privately Held**
WEB: www.goodcook.com
SIC: 5023 Kitchenware
PA: Oncap Ii L.P.
161 Bay St
Toronto ON M5J 2
416 214-4300

(P-6548)
BREVILLE USA INC
19400 S Western Ave, Torrance
(90501-1119)
PHONE................................310 755-3000
Damian Baden Court, *CEO*
Simon Schober, *CFO*
Henry Hsu, *Technical Mgr*
Chun Ip, *Opers Mgr*
Ally Barajas, *Marketing Staff*
◆ EMP: 50
SQ FT: 135,000
SALES (est): 29.3MM **Privately Held**
SIC: 5023 5064 Home furnishings: appliance parts, household
HQ: Breville Holdings Pty Limited
G Se 2 170 Bourke Rd
Alexandria NSW 2015

(P-6549)
BYTHEWAYS MANUFACTURING INC
Also Called: B T W
2080 Enterprise Blvd, West Sacramento
(95691-5051)
PHONE................................916 453-1212
Mervin Bytheway Jr, *President*
Jann Bytheway, *Corp Secy*
EMP: 300
SALES (est): 20.2MM **Privately Held**
SIC: 5023 Window furnishings

PA: Hunter Douglas N.V.
Dokweg 19
Willemstad

(P-6550)
COA INC (PA)
Also Called: Coaster Company of America
12928 Sandoval St, Santa Fe Springs
(90670-4061)
PHONE.................................562 944-7899
Michael Yeh, *President*
Marc Alters, *Vice Pres*
Larry Furiani, *Vice Pres*
Lisa KAO, *Admin Sec*
Marlene Vidal, *Administration*
◆ EMP: 200
SQ FT: 210,000
SALES (est): 248.9MM **Privately Held**
WEB: www.coa.net
SIC: 5023 Home furnishings

(P-6551)
CONRAD IMPORTS INC
540 Barneveld Ave Ste H, San Francisco
(94124-1805)
PHONE.................................415 626-3303
Ruth M Holland, *President*
Timothy Moran, *CFO*
Janice Holland, *Vice Pres*
Ed Fernandez, *Info Tech Dir*
Sara Manning, *Technical Staff*
EMP: 93 EST: 1956
SALES (est): 25.2MM **Privately Held**
WEB: www.conradshades.com
SIC: 5023 Window furnishings

(P-6552)
CONTRACTORS FLRG SVC CAL
INC
300 E Dyer Rd, Santa Ana (92707-3740)
P.O. Box 15106 (92735-0106)
PHONE.................................714 556-6100
Joseph J Ott, *President*
EMP: 110
SQ FT: 10,000
SALES: 16.6MM **Privately Held**
WEB: www.conflorsvcofca.com
SIC: 5023 Floor coverings

(P-6553)
E & E CO LTD (PA)
Also Called: Jla Home
45875 Northport Loop E, Fremont
(94538-6414)
PHONE.................................510 490-9788
Edmund Jin, *CEO*
Rusty Ortiz, *COO*
Nancy Hattersley, *Chairman*
Michael Mullen, *Exec VP*
Hellen Xu, *Exec VP*
◆ EMP: 180
SQ FT: 60,000
SALES (est): 303.3MM **Privately Held**
WEB: WWW.ESHEER.COM
SIC: 5023 Sheets, textile

(P-6554)
ELEGANCE WOOD PRODUCTS
INC
Also Called: Elegance Exotic Wood Flooring
7351 Mcguire Ave, Fontana (92336-1668)
PHONE.................................909 484-7676
Jean Tong, *CEO*
Michael Liu, *Accountant*
Karen Peng, *Controller*
▲ EMP: 60 EST: 2000
SQ FT: 500,000
SALES (est): 12.7MM **Privately Held**
SIC: 5023 Wood flooring

(P-6555)
ELIJAH TEXTILES INC
Also Called: Sharp Fabric
1251 E Olympic Blvd, Los Angeles
(90021-1837)
PHONE.................................310 666-3443
Kourosh Amirianfar, *President*
EMP: 82
SQ FT: 100,000
SALES: 34MM **Privately Held**
SIC: 5023 5949 Sheets, textile; fabric
stores piece goods

(P-6556)
EV RAY INC
6400 Variel Ave, Woodland Hills
(91367-2577)
PHONE.................................818 346-5381
Lee Brown, *President*
Helen Kim, *Finance Mgr*
Diana Villa, *Purchasing*
Beatrice Gomes, *Manager*
EMP: 50
SQ FT: 22,000
SALES (est): 6.5MM **Privately Held**
WEB: www.rayev.com
SIC: 5023 2211 2591 2391 Draperies;
draperies & drapery fabrics, cotton; drap-
ery hardware & blinds & shades; curtains
& draperies

(P-6557)
EVRIHOLDER PRODUCTS LLC
(HQ)
1500 S Lewis St, Anaheim (92805-6423)
PHONE.................................714 490-7878
Ivan Stein, *CEO*
Scott Neamand, *CFO*
▲ EMP: 50
SQ FT: 45,000
SALES (est): 29.6MM
SALES (corp-wide): 68.4MM **Privately
Held**
WEB: www.evriholder.com
SIC: 5023 5085 5087 Kitchenware; bins &
containers, storage; cleaning & mainte-
nance equipment & supplies
PA: Clearlight Partners, Llc
100 Bayview Cir Ste 5000
Newport Beach CA 92660
949 725-6616

(P-6558)
GALLEHER LLC (PA)
9303 Greenleaf Ave, Santa Fe Springs
(90670-3029)
PHONE.................................562 944-8885
Jeff Hamar, *CEO*
Rick Coates, *COO*
Ray Iodice, *CFO*
Todd Hamar, *Senior VP*
Kyle Sherman, *Division Mgr*
▲ EMP: 110 EST: 2018
SQ FT: 100,000
SALES (est): 103.3MM **Privately Held**
WEB: www.galleher.com
SIC: 5023 Wood flooring

(P-6559)
GATE FIVE GROUP LLC
Also Called: Roost
200 Gate 5 Rd Ste 116, Sausalito
(94965-1456)
PHONE.................................415 339-9500
Scott Donnellan,
Sarah Lukenbill, *Human Res Dir*
Kim Lee, *Merchandising*
Adrienne Tribolet, *Sales Staff*
Lisa Grundy, *Director*
▲ EMP: 50
SQ FT: 1,500
SALES (est): 17.7MM **Privately Held**
SIC: 5023 Decorative home furnishings
supplies

(P-6560)
GIBSON OVERSEAS INC
2410 Yates Ave, Commerce (90040-1918)
PHONE.................................323 832-8900
Sohail Gabbay, *CEO*
Syed Haneef, *Vice Pres*
Kevin Notrica, *Vice Pres*
Sona Chui, *Department Mgr*
Cruz Mark, *Comp Spec*
◆ EMP: 510
SQ FT: 850,000
SALES (est): 221.8MM **Privately Held**
WEB: www.gibsonusa.com
SIC: 5023 Glassware; china; kitchen tools
& utensils

(P-6561)
GINA B LTD INC
Also Called: Gina B Showroom
1601 W 134th St, Gardena (90249-2013)
PHONE.................................310 366-7926
Rolf Berschneider, *President*
Gina Berschneider, *Vice Pres*
EMP: 62 EST: 1968

SALES (est): 5.7MM **Privately Held**
SIC: 5023 2599 2542 2273 Home furnishings; factory furniture & fixtures; partitions & fixtures, except wood; carpets &
rugs

(P-6562)
GLOBAL ACCENTS INC
19808 Normandie Ave, Torrance
(90502-1112)
PHONE.................................310 639-2600
Danny Partielli, *President*
▲ EMP: 110
SQ FT: 50,000
SALES (est): 10.6MM **Privately Held**
SIC: 5023 Rugs; bedspreads

(P-6563)
HORNER-HALLEHER HOLDING
CO (PA)
9303 Greenleaf Ave, Santa Fe Springs
(90670-3029)
PHONE.................................562 944-8885
Michelle Credit, *Analyst*
Jonathan Leon, *Buyer*
David Goodman, *Post Master*
EMP: 149
SQ FT: 100,000
SALES (est): 10.4MM **Privately Held**
SIC: 5023 Floor coverings

(P-6564)
INTERNTONAL WIN
TREATMENTS INC (PA)
Also Called: Custom Craft Company
12301 Hawkins St, Santa Fe Springs
(90670-3366)
PHONE.................................562 236-2120
Tsong Shih, *President*
Hsawn Shih, *Shareholder*
◆ EMP: 100
SQ FT: 30,000
SALES (est): 16.7MM **Privately Held**
SIC: 5023 Venetian blinds

(P-6565)
K T W PRODUCTIONS INC
6303 E Cedarbrooks Rd, Orange
(92867-2491)
PHONE.................................714 685-0428
Lola Wang, *President*
Rex Wang, *Vice Pres*
▲ EMP: 800
SALES (est): 64.7MM **Privately Held**
SIC: 5023 Home furnishings

(P-6566)
KEECO LLC (PA)
30736 Wiegman Rd, Hayward
(94544-7819)
PHONE.................................510 324-8800
Christopher Grassi,
Martin Berry, *VP Finance*
Joe Lillie, *Warehouse Mgr*
Kristine Igoe,
Ben Steingl,
◆ EMP: 70
SQ FT: 500,000
SALES (est): 64.7MM **Privately Held**
WEB: www.lkeeco.com
SIC: 5023 Linens & towels; linens, table

(P-6567)
LE CROCHET BY SARO INC (PA)
Also Called: Saro Lifestyle
3333 W Pacific Ave, Burbank (91505-1553)
PHONE.................................818 846-3314
Kevork Kalenderian, *President*
Betty Barsoumian, *Director*
◆ EMP: 50
SQ FT: 6,000
SALES (est): 13MM **Privately Held**
SIC: 5023 5131 Linens & towels; linen
piece goods, woven

(P-6568)
LEDRA BRANDS INC
Also Called: Bruck Lighting Systems
15774 Gateway Cir, Tustin (92780-6469)
PHONE.................................714 259-9959
Alex Ladjevardi, *President*
Farah Emami, *COO*
Jade Turney, *Vice Pres*
Jason Luckenbill, *Graphic Designe*
Matt Samuel, *Project Engr*
▲ EMP: 55 EST: 1993

SQ FT: 30,000
SALES (est): 25.4MM **Privately Held**
WEB: www.brucklightingsystems.com
SIC: 5023 Lamps: floor, boudoir, desk

(P-6569)
LONGUST DISTRIBUTING LLC
1206 N Miller St Unit A, Anaheim
(92806-1960)
PHONE.................................480 820-6244
John Trujillo, *Branch Mgr*
Carol Terrazas, *Buyer*
Evelyn Gregorian, *Sales Mgr*
Debbie McGrath, *Manager*
EMP: 50
SALES (corp-wide): 60MM **Privately
Held**
SIC: 5023 Floor coverings; resilient floor
coverings: tile or sheet; carpets; wood
flooring
PA: Longust Distributing, Llc
2432 W Birchwood Ave
Mesa AZ 85202
480 820-6244

(P-6570)
MARIAK INDUSTRIES INC
Also Called: Mariak Window Fashion
575 W Manville St, Rancho Dominguez
(90220-5509)
PHONE.................................310 661-4400
Leo Elinson, *CEO*
▲ EMP: 380
SQ FT: 80,000
SALES (est): 110.1MM
SALES (corp-wide): 3B **Privately Held**
SIC: 5023 2591 Vertical blinds; blinds ver-
tical
HQ: Springs Window Fashions, Llc
7549 Graber Rd
Middleton WI 53562
608 836-1011

(P-6571)
MEYER CORPORATION US
Also Called: Faberware Div
2001 Meyer Way, Fairfield (94533-6802)
PHONE.................................707 399-2100
Stuart Levine, *Manager*
EMP: 100 **Privately Held**
WEB: www.meyer.com
SIC: 5023 3469 1541 5046 Kitchenware;
cooking ware, except porcelain enam-
elled; industrial buildings & warehouses;
commercial equipment; pressed & blown
glass
HQ: Meyer Corporation, U.S.
1 Meyer Plz
Vallejo CA 94590
707 551-2800

(P-6572)
NEUBERG NUBERG IMPORTERS
GROUP
Also Called: Framing Fabrics
6001 Santa Monica Blvd, Los Angeles
(90038-1807)
PHONE.................................800 832-2742
Larry Neuberg, *President*
▲ EMP: 50
SQ FT: 15,000
SALES (est): 5.7MM **Privately Held**
SIC: 5023 Frames & framing, picture &
mirror

(P-6573)
NEXGRILL INDUSTRIES INC
(PA)
14050 Laurelwood Pl, Chino (91710-5454)
PHONE.................................909 598-8799
Sherman Lin, *President*
Pak LI, *IT/INT Sup*
Phillip Leary, *Technical Staff*
Sue Lim, *Accounting Mgr*
Annette Ho, *Opers Mgr*
▲ EMP: 53
SQ FT: 50,000
SALES (est): 28.3MM **Privately Held**
WEB: www.nexgrill.com
SIC: 5023 3631 Grills, barbecue; barbe-
cues, grills & braziers (outdoor cooking)

(PA)=Parent Co (HQ)=Headquarters (DH)=Div Headquarters
✪ = New Business established in last 2 years

(P-6574)
NORMAN INTERNATIONAL INC
Also Called: Norman Charter
12301 Hawkins St, Santa Fe Springs
(90670-3366)
PHONE.....................................562 946-0420
Ranjan Mada, *CEO*
Paul Shih, *Vice Pres*
James Wang, *Info Tech Mgr*
Erica Ching, *Webmaster*
Susan Huang, *Business Mgr*
◆ EMP: 70
SALES (est): 53.5MM Privately Held
WEB: www.normanintlusa.com
SIC: 5023 Home furnishings

(P-6575)
OLDE THOMPSON LLC
3250 Camino Del Sol, Oxnard
(93030-8998)
PHONE.....................................805 983-0388
Jeffrey M Shumway, *CEO*
Steve Rowe, *CFO*
Heidi Slocumb, *Vice Pres*
Larry Valenzuela, *General Mgr*
Doug McKenzie, *Safety Mgr*
◆ EMP: 225 EST: 1917
SQ FT: 88,000
SALES (est): 100.1MM Privately Held
WEB: www.oldethompson.com
SIC: 5023 2631 5149 Kitchenware; container, packaging & boxboard; spices & seasonings

(P-6576)
OMEGA MOULDING WEST LLC
5500 Lindbergh Ln, Bell (90201-6410)
PHONE.....................................323 261-3510
Bernard Portnoy, *Mng Member*
David Merzin,
Anastasia Portnoy,
◆ EMP: 130
SQ FT: 130,000
SALES (est): 18.2MM Privately Held
WEB: www.omegamoulding.com
SIC: 5023 Frames & framing, picture & mirror

(P-6577)
PAVIGYM AMERICA CORP
1902 Wright Pl Fl 2, Carlsbad
(92008-6583)
PHONE.....................................858 414-8624
Marcos Requena Penat, *CEO*
◆ EMP: 100
SALES (est): 12.5MM Privately Held
SIC: 5023 Floor coverings

(P-6578)
PEKING HANDICRAFT INC (PA)
Also Called: P H I
1388 San Mateo Ave, South San Francisco
(94080-6501)
PHONE.....................................650 871-3788
Derrick Lo, *CEO*
Clinton Chien, *COO*
Laura Donald, *Vice Pres*
Jenny Xie, *Business Anlyst*
Yuliya Song, *Sales Executive*
◆ EMP: 120
SQ FT: 150,000
SALES: 113.4MM Privately Held
WEB: www.pkhc.com
SIC: 5023 Linens & towels; bedspreads; sheets, textile; decorative home furnishings & supplies

(P-6579)
PSI3G INC
2979 Promenade St Ste 100, West Sacramento (95691-6410)
PHONE.....................................916 803-2879
Shawn Still, *Branch Mgr*
EMP: 58
SALES (corp-wide): 16.8MM Privately
Held
SIC: 5023 5713 Floor coverings; floor covering stores
PA: Psi3g, Inc.
    505 San Marin Dr Ste A120
    Novato CA 94945
    415 493-3854

(P-6580)
R&S CARPET SERVICES INC
Also Called: R & S Floor Covering
1485 Spruce St Ste C106, Riverside
(92507-2445)
PHONE.....................................909 740-6645
Roy Paswaters, *President*
Steven Birito, *Vice Pres*
Marcos Carrasco, *Vice Pres*
EMP: 61
SQ FT: 9,000
SALES (est): 7MM Privately Held
SIC: 5023 1752 Carpets; carpet laying

(P-6581)
SHAW INDUSTRIES GROUP INC
Also Called: Tuftex Carpet Mills
15305 Valley View Ave, Santa Fe Springs
(90670-5325)
PHONE.....................................562 921-7209
Jim Cusack, *Director*
Michael Arai, *Accounting Mgr*
Edward Zaldana, *Manager*
EMP: 271
SALES (corp-wide): 225.3B Publicly
Held
SIC: 5023 Floor coverings
HQ: Shaw Industries Group, Inc.
    616 E Walnut Ave
    Dalton GA 30721
    800 446-9332

(P-6582)
SIERRA LIVING CONCEPTS INC
46560 Fremont Blvd # 414, Fremont
(94538-6482)
PHONE.....................................510 402-4906
Chetna Nathawat, *President*
Leslie Riekena, *Marketing Staff*
Raj Nathawat, *Director*
▲ EMP: 55
SALES (est): 1MM Privately Held
SIC: 5023 Decorative home furnishings & supplies

(P-6583)
SIMPLEHUMAN LLC (PA)
19850 Magellan Dr, Torrance (90502-1106)
PHONE.....................................310 436-2250
Frank Yang, *Mng Member*
Jenni Lain, *Executive*
Sean Byun, *VP Sales*
Susan Ahn, *Sales Staff*
Jackson Yang,
◆ EMP: 55
SQ FT: 55,000
SALES (est): 47.4MM Privately Held
WEB: www.simplehuman.net
SIC: 5023 Kitchenware

(P-6584)
SOTO PROVISION INC
Also Called: Soto Food Service
488 Parriott Pl W, City of Industry
(91745-1015)
PHONE.....................................626 458-4600
John R Renna Sr, *President*
John R Renna Jr, *Vice Pres*
EMP: 70
SQ FT: 35,000
SALES (est): 55.9MM Privately Held
WEB: www.sotofoodservice.com
SIC: 5023 5046 Kitchen tools & utensils; kitchenware; commercial cooking & food service equipment

(P-6585)
SUNDAY BAZAAR INC
Also Called: Lunares
495 Barneveld Ave, San Francisco
(94124-1501)
PHONE.....................................415 621-0764
Nimerta Oberoi, *President*
Sunena Balain, *Marketing Staff*
▲ EMP: 87
SQ FT: 4,000
SALES (est): 13.6MM Privately Held
WEB: www.lunares.com
SIC: 5023 5199 Decorative home furnishings & supplies; gifts & novelties

(P-6586)
TABLETOPS UNLIMITED INC
(PA)
23000 Avalon Blvd, Carson (90745-5017)
PHONE.....................................310 549-6000
Javad Asgari, *CEO*
Mohsen Asgari, *President*
Hamid Ebrahimi, *President*
Fred Rabizadeh, *COO*
Daryoush Molayem, *Vice Pres*
◆ EMP: 70
SQ FT: 350,000
SALES (est): 37.9MM Privately Held
WEB: www.tabletopsunltd.com
SIC: 5023 China; glassware; stainless steel flatware

(P-6587)
TEST-RITE PRODUCTS CORP
(DH)
1900 Burgundy Pl, Ontario (91761-2308)
PHONE.....................................909 605-9899
Jack Ho, *Treasurer*
Vivian Huang, *Accounts Mgr*
▲ EMP: 80
SQ FT: 400,000
SALES: 133.6MM Privately Held
SIC: 5023 Home furnishings

(P-6588)
THUNDER GROUP INC (PA)
780 Nogales St Ste C, City of Industry
(91748-1380)
PHONE.....................................626 935-1605
Eddie Liu, *CEO*
Chun Chieh Liu, *President*
Ralph Liu, *Vice Pres*
Lin CHI Liu, *Admin Sec*
Cindy Tung, *IT Specialist*
◆ EMP: 50
SQ FT: 340,000
SALES (est): 27.2MM Privately Held
SIC: 5023 Kitchenware

(P-6589)
TIFFANY DALE INC (PA)
14765 Industry Cir, La Mirada
(90638-5818)
PHONE.....................................714 739-2700
Ye H Chung, *CEO*
Garbiel Chung, *Vice Pres*
Connie Chung, *Admin Sec*
Griselda Ceballos, *Administration*
Serina Chung, *Administration*
▲ EMP: 83
SQ FT: 88,480
SALES (est): 14.4MM Privately Held
SIC: 5023 Lamps: floor, boudoir, desk

(P-6590)
TOM RAY INDUSTRIES INC
Also Called: Thefloorstore/Flor Stor
23182 Alcalde Dr Ste G, Laguna Hills
(92653-1450)
PHONE.....................................949 380-8333
Thomas Ray, *President*
EMP: 100
SQ FT: 700,000
SALES (est): 15.5MM Privately Held
WEB: www.florstor.com
SIC: 5023 5211 1752 5713 Floor coverings; flooring, wood; wood floor installation & refinishing; floor tile; specialty cleaning & sanitation preparations; interior decorating

(P-6591)
TRI - STAR WIN COVERINGS INC
Also Called: Carpet Care By Tri-Star
19555 Prairie St, Northridge (91324-2424)
PHONE.....................................818 718-3188
Bernard Warshauer, *CEO*
Deborah Newhouse, *Controller*
Bob Lewis, *Director*
EMP: 50
SQ FT: 22,000
SALES (est): 24.5MM Privately Held
WEB: www.tsinteriors.com
SIC: 5023 5719 Floor coverings; window furnishings; window furnishings

(P-6592)
TRI-WEST LTD (PA)
12005 Pike St, Santa Fe Springs
(90670-6100)
PHONE.....................................562 692-9166
Allen Gage, *Partner*
John Lubinxki, *Partner*
Randy Sims, *Partner*
John Lubinski, *COO*
Jim Johnston, *CFO*
▲ EMP: 200 EST: 1976
SQ FT: 300,000
SALES (est): 182.6MM Privately Held
WEB: www.triwestltd.com
SIC: 5023 Floor coverings; resilient floor coverings: tile or sheet; wood flooring

(P-6593)
UMA ENTERPRISES INC (PA)
350 W Apra St, Compton (90220-5529)
PHONE.....................................310 631-1166
James Buch, *CEO*
Melissa Dench, *Vice Pres*
Robert Rich, *Vice Pres*
Uma Agarwal, *Admin Sec*
Arman Ekmekci, *Natl Sales Mgr*
◆ EMP: 140
SQ FT: 460,000
SALES (est): 92.3MM Privately Held
WEB: www.umainc.com
SIC: 5023 Decorative home furnishings & supplies

(P-6594)
UNIQUE CARPETS LTD
7360 Jurupa Ave, Riverside (92504-1025)
PHONE.....................................951 352-8125
Bill D Graves, *President*
Robert L Binford, *Exec VP*
Martin Lopez, *Vice Pres*
Jimmy Apple, *Opers Mgr*
Christina Murray, *Production*
▲ EMP: 55
SALES (est): 18.4MM Privately Held
WEB: www.uniquecarpets.com
SIC: 5023 2273 Carpets; carpets & rugs

(P-6595)
UNIVERSAL WOOD MOULDING
INC (PA)
Also Called: Universal Framing Products
21139 Centre Pointe Pkwy, Santa Clarita
(91350-2994)
PHONE.....................................661 362-6262
Jon M Bromberg, *CEO*
AVI Feibenlatt, *Ch of Bd*
Mark Gottlieb, *President*
Jonathan Glassick, *Opers Staff*
Alicia Costin, *Mktg Coord*
▲ EMP: 62
SALES (est): 21.8MM Privately Held
WEB: www.universalframing.com
SIC: 5023 3999 Frames & framing, picture & mirror; atomizers; toiletry; advertising curtains

(P-6596)
VALLEY WHOLESALE SUPPLY
CORP (PA)
Also Called: Valley Molding & Frame
10708 Vanowen St, North Hollywood
(91605-6401)
PHONE.....................................818 769-5656
Charles Aaron, *Ch of Bd*
Michelle Merritt, *Shareholder*
David A Labowitz, *President*
Suzanne Ehrmann, *Vice Pres*
▲ EMP: 57
SQ FT: 30,000
SALES (est): 21.9MM Privately Held
WEB: www.valleymoulding.com
SIC: 5023 5031 Frames & framing, picture & mirror; decorating supplies; molding, all materials

(P-6597)
VALYRIA LLC (HQ)
Also Called: Transpac
1050 Aviator Dr, Vacaville (95688-8900)
PHONE.....................................707 452-0600
Laurie Gilner, *President*
Craig Mackley, *Vice Pres*
Bhavik Patel, *Administration*
Jose Gomez, *Technology*
Karen Goodlow, *Sales Staff*
▲ EMP: 60 EST: 2016
SQ FT: 175,000
SALES: 7.7MM
SALES (corp-wide): 56.5MM Privately
Held
SIC: 5023 Decorative home furnishings & supplies
PA: C & F Enterprises, Inc.
    819 Bluecrab Rd
    Newport News VA 23606
    757 310-6100

(P-6598)
VENUS GROUP INC
Also Called: Venus Textiles
25861 Wright, Foothill Ranch (92610-3504)
PHONE..................................949 609-1299
Kirit D Patel, *CEO*
Rajni D Patel, *Vice Pres*
Rita Epperson, *Executive Asst*
Cecilia Henson, *Mfg Mgr*
Garry Stoltenberg, *Sales Staff*
◆ **EMP:** 85
SALES (est): 58.6MM **Privately Held**
WEB: www.venusgroup.com
SIC: 5023 2392 5719 Towels; towels, fabric & nonwoven: made from purchased materials; towels

(P-6599)
W DIAMOND SUPPLY CO (DH)
Also Called: Diamond W Floorcovering
19321 E Walnut Dr N, City of Industry
(91748-1436)
PHONE..................................909 859-8939
Louis J Bettitta, *CEO*
Mike Klingele, *President*
Kandi Anderson, *COO*
Daniel Erickson, *CFO*
Eric Erman, *Purchasing*
▲ **EMP:** 60
SQ FT: 106,000
SALES (est): 20.2MM
SALES (corp-wide): 589.6K **Privately Held**
WEB: www.diamondw.com
SIC: 5023 Floor coverings
HQ: Tarkett, Inc.
30000 Aurora Rd
Solon OH 44139
800 899-8916

(P-6600)
ZODAX LP (PA)
14040 Arminta St, Panorama City
(91402-6080)
PHONE..................................818 785-5626
Philip Cohanim, *Managing Prtnr*
Edward Cohanim, *Partner*
Ginalin Tan, *COO*
Eddie Kohan, *Vice Pres*
Carmela Donato Pineda, *Accountant*
▲ **EMP:** 75
SQ FT: 100,000
SALES (est): 2.2MM **Privately Held**
SIC: 5023 Decorative home furnishings & supplies

5031 Lumber, Plywood & Millwork Wholesale

(P-6601)
ALLIED BUILDING PRODUCTS CORP
Also Called: AMS
456 Industrial Rd, San Bernardino
(92408-3716)
PHONE..................................909 796-6926
Paul Lynd, *Manager*
Nancy Wetzel, *Project Mgr*
Josh Bejarano, *Traffic Dir*
Kami Gonzalez, *Sales Associate*
EMP: 50
SQ FT: 25,000
SALES (corp-wide): 6.4B **Publicly Held**
WEB: www.a-m-s.com
SIC: 5031 Lumber, plywood & millwork
HQ: Allied Building Products Corp.
15 E Union Ave
East Rutherford NJ 07073
201 507-8400

(P-6602)
AMERICAN BUILDING SUPPLY INC (HQ)
Also Called: Abs-American Building Supply
8360 Elder Creek Rd, Sacramento
(95828-1705)
P.O. Box 293030 (95829-3030)
PHONE..................................916 503-4100
Mark Ballantyne, *CEO*
Dave Baker, *President*
Jan Leonard, *Vice Pres*
Jake Pronio, *Vice Pres*
Son Nguyen, *CTO*
▲ **EMP:** 250

SQ FT: 230,000
SALES (est): 368.3MM **Publicly Held**
WEB: www.infinitydoor.com
SIC: 5031 3231 Doors; door frames, all materials; doors, glass: made from purchased glass

(P-6603)
AMERICAN BUILDING SUPPLY INC
1488 Tillie Lewis Dr, Stockton
(95206-1131)
PHONE..................................209 941-8852
Randy Neto, *Branch Mgr*
EMP: 100 **Publicly Held**
WEB: www.infinitydoor.com
SIC: 5031 Doors
HQ: American Building Supply, Inc.
8360 Elder Creek Rd
Sacramento CA 95828
916 503-4100

(P-6604)
ANFINSON LUMBER SALES INC (PA)
13041 Union Ave, Fontana (92337-6952)
PHONE..................................951 681-4707
Richard Anfinson, *President*
Patricia J Anfinson, *Admin Sec*
EMP: 60
SQ FT: 48,000
SALES (est): 11.2MM **Privately Held**
WEB: www.anfinson.com
SIC: 5031 Lumber: rough, dressed & finished

(P-6605)
ATRIUM DOOR & WIN CO ARIZ INC
5455 E La Palma Ave Ste A, Anaheim
(92807-2006)
PHONE..................................714 693-0601
Gregory T Faherty, *President*
Randall S Fojtasek, *President*
Jeff Hull, *CEO*
EMP: 300
SQ FT: 220,000
SALES (est): 24.6MM
SALES (corp-wide): 2B **Publicly Held**
SIC: 5031 Windows
HQ: Atrium Windows And Doors, Inc.
959 Profit Dr
Dallas TX 75247
214 583-1840

(P-6606)
B B & T MANAGEMENT CORP
Also Called: Blomberg Window
1453 Blair Ave, Sacramento (95822-3410)
PHONE..................................916 428-8060
J Philip Collier, *President*
Ralph S Blomberg, *Vice Pres*
EMP: 200
SALES (est): 20.4MM **Privately Held**
SIC: 5031 Windows

(P-6607)
BMC STOCK HOLDINGS INC
Also Called: Heritage One Door & Carpentry
4300 Jetway Ct, North Highlands
(95660-5702)
PHONE..................................916 481-5030
John Dutter, *Branch Mgr*
EMP: 350 **Publicly Held**
SIC: 5031 2431 Doors & windows; windows & window parts & trim, wood
PA: Bmc Stock Holdings, Inc.
8020 Arco Corp Dr Ste 400
Raleigh NC 27617

(P-6608)
BUILDERS FIRSTSOURCE INC
1262 E Main St, El Cajon (92021-7250)
PHONE..................................619 440-7711
Tom Iannacone, *Executive*
Debbie Conro, *Sales Staff*
EMP: 50
SALES (corp-wide): 7.7B **Publicly Held**
WEB: www.hopelumber.com
SIC: 5031 5072 Lumber: rough, dressed & finished; hardware

PA: Builders Firstsource, Inc.
2001 Bryan St Ste 1600
Dallas TX 75201
214 880-3500

(P-6609)
BUILDERS FIRSTSOURCE INC
3450 Highland Ave, National City
(91950-7420)
PHONE..................................619 425-6660
Ted Teran, *Manager*
EMP: 50
SALES (corp-wide): 7.7B **Publicly Held**
WEB: www.hopelumber.com
SIC: 5031 Lumber, plywood & millwork
PA: Builders Firstsource, Inc.
2001 Bryan St Ste 1600
Dallas TX 75201
214 880-3500

(P-6610)
BUILDING MATERIAL DISTRS INC (PA)
Also Called: B M D
225 Elm Ave, Galt (95632-1558)
P.O. Box 606 (95632-0606)
PHONE..................................209 745-3001
Mike Garrison, *Chairman*
Jeff Gore, *President*
Cynthia Thompson, *CFO*
Steven Ellinwood, *Chairman*
Amber Blackman, *Sales Staff*
◆ **EMP:** 170
SQ FT: 100,000
SALES (est): 161.1MM **Privately Held**
WEB: www.bmdusa.com
SIC: 5031 Building materials, exterior; building materials, interior; window frames, all materials; door frames, all materials

(P-6611)
CERTAINTEED GYPSUM INC
27442 Portola Pkwy # 100, El Toro
(92610-2823)
PHONE..................................949 282-5300
Jeff Dushack, *Manager*
EMP: 50
SALES (corp-wide): 215.9MM **Privately Held**
WEB: www.bpb-na.com
SIC: 5031 Wallboard
HQ: Certainteed Gypsum, Inc.
20 Moores Rd
Malvern PA 19355

(P-6612)
COLLIER WAREHOUSE INC
Also Called: Cwi
90 Dorman Ave, San Francisco
(94124-1807)
PHONE..................................415 920-9720
Paul C Akin, *CEO*
David C Freer, *President*
Christy Akin, *Admin Sec*
Ryan Macphee, *Human Resources*
Jesus Lopez, *Warehouse Mgr*
▼ **EMP:** 50
SQ FT: 8,000
SALES (est): 34.1MM **Privately Held**
WEB: www.collier-sf.com
SIC: 5031 1751 Windows; doors; skylights, all materials; window & door (prefabricated) installation

(P-6613)
COMPLETE MILLWORK SERVICES INC
405 Aldo Ave, Santa Clara (95054-2302)
PHONE..................................408 567-9664
Isaiah Clapp, *Project Mgr*
EMP: 75
SALES (corp-wide): 74.7MM **Privately Held**
SIC: 5031 Millwork
PA: Complete Millwork Services, Inc.
4909 Goni Rd Ste A
Carson City NV 89706
775 246-0485

(P-6614)
COUNTY BUILDING MATERIALS INC
Also Called: Payless Patio & Rockery
2927 S King Rd, San Jose (95122-1597)
PHONE..................................408 274-4920
Jay Robert Williams Jr, *CEO*
Jay R William Sr, *President*
Harry Glaze, *Vice Pres*
▲ **EMP:** 60
SQ FT: 26,000
SALES (est): 10.9MM **Privately Held**
SIC: 5031 5032 5261 5193 Building materials, exterior; building materials, interior; brick, stone & related material; nursery stock, seeds & bulbs; nursery stock; masonry materials & supplies

(P-6615)
DISCOUNT BUILDERS SUPPLY
1695 Mission St, San Francisco
(94103-2432)
PHONE..................................415 285-2800
Charles Goodman, *President*
▲ **EMP:** 69
SQ FT: 40,000
SALES (est): 29.9MM **Privately Held**
SIC: 5031 5211 Building materials, exterior; lumber & other building materials

(P-6616)
EMPIRE COMPANY LLC
31 Heron Ln, Riverside (92507-1243)
PHONE..................................951 742-5273
Scott Price, *Branch Mgr*
EMP: 82
SALES (corp-wide): 227.6MM **Privately Held**
SIC: 5031 Lumber, plywood & millwork
HQ: The Empire Company Llc
8181 Logistics Dr
Zeeland MI 49464
800 253-9000

(P-6617)
FOREST PRODUCTS DISTRS INC
1090 W Waterfront Dr, Eureka
(95501-0169)
P.O. Box 8088, Rapid City SD (57709-8088)
PHONE..................................707 443-7024
Carroll Korb, *President*
Jeff Plooster, *Controller*
EMP: 65
SALES: 950K **Privately Held**
SIC: 5031 Doors

(P-6618)
FOUNDATION BUILDING MTLS INC (PA)
Also Called: FMB
2741 Walnut Ave Ste 200, Tustin
(92780-7063)
PHONE..................................714 380-3127
Ruben Mendoza, *President*
John Gorey, *CFO*
Kirby Thompson, *Senior VP*
Jim Carpenter, *Vice Pres*
Scott Evans, *Vice Pres*
EMP: 67 **EST:** 2011
SALES: 2B **Publicly Held**
SIC: 5031 5033 5039 Building materials, interior; wallboard; roofing, siding & insulation; insulation materials; ceiling systems & products

(P-6619)
GOLDEN STATE LUMBER INC
3033 S Airport Way, Stockton
(95206-3899)
P.O. Box 31810 (95213-1810)
PHONE..................................209 234-7700
Ralph Panttaja, *Branch Mgr*
Renae Gunkel, *Credit Mgr*
Andi Doughty, *Analyst*
EMP: 200
SALES (corp-wide): 235MM **Privately Held**
WEB: www.goldenstatelumber.com
SIC: 5031 5211 Lumber: rough, dressed & finished; lumber & other building materials

P R O D U C T S & S V C S

PA: Golden State Lumber, Inc.
855 Lakeville St Ste 200
Petaluma CA 94952
707 206-4100

(P-6620)
GROVE LUMBER & BLDG SUPS INC (PA)
1300 S Campus Ave, Ontario (91761-4378)
PHONE.................................909 947-0277
Raymond G Croll Jr, *CEO*
Jim Armas, *Store Mgr*
EMP: 240 **EST:** 1979
SQ FT: 3,000
SALES (est): 132.1MM **Privately Held**
SIC: 5031 5211 Lumber: rough, dressed & finished; lumber products

(P-6621)
HARDY WINDOW COMPANY (PA)
1639 E Miraloma Ave, Placentia (92870-6623)
PHONE.................................714 996-1807
Chance P Hardy, *President*
Diana Gonzalez, *Human Resources*
Darin Edmonds, *Sales Staff*
Holly Hanson, *Sales Staff*
Gary Prahl, *Sales Staff*
EMP: 141
SQ FT: 14,000
SALES (est): 30.5MM **Privately Held**
WEB: www.hardywindows.com
SIC: 5031 Windows

(P-6622)
HEPPNER HARDWOODS INC
555 W Danlee St, Azusa (91702-2342)
PHONE.................................626 969-7983
Lorraine Heppner, *President*
Brent Heppner, *COO*
Jack Bogle, *CFO*
Brian Giertz, *Executive Asst*
▲ **EMP:** 60
SQ FT: 217,800
SALES (est): 31.7MM **Privately Held**
WEB: www.heppnerhardwoods.com
SIC: 5031 Lumber: rough, dressed & finished

(P-6623)
HERITAGE 1 WINDOW AND BUILDING
4300 Jetway Ct, North Highlands (95660-5702)
P.O. Box 214609, Sacramento (95821-0609)
PHONE.................................916 481-5030
Charles Gardemeyer, *CEO*
Stephen Beckham, *COO*
Geoff Hughes, *CFO*
John Ballou, *Sales Mgr*
Tyler Randolth, *Manager*
EMP: 171
SQ FT: 80,000
SALES: 24MM
SALES (corp-wide): 89.5MM **Privately Held**
SIC: 5031 Doors & windows
PA: Heritage Interests, Llc
4300 Jetway Ct
North Highlands CA 95660
916 481-5030

(P-6624)
HERITAGE ONE CARPENTRY INC
2107 Forest Ave Ste 100, Chico (95928-7696)
PHONE.................................530 345-6622
Charles Gardemeyer, *President*
Stephen Beckham, *Shareholder*
Geoffrey Hughes, *CFO*
EMP: 162 **EST:** 2012
SQ FT: 3,000
SALES: 33.9MM
SALES (corp-wide): 89.5MM **Privately Held**
SIC: 5031 1751 Lumber, plywood & millwork; cabinet & finish carpentry
PA: Heritage Interests, Llc
4300 Jetway Ct
North Highlands CA 95660
916 481-5030

(P-6625)
HERITAGE ONE DOOR AND BUILDING
4300 Jetway Ct, North Highlands (95660-5702)
P.O. Box 214609, Sacramento (95821-0609)
PHONE.................................916 481-5030
Charles Gardemeyer, *Mng Member*
John Dutter, *COO*
Geoff Hughes, *CFO*
John Ballou, *Sales Mgr*
Tyler Randolth, *Manager*
EMP: 86
SQ FT: 80,000
SALES: 31.6MM
SALES (corp-wide): 89.5MM **Privately Held**
SIC: 5031 2431 Doors & windows; windows & window parts & trim, wood
PA: Heritage Interests, Llc
4300 Jetway Ct
North Highlands CA 95660
916 481-5030

(P-6626)
HIGH COUNTRY LUMBER INC (PA)
Also Called: Ace Hardware
444 S Main St, Bishop (93514-3421)
PHONE.................................760 873-5874
Steven Joseph, *President*
Scott Piercey, *Corp Secy*
Wyatt Gaunt, *Sales Mgr*
Ivan Garcia, *Sales Staff*
Trevor Newcomb, *Sales Staff*
EMP: 50
SQ FT: 10,000
SALES (est): 29.4MM **Privately Held**
SIC: 5031 5211 Lumber, plywood & millwork; lumber & other building materials

(P-6627)
HIGHLAND LUMBER SALES INC
300 E Santa Ana St, Anaheim (92805-3953)
PHONE.................................714 778-2293
Ken Lobue, *President*
Richard Phillips, *President*
Richard J Phillips, *CEO*
Alan Arbiso, *Relg Ldr*
▲ **EMP:** 60
SQ FT: 2,000
SALES (est): 24MM **Privately Held**
SIC: 5031 2493 2431 5211 Lumber: rough, dressed & finished; reconstituted wood products; millwork; lumber products

(P-6628)
HUMBOLDT REDWOOD COMPANY LLC (HQ)
125 Main St, Scotia (95565)
P.O. Box 712 (95565-0712)
PHONE.................................707 764-4472
Bob Mertz,
Mike Jani,
Marty Olhiser,
EMP: 300
SALES (est): 103MM
SALES (corp-wide): 81.8MM **Privately Held**
SIC: 5031 Lumber: rough, dressed & finished
PA: Mendocino Redwood Company, Llc
850 Kunzler Ranch Rd
Ukiah CA 95482
707 463-5110

(P-6629)
HUTTIG BUILDING PRODUCTS INC
Also Called: Huttig Sash & Door Co
8120 Pwr Rdge Rd Bldg 100, Sacramento (95826)
PHONE.................................916 383-3721
Doug Brian, *General Mgr*
EMP: 60
SALES (corp-wide): 839.6MM **Publicly Held**
WEB: www.huttig.com
SIC: 5031 Building materials, exterior
PA: Huttig Building Products, Inc.
555 Mryvlle Univ Dr Ste 4
Saint Louis MO 63141
314 216-2600

(P-6630)
JAMES HARDIE BUILDING PDTS INC
10901 Elm Ave, Fontana (92337-7327)
PHONE.................................909 355-6500
Bob Mussleman, *Branch Mgr*
EMP: 190 **Privately Held**
SIC: 5031 3272 Building materials, exterior; areaways, basement window: concrete
HQ: James Hardie Building Products Inc.
231 S La Salle St # 2000
Chicago IL 60604
312 291-5072

(P-6631)
JELD-WEN INC
Also Called: Jeld-Wen Windows
2760 Progress St Ste B, Vista (92081-8449)
PHONE.................................760 597-4201
Clint Honeycutt, *Vice Pres*
Bill Maschmeier, *General Mgr*
Will Elchrick, *Technology*
Craig Nath, *Manager*
EMP: 300 **Publicly Held**
SIC: 5031 Doors & windows
HQ: Jeld-Wen, Inc.
2645 Silver Crescent Dr
Charlotte NC 28273
800 535-3936

(P-6632)
MENDOCINO FOREST PDTS CO LLC
Also Called: Sawmill
850 Kunzler Ranch Rd, Ukiah (95482-7294)
P.O. Box 996 (95482-0996)
PHONE.................................707 468-1431
Dean Kerstetter, *Exec VP*
EMP: 200
SALES (est): 13.7MM
SALES (corp-wide): 134.9MM **Privately Held**
SIC: 5031 2421 2499 Lumber: rough, dressed & finished; fencing, wood; sawmills & planing mills, general; fencing, docks & other outdoor wood structural products
PA: Mendocino Forest Products Company Llc
3700 Old Redwood Hwy # 200
Santa Rosa CA 95403
707 620-2961

(P-6633)
MENDOCINO FOREST PDTS CO LLC (PA)
3700 Old Redwood Hwy # 200, Santa Rosa (95403-5739)
P.O. Box 390, Calpella (95418-0390)
PHONE.................................707 620-2961
Sandy Dean, *CEO*
John Russell, *President*
Bob Mertz, *CEO*
Jim Pelkey, *CFO*
EMP: 400
SQ FT: 5,000
SALES (est): 134.9MM **Privately Held**
SIC: 5031 2421 Lumber: rough, dressed & finished; sawmills & planing mills, general

(P-6634)
MENDOCINO FOREST PDTS CO LLC
Also Called: Calpella Distribution Center
6375 N State St, Calpella (95418)
P.O. Box 336 (95418-0336)
PHONE.................................707 485-6800
Mike Benetti, *Branch Mgr*
EMP: 94
SALES (est): 6.7MM
SALES (corp-wide): 134.9MM **Privately Held**
SIC: 5031 2421 Lumber: rough, dressed & finished; sawmills & planing mills, general
PA: Mendocino Forest Products Company Llc
3700 Old Redwood Hwy # 200
Santa Rosa CA 95403
707 620-2961

(P-6635)
NICHOLS LUMBER & HARDWARE CO
13470 Dalewood St, Baldwin Park (91706-5883)
PHONE.................................626 960-4802
Judith A Nichols, *President*
Rick Dean, *Vice Pres*
Judy Nichols, *Executive*
Charles Nichols, *Admin Sec*
Jose Jimenez, *Sales Staff*
EMP: 75
SALES (est): 46.5MM **Privately Held**
SIC: 5031 5251 2421 Lumber: rough, dressed & finished; hardware; sawmills & planing mills, general

(P-6636)
OAKLAND PALLET COMPANY INC (PA)
2500 Grant Ave, San Lorenzo (94580-1810)
PHONE.................................510 278-1291
Jose G Padilla, *President*
Javier Padilla, *Corp Secy*
Carlos Padilla, *Vice Pres*
Cesar Gonzalez, *Executive*
Manuel Padillia, *VP Sales*
EMP: 130
SALES (est): 50.2MM **Privately Held**
SIC: 5031 7699 Pallets, wood; pallet repair

(P-6637)
OREGON PCF BLDG PDTS CALIF INC
Also Called: Orepac Building Products
8185 Signal Ct Ste A, Sacramento (95824-2354)
PHONE.................................916 381-8051
John Dutter, *Site Mgr*
Cesar Moreno, *Manager*
EMP: 87
SALES (corp-wide): 557.2MM **Privately Held**
SIC: 5031 Building materials, exterior; building materials, interior; lumber: rough, dressed & finished; millwork
HQ: Oregon Pacific Building Products (Calif.), Inc.
30170 Sw Ore Pac Ave
Wilsonville OR 97070
503 685-5499

(P-6638)
OREGON PCF BLDG PDTS MAPLE INC
Also Called: Orepac Millwork Products
2401 E Philadelphia St, Ontario (91761-7743)
PHONE.................................909 627-4043
Douglas Hart, *President*
Kristopher Schroeder, *General Mgr*
Mark Calhoun, *Director*
▲ **EMP:** 125
SALES (est): 27.8MM
SALES (corp-wide): 557.2MM **Privately Held**
SIC: 5031 5032 Lumber, plywood & millwork; brick, stone & related material
PA: Orepac Holding Company
30170 Sw Ore Pac Ave
Wilsonville OR 97070
503 685-5499

(P-6639)
PACIFIC COAST SUPPLY LLC
Also Called: Weyrick Pacific
626 N Main St, Templeton (93465-9010)
PHONE.................................805 434-4800
Colin Weyrick, *Branch Mgr*
EMP: 81
SALES (corp-wide): 1.5B **Privately Held**
SIC: 5031 Lumber, plywood & millwork
HQ: Pacific Coast Supply, Llc
4290 Roseville Rd
North Highlands CA 95660
916 971-2301

(P-6640)
PACIFIC COAST SUPPLY LLC
Also Called: Anderson Lumber
4290 Roseville Rd, North Highlands (95660-5710)
PHONE.................................916 481-2220

▲ = Import ▼ =Export
◆ =Import/Export

Chris Lucchetti, *Branch Mgr*
EMP: 150
SALES (corp-wide): 1.5B **Privately Held**
SIC: 5031 5211 Lumber, plywood & millwork; lumber & other building materials
HQ: Pacific Coast Supply, Llc
4290 Roseville Rd
North Highlands CA 95660
916 971-2301

(P-6641)
PACIFIC COAST SUPPLY LLC (HQ)
4290 Roseville Rd, North Highlands (95660-5710)
PHONE..................................916 971-2301
Curt Gomes, *President*
Robert Ramos, *COO*
Lisa Goeppner, *CFO*
Walter Payne, *Bd of Directors*
Joe Gower, *Vice Pres*
EMP: 153
SALES (est): 443.6MM
SALES (corp-wide): 1.5B **Privately Held**
WEB: www.paccoast.com
SIC: 5031 Lumber, plywood & millwork
PA: Pacific Coast Building Products, Inc.
10600 White Rock Rd # 100
Rancho Cordova CA 95670
916 631-6500

(P-6642)
PACIFIC STATES INDUSTRIES INC
Also Called: Redwood Empire Division
31401 Mccray Rd, Cloverdale (95425)
P.O. Box 156 (95425-0156)
PHONE..................................707 894-4242
Nolan Schweikl, *General Mgr*
EMP: 250
SALES (corp-wide): 161.8MM **Privately Held**
SIC: 5031 Lumber: rough, dressed & finished
PA: Pacific States Industries, Incorporated
10 Madrone Ave
Morgan Hill CA 95037
408 779-7354

(P-6643)
PHILLIPS PLYWOOD CO INC
Also Called: Quality Laminating
13599 Desmond St, Pacoima (91331-2300)
P.O. Box 51396, Los Angeles (90051-5696)
PHONE..................................818 897-7736
Douglas F Madsen, *CEO*
Shawn Carlisle, *President*
Lynne Corwin, *VP Finance*
Jeanne Wilson, *Personnel*
Roberto Perez, *Sales Staff*
EMP: 55 **EST:** 1986
SQ FT: 100,000
SALES (est): 29.7MM **Privately Held**
WEB: www.phillipsplywood.com
SIC: 5031 Plywood

(P-6644)
PINE TREE LUMBER COMPANY LP (PA)
707 N Andreasen Dr, Escondido (92029-1497)
PHONE..................................760 745-0411
Jacob Brouwer, *Partner*
Betty Lipton, *Controller*
Gail Psqueda, *Human Res Mgr*
Marvin Newton, *Sales Staff*
Clay Rosman, *Sales Staff*
EMP: 56
SQ FT: 45,000
SALES (est): 43.2MM **Privately Held**
WEB: www.pinetreelumber.com
SIC: 5031 5211 Building materials, interior; building materials, exterior; lumber & other building materials

(P-6645)
PJS LUMBER INC
Also Called: P J'S Construction Supplies
45055 Fremont Blvd, Fremont (94538-6318)
PHONE..................................510 743-5300
Shane McMillan, *CEO*
Carlton J McMillan, *President*
Terry W Protto, *CEO*
Jeff Veilleux, *Vice Pres*

Bill Bryan, *Maint Spvr*
EMP: 145
SQ FT: 2,000
SALES (est): 101.3MM **Privately Held**
SIC: 5031 5051 Lumber: rough, dressed & finished; steel

(P-6646)
PLY GEM PACIFIC WINDOWS CORP
235 Radio Rd, Corona (92879-1725)
PHONE..................................951 272-1300
Randy Dasalla, *Branch Mgr*
EMP: 100
SALES (corp-wide): 2B **Publicly Held**
SIC: 5031 Windows
HQ: Ply Gem Pacific Windows Corporation
2600 Grand Blvd Ste 900
Kansas City MO 64108
816 426-8200

(P-6647)
POTTER ROEMER LLC (HQ)
17451 Hurley St, City of Industry (91744-5106)
P.O. Box 3527 (91744-0527)
PHONE..................................626 855-4890
Donald E Morris, *Mng Member*
Jeff Herne, *Regional Mgr*
Eva Ramirez, *Credit Mgr*
Dale Nakatani, *Purch Agent*
Katherine Song, *Export Mgr*
▲ **EMP:** 95
SQ FT: 110,000
SALES: 26.2MM
SALES (corp-wide): 85MM **Privately Held**
WEB: www.potterroemer.com
SIC: 5031 3569 2542 Skylights, all materials; firefighting apparatus & related equipment; partitions & fixtures, except wood
PA: Acorn Engineering Company
15125 Proctor Ave
City Of Industry CA 91746
800 488-8999

(P-6648)
REDWOOD PRODUCTS CHINO INC
Also Called: Rancho Wholesale
9301 Remington Ave, Chino (91710-9346)
P.O. Box 2662, Corona (92878-2662)
PHONE..................................909 923-5656
Jaime Carlos, *President*
Maricela Rodriguez, *Vice Pres*
EMP: 60 **EST:** 2000
SALES (est): 23.1MM **Privately Held**
WEB: www.redwoodproductschino.com
SIC: 5031 Lumber: rough, dressed & finished

(P-6649)
RELIABLE WHOLESALE LUMBER INC (PA)
7600 Redondo Cir, Huntington Beach (92648-1303)
P.O. Box 191 (92648-0191)
PHONE..................................714 848-8222
Jerome M Higman, *President*
Will Higman, *COO*
David Higman, *CFO*
Bogie Nicols, *Exec VP*
Scott Nicols, *Vice Pres*
EMP: 90
SQ FT: 4,500
SALES (est): 159.3MM **Privately Held**
WEB: www.rwli.net
SIC: 5031 2421 Lumber: rough, dressed & finished; sawmills & planing mills, general

(P-6650)
ROBERTS LUMBER SALES INC
Also Called: Robert's Lumber
2661 S Lilac Ave, Bloomington (92316-3211)
PHONE..................................909 350-9164
Robert Cantero Jr, *CEO*
Lori Cantero, *Principal*
EMP: 57 **EST:** 1997
SALES (est): 15.1MM **Privately Held**
SIC: 5031 2448 Lumber: rough, dressed & finished; wood pallets & skids

(P-6651)
ROSEBURG FOREST PRODUCTS CO
98 Mill St, Weed (96094-2251)
PHONE..................................530 938-2721
Tom Didgs, *Manager*
Robin Styers, *Opers Staff*
Kent Hubbard, *Maintence Staff*
EMP: 161
SQ FT: 180,000
SALES (corp-wide): 960.2MM **Privately Held**
WEB: www.rfpco.com
SIC: 5031 Lumber: rough, dressed & finished
HQ: Roseburg Forest Products Co
3660 Gateway St Ste A
Springfield OR 97477
541 679-3311

(P-6652)
ROYAL PLYWOOD COMPANY LLC
6003 88th St Ste 100, Sacramento (95828-1143)
P.O. Box 728, La Mirada (90637-0728)
PHONE..................................916 426-3292
Gabriel N Marshi, *Mng Member*
EMP: 78
SALES (corp-wide): 67.9MM **Privately Held**
SIC: 5031 Plywood
PA: Royal Plywood Company, Llc
14171 Park Pl
Cerritos CA 90703
562 404-2989

(P-6653)
ROYAL PLYWOOD COMPANY LLC (PA)
14171 Park Pl, Cerritos (90703-2463)
P.O. Box 728, La Mirada (90637-0728)
PHONE..................................562 404-2989
Gabriel N Marshi,
Brian McMaster, *Info Tech Mgr*
Linda Ramirez, *Credit Staff*
Stephen Fuller,
▲ **EMP:** 78
SQ FT: 120,000
SALES (est): 67.9MM **Privately Held**
WEB: www.royalplywood.com
SIC: 5031 Building materials, exterior

(P-6654)
SAROYAN LUMBER COMPANY INC (PA)
Also Called: Saroyan Lumber and Moulding Co
6230 S Alameda St, Huntington Park (90255-3503)
PHONE..................................800 624-9309
Richard Saroyan, *President*
Dorothy A Robinson, *Shareholder*
Marylne Nahery, *CFO*
John Saroyan, *Corp Secy*
Robert Lemke, *Vice Pres*
▲ **EMP:** 66
SQ FT: 144,000
SALES (est): 36.9MM **Privately Held**
WEB: www.saroyanlumber.com
SIC: 5031 Lumber: rough, dressed & finished; millwork

(P-6655)
SHAPP INTERNATIONAL TRDG INC
Also Called: Shapp Internatioonal
6000 Reseda Blvd, Tarzana (91356-1500)
P.O. Box 893, Woodland Hills (91365-0893)
PHONE..................................818 348-3000
Allan Shapiro, *President*
Louis Justin, *Treasurer*
EMP: 118
SQ FT: 8,000
SALES (est): 33.2MM **Privately Held**
SIC: 5031 5064 5112 5021 Lumber, plywood & millwork; electrical appliances, major; stationery & office supplies; furniture

(P-6656)
SIERRA FOREST PRODUCTS
9000 Road 234, Terra Bella (93270-9560)
P.O. Box 10060 (93270-0060)
PHONE..................................559 535-4893
Kent Duysen, *CEO*
Glenn Duysen, *Treasurer*
EMP: 110 **EST:** 1964
SQ FT: 3,000
SALES (est): 29.8MM **Privately Held**
SIC: 5031 Lumber, plywood & millwork

(P-6657)
SINGLEY ENTERPRISES (PA)
Also Called: Garage Door Specialists
121 Main Ave, Sacramento (95838-2041)
P.O. Box 572, West Sacramento (95691-0572)
PHONE..................................866 890-1776
Gary B Singley, *CEO*
Charlene Singley, *Treasurer*
▲ **EMP:** 50
SQ FT: 14,400
SALES (est): 21.7MM **Privately Held**
SIC: 5031 Doors, garage

(P-6658)
SLIDING DOOR COMPANY (PA)
Also Called: Sliding Door Co, The
20235 Bahama St, Chatsworth (91311-6204)
PHONE..................................818 997-7855
Doron Polus, *President*
Eyal Salpeter, *Info Tech Mgr*
Leilani Garcia, *Graphic Designe*
Suzanne Petersen, *Accounting Mgr*
Dayna Petersen, *Recruiter*
▲ **EMP:** 92
SQ FT: 22,000
SALES (est): 27.6MM **Privately Held**
WEB: www.slidingdoorco.com
SIC: 5031 Windows

(P-6659)
STATES DRAWER BOX SPC LLC
1482 N Batavia St, Orange (92867-3505)
PHONE..................................714 744-4247
Cathy Blankenship, *President*
EMP: 60
SALES (est): 15.6MM **Privately Held**
WEB: www.dbsdrawers.com
SIC: 5031 Lumber: rough, dressed & finished
PA: States Industries, Llc
29545 E Enid Rd
Eugene OR 97402

(P-6660)
SUNBURST SHUTTERS CAL INC (PA)
1037 S Melrose St Ste B, Placentia (92870-7132)
PHONE..................................714 997-0800
Greg Arnett, *President*
EMP: 70
SQ FT: 3,000
SALES (est): 8.7MM **Privately Held**
WEB: www.sunburstshutters.com
SIC: 5031 Windows

(P-6661)
SUNSET MOULDING CO
2200 Paseo Rd, Live Oak (95953-9721)
PHONE..................................530 695-3379
Jim Perigo, *Branch Mgr*
Howard Little, *Branch Mgr*
EMP: 60
SALES (corp-wide): 24.3MM **Privately Held**
WEB: www.sunsetmoulding.com
SIC: 5031 Lumber, plywood & millwork
PA: Sunset Moulding Co.
2231 Paseo Rd
Live Oak CA 95953
530 790-2700

(P-6662)
T M COBB COMPANY
Also Called: Tom Ray
8490 Rovana Cir, Sacramento (95828-2529)
PHONE..................................916 381-7330
Steve Grambush, *Manager*
EMP: 70
SQ FT: 40,000

P R O D U C T S & S V C S

SALES (corp-wide): 92.5MM **Privately Held**
WEB: www.tmcobbco.com
SIC: **5031** 5032 2431 Doors; door frames, all materials; masons' materials; millwork
PA: T. M. Cobb Company
500 Palmyrita Ave
Riverside CA 92507
951 248-2400

(P-6663)
TABER COMPANY INC
1442 Ritchey St, Santa Ana (92705-4717)
PHONE.....................714 543-7100
Brian Taber, *President*
Don Cox, *Project Mgr*
Andre Alex, *Supervisor*
EMP: 65
SQ FT: 11,000
SALES (est): 27.8MM **Privately Held**
WEB: www.taberco.net
SIC: **5031** Building materials, interior

(P-6664)
TRIM TECH INDUSTRIES INC
1724 Ringwood Ave, San Jose (95131-1711)
PHONE.....................408 573-4514
Ellen Medeiros, *President*
Andy Medeiros, *Project Mgr*
Ted Stieber, *Technology*
Cyndy Thomas, *Purch Mgr*
Virginia Salas, *Purch Agent*
EMP: 50 EST: 1992
SALES (est): 8.9MM **Privately Held**
SIC: **5031** Doors, combination, screen-storm

(P-6665)
USG INTERIORS LLC
2575 Loomis Rd, Stockton (95205-8045)
PHONE.....................209 466-4636
Sandy Hirzel, *Manager*
EMP: 70
SALES (corp-wide): 8.2B **Privately Held**
SIC: **5031** Building materials, exterior
HQ: Usg Interiors, Llc
125 S Franklin St
Chicago IL 60606
800 874-4968

(P-6666)
VIRGINIA HARDWOOD COMPANY (PA)
1000 W Foothill Blvd, Azusa (91702-2840)
PHONE.....................626 815-0540
David V Ferrari, *Chairman*
Gary Henzie, *President*
Robin Ezzo, *Corp Secy*
Jeannette Ferrari, *Vice Pres*
Mike Ferrari, *Vice Pres*
▲ EMP: 56 EST: 1946
SQ FT: 60,000
SALES (est): 27.2MM **Privately Held**
WEB: www.virginiahardwood.com
SIC: **5031** Hardboard

(P-6667)
WEYERHAEUSER COMPANY
Also Called: Marketing Sales & Dist Div
17400 Slover Ave, Fontana (92337-8004)
P.O. Box 487 (92334-0487)
PHONE.....................909 877-6100
Mark Davis, *Branch Mgr*
EMP: 65
SQ FT: 85,000
SALES (corp-wide): 7.4B **Publicly Held**
SIC: **5031** Lumber: rough, dressed & finished
PA: Weyerhaeuser Company
220 Occidental Ave S
Seattle WA 98104
206 539-3000

5032 Brick, Stone & Related Construction Mtrls Wholesale

(P-6668)
A TEICHERT & SON INC (HQ)
Also Called: Teichert Construction
3500 American River Dr, Sacramento (95864-5893)
P.O. Box 15002 (95851-0002)
PHONE.....................916 484-3011
Judson T Riggs, *President*
Dana M Davis, *President*
Kenneth A Kayser, *President*
Narendra M Pathipati, *CFO*
Terri A Bakken, *Vice Pres*
▼ EMP: 136
SALES (est): 775.9MM
SALES (corp-wide): 784MM **Privately Held**
SIC: **5032** 3273 1611 1442 Brick, stone & related material; ready-mixed concrete; highway & street construction; construction sand & gravel; single-family housing construction
PA: Teichert, Inc.
3500 American River Dr
Sacramento CA 95864
916 484-3011

(P-6669)
ARIZONA TILE LLC
1620 S Lewis St, Anaheim (92805-6436)
PHONE.....................714 978-6403
EMP: 100
SALES (corp-wide): 322.1MM **Privately Held**
SIC: **5032**
PA: Arizona Tile, L.L.C.
8829 S Priest Dr
Tempe AZ 85284
480 893-9393

(P-6670)
ARRIAGA USA INC (PA)
Also Called: Stoneland
12000 Sherman Way, North Hollywood (91605-3727)
PHONE.....................818 982-9559
Shalom Rubin, *President*
◆ EMP: 60
SALES (est): 31.9MM **Privately Held**
SIC: **5032** Marble building stone

(P-6671)
ATLAS CONSTRUCTION SUPPLY INC (PA)
4640 Brinnell St, San Diego (92111-2302)
PHONE.....................858 277-2100
Brian Quinn, *President*
James E Wright, *Corp Secy*
Tom Vargas, *Exec VP*
Walt Borkert, *Technology*
Debbie Lopez, *Credit Mgr*
▲ EMP: 75
SQ FT: 30,000
SALES (est): 85.2MM **Privately Held**
WEB: www.atlasform.com
SIC: **5032** Concrete building products

(P-6672)
CARRARA MARBLE CO AMER INC (PA)
15939 Phoenix Dr, City of Industry (91745-1624)
PHONE.....................626 961-6010
William Cordova, *President*
James Hogan, *Senior VP*
Dirk Wietstock, *Vice Pres*
Eloise Paz, *Controller*
Steve Barron, *Opers Staff*
▲ EMP: 70
SQ FT: 30,000
SALES (est): 30.7MM **Privately Held**
SIC: **5032** 1743 1741 Ceramic wall & floor tile; marble installation, interior; masonry & other stonework

(P-6673)
CEMEX CNSTR MTLS PCF LLC
Also Called: Cem - Victorville River Plant
16888 E St, Victorville (92394-2999)
PHONE.....................760 381-7600
Don Kelly, *Manager*
EMP: 234
SQ FT: 2,684 **Privately Held**
SIC: **5032** Cement
HQ: Cemex Construction Materials Pacific, Llc
1501 Belvedere Rd
West Palm Beach FL 33406
561 833-5555

(P-6674)
CLARK - PACIFIC CORPORATION (PA)
Also Called: Clark Pacific
1980 S River Rd, West Sacramento (95691-2817)
PHONE.....................916 371-0305
Robert Clark, *President*
Don Clark, *President*
Geene Alhady, *Exec Dir*
Brad Williams, *General Mgr*
Vanessa Borrero, *Executive Asst*
▲ EMP: 300
SQ FT: 20,000
SALES (est): 229.7MM **Privately Held**
WEB: www.clarkpacific.com
SIC: **5032** 3272 Brick, stone & related material; concrete products, precast

(P-6675)
CLASSIC TILE & MOSAIC INC (PA)
Also Called: Ctm
14463 S Broadway, Gardena (90248-1807)
PHONE.....................310 538-9605
Vincent Cullinan, *CEO*
Bonnie Daland, *Vice Pres*
▲ EMP: 60
SALES (est): 27.8MM **Privately Held**
WEB: www.classictileandmosaic.com
SIC: **5032** 5211 Tile, clay or other ceramic, excluding refractory; tile, ceramic

(P-6676)
CONCRETE TIE INDUSTRIES INC (PA)
130 E Oris St, Compton (90222-2714)
P.O. Box 5406 (90224-5406)
PHONE.....................310 628-2328
Paul J Schoendienst, *President*
Martin Schoendienst, *Vice Pres*
Steve Sim, *Admin Sec*
Steve Sims, *Controller*
EMP: 83
SQ FT: 280,000
SALES (est): 15.1MM **Privately Held**
WEB: www.concretetie.com
SIC: **5032** 3452 Concrete & cinder building products; bolts, nuts, rivets & washers

(P-6677)
COUNTRY FLOORS AMERICA LLC (PA)
8735 Melrose Ave, Vernon (90058)
PHONE.....................310 657-0510
Munir Turumc,
Ron Pentz, *Consultant*
▲ EMP: 75
SALES (est): 7MM **Privately Held**
WEB: www.countryfloors.com
SIC: **5032** 5713 Tile, clay or other ceramic, excluding refractory; terra cotta; floor tile

(P-6678)
CPC SERVICES INC
2025 E Fincl Way Ste 200, Glendora (91741)
PHONE.....................626 852-6200
James Repman, *President*
David Hatcher, *Admin Asst*
Ron White, *Info Tech Mgr*
Jim Macias, *Technology*
Alice Maupin, *Engineer*
EMP: 75
SALES (est): 3.2MM **Privately Held**
SIC: **5032** Brick, stone & related material

(P-6679)
D & D READY MIX INC
5353 Byron Hot Springs Rd, Byron (94514-1624)
PHONE.....................209 627-7224
Juan Carlos G Gonzalez, *CEO*
Rosa Gaona, *Principal*
EMP: 59
SALES (est): 15.4MM **Privately Held**
SIC: **5032** Concrete mixtures

(P-6680)
DAL-TILE CORPORATION
1132 Duryea Ave, Irvine (92614-5520)
PHONE.....................949 260-0488
Terri M Girr, *Branch Mgr*
EMP: 68
SALES (corp-wide): 9.9B **Publicly Held**
WEB: www.mohawk.com
SIC: **5032** Ceramic wall & floor tile
HQ: Dal-Tile Corporation
7834 C F Hawn Fwy
Dallas TX 75217
214 398-1411

(P-6681)
DAL-TILE CORPORATION
4201 Technology Dr, Modesto (95356-9493)
PHONE.....................209 543-0924
Gwen Kemple, *Manager*
EMP: 68
SALES (corp-wide): 9.9B **Publicly Held**
WEB: www.mohawk.com
SIC: **5032** Ceramic wall & floor tile
HQ: Dal-Tile Corporation
7834 C F Hawn Fwy
Dallas TX 75217
214 398-1411

(P-6682)
ELEGANT SURFACES
3640 Amrcn Rver Dr 150, Sacramento (95864)
P.O. Box 705, Byron (94514-0705)
PHONE.....................209 823-9388
John Polimeno, *CEO*
Dan Thompson, *President*
Kristie Polimeno, *Vice Pres*
▲ EMP: 100 EST: 1967
SQ FT: 48,000
SALES (est): 11.3MM **Privately Held**
WEB: www.elegantsurfaces.com
SIC: **5032** 3281 Marble building stone; marble, building: cut & shaped

(P-6683)
EMSER INTERNATIONAL LLC (PA)
8431 Santa Monica Blvd, Los Angeles (90069-4294)
PHONE.....................323 650-2000
Sam Ghodsian, *Mng Member*
Cindy Dalessio, *Branch Mgr*
David Hille, *Branch Mgr*
Jessica Gherna, *Sales Staff*
Ehsan Ghodsian,
▲ EMP: 70
SQ FT: 50,000
SALES (est): 104.9MM **Privately Held**
SIC: **5032** Ceramic wall & floor tile

(P-6684)
FRANK SCIARRINO MARBLE G
7505 Trade St, San Diego (92121-2411)
P.O. Box 600265 (92160-0265)
PHONE.....................858 695-8030
Frank Sciarrino, *President*
Anna Maria, *Vice Pres*
▲ EMP: 80
SQ FT: 20,000
SALES (est): 8MM **Privately Held**
WEB: www.fsmarble.com
SIC: **5032** 5211 1799 1743 Marble building stone; cabinets, kitchen; counter top installation; tile installation, ceramic

(P-6685)
FST SAND & GRAVEL INC
21780 Temescal Canyon Rd, Corona (92883-5669)
P.O. Box 2798 (92878-2798)
PHONE.....................951 277-8440
Frank Smith, *President*
Jennifer Reece, *Office Mgr*
Frances Martinez, *Sales Staff*

EMP: 50
SQ FT: 1,078
SALES (est): 29.3MM **Privately Held**
WEB: www.fstsand.com
SIC: 5032 Sand, construction; gravel

(P-6686)
GBI TILE & STONE INC (PA)
Also Called: Quarry Collection
5900 Skylab Rd Ste 150, Huntington Beach
(92647-2075)
PHONE..................949 567-1880
Marco A Gonzalez, *Vice Pres*
Marco Gonzalez, *Vice Pres*
Jeff Jonas, *Principal*
Dale Sison, *Info Tech Mgr*
Lorna Irvine-Thomas, *Purch Mgr*
◆ EMP: 50
SALES (est): 20MM **Privately Held**
SIC: 5032 Brick, stone & related material

(P-6687)
GOLDEN STATE PLASTERING
7082 N Harrison Ave, Fresno (93650-1008)
P.O. Box 3452 (93650-3452)
PHONE..................559 439-3920
Monty Bound, *Manager*
Monty Bounds, *Manager*
EMP: 90
SQ FT: 4,920
SALES (est): 4.5MM **Privately Held**
SIC: 5032 Stucco

(P-6688)
GRANITE ROCK CO
Also Called: A R Wilson Quarry & Asp Plant
End Of Quarry Rd, Aromas (95004)
P.O. Box 699 (95004-0699)
PHONE..................831 392-3780
Bruce Woolpert, *President*
EMP: 200
SALES (corp-wide): 992MM **Privately Held**
WEB: www.graniterock.com
SIC: 5032 Brick, stone & related material
PA: Granite Rock Co.
350 Technology Dr
Watsonville CA 95076
831 768-2000

(P-6689)
HOLLIDAY ROCK CO INC (PA)
1401 N Benson Ave, Upland (91786-2166)
PHONE..................909 982-1553
Penny Holliday, *CEO*
Ethel Holliday, *President*
Fredrick N Holliday, *Vice Pres*
John Holliday, *Vice Pres*
Joe Hanlon, *Accounting Mgr*
EMP: 54
SQ FT: 2,000
SALES (est): 49.1MM **Privately Held**
WEB: www.hollidayrock.com
SIC: 5032 Asphalt mixture; concrete mixtures; stone, crushed or broken; sand, construction

(P-6690)
L & W SUPPLY CORPORATION
Also Called: Calply
7750 Convoy Ct, San Diego (92111-1106)
PHONE..................858 627-0811
Donald Smith, *Manager*
EMP: 50
SALES (corp-wide): 457.2MM **Privately Held**
WEB: www.calply.com
SIC: 5032 Drywall materials
HQ: L & W Supply Corporation
300 S Riverside Plz # 200
Chicago IL 60606
312 606-4000

(P-6691)
LYNGSO GARDEN MATERIALS INC
345 Shoreway Rd, San Carlos
(94070-2708)
PHONE..................650 364-1730
Theresa Lyngso, *President*
Linda K Lyngso, *Vice Pres*
Pamela Parkinson, *Admin Sec*
James Kolter, *Opers Mgr*
Steve Powers, *Manager*
▲ EMP: 50

SALES (est): 24.6MM **Privately Held**
WEB: www.lyngso.net
SIC: 5032 5261 5211 5191 Brick, stone & related material; nurseries & garden centers; lumber & other building materials; greenhouse equipment & supplies

(P-6692)
M S INTERNATIONAL INC (PA)
Also Called: MSI
2095 N Batavia St, Orange (92865-3101)
PHONE..................714 685-7500
Manahar Shah, *CEO*
Rajesh Shah, *President*
Chandrika Shah, *Corp Secy*
Marlene Ramirez, *Officer*
Phil Caudillo, *Vice Pres*
◆ EMP: 300
SQ FT: 500,000
SALES (est): 582MM **Privately Held**
WEB: www.msistone.com
SIC: 5032 Granite building stone

(P-6693)
PACIFIC CLAY PRODUCTS INC
14741 Lake St, Lake Elsinore
(92530-1610)
PHONE..................661 857-1401
Barry Coley, *President*
Kai Chin, *Vice Pres*
Dale Kline, *Vice Pres*
Brenna Deparis, *Administration*
Vince Tannahill, *Administration*
▲ EMP: 160 EST: 1930
SQ FT: 200,000
SALES (est): 46.7MM **Privately Held**
WEB: www.pacificclay.com
SIC: 5032 3251 Tile & clay products; paving brick, clay

(P-6694)
PARAGON INDUSTRIES INC
Also Called: Bedrosian's Tile & Marble
1235 S State College Blvd, Anaheim
(92806-5145)
PHONE..................714 778-8453
Lonnie Martinez, *Branch Mgr*
Felicia Clark, *Creative Dir*
Grace Nguyen, *Business Mgr*
EMP: 60
SALES (corp-wide): 293.9MM **Privately Held**
SIC: 5032 5211 Tile, clay or other ceramic, excluding refractory; tile, ceramic
PA: Paragon Industries Inc.
4285 N Golden State Blvd
Fresno CA 93722
559 275-5000

(P-6695)
PATRICK INDUSTRIES INC
Also Called: Custom Vinyls
13414 Slover Ave, Fontana (92337-6977)
PHONE..................909 350-4440
Vince Fergan, *Branch Mgr*
EMP: 150
SALES (corp-wide): 2.2B **Publicly Held**
WEB: www.patrickind.com
SIC: 5032 1799 2435 3083 Brick, stone & related material; building site preparation; hardwood veneer & plywood; laminated plastics plate & sheet
PA: Patrick Industries, Inc.
107 W Franklin St
Elkhart IN 46516
574 294-7511

(P-6696)
PLAYMAR INC
2502 Channing Ave, San Jose
(95131-1004)
PHONE..................408 324-1930
EMP: 70
SALES (est): 1.1MM **Privately Held**
SIC: 5032 Granite building stone

(P-6697)
SYAR INDUSTRIES INC
13666 Healdsburg Ave, Healdsburg
(95448-9234)
P.O. Box 325 (95448-0325)
PHONE..................707 433-3366
Dick Love, *Manager*
EMP: 65

SALES (corp-wide): 100.2MM **Privately Held**
WEB: www.syar.com
SIC: 5032 Gravel; sand, construction; stone, crushed or broken
PA: Syar Industries, Inc.
2301 Napa Vallejo Hwy
Napa CA 94558
707 252-8711

(P-6698)
THOMPSON BUILDING MTLS INC
6618 Federal Blvd, Lemon Grove
(91945-1312)
PHONE..................619 287-9410
Kenneth R Thompson, *President*
EMP: 50
SQ FT: 15,000
SALES (est): 12.1MM
SALES (corp-wide): 77.9MM **Privately Held**
SIC: 5032 5211 Plastering materials; lime & plaster
PA: Opal Service, Inc.
282 S Anita Dr
Orange CA 92868
714 935-0900

(P-6699)
UGM CITATAH INC (PA)
Also Called: Ugmc
13220 Cambridge St, Santa Fe Springs
(90670-4902)
PHONE..................562 921-9549
Viken Dave Yaghjian, *President*
Bruce Feaster, *Exec VP*
Irmen Yaghjian, *Admin Sec*
▲ EMP: 125
SQ FT: 46,000
SALES (est): 31.4MM **Privately Held**
WEB: www.ugmcstone.com
SIC: 5032 1741 1743 Marble building stone; stone masonry; terrazzo, tile, marble, mosaic work

(P-6700)
UNITED MARBLE & GRANITE INC
2163 Martin Ave, Santa Clara
(95050-2701)
PHONE..................408 347-3300
Manuel De Oliveira, *President*
Velma De Oliveira, *Executive*
Joseph Enos, *Purchasing*
▲ EMP: 80
SALES (est): 254.7K **Privately Held**
WEB: www.umglabs.com
SIC: 5032 Marble building stone

(P-6701)
VALORI SAND & GRAVEL COMPANY (PA)
Also Called: Thompson Building Materials
141 W Taft Ave, Orange (92865-4217)
PHONE..................714 637-0104
Kenneth R Thompson, *President*
▲ EMP: 100
SALES (est): 49.5MM **Privately Held**
SIC: 5032 Sand, construction

(P-6702)
VALORI SAND & GRAVEL COMPANY
Also Called: Thompson Building Materials
11027 Cherry Ave, Fontana (92337-7118)
P.O. Box 950 (92334-0950)
PHONE..................909 350-3000
Tom Rievley, *Branch Mgr*
EMP: 150
SALES (corp-wide): 49.5MM **Privately Held**
SIC: 5032 5211 Brick, stone & related material; cement
PA: Valori Sand & Gravel Company Inc
141 W Taft Ave
Orange CA 92865
714 637-0104

(P-6703)
WALKER & ZANGER INC (PA)
16719 Schoenborn St, North Hills
(91343-6115)
PHONE..................818 280-8300
Jonathan Zanger, *CEO*

Pat Petrocelli, *COO*
Kim Bernard, *Exec Dir*
Drew Rust, *Branch Mgr*
Fernando Decipeda, *Asst Controller*
◆ EMP: 60
SQ FT: 30,000
SALES (est): 69.7MM **Privately Held**
SIC: 5032 Marble building stone; ceramic wall & floor tile

(P-6704)
WEST COAST SAND AND GRAVEL INC (PA)
Also Called: West Coast Materials
7282 Orangethorpe Ave, Buena Park
(90621-3331)
P.O. Box 5067 (90622-5067)
PHONE..................714 522-0282
Daniel C Reyneveld, *CEO*
Marvin J Struiksma, *President*
John Struiksma, *Vice Pres*
James Slater, *General Mgr*
Bob Struiksma, *Admin Sec*
EMP: 71
SQ FT: 4,200
SALES (est): 38.2MM **Privately Held**
WEB: www.wcsg.com
SIC: 5032 Sand, construction; gravel

(P-6705)
WESTERN PACIFIC DISTRG LLC
Also Called: Westpac Materials
341 W Meats Ave, Orange (92865-2623)
PHONE..................714 974-6837
Mark Hamilton, *Mng Member*
Leslie Dickson, *Manager*
EMP: 150
SALES (est): 37.1MM **Privately Held**
WEB: www.westernpacificdistributing.com
SIC: 5032 Drywall materials

5033 Roofing, Siding & Insulation Mtrls Wholesale

(P-6706)
ALLIED BUILDING PRODUCTS CORP
1201 E Mcfadden Ave, Santa Ana
(92705-4101)
PHONE..................714 647-9792
Stephen Rhorer, *Manager*
EMP: 50
SALES (corp-wide): 6.4B **Publicly Held**
WEB: www.alliedbuilding.com
SIC: 5033 Roofing, asphalt & sheet metal
HQ: Allied Building Products Corp.
15 E Union Ave
East Rutherford NJ 07073
201 507-8400

(P-6707)
ALLIED BUILDING PRODUCTS CORP
4159 Santa Rosa Ave, Santa Rosa
(95407-8276)
PHONE..................707 584-7599
Jim Brenton, *Manager*
EMP: 50
SALES (corp-wide): 6.4B **Publicly Held**
WEB: www.alliedbuilding.com
SIC: 5033 5211 Roofing & siding materials; roofing material
HQ: Allied Building Products Corp.
15 E Union Ave
East Rutherford NJ 07073
201 507-8400

(P-6708)
ALLIED BUILDING PRODUCTS CORP
Also Called: AMS
1620 S Maple Ave, Montebello
(90640-6510)
PHONE..................323 721-9011
Bill Wick, *Branch Mgr*
Marta Higginbotham, *Admin Asst*
Larry Cain, *Sales Staff*
Oj Dutcher, *Sales Staff*
Jeff Fedderson, *Sales Staff*
EMP: 100

SALES (corp-wide): 6.4B **Publicly Held**
WEB: www.a-m-s.com
SIC: **5033** Roofing, siding & insulation
HQ: Allied Building Products Corp.
15 E Union Ave
East Rutherford NJ 07073
201 507-8400

(P-6709)
BEACON ROOFING SUPPLY INC
200 San Jose Ave, San Jose (95125-1008)
PHONE..................408 293-5947
EMP: 99
SALES (corp-wide): 6.4B **Publicly Held**
SIC: **5033** Roofing & siding materials
PA: Beacon Roofing Supply, Inc.
505 Huntmar Park Dr # 300
Herndon VA 20170
571 323-3939

(P-6710)
BEACON SALES ACQUISITION INC
Also Called: Pacific Supply
1201 E Mcfadden Ave, Santa Ana (92705-4101)
PHONE..................714 288-1974
Amber Williams, *Sales Associate*
EMP: 110
SALES (corp-wide): 6.4B **Publicly Held**
SIC: **5033** 5211 Roofing, asphalt & sheet metal; roofing material
HQ: Beacon Sales Acquisition, Inc.
50 Webster Ave
Somerville MA 02143
877 645-7663

(P-6711)
BURLINGAME INDUSTRIES INC
Also Called: Eagle Roofing Products
4555 Mckinley Ave, Stockton (95206-4008)
PHONE..................209 464-9001
Hersch Beahm, *Manager*
EMP: 100
SALES (corp-wide): 81.5MM **Privately Held**
SIC: **5033** Roofing, siding & insulation
PA: Burlingame Industries, Incorporated
3546 N Riverside Ave
Rialto CA 92377
909 355-7000

(P-6712)
CARLISLE CONSTRUCTION MTLS INC
Also Called: Western Insulfoam
5635 Schaefer Ave, Chino (91710-9048)
PHONE..................909 591-7425
Tom Tartaglione, *Manager*
Chris Brown, *General Mgr*
EMP: 100
SQ FT: 45,464
SALES (corp-wide): 4.4B **Publicly Held**
WEB: www.insulfoam.com
SIC: **5033** 3086 Insulation materials; cups & plates, foamed plastic
HQ: Carlisle Construction Materials, Llc
1285 Ritner Hwy
Carlisle PA 17013

(P-6713)
CARLISLE CONSTRUCTION MTLS INC
Also Called: Insulfoam
1155 Business Park Dr, Dixon (95620-4303)
PHONE..................707 678-6900
Rick Canady, *Manager*
EMP: 55
SALES (corp-wide): 4.4B **Publicly Held**
WEB: www.insulfoam.com
SIC: **5033** 3086 Insulation materials; plastics foam products
HQ: Carlisle Construction Materials, Llc
1285 Ritner Hwy
Carlisle PA 17013

(P-6714)
EXTERIOR SOLUTIONS INC
25752 Simpson Pl, Calabasas (91302-3154)
PHONE..................310 400-3510
Craig Carson, *CEO*

EMP: 70
SALES (est): 11.2MM **Privately Held**
SIC: **5033** Roofing, siding & insulation

(P-6715)
MAC ARTHUR CO
1420b Enterprise Blvd, West Sacramento (95691-3485)
PHONE..................916 226-5706
EMP: 248
SALES (corp-wide): 190.3MM **Privately Held**
SIC: **5033** Roofing, siding & insulation
PA: Mac Arthur Co.
2400 Wycliff St
Saint Paul MN 55114
651 646-2773

(P-6716)
OWENS CORNING SALES LLC
960 Central Expy, Santa Clara (95050-2665)
PHONE..................408 235-1351
Chris Rukman, *Branch Mgr*
Mark Bauman, *Info Tech Dir*
EMP: 400 **Publicly Held**
WEB: www.owenscorning.com
SIC: **5033** 3296 Fiberglass building materials; mineral wool
HQ: Owens Corning Sales, Llc
1 Owens Corning Pkwy
Toledo OH 43659
419 248-8000

(P-6717)
REVCHEM COMPOSITES INC (PA)
Also Called: Revchem Plastics
2720 S Willow Ave B, Bloomington (92316-3259)
P.O. Box 333 (92316-0333)
PHONE..................909 877-8477
Douglas L Dennis, *CEO*
Gina L Dennis, *Principal*
▲ EMP: 60
SALES (est): 30.7MM **Privately Held**
WEB: www.revchem.com
SIC: **5033** Fiberglass building materials

(P-6718)
ROOFING SUPPLY GROUP LLC
14128 Kornblum Ave, Hawthorne (90250-8114)
PHONE..................424 269-7330
EMP: 68
SALES (corp-wide): 6.4B **Publicly Held**
SIC: **5033** Roofing & siding materials
HQ: Roofing Supply Group, Llc
505 Huntmar Park Dr # 300
Herndon VA 20170

(P-6719)
ROOFING WHOLESALE CO INC
118 Commercial Rd, San Bernardino (92408-4148)
PHONE..................909 825-8440
Rick Knudsen, *Branch Mgr*
Pat Paszternak, *Manager*
EMP: 60
SALES (corp-wide): 148.8MM **Privately Held**
WEB: www.rwc.org
SIC: **5033** Roofing, asphalt & sheet metal
PA: Roofing Wholesale Co., Inc.
1918 W Grant St
Phoenix AZ 85009
602 258-3794

(P-6720)
STANDARD INDUSTRIES INC
Also Called: GAF Materials
3301 Navone Rd, Stockton (95215-9312)
PHONE..................209 242-5000
David Kirkham, *Director*
EMP: 50
SQ FT: 30,000
SALES (corp-wide): 2.5B **Privately Held**
SIC: **5033** Roofing & siding materials
HQ: Standard Industries Inc.
1 Campus Dr
Parsippany NJ 07054

(P-6721)
STANDARD INDUSTRIES INC
Also Called: GAF Materials
6505 S Zerker Rd, Shafter (93263-9614)
PHONE..................661 387-1110
Phil Halpin, *General Mgr*
EMP: 100
SALES (corp-wide): 2.5B **Privately Held**
SIC: **5033** Roofing & siding materials
HQ: Standard Industries Inc.
1 Campus Dr
Parsippany NJ 07054

(P-6722)
TRI-VALLEY SUPPLY INC (PA)
Also Called: Tri Valley Wholesale
1705 Enterprise Dr, Fairfield (94533-5801)
PHONE..................707 469-7470
James P Petersen, *President*
Joe Dean, *Vice Pres*
David Van Beek, *Vice Pres*
▲ EMP: 85 EST: 1993
SQ FT: 15,000
SALES (est): 39.6MM **Privately Held**
WEB: www.trivalleysupply.com
SIC: **5033** Roofing & siding materials

5039 Construction Materials, NEC Wholesale

(P-6723)
JENSEN ENTERPRISES INC
Also Called: Jensen Precast
5400 Raley Blvd, Sacramento (95838-1700)
PHONE..................916 992-8301
Mark Voiselle, *General Mgr*
Miles Bennett, *President*
Sammy Ramos, *Foreman/Supr*
Digna Barton, *Sales Staff*
Jay Devries, *Sales Staff*
EMP: 70
SALES (corp-wide): 186.5MM **Privately Held**
SIC: **5039** 5211 Septic tanks; masonry materials & supplies
PA: Jensen Enterprises, Inc.
825 Steneri Way
Sparks NV 89431
775 352-2700

(P-6724)
LA CANTINA DOORS INC
1875 Ord Way, Oceanside (92056-3589)
PHONE..................888 221-0141
Matthew Power, *CEO*
Toby Jones, *Vice Pres*
Dustin Abrams, *Prdtn Mgr*
Benjamin Woo, *Marketing Mgr*
Sara Healy, *Marketing Staff*
◆ EMP: 50
SALES (est): 39.5MM **Privately Held**
WEB: www.lacantinadoors.com
SIC: **5039** Doors, sliding

(P-6725)
LSF9 CYPRESS HOLDINGS LLC
2741 Walnut Ave Ste 200, Tustin (92780-7063)
PHONE..................714 380-3127
Ruben Mendoza, *President*
EMP: 3398 EST: 2015
SALES (est): 28.3MM
SALES (corp-wide): 2B **Publicly Held**
SIC: **5039** 5031 5033 Ceiling systems & products; wallboard; insulation materials
HQ: Lsf9 Cypress Parent, Llc
2741 Walnut Ave Ste 200
Tustin CA 92780
714 380-3127

(P-6726)
SECURITY CONTRACTOR SVCS INC (PA)
Also Called: S C S
5339 Jackson St, North Highlands (95660-5004)
PHONE..................916 338-4200
Barry J Marrs, *CEO*
Ron Kyewski, *CFO*
Steve Mann, *Branch Mgr*
Laurie Sullivan, *Credit Staff*
Rick Marrs, *Sales Staff*

EMP: 60 EST: 1961
SQ FT: 50,000
SALES (est): 37.6MM **Privately Held**
WEB: www.scsfence.com
SIC: **5039** 7359 3315 Wire fence, gates & accessories; equipment rental & leasing; steel wire & related products

(P-6727)
SOUTHGATE GLASS & SCREEN INC (PA)
6852 Franklin Blvd, Sacramento (95823-1810)
PHONE..................916 476-8396
Scott Davis, *President*
Tim Wolhart, *Division Mgr*
Jim Boller, *Project Mgr*
Melissa Robinson, *Mktg Coord*
Brian Moen, *Manager*
EMP: 50
SQ FT: 5,000
SALES: 10MM **Privately Held**
SIC: **5039** 5231 Glass construction materials; glass

(P-6728)
SOUTHGATE GLASS & SCREEN INC
6199 Warehouse Way, Sacramento (95826-4907)
PHONE..................916 476-8396
Dave Megeary, *Branch Mgr*
EMP: 50
SALES (corp-wide): 10MM **Privately Held**
SIC: **5039** 5231 Glass construction materials; glass
PA: Southgate Glass & Screen, Inc.
6852 Franklin Blvd
Sacramento CA 95823
916 476-8396

5043 Photographic Eqpt & Splys Wholesale

(P-6729)
ADOLPH GASSER INC
Also Called: Adolph Gasser Photography
4340 Redwood Hwy Ste 227, San Rafael (94903-2104)
PHONE..................415 495-3852
John Gasser, *President*
EMP: 137
SALES (est): 765.2K **Privately Held**
WEB: www.adolphgasser.com
SIC: **5043** 5946 7359 5731 Photographic cameras, projectors, equipment & supplies; cameras; photographic supplies; audio-visual equipment & supply rental; video cameras & accessories

(P-6730)
CANON USA INC
15955 Alton Pkwy, Irvine (92618-3731)
PHONE..................949 753-4000
Glen Takahashi, *Manager*
Chuck Arnold, *Executive*
Jennifer Mathews, *Executive*
Paul Fynan, *Admin Sec*
Carlos N Mendoa, *IT/INT Sup*
EMP: 350 **Privately Held**
WEB: www.usa.canon.com
SIC: **5043** 5044 5045 8741 Photographic cameras, projectors, equipment & supplies; office equipment; computers; management services
HQ: Canon U.S.A., Inc.
1 Canon Park
Melville NY 11747
516 328-5000

(P-6731)
CHRISTIE DGTAL SYSTEMS USA INC (DH)
10550 Camden Dr, Cypress (90630-4600)
PHONE..................714 527-7056
Jack Kline, *President*
◆ EMP: 97
SQ FT: 85,000
SALES (est): 81.2MM **Privately Held**
SIC: **5043** Projection apparatus, motion picture & slide

HQ: Christie Digital Systems, Inc.
10550 Camden Dr
Cypress CA 90630
714 236-8610

(P-6732)
FUJIFILM NORTH AMERICA CORP
Also Called: Fuji Photo Film
6200 Phyllis Dr, Cypress (90630-5239)
PHONE..................714 372-4200
Bobby Bruce, *Manager*
Carlos Cabral, *Info Tech Dir*
George Bouchard, *Business Mgr*
Jeff Ash, *VP Mktg*
Jim Riekert, *Mktg Dir*
EMP: 150 **Privately Held**
SIC: 5043 Photographic equipment & supplies
HQ: Fujifilm North America Corporation
200 Summit Lake Dr Fl 2
Valhalla NY 10595
914 789-8100

(P-6733)
JK IMAGING LTD
17239 S Main St, Gardena (90248-3129)
PHONE..................310 755-6848
Joe Atick, *CEO*
Shu-Ping Wu, *CFO*
Mike Feng, *Admin Sec*
▲ EMP: 100
SQ FT: 6,000
SALES (est): 100MM **Privately Held**
SIC: 5043 Cameras & photographic equipment

(P-6734)
KYOCERA INTERNATIONAL INC
222 N Pacific Coast Hwy, El Segundo (90245-5648)
PHONE..................310 647-2805
Steve Clark, *Manager*
EMP: 60 **Publicly Held**
SIC: 5043 Cameras & photographic equipment
HQ: Kyocera International, Inc.
8611 Balboa Ave
San Diego CA 92123
858 492-1456

(P-6735)
NORITSU AMERICA CORPORATION (HQ)
6900 Noritsu Ave, Buena Park (90620-1372)
P.O. Box 5039 (90622-5039)
PHONE..................714 521-9040
Michiro Niikura, *CEO*
Kanichi Nishimoto, *Ch of Bd*
Frank Morrow, *Vice Pres*
Patrik Norrby, *Vice Pres*
Akihiko Kuwabara, *Principal*
◆ EMP: 115 **EST:** 1978
SQ FT: 27,500
SALES (est): 66.4MM **Privately Held**
WEB: www.noritsu.com
SIC: 5043 Photographic processing equipment

(P-6736)
PILGRIM OPERATIONS LLC
Also Called: Tailbroom Media Grop
12020 Chanl Blvd Ste 200, North Hollywood (91607)
PHONE..................818 478-4500
Douglas Liechty, *Mng Member*
Matthew Ducey, *Personnel*
EMP: 400
SALES (est): 319.5K **Privately Held**
SIC: 5043 Motion picture studio & theater equipment

5044 Office Eqpt Wholesale

(P-6737)
ACM TECHNOLOGIES INC (PA)
Also Called: Allstate
2535 Research Dr, Corona (92882-7607)
PHONE..................951 738-9898
Stan Shue Lin, *CEO*
Monica Lin, *Corp Secy*
Clarence Perera, *Business Anlyst*
Elly Lai, *Purch Agent*

Carolyne Chu, *Marketing Mgr*
◆ EMP: 52
SALES (est): 28.6MM **Privately Held**
WEB: www.acmtech.com
SIC: 5044 Copying equipment; photocopy machines

(P-6738)
ALLSTATE IMAGING INC (PA)
21621 Nordhoff St, Chatsworth (91311-5828)
PHONE..................818 678-4550
Alan Jurick, *President*
Russel Leventhal, *CEO*
Richard Shapiro, *CFO*
EMP: 80
SALES (est): 42.5MM **Privately Held**
SIC: 5044 Office equipment

(P-6739)
BANKCARD USA MERCHANT SRVC
5701 Lindero Canyon Rd, Westlake Village (91362-4060)
PHONE..................818 597-7000
Shawn Skelton, *President*
Alan Griefer, *Exec VP*
EMP: 85
SQ FT: 20,000
SALES (est): 16.4MM **Privately Held**
WEB: www.busams.com
SIC: 5044 Check writing, signing & endorsing machines

(P-6740)
CANON BUS SOLUTIONS-WEST INC
110 W Walnut St, Gardena (90248-3100)
P.O. Box 51075, Los Angeles (90074-1075)
PHONE..................310 217-3000
Bill Joseph, *President*
Keiko Brockel, *Vice Pres*
John Murphy, *Director*
EMP: 450
SQ FT: 100,000
SALES (est): 34.4MM **Privately Held**
WEB: www.usa.canon.com
SIC: 5044 Office equipment
HQ: Canon U.S.A., Inc.
1 Canon Park
Melville NY 11747
516 328-5000

(P-6741)
CANON SOLUTIONS AMERICA INC
203 S Waterman Ave, El Centro (92243-2228)
PHONE..................800 323-4827
EMP: 80 **Privately Held**
SIC: 5044 Office equipment
HQ: Canon Solutions America, Inc.
1 Canon Park
Melville NY 11747
631 330-5000

(P-6742)
CANON SOLUTIONS AMERICA INC
3237 E Guasti Rd Ste 200, Ontario (91761-1243)
PHONE..................909 390-7400
Larry Candejas, *Branch Mgr*
Marcy Weiner, *Accounts Exec*
EMP: 65 **Privately Held**
SIC: 5044 Office equipment
HQ: Canon Solutions America, Inc.
1 Canon Park
Melville NY 11747
631 330-5000

(P-6743)
CANON SOLUTIONS AMERICA INC
201 California St Ste 100, San Francisco (94111-5003)
PHONE..................415 743-7300
Kim Haydel, *Vice Pres*
Jeff Le, *Software Dev*
John Focarino, *Director*
Jim Otzko, *Manager*
Andrew Mergenthaler, *Accounts Exec*
EMP: 51 **Privately Held**
SIC: 5044 Copying equipment

HQ: Canon Solutions America, Inc.
1 Canon Park
Melville NY 11747
631 330-5000

(P-6744)
CANON SOLUTIONS AMERICA INC
123 Paularino Ave, Costa Mesa (92626-3311)
PHONE..................949 753-4200
Mark Hix, *Branch Mgr*
EMP: 80 **Privately Held**
SIC: 5044 Photocopy machines
HQ: Canon Solutions America, Inc.
1 Canon Park
Melville NY 11747
631 330-5000

(P-6745)
COAST TO COAST BUS EQP INC (PA)
8 Vanderbilt Ste 200, Irvine (92618-2080)
PHONE..................949 457-7300
Paul M Faus, *President*
Julie Davis, *Treasurer*
Marla Gastelum, *Executive*
Susanna Lee, *Administration*
Zach Reeves, *Director*
EMP: 55
SQ FT: 20,100
SALES (est): 13.7MM **Privately Held**
WEB: www.ctcbe.com
SIC: 5044 5065 Photocopy machines; teletype equipment

(P-6746)
COPIER SOURCE INC (PA)
Also Called: Image Source
650 E Hospitality Ln # 500, San Bernardino (92408-3535)
PHONE..................909 890-4040
David Bradley Craft, *CEO*
Jill Craft, *Corp Secy*
EMP: 65
SALES (est): 49MM **Privately Held**
SIC: 5044 Office equipment

(P-6747)
CUSTOM BUSINESS SOLUTIONS INC (PA)
Also Called: Northstar
12 Morgan, Irvine (92618-2003)
PHONE..................949 380-7674
Art Julian, *CEO*
Colleen Julian, *President*
Rom Krupp, *President*
Michael Block, *CFO*
Joseph Castillo, *Vice Pres*
◆ EMP: 68
SQ FT: 21,000
SALES (est): 64.4MM **Privately Held**
WEB: www.cbs-posi.com
SIC: 5044 Cash registers

(P-6748)
DUPLO USA CORPORATION (PA)
3050 Daimler St, Santa Ana (92705-5813)
PHONE..................949 752-8222
Peter Tu, *President*
Jim Peffer, *COO*
Barry Shultis, *Executive*
Kevin Stevenson, *Technical Staff*
Bradley Mathews, *Engineer*
◆ EMP: 80
SQ FT: 30,000
SALES (est): 33.6MM **Privately Held**
WEB: www.duplousa.com
SIC: 5044 Duplicating machines

(P-6749)
IMAGE IV SYSTEMS INC (PA)
512 S Varney St, Burbank (91502-2196)
PHONE..................323 849-3049
Ronald Warren, *President*
Sue Warren, *Vice Pres*
Walter Martinez, *Technician*
Kevin Nguyen, *Technician*
Juan Ramirez, *Technology*
EMP: 79
SQ FT: 4,000
SALES (est): 22.9MM **Privately Held**
WEB: www.imageiv.com
SIC: 5044 Photocopy machines; copying equipment

(P-6750)
INTEGRATED OFFICE TECH LLC (PA)
Also Called: Iotec
12150 Mora Dr Ste 2, Santa Fe Springs (90670-3700)
PHONE..................562 236-9200
Robert Zieman,
Matt Zieman, *Sales Staff*
Doug Lu,
Dana Ruf,
EMP: 70
SQ FT: 30,000
SALES: 20MM **Privately Held**
WEB: www.iotecdigital.com
SIC: 5044 7371 7379 Copying equipment; computer software systems analysis & design, custom; computer related maintenance services

(P-6751)
INTEGRUS LLC
Also Called: Advanced Office
14370 Myford Rd Ste 100, Irvine (92606-1015)
PHONE..................714 547-9500
Mike Dixon, *CEO*
Richard Van Dyke, *President*
Tim Wickers, *Vice Pres*
Nicole Filtz, *Administration*
Scott Daub, *Manager*
EMP: 100 **EST:** 2011
SALES: 18MM **Privately Held**
SIC: 5044 Office equipment

(P-6752)
INTERNATIONAL BUS MCHS CORP
Also Called: IBM
425 Market St, San Francisco (94105-2532)
PHONE..................415 545-4747
Wirt Cook, *CEO*
Craig Silverman, *Partner*
Judy Warmington, *Partner*
Brigett Lindberg, *Vice Pres*
Christopher C Rimer, *Vice Pres*
EMP: 208
SALES (corp-wide): 79.5B **Publicly Held**
WEB: www.ibm.com
SIC: 5044 5045 3571 Office equipment; computers, peripherals & software; electronic computers
PA: International Business Machines Corporation
1 New Orchard Rd Ste 1 # 1
Armonk NY 10504
914 499-1900

(P-6753)
INTERNATIONAL BUS MCHS CORP
Also Called: IBM
2077 Gateway Pl, San Jose (95110-1090)
P.O. Box 49015 (95161)
PHONE..................408 452-4800
Barry Gafner, *Principal*
EMP: 200
SALES (corp-wide): 79.5B **Publicly Held**
WEB: www.ibm.com
SIC: 5044 5045 Office equipment; computers, peripherals & software
PA: International Business Machines Corporation
1 New Orchard Rd Ste 1 # 1
Armonk NY 10504
914 499-1900

(P-6754)
INTERNATIONAL LITIGATION SVCS
65 Enterprise, Aliso Viejo (92656-2705)
PHONE..................888 313-4457
Joseph Thorpe, *CEO*
Mark Liekkio, *Senior VP*
Tony Chu, *Litigation*
Mariette Wilkinson, *Sr Consultant*
EMP: 50
SQ FT: 7,000
SALES (est): 10.7MM **Privately Held**
SIC: 5044 Office equipment

(P-6755)
KONICA MINOLTA BUSINESS SOLUTI
1831 Commercenter W, San Bernardino (92408-3303)
PHONE..................................909 824-2000
Linda F Turner, *Manager*
EMP: 69
SQ FT: 13,000 **Privately Held**
WEB: www.konicabt.com
SIC: 5044 5065 5943 Photocopy machines; facsimile equipment; office forms & supplies
HQ: Konica Minolta Business Solutions U.S.A., Inc.
100 Williams Dr
Ramsey NJ 07446
201 825-4000

(P-6756)
KONICA MINOLTA BUSINESS SOLUTI
Also Called: Minolta Business Systems
879 W 190th St Ste 200, Gardena (90248-4223)
PHONE..................................310 214-6696
Brian Shaw, *General Mgr*
Tom Devico, *Branch Mgr*
Craig Grammer, *Manager*
EMP: 50 **Privately Held**
WEB: www.konicabt.com
SIC: 5044 Photocopy machines
HQ: Konica Minolta Business Solutions U.S.A., Inc.
100 Williams Dr
Ramsey NJ 07446
201 825-4000

(P-6757)
KYOCERA DCMENT SLTONS AMER INC
Also Called: Kyocera Technology Development
1855 Gateway Blvd Ste 400, Concord (94520-3289)
PHONE..................................925 849-3300
Atsushi Yuki, *Manager*
EMP: 70 **Publicly Held**
SIC: 5044 Photocopy machines
HQ: Kyocera Document Solutions America, Inc.
225 Sand Rd
Fairfield NJ 07004
973 808-8444

(P-6758)
M-S CASH DRAWER CORPORATION (PA)
2085 E Foothill Blvd B, Pasadena (91107-6400)
PHONE..................................626 792-2111
Paul R Masson, *President*
◆ EMP: 64 EST: 1974
SQ FT: 50,000
SALES (est): 8.7MM **Privately Held**
WEB: www.mscashdrawer.com
SIC: 5044 Cash registers

(P-6759)
MICROTEK LAB INC (HQ)
13337 South St, Cerritos (90703-7308)
PHONE..................................310 687-5823
Clark Hsu, *President*
Stewart Chow, *President*
▲ EMP: 110 EST: 1980
SQ FT: 126,000
SALES (est): 27.5MM **Privately Held**
WEB: www.microtek.com
SIC: 5044 Copying equipment

(P-6760)
MR COPY INC (DH)
Also Called: Mrc, Smart Tech Solutions
5657 Copley Dr, San Diego (92111-7903)
PHONE..................................858 573-6300
Bob Leone, *President*
Kevin McCarty, *Financial Exec*
EMP: 75
SQ FT: 18,000
SALES (est): 136.2MM
SALES (corp-wide): 405.1MM **Publicly Held**
SIC: 5044 Copying equipment; photocopy machines

(P-6761)
NATIONAL LINK INCORPORATED
2235 Auto Centre Dr, Glendora (91740-6721)
PHONE..................................909 670-1900
Sam Kandah, *President*
Jim Scott, *CFO*
Carol Kandah, *Admin Sec*
Christa Dominguez, *Sales Staff*
Mark Wasilow, *Director*
EMP: 68
SQ FT: 5,000
SALES (est): 24.8MM **Privately Held**
SIC: 5044 7389 7359 Bank automatic teller machines; credit card service; electronic equipment rental, except computers

(P-6762)
OFFICE DEPOT INC
7531 Quail Vista Ln, Citrus Heights (95610-8804)
PHONE..................................916 927-0171
Dennise Moran, *Principal*
EMP: 100
SALES (corp-wide): 11B **Publicly Held**
WEB: www.officedepot.com
SIC: 5044 5045 5112 Office equipment; computers, peripherals & software; computers; office supplies
PA: Office Depot, Inc.
6600 N Military Trl
Boca Raton FL 33496
561 438-4800

(P-6763)
RICOH USA INC
Also Called: Data-Image Systems
3046 Prospect Park Dr # 100, Rancho Cordova (95670-6356)
PHONE..................................916 638-3333
Merlin Shoemaker, *CEO*
Jack Fisher, *General Mgr*
EMP: 75 **Privately Held**
WEB: www.ikon.com
SIC: 5044 Office equipment
HQ: Ricoh Usa, Inc.
300 Eagleview Blvd # 200
Exton PA 19341
610 296-8000

(P-6764)
RICOH USA INC
460 E Brokaw Rd, San Jose (95112-1015)
PHONE..................................408 436-1000
John Reed, *Sales & Mktg St*
Terry Young, *MIS Dir*
Kahing Sit, *Manager*
EMP: 72 **Privately Held**
WEB: www.ikon.com
SIC: 5044 5065 Photocopy machines; facsimile equipment
HQ: Ricoh Usa, Inc.
300 Eagleview Blvd # 200
Exton PA 19341
610 296-8000

(P-6765)
RICOH USA INC
9430 Topanga Canyon Blvd # 100, Chatsworth (91311-5765)
PHONE..................................818 294-8601
Daniel Walsh, *Manager*
EMP: 50 **Privately Held**
SIC: 5044 Photocopy machines
HQ: Ricoh Usa, Inc.
300 Eagleview Blvd # 200
Exton PA 19341
610 296-8000

(P-6766)
RICOH USA INC
Also Called: Ricoh Business Solutions
17011 Beach Blvd Ste 1000, Huntington Beach (92647-7402)
PHONE..................................714 396-0568
Tracy Wood, *Manager*
EMP: 50 **Privately Held**
SIC: 5044 5112 3861 3661 Copying equipment; photocopying supplies; photographic equipment & supplies; telephone & telegraph apparatus
HQ: Ricoh Usa, Inc.
300 Eagleview Blvd # 200
Exton PA 19341
610 296-8000

(P-6767)
RICOH USA INC
6330 Variel Ave, Woodland Hills (91367-2543)
PHONE..................................213 629-1838
Steve Smith, *Exec VP*
EMP: 100 **Privately Held**
WEB: www.ikon.com
SIC: 5044 Photocopy machines
HQ: Ricoh Usa, Inc.
300 Eagleview Blvd # 200
Exton PA 19341
610 296-8000

(P-6768)
RICOH USA INC
Also Called: Nightrider Overnite Copy Svc
333 Bush St Ste 2500, San Francisco (94104-2862)
PHONE..................................415 392-6850
John Wilkinson, *Manager*
EMP: 60 **Privately Held**
WEB: www.ikon.com
SIC: 5044 Photocopy machines
HQ: Ricoh Usa, Inc.
300 Eagleview Blvd # 200
Exton PA 19341
610 296-8000

(P-6769)
RICOH USA INC
21820 Burbank Blvd # 229, Woodland Hills (91367-6476)
PHONE..................................818 703-0265
David Burton, *Manager*
EMP: 50 **Privately Held**
SIC: 5044 Photocopy machines
HQ: Ricoh Usa, Inc.
300 Eagleview Blvd # 200
Exton PA 19341
610 296-8000

(P-6770)
RICOH USA INC
Also Called: Nightrider Overnite Copy Svc
1300 Clay St Ste 165, Oakland (94612-1421)
PHONE..................................510 839-6399
Charles Dickinson, *Manager*
EMP: 50 **Privately Held**
WEB: www.ikon.com
SIC: 5044 Office equipment
HQ: Ricoh Usa, Inc.
300 Eagleview Blvd # 200
Exton PA 19341
610 296-8000

(P-6771)
RICOH USA INC
1390 Willow Pass Rd # 480, Concord (94520-7905)
PHONE..................................925 988-4000
Renee Faxton, *Branch Mgr*
EMP: 150 **Privately Held**
WEB: www.ikon.com
SIC: 5044 5065 7629 7359 Photocopy machines; typewriters; facsimile equipment; electronic equipment repair; office machine rental, except computers; stationery stores; computer rental & leasing
HQ: Ricoh Usa, Inc.
300 Eagleview Blvd # 200
Exton PA 19341
610 296-8000

(P-6772)
RICOH USA INC
16969 Von Karman Ave, Irvine (92606-4948)
PHONE..................................949 225-2300
Steve Bastien, *Manager*
EMP: 75 **Privately Held**
WEB: www.ikon.com
SIC: 5044 Photocopy machines
HQ: Ricoh Usa, Inc.
300 Eagleview Blvd # 200
Exton PA 19341
610 296-8000

(P-6773)
SOURCECORP BPS NTHRN CAL INC
900 Fortress St, Chico (95973-9514)
PHONE..................................530 893-7900
Steve Grieco, *CEO*
Katy Murray, *CFO*

Russel Birk, *Treasurer*
Charles Gilbert, *General Counsel*
EMP: 92
SALES (est): 4.4MM
SALES (corp-wide): 1.5B **Publicly Held**
SIC: 5044 7389 Microfilm equipment; microfilm recording & developing service
HQ: Sourcecorp Bps Inc.
2701 E Grauwyler Rd
Irving TX 75061
866 321-5854

(P-6774)
TOSHIBA AMER BUS SOLUTIONS INC (HQ)
25530 Commercentre Dr, Lake Forest (92630-8855)
PHONE..................................949 462-6000
Scott Maccabe, *CEO*
Matt Barnes, *President*
Mark Mathews, *President*
Desmond Allen, *CFO*
Larry White, *Officer*
◆ EMP: 350
SQ FT: 90,000
SALES (est): 1.3B **Privately Held**
WEB: www.levenstein.com
SIC: 5044 Copying equipment

(P-6775)
ULTREX MANAGEMENT SERVICES (PA)
712 Fiero Ln Ste 33, San Luis Obispo (93401-7979)
PHONE..................................805 783-1234
Rolf W Berkfeld, *CEO*
Caroline Berkfeld, *Admin Sec*
Karoline Berkseld, *Human Res Dir*
Grant Berkefeld, *Sales Staff*
Jose Najera, *Manager*
EMP: 60
SALES (est): 15.8MM **Privately Held**
WEB: www.ultrex.net
SIC: 5044 Copying equipment

(P-6776)
UNITED MERCHANT SVCS CAL INC
Also Called: Ums Banking
750 Fairmont Ave Ste 201, Glendale (91203-1074)
PHONE..................................818 246-6767
Joyce Gaines, *President*
Lynda Neuman, *CFO*
Karen Brown, *Officer*
Bruce Ferguson, *Exec VP*
Chris Lake, *Exec VP*
EMP: 72
SQ FT: 8,580
SALES (est): 33.2MM **Privately Held**
WEB: www.umsbanking.com
SIC: 5044 5065 7629 Office equipment; electronic parts & equipment; electronic equipment repair

(P-6777)
UNITED RIBBON COMPANY INC
Also Called: United Imaging
21201 Oxnard St, Woodland Hills (91367-5015)
PHONE..................................818 716-1515
Michael Cohen, *President*
Yigal Avrahamy, *Vice Pres*
Arturo Jimenez, *Executive*
Antonio Flores, *Sales Staff*
Tyler Kendrick, *Accounts Exec*
EMP: 85
SQ FT: 22,000
SALES (est): 57.7MM **Privately Held**
WEB: www.unitedimaging.com
SIC: 5044 5943 5021 7699 Office equipment; office forms & supplies; office & public building furniture; office equipment & accessory customizing; computer & photocopying supplies

(P-6778)
XEROX CORPORATION
914 S Victory Blvd, Burbank (91502-2429)
PHONE..................................818 848-8676
Michael Simenian, *Branch Mgr*
EMP: 77
SALES (corp-wide): 405.1MM **Publicly Held**
WEB: www.xerox.com
SIC: 5044 Office equipment

▲ = Import ▼=Export
◆ =Import/Export

HQ: Xerox Corporation
    201 Merritt 7
    Norwalk CT 06851
    203 968-3000

(P-6779)
XEROX CORPORATION
2118 Wilshire Blvd, Santa Monica
(90403-5704)
PHONE..................310 526-3940
Kalika Marina, *Principal*
Stephen J Kania, *Med Doctor*
EMP: 84
SALES (corp-wide): 405.1MM **Publicly Held**
SIC: 5044 Office equipment
HQ: Xerox Corporation
    201 Merritt 7
    Norwalk CT 06851
    203 968-3000

(P-6780)
XEROX CORPORATION
478 Ferne Ave, Palo Alto (94306-4620)
PHONE..................650 813-6787
EMP: 80
SALES (corp-wide): 405.1MM **Publicly Held**
SIC: 5044 Office equipment
HQ: Xerox Corporation
    201 Merritt 7
    Norwalk CT 06851
    203 968-3000

(P-6781)
XEROX CORPORATION
3333 Coyote Hill Rd, Palo Alto
(94304-1314)
PHONE..................650 813-7138
David Smith, *Vice Pres*
Rob McHenry, *Vice Pres*
Patrick Maeda, *Executive*
Larry Cowart, *Engineer*
Julie Zinker, *Purch Mgr*
EMP: 150
SALES (corp-wide): 405.1MM **Publicly Held**
WEB: www.xerox.com
SIC: 5044 Office equipment
HQ: Xerox Corporation
    201 Merritt 7
    Norwalk CT 06851
    203 968-3000

(P-6782)
XEROX EDUCATION SERVICES LLC (DH)
2277 E 220th St, Long Beach
(90810-1639)
PHONE..................310 830-9847
J M Peffer, *Mng Member*
Mike R Festa, *Mng Member*
EMP: 90 EST: 1970
SALES (est): 270.6MM
SALES (corp-wide): 5.3B **Publicly Held**
WEB: www.acseducationservices.com
SIC: 5044 Office equipment
HQ: Conduent Business Services, Llc
    100 Campus Dr Ste 200
    Florham Park NJ 07932
    973 261-7100

(P-6783)
YOUNG SYSTEMS CORPORATION
Also Called: Nuworld Business Systems
13125 Midway Pl, Cerritos (90703-2232)
PHONE..................562 921-2256
Young H Lee, *President*
Claudia Reed, *Executive*
June S Lee, *Admin Sec*
Lian Nguyen, *Admin Asst*
Chris Chang, *Info Tech Dir*
◆ **EMP:** 53
SQ FT: 46,000
SALES (est): 24.5MM **Privately Held**
WEB: www.nuworldinc.com
SIC: 5044 5999 Photocopy machines; business machines & equipment

(P-6784)
YUBICO INC
530 Lytton Ave Ste 301, Palo Alto
(94301-1541)
PHONE..................408 774-4064

Stina Ehrensvard, *CEO*
Mattias Danielsson, *CFO*
Kurt Lennartsson, *Officer*
Rick O'Rourke, *Officer*
Jesper Johansson, *Vice Pres*
EMP: 150
SALES (est): 53.1MM **Privately Held**
SIC: 5044 7379 Office equipment;

5045 Computers & Peripheral Eqpt & Software Wholesale

(P-6785)
ACROSS SYSTEMS INC
100 N Brand Blvd Ste 100, Glendale
(91203-2636)
PHONE..................877 922-7677
Daniel Nackovski, *President*
EMP: 70
SALES (est): 5.7MM **Privately Held**
SIC: 5045 Computer software

(P-6786)
ADESSO INC
Also Called: ADS Techonlogy
160 Commerce Way, Walnut (91789-2714)
PHONE..................909 839-2929
Allen Ku, *President*
▲ **EMP:** 200
SQ FT: 31,000
SALES (est): 12.7MM **Privately Held**
WEB: www.adesso.com
SIC: 5045 Computer peripheral equipment

(P-6787)
ADVANCED INDUSTRIAL CMPT INC (PA)
Also Called: Aic Inc USA
21808 Garcia Ln, City of Industry
(91789-0941)
PHONE..................909 895-8989
Michael Liang, *Ch of Bd*
Shun Ying Liang, *CEO*
Belle Wang, *CFO*
Kit Chui, *Vice Pres*
Kevin Tung, *Business Mgr*
▲ **EMP:** 57
SQ FT: 65,000
SALES (est): 24.1MM **Privately Held**
WEB: www.aicipc.com
SIC: 5045 Mainframe computers

(P-6788)
ADVANTECH CORPORATION (HQ)
380 Fairview Way, Milpitas (95035-3062)
P.O. Box 45895, San Francisco (94145-0895)
PHONE..................408 519-3800
Ke-Cheng Liu, *CEO*
Chaney Ho, *President*
Edna Garcia, *Senior VP*
Eric Chen, *Vice Pres*
Deryu Yin, *Vice Pres*
▲ **EMP:** 126
SQ FT: 100,000
SALES: 355MM **Privately Held**
SIC: 5045 7379 Computers, peripherals & software; computer hardware requirements analysis

(P-6789)
AGILYSYS INC
5383 Hollister Ave # 120, Santa Barbara
(93111-2304)
PHONE..................805 692-6339
Michael Hinojosa, *Principal*
Nancy Naretto, *Marketing Staff*
Tim Hansen, *Sales Staff*
EMP: 108
SALES (corp-wide): 140.8MM **Publicly Held**
WEB: www.pios.com
SIC: 5045 Computer software
PA: Agilysys, Inc.
    1000 Windward Conc # 250
    Alpharetta GA 30005
    770 810-7800

(P-6790)
AGILYSYS INC
1900 Powell St Ste 230, Emeryville
(94608-1837)
PHONE..................702 759-4879
Christian Fisher, *Manager*
EMP: 50
SALES (corp-wide): 140.8MM **Publicly Held**
WEB: www.pios.com
SIC: 5045 7371 Computer software; computer software development & applications
PA: Agilysys, Inc.
    1000 Windward Conc # 250
    Alpharetta GA 30005
    770 810-7800

(P-6791)
ALTAMETRICS LLC
3191 Red Hill Ave Ste 100, Costa Mesa
(92626-3451)
PHONE..................800 676-1281
Mitesh Gala, *President*
Anand Gala, *CFO*
Kimberly Lebish, *Administration*
Ajay Shiv, *CIO*
Narinder Kumar, *Info Tech Mgr*
EMP: 140
SQ FT: 6,000
SALES (est): 31.7MM **Privately Held**
WEB: www.altametrics.com
SIC: 5045 Computer software

(P-6792)
AMAX ENGINEERING CORPORATION (PA)
Also Called: Amax Computer
1565 Reliance Way, Fremont (94539-6103)
PHONE..................510 651-8886
Jerry Kc Shih, *CEO*
CHI-Lei Ni, *CFO*
Jean Shih, *Vice Pres*
Jennifer Xu, *Manager*
▲ **EMP:** 150
SQ FT: 110,000
SALES (est): 193.8MM **Privately Held**
WEB: www.amaxit.com
SIC: 5045 Computer peripheral equipment; computer software

(P-6793)
AMBERFIN LIMITED
7590 N Glenoaks Blvd # 101, Burbank
(91504-1011)
PHONE..................818 768-8948
Jeremy Mh Deaner, *President*
EMP: 50
SALES (est): 2.3MM **Privately Held**
SIC: 5045 Computers, peripherals & software

(P-6794)
AMERICAN FUTURE TECH CORP
Also Called: Ibuypower
529 Baldwin Park Blvd, City of Industry
(91746-1419)
PHONE..................888 462-3899
Alex Hou, *CEO*
Darren Su, *Vice Pres*
▲ **EMP:** 120
SQ FT: 25,000
SALES (est): 115.3MM **Privately Held**
WEB: www.aftcorp.com
SIC: 5045 Computer peripheral equipment

(P-6795)
AMERICAN PORTWELL TECH INC (PA)
Also Called: AP Tech
44200 Christy St, Fremont (94538-3179)
PHONE..................510 403-3399
Allen Lee, *CEO*
Kevin Lee, *Vice Pres*
Jacob Siu, *Info Tech Mgr*
Jason Chen, *Project Mgr*
Ken Smyth, *Business Mgr*
▲ **EMP:** 90 EST: 1999
SQ FT: 42,515
SALES (est): 74MM **Privately Held**
WEB: www.portwell.com
SIC: 5045 Computer peripheral equipment

(P-6796)
AOPEN AMERICA INCORPORATED
2150 N 1st St Ste 300, San Jose
(95131-2044)
PHONE..................408 586-1200
Dale Tsai, *President*
James Huang, *Vice Pres*
Chad Wu, *Human Resources*
Brett McCarthy, *Natl Sales Mgr*
▲ **EMP:** 70 EST: 1997
SQ FT: 50,000
SALES: 13MM **Privately Held**
SIC: 5045 Computer software
PA: Aopen Incorporated
    21f, No. 92, Xintai 5th Rd., Sec. 1
    New Taipei City TAP 22102

(P-6797)
ARBITECH LLC
64 Fairbanks, Irvine (92618-1602)
PHONE..................949 376-6650
Francisco Llaca, *President*
David Walker, *CFO*
James Whalen Becomes, *Exec VP*
Jimmy Whalen, *Exec VP*
Stuart Jeffries, *Vice Pres*
▲ **EMP:** 74
SQ FT: 40,000
SALES: 116.1MM **Privately Held**
WEB: www.arbitech.com
SIC: 5045 Computer peripheral equipment

(P-6798)
ASI COMPUTER TECHNOLOGIES INC (PA)
Also Called: A S I
48289 Fremont Blvd, Fremont
(94538-6510)
PHONE..................510 226-8000
Christine Liang, *President*
Marcel Liang, *CEO*
Kelvin Smith, *Administration*
Joseph Cox, *Credit Staff*
◆ **EMP:** 200
SQ FT: 155,000
SALES (est): 468.9MM **Privately Held**
WEB: www.asipartner.com
SIC: 5045 3577 Disk drives; keying equipment; printers, computer; terminals, computer; computer output to microfilm units

(P-6799)
ASUS COMPUTER INTERNATIONAL
48720 Kato Rd, Fremont (94538-7312)
PHONE..................510 739-3777
Steve Chang, *CEO*
Charles Kuang,
Ivan Hoe, *President*
Raymond Chen, *Vice Pres*
Alan Hsieh, *Vice Pres*
▲ **EMP:** 130
SQ FT: 13,000
SALES (est): 139.7MM **Privately Held**
WEB: www.asus.com
SIC: 5045 3577 Computer peripheral equipment; computer peripheral equipment
PA: Asustek Computer Incorporation
    15, Lide Rd.,
    Taipei City TAP 11259

(P-6800)
ATEN TECHNOLOGY INC
Also Called: Iogear
15365 Barranca Pkwy, Irvine (92618-2216)
PHONE..................949 428-1111
Kevin Sun-Chung Chen, *President*
Holly Garcia, *Vice Pres*
Richard Cheng, *Info Tech Mgr*
Chris Wdowiak, *Info Tech Mgr*
Larry Levy, *Technician*
▲ **EMP:** 80
SALES (est): 54.8MM **Privately Held**
SIC: 5045 Computers & accessories, personal & home entertainment
PA: Aten International Co., Ltd.
    3f, No. 125, Datong Rd., Sec. 2
    New Taipei City TAP 22183

(P-6801)
AUTOMATION ANYWHERE INC (PA)
633 River Oaks Pkwy, San Jose (95134-1907)
P.O. Box 640007 (95164-0007)
PHONE...................................888 484-3535
Mihir Shukla, *CEO*
Richard French, *COO*
Ankur Kothari, *CFO*
Riadh Dridi, *Chief Mktg Ofcr*
Milan Sheth, *Exec VP*
EMP: 65
SQ FT: 14,000
SALES (est): 271.7MM **Privately Held**
WEB: www.tethyssolutions.com
SIC: 5045 7371 Computer software; computer software writing services

(P-6802)
AVANQUEST NORTH AMERICA LLC (HQ)
Also Called: Nova Development
23801 Calabasas Rd # 2005, Calabasas (91302-1547)
PHONE...................................818 591-9600
Roger Bloxberg, *CEO*
Todd Helfstein, *President*
Sharon Chiu, *CFO*
Cynthia Esters, *Officer*
Erica Nasser, *Vice Pres*
▲ **EMP:** 80
SQ FT: 12,000
SALES (est): 58.6MM
SALES (corp-wide): 1.4MM **Privately Held**
WEB: www.novareg.com
SIC: 5045 Computer software
PA: Claranova S.E.
　　Avanquest Blue Squad Bvrp Software
　　Immeuble Vision Defense
　　La Garenne-Colombes 92250
　　962 557-603

(P-6803)
AVER INFORMATION INC
668 Mission Ct, Fremont (94539-8206)
PHONE...................................408 263-3828
Arthur S Pait, *President*
Sinar Pait, *CEO*
Jeff McNall, *Business Mgr*
David KAO, *Sales Dir*
▲ **EMP:** 50
SQ FT: 15,000
SALES (est): 17.4MM **Privately Held**
SIC: 5045 7382 5099 Computer software; computers & accessories, personal & home entertainment; security systems services; confinement surveillance systems maintenance & monitoring; video & audio equipment
PA: Aver Information Inc.
　　8f, 157, Da'an Rd,
　　New Taipei City TAP 23673

(P-6804)
AXIOM MEMORY SOLUTIONS INC
16 Goodyear Ste 120, Irvine (92618-3757)
PHONE...................................949 581-1450
Keith Carpenter, *President*
Jennifer Gowers, *Executive*
Josh Tarin, *Executive Asst*
John Brock, *Marketing Mgr*
Ann Millard, *Sales Staff*
EMP: 75 **EST:** 1995
SALES: 26MM **Privately Held**
WEB: www.axiommemory.com
SIC: 5045 Computer peripheral equipment

(P-6805)
BACKWEB TECHNOLOGIES INC
2727 Walsh Ave Ste 102, Santa Clara (95051-0956)
PHONE...................................408 933-1700
Eli Barkat, *Ch of Bd*
Daniel Platzker, *Vice Pres*
EMP: 50
SQ FT: 16,000
SALES (est): 4.4MM **Privately Held**
WEB: www.backweb.com
SIC: 5045 Computer software

(P-6806)
BAYNOTE INC
75 E Santa Clara St # 600, San Jose (95113-1826)
PHONE...................................866 921-0919
Bill Hustad, *President*
Dario Calia, *Engineer*
Dan Darnell, *Marketing Staff*
EMP: 55
SALES (est): 8.3MM
SALES (corp-wide): 58.1MM **Privately Held**
SIC: 5045 Computer software
PA: Kibo Software, Inc.
　　717 N Harwood St Ste 1800
　　Dallas TX 75201
　　707 780-1600

(P-6807)
BENQ AMERICA CORP (HQ)
3200 Park Center Dr # 150, Costa Mesa (92626-7163)
PHONE...................................714 559-4900
KY Lee, *Chairman*
Lars Yoder, *President*
Ellin Lee, *CFO*
Peter Chen, *Vice Pres*
Kalai Raman, *Info Tech Dir*
◆ **EMP:** 65 **EST:** 1997
SALES (est): 40.2MM **Privately Held**
SIC: 5045 Computer peripheral equipment

(P-6808)
BIZCOM ELECTRONICS INC (HQ)
1171 Montague Expy, Milpitas (95035-6845)
PHONE...................................408 262-7877
Ray Chen, *CEO*
Duan Wang, *President*
Gary Lu, *CFO*
Shikuan Chen, *Vice Pres*
Tony Cheng, *Vice Pres*
▲ **EMP:** 140
SQ FT: 50,000
SALES (est): 36.3MM **Privately Held**
WEB: www.bizcom-us.com
SIC: 5045 7629 7378 Computers; telecommunication equipment repair (except telephones); computer maintenance & repair

(P-6809)
BRAMASOL INC
3979 Freedom Cir Ste 620, Santa Clara (95054-1262)
PHONE...................................408 831-0046
Dave Fellers, *CEO*
Jonathan Bell, *CFO*
EMP: 80
SQ FT: 2,000
SALES (est): 22.4MM **Privately Held**
WEB: www.bramasol.com
SIC: 5045 Computer software

(P-6810)
BROADWAY TYPEWRITER CO INC
Also Called: AREY JONES EDUCATIONAL SOLUTIO
1055 6th Ave Ste 101, San Diego (92101-5229)
PHONE...................................800 998-9199
Michael Scarpella, *President*
David Scarpella, *CFO*
Peter Scarpella, *Vice Pres*
Margaret Scarpella, *Admin Sec*
Erik Pitti, *Technology*
EMP: 80 **EST:** 1968
SQ FT: 40,000
SALES: 98.1MM **Privately Held**
SIC: 5045 7378 Computers, peripherals & software; computer maintenance & repair

(P-6811)
C9 EDGE INC
177 Bovet Rd Ste 520, San Mateo (94402-3144)
PHONE...................................650 561-7855
Michael Howard, *CEO*
Stephen Lucas, *CFO*
David Thompson, *Vice Pres*
Andy Twigg, *CTO*
Justin Shriber, *VP Prdtn*
EMP: 60

SQ FT: 10,000
SALES (est): 7.5MM **Privately Held**
SIC: 5045 Computer software

(P-6812)
CACI NSS INC
Also Called: Enganering and Technical Svcs
3201 Airpark Dr Ste 109, Santa Maria (93455-1834)
PHONE...................................703 841-7800
Brad Bush, *Senior VP*
Erin Pfarner, *Director*
Andrew McKay, *Manager*
EMP: 150
SALES (corp-wide): 4.9B **Publicly Held**
SIC: 5045 3663 Computers, peripherals & software; radio & TV communications equipment
HQ: Caci Nss, Inc.
　　11955 Freedom Dr Fl 2
　　Reston VA 20190
　　703 434-4000

(P-6813)
CASEWISE SYSTEMS INC (DH)
9465 Wilshire Blvd # 300, Beverly Hills (90212-2612)
PHONE...................................424 284-4101
Alexandre Wentzo, *CEO*
Michael R Hodes, *CFO*
EMP: 85
SQ FT: 5,000
SALES: 9.7MM **Privately Held**
WEB: www.casewise.com
SIC: 5045 8742 7372 Computer software; management consulting services; business oriented computer software
HQ: Casewise Systems Limited
　　Casewise Systems Ltd, 6
　　Birmingham W MIDLANDS B1 2J
　　203 884-0121

(P-6814)
COMMERCIAL INDUS DESIGN CO INC
Also Called: C I Design
20372 N Sea Cir, Lake Forest (92630-8806)
PHONE...................................949 273-6199
Jeff Wu, *CEO*
Kae J Lee, *President*
▲ **EMP:** 60
SALES (est): 12.5MM **Privately Held**
WEB: www.cidesign.com
SIC: 5045 Computer peripheral equipment

(P-6815)
CONTEC MICROELECTRONICS USA
Also Called: Contec USA
17811 Gillette Ave Fl 1, Irvine (92614-6501)
PHONE...................................949 250-4025
Fax: 408 400-9115
▲ **EMP:** 52
SQ FT: 4,500
SALES: 3.2MM **Privately Held**
SIC: 5045

(P-6816)
CONVRGD DATA TECH INC
999 Commercial St Ste 202, Palo Alto (94303-4909)
PHONE...................................650 461-4488
Akash Rajkumar Saraf, *CEO*
EMP: 110
SALES (est): 8.5MM **Privately Held**
SIC: 5045 Computers, peripherals & software

(P-6817)
CREATIVE LABS INC (DH)
1901 Mccarthy Blvd, Milpitas (95035-7427)
PHONE...................................408 428-6600
Keh Long Ng, *CEO*
Danielle Dunlap, *Executive Asst*
MAI Cheng, *Info Tech Mgr*
Arlene Hodges, *Accounting Mgr*
Robert Gilsdorf, *Director*
▲ **EMP:** 200
SQ FT: 57,000

SALES (est): 81.7MM
SALES (corp-wide): 54.9MM **Privately Held**
WEB: www.creativelabs.com
SIC: 5045 5734 3577 Computer peripheral equipment; computer & software stores; computer peripheral equipment

(P-6818)
CURVATURE LLC (DH)
6500 Hollister Ave # 210, Santa Barbara (93117-3011)
PHONE...................................800 230-6638
Sachi Thompson, *Exec VP*
Mark Kelly, *Vice Pres*
Holger Peters, *Vice Pres*
Edwin Toh, *Vice Pres*
Daniel Chua, *Executive*
◆ **EMP:** 300
SQ FT: 59,000
SALES (est): 321.8MM
SALES (corp-wide): 359.7MM **Privately Held**
WEB: www.networkhardware.com
SIC: 5045 7379 Computer peripheral equipment; computer related maintenance services
HQ: Nhr Newco Holdings Llc
　　6500 Hollister Ave # 210
　　Santa Barbara CA 93117
　　805 964-9975

(P-6819)
CYARA SOLUTIONS CORP
805 Veterans Blvd Ste 105, Redwood City (94063-1750)
PHONE...................................650 549-8522
Alok Kulkarni, *CEO*
James Isaacs, *President*
Mark Verbeck, *Vice Pres*
George Skaryak, *Exec VP*
Matt Melymuka, *Vice Pres*
EMP: 143
SALES (est): 5.7MM **Privately Held**
SIC: 5045 Computer software

(P-6820)
CYBERCSI INC
3511 Thomas Rd Ste 5, Santa Clara (95054-2039)
PHONE...................................408 727-2900
Dave Sanders, *CEO*
David Wurfer, *Vice Pres*
Mike Saloman, *CTO*
Chris Herring, *Software Dev*
Tim Markos, *Technology*
EMP: 95
SQ FT: 11,000
SALES (est): 35.6MM **Privately Held**
SIC: 5045 7378 Computers, peripherals & software; computer maintenance & repair

(P-6821)
CYBERPOWER INC
730 Baldwin Park Blvd, City of Industry (91746-1503)
PHONE...................................626 813-7730
Stanley Kwong Ho, *CEO*
Eric Cheung, *President*
Judy Chen, *CFO*
Bobby Wang, *Vice Pres*
Tjandra Afandi, *Information Mgr*
▲ **EMP:** 91
SQ FT: 100,000
SALES (est): 120.9MM **Privately Held**
WEB: www.cyberpowerpc.com
SIC: 5045 Computer peripheral equipment

(P-6822)
CYPHORT INC
1133 Innovation Way, Sunnyvale (94089-1228)
PHONE...................................408 841-4665
Manoj B Leelanivas, *CEO*
Gord Boyce, *Ch Credit Ofcr*
Fengmin Gong, *Officer*
Denis Eversen, *Vice Pres*
Anthony James, *Vice Pres*
EMP: 50
SQ FT: 10,000
SALES (est): 13.7MM **Privately Held**
SIC: 5045 Computer software

(P-6823)
D-LINK SYSTEMS INCORPORATED
Also Called: D - Link
17595 Mount Herrmann St, Fountain Valley
(92708-4160)
PHONE....................714 885-6000
Steven Joe, *President*
Carlos Casassus Fontecilla, *President*
A J Wang, *President*
Mellani Stainbrook, *Officer*
Raman Bridwell, *Assoc VP*
▲ EMP: 164
SQ FT: 120,000
SALES: 122MM **Privately Held**
WEB: www.dlink.com
SIC: 5045 3577 Computers; computer peripheral equipment
PA: D-Link Corporation
289, Sinhu 3rd Rd.,
Taipei City TAP 11494

(P-6824)
DATA EXCHANGE CORPORATION (PA)
Also Called: D E X
3600 Via Pescador, Camarillo
(93012-5035)
PHONE....................805 388-1711
Sheldon Malchicoff, *CEO*
Shawn Howie, *CFO*
Paul Gettings, *Exec VP*
▲ EMP: 300
SQ FT: 100,000
SALES (est): 119.2MM **Privately Held**
SIC: 5045 7378 Computers, peripherals & software; computer & data processing equipment repair/maintenance; computer peripheral equipment repair & maintenance

(P-6825)
DATALLEGRO INC
85 Enterprise Ste 200, Aliso Viejo
(92656-2614)
PHONE....................949 680-3000
Stuart Frost, *Ch of Bd*
Mark Theissen, *Vice Pres*
EMP: 100
SQ FT: 16,000
SALES (est): 10MM
SALES (corp-wide): 125.8B **Publicly Held**
WEB: www.datallegro.com
SIC: 5045 Computer software
PA: Microsoft Corporation
1 Microsoft Way
Redmond WA 98052
425 882-8080

(P-6826)
DIGIQUEST CORP
989 Talcey Ter, Riverside (92506-7517)
PHONE....................951 776-4344
K B Reddy, *President*
EMP: 50
SALES (est): 3.5MM **Privately Held**
WEB: www.digiquestindia.com
SIC: 5045 7379 Computer peripheral equipment; computer related consulting services

(P-6827)
ELITEGROUP CMPT SYSTEMS INC
6851 Mowry Ave, Newark (94560-4925)
PHONE....................510 226-7333
Ray Lin, *CEO*
Lena Ruan, *Corp Secy*
See See Lo, *Principal*
Shirley Peng, *Purch Mgr*
Brenda Riveros, *Sales Executive*
▲ EMP: 200
SQ FT: 60,000
SALES (est): 50.2MM **Privately Held**
SIC: 5045 Computer peripheral equipment
HQ: Elitegroup Computer Systems Holding Company (Inc)
6851 Mowry Ave
Newark CA 94560
510 794-2952

(P-6828)
ELO TOUCH SOLUTIONS INC (HQ)
670 N Mccarthy Blvd # 100, Milpitas
(95035-5119)
PHONE....................408 597-8000
Craig A Witsoe, *CEO*
Michael Duong, *Partner*
Dan Ludwick, *President*
Roxi Wen, *CFO*
Kevin Cole, *Vice Pres*
◆ EMP: 149
SQ FT: 75,000
SALES (est): 203.9MM
SALES (corp-wide): 3.8B **Privately Held**
SIC: 5045 Computers, peripherals & software
PA: The Gores Group Llc
9800 Wilshire Blvd
Beverly Hills CA 90212
310 209-3010

(P-6829)
EN POINTE TECHNOLOGIES SLS LLC
1940 E Mariposa Ave, El Segundo
(90245-3457)
PHONE....................310 337-6151
Frank Khulusi, *CEO*
Robert Miley, *President*
Brandon Laverne, *CFO*
EMP: 200
SQ FT: 29,032
SALES (est): 20.3MM **Publicly Held**
SIC: 5045 Computer peripheral equipment; computers
HQ: Pcm, Inc.
1940 E Mariposa Ave
El Segundo CA 90245
310 354-5600

(P-6830)
ENDORSE CORP
60 E 3rd Ave, San Mateo (94401-4030)
PHONE....................617 470-8332
Steven Carpenter, *CEO*
EMP: 917
SALES (est): 245.9K **Publicly Held**
SIC: 5045 Computer software
PA: Dropbox, Inc.
1800 Owens St Ste 200
San Francisco CA 94158

(P-6831)
ENVIRONMENTAL SYSTEMS RESEARCH
1600 K St Ste 4c, Sacramento
(95814-4022)
PHONE....................916 448-2412
EMP: 76
SALES (corp-wide): 1.1B **Privately Held**
SIC: 5045 Computer software
PA: Environmental Systems Research Institute, Inc.
380 New York St
Redlands CA 92373
909 793-2853

(P-6832)
EON REALITY INC (PA)
39 Parker Ste 100, Irvine (92618-1605)
PHONE....................949 460-2000
Mats Johansson, *President*
Simon Law, *Technical Mgr*
Haskell H Gray, *Business Mgr*
Nancy Johansson, *Purch Mgr*
Mark Cheben, *Marketing Staff*
EMP: 50
SQ FT: 16,000
SALES (est): 25.5MM **Privately Held**
WEB: www.eonreality.com
SIC: 5045 5734 Computer software; computer software & accessories

(P-6833)
ESET LLC (HQ)
Also Called: Eset North America
610 W Ash St Ste 1700, San Diego
(92101-3373)
PHONE....................619 876-5400
Anton Zajac, *President*
Amelia Foss, *Partner*
Robert Lammert, *Partner*
Tessa Prophet, *Partner*

Andrew Lee, *CEO*
EMP: 76
SQ FT: 57,000
SALES (est): 75.2MM
SALES (corp-wide): 555.7MM **Privately Held**
WEB: www.nod32.com
SIC: 5045 Computer software
PA: Eset, Spol. S R.O.
Einsteinova 24
Bratislava 85101
232 244-111

(P-6834)
EVGA CORPORATION (PA)
408 Saturn St, Brea (92821-1710)
PHONE....................714 528-4500
Taisheng Han, *President*
Bob Klase, *Vice Pres*
Sean Lee, *Software Engr*
Jack Nguyen, *Webmaster*
David Risser, *Technology*
▲ EMP: 50
SALES (est): 71.8MM **Privately Held**
WEB: www.evga.com
SIC: 5045 Computers & accessories, personal & home entertainment

(P-6835)
EWORKPLACE SOLUTIONS INC
Also Called: Batchmaster Software
9861 Irvine Center Dr, Irvine (92618-4307)
PHONE....................949 583-1646
Sahib Dudani, *President*
Laura Spingler, *Vice Pres*
Bryan Forte, *Program Mgr*
Maria Figueroa, *Office Mgr*
Amit Goyal, *Sr Software Eng*
EMP: 200
SQ FT: 5,000
SALES (est): 72.6MM **Privately Held**
WEB: www.batchmaster.com
SIC: 5045 Computer software

(P-6836)
F-SECURE INC
470 Ramona St, Palo Alto (94301-1707)
PHONE....................888 432-8233
Risto Siilasmaa, *Ch of Bd*
Ilkka Starck, *Exec VP*
Janne Jarvinen, *Vice Pres*
Sean Obrey, *Vice Pres*
Pirkka Palomaki, *CTO*
EMP: 50
SALES (est): 13.4MM
SALES (corp-wide): 218.3MM **Privately Held**
WEB: www.f-secure.com
SIC: 5045 Computer software
PA: F-Secure Oyj
Tammasaarenkatu 7
Helsinki 00180
925 200-700

(P-6837)
FORGEROCK INC (PA)
201 Mission St Ste 2900, San Francisco
(94105-1858)
PHONE....................415 599-1100
Francis C Rosch, *CEO*
Priya Sharma, *Partner*
Doron Baruth, *COO*
John Fernandez, *CFO*
Jonathan Scudder, *Founder*
EMP: 91
SQ FT: 15,000
SALES (est): 89.9MM **Privately Held**
SIC: 5045 7372 Computer software; prepackaged software

(P-6838)
FRYS ELECTRONICS INC
3600 N Sepulveda Blvd, Manhattan Beach
(90266-3633)
PHONE....................310 364-3797
Joel Byer, *Manager*
EMP: 200
SALES (corp-wide): 26.9MM **Privately Held**
WEB: www.frys.com
SIC: 5045 5731 Computers, peripherals & software; radio, television & electronic stores

PA: Fry's Electronics, Inc.
600 E Brokaw Rd
San Jose CA 95112
408 487-4500

(P-6839)
FUJITSU COMPUTER PDTS AMER INC (HQ)
1250 E Arques Ave, Sunnyvale
(94085-5401)
PHONE....................800 626-4686
Etsuro Sato, *President*
Victor Kan, *COO*
Motoyasu Matsuzaki, *CFO*
Carlos Huang, *Accountant*
▲ EMP: 340
SQ FT: 75,335
SALES (est): 83.7MM **Privately Held**
WEB: www.fcpa.com
SIC: 5045 Computer peripheral equipment

(P-6840)
GAR ENTERPRISES (PA)
Also Called: K G S Electronics
418 E Live Oak Ave, Arcadia (91006-5619)
PHONE....................626 574-1175
Nathan Sugimoto, *CEO*
Hidayat Sukandhi, *Engineer*
Cory Soto, *Sales Mgr*
Brad McKibbin, *Sales Staff*
Kazuo G Sugimoto, *Pastor*
EMP: 100 EST: 1960
SQ FT: 17,000
SALES (est): 34.4MM **Privately Held**
WEB: www.kgselectronics.com
SIC: 5045 3728 Anti-static equipment & devices; aircraft assemblies, subassemblies & parts

(P-6841)
GBT INC
Also Called: Gigabyte Technology
17358 Railroad St, City of Industry
(91748-1023)
PHONE....................626 854-9338
Eric C Lu, *President*
James Liao, *Principal*
Olga Veko, *Marketing Mgr*
▲ EMP: 80
SQ FT: 35,000
SALES (est): 30.6MM **Privately Held**
WEB: www.giga-byte.com
SIC: 5045 Computers & accessories, personal & home entertainment
PA: Giga-Byte Technology Co., Ltd.
5f, 6, Baoqiang Rd.,
New Taipei City TAP 23144

(P-6842)
GENERAL MICRO SYSTEMS INC (PA)
Also Called: G M S
8358 Maple Pl, Rancho Cucamonga
(91730-3839)
P.O. Box 3689 (91729-3689)
PHONE....................909 980-4863
Benjamin K Sharfi, *President*
Clive Souter, *Sr Software Eng*
Melinda Mejia, *Info Tech Mgr*
Tom Hanson, *Engineer*
EMP: 80
SQ FT: 20,000
SALES (est): 40.5MM **Privately Held**
WEB: www.gms4sbc.com
SIC: 5045 Computers, peripherals & software

(P-6843)
GENERAL PROCUREMENT INC (PA)
Also Called: Connect Computers
2601 Walnut Ave, Tustin (92780-7005)
PHONE....................949 679-7960
Imad Boukai, *President*
Sam Boukai, *Vice Pres*
Jahanvi Solanki, *Manager*
▲ EMP: 68
SQ FT: 2,800
SALES (est): 134.4MM **Privately Held**
WEB: www.connect-computers.com
SIC: 5045 5065 Computers, peripherals & software; electronic parts

(P-6844)
GENTEK MEDIA INC
12246 Colony Ave, Chino (91710-2095)
PHONE................................909 476-3818
Gene Seto, *CEO*
◆ **EMP:** 50
SALES (est): 10.3MM **Privately Held**
WEB: www.gentekmedia.com
SIC: **5045** Computers, peripherals & software

(P-6845)
GETAC INC
15495 Sand Canyon Ave # 300, Irvine
(92618-3153)
PHONE................................949 681-2900
Ming-Hang Hwang, *CEO*
Jim Rimay, *President*
Scott Shainman, *General Mgr*
Hj Lu, *Info Tech Mgr*
Leslie Abbott, *Human Res Mgr*
▲ **EMP:** 90
SQ FT: 12,000
SALES (est): 22.2MM **Privately Held**
WEB: www.getac.com
SIC: **5045** Mainframe computers
HQ: Mitac International Corporation
No. 1, Yanfa 2nd Rd., Hsinchu Science Industrial Park Science Ba
Paoshan Hsiang HSI 30076

(P-6846)
HITACHI VANTARA
CORPORATION
15231 Ave Of Science # 100, San Diego
(92128-3449)
PHONE................................858 537-3000
Hicham Abdessanad, *Vice Pres*
Rebecca Martin, *Human Resources*
Dale Hoberg, *Director*
Paul Coumans, *Supervisor*
EMP: 200 **Privately Held**
WEB: www.hds.com
SIC: **5045** 7378 Computers; computer maintenance & repair
HQ: Hitachi Vantara Corporation
2535 Augustine Dr
Santa Clara CA 95054
408 970-1000

(P-6847)
HON HAI PRECISION INDUST
LTD
500 S Kraemer Blvd # 100, Brea
(92821-6728)
PHONE................................714 988-9388
Vincent Ho, *Manager*
EMP: 70 **Privately Held**
SIC: **5045** Computers & accessories, personal & home entertainment
PA: Hon Hai Precision Industry Co., Ltd.
66, Zhongshan Rd.,
New Taipei City TAP 23680

(P-6848)
HONEYWELL INTERNATIONAL
INC
1099 Sneath Ln, San Bruno (94066-2311)
PHONE................................650 918-3229
Cathy Ward, *Regional Mgr*
EMP: 60
SQ FT: 16,400
SALES (corp-wide): 41.8B **Publicly Held**
WEB: www.honeywell.com
SIC: **5045** 7382 7381 Computer peripheral equipment; security systems services; detective & armored car services
PA: Honeywell International Inc.
300 S Tryon St
Charlotte NC 28202
973 455-2000

(P-6849)
HORIZON TECHNOLOGIES INC
Also Called: Horizon Systems
1270 Oakmead Pkwy Ste 115, Sunnyvale
(94085-4031)
PHONE................................408 733-1530
Santosh Addagulla, *President*
EMP: 213

SALES (est): 27.1MM **Privately Held**
WEB: www.horizontechnol.com
SIC: **5045** Computers, peripherals & software

(P-6850)
I2C INC
100 Redwood Shores Pkwy, Redwood City
(94065-1155)
PHONE................................650 593-5400
Amir Wain, *CEO*
Ted Dargan, *Partner*
Charlie Noreen, *CFO*
Joseph Derosa, *Exec VP*
Peg Johnson, *Exec VP*
EMP: 400 **EST:** 2000
SALES (est): 126.6MM **Privately Held**
WEB: www.i2cinc.com
SIC: **5045** Computer software

(P-6851)
IMAGESTAT CORPORATION
2950 28th St, Santa Monica (90405)
P.O. Box 3155, Culver City (90231-3155)
PHONE................................310 392-1100
Robert G Milne III, *President*
EMP: 120
SQ FT: 8,000
SALES (est): 10.3MM **Privately Held**
WEB: www.imagestat.com
SIC: **5045** 7334 Computers, peripherals & software; photocopying & duplicating services

(P-6852)
INFRASCALE INC (PA)
Also Called: SOS Hosting
999 N Pacific Coast Hwy # 100, El Segundo (90245-2714)
PHONE................................310 878-2621
Ken Shaw Jr, *Principal*
Michael Bell, *President*
Kenneth Shaw, *CEO*
Hardy Parungao, *CFO*
Bill Falk, *Risk Mgmt Dir*
EMP: 56
SQ FT: 8,000
SALES: 14MM **Privately Held**
SIC: **5045** 7372 Computers, peripherals & software; computer software; business oriented computer software

(P-6853)
INGRAM MICRO INC (HQ)
3351 Michelson Dr Ste 100, Irvine
(92612-0697)
PHONE................................714 566-1000
Alain Monie, *CEO*
Gina Mastantuono, *CFO*
Ramesh Nair, *CFO*
Augusto P Aragone, *Exec VP*
Paul Bay, *Exec VP*
◆ **EMP:** 4000 **EST:** 1979
SALES (est): 39.8B
SALES (corp-wide): 48.4B **Privately Held**
WEB: www.ingrammicro.com
SIC: **5045** Computer software
PA: Hna Technology Co., Ltd.
803, Huaying Building, Central Avenue, (Airport Economic Zone) P
Tianjin 30038
225 867-9088

(P-6854)
IRON SYSTEMS INC
980 Mission Ct, Fremont (94539-8202)
PHONE................................408 943-8000
Billy Bath, *President*
Harvey Bath, *Vice Pres*
George Davidson, *Vice Pres*
Bob Sidhu, *Vice Pres*
Harpreet Singh, *Vice Pres*
▲ **EMP:** 75
SQ FT: 43,000
SALES (est): 64.7MM **Privately Held**
WEB: www.ironsystems.com
SIC: **5045** Computers, peripherals & software

(P-6855)
IXOS SOFTWARE INC (PA)
8717 Research Dr, Irvine (92618-4200)
PHONE................................949 784-8000
Mark Smith, *CFO*
Da-Thao Becker, *Opers Staff*
EMP: 100

SQ FT: 30,000
SALES (est): 40.1MM **Privately Held**
WEB: www.ixos.com
SIC: **5045** Computer software

(P-6856)
JAG SOFTWARE INC
2235 Skyline Dr, Milpitas (95035-6682)
PHONE................................408 262-0572
Suresh Kottapalli, *President*
EMP: 69
SQ FT: 2,400
SALES (est): 7.1MM **Privately Held**
WEB: www.jagsoftware.com
SIC: **5045** Computer software

(P-6857)
JAGUAR COMPUTER SYSTEMS
INC
4135 Indus Way, Riverside (92503-4848)
PHONE................................951 273-7950
Joan E Hoanzl, *President*
George Hoanzl, *Vice Pres*
Linda Bowman, *Accounting Dir*
EMP: 50
SQ FT: 17,000
SALES (est): 6.6MM **Privately Held**
WEB: www.jaguarcomputersystems.com
SIC: **5045** 8742 7378 Computer peripheral equipment; marketing consulting services; computer maintenance & repair

(P-6858)
K-MICRO INC
Also Called: Corpinfo Services
1618 Stanford St, Santa Monica
(90404-4114)
PHONE................................310 442-3200
Michael Sabourian, *President*
Ahmad Gramian, *Vice Pres*
EMP: 96
SQ FT: 25,000
SALES: 16.6MM **Privately Held**
SIC: **5045** 7378 7373 7371 Computers & accessories, personal & home entertainment; computer maintenance & repair; computer integrated systems design; custom computer programming services

(P-6859)
LASERTECH COMPUTER DISTR
INC
139 N Sunset Ave, City of Industry
(91744-1850)
PHONE................................626 435-2800
Tony Ho, *President*
Annie Ho, *Admin Sec*
▲ **EMP:** 70
SQ FT: 28,000
SALES (est): 9.1MM **Privately Held**
WEB: www.ltcom.com
SIC: **5045** 5734 Computer peripheral equipment; computer & software stores

(P-6860)
LD PRODUCTS INC
Also Called: 4inkjets.com
3700 Cover St, Long Beach (90808-1782)
PHONE................................562 986-6940
Aaron Leon, *CEO*
Patrick Devane, *Senior VP*
◆ **EMP:** 150
SQ FT: 25,000
SALES (est): 119.3MM **Privately Held**
WEB: www.ldproducts.com
SIC: **5045** 2621 Printers, computer; stationery, envelope & tablet papers

(P-6861)
LITE-ON SALES AND DIST INC
726 S Hillview Dr, Milpitas (95035-5455)
PHONE................................510 687-1800
Ren-Wu Gong, *President*
Lando Lin, *CEO*
Chin-Sou Tsai Hong, *CFO*
Norlis Amaya, *Engineer*
Yung-Huei Chen, *Director*
▲ **EMP:** 100
SQ FT: 8,100
SALES (est): 15.1MM **Privately Held**
SIC: **5045** Computer peripheral equipment
PA: Lite-On Technology Corporation
22f, 392, Ruey Kuang Rd.,
Taipei City TAP 11492

(P-6862)
LIVESCRIBE INC
930 Roosevelt, Irvine (92620-3664)
PHONE................................503 290-4029
Gilles Bouchard, *CEO*
Ken Cucarola, *CFO*
Paul Machle, *CFO*
Brett Halle, *Senior VP*
Sherri Schultz, *Administration*
▲ **EMP:** 50
SQ FT: 24,000
SALES (est): 22.2MM
SALES (corp-wide): 12.8MM **Privately Held**
WEB: www.livescribe.com
SIC: **5045** Computer software
PA: Anoto Group Ab
Traktorvagen 11
Lund 226 6
465 401-200

(P-6863)
MA LABORATORIES INC
Also Called: MA Labs
18725 San Jose Ave, City of Industry
(91748-1324)
PHONE................................626 820-8988
Christine Pan, *Manager*
EMP: 55
SALES (corp-wide): 569.1MM **Privately Held**
SIC: **5045** Computers, peripherals & software
PA: Ma Laboratories, Inc.
2075 N Capitol Ave
San Jose CA 95132
408 941-0808

(P-6864)
MAGNELL ASSOCIATE INC (DH)
Also Called: A B S
17560 Rowland St, City of Industry
(91748-1114)
PHONE................................626 271-9700
James Wu, *CEO*
Craig Hayes, *Vice Pres*
William Slusher, *Info Tech Dir*
Albert Chong, *Info Tech Mgr*
Sam Liu, *Mfg Dir*
◆ **EMP:** 130
SALES (est): 1.8B
SALES (corp-wide): 2B **Privately Held**
SIC: **5045** Computers & accessories, personal & home entertainment
HQ: Newegg Inc.
17560 Rowland St
City Of Industry CA 91748
626 271-9700

(P-6865)
MAGNELL ASSOCIATE INC
Also Called: ABS Computer Technologies
18045 Rowland St, City of Industry
(91748-1205)
PHONE................................626 271-1580
Fred Chang, *President*
EMP: 100
SALES (corp-wide): 2B **Privately Held**
SIC: **5045** Computers & accessories, personal & home entertainment
HQ: Magnell Associate, Inc.
17560 Rowland St
City Of Industry CA 91748
626 271-9700

(P-6866)
MARIADB USA INC
350 Bay St Ste 100-319, San Francisco
(94133-1966)
PHONE................................847 562-9000
Michael Howard, *CEO*
Juha Aropaltio, *Controller*
EMP: 100
SALES: 34MM **Privately Held**
SIC: **5045** Computer software

(P-6867)
MATTERPORT INC (PA)
352 E Java Dr, Sunnyvale (94089-1328)
PHONE................................888 993-8990
Rj Pittman, *CEO*
JD Fay, *CFO*
Chris Bell, *Officer*
Carol Mackinlay, *Officer*
Jean Barbagelata, *Vice Pres*
EMP: 181

SALES (est): 3.5MM **Privately Held**
SIC: 5045 Computer software

(P-6868)
MAX GROUP CORPORATION (PA)
17011 Green Dr, City of Industry
(91745-1800)
PHONE..........................626 935-0050
Su-Tzu Tsai, *CEO*
Chung-Jen Tsai, *President*
Jonathan Min, *Finance Mgr*
◆ EMP: 65
SQ FT: 120,000
SALES (est): 87.9MM **Privately Held**
WEB: www.maxgroup.com
SIC: 5045 Computer peripheral equipment;
disk drives; keying equipment; printers;
computer

(P-6869)
MBH ENTERPRISES INC
1430 Franklin St Ste 201, Oakland
(94612-3209)
PHONE..........................510 302-6680
Michael B Hudson, *CEO*
David Rubin, *Exec VP*
EMP: 55
SALES (est): 3.7MM **Privately Held**
SIC: 5045 Computers, peripherals & soft-
ware

(P-6870)
MEMORY TO GO
10801 National Blvd # 101, Los Angeles
(90064-4139)
PHONE..........................310 446-0111
Isaac Faliz, *President*
EMP: 100
SALES (est): 11.3MM **Privately Held**
WEB: www.memorytogo.com
SIC: 5045 Computers, peripherals & soft-
ware

(P-6871)
MEMORYTEN INC (PA)
Also Called: Memoryx
2995 Mead Ave, Santa Clara (95051-0818)
PHONE..........................408 516-4141
Kenneth Olsen, *President*
Gergia Law, *CFO*
Charles Kim, *Info Tech Mgr*
Veronica Anderson, *Technology*
Jacqueline Ip, *Accountant*
▲ EMP: 56
SALES (est): 18.9MM **Privately Held**
WEB: www.memoryx.net
SIC: 5045 Computers, peripherals & soft-
ware

(P-6872)
MICRO-TECHNOLOGY CONCEPTS INC
Also Called: M T C
17837 Rowland St, City of Industry
(91748-1122)
PHONE..........................626 839-6800
Roy Han, *President*
Richard Shyu, *Senior VP*
Alan Djen, *Mktg Dir*
▲ EMP: 85
SQ FT: 42,500
SALES (est): 59.7MM
SALES (corp-wide): 16.3MM **Privately
Held**
WEB: www.mtcusa.com
SIC: 5045 Computer peripheral equipment
PA: Mtc Direct, Inc.
17837 Rowland St
City Of Industry CA 91748
626 839-6800

(P-6873)
MICROMENDERS INC (PA)
1388 Sutter St Ste 650, San Francisco
(94109-5452)
PHONE..........................415 344-0917
Toll Free:..........................888 -
Dave Sperry, *CEO*
Scott Estrella, *Partner*
Corey Choi, *Vice Pres*
Audel Barocio, *Administration*
Miguel Hundelt, *Administration*
EMP: 55
SQ FT: 5,375

SALES (est): 18.9MM **Privately Held**
SIC: 5045 7373 7371 4813 Computers,
peripherals & software; local area network
(LAN) systems integrator; computer software systems analysis & design, custom;

(P-6874)
MITSUBA CORPORATION
2509 Reata Pl, Diamond Bar (91765-3661)
PHONE..........................909 374-2631
Jen Jon Chen, *President*
Monica Chen, *Corp Secy*
Robin Chang, *Purch Agent*
EMP: 75
SQ FT: 40,000
SALES (est): 6.7MM **Privately Held**
SIC: 5045 Computer peripheral equipment;
computers; computer software

(P-6875)
MSI COMPUTER CORP (HQ)
901 Canada Ct, City of Industry
(91748-1136)
PHONE..........................626 913-0828
Andy Tung, *CEO*
Connie Chang, *CFO*
Tom Carney, *Vice Pres*
David Wu, *Vice Pres*
Renee Gastellum, *Office Mgr*
◆ EMP: 90
SQ FT: 77,500
SALES (est): 31.8MM **Privately Held**
WEB: www.msicomputer.com
SIC: 5045 Computer peripheral equipment

(P-6876)
MTC WORLDWIDE CORP
17837 Rowland St, City of Industry
(91748-1122)
PHONE..........................626 839-6800
Roy Han, *Principal*
▲ EMP: 79
SQ FT: 42,500
SALES (est): 26.5MM
SALES (corp-wide): 80.3MM **Privately
Held**
WEB: www.mtcdirect.com
SIC: 5045 3577 Computer peripheral
equipment; computer peripheral equip-
ment
PA: Mtc Direct, Inc.
17837 Rowland St
City Of Industry CA 91748
626 839-6800

(P-6877)
NEXINFO SOLUTIONS INC
8502 E Chapman Ave # 364, Orange
(92869-2461)
PHONE..........................714 368-1452
Arun Cavale, *President*
Sahil Gupta, *Technical Staff*
Wilma Flanagan, *Director*
Mahesh Naalla, *Consultant*
EMP: 50
SALES (est): 5MM **Privately Held**
SIC: 5045 8742 Computer software; man-
agement consulting services

(P-6878)
NHR NEWCO HOLDINGS LLC (HQ)
6500 Hollister Ave # 210, Santa Barbara
(93117-3011)
PHONE..........................805 964-9975
Sachi Thompson, *COO*
Sanford Tassel, *CFO*
Mike Sheldon, *Bd of Directors*
Mark Kelly, *Vice Pres*
Kelly Mark, *Vice Pres*
EMP: 94
SALES (est): 321.8MM
SALES (corp-wide): 359.7MM **Privately
Held**
SIC: 5045 Computers, peripherals & soft-
ware
PA: Curvature, Inc.
2810 Coliseum Centre Dr # 600
Charlotte NC 28217
704 921-1620

(P-6879)
ORACLE AMERICA INC
500 Oracle Pkwy, Redwood City
(94065-1677)
PHONE..........................800 633-0584

EMP: 58
SALES (corp-wide): 39.5B **Publicly Held**
SIC: 5045 8731 Computer software; com-
puter (hardware) development
HQ: Oracle America, Inc.
500 Oracle Pkwy
Redwood City CA 94065
650 506-7000

(P-6880)
PARASOFT CORPORATION (PA)
101 E Huntington Dr Fl 2, Monrovia
(91016-3496)
PHONE..........................626 256-3680
Elzbieta Kolawa, *President*
Nicole Marsh, *Info Tech Mgr*
EMP: 50
SALES (est): 25.5MM **Privately Held**
WEB: www.foodmagic.com
SIC: 5045 8711 8748 Computers; com-
puter software development; systems en-
gineering consultant, ex. computer or
professional

(P-6881)
PAYDARFAR INDUSTRIES INC
Also Called: Saratech
26054 Acero, Mission Viejo (92691-2768)
PHONE..........................949 481-3267
Saeed Paydarfar PHD, *CEO*
Robert McLoughlin, *Vice Pres*
Sara Paydarfar, *Admin Asst*
Caden Reiman, *Info Tech Mgr*
Mimi Lan, *Engineer*
EMP: 60
SQ FT: 5,930
SALES (est): 35.5MM **Privately Held**
SIC: 5045 8711 7372 7373 Computer
software; engineering services; prepack-
aged software; value-added resellers,
computer systems; computer-aided de-
sign (CAD) systems service; computer-
aided engineering (CAE) systems service

(P-6882)
PCM SALES INC (DH)
Also Called: Micro P Technologies
1940 E Mariposa Ave, El Segundo
(90245-3457)
PHONE..........................310 354-5600
Joseph Hayek, *CEO*
Mike M Mogavero, *President*
Peter Freix, *CEO*
Greg Richey, *CEO*
Brandon H Laverne, *CFO*
▼ EMP: 153
SALES (est): 1.4B **Publicly Held**
WEB: www.pcmall.com
SIC: 5045 Computers, peripherals & soft-
ware
HQ: Pcm, Inc.
1940 E Mariposa Ave
El Segundo CA 90245
310 354-5600

(P-6883)
PENGUIN COMPUTING INC (DH)
45800 Northport Loop W, Fremont
(94538-6413)
PHONE..........................415 954-2800
Tom Coull, *President*
Lisa Cummins, *CFO*
Dan Dowling, *Vice Pres*
Dan Stuart, *Vice Pres*
Barbara Fernandez, *Executive Asst*
▲ EMP: 85
SQ FT: 86,000
SALES: 166.5MM
SALES (corp-wide): 1.2B **Publicly Held**
WEB: www.penguincomputing.com
SIC: 5045 7371 7379 Computer software;
custom computer programming services;
computer related maintenance services

(P-6884)
PHELPS UNITED LLC
Also Called: Sourcing Solutions
3183 Red Hill Ave, Costa Mesa
(92626-3401)
PHONE..........................657 212-8050
Larry Weng, *CEO*
Ken Bast, *COO*
Greg Dalby, *General Mgr*
Chris Raub, *General Mgr*
Lloyd Seeley, *CTO*
EMP: 55

SQ FT: 31,000
SALES: 50MM **Privately Held**
SIC: 5045 Computers, peripherals & soft-
ware

(P-6885)
PHIHONG USA CORP (HQ)
47800 Fremont Blvd, Fremont
(94538-6551)
PHONE..........................510 445-0100
Fei Hung Alex Lin, *President*
Emily Tsai, *Finance*
▲ EMP: 58
SQ FT: 33,000
SALES (est): 118.8MM **Privately Held**
WEB: www.phihong.com
SIC: 5045 3572 Computer peripheral
equipment; computer disk & drum drives
& components

(P-6886)
PRIVATE LABEL PC LLC
Also Called: Plpc
748 Epperson Dr Ste B, City of Industry
(91748-1336)
PHONE..........................626 965-8686
Rachel Luke, *Mng Member*
Chris Luke, *Treasurer*
Jonathan Wang, *Vice Pres*
Caroline Lin, *Manager*
Gerson Montes, *Manager*
▲ EMP: 120
SALES (est): 73.3MM **Privately Held**
WEB: www.vistapc.com
SIC: 5045 Computer peripheral equipment

(P-6887)
PROFICIO INC (PA)
3264 Grey Hawk Ct, Carlsbad
(92010-6651)
PHONE..........................800 779-5042
Brad Taylor, *President*
Tim McElwee, *COO*
Dustin Ritter, *Chief Mktg Ofcr*
Dickon Smart-Gill, *Senior VP*
Ken Adamson, *Vice Pres*
EMP: 50
SQ FT: 5,000
SALES (est): 29.3MM **Privately Held**
SIC: 5045 Computer software

(P-6888)
PROMISE TECHNOLOGY INC
580 Cottonwood Dr, Milpitas (95035-7403)
PHONE..........................408 228-1400
Tung-Hsu Lin, *CEO*
Bhakti Panchal, *Administration*
Corrina Villalovos, *Administration*
David Bautista, *Info Tech Mgr*
Esteban Guzman Ptu, *Technician*
▲ EMP: 80
SQ FT: 40,000
SALES (est): 60.2MM **Privately Held**
WEB: www.promise.com
SIC: 5045 7379 Computers, peripherals &
software; data processing consultant
PA: Promise Technology Inc.
2f, No. 30, Gongye E. 9th Rd.,
Xinzhukexuegongyexueyuan District
Paoshan Hsiang HSI 30075

(P-6889)
QUADRANT COMPONENTS INC
46567 Fremont Blvd, Fremont
(94538-6409)
PHONE..........................510 656-9988
Chad Yau, *Ch of Bd*
Wenli Yau, *CFO*
▲ EMP: 80
SQ FT: 30,000
SALES (est): 9MM **Privately Held**
WEB: www.quadrant.com
SIC: 5045 3679 Computers, peripherals &
software; electronic circuits

(P-6890)
RAVIG INC
Also Called: Salient Global Technologies
510 Garcia Ave Ste E, Pittsburg
(94565-7405)
PHONE..........................925 526-1234
Ravikanth Ganaparvapu, *CEO*
Ravi Ganapa, *General Mgr*
William Lee, *Director*
EMP: 60

P
R
O
D
U
C
T
S

&

S
V
C
S

SQ FT: 34,000
SALES: 2.7MM **Privately Held**
SIC: 5045 7373 3571 Computers, peripherals & software; systems software development services; electronic computers

(P-6891)
RIVERBED TECHNOLOGY INC (HQ)
680 Folsom St Ste 500, San Francisco
(94107-2160)
PHONE........................415 247-8800
Rich McBee, *President*
Laura Padilla, *Partner*
John Tyler, *CFO*
Don Smoot, *Ch Credit Ofcr*
Subbu Iyer, *Chief Mktg Ofcr*
▲ **EMP:** 70
SQ FT: 167,000
SALES (est): 876.6MM
SALES (corp-wide): 1.3B **Privately Held**
WEB: www.riverbed.com
SIC: 5045 3577 Computer software; com-
puter peripheral equipment
PA: Riverbed Holdings, Inc.
300 N La Salle Dr # 4350
Chicago IL 60654
312 254-3300

(P-6892)
ROLAND DGA CORPORATION (HQ)
15363 Barranca Pkwy, Irvine (92618-2216)
PHONE........................949 727-2100
Andrew Oransky, *CEO*
Bruce Lauper, *CFO*
David Goward, *Exec VP*
Connie Caigoy, *Executive*
Patrick Kersey, *Creative Dir*
◆ **EMP:** 105
SQ FT: 53,000
SALES: 119.4MM **Privately Held**
WEB: www.rolanddga.com
SIC: 5045 8741 Computer peripheral
equipment; management services

(P-6893)
SANYO DENKI AMERICA INC (HQ)
468 Amapola Ave, Torrance (90501-1474)
PHONE........................310 783-5400
Stan Kato, *CEO*
Tin Tran, *CFO*
Rieko Suzuki, *Executive*
Daisuke Kanamatsu, *Engineer*
Henry Takeishi, *Engineer*
▲ **EMP:** 52
SQ FT: 45,000
SALES (est): 30MM **Privately Held**
WEB: www.sanyo-denki.com
SIC: 5045 7373 Computers & acces-
sories, personal & home entertainment;
computer-aided system services

(P-6894)
SIGMANET INC (HQ)
4290 E Brickell St, Ontario (91761-1524)
PHONE........................909 230-7500
Ahmed Al Khatib, *CEO*
Neil Wada, *President*
Apo Hagopian, *Senior VP*
Stephen Monteros, *Vice Pres*
Sam Garrison, *Business Mgr*
EMP: 125
SQ FT: 100,000
SALES (est): 240.2MM **Privately Held**
WEB: www.sigmanet.com
SIC: 5045 7373 Computers, peripherals &
software; computer integrated systems
design

(P-6895)
SK HYNIX AMERICA INC (HQ)
3101 N 1st St, San Jose (95134-1934)
PHONE........................408 232-8000
Kun Chul Suh, *CEO*
Jae H Park, *President*
Lisa Schmidt, *Vice Pres*
Heeseung Cho, *Administration*
C Charles Cho, *Info Tech Mgr*
▲ **EMP:** 80
SQ FT: 190,000
SALES (est): 271.7MM **Privately Held**
SIC: 5045 5065 Computer peripheral
equipment; semiconductor devices

(P-6896)
SMC NETWORKS INC (HQ)
20 Mason, Irvine (92618-2706)
PHONE........................949 679-8029
Alex Kim, *CEO*
Inho Kim, *President*
Frank Kuo, *President*
Lane Ruoff, *CFO*
Vivian Hsu, *Accountant*
▲ **EMP:** 80 **EST:** 1971
SQ FT: 22,650
SALES (est): 25.3MM **Privately Held**
WEB: www.smc.com
SIC: 5045 Computer peripheral equipment

(P-6897)
SOLID OAK SOFTWARE INC (PA)
1209 De La Vina St Ste B, Santa Barbara
(93101-5173)
P.O. Box 6826 (93160-6826)
PHONE........................805 568-5415
Brian Milburn, *President*
Mark Kanter, *Vice Pres*
EMP: 55
SALES (est): 9.4MM **Privately Held**
WEB: www.solidoak.com
SIC: 5045 7372 Computer software;
prepackaged software

(P-6898)
SOLVER INC
10780 Santa Monica Blvd # 370, Los Ange-
les (90025-4779)
PHONE........................310 691-5300
Nils Rasmussen, *President*
Corey Barak, *COO*
Hadrian Knotz, *CIO*
Michael Applegate, *CTO*
EMP: 50
SQ FT: 5,000
SALES: 10.5MM **Privately Held**
WEB: www.solverusa.com
SIC: 5045 7379 7374 Computer software;
computer related consulting services;
data processing & preparation

(P-6899)
SOMANSA TECHNOLOGIES INC
3003 N 1st St 301, San Jose (95134-2004)
PHONE........................408 297-1234
Suk Won Kwon, *CEO*
EMP: 60
SALES (est): 1.5MM **Privately Held**
SIC: 5045 Computers, peripherals & soft-
ware

(P-6900)
SOUTHLAND TECHNOLOGY INC
8053 Vickers St, San Diego (92111-1917)
PHONE........................858 694-0932
Grace Pedigo, *CEO*
Robert Pedigo, *President*
Daniel Abrams, *Vice Pres*
Ben Keepper, *CTO*
Josh Armstrong, *Technician*
EMP: 65
SQ FT: 16,000
SALES (est): 60.1MM **Privately Held**
WEB: www.southlandtechnology.com
SIC: 5045 8748 7373 7379 Computer
peripheral equipment; systems engineer-
ing consultant, ex. computer or profes-
sional; computer integrated systems
design; computer related maintenance
services; home entertainment computer
software

(P-6901)
SPACE AGE METAL PRODUCTS INC
23605 Telo Ave, Torrance (90505-4028)
PHONE........................310 539-5500
Arnold Klein, *CEO*
Emma Klein, *Corp Secy*
EMP: 200
SQ FT: 20,000
SALES (est): 16.4MM **Privately Held**
SIC: 5045 Computer peripheral equipment

(P-6902)
SPOTCUES INC
Also Called: Smartcues Inc
1975 W El Cmno Real 301, Mountain View
(94040)
PHONE........................408 435-2700
Jay Pullur, *President*
Vijay Pullur, *President*
K V Prasad, *Vice Pres*
Dimple Pandya, *Executive*
Narasimha Gadepalli, *Info Tech Dir*
EMP: 700 **EST:** 2001
SALES: 6MM **Privately Held**
WEB: www.pramati.com
SIC: 5045 Computer peripheral equipment
PA: Pramati Technologies Private Limited
No-301, Block-1,
Hyderabad TS 50001
-

(P-6903)
SQUARE ENIX INC
999 N Pacific Coast Hwy # 3, El Segundo
(90245-2731)
PHONE........................310 846-0400
Mike Fischer, *President*
Michihiro Sasaki, *Officer*
Jim Burley, *Vice Pres*
Phil Rogers, *Principal*
Stephen Ross, *Principal*
▲ **EMP:** 110
SALES (est): 60.5MM **Privately Held**
SIC: 5045 7372 Computer software; pub-
lishers' computer software
HQ: Square Enix Of America Holdings, Inc.
999 N Pacific Coast Hwy # 3
El Segundo CA 90245

(P-6904)
SUPER TALENT TECHNOLOGY CORP
2077 N Capitol Ave, San Jose
(95132-1009)
PHONE........................408 957-8133
Abraham MA, *President*
◆ **EMP:** 670
SALES (est): 91MM **Privately Held**
WEB: www.superlightwave.com
SIC: 5045 Computer peripheral equipment

(P-6905)
SWITCHFLY INC (PA)
500 3rd St Ste 440, San Francisco
(94107-1889)
PHONE........................415 541-9100
Craig Brennan, *CEO*
Graham Blankenbaker, *CTO*
EMP: 120
SALES (est): 39.6MM **Privately Held**
SIC: 5045 Computer software

(P-6906)
SYSPRO IMPACT SOFTWARE INC
959 S Coast Dr Ste 100, Costa Mesa
(92626-1786)
PHONE........................714 437-1000
Brian Stein, *CEO*
Joey Benadretti, *President*
Piero Broccardo, *CFO*
Sandra Fraga, *Chief Mktg Ofcr*
Kristin Valentyn, *Risk Mgmt Dir*
EMP: 200
SALES (est): 70.3MM **Privately Held**
WEB: www.syspro.com
SIC: 5045 7372 7371 Computer software;
prepackaged software; custom computer
programming services

(P-6907)
TIDEBREAK INC
958 San Leandro Ave # 500, Mountain View
(94043-1995)
P.O. Box 855, Palo Alto (94302-0855)
PHONE........................650 289-9869
Andrew J Milne, *CEO*
Celeste Montalvo, *Executive Asst*
Brad Johanson, *CTO*
Thomas Mallen, *Sales Staff*
EMP: 80
SALES (est): 6.6MM **Privately Held**
SIC: 5045 Computers, peripherals & soft-
ware

(P-6908)
TONER SUPPLY USA INC
Also Called: Tsu Corporate Services
8055 Lankershim Blvd # 11, North Holly-
wood (91605-1628)
PHONE........................818 504-6540
Omar Bian, *President*
Gus Obregon, *Vice Pres*
▲ **EMP:** 50
SQ FT: 120,000
SALES (est): 7.6MM **Privately Held**
SIC: 5045 7378 Computer peripheral
equipment; computer peripheral equip-
ment repair & maintenance

(P-6909)
TRANQUILMONEY INC
5823 Ruddy Duck Ct, Stockton
(95207-4518)
PHONE........................800 979-6739
EMP: 75
SALES (corp-wide): 10.9MM **Privately
Held**
SIC: 5045 Computers, peripherals & soft-
ware
PA: Tranquilmoney Inc.
461 Vose Ave
South Orange NJ 07079
212 494-0383

(P-6910)
TREND MICRO INCORPORATED
10101 N De Anza Blvd, Cupertino
(95014-2264)
PHONE........................408 257-1500
Anrew Lai, *Branch Mgr*
EMP: 67 **Privately Held**
SIC: 5045 7382 7372 Computer software;
security systems services; prepackaged
software
HQ: Trend Micro Incorporated
225 E John Carpenter Fwy # 1500
Irving TX 75062
408 257-1500

(P-6911)
TRENDNET INC (PA)
20675 Manhattan Pl, Torrance
(90501-1827)
PHONE........................310 961-5500
Pei Cheng Huang, *President*
Peggy Huang, *CFO*
Jaime Castro, *General Mgr*
Denise Shaw, *Sales Mgr*
Amilkar Garcia, *Manager*
◆ **EMP:** 80
SQ FT: 90,000
SALES (est): 23.3MM **Privately Held**
WEB: www.trendware.com
SIC: 5045 Computer peripheral equipment

(P-6912)
TRIVAD INC
1350 Bayshore Hwy Ste 450, Burlingame
(94010-1833)
PHONE........................650 286-1086
Jenna Lim, *CEO*
Gayle Godkin, *Executive*
Justin Smith, *Executive*
Zac Zuckerman, *Executive*
Jane Reyner, *Accountant*
EMP: 150
SQ FT: 6,000
SALES (est): 81.3MM **Privately Held**
WEB: www.trivad.com
SIC: 5045 7373 5734 3721 Computers,
peripherals & software; computer inte-
grated systems design; computer & soft-
ware stores; airplanes, fixed or rotary
wing; airborne radio communications
equipment; search & navigation equip-
ment; aircraft control systems, electronic;
navigational systems & instruments

(P-6913)
TW SECURITY CORP (DH)
5 Park Plz Ste 400, Irvine (92614-8524)
PHONE........................949 932-1000
John Vigouroux, *CEO*
Bruce Green, *COO*
Rodney S Miller, *CFO*
William Kilmer, *Chief Mktg Ofcr*
Paul D Myer, *Senior VP*
EMP: 120
SQ FT: 28,000

SALES (est): 26.5MM
SALES (corp-wide): 13MM **Privately Held**
WEB: www.marhsa18e6.com
SIC: **5045** Computer software
HQ: Trustwave Holdings, Inc.
70 W Madison St Ste 600
Chicago IL 60602
312 750-0950

(P-6914)
TYAN COMPUTER CORPORATION
3288 Laurelview Ct, Fremont (94538-6535)
PHONE................................510 651-8868
Jhi-Wu Ho, *CEO*
James Sytwu, *Exec VP*
Eric Cho, *Senior VP*
Danny Hsu, *Vice Pres*
George Koivun, *Vice Pres*
◆ EMP: 85
SALES (est): 23.6MM **Privately Held**
WEB: www.tyan.com
SIC: **5045** Computers, peripherals & software
HQ: Mitac Computing Technology Corporation
3f, No. 1, R&D 2nd Rd., Hsinchu Science Industrial Park
Paoshan Hsiang HSI 30076

(P-6915)
UNICAL ENTERPRISES INC
Also Called: Northwestern Bell Telephones
16960 Gale Ave, City of Industry (91745-1805)
PHONE................................626 965-5588
Frank Liu, *President*
Rebecca Tsui, *Vice Pres*
▲ EMP: 65
SQ FT: 72,000
SALES (est): 8.5MM **Privately Held**
WEB: www.unical-usa.com
SIC: **5045** 5065 Terminals, computer; telephone & telegraphic equipment

(P-6916)
VALGENESIS INC
395 Oyster Point Blvd # 228, South San Francisco (94080-1930)
PHONE................................510 445-0505
Siva Samy, *President*
Shanti Mulyadi, *Manager*
▼ EMP: 50
SQ FT: 1,000
SALES (est): 7.8MM **Privately Held**
SIC: **5045** 7371 Computer software; computer software development & applications

(P-6917)
VIEWSONIC CORPORATION (PA)
10 Pointe Dr Ste 200, Brea (92821-7620)
PHONE................................909 444-8888
James Chu, *Ch of Bd*
Brian Igoe, *Vice Pres*
Caroline Lin, *Vice Pres*
Myrna Jones, *Exec Dir*
Bonny Cheng, *General Mgr*
◆ EMP: 140
SQ FT: 298,050
SALES (est): 541.8MM **Privately Held**
WEB: www.viewsonic.com
SIC: **5045** Computer peripheral equipment

(P-6918)
VISCIRA LLC
200 Vallejo St, San Francisco (94111-1512)
PHONE................................415 848-8010
Dave Gulezian, *President*
Rick Barker, *COO*
Hagop Kane Kaneboughazian, *Vice Pres*
Katherine Cusguen-Garcia, *Office Mgr*
EMP: 100
SQ FT: 10,000
SALES (est): 36.6MM
SALES (corp-wide): 20B **Privately Held**
SIC: **5045** 7371 Computer software; computer software development & applications
HQ: Sudler & Hennessey, Llc
3 Columbus Cir Fl 7
New York NY 10019
212 614-4100

(P-6919)
WONDERWARE CORPORATION (DH)
26561 Rancho Pkwy S, Lake Forest (92630-8301)
PHONE................................949 727-3200
Rick Bullotta, *Vice Pres*
Peter Kent, *Senior VP*
Dave Pickett, *Senior VP*
Alfredo Blumenthal, *Vice Pres*
Dottie Sargent, *Vice Pres*
EMP: 300
SQ FT: 32,000
SALES (est): 61.3MM **Privately Held**
WEB: www.wonderware.com
SIC: **5045** Computer software

(P-6920)
WORLD WIDE TECHNOLOGY LLC
1165 W Walnut St, Compton (90220-5113)
PHONE................................310 537-8335
Rob Macphee, *Manager*
EMP: 50
SALES (corp-wide): 4.8B **Privately Held**
SIC: **5045** 5065 Computers, peripherals & software; communication equipment
HQ: World Wide Technology, Llc
1 World Wide Way
Saint Louis MO 63146
314 569-7000

(P-6921)
XTRAPLUS CORPORATION
Also Called: Zipzoomfly
39889 Eureka Dr, Newark (94560-4811)
PHONE................................510 897-1890
MEI F Chan, *President*
▲ EMP: 90 EST: 1998
SALES (est): 9.9MM **Privately Held**
WEB: www.zipzoomfly.com
SIC: **5045** 3577 Computer peripheral equipment; computer peripheral equipment

---

5046 Commercial Eqpt, NEC Wholesale

(P-6922)
BUYEFFICIENT LLC
903 Calle Amanecer # 200, San Clemente (92673-6251)
PHONE................................949 382-3129
Dennis Baker, *President*
EMP: 76
SALES (est): 7.7MM **Publicly Held**
SIC: **5046** Hotel equipment & supplies
HQ: Avendra, Llc
540 Gaither Rd Ste 200
Rockville MD 20850
301 825-0500

(P-6923)
CLIPPER CORPORATION (PA)
21124 Figueroa St, Carson (90745-1938)
PHONE................................310 533-8585
Lina Hu, *CEO*
Nancy Hejran, *CFO*
Ashley LI, *Director*
◆ EMP: 50 EST: 1994
SQ FT: 59,810
SALES (est): 39MM **Privately Held**
WEB: www.clipper-corp.com
SIC: **5046** Restaurant equipment & supplies; cooking equipment, commercial

(P-6924)
HANNAM CHAIN USA INC (PA)
Also Called: Hannam Chain Super 1 Market
2740 W Olympic Blvd, Los Angeles (90006-2633)
PHONE................................213 382-2922
Kee W Ha, *CEO*
Perry King, *General Mgr*
▲ EMP: 105
SQ FT: 22,000
SALES (est): 72MM **Privately Held**
SIC: **5046** 5411 Restaurant equipment & supplies; supermarkets, independent

(P-6925)
INTERSTATE ELECTRIC CO INC (PA)
Also Called: IEC
2240 Yates Ave, Commerce (90040-1914)
PHONE................................323 724-0420
Edward Urlik, *President*
Arnie Binter, *Branch Mgr*
Ed Brent, *Branch Mgr*
George Haberstroh, *General Mgr*
Manual Gonzales, *Credit Staff*
▲ EMP: 94 EST: 1966
SQ FT: 72,000
SALES (est): 70.5MM **Privately Held**
WEB: www.interstateelectric.com
SIC: **5046** Signs, electrical

(P-6926)
JC FOODSERVICE INC (PA)
Also Called: Action Sales
415 S Atlantic Blvd, Monterey Park (91754-3209)
PHONE................................626 299-3800
Joel Chang, *President*
Jack Chang, *Vice Pres*
Eva Lau, *Business Mgr*
Daisuke Hattori, *Sales Staff*
Domanic Lau, *Sales Staff*
◆ EMP: 55
SQ FT: 25,000
SALES (est): 47.3MM **Privately Held**
WEB: www.actionsales.com
SIC: **5046** Restaurant equipment & supplies

(P-6927)
JONES SIGN CO INC
Also Called: Ultrasigns Electrical Advg
9025 Balboa Ave Ste 150, San Diego (92123-1522)
PHONE................................858 569-1400
John Mortensen, *President*
Mary Jo Wenzel, *Controller*
Juan Rodriguez, *Manager*
EMP: 120
SALES (corp-wide): 73MM **Privately Held**
SIC: **5046** Signs, electrical
PA: Jones Sign Co., Inc.
1711 Scheuring Rd
De Pere WI 54115
920 983-6700

(P-6928)
JUSTMAN PACKAGING & DISPLAY
5819 Telegraph Rd, Commerce (90040-1515)
PHONE................................323 728-8888
Morley Justman, *President*
Barbara Cabaret, *CFO*
Russell Justman, *Vice Pres*
▲ EMP: 70
SQ FT: 125,000
SALES (est): 64.8MM **Privately Held**
WEB: www.justman.com
SIC: **5046** 5113 2752 Display equipment, except refrigerated; corrugated & solid fiber boxes; commercial printing, lithographic

(P-6929)
PBI-BIRKENWALD MARKET EQP INC (PA)
Also Called: P B I
2667 Gundry Ave, Long Beach (90755-1808)
P.O. Box 6097 (90806-0097)
PHONE................................562 595-4785
Thomas L Everson, *President*
Kim Everson, *COO*
Jim Ennis, *CFO*
Laurie Stone, *Senior VP*
Erik Everson, *Vice Pres*
▲ EMP: 50 EST: 1949
SQ FT: 85,000
SALES (est): 25.1MM **Privately Held**
WEB: www.pbimarketing.com
SIC: **5046** Store equipment; scales, except laboratory; shelving, commercial & industrial; cooking equipment, commercial

(P-6930)
PETERSON MACHINERY CO (PA)
Also Called: Peterson Cat
955 Marina Blvd, San Leandro (94577-3440)
P.O. Box 5258 (94577-0610)
PHONE................................541 302-9199
Duane S Doyle, *CEO*
Mark Ehni, *President*
Keith Davidge, *CFO*
Kevin Goodwin, *Branch Mgr*
Bill Bean, *General Mgr*
EMP: 83
SALES (est): 362.2MM **Privately Held**
WEB: www.petersonholding.com
SIC: **5046** Commercial equipment

(P-6931)
SHOPPER INC
3987 Heritage Oak Ct, Simi Valley (93063-6711)
PHONE................................805 527-6700
Bill Bieda, *CEO*
Sally Quioan, *CFO*
Elliot Bieda, *Vice Pres*
Howard Bieda, *Vice Pres*
Brock Helvie, *Executive*
◆ EMP: 300
SQ FT: 80,000
SALES (est): 74.7MM **Privately Held**
WEB: www.shopperinc.com
SIC: **5046** Store fixtures & display equipment

(P-6932)
STEUBER CORPORATION (PA)
Also Called: Foodcraft Cof Refreshment Svcs
20425 S Susana Rd, Long Beach (90810-1136)
PHONE................................310 632-8255
Robert A Steuber, *President*
Cathy H Steuber, *Corp Secy*
Stuart Harris, *Vice Pres*
Philip Steuber, *Vice Pres*
EMP: 85
SQ FT: 18,000
SALES (est): 23.9MM **Privately Held**
SIC: **5046** 5963 5149 5411 Coffee brewing equipment & supplies; direct selling establishments; groceries & related products; convenience stores; medicine cabinet sundries

(P-6933)
TOM DREHER SALES INC
Beach Cities Wholesalers
2021 W 17th St, Long Beach (90813-1011)
P.O. Box 41386 (90853-1386)
PHONE................................562 355-4074
Tom Dreher, *President*
EMP: 87
SALES (corp-wide): 1.2MM **Privately Held**
SIC: **5046** 5145 Restaurant equipment & supplies; popcorn & supplies
PA: Tom Dreher Sales Inc.
2021 W 17th St
Long Beach CA
562 355-4074

5047 Medical, Dental & Hospital Eqpt & Splys Wholesale

(P-6934)
AAXIS PHARMACEUTICALS INC
Also Called: Aaxis Pacific
1835 262nd St, Lomita (90717-3346)
PHONE................................424 263-5294
Soa Sher, *CEO*
EMP: 101
SALES (est): 1.8MM **Privately Held**
SIC: **5047** 7389 Medical equipment & supplies;

(P-6935)
ACON LABORATORIES INC (PA)
10125 Mesa Rim Rd, San Diego (92121-2915)
PHONE................................858 875-8000
Jinn-Nan Lin, *President*
Leigh Thorup, *Info Tech Mgr*
Todd Nguyen, *IT/INT Sup*

Kristi Gayagoy, *Research*
Maxwell Kum, *Research*
▲ **EMP:** 65
SQ FT: 36,000
SALES (est): 17.9MM **Privately Held**
WEB: www.aconlabs.com
SIC: 5047 Medical equipment & supplies

(P-6936)
ADVANCED REHABILITATION TECH
7950 Dunbrook Rd, San Diego
(92126-4371)
P.O. Box 915, Cardiff By The Sea (92007-0915)
PHONE...................858 621-5959
Richard M Harris, *President*
Jack Bailey, *Shareholder*
Darrel Blomberg, *Shareholder*
Stan Dunlap, *Vice Pres*
Chet Teklinski, *Vice Pres*
EMP: 57
SQ FT: 12,000
SALES (est): 11.3MM **Privately Held**
SIC: 5047 Medical equipment & supplies

(P-6937)
ALPHAEON CORPORATION (HQ)
17901 Von Karman Ave # 150, Irvine
(92614-5245)
PHONE...................949 284-4555
Murthy Simhambhatla, *CEO*
Clint Carnell, *President*
Jeff Castillo, *President*
Kuntal Joshi, *President*
Bob Rhatigan, *COO*
EMP: 51 **EST:** 2012
SALES (est): 36.4MM
SALES (corp-wide): 36.8MM **Publicly Held**
SIC: 5047 Hospital equipment & furniture
PA: Strathspey Crown Holdings Llc
4040 Macarthur Blvd # 210
Newport Beach CA 92660
949 260-1700

(P-6938)
AMERICAN MEDICAL TECH INC
17595 Cartwright Rd, Irvine (92614-5847)
PHONE...................949 553-0359
Jean Signore, *President*
Jerry Signore, *Vice Pres*
Pamela Scarborough, *Education*
Sidney Felczer, *Director*
Tessa Hammond, *Director*
EMP: 100
SALES (est): 24.4MM **Privately Held**
SIC: 5047 Medical equipment & supplies

(P-6939)
AMPRONIX INC
15 Whatney, Irvine (92618-2808)
PHONE...................949 273-8000
Nausser Fathollahi, *President*
Aladdin Doroudi, *CFO*
Gennie Bui, *Admin Asst*
Jessica Cumpian, *Admin Asst*
Evelyn Navarro, *Admin Asst*
▲ **EMP:** 78
SQ FT: 58,000
SALES (est): 49.9MM **Privately Held**
WEB: www.ampronix.com
SIC: 5047 Diagnostic equipment, medical

(P-6940)
ANGIOSCORE INC
5055 Brandin Ct, Fremont (94538-3140)
PHONE...................510 933-7900
Thomas R Trotter, *President*
EMP: 140
SQ FT: 44,000
SALES (est): 45.2MM
SALES (corp-wide): 20.8B **Privately Held**
SIC: 5047 Medical equipment & supplies
HQ: Spectranetics Corporation
9965 Federal Dr Ste 100
Colorado Springs CO 80921
719 447-2000

(P-6941)
APRIA HEALTHCARE LLC
480 Carlton Ct, South San Francisco
(94080-2012)
PHONE...................650 588-9744
Geronimo Jimenez, *Manager*
Gerardo Noria, *Manager*

EMP: 56 **Privately Held**
WEB: www.apria.com
SIC: 5047 7352 5999 Hospital equipment & furniture; dental equipment & supplies; medical equipment & supplies; medical equipment rental; medical apparatus & supplies
HQ: Apria Healthcare Llc
26220 Enterprise Ct
Lake Forest CA 92630
949 639-2000

(P-6942)
APRIA HEALTHCARE LLC
1450 Expo Pkwy Ste D, Sacramento
(95815-4231)
PHONE...................530 677-2713
Jim Hay, *Branch Mgr*
David Russell, *General Mgr*
EMP: 192 **Privately Held**
WEB: www.apria.com
SIC: 5047 Hospital equipment & furniture
HQ: Apria Healthcare Llc
26220 Enterprise Ct
Lake Forest CA 92630
949 639-2000

(P-6943)
APRIA HEALTHCARE LLC (HQ)
26220 Enterprise Ct, Lake Forest
(92630-8405)
P.O. Box 610 (92609-0610)
PHONE...................949 639-2000
Daniel J Starck, *CEO*
Donna Blake, *President*
Matt Gallagher, *President*
Debra Morris, *CFO*
Raoul Smyth, *Exec VP*
◆ **EMP:** 350
SALES (est): 1.1B **Privately Held**
WEB: www.apria.com
SIC: 5047 7352 5999 Hospital equipment & furniture; dental equipment & supplies; medical equipment & supplies; medical equipment rental; medical apparatus & supplies

(P-6944)
APRIA HEALTHCARE LLC
2510 Dean Lesher Dr Ste D, Concord
(94520-1368)
PHONE...................925 827-8800
Dencio Chua, *Manager*
EMP: 63
SQ FT: 2,400 **Privately Held**
WEB: www.apria.com
SIC: 5047 7352 Hospital equipment & furniture; medical equipment rental
HQ: Apria Healthcare Llc
26220 Enterprise Ct
Lake Forest CA 92630
949 639-2000

(P-6945)
AVITA MEDICAL AMERICAS LLC
28159 Ave Stnford Ste 220, Valencia
(91355)
PHONE...................661 367-9170
Michael S Perry, *Mng Member*
David Fencil, *Vice Pres*
Debbie Garner, *Vice Pres*
Sean Ekins, *Controller*
Timothy Rooney,
▲ **EMP:** 71
SQ FT: 23,000
SALES (est): 3.6MM **Publicly Held**
SIC: 5047 Medical & hospital equipment
PA: Avita Medical Ltd
L 7 330 Collins St
Melbourne VIC 3000

(P-6946)
B BRAUN MEDICAL INC
1151 Mildred St Ste B, Ontario
(91761-3504)
PHONE...................909 906-7575
Didi Paano, *Sales Staff*
Peter McGregor, *Director*
Soheil Taghavi, *Manager*
Dennis Johnson, *Supervisor*
EMP: 1300
SALES (corp-wide): 2.6MM **Privately Held**
SIC: 5047 Medical equipment & supplies

HQ: B. Braun Medical Inc.
824 12th Ave
Bethlehem PA 18018
610 691-5400

(P-6947)
BACKPROJECT CORPORATION
170 N Wolfe Rd, Sunnyvale (94086-5211)
PHONE...................408 730-1111
Steve Hoffman, *President*
◆ **EMP:** 66
SQ FT: 18,000
SALES (est): 7.6MM **Privately Held**
WEB: www.backproject.com
SIC: 5047 Medical equipment & supplies

(P-6948)
BALT USA LLC
Also Called: Blockade Medical
29 Parker Ste 100, Irvine (92618-1667)
PHONE...................949 788-1443
David A Ferrera, *President*
Billy Mitchell, *VP Opers*
Dawson Le, *Mfg Staff*
Robert Austin, *Regl Sales Mgr*
Ryan Solomon, *Marketing Staff*
EMP: 90
SQ FT: 47,000
SALES: 5.2MM
SALES (corp-wide): 1.3MM **Privately Held**
SIC: 5047 3841 Medical equipment & supplies; surgical & medical instruments
HQ: Balt International
10 Rue De La Croix Vigneron
Montmorency 95160
139 894-641

(P-6949)
BECTON DICKINSON AND COMPANY
Also Called: Bdc Distribution Center
2200 W San Bernardino Ave, Redlands
(92374-5008)
PHONE...................909 748-7300
Ricardo Frias, *Branch Mgr*
EMP: 100
SALES (corp-wide): 15.9B **Publicly Held**
SIC: 5047 Medical equipment & supplies
PA: Becton, Dickinson And Company
1 Becton Dr
Franklin Lakes NJ 07417
201 847-6800

(P-6950)
BENCO DENTAL SUPPLY CO
3590 Harbor Gtwy N, Costa Mesa
(92626-1425)
PHONE...................714 424-0977
Bret McCarroll, *Accounts Mgr*
EMP: 98
SALES (corp-wide): 591.4MM **Privately Held**
SIC: 5047 Dental equipment & supplies
PA: Benco Dental Supply Co.
295 Centerpoint Blvd
Pittston PA 18640
570 602-7781

(P-6951)
BINDING SITE INC (PA)
6730 Mesa Ridge Rd Ste B, San Diego
(92121-2951)
PHONE...................858 453-9177
Doug Kurth, *President*
Doug Anderson, *Exec VP*
Alan Alcuaz, *Technical Staff*
Katie Brentzel, *Technical Staff*
▲ **EMP:** 62
SQ FT: 23,000
SALES (est): 24.6MM **Privately Held**
WEB: www.thebindingsite.com
SIC: 5047 Diagnostic equipment, medical

(P-6952)
BIOSITE INC
9975 Summers Ridge Rd, San Diego
(92121-2997)
PHONE...................510 683-9063
Yonkin John, *President*
Lisa Wikstrom, *Executive*
Emily Parker, *Associate Dir*
Gillian Parker, *Info Tech Mgr*
Danae Monroe, *Research*
EMP: 62 **EST:** 2011

SALES (est): 17.2MM **Privately Held**
SIC: 5047 Medical equipment & supplies

(P-6953)
BONGMI INC
68 Harriet St Unit 3, San Francisco
(94103-4094)
PHONE...................415 823-8595
Snow LI, *Director*
EMP: 50
SALES: 20K **Privately Held**
SIC: 5047 7389 Medical equipment & supplies;

(P-6954)
BRADEN PARTNERS LP A CALIF
7500 District Blvd, Bakersfield
(93313-4832)
PHONE...................661 632-1979
Patrick Sullivan, *Manager*
EMP: 87
SALES (corp-wide): 91.7MM **Privately Held**
SIC: 5047 Medical equipment & supplies
HQ: Braden Partners, L.P., A California Limited Partnership
1304 Sthpint Blvd Ste 130
Petaluma CA 94954

(P-6955)
BRENTWOOD MEDICAL TECH CORP
Also Called: Midmark Diagnostics Group
1125 W 190th St, Gardena (90248-4303)
PHONE...................800 624-8950
Rebecca Mabry, *President*
Gary Bullington, *Director*
EMP: 60
SQ FT: 27,000
SALES (est): 7.3MM
SALES (corp-wide): 389.2MM **Privately Held**
WEB: www.midmarkdiagnostics.com
SIC: 5047 Medical equipment & supplies
PA: Midmark Corporation
10170 Penny Ln Ste 300
Miamisburg OH 45342
937 526-8472

(P-6956)
CANON MEDICAL SYSTEMS USA INC (DH)
Also Called: Video Sensing Division
2441 Michelle Dr, Tustin (92780-7047)
P.O. Box 2068 (92781-2068)
PHONE...................714 730-5000
Shuzo Yamamoto, *President*
John Patterson, *CFO*
Peter N S Annand, *Senior VP*
Calum G Cunningham, *Vice Pres*
Christopher Federoff, *Vice Pres*
◆ **EMP:** 300
SQ FT: 135,000
SALES (est): 5.6MM **Privately Held**
WEB: www.tams.com
SIC: 5047 X-ray machines & tubes; medical equipment & supplies

(P-6957)
CARDINAL HEALTH INC
1100 Bird Center Dr, Palm Springs
(92262-8000)
PHONE...................951 360-2199
EMP: 52
SALES (corp-wide): 102.5B **Publicly Held**
SIC: 5047
PA: Cardinal Health, Inc.
7000 Cardinal Pl
Dublin OH 43017
614 757-5000

(P-6958)
CARDINAL HEALTH 200 LLC
3750 Torrey View Ct, San Diego
(92130-2622)
PHONE...................951 686-8900
Michael McMahon, *Manager*
Geoffrey Healthcare, *Engineer*
EMP: 210
SQ FT: 28,000

SALES (corp-wide): 145.5B **Publicly Held**
WEB: www.allegiancehealth.com
SIC: **5047** 3845 3672 Medical equipment & supplies; electromedical equipment; printed circuit boards
HQ: Cardinal Health 200, Llc
3651 Birchwood Dr
Waukegan IL 60085

(P-6959)
CARDIOMART INC
11715 Avenida Del Sol, Northridge (91326-1501)
P.O. Box 8224 (91327-8224)
PHONE.................310 572-6724
Alex Tajyar, *President*
▲ EMP: 50
SALES (est): 5.1MM **Privately Held**
SIC: **5047** 3842 Medical & hospital equipment; surgical appliances & supplies

(P-6960)
CAREFUSION SOLUTIONS LLC (DH)
3750 Torrey View Ct, San Diego (92130-2622)
PHONE.................858 617-2100
Keiran Gallahue, *CEO*
Tom Leonard, *President*
James Hinrichs, *CFO*
Don Abbey, *Exec VP*
Scott Bostick, *Senior VP*
EMP: 600
SALES (est): 327.2MM
SALES (corp-wide): 15.9B **Publicly Held**
SIC: **5047** Medical equipment & supplies

(P-6961)
CHEN DVID MD DGNSTC MED GROUP
Also Called: Diagnstic Med Group Sthern Cal
25 N Santa Anita Ave, Arcadia (91006-3111)
PHONE.................626 566-3900
EMP: 101 **Privately Held**
SIC: **5047** Medical & hospital equipment
PA: Chen, David Md Diagnostic Medical Group Inc
1129 S San Gabriel Blvd
San Gabriel CA 91776

(P-6962)
CHINA YNGXIN PHRMCEUTICALS INC
927 Canada Ct, City of Industry (91748-1136)
PHONE.................626 581-9098
Yongxin Liu, *Ch of Bd*
Ning Liu, *President*
Harry Zhang, *CFO*
EMP: 673
SALES: 47.5MM **Privately Held**
SIC: **5047** Medical equipment & supplies

(P-6963)
CONSENSUS ORTHOPEDICS INC
1115 Windfield Way # 100, El Dorado Hills (95762-9835)
PHONE.................916 355-7123
Collen Gray, *President*
Curt Wiedenhoefer, *President*
Gail V Dalen, *Exec VP*
Carolyn Hayes, *Vice Pres*
Dan Richards, *Vice Pres*
EMP: 82
SQ FT: 25,000
SALES (est): 43MM **Privately Held**
WEB: www.hayesmed.com
SIC: **5047** 3841 Medical equipment & supplies; surgical & medical instruments

(P-6964)
EDGE SYSTEMS LLC (PA)
Also Called: Hydrafacial Company, The
2165 E Spring St, Long Beach (90806-2114)
PHONE.................800 603-4996
Clint Carnell, *CEO*
Jeff Nardoci, *COO*
Randy Sieve, *CFO*
Karol Ferrin, *Executive Asst*

Teresa Gutierrez, *Administration*
▲ EMP: 170
SQ FT: 22,515
SALES (est): 108.8MM **Privately Held**
WEB: www.edgesystem.net
SIC: **5047** Medical equipment & supplies

(P-6965)
FISHER & PAYKEL HEALTHCARE INC
173 Technology Dr Ste 100, Irvine (92618-2489)
PHONE.................949 453-4000
Justin Callahan, *President*
Tony Barclay, *CFO*
Bryan Goudzwaard, *Vice Pres*
Ross Ferguson, *Sales Staff*
Susan Hoefs, *Sales Staff*
▲ EMP: 150
SQ FT: 5,000
SALES (est): 79.9MM **Privately Held**
SIC: **5047** Medical equipment & supplies
PA: Fisher & Paykel Healthcare Corporation Limited
15 Maurice Paykel Place
Auckland 1061

(P-6966)
GENERAL HOME MEDICAL SUP INC
4607 Lakeview Canyon Rd # 584, Westlake Village (91361-4028)
PHONE.................805 449-1559
Kambiz Yadidi, *CEO*
▲ EMP: 88
SQ FT: 5,700
SALES (est): 8.6MM **Privately Held**
WEB: www.sinusdynamics.com
SIC: **5047** Medical equipment & supplies

(P-6967)
GOLDEN STATE MEDICAL SUP INC
5187 Camino Ruiz, Camarillo (93012-8601)
PHONE.................805 477-9866
Benjamin Hall, *CEO*
Shiela Curran, *COO*
Thomas S Weaver, *CFO*
Dave Arnold, *Senior VP*
Jim McManimie, *Senior VP*
EMP: 150
SQ FT: 95,500
SALES (est): 128.2MM **Privately Held**
WEB: www.gsms.us
SIC: **5047** Medical equipment & supplies
PA: Gsms, Inc.
5187 Camino Ruiz
Camarillo CA 93012
805 477-9866

(P-6968)
GORDIAN MEDICAL INC
Also Called: American Medical Technologies
17595 Cartwright Rd, Irvine (92614-5847)
PHONE.................714 556-0200
Joseph Del Signore, *President*
Gerald Del Signore, *CEO*
David Simon, *Vice Pres*
EMP: 290
SALES (est): 86.7MM **Privately Held**
SIC: **5047** Medical equipment & supplies

(P-6969)
HARDY DIAGNOSTICS (PA)
1430 W Mccoy Ln, Santa Maria (93455-1005)
P.O. Box 645264, Cincinnati OH (45264-5264)
PHONE.................805 346-2766
Jay R Hardy, *President*
Darla Prevish, *CFO*
Kathleen Salazar, *Technician*
Christopher Massey, *Research*
Anthony Mendoza, *Technology*
◆ EMP: 300
SQ FT: 75,000
SALES: 45MM **Privately Held**
WEB: www.hardydiagnostics.com
SIC: **5047** 2836 Medical equipment & supplies; agar culture media

(P-6970)
HONEY LAKE HOSPICE INC
60 S Lassen St, Susanville (96130-4363)
P.O. Box 1166 (96130-1166)
PHONE.................530 257-3137
EMP: 60
SALES (est): 4.2MM **Privately Held**
SIC: **5047** Medical equipment & supplies

(P-6971)
ICRCO INC (PA)
Also Called: Image Capture Review
26 Coromar Dr, Goleta (93117-3024)
PHONE.................310 921-9559
Stephen Neushul, *CEO*
Linda Pahl, *CFO*
Dhaval Joshi, *Sr Software Eng*
MA Vang, *Human Res Mgr*
Jason Trump, *Med Doctor*
▲ EMP: 50
SQ FT: 11,000
SALES (est): 18.6MM **Privately Held**
WEB: www.icrcompany.com
SIC: **5047** Medical & hospital equipment

(P-6972)
JB DENTAL SUPPLY CO INC (PA)
17000 Kingsview Ave, Carson (90746-1230)
PHONE.................310 202-8855
Joseph Berman, *President*
Manny Chada, *Vice Pres*
Kimberly A Arana, *Director*
EMP: 120 **EST:** 1973
SQ FT: 26,000
SALES (est): 36.3MM **Privately Held**
SIC: **5047** Dental equipment & supplies

(P-6973)
JOERNS LLC (HQ)
19748 Dearborn St, Chatsworth (91311-6509)
PHONE.................800 966-6662
Mark Ludwig, *CEO*
Mark Urbania, *CFO*
Kevin Conway, *Officer*
EMP: 150
SQ FT: 28,000
SALES (est): 54.3MM
SALES (corp-wide): 163MM **Privately Held**
WEB: www.trilinemedical.com
SIC: **5047** Hospital equipment & furniture
PA: Quad-C Jh Holdings Inc.
2430 Whitehall Park Dr
Charlotte NC 28273
800 826-0270

(P-6974)
KLM ORTHOTIC LABORATORIES INC
28280 Alta Vista Ave, Valencia (91355-0958)
PHONE.................661 295-2600
Kirk Marshall, *President*
Scott Marshall, *Corp Secy*
Kent Marshall, *Vice Pres*
EMP: 100
SQ FT: 35,000
SALES (est): 24.3MM **Privately Held**
SIC: **5047** 3842 Medical laboratory equipment; foot appliances, orthopedic

(P-6975)
MARDX DIAGNOSTICS INC
5919 Farnsworth Ct, Carlsbad (92008-7303)
P.O. Box 1059, Jamestown NY (14702-1059)
PHONE.................760 929-0500
Ian Woodwards, *CEO*
EMP: 53
SQ FT: 21,500
SALES (est): 9.2MM **Privately Held**
SIC: **5047** Diagnostic equipment, medical
HQ: Trinity Biotech, Inc.
2823 Girts Rd
Jamestown NY 14701
800 325-3424

(P-6976)
MENTOR WORLDWIDE LLC
5425 Hollister Ave, Santa Barbara (93111-3341)
PHONE.................805 681-6000
Diane Becker, *Manager*
Troy Hinshaw, *Analyst*
Greg Lynch, *Sales Staff*
Grenham William, *Director*
EMP: 500
SALES (corp-wide): 81.5B **Publicly Held**
WEB: www.mentordirect.com
SIC: **5047** Medical & hospital equipment
HQ: Mentor Worldwide Llc
31 Technology Dr Ste 200
Irvine CA 92618
800 636-8678

(P-6977)
MERRY X-RAY CHEMICAL CORP (PA)
Also Called: M X R
4909 Murphy Canyon Rd # 120, San Diego (92123-4300)
PHONE.................858 565-4472
Ted Sloan, *CEO*
Bernard Amato, *CFO*
Butch Davis, *Regional Mgr*
Joseph Gallagher, *General Mgr*
Sondra Beith, *Admin Sec*
EMP: 153 **EST:** 1958
SQ FT: 10,000
SALES (est): 98.8MM **Privately Held**
SIC: **5047** X-ray machines & tubes; X-ray film & supplies

(P-6978)
MILTENYI BIOTEC INC (HQ)
2303 Lindbergh St, Auburn (95602-9562)
PHONE.................530 745-2800
Stefan Miltenyi, *President*
Barbara Malerstein, *Research*
Sarah Steimer, *Technical Staff*
Christina Stillwell, *Technical Staff*
Joan Blynn, *Accounting Mgr*
▲ EMP: 66
SQ FT: 20,000
SALES (est): 37.5MM
SALES (corp-wide): 423.2MM **Privately Held**
WEB: www.miltenyibiotec.com
SIC: **5047** 8731 Medical & hospital equipment; biotechnical research, commercial
PA: Miltenyi Gmbh
Friedrich-Ebert-Str. 68
Bergisch Gladbach 51429
220 483-060

(P-6979)
MORIGON TECHNOLOGIES LLC
Also Called: Medstop Medical
7615 Fulton Ave, North Hollywood (91605-1805)
PHONE.................818 764-8880
Amaury J Agoncillo, *CEO*
EMP: 50
SQ FT: 8,000
SALES: 2.6MM **Privately Held**
SIC: **5047** Medical equipment & supplies

(P-6980)
NANTBIOSCIENCE INC
9920 Jefferson Blvd, Culver City (90232-3506)
PHONE.................310 883-1300
Patrick Soon-Shiong, *CEO*
EMP: 74
SALES (est): 480.7K
SALES (corp-wide): 154.7MM **Publicly Held**
SIC: **5047** 8099 Medical laboratory equipment; blood related health services
PA: Nantworks, Llc
9920 Jefferson Blvd
Culver City CA 90232
310 883-1300

(P-6981)
NDS SURGICAL IMAGING LLC
5750 Hellyer Ave, San Jose (95138-1000)
PHONE.................408 776-0085
Karim Khadr, *President*
Sam Brown, *CFO*
Dave Cantin, *Vice Pres*
Rainer Scholl, *Vice Pres*
Darko Spoljaric, *Vice Pres*

◆ **EMP:** 215
SQ FT: 73,000
SALES (est): 76.1MM **Publicly Held**
WEB: www.ndssi.com
SIC: 5047 Patient monitoring equipment
HQ: Novanta Corporation
 125 Middlesex Tpke
 Bedford MA 01730
 781 266-5700

(P-6982)
NIHON KOHDEN AMERICA INC (HQ)
15353 Barranca Pkwy, Irvine (92618-2216)
PHONE....................949 580-1555
Fumio Izumida, *CEO*
Barry Klegerman, *President*
Josh Lewis, *President*
Eiichi Tanaka, *President*
Wilson Constantine, *COO*
▲ **EMP:** 60
SQ FT: 35,000
SALES (est): 72.4MM **Privately Held**
WEB: www.nkusa.com
SIC: 5047 Electro-medical equipment

(P-6983)
NOVA ORTHO-MED INC (PA)
1470 Beachey Pl, Carson (90746-4002)
PHONE....................310 352-3600
Sue Chen, *Principal*
Ronald Gaudiano, *Vice Pres*
Robin Castillo, *Warehouse Mgr*
▲ **EMP:** 50
SQ FT: 5,500
SALES (est): 19.6MM **Privately Held**
WEB: www.novaorthomed.com
SIC: 5047 Medical equipment & supplies

(P-6984)
NUVI GLOBAL
518 W Henderson Ave Apt 9, Porterville (93257-1769)
P.O. Box 2568 (93258-2568)
PHONE....................559 306-2646
Herlinda Ruelas, *Owner*
EMP: 600 **EST:** 2014
SALES (est): 16.4MM **Privately Held**
SIC: 5047 Incontinent care products & supplies

(P-6985)
OLYMPUS AMERICA INC
Also Called: OLYMPUS AMERICA INC.
23342 Madero, Mission Viejo (92691-2796)
PHONE....................949 466-3548
EMP: 110 **Privately Held**
SIC: 5047 Medical equipment & supplies; diagnostic equipment, medical
HQ: Olympus America Inc
 3500 Corporate Pkwy
 Center Valley PA 18034
 484 896-5000

(P-6986)
ORCHID MPS
3233 W Harvard St, Santa Ana (92704-3917)
PHONE....................714 549-9203
Mark Deischter, *Vice Pres*
EMP: 100
SALES (est): 12.6MM **Privately Held**
SIC: 5047 Medical equipment & supplies

(P-6987)
OWENS & MINOR INC
5125 Ontario Mills Pkwy, Ontario (91764-5103)
PHONE....................909 944-2100
Tom Kelly, *Branch Mgr*
EMP: 57 **Publicly Held**
WEB: www.owens-minor.com
SIC: 5047 Medical equipment & supplies
PA: Owens & Minor, Inc.
 9120 Lockwood Blvd
 Mechanicsville VA 23116

(P-6988)
OWENS & MINOR INC
18520 Stanford Rd, Tracy (95377-9708)
PHONE....................209 833-4600
Jim Bierman, *President*
EMP: 57 **Publicly Held**
SIC: 5047 Medical equipment & supplies

PA: Owens & Minor, Inc.
 9120 Lockwood Blvd
 Mechanicsville VA 23116

(P-6989)
PATTERSON DENTAL SUPPLY INC
Also Called: Patterson Dental 426
185 S Douglas St Ste 100, El Segundo (90245-4673)
PHONE....................310 426-3100
Ken Sartin, *Manager*
EMP: 75
SALES (corp-wide): 5.5B **Publicly Held**
WEB: www.pattersondentalsupply.com
SIC: 5047 Dental equipment & supplies
HQ: Patterson Dental Supply, Inc.
 1031 Mendota Heights Rd
 Saint Paul MN 55120
 651 686-1600

(P-6990)
PATTERSON DENTAL SUPPLY INC
Also Called: Patterson Dental 454
1030 Winding Creek Rd # 150, Roseville (95678-7045)
PHONE....................916 780-5100
James Ryan, *Manager*
EMP: 69
SALES (corp-wide): 5.5B **Publicly Held**
WEB: www.pattersondentalsupply.com
SIC: 5047 Dental equipment & supplies
HQ: Patterson Dental Supply, Inc.
 1031 Mendota Heights Rd
 Saint Paul MN 55120
 651 686-1600

(P-6991)
PATTERSON DENTAL SUPPLY INC
Also Called: Patterson Dental 590
800 Monte Vista Dr, Dinuba (93618-9117)
PHONE....................559 595-1450
Ceasar Lopez, *Manager*
David Cervantes, *Sales Staff*
EMP: 58
SALES (corp-wide): 5.5B **Publicly Held**
WEB: www.pattersondentalsupply.com
SIC: 5047 Dental equipment & supplies
HQ: Patterson Dental Supply, Inc.
 1031 Mendota Heights Rd
 Saint Paul MN 55120
 651 686-1600

(P-6992)
PHILIPS MEDICAL SYSTEMS CLEVEL
1 Marconi, Irvine (92618-2520)
PHONE....................949 699-2300
David Carter, *Branch Mgr*
EMP: 100
SALES (corp-wide): 20.8B **Privately Held**
SIC: 5047 X-ray machines & tubes; diagnostic equipment, medical; X-ray film & supplies
HQ: Philips Medical Systems (Cleveland), Inc.
 595 Miner Rd
 Cleveland OH 44143
 440 247-2652

(P-6993)
POLESTAR LABS INC
1223 Pacific Oaks Pl # 102, Escondido (92029-2913)
P.O. Box 460249 (92046-0249)
PHONE....................760 480-2600
Michael Dunaway, *CEO*
Charles Chuck Fabijanic, *Senior VP*
Trudy Dunaway, *Admin Sec*
EMP: 70
SALES: 5MM **Privately Held**
SIC: 5047 5999 7699 7363 Medical laboratory equipment; medical apparatus & supplies; laboratory instrument repair; medical help service; management services

(P-6994)
POM MEDICAL LLC
11959 Discovery Ct, Moorpark (93021-7120)
PHONE....................805 306-2105

Jeff Voss,
EMP: 99
SQ FT: 3,000
SALES (est): 774.2K **Privately Held**
SIC: 5047 Oxygen therapy equipment

(P-6995)
PORTERVILLE SHELTERED WORKSHOP
1853 E Cross Ave, Tulare (93274-7388)
PHONE....................559 684-9168
EMP: 59
SALES (corp-wide): 10.4MM **Privately Held**
SIC: 5047
PA: Porterville Sheltered Workshop
 194 W Poplar Ave
 Porterville CA 93257
 559 784-7187

(P-6996)
PRACTICE WARES INC
Also Called: Practicewares Dental Supply
2377 Gold Meadow Way, Gold River (95670-4405)
PHONE....................916 526-2674
EMP: 50
SALES (corp-wide): 12.5MM **Privately Held**
SIC: 5047
PA: Practice Wares, Inc
 3400 E Mcdowell Rd
 Phoenix AZ
 602 225-9090

(P-6997)
PRI MEDICAL TECHNOLOGIES INC (DH)
Also Called: UHS Surgical Services
10939 Pendleton St, Sun Valley (91352-1522)
PHONE....................818 394-2800
Bradley Jacobsen, *CEO*
Louis Buther, *President*
William M McKay, *Treasurer*
Lee Pulju, *Treasurer*
Gary Blackford, *Director*
EMP: 55
SQ FT: 14,500
SALES (est): 18.6MM
SALES (corp-wide): 242.6MM **Privately Held**
SIC: 5047 7352 8741 Instruments, surgical & medical; medical equipment rental; administrative management; financial management for business; personnel management
HQ: Agiliti Health, Inc.
 6625 W 78th St Ste 300
 Minneapolis MN 55439
 952 893-3200

(P-6998)
PROFESSIONAL HOSPITAL SUP INC (HQ)
42500 Winchester Rd, Temecula (92590-2570)
PHONE....................951 699-5000
Jenise Luttgens, *CEO*
John Augustine, *CFO*
Doug Hoffee, *Exec VP*
Rebecca Brown, *Administration*
Cory Dacio, *Info Tech Dir*
▲ **EMP:** 1200
SQ FT: 300,000
SALES (est): 551.2MM
SALES (corp-wide): 5.7B **Privately Held**
WEB: www.phsyes.com
SIC: 5047 Medical equipment & supplies
PA: Medline Industries, Inc.
 3 Lakes Dr
 Northfield IL 60093
 847 949-5500

(P-6999)
RADIOMETER AMERICA INC (HQ)
250 S Kraemer Blvd Ms, Brea (92821-6232)
PHONE....................800 736-0600
Torben Neilson, *President*
Frank T McFaden, *Treasurer*
Cathy Yang, *Vice Pres*
Michaela Koeck, *Administration*
Maryrose Luna, *Technical Staff*

▲ **EMP:** 103
SQ FT: 35,000
SALES (est): 57.6MM
SALES (corp-wide): 19.8B **Publicly Held**
WEB: www.radiometeramerica.com
SIC: 5047 Medical equipment & supplies
PA: Danaher Corporation
 2200 Penn Ave Nw Ste 800w
 Washington DC 20037
 202 828-0850

(P-7000)
RASHMAN CORPORATION
Also Called: Uniform Accessories
8600 Wilbur Ave, Northridge (91324-4438)
PHONE....................818 993-3030
Richard Rashman, *CEO*
Roger Rashman, *Vice Pres*
Cathi Eicher, *Director*
▲ **EMP:** 65 **EST:** 1969
SQ FT: 50,000
SALES (est): 19.3MM **Privately Held**
WEB: www.neve.com
SIC: 5047 Medical equipment & supplies

(P-7001)
SAKURA FINETEK USA INC (HQ)
1750 W 214th St, Torrance (90501-2857)
PHONE....................310 972-7800
Takashi Tsuzuki, *Ch of Bd*
Anthony C Marotti, *President*
Kenichi Matsumoto, *Chm Emeritus*
Kam Patel, *Corp Secy*
◆ **EMP:** 109
SQ FT: 68,000
SALES (est): 60.6MM **Privately Held**
WEB: www.sakura-americas.com
SIC: 5047 Medical laboratory equipment

(P-7002)
SAN JOSE SURGICAL SUPPLY INC (PA)
902 S Bascom Ave, San Jose (95128-3599)
PHONE....................408 293-9033
Dennis J Collins, *President*
Emile Fatha, *Director*
Bob Reggiani, *Accounts Exec*
▲ **EMP:** 50
SQ FT: 15,000
SALES (est): 18.6MM **Privately Held**
WEB: www.sjsurgical.com
SIC: 5047 5122 Surgical equipment & supplies; pharmaceuticals

(P-7003)
SENDX MEDICAL INC (DH)
1945 Palomar Oaks Way # 100, Carlsbad (92011-1300)
PHONE....................760 930-6300
Todd Fletcher, *President*
Doreen Milford, *President*
Matt Leader, *Vice Pres*
John Worley, *Vice Pres*
▲ **EMP:** 53 **EST:** 1998
SQ FT: 35,000
SALES (est): 45.1MM
SALES (corp-wide): 19.8B **Publicly Held**
WEB: www.danaher-dps.com
SIC: 5047 Medical equipment & supplies
HQ: Dhcdan Holding Aps
 Akandevej 21
 BrOnshOj 2700
 382 738-27

(P-7004)
SHIELD-DENVER HEALTH CARE CTR (HQ)
Also Called: Shield Healthcare
27911 Franklin Pkwy, Valencia (91355-4110)
PHONE....................661 294-4200
Jim Snell, *President*
Jeffery Thompson, *Corp Secy*
Tina Borella, *Admin Asst*
Robert Davey, *Info Tech Mgr*
Cheryl Hornberger, *VP Sales*
EMP: 200
SQ FT: 95,000
SALES (est): 37.7MM **Privately Held**
SIC: 5047 Medical & hospital equipment

▲ = Import ▼=Export
◆ =Import/Export

(P-7005)
SHIMADZU PRECISION INSTRS INC
Shimadzu Medical Systems
20101 S Vermont Ave, Torrance
(90502-1328)
PHONE..................310 217-8855
Akinori Yamaguchi, *President*
Annette Carlisle, *Administration*
Chiho Lynch, *Accountant*
Christina Gonzalez, *HR Admin*
EMP: 80 **Privately Held**
WEB: www.spi-inc.com
SIC: 5047 Medical equipment & supplies
HQ: Shimadzu Precision Instruments, Inc.
3645 N Lakewood Blvd
Long Beach CA 90808
562 420-6226

(P-7006)
SIEMENS MED SOLUTIONS USA INC
Ultra Sound Division
685 E Middlefield Rd, Mountain View
(94043-4045)
P.O. Box 7393 (94039-7393)
PHONE..................650 694-5747
Franz Wiehler, *CFO*
Gayatri James, *Admin Asst*
Henry Lai, *Director*
Shelly Pearce, *Manager*
EMP: 300
SQ FT: 373,000
SALES (corp-wide): 95B **Privately Held**
WEB: www.siemensmedical.com
SIC: 5047 Diagnostic equipment, medical
HQ: Siemens Medical Solutions Usa, Inc.
40 Liberty Blvd
Malvern PA 19355
888 826-9702

(P-7007)
SOUND TECHNOLOGIES INC
Also Called: Sound-Eklin
5810 Van Allen Way, Carlsbad
(92008-7300)
PHONE..................760 918-9626
Robert Antin, *President*
Craig Hamasaki, *Manager*
Robert Jacobi, *Manager*
Linda Zalewski, *Manager*
▼ EMP: 52
SQ FT: 11,933
SALES (est): 40.7MM
SALES (corp-wide): 37.6B **Privately Held**
WEB: www.soundvet.com
SIC: 5047 Veterinarians' equipment & supplies
HQ: Vca Inc.
12401 W Olympic Blvd
Los Angeles CA 90064
310 571-6500

(P-7008)
SUPER CARE INC
12176 Industrial Blvd, Victorville
(92395-5879)
PHONE..................760 245-2034
EMP: 80
SALES (corp-wide): 64MM **Privately Held**
SIC: 5047 Instruments, surgical & medical
PA: Super Care, Inc.
8345 Firestone Blvd # 210
Downey CA 90241
800 206-4880

(P-7009)
TEAM MAKENA LLC (PA)
Also Called: Restore Motion
27051 Towne Centre Dr # 180, Foothill Ranch (92610-2819)
PHONE..................949 474-1753
Mark Tymchenko, *Sales Staff*
Jim Schuerger,
EMP: 53
SALES: 14.6MM **Privately Held**
SIC: 5047 Hospital equipment & supplies

(P-7010)
TEAM POST-OP INC (DH)
17256 Red Hill Ave, Irvine (92614-5628)
P.O. Box 650846, Dallas TX (75265-0846)
PHONE..................949 253-5500
Jeffrey Salamon, *President*

Lisa Salamon, *Admin Sec*
EMP: 60
SQ FT: 1,400
SALES (est): 14MM
SALES (corp-wide): 1B **Publicly Held**
SIC: 5047 Orthopedic equipment & supplies
HQ: Hanger Prosthetics & Orthotics, Inc.
10910 Domain Dr Ste 300
Austin TX 78758
512 777-3800

(P-7011)
THERAPAK LLC (DH)
651 Wharton Dr, Claremont (91711-4819)
PHONE..................909 267-2000
Todd Gates, *President*
Arbi Harootoonian, *Vice Pres*
Fanie Bernardo, *General Mgr*
Brent Dixon, *Project Mgr*
Charlotte Wiltshire, *Project Mgr*
◆ EMP: 70
SQ FT: 24,000
SALES (est): 296.1MM
SALES (corp-wide): 1.4B **Publicly Held**
WEB: www.therapak.com
SIC: 5047 Medical equipment & supplies; diagnostic equipment, medical
HQ: Vwr Corporation
Radnor Corp Ctr 1 200
Radnor PA 19087
610 386-1700

(P-7012)
TOSOH BIOSCIENCE INC
Also Called: Tosoh USA
6000 Shoreline Ct Ste 101, South San Francisco (94080-7606)
PHONE..................650 615-4970
Max Yamata, *President*
▲ EMP: 75
SQ FT: 13,917
SALES (est): 16.5MM **Privately Held**
WEB: www.tosohbioscience.com
SIC: 5047 Diagnostic equipment, medical
HQ: Tosoh America, Inc.
3600 Gantz Rd
Grove City OH 43123
614 539-8622

(P-7013)
TRADECOM MED TRANSCRIPTION INC
363 Piercy Rd, San Jose (95138-1403)
PHONE..................408 225-9200
Samit Shah, *President*
Dhaval Patel, *CFO*
Ram Mankad, *Vice Pres*
Deval Nanavati, *Vice Pres*
Deanna De Guzman, *Opers Mgr*
EMP: 110 EST: 1997
SQ FT: 1,500
SALES: 850K **Privately Held**
WEB: www.tradecomusa.com
SIC: 5047 X-ray machines & tubes; diagnostic equipment, medical

(P-7014)
TWIN MED LLC (PA)
11333 Greenstone Ave, Santa Fe Springs (90670-4618)
PHONE..................323 582-9900
David Blonder, *Mktg Dir*
Michael Lawler, *COO*
David Klarner, *CFO*
Jason Goulding, *Vice Pres*
ARI Landau, *Vice Pres*
EMP: 79
SALES (est): 217.2MM **Privately Held**
SIC: 5047 8082 8093 Medical equipment & supplies; home health care services; specialty outpatient clinics

(P-7015)
ULTRA SOLUTIONS LLC
1137 E Philadelphia St, Ontario (91761-5611)
PHONE..................909 628-1778
Sterling Peloso, *CEO*
Tommy Ly, *Vice Pres*
Felix Hoang, *Engineer*
Michelle York, *Analyst*
Bang Nguyen, *Opers Mgr*
▲ EMP: 50
SQ FT: 7,500

SALES (est): 19.8MM **Privately Held**
SIC: 5047 Diagnostic equipment, medical; medical equipment & supplies

(P-7016)
VETERINARY SERVICE INC
935 Palmyrita Ave, Riverside (92507-1819)
PHONE..................951 328-4900
Colin Anderson, *Branch Mgr*
EMP: 57
SALES (corp-wide): 180.1MM **Privately Held**
WEB: www.vsi.cc
SIC: 5047 5199 5083 Veterinarians' equipment & supplies; pet supplies; poultry equipment
PA: Veterinary Service, Inc.
4100 Bangs Ave
Modesto CA 95356
209 545-5100

(P-7017)
VIDENT
Also Called: Vita North America
22705 Savi Ranch Pkwy # 100, Yorba Linda (92887-4604)
PHONE..................714 221-6700
Emanuel Rauter, *CEO*
Jobe Dubbs, *Vice Pres*
Greg Romeo, *Vice Pres*
Janet Siwinski, *Business Dir*
Nhi Nguyen, *General Mgr*
▲ EMP: 70
SQ FT: 43,000
SALES (est): 24.6MM
SALES (corp-wide): 127.5MM **Privately Held**
WEB: www.vident.com
SIC: 5047 Dental equipment & supplies
HQ: Vita - Zahnfabrik H. Rauter Gesellschaft Mit Beschrankter Haftung & Co Kg
Spitalgasse 3
Bad Sackingen 79713
776 156-20

(P-7018)
VIEWRAY TECHNOLOGIES INC
815 E Middlefield Rd, Mountain View (94043-4025)
PHONE..................650 252-0920
EMP: 75
SALES (corp-wide): 80.9MM **Publicly Held**
SIC: 5047 Medical & hospital equipment
HQ: Viewray Technologies, Inc.
2 Thermo Fisher Way
Oakwood Village OH 44146
440 703-3210

5048 Ophthalmic Goods Wholesale

(P-7019)
ABB/CON-CISE OPTICAL GROUP LLC
Also Called: Primary Eyecare Network
1750 N Loop Rd Ste 150, Alameda (94502-8013)
PHONE..................800 852-8089
EMP: 80
SALES (corp-wide): 1.3B **Privately Held**
SIC: 5048 5044
HQ: Abb/Con-Cise Optical Group Llc
12301 Nw 39th St
Coral Springs FL 33065
800 852-8089

(P-7020)
ABB/CON-CISE OPTICAL GROUP LLC
Also Called: ABB Optical Group
1750 N Loop Rd Ste 150, Alameda (94502-8013)
PHONE..................510 483-9400
Angel Alvarez, *CEO*
Shelley Farley, *Executive*
Christine Goepp, *Accounts Exec*
EMP: 80
SALES (corp-wide): 353MM **Privately Held**
SIC: 5048 5049 Ophthalmic goods; optical goods

HQ: Abb/Con-Cise Optical Group Llc
12301 Nw 39th St
Coral Springs FL 33065

(P-7021)
ATLANTIC OPTICAL CO INC
Also Called: Ltd Eyewear
9747 Independence Ave, Chatsworth (91311-4318)
P.O. Box 3519 (91313-3519)
PHONE..................818 407-1890
Sheldon H Lehrer, *President*
Chett Lehrer, *Corp Secy*
Keith Lehrer, *Vice Pres*
Rob Blatt, *Regl Sales Mgr*
▲ EMP: 80 EST: 1950
SALES (est): 11.1MM **Privately Held**
SIC: 5048 Frames, ophthalmic

(P-7022)
ESSILOR LABORATORIES AMER INC
Also Called: Bartley Optical
1300 W Optical Dr, Irwindale (91702-3282)
PHONE..................626 969-6181
Robert Babcock, *Manager*
EMP: 70
SALES (corp-wide): 1.4MM **Privately Held**
WEB: www.crizal.com
SIC: 5048 3851 Frames, ophthalmic; lenses, ophthalmic; ophthalmic goods
HQ: Essilor Laboratories Of America, Inc.
13515 N Stemmons Fwy
Dallas TX 75234
972 241-4141

(P-7023)
MARCOLIN USA INC
Also Called: Viva International
6 Janet Way Apt 116, Belvedere Tiburon (94920-2164)
PHONE..................415 383-6348
EMP: 66 **Privately Held**
SIC: 5048 5099
HQ: Marcolin U.S.A., Inc.
3140 Us Highway 22
Branchburg NJ 08876
800 345-8482

(P-7024)
NEOSTYLE EYEWEAR CORPORATION
2651 La Mirada Dr Ste 150, Vista (92081-8435)
PHONE..................760 305-4004
Helmuth Igel, *President*
Helga Igel, *Corp Secy*
EMP: 70
SQ FT: 17,000
SALES (est): 9.4MM **Privately Held**
WEB: www.neostyle.com
SIC: 5048 Frames, ophthalmic

(P-7025)
NIDEK INCORPORATED
2040 Corporate Ct, San Jose (95131-1753)
PHONE..................510 226-5700
Motoki Ozawa, *CEO*
Hideo Ozawa, *Ch of Bd*
Jun Iwata, *COO*
Gary Mikaelian, *Research*
Faye Custodio, *Technology*
◆ EMP: 50
SALES (est): 18.1MM **Privately Held**
SIC: 5048 8011 3845 3841 Optometric equipment & supplies; offices & clinics of medical doctors; electromedical equipment; surgical & medical instruments; electrical equipment & supplies
PA: Nidek Co.,Ltd.
34-14, Maehama, Hiroishicho
Gamagori AIC 443-0

P
R
O
D
U
C
T
S

&

S
V
C
S

5049 Professional Eqpt & Splys, NEC Wholesale

(P-7026)
ABC SCHOOL EQUIPMENT INC
Also Called: Platinum Visual Systems
1451 E 6th St, Corona (92879-1715)
PHONE..................................951 817-2200
Gary P Stell Jr, *CEO*
Thomas Mendez, *CFO*
Demiris Reid, *Project Mgr*
Tom Mendez, *Controller*
Tim Brantley, *VP Sales*
EMP: 70
SQ FT: 35,000
SALES (est): 29.7MM **Privately Held**
WEB: www.abcschoolequipment.com
SIC: 5049 3861 2531 School supplies;
  photographic equipment & supplies; public building & related furniture

(P-7027)
CPI INTERNATIONAL
5580 Skylane Blvd, Santa Rosa
(95403-1030)
PHONE..................................707 521-6327
Ryan Vice, *CEO*
Joseph Phillips, *CFO*
Tommy Mitchell, *Vice Pres*
▲ EMP: 70
SQ FT: 20,000
SALES (est): 18.7MM **Privately Held**
WEB: www.colitag.com
SIC: 5049 3826 Analytical instruments;
  analytical instruments

(P-7028)
FACTORY R D
23192 Verdugo Dr, Laguna Hills
(92653-1377)
PHONE..................................949 900-3460
Tom Swanecamp, *Owner*
EMP: 60
SALES (est): 1.7MM **Privately Held**
SIC: 5049 Engineers' equipment & supplies

(P-7029)
FISHER SCIENTIFIC COMPANY LLC
6722 Bickmore Ave, Chino (91708-9101)
PHONE..................................909 393-2100
John Pouk, *Vice Pres*
EMP: 100
SALES (corp-wide): 24.3B **Publicly Held**
WEB: www.fishersci.com
SIC: 5049 Laboratory equipment, except
  medical or dental
HQ: Fisher Scientific Company Llc
  300 Industry Dr
  Pittsburgh PA 15275
  724 517-1500

(P-7030)
INTERLAB INC
636 Broadway Ste 322, San Diego
(92101-5410)
PHONE..................................619 302-3095
Alexander Vedemin, *President*
Boris Urslts, *Admin Sec*
▼ EMP: 50
SALES (est): 18MM **Privately Held**
SIC: 5049 Laboratory equipment, except
  medical or dental

(P-7031)
R C I ENTERPRISES INC
Also Called: R C I Image Systems
3848 Del Amo Blvd Ste 301, Torrance
(90503-7711)
PHONE..................................310 370-5900
Richard Corrales, *President*
Lynda Deibner, *Corp Secy*
Lyla Corrales, *Vice Pres*
Vickie Corrales, *Vice Pres*
Eric Gungab, *Info Tech Mgr*
EMP: 50
SQ FT: 12,000
SALES (est): 7.8MM **Privately Held**
SIC: 5049 7389 Optical goods; microfilm
  recording & developing service

(P-7032)
REM OPTICAL COMPANY INC
Also Called: REM Eye Wear
10941 La Tuna Canyon Rd, Sun Valley
(91352-2012)
PHONE..................................818 504-3950
Michael L Hundert, *CEO*
Steve Horowitz, *President*
Donna Gindy, *COO*
Gerry Hundert, *Chairman*
Donna Nakawaki, *Senior VP*
◆ EMP: 100
SQ FT: 42,000
SALES (est): 50.9MM **Privately Held**
WEB: www.remeyewear.com
SIC: 5049 Optical goods

(P-7033)
RINCON TECHNOLOGY INC (PA)
810 E Montecito St, Santa Barbara
(93103-3221)
P.O. Box 123081, Dallas TX (75312-3081)
PHONE..................................805 684-8100
Jason Kelly, *President*
Jody Hearron, *President*
Michael J Bartling, *Vice Pres*
Matt Flanagan, *Executive*
Ken Clark, *Business Dir*
EMP: 50
SQ FT: 15,000
SALES (est): 38.5MM **Privately Held**
WEB: www.rincontechnology.com
SIC: 5049 3825 Scientific & engineering
  equipment & supplies; network analyzers

(P-7034)
SOCIAL STUDIES SCHOOL SERVICE
Also Called: Writing Company
10200 Jefferson Blvd, Culver City
(90232-3524)
P.O. Box 802 (90232-0802)
PHONE..................................310 839-2436
David M Weigner, *CEO*
Irwin Ledin, *President*
Sanford Weiner, *President*
Dawn Dawson, *Director*
▲ EMP: 65 EST: 1967
SALES (est): 34.2MM **Privately Held**
WEB: www.socialstudies.com
SIC: 5049 School supplies

(P-7035)
TECAN SP INC
14180 Live Oak Ave, Baldwin Park
(91706-1350)
P.O. Box 1608 (91706-7608)
PHONE..................................626 962-0010
Philip A Dimson, *CEO*
Christian Herr, *CFO*
Nancy Dimson, *Train & Dev Mgr*
▲ EMP: 84
SALES (est): 2.5MM
SALES (corp-wide): 597.4MM **Privately Held**
WEB: www.speware.com
SIC: 5049 Laboratory equipment, except
  medical or dental
PA: Tecan Group Ag
  Seestrasse 103
  MAnnedorf ZH 8708
  449 228-888

(P-7036)
VWR INTERNATIONAL LLC
Also Called: VWR Scientific
6609 Mount Whitney Dr, Buena Park
(90620-4237)
PHONE..................................714 220-2615
Jenny Nelson, *Branch Mgr*
Devin Davis, *Vice Pres*
Aguilar Debbie, *Area Spvr*
Joell Aubrey, *Technician*
Tim Litchfield, *Project Mgr*
EMP: 50
SALES (corp-wide): 1.4B **Publicly Held**
WEB: www.vwrsp.com
SIC: 5049 5169 Laboratory equipment,
  except medical or dental; chemicals & allied products
HQ: Vwr International, Llc
  100 W Matsonford Rd # 1
  Radnor PA 19087
  610 386-1700

5051 Metals Service Centers

(P-7037)
ACME METALS & STEEL SUPPLY
14930 S San Pedro St, Gardena
(90248-2036)
PHONE..................................310 329-2263
Jack Goldberg, *Chairman*
Avelino Garcia, *General Mgr*
Cristina Martinez, *Controller*
◆ EMP: 60
SQ FT: 265,000
SALES (est): 42.5MM **Privately Held**
SIC: 5051 Steel

(P-7038)
ACME METALS LLC
Also Called: Acme Metals & Steel Supply
14930 S San Pedro St, Gardena
(90248-2036)
PHONE..................................310 329-2263
Howard Brand, *CEO*
EMP: 60
SQ FT: 240,000
SALES (est): 38MM **Privately Held**
SIC: 5051 Pipe & tubing, steel

(P-7039)
AJ OSTER WEST LLC
Also Called: Ajo
22833 La Palma Ave, Yorba Linda
(92887-4767)
PHONE..................................714 692-1000
Aaron Baldridge, *General Mgr*
Marc R Bacon, *CFO*
Robert M James, *Vice Pres*
Joseph T Woo, *Vice Pres*
Jorge Nieves, *Plant Mgr*
▲ EMP: 57
SQ FT: 55,000
SALES (est): 22MM
SALES (corp-wide): 4.8MM **Privately Held**
WEB: www.olinbrass.com
SIC: 5051 Metals service centers & offices
HQ: Wieland Metal Services, Llc
  301 Metro Center Blvd # 204
  Warwick RI 02886
  401 736-2600

(P-7040)
ALPERT & ALPERT IRON & MET INC
2350 W 16th St, Long Beach (90813-1044)
PHONE..................................562 624-8833
George Soto, *Branch Mgr*
EMP: 50
SALES (corp-wide): 51.1MM **Privately Held**
SIC: 5051 Iron & steel (ferrous) products;
  miscellaneous nonferrous products
PA: Alpert & Alpert Iron & Metal, Inc.
  1815 S Soto St
  Los Angeles CA 90023
  323 265-4040

(P-7041)
ALUMINUM PRECISION PDTS INC (PA)
3333 W Warner Ave, Santa Ana
(92704-5898)
PHONE..................................714 546-8125
Gregory S Keeler, *President*
Simona Manoiu, *CFO*
Greg Keeler, *Vice Pres*
Roark Keeler, *Vice Pres*
David P Silva, *Vice Pres*
◆ EMP: 550
SALES (est): 212MM **Privately Held**
WEB: www.aluminumprecision.com
SIC: 5051 Metals service centers & offices

(P-7042)
AM PRODUCTS INC
1661 Palm St, Santa Ana (92701-5189)
PHONE..................................714 662-4454
Tim Van Mechelen, *President*
Case Van Mechelen, *CEO*
EMP: 50
SALES (est): 6.6MM **Privately Held**
WEB: www.amproducts.net
SIC: 5051 5072 Sheets, metal; structural
  shapes, iron or steel; power tools & accessories

(P-7043)
AMERICAN METALS CORPORATION (HQ)
1499 Parkway Blvd, West Sacramento
(95691-5019)
P.O. Box 980100 (95798-0100)
PHONE..................................916 371-7700
Nicole Heater, *CEO*
Thomas Gimbel, *Bd of Directors*
John Walls, *Safety Mgr*
Teisha Duffey, *Sales Staff*
Robert Falcone, *Sales Staff*
▲ EMP: 105
SALES (est): 94.7MM
SALES (corp-wide): 11.5B **Publicly Held**
WEB: www.rsac.com
SIC: 5051 Iron or steel flat products; castings, rough: iron or steel; steel; aluminum
  bars, rods, ingots, sheets, pipes, plates,
  etc.
PA: Reliance Steel & Aluminum Co.
  350 S Grand Ave Ste 5100
  Los Angeles CA 90071
  213 687-7700

(P-7044)
AOC TECHNOLOGIES INC
5960 Inglewood Dr, Pleasanton
(94588-8610)
PHONE..................................925 875-0808
Gordon Gu, *President*
▲ EMP: 315
SALES (est): 124.4MM **Privately Held**
WEB: www.aoctech.com
SIC: 5051 3357 Metal wires, ties, cables &
  screening; fiber optic cable (insulated)

(P-7045)
ARCHITECTURAL GL & ALUM CO INC (PA)
6400 Brisa St, Livermore (94550-2550)
PHONE..................................925 583-2460
Joseph Brescia, *CEO*
John Buckley, *President*
William Coll Jr, *Vice Pres*
Dan Romine, *Vice Pres*
William Coll Sr, *Admin Sec*
▲ EMP: 155 EST: 1970
SQ FT: 33,000
SALES (est): 145.6MM **Privately Held**
SIC: 5051 1793 1791 3442 Aluminum
  bars, rods, ingots, sheets, pipes, plates,
  etc.; glass & glazing work; exterior wall
  system installation; sash, door or window:
  metal

(P-7046)
ASC PROFILES LLC (DH)
Also Called: ASC Building Products
2110 Enterprise Blvd, West Sacramento
(95691-3428)
PHONE..................................916 376-2800
Sarah Deukmejian, *CEO*
Paul Warme, *CFO*
Marie Ortega, *Info Tech Dir*
Shane Smith, *Info Tech Mgr*
Scott Sonneborn, *Project Mgr*
EMP: 85 EST: 1972
SQ FT: 87,120
SALES (est): 92.1MM **Privately Held**
WEB: www.ascpacific.com
SIC: 5051 Steel

(P-7047)
B & B SURPLUS INC (PA)
Also Called: B & B Specialty Metals
7020 Rosedale Hwy, Bakersfield
(93308-5842)
PHONE..................................661 589-0381
Donice Boylan, *President*
Mike Georgino, *Vice Pres*
Allen Arrington, *Admin Sec*
Michael Arrington, *Credit Mgr*
Katherine Johansen, *Credit Mgr*
▲ EMP: 65 EST: 1964
SQ FT: 20,000
SALES (est): 49.6MM **Privately Held**
SIC: 5051 Steel

(P-7048)
BLUE CHIP STAMPS
301 E Colo Blvd Ste 300, Pasadena
(91101)
PHONE..................................626 585-6700
Robert H Bird, *CEO*
Charles T Munger, *CEO*
Jeffrey L Jacobson, *CFO*
Kenneth E Wittmeyer, *Vice Pres*
EMP: 3074 **EST:** 1956
SQ FT: 123,732
SALES (est): 221.8MM
SALES (corp-wide): 225.3B **Publicly
Held**
WEB: www.bluechipstamps.com
SIC: 5051 Steel
PA: Berkshire Hathaway Inc.
3555 Farnam St Ste 1140
Omaha NE 68131
402 346-1400

(P-7049)
BORRMANN METAL CENTER
(PA)
110 W Olive Ave, Burbank (91502-1822)
PHONE..................................818 846-7171
Robert Wedeen, *President*
Bob Persson, *President*
Jane Borrmann, *CEO*
William L Todd, *Corp Secy*
Lisa Castillo, *Human Resources*
▲ **EMP:** 60 **EST:** 1946
SQ FT: 75,000
SALES: 43MM **Privately Held**
WEB: www.borrmannmetalcenter.com
SIC: 5051 Steel

(P-7050)
BPS SUPPLY GROUP (PA)
Also Called: Imperial Pipe & Supply
3301 Zachary Ave, Shafter (93263-9424)
P.O. Box 639, Bakersfield (93302-0639)
PHONE..................................661 589-9141
Dwight Byrum, *Chairman*
Dan Byrum, *President*
John Byrum, *COO*
Cary Evans, *CFO*
Dwight Byrumm, *Chairman*
◆ **EMP:** 60 **EST:** 1968
SQ FT: 20,000
SALES (est): 152.7MM **Privately Held**
SIC: 5051 5085 Pipe & tubing, steel;
valves & fittings

(P-7051)
CALIFORNIA STEEL AND TUBE
LLC
16049 Stephens St, City of Industry
(91745-1717)
PHONE..................................626 968-5511
Rick Hirsch, *President*
Ron Prichard, *Vice Pres*
James Udell, *Info Tech Mgr*
EMP: 108 **EST:** 1952
SQ FT: 108,000
SALES (est): 27.5MM
SALES (corp-wide): 7.7B **Privately Held**
WEB: www.californiasteelandtube.com
SIC: 5051 Steel
HQ: Kloeckner Metals Corporation
500 Colonial Center Pkwy # 500
Roswell GA 30076

(P-7052)
CALPIPE INDUSTRIES LLC (HQ)
Also Called: Calbond
19440 S Dminguez Hills Dr, Rancho
Dominguez (90220-6417)
PHONE..................................562 803-4388
Daniel J Markus, *CEO*
Fred Arjani, *CFO*
Sheri Caine-Markus, *Admin Sec*
▲ **EMP:** 150
SQ FT: 60,000
SALES (est): 79.8MM **Publicly Held**
SIC: 5051 3498 Metals service centers &
offices; fabricated pipe & fittings; tube fab-
ricating (contract bending & shaping)

(P-7053)
CHROME DEPOSIT CORP
Also Called: Roll Technology West
900 Loveridge Rd, Pittsburg (94565-2808)
P.O. Box 472 (94565-0047)
PHONE..................................925 432-4507
Jim Goehring, *General Mgr*
EMP: 91
SALES (est): 15.8MM **Privately Held**
SIC: 5051 Steel

(P-7054)
CLEMENT SUPPORT SERVICES
INC
1001 Yosemite Dr, Milpitas (95035-5409)
PHONE..................................408 227-1171
Anthony Clement, *CEO*
John White, *CFO*
Michelle Clement, *Vice Pres*
Mike Golini, *Vice Pres*
EMP: 54
SQ FT: 36,000
SALES (est): 36.7MM **Privately Held**
WEB: www.clementsupport.com
SIC: 5051 Nonferrous metal sheets, bars,
rods, etc.

(P-7055)
CMC STEEL FABRICATORS INC
5425 Industrial Pkwy, San Bernardino
(92407-1803)
PHONE..................................909 713-1130
Lee Albright, *Manager*
EMP: 65 **Privately Held**
SIC: 5051 Steel
HQ: Cmc Steel Fabricators, Inc.
3880 Murphy Canyon Rd # 100
San Diego CA 92123

(P-7056)
COAST ALUM &
ARCHITECTURAL INC (PA)
10628 Fulton Wells Ave, Santa Fe Springs
(90670-3740)
P.O. Box 2144 (90670-0440)
PHONE..................................562 946-6061
Thomas C Clark, *President*
Bonnie Clark, *Shareholder*
Julio Marrero, *COO*
Charley Holton, *Branch Mgr*
Raul Colindres, *IT/INT Sup*
▲ **EMP:** 125
SQ FT: 112,000
SALES (est): 198.4MM **Privately Held**
SIC: 5051 Miscellaneous nonferrous prod-
ucts; nonferrous metal sheets, bars, rods,
etc.

(P-7057)
CONCORD IRON WORKS INC
Also Called: C I W
1501 Loveridge Rd Ste 15, Pittsburg
(94565-2812)
PHONE..................................925 432-0136
Jill Lee, *President*
Rita Gonsalves, *Corp Secy*
Jill M Lee, *Vice Pres*
David Maggi, *Vice Pres*
Rosa Cendejas, *Office Mgr*
EMP: 50
SQ FT: 65,000
SALES (est): 30.5MM **Privately Held**
WEB: www.concordiron.com
SIC: 5051 Steel

(P-7058)
CREST STEEL CORPORATION
6580 General Rd, Riverside (92509-0103)
PHONE..................................310 830-2651
James D Hoffman, *CEO*
Kris Farris, *President*
David Vercuche, *CFO*
Dave Zertuche, *CFO*
George Morris, *General Mgr*
▲ **EMP:** 90
SQ FT: 12,000
SALES (est): 118.8MM
SALES (corp-wide): 11.5B **Publicly Held**
SIC: 5051 Steel
PA: Reliance Steel & Aluminum Co.
350 S Grand Ave Ste 5100
Los Angeles CA 90071
213 687-7700

(P-7059)
DANIEL GERARD WORLDWIDE
INC
Also Called: City Wire Cloth
13055 Jurupa Ave, Fontana (92337-6982)
PHONE..................................951 361-1111
Todd Snelbaker, *Manager*
EMP: 71
SQ FT: 50,000
SALES (corp-wide): 77.9MM **Privately
Held**
WEB: www.gerarddaniels.com
SIC: 5051 3496 3356 3315 Wire; mesh,
made from purchased wire; nonferrous
rolling & drawing; steel wire & related
products
PA: Daniel Gerard Worldwide Inc
34 Barnhart Dr
Hanover PA 17331
800 232-3332

(P-7060)
DIX METALS INC
14801 Able Ln Ste 101, Huntington Beach
(92647-2059)
PHONE..................................714 677-0777
Donald Carr, *Vice Pres*
Stefanie Salazar, *COO*
Bob Dix Sr, *Vice Pres*
Jon Nutter, *Sales Associate*
▲ **EMP:** 59
SQ FT: 111,000
SALES (est): 28.9MM **Privately Held**
WEB: www.dixmetals.com
SIC: 5051 Ferrous metals; nonferrous
metal sheets, bars, rods, etc.

(P-7061)
DOUGLAS STEEL SUPPLY INC
(PA)
Also Called: Douglas Steel Supply Co.
4804 Laurel Canyon Blvd, Valley Village
(91607-3717)
PHONE..................................323 587-7676
Douglas Stein, *CEO*
Don Hecht, *Vice Pres*
Donal Hecht, *Vice Pres*
Theresa Gomez, *Sales Associate*
Ken Mc Dermott, *Director*
EMP: 67
SQ FT: 100,000
SALES (est): 33.6MM **Privately Held**
WEB: www.douglassteelsupply.com
SIC: 5051 Steel; sheets, metal

(P-7062)
E JORDAN BROOKES CO INC
(PA)
Also Called: E Jordan Brookes Co.
10634 Shoemaker Ave, Santa Fe Springs
(90670-4038)
PHONE..................................562 968-2100
Robert Brooke, *CEO*
R J Brookes Jr, *President*
Robert J Brookes Jr, *President*
Valentine Brookes, *Corp Secy*
Stephen Johnson, *Business Mgr*
◆ **EMP:** 69
SQ FT: 75,000
SALES (est): 47.5MM **Privately Held**
WEB: www.ejbco.com
SIC: 5051 Metals service centers & offices

(P-7063)
EARLE M JORGENSEN
COMPANY
Also Called: EMJ Hayward
31100 Wiegman Rd, Hayward
(94544-7850)
PHONE..................................510 487-2700
Barbara Nemeth, *Branch Mgr*
Richard Kotalik, *Sales Associate*
EMP: 54
SQ FT: 91,982
SALES (corp-wide): 11.5B **Publicly Held**
WEB: www.emjmetals.com
SIC: 5051 Steel
HQ: Earle M. Jorgensen Company
10650 Alameda St
Lynwood CA 90262
323 567-1122

(P-7064)
EARLE M JORGENSEN
COMPANY
350 S Grand Ave Ste 5100, Los Angeles
(90071-3421)
PHONE..................................323 567-1122
Janice Day, *Manager*
Steve Munro, *Manager*
EMP: 54
SALES (corp-wide): 11.5B **Publicly Held**
SIC: 5051 Steel
HQ: Earle M. Jorgensen Company
10650 Alameda St
Lynwood CA 90262
323 567-1122

(P-7065)
FALLON LAND COMPANY INC
Also Called: Southland Steel
4 Corporate Plaza Dr # 210, Newport
Beach (92660-7906)
P.O. Box 1755 (92659-0755)
PHONE..................................213 880-1279
Robert Fallon, *President*
EMP: 50
SQ FT: 48,000
SALES (est): 9.9MM **Privately Held**
SIC: 5051 Metals service centers & offices

(P-7066)
GEORG FISCHER LLC (DH)
Also Called: Georg Fischer Piping
9271 Jeronimo Rd, Irvine (92618-1906)
PHONE..................................714 731-8800
James Jackson,
Daniel Vaterlaus, *Officer*
Max Holloway, *Vice Pres*
Thomas Sixsmith, *Vice Pres*
Kuno Lischer, *General Mgr*
◆ **EMP:** 70
SQ FT: 55,000
SALES: 69.3MM
SALES (corp-wide): 4.6B **Privately Held**
WEB: www.us.piping.georgefischer.com
SIC: 5051 5085 Pipe & tubing, steel;
valves & fittings
HQ: George Fischer, Inc.
3401 Aero Jet Ave
El Monte CA 91731
626 571-2770

(P-7067)
GLOBAL STAINLESS SUPPLY
17006 S Figueroa St, Gardena
(90248-3019)
PHONE..................................310 525-1865
Art Shelton, *President*
Michelle Brunlehler, *Exec Sec*
▲ **EMP:** 300
SALES (est): 19.8MM **Privately Held**
SIC: 5051 Steel

(P-7068)
GVS ITALY
8616 La Tijera Blvd, Los Angeles
(90045-3944)
PHONE..................................424 382-4343
Bruno Montesano, *Manager*
EMP: 100
SALES: 30MM **Privately Held**
SIC: 5051 Aluminum bars, rods, ingots,
sheets, pipes, plates, etc.

(P-7069)
HARBOR PIPE AND STEEL INC
Also Called: James Metals
1495 Columbia Ave Bldg 10, Riverside
(92507-2074)
PHONE..................................951 369-3990
Joseph W Beattie, *President*
Martha Fournier, *Corp Secy*
Joe Beattie, *Principal*
Tom Liljegren, *Principal*
P Jay Peterson, *Principal*
▲ **EMP:** 150 **EST:** 1962
SALES (est): 134.5MM **Privately Held**
SIC: 5051 Steel

(P-7070)
HARTMAN INDUSTRIES
Also Called: Commercial Casting Co
14933 Whittram Ave, Fontana
(92335-3186)
PHONE..................................909 428-0114
Brad J Hartman, *CEO*
Brett Hartman, *Vice Pres*

P
R
O
D
U
C
T
S

&

S
V
C
S

Sean Hartman, *Vice Pres*
Russ Hartman, *Manager*
▲ **EMP:** 60
SQ FT: 73,000
SALES: 8MM **Privately Held**
WEB: www.cmeworkholding.com
SIC: 5051 Castings, rough: iron or steel

(P-7071)
HUBBARD IRON DOORS INC
7407 Telegraph Rd, Montebello
(90640-6515)
PHONE..................323 724-6500
Ron Hubbard, *President*
EMP: 50
SQ FT: 20,000
SALES (est): 12MM **Privately Held**
WEB: www.hubbardirondoors.com
SIC: 5051 Iron or steel semifinished products

(P-7072)
INFINITY METALS INC
600 E Lambert Rd, La Habra (90631-6141)
PHONE..................562 697-8826
Kevin Ufholtz, *President*
EMP: 50
SQ FT: 2,000
SALES (est): 35MM **Privately Held**
SIC: 5051 Steel

(P-7073)
JFE SHOJI TRADE AMERICA INC (HQ)
301 E Ocean Blvd Ste 1750, Long Beach
(90802-4879)
PHONE..................562 637-3500
Toshihiro Kabasawa, *Exec VP*
Hidehiko Ogawa, *Exec VP*
▲ **EMP:** 85
SQ FT: 7,500
SALES (est): 294.2MM **Privately Held**
SIC: 5051 Steel

(P-7074)
JIMS SUPPLY CO INC (PA)
3500 Buck Owens Blvd, Bakersfield
(93308-4920)
P.O. Box 668 (93302-0668)
PHONE..................661 616-6977
Doreen M Boylan, *CEO*
Bryan Boylan, *CFO*
Jonathan Thomas, *CFO*
Jennifer Drake, *Treasurer*
Jennice Boylan, *Vice Pres*
▲ **EMP:** 82 **EST:** 1960
SQ FT: 25,300
SALES (est): 53.7MM **Privately Held**
WEB: www.jimssupply.com
SIC: 5051 Steel

(P-7075)
JOSEPH T RYERSON & SON INC
4310 Bandini Blvd, Vernon (90058-4308)
P.O. Box 513817, Los Angeles (90051-1817)
PHONE..................323 267-6000
Steve Bosway, *Branch Mgr*
Edward J Lehner, *CEO*
Rod Newcombe, *Project Mgr*
EMP: 80 **Publicly Held**
SIC: 5051 5162 5085 Aluminum bars, rods, ingots, sheets, pipes, plates, etc.; iron & steel (ferrous) products; plastics materials & basic shapes; industrial supplies
HQ: Joseph T. Ryerson & Son, Inc.
227 W Monroe St Fl 27
Chicago IL 60606
312 292-5000

(P-7076)
KLOECKNER METALS CORPORATION
Also Called: Gary Steel Division
9804 Norwalk Blvd Ste A, Santa Fe Springs
(90670-2901)
PHONE..................562 906-2020
Bob Tripp, *Vice Pres*
Sergio Torres, *General Mgr*
Scott Britt, *Opers Staff*
Stella Trujillo, *Sales Staff*
EMP: 75

SALES (corp-wide): 7.7B **Privately Held**
SIC: 5051 Steel
HQ: Kloeckner Metals Corporation
500 Colonial Center Pkwy # 500
Roswell GA 30076

(P-7077)
KLOECKNER METALS CORPORATION
9804 Norwalk Blvd Ste A, Santa Fe Springs
(90670-2901)
PHONE..................562 906-2020
Marshall Katz, *Branch Mgr*
EMP: 50
SALES (corp-wide): 7.7B **Privately Held**
WEB: www.macsteelusa.com
SIC: 5051 Steel
HQ: Kloeckner Metals Corporation
500 Colonial Center Pkwy # 500
Roswell GA 30076

(P-7078)
KLOECKNER METALS CORPORATION
2000 S O St, Tulare (93274-6852)
PHONE..................559 688-7980
Bob Kyle, *Branch Mgr*
Gary Hinchey, *Purch Agent*
EMP: 52
SALES (corp-wide): 7.7B **Privately Held**
SIC: 5051 Steel
HQ: Kloeckner Metals Corporation
500 Colonial Center Pkwy # 500
Roswell GA 30076

(P-7079)
MAXX METALS INC
355 Quarry Rd, San Carlos (94070-6217)
P.O. Box 10963, Pleasanton (94588-0963)
PHONE..................650 654-1500
Paul A Wallace, *President*
EMP: 68
SQ FT: 13,000
SALES (est): 5.2MM **Privately Held**
SIC: 5051 Steel

(P-7080)
MITSUI & CO (USA) INC
Also Called: Mitsui USA
601 S Figueroa St # 1900, Los Angeles
(90017-5704)
PHONE..................213 896-1100
Shozaburo Marayama, *Manager*
EMP: 52 **Privately Held**
WEB: www.mitsui.com
SIC: 5051 5094 Steel; bullion, precious metals
HQ: Mitsui & Co. (U.S.A.), Inc.
200 Park Ave Fl 36
New York NY 10166
212 878-4000

(P-7081)
MONICO ALLOYS INC (PA)
3039 E Ana St, Compton (90221-5604)
PHONE..................310 928-0168
Jason Zenk, *President*
Jason D Zenk, *President*
Saul Zenk, *CFO*
Ken Larson, *Senior VP*
Bruce Botansky, *Vice Pres*
◆ **EMP:** 98
SQ FT: 60,000
SALES (est): 59.8MM **Privately Held**
WEB: www.monicoalloys.com
SIC: 5051 Metals service centers & offices

(P-7082)
MWS PRECISION WIRE INDS INC
Also Called: Mws Wire Industries
31200 Cedar Valley Dr, Westlake Village
(91362-4035)
PHONE..................818 991-8553
Toll Free:.................888
Darrell H Friedman, *President*
Alan Friedman, *President*
Lois J Friedman, *Admin Sec*
Tomm Carlson, *Info Tech Mgr*
Denis Goss, *Controller*
EMP: 52
SQ FT: 32,000

SALES (est): 48.1MM **Privately Held**
WEB: www.mwswire.com
SIC: 5051 3351 3357 Copper sheets, plates, bars, rods, pipes, etc.; wire, copper & copper alloy; nonferrous wiredrawing & insulating

(P-7083)
NORMAN INDUSTRIAL MTLS INC (PA)
Also Called: Industrial Metal Supply Co
8300 San Fernando Rd, Sun Valley
(91352-3222)
PHONE..................818 729-3333
Eric Steinhauer, *CEO*
David Pace, *President*
Dave Cohen, *COO*
David Berkey, *CFO*
Jennifer Vitale, *Executive Asst*
◆ **EMP:** 125
SQ FT: 70,000
SALES (est): 158.7MM **Privately Held**
WEB: www.industrialmetalsupply.com
SIC: 5051 3441 3449 Metals service centers & offices; fabricated structural metal; miscellaneous metalwork

(P-7084)
NORMAN INDUSTRIAL MTLS INC
Also Called: Industrial Metal Supply Co Eba
7550 Ronson Rd, San Diego (92111-1500)
PHONE..................858 277-8200
Wesley Sykes, *Manager*
EMP: 50
SALES (est): 6.1MM
SALES (corp-wide): 158.7MM **Privately Held**
WEB: www.industrialmetalsupply.com
SIC: 5051 5211 Steel; lumber & other building materials
PA: Norman Industrial Materials, Inc.
8300 San Fernando Rd
Sun Valley CA 91352
818 729-3333

(P-7085)
PACIFIC METALS GROUP LLC
Also Called: Pacmet Aerospace
787 S Wanamaker Ave, Ontario
(91761-8116)
PHONE..................909 218-8889
David A Janes Jr,
◆ **EMP:** 50
SQ FT: 45,000
SALES (est): 34.4MM **Privately Held**
WEB: www.cmemetalstamping.com
SIC: 5051 Metals service centers & offices

(P-7086)
PACIFIC STEEL GROUP
2755 S Willow Ave, Bloomington
(92316-3260)
PHONE..................858 449-7219
EMP: 212
SALES (corp-wide): 147.6MM **Privately Held**
SIC: 5051 Iron & steel (ferrous) products
PA: Pacific Steel Group
4805 Murphy Canyon Rd
San Diego CA 92123
858 251-1100

(P-7087)
PACIFIC STEEL GROUP
Gilmore Ave Bldg 411, Stockton (95203)
PHONE..................707 297-8922
EMP: 71
SALES (corp-wide): 147.6MM **Privately Held**
SIC: 5051 Iron & steel (ferrous) products
PA: Pacific Steel Group
4805 Murphy Canyon Rd
San Diego CA 92123
858 251-1100

(P-7088)
PATTON SALES CORP (PA)
Also Called: Patton's Steel
1095 E California St, Ontario (91761-1909)
P.O. Box 273 (91762-8273)
PHONE..................909 988-0661
Jonathan Novack, *CEO*
Louie Lucero, *Administration*
Kristina Amaro, *Credit Mgr*
Dani Novack, *Advt Staff*
Crystal Mason, *Sales Staff*

◆ **EMP:** 120
SQ FT: 16,000
SALES (est): 136.8MM **Privately Held**
WEB: www.pattonscorp.com
SIC: 5051 5084 5712 5211 Steel; industrial machinery & equipment; office furniture; lumber & other building materials

(P-7089)
PDM STEEL SERVICE CENTERS
3500 Bassett St, Santa Clara (95054-2704)
P.O. Box 329 (95052-0329)
PHONE..................408 988-3000
John Norman, *General Mgr*
Lee Webber, *Marketing Staff*
Paul Lowe, *Sales Staff*
EMP: 65
SQ FT: 46,080
SALES (corp-wide): 11.5B **Publicly Held**
WEB: www.pdmsteel.com
SIC: 5051 3444 3272 Steel; sheet metalwork; concrete products
HQ: Pdm Steel Service Centers, Inc
3535 E Myrtle St
Stockton CA 95205

(P-7090)
PDM STEEL SERVICE CENTERS
4005 E Church Ave, Fresno (93725-1415)
P.O. Box 11188 (93772-1188)
PHONE..................559 442-1410
Mike Hill, *Branch Mgr*
EMP: 50
SALES (corp-wide): 11.5B **Publicly Held**
WEB: www.pdmsteel.com
SIC: 5051 Steel
HQ: Pdm Steel Service Centers, Inc
3535 E Myrtle St
Stockton CA 95205

(P-7091)
PDM STEEL SERVICE CENTERS
Also Called: Ferralloy PDM Steel Service
936 Performance Dr, Stockton
(95206-4930)
PHONE..................209 234-0548
Frances Espinosa, *Branch Mgr*
EMP: 60
SALES (corp-wide): 11.5B **Publicly Held**
WEB: www.ferralloy.com
SIC: 5051 Steel
HQ: Pdm Steel Service Centers, Inc
3535 E Myrtle St
Stockton CA 95205

(P-7092)
RAMCAST ORNAMENTAL SUP CO INC (PA)
2201 Firestone Blvd, Los Angeles
(90002-1547)
PHONE..................323 585-1625
Rosalba R Warschaw, *CEO*
Ismael Ramirez, *President*
Hector Ramirez, *Treasurer*
Juan Ramirez, *Vice Pres*
Ricardo Ramirez, *Director*
▲ **EMP:** 105
SQ FT: 30,000
SALES: 47.9MM **Privately Held**
WEB: www.ramcast.net
SIC: 5051 Steel

(P-7093)
RELIANCE STEEL & ALUMINUM CO (PA)
350 S Grand Ave Ste 5100, Los Angeles
(90071-3421)
PHONE..................213 687-7700
Gregg J Mollins, *President*
Mark V Kaminski, *Ch of Bd*
James D Hoffman, *COO*
Karla R Lewis, *CFO*
William K Sales Jr, *Exec VP*
◆ **EMP:** 82 **EST:** 1939
SALES: 11.5B **Publicly Held**
WEB: www.rsac.com
SIC: 5051 Structural shapes, iron or steel

(P-7094)
RELIANCE STEEL & ALUMINUM CO
Reliance Metal Center
33201 Western Ave, Union City
(94587-2208)
PHONE.................................510 476-4400
Dave Buchanan, *Manager*
Briana Cash, *Administration*
Mike Waller, *Warehouse Mgr*
EMP: 90
SQ FT: 137,757
SALES (corp-wide): 11.5B **Publicly Held**
WEB: www.rsac.com
SIC: 5051 Steel; aluminum bars, rods, ingots, sheets, pipes, plates, etc.; bars, metal; copper
PA: Reliance Steel & Aluminum Co.
350 S Grand Ave Ste 5100
Los Angeles CA 90071
213 687-7700

(P-7095)
RELIANCE STEEL & ALUMINUM CO
Tube Service
9351 Norwalk Blvd, Santa Fe Springs
(90670-2925)
P.O. Box 2728 (90670-0728)
PHONE.................................562 695-0467
Jan Hollar, *Branch Mgr*
Maria Munoz, *Credit Staff*
Dorothy Kinsey, *Human Res Dir*
Karen Hansen, *Purch Mgr*
John Rede, *Purch Mgr*
EMP: 58
SQ FT: 40,000
SALES (corp-wide): 11.5B **Publicly Held**
WEB: www.rsac.com
SIC: 5051 Steel
PA: Reliance Steel & Aluminum Co.
350 S Grand Ave Ste 5100
Los Angeles CA 90071
213 687-7700

(P-7096)
RELIANCE STEEL & ALUMINUM CO
Bralco Metals
15090 Northam St, La Mirada
(90638-5757)
PHONE.................................714 736-4800
Michael Hubbart, *Branch Mgr*
Dee Beard, *Credit Mgr*
Tracie Ichikawa, *Credit Staff*
Denise Williams, *Buyer*
Laureano Gomez, *Production*
EMP: 118
SALES (corp-wide): 11.5B **Publicly Held**
WEB: www.rsac.com
SIC: 5051 Steel; ferrous metals
PA: Reliance Steel & Aluminum Co.
350 S Grand Ave Ste 5100
Los Angeles CA 90071
213 687-7700

(P-7097)
RELIANCE STEEL & ALUMINUM CO
Also Called: Reliance Steel Company
2537 E 27th St, Vernon (90058-1284)
PHONE.................................323 583-6111
John Becknell, *Branch Mgr*
Mario Campos, *Plant Mgr*
EMP: 200
SALES (corp-wide): 11.5B **Publicly Held**
WEB: www.rsac.com
SIC: 5051 Steel
PA: Reliance Steel & Aluminum Co.
350 S Grand Ave Ste 5100
Los Angeles CA 90071
213 687-7700

(P-7098)
RELIANCE STEEL & ALUMINUM CO
Metalcenter
12034 Greenstone Ave, Santa Fe Springs
(90670-4727)
P.O. Box 2101 (90670-0013)
PHONE.................................562 944-3322
Jay Rose, *Branch Mgr*
Al Cawley, *Opers Mgr*
EMP: 80
SQ FT: 142,000

SALES (corp-wide): 11.5B **Publicly Held**
WEB: www.rsac.com
SIC: 5051 Steel
PA: Reliance Steel & Aluminum Co.
350 S Grand Ave Ste 5100
Los Angeles CA 90071
213 687-7700

(P-7099)
ROLLED STEEL PRODUCTS CORP (PA)
Also Called: R S P
2187 Garfield Ave, Commerce
(90040-1855)
PHONE.................................323 723-8836
Robert Alperson, *Ch of Bd*
Steven Alperson, *President*
Lonnie Alperson, *CFO*
Dennis Moslenko, *MIS Dir*
Hector Vasquez, *Purch Mgr*
EMP: 68
SQ FT: 125,000
SALES (est): 25MM **Privately Held**
WEB: www.rolledsteel.com
SIC: 5051 3316 Steel; cold finishing of steel shapes

(P-7100)
ROSSIN STEEL INC
2660 Cactus Rd, San Diego (92154-8022)
PHONE.................................619 656-9200
Ted F Rossin, *CEO*
Jeffrey Clinkscleas, *Vice Pres*
EMP: 110
SALES: 30MM **Privately Held**
WEB: www.rossinsteel.com
SIC: 5051 Steel

(P-7101)
SAC INTERNATIONAL STEEL INC (PA)
6130 Avalon Blvd, Los Angeles
(90003-1633)
PHONE.................................323 232-2467
Shaukat A Chohan, *President*
Shaukaj Ali Chohan, *President*
Omar Chohan, *Vice Pres*
Mahmooda Chohan, *Admin Sec*
◆ **EMP:** 74
SQ FT: 100,000
SALES (est): 20.4MM **Privately Held**
WEB: www.sacintl.com
SIC: 5051 Sheets, metal

(P-7102)
SAMUEL SON & CO (USA) INC
12389 Lower Azusa Rd, Arcadia
(91006-5889)
PHONE.................................323 722-0300
David Olivia, *Branch Mgr*
Kurt Perine, *Sales Staff*
EMP: 50
SALES (corp-wide): 1.8B **Privately Held**
SIC: 5051 Ferroalloys; steel
HQ: Samuel, Son & Co. (Usa) Inc.
1401 Davey Rd Ste 300
Woodridge IL 60517
630 783-8900

(P-7103)
SIMPSON STRONG-TIE INTL INC
Simpson Strong-Tie Anchor Syst
5956 W Las Positas Blvd, Pleasanton
(94588-8540)
PHONE.................................925 560-9000
Undetermin BR, *Manager*
EMP: 100
SALES (corp-wide): 1B **Publicly Held**
SIC: 5051 Forms, concrete construction (steel)
HQ: Simpson Strong-Tie International, Inc.
5956 W Las Positas Blvd
Pleasanton CA 94588

(P-7104)
SLAKEY BROTHERS INC
1001 Oates Ct, Modesto (95358-5818)
P.O. Box 4099 (95352-4099)
PHONE.................................209 556-1100
Bob Wirowek, *Manager*
EMP: 50

SALES (corp-wide): 197MM **Privately Held**
WEB: www.slakey.com
SIC: 5051 5084 5078 5064 Sheets, metal; industrial machine parts; fixtures, refrigerated; air conditioning room units, self-contained; heating & air conditioning contractors; heating equipment (hydronic)
PA: Slakey Brothers, Inc.
2215 Kausen Dr Ste 1
Elk Grove CA 95758
916 478-2000

(P-7105)
SPECIALTY STEEL SERVICE CO INC (HQ)
3300 Douglas Blvd Ste 128, Roseville
(95661-3897)
PHONE.................................916 771-4737
Fax: 916 771-8658
▲ **EMP:** 70
SQ FT: 3,000
SALES (est): 24.4MM
SALES (corp-wide): 10.4B **Publicly Held**
WEB: www.specialtysteel.net
SIC: 5051
PA: Reliance Steel & Aluminum Co.
350 S Grand Ave Ste 5100
Los Angeles CA 90071
213 687-7700

(P-7106)
STATE PIPE & SUPPLY INC (DH)
183 S Cedar Ave, Rialto (92376-9011)
PHONE.................................909 877-9999
Byung Joon Lee, *CEO*
Honggie Kim, *President*
Gary Knoroski, *Vice Pres*
Howard W Lee, *Admin Sec*
Erik Estrada, *Sales Staff*
EMP: 55
SQ FT: 20,000
SALES (est): 42.9MM **Privately Held**
WEB: www.statepipe.com
SIC: 5051 5085 Pipe & tubing, steel; industrial supplies
HQ: Seah Steel California, Llc
2100 Main St Ste 100
Irvine CA 92614
949 655-8000

(P-7107)
TA CHEN INTERNATIONAL INC (HQ)
Also Called: Sunland Shutters
5855 Obispo Ave, Long Beach
(90805-3715)
PHONE.................................562 808-8000
Johnny Hsieh, *CEO*
Andrew Chang, *CFO*
James Chang, *Vice Pres*
John Hellighausen, *Vice Pres*
William Pines, *Branch Mgr*
◆ **EMP:** 172
SQ FT: 200,000
SALES: 1.2B **Privately Held**
WEB: www.tachen.com
SIC: 5051 Metals service centers & offices

(P-7108)
TCI ALUMINUM/NORTH INC
2353 Davis Ave, Hayward (94545-1111)
PHONE.................................510 786-3750
Jeff Bordalampe, *President*
Jim Clifton, *Vice Pres*
Mark Oatley, *Sales Engr*
John Bordalampe, *Sales Staff*
EMP: 60
SQ FT: 60,000
SALES (est): 40.3MM **Privately Held**
WEB: www.tcialuminum.com
SIC: 5051 Aluminum bars, rods, ingots, sheets, pipes, plates, etc.

(P-7109)
TELL STEEL INC
2345 W 17th St, Long Beach (90813-1097)
PHONE.................................562 435-4826
Greg More, *President*
Pete V Trigt, *Admin Sec*
Donna Hansen, *Human Res Dir*
Greg Moore, *VP Opers*
Kevin McClister, *Sales Executive*
▲ **EMP:** 60
SQ FT: 100,000

SALES (est): 58.7MM
SALES (corp-wide): 68.2MM **Privately Held**
WEB: www.tellsteel.com
SIC: 5051 Steel; aluminum bars, rods, ingots, sheets, pipes, plates, etc.
PA: Tuffli Company Incorporated
2780 Skypark Dr Ste 460
Torrance CA 90505
310 326-5500

(P-7110)
TMX AEROSPACE
12821 Carmenita Rd Unit F, Santa Fe Springs (90670-4805)
PHONE.................................562 215-4410
EMP: 120
SALES (est): 12.6MM **Privately Held**
SIC: 5051 Metals service centers & offices

(P-7111)
TOTTEN TUBES INC (PA)
500 W Danlee St, Azusa (91702-2341)
PHONE.................................626 812-0220
Tracy N Totten, *CEO*
Linda Furse, *Owner*
David Totten, *Chairman*
Jeffrey Totten, *Treasurer*
Laura Morick, *Vice Pres*
EMP: 60
SQ FT: 73,000
SALES (est): 51.2MM **Privately Held**
WEB: www.tottentubes.com
SIC: 5051 3498 Pipe & tubing, steel; steel; coils, pipe: fabricated from purchased pipe

(P-7112)
VER SALES INC (PA)
2509 N Naomi St, Burbank (91504-3236)
PHONE.................................818 567-3000
Gloria Ryan, *CEO*
James J Ryan, *CEO*
Craig Ryan, *Vice Pres*
Patrick Ryan, *Vice Pres*
Paul Ryan, *Vice Pres*
▲ **EMP:** 54
SQ FT: 30,000
SALES (est): 22.9MM **Privately Held**
WEB: www.versales.com
SIC: 5051 5099 3357 Metal wires, ties, cables & screening; safety equipment & supplies; nonferrous wiredrawing & insulating

(P-7113)
WINDY CITY WIRE AND CONNECTIVI
8024 Central Ave, Newark (94560-3450)
PHONE.................................510 284-3956
EMP: 217 **Privately Held**
SIC: 5051 Metal wires, ties, cables & screening
PA: Windy City Wire Cable And Technology Products, Llc
386 Internationale Dr H
Bolingbrook IL 60440

5052 Coal & Other Minerals & Ores Wholesale

(P-7114)
MORRISON LANDSCAPE
Also Called: Earthco
1225 E Wakeham Ave, Santa Ana
(92705-4145)
PHONE.................................714 571-0455
Robert Morrison, *President*
Denise Morrison, *Vice Pres*
Dan Morrison, *Manager*
EMP: 50
SALES (est): 4.4MM **Privately Held**
SIC: 5052 Coal & other minerals & ores

5063 Electrl Apparatus, Eqpt, Wiring Splys Wholesale

(P-7115)
ACT LIGHTING INC
2313 N Valley St, Burbank (91505-1114)
PHONE..................................818 707-0884
Mario Collazo, *Vice Pres*
Desiree Asanger, *Administration*
Lauren Perez, *Administration*
Spencer Michaels, *Technical Staff*
Aaron Hubbard, *Sales Staff*
EMP: 558
SALES (corp-wide): 59MM **Privately Held**
WEB: www.aclighting.com
SIC: 5063 Lighting fixtures
PA: A.C.T. Lighting, Inc.
　122 John St
　Hackensack NJ 07601
　844 996-0884

(P-7116)
ADEMCO INC
Also Called: ADI Global Distribution
1635 N Batavia St, Orange (92867-3508)
PHONE..................................714 283-0110
Mary Peterson, *Manager*
EMP: 50
SALES (corp-wide): 4.8B **Publicly Held**
WEB: www.adilink.com
SIC: 5063 3669 3822 Electrical apparatus
　& equipment; emergency alarms; auto
　controls regulating residntl & coml envi-
　ronmt & applncs
HQ: Ademco Inc.
　1985 Douglas Dr N
　Golden Valley MN 55422
　800 468-1502

(P-7117)
ADEMCO INC
Also Called: ADI Global Distribution
487 Mathew St, Santa Clara (95050-3105)
PHONE..................................408 986-8200
Dave Nash, *Owner*
EMP: 57
SALES (corp-wide): 4.8B **Publicly Held**
SIC: 5063 3669 3822 Electrical apparatus
　& equipment; emergency alarms; auto
　controls regulating residntl & coml envi-
　ronmt & applncs
HQ: Ademco Inc.
　1985 Douglas Dr N
　Golden Valley MN 55422
　800 468-1502

(P-7118)
ADJ PRODUCTS LLC (PA)
6122 S Eastern Ave, Commerce
(90040-3402)
PHONE..................................323 582-2650
Charles J Davies, *CEO*
Toby Velasquez, *President*
EMP: 120
SALES (est): 38MM **Privately Held**
SIC: 5063 Lighting fixtures

(P-7119)
ALLIED ELECTRIC MOTOR SVC INC (PA)
4690 E Jensen Ave, Fresno (93725-1698)
PHONE..................................559 486-4222
Salvatore Rome, *Ch of Bd*
Gail Mandal, *President*
Joyce Barnes, *Treasurer*
Henry Mandal, *Senior VP*
Richard Johnson, *Vice Pres*
EMP: 65
SQ FT: 100,000
SALES (est): 43.9MM **Privately Held**
WEB: www.alliedelectric.net
SIC: 5063 7694 Electrical supplies; elec-
　tric motor repair

(P-7120)
ALLSALE ELECTRIC INC
9240 Jordan Ave, Chatsworth
(91311-5709)
PHONE..................................818 715-0181
Evan Joel Regenstreif, *President*

Hannah Devos, *Office Mgr*
Kyle Adams, *Purch Mgr*
Edward Ratzlaff, *Marketing Mgr*
Manny Lopez, *Sales Staff*
EMP: 56
SQ FT: 30,000
SALES (est): 45.5MM **Privately Held**
WEB: www.allsaleelectric.com
SIC: 5063 Electrical supplies

(P-7121)
AMERICAN DE ROSA LAMPARTS LLC (PA)
Also Called: Luminance
1945 S Tubeway Ave, Commerce
(90040-1611)
PHONE..................................800 777-4440
Christopher M Larocca, *Mng Member*
Lilli Rodriguez, *Human Res Dir*
Adolfo Lopez, *Natl Sales Mgr*
Miguel Galicia, *Regl Sales Mgr*
Linda Gleason, *Regl Sales Mgr*
◆ **EMP:** 85
SQ FT: 155,000
SALES (est): 59.6MM **Privately Held**
SIC: 5063 3364 3229 Lighting fixtures;
　light bulbs & related supplies; lighting fit-
　tings & accessories; brass & bronze die-
　castings; bulbs for electric lights

(P-7122)
AMERICAN ELECTRIC SUPPLY INC (PA)
361 S Maple St, Corona (92880-6907)
P.O. Box 2710 (92878-2710)
PHONE..................................951 734-7910
Michael Pratt, *CEO*
Jerry Empson, *Treasurer*
Barry Van Fossan, *Vice Pres*
Kevin Klinzing, *Admin Sec*
Steve Pratt, *IT/INT Sup*
▲ **EMP:** 99
SQ FT: 13,086
SALES (est): 113MM **Privately Held**
WEB: www.amelect.com
SIC: 5063 Electrical supplies; wire & cable;
　lighting fixtures

(P-7123)
ANIXTER INC
855 National Dr Ste 103, Sacramento
(95834-1195)
PHONE..................................916 563-7560
Rich Westphal, *Manager*
Brian Beltran, *Branch Mgr*
Sean Webb, *Branch Mgr*
Garrett Okusako, *Manager*
EMP: 100
SALES (corp-wide): 8.4B **Publicly Held**
SIC: 5063 Electrical apparatus & equip-
　ment
HQ: Anixter Inc.
　2301 Patriot Blvd
　Glenview IL 60026
　800 323-8167

(P-7124)
ANIXTER INC
30061 Ahern Ave, Union City (94587-1234)
PHONE..................................510 477-2400
Willie Rivera, *Principal*
Eric Elsenbroek, *Technology*
EMP: 60
SALES (corp-wide): 8.4B **Publicly Held**
SIC: 5063 Wire & cable
HQ: Anixter Inc.
　2301 Patriot Blvd
　Glenview IL 60026
　800 323-8167

(P-7125)
ANIXTER INC
5000 Franklin Dr 200, Pleasanton
(94588-3354)
PHONE..................................925 469-8500
Sabrina Vasquez, *Manager*
EMP: 50
SALES (corp-wide): 8.4B **Publicly Held**
SIC: 5063 Wire & cable
HQ: Anixter Inc.
　2301 Patriot Blvd
　Glenview IL 60026
　800 323-8167

(P-7126)
ARROW WIRE & CABLE INC (PA)
13911 Yorba Ave, Chino (91710-5521)
PHONE..................................909 282-1940
Zahid Karim, *President*
Jim Morales, *Vice Pres*
Steve Sandys, *Opers Mgr*
Anthony Morales, *Sales Executive*
Ronna Warnders, *Sales Staff*
▲ **EMP:** 50
SQ FT: 26,000
SALES (est): 34.2MM **Privately Held**
WEB: www.arrow-wc.com
SIC: 5063 Electronic wire & cable; wire &
　cable

(P-7127)
BARTCO LIGHTING INC
5761 Research Dr, Huntington Beach
(92649-1616)
PHONE..................................714 230-3200
Robert Barton, *CEO*
Daniel Barton, *Exec VP*
Dana B McKe, *Exec VP*
Brian Labbe, *Vice Pres*
Rebecca Mendez, *Executive*
▲ **EMP:** 70
SALES (est): 20MM **Privately Held**
WEB: www.bartcolighting.com
SIC: 5063 3648 Lighting fixtures, commer-
　cial & industrial; lighting fixtures; airport
　lighting fixtures: runway approach, taxi or
　ramp

(P-7128)
BAY CITY EQUIPMENT INDS INC
Also Called: John Deere Authorized Dealer
13625 Danielson St, Poway (92064-6829)
PHONE..................................619 938-8200
Mark Loftin, *CEO*
Rodney Lee, *President*
Charles Loftin, *Corp Secy*
Ej Ochoa, *Opers Mgr*
Denny Keeler, *Manager*
EMP: 100
SQ FT: 20,000
SALES (est): 32.8MM **Privately Held**
WEB: www.bcew.com
SIC: 5063 5082 Generators; motors, elec-
　tric; construction & mining machinery

(P-7129)
BEL AIR LIGHTING INC (PA)
Also Called: Trans Globe Lighting
28104 Witherspoon Pkwy, Valencia
(91355-4175)
PHONE..................................818 768-5511
Eli Haber, *CEO*
Cary Haber, *President*
Nazanine Amiri, *CFO*
David Ziv, *Exec VP*
Scott Smith, *Sales Staff*
◆ **EMP:** 102
SQ FT: 200,000
SALES (est): 55.9MM **Privately Held**
WEB: www.tglighting.com
SIC: 5063 Lighting fixtures

(P-7130)
BRITHINEE ELECTRIC
620 S Rancho Ave, Colton (92324-3296)
PHONE..................................909 825-7971
Wallace P Brithinee, *President*
Donald P Brithinee, *Vice Pres*
Craig Slape, *Department Mgr*
Carlos Mazariegos, *Design Engr*
Brian Wilkinson, *Project Mgr*
EMP: 57
SALES (est): 33.2MM **Privately Held**
WEB: www.brithinee.com
SIC: 5063 7694 Motors, electric; electric
　motor repair

(P-7131)
CABLECONN INDUSTRIES INC
7198 Convoy Ct, San Diego (92111-1019)
PHONE..................................858 571-7111
Lisa Coffman, *President*
Rod Coffman, *Vice Pres*
Roger Newman, *Vice Pres*
Kimm Bronk, *Purch Mgr*
Aaron Yip, *Prdtn Mgr*
EMP: 65
SQ FT: 20,000

SALES: 9.1MM **Privately Held**
WEB: www.cableconn-sd.com
SIC: 5063 3678 3643 Building wire &
　cable; electronic connectors; current-car-
　rying wiring devices

(P-7132)
CALIFORNIA LIGHTING SALES INC (PA)
4900 Rivergrade Rd D110, Baldwin Park
(91706-1459)
PHONE..................................626 775-6000
Roger David, *President*
Marcus Cone, *CFO*
Norma Cortez, *Project Mgr*
Michael David, *Sales Staff*
Matthew Ghobadi, *Sales Staff*
EMP: 59 **EST:** 1965
SQ FT: 16,000
SALES (est): 8.6MM **Privately Held**
WEB: www.californialightingsales.com
SIC: 5063 Lighting fixtures, commercial &
　industrial; lighting fixtures

(P-7133)
CENTURY COMMERCIAL SERVICE
12820 Earhart Ave, Auburn (95602-9027)
P.O. Box 6793 (95604-6793)
PHONE..................................530 823-1004
Keith Estes, *President*
Brent Estes, *Vice Pres*
Traci Estes, *Vice Pres*
Lorin Estes, *Technician*
Anna Giovacchini, *Sales Staff*
EMP: 50
SQ FT: 6,500
SALES (est): 31.9MM **Privately Held**
WEB: www.centurylighting.com
SIC: 5063 1731 8748 Light bulbs & re-
　lated supplies; lighting contractor; energy
　conservation consultant

(P-7134)
CHESTER C LEHMANN CO INC (PA)
Also Called: Electrical Distributors Co
1135 Auzerais Ave, San Jose (95126-3402)
P.O. Box 26830 (95159-6830)
PHONE..................................408 293-5818
Chester C Lehmann III, *CEO*
Scott Lehmann, *President*
Melissa Lankford, *Project Mgr*
Teresa T Nielsen, *Project Mgr*
Steve Soliz, *Train & Dev Mgr*
▼ **EMP:** 65
SQ FT: 80,000
SALES (est): 149.7MM **Privately Held**
WEB: www.electdist.com
SIC: 5063 Electrical supplies

(P-7135)
COASTAL TRAFFIC SYSTEMS INC
9391 Power Dr, Huntington Beach
(92646-7236)
PHONE..................................714 641-3744
Steven Beiber, *President*
Paul Beiber, *Treasurer*
Tito Tigno, *Principal*
EMP: 58
SALES (est): 8.1MM **Privately Held**
SIC: 5063 Signaling equipment, electrical

(P-7136)
COMMERCIAL LIGHTING INDS INC
Also Called: Cli
81161 Indio Blvd, Indio (92201-1931)
PHONE..................................800 755-0155
Frank Halcovich, *CEO*
Jennifer Johnson, *Manager*
▼ **EMP:** 74
SQ FT: 81,000
SALES (est): 46.1MM **Privately Held**
WEB: www.commercial-lighting.net
SIC: 5063 Light bulbs & related supplies;
　lighting fixtures

(P-7137)
CONSOLIDATED ELEC DISTRS INC
5457 Ruffin Rd, San Diego (92123-1312)
PHONE..................................858 268-1020
Scott Branstetter, *Manager*

▲ = Import ▼=Export
◆ =Import/Export

Aj Egoian, *Opers Mgr*
Kaity Elliott, *Sales Associate*
Blake Dmochowski, *Sales Staff*
Greg Furton, *Sales Staff*
EMP: 51
SQ FT: 30,000
SALES (est): 3.8B **Privately Held**
SIC: 5063 Electrical supplies
PA: Consolidated Electrical Distributors,
Inc.
1920 Westridge Dr
Irving TX 75038
972 582-5300

(P-7138)
CONSOLIDATED ELEC DISTRS INC
Also Called: All-Phase Electric Supply
3020 W Empire Ave, Burbank
(91504-3109)
PHONE..................626 345-0000
Ed Carney, *Branch Mgr*
Robert Feller, *Principal*
Carol Stiekaley, *Principal*
EMP: 53
SALES (corp-wide): 3.8B **Privately Held**
SIC: 5063 Electrical supplies
PA: Consolidated Electrical Distributors,
Inc.
1920 Westridge Dr
Irving TX 75038
972 582-5300

(P-7139)
CORDELIA LIGHTING INC
20101 S Santa Fe Ave, Compton
(90221-5917)
PHONE..................310 886-3490
James Keng, *President*
Jay Spowart, *Vice Pres*
Li-WEI Wang, *Vice Pres*
Singh Chang, *Data Proc Staff*
Mike Reis, *Sales Staff*
▲ **EMP:** 106
SQ FT: 200,000
SALES (est): 28.2MM **Privately Held**
WEB: www.cordelia.com
SIC: 5063 Lighting fixtures

(P-7140)
COUNTY WHL ELC CO LOS ANGELES
Also Called: C E D
560 N Main St, Orange (92868-1102)
PHONE..................714 633-3801
Joe Mihelich, *Principal*
Craig Peters, *Branch Mgr*
Fernando Yazon, *Purchasing*
Dan Caballero, *Sales Mgr*
Ralph Padilla, *Accounts Mgr*
EMP: 76 **EST:** 1986
SALES (est): 24.8MM
SALES (corp-wide): 3.8B **Privately Held**
SIC: 5063 Electrical supplies
PA: Consolidated Electrical Distributors,
Inc.
1920 Westridge Dr
Irving TX 75038
972 582-5300

(P-7141)
DAHL-BECK ELECTRIC CO
2775 Goodrick Ave, Richmond
(94801-1109)
PHONE..................510 237-2325
Roger Beck, *CEO*
William R Beck, *President*
James Ross, *Corp Secy*
Gerald Vaio, *Vice Pres*
▲ **EMP:** 65 **EST:** 1932
SQ FT: 75,000
SALES (est): 24.3MM **Privately Held**
WEB: www.dahl-beck.com
SIC: 5063 1731 Electrical supplies; general electrical contractor

(P-7142)
DELAWARE ELECTRO INDS INC (PA)
Also Called: Liberty Engineering
9248 Eton Ave, Chatsworth (91311-5807)
PHONE..................818 786-8111
Steven D Hollopeter, *President*
Anshuman Kumar, *Executive*
Tim Church, *Admin Sec*
Alexander M Milley, *Admin Sec*

Vic Neil, *CIO*
EMP: 56
SQ FT: 19,000
SALES (est): 43.4MM **Privately Held**
WEB: www.fusesunlimited.com
SIC: 5063 5072 5065 Fuses & accessories; circuit breakers; hardware; rivets; miscellaneous fasteners; electronic parts & equipment

(P-7143)
DLIGHT DESIGN INC
2100 Geng Rd Ste 210, Palo Alto
(94303-3307)
PHONE..................415 872-6136
Ned Tozun, *CEO*
Sam Goldman, *President*
Marco Galfre, *Engineer*
Jacob Okoth, *Director*
▲ **EMP:** 800
SALES: 1.6MM **Privately Held**
SIC: 5063 Electrical supplies

(P-7144)
DMF INC
Also Called: Dmf Lighting
1118 E 223rd St, Carson (90745-4210)
PHONE..................323 934-7779
Morteza Danesh, *CEO*
Fariba Danesh, *Vice Pres*
Michael Danesh, *Vice Pres*
Andrew Wakefield, *Vice Pres*
Fred Kopitzke, *Engineer*
▲ **EMP:** 80
SQ FT: 8,000
SALES (est): 103MM **Privately Held**
WEB: www.dmflighting.com
SIC: 5063 Lighting fixtures, commercial & industrial

(P-7145)
EATON AEROSPACE LLC
4690 Colorado Blvd, Los Angeles
(90039-1106)
PHONE..................818 409-0200
Stephanie Stewart, *Branch Mgr*
Steve Thornock, *Technician*
Arthur Gryszkiewicz, *Design Engr*
Hai Nguyen, *Design Engr*
Rowena Garcia, *Project Engr*
EMP: 376
SQ FT: 41,117 **Privately Held**
WEB: www.eaton.com
SIC: 5063 Electrical apparatus & equipment
HQ: Eaton Aerospace Llc
1000 Eaton Blvd
Cleveland OH 44122
216 523-5000

(P-7146)
EDGES ELECTRICAL GROUP LLC (HQ)
1135 Auzerais Ave, San Jose (95126-3402)
P.O. Box 26830 (95159-6830)
PHONE..................408 293-5818
Mark Arndt, *CFO*
Leah Dillard, *Project Mgr*
John Slattery, *Purchasing*
John Russ, *Marketing Mgr*
Mike Flynn, *Sales Mgr*
EMP: 73
SALES (est): 149.7MM **Privately Held**
SIC: 5063 Electrical supplies
PA: Chester C. Lehmann Co., Inc.
1135 Auzerais Ave
San Jose CA 95126
408 293-5818

(P-7147)
ELECTRIC MOTOR SHOP
Also Called: Electric Motor & Supply Co.
250 Broadway St, Fresno (93721-3103)
P.O. Box 446 (93709-0446)
PHONE..................559 233-1153
Dicks Caglia, *President*
Kelly Martin, *Superintendent*
EMP: 80
SQ FT: 1,296
SALES (est): 6.5MM
SALES (corp-wide): 127.8MM **Privately Held**
WEB: www.electricmotorshop.com
SIC: 5063 Electrical supplies

PA: Electric Motor Shop
253 Fulton St
Fresno CA 93721
559 233-1153

(P-7148)
ELECTRIC SALES UNLIMITED
9023 Norwalk Blvd, Santa Fe Springs
(90670-2531)
PHONE..................562 463-8300
John J Defazio Jr, *President*
Chuck Beadle, *Vice Pres*
J Defazio, *Vice Pres*
Chuck Henze, *Info Tech Dir*
Hannah Terflinger, *Project Mgr*
▲ **EMP:** 50
SQ FT: 75,000
SALES (est): 17.5MM **Privately Held**
WEB: www.esu.com
SIC: 5063 Electrical supplies

(P-7149)
ERS SEC ALARM SYSTEMS INC
Also Called: Emergency Reporting Systems
4538 Santa Anita Ave, El Monte
(91731-1318)
PHONE..................626 579-2525
David Chao, *President*
EMP: 53
SQ FT: 15,000
SALES (est): 18.8MM **Privately Held**
WEB: www.erssecurity.com
SIC: 5063 1731 Burglar alarm systems; fire detection & burglar alarm systems specialization

(P-7150)
FACILITY SOLUTIONS GROUP INC
801 Richfield Rd, Placentia (92870-6731)
PHONE..................714 993-3966
Jeff Johnson, *District Mgr*
EMP: 64
SALES (corp-wide): 1B **Privately Held**
WEB: www.americanlight.com
SIC: 5063 1731 Lighting fixtures, commercial & industrial; light bulbs & related supplies; electrical work; lighting contractor
PA: Facility Solutions Group, Inc.
4401 West Gate Blvd # 310
Austin TX 78745
512 440-7985

(P-7151)
GRAYBAR ELECTRIC COMPANY INC
1370 Valley Vista Dr # 100, Diamond Bar
(91765-3921)
PHONE..................909 451-4300
Bruce Spencer, *Engr R&D*
Lindsay Salmons, *Project Mgr*
Franco Sabalones, *Business Mgr*
Jennifer Caldera, *Finance Mgr*
Kimberly Morris, *Human Res Dir*
EMP: 153
SALES (corp-wide): 7.2B **Privately Held**
WEB: www.graybar.com
SIC: 5063 5065 Electrical supplies; telephone equipment
PA: Graybar Electric Company, Inc.
34 N Meramec Ave
Saint Louis MO 63105
314 573-9200

(P-7152)
GRAYBAR ELECTRIC COMPANY INC
3089 Whipple Rd, Union City (94587-1236)
PHONE..................925 557-3000
Eric Ortega, *Branch Mgr*
EMP: 74
SQ FT: 117,648
SALES (corp-wide): 7.2B **Privately Held**
WEB: www.graybar.com
SIC: 5063 5065 Electrical supplies; telephone equipment
PA: Graybar Electric Company, Inc.
34 N Meramec Ave
Saint Louis MO 63105
314 573-9200

(P-7153)
HOCHIKI AMERICA CORPORATION
7051 Village Dr Ste 100, Buena Park
(90621-2268)
P.O. Box 514689, Los Angeles (90051-4689)
PHONE..................714 522-2246
Hisham Harake, *CEO*
Hiroshi Kamei, *CFO*
Rick Boisclair, *Vice Pres*
Sunichi Shoji, *Vice Pres*
Rocio Barba, *Regional Mgr*
◆ **EMP:** 104
SQ FT: 30,000
SALES (est): 66.7MM **Privately Held**
WEB: www.hochiki.com
SIC: 5063 3669 Fire alarm systems; fire detection systems, electric
PA: Hochiki Corporation
2-10-43, Kamiosaki
Shinagawa-Ku TKY 141-0

(P-7154)
HUBBELL LIGHTING INC
2498 Roll Dr, San Diego (92154-7213)
PHONE..................619 946-1800
EMP: 252
SALES (corp-wide): 4.4B **Publicly Held**
SIC: 5063 Electrical apparatus & equipment
HQ: Hubbell Lighting, Inc.
701 Millennium Blvd
Greenville SC 29607

(P-7155)
INDEPENDENT ELECTRIC SUP INC (DH)
2001 Marina Blvd, San Leandro
(94577-3204)
PHONE..................510 877-9850
David Jones, *President*
Rick Crew, *Branch Mgr*
Brett Massip, *Branch Mgr*
Pete Schneider, *Branch Mgr*
Matt Christ, *Project Mgr*
EMP: 153 **EST:** 1973
SALES (est): 600MM
SALES (corp-wide): 11.7MM **Privately Held**
WEB: www.iesupply.com
SIC: 5063 Electrical supplies; wiring devices; electrical construction materials; cable conduit
HQ: Sonepar Management Us, Inc.
510 Walnut St Ste 400
Philadelphia PA 19106
215 399-5900

(P-7156)
INSULATION SOURCES INC (PA)
Also Called: ICO Rally
2575 E Bayshore Rd, Palo Alto
(94303-3210)
PHONE..................650 856-8378
Edwina M Cioffi, *CEO*
Esther Constantakis, *Info Tech Mgr*
Cecil Dyer, *Director*
▲ **EMP:** 90
SQ FT: 15,000
SALES (est): 46.5MM **Privately Held**
SIC: 5063 5065 3671 Wire & cable; electronic parts; cathode ray tubes, including rebuilt

(P-7157)
JELIGHT COMPANY INC
2 Mason, Irvine (92618-2513)
PHONE..................949 380-8774
Marinko Jelic, *President*
Renata Jelic, *Admin Sec*
▲ **EMP:** 65
SQ FT: 27,000
SALES (est): 25MM **Privately Held**
WEB: www.jelight.com
SIC: 5063 Electrical apparatus & equipment

(P-7158)
JME INC (PA)
Also Called: T M B
527 Prk Ave San Fernando, San Fernando
(91340)
PHONE...............................201 896-8600
Colin R Waters, CEO
Thomas M Bissett, President
Luis V De Dios, Administration
Raul Ortega, Sales Staff
Nicole Rizzo, Sales Staff
◆ EMP: 136
SQ FT: 34,000
SALES (est): 105.8MM Privately Held
WEB: www.tmb.com
SIC: 5063 Lighting fittings & accessories

(P-7159)
**JOHN SHANNON MC GEE CO
INC**
Also Called: McGee Company
8190 Byron Rd, Whittier (90606-2616)
PHONE...............................562 789-1777
Glenn Hitomi, President
Tracey Miller, CFO
Lee Hatcher, Vice Pres
Ken Porter, Vice Pres
Mark Schlueter, Vice Pres
▲ EMP: 50 EST: 1963
SQ FT: 74,000
SALES (est): 7.9MM Privately Held
WEB: www.mcgeeco.com
SIC: 5063 Electrical apparatus & equip-
ment

(P-7160)
**KOFFLER ELEC MECH APPRTS
REPAI**
527 Whitney St, San Leandro (94577-1113)
PHONE...............................510 567-0630
Lari Koffler, President
Charles H Koffler, Vice Pres
Kerry Koffler, Admin Sec
Wayne Berner, Controller
▲ EMP: 80
SQ FT: 77,548
SALES (est): 21.4MM Privately Held
WEB: www.koffler.com
SIC: 5063 7694 Motors, electric; electric
motor repair

(P-7161)
**LIGHTING TECHNOLOGIES INTL
LLC**
13700 Live Oak Ave, Baldwin Park
(91706-1319)
PHONE...............................626 480-0755
Ken Luttio,
Thomas Hardenburger, Mktg Dir
▲ EMP: 220
SALES (est): 75.7MM Privately Held
SIC: 5063 3648 Lighting fixtures; lighting
equipment

(P-7162)
LUMENS LLC (HQ)
2020 L St Ste Ll10, Sacramento
(95811-4260)
PHONE...............................916 444-5585
Ken Plumlee, President
Peter Weight, Admin Sec
Brian Del Vecchio, Sr Software Eng
Sarah Schaale, Marketing Staff
Richard Tawney, Marketing Staff
◆ EMP: 52
SQ FT: 5,700
SALES (est): 31.7MM Privately Held
SIC: 5063 5712 Lighting fixtures; furniture
stores

(P-7163)
MAGNETIKA INC (PA)
2041 W 139th St, Gardena (90249-2409)
PHONE...............................310 527-8100
Francis Ishida, President
Basil P Caloyeras, CEO
Nagui Guirgis, COO
Basil Caloyeras, CFO
Ameet Butala, Exec VP
EMP: 80
SQ FT: 40,000

SALES (est): 40.4MM Privately Held
SIC: 5063 3612 Transformers, electric;
power transmission equipment, electric;
ballasts for lighting fixtures; power transformers, electric

(P-7164)
**MAIN ELECTRIC SUPPLY CO
LLC (PA)**
3600 W Segerstrom Ave, Santa Ana
(92704-6408)
P.O. Box 25750 (92799-5750)
PHONE...............................949 833-3052
Scott R Germann, President
Paul Vowels, COO
Karen Morris, CFO
Christine Baeza, Department Mgr
Josh Lajoie, Branch Mgr
▲ EMP: 69
SQ FT: 35,000
SALES (est): 434.5MM Privately Held
WEB: www.mainelectricsupply.com
SIC: 5063 Electrical supplies

(P-7165)
**MAIN ELECTRIC SUPPLY CO
LLC**
461 Main St, Riverside (92501-1029)
PHONE...............................951 784-2900
Rich Ramirez, Sales Staff
EMP: 78
SALES (corp-wide): 434.5MM Privately
Held
SIC: 5063 Electrical supplies
PA: Main Electric Supply Company Llc
3600 W Segerstrom Ave
Santa Ana CA 92704
949 833-3052

(P-7166)
MAXIM LIGHTING
253 Vineland Ave, City of Industry
(91746-2319)
PHONE...............................626 956-4200
Jacob Sperling, President
Zvi Sperling, Vice Pres
▲ EMP: 103
SQ FT: 285,000
SALES (est): 7.5MM Privately Held
WEB: www.maximlighting.com
SIC: 5063 Lighting fixtures

(P-7167)
MINKA LIGHTING INC (PA)
Also Called: Minka Group
1151 Bradford Cir, Corona (92882-7166)
PHONE...............................951 735-9220
Marian Tang, CEO
Kurt Schulzman, Principal
◆ EMP: 70
SQ FT: 350,000
SALES (est): 82.8MM Privately Held
WEB: www.minka.com
SIC: 5063 Lighting fixtures

(P-7168)
MOTIVE ENERGY INC (PA)
125 E Coml St Bldg B, Anaheim (92801)
PHONE...............................714 888-2525
Robert J Istwan, President
Gerard Mangan, CFO
Tom Quinn, General Mgr
Edith Gutierrez, Accounting Mgr
Tony Capolino, VP Sales
▼ EMP: 85
SQ FT: 35,000
SALES (est): 89MM Privately Held
SIC: 5063 Storage batteries, industrial

(P-7169)
MULTIQUIP INC (DH)
Also Called: Mq Power
6141 Katella Ave Ste 200, Cypress
(90630-5202)
PHONE...............................310 537-3700
Robert J Graydon, CEO
Jim Henehan, CFO
Mike Schick, District Mgr
Luis Torres, Regl Sales Mgr
Melissa Hull, Sales Staff
◆ EMP: 300

SALES (est): 245.5MM Privately Held
WEB: www.multiquip.com
SIC: 5063 5082 3645 Generators; general construction machinery & equipment;
garden, patio, walkway & yard lighting fixtures: electric
HQ: Itochu International Inc.
1251 Ave Of The Amrcas 51
New York NY 10020
212 818-8000

(P-7170)
**MYERS POWER PRODUCTS INC
(PA)**
Also Called: Myers FSI
2950 E Philadelphia St, Ontario
(91761-8545)
PHONE...............................909 923-1800
Diana Grootonk, CEO
Jose Cudal, CFO
Conrad Pecile, Executive
George Hodous, General Mgr
Robert Hodous, Planning Mgr
▲ EMP: 130
SQ FT: 40,000
SALES (est): 199.8MM Privately Held
WEB: www.myerspower.com
SIC: 5063 Electrical apparatus & equip-
ment

(P-7171)
NELSON & ASSOCIATES INC
12816 Leffingwell Ave, Santa Fe Springs
(90670-6343)
PHONE...............................562 921-4423
Todd James Nelson, CEO
Brian Haupt, Exec VP
Kurt Nelson, Principal
▲ EMP: 75
SQ FT: 120,000
SALES (est): 32.2MM Privately Held
WEB: www.nelsonreps.com
SIC: 5063 Electrical supplies; telephone &
telegraph wire & cable

(P-7172)
NORA LIGHTING INC
6505 Gayhart St, Commerce (90040-2507)
PHONE...............................800 686-6672
Fred Farzan, CEO
Jill Farzan, Exec VP
Mickey Majchrzak, Sales Staff
▲ EMP: 72
SQ FT: 150,000
SALES (est): 65MM Privately Held
WEB: www.noralighting.com
SIC: 5063 3648 5719 Lighting fixtures;
lighting fixtures, except electric: residen-
tial; lighting fixtures

(P-7173)
**ONESOURCE DISTRIBUTORS
LLC**
Also Called: One Source Supply Solutions
6530 Altura Blvd, Buena Park
(90620-1040)
PHONE...............................714 685-5378
William Mourtinzen, Mng Member
EMP: 59
SALES (corp-wide): 11.7MM Privately
Held
WEB: www.1sourcedist.com
SIC: 5063 5065 Electrical apparatus &
equipment; electronic parts & equipment
HQ: Onesource Distributors, Llc
3951 Oceanic Dr
Oceanside CA 92056
760 966-4500

(P-7174)
**ORIENTAL MOTOR USA
CORPORATION (DH)**
570 Alaska Ave, Torrance (90503-3904)
PHONE...............................310 715-3300
Ryan Kanemura, President
Kulie Fintak, President
Pete Derose, Exec VP
Greg Johnston, Exec VP
Jake Kitayama, Principal
◆ EMP: 60
SQ FT: 31,600
SALES (est): 45.6MM Privately Held
SIC: 5063 Motors, electric

(P-7175)
PACIFIC LIGHTING MFR INC
Also Called: Utopia Lighting
2329 E Pacifica Pl, Compton (90220-6210)
PHONE...............................310 327-7711
▲ EMP: 62
SQ FT: 100,000
SALES: 12.5MM Privately Held
SIC: 5063

(P-7176)
PACIFIC LIGHTING MFR INC
Also Called: Utopia Lighting
2329 E Pacifica Pl, Rancho Dominguez
(90220-6210)
PHONE...............................310 327-7711
Soon Goo Hong, CEO
David Kim, President
Bohi Hong, Admin Sec
EMP: 56
SALES: 14.1MM Privately Held
SIC: 5063 Lighting fixtures

(P-7177)
POWER PLUS LLC
1210 N Red Gum St, Anaheim
(92806-1820)
PHONE...............................714 507-1881
Steven Bray,
EMP: 57
SALES (est): 10.1MM Privately Held
SIC: 5063 Generators

(P-7178)
PQL INC (PA)
Also Called: Premium Quality Lighting
2285 Ward Ave, Simi Valley (93065-1863)
PHONE...............................805 579-8279
Andy Sreden, President
Barbara Gonzales, Credit Mgr
Hank Bachman, VP Sales
Milton Edwards, Supervisor
▲ EMP: 50
SQ FT: 15,000
SALES (est): 33.5MM Privately Held
SIC: 5063 Light bulbs & related supplies;
lighting fixtures

(P-7179)
**REGENCY ENTERPRISES INC
(PA)**
Also Called: Regency Lighting
9261 Jordan Ave, Chatsworth
(91311-5739)
PHONE...............................:818 901-0255
Ron Regenstreif, CEO
Scott Anderson, President
Isaac Regenstreif, President
Judah Regenstreif, President
Michael Goldstone, COO
◆ EMP: 272
SALES: 150MM Privately Held
WEB: www.regencylighting.com
SIC: 5063 Light bulbs & related supplies;
lighting fixtures

(P-7180)
SCHNEIDER ELECTRIC USA INC
Also Called: Schneider Electric 600
6160 Stoneridge Mall Rd # 200, Pleasanton
(94588-3285)
PHONE...............................925 462-0986
Scott Day, Manager
David Jerome, Program Mgr
Vicki Giusti, Executive Asst
Lynnette Rennon, Executive Asst
Oscar Esquer, Technician
EMP: 55
SALES (corp-wide): 177.9K Privately
Held
WEB: www.squared.com
SIC: 5063 Electrical apparatus & equip-
ment
HQ: Schneider Electric Usa, Inc.
201 Wshington St Ste 2700
Boston MA 02108
978 975-9600

(P-7181)
SCHNEIDER ELECTRIC USA INC
Also Called: Schneider Electric 650
21680 Gateway Center Dr # 300, Diamond
Bar (91765-2453)
PHONE...............................909 612-5400
Scott Forry, Manager
Orlando Perez, Vice Pres

Spencer Brown, *Engineer*
Rick Hendrix, *Manager*
EMP: 51
SALES (corp-wide): 177.9K **Privately Held**
WEB: www.squared.com
SIC: 5063 Electrical apparatus & equipment
HQ: Schneider Electric Usa, Inc.
    201 Wshington St Ste 2700
    Boston MA 02108
    978 975-9600

(P-7182)
SELECTA PRODUCTS INC (PA)
Also Called: Selecta Switch
1200 E Tehachapi Blvd, Tehachapi (93561-8129)
P.O. Box 888 (93581-0888)
PHONE.................................661 823-7050
John Kenyon, *President*
Charles Kenyon, *Ch of Bd*
James Kenyon, *President*
Dorothy Kenyon, *Vice Pres*
Charlotte Tathwell, *Vice Pres*
▼ **EMP:** 85
SQ FT: 20,000
SALES (est): 48.2MM **Privately Held**
WEB: www.selectaproductsinc.com
SIC: 5063 5065 Electrical supplies; electronic parts

(P-7183)
SIEMENS INDUSTRY INC
2525 Barrington Ct, Hayward (94545-1167)
PHONE.................................510 783-6000
John P Nichols, *Manager*
Manny Monje, *Executive*
Mike Volckaert, *Engineer*
EMP: 300
SALES (corp-wide): 95B **Privately Held**
SIC: 5063 Electrical apparatus & equipment
HQ: Siemens Industry, Inc.
    1000 Deerfield Pkwy
    Buffalo Grove IL 60089
    847 215-1000

(P-7184)
SIEMENS INDUSTRY INC
2420 S Reservoir St, Pomona (91766-6412)
PHONE.................................909 627-6141
Gary Rowe, *Branch Mgr*
EMP: 60
SALES (corp-wide): 95B **Privately Held**
WEB: www.sea.siemens.com
SIC: 5063 Electrical apparatus & equipment
HQ: Siemens Industry, Inc.
    1000 Deerfield Pkwy
    Buffalo Grove IL 60089
    847 215-1000

(P-7185)
SIEMENS INDUSTRY INC
6141 Katella Ave, Cypress (90630-5202)
PHONE.................................714 761-2200
Eric Ackerman, *General Mgr*
Joseph Wurzelbacher, *Business Dir*
Diana Young, *Office Mgr*
Asif Shaikh, *Purchasing*
Thomas Murray, *Opers Staff*
EMP: 122
SALES (corp-wide): 95B **Privately Held**
WEB: www.sibt.com
SIC: 5063 Electrical apparatus & equipment
HQ: Siemens Industry, Inc.
    1000 Deerfield Pkwy
    Buffalo Grove IL 60089
    847 215-1000

(P-7186)
SILICONSYSTEMS INC
26840 Aliso Viejo Pkwy # 1, Aliso Viejo (92656-2624)
PHONE.................................949 900-9400
Michael Hajeck, *CEO*
Andrew Talbot, *CFO*
David Merry, *CTO*
▲ **EMP:** 85

SALES (est): 11.1MM
SALES (corp-wide): 16.5B **Publicly Held**
WEB: www.siliconsystems.com
SIC: 5063 Electrical apparatus & equipment
PA: Western Digital Corporation
    5601 Great Oaks Pkwy
    San Jose CA 95119
    408 717-6000

(P-7187)
SOUTHWIRE COMPANY LLC
Southwire Master Service Ctr
9199 Cleveland Ave # 100, Rancho Cucamonga (91730-8559)
PHONE.................................909 989-2888
David Jordan, *Branch Mgr*
Turner Thomason, *Sales Dir*
Michael Sutton, *Manager*
EMP: 60
SALES (corp-wide): 2.2B **Privately Held**
WEB: www.southwire.com
SIC: 5063 Electrical supplies
PA: Southwire Company, Llc
    1 Southwire Dr
    Carrollton GA 30119
    770 832-4242

(P-7188)
STEVEN ENGINEERING INC
230 Ryan Way, South San Francisco (94080-6370)
PHONE.................................650 588-9200
Bonnie A Walter, *CEO*
Kenneth D Walter, *President*
Bryan J Woifgram, *Exec VP*
Bryan Wolfgram, *Exec VP*
Paul E Burk III, *Vice Pres*
◆ **EMP:** 110
SQ FT: 66,000
SALES (est): 140.5MM **Privately Held**
WEB: www.stevenengineering.com
SIC: 5063 Electrical apparatus & equipment

(P-7189)
USHIO AMERICA INC (HQ)
5440 Cerritos Ave, Cypress (90630-4567)
PHONE.................................714 236-8600
Shinji Kameda, *President*
Yuichi Asaka, *CFO*
Yuki Graham, *Executive*
Paul Iverson, *Executive*
Julie Dixon, *Office Admin*
◆ **EMP:** 90
SQ FT: 70,000
SALES (est): 69.6MM **Privately Held**
WEB: www.ushio.com
SIC: 5063 Lighting fixtures, commercial & industrial

(P-7190)
WALTERS WHOLESALE ELECTRIC CO (HQ)
2825 Temple Ave, Signal Hill (90755-2212)
PHONE.................................562 988-3100
John L Walter, *CEO*
Bill Durkee, *President*
Roland Wood, *CFO*
Nancy Nielsen, *Treasurer*
John Berumen, *Branch Mgr*
▼ **EMP:** 50
SQ FT: 10,000
SALES (est): 462.5MM
SALES (corp-wide): 3.8B **Privately Held**
WEB: www.walterswholesale.com
SIC: 5063 3699 1731 Wire & cable; electrical equipment & supplies; lighting contractor
PA: Consolidated Electrical Distributors, Inc.
    1920 Westridge Dr
    Irving TX 75038
    972 582-5300

(P-7191)
WALTERS WHOLESALE ELECTRIC CO
200 N Berry St, Brea (92821-3903)
PHONE.................................714 784-1900
Ron Byrd, *Branch Mgr*
EMP: 140
SALES (corp-wide): 3.8B **Privately Held**
WEB: www.walterswholesale.com
SIC: 5063 Electrical supplies

HQ: Walters Wholesale Electric Co.
    2825 Temple Ave
    Signal Hill CA 90755
    562 988-3100

(P-7192)
WW GRAINGER INC
Also Called: Grainger 732
2261 Ringwood Ave, San Jose (95131-1792)
PHONE.................................408 432-8200
Alicia Bugos, *Manager*
Marina Kisseleva, *Opers Mgr*
Judith Stein, *Counsel*
Jeff Cole, *Manager*
EMP: 120
SQ FT: 38,082
SALES (corp-wide): 11.2B **Publicly Held**
WEB: www.grainger.com
SIC: 5063 5084 5075 5078 Motors, electric; motor controls, starters & relays: electric; power transmission equipment, electric; generators; fans, industrial; pumps & pumping equipment; compressors, except air conditioning; pneumatic tools & equipment; warm air heating equipment & supplies; air conditioning equipment, except room units; refrigeration equipment & supplies; electric tools; power tools & accessories; hand tools
PA: W.W. Grainger, Inc.
    100 Grainger Pkwy
    Lake Forest IL 60045
    847 535-1000

(P-7193)
YASKAWA AMERICA INC
4101 Burton Dr, Santa Clara (95054-1510)
PHONE.................................408 748-4400
Jody Kurtzhalts, *CEO*
EMP: 225 **Privately Held**
WEB: www.methodsmachine.com
SIC: 5063 Electrical apparatus & equipment
HQ: Yaskawa America, Inc.
    2121 Norman Dr
    Waukegan IL 60085
    847 887-7000

(P-7194)
YDESIGN GROUP LLC (PA)
Also Called: Yliving
1850 Mt Diablo Blvd # 210, Walnut Creek (94596-4428)
PHONE.................................866 842-6209
Graham C Weaver,
Sean Callahan,
◆ **EMP:** 50
SALES (est): 38.4MM **Privately Held**
SIC: 5063 5031 Lighting fixtures; lighting fittings & accessories; lighting fixtures, commercial & industrial; lighting fixtures, residential; building materials, interior

(P-7195)
ZIPPY USA INC
Also Called: Kpower Sup McRswitch Inverters
1 Morgan, Irvine (92618-1917)
PHONE.................................949 366-9525
Chin W Chou, *President*
Chin S Tsai, *Treasurer*
Frank Lee, *Admin Mgr*
Kevin Lai, *Prdtn Mgr*
Amy Mewherter, *Sales Staff*
▲ **EMP:** 54 **EST:** 1996
SQ FT: 19,000
SALES (est): 11MM **Privately Held**
WEB: www.zippyusa.com
SIC: 5063 Motor controls, starters & relays: electric
PA: Zippy Technology Corp.
    10f, No. 50, Minquan Rd.,
    New Taipei City TAP 23141

(P-7196)
ZSPACE INC
2728 Orchard Pkwy, San Jose (95134-2012)
PHONE.................................408 498-4050
Paul Kellenberger, *CEO*
Joseph Powers, *CFO*
EMP: 100
SALES (est): 47.7MM **Privately Held**
SIC: 5063 Transformers, electric

5064 Electrical Appliances, TV & Radios Wholesale

(P-7197)
ALPINE ELECTRONICS AMERICA INC
2012 Abalone Ave Ste D, Torrance (90501-3726)
PHONE.................................310 783-7391
James Doboe, *Branch Mgr*
EMP: 102 **Privately Held**
SIC: 5064 Radios, motor vehicle
HQ: Alpine Electronics Of America, Inc.
    1500 Atlantic Blvd
    Auburn Hills MI 48326
    248 409-9444

(P-7198)
AVA ENTERPRISES INC
Also Called: Boss Audio Systems
3451 Lunar Ct, Oxnard (93030-8976)
PHONE.................................805 988-0192
Soheil Rabbani, *President*
Kam Mobini, *Shareholder*
Sheila Rabbani, *Vice Pres*
◆ **EMP:** 50
SQ FT: 70,000
SALES (est): 22.5MM **Privately Held**
WEB: www.bossaudio.com
SIC: 5064 Radios, motor vehicle

(P-7199)
CLARION CORPORATION AMERICA (HQ)
6200 Gateway Dr, Cypress (90630-4842)
PHONE.................................310 327-9100
Chris Honma, *President*
Bobby Song, *CFO*
Jeff Lehnhardt, *Admin Sec*
◆ **EMP:** 77 **EST:** 1966
SQ FT: 53,208
SALES (est): 423.7MM **Privately Held**
SIC: 5064 Radios, motor vehicle

(P-7200)
CONCEPT ENTERPRISES INC
152 S Brent Cir, Walnut (91789-3050)
PHONE.................................626 968-8827
Edward Liu, *CEO*
Calvin Liu, *Exec VP*
Willie Liu, *Vice Pres*
▲ **EMP:** 60 **EST:** 1976
SALES (est): 14.3MM **Privately Held**
SIC: 5064 Electrical entertainment equipment; radios, motor vehicle

(P-7201)
E & S INTERNATIONAL ENTPS INC (PA)
Also Called: Import Direct
7801 Hayvenhurst Ave, Van Nuys (91406-1712)
PHONE.................................818 887-0700
Philip Asherian, *CEO*
Farshad Asherian, *President*
Michael RAD, *COO*
Mike RAD, *COO*
Mark W Barron, *CFO*
◆ **EMP:** 136
SQ FT: 60,000
SALES (est): 194.9MM **Privately Held**
WEB: www.esintl.com
SIC: 5064 Electrical appliances, television & radio

(P-7202)
EXPRESCOM LLC
Also Called: Exprescom S.A. De C.V.
10145 Via De La Amistad, San Diego (92154-5216)
PHONE.................................619 271-0531
EMP: 58
SALES (corp-wide): 4.1MM **Privately Held**
SIC: 5064 5065
PA: Exprescom, Llc
    3753 Howard Hughes Pkwy
    Las Vegas NV 89169
    702 943-1859

(P-7203)
F O C ELECTRONICS CORPORATION
Also Called: Crazy Gideons
830 Traction Ave, Los Angeles
(90013-1816)
PHONE..................213 625-5775
Gideon Kotzer, *President*
Leonie Kotzer, *Corp Secy*
EMP: 50
SQ FT: 50,000
SALES (est): 6.1MM **Privately Held**
WEB: www.crazygideons.com
SIC: 5064 5731 Electrical entertainment
  equipment; television sets; video cassette
  recorders & accessories; radios; radio,
  television & electronic stores

(P-7204)
FLW INC
5672 Bolsa Ave, Huntington Beach
(92649-1113)
PHONE..................714 751-7512
Andrew Peek, *President*
Andy Peek, *Vice Pres*
Matthew Peek, *Controller*
EMP: 55
SALES (est): 2.5MM **Privately Held**
SIC: 5064 Electrical appliances, major

(P-7205)
FUJITSU TEN CORP OF AMERICA
19600 S Vermont Ave, Torrance
(90502-1140)
PHONE..................310 327-2151
Masami Yamamoto, *President*
Ken Nakasuji, *Electrical Engi*
James Davis, *Senior Mgr*
Alden Salazar, *Manager*
EMP: 120 **Privately Held**
SIC: 5064 7539 Radios, motor vehicle; ra-
  dios; automotive repair shops
HQ: Denso Ten Limited
  1-2-28, Goshodori, Hyogo-Ku
  Kobe HYO 652-0

(P-7206)
HOMELAND HOUSEWARES LLC
Also Called: Magic Bullet
11601 Wilshire Blvd Fl 23, Los Angeles
(90025-1759)
PHONE..................310 996-7200
Rich Krause, *CEO*
▲ EMP: 80
SALES (est): 37MM
SALES (corp-wide): 9.4MM **Privately Held**
SIC: 5064 5963 Electrical appliances,
  major; appliance sales, house-to-house
HQ: Capital Brands, Llc
  11601 Wilshire Blvd Fl 23
  Los Angeles CA 90025

(P-7207)
JVCKENWOOD USA CORPORATION (HQ)
2201 E Dominguez St, Long Beach
(90810-1009)
P.O. Box 22745 (90801-5745)
PHONE..................310 639-9000
Kuhiro Aigami, *President*
Kazuhiro Aigami, *President*
Joseph Glassett, *CEO*
Dilip Patki, *CFO*
Craig Geiger, *Exec VP*
◆ EMP: 160
SQ FT: 238,000
SALES (est): 86.3MM **Privately Held**
WEB: www.kenwoodusa.com
SIC: 5064 High fidelity equipment

(P-7208)
MEMOREX PRODUCTS INC
17777 Center Court Dr N S, Cerritos
(90703-9320)
PHONE..................562 653-2800
Michael Golacinski, *President*
Allan Yap, *Ch of Bd*
Kevin McDonnell, *CFO*
Mae Higa, *Admin Sec*
▲ EMP: 159
SQ FT: 212,000

SALES (est): 6.6MM **Publicly Held**
WEB: www.memorex.com
SIC: 5064 5065 5045 3652 Electrical entertainment equipment; radio & television
  equipment & parts; computer peripheral
  equipment; pre-recorded records & tapes;
  household audio & video equipment
PA: Glassbridge Enterprises, Inc.
  1099 Helmo Ave N Ste 250
  Oakdale MN 55128

(P-7209)
NEW AIR LLC
6600 Katella Ave, Cypress (90630-5104)
PHONE..................657 257-4349
Luke S Peters, *Mng Member*
Mariella L Peters,
EMP: 50
SQ FT: 130,000
SALES (est): 413.9K **Privately Held**
SIC: 5064 Air conditioning appliances

(P-7210)
PANASONIC
26160 Enterprise Way, Lake Forest
(92630-8403)
PHONE..................949 581-0661
Susan Hall, *President*
Scott Sebek, *Program Mgr*
Tom Turney, *Program Mgr*
James Wong, *Program Mgr*
Bertha Gollaz, *Admin Sec*
EMP: 149 EST: 2014
SALES (est): 19.5MM **Privately Held**
SIC: 5064 Electrical appliances, television
  & radio

(P-7211)
PANASONIC CORP NORTH AMERICA
Also Called: Panasonic Broadcast TV Sys-
tems
3330 Chnga Blvd W Ste 505, Los Angeles
(90068-1355)
PHONE..................323 436-3500
Russ Walker, *Manager*
EMP: 125 **Privately Held**
WEB: www.panasonic.com
SIC: 5064 Electrical appliances, television
  & radio
HQ: Panasonic Corporation Of North Amer-
  ica
  2 Riverfront Plz Ste 200
  Newark NJ 07102
  201 348-7000

(P-7212)
PANASONIC CORP NORTH AMERICA
Also Called: TV Group
2001 Sanyo Ave, San Diego (92154-6212)
P.O. Box 2000, Forrest City AR (72336-
2000)
PHONE..................619 661-1134
Joji Sewa, *Branch Mgr*
EMP: 50 **Privately Held**
WEB: www.sanyoctv.com
SIC: 5064 Electrical appliances, television
  & radio
HQ: Panasonic Corporation Of North Amer-
  ica
  2 Riverfront Plz Ste 200
  Newark NJ 07102
  201 348-7000

(P-7213)
PANASONIC CORP NORTH AMERICA
2033 Gateway Pl Ste 200, San Jose
(95110-3714)
PHONE..................201 348-7000
Shauna Peterson, *Director*
EMP: 54 **Privately Held**
WEB: www.panasonic.com
SIC: 5064 Electrical appliances, television
  & radio
HQ: Panasonic Corporation Of North Amer-
  ica
  2 Riverfront Plz Ste 200
  Newark NJ 07102
  201 348-7000

(P-7214)
PANASONIC CORP NORTH AMERICA
Panasonic Avc Networks Company
7625 Panasonic Way, San Diego
(92154-8204)
PHONE..................619 661-1134
EMP: 54 **Privately Held**
SIC: 5064 Television sets
HQ: Panasonic Corporation Of North Amer-
  ica
  2 Riverfront Plz Ste 200
  Newark NJ 07102
  201 348-7000

(P-7215)
R & B WHOLESALE DISTRS INC (PA)
2350 S Milliken Ave, Ontario (91761-2332)
PHONE..................909 230-5400
Robert O Burggraf, *President*
Shamsul Hyder, *CFO*
Robert Burggrat, *Treasurer*
Masako Burggraf, *Vice Pres*
Connie Espina, *General Mgr*
▲ EMP: 135
SQ FT: 72,000
SALES (est): 96.4MM **Privately Held**
WEB: www.rbdist.com
SIC: 5064 Electrical appliances, major;
  electrical entertainment equipment

(P-7216)
REPUBLIC SVCS VSCO RD LANDFILL
4001 N Vasco Rd, Livermore (94551-9766)
PHONE..................925 447-0491
Kevin Finn, *President*
Eric Horton, *General Mgr*
H Wayne Huizenga,
EMP: 50
SQ FT: 600
SALES (est): 5.9MM
SALES (corp-wide): 10B **Publicly Held**
WEB: www.republicservices.com
SIC: 5064 Garbage disposals
PA: Republic Services, Inc.
  18500 N Allied Way # 100
  Phoenix AZ 85054
  480 627-2700

(P-7217)
SAMSUNG ELECTRONICS AMER INC
18600 S Broadwick St, Rancho Dominguez
(90220-6434)
PHONE..................310 537-7000
K Hilm, *General Mgr*
James MO, *Sales Staff*
David Caldwell, *Supervisor*
EMP: 100 **Privately Held**
WEB: www.samsung.com
SIC: 5064 5065 Electrical appliances, tele-
  vision & radio; communication equipment
HQ: Samsung Electronics America, Inc.
  85 Challenger Rd Fl 7
  Ridgefield Park NJ 07660
  201 229-4000

(P-7218)
SIERRA SELECT DISTRIBUTORS INC
4320 Roseville Rd, North Highlands
(95660-5711)
PHONE..................916 483-9295
Patrick Russell Tatro, *CEO*
John Tatro, *Vice Pres*
Michael W Tatro, *General Mgr*
▲ EMP: 65 EST: 1982
SQ FT: 54,000
SALES (est): 47.9MM **Privately Held**
WEB: www.sierraselect.com
SIC: 5064 Radios; television sets; video
  cassette recorders & accessories; mi-
  crowave ovens, non-commercial

(P-7219)
SONY ELECTRONICS INC
Also Called: Sony Logistics
2201 E Carson St, Carson (90810-1227)
PHONE..................310 835-6121
Alan Schwab, *Manager*
EMP: 127 **Privately Held**

SIC: 5064 5065 Electrical appliances, television & radio; electronic parts & equipment
HQ: Sony Electronics Inc.
  16535 Via Esprillo Bldg 1
  San Diego CA 92127
  858 942-2400

(P-7220)
TV GUIDE ENTRMT GROUP LLC
2700 Colorado Ave Ste 200, Santa Monica
(90404-5502)
PHONE..................310 360-1441
EMP: 57
SALES: 78.4MM
SALES (corp-wide): 25.9B **Publicly Held**
SIC: 5064 Electrical entertainment equip-
  ment
HQ: Cbs Interactive Inc.
  235 2nd St
  San Francisco CA 94105

(P-7221)
WATER HEATERS ONLY INC
3620 Haven Ave, Redwood City
(94063-4640)
PHONE..................650 368-9998
Tom Crabtree, *President*
Michelle Dean, *Admin Asst*
Tony Edwards, *Technician*
Bill Lee, *Sales Associate*
Yana Carpenter, *Sales Staff*
EMP: 90
SALES (est): 8.2MM **Privately Held**
SIC: 5064 5999 1711 Water heaters,
  electric; plumbing & heating supplies;
  heating systems repair & maintenance

5065 Electronic Parts & Eqpt Wholesale

(P-7222)
7DAYS INC
3503 Jack Northrop Ave, Hawthorne
(90250-4433)
PHONE..................424 255-5872
Shiu Hou Sing, *President*
Hong Xia LI, *Manager*
EMP: 200
SALES: 13MM **Privately Held**
SIC: 5065 Electronic parts & equipment

(P-7223)
ABX ENGINEERING INC
875 Stanton Rd, Burlingame (94010-1403)
PHONE..................650 552-2300
Paul Leininger, *CEO*
Brian Helm, *Vice Pres*
Gil Galvan, *Program Mgr*
Rigo Alonso, *Project Mgr*
Hector Scritzky, *Engineer*
EMP: 100
SQ FT: 16,000
SALES (est): 54MM **Privately Held**
WEB: www.abxengr.com
SIC: 5065 7373 3672 Electronic parts;
  turnkey vendors, computer systems;
  printed circuit boards

(P-7224)
ADVANCED MNLYTHIC CERAMICS INC
Also Called: AMC
15191 Bledsoe St, Sylmar (91342-2710)
PHONE..................818 364-9800
N Eric Johanson, *Ch of Bd*
Phu Luu, *President*
Steve Makl, *Principal*
Richard Donovan, *Controller*
▲ EMP: 130
SQ FT: 35,000
SALES (est): 11.6MM **Privately Held**
WEB: www.amccaps.com
SIC: 5065 Electronic parts & equipment
HQ: Johanson Dielectrics, Inc.
  4001 Calle Tecate
  Sylmar CA 93012
  805 389-1166

▲ = Import ▼=Export
◆ =Import/Export

(P-7225)
ADVANCED MP TECHNOLOGY LLC (DH)
1010 Calle Sombra, San Clemente (92673-6227)
PHONE..........................800 492-3113
Homayoun Shorooghi, *President*
Ivy LI, *Purchasing*
Michele Anderson, *Manager*
Florence Kong, *Manager*
Erez Mosuchi, *Manager*
◆ EMP: 126
SQ FT: 86,000
SALES (est): 120MM **Privately Held**
WEB: www.advancedmp.com
SIC: 5065 Electronic parts
HQ: America Ii Electronics, Llc
2600 118th Ave N
Saint Petersburg FL 33716
727 573-0900

(P-7226)
ALTURA COMM SOLUTIONS LLC (DH)
1540 S Lewis St, Anaheim (92805-6423)
PHONE..........................714 948-8400
Robert Blazek, *CEO*
Tim Henion, *President*
David Key, *CFO*
Ron Enos, *Vice Pres*
Lance Flores, *Opers Staff*
EMP: 55
SQ FT: 25,000
SALES (est): 71.5MM **Privately Held**
WEB: www.alturacs.com
SIC: 5065 Electronic parts & equipment

(P-7227)
ALTURA COMM SOLUTIONS LLC
1840 Gateway Dr Ste 100, San Mateo (94404-4066)
PHONE..........................650 513-5100
Jobie Soliman, *Manager*
EMP: 70
SALES (corp-wide): 71.5MM **Privately Held**
WEB: www.alturacs.com
SIC: 5065 3661 1731 Electronic parts & equipment; telephone & telegraph apparatus; electrical work
HQ: Altura Communication Solutions, Llc
1540 S Lewis St
Anaheim CA 92805
714 948-8400

(P-7228)
ALVARION INC (HQ)
555 N Mathilda Ave # 210, Sunnyvale (94085-3503)
PHONE..........................650 314-2500
Zvi Slonimsky, *President*
Amir Rosenzweg, *President*
Joshua Mony, *VP Sales*
▲ EMP: 50
SQ FT: 16,000
SALES (est): 8.5MM
SALES (corp-wide): 5.6MM **Privately Held**
WEB: www.alvarion-usa.com
SIC: 5065 Communication equipment
PA: Alvarion Ltd
21 Habarzel
Tel Aviv-Jaffa 69710
364 562-62

(P-7229)
AMERICAN ZETTLER INC (HQ)
75 Columbia, Aliso Viejo (92656-4115)
PHONE..........................949 831-5000
Michael P Morgan, *President*
Rainer Moegling, *CFO*
Scott Peavey, *Vice Pres*
▲ EMP: 60
SQ FT: 63,000
SALES (est): 33.8MM **Privately Held**
WEB: www.azettler.com
SIC: 5065 Communication equipment

(P-7230)
AP GLOBAL INC
Also Called: Accessory Power
31352 Via Colinas Ste 101, Westlake Village (91362-6810)
PHONE..........................818 707-3167
Robert Breines, *President*

Gail Breines, *Vice Pres*
Pascale Malevez, *Office Mgr*
Michael Fetchet, *Administration*
EMP: 60 EST: 2013
SALES (est): 28.3MM **Privately Held**
SIC: 5065 Electronic parts & equipment

(P-7231)
APUMAC LLC
Also Called: Apumac.com
6404 Wilshire Blvd # 106, Los Angeles (90048-5501)
PHONE..........................888 248-7775
Lilyane Bensimon, *President*
EMP: 214
SQ FT: 1,500
SALES (est): 21.7MM **Privately Held**
SIC: 5065 Mobile telephone equipment

(P-7232)
ARCONIX/USA INC
Also Called: Arconix USA
880 Avenida Acaso Ste 100, Camarillo (93012-8721)
PHONE..........................805 388-2525
Allen Kay, *President*
Mark G Harris, *Vice Pres*
Cameron Hill, *Vice Pres*
John R Danzi, *Controller*
EMP: 52 EST: 1948
SALES (est): 5.5MM
SALES (corp-wide): 483.7MM **Privately Held**
WEB: www.penn-eng.com
SIC: 5065 Electronic parts & equipment
HQ: Penn Engineering & Manufacturing Corp.
5190 Old Easton Rd
Danboro PA 18916
215 766-8853

(P-7233)
ARROW ELECTRONICS INC
Also Called: Arrow Bell
20935 Warner Center Ln A, Woodland Hills (91367-6581)
PHONE..........................818 932-1022
Mike Jerworski, *General Mgr*
Paul Shewring, *General Mgr*
Vito Farello, *Manager*
EMP: 85
SALES (corp-wide): 29.6B **Publicly Held**
WEB: www.arrow.com
SIC: 5065 Electronic parts
PA: Arrow Electronics, Inc.
9201 E Dry Creek Rd
Centennial CO 80112
303 824-4000

(P-7234)
AVI SYSTEMS INC
44150 S Grimmer Blvd, Fremont (94538-6310)
PHONE..........................415 915-2070
EMP: 328
SALES (corp-wide): 250.2MM **Privately Held**
SIC: 5065 Sound equipment, electronic
PA: Avi Systems, Inc.
9675 W 76th St Ste 200
Eden Prairie MN 55344
952 949-3700

(P-7235)
AVNET INC
Also Called: Avnet Computers
220 Commerce Ste 100, Irvine (92602-1346)
PHONE..........................949 789-4100
Tony Coletto, *Branch Mgr*
Brian Stroud, *Technical Staff*
Sherina Chan, *Director*
Greg Vickrey, *Manager*
EMP: 75
SALES (corp-wide): 19.5B **Publicly Held**
WEB: www.avnet.com
SIC: 5065 Semiconductor devices; electronic parts
PA: Avnet, Inc.
2211 S 47th St
Phoenix AZ 85034
480 643-2000

(P-7236)
AVNET INC
Also Called: Avnet Computers
20951 Burbank Blvd Ste A, Woodland Hills (91367-6696)
PHONE..........................818 594-8310
James Williams, *Manager*
Ian Bryan, *Marketing Mgr*
Mehrdad Bradaran, *Accounts Mgr*
EMP: 60
SALES (corp-wide): 19.5B **Publicly Held**
WEB: www.avnet.com
SIC: 5065 Electronic parts
PA: Avnet, Inc.
2211 S 47th St
Phoenix AZ 85034
480 643-2000

(P-7237)
AVNET INC
Also Called: Avnet Computers
2580 Junction Ave, San Jose (95134-1902)
PHONE..........................408 501-3925
Dan Weiss, *Director*
EMP: 86
SALES (corp-wide): 19.5B **Publicly Held**
SIC: 5065 Semiconductor devices
PA: Avnet, Inc.
2211 S 47th St
Phoenix AZ 85034
480 643-2000

(P-7238)
AVNET INC
Electronics Div.
1400 Montefino Ave # 110, Diamond Bar (91765-5500)
PHONE..........................760 946-5030
Beth Boedeke, *Branch Mgr*
EMP: 270
SALES (corp-wide): 19.5B **Publicly Held**
WEB: www.avnet.com
SIC: 5065 Electronic parts
PA: Avnet, Inc.
2211 S 47th St
Phoenix AZ 85034
480 643-2000

(P-7239)
AVNET INC
Also Called: Avnet Computers
13500 Evening Creek Dr N # 400, San Diego (92128-8125)
PHONE..........................858 385-7500
Mark Goodding, *Branch Mgr*
Erik West, *Partner*
EMP: 400
SALES (corp-wide): 19.5B **Publicly Held**
SIC: 5065 5045 7379 Semiconductor devices; computers, peripherals & software; computer related consulting services
PA: Avnet, Inc.
2211 S 47th St
Phoenix AZ 85034
480 643-2000

(P-7240)
BELKIN INTERNATIONAL INC (DH)
Also Called: Belkin Components
12045 Waterfront Dr, Playa Vista (90094-2999)
PHONE..........................310 751-5100
Chester J Pipkin, *President*
George C Platisa, *CFO*
Janice Pipkin, *Treasurer*
D Thomas Triggs,
Jean Cook, *Admin Asst*
◆ EMP: 450 EST: 1983
SQ FT: 218,000
SALES (est): 434.3MM **Privately Held**
WEB: www.belkin.com
SIC: 5065 5045 Intercommunication equipment, electronic; communication equipment; computers & accessories, personal & home entertainment

(P-7241)
BRIX GROUP INC (PA)
Also Called: Pana-Pacific
838 N Laverne Ave, Fresno (93727-6868)
PHONE..........................559 457-4700
Harrison Brix, *CEO*
Kristina Reed, *President*
John Trenberth, *President*
Ron Dodds, *Executive*

Charlie Nguyen, *Admin Mgr*
▲ EMP: 80 EST: 1973
SQ FT: 35,000
SALES (est): 144.1MM **Privately Held**
WEB: www.brixcom.com
SIC: 5065 5013 Mobile telephone equipment; paging & signaling equipment; motor vehicle supplies & new parts

(P-7242)
BT AMERICAS INC
2160 E Grand Ave, El Segundo (90245-5024)
PHONE..........................646 487-7400
EMP: 100
SALES (corp-wide): 33.2B **Privately Held**
SIC: 5065
HQ: Bt Americas Inc.
8951 Cypress Waters Blvd # 200
Coppell TX 75019
877 272-0832

(P-7243)
BUYERS CONSULTATION SVC INC (PA)
Also Called: B C S
8735 Remmet Ave, Canoga Park (91304-1519)
P.O. Box 8427, Calabasas (91372-8427)
PHONE..........................818 341-4820
Jo Manhan, *President*
Larry Manhan, *Technology*
Kyle Regal, *Opers Mgr*
▲ EMP: 75
SQ FT: 40,000
SALES (est): 57.9MM **Privately Held**
SIC: 5065 7389 5093 4953 Electronic parts & equipment; auctioneers, fee basis; metal scrap & waste materials; recycling, waste materials

(P-7244)
CAL SOUTHERN SOUND IMAGE INC (PA)
2425 Auto Park Way, Escondido (92029-1222)
PHONE..........................760 737-3900
David R Shadoan, *CEO*
Ralph Wagner, *CFO*
Larry Itatlia, *Vice Pres*
Mike Martin, *Vice Pres*
Kyle Anderson, *Department Mgr*
EMP: 65
SQ FT: 28,000
SALES (est): 50.5MM **Privately Held**
SIC: 5065 3651 5064 Sound equipment, electronic; speaker systems; electrical appliances, television & radio

(P-7245)
CALIFORNIA EASTERN LABS INC (PA)
4590 Patrick Henry Dr, Santa Clara (95054-1817)
PHONE..........................408 919-2500
Jerry A Arden, *Ch of Bd*
Paul A S Minton, *President*
Mark A Sargent, *CFO*
Kevin Beber, *Vice Pres*
Masaru Kaneko, *Vice Pres*
▲ EMP: 80
SQ FT: 42,000
SALES (est): 27.5MM **Privately Held**
WEB: www.cel.com
SIC: 5065 Semiconductor devices

(P-7246)
CAVENDISH KINETICS INC
2960 N 1st St, San Jose (95134-2021)
PHONE..........................408 627-4504
Paul Dal Santo, *President*
Dan Smith, *Exec VP*
Atul P Shingal, *Vice Pres*
Paul Tornatta, *Vice Pres*
Rose Reilly, *Admin Mgr*
EMP: 50
SALES (est): 1MM
SALES (corp-wide): 3B **Publicly Held**
SIC: 5065 Semiconductor devices
PA: Qorvo, Inc.
7628 Thorndike Rd
Greensboro NC 27409
336 664-1233

(P-7247)
CBOL CORPORATION
19850 Plummer St, Chatsworth
(91311-5652)
PHONE....................818 704-8200
Howard Nam, *COO*
Spencer H Kim, *CEO*
Kenneth Cheung, *Officer*
Lynn Turk, *Admin Sec*
Elizabeth Ahn, *Project Mgr*
◆ **EMP:** 131
SQ FT: 69,820
SALES (est): 151.4MM **Privately Held**
WEB: www.cbolcorp.com
SIC: 5065 5072 5013 5088 Electronic
parts & equipment; hardware; staples;
motor vehicle supplies & new parts; trans-
portation equipment & supplies; industrial
machinery & equipment; plastics materi-
als & basic shapes

(P-7248)
CELESTICA LLC
895 S Rockefeller Ave # 102, Ontario
(91761-8182)
PHONE....................909 418-6986
James Rodriguez, *Branch Mgr*
EMP: 400
SALES (corp-wide): 23.7B **Privately Held**
SIC: 5065 7629 Electronic parts & equip-
ment; electronic equipment repair
HQ: Celestica Llc
11 Continental Blvd # 103
Merrimack NH 03054

(P-7249)
CELLULAR PALACE INC
Also Called: Wireless Lines
10435 Santa Monica Blvd F, Los Angeles
(90025-6936)
PHONE....................310 278-2007
Rahim Bobby Malmed, *President*
Shahram Javidzad, *Officer*
▲ **EMP:** 89
SALES (est): 11.4MM **Privately Held**
SIC: 5065 5064 5999 5731 Telephone &
telegraphic equipment; paging & signaling
equipment; high fidelity equipment; alarm
signal systems; telephone & communication equipment; high fidelity stereo equipment; radios, two-way, citizens' band,
weather, short-wave, etc.

(P-7250)
CELLUPHONE LLC
6119 E Wash Blvd Ste 200, Commerce
(90040-2452)
PHONE....................323 727-9131
EMP: 99
SALES (est): 10MM **Privately Held**
SIC: 5065 5999 Electronic parts & equip-
ment; telephone equipment & systems

(P-7251)
CICOIL LLC
24960 Avenue Tibbitts, Valencia
(91355-3426)
PHONE....................661 295-1295
Howard Lind, *CEO*
Robert Newbrey, *Engineer*
Donnita Trujillo, *Purch Mgr*
Johnathan Hinkley, *Director*
EMP: 80
SQ FT: 16,000
SALES: 12.2MM **Privately Held**
WEB: www.cicoil.com
SIC: 5065 Electronic parts & equipment

(P-7252)
**CNET TECHNOLOGY
CORPORATION (HQ)**
26291 Prod Ave Ste 205, Hayward (94545)
PHONE....................408 392-9966
Simon J Chang, *President*
▲ **EMP:** 179
SQ FT: 50,000
SALES (est): 30MM **Privately Held**
WEB: www.cnetusa.com
SIC: 5065 3661 3577 Communication
equipment; modems, computer; tele-
phone & telegraph apparatus; computer
peripheral equipment

(P-7253)
CORNER PRODUCTS COMPANY
Also Called: CP Technologies
17110 Armstrong Ave, Irvine (92614-5718)
PHONE....................800 876-8889
Chao-Jen Lin, *CEO*
Rick Hsu, *CEO*
Michael Hsu, *Principal*
▲ **EMP:** 55
SQ FT: 17,000
SALES (est): 17.2MM **Privately Held**
SIC: 5065 5045 Telephone equipment;
computer peripheral equipment

(P-7254)
DAVID LEVY CO INC
Also Called: Dlc
12753 Moore St, Cerritos (90703-2136)
PHONE....................562 404-9998
David Levy, *CEO*
John Latino, *Vice Pres*
Gordon Schaer, *Admin Sec*
Dale Lincoln, *Sales Staff*
▲ **EMP:** 50 EST: 1978
SQ FT: 25,000
SALES (est): 14.7MM **Privately Held**
WEB: www.cybertraklocate.com
SIC: 5065 Electronic parts

(P-7255)
DB ROBERTS INC
880 Avenida Acaso Ste 100, Camarillo
(93012-8721)
PHONE....................805 988-4882
Mark Harris, *Vice Pres*
EMP: 52
SALES (corp-wide): 82.3MM **Privately
Held**
WEB: www.dbroberts.com
SIC: 5065 Electronic parts & equipment
PA: D.B. Roberts, Inc.
58 Jonspin Rd
Wilmington MA 01887
978 657-4870

(P-7256)
**DECISION SCIENCES INTL
CORP**
12345 First American Way # 100, Poway
(92064-6828)
PHONE....................858 571-1900
Dwight Johnson, *President*
Brian Gallagher, *President*
Mike Goll, *CFO*
Eric Fleckten, *Senior VP*
Michael Sossong, *CTO*
▼ **EMP:** 60 EST: 2009
SALES (est): 19.6MM **Privately Held**
SIC: 5065 Radar detectors

(P-7257)
DELTA AMERICA LTD (HQ)
Also Called: Delta Products
46101 Fremont Blvd, Fremont
(94538-6468)
PHONE....................510 668-5100
Ming H Huang, *President*
Wayne Brown, *Office Mgr*
Yao Chou, *Admin Sec*
Bin Su, *Info Tech Dir*
◆ **EMP:** 130
SALES (est): 73.2MM **Privately Held**
SIC: 5065 3679 8731 Electronic parts &
equipment; switches, stepping; power
supplies, all types: static; electronic re-
search

(P-7258)
DIALOG SEMICONDUCTOR INC
1515 Wyatt Dr, Santa Clara (95054-1586)
PHONE....................408 327-8800
EMP: 235
SALES (corp-wide): 1.4B **Privately Held**
SIC: 5065 Semiconductor devices
HQ: Dialog Semiconductor, Inc.
2560 Mission College Blvd # 110
Santa Clara CA 95054
408 845-8500

(P-7259)
**EDGEWISE MEDIA SERVICES
INC (PA)**
Also Called: Comtel Pro Media
4518 W Vanowen St, Burbank
(91505-1135)
PHONE....................714 919-2020
David Cohen, *President*
▲ **EMP:** 84
SQ FT: 33,000
SALES (est): 11.4MM **Privately Held**
SIC: 5065 Tapes, audio & video recording

(P-7260)
EFORCITY CORP - NFM
Also Called: Ascend Distribution
18525 Railroad St, City of Industry
(91748-1316)
PHONE....................626 442-3168
Michael Wong, *Manager*
Jack Sheng, *CEO*
Eugene Wong, *CFO*
Tiffany Wu, *CIO*
Bolan You, *Info Tech Dir*
◆ **EMP:** 60
SQ FT: 100,000
SALES (est): 43.6MM **Privately Held**
WEB: www.eforcity.com
SIC: 5065 Telephone equipment

(P-7261)
ELMA ELECTRONIC INC
17700 Shideler Pkwy, Lathrop
(95330-9356)
PHONE....................209 858-2411
Badri Rajan, *VP Mfg*
Marc Gaillant, *Prgrmr*
Marc Gallant, *Manager*
EMP: 50
SALES (corp-wide): 146.8MM **Privately
Held**
SIC: 5065 Electronic parts & equipment
HQ: Elma Electronic Inc.
44350 S Grimmer Blvd
Fremont CA 94538

(P-7262)
ELROB INC
Also Called: El-Com Cabletek
12691 Monarch St, Garden Grove
(92841-3918)
PHONE....................714 230-6100
Elie Vrobel, *CEO*
Arik Vrobel, *President*
Dan Balentine, *Vice Pres*
Ken Chau, *Purch Agent*
▲ **EMP:** 54
SQ FT: 38,500
SALES (est): 47.6MM **Privately Held**
WEB: www.elcomcabletek.com
SIC: 5065 3679 3613 3643 Electronic
parts; harness assemblies for electronic
use: wire or cable; switchgear & switch-
board apparatus; current-carrying wiring
devices

(P-7263)
EURASIA POWER LLC
4022 Cmino Ranchero Ste D, Camarillo
(93012)
PHONE....................805 383-1234
Marilou Erb,
Dan Erb,
▲ **EMP:** 50
SALES (est): 14.7MM **Privately Held**
WEB: www.eurasiapower.com
SIC: 5065 Electronic parts & equipment

(P-7264)
**EVER WIN INTERNATIONAL
CORP**
17579 Railroad St, City of Industry
(91748-1125)
PHONE....................626 810-8218
Charles Chen, *CEO*
Henry Chen, *President*
Christine Cheng, *CFO*
Mae Hsu, *Exec VP*
Jim O'Brien, *Vice Pres*
▲ **EMP:** 50
SQ FT: 90,000

SALES (est): 39.9MM **Privately Held**
WEB: www.everwin.com
SIC: 5065 Telephone & telegraphic equip-
ment

(P-7265)
EWING-FOLEY INC (PA)
10061 Bubb Rd Ste 100, Cupertino
(95014-4162)
PHONE....................408 342-1201
Richard Foley, *Ch of Bd*
Todd Henry, *Partner*
Gary Lessing, *President*
Robert Lessing, *Corp Secy*
Jarred Flores, *District Mgr*
EMP: 50 EST: 1964
SQ FT: 13,000
SALES (est): 16.7MM **Privately Held**
WEB: www.ewingfoley.com
SIC: 5065 Electronic parts

(P-7266)
EXIS INC
1570 The Alameda Ste 150, San Jose
(95126-2331)
PHONE....................408 944-4600
Jim Bailey, *President*
Ralph Haar, *Vice Pres*
Suzie Ferreira, *Sales Staff*
EMP: 50
SQ FT: 22,000
SALES (est): 7.4MM **Privately Held**
WEB: www.exisinc.com
SIC: 5065 Electronic parts

(P-7267)
FIBERTRON CORPORATION
6400 Artesia Blvd, Buena Park
(90620-1006)
P.O. Box 5220 (90622-5220)
PHONE....................714 670-7711
Marlene Spiegel, *President*
Eileen Cohen, *Treasurer*
Henry J Cohen, *Finance Other*
▼ **EMP:** 75
SQ FT: 104,000
SALES (est): 34MM **Privately Held**
SIC: 5065 Communication equipment

(P-7268)
**FLIR COMMERCIAL SYSTEMS
INC (HQ)**
6769 Hollister Ave # 100, Goleta
(93117-5572)
PHONE....................805 964-9797
James J Cannon, *President*
Carol P Lowe, *CFO*
Tim Fitzgibbons, *General Mgr*
Darren Haley, *Manager*
▲ **EMP:** 350
SALES (est): 507.8MM
SALES (corp-wide): 1.7B **Publicly Held**
SIC: 5065 3699 Security control equip-
ment & systems; security devices
PA: Flir Systems, Inc.
27700 Sw Parkway Ave
Wilsonville OR 97070
503 498-3547

(P-7269)
FRONTIER CALIFORNIA INC
112 S Lakeview Canyon Rd, Westlake Vil-
lage (91362-3925)
PHONE....................805 372-6000
Deb Anders, *President*
EMP: 650
SALES (corp-wide): 8.6B **Publicly Held**
SIC: 5065 4813 4812 Telephone equip-
ment; telephone communication, except
radio; radio telephone communication
HQ: Frontier California Inc.
140 West St
New York NY 10007
212 395-1000

(P-7270)
FULL CIRCLE WIRELESS INC
8900 Research Dr, Irvine (92618-4245)
PHONE....................949 783-7979
Shelton Basham, *CEO*
EMP: 50
SALES (est): 7MM **Privately Held**
WEB: www.fullcirclewireless.com
SIC: 5065 Mobile telephone equipment

(P-7271)
FUMAI INDUSTRIAL INC
735 W Duarte Rd, Arcadia (91007-7522)
PHONE..................................626 272-1788
John Whang, *Branch Mgr*
EMP: 75
SALES (corp-wide): 7.5MM **Privately Held**
SIC: **5065** Communication equipment
PA: Shanghai Pudong Fumei Industry & Trade Co., Ltd.
No.5, Xinchun Road, Xinchun Village, Huanglou, Chuansha Town, Pu Shanghai 20120
215 894-4666

(P-7272)
GENERAL TRANSISTOR CORPORATION (PA)
Also Called: G T C
12449 Putnam St, Whittier (90602-1023)
PHONE..................................310 578-7344
Albert A Barrios, *President*
Ilan Israely, *Vice Pres*
EMP: 52
SALES (est): 15.9MM **Privately Held**
WEB: www.gtcelectronics.com
SIC: **5065** 3674 Semiconductor devices; semiconductor circuit networks

(P-7273)
GGEC AMERICA INC
20450 Stevens Creek Blvd # 220, Cupertino (95014-6812)
PHONE..................................714 750-2280
Dave Cox, *President*
Jiaxi Huang, *President*
Kobe Zhang, *Vice Pres*
▲ EMP: 72
SQ FT: 2,700
SALES (est): 10.2MM
SALES (corp-wide): 582.2MM **Privately Held**
WEB: www.gabrielkoneta.com
SIC: **5065** Electronic parts
PA: Guoguang Electric Limited
No.8, Jinghu Ave., Xinya Street, Huadu District
Guangzhou 51080
202 267-5743

(P-7274)
GRIFFIN TECHNOLOGY LLC (HQ)
3347 Michelson Dr Ste 100, Irvine (92612-0661)
PHONE..................................949 250-4929
Paul Griffin, *CEO*
▲ EMP: 70
SALES (est): 39.9MM
SALES (corp-wide): 47.6MM **Privately Held**
WEB: www.griffintechnology.com
SIC: **5065** Communication equipment
PA: Incipio Technologies, Inc.
3347 Michelson Dr Ste 100
Irvine CA 92612
949 250-4929

(P-7275)
H M ELECTRONICS INC (PA)
Also Called: H M E
2848 Whiptail Loop, Carlsbad (92010-6708)
PHONE..................................858 535-6000
Harrison Y Miyahira, *Ch of Bd*
Charles Miyahira, *CEO*
Michael Featheringham, *Vice Pres*
Paul Foley, *Vice Pres*
Mike Garrett, *Vice Pres*
◆ EMP: 315 EST: 1971
SQ FT: 73,000
SALES (est): 509.9MM **Privately Held**
WEB: www.hme.com
SIC: **5065** Electronic parts & equipment

(P-7276)
HEILIND ELECTRONICS INC
Also Called: Force Electronics
700 N Plaza Dr, Visalia (93291-9327)
PHONE..................................559 651-0168
Mark Adams, *Manager*
EMP: 55

SALES (corp-wide): 730.7MM **Privately Held**
WEB: www.heilind.com
SIC: **5065** Electronic parts
PA: Heilind Electronics, Inc
58 Jonspin Rd
Wilmington MA 01887
978 657-4870

(P-7277)
HIRSCH ELECTRONICS LLC
1900 Carnegie Ave Ste B, Santa Ana (92705-5557)
PHONE..................................949 250-8888
John Picc, *Mng Member*
Diana Midland, *Info Tech Mgr*
Vouy Yeng, *Technology*
Stephen D Healy, *Mng Member*
John Piccininni, *Mng Member*
EMP: 85 EST: 1981
SQ FT: 34,600
SALES (est): 15.7MM **Publicly Held**
WEB: www.hirschelectronics.com
SIC: **5065** Security control equipment & systems
PA: Identiv, Inc.
2201 Walnut Ave Ste 100
Fremont CA 94538

(P-7278)
HITACHI HIGH TECH AMER INC
5960 Inglewood Dr Ste 200, Pleasanton (94588-8611)
PHONE..................................925 218-2800
Bob Gordon, *Manager*
Robert Gordon, *Vice Pres*
Tom Heiser, *Vice Pres*
John Giudicessi, *Executive*
Donna Armanino, *Managing Dir*
EMP: 70 **Privately Held**
WEB: www.hitachi-hhta.com
SIC: **5065** Electronic parts
HQ: Hitachi High Technologies America, Inc.
10 N Martingale Rd # 500
Schaumburg IL 60173
847 273-4141

(P-7279)
HONEYWELL INTERNATIONAL INC
1349 Moffett Park Dr, Sunnyvale (94089-1134)
PHONE..................................408 962-2000
Barry Russell, *Manager*
EMP: 60
SALES (corp-wide): 41.8B **Publicly Held**
WEB: www.honeywell.com
SIC: **5065** 3674 Electronic parts; semiconductors & related devices
PA: Honeywell International Inc.
300 S Tryon St
Charlotte NC 28202
973 455-2000

(P-7280)
HP INC
16399 W Bernardo Dr # 61, San Diego (92127-1801)
PHONE..................................858 924-5117
Philip Liebscher, *Branch Mgr*
David Collom, *Software Engr*
Paul Hunter, *Project Mgr*
Marsi Bennett, *Research*
Anne Kadonaga, *Research*
EMP: 350
SALES (corp-wide): 58.4B **Publicly Held**
SIC: **5065** Electronic parts & equipment
PA: Hp, Inc.
1501 Page Mill Rd
Palo Alto CA 94304
650 857-1501

(P-7281)
I C CLASS COMPONENTS CORP (PA)
Also Called: Classic
23605 Telo Ave, Torrance (90505-4028)
PHONE..................................310 539-5500
Jeffrey Klein, *President*
Chris Klein, *COO*
Kris Klein, *COO*
Emma Klein, *Treasurer*
Perry Klein, *Vice Pres*
▲ EMP: 100

SQ FT: 53,000
SALES (est): 87MM **Privately Held**
WEB: www.connxx.com
SIC: **5065** Electronic parts

(P-7282)
IDEC CORPORATION (HQ)
1175 Elko Dr, Sunnyvale (94089-2209)
PHONE..................................408 747-0550
Toshiyuki Funaki, *CEO*
Mikio Funaki, *President*
Donald L Scriver, *CFO*
Donald Scrivner, *CFO*
Juan Moreno, *Chief Mktg Ofcr*
▲ EMP: 89
SQ FT: 84,000
SALES (est): 45.2MM **Privately Held**
WEB: www.idec.com
SIC: **5065** Electronic parts

(P-7283)
INDUCTORS INC
Also Called: Central Technologies
1740 W Collins Ave, Orange (92867-5423)
PHONE..................................949 623-2460
Judy Macdonald, *CEO*
▲ EMP: 50
SALES (est): 19.7MM **Privately Held**
WEB: www.inductor.com
SIC: **5065** Electronic parts

(P-7284)
INSULECTRO (PA)
20362 Windrow Dr Ste 100, Lake Forest (92630-8140)
PHONE..................................949 587-3200
Timothy P Redfern, *CEO*
Patrick Redfern, *President*
Brad Biddle, *CFO*
Chris Hunrath, *Vice Pres*
Kathy Linares, *Vice Pres*
▲ EMP: 70 EST: 1991
SQ FT: 40,000
SALES (est): 128.6MM **Privately Held**
WEB: www.cac-inc.com
SIC: **5065** Electronic parts

(P-7285)
JIT CORPORATION
Also Called: J I T
2790 Valley View Ave, Norco (92860-2349)
PHONE..................................805 238-5000
Brent Smith, *President*
Sharon Smith, *Corp Secy*
EMP: 60
SQ FT: 30,000
SALES (est): 55.7MM **Privately Held**
WEB: www.jitmfg.com
SIC: **5065** Electronic parts

(P-7286)
JOHNSON CONTROLS INC
1757 Tapo Canyon Rd # 120, Simi Valley (93063-3390)
PHONE..................................805 522-5555
Patrick Young, *Regional Mgr*
Dimitri Dorfman, *Information Mgr*
EMP: 60 **Privately Held**
SIC: **5065** Security control equipment & systems
HQ: Johnson Controls, Inc.
5757 N Green Bay Ave
Milwaukee WI 53209
414 524-1200

(P-7287)
JRI INC
Also Called: J R Industries
31280 La Baya Dr, Westlake Village (91362-4005)
PHONE..................................818 706-2424
Kathy Becker, *President*
▲ EMP: 50
SQ FT: 20,000
SALES (est): 25.8MM **Privately Held**
WEB: www.jri.com
SIC: **5065** 3679 Electronic parts; harness assemblies for electronic use: wire or cable

(P-7288)
KIOXIA AMERICA INC (DH)
Also Called: Toshiba Memory America, Inc.
2610 Orchard Pkwy, San Jose (95134-2020)
PHONE..................................408 526-2400

Takanori Nakazawa, *CFO*
EMP: 200
SQ FT: 60,000
SALES: 3B **Privately Held**
SIC: **5065** Semiconductor devices
HQ: Toshiba America Electronic Components Inc
5231 California Ave
Irvine CA 92617
949 462-7700

(P-7289)
KYOCERA INTERNATIONAL INC
3565 Cadillac Ave, Costa Mesa (92626-1401)
PHONE..................................714 428-3600
EMP: 50 **Publicly Held**
SIC: **5065** 5013 5085 Electronic parts; heaters, motor vehicle; industrial tools
HQ: Kyocera International, Inc.
8611 Balboa Ave
San Diego CA 92123
858 492-1456

(P-7290)
LBF ENTERPRISES (PA)
Also Called: Powermatic Associates
1264 Stealth St, Livermore (94551-9354)
PHONE..................................925 461-7171
Frank Nudo, *CEO*
Rudy Solis Jr, *CFO*
Moore Kevin, *Sales Engr*
Carol Bayer, *Sales Staff*
Laura Bruce, *Sales Staff*
EMP: 70
SALES (est): 38.2MM **Privately Held**
WEB: www.powermatic.net
SIC: **5065** Electronic parts & equipment

(P-7291)
LEGACY FRAMES
11220 Wright Rd, Lynwood (90262-3124)
PHONE..................................310 537-4210
Angelica Serrano, *CEO*
EMP: 54
SALES: 5MM **Privately Held**
SIC: **5065** Mobile telephone equipment

(P-7292)
LEMO USA INC
635 Park Ct, Rohnert Park (94928-7940)
P.O. Box 2408 (94927-2408)
PHONE..................................707 206-3700
Dinshaw Pohwala, *CEO*
Michael Grieco, *COO*
Farhad Kashani, *General Mgr*
Wendy Christiansen, *Executive Asst*
Marian Johnson, *Administration*
EMP: 100
SQ FT: 55,000
SALES (est): 58.1MM
SALES (corp-wide): 124.5MM **Privately Held**
WEB: www.lemousa.com
SIC: **5065** 3678 Connectors, electronic; electronic connectors
HQ: Interlemo U.S.A. Inc.
635 Park Ct
Rohnert Park CA 94928
707 578-8811

(P-7293)
LG DISPLAY AMERICA INC
2791 Loker Ave W, Carlsbad (92010-6601)
PHONE..................................760 692-0900
Byungdo Park, *Branch Mgr*
Michael Kim, *President*
Thomas Schauneweg, *Vice Pres*
Dawit Kim, *Administration*
Kim Chanelle, *Human Resources*
EMP: 50 **Privately Held**
SIC: **5065** Modems, computer
HQ: Lg Display America, Inc.
2540 N 1st St Ste 400
San Jose CA 95131
408 350-0190

(P-7294)
LG DISPLAY AMERICA INC (HQ)
2540 N 1st St Ste 400, San Jose (95131-1016)
PHONE..................................408 350-0190
Chris Min, *President*
Davis Lee, *President*
James Jeong, *CFO*
Yong Kee Huang, *Senior VP*

Cheol D Ong Jeong, *Principal*
▲ **EMP:** 70
SQ FT: 1,000
SALES (est): 46.7MM **Privately Held**
SIC: 5065 Modems, computer

(P-7295)
LINKSYS LLC
12045 Waterfront Dr, Playa Vista (90094-2999)
PHONE.............................310 751-5100
Dang Nguyen, *Manager*
EMP: 110 **Privately Held**
SIC: 5065 Electronic parts & equipment
HQ: Linksys Llc
121 Theory
Irvine CA 92617
949 270-8500

(P-7296)
LINKSYS LLC (DH)
121 Theory, Irvine (92617-3209)
P.O. Box 91830, Los Angeles (90009-1830)
PHONE.............................949 270-8500
Chet Pipkin, *Mng Member*
Wiener Mondesir, *Senior Mgr*
◆ **EMP:** 275
SQ FT: 20,000
SALES (est): 314.4MM **Privately Held**
WEB: www.cisco.com
SIC: 5065 Communication equipment
HQ: Belkin International, Inc.
12045 Waterfront Dr
Playa Vista CA 90094
310 751-5100

(P-7297)
LITE-ON INC (HQ)
Also Called: Lite-On U S A
720 S Hillview Dr, Milpitas (95035-5455)
PHONE.............................408 946-4873
Sonny Hsuen-Ching Chao, *President*
Anson Chiu, *General Mgr*
Jing Shao, *Sr Software Eng*
Julie Huang, *Accountant*
Jennifer Y Chen, *Human Resources*
▲ **EMP:** 50
SQ FT: 25,000
SALES (est): 17.7MM **Privately Held**
WEB: www.liteonus.com
SIC: 5065 Semiconductor devices

(P-7298)
LTS ASSOCIATE INC (PA)
18738 San Jose Ave, City of Industry (91748-1323)
PHONE.............................626 435-2838
Grant Long, *CEO*
Kai Yang, *Co-CEO*
Carlo Yu, *Admin Sec*
EMP: 50
SALES (est): 27.9MM **Privately Held**
SIC: 5065 Security control equipment & systems

(P-7299)
MACRONIX AMERICA INC (HQ)
Also Called: Mxic
680 N Mccarthy Blvd # 200, Milpitas (95035-5120)
PHONE.............................408 262-8887
Arthur Yang, *CEO*
Rudy Prochivina, *Vice Pres*
Richard Culver, *CTO*
Wilvin Lee, *MIS Staff*
Samuel Su, *Regl Sales Mgr*
EMP: 53
SQ FT: 20,000
SALES (est): 18.9MM **Privately Held**
WEB: www.macronix.com
SIC: 5065 3674 Semiconductor devices; semiconductors & related devices

(P-7300)
MDE SEMICONDUCTOR INC
201 Shipyard Way Ste C, Newport Beach (92663-4452)
PHONE.............................760 564-8656
Bill Morgan, *President*
▲ **EMP:** 75
SALES (est): 7.3MM **Privately Held**
WEB: www.mdesemiconductor.com
SIC: 5065 Electronic parts & equipment

(P-7301)
METRIC EQUIPMENT SALES INC
Also Called: Microlease
25841 Industrial Blvd # 200, Hayward (94545-2991)
PHONE.............................510 264-0887
Nigel Brown, *CEO*
Mike Clark, *CEO*
Nathan Hurst, *CFO*
David Sherve, *Senior VP*
Gordon Curwen, *Vice Pres*
EMP: 70
SQ FT: 25,000
SALES (est): 51.9MM
SALES (corp-wide): 122.9MM **Privately Held**
WEB: www.metrictest.com
SIC: 5065 5084 7359 3825 Electronic parts; measuring & testing equipment, electrical; electronic equipment rental, except computers; instruments to measure electricity
HQ: Microlease Inc.
6060 Sepulveda Blvd
Van Nuys CA 91411
866 520-0200

(P-7302)
MICRO-MECHANICS INC
465 Woodview Ave, Morgan Hill (95037-2800)
PHONE.............................408 779-2927
Christopher R Borch, *President*
Michael Maguire, *Engineer*
Shirley Bautista, *Sales Engr*
Kathleen Edmiston,
Carol Bean, *Manager*
EMP: 50
SQ FT: 42,000
SALES (est): 24.7MM **Privately Held**
WEB: www.micromechanics.com
SIC: 5065 3674 Semiconductor devices; semiconductors & related devices
PA: Micro-Mechanics (Holdings) Ltd.
31 Kaki Bukit Place
Singapore 41620

(P-7303)
MINIMATICS INC (PA)
3445 De La Cruz Blvd, Santa Clara (95054-2110)
PHONE.............................650 969-5630
Walter Chew, *President*
Charles R Fowler, *Shareholder*
Siegfried Waaga, *General Mgr*
Marjorie Chew, *Admin Sec*
EMP: 57 **EST:** 1973
SALES (est): 19.2MM **Privately Held**
WEB: www.minimatics.com
SIC: 5065 3599 Semiconductor devices; machine shop, jobbing & repair

(P-7304)
MITSUBISHI ELECTRIC US INC
7345 Orangewood Ave, Garden Grove (92841-1411)
PHONE.............................714 934-5300
EMP: 60
SALES (corp-wide): 36.3B **Privately Held**
SIC: 5065 5045
HQ: Mitsubishi Electric Us, Inc.
5900 Katella Ave Ste A
Cypress CA 90630
714 220-2500

(P-7305)
MOBILYGEN CORPORATION
160 Rio Robles, San Jose (95134-1813)
PHONE.............................408 601-1000
Joseph Perl, *Ch of Bd*
Chris Day, *President*
EMP: 60
SQ FT: 13,000
SALES (est): 6.2MM
SALES (corp-wide): 2.3B **Publicly Held**
WEB: www.mobilygen.com
SIC: 5065 Semiconductor devices
PA: Maxim Integrated Products, Inc.
160 Rio Robles
San Jose CA 95134
408 601-1000

(P-7306)
MOSCHIP SEMICONDUCTOR TECH USA
3335 Kifer Rd, Santa Clara (95051-0719)
PHONE.............................408 737-7141
Ram K Reddey, *CEO*
Shiri Kadambi, *President*
Ashok Kumar, *Vice Pres*
Dayakar Reddy, *Managing Dir*
Sam Sanyal, *Marketing Staff*
EMP: 120
SQ FT: 4,000
SALES (est): 15.9MM **Privately Held**
WEB: www.moschip.com
SIC: 5065 Semiconductor devices
PA: Moschip Technologies Limited
Plot No. 83 & 84, 2nd Floor,
Hyderabad TS 50003

(P-7307)
MOTOROLA MOBILITY LLC
6450 Sequence Dr, San Diego (92121-4376)
PHONE.............................858 455-1500
Rick Neal, *Branch Mgr*
Arsalan Khan, *Software Engr*
Rebecca Burbrink, *Project Mgr*
Yang Jenny, *Engineer*
EMP: 80
SQ FT: 30,000 **Privately Held**
WEB: www.motorola-labs.com
SIC: 5065 3663 Communication equipment; radio & TV communications equipment
HQ: Motorola Mobility Llc
222 Mdse Mart Plz # 1800
Chicago IL 60654

(P-7308)
NALLATECH INC
741 Flynn Rd, Camarillo (93012-8056)
PHONE.............................805 383-8997
Colin Rutherford, *Chairman*
Allan Cantle, *President*
William P Miller, *CEO*
Ed Hennessy, *Vice Pres*
EMP: 64
SALES (est): 24.3MM
SALES (corp-wide): 40.6B **Privately Held**
WEB: www.nallatech.com
SIC: 5065 Electronic parts & equipment
HQ: Interconnect Systems, Inc.
741 Flynn Rd
Camarillo CA 93012
805 482-2870

(P-7309)
NEST LABS INC
3400 Hillview Ave, Palo Alto (94304-1346)
PHONE.............................855 469-6378
Tony Fadell, *CEO*
Matthew Rogers, *Principal*
Kathy Vick, *Executive Asst*
James Lyons, *Software Engr*
Ajay Ravindra, *Software Engr*
◆ **EMP:** 70
SALES (est): 61.8MM
SALES (corp-wide): 136.8B **Publicly Held**
SIC: 5065 5999 Electronic parts & equipment; electronic parts & equipment
HQ: Google Llc
1600 Amphitheatre Pkwy
Mountain View CA 94043
650 253-0000

(P-7310)
NOVACAP LLC
25111 Anza Dr, Valencia (91355-3478)
PHONE.............................661 295-5920
Mark Skoog, *CEO*
Shelley Mears, *Info Tech Mgr*
Paco Sarmiento, *Engineer*
Teri Servera, *Human Res Dir*
Novacap Syfer, *Mfg Staff*
▲ **EMP:** 280
SQ FT: 38,000
SALES (est): 120.3MM
SALES (corp-wide): 826.9MM **Publicly Held**
WEB: www.novacap.com
SIC: 5065 Electronic parts & equipment

PA: Knowles Corporation
1151 Maplewood Dr
Itasca IL 60143
630 250-5100

(P-7311)
NU HORIZONS ELECTRONICS CORP
890 N Mccarthy Blvd, San Jose (95131)
PHONE.............................408 946-4154
EMP: 50
SALES (corp-wide): 23.2B **Publicly Held**
SIC: 5065
HQ: Nu Horizons Electronics Corp.
70 Maxess Rd
Melville NY 11747
631 396-5000

(P-7312)
NUCOURSE DISTRIBUTION INC
22342 Avenida Empresa # 200, Rcho STA Marg (92688-2140)
PHONE.............................866 655-4366
Nicholas Troy Seedorf, *CEO*
Brandon Seedorf, *Vice Pres*
Ian Shiry, *Finance*
EMP: 55
SALES (est): 89MM **Privately Held**
SIC: 5065 Electronic parts & equipment

(P-7313)
NUVOTON TECHNOLOGY CORP AMER
2727 N 1st St, San Jose (95134-2029)
PHONE.............................408 544-1718
Arthur Yu-Cheng Chiao, *Chairman*
Robert Hsu, *President*
Mark Hemming, *Chief Mktg Ofcr*
Stephen Rei-Min Huang, *Vice Pres*
Bor-Yuan Hwang, *Vice Pres*
EMP: 60
SALES (est): 24.3MM **Privately Held**
SIC: 5065 Semiconductor devices
HQ: Nuvoton Technology Corporation
4, Creation 3rd Rd.,
Hsinchu City 30077

(P-7314)
ODU-USA INC (HQ)
300 Camarillo Ranch Rd A, Camarillo (93012-5208)
PHONE.............................805 484-0540
Michael Savage, *CEO*
Joseph Cisi, *President*
Kurt Woelfl, *CEO*
▲ **EMP:** 60
SQ FT: 20,000
SALES (est): 40MM
SALES (corp-wide): 139.7MM **Privately Held**
WEB: www.odu-usa.com
SIC: 5065 Connectors, electronic
PA: Odu Gmbh & Co. Kg
Pregelstr. 11
Muhldorf A. Inn 84453
863 161-560

(P-7315)
ORGANIC AFFINITY LLC
3980 Hopevale Dr, Sherman Oaks (91403-4414)
PHONE.............................801 870-7433
David Surber, *Mng Member*
EMP: 65
SALES (est): 2.6MM **Privately Held**
SIC: 5065 Electronic parts & equipment

(P-7316)
OSRAM OPTO SEMICONDUCTORS INC
1150 Kifer Rd Ste 100, Sunnyvale (94086-5302)
PHONE.............................408 588-3800
Tom Shottes, *Manager*
EMP: 52
SALES (corp-wide): 4.7B **Privately Held**
WEB: www.osram-os.com
SIC: 5065 Semiconductor devices
HQ: Osram Opto Semiconductors Inc.
1150 Kifer Rd Ste 100
Sunnyvale CA 94086

(P-7317)
OSRAM OPTO SEMICONDUCTORS INC (HQ)
1150 Kifer Rd Ste 100, Sunnyvale (94086-5302)
PHONE............................408 962-3736
Olaf Berlien, *CEO*
▲ **EMP:** 50
SALES (est): 29MM
SALES (corp-wide): 4.7B **Privately Held**
WEB: www.osram-os.com
SIC: 5065 Semiconductor devices
PA: Osram Licht Ag
Marcel-Breuer-Str. 6
Munchen 80807
896 213-0

(P-7318)
PARTSEARCH TECHNOLOGIES INC
Also Called: Andrews Electronics
25158 Avenue Stanford, Santa Clarita (91355-1226)
PHONE............................661 257-7700
John Zeitlin, *Manager*
EMP: 50
SALES (corp-wide): 42.8B **Publicly Held**
SIC: 5065 3679 Electronic parts; commutators, electronic
HQ: Partsearch Technologies Inc.
27460 Avenue Scott D
Valencia CA 91355
800 289-0300

(P-7319)
PERILLO INDUSTRIES INC
Also Called: Century Electronics
2150 Anchor Ct Ste A, Newbury Park (91320-1609)
PHONE............................805 498-9838
Mary Perillo, *President*
Clint Wilder, *Research*
Grace Abaya, *Human Resources*
EMP: 50 **EST:** 1973
SQ FT: 20,000
SALES (est): 26MM **Privately Held**
SIC: 5065 Electronic parts & equipment

(P-7320)
PHASE MATRIX INC
Also Called: Ni Microwave Components
4600 Patrick Henry Dr, Santa Clara (95054-1817)
PHONE............................954 490-9429
Pete Pragastis, *President*
George Clark, *Administration*
Rick Kraft, *Info Tech Mgr*
Raj Johal, *Senior Buyer*
Gary Gerlinger, *Materials Mgr*
EMP: 50
SQ FT: 24,000
SALES (est): 25.1MM
SALES (corp-wide): 1.3B **Publicly Held**
WEB: www.phasematrix.com
SIC: 5065 Electronic parts & equipment
PA: National Instruments Corporation
11500 N Mopac Expy
Austin TX 78759
512 683-0100

(P-7321)
PRESIDIO COMPONENTS INC
7169 Construction Ct, San Diego (92121-2615)
PHONE............................858 578-9390
Violet Devoe, *President*
Alan Devoe, *Vice Pres*
Daniel Devoe, *Vice Pres*
Lambert Devoe, *Vice Pres*
▲ **EMP:** 120 **EST:** 1980
SQ FT: 35,000
SALES (est): 66.8MM **Privately Held**
WEB: www.presidiocomponents.com
SIC: 5065 Electronic parts & equipment

(P-7322)
PRISM ELECTRONICS CORP (PA)
900 Lightpost Way 100, Morgan Hill (95037-2869)
PHONE............................408 778-7050
John Jules Mauro, *CEO*
Sofia Fedotova, *Admin Sec*
◆ **EMP:** 50
SQ FT: 21,373

SALES (est): 12.3MM **Privately Held**
SIC: 5065 Electronic parts

(P-7323)
PROJECTIONS UNLIMITED INC (PA)
Also Called: P U I
15311 Barranca Pkwy, Irvine (92618-2216)
PHONE............................714 544-2700
David Herring, *CEO*
Andrew Salas, *CFO*
Dave Burgener, *Vice Pres*
Robert Gau, *Vice Pres*
Kurt Oliver, *Admin Sec*
▲ **EMP:** 50
SQ FT: 17,500
SALES: 21.1MM **Privately Held**
SIC: 5065 Electronic parts & equipment

(P-7324)
PURISM SPC
5670 El Camino Real Ste E, Carlsbad (92008-7125)
PHONE............................415 555-1212
Todd Weaver, *CEO*
EMP: 50
SALES (est): 7.1MM **Privately Held**
SIC: 5065 Telephone equipment

(P-7325)
QMADIX INC
14350 Arminta St, Panorama City (91402-6869)
PHONE............................818 988-4300
Ezra Soumekh, *CEO*
David Khalepari, *CEO*
Richard Mertz, *COO*
Heidi Dianaty, *CFO*
Cesar Cerritos, *Executive*
▲ **EMP:** 51
SQ FT: 30,000
SALES (est): 15.5MM **Privately Held**
WEB: www.paramountwireless.com
SIC: 5065 Mobile telephone equipment

(P-7326)
QUEST COMPONENTS INC
14711 Clark Ave, City of Industry (91745-1307)
PHONE............................626 333-5858
Dave A Hozen, *CEO*
Elaine Bowker, *CFO*
Andre A Hozen, *Treasurer*
John Haproff, *Sales Staff*
Linda Olivas, *Sales Staff*
▲ **EMP:** 50
SQ FT: 32,000
SALES (est): 26.1MM **Privately Held**
WEB: www.quest-comp.com
SIC: 5065 Electronic parts

(P-7327)
QUINSTAR TECHNOLOGY INC
24085 Garnier St, Torrance (90505-5319)
PHONE............................310 320-1111
Leo Fong, *President*
John Kuno, *Exec VP*
Hj Kuno, *Vice Pres*
▲ **EMP:** 72
SALES (est): 37.8MM **Privately Held**
WEB: www.quinstar.com
SIC: 5065 Electronic parts & equipment

(P-7328)
R&M USA INC
Also Called: REALM
840 Yosemite Way, Milpitas (95035-6360)
PHONE............................408 945-6626
Christopher Stratas, *President*
Michel Riva, *Director*
Patrick Steiner, *Director*
▲ **EMP:** 80
SQ FT: 34,865
SALES: 20.2MM
SALES (corp-wide): 106.7MM **Privately Held**
WEB: www.rcgoptic.com
SIC: 5065 Communication equipment
HQ: Reichle & De-Massari Ag
Binzstrasse 32
Wetzikon ZH 8620
449 319-777

(P-7329)
RAKON AMERICA LLC
7600 Dublin Blvd Ste 220, Dublin (94568-2944)
PHONE............................847 930-5100
Dean Ransom,
EMP: 600
SALES (est): 42.4MM
SALES (corp-wide): 77.6MM **Privately Held**
WEB: www.rakon.com
SIC: 5065 Electronic parts & equipment
PA: Rakon Limited
8 Sylvia Park Road
Auckland 1060
957 355-54

(P-7330)
RAND TECHNOLOGY LLC (PA)
15225 Alton Pkwy Unit 100, Irvine (92618-2351)
PHONE............................949 255-5700
Andrea Klein, *President*
Paul Bockstedt, *President*
Tawnie Bassett-Parkins, *CFO*
Sean Sloan, *CFO*
Jeffrey Wasserman, *Vice Pres*
EMP: 67
SQ FT: 25,000
SALES (est): 66.6MM **Privately Held**
WEB: www.randtech.com
SIC: 5065 Semiconductor devices

(P-7331)
RANTEC POWER SYSTEMS INC (HQ)
1173 Los Olivos Ave, Los Osos (93402-3230)
PHONE............................805 596-6000
Michael C Bickel, *President*
Frank Janku, *CFO*
Robert Judd, *General Mgr*
Alan Garton, *Design Engr*
Jacob Cope, *Engineer*
EMP: 98
SQ FT: 40,000
SALES: 35.5MM
SALES (corp-wide): 33.3MM **Privately Held**
WEB: www.rantec.com
SIC: 5065 Electronic parts & equipment
PA: Rps Holdings, Inc.
1173 Los Olivos Ave
Los Osos CA 93402
805 596-6000

(P-7332)
RAYTHEON COMMAND AND CONTROL
2000 E El Segundo Blvd, El Segundo (90245-4501)
PHONE............................714 446-3232
Ron Levesque, *Branch Mgr*
EMP: 50
SALES (corp-wide): 27B **Publicly Held**
SIC: 5065 Security control equipment & systems
HQ: Raytheon Command And Control Solutions Llc
1801 Hughes Dr
Fullerton CA 92833

(P-7333)
RAYTHEON COMMAND AND CONTROL (HQ)
1801 Hughes Dr, Fullerton (92833-2200)
P.O. Box 34055 (92834-9455)
PHONE............................714 446-3118
Peter W Chiarelli,
Alex Cresswell,
Don Johnson,
▲ **EMP:** 700
SALES (est): 295MM
SALES (corp-wide): 27B **Publicly Held**
SIC: 5065 Security control equipment & systems
PA: Raytheon Company
870 Winter St
Waltham MA 02451
781 522-3000

(P-7334)
RENESAS ELECTRONICS AMER INC
Also Called: Intersil Techwell
1541 Rollins Rd, Burlingame (94010-2305)
PHONE............................408 588-6750
Richard Turner, *Director*
EMP: 600 **Privately Held**
SIC: 5065 Electronic parts & equipment
HQ: Renesas Electronics America Inc.
1001 Murphy Ranch Rd
Milpitas CA 95035
408 432-8888

(P-7335)
SAMSUNG ELECTRONICS AMER INC
665 Clyde Ave, Mountain View (94043-2235)
PHONE............................650 210-1000
Evan Maxei, *Director*
Adriana Park, *Bd of Directors*
George Apostol, *Vice Pres*
Helen Ong, *Vice Pres*
James Ting, *Vice Pres*
EMP: 1000
SQ FT: 395 **Privately Held**
WEB: www.samsung.com
SIC: 5065 Electronic parts & equipment
HQ: Samsung Electronics America, Inc.
85 Challenger Rd Fl 7
Ridgefield Park NJ 07660
201 229-4000

(P-7336)
SAMSUNG INTERNATIONAL INC (DH)
333 H St Ste 6000, Chula Vista (91910-5565)
PHONE............................619 671-6859
Jong Hyun Won, *CEO*
Hyunsik Lee, *Senior Mgr*
Paul Yun, *Asst Mgr*
◆ **EMP:** 50
SALES (est): 138.2MM **Privately Held**
SIC: 5065 Electronic parts & equipment
HQ: Samsung Electronics America, Inc.
85 Challenger Rd Fl 7
Ridgefield Park NJ 07660
201 229-4000

(P-7337)
SAMSUNG SEMICONDUCTOR INC (DH)
3655 N 1st St, San Jose (95134-1707)
PHONE............................408 544-4000
Young Chang Bae, *President*
Damian Huh, *CFO*
Tom Quinn, *Senior VP*
Chris Byrne, *Vice Pres*
Jim Elliott, *Vice Pres*
◆ **EMP:** 216
SQ FT: 206,816
SALES (est): 915.4MM **Privately Held**
SIC: 5065 5045 Semiconductor devices; computers, peripherals & software
HQ: Samsung Electronics America, Inc.
85 Challenger Rd Fl 7
Ridgefield Park NJ 07660
201 229-4000

(P-7338)
SARCO INC
Also Called: 123ewireless
30412 Esperanza, Rcho STA Marg (92688-2144)
PHONE............................949 888-5548
Ali Sar, *President*
Megan Flower, *Exec VP*
Claudia Hernandez, *Accounting Mgr*
Eleanor Jackson, *Human Res Mgr*
Mike Vela, *Production*
◆ **EMP:** 50
SQ FT: 30,000
SALES (est): 17.1MM **Privately Held**
WEB: www.123edistribution.com
SIC: 5065 Electronic parts & equipment

(P-7339)
SCREEN SPE USA LLC (DH)
Also Called: Dns Electronics
820 Kifer Rd Ste B, Sunnyvale (94086-5200)
PHONE............................408 523-9140
Tadahiro Suhara, *CEO*

James Beard, *President*
Kirk Kitaguchi, *Senior VP*
Scott Gallar, *VP Finance*
▲ **EMP:** 177
SQ FT: 28,400
SALES (est): 75.1MM **Privately Held**
WEB: www.dnse.com
SIC: 5065 7629 Electronic parts; electrical repair shops
HQ: Screen North America Holdings, Inc.
5110 Tollview Dr
Rolling Meadows IL 60008
847 870-7400

(P-7340)
SILICONWARE USA INC (DH)
1735 Tech Dr Ste 300 Fl 3, San Jose (95110)
PHONE..........................408 573-5500
Bough Lin, *Ch of Bd*
Randy Hsiao Yu Lo, *President*
Yi Hsin Lin, *CFO*
EMP: 50 **EST:** 1996
SQ FT: 8,000
SALES (est): 13.2MM **Privately Held**
WEB: www.spilca.com
SIC: 5065 Semiconductor devices

(P-7341)
SL POWER ELECTRONICS CORP (PA)
6050 King Dr Ste A, Ventura (93003-7176)
PHONE..........................800 235-5929
Jim Taylor, *President*
Ken Owens, *CEO*
Steven Miller, *Vice Pres*
Tammy Matteson, *Executive Asst*
Derek Martin, *IT/INT Sup*
◆ **EMP:** 65 **EST:** 1978
SQ FT: 36,480
SALES (est): 182.7MM **Privately Held**
SIC: 5065 Electronic parts & equipment

(P-7342)
SMA SOLAR TECHNOLOGY AMER LLC (HQ)
Also Called: SMA America
6020 West Oaks Blvd, Rocklin (95765-5472)
PHONE..........................916 625-0870
Jurgen Krehnke,
King Peter, *IT Specialist*
Renzo Morante, *Project Mgr*
Aaron Wurst, *Project Mgr*
Chris Bounds, *Technology*
◆ **EMP:** 79 **EST:** 2000
SQ FT: 25,000
SALES (est): 247.2MM
SALES (corp-wide): 871.1MM **Privately Held**
WEB: www.sma-america.com
SIC: 5065 Electronic parts
PA: Sma Solar Technology Ag
Sonnenallee 1
Niestetal 34266
561 952-20

(P-7343)
SOLIGENT DISTRIBUTION LLC (HQ)
1400 N Mcdowell Blvd # 201, Petaluma (94954-6553)
PHONE..........................707 992-3100
Jonathan Doochin, *CEO*
Thomas Enzendorfer, *President*
Mark Laabs, *COO*
Eric Von Dermehden, *Vice Pres*
Jeremy Doochin, *VP Bus Dvlpt*
▼ **EMP:** 57 **EST:** 2013
SALES (est): 122.8MM
SALES (corp-wide): 154.6MM **Privately Held**
SIC: 5065 8711 Electronic parts & equipment; engineering services
PA: Soligent Holdings Inc.
1500 Valley House Dr # 210
Rohnert Park CA 94928
707 992-3100

(P-7344)
SOURCE PHOTONICS USA INC (PA)
8521 Fllbrook Ave Ste 200, West Hills (91304)
PHONE..........................818 773-9044

Doug Wright, *CEO*
EMP: 249
SALES (est): 40.7MM **Privately Held**
WEB: www.luminentinc.com
SIC: 5065 Electronic parts & equipment

(P-7345)
STELLAR MICROELECTRONICS INC
9340 Owensmouth Ave, Chatsworth (91311-6915)
PHONE..........................661 775-3500
Sudesh Arora, *President*
V U Ngyen, *Engineer*
Noel Santos, *Engineer*
David Ford, *Sales Staff*
EMP: 239
SQ FT: 140,000
SALES (est): 124.8MM
SALES (corp-wide): 1.1B **Privately Held**
WEB: www.stellarmicro.com
SIC: 5065 Semiconductor devices
PA: Natel Engineering Company, Llc
9340 Owensmouth Ave
Chatsworth CA 91311
818 495-8617

(P-7346)
STEREN ELECTRONICS INTL LLC (PA)
6910 Carroll Rd Ste 200, San Diego (92121-2211)
PHONE..........................800 266-3333
Leon Shteremberg Ttee,
Teresa Morton, *Sales Staff*
David Shteremberg,
Vick Soffer,
Jose Zyman,
◆ **EMP:** 100
SQ FT: 75,000
SALES (est): 41.4MM **Privately Held**
WEB: www.steren.com
SIC: 5065 Connectors, electronic

(P-7347)
STMICROELECTRONICS INC
2755 Great America Way, Santa Clara (95054-1166)
PHONE..........................408 452-8585
EMP: 140
SALES (corp-wide): 8.3B **Privately Held**
SIC: 5065
HQ: Stmicroelectronics, Inc
750 Canyon Dr Ste 300
Coppell TX 75019
972 466-6000

(P-7348)
SUMITOMO ELECTRIC DEVICE INNOV
2355 Zanker Rd, San Jose (95131-1109)
PHONE..........................408 232-9500
Mike Nishiguchi, *CEO*
John Wyatt, *CFO*
Eddie Tsumura, *Vice Pres*
Chris Wiggins, *Vice Pres*
Ed Wilson, *Vice Pres*
▲ **EMP:** 80
SQ FT: 52,600
SALES (est): 28.6MM **Privately Held**
WEB: www.sei-device.com
SIC: 5065 Electronic parts
PA: Sumitomo Electric Industries, Ltd.
4-5-33, Kitahama, Chuo-Ku
Osaka OSK 541-0

(P-7349)
SUPERIOR COMMUNICATIONS INC (PA)
Also Called: Puregear
5027 Irwindale Ave # 900, Irwindale (91706-2187)
PHONE..........................877 522-4727
Solomon Chen, *Ch of Bd*
Michael Cavanah, *Shareholder*
Jeffrey Banks, *President*
Mike Cavah, *President*
Mike Cost, *COO*
▲ **EMP:** 248
SQ FT: 11,000
SALES (est): 746.4MM **Privately Held**
WEB: www.scp4me.com
SIC: 5065 Communication equipment

(P-7350)
SURVEILLANCE SYSTEMS
Also Called: Ssi
4465 Granite Dr Ste 700, Rocklin (95677-2143)
PHONE..........................800 508-6981
Michael T Flowers, *CEO*
Jon Ward, *President*
Mark Haney, *Chairman*
Olga Suarez, *Accounting Mgr*
Kellie Vogel, *Sales Staff*
EMP: 50
SQ FT: 15,000
SALES (est): 20MM **Privately Held**
WEB: www.ssicctv.com
SIC: 5065 Video equipment, electronic; security control equipment & systems

(P-7351)
SWANN COMMUNICATIONS USA INC
12636 Clark St, Santa Fe Springs (90670-3950)
PHONE..........................562 777-2551
Michael Lucas, *CEO*
Jason Carrington, *CFO*
Dennis McTighe, *Vice Pres*
Geoffrey Schorz, *Technical Staff*
Ann Cook, *Human Res Dir*
◆ **EMP:** 87
SQ FT: 45,000
SALES (est): 108MM **Privately Held**
WEB: www.swann.com
SIC: 5065 Video equipment, electronic

(P-7352)
TABULA INC
1100 La Avenida St Ste A, Mountain View (94043-1453)
PHONE..........................408 986-9140
Dennis Segers, *CEO*
Steven Teig, *President*
EMP: 100
SALES (est): 57.3MM **Privately Held**
WEB: www.tabula.com
SIC: 5065 Semiconductor devices

(P-7353)
TALLEY INC (PA)
Also Called: Talley & Associates
12976 Sandoval St, Santa Fe Springs (90670-4061)
P.O. Box 3123 (90670-0123)
PHONE..........................562 906-8000
John R Talley, *CEO*
Mark D Talley, *President*
George R Hulbert, *CFO*
Karen Frankenberg, *Officer*
Elizabeth J Talley, *Exec VP*
◆ **EMP:** 110
SQ FT: 80,000
SALES (est): 113.9MM **Privately Held**
WEB: www.talleycom.com
SIC: 5065 Communication equipment; amateur radio communications equipment

(P-7354)
TDK-LAMBDA AMERICAS INC
401 Mile Of Cars Way # 3, National City (91950-6610)
PHONE..........................619 575-4400
Pascal Shauson, *CEO*
Vinod Bapat, *President*
George Bees, *President*
Lynette Toves, *Admin Sec*
Tom Wichert, *VP Sales*
EMP: 200 **Privately Held**
WEB: www.lambdapower.com
SIC: 5065 Electronic parts & equipment
HQ: Tdk-Lambda Americas Inc.
405 Essex Rd
Tinton Falls NJ 07753
732 922-9300

(P-7355)
TECH SYSTEMS INC
7372 Walnut Ave Ste J, Buena Park (90620-1718)
PHONE..........................714 523-5404
Raymond Downs, *Manager*
EMP: 120
SALES (corp-wide): 33.8MM **Privately Held**
SIC: 5065 Closed circuit television

PA: Tech Systems, Inc.
4942 Summer Oak Dr
Buford GA 30518
770 495-8700

(P-7356)
TRAK MICROWAVE CORPORATION
375 Conejo Ridge Ave, Thousand Oaks (91361-4928)
PHONE..........................805 267-0100
◆ **EMP:** 160 **EST:** 1971
SQ FT: 67,000
SALES (est): 4MM
SALES (corp-wide): 4.2B **Privately Held**
WEB: www.tecom-ind.com
SIC: 5065 Electronic parts
HQ: Smiths Interconnect, Inc.
4726 Eisenhower Blvd
Tampa FL 33634
813 901-7200

(P-7357)
TTI INC
Also Called: Rfmw
188 Martinvale Ln, San Jose (95119-1356)
PHONE..........................408 414-1450
Joel Levine, *Branch Mgr*
EMP: 80
SALES (corp-wide): 225.3B **Publicly Held**
SIC: 5065 Electronic parts
HQ: Tti, Inc.
2441 Northeast Pkwy
Fort Worth TX 76106
817 740-9000

(P-7358)
U-2 HOME ENTERTAINMENT INC
Also Called: Tai Seng Entertainment
170 S Spruce Ave Ste 200, South San Francisco (94080-4557)
P.O. Box 818, San Bruno (94066-0818)
PHONE..........................650 871-8118
▲ **EMP:** 50
SALES (est): 10.2MM **Privately Held**
SIC: 5065

(P-7359)
UNIFIED TELDATA INC
Also Called: Utdi
126 Neider Ln, Mill Valley (94941-2474)
PHONE..........................415 888-8940
Toll Free:..........................888 -
Lyhn Haller, *President*
EMP: 52
SQ FT: 3,500
SALES (est): 6.9MM **Privately Held**
WEB: www.utdi.com
SIC: 5065 Telephone equipment; communication equipment; intercommunication equipment, electronic

(P-7360)
UNION TECHNOLOGY CORP
718 Monterey Pass Rd, Monterey Park (91754-3607)
PHONE..........................323 266-6871
David I Chu, *CEO*
John Yang, *Shareholder*
Lori Chu, *CFO*
▲ **EMP:** 50
SQ FT: 21,800
SALES (est): 11.2MM **Privately Held**
WEB: www.uniontechcorp.com
SIC: 5065 3675 Electronic parts; electronic capacitors

(P-7361)
VIA TECHNOLOGIES INC
Also Called: Via Embedded Store
940 Mission Ct, Fremont (94539-8202)
PHONE..........................510 683-3300
Wenchi Chen, *President*
Cher Wang, *CFO*
Fan Lu, *Project Mgr*
Andy Hwang, *Technical Staff*
Bihua Gao, *Engineer*
▲ **EMP:** 130
SQ FT: 55,000
SALES (est): 49.3MM **Privately Held**
WEB: www.via.com.tw
SIC: 5065 Electronic parts

PA: Via Usa Inc
940 Mission Ct
Fremont CA 94539
510 683-3300

(P-7362)
WDPT FILM DISTRIBUTION LLC
500 S Buena Vista St, Burbank
(91521-0001)
PHONE..............................818 560-1000
Walt Disney Pictures, *Mng Member*
EMP: 176
SALES (est): 94.1MM **Privately Held**
SIC: 5065 Video equipment, electronic

(P-7363)
WENZLAU ENGINEERING INC
2950 E Harcourt St, Compton
(90221-5502)
PHONE..............................310 604-3400
William D Wenzlau Jr, *CEO*
◆ **EMP:** 64
SQ FT: 40,000
SALES (est): 20MM **Privately Held**
WEB: www.wenzlau.com
SIC: 5065 8711 5511 Electronic parts &
equipment; consulting engineer; trucks,
tractors & trailers: new & used

(P-7364)
WINBOND ELECTRONICS CORP AMER
2727 N 1st St, San Jose (95134-2029)
PHONE..............................408 943-6666
Yuan Mou Shu, *Principal*
Yung Chin, *Treasurer*
Jun-WEI Chen, *Vice Pres*
Pei-Ming Cheng, *Vice Pres*
Ming-Huei Shieh, *Executive*
▲ **EMP:** 60
SQ FT: 50,000
SALES (est): 23.9MM **Privately Held**
WEB: www.winbond-usa.com
SIC: 5065 8731 3674 Electronic parts;
commercial physical research; semicon-
ductors & related devices
PA: Winbond Electronics Corp.
8, Keya 1st Rd.,
Taichung City 42881

(P-7365)
WURLDTECH SECURITY TECH LTD
2623 Camino Ramon, San Ramon
(94583-9130)
PHONE..............................604 669-6674
William Ruh, *CEO*
EMP: 75 **EST:** 2016
SALES (est): 26MM **Privately Held**
SIC: 5065 Security control equipment &
systems

(P-7366)
XCERRA CORPORATION
Also Called: Western Region
880 N Mccarthy Blvd # 100, Milpitas
(95035-5126)
PHONE..............................408 635-4300
Ken Daub, *Branch Mgr*
Steve Blanchette, *Info Tech Mgr*
Jill Barres, *Human Res Dir*
Steve Wigley, *VP Mktg*
Mark Belanger, *Manager*
EMP: 200
SALES (corp-wide): 451.7MM **Publicly
Held**
WEB: www.ltx.com
SIC: 5065 Semiconductor devices
HQ: Xcerra Corporation
825 University Ave
Norwood MA 02062
781 461-1000

(P-7367)
XMULTIPLE TECHNOLOGIES
1919 Williams St Ste 325, Simi Valley
(93065-7848)
PHONE..............................805 579-1100
Alan Pocrass, *CEO*
Jeremy Chu, *President*
Mr Drew Stoiberg, *VP Sales*
Mike Basowski, *Manager*
Don Diamond, *Manager*
EMP: 1500 **EST:** 2001

SALES (est): 81.3MM **Privately Held**
WEB: www.starbursthomepage.com
SIC: 5065 Electronic parts & equipment

(P-7368)
XP POWER LLC
Also Called: Emco High Voltage
11383 Prospect Dr, Jackson (95642-9311)
PHONE..............................209 267-1630
Michael Doherty, *Vice Pres*
EMP: 60 **Privately Held**
SIC: 5065 Electronic parts & equipment
HQ: Xp Power Llc
990 Benecia Ave
Sunnyvale CA 94085
408 732-7777

(P-7369)
XP POWER LLC (DH)
990 Benecia Ave, Sunnyvale (94085-2804)
PHONE..............................408 732-7777
Mike Laver, *Mng Member*
Frank Bidwell, *President*
Hiren Shah, *Exec VP*
Mike Doherty, *Vice Pres*
Peter Nguyen, *Program Mgr*
▲ **EMP:** 60
SQ FT: 58,000
SALES (est): 90.3MM **Privately Held**
SIC: 5065 Electronic parts & equipment
HQ: Xp Power Plc
16 Horseshoe Park
Reading BERKS
118 984-5515

(P-7370)
YUNEEC USA INC
9227 Haven Ave Ste 210, Rancho Cuca-
monga (91730-5473)
PHONE..............................855 284-8888
Mike Kahn, *CEO*
Ryan Borders, *COO*
Larry Liu, *CFO*
Min Fu, *Controller*
▲ **EMP:** 70 **EST:** 2013
SALES: 54MM **Privately Held**
SIC: 5065 7629 Video equipment, elec-
tronic; electrical equipment repair serv-
ices
PA: Yuneec International Co., Limited
Rm 2301 23/F
Kwun Tong KLN

(P-7371)
ZETTLER COMPONENTS INC (PA)
75 Columbia, Orange (92868)
PHONE..............................949 831-5000
Kurt Rexius, *General Mgr*
▲ **EMP:** 250
SQ FT: 27,000
SALES (est): 35.8MM **Privately Held**
WEB: www.zettlercomponents.com
SIC: 5065 3669 5087 Intercommunication
equipment, electronic; intercommunica-
tion systems, electric; firefighting equip-
ment

(P-7372)
ZMODO TECHNOLOGY CORP LTD
17870 Castleton St # 200, City of Industry
(91748-1755)
PHONE..............................217 903-5673
Kejia Wan, *President*
EMP: 700
SALES (est): 47.5MM **Privately Held**
SIC: 5065 Mobile telephone equipment

5072 Hardware Wholesale

(P-7373)
ACF COMPONENTS & FASTENERS INC
Also Called: A C F
742 Arrow Grand Cir, Covina (91722-2147)
PHONE..............................949 833-0506
Jill Alvarez, *Manager*
Rocky Thauberger, *Sales Staff*
EMP: 55
SQ FT: 20,000

SALES (est): 5.1MM
SALES (corp-wide): 26.3MM **Privately
Held**
WEB: www.acfcom.com
SIC: 5072 5065 5085 Miscellaneous fas-
teners; electronic parts; fasteners, indus-
trial: nuts, bolts, screws, etc.
PA: Acf Components & Fasteners, Inc.
31012 Huntwood Ave
Hayward CA 94544
510 487-2100

(P-7374)
ADEPT FASTENERS INC (PA)
28709 Industry Dr, Valencia (91355-5414)
P.O. Box 579, Castaic (91310-0579)
PHONE..............................661 257-6600
Gary Young, *President*
Don List, *Vice Pres*
Keith McDonald, *Executive*
Cheryl Odermatt, *Program Mgr*
Elaine Young, *Office Mgr*
EMP: 57
SQ FT: 40,000
SALES (est): 91.9MM **Privately Held**
WEB: www.adeptfasteners.com
SIC: 5072 Miscellaneous fasteners

(P-7375)
ALLFAST FASTENING SYSTEMS LLC
15200 Don Julian Rd, City of Industry
(91745-1098)
P.O. Box 3166 (91744-0166)
PHONE..............................626 968-9388
James H Randall,
Tiancheng Tan, *Engineer*
◆ **EMP:** 58 **EST:** 1971
SALES (est): 45.2MM
SALES (corp-wide): 877.1MM **Publicly
Held**
WEB: www.allfastinc.com
SIC: 5072 Hardware
PA: Trimas Corporation
38505 Woodward Ave # 200
Bloomfield Hills MI 48304
248 631-5450

(P-7376)
ALLTRADE TOOLS LLC
6122 Katella Ave, Cypress (90630-5203)
PHONE..............................310 522-9008
Dennis Hale, *Principal*
Robert Ellis, *CFO*
Annie Fung, *Asst Treas*
Sue McNeese, *Human Res Mgr*
Eric Hennings, *Manager*
◆ **EMP:** 50
SQ FT: 140,000
SALES (est): 29.4MM **Privately Held**
SIC: 5072 Hand tools

(P-7377)
AMERICAN BOLT & SCREW MFG CORP (PA)
14650 Miller Ave Ste 200, Fontana
(92336-1694)
P.O. Box 4300, Ontario (91761-8800)
PHONE..............................909 390-0522
Jimmie W Hooper, *President*
Cynthia Alvarez, *Vice Pres*
Jerry Alvarez, *Technician*
Nancy Vega, *Technology*
David Klesser, *Analyst*
▲ **EMP:** 52 **EST:** 1970
SQ FT: 110,000
SALES: 54.8MM **Privately Held**
SIC: 5072 Bolts, nuts & screws

(P-7378)
AMERICAN KAL ENTERPRISES INC (PA)
Also Called: Pro America Premium Tools
4265 Puente Ave, Baldwin Park
(91706-3420)
PHONE..............................626 338-7308
John Toshima, *President*
Mila Birotte, *Admin Sec*
J R Spotswood, *Sales Executive*
▲ **EMP:** 90
SQ FT: 32,000
SALES (est): 23.1MM **Privately Held**
SIC: 5072 3546 3463 3462 Hand tools;
power-driven handtools; nonferrous forg-
ings; iron & steel forgings; hand & edge
tools

(P-7379)
AMERIWEST INDUSTRIES INC
Also Called: Tenpo Hardware
2910 S Archibald Ave A, Ontario
(91761-7323)
PHONE..............................909 930-1898
Weidan Wu, *CEO*
▲ **EMP:** 50
SQ FT: 112,000
SALES (est): 10.1MM **Privately Held**
WEB: www.ameriwestindustries.com
SIC: 5072 Hardware

(P-7380)
ARCONIC GLOBAL FAS & RINGS INC
Also Called: Arconic Fastening Systems
1925 N Macarthur Dr # 200, Tracy
(95376-2835)
PHONE..............................209 839-3005
Rod Alavi, *Director*
EMP: 60
SALES (corp-wide): 14B **Publicly Held**
WEB: www.alcoafasteners.com
SIC: 5072 Hardware
HQ: Arconic Global Fasteners & Rings, Inc.
3990a Heritage Oak Ct
Simi Valley CA 93063
805 527-3600

(P-7381)
ARROW TOOLS FAS & SAW INC
7635 Burnet Ave, Van Nuys (91405-1006)
PHONE..............................818 780-1464
Jeffrey S Silverman, *CEO*
Stewart Epstein, *President*
Susan Epstein, *Corp Secy*
Jeff Burch, *Branch Mgr*
Mike Glazier, *Project Mgr*
EMP: 50
SQ FT: 25,000
SALES (est): 55MM **Privately Held**
WEB: www.arrowtools.com
SIC: 5072 Hand tools

(P-7382)
ASSA ABLOY RSDENTIAL GROUP INC (HQ)
15250 Stafford St, City of Industry
(91744-4418)
PHONE..............................626 961-0413
Thomas Millar, *President*
Ping Tsai, *Engineer*
Erika Berglund, *Human Res Mgr*
◆ **EMP:** 200
SQ FT: 38,000
SALES (est): 159.3MM
SALES (corp-wide): 9.3B **Privately Held**
WEB: www.emtek.com
SIC: 5072 Hardware
PA: Assa Abloy Ab
Klarabergsviadukten 90
Stockholm 111 6
850 648-500

(P-7383)
ASSA ABLOY RSDENTIAL GROUP INC
600 Balwin Park Blvd, City of Industry
(91746)
PHONE..............................626 369-4718
Birk Sorennsen, *Manager*
EMP: 400
SALES (corp-wide): 9.3B **Privately Held**
WEB: www.emtek.com
SIC: 5072 Hardware
HQ: Assa Abloy Residential Group, Inc.
15250 Stafford St
City Of Industry CA 91744
626 961-0413

(P-7384)
AWI ACQUISITION COMPANY (PA)
Also Called: Allied International
28955 Ave Sherman, Valencia (91355)
PHONE..............................818 364-2333
Timothy Florian, *Ch of Bd*
Melissa Berninger, *CFO*
Greg Holdridge, *Natl Sales Mgr*
Dave Watters, *Natl Sales Mgr*
Geraldine Becker, *Sales Staff*
▲ **EMP:** 68
SQ FT: 106,000

SALES (est): 21.4MM Privately Held
WEB: www.alliedtools.com
SIC: 5072 3499 Hand tools; stabilizing bars (cargo), metal

(P-7385)
B & B SPECIALTIES INC
G S Aerospace Division
4321 E La Palma Ave, Anaheim (92807-1887)
PHONE.....................714 985-3075
Tom Rutan, Manager
EMP: 100
SALES (est): 3.9MM
SALES (corp-wide): 40.3MM Privately Held
WEB: www.bbspecialties.com
SIC: 5072 3429 Miscellaneous fasteners; manufactured hardware (general)
PA: B & B Specialties, Inc.
    4321 E La Palma Ave
    Anaheim CA 92807
    714 985-3000

(P-7386)
CAMSTAR INTERNATIONAL INC
939 W 9th St, Upland (91786-4543)
PHONE.....................909 931-2540
Bingqing LI, President
Eric De La Cruz, Sales Executive
Jason Jaime, Sales Staff
▲ EMP: 75
SQ FT: 1,500
SALES (est): 12.5MM
SALES (corp-wide): 134.9K Privately Held
SIC: 5072 Security devices, locks
PA: Yuxin Technology Company
    Dayao Village
    Weifang
    536 784-8108

(P-7387)
CENTRAL INDIANA HDWR CO INC (PA)
Also Called: Schricker
3512 Seagate Way Ste 190, Oceanside (92056-2689)
P.O. Box 501850, Indianapolis IN (46250-6850)
PHONE.....................317 558-5700
Ron Couch, President
Norman L Bristley, Ch of Bd
Rondal Couch, President
Gary Wilson, Senior VP
▲ EMP: 77
SQ FT: 129,000
SALES (est): 31.3MM Privately Held
WEB: www.cih-indy.com
SIC: 5072 5031 5211 Builders' hardware; metal doors, sash & trim; door frames, all materials; doors; lumber & other building materials

(P-7388)
CHARLES MCMURRAY CO (PA)
2520 N Argyle Ave, Fresno (93727-1399)
P.O. Box 569 (93709-0569)
PHONE.....................559 292-5751
Charles McMurray, CEO
Louis Mc Murray, President
Cassie Mc Murray, Admin Sec
Kathy Earnhart, Credit Mgr
▲ EMP: 108
SQ FT: 58,000
SALES (est): 52.5MM Privately Held
SIC: 5072 Builders' hardware

(P-7389)
CLARENDON SPECIALTY FAS INC
16761 Burke Ln, Huntington Beach (92647-4560)
PHONE.....................714 842-2603
Michael Lang, President
Jeff Heywood, Executive
Arnaud Zemmour, Business Dir
Matthew Blackburn, Controller
Simon Martin, Opers Dir
▲ EMP: 90
SQ FT: 4,000
SALES (est): 5.7MM Privately Held
WEB: www.coastfab.com
SIC: 5072 3444 Miscellaneous fasteners; sheet metalwork

(P-7390)
CORONA CLIPPER INC
22440 Temescal Canyon Rd # 102, Corona (92883-4200)
PHONE.....................951 737-6515
Stephen J Erickson, CEO
Al Schulten, CFO
John Reisveck, Exec VP
Michael Dickson, Materials Mgr
Tim Atnip, Mfg Staff
◆ EMP: 70
SQ FT: 85,000
SALES (est): 40.8MM
SALES (corp-wide): 26.9MM Privately Held
WEB: www.coronaclipper.com
SIC: 5072 3524 Hand tools; lawn & garden equipment
PA: Natt Tools Group Inc
    460 Sherman Ave N
    Hamilton ON L8L 8
    905 549-7433

(P-7391)
CPO COMMERCE LLC
120 W Bellevue Dr Ste 300, Pasadena (91105-2579)
PHONE.....................626 585-3600
Robert H Tolleson, President
Girisha Chandraraj, COO
Todd A Shelton, CFO
Robert J Kelderhouse, Treasurer
Eric A Blanchard, Senior VP
▼ EMP: 81
SALES (est): 74.7MM Privately Held
SIC: 5072 Power tools & accessories
HQ: Essendant Co.
    1 Parkway North Blvd # 100
    Deerfield IL 60015
    847 627-7000

(P-7392)
G K TOOL CORP
Also Called: Kal Tool Co
4265 Puente Ave, Baldwin Park (91706-3420)
PHONE.....................626 338-7300
EMP: 90
SQ FT: 32,000
SALES (est): 8.6MM
SALES (corp-wide): 24.9MM Privately Held
SIC: 5072
PA: American Kal Enterprises, Inc.
    4265 Puente Ave
    Baldwin Park CA 91706
    626 338-7308

(P-7393)
HD SUPPLY CONSTRUCTION SUPPLY
Also Called: White Cap 24
1995 W Cordelia Rd, Fairfield (94534-1661)
PHONE.....................707 863-8282
Marcelus Joanes, Principal
EMP: 53 Publicly Held
SIC: 5072 Hardware
HQ: Hd Supply Construction Supply, Ltd (Lp)
    3400 Cumberland Blvd Se
    Atlanta GA 30339
    770 852-9000

(P-7394)
HD SUPPLY CONSTRUCTION SUPPLY
Also Called: White Cap 35
595 Brennan St, San Jose (95131-1202)
P.O. Box 610640 (95161-0640)
PHONE.....................408 428-2000
Larry Holloway, Manager
Mark Charon, Branch Mgr
EMP: 50 Publicly Held
SIC: 5072 Hardware
HQ: Hd Supply Construction Supply, Ltd (Lp)
    3400 Cumberland Blvd Se
    Atlanta GA 30339
    770 852-9000

(P-7395)
JACKSONS HARDWARE INC
Also Called: Marin Industrial Distributors
435 Du Bois St, San Rafael (94901-3910)
P.O. Box 10247 (94912-0247)
PHONE.....................415 870-4083
Matthew R Olson, President
Anna Buss, Treasurer
EMP: 61
SQ FT: 50,000
SALES (est): 24.9MM Privately Held
WEB: www.jacksonshardware.com
SIC: 5072 5251 Hardware; hardware

(P-7396)
LEIGHT SALES CO INC
1611 S Catalina Ave L45, Redondo Beach (90277-5299)
PHONE.....................310 223-1000
Bryan Moskowitz, CEO
Helene Moskowitz, Corp Secy
Alan Moskowitz, Principal
▲ EMP: 75
SQ FT: 60,000
SALES (est): 41.2MM Privately Held
WEB: www.leightsales.com
SIC: 5072 Miscellaneous fasteners

(P-7397)
LIBERTY HARDWARE MFG CORP
5555 Jurupa St, Ontario (91761-3606)
PHONE.....................909 605-2300
Kevin Buckner, Branch Mgr
EMP: 51
SALES (corp-wide): 8.3B Publicly Held
WEB: www.libertyhardware.com
SIC: 5072 Hardware
HQ: Liberty Hardware Mfg. Corp.
    140 Business Park Dr
    Winston Salem NC 27107
    336 769-4077

(P-7398)
LONG-LOK FASTENERS CORPORATION
20501 Belshaw Ave, Carson (90746-3505)
PHONE.....................310 667-4200
Robert M Bennett, CEO
EMP: 50
SALES (est): 5.4MM Privately Held
SIC: 5072 Miscellaneous fasteners

(P-7399)
LOUIS WURTH AND COMPANY (DH)
895 Columbia St, Brea (92821-2917)
P.O. Box 2253 (92822-2253)
PHONE.....................714 529-1771
Vito Mancini, President
Tom Mauss, President
Ed McGraw, CFO
Jeremy Mitchell, Branch Mgr
Kim Schnurstein, Accountant
▲ EMP: 90
SQ FT: 116,000
SALES (est): 95.4MM
SALES (corp-wide): 15.5B Privately Held
WEB: www.louisandcompany.com
SIC: 5072 5198 Furniture hardware; stain
HQ: Wurth Group Of North America Inc.
    93 Grant St
    Ramsey NJ 07446
    201 818-8877

(P-7400)
MAKITA USA INC (HQ)
14930 Northam St, La Mirada (90638-5753)
PHONE.....................714 522-8088
Hiroshi Tsujimura, CEO
Randy D Caillier, Vice Pres
Rich Chapman, Vice Pres
Ron Schachter, Vice Pres
Dennis Stauch, Vice Pres
◆ EMP: 250
SQ FT: 130,000
SALES: 1B Privately Held
WEB: www.makita.com
SIC: 5072 Power handtools; power tools & accessories

(P-7401)
MILSPEC INDUSTRIES INC (DH)
5825 Greenwood Ave, Commerce (90040-3846)
P.O. Box 60887, Los Angeles (90060-0887)
PHONE.....................213 680-9690
David Lifschitz, CEO
Galen Ho'o, President
Saleem Baakza, Vice Pres
Anthony Batista, Vice Pres
Ken Hunter, Executive
▼ EMP: 70
SALES (est): 21.9MM
SALES (corp-wide): 84.8MM Privately Held
WEB: www.milspecind.com
SIC: 5072 5085 Hardware; industrial supplies
HQ: Gehr Industries, Inc.
    7400 E Slauson Ave
    Commerce CA 90040
    323 728-5558

(P-7402)
PORTEOUS ENTERPRISES INC
22795 Utility Way, Carson (90745-5012)
PHONE.....................310 549-9180
John B Porteous, Principal
EMP: 200 Privately Held
WEB: www.porteousfastener.com
SIC: 5072 Nuts (hardware); bolts; screws; washers (hardware)
HQ: Porteous Enterprises, Inc.
    1040 E Watson Center Rd
    Carson CA 90745
    310 549-9180

(P-7403)
PRIME-LINE PRODUCTS COMPANY (DH)
Also Called: Slide Go
26950 San Bernardino Ave, Redlands (92374-5022)
PHONE.....................909 887-8118
Ronald F Turk, President
Bryan Aernan, Vice Pres
Paul Entwisele, Vice Pres
Jeff Grande, Vice Pres
Howard Kauffman, Vice Pres
◆ EMP: 325
SQ FT: 100,000
SALES (est): 6.1MM
SALES (corp-wide): 854.8MM Privately Held
WEB: www.prime-line-products.com
SIC: 5072 Builders' hardware
HQ: Great Star Industrial Usa, Llc
    9836 Northcross Center Ct
    Huntersville NC 28078
    704 892-4965

(P-7404)
SEREC ENTERTAINMENT LLC
1671 N Rocky Rd, Upland (91784-2500)
PHONE.....................626 893-0600
Steven A Ferraiuolo, President
EMP: 50
SALES (est): 5MM Privately Held
SIC: 5072 7389 Hardware;

(P-7405)
SHAMROCK SUPPLY COMPANY INC (PA)
Also Called: Shamrock Companies, The
3366 E La Palma Ave, Anaheim (92806-2814)
PHONE.....................714 575-1800
John J O'Connor, Ch of Bd
Michael O'Connor, President
Juan Ossa, Info Tech Dir
Fanny McShane, Info Tech Mgr
Megan Peters, Purchasing
▲ EMP: 52
SQ FT: 45,000
SALES (est): 74.4MM Privately Held
WEB: www.shamrocksupply.com
SIC: 5072 5084 3842 Hand tools; industrial machinery & equipment; personal safety equipment

(P-7406)
SNAP-ON INCORPORATED
Also Called: Snap-On Tools
19220 San Jose Ave, City of Industry
(91748-1417)
PHONE..............................626 965-0668
Michael King, *Branch Mgr*
EMP: 95
SALES (corp-wide): 3.7B **Publicly Held**
WEB: www.snapon.com
SIC: 5072 Hand tools
PA: Snap-On Incorporated
2801 80th St
Kenosha WI 53143
262 656-5200

(P-7407)
SOFFIETTI CO
236 W Orange Show, San Bernardino
(92408)
PHONE..............................909 907-2277
EMP: 65 **EST:** 2009
SQ FT: 2,700
SALES (est): 200K **Privately Held**
SIC: 5072 5084 5511

(P-7408)
SUNKIST ENTERPRISES
1308 Rollins Rd, Burlingame (94010-2410)
PHONE..............................650 347-3900
Ali Husain, *Owner*
EMP: 75
SQ FT: 6,000
SALES (est): 6.9MM **Privately Held**
WEB: www.sunkistenterprises.com
SIC: 5072 5031 Hardware; lumber, ply-
wood & millwork

(P-7409)
TOMARCO CONTRACTOR SPC INC (PA)
Also Called: Tomarco Fastening Systems
14848 Northam St, La Mirada
(90638-5747)
PHONE..............................714 523-1771
William Thompson, *CEO*
Keith Watkins, *President*
Dave Lewis, *COO*
Patrick Armstrong, *Vice Pres*
Nick Ciminello, *Regional Mgr*
▲ EMP: 60
SQ FT: 33,000
SALES (est): 68.6MM **Privately Held**
WEB: www.tomarco.com
SIC: 5072 Hand tools; power handtools;
builders' hardware

(P-7410)
VENTURE PACIFIC TOOLS INC
17152 Daimler St, Irvine (92614-5509)
PHONE..............................949 475-5505
Daniel Congellieri, *President*
▲ EMP: 61
SALES (est): 2.3MM **Privately Held**
SIC: 5072 Power tools & accessories

(P-7411)
VIAWORLD ADVANCED PRODUCTS
920 Saratoga Ave Ste 103, San Jose
(95129-3445)
PHONE..............................408 597-7051
John Xingqiang Wu, *President*
EMP: 56
SALES: 5MM **Privately Held**
WEB: www.viaworld.com
SIC: 5072 Power tools & accessories

(P-7412)
WILDENRADT-MCMURRAY INC
Also Called: Macmurray Pacific
568 7th St, San Francisco (94103-4710)
PHONE..............................510 835-5500
Eric Wildenradt, *CEO*
Theodore Wildenradt, *President*
Vernelle Wildenradt, *Corp Secy*
Adrian Restauro, *Sales Staff*
▲ EMP: 70
SQ FT: 25,000
SALES (est): 31.5MM **Privately Held**
WEB: www.macmurraypacific.com
SIC: 5072 Builders' hardware

5074 Plumbing & Heating Splys Wholesale

(P-7413)
BRITA PRODUCTS COMPANY
1221 Broadway Ste 290, Oakland
(94612-1838)
P.O. Box 24305 (94623-1305)
PHONE..............................510 271-7000
Greg Frank, *President*
EMP: 85
SALES (est): 43.8MM
SALES (corp-wide): 6.2B **Publicly Held**
WEB: www.brita.com
SIC: 5074 Water purification equipment
PA: The Clorox Company
1221 Broadway Ste 1300
Oakland CA 94612
510 271-7000

(P-7414)
BUILDCOM INC
Also Called: Faucetdirect.com
402 Otterson Dr Ste 100, Chico
(95928-8247)
PHONE..............................800 375-3403
Christian B Friedland, *President*
Erik Lukasek, *President*
Danielle Porto Mohn, *Chief Mktg Ofcr*
Dan Davis, *Vice Pres*
Lindsay Fee, *Vice Pres*
▼ EMP: 380
SQ FT: 22,100
SALES (est): 221.8MM
SALES (corp-wide): 20.7B **Privately Held**
WEB: www.improvementdirect.com
SIC: 5074 5999 Plumbing fittings & sup-
plies; plumbing & heating supplies
HQ: Ferguson Enterprises, Llc
12500 Jefferson Ave
Newport News VA 23602
757 874-7795

(P-7415)
BUILDINGS IOT INC (PA)
Also Called: Johnson Contrls Authorized Dlr
3451 Vincent Rd Ste C, Pleasant Hill
(94523-7317)
PHONE..............................800 800-7126
Terry L Turner, *President*
Clint Bradford, *Vice Pres*
Chip Cummins, *Vice Pres*
Jason Dewar, *Vice Pres*
Bridgette Ann T Davies, *Principal*
EMP: 75 **EST:** 1962
SQ FT: 10,000
SALES (est): 179MM **Privately Held**
WEB: www.controlco.com
SIC: 5074 5084 8742 Plumbing & hy-
dronic heating supplies; controlling instru-
ments & accessories; automation &
robotics consultant

(P-7416)
ELMCO SALES INC (PA)
15070 Proctor Ave, City of Industry
(91746-3305)
P.O. Box 3787 (91744-0787)
PHONE..............................626 855-4831
Donald E Morris, *Ch of Bd*
Kristin E Kahle, *Corp Secy*
Adelina Cisneros, *Executive Asst*
Mike Barry, *Purch Agent*
Joe Joyce, *Sales Associate*
EMP: 90
SQ FT: 49,650
SALES (est): 37.2MM **Privately Held**
SIC: 5074 Plumbing fittings & supplies

(P-7417)
ELMCO/DUDDY INC (HQ)
Also Called: Elmco Stewart
15070 Proctor Ave, City of Industry
(91746-3305)
P.O. Box 3787 (91744-0787)
PHONE..............................626 333-9942
Donald E Morris, *CEO*
Rondall Stewart, *President*
Ron Samuelson, *Branch Mgr*
John Plowman, *Controller*
Brendon St Claire, *Sales Associate*
EMP: 50
SQ FT: 49,650

SALES (est): 35.5MM
SALES (corp-wide): 37.2MM **Privately Held**
WEB: www.elmcoduddy.com
SIC: 5074 Plumbers' brass goods & fittings
PA: Elmco Sales Inc.
15070 Proctor Ave
City Of Industry CA 91746
626 855-4831

(P-7418)
EPS CORPORATE HOLDINGS INC
1235 S Lewis St, Anaheim (92805-6429)
PHONE..............................714 635-3131
Greg Boiko, *Manager*
EMP: 60 **Privately Held**
SIC: 5074 1711 Plumbing & hydronic heat-
ing supplies; plumbing contractors
HQ: Eps Corporate Holdings, Inc.
3100 Donald Douglas
Santa Monica CA 90405
-

(P-7419)
FERGUSON ENTERPRISES INC
Also Called: Cal-Steam
898 Pennsylvania Ave, San Francisco
(94107-3441)
PHONE..............................408 441-7276
Stew Corbin, *Manager*
Karen Hsu, *Manager*
EMP: 75
SALES (corp-wide): 20.7B **Privately Held**
SIC: 5074 Plumbing & hydronic heating
supplies
HQ: Ferguson Enterprises, Llc
12500 Jefferson Ave
Newport News VA 23602
757 874-7795

(P-7420)
FERGUSON ENTERPRISES INC
Also Called: Lincoln Products
18825 San Jose Ave, City of Industry
(91748-1326)
PHONE..............................626 965-0724
Michael Aucoin, *Branch Mgr*
Brad Blakeley, *Opers Mgr*
EMP: 80
SALES (corp-wide): 20.7B **Privately Held**
WEB: www.ferguson.com
SIC: 5074 Plumbing fittings & supplies
HQ: Ferguson Enterprises, Llc
12500 Jefferson Ave
Newport News VA 23602
757 874-7795

(P-7421)
FERGUSON ENTERPRISES INC
704 N Laverne Ave, Fresno (93727-6850)
PHONE..............................559 253-2900
Greg Lourente, *Branch Mgr*
Greg Lourence, *General Mgr*
EMP: 50
SALES (corp-wide): 20.7B **Privately Held**
SIC: 5074 Plumbing fittings & supplies
HQ: Ferguson Enterprises, Llc
12500 Jefferson Ave
Newport News VA 23602
757 874-7795

(P-7422)
FERGUSON ENTERPRISES INC
Also Called: Ferguson 667
3280 Market St, San Diego (92102-3334)
PHONE..............................619 515-0300
Louie Armstrong, *Branch Mgr*
EMP: 70
SQ FT: 45,000
SALES (corp-wide): 20.7B **Privately Held**
WEB: www.ferguson.com
SIC: 5074 Plumbing fittings & supplies
HQ: Ferguson Enterprises, Llc
12500 Jefferson Ave
Newport News VA 23602
757 874-7795

(P-7423)
FERGUSON ENTERPRISES INC
9750 S Town Ave, Pomona (91766)
PHONE..............................909 364-8700
Brian Hohn, *Manager*
EMP: 115

SALES (corp-wide): 20.7B **Privately Held**
WEB: www.ferguson.com
SIC: 5074 Plumbing fittings & supplies
HQ: Ferguson Enterprises, Llc
12500 Jefferson Ave
Newport News VA 23602
757 874-7795

(P-7424)
FERGUSON ENTERPRISES INC
Also Called: Ferguson 677
6421 Industry Way, Westminster
(92683-3696)
PHONE..............................714 893-1936
Matthew Moore, *Manager*
EMP: 250
SALES (corp-wide): 20.7B **Privately Held**
WEB: www.ferguson.com
SIC: 5074 Plumbing fittings & supplies
HQ: Ferguson Enterprises, Llc
12500 Jefferson Ave
Newport News VA 23602
757 874-7795

(P-7425)
FERGUSON ENTERPRISES INC
Also Called: Ferguson 601
7651 Woodman Ave, Van Nuys
(91402-6536)
PHONE..............................818 786-9720
Fred Raviol, *Branch Mgr*
Jeff Van Wagesen, *Vice Pres*
Jon Balano, *Opers Mgr*
EMP: 50
SALES (corp-wide): 20.7B **Privately Held**
WEB: www.ferguson.com
SIC: 5074 Plumbing fittings & supplies
HQ: Ferguson Enterprises, Llc
12500 Jefferson Ave
Newport News VA 23602
757 874-7795

(P-7426)
FERGUSON FIRE FABRICATION INC (DH)
Also Called: Pacific Fire Safety
2750 S Towne Ave, Pomona (91766-6205)
PHONE..............................909 517-3085
Leo J Klien, *President*
Leo J Klein, *President*
Dave Keltner, *CFO*
▲ EMP: 100
SQ FT: 120,000
SALES (est): 160.5MM
SALES (corp-wide): 20.7B **Privately Held**
WEB: www.sierracraft.com
SIC: 5074 5099 Plumbing fittings & sup-
plies; safety equipment & supplies; fire
extinguishers
HQ: Ferguson Enterprises, Llc
12500 Jefferson Ave
Newport News VA 23602
757 874-7795

(P-7427)
GCO INC (PA)
27750 Industrial Blvd, Hayward
(94545-4043)
PHONE..............................510 786-3333
Michael H Groeniger, *Ch of Bd*
Beverly J Groeniger, *Treasurer*
Richard Alexander, *Exec VP*
Richard Old, *Vice Pres*
James Wunsche, *Vice Pres*
EMP: 50
SQ FT: 15,000
SALES (est): 118.9MM **Privately Held**
WEB: www.groeniger.com
SIC: 5074 5087 Pipe & boiler covering;
pipes & fittings, plastic; plumbing & heat-
ing valves; firefighting equipment; sprin-
kler systems

(P-7428)
GREEN CONVERGENCE (PA)
Also Called: Sunpower By Green Conver-
gence
28490 Wstnghuse Pl Ste 16, Valencia
(91355)
PHONE..............................661 294-9495
Mark Clinton Figearo, *CEO*
Donald Schramm, *President*
Stacy Hitt, *CFO*
Pablo Padilla, *Department Mgr*
Alyssia Johnson, *Receptionist*
EMP: 53 **EST:** 2008

SQ FT: 6,000
SALES: 1MM **Privately Held**
SIC: **5074** 1711 2493 2621 Heating equipment & panels, solar; solar energy contractor; roofing board, unsaturated; roofing felt stock; building & roofing paper, felts & insulation siding; roofing & gutter work; roofing contractor; battery service & repair

(P-7429)
HARRINGTON INDUSTRIAL PLAS LLC (HQ)
14480 Yorba Ave, Chino (91710-5766)
P.O. Box 5128 (91708-5128)
PHONE...............................909 597-8641
James W Swanson, *Mng Member*
James Kasprick, *Regional Mgr*
Ken Lang, *Branch Mgr*
Bill Reilly, *Branch Mgr*
Jeff Johnson, *Office Mgr*
▼ EMP: 85
SQ FT: 50,000
SALES (est): 210MM
SALES (corp-wide): 7MM **Privately Held**
WEB: www.harringtonplastics.com
SIC: **5074** Pipes & fittings, plastic; plumbing & heating valves
PA: Aliaxis
Avenue Arnaud Fraiteur 1523
Bruxelles 1050
277 550-50

(P-7430)
LARSEN SUPPLY CO (PA)
Also Called: Lasco
12055 Slauson Ave, Santa Fe Springs (90670-2601)
PHONE...............................562 698-0731
Richard Larsen, *Ch of Bd*
Ruth Larsen, *Shareholder*
Rella Bodinus, *Vice Pres*
Danny Pro, *Technology*
Joel Drake, *Marketing Mgr*
◆ EMP: 100
SQ FT: 60,000
SALES (est): 33.3MM **Privately Held**
WEB: www.lasco.net
SIC: **5074** 5075 Plumbing fittings & supplies; warm air heating & air conditioning

(P-7431)
MERIDIAN HOLDINGS
2580 El Camino Real, Atascadero (93422-1916)
PHONE...............................805 539-2752
Jason Devries, *President*
EMP: 55
SALES (est): 16.6MM **Privately Held**
SIC: **5074** Plumbing & hydronic heating supplies

(P-7432)
NEXTRACKER INC (DH)
6200 Paseo Padre Pkwy, Fremont (94555-3601)
PHONE...............................510 270-2500
Daniel Shugar, *CEO*
Bruce Ledesma, *President*
Tyroan Hardy, *COO*
Marco Garcia, *Ch Credit Ofcr*
Mike Mehawich, *Chief Mktg Ofcr*
◆ EMP: 53
SQ FT: 30,000
SALES (est): 269.2MM
SALES (corp-wide): 26.2B **Privately Held**
SIC: **5074** Heating equipment & panels, solar

(P-7433)
OATEY SUPPLY CHAIN SVCS INC
6600 Smith Ave, Newark (94560-4220)
PHONE...............................510 797-4677
Armando Romo, *Manager*
EMP: 50
SALES (corp-wide): 470MM **Privately Held**
SIC: **5074** Plumbing & hydronic heating supplies
HQ: Oatey Supply Chain Services, Inc.
20600 Emerald Pkwy
Cleveland OH 44135
216 267-7100

(P-7434)
PACE SUPPLY CORP (PA)
6000 State Farm Dr # 200, Rohnert Park (94928-2226)
P.O. Box 6407 (94927-6407)
PHONE...............................707 755-2499
Ron Bohannon, *President*
Ted M Green, *Ch of Bd*
Albert Bacci, *Admin Sec*
Lynette Sisemore, *Accounting Mgr*
Krista Shirley, *Credit Staff*
▲ EMP: 80
SQ FT: 10,000
SALES (est): 193.4MM **Privately Held**
WEB: www.pacesupply.com
SIC: **5074** Plumbing fittings & supplies

(P-7435)
PURCELL-MURRAY COMPANY INC (PA)
1744 Rollins Rd, Burlingame (94010-2208)
PHONE...............................415 468-6620
Timothy J Murray, *President*
Laurence D Purcell, *Vice Pres*
Cristina Lintoco, *Executive*
Kevin Murray, *Executive*
Brigitte Castillo, *Administration*
▲ EMP: 67
SALES (est): 54.9MM **Privately Held**
SIC: **5074** 5064 Plumbing fittings & supplies; electrical appliances, major

(P-7436)
RYAN HERCO PRODUCTS CORP (DH)
Also Called: Ryan Herco Flow Solutions
3010 N San Fernando Blvd, Burbank (91504-2524)
PHONE...............................818 841-1141
Randy Beckwith, *CEO*
Rob Caccamo, *Administration*
Merlin Landaverde, *Administration*
Simon Artoonabedi, *Planning*
Wade Aldridge, *Technical Staff*
◆ EMP: 60 EST: 1948
SQ FT: 48,000
SALES (est): 167.6MM **Privately Held**
WEB: www.ryanherco.com
SIC: **5074** 5162 Pipes & fittings, plastic; plastics materials & basic shapes

(P-7437)
SLAKEY BROTHERS INC
1480 Nicora Ave, San Jose (95133-1639)
PHONE...............................408 494-0460
Tom Trapani, *Sales/Mktg Mgr*
James Hawkins, *Branch Mgr*
Diane Blythe, *Financial Exec*
EMP: 50
SALES (corp-wide): 197MM **Privately Held**
WEB: www.slakey.com
SIC: **5074** Plumbing & hydronic heating supplies
PA: Slakey Brothers, Inc.
2215 Kausen Dr Ste 1
Elk Grove CA 95758
916 478-2000

(P-7438)
SOUTH WEST SUN SOLAR INC
13752 Harbor Blvd, Garden Grove (92843-4009)
PHONE...............................714 582-3909
Hieu Nguyen, *CEO*
Mimi Ngo, *President*
EMP: 50
SALES (est): 7.1MM **Privately Held**
SIC: **5074** Heating equipment & panels, solar

(P-7439)
SUEZ WTS SYSTEMS USA INC
Also Called: Apollo Div Ionics Ultrapure
5900 Silvercreek Vly Rd, San Jose (95138-1083)
PHONE...............................408 360-5900
Tim Addleman, *Manager*
EMP: 80
SALES (corp-wide): 94.7MM **Privately Held**
WEB: www.ionics.com
SIC: **5074** Plumbing & hydronic heating supplies

HQ: Suez Wts Systems Usa, Inc.
4636 Somerton Rd
Trevose PA 19053
781 359-7000

(P-7440)
SUNERGY CALIFORNIA LLC
4801 Urbani Ave, McClellan (95652-2000)
PHONE...............................916 550-5370
Xiaoli Zhou,
EMP: 50 EST: 2017
SALES (est): 99.6K **Privately Held**
SIC: **5074** Heating equipment & panels, solar

(P-7441)
TA INDUSTRIES INC (PA)
Also Called: Truaire
11130 Bloomfield Ave, Santa Fe Springs (90670-4603)
P.O. Box 4448 (90670-1460)
PHONE...............................562 466-1000
Yongki Yi, *Principal*
Janice Kim, *CFO*
Alex Yi, *Vice Pres*
Elizabeth Yi, *Vice Pres*
Tim McDonald, *Managing Dir*
▲ EMP: 69
SQ FT: 86,000
SALES (est): 32.7MM **Privately Held**
WEB: www.truaire.com
SIC: **5074** 5075 3567 Heating equipment (hydronic); air conditioning & ventilation equipment & supplies; heating units & devices, industrial: electric

(P-7442)
WESTERN NEVADA SUPPLY CO
10990 Industrial Way A, Truckee (96161-0257)
PHONE...............................530 582-5009
Theodore Reviglio, *Branch Mgr*
EMP: 237
SALES (corp-wide): 284.8MM **Privately Held**
SIC: **5074** Plumbing fittings & supplies
PA: Western Nevada Supply Co.
950 S Rock Blvd
Sparks NV 89431
775 359-5800

5075 Heating & Air Conditioning Eqpt & Splys Wholesale

(P-7443)
AIR TREATMENT CORPORATION (PA)
640 N Puente St, Brea (92821-2830)
PHONE...............................909 869-7975
Mark Hartman, *Ch of Bd*
Deborah Hudson, *CFO*
Meela Shah, *Office Admin*
Dayna Jones, *Executive Asst*
Tiffany Hamp, *Admin Asst*
▲ EMP: 65
SQ FT: 45,000
SALES (est): 95.9MM **Privately Held**
SIC: **5075** Electrical heating equipment; air conditioning equipment, except room units

(P-7444)
BAKER DISTRIBUTING COMPANY LLC
241 Market Pl, Escondido (92029-1301)
P.O. Box 848459, Dallas TX (75284-8459)
PHONE...............................760 708-4201
Rhonda Waag, *Branch Mgr*
EMP: 99
SQ FT: 12,000
SALES (corp-wide): 4.5B **Publicly Held**
SIC: **5075** Warm air heating & air conditioning
HQ: Baker Distributing Company Llc
14610 Breakers Dr Ste 100
Jacksonville FL 32258
904 407-4500

(P-7445)
CALIFORNIA HYDRONICS CORP (PA)
Also Called: Columbia Hydronics Co.
2293 Tripaldi Way, Hayward (94545-5024)
P.O. Box 5049 (94540-5049)
PHONE...............................510 293-1993
David Attard, *President*
John Arthur, *CFO*
Kevin McCloud, *Treasurer*
James A Attard, *Vice Pres*
Mark Copeland, *Executive*
EMP: 50
SQ FT: 50,000
SALES (est): 61.1MM **Privately Held**
WEB: www.calhydro.com
SIC: **5075** 3585 Warm air heating equipment & supplies; refrigeration & heating equipment

(P-7446)
EDWARD B WARD & COMPANY INC (DH)
Also Called: Ward, E B
99 S Hill Dr Ste B, Brisbane (94005-1282)
PHONE...............................415 330-6600
James Lazor, *President*
John Ward, *Ch of Bd*
Robert McDonough, *CEO*
Edward B Ward, *COO*
Paul Caputi, *Vice Pres*
▲ EMP: 50
SQ FT: 45,000
SALES (est): 11.9MM
SALES (corp-wide): 66.5B **Publicly Held**
WEB: www.valair.com
SIC: **5075** Air conditioning equipment, except room units
HQ: Carrier Corporation
13995 Pasteur Blvd
Palm Beach Gardens FL 33418
800 379-6484

(P-7447)
EL CAJON PLUMBING & HTG SUP CO
4360 Mensha Pl, San Diego (92130-2443)
PHONE...............................619 449-7300
Morton B Hirshman, *CEO*
Naomi Hirshman, *Vice Pres*
Loni Olsher, *Vice Pres*
Shelly Olsher, *Principal*
Susy Perez, *Pub Rel Mgr*
EMP: 50 EST: 1973
SALES (est): 15.3MM **Privately Held**
WEB: www.elcajonplumbing.com
SIC: **5075** 5074 Dust collecting equipment; plumbing & hydronic heating supplies

(P-7448)
FLORENCE FILTER CORPORATION
530 W Manville St, Compton (90220-5587)
PHONE...............................310 637-1137
Adrian M Anhood, *CEO*
Erika A Anhood, *President*
Floriana A Anhood, *CEO*
Albert Han, *Recruiter*
▲ EMP: 60
SQ FT: 55,000
SALES (est): 20.7MM **Privately Held**
WEB: www.florencefilter.com
SIC: **5075** 3564 5211 Air filters; filters, air: furnaces, air conditioning equipment, etc.; lumber & other building materials

(P-7449)
GOODMAN MANUFACTURING CO LP
41670 Reagan Way, Murrieta (92562-6930)
PHONE...............................951 304-7402
EMP: 292 **Privately Held**
WEB: www.goodmanmfg.com
SIC: **5075** Warm air heating & air conditioning
HQ: Goodman Manufacturing Company, Lp
5151 San Felipe St # 500
Houston TX 77056
713 861-2500

(P-7450)
GOODMAN MANUFACTURING CO LP
3562 Ruffin Rd, San Diego (92123-2596)
PHONE..................................858 569-1715
Steve Thoreson, *Manager*
EMP: 266 Privately Held
SIC: 5075 Warm air heating & air conditioning
HQ: Goodman Manufacturing Company, Lp
5151 San Felipe St # 500
Houston TX 77056
713 861-2500

(P-7451)
HKF INC (PA)
Also Called: Therm Pacific
5983 Smithway St, Commerce (90040-1607)
PHONE..................................323 225-1318
James P Hartfield, *President*
▲ **EMP: 450**
SALES (est): 116.6MM Privately Held
SIC: 5075 3873 5064 3567 Warm air heating & air conditioning; watches, clocks, watchcases & parts; electrical appliances, television & radio; industrial furnaces & ovens; current-carrying wiring devices

(P-7452)
HONEYWELL INTERNATIONAL INC
514 S Lyon St, Santa Ana (92701-6362)
PHONE..................................714 796-7500
Emily McCue, *Manager*
Christine Bolinger, *Director*
EMP: 115
SALES (corp-wide): 41.8B Publicly Held
WEB: www.honeywell.com
SIC: 5075 8748 7382 Warm air heating & air conditioning; business consulting; security systems services
PA: Honeywell International Inc.
300 S Tryon St
Charlotte NC 28202
973 455-2000

(P-7453)
LENNOX INDUSTRIES INC
19801 Nordhoff Pl Ste 109, Chatsworth (91311-6612)
PHONE..................................818 739-1616
EMP: 140
SALES (corp-wide): 3.8B Publicly Held
SIC: 5075 Warm air heating & air conditioning
HQ: Lennox Industries Inc.
2100 Lake Park Blvd
Richardson TX 75080
972 497-5000

(P-7454)
NORITZ AMERICA CORPORATION (HQ)
11160 Grace Ave, Fountain Valley (92708-5436)
PHONE..................................714 433-2905
Hisashi Uryu, *CEO*
Toshiyuki Otaki, *CEO*
Jason Fleming, *Vice Pres*
Akie Kurakata, *Planning*
Alex Pena, *Technology*
▲ **EMP: 56**
SALES (est): 29.7MM Privately Held
SIC: 5075 Warm air heating equipment & supplies

(P-7455)
NORMAN S WRIGHT MECH EQP CORP (PA)
99 S Hill Dr Ste A, Brisbane (94005-1282)
PHONE..................................415 467-7600
Richard F Leao, *President*
Robert L Beyer, *Exec VP*
Salvatore M Giglio, *Exec VP*
Pauline Vela, *Human Res Mgr*
Gregory Chan, *Sales Staff*
EMP: 80
SQ FT: 50,000

SALES (est): 157.8MM Privately Held
WEB: www.norman-wright.com
SIC: 5075 1711 Warm air heating equipment & supplies; air conditioning & ventilation equipment & supplies; heating & air conditioning contractors

(P-7456)
SIERRA PCF HM & COMFORT INC
Also Called: Sierra Pacific Htg & Air-Solar
2550 Mercantile Dr Ste D, Rancho Cordova (95742-8202)
PHONE..................................916 638-0543
Jason Hanson, *President*
Mike Loer, *Vice Pres*
Lynne Bertolino, *Accounting Mgr*
Lynne Lockwood, *Accounting Mgr*
Kathleen Webster, *Finance Mgr*
EMP: 75
SALES (est): 48.2MM Privately Held
WEB: www.sierrapacifichome.com
SIC: 5075 5074 Warm air heating & air conditioning; heating equipment & panels, solar

(P-7457)
TRANE US INC
4145 Delmar Ave Ste 2, Rocklin (95677-4041)
PHONE..................................916 577-1100
Tyler Clemmer, *Manager*
EMP: 90 Privately Held
SIC: 5075 Air conditioning & ventilation equipment & supplies
HQ: Trane U.S. Inc.
3600 Pammel Creek Rd
La Crosse WI 54601
608 787-2000

(P-7458)
TUCKER DISTRIBUTORS
Also Called: Tucker Sheet Metal Distr
5380 E Hunter Ave, Anaheim (92807-2053)
PHONE..................................714 970-5742
Tom Tucker, *Partner*
Sue Tucker, *Partner*
EMP: 50
SQ FT: 16,000
SALES: 12.6MM Privately Held
SIC: 5075 5051 5084 Ventilating equipment & supplies; tin & tin base metals, shapes, forms, etc.; metalworking machinery

(P-7459)
ULTRAVIOLET DEVICES INC
26145 Technology Dr, Valencia (91355-1138)
PHONE..................................661 295-8140
Peter Veloz, *CEO*
David Veloz, *Shareholder*
Richard Hayes, *Vice Pres*
Ashish Mathur, *Vice Pres*
Lev Rotkop, *Vice Pres*
▲ **EMP: 53**
SQ FT: 45,000
SALES (est): 34.7MM Privately Held
WEB: www.uvdi.com
SIC: 5075 5074 Air filters; water purification equipment

5078 Refrigeration Eqpt & Splys Wholesale

(P-7460)
ALLIED BEVERAGE LLC
13235 Golden State Rd, Sylmar (91342-1129)
PHONE..................................818 493-6400
Mark Smith, *CEO*
Kimberly Clift, *CFO*
Jozsef Locsmandi, *Principal*
Erin Gabler,
Steve Miller, *Director*
EMP: 500
SALES (est): 27.3MM Privately Held
SIC: 5078 Beverage coolers

(P-7461)
CUSTOM COOLER INC (HQ)
420 E Arrow Hwy, San Dimas (91773-3340)
PHONE..................................909 592-1111

Sangyup Steve Lee, *President*
Young G Kim, *Vice Pres*
Ray Tolcher, *Vice Pres*
▲ **EMP: 80**
SALES (est): 46.6MM
SALES (corp-wide): 213.6MM Privately Held
SIC: 5078 Refrigeration equipment & supplies
PA: Kps Global Llc
4201 N Beach St
Fort Worth TX 76137
817 281-5121

(P-7462)
OMNITEAM INC
9300 Hall Rd, Downey (90241-5309)
PHONE..................................562 923-9660
Kans Haasis Jr, *CEO*
Robert Davis, *Vice Pres*
Don Hyatt Sr, *Vice Pres*
EMP: 125
SQ FT: 100,000
SALES (est): 49.9MM Privately Held
WEB: www.omniteam.com
SIC: 5078 Commercial refrigeration equipment

(P-7463)
PEPSI-COLA METRO BTLG CO INC
6659 Sycamore Canyon Blvd, Riverside (92507-0733)
PHONE..................................951 697-3200
Jerry Sime, *Manager*
EMP: 500
SALES (corp-wide): 64.6B Publicly Held
WEB: www.joy-of-cola.com
SIC: 5078 2086 5149 Refrigerated beverage dispensers; bottled & canned soft drinks; soft drinks
HQ: Pepsi-Cola Metropolitan Bottling Company, Inc.
1111 Westchester Ave
White Plains NY 10604
914 767-6000

(P-7464)
REFRIGERATION HDWR SUP CORP
9021 Norris Ave, Sun Valley (91352-2618)
PHONE..................................818 768-3636
Pamela Sylvester, *Branch Mgr*
EMP: 50
SALES (corp-wide): 24.7MM Privately Held
SIC: 5078 5722 3585 7699 Refrigeration equipment & supplies; household appliance stores; refrigeration & heating equipment; restaurant equipment repair
PA: Refrigeration Hardware Supply Corporation
632 Foresight Cir
Grand Junction CO 81505
970 241-2800

(P-7465)
UNITED REFRIGERATION INC
3573a Hayden Ave, Culver City (90232-2412)
PHONE..................................310 204-2500
John Nunez, *President*
EMP: 99
SQ FT: 2,000
SALES (corp-wide): 50MM Privately Held
SIC: 5078 Refrigeration equipment & supplies
PA: United Refrigeration, Inc.
11401 Roosevelt Blvd
Philadelphia PA 19154
215 698-9100

5082 Construction & Mining Mach & Eqpt Wholesale

(P-7466)
BRAND SERVICES INC
Also Called: Brand Services of California
535 Watt Dr, Fairfield (94534-1790)
PHONE..................................707 603-3400

Paul Wood, *President*
EMP: 50
SALES (est): 16MM Privately Held
SIC: 5082 Scaffolding

(P-7467)
CALIFORNIA CONTRS SUPS INC
7729 Burnet Ave, Van Nuys (91405-1008)
PHONE..................................818 785-8823
David Rogal, *CEO*
Phil Kaufmann, *President*
Al Lester, *Corp Secy*
EMP: 55
SQ FT: 16,000
SALES (est): 12.8MM Privately Held
SIC: 5082 Contractors' materials; general construction machinery & equipment

(P-7468)
CAMERON WEST COAST INC
Also Called: Cameron Surface Systems
4316 Yeager Way, Bakersfield (93313)
PHONE..................................661 837-4980
Stefan Radwanski, *Principal*
▲ **EMP: 90 EST: 1992**
SQ FT: 48,000
SALES (est): 42.1MM Publicly Held
SIC: 5082 1389 7353 Oil field equipment; oil field services; oil field equipment, rental or leasing
HQ: Cameron International Corporation
4646 W Sam Houston Pkwy N
Houston TX 77041

(P-7469)
CNH INDUSTRIAL AMERICA LLC
1919 Williams St, San Leandro (94577-2303)
PHONE..................................510 351-2015
Norma Smith, *Manager*
EMP: 50
SALES (corp-wide): 49.5MM Privately Held
SIC: 5082 General construction machinery & equipment
PA: Cnh Industrial America Llc
700 State St
Racine WI 53404
262 636-6011

(P-7470)
EMPIRE SOUTHWEST LLC
Also Called: Caterpillar Authorized Dealer
3393 Us Highway 86, Imperial (92251-9527)
P.O. Box 936 (92251-0936)
PHONE..................................760 545-6200
Diane Madrigal, *Manager*
EMP: 300
SALES (corp-wide): 881.9MM Privately Held
WEB: www.empire-cat.com
SIC: 5082 General construction machinery & equipment
PA: Empire Southwest, Llc
1725 S Country Club Dr
Mesa AZ 85210
480 633-4000

(P-7471)
FLUOR ENTERPRISES INC
3 Polaris Way, Aliso Viejo (92656-5338)
PHONE..................................949 349-2000
Ronald Albright, *Branch Mgr*
EMP: 200
SALES (corp-wide): 19.1B Publicly Held
SIC: 5082 Construction & mining machinery
HQ: Fluor Enterprises, Inc.
6700 Las Colinas Blvd
Irving TX 75039
469 398-7000

(P-7472)
GAMA CONTRACTING SERVICES INC
1835 Floradale Ave, South El Monte (91733-3605)
PHONE..................................626 442-7200
Jose Sergio Duenas, *President*
EMP: 140
SALES (est): 8.5MM Privately Held
SIC: 5082 1795 8744 General construction machinery & equipment; wrecking & demolition work;

(P-7473)
GOTTSTEIN CONTRACTING CORP
4114 Armour Ave, Bakersfield
(93308-4509)
PHONE....................661 322-8934
Scott Gottstein, *Branch Mgr*
EMP: 60
SALES (corp-wide): 18.7MM **Privately Held**
SIC: 5082 General construction machinery & equipment
PA: Gottstein Corporation
39 Elm Rd
Hazle Township PA 18202
570 454-7162

(P-7474)
HAWTHORNE MACHINERY CO
Also Called: Caterpillar Authorized Dealer
8050 Othello Ave, San Diego (92111-3714)
PHONE....................858 974-6800
Bob Price, *Manager*
EMP: 100
SALES (corp-wide): 195.6MM **Privately Held**
SIC: 5082 General construction machinery & equipment
PA: Hawthorne Machinery Co.
16945 Camino San Bernardo
San Diego CA 92127
858 674-7000

(P-7475)
HERCA TELECOMM SERVICES INC
Also Called: Herca Construction Services
18610 Beck St, Perris (92570-9185)
PHONE....................951 940-5941
Hector R Castellon, *President*
Tracy Hertel, *CFO*
Raul Castellon, *Opers Staff*
Alfredo Castellon, *Director*
Alfonso Catellon, *Director*
EMP: 56
SQ FT: 67,900
SALES: 16.2MM **Privately Held**
WEB: www.hercatelecomm.com
SIC: 5082 1623 1731 3663 General construction machinery & equipment; communication line & transmission tower construction; general electrical contractor; antennas, transmitting & communications

(P-7476)
HOLT OF CALIFORNIA (HQ)
Also Called: Holt CA
7310 Pacific Ave, Pleasant Grove (95668-9708)
PHONE....................916 991-8200
Victor Wykoff Jr, *Ch of Bd*
Kenneth Monroe, *President*
Daniel Johns, *CFO*
Gordon Beatie, *Vice Ch Bd*
Ronald Monroe, *Exec VP*
▲ EMP: 155
SQ FT: 160,000
SALES (est): 326.6MM
SALES (corp-wide): 356MM **Privately Held**
WEB: www.holtcausedparts.com
SIC: 5082 5084 5083 7359 General construction machinery & equipment; tractors, construction; materials handling machinery; agricultural machinery; equipment rental & leasing
PA: Hoc Holdings, Inc.
7310 Pacific Ave
Pleasant Grove CA 95668
916 921-8950

(P-7477)
HOLT OF CALIFORNIA
Also Called: Caterpillar Authorized Dealer
3850 Channel Dr, West Sacramento (95691-3466)
PHONE....................916 373-4100
Toll Free:....................888 -
Carry Roulet, *Manager*
Bob Wolfe, *Vice Pres*
Dave Dobberteen, *Accounts Mgr*
EMP: 150

SALES (corp-wide): 356MM **Privately Held**
WEB: www.holtcausedparts.com
SIC: 5082 5083 5084 General construction machinery & equipment; agricultural machinery & equipment; materials handling machinery
HQ: Holt Of California
7310 Pacific Ave
Pleasant Grove CA 95668
916 991-8200

(P-7478)
HOLT OF CALIFORNIA
1234 W Charter Way, Stockton (95206-1109)
PHONE....................209 462-3660
Ken Monroe, *Owner*
EMP: 108
SALES (corp-wide): 356MM **Privately Held**
SIC: 5082 Tractors, construction
HQ: Holt Of California
7310 Pacific Ave
Pleasant Grove CA 95668
916 991-8200

(P-7479)
HUB CONSTRUCTION SPC INC
1856 S Bon View Ave, Ontario (91761-5501)
PHONE....................909 947-4669
Tim Robuck, *Manager*
EMP: 50
SALES (corp-wide): 35.1MM **Privately Held**
SIC: 5082 3444 Concrete processing equipment; concrete forms, sheet metal
PA: Hub Construction Specialties, Inc.
379 S I St
San Bernardino CA 92410
909 889-0161

(P-7480)
J M EQUIPMENT COMPANY INC
3751 E Calwa Ave, Fresno (93725-2002)
P.O. Box 2400 (93745-2400)
PHONE....................559 233-0187
Scott Anderson, *Manager*
Rod Kiser, *Manager*
EMP: 50
SQ FT: 900
SALES (corp-wide): 42.2MM **Privately Held**
WEB: www.jmequipment.com
SIC: 5082 7353 5084 General construction machinery & equipment; heavy construction equipment rental; materials handling machinery
PA: J. M. Equipment Company, Inc.
321 Spreckels Ave
Manteca CA 95336
209 522-3271

(P-7481)
JOHNSON MACHINERY CO (PA)
Also Called: Caterpillar Authorized Dealer
800 E La Cadena Dr, Riverside (92507-8715)
P.O. Box 351 (92502-0351)
PHONE....................951 686-4560
William Johnson Jr, *President*
Kevin Kelly, *Exec VP*
Matt Merickel, *Exec VP*
Rebecca Palmer, *Accountant*
Greg Bindl, *Sales Staff*
◆ EMP: 175
SQ FT: 70,000
SALES (est): 205.9MM **Privately Held**
WEB: www.johnson-machinery.com
SIC: 5082 General construction machinery & equipment

(P-7482)
PAPE MACHINERY INC
Also Called: John Deere Authorized Dealer
2850 El Centro Rd, Sacramento (95833-9602)
P.O. Box 15017 (95851-0017)
PHONE....................916 922-7181
Josh Juenger, *Branch Mgr*
Jordan Pape, *CEO*
EMP: 82

SALES (corp-wide): 640.9MM **Privately Held**
WEB: www.papemh.com
SIC: 5082 General construction machinery & equipment
HQ: Pape' Machinery, Inc.
355 Goodpasture Island Rd # 300
Eugene OR 97401
541 683-5073

(P-7483)
PEARCE INDUSTRIES INC
6558 Meany Ave, Bakersfield (93308-5124)
PHONE....................661 695-3420
EMP: 63
SALES (corp-wide): 396MM **Privately Held**
SIC: 5082 Construction & mining machinery
PA: Pearce Industries, Inc.
12320 Main St
Houston TX 77035
713 723-1050

(P-7484)
QUINN COMPANY
13275 Golden State Rd, Sylmar (91342-1129)
PHONE....................818 767-7171
Brock Phil, *Sales Executive*
EMP: 61
SALES (corp-wide): 455MM **Privately Held**
SIC: 5082 General construction machinery & equipment
HQ: Quinn Company
10006 Rose Hills Rd
City Of Industry CA 90601
562 463-4000

(P-7485)
QUINN COMPANY
Also Called: Caterpillar Authorized Dealer
2200 Pegasus Dr, Bakersfield (93308-6801)
PHONE....................661 393-5800
Steve Eucce, *Branch Mgr*
EMP: 62
SALES (corp-wide): 455MM **Privately Held**
WEB: www.quinngroup.net
SIC: 5082 5083 5084 7353 General construction machinery & equipment; farm & garden machinery; industrial machinery & equipment; heavy construction equipment rental
HQ: Quinn Company
10006 Rose Hills Rd
City Of Industry CA 90601
562 463-4000

(P-7486)
QUINN COMPANY
Also Called: Caterpillar Authorized Dealer
801 Del Norte Blvd, Oxnard (93030-8966)
PHONE....................805 485-2171
Jay Ervine, *Branch Mgr*
Debbie Payne, *Credit Mgr*
EMP: 62
SALES (corp-wide): 455MM **Privately Held**
WEB: www.quinngroup.net
SIC: 5082 5083 5084 7353 General construction machinery & equipment; farm & garden machinery; industrial machinery & equipment; heavy construction equipment rental
HQ: Quinn Company
10006 Rose Hills Rd
City Of Industry CA 90601
562 463-4000

(P-7487)
QUINN COMPANY
Also Called: Caterpillar Authorized Dealer
1655 Carlotti Dr, Santa Maria (93454-1503)
PHONE....................805 925-8611
Dan Hunt, *Manager*
Monty Baker, *General Mgr*
EMP: 62

SALES (corp-wide): 455MM **Privately Held**
WEB: www.quinngroup.net
SIC: 5082 5083 5084 7353 General construction machinery & equipment; farm & garden machinery; industrial machinery & equipment; heavy construction equipment rental
HQ: Quinn Company
10006 Rose Hills Rd
City Of Industry CA 90601
562 463-4000

(P-7488)
QUINN GROUP INC
Also Called: Caterpillar Authorized Dealer
1300 Abbott St, Salinas (93901-4507)
PHONE....................831 758-8461
Kelly Francis, *Store Mgr*
Jesse Sandoval, *Manager*
EMP: 1000
SALES (corp-wide): 455MM **Privately Held**
WEB: www.quinnengines.com
SIC: 5082 General construction machinery & equipment
PA: Quinn Group, Inc.
10006 Rose Hills Rd
City Of Industry CA 90601
562 463-4000

(P-7489)
QUINN SHEPHERD MACHINERY
Also Called: Caterpillar Authorized Dealer
10006 Rose Hills Rd, City of Industry (90601-1702)
P.O. Box 226789, Los Angeles (90022-6789)
PHONE....................562 463-6000
Blake Quinn, *President*
▲ EMP: 287
SQ FT: 163,000
SALES (est): 99.9MM
SALES (corp-wide): 455MM **Privately Held**
SIC: 5082 5084 General construction machinery & equipment; excavating machinery & equipment; mining machinery & equipment, except petroleum; industrial machinery & equipment
PA: Quinn Group, Inc.
10006 Rose Hills Rd
City Of Industry CA 90601
562 463-4000

(P-7490)
RDO VERMEER LLC
Also Called: Vermeer Pacific
3980 Research Dr, Sacramento (95838-3257)
PHONE....................916 643-0999
Christi Offutt,
EMP: 99
SALES (est): 8.4MM **Privately Held**
SIC: 5082 Contractors' materials

(P-7491)
SAFWAY SERVICES LP
1660 Gilbreth Rd, Burlingame (94010-1408)
PHONE....................650 652-9255
Fax: 650 652-9255
EMP: 50
SALES (corp-wide): 1.7B **Privately Held**
SIC: 5082
HQ: Safway Services, L.P.
N19w24200 Riverwood Dr # 200
Waukesha WI 53188
262 523-6500

(P-7492)
SAFWAY SERVICES LP
4072b Teal Ct, Benicia (94510-1238)
PHONE....................707 745-2000
Sully Cittadino, *Manager*
Kathy Perotti, *Executive*
EMP: 50
SALES (corp-wide): 855.2MM **Privately Held**
WEB: www.safway.com
SIC: 5082 Scaffolding
HQ: Safway Services, L.P.
N19w24200 Riverwood Dr # 200
Waukesha WI 53188
262 523-6500

(P-7493)
SOUND-CRETE CONTRACTORS INC
530 Opper St Ste A, Escondido
(92029-1034)
PHONE......................760 291-1240
Louis Fisher, *President*
Terry Russo, *Vice Pres*
Jim Dorsey, *Manager*
EMP: 65
SALES (est): 7.4MM **Privately Held**
SIC: 5082 General construction machinery & equipment

(P-7494)
SOUTHWEST GENERAL CONTRS INC
912 S Andreasen Dr # 101, Escondido
(92029-1900)
PHONE......................760 480-8747
Dane Crown, *President*
EMP: 50
SQ FT: 4,500
SALES (est): 10.4MM **Privately Held**
SIC: 5082 General construction machinery & equipment

(P-7495)
TOM MALLOY CORPORATION (PA)
Also Called: Trench Shoring Company
206 N Central Ave, Compton (90220-1463)
PHONE......................310 327-5554
Thomas E Malloy, *CEO*
Kevin Malloy, *President*
Kelley Malloy, *Vice Pres*
Greg Holm, *Branch Mgr*
Karen Lopez, *Branch Mgr*
▲ **EMP:** 50 **EST:** 1973
SALES (est): 43.7MM **Privately Held**
SIC: 5082 7353 Construction & mining machinery; heavy construction equipment rental

(P-7496)
WHITE CAP CONSTRUCTION SUPPLY
1815 Ritchey St, Santa Ana (92705-5127)
PHONE......................949 794-5300
Jack Karg, *Principal*
Kevin Burns, *Branch Mgr*
Brad Jones, *District Mgr*
Okelly Shane, *Project Mgr*
Jim Dierker, *VP Finance*
EMP: 1033
SALES (est): 20.6MM **Publicly Held**
SIC: 5082 Construction & mining machinery
HQ: White Cap Construction Supply, Inc.
3100 Cumberland Blvd Se # 1700
Atlanta GA 30339
404 879-7740

5083 Farm & Garden Mach & Eqpt Wholesale

(P-7497)
ALSCO - GEYER IRRIGATION INC
700 5th St, Arbuckle (95912-9550)
P.O. Box 111 (95912-0111)
PHONE......................530 476-2253
Charles Geyer, *President*
Marjoria Martinez, *Admin Sec*
Andrew Geyer, *Sales Staff*
Rocio Hernandez, *Cashier*
EMP: 90
SQ FT: 3,000
SALES (est): 64.5MM **Privately Held**
WEB: www.alscogeyer.com
SIC: 5083 Irrigation equipment

(P-7498)
ATI MACHINERY INC
Also Called: NAPA West
21436 S Lassen Ave, Five Points (93624)
P.O. Box 445 (93624-0445)
PHONE......................559 884-2471
Toll Free:......................888 -
Leo A Marihart, *Ch of Bd*
Mark Moorhead, *President*
Richard Demler, *Admin Sec*
EMP: 50

SQ FT: 22,000
SALES (est): 17.3MM **Privately Held**
WEB: www.atimachinery.com
SIC: 5083 7699 7359 Farm equipment parts & supplies; farm machinery repair; equipment rental & leasing

(P-7499)
EURODRIP USA INC
1850 W Almond Ave, Madera (93637-5214)
PHONE......................559 674-2670
Rowland Wilkinson, *CEO*
◆ **EMP:** 80
SQ FT: 33,180
SALES: 76MM
SALES (corp-wide): 462.2K **Privately Held**
WEB: www.eurodripusa.com
SIC: 5083 3084 Irrigation equipment; plastics pipe
HQ: Eurodrip S.A.
Athinon - Lamias National Rd (55th Km), P.O. Box 34
Oinofyta 32011
-

(P-7500)
GREEN ACRES NURSERY & SUP LLC
604 Sutter St, Folsom (95630-2575)
PHONE......................916 782-2273
Mark Gill,
▲ **EMP:** 90
SALES (est): 52.3MM **Privately Held**
SIC: 5083 5261 Irrigation equipment; nursery stock, seeds & bulbs

(P-7501)
KRC EQUIPMENT LLC
700 N Twin Oaks Valley Rd, San Marcos
(92069-1714)
P.O. Box 729 (92079-0729)
PHONE......................760 744-1036
Gerald Sebby, *President*
Cathy Sebby,
EMP: 58 **EST:** 1998
SALES (est): 5.2MM **Privately Held**
SIC: 5083 Landscaping equipment

(P-7502)
LAWRENCE TRACTOR COINC (PA)
Also Called: John Deere Authorized Dealer
2436 E Valley Oaks Dr, Visalia
(93292-6713)
PHONE......................559 734-7406
Mark Lawrence, *President*
Angie Lawrence, *Shareholder*
Richard Nunes, *Corp Secy*
Steven Lawrence, *Vice Pres*
Neil Walden, *Foreman/Supr*
▲ **EMP:** 98 **EST:** 1970
SQ FT: 72,000
SALES (est): 51.6MM **Privately Held**
WEB: www.lawrencetractor.com
SIC: 5083 7699 Agricultural machinery; farm implements; farm equipment parts & supplies; farm machinery repair

(P-7503)
NETAFIM IRRIGATION INC (HQ)
5470 E Home Ave, Fresno (93727-2107)
PHONE......................559 453-6800
Igal Aisenberg, *President*
Lauri Hanover, *CFO*
Iris Ron, *Officer*
Aletta Froticks, *Vice Pres*
Hila Mukevisius, *Vice Pres*
▲ **EMP:** 110 **EST:** 1965
SQ FT: 100,000
SALES (est): 91.1MM
SALES (corp-wide): 365.7MM **Privately Held**
WEB: www.netafimusa.com
SIC: 5083 3523 Irrigation equipment; irrigation equipment, self-propelled
PA: Netafim Ltd
10 Hashalom Rd.
Tel Aviv-Jaffa 67892
864 747-47

(P-7504)
QUINN GROUP INC
Also Called: Caterpillar Authorized Dealer
801 Del Norte Blvd, Oxnard (93030-8966)
PHONE......................805 485-2171

Jim Barr, *Manager*
EMP: 80
SQ FT: 5,000
SALES (corp-wide): 455MM **Privately Held**
WEB: www.catpower.com
SIC: 5083 5082 5084 Agricultural machinery & equipment; construction & mining machinery; industrial machinery & equipment
PA: Quinn Group, Inc.
10006 Rose Hills Rd
City Of Industry CA 90601
562 463-4000

(P-7505)
QUINN GROUP INC
2200 Pegasus Dr, Bakersfield
(93308-6801)
PHONE......................661 393-5800
Mike Ford, *Branch Mgr*
Robin Camp, *Sales Staff*
EMP: 110
SALES (corp-wide): 455MM **Privately Held**
WEB: www.catpower.com
SIC: 5083 5084 7359 Tractors, agricultural; tractors, industrial; industrial truck rental
PA: Quinn Group, Inc.
10006 Rose Hills Rd
City Of Industry CA 90601
562 463-4000

(P-7506)
RDO CONSTRUCTION EQUIPMENT CO
Also Called: John Deere Authorized Dealer
20 Iowa Ave, Riverside (92507-1028)
PHONE......................951 778-3700
Greg Burgman, *General Mgr*
EMP: 50
SALES (corp-wide): 2.3B **Privately Held**
SIC: 5083 Farm & garden machinery
HQ: Rdo Construction Equipment Co.
2000 Industrial Dr
Bismarck ND 58501
701 223-5798

(P-7507)
S A CAMP COMPANIES (PA)
17876 Zerker Rd, Bakersfield
(93308-9221)
PHONE......................661 399-4451
James S Camp, *President*
D M Hart, *Vice Pres*
Kurt Eilers, *Sales Engr*
Don Pedersen, *Sales Engr*
EMP: 50
SQ FT: 10,000
SALES (est): 18.1MM **Privately Held**
WEB: www.sacamp.net
SIC: 5083 0191 6552 Agricultural machinery; general farms, primarily crop; subdividers & developers

(P-7508)
SPEARS MANUFACTURING CO (PA)
15853 Olden St, Sylmar (91342-1293)
P.O. Box 9203 (91392-9203)
PHONE......................818 364-1611
Robert Wayne Spears, *CEO*
Wayne Spears, *President*
Ken Ruggles, *Corp Secy*
Michael Valasquez, *Vice Pres*
Mike Velasquez, *Vice Pres*
◆ **EMP:** 134 **EST:** 1970
SQ FT: 119,088
SALES (est): 1.5B **Privately Held**
WEB: www.spearsmfg.com
SIC: 5083 3494 Irrigation equipment; valves & pipe fittings

(P-7509)
THOMASON TRACTOR CO CALIFORNIA
Also Called: John Deere Authorized Dealer
985 12th St, Firebaugh (93622)
P.O. Box 97 (93622-0097)
PHONE......................559 659-2039
Audrey Thomason, *President*
Rodney Thomason, *Vice Pres*
Jessica Diaz, *Office Admin*
Don York Jr, *Sales Mgr*
Veronica Munguia, *Asst Office Mgr*

EMP: 50 **EST:** 1967
SQ FT: 33,000
SALES (est): 29MM **Privately Held**
WEB: www.thomasontractor.com
SIC: 5083 Agricultural machinery & equipment

(P-7510)
TURF STAR INC
Also Called: Turfstar
79253 Country Club Dr, Bermuda Dunes
(92203-1229)
PHONE......................760 772-3575
Leonard Gregory, *President*
EMP: 100
SALES (corp-wide): 86.8MM **Privately Held**
WEB: www.turfstar.com
SIC: 5083 Garden machinery & equipment
PA: Turf Star, Inc.
2438 Radley Ct
Hayward CA 94545
800 585-8001

(P-7511)
TURLOCK DAIRY & RFRGN INC
Also Called: T D R
1819 S Walnut Rd, Turlock (95380-9219)
P.O. Box 1530 (95381-1530)
PHONE......................209 667-6455
Mathew Anthony Bruno, *CEO*
Tony Bruno, *President*
EMP: 100 **EST:** 1972
SQ FT: 10,000
SALES (est): 69.9MM **Privately Held**
WEB: www.turlockdairy.com
SIC: 5083 7699 1542 Dairy machinery & equipment; industrial equipment services; nonresidential construction

(P-7512)
VUCOVICH INC (PA)
Also Called: John Deere Authorized Dealer
4288 S Bagley Ave, Fresno (93725-9014)
P.O. Box 2513 (93745-2513)
PHONE......................559 486-8020
Marsha Vucovich, *President*
Brad Wood, *Executive*
Bill Kidd, *General Mgr*
Reid Pinion, *Controller*
John Laemmlen, *Sales Staff*
EMP: 60
SQ FT: 42,800
SALES: 50MM **Privately Held**
WEB: www.fresnoequipment.com
SIC: 5083 Farm equipment parts & supplies; agricultural machinery & equipment

5084 Industrial Mach & Eqpt Wholesale

(P-7513)
A MEISSNERS HHLD & INDUS SVC
2417 Cormorant Way, Sacramento
(95815-2714)
PHONE......................916 920-2121
Jim Meissners, *Owner*
EMP: 57 **EST:** 2001
SALES (est): 2.8MM **Privately Held**
SIC: 5084 Sewing machines, industrial

(P-7514)
AIRGAS INC
653 N Market St, Redding (96003-3609)
PHONE......................530 241-1544
John Sabo, *Branch Mgr*
EMP: 281
SALES (corp-wide): 125.9MM **Privately Held**
SIC: 5084 Welding machinery & equipment
HQ: Airgas, Inc.
259 N Radnor Chester Rd # 100
Radnor PA 19087
610 687-5253

(P-7515)
AIRGAS INC
9010 Clairemont Mesa Blvd, San Diego
(92123-1208)
PHONE......................858 279-8200
Leigh Hart, *Branch Mgr*
EMP: 110

SALES (corp-wide): 125.9MM **Privately Held**
WEB: www.airgas.com
SIC: **5084** Welding machinery & equipment
HQ: Airgas, Inc.
259 N Radnor Chester Rd # 100
Radnor PA 19087
610 687-5253

(P-7516)
AIRGAS SAFETY INC
2355 Workman Mill Rd, City of Industry
(90601-1459)
PHONE......................562 699-5239
Olaya Rivera, *Branch Mgr*
Darryl Langdon, *Accounts Mgr*
EMP: 80
SALES (corp-wide): 125.9MM **Privately Held**
WEB: www.airgassafety.com
SIC: **5084** 5085 3561 3841 Safety equipment; welding supplies; cylinders, pump; surgical & medical instruments
HQ: Airgas Safety, Inc.
2501 Green Ln
Levittown PA 19057

(P-7517)
AIRGAS USA LLC
11711 S Alameda St, Los Angeles
(90059-2130)
PHONE......................323 568-2244
Dennis Beukelmau, *Branch Mgr*
EMP: 58
SALES (corp-wide): 125.9MM **Privately Held**
WEB: www.airgaswest.com
SIC: **5084** Welding machinery & equipment
HQ: Airgas Usa, Llc
259 N Radnor Chester Rd
Radnor PA 19087

(P-7518)
AIRGAS USA LLC
5121 Brandin Ct, Fremont (94538-5109)
PHONE......................510 659-0162
Gita Parobek, *Manager*
Eric Kleinschmidt, *Plant Engr*
EMP: 50
SQ FT: 24,000
SALES (corp-wide): 125.9MM **Privately Held**
WEB: www.asgemail.com
SIC: **5084** Welding machinery & equipment
HQ: Airgas Usa, Llc
259 N Radnor Chester Rd
Radnor PA 19087
610 687-5253

(P-7519)
AIRGAS USA LLC
441 Hobson St, San Jose (95110-2016)
PHONE......................408 998-6380
Al Shull, *Manager*
Max Hooper, *President*
Peter McCausland, *CEO*
EMP: 65
SQ FT: 7,200
SALES (corp-wide): 125.9MM **Privately Held**
SIC: **5084** 5169 Welding machinery & equipment; industrial gases
HQ: Airgas Usa, Llc
259 N Radnor Chester Rd
Radnor PA 19087
610 687-5253

(P-7520)
ALLTEK COMPANY U S A INC
18281 Gothard St Ste 102, Huntington Beach (92648-1205)
PHONE......................714 375-9785
Weishui W Zhang, *President*
Joline Yin, *Vice Pres*
John Zhang, *Vice Pres*
Linda Zhu, *Vice Pres*
EMP: 50
SQ FT: 2,000
SALES (est): 16.9MM **Privately Held**
WEB: www.alltekusa.com
SIC: **5084** 5065 Industrial machinery & equipment; semiconductor devices

(P-7521)
AMADA AMERICA INC (HQ)
7025 Firestone Blvd, Buena Park
(90621-1869)
PHONE......................714 739-2111
Mike Guarin, *CEO*
Jerry Rush, *COO*
KOA Nakata, *CFO*
Koji Tsuchimoto, *CFO*
Yukihiro Fukui, *Officer*
◆ EMP: 75
SQ FT: 103,000
SALES (est): 191.2MM **Privately Held**
SIC: **5084** 6159 Metalworking machinery; metalworking tools (such as drills, taps, dies, files); machinery & equipment finance leasing

(P-7522)
ANA TRADING CORP USA (DH)
3625 Del Amo Blvd Ste 300, Torrance
(90503-1693)
PHONE......................310 542-2500
Hideto Osada, *President*
Brent Johnson, *Exec VP*
Hisato Teruyama, *Exec VP*
Takashi Kinoshita, *Vice Pres*
Noriyuki Shibata, *Vice Pres*
◆ EMP: 58
SQ FT: 11,000
SALES: 23.5MM **Privately Held**
SIC: **5084** 5088 0173 0175 Industrial machine parts; aircraft & parts; walnut grove; prune orchard

(P-7523)
ANHEUSER-BUSCH LLC
3101 Busch Dr, Fairfield (94534-9726)
PHONE......................707 429-7595
Kevin Finger, *Manager*
Sean Williams, *Engineer*
Sean Connors, *Opers Mgr*
EMP: 450
SALES (corp-wide): 1.5B **Privately Held**
WEB: www.hispanicbud.com
SIC: **5084** Brewery products manufacturing machinery, commercial
HQ: Anheuser-Busch, Llc
1 Busch Pl
Saint Louis MO 63118
800 342-5283

(P-7524)
ANRITSU AMERICAS SALES COMPANY
490 Jarvis Dr, Morgan Hill (95037-2834)
PHONE......................408 778-2000
Hirokazu Hamada, *CEO*
EMP: 540
SQ FT: 250,000
SALES (est): 54.1MM **Privately Held**
SIC: **5084** Measuring & testing equipment, electrical
HQ: Anritsu U.S. Holding, Inc.
490 Jarvis Dr
Morgan Hill CA 95037
408 778-2000

(P-7525)
B C RENTALS LLC (HQ)
Also Called: Bc Traffic Specialists
638 W Southern Ave, Orange
(92865-3219)
PHONE......................714 974-1190
Robert Carson, *President*
Rick Webb, *General Mgr*
Sally Carson, *Admin Sec*
Maria Gomez, *Accountant*
Jeff Airhart, *Sales Associate*
▲ EMP: 80
SQ FT: 3,000
SALES: 15MM **Privately Held**
SIC: **5084** 5999 7359 Safety equipment; safety supplies & equipment; equipment rental & leasing
PA: Infrastripe, Llc
11121 Carmel Commons Blvd
Charlotte NC 28226
704 936-0125

(P-7526)
BARDEX CORPORATION
6338 Lindmar Dr, Goleta (93117-3112)
PHONE......................805 964-7747
Thomas Miller, *CEO*
Kusnadhi Sidikpramana, *CFO*

Tom Miller, *Vice Pres*
Anita Elovitz, *Admin Asst*
Charlie Orourke, *Info Tech Dir*
◆ EMP: 62
SQ FT: 80,000
SALES (est): 35.5MM **Privately Held**
WEB: www.bardex.com
SIC: **5084** Industrial machinery & equipment

(P-7527)
BAY ADVANCED TECHNOLOGIES LLC
Also Called: Bay Advanced Tech 0045
8100 Central Ave, Newark (94560-3449)
PHONE......................510 857-0900
Mike Stimson, *Branch Mgr*
EMP: 88
SALES (corp-wide): 3.4B **Publicly Held**
SIC: **5084** Pneumatic tools & equipment
HQ: Bay Advanced Technologies, Llc
8100 Central Ave
Newark CA 94560
510 857-0900

(P-7528)
BEJAC CORPORATION (PA)
569 S Van Buren St, Placentia
(92870-6613)
PHONE......................714 528-6224
Ron Barlet, *President*
Kim Smith-Grime, *CFO*
Peggy Barlet, *Treasurer*
Robert Cycon, *Vice Pres*
Tyler Decamp, *Technician*
▼ EMP: 66 EST: 1953
SQ FT: 2,000
SALES (est): 37MM **Privately Held**
WEB: www.bejac.com
SIC: **5084** 7353 Industrial machinery & equipment; heavy construction equipment rental

(P-7529)
BIG JOE CALIFORNIA NORTH INC (PA)
Also Called: Big Joe Handling Systems
25932 Eden Landing Rd, Hayward
(94545-3816)
PHONE......................510 785-6900
Boyd J Kiefus, *CEO*
Rod D Kiefus, *CFO*
Rod Kiefus, *Manager*
EMP: 125
SQ FT: 52,000
SALES (est): 95.1MM **Privately Held**
SIC: **5084** 5999 7359 8331 Lift trucks & parts; business machines & equipment; equipment rental & leasing; job training services

(P-7530)
BLAKE H BROWN INC (DH)
Also Called: John Tillman Company
1300 W Artesia Blvd, Compton
(90220-5307)
P.O. Box 6257 (90224-6257)
PHONE......................310 764-0110
Blake H Brown, *CEO*
▲ EMP: 100 EST: 1928
SQ FT: 25,000
SALES (corp-wide): 11.6B **Privately Held**
WEB: www.jtillman.com
SIC: **5084** 3842 3548 Safety equipment; personal safety equipment; welding apparatus

(P-7531)
BORETECH RESRCE RECOVRY ENGINE
Also Called: Boretech Rsource Recovery Engrg
5546 Vintage Cir, Stockton (95219-2510)
PHONE......................209 373-2588
Jo Hua Lee, *President*
Alice KAO, *Vice Pres*
▲ EMP: 50
SALES: 24MM **Privately Held**
SIC: **5084** 2611 Recycling machinery & equipment; pulp manufactured from waste or recycled paper

(P-7532)
BUCKEYE FIRE EQUIPMENT COMPANY
2416 Teagarden St, San Leandro
(94577-4336)
PHONE......................510 483-1815
Mark Libardos, *Principal*
EMP: 291
SALES (corp-wide): 108.3MM **Privately Held**
SIC: **5084** Industrial machinery & equipment
PA: Buckeye Fire Equipment Company
110 Kings Rd
Kings Mountain NC 28086
704 739-7415

(P-7533)
BUCKLES-SMITH ELECTRIC COMPANY (PA)
540 Martin Ave, Santa Clara (95050-2954)
PHONE......................408 280-7777
Art Cook, *CEO*
Pat Berry, *Vice Pres*
Roger Stanger, *Vice Pres*
Ron Zimmerman, *Admin Sec*
EMP: 55
SALES (est): 125.9MM **Privately Held**
WEB: www.geindustrial.com
SIC: **5084** 5063 Industrial machinery & equipment; electrical supplies

(P-7534)
CAL-LIFT INC
13027 Crossroads Pkwy S, La Puente
(91746-3406)
PHONE......................562 566-1400
Mark T Maechling, *CEO*
Michele Suire, *Executive*
Veronica Aceves, *Human Res Dir*
Robert Bey, *VP Sales*
Rick Zaklan, *Accounts Mgr*
EMP: 55
SQ FT: 40,000
SALES (est): 34.6MM **Privately Held**
SIC: **5084** 7699 7359 Materials handling machinery; industrial equipment services; industrial machinery & equipment repair; equipment rental & leasing

(P-7535)
CDS MOVING EQUIPMENT INC (PA)
375 W Manville St, Rancho Dominguez
(90220-5617)
PHONE......................310 631-1100
Allen J Sidor, *President*
Margo Castillo, *Office Mgr*
Lou Morales, *Purchasing*
▲ EMP: 80
SQ FT: 100,000
SALES (est): 53.3MM **Privately Held**
WEB: www.cds-usa.com
SIC: **5084** Materials handling machinery

(P-7536)
CHALLENGER INDUSTRIES INC
Also Called: Challenger Ent
2971 E White Star Ave, Anaheim
(92806-2630)
PHONE......................714 630-4344
Gregory Joseph Martin, *President*
Ron Flicker, *Exec VP*
▲ EMP: 60
SQ FT: 4,000
SALES (est): 7.5MM **Privately Held**
WEB: www.challengerenterprises.com
SIC: **5084** Materials handling machinery

(P-7537)
CLARKLIFT-WEST INC
Also Called: Team Power Forklift
4750 Illinois Ave, Fair Oaks (95628-6313)
PHONE......................916 381-5674
Joe Hensler, *President*
Pete Thomas, *Vice Pres*
Dean Walker, *Vice Pres*
▲ EMP: 121
SQ FT: 50,000
SALES (est): 22.1MM **Privately Held**
WEB: www.teampowerforklift.com
SIC: **5084** 7699 7359 Lift trucks & parts; materials handling machinery; industrial truck repair; industrial machinery & equipment repair; industrial truck rental

(P-7538)
CLAUDE LAVAL CORPORATION
Also Called: Lakos
1365 N Clovis Ave, Fresno (93727-2295)
P.O. Box 6119 (93703-6119)
PHONE...................................559 255-1601
Scott Marion, *CEO*
Brian Ketcham, *CFO*
Kathy Colby, *Exec VP*
Eric Arneson, *Admin Sec*
Cindy Reiter, *Administration*
◆ EMP: 90
SQ FT: 100,000
SALES (est): 74.8MM
SALES (corp-wide): 4.4MM **Privately Held**
WEB: www.lakos.com
SIC: 5084 Industrial machinery & equipment
PA: Lakos Acquisition Holdco, Llc
1365 N Clovis Ave
Fresno CA 93727
559 255-1601

(P-7539)
CUMMINS PACIFIC LLC
14775 Wicks Blvd, San Leandro
(94577-6717)
PHONE...................................510 351-6101
EMP: 270
SALES (corp-wide): 23.7B **Publicly Held**
SIC: 5084 Engines & parts, diesel
HQ: Cummins Pacific, Llc
1939 Deere Ave
Irvine CA 92606

(P-7540)
CUSTOM BILT HOLDINGS LLC
15133 Sierra Bonita Ln, Chino
(91710-8904)
PHONE...................................909 664-1587
Neil Goldstein, *Manager*
Jorge Jimenez, *Opers Mgr*
EMP: 90
SALES (corp-wide): 40MM **Privately Held**
SIC: 5084 1761 Metalworking machinery; roofing contractor
PA: Custom Bilt Holdings, Llc
3001 Skyway Cir N Ste 160
Irving TX 75038
214 699-4876

(P-7541)
E & M ELECTRIC AND MCHY INC (PA)
Also Called: E&M
126 Mill St, Healdsburg (95448-4438)
PHONE...................................707 433-5578
Steven Edgar Deas, *CEO*
Steven Deas, *Vice Pres*
Dan Mossberg, *Office Admin*
Daniel Nicholas, *Engineer*
Ed Silver, *Sales Staff*
▲ EMP: 50 EST: 1972
SQ FT: 25,000
SALES (est): 78.4MM **Privately Held**
WEB: www.enm.com
SIC: 5084 5999 5063 7694 Instruments & control equipment; motors, electric; motors, electric; electric motor repair

(P-7542)
EAST BAY CLARKLIFT INC
4646 E Jensen Ave, Fresno (93725-1603)
P.O. Box 2808 (93745-2808)
PHONE...................................559 268-6621
Kerry Perez, *General Mgr*
EMP: 73
SALES (corp-wide): 44.3MM **Privately Held**
SIC: 5084 7359 7699 Materials handling machinery; equipment rental & leasing; industrial equipment services
PA: East Bay Clarklift, Inc.
4701 Oakport St
Oakland CA 94601
510 534-6566

(P-7543)
ELEVATOR EQUIPMENT CORPORATION (PA)
Also Called: Eeco
4035 Goodwin Ave, Los Angeles
(90039-1190)
P.O. Box 39714 (90039-0714)
PHONE...................................323 245-0147
Abe Salehpour, *CEO*
Abdul Mozayeni, *CFO*
◆ EMP: 75
SQ FT: 20,000
SALES (est): 37.3MM **Privately Held**
WEB: www.eecovalves.com
SIC: 5084 Elevators

(P-7544)
ELLISON MACHINERY CO (DH)
Also Called: Ellison Technologies
9912 Pioneer Blvd, Santa Fe Springs
(90670-3257)
PHONE...................................562 949-8311
W J Ellison, *President*
Donald Bendix, *Corp Secy*
Leonard C Atkins, *Vice Pres*
Klaus Rindt, *Vice Pres*
John Schwartz, *Vice Pres*
EMP: 75
SQ FT: 45,000
SALES (est): 69.1MM **Privately Held**
WEB: www.ellisontechnologies.com
SIC: 5084 Metalworking machinery
HQ: Ellison Technologies, Inc.
9912 Pioneer Blvd
Santa Fe Springs CA 90670
562 949-8311

(P-7545)
ELLISON TECHNOLOGIES INC
9912 Pioneer Blvd, Santa Fe Springs
(90670-3250)
PHONE...................................562 949-8311
EMP: 61 **Privately Held**
SIC: 5084 Metalworking machinery
HQ: Ellison Technologies, Inc.
9912 Pioneer Blvd
Santa Fe Springs CA 90670
562 949-8311

(P-7546)
FARM PUMP & IRRIGATION CO INC (PA)
Also Called: F P I
535 N Shafter Ave, Shafter (93263-1900)
P.O. Box 1477 (93263-1477)
PHONE...................................661 589-6901
John Gargan, *CEO*
Kathy Gargan, *Corp Secy*
EMP: 60
SQ FT: 4,000
SALES (est): 22.9MM **Privately Held**
WEB: www.fpi-co.com
SIC: 5084 5083 Pumps & pumping equipment; irrigation equipment

(P-7547)
FUELING AND SERVICE TECH INC
Also Called: Fastech
7050 Village Dr Ste D, Buena Park
(90621-2281)
PHONE...................................714 523-0194
M Dan McGill, *CEO*
Christine Hawley, *Vice Pres*
Glen Ragle, *Program Mgr*
Krol Lee, *Technician*
Jose Dethier, *Project Mgr*
EMP: 75
SQ FT: 15,000
SALES (est): 59.7MM **Privately Held**
SIC: 5084 Petroleum industry machinery

(P-7548)
GENMARK AUTOMATION (HQ)
46723 Lakeview Blvd, Fremont
(94538-6528)
PHONE...................................510 897-3400
Yuji Shioga, *CEO*
Danny Hinckley, *QC Mgr*
▼ EMP: 98
SQ FT: 86,000
SALES (est): 31.6MM **Privately Held**
WEB: www.genmarkautomation.com
SIC: 5084 3674 Industrial machinery & equipment; wafers (semiconductor devices)

(P-7549)
HARBOR DIESEL AND EQP INC
Also Called: Diesel Parts and Service
537 W Anaheim St, Long Beach
(90813-2895)
P.O. Box 21399 (90801-4399)
PHONE...................................562 591-5665
James V Zupanovich, *Ch of Bd*
Mike Zupanovich, *President*
David Hively, *CFO*
Thomas Weersing, *Vice Pres*
▲ EMP: 51 EST: 1971
SALES (est): 26.7MM **Privately Held**
WEB: www.harbordiesel.com
SIC: 5084 5531 7538 Engines & parts, diesel; truck equipment & parts; diesel engine repair: automotive

(P-7550)
INDUSTRIAL PARTS DEPOT LLC (HQ)
Also Called: Ipd
23231 Normandie Ave, Torrance
(90501-5096)
PHONE...................................310 530-1900
Russell Kneipp, *President*
Michelle Hoehn, *Vice Pres*
Richard Ward, *Vice Pres*
Mark Tu, *Information Mgr*
Dave Simpson, *Engineer*
◆ EMP: 70
SQ FT: 40,000
SALES (est): 40.1MM
SALES (corp-wide): 75.9MM **Privately Held**
WEB: www.ipdparts.com
SIC: 5084 3519 Engines & parts, diesel; parts & accessories, internal combustion engines
PA: Storm Industries, Inc.
23223 Normandie Ave
Torrance CA 90501
310 534-5232

(P-7551)
INOXPA USA INC
3721 Santa Rosa Ave B4, Santa Rosa
(95407-8240)
PHONE...................................707 585-3900
Candi Granes Campasol, *President*
▲ EMP: 300
SQ FT: 1,600
SALES (est): 29.8MM **Privately Held**
SIC: 5084 Pumps & pumping equipment

(P-7552)
INTERNATIONAL THERMOPRODUCTS
11015 Mission Park Ct, Santee
(92071-5601)
PHONE...................................619 562-7001
Randall Newcomb, *Owner*
EMP: 50
SALES (est): 3.7MM **Privately Held**
SIC: 5084 3567 Heat exchange equipment, industrial; electrical furnaces, ovens & heating devices, exc. induction

(P-7553)
JA AUTOMATION & CONTROL LLC
6965 Cmino Mqladora Ste H, San Diego
(92154)
PHONE...................................619 661-2591
Jose A Fernandez, *Mng Member*
EMP: 50
SALES (est): 6.4MM **Privately Held**
SIC: 5084 Industrial machinery & equipment

(P-7554)
KENTMASTER MFG CO INC (PA)
1801 S Mountain Ave, Monrovia
(91016-4270)
PHONE...................................626 359-8888
Ralph Karubian, *CEO*
▲ EMP: 50 EST: 1948
SQ FT: 50,000
SALES (est): 19.1MM **Privately Held**
WEB: www.kentmaster.com
SIC: 5084 Industrial machinery & equipment

(P-7555)
LABORATORY SPECIALTY GASES
Also Called: Westair Gas and Equipment
2506 Market St, San Diego (92102-3010)
PHONE...................................619 234-6060
Steve Castiglione, *President*
EMP: 110
SALES (est): 13.1MM **Privately Held**
SIC: 5084 Welding machinery & equipment

(P-7556)
LINDSAY TRANSPORTATION
Also Called: Lindsay Trnsp Solutions
180 River Rd, Rio Vista (94571-1208)
PHONE...................................707 374-6800
Bill Cooley, *President*
Kristel Flores,
EMP: 250
SALES (est): 30.1MM
SALES (corp-wide): 444MM **Publicly Held**
SIC: 5084 Safety equipment
HQ: Lindsay Transportation Solutions, Inc.
180 River Rd
Rio Vista CA 94571
707 374-6800

(P-7557)
LMC WEST INC
5300 Claus Rd, Riverbank (95367)
P.O. Box 325 (95367-0325)
PHONE...................................209 869-0144
Fax: 209 869-0258
EMP: 50
SQ FT: 50,000
SALES (est): 10.3MM
SALES (corp-wide): 2.3B **Publicly Held**
SIC: 5084
PA: Donaldson Company, Inc.
1400 W 94th St
Minneapolis MN 55431
952 887-3131

(P-7558)
LORING SMART ROAST INC
3200 Dutton Ave Ste 413, Santa Rosa
(95407-5736)
PHONE...................................707 526-7215
Mark Ludwig, *Founder*
Scott Robinson, *Mfg Dir*
Dennis Vogel, *Marketing Staff*
EMP: 54
SQ FT: 19,000
SALES (est): 12MM **Privately Held**
SIC: 5084 Food industry machinery

(P-7559)
MACHINING TIME SAVERS INC
Also Called: Haas Factory Outlet
1338 S State College Pkwy, Anaheim
(92806-5241)
PHONE...................................714 635-7373
Donald Martin, *President*
EMP: 53
SQ FT: 10,000
SALES (est): 22.5MM **Privately Held**
WEB: www.mtscnc.com
SIC: 5084 7699 Machine tools & accessories; metalworking machinery; industrial machinery & equipment repair

(P-7560)
MASON-WEST INC
3910 Chapman St Ste D, San Diego
(92110-5644)
PHONE...................................619 226-8253
Joe Hastings, *Manager*
EMP: 50
SALES (corp-wide): 17.5MM **Privately Held**
SIC: 5084 Controlling instruments & accessories
PA: Mason-West, Inc.
1601 E Miraloma Ave
Placentia CA 92870
714 630-0701

(P-7561)
MATERIAL HANDLING SUPPLY INC (HQ)
12900 Firestone Blvd, Santa Fe Springs (90670-5405)
PHONE.....................562 921-7715
Alexander Stephen Lynn, *CEO*
Donn C Lynn Jr, *Ch of Bd*
John Hanson, *Corp Secy*
Brian Challoner, *Marketing Staff*
Steve Birdsall, *Director*
EMP: 80 **EST:** 1962
SQ FT: 85,000
SALES (est): 33.8MM
SALES (corp-wide): 8.2MM **Privately Held**
SIC: 5084 7629 5046 Food industry machinery; engines & transportation equipment; materials handling machinery; electrical repair shops; commercial equipment
PA: Envicor
12900 Firestone Blvd
Santa Fe Springs CA 90670
562 921-7715

(P-7562)
MAXON LIFT CORPORATION
11921 Slauson Ave, Santa Fe Springs (90670-2221)
PHONE.....................562 464-0099
Casey Lugash, *President*
Larry Lugash, *Exec VP*
Brian Hufnagl, *Vice Pres*
Raymundo Sidon, *Vice Pres*
Lawrence Jones, *Administration*
▲ **EMP:** 110
SQ FT: 30,000
SALES (est): 179.7MM **Privately Held**
WEB: www.maxonlift.com
SIC: 5084 3537 3534 Lift trucks & parts; industrial trucks & tractors; elevators & moving stairways

(P-7563)
MCCAIN INC (DH)
2365 Oak Ridge Way, Vista (92081-8348)
PHONE.....................760 727-8100
Michael Schuch, *CEO*
Carl McCollum, *CFO*
▲ **EMP:** 250
SQ FT: 6,700
SALES (est): 157.6MM
SALES (corp-wide): 177.9K **Privately Held**
WEB: www.mccaintraffic.com
SIC: 5084 3444 3669 Industrial machinery & equipment; sheet metalwork; traffic signals, electric
HQ: Swarco Ag
Blattenwaldweg 8
Wattens 6112
522 458-770

(P-7564)
MCGRATH RENTCORP
Also Called: Mobile Modular
5700 Las Positas Rd, Livermore (94551-7806)
PHONE.....................877 221-2813
M Richard Smith, *Bd of Directors*
Ronald Zech, *Bd of Directors*
Philip Hawkins, *Vice Pres*
Kristina Vantrease, *Vice Pres*
Chris Snyder, *Surgery Dir*
EMP: 102
SALES (corp-wide): 498.3MM **Publicly Held**
SIC: 5084 7359 Measuring & testing equipment, electrical; electronic equipment rental, except computers
PA: Mcgrath Rentcorp
5700 Las Positas Rd
Livermore CA 94551
925 606-9200

(P-7565)
MCGRATH RENTCORP (PA)
5700 Las Positas Rd, Livermore (94551-7806)
PHONE.....................925 606-9200
Joseph F Hanna, *President*
Keith E Pratt, *CFO*
John P Skenesky, *Treasurer*
Philip B Hawkins, *Vice Pres*
John P Lieffrig, *Vice Pres*

EMP: 153 **EST:** 1979
SQ FT: 26,000
SALES: 498.3MM **Publicly Held**
SIC: 5084 7359 Measuring & testing equipment, electrical; electronic equipment rental, except computers

(P-7566)
MCKINLEY EQUIPMENT CORPORATION (PA)
17611 Armstrong Ave, Irvine (92614-5760)
PHONE.....................800 770-6094
W Michael Mc Kinley, *President*
Kevin Rusin, *CFO*
William White Mc Kinley, *Vice Pres*
Thomas Beardshear, *Info Tech Mgr*
Morgan Andrade, *Technician*
▲ **EMP:** 67 **EST:** 1948
SQ FT: 12,000
SALES (est): 56MM **Privately Held**
WEB: www.mckinleyequipment.com
SIC: 5084 Materials handling machinery

(P-7567)
MIGHTY ENTERPRISES INC
Also Called: Mighty USA
19706 Normandie Ave, Torrance (90502-1111)
PHONE.....................310 516-7478
Peter Th Tsai, *President*
Daniel Huang, *Vice Pres*
Gloria Zuniga, *Admin Sec*
Ron Dumas, *Engineer*
Kelly Lee, *Accountant*
▲ **EMP:** 55
SQ FT: 18,000
SALES (est): 26.1MM **Privately Held**
SIC: 5084 Machine tools & accessories

(P-7568)
NAGRA USA INC (HQ)
841 Apollo St Ste 300, El Segundo (90245-4769)
PHONE.....................310 335-5225
Virginio Trevisan, *President*
Ray Ruemmele, *Partner*
EMP: 85
SQ FT: 1,100
SALES (est): 57.8MM
SALES (corp-wide): 919.6MM **Privately Held**
WEB: www.nagra.com
SIC: 5084 Safety equipment
PA: Kudelski S.A.
Route De Geneve 22-24
Cheseaux-Sur-Lausanne VD 1033
217 320-101

(P-7569)
NAN FANG DIST GROUP INC
2100 Williams St, San Leandro (94577-3225)
PHONE.....................510 297-5382
Ze Pan, *CEO*
Zhen Poon, *Vice Pres*
▲ **EMP:** 100
SALES (est): 32.3MM **Privately Held**
SIC: 5084 Engines & parts, diesel

(P-7570)
NAUMANN/HOBBS MATERIAL
Also Called: Hawthorne Lift Systems
8575 Cherry Ave, Fontana (92335-3029)
PHONE.....................909 427-0125
Ed Gen, *Manager*
EMP: 105
SALES (corp-wide): 90MM **Privately Held**
SIC: 5084 Materials handling machinery
PA: Naumann/Hobbs Material Handling Corporation Ii, Inc.
4335 E Wood St
Phoenix AZ 85040
602 437-1331

(P-7571)
NAUMANN/HOBBS MATERIAL
Also Called: Hawthorne Lift Systems
1600 E Mission Rd, San Marcos (92069-4564)
PHONE.....................858 207-6274
Jim Ventors, *Branch Mgr*
Jim Venters, *Branch Mgr*
Dan Kennedy, *Technician*
Richard Torres, *Technician*
Gary Stark, *Mfg Mgr*

EMP: 105
SALES (corp-wide): 90MM **Privately Held**
SIC: 5084 Materials handling machinery
PA: Naumann/Hobbs Material Handling Corporation Ii, Inc.
4335 E Wood St
Phoenix AZ 85040
602 437-1331

(P-7572)
NIKON PRECISION INC (DH)
1399 Shoreway Rd, Belmont (94002-4107)
PHONE.....................650 508-4674
Toyohiro Takamine, *CEO*
Takao Naito, *President*
Mayumi Takahashi, *Analyst*
Russell Black, *Site Mgr*
Michelle Brogan, *Production*
▲ **EMP:** 250
SQ FT: 30,000
SALES (est): 179.1MM **Privately Held**
WEB: www.nikonprecision.com
SIC: 5084 5065 Industrial machinery & equipment; electronic parts & equipment

(P-7573)
OTIS ELEVATOR COMPANY
2701 Media Center Dr # 2, Los Angeles (90065-1700)
PHONE.....................323 342-4500
Marcus Burten, *Manager*
Cynthia Armijos, *Human Resources*
EMP: 50
SALES (corp-wide): 66.5B **Publicly Held**
WEB: www.otis.com
SIC: 5084 Elevators
HQ: Otis Elevator Company
1 Carrier Pl
Farmington CT 06032
860 674-3000

(P-7574)
PAPE MATERIAL HANDLING INC
47132 Kato Rd, Fremont (94538-7333)
PHONE.....................510 659-4100
Ken Mader, *Branch Mgr*
Chris Wetle, *President*
Jordan Pape, *CEO*
EMP: 80
SQ FT: 37,536
SALES (corp-wide): 640.9MM **Privately Held**
SIC: 5084 8743 7359 5082 Materials handling machinery; sales promotion; stores & yards equipment rental; contractors' materials
HQ: Pape' Material Handling, Inc.
355 Goodpasture Island Rd
Eugene OR 97401
541 683-5073

(P-7575)
POWELL WORKS INC
17807 Maclaren St Ste B, La Puente (91744-5700)
PHONE.....................909 861-6699
Jerry Wang, *President*
▲ **EMP:** 256
SQ FT: 2,500
SALES (est): 18.8MM **Privately Held**
SIC: 5084 Compressors, except air conditioning

(P-7576)
POWER GENERATION ENTPS INC
11411 Cumpston St Ste 104, North Hollywood (91601-2674)
PHONE.....................818 484-8550
Vartan Seropian, *CEO*
Victor Seropian, *Sales Staff*
EMP: 110
SALES (est): 23.2MM **Privately Held**
SIC: 5084 Industrial machinery & equipment

(P-7577)
PRAXAIR INC
2677 Signal Pkwy, Long Beach (90755-2260)
PHONE.....................562 427-0099
Mike Alives, *Manager*
EMP: 60 **Privately Held**
SIC: 5084 Welding machinery & equipment

HQ: Praxair, Inc.
10 Riverview Dr
Danbury CT 06810
203 837-2000

(P-7578)
PROGAUGE TECHNOLOGIES INC
2331 Cepheus Ct, Bakersfield (93308-6944)
P.O. Box 1312 (93302-1312)
PHONE.....................661 392-9600
Donald C Nelson, *CEO*
Danny B Henderson, *Admin Sec*
EMP: 50
SQ FT: 9,000
SALES (est): 16MM **Privately Held**
SIC: 5084 Industrial machinery & equipment

(P-7579)
PROPROCESS CORPORATION
Also Called: Doughpro
20281 Harvill Ave, Perris (92570-7235)
P.O. Box 869, Paramount (90723-0869)
PHONE.....................800 624-6717
Eugene Raio, *President*
Dan Raio, *Vice Pres*
EMP: 70
SQ FT: 7,000
SALES (est): 10.2MM **Privately Held**
WEB: www.doughpro.com
SIC: 5084 Food product manufacturing machinery

(P-7580)
PROVOAST AUTOMATION CONTROLS (PA)
12635 Danielson Ct # 205, Poway (92064-8806)
PHONE.....................858 748-2237
Mitch Provoast, *President*
Kathy Provoast, *Treasurer*
Ron Mayhew, *Vice Pres*
EMP: 100
SQ FT: 5,000
SALES (est): 33MM **Privately Held**
WEB: www.proautocon.com
SIC: 5084 5085 Industrial machinery & equipment; valves & fittings

(P-7581)
QUINN LIFT INC
Also Called: Caterpillar Authorized Dealer
1300 Abbott St, Salinas (93901-4507)
P.O. Box 1908 (93902-1908)
PHONE.....................831 758-4086
Mike Gularte, *Manager*
EMP: 68
SALES (corp-wide): 455MM **Privately Held**
WEB: www.altalift.net
SIC: 5084 Lift trucks & parts
HQ: Quinn Lift, Inc.
10273 S Golden State Blvd
Selma CA 93662

(P-7582)
R B INTERNATIONAL INC (PA)
Also Called: Rbi Bearings
109 N Ivy Ave Ste D, Monrovia (91016-2295)
PHONE.....................626 357-7652
Rubien Hao Chen, *CEO*
Mike Kenney, *Vice Pres*
Darren Meeks, *Manager*
◆ **EMP:** 50
SALES (est): 12.1MM **Privately Held**
SIC: 5084 5085 Industrial machine parts; bearings

(P-7583)
R F MACDONALD CO (PA)
25920 Eden Landing Rd, Hayward (94545-3816)
PHONE.....................510 784-0110
Michael D Macdonald, *Co-President*
James T Macdonald, *President*
Chris Sentner, *Vice Pres*
Robert Sygiel, *Vice Pres*
Jim Swan, *Executive*
EMP: 153
SQ FT: 25,000

▲ = Import ▼=Export
◆ =Import/Export

SALES (est): 97.1MM **Privately Held**
SIC: **5084** 7699 5074 Pumps & pumping equipment; industrial machinery & equipment repair; boilers, power (industrial)

(P-7584)
RAYMOND HANDLING SOLUTIONS INC (DH)
9939 Norwalk Blvd, Santa Fe Springs (90670-3321)
P.O. Box 3683 (90670-1683)
PHONE......................................562 944-8067
James Wilcox, *CEO*
Joseph Bustamante, *Partner*
Adrian Castelan, *District Mgr*
Mike Slater, *District Mgr*
Edwin Funes, *Admin Asst*
EMP: 111
SQ FT: 5,000
SALES (est): 124.5MM **Privately Held**
WEB: www.raymondhandlingsolutions.com
SIC: **5084** 7699 7359 Materials handling machinery; industrial machinery & equipment repair; industrial truck rental
HQ: The Raymond Corporation
22 S Canal St
Greene NY 13778
607 656-2311

(P-7585)
RAYMOND HANDLING SOLUTIONS INC
4602 E Brickell St, Ontario (91761-1573)
PHONE......................................909 930-9399
James Wilcox, *President*
EMP: 83 **Privately Held**
SIC: **5084** Materials handling machinery
HQ: Raymond Handling Solutions, Inc.
9939 Norwalk Blvd
Santa Fe Springs CA 90670
562 944-8067

(P-7586)
REBAS INC
Also Called: Toyota-Lift of Los Angeles
12907 Imperial Hwy, Santa Fe Springs (90670-4715)
PHONE......................................562 941-4155
Shankar Basu, *Ch of Bd*
Simon Walker, *COO*
Mark Clark, *Vice Pres*
Ahmed Mukhtar, *IT/INT Sup*
Bo Hansson Holmquist, *Technology*
▲ EMP: 104
SQ FT: 103,000
SALES (est): 129.2MM **Privately Held**
WEB: www.toyota-lift.com
SIC: **5084** Industrial machinery & equipment

(P-7587)
RKI INSTRUMENTS INC (PA)
Also Called: R K I
33248 Central Ave, Union City (94587-2010)
PHONE......................................510 441-5656
Robert Pellissier, *President*
Syed Hashim, *Partner*
Sandra Gallagher, *Vice Pres*
Marco Negrete, *Technical Mgr*
Steve Peluffo, *Technical Mgr*
▲ EMP: 55
SQ FT: 10,000
SALES (est): 28.9MM **Privately Held**
WEB: www.rkiinstruments.com
SIC: **5084** Industrial machinery & equipment; on-stream gas/liquid analysis instruments, industrial

(P-7588)
SIEMENS INDUSTRY INC
25821 Industrial Blvd # 300, Hayward (94545-2919)
PHONE......................................510 783-6000
John P Nichols, *Manager*
EMP: 150
SALES (corp-wide): 95B **Privately Held**
WEB: www.sibt.com
SIC: **5084** Instruments & control equipment
HQ: Siemens Industry, Inc.
1000 Deerfield Pkwy
Buffalo Grove IL 60089
847 215-1000

(P-7589)
SIEMENS INDUSTRY INC
9835 Carroll Ctre Rd 10, San Diego (92126)
PHONE......................................858 693-8711
Majd Khleis, *Manager*
EMP: 75
SQ FT: 3,300
SALES (corp-wide): 95B **Privately Held**
WEB: www.sibt.com
SIC: **5084** 1711 3822 3825 Pneumatic tools & equipment; mechanical contractor; auto controls regulating residntl & coml environmt & applncs; instruments to measure electricity; industrial instrmnts msrmnt display/control process variable
HQ: Siemens Industry, Inc.
1000 Deerfield Pkwy
Buffalo Grove IL 60089
847 215-1000

(P-7590)
SMC CORPORATION OF AMERICA
2841 Junction Ave Ste 110, San Jose (95134-1921)
PHONE......................................408 943-9600
Joe Hanna, *Manager*
EMP: 50 **Privately Held**
WEB: www.smcusa.com
SIC: **5084** Pneumatic tools & equipment
HQ: Smc Corporation Of America
10100 Smc Blvd
Noblesville IN 46060
317 899-4440

(P-7591)
SOUTHERN CALIFORNIA MTL HDLG
Also Called: Southern Calif Mtl Hdlg Co
19755 Bahama St, Northridge (91324-3304)
PHONE......................................805 650-6000
Toni Edgar, *Manager*
EMP: 65 **Privately Held**
WEB: www.scmh.com
SIC: **5084** Materials handling machinery
HQ: Southern California Material Handling Inc
12393 Slauson Ave
Whittier CA 90606
562 949-1006

(P-7592)
SOUTHERN CALIFORNIA MTL HDLG
8124 Deering Ave, Canoga Park (91304-5013)
PHONE......................................818 349-1220
S Handling, *Branch Mgr*
EMP: 61 **Privately Held**
SIC: **5084** Conveyor systems
HQ: Southern California Material Handling Inc
12393 Slauson Ave
Whittier CA 90606
562 949-1006

(P-7593)
SOUTHERN CALIFORNIA MTL HDLG (DH)
Also Called: Scmh
12393 Slauson Ave, Whittier (90606-2824)
P.O. Box 80770, San Marino (91118-8770)
PHONE......................................562 949-1006
Tim Cleary, *President*
Mike Wolfe, *COO*
Ellen Laurente, *Administration*
Angela Fuller, *Office Spvr*
Cindy Bautista, *Controller*
▲ EMP: 140
SALES (est): 47.9MM **Privately Held**
WEB: www.scmh.com
SIC: **5084** Conveyor systems; materials handling machinery

(P-7594)
SPECIALIZED ELEVATOR SVCS LLC
14320 Iseli Rd, Santa Fe Springs (90670-5204)
PHONE......................................562 407-1200
Don Webster, *President*
Jeff Feltch, *CFO*
Barry Meacham, *Treasurer*

Robert Baehr, *Admin Sec*
Amanda Rubio, *Administration*
EMP: 100
SQ FT: 6,000
SALES: 11.7MM **Privately Held**
WEB: www.specializedelevator.com
SIC: **5084** Elevators

(P-7595)
SSTMAS Y ARANDA EQPOS HDRLICOS
280 Campillo St Ste L, Calexico (92231-3200)
PHONE......................................619 245-4502
Armando Aranda, *President*
Carlos Verdugo, *Principal*
Roberto Pena, *Director*
EMP: 50
SALES: 15MM **Privately Held**
SIC: **5084** Hydraulic systems equipment & supplies
PA: Aranda Sistemas Y Equipos Hidraulicos, S. De R.L. De C.V.
Blvd. Lazaro Cardenas No. 1159
Mexicali B.C. 21190

(P-7596)
STAINLESS STL FABRICATORS INC
Also Called: Cook King
15120 Desman Rd, La Mirada (90638-5737)
PHONE......................................714 739-9904
Craig Miller, *President*
Glenna Miller, *CFO*
Dave Hart, *Vice Pres*
EMP: 60
SQ FT: 11,204
SALES (est): 23.4MM **Privately Held**
SIC: **5084** 3444 Industrial machinery & equipment; restaurant sheet metalwork

(P-7597)
SURFACE PUMPS INC (PA)
3301 Unicorn Rd, Bakersfield (93308-6852)
P.O. Box 5757 (93388-5757)
PHONE......................................661 393-1545
Steven J Durrett, *President*
Marty Rushing, *Corp Secy*
David Cook, *Vice Pres*
Carly Collins, *Human Resources*
Larry Conner, *Sales Staff*
EMP: 51 EST: 1970
SQ FT: 14,000
SALES (est): 57MM **Privately Held**
SIC: **5084** 7699 8711 3519 Pumps & pumping equipment; pumps & pumping equipment repair; engineering services; parts & accessories; internal combustion engines

(P-7598)
THYSSENKRUPP ELEVATOR CORP
14400 Catalina St, San Leandro (94577-5516)
PHONE......................................510 476-1900
Ed Persico, *Manager*
Robert Dotson, *General Mgr*
Mike Dugan, *Senior Engr*
EMP: 100
SALES (corp-wide): 39.8B **Privately Held**
WEB: www.thyssenkruppelevator.com
SIC: **5084** 1796 3534 Elevators; elevator installation & conversion; elevators & moving stairways
HQ: Thyssenkrupp Elevator Corporation
11605 Haynes Bridge Rd # 650
Alpharetta GA 30009
678 319-3240

(P-7599)
THYSSENKRUPP ELEVATOR CORP
1965 Gillespie Way # 101, El Cajon (92020-0500)
PHONE......................................619 596-7220
Jeff Hansen, *Manager*
Alisa Bradford, *Admin Sec*
EMP: 100
SALES (corp-wide): 39.8B **Privately Held**
WEB: www.tyssenkrupp.com
SIC: **5084** Elevators

HQ: Thyssenkrupp Elevator Corporation
11605 Haynes Bridge Rd # 650
Alpharetta GA 30009
678 319-3240

(P-7600)
THYSSENKRUPP ELEVATOR CORP
2850 N California St, Burbank (91504-2560)
PHONE......................................818 847-2568
Christina Siebold, *Manager*
EMP: 58
SALES (corp-wide): 39.8B **Privately Held**
WEB: www.tyssenkrupp.com
SIC: **5084** Elevators
HQ: Thyssenkrupp Elevator Corporation
11605 Haynes Bridge Rd # 650
Alpharetta GA 30009
678 319-3240

(P-7601)
TOYOTALIFT INC (PA)
1850 John Towers Ave, El Cajon (92020-1134)
P.O. Box 710280, Santee (92072-0280)
PHONE......................................619 562-5438
Garland Pierce, *CEO*
Alice Pierce, *Admin Sec*
Norma Caro, *Human Resources*
▲ EMP: 50 EST: 1976
SALES (est): 38.8MM **Privately Held**
WEB: www.toyotaliftinc.com
SIC: **5084** 7359 Materials handling machinery; equipment rental & leasing

(P-7602)
TRI TOOL INC (PA)
3041 Sunrise Blvd, Rancho Cordova (95742-6502)
PHONE......................................916 288-6100
George J Wernette III, *CEO*
George J Wernette, *President*
Chris Soriano, *CFO*
Minh Transon, *Vice Pres*
Ken Boden, *Regional Mgr*
▲ EMP: 163 EST: 1972
SQ FT: 125,000
SALES (est): 99.2MM **Privately Held**
WEB: www.tritool.com
SIC: **5084** 3548 3541 Industrial machinery & equipment; welding apparatus; pipe cutting & threading machines

(P-7603)
UNITED MATERIAL HANDLING INC
23900 Brodiaea Ave, Moreno Valley (92553-8841)
PHONE......................................951 657-4900
Ryan Bartlett, *President*
Brook Bartlett, *Vice Pres*
Mike Goritz, *Accounts Mgr*
▲ EMP: 61
SALES (est): 24.7MM **Privately Held**
SIC: **5084** Materials handling machinery

(P-7604)
UTILITY TRLR SLS OF CENTL CAL
2680 S East Ave, Fresno (93706-5400)
P.O. Box 11845 (93775-1845)
PHONE......................................559 237-2001
Michael Sutherland, *Manager*
EMP: 50
SALES (corp-wide): 35.5MM **Privately Held**
WEB: www.utilitycc.com
SIC: **5084** Trailers, industrial
PA: Utility Trailer Sales Of Central California, Inc
2680 S East Ave
Lathrop CA 95330
209 444-8800

(P-7605)
VALIN CORPORATION (PA)
5225 Hellyer Ave Ste 220, San Jose (95138-1021)
PHONE......................................408 730-9850
Joseph C Nettemeyer, *CEO*
John Pregenzer, *CFO*
David Hefler, *CFO*
Eric Nealon, *Project Mgr*
Bill Kropp, *Technical Staff*

PRODUCTS & SVCS

◆ **EMP:** 96
SALES (est): 5.7MM **Privately Held**
WEB: www.valinonline.com
SIC: 5084 Materials handling machinery;
processing & packaging equipment

(P-7606)
VALLEY POWER SYSTEMS INC
Also Called: Valley Detroit Diesel
4000 Rosedale Hwy, Bakersfield
(93308-6131)
PHONE.....................661 325-9001
Ken Relyea, *Branch Mgr*
EMP: 50
SALES (corp-wide): 181.2MM **Privately Held**
WEB: www.valleypowersystems.com
SIC: 5084 Engines & parts, diesel
PA: Valley Power Systems, Inc.
425 S Hacienda Blvd
City Of Industry CA 91745
626 333-1243

(P-7607)
VERITIV OPERATING COMPANY
Also Called: International Paper
7337 Las Positas Rd, Livermore
(94551-5110)
PHONE.....................925 245-6075
Elizabeth Richman, *Executive*
EMP: 151
SALES (corp-wide): 8.7B **Publicly Held**
SIC: 5084 Processing & packaging equipment; printing trades machinery, equipment & supplies
HQ: Veritiv Operating Company
1000 Abernathy Rd Bldg 4
Atlanta GA 30328
770 391-8200

(P-7608)
WASSER FILTRATION INC
Also Called: Force Measurement Systems
1215 N Fee Ana St, Anaheim (92807-1804)
PHONE.....................714 525-0630
Greg Stewart, *Vice Pres*
EMP: 70
SALES (corp-wide): 18.4MM **Privately Held**
WEB: www.pacpress.com
SIC: 5084 Industrial machinery & equipment
PA: Wasser Filtration, Inc.
1215 N Fee Ana St
Anaheim CA 92807
714 982-5600

(P-7609)
WESTAIR GASES & EQUIPMENT INC
2300 Haffley Ave, National City
(91950-6419)
PHONE.....................619 474-0079
Pat Dalton, *Branch Mgr*
Daisy Pait, *Associate*
EMP: 60
SALES (corp-wide): 70.4MM **Privately Held**
WEB: www.westairgases.com
SIC: 5084 Welding machinery & equipment
PA: Westair Gases & Equipment, Inc.
2506 Market St
San Diego CA 92102
866 937-8247

(P-7610)
WESTAIR GASES & EQUIPMENT INC (PA)
Also Called: San Diego Welders Supply
2506 Market St, San Diego (92102-3010)
P.O. Box 131902 (92170-1902)
PHONE.....................866 937-8247
Andrew J Castiglione, *CEO*
Steve Castiglione, *President*
Tim Van Linge, *CFO*
Sue Castiglione, *Corp Secy*
Austin Zoutis, *Vice Pres*
EMP: 50
SQ FT: 10,000
SALES (est): 70.4MM **Privately Held**
WEB: www.westairgases.com
SIC: 5084 Welding machinery & equipment

(P-7611)
YALE/CHASE EQP & SVCS INC (PA)
2615 Pellissier Pl, City of Industry
(90601-1508)
P.O. Box 1231, La Puente (91749-1231)
PHONE.....................562 463-8000
Roger Ketelsleger, *President*
Duc Nguyen, *Administration*
John Rosser, *MIS Dir*
Jana Jamson, *Info Tech Dir*
Mike Barraza, *Technician*
◆ **EMP:** 116
SQ FT: 33,000
SALES (est): 94.9MM **Privately Held**
WEB: www.yalechase.com
SIC: 5084 7699 7359 Lift trucks & parts;
industrial machinery & equipment repair;
industrial truck rental

(P-7612)
ZEMARC CORPORATION (PA)
6431 Flotilla St, Commerce (90040-1597)
PHONE.....................323 721-5598
Viren Patel, *CEO*
Dave Manzi, *President*
Abdul Zeke Zahid, *Founder*
Irma K Zahid, *Vice Pres*
Irma Zahid, *Vice Pres*
EMP: 50
SQ FT: 50,000
SALES (est): 30.7MM **Privately Held**
SIC: 5084 Hydraulic systems equipment & supplies; pneumatic tools & equipment

---

5085 Industrial Splys Wholesale

(P-7613)
ACHEM INDUSTRY AMERICA INC (PA)
4250 N Harbor Blvd, Fullerton
(92835-1017)
PHONE.....................562 802-0998
Joseph Lin, *CEO*
Shin Pai Kuei, *President*
Alex Chen, *General Mgr*
Benedict Chen, *Controller*
Bob Kuminski, *Natl Sales Mgr*
◆ **EMP:** 65
SALES (est): 34.6MM **Privately Held**
WEB: www.achem.com
SIC: 5085 Industrial supplies

(P-7614)
ADCO CONTAINER COMPANY
9959 Canoga Ave, Chatsworth
(91311-3090)
PHONE.....................818 998-2565
Fax: 818 998-3648
EMP: 50
SQ FT: 24,000
SALES (est): 12.2MM **Privately Held**
WEB: www.adcocontainer.com
SIC: 5085 7336

(P-7615)
ALLIED HIGH TECH PRODUCTS INC
2376 E Pacifica Pl, Rancho Dominguez
(90220-6214)
P.O. Box 4608, Compton (90224-4608)
PHONE.....................310 635-2466
Robert C Smith, *Ch of Bd*
Shirley A Smith, *Corp Secy*
Eddie Padilla, *General Mgr*
Shirley Smith, *CTO*
Betsy O'Connell, *Technology*
▲ **EMP:** 70
SQ FT: 34,000
SALES (est): 71.2MM **Privately Held**
WEB: www.alliedhightech.com
SIC: 5085 Abrasives

(P-7616)
ARC FASTENER SUPPLY & MFG
Also Called: A R C Fastener Supply
2104 Wembley Ln, Corona (92881-7441)
PHONE.....................909 481-8171
Joseph Myers, *President*
▲ **EMP:** 78
SQ FT: 70,000

SALES (est): 13.4MM **Privately Held**
WEB: www.arcfasteners.com
SIC: 5085 5072 Fasteners, industrial:
nuts, bolts, screws, etc.; hardware

(P-7617)
ARCONIC GLOBAL FAS & RINGS INC
Also Called: Arconic Fstening Systems Rings
135 N Unruh Ave, City of Industry
(91744-4427)
PHONE.....................626 968-3831
Hatty Ao, *Director*
Kelly Liao, *Engineer*
George Cameron, *Manager*
Steve Martin, *Manager*
Sandra Perez, *Manager*
EMP: 350
SQ FT: 58,400
SALES (corp-wide): 14B **Publicly Held**
WEB: www.alcoafasteners.com
SIC: 5085 Fasteners & fastening equipment
HQ: Arconic Global Fasteners & Rings, Inc.
3990a Heritage Oak Ct
Simi Valley CA 93063
805 527-3600

(P-7618)
ARCONIC GLOBAL FAS & RINGS INC
Also Called: Arconic Fstening Systems Rings
3000 Lomita Blvd, Torrance (90505-5103)
PHONE.....................310 784-0700
Kenneth Paine, *Manager*
Eleanor Wang, *Controller*
David Lawton, *Maintence Staff*
Scott Ryan, *Manager*
EMP: 60
SALES (corp-wide): 14B **Publicly Held**
WEB: www.alcoafasteners.com
SIC: 5085 Fasteners & fastening equipment
HQ: Arconic Global Fasteners & Rings, Inc.
3990a Heritage Oak Ct
Simi Valley CA 93063
805 527-3600

(P-7619)
ARCONIC GLOBAL FAS & RINGS INC
Also Called: Arconic Fastening Systems
3014 Lomita Blvd, Torrance (90505-5103)
PHONE.....................310 530-2220
Oliver Jarraolt, *President*
EMP: 500
SALES (corp-wide): 14B **Publicly Held**
WEB: www.alcoafasteners.com
SIC: 5085 Industrial supplies
HQ: Arconic Global Fasteners & Rings, Inc.
3990a Heritage Oak Ct
Simi Valley CA 93063
805 527-3600

(P-7620)
ARCONIC GLOBAL FAS & RINGS INC (HQ)
Also Called: Arconic Fastening Systems
3990a Heritage Oak Ct, Simi Valley
(93063-6715)
PHONE.....................805 527-3600
Olivier Jarrault, *President*
Karen Harlan, *Human Res Mgr*
Lisa Robertson, *Director*
▲ **EMP:** 120
SQ FT: 37,000
SALES (est): 1.8B
SALES (corp-wide): 14B **Publicly Held**
WEB: www.alcoafasteners.com
SIC: 5085 5072 5065 Fasteners & fastening equipment; hardware; electronic parts & equipment
PA: Arconic Inc.
201 Isabella St Ste 200
Pittsburgh PA 15212
412 553-1950

(P-7621)
ARCONIC GLOBAL FAS & RINGS INC
Also Called: Arconic Fastening Systems
800 S State College Blvd, Fullerton
(92831-5334)
PHONE.....................714 871-1550
Craig Brown, *Manager*

Joe Crumpler, *Info Tech Mgr*
Virginia Camarillo, *Engineer*
Michael Caton, *Engineer*
Frank Inman, *Engineer*
EMP: 100
SQ FT: 153,604
SALES (corp-wide): 14B **Publicly Held**
WEB: www.alcoafasteners.com
SIC: 5085 Fasteners & fastening equipment
HQ: Arconic Global Fasteners & Rings, Inc.
3990a Heritage Oak Ct
Simi Valley CA 93063
805 527-3600

(P-7622)
ARCONIC GLOBAL FAS & RINGS INC
Also Called: Arconic Fastening Systems
3000 Lomita Blvd, Torrance (90505-5103)
PHONE.....................310 530-2220
William Hart, *Director*
EMP: 50
SALES (corp-wide): 14B **Publicly Held**
SIC: 5085 Industrial supplies
HQ: Arconic Global Fasteners & Rings, Inc.
3990a Heritage Oak Ct
Simi Valley CA 93063
805 527-3600

(P-7623)
ARCONIC GLOBAL FAS & RINGS INC
Also Called: Arconic Fastening Systems
3018 Lomita Blvd, Torrance (90505-5103)
PHONE.....................310 530-2220
Melanie Brooks, *Branch Mgr*
EMP: 1000
SALES (corp-wide): 14B **Publicly Held**
WEB: www.alcoafasteners.com
SIC: 5085 Fasteners & fastening equipment
HQ: Arconic Global Fasteners & Rings, Inc.
3990a Heritage Oak Ct
Simi Valley CA 93063
805 527-3600

(P-7624)
ARIES FILTERWORKS
13850 Van Ness Ave, Gardena
(90249-2476)
PHONE.....................323 262-1600
Jeffrey Gottlieb, *President*
▲ **EMP:** 50
SQ FT: 20,000
SALES (est): 4MM **Privately Held**
SIC: 5085 Filters, industrial

(P-7625)
BAY STANDARD INC
24485 Marsh Creek Rd, Brentwood
(94513-4319)
P.O. Box 801 (94513-0801)
PHONE.....................925 634-1181
Gary W Landgraf, *President*
Karen Landgraf, *Treasurer*
Tom Landgraf, *Vice Pres*
▲ **EMP:** 100
SALES: 13MM **Privately Held**
SIC: 5085 3965 Fasteners & fastening equipment; fasteners

(P-7626)
BEACON ROOFING SUPPLY INC
8501 Telfair Ave, Sun Valley (91352-3928)
PHONE.....................818 768-4661
EMP: 60
SALES (corp-wide): 6.4B **Publicly Held**
SIC: 5085 5169 Industrial supplies;
sealants
PA: Beacon Roofing Supply, Inc.
505 Huntmar Park Dr # 300
Herndon VA 20170
571 323-3939

(P-7627)
BEARING ENGINEERS INC (PA)
Also Called: Motion Solutions
27 Argonaut, Aliso Viejo (92656-1423)
PHONE.....................949 586-7442
Scott Depenbrok, *President*
Elizabeth Gordon, *CFO*
Henry Kim, *Vice Pres*
Wallis Logan, *Vice Pres*
Wally Logan, *Vice Pres*
▲ **EMP:** 57

SQ FT: 22,000
SALES: 32MM **Privately Held**
WEB: www.bearingengineers.com
SIC: 5085 Bearings

(P-7628)
BELL PIPE & SUPPLY CO
215 E Ball Rd, Anaheim (92805-6394)
P.O. Box 151 (92815-0151)
PHONE.....................................714 772-3200
Franklin M Bell III, *CEO*
Kristin C Bell, *Corp Secy*
Larry Harper, *Sales Associate*
Manuel Mejia, *Sales Staff*
▲ EMP: 50 EST: 1956
SQ FT: 35,000
SALES (est): 58.4MM **Privately Held**
WEB: www.bellpipe.com
SIC: 5085 Valves & fittings

(P-7629)
BOYD CORPORATION
Also Called: Specialty Sealing
4990 E Hunter Ave, Anaheim (92807-2057)
PHONE.....................................714 777-5995
Mitch Aiello, *Manager*
EMP: 144
SALES (corp-wide): 11.3MM **Privately Held**
SIC: 5085 Seals, industrial
PA: The Boyd Corporation
5832 Ohio St
Yorba Linda CA 92886
714 533-2375

(P-7630)
CENTRAL PURCHASING LLC (PA)
Also Called: Harbor Freight Tools
3491 Mission Oaks Blvd, Camarillo (93012-5034)
P.O. Box 6010 (93011-6010)
PHONE.....................................800 444-3353
Eric L Smidt, *President*
Robert Rene, *COO*
Ben Adelstein, *Exec VP*
Roger Sheaves, *Vice Pres*
Trey Feiler, *VP Bus Dvlpt*
◆ EMP: 500
SQ FT: 277,000
SALES (est): 2.4B **Privately Held**
WEB: www.harborfreight.com
SIC: 5085 5961 5251 Tools; tools & hardware, mail order; tools

(P-7631)
CONTINENTAL WESTERN CORP (PA)
Also Called: C W C
2950 Merced St Ste 200, San Leandro (94577-5641)
P.O. Box 2418 (94577-0241)
PHONE.....................................510 352-3133
Frederick J Oshay, *President*
Greg Lewis, *Branch Mgr*
Daniel Casper, *Info Tech Mgr*
Craig Steinke, *Controller*
Justin Spangler, *Purch Mgr*
◆ EMP: 50
SQ FT: 25,000
SALES: 60MM **Privately Held**
WEB: www.cwestern.com
SIC: 5085 3069 Twine; cordage; rope, cord & thread; rapping, rubber

(P-7632)
CRANE CO
3201 Walnut Ave, Long Beach (90755-5225)
PHONE.....................................562 426-2531
Kevin McKown, *Manager*
EMP: 110
SALES (corp-wide): 3.3B **Publicly Held**
WEB: www.craneco.com
SIC: 5085 Valves & fittings
PA: Crane Co.
100 1st Stamford Pl # 300
Stamford CT 06902
203 363-7300

(P-7633)
DHV INDUSTRIES INC
3451 Pegasus Dr, Bakersfield (93308-6827)
PHONE.....................................661 392-8948
Tingchun Huang, *President*

◆ EMP: 52
SQ FT: 180,000
SALES (est): 15MM **Privately Held**
WEB: www.dhvindustries.com
SIC: 5085 3491 Valves & fittings; industrial valves

(P-7634)
G W MAINTENANCE INC (PA)
Also Called: Petroquip
1101 E 6th St, Santa Ana (92701-4912)
P.O. Box 10696 (92711-0696)
PHONE.....................................714 541-2211
Kami Keshmiri, *President*
Barry F Branin, *Ch of Bd*
Vivian Branin, *Treasurer*
EMP: 59
SQ FT: 24,000
SALES (est): 7.1MM **Privately Held**
WEB: www.gwmaintenance.com
SIC: 5085 5084 Valves & fittings; gas equipment, parts & supplies; instruments & control equipment; hoists; pumps & pumping equipment

(P-7635)
GENERAL TOOL INC
Also Called: Gt Diamond
2025 Alton Pkwy, Irvine (92606-4904)
PHONE.....................................949 261-2322
Jae Woo Kim, *CEO*
Juan Montejano, *Regl Sales Mgr*
▲ EMP: 90
SQ FT: 40,000
SALES (est): 26.8MM **Privately Held**
WEB: www.gtdiamond.com
SIC: 5085 Diamonds, industrial: natural, crude

(P-7636)
GRISWOLD INDUSTRIES
Also Called: Griswald Industries
24100 Water Ave, Perris (92570-6738)
PHONE.....................................951 657-1718
Fred Zimmer, *Manager*
EMP: 55
SQ FT: 25,000
SALES (corp-wide): 126.5MM **Privately Held**
SIC: 5085 3494 Valves & fittings; valves & pipe fittings
PA: Griswold Industries
1701 Placentia Ave
Costa Mesa CA 92627
949 722-4800

(P-7637)
INDUSTRIAL CONTAINER SERVICES
Also Called: Ics-CA North
749 Galleria Blvd, Roseville (95678-1331)
PHONE.....................................916 781-2775
Charles Veniez, *CEO*
Gerald Butler,
Alain G Magnan,
Kay Rykowski,
Calvin G Lee, *Mng Member*
EMP: 52
SQ FT: 10,000
SALES (est): 16.9MM
SALES (corp-wide): 1.2B **Privately Held**
WEB: www.capitaldrum.com
SIC: 5085 2655 Commercial containers; fiber cans, drums & similar products
HQ: Industrial Container Services Llc
2600 Mtland Ctr Pkwy 20 # 200
Maitland FL 32751
407 930-4182

(P-7638)
KIRKHILL RUBBER COMPANY
2500 E Thompson St, Long Beach (90805-1836)
PHONE.....................................562 803-1117
David Schlothauer, *President*
Edward Reker, *President*
EMP: 99
SALES (est): 8.2MM
SALES (corp-wide): 1.5B **Privately Held**
SIC: 5085 Rubber goods, mechanical
HQ: Hexpol Holding Inc.
14330 Kinsman Rd
Burton OH 44021
440 834-4644

(P-7639)
LEWIS-GOETZ AND COMPANY INC
Also Called: Valley Rubber & Gasket
10182 Croydon Way, Sacramento (95827-2102)
PHONE.....................................916 366-9340
Les A Shively, *CEO*
Debbie Herbers, *Technology*
EMP: 98 **Privately Held**
SIC: 5085 3053 3052 Hose, belting & packing; gaskets & seals; gaskets, packing & sealing devices; rubber & plastics hose & beltings
HQ: Eriks North America, Inc.
650 Washington Rd Ste 500
Pittsburgh PA 15228
800 937-9070

(P-7640)
LINEAR INDUSTRIES LTD (PA)
1850 Enterprise Way, Monrovia (91016-4271)
PHONE.....................................626 303-1130
Anthony Dell Angelica, *President*
Jean Cade, *CFO*
Savonia Angelica, *Vice Pres*
▲ EMP: 62
SQ FT: 45,000
SALES (est): 29MM **Privately Held**
WEB: www.linearindustries.com
SIC: 5085 3625 5065 5072 Bearings; positioning controls, electric; electronic parts; hardware; power transmission equipment; machine tool accessories

(P-7641)
LONESTAR SIERRA LLC
1820 W Orangewood Ave, Orange (92868-2043)
PHONE.....................................866 575-5680
David Wood,
EMP: 225
SALES: 15MM **Privately Held**
SIC: 5085 Refractory material

(P-7642)
LOS ANGELES RUBBER COMPANY (PA)
Also Called: Mechanical Drives and Belting
2915 E Washington Blvd, Los Angeles (90023-4218)
PHONE.....................................323 263-4131
Carol A Durst, *CEO*
David Durst, *Vice Pres*
Michael Durst, *Vice Pres*
Wayne Roberts, *Vice Pres*
▲ EMP: 55
SQ FT: 31,000
SALES (est): 37.7MM **Privately Held**
SIC: 5085 Industrial supplies

(P-7643)
MECHANICAL DRIVES CO (PA)
Also Called: L A Rubber Co
2915 E Washington Blvd, Los Angeles (90023-4218)
PHONE.....................................323 263-4131
Michael Durst, *CEO*
T Wayne Gehan, *CEO*
David Durst, *Vice Pres*
EMP: 54
SQ FT: 33,000
SALES (est): 27.4MM **Privately Held**
SIC: 5085 Bearings

(P-7644)
MILLENNIA STAINLESS INC
10016 Romandel Ave, Santa Fe Springs (90670-3424)
PHONE.....................................562 946-3545
Ching-PO LI, *CEO*
Lisa Chen, *Accounting Mgr*
Herlinda LI, *Sales Associate*
▲ EMP: 75
SQ FT: 10,500
SALES (est): 26.2MM **Privately Held**
SIC: 5085 5065 5051 Industrial supplies; coils, electronic; steel
PA: Chain Chon Industrial Co., Ltd.
No. 178, Daguan Rd.
Taoyuan City TAY 33753

(P-7645)
MT SUPPLY INC (DH)
Also Called: Machine Tools Supply
3505 Cadillac Ave Ste K2, Costa Mesa (92626-1432)
PHONE.....................................800 938-6658
George H Ponce Jr, *CEO*
Joseph Custer, *Principal*
Steve Pixley, *Principal*
George Ponce, *General Mgr*
David Ramos, *Admin Asst*
EMP: 163
SALES (est): 195.9MM
SALES (corp-wide): 3.1B **Publicly Held**
SIC: 5085 5084 Industrial supplies; materials handling machinery
HQ: Dnow L.P.
7402 N Eldridge Pkwy
Houston TX 77041
281 823-4700

(P-7646)
PACIFIC COAST DRUM COMPANY
Also Called: Gene's Cooperage
2200 Rosemead Blvd 2204, El Monte (91733-1520)
P.O. Box 3593 (91733-0593)
PHONE.....................................626 443-3096
Darryl Bartolotti, *President*
Gene Bartolotti, *Ch of Bd*
EMP: 80 EST: 1961
SQ FT: 50,000
SALES: 11.5MM **Privately Held**
SIC: 5085 Drums, new or reconditioned

(P-7647)
PACIFIC ECHO INC
23540 Telo Ave, Torrance (90505-4098)
PHONE.....................................310 539-1822
Yasuo Ogami, *CEO*
▲ EMP: 90
SQ FT: 110,000
SALES (est): 39MM **Privately Held**
WEB: www.pacificecho.com
SIC: 5085 Hose, belting & packing
HQ: Kakuichi Co., Ltd.
1415, Midoricho, Tsuruga
Nagano NAG 380-0

(P-7648)
PRH PRO INC
13089 Peyton Dr Ste C362, Chino Hills (91709-6018)
PHONE.....................................714 510-7226
Wayman Bill Peng, *President*
EMP: 161
SQ FT: 2,000
SALES: 100MM **Privately Held**
SIC: 5085 Cooperage stock

(P-7649)
PRINTING TECHNOLOGY INC
Also Called: Pti
9831 Independence Ave, Chatsworth (91311-4320)
PHONE.....................................818 576-9220
Peter De Salay, *President*
Julian Desalay, *Vice Pres*
Tim Purugganan, *Vice Pres*
◆ EMP: 160
SALES (est): 35.4MM **Privately Held**
WEB: www.ptiimaging.com
SIC: 5085 5084 5111 Ink, printers'; printing trades machinery, equipment & supplies; printing paper

(P-7650)
PROGRESSIVE TRNSP SVCS INC
19500 S Alameda St, Compton (90221-6204)
PHONE.....................................510 268-3776
Edgar Tafolla, *Branch Mgr*
EMP: 56 **Privately Held**
SIC: 5085 Commercial containers
PA: Progressive Transportation Services, Llc
1360 W Pacific Coast Hwy
Long Beach CA 90810

(P-7651)
RBC TRANSPORT DYNAMICS CORP
3131 W Segerstrom Ave, Santa Ana (92704-5811)
PHONE.....................203 267-7001
Michael Harnett, *President*
Charles Bliss, *General Mgr*
Saul Murillo, *Design Engr*
Daryl Cousins, *Engineer*
Zacharie Fowler, *Engineer*
▲ EMP: 185
SQ FT: 75,000
SALES (est): 82.3MM
SALES (corp-wide): 702.5MM **Publicly Held**
SIC: 5085 Bearings
HQ: Roller Bearing Company Of America, Inc.
102 Willenbrock Rd
Oxford CT 06478
203 267-7001

(P-7652)
ROPE PARTNER INC
125 Mcpherson St Ste B, Santa Cruz (95060-5883)
PHONE.....................831 460-9448
Eric Stanfield, *President*
Chris Bley, *Founder*
Linda Benko, *Technician*
Grant Deitchman, *Technician*
Shayd Otis, *Technician*
EMP: 65
SQ FT: 1,900
SALES: 950K **Privately Held**
WEB: www.ropepartner.com
SIC: 5085 Rope, cord & thread

(P-7653)
RUBY INDUSTRIAL TECH LLC
910 S Wanamaker Ave, Ontario (91761-8151)
PHONE.....................909 390-7919
Tom Serafin, *Branch Mgr*
EMP: 50
SALES (corp-wide): 781.2MM **Privately Held**
SIC: 5085 Bearings
PA: Ruby Industrial Technologies, Llc
1 Vision Way
Bloomfield CT 06002
860 687-5000

(P-7654)
RUTLAND TOOL & SUPPLY CO (HQ)
Also Called: MSC Metalworking
2225 Workman Mill Rd, City of Industry (90601-1437)
PHONE.....................562 566-5000
Thomas J Neri, *CEO*
Andrew Verey, *President*
Dustin Meyers, *Accounts Exec*
▲ EMP: 140
SALES (est): 27.6MM **Publicly Held**
SIC: 5085 5251 Industrial supplies; tools

(P-7655)
S & S TOOL & SUPPLY INC (HQ)
Also Called: S & S Supplies and Solutions
2700 Maxwell Way, Fairfield (94534-9708)
P.O. Box 1111, Martinez (94553-0111)
PHONE.....................925 313-0360
Tracy Tomkovicz, *CEO*
Tanya Powell, *CFO*
Phil Jones, *Info Tech Mgr*
Andrew Thompson, *Technology*
Daniel Adams, *Buyer*
▲ EMP: 100
SQ FT: 90,000
SALES: 153.2MM
SALES (corp-wide): 974.6MM **Privately Held**
WEB: www.sns-tool.com
SIC: 5085 7699 5072 7359 Industrial tools; industrial equipment services; tool repair services; hand tools; power tools; equipment rental & leasing; tool rental
PA: Total Safety U.S., Inc.
3151 Briarpark Dr Ste 500
Houston TX 77042
713 353-7100

(P-7656)
SEGUIN MREAU NAPA COPERAGE INC
Also Called: Fine Northern Oak
151 Camino Dorado, NAPA (94558-6213)
PHONE.....................707 252-3408
Nicolas Mahler-Besse, *Principal*
◆ EMP: 57
SQ FT: 40,000
SALES (est): 15.5MM **Privately Held**
SIC: 5085 2449 Barrels, new or reconditioned; barrels, wood: coopered
PA: Seguin Moreau Holdings Inc
151 Camino Dorado
Napa CA 94558

(P-7657)
SO CAL SANDBAGS INC
12620 Bosley Ln, Corona (92883-6358)
PHONE.....................951 277-3404
Peter Rasinski, *President*
Wanda Chavez, *Controller*
Nina Sosinski, *Manager*
EMP: 100
SALES (est): 54.1MM **Privately Held**
WEB: www.socalsandbags.com
SIC: 5085 5999 Industrial supplies; safety supplies & equipment

(P-7658)
SOLAR LINK INTERNATIONAL INC
4652 E Brickell St Ste A, Ontario (91761-1593)
P.O. Box 56, San Dimas (91773-0056)
PHONE.....................909 605-7789
Johnny Tsai, *Vice Pres*
▲ EMP: 218 EST: 1998
SALES (est): 55.5MM **Privately Held**
SIC: 5085 Industrial supplies

(P-7659)
SUNNYVALE FLUID SYS TECH INC
Also Called: Swagelok Northern California
3393 W Warren Ave, Fremont (94538-6424)
PHONE.....................510 933-2500
Rod Fallow, *CEO*
Victor Jung, *Cust Mgr*
Les McElwain, *Director*
Jeff Hopkins, *Manager*
Josh Herndon, *Accounts Mgr*
EMP: 50
SQ FT: 14,000
SALES (est): 26.7MM **Privately Held**
WEB: www.sunnyvale.swagelok.com
SIC: 5085 3492 Valves.& fittings; fluid power valves & hose fittings

(P-7660)
TCT CIRCUIT SUPPLY INC
560 S Melrose St, Placentia (92870-6327)
PHONE.....................714 644-9700
Ian Hemmings, *President*
Kathy Chen, *Principal*
Amie Chien Chien, *Principal*
Tim Derrick, *Sales Staff*
EMP: 55
SALES (est): 1.8MM **Privately Held**
SIC: 5085 Tools

(P-7661)
VAT INCORPORATED (DH)
655 River Oaks Pkwy, San Jose (95134-1907)
PHONE.....................781 935-1446
Andrew Witken, *President*
Robert Campbell, *President*
Simon Mansbridge, *President*
Brian J Darcy, *Treasurer*
Bobby Choo, *Info Tech Mgr*
▲ EMP: 50
SALES: 13.2MM
SALES (corp-wide): 702.4MM **Privately Held**
WEB: www.vat.com
SIC: 5085 7699 3491 Valves & fittings; valve repair, industrial; industrial valves
HQ: Vat Holding Ag
Seelistrasse 1
Haag (Rheintal) SG 9469
817 716-161

(P-7662)
WEST-SPEC PARTNERS
20525 Nordhoff St Ste 42, Chatsworth (91311-6135)
PHONE.....................818 725-7000
Dave Kukanek, *Partner*
EMP: 50
SALES (est): 4.8MM **Privately Held**
WEB: www.vertexdistribution.com
SIC: 5085 Fasteners & fastening equipment

(P-7663)
WW GRAINGER INC
4700 Hamner Ave, Eastvale (91752-1018)
PHONE.....................951 727-2300
Brian Williams, *Opers-Prdtn-Mfg*
EMP: 220
SQ FT: 20,000
SALES (corp-wide): 11.2B **Publicly Held**
WEB: www.grainger.com
SIC: 5085 Industrial supplies
PA: W.W. Grainger, Inc.
100 Grainger Pkwy
Lake Forest IL 60045
847 535-1000

5087 Service Establishment Eqpt & Splys Wholesale

(P-7664)
AMERICAN SANITARY SUPPLY INC
Also Called: American Chemical & Sanitary
592 Explorer St, Brea (92821-3108)
P.O. Box 6436, Anaheim (92816-0436)
PHONE.....................714 632-3010
Luis Salazar, *CEO*
Tammy Zingmark, *CFO*
Silvia Salazar, *Vice Pres*
▲ EMP: 50
SQ FT: 20,000
SALES: 15MM **Privately Held**
SIC: 5087 Janitors' supplies

(P-7665)
ARROW USA
1105 Highland Ct, Beaumont (92223-7091)
PHONE.....................951 845-6144
Sam Chang, *President*
Zuhair Klenzi, *President*
Wen Zhang, *Treasurer*
S Kalanzeh, *Vice Pres*
Susan Chen, *Director*
EMP: 75
SQ FT: 3,000
SALES: 500MM **Privately Held**
SIC: 5087 Beauty salon & barber shop equipment & supplies

(P-7666)
BEAUTITUDES BEAUTY SUPPLY LLC
7850 White Ln Ste E, Bakersfield (93309-7699)
PHONE.....................800 830-6076
Jaime Hecht, *President*
EMP: 51 EST: 2015
SQ FT: 1,500
SALES (est): 4.1MM **Privately Held**
SIC: 5087 Beauty parlor equipment & supplies

(P-7667)
BENEX LLC
169 Saxony Rd Ste 111, Encinitas (92024-6779)
PHONE.....................310 675-6200
EMP: 62
SALES (est): 996.5K **Privately Held**
SIC: 5087

(P-7668)
CHIRO INC (PA)
Also Called: Mr Clean Maintenance Systems
2260 S Vista Ave, Bloomington (92316-2908)
P.O. Box 31, Colton (92324-0031)
PHONE.....................909 879-1160
Arthur Rose, *President*
Carbajal Ray, *CFO*

Timothy Russell, *Vice Pres*
Denise Peters, *Human Res Dir*
Duane Chandler, *Sales Mgr*
EMP: 75
SQ FT: 10,000
SALES (est): 79.2MM **Privately Held**
WEB: www.mrcleansystems.com
SIC: 5087 7349 5169 Cleaning & maintenance equipment & supplies; cleaning service, industrial or commercial; chemicals & allied products

(P-7669)
DISH FACTORY INC (PA)
333 E Valley Blvd, Colton (92324-3048)
PHONE.....................213 687-9500
Charles Wyatt, *President*
Leo Perez, *Purch Mgr*
◆ EMP: 55
SALES (est): 11.9MM **Privately Held**
WEB: www.dishfactory.com
SIC: 5087 7699 Restaurant supplies; restaurant equipment repair

(P-7670)
FISHMAN SUPPLY COMPANY
1345 Industrial Ave, Petaluma (94952-6500)
P.O. Box 750279 (94975-0279)
PHONE.....................707 763-8161
Leland Fishman, *President*
Valerie Gossage, *Corp Secy*
Andrew Fishman, *Vice Pres*
Julie Fishman, *Vice Pres*
Jeanie Berry, *Purch Mgr*
EMP: 52
SQ FT: 26,000
SALES: 12.9MM **Privately Held**
WEB: www.fishmansupply.com
SIC: 5087 5113 5112 Janitors' supplies; shipping supplies; office filing supplies

(P-7671)
GLAMOUR INDUSTRIES CO
100 Wilshire Blvd Ste 700, Santa Monica (90401-3602)
PHONE.....................213 687-8600
EMP: 100
SALES (est): 1.1MM
SALES (corp-wide): 100.2MM **Privately Held**
SIC: 5087 Beauty parlor equipment & supplies; barber shop equipment & supplies
PA: Glamour Industries, Co.
2220 Gaspar Ave
Commerce CA 90040
323 728-2999

(P-7672)
HYDRO TEK SYSTEMS INC
2353 Almond Ave, Redlands (92374-2035)
PHONE.....................909 799-9222
John S Koen, *President*
Andrea S Koen, *Admin Sec*
◆ EMP: 63
SQ FT: 45,000
SALES (est): 14MM
SALES (corp-wide): 1.2B **Privately Held**
WEB: www.hydroteksystems.com
SIC: 5087 3589 5084 Service establishment equipment; commercial cleaning equipment; industrial machinery & equipment
HQ: Nilfisk A/S
Kornmarksvej 1
BrOndby 2605
721 821-20

(P-7673)
JWDANGELO COMPANY INC
601 S Harbor Blvd, La Habra (90631-6187)
P.O. Box 3744 (90632-3744)
PHONE.....................562 690-1000
John W D Angelo, *CEO*
Jack Giguere, *Vice Pres*
Cathy Lite, *Vice Pres*
Shannon Smith, *Admin Asst*
Rodney Gifford, *Info Tech Mgr*
EMP: 50
SQ FT: 35,000
SALES (est): 17.3MM **Privately Held**
WEB: www.jwdangelo.com
SIC: 5087 Firefighting equipment

(P-7674)
LN CURTIS AND SONS (PA)
1800 Peralta St, Oakland (94607-1609)
P.O. Box 60000, San Francisco (94160-0001)
PHONE..................510 839-5111
John Viboch, *Treasurer*
Jeff Curtis, *Vice Pres*
Tim Henderson, *Vice Pres*
Troy Garside, *Branch Mgr*
Roger Curtis, *Division Mgr*
▲ EMP: 65
SQ FT: 25,000
SALES (est): 70.1MM **Privately Held**
SIC: 5087 5099 Firefighting equipment;
safety equipment & supplies

(P-7675)
NAIL EMPORIUM
Also Called: Nail Emporium Beauty Supply
1517 N Harmony Cir, Anaheim
(92807-6003)
PHONE..................714 779-9889
James George, *Owner*
Garret Kellenberger, *Manager*
EMP: 50
SALES (est): 2.3MM **Privately Held**
SIC: 5087 5122 Beauty parlor equipment
& supplies; cosmetics, perfumes & hair
products

(P-7676)
NAIMIES BEAUTY CENTER INC (PA)
Also Called: Naimies Film & TV Beauty Sup
12640 Riverside Dr, Valley Village
(91607-3411)
PHONE..................818 655-9933
Naimie Ojeil, *President*
Samuel Ishk, *Vice Pres*
ARI Derbedrossian, *Opers Staff*
Aram Kalustian, *Sales Executive*
Nicole Fischer, *Cust Mgr*
▲ EMP: 60
SQ FT: 7,000
SALES (est): 11.2MM **Privately Held**
WEB: www.naimies.com
SIC: 5087 5999 Beauty parlor equipment
& supplies; toiletries, cosmetics & per-
fumes

(P-7677)
NIKKEN GLOBAL INC (HQ)
18301 Von Karman Ave # 120, Irvine
(92612-1009)
PHONE..................949 789-2000
Tom Toshizo Watanabe, *Ch of Bd*
Kendall Cho, *President*
Ruth Ann Bellino, *Accountant*
▲ EMP: 155
SALES (est): 32.6MM
SALES (corp-wide): 54.2MM **Privately Held**
SIC: 5087 5023 5013 5122 Stress reduc-
ing equipment, electric; bedspreads; seat
covers; vitamins & minerals; long distance
telephone communications
PA: Nikken International, Inc.
18301 Von Karman Ave # 120
Irvine CA 92612
949 789-2000

(P-7678)
O P I PRODUCTS INC (HQ)
13034 Saticoy St, North Hollywood
(91605-3510)
PHONE..................818 759-8688
Jules Kaufman, *CEO*
John Heffner, *President*
Eric Schwartz, *COO*
William Halfacre, *Exec VP*
Susan Weiss-Fischmann, *Exec VP*
◆ EMP: 500
SQ FT: 250,000
SALES (est): 184.4MM **Publicly Held**
SIC: 5087 2844 Beauty parlor equipment
& supplies; toilet preparations

(P-7679)
PAGE FRONT CATERING
Also Called: Pacific Dining Food Svc MGT
34793 Ardentech Ct, Fremont
(94555-3657)
P.O. Box 32761, San Jose (95152-2761)
PHONE..................408 406-8487
Richard McMahon, *Owner*

EMP: 57
SALES (est): 4.6MM **Privately Held**
SIC: 5087 5812 7389 Vending machines
& supplies; caterers; coffee service

(P-7680)
PUREBEAUTY INC
Also Called: Pure Beauty-A Freeman Com-
pany
32920 Alvarado Niles Rd # 220, Union City
(94587-8102)
PHONE..................510 477-7950
Jeno Reynoso, *General Mgr*
EMP: 50
SALES (corp-wide): 161.4MM **Privately Held**
WEB: www.embarcaderoshop.com
SIC: 5087 Beauty parlor equipment & sup-
plies
HQ: Purebeauty, Inc.
10610 E 26th Cir N
Wichita KS

(P-7681)
PWS INC (PA)
12020 Garfield Ave, South Gate
(90280-7823)
PHONE..................323 721-8832
Morton E Pollack, *Chairman*
Brad Pollack, *President*
Eric Steinberg, *CEO*
Yumi Ryoo, *Sales Staff*
▲ EMP: 51 EST: 1966
SQ FT: 50,000
SALES (est): 51.8MM **Privately Held**
WEB: www.pwslaundry.com
SIC: 5087 Laundry equipment & supplies

(P-7682)
SWEIS INC (PA)
23760 Hawthorne Blvd, Torrance
(90505-5906)
PHONE..................310 375-0558
Karl Sweis, *President*
Jason Hilt, *Controller*
Denise Jones, *Manager*
Tanya Del Pozzo, *Consultant*
EMP: 125
SQ FT: 4,200
SALES (est): 23.3MM **Privately Held**
WEB: www.sweisinc.com
SIC: 5087 2844 Beauty parlor equipment
& supplies; hair preparations, including
shampoos

(P-7683)
UNITED FABRICARE SUPPLY INC (PA)
1237 W Walnut St, Compton (90220-5009)
P.O. Box 1796, Los Angeles (90001-0796)
PHONE..................310 886-3790
Steve S Hong, *CEO*
Hae S Hong, *Corp Secy*
Mike Fahar, *Exec VP*
Kirby Schnebly, *Exec VP*
W David Weimer, *Exec VP*
▲ EMP: 75
SQ FT: 50,000
SALES (est): 43.5MM **Privately Held**
WEB: www.unitedfabricaresupply.com
SIC: 5087 Laundry & dry cleaning equip-
ment & supplies

(P-7684)
WAXIES ENTERPRISES INC
905 Wineville Ave, Ontario (91764-5595)
P.O. Box 5926, San Bernardino (92412)
PHONE..................909 942-3100
Jeff Roberts, *General Mgr*
Duke Ordaz, *COO*
EMP: 115
SALES (corp-wide): 390MM **Privately Held**
WEB: www.waxie.com
SIC: 5087 Janitors' supplies
PA: Waxie's Enterprises, Inc.
9353 Waxie Way
San Diego CA 92123
800 995-4466

(P-7685)
WAXIES ENTERPRISES INC
901 N Canyon Pkwy, Livermore (94551)
PHONE..................925 454-2900
John Bielenberg, *General Mgr*

Tiffany McLaughlin, *Sales Mgr*
EMP: 50
SALES (corp-wide): 390MM **Privately Held**
WEB: www.waxie.com
SIC: 5087 Janitors' supplies
PA: Waxie's Enterprises, Inc.
9353 Waxie Way
San Diego CA 92123
800 995-4466

(P-7686)
WINCO INDUSTRIES COMPANY
Also Called: Winco Dwl Industries Co
14950 Valley View Ave, La Mirada
(90638-5224)
PHONE..................562 926-5600
David LI, *President*
Lilly Song, *Purch Mgr*
Angela Black, *Traffic Mgr*
Bob Burzin, *Natl Sales Mgr*
▲ EMP: 50
SALES (est): 9.2MM **Privately Held**
SIC: 5087 Restaurant supplies

(P-7687)
WORLDWIDE INTGRTED RSRCES INC
7171 Telegraph Rd, Montebello
(90640-6511)
PHONE..................323 838-8938
Fred Morad, *President*
Sina Salamat, *CFO*
Susan Morad, *Admin Sec*
◆ EMP: 60
SQ FT: 20,000
SALES (est): 10.6MM **Privately Held**
WEB: www.wwir.com
SIC: 5087 Janitors' supplies

┌─────────────────────────┐
│ **5088 Transportation Eqpt &**
│ **Splys, Except Motor**
│ **Vehicles Wholesale**
└─────────────────────────┘

(P-7688)
AIREY ENTERPRISES LLC
Also Called: A Transportation
5530 Corbin Ave Ste 325, Tarzana
(91356-6037)
P.O. Box 17328, Encino (91416-7328)
PHONE..................818 530-3362
Latasha George,
EMP: 160
SALES (est): 8.8MM **Privately Held**
SIC: 5088 Transportation equipment &
supplies

(P-7689)
APICAL INDUSTRIES INC
Also Called: Dart Aerospace
3030 Enterprise Ct Ste A, Vista
(92081-8358)
PHONE..................760 724-5300
Alain Madore, *CEO*
Daniela Delarosa, *Office Mgr*
EMP: 100
SQ FT: 30,000
SALES (est): 41.7MM
SALES (corp-wide): 221.6MM **Publicly Held**
WEB: www.apicalindustries.com
SIC: 5088 3728 Helicopter parts; aircraft
landing assemblies & brakes
HQ: Dart Aerospace Ltd
1270 Aberdeen St
Hawkesbury ON K6A 1
613 632-5200

(P-7690)
BOEING DISTRIBUTION SVCS INC
1351 Charles Willard St, Carson
(90746-4023)
PHONE..................310 900-1300
Chris Caudana, *Branch Mgr*
Sherry Hancock, *Sales Staff*
EMP: 246
SALES (corp-wide): 101.1B **Publicly Held**
SIC: 5088 Aircraft equipment & supplies

HQ: Boeing Distribution Services, Inc.
3760 W 108th St Unit 1
Hialeah FL 33018
561 383-5100

(P-7691)
BOEING SATELLITE SYSTEMS
200 N Pacific Coast Hwy, El Segundo
(90245-4340)
PHONE..................310 326-3100
S D Dorfman, *Manager*
EMP: 94
SALES (corp-wide): 101.1B **Publicly Held**
SIC: 5088 4899 Aircraft & space vehicle
supplies & parts; satellite earth stations
HQ: Boeing Satellite Systems International,
Inc.
2260 E Imperial Hwy
El Segundo CA 90245
310 364-4000

(P-7692)
JCM ENGINEERING CORP
2690 E Cedar St, Ontario (91761-8533)
PHONE..................909 923-3730
Carlo A Moyano, *Founder*
William Durante, *President*
Robert Schenkkan, *President*
Myrna Lamar, *COO*
Jay Gross, *CFO*
EMP: 95
SQ FT: 140,000
SALES (est): 66MM **Privately Held**
WEB: www.jcmcorp.com
SIC: 5088 Aeronautical equipment & sup-
plies

(P-7693)
KELLSTROM HOLDING CORPORATION (PA)
Also Called: Merex Group
100 N Pcf Cast Hwy Ste 19, El Segundo
(90245)
PHONE..................561 222-7455
Christopher R Celtruda, *President*
Michael P Hompesch, *Partner*
Frank J Pados Jr, *Partner*
Thomas J Caracciolo, *Managing Prtnr*
Jikun Kim, *CFO*
EMP: 54 EST: 2011
SQ FT: 25,821
SALES (est): 154.1MM **Privately Held**
SIC: 5088 Aircraft engines & engine parts

(P-7694)
KIRKHILL AIRCRAFT PARTS CO (PA)
Also Called: Proponent
3120 Enterprise St, Brea (92821-6236)
PHONE..................323 216-9136
Andrew Todhunter, *CEO*
Scott Joynt, *President*
Steven Frields, *CFO*
Lynann Collins, *Vice Pres*
Chris Mercier, *Vice Pres*
▲ EMP: 175
SQ FT: 177,000
SALES (est): 141MM **Privately Held**
WEB: www.kapcovaltec.com
SIC: 5088 3728 Aircraft & parts; aircraft
parts & equipment

(P-7695)
LJ WALCH CO INC
6600 Preston Ave, Livermore (94551-5132)
P.O. Box 2798 (94551-2798)
PHONE..................925 449-9252
Ron Luty, *CEO*
Tony Ippolito, *President*
Mark Nelson, *Senior VP*
Bill Luty, *Vice Pres*
Tom Walch, *Vice Pres*
▲ EMP: 60
SQ FT: 38,500
SALES (est): 22.7MM **Privately Held**
WEB: www.ljwalch.com
SIC: 5088 7629 Aircraft & parts; aircraft
electrical equipment repair

(P-7696)
LOGISTICAL SUPPORT LLC
Also Called: RTC Aerospace
20409 Prairie St, Chatsworth (91311-6029)
PHONE..................818 341-3344
Joseph Lucan,

William Hart, *Vice Pres*
Jerry Hill, *Vice Pres*
EMP: 120
SQ FT: 14,600
SALES (est): 10.7MM
SALES (corp-wide): 28.7MM **Privately Held**
WEB: www.logisticalsupport.com
SIC: 5088 Aircraft & parts
PA: Rtc Aerospace Llc
    7215 45th Street Ct E
    Fife WA 98424
    918 407-0291

(P-7697)
ONTIC ENGINEERING AND MFG INC (HQ)
20400 Plummer St, Chatsworth (91311-5372)
P.O. Box 2424 (91313-2424)
PHONE..................818 678-6555
Greth Hall, *CEO*
Peg Billson, *President*
Terry Streb, *Program Mgr*
Susan Hunt, *Administration*
Carmin Ortiz, *Administration*
EMP: 269
SQ FT: 54,000
SALES (est): 173.8MM
SALES (corp-wide): 2.3B **Privately Held**
SIC: 5088 3728 3812 Aircraft equipment & supplies; aircraft parts & equipment; search & navigation equipment
PA: Bba Aviation Plc
    105 Wigmore Street
    London W1U 1
    207 514-3999

(P-7698)
PACIFIC CONTOURS CORPORATION (PA)
5340 E Hunter Ave, Anaheim (92807-2053)
PHONE..................714 693-1260
Michael Rapacz, *CEO*
Tim Anderson, *CFO*
EMP: 60
SQ FT: 32,000
SALES (est): 18MM **Privately Held**
WEB: www.pacificcontours.com
SIC: 5088 3728 Aircraft & parts; aircraft assemblies, subassemblies & parts

(P-7699)
SHIMADZU PRECISION INSTRS INC (DH)
Also Called: Shimadzu Medical Systems USA
3645 N Lakewood Blvd, Long Beach (90808-1797)
PHONE..................562 420-6226
Yutaka Nakamura, *CEO*
Koki Aoyama, *President*
Atsushi Nishizaki, *President*
Akira Watanabe, *President*
▲ **EMP:** 70
SQ FT: 60,000
SALES (est): 157.7MM **Privately Held**
WEB: www.spi-inc.com
SIC: 5088 5047 5084 Aircraft equipment & supplies; medical equipment & supplies; industrial machinery & equipment

(P-7700)
STRECH PLASTICS INCORPORATED
900 John St Ste J, Banning (92220-6204)
PHONE..................951 922-2224
James M Strech, *CEO*
Jim Underwood, *Info Tech Dir*
Aaron Tacchia, *Sales Staff*
▲ **EMP:** 50
SQ FT: 52,000
SALES (est): 22.8MM **Privately Held**
WEB: www.strechplastics.com
SIC: 5088 3949 Golf carts; sporting & athletic goods

(P-7701)
TPS AVIATION INC (PA)
1515 Crocker Ave, Hayward (94544-7038)
PHONE..................510 475-1010
George Sozaburo Kujiraoka, *CEO*
Chris Ybarra, *Info Tech Mgr*
Jane Milanes, *Controller*
David Lim, *Purch Mgr*
Kevin Suyeyasu, *Purch Mgr*

◆ **EMP:** 100 **EST:** 1963
SQ FT: 58,700
SALES: 48.7MM **Privately Held**
WEB: www.tpsaviation.com
SIC: 5088 5065 3728 3429 Aircraft & parts; aircraft engines & engine parts; aircraft equipment & supplies; guided missiles & space vehicles; electronic parts; aircraft parts & equipment; manufactured hardware (general)

(P-7702)
WESCO AIRCRAFT HARDWARE CORP (HQ)
24911 Avenue Stanford, Valencia (91355-1281)
PHONE..................661 775-7200
Dave Currence, *CIO*
Alex Murray, *COO*
Richard Weller, *CFO*
Todd Renehan, *Ch Credit Ofcr*
John Holland,
▲ **EMP:** 370 **EST:** 1953
SALES (est): 411.3MM **Publicly Held**
SIC: 5088 3728 Aircraft & parts; research & dev by manuf., aircraft parts & auxiliary equip

(P-7703)
WESCO AIRCRAFT HARDWARE CORP
27727 Avenue Scott, Valencia (91355-3909)
PHONE..................661 775-7200
Steve Halford, *Opers Mgr*
Viktoria Kravchenko, *Engineer*
Brandi Marino, *Buyer*
Chad Rowe, *Sales Staff*
Bruce Weinstein, *Director*
EMP: 400 **Publicly Held**
SIC: 5088 Aircraft & parts
HQ: Wesco Aircraft Hardware Corp.
    24911 Avenue Stanford
    Valencia CA 91355
    661 775-7200

5091 Sporting & Recreational Goods & Splys Wholesale

(P-7704)
BAUER HOCKEY INC
Also Called: Easton Hockey
3500 Willow Ln, Thousand Oaks (91361-4921)
PHONE..................818 782-6445
Bernard McDonell, *Ch of Bd*
Paul E Harrington, *Principal*
Ryan Weller, *Sales Mgr*
EMP: 423
SALES (corp-wide): 149.6MM **Privately Held**
SIC: 5091 Sporting & recreation goods
PA: Old Bh Inc.
    100 Domain Dr
    Exeter NH 03833
    603 430-2111

(P-7705)
CALLAWAY GOLF BALL OPRTONS INC (HQ)
2180 Rutherford Rd, Carlsbad (92008-7328)
PHONE..................760 931-1771
Chip Brewer, *CEO*
EMP: 1700 **EST:** 2003
SALES (est): 635.3K
SALES (corp-wide): 1.2B **Publicly Held**
SIC: 5091 Golf equipment
PA: Callaway Golf Company
    2180 Rutherford Rd
    Carlsbad CA 92008
    760 931-1771

(P-7706)
CHEM QUIP INC
Also Called: White House Sales
2551 Land Ave, Sacramento (95815-2363)
PHONE..................800 821-1678
Don Aston, *CEO*
Greg Durkee, *President*
Steve Hubbard, *CFO*

Brain Long, *Admin Sec*
Chris Sanders, *Project Mgr*
EMP: 62
SQ FT: 20,000
SALES: 24MM **Privately Held**
WEB: www.chemquip.com
SIC: 5091 5169 Swimming pools, equipment & supplies; chlorine

(P-7707)
DAIWA CORPORATION
Also Called: Daiwa Golf Company Division
11137 Warland Dr, Cypress (90630-5034)
P.O. Box 6600 (90630-0066)
PHONE..................562 375-6800
Tomoaki Komatsu, *CEO*
Tad Suzuki, *President*
William Steiner, *Vice Pres*
Cynthia Young, *Vice Pres*
Curt Arakawa, *Marketing Mgr*
◆ **EMP:** 58
SALES (est): 25MM **Privately Held**
WEB: www.daiwa.com
SIC: 5091 3949 Fishing tackle; golf equipment
PA: Globeride, Inc.
    3-14-16, Maesawa
    Higashi Kurume TKY 203-0

(P-7708)
EVIKECOM INC
2801 W Mission Rd, Alhambra (91803-1223)
PHONE..................626 286-0360
Evike Change, *CEO*
Julie Chang, *COO*
George Melahn, *Marketing Staff*
Maria Gao, *Retailers*
Evike RMA, *Retailers*
▲ **EMP:** 70
SALES (est): 24MM **Privately Held**
SIC: 5091 5941 Sporting & recreation goods; sporting goods & bicycle shops

(P-7709)
FESTIVAL FUN PARKS LLC
Also Called: Raging Waters San Dimas 703
111 Raging Waters Dr, San Dimas (91773-3928)
PHONE..................909 802-2200
Robert Zues, *General Mgr*
EMP: 700 **Privately Held**
SIC: 5091 Water slides (recreation park)
HQ: Festival Fun Parks, Llc
    4590 Macarthur Blvd # 400
    Newport Beach CA 92660
    949 261-0404

(P-7710)
GENERAL POOL & SPA SUPPLY INC (PA)
11285 Sunco Dr, Rancho Cordova (95742-6517)
PHONE..................916 853-2401
Philip Gelhaus, *President*
Patty Gelhaus, *Corp Secy*
Mark Yomogida, *Vice Pres*
Carlos Sorto, *Site Mgr*
▼ **EMP:** 55
SQ FT: 25,000
SALES (est): 27.4MM **Privately Held**
WEB: www.gpspool.com
SIC: 5091 Swimming pools, equipment & supplies; spa equipment & supplies

(P-7711)
GIANT BICYCLE INC (DH)
3587 Old Conejo Rd, Newbury Park (91320-2122)
PHONE..................805 267-4600
Elysa Walk, *Principal*
Jean Scott, *Technology*
John Thompson, *Sales Dir*
Reuben Hernandez, *Merchandising*
Andrew Juskaitis, *Marketing Staff*
◆ **EMP:** 55
SQ FT: 75,000
SALES (est): 34.7MM **Privately Held**
SIC: 5091 Bicycles
HQ: Gaiwin B.V.
    Pascallaan 66
    Lelystad 8218
    320 296-296

(P-7712)
INTER VALLEY POOL SUPPLY INC
Also Called: Intervalley Pools
1415 E 3rd St, Pomona (91766-2241)
PHONE..................626 969-5657
John A Fry, *President*
EMP: 60
SQ FT: 23,000
SALES (est): 9.7MM
SALES (corp-wide): 72.3MM **Privately Held**
SIC: 5091 5963 Swimming pools, equipment & supplies; bottled water delivery
PA: Hasa, Inc.
    23119 Drayton St
    Santa Clarita CA 91350
    661 259-5848

(P-7713)
INTEX RECREATION CORP (PA)
4001 Via Oro Ave Ste 210, Long Beach (90810-1400)
PHONE..................310 549-5400
Tien P Zee, *President*
Wayne Farmer, *Info Tech Dir*
Rosevilla Tan, *Credit Staff*
Liz Botek, *Analyst*
Rick Oster, *Sales Mgr*
◆ **EMP:** 58
SQ FT: 80,000
SALES (est): 171.8MM **Privately Held**
WEB: www.intexcorp.net
SIC: 5091 5092 5021 3081 Watersports equipment & supplies; toys; waterbeds; vinyl film & sheet; polyethylene film

(P-7714)
JUPITER HOLDING I CORP (HQ)
13925 City Center Dr # 200, Chino Hills (91709-5437)
PHONE..................909 606-1416
Charles Huebner, *CEO*
EMP: 4948
SALES (est): 1.5B **Privately Held**
SIC: 5091 7991 5719 Spa equipment & supplies; spas; bath accessories

(P-7715)
MANDUKA LLC (HQ)
2121 Park Pl Ste 250, El Segundo (90245-4843)
PHONE..................310 426-1495
Sky Meltzer, *CEO*
Beau Swenson, *CFO*
Cathy Quain, *Vice Pres*
Erica Shaw, *Graphic Designe*
Ramiro Castillo, *Accountant*
▲ **EMP:** 50
SALES (est): 32.2MM
SALES (corp-wide): 58.4MM **Privately Held**
SIC: 5091 5941 5699 Sporting & recreation goods; specialty sport supplies; golf, tennis & ski shops; sports apparel
PA: Valor Equity Partner Holdings, Llc
    875 N Michigan Ave # 3214
    Chicago IL 60611
    312 683-1900

(P-7716)
NATIONAL LIQUIDATORS
2715 W Coast Hwy, Newport Beach (92663-4723)
PHONE..................949 631-6715
Robert G Tony, *Director*
Robert Tony, *President*
EMP: 50
SALES (est): 3.3MM **Privately Held**
WEB: www.yachtauctions.com
SIC: 5091 Boats, canoes, watercrafts & equipment

(P-7717)
NEW CENTURY SCIENCE & TECH
18031 Cortney Ct, City of Industry (91748-1203)
PHONE..................626 581-5500
Carson Cheng, *President*
EMP: 60
SALES: 5MM **Privately Held**
SIC: 5091 Sporting & recreation goods

(P-7718)
RAZOR USA LLC (PA)
12723 166th St, Cerritos (90703-2102)
P.O. Box 3610 (90703-3610)
PHONE......................562 345-6000
Carlton Calvin, *Mng Member*
Erin Bitar, *Vice Pres*
Ian Desberg, *Vice Pres*
David Kim, *Planning*
Dong Lam, *Technician*
◆ EMP: 70
SQ FT: 50,000
SALES (est): 40.6MM **Privately Held**
WEB: www.razor.com
SIC: 5091 Sporting & recreation goods

(P-7719)
REC CENTER
501 Stanyan St, San Francisco
(94117-1898)
PHONE......................415 831-6818
Elizabeth Goldstein, *Director*
Peter Silva, *Officer*
Armando Domine, *Administration*
Anne Donnelly, *Business Mgr*
Connie Fontanilla, *Analyst*
EMP: 144 EST: 2011
SALES (est): 7.1MM **Privately Held**
SIC: 5091 Water slides (recreation park)

(P-7720)
SHIMANO NORTH AMER HOLDG INC (HQ)
1 Holland, Irvine (92618-2506)
PHONE......................949 951-5003
David Pfeiffer, *President*
Jim Lafrance, *CFO*
Chiam Teng, *Vice Pres*
Robert Bakker, *Area Mgr*
Robert Milne, *Area Mgr*
▲ EMP: 150
SQ FT: 122,000
SALES (est): 52.6MM **Privately Held**
SIC: 5091 Bicycle parts & accessories; fishing equipment & supplies

(P-7721)
TROY LEE DESIGNS LLC (PA)
155 E Rincon St, Corona (92879-1328)
PHONE......................951 371-5219
Dave Bertran, *CEO*
Troy Michael Lee, *President*
Ricardo Gonzalez, *Vice Pres*
Maki Ushiroyama, *Creative Dir*
Bill Keefe, *General Mgr*
▲ EMP: 79
SQ FT: 6,000
SALES (est): 28.3MM **Privately Held**
WEB: www.troyleedesigns.com
SIC: 5091 7336 Sporting & recreation goods; graphic arts & related design

(P-7722)
TUM YETO INC
Also Called: Foundation Super Skateboard
2001 Commercial St, San Diego
(92113-1109)
PHONE......................619 232-7523
Tod Swank, *CEO*
Tara Lewis, *Controller*
▲ EMP: 50
SQ FT: 29,000
SALES (est): 10.3MM **Privately Held**
WEB: www.tumyeto.com
SIC: 5091 5137 Sporting & recreation goods; sportswear, women's & children's

(P-7723)
WARRIOR CUSTOM GOLF INC (PA)
Also Called: Warrior Golf
15 Mason, Irvine (92618-2707)
PHONE......................949 699-2499
Jeremy Rosenthal, *Risk Mgmt Dir*
Brendan M Flaherty, *CEO*
Jorge Festini, *Vice Pres*
Pete Wheelahan, *Vice Pres*
Star Festini, *Executive*
▲ EMP: 118
SQ FT: 20,000
SALES (est): 46.7MM **Privately Held**
WEB: www.warriorcustomgolf.com
SIC: 5091 5941 Golf equipment; sporting goods & bicycle shops

---

5092 Toys & Hobby Goods & Splys Wholesale

(P-7724)
A L S INDUSTRIES INC
1942 Artesia Blvd, Torrance (90504-3599)
PHONE......................310 532-9262
Richard D Smith, *President*
David Albert, *Vice Pres*
▲ EMP: 50 EST: 1970
SQ FT: 70,000
SALES (est): 10.8MM **Privately Held**
SIC: 5092 Video games

(P-7725)
AURORA WORLD INC
8820 Mercury Ln, Pico Rivera
(90660-6706)
PHONE......................562 205-1222
Heui-Yul Noh, *CEO*
Kee Sun Hong, *Exec VP*
Daniel Rah, *CIO*
Maline Sip, *Credit Staff*
Ellie Kim, *Purchasing*
◆ EMP: 110
SQ FT: 100,000
SALES (est): 68.4MM **Privately Held**
WEB: www.auroragift.com
SIC: 5092 Toys
PA: Aurora World Corporation
624 Teheran-Ro, Gangnam-Gu
Seoul 06175

(P-7726)
AZUBU NORTH AMERICA INC
15303 Ventura Blvd # 900, Sherman Oaks
(91403-3199)
PHONE......................310 759-9529
Ian Sharpe, *CEO*
Jason Katz, *COO*
Abe Gottesman, *Vice Pres*
Andrew Greaves, *Vice Pres*
EMP: 50
SALES (est): 10.2MM **Privately Held**
SIC: 5092 5734 Video games; software, computer games

(P-7727)
BANDAI NAMCO ENTRMT AMER INC (DH)
Also Called: Ndga
2051 Mission College Blvd, Santa Clara
(95054-1519)
PHONE......................408 235-2000
Naoki Katashima, *CEO*
Masaaki Tsuji, *President*
Hide Irie, *COO*
Arnaud Muller, *COO*
Shuji Nakata, *CFO*
▲ EMP: 200
SQ FT: 51,118
SALES (est): 119.7MM **Privately Held**
WEB: www.namcobandaigames.com
SIC: 5092 Video games

(P-7728)
BLUE BOX OPCO LLC (DH)
Also Called: Infantino
10025 Mesa Rim Rd, San Diego
(92121-2913)
PHONE......................800 840-4916
Alex Chan, *
Justin Hagert, *CFO*
Blaine Maas, *Controller*
Ricardo Meza, *Manager*
▲ EMP: 52 EST: 2014
SALES (est): 26.6MM **Privately Held**
SIC: 5092 Toys & hobby goods & supplies

(P-7729)
CAPCOM ENTERTAINMENT INC
Also Called: Capcom U.S.a
185 Berry St Ste 1200, San Francisco
(94107-1794)
PHONE......................650 350-6500
Kazuhiro Abe, *CEO*
Mark Beaumont, *COO*
Kiichiro Urata, *COO*
Jason Mueller, *Senior VP*
Ian Atkinson, *Vice Pres*
▲ EMP: 80
SALES (est): 25.1MM **Privately Held**
SIC: 5092 Video games

HQ: Capcom U.S.A. Inc
185 Berry St Ste 1200
San Francisco CA 94107
650 350-6500

(P-7730)
CAPCOM U S A INC (HQ)
185 Berry St Ste 1200, San Francisco
(94107-1794)
PHONE......................650 350-6500
Koko Ishikawa, *President*
Rob Dyer, *COO*
Edmund Wong, *Purchasing*
Bao Le, *Manager*
▲ EMP: 180
SALES (est): 51.9MM **Privately Held**
SIC: 5092 7993 7372 Video games; arcades; prepackaged software

(P-7731)
DELTA CREATIVE INC
2690 Pellissier Pl, City of Industry
(90601-1507)
PHONE......................800 423-4135
William B George, *President*
Martina Mueller, *CEO*
Alexander Ritchie, *Vice Pres*
▲ EMP: 105 EST: 1974
SQ FT: 112,000
SALES (est): 13.3MM
SALES (corp-wide): 11.3B **Privately Held**
WEB: www.deltacreative.com
SIC: 5092 5198 Arts & crafts equipment & supplies; paints
HQ: Dk Household Brands Holding Ag
Muhlebachstrasse 20
ZUrich ZH 8008

(P-7732)
FAO ROC HOLDINGS LLC
Also Called: Fao Schwarz
15 Cushing, Irvine (92618-4220)
PHONE......................949 900-6501
David Conn, *CEO*
David Niggli, *Chief Mktg Ofcr*
Robert Tuscano, *VP Opers*
EMP: 170
SALES (est): 41.7K **Privately Held**
SIC: 5092 7371 Toys & hobby goods & supplies; computer software development & applications

(P-7733)
GROW BRAINS SYSTEM INC
2324 Ocean Park Blvd D, Santa Monica
(90405-5166)
PHONE......................310 428-6445
Bruce Ward, *CEO*
EMP: 50
SALES (est): 1.9MM **Privately Held**
SIC: 5092 Video games

(P-7734)
INTERNATIONAL TOY INC
17682 Cowan Ste 100, Irvine (92614-1609)
PHONE......................949 333-3777
Steve Asher, *President*
EMP: 50
SQ FT: 2,500
SALES (est): 17.5MM **Privately Held**
SIC: 5092 Toys & hobby goods & supplies

(P-7735)
JAKKS SALES CORPORATION
2951 28th St Ste 51, Santa Monica
(90405-2961)
PHONE......................424 268-9444
Stephen Berman, *President*
Joel Bennett, *CFO*
EMP: 50
SALES (est): 5.8MM **Publicly Held**
SIC: 5092 Toys
PA: Jakks Pacific, Inc.
2951 28th St
Santa Monica CA 90405

(P-7736)
JINX INC (PA)
Also Called: Jinx Hackwear/Jinx.com
13465 Gregg St, Poway (92064-7135)
PHONE......................888 546-9266
Sean Gailey, *CEO*
Tim Norris, *COO*
Billy Baggins, *Vice Pres*

Doug Treese, *Vice Pres*
Hope Chris, *Creative Dir*
◆ EMP: 57
SALES (est): 37.1MM **Privately Held**
WEB: www.jinx.com
SIC: 5092 5136 5137 Video games; men's & boys' clothing; women's & children's clothing

(P-7737)
KELLYTOY WORLDWIDE INC
4811 S Alameda St, Vernon (90058-2805)
PHONE......................323 923-1300
Jonathan Kelly, *President*
▲ EMP: 74
SALES (est): 9.6MM **Privately Held**
SIC: 5092 Toys

(P-7738)
MERCHSOURCE LLC (PA)
Also Called: Threesixty Group
7755 Irvine Center Dr, Irvine (92618-2903)
PHONE......................800 374-2744
Johann Clapp, *Managing Prtnr*
Jolene Myers, *CFO*
Paul Sunny, *Finance Dir*
Kirk McLean, *
Mike Roberts, *
◆ EMP: 80
SALES (est): 87.7MM **Privately Held**
WEB: www.merchsource.com
SIC: 5092 Toys & hobby goods & supplies

(P-7739)
MGA ENTERTAINMENT INC (PA)
9220 Winnetka Ave, Chatsworth
(91311-8172)
PHONE......................818 894-2525
Isaac Larian, *President*
Stuart Russell, *Broker*
Trevor Benson, *Purchasing*
AME Cameron, *VP Mktg*
◆ EMP: 300 EST: 1980
SALES (est): 617.7MM **Privately Held**
WEB: www.mgae.com
SIC: 5092 Toys; toys & games

(P-7740)
PERFORMANCE DESIGNED PDTS LLC (HQ)
9179 Aero Dr, San Diego (92123-2411)
PHONE......................323 234-9911
Chris Richards, *
Kathryn Browne, *President*
Todd Koniares, *Vice Pres*
Storm Orion, *Vice Pres*
Bob Picunko, *Vice Pres*
◆ EMP: 64
SQ FT: 18,000
SALES (est): 136.8MM
SALES (corp-wide): 4.1B **Privately Held**
WEB: www.pelicanacc.com
SIC: 5092 Toys & games; video games
PA: Patriarch Partners, Llc
1 Liberty Plz Rm 3500
New York NY 10006
212 825-0550

(P-7741)
RADICA ENTERPRISES LTD
Also Called: Radica USA
333 Continental Blvd, El Segundo
(90245-5032)
PHONE......................310 252-2000
Patrick Feely, *CEO*
◆ EMP: 57
SQ FT: 24,000
SALES (est): 3.6MM
SALES (corp-wide): 4.5B **Publicly Held**
SIC: 5092 Toy novelties & amusements
HQ: Radica Games Limited
C/O Appleby Spurling Hunter
Hamilton

(P-7742)
SOLUTIONS 2 GO LLC
20091 Ellipse, Lake Forest (92610-3001)
PHONE......................949 825-7700
Nima Taghavi, *Mng Member*
Wayne Yodzio, *President*
Michael Maas, *
▲ EMP: 56
SQ FT: 14,000
SALES (est): 243MM **Privately Held**
SIC: 5092 Toys & hobby goods & supplies

P
R
O
D
U
C
T
S
&
S
V
C
S

(P-7743)
STK INTERNATIONAL INC
6160 Peach Tree St, Compton (90220)
PHONE..................................310 720-1277
Stuart Kole, *President*
◆ **EMP:** 70
SQ FT: 120,000
SALES: 12MM **Privately Held**
WEB: www.stkinternational.com
SIC: 5092 5072 5023 Toys; hand tools;
power tools & accessories; home furnishings; kitchenware

(P-7744)
WHAM-O INC
6301 Owensmouth Ave # 700, Woodland
Hills (91367-2265)
PHONE..................................818 963-4200
Raylin Hsieh, *CEO*
Jeff Hsieh, *Chairman*
Todd Richards, *VP Sales*
Thomas Lindahl, *Sales Staff*
Helen Puyot, *Sales Staff*
◆ **EMP:** 59
SALES (est): 16.3MM **Privately Held**
WEB: www.wham-o.com
SIC: 5092 5091 3944 3949 Toys &
games; surfing equipment & supplies; toy
trains, airplanes & automobiles; sporting
& athletic goods

5093 Scrap & Waste Materials Wholesale

(P-7745)
AADLEN BROTHERS AUTO WRECKING (PA)
11590 Tuxford St, Sun Valley (91352-3112)
PHONE..................................323 875-1400
Sam Adlen, *President*
Samuel Lewinstein, *Corp Secy*
Jorge Trujillo, *Opers Mgr*
EMP: 79 EST: 1951
SALES (est): 19.5MM **Privately Held**
WEB: www.aadlenbros.com
SIC: 5093 Metal scrap & waste materials

(P-7746)
ALCO IRON & METAL CO (PA)
2140 Davis St, San Leandro (94577-1062)
PHONE..................................510 562-1107
Kem Kantor, *President*
Michael Bercovich, *COO*
Keith Kantor, *Vice Pres*
Kevin Kantor, *Vice Pres*
Tony Nam, *Vice Pres*
◆ **EMP:** 100
SQ FT: 35,000
SALES (est): 74MM **Privately Held**
SIC: 5093 5051 Metal scrap & waste materials; steel

(P-7747)
AMERICA CHUNG NAM (GROUP) (PA)
1163 Fairway Dr, City of Industry
(91789-2846)
PHONE..................................909 839-8383
Teresa Cheung, *CEO*
Sam Liu, *COO*
Kevin Zhao, *CFO*
Ken Liu, *Vice Pres*
John Wong, *Vice Pres*
▼ **EMP:** 125
SQ FT: 30,000
SALES (est): 200.6MM **Privately Held**
WEB: www.acni.net
SIC: 5093 Waste paper

(P-7748)
AMERICA CHUNG NAM LLC (HQ)
Also Called: A C N
1163 Fairway Dr Fl 3, City of Industry
(91789-2851)
PHONE..................................909 839-8383
Teresa Cheung, *CEO*
Sam Liu, *COO*
Xue Bai, *CFO*
Kevin Zhao, *CFO*
Scott Taylor, *Vice Pres*
◆ **EMP:** 200

SALES (est): 199.7MM
SALES (corp-wide): 200.6MM **Privately Held**
SIC: 5093 Waste paper
PA: America Chung Nam (Group) Holdings
Llc
1163 Fairway Dr
City Of Industry CA 91789
909 839-8383

(P-7749)
AMERICAN METAL & IRON INC
2377 Tulip Rd, San Jose (95128-1141)
P.O. Box 610 (95106-0610)
PHONE..................................408 452-0777
Howard Misle, *President*
Debra L Ginestra, *Principal*
◆ **EMP:** 55
SQ FT: 10,000
SALES (est): 5.8MM **Privately Held**
WEB: www.amerimetals.com
SIC: 5093 Metal scrap & waste materials

(P-7750)
ANGELUS WESTERN PPR FIBERS INC
2474 Porter St, Los Angeles (90021-2511)
PHONE..................................213 623-9221
Greg Rouchon, *President*
Steve Young, *Treasurer*
Tom Rouchon, *Vice Pres*
David Jones, *Admin Sec*
EMP: 51 EST: 1977
SQ FT: 10,000
SALES: 25MM **Privately Held**
SIC: 5093 Waste paper

(P-7751)
B & B PLASTICS RECYCLERS INC (PA)
3040 N Locust Ave, Rialto (92377-3706)
PHONE..................................909 829-3606
Baltasar Mejia, *President*
Bacilio Mejia, *Vice Pres*
Phillip Booker, *Sales Staff*
Martha Martinez, *Sales Staff*
Maria Carreon, *Accounts Exec*
EMP: 66
SQ FT: 100,000
SALES (est): 128.9MM **Privately Held**
SIC: 5093 2673 Plastics scrap; bags: plastic, laminated & coated

(P-7752)
BESTWAY RECYCLING COMPANY INC (PA)
2268 Firestone Blvd, Los Angeles
(90002-1546)
P.O. Box 109, South Gate (90280-0109)
PHONE..................................323 588-8157
Edward Young Kim, *President*
Nam Sook Kim, *Treasurer*
Dong Kim, *Opers Mgr*
▼ **EMP:** 52 EST: 1963
SQ FT: 165,000
SALES (est): 17.4MM **Privately Held**
SIC: 5093 Waste paper; nonferrous metals
scrap; bottles, waste; plastics scrap

(P-7753)
CASS INC (PA)
2730 Peralta St, Oakland (94607-1707)
P.O. Box 24222 (94623-1222)
PHONE..................................510 893-6476
Edward B Kangeter IV, *CEO*
Chal Sulprizio, *President*
Carmen Zeng, *CFO*
William Inman, *Commercial*
◆ **EMP:** 120
SQ FT: 20,000
SALES (est): 56.5MM **Privately Held**
SIC: 5093 Nonferrous metals scrap

(P-7754)
CEDARWOOD-YOUNG COMPANY
Also Called: Allan Company
14618 Arrow Hwy, Baldwin Park
(91706-1733)
PHONE..................................626 962-4047
Ernesto Lopez, *Branch Mgr*
EMP: 55
SQ FT: 10,664

SALES (corp-wide): 299.9MM **Privately
Held**
WEB: www.allancompany.com
SIC: 5093 2611 Waste paper; pulp mills
PA: Cedarwood-Young Company
14620 Joanbridge St
Baldwin Park CA 91706
626 962-4047

(P-7755)
CITY FIBERS INC (PA)
2500 S Santa Fe Ave, Vernon
(90058-1116)
P.O. Box 58646, Los Angeles (90058-0646)
PHONE..................................323 583-1013
David T Jones, *President*
Kipp Jones, *Vice Pres*
Veronika Trujillo, *Executive Asst*
Maria Quiane, *Asst Mgr*
Vanessa Acosta, *Advisor*
EMP: 60
SQ FT: 55,000
SALES (est): 27.2MM **Privately Held**
SIC: 5093 4953 Waste paper; recycling,
waste materials

(P-7756)
CUSTOM ALLOY SCRAP SALES INC (HQ)
2730 Peralta St, Oakland (94607-1707)
P.O. Box 24222 (94623-1222)
PHONE..................................510 893-6476
Chal Sulprizio, *President*
Martha Bisso, *Buyer*
Anne Lee, *Mktg Dir*
Chad Mueller, *Marketing Staff*
Mitchell Donovan, *Maintence Staff*
EMP: 50
SQ FT: 1,000
SALES (est): 7.3MM
SALES (corp-wide): 56.5MM **Privately
Held**
SIC: 5093 Metal scrap & waste materials;
nonferrous metals scrap
PA: Cass, Inc.
2730 Peralta St
Oakland CA 94607
510 893-6476

(P-7757)
FIRMA PLASTIC CO INC
9309 Rayo Ave, South Gate (90280-3612)
PHONE..................................323 567-7767
David A Carpenter, *Vice Pres*
EMP: 434
SALES (est): 8.6MM **Privately Held**
WEB: www.mtlm.com
SIC: 5093 Metal scrap & waste materials
HQ: Metal Management, Inc.
200 W Madison St Ste 3600
Chicago IL 60606
312 645-0700

(P-7758)
GEORGIA-PACIFIC LLC
15500 Valley View Ave, La Mirada
(90638-5230)
PHONE..................................562 926-8888
Jeff McCranie, *Manager*
EMP: 81
SALES (corp-wide): 40.6B **Privately Held**
SIC: 5093 Waste paper
HQ: Georgia-Pacific Llc
133 Peachtree St Nw
Atlanta GA 30303
404 652-4000

(P-7759)
GLOBAL PLASTICS INC
145 Malbert St, Perris (92570-8624)
PHONE..................................951 657-5466
Nadim Salim Bahou, *President*
Patti Gilmour, *CFO*
▲ **EMP:** 120
SQ FT: 55,000
SALES (est): 25MM **Privately Held**
WEB: www.globalpet.com
SIC: 5093 4953 3053 Plastics scrap; recycling, waste materials; packing materials

(P-7760)
GREEN PLANET 21 INC (PA)
336 Adeline St, Oakland (94607-2520)
PHONE..................................510 873-8777
Stephen Sutta, *President*

▲ **EMP:** 50
SQ FT: 10,000
SALES (est): 15.7MM **Privately Held**
SIC: 5093 Waste paper

(P-7761)
GREENPATH RECOVERY WEST INC
Also Called: Greenpath Recovery Recycl
Svcs
330 W Citrus St Ste 250, Colton
(92324-1422)
PHONE..................................909 954-0686
Joe Castro, *President*
Rebecca Somerville, *Opers Staff*
EMP: 60
SQ FT: 90,000
SALES (est): 31.1MM **Privately Held**
SIC: 5093 3089 2821 Scrap & waste materials; plastic processing; injection molding of plastics; plastics materials & resins;
molding compounds, plastics

(P-7762)
JACK ENGLE & CO (PA)
8440 S Alameda St, Los Angeles
(90001-4112)
P.O. Box 1705 (90001-0705)
PHONE..................................323 589-8111
Alan M Engle, *CEO*
Jack Engle, *CEO*
Jason Engle, *Vice Pres*
Julius Miller, *General Mgr*
Sabrina Robinson, *Finance Mgr*
◆ **EMP:** 55 EST: 1965
SQ FT: 25,000
SALES (est): 35MM **Privately Held**
WEB: www.jackengleco.com
SIC: 5093 Ferrous metal scrap & waste;
metal scrap & waste materials

(P-7763)
KINSBURSKY BROS SUPPLY INC (PA)
Also Called: K B I
125 E Commercial St Ste A, Anaheim
(92801-1214)
PHONE..................................714 738-8516
Steven Kinsbursky, *President*
Aaron Zisman, *CFO*
Scott Kinsbursky, *Vice Pres*
Todd Coy, *Admin Sec*
Trevor Henderson, *Software Dev*
▲ **EMP:** 75
SQ FT: 35,000
SALES (est): 37MM **Privately Held**
WEB: www.kinsbursky.com
SIC: 5093 Metal scrap & waste materials

(P-7764)
MIDNIGHT AUTO RECYCLING LLC
434 E 6th St, San Bernardino
(92410-4507)
P.O. Box 24003 (92406-0503)
PHONE..................................909 884-5308
Ted Smith, *Administration*
EMP: 50 EST: 1998
SALES (est): 6.3MM **Privately Held**
SIC: 5093 Automotive wrecking for scrap

(P-7765)
NEW NGC INC
Also Called: Gold Bond Building Products
1040 Canal Blvd, Richmond (94804-3550)
PHONE..................................510 234-6745
John Phillips, *Principal*
JD Cohen, *Marketing Staff*
EMP: 50
SALES (corp-wide): 723.5MM **Privately
Held**
WEB: www.natgyp.com
SIC: 5093 3275 Scrap & waste materials;
gypsum products
HQ: New Ngc, Inc.
2001 Rexford Rd
Charlotte NC 28211

(P-7766)
NEWPORT CH INTERNATIONAL LLC (PA)
1100 W Town And Country R, Orange
(92868-4662)
PHONE..................................714 572-8881

▲ = Import ▼=Export
◆ =Import/Export

Clark Hahne,
Roberts Jesse, *Purchasing*
McCallum Michael, *Purchasing*
Jessica Chavez, *Sales Staff*
Eddy Kuo, *Sales Staff*
◆ **EMP:** 58
SQ FT: 8,300
SALES (est): 207MM **Privately Held**
WEB: www.newportchintl.com
SIC: 5093 Waste paper; plastics scrap

(P-7767)
PAVEMENT RECYCLING SYSTEMS INC (PA)
Also Called: Prsi
10240 San Sevaine Way, Jurupa Valley
(91752-1100)
PHONE..............................951 682-1091
Richard W Gove, *President*
Stephen Concannon, *President*
Debbie Whitson, *COO*
Nathan Beyler, *CFO*
Steve Concannon, *Regional Mgr*
▲ **EMP:** 125
SQ FT: 40,000
SALES (est): 126.7MM **Privately Held**
SIC: 5093 1611 Scrap & waste materials;
surfacing & paving

(P-7768)
PICK-A-PART AUTO WRECKING
9445 Cambridge St, Cypress (90630-2705)
PHONE..............................559 485-3071
Christopher L McElroy, *CEO*
EMP: 70
SQ FT: 1,200
SALES (est): 16.2MM
SALES (corp-wide): 11.8B **Publicly Held**
WEB: www.pickapart.com
SIC: 5093 5531 5015 Automotive wreck-
ing for scrap; automotive parts; automo-
tive parts & supplies, used
HQ: Pick-Your-Part Auto Wrecking
1235 S Beach Blvd
Anaheim CA 92804
800 962-2277

(P-7769)
RALISON INTERNATIONAL INC
15328 Central Ave, Chino (91710-7658)
PHONE..............................909 393-0008
Jihong Luo, *President*
Eric Lao, *Vice Pres*
Garrett Nicco, *Business Mgr*
Joyce Chan, *Purch Mgr*
Eddie Lam, *Manager*
▼ **EMP:** 50
SQ FT: 6,000
SALES (est): 28MM **Privately Held**
SIC: 5093 Waste paper

(P-7770)
RIVERSIDE SCRAP IR & MET CORP (PA)
Also Called: Redlands Recycling
2993 6th St, Riverside (92507-4131)
P.O. Box 5288 (92517-5288)
PHONE..............................951 686-2120
Samuel Frankel, *Ch of Bd*
Daniel Jay Frankel, *President*
Raj Gandhi, *Exec VP*
Muriel K Frankel, *Vice Pres*
EMP: 50
SQ FT: 22,275
SALES (est): 17.2MM **Privately Held**
SIC: 5093 Nonferrous metals scrap; waste
paper; bottles, waste; plastics scrap

(P-7771)
SCHNITZER STEEL INDUSTRIES INC
1101 Embarcadero W, Oakland
(94607-2536)
P.O. Box 747 (94604-0747)
PHONE..............................510 444-3919
Gary Schnitzer, *Vice Pres*
EMP: 100
SALES (corp-wide): 2.1B **Publicly Held**
WEB: www.schn.com
SIC: 5093 Ferrous metal scrap & waste
PA: Schnitzer Steel Industries, Inc.
299 Sw Clay St Ste 350
Portland OR 97201
503 224-9900

(P-7772)
SIERRA INTERNATIONAL MCHY LLC
1620 E Brundage Ln Frnt, Bakersfield
(93307-2756)
P.O. Box 1340 (93302-1340)
PHONE..............................661 327-7073
Phillip Sacco, *Mng Member*
Dean Carpenter, *CFO*
Felipe Guerra, *Officer*
Deanna Perkins, *Human Resources*
Jeff Hannah, *Plant Mgr*
◆ **EMP:** 65
SQ FT: 15,000
SALES (est): 51.1MM **Privately Held**
SIC: 5093 5084 Nonferrous metals scrap;
ferrous metal scrap & waste; industrial
machinery & equipment

(P-7773)
SIMS GROUP USA CORPORATION
Also Called: Sims/LMC Recyclers
1900 Monterey Hwy, San Jose
(95112-6100)
PHONE..............................408 494-4242
Tom Sorci, *Manager*
EMP: 100 **Privately Held**
SIC: 5093 4953 3231 Ferrous metal
scrap & waste; refuse systems; products
of purchased glass
HQ: Sims Group Usa Corporation
600 S 4th St
Richmond CA 94804
510 412-5300

(P-7774)
SIMS GROUP USA CORPORATION (DH)
Also Called: Simsmetal America
600 S 4th St, Richmond (94804-3504)
PHONE..............................510 412-5300
Galdino Claro, *CEO*
Bob Kelman, *President*
Myles Partridge, *CFO*
Jimmie Buckland, *Exec VP*
John Crabb, *Principal*
◆ **EMP:** 100
SQ FT: 4,000
SALES (est): 157.9MM **Privately Held**
SIC: 5093 4953 Ferrous metal scrap &
waste; recycling, waste materials
HQ: Sims Group Usa Holdings Corp
16 W 22nd St Fl 10
New York NY 10010
212 604-0710

(P-7775)
SOS METALS INC (DH)
201 E Gardena Blvd, Gardena
(90248-2813)
PHONE..............................310 217-8848
Kenneth Buck, *CEO*
◆ **EMP:** 165
SQ FT: 115,000
SALES (est): 90.3MM
SALES (corp-wide): 225.3B **Publicly Held**
WEB: www.sosmetals.com
SIC: 5093 5051 Ferrous metal scrap &
waste; ferroalloys
HQ: Precision Castparts Corp.
4650 Sw Mcdam Ave Ste 300
Portland OR 97239
503 946-4800

(P-7776)
SPECIALTY FIBRES LLC (PA)
3201 Dnville Blvd Ste 265, Alamo (94507)
PHONE..............................925 934-8700
Joseph B Scherman, *Mng Member*
◆ **EMP:** 64
SALES (est): 9.4MM **Privately Held**
WEB: www.specialtyfibres.com
SIC: 5093 Waste paper

(P-7777)
STANDARD IRON & METALS CO
4525 San Leandro St, Oakland
(94601-4449)
PHONE..............................510 535-0222
Jason Allen, *Principal*
Lloyd Weinstein, *Corp Secy*
Carolina Garcia, *Traffic Mgr*
▼ **EMP:** 50

SQ FT: 20,000
SALES (est): 22.5MM **Privately Held**
WEB: www.standardiron.net
SIC: 5093 Ferrous metal scrap & waste;
nonferrous metals scrap

(P-7778)
TST INC
Tandem Division
11601 Etiwanda Ave, Fontana
(92337-6929)
PHONE..............................909 590-1098
Andrew D Stein, *CEO*
EMP: 75
SALES (corp-wide): 64.6MM **Privately
Held**
SIC: 5093 Metal scrap & waste materials
PA: Tst, Inc.
13428 Benson Ave
Chino CA 91710
951 737-3169

5094 Jewelry, Watches, Precious Stones Wholesale

(P-7779)
A-MARK PRECIOUS METALS INC (PA)
2121 Rosecrans Ave # 6300, El Segundo
(90245-7528)
PHONE..............................310 587-1477
Gregory N Roberts, *CEO*
Jeffrey D Benjamin, *Ch of Bd*
Thor G Gjerdrum, *President*
Kathleen Simpson Taylor, *CFO*
Carol Meltzer, *Exec VP*
▲ **EMP:** 56
SQ FT: 9,000
SALES (est): 4.7B **Publicly Held**
SIC: 5094 Jewelry; precious metals

(P-7780)
BASK JEWELRY INC
2607 S Main St, Soquel (95073-2409)
PHONE..............................831 479-8849
Steve Battelle, *President*
▼ **EMP:** 100
SQ FT: 2,400
SALES (est): 9.9MM **Privately Held**
WEB: www.bask.com
SIC: 5094 Jewelry & precious stones

(P-7781)
BJS RESTAURANTS INC
3401 Dale Rd Ste 840, Modesto
(95356-0549)
PHONE..............................209 526-8850
Brandon Mynear, *Principal*
EMP: 147
SALES (corp-wide): 1.1B **Publicly Held**
SIC: 5094 Jewelry
PA: Bj's Restaurants, Inc.
7755 Center Ave Ste 300
Huntington Beach CA 92647
714 500-2400

(P-7782)
BUNGALOW 16 ENTERTAINMENT LLC
8113 Melrose Ave, Los Angeles
(90046-7011)
PHONE..............................310 226-7870
▲ **EMP:** 50
SQ FT: 2,000
SALES (est): 4.2MM **Privately Held**
SIC: 5094

(P-7783)
C&C JEWELRY MFG INC
323 W 8th St Fl 4, Los Angeles
(90014-3109)
PHONE..............................213 623-6800
Mikhail Chekhman, *President*
Robert Connolly, *Vice Pres*
▲ **EMP:** 56
SQ FT: 3,000
SALES (est): 28.3MM **Privately Held**
SIC: 5094 3911 Jewelry & precious
stones; jewelry, precious metal

(P-7784)
CHAIN & CHARM INC
Also Called: Chain & Charm Jewelry Mfg
817 San Julian St Ph 1, Los Angeles
(90014-2400)
PHONE..............................213 683-1039
Cheo K Chia, *President*
Meang K Chia, *Vice Pres*
EMP: 75
SQ FT: 26,000
SALES (est): 14.7MM **Privately Held**
WEB: www.chainandcharm.com
SIC: 5094 Jewelry

(P-7785)
CHATHAM INC
300 Rancheros Dr Ste 360, San Marcos
(92069-2970)
PHONE..............................800 222-2002
Harry Stubbert, *CEO*
EMP: 50
SALES (est): 2.1MM **Privately Held**
SIC: 5094 Jewelry & precious stones

(P-7786)
CPI LUXURY GROUP
Also Called: China Pearl
10220 Norris Ave, Pacoima (91331-2217)
PHONE..............................818 249-9888
Harold Jabarian, *CEO*
Kevork Hasbanian, *Vice Pres*
Harry Karagozian, *Accounting Mgr*
▲ **EMP:** 54
SQ FT: 15,000
SALES: 23MM **Privately Held**
WEB: www.chinapearl-usa.com
SIC: 5094 Pearls

(P-7787)
CW WELDING SERVICE INC
761 Majors Ct, Bakersfield (93308-9436)
PHONE..............................661 399-5422
Ellis Firatt, *Branch Mgr*
Rocky Marquez, *General Mgr*
EMP: 51 **Privately Held**
SIC: 5094 5051 1761 Precious stones &
metals; metals service centers & offices;
sheet metalwork
PA: C.W. Welding Service, Inc.
1735 Santa Fe Ave
Long Beach CA 90813

(P-7788)
EMMI INC
Also Called: Emmi Universal Fine Jeweller
631 S Olive St Ste 302, Los Angeles
(90014-3656)
PHONE..............................213 622-7234
Edward Zohrabian, *President*
Isabel Zohrabian, *Treasurer*
▲ **EMP:** 60
SQ FT: 20,000
SALES (est): 12.2MM **Privately Held**
SIC: 5094 Jewelry

(P-7789)
GOLDCO DIRECT LLC
21215 Burbank Blvd # 600, Woodland Hills
(91367-7090)
PHONE..............................818 343-0186
Trevor Gerszt,
Gardiner Adam, *Officer*
Kc Derian, *Executive*
Ben Monaci, *Executive*
Todd Turpin, *Broker*
EMP: 80
SQ FT: 20,000
SALES: 40MM **Privately Held**
SIC: 5094 Precious metals

(P-7790)
MEL BERNIE AND COMPANY INC (PA)
Also Called: 1928 Jewelry Company
3000 W Empire Ave, Burbank
(91504-3109)
PHONE..............................818 841-1928
Melvyn Bernie, *CEO*
▲ **EMP:** 250
SQ FT: 65,000
SALES (est): 55.6MM **Privately Held**
WEB: www.1928.com
SIC: 5094 Jewelry

(P-7791)
NER PRECIOUS METALS INC
640 St Hill St Ste 450, Los Angeles (90014)
PHONE..................310 367-3179
Pedram Shamekh, *CEO*
▲ **EMP:** 60
SQ FT: 900
SALES (est): 5.5MM **Privately Held**
SIC: 5094 5131 5085 Precious metals; piece goods & other fabrics; industrial supplies

(P-7792)
NIXON INC (PA)
Also Called: Nixon Watches
701 S Coast Highway 101, Encinitas (92024-4441)
PHONE..................760 944-0900
Nicholas Stowe, *CEO*
Andrus Laats, *President*
Brian White, *Vice Pres*
Chad Dinenna, *Admin Sec*
Sherman Kori, *Accounting Mgr*
▲ **EMP:** 120
SQ FT: 3,000
SALES (est): 56.3MM **Privately Held**
WEB: www.nixonnow.com
SIC: 5094 5611 5136 Watches & parts; clothing accessories: men's & boys'; leather & sheep lined clothing, men's & boys'

(P-7793)
SWEDA COMPANY LLC
17411 E Valley Blvd, City of Industry (91744-5159)
PHONE..................626 357-9999
Jim Hagan, *CEO*
Kellie Claudio, *Vice Pres*
Scott Pearson, *Vice Pres*
Paul Beck,
Seidler Sweda,
▲ **EMP:** 200
SQ FT: 350,000
SALES (est): 121.4MM **Privately Held**
WEB: www.sweda.com
SIC: 5094 5044 Watches & parts; clocks; calcvlators, electronic

(P-7794)
TACORI ENTERPRISES
Also Called: Tacori By B & T Jewelers
1736 Gardena Ave, Glendale (91204-2907)
PHONE..................818 863-1536
Haig Tacorian, *CEO*
Alred Margousian, *CFO*
Gilda Tacorian, *Vice Pres*
Jocelyn Stock, *Credit Mgr*
Lydia Andonian, *Controller*
▲ **EMP:** 58
SQ FT: 16,000
SALES (est): 65MM **Privately Held**
WEB: www.tacori.com
SIC: 5094 Jewelry

(P-7795)
TOUCAN INC (PA)
Also Called: Tomas Jewelry
824 L St Ste 6, Arcata (95521-5766)
P.O. Box 4899 (95518-4899)
PHONE..................707 822-6662
Thomas S Perrett, *President*
Margaret Carey, *Manager*
▲ **EMP:** 80
SQ FT: 25,000
SALES (est): 18.5MM **Privately Held**
WEB: www.tomasjewelry.com
SIC: 5094 Jewelry; precious metals

5099 Durable Goods: NEC Wholesale

(P-7796)
AGRITEC INTERNATIONAL LTD
Also Called: Cleantech Environmental
5820 Martin Rd, Irwindale (91706-6213)
PHONE..................626 812-7200
Robert Eldon Brown III, *President*
Loretta Ventura, *Office Mgr*
EMP: 50
SQ FT: 5,000

SALES (est): 24MM **Privately Held**
WEB: www.cleantechnv.com
SIC: 5099 Safety equipment & supplies

(P-7797)
ALPHA SYSTEMS FIRE PROTECTION
7356 Fulton Ave, North Hollywood (91605-4113)
P.O. Box 331027, Pacoima (91333-1027)
PHONE..................323 227-0700
Jerry Pivnik, *President*
Jill Pivnik, *Principal*
EMP: 50
SQ FT: 2,776
SALES (est): 5MM **Privately Held**
SIC: 5099 Fire extinguishers

(P-7798)
ARTISAN PICTURES INC
Also Called: Live International
2700 Colorado Ave Fl 2, Santa Monica (90404-5502)
PHONE..................310 449-9200
Jon Feltheimer, *CEO*
Anthony J Scotti, *Ch of Bd*
Steve Beeks, *President*
Amir Malin, *President*
Ronald B Cushey, *CFO*
EMP: 150
SALES (est): 26.9MM
SALES (corp-wide): 3.6B **Privately Held**
SIC: 5099 Video cassettes, accessories & supplies
HQ: Lions Gate Entertainment Inc.
2700 Colorado Ave Ste 200
Santa Monica CA 90404
310 449-9200

(P-7799)
BAY MARINE & INDUS SUP LLC
2900 Main St, Alameda (94501-7522)
PHONE..................510 337-9122
Bill Elliott, *Principal*
James Whitman, *Principal*
EMP: 50
SALES (est): 4.8MM **Privately Held**
SIC: 5099 Durable goods

(P-7800)
BOSSA NOVA ROBOTICS INC (HQ)
610 22nd St Ste 250, San Francisco (94107-3576)
PHONE..................415 234-5136
Bruce McWilliams, *CEO*
Amy Han, *Vice Pres*
Kyle Stanhouse, *Software Engr*
Alex Henning, *Engineer*
Richard Won, *Controller*
▼ **EMP:** 180
SQ FT: 5,000
SALES (est): 4.5MM **Privately Held**
SIC: 5099 Robots, service or novelty

(P-7801)
BRETHREN INC
Also Called: Fire Safety First
1170 E Fruit St, Santa Ana (92701-4205)
PHONE..................714 836-4800
Al Saia, *CEO*
Mike Saia, *Vice Pres*
Peggy Saia, *Admin Sec*
EMP: 50 **EST:** 1984
SQ FT: 4,000
SALES (est): 18.2MM **Privately Held**
WEB: www.firesafetyfirst.com
SIC: 5099 7389 Fire extinguishers; fire extinguisher servicing

(P-7802)
CELLMARK INC (DH)
Also Called: United International
88 Rowland Way Ste 300, Novato (94945-5049)
PHONE..................415 927-1700
Fredrik Anderson, *CEO*
Michael J Cussen, *CFO*
Anthony Costanzo, *Controller*
Junko Bice, *Sales Staff*
◆ **EMP:** 65
SQ FT: 13,000
SALES (est): 142.1MM
SALES (corp-wide): 3.1B **Privately Held**
SIC: 5099 5093 5111 Pulpwood; waste paper; fine paper

HQ: Cellmark Ab
Lilla Bommen 3c
Goteborg 411 0
311 900-07

(P-7803)
CENTERLINE WOOD PRODUCTS
10007 Yucca Rd, Adelanto (92301-2242)
PHONE..................760 246-4530
Michael Rodriguez, *President*
EMP: 99
SALES (est): 2.5MM **Privately Held**
SIC: 5099 Wood & wood by-products

(P-7804)
D J AMERICAN SUPPLY INC
Also Called: American Dj Group of Companies
6122 S Eastern Ave, Commerce (90040-3402)
PHONE..................323 582-2650
Charles Davies, *President*
Alfred Gonzales, *President*
Toby Velazquez, *President*
Jimmy Kan, *IT Specialist*
Ernie Velazquez, *Sales Mgr*
◆ **EMP:** 126
SQ FT: 100,000
SALES (est): 52.1MM **Privately Held**
SIC: 5099 5719 5999 Firearms & ammunition, except sporting; lighting fixtures; theatrical equipment & supplies

(P-7805)
DAMAO LUGGAGE INTL INC
Also Called: Chariot Travelware
1909 S Vineyard Ave, Ontario (91761-7747)
PHONE..................909 923-6531
Moon Woo, *President*
Wendy Fan, *CFO*
Abby Kee, *Director*
Jian Kee, *Director*
Wilson Xu, *Director*
▲ **EMP:** 3014
SQ FT: 60,000
SALES (est): 161.4MM **Privately Held**
SIC: 5099 3161 Luggage; luggage

(P-7806)
DAW INDUSTRIES INC
6610 Nncy Rdge Dr Ste 100, San Diego (92121)
PHONE..................858 622-4955
Hugo Belzidsky, *President*
Stuart Marquette, *Vice Pres*
Nick Burrow, *Human Res Mgr*
▲ **EMP:** 50
SALES (est): 9.4MM **Privately Held**
WEB: www.daw-usa.com
SIC: 5099 Safety equipment & supplies; fire extinguishers

(P-7807)
DZ TRADING LTD
12492 Feather Dr, Eastvale (91752-1483)
PHONE..................951 479-5700
Berenice Monay, *Manager*
EMP: 152
SALES (corp-wide): 59MM **Privately Held**
SIC: 5099 Brass goods
PA: Dz Trading, Ltd.
58 W 40th St Fl 8
New York NY 10018
212 869-3939

(P-7808)
EASTMAN MUSIC COMPANY (PA)
Also Called: Eastmans Guitars
2158 Pomona Blvd, Pomona (91768-3332)
PHONE..................909 868-1777
Saul Friedgood, *CEO*
Qian Ni, *CEO*
Zachary Maltzman, *CFO*
Julie Liu, *Purchasing*
▲ **EMP:** 51 **EST:** 2001
SALES (est): 18.6MM **Privately Held**
WEB: www.eastmanstrings.com
SIC: 5099 3931 Musical instruments; accordions & parts

(P-7809)
FOX LUGGAGE INC
5353 E Slauson Ave, Commerce (90040-2916)
PHONE..................323 588-1688
Wayne Wang, *CEO*
Sherrishan H Lee, *President*
Skip She, *Manager*
▲ **EMP:** 65
SQ FT: 80,000
SALES (est): 10.6MM **Privately Held**
WEB: www.foxluggage.com
SIC: 5099 Luggage

(P-7810)
FRESH PICK PRODUCE
195 San Pedro Ave Ste D, Morgan Hill (95037-5142)
PHONE..................408 315-4612
Stephanie Tsigaris,
EMP: 50
SALES (est): 777.2K **Privately Held**
SIC: 5099 Durable goods

(P-7811)
GENIUS PRODUCTS INC
3301 Expo Blvd Ste 100, Santa Monica (90404)
PHONE..................310 453-1222
Trevor Drinkwater, *President*
Stephen K Bannon, *Ch of Bd*
Edward J Byrnes, *CFO*
▲ **EMP:** 222
SQ FT: 40,520
SALES (est): 132.2K **Privately Held**
SIC: 5099 3652 7819 Video & audio equipment; pre-recorded records & tapes; video tape or disk reproduction

(P-7812)
GOLDEN STATE MEDICAL SUPPLY
5247 Camino Ruiz, Camarillo (93012-8602)
PHONE..................805 477-8966
Benjamin Hall, *CEO*
Thomas Weaver, *CFO*
EMP: 99
SALES (est): 1.4MM **Privately Held**
SIC: 5099 Durable goods

(P-7813)
GOLDEN WEST CUSTOM WD SHUTTERS
20561 Pascal Way, Lake Forest (92630-8119)
PHONE..................949 951-0600
Fax: 949 595-0363
EMP: 50
SALES (est): 3.4MM **Privately Held**
SIC: 5099

(P-7814)
GUTHY-RENKER LLC (PA)
Also Called: Proactiv
100 N Pacific Coast Hwy, El Segundo (90245-4359)
P.O. Box 13670, Palm Desert (92255-3670)
PHONE..................760 773-9022
Greg Renker, *President*
Felipe Jimenez, *Vice Pres*
Laura Lum, *Vice Pres*
Joel Schaeffer, *Vice Pres*
Sam Sheard, *Vice Pres*
▲ **EMP:** 60
SQ FT: 15,000
SALES (est): 270.2MM **Privately Held**
WEB: www.sheercover.com
SIC: 5099 7812 5999 7389 Tapes & cassettes, prerecorded; commercials, television: tape or film; cosmetics; telemarketing services

(P-7815)
GUTHY-RENKER LLC
Also Called: Guthy-Renker Direct
3340 Ocean Park Blvd Fl 2, Santa Monica (90405-3204)
PHONE..................310 581-6250
Bill Guthy, *President*
Jenna Cerone, *Marketing Staff*
EMP: 80

SALES (corp-wide): 270.2MM **Privately Held**
WEB: www.sheercover.com
SIC: 5099 7812 5999 Tapes & cassettes, prerecorded; commercials, television: tape or film; cosmetics
PA: Guthy-Renker Llc
100 N Pacific Coast Hwy
El Segundo CA 90245
760 773-9022

(P-7816)
GYPSUM DRY WALL SUPPLY CO
2049 Senter Rd, San Jose (95112-2600)
PHONE..................408 993-9710
Denise Willis, *Manager*
EMP: 50
SALES (est): 195.5K **Privately Held**
SIC: 5099 Firearms & ammunition, except sporting

(P-7817)
H AND H DRUG STORES INC
Also Called: Western Drug Medical Supply
4692 E Waterloo Rd, Stockton (95215-2309)
PHONE..................209 931-5200
Haig J Youredjian, *Principal*
EMP: 86
SALES (corp-wide): 52.8MM **Privately Held**
SIC: 5099 Brass goods
PA: H And H Drug Stores, Inc.
3604 San Fernando Rd
Glendale CA 91204
818 956-6691

(P-7818)
ICU EYEWEAR INC
Also Called: Cable Car Eyewear
1900 Shelton Dr, Hollister (95023-9498)
PHONE..................831 637-9300
Rick Allen, *Manager*
EMP: 60
SALES (corp-wide): 16.7MM **Privately Held**
SIC: 5099 Sunglasses
PA: Icu Eyewear, Inc.
1900 Shelton Dr
Hollister CA 95023
831 637-9300

(P-7819)
JORGENSEN & SONS INC (PA)
Also Called: Jorgensen & Co
2467 Foundry Park Ave, Fresno (93706-4531)
PHONE..................559 268-6241
Darrell Hefley, *CEO*
Donald Jorgensen, *Ch of Bd*
Leon Young, *President*
Jim Rushing, *Treasurer*
Al V Jorgensen, *Vice Ch Bd*
EMP: 55
SQ FT: 28,000
SALES (est): 30.4MM **Privately Held**
SIC: 5099 1731 Safety equipment & supplies; fire detection & burglar alarm systems specialization

(P-7820)
KAWAI AMERICA CORPORATION (HQ)
2055 E University Dr, Compton (90220-6411)
PHONE..................310 631-1771
Hirotaka Kawai, *President*
Naoki Mori, *President*
Yoshiro Kataoka, *Admin Sec*
Don Mannino, *Master*
Joel Bonifacio, *Manager*
◆ **EMP:** 50
SQ FT: 73,000
SALES (est): 24MM **Privately Held**
SIC: 5099 Pianos

(P-7821)
MENDOCINO FOREST PDTS CO LLC
6500 Durable Mill Rd, Calpella (95418)
PHONE..................707 620-2961
Jon Roi, *Branch Mgr*
EMP: 52
SALES (corp-wide): 134.9MM **Privately Held**
SIC: 5099 Wood & wood by-products

PA: Mendocino Forest Products Company Llc
3700 Old Redwood Hwy # 200
Santa Rosa CA 95403
707 620-2961

(P-7822)
MONOPRICE INC (HQ)
Also Called: Monoprice.com
1 Pointe Dr Ste 400, Brea (92821-7634)
PHONE..................909 989-6887
Bernard Luthi, *CEO*
◆ **EMP:** 115
SQ FT: 30,000
SALES (est): 144.7MM **Privately Held**
SIC: 5099 Video & audio equipment

(P-7823)
MONSTER INC (PA)
Also Called: Monster Products
601 Gateway Blvd Ste 900, South San Francisco (94080-7070)
P.O. Box 435, Brisbane (94005-0435)
PHONE..................415 840-2000
Noel Lee, *President*
Irene Baron, *Vice Pres*
Cris Alqueza, *Technology*
James Takenouchi, *Technology*
Emma Barton, *Recruiter*
▲ **EMP:** 330
SQ FT: 50,000
SALES (est): 229.6MM **Privately Held**
WEB: www.monstercable.com
SIC: 5099 4841 3679 Video & audio equipment; cable & other pay television services; headphones, radio

(P-7824)
MSC CHATSWORTH
9324 Corbin Ave, Northridge (91324-2405)
PHONE..................818 718-7696
Wendy Araiza, *Principal*
EMP: 89
SALES (est): 11.5MM **Privately Held**
SIC: 5099 Durable goods

(P-7825)
NEW CENTURY MEDIA CORP
2727 Pellissier Pl, City of Industry (90601-1510)
PHONE..................562 695-1000
Carson Yu, *President*
Andy Forman, *Vice Pres*
Jennifer Yu, *Vice Pres*
▲ **EMP:** 50
SQ FT: 21,000
SALES (est): 17.8MM **Privately Held**
WEB: www.newcenturymediausa.com
SIC: 5099 Video cassettes, accessories & supplies

(P-7826)
OLIVET INTERNATIONAL INC (PA)
11015 Hopkins St, Jurupa Valley (91752-3248)
PHONE..................951 681-8888
Lydia Hsu, *President*
Andrew Bomes, *President*
David Yu, *CFO*
Jeanelle Harris, *Vice Pres*
Neal Weinstein, *Vice Pres*
▲ **EMP:** 89
SQ FT: 456,000
SALES (est): 180.5MM **Privately Held**
WEB: www.olivetintl.com
SIC: 5099 Luggage

(P-7827)
PRAJIN 1 STOP DISTRIBUTORS INC (PA)
Also Called: Prajin Discount Distributors
5701 Pacific Blvd 5711, Huntington Park (90255-2615)
PHONE..................323 395-5302
Antonio Prajin, *President*
Maria Gina Prajin, *Shareholder*
George Prajin, *Corp Secy*
Anthony Prajin Jr, *Vice Pres*
Peter Prajin, *General Mgr*
EMP: 50
SQ FT: 1,000
SALES (est): 14.1MM **Privately Held**
WEB: www.prajin1stop.com
SIC: 5099 5735 Compact discs; compact discs

(P-7828)
QUEST GROUP (PA)
Also Called: Audioquest
2621 White Rd, Irvine (92614-6247)
PHONE..................949 585-0111
William E Low, *CEO*
Mike McConnell, *CFO*
Joe Anzenberger, *Vice Pres*
David Nichols, *Vice Pres*
Adri Meesters, *Office Mgr*
▲ **EMP:** 66
SQ FT: 45,000
SALES (est): 24.2MM **Privately Held**
WEB: www.audioquest.com
SIC: 5099 Video & audio equipment

(P-7829)
READY AMERICA INC (PA)
Also Called: Quakehold
1399 Specialty Dr, Vista (92081-8521)
PHONE..................760 295-0234
Dean H Reese, *CEO*
▲ **EMP:** 53
SALES (est): 14.5MM **Privately Held**
WEB: www.marlyco.com
SIC: 5099 Safety equipment & supplies

(P-7830)
RGGD INC (PA)
Also Called: Crystal Art of Florida
4950 S Santa Fe Ave, Vernon (90058-2106)
PHONE..................323 581-6617
Randy Greenberg, *CEO*
Douglass Song, *President*
Glenn Knecht, *Admin Sec*
▲ **EMP:** 80
SQ FT: 120,000
SALES (est): 32.4MM **Privately Held**
SIC: 5099 3441 Wood & wood by-products; fabricated structural metal

(P-7831)
ROLAND CORPORATION US (HQ)
5100 S Eastern Ave, Los Angeles (90040-2950)
P.O. Box 910921 (90091-0921)
PHONE..................323 890-3700
Christopher Bristol, *CEO*
Dennis M Houlihan, *Vice Pres*
Mark S Malbon, *Vice Pres*
Charles L Wright, *Vice Pres*
Jun Yamato, *Vice Pres*
◆ **EMP:** 165
SQ FT: 50,000
SALES (est): 82MM **Privately Held**
SIC: 5099 5045 3931 Musical instruments; computer peripheral equipment; organs, all types: pipe, reed, hand, electronic, etc.

(P-7832)
ROSEN ELECTRONICS LLC
2500 E Francis St, Ontario (91761-7730)
PHONE..................951 898-9808
W Thomas Clements, *President*
▲ **EMP:** 75
SALES (est): 15.3MM
SALES (corp-wide): 34.1MM **Privately Held**
WEB: www.rosenentertainment.com
SIC: 5099 3679 Video & audio equipment; liquid crystal displays (LCD)
PA: Aamp Of Florida, Inc.
15500 Lightwave Dr # 202
Clearwater FL 33760
727 572-9255

(P-7833)
RWP TRANSFER INC
Also Called: Recycled Wood Products
1313 E Phillips Blvd, Pomona (91766-5431)
PHONE..................909 868-6882
Chris Kiralla, *President*
EMP: 50
SQ FT: 1,100
SALES (est): 14.1MM **Privately Held**
SIC: 5099 5083 Wood & wood by-products; landscaping equipment

(P-7834)
SAN DIMAS LUGGAGE COMPANY
2095 S Archibald Ave, Ontario (91761-8579)
PHONE..................909 510-8820
Laurent Kabbabe, *Controller*
Vovoama Castro, *Human Res Mgr*
EMP: 60 **EST:** 1977
SALES (est): 12.8MM **Privately Held**
SIC: 5099 Luggage

(P-7835)
SCOPE SEVEN LLC
2201 Park Pl Ste 100, El Segundo (90245-5167)
PHONE..................310 220-3939
Gordon Doran, *Mng Member*
EMP: 62
SALES (est): 6.8MM **Privately Held**
SIC: 5099 Compact discs

(P-7836)
SONY MUSIC ENTERTAINMENT INC
Also Called: Sony Publishers
9830 Wilshire Blvd, Beverly Hills (90212-1804)
PHONE..................310 272-2555
EMP: 250 **Privately Held**
WEB: www.sonymusic.com
SIC: 5099 Phonograph records
HQ: Sony Music Entertainment, Inc.
25 Madison Ave Fl 19
New York NY 10010
212 833-8000

(P-7837)
SUN COAST MERCHANDISE CORP
6315 Bandini Blvd, Commerce (90040-3115)
PHONE..................323 720-9700
Kumar C Bhavnani, *President*
Vinay Arora, *Officer*
Dilip Bhavnani, *Vice Pres*
Vidya Bhavnani, *Admin Sec*
Mukhtar Ahmed, *Technology*
▲ **EMP:** 250 **EST:** 1943
SQ FT: 120,000
SALES (est): 79.5MM **Privately Held**
SIC: 5099 Brass goods

(P-7838)
SUNSCAPE EYEWEAR INC
17526 Von Karman Ave A, Irvine (92614-4258)
PHONE..................949 553-0590
Ali Adam Rizza, *President*
Adam Rizza, *CFO*
Wally Rizza, *Vice Pres*
▲ **EMP:** 78
SQ FT: 10,500
SALES (est): 9.8MM **Privately Held**
WEB: www.isunscape.com
SIC: 5099 Sunglasses

(P-7839)
TRAVELERS CLUB LUGGAGE INC
5911 Fresca Dr, La Palma (90623-1056)
PHONE..................714 523-8808
Peter D Yu, *CEO*
◆ **EMP:** 54
SQ FT: 120,000
SALES (est): 23MM **Privately Held**
WEB: www.travelersclub.com
SIC: 5099 Luggage

(P-7840)
TREEFROG DEVELOPMENTS INC
Also Called: Lifeproof
15110 Ave Of Science, San Diego (92128-3440)
PHONE..................619 324-7755
Gary Rayner, *CEO*
Kevin Morse, *CFO*
Dan Koziol, *Vice Pres*
◆ **EMP:** 75 **EST:** 2009
SQ FT: 20,000

SALES (est): 32.2MM
SALES (corp-wide): 228MM Privately Held
SIC: 5099 Cases, carrying
PA: Otter Products, Llc
   209 S Meldrum St
   Fort Collins CO 80521
   855 688-7269

(P-7841)
TRENDSETTAH USA INC
1420 S Highland Ave L203, Fullerton
(92832-3514)
PHONE..................................888 775-4881
Akrum Alrahib, *CEO*
Sal Kureh, *CFO*
Ramzy Rahib, *Treasurer*
Mousa Rahib, *Admin Sec*
▼ EMP: 63
SQ FT: 40,000
SALES (est): 13.9MM Privately Held
SIC: 5099 Novelties, durable

(P-7842)
TUMI INC
333 Santana Row Apt 230, San Jose
(95128-2007)
PHONE..................................408 244-6512
Laurence Franklin, *President*
EMP: 70
SALES (corp-wide): 177.9K Privately Held
SIC: 5099 Luggage
HQ: Tumi, Inc.
   499 Thornall St Ste 10
   Edison NJ 08837
   908 756-4400

(P-7843)
UNIVERSAL MUS GROUP HLDNGS INC
21301 Burbank Blvd # 100, Woodland Hills
(91367-6679)
PHONE..................................317 871-0319
Steven Margeotes, *Vice Pres*
EMP: 600
SALES (corp-wide): 78.1MM Privately Held
SIC: 5099 Video & audio equipment
HQ: Universal Music Group Holdings, Inc.
   1755 Broadway Fl 6
   New York NY 10019
   212 333-8000

(P-7844)
YALEY ENTERPRISES INC
7664 Avianca Dr, Redding (96002-9703)
P.O. Box 1426, Anderson (96007-1426)
PHONE..................................530 365-5252
Patricia J Yaley, *CEO*
Thomas O'Rourke, *Corp Secy*
Thomas J Yaley, *Vice Pres*
▲ EMP: 50
SQ FT: 30,000
SALES (est): 10.9MM Privately Held
SIC: 5099 3544 Brass goods; special dies, tools, jigs & fixtures

(P-7845)
YAMAHA CORPORATION OF AMERICA (HQ)
Also Called: Yamaha Music Corporation U S A
6600 Orangethorpe Ave, Buena Park
(90620-1396)
PHONE..................................714 522-9011
Hitoshi Fukutome, *CEO*
Terry Lewis, *Senior VP*
Douglas Penstone-Smith, *Vice Pres*
Kevin Mushel, *District Mgr*
Tracy Bargielski, *General Mgr*
◆ EMP: 300
SALES (est): 298.1MM Privately Held
WEB: www.yamaha.com
SIC: 5099 5065 5091 3931 Musical instruments; pianos; sound equipment, electronic; sporting & recreation goods; golf equipment; musical instruments

---

5111 Printing & Writing Paper Wholesale

(P-7846)
DOT LEASING COMPANY
2424 Mcgaw Ave, Irvine (92614-5834)
PHONE..................................949 474-1100
Bruce Carson, *Managing Prtnr*
William Clark, *Partner*
Charles Massingill, *Partner*
Eric Pepys, *Partner*
Bruce M Carson, *Managing Prtnr*
EMP: 151
SQ FT: 40,000
SALES (est): 9.5MM Privately Held
SIC: 5111 Printing & writing paper

(P-7847)
KELLY PAPER COMPANY (HQ)
288 Brea Canyon Rd, Walnut
(91789-3087)
PHONE..................................909 859-8200
Janice Gottesman, *President*
Rick Anderson, *Vice Pres*
Luis Arevalos, *Branch Mgr*
Kyle Domene, *Branch Mgr*
Gary Edwards, *Branch Mgr*
▲ EMP: 50 EST: 1936
SALES (est): 315.7MM
SALES (corp-wide): 4.3B Privately Held
WEB: www.kellypaper.com
SIC: 5111 5943 Printing paper; office forms & supplies
PA: Central National Gottesman Inc.
   3 Manhattanville Rd # 301
   Purchase NY 10577
   914 696-9000

(P-7848)
SPICERS PAPER INC (HQ)
12310 Slauson Ave, Santa Fe Springs
(90670-2629)
PHONE..................................562 698-1199
Janice L Gottesman, *CEO*
Anthony Kennedy, *VP Finance*
Jeff Penney, *Buyer*
Andrew Wylder, *VP Sales*
Terri Wensley, *Marketing Mgr*
▲ EMP: 180
SQ FT: 365,000
SALES (est): 511.3MM
SALES (corp-wide): 4.3B Privately Held
WEB: www.spicers.com
SIC: 5111 Fine paper; printing paper; writing paper
PA: Central National Gottesman Inc.
   3 Manhattanville Rd # 301
   Purchase NY 10577
   914 696-9000

5112 Stationery & Office Splys Wholesale

(P-7849)
5 DAY BUSINESS FORMS MFG INC (PA)
2910 E La Cresta Ave, Anaheim
(92806-1818)
P.O. Box 6269 (92816-0269)
PHONE..................................213 623-3577
Leslie Messick, *President*
Walter Messick, *Shareholder*
EMP: 54 EST: 1976
SQ FT: 22,500
SALES: 11.8MM Privately Held
WEB: 5daybf.com
SIC: 5112 Business forms

(P-7850)
5 DAY BUSINESS FORMS MFG INC
2921 E La Cresta Ave, Anaheim
(92806-1873)
PHONE..................................714 632-8674
Lesley Messick, *Branch Mgr*
Norman Hamamoto, *Chief Mktg Ofcr*
Wendy Schul, *Human Res Mgr*
Scott Kirschner, *Purch Agent*
Todd Kirschner, *Sales Executive*
EMP: 62

SALES (corp-wide): 11.8MM Privately Held
SIC: 5112 Business forms
PA: 5 Day Business Forms Mfg., Inc.
   2910 E La Cresta Ave
   Anaheim CA 92806
   213 623-3577

(P-7851)
A YAFA PEN COMPANY
21306 Gault St, Canoga Park
(91303-2123)
PHONE..................................818 704-8888
Yair Greenberg, *CEO*
Niv Avidan, *Exec VP*
Ken Jones, *Vice Pres*
Anita Sebetic, *General Mgr*
Eddie Olague, *Webmaster*
▲ EMP: 50 EST: 1978
SQ FT: 25,000
SALES (est): 16.1MM Privately Held
WEB: www.aldodomani.com
SIC: 5112 5199 Office supplies; advertising specialties

(P-7852)
ALL PHASE BUSINESS SUPPLIES
1920 E Gladwick St, Compton
(90220-6201)
PHONE..................................310 631-1900
Jeffrey Kraus, *President*
EMP: 50
SQ FT: 10,000
SALES (est): 4.8MM Privately Held
SIC: 5112 5943 Office supplies; office forms & supplies

(P-7853)
BANGKIT (USA) INC
Also Called: Bazic Product
10511 Valley Blvd, El Monte (91731-2403)
PHONE..................................626 672-0888
Handy Hioe, *CEO*
Eric Concepcion, *Vice Pres*
Anita Handojo, *Vice Pres*
Susiana Widyaya, *Office Mgr*
Susy Widjaja, *Credit Mgr*
◆ EMP: 80
SQ FT: 195,000
SALES (est): 49.6MM Privately Held
SIC: 5112 Office supplies

(P-7854)
CARTRIDGE FAMILY INC
Also Called: Cartridge Family Ink
1940 Union St Ste 29, Oakland
(94607-2352)
PHONE..................................510 658-0400
Nate Laskin, *CEO*
EMP: 148
SQ FT: 2,750
SALES (est): 15.5MM Privately Held
WEB: www.cartridgefamily.com
SIC: 5112 5065 5044 7389 Laserjet supplies; facsimile equipment; copying equipment; printers' services: folding, collating

(P-7855)
DIETRICH POST CO INC
945 Bryant St, San Francisco
(94103-4523)
PHONE..................................510 596-0080
EMP: 50
SALES (est): 4.1MM Privately Held
SIC: 5112

(P-7856)
ESSENDANT CO
Also Called: United Stationers
918 S Stimson Ave, City of Industry
(91745-1640)
PHONE..................................626 961-0011
Terry Deines, *Manager*
EMP: 230 Privately Held
WEB: www.ussco.com
SIC: 5112 5044 5021 5943 Office supplies; office equipment; furniture; office forms & supplies
HQ: Essendant Co.
   1 Parkway North Blvd # 100
   Deerfield IL 60015
   847 627-7000

(P-7857)
ESSENDANT CO
5440 Stationers Way, Sacramento
(95842-1900)
PHONE..................................916 344-6707
Greg Birdsall, *Branch Mgr*
Carl Murphy, *General Mgr*
Sheryl Weber, *Safety Mgr*
Kurt Standen, *Opers Staff*
Ted Pinnow, *Facilities Mgr*
EMP: 200 Privately Held
WEB: www.ussco.com
SIC: 5112 Office supplies
HQ: Essendant Co.
   1 Parkway North Blvd # 100
   Deerfield IL 60015
   847 627-7000

(P-7858)
IMAGING TECHNOLOGIES GROUP LLC
Also Called: ltd Print Solutions
5220 Pacific Concourse Dr, Los Angeles
(90045-6277)
PHONE..................................310 638-2500
Benjamin Alexander,
Alyson Zgrabik, *Purchasing*
David Mullen, *Sales Staff*
▼ EMP: 50 EST: 1980
SQ FT: 7,000
SALES (est): 10MM Privately Held
WEB: www.rhinotek.com
SIC: 5112 Computer & photocopying supplies

(P-7859)
JOHN A MAIDA ENTERPRISES
Also Called: Maida Specialties Co
P.O. Box 6144 (95150-6144)
PHONE..................................408 254-3100
Neil Callahan, *President*
Sandra Callahan, *Vice Pres*
EMP: 50 EST: 1968
SQ FT: 17,000
SALES (est): 7.7MM Privately Held
SIC: 5112 5199 5099 Greeting cards; party favors, balloons, hats, etc.; sunglasses

(P-7860)
NAT SIM CORP
Also Called: U S Office & Industry Supply
7405 Woodley Ave, Van Nuys
(91406-2924)
P.O. Box 10540, Canoga Park (91309-1540)
PHONE..................................818 705-3131
Yzes Yallouz, *President*
EMP: 53
SQ FT: 3,000
SALES (est): 6.3MM Privately Held
SIC: 5112 5085 Office supplies; industrial tools

(P-7861)
PENTEL OF AMERICA LTD (HQ)
2715 Columbia St, Torrance (90503-3861)
PHONE..................................310 320-3831
Chotaro Koumi, *President*
Norikazu Hasegama, *CFO*
Nobuo Aihara, *Chief Mktg Ofcr*
Atsumi Nakayama, *Officer*
Minoru Mike Osada, *Exec VP*
▲ EMP: 132 EST: 1966
SQ FT: 46,000
SALES (est): 105MM Privately Held
WEB: www.pentel.com
SIC: 5112 3951 5199 3952 Pens &/or pencils; pens & mechanical pencils; artists' materials; artists' materials, except pencils & leads

(P-7862)
PENTEL OF AMERICA LTD
4000 E Airport Dr Ste C, Ontario
(91761-1592)
PHONE..................................909 975-2200
Steve Mukai, *Manager*
Sean Palmer, *Business Anlyst*
EMP: 50 Privately Held
SIC: 5112 Pens &/or pencils
HQ: Pentel Of America, Ltd.
   2715 Columbia St
   Torrance CA 90503
   310 320-3831

(P-7863)
PUNCH STUDIO LLC (PA)
6025 W Slauson Ave, Culver City
(90230-6507)
P.O. Box 3663 (90231-3663)
PHONE..........................310 390-9900
Todd Kirshner, *Mng Member*
Nathalie Carrer, *CFO*
◆ **EMP:** 230
SQ FT: 106,000
SALES (est): 55MM **Privately Held**
WEB: www.punchstudio.com
SIC: 5112 Greeting cards

(P-7864)
RR DONNELLEY & SONS COMPANY
Also Called: Moore Business Forms
40610 County Center Dr # 100, Temecula
(92591-6021)
PHONE..........................951 296-2890
Rick Budge, *Manager*
EMP: 100
SALES (corp-wide): 6.8B **Publicly Held**
WEB: www.moore.com
SIC: 5112 2761 2752 Business forms;
manifold business forms; color lithography
PA: R. R. Donnelley & Sons Company
35 W Wacker Dr
Chicago IL 60601
312 326-8000

(P-7865)
S P RICHARDS COMPANY
Also Called: S.p Richards
10235 San Sevaine Way # 120, Jurupa Valley (91752-1153)
PHONE..........................951 681-3114
Jay Brooks, *Branch Mgr*
Dennis Brunet, *Accounts Mgr*
EMP: 100
SALES (corp-wide): 18.7B **Publicly Held**
WEB: www.sprichards.com
SIC: 5112 5021 Stationery & office supplies; office furniture
HQ: S. P. Richards Company
6300 Highlands Pkwy Se
Smyrna GA 30082
770 434-4571

(P-7866)
SAFEGUARD BUSINESS SYSTEMS INC
414 N A St, Oxnard (93030)
PHONE..........................805 486-9769
Greg Cook, *Branch Mgr*
EMP: 110
SALES (corp-wide): 2B **Publicly Held**
WEB: www.gosafeguard.com
SIC: 5112 Business forms
HQ: Safeguard Business Systems, Inc.
8585 N Stemmons Fwy 600n
Dallas TX 75247
800 523-2422

(P-7867)
TROWBRIDGE ENTERPRISES (PA)
Also Called: Palace Business Solutions
2606 Chanticleer Ave, Santa Cruz
(95065-1810)
PHONE..........................831 476-3815
Toll Free:..........................888 -
Roy M Trowbridge, *CEO*
Frank H Trowbridge III, *CFO*
Margaret Trowbridge, *Corp Secy*
Todd Trowbridge, *Officer*
Neal Heckman, *Vice Pres*
EMP: 80
SQ FT: 11,000
SALES (est): 32.3MM **Privately Held**
WEB: www.gopalace.com
SIC: 5112 5943 5999 Office supplies; stationery stores; artists' supplies & materials

(P-7868)
VIKING OFFICE PRODUCTS INC (HQ)
3366 E Willow St, Signal Hill (90755-2311)
PHONE..........................562 490-1000
M Bruce Nelson, *President*
Ronald W Weissman, *Senior VP*
Mark R Brown, *Vice Pres*

▲ **EMP:** 292
SQ FT: 187,000
SALES (est): 1.9B
SALES (corp-wide): 11B **Publicly Held**
SIC: 5112 5021 5045 5087 Office supplies; business forms; stationery; office furniture; computers, peripherals & software; janitors' supplies; photographic equipment & supplies; catalog & mail-order houses
PA: Office Depot, Inc.
6600 N Military Trl
Boca Raton FL 33496
561 438-4800

(P-7869)
WARDENS OFFICE INC (PA)
Also Called: Office Furniture Outlet
4101 Technology Dr, Modesto
(95356-9051)
PHONE..........................949 916-5771
Patrick G Warden, *Ch of Bd*
Joe Cunningham, *President*
Chris Peterson, *President*
Jennifer Viss, *COO*
Rochelle Sise, *CFO*
EMP: 52
SALES (est): 18.9MM **Privately Held**
WEB: www.wardensopc.com
SIC: 5112 5021 5199 Office supplies; office furniture; gifts & novelties

---
5113 Indl & Personal Svc Paper Wholesale

(P-7870)
AMERICAN PAPER & PLASTICS INC
Also Called: American Paper & Provisions
550 S 7th Ave, City of Industry
(91746-3120)
PHONE..........................626 444-0000
Daniel Emrani, *CEO*
Rhonda Smith, *President*
Rod Lynch, *Vice Pres*
Dennis Tye, *Vice Pres*
Angel Herandez, *Admin Sec*
EMP: 119
SQ FT: 300,000
SALES (est): 130.1MM **Privately Held**
WEB: www.appinc.com
SIC: 5113 Bags, paper & disposable plastic

(P-7871)
ANDWIN CORPORATION (PA)
Also Called: Andwin Scientific
167 W Cochran St, Simi Valley
(93065-6217)
P.O. Box 689, Woodland Hills (91365-0689)
PHONE..........................818 999-2828
Natalie Sarraf, *CEO*
Abner Levy, *President*
Andrew Fox, *Vice Pres*
Madel Amiscaray, *Executive*
Dave Baltes, *General Mgr*
▲ **EMP:** 110
SALES (est): 60.7MM **Privately Held**
WEB: www.andwin.com
SIC: 5113 5199 5087 5047 Shipping supplies; art goods & supplies; packaging materials; janitors' supplies; hospital equipment & furniture; barium diagnostic agents

(P-7872)
BUNZL DISTRIBUTION CAL LLC (DH)
3310 E Miraloma Ave, Anaheim
(92806-1911)
PHONE..........................714 688-1900
Patrick L Larmon, *President*
Scot Gregory, *General Mgr*
Charles Price, *Auditor*
◆ **EMP:** 98
SQ FT: 150,000
SALES (est): 113.4MM
SALES (corp-wide): 11.6B **Privately Held**
SIC: 5113 Paper & products, wrapping or coarse

HQ: Bunzl Distribution Usa, Llc
1 Cityplace Dr Ste 200
Saint Louis MO 63141
314 997-5959

(P-7873)
BUNZL RETAIL SERVICES LLC
8449 Milliken Ave Ste 102, Rancho Cucamonga (91730-5540)
PHONE..........................909 476-2457
EMP: 87
SALES (corp-wide): 11.6B **Privately Held**
SIC: 5113 Paper & products, wrapping or coarse
HQ: Bunzl Retail Services, Llc
8338 Austin Ave
Morton Grove IL 60053
847 733-1469

(P-7874)
BUNZL USA INC
Also Called: Papercraft Los Angeles
15959 Piuma Ave, Cerritos (90703-1526)
PHONE..........................314 997-5959
Jeff McElroy, *Principal*
EMP: 66
SALES (corp-wide): 11.6B **Privately Held**
SIC: 5113 Industrial & personal service paper
HQ: Bunzl Usa, Inc.
1 Cityplace Dr Ste 200
Saint Louis MO 63141
314 997-5959

(P-7875)
CALIFORNIA SUPPLY INC (PA)
491 E Compton Blvd, Gardena
(90248-2078)
P.O. Box 3906 (90247-7598)
PHONE..........................310 532-2500
Mark Weinstein, *CEO*
Art Gaford, *CFO*
Michael Rosson, *Exec VP*
Mike McMillen, *Vice Pres*
Michel Rosson, *Vice Pres*
▲ **EMP:** 69 **EST:** 1975
SQ FT: 75,000
SALES (est): 70.4MM **Privately Held**
WEB: www.calsupply.com
SIC: 5113 5087 Industrial & personal service paper; janitors' supplies

(P-7876)
CALVEY INCORPORATED
Also Called: Ernest Packaging Solutions
8670 Fruitridge Rd # 300, Sacramento
(95826-9735)
PHONE..........................916 681-4800
A Charles Wilson, *Chairman*
Tim Wilson, *President*
▲ **EMP:** 60
SQ FT: 155,000
SALES (est): 36.1MM
SALES (corp-wide): 240.9MM **Privately Held**
SIC: 5113 Boxes, paperboard & disposable plastic; corrugated & solid fiber boxes
PA: Ernest Packaging
5777 Smithway St
Commerce CA 90040
800 233-7788

(P-7877)
ELKAY PLASTICS CO INC (PA)
6000 Sheila St, Commerce (90040-2405)
PHONE..........................323 722-7073
Louis Chertkow, *President*
Geoffrey Pankau, *CFO*
Noopur Vyas, *Programmer Anys*
Juan Battini, *Technician*
Doron Chertkow, *Project Mgr*
▲ **EMP:** 100 **EST:** 1966
SQ FT: 175,000
SALES (est): 98.2MM **Privately Held**
WEB: www.elkayplastics.com
SIC: 5113 Bags, paper & disposable plastic

(P-7878)
FRICK PAPER COMPANY
Also Called: Paper Mart Indus & Ret Packg
2164 N Batavia St, Orange (92865-3104)
PHONE..........................323 726-8200
John Frick, *Partner*
Thomas Frick, *Partner*
Tom Frick, *Partner*

Carlos Sandoval, *Database Admin*
Calvin Lim, *Technical Staff*
▲ **EMP:** 106
SQ FT: 210,000
SALES (est): 61.1MM **Privately Held**
WEB: www.papermart.com
SIC: 5113 Paper & products, wrapping or coarse

(P-7879)
GAHVEJIAN ENTERPRISES INC
Also Called: Mid Valley Packaging & Sup Co
2004 S Temperance Ave, Fowler
(93625-9759)
P.O. Box 96 (93625-0096)
PHONE..........................559 834-5956
Carrie L Gahvejian, *President*
John Gahvejian, *President*
Lorrie Gahvejian, *Corp Secy*
Erik Creede, *Principal*
Dwayne Harris, *Controller*
◆ **EMP:** 50
SQ FT: 150,000
SALES (est): 54.9MM **Privately Held**
SIC: 5113 Bags, paper & disposable plastic; boxes, paperboard & disposable plastic; folding paperboard boxes

(P-7880)
GEORGIA-PACIFIC LLC
9525 W Nicholas Ct, Visalia (93291-9468)
PHONE..........................559 651-5500
Barbera Fox, *Branch Mgr*
EMP: 150
SALES (corp-wide): 40.6B **Privately Held**
WEB: www.gp.com
SIC: 5113 Corrugated & solid fiber boxes
HQ: Georgia-Pacific Llc
133 Peachtree St Nw
Atlanta GA 30303
404 652-4000

(P-7881)
GEORGIA-PACIFIC LLC
9206 Santa Fe Springs Rd, Santa Fe Springs (90670-2618)
PHONE..........................562 861-6226
EMP: 275
SALES (corp-wide): 40.6B **Privately Held**
SIC: 5113 2653 Corrugated & solid fiber boxes; bags, paper & disposable plastic; boxes, corrugated: made from purchased materials; display items, corrugated: made from purchased materials
HQ: Georgia-Pacific Llc
133 Peachtree St Nw
Atlanta GA 30303
404 652-4000

(P-7882)
GREENLEAF PAPER PRODUCTS
Also Called: Moor Products
26431 Crown Valley Pkwy # 150, Mission Viejo (92691-7201)
PHONE..........................949 348-0048
Greg Mosby, *President*
EMP: 60
SALES (est): 245.7K **Privately Held**
SIC: 5113 Industrial & personal service paper

(P-7883)
MAXCO SUPPLY INC (PA)
605 S Zediker Ave, Parlier (93648-2033)
P.O. Box 814 (93648-0814)
PHONE..........................559 646-8449
Max Flaming, *President*
David Bryant, *COO*
Mike Reitz, *Engineer*
Robert Grote, *VP Mfg*
Jesse Sanders, *Prdtn Mgr*
▲ **EMP:** 200 **EST:** 1972
SQ FT: 8,500
SALES (est): 149.5MM **Privately Held**
SIC: 5113 2436 3554 Shipping supplies; softwood veneer & plywood; box making machines, paper

(P-7884)
MAXCO SUPPLY INC
8419 Di Giorgio Rd, Lamont (93241-2547)
PHONE..........................559 646-6700
Steve Grote, *Principal*
EMP: 83

P R O D U C T S   &   S V C S

SALES (corp-wide): 149.5MM **Privately Held**
SIC: 5113 Bags, paper & disposable plastic
PA: Maxco Supply, Inc.
605 S Zediker Ave
Parlier CA 93648
559 646-8449

(P-7885)
MICHAEL MADDEN CO INC
Also Called: Paper Company, The
2825 Warner Ave, Irvine (92606-4443)
P.O. Box 17807 (92623-7807)
PHONE................................800 834-6248
Jason Tillis, *President*
Jody Madden, *Vice Pres*
Michael Madden, *Vice Pres*
Julie Scheibe, *Vice Pres*
Julie K Scheide, *Vice Pres*
◆ **EMP:** 70
SQ FT: 75,000
SALES (est): 62.2MM
SALES (corp-wide): 1.2B **Privately Held**
SIC: 5113 Industrial & personal service paper
PA: Imperial Bag & Paper Co. Llc
255 Route 1 And 9
Jersey City NJ 07306
201 437-7440

(P-7886)
NEWAY PACKAGING CORP (PA)
1973 E Via Arado, Rancho Dominguez
(90220-6102)
PHONE................................602 454-9000
Russell E Freebury, *President*
Sarah D Giles-Bell, *Vice Pres*
Carole Freebury, *Controller*
Robert Hayward, *Sales Executive*
◆ **EMP:** 60
SQ FT: 36,000
SALES (est): 79.7MM **Privately Held**
WEB: www.newaypackaging.com
SIC: 5113 5084 Shipping supplies; packaging machinery & equipment

(P-7887)
OAK PAPER PRODUCTS CO INC (PA)
Also Called: Oak Distribution
3686 E Olympic Blvd, Los Angeles
(90023-3146)
P.O. Box 23965 (90023-0965)
PHONE................................323 268-0507
Max Weissberg, *President*
Richard Seff, *Ch of Bd*
David Weissberg, *CEO*
David Karr, *COO*
Dick Seff, *Chairman*
▲ **EMP:** 174
SQ FT: 250,000
SALES (est): 141.8MM **Privately Held**
WEB: www.oakdistribution.com
SIC: 5113 5199 5087 2653 Shipping supplies; packaging materials; janitors' supplies; corrugated & solid fiber boxes

(P-7888)
OASIS BRANDS INC
100 S Anaheim Blvd # 280, Anaheim
(92805-3848)
PHONE................................540 658-2830
Lee Shuchun, *Director*
Michelle Wu, *Accountant*
John Bartow, *Sales Staff*
▲ **EMP:** 75
SALES: 156MM **Privately Held**
SIC: 5113 Napkins, paper

(P-7889)
ORORA NORTH AMERICA
Also Called: Mpp San Diego Div 6064
664 N Twin Oaks Valley Rd, San Marcos
(92069-1712)
PHONE................................760 510-7170
Scott Romagnoli, *Manager*
Brian Reynolds, *General Mgr*
Mike Galusky, *Human Res Mgr*
Geraldine Saalfeld, *Purchasing*
Hailing Gu, *Opers Spvr*
EMP: 63 **Privately Held**
SIC: 5113 2653 Paper & products, wrapping or coarse; boxes, corrugated: made from purchased materials

HQ: Orora Packaging Solutions
6600 Valley View St
Buena Park CA 90620
714 562-6000

(P-7890)
ORORA NORTH AMERICA
Mpp Los Angeles Div 6060
3201 W Mission Rd, Alhambra
(91803-1113)
PHONE................................626 284-9524
Marc Fenster, *Manager*
EMP: 140 **Privately Held**
SIC: 5113 2653 Paper & products, wrapping or coarse; boxes, corrugated: made from purchased materials
HQ: Orora Packaging Solutions
6600 Valley View St
Buena Park CA 90620
714 562-6000

(P-7891)
ORORA NORTH AMERICA
Also Called: Landsberg San Diego Div 1007
664 N Twin Oaks Valley Rd, San Marcos
(92069-1712)
PHONE................................760 510-7000
Brian Reynolds, *Branch Mgr*
EMP: 62
SQ FT: 5,000 **Privately Held**
SIC: 5113 2653 Paper & products, wrapping or coarse; boxes, corrugated: made from purchased materials
HQ: Orora Packaging Solutions
6600 Valley View St
Buena Park CA 90620
714 562-6000

(P-7892)
ORORA NORTH AMERICA
Also Called: Corru Kraft Buena Pk Div 5058
6200 Caballero Blvd, Buena Park
(90620-1124)
PHONE................................714 562-6002
Jim Wilczek, *Branch Mgr*
Jim Mers, *Opers Mgr*
John Homolak, *Manager*
EMP: 149 **Privately Held**
SIC: 5113 2653 Paper & products, wrapping or coarse; boxes, corrugated: made from purchased materials
HQ: Orora Packaging Solutions
6600 Valley View St
Buena Park CA 90620
714 562-6000

(P-7893)
ORORA PACKAGING SOLUTIONS (HQ)
Also Called: Landsberg Orora
6600 Valley View St, Buena Park
(90620-1145)
PHONE................................714 562-6000
Bernardino Salvatore, *President*
Bernardino Salvatorre, *President*
David Conley, *CFO*
Steve Monschau, *Vice Pres*
Michael Quigley, *Division Mgr*
▲ **EMP:** 100 **EST:** 1951
SQ FT: 300,000
SALES (est): 2.3B **Privately Held**
WEB: www.amcor.com
SIC: 5113 2653 Paper & products, wrapping or coarse; sanitary food containers; boxes, corrugated: made from purchased materials

(P-7894)
ORORA PACKAGING SOLUTIONS
Also Called: Mpp Brea Div 6079
3200 Enterprise St, Brea (92821-6238)
PHONE................................714 984-2300
Carol Hortick, *Manager*
EMP: 84 **Privately Held**
SIC: 5113 2653 Paper & products, wrapping or coarse; boxes, corrugated: made from purchased materials
HQ: Orora Packaging Solutions
6600 Valley View St
Buena Park CA 90620
714 562-6000

(P-7895)
ORORA PACKAGING SOLUTIONS
Mpp Union City Div 6062
33463 Western Ave, Union City
(94587-3201)
P.O. Box 60000, San Francisco (94160-0001)
PHONE................................510 487-1211
Nafiz Korustan, *Manager*
James Sweeney, *Cust Mgr*
EMP: 95 **Privately Held**
SIC: 5113 2653 Paper & products, wrapping or coarse; boxes, corrugated: made from purchased materials
HQ: Orora Packaging Solutions
6600 Valley View St
Buena Park CA 90620
714 562-6000

(P-7896)
ORORA PACKAGING SOLUTIONS
Also Called: Landsberg Los Angeles Div 1001
1640 S Greenwood Ave, Montebello
(90640-6538)
PHONE................................323 832-2000
Jed Wockenfuss, *Manager*
David Conley, *Finance Mgr*
Mike Hallstrom, *Sales Staff*
EMP: 168 **Privately Held**
SIC: 5113 2653 Paper & products, wrapping or coarse; boxes, corrugated: made from purchased materials
HQ: Orora Packaging Solutions
6600 Valley View St
Buena Park CA 90620
714 562-6000

(P-7897)
ORORA PACKAGING SOLUTIONS
Also Called: Mpp Fullerton Div 6061
1901 E Rosslynn Ave, Fullerton
(92831-5141)
PHONE................................714 278-6000
Carol Hortick, *Branch Mgr*
Bob Deshazo, *VP Sales*
Tony Visciotti, *Maintence Staff*
EMP: 101 **Privately Held**
SIC: 5113 2653 Paper & products, wrapping or coarse; boxes, corrugated: made from purchased materials
HQ: Orora Packaging Solutions
6600 Valley View St
Buena Park CA 90620
714 562-6000

(P-7898)
ORORA PACKAGING SOLUTIONS
Also Called: Corru Kraft Fullerton Div 5068
1911 E Rosslynn Ave, Fullerton
(92831-5141)
PHONE................................714 773-0124
Ron Crawford, *Manager*
Frank McDonald, *Maint Spvr*
EMP: 85 **Privately Held**
SIC: 5113 2653 Paper & products, wrapping or coarse; boxes, corrugated: made from purchased materials
HQ: Orora Packaging Solutions
6600 Valley View St
Buena Park CA 90620
714 562-6000

(P-7899)
P & R PAPER SUPPLY CO INC (PA)
1898 E Colton Ave, Redlands
(92374-9798)
P.O. Box 590 (92373-0201)
PHONE................................909 389-1811
Mark S Maiberger, *CEO*
Joe Maiberger, *CFO*
Luke Maiberger, *Vice Pres*
Amanda Stromsheim, *Branch Mgr*
Renee Berry, *Executive Asst*
▲ **EMP:** 103
SQ FT: 75,000

SALES (est): 102.2MM **Privately Held**
WEB: www.prpaper.com
SIC: 5113 5169 5149 5072 Paper & products, wrapping or coarse; chemicals & allied products; groceries & related products; hardware; commercial equipment

(P-7900)
PACIFIC PAPER CONVERTING INC (PA)
Also Called: Paper Cutters
6023 Bandini Blvd, Los Angeles
(90040-2904)
PHONE................................323 888-1330
Susan Feinstein, *President*
Beth Feinstein Thurber, *Vice Pres*
EMP: 70
SQ FT: 150,000
SALES (est): 20.1MM **Privately Held**
SIC: 5113 Industrial & personal service paper

(P-7901)
PACKAGING INNOVATORS LLC
6650 National Dr, Livermore (94550-8802)
P.O. Box 1110 (94551-1110)
PHONE................................925 371-2000
William E Mazzocco, *President*
Beverly J Flynt, *Corp Secy*
Mark Andrew Mazzocco, *Vice Pres*
Mark Mazzocco, *Vice Pres*
Ignacio Maciel, *Plant Supt*
▲ **EMP:** 90
SQ FT: 114,000
SALES (est): 53.3MM
SALES (corp-wide): 222.8MM **Privately Held**
WEB: www.callpic.com
SIC: 5113 2653 3993 Shipping supplies; corrugated & solid fiber boxes; display items, solid fiber: made from purchased materials; signs & advertising specialties
PA: Golden West Packaging Group Llc
8333 24th Ave
Sacramento CA 95826
404 345-8365

(P-7902)
ROYAL PAPER CORP (PA)
Also Called: Royal Supply Midwest
10232 Palm Dr, Santa Fe Springs
(90670-3368)
PHONE................................562 903-9030
Michael Rashtchi, *CEO*
George ABI-Aad, *President*
Marianne ABI-Aad, *Exec VP*
John Soon, *Vice Pres*
Johnathan Soon, *Vice Pres*
▲ **EMP:** 60
SQ FT: 65,000
SALES (est): 53.2MM **Privately Held**
WEB: www.royal-paper.com
SIC: 5113 5087 Containers, paper & disposable plastic; paper & products, wrapping or coarse; cleaning & maintenance equipment & supplies

(P-7903)
SOLARIS PAPER INC (PA)
100 S Anaheim Blvd # 280, Anaheim
(92805-3807)
PHONE................................562 653-1680
Stephen Maher, *CEO*
Andre Soetjahja, *COO*
Steve KAO, *Vice Pres*
Corey Rodriguez, *Vice Pres*
Chia-Shih Yoh, *Info Tech Dir*
▲ **EMP:** 84
SQ FT: 200,000
SALES (est): 244.8MM **Privately Held**
SIC: 5113 Industrial & personal service paper

(P-7904)
UNISOURCE PACKAGING INC
4225 Hacienda Dr Ste A, Pleasanton
(94588-2720)
P.O. Box 8803 (94588)
PHONE................................925 227-6000
Allan Dragone, *CEO*
▲ **EMP:** 112
SALES (est): 21.8MM
SALES (corp-wide): 8.7B **Publicly Held**
WEB: www.unisourcelink.com
SIC: 5113 Shipping supplies

HQ: Veritiv Operating Company
1000 Abernathy Rd Bldg 4
Atlanta GA 30328
770 391-8200

(P-7905)
VERITIV OPERATING COMPANY
Northern California Mkt Area
4395 S Minnewawa Ave # 101, Fresno
(93725-9479)
P.O. Box 11368 (93773-1368)
PHONE.................................559 268-0467
Fax: 559 233-9136
EMP: 90
SALES (corp-wide): 8.3B Publicly Held
SIC: 5113
HQ: Veritiv Operating Company
1000 Abernathy Rd
Atlanta GA 30328
770 391-8200

(P-7906)
VERITIV OPERATING COMPANY
Also Called: International Paper
15005 Northam St, La Mirada
(90638-5759)
PHONE.................................714 690-4000
Dale Alby, Manager
EMP: 100
SALES (corp-wide): 8.7B Publicly Held
WEB: www.internationalpaper.com
SIC: 5113 5111 Industrial & personal service paper; printing & writing paper
HQ: Veritiv Operating Company
1000 Abernathy Rd Bldg 4
Atlanta GA 30328
770 391-8200

(P-7907)
VERITIV OPERATING COMPANY
Also Called: Northern California Mkt Area
1701 National Dr Ste 110, Sacramento
(95834-2915)
PHONE.................................916 283-2160
Rich Griffin, Manager
EMP: 100
SALES (corp-wide): 8.7B Publicly Held
WEB: www.unisourcelink.com
SIC: 5113 Industrial & personal service paper
HQ: Veritiv Operating Company
1000 Abernathy Rd Bldg 4
Atlanta GA 30328
770 391-8200

(P-7908)
VERITIV OPERATING COMPANY
International Paper
345 Schwerin St, San Francisco
(94134-3246)
PHONE.................................415 586-9160
Jim Teahan, Manager
EMP: 63
SALES (corp-wide): 8.7B Publicly Held
WEB: www.internationalpaper.com
SIC: 5113 Industrial & personal service paper
HQ: Veritiv Operating Company
1000 Abernathy Rd Bldg 4
Atlanta GA 30328
770 391-8200

(P-7909)
VERITIV OPERATING COMPANY
Also Called: Southern California Mkt Area
13217 S Figueroa St, Los Angeles
(90061-1139)
PHONE.................................310 527-3000
Chris Hendrix, Manager
EMP: 200
SQ FT: 13,000
SALES (corp-wide): 8.7B Publicly Held
WEB: www.unisourcelink.com
SIC: 5113 Industrial & personal service paper
HQ: Veritiv Operating Company
1000 Abernathy Rd Bldg 4
Atlanta GA 30328
770 391-8200

(P-7910)
VERITIV OPERATING COMPANY
Also Called: Southern California Mkt Area
2600 Commerce Way, Commerce
(90040-1413)
P.O. Box 910907, Los Angeles (90091-0907)
PHONE.................................323 725-3700
Garryl Lasayette, Manager
EMP: 200
SALES (corp-wide): 8.7B Publicly Held
WEB: www.unisourcelink.com
SIC: 5113 Industrial & personal service paper
HQ: Veritiv Operating Company
1000 Abernathy Rd Bldg 4
Atlanta GA 30328
770 391-8200

(P-7911)
VERITIV OPERATING COMPANY
Also Called: Unisource Maint Sup Systems
20 Centerpointe Dr # 130, La Palma
(90623-2505)
PHONE.................................714 690-6600
Jim Speights, Manager
EMP: 300
SALES (corp-wide): 8.7B Publicly Held
WEB: www.unisourcelink.com
SIC: 5113 Industrial & personal service paper
HQ: Veritiv Operating Company
1000 Abernathy Rd Bldg 4
Atlanta GA 30328
770 391-8200

(P-7912)
VITCO DISTRIBUTORS INC
Also Called: Vitco Food Service
715 E California St, Ontario (91761-1814)
PHONE.................................909 355-1300
Kostas Vitakis, President
Emmanuel Vitakis, Treasurer
Deeann Combs, Vice Pres
Terry Morvan, Vice Pres
Scott Seward, Purch Mgr
EMP: 60
SQ FT: 20,000
SALES (est): 65.4MM Privately Held
SIC: 5113 Disposable plates, cups, napkins & eating utensils

5122 Drugs, Drug Proprietaries & Sundries Wholesale

(P-7913)
ACCESS BIOLOGICALS LLC
995 Park Center Dr, Vista (92081-8312)
PHONE.................................760 931-8444
Barry Plost, Mng Member
Roger Weiss, Lab Dir
Susan Mills, Accounting Dir
Kathleen Nelson, Asst Controller
Ed Marsh, Opers Staff
EMP: 71
SQ FT: 1,000
SALES (est): 37.8MM Privately Held
SIC: 5122 Biologicals & allied products

(P-7914)
AGILENT TECHNOLOGIES INC
6392 Via Real, Carpinteria (93013-2921)
PHONE.................................805 566-6655
Nelly Risdon, Manager
EMP: 225
SALES (corp-wide): 4.9B Publicly Held
SIC: 5122 3841 Biologicals & allied products; diagnostic apparatus, medical
PA: Agilent Technologies, Inc.
5301 Stevens Creek Blvd
Santa Clara CA 95051
408 345-8886

(P-7915)
AMERISOURCEBERGEN CORPORATION
500 N State College Blvd # 900, Orange
(92868-1604)
P.O. Box 5915 (92863-5915)
PHONE.................................714 704-4407
John McAlpine, Branch Mgr

Liz Carbon, Vice Pres
Tamara Andervich, Technical Staff
Wesley Behar, Sales Staff
EMP: 122
SALES (corp-wide): 167.9B Publicly Held
SIC: 5122 Pharmaceuticals
PA: Amerisourcebergen Corporation
1300 Morris Dr Ste 100
Chesterbrook PA 19087
610 727-7000

(P-7916)
AMERISOURCEBERGEN CORPORATION
215 Deininger Cir, Corona (92880-1707)
PHONE.................................951 493-2339
EMP: 122
SALES (corp-wide): 167.9B Publicly Held
SIC: 5122 Drugs & drug proprietaries
PA: Amerisourcebergen Corporation
1300 Morris Dr Ste 100
Chesterbrook PA 19087
610 727-7000

(P-7917)
AMERISOURCEBERGEN DRUG CORP
Also Called: ABC Valencia
24903 Avenue Kearny, Valencia
(91355-1252)
PHONE.................................661 257-6400
Ron Green, Manager
Henry McGee, Bd of Directors
Mike Quick, Vice Pres
Douglas Robinson, Vice Pres
Tina Peterson, Program Mgr
EMP: 150
SALES (corp-wide): 167.9B Publicly Held
WEB: www.amerisourcebergen.net
SIC: 5122 4225 Pharmaceuticals; general warehousing & storage
HQ: Amerisourcebergen Drug Corporation
1300 Morris Dr Ste 100
Chesterbrook PA 19087
610 727-7000

(P-7918)
AMERISOURCEBERGEN DRUG CORP
Also Called: ABC Sacramento Striker
1325 Striker Ave, Sacramento
(95834-1164)
PHONE.................................916 830-4500
Bruce Bennett, Branch Mgr
Randy Howery, Research
Ida Henson, Technical Staff
Sandy Bones, Finance
EMP: 102
SALES (corp-wide): 167.9B Publicly Held
WEB: www.amerisourcebergen.net
SIC: 5122 Pharmaceuticals
HQ: Amerisourcebergen Drug Corporation
1300 Morris Dr Ste 100
Chesterbrook PA 19087
610 727-7000

(P-7919)
AMERISOURCEBERGEN DRUG CORP
Also Called: ABC Corona
1851 California Ave, Corona (92881-6477)
PHONE.................................951 371-2000
Joe Cheney, Manager
Mark Brown, Executive
Lori Bunton, Technology
David Ammeraal, Manager
EMP: 200
SALES (corp-wide): 167.9B Publicly Held
WEB: www.amerisourcebergen.net
SIC: 5122 4225 Pharmaceuticals; general warehousing & storage
HQ: Amerisourcebergen Drug Corporation
1300 Morris Dr Ste 100
Chesterbrook PA 19087
610 727-7000

(P-7920)
BAXTER HEALTHCARE CORPORATION
1 Baxter Way Ste 100, Westlake Village
(91362-3813)
PHONE.................................805 372-3000
John Bacich, President
Barry Deutsch, President
Simon Bhasin, Director
Patrick Gavit, Director
Bill Krosky, Manager
EMP: 1000
SALES (corp-wide): 11.1B Publicly Held
SIC: 5122 2834 2836 5047 Drugs, proprietaries & sundries; solutions, pharmaceutical; biological products, except diagnostic; medical equipment & supplies
HQ: Baxter Healthcare Corporation
1 Baxter Pkwy
Deerfield IL 60015
224 948-2000

(P-7921)
BEAUTY 21 COSMETICS INC
Also Called: L A Girl
2021 S Archibald Ave, Ontario
(91761-8535)
PHONE.................................909 945-2220
Chafe Trinh, Principal
Kim Hamilton, Manager
◆ EMP: 105
SQ FT: 250,000
SALES (est): 80.9MM Privately Held
WEB: www.lagirlusa.com
SIC: 5122 2844 Cosmetics; toilet preparations

(P-7922)
BERGEN BRUNSWIG DRUG COMPANY
4000 W Metropolitan Dr # 200, Orange
(92868-3503)
PHONE.................................714 385-4000
Brent Martini, President
John H Mc Alpine, CFO
John McAlpine, CFO
Doug Batezel,
EMP: 2845
SALES (est): 177.9MM Privately Held
SIC: 5122 Pharmaceuticals

(P-7923)
BRIGHT PHARMACEUTICAL SERVICES
4570 Van Nuys Blvd, Sherman Oaks
(91403)
PHONE.................................818 981-9100
Alison Macpherson, President
Kadam Freeman, Managing Prtnr
EMP: 55
SQ FT: 2,500
SALES (est): 12.7MM Privately Held
WEB: www.brightps.com
SIC: 5122 Pharmaceuticals

(P-7924)
BRYANT RANCH PREPACK
1919 N Victory Pl, Burbank (91504-3425)
PHONE.................................818 764-7225
Sanjay Anand, President
EMP: 50
SALES (est): 20.7MM Privately Held
SIC: 5122 Pharmaceuticals

(P-7925)
CALIFORNIA SUNCARE INC
Also Called: California Tan
12777 W Jefferson Blvd, Los Angeles
(90066-7048)
PHONE.................................310 578-4400
Duncan Robins, CEO
Sandy Kagan, CFO
EMP: 77
SALES (est): 7.1MM Privately Held
WEB: www.californiatan.com
SIC: 5122 5199 Cosmetics, perfumes & hair products; pet supplies

(P-7926)
CARDINAL HEALTH INC
793 Via Lata, Colton (92324-3930)
PHONE.................................909 824-1820
Dennis Kephert, Manager
John A Fiacco, Treasurer
Rebecca McGrath, Vice Pres

Steve Grzymkowski, *Business Dir*
Michael Clark, *Engineer*
EMP: 74
SALES (corp-wide): 145.5B **Publicly Held**
SIC: 5122 Pharmaceuticals
PA: Cardinal Health, Inc.
　　7000 Cardinal Pl
　　Dublin OH 43017
　　614 757-5000

(P-7927)
CARDINAL HEALTH INC
3238 Dwight Rd, Elk Grove (95758-6439)
PHONE..........................916 372-9880
Trey Almonza, *Manager*
Craig Sitze, *Analyst*
Norma Garcia, *Opers Staff*
EMP: 200
SALES (corp-wide): 145.5B **Publicly Held**
SIC: 5122 Pharmaceuticals
PA: Cardinal Health, Inc.
　　7000 Cardinal Pl
　　Dublin OH 43017
　　614 757-5000

(P-7928)
CARDINAL HEALTH INC
700 Vaughn Rd, Dixon (95620-9226)
PHONE..........................530 406-3600
Dan Evert, *Branch Mgr*
Rhonda Elliott, *Sales Staff*
EMP: 230
SALES (corp-wide): 145.5B **Publicly Held**
SIC: 5122 Drugs, proprietaries & sundries
PA: Cardinal Health, Inc.
　　7000 Cardinal Pl
　　Dublin OH 43017
　　614 757-5000

(P-7929)
CARDINAL HEALTH INC
1007 Canal Blvd, Richmond (94804-3549)
PHONE..........................510 232-2030
Alan Kim, *Branch Mgr*
Shannon Byrne, *Administration*
EMP: 74
SALES (corp-wide): 145.5B **Publicly Held**
SIC: 5122 Pharmaceuticals
PA: Cardinal Health, Inc.
　　7000 Cardinal Pl
　　Dublin OH 43017
　　614 757-5000

(P-7930)
CARDINAL HEALTH INC
7330 N Palm Ave Ste 104, Fresno
(93711-5768)
PHONE..........................559 448-0788
Mark Stassen, *Branch Mgr*
Laurel Bejeckian, *Vice Pres*
Evelyn Lvas, *Purchasing*
Marsha Aragon, *Opers Staff*
Steven Grant, *Sales Mgr*
EMP: 74
SALES (corp-wide): 145.5B **Publicly Held**
SIC: 5122 Pharmaceuticals
PA: Cardinal Health, Inc.
　　7000 Cardinal Pl
　　Dublin OH 43017
　　614 757-5000

(P-7931)
CARDINAL HEALTH INC
1935 Pine St, Redding (96001-1921)
PHONE..........................530 225-8735
Kurt Dunphy, *Branch Mgr*
EMP: 74
SALES (corp-wide): 145.5B **Publicly Held**
SIC: 5122 Pharmaceuticals
PA: Cardinal Health, Inc.
　　7000 Cardinal Pl
　　Dublin OH 43017
　　614 757-5000

(P-7932)
CARDINAL HEALTH INC
4551 E Philadelphia St, Ontario
(91761-2316)
PHONE..........................909 605-0900
Mark Summers, *Manager*

Bran-Silva Vanessa, *Analyst*
Robin Lockwood, *Human Res Mgr*
Jeremy Fortune, *Opers Mgr*
Brian Merrill, *Warehouse Mgr*
EMP: 73
SALES (corp-wide): 145.5B **Publicly Held**
SIC: 5122 Pharmaceuticals
PA: Cardinal Health, Inc.
　　7000 Cardinal Pl
　　Dublin OH 43017
　　614 757-5000

(P-7933)
CARDINAL HEALTH INC
Also Called: Whitmire Distribution
27680 Avenue Mentry, Valencia
(91355-1200)
PHONE..........................661 295-6100
Stewert Levin, *Manager*
EMP: 120
SALES (corp-wide): 145.5B **Publicly Held**
SIC: 5122 Pharmaceuticals
PA: Cardinal Health, Inc.
　　7000 Cardinal Pl
　　Dublin OH 43017
　　614 757-5000

(P-7934)
CC WELLNESS LLC (HQ)
Also Called: United Consortium
29000 Hancock Pkwy, Valencia
(91355-1007)
PHONE..........................661 295-1700
Marek Jan Olszewski, *CEO*
Joe Walls, *COO*
Octavio Cervantes, *Prdtn Mgr*
▲ **EMP:** 55 **EST:** 1999
SQ FT: 38,000
SALES (est): 15MM **Privately Held**
SIC: 5122 Pharmaceuticals
PA: Cc Wellness Acquisition Llc
　　29000 Hancock Pkwy
　　Valencia CA 91355
　　661 295-1700

(P-7935)
CELGENE CORPORATION
Also Called: Celgene Signal Research
10300 Campus Point Dr # 100, San Diego
(92121-1504)
PHONE..........................858 677-0034
EMP: 134
SALES (corp-wide): 11.2B **Publicly Held**
SIC: 5122
PA: Celgene Corporation
　　86 Morris Ave
　　Summit NJ 07901
　　908 673-9000

(P-7936)
CELL DESIGN LABS INC
5858 Horton St Ste 240, Emeryville
(94608-2018)
PHONE..........................510 398-0501
Brian Atwood, *CEO*
Peter Emtage, *Officer*
Roger Sidhu, *Officer*
EMP: 50
SQ FT: 19,000
SALES: 1MM
SALES (corp-wide): 22.1B **Publicly Held**
SIC: 5122 Biotherapeutics
PA: Gilead Sciences, Inc.
　　333 Lakeside Dr
　　Foster City CA 94404
　　650 574-3000

(P-7937)
CENTRAL REFILL PHARMACEUTICALS
Also Called: Central Retail Pharmaceuticals
9521 Dalen St, Downey (90242-4847)
PHONE..........................562 401-4214
Benjamin Chu, *Owner*
EMP: 100 **EST:** 2008
SALES (est): 5.3MM **Privately Held**
SIC: 5122 Pharmaceuticals

(P-7938)
COLORESCIENCE INC
2141 Palomar Airport Rd R, Carlsbad
(92011-1423)
PHONE..........................866 426-5673
Mary Fisher, *CEO*

Steve P Loomis, *CFO*
Steve Loomis, *CFO*
Josie Juncal, *Ch Credit Ofcr*
Ted Ebel, *Officer*
▲ **EMP:** 111
SQ FT: 15,000
SALES (est): 2.1MM **Privately Held**
WEB: www.colorescience.com
SIC: 5122 2844 Cosmetics; cosmetic preparations

(P-7939)
COUNTER BRANDS LLC (PA)
Also Called: Beautycounter
1733 Ocean Ave, Santa Monica
(90401-3223)
PHONE..........................310 828-0111
Gregg Renfrew, *CEO*
Ana Badell, *COO*
Tony Prudhomme, *CFO*
Patty Wu, *Ch Credit Ofcr*
Don Florence, *Officer*
▲ **EMP:** 57
SALES (est): 106.8MM **Privately Held**
SIC: 5122 Cosmetics

(P-7940)
COUNTY OF LOS ANGELES
Also Called: Health Services, Dept of
1000 W Crson St Bsmnt 404 Basement,
Torrance (90502)
PHONE..........................310 222-2357
Wes Kamikawa, *Director*
EMP: 95 **Privately Held**
WEB: www.co.la.ca.us
SIC: 5122 9431 Pharmaceuticals; administration of public health programs;
PA: County Of Los Angeles
　　500 W Temple St Ste 437
　　Los Angeles CA 90012
　　213 974-1101

(P-7941)
DR FRESH LLC
Also Called: High Ridge Brands
6 Centerpointe Dr Ste 640, La Palma
(90623-2587)
PHONE..........................714 690-1573
Doug Corbett, *CEO*
Mark Walsh, *Officer*
Daniel Enriquez, *Vice Pres*
Nikhil Jindal, *Accounting Mgr*
Marcus Pease, *Sales Staff*
◆ **EMP:** 100 **EST:** 2012
SQ FT: 55,000
SALES (est): 89.3MM **Privately Held**
SIC: 5122 Toothbrushes, except electric
PA: High Ridge Brands Co.
　　333 Ludlow St Ste 2
　　Stamford CT 06902

(P-7942)
FENTY BEAUTY LLC
425 Market St Fl 19, San Francisco
(94105-2425)
PHONE..........................818 973-2709
David Suliteanu, *Mng Member*
Andrea Freedman, *VP Finance*
Kristin Walcott,
Jean Vazquez, *Senior Mgr*
Michelle Liu, *Director*
EMP: 200
SALES (est): 10.7MM **Privately Held**
SIC: 5122 Cosmetics

(P-7943)
FFF ENTERPRISES INC (PA)
44000 Winchester Rd, Temecula
(92590-2578)
PHONE..........................951 296-2500
Patrick M Schmidt, *CEO*
Richard Bagley, *Vice Pres*
Bob Coates, *Vice Pres*
Vanessa Koch, *Vice Pres*
Philip Quarles, *Executive*
EMP: 300
SQ FT: 162,000
SALES (est): 230.5MM **Privately Held**
WEB: www.fffenterprises.com
SIC: 5122 Pharmaceuticals

(P-7944)
GALE LINA INC
230 S 9th Ave, City of Industry
(91746-3309)
PHONE..........................909 595-8898
John Chen, *CEO*
Lina Chen, *CFO*
▲ **EMP:** 100 **EST:** 1991
SALES (est): 49MM **Privately Held**
SIC: 5122 Cosmetics

(P-7945)
GLAXOSMITHKLINE LLC
3366 N Torrey Pines Ct, La Jolla
(92037-1025)
PHONE..........................858 260-5900
Nitsan Kolikant, *Sales Staff*
Diane Dire, *Accounts Mgr*
EMP: 50
SALES (corp-wide): 39.5B **Privately Held**
SIC: 5122 2834 Toothbrushes, except electric; pharmaceutical preparations
HQ: Glaxosmithkline Llc
　　5 Crescent Dr
　　Philadelphia PA 19112
　　215 751-4000

(P-7946)
GOLDEN N-LIFE DIAMITE INTL INC (PA)
3500 Gateway Blvd, Fremont
(94538-6584)
PHONE..........................510 651-0405
Roget Uys, *CEO*
Daniel L Lewis, *COO*
Robert Galano, *Vice Pres*
▲ **EMP:** 80
SQ FT: 66,000
SALES (est): 40.5MM **Privately Held**
WEB: www.us.gnld.com
SIC: 5122 Cosmetics, perfumes & hair products

(P-7947)
GREEN WAVE INGREDIENTS INC
Also Called: Ingredientsonline.com
14821 Northam St, La Mirada
(90638-5748)
PHONE..........................562 207-9770
Sherry Wang, *President*
Steven Cornejo, *Executive*
Charles Ortiz, *Controller*
Daniel Aldaz, *Warehouse Mgr*
Alice Chin, *Director*
▲ **EMP:** 50
SQ FT: 50,000
SALES (est): 17.6MM **Privately Held**
SIC: 5122 Vitamins & minerals

(P-7948)
GRIFOLS SHARED SVCS N AMER INC (HQ)
2410 Lillyvale Ave, Los Angeles
(90032-3514)
PHONE..........................323 225-2221
Gregory Rich, *CEO*
Max Debrouwer, *CFO*
Thomas Glanzmann, *Chairman*
Bill Barnett, *Vice Pres*
David Bell, *Vice Pres*
▲ **EMP:** 153
SALES (est): 3.8B
SALES (corp-wide): 741MM **Privately Held**
WEB: www.grifolsusa.com
SIC: 5122 2834 Drugs, proprietaries & sundries; druggists' preparations (pharmaceuticals)
PA: Grifols Sa
　　Calle Jesus I Maria 6
　　Barcelona 08022
　　935 710-196

(P-7949)
H D SMITH LLC
1370 E Victoria St, Carson (90746-7501)
P.O. Box 6231 (90749-6231)
PHONE..........................310 641-1885
Bob Schwartz, *Manager*
Angelo Grande, *Vice Pres*
Maureen Alcantara, *Executive*
Dave Durecki, *Sales Staff*
EMP: 100

▲ = Import ▼=Export
◆ =Import/Export

SALES (corp-wide): 167.9B **Publicly Held**
WEB: www.hdsmith.com
SIC: 5122 5047 Pharmaceuticals; medical & hospital equipment
HQ: H. D. Smith, Llc
1300 Morris Dr
Chesterbrook PA 19087
866 232-1222

(P-7950)
HATCHBEAUTY PRODUCTS LLC (PA)
10951 W Pico Blvd Ste 300, Los Angeles (90064-2188)
P.O. Box 641415 (90064-6415)
PHONE..................310 396-7070
Ben Bennett, *Managing Prtnr*
Benjamin Bennett, *Partner*
Tracy Holland, *Managing Prtnr*
Dena Watson, *Executive*
◆ EMP: 83 EST: 2010
SQ FT: 1,500
SALES (est): 74.6MM **Privately Held**
SIC: 5122 Cosmetics, perfumes & hair products

(P-7951)
HOYU AMERICA CO
Also Called: Samy Co
6265 Phyllis Dr, Cypress (90630-5240)
PHONE..................714 230-3000
Yoshihiro Sasaki, *President*
▲ EMP: 58
SALES (est): 35MM **Privately Held**
SIC: 5122 5999 Cosmetics, perfumes & hair products; hair care products
HQ: Hoyu Co.,Ltd.
1-501, Tokugawa, Higashi-Ku
Nagoya AIC 461-0
-

(P-7952)
IRWIN NATURALS
5310 Beethoven St, Los Angeles (90066-7015)
PHONE..................310 306-3636
Timothy Toll, *CEO*
Klee Irwin, *President*
Jeffrey Sugawara, *Senior VP*
Rebecca Pearman, *Vice Pres*
Mark Greene, *Creative Dir*
▼ EMP: 80
SQ FT: 52,000
SALES (est): 48.6MM **Privately Held**
SIC: 5122 Vitamins & minerals

(P-7953)
J T R COMPANY INC (PA)
Also Called: Area Distributing Co
1102 S 3rd St, San Jose (95112-5918)
P.O. Box 8589 (95155-8589)
PHONE..................408 975-7733
Josy T Ryan, *President*
Louis Ryan, *Corp Secy*
Kelly Ryan, *Vice Pres*
Kevin Ryan, *Vice Pres*
Gary G Smith, *Vice Pres*
EMP: 80
SQ FT: 130,000
SALES (est): 41.9MM **Privately Held**
WEB: www.jtrsport.com
SIC: 5122 5199 5113 Toilet articles; packaging materials; towels, paper

(P-7954)
JARROW FORMULAS INC (PA)
1824 S Robertson Blvd, Los Angeles (90035-4317)
PHONE..................310 204-6936
Ben Khowong, *CEO*
Jarrow L Rogovin, *President*
Clayton Dubose, *Treasurer*
Michael Jacobs, *Vice Pres*
ARA Soghomonian, *Creative Dir*
◆ EMP: 90
SQ FT: 37,000
SALES (est): 112.7MM **Privately Held**
SIC: 5122 Vitamins & minerals

(P-7955)
JESSICA COSMETICS INTL INC
Also Called: Jessica's Cosmetics
13209 Saticoy St, North Hollywood (91605-3405)
PHONE..................818 759-1050

Jessica Vartoughian, *President*
Peter Sarkissian, *Sales Staff*
◆ EMP: 60 EST: 1968
SALES (est): 24MM **Privately Held**
SIC: 5122 7231 Cosmetics; beauty shops

(P-7956)
JORDANA COSMETICS LLC
2035 E 49th St, Vernon (90058-2801)
P.O. Box 8382, Los Angeles (90008-0382)
PHONE..................310 730-4400
Laurie Minc, *President*
Ralph Bijou, *Principal*
Anabel Sagrero, *Office Mgr*
Ericka Molina, *Director*
◆ EMP: 65
SQ FT: 30,000
SALES (est): 40.9MM **Privately Held**
WEB: www.jordanacosmetics.com
SIC: 5122 5961 Cosmetics; catalog & mail-order houses

(P-7957)
KATE SOMERVILLE HOLDINGS LLC
144 S Beverly Dr Ste 500, Beverly Hills (90212-3023)
PHONE..................323 655-4170
Kate Somerville, *Mng Member*
▲ EMP: 51 EST: 2007
SALES (est): 22.7MM
SALES (corp-wide): 58.3B **Privately Held**
SIC: 5122 Toiletries; cosmetics; perfumes
PA: Unilever N.V.
Weena 455
Rotterdam
102 174-000

(P-7958)
M P O INC (HQ)
3760 Kilroy Airport Way # 5, Long Beach (90806-2443)
PHONE..................562 628-1007
Al Hummel, *President*
Preston Romm, *CFO*
David Goldstein, *Exec VP*
Albert F Hummel, *Principal*
Alex Daza, *Technical Staff*
EMP: 72
SQ FT: 16,000
SALES (est): 31.7MM **Privately Held**
WEB: www.obagi.com
SIC: 5122 Cosmetics

(P-7959)
MARKWINS BEAUTY PRODUCTS INC
22067 Ferrero, City of Industry (91789-5214)
PHONE..................909 595-8898
Eric Chen, *President*
Stefano Curti, *President*
Michael Shaw, *COO*
Shawn Haynes, *Senior VP*
James Koeppl, *Senior VP*
▲ EMP: 66
SQ FT: 200,000
SALES (est): 40.3MM
SALES (corp-wide): 283.8MM **Privately Held**
WEB: www.markwins.com
SIC: 5122 Cosmetics
PA: Markwins International Corp
22067 Ferrero
Walnut CA 91789
909 595-8898

(P-7960)
MARKWINS INTERNATIONAL CORP (PA)
22067 Ferrero, Walnut (91789-5214)
PHONE..................909 595-8898
Sung-Tsei Eric Chen, *President*
Jeff Rogers, *President*
Leslie H Hernandez, *CFO*
Lina Chen,
Stan Walker, *Regional Mgr*
▲ EMP: 150
SQ FT: 320,000
SALES (est): 283.8MM **Privately Held**
SIC: 5122 Cosmetics

(P-7961)
MCKESSON CORPORATION
6969 Brockton Ave Ste B, Riverside (92506-3813)
PHONE..................951 686-3575
Robert Bourne, *Branch Mgr*
EMP: 65
SALES (corp-wide): 214.3B **Publicly Held**
WEB: www.imckesson.com
SIC: 5122 5047 5199 7372 Pharmaceuticals; proprietary (patent) medicines; toiletries; druggists' sundries; medical equipment & supplies; first aid supplies; general merchandise, non-durable; prepackaged software
PA: Mckesson Corporation
6555 State Highway 161
Irving TX 75039
972 446-4800

(P-7962)
MCKESSON CORPORATION
3000 Colby St, Berkeley (94705-2083)
PHONE..................510 666-0854
Micah Wakamatsu, *Branch Mgr*
EMP: 66
SALES (corp-wide): 214.3B **Publicly Held**
SIC: 5122 Pharmaceuticals
PA: Mckesson Corporation
6555 State Highway 161
Irving TX 75039
972 446-4800

(P-7963)
MCKESSON CORPORATION
Also Called: McKesson Drug
9501 Norwalk Blvd, Santa Fe Springs (90670-2929)
P.O. Box 2116 (90670-0116)
PHONE..................562 463-2100
Todd Kleinow, *Manager*
Marcus Mandagie, *Manager*
EMP: 120
SALES (corp-wide): 214.3B **Publicly Held**
WEB: www.imckesson.com
SIC: 5122 Pharmaceuticals
PA: Mckesson Corporation
6555 State Highway 161
Irving TX 75039
972 446-4800

(P-7964)
MCKESSON CORPORATION
Also Called: Drohan Trade Center
11000 Trade Center Dr, Rancho Cordova (95670-6153)
PHONE..................916 636-8700
Donna Draher, *Branch Mgr*
Jackie Haines, *Administration*
Ramdas Sankarnarayan, *Administration*
John Keeling, *Technology*
Mark Rissing, *Opers Staff*
EMP: 53
SQ FT: 3,000
SALES (corp-wide): 214.3B **Publicly Held**
WEB: www.imckesson.com
SIC: 5122 Pharmaceuticals
PA: Mckesson Corporation
6555 State Highway 161
Irving TX 75039
972 446-4800

(P-7965)
MCKESSON MEDICAL-SURGICAL INC
16043 El Prado Rd, Chino (91708-9144)
PHONE..................800 767-6339
Stanton McComb, *Branch Mgr*
EMP: 78
SALES (corp-wide): 214.3B **Publicly Held**
SIC: 5122 Pharmaceuticals
HQ: Mckesson Medical-Surgical Inc.
9954 Mayland Dr Ste 4000
Richmond VA 23233
804 264-7500

(P-7966)
MCKESSON MEDICAL-SURGICAL INC
1525 Rnch Conejo Blvd # 104, Newbury Park (91320-1441)
PHONE..................805 375-8800
Mike Douglas, *Branch Mgr*
Garrett Muramoto, *Senior Mgr*
EMP: 54
SALES (corp-wide): 214.3B **Publicly Held**
WEB: www.gmholdings.com
SIC: 5122 Pharmaceuticals
HQ: Mckesson Medical-Surgical Inc.
9954 Mayland Dr Ste 4000
Richmond VA 23233
804 264-7500

(P-7967)
METAGENICS INC (DH)
25 Enterprise Ste 200, Aliso Viejo (92656-2713)
PHONE..................949 366-0818
Brent Eck, *President*
Jean M Bellin, *President*
Dave Tuit, *CFO*
Sara Gottfried, *Chief Mktg Ofcr*
John Troup, *Officer*
◆ EMP: 150
SQ FT: 88,000
SALES (est): 188.5MM
SALES (corp-wide): 8.7B **Privately Held**
WEB: www.ethicalnutrients.com
SIC: 5122 Vitamins & minerals; medicinals & botanicals
HQ: Alticor Inc.
7575 Fulton St E
Ada MI 49355
616 787-1000

(P-7968)
METAGENICS INC
100 Avenida La Pata, San Clemente (92673-6305)
PHONE..................800 692-9400
Carol Perkovich, *Manager*
EMP: 100
SALES (corp-wide): 8.7B **Privately Held**
WEB: www.ethicalnutrients.com
SIC: 5122 5047 Vitamins & minerals; physician equipment & supplies
HQ: Metagenics, Inc.
25 Enterprise Ste 200
Aliso Viejo CA 92656
949 366-0818

(P-7969)
MISSION SERIES INC
1585 W Mission Blvd, Pomona (91766-1233)
PHONE..................714 736-1000
Robert Friedland, *President*
EMP: 50
SALES (est): 1MM **Privately Held**
SIC: 5122 Cosmetics

(P-7970)
N QIAGEN AMERCN HOLDINGS INC (HQ)
27220 Turnberry Ln # 200, Valencia (91355-1018)
PHONE..................800 426-8157
Peer Schatz, *President*
Thierry Bernard, *Vice Pres*
Rainer Metzger, *Vice Pres*
Edelstein Gloria, *Associate Dir*
Prashant Vaidya, *Info Tech Mgr*
EMP: 250
SALES (est): 205.5MM
SALES (corp-wide): 1.5B **Privately Held**
SIC: 5122 Biologicals & allied products
PA: Qiagen N.V.
Hulsterweg 82
Venlo 5912
773 556-600

(P-7971)
OMNICARE INC
20967 Cabot Blvd, Hayward (94545-1155)
PHONE..................510 293-9663
EMP: 99
SALES (corp-wide): 194.5B **Publicly Held**
SIC: 5122 Pharmaceuticals

P R O D U C T S & S V C S

HQ: Omnicare, Inc.
900 Omnicare Ctr 201e4t
Cincinnati OH 45202
513 719-2600

(P-7972)
PACIFIC PHARMA INC
18600 Von Karman Ave, Irvine
(92612-1513)
PHONE..................714 246-4600
EMP: 2000
SALES (est): 108.7MM Privately Held
SIC: 5122
HQ: Allergan, Inc.
400 Interpace Pkwy
Parsippany NJ 07940
862 261-7000

(P-7973)
PACIRA PHARMACEUTICALS INC
Also Called: Research & Dev & Mfg Site
10578 Science Center Dr, San Diego
(92121-1143)
PHONE..................858 625-2424
EMP: 125 Publicly Held
SIC: 5122 Pharmaceuticals
PA: Pacira Pharmaceuticals, Inc.
5 Sylvan Way Ste 300
Parsippany NJ 07054

(P-7974)
PAUL MITCHELL JOHN SYSTEMS (PA)
20705 Centre Pointe Pkwy, Santa Clarita
(91350-2967)
P.O. Box 10597, Beverly Hills (90213-3597)
PHONE..................310 248-3888
John Paul Dejoria, CEO
Rick Battaglini, Officer
Julia Provost, Vice Pres
Angela Hauk, Program Mgr
Briana Wolfe, Administration
◆ EMP: 80
SQ FT: 90,000
SALES (est): 132.2MM Privately Held
SIC: 5122 Hair preparations

(P-7975)
PHARMERICA LONG-TERM CARE LLC
Also Called: Ltc Pharmacy
1130 Palmyrita Ave # 350, Riverside
(92507-1742)
PHONE..................951 784-1616
Kim Young, Branch Mgr
EMP: 60
SALES (corp-wide): 2B Privately Held
WEB: www.pharmerica.com
SIC: 5122 Pharmaceuticals
HQ: Pharmerica Long-Term Care, Llc
3625 Queen Palm Dr
Tampa FL 33619
877 975-2273

(P-7976)
PIXI INC
Also Called: Pixi Beauty
10351 Santa Monica Blvd # 410, Los Angeles (90025-6937)
PHONE..................310 670-7767
Felix Strand, President
Anthony Oppe, CEO
Petra Strand Oppe, Founder
Shawna Skowrup, Accountant
EMP: 64
SQ FT: 8,400
SALES (est): 6.5MM Privately Held
SIC: 5122 Cosmetics

(P-7977)
PPHM INC
Also Called: Avid Bioservices
14282 Franklin Ave, Tustin (92780-7009)
PHONE..................714 508-6100
Steve King, CEO
Paul Lytle, CFO
Tracy L Kinjerski, Vice Pres
Jeffrey Masten, Vice Pres
EMP: 100

SALES (est): 36.8MM
SALES (corp-wide): 53.6MM Publicly Held
WEB: www.avidbioservices.com
SIC: 5122 Pharmaceuticals
PA: Avid Bioservices, Inc.
2642 Michelle Dr Ste 200
Tustin CA 92780
714 508-6000

(P-7978)
PRIMAL ELEMENTS INC
18062 Redondo Cir, Huntington Beach
(92648-1326)
PHONE..................714 899-0757
Faith Freeman, CEO
Scott Freeman, President
▲ EMP: 99
SQ FT: 56,500
SALES (est): 38.7MM Privately Held
WEB: www.primalelements.com
SIC: 5122 2841 Cosmetics; detergents, synthetic organic or inorganic alkaline

(P-7979)
PRIMAL NUTRITION LLC
Also Called: Primal Blueprint
1631 S Rose Ave, Oxnard (93033-2470)
P.O. Box 145, Malibu (90265-0145)
PHONE..................310 317-4414
Mark Sisson, CEO
Morgan Zanoti, President
Adrian Vasquez, Opers Staff
EMP: 50
SQ FT: 3,500
SALES (est): 11.4MM
SALES (corp-wide): 26.2B Publicly Held
WEB: www.primalnutrition.com
SIC: 5122 5149 Vitamins & minerals; health foods
PA: The Kraft Heinz Company
1 Ppg Pl Fl 34
Pittsburgh PA 15222
412 456-5700

(P-7980)
RUGBY LABORATORIES INC (DH)
311 Bonnie Cir, Corona (92880-2882)
PHONE..................951 270-1400
David C Hsia PHD, President
Michael E Boser, CFO
Michel J Feldman, Officer
Frederick Wilkinson, Vice Pres
Chato Abad, VP Finance
EMP: 90
SALES (est): 20.8MM
SALES (corp-wide): 145.5B Publicly Held
WEB: www.watsonpharm.com
SIC: 5122 2834 Pharmaceuticals; pharmaceutical preparations
HQ: The Harvard Drug Group L L C
17177 N Laurel Park Dr # 233
Livonia MI 48152
734 525-8700

(P-7981)
SCIENCE OF SKINCARE LLC
Also Called: Innovative Skin Care
3333 N San Fernando Blvd, Burbank
(91504-2531)
PHONE..................818 254-7961
C B Johns, Mng Member
Katherine Medina, Business Mgr
Patty Myers, Business Mgr
Ruben Gayon, Accountant
Pierre Pethrus, Plant Mgr
▲ EMP: 97
SQ FT: 36,000
SALES (est): 53.9MM Privately Held
WEB: www.innovativeskincare.com
SIC: 5122 Cosmetics

(P-7982)
SCILEX HOLDING COMPANY (HQ)
4955 Directors Pl, San Diego (92121-3836)
PHONE..................858 203-4100
Jaisim Shah, CEO
EMP: 66
SALES (est): 5.8MM
SALES (corp-wide): 21.1MM Publicly Held
SIC: 5122 Pharmaceuticals

PA: Sorrento Therapeutics, Inc.
4955 Directors Pl
San Diego CA 92121
858 203-4100

(P-7983)
SGII INC
Also Called: Senegence International
19651 Alter, Foothill Ranch (92610-2507)
PHONE..................949 521-6161
Joni Rogers Kante, CEO
Philippe Guerreau, President
Ben Kante, COO
James Roh, Officer
Kirsten Aguilar, Vice Pres
▲ EMP: 250
SQ FT: 49,415
SALES (est): 20.8MM Privately Held
WEB: www.senegence.com
SIC: 5122 Cosmetics; vitamins & minerals

(P-7984)
STAR NAIL PRODUCTS INC
Also Called: Star Nail International
29120 Avenue Paine, Valencia
(91355-5402)
PHONE..................661 257-3376
Tony Cuccio, CEO
Anthony Cuccio, President
Roberta Cuccio, Vice Pres
Elaine Watson, Vice Pres
Shelley Cassulo, Marketing Staff
◆ EMP: 55
SQ FT: 14,000
SALES (est): 28.2MM Privately Held
WEB: www.allseasonnails.com
SIC: 5122 2844 7231 Cosmetics; toilet preparations; beauty shops

(P-7985)
STARLIGHT INTERNATIONAL LTD LP
38 Saint Joseph Ave, Long Beach
(90803-3156)
PHONE..................562 439-5740
Pat Ellington, Agent
EMP: 52 Privately Held
WEB: www.starlighttint.com
SIC: 5122 Vitamins & minerals
PA: Starlight International, Ltd. Lp
22131 Burbank Blvd Unit 3
Woodland Hills CA 91367

(P-7986)
SUPERBALIFE INTERNATIONAL LLC
Also Called: Prostavar Rx
1171 S Robertson Blvd # 525, Los Angeles
(90035-1403)
PHONE..................310 553-7400
Fred Buckley, President
Corrine Buckley, Mng Member
EMP: 62
SALES (est): 22MM Privately Held
SIC: 5122 Vitamins & minerals

(P-7987)
UNITE EUROTHERAPY INC
2870 Whiptail Loop, Carlsbad
(92010-6709)
PHONE..................760 585-1800
Andrew Dale, President
Jerry Trombetta, President
Chris Hlavaty, CFO
▲ EMP: 80
SALES (est): 23MM Privately Held
SIC: 5122 Hair preparations

(P-7988)
VALLEY OF SUN COSMETICS LLC
Also Called: Valley of The Sun Labs
535 Patrice Pl, Gardena (90248-4232)
PHONE..................310 327-9062
Jimmy Ajmal,
Ajmal Shehzad,
◆ EMP: 156
SQ FT: 10,000
SALES (est): 48.5MM Privately Held
WEB: www.cosmeticusa.com
SIC: 5122 Cosmetics

(P-7989)
VALLEY WHOLESALE DRUG CO LLC
1401 W Fremont St, Stockton
(95203-2627)
P.O. Box 247, Thorofare NJ (08086-0247)
PHONE..................209 466-0131
Henry Dale Smith, CEO
Dan Matteoli, Vice Pres
Angelo Grande, Principal
EMP: 75 EST: 1948
SQ FT: 10,000
SALES (est): 52.6MM
SALES (corp-wide): 167.9B Publicly Held
SIC: 5122 Pharmaceuticals; cosmetics; druggists' sundries
HQ: H. D. Smith, Llc
1300 Morris Dr
Chesterbrook PA 19087
866 232-1222

(P-7990)
VETERINARY PHARMACEUTICALS INC
13159 Hanford Armona Rd, Hanford
(93230)
PHONE..................559 582-6800
Harold Des Jardins, CEO
Alice Des Jardins, Vice Pres
▲ EMP: 52
SALES (est): 18.9MM Privately Held
SIC: 5122 Pharmaceuticals

(P-7991)
VICTORY PHARMA INC
11682 El Camino Real # 250, San Diego
(92130-2092)
PHONE..................858 720-4500
James W Newman, Ch of Bd
Matthew Heck, President
Daniel Stokely, COO
David Parker, CFO
Ana Adam, Vice Pres
EMP: 150
SALES (est): 17.4MM Privately Held
WEB: www.victorypharma.com
SIC: 5122 Pharmaceuticals

(P-7992)
VIVA LIFE SCIENCE INC
350 Paularino Ave, Costa Mesa
(92626-4616)
PHONE..................949 645-6100
David Fan, President
Millie Hardi, Purchasing
Nasim Moradi, Mktg Dir
EMP: 100
SQ FT: 60,000
SALES (est): 14.6MM Privately Held
SIC: 5122 2833 Vitamins & minerals; cosmetics; medicinals & botanicals

(P-7993)
WITHROW PHRM & HLTH SPC LAB
2235 Via Puerta Unit A, Laguna Woods
(92637-8114)
PHONE..................323 721-4281
Sergio Quinones, President
Selma Quinones, Controller
EMP: 100 EST: 1928
SALES (est): 10.9MM Privately Held
WEB: www.withrow-pharm.com
SIC: 5122 7231 Pharmaceuticals; beauty shops

5131 Piece Goods, Notions & Dry Goods Wholesale

(P-7994)
CHARMING TRIM & PACKAGING
28 Brookside Ct, Novato (94947-3847)
PHONE..................415 302-7021
Richard Ringeisen, President
Jeremy Van Houten, Executive
Barry Chan, Exec Dir
EMP: 1000
SALES (est): 53.6MM Privately Held
SIC: 5131 3111 Trimmings, apparel; garment leather

(P-7995)
DAZIAN LLC
Also Called: Dazian's
10671 Lorne St, Sun Valley (91352-4642)
PHONE..................................818 287-3800
Chris Diaz, *Branch Mgr*
Denise McCarthy, *Finance Mgr*
Ashley Brown, *Sales Staff*
Adriana Vilar, *Sales Staff*
EMP: 60
SALES (est): 7.4MM
SALES (corp-wide): 60.2MM **Privately Held**
WEB: www.dazian.com
SIC: 5131 Piece goods & other fabrics
PA: Dazian, Llc
        18 Central Blvd
        South Hackensack NJ 07606
        877 232-9426

(P-7996)
DESIGN COLLECTION INC
Also Called: Global Garments
2209 S Santa Fe Ave, Los Angeles
(90058-1109)
PHONE..................................323 277-9200
Simon Barlava, *CEO*
Sohail Hussain, *CFO*
Sohaila Hussaini, *CFO*
Morris Barlava, *Vice Pres*
Nasser Barlava, *Admin Sec*
◆ **EMP:** 60
SQ FT: 67,000
SALES (est): 20.8MM **Privately Held**
WEB: www.designcollection.com
SIC: 5131 5023 Trimmings, apparel;
        sheets, textile

(P-7997)
FABRIC BARN
3123 E Anaheim St, Long Beach
(90804-3862)
PHONE..................................562 494-3450
Jay Keegan, *Partner*
Linda Hanna, *Partner*
Veronica Molina, *Manager*
▲ **EMP:** 230
SQ FT: 8,000
SALES (est): 18.7MM **Privately Held**
SIC: 5131 5092 Lace fabrics; ribbons; toys
        & hobby goods & supplies

(P-7998)
INNOVO AZTECA APPAREL INC
5901 S Eastern Ave 104, Commerce
(90040-4003)
PHONE..................................323 837-3700
Marc Crossman, *President*
Hamish Sandhu, *CFO*
▲ **EMP:** 80
SALES (est): 9.8MM
SALES (corp-wide): 596.6MM **Publicly Held**
WEB: www.innovogroup.com
SIC: 5131 Trimmings, apparel
PA: Centric Brands Inc.
        350 5th Ave Fl 6
        New York NY 10118
        646 582-6000

(P-7999)
L & R DISTRIBUTORS INC
9292 9th St, Rancho Cucamonga
(91730-4407)
PHONE..................................909 980-3807
EMP: 275
SALES (corp-wide): 985.9MM **Privately Held**
SIC: 5131 Notions
PA: L. & R. Distributors, Inc.
        88 35th St Ste 5
        Brooklyn NY 11232
        718 272-2100

(P-8000)
LAFAYETTE TEXTILE INDS LLC
2051 E 55th St, Vernon (90058-3441)
PHONE..................................323 264-2212
Ali Reza Zahedi, *CEO*
Ali Dehbahani, *COO*
Moshan Dibaei, *CFO*
Carol Ueng, *Accounting Mgr*
Ali Behbahani, *Manager*
▲ **EMP:** 85
SQ FT: 68,000

SALES (est): 27.8MM **Privately Held**
WEB: www.lafayettetextiles.com
SIC: 5131 Piece goods & notions

(P-8001)
M M FAB INC
Also Called: South Seas Imports
2300 E Gladwick St, Compton
(90220-6208)
PHONE..................................310 763-3800
Richard Friedman, *Principal*
Al Mass, *VP Finance*
Sergio Garcia, *Sales Mgr*
Renshaw Justin, *Sales Staff*
▲ **EMP:** 85
SQ FT: 110,000
SALES (est): 23.5MM **Privately Held**
SIC: 5131 Textiles, woven

(P-8002)
MERIDIAN TEXTILES INC (PA)
6415 Canning St, Commerce (90040-3121)
PHONE..................................323 869-5700
Howard Deutchman, *President*
▲ **EMP:** 74
SQ FT: 36,000
SALES (est): 39.8MM **Privately Held**
WEB: www.markfabrics.com
SIC: 5131 Textile converters

(P-8003)
MODERN BUTTON COMPANY OF CAL
3957 S Hill St, Los Angeles (90037-1313)
PHONE..................................213 747-7431
Alan Failo, *President*
Virginia Acosta, *Vice Pres*
EMP: 50
SQ FT: 4,400
SALES (est): 4.8MM **Privately Held**
SIC: 5131 Buttons

(P-8004)
MORGAN FABRICS CORPORATION (PA)
Also Called: Michael Jon Designs
4265 Exchange Ave, Vernon (90058-2604)
P.O. Box 58523, Los Angeles (90058-0523)
PHONE..................................323 583-9981
Arnold Gittelson, *Chairman*
Michael Gittelson, *President*
Ken Yang, *CFO*
Robert Gittelson, *Vice Pres*
Paulina Muzekari, *Vice Pres*
▲ **EMP:** 60 EST: 1956
SQ FT: 50,000
SALES: 47MM **Privately Held**
WEB: www.morganfabrics.com
SIC: 5131 Textiles, woven; upholstery fab-
        rics, woven

(P-8005)
PHOENIX TEXTILE INC (PA)
Also Called: Level 99
14600 S Broadway, Gardena (90248-1812)
PHONE..................................310 715-7090
Dominic Poon, *President*
Joseph TSE, *Treasurer*
Lucia Wang, *Vice Pres*
Charlton Wang, *Info Tech Mgr*
Robert Jones, *Regl Sales Mgr*
▲ **EMP:** 100
SQ FT: 39,000
SALES (est): 29.4MM **Privately Held**
SIC: 5131 7389 Textiles, woven; sewing
        contractor; textile designers

(P-8006)
PINDLER & PINDLER INC (PA)
11910 Poindexter Ave, Moorpark
(93021-1748)
P.O. Box 8007 (93020-8007)
PHONE..................................805 531-9090
Curt R Pindler, *President*
Sean Quinn, *CFO*
S L Crawford Jr, *Exec VP*
Kelby Gleghorn, *General Mgr*
Barbara Bick, *Admin Sec*
▲ **EMP:** 95 EST: 1939
SQ FT: 75,000
SALES (est): 101MM **Privately Held**
WEB: www.pindler.com
SIC: 5131 Drapery material, woven; uphol-
        stery fabrics, woven

(P-8007)
RADIX TEXTILE INC
745 Kohler St, Los Angeles (90021-1517)
PHONE..................................323 234-1667
Arad Shemirani, *CEO*
▲ **EMP:** 99 EST: 2007
SALES (est): 5.5MM **Privately Held**
SIC: 5131 2211 Piece goods & other fab-
        rics; broadwoven fabric mills, cotton

(P-8008)
ROBERT KAUFMAN CO INC
135 W 132nd St, Los Angeles
(90061-1682)
P.O. Box 59266 (90059-0266)
PHONE..................................310 538-3482
Eric Thompson, *Manager*
Jessica Meza, *Technology*
EMP: 50
SALES (corp-wide): 55.6MM **Privately Held**
WEB: www.robertkaufman.com
SIC: 5131 Piece goods & other fabrics
PA: Robert Kaufman Co., Inc.
        129 W 132nd St
        Los Angeles CA 90061
        310 538-3482

(P-8009)
ROMEX TEXTILES INC (PA)
785 E 14th Pl, Los Angeles (90021-2117)
PHONE..................................213 749-9090
Shahab Binafard, *CEO*
Soleyman Binafard, *Admin Sec*
Grethelle Simon, *Opers Mgr*
▲ **EMP:** 50
SQ FT: 10,000
SALES (est): 17.7MM **Privately Held**
SIC: 5131 2211 Textiles, woven; apparel &
        outerwear fabrics, cotton

(P-8010)
SAM JUNG USA INC
Also Called: S & J
843 E 31st St, Los Angeles (90011-2006)
PHONE..................................323 231-0811
Joung Ha Lee, *President*
◆ **EMP:** 60
SQ FT: 50,000
SALES (est): 7.8MM **Privately Held**
SIC: 5131 Piece goods & notions

(P-8011)
SEXY HAIR CONCEPTS
9232 Eton Ave, Chatsworth (91311-5807)
PHONE..................................800 848-3383
Carl Heinzsch, *President*
◆ **EMP:** 100
SALES (est): 13.6MM **Privately Held**
SIC: 5131 Hair accessories

(P-8012)
SHASON INC (PA)
Also Called: Dream River
5525 S Soto St, Vernon (90058-3622)
PHONE..................................323 269-6666
Barok Shahery, *President*
Henry Shahery, *Vice Pres*
Vic Japson, *Manager*
▲ **EMP:** 52
SALES (est): 22.7MM **Privately Held**
WEB: www.shasoninc.com
SIC: 5131 Textiles, woven

(P-8013)
STAR FABRICS INC (PA)
1440 Walnut St, Los Angeles (90011-1351)
PHONE..................................213 688-2871
Elias Haroni, *President*
Soussan Heroni, *Vice Pres*
Debra Grauten, *Sales Executive*
Marylou Manzo, *Sales Mgr*
Brenda Castellanos, *Manager*
▲ **EMP:** 70
SQ FT: 100,000
SALES (est): 11MM **Privately Held**
SIC: 5131 Textiles, woven

(P-8014)
TALON INTERNATIONAL INC (PA)
21900 Burbank Blvd # 270, Woodland Hills
(91367-6469)
PHONE..................................818 444-4100
Mark Dyne, *Ch of Bd*

Larry Dyne, *CEO*
James Reeder, *COO*
Daniel Ryu, *Officer*
Gary Dyne, *Exec VP*
EMP: 69
SALES: 48.2MM **Publicly Held**
SIC: 5131 3965 Sewing supplies & no-
        tions; zipper

(P-8015)
UNITED FABRICS INTL INC
1723 S Central Ave, Los Angeles
(90021-3030)
PHONE..................................213 749-8200
Shahariar S Simantob, *President*
Ramin Simantob, *Vice Pres*
Arbi Rostami, *Technology*
▲ **EMP:** 51
SQ FT: 35,000
SALES: 16.5MM **Privately Held**
WEB: www.unitedfabric.com
SIC: 5131 5949 Textiles, woven; fabric
        stores piece goods

(P-8016)
ZABIN INDUSTRIES INC (PA)
3957 S Hill St Ste A, Los Angeles
(90037-1343)
P.O. Box 15218 (90015-0218)
PHONE..................................213 749-1215
Alan Faiola, *President*
Virginia Acosta, *Vice Pres*
Eric Sebso, *Vice Pres*
Manolo Alvaro, *Human Res Mgr*
Fernando F Garcia, *Manager*
▲ **EMP:** 78
SQ FT: 43,000
SALES (est): 11MM **Privately Held**
WEB: www.zabin.com
SIC: 5131 Zippers; textile converters; but-
        tons; net goods

5136 Men's & Boys' Clothing & Furnishings Wholesale

(P-8017)
AG ADRIANO GOLDSCHMIED INC (PA)
Also Called: AG Jeans
2741 Seminole Ave, South Gate
(90280-5550)
PHONE..................................323 357-1111
U Yul Ku, *President*
Adriano Suarez, *Vice Pres*
Vanessa Choi, *Executive Asst*
Sophia Huynh, *Admin Sec*
Paul Kim, *Director*
▲ **EMP:** 56
SQ FT: 150,000
SALES (est): 38.5MM **Privately Held**
WEB: www.bluelement.com
SIC: 5136 5137 5699 Apparel belts,
        men's & boys'; apparel belts, women's &
        children's; designers, apparel

(P-8018)
ARTICOUTURE INC
1265 S Johnson Dr, City of Industry
(91745-2409)
PHONE..................................626 336-7299
Kuei-Lin Hsieh, *CEO*
EMP: 50
SALES (est): 4.8MM **Privately Held**
SIC: 5136 5137 Men's & boys' clothing;
        women's & children's clothing

(P-8019)
ARTWEAR INC
13621 S Main St, Los Angeles
(90061-2163)
PHONE..................................310 217-1393
Ora Ketpongsuda, *President*
Paul Ketpongsuda, *Vice Pres*
Leo Cantinbuhan, *Technology*
▲ **EMP:** 50
SQ FT: 48,000

P R O D U C T S & S V C S

SALES (est): 11.2MM **Privately Held**
WEB: www.lesliejordan.com
SIC: **5136** 5137 2396 2331 Shirts, men's & boys'; women's & children's sportswear & swimsuits; automotive & apparel trimmings; women's & misses' blouses & shirts; men's & boys' furnishings; finishing plants, cotton

(P-8020)
BRAD RAMBO & ASSOCIATES INC (PA)
Also Called: Independent Trading Company
1341 Calle Avanzado, San Clemente (92673-6351)
PHONE.............................949 366-9911
Brad Rambo, *President*
Brandon Rambo, *Principal*
Dena Marques, *Info Tech Dir*
Alia Ahmed, *Human Res Mgr*
Jeff Bush, *Sales Staff*
▲ EMP: 55
SQ FT: 20,500
SALES (est): 25.7MM **Privately Held**
WEB: www.independenttradingco.com
SIC: **5136** Shirts, men's & boys'

(P-8021)
BRODER BROS CO
3443 E Central Ave, Fresno (93725-2542)
PHONE.............................559 233-9900
Keith Hamilton, *Manager*
EMP: 59
SALES (corp-wide): 3.7B **Privately Held**
WEB: www.broderbros.com
SIC: **5136** 5137 Sportswear, men's & boys'; sportswear, women's & children's
PA: Broder Bros., Co.
6 Neshaminy Interplex Dr
Trevose PA 19053
215 291-0300

(P-8022)
CHEF WORKS INC (PA)
12325 Kerran St A, Poway (92064-6801)
PHONE.............................858 643-5600
Neil R Gross, *CEO*
Diane Harnly, *Exec VP*
Jeffrey Abelsohn, *Vice Pres*
Eddie Laird, *Vice Pres*
Ann Malk, *Vice Pres*
▲ EMP: 120
SQ FT: 50,000
SALES (est): 98.5MM **Privately Held**
WEB: www.chefwork.com
SIC: **5136** 5137 Uniforms, men's & boys'; uniforms, women's & children's

(P-8023)
COLOSSEUM ATHLETICS CORP
2400 S Wilmington Ave, Compton (90220-5403)
PHONE.............................310 667-8341
Stuart Whang, *CEO*
Alphan Tsoi, *Exec VP*
Ana Benedicto, *Human Resources*
Joann Mun, *Purchasing*
Kwon Richard, *Merchandising*
◆ EMP: 85
SQ FT: 64,227
SALES (est): 44.6MM **Privately Held**
SIC: **5136** 5137 Sportswear, men's & boys'; sportswear, women's & children's

(P-8024)
DECKY CO INC (PA)
2121 S Wilmington Ave, Compton (90220-5447)
PHONE.............................310 608-2726
John Whang, *President*
Sun Wook Whang, *Shareholder*
Felicia Guardado, *Sales Mgr*
▲ EMP: 55
SQ FT: 20,000
SALES (est): 9.3MM **Privately Held**
WEB: www.decky.net
SIC: **5136** Sportswear, men's & boys'; hats, men's & boys'

(P-8025)
DORFMAN-PACIFIC CO (HQ)
Also Called: Dorfman Pacific
2615 Boeing Way, Stockton (95206-3984)
P.O. Box 213005 (95213-9005)
PHONE............................209 982-1400
Douglas Edward Highsmith, *CEO*

Bakul Patel, *CFO*
Debra Highsmith, *Admin Sec*
◆ EMP: 140
SQ FT: 275,000
SALES (est): 67.8MM **Privately Held**
WEB: www.dorfman-pacific.com
SIC: **5136** 5137 Caps, men's & boys'; hats, men's & boys'; men's & boys' outerwear; caps & gowns; hats: women's, children's & infants'; women's & children's outerwear

(P-8026)
DREAM LOUNGE INC
11271 Ventura Blvd 456, Studio City (91604-3136)
PHONE............................213 688-7888
John Vorzimer, *CEO*
EMP: 2210 EST: 2011
SALES (est): 225MM **Privately Held**
SIC: **5136** 5137 Hosiery, men's & boys'; hosiery: women's, children's & infants'

(P-8027)
EISENBERG INTERNATIONAL CORP (PA)
9128 Jordan Ave, Chatsworth (91311-5707)
PHONE............................818 365-8161
Joel Eisenberg, *President*
Lynn Eisenberg, *Corp Secy*
Richard Eisenberg, *Vice Pres*
▲ EMP: 55
SQ FT: 36,000
SALES (est): 13.4MM **Privately Held**
WEB: www.eisenbergintl.com
SIC: **5136** Coats, men's & boys'; sportswear, men's & boys'; suits, men's & boys'; trousers, men's & boys'

(P-8028)
FAM LLC
Also Called: Fam Brands
5553 Bandini Blvd Ste B, Bell (90201-6421)
PHONE............................323 888-7755
Frank Zarabi,
Patrick Chow, *CFO*
Norah Emamjomeh, *Senior VP*
Steve Ryan, *Info Tech Dir*
Olivia Sanchez, *Prdtn Mgr*
▲ EMP: 75
SQ FT: 75,000
SALES (est): 71.6MM **Privately Held**
WEB: www.fambrands.com
SIC: **5136** 5137 Sportswear, men's & boys'; women's & children's sportswear & swimsuits

(P-8029)
FAMMA GROUP INC (PA)
4510 Loma Vista Ave, Vernon (90058-2602)
PHONE............................323 826-9600
Don X Ho, *CEO*
Joe Kamari, *President*
Jack Luk, *Controller*
EMP: 100
SQ FT: 30,288
SALES (est): 47.8MM **Privately Held**
SIC: **5136** 5137 Men's & boys' clothing; women's & children's clothing

(P-8030)
FOX HEAD INC (PA)
Also Called: Fox Racing
16752 Armstrong Ave, Irvine (92606-4912)
PHONE............................888 369-7223
Peter Fox, *Chairman*
Pete Fox, *President*
Paul E Harrington, *CEO*
Brian Woods, *Officer*
Geoffrey T Fox, *Vice Pres*
◆ EMP: 200 EST: 1975
SALES (est): 252.5MM **Privately Held**
WEB: www.foxbmx.com
SIC: **5136** 5137 5961 5699 Sportswear, men's & boys'; sportswear, women's & children's; mail order house; sports apparel

(P-8031)
GONZALES PARK LLC
Also Called: Aztlan Graphics
495 Ryan Ave, Chico (95973-8846)
PHONE............................530 343-8725

Daniel Gonzales,
Dawn Gonzales, *Treasurer*
▲ EMP: 174
SQ FT: 26,000
SALES (est): 152.6MM **Privately Held**
WEB: www.5sun.com
SIC: **5136** 2326 Shirts, men's & boys'; men's & boys' work clothing

(P-8032)
HELMET HOUSE INC (PA)
Also Called: Tour Master
26855 Malibu Hills Rd, Calabasas Hills (91301-5100)
PHONE............................800 421-7247
Robert M Miller, *CEO*
Randy Hutchings, *CFO*
Richard Kimes, *Chief Mktg Ofcr*
Philip Bellomy, *Vice Pres*
Helen Ivener, *Admin Asst*
▲ EMP: 73
SQ FT: 80,000
SALES (est): 73.6MM **Privately Held**
WEB: www.helmethouse.com
SIC: **5136** 3949 Men's & boys' clothing; helmets, athletic

(P-8033)
HWMM (HQ)
Also Called: Lifted Research Group
7 Studebaker, Irvine (92618-2013)
P.O. Box 4743, Laguna Beach (92652-4743)
PHONE............................949 581-1144
Robert D Wright, *President*
Luis Valladares, *Sales Staff*
◆ EMP: 51
SALES (est): 71.6MM
SALES (corp-wide): 173MM **Privately Held**
WEB: www.liftedresearchgroup.com
SIC: **5136** Sportswear, men's & boys'
PA: Mad Engine, Llc
6740 Cobra Way Ste 100
San Diego CA 92121
858 558-5270

(P-8034)
HYBRID PROMOTIONS LLC (PA)
10711 Walker St, Cypress (90630-4720)
PHONE............................714 952-3866
David Lederman, *Mng Member*
Brad Shapiro, *CFO*
Sara Matthews, *Vice Pres*
Kenneth Ruzic, *Creative Dir*
Carre Perkins, *Business Anlyst*
▲ EMP: 130
SQ FT: 100,000
SALES (est): 670.2MM **Privately Held**
WEB: www.hybridtees.com
SIC: **5136** 5137 5611 Sportswear, men's & boys'; women's & children's clothing; men's & boys' clothing stores

(P-8035)
L A CSTM AP & PROMOTIONS INC (PA)
2680 Temple Ave, Long Beach (90806-2209)
PHONE............................562 595-1770
Chris Roybal, *President*
Peter Calderon, *Purch Mgr*
EMP: 56
SQ FT: 10,000
SALES (est): 14.5MM **Privately Held**
WEB: www.lacustomapparel.com
SIC: **5136** Men's & boys' clothing

(P-8036)
LA BRANDS LLC
Also Called: US Blanks
4726 Loma Vista Ave, Vernon (90058-3215)
PHONE............................323 234-5070
Greg Baxter, *Manager*
EMP: 50
SALES (corp-wide): 1.4MM **Privately Held**
SIC: **5136** 5137 Men's & boys' sportswear & work clothing; women's & children's clothing
PA: L.A. Brands Llc
1717 N Naper Blvd Ste 203
Naperville IL

(P-8037)
LANDMARK PROTECTION INC
675 N 1st St Ste 620, San Jose (95112-5145)
PHONE............................408 293-6300
Daniel Miranda, *President*
EMP: 300
SQ FT: 6,000
SALES (est): 10MM **Privately Held**
WEB: www.landmarkprotection.com
SIC: **5136** 5099 7381 Uniforms, men's & boys'; safety equipment & supplies; guard services; security guard service

(P-8038)
LIQUIDITY SERVICES INC
Str
741 E Ball Rd Ste 200, Anaheim (92805-5952)
PHONE............................714 738-6446
Carl Jones, *Branch Mgr*
EMP: 100 **Publicly Held**
WEB: www.liquidation.com
SIC: **5136** 5137 5139 5611 Men's & boys' clothing; women's & children's clothing; footwear; men's & boys' clothing stores; radio, television & electronic stores; salvaging of damaged merchandise, service only
PA: Liquidity Services, Inc.
6931 Arlington Rd Ste 200
Bethesda MD 20814

(P-8039)
M & S TRADING INC
Also Called: 7 Diamonds Clothing
15778 Gateway Cir, Tustin (92780-6469)
PHONE............................714 241-7190
Sami Khalil, *CEO*
Christopher Vicente, *Graphic Designe*
▲ EMP: 71
SQ FT: 36,000
SALES (est): 13.2MM **Privately Held**
WEB: www.7diamonds.com
SIC: **5136** 5137 Sportswear, men's & boys'; women's & children's clothing

(P-8040)
MOUNTAIN GEAR CORPORATION
Also Called: Tri-Mountain
4889 4th St, Irwindale (91706-2194)
PHONE............................626 851-2488
Daniel Tsai, *CEO*
Sandy Treagus, *CFO*
Jennifer Tsai, *Vice Pres*
Rosie Tsai, *Vice Pres*
Olga Duran, *CTO*
▲ EMP: 125
SQ FT: 300,000
SALES (est): 48.3MM **Privately Held**
WEB: www.trimountain.com
SIC: **5136** Sportswear, men's & boys'

(P-8041)
NORTH BAY DISTRIBUTION INC
2029 E Monte Vista Ave, Vacaville (95688-3100)
PHONE............................707 450-1219
Lee Perry, *Branch Mgr*
EMP: 70
SQ FT: 250,000
SALES (corp-wide): 40MM **Privately Held**
SIC: **5136** Men's & boys' clothing
PA: North Bay Distribution, Inc.
2050 Cessna Dr
Vacaville CA 95688
707 452-9984

(P-8042)
OTTO INTERNATIONAL INC (PA)
Also Called: Otto Cap
3550 Jurupa St Ste A, Ontario (91761-2946)
PHONE............................909 937-1998
Razgo Lee, *President*
Frank Jou, *CFO*
Heidi Soria, *Sales Associate*
◆ EMP: 100
SQ FT: 136,000
SALES (est): 47.8MM **Privately Held**
WEB: www.ottocap.com
SIC: **5136** Caps, men's & boys'

▲ = Import ▼ =Export
◆ =Import/Export

(P-8043)
PIEGE CO (PA)
Also Called: Felina Lingerie
20120 Plummer St, Chatsworth
(91311-5448)
PHONE..............................818 727-9100
Kambiz Zarabi, *President*
Morad Zarabi, *Ch of Bd*
Michael Zarabi, *Exec VP*
Nara Estepani, *Controller*
Sherri Kamali, *Human Res Mgr*
▲ EMP: 195
SQ FT: 48,000
SALES (est): 78.4MM **Privately Held**
WEB: www.felinausa.com
SIC: 5136 5137 Men's & boys' suits &
trousers; lingerie

(P-8044)
PRANA LIVING LLC (HQ)
3209 Lionshead Ave, Carlsbad
(92010-4710)
PHONE..............................866 915-6457
Scott Kerslake, *CEO*
Larry Callette, *CFO*
Jessica Mahoney, *Vice Pres*
Jeff Haack, *Creative Dir*
Molly Reimers, *Financial Analy*
▲ EMP: 90
SALES (est): 55.3MM
SALES (corp-wide): 2.8B **Publicly Held**
SIC: 5136 5137 Men's & boys' clothing;
women's & children's clothing
PA: Columbia Sportswear Company
14375 Nw Science Park Dr
Portland OR 97229
503 985-4000

(P-8045)
QUAKE CITY CASUALS INC
Also Called: Quake City Caps
1800 S Flower St, Los Angeles
(90015-3424)
PHONE..............................213 746-0540
John Glucksman, *CEO*
Steve De Mars, *President*
Soledad Wong, *Chief Mktg Ofcr*
Priscilla Hill, *Vice Pres*
Nathan Munoz, *Accountant*
▲ EMP: 125
SQ FT: 11,500
SALES (est): 23.6MM **Privately Held**
WEB: www.capstoneheadwear.com
SIC: 5136 Men's & boys' clothing

(P-8046)
RICK SOLOMON ENTERPRISES INC (PA)
Also Called: Axis
8460 Higuera St, Culver City (90232-2520)
P.O. Box 266, Los Angeles (90078-0266)
PHONE..............................310 280-3700
Richard Solomon, *President*
Barbara Baskin, *CFO*
◆ EMP: 70
SQ FT: 14,058
SALES (est): 12.1MM **Privately Held**
WEB: www.axisclothing.com
SIC: 5136 Sportswear, men's & boys'

(P-8047)
STUSSY INC
17426 Daimler St, Irvine (92614-5514)
PHONE..............................949 474-9255
Frank Sinatra, *CEO*
Andy Tirpstra, *General Mgr*
Mindy Cook, *Admin Sec*
Desiree Hardy, *Admin Asst*
Chad Naylor, *Planning*
▲ EMP: 90
SQ FT: 30,000
SALES (est): 40MM **Privately Held**
SIC: 5136 Men's & boys' clothing

(P-8048)
TOPWIN CORPORATION (PA)
Also Called: People's Place
1808 Abalone Ave, Torrance (90501-3703)
PHONE..............................310 325-2255
Tomokazu Yoshimura, *CEO*
Kacey Abe, *Manager*
▲ EMP: 60
SQ FT: 22,000

SALES (est): 35.9MM **Privately Held**
WEB: www.topwin.com
SIC: 5136 5137 5611 5621 Men's &
boys' clothing; women's & children's
clothing; men's & boys' clothing stores;
women's clothing stores; mannequins

(P-8049)
UNI HOSIERY CO INC (PA)
1911 E Olympic Blvd, Los Angeles
(90021-2421)
PHONE..............................213 228-0100
Harry Chung, *CEO*
Eric Park, *Accountant*
Kim Richard, *Sales Mgr*
Michelle Choi, *Sales Staff*
Hilida Lee, *Sales Staff*
◆ EMP: 120
SQ FT: 500,000
SALES (est): 45.3MM **Privately Held**
WEB: www.unihosiery.com
SIC: 5136 5137 Hosiery, men's & boys';
hosiery: women's, children's & infants';
lingerie

(P-8050)
VOLCOM LLC
1725 Monrovia Ave, Costa Mesa
(92627-4401)
PHONE..............................949 646-2175
Richard R Woolcott, *Branch Mgr*
EMP: 200 **Privately Held**
SIC: 5136 Men's & boys' clothing
PA: Volcom, Llc
1740 Monrovia Ave
Costa Mesa CA 92627

(P-8051)
WOR INTERNATIONAL INC
Also Called: Nick and MO
15612 1st St, Irwindale (91706-6220)
P.O. Box 1631, Walnut (91788-1631)
PHONE..............................626 812-8888
Hsu WEI Wang, *President*
Roger Liang, *Vice Pres*
◆ EMP: 50
SQ FT: 30,000
SALES: 13.2MM **Privately Held**
WEB: www.worusa.com
SIC: 5136 Men's & boys' clothing

┌─────────────────────────────┐
│ **5137 Women's, Children's &** │
│ **Infants Clothing Wholesale** │
└─────────────────────────────┘

(P-8052)
2253 APPAREL INC (PA)
Also Called: Celebrity Pink USA
1708 Aeros Way, Montebello (90640-6504)
PHONE..............................323 837-9800
Doron Kadosh, *President*
Holly Arnesen-Sileo, *Exec VP*
Benny Goldstein, *Admin Sec*
David Kadosh,
Michelle Jacobsen, *Manager*
▲ EMP: 80
SQ FT: 50,000
SALES (est): 100MM **Privately Held**
WEB: www.2253apparel.com
SIC: 5137 Women's & children's clothing

(P-8053)
ALSTYLE AP & ACTIVEWEAR MGT CO (HQ)
1501 E Cerritos Ave, Anaheim
(92805-6400)
PHONE..............................714 765-0400
Rauf Gajiani, *CEO*
Amin Amdani, *Vice Pres*
Richard Travis, *Vice Pres*
Omer Hasan, *Technical Staff*
Mohammad Meah, *Purchasing*
◆ EMP: 1800 EST: 2001
SQ FT: 715,000
SALES (est): 526.2MM
SALES (corp-wide): 2.9B **Privately Held**
WEB: www.alstyle.com
SIC: 5137 Women's & children's clothing

PA: Gildan Activewear Inc
600 Boul De Maisonneuve O 33eme
etage
Montreal QC H3A 3
514 735-2023

(P-8054)
AMOUR VERT INC
1278 Minnesota St Ste A, San Francisco
(94107-3408)
PHONE..............................650 388-4284
Aaron Hoey, *CEO*
Amanda Halper, *Marketing Staff*
Cooper Lauren, *Manager*
Jordan Marks, *Retailers*
EMP: 64
SALES: 13MM **Privately Held**
SIC: 5137 Women's & children's clothing

(P-8055)
BABY TREND INC (HQ)
13048 Valley Blvd, Fontana (92335-2602)
PHONE..............................909 773-0018
Jiangfeng Su, *CEO*
Betty Tsai, *Vice Pres*
Brad Mattarocci, *General Mgr*
Yong Kim, *Executive Asst*
Kim Yong, *Executive Asst*
◆ EMP: 61
SQ FT: 67,000
SALES (est): 19MM **Privately Held**
WEB: www.babytrend.com
SIC: 5137 Baby goods

(P-8056)
BCBG MAX AZRIA GROUP LLC
2761 Fruitland Ave, Vernon (90058-3607)
PHONE..............................323 589-2224
EMP: 69 EST: 2014
SALES (est): 1.1MM
SALES (corp-wide): 1.5B **Privately Held**
SIC: 5137 5621 2335
PA: Guggenheim Partners, Llc
330 Madison Ave Rm 201
New York NY 10017
212 739-0700

(P-8057)
BCTC CORPORATION
5500 E Olympic Blvd Ste B, Commerce
(90022-5130)
PHONE..............................323 888-9388
Shirley Bao, *Chairman*
Even Chew, *President*
Sally Bao, *Vice Pres*
Edward Hu, *Vice Pres*
Alex Kang, *Finance*
▲ EMP: 80 EST: 1973
SQ FT: 75,000
SALES: 18.9MM **Privately Held**
WEB: www.bctccorp.com
SIC: 5137 Women's & children's clothing

(P-8058)
BLUE PLANET INTERNATIONAL INC
Also Called: Boom-Boom Jeans
2945 E 12th St, Los Angeles (90023-3623)
PHONE..............................323 526-9999
Simon Parsakar, *President*
Ezra Parsakar, *Vice Pres*
◆ EMP: 50
SQ FT: 30,000
SALES (est): 45MM **Privately Held**
WEB: www.boomboomjeans.com
SIC: 5137 Women's & children's clothing

(P-8059)
BRUML MANAGEMENT LLC
Also Called: Techstyles Sportswear
2051 Alpine Way, Hayward (94545-1703)
PHONE..............................800 733-3629
Jonathan Bruml, *Mng Member*
Lisa Bruml,
EMP: 50
SQ FT: 20,000
SALES (est): 12MM **Privately Held**
SIC: 5137 5136 Women's & children's
clothing; men's & boys' clothing

(P-8060)
BUNNY BEACH SWIMWEAR INC (PA)
Also Called: Beach Bunny Swimwear
555 Anton Blvd Ste 150, Costa Mesa
(92626-7036)
PHONE..............................949 336-6300
Angela A Chittenden, *Mng Member*
Stephanie Weber, *Manager*
▲ EMP: 59
SALES (est): 14MM **Privately Held**
WEB: www.beachbunnyswimwear.com
SIC: 5137 Swimsuits: women's, children's
& infants'

(P-8061)
CALIFORNIA RAIN COMPANY INC
1213 E 14th St, Los Angeles (90021-2215)
PHONE..............................213 623-6061
Jack Jhy C Jang, *Prdtn Mgr*
Cita Panorama, *Prdtn Mgr*
◆ EMP: 90
SQ FT: 8,600
SALES (est): 33.2MM **Privately Held**
WEB: www.californiarainla.com
SIC: 5137 5136 5699 Sportswear,
women's & children's; sportswear, men's
& boys'; customized clothing & apparel

(P-8062)
CECICO INC
Also Called: Cecico Town
1016 Towne Ave Unit 110, Los Angeles
(90021-2078)
PHONE..............................323 269-7000
Kelly Kyung Lie Ahn, *Principal*
Kelly K Ahn, *Principal*
▲ EMP: 55
SALES (est): 8.7MM **Privately Held**
SIC: 5137 2339 Women's & children's
clothing; women's & misses' accessories

(P-8063)
CHANCE GROUP LLC
911 E 106th St, Los Angeles (90002-3442)
PHONE..............................310 343-3766
Shaunt Khandamian, *CEO*
EMP: 50
SALES: 15MM **Privately Held**
SIC: 5137 Women's & children's dresses,
suits, skirts & blouses

(P-8064)
CHILDRENS BTQ AT STEVENS HOPE
Also Called: Childrens Botique, The
10730 Fthill Blvd Ste 170, Rancho Cuca-
monga (91730)
PHONE..............................909 256-0100
Tony Campbell, *Owner*
EMP: 50
SALES (est): 2.4MM **Privately Held**
SIC: 5137 3949 8699 Women's & chil-
dren's clothing; sporting & athletic goods;
charitable organization

(P-8065)
CLAUDIA RICHARD INC
4871 S Santa Fe Ave, Vernon
(90058-2103)
PHONE..............................323 264-3915
Benjamin Boston, *President*
Ram Kundani, *Vice Pres*
◆ EMP: 59
SALES (est): 15.9MM **Privately Held**
SIC: 5137 Women's & children's clothing

(P-8066)
COLLECTED GROUP COMPANY LLC
Also Called: Joie
5300 S Santa Fe Ave, Vernon
(90058-3520)
PHONE..............................323 277-3900
Serge Azria, *Branch Mgr*
EMP: 50
SALES (corp-wide): 170.1MM **Privately Held**
SIC: 5137 Women's & children's clothing
HQ: Dutch, Llc
5301 S Santa Fe Ave
Vernon CA 90058
323 277-3900

P R O D U C T S & S V C S

(P-8067)
COMAK TRADING INC A CAL CORP
2550 S Soto St, Vernon (90058-8013)
PHONE...................................323 261-3404
EMP: 100
SALES (est): 12.6MM **Privately Held**
SIC: 5137 5136 5139

(P-8068)
DELTA GALIL USA INC
Also Called: Loomworks Apparel
16912 Von Karman Ave, Irvine (92606-4972)
PHONE...................................949 296-0380
EMP: 54
SALES (corp-wide): 389.2MM **Privately Held**
SIC: 5137 Women's & children's lingerie & undergarments
HQ: Delta Galil Usa Inc.
1 Harmon Plz Fl 5
Secaucus NJ 07094
201 902-0055

(P-8069)
DUTCH LLC (DH)
Also Called: Current Elliot
5301 S Santa Fe Ave, Vernon (90058-3519)
PHONE...................................323 277-3900
Serge K Azria, *Mng Member*
Morgan Dreyer, *Executive Asst*
Florence Azria,
▲ EMP: 133
SQ FT: 40,000
SALES (est): 170.1MM
SALES (corp-wide): 170.1MM **Privately Held**
SIC: 5137 Women's & children's clothing
HQ: The Collected Group Llc
5301 S Santa Fe Ave
Vernon CA 90058
323 277-3900

(P-8070)
EDGEMINE INC
Also Called: Mine Fashion
1801 E 50th St, Los Angeles (90058-1940)
PHONE...................................323 267-8222
Kevin Chang Kang, *President*
Kristen Han, *Exec VP*
▲ EMP: 120 EST: 1994
SQ FT: 45,000
SALES (est): 630.8K **Privately Held**
SIC: 5137 Women's & children's clothing

(P-8071)
EIGHTY ONE ENTERPRISE INC
9401 Whitmore St, El Monte (91731-2821)
PHONE...................................626 371-1980
May Sayphraraj, *President*
Darren Sayphraraj, *Treasurer*
◆ EMP: 50 EST: 2012
SQ FT: 60,000
SALES (est): 18MM **Privately Held**
SIC: 5137 Lingerie

(P-8072)
ESP GROUP LTD
2397 Bateman Ave, Duarte (91010-3313)
PHONE...................................626 301-0280
Yan Wang, *CEO*
David Ouyang, *President*
William Yue, *CFO*
Joseph Buonfiglio, *Vice Pres*
◆ EMP: 68
SQ FT: 150,000
SALES (est): 28.7MM **Privately Held**
SIC: 5137 Women's & children's clothing

(P-8073)
FACTORY 2-U IMPORT EXPORT INC
Also Called: Oren's Replay
13034 Delano St, Van Nuys (91401-3209)
PHONE...................................323 587-9900
Liat Madar, *CEO*
EMP: 60
SALES (est): 2.1MM **Privately Held**
WEB: www.youimport.com
SIC: 5137 5136 Women's & children's clothing; men's & boys' clothing

(P-8074)
GURU DENIM LLC (DH)
Also Called: True Religion Brand Jeans
1888 Rosecrans Ave, Manhattan Beach (90266-3712)
PHONE...................................323 266-3072
John Ermatinger, *Mng Member*
Eric Bauer, *CFO*
Alan Weiss, *Controller*
▲ EMP: 150
SQ FT: 19,300
SALES (est): 549.2MM
SALES (corp-wide): 350MM **Privately Held**
WEB: www.gurudenim.com
SIC: 5137 5611 Women's & children's clothing; clothing accessories: men's & boys'
HQ: True Religion Apparel, Inc.
1888 Rosecrans Ave # 1000
Manhattan Beach CA 90266
323 266-3072

(P-8075)
HARVEYS INDUSTRIES INC
Also Called: Original Seatbeltbag , The
724 N Poinsettia St, Santa Ana (92701-3941)
PHONE...................................714 277-4700
Dana Harvey, *CEO*
Melanie Harvey, *Admin Sec*
Jessica Rice, *Human Res Mgr*
Chris Harvey, *Manager*
Addrienne Matheny, *Manager*
▲ EMP: 55
SQ FT: 12,000
SALES (est): 22.8MM **Privately Held**
WEB: www.harveysboutique.com
SIC: 5137 5632 Handbags; women's accessory & specialty stores

(P-8076)
HIBSHMAN TRADING CORPORATION
Also Called: Mattress Liqidation
9843 6th St Ste 103, Rancho Cucamonga (91730-5741)
PHONE...................................909 581-1800
Erik D Hibshman, *President*
EMP: 60
SQ FT: 65,000
SALES: 7.5MM **Privately Held**
SIC: 5137 5136 5021 Women's & children's clothing; men's & boys' clothing; mattresses

(P-8077)
HOUSTON SALEM INC
Also Called: Chaser
217 E 157th St, Gardena (90248-2510)
PHONE...................................310 719-7004
Stephen Martin Kayne, *CEO*
Jackie Sique Molina, *Controller*
▲ EMP: 50
SQ FT: 70,000
SALES (est): 23.7MM **Privately Held**
WEB: www.bhcompany.com
SIC: 5137 5136 Women's & children's clothing; men's & boys' clothing

(P-8078)
INCREMENTO INC
Also Called: Peach Love California
2670 Leonis Blvd, Vernon (90058-2204)
PHONE...................................213 624-7777
Su Hee Choi, *CEO*
EMP: 60
SQ FT: 50,000
SALES (est): 8.2MM **Privately Held**
SIC: 5137 Women's & children's clothing

(P-8079)
ISABEL GARRETON INC (PA)
770 Miraflores, San Pedro (90731-1437)
PHONE...................................310 833-7768
Isabel Garreton, *President*
Michael Juneau, *Data Proc Dir*
Erika Whitham, *Software Dev*
EMP: 125
SALES (est): 15.3MM **Privately Held**
WEB: www.isabelgarreton.com
SIC: 5137 Women's & children's clothing

(P-8080)
JEAN MART INC
6700 Avalon Blvd, Los Angeles (90003-1920)
PHONE...................................323 752-7775
Arnold Yu, *Principal*
Helen C Yi, *President*
▲ EMP: 100
SQ FT: 5,000
SALES (est): 50.3MM **Privately Held**
SIC: 5137 7389 Women's & children's clothing; sewing contractor

(P-8081)
KAREN KANE INC (PA)
2275 E 37th St, Vernon (90058-1435)
PHONE...................................323 588-0000
Lonnie Kane, *President*
Cecelia Jenkins, *Treasurer*
Karen Kane, *Vice Pres*
Donna Ancheta, *Accountant*
Livia Medina, *Human Res Dir*
▲ EMP: 130
SQ FT: 96,000
SALES (est): 87.1MM **Privately Held**
SIC: 5137 Women's & children's clothing; women's & children's accessories

(P-8082)
KASH APPAREL LLC
Also Called: Socialite Clothing
1437 E 20th St, Los Angeles (90011-1301)
PHONE...................................213 747-8885
Stephanie Kleinjan, *Mng Member*
Adir Haroni,
▲ EMP: 68
SQ FT: 10,000
SALES (est): 22.8MM **Privately Held**
SIC: 5137 Women's & children's accessories

(P-8083)
KBL GROUP INTERNATIONAL LTD
Also Called: Kbl International
9142 9150 Norwalk Blvd, Santa Fe Springs (90670)
PHONE...................................562 699-9995
Thomas Ko, *Branch Mgr*
EMP: 50
SALES (corp-wide): 47.2MM **Privately Held**
WEB: www.crystalk.com
SIC: 5137 Sportswear, women's & children's
PA: Kbl Group International Ltd.
1441 Broadway Fl 17th
New York NY 10018
212 391-1551

(P-8084)
KELLWOOD COMPANY LLC
Also Called: Xoxo
13085 Temple Ave, City of Industry (91746-1418)
PHONE...................................626 934-4155
Sherri Akers, *Branch Mgr*
EMP: 150
SALES (corp-wide): 594MM **Privately Held**
SIC: 5137 Women's & children's clothing
PA: Kellwood Company, Llc
600 Kellwood Pkwy Ste 110
Chesterfield MO 63017
314 576-3100

(P-8085)
KOS-USA
3434 S Broadway, Los Angeles (90007-4409)
PHONE...................................213 747-2591
Donna Shin, *President*
Charlie Shin, *Vice Pres*
EMP: 60 EST: 1991
SALES (est): 7.7MM **Privately Held**
WEB: www.kosusa.com
SIC: 5137 Women's & children's clothing

(P-8086)
LDLA CLOTHING LLC
Also Called: Living Doll
13071 Temple Ave, La Puente (91746-1418)
PHONE...................................323 312-2805
Amy Powers, *Owner*
Richard Swartz, *CFO*

EMP: 60
SALES: 50MM **Privately Held**
SIC: 5137 Women's & children's clothing

(P-8087)
LIMS INC
2880 Zanker Rd, San Jose (95134-2117)
PHONE...................................925 803-7795
Roberto Lim, *President*
EMP: 80
SQ FT: 9,000
SALES: 8MM **Privately Held**
WEB: www.china-usa-lims.com
SIC: 5137 Women's & children's clothing

(P-8088)
LYMI INC (PA)
Also Called: Reformation, The
2263 E Vernon Ave, Vernon (90058-1631)
PHONE...................................213 434-2772
Yael Aflalo, *CEO*
Jennifer Loo, *CFO*
Holly Rogers, *Controller*
Kate Rockwell, *Buyer*
Kathleen Talbot, *Opers Mgr*
▲ EMP: 100
SQ FT: 120,000
SALES (est): 249.2MM **Privately Held**
SIC: 5137 Women's & children's clothing

(P-8089)
MAD DOGG ATHLETICS INC (PA)
Also Called: Spinning
2111 Narcissus Ct, Venice (90291-4818)
PHONE...................................310 823-7008
John R Baudhuin, *President*
Aerin Shaw, *COO*
Jonathan Goldberg, *Admin Sec*
Michele McDonnell, *Prdtn Mgr*
◆ EMP: 77
SALES (est): 50.3MM **Privately Held**
WEB: www.spinning.com
SIC: 5137 5122 7812 Sportswear, women's & children's; vitamins & minerals; video tape production

(P-8090)
MADALUXE GROUP LLC (PA)
1760 Apollo Ct, Seal Beach (90740-5617)
PHONE...................................562 296-1055
Sandra Sholl, *Mng Member*
Delynn Lane, *Treasurer*
Adam Freede, *Vice Pres*
Elizabeth Jalonschi, *Project Mgr*
Matthew Polisciuc, *Accountant*
◆ EMP: 50
SQ FT: 64,000
SALES: 60MM **Privately Held**
SIC: 5137 5136 Women's & children's clothing; men's & boys' clothing

(P-8091)
MALIBU DESIGN GROUP
Also Called: Ocean Dream
5445 Jillson St, Commerce (90040-2117)
PHONE...................................323 271-1700
Mollie Cha, *CEO*
Mary Chung, *Admin Sec*
◆ EMP: 50
SQ FT: 60,000
SALES (est): 22.8MM **Privately Held**
SIC: 5137 Swimsuits: women's, children's & infants'

(P-8092)
MARIKA GROUP INC
Also Called: Shiva-Shakthi
8960 Carroll Way, San Diego (92121-2429)
PHONE...................................858 537-5300
Donald Schumacher, *Vice Pres*
Scott Kalman, *President*
Lew Corpuz, *Vice Pres*
▲ EMP: 60
SQ FT: 60,000
SALES (est): 11.4MM **Privately Held**
SIC: 5137 2339 Sportswear, women's & children's; women's & misses' outerwear

(P-8093)
MATESTA CORPORATION
5620 Knott Ave, Buena Park (90621-1808)
P.O. Box 5395 (90622-5395)
PHONE...................................949 874-6052
Salim Saeed, *CEO*
Robert Abraham, *CFO*

▲ = Import ▼=Export
◆ =Import/Export

EMP: 106
SALES: 62MM **Privately Held**
SIC: 5137 5136 Women's & children's
clothing; men's & boys' clothing

(P-8094)
MEL BERNIE AND COMPANY INC
Edgar Berebi A Div 1928 Jwly
3000 W Empire Ave, Burbank
(91504-3109)
PHONE..................................818 841-1928
Mel Bernie, *Branch Mgr*
EMP: 150
SALES (corp-wide): 55.6MM **Privately
Held**
WEB: www.1928.com
SIC: 5137 Women's & children's acces-
sories
PA: Mel Bernie And Company, Inc.
    3000 W Empire Ave
    Burbank CA 91504
    818 841-1928

(P-8095)
MIAS FASHION MFG CO INC
Also Called: California Basic
12623 Cisneros Ln, Santa Fe Springs
(90670-3373)
PHONE..................................562 906-1060
Peter D Anh, *President*
Brian Song, *CFO*
◆ EMP: 252 EST: 1999
SALES: 163MM **Privately Held**
WEB: www.mfmcoinc.com
SIC: 5137 Women's & children's clothing

(P-8096)
MIKEN SALES INC (PA)
Also Called: Miken Clothing
7230 Oxford Way, Commerce
(90040-3643)
PHONE..................................323 266-2560
Michael Bobbitt, *CEO*
Kenny Landy, *Vice Pres*
Jonathan Namm, *VP Opers*
◆ EMP: 53
SQ FT: 23,000
SALES (est): 21.1MM **Privately Held**
SIC: 5137 Women's & children's clothing

(P-8097)
MOLA INC
2957 E 46th St, Vernon (90058-2423)
PHONE..................................323 582-0088
▲ EMP: 150
SALES (est): 45.2MM **Privately Held**
SIC: 5137

(P-8098)
MS BUBBLES INC (PA)
Also Called: Eighty Eight
2731 S Alameda St, Los Angeles
(90058-1311)
PHONE..................................323 544-0300
Aneeta Chopra, *CEO*
Sanjiv Chopra, *Treasurer*
Renu Chopra, *Vice Pres*
Rajeshwar Chopra, *Admin Sec*
▲ EMP: 75
SQ FT: 50,000
SALES (est): 29.4MM **Privately Held**
WEB: www.msbubbles.com
SIC: 5137 Women's & children's clothing

(P-8099)
MYSTIC INC (PA)
2444 Porter St, Los Angeles (90021-2511)
PHONE..................................213 746-8538
Haejin Han, *President*
Hae Han, *CEO*
Daniel Priano, *COO*
▲ EMP: 55
SQ FT: 45,000
SALES: 15.3MM **Privately Held**
SIC: 5137 2339 Women's & children's
clothing; athletic clothing: women's,
misses' & juniors'

(P-8100)
NEW PRIDE CORPORATION
Also Called: Belinda
5101 Pacific Blvd, Vernon (90058-2217)
PHONE..................................323 584-6608
Miran Byun, *CEO*
Ho Lee, *President*

EMP: 55
SQ FT: 5,000
SALES (est): 5.6MM **Privately Held**
SIC: 5137 2331 Women's & children's
clothing; women's & misses' blouses &
shirts

(P-8101)
NEWPORT APPAREL CORPORATION (PA)
Also Called: I N G
1215 W Walnut St, Compton (90220-5009)
PHONE..................................310 605-1900
James Kim, *President*
Kimberly Kim, *CFO*
Joyce Cho, *Executive*
Esther Kim, *Info Tech Mgr*
▲ EMP: 62
SQ FT: 38,500
SALES (est): 27.7MM **Privately Held**
WEB: www.newporting.com
SIC: 5137 Sportswear, women's & chil-
dren's

(P-8102)
NHN GLOBAL INC (PA)
Also Called: Fashiongo.com
3530 Wilshire Blvd Ste 16, Los Angeles
(90010-2328)
PHONE..................................424 672-1177
Daniel Lee, *CEO*
Ron Hao, *Sales Staff*
EMP: 118
SALES (est): 768.1K **Privately Held**
SIC: 5137 7389 Women's & children's
clothing;

(P-8103)
NYDJ APPAREL LLC
Also Called: Not Your Daughters Jeans
5401 S Soto St, Vernon (90058-3618)
PHONE..................................323 581-9040
Lisa Collier,
Jennifer Adams, *COO*
Rosella Giuliani, *Vice Pres*
Helen Rhim, *Vice Pres*
Eric Ueno, *Vice Pres*
▲ EMP: 200
SQ FT: 6,000
SALES (est): 148.4MM **Privately Held**
WEB: www.lls.com
SIC: 5137 Women's & children's clothing

(P-8104)
NYGARD INC
Also Called: Tan Jay-Nygard Outlet Store
14401 S San Pedro St, Gardena
(90248-2026)
PHONE..................................310 776-8900
Murray Batte, *President*
Katrina Cortez, *Manager*
EMP: 63
SALES (corp-wide): 419.3K **Privately
Held**
SIC: 5137 Women's & children's clothing
HQ: Nygard Inc.
    1435 Broadway
    New York NY 10018
    646 520-2000

(P-8105)
ONE 3 TWO INC
Also Called: Obey Clothing
17353 Derian Ave, Irvine (92614-5801)
PHONE..................................949 596-8400
Regan Don Juncal, *CEO*
Don Junkal, *President*
Steve Melgren, *CFO*
Chris Broder, *Vice Pres*
Peraza Adrian, *Controller*
▲ EMP: 106 EST: 2000
SALES (est): 46.2MM **Privately Held**
WEB: www.obey.com
SIC: 5137 Women's & children's clothing

(P-8106)
PARAGON TEXTILES INC
Also Called: Samiyatex
13003 S Figueroa St, Los Angeles
(90061-1136)
PHONE..................................310 323-7500
Murtaza Haji, *President*
Farhana Haji, *Treasurer*
▼ EMP: 45
SQ FT: 42,500

SALES (est): 29.6MM **Privately Held**
WEB: www.samiyatex.com
SIC: 5137 Women's & children's clothing

(P-8107)
RUNWAY LIQUIDATION LLC (HQ)
Also Called: Bcbg Max Azria Group, LLC
2761 Fruitland Ave, Vernon (90058-3607)
PHONE..................................323 589-2224
Max Azria,
Bernd Kroeber, *Exec VP*
Martine Melloul, *Exec VP*
◆ EMP: 153
SQ FT: 500,000
SALES (est): 576.5MM
SALES (corp-wide): 570.1MM **Privately
Held**
WEB: www.bcbg.com
SIC: 5137 5621 2335 Women's & chil-
dren's clothing; women's clothing stores;
women's, juniors' & misses' dresses
PA: Marquee Brands Llc
    50 W 57th St
    New York NY 10019
    212 203-8135

(P-8108)
SAME SWIM LLC
2333 E 49th St, Vernon (90058-2820)
PHONE..................................323 582-2588
Shea Petranovic,
Ryan Horne,
EMP: 90
SALES (est): 110.7K **Privately Held**
SIC: 5137 Women's & children's sports-
wear & swimsuits

(P-8109)
SECRET CHARM LLC (PA)
1433 Walnut St, Los Angeles (90011-1314)
PHONE..................................213 742-7744
Adir Haroni, *Mng Member*
Eran Haroni, *President*
Janette Edwards, *CFO*
Elias Haroni,
Soussan Haroni,
▲ EMP: 230
SALES (est): 99.3MM **Privately Held**
SIC: 5137 Children's goods

(P-8110)
SEVEN LICENSING COMPANY LLC
Also Called: Seven7 Brands
801 S Figueroa St # 2500, Los Angeles
(90017-5504)
PHONE..................................323 881-0308
Jacqueline Rose Guez, *Mng Member*
Gerald Guez,
▲ EMP: 80
SQ FT: 10,000
SALES (est): 26.5MM **Privately Held**
SIC: 5137 Women's & children's acces-
sories
PA: Sunrise Brands, Llc
    801 S Figueroa St # 2500
    Los Angeles CA 90017

(P-8111)
SEYMOUR GALE & ASSOCIATES
4501 Cedros Ave Unit 118, Sherman Oaks
(91403-2839)
PHONE..................................213 622-5361
Seymour Gale, *Owner*
EMP: 50
SQ FT: 1,500
SALES (est): 12.1MM **Privately Held**
SIC: 5137 Women's & children's clothing

(P-8112)
SUNRISE BRANDS LLC (PA)
801 S Figueroa St # 2500, Los Angeles
(90017-5504)
PHONE..................................323 780-8250
Gerard Guez, *CEO*
Don Waldman, *COO*
Peter Akaragian, *CFO*
Donald Waldman, *CFO*
Linda Cohen, *Vice Pres*
EMP: 50
SALES (est): 87.5MM **Privately Held**
SIC: 5137 5136 Women's & children's
clothing; men's & boys' clothing

(P-8113)
SWATFAME INC (PA)
Also Called: Kut From The Kloth
16425 Gale Ave, City of Industry
(91745-1722)
PHONE..................................626 961-7928
Bruce Stern, *Ch of Bd*
Jonathan Greenberg, *President*
Mitchell Quaranta, *CEO*
J P Wolk, *CFO*
Joseph Wolk, *CFO*
▲ EMP: 290
SQ FT: 233,000
SALES: 185.4MM **Privately Held**
WEB: www.swatfame.com
SIC: 5137 2211 2339 Dresses; sports-
wear, women's & children's; denims;
women's & misses' outerwear

(P-8114)
TARRANT APPAREL GROUP
Also Called: Fashion Resources
801 S Figueroa St # 2500, Los Angeles
(90017-5504)
PHONE..................................323 780-8250
Gerard Guez, *Ch of Bd*
Peter Akaradian, *CFO*
Todd Kay, *Vice Ch Bd*
▲ EMP: 250
SALES (est): 57.3MM **Privately Held**
SIC: 5137 Women's & children's clothing
PA: Sunrise Brands, Llc
    801 S Figueroa St # 2500
    Los Angeles CA 90017

(P-8115)
TOPSON DOWNS CALIFORNIA INC (PA)
3840 Watseka Ave, Culver City
(90232-2633)
PHONE..................................310 558-0300
John Poyer, *President*
Kelly Gordon, *COO*
Kristopher Scott, *CFO*
Joe Wirht, *Admin Sec*
Jesseka McGee, *Human Resources*
▲ EMP: 250
SQ FT: 42,000
SALES (est): 280.2MM **Privately Held**
WEB: www.topsondowns.com
SIC: 5137 Women's & children's clothing

(P-8116)
TYR SPORT INC
Also Called: T Y R
1790 Apollo Ct, Seal Beach (90740-5617)
P.O. Box 1930, Huntington Beach (92647-
1930)
PHONE..................................562 430-1380
Matthew Dilorenzo, *CEO*
Steven Locke, *COO*
Joe Roehrig, *CFO*
David Melendez, *Info Tech Mgr*
Chris Sacco, *Controller*
◆ EMP: 60
SQ FT: 80,000
SALES (est): 28.8MM
SALES (corp-wide): 52MM **Privately
Held**
WEB: www.tyr.com
SIC: 5137 5136 5091 2329 Sportswear,
women's & children's; swimsuits:
women's, children's & infants'; women's
& children's accessories; beachwear,
men's & boys'; sporting & recreation
goods; bathing suits & swimwear: men's
& boys'; basketball uniforms: men's,
youths' & boys'
PA: Swimwear Anywhere, Inc.
    85 Sherwood Ave
    Farmingdale NY 11735
    631 420-1400

(P-8117)
YOUNG BAE FASHIONS INC
4811 Hampton St, Vernon (90058-2135)
P.O. Box 58187, Los Angeles (90058-0187)
PHONE..................................323 583-8684
Young Bae, *President*
Chung Bae, *Admin Sec*
▲ EMP: 75 EST: 1976
SQ FT: 40,000
SALES: 12MM **Privately Held**
SIC: 5137 Women's & children's clothing

(PA)=Parent Co (HQ)=Headquarters (DH)=Div Headquarters
✪ = New Business established in last 2 years

2019 Directory of California
Wholesalers and Services Companies

349

PRODUCTS & SVCS

5139 Footwear Wholesale

(P-8118)
ACI INTERNATIONAL (PA)
844 Moraga Dr, Los Angeles (90049-1632)
PHONE..........................310 889-3400
Steve Jackson, *CEO*
Jay Jackson, *President*
David Mankowitz, *CFO*
Scott Coble, *Exec VP*
Jeffrey Glazier, *Exec VP*
▲ **EMP:** 79 **EST:** 1952
SQ FT: 40,000
SALES (est): 39.2MM **Privately Held**
WEB: www.aciint.com
SIC: 5139 Shoes; slippers, house

(P-8119)
AHA SHOES INC
72 S Main St Ste A, Templeton
(93465-9787)
PHONE..........................805 434-9891
Christopher A Takken, *CEO*
Marc Takken, *Principal*
EMP: 60
SQ FT: 3,000
SALES: 8.2MM **Privately Held**
SIC: 5139 Shoes

(P-8120)
ASICS AMERICA CORPORATION (HQ)
Also Called: Asics Tiger
80 Technology Dr, Irvine (92618-2301)
PHONE..........................949 453-8888
Kevin Wulff, *CEO*
Seiho Gohashi, *Ch of Bd*
Richard Bourne, *President*
Kenji Sakai, *CFO*
Craig Gillan, *Vice Pres*
▲ **EMP:** 109 **EST:** 1973
SQ FT: 45,000
SALES (est): 237.3MM **Privately Held**
WEB: www.onitsukatiger.com
SIC: 5139 5136 5137 2369 Footwear, athletic; sportswear, men's & boys'; men's & boys' furnishings; sportswear, women's & children's; women's & children's accessories; girls' & children's outerwear; women's & misses' outerwear; men's & boys' furnishings

(P-8121)
AYLESVA INC
14537 Garfield Ave, Paramount
(90723-3425)
PHONE..........................562 688-0592
Jose Luis Solorcano, *President*
EMP: 120
SALES: 24MM **Privately Held**
SIC: 5139 5661 5651 5137 Shoes; shoe stores; family clothing stores; coordinate sets: women's, children's & infants'

(P-8122)
BIRKENSTOCK USA LP (DH)
8171 Redwood Blvd, Novato (94945-1403)
PHONE..........................415 884-3200
Stephan Birkenstock, *Partner*
Bernd Hillen, *Partner*
Christa Skov, *Partner*
Michael Hoessl, *Vice Pres*
Nancy Moock, *Executive*
▲ **EMP:** 62
SQ FT: 15,000
SALES (est): 30.6MM
SALES (corp-wide): 742MM **Privately Held**
WEB: www.birkenstockusa.com
SIC: 5139 Footwear

(P-8123)
BUFFALO DISTRIBUTION
Also Called: Keen Account
1624 Pacific St, Union City (94587-2028)
PHONE..........................510 475-9810
Lee Perry, *President*
▲ **EMP:** 50 **EST:** 1999
SALES (est): 6MM **Privately Held**
WEB: www.buffalodistribution.com
SIC: 5139 Footwear

(P-8124)
CAPE ROBBIN INC
1943 W Mission Blvd, Pomona
(91766-1037)
PHONE..........................626 810-8080
Michael Chen, *CEO*
Cindy Chang, *Sales Mgr*
Sandy Mancuso, *Sales Staff*
Jean Yang, *Manager*
▲ **EMP:** 50
SQ FT: 20,000
SALES (est): 911.8K **Privately Held**
SIC: 5139 3171 Shoes; handbags, women's

(P-8125)
CELS ENTERPRISES INC (PA)
Also Called: Chinese Laundry Shoes
3485 S La Cienega Blvd A, Los Angeles
(90016-4497)
PHONE..........................310 838-2103
Robert Goldman, *CEO*
Derek Bordeaux, *Vice Pres*
Ellen Schiff, *Vice Pres*
Christine Sung, *Vice Pres*
Jenna Roll, *Executive*
◆ **EMP:** 62
SQ FT: 72,000
SALES (est): 35.7MM **Privately Held**
WEB: www.chineselaundry.com
SIC: 5139 Shoes

(P-8126)
CHINESE LAUNDRY INC
Also Called: Chinese Laundry Shoes
3485 S La Cienega Blvd, Los Angeles
(90016-4497)
PHONE..........................310 945-3299
Robert Goldman, *President*
Stewart Goldman, *Exec VP*
Christine Sung, *Vice Pres*
Sean Corpuz, *Programmer Anys*
Kyler Jafari, *Buyer*
EMP: 50 **EST:** 1985
SQ FT: 72,000
SALES (est): 20MM **Privately Held**
SIC: 5139 Shoes

(P-8127)
CONVERSE INC
2150 E Montclair Plaza Ln, Montclair
(91763-1535)
PHONE..........................909 625-6655
EMP: 90
SALES (corp-wide): 39.1B **Publicly Held**
SIC: 5139 Footwear, athletic
HQ: Converse Inc.
1 Lovejoy Wharf
Boston MA 02114
978 983-3300

(P-8128)
CONVERSE INC
1437-39 3rd St Promenade, Santa Monica
(90401)
PHONE..........................310 451-0314
EMP: 89
SALES (corp-wide): 39.1B **Publicly Held**
SIC: 5139 5661 Footwear, athletic; footwear, athletic
HQ: Converse Inc.
1 Lovejoy Wharf
Boston MA 02114
978 983-3300

(P-8129)
CONVERSE INC
Also Called: Distritution Center
4450 E Lowell St, Ontario (91761-2220)
PHONE..........................909 974-5695
Samone Carrollin, *Manager*
EMP: 90
SALES (corp-wide): 39.1B **Publicly Held**
SIC: 5139 Footwear
HQ: Converse Inc.
1 Lovejoy Wharf
Boston MA 02114
978 983-3300

(P-8130)
E M S TRADING INC
Also Called: Michael-Antonio Studio
5161 Richton St, Montclair (91763-1310)
PHONE..........................909 581-7800
Michael C Su, *CEO*
Ruby Su, *CFO*

Alice Su, *Vice Pres*
Jack Su, *Admin Sec*
◆ **EMP:** 50
SQ FT: 150,000
SALES (est): 14MM **Privately Held**
SIC: 5139 Shoes

(P-8131)
EAST LION CORPORATION
Also Called: Qupid Shoe
318 Brea Canyon Rd, Walnut
(91789-3093)
PHONE..........................626 912-1818
Ben Yi Kuo, *CEO*
Julie Kuo, *Vice Pres*
Connie Kuo, *Creative Dir*
Hanson Zhao, *Technology*
Julia Cho, *CPA*
◆ **EMP:** 50
SALES (est): 23.6MM **Privately Held**
WEB: www.eastlioncorp.com
SIC: 5139 Shoes

(P-8132)
FOREVER LINK INTERNATIONAL INC
888 S Azusa Ave, City of Industry
(91748-1028)
PHONE..........................877 839-9899
Charles Hailongcui, *CEO*
Nicole Chen, *Purchasing*
Jason Lee, *Sales Associate*
◆ **EMP:** 50
SALES (est): 8.3MM **Privately Held**
SIC: 5139 Shoes

(P-8133)
FORTUNE DYNAMIC INC
21923 Ferrero, City of Industry
(91789-5210)
PHONE..........................909 979-8318
Carol Lee, *President*
James Lee, *Vice Pres*
◆ **EMP:** 90
SQ FT: 150,000
SALES (est): 50MM **Privately Held**
WEB: www.fortunedynamic.com
SIC: 5139 Shoes

(P-8134)
HI-TEC SPORTS USA INC (DH)
Also Called: Magnum USA
5990 Sepulvda Blvd # 600, Van Nuys
(91411-2523)
PHONE..........................209 545-1111
Simon Bonham, *CEO*
Ed Van Wezel, *CEO*
William Berta, *CFO*
Frank Van Wezel, *Chairman*
Brad Gebhard, *Principal*
▲ **EMP:** 57 **EST:** 1978
SQ FT: 120,000
SALES (est): 30.3MM
SALES (corp-wide): 24.4MM **Publicly Held**
WEB: www.magnumboots.com
SIC: 5139 Footwear, athletic
HQ: Hi-Tec Sports Public Limited Company
Aviation Way
Southend-On-Sea
170 254-1741

(P-8135)
J P ORIGINAL CORP (PA)
Also Called: Doll House Footwear
19101 E Walnut Dr N, City of Industry
(91748-1429)
PHONE..........................626 839-4300
C H Hsueh, *Ch of Bd*
Si-Tuo Hsu, *President*
Nina Hsu, *Purch Mgr*
Kenny Hsu, *Purchasing*
◆ **EMP:** 60
SQ FT: 67,000
SALES (est): 27.8MM **Privately Held**
WEB: www.jpo.com
SIC: 5139 Shoes

(P-8136)
KOMMONWEALTH INC
Also Called: Creative Recreation
6420 Wilshire Blvd, Los Angeles
(90048-5502)
PHONE..........................310 278-7328
Robert Nand, *CEO*
▲ **EMP:** 50

SALES (est): 12.9MM **Privately Held**
SIC: 5139 Shoes

(P-8137)
L & L LOGIC AND LOGISTICS LP
6 Hamilton Landing # 250, Novato
(94949-8264)
PHONE..........................707 795-2475
▲ **EMP:** 50
SALES (est): 3.9MM **Privately Held**
WEB: www.ll-logistics.com
SIC: 5139

(P-8138)
MILLENNIAL BRANDS LLC (PA)
Also Called: Rocket Dog Brands
2000 Crow Canyon Pl # 300, San Ramon
(94583-4633)
PHONE..........................866 938-4806
Scott Briskie, *Mng Member*
Doug Younce, *Treasurer*
Carly Marie, *Vice Pres*
Yoni Feliciano, *Office Mgr*
Andy Petersen, *VP Sales*
▲ **EMP:** 90
SQ FT: 20,000
SALES (est): 30.1MM **Privately Held**
SIC: 5139 Footwear

(P-8139)
NIKEWOMAN
447 Great Mall Dr, Milpitas (95035-8041)
PHONE..........................408 942-6457
Jason Cablag, *Manager*
EMP: 50
SALES (est): 1.9MM **Privately Held**
SIC: 5139 Shoes

(P-8140)
OSATA ENTERPRISES INC
Also Called: Globe Shoes
225 S Aviation Blvd, El Segundo
(90245-4604)
PHONE..........................888 445-6237
Matthew Hill, *President*
Gary Valentine, *Vice Pres*
▲ **EMP:** 100 **EST:** 1997
SQ FT: 30,000
SALES (est): 33.5MM **Privately Held**
WEB: www.globeshoes.com
SIC: 5139 Shoes
PA: Globe International Limited
1 Fennellst
Port Melbourne VIC 3207

(P-8141)
PRIMA ROYALE ENTERPRISES LTD
Also Called: Prima Royale
150 S Los Robles Ave # 100, Pasadena
(91101-2456)
PHONE..........................626 960-8388
Ing Nan Yu, *CEO*
Harry K T Chow, *President*
Judy Chow, *COO*
Bobby Bruce Levy, *Vice Pres*
Katherine Nelson, *Vice Pres*
◆ **EMP:** 55
SQ FT: 55,000
SALES (est): 8.7MM **Privately Held**
WEB: www.primaroyale.com
SIC: 5139 3143 Shoes; men's footwear, except athletic

(P-8142)
RAINBOW SANDALS INC
900 Calle Negocio, San Clemente
(92673-6201)
PHONE..........................949 276-4431
Jay Longley Jr, *President*
Tony Bordeaux, *Technology*
Pat Huber, *Mktg Dir*
Kirby Keeter,
Sabrina Sexton, *Cust Mgr*
◆ **EMP:** 50
SQ FT: 5,000
SALES: 48.7K **Privately Held**
WEB: www.rainbowsandals.com
SIC: 5139 Shoes

(P-8143)
REALLY LIKEABLE PEOPLE INC
2251 Las Palmas Dr, Carlsbad
(92011-1527)
P.O. Box 131750 (92013-1750)
PHONE..................................760 431-5577
Jon W Humphrey, *President*
Diana Crawford, *CFO*
EMP: 50
SQ FT: 15,000
SALES (est): 8.6MM **Privately Held**
SIC: 5139 Footwear

5141 Groceries, General Line Wholesale

(P-8144)
ABACUS BUSINESS CAPITAL INC
Also Called: Island Pacific Supermarket
738 Epperson Dr, City of Industry
(91748-1336)
PHONE..................................909 594-8080
Chengbiao Xue, *CEO*
Mina Hong, *General Mgr*
EMP: 50 **EST:** 2018
SALES (est): 1.3MM **Privately Held**
SIC: 5141 Groceries, general line

(P-8145)
ACOSTA INC
Also Called: Acosta Sales & Marketing
915 W Imperial Hwy # 200, Brea
(92821-3851)
PHONE..................................714 988-1500
Rick Nist, *Branch Mgr*
Raymond Hudash, *Manager*
EMP: 150
SALES (corp-wide): 5.8B **Privately Held**
WEB: www.acosta.com
SIC: 5141 Food brokers
PA: Acosta Inc.
6600 Corporate Ctr Pkwy
Jacksonville FL 32216
904 332-7986

(P-8146)
ACOSTA INC
Acosta Sales & Marketing
5735 W Las Positas Blvd # 300, Pleasanton
(94588-4002)
P.O. Box 9039 (94566-9039)
PHONE..................................925 600-3500
Tony Mello, *Director*
Deborah Karst, *Vice Pres*
Vicki Devitt, *Business Mgr*
Rick Mallmans, *Business Mgr*
Renee Mulcahy, *Business Mgr*
EMP: 85
SQ FT: 10,000
SALES (corp-wide): 5.8B **Privately Held**
WEB: www.acosta.com
SIC: 5141 Food brokers
PA: Acosta Inc.
6600 Corporate Ctr Pkwy
Jacksonville FL 32216
904 332-7986

(P-8147)
ADVANTAGE SALES & MARKETING
5064 Franklin Dr, Pleasanton (94588-3354)
PHONE..................................925 463-5600
Clyde Le Baron, *President*
Steve Derking, *Exec VP*
Dale Hensley, *Sales Mgr*
Gary East, *Sales Staff*
Chip Krueger, *Sales Staff*
EMP: 250 **EST:** 1945
SQ FT: 27,000
SALES (est): 23.1MM **Privately Held**
SIC: 5141 5142 5122 Food brokers; packaged frozen goods; druggists' sundries

(P-8148)
ADVANTAGE SALES & MKTG INC
200 N Pacific Coast Hwy # 1000, El Segundo (90245-5606)
PHONE..................................310 321-6869
S D Dorfman, *Branch Mgr*
Victoria Beam, *Analyst*
Daniel Kim, *Manager*
EMP: 123
SALES (corp-wide): 11.4B **Privately Held**
SIC: 5141 Food brokers
PA: Advantage Sales & Marketing Inc.
18100 Von Karman Ave # 900
Irvine CA 92612
949 797-2900

(P-8149)
ADVANTAGE SALES & MKTG INC (PA)
Also Called: Advantage Solutions
18100 Von Karman Ave # 900, Irvine
(92612-7195)
PHONE..................................949 797-2900
Sonny King, *Chairman*
Chris Cuello, *President*
Dave Thurman, *President*
Tanya Domier, *CEO*
Brian Stevens, *COO*
◆ **EMP:** 250
SQ FT: 48,000
SALES (est): 11.4B **Privately Held**
WEB: www.asmnet.com
SIC: 5141 Food brokers

(P-8150)
ADVANTAGE SALES & MKTG LLC
6700 Koll Center Pkwy # 300, Pleasanton
(94566-7060)
PHONE..................................925 463-5600
Barry Johnson, *President*
EMP: 72
SALES (corp-wide): 11.4B **Privately Held**
SIC: 5141 5142 Food brokers; packaged frozen goods
HQ: Advantage Sales & Marketing Llc
18100 Von Karman Ave # 900
Irvine CA 92612
949 797-2900

(P-8151)
ADVANTAGE WAYPOINT LLC
2642 Michelle Dr, Tustin (92780-7019)
PHONE..................................717 424-4973
Angelica Harris, *Admin Mgr*
Martin Evans, *President*
Kristopher Bloom, *General Mgr*
Shawn Irvine, *General Mgr*
Kim Hoffman, *Administration*
EMP: 81
SALES (corp-wide): 200MM **Privately Held**
SIC: 5141 Food brokers
PA: Advantage Waypoint Llc
13521 Prestige Pl
Tampa FL 33635
813 358-5900

(P-8152)
ADVANTAGE-CROWN SLS & MKTG LLC (DH)
1400 S Douglass Rd # 200, Anaheim
(92806-6904)
P.O. Box 66010 (92816-6010)
PHONE..................................714 780-3000
Sonny King, *CEO*
Aj Stukenborg, *General Mgr*
Jeannette Marston, *Administration*
Greg Duda, *Business Mgr*
Gail Degeorge, *Broker*
▲ **EMP:** 1100
SALES (est): 379.3MM
SALES (corp-wide): 11.4B **Privately Held**
SIC: 5141 Food brokers
HQ: Advantage Sales & Marketing Llc
18100 Von Karman Ave # 900
Irvine CA 92612
949 797-2900

(P-8153)
AFC DISTRIBUTION CORP
19205 S Laurel Park Rd, Rancho Dominguez (90220-6032)
PHONE..................................310 604-3630
Ryuji Ishii, *President*
Jeffery Seiler, *Vice Pres*
EMP: 50 **EST:** 2016
SALES (est): 1.5MM
SALES (corp-wide): 34MM **Privately Held**
SIC: 5141 Groceries, general line

PA: Advanced Fresh Concepts Corp.
19205 S Laurel Park Rd
Rancho Dominguez CA 90220
310 604-3630

(P-8154)
AMERICAN ACE INTERNATIONAL CO
Also Called: American Ace Intl Trdg Co
313 Newquist Pl Ste A, City of Industry
(91745-1091)
PHONE..................................626 937-6116
Jimmy S T Young, *Vice Pres*
Walter Kang Young, *President*
EMP: 55
SALES (est): 7.9MM **Privately Held**
SIC: 5141 5012 5064 Groceries, general line; automobiles; television sets; video cassette recorders & accessories

(P-8155)
AMK FOODSERVICES INC
Also Called: Kaney Foods
830 Capitolio Way, San Luis Obispo
(93401-7122)
P.O. Box 1188 (93406-1188)
PHONE..................................805 544-7600
John P Kaney, *CEO*
EMP: 130
SQ FT: 35,000
SALES (est): 37.3MM **Privately Held**
SIC: 5141 Food brokers

(P-8156)
BAY BROKERAGE INC
17 Woodleaf Ave, Redwood City
(94061-1823)
PHONE..................................650 413-1721
Richard Hoadley, *President*
Kevin Pope, *CFO*
Robert Crane, *Vice Pres*
Michael Fouch, *Vice Pres*
EMP: 50 **EST:** 1978
SQ FT: 8,000
SALES (est): 11MM **Privately Held**
WEB: www.baybrokerage.com
SIC: 5141 Food brokers

(P-8157)
BI-RITE RESTAURANT SUP CO INC
Also Called: BI-RITE FOODSERVICE DISTRIBUTO
123 S Hill Dr, Brisbane (94005-1203)
PHONE..................................415 656-0187
William Barulich, *CEO*
Steve Barulich, *President*
Zachary Barulich, *CFO*
Zack Barulich, *CFO*
Tom Whiteside, *Exec VP*
◆ **EMP:** 300 **EST:** 1941
SQ FT: 220,000
SALES: 324MM **Privately Held**
WEB: www.biritefoodservice.com
SIC: 5141 5147 5148 5023 Groceries, general line; meats & meat products; fresh fruits & vegetables; kitchenware; linens, table; towels; commercial equipment; direct selling establishments

(P-8158)
C&S WHOLESALE GROCERS INC
2797 S Orange Ave, Fresno (93725-1919)
P.O. Box 11097 (93771-1097)
PHONE..................................559 442-4700
Randy Wood, *Branch Mgr*
Venkata Sreepada, *Executive*
EMP: 475
SALES (corp-wide): 3.9B **Privately Held**
SIC: 5141 Food brokers
PA: C&S Wholesale Grocers, Inc.
7 Corporate Dr
Keene NH 03431
603 354-7000

(P-8159)
CANTON FOOD CO INC
750 S Alameda St, Los Angeles
(90021-1624)
PHONE..................................213 688-7707
Shiu Lit Kwan, *CEO*
Cho W Kwan, *President*
Shui Lit Kwan, *CEO*
Cho Kwan, *Vice Pres*

Wai Kam Kwan, *Vice Pres*
▲ **EMP:** 106
SQ FT: 96,000
SALES (est): 90.2MM **Privately Held**
WEB: www.cantonfoodco.com
SIC: 5141 5146 5411 5421 Food brokers; seafoods; grocery stores; seafood markets; groceries & related products; refrigerated warehousing & storage

(P-8160)
CERENZIA FOODS INC
8585 White Oak Ave, Rancho Cucamonga
(91730-5146)
P.O. Box 3719 (91729-3719)
PHONE..................................909 989-4000
Joseph F Annunziato, *CEO*
Armando Curiel, *Sales Staff*
▲ **EMP:** 60
SQ FT: 75,000
SALES (est): 70.3MM **Privately Held**
WEB: www.cerenziafoods.com
SIC: 5141 Food brokers

(P-8161)
CHEFS WAREHOUSE WESTCOAST LLC (HQ)
16633 Gale Ave, City of Industry
(91745-1802)
PHONE..................................626 465-4200
Chris Pappas, *President*
Tom Burghardt, *Finance*
Pedro Trejo, *Human Res Dir*
Ken Clark, *Mng Member*
John Pappas, *Mng Member*
▲ **EMP:** 59
SALES (est): 44.1MM **Publicly Held**
WEB: www.chefswarehouse.com
SIC: 5141 Food brokers

(P-8162)
CONCORD FOODS INC (PA)
4601 E Guasti Rd, Ontario (91761-8105)
PHONE..................................909 975-2000
Nick J Sciortino Jr, *President*
Roy Sciortino, *CFO*
John Sciortino, *Vice Pres*
Christy Santiago, *Credit Mgr*
John Bernieri, *Purchasing*
EMP: 72
SQ FT: 67,000
SALES (est): 90.5MM **Privately Held**
WEB: www.concordfoodsinc.com
SIC: 5141 Food brokers

(P-8163)
CORE-MARK CORONA 2
1550 Magnolia Ave, Corona (92879-2094)
PHONE..................................800 622-1206
Thomas Perkins, *President*
Christopher Miller, *CFO*
EMP: 50
SQ FT: 60,000
SALES (est): 1.2MM **Privately Held**
SIC: 5141 Groceries, general line

(P-8164)
CORE-MARK SACRAMENTO 2
2959 Thomas Pl Ste 150, West Sacramento
(95691-5751)
PHONE..................................866 791-4210
Thomas Perkins, *President*
Christopher Miller, *CFO*
EMP: 50
SQ FT: 79,000
SALES (est): 1.3MM **Privately Held**
SIC: 5141 Groceries, general line

(P-8165)
CROSSMARK INC
2401 E Katella Ave # 625, Anaheim
(92806-5939)
PHONE..................................714 464-6318
John Owen, *Exec VP*
EMP: 57 **Privately Held**
SIC: 5141 Food brokers
PA: Crossmark, Inc.
5100 Legacy Dr
Plano TX 75024

(P-8166)
CROSSMARK INC
Also Called: Crossmark Sales & Marketing
3875 Hopyard Rd Ste 250, Pleasanton
(94588-2784)
PHONE.....................925 463-3555
Jeff Nanna, *Director*
Marc Matthiesen, *Sales Staff*
Sean Hedrick, *Accounts Exec*
EMP: 300 **Privately Held**
WEB: www.crossmark.com
SIC: 5141 Food brokers
PA: Crossmark, Inc.
5100 Legacy Dr
Plano TX 75024

(P-8167)
D&A ENTERPRISES INC
34943 Newark Blvd, Newark (94560-1215)
PHONE.....................510 445-1600
Afit Vyas, *President*
EMP: 300
SALES (est): 29.6MM **Privately Held**
SIC: 5141 Food brokers

(P-8168)
DEL MONACO SPECIALTY FOODS INC
18675 Madrone Pkwy # 150, Morgan Hill
(95037-2868)
PHONE.....................408 500-4100
Ernestine Del Monaco, *Ch of Bd*
Vic Del Monaco, *CEO*
Tony Del Monaco, *Vice Pres*
Tony D Monaco, *Vice Pres*
Stephanie Del Monaco, *Research*
EMP: 88
SQ FT: 18,000
SALES (est): 28.3MM
SALES (corp-wide): 105MM **Privately Held**
WEB: www.delmonacofoods.com
SIC: 5141 Food brokers
PA: Kettle Cuisine, Llc
330 Lynnway
Lynn MA 01901
617 409-1100

(P-8169)
DOT FOODS INC
2200 Nickerson Dr, Modesto (95358-9489)
PHONE.....................209 581-9090
Fax: 209 581-9082
EMP: 134
SALES (corp-wide): 5.4B **Privately Held**
SIC: 5141
PA: Dot Foods, Inc.
1 Dot Way
Mount Sterling IL 62353
217 773-4411

(P-8170)
DPI SPECIALTY FOODS WEST INC (DH)
601 S Rockefeller Ave, Ontario
(91761-7871)
PHONE.....................909 975-1019
John Jordan, *CEO*
James De Keyser, *President*
Donna Robbins, *President*
Francis Haren, *COO*
Conor Crowley, *CFO*
◆ EMP: 122 EST: 1951
SQ FT: 250,000
SALES (est): 502.8MM
SALES (corp-wide): 988.6MM **Privately Held**
WEB: www.dpi-west.com
SIC: 5141 Food brokers
HQ: Dpi Specialty Foods, Inc.
601 S Rockefeller Ave
Ontario CA 91761
909 390-0892

(P-8171)
E G AYERS DISTRIBUTING INC
5819 S Broadway St, Eureka (95503-6906)
PHONE.....................707 445-2077
Paul A Ayers, *CEO*
Phillip Ayers, *Corp Secy*
Pat Gillmore, *Manager*
EMP: 50
SQ FT: 15,000

SALES (est): 22.4MM **Privately Held**
WEB: www.ayersdistributing.com
SIC: 5141 5149 Food brokers; beverages,
except coffee & tea

(P-8172)
EXANDAL CORPORATION
Also Called: Colorexa
17620 Sherman Way Ste 207, Van Nuys
(91406-3527)
PHONE.....................818 705-9497
Carlos Alvaro, *President*
Alejandro Hinostroza, *Sales Executive*
Andrea Alvaro, *Director*
▲ EMP: 150
SALES (est): 27.7MM **Privately Held**
WEB: www.exandal.com
SIC: 5141 Food brokers
PA: Exandal S.A.C.
Av. Los Alamos Mz. I Lt. 8
Lima LM 22

(P-8173)
FOOD SALES WEST INC (PA)
235 Baker St, Costa Mesa (92626-4521)
P.O. Box 19738, Irvine (92623-9738)
PHONE.....................714 966-2900
David Lyons, *CEO*
Carl Scharffenberger, *President*
Mary Ellen Scharffenberger, *Corp Secy*
Michael Berkson, *Vice Pres*
Robert Watkins, *Vice Pres*
EMP: 85 EST: 1973
SQ FT: 12,000
SALES (est): 16.1MM **Privately Held**
WEB: www.foodsaleswest.com
SIC: 5141 Food brokers

(P-8174)
FOOTHILL PACKING INC
2255 S Broadway, Santa Maria
(93454-7871)
PHONE.....................805 925-7900
Jorge Rivera, *President*
EMP: 489
SALES (corp-wide): 46.8MM **Privately Held**
SIC: 5141 Groceries, general line
PA: Foothill Packing, Inc.
1582 Moffett St
Salinas CA 93905
831 784-1453

(P-8175)
FORTUNE AVENUE FOODS INC
2117 Pointe Ave, Ontario (91761-8529)
PHONE.....................909 930-5989
Daniel C Yang, *CEO*
Fula Yang, *Vice Pres*
▲ EMP: 55
SQ FT: 27,000
SALES (est): 23.2MM **Privately Held**
WEB: www.fortuneavenuefoods.com
SIC: 5141 Food brokers

(P-8176)
GOURMET FOODS
Also Called: H.U.G. Company
2557 Barrington Ct, Hayward (94545-1174)
PHONE.....................510 887-0340
Uwe Henze, *President*
Edgar Mayorquin, *Prdtn Mgr*
EMP: 90
SALES (est): 27.5MM
SALES (corp-wide): 100.3MM **Privately Held**
SIC: 5141 Food brokers
PA: Gourmet Foods, Inc.
2910 E Harcourt St
Compton CA 90221
310 632-3300

(P-8177)
GOURMET FOODS INC (PA)
2910 E Harcourt St, Compton
(90221-5502)
PHONE.....................310 632-3300
Heinz Naef, *President*
Gary David, *CFO*
Ursina Naef, *Corp Secy*
Karen McCullough, *CIO*
Michael Baumgart, *CTO*
◆ EMP: 83
SQ FT: 35,000

SALES (est): 100.3MM **Privately Held**
WEB: www.gourmetfoodsinc.com
SIC: 5141 5812 2099 Food brokers; eat-
ing places; food preparations

(P-8178)
GRAND SUPERCENTER INC
8550 Chetle Ave Ste B, Whittier
(90606-2662)
PHONE.....................562 318-3451
Ilyeon Kwon, *CEO*
EMP: 70
SALES (corp-wide): 17.4MM **Privately Held**
SIC: 5141 5499 Groceries, general line;
juices, fruit or vegetable
HQ: Grand Supercenter Inc.
300 Chubb Ave
Lyndhurst NJ 07071
201 507-9900

(P-8179)
GROCERS SPECIALTY COMPANY (DH)
Also Called: G S C Ball
5200 Sheila St, Commerce (90040-3906)
P.O. Box 513396, Los Angeles (90051-1396)
PHONE.....................323 264-5200
Joe Falvey, *President*
Rich Martin, *CFO*
Christine Neal, *Treasurer*
Bob Ling, *Admin Sec*
▲ EMP: 50 EST: 1981
SQ FT: 106,000
SALES (est): 124.9MM **Publicly Held**
SIC: 5141 Groceries, general line
HQ: Unified Grocers, Inc.
5200 Sheila St
Commerce CA 90040
323 264-5200

(P-8180)
HOMEGROWN NATURAL FOODS INC
Also Called: Consorzio
1610 5th St, Berkeley (94710-1715)
PHONE.....................510 558-7500
John Foraker, *President*
Marc Van Valen, *Controller*
EMP: 75
SQ FT: 10,000
SALES (est): 16.8MM
SALES (corp-wide): 16.8B **Publicly Held**
SIC: 5141 5149 Groceries, general line;
natural & organic foods
HQ: Annie's, Inc.
1610 5th St
Berkeley CA 94710

(P-8181)
ICPK CORPORATION
Also Called: Hpp Food Services
1130 W C St, Wilmington (90744-5102)
PHONE.....................310 830-8020
EMP: 70
SALES (corp-wide): 4MM **Privately Held**
SIC: 5141 Groceries, general line
PA: Icpk Corporation
4380 Cerritos Ave
Los Alamitos CA 90720
714 321-7025

(P-8182)
IMPACT GROUP LLC
Also Called: Co-Sales
7133 Koll Center Pkwy # 200, Pleasanton
(94566-3203)
PHONE.....................925 327-7322
Kathy Jean McOmber, *Administration*
EMP: 59
SALES (corp-wide): 33.8MM **Privately Held**
SIC: 5141 Food brokers
PA: Impact Group, Llc
950 W Bannock St Ste 500
Boise ID 83702
208 343-5800

(P-8183)
JETRO CASH AND CARRY ENTPS LLC
Also Called: Restaurant Depot
1275 Vine St, Sacramento (95811-0427)
PHONE.....................916 492-2305
MI Thao, *Controller*
EMP: 95
SALES (corp-wide): 24.5B **Privately Held**
SIC: 5141 5046 Groceries, general line;
restaurant equipment & supplies
HQ: Jetro Cash And Carry Enterprises, Llc
1524 132nd St
College Point NY 11356
718 939-6400

(P-8184)
LASSEN CANYON NURSERY INC (PA)
1300 Salmon Creek Rd, Redding
(96003-9641)
P.O. Box 992400 (96099-2400)
PHONE.....................530 223-1075
Elizabeth Elwood Ponce, *CEO*
Kenneth Elwood Jr, *President*
Crystal Amen, *Sales Mgr*
Mel Fernandez, *Marketing Staff*
Wade Bunn, *Sales Staff*
▼ EMP: 125
SQ FT: 3,000
SALES (est): 93.1MM **Privately Held**
WEB: www.lassencanyonnursery.com
SIC: 5141 5191 0171 Groceries, general
line; hay; raspberry farm

(P-8185)
LAX-C INC
1100 N Main St, Los Angeles (90012-1832)
PHONE.....................323 343-9000
Suprata Bovornsivamoon, *President*
▲ EMP: 50
SALES (est): 24.9MM **Privately Held**
WEB: www.lax-c.com
SIC: 5141 Groceries, general line

(P-8186)
LEE BROS FOODSERVICES INC (PA)
Also Called: Lee Industrial Catering
660 E Gish Rd, San Jose (95112-2707)
PHONE.....................408 275-0700
Chieu Van Le, *CEO*
Tu Lee, *COO*
Huong Le, *Vice Pres*
Carol Lee, *Vice Pres*
Jimmy Lee, *Vice Pres*
◆ EMP: 150
SQ FT: 15,000
SALES (est): 93MM **Privately Held**
SIC: 5141 5142 Food brokers; packaged
frozen goods

(P-8187)
MARQUEZ BROTHERS ENTPS INC
15480 Valley Blvd, City of Industry
(91746-3325)
PHONE.....................626 330-3310
Gustavo Marquez, *President*
Jaime Marquez, *Vice Pres*
Juan Marquez, *Vice Pres*
◆ EMP: 200
SQ FT: 200,000
SALES (est): 84.3MM **Privately Held**
SIC: 5141 Food brokers

(P-8188)
MARQUEZ BROTHERS INTL INC (PA)
Also Called: M B
5801 Rue Ferrari, San Jose (95138-1857)
PHONE.....................408 960-2700
Gustavo Marquez, *CEO*
Jaime Marquez, *Exec VP*
Mari Marquez, *Executive*
Angel Garza, *General Mgr*
Roberto Montes, *Opers Staff*
▲ EMP: 150
SQ FT: 160,000
SALES (est): 345.8MM **Privately Held**
WEB: www.elmexicano.net
SIC: 5141 Groceries, general line

▲ = Import ▼=Export
◆ =Import/Export

(P-8189)
MARQUEZ BROTHERS INTL INC
Also Called: El Mexicano
1329 W Olympic Blvd, Montebello
(90640-5010)
PHONE.................................323 722-8103
Sal Alcaraz, *Manager*
EMP: 58
SALES (corp-wide): 345.8MM **Privately Held**
WEB: www.elmexicano.net
SIC: 5141 Food brokers
PA: Marquez Brothers International, Inc.
5801 Rue Ferrari
San Jose CA 95138
408 960-2700

(P-8190)
MARQUEZ BROTHERS INTL INC
Also Called: Cheese Plant
179 S 11th Ave, Hanford (93230-5056)
PHONE.................................559 584-8000
Jaun Marquez, *Vice Pres*
EMP: 152
SALES (corp-wide): 345.8MM **Privately Held**
WEB: www.elmexicano.net
SIC: 5141 2022 Groceries, general line;
natural cheese
PA: Marquez Brothers International, Inc.
5801 Rue Ferrari
San Jose CA 95138
408 960-2700

(P-8191)
MARTIN-BROWER COMPANY LLC
4704 Fite Ct, Stockton (95215-8308)
P.O. Box 547, Sheridan OR (97378-0547)
PHONE.................................209 466-2980
Mark Peterson, *Principal*
EMP: 138 **Privately Held**
SIC: 5141 Food brokers
HQ: The Martin-Brower Company L L C
6250 N River Rd Ste 9000
Rosemont IL 60018
847 227-6500

(P-8192)
MCLANE COMPANY INC
800 E Pescadero Ave, Tracy (95304-9799)
PHONE.................................209 221-7500
Bruce Bravo, *Manager*
EMP: 217
SALES (corp-wide): 225.3B **Publicly Held**
SIC: 5141 Groceries, general line
HQ: Mclane Company, Inc.
4747 Mclane Pkwy
Temple TX 76504
254 771-7500

(P-8193)
MCLANE FOODSERVICE DIST INC
Also Called: Mbm
17872 Cartwright Rd, Irvine (92614)
PHONE.................................714 863-0163
Ken McDonald, *Branch Mgr*
EMP: 100
SALES (corp-wide): 225.3B **Publicly Held**
WEB: www.mbmlc.com
SIC: 5141 5142 5144 Groceries, general line; packaged frozen goods; poultry & poultry products
HQ: Mclane Foodservice Distribution, Inc.
2641 Meadowbrook Rd
Rocky Mount NC 27801
252 985-7200

(P-8194)
MCLANE/PACIFIC INC
3876 E Childs Ave, Merced (95341-9520)
P.O. Box 2107 (95344-0107)
PHONE.................................209 725-2500
William G Rosier, *CEO*
Mike Youngblood, *President*
Kevin Koch, *Treasurer*
Jim Kent, *Exec VP*
Ramiro Bautista, *Manager*
▲ **EMP:** 498
SQ FT: 220,000

SALES (est): 158.9MM
SALES (corp-wide): 225.3B **Publicly Held**
WEB: www.mclaneco.com
SIC: 5141 Groceries, general line
HQ: Mclane Company, Inc.
4747 Mclane Pkwy
Temple TX 76504
254 771-7500

(P-8195)
MERCADO LATINO INC (PA)
245 Baldwin Park Blvd, City of Industry (91746-1404)
P.O. Box 6168, El Monte (91734-6168)
PHONE.................................626 333-6862
Graciliano Rodriguez, *President*
George Rodriguez, *CFO*
Richard Rodriguez, *Senior VP*
Angelita Rodriguez, *Admin Sec*
◆ **EMP:** 100 **EST:** 1963
SQ FT: 105,000
SALES (est): 227.6MM **Privately Held**
WEB: www.mercadolatinoinc.com
SIC: 5141 5148 Food brokers; fresh fruits & vegetables

(P-8196)
MERCADO LATINO INC
33430 Western Ave, Union City (94587-3202)
PHONE.................................510 475-5500
Robert Rodriguez, *Principal*
EMP: 50
SALES (corp-wide): 227.6MM **Privately Held**
WEB: www.mercadolatinoinc.com
SIC: 5141 Food brokers
PA: Mercado Latino, Inc.
245 Baldwin Park Blvd
City Of Industry CA 91746
626 333-6862

(P-8197)
MISHIMA FOODS USA INC (PA)
2340 Plaza Del Amo # 105, Torrance (90501-3445)
PHONE.................................310 787-1533
Yutaka Mishima, *President*
Tsukasa Hatsukade, *Vice Pres*
Yuho Quintero, *Marketing Staff*
▲ **EMP:** 76
SALES (est): 22.8MM **Privately Held**
SIC: 5141 Food brokers

(P-8198)
NAFTA DISTRIBUTORS
5120 Santa Ana St, Ontario (91761-8632)
PHONE.................................909 605-7515
Samuel Madikians, *CEO*
▲ **EMP:** 50
SQ FT: 12,000
SALES (est): 31.3MM **Privately Held**
WEB: www.naftadist.com
SIC: 5141 Food brokers

(P-8199)
NASSER COMPANY INC (PA)
Also Called: Nasser Company of Arizona
22720 Savi Ranch Pkwy, Yorba Linda (92887-4614)
PHONE.................................714 279-2100
Burhan Nasser, *President*
Bill Arink, *President*
Mary Beth Nasser, *Corp Secy*
Becky Salazar, *VP Admin*
Ana Cerna, *Human Res Mgr*
EMP: 60
SQ FT: 17,445
SALES (est): 133.7MM **Privately Held**
SIC: 5141 Food brokers

(P-8200)
NONGSHIM AMERICA INC (HQ)
12155 6th St, Rancho Cucamonga (91730-6115)
PHONE.................................909 481-3698
Dong Y Shin, *CEO*
Kevin Chang, *CFO*
Chris Gepford, *Principal*
Eugene Shin, *Branch Mgr*
Hector Tejeda, *Branch Mgr*
◆ **EMP:** 250

SALES (est): 232.1MM **Privately Held**
WEB: www.nongshim.us
SIC: 5141 2098 Groceries, general line; noodles (e.g. egg, plain & water), dry

(P-8201)
NZG SPECIALTIES INC (PA)
Also Called: Gourmet Trading Company
2580 Santa Fe Ave, Redondo Beach (90278-1116)
P.O. Box 88432, Los Angeles (90009-8432)
PHONE.................................310 216-7575
Peter Lineen, *President*
Trent Grose, *CFO*
Scott Hulsey, *Vice Pres*
Marisala Morlett, *Admin Sec*
Chris Capelton, *Info Tech Mgr*
◆ **EMP:** 57
SQ FT: 55,000
SALES (est): 131.2MM **Privately Held**
WEB: www.gourmettrading.net
SIC: 5141 Food brokers

(P-8202)
OAKHURST INDUSTRIES INC
Also Called: Freund Baking Co
3265 Investment Blvd, Hayward (94545-3806)
PHONE.................................510 265-2400
Jim Freund, *Principal*
Larry Lumley, *Plant Mgr*
EMP: 80
SQ FT: 67,896
SALES (corp-wide): 88.4MM **Privately Held**
WEB: www.oakhurstproperties.com
SIC: 5141 2051 Groceries, general line; bread, cake & related products
PA: Oakhurst Industries, Inc.
2050 S Tubeway Ave
Commerce CA 90040
323 724-3000

(P-8203)
PALISADES RANCH INC
Also Called: Goldberg and Solovy Foods Inc
5925 Alcoa Ave, Vernon (90058-3920)
PHONE.................................323 581-6161
Paul Paget, *CEO*
Earl Goldberg, *President*
EMP: 285
SQ FT: 70,000
SALES (est): 117MM
SALES (corp-wide): 60.1B **Publicly Held**
WEB: www.gsfoods.com
SIC: 5141 5149 5046 5169 Food brokers; groceries & related products; restaurant equipment & supplies; chemicals & allied products
PA: Sysco Corporation
1390 Enclave Pkwy
Houston TX 77077
281 584-1390

(P-8204)
PALO ALTO EGG AND FOOD SVC CO
Also Called: Palo Alto Food Company
6691 Clark Ave, Newark (94560-3925)
P.O. Box 327 (94560-0327)
PHONE.................................510 456-2420
Eric Jensen, *CEO*
Paul Jensen, *Vice Pres*
EMP: 50
SQ FT: 15,000
SALES (est): 20.8MM **Privately Held**
WEB: www.paloaltoegg.com
SIC: 5141 Food brokers

(P-8205)
PERFORMANCE FOOD GROUP INC
Also Called: Performance Roma Southern Cal
16639 Gale Ave, City of Industry (91745-1802)
P.O. Box 5146, Denver CO (80217-5146)
PHONE.................................800 697-7662
Doug Freitas, *Branch Mgr*
Pete Lerma, *Facilities Mgr*
Jacquie Dicicco, *Manager*
EMP: 65
SALES (corp-wide): 19.7B **Publicly Held**
WEB: www.romafood.com
SIC: 5141 Food brokers

HQ: Performance Food Group, Inc.
12500 West Creek Pkwy
Richmond VA 23238
804 484-7700

(P-8206)
PERFORMANCE FOOD GROUP INC
Also Called: Performnce Foodservice-Ledyard
1047 17th Ave, Santa Cruz (95062-3033)
PHONE.................................831 462-4400
Steve Rebottaro, *Branch Mgr*
Cody Walz, *General Mgr*
Michael McGee, *Buyer*
EMP: 101
SALES (corp-wide): 19.7B **Publicly Held**
SIC: 5141 5046 5087 Food brokers; restaurant equipment & supplies; janitors' supplies
HQ: Performance Food Group, Inc.
12500 West Creek Pkwy
Richmond VA 23238
804 484-7700

(P-8207)
PERRIN BERNARD SUPOWITZ LLC (PA)
Also Called: Fergadis Enterprises
5496 Lindbergh Ln, Bell (90201-6409)
PHONE.................................323 981-2800
Jeremy Shapiro, *CEO*
Ron Margolis, *CFO*
Heidi Palikan, *CFO*
James Borillo, *Technology*
Steven Silver, *Business Mgr*
EMP: 79
SQ FT: 175,000
SALES (est): 117.5MM **Privately Held**
WEB: www.fergadis.com
SIC: 5141 Groceries, general line

(P-8208)
PITTSBURG WHOLESALE GROC INC
1670 Overland Ct, West Sacramento (95691-3490)
PHONE.................................916 372-7772
Farzam Hariri, *Manager*
Rashad Alkobadi, *Sales Staff*
EMP: 65
WEB: www.pitcofoods.com
SIC: 5141 Food brokers
PA: Pittsburg Wholesale Grocers, Inc.
567 Cinnabar St
San Jose CA 95110

(P-8209)
PITTSBURG WHOLESALE GROC INC (PA)
Also Called: Pitco Foods
567 Cinnabar St, San Jose (95110-2306)
PHONE.................................916 372-7772
Pericles Navab, *CEO*
David Luttway, *President*
Ryan Anhari, *Opers Staff*
Michael Perry, *Sales Staff*
Armondo Neyra, *Supervisor*
▼ **EMP:** 190
SQ FT: 160,000
SALES (est): 181.5MM **Privately Held**
WEB: www.pitcofoods.com
SIC: 5141 Food brokers

(P-8210)
RELIANCE INTERMODAL INC
1919 Martin Luther King, Stockton (95210)
P.O. Box 31238 (95213-1238)
PHONE.................................209 946-0200
Lakhbir S Deol, *CEO*
EMP: 65
SALES: 9.7MM **Privately Held**
SIC: 5141 Groceries, general line

(P-8211)
RESTAURANT DEPOT
17332 Gothard St, Huntington Beach (92647-6203)
PHONE.................................714 378-3535
EMP: 50
SQ FT: 42,000
SALES (est): 8.5MM **Privately Held**
SIC: 5141 Groceries, general line

(P-8212)
RIO VISTA VENTURES LLC (PA)
Also Called: Giumarra Companies
15651 Old Milky Way, Escondido
(92027-7104)
P.O. Box 861449, Los Angeles (90086-
1449)
PHONE..............................760 480-8502
Don Corsaro, *Chairman*
Timothy Riley, *President*
Craig Uchizono, *Vice Pres*
Chuck Anunciation, *Division Mgr*
Tom Wilson, *Sales Mgr*
▲ EMP: 50 EST: 1975
SALES (est): 92.6MM **Privately Held**
SIC: 5141 Food brokers

(P-8213)
RIO VISTA VENTURES LLC
Also Called: Giumarra Company, The
3646 Avenue 416, Reedley (93654-9111)
PHONE..............................559 897-6730
Donald Corsaro, *President*
EMP: 50
SALES (corp-wide): 92.6MM **Privately
Held**
SIC: 5141 Food brokers
PA: Rio Vista Ventures Llc
    15651 Old Milky Way
    Escondido CA 92027
    760 480-8502

(P-8214)
ROBERT KINSELLA INC
15375 Barranca Pkwy G107, Irvine
(92618-2217)
PHONE..............................949 453-9533
Robert Kinsella, *Owner*
EMP: 77
SALES (corp-wide): 14.3MM **Privately
Held**
WEB: www.premierbakers.com
SIC: 5141 Food brokers
PA: Robert Kinsella, Inc.
    535 S Nolen Dr Ste 100
    Southlake TX 76092
    214 260-8670

(P-8215)
SALADINOS INC (PA)
3325 W Figarden Dr, Fresno (93711-3909)
P.O. Box 12266 (93777-2266)
PHONE..............................559 271-3700
Craig A Saladino, *CEO*
Owen Escola, *President*
Patrick Peters, *COO*
Don Saladino, *Chairman*
John Muro, *Vice Pres*
EMP: 113
SQ FT: 40,000
SALES (est): 338.2MM **Privately Held**
WEB: www.saladinos.com
SIC: 5141 2099 Food brokers; food prepa-
rations

(P-8216)
SHOEI FOODS USA INC
1900 Feather River Blvd, Olivehurst
(95961-9627)
PHONE..............................530 742-7866
Don Soetaert, *CEO*
Sumio Kawanabe, *President*
Tall Matsushima, *President*
◆ EMP: 100
SQ FT: 68,000
SALES (est): 88.3MM **Privately Held**
SIC: 5141 Food brokers
PA: Shoei Foods Corporation
    5-7, Akihabara
    Taito-Ku TKY 110-0

(P-8217)
SMART & FINAL STORES INC
12339 Poway Rd, Poway (92064-4218)
PHONE..............................858 748-0101
David Hirz, *Branch Mgr*
EMP: 534
SALES (corp-wide): 4.7B **Privately Held**
SIC: 5141 Groceries, general line
PA: Smart & Final Stores, Inc.
    600 Citadel Dr
    Commerce CA 90040
    323 869-7500

(P-8218)
SMART & FINAL STORES INC
3049 E Coast Hwy, Corona Del Mar
(92625-2234)
PHONE..............................949 675-2396
Layne Bob, *Branch Mgr*
EMP: 267
SALES (corp-wide): 4.7B **Privately Held**
SIC: 5141 Groceries, general line
PA: Smart & Final Stores, Inc.
    600 Citadel Dr
    Commerce CA 90040
    323 869-7500

(P-8219)
SMART & FINAL STORES INC
9870 N Magnolia Ave, Santee
(92071-1901)
PHONE..............................619 449-2396
EMP: 326
SALES (corp-wide): 4.7B **Privately Held**
SIC: 5141 Groceries, general line
PA: Smart & Final Stores, Inc.
    600 Citadel Dr
    Commerce CA 90040
    323 869-7500

(P-8220)
SMART & FINAL STORES INC
4550 W Pico Blvd, Los Angeles
(90019-4257)
PHONE..............................323 549-9586
EMP: 334
SALES (corp-wide): 4.7B **Privately Held**
SIC: 5141 Groceries, general line
PA: Smart & Final Stores, Inc.
    600 Citadel Dr
    Commerce CA 90040
    323 869-7500

(P-8221)
SMART & FINAL STORES INC
1005 W Arrow Hwy, San Dimas
(91773-2422)
PHONE..............................909 592-2190
EMP: 267
SALES (corp-wide): 4.7B **Privately Held**
SIC: 5141 Groceries, general line
PA: Smart & Final Stores, Inc.
    600 Citadel Dr
    Commerce CA 90040
    323 869-7500

(P-8222)
SMART & FINAL STORES INC
13346 Limonite Ave, Eastvale
(92880-3360)
PHONE..............................909 773-1813
EMP: 196
SALES (corp-wide): 4.7B **Privately Held**
SIC: 5141 Groceries, general line
PA: Smart & Final Stores, Inc.
    600 Citadel Dr
    Commerce CA 90040
    323 869-7500

(P-8223)
SMART & FINAL STORES INC
150 B Ave, Coronado (92118-1511)
PHONE..............................619 522-2014
EMP: 267
SALES (corp-wide): 4.7B **Privately Held**
SIC: 5141 Groceries, general line
PA: Smart & Final Stores, Inc.
    600 Citadel Dr
    Commerce CA 90040
    323 869-7500

(P-8224)
SMART & FINAL STORES INC
7223 Fair Oaks Blvd, Carmichael
(95608-6410)
PHONE..............................916 486-6315
EMP: 267
SALES (corp-wide): 4.7B **Privately Held**
SIC: 5141 Groceries, general line
PA: Smart & Final Stores, Inc.
    600 Citadel Dr
    Commerce CA 90040
    323 869-7500

(P-8225)
SMART & FINAL STORES INC
1464 E Grand Ave, Arroyo Grande
(93420-2448)
PHONE..............................805 574-1599

EMP: 334
SALES (corp-wide): 4.7B **Privately Held**
SIC: 5141 Groceries, general line
PA: Smart & Final Stores, Inc.
    600 Citadel Dr
    Commerce CA 90040
    323 869-7500

(P-8226)
SMART & FINAL STORES INC
850 Linden Ave, Carpinteria (93013-2043)
PHONE..............................805 566-2174
EMP: 326
SALES (corp-wide): 4.7B **Privately Held**
SIC: 5141 Groceries, general line
PA: Smart & Final Stores, Inc.
    600 Citadel Dr
    Commerce CA 90040
    323 869-7500

(P-8227)
SMART & FINAL STORES INC
1308 W Edinger Ave, Santa Ana
(92704-4306)
PHONE..............................714 549-2362
EMP: 334
SALES (corp-wide): 4.7B **Privately Held**
SIC: 5141 Groceries, general line
PA: Smart & Final Stores, Inc.
    600 Citadel Dr
    Commerce CA 90040
    323 869-7500

(P-8228)
SMART & FINAL STORES INC
13439 Camino Canada, El Cajon
(92021-8811)
PHONE..............................619 390-1738
EMP: 326
SALES (corp-wide): 4.7B **Privately Held**
SIC: 5141 Groceries, general line
PA: Smart & Final Stores, Inc.
    600 Citadel Dr
    Commerce CA 90040
    323 869-7500

(P-8229)
SMART & FINAL STORES INC
15427 Amar Rd, La Puente (91744-2803)
PHONE..............................626 330-2495
Robert Terry, *Branch Mgr*
EMP: 326
SALES (corp-wide): 4.7B **Privately Held**
SIC: 5141 Groceries, general line
PA: Smart & Final Stores, Inc.
    600 Citadel Dr
    Commerce CA 90040
    323 869-7500

(P-8230)
SMART & FINAL STORES INC
18555 Devonshire St, Northridge
(91324-1308)
PHONE..............................818 368-6409
Marie Teolis, *Branch Mgr*
EMP: 401
SALES (corp-wide): 4.7B **Privately Held**
SIC: 5141 Groceries, general line
PA: Smart & Final Stores, Inc.
    600 Citadel Dr
    Commerce CA 90040
    323 869-7500

(P-8231)
SMART & FINAL STORES INC
1180 S King Rd, San Jose (95122-2143)
PHONE..............................408 251-0109
EMP: 261
SALES (corp-wide): 4.7B **Privately Held**
SIC: 5141 Groceries, general line
PA: Smart & Final Stores, Inc.
    600 Citadel Dr
    Commerce CA 90040
    323 869-7500

(P-8232)
SMART & FINAL STORES INC
644 Redondo Ave, Long Beach
(90814-1453)
PHONE..............................562 438-0450
EMP: 261
SALES (corp-wide): 4.7B **Privately Held**
SIC: 5141 Groceries, general line

PA: Smart & Final Stores, Inc.
    600 Citadel Dr
    Commerce CA 90040
    323 869-7500

(P-8233)
SMART & FINAL STORES INC
1845 W Vista Way, Vista (92083-6119)
PHONE..............................760 732-1480
EMP: 267
SALES (corp-wide): 4.7B **Privately Held**
SIC: 5141 Groceries, general line
PA: Smart & Final Stores, Inc.
    600 Citadel Dr
    Commerce CA 90040
    323 869-7500

(P-8234)
SMART & FINAL STORES INC
2121 Spring St, Paso Robles (93446-1455)
PHONE..............................805 237-0323
EMP: 326
SALES (corp-wide): 4.7B **Privately Held**
SIC: 5141 Groceries, general line
PA: Smart & Final Stores, Inc.
    600 Citadel Dr
    Commerce CA 90040
    323 869-7500

(P-8235)
SMART & FINAL STORES INC
955 Carlsbad Village Dr, Carlsbad
(92008-1802)
PHONE..............................760 434-2449
EMP: 267
SALES (corp-wide): 4.7B **Privately Held**
SIC: 5141 Groceries, general line
PA: Smart & Final Stores, Inc.
    600 Citadel Dr
    Commerce CA 90040
    323 869-7500

(P-8236)
SMART & FINAL STORES INC
933 Sweetwater Rd, Spring Valley
(91977-4837)
PHONE..............................619 668-9039
EMP: 196
SALES (corp-wide): 4.7B **Privately Held**
SIC: 5141 Groceries, general line
PA: Smart & Final Stores, Inc.
    600 Citadel Dr
    Commerce CA 90040
    323 869-7500

(P-8237)
SMART & FINAL STORES INC
26911 Trabuco Rd, Mission Viejo
(92691-3506)
PHONE..............................949 581-1212
EMP: 267
SALES (corp-wide): 4.7B **Privately Held**
SIC: 5141 Groceries, general line
PA: Smart & Final Stores, Inc.
    600 Citadel Dr
    Commerce CA 90040
    323 869-7500

(P-8238)
SMART & FINAL STORES INC
2825 Grass Valley Hwy, Auburn
(95603-2542)
PHONE..............................530 823-1205
EMP: 200
SALES (corp-wide): 4.7B **Privately Held**
SIC: 5141 Groceries, general line
PA: Smart & Final Stores, Inc.
    600 Citadel Dr
    Commerce CA 90040
    323 869-7500

(P-8239)
SMART & FINAL STORES INC
2235 University Ave, San Diego
(92104-2717)
PHONE..............................619 291-1842
EMP: 267
SALES (corp-wide): 4.7B **Privately Held**
SIC: 5141 Groceries, general line
PA: Smart & Final Stores, Inc.
    600 Citadel Dr
    Commerce CA 90040
    323 869-7500

(P-8240)
SMART & FINAL STORES INC
615 N Pacific Coast Hwy, Redondo Beach
(90277-2107)
PHONE.....................................323 497-8528
EMP: 326
SALES (corp-wide): 4.7B Privately Held
SIC: 5141 Groceries, general line
PA: Smart & Final Stores, Inc.
    600 Citadel Dr
    Commerce CA 90040
    323 869-7500

(P-8241)
SMART & FINAL STORES INC
240 S Diamond Bar Blvd, Diamond Bar
(91765-1605)
PHONE.....................................323 855-8434
EMP: 267
SALES (corp-wide): 4.7B Privately Held
SIC: 5141 Groceries, general line
PA: Smart & Final Stores, Inc.
    600 Citadel Dr
    Commerce CA 90040
    323 869-7500

(P-8242)
SMART & FINAL STORES INC
3830 W Verdugo Ave, Burbank
(91505-3441)
PHONE.....................................818 954-8631
EMP: 261
SALES (corp-wide): 4.7B Privately Held
SIC: 5141 Groceries, general line
PA: Smart & Final Stores, Inc.
    600 Citadel Dr
    Commerce CA 90040
    323 869-7500

(P-8243)
SMART & FINAL STORES INC
5038 W Avenue N, Palmdale (93551-5729)
PHONE.....................................661 722-6210
Danny Omada, *Branch Mgr*
EMP: 267
SALES (corp-wide): 4.7B Privately Held
SIC: 5141 Groceries, general line
PA: Smart & Final Stores, Inc.
    600 Citadel Dr
    Commerce CA 90040
    323 869-7500

(P-8244)
SMART & FINAL STORES INC
5770 Lindero Canyon Rd, Westlake Village
(91362-4088)
PHONE.....................................818 889-8253
EMP: 261
SALES (corp-wide): 4.7B Privately Held
SIC: 5141 Groceries, general line
PA: Smart & Final Stores, Inc.
    600 Citadel Dr
    Commerce CA 90040
    323 869-7500

(P-8245)
SMART & FINAL STORES INC
7800 Telegraph Rd, Ventura (93004-1503)
PHONE.....................................805 647-4276
Brian Gillman, *Branch Mgr*
EMP: 261
SALES (corp-wide): 4.7B Privately Held
SIC: 5141 Groceries, general line
PA: Smart & Final Stores, Inc.
    600 Citadel Dr
    Commerce CA 90040
    323 869-7500

(P-8246)
SMART & FINAL STORES INC
2800 Fletcher Pkwy, El Cajon (92020-2111)
PHONE.....................................619 589-7000
EMP: 200
SALES (corp-wide): 4.7B Privately Held
SIC: 5141 Groceries, general line
PA: Smart & Final Stores, Inc.
    600 Citadel Dr
    Commerce CA 90040
    323 869-7500

(P-8247)
SMART & FINAL STORES INC
10740 Westview Pkwy, San Diego
(92126-2962)
PHONE.....................................858 578-7343
EMP: 267

SALES (corp-wide): 4.7B Privately Held
SIC: 5141 Groceries, general line
PA: Smart & Final Stores, Inc.
    600 Citadel Dr
    Commerce CA 90040
    323 869-7500

(P-8248)
**SMART & FINAL STORES INC
(PA)**
600 Citadel Dr, Commerce (90040-1562)
PHONE.....................................323 869-7500
David G Hirz, *President*
David B Kaplan, *Ch of Bd*
Richard N Phegley, *CFO*
Andrew Greenebaum, *Officer*
Leland P Smith, *Senior VP*
EMP: 447 EST: 2012
SQ FT: 81,000
SALES: 4.7B Privately Held
SIC: 5141 Groceries, general line

(P-8249)
SMART & FINAL STORES INC
13003 Whittier Blvd, Whittier (90602-3046)
PHONE.....................................562 907-7037
David Hirs, *Branch Mgr*
EMP: 334
SALES (corp-wide): 4.7B Privately Held
SIC: 5141 Groceries, general line
PA: Smart & Final Stores, Inc.
    600 Citadel Dr
    Commerce CA 90040
    323 869-7500

(P-8250)
SMART & FINAL STORES INC
303 E Foothill Blvd, Azusa (91702-2516)
PHONE.....................................626 334-5189
EMP: 261
SALES (corp-wide): 4.7B Privately Held
SIC: 5141 Groceries, general line
PA: Smart & Final Stores, Inc.
    600 Citadel Dr
    Commerce CA 90040
    323 869-7500

(P-8251)
SMART & FINAL STORES INC
2425 N Blackstone Ave, Fresno
(93703-1748)
PHONE.....................................559 229-2944
EMP: 261
SALES (corp-wide): 4.7B Privately Held
SIC: 5141 Groceries, general line
PA: Smart & Final Stores, Inc.
    600 Citadel Dr
    Commerce CA 90040
    323 869-7500

(P-8252)
SMART & FINAL STORES INC
401 Jacklin Rd, Milpitas (95035-3226)
PHONE.....................................408 941-9642
EMP: 326
SALES (corp-wide): 4.7B Privately Held
SIC: 5141 Groceries, general line
PA: Smart & Final Stores, Inc.
    600 Citadel Dr
    Commerce CA 90040
    323 869-7500

(P-8253)
SMART & FINAL STORES INC
790 W Shaw Ave, Clovis (93612-3216)
PHONE.....................................559 297-9376
EMP: 261
SALES (corp-wide): 4.7B Privately Held
SIC: 5141 Groceries, general line
PA: Smart & Final Stores, Inc.
    600 Citadel Dr
    Commerce CA 90040
    323 869-7500

(P-8254)
SMART & FINAL STORES LLC
4439 Genesee Ave, San Diego
(92117-3005)
PHONE.....................................858 268-2400
Denis Clyde, *Manager*
EMP: 70
SALES (corp-wide): 4.7B Privately Held
SIC: 5141 Groceries, general line

HQ: Smart & Final Stores Llc
    600 Citadel Dr
    Commerce CA 90040
    323 869-7500

(P-8255)
SMART & FINAL STORES LLC
1260 Garnet Ave, San Diego (92109-2912)
PHONE.....................................858 270-8200
David Schrock, *Manager*
EMP: 80
SALES (corp-wide): 4.7B Privately Held
SIC: 5141 Groceries, general line
HQ: Smart & Final Stores Llc
    600 Citadel Dr
    Commerce CA 90040
    323 869-7500

(P-8256)
SMART & FINAL STORES LLC
3315 Rosecrans St Ste B, San Diego
(92110-4224)
PHONE.....................................619 523-3640
Kevin King, *Director*
EMP: 70
SALES (corp-wide): 4.7B Privately Held
SIC: 5141 Groceries, general line
HQ: Smart & Final Stores Llc
    600 Citadel Dr
    Commerce CA 90040
    323 869-7500

(P-8257)
**SMART & FINAL STORES LLC
(DH)**
600 Citadel Dr, Commerce (90040-1562)
PHONE.....................................323 869-7500
Etienne P Snollaerts, *CEO*
Ross E Roeder, *Ch of Bd*
Diane Godfrey, *President*
Martin Lynch, *CFO*
Dennis L Chiavelli, *Exec VP*
EMP: 153
SALES (est): 4.2B
SALES (corp-wide): 4.7B Privately Held
SIC: 5141 Groceries, general line
HQ: Smart & Final, Inc.
    600 Citadel Dr
    Commerce CA 90040
    323 869-7500

(P-8258)
SMART & FINAL STORES LLC
471 College Blvd, Oceanside (92057-5435)
PHONE.....................................760 726-7274
Jordan Kelly, *Director*
EMP: 60
SALES (corp-wide): 4.7B Privately Held
SIC: 5141 Groceries, general line
HQ: Smart & Final Stores Llc
    600 Citadel Dr
    Commerce CA 90040
    323 869-7500

(P-8259)
SMART & FINAL STORES LLC
4175 Park Blvd, San Diego (92103-2510)
PHONE.....................................619 291-8287
Dennis Gross, *Manager*
EMP: 80
SALES (corp-wide): 4.7B Privately Held
SIC: 5141 Food brokers
HQ: Smart & Final Stores Llc
    600 Citadel Dr
    Commerce CA 90040
    323 869-7500

(P-8260)
SMART & FINAL STORES LLC
659 Lomas Santa Fe Dr, Solana Beach
(92075-1412)
PHONE.....................................858 350-7900
Davis Sparano, *Manager*
EMP: 100
SALES (corp-wide): 4.7B Privately Held
SIC: 5141 Groceries, general line
HQ: Smart & Final Stores Llc
    600 Citadel Dr
    Commerce CA 90040
    323 869-7500

(P-8261)
**SOUTHWEST TRADERS
INCORPORATED**
4747 Frontier Way, Stockton (95215-9671)
PHONE.....................................209 462-1607

Jerry Alestra, *Branch Mgr*
EMP: 91
SALES (corp-wide): 398.7MM Privately Held
SIC: 5141 Food brokers
PA: Southwest Traders Incorporated
    27565 Diaz Rd
    Temecula CA 92590
    951 699-7800

(P-8262)
**SOUTHWEST TRADERS
INCORPORATED (PA)**
Also Called: Swt Stockton
27565 Diaz Rd, Temecula (92590-3411)
PHONE.....................................951 699-7800
Ken Smith, *CEO*
Lynne Bredemeier, *CFO*
Daniel Ruckel, *Info Tech Mgr*
Steve Mays, *IT/INT Sup*
Angela Bergeron, *Human Res Dir*
▲ EMP: 180
SQ FT: 130,000
SALES (est): 398.7MM Privately Held
SIC: 5141 Food brokers

(P-8263)
**SPROUTS FARMERS MARKET
INC**
Also Called: Sprouts 252
820 N Western Ave, San Pedro
(90732-2426)
PHONE.....................................310 831-7836
Khoi Tran, *Director*
EMP: 72
SALES (corp-wide): 5.2B Publicly Held
SIC: 5141 Groceries, general line
PA: Sprouts Farmers Market, Inc.
    5455 E High St Ste 111
    Phoenix AZ 85054
    480 814-8016

(P-8264)
SUNFOODS LLC (HQ)
Also Called: Hinode
1620 E Kentucky Ave, Woodland
(95776-6110)
P.O. Box 8729 (95776-8729)
PHONE.....................................530 661-1923
Matt Alonso, *CEO*
Jacqueline Hartshorn,
John Koury,
Clyde Uchida,
◆ EMP: 70
SQ FT: 1,600
SALES: 22MM Privately Held
SIC: 5141 Food brokers

(P-8265)
SYGMA NETWORK INC
3741 Gold River Ln, Stockton
(95215-9669)
PHONE.....................................209 932-5300
John Rivers, *Vice Pres*
Don Thornburg, *Executive*
EMP: 125
SALES (corp-wide): 60.1B Publicly Held
WEB: www.sygmanetwork.com
SIC: 5141 Food brokers
HQ: The Sygma Network Inc
    5550 Blazer Pkwy Ste 300
    Dublin OH 43017

(P-8266)
**SYSCO CENTRAL CALIFORNIA
INC**
136 Mariposa Rd, Modesto (95354-4122)
P.O. Box 729 (95353-0729)
PHONE.....................................209 527-7700
Elizabeth Aspray, *President*
Robin Kawashima, *CFO*
Patrick Kissee, *Vice Pres*
Simon To, *Vice Pres*
Jason Boyd, *Buyer*
▲ EMP: 312
SQ FT: 177,000
SALES (corp-wide): 60.1B Publicly Held
SIC: 5141 5142 5046 5148 Food bro-
    kers; meat, frozen: packaged; vegetables,
    frozen; restaurant equipment & supplies;
    fruits, fresh; vegetables, fresh
PA: Sysco Corporation
    1390 Enclave Pkwy
    Houston TX 77077
    281 584-1390

(P-8267)
SYSCO LOS ANGELES INC
20701 Currier Rd, Walnut (91789-2904)
PHONE.............................909 595-9595
Daniel S Haag, *CEO*
John KAO, *Senior VP*
Fred Guibara, *Vice Pres*
Janice Puket, *Comp Tech*
Peter Gatto, *Buyer*
◆ **EMP:** 1000
SALES (est): 221.8MM
SALES (corp-wide): 60.1B **Publicly Held**
WEB: www.syscola.com
SIC: **5141** 5084 Groceries, general line;
food industry machinery
PA: Sysco Corporation
1390 Enclave Pkwy
Houston TX 77077
281 584-1390

(P-8268)
SYSCO RIVERSIDE INC
15750 Meridian Pkwy, Riverside
(92518-3001)
PHONE.............................951 601-5300
Saul Adelsberg, *CEO*
Nancy Drake, *Credit Staff*
EMP: 375
SALES (est): 205.7MM
SALES (corp-wide): 60.1B **Publicly Held**
SIC: **5141** 5142 5143 5144 Food bro-
kers; packaged frozen goods; dairy prod-
ucts, except dried or canned; poultry &
poultry products; confectionery; fish &
seafoods
PA: Sysco Corporation
1390 Enclave Pkwy
Houston TX 77077
281 584-1390

(P-8269)
SYSCO SACRAMENTO INC
7062 Pacific Ave, Pleasant Grove
(95668-9731)
P.O. Box 138007, Sacramento (95813-
8007)
PHONE.............................916 275-2714
Jackie L Ward, *Ch of Bd*
Bill Delaney, *President*
Delmer Schnuelle, *President*
Tom Bene, *Exec VP*
Brian Beach, *Senior VP*
▼ **EMP:** 393
SQ FT: 350,000
SALES (est): 221.8MM
SALES (corp-wide): 60.1B **Publicly Held**
WEB: www.sac.sysco.com
SIC: **5141** 5142 Food brokers; packaged
frozen goods
PA: Sysco Corporation
1390 Enclave Pkwy
Houston TX 77077
281 584-1390

(P-8270)
SYSCO SAN DIEGO INC
12180 Kirkham Rd, Poway (92064-6879)
PHONE.............................858 513-7300
Kevin Mangan, *CEO*
Howard Poole, *President*
Debra Morey, *Vice Pres*
Jaime Maldonado, *Buyer*
Michael Okuma, *Mktg Dir*
◆ **EMP:** 370 **EST:** 1996
SQ FT: 250,000
SALES (est): 221.8MM
SALES (corp-wide): 60.1B **Publicly Held**
SIC: **5141** 5142 5147 5148 Food bro-
kers; packaged frozen goods; meats &
meat products; fresh fruits & vegetables;
food industry machinery
PA: Sysco Corporation
1390 Enclave Pkwy
Houston TX 77077
281 584-1390

(P-8271)
SYSCO SAN FRANCISCO INC
5900 Stewart Ave, Fremont (94538-3147)
P.O. Box 697 (94537-0697)
PHONE.............................510 226-3000
James Ehlers, *President*
Glory Law, *Officer*
Bruce Luong, *Vice Pres*
Wesley Wilson, *Vice Pres*
Patrick Bily, *Principal*

▼ **EMP:** 650
SQ FT: 470,000
SALES (est): 221.8MM
SALES (corp-wide): 60.1B **Publicly Held**
WEB: www.syscosf.com
SIC: **5141** 5147 5142 Groceries, general
line; meats, fresh; packaged frozen goods
PA: Sysco Corporation
1390 Enclave Pkwy
Houston TX 77077
281 584-1390

(P-8272)
SYSCO VENTURA INC
3100 Sturgis Rd, Oxnard (93030-7276)
PHONE.............................805 205-7000
Jerry L Barash, *President*
Manny Fernandez, *Ch of Bd*
Bill Delaney, *President*
William Mastrosimone, *CFO*
Brian Beach, *Vice Pres*
EMP: 300
SQ FT: 370,000
SALES (est): 183.1MM
SALES (corp-wide): 60.1B **Publicly Held**
SIC: **5141** Food brokers
PA: Sysco Corporation
1390 Enclave Pkwy
Houston TX 77077
281 584-1390

(P-8273)
TAPIA ENTERPRISES INC (PA)
Also Called: Tapia Brothers Co
6067 District Blvd, Maywood (90270-3560)
PHONE.............................323 560-7415
Raul Tapia, *CEO*
Francisco Tapia, *Treasurer*
Ramon Tapia, *Admin Sec*
Sergio Vasquez, *Purchasing*
Ramiro Rubalcava, *Marketing Staff*
▲ **EMP:** 95
SQ FT: 40,000
SALES (est): 266.4MM **Privately Held**
WEB: www.tapiabrothers.com
SIC: **5141** Groceries, general line

(P-8274)
UNIFIED GROCERS INC
Also Called: Market Centre
455 N Canyons Pkwy, Livermore
(94551-7681)
PHONE.............................323 264-5200
Joe Falvey, *Exec VP*
Christine Parra, *Manager*
Marissa Ruelas, *Manager*
EMP: 100 **EST:** 2015
SALES (est): 3.4MM **Publicly Held**
SIC: **5141** Groceries, general line
HQ: Unified Grocers, Inc.
5200 Sheila St
Commerce CA 90040
323 264-5200

(P-8275)
UNION SUPPLY GROUP INC (PA)
Also Called: Union Supply Company
2301 E Pacifica Pl, Rancho Dominguez
(90220-6210)
P.O. Box 7006 (90224-7006)
PHONE.............................310 603-8899
Tom Thomas, *CEO*
Scott Schaldenbrand, *CFO*
Lyndel Hay, *Exec VP*
John Son, *Vice Pres*
Jasmine Awadallah, *Program Mgr*
▲ **EMP:** 115
SQ FT: 24,000
SALES (est): 117.3MM **Privately Held**
SIC: **5141** 5139 5136 Groceries, general
line; footwear; men's & boys' clothing

(P-8276)
US FOODS INC
1283 Sherborn St Ste 102, Corona
(92879-5003)
PHONE.............................951 256-2400
Brad Bastyr, *Branch Mgr*
Cheryl Kuks, *Executive Asst*
Carina Arciga, *Cust Mgr*
Don Loessberg, *Manager*
Jason Mead, *Manager*
EMP: 155 **Publicly Held**
SIC: **5141** Food brokers

HQ: Us Foods, Inc.
9399 W Higgins Rd # 100
Rosemont IL 60018

(P-8277)
US FOODS INC
300 Lawrence Dr Frnt, Livermore
(94551-5139)
PHONE.............................925 606-3525
Phil Collins, *Branch Mgr*
Rob West, *Warehouse Mgr*
Nelson Lum, *Manager*
Cat Lindquist, *Accounts Exec*
EMP: 500 **Publicly Held**
WEB: www.usfoodservice.com
SIC: **5141** Food brokers
HQ: Us Foods, Inc.
9399 W Higgins Rd # 100
Rosemont IL 60018
-

(P-8278)
US FOODS INC
15155 Northam St, La Mirada
(90638-5754)
P.O. Box 29283, Phoenix AZ (85038-9283)
PHONE.............................714 670-3500
David Patterson, *Branch Mgr*
EMP: 172 **Publicly Held**
WEB: www.usfoodservice.com
SIC: **5141** 5046 3556 2099 Food bro-
kers; commercial equipment; food prod-
ucts machinery; food preparations;
restaurant equipment repair
HQ: Us Foods, Inc.
9399 W Higgins Rd # 100
Rosemont IL 60018

(P-8279)
US FOODS INC
Also Called: U S Foods
392 W Walnut Ave, Fullerton (92832-2351)
PHONE.............................714 670-3500
Gene McHugh, *General Mgr*
EMP: 50 **Publicly Held**
WEB: www.usfoodservice.com
SIC: **5141** 5142 Food brokers; packaged
frozen goods
HQ: Us Foods, Inc.
9399 W Higgins Rd # 100
Rosemont IL 60018

(P-8280)
USFI INC
110 W Walnut St 221, Gardena
(90248-3100)
PHONE.............................310 768-1937
Gary Place, *President*
William Baek, *CFO*
Steven Choi, *Vice Pres*
Byung Hak Erick Yoo, *Director*
▲ **EMP:** 75 **EST:** 1998
SQ FT: 4,000
SALES (est): 47.5MM **Privately Held**
WEB: www.usfifoods.com
SIC: **5141** 5149 Food brokers; groceries &
related products

(P-8281)
USTOV INC
Also Called: U.S. Trading Company
21118 Cabot Blvd, Hayward (94545-1130)
PHONE.............................510 781-1818
Paul M Tov, *CEO*
◆ **EMP:** 50
SQ FT: 132,000
SALES (est): 33.5MM **Privately Held**
SIC: **5141** Food brokers

(P-8282)
VIELE & SONS INC
Also Called: Viele & Sons Instnl Groc
1820 E Valencia Dr, Fullerton (92831-4847)
PHONE.............................714 447-3663
Anthony J Viele, *President*
Jim Viele, *Shareholder*
Nancy Montez Viele, *Shareholder*
Joseph Viele, *Treasurer*
Anthony Viele Jr, *Vice Pres*
EMP: 90
SQ FT: 95,000

SALES (est): 111MM **Privately Held**
WEB: www.vieleandsons.com
SIC: **5141** Groceries, general line

(P-8283)
WEST PICO DISTRIBUTORS LLC
5201 S Downey Rd, Vernon (90058-3703)
P.O. Box 58107 (90058-0107)
PHONE.............................323 586-9050
Mordy Herzog,
David Kagan,
EMP: 55
SALES (est): 2.1MM **Privately Held**
SIC: **5141** Food brokers

(P-8284)
WISMETTAC ASIAN FOODS INC (HQ)
Also Called: Wismettac Fresh Fish
13409 Orden Dr, Santa Fe Springs
(90670-6336)
PHONE.............................562 802-1900
Takayuki Kanai, *CEO*
Tom Kawaguchi, *CFO*
Teijiro Sho, *Officer*
Toshiyoki Nishikawa, *Vice Pres*
Yuji Sasa, *Vice Pres*
◆ **EMP:** 200
SQ FT: 225,000
SALES (est): 556.5MM **Privately Held**
WEB: www.nishimototrading.com
SIC: **5141** Groceries, general line

5142 Packaged Frozen Foods Wholesale

(P-8285)
CALBEE NORTH AMERICA LLC
2600 Maxwell Way, Fairfield (94534-1915)
PHONE.............................707 427-2500
Gene Jensen, *Branch Mgr*
Fumie Mihaly, *Manager*
EMP: 50 **Privately Held**
SIC: **5142** 5145 2038 Packaged frozen
goods; snack foods; snacks, including
onion rings, cheese sticks, etc.
HQ: Calbee North America, Llc
72600 Lewis & Clark Dr
Boardman OR 97818
-

(P-8286)
GOLD STAR FOODS INC (HQ)
3781 E Airport Dr, Ontario (91761-1558)
P.O. Box 4328 (91761-8828)
PHONE.............................909 843-9600
Sean Leer, *President*
Les Wong, *COO*
Greg Johnson, *CFO*
Mahvash Howell, *Senior VP*
Frank Manzano, *Vice Pres*
▲ **EMP:** 123
SQ FT: 38,000
SALES (est): 365.8MM
SALES (corp-wide): 431MM **Privately
Held**
WEB: www.goldstarfoods.com
SIC: **5142** Packaged frozen goods
PA: Highview Capital, Llc
11755 Wilshire Blvd # 14
Los Angeles CA 90025
310 806-9780

(P-8287)
INTERSTATE MEAT & PROVISION
Also Called: Sterling Pacific Meat Company
6114 Scott Way, Commerce (90040-3518)
PHONE.............................323 838-9400
Jim Asher, *CEO*
Roya Galindo, *Director*
▲ **EMP:** 100
SQ FT: 25,038
SALES (est): 85.9MM **Privately Held**
SIC: **5142** 5147 Packaged frozen goods;
meat brokers

(P-8288)
J AND J WALL BAKING CO INC
8806 Fruitridge Rd, Sacramento
(95826-9708)
PHONE.............................916 381-1410

John Wall, *CEO*
EMP: 55
SQ FT: 50,000
SALES (est): 16.2MM **Privately Held**
SIC: 5142 Bakery products, frozen

(P-8289)
JETRO CASH AND CARRY ENTPS LLC
1265 N Kraemer Blvd, Anaheim (92806-1921)
PHONE......................714 666-8211
Stanley Fleishman,
Pat Rosica, *President*
EMP: 130
SALES (corp-wide): 24.5B **Privately Held**
SIC: 5142 5046 5181 5147 Packaged frozen goods; restaurant equipment & supplies; beer & other fermented malt liquors; meats, fresh; grocery stores
HQ: Jetro Cash And Carry Enterprises, Llc
1524 132nd St
College Point NY 11356
718 939-6400

(P-8290)
L & T MEAT CO
3050 E 11th St, Los Angeles (90023-3606)
PHONE......................323 262-2815
Chak Por Tea, *President*
Bobby Lu, *Vice Pres*
EMP: 80
SQ FT: 20,000
SALES (est): 30.8MM **Privately Held**
WEB: www.ltmeat.com
SIC: 5142 Frozen fish, meat & poultry

(P-8291)
MARIE CLLENDER WHOLESALERS INC
170 E Rincon St, Corona (92879-1327)
PHONE......................951 737-6760
Phillip Ratner, *President*
Gerald Tanaka, *Senior VP*
Kurt Schweickhart, *Vice Pres*
EMP: 65
SQ FT: 28,000
SALES (est): 22.3MM
SALES (corp-wide): 836.5MM **Privately Held**
WEB: www.castleharlan.com
SIC: 5142 Bakery products, frozen
HQ: Castle Harlan Partners Iii Lp
150 E 58th St Fl 38
New York NY 10155
212 644-8600

(P-8292)
MCLANE FOODSERVICE DIST INC
Also Called: M B M
5675 Sunol Blvd, Pleasanton (94566-7765)
PHONE......................252 985-7200
Al Monceaux, *Manager*
EMP: 65
SALES (corp-wide): 225.3B **Publicly Held**
WEB: www.mbmlc.com
SIC: 5142 Packaged frozen goods
HQ: Mclane Foodservice Distribution, Inc.
2641 Meadowbrook Rd
Rocky Mount NC 27801
252 985-7200

(P-8293)
OTASTY FOODS INC
160 S Hacienda Blvd, City of Industry (91745-1101)
PHONE......................626 330-1229
Ming Chao Huang, *President*
Ken Chen, *Vice Pres*
◆ **EMP:** 91
SQ FT: 58,000
SALES (est): 40.8MM **Privately Held**
WEB: www.otasty.com
SIC: 5142 Packaged frozen goods

(P-8294)
PACIFIC FRESH SEA FOOD COMPANY (HQ)
Also Called: Pacific Seafood Sacramento
1420 National Dr, Sacramento (95834-1967)
PHONE......................916 419-5500
Frank Dominic Dulcich, *President*

Tim Horgan, *COO*
Andrea Greene, *Credit Mgr*
Marty Martinez, *Sales Mgr*
Cynthia Geddis, *Marketing Staff*
◆ **EMP:** 178
SQ FT: 50,000
SALES (est): 94.8MM
SALES (corp-wide): 569.5MM **Privately Held**
SIC: 5142 5146 Fish, frozen: packaged; fish, fresh
PA: Dulcich, Inc.
16797 Se 130th Ave
Clackamas OR 97015
503 226-2200

(P-8295)
PRODUCERS DAIRY FOODS INC (PA)
250 E Belmont Ave, Fresno (93701-1405)
PHONE......................559 264-6583
Lawrence A Shehadey, *Ch of Bd*
Richard Shehadey, *CEO*
Scott Shehadey, *Vice Pres*
Williams Brandi, *Executive*
Ted Enea, *Branch Mgr*
▲ **EMP:** 200
SALES (est): 181.6MM **Privately Held**
WEB: www.producersdairy.com
SIC: 5142 5143 Fruit juices, frozen; dairy products, except dried or canned

(P-8296)
RESTAURANT DEPOT LLC
520 Brennan St, San Jose (95131-1201)
PHONE......................408 344-0107
Ron McGill, *Branch Mgr*
EMP: 150
SALES (corp-wide): 24.5B **Privately Held**
WEB: www.jrdtuning.com
SIC: 5142 5147 5141 5181 Packaged frozen goods; meats, fresh; groceries, general line; beer & other fermented malt liquors; tobacco & tobacco products
HQ: Restaurant Depot, Llc
1524 132nd St
College Point NY 11356

(P-8297)
RESTAURANT DEPOT LLC
180 N San Gabriel Blvd, Pasadena (91107-3426)
PHONE......................626 744-0204
Dan Mihal, *Manager*
EMP: 150
SALES (corp-wide): 24.5B **Privately Held**
WEB: www.jrdtuning.com
SIC: 5142 5141 5194 5181 Packaged frozen goods; groceries, general line; tobacco & tobacco products; beer & other fermented malt liquors; meats, fresh
HQ: Restaurant Depot, Llc
1524 132nd St
College Point NY 11356

(P-8298)
RESTAURANT DEPOT LLC
400 High St, Oakland (94601-3904)
PHONE......................510 628-0600
John Derosa, *Branch Mgr*
EMP: 150
SALES (corp-wide): 24.5B **Privately Held**
WEB: www.jrdtuning.com
SIC: 5142 5147 5141 5181 Packaged frozen goods; meats, fresh; groceries, general line; beer & other fermented malt liquors; tobacco & tobacco products
HQ: Restaurant Depot, Llc
1524 132nd St
College Point NY 11356

(P-8299)
RESTAURANT DEPOT LLC
17332 Gothard St, Huntington Beach (92647-6203)
PHONE......................714 378-3535
Alan Cummins, *Manager*
EMP: 150

SALES (corp-wide): 24.5B **Privately Held**
WEB: www.jrdtuning.com
SIC: 5142 5194 5147 5181 Packaged frozen goods; tobacco & tobacco products; meats, fresh; beer & other fermented malt liquors; groceries, general line
HQ: Restaurant Depot, Llc
1524 132nd St
College Point NY 11356

(P-8300)
RESTAURANT DEPOT LLC
2300 E 68th St, Long Beach (90805-1728)
PHONE......................562 634-6771
Adrian Padilla, *Branch Mgr*
EMP: 92
SALES (corp-wide): 24.5B **Privately Held**
WEB: www.jrdtuning.com
SIC: 5142 5147 5141 5181 Packaged frozen goods; meats, fresh; groceries, general line; beer & other fermented malt liquors; tobacco & tobacco products
HQ: Restaurant Depot, Llc
1524 132nd St
College Point NY 11356
-

(P-8301)
S J S LINK INTERNATIONAL INC (PA)
468 N Camden Dr Ste 311, Beverly Hills (90210-4507)
PHONE......................310 860-7666
Shiraz Mamedov, *CEO*
Olga Sedova, *CFO*
Alex Zimmer, *Treasurer*
▼ **EMP:** 50
SALES (est): 8.5MM **Privately Held**
WEB: www.sjsusa.com
SIC: 5142 Frozen fish, meat & poultry

(P-8302)
SJ DISTRIBUTORS INC (PA)
625 Vista Way, Milpitas (95035-5433)
P.O. Box 1202, Santa Clara (95052-1202)
PHONE......................888 988-2328
Scott Chun Ho Suen, *CEO*
Jerry Yeung, *CFO*
Jenny Lin, *Admin Sec*
EMP: 71
SQ FT: 60,000
SALES (est): 171.3MM **Privately Held**
SIC: 5142 5149 5148 5146 Meat, frozen: packaged; canned goods: fruit, vegetables, seafood, meats, etc.; fresh fruits & vegetables; seafoods

(P-8303)
SUPERIOR FOODS INC
Also Called: Superior Foods Companies, The
275 Westgate Dr, Watsonville (95076-2470)
PHONE......................831 728-3691
David E Moore, *Ch of Bd*
Mateo Lettunich, *President*
R Neil Happee, *CEO*
Neil Happee, *COO*
H Monroe Howser III, *CFO*
◆ **EMP:** 100
SQ FT: 10,782
SALES (est): 90MM **Privately Held**
SIC: 5142 Fruits, frozen

(P-8304)
VPS COMPANIES INC (PA)
310 Walker St, Watsonville (95076-4525)
P.O. Box 118 (95077-0118)
PHONE......................831 724-7551
Jack Randle, *Ch of Bd*
Ronald Marker, *CFO*
Fred J Haas, *Corp Secy*
▲ **EMP:** 50
SQ FT: 10,000
SALES (est): 384MM **Privately Held**
WEB: www.us-foods.com
SIC: 5142 0723 4731 Fruits, frozen; vegetables, frozen; crop preparation services for market; freight transportation arrangement

(P-8305)
VPS COMPANIES INC
Also Called: Central Cold Storage
13526 Blackie Rd, Castroville (95012-3212)
P.O. Box 610 (95012-0610)
PHONE......................831 633-4011
Jonathon Thorton, *President*
EMP: 50
SALES (corp-wide): 384MM **Privately Held**
WEB: www.us-foods.com
SIC: 5142 Fruits, frozen
PA: The Vps Companies Inc
310 Walker St
Watsonville CA 95076
831 724-7551

(P-8306)
WEI-CHUAN USA INC (PA)
6655 Garfield Ave, Bell Gardens (90201-1807)
PHONE......................626 225-7168
Steve Lin, *President*
William Huang, *Treasurer*
Andrew Chang, *Branch Mgr*
Benny Chang, *Admin Sec*
Robert Hsu, *Purch Mgr*
◆ **EMP:** 120
SQ FT: 38,000
SALES (est): 100.2MM **Privately Held**
SIC: 5142 2038 Packaged frozen goods; dinners, frozen & packaged; ethnic foods, frozen

(P-8307)
WEST PICO FOODS INC
5201 S Downey Rd, Vernon (90058-3703)
P.O. Box 58107 (90058-0107)
PHONE......................323 586-9050
Elias Naghi, *President*
Don Lubitz, *Treasurer*
Evelyn Cruz, *Executive*
Jason Schultz, *Buyer*
▲ **EMP:** 125
SQ FT: 42,000
SALES (est): 101.9MM **Privately Held**
WEB: www.westpicofoods.com
SIC: 5142 5144 Packaged frozen goods; poultry: live, dressed or frozen (unpackaged)

5143 Dairy Prdts, Except Dried Or Canned Wholesale

(P-8308)
ALTA-DENA CERTIFIED DAIRY LLC
4656 Cardin St, San Diego (92111-1419)
PHONE......................858 292-6930
Frank Reimhard, *General Mgr*
EMP: 75
SALES (corp-wide): 941.7MM **Privately Held**
WEB: www.altadenadairy.com
SIC: 5143 Dairy depot
HQ: Alta-Dena Certified Dairy, Llc
17637 E Valley Blvd
City Of Industry CA 91744
626 964-6401

(P-8309)
ARYA ICE CREAM DISTRG CO INC
914 E 31st St, Los Angeles (90011-2502)
P.O. Box 456, Harbor City (90710-0456)
PHONE......................323 234-2994
Ali Pakravan, *CEO*
Mansour Azizian, *Shareholder*
Farhad Karamati, *Shareholder*
Mansour Sahabi, *Shareholder*
Hossein Sahabi, *Vice Pres*
▲ **EMP:** 60
SQ FT: 46,000
SALES (est): 70.2MM **Privately Held**
WEB: www.aryaicecream.com
SIC: 5143 Ice cream & ices

P R O D U C T S & S V C S

(P-8310)
CACIQUE INC
14923 Proctor Ave, La Puente
(91746-3206)
P.O. Box 1047, Monrovia (91017-1047)
PHONE..............................626 961-3399
Mac Moore, *Director*
Michael Schmidt, *Regional*
EMP: 240
SALES (corp-wide): 100.8MM **Privately Held**
SIC: 5143 Cheese
PA: Cacique, Inc.
800 Royal Oaks Dr Ste 200
Monrovia CA 91016
626 961-3399

(P-8311)
CALIFIA FARMS LLC (PA)
1321 Palmetto St, Los Angeles
(90013-2228)
PHONE..............................213 694-4667
Greg Stelpenpoho, *CEO*
Demir Vangelov, *CFO*
Robert Adriaansen, *Engineer*
Jim Whitaker, *VP Sales*
Andrew Fendelman, *Sales Mgr*
▼ **EMP:** 50 **EST:** 2010
SALES: 100MM **Privately Held**
SIC: 5143 5149 Milk & cream, fluid; coffee, green or roasted

(P-8312)
CENTRAL VALLEY CHEESE INC
115 S Kilroy Rd, Turlock (95380-9531)
PHONE..............................209 664-1080
Antranik Baghdassarian, *CEO*
EMP: 70
SALES (est): 62.5MM **Privately Held**
WEB: www.karouncheese.com
SIC: 5143 Cheese
PA: Karoun Dairies, Inc.
13023 Arroyo St
San Fernando CA 91340

(P-8313)
CHALLENGE DAIRY PRODUCTS INC
5741 Smithway St, Commerce
(90040-1507)
PHONE..............................323 724-3130
Dan Bollinger, *Principal*
Jake Carden, *Manager*
EMP: 50
SALES (corp-wide): 253.1MM **Privately Held**
WEB: www.challengedairy.com
SIC: 5143 2023 2021 Dairy depot; dry, condensed, evaporated dairy products; creamery butter
HQ: Challenge Dairy Products, Inc
6701 Donlon Way
Dublin CA 94568
925 828-6160

(P-8314)
CHALLENGE DAIRY PRODUCTS INC (HQ)
6701 Donlon Way, Dublin (94568-2850)
P.O. Box 2369 (94568-0706)
PHONE..............................925 828-6160
Irvin Holmes, *President*
Jason Morris, *President*
Stanford Alan Maag, *CFO*
Tim Anderson, *Vice Pres*
Tom Ditto, *Vice Pres*
▲ **EMP:** 57 **EST:** 1976
SQ FT: 8,500
SALES (est): 192.9MM
SALES (corp-wide): 253.1MM **Privately Held**
WEB: www.challengedairy.com
SIC: 5143 5149 Butter; milk, canned or dried
PA: California Dairies, Inc.
2000 N Plaza Dr
Visalia CA 93291
559 625-2200

(P-8315)
DREYERS GRAND ICE CREAM HOLD (DH)
5929 College Ave, Oakland (94618-1325)
PHONE..............................510 652-8187

Michael T Mitchell, *CEO*
Sherri Bjelka, *Officer*
Suzanne Saltzman, *Principal*
Sammy Yoshida, *Technical Staff*
Roseanna Garcia, *Analyst*
◆ **EMP:** 230
SQ FT: 64,000
SALES (est): 612MM
SALES (corp-wide): 92B **Privately Held**
SIC: 5143 5451 2024 Frozen dairy desserts; ice cream & ices; ice cream (packaged); ice cream & frozen desserts; ice cream, packaged: molded, on sticks, etc.; ice cream, bulk; yogurt desserts, frozen
HQ: Nestle Prepared Foods Company
30003 Bainbridge Rd
Solon OH 44139
440 248-3600

(P-8316)
DRIFTWOOD DAIRY INC
10724 Lower Azusa Rd, El Monte
(91731-1390)
P.O. Box 5508 (91734-1508)
PHONE..............................626 444-9591
P Kelly Olds, *CEO*
Monty Zwieg, *Vice Pres*
Gary Bardakji, *Regl Sales Mgr*
Mark Brown, *Sales Mgr*
Steve Nuckolls, *Facilities Mgr*
EMP: 215
SALES (est): 193.3MM **Privately Held**
WEB: www.driftwooddairy.com
SIC: 5143 Dairy products, except dried or canned

(P-8317)
FOSTER DAIRY PRODUCTS DISTRG (PA)
529 Kansas Ave, Modesto (95351-1515)
PHONE..............................209 576-3400
Jeff Foster, *President*
EMP: 620
SALES (est): 91MM **Privately Held**
SIC: 5143 2026 Dairy products, except dried or canned; fluid milk

(P-8318)
KLM MANAGEMENT COMPANY
Also Called: Amcom Food Service
14120 Valley Blvd, City of Industry
(91746-2802)
PHONE..............................626 330-3479
Ted Degroot, *President*
VA Mechelen David, *Vice Pres*
Jose Gonzalez, *Principal*
Khalid Mehmood, *Principal*
Curtis Degroot, *Admin Sec*
▼ **EMP:** 70
SQ FT: 91,000
SALES (est): 45.4MM **Privately Held**
SIC: 5143 Dairy products, except dried or canned

(P-8319)
LOS ALTOS FOOD PRODUCTS INC
450 Baldwin Park Blvd, City of Industry
(91746-1407)
PHONE..............................626 330-6555
Raul Andrade, *President*
Alln Andrade, *Vice Pres*
Gloria Andrade, *Vice Pres*
EMP: 105
SQ FT: 38,000
SALES (est): 102MM **Privately Held**
WEB: www.losaltosfoods.com
SIC: 5143 Cheese

(P-8320)
NESTLE DREYERS ICE CREAM CO
Also Called: Dreyer's Grand Ice Cream
351 Cheryl Ln, Walnut (91789-3003)
PHONE..............................909 595-0677
Mike Stamper, *Manager*
EMP: 175
SALES (corp-wide): 92B **Privately Held**
WEB: www.dreyersinc.com
SIC: 5143 2024 4222 Ice cream & ices; ice cream & frozen desserts; refrigerated warehousing & storage

HQ: Nestle Dreyer's Ice Cream Company
5929 College Ave
Oakland CA 94618

(P-8321)
NESTLE ICE CREAM COMPANY
7301 District Blvd, Bakersfield
(93313-2042)
PHONE..............................661 398-3500
James L Dintaman, *CEO*
▲ **EMP:** 1920
SALES (est): 221.8MM
SALES (corp-wide): 92B **Privately Held**
WEB: www.haagendazsrewards.com
SIC: 5143 5451 Ice cream & ices; ice cream (packaged)
HQ: Dreyer's Grand Ice Cream Holdings, Inc.
5929 College Ave
Oakland CA 94618
510 652-8187

(P-8322)
NESTLE USA INC
6205 Engel Way, Gilroy (95020-7016)
PHONE..............................408 846-6892
Chris Pedro, *Branch Mgr*
EMP: 135
SALES (corp-wide): 92B **Privately Held**
SIC: 5143 Ice cream & ices
HQ: Nestle Usa, Inc.
1812 N Moore St Ste 118
Rosslyn VA 22209
818 549-6000

(P-8323)
PACIFIC CHEESE CO INC (PA)
21090 Cabot Blvd, Hayward (94545-1110)
P.O. Box 56598 (94545-6598)
PHONE..............................510 784-8800
Stephen B Gaddis, *President*
Dale Tate, *CFO*
June M Gaddis, *Corp Secy*
Rechelle Garza, *Human Res Dir*
Denise Kobzoff, *Export Mgr*
▲ **EMP:** 153
SQ FT: 107,000
SALES: 800MM **Privately Held**
WEB: www.pacific-cheese.com
SIC: 5143 Cheese

(P-8324)
SVD INC
Also Called: Sun Valley Dairy
8088 San Fernando Rd, Sun Valley
(91352-4001)
PHONE..............................818 504-1775
Jack Galadjian, *CEO*
ARA Kozanian, *President*
▲ **EMP:** 55
SQ FT: 40,000
SALES (est): 43.4MM **Privately Held**
WEB: www.voskos.com
SIC: 5143 Yogurt

┌─────────────────────────────────┐
5144 Poultry & Poultry Prdts Wholesale
└─────────────────────────────────┘

(P-8325)
GOOD EGGS INC (PA)
901 Rankin St, San Francisco
(94124-1626)
PHONE..............................415 483-7344
Rob Spiro, *Chairman*
Nate Jordan, *Buyer*
Jane Stecyk, *Director*
EMP: 91
SALES (est): 53.4MM **Privately Held**
SIC: 5144 2099 Eggs; ready-to-eat meals, salads & sandwiches

(P-8326)
HIDDEN VILLA RANCH PRODUCE INC
310 N Harbor Blvd Ste 205, Fullerton
(92832-1954)
P.O. Box 34001 (92834-9411)
PHONE..............................714 680-3447
Tim E Luberski, *President*
Don Lawson, *CFO*
Robert J Kelly, *Exec VP*
Greg Schneider, *Exec VP*
Michael Sencer, *Exec VP*

◆ **EMP:** 270
SQ FT: 21,619
SALES: 410MM
SALES (corp-wide): 350MM **Privately Held**
WEB: www.hiddenvillaranch.com
SIC: 5144 Eggs
PA: Luberski, Inc.
310 N Harbor Blvd Ste 205
Fullerton CA 92832
714 680-3447

(P-8327)
INTERSTATE FOODS INC
310 S Long Beach Blvd, Compton
(90221-3448)
PHONE..............................310 635-0426
Carlos Velasco, *CEO*
EMP: 145 **EST:** 2000
SQ FT: 13,000
SALES (est): 38.7MM **Privately Held**
SIC: 5144 Poultry products

(P-8328)
LEHAR SALES CO
477 Forbes Blvd, South San Francisco
(94080-2017)
PHONE..............................510 465-3255
Harold J De Luca, *CEO*
Rick Charles, *President*
Hariette Young, *Treasurer*
Tarry Winfrey, *Vice Pres*
Claire Venturini, *Admin Sec*
EMP: 55
SALES (est): 6.9MM
SALES (corp-wide): 71.8MM **Privately Held**
WEB: www.pacagri.com
SIC: 5144 Poultry: live, dressed or frozen (unpackaged); poultry products
PA: Pacific Agri-Products, Inc.
477 Forbes Blvd
South San Francisco CA 94080
650 873-0440

(P-8329)
LUBERSKI INC
Also Called: Hidden Villa Ranch
1811 Mountain Ave, Norco (92860-2863)
PHONE..............................951 271-3866
Tim Luberski, *Branch Mgr*
EMP: 70
SALES (corp-wide): 350MM **Privately Held**
WEB: www.calsunshine.com
SIC: 5144 Eggs
PA: Luberski, Inc.
310 N Harbor Blvd Ste 205
Fullerton CA 92832
714 680-3447

(P-8330)
NEW STOCKTON POULTRY INC
302 S San Joaquin St, Stockton
(95203-3536)
P.O. Box 2129 (95201-2129)
PHONE..............................209 466-1952
William P K Chan, *CEO*
John Luu, *President*
Ming Luu, *Vice Pres*
▲ **EMP:** 50
SALES (est): 7.7MM **Privately Held**
SIC: 5144 5499 2015 5421 Poultry: live, dressed or frozen (unpackaged); eggs & poultry; poultry, processed: fresh; meat & fish markets

(P-8331)
NULAID FOODS INC (PA)
200 W 5th St, Ripon (95366-2793)
PHONE..............................209 599-2121
David K Crockett, *President*
Scott Hennecke, *CFO*
Amy Parsons, *Accounting Mgr*
Sonja Murray, *QC Dir*
Linda Coss, *Opers Staff*
EMP: 76
SQ FT: 5,000
SALES (est): 43.2MM **Privately Held**
WEB: www.nulaid.com
SIC: 5144 2047 2015 2023 Eggs; eggs: cleaning, oil treating, packing & grading; dog food; egg processing; cream substitutes

▲ = Import ▼=Export
◆ =Import/Export

(P-8332)
RACE STREET PARTNERS INC (PA)
967 W Hedding St, San Jose (95126-1257)
PHONE.................408 294-6161
Gino Barsanti, *Chairman*
Michael Barsanti, *Corp Secy*
Dan Barsanti, *Vice Pres*
David Riparbelli, *Vice Pres*
James Riparbelli, *Vice Pres*
EMP: 80
SQ FT: 63,000
SALES (est): 20.5MM **Privately Held**
WEB: www.racestreetfoods.com
SIC: 5144 5146 5147 5142 Poultry & poultry products; fish & seafoods; meats & meat products; packaged frozen goods; frozen fish, meat & poultry

(P-8333)
ROGERS POULTRY CO (PA)
5050 S Santa Fe Ave, Vernon (90058-2124)
PHONE.................323 585-0802
George V Saffarrans, *CEO*
John C Butler, *COO*
Ken Hayashi, *Executive*
Koen Hennon, *Executive*
Ralph Schemel, *Administration*
EMP: 100
SQ FT: 15,000
SALES: 56.7MM **Privately Held**
WEB: www.rogerspoultry.com
SIC: 5144 Poultry products

(P-8334)
ROGERS POULTRY CO
2020 E 67th St, Los Angeles (90001-2169)
PHONE.................800 585-0802
John C Butler, *COO*
EMP: 80
SALES (est): 4.2MM
SALES (corp-wide): 56.7MM **Privately Held**
SIC: 5144 Poultry products
PA: Roger's Poultry Co.
5050 S Santa Fe Ave
Vernon CA 90058
323 585-0802

(P-8335)
SQUAB PRODUCERS CALIF INC
409 Primo Way, Modesto (95358-5721)
PHONE.................209 537-4744
Robert Shipley, *President*
EMP: 55 **EST:** 1943
SQ FT: 11,000
SALES (est): 8.4MM **Privately Held**
WEB: www.squab.com
SIC: 5144 2015 Poultry: live, dressed or frozen (unpackaged); poultry slaughtering & processing

(P-8336)
SUNRISE FARMS LLC
395 Liberty Rd, Petaluma (94952-8104)
PHONE.................707 778-6450
James Carlson, *Manager*
Larry Johnson,
Al Nissen,
Arnold Riebli,
Richard Weber,
▲ **EMP:** 65
SQ FT: 10,000
SALES (est): 14.7MM **Privately Held**
SIC: 5144 2015 Eggs: cleaning, oil treating, packing & grading; poultry slaughtering & processing

```
5145 Confectionery
Wholesale
```

(P-8337)
A & R WHOLESALE DISTRS INC
1765 W Penhall Way, Anaheim (92801-6728)
PHONE.................714 777-7742
Martin R Alsobrooks, *CEO*
Ron Paz, *President*
Jeff Kuriel, *CEO*
EMP: 60

SALES (est): 36.8MM
SALES (corp-wide): 431MM **Privately Held**
SIC: 5145 Snack foods
HQ: Gold Star Foods, Inc.
3781 E Airport Dr
Ontario CA 91761
909 843-9600

(P-8338)
B B G MANAGEMENT GROUP (PA)
Also Called: Granlund Candies
12164 California St, Yucaipa (92399-4333)
PHONE.................909 797-9581
R Scott Burkle, *President*
Margie Rogan, *Vice Pres*
EMP: 58 **EST:** 1961
SQ FT: 10,000
SALES (est): 7.1MM **Privately Held**
SIC: 5145 2064 Candy; candy & other confectionery products

(P-8339)
CANTEEN VENDING - SAN DIEGO
Also Called: Rainbow Vending & Distributing
5515 Market St, San Diego (92114-2218)
PHONE.................619 527-1900
Greg Karron, *President*
Greg Carron, *President*
Don Martin, *CFO*
EMP: 53 **EST:** 1968
SQ FT: 10,300
SALES (est): 16MM
SALES (corp-wide): 29.6B **Privately Held**
WEB: www.rainbowvending.com
SIC: 5145 5149 5962 Snack foods; soft drinks; candy & snack food vending machines
HQ: Compass Group Usa, Inc.
2400 Yorkmont Rd
Charlotte NC 28217
704 328-4000

(P-8340)
CENTURY SNACKS LLC
5560 E Slauson Ave, Commerce (90040-2921)
PHONE.................323 278-9578
Valerie Oswalt, *CEO*
Stephen Famolaro, *CFO*
David Lowe, *Chairman*
Tiffany Obenchain, *Vice Pres*
Russ McDonough, *CIO*
EMP: 330 **EST:** 1999
SQ FT: 280,000
SALES (est): 120MM
SALES (corp-wide): 177.6MM **Privately Held**
SIC: 5145 2064 Nuts, salted or roasted; nuts, candy covered; nuts, glace
HQ: Scncs, Llc
5560 E Slauson Ave
Commerce CA 90040
323 278-9578

(P-8341)
FRITO-LAY NORTH AMERICA INC
401 Burns Dr, Yuba City (95991-7233)
PHONE.................530 671-7854
Randy Meyers, *Branch Mgr*
EMP: 164
SALES (corp-wide): 64.6B **Publicly Held**
SIC: 5145 Snack foods
HQ: Frito-Lay North America, Inc.
7701 Legacy Dr
Plano TX 75024

(P-8342)
FRITO-LAY NORTH AMERICA INC
14600 Proctor Ave, City of Industry (91746-3249)
PHONE.................626 855-1300
Marty McFadden, *Principal*
EMP: 400
SQ FT: 54,844
SALES (corp-wide): 64.6B **Publicly Held**
WEB: www.fritolay.com
SIC: 5145 Snack foods

HQ: Frito-Lay North America, Inc.
7701 Legacy Dr
Plano TX 75024

(P-8343)
FRITO-LAY NORTH AMERICA INC
28801 Highway 58, Bakersfield (93314-9000)
PHONE.................661 328-6034
Jason Audler, *Manager*
Terry Bartz, *Manager*
EMP: 188
SALES (corp-wide): 64.6B **Publicly Held**
SIC: 5145 Snack foods
HQ: Frito-Lay North America, Inc.
7701 Legacy Dr
Plano TX 75024

(P-8344)
FRITO-LAY NORTH AMERICA INC
3630 N Hazel Ave, Fresno (93722-4594)
PHONE.................559 226-8153
Cregg Jerri, *Branch Mgr*
EMP: 150
SALES (corp-wide): 64.6B **Publicly Held**
WEB: www.fritolay.com
SIC: 5145 5149 2096 Snack foods; groceries & related products; potato chips & similar snacks
HQ: Frito-Lay North America, Inc.
7701 Legacy Dr
Plano TX 75024

(P-8345)
FRITO-LAY NORTH AMERICA INC
751 W Avenue L8, Lancaster (93534-7103)
PHONE.................661 951-1399
Glenn Kliewer, *General Mgr*
Lori Jensen, *Regl Sales Mgr*
Zanetta Robinson, *Sales Staff*
EMP: 65
SALES (corp-wide): 64.6B **Publicly Held**
WEB: www.fritolay.com
SIC: 5145 Snack foods
HQ: Frito-Lay North America, Inc.
7701 Legacy Dr
Plano TX 75024

(P-8346)
FRITO-LAY NORTH AMERICA INC
1774 Automation Pkwy, San Jose (95131-1873)
PHONE.................559 312-8553
EMP: 80
SQ FT: 48,250
SALES (corp-wide): 64.6B **Publicly Held**
WEB: www.fritolay.com
SIC: 5145 Snack foods
HQ: Frito-Lay North America, Inc.
7701 Legacy Dr
Plano TX 75024

(P-8347)
FRITO-LAY NORTH AMERICA INC
151 W Hill Pl, Brisbane (94005-1221)
PHONE.................415 467-1860
Luis Andrade, *Manager*
EMP: 85
SALES (corp-wide): 64.6B **Publicly Held**
WEB: www.fritolay.com
SIC: 5145 5149 Snack foods; groceries & related products
HQ: Frito-Lay North America, Inc.
7701 Legacy Dr
Plano TX 75024

(P-8348)
FRITO-LAY NORTH AMERICA INC
3810 Seaport Blvd, West Sacramento (95691-3449)
PHONE.................916 372-5400
Troy Shea, *Manager*
EMP: 150

HQ: Frito-Lay North America, Inc.
7701 Legacy Dr
Plano TX 75024

SALES (corp-wide): 64.6B **Publicly Held**
WEB: www.fritolay.com
SIC: 5145 5149 Snack foods; groceries & related products
HQ: Frito-Lay North America, Inc.
7701 Legacy Dr
Plano TX 75024

(P-8349)
FRITO-LAY NORTH AMERICA INC
6320 District Blvd, Bakersfield (93313-2142)
PHONE.................661 835-0347
Tim King, *Manager*
EMP: 50
SQ FT: 18,000
SALES (corp-wide): 64.6B **Publicly Held**
WEB: www.fritolay.com
SIC: 5145 5149 Snack foods; groceries & related products
HQ: Frito-Lay North America, Inc.
7701 Legacy Dr
Plano TX 75024

(P-8350)
FRITO-LAY NORTH AMERICA INC
1450 S Loop Rd, Alameda (94502-2702)
PHONE.................510 769-5000
Steve Pahara, *Principal*
EMP: 62
SALES (corp-wide): 64.6B **Publicly Held**
WEB: www.fritolay.com
SIC: 5145 Snack foods
HQ: Frito-Lay North America, Inc.
7701 Legacy Dr
Plano TX 75024

(P-8351)
FRITO-LAY NORTH AMERICA INC
1390 Vantage Ct, Vista (92081-8524)
PHONE.................760 727-6022
Fred Schmidt, *Manager*
EMP: 100
SQ FT: 19,836
SALES (corp-wide): 64.6B **Publicly Held**
WEB: www.fritolay.com
SIC: 5145 5149 Snack foods; groceries & related products
HQ: Frito-Lay North America, Inc.
7701 Legacy Dr
Plano TX 75024

(P-8352)
FRITO-LAY NORTH AMERICA INC
Also Called: El Toro DC
26962 Vista Ter, El Toro (92630-8123)
PHONE.................949 586-4644
Tyrone Suruta, *Manager*
EMP: 75
SQ FT: 14,356
SALES (corp-wide): 64.6B **Publicly Held**
WEB: www.fritolay.com
SIC: 5145 Snack foods
HQ: Frito-Lay North America, Inc.
7701 Legacy Dr
Plano TX 75024

(P-8353)
FRITO-LAY NORTH AMERICA INC
8316 W Elowin Ct, Visalia (93291-9262)
PHONE.................559 651-1334
Jim Johnson, *Manager*
EMP: 70
SQ FT: 19,800
SALES (corp-wide): 64.6B **Publicly Held**
WEB: www.fritolay.com
SIC: 5145 Potato chips
HQ: Frito-Lay North America, Inc.
7701 Legacy Dr
Plano TX 75024

PRODUCTS & SVCS

(P-8354)
FRITO-LAY NORTH AMERICA INC
4029 Leckron Rd, Modesto (95357-0516)
PHONE....................................209 544-5424
EMP: 187
SALES (corp-wide): 64.6B **Publicly Held**
SIC: 5145 Snack foods
HQ: Frito-Lay North America, Inc.
   7701 Legacy Dr
   Plano TX 75024

(P-8355)
FRITO-LAY NORTH AMERICA INC
1924 E Maple Ave, El Segundo (90245-3411)
PHONE....................................310 322-5001
Ed Castro, *Branch Mgr*
EMP: 50
SALES (corp-wide): 64.6B **Publicly Held**
WEB: www.fritolay.com
SIC: 5145 Snack foods
HQ: Frito-Lay North America, Inc.
   7701 Legacy Dr
   Plano TX 75024

(P-8356)
GICO MANAGEMENT
23073 S Frederick Rd, Ripon (95366-9616)
PHONE....................................209 599-7131
Steve Gikas, *Owner*
▲ EMP: 75
SQ FT: 100,000
SALES (est): 20.3MM **Privately Held**
SIC: 5145 Confectionery

(P-8357)
INNER CIRCLE ENTERTAINMENT
Also Called: Ruby Sky
464 Monterey Ave Ste A, Los Gatos (95030-5326)
PHONE....................................415 693-0777
George Karpaty, *President*
Frank Finelli, *Principal*
EMP: 60
SQ FT: 17,500
SALES (est): 12.8MM **Privately Held**
SIC: 5145 Snack foods

(P-8358)
MONTPELIER NUT COMPANY INC (PA)
1518 K St, Modesto (95354-1108)
PHONE....................................209 566-9084
Kenfield Alldrin, *CEO*
Steve Zeff, *CFO*
◆ EMP: 55
SALES (est): 15.8MM **Privately Held**
SIC: 5145 Nuts, salted or roasted

(P-8359)
R W GARCIA CO INC (PA)
100 Enterprise Way C230, Scotts Valley (95066-3274)
P.O. Box 8290, San Jose (95155-8290)
PHONE....................................408 287-4616
Robert W Garcia, *President*
Margaret Garcia, *Vice Pres*
Janette Rosales, *Office Mgr*
Alicia Henry, *Controller*
Cody Howell, *QC Mgr*
◆ EMP: 50
SQ FT: 30,000
SALES (est): 105.1MM **Privately Held**
WEB: www.rwgarcia.com
SIC: 5145 2096 2099 Snack foods; tortilla chips; food preparations

(P-8360)
S&E GOURMET CUTS INC
Also Called: Country Archer Jerky
379 Industrial Rd, San Bernardino (92408-3713)
PHONE....................................909 370-0155
Eugene Kang, *CEO*
Tim Bateman, *Vice Pres*
Susan Kang, *Vice Pres*
Daniel Palacios, *Graphic Designe*
Jeff Wong, *VP Mktg*
EMP: 150 EST: 2011

SALES (est): 22MM **Privately Held**
SIC: 5145 Snack foods

5146 Fish & Seafood Wholesale

(P-8361)
ANOVA FOOD LLC
280 10th Ave, San Diego (92101-7406)
PHONE....................................813 902-9003
Jan Tharp, *CEO*
▲ EMP: 100
SALES (est): 4.6MM **Privately Held**
SIC: 5146 Seafoods
HQ: Bee Bumble Foods Llc
   280 10th Ave
   San Diego CA 92101
   858 715-4000

(P-8362)
ANTHONYS FISH GROTTO
Also Called: Ghio Seafood Products
9530 Murray Dr, La Mesa (91942-3924)
PHONE....................................619 713-1853
Anthony A Ghio, *Partner*
Cottardo Ghio, *Partner*
Adele Weber, *Partner*
Dan Shehan, *Controller*
EMP: 60 EST: 1946
SQ FT: 11,000
SALES (est): 6.9MM **Privately Held**
SIC: 5146 5141 Seafoods; groceries, general line

(P-8363)
ATLANTA SEAFOODS LLC
Also Called: Sea Catch Seafoods
10501 Valley Blvd # 1820, El Monte (91731-2461)
PHONE....................................626 626-4900
Wayne Berman, *Mng Member*
▲ EMP: 65
SQ FT: 48,000
SALES (est): 32.1MM **Privately Held**
SIC: 5146 Fish & seafoods

(P-8364)
BLUE RIVER SEAFOOD INC
Also Called: Joe Pucci & Sons Seafoods
25447 Industrial Blvd, Hayward (94545-2931)
PHONE....................................510 300-6800
Chris Lam, *President*
Sean Nguyen, *General Mgr*
Myrla Best, *Controller*
Colleen Laa, *Buyer*
Lam Tony, *Manager*
▲ EMP: 50
SQ FT: 53,000
SALES (est): 30.5MM **Privately Held**
SIC: 5146 2092 Fish, fresh; fish, frozen, unpackaged; fresh or frozen packaged fish

(P-8365)
BSM UNI
712 Ceres Ave, Los Angeles (90021-1516)
PHONE....................................213 626-2557
Shigeru Matsushita, *President*
Darlene Matsushita, *Vice Pres*
EMP: 50
SQ FT: 8,000
SALES (est): 7.3MM **Privately Held**
WEB: www.smuni.com
SIC: 5146 Seafoods

(P-8366)
CAITO FISHERIES INC (PA)
19400 Harbor Ave, Fort Bragg (95437-5615)
P.O. Box 1370 (95437-1370)
PHONE....................................707 964-6368
Joseph A Caito, *CEO*
James G Caito, *Vice Pres*
EMP: 100 EST: 1975
SQ FT: 10,000
SALES (est): 23.1MM **Privately Held**
WEB: www.caitofisheries.com
SIC: 5146 Seafoods

(P-8367)
CALIFORNIA SHELLFISH CO INC
Point St George Fisheries
1280 Columbus Ave 300r, San Francisco (94133-1302)
P.O. Box 1386, Santa Rosa (95402-1386)
PHONE....................................707 542-9490
Tony Delima, *Branch Mgr*
EMP: 350
SALES (corp-wide): 105.4MM **Privately Held**
SIC: 5146 Fish, fresh; fish, frozen, unpackaged
PA: California Shellfish Company, Inc.
   818 E Broadway C
   San Gabriel CA 91776
   415 923-7400

(P-8368)
DEL MAR SEAFOODS INC
1449 Spinnaker Dr, Ventura (93001-4355)
PHONE....................................805 850-0421
EMP: 185
SALES (corp-wide): 38.3MM **Privately Held**
SIC: 5146 Seafoods
PA: Del Mar Seafoods, Inc.
   331 Ford St
   Watsonville CA 95076
   831 763-3000

(P-8369)
H & N FOODS INTERNATIONAL INC (HQ)
Also Called: H & N Fish Co.
5580 S Alameda St, Vernon (90058-3426)
PHONE....................................323 586-9300
Hua Thanh Ngo, *President*
Christine Ngo, *Exec VP*
Bobby Ngo, *Vice Pres*
Dat Trieu, *Vice Pres*
Mario Guardado, *General Mgr*
◆ EMP: 125
SQ FT: 45,000
SALES (est): 69.9MM
SALES (corp-wide): 162.3MM **Privately Held**
SIC: 5146 Fish, fresh; fish, frozen, unpackaged
PA: H & N Group, Inc.
   5580 S Alameda St
   Vernon CA 90058
   323 586-9388

(P-8370)
INTERNATIONAL MARINE PDTS INC (HQ)
500 E 7th St, Los Angeles (90014-2410)
PHONE....................................213 893-6123
James Ho, *CEO*
Hector Esparza, *Opers Staff*
Yoshihiro Momose, *Manager*
Shota Tanaka, *Supervisor*
▲ EMP: 50
SQ FT: 10,000
SALES (est): 36.8MM **Privately Held**
WEB: www.intmarine.com
SIC: 5146 Fish, fresh; fish, frozen, unpackaged

(P-8371)
KINGS SEAFOOD COMPANY LLC
7691 Edinger Ave, Huntington Beach (92647-3604)
PHONE....................................714 793-1177
Malia Cappuccio, *Branch Mgr*
EMP: 100
SALES (corp-wide): 75.2MM **Privately Held**
SIC: 5146 Seafoods
PA: King's Seafood Company, Llc
   3185 Airway Ave Ste J
   Costa Mesa CA 92626

(P-8372)
KINGS SEAFOOD COMPANY LLC
1521 W Katella Ave, Orange (92867-3410)
PHONE....................................714 771-6655
Fred Belez, *Branch Mgr*
EMP: 100

SALES (corp-wide): 75.2MM **Privately Held**
SIC: 5146 Seafoods
PA: King's Seafood Company, Llc
   3185 Airway Ave Ste J
   Costa Mesa CA 92626

(P-8373)
M & J SEAFOOD COMPANY INC
6859 Walthall Way, Paramount (90723-2028)
PHONE....................................562 529-2786
J Jesus Rodriguez, *CEO*
Wendy McDonalds, *COO*
EMP: 55
SALES: 75MM **Privately Held**
SIC: 5146 5147 Seafoods; meats & meat products

(P-8374)
NORTH COAST FISHERIES LLC
Also Called: Alca Trax Sea Foods
2255 Challenger Way # 101, Santa Rosa (95407-5423)
PHONE....................................707 579-0679
Michael Lucas, *Mng Member*
EMP: 65
SQ FT: 10,000
SALES (est): 32.3MM **Privately Held**
WEB: www.northcoastfisheries.com
SIC: 5146 2091 Seafoods; fish, cured; fish, fresh; fish, frozen, unpackaged; canned & cured fish & seafoods

(P-8375)
OCEAN GROUP INC (PA)
Also Called: Ocean Fresh Fish Seafood Mktg
1100 S Santa Fe Ave, Los Angeles (90021-1743)
PHONE....................................213 622-3677
Young Won Kim, *President*
Hyojin Ahn, *CFO*
Katie Yeh, *Officer*
Tae S Kim, *Admin Sec*
◆ EMP: 60
SQ FT: 20,000
SALES: 40MM **Privately Held**
SIC: 5146 Seafoods

(P-8376)
OCEAN QUEEN 87 INC
4511 Everett Ave, Vernon (90058-2621)
PHONE....................................323 585-1200
Yuho Nagata, *President*
Justin Genochio, *Opers Mgr*
EMP: 50
SQ FT: 3,700
SALES (est): 13.1MM **Privately Held**
SIC: 5146 Seafoods

(P-8377)
ORE-CAL CORP (PA)
Also Called: Harvest of The Sea
634 Crocker St, Los Angeles (90021-1002)
P.O. Box 21832 (90021-0832)
PHONE....................................213 623-8493
Mark Shinbane, *President*
Sandra Shinbane, *Corp Secy*
Charlie Molinelli, *Vice Pres*
David Rovner, *Info Tech Dir*
Tony Tuck, *Controller*
◆ EMP: 55
SQ FT: 80,000
SALES: 260MM **Privately Held**
SIC: 5146 5142 Fish & seafoods; packaged frozen goods

(P-8378)
ORIENT FISHERIES INC
Also Called: Ofi Markesa International
1912 E Vernon Ave Ste 110, Vernon (90058-1611)
PHONE....................................323 588-4185
Ming Shin Kou, *President*
David L Prince,
▲ EMP: 52
SQ FT: 3,000
SALES (est): 9.6MM **Privately Held**
SIC: 5146 Seafoods

▲ = Import ▼=Export
◆ =Import/Export

(P-8379)
PACIFIC AMERICAN FISH CO INC (PA)
Also Called: Pafco
5525 S Santa Fe Ave, Vernon
(90058-3523)
PHONE...................................323 319-1551
Peter Huh, *CEO*
Paul Huh, *Exec VP*
Rick Corl, *Opers Staff*
◆ EMP: 300
SQ FT: 100,000
SALES (est): 180.6MM **Privately Held**
WEB: www.pafco.net
SIC: 5146 2091 Fish, fresh; fish, frozen,
unpackaged; seafoods; fish, filleted
(boneless)

(P-8380)
PACIFIC CHOICE SEAFOOD COMPANY
1 Commercial St, Eureka (95501-0241)
PHONE...................................707 442-2981
Rick Harris, *Manager*
EMP: 300
SALES (corp-wide): 569.5MM **Privately Held**
SIC: 5146 Seafoods
HQ: Pacific Choice Seafood Company
3220 Sw 1st Ave
Portland OR 97239
503 226-2200

(P-8381)
PACIFIC SEA FOOD CO INC
Also Called: Jakes Crawfish & Seafood
1420 National Dr, Sacramento
(95834-1967)
PHONE...................................916 419-5500
Barb Pacella, *Branch Mgr*
George Pisano, *Purchasing*
EMP: 100
SALES (corp-wide): 569.5MM **Privately Held**
WEB: www.pacificseafoodco.com
SIC: 5146 5142 5143 Fish, fresh; fish,
frozen, unpackaged; seafoods; fish,
frozen: packaged; meat, frozen: pack-
aged; poultry, frozen: packaged; cheese
HQ: Pacific Seafood - Portland, Llc
16797 Se 130th Ave
Clackamas OR 97015
503 905-4500

(P-8382)
PACIFIC SEA FOOD CO INC
Also Called: Pacific Fresh Seafood Company
605 Flint Ave, Wilmington (90744-6110)
PHONE...................................310 835-4343
James Lanter, *General Mgr*
EMP: 50
SALES (corp-wide): 569.5MM **Privately Held**
WEB: www.pacificseafoodco.com
SIC: 5146 Fish & seafoods
HQ: Pacific Seafood - Portland, Llc
16797 Se 130th Ave
Clackamas OR 97015
503 905-4500

(P-8383)
PLD ENTERPRISES INC
Also Called: Superior Seafood Co
440 Stanford Ave, Los Angeles
(90013-2121)
PHONE...................................213 626-4444
Chip Mezin, *General Mgr*
EMP: 61
SALES (est): 5.8MM **Privately Held**
SIC: 5146 Fish & seafoods
PA: P.L.D. Enterprises, Inc.
1621 W 25th St Ste 228
San Pedro CA 90732

(P-8384)
PLD ENTERPRISES INC (PA)
Also Called: Superior Seafood Co
1621 W 25th St Ste 228, San Pedro
(90732-4301)
PHONE...................................310 547-3366
Paul Di Girolamo, *CEO*
Dannesh Alam, *Sales Mgr*
▲ EMP: 72
SQ FT: 10,000

SALES (est): 37.5MM **Privately Held**
SIC: 5146 Fish & seafoods

(P-8385)
PROSPECT ENTERPRISES INC (PA)
Also Called: American Fish and Seafood
625 Kohler St, Los Angeles (90021-1023)
PHONE...................................213 599-5700
Ernest Y Doizaki, *Ch of Bd*
Jack King, *President*
Paula Eberhardt, *CFO*
Robert Sigur, *Chief Mktg Ofcr*
Peter Alvino, *Purchasing*
▲ EMP: 160
SQ FT: 20,000
SALES (est): 215.8MM **Privately Held**
WEB: www.americanfish.com
SIC: 5146 2092 Fish, fresh; fish, frozen,
unpackaged; seafoods; fresh or frozen
packaged fish

(P-8386)
RED CHAMBER CO (PA)
1912 E Vernon Ave, Vernon (90058-1611)
PHONE...................................323 234-9000
Shan Chun Kou, *Ch of Bd*
Shu Chin Kou, *Ch of Bd*
Ming Bin Kou, *CEO*
Mingbin Kou, *COO*
Sharon Chao, *Controller*
◆ EMP: 341
SQ FT: 15,000
SALES (est): 393MM **Privately Held**
WEB: www.redchamber.com
SIC: 5146 4222 Seafoods; warehousing,
cold storage or refrigerated

(P-8387)
SANTA MONICA SEAFOOD COMPANY
1000 Wilshire Blvd, Santa Monica
(90401-1907)
PHONE...................................310 393-5244
Vince Cigiliano, *Director*
EMP: 156
SALES (corp-wide): 129.2MM **Privately Held**
SIC: 5146 Seafoods
PA: Santa Monica Seafood Company
18531 S Broadwick St
Rancho Dominguez CA 90220
310 886-7900

(P-8388)
SEA WIN INC
526 Stanford Ave, Los Angeles
(90013-2123)
PHONE...................................213 688-2899
Nam Tran, *CEO*
Frances Tran, *Admin Sec*
▲ EMP: 50
SQ FT: 29,000
SALES (est): 22.2MM **Privately Held**
SIC: 5146 Fish, fresh; fish, frozen, unpack-
aged

(P-8389)
SHOWA MARINE INC (PA)
668 S Alameda St Ste A, Los Angeles
(90021-1270)
PHONE...................................213 627-4091
Taro John Ikeda, *CEO*
Goro Ikeda, *President*
Dennis Kimoshita, *Corp Secy*
Kumiko Ikeda, *Vice Pres*
Caz Kitani, *Principal*
▲ EMP: 60
SQ FT: 100,000
SALES (est): 25.7MM **Privately Held**
SIC: 5146 5149 Seafoods; specialty food
items

(P-8390)
SLADE GORTON & CO INC
1 Centerpointe Dr Ste 311, La Palma
(90623-2512)
PHONE...................................714 676-4200
EMP: 66 **Privately Held**
SIC: 5146
HQ: Gorton Slade & Co Inc
225 Southampton St
Boston MA 02118
617 442-5800

(P-8391)
SOUTHWIND FOODS LLC (PA)
Also Called: Great Amercn Seafood Import
Co
20644 S Fordyce Ave, Carson
(90810-1018)
P.O. Box 86021, Los Angeles (90086-0021)
PHONE...................................323 262-8222
Buddy Galletti, *President*
Sam Galletti, *CEO*
Scott Fernandez, *COO*
Jim Lee, *CFO*
Jennifer Castania, *Vice Pres*
▲ EMP: 100
SQ FT: 80,000
SALES (est): 188.7MM **Privately Held**
SIC: 5146 5147 Seafoods; meats & meat
products

(P-8392)
STAGNARO BROTHERS SEAFOOD INC
320 Washington St, Santa Cruz
(95060-4929)
PHONE...................................831 423-1188
Giovanni Stagnaro, *Ch of Bd*
Robert Tara, *President*
Virginia Stagnaro, *Treasurer*
Ernest M Stagnaro, *Vice Ch Bd*
Robert Mc Pherson, *Vice Pres*
EMP: 73
SQ FT: 12,000
SALES (est): 19.7MM **Privately Held**
WEB: www.stagnarobros.com
SIC: 5146 5812 5421 Seafoods; seafood
restaurants; seafood markets

(P-8393)
STAR FISHERIES
Also Called: Seaport Fish Company
841 Watson Ave, Wilmington (90744-3732)
P.O. Box 1150, San Pedro (90733-1150)
PHONE...................................310 549-4992
Anthony Di Maggio, *President*
EMP: 55
SALES (est): 3.9MM
SALES (corp-wide): 58.9MM **Privately Held**
SIC: 5146 Seafoods
PA: Star Fisheries
222 W 6th St Ste 500
San Pedro CA 90731
310 832-8395

(P-8394)
STAR FISHERIES (PA)
222 W 6th St Ste 500, San Pedro
(90731-3646)
P.O. Box 1150 (90733-1150)
PHONE...................................310 832-8395
Jolene Dimaggio, *President*
Anthony Di Maggio, *President*
Louie J Bozanich, *Vice Pres*
Melissa Castagnola, *Plant Mgr*
Marissa Dimaggio, *Marketing Staff*
▲ EMP: 90
SQ FT: 8,000
SALES (est): 56.5MM **Privately Held**
WEB: www.starfisheries.com
SIC: 5146 Seafoods

(P-8395)
TRADEWIND SEAFOOD INC
1505 Mountain View Ave, Oxnard
(93030-5107)
PHONE...................................805 483-8555
Mack Demachi, *President*
Hiromi Demachi, *Vice Pres*
EMP: 50
SQ FT: 5,000
SALES (est): 9.4MM **Privately Held**
SIC: 5146 Seafoods

(P-8396)
TRI-MARINE FISH COMPANY LLC
220 Cannery St, San Pedro (90731-7308)
PHONE...................................310 547-1144
Vince Torre, *Mng Member*
Walt Hadlow, *Plant Engr*
◆ EMP: 75
SQ FT: 30,000
SALES (est): 25.1MM **Privately Held**
SIC: 5146 Seafoods

(P-8397)
TRI-UNION SEAFOODS LLC (DH)
Also Called: Chicken of Sea International
2150 E Grand Ave, El Segundo
(90245-5024)
P.O. Box 85568, San Diego (92186-5568)
PHONE...................................858 558-9662
Shue Wing Chan, *President*
David E Roszmann, *COO*
Jim Cox, *Senior VP*
Christie Fleming, *Senior VP*
Brenden Beck, *Vice Pres*
◆ EMP: 69
SQ FT: 24,000
SALES (est): 63.4MM **Privately Held**
SIC: 5146 2091 Seafoods; tuna fish: pack-
aged in cans, jars, etc.; salmon: pack-
aged in cans, jars, etc.
HQ: Thai Union North America, Inc.
9330 Scranton Rd Ste 500
El Segundo CA 90245
424 397-8556

(P-8398)
TRUE WRLD FODS LOS ANGELES LLC
4200 S Alameda St, Vernon (90058-1602)
PHONE...................................323 846-3300
Jang Hoee Kim, *President*
Scott Howard, *General Mgr*
Susan Madden, *Human Res Mgr*
▲ EMP: 55
SQ FT: 55,000
SALES (est): 22.7MM
SALES (corp-wide): 598.4MM **Privately Held**
SIC: 5146 Fish, frozen, unpackaged; fish,
fresh
HQ: True World Foods New York Llc
32-34 Papetti Plz
Elizabeth NJ 07206
908 351-9090

(P-8399)
TRUE WRLD FODS SAN FRNCSCO LLC
1815 Williams St, San Leandro
(94577-2301)
PHONE...................................510 352-8140
Shinryo Shimada, *Mng Member*
Makoto Kikuchi,
David Miller,
◆ EMP: 62
SQ FT: 27,000
SALES (est): 21.1MM
SALES (corp-wide): 598.4MM **Privately Held**
SIC: 5146 Fish & seafoods
HQ: True World Holdings Llc
24 Link Dr Unit D
Rockleigh NJ 07647
201 750-0024

5147 Meats & Meat Prdts Wholesale

(P-8400)
BICARA LTD
318 Avenue I Ste 65, Redondo Beach
(90277-5601)
PHONE...................................310 316-6222
William Jeffrey Hughes, *CEO*
William D Hughes, *President*
Raymond Rosenthal, *Vice Pres*
◆ EMP: 300
SQ FT: 105,000
SALES (est): 64.5MM **Privately Held**
WEB: www.bicara.net
SIC: 5147 5146 5141 Meats & meat prod-
ucts; seafoods; groceries, general line

(P-8401)
BRIDGFORD MARKETING COMPANY (DH)
1308 N Patt St, Anaheim (92801-2551)
P.O. Box 3773 (92803-3773)
PHONE...................................714 526-5533
Allan L Bridgford, *Chairman*
John Simmons, *President*
Ray Lancey, *CFO*
William L Bridgford, *Chairman*
EMP: 89

P
R
O
D
U
C
T
S
&
S
V
C
S

SQ FT: 100,000
SALES (est): 40.1MM
SALES (corp-wide): 174.2MM **Publicly Held**
SIC: 5147 5149 Meats & meat products; bakery products
HQ: Bridgford Foods Corporation
1308 N Patt St
Anaheim CA 92801
714 526-5533

(P-8402)

CALIFORNIA FARMS MEAT CO INC
4401 S Downey Rd, Vernon (90058-2518)
PHONE..................................323 581-3663
Erik Litmanovich, *CEO*
EMP: 61 EST: 2013
SALES (est): 1.6MM
SALES (corp-wide): 18.8MM **Privately Held**
SIC: 5147 Meats & meat products
PA: Golden West Food Group, Inc.
4401 S Downey Rd
Vernon CA 90058
888 807-3663

(P-8403)

DANIELS WESTERN MEAT PACKERS
5217 Industry Ave, Pico Rivera (90660-2505)
PHONE..................................562 948-2254
Alfred Santos, *CEO*
Daniel Caloca, *Purch Mgr*
Denise Verdugo, *Purchasing*
Jackie Aguayo, *Sales Staff*
▲ EMP: 80
SQ FT: 12,000
SALES (est): 44.9MM **Privately Held**
WEB:
www.danielswesternmeatpackers.com
SIC: 5147 Meats, fresh

(P-8404)

DEL MAR HOLDING LLC
1022 Bay Marina Dr 10, National City (91950-6398)
PHONE..................................313 659-7300
Leon Bergmann, *CEO*
Joel Jorgensen, *CFO*
EMP: 1600
SQ FT: 9,700
SALES: 3.5B **Privately Held**
SIC: 5147 Meats & meat products

(P-8405)

GOLDEN WEST TRADING INC
Also Called: Royal Poultry
4401 S Downey Rd, Vernon (90058-2518)
P.O. Box 58161 (90058-0161)
PHONE..................................323 581-3663
Erik Litmanovich, *CEO*
Levi Litmanovich, *Ch of Bd*
Tony Cimolino, *President*
Josh Solovy, *President*
Richard Lunsford, *CFO*
▲ EMP: 180
SQ FT: 40,000
SALES (est): 211.9MM **Privately Held**
WEB: www.gwtinc.com
SIC: 5147 5142 Meats & meat products; meat, frozen: packaged

(P-8406)

HARVEST MEAT COMPANY INC (HQ)
Also Called: Harvest Food Distributors
1022 Bay Marina Dr # 106, National City (91950-6327)
PHONE..................................619 477-0185
John J Leavy, *CEO*
Kevin Leavy, *President*
Eric Doan, *CFO*
Dennis Kevin, *Principal*
◆ EMP: 80
SQ FT: 60,000
SALES (est): 223.5MM
SALES (corp-wide): 294.5MM **Privately Held**
WEB: www.harvestmeat.com
SIC: 5147 Meats & meat products
PA: Sand Dollar Holdings, Inc.
1022 Bay Marina Dr # 106
National City CA 91950
619 477-0185

(P-8407)

HEARTLAND MEAT COMPANY INC
Also Called: H M C
3461 Main St, Chula Vista (91911-5828)
PHONE..................................619 407-3668
Joseph E Stidman, *CEO*
Stephanie Stidman, *Corp Secy*
James Methey, *Vice Pres*
Blanca Lowery, *Human Res Mgr*
Pat Stidman, *Buyer*
EMP: 70
SQ FT: 49,000
SALES (est): 35.5MM **Privately Held**
WEB: www.heartlandmeat.com
SIC: 5147 2013 Meats, fresh; sausages & other prepared meats

(P-8408)

HOLIDAY MEAT & PROVISION CORP
405 Centinela Ave, Inglewood (90302-3294)
PHONE..................................310 674-0541
Nat Rocker, *President*
Sue Rocker, *Admin Sec*
EMP: 200
SQ FT: 14,000
SALES: 60MM **Privately Held**
SIC: 5147 5144 5146 Meats, fresh; poultry products; seafoods

(P-8409)

JETRO CASH AND CARRY ENTPS LLC
Also Called: Restaurant Depot
2045 Evans Ave, San Francisco (94124-1022)
PHONE..................................415 920-2888
Bob Britton, *Branch Mgr*
EMP: 100
SALES (corp-wide): 24.5B **Privately Held**
WEB: www.jetro.com
SIC: 5147 5141 5142 5181 Meats, fresh; groceries, general line; packaged frozen goods; beer & other fermented malt liquors; tobacco & tobacco products
HQ: Jetro Cash And Carry Enterprises, Llc
1524 132nd St
College Point NY 11356
718 939-6400

(P-8410)

MACSEI INDUSTRIES CORPORATION
1784 E Vernon Ave, Vernon (90058-1526)
PHONE..................................323 233-7864
Seiichi Shibata, *President*
◆ EMP: 52
SQ FT: 8,913
SALES (est): 8.6MM **Privately Held**
SIC: 5147 Meat brokers

(P-8411)

MCLANE FOODSERVICE DIST INC
3051 N Church St, Rancho Cucamonga (91730)
PHONE..................................909 484-6100
EMP: 153
SALES (corp-wide): 225.3B **Publicly Held**
SIC: 5147 5113 5149 5142 Lard; cardboard & products; breakfast cereals; bakery products, frozen
HQ: Mclane Foodservice Distribution, Inc.
2641 Meadowbrook Rd
Rocky Mount NC 27801
252 985-7200

(P-8412)

NEWPORT MEAT SOUTHERN CAL INC
Also Called: Newport Meat Company
16691 Hale Ave, Irvine (92606-5025)
PHONE..................................949 399-4200
Timothy K Hussman, *CEO*
Denise Van Voorhis, *CFO*
Vincent Ariel, *Sales Staff*
Nicholas Ferrara, *Sales Staff*
Chad Hattery, *Transptn Dir*
EMP: 227 EST: 1976
SQ FT: 92,000

SALES (est): 134.4MM
SALES (corp-wide): 60.1B **Publicly Held**
WEB: www.newportmeat.com
SIC: 5147 5142 Meats, fresh; packaged frozen goods
PA: Sysco Corporation
1390 Enclave Pkwy
Houston TX 77077
281 584-1390

(P-8413)

ORITZ CORPORATION (PA)
1555 Old Bayshore Hwy # 400, Burlingame (94010-1617)
P.O. Box 4646 (94011-4646)
PHONE..................................650 692-8000
Vladimir R Grave, *President*
◆ EMP: 103
SQ FT: 45,000
SALES (est): 48.6MM **Privately Held**
WEB: www.oritz.com
SIC: 5147 Meats & meat products

(P-8414)

PNC INC
Also Called: SEAPORT MEAT COMPANY
2533 Folex Way, Spring Valley (91978-2038)
P.O. Box 1159 (91979-1159)
PHONE..................................619 713-2278
Nancy Camarda, *CEO*
Pete Camarda, *Admin Sec*
EMP: 51
SQ FT: 17,995
SALES: 23.9MM **Privately Held**
SIC: 5147 Meats, fresh

(P-8415)

R W ZANT CO (PA)
1470 E 4th St, Los Angeles (90033-4288)
PHONE..................................323 980-5457
Robert W Zant, *President*
Paul Olsen, *Officer*
William Zant, *Principal*
Mary Zant, *Admin Sec*
Ibrahim El-Helou, *Info Tech Dir*
▲ EMP: 90 EST: 1950
SQ FT: 42,000
SALES: 301MM **Privately Held**
SIC: 5147 5146 5144 4222 Meats, fresh; fish & seafoods; poultry & poultry products; cheese warehouse

(P-8416)

RANCHO FOODS INC
2528 E 37th St, Vernon (90058-1725)
P.O. Box 58504, Los Angeles (90058-0504)
PHONE..................................323 585-0503
Annette Mac Donald, *President*
John Mac Donald, *Vice Pres*
Scott Dean, *Sales Executive*
EMP: 100
SQ FT: 26,000
SALES (est): 81.5MM **Privately Held**
WEB: www.ranchofoods.com
SIC: 5147 2013 Meats, fresh; sausages & other prepared meats

(P-8417)

RICHMOND WHOLESALE MEAT CO
Also Called: Richmond Peak Quality
2920 Regatta Blvd, Richmond (94804-4528)
PHONE..................................510 233-5111
Richard Doellstedt, *President*
Alan Bell, *CFO*
Jon Doellstedt, *Officer*
Carl Doellstedt, *Vice Pres*
Paul Guess, *Vice Pres*
◆ EMP: 85
SQ FT: 100,000
SALES: 100MM **Privately Held**
WEB: www.rwm.biz
SIC: 5147 Meats, fresh

(P-8418)

RITE-WAY MEAT PACKERS INC
5151 Alcoa Ave, Vernon (90058-3715)
PHONE..................................323 826-2144
Irwin Miller, *President*
Carol Miller, *Corp Secy*
▲ EMP: 69
SQ FT: 64,000
SALES (est): 33.1MM **Privately Held**
SIC: 5147 Meats, fresh

(P-8419)

RONGCHENG TRADING LLC
Also Called: Always Best
19319 Arenth Ave, City of Industry (91748-1401)
PHONE..................................626 338-1090
MEI Lan Liang, *Mng Member*
Fannie Yang, *COO*
Angie Lee, *CFO*
Tim Chen, *Buyer*
Xiao Mou Zhang, *Mng Member*
▲ EMP: 50
SQ FT: 80,000
SALES (est): 42.3MM **Privately Held**
SIC: 5147 Meats, fresh

(P-8420)

SAND DOLLAR HOLDINGS INC (PA)
1022 Bay Marina Dr # 106, National City (91950-6398)
PHONE..................................619 477-0185
John Leavy, *President*
Eric Doan, *CFO*
Kevin Leavy, *Vice Pres*
▲ EMP: 80
SALES (est): 302.4MM
SALES (corp-wide): 294.5MM **Privately Held**
SIC: 5147 Meats, fresh

(P-8421)

THREE SONS INC
Also Called: American Companies
5201 Industry Ave, Pico Rivera (90660-2505)
P.O. Box 6 (90660-0006)
PHONE..................................562 801-4100
Michael Shannon Day, *CEO*
David Day, *Shareholder*
Mariellen Day, *Shareholder*
Michael Day, *Shareholder*
John Brenan, *Vice Pres*
▲ EMP: 87
SQ FT: 40,000
SALES (est): 47MM **Privately Held**
WEB: www.threesons.com
SIC: 5147 2013 2011 Meats, cured or smoked; meats, fresh; sausages & other prepared meats; meat packing plants

(P-8422)

WAYNE PROVISION CO INC (PA)
Also Called: Premier Meat Company
5030 Gifford Ave, Vernon (90058-2726)
P.O. Box 58183, Los Angeles (90058-0183)
PHONE..................................323 277-5888
Naftali Greenberg, *CEO*
Terry Hanks, *Shareholder*
Eldad Hadar, *Vice Pres*
Leeann Candelaria, *Credit Mgr*
Andy Rocker, *Sales Mgr*
▼ EMP: 70
SQ FT: 7,822
SALES (est): 53.1MM **Privately Held**
WEB: www.premiermeats.com
SIC: 5147 5144 Meats, fresh; poultry & poultry products

(P-8423)

WEBERS QUALITY MEATS INC
Also Called: Butcher's Brand
990 Carden St, San Leandro (94577-1164)
PHONE..................................510 635-9892
Stefan Weber, *President*
Linda Weber, *Corp Secy*
EMP: 60
SQ FT: 10,000
SALES (est): 34.6MM **Privately Held**
WEB: www.webersqualitymeats.com
SIC: 5147 5142 Meats, fresh; meat, frozen: packaged

(P-8424)

WEST COAST PRIME MEATS LLC
344 Cliffwood Park St, Brea (92821-4103)
PHONE..................................714 255-8560
William H Hustedt, *Mng Member*
Bill Hustedt, *Managing Prtnr*
Amy Nickoloff, *Managing Prtnr*
Samuel Rachal, *QA Dir*
Nathan Bennett, *VP Finance*
EMP: 120

▲ = Import ▼=Export
◆ =Import/Export

SALES (est): 71.9MM **Privately Held**
SIC: 5147 Meats, fresh

(P-8425)

YOSEMITE MEAT COMPANY INC
601 Zeff Rd, Modesto (95351-3942)
P.O. Box 580008 (95358-0001)
PHONE..................................209 524-5117
Johnnie F Lau, *President*
Gay Lau, *Vice Pres*
Chance Reeder, *Plant Supt*
▲ EMP: 100
SQ FT: 3,600
SALES (est): 58MM **Privately Held**
WEB: www.yosemitemeat.com
SIC: 5147 2013 Meats, fresh; bacon, side
& sliced: from purchased meat

5148 Fresh Fruits & Vegetables Wholesale

(P-8426)

4 EARTH FARMS INC (PA)
5555 E Olympic Blvd, Commerce
(90022-5129)
PHONE..................................323 201-5800
David Lake, *CEO*
Robert Lake, *COO*
Kevin Whiteman, *Executive*
Hakob Sadoyan, *Director*
▼ EMP: 79
SQ FT: 165,000
SALES: 230.3MM **Privately Held**
WEB: www.mclproduce.com
SIC: 5148 Fresh fruits & vegetables

(P-8427)

ABP LIQUIDATING CORP
299 Lawrence Ave, South San Francisco
(94080-6818)
PHONE..................................650 871-7689
Brett Besser, *CEO*
Ardynne Besser, *Principal*
EMP: 50 EST: 1971
SQ FT: 11,000
SALES (est): 12.8MM **Privately Held**
WEB: www.abproduce.com
SIC: 5148 5144 Fruits, fresh; vegetables,
fresh; eggs

(P-8428)

ADVANTAGE PRODUCE INC
1511 Bay St, Los Angeles (90021-1634)
P.O. Box 86388 (90086-0388)
PHONE..................................213 627-2777
Steven A Beck, *President*
Don Beck, *Vice Pres*
EMP: 50
SQ FT: 27,000
SALES: 40MM **Privately Held**
SIC: 5148 Fruits; vegetables

(P-8429)

AMS - EXOTIC LLC
720 S Alameda St, Los Angeles
(90021-1616)
PHONE..................................213 612-5888
Sinera Chau-Pech, *Mng Member*
Thierry Delappe,
Martin Seymour,
◆ EMP: 55
SQ FT: 14,000
SALES: 20MM **Privately Held**
WEB: www.ams-exotic.com
SIC: 5148 Fruits

(P-8430)

ANDREW AND WILLIAMSON SALES CO (PA)
Also Called: Andrew Williamson Fresh Prod
9940 Marconi Dr, San Diego (92154-7270)
PHONE..................................619 661-6000
Fred M Williamson, *CEO*
Ira Gershow, *CFO*
John King, *Vice Pres*
Mitch Williamson, *Vice Pres*
Byron Ponce, *Info Tech Dir*
▲ EMP: 60
SQ FT: 20,000
SALES (est): 65.6MM **Privately Held**
WEB: www.andrew-williamson.com
SIC: 5148 Fruits, fresh; vegetables

(P-8431)

BLAZER WILKINSON LP
19040 Portola Dr, Salinas (93908-1213)
P.O. Box 7428, Spreckels (93962-7428)
PHONE..................................831 455-3700
John Wilkinson, *General Ptnr*
Scott Blazer, *Partner*
Paige Hufford, *Accounting Mgr*
Makayla McKinley, *Business Mgr*
Kiana Amaral, *Controller*
EMP: 300
SQ FT: 25,000
SALES (est): 88MM **Privately Held**
SIC: 5148 Fresh fruits & vegetables

(P-8432)

BONTADELLI INC
2611 Mission St, Santa Cruz (95060-5702)
P.O. Box 879 (95061-0879)
PHONE..................................831 423-8572
Ernest J Bontadelli, *President*
Steven Bontadelli, *Vice Pres*
EMP: 60 EST: 1971
SALES (est): 10.7MM **Privately Held**
SIC: 5148 Vegetables, fresh

(P-8433)

BUY FRESH PRODUCE INC
6636 E 26th St, Commerce (90040-3216)
PHONE..................................323 796-0127
Ted Kasnetsis, *President*
Traci Kasnetsis, *CFO*
Ashley Kasnetsis, *Sales Associate*
EMP: 80
SQ FT: 23,500
SALES (est): 1.8MM **Privately Held**
WEB: www.buyfreshproduceinc.com
SIC: 5148 Fruits, fresh

(P-8434)

CAL FRESCO LLC
6850 Artesia Blvd, Buena Park
(90620-1015)
PHONE.................../......714 690-7700
Fernando Vargas, *President*
David Ruada, *Opers Mgr*
Alex Vargas, *Manager*
▼ EMP: 112
SQ FT: 75,000
SALES: 51.8MM **Privately Held**
WEB: www.calfresco.com
SIC: 5148 Fruits, fresh

(P-8435)

CALAVO GROWERS INC
28410 Vincent Moraga Dr, Temecula
(92590-3654)
PHONE..................................951 676-7331
Gerry Watts, *Vice Pres*
EMP: 50
SALES (corp-wide): 1B **Publicly Held**
WEB: www.calavo.com
SIC: 5148 5142 Fruits, fresh; frozen veg-
etables & fruit products
PA: Calavo Growers, Inc.
   1141 Cummings Rd Ste A
   Santa Paula CA 93060
   805 525-1245

(P-8436)

CALIFORNIA FRUIT EXCHANGE LLC (PA)
Also Called: Farmstead Gourmet
6011 E Pine St, Lodi (95240-0815)
P.O. Box 1264 (95241-1264)
PHONE..................................209 334-2988
Paul Marchand,
Suzanne Hernandez, *Mktg Dir*
▲ EMP: 150
SQ FT: 47,200
SALES (est): 142.8MM **Privately Held**
SIC: 5148 5499 Fruits; food gift baskets

(P-8437)

CALIFORNIA PRODUCE WHOLSALERS
6818 Watcher St, Commerce (90040-3715)
P.O. Box 911397, Los Angeles (90091-1237)
PHONE..................................562 776-5770
Alex Pappas, *CEO*
Harry Pappas, *Treasurer*
EMP: 50
SQ FT: 18,000

(P-8438)

CALIFORNIA VEGETABLE SPC INC
Also Called: California Endive Farm
15 Poppy House Rd, Rio Vista
(94571-1201)
P.O. Box 638 (94571-0638)
PHONE..................................707 374-2111
Alexandre Pierron-Darbonne, *CEO*
Richard Collins, *President*
Luc Darbonne, *CEO*
Jose Arias, *Vice Pres*
▲ EMP: 70
SQ FT: 11,000
SALES (est): 8MM **Privately Held**
WEB: www.endive.com
SIC: 5148 Fresh fruits & vegetables

(P-8439)

CAPAY INCORPORATED (PA)
Also Called: Capay Fruits and Vegetables
3880 Seaport Blvd, West Sacramento
(95691-3449)
PHONE..................................530 796-0730
Thaddeus Barsotti, *CEO*
Noah Barnes, *President*
Javier Vargas, *Vice Pres*
Moyra Barsotti, *Admin Sec*
EMP: 99
SALES (est): 65.6MM **Privately Held**
WEB: www.capay.com
SIC: 5148 Fresh fruits & vegetables

(P-8440)

CAPURRO MARKETING LLC
Also Called: Capurro Farms
2250 Highway 1, Moss Landing
(95039-9631)
P.O. Box 450 (95039-0450)
PHONE..................................831 728-1767
Frank L Capurro,
Kristofer Capurro,
John Manfre,
Michael Manfre,
EMP: 60 EST: 2000
SQ FT: 70,000
SALES (est): 15.7MM **Privately Held**
WEB: www.capurromkt.com
SIC: 5148 Fresh fruits & vegetables

(P-8441)

CECELIA PACKING CORPORATION
24780 E South Ave, Orange Cove
(93646-9426)
PHONE..................................559 626-5000
James J Cotter, *CEO*
David G Roth, *President*
Randy Jacobson, *Sales Staff*
◆ EMP: 130
SQ FT: 55,000
SALES (est): 44.7MM **Privately Held**
SIC: 5148 Fresh fruits & vegetables

(P-8442)

CHICO PRODUCE INC (PA)
Also Called: Pro Pacific Fresh
70 Pepsi Way, Durham (95938-9798)
P.O. Box 1069 (95938-1069)
PHONE..................................530 893-0596
Terry Richardson, *CEO*
Bruce Parks, *Ch of Bd*
Dave Deuel, *Technology*
Mike Ayers, *Marketing Staff*
Nathan Parks, *Sales Staff*
▼ EMP: 141
SQ FT: 70,000
SALES (est): 60MM **Privately Held**
WEB: www.propacificfresh.com
SIC: 5148 5149 Fruits, fresh; dried or
canned foods

(P-8443)

CHIQUITA BRANDS INTL INC
746 Market Ct, Los Angeles (90021-1103)
PHONE..................................213 488-0925
Jay Jebbia, *President*
EMP: 60
SALES (corp-wide): 3B **Privately Held**
WEB: www.chiquita.com
SIC: 5148 Fruits, fresh

HQ: Chiquita Brands International, Inc.
   1855 Griffin Rd Ste C436
   Dania FL 33004
   954 924-5700

(P-8444)

CHRISTOPHER RANCH LLC
Also Called: California Produce
1690 Freitas Rd, San Juan Bautista
(95045-9530)
PHONE..................................831 636-8722
Steve Moss, *Manager*
EMP: 65
SALES (est): 5.6MM
SALES (corp-wide): 103.5MM **Privately Held**
WEB: www.christopher-ranch.com
SIC: 5148 Fresh fruits & vegetables
PA: Christopher Ranch, Llc
   305 Bloomfield Ave
   Gilroy CA 95020
   408 847-1100

(P-8445)

CHURCH BROTHERS LLC (PA)
19065 Portola Dr Ste C, Salinas
(93908-1250)
P.O. Box 509 (93902-0509)
PHONE..................................831 796-1000
Tom Church,
Jay Brown, *CFO*
Merritt Bruce, *Vice Pres*
Paula Crabtree, *Executive*
Linda Schroeder, *Credit Mgr*
EMP: 100
SQ FT: 1,000
SALES: 505MM **Privately Held**
SIC: 5148 Fresh fruits & vegetables

(P-8446)

COAST CITRUS DISTRIBUTORS (PA)
Also Called: COAST TROPICAL
7597 Bristow Ct, San Diego (92154-7419)
P.O. Box 530369 (92153-0369)
PHONE..................................619 661-7950
James M Alvarez, *Ch of Bd*
Isabel Freeland, *CFO*
Nick Alvarez, *Officer*
Margarita Alvarez, *Admin Sec*
Mica Simpson, *Administration*
◆ EMP: 100
SQ FT: 80,000
SALES: 306.9MM **Privately Held**
WEB: www.coastcitrus.com
SIC: 5148 Fruits, fresh

(P-8447)

COAST CITRUS DISTRIBUTORS
Also Called: Olympic Frt & Vegatable Distr
1601 E Olympic Blvd, Los Angeles
(90021-1936)
PHONE..................................213 955-3444
Tom Hall, *Vice Pres*
EMP: 150
SALES (corp-wide): 306.9MM **Privately Held**
WEB: www.coastcitrus.com
SIC: 5148 Fruits, fresh
PA: Coast Citrus Distributors
   7597 Bristow Ct
   San Diego CA 92154
   619 661-7950

(P-8448)

COAST CITRUS DISTRIBUTORS
Also Called: Coast Tropical
131 Terminal Ct 13, South San Francisco
(94080-6526)
P.O. Box 2884 (94083)
PHONE..................................650 588-0707
Patrick Graham, *Manager*
EMP: 50
SALES (corp-wide): 306.9MM **Privately Held**
WEB: www.coastcitrus.com
SIC: 5148 Fruits, fresh
PA: Coast Citrus Distributors
   7597 Bristow Ct
   San Diego CA 92154
   619 661-7950

(P-8449)
COAST PRODUCE COMPANY (PA)
1791 Bay St, Los Angeles (90021-1655)
P.O. Box 86468 (90086-0468)
PHONE...................................213 955-4900
Mike Ito, *CEO*
Rick Uyeno, *CFO*
John K Dunn, *Principal*
Rafael Elizalde, *Buyer*
Vicki Wong, *Director*
▲ **EMP:** 165
SQ FT: 80,000
SALES (est): 73MM **Privately Held**
WEB: www.coastpro.com
SIC: 5148 Fruits, fresh

(P-8450)
COHN WHOLESALE FRUIT & GROCERY (PA)
3511 Camino Del Rio S # 306, San Diego (92108-4020)
PHONE 619 528-1113
Phillip L Cohn, *President*
Alice Cohn, *Treasurer*
Aaron Cohn, *Vice Pres*
EMP: 201
SALES (est): 32.3MM **Privately Held**
WEB: www.cohngrocery.com
SIC: 5148 Fruits

(P-8451)
CUSTOM PRODUCE SALES (PA)
13475 E Progress Dr, Parlier (93648-9674)
P.O. Box 977, Kingsburg (93631-0977)
PHONE...................................559 254-5800
Marvin Farris, *CEO*
Tony Bozzo, *Marketing Staff*
Katie Morisson, *Sales Staff*
▲ **EMP:** 180
SALES (est): 28MM **Privately Held**
WEB: www.customproducesales.com
SIC: 5148 Fresh fruits & vegetables

(P-8452)
D & D WHOLESALE DISTRS INC
777 Baldwin Park Blvd, City of Industry (91746-1504)
PHONE...................................626 333-2111
Joe Dupree, *President*
Pamela Dupree, *Corp Secy*
EMP: 90
SQ FT: 20,000
SALES (est): 58.8MM **Privately Held**
SIC: 5148 5143 Fruits, fresh; dairy products, except dried or canned

(P-8453)
DAVALAN SALES INC
Also Called: Davalan Fresh
1601 E Olympic Blvd # 325, Los Angeles (90021-1957)
PHONE...................................213 623-2500
Alan Frick, *President*
Dave Bouton, *CEO*
Andy Miller, *General Mgr*
Bob Morse, *Sales Staff*
▲ **EMP:** 200
SQ FT: 15,000
SALES (est): 107.1MM **Privately Held**
SIC: 5148 Fruits; vegetables

(P-8454)
DAYLIGHT FOODS INC
30200 Whipple Rd, Union City (94587-1524)
PHONE...................................408 284-7300
Chris Vlahopouliotis, *President*
Paul Jennings, *Vice Pres*
▲ **EMP:** 120
SALES: 49.5MM **Privately Held**
SIC: 5148 Fruits, fresh; vegetables, fresh

(P-8455)
DEARDORFF-JACKSON CO
Also Called: Deardorff Family Farm
400 Lombard St, Oxnard (93030-5100)
P.O. Box 1188 (93032-1188)
PHONE...................................805 487-7801
Tom Deardorff Jr, *President*
Scott Deardorff, *Admin Sec*
Doug Lowthorp, *Sales Mgr*
Geremy Olsen, *Manager*
EMP: 50 **EST:** 1954
SQ FT: 115,000

SALES (est): 44MM **Privately Held**
WEB: www.deardorffjackson.com
SIC: 5148 Fresh fruits & vegetables

(P-8456)
DIMARE FRESH
4050 Pell Cir, Sacramento (95838-2527)
P.O. Box 340188 (95834-0188)
PHONE...................................916 921-6302
Jerry Just, *General Mgr*
John Jarin, *Manager*
EMP: 300
SALES (est): 64.4MM **Privately Held**
SIC: 5148 Fruits, fresh

(P-8457)
DOLE FRESH FRUIT COMPANY (HQ)
1 Dole Dr, Westlake Village (91362-7300)
P.O. Box 5700, Thousand Oaks (91359-5700)
PHONE...................................818 874-4000
Johan Linden, *President*
John Trummel, *President*
Johan L Malmqvist, *Treasurer*
Johan Malmqvist, *Treasurer*
Ronald D Bouchard, *Vice Pres*
◆ **EMP:** 460
SQ FT: 57,000
SALES (est): 961MM
SALES (corp-wide): 1.1B **Privately Held**
SIC: 5148 Fruits, fresh; banana ripening
PA: Dole Food Company, Inc.
　1 Dole Dr
　Westlake Village CA 91362
　818 874-4000

(P-8458)
DOLE FRESH VEGETABLES INC
32655 Camphora Rd, Soledad (93960-9600)
PHONE...................................831 678-5030
Sheila Lee, *Manager*
Arturo Castro, *Technician*
Mario Martinez, *Maint Spvr*
EMP: 210
SQ FT: 1,664
SALES (corp-wide): 1.1B **Privately Held**
SIC: 5148 Fresh fruits & vegetables
HQ: Dole Fresh Vegetables, Inc.
　2959 Salinas Hwy
　Monterey CA 93940
　831 422-8871

(P-8459)
DOLE HOLDINGS INC (PA)
1 Dole Dr, Westlake Village (91362-7300)
PHONE...................................818 879-6600
David Delorenzo, *President*
Lawrence Henrard, *Vice Pres*
Bonnie Rothstein, *Admin Mgr*
Amanda France, *Technology*
Rosemary Johansson, *Technology*
◆ **EMP:** 51
SALES (est): 11.4MM **Privately Held**
SIC: 5148 0161 0174 0175 Fresh fruits & vegetables; vegetables & melons; citrus fruits; deciduous tree fruits; canned fruits & specialties

(P-8460)
DRISCOLLS INC (PA)
345 Westridge Dr, Watsonville (95076-4169)
P.O. Box 50045 (95077-5045)
PHONE...................................831 424-0506
Miles Reiter, *CEO*
Joseph Miles Reiter, *Ch of Bd*
Sean Martin, *CFO*
Elly Hoever, *Treasurer*
Soren Bjorn, *Vice Pres*
◆ **EMP:** 60
SQ FT: 19,932
SALES (est): 453.8MM **Privately Held**
WEB: www.driscolls.com
SIC: 5148 5431 Fruits, fresh; fruit & vegetable markets

(P-8461)
DRISCOLLS INC
150 Westridge Dr, Watsonville (95076-6709)
PHONE...................................800 871-3333
Rick Harrison, *Vice Pres*
Rekha Vaddi, *Software Dev*
Luis Garcia, *Opers Staff*

Shannon Corbin, *Director*
EMP: 75
SALES (corp-wide): 453.8MM **Privately Held**
SIC: 5148 Fruits, fresh
PA: Driscoll's, Inc.
　345 Westridge Dr
　Watsonville CA 95076
　831 424-0506

(P-8462)
DRISCOLLS INC
1750 San Juan Rd, Aromas (95004-9027)
P.O. Box 50045, Watsonville (95077-5045)
PHONE...................................831 763-5100
Rick Reyes, *Branch Mgr*
EMP: 50
SALES (corp-wide): 453.8MM **Privately Held**
WEB: www.driscolls.com
SIC: 5148 Fruits, fresh
PA: Driscoll's, Inc.
　345 Westridge Dr
　Watsonville CA 95076
　831 424-0506

(P-8463)
EARLS ORGANIC
Also Called: Earl's Organic Produce
2101 Jerrold Ave Ste 100, San Francisco (94124-1009)
PHONE...................................415 824-7419
Earl Herrick, *Principal*
Katherine Vining, *Admin Sec*
Jose Cruz, *Administration*
Michele Smith-Jefferies, *Accounting Dir*
Robert Lichtenberg, *Purchasing*
▲ **EMP:** 78
SALES (est): 50MM **Privately Held**
SIC: 5148 Fresh fruits & vegetables

(P-8464)
ECO FARMS AVOCADOS INC (PA)
28790 Las Haciendas St, Temecula (92590-2614)
PHONE...................................951 694-3013
Steve Taft, *CEO*
Norman Traner, *Corp Secy*
Gahl Crane, *Sales Dir*
Miguel Hernandez, *Manager*
▲ **EMP:** 140
SQ FT: 20,000
SALES (est): 38MM **Privately Held**
SIC: 5148 Fresh fruits & vegetables

(P-8465)
ECO FARMS SALES INC (PA)
28790 Las Haciendas St, Temecula (92590-2614)
PHONE...................................951 694-3013
Steve Taft, *President*
▲ **EMP:** 50
SQ FT: 20,000
SALES (est): 28.3MM **Privately Held**
SIC: 5148 Fresh fruits & vegetables

(P-8466)
EVOLUTION FRESH INC (HQ)
Also Called: Evolution Juice
11655 Jersey Blvd, Rancho Cucamonga (91730-4903)
PHONE...................................800 794-9986
Chris Bruzzo, *CEO*
James Rosenberg, *Ch of Bd*
Ricki Reves, *CFO*
▲ **EMP:** 65
SQ FT: 70,000
SALES (est): 250.9MM
SALES (corp-wide): 24.7B **Publicly Held**
SIC: 5148 2037 Fruits, fresh; vegetables, fresh; frozen fruits & vegetables
PA: Starbucks Corporation
　2401 Utah Ave S
　Seattle WA 98134
　206 447-1575

(P-8467)
FAMILY TREE PRODUCE INC
5510 E La Palma Ave, Anaheim (92807-2108)
PHONE...................................714 693-5688
Fidel Guzman, *President*
Christy Guzman, *Corp Secy*
Frank Guzman, *Controller*
Carlos Villa, *Accounts Exec*

EMP: 115
SQ FT: 33,000
SALES: 37.4MM **Privately Held**
WEB: www.ftproduce.com
SIC: 5148 Fruits, fresh; potatoes, fresh; vegetables, fresh

(P-8468)
FAMOUS VINEYARDS LLC
20715 Ave 8, Richgrove (93261)
PHONE...................................661 392-5000
Joe Butkiewicz, *Mng Member*
EMP: 100
SALES (est): 5.7MM **Privately Held**
SIC: 5148 Fruits, fresh

(P-8469)
FIELD FRESH FARMS LLC
320 Industrial Rd, Watsonville (95076-5116)
P.O. Box 2731 (95077-2731)
PHONE...................................831 722-1422
Mike Dobler, *President*
Paul Betancourt, *Controller*
Cary Lee, *Opers Staff*
Fernando Ramirez, *Sales Mgr*
Manny Diaz, *Sales Staff*
EMP: 80
SQ FT: 66,000
SALES: 49MM **Privately Held**
SIC: 5148 Vegetables, fresh

(P-8470)
FRESHKO PRODUCE SERVICES INC
2155 E Muscat Ave, Fresno (93725-2326)
P.O. Box 11097 (93771-1097)
PHONE...................................559 497-7000
Manny Robles, *Principal*
Randall Shepherd, *Principal*
EMP: 142
SQ FT: 47,000
SALES (est): 62.4MM
SALES (corp-wide): 3.9B **Privately Held**
WEB: www.freshkoproduce.com
SIC: 5148 5499 Fruits, fresh; juices, fruit or vegetable
PA: C&S Wholesale Grocers, Inc.
　7 Corporate Dr
　Keene NH 03431
　603 354-7000

(P-8471)
FRESHPOINT INC
30336 Whipple Rd, Union City (94587-1525)
PHONE...................................510 476-5900
Robert Gordon, *Branch Mgr*
EMP: 135
SALES (corp-wide): 60.1B **Publicly Held**
SIC: 5148 Fresh fruits & vegetables
HQ: Freshpoint, Inc.
　1390 Enclave Pkwy
　Houston TX 77077

(P-8472)
FRESHPOINT INC
Also Called: Freshpoint Las Vegas
155 N Orange Ave, City of Industry (91744-3432)
PHONE...................................626 855-1400
Terry Owen, *President*
James Ashe, *Opers Mgr*
EMP: 136
SALES (corp-wide): 60.1B **Publicly Held**
SIC: 5148 Fresh fruits & vegetables
HQ: Freshpoint, Inc.
　1390 Enclave Pkwy
　Houston TX 77077

(P-8473)
FRESHPOINT CENTRAL CALIFORNIA
5900 N Golden State Blvd, Turlock (95382-9671)
PHONE...................................209 216-0200
Brian M Sturgeon, *President*
Jeffrey A Sacchini, *CEO*
Melissa Gaffaney, *Purchasing*
EMP: 150
SQ FT: 54,000

SALES (est): 53.4MM
SALES (corp-wide): 60.1B **Publicly Held**
WEB: www.piranhaproduce.com
SIC: **5148** Fresh fruits & vegetables
HQ: Freshpoint, Inc.
1390 Enclave Pkwy
Houston TX 77077

(P-8474)
FRESHPOINT SOUTHERN CAL INC
Also Called: Freshpoint Southern California
155 N Orange Ave, City of Industry
(91744-3432)
PHONE..................626 855-1400
Verne L Lusby, *CEO*
Jeff Ronk, *Exec VP*
Jon Greco, *Vice Pres*
Joel Barker, *Director*
Rich Dachman, *Director*
EMP: 208 EST: 1921
SQ FT: 97,000
SALES (est): 98.8MM
SALES (corp-wide): 60.1B **Publicly Held**
WEB: www.theproducehunter.com
SIC: **5148** 5142 Fruits, fresh; vegetables, fresh; packaged frozen goods
PA: Sysco Corporation
1390 Enclave Pkwy
Houston TX 77077
281 584-1390

(P-8475)
FRIEDAS INC
Also Called: Friedas Specialty Produce
4465 Corporate Center Dr, Los Alamitos
(90720-2561)
PHONE..................714 826-6100
Karen Caplan, *President*
Jackie Caplan-Wiggins, *COO*
Jackie Caplan, *Vice Pres*
Brittany Laukat, *Human Res Mgr*
Ryan Birkett, *Buyer*
▲ EMP: 75
SQ FT: 81,306
SALES (est): 56.1MM **Privately Held**
WEB: www.friedas.com
SIC: **5148** 5499 7389 Vegetables, fresh; fruits, fresh; dried fruit; labeling bottles, cans, cartons, etc.

(P-8476)
FRUIT GROWERS SUPPLY COMPANY
225 S Wineville Ave, Ontario (91761-7891)
PHONE..................909 390-0190
Steve Moore, *Sales/Mktg Mgr*
Stephen Moore, *General Mgr*
Chad Cox, *Technology*
Jolina Yoo, *Accounting Mgr*
Sue Fisher, *Buyer*
EMP: 80
SALES (corp-wide): 222.6MM **Privately Held**
SIC: **5148** Fresh fruits & vegetables
PA: Fruit Growers Supply Company Inc
27770 N Entrmt Dr Fl 3 Flr 3
Valencia CA 91355
661 290-8704

(P-8477)
FRUIT GUYS
4465 Corporate Center Dr, Los Alamitos
(90720-2540)
PHONE..................714 826-2993
Nicole Joseph, *General Mgr*
EMP: 60 EST: 2014
SALES (est): 3.7MM **Privately Held**
SIC: **5148** Fruits

(P-8478)
FRUIT PATCH SALES LLC
38773 Road 48, Dinuba (93618-9718)
PHONE..................559 591-1170
Dennis Bergquist, *Mng Member*
Doug Reader, *Treasurer*
William L Byers,
Jim Gallagher,
Scott Wallace,
▼ EMP: 500
SQ FT: 3,000
SALES (est): 162.5MM **Privately Held**
SIC: **5148** Fruits

(P-8479)
GALLI PRODUCE COMPANY
1650 Old Bayshore Hwy, San Jose
(95112-4304)
P.O. Box 612620 (95161-2620)
PHONE..................408 436-6100
Gerald Pieracci, *President*
Kristin Killin, *Corp Secy*
Jeff Pieracci, *Vice Pres*
Dennis Tinucci, *Vice Pres*
Joseph Vanni, *Vice Pres*
EMP: 60
SQ FT: 10,000
SALES (est): 22.3MM **Privately Held**
WEB: www.galliproduce.com
SIC: **5148** 5142 Fruits, fresh; vegetables, fresh; fruits, frozen; vegetables, frozen

(P-8480)
GENERAL PROD A CAL LTD PARTNR (PA)
1330 N B St, Sacramento (95811-0605)
P.O. Box 308 (95812-0308)
PHONE..................916 441-6431
Jeff Sacchini, *CEO*
Dan Chan, *President*
Don Weersing, *Vice Pres*
Sheryl Weichert, *Vice Pres*
Chan Van, *Accountant*
◆ EMP: 225 EST: 1933
SQ FT: 110,000
SALES (est): 137.7MM **Privately Held**
WEB: www.generalprod.com
SIC: **5148** Fruits, fresh; vegetables, fresh

(P-8481)
GILLS ONIONS LLC
1051 Pacific Ave, Oxnard (93030-7254)
PHONE..................805 240-1983
Steve Gill, *Mng Member*
Jaime Cota, *Purchasing*
Arturo Coronado, *Plant Mgr*
Teri Trost, *Regl Sales Mgr*
Jessica Ortega, *Sales Staff*
▲ EMP: 55
SALES (est): 34MM **Privately Held**
WEB: www.gillsonions.com
SIC: **5148** Fresh fruits & vegetables

(P-8482)
GIUMARRA BROS FRUIT CO INC (PA)
Also Called: Giumarra International Berry
1601 E Olympic Blvd # 408, Los Angeles
(90021-1943)
P.O. Box 861449 (90086-1449)
PHONE..................213 627-2900
Donald Corsaro, *CEO*
John Corsaro, *President*
John Giumarra Jr, *Treasurer*
John H Corsaro, *Vice Pres*
TI Riley, *Vice Pres*
◆ EMP: 74 EST: 1950
SQ FT: 8,000
SALES (est): 67.9MM **Privately Held**
WEB: www.giumarra.com
SIC: **5148** Fresh fruits & vegetables

(P-8483)
GOURMET SPECIALTIES INC
2120 E 25th St, Vernon (90058-1126)
PHONE..................323 587-1734
Abundio Ruiz, *CEO*
Michelle Medina, *Office Mgr*
EMP: 75
SALES (est): 8.2MM **Privately Held**
SIC: **5148** Fresh fruits & vegetables

(P-8484)
GREEN FARMS INC
Also Called: Worldwide Produce
2652 Long Beach Ave, Los Angeles
(90058-1323)
PHONE..................858 831-7701
Abbas Ghulam, *Branch Mgr*
EMP: 293 **Privately Held**
SIC: **5148** Fresh fruits & vegetables
PA: Green Farms California, Llc
2652 Long Beach Ave Ste 2
Los Angeles CA 90058

(P-8485)
GREEN FARMS CALIFORNIA LLC (PA)
Also Called: Worldwide Produce
2652 Long Beach Ave Ste 2, Los Angeles
(90058-1323)
P.O. Box 54399 (90054-0399)
PHONE..................213 747-4411
Stuart Weisfeld, *CEO*
Ron Warenkiewicz, *CFO*
Laura Ramos, *General Mgr*
Silvia Macias, *Human Res Mgr*
▼ EMP: 107
SQ FT: 150
SALES (est): 304.7MM **Privately Held**
WEB: www.worldwideproduce.com
SIC: **5148** Fresh fruits & vegetables

(P-8486)
GREEN THUMB PRODUCE INC
2648 W Ramsey St, Banning (92220-3716)
P.O. Box 1357 (92220-0010)
PHONE..................951 849-4711
Lonnie Saverino, *President*
Jeff Young, *Buyer*
EMP: 250
SALES (est): 87.2MM **Privately Held**
SIC: **5148** Fresh fruits & vegetables

(P-8487)
GRIMMWAY ENTERPRISES INC
Also Called: Cal-Organic Farms
12000 Main St, Lamont (93241-2836)
P.O. Box 81498, Bakersfield (93380-1498)
PHONE..................661 845-3758
Roodzant Steve, *General Mgr*
Imelda Vidaurri, *Production*
Joanne Ford, *Sales Staff*
EMP: 339
SALES (corp-wide): 1.8B **Privately Held**
SIC: **5148** Vegetables, fresh
PA: Grimmway Enterprises, Inc.
14141 Di Giorgio Rd
Arvin CA 93203
800 301-3101

(P-8488)
GROWERS EXPRESS LLC (PA)
150 Main St Ste 210, Salinas (93901-3439)
P.O. Box 948 (93902-0948)
PHONE..................831 757-9951
David L Gill, *Mng Member*
▼ EMP: 153
SQ FT: 10,000
SALES (est): 307.1MM **Privately Held**
SIC: **5148** Vegetables

(P-8489)
HARVEST SENSATIONS LLC (PA)
3030 E Washington Blvd, Los Angeles
(90023-4220)
PHONE..................213 895-6968
Chris Coffman, *Mng Member*
Charles Gilbert, *Ch of Bd*
Bob Kiehnle, *CFO*
Diana Rios, *Administration*
Delma Mendoza, *Sales Staff*
▲ EMP: 51
SALES (est): 40MM **Privately Held**
SIC: **5148** Fruits

(P-8490)
JACK H CALDWELL & SONS INC
Also Called: Choice Pak Products
4035 E 52nd St, Maywood (90270-2205)
PHONE..................323 589-4008
Harry Caldwell, *President*
Duke Caldwell, *Vice Pres*
EMP: 60
SQ FT: 5,000
SALES (est): 35.7MM **Privately Held**
SIC: **5148** Vegetables, fresh

(P-8491)
JHP PRODUCE INC
1601 E Olympic Blvd # 200, Los Angeles
(90021-1936)
PHONE..................213 627-1093
Chuck Johnson, *President*
Breccia Hellman, *Shareholder*
Tracy Hellman, *Corp Secy*
EMP: 55
SQ FT: 21,000

SALES (est): 15.6MM **Privately Held**
SIC: **5148** Vegetables; potatoes, fresh; vegetables, fresh; fruits, fresh

(P-8492)
KINGSBURG APPLE PACKERS INC
Also Called: Kingsburg Orchards
10363 Davis Ave, Kingsburg (93631-9539)
P.O. Box 38 (93631-0038)
PHONE..................559 897-5132
George H Jackson, *President*
Colleen Jackson, *Corp Secy*
Becky Stark, *Controller*
Brian Keavy, *Export Mgr*
◆ EMP: 450
SQ FT: 10,000
SALES (est): 111.2MM **Privately Held**
SIC: **5148** Fruits, fresh

(P-8493)
LA SPECIALTY PRODUCE CO (PA)
Also Called: San Fransisco Speciality Prod
13527 Orden Dr, Santa Fe Springs
(90670-6338)
P.O. Box 2293 (90670-0293)
PHONE..................562 741-2200
Michael Glick, *President*
Kathleen Glick, *Vice Pres*
Joycee Del Toro, *Executive*
Peter Saucedo, *Representative*
Saul Slotnick, *Representative*
EMP: 375
SQ FT: 188,000
SALES (est): 418MM **Privately Held**
WEB: www.laspecialtyproduce.com
SIC: **5148** Fruits, fresh

(P-8494)
LEGACY FARMS LLC
1765 W Penhall Way, Anaheim
(92801-6728)
PHONE..................714 736-1800
Nick Cancellieri, *Managing Prtnr*
Richard Tansley, *CFO*
Rick Baxter, *Principal*
Vince Mendoza, *Principal*
Ron Shimizu, *Principal*
▲ EMP: 120
SQ FT: 95,000
SALES (est): 74.4MM **Privately Held**
SIC: **5148** Fruits, fresh

(P-8495)
LIBERTY PACKING COMPANY LLC (PA)
Also Called: Morning Star Company The
724 Main St, Woodland (95695-3491)
PHONE..................209 826-7100
Chris Rufer,
▲ EMP: 120
SALES (est): 71.7MM **Privately Held**
SIC: **5148** 2033 Vegetables; tomato products: packaged in cans, jars, etc.

(P-8496)
LJ DISTRIBUTORS INC
Also Called: Team Tomato
12840 Leyva St, Norwalk (90650-6852)
P.O. Box 610, Bellflower (90707-0610)
PHONE..................562 229-7660
Lute Miyazaki, *President*
Marlene Castro, *Vice Pres*
◆ EMP: 54
SQ FT: 115,000
SALES (est): 13.1MM **Privately Held**
WEB: www.teamtomato.com
SIC: **5148** Fruits; vegetables

(P-8497)
LOEWY ENTERPRISES
Also Called: Sunrise Produce Company
500 Burning Tree Rd, Fullerton
(92833-1400)
PHONE..................323 726-3838
Paul Carone, *President*
Ron Alderete, *Exec Dir*
John Akin, *QC Mgr*
April Berlanga, *Manager*
EMP: 90
SQ FT: 41,000
SALES (est): 67.8MM **Privately Held**
SIC: **5148** Fruits, fresh

(P-8498)
MISSION PRODUCE INC
3803 Dufau Rd, Oxnard (93033-8296)
P.O. Box 5267 (93031-5267)
PHONE...........................805 981-3650
Steven J Barnard, *President*
David Estes, *CTO*
David Hall, *Manager*
EMP: 75
SALES (corp-wide): 115MM **Privately Held**
WEB: www.missionpro.com
SIC: 5148 Fruits, fresh
PA: Mission Produce, Inc.
2500 E Vineyard Ave # 300
Oxnard CA 93036
805 981-3650

(P-8499)
MONSANTO COMPANY
37437 State Highway 16, Woodland (95695-9353)
PHONE...........................530 669-6224
Rusty Myer, *Branch Mgr*
Terry Berke, *Associate*
EMP: 300
SALES (corp-wide): 45.3B **Privately Held**
SIC: 5148 Vegetables
HQ: Monsanto Company
800 N Lindbergh Blvd
Saint Louis MO 63167
314 694-1000

(P-8500)
MOONLIGHT PACKING CORPORATION (PA)
Also Called: Moonlight Companies
17719 E Huntsman Ave, Reedley (93654-9205)
P.O. Box 846 (93654-0846)
PHONE...........................559 638-7799
Russell Tavlan, *President*
Ty Tavlan, *CFO*
Jim Jones, *Executive*
Jared Riley, *CTO*
Jay Reimer, *Info Tech Dir*
EMP: 185
SQ FT: 80,000
SALES (est): 437.1MM **Privately Held**
WEB: www.moonlightcompanies.com
SIC: 5148 4783 Fruits, fresh; packing & crating

(P-8501)
NATURES PRODUCE COMPANY
3305 Bandini Blvd, Vernon (90058-4130)
P.O. Box 58366 (90058-0366)
PHONE...........................323 235-4343
Rick Polisky, *CEO*
Luis Orendain, *Opers Spvr*
Michael Feuerstein, *Sales Staff*
▲ EMP: 80
SALES (est): 47.4MM **Privately Held**
WEB: www.naturesproducecompany.com
SIC: 5148 Fruits, fresh

(P-8502)
NEWSTAR FRESH FOODS LLC (PA)
850 Work St Ste 101, Salinas (93901-4378)
P.O. Box 2627 (93902-2627)
PHONE...........................888 782-7220
Anthony Vasquez, *CEO*
Carl Wiseman, *CFO*
Loui Barriga, *Vice Pres*
Mitch Secondo, *Vice Pres*
Greg Zelei, *Vice Pres*
▼ EMP: 200
SQ FT: 1,300,000
SALES (est): 75MM **Privately Held**
WEB: www.newstarfreshfoods.com
SIC: 5148 Fresh fruits & vegetables

(P-8503)
NUNES COMPANY INC (PA)
Also Called: Foxy
925 Johnson Ave, Salinas (93901-4327)
P.O. Box 673 (93902-0673)
PHONE...........................831 751-7510
Tom P Nunes Jr, *CEO*
Mike Scarr, *CFO*
Enos Barera, *Treasurer*
Mark Crossgrove, *Vice Pres*
Frank R Nunes, *Vice Pres*

▼ EMP: 50 EST: 1976
SALES (est): 38.5MM **Privately Held**
WEB: www.foxy.com
SIC: 5148 Vegetables

(P-8504)
OAKVILLE PRODUCE PARTNERS LLC
Also Called: Greenleaf Produce
453 Valley Dr, Brisbane (94005-1209)
PHONE...........................415 647-2991
William F Wilkinson, *Mng Member*
Frank Ballentine, *President*
Mark Natividad, *Finance Dir*
Huy Tran, *Credit Mgr*
Nick Salas, *Opers Mgr*
EMP: 150
SQ FT: 32,000
SALES (est): 99.5MM **Privately Held**
WEB: www.greenleafsf.com
SIC: 5148 5451 Fruits, fresh; vegetables, fresh; dairy products stores

(P-8505)
PACIFIC COAST PRODUCE INC
950 Mountain View Ave # 1, Oxnard (93030-6201)
PHONE...........................805 240-3385
Carlos Marez, *CEO*
Uvence Cortez, *Treasurer*
Maribelle Cortez, *Vice Pres*
EMP: 50
SQ FT: 16,000
SALES (est): 25.5MM **Privately Held**
WEB: www.pacificcoastproduce.com
SIC: 5148 5149 5812 5142 Fruits, fresh; canned goods: fruit, vegetables, seafood, meats, etc.; contract food services; frozen fish, meat & poultry; frozen dairy desserts

(P-8506)
PACIFIC INTL VGETABLE MKTG INC (PA)
Also Called: Pacific International Mktg
740 Airport Blvd, Salinas (93901-4510)
P.O. Box 3737 (93912-3737)
PHONE...........................831 422-3745
Dave L Johnson, *CEO*
David Black, *Vice Pres*
Steve Tripp, *Admin Sec*
Henry Dill, *Sales Mgr*
John Chobanian, *Sales Staff*
◆ EMP: 75
SQ FT: 1,800
SALES (est): 35.1MM **Privately Held**
WEB: www.purepacificorganic.com
SIC: 5148 Fresh fruits & vegetables

(P-8507)
PACIFIC TRELLIS FRUIT LLC (PA)
Also Called: Dulcinea Farms
2301 E 7th St Ste C200, Los Angeles (90023-1041)
PHONE...........................323 859-9600
Linda Chen, *President*
Josh Leichter, *General Mgr*
Patricia Medina, *Controller*
Angela Eastham, *Sales Staff*
David Sullivan,
▲ EMP: 130
SQ FT: 10,000
SALES (est): 187.8MM **Privately Held**
WEB: www.pacifictrellisfruit.com
SIC: 5148 Fruits, fresh

(P-8508)
PARAMOUNT EXPORT COMPANY
5875 Lamas St, San Diego (92122-3146)
PHONE...........................858 452-8101
James Galagan, *Principal*
Melanie McNeil, *Sales Staff*
EMP: 55
SALES (corp-wide): 76.6MM **Privately Held**
SIC: 5148 5149 Fruits, fresh; specialty food items
PA: Paramount Export Company
175 Filbert St Ste 201
Oakland CA 94607
510 839-0150

(P-8509)
PREMIER MUSHROOMS LP (PA)
2880 Niagara Ave, Colusa (95932)
PHONE...........................530 458-2700
John Ashbaugh, *Partner*
Rex Pugh, *CFO*
▲ EMP: 170
SQ FT: 10,000
SALES (est): 96.3MM **Privately Held**
SIC: 5148 Fresh fruits & vegetables

(P-8510)
PRIMETIME INTERNATIONAL INC
86705 Avenue 54 Ste A, Coachella (92236-3814)
PHONE...........................760 399-4166
Carl Sam Maggio, *CEO*
Jim Detty, *Credit Mgr*
Mark Nickerson, *Mng Member*
Jeff Taylor, *Mng Member*
Mike Way, *Mng Member*
▲ EMP: 95
SQ FT: 4,000
SALES: 200MM
SALES (corp-wide): 123.9MM **Privately Held**
WEB: www.primetimeproduce.com
SIC: 5148 4783 Vegetables, fresh; packing goods for shipping
PA: Sun And Sands Enterprises, Llc
86705 Avenue 54 Ste A
Coachella CA 92236
760 399-4278

(P-8511)
PRO ACT LLC
40 Ragsdale Dr Ste 200, Monterey (93940-5774)
PHONE...........................831 655-4250
Max Yeater, *CEO*
Steve Grinstead, *CEO*
Bob Kiehnle, *CFO*
Kelly Jacob, *Vice Pres*
Anthony Molinaro, *Vice Pres*
▲ EMP: 80
SALES (est): 55.4MM **Privately Held**
WEB: www.proactusa.com
SIC: 5148 Vegetables

(P-8512)
PRODUCE COMPANY
Also Called: Finest Produce
16809 Bellflower Blvd # 32, Bellflower (90706-5901)
PHONE...........................310 508-7760
Edward L Puppo, *President*
Steven Morris, *Vice Pres*
EMP: 130
SQ FT: 2,000
SALES: 5.5MM **Privately Held**
SIC: 5148 Fresh fruits & vegetables

(P-8513)
PRODUCE EXCHANGE INCORPORATED (DH)
7407 Southfront Rd, Livermore (94551-8224)
PHONE...........................925 454-8700
Marty Mazzanti, *Manager*
Samuel E Jones Jr, *President*
Martin Moreno, *Buyer*
Alison Contois, *Sales Staff*
Jason Lind, *Sales Staff*
▲ EMP: 65
SQ FT: 10,000
SALES (est): 10MM
SALES (corp-wide): 238.9MM **Privately Held**
WEB: www.tpemail.com
SIC: 5148 Fruits, fresh; vegetables
HQ: Lipman-Texas, Llc
315 New Market Rd E
Immokalee FL 34142
239 657-4421

(P-8514)
PROFESSIONAL PRODUCE
2570 E 25th St, Los Angeles (90058-1211)
P.O. Box 58308 (90058-0308)
PHONE...........................323 277-1550
Ted Kaplan, *CEO*
Maribel Reyes, *CFO*
Zackary Pregent, *Sales Staff*
◆ EMP: 99

SQ FT: 5,000
SALES (est): 76MM **Privately Held**
WEB: www.profproduce.com
SIC: 5148 Fruits, fresh

(P-8515)
PROGRESSIVE PRODUCE LLC (HQ)
Also Called: Progressive Marketing Group
5790 Peachtree St, Commerce (90040-4000)
PHONE...........................323 890-8100
James K Leimkuhler, *President*
Howard Nager, *Vice Pres*
Victor Rte, *Vice Pres*
Jamie Simon, *Principal*
Don Hessel, *General Mgr*
▲ EMP: 104
SQ FT: 106,000
SALES (est): 75.5MM **Privately Held**
WEB: www.progressiveproduce.com
SIC: 5148 4213 7389 Fruits, fresh; vegetables, fresh; refrigerated products transport; packaging & labeling services

(P-8516)
REGATTA TROPICALS LTD (PA)
1742 Manhattan Ave Ste C, Grover Beach (93433-2500)
PHONE...........................805 473-1320
Steven J Matych, *President*
Teresa Barnes-Matych, *Corp Secy*
◆ EMP: 80
SQ FT: 1,000
SALES (est): 57.1MM **Privately Held**
SIC: 5148 Fruits, fresh

(P-8517)
RIVER RANCH FRESH FOODS LLC (HQ)
911 Blanco Cir Ste B, Salinas (93901-4449)
PHONE...........................831 758-1390
Bruce Knobeloch, *CEO*
John Bowman, *President*
Tom Welch, *CFO*
W Baxley, *Vice Pres*
Ped Mills,
▲ EMP: 450
SALES (est): 124.1MM **Privately Held**
WEB: www.rrff.com
SIC: 5148 Vegetables, fresh

(P-8518)
SAMBAZON INC (PA)
209 Avenida Fabricante # 200, San Clemente (92672-7544)
PHONE...........................877 726-2296
Ryan Black, *CEO*
Bruce Peasland, *CFO*
Jeremy Black, *Vice Pres*
Ed Nichols, *Vice Pres*
Travis Baumgardner, *Director*
◆ EMP: 60
SQ FT: 10,000
SALES (est): 50.8MM **Privately Held**
WEB: www.sambazon.com
SIC: 5148 5499 Fruits; juices, fruit or vegetable

(P-8519)
SEASON PRODUCE CO INC
1601 E Olympic Blvd # 315, Los Angeles (90021-1942)
PHONE...........................213 689-0008
Patrick R Horwath, *President*
Daniel Horwath, *Vice Pres*
Timothy R Horwath, *Vice Pres*
EMP: 353
SQ FT: 20,000
SALES (est): 78.1MM **Privately Held**
WEB: www.s-hpacking.com
SIC: 5148 Fresh fruits & vegetables
PA: S & H Packing & Sales Co., Inc.
2590 Harriet St
Vernon CA 90058
323 581-7172

(P-8520)
SEQUOIA ENTERPRISES INC
Also Called: Sequoia Orange
150 W Pine St, Exeter (93221-1613)
PHONE...........................559 592-9455
James Wilson, *CEO*
Marvin L Wilson, *President*
Jan Lee, *Manager*

2019 Directory of California
Wholesalers and Services Companies

▲ = Import ▼=Export
◆ =Import/Export

▼ **EMP:** 70 **EST:** 1975
SQ FT: 5,100
SALES (est): 16.6MM **Privately Held**
SIC: 5148 Fruits, fresh

(P-8521)
SGF PRODUCE HOLDING CORP
701 W Kimberly Ave # 210, Placentia
(92870-6342)
PHONE..........................714 630-6292
Ed Haft, *CEO*
Joe McCarthy, *CFO*
EMP: 360 **EST:** 2008
SALES (est): 56.2MM **Privately Held**
SIC: 5148 2037 0191 Fruits; vegetables;
frozen fruits & vegetables; general farms,
primarily crop

(P-8522)
SHAPIRO-GILMAN-SHANDLER CO (PA)
Also Called: S G S Produce
739 Decatur St, Los Angeles (90021-1649)
PHONE..........................213 593-1200
Carol C Shandler, *President*
Muriel Shandler, *Vice Pres*
Morris Shander, *Principal*
▲ **EMP:** 101
SQ FT: 50,000
SALES (est): 37.9MM **Privately Held**
WEB: www.sgsproduce.com
SIC: 5148 Fruits, fresh; vegetables

(P-8523)
SIMPLY FRESH FRUIT INC
4383 Exchange Ave, Vernon (90058-2619)
PHONE..........................323 586-0000
Gustavo Fernandez, *CEO*
William Sander, *President*
Jaxon Potter, *Vice Pres*
Bruce Spiro, *Vice Pres*
◆ **EMP:** 99
SQ FT: 60,000
SALES (est): 20.2MM
SALES (corp-wide): 26.8MM **Privately Held**
WEB: www.simplyfreshfruit.com
SIC: 5148 Fresh fruits & vegetables
PA: Sffi Company, Inc.
4383 Exchange Ave
Vernon CA 90058
323 586-0000

(P-8524)
SOUTHERN FRESH PROD PROVS INC
11954 Washington Blvd, Whittier
(90606-2608)
PHONE..........................562 236-2784
Daniel Meza, *President*
Daniel Silverman, *CFO*
Naomi Silverman, *Treasurer*
Sanford Deutsch, *Vice Pres*
Tracey Goldstein, *Admin Sec*
EMP: 65
SALES (est): 29.9MM **Privately Held**
SIC: 5148 Fresh fruits & vegetables

(P-8525)
STELLAR DISTRIBUTING INC
21801 Ave Ste 16, Madera (93637)
PHONE..........................559 664-8400
Paul Catania Jr, *President*
Robert Farnam, *CFO*
Kurt Cappelluti, *Manager*
◆ **EMP:** 350
SQ FT: 30,000
SALES: 61.6MM **Privately Held**
WEB: www.stellardistributing.com
SIC: 5148 Vegetables, fresh; fruits, fresh

(P-8526)
SUN PACIFIC MARKETING COOP INC
Also Called: Sun Pacific Farming
31452 Old River Rd, Bakersfield
(93311-9621)
PHONE..........................661 847-1015
Bob Dipiazza, *Branch Mgr*
Chris Bradley, *Controller*
EMP: 316
SALES (corp-wide): 336MM **Privately Held**
SIC: 5148 Fresh fruits & vegetables

PA: Sun Pacific Marketing Cooperative, Inc.
1095 E Green St
Pasadena CA 91106
213 612-9957

(P-8527)
SUNBERRY GROWERS LLC
710 La Guardia St Ste A, Salinas
(93905-3354)
PHONE..........................805 922-9888
Carlos Ramirez, *Mng Member*
EMP: 991
SALES (est): 30.9MM
SALES (corp-wide): 85MM **Privately Held**
SIC: 5148 Fresh fruits & vegetables
PA: Ramco Enterprises, L.P.
710 La Guardia St
Salinas CA 93905
831 758-5272

(P-8528)
SUNKIST GROWERS INC (PA)
27770 Entertainment Dr, Valencia
(91355-1092)
PHONE..........................661 290-8900
Russell Hanlin II, *President*
Christian Harris, *COO*
Richard G French, *CFO*
Kevin Fiori, *Exec VP*
Michael Wootton, *Senior VP*
◆ **EMP:** 223 **EST:** 1893
SQ FT: 50,000
SALES: 1.3B **Privately Held**
WEB: www.sunkist.com
SIC: 5148 2033 2037 2899 Fruits, fresh;
fruit juices: packaged in cans, jars, etc.;
fruit juice concentrates, frozen; lemon oil
(edible); orange oil; grapefruit oil; copy-
right buying & licensing; display equip-
ment, except refrigerated

(P-8529)
SUNRISE GROWERS INC (HQ)
Also Called: Sunrise Growers-Frozsun Foods
701 W Kimberly Ave # 210, Placentia
(92870-6354)
PHONE..........................714 630-2170
Edward Haft, *President*
Don Guthrie, *Vice Pres*
Maria Gonzalez, *General Mgr*
Melissa Messerli, *Manager*
◆ **EMP:** 300
SALES (est): 340.7MM
SALES (corp-wide): 1.2B **Privately Held**
WEB: www.frozsun.com
SIC: 5148 2037 Fruits, fresh; frozen fruits
& vegetables
PA: Sunopta Inc
2233 Argentia Rd Suite 401
Mississauga ON L5N 2
905 821-9669

(P-8530)
TOMATOES EXTRAORDINAIRE INC
Also Called: Specialty Produce
1929 Hancock St Ste 150, San Diego
(92110-2062)
P.O. Box 82066 (92138-2066)
PHONE..........................619 295-3172
Robert Harrington, *President*
Richard Harrington, *Vice Pres*
Cilley Christopher, *Technology*
Alan Guevara, *Technology*
Janet Harrington, *Accountant*
EMP: 150
SQ FT: 26,000
SALES (est): 73.6MM **Privately Held**
SIC: 5148 Fresh fruits & vegetables

(P-8531)
TURLOCK FRUIT CO (PA)
500 S Tully Rd, Turlock (95380-5121)
P.O. Box 130 (95381-0130)
PHONE..........................209 634-7207
Donald J Smith, *President*
Stephen H Smith, *Admin Sec*
EMP: 50
SQ FT: 1,500
SALES (est): 19.3MM **Privately Held**
SIC: 5148 Fruits

(P-8532)
UMINA BROS INC (PA)
1601 E Olympic Blvd # 403, Los Angeles
(90021-1943)
P.O. Box 861146 (90086-1146)
PHONE..........................213 622-9206
Richard Flamminio, *President*
Marie Mastrangelo, *COO*
Mark Golden, *Vice Pres*
Vic Grosso, *Executive*
Matt Beltran, *General Mgr*
◆ **EMP:** 100
SQ FT: 24,800
SALES (est): 54.6MM **Privately Held**
SIC: 5148 Fruits, fresh

(P-8533)
V & L PRODUCE INC
Also Called: General Produce
2550 E 25th St, Vernon (90058-1211)
PHONE..........................323 589-3125
Victor Mendoza, *President*
▲ **EMP:** 140
SQ FT: 12,000
SALES (est): 61.5MM **Privately Held**
SIC: 5148 Fresh fruits & vegetables

(P-8534)
VAL-PRO INC
Also Called: Continental Sales Co.
1661 Mcgarry St, Los Angeles
(90021-3116)
PHONE..........................213 689-0844
Joe Vidal, *Branch Mgr*
EMP: 60
SALES (corp-wide): 202.8MM **Privately Held**
SIC: 5148 Fruits, fresh
PA: Val-Pro, Inc.
1601 E Olympic Blvd # 300
Los Angeles CA 90021
213 627-8736

(P-8535)
VEG-FRESH FARMS LLC
1400 W Rincon St, Corona (92880-9205)
PHONE..........................800 422-5535
Lawrence Cancellieri Jr,
Mark Resnikoff,
Mark C Widder,
EMP: 220
SQ FT: 94,000
SALES (est): 189.6MM **Privately Held**
WEB: www.vegfresh.com
SIC: 5148 Vegetables, fresh; fruits

(P-8536)
VEGIWORKS INC
2101 Jerrold Ave, San Francisco
(94124-1009)
PHONE..........................415 643-8686
Shing Ho, *CFO*
Calvin Leong, *Vice Pres*
Phillip Woo, *Admin Sec*
EMP: 65
SQ FT: 16,000
SALES (est): 27.9MM **Privately Held**
WEB: www.vegiworks.com
SIC: 5148 Fresh fruits & vegetables

(P-8537)
VERITABLE VEGETABLE INC
1100 Cesar Chavez, San Francisco
(94124-1214)
PHONE..........................415 641-3500
Maryjane Evans, *President*
Gerilyn Botting, *CFO*
Shira Tannor, *Officer*
Ruth Lalputan, *Administration*
Keith Wall, *Business Mgr*
EMP: 57
SQ FT: 8,000
SALES (est): 38.5MM **Privately Held**
WEB: www.veritablevegetable.com
SIC: 5148 Fruits, fresh; vegetables

(P-8538)
WATSONVILLE COAST PRODUCE INC
275 Kearney Ext Frnt, Watsonville
(95076-4463)
P.O. Box 490 (95077-0490)
PHONE..........................831 722-3851
Gary L Manfre, *CEO*
Douglas Peterson, *Treasurer*
John Burkett, *Vice Pres*

Frank L Capurro, *Vice Pres*
Sergio Gomez, *Human Res Mgr*
EMP: 105
SQ FT: 40,000
SALES: 31MM **Privately Held**
SIC: 5148 Fruits, fresh

(P-8539)
WIEMAR DISTRIBUTORS INC
Also Called: M & M Distributors
1953 S Alameda St, Los Angeles
(90058-1013)
PHONE..........................213 747-7036
Marco Moreno, *President*
Rosa Moreno, *Vice Pres*
Margarita Orduno, *Controller*
▲ **EMP:** 65
SQ FT: 31,000
SALES: 34.6MM **Privately Held**
WEB: www.mmdistributors.org
SIC: 5148 Fruits, fresh

(P-8540)
WILLIAM BRAMMER
Also Called: Be Wise Ranch
20505 San Pasqual Rd, Escondido
(92025-7821)
PHONE..........................760 746-6006
William Brammer, *Owner*
Bill Brammer, *Telecomm Mgr*
EMP: 115
SALES (est): 11.5MM **Privately Held**
WEB: www.bewiseranch.com
SIC: 5148 0161 Fresh fruits & vegetables;
vegetables & melons

(P-8541)
WORLD VARIETY PRODUCE INC
Also Called: Melissas World Variety Produce
5325 S Soto St, Vernon (90058-3624)
P.O. Box 514599, Los Angeles (90051-2599)
PHONE..........................800 588-0151
Anna Raya, *Principal*
Joe V Hernandez, *President*
Sharon Hernandez, *Treasurer*
Samuel Rodriguez, *Executive*
Matt Bergholz, *Regional Mgr*
▲ **EMP:** 325
SQ FT: 244,000
SALES (est): 205.9MM **Privately Held**
SIC: 5148 Fruits, fresh

5149 Groceries & Related Prdts, NEC Wholesale

(P-8542)
ANNIES HOMEGROWN INC
1610 5th St, Berkeley (94710-1715)
PHONE..........................510 558-7500
John Foraker, *CEO*
Stephen Palmer, *Admin Sec*
David Tran, *VP Sales*
Sandy Cortez, *Manager*
John Farrell, *Manager*
▼ **EMP:** 75
SQ FT: 10,000
SALES (est): 18.4MM
SALES (corp-wide): 16.8B **Publicly Held**
SIC: 5149 Natural & organic foods
HQ: Annie's, Inc.
1610 5th St
Berkeley CA 94710

(P-8543)
APP WHOLESALE LLC
3686 E Olympic Blvd, Los Angeles
(90023-3146)
PHONE..........................323 980-3746
David Weissberg,
EMP: 500 **EST:** 2013
SQ FT: 220,000
SALES (est): 217MM **Privately Held**
SIC: 5149 2741 Specialty food items;
business service newsletters: publishing
& printing

PRODUCTS & SVCS

(P-8544)
ARCHER-DANIELS-MIDLAND COMPANY
ADM
3390 S Chestnut Ave, Fresno
(93725-2609)
PHONE.................................559 233-6262
Bob Rogers, *Plant Mgr*
EMP: 80
SQ FT: 25,000
SALES (corp-wide): 64.3B **Publicly Held**
WEB: www.admworld.com
SIC: 5149 2041 Oleomargarine; pancake batter, frozen or refrigerated
PA: Archer-Daniels-Midland Company
    77 W Wacker Dr Ste 4600
    Chicago IL 60601
    312 634-8100

(P-8545)
ARTISAN BAKERS
21684 8th St E Ste 400, Sonoma
(95476-2816)
PHONE.................................707 939-1765
Bill Dozier, *CEO*
Craig Ponsford, *President*
Elizabeth Ponsford, *Treasurer*
Sharon Ponsford, *Vice Pres*
Chris Jones, *Admin Sec*
EMP: 60
SQ FT: 4,400
SALES (est): 25.8MM **Privately Held**
WEB: www.artisanbakers.com
SIC: 5149 5461 Bakery products; bakeries

(P-8546)
ARYZTA LLC
Also Called: Fresh Start Bakeries
920 Shaw Rd, Stockton (95215-4014)
PHONE.................................209 469-4920
Dan Bailey, *Mng Officer*
Richard Sielman, *COO*
Steve Mills, *Vice Pres*
Shawn Damm, *Analyst*
Debbie Taylor, *Maintence Staff*
EMP: 50
SALES (corp-wide): 3.9B **Privately Held**
WEB: www.fsbglobal.net
SIC: 5149 Bakery products
HQ: Aryzta Llc
    6080 Center Dr Ste 900
    Los Angeles CA 90045
    310 417-4700

(P-8547)
ASHBURY MARKET INC
Also Called: Raison D'Etre Bakery
179 Starlite St, South San Francisco
(94080-6313)
PHONE.................................650 952-8889
Arnold E Wong, *President*
Richard Wong, *CEO*
Mary Wong, *CFO*
David Brogan, *Consultant*
EMP: 80
SQ FT: 10,000
SALES (est): 19.1MM **Privately Held**
SIC: 5149 Bakery products

(P-8548)
BAKERY EX SOUTHERN CAL LLC
1910 W Malvern Ave, Fullerton
(92833-2105)
PHONE.................................714 446-9470
Charles Burman,
Ronald Currie, *General Mgr*
EMP: 100
SQ FT: 28,000
SALES (est): 28MM **Privately Held**
SIC: 5149 Bakery products

(P-8549)
BAKKAVOR FOODS USA INC (DH)
18201 Central Ave, Carson (90746-4007)
PHONE.................................704 522-1977
Ivan Clingan, *CEO*
Jolyon Punnett, *CFO*
Joe Alonso, *CIO*
Christopher Cervantes, *Research*
Ron Pearson, *Engineer*
▲ EMP: 300
SQ FT: 100,000

SALES (est): 383.4MM
SALES (corp-wide): 2.3B **Privately Held**
WEB: www.twochefsonaroll.com
SIC: 5149 2051 Bakery products; bread, cake & related products

(P-8550)
BAY BREAD LLC
Also Called: La Boulange
2325 Pine St, San Francisco (94115-2714)
PHONE.................................415 440-0356
Pascal Rigo, *Mng Member*
Fred Estrada,
Lori Goodman,
EMP: 70
SALES (est): 14.4MM
SALES (corp-wide): 24.7B **Publicly Held**
SIC: 5149 Breading mixes
PA: Starbucks Corporation
    2401 Utah Ave S
    Seattle WA 98134
    206 447-1575

(P-8551)
BUENA VISTA FOOD PRODUCTS INC (DH)
823 W 8th St, Azusa (91702-2247)
PHONE.................................626 815-8859
Laura Trujillo, *President*
Norma Flores, *CFO*
Marta Nava, *Human Res Mgr*
Philippe Francoz, *VP Opers*
Brian Dedick, *Plant Mgr*
EMP: 115
SALES (est): 102MM **Privately Held**
WEB: www.dvfoods.com
SIC: 5149 Bakery products
HQ: Sterling Foods, Llc
    1075 Arion Pkwy
    San Antonio TX 78216
    210 490-1669

(P-8552)
CALIFORNIA BAKING COMPANY
Also Called: California Bread Co.
681 Anita St, Chula Vista (91911-4663)
PHONE.................................619 591-8289
Abraham Levy, *President*
EMP: 300
SALES (est): 31.2MM **Privately Held**
SIC: 5149 2051 Bakery products; sponge goods, bakery: except frozen

(P-8553)
CAMPANILE II LP
Also Called: Campanile Restaurant
13721 Ventura Blvd, Sherman Oaks
(91423-3023)
PHONE.................................323 939-6813
Lawrence E Silverton, *Partner*
EMP: 280
SALES (est): 17.3MM **Privately Held**
SIC: 5149 5812 Bakery products; American restaurant

(P-8554)
CAPITAL BRANDS LLC (HQ)
11601 Wilshire Blvd Fl 23, Los Angeles
(90025-1759)
P.O. Box 4564, Pacoima (91333-4564)
PHONE.................................310 996-7200
Rich Krause, *CEO*
Nick Sternberg, *COO*
Jeff Klausner, *Officer*
Bob Finnance, *Exec VP*
Richard Kam, *Exec VP*
EMP: 72
SALES (est): 65.1MM
SALES (corp-wide): 9.4MM **Privately Held**
SIC: 5149 Groceries & related products
PA: Capital Brands Holdings Inc.
    11601 Wilshire Blvd Fl 23
    Los Angeles CA 90025
    310 996-7200

(P-8555)
CHOOLJIAN BROS PACKING CO INC
3192 S Indianola Ave, Sanger
(93657-9716)
P.O. Box 395 (93657-0395)
PHONE.................................559 875-5501
Michael Chuoolgin, *CEO*
Darrell Smith, *Controller*
Dannie Cantos, *Director*

◆ EMP: 50
SQ FT: 1,800
SALES (est): 20.7MM **Privately Held**
SIC: 5149 Dried or canned foods

(P-8556)
CIXTA ENTERPRISES INC
21208 Sherman Way, Canoga Park
(91303-1512)
PHONE.................................818 346-1665
Miguel Gonzales, *President*
Ezequiel De Luna, *Manager*
EMP: 103
SALES (est): 5.5MM **Privately Held**
SIC: 5149 Groceries & related products

(P-8557)
CJ AMERICA INC (HQ)
Also Called: C J Foods
5700 Wilshire Blvd # 540, Los Angeles
(90036-3819)
PHONE.................................213 427-5566
Jin Won Kim, *President*
Soohee Lee, *CFO*
Hoongoo Jung, *Human Res Dir*
Glen Choi, *Human Res Mgr*
Mina Kang, *Marketing Staff*
◆ EMP: 54
SQ FT: 6,000
SALES (est): 55.9MM
SALES (corp-wide): 5.3B **Privately Held**
SIC: 5149 1541 3556 5169 Groceries & related products; food products manufacturing or packing plant construction; food products machinery; food additives & preservatives
PA: Cj Cheiljedang Corp.
    330 Dongho-Ro, Jung-Gu
    Seoul 04560
    822 674-0111

(P-8558)
CLIF BAR & COMPANY (PA)
1451 66th St, Emeryville (94608-1004)
PHONE.................................510 596-6300
Kevin Cleary, *CEO*
Kit Crawform, *Co-COB*
Rich Borango, *Vice Pres*
Randy Erickson, *Vice Pres*
Lynn Ineson, *Vice Pres*
▲ EMP: 153
SQ FT: 120,000
SALES (est): 2.3B **Privately Held**
WEB: www.clifbar.com
SIC: 5149 Specialty food items

(P-8559)
CLOVER-STORNETTA FARMS INC (PA)
Also Called: Clover Sonoma
1800 S Mcdowell Blvd, Petaluma
(94954-6962)
P.O. Box 750369 (94975-0369)
PHONE.................................707 769-3282
Marcus Benedetti, *President*
Dan Benedetti, *Ch of Bd*
Ken Gott, *COO*
Gene Benedetti, *Vice Pres*
Mkulima Britt, *Vice Pres*
EMP: 180
SQ FT: 80,000
SALES (est): 142.3MM **Privately Held**
WEB: www.clo-cow.com
SIC: 5149 5143 2026 Juices; dairy products, except dried or canned; milk & cream, except fermented, cultured & flavored

(P-8560)
COLUSA PRODUCE CORPORATION
1954 Progress Rd, Meridian (95957-9643)
PHONE.................................530 696-0121
Jim Wallace, *President*
Barbara Overton, *Office Mgr*
Joe Wallace, *Director*
◆ EMP: 78
SQ FT: 5,000
SALES (est): 16.7MM **Privately Held**
SIC: 5149 5159 5148 Spices & seasonings; broomcorn; fresh fruits & vegetables

(P-8561)
COMPLETE FOOD SERVICE INC
3815 Wabash Dr, Jurupa Valley
(91752-1143)
PHONE.................................951 685-8490
Keith Kahn, *President*
Mitchell Kahn, *Vice Pres*
Mark Kahn, *Admin Sec*
EMP: 90
SQ FT: 40,000
SALES (est): 17.5MM **Privately Held**
SIC: 5149 5722 Groceries & related products; sewing machines

(P-8562)
COMPLETELY FRESH FOODS INC
4401 S Downey Rd, Vernon (90058-2518)
P.O. Box 58667, Los Angeles (90058-0667)
PHONE.................................323 722-9136
Josh Solovy, *President*
Eric Litmanovich, *Vice Pres*
Levi Litmanovich, *Vice Pres*
EMP: 200
SQ FT: 15,000
SALES (est): 61.5MM **Privately Held**
SIC: 5149 5046 Specialty food items; commercial equipment; commercial cooking & food service equipment

(P-8563)
CORE NUTRITION LLC
100 N Pacific Coast Hwy, El Segundo
(90245-4359)
PHONE.................................310 640-0500
Lance Collins, *Mng Member*
Fred Pinczuk,
EMP: 82
SALES (est): 12.9MM **Publicly Held**
SIC: 5149 Mineral or spring water bottling
PA: Keurig Dr Pepper Inc.
    53 South Ave
    Burlington MA 01803

(P-8564)
CORE NUTRITION LLC
1222 E Grand Ave Ste 102, El Segundo
(90245-4219)
PHONE.................................310 640-0500
EMP: 50 EST: 2014
SALES (est): 4MM **Privately Held**
SIC: 5149 2834

(P-8565)
CORE-MARK INTERNATIONAL INC
200 Coremark Ct, Bakersfield
(93307-8402)
P.O. Box 70458 (93387-0458)
PHONE.................................661 366-2673
Caral Parker, *President*
EMP: 107
SALES (corp-wide): 16.4B **Publicly Held**
WEB: www.core-mark.com
SIC: 5149 Groceries & related products
HQ: Core-Mark International, Inc.
    1500 Solana Blvd Ste 3400
    Westlake TX 76262
    650 589-9445

(P-8566)
CORE-MARK INTERNATIONAL INC
2311 E 48th St, Vernon (90058-2007)
PHONE.................................323 583-6531
Julian Puentes, *Branch Mgr*
EMP: 150
SALES (corp-wide): 16.4B **Publicly Held**
WEB: www.core-mark.com
SIC: 5149 5194 5145 Groceries & related products; tobacco & tobacco products; confectionery
HQ: Core-Mark International, Inc.
    1500 Solana Blvd Ste 3400
    Westlake TX 76262
    650 589-9445

(P-8567)
CORE-MARK INTERNATIONAL INC
3970 Pell Cir, Sacramento (95838-2511)
PHONE.................................509 535-9768
Christopher Ladesich, *Principal*
EMP: 150

SQ FT: 25,000
SALES (corp-wide): 16.4B **Publicly Held**
WEB: www.core-mark.com
SIC: 5149 5194 5141 Groceries & related
   products; tobacco & tobacco products;
   groceries, general line
HQ: Core-Mark International, Inc.
   1500 Solana Blvd Ste 3400
   Westlake TX 76262
   650 589-9445

(P-8568)
CORE-MARK INTERNATIONAL INC
31300 Medallion Dr, Hayward
(94544-7902)
PHONE..................................510 487-3000
Bob Norton, *Manager*
EMP: 150
SALES (corp-wide): 16.4B **Publicly Held**
WEB: www.core-mark.com
SIC: 5149 5194 5145 5141 Groceries &
   related products; tobacco & tobacco prod-
   ucts; confectionery; groceries, general
   line
HQ: Core-Mark International, Inc.
   1500 Solana Blvd Ste 3400
   Westlake TX 76262
   650 589-9445

(P-8569)
CORNER BAKERY STORE
1040 W Imperial Hwy Ste A, La Habra
(90631-0608)
PHONE..................................714 459-1420
Jim Vinz, *CEO*
EMP: 50
SALES (est): 2MM **Privately Held**
SIC: 5149 Bakery products

(P-8570)
CREATIVE ENERGY FOODS INC
9957 Medford Ave Ste 4, Oakland
(94603-2360)
PHONE..................................510 638-8668
Richard C Dwinell, *CEO*
George Jewell, *President*
Bennet Marv, *CFO*
Jacker Wong, *CFO*
Drew Goldberg, *Vice Pres*
▲ **EMP:** 95
SQ FT: 105,000
SALES (est): 56.2MM **Privately Held**
WEB: www.energybar.com
SIC: 5149 2026 Health foods; dips, sour
   cream based

(P-8571)
CTC FOOD INTERNATIONAL INC (PA)
Also Called: Oriental Trading Co
50 W Ohio Ave, Richmond (94804-2039)
PHONE..................................650 873-7600
Ike Fukmoto, *President*
Yoichi Kadona, *Shareholder*
Morihiro Ogawa, *Shareholder*
Hideki Otani, *Ch of Bd*
Lawrence Tanita, *CFO*
◆ **EMP:** 50
SQ FT: 40,000
SALES (est): 16.9MM **Privately Held**
SIC: 5149 5182 Specialty food items; wine

(P-8572)
CULINARY HISPANIC FOODS INC
Also Called: Productos Chata
805 Bow St, Chula Vista (91914)
PHONE..................................619 955-6101
Jorge Aguilar, *CEO*
Carlos Machado, *Principal*
▲ **EMP:** 1458
SQ FT: 4,000
SALES: 1MM **Privately Held**
SIC: 5149 Canned goods: fruit, vegetables,
   seafood, meats, etc.

(P-8573)
DS SERVICES OF AMERICA INC
Also Called: Sparkletts
4548 Azusa Canyon Rd, Irwindale
(91706-2742)
PHONE..................................626 472-7201
Linda Gonzales, *Manager*
Mark Iwasaki, *Info Tech Mgr*

EMP: 200
SQ FT: 67,508
SALES (corp-wide): 2.2B **Privately Held**
WEB: www.suntorywatergroup.com
SIC: 5149 5963 Water, distilled; direct sell-
   ing establishments
HQ: Ds Services Of America, Inc.
   2300 Windy Ridge Pkwy Se 500n
   Atlanta GA 30339
   770 933-1400

(P-8574)
EL GUAPO SPICES INC (PA)
Also Called: El Guapo Spices and Herbs Pkg
6200 E Slauson Ave, Commerce
(90040-3012)
PHONE..................................213 312-1300
Dan Terrazas, *President*
EMP: 100
SALES (est): 11.8MM **Privately Held**
SIC: 5149 Spices & seasonings

(P-8575)
FALCON TRADING COMPANY (PA)
Also Called: Sunridge Farms
423 Salinas Rd, Royal Oaks (95076-5232)
PHONE..................................831 786-7000
Morty Cohen, *CEO*
Rebecca Cohen, *Vice Pres*
Bruce Brinker, *Executive*
Denise Markowitz, *Executive*
Robin Van Soest, *Executive*
◆ **EMP:** 215 **EST:** 1977
SQ FT: 24,500
SALES (est): 108.7MM **Privately Held**
WEB: www.sunridgefarms.com
SIC: 5149 Natural & organic foods

(P-8576)
FAMOUS RAMONA WATER INC
250 Aqua Ln, Ramona (92065-2024)
P.O. Box 1195 (92065-0860)
PHONE..................................760 789-0174
Julian C Filer, *CEO*
Joe Bruni, *President*
Mark Filer, *Exec VP*
Debbie Bruni, *Admin Sec*
EMP: 50
SQ FT: 48,000
SALES (est): 14.1MM **Privately Held**
WEB: www.famousramonawater.com
SIC: 5149 5085 Mineral or spring water
   bottling; commercial containers

(P-8577)
FIJI WATER COMPANY LLC (HQ)
11444 W Olympic Blvd # 250, Los Angeles
(90064-1534)
PHONE..................................310 966-5700
Stewart A Resnick, *Ch of Bd*
Kim Katzenberger, *CFO*
William Foltz, *Senior VP*
Scott Parido, *Vice Pres*
Julie Silver, *Vice Pres*
◆ **EMP:** 50
SQ FT: 12,000
SALES (est): 43MM
SALES (corp-wide): 1.5B **Privately Held**
WEB: www.fijiwater.com
SIC: 5149 Mineral or spring water bottling
PA: The Wonderful Company Llc
   11444 W Olympic Blvd # 210
   Los Angeles CA 90064
   310 966-5700

(P-8578)
FRESH GRILL LLC
111 E Garry Ave, Santa Ana (92707-4201)
PHONE..................................714 444-2126
Jeff Heavirland, *Mng Member*
Diana Rodriguez, *Human Res Dir*
Iris Rodriguez, *Purch Mgr*
Phil Abreo, *Sales Staff*
▲ **EMP:** 200
SQ FT: 27,000
SALES (est): 62.3MM
SALES (corp-wide): 10.8MM **Privately Held**
WEB: www.freshgrillfoods.com
SIC: 5149 8742 Specialty food items; food
   & beverage consultant
PA: Fb Holding Company, Llc
   111 E Garry Ave
   Santa Ana CA 92707
   714 444-2126

(P-8579)
FRESHOLOGY INC
12400 Wilshire Blvd # 1180, Los Angeles
(90025-1058)
PHONE..................................818 847-1888
Todd Demann, *Principal*
▲ **EMP:** 71
SQ FT: 15,500
SALES (est): 15.5MM **Privately Held**
WEB: www.freshology.com/
SIC: 5149 Diet foods

(P-8580)
FUJI FOOD PRODUCTS INC (PA)
14420 Bloomfield Ave, Santa Fe Springs
(90670-5410)
PHONE..................................562 404-2590
Farrell Hirsch, *CEO*
Humberto Villagomez, *COO*
Javier Aceves, *CFO*
Diana Alonso, *Admin Asst*
Deeda Arellano, *Admin Asst*
▲ **EMP:** 100 **EST:** 2010
SQ FT: 90,000
SALES (est): 405.9MM **Privately Held**
WEB: www.fujifood.com
SIC: 5149 Groceries & related products

(P-8581)
FUJI FOOD PRODUCTS INC
8660 Miramar Rd Ste N, San Diego
(92126-4362)
PHONE..................................619 268-3118
Kenny Sung, *Branch Mgr*
EMP: 125
SALES (corp-wide): 405.9MM **Privately Held**
WEB: www.fujifood.com
SIC: 5149 Specialty food items
PA: Fuji Food Products, Inc.
   14420 Bloomfield Ave
   Santa Fe Springs CA 90670
   562 404-2590

(P-8582)
GALASSOS BAKERY (PA)
10820 San Sevaine Way, Jurupa Valley
(91752-1116)
PHONE..................................951 360-1211
Jeannette Galasso, *President*
Mark Bailey, *Treasurer*
Rick Vargas, *Vice Pres*
Pearl Denault, *Project Mgr*
Maryann Sclifo, *Supervisor*
EMP: 180
SQ FT: 110,000
SALES (est): 120.6MM **Privately Held**
WEB: www.galassos.com
SIC: 5149 Bakery products

(P-8583)
GIANNAS BAKING COMPANY
11165 Commercial Pkwy, Castroville
(95012-3207)
PHONE..................................831 633-3700
Peter Uli, *President*
EMP: 54
SALES (est): 12.6MM **Privately Held**
WEB: www.giannas.com
SIC: 5149 Bakery products

(P-8584)
GOLDA & I CHOCOLATIERS INC
23052 Alicia Pkwy Ste H, Mission Viejo
(92692-1661)
PHONE..................................949 660-9581
EMP: 55
SQ FT: 3,000
SALES (est): 6.5MM **Privately Held**
WEB: www.crowncityconfections.com
SIC: 5149

(P-8585)
GOURMET INDIA FOOD COMPANY LLC
12220 Rivera Rd Ste A, Whittier
(90606-6206)
PHONE..................................562 698-9763
Sam Jeevan,
Saleem Hai,
▲ **EMP:** 75
SALES (est): 12.8MM **Privately Held**
SIC: 5149 Bakery products

(P-8586)
HARRIS FREEMAN & CO INC (PA)
Also Called: Harris Tea Company
3110 E Miraloma Ave, Anaheim
(92806-1906)
PHONE..................................714 765-1190
Anil J Shah, *CEO*
Kevin Shah, *President*
Martin Clay, *CFO*
Meena Shah, *Treasurer*
Richard Haas, *Vice Pres*
◆ **EMP:** 500
SQ FT: 58,000
SALES (est): 292.1MM **Privately Held**
SIC: 5149 2099 Tea; spices, including
   grinding

(P-8587)
HEALTH VALLEY FOODS INC
16007 Cmino De La Cantera, Irwindale
(91702)
PHONE..................................626 334-3241
▲ **EMP:** 300
SALES (est): 14.2MM **Publicly Held**
WEB: www.hain-celestial.com
SIC: 5149 Health foods; natural & organic
   foods
PA: The Hain Celestial Group Inc
   1111 Marcus Ave Ste 100
   New Hyde Park NY 11042

(P-8588)
INTERBAKE FOODS LLC
Also Called: Norse Dairy Systems
1910 W Temple St, Los Angeles
(90026-4929)
P.O. Box 26338 (90026-0338)
PHONE..................................213 484-8161
Randy Obrien, *Branch Mgr*
Jack Frysvtak, *Plant Mgr*
EMP: 60
SALES (corp-wide): 36.8B **Privately Held**
WEB: www.interbake.com
SIC: 5149 Bakery products
HQ: Interbake Foods Llc
   3951 Westerre Pkwy # 200
   Henrico VA 23233
   804 755-7107

(P-8589)
IONICS ALTRPURE WTR CRPARATION
Also Called: Apollo Cpr
7777 Industry Ave, Pico Rivera
(90660-4303)
PHONE..................................562 948-2188
Winston Mar, *Vice Pres*
EMP: 95
SQ FT: 12,000
SALES (est): 7.4MM **Privately Held**
SIC: 5149 5999 Mineral or spring water
   bottling; water purification equipment

(P-8590)
ITALFOODS INC
205 Shaw Rd, South San Francisco
(94080-6605)
P.O. Box 2563 (94083-2563)
PHONE..................................650 877-0724
Georgette Guerra, *CEO*
Donald Raphael, *General Mgr*
Ahliza Wong, *Analyst*
Richard Degaetano, *Purchasing*
Lorenzo Chiostri, *Sales Staff*
▲ **EMP:** 80 **EST:** 1978
SQ FT: 114,000
SALES (est): 31.3MM **Privately Held**
WEB: www.italfoods.com
SIC: 5149 Specialty food items

(P-8591)
J & D MEAT COMPANY
Also Called: JD Food
4671 E Edgar Ave, Fresno (93725)
P.O. Box 12051 (93776-2051)
PHONE..................................559 445-1123
Mark K Ford, *President*
Robert Maxey, *CFO*
Jon Trueblood, *General Mgr*
Steven Maxey, *Admin Sec*
Steve Lloyd, *Human Res Mgr*
EMP: 115
SQ FT: 51,000

PRODUCTS & SVCS

SALES (est): 81.1MM **Privately Held**
WEB: www.jdfoodservice.com
SIC: 5149 5147 5148 5143 Groceries & related products; meats & meat products; fresh fruits & vegetables; dairy products, except dried or canned; packaged frozen goods

(P-8592)
JACMAR DDC LLC
Also Called: Jacmar Food Service Dist
3057 Promenade St, West Sacramento (95691-5941)
PHONE..................916 372-9795
James A Dalpozzo, *Mng Member*
David Reid,
EMP: 55
SQ FT: 100,000
SALES (est): 19.8MM
SALES (corp-wide): 68.2MM **Privately Held**
WEB: www.jacmar.com
SIC: 5149 Natural & organic foods
PA: The Jacmar Companies
300 Baldwin Park Blvd
City Of Industry CA 91746
800 834-8806

(P-8593)
JAGPREET ENTERPRISES LLC
Also Called: Quick-N-Ezee Indian Foods
25823 Clawiter Rd, Hayward (94545-3217)
PHONE..................510 336-8376
Sukhjeet K Singh, *CEO*
Cecilia Huffstutler, *Vice Pres*
Bonnie Chimni, *Opers Staff*
Dalbir Singh, *Director*
Joe Vitale, *Manager*
▲ **EMP:** 150
SQ FT: 30,000
SALES (est): 63.2MM **Privately Held**
WEB: www.sukhis.com
SIC: 5149 Groceries & related products

(P-8594)
JFC INTERNATIONAL INC (HQ)
7101 E Slauson Ave, Commerce (90040-3622)
P.O. Box 875349, Los Angeles (90087-0449)
PHONE..................323 721-6100
Yoshiyuki Ishigaki, *CEO*
Hiroyuki Enomoto, *President*
Masanori Takenaka, *Vice Pres*
Ichiro Komatsubara, *Branch Mgr*
Kiyoshi Tamai, *Branch Mgr*
◆ **EMP:** 203 **EST:** 1948
SALES (est): 410.4MM **Privately Held**
WEB: www.jfc.com
SIC: 5149 7389 Specialty food items; labeling bottles, cans, cartons, etc.

(P-8595)
JFC INTERNATIONAL INC
Also Called: Los Angeles Branch
7101 E Slauson Ave, Commerce (90040-3622)
PHONE..................323 721-6900
Shoso Ota, *Branch Mgr*
EMP: 165 **Privately Held**
SIC: 5149 Specialty food items
HQ: Jfc International Inc.
7101 E Slauson Ave
Commerce CA 90040
323 721-6100

(P-8596)
JOHNS DOG FOOD DISTRIBUTING
Also Called: John's Pet Products
1633 Monterey Hwy, San Jose (95112-6111)
PHONE..................408 275-1943
Johannes G Rademakers, *Owner*
EMP: 60 **EST:** 1970
SQ FT: 7,000
SALES (est): 2.8MM **Privately Held**
SIC: 5149 5999 Pet foods; pet supplies

(P-8597)
JOYRIDE COFFEE DISTRS LLC
1485 Yosemite Ave, San Francisco (94124-3321)
PHONE..................718 841-7206
EMP: 78

SALES (corp-wide): 10MM **Privately Held**
SIC: 5149 Coffee & tea
PA: Joyride Coffee Distributors, Llc
3712 56th St
Woodside NY 11377
917 670-3314

(P-8598)
K T LUCKY CO INC
10925 Schmidt Rd, El Monte (91733-2707)
PHONE..................626 579-7272
Hang Huynh, *President*
▲ **EMP:** 70
SQ FT: 12,000
SALES (est): 11.9MM **Privately Held**
SIC: 5149 Macaroni; rice, polished

(P-8599)
KRADJIAN IMPORTING COMPANY INC (PA)
5018 San Fernando Rd, Glendale (91204-1114)
PHONE..................818 502-1313
Raffi Kradjian, *President*
Viken Kradjian, *Vice Pres*
Ram Sethuram, *Controller*
Sahag Arabian, *Marketing Staff*
◆ **EMP:** 61 **EST:** 1987
SQ FT: 50,000
SALES (est): 34.7MM **Privately Held**
SIC: 5149 Specialty food items

(P-8600)
KRAFT HEINZ FOODS COMPANY
5000 Hopyard Rd Ste 235, Pleasanton (94588-3314)
PHONE..................925 469-0057
Carroll Wine, *Branch Mgr*
EMP: 500
SALES (corp-wide): 26.2B **Publicly Held**
SIC: 5149 Groceries & related products
HQ: Kraft Heinz Foods Company
1 Ppg Pl Fl 34
Pittsburgh PA 15222
412 456-5700

(P-8601)
KRAFT HEINZ FOODS COMPANY
Also Called: Kraft Foods
1055 E North Ave, Fresno (93725-1914)
PHONE..................559 499-5300
Tony Lacerva, *General Mgr*
EMP: 50
SALES (corp-wide): 26.2B **Publicly Held**
WEB: www.kraftfoods.com
SIC: 5149 Groceries & related products
HQ: Kraft Heinz Foods Company
1 Ppg Pl Fl 34
Pittsburgh PA 15222
412 456-5700

(P-8602)
KRONOS FOODS CORP
Also Called: Rain Creek Baking
2401 W Almond Ave, Madera (93637-4807)
PHONE..................559 674-4445
Michael Austin, *CEO*
EMP: 75
SALES (corp-wide): 120MM **Privately Held**
SIC: 5149 Bakery products
PA: Kronos Foods Corp.
1 Kronos
Glendale Heights IL 60139

(P-8603)
LA PROVENCE INC
Also Called: La Provence Bakery
1370 W San Marcos Blvd # 130, San Marcos (92078-1601)
PHONE..................760 736-3299
Philip Dardaine, *CEO*
Karen Dardaine, *Corp Secy*
Thierry Bouchereau, *Vice Pres*
EMP: 95
SQ FT: 6,000
SALES (est): 25.5MM **Privately Held**
SIC: 5149 Bakery products

(P-8604)
LA TORTILLA FACTORY INC (PA)
3300 Westwind Blvd, Santa Rosa (95403-8273)
PHONE..................707 586-4000

Samuel Carlos Tamayo, *CEO*
Carlos G Tamayo, *President*
Carlos Tamayo, *President*
Dave Davis, *COO*
Willie Tamayo, *Exec VP*
EMP: 280 **EST:** 1977
SALES (est): 157.8MM **Privately Held**
WEB: www.latortillafactory.com
SIC: 5149 2051 Specialty food items; bakery products; bread, cake & related products

(P-8605)
LENORE JOHN & CO (PA)
1250 Delevan Dr, San Diego (92102-2437)
PHONE..................619 232-6136
John G Lenore, *CEO*
Jamie Lenore, *President*
Doris Anthony, *Human Res Dir*
Alfonzo Hernandez, *Sales Staff*
Zach Leeds, *Warehouse Mgr*
◆ **EMP:** 120
SQ FT: 50,000
SALES (est): 173.8MM **Privately Held**
WEB: www.johnlenore.com
SIC: 5149 5182 5181 Soft drinks; mineral or spring water bottling; wine; liquor; beer & other fermented malt liquors

(P-8606)
MHH HOLDINGS INC
5653 Alton Pkwy, Irvine (92618-4058)
PHONE..................949 651-9903
Cynthia Espere, *Branch Mgr*
EMP: 177
SALES (corp-wide): 68.2MM **Privately Held**
SIC: 5149 Tea
PA: Mhh Holdings, Inc.
4580 Calle Alto
Camarillo CA 93012
805 484-7924

(P-8607)
MHH HOLDINGS INC
415 S Lake Ave Ste 108, Pasadena (91101-5047)
PHONE..................626 744-9370
Xiomara Bellido, *Principal*
EMP: 118
SALES (corp-wide): 68.2MM **Privately Held**
SIC: 5149 Tea
PA: Mhh Holdings, Inc.
4580 Calle Alto
Camarillo CA 93012
805 484-7924

(P-8608)
MIGHTY LEAF TEA
100 Smith Ranch Rd # 120, San Rafael (94903-1979)
PHONE..................415 491-2650
Shiela Stanziale, *CEO*
Jill Portman, *President*
Bliss Dake, *Vice Pres*
◆ **EMP:** 65
SQ FT: 5,000
SALES (est): 26.2MM
SALES (corp-wide): 2.4B **Privately Held**
WEB: www.mightyleaf.com
SIC: 5149 5499 Tea; tea
HQ: Peet's Coffee & Tea, Llc
1400 Park Ave
Emeryville CA 94608
510 594-2100

(P-8609)
MONDELEZ GLOBAL LLC
Also Called: Nabisco
5815 Clark St, Ontario (91761-3676)
PHONE..................909 605-0140
Botie Magee, *Branch Mgr*
EMP: 70 **Publicly Held**
WEB: www.kraftfoods.com
SIC: 5149 2099 2052 Crackers, cookies & bakery products; food preparations; cookies & crackers
HQ: Mondelez Global Llc
3 N Pkwy Ste 300
Deerfield IL 60015
847 943-4000

(P-8610)
MONSTER ENERGY COMPANY (HQ)
1 Monster Way, Corona (92879-7101)
PHONE..................951 739-6200
Rodney C Sacks, *CEO*
Hilton H Scholsberg, *Vice Ch Bd*
Mark Hall, *Bd of Directors*
John Beasley, *Vice Pres*
Paul Dechary, *Vice Pres*
◆ **EMP:** 153
SQ FT: 300,000
SALES (est): 1.1B
SALES (corp-wide): 3.8B **Publicly Held**
WEB: www.hansens.com
SIC: 5149 Juices; soft drinks
PA: Monster Beverage Corporation
1 Monster Way
Corona CA 92879
951 739-6200

(P-8611)
MORRIS NATIONAL INC (HQ)
Also Called: McGreever and Danlee Very
760 N Mckeever Ave, Azusa (91702-2349)
PHONE..................626 385-2000
Gerry Morris Zubatoff, *CEO*
Gerald Morris, *President*
David Kiel, *CFO*
Bram Zubatoff, *Admin Sec*
◆ **EMP:** 56
SQ FT: 125,000
SALES (est): 173.2MM
SALES (corp-wide): 143.3MM **Privately Held**
WEB: www.morrisnational.com
SIC: 5149 5145 Chocolate; confectionery
PA: Morris National Inc
100 Jacob Keffer Pky
Concord ON L4K 4
905 879-7777

(P-8612)
MUTUAL TRADING CO INC (HQ)
Also Called: M T C
431 Crocker St, Los Angeles (90013-2180)
PHONE..................213 626-9458
Kosei Yamamoto, *CEO*
Noritoshi Kanai, *President*
Seicho Fujikawa, *Vice Pres*
Kotaro Hoshizaki, *Principal*
Keita Yagai, *Info Tech Dir*
◆ **EMP:** 105
SQ FT: 100,000
SALES (est): 152.6MM **Privately Held**
WEB: www.lamtc.com
SIC: 5149 5141 5023 Groceries & related products; groceries, general line; home furnishings

(P-8613)
MUTUAL TRADING CO INC
Also Called: San Diego Mutual Trading
13790 Stowe Dr Ste A, Poway (92064-8841)
PHONE..................858 748-9458
Min Lee, *General Mgr*
EMP: 50
SQ FT: 61,639 **Privately Held**
SIC: 5149 5023 5141 Groceries & related products; home furnishings; groceries, general line
HQ: Mutual Trading Co., Inc.
431 Crocker St
Los Angeles CA 90013
213 626-9458

(P-8614)
NAVITAS LLC
Also Called: Navitas Naturals
15 Pamaron Way, Novato (94949-6231)
PHONE..................415 883-8116
Zachary Adelman, *Mng Member*
Ira Haber, *COO*
Mary Gadd, *Sales Staff*
◆ **EMP:** 50
SALES (est): 19.2MM **Privately Held**
WEB: www.navitasnaturals.com
SIC: 5149 Health foods

(P-8615)
NESTLE WATERS NORTH AMER INC
Also Called: Arrowhead Water
619 N Main St, Orange (92868-1103)
PHONE.................................714 532-6220
Dan Miller, *Sales/Mktg Mgr*
EMP: 135
SQ FT: 16,312
SALES (corp-wide): 92B **Privately Held**
WEB: www.zephyronline.com
SIC: 5149 5499 5963 5078 Water, distilled; water: distilled mineral or spring; bottled water delivery; refrigeration equipment & supplies; plumbing & hydronic heating supplies
HQ: Nestle Waters North America Inc.
900 Long Ridge Rd Bldg 2
Stamford CT 06902

(P-8616)
NEUROBRANDS LLC
Also Called: Neuro Drinks
15303 Ventura Blvd # 675, Sherman Oaks (91403-6608)
PHONE.................................310 393-6444
Diana Jenkins, *CEO*
Scott Laporta, *President*
Rigo De Leon, *Area Mgr*
Armando Lassale, *Area Mgr*
David O'Connor, *Area Mgr*
▲ EMP: 125
SALES (est): 82.3MM **Privately Held**
SIC: 5149 Soft drinks

(P-8617)
NEW DESSERTS INC
Also Called: Just Desserts
5000 Fulton Dr, Fairfield (94534-1677)
PHONE.................................415 780-6860
Michael Mendes, *CEO*
Marc Cabi, *Technology*
Leighton Mue, *VP Finance*
John Wohlgemuth, *VP Opers*
EMP: 93
SQ FT: 73,500
SALES (est): 54.8MM **Privately Held**
SIC: 5149 2024 Bakery products; ice cream & frozen desserts

(P-8618)
NGS GROUP INC
4152 W Washington Blvd, Los Angeles (90018-1054)
PHONE.................................323 735-1700
Steven Ngu, *President*
EMP: 54
SQ FT: 1,500
SALES (est): 5.9MM **Privately Held**
WEB: www.pacificfrenchbakery.com
SIC: 5149 Bakery products

(P-8619)
NICOLA INTERNATIONAL INC
11119 Dora St, Sun Valley (91352-3339)
PHONE.................................818 767-1133
Nicola Khachatoorian, *President*
Adik Khachatoorian, *Corp Secy*
Alice Toomanian, *Exec VP*
▲ EMP: 125
SQ FT: 150,000
SALES (est): 11.1MM **Privately Held**
WEB: www.nicolainternational.com
SIC: 5149 5148 Cooking oils & shortenings; vegetables

(P-8620)
NOWHER PARTNERS LLC
Also Called: Erewhon Natural Foods Market
26767 Agoura Rd Ste A, Calabasas (91302-1992)
PHONE.................................818 857-3366
Victor Grenner, *Branch Mgr*
EMP: 100
SALES (corp-wide): 21.6MM **Privately Held**
SIC: 5149 Natural & organic foods
PA: Nowhere Partners Corp.
7600 Beverly Blvd
Los Angeles CA 90036
818 857-3366

(P-8621)
OH MY GREEN INC
1845 Rollins Rd, Burlingame (94010-2209)
PHONE.................................650 989-8181
Michael Heinrich, *CEO*
Craig Simmons,
Jennifer Sassenus, *Executive Asst*
Brian Maloney, *Warehouse Mgr*
EMP: 80 EST: 2013
SALES (est): 29.8MM **Privately Held**
SIC: 5149 Health foods

(P-8622)
ORWICK FRESH FOODS INC
7940 Cherry Ave Ste 203, Fontana (92336-4021)
PHONE.................................909 985-5604
Richard V Orwick, *President*
EMP: 50 EST: 2000
SALES (est): 7.1MM **Privately Held**
SIC: 5149 Natural & organic foods

(P-8623)
PACIFIC FOODS & DIST INC
3431 W Carriage Dr, Santa Ana (92704-6411)
PHONE.................................714 547-0787
James H Loftus Jr, *President*
EMP: 100
SALES (est): 32.1MM **Privately Held**
WEB: www.pacificfoodsdistribution.com
SIC: 5149 Bakery products

(P-8624)
PASADENA BAKING CO
70 W Pal Meto Ave, Pasadena (91105)
PHONE.................................626 796-5093
Armen Shirvanian, *Partner*
Akis Markoutsis, *Partner*
Gonzalo Wieler, *Sales Mgr*
EMP: 50
SQ FT: 10,000
SALES (est): 7.9MM **Privately Held**
WEB: www.pasadenabaking.com
SIC: 5149 Bakery products

(P-8625)
PASTA PICCININI INC
950 N Fair Oaks Ave, Pasadena (91103-3009)
PHONE.................................626 798-0841
Stefano Piccinini, *Principal*
William Coulvane, *Admin Mgr*
Sandra Bane, *Finance Mgr*
Peggy Flores, *Human Res Mgr*
▲ EMP: 65
SQ FT: 30,000
SALES (est): 20.5MM **Privately Held**
WEB: www.gourmetpasta.com
SIC: 5149 5812 Pasta & rice; eating places

(P-8626)
PASTA SHOP (PA)
Also Called: Market Hall Foods
5655 College Ave Ste 201, Oakland (94618-1583)
PHONE.................................510 250-6005
Sara Wilson, *Managing Prtnr*
Anthony Wilson, *Partner*
Peter Wilson, *Partner*
Nel Da Silva, *Executive*
Asha Loupy, *Administration*
▲ EMP: 80
SQ FT: 4,500
SALES (est): 65.7MM **Privately Held**
WEB: www.rockridgemarkethall.com
SIC: 5149 5411 5812 5431 Pasta & rice; delicatessens; caterers; fruit & vegetable markets

(P-8627)
PEPSI-COLA METRO BTLG CO INC
3029 Coffey Ln, Santa Rosa (95403-2513)
PHONE.................................707 535-4560
Brad Pighin, *General Mgr*
EMP: 80
SQ FT: 32,000
SALES (corp-wide): 64.6B **Publicly Held**
WEB: www.joy-of-cola.com
SIC: 5149 4225 2086 Soft drinks; general warehousing & storage; bottled & canned soft drinks
HQ: Pepsi-Cola Metropolitan Bottling Company, Inc.
1111 Westchester Ave
White Plains NY 10604
914 767-6000

(P-8628)
PEPSI-COLA METRO BTLG CO INC
200 River Rd, Modesto (95351-3912)
PHONE.................................209 557-5100
Jake Aigen, *Sales/Mktg Mgr*
Brian Ollar, *Sales Associate*
Paul Trisler, *Manager*
EMP: 150
SQ FT: 5,000
SALES (corp-wide): 64.6B **Publicly Held**
WEB: www.joy-of-cola.com
SIC: 5149 2086 Soft drinks; bottled & canned soft drinks
HQ: Pepsi-Cola Metropolitan Bottling Company, Inc.
1111 Westchester Ave
White Plains NY 10604
914 767-6000

(P-8629)
PERFECT BAR LLC
Also Called: Perfect Snacks
3931 Sorrento Valley Blvd, San Diego (92121-1402)
PHONE.................................866 628-8548
Bill Keith, *CEO*
Allison Jennings, *Human Res Mgr*
EMP: 95
SQ FT: 16,000
SALES (est): 55.9MM **Publicly Held**
SIC: 5149 Health foods
PA: Mondelez International, Inc.
3 Parkway North Blvd # 300
Deerfield IL 60015

(P-8630)
PERFORMANCE FOOD GROUP INC
Also Called: Performance Foodservice
6211 Las Positas Rd, Livermore (94551-5101)
PHONE.................................925 456-8664
Bill Bolton, *Branch Mgr*
EMP: 90
SALES (corp-wide): 19.7B **Publicly Held**
WEB: www.romafood.com
SIC: 5149 5141 Pizza supplies; groceries, general line
HQ: Performance Food Group, Inc.
12500 West Creek Pkwy
Richmond VA 23238
804 484-7700

(P-8631)
POMWONDERFUL LLC (DH)
11444 W Olympic Blvd, Los Angeles (90064-1549)
PHONE.................................310 966-5800
Richard Cottrell, *CEO*
Matt Tupper, *President*
Bradley Gillespie, *Vice Pres*
Kurt Vetter, *Vice Pres*
Leon Tin Change, *Controller*
◆ EMP: 116
SALES (est): 500.4MM
SALES (corp-wide): 1.5B **Privately Held**
WEB: www.pomwonderful.com
SIC: 5149 5148 5085 Beverage concentrates; juices; tea; fruits, fresh; plastic bottles
HQ: Pom Wonderful Holdings Llc
11444 W Olympic Blvd # 210
Los Angeles CA 90064
310 966-5800

(P-8632)
POMWONDERFUL LLC
900 Airport Blvd, Mendota (93640-2441)
PHONE.................................310 966-5800
Larry Isonio, *Branch Mgr*
EMP: 100
SALES (corp-wide): 1.5B **Privately Held**
SIC: 5149 5148 5085 Beverage concentrates; fruits, fresh; plastic bottles
HQ: Pomwonderful Llc
11444 W Olympic Blvd
Los Angeles CA 90064
310 966-5800

(P-8633)
POSH BAGEL INC (PA)
445 Nelo St, Santa Clara (95054-2145)
PHONE.................................408 980-8451
Jeff Ottoveggio, *President*
Sergio Donoso, *Vice Pres*
EMP: 75
SQ FT: 15,000
SALES (est): 38.3MM **Privately Held**
WEB: www.theposhbagel.com
SIC: 5149 Bakery products

(P-8634)
PRESSED JUICERY INC
3530 E Church Ave, Fresno (93725-1337)
PHONE.................................559 777-8900
Hayden Slater, *President*
EMP: 50
SALES (corp-wide): 106.8MM **Privately Held**
SIC: 5149 2033 Water, distilled; fruit juices: packaged in cans, jars, etc.
PA: Pressed Juicery, Inc.
1550 17th St
Santa Monica CA 90404
310 477-7171

(P-8635)
PRESTIGE SALES II LLC
1038 E Bastanchury Rd, Fullerton (92835-2786)
PHONE.................................714 632-8020
Greg Zail, *Mng Member*
Bernie Barrad,
▲ EMP: 75
SQ FT: 27,000
SALES (est): 4.4MM **Privately Held**
WEB: www.psana.com
SIC: 5149 5181 Soft drinks; beer & ale

(P-8636)
QUEST NUTRITION LLC (PA)
777 S Avi Blvd Ste 100, El Segundo (90245)
PHONE.................................562 272-0180
Michael Osborn, *Mng Member*
Mike Osborn, *CFO*
Reza Mazloumi, *Vice Pres*
Derek Ito, *Info Tech Dir*
Sam Vargas, *Technician*
▲ EMP: 150
SQ FT: 43,728
SALES (est): 196.1MM **Privately Held**
SIC: 5149 Beverages, except coffee & tea; health foods; cookies

(P-8637)
REAL GOOD FOOD COMPANY LLC
111 N Artsakh St Ste 201, Glendale (91206-4097)
PHONE.................................909 744-0073
Josh Schreider,
Mista Asbury,
EMP: 200 EST: 2016
SALES (est): 22MM **Privately Held**
SIC: 5149 Specialty food items

(P-8638)
RED BULL DISTRIBUTION CO INC (HQ)
Also Called: Redbull Distribution Co Colo
1740 Stewart St, Santa Monica (90404-4022)
PHONE.................................916 515-3501
Selin Chidiak, *CEO*
Peter Kwon, *Admin Sec*
EMP: 84
SALES (est): 103.7MM
SALES (corp-wide): 3.9B **Privately Held**
SIC: 5149 Beverage concentrates
PA: Red Bull Gmbh
Am Brunnen 1
Fuschl Am See 5330
662 658-20

(P-8639)
REYES COCA-COLA BOTTLING LLC
12925 Bradley Ave, Sylmar (91342-3830)
PHONE.................................818 362-4307
Larry Campbell, *Branch Mgr*
EMP: 75

SALES (corp-wide): 785.2MM Privately Held
SIC: **5149** 4225 2086 Soft drinks; general warehousing; bottled & canned soft drinks
PA: Reyes Coca-Cola Bottling, L.L.C.
3 Park Plz Ste 600
Irvine CA 92614
213 744-8616

(P-8640)
ROCKVIEW DAIRIES INC (PA)
Also Called: Motive Nation
7011 Stewart And Gray Rd, Downey (90241-4347)
P.O. Box 668 (90241-0668)
PHONE..................562 927-5511
Egbert Jim Degroot, *CEO*
Valarie Cooke, *President*
Edgar Del Rio, *CFO*
Joe Valadez, *CFO*
Carlos Lopez, *Lab Dir*
◆ EMP: 106
SALES (est): 163.6MM Privately Held
WEB: www.rockviewfarms.com
SIC: **5149** 5143 2026 Dried or canned foods; milk; fluid milk

(P-8641)
SADIE ROSE BAKING CO
2614 Temple Heights Dr, Oceanside (92056-3512)
PHONE..................619 718-9532
Jennifer Ann Curran, *CEO*
Michael Lipman, *President*
Cassie Polley, *QC Mgr*
Therese Wootton, *Regl Sales Mgr*
Stefany Dybeck, *Sales Mgr*
◆ EMP: 70
SQ FT: 23,000
SALES (est): 19.2MM Privately Held
SIC: **5149** Bakery products

(P-8642)
SEMIFREDDIS INC (PA)
Also Called: Semifreddi's Bakery
1980 N Loop Rd, Alameda (94502-3540)
PHONE..................510 596-9930
Thomas Frainier, *President*
Michael Rose, *Admin Sec*
Cary Weigle, *Engrg Dir*
Jorge Blancas, *Senior Mgr*
John Tredgold, *Director*
EMP: 110
SQ FT: 36,000
SALES (est): 51.4MM Privately Held
WEB: www.semifreddis.com
SIC: **5149** 5461 Bakery products; bakeries

(P-8643)
SETTON PSTCHIO TERRA BELLA INC (HQ)
9370 Road 234, Terra Bella (93270-9226)
P.O. Box 11089 (93270-1089)
PHONE..................559 535-6050
Joshua Setton, *President*
Morris Setton, *Vice Pres*
▲ EMP: 70
SQ FT: 133,000
SALES (est): 37MM
SALES (corp-wide): 22.9MM Privately Held
SIC: **5149** 5145 0173 2068 Fruits, dried; nuts, salted or roasted; pistachio grove; salted & roasted nuts & seeds
PA: Setton's International Foods, Inc.
85 Austin Blvd
Commack NY 11725
631 543-8090

(P-8644)
SHAW BAKERS LLC
320b Shaw Rd Ste B, South San Francisco (94080-6623)
PHONE..................650 273-1440
Darrell Smith, *Mng Member*
EMP: 100
SALES: 10MM Privately Held
SIC: **5149** Bakery products

(P-8645)
SOOFER CO INC
Also Called: Sadaf Foods
2828 S Alameda St, Vernon (90058-1347)
PHONE..................323 234-6666
Dariush Soofer, *CEO*
Jamshid Soofer, *President*

Behrooz David Soofer, *COO*
George Melikian, *Officer*
Ramon Sentimental, *Principal*
▲ EMP: 75 EST: 1981
SQ FT: 70,000
SALES (est): 55.3MM Privately Held
WEB: www.sadaf.com
SIC: **5149** Spices & seasonings

(P-8646)
STAPLETON - SPENCE PACKING CO (PA)
1900 State Highway 99, Gridley (95948-9401)
P.O. Box 948 (95948-0948)
PHONE..................408 297-8815
Martin Bradley Stapleton, *CEO*
Tom Thornton, *Vice Pres*
Gavin Heitman, *Admin Sec*
Deborah Reynolds, *Accountant*
Stacey Sallaberry, *Human Res Mgr*
◆ EMP: 79 EST: 1951
SQ FT: 105,000
SALES (est): 58.9MM Privately Held
WEB: www.stapleton-spence.com
SIC: **5149** Groceries & related products

(P-8647)
STARWEST BOTANICALS INC (PA)
161 Main Ave, Sacramento (95838-2080)
PHONE..................916 638-8100
Van Joerger, *President*
Jeani Fernland, *Executive*
Bonnie Sadkowski, *Purch Mgr*
Steven Riccardelli, *VP Sls/Mktg*
Melissa Waters, *Mktg Dir*
◆ EMP: 95 EST: 1975
SQ FT: 68,400
SALES: 37.3MM Privately Held
WEB: www.starwestherb.com
SIC: **5149** Tea; spices & seasonings

(P-8648)
SUJA LIFE LLC
Also Called: Suja Juice
3831 Ocean Ranch Blvd, Oceanside (92056-2647)
PHONE..................855 879-7852
Jeffrey Church, *CEO*
James Brennan, *President*
Alicia Conforti, *Office Mgr*
Mike Cifone, *Controller*
Clarissa Longo, *Marketing Staff*
▲ EMP: 205
SALES (est): 135.6MM Privately Held
SIC: **5149** Fruit peel

(P-8649)
SUN CHLORELLA USA CORP
3305 Kashiwa St, Torrance (90505-4022)
PHONE..................310 891-0600
Futoshi Nakayama, *CEO*
Yoshihito Nishimaki, *President*
Rose Straub, *COO*
Ellen Kubijanto, *CFO*
Colette Sweeny,
▲ EMP: 54
SQ FT: 20,000
SALES (est): 13MM Privately Held
WEB: www.sunchlorellausa.com
SIC: **5149** Health foods
PA: Sun Chlorella Corp.
369, Osakacho, Karasumadori Gojo Sagaru
Shimogyo-Ku, Kyoto KYO 600-8

(P-8650)
SUN TEN LABS LIQUIDATION CO
9250 Jeronimo Rd, Irvine (92618-1905)
PHONE..................949 587-0509
Charleson C Hsu, *CEO*
▲ EMP: 60
SALES (est): 14.2MM Privately Held
WEB: www.sunten.com
SIC: **5149** 2834 2833 Spices & seasonings; pharmaceutical preparations; medicinals & botanicals

(P-8651)
SUN-MAID GROWERS CALIFORNIA (PA)
13525 S Bethel Ave, Kingsburg (93631-9232)
PHONE..................559 897-6235
Harry J Overly, *President*
Braden Bender, *CFO*
Kayhan Hazrati, *Vice Pres*
Tim Renna, *Executive*
Rick Stark, *Admin Sec*
◆ EMP: 750
SALES: 362.1MM Privately Held
SIC: **5149** Groceries & related products

(P-8652)
SUN-MAID GROWERS CALIFORNIA
Also Called: Sun Maid Growers
15628 E Nebraska Ave, Kingsburg (93631-9714)
PHONE..................559 897-8900
EMP: 273
SALES (corp-wide): 362.1MM Privately Held
SIC: **5149** Groceries & related products
PA: Sun-Maid Growers Of California
13525 S Bethel Ave
Kingsburg CA 93631
559 897-6235

(P-8653)
SUPER STORE INDUSTRIES
Also Called: Ssi
2800 W March Ln Ste 210, Stockton (95219-8200)
P.O. Box 549, Lathrop (95330-0549)
PHONE..................209 858-3365
Tom Hughes, *Branch Mgr*
EMP: 400
SALES (corp-wide): 293.7MM Privately Held
SIC: **5149** 5141 4225 Groceries & related products; groceries, general line; general warehousing & storage
PA: Super Store Industries
16888 Mckinley Ave
Lathrop CA 95330
209 858-3365

(P-8654)
SURVIVALCAVE INC
10620 Treena St Ste 230, San Diego (92131-1140)
PHONE..................800 719-7650
J R Fisher, *President*
EMP: 50 EST: 2010
SALES (est): 7.8MM Privately Held
SIC: **5149** Canned goods: fruit, vegetables, seafood, meats, etc.

(P-8655)
SYGMA NETWORK INC
46905 47th St W, Lancaster (93536-8527)
PHONE..................661 723-0405
Mike Wren, *Branch Mgr*
EMP: 200
SALES (corp-wide): 60.1B Publicly Held
WEB: www.sygmanetwork.com
SIC: **5149** Specialty food items
HQ: The Sygma Network Inc
5550 Blazer Pkwy Ste 300
Dublin OH 43017

(P-8656)
TAMA TRADING COMPANY
1920 E 20th St, Vernon (90058-1076)
PHONE..................213 748-8262
William A Sauro, *CEO*
Sandra Sauro, *Corp Secy*
◆ EMP: 61
SQ FT: 60,000
SALES (est): 24.4MM Privately Held
SIC: **5149** 5143 5147 5145 Specialty food items; seasonings, sauces & extracts; pasta & rice; cheese; meats & meat products; candy

(P-8657)
TANAKA FARMS
5380 University Dr, Irvine (92612-2944)
PHONE..................949 653-2100
Glenn Tannaka, *Owner*
EMP: 60 EST: 1975

SALES (est): 5.1MM Privately Held
WEB: www.tanakafarms.com
SIC: **5149** Groceries & related products

(P-8658)
TASTEFUL SELECTIONS LLC
13003 Di Giorgio Rd, Arvin (93203-9529)
PHONE..................661 588-1053
Robert Bender, *Mng Member*
Aimee Rabanal, *Accountant*
EMP: 56
SALES (est): 16.7MM Privately Held
SIC: **5149** 5812 Condiments; eating places

(P-8659)
TAWA SERVICES INC (PA)
6338 Regio Ave, Buena Park (90620)
PHONE..................714 521-8899
Jonson Chen, *CEO*
Young You, *Principal*
▼ EMP: 270
SALES (est): 101.7MM Privately Held
SIC: **5149** 5411 Groceries & related products; grocery stores

(P-8660)
TOO GOOD GOURMET INC (PA)
2380 Grant Ave, San Lorenzo (94580-1806)
PHONE..................510 317-8150
Amie G Watson, *CEO*
Jennifer Finley, *President*
Joe Waldrep, *Plant Mgr*
Denise Zerbini, *Manager*
Emily Melo, *Clerk*
▲ EMP: 71
SQ FT: 50,000
SALES (est): 6.6MM Privately Held
WEB: www.toogoodgourmet.com
SIC: **5149** 5461 2052 Cookies; crackers, cookies & bakery products; cookies; cookies

(P-8661)
TRAINA DRIED FRUIT INC
Also Called: Traina Foods
337 1/2 Lemon Ave, Patterson (95363-9634)
P.O. Box 157 (95363-0157)
PHONE..................209 892-5472
William Traina, *CEO*
Joseph Traina, *CFO*
Justin A Traina, *Vice Pres*
Josephine Traina, *Admin Sec*
▲ EMP: 240
SQ FT: 5,000
SALES (est): 18.9MM Privately Held
WEB: www.trainadriedfruit.com
SIC: **5149** Fruits, dried

(P-8662)
TRINITY FRESH DISTRIBUTION LLC
8200 Berry Ave Ste 140, Sacramento (95828-1612)
P.O. Box 619, Sloughhouse (95683-0619)
PHONE..................916 714-7368
Paul Abess,
EMP: 70
SALES (est): 15.6MM Privately Held
SIC: **5149** Dairy products, dried or canned

(P-8663)
UNITED NATURAL FOODS INC
2450 17th Ave Ste 250, Santa Cruz (95062-1987)
PHONE..................831 462-5870
Melody Meyer, *Branch Mgr*
EMP: 133 **Publicly Held**
SIC: **5149** 5122 5142 Organic & diet foods; health foods; natural & organic foods; cosmetics, perfumes & hair products; vitamins & minerals; packaged frozen goods
PA: United Natural Foods, Inc.
313 Iron Horse Way
Providence RI 02908

(P-8664)
US FOODS INC
US Foods Corona
1283 Sherborn St Ste 102, Corona (92879-5003)
PHONE..................800 888-3147

Graylon Macfall, *Division Pres*
EMP: 250 Publicly Held
SIC: 5149 Dried or canned foods
HQ: Us Foods, Inc.
9399 W Higgins Rd # 100
Rosemont IL 60018

(P-8665)
US FOODS INC
1283 Sherborn St Ste 102, Corona
(92879-5003)
PHONE..................................951 582-8500
Patrick Waller, *Manager*
EMP: 150 Publicly Held
WEB: www.usfoodservice.com
SIC: 5149 Groceries & related products
HQ: Us Foods, Inc.
9399 W Higgins Rd # 100
Rosemont IL 60018

(P-8666)
US FOODS INC
Also Called: Mesa Cold Strg 4145
700 S Raymond Ave, Fullerton
(92831-5233)
PHONE..................................714 449-9990
Ed Libel, *Branch Mgr*
EMP: 161 Publicly Held
SIC: 5149 Dried or canned foods
HQ: Us Foods, Inc.
9399 W Higgins Rd # 100
Rosemont IL 60018

(P-8667)
US FOODS INC
Also Called: Sierra Pacific 4117
4300 Finch Rd, Modesto (95357-4102)
PHONE..................................209 572-2882
EMP: 159 Publicly Held
SIC: 5149 Dried or canned foods
HQ: Us Foods, Inc.
9399 W Higgins Rd # 100
Rosemont IL 60018

(P-8668)
US FOODS INC
Also Called: Csi Cold Storage 4150
1415 N Raymond Ave, Anaheim
(92801-1111)
PHONE..................................714 449-2880
EMP: 159 Publicly Held
SIC: 5149 Dried or canned foods
HQ: Us Foods, Inc.
9399 W Higgins Rd # 100
Rosemont IL 60018

(P-8669)
US FOODS INC
Also Called: USF-La Mirada 4150
15155 Northam St, La Mirada
(90638-5754)
PHONE..................................714 670-3500
David Patterson, *Branch Mgr*
EMP: 159 Publicly Held
SIC: 5149 Dried or canned foods
HQ: Us Foods, Inc.
9399 W Higgins Rd # 100
Rosemont IL 60018

(P-8670)
US FOODS INC
Also Called: San Diego CLD Stg 4140
1240 W 28th St, National City
(91950-6319)
PHONE..................................619 474-6525
EMP: 159 Publicly Held
SIC: 5149 Dried or canned foods
HQ: Us Foods, Inc.
9399 W Higgins Rd # 100
Rosemont IL 60018

(P-8671)
US FOODS INC
Also Called: USF Import FWD Wh 4150
1283 Sherborn St Ste 102, Corona
(92879-5003)
PHONE..................................951 256-2400
EMP: 159 Publicly Held
SIC: 5149 Dried or canned foods

HQ: Us Foods, Inc.
9399 W Higgins Rd # 100
Rosemont IL 60018

(P-8672)
VISTA VERDE FARMS
11251 Melcher Rd, Delano (93215-9310)
PHONE..................................661 720-9733
Santos Montmayor, *Owner*
EMP: 50
SALES (est): 2.4MM Privately Held
SIC: 5149 Groceries & related products

(P-8673)
WALONG MARKETING INC (PA)
Also Called: Foods and Produce
6281 Regio Ave, Buena Park (90620-1023)
PHONE..................................714 670-8899
Chang Hua K Chen, *CEO*
Roger Chen, *Ch of Bd*
Philip Yang, *Buyer*
Danny Wong, *Sales Associate*
Jonson Chen, *Manager*
◆ **EMP: 100**
SALES (est): 63.9MM Privately Held
SIC: 5149 5411 Groceries & related products; grocery stores

(P-8674)
YAMAMOTO OF ORIENT INC (HQ)
Also Called: Yamamotoyama of America
122 Voyager St, Pomona (91768-3252)
PHONE..................................909 594-7356
Kahei Yamamoto, *Ch of Bd*
Hisayuki Nakagawa, *President*
Daniel Goldstein, *COO*
Kazumi Ikeda, *Treasurer*
Kaichiro Yamamoto, *Admin Sec*
▲ **EMP: 130 EST: 1975**
SQ FT: 60,000
SALES (est): 62.8MM Privately Held
WEB: www.yamamotoyama.com
SIC: 5149 6512 5812 Tea; shopping center, property operation only; eating places

---

5153 Grain & Field Beans Wholesale

(P-8675)
A L GILBERT COMPANY
Also Called: Berry Seed & Feed
4431 Jessup Rd, Keyes (95328)
P.O. Box 459 (95328-0459)
PHONE..................................209 537-0766
Edwin Gallagher, *Branch Mgr*
EMP: 60
SALES (corp-wide): 335.5MM Privately Held
SIC: 5153 Grains
PA: A. L. Gilbert Company
304 N Yosemite Ave
Oakdale CA 95361
209 847-1721

(P-8676)
ANDERSON HAY & GRAIN CO INC
915 E Colon St, Wilmington (90744-2101)
PHONE..................................509 925-9818
EMP: 105
SALES (corp-wide): 1.7MM Privately Held
SIC: 5153 Grains
PA: Anderson Hay & Grain Co., Inc.
910 Anderson Rd
Ellensburg WA 98926
509 925-9818

(P-8677)
BUNGE MILLING INC
845 Kentucky Ave, Woodland
(95695-2744)
PHONE..................................530 666-1691
EMP: 139 Privately Held
SIC: 5153 Grains
HQ: Bunge Milling, Inc.
1391 Timberlake Manor Pkw
Chesterfield MO 63017
314 292-2000

(P-8678)
CALIFORNIA CEREAL PRODUCTS INC (PA)
1267 14th St, Oakland (94607-2246)
PHONE..................................510 452-4500
Robert Sterling Savely, *CEO*
Mark Graham, *President*
David Hernick, *QC Mgr*
Nestor Pajuleras, *Products*
Phil Gunter, *Manager*
◆ **EMP: 56**
SQ FT: 120,000
SALES (est): 45.4MM Privately Held
SIC: 5153 Grains

(P-8679)
PACIFIC GRAIN & FOODS LLC (PA)
Also Called: Pacific Grain and Foods
4067 W Shaw Ave Ste 116, Fresno
(93722-6214)
P.O. Box 3928, Pinedale (93650-3928)
PHONE..................................559 276-2580
Lee Perkins, *President*
Karen Perkins, *Vice Pres*
Jose M Alvarado, *Executive*
Craig Roberts, *Plant Mgr*
Rita Garcia, *Director*
◆ **EMP: 135**
SQ FT: 172,000
SALES (est): 30MM Privately Held
WEB: www.pacificgrainfoods.com
SIC: 5153 7389 5149 Grains; packaging & labeling services; spices & seasonings

---

5154 Livestock Wholesale

(P-8680)
SHASTA LIVESTOCK AUCTION YARD
3917 Main St, Cottonwood (96022)
P.O. Box 558 (96022-0558)
PHONE..................................530 347-3793
Ellington Peek, *President*
Beatrice Peek, *Vice Pres*
EMP: 60
SQ FT: 15,000
SALES (est): 9.3MM Privately Held
SIC: 5154 Auctioning livestock

5159 Farm-Prdt Raw Mtrls, NEC Wholesale

(P-8681)
SELECT HARVEST USA LLC (PA)
Also Called: Spycher Brothers
14827 W Harding Rd, Turlock
(95380-9012)
PHONE..................................209 668-2471
Robert L Nunes, *Mng Member*
Maria Medina, *Purchasing*
Sheryl Wheeler, *Sales Staff*
Juan-Carlos Veraza, *Director*
◆ **EMP: 87 EST: 2008**
SQ FT: 100,000
SALES (est): 54MM Privately Held
SIC: 5159 0173 Nuts & nut by-products; almond grove

(P-8682)
SOUTH VALLEY ALMOND CO LLC
Also Called: South Valley Farms
15443 Beech Ave, Wasco (93280-7604)
PHONE..................................661 391-9000
Paul C Genho, *Mng Member*
Bobbie Sanocki, *Purch Mgr*
Daryl Wilkendorf,
Merrill Dibble, *Mng Member*
▼ **EMP: 200**
SQ FT: 4,000
SALES (est): 60.8MM Privately Held
SIC: 5159 Nuts & nut by-products

5162 Plastics Materials & Basic Shapes Wholesale

(P-8683)
CIRRUS ENTERPRISES LLC
Also Called: E.V. Roberts
18027 Bishop Ave, Carson (90746-4019)
PHONE..................................310 204-6159
Ron Cloud, *CEO*
John Vogt, *Vice Pres*
Donna Knapp, *Executive Asst*
Keiko Clark, *Administration*
Seth Arnold, *Technical Staff*
▲ **EMP: 52**
SQ FT: 26,000
SALES (est): 40.5MM Privately Held
WEB: www.evroberts.com
SIC: 5162 2821 2891 5198 Plastics products; epoxy resins; adhesives & sealants; paints, varnishes & supplies; chemicals & allied products

(P-8684)
CONSOLIDATED PLASTICS CORP (PA)
Also Called: Paragon Plastics Co Div
14954 La Palma Dr, Chino (91710-9695)
PHONE..................................909 393-8222
Jean Bouris, *President*
Gloria Jean Bouris, *CEO*
EMP: 55
SQ FT: 45,000
SALES (est): 14.4MM Privately Held
WEB: www.planetplastics.com
SIC: 5162 3599 Plastics sheets & rods; machine shop, jobbing & repair

(P-8685)
DONGALEN ENTERPRISES INC (PA)
Also Called: Interstate Plastics
330 Commerce Cir, Sacramento
(95815-4213)
P.O. Box 130027 (95853-0027)
PHONE..................................916 422-3110
Mark Courtright, *President*
Cole Klokkevold, *CFO*
Lori O'Hara, *Sales Staff*
Sean Tinney, *Sales Staff*
John Schwenck, *Director*
▲ **EMP: 50**
SQ FT: 33,000
SALES (est): 94.7MM Privately Held
WEB: www.interstateplastics.com
SIC: 5162 Plastics products

(P-8686)
VPET USA INC (PA)
12925 Marlay Ave, Fontana (92337-6939)
PHONE..................................909 605-1668
Henry Lee, *CEO*
Deedee Kerr, *Vice Pres*
Benson Liu, *Vice Pres*
Penson Liu, *Vice Pres*
Pan Eirleen, *Technology*
◆ **EMP: 60**
SALES (est): 67.6MM Privately Held
WEB: www.vpetusa.com
SIC: 5162 Plastics basic shapes

5169 Chemicals & Allied Prdts, NEC Wholesale

(P-8687)
AIRGAS USA LLC
9010 Clairemont Mesa Blvd, San Diego
(92123-1208)
P.O. Box 6030, Lakewood (90714-6030)
PHONE..................................858 279-8200
Pat Muller, *Vice Pres*
EMP: 110
SALES (corp-wide): 125.9MM Privately Held
WEB: www.airgaswest.com
SIC: 5169 5084 5047 5046 Industrial gases; industrial machinery & equipment; medical & hospital equipment; commercial equipment

---

HQ: Airgas Usa, Llc
259 N Radnor Chester Rd
Radnor PA 19087
610 687-5253

(P-8688)
AMERICAN VANGUARD CORPORATION
Also Called: Amvac Chemical
4100 E Washington Blvd, Commerce
(90023-4406)
PHONE..................................323 264-3910
Arun Malik, *Manager*
EMP: 200
SALES (corp-wide): 454.2MM **Publicly Held**
WEB: www.amvac-chemical.com
SIC: 5169 2879 Chemicals & allied products; pesticides, agricultural or household
PA: American Vanguard Corporation
4695 Macarthur Ct
Newport Beach CA 92660
949 260-1200

(P-8689)
AQUA-SERV ENGINEERS INC (HQ)
13560 Colombard Ct, Fontana
(92337-7702)
PHONE..................................951 681-9696
Earl L Harper, *CEO*
Garland Rachels, *President*
Buck Long, *Senior VP*
Chris Long, *Area Mgr*
Kent Duncan, *Technical Staff*
EMP: 56 **EST:** 1958
SQ FT: 63,000
SALES (est): 32.4MM **Privately Held**
WEB: www.aqua-serv.com
SIC: 5169 Chemicals & allied products

(P-8690)
ASHLAND LLC
Also Called: Ashland Performance Materials
20915 S Wilmington Ave, Carson
(90810-1039)
PHONE..................................310 223-3505
Randy Weld, *Manager*
EMP: 90
SALES (corp-wide): 3.7B **Publicly Held**
WEB: www.ashland.com
SIC: 5169 Alkalines & chlorine
HQ: Ashland Llc
50 E Rivercenter Blvd # 1600
Covington KY 41011
859 815-3333

(P-8691)
BRENNTAG PACIFIC INC (DH)
10747 Patterson Pl, Santa Fe Springs
(90670-4043)
PHONE..................................562 903-9626
William A Fidler, *CEO*
Steven Pozzi, *President*
H Edward Boyadjian, *CFO*
Julia Tu, *Controller*
▲ **EMP:** 153
SALES (est): 431.8MM
SALES (corp-wide): 14.3B **Privately Held**
SIC: 5169 Chemicals, industrial & heavy; industrial chemicals
HQ: Brenntag North America, Inc.
5083 Pottsville Pike
Reading PA 19605
610 926-6100

(P-8692)
CARGILL INCORPORATED
7220 Central Ave, Newark (94560-4205)
PHONE..................................510 797-1820
Warren Staley, *CEO*
EMP: 250
SALES (corp-wide): 114.7B **Privately Held**
WEB: www.cargill.com
SIC: 5169 Chemicals & allied products
PA: Cargill, Incorporated
15407 Mcginty Rd W
Wayzata MN 55391
952 742-7575

(P-8693)
CHEMICAL DEPENDENCY RECOVERY
2829 Watt Ave Ste 150, Sacramento
(95821-6245)
PHONE..................................916 482-1132
Melissa Rose, *Director*
EMP: 50
SALES (est): 2.3MM **Privately Held**
SIC: 5169 Chemicals & allied products

(P-8694)
CZECH COMMERCE LTD
3063 Larkin Rd, Pebble Beach
(93953-2910)
PHONE..................................831 649-4633
Jaroslav Stepanek, *President*
EMP: 53
SQ FT: 450
SALES (est): 2MM **Privately Held**
SIC: 5169 5031 Alcohols; building materials, exterior

(P-8695)
DAICEL SAFETY SYSTEMS
2655 1st St Ste 300, Simi Valley
(93065-1580)
PHONE..................................805 387-1004
Nick Bruge, *President*
Mark Harper, *CFO*
EMP: 170
SALES (est): 2.7MM **Privately Held**
SIC: 5169 Industrial chemicals
HQ: Daicel America Holdings, Inc.
1 Parker Plz
Fort Lee NJ 07024
201 461-4466

(P-8696)
DESERT STAR CO
23119 Drayton St, Saugus (91350-2547)
PHONE..................................661 259-5848
Mary Flynn, *Vice Pres*
EMP: 50
SALES (est): 2.3MM **Privately Held**
WEB: www.desertstar.net
SIC: 5169 Chemicals & allied products

(P-8697)
E T HORN COMPANY (PA)
16050 Canary Ave, La Mirada
(90638-5585)
P.O. Box 1238 (90637-1238)
PHONE..................................714 523-8050
Jeffrey Martin, *CEO*
Kevin Salerno, *President*
Julie Wubbena, *CFO*
Roger Clemens, *Officer*
Vince Anderson, *Vice Pres*
▲ **EMP:** 70 **EST:** 1961
SQ FT: 1,200
SALES (est): 319MM **Privately Held**
SIC: 5169 Industrial chemicals

(P-8698)
ENVIRO TECH CHEMICAL SVCS INC (PA)
500 Winmoore Way, Modesto
(95358-5750)
PHONE..................................209 581-9576
Michael S Harvey, *President*
Michael B Archibald, *Vice Pres*
Charlie Lucas, *Maintence Staff*
◆ **EMP:** 102
SQ FT: 136,551
SALES: 53.2MM **Privately Held**
WEB: www.amcor.com.au
SIC: 5169 2842 Industrial chemicals; specialty cleaning preparations

(P-8699)
HILL BROTHERS CHEMICAL COMPANY (PA)
1675 N Main St, Orange (92867-3499)
PHONE..................................714 998-8800
Ronald R Hill, *President*
Thomas F James, *CFO*
Kathryn J Waters, *Corp Secy*
Matthew Thorne, *Exec VP*
Ashley Crispell, *Administration*
▲ **EMP:** 153

SALES (est): 110.9MM **Privately Held**
WEB: www.durafiber.com
SIC: 5169 2819 Acids; calcium chloride & hypochlorite; magnesium compounds or salts, inorganic

(P-8700)
INEOS COMPOSITES US LLC
6608 E 26th St, Commerce (90040-3216)
P.O. Box 22118, Los Angeles (90022-0118)
PHONE..................................323 767-1300
Reid Mork, *Branch Mgr*
Grant Needham, *Plant Mgr*
Fernando Celaya, *Maintence Staff*
EMP: 60
SQ FT: 45,845
SALES (corp-wide): 352.2K **Privately Held**
WEB: www.ashland.com
SIC: 5169 Alkalines & chlorine
HQ: Ineos Composites Us, Llc
5220 Blazer Pkwy
Dublin OH 43017
614 790-3333

(P-8701)
K R ANDERSON INC (PA)
Also Called: Krayden
18330 Sutter Blvd, Morgan Hill
(95037-2841)
PHONE..................................408 825-1800
Dennis Wagner, *CEO*
Jim Caviglia, *Treasurer*
Doreen Oroshnik, *Administration*
Lisa Cummings, *Asst Controller*
Samantha Wagner, *Purch Agent*
▲ **EMP:** 60
SQ FT: 60,000
SALES (est): 43.3MM **Privately Held**
WEB: www.andfab.com
SIC: 5169 Synthetic resins, rubber & plastic materials

(P-8702)
MCP INDUSTRIES INC
Also Called: Purosil Division
10039 Norwalk Blvd, Santa Fe Springs
(90670-3323)
P.O. Box 2467, Corona (92878-2467)
PHONE..................................562 944-5511
Surrender Marwaha, *Manager*
EMP: 100
SALES (corp-wide): 126.4MM **Privately Held**
WEB: www.missionrubber.com
SIC: 5169 Silicon lubricants
PA: Mcp Industries, Inc.
708 S Temescal St Ste 101
Corona CA 92879
951 736-1881

(P-8703)
NALCO COMPANY LLC
1320 Arnold Dr Ste 246, Martinez
(94553-6537)
PHONE..................................925 957-9720
Bob Smith, *District Mgr*
Matt Del Bonta, *Area Mgr*
EMP: 100
SALES (corp-wide): 14.6B **Publicly Held**
WEB: www.nalco.com
SIC: 5169 Industrial chemicals
HQ: Nalco Company Llc
1601 W Diehl Rd
Naperville IL 60563
630 305-1000

(P-8704)
NORAC ADDITIVES LLC
813 Towne Center Dr, Pomona
(91767-5901)
PHONE..................................909 321-5952
Mike Connor, *Mng Member*
EMP: 55
SALES (est): 89.5K **Privately Held**
SIC: 5169 Chemical additives

(P-8705)
PMC LEADERS IN CHEMICALS INC (HQ)
12243 Branford St, Sun Valley
(91352-1010)
PHONE..................................818 896-1101
Gary Kamins, *President*
EMP: 200
SQ FT: 180,000

SALES: 300MM
SALES (corp-wide): 2.5B **Privately Held**
SIC: 5169 3086 Chemicals & allied products; plastics foam products
PA: Pmc Global, Inc.
12243 Branford St
Sun Valley CA 91352
818 896-1101

(P-8706)
PRAXAIR INC
2300 E Pacific Coast Hwy, Wilmington
(90744-2919)
P.O. Box 1309 (90748)
PHONE..................................562 983-2100
Ted Mayberry, *Branch Mgr*
EMP: 96 **Privately Held**
SIC: 5169 2813 Industrial gases; industrial gases
HQ: Praxair, Inc.
10 Riverview Dr
Danbury CT 06810
203 837-2000

(P-8707)
PROCTER & GAMBLE DISTRG LLC
1992 Rockefeller Dr, Ceres (95307-7274)
PHONE..................................209 538-3987
Michael Wheatley, *Branch Mgr*
EMP: 273
SALES (corp-wide): 67.6B **Publicly Held**
SIC: 5169 Detergents
HQ: Procter & Gamble Distributing Llc
1 Procter And Gamble Plz
Cincinnati OH 45202
513 983-1100

(P-8708)
PROCTER & GAMBLE DISTRG LLC
2010 Crow Canyon Pl # 230, San Ramon
(94583-1344)
PHONE..................................925 867-4900
Virginia Cavlin, *Manager*
EMP: 273
SALES (corp-wide): 67.6B **Publicly Held**
SIC: 5169 5122 5149 5113 Detergents; laundry soap chips & powder; drugs, proprietaries & sundries; groceries & related products; coffee, green or roasted; napkins, paper; towels, paper; dishes, disposable plastic & paper; diapers; service establishment equipment
HQ: Procter & Gamble Distributing Llc
1 Procter And Gamble Plz
Cincinnati OH 45202
513 983-1100

(P-8709)
UNITED PETROCHEMICALS INC
3000 W Macarthur Blvd # 300, Santa Ana
(92704-6916)
PHONE..................................949 629-8736
Lynne Vanderwall, *CEO*
Zach Smith, *Vice Pres*
EMP: 75
SQ FT: 25,000
SALES (est): 2.8MM **Privately Held**
SIC: 5169 Industrial chemicals

(P-8710)
UNIVAR SOLUTIONS USA INC
2600 Garfield Ave, Commerce
(90040-2608)
P.O. Box 512062 (90040)
PHONE..................................323 727-7005
Gary Cramer, *Branch Mgr*
Aaron Cervantes, *Planning*
Jim Foley, *Train & Dev Mgr*
Christina Nassralla, *Purchasing*
Mark Vetter, *Sales Mgr*
EMP: 175
SALES (corp-wide): 8.6B **Publicly Held**
SIC: 5169 Industrial chemicals
HQ: Univar Solutions Usa Inc.
3075 Highland Pkwy # 200
Downers Grove IL 60515
331 777-6000

(P-8711)
UNIVAR SOLUTIONS USA INC
2256 Junction Ave, San Jose (95131-1216)
PHONE..................................408 435-8649
Dan Manners, *Branch Mgr*
Carly Richard, *Opers Staff*

Craig Colbert, *Sales Mgr*
James Rogers, *Manager*
EMP: 80
SALES (corp-wide): 8.6B **Publicly Held**
SIC: 5169 5191 Industrial chemicals; farm supplies
HQ: Univar Solutions Usa Inc.
3075 Highland Pkwy # 200
Downers Grove IL 60515
331 777-6000

(P-8712)
VALEANT BIOMEDICALS INC (DH)
1 Enterprise, Aliso Viejo (92656-2606)
PHONE..............................949 461-6000
Tim Tyson, *President*
Laurie W Little, *Vice Pres*
Denise Raimondo, *Associate Dir*
Christine Novitski, *Executive Asst*
Emily Seliskar, *Planning*
EMP: 100
SQ FT: 55,000
SALES (est): 62.9MM
SALES (corp-wide): 8.3B **Privately Held**
SIC: 5169 2835 8731 3826 Chemicals & allied products; in vitro & in vivo diagnostic substances; blood derivative diagnostic agents; biotechnical research, commercial; analytical instruments; liquid testing apparatus; medical equipment & supplies
HQ: Bausch Health Americas, Inc.
400 Somerset Corp Blvd
Bridgewater NJ 08807
908 927-1400

5171 Petroleum Bulk Stations & Terminals

(P-8713)
BP WEST COAST PRODUCTS LLC
Also Called: BP Products W Coast Refinery
1801 E Sepulveda Blvd, Carson (90745-6121)
PHONE..............................310 549-6204
George Nicolaides, *Plant Mgr*
EMP: 250
SALES (corp-wide): 298.7B **Privately Held**
SIC: 5171 Petroleum bulk stations & terminals
HQ: Bp West Coast Products Llc
4519 Grandview Rd
Blaine WA 98230
310 549-6204

(P-8714)
C L BRYANT INC
7401 Del Cielo Way, Modesto (95356-8874)
PHONE..............................209 566-5000
Toll Free:.....................................877 -
Charles L Bryant Jr, *President*
EMP: 159
SQ FT: 16,164
SALES (est): 32.4MM **Privately Held**
SIC: 5171 5541 Petroleum bulk stations; filling stations, gasoline

(P-8715)
GENERAL PETROLEUM CORPORATION
237 E Whitmore Ave, Modesto (95358-9411)
PHONE..............................209 537-1056
EMP: 70
SALES (corp-wide): 1.1B **Privately Held**
SIC: 5171
HQ: General Petroleum Corporation
19501 S Santa Fe Ave
Compton CA 90221
562 983-7300

(P-8716)
SOUTHERN COUNTIES OIL CO (PA)
Also Called: SC Fuels
1800 W Katella Ave # 400, Orange (92867-3449)
P.O. Box 4159 (92863-4159)
PHONE..............................714 744-7140

Frank P Greinke, *CEO*
Steve Greinke, *President*
David Larimer, *COO*
Mimi Taylor, *CFO*
Timothy Wolthuis, *Senior VP*
EMP: 95 **EST:** 1969
SALES (est): 1.2B **Privately Held**
SIC: 5171 5541 5172 Petroleum bulk stations; gasoline service stations; petroleum products

5172 Petroleum & Petroleum Prdts Wholesale

(P-8717)
ALL-POINTS PETROLEUM LLC
640 Noyes Ct, Benicia (94510-1229)
P.O. Box 2658, Grants Pass OR (97528-0240)
PHONE..............................707 745-1116
Ronald Myska,
EMP: 61
SQ FT: 4,000
SALES (est): 44.9MM **Privately Held**
WEB: www.allpointspetroleum.com
SIC: 5172 Gasoline

(P-8718)
AMERIGAS PROPANE LP
11030 White Rock Rd # 100, Rancho Cordova (95670-6011)
PHONE..............................916 852-7400
Fax: 916 631-3180
EMP: 100 **Publicly Held**
SIC: 5172 7374
HQ: Amerigas Propane, L.P.
460 N Gulph Rd Ste 100
King Of Prussia PA 19406

(P-8719)
AMYRIS FUELS LLC
5885 Hollis St Ste 100, Emeryville (94608-2405)
PHONE..............................510 450-0761
John G Melo,
Benedict Tanjoco, *Manager*
EMP: 159
SALES (est): 6.1MM
SALES (corp-wide): 63.6MM **Publicly Held**
SIC: 5172 Fuel oil
PA: Amyris, Inc.
5885 Hollis St Ste 100
Emeryville CA 94608
510 450-0761

(P-8720)
BAY AREA/DIABLO PETROLEUM CO (HQ)
1340 Arnold Dr Ste 231, Martinez (94553-4189)
P.O. Box 4450, San Francisco (94144-0001)
PHONE..............................925 228-2222
Dennis M O'Keefe, *CEO*
Patrick O'Keefe, *Vice Pres*
EMP: 125 **EST:** 1970
SQ FT: 6,000
SALES (est): 111.6MM **Privately Held**
SIC: 5172 Gasoline
PA: Golden Gate Petroleum Co.
1340 Arnold Dr Ste 231
Martinez CA 94553
925 335-3700

(P-8721)
BAY AREA/DIABLO PETROLEUM CO
1800 Sutter St, Concord (94520-2563)
P.O. Box 44550, San Francisco (94144-0001)
PHONE..............................925 228-2222
Russell Mederios, *Manager*
EMP: 130
SALES (corp-wide): 111.6MM **Privately Held**
SIC: 5172 Gases, liquefied petroleum (propane)
HQ: Bay Area/Diablo Petroleum, Co.
1340 Arnold Dr Ste 231
Martinez CA 94553
925 228-2222

(P-8722)
CASEY COMPANY (PA)
180 E Ocean Blvd Ste 1010, Long Beach (90802-4711)
PHONE..............................562 436-9685
Larry Delpit Sr, *Chairman*
Barbara Odom, *Treasurer*
Neil Walker, *Executive*
EMP: 129
SQ FT: 4,000
SALES (est): 39.4MM **Privately Held**
SIC: 5172 Petroleum products

(P-8723)
DASSELS PETROLEUM INC
340 El Camino Real S, Salinas (93901-4553)
PHONE..............................831 636-5100
Graham Mackie, *Branch Mgr*
EMP: 50
SALES (corp-wide): 33MM **Privately Held**
WEB: www.dassels.com
SIC: 5172 Gases, liquefied petroleum (propane)
PA: Dassel's Petroleum, Inc.
31 Wright Rd
Hollister CA 95023
831 636-5100

(P-8724)
DOWNS FUEL TRANSPORT INC
1296 Magnolia Ave, Corona (92879-2027)
PHONE..............................951 256-8286
Michael J Downs, *President*
EMP: 50
SALES (est): 13.3MM **Privately Held**
SIC: 5172 Engine fuels & oils

(P-8725)
ED STAUB & SONS PETROLEUM INC
406 W 8th St, Alturas (96101-3205)
P.O. Box 1684 (96101-1684)
PHONE..............................530 233-2610
Sam Lutz, *Manager*
EMP: 53
SALES (corp-wide): 327.9MM **Privately Held**
SIC: 5172 Petroleum products
PA: Ed Staub & Sons Petroleum, Inc.
1301 Esplanade Ave
Klamath Falls OR 97601
541 887-8900

(P-8726)
EFUEL LLC
Also Called: Easy Fuel
65 Enterprise Fl 3, Aliso Viejo (92656-2705)
PHONE..............................949 330-7145
Donald Harper, *CEO*
EMP: 90
SALES (est): 65MM **Privately Held**
SIC: 5172 Petroleum products

(P-8727)
EMPIRE OIL CO
2756 S Riverside Ave, Bloomington (92316-3500)
PHONE..............................909 877-0226
Richard Alden Sr, *CEO*
Richard Scott Alden Jr, *President*
Donald Welker, *CFO*
EMP: 52
SQ FT: 2,300
SALES (est): 51.8MM **Publicly Held**
WEB: www.empireoil.com
SIC: 5172 Diesel fuel; lubricating oils & greases
HQ: Northern Tier Energy Lp
1250 W Washington St # 101
Tempe AZ 85281
602 302-5450

(P-8728)
FLYERS ENERGY LLC
4200 Buck Owens Blvd, Bakersfield (93308-4935)
PHONE..............................661 321-9961
Henry Medina, *President*
EMP: 320
SALES (corp-wide): 263.9MM **Privately Held**
SIC: 5172 Engine fuels & oils

PA: Flyers Energy, Llc
2360 Lindbergh St
Auburn CA 95602
530 885-0401

(P-8729)
FLYERS ENERGY LLC
571 W Slover Ave, Bloomington (92316-2454)
PHONE..............................909 877-2441
David Larimer, *Branch Mgr*
EMP: 118
SALES (corp-wide): 263.9MM **Privately Held**
SIC: 5172 Engine fuels & oils
PA: Flyers Energy, Llc
2360 Lindbergh St
Auburn CA 95602
530 885-0401

(P-8730)
GENERAL PETROLEUM CORPORATION (DH)
Also Called: G P Resources
19501 S Santa Fe Ave, Compton (90221-5913)
PHONE..............................562 983-7300
James A Halsam III, *CEO*
Michael Ruehring, *President*
Sean Kha, *Vice Pres*
Charles McDaniels, *Vice Pres*
Tracy Mausser, *Human Res Mgr*
▲ **EMP:** 150
SQ FT: 5,000
SALES (est): 75MM
SALES (corp-wide): 1.2B **Privately Held**
SIC: 5172 Crude oil
HQ: Pecos, Inc.
19501 S Santa Fe Ave
Compton CA 90221
310 356-2300

(P-8731)
INTER-STATE OIL CO (PA)
8221 Alpine Ave, Sacramento (95826-4708)
PHONE..............................916 457-6572
Brent Andrews, *President*
Terrance W Andrews, *President*
Laurie Andrews, *CFO*
Glen Jager, *Branch Mgr*
BDB Matthews, *Division Mgr*
EMP: 65
SQ FT: 20,000
SALES (est): 100.1MM **Privately Held**
WEB: www.interstateoil.com
SIC: 5172 Lubricating oils & greases

(P-8732)
INTERSTATE FUEL SYSTEMS INC
8221 Alpine Ave, Sacramento (95826-4708)
PHONE..............................916 457-6572
Terrance Andrews, *President*
Laurene Andrews, *Treasurer*
Dan Dalio, *Admin Sec*
Jason Ware, *Sales Staff*
EMP: 100
SQ FT: 20,000
SALES (est): 21.5MM **Privately Held**
SIC: 5172 Fuel oil

(P-8733)
IPC (USA) INC (HQ)
4 Hutton Cntre Dr Ste 700, Santa Ana (92707)
PHONE..............................949 648-5600
Hiroki Okinaga, *CEO*
EMP: 65
SQ FT: 9,450
SALES (est): 172.4MM **Privately Held**
WEB: www.usipc.com
SIC: 5172 Aircraft fueling services; diesel fuel; gasoline

(P-8734)
M O DION & SONS INC (PA)
1543 W 16th St, Long Beach (90813-1210)
PHONE..............................562 432-3946
Toll Free:.....................................888 -
Pat Cullen, *CEO*
Matt Cullen, *President*
Patrick B Cullen, *CEO*
Bill Frank, *CFO*
EMP: 60 **EST:** 1930

P R O D U C T S & S V C S

SQ FT: 85,000
SALES: 201.9MM **Privately Held**
WEB: www.dionandsons.com
SIC: 5172 Gasoline; diesel fuel; lubricating oils & greases

(P-8735)
SOUTHERN COUNTIES OIL CO
2075 Alum Rock Ave, San Jose (95116-2006)
PHONE..............................408 251-0811
Kathy Demarco, *Manager*
EMP: 50
SALES (corp-wide): 1.2B **Privately Held**
WEB: www.coastoil.com
SIC: 5172 Petroleum products
PA: Southern Counties Oil Co.
1800 W Katella Ave # 400
Orange CA 92867
714 744-7140

(P-8736)
STURDY OIL COMPANY
721 Vertin Ave, Salinas (93901-4526)
PHONE..............................831 970-9897
EMP: 72
SALES (corp-wide): 77.4MM **Privately Held**
SIC: 5172 Gasoline
PA: Sturdy Oil Company
1511 Abbott St
Salinas CA 93901
831 422-8801

(P-8737)
SWISSPORT FUELING INC
1 Edward White Way, Oakland (94621-4553)
P.O. Box 6366 (94603-0366)
PHONE..............................510 562-1701
Ken Carlson, *Manager*
Patrick Chan, *Finance Mgr*
EMP: 72
SALES (corp-wide): 175.4MM **Privately Held**
SIC: 5172 4925 Aircraft fueling services; gas production and/or distribution
PA: Swissport Fueling, Inc.
45025 Aviation Dr Ste 350
Dulles VA 20166
703 742-4338

(P-8738)
TOWER ENERGY GROUP (PA)
1983 W 190th St Ste 100, Torrance (90504-6240)
PHONE..............................310 538-8000
John Rogers, *Principal*
Twanna Rogers, *Vice Pres*
Nick Battaglia, *General Mgr*
Siamak Heshmati, *Admin Asst*
John Hendrick, *Opers Mgr*
EMP: 91
SQ FT: 22,702
SALES (est): 160.5MM **Privately Held**
SIC: 5172 Gasoline

(P-8739)
VALLEY PACIFIC PETRO SVCS INC
9521 Enos Ln, Bakersfield (93314-8007)
PHONE..............................661 746-7737
Kat Bowen, *Branch Mgr*
EMP: 103
SALES (corp-wide): 98.7MM **Privately Held**
SIC: 5172 Gasoline
PA: Valley Pacific Petroleum Services, Inc.
152 Frank West Cir # 100
Stockton CA 95206
209 948-9412

(P-8740)
VAN DE POL ENTERPRISES INC (PA)
4895 S Airport Way, Stockton (95206-3915)
P.O. Box 1107 (95201-1107)
PHONE..............................209 465-3421
Lee Atwater, *Ch of Bd*
Paul Gosal, *Owner*
Ted Wysoki, *Owner*
Ronald M Vandepol, *CEO*
Scott Macewan, *CFO*
EMP: 75
SQ FT: 10,000

SALES (est): 132.1MM **Privately Held**
SIC: 5172 Gasoline

(P-8741)
WARREN E&P INC
Also Called: Warren E & P
400 Oceangate Ste 200, Long Beach (90802-4306)
PHONE..............................877 587-9494
James A Watt, *CEO*
EMP: 67
SQ FT: 7,000
SALES (est): 1.9MM **Publicly Held**
SIC: 5172 Gasoline
PA: Warren Resources, Inc.
5420 Lbj Fwy Ste 600
Dallas TX 75240

(P-8742)
WHOLESALE FUELS INC
2200 E Brundage Ln, Bakersfield (93307-3066)
P.O. Box 82277 (93380-2277)
PHONE..............................661 327-4900
Charles McCan, *Officer*
Brian Bucassa, *CFO*
Tom Jamieson, *Corp Secy*
EMP: 63 EST: 1982
SQ FT: 5,000
SALES: 54.2MM **Privately Held**
WEB: www.wholesalefuels.com
SIC: 5172 Gasoline

5181 Beer & Ale Wholesale

(P-8743)
ACE BEVERAGE CO
550 S Mission Rd, Los Angeles (90033-4234)
P.O. Box 33256 (90033-0256)
PHONE..............................323 266-6238
Dan Holland, *Principal*
John Lavarias, *Manager*
EMP: 100
SALES (corp-wide): 433.6MM **Privately Held**
SIC: 5181 Beer & ale
HQ: Ace Beverage Co.
401 S Anderson St
Los Angeles CA 90033
323 264-6001

(P-8744)
ADVANCE BEVERAGE CO INC
5200 District Blvd, Bakersfield (93313-2330)
P.O. Box 9517 (93389-9517)
PHONE..............................661 833-3783
William K Lazzerini Sr, *Ch of Bd*
William K Lazzerini Jr, *President*
Anthony Lazzerini, *Vice Pres*
Terrie Brewer, *Human Res Mgr*
Mike Lazzerini, *Manager*
▲ EMP: 90
SQ FT: 93,000
SALES (est): 49.6MM **Privately Held**
WEB: www.advancebeverage.com
SIC: 5181 5182 Beer & other fermented malt liquors; wine

(P-8745)
ALLIED COMPANY HOLDINGS INC (PA)
Also Called: Best-Way Distributing Co
13235 Golden State Rd, Sylmar (91342-1129)
PHONE..............................818 493-6400
Kevin Williams, *CEO*
Erin S Gabler, *CFO*
William L Larson, *Vice Pres*
Earl J Whitehead, *Admin Sec*
Terry Parco, *Human Resources*
◆ EMP: 295
SQ FT: 240,000
SALES (est): 88.7MM **Privately Held**
WEB: www.alliedbeverages.com
SIC: 5181 Beer & other fermented malt liquors

(P-8746)
ANHEUSER-BUSCH LLC
1400 Marlborough Ave, Riverside (92507-2097)
PHONE..............................951 782-3935
Yo Sanchez, *Manager*
EMP: 150
SQ FT: 100,000
SALES (corp-wide): 1.5B **Privately Held**
WEB: www.hispanicbud.com
SIC: 5181 Beer & other fermented malt liquors
HQ: Anheuser-Busch, Llc
1 Busch Pl
Saint Louis MO 63118
800 342-5283

(P-8747)
ANHEUSER-BUSCH LLC
20499 S Reeves Ave, Carson (90810-1011)
PHONE..............................310 761-4600
Damian Bonnenfant, *Manager*
EMP: 115
SALES (corp-wide): 1.5B **Privately Held**
WEB: www.hispanicbud.com
SIC: 5181 Beer & other fermented malt liquors
HQ: Anheuser-Busch, Llc
1 Busch Pl
Saint Louis MO 63118
800 342-5283

(P-8748)
ANHEUSER-BUSCH LLC
18952 Macarthur Blvd, Irvine (92612-1432)
PHONE..............................949 263-9270
EMP: 111
SALES (corp-wide): 1.9B **Privately Held**
SIC: 5181
HQ: Anheuser-Busch, Llc
1 Busch Pl
Saint Louis MO 63118
314 632-6777

(P-8749)
BAY AREA DISTRIBUTING CO INC
1061 Factory St, Richmond (94801-2161)
PHONE..............................510 232-8554
Kenneth G Sodo, *President*
Michael Bosnich, *Vice Pres*
Janice Kwiatkowski, *Admin Asst*
Jeanine Mills, *Human Res Mgr*
Chris Baker, *Sales Staff*
▲ EMP: 50 EST: 1973
SQ FT: 22,000
SALES (est): 18.3MM **Privately Held**
SIC: 5181 5149 Beer & other fermented malt liquors; mineral or spring water bottling; soft drinks

(P-8750)
BEAUCHAMP DISTRIBUTING COMPANY
1911 S Santa Fe Ave, Compton (90221-5306)
PHONE..............................310 639-5320
Patrick L Beauchamp, *President*
Peter J Gumpert, *CFO*
Mary S Beauchamp, *Treasurer*
Stacee L Beauchamp, *Vice Pres*
Boomer Reisingerbeauch, *Sales Staff*
▲ EMP: 100
SQ FT: 100,000
SALES (est): 62.5MM **Privately Held**
SIC: 5181 5149 Beer & other fermented malt liquors; groceries & related products

(P-8751)
BOTTOMLEY DISTRIBUTING CO INC
755 Yosemite Dr, Milpitas (95035-5463)
PHONE..............................408 945-0660
Donald A Bottomley, *President*
Michael Santos, *Sales Mgr*
Craig Shore, *Sales Mgr*
Javier Arevalo, *Sales Associate*
Tony Sanfilippo, *Sales Staff*
▲ EMP: 90
SQ FT: 96,000
SALES (est): 21.6MM **Privately Held**
SIC: 5181 Beer & other fermented malt liquors

(P-8752)
CAPITAL BEVERAGE COMPANY (PA)
2500 Del Monte St, West Sacramento (95691-3835)
P.O. Box 914 (95691-0914)
PHONE..............................916 371-8164
Kenneth M Adamson, *President*
◆ EMP: 110 EST: 1960
SQ FT: 130,000
SALES (est): 28.7MM **Privately Held**
SIC: 5181 5182 5149 Beer & other fermented malt liquors; wine coolers, alcoholic; juices; mineral or spring water bottling

(P-8753)
CENTRAL COAST DISTRIBUTING LLC
815 S Blosser Rd, Santa Maria (93458-4915)
PHONE..............................805 922-2108
Michael Larrabee Jr, *President*
Gary Rudolph, *CFO*
Moises Gomez, *Executive*
Gil Fierros, *Area Mgr*
▲ EMP: 90
SQ FT: 51,651
SALES (est): 40.5MM **Privately Held**
SIC: 5181 Beer & other fermented malt liquors

(P-8754)
CLASSIC DISTRG & BEV GROUP INC
120 Puente Ave, City of Industry (91746-2301)
PHONE..............................626 934-3700
Carlos Joseph Sanchez, *President*
John Thomas, *CFO*
Alex Hernandez, *Manager*
Mike Sanchez, *Manager*
▲ EMP: 261
SQ FT: 102,000
SALES (est): 138.9MM **Privately Held**
WEB: www.classicdist.com
SIC: 5181 Beer & other fermented malt liquors

(P-8755)
COUCH DISTRIBUTING COMPANY INC
104 Lee Rd, Watsonville (95076-9448)
P.O. Box 50004 (95077-5004)
PHONE..............................831 724-0649
George W Couch III, *CEO*
Bonte Eugene, *Exec VP*
Geoffrey A Couch, *Vice Pres*
Rod Crowell, *Vice Pres*
Louie Pieracci, *Vice Pres*
▲ EMP: 160
SQ FT: 72,000
SALES (est): 75.2MM **Privately Held**
WEB: www.couchdistributing.com
SIC: 5181 Beer & other fermented malt liquors

(P-8756)
CREST BEVERAGE COMPANY INC
3840 Via De La Valle, Del Mar (92014-4268)
P.O. Box 9160, Rancho Santa Fe (92067-4160)
PHONE..............................858 452-2300
Steven S Sourapas Sr, *President*
▲ EMP: 170
SQ FT: 160,000
SALES (est): 57.4MM **Privately Held**
WEB: www.crestbeverage.com
SIC: 5181 5182 5149 Beer & other fermented malt liquors; wine; groceries & related products

(P-8757)
DBI BEVERAGE INC
4140 Brew Master Dr, Ceres (95307-7583)
PHONE..............................209 524-2477
Alexander Sweet, *Vice Pres*
Oke Ransome, *Manager*
Victor Ruiz, *Supervisor*
EMP: 75

▲ = Import ▼ =Export
◆ =Import/Export

SALES (corp-wide): 172.5MM **Privately Held**
SIC: **5181** Beer & other fermented malt liquors
PA: Dbi Beverage Inc.
2 Ingram Blvd
La Vergne TN 37089
615 793-2337

(P-8758)
DBI BEVERAGE SAN FRANCISCO
245 S Spruce Ave Ste 100, South San Francisco (94080-4597)
PHONE..................415 643-9900
David Ingram, *Ch of Bd*
Bob Stahl, *Co-President*
Stan J Butkowski, *Vice Pres*
Sergio Serrano, *District Mgr*
Rick Guida, *General Mgr*
▲ EMP: 250
SALES (est): 32.4MM
SALES (corp-wide): 172.5MM **Privately Held**
WEB: www.goldenbrands.com
SIC: **5181 5149** Beer & other fermented malt liquors; soft drinks; mineral or spring water bottling
PA: Dbi Beverage Inc.
2 Ingram Blvd
La Vergne TN 37089
615 793-2337

(P-8759)
DONAGHY SALES INC
2363 S Cedar Ave, Fresno (93725-1078)
PHONE..................(559 486-0901
Edward Donaghy, *CEO*
Janis Donaghy, *Admin Sec*
▲ EMP: 150
SQ FT: 75,000
SALES (est): 74.4MM **Privately Held**
SIC: **5181** Beer & other fermented malt liquors

(P-8760)
ELYXIR DISTRIBUTING LLC
270 W Riverside Dr, Watsonville (95076-5106)
PHONE..................831 761-6400
Paul C Ely III,
Kym Dewitt, *CFO*
Frederick Martinez, *District Mgr*
Skip Ely, *CIO*
Michelle Perry, *Human Res Mgr*
EMP: 103
SQ FT: 35,000
SALES (est): 58.7MM **Privately Held**
WEB: www.elyxir.com
SIC: **5181 5149** Beer & other fermented malt liquors; beverages, except coffee & tea

(P-8761)
FOOTHILL DISTRIBUTING CO INC
1530 Beltline Rd, Redding (96003-1408)
P.O. Box 492800 (96049-2800)
PHONE..................530 243-3932
Lance Goble, *President*
Lynn Goble, *Corp Secy*
Gary Burks, *Vice Pres*
Andi Fox, *Office Mgr*
▲ EMP: 101
SQ FT: 33,000
SALES (est): 39MM **Privately Held**
WEB: www.foothilldistributing.com
SIC: **5181 5182** Beer & other fermented malt liquors; wine

(P-8762)
FRESNO BEVERAGE COMPANY INC
Also Called: Valley Wide Beverage Company
3525 S East Ave, Fresno (93725-9000)
PHONE..................559 650-1500
Louis J Amendola, *CEO*
Michelle Smith, *Executive*
Brian Kennedy, *VP Admin*
Junior Cazares, *District Mgr*
Jeff Beal, *Sales Mgr*
◆ EMP: 180
SQ FT: 140,000

SALES (est): 90.1MM **Privately Held**
WEB: www.valleywidebeverage.com
SIC: **5181** Beer & other fermented malt liquors

(P-8763)
GATE CITY BEVERAGE DISTRS (PA)
2505 Steele Rd, San Bernardino (92408-3913)
PHONE..................909 799-0281
Leona Aronoff, *President*
Barry Aronoff, *CFO*
Charles Watts, *VP Opers*
Berg Marty, *Marketing Mgr*
▲ EMP: 294 EST: 1940
SQ FT: 280,000
SALES (est): 72.4MM **Privately Held**
WEB: www.gcbev.com
SIC: **5181 5149 5145** Beer & other fermented malt liquors; soft drinks; mineral or spring water bottling; confectionery

(P-8764)
GATE CITY BEVERAGE DISTRS
31315 Plantation Dr, Thousand Palms (92276-6602)
PHONE..................760 775-5483
Barry J Aronoff, *Owner*
EMP: 294
SQ FT: 10,000
SALES (corp-wide): 72.4MM **Privately Held**
WEB: www.gcbev.com
SIC: **5181 5149** Beer & other fermented malt liquors; water, distilled
PA: Gate City Beverage Distributors
2505 Steele Rd
San Bernardino CA 92408
909 799-0281

(P-8765)
HARALAMBOS BEVERAGE COMPANY (PA)
2300 Pellissier Pl, City of Industry (90601-1500)
P.O. Box 6005, El Monte (91734-2005)
PHONE..................562 347-4300
H T Haralambos, *CEO*
Anthony Haralambos, *President*
Thomas Haralambos, *Vice Pres*
Sally Haralambos, *Admin Sec*
Charles Mavudzi, *Info Tech Dir*
▲ EMP: 300 EST: 1933
SQ FT: 270,000
SALES (est): 199.8MM **Privately Held**
WEB: www.haralambos.com
SIC: **5181 5149** Beer & other fermented malt liquors; beverages, except coffee & tea

(P-8766)
HARBOR DISTRIBUTING LLC (HQ)
5901 Bolsa Ave, Huntington Beach (92647-2053)
PHONE..................714 933-2400
David K Reyes,
Tim McGuire,
Chris Reyes,
Jude Reyes,
▲ EMP: 200
SQ FT: 150,000
SALES (est): 135.8MM **Privately Held**
SIC: **5181** Beer & other fermented malt liquors

(P-8767)
HARBOR DISTRIBUTING LLC
Also Called: Golden Brands
3500 Carlin Dr, West Sacramento (95691-5872)
PHONE..................916 373-5700
Kimberly Clift, *Branch Mgr*
EMP: 300 **Privately Held**
SIC: **5181** Beer & other fermented malt liquors
HQ: Harbor Distributing, Llc
5901 Bolsa Ave
Huntington Beach CA 92647
714 933-2400

(P-8768)
HARBOR DISTRIBUTING LLC
Also Called: Harbor Distributing Co
16407 S Main St, Gardena (90248-2823)
PHONE..................310 538-5483
David Reyes, *Branch Mgr*
EMP: 300 **Privately Held**
SIC: **5181** Beer & other fermented malt liquors
HQ: Harbor Distributing, Llc
5901 Bolsa Ave
Huntington Beach CA 92647
714 933-2400

(P-8769)
HORIZON BEVERAGE COMPANY
8380 Pardee Dr, Oakland (94621-1481)
P.O. Box 6639 (94603-0639)
PHONE..................800 332-8358
Ces Butner, *Partner*
Denny Suzuki, *Partner*
EMP: 80
SQ FT: 20,000
SALES (est): 8.6MM **Privately Held**
SIC: **5181** Beer & other fermented malt liquors

(P-8770)
HORIZON BEVERAGE COMPANY LP
8380 Pardee Dr, Oakland (94621-1481)
P.O. Box 6639 (94603-0639)
PHONE..................510 465-2212
Gary Shinn,
Mike Thomas, *President*
Bonnie Medina, *Manager*
▲ EMP: 94
SALES (est): 21.7MM **Privately Held**
SIC: **5181** Beer & other fermented malt liquors

(P-8771)
JETRO CASH AND CARRY ENTPS LLC
5333 W Jefferson Blvd, Los Angeles (90016-3713)
PHONE..................323 964-1200
Enrique Gallard, *Principal*
EMP: 100
SALES (corp-wide): 24.5B **Privately Held**
WEB: www.jetro.com
SIC: **5181 5142 5194 5147** Beer & other fermented malt liquors; packaged frozen goods; tobacco & tobacco products; meats, fresh; groceries, general line
HQ: Jetro Cash And Carry Enterprises, Llc
1524 132nd St
College Point NY 11356
718 939-6400

(P-8772)
JORDANOS INC (PA)
Also Called: Jordano's Food Service
550 S Patterson Ave, Santa Barbara (93111-2498)
P.O. Box 6803 (93160-6803)
PHONE..................805 964-0611
Peter Jordano, *CEO*
Michael F Sieckowski, *CFO*
Jeffrey S Jordano, *Exec VP*
▲ EMP: 250
SQ FT: 80,000
SALES (est): 350.6MM **Privately Held**
WEB: www.jordanos.com
SIC: **5181 5182 5149 5141** Beer & other fermented malt liquors; wine; soft drinks; groceries, general line; packaged frozen goods; fresh fruits & vegetables

(P-8773)
LARRABEE BROTHRS DISTRIBTNG CO
815 S Blosser Rd, Santa Maria (93458-4915)
PHONE..................805 922-2108
Michael Larrabee, *President*
Margaret Larrabee, *Vice Pres*
EMP: 100
SQ FT: 51,651
SALES (est): 12.3MM **Privately Held**
SIC: **5181** Beer & other fermented malt liquors

(P-8774)
LE VECKE CORPORATION (PA)
Also Called: Le Vecke Group
10810 Inland Ave, Jurupa Valley (91752-3235)
PHONE..................951 681-8600
Joseph Neil Levecke, *CEO*
Neil Levecke, *President*
Luc Vanhal, *CFO*
Danny Orozco, *Admin Asst*
Maggie Weaver, *Human Resources*
◆ EMP: 62
SALES (est): 64.6MM
SALES (corp-wide): 71.1MM **Privately Held**
WEB: www.levecke.com
SIC: **5181** Beer & other fermented malt liquors

(P-8775)
LIQUID INVESTMENTS INC (PA)
3840 Via De La Valle # 300, Del Mar (92014-4268)
PHONE..................858 509-8510
Ron L Fowler, *CEO*
Mark Herculson, *Exec VP*
Terry L Harris, *VP Finance*
Terry Smith, *Finance*
▲ EMP: 170 EST: 1981
SQ FT: 190,000
SALES (est): 202.6MM **Privately Held**
WEB: www.lqdinv.com
SIC: **5181 5145 5182** Beer & other fermented malt liquors; fountain supplies; wine

(P-8776)
MARKSTEIN BEV CO SACRAMENTO
Also Called: Markstein Beverage Company
60 Main Ave, Sacramento (95838-2034)
P.O. Box 15379 (95851-0379)
PHONE..................916 920-3911
Hayden Markstein, *CEO*
Richard Markstein, *Ch of Bd*
Steve Markstein, *President*
Barbara Sady, *IT/INT Sup*
▲ EMP: 150
SALES (est): 97.6MM **Privately Held**
WEB: www.marksteinbev.com
SIC: **5181 5149** Beer & other fermented malt liquors; soft drinks; mineral or spring water bottling

(P-8777)
MARKSTEIN BEVERAGE CO
505 S Pacific St, San Marcos (92078-4049)
P.O. Box 6902 (92079-6902)
PHONE..................760 744-9100
Kenneth W Markstein, *CEO*
Steven Markstein, *Vice Pres*
▲ EMP: 120
SQ FT: 118,000
SALES (est): 57.5MM **Privately Held**
WEB: www.abwholesaler.com
SIC: **5181** Beer & other fermented malt liquors

(P-8778)
MATAGRANO INC
440 Forbes Blvd, South San Francisco (94080-2015)
P.O. Box 2588 (94083-2588)
PHONE..................650 829-4829
Louis Matagrano, *President*
William Hill, *CFO*
Tom Haas, *Vice Pres*
Frank Matagrano Jr, *Vice Pres*
Gary Nagle, *Division Mgr*
▲ EMP: 175
SQ FT: 100,000
SALES (est): 123.9MM **Privately Held**
WEB: www.matagrano.com
SIC: **5181 5149** Beer & other fermented malt liquors; mineral or spring water bottling; juices

(P-8779)
ME FOX & COMPANY INC
128 Component Dr, San Jose (95131-1180)
P.O. Box 2336, Saratoga (95070-0336)
PHONE..................408 435-8510
Michael E Fox Sr, *Ch of Bd*
Terence Fox, *President*

P
R
O
D
U
C
T
S

&

S
V
C
S

Doug Webenbauer, *CFO*
Catherine Fox, *Treasurer*
Mary Ellen Fox, *Exec VP*
▲ **EMP:** 100
SQ FT: 126,000
SALES (est): 75.4MM **Privately Held**
SIC: 5181 5149 Beer & other fermented
malt liquors; soft drinks; mineral or spring
water bottling; juices

(P-8780)
MESA DISTRIBUTING COINC
(HQ)
3840 Via De La Valle # 300, Del Mar
(92014-4268)
PHONE..............................858 452-2300
Ronald Fowler, *Ch of Bd*
Ron L Fowler, *Ch of Bd*
Jack F Studebaker, *Admin Sec*
EMP: 225
SQ FT: 190,000
SALES (est) 27.6MM
SALES (corp-wide): 202.6MM **Privately
Held**
WEB: www.mesadistributing.com
SIC: 5181 0182 5182 Beer & other fer-
mented malt liquors; vegetable crops
grown under cover; wine & distilled bever-
ages
PA: Liquid Investments, Inc.
3840 Via De La Valle # 300
Del Mar CA 92014
858 509-8510

(P-8781)
MISSION BEVERAGE CO (HQ)
550 S Mission Rd, Los Angeles
(90033-4256)
P.O. Box 33256 (90033-0256)
PHONE..............................323 266-6238
John E Anderson Sr, *Ch of Bd*
Don Holland, *President*
Therese D Curtis, *Corp Secy*
◆ **EMP:** 210
SALES (est) 47.7MM
SALES (corp-wide): 433.6MM **Privately
Held**
SIC: 5181 5149 Beer & other fermented
malt liquors; soft drinks
PA: Topa Equities, Ltd.
1800 Ave Of The
Los Angeles CA 90067
310 203-9199

(P-8782)
MORRIS DISTRIBUTING INC
3800a Lakeville Hwy, Petaluma
(94954-5673)
P.O. Box 5699 (94955-5699)
PHONE..............................707 769-7294
Ronald L Morris, *CEO*
Joe Netter, *Corp Secy*
▲ **EMP:** 80
SQ FT: 13,500
SALES (est): 25.7MM **Privately Held**
SIC: 5181 5149 Beer & other fermented
malt liquors; mineral or spring water bot-
tling

(P-8783)
NOR-CAL BEVERAGE CO INC
(PA)
2150 Stone Blvd, West Sacramento
(95691-4049)
PHONE..............................916 372-0600
Shannon Deary-Bell, *President*
Donald Deary, *Ch of Bd*
Grant Deary, *President*
Tim Deary, *President*
Mike Montroni, *CFO*
◆ **EMP:** 280
SQ FT: 152,000
SALES (est): 248.5MM **Privately Held**
SIC: 5181 2086 Beer & other fermented
malt liquors; soft drinks: packaged in
cans, bottles, etc.; fruit drinks (less than
100% juice): packaged in cans, etc.

(P-8784)
OB USA INC
Also Called: Bws Group Co.
931 S Cypress St, La Habra (90631-6833)
PHONE..............................213 465-4876
James Ha, *CEO*
EMP: 120

SALES (est): 24.5MM **Privately Held**
SIC: 5181 Beer & other fermented malt
liquors

(P-8785)
RESTAURANT DEPOT LLC
1265 N Kraemer Blvd, Anaheim
(92806-1921)
PHONE..............................714 666-9205
Ralph Vasquez, *Manager*
EMP: 150
SALES (corp-wide): 24.5B **Privately Held**
WEB: www.jrdtuning.com
SIC: 5181 5141 5194 5142 Beer & other
fermented malt liquors; groceries, general
line; tobacco & tobacco products; pack-
aged frozen goods; meats, fresh
HQ: Restaurant Depot, Llc
1524 132nd St
College Point NY 11356

(P-8786)
RESTAURANT DEPOT LLC
19901 Hamilton Ave Ste A, Torrance
(90502-1367)
PHONE..............................310 516-7400
Sue Greene, *Branch Mgr*
EMP: 60
SALES (corp-wide): 24.5B **Privately Held**
WEB: www.jrdtuning.com
SIC: 5181 5141 5194 5142 Beer & other
fermented malt liquors; groceries, general
line; tobacco & tobacco products; pack-
aged frozen goods; meats, fresh
HQ: Restaurant Depot, Llc
1524 132nd St
College Point NY 11356

(P-8787)
RESTAURANT DEPOT LLC
2045 Evans Ave, San Francisco
(94124-1022)
PHONE..............................415 920-2888
Samuel Cortez, *Branch Mgr*
EMP: 150
SALES (corp-wide): 24.5B **Privately Held**
WEB: www.jrdtuning.com
SIC: 5181 5141 5194 5142 Beer & other
fermented malt liquors; groceries, general
line; tobacco & tobacco products; pack-
aged frozen goods; meats, fresh
HQ: Restaurant Depot, Llc
1524 132nd St
College Point NY 11356

(P-8788)
RESTAURANT DEPOT LLC
5333 W Jefferson Blvd, Los Angeles
(90016-3713)
PHONE..............................323 964-1220
Enrique Gallard, *Manager*
EMP: 150
SALES (corp-wide): 24.5B **Privately Held**
WEB: www.jrdtuning.com
SIC: 5181 5194 5147 5142 Beer & other
fermented malt liquors; tobacco & to-
bacco products; meats, fresh; packaged
frozen goods; groceries, general line
HQ: Restaurant Depot, Llc
1524 132nd St
College Point NY 11356

(P-8789)
RESTAURANT DEPOT LLC
15853 Strathern St, Van Nuys
(91406-1310)
PHONE..............................818 376-7687
Dan Mihal, *Manager*
EMP: 150
SALES (corp-wide): 24.5B **Privately Held**
WEB: www.jrdtuning.com
SIC: 5181 5147 5141 5142 Beer & other
fermented malt liquors; meats, fresh; gro-
ceries, general line; packaged frozen
goods; tobacco & tobacco products
HQ: Restaurant Depot, Llc
1524 132nd St
College Point NY 11356

(P-8790)
SACCANI DISTRIBUTING
COMPANY
2600 5th St, Sacramento (95818-2899)
P.O. Box 1764 (95812-1764)
PHONE..............................916 441-0213
Gary Saccani, *President*
Steven Fishman, *Corp Secy*
Roland Saccani, *Vice Pres*
Neal Banyard, *District Mgr*
Bise Rod, *District Mgr*
▲ **EMP:** 90
SQ FT: 40,000
SALES (est): 37.9MM **Privately Held**
SIC: 5181 5149 Beer & other fermented
malt liquors; soft drinks

(P-8791)
SEQUOIA BEVERAGE
COMPANY LP
2122 N Plaza Dr, Visalia (93291-9358)
P.O. Box 5025 (93278-5025)
PHONE..............................559 651-2444
Dan Bueno, *Partner*
Rose Bueno, *Partner*
Joan Carpenter, *Partner*
Bill McAlister, *Administration*
Laurie Zuniga, *Administration*
EMP: 101
SQ FT: 100,000
SALES (est): 77.2MM **Privately Held**
WEB: www.sequoia-beverage.com
SIC: 5181 Beer & other fermented malt
liquors

(P-8792)
STRAUB DISTRIBUTING CO LTD
(PA)
4633 E La Palma Ave, Anaheim
(92807-1909)
PHONE..............................714 779-4000
Michael L Cooper, *General Ptnr*
Robert K Adams, *Partner*
Don Beightol, *Partner*
▲ **EMP:** 150
SQ FT: 32,000
SALES (est): 136MM **Privately Held**
WEB: www.sdcoc.net
SIC: 5181 Beer & other fermented malt
liquors

(P-8793)
T F LOUDERBACK INC (PA)
Also Called: Bay Area Beverage
700 National Ct, Richmond (94804-2008)
PHONE..............................510 965-6120
Thomas J Louderback, *President*
Ron Bishop, *CFO*
Chris Reed, *Division Mgr*
Todd Rovelstad, *Admin Sec*
Juan Maciel, *Graphic Designe*
▲ **EMP:** 102
SQ FT: 65,000
SALES (est): 68.2MM **Privately Held**
WEB: www.bayareabev.com
SIC: 5181 5149 2037 2033 Beer & other
fermented malt liquors; beverages, except
coffee & tea; juices; frozen fruits & veg-
etables; canned fruits & specialties

(P-8794)
TRIANGLE DISTRIBUTING CO
(PA)
Also Called: Heimark Distributing
12065 Pike St, Santa Fe Springs
(90670-2964)
PHONE..............................562 699-3424
Donald Heimark, *Ch of Bd*
Peter H Heimark, *President*
Mike Crow, *Corp Secy*
▲ **EMP:** 170
SQ FT: 150,000
SALES (est): 86.8MM **Privately Held**
WEB: www.triangle-dist.com
SIC: 5181 Beer & other fermented malt
liquors

(P-8795)
TRIANGLE DISTRIBUTING CO
Also Called: Hallmark Distributing
82851 Avenue 45, Indio (92201-2379)
P.O. Box 3108 (92202-3108)
PHONE..............................760 347-4052
Bill Shiner, *General Mgr*
James B Fleming, *President*

EMP: 55
SALES (corp-wide): 86.8MM **Privately
Held**
WEB: www.triangle-dist.com
SIC: 5181 Beer & other fermented malt
liquors
PA: Triangle Distributing Co.
12065 Pike St
Santa Fe Springs CA 90670
562 699-3424

**5182 Wine & Distilled
Alcoholic Beverages
Wholesale**

(P-8796)
AV BRANDS INC
Also Called: Aveniu Brands
635 Broadway Ste 2, Sonoma
(95476-7004)
PHONE..............................410 884-9463
Andrew Mansinne, *President*
▲ **EMP:** 50
SQ FT: 7,000
SALES (est): 20.6MM **Privately Held**
WEB: www.avimports.com
SIC: 5182 Wine

(P-8797)
BARREL TEN QUARTER CIRCLE
INC
33 Harlow Ct, NAPA (94558-7520)
P.O. Box 3400 (94558-0551)
PHONE..............................707 265-4000
Fred T Franzia, *CEO*
John G Franzia Jr, *Co-President*
Joseph S Franzia, *Co-President*
Daniel Leonard, *Vice Pres*
EMP: 300
SALES (est): 45.5MM
SALES (corp-wide): 196.9MM **Privately
Held**
SIC: 5182 Bottling wines & liquors
PA: Bronco Wine Company
6342 Bystrum Rd
Ceres CA 95307
209 538-3131

(P-8798)
BAY AREA BEVERAGE CO
700 National Ct, Richmond (94804-2008)
PHONE..............................510 965-6120
Tj Louderback, *President*
Ciaran Byrne, *CFO*
Larry Green, *Vice Pres*
EMP: 205
SALES (est): 49.8MM **Privately Held**
SIC: 5182 Wine

(P-8799)
BEN MYERSON CANDY CO INC
(PA)
Also Called: Wine Warehouse
6550 E Washington Blvd, Commerce
(90040-1822)
P.O. Box 910900, Los Angeles (90091-
0900)
PHONE..............................800 331-2829
James P Myerson, *President*
Linda Perez, *President*
Robert Myerson, *Treasurer*
James Myerson, *Corp Secy*
Trevor Thiret, *Exec VP*
◆ **EMP:** 350
SQ FT: 135,000
SALES (est): 363.7MM **Privately Held**
SIC: 5182 5023 Wine; glassware

(P-8800)
BEN MYERSON CANDY CO INC
Also Called: Wine Warehouse
3463 Collins Ave, Richmond (94806-2000)
P.O. Box 45616, San Francisco (94145-
0616)
PHONE..............................510 236-2233
Michael Cimino, *Manager*
Keith Smith, *CFO*
Linda Myerson, *Vice Pres*
Christopher Giordano, *Manager*
Brendan Sinclair, *Manager*
EMP: 95
SQ FT: 2,000

SALES (corp-wide): 363.7MM **Privately Held**
SIC: 5182 5181 Liquor; neutral spirits; beer & ale
PA: Ben Myerson Candy Co., Inc.
    6550 E Washington Blvd
    Commerce CA 90040
    800 331-2829

(P-8801)
CRIMSON WINE GROUP LTD (PA)
2700 Napa Vly Corp Dr B, NAPA (94558)
PHONE.....................800 486-0503
Nicolas Quille, *CEO*
John D Cumming, *Ch of Bd*
Karen L Diepholz, *CFO*
Lisa H Kislak, *Chief Mktg Ofcr*
Mike S Cekay, *Senior VP*
▲ EMP: 178
SQ FT: 13,200
SALES: 67.7MM **Publicly Held**
SIC: 5182 Wine

(P-8802)
DBI BEVERAGE SACRAMENTO (HQ)
3500 Carlin Dr, West Sacramento (95691-5872)
PHONE.....................916 373-5700
Jeff Skinner, *CEO*
Kim Paulk, *Vice Pres*
Ryan Bosch, *Branch Mgr*
Bob Beviacqua, *District Mgr*
Tom Grace, *District Mgr*
▲ EMP: 56 EST: 2007
SQ FT: 200,000
SALES (est): 93.7MM
SALES (corp-wide): 172.5MM **Privately Held**
SIC: 5182 5149 Wine & distilled beverages; beverages, except coffee & tea
PA: Dbi Beverage Inc.
    2 Ingram Blvd
    La Vergne TN 37089
    615 793-2337

(P-8803)
DIAGEO NORTH AMERICA INC
21468 8th St E, Sonoma (95476-9767)
PHONE.....................707 939-6200
Claudia Schubert, *Branch Mgr*
EMP: 65
SALES (corp-wide): 16.3B **Privately Held**
SIC: 5182 Wine
HQ: Diageo North America Inc.
    801 Main Ave
    Norwalk CT 06851
    203 229-2100

(P-8804)
DIAGEO NORTH AMERICA INC
30 Journey, Aliso Viejo (92656-3317)
PHONE.....................949 421-3974
Chris Turbeville, *Branch Mgr*
EMP: 69
SALES (corp-wide): 16.3B **Privately Held**
SIC: 5182 Wine
HQ: Diageo North America Inc.
    801 Main Ave
    Norwalk CT 06851
    203 229-2100

(P-8805)
DRINKS HOLDINGS INC
1125 E Broadway 173, Glendale (91205-1315)
PHONE.....................310 441-8400
EMP: 90
SALES (corp-wide): 102.8MM **Privately Held**
SIC: 5182 Wine
PA: Drinks Holdings, Inc.
    11175 Santa Monica Blvd # 400
    Los Angeles CA 90025
    310 441-8400

(P-8806)
FOLIO WINE COMPANY LLC (PA)
Also Called: Folio Wine Company Imports
550 Gateway Dr Ste 220, NAPA (94558-7578)
PHONE.....................707 254-9885
R Michael Mondavi, *Mng Member*

Jamie Conahan, *Partner*
Holly Delucchi, *Partner*
Jennifer Hornor, *Partner*
Clint Wilsey, *Vice Pres*
▲ EMP: 105
SALES (est): 35.9MM **Privately Held**
WEB: www.foliowine.com
SIC: 5182 Wine

(P-8807)
FOLIO WINE COMPANY LLC
1285 Dealy Ln, NAPA (94559-9706)
PHONE.....................707 256-2757
Rick Choate, *Branch Mgr*
EMP: 65
SALES (corp-wide): 35.9MM **Privately Held**
SIC: 5182 Wine
PA: Folio Wine Company, Llc
    550 Gateway Dr Ste 220
    Napa CA 94558
    707 254-9885

(P-8808)
FRANK-LIN DISTILLERS PDTS LTD (PA)
2455 Huntington Dr, Fairfield (94533-9734)
PHONE.....................408 259-8900
Frank J Maestri, *President*
Anthony Demaria, *CFO*
Mark S Pechusick, *Exec VP*
Lindley Maestri, *Vice Pres*
Michael Maestri, *Vice Pres*
◆ EMP: 110 EST: 1966
SQ FT: 54,216
SALES (est): 78.1MM **Privately Held**
SIC: 5182 2085 Wine; distilled & blended liquors

(P-8809)
FREIXENET USA INC
Also Called: Gloria Ferrer
23555 Arnold Dr, Sonoma (95476-9285)
P.O. Box 1949 (95476-1949)
PHONE.....................707 996-7256
Jose Maria Ferrer, *President*
Eva Bertran, *Exec VP*
David Brown, *VP Mktg*
▲ EMP: 54
SQ FT: 4,000
SALES (est): 29.8MM
SALES (corp-wide): 242.4MM **Privately Held**
WEB: www.freixenetusa.com
SIC: 5182 Wine
PA: Freixenet Sa
    Plaza Joan Sala 2
    Sant Sadurni D Anoia 08770
    938 917-000

(P-8810)
GALLO SALES COMPANY INC (DH)
30825 Wiegman Rd, Hayward (94544-7893)
P.O. Box 1266, Union City (94587-6266)
PHONE.....................510 476-5000
Joseph E Gallo, *President*
Andrew Sanchez, *Sales Staff*
EMP: 225
SQ FT: 59,000
SALES (est): 42.1MM
SALES (corp-wide): 2.3B **Privately Held**
SIC: 5182 Wine
HQ: Gallo Glass Company
    605 S Santa Cruz Ave
    Modesto CA 95354
    209 341-3710

(P-8811)
GUARACHI WINE PARTNERS INC
Also Called: Parker Station
22837 Ventura Blvd # 300, Woodland Hills (91364-1224)
PHONE.....................818 225-5100
Alejandro Guarachi, *CEO*
Daniel Lyons, *President*
Travis Arnesen, *Vice Pres*
James Eder, *Area Mgr*
Maria Cordova, *Human Resources*
▲ EMP: 80
SQ FT: 5,000
SALES (est): 37MM **Privately Held**
WEB: www.tgicimporters.com
SIC: 5182 Wine

(P-8812)
HENRY WINE GROUP LLC (HQ)
Also Called: Henry Wine Group of C.A., The
4301 Industrial Way, Benicia (94510-1227)
PHONE.....................707 745-8500
Ed Hogan, *President*
Kent Fitzgerald, *President*
Stephanie O'Brien, *CFO*
Amoreena Anker, *Vice Pres*
Ron Lastinger, *Vice Pres*
▲ EMP: 297
SALES (est): 80.3MM
SALES (corp-wide): 604.4MM **Privately Held**
SIC: 5182 Wine
PA: The Winebow Group Llc
    4800 Cox Rd Ste 300
    Glen Allen VA 23060
    804 752-3670

(P-8813)
JACKSON FAMILY WINES INC
Regal Wine Company, The
1190 Kittyhawk Blvd Ste A, Santa Rosa (95403-1013)
PHONE.....................415 819-0301
John Grant, *Branch Mgr*
EMP: 150
SQ FT: 20,746
SALES (corp-wide): 329.7MM **Privately Held**
WEB: www.cambriawines.com
SIC: 5182 Wine
PA: Jackson Family Wines, Inc.
    421 And 425 Aviation Blvd
    Santa Rosa CA 95403
    707 544-4000

(P-8814)
MAGAVE TEQUILA INC
6 Park Pl, Belvedere Tiburon (94920-1048)
PHONE.....................415 515-3536
Michael Patane, *CEO*
▲ EMP: 50
SALES (est): 13.4MM **Privately Held**
SIC: 5182 Liquor

(P-8815)
MONTESQUIEU CORP
Also Called: Montesquieu Vins & Domaines
8929 Aero Dr Ste C, San Diego (92123-2231)
PHONE.....................877 705-5669
Fonda Hopkins, *President*
Frank Kryger, *Director*
▲ EMP: 100
SQ FT: 28,800
SALES (est): 18.2MM **Privately Held**
WEB: www.gerhardtwines.com
SIC: 5182 8743 Wine; promotion service

(P-8816)
SOUTHERN GLAZERS WINE
Also Called: Sgws of CA
33321 Dowe Ave, Union City (94587-2033)
P.O. Box 5001 (94587-8501)
PHONE.....................510 477-5500
Gary Nedd, *Manager*
Gunnar Brekke, *Executive*
Gina Chai, *Executive*
Tommy Sotiropulos, *Executive*
Elizabeth Duran, *Executive Asst*
EMP: 350
SALES (corp-wide): 13.8B **Privately Held**
WEB: www.southernwine.com
SIC: 5182 Wine
PA: Southern Glazer's Wine And Spirits, Llc
    1600 Nw 163rd St
    Miami FL 33169
    305 625-4171

(P-8817)
SOUTHERN GLAZERS WINE
723 Palmyrita Ave, Riverside (92507-1811)
PHONE.....................951 274-2420
Ryan Okeese, *Manager*
Ivan Rouse, *Manager*
EMP: 50
SALES (corp-wide): 13.8B **Privately Held**
WEB: www.southernwine.com
SIC: 5182 Wine
PA: Southern Glazer's Wine And Spirits, Llc
    1600 Nw 163rd St
    Miami FL 33169
    305 625-4171

(P-8818)
SOUTHERN GLAZERS WINE
10730 Scripps Ranch Blvd, San Diego (92131-1003)
PHONE.....................858 537-3912
Craig Fontaine, *Manager*
EMP: 110
SALES (corp-wide): 13.8B **Privately Held**
WEB: www.southernwine.com
SIC: 5182 Wine
PA: Southern Glazer's Wine And Spirits, Llc
    1600 Nw 163rd St
    Miami FL 33169
    305 625-4171

(P-8819)
SOUTHERN GLAZERS WINE
2320 Kruse Dr, San Jose (95131-1231)
PHONE.....................408 750-3540
Julie Long, *Branch Mgr*
Kelsea Rehs, *Sales Staff*
EMP: 75
SALES (corp-wide): 13.8B **Privately Held**
WEB: www.southernwine.com
SIC: 5182 Bottling wines & liquors; wine
PA: Southern Glazer's Wine And Spirits, Llc
    1600 Nw 163rd St
    Miami FL 33169
    305 625-4171

(P-8820)
SOUTHERN GLAZERS WINE
17101 Valley View Ave, Cerritos (90703-2413)
PHONE.....................562 926-2000
Steve Slader, *Branch Mgr*
Stephen Magliocco, *Vice Pres*
Dane Meza, *Area Mgr*
Andre Surma, *Purchasing*
Steve Chapman, *Sales Staff*
EMP: 500
SALES (corp-wide): 13.8B **Privately Held**
WEB: www.southernwine.com
SIC: 5182 5181 Wine; liquor; beer & ale
PA: Southern Glazer's Wine And Spirits, Llc
    1600 Nw 163rd St
    Miami FL 33169
    305 625-4171

(P-8821)
VINO FARMS LLC
1377 E Lodi Ave, Lodi (95240-0840)
PHONE.....................209 334-6975
James Ledbetter,
John Ledbetter,
EMP: 700
SQ FT: 5,000
SALES (est): 123MM **Privately Held**
SIC: 5182 Wine

(P-8822)
VINWOOD CELLARS INC
18700 Geyserville Ave, Geyserville (95441-9526)
P.O. Box 1341, Healdsburg (95448-1341)
PHONE.....................707 857-4011
Alan Hemphill, *President*
EMP: 50
SALES (est): 8MM **Privately Held**
SIC: 5182 2084 Wine & distilled beverages; wines

(P-8823)
WINE GROUP INC
Also Called: Franza Sanger Winery
2916 S Reed Ave, Sanger (93657-9526)
PHONE.....................559 638-3511
Gary Nakagawa, *Manager*
EMP: 95
SALES (corp-wide): 148.2MM **Privately Held**
SIC: 5182 Wine
HQ: The Wine Group Inc
    17000 E State Highway 120
    Ripon CA 95366
    209 599-4111

(P-8824)
WINERY EXCHANGE INC (PA)
Also Called: Wx Brands
500 Redwood Blvd Ste 200, Novato (94947-6921)
PHONE.....................415 382-6900
Peter Byck, *CEO*
John Gilmer, *Senior VP*
Bryan Moreno, *Senior VP*

P R O D U C T S & S V C S

Peter Arbios, *Vice Pres*
Richard Bartlett, *Vice Pres*
▲ **EMP:** 50
SQ FT: 8,300
SALES (est): 74.1MM **Privately Held**
WEB: www.wineryexchange.com
SIC: 5182 Wine

(P-8825)
WINIARSKI MANAGEMENT INC
5766 Silverado Trl, NAPA (94558-9413)
PHONE..................707 944-2020
Warren P Winiarski, *President*
EMP: 100
SALES (est): 10MM **Privately Held**
SIC: 5182 0172 Wine; grapes

(P-8826)
YOUNGS HOLDINGS INC (PA)
14402 Franklin Ave, Tustin (92780-7013)
PHONE..................714 368-4615
Chris Underwood, *CEO*
Vernon Underwood Jr, *Ch of Bd*
John Barton, *Vice Pres*
Scott Blackburn, *Vice Pres*
Robert Cernius, *Vice Pres*
EMP: 100
SALES (est): 1.2B **Privately Held**
SIC: 5182 Wine; neutral spirits

(P-8827)
YOUNGS MARKET COMPANY LLC (HQ)
14402 Franklin Ave, Tustin (92780-7013)
PHONE..................800 317-6150
Chris Underwood, *CEO*
Dennis Hamann, *CFO*
Kevin Manion, *CFO*
Vern Underwood, *Chairman*
Kevin Perez, *Treasurer*
◆ **EMP:** 350
SQ FT: 250,000
SALES (est): 981MM
SALES (corp-wide): 1.2B **Privately Held**
SIC: 5182 Wine; neutral spirits
PA: Young's Holdings, Inc.
14402 Franklin Ave
Tustin CA 92780
714 368-4615

(P-8828)
YOUNGS MARKET COMPANY LLC
850 Jarvis Dr, Morgan Hill (95037-2846)
PHONE..................408 782-3121
Ken Feroli, *Manager*
EMP: 100
SALES (corp-wide): 1.2B **Privately Held**
SIC: 5182 Liquor
HQ: Young's Market Company, Llc
14402 Franklin Ave
Tustin CA 92780
800 317-6150

(P-8829)
YOUNGS MARKET COMPANY LLC
5100 Franklin Dr, Pleasanton (94588-3355)
PHONE..................510 475-2200
Chris Nicks, *Manager*
Regan Martinez, *Human Res Mgr*
Nicholas Westbrook, *Merchandising*
Wayne West, *Sales Staff*
Scott Allen, *Manager*
EMP: 400
SQ FT: 20,000
SALES (corp-wide): 1.2B **Privately Held**
SIC: 5182 Wine; liquor
HQ: Young's Market Company, Llc
14402 Franklin Ave
Tustin CA 92780
800 317-6150

(P-8830)
YOUNGS MARKET COMPANY LLC
Also Called: Wine Dept
500 S Central Ave, Los Angeles (90013-1715)
PHONE..................213 629-3929
Mark Sneed, *Branch Mgr*
Scott Senatore, *Vice Pres*
Ponder Zach, *Technology*
Jamie Van Hoorn, *Sales Staff*
EMP: 450

SALES (corp-wide): 1.2B **Privately Held**
SIC: 5182 Liquor
HQ: Young's Market Company, Llc
14402 Franklin Ave
Tustin CA 92780
800 317-6150

(P-8831)
YOUNGS MARKET COMPANY LLC
256 Sutton Pl Ste 106, Santa Rosa (95407-8163)
PHONE..................707 584-5170
Mark Delbenny, *Manager*
EMP: 65
SALES (corp-wide): 1.2B **Privately Held**
SIC: 5182 Wine
HQ: Young's Market Company, Llc
14402 Franklin Ave
Tustin CA 92780
800 317-6150

(P-8832)
YOUNGS MARKET COMPANY LLC
3620 Industrial Blvd # 10, West Sacramento (95691-6518)
PHONE..................916 617-4402
Jim Morris, *Branch Mgr*
Jon Scriven, *Exec VP*
Todd Kamla, *Sales Staff*
EMP: 50
SALES (corp-wide): 1.2B **Privately Held**
SIC: 5182 Liquor; wine
HQ: Young's Market Company, Llc
14402 Franklin Ave
Tustin CA 92780
800 317-6150

5191 Farm Splys Wholesale

(P-8833)
AG RX (PA)
751 S Rose Ave, Oxnard (93030-5146)
P.O. Box 2008 (93034-2008)
PHONE..................805 487-0696
Ken Burdullis, *President*
EMP: 92
SQ FT: 45,000
SALES (est): 79.5MM **Privately Held**
WEB: www.agrx.com
SIC: 5191 Fertilizer & fertilizer materials

(P-8834)
ASSOCIATED FEED & SUPPLY CO (PA)
Also Called: Farwest Trading
5213 W Main St, Turlock (95380-9413)
P.O. Box 2367 (95381-2367)
PHONE..................209 667-2708
Matt Swanson, *President*
Jim Hyer, *Exec VP*
Kurt Hertlein, *Vice Pres*
▲ **EMP:** 125
SQ FT: 1,800
SALES (est): 99.9MM **Privately Held**
SIC: 5191 Animal feeds

(P-8835)
BORDER VALLEY TRADING LTD
604 Mead Rd, Brawley (92227-9748)
P.O. Box 62 (92227-0062)
PHONE..................760 344-6700
EMP: 56 **Privately Held**
SIC: 5191
PA: Border Valley Trading, Ltd.
14503 W Harding Rd
Turlock CA 92227

(P-8836)
BORDER VALLEY TRADING LTD
604 Mead Rd, Brawley (92227-9748)
P.O. Box 62 (92227-0062)
PHONE..................760 344-6700
Greg Braun, *President*
Paul Cameron, *Corp Secy*
Robert Presley, *Vice Pres*
◆ **EMP:** 68
SQ FT: 1,200
SALES (est): 61.8MM **Privately Held**
SIC: 5191 Hay

(P-8837)
BRITZ FERTILIZERS INC
Also Called: Bsgs Five Points
21817 S Frsno Coalinga Rd, Five Points (93624)
PHONE..................559 884-2421
Ken Walls, *Manager*
EMP: 100
SALES (corp-wide): 297.6MM **Privately Held**
WEB: www.britzinc.com
SIC: 5191 Chemicals, agricultural; fertilizer & fertilizer materials
HQ: Britz Fertilizers Inc.
3265 W Figarden Dr
Fresno CA 93711
559 448-8000

(P-8838)
BUTTONWILLOW WAREHOUSE CO INC (HQ)
3430 Unicorn Rd, Bakersfield (93308-6829)
P.O. Box 98, Buttonwillow (93206-0098)
PHONE..................661 695-6500
Donald Houchin, *President*
Brad Crowder, *COO*
Scott Stanley, *CFO*
Wallace Houchin, *Vice Pres*
Dean Dominguez, *Manager*
EMP: 75
SALES (est): 80.3MM
SALES (corp-wide): 89MM **Privately Held**
SIC: 5191 Fertilizer & fertilizer materials
PA: Tech Agricultural, Inc.
125 Front St
Buttonwillow CA 93206
661 764-5234

(P-8839)
E B STONE & SON INC
Also Called: Greenall
6111 Lambie Rd, Suisun City (94585-9789)
P.O. Box 550 (94585-0550)
PHONE..................707 426-2500
Bradford G Crandall, *CEO*
Bradford G Crandall Jr, *President*
Lynne Crandall, *Admin Sec*
EMP: 65
SQ FT: 79,000
SALES (est): 42.2MM **Privately Held**
WEB: www.ebstone.org
SIC: 5191 2873 2875 3423 Fertilizer & fertilizer materials; garden supplies; nitrogenous fertilizers; fertilizers, mixing only; hand & edge tools

(P-8840)
FOSTER POULTRY FARMS
4107 Ave 360, Traver (93673)
PHONE..................559 457-6509
Larry Ficken, *Plant Mgr*
EMP: 927
SALES (corp-wide): 3B **Privately Held**
SIC: 5191 Farm supplies
PA: Foster Poultry Farms
1000 Davis St
Livingston CA 95334
209 394-6914

(P-8841)
JR SIMPLOT COMPANY
3265 W Figarden Dr, Fresno (93711-3912)
P.O. Box 28955 (93729-8955)
PHONE..................559 439-3900
EMP: 178
SALES (corp-wide): 4.8B **Privately Held**
SIC: 5191 Fertilizer & fertilizer materials
PA: J.R. Simplot Company
1099 W Front St
Boise ID 83702
208 780-3287

(P-8842)
JR SIMPLOT COMPANY
Also Called: Simplot Growers Solutions
35836 W Bullard Ave, Firebaugh (93622-9714)
P.O. Box 725 (93622-0725)
PHONE..................559 659-2033
Johnny Valov, *Branch Mgr*
EMP: 50
SALES (corp-wide): 4.8B **Privately Held**
SIC: 5191 Fertilizer & fertilizer materials

PA: J.R. Simplot Company
1099 W Front St
Boise ID 83702
208 780-3287

(P-8843)
L & L NURSERY SUPPLY INC (PA)
Also Called: Unigro
2552 Shenandoah Way, San Bernardino (92407-1845)
PHONE..................909 591-0461
Lloyd Swindell, *Ch of Bd*
Harvey Luth, *President*
Tom Medhurst, *President*
Mike Fuson, *Vice Pres*
Larry Tabert, *Info Tech Mgr*
▲ **EMP:** 150 **EST:** 1953
SQ FT: 107,000
SALES (est): 184.4MM **Privately Held**
WEB: www.llnurserysupply.com
SIC: 5191 2875 2449 5193 Insecticides; fertilizer & fertilizer materials; soil, potting & planting; potting soil, mixed; wood containers; flowers & florists' supplies

(P-8844)
L A HEARNE COMPANY (PA)
512 Metz Rd, King City (93930-2503)
PHONE..................831 385-5441
Francis Giudici, *President*
Dennis Hearne, *Ch of Bd*
Frank Hearne, *Vice Pres*
Mike Hearne, *Vice Pres*
Tim Hearne, *Vice Pres*
▲ **EMP:** 70 **EST:** 1938
SQ FT: 220,000
SALES (est): 75.1MM **Privately Held**
WEB: www.hearneco.com
SIC: 5191 0723 5699 4214 Fertilizers & agricultural chemicals; bean cleaning services; grain drying services; seed cleaning; western apparel; local trucking with storage; livestock feeds; lawn & garden supplies

(P-8845)
LANTING HAY DEALER INC
9032 Merrill Ave, Ontario (91762-7234)
P.O. Box 747, Chino (91708-0747)
PHONE..................909 563-5601
Ronald J Lanting, *President*
Lorraine Lanting, *Corp Secy*
Bradley M Lanting, *Vice Pres*
Curtis J Lanting, *Vice Pres*
Ronald P Lanting, *Vice Pres*
EMP: 75
SQ FT: 40,000
SALES (est): 18.9MM **Privately Held**
SIC: 5191 Hay

(P-8846)
MANN LAKE LTD
500 Santa Anita Dr, Woodland (95776-6117)
PHONE..................530 662-4061
Eric Foster, *Branch Mgr*
Katie Doyle, *Sales Staff*
Troy Martinson, *Sales Staff*
EMP: 50
SALES (corp-wide): 331.8MM **Privately Held**
SIC: 5191 5149 Beekeeping supplies (non-durable); sugar, refined
HQ: Mann Lake, Ltd.
501 1st St S
Hackensack MN 56452
800 880-7694

(P-8847)
MILHOUS FEED
24077 State Highway 49, Nevada City (95959-8519)
PHONE..................530 292-3242
Oliver Milhous, *Partner*
Franklin Milhous, *Partner*
Richard Milhous, *Partner*
EMP: 150
SQ FT: 1,280
SALES: 1.5MM **Privately Held**
SIC: 5191 Feed

(P-8848)
NEWCO DISTRIBUTORS INC
9060 Rochester Ave, Rancho Cucamonga
(91730-5522)
P.O. Box 1449 (91729-1449)
PHONE..............................909 291-2240
Randall Barb, *CEO*
Rob Chell, *Officer*
Melina White, *Vice Pres*
Carlos Elgueta, *Network Enginr*
Jodi Barb, *Technology*
EMP: 60
SQ FT: 60,000
SALES (est): 51.4MM **Privately Held**
WEB: www.newcodistributors.com
SIC: 5191 5149 Animal feeds; pet foods

(P-8849)
NUTRIEN AG SOLUTIONS INC
305 Larsen Rd, Imperial (92251-9757)
P.O. Box 698 (92251-0698)
PHONE..............................760 355-1133
Shane Brady, *Manager*
EMP: 59 **Privately Held**
WEB: www.cropproductionservices.com
SIC: 5191 Fertilizer & fertilizer materials;
chemicals, agricultural; herbicides; insec-
ticides
HQ: Nutrien Ag Solutions, Inc.
3005 Rocky Mountain Ave
Loveland CO 80538
970 685-3300

(P-8850)
NUTRIEN AG SOLUTIONS INC
1335 W Main St, Santa Maria
(93458-4903)
P.O. Box 669 (93456-0669)
PHONE..............................805 922-5848
Joe Wickham, *Manager*
EMP: 80
SQ FT: 32,165 **Privately Held**
WEB: www.cropproductionservices.com
SIC: 5191 Fertilizer & fertilizer materials;
chemicals, agricultural; herbicides; insec-
ticides
HQ: Nutrien Ag Solutions, Inc.
3005 Rocky Mountain Ave
Loveland CO 80538
970 685-3300

(P-8851)
NUTRIEN AG SOLUTIONS INC
21929 S Lassen, Five Points (93624)
P.O. Box 338 (93624-0338)
PHONE..............................559 884-6010
Scott Desmond, *Manager*
EMP: 50
SQ FT: 5,670 **Privately Held**
WEB: www.cropproductionservices.com
SIC: 5191 Fertilizer & fertilizer materials;
chemicals, agricultural; herbicides; insec-
ticides
HQ: Nutrien Ag Solutions, Inc.
3005 Rocky Mountain Ave
Loveland CO 80538
970 685-3300

(P-8852)
NUTRIEN AG SOLUTIONS INC
1143 Terven Ave, Salinas (93901-4522)
P.O. Box 657 (93902-0657)
PHONE..............................831 757-5391
John Patinl, *Manager*
Lon Lanini, *Branch Mgr*
EMP: 60 **Privately Held**
WEB: www.cropproductionservices.com
SIC: 5191 Fertilizer & fertilizer materials;
chemicals, agricultural; herbicides; insec-
ticides
HQ: Nutrien Ag Solutions, Inc.
3005 Rocky Mountain Ave
Loveland CO 80538
970 685-3300

(P-8853)
PLANTERS HAY INC
1295 E St 78, Brawley (92227)
PHONE..............................760 344-0620
Stephen Benson, *CEO*
◆ **EMP:** 52
SALES (est): 15.3MM **Privately Held**
SIC: 5191 7389 Hay; styling of fashions,
apparel, furniture, textiles, etc.

(P-8854)
**PROFESSIONALS CHOICE
SPORT**
2025 Gillespie Way # 106, El Cajon
(92020-0924)
PHONE..............................619 873-1100
Nina Scott, *CEO*
Igor Prokopenko, *Technology*
Brian O'Connor, *Controller*
Brian Oconnor, *Controller*
Cynthia Jacobo, *Prdtn Mgr*
▲ **EMP:** 80
SQ FT: 20,000
SALES: 15MM **Privately Held**
WEB: www.profchoice.com
SIC: 5191 Equestrian equipment

(P-8855)
**RENTOKIL NORTH AMERICA
INC**
Also Called: Target Specialty Products
15415 Marquardt Ave, Santa Fe Springs
(90670-5711)
PHONE..............................562 802-2238
Bonnie Fallon, *Manager*
EMP: 100
SALES (corp-wide): 3.1B **Privately Held**
SIC: 5191 Chemicals, agricultural
HQ: Rentokil North America, Inc.
1125 Berkshire Blvd # 15
Wyomissing PA 19610
610 372-9700

(P-8856)
**SAKATA SEED AMERICA INC
(HQ)**
18095 Serene Dr, Morgan Hill
(95037-2833)
P.O. Box 880 (95038-0880)
PHONE..............................408 778-7758
David Armstrong, *CEO*
Koichi Matsunaga, *Vice Pres*
Randy Johnson, *Branch Mgr*
Anne-Claire Lales, *Admin Sec*
Philip Brown, *Technical Mgr*
▲ **EMP:** 90
SQ FT: 48,000
SALES (est): 91.2MM **Privately Held**
WEB: www.sakata.com
SIC: 5191 0182 Seeds: field, garden &
flower; vegetable crops grown under
cover

(P-8857)
SEEDS OF CHANGE INC
Also Called: Sustainable Agriculture
2555 S Dominguez Hills Dr, Rancho
Dominguez (90220-6402)
P.O. Box 4908 (90224-4908)
PHONE..............................310 764-7700
Will Righeimer, *CEO*
◆ **EMP:** 120
SQ FT: 25,411
SALES (est): 46.8MM
SALES (corp-wide): 37.6B **Privately Held**
SIC: 5191 0723 Seeds: field, garden &
flower; crop preparation services for mar-
ket
HQ: Mars Food Us, Llc
2001 E Cashdan Ste 201
Rancho Dominguez CA 90220
310 933-0670

(P-8858)
**SEMINIS VEGETABLE SEEDS
INC (DH)**
2700 Camino Del Sol, Oxnard
(93030-7967)
PHONE..............................855 733-3834
Michael J Frank, *CEO*
Kerry Preete, *President*
◆ **EMP:** 600 **EST:** 1962
SQ FT: 370,000
SALES (est): 526.4MM
SALES (corp-wide): 45.3B **Privately Held**
WEB: www.bruinsma.com
SIC: 5191 0723 Seeds: field, garden &
flower; crop preparation services for mar-
ket
HQ: Monsanto Company
800 N Lindbergh Blvd
Saint Louis MO 63167
314 694-1000

(P-8859)
**STANISLAUS FARM SUPPLY
COMPANY (PA)**
Also Called: Stan Farm
624 E Service Rd, Modesto (95358-9451)
PHONE..............................209 538-7070
Nickolas J Biscay, *CEO*
Espiridion Ixta, *CFO*
Ed Tobler, *Manager*
Mike Ray, *Supervisor*
EMP: 65
SQ FT: 4,000
SALES (est): 90.8MM **Privately Held**
SIC: 5191 Fertilizer & fertilizer materials;
insecticides; seeds: field, garden & flower

(P-8860)
SYNGENTA SEEDS INC
5653 Monterey Frontage Rd, Gilroy
(95020-9588)
PHONE..............................408 847-4242
Ed Merrell, *Branch Mgr*
Michael McMillen, *Research*
Doug Foster, *Associate*
EMP: 50
SALES (corp-wide): 64.2B **Privately Held**
SIC: 5191 Seeds: field, garden & flower
HQ: Syngenta Seeds, Llc
11055 Wayzata Blvd
Hopkins MN 55305
612 656-8600

(P-8861)
VOLOAGRI INC
3424 Roberto Ct, San Luis Obispo
(93401-7126)
PHONE..............................805 547-9391
Alois Van Vliet, *CEO*
EMP: 150 **EST:** 2012
SALES (est): 24.9MM **Privately Held**
SIC: 5191 Seeds & bulbs

(P-8862)
WESTERN MILLING LLC (HQ)
Also Called: O.H. Kruse Grain and Milling
31120 West St, Goshen (93227)
P.O. Box 1029 (93227-1029)
PHONE..............................559 302-1000
Kevin Kruse, *Mng Member*
Mark Labounty, *COO*
Mike Rosa, *Vice Pres*
Dave Spaulding, *Division Mgr*
Janet Cassidy, *Office Mgr*
◆ **EMP:** 243
SALES (est): 553.7MM **Privately Held**
WEB: www.westernmilling.com
SIC: 5191 Animal feeds
PA: Kruse Investment Company, Inc.
31120 W St
Goshen CA 93227
559 302-1000

(P-8863)
WILBUR-ELLIS COMPANY LLC
12550 S Colorado Ave, Helm (93627)
PHONE..............................559 866-5667
Tim Doss, *General Mgr*
EMP: 60
SALES (corp-wide): 2.7B **Privately Held**
WEB: www.wilbur-ellis.com
SIC: 5191 Fertilizer & fertilizer materials
HQ: Wilbur-Ellis Company Llc
345 California St Fl 27
San Francisco CA 94104
415 772-4000

(P-8864)
**WILBUR-ELLIS COMPANY LLC
(DH)**
345 California St Fl 27, San Francisco
(94104-2644)
PHONE..............................415 772-4000
John P Thacher, *Ch of Bd*
Daniel R Vradenburg, *President*
Michael J Hunter, *CFO*
Alison J Amonette, *Treasurer*
Nick Braden, *Vice Pres*
EMP: 300
SALES (est): 2.4B
SALES (corp-wide): 2.7B **Privately Held**
SIC: 5191 0711 Farm supplies; fertilizer &
fertilizer materials; insecticides; fertilizer
application services

HQ: Wilbur-Ellis Holdings Ii, Inc.
345 California St Fl 27
San Francisco CA 94104
415 772-4000

(P-8865)
WILBUR-ELLIS COMPANY LLC
Also Called: Weco - Us.ca. El Centro
45 Danenberg Dr, El Centro (92243-9447)
PHONE..............................760 352-2847
Dan Wray, *Manager*
EMP: 58
SALES (corp-wide): 2.7B **Privately Held**
WEB: www.wilbur-ellis.com
SIC: 5191 Feed
HQ: Wilbur-Ellis Company Llc
345 California St Fl 27
San Francisco CA 94104
415 772-4000

> **5192 Books, Periodicals &
> Newspapers Wholesale**

(P-8866)
ANDERSON NEWS LLC
15172 Goldenwest Cir, Westminster
(92683-5222)
P.O. Box 8401 (92684-8401)
PHONE..............................714 892-7766
Dave Schultz, *Branch Mgr*
EMP: 74
SALES (corp-wide): 178.9MM **Privately
Held**
WEB: www.kadsi.com
SIC: 5192 Magazines
PA: Anderson News, Llc
265 Brookview Town Ste
Knoxville TN 37919
865 584-9765

(P-8867)
BAKER & TAYLOR LLC
10350 Barnes Canyon Rd # 100, San
Diego (92121-2708)
PHONE..............................858 457-2500
James Leidich, *Director*
EMP: 187
SALES (corp-wide): 6.4B **Privately Held**
WEB: www.accupackinc.com
SIC: 5192 5099 5199 5045 Books; tapes
& cassettes, prerecorded; video cas-
settes, accessories & supplies; calendars;
computer software; book stores; audio
tapes, prerecorded; video tapes, prere-
corded
HQ: Baker & Taylor, Llc
2550 W Tyvola Rd Ste 300
Charlotte NC 28217

(P-8868)
CLASSIFIED ADVERTISING
715 Anacapa St, Santa Barbara
(93101-2203)
P.O. Box 1359 (93102-1359)
PHONE..............................805 564-5200
Sarah Sinclair, *Manager*
EMP: 85
SALES (est): 403.4K **Privately Held**
SIC: 5192 7311 Newspapers; advertising
agencies

(P-8869)
**CONTRA COSTA NEWSPAPERS
INC**
1650 Cavallo Rd, Antioch (94509-1928)
PHONE..............................925 757-2525
Debbie Mathias, *Manager*
EMP: 50
SQ FT: 24,534
SALES (corp-wide): 4.2B **Privately Held**
WEB: www.contracostatimes.com
SIC: 5192 Newspapers
HQ: Contra Costa Newspapers, Inc.
175 Lennon Ln Ste 100
Walnut Creek CA 94598
925 935-2525

(P-8870)
EL AVISO MAGAZINE
4850 Gage Ave, Bell (90201-1409)
P.O. Box 127, Huntington Park (90255-
0127)
PHONE..............................323 586-9199

PRODUCTS & SVCS

Jose Zepeda, *CEO*
Martha Ramirez, *Office Admin*
Yazmin Gonzalez, *Opers Mgr*
Pedro Diaz, *Advt Staff*
Miguel Gabrielli, *Advt Staff*
EMP: 300
SALES (est): 35.1MM **Privately Held**
SIC: 5192 2721 Magazines; magazines: publishing & printing

(P-8871)
EMMIS PUBLISHING CORPORATION
Also Called: Los Angeles Magazine
5900 Wilshire Blvd Fl 10, Los Angeles (90036-5024)
PHONE................323 801-0100
Kristy Day, *Sales Staff*
Rose Demaria, *Director*
Bonnie Magid, *Manager*
Lesley Suter, *Editor*
EMP: 55
SALES (corp-wide): 114.1MM **Publicly Held**
SIC: 5192 Magazines
HQ: Emmis Publishing Corporation
40 Monument Cir Ste 700
Indianapolis IN 46204
317 266-0100

(P-8872)
HAY HOUSE INC (PA)
2776 Loker Ave W, Carlsbad (92010-6611)
P.O. Box 5100 (92018-5100)
PHONE................760 431-7695
Louise L Hay, *Ch of Bd*
Reid Tracy, *President*
◆ **EMP:** 92
SQ FT: 20,000
SALES (est): 52.4MM **Privately Held**
WEB: www.hayhouse.com
SIC: 5192 5099 5942 5735 Books; tapes & cassettes, prerecorded; book stores; audio tapes, prerecorded

(P-8873)
ICONIC CHRONICLES MAGAZINE LLC
5120 Monetta Ln, Sacramento (95835-2030)
PHONE................707 712-2097
EMP: 57
SALES (est): 62K **Privately Held**
SIC: 5192 Magazines

(P-8874)
MADER NEWS INC
913 Ruberta Ave, Glendale (91201-2346)
PHONE................818 551-5000
Avan Mader, *President*
Steven Chia, *Human Res Dir*
Rafael Sotomayor, *Opers Mgr*
EMP: 100
SQ FT: 2,400
SALES (est): 26.1MM **Privately Held**
SIC: 5192 Newspapers

(P-8875)
NEWSWAYS SERVICES INC
Also Called: Newsways Distributors
1324 Cypress Ave, Los Angeles (90065-1220)
PHONE................323 258-6000
John Dorman, *President*
Christine Du, *Marketing Mgr*
▲ **EMP:** 135
SQ FT: 8,500
SALES (est): 53.6MM **Privately Held**
SIC: 5192 Magazines

(P-8876)
SCHOLASTIC BOOK FAIRS INC
2890 E White Star Ave, Anaheim (92806-2632)
PHONE................714 237-1100
Jim Wind, *Branch Mgr*
EMP: 75
SALES (corp-wide): 1.6B **Publicly Held**
WEB: www.scholasticbookfairs.com
SIC: 5192 Books
HQ: Scholastic Book Fairs, Inc.
1080 Greenwood Blvd
Lake Mary FL 32746
407 829-7300

(P-8877)
SCHOLASTIC BOOK FAIRS INC
42001 Christy St, Fremont (94538-3163)
PHONE................510 771-1700
Caesey Ryan, *Branch Mgr*
EMP: 100
SALES (corp-wide): 1.6B **Publicly Held**
WEB: www.scholasticbookfairs.com
SIC: 5192 Books
HQ: Scholastic Book Fairs, Inc.
1080 Greenwood Blvd
Lake Mary FL 32746
407 829-7300

(P-8878)
TEN ENTHUSIAST NETWORK LLC
Also Called: TEN ENTHUSIAST NETWORK, LLC
1821 E Dyer Rd Ste 150, Santa Ana (92705-5730)
PHONE................714 709-9021
Scott Bailey, *Branch Mgr*
Ryan Manson, *Editor*
EMP: 210
SQ FT: 59,000 **Privately Held**
SIC: 5192 Books, periodicals & newspapers
PA: Ten Publishing Media, Llc
831 S Douglas St Ste 100
El Segundo CA 90245
-

(P-8879)
WHITE DIGITAL MEDIA INC
Also Called: Wdm Group
3394 Carmel Mountain Rd # 250, San Diego (92121-1072)
PHONE................760 827-7800
Brian Smith, *CEO*
Glen White, *President*
Matthew P Melucci, *Officer*
Andy Turner, *Officer*
Keith Amber, *Office Mgr*
EMP: 150
SALES (est): 38.3MM **Privately Held**
SIC: 5192 Magazines

5193 Flowers, Nursery Stock & Florists' Splys Wholesale

(P-8880)
ALTMAN SPECIALTY PLANTS LLC (PA)
Also Called: Altman Plants
3742 Blue Bird Canyon Rd, Vista (92084-7432)
PHONE................800 348-4881
Ken Altman, *CEO*
Deena Altman, *Vice Pres*
Erin McCarthy, *Vice Pres*
Rhonda Humphrey, *Opers Mgr*
Kathy Nyquist, *Natl Sales Mgr*
▲ **EMP:** 800
SQ FT: 4,000
SALES (est): 693MM **Privately Held**
WEB: www.altmanplants.com
SIC: 5193 3999 Nursery stock; atomizers, toiletry

(P-8881)
B & B NURSERIES INC
Also Called: Landscape Center
9505 Cleveland Ave, Riverside (92503-6241)
P.O. Box 7399 (92513-7399)
PHONE................951 352-8383
Mark Barrett, *CEO*
EMP: 109
SQ FT: 2,100
SALES (est): 16.7MM **Privately Held**
SIC: 5193 0781 Flowers & nursery stock; landscape counseling services

(P-8882)
BAMBOO PIPELINE INC
9959 Calaveras Rd, Sunol (94586-9523)
PHONE................925 862-1904
Matt Fay, *President*
Mike Cornell, *Vice Pres*
EMP: 50

SALES (est): 866.1K **Privately Held**
SIC: 5193 Plants, potted

(P-8883)
BAY CITY FLOWER CO (PA)
2265 Cabrillo Hwy S, Half Moon Bay (94019-2250)
P.O. Box 186 (94019-0186)
PHONE................650 726-5535
Harrison Higaki, *Ch of Bd*
Naomi Higaki, *Shareholder*
Sam Hasegawa, *CFO*
Samuel Hasegawa, *CFO*
Scott Cornwell, *Engineer*
▲ **EMP:** 300
SQ FT: 2,000
SALES (est): 79.2MM **Privately Held**
WEB: www.baycityflower.com
SIC: 5193 Flowers, fresh

(P-8884)
BRAND FLOWER FARMS INC (PA)
Also Called: Farmers W Flowers & Bouquets
5300 Foothill Rd, Carpinteria (93013-3017)
P.O. Box 600 (93014-0600)
PHONE................805 684-5531
Wilja Happ, *CEO*
Maximino Santillon, *President*
Tom Lemus, *COO*
Monica Preciado, *CFO*
Will Stewart, *Vice Pres*
▲ **EMP:** 200
SQ FT: 500,000
SALES (est): 18.5MM **Privately Held**
WEB: www.brandflowers.com
SIC: 5193 Flowers, fresh

(P-8885)
BUSHNELL GARDENS
Also Called: Bushnell's Landscape Creations
5255 Douglas Blvd, Granite Bay (95746-6204)
PHONE................916 791-4199
David Bushnell, *Owner*
EMP: 80
SQ FT: 1,040
SALES (est): 6.7MM **Privately Held**
SIC: 5193 0781 0782 5261 Nursery stock; landscape architects; lawn & garden services; landscape contractors; nurseries

(P-8886)
CAL COLOR GROWERS LLC
330 Peebles Ave, Morgan Hill (95037-2712)
P.O. Box 550 (95038-0550)
PHONE................408 778-0835
David Vincent, *Mng Member*
Michelle Vincnet,
▲ **EMP:** 73
SQ FT: 478,000
SALES (est): 6MM **Privately Held**
SIC: 5193 Nursery stock

(P-8887)
CAMFLOR INC
2364 Riverside Rd, Watsonville (95076-9430)
PHONE................831 726-1330
Daniel Campos, *President*
Zandra Campos, *CFO*
Gil Campos, *Info Tech Mgr*
Jose Campos, *Financial Exec*
▲ **EMP:** 110
SALES (est): 14.7MM **Privately Held**
WEB: www.camflor.com
SIC: 5193 Flowers & florists' supplies

(P-8888)
COLOR SPOT NURSERIES INC
321 W Sepulveda Blvd, Carson (90745-6313)
PHONE................310 549-7470
Fax: 310 549-7312
EMP: 98
SALES (corp-wide): 3.2B **Privately Held**
SIC: 5193
HQ: Color Spot Nurseries, Inc.
27368 Via
Temecula CA 92590
-

(P-8889)
COREY NURSERY CO INC (PA)
1650 Monte Vista Ave, Claremont (91711-2999)
P.O. Box 609 (91711-0609)
PHONE................909 621-6886
Jeffrey E Corey, *CEO*
Brian Corey, *Shareholder*
Ken Corey, *Shareholder*
Gene Corey, *Ch of Bd*
Eugene K Corey, *President*
▲ **EMP:** 60 EST: 1978
SQ FT: 170,000
SALES (est): 31.9MM **Privately Held**
WEB: www.coreynursery.com
SIC: 5193 Nursery stock

(P-8890)
COUNTRY FLORAL SUPPLY INC (PA)
Also Called: Country Furnishings
3802 Weatherly Cir, Westlake Village (91361-3821)
PHONE................805 520-8026
Mark Reese, *President*
Debbie Reese, *Vice Pres*
▲ **EMP:** 80
SQ FT: 60,000
SALES (est): 48.5MM **Privately Held**
WEB: www.countryfloralsupply.com
SIC: 5193 5999 Artificial flowers; artificial flowers

(P-8891)
DELTA FLORAL DISTRIBUTORS INC
6810 West Blvd, Los Angeles (90043-4668)
PHONE................323 751-8116
Foti Defterios, *President*
Heidi Hansen, *Controller*
▲ **EMP:** 200
SQ FT: 30,000
SALES (est): 23.1MM **Privately Held**
SIC: 5193 Flowers, fresh

(P-8892)
FISHERS NURSERY
24081 S Austin Rd, Ripon (95366-9646)
P.O. Box 657 (95366-0657)
PHONE................209 599-3412
Jerry Fisher, *President*
Mary Fisher, *Corp Secy*
▲ **EMP:** 75 EST: 1968
SQ FT: 450,000
SALES (est): 5.8MM **Privately Held**
WEB: www.fishersnursery.com
SIC: 5193 Nursery stock

(P-8893)
G M FLORAL COMPANY
Also Called: G M Floral Supply
740 Maple Ave, Los Angeles (90014-2261)
PHONE................213 489-7055
Mas Yoshida, *Principal*
Mark Mukai, *Controller*
EMP: 50
SALES (corp-wide): 11.2MM **Privately Held**
WEB: www.gmfloral.com
SIC: 5193 Florists' supplies
PA: G M Floral Company
531 E Evelyn Ave
Mountain View CA
-

(P-8894)
GREEN THUMB INTERNATIONAL INC
21812 Sherman Way, Canoga Park (91303-1940)
PHONE................818 340-6400
Del Berquist, *Principal*
EMP: 100
SALES (corp-wide): 60.5MM **Privately Held**
WEB: www.greenthumbinternational.com
SIC: 5193 5261 0782 0181 Nursery stock; nurseries & garden centers; lawn & garden services; ornamental nursery products
PA: Green Thumb International Inc
7105 Jordan Ave
Canoga Park CA 91303
818 340-6400

(P-8895)
GREEN TREE NURSERY
Also Called: Linwood Nursery
23979 Lake Rd, La Grange (95329-9505)
PHONE..................................209 874-9100
Jason Hall, *Partner*
Chris Torres, *Office Mgr*
EMP: 50
SQ FT: 6,000
SALES (est): 3.3MM **Privately Held**
SIC: 5193 Nursery stock

(P-8896)
GROLINK PLANT COMPANY INC
(PA)
4107 W Gonzales Rd, Oxnard
(93036-7783)
P.O. Box 5506 (93031-5506)
PHONE..................................805 984-7958
Anthony Vollering, *CEO*
Harry Van Wingerden, *Shareholder*
Jerry Van Wingerden, *Corp Secy*
Yasmin Jafroodi, *Executive*
Art Gordijin, *Principal*
▲ EMP: 150
SQ FT: 400,000
SALES (est): 21.3MM **Privately Held**
WEB: www.grolink.com
SIC: 5193 0181 Nursery stock; ornamental nursery products

(P-8897)
HEADSTART NURSERY INC (PA)
4860 Monterey Rd, Gilroy (95020-9511)
PHONE..................................408 842-3030
Steven H Costa, *President*
Don Christopher, *Vice Pres*
Randy Costa, *Vice Pres*
Chris Peck, *General Mgr*
William A Christopher, *Admin Sec*
▲ EMP: 85
SQ FT: 3,000
SALES (est): 66.7MM **Privately Held**
WEB: www.headstartnursery.com
SIC: 5193 5261 Plants, potted; nursery stock; nurseries & garden centers

(P-8898)
HINES NURSERIES LLC
22941 Mill Creek Dr, Laguna Hills
(92653-1264)
PHONE..................................602 254-2831
Phil Wayne, *Manager*
EMP: 100 **Privately Held**
WEB: www.hineshort.com
SIC: 5193 Nursery stock
PA: Hines Nurseries Llc
1700 E Putnam Ave Ste 401
Old Greenwich CT

(P-8899)
HOLLAND FLOWER MARKET
INC (PA)
755 Wall St Ste 7g, Los Angeles
(90014-2315)
PHONE..................................213 627-9900
Jaap Haverkate, *President*
▲ EMP: 51
SQ FT: 11,000
SALES (est): 26MM **Privately Held**
SIC: 5193 Flowers, fresh

(P-8900)
KENDAL FLORAL SUPPLY LLC
(PA)
Also Called: Kendal North Bouquet Co
1960 Kellogg Ave, Carlsbad (92008-6581)
PHONE..................................760 431-4910
Kenneth X Baca, *President*
Lynn Schmierer, *Marketing Staff*
▲ EMP: 80
SALES (est): 66.6MM **Privately Held**
WEB: www.kendalfloral.com
SIC: 5193 Flowers, fresh

(P-8901)
LOMA VISTA NURSERY
Also Called: Loma Vista Nursery 2
18272 Bastanchury Rd, Yorba Linda
(92886)
PHONE..................................714 779-5583
Norman Van Ginkel, *President*
EMP: 57

SALES (est): 4MM **Privately Held**
SIC: 5193 5261 Nursery stock; nursery stock, seeds & bulbs

(P-8902)
MAYESH WHOLESALE FLORIST
INC (PA)
5401 W 104th St, Los Angeles
(90045-6011)
PHONE..................................310 342-0980
Patrick Dahlson, *CEO*
Cindie Boer, *COO*
Ben Henderson, *Branch Mgr*
Victor Demetriou, *Asst Controller*
Tracy Olmedo, *Personnel Assit*
▲ EMP: 50
SQ FT: 20,000
SALES (est): 85.2MM **Privately Held**
WEB: www.mayeshwholesale.com
SIC: 5193 5992 Flowers, fresh; florists

(P-8903)
MELLANO & CO (PA)
Also Called: Mellano Enterprises
766 Wall St, Los Angeles (90014-2316)
P.O. Box 100, San Luis Rey (92068-0100)
PHONE..................................213 622-0796
John Mellano, *President*
Michael Matthew Mellano, *President*
Battista Castellano, *Corp Secy*
Michelle Castellano, *Vice Pres*
Bob Mellano, *Vice Pres*
EMP: 275
SALES (est): 50.9MM **Privately Held**
WEB: www.mellano.com
SIC: 5193 Flowers, fresh

(P-8904)
MELLANO & CO
Also Called: Melano Enterprises
734 Wilshire Rd, Oceanside (92057-2111)
P.O. Box 100, San Luis Rey (92068-0100)
PHONE..................................760 433-9550
Harry M Mellano, *Owner*
Rosa Mendoza, *Office Mgr*
Amy Morton, *Human Resources*
Ellie Ellsworth, *Sales Staff*
Cathy Hickman-Frost, *Sales Staff*
EMP: 170
SALES (est): 6.8MM
SALES (corp-wide): 50.9MM **Privately Held**
WEB: www.mellano.com
SIC: 5193 Flowers, fresh
PA: Mellano & Co.
766 Wall St
Los Angeles CA 90014
213 622-0796

(P-8905)
MONTEREY BAY BOUQUET
ACQUISIT
481 San Andreas Rd, Watsonville
(95076-9524)
P.O. Box 1778 (95077-1778)
PHONE..................................831 786-2700
Phil Buran, *Mng Member*
EMP: 170
SALES (est): 10.4MM **Privately Held**
SIC: 5193 Flowers & florists' supplies

(P-8906)
MYRIAD FLOWERS
INTERNATIONAL
4601 Foothill Rd, Carpinteria (93013-3097)
PHONE..................................805 684-8079
Harry Van Wingerden, *President*
Michelle Van Wingerden, *Vice Pres*
Erik Van Winderden, *Executive*
▲ EMP: 65
SQ FT: 2,000
SALES: 5MM **Privately Held**
WEB: www.myriadflowers.com
SIC: 5193 Flowers, fresh

(P-8907)
NAKASE BROTHERS
WHOLESALE NURS (PA)
9441 Krepp Dr, Huntington Beach
(92646-2799)
PHONE..................................949 855-4388
Shigeo Gary Nakase, *Principal*
Jun Turalba, *Executive Asst*
▲ EMP: 100

SALES (est): 31.5MM **Privately Held**
WEB: www.nakasebros.com
SIC: 5193 Nursery stock

(P-8908)
NAKASE BROTHERS
WHOLESALE NURS
20621 Lake Forest Dr, Lake Forest (92630)
PHONE..................................949 855-4388
Joann Shurlock, *Manager*
EMP: 200
SALES (corp-wide): 31.5MM **Privately Held**
WEB: www.nakasebros.com
SIC: 5193 Nursery stock
PA: Nakase Brothers Wholesale Nursery
9441 Krepp Dr
Huntington Beach CA 92646
949 855-4388

(P-8909)
NORMANS NURSERY INC (PA)
8665 Duarte Rd, San Gabriel (91775-1139)
PHONE..................................626 285-9795
Charles Norman, *President*
Caroline Norman, *Treasurer*
Barbara Hayes, *Buyer*
▼ EMP: 50
SQ FT: 4,000
SALES (est): 160MM **Privately Held**
WEB: www.nngrower.com
SIC: 5193 0181 Nursery stock; nursery stock, growing of

(P-8910)
NORMANS NURSERY INC
5800 Via Real, Carpinteria (93013-2610)
PHONE..................................805 684-5442
EMP: 310
SALES (corp-wide): 160MM **Privately Held**
SIC: 5193 Nursery stock
PA: Norman's Nursery, Inc.
8665 Duarte Rd
San Gabriel CA 91775
626 285-9795

(P-8911)
NORMANS NURSERY INC
6250 N Escalon Bellota Rd, Linden
(95236-9428)
P.O. Box 959 (95236-0959)
PHONE..................................209 887-2033
Barbara Hayes, *Manager*
EMP: 200
SALES (corp-wide): 160MM **Privately Held**
WEB: www.nngrower.com
SIC: 5193 0181 Nursery stock; nursery stock, growing of
PA: Norman's Nursery, Inc.
8665 Duarte Rd
San Gabriel CA 91775
626 285-9795

(P-8912)
PACIFIC COAST NURSERY INC
2885 E La Cresta Ave, Anaheim
(92806-1817)
PHONE..................................714 630-4868
Richard F Buccola, *President*
Dennis Buccola, *Corp Secy*
EMP: 70
SALES (est): 8.5MM **Privately Held**
WEB: www.pacificcoastnursery.com
SIC: 5193 Nursery stock

(P-8913)
PARDEE TREE NURSERY
30970 Via Puerta Del Sol, Oceanside
(92057)
P.O. Box 240, Bonsall (92003-0240)
PHONE..................................760 630-5400
Lauren Davis, *President*
EMP: 75
SALES (est): 16.3MM **Privately Held**
WEB: www.pardeetree.com
SIC: 5193 Nursery stock

(P-8914)
PLANT SCIENCES INC
234 Juniper Knoll Rd, Macdoel (96058)
P.O. Box 269 (96058-0269)
PHONE..................................530 398-4042
Tom Alvin, *Manager*
EMP: 50

SALES (corp-wide): 35MM **Privately Held**
WEB: www.plantsciences.com
SIC: 5193 Nursery stock
PA: Plant Sciences, Inc.
342 Green Valley Rd
Watsonville CA 95076
831 728-7771

(P-8915)
PLANTEL NURSERIES INC
2775 E Clark Ave, Santa Maria
(93455-5813)
PHONE..................................805 349-8952
EMP: 255
SALES (corp-wide): 8MM **Privately Held**
SIC: 5193 Nursery stock
PA: Plantel Nurseries Inc
2775 E Clark Ave
Santa Maria CA 93455
805 349-8952

(P-8916)
PONTO NURSERY INC
2545 Ramona Dr, Vista (92084-1632)
P.O. Box 536 (92085-0536)
PHONE..................................760 724-6003
William Ponto, *President*
Judy Ponto, *Corp Secy*
EMP: 70
SQ FT: 2,000
SALES: 3.5MM **Privately Held**
SIC: 5193 Nursery stock

(P-8917)
RIVERSIDE NURSERY & LDSCP
INC
4763 W Spruce Ave Ste 111, Fresno
(93722-3572)
PHONE..................................559 275-1891
Mitchel Hutcheson, *President*
Anglea Hutchenson, *Vice Pres*
James Hutchenson, *Admin Sec*
EMP: 60
SQ FT: 4,000
SALES (est): 5.5MM **Privately Held**
WEB: www.riversidelandscape.com
SIC: 5193 0781 Nursery stock; landscape architects

(P-8918)
SCHUBERT NURSERY (PA)
139 Zabala Rd, Salinas (93908-9753)
PHONE..................................831 753-0144
Karl Faigle, *President*
Arlene Faigle, *Corp Secy*
EMP: 86
SQ FT: 2,000
SALES (est): 5.8MM **Privately Held**
WEB: www.schubertnursery.com
SIC: 5193 5261 Nursery stock; nurseries & garden centers

(P-8919)
SPECTRUM EQUIPMENT LLC
Also Called: Spectrum Floral Service
2505 Commerce Way, Vista (92081-8420)
PHONE..................................760 599-8849
Gene Aschbrenner, *Mng Member*
Sarah Aschbrenner,
William Simon,
EMP: 80
SQ FT: 16,000
SALES (est): 16MM **Privately Held**
SIC: 5193 Flowers, fresh

(P-8920)
SUNCREST NURSERIES INC
400 Casserly Rd, Watsonville
(95076-9700)
PHONE..................................831 728-2595
Stan Iversen, *President*
Maria Torres, *Executive*
EMP: 55
SQ FT: 1,000
SALES (est): 6.2MM **Privately Held**
WEB: www.suncrestnurseries.com
SIC: 5193 Nursery stock

(P-8921)
SUNNYSLOPE TREE FARM INC
Also Called: Sunnyslope Trees
1545 N Glassell St, Orange (92867)
PHONE..................................714 532-1440
Todd Flammer, *President*
Jack W Flammer Sr, *Ch of Bd*

(PA)=Parent Co (HQ)=Headquarters (DH)=Div Headquarters
✪ = New Business established in last 2 years

EMP: 100
SQ FT: 1,000
SALES (est): 14.8MM **Privately Held**
WEB: www.sunnyslope.net
SIC: 5193 Nursery stock

(P-8922)
SUNSHINE FLORAL INC
4595 Foothill Rd, Carpinteria (93013-3096)
PHONE.............................805 684-1177
Henry Vanwingerden, *President*
Anthony Vollering, *Vice Pres*
▲ EMP: 70
SALES (est): 5.8MM **Privately Held**
SIC: 5193 Flowers, fresh

(P-8923)
SUNSHINE FLORAL LLC
1070 S Rice Ave Ste 1, Oxnard
(93033-2110)
PHONE.............................805 982-8822
Anthony Vollering, *Mng Member*
Ed Lozano, *General Mgr*
Henry Van Wingerden, *Mng Member*
Ton Vollering, *Mng Member*
▲ EMP: 60 EST: 1985
SQ FT: 10,000
SALES (est): 5.6MM **Privately Held**
WEB: www.sunshinefloral.com
SIC: 5193 Flowers, fresh

(P-8924)
SUPER GARDEN CENTERS INC
Also Called: Green Thumb Nursery
7659 Topanga Canyon Blvd, Canoga Park
(91304-5535)
P.O. Box 111 (91305-0111)
PHONE.............................818 348-9266
Nancy Bergquist, *Manager*
EMP: 50
SALES (corp-wide): 28.6MM **Privately Held**
SIC: 5193 5261 Nursery stock; fertilizer; nursery stock, seeds & bulbs
PA: Super Garden Centers, Inc.
21812 Sherman Way
Canoga Park CA 91303
818 340-6400

(P-8925)
T - Y NURSERY INC
15335 Highway 76, Pauma Valley
(92061-9583)
P.O. Box 424 (92061-0424)
PHONE.............................760 742-2151
Alfonso Ramos, *Manager*
EMP: 200
SALES (corp-wide): 1.2MM **Privately Held**
SIC: 5193 5261 Plants, potted; nurseries
PA: T - Y Nursery, Inc.
5221 Arvada St
Torrance CA 90503
310 370-2561

(P-8926)
TELAFLORA LLC
11444 W Olympic Blvd Fl 4, Los Angeles
(90064-1546)
PHONE.............................310 231-9199
Stewart Resnick,
Lynda Resnick,
EMP: 450
SALES (est): 26.3MM **Privately Held**
SIC: 5193 Flowers & florists' supplies

(P-8927)
TORO NURSERY INC
17585 Crenshaw Blvd, Torrance
(90504-3403)
PHONE.............................310 715-1982
Salvador Sanchez, *President*
Antonio Gomez, *Vice Pres*
EMP: 60
SALES (est): 4.6MM **Privately Held**
SIC: 5193 Nursery stock

(P-8928)
UNITED FLORAL EXCHANGE INC
Also Called: Cal Americas Wholesale Florist
2834 La Mirada Dr Ste B, Vista
(92081-8440)
PHONE.............................760 597-1940
Jim Dionne, *President*
Thayis Dionne, *Vice Pres*

EMP: 75
SQ FT: 30,000
SALES (est): 4.1MM **Privately Held**
WEB: www.calamericas.com
SIC: 5193 Flowers, fresh

(P-8929)
USA BOUQUET LLC
2834 La Mirada Dr Ste B, Vista
(92081-8440)
PHONE.............................800 878-9909
Edgar Lozano,
EMP: 88
SALES (corp-wide): 319.1MM **Privately Held**
SIC: 5193 Flowers, fresh
HQ: Usa Bouquet Llc
1500 Nw 95th Ave
Doral FL 33172
786 437-6500

(P-8930)
VALLEY FLOWERS INC
3920 Via Real, Carpinteria (93013-1266)
P.O. Box 1279 (93014-1279)
PHONE.............................805 684-6651
Walter Vanwingerden, *President*
John Vanwingerden, *Vice Pres*
▲ EMP: 60
SALES (est): 4.1MM **Privately Held**
WEB: www.valleyflowers.com
SIC: 5193 Flowers & nursery stock

(P-8931)
VILLAGE NURSERIES WHL LLC (PA)
1589 N Main St, Orange (92867-3439)
PHONE.............................714 279-3100
David House, *Mng Member*
Rick Rehm, *CFO*
Dave Hill, *Sales Staff*
Wayne Johnson,
EMP: 50
SQ FT: 12,321
SALES (est): 188.4MM **Privately Held**
SIC: 5193 Nursery stock

(P-8932)
VILLAGE NURSERIES WHL LLC
6901 Bradshaw Rd, Sacramento
(95829-9303)
PHONE.............................916 993-2292
Steve Sawyer, *Branch Mgr*
EMP: 367
SALES (corp-wide): 188.4MM **Privately Held**
SIC: 5193 Nursery stock
PA: Village Nurseries Wholesale, Llc
1589 N Main St
Orange CA 92867
714 279-3100

(P-8933)
VILLAGE NURSERIES WHL LLC
20099 Santa Rosa Mine Rd, Perris
(92570-7774)
PHONE.............................951 657-3940
Joseph Jensen, *Branch Mgr*
Luis Verdoza, *Supervisor*
EMP: 183
SALES (corp-wide): 188.4MM **Privately Held**
SIC: 5193 Nursery stock
PA: Village Nurseries Wholesale, Llc
1589 N Main St
Orange CA 92867
714 279-3100

(P-8934)
WESTERN STAR NURSERIES LLC
9394 Robson Rd, Galt (95632-8841)
P.O. Box 725 (95632-0725)
PHONE.............................209 744-2552
Robert Painter,
Sally B Painter,
EMP: 50
SALES (est): 1.7MM **Privately Held**
SIC: 5193 Nursery stock

(P-8935)
WESTLAND FLRAL CARPINTERIA INC
1400 Cravens Ln, Carpinteria
(93013-3166)
PHONE.............................805 684-4011
Case Van Wingerden, *CEO*
EMP: 50
SALES (est): 11.9MM **Privately Held**
SIC: 5193 Flowers, fresh

(P-8936)
WESTLAND ORCHIDS INC
Also Called: Westland Floral
1400 Cravens Ln, Carpinteria
(93013-3166)
PHONE.............................805 684-1436
David Van Wingerden, *CEO*
Diana Filippin, *Technology*
Ellie Ramirez, *Human Resources*
Kelly Gomez, *Sales Staff*
Diane Leforge, *Manager*
▲ EMP: 50
SALES (est): 12.6MM **Privately Held**
SIC: 5193 Flowers & florists' supplies

(P-8937)
WINWARD INTERNATIONAL INC (PA)
Also Called: Winward Silks
42760 Albrae St, Fremont (94538-3390)
PHONE.............................510 487-8686
Patrick Tai, *President*
Garrison Tai, *President*
▲ EMP: 80
SQ FT: 10,000
SALES (est): 12.9MM **Privately Held**
SIC: 5193 5023 Artificial flowers; decorative home furnishings & supplies

---

5194 Tobacco & Tobacco Prdts Wholesale

(P-8938)
CORE-MARK INTERNATIONAL INC
8333 Edison Hwy, Bakersfield
(93307-9173)
PHONE.............................661 366-2673
Caral Parker, *Principal*
EMP: 121
SALES (corp-wide): 16.4B **Publicly Held**
SIC: 5194 Tobacco & tobacco products
HQ: Core-Mark International, Inc.
1500 Solana Blvd Ste 3400
Westlake TX 76262
650 589-9445

(P-8939)
FLAWLESS VAPE WHOLESALE DIST
1021 E Orangethorpe Ave, Anaheim
(92801-1135)
PHONE.............................714 768-7928
Jason Grace, *President*
EMP: 60
SALES: 30MM **Privately Held**
SIC: 5194 Cigarettes

(P-8940)
KRETEK INTERNATIONAL INC (DH)
5449 Endeavour Ct, Moorpark
(93021-1712)
PHONE.............................805 531-8888
Hugh R Cassar, *CEO*
Sean Cassar, *COO*
Donald Gormley, *CFO*
Lynn K Cassar, *Corp Secy*
Eliot Suied, *VP Sales*
◆ EMP: 90
SQ FT: 80,000
SALES (est): 51.1MM **Privately Held**
WEB: www.kretek.com
SIC: 5194 Cigarettes; smoking tobacco; cigars

(P-8941)
MTC DISTRIBUTING (PA)
4900 Stoddard Rd, Modesto (95356-9389)
P.O. Box 3776 (95352-3776)
PHONE.............................209 523-6449

Todd E Manss, *Principal*
Todd Manss, *CFO*
John Subia, *Executive*
Robert Bettencourt, *Info Tech Mgr*
Daniel Borras, *Programmer Anys*
EMP: 200 EST: 1921
SQ FT: 100,000
SALES (est): 144.8MM **Privately Held**
SIC: 5194 5145 5149 Cigarettes; candy; groceries & related products

(P-8942)
PACIFIC GROSERVICE INC
Also Called: Pitco Foods
567 Cinnabar St, San Jose (95110-2306)
PHONE.............................408 727-4826
Pericles Navab, *Ch of Bd*
Azadeh Hariri, *Shareholder*
Frank Hariri, *Shareholder*
Esmael Maboudi, *Shareholder*
Parviz Maboudi, *Shareholder*
▲ EMP: 360
SQ FT: 85,000
SALES (est): 198.7MM **Privately Held**
SIC: 5194 5145 5141 5113 Tobacco & tobacco products; candy; groceries, general line; industrial & personal service paper; service establishment equipment

(P-8943)
TREPCO IMPORTS & DIST LTD
Trepco West
11860 Cmnty Rd Ste 150, Poway (92064)
PHONE.............................619 690-7999
Wiam Paulus, *Branch Mgr*
Greg Schaad, *Vice Pres*
EMP: 50
SALES (corp-wide): 69.8MM **Privately Held**
SIC: 5194 5141 Tobacco & tobacco products; groceries, general line
PA: Trepco Imports & Distribution, Ltd.
1201 E Lincoln Ave
Madison Heights MI 48071
248 546-3661

5198 Paints, Varnishes & Splys Wholesale

(P-8944)
BERG LACQUER CO (PA)
Also Called: Pacific Coast Lacquer
3150 E Pico Blvd, Los Angeles
(90023-3632)
PHONE.............................323 261-8114
Sandra Berg, *President*
Robert O Berg, *Ch of Bd*
Donna Berg, *Treasurer*
Joanna Guzman, *Manager*
▼ EMP: 65 EST: 1934
SQ FT: 85,000
SALES (est): 59MM **Privately Held**
WEB: www.ellispaint.com
SIC: 5198 2851 Paints, varnishes & supplies; paints & paint additives

(P-8945)
SHILPARK PAINT CORPORATION (PA)
Also Called: Shilpark Paint Automotive
1640 S Vermont Ave, Los Angeles
(90006-4522)
PHONE.............................323 732-7093
Shil Kyoung Park, *CEO*
Mina Park, *Treasurer*
Christine Sihn, *Accountant*
Corman Park, *Manager*
Robert Park, *Manager*
EMP: 70
SALES (est): 25.1MM **Privately Held**
SIC: 5198 5231 5013 Paints; paint & painting supplies; body repair or paint shop supplies, automotive

(P-8946)
TCP GLOBAL CORPORATION
Also Called: Autobody Depot
6695 Rasha St, San Diego (92121-2240)
PHONE.............................858 909-2110
Dean A Faucett, *President*
Dean Faucett, *President*
Rick Faucett, *Vice Pres*
Todd Faucett, *Vice Pres*
Matt Herring, *Store Mgr*

◆ **EMP:** 67
SQ FT: 38,000
SALES (est): 66.8MM **Privately Held**
SIC: 5198 5231 Paints; paint

5199 Nondurable Goods, NEC Wholesale

(P-8947)
AJM PACKAGING CORPORATION
1160 Vernon Way, El Cajon (92020-1837)
PHONE..........................619 448-4007
Joe Marcelynas, *Principal*
EMP: 97
SALES (corp-wide): 351.1MM **Privately Held**
SIC: 5199 Packaging materials
PA: A.J.M. Packaging Corporation
     E-4111 Andover Rd
     Bloomfield Hills MI 48302
     248 901-0040

(P-8948)
ALLAQUARIA LLC
Also Called: Quality Marine
5420 W 104th St, Los Angeles (90045-6012)
P.O. Box 2439 (90051-0439)
PHONE..........................310 645-1107
G Christopher Bverner, *Mng Member*
Sophie Lam, *Controller*
Oscar Velazquez, *Opers Mgr*
Thomas Troy, *Production*
Mary L Buerner,
▲ **EMP:** 60
SQ FT: 45,000
SALES (est): 19.4MM **Privately Held**
SIC: 5199 Tropical fish

(P-8949)
AMD TRADING COMPANY INC
1021 Stockton St, San Francisco (94108-1109)
PHONE..........................415 391-0601
Amanda Ho, *Principal*
▲ **EMP:** 128 **EST:** 2008
SALES (est): 10.5MM **Privately Held**
SIC: 5199 Nondurable goods

(P-8950)
ARMINAK & ASSOCIATES LLC
4832 Azusa Canyon Rd A, Irwindale (91706-1904)
P.O. Box 2245, Baldwin Park (91706-1141)
PHONE..........................626 358-4804
Thomas A Amanto, *President*
▲ **EMP:** 55
SQ FT: 50,000
SALES (est): 22.7MM
SALES (corp-wide): 877.1MM **Publicly Held**
WEB: www.arminak-associates.com
SIC: 5199 Packaging materials
PA: Trimas Corporation
     38505 Woodward Ave # 200
     Bloomfield Hills MI 48304
     248 631-5450

(P-8951)
ART SUPPLY ENTERPRISES INC (PA)
Also Called: Macpherson's
1375 Ocean Ave, Emeryville (94608-1128)
PHONE..........................510 428-9011
David Schofield, *CEO*
Corinne Smith, *Graphic Designe*
Mike Chen, *Accountant*
Eric Matthews, *Controller*
Jennifer Spotswood, *Personnel Assit*
◆ **EMP:** 215
SQ FT: 16,000
SALES (est): 161.3MM **Privately Held**
WEB: www.arts-and-crafts-supplies-whole-sale.a2zyp
SIC: 5199 Artists' materials

(P-8952)
BLOWER-DEMPSAY CORPORATION (PA)
Also Called: Pak West Paper & Packaging
4042 W Garry Ave, Santa Ana (92704-6300)
PHONE..........................714 481-3800
James F Blower, *President*
Serge Poirier, *CFO*
Linda B Dempsay, *Admin Sec*
Gary Smith, *Opers Mgr*
James Fleming, *Director*
▲ **EMP:** 217
SQ FT: 190,000
SALES (est): 142.6MM **Privately Held**
SIC: 5199 Packaging materials

(P-8953)
BRANDVIA ALLIANCE INC (PA)
2159 Bering Dr, San Jose (95131-2014)
PHONE..........................408 955-0500
James David Childers, *President*
Diane Garretson, *Partner*
Shirley Doxtad, *President*
Cindy Kahl, *Corp Secy*
Doug Kahl, *Vice Pres*
◆ **EMP:** 102
SQ FT: 21,000
SALES (est): 82.8MM **Privately Held**
SIC: 5199 Advertising specialties

(P-8954)
BUBBLA INC
7931 Deering Ave, Canoga Park (91304-5008)
PHONE..........................818 884-2000
Andrew Cooper, *President*
EMP: 50
SQ FT: 23,500
SALES (est): 4.9MM **Privately Held**
WEB: www.bubbla.com
SIC: 5199 Packaging materials

(P-8955)
CALICO BRANDS INC
Also Called: Scripto
2055 S Haven Ave, Ontario (91761-0736)
PHONE..........................909 930-5000
Felix M Hon, *CEO*
Laurie Hon, *Director*
▲ **EMP:** 50
SQ FT: 125,000
SALES (est): 14.6MM
SALES (corp-wide): 11.3MM **Privately Held**
SIC: 5199 Lighters, cigarette & cigar
PA: Tokai International Holdings, Inc.
     2055 S Haven Ave
     Ontario CA 91761
     909 930-5000

(P-8956)
CELMOL INC
Also Called: Mark Roberts
1611 E Saint Andrew Pl, Santa Ana (92705-4932)
PHONE..........................714 259-1000
Mark Rees, *President*
Norine Anson, *Analyst*
▲ **EMP:** 60
SQ FT: 36,000
SALES (est): 10.8MM **Privately Held**
WEB: www.xmas-magic.com
SIC: 5199 5193 Christmas novelties; gifts & novelties; flowers, fresh

(P-8957)
CENTRAL GARDEN & PET COMPANY
9235 Activity Rd, San Diego (92126-4440)
PHONE..........................858 695-0743
EMP: 59
SALES (corp-wide): 2.2B **Publicly Held**
WEB: www.centralgardenandpet.com
SIC: 5199 2048 Pet supplies; prepared feeds
PA: Central Garden & Pet Company
     1340 Treat Blvd Ste 600
     Walnut Creek CA 94597
     925 948-4000

(P-8958)
CENTRAL GARDEN & PET COMPANY
Also Called: Breeders Choice Pet Foods
16321 Arrow Hwy, Irwindale (91706-2018)
PHONE..........................626 334-9301
Jeff Sutherland, *President*
Clint Hammond, *Cust Mgr*
EMP: 80
SALES (corp-wide): 2.2B **Publicly Held**
SIC: 5199 Pet supplies
PA: Central Garden & Pet Company
     1340 Treat Blvd Ste 600
     Walnut Creek CA 94597
     925 948-4000

(P-8959)
CINTAS CORPORATION NO 2
4320 E Miraloma Ave, Anaheim (92807-1886)
PHONE..........................714 288-8400
Robert Sklar, *Branch Mgr*
EMP: 88
SALES (corp-wide): 6.8B **Publicly Held**
WEB: www.cintas-corp.com
SIC: 5199 First aid supplies
HQ: Cintas Corporation No. 2
     6800 Cintas Blvd
     Mason OH 45040

(P-8960)
CLASSIC SOFT TRIM INC
3201 Diablo Ave, Hayward (94545-2701)
PHONE..........................510 782-4911
Steve Robinson, *Manager*
EMP: 75 **Privately Held**
WEB: www.cstdi.com
SIC: 5199 Automobile fabrics
PA: Classic Soft Trim, Inc.
     4516 Seton Center Pkwy # 135
     Austin TX 78759

(P-8961)
CLOUDRADIANT CORP (PA)
Also Called: Enbiz International
12 Fuchsia, Lake Forest (92630-1431)
PHONE..........................408 256-1527
Anil RAO, *President*
◆ **EMP:** 128 **EST:** 2010
SALES (est): 202.8MM **Privately Held**
SIC: 5199 8748 7371 8711 General merchandise, non-durable; business consulting; computer software systems analysis & design, custom; consulting engineer; general management consultant

(P-8962)
CLOUDRADIANT CORP
Also Called: Enbiz International
1111 Di Napoli Dr, San Jose (95129-4014)
PHONE..........................408 256-1527
Anil RAO, *President*
EMP: 726
SALES (corp-wide): 202.8MM **Privately Held**
SIC: 5199 8748 General merchandise, non-durable; business consulting
PA: Cloudradiant Corp.
     12 Fuchsia
     Lake Forest CA 92630
     408 256-1527

(P-8963)
COSTCO WHOLESALE CORPORATION
16505 Sierra Lakes Pkwy, Fontana (92336-1256)
PHONE..........................909 823-8270
EMP: 196
SALES (corp-wide): 116.2B **Publicly Held**
SIC: 5199
PA: Costco Wholesale Corporation
     999 Lake Dr Ste 200
     Issaquah WA 98027
     425 313-8100

(P-8964)
CROSSROAD SERVICES INC
2360 Alvarado St, San Leandro (94577-4314)
PHONE..........................714 728-3915
Steven Scheiner, *President*

Feroun Khan, *Vice Pres*
EMP: 419
SQ FT: 5,000
SALES: 21MM **Privately Held**
SIC: 5199 Variety store merchandise

(P-8965)
DEJUNO CORPORATION
6275 Providence Way, Eastvale (92880-9635)
PHONE..........................909 230-6744
Yuanzhe Gao, *President*
Fei Hong, *Vice Pres*
EMP: 59
SQ FT: 30,000
SALES: 2MM **Privately Held**
SIC: 5199 Leather goods, except footwear, gloves, luggage, belting

(P-8966)
DIRECT PACK INC
1025 W 8th St, Azusa (91702-2248)
PHONE..........................626 380-2360
Gandhi Sifuentes, *Vice Pres*
EMP: 87
SALES (corp-wide): 2.5B **Privately Held**
SIC: 5199 Packaging materials
HQ: Direct Pack, Inc.
     12243 Branford St
     Sun Valley CA 91352

(P-8967)
DOLPHIN HKG LTD (PA)
Also Called: Dolphin International
1125 W Hillcrest Blvd, Inglewood (90301-2021)
P.O. Box 91081, Los Angeles (90009-1081)
PHONE..........................310 215-3356
Steven Lundblad, *President*
Helen Lundblad, *Vice Pres*
▲ **EMP:** 70
SQ FT: 12,000
SALES (est): 41.3MM **Privately Held**
WEB: www.dolphin-int.com
SIC: 5199 Tropical fish

(P-8968)
EMERALD PACKAGING INC
Also Called: E P
33050 Western Ave, Union City (94587-2157)
PHONE..........................510 429-5700
Kevin Kelly, *CEO*
James P Kelly Sr, *Ch of Bd*
James M Kelly Jr, *Exec VP*
Jim Kelly, *Vice Pres*
Maura Kelly Koberlein, *Vice Pres*
▲ **EMP:** 250
SQ FT: 80,000
SALES (est): 132MM **Privately Held**
SIC: 5199 Packaging materials

(P-8969)
ERNEST PACKAGING (PA)
Also Called: Ernest Paper
5777 Smithway St, Commerce (90040-1507)
PHONE..........................800 233-7788
Charles Wilson, *Ch of Bd*
Timothy Wilson, *President*
▲ **EMP:** 130 **EST:** 1947
SQ FT: 300,000
SALES (est): 240.9MM **Privately Held**
WEB: www.ipdpkg.com
SIC: 5199 7389 5113 Packaging materials; cosmetic kits, assembling & packaging; shipping supplies

(P-8970)
FIGI ACQUISITION COMPANY LLC
3636 Gateway Center Ave, San Diego (92102-4524)
PHONE..........................800 678-3444
Woody Laforge,
EMP: 200
SQ FT: 216,000
SALES (est): 10.2MM **Privately Held**
SIC: 5199 Gifts & novelties

(P-8971)
FOAM DISTRIBUTORS INCORPORATED
Also Called: Foam Fabrication For Packaging
31009 San Antonio St, Hayward
(94544-7903)
PHONE......................510 441-8377
Stephanie Wright, CFO
Steve M Doyle, CEO
James Doyle, General Mgr
David Brown, CTO
Mark David, Technology
EMP: 75
SQ FT: 72,000
SALES: 11.6MM Privately Held
WEB: www.foamdist.com
SIC: 5199 Packaging materials

(P-8972)
FOLAND GROUP INC
1500 S Hellman Ave, Ontario (91761-7634)
PHONE......................909 930-9900
Dennis Foland, President
EMP: 52
SALES (est): 1.1MM
SALES (corp-wide): 39MM Privately Held
SIC: 5199 General merchandise, non-durable
PA: Dennis Foland, Inc.
1500 S Hellman Ave
Ontario CA 91761
909 930-9900

(P-8973)
FREE STREAM MEDIA CORP (PA)
Also Called: Samba TV
123 Townsend St 5, San Francisco
(94107-1907)
PHONE......................415 854-0073
Ashwin Navin, CEO
Jackson Huynh, COO
Dan Ackerman, Officer
Jay Wolff, Vice Pres
Rahul Modi, Sr Software Eng
EMP: 80
SQ FT: 11,000
SALES (est): 53.4MM Privately Held
SIC: 5199 Advertising specialties

(P-8974)
GAJU MARKET CORPORATION
450 S Western Ave, Los Angeles
(90020-4120)
PHONE......................213 382-9444
David Rhee, CEO
EMP: 135
SQ FT: 2,000
SALES: 2MM Privately Held
SIC: 5199 General merchandise, non-durable

(P-8975)
GEORGE P JOHNSON COMPANY
999 Skyway Rd Ste 300, San Carlos
(94070-2722)
PHONE......................650 226-0600
Chris Meyer, CEO
Randy Oline, Opers Staff
Ann Fabiano, Director
Jennifer Kasick, Director
Sonearra E Cross, Manager
EMP: 120
SALES (corp-wide): 285.9MM Privately Held
SIC: 5199 8742 Advertising specialties; marketing consulting services
HQ: George P Johnson Company
3600 Giddings Rd
Auburn Hills MI 48326
248 475-2500

(P-8976)
GRAHAM PACKAGING COMPANY LP
4500 Finch Rd, Modesto (95357-4145)
PHONE......................209 572-5187
Tom Sponder, Executive
Robert Jimenez, Technician
EMP: 168
SALES (corp-wide): 14.1MM Privately Held
SIC: 5199 Packaging materials

HQ: Graham Packaging Company, L.P.
700 Indian Springs Dr # 100
Lancaster PA 17601
717 849-8500

(P-8977)
GRHT INC
Also Called: Foam Co, The
14818 Raymer St, Van Nuys (91405-1219)
PHONE......................323 873-6393
Gil Rosky, President
Hossein Tehrani, Vice Pres
EMP: 60
SQ FT: 11,000
SALES (est): 11.5MM Privately Held
SIC: 5199 Foam rubber

(P-8978)
HAY KUHN INC
1880 Jeffrey Rd, El Centro (92243-9532)
P.O. Box 338 (92244-0338)
PHONE......................760 353-0124
Felipe Irigoyen, President
Terry Allegranza, Controller
Janet Franklin, Clerk
◆ EMP: 50
SQ FT: 1,500
SALES (est): 12.8MM Privately Held
SIC: 5199 4789 Packaging materials; car loading

(P-8979)
IMPORT COLLECTION (PA)
Also Called: Tic
7885 Nelson Rd, Panorama City
(91402-6829)
PHONE......................818 782-3060
David Mehdyzadeh, CEO
Sina Mehdyzadeh, Corp Secy
Sammy Mehdizadeh, Vice Pres
Jennifer McMorris, Clerk
◆ EMP: 65 EST: 1971
SQ FT: 160,000
SALES (est): 29.8MM Privately Held
WEB: www.importcollection.com
SIC: 5199 5023 Gifts & novelties; decorative home furnishings & supplies

(P-8980)
INTERNTIONAL PET SUPS DIST INC
Also Called: Petco
10850 Via Frontera, San Diego
(92127-1705)
PHONE......................858 453-7845
James Myers, CEO
Benjamin Foos, Art Dir
◆ EMP: 100
SQ FT: 70,000
SALES (est): 36.1MM
SALES (corp-wide): 264.1K Privately Held
WEB: www.petco.com
SIC: 5199 Pet supplies
HQ: Petco Animal Supplies, Inc.
10850 Via Frontera
San Diego CA 92127
858 453-7845

(P-8981)
KATZKIN LEATHER INC (PA)
6868 W Acco St, Montebello (90640-5441)
PHONE......................323 725-1243
Brook Mayberry, President
Miles Hubbard, Marketing Staff
▲ EMP: 200
SQ FT: 50,000
SALES (est): 83.4MM Privately Held
WEB: www.katzkin.com
SIC: 5199 2531 Leather & cut stock; seats, automobile

(P-8982)
KOLE IMPORTS
Also Called: Basket Basics
24600 Main St, Carson (90745-6332)
PHONE......................310 834-0004
Robert Kole, CEO
Alma A Corral, Vice Pres
Dan Kole, Vice Pres
Ty Yolac, Marketing Staff
Henry Lopez, Manager
◆ EMP: 84
SQ FT: 150,000

SALES (est): 35.6MM Privately Held
WEB: www.koleimports.com
SIC: 5199 Gifts & novelties; general merchandise, non-durable

(P-8983)
LEE-MAR AQUARIUM & PET SUPS
Also Called: Lee Mar Aquarium & Pet Sups
2459 Dogwood Way, Vista (92081-8421)
PHONE......................760 727-1300
Terran R Boyd, President
Jeff Boyd, VP Sales
▲ EMP: 100
SQ FT: 67,000
SALES (est): 25.7MM Privately Held
WEB: www.leemarpet.com
SIC: 5199 3999 Pet supplies; pet supplies

(P-8984)
LIFESTREET CORPORATION
Also Called: Lifestreet Media
98 Battery St St 504, San Carlos (94070)
PHONE......................650 508-2220
Mitchell Wiesman, CEO
EMP: 75 EST: 2008
SALES (est): 15.6MM Privately Held
SIC: 5199 Advertising specialties

(P-8985)
LIVE NATION MERCHANDISE INC (HQ)
Also Called: Signatures Sni
450 Mission St Ste 300, San Francisco
(94105-2518)
PHONE......................415 247-7400
Dell Furano, CEO
Ron Bension, President
Michael Rapino, President
John Reid, President
Arthur Fogel, Chairman
▲ EMP: 50
SQ FT: 27,000
SALES (est): 86.9MM
SALES (corp-wide): 10.7B Publicly Held
WEB: www.signaturesnet.com
SIC: 5199 Advertising specialties
PA: Live Nation Entertainment, Inc.
9348 Civic Center Dr Lbby
Beverly Hills CA 90210
800 653-8000

(P-8986)
LOGOMARK INC
1201 Bell Ave, Tustin (92780-6420)
PHONE......................714 675-6100
Trevor Gnesin, President
◆ EMP: 250
SQ FT: 200,000
SALES (est): 148.2MM Privately Held
WEB: www.logomark.com
SIC: 5199 Advertising specialties

(P-8987)
MAX LEATHER
8533 Washington Blvd, Culver City
(90232-7462)
PHONE......................310 841-6990
Max Khansefid, President
EMP: 50
SALES (est): 6.6MM Privately Held
WEB: www.maxleatherinc.com
SIC: 5199 Leather & cut stock; leather, leather goods & furs

(P-8988)
MIDWAY INTERNATIONAL INC
13131 166th St, Cerritos (90703-2202)
PHONE......................562 921-2255
Ha Suk Chung, President
◆ EMP: 50
SQ FT: 32,700
SALES (est): 16.6MM Privately Held
SIC: 5199 Wigs

(P-8989)
MISSION PETS INC
986 Mission St Fl 5, San Francisco
(94103-2970)
PHONE......................415 904-9914
Carmine Petruzello, CEO
Jannita Hanson, CFO
Dan Brown, Vice Pres
Michelle Elliot, Vice Pres
Nancy Agger Nielsen, Controller
▲ EMP: 50

SQ FT: 10,000
SALES (est): 11.3MM Privately Held
SIC: 5199 Pet supplies

(P-8990)
NATIONAL SALES CORP
7250 Oxford Way, Commerce
(90040-3643)
PHONE......................323 586-0200
Karmel Nazarian, President
Ehsanollah Eshaghian, Treasurer
▲ EMP: 52
SQ FT: 55,000
SALES: 25MM Privately Held
WEB: www.e-nsc.com
SIC: 5199 General merchandise, non-durable

(P-8991)
NW PACKAGING LLC (PA)
1201 E Lexington Ave, Pomona
(91766-5520)
P.O. Box 357, Placentia (92871-0357)
PHONE......................909 706-3627
Robert E Sliter, Administration
EMP: 100
SALES (est): 49.8MM Privately Held
SIC: 5199 Packaging materials

(P-8992)
OXGORD INCORPORATED
16325 S Avalon Blvd, Gardena
(90248-2909)
PHONE......................800 221-0718
Akiva Nourollah, President
▲ EMP: 150 EST: 2012
SALES (est): 3.2MM Privately Held
SIC: 5199 General merchandise, non-durable

(P-8993)
PACIFIC EASTERN INTL PDTS
Also Called: Pacific Eastern Intl Pdts I
12551 Barrett Ln, Santa Ana (92705-1306)
PHONE......................714 538-3434
Thomas Osbourne, President
Teri Osbourne, Admin Sec
EMP: 90
SALES (est): 4.2MM Privately Held
SIC: 5199 General merchandise, non-durable

(P-8994)
PACIFIC METRO LLC (PA)
Also Called: Thomas Kinkade Company, The
18715 Madrone Pkwy, Morgan Hill
(95037-2876)
PHONE......................408 201-5000
Eric H Halvorson, President
Steve Paszkiewicz, President
Herbert D Montgomery, CFO
Anthony D Thomopoulos, Chairman
Daniel Byrne, Exec VP
▲ EMP: 350
SQ FT: 400,000
SALES (est): 74MM Privately Held
SIC: 5199 Art goods

(P-8995)
PACIFIC WESTERN SALES (PA)
Also Called: Pbfy Flexible Packaging
2980 Enterprise St Ste A, Brea
(92821-6283)
PHONE......................714 572-6730
Lyndsey William Tidwell, President
Jimmy Hou, President
Lorraine Clements, Treasurer
Jay Johnson, Vice Pres
Andrea Pennington, Vice Pres
◆ EMP: 51
SQ FT: 49,000
SALES: 16MM Privately Held
WEB: www.pacificwesternsales.com
SIC: 5199 7336 Packaging materials; package design

(P-8996)
PACKAGING MANUFACTURING INC
2475 Pseo De Las Americas, San Diego
(92154-7255)
PHONE......................619 498-9199
Salvatore Anza, CEO
EMP: 250 EST: 2009
SALES (est): 30.8MM Privately Held
SIC: 5199 Packaging materials

(P-8997)
PACTIV LLC
5370 E Home Ave, Fresno (93727-2104)
PHONE..................................559 251-7351
Chris Verard, *Manager*
Shaun Thompson, *Controller*
Ricky Bland, *Manager*
EMP: 110
SQ FT: 5,000
SALES (corp-wide): 14.1MM **Privately Held**
WEB: www.pactiv.com
SIC: 5199 Packaging materials
HQ: Pactiv Llc
1900 W Field Ct
Lake Forest IL 60045
847 482-2000

(P-8998)
PACTIV LLC
1 Diamond Ave, Red Bluff (96080)
PHONE..................................530 529-3340
William Haser, *Branch Mgr*
Vl Lindsey, *President*
Laura Daniel, *Human Res Dir*
V Lindsey, *Human Resources*
EMP: 100
SALES (corp-wide): 14.1MM **Privately Held**
WEB: www.pactiv.com
SIC: 5199 Packaging materials
HQ: Pactiv Llc
1900 W Field Ct
Lake Forest IL 60045
847 482-2000

(P-8999)
PACTIV PACKAGING INC (DH)
Also Called: Pwp
3751 Seville Ave, Vernon (90058-1741)
PHONE..................................323 513-9000
Ira Maroofion, *President*
Peter J Lazaredes, *President*
Will Durall, *Project Mgr*
John Bussey, *Engineer*
Deepak Vakil, *Controller*
◆ **EMP:** 60
SALES (est): 94.4MM
SALES (corp-wide): 14.1MM **Privately Held**
WEB: www.pwpc.com
SIC: 5199 Packaging materials
HQ: Pactiv Llc
1900 W Field Ct
Lake Forest IL 60045
847 482-2000

(P-9000)
PD LIQUIDATION INC
Also Called: Pipe Dream Products
21350 Lassen St, Chatsworth (91311-4254)
PHONE..................................818 772-0100
David Feldman, *CEO*
Robert Feldman, *President*
Brian Flowers, *CFO*
Steve Sav, *Vice Pres*
Hernan Zegarra, *Accountant*
◆ **EMP:** 150
SALES (est): 45.9MM
SALES (corp-wide): 29.6MM **Privately Held**
WEB: www.pipedreamproducts.com
SIC: 5199 Gifts & novelties
PA: Diamond Products, Llc
21350 Lassen St
Chatsworth CA 91311
818 772-0100

(P-9001)
PHD MARKETING INC
1373 Ridgeway St, Pomona (91768-2701)
PHONE..................................909 620-1000
Thaer Ahmad, *President*
John Kamar, *Treasurer*
▲ **EMP:** 60
SQ FT: 20,000
SALES (est): 8.6MM **Privately Held**
SIC: 5199 5399 General merchandise, non-durable; Army-Navy goods

(P-9002)
POLYVORE INC
701 First Ave, Sunnyvale (94089-1019)
PHONE..................................650 968-1195
Jessica Lee, *CEO*

Jen Matteucci, *Partner*
Pasha Sadri, *CTO*
Yue Wu, *Software Dev*
Greg Palmer, *Software Engr*
EMP: 60
SALES (est): 9.6MM
SALES (corp-wide): 2.1MM **Privately Held**
SIC: 5199 Advertising specialties
HQ: Groupe Atallah Inc
333 Rue Chabanel O Bureau 900
Montreal QC H2N 2
514 600-5818

(P-9003)
PRATT INDUSTRIES INC
1051 S Rose Ave, Oxnard (93030-5180)
PHONE..................................805 483-5331
Richard Meyers, *Manager*
EMP: 50
SALES (corp-wide): 2.5B **Privately Held**
WEB: www.rmp.com
SIC: 5199 Packaging materials
PA: Pratt Industries, Inc.
1800 Sarasot Bus Pkwy Ne C
Conyers GA 30013
770 918-5678

(P-9004)
PREGIS LLC
33340 Central Ave, Union City (94587-2044)
PHONE..................................510 404-1360
Steve Nau, *Manager*
EMP: 65
SALES (corp-wide): 4.7B **Privately Held**
SIC: 5199 Packaging materials
HQ: Pregis Llc
1650 Lake Cook Rd Ste 400
Deerfield IL 60015
847 597-2200

(P-9005)
PRO SPECIALTIES GROUP INC
8221 Arjons Dr Ste F, San Diego (92126-6319)
PHONE..................................858 541-1100
Cheng Shun LI, *President*
Sin Ghim, *Vice Pres*
I Chin LI, *Admin Sec*
Aprilyn Diaz, *Graphic Designe*
Jennie Ryan, *Graphic Designe*
▲ **EMP:** 70
SQ FT: 23,000
SALES: 35MM **Privately Held**
WEB: www.psginc.com
SIC: 5199 Advertising specialties

(P-9006)
QUAKER PET GROUP INC
160 Mitchell Blvd, San Rafael (94903-2044)
PHONE..................................415 721-7400
Kevin Fick, *CEO*
Mike Trott, *CFO*
▲ **EMP:** 100
SQ FT: 11,000
SALES: 67MM **Privately Held**
SIC: 5199 Pet supplies
HQ: Worldwise, Inc.
6 Hamilton Landing # 150
Novato CA 94949

(P-9007)
QUETICO LLC (PA)
5521 Schaefer Ave, Chino (91710-9070)
PHONE..................................909 628-6200
Thomas Fenchel, *Mng Member*
Nick Agakanian, *Vice Pres*
Ivan Spiers, *Human Res Mgr*
Janet Guerrero, *Personnel Assit*
▲ **EMP:** 60
SQ FT: 278,500
SALES (est): 334.1MM **Privately Held**
WEB: www.quetico.net
SIC: 5199 7389 General merchandise, non-durable; packaging & labeling services

(P-9008)
R M B PACKAGING CO INC
9667 Canoga Ave, Chatsworth (91311-4115)
PHONE..................................818 998-0658
Paul Thomas, *CEO*

EMP: 50
SALES (est): 6MM **Privately Held**
SIC: 5199 Packaging materials

(P-9009)
REDBARN PET PRODUCTS INC (PA)
Also Called: Redbarn Premium Pet Products
3229 E Spring St Ste 310, Long Beach (90806-2478)
PHONE..................................562 495-7315
Jeff Baikie, *CEO*
Howard Bloxam, *President*
Phillip Kim, *CFO*
Joe Martinez, *Principal*
Javier Solorzano, *Graphic Designe*
▼ **EMP:** 123
SQ FT: 50,000
SALES (est): 122MM **Privately Held**
WEB: www.redbarninc.com
SIC: 5199 2047 Pet supplies; dog & cat food

(P-9010)
SCHROFF INC
7328 Trade St, San Diego (92121-3435)
PHONE..................................858 740-2400
Robert Bradley, *Branch Mgr*
William Monahan, *Director*
EMP: 120 **Privately Held**
SIC: 5199 Packaging materials
HQ: Schroff, Inc.
170 Commerce Dr
Warwick RI 02886
763 204-7700

(P-9011)
SHIMS BARGAIN INC (PA)
Also Called: J C Sales
2600 S Soto St, Vernon (90058-8015)
PHONE..................................323 881-0099
K Kenneth Suh, *President*
BJ Chang, *CFO*
James Shim, *Chairman*
Sena OH, *Bookkeeper*
◆ **EMP:** 100
SQ FT: 420,000
SALES (est): 177.5MM **Privately Held**
SIC: 5199 General merchandise, non-durable

(P-9012)
SONORA TRADE COMPANY INC
2127 Olympic Pkwy, Chula Vista (91915-1359)
PHONE..................................619 878-5848
Hanna Shayota, *CEO*
▲ **EMP:** 55
SALES (est): 8.6MM **Privately Held**
SIC: 5199 Art goods & supplies

(P-9013)
SPECIALTY MERCHANDISE CORP (PA)
Also Called: Smart Living Company
4100 Guardian St Ste 112, Simi Valley (93063-6727)
PHONE..................................805 578-5500
Mark Schelbert, *CEO*
Scott Palladino, *CFO*
Charles Serian, *CTO*
Kevin Kiely, *Controller*
Tom Krutilek, *Marketing Staff*
▲ **EMP:** 50
SALES (est): 95.2MM **Privately Held**
WEB: www.onlinesmc.com
SIC: 5199 Gifts & novelties

(P-9014)
TARGUS INTERNATIONAL LLC (PA)
1211 N Miller St, Anaheim (92806-1933)
PHONE..................................714 765-5555
Mikel H Williams, *CEO*
Bill Oppenlander, *President*
Victor C Streufert, *CFO*
Andrew Corkill, *Vice Pres*
Allen H Gharapetian, *Vice Pres*
◆ **EMP:** 175
SQ FT: 200,656
SALES (est): 172.1MM **Privately Held**
WEB: www.targus.com
SIC: 5199 Bags, baskets & cases

(P-9015)
THORO—PACKAGING (DH)
1467 Davril Cir, Corona (92880-6957)
PHONE..................................951 278-2100
Janet Dabek Steiner, *President*
EMP: 75
SQ FT: 56,000
SALES: 64.8MM
SALES (corp-wide): 6.9MM **Privately Held**
WEB: www.thoropkg.com
SIC: 5199 Packaging materials
HQ: Autajon Cs
Petit Pelican Petit Pelican
Montelimar 26200
475 002-000

(P-9016)
ULINE INC
2950 Jurupa St, Ontario (91761-2936)
PHONE..................................909 605-7090
Toll Free:..................................877 -
Israel Baluja, *Branch Mgr*
Will Reilly, *Sales Dir*
Billy Cockrell, *Representative*
EMP: 57
SALES (corp-wide): 3.9B **Privately Held**
WEB: www.uline.com
SIC: 5199 Packaging materials
PA: Uline, Inc.
12575 Uline Dr
Pleasant Prairie WI 53158
262 612-4200

(P-9017)
US FOODS INC
1201 Park Center Dr, Vista (92081-8313)
PHONE..................................760 599-6200
Gary Graig, *Branch Mgr*
Maurice Callen, *Supervisor*
EMP: 375 **Publicly Held**
WEB: www.usfoodservice.com
SIC: 5199 5147 5144 5142 General merchandise, non-durable; meats & meat products; poultry & poultry products; packaged frozen goods; groceries, general line
HQ: Us Foods, Inc.
9399 W Higgins Rd # 100
Rosemont IL 60018

(P-9018)
VEGETABLE GROWERS SUPPLY CO (PA)
Also Called: V G S
1360 Merrill St, Salinas (93901-4432)
P.O. Box 757 (93902-0757)
PHONE..................................831 759-4600
Ron Huff, *CEO*
William J Locke III, *President*
Lisa Erling, *CFO*
Susan Gong, *Administration*
Nancy Bauer, *Credit Mgr*
▲ **EMP:** 50
SQ FT: 38,000
SALES (est): 83.1MM **Privately Held**
WEB: www.veggrow.com
SIC: 5199 2449 Packaging materials; rectangular boxes & crates, wood

(P-9019)
VIA TRADING CORPORATION
2520 Industry Way, Lynwood (90262-4015)
PHONE..................................877 202-3616
Jacques Stambouli, *CEO*
Alain Stambouli, *President*
Alex Antypas, *COO*
Edwin Cortez, *Administration*
Ramses Cobian, *Controller*
◆ **EMP:** 57
SQ FT: 240,000
SALES: 39.3MM **Privately Held**
WEB: www.viatrading.com
SIC: 5199 General merchandise, non-durable

(P-9020)
VICTORY FOAM INC (PA)
3 Holland, Irvine (92618-2506)
PHONE..................................949 474-0690
Frank M Comerford, *CEO*
Helen Comerford, *Corp Secy*
Myles Comerford, *Vice Pres*
Shea Oddo, *Technology*
Alejandro Alarcon, *Engineer*

P R O D U C T S & S V C S

▲ EMP: 95
SQ FT: 53,000
SALES (est): 43.7MM **Privately Held**
WEB: www.victoryfoam.com
SIC: 5199 Packaging materials

(P-9021)
VIPSTORE USA CO
13674 Star Ruby Ave, Eastvale
(92880-5557)
PHONE..........................626 934-7880
Hongjie Yang, *President*
EMP: 400
SALES: 12MM **Privately Held**
SIC: 5199 General merchandise, non-durable

(P-9022)
WARREN AUTO DE MEXICO LLC
517 S Cedros Ave, Solana Beach
(92075-1922)
PHONE..........................858 794-7947
EMP: 100
SALES (est): 1.3MM **Privately Held**
SIC: 5199

(P-9023)
WEBB SUNRISE INC
3320 Kemper St Ste 201, San Diego
(92110-4905)
PHONE..........................619 220-7050
Lawrence R Webb Sr, *President*
Joji Mangubat, *Vice Pres*
Donna Webb, *Vice Pres*
EMP: 50
SQ FT: 10,000
SALES (est): 4.6MM **Privately Held**
SIC: 5199 Advertising specialties

(P-9024)
WONDERTREATS INC
2200 Lapham Dr, Modesto (95354-3911)
PHONE..........................209 521-8881
Jocelyn Yu Hall, *CEO*
Greg Hall, *President*
Aileen Ong, *Admin Asst*
Louise Xiao, *Purch Dir*
Don Greenland, *Sales Mgr*
▲ EMP: 315
SQ FT: 230,000
SALES (est): 135.8MM **Privately Held**
SIC: 5199 5947 Gift baskets; gift baskets

6011 Federal Reserve Banks

(P-9025)
FEDERAL RSRVE BNK SAN FRNCISCO (HQ)
101 Market St, San Francisco
(94105-1530)
P.O. Box 7702 (94120-7702)
PHONE..........................415 974-2000
John C Williams, *President*
Alexander R Mehran, *Ch of Bd*
Patricia E Yarrington, *Ch of Bd*
John F Moore, *COO*
Barry M Meyer, *Chairman*
◆ EMP: 1397
SQ FT: 471,543
SALES (est): 4MM **Privately Held**
SIC: 6011 Federal reserve banks
PA: Board Of Governors Of The Federal
Reserve System
20th St Cnsttution Ave Nw
Washington DC 20551
202 452-3000

(P-9026)
FEDERAL RSRVE BNK SAN FRNCISCO
Also Called: Los Angeles Branch
950 S Grand Ave, Los Angeles
(90015-4202)
P.O. Box 512077 (90051-0077)
PHONE..........................213 683-2300
Mark Mullinix, *Manager*
Tomi Barker, *Administration*
EMP: 640 **Privately Held**
SIC: 6011 Federal reserve branches
HQ: Federal Reserve Bank Of San Francisco
101 Market St
San Francisco CA 94105
415 974-2000

6021 National Commercial Banks

(P-9027)
AMERICAN BUSINESS BANK
3633 Inland Empire Blvd # 720, Ontario
(91764-4922)
PHONE..........................909 919-2040
Elaine Lopez, *Branch Mgr*
EMP: 89
SALES (corp-wide): 74MM **Publicly Held**
SIC: 6021 National commercial banks
PA: American Business Bank
400 S Hope St Ste 300
Los Angeles CA 90071
949 261-1122

(P-9028)
AMERICAN PLUS BANK (PA)
630 W Duarte Rd, Arcadia (91007-9205)
PHONE..........................626 821-9188
Julian Liu, *Ch Credit Ofcr*
Eric Feder, *Officer*
Kenneth Lo, *Officer*
Sandra Ip, *Executive Asst*
EMP: 50
SALES: 22.5MM **Privately Held**
SIC: 6021 National commercial banks

(P-9029)
BANA HOME LOAN SERVICING
31303 Agoura Rd, Westlake Village
(91361-4635)
PHONE..........................213 345-7975
Rachel Fiorillo, *Senior VP*
EMP: 900
SALES (est): 301.6K **Privately Held**
SIC: 6021 National commercial banks

(P-9030)
BANC CALIFORNIA NATIONAL ASSN (HQ)
3 Macarthur Pl, Santa Ana (92707-6067)
PHONE..........................877 770-2262
Robert Franko, *President*
Hamid Hussain, *President*
Tigran Karavardanyan, *President*
Sharon Murray, *President*
Neal Mendelsohn, *Officer*
EMP: 95
SALES: 416.1MM
SALES (corp-wide): 446.7MM **Publicly Held**
SIC: 6021 National commercial banks
PA: Banc Of California, Inc.
3 Macarthur Pl Ste 100
Santa Ana CA 92707
855 361-2262

(P-9031)
BANC OF CALIFORNIA INC (PA)
3 Macarthur Pl Ste 100, Santa Ana
(92707-6068)
P.O. Box 61452, Irvine (92602-6048)
PHONE..........................855 361-2262
Douglas H Bowers, *President*
Robert D Sznewajs, *Ch of Bd*
John A Bogler, *CFO*
Rita H Dailey, *Treasurer*
Kris A Gagnon, *Ch Credit Ofcr*
EMP: 120
SALES: 446.7MM **Publicly Held**
SIC: 6021 National commercial banks

(P-9032)
BANK AMERICA NATIONAL ASSN
5292 N Palm Ave, Fresno (93704-2209)
PHONE..........................559 445-7731
Kim Garcia, *Manager*
EMP: 80
SALES (corp-wide): 110.5B **Publicly Held**
WEB: www.bofa.com
SIC: 6021 National commercial banks
HQ: Bank Of America, National Association
100 S Tryon St
Charlotte NC 28202
704 386-5681

(P-9033)
BANK AMERICA NATIONAL ASSN
1525 Market St, San Francisco
(94103-1289)
PHONE..........................800 432-1000
John Watson, *Branch Mgr*
Duane Miller, *Vice Pres*
EMP: 50
SALES (corp-wide): 110.5B **Publicly Held**
WEB: www.bofa.com
SIC: 6021 National commercial banks
HQ: Bank Of America, National Association
100 S Tryon St
Charlotte NC 28202
704 386-5681

(P-9034)
BANK AMERICA NATIONAL ASSN
345 Montgomery St, San Francisco
(94104-1898)
P.O. Box 37000 (94137-0001)
PHONE..........................415 913-5891
Thomas Sidon, *Sales/Mktg Mgr*
H Anton Tucher, *Managing Dir*
EMP: 120
SALES (corp-wide): 110.5B **Publicly Held**
WEB: www.bofa.com
SIC: 6021 National commercial banks
HQ: Bank Of America, National Association
100 S Tryon St
Charlotte NC 28202
704 386-5681

(P-9035)
BANK AMERICA NATIONAL ASSN
400 Broadway St, Chico (95928-5323)
P.O. Box 1289 (95927-1289)
PHONE..........................530 891-7019
Mark Francis, *Manager*
EMP: 60
SQ FT: 15,763
SALES (corp-wide): 110.5B **Publicly Held**
WEB: www.bofa.com
SIC: 6021 National commercial banks
HQ: Bank Of America, National Association
100 S Tryon St
Charlotte NC 28202
704 386-5681

(P-9036)
BANK AMERICA NATIONAL ASSN
345 N Brand Blvd, Glendale (91203-2368)
PHONE..........................800 432-1000
Don Nodell, *Manager*
EMP: 60
SALES (corp-wide): 110.5B **Publicly Held**
WEB: www.bofa.com
SIC: 6021 National commercial banks
HQ: Bank Of America, National Association
100 S Tryon St
Charlotte NC 28202
704 386-5681

(P-9037)
BANK AMERICA NATIONAL ASSN
6351 E Spring St, Long Beach
(90808-4021)
P.O. Box 409 (90801-0409)
PHONE..........................562 624-4330
Jennifer Davis, *Branch Mgr*
EMP: 50
SALES (corp-wide): 110.5B **Publicly Held**
WEB: www.bofa.com
SIC: 6021 National commercial banks
HQ: Bank Of America, National Association
100 S Tryon St
Charlotte NC 28202
704 386-5681

(P-9038)
BANK AMERICA NATIONAL ASSN
120 S Brand Blvd, San Fernando
(91340-3377)
PHONE..........................818 898-3033
Janice Musgrove, *Branch Mgr*
EMP: 60
SALES (corp-wide): 110.5B **Publicly Held**
WEB: www.bofa.com
SIC: 6021 National commercial banks
HQ: Bank Of America, National Association
100 S Tryon St
Charlotte NC 28202
704 386-5681

(P-9039)
BANK AMERICA NATIONAL ASSN
212 E Main St, Visalia (93291-6356)
P.O. Box 551 (93279-0551)
PHONE..........................800 432-1000
Gordon Young, *President*
Bobbie Roth, *Customer Svc Re*
EMP: 50
SALES (corp-wide): 110.5B **Publicly Held**
WEB: www.bofa.com
SIC: 6021 National commercial banks
HQ: Bank Of America, National Association
100 S Tryon St
Charlotte NC 28202
704 386-5681

(P-9040)
BANK AMERICA NATIONAL ASSN
550 S Hill St Ste 101, Los Angeles
(90013-2403)
PHONE..........................310 384-4562
Stacy Young, *Manager*
Gregg Hall, *Vice Pres*
Manohara Maddineni, *Vice Pres*
EMP: 65
SALES (corp-wide): 110.5B **Publicly Held**
WEB: www.bofa.com
SIC: 6021 National commercial banks
HQ: Bank Of America, National Association
100 S Tryon St
Charlotte NC 28202
704 386-5681

(P-9041)
BANK AMERICA NATIONAL ASSN
13220 Harbor Blvd, Garden Grove
(92843-1737)
P.O. Box 758 (92842-0758)
PHONE..........................714 973-8495
Rita Castro, *Branch Mgr*
Linda Ropp, *Cust Mgr*
Martha Albert, *Manager*
EMP: 50
SALES (corp-wide): 110.5B **Publicly Held**
WEB: www.bofa.com
SIC: 6021 National commercial banks
HQ: Bank Of America, National Association
100 S Tryon St
Charlotte NC 28202
704 386-5681

(P-9042)
BANK AMERICA NATIONAL ASSN
275 Valencia Ave, Brea (92823-6340)
PHONE..........................949 474-8801
Pearl Bfar, *Administration*
EMP: 60
SALES (corp-wide): 110.5B **Publicly Held**
SIC: 6021 National commercial banks
HQ: Bank Of America, National Association
100 S Tryon St
Charlotte NC 28202
704 386-5681

(P-9043)
BANK AMERICA NATIONAL ASSN
1687 E Florida Ave, Hemet (92544-8646)
P.O. Box 1406 (92546-1406)
PHONE..................................951 929-8614
John Borah, *Branch Mgr*
EMP: 50
SALES (corp-wide): 110.5B **Publicly Held**
WEB: www.bofa.com
SIC: 6021 National commercial banks
HQ: Bank Of America, National Association
100 S Tryon St
Charlotte NC 28202
704 386-5681

(P-9044)
BANK AMERICA NATIONAL ASSN
1450 W Redondo Beach Blvd, Gardena (90247-3399)
PHONE..................................800 432-1000
Rosa Caldera, *Branch Mgr*
EMP: 75
SALES (corp-wide): 110.5B **Publicly Held**
WEB: www.bofa.com
SIC: 6021 National commercial banks
HQ: Bank Of America, National Association
100 S Tryon St
Charlotte NC 28202
704 386-5681

(P-9045)
BANK AMERICA NATIONAL ASSN
5901 Canoga Ave, Woodland Hills (91367-5010)
PHONE..................................818 577-2000
Albert Welch, *Sales/Mktg Mgr*
EMP: 60
SALES (corp-wide): 110.5B **Publicly Held**
WEB: www.bofa.com
SIC: 6021 National commercial banks
HQ: Bank Of America, National Association
100 S Tryon St
Charlotte NC 28202
704 386-5681

(P-9046)
BANK AMERICA NATIONAL ASSN
4100 Chino Hills Pkwy, Chino Hills (91709-2611)
P.O. Box 727, Chino (91708-0727)
PHONE..................................909 393-3002
Kathleen Mossbarger, *Branch Mgr*
EMP: 99
SALES (corp-wide): 110.5B **Publicly Held**
WEB: www.bofa.com
SIC: 6021 National commercial banks
HQ: Bank Of America, National Association
100 S Tryon St
Charlotte NC 28202
704 386-5681

(P-9047)
BANK AMERICA NATIONAL ASSN
27489 Ynez Rd, Temecula (92591-4612)
PHONE..................................951 676-4114
Theresa Fukuda, *Branch Mgr*
EMP: 53
SALES (corp-wide): 110.5B **Publicly Held**
WEB: www.bofa.com
SIC: 6021 National commercial banks
HQ: Bank Of America, National Association
100 S Tryon St
Charlotte NC 28202
704 386-5681

(P-9048)
BANK LEUMI USA
Also Called: Bank Leumi Le
555 W 5th St Fl 33, Los Angeles (90013-1050)
PHONE..................................323 966-4700
Toll Free:..................................877
Abraham Maoz, *Exec VP*
Ana Alexander, *Manager*
Chagit Raskin, *Assistant VP*

EMP: 61
SALES (corp-wide): 3.7B **Privately Held**
SIC: 6021 National commercial banks
HQ: Bank Leumi Usa
579 5th Ave Frnt A
New York NY 10017
917 542-2343

(P-9049)
BANK OF HOPE (HQ)
3200 Wilshire Blvd # 1400, Los Angeles (90010-1325)
PHONE..................................213 639-1700
Kevin S Kim, *CEO*
Scott Yoon-Suk Whang, *Ch of Bd*
Min J Kim, *President*
Chung Lee, *Bd of Directors*
Timothy Christensen, *Officer*
▲ **EMP:** 108
SALES (est): 377.7MM
SALES (corp-wide): 710.3MM **Publicly Held**
WEB: www.narabank.com
SIC: 6021 National commercial banks
PA: Hope Bancorp, Inc.
3200 Wilshire Blvd # 1400
Los Angeles CA 90010
213 639-1700

(P-9050)
BANK OF SIERRA
Also Called: Bank of Sierra
500 Marsh St, San Luis Obispo (93401-3955)
PHONE..................................805 541-0400
Kevin McPhaill, *Principal*
EMP: 60
SALES (corp-wide): 123.2MM **Publicly Held**
SIC: 6021 National commercial banks
HQ: Bank Of The Sierra
90 N Main St
Porterville CA 93257
559 782-4300

(P-9051)
BANNER BANK
9340 E Stockton Blvd, Elk Grove (95624-1456)
PHONE..................................916 685-6546
Scott A Kisting, *CEO*
EMP: 60 **Publicly Held**
WEB: www.premierwestbank.com
SIC: 6021 6029 National commercial banks; commercial banks
HQ: Banner Bank
10 S 1st Ave
Walla Walla WA 99362
800 272-9933

(P-9052)
BBVA USA
Also Called: Compass Bank
27851 Bradley Rd Ste 125, Sun City (92586-2282)
PHONE..................................951 672-4829
EMP: 337
SALES (corp-wide): 1.4B **Privately Held**
SIC: 6021 National commercial banks
HQ: Bbva Usa
15 20th St S Ste 100
Birmingham AL 35233
205 297-1986

(P-9053)
CANADIAN IMPERIAL BANK
620 Newport Center Dr, Newport Beach (92660-6420)
PHONE..................................949 759-4718
Robert Ctvrtlik, *Principal*
Kasandra Schindler, *Vice Pres*
EMP: 78
SALES (corp-wide): 13.7B **Privately Held**
WEB: www.cibc.com
SIC: 6021 National commercial banks
PA: Canadian Imperial Bank Of Commerce
199 Bay St Commerce Crt W
Toronto ON M5L 1
416 980-3096

(P-9054)
CARPENTER FUND MANAGER GP LLC
5 Park Plz Ste 950, Irvine (92614-8527)
PHONE..................................949 261-8888
Edward J Carpenter,

Arthur Hidalgo, *Exec VP*
Howard Gould, *Vice Pres*
EMP: 188
SALES (est): 13.1MM **Privately Held**
SIC: 6021 National commercial banks

(P-9055)
CIT BANK NA
78010 Main St, La Quinta (92253-3408)
PHONE..................................760 771-3498
Robert Kehrberg, *Branch Mgr*
EMP: 65
SALES (corp-wide): 3.2B **Publicly Held**
SIC: 6021 National commercial banks
HQ: Cit Bank, N.A.
75 N Fair Oaks Ave Ste C
Pasadena CA 91103

(P-9056)
CIT BANK NA
1570 Rosecrans Ave, Manhattan Beach (90266-3718)
PHONE..................................310 727-5660
EMP: 63
SALES (corp-wide): 3.2B **Publicly Held**
SIC: 6021 National commercial banks
HQ: Cit Bank, N.A.
75 N Fair Oaks Ave Ste C
Pasadena CA 91103

(P-9057)
CIT BANK NA
3410 Grand Ave Ste A, Chino Hills (91709-1473)
PHONE..................................909 631-2560
Jennifer Ferguson, *Branch Mgr*
EMP: 63
SALES (corp-wide): 3.2B **Publicly Held**
SIC: 6021 National commercial banks
HQ: Cit Bank, N.A.
75 N Fair Oaks Ave Ste C
Pasadena CA 91103

(P-9058)
CIT BANK NA
2920 N Beverly Glen Cir, Los Angeles (90077-1724)
PHONE..................................310 475-4594
Diane Thomas, *Principal*
Jeffrey Rose, *Site Mgr*
EMP: 56
SALES (corp-wide): 3.2B **Publicly Held**
SIC: 6021 National commercial banks
HQ: Cit Bank, N.A.
75 N Fair Oaks Ave Ste C
Pasadena CA 91103

(P-9059)
CIT BANK NA
1111 N Brand Blvd Ste A, Glendale (91202-3072)
PHONE..................................818 502-8400
George Lazar, *Principal*
EMP: 59
SALES (corp-wide): 3.2B **Publicly Held**
SIC: 6021 National commercial banks
HQ: Cit Bank, N.A.
75 N Fair Oaks Ave Ste C
Pasadena CA 91103

(P-9060)
CIT BANK NA
1750 Ocean Park Blvd, Santa Monica (90405-4938)
PHONE..................................310 452-3802
Art Bikidjian, *Branch Mgr*
Marinthia Thomas, *Surgery Dir*
EMP: 65
SALES (corp-wide): 3.2B **Publicly Held**
SIC: 6021 National commercial banks
HQ: Cit Bank, N.A.
75 N Fair Oaks Ave Ste C
Pasadena CA 91103

(P-9061)
CIT BANK NA
3500 E 7th St, Long Beach (90804-5137)
PHONE..................................562 433-0972
Nicole Graves, *Branch Mgr*
EMP: 65

(P-9062)
CIT BANK NA
17050 Ventura Blvd # 100, Encino (91316-4143)
PHONE..................................818 817-5320
Noel Youcefi, *Branch Mgr*
EMP: 63
SALES (corp-wide): 3.2B **Publicly Held**
SIC: 6021 National commercial banks
HQ: Cit Bank, N.A.
75 N Fair Oaks Ave Ste C
Pasadena CA 91103

(P-9063)
CIT BANK NA
1727 E Daily Dr, Camarillo (93010-6202)
PHONE..................................805 465-1053
Susan Anderson, *Manager*
EMP: 64
SALES (corp-wide): 3.2B **Publicly Held**
SIC: 6021 National commercial banks
HQ: Cit Bank, N.A.
75 N Fair Oaks Ave Ste C
Pasadena CA 91103

(P-9064)
CIT BANK NA
5573 Sepulveda Blvd, Culver City (90230-5513)
PHONE..................................310 390-7745
Millie Davis, *Vice Pres*
EMP: 63
SALES (corp-wide): 3.2B **Publicly Held**
SIC: 6021 National commercial banks
HQ: Cit Bank, N.A.
75 N Fair Oaks Ave Ste C
Pasadena CA 91103

(P-9065)
CIT BANK NA
Also Called: Onewest Bank
10784 Jefferson Blvd, Culver City (90230-4933)
PHONE..................................310 559-7222
Peter Smith, *Branch Mgr*
EMP: 63
SALES (corp-wide): 3.2B **Publicly Held**
SIC: 6021 National commercial banks
HQ: Cit Bank, N.A.
75 N Fair Oaks Ave Ste C
Pasadena CA 91103

(P-9066)
CIT BANK NA
3000 S Sepulveda Blvd, Los Angeles (90034-4202)
PHONE..................................310 477-0546
Delmy Martinez, *Branch Mgr*
EMP: 63
SALES (corp-wide): 3.2B **Publicly Held**
SIC: 6021 National commercial banks
HQ: Cit Bank, N.A.
75 N Fair Oaks Ave Ste C
Pasadena CA 91103

(P-9067)
CIT BANK NA
1001 N San Fernando Blvd, Burbank (91504-4303)
PHONE..................................818 525-3760
EMP: 64
SALES (corp-wide): 3.2B **Publicly Held**
SIC: 6021 National commercial banks
HQ: Cit Bank, N.A.
75 N Fair Oaks Ave Ste C
Pasadena CA 91103

(P-9068)
CIT BANK NA
27620 Marguerite Pkwy B, Mission Viejo (92692-3607)
PHONE..................................949 347-7014
Dagmar Richter, *Branch Mgr*

PRODUCTS & SVCS

EMP: 63
SALES (corp-wide): 3.2B **Publicly Held**
SIC: 6021 National commercial banks
HQ: Cit Bank, N.A.
  75 N Fair Oaks Ave Ste C
  Pasadena CA 91103

(P-9069)
CIT BANK NA
3700 E Coast Hwy, Corona Del Mar
(92625-2520)
PHONE...........................949 675-2890
Rodney Holder, *Branch Mgr*
EMP: 56
SALES (corp-wide): 3.2B **Publicly Held**
SIC: 6021 National commercial banks
HQ: Cit Bank, N.A.
  75 N Fair Oaks Ave Ste C
  Pasadena CA 91103
  -

(P-9070)
CIT BANK NA (HQ)
75 N Fair Oaks Ave Ste C, Pasadena
(91103-3647)
P.O. Box 7056 (91109-7056)
PHONE...........................626 859-5400
Ellen R Alemany, *Ch of Bd*
James P Broom, *President*
James L Hudak, *President*
C Jeffrey Knittel, *President*
Joseph Otting, *President*
EMP: 72
SALES: 2.4B
SALES (corp-wide): 3.2B **Publicly Held**
WEB: www.loanworks.com
SIC: 6021 National commercial banks
PA: Cit Group Inc.
  11 W 42nd St
  New York NY 10036
  212 461-5200

(P-9071)
CIT BANK NA
199 E Thousand Oaks Blvd, Thousand
Oaks (91360-5710)
PHONE...........................805 379-5520
Tracey Sirkus, *Branch Mgr*
EMP: 56
SALES (corp-wide): 3.2B **Publicly Held**
SIC: 6021 National commercial banks
HQ: Cit Bank, N.A.
  75 N Fair Oaks Ave Ste C
  Pasadena CA 91103

(P-9072)
CIT BANK NATIONAL
ASSOCIATION
20505 Devonshire St, Chatsworth
(91311-3208)
PHONE...........................818 885-9065
Phyllis Barber, *Branch Mgr*
Wendell Grayson, *Marketing Staff*
EMP: 56
SALES (corp-wide): 3.2B **Publicly Held**
SIC: 6021 National commercial banks
HQ: Cit Bank, N.A.
  75 N Fair Oaks Ave Ste C
  Pasadena CA 91103

(P-9073)
CIT BANK NATIONAL
ASSOCIATION
220 N Hacienda Blvd, City of Industry
(91744-4403)
PHONE...........................626 435-2260
Blanca Deanda, *Manager*
EMP: 64
SALES (corp-wide): 3.2B **Publicly Held**
SIC: 6021 National commercial banks
HQ: Cit Bank, N.A.
  75 N Fair Oaks Ave Ste C
  Pasadena CA 91103

(P-9074)
CIT BANK NATIONAL
ASSOCIATION
401 Wilshire Blvd, Santa Monica
(90401-1416)
PHONE...........................310 394-1640
Farooq Ganatra, *Branch Mgr*

EMP: 63
SALES (corp-wide): 3.2B **Publicly Held**
SIC: 6021 National commercial banks
HQ: Cit Bank, N.A.
  75 N Fair Oaks Ave Ste C
  Pasadena CA 91103

(P-9075)
CIT BANK NATIONAL
ASSOCIATION
12401 Wilshire Blvd, Los Angeles
(90025-1085)
PHONE...........................310 820-9650
Leonard Rampulla, *Branch Mgr*
EMP: 56
SALES (corp-wide): 3.2B **Publicly Held**
SIC: 6021 National commercial banks
HQ: Cit Bank, N.A.
  75 N Fair Oaks Ave Ste C
  Pasadena CA 91103

(P-9076)
CIT BANK NATIONAL
ASSOCIATION
13405 Washington Blvd, Marina Del Rey
(90292-5658)
PHONE...........................310 577-6142
Chris Young, *Branch Mgr*
EMP: 56
SALES (corp-wide): 3.2B **Publicly Held**
SIC: 6021 National commercial banks
HQ: Cit Bank, N.A.
  75 N Fair Oaks Ave Ste C
  Pasadena CA 91103

(P-9077)
CIT BANK NATIONAL
ASSOCIATION
1630 Montana Ave, Santa Monica
(90403-1808)
PHONE...........................310 829-4477
Euzene Brink, *Manager*
EMP: 56
SALES (corp-wide): 3.2B **Publicly Held**
SIC: 6021 National commercial banks
HQ: Cit Bank, N.A.
  75 N Fair Oaks Ave Ste C
  Pasadena CA 91103

(P-9078)
CIT BANK NATIONAL
ASSOCIATION
5701 S Eastrn Ave Ste 108, Commerce
(90040)
PHONE...........................323 838-6881
Jonathan Silva, *Branch Mgr*
EMP: 56
SALES (corp-wide): 3.2B **Publicly Held**
SIC: 6021 National commercial banks
HQ: Cit Bank, N.A.
  75 N Fair Oaks Ave Ste C
  Pasadena CA 91103

(P-9079)
CIT BANK NATIONAL
ASSOCIATION
30019 Hawthorne Blvd, Rancho Palos
Verdes (90275-5453)
PHONE...........................310 265-1656
Miguel Gonzalez, *Branch Mgr*
EMP: 56
SALES (corp-wide): 3.2B **Publicly Held**
SIC: 6021 National commercial banks
HQ: Cit Bank, N.A.
  75 N Fair Oaks Ave Ste C
  Pasadena CA 91103

(P-9080)
CITIBANK NATIONAL
ASSOCIATION
3967 E Thousand Oaks Blvd, Westlake Vil-
lage (91362-3628)
PHONE...........................805 497-7361
EMP: 132
SALES (corp-wide): 72.8B **Publicly Held**
SIC: 6021 National commercial banks

HQ: Citibank, National Association
  701 E 60th St N
  Sioux Falls SD 57104
  605 331-2626

(P-9081)
CITIBANK NATIONAL
ASSOCIATION
3580 Tyler St, Riverside (92503-4133)
PHONE...........................800 627-3999
Dawn Latshaw, *Branch Mgr*
EMP: 132
SALES (corp-wide): 72.8B **Publicly Held**
SIC: 6021 National commercial banks
HQ: Citibank, National Association
  701 E 60th St N
  Sioux Falls SD 57104
  605 331-2626

(P-9082)
CITIBANK NATIONAL
ASSOCIATION
Also Called: Otay Lakes Road Branch
2240 Otay Lakes Rd 304-3, Chula Vista
(91915-1003)
PHONE...........................619 870-0609
EMP: 211
SALES (corp-wide): 72.8B **Publicly Held**
SIC: 6021 National commercial banks
HQ: Citibank, National Association
  701 E 60th St N
  Sioux Falls SD 57104
  605 331-2626

(P-9083)
CITIBANK NATIONAL
ASSOCIATION
Also Called: Sf-Potrero Hill
150 Pennsylvania Ave, San Francisco
(94107-2525)
PHONE...........................415 431-6940
EMP: 211
SALES (corp-wide): 72.8B **Publicly Held**
SIC: 6021 National commercial banks
HQ: Citibank, National Association
  701 E 60th St N
  Sioux Falls SD 57104
  605 331-2626

(P-9084)
CITIGROUP INC
325 E Hillcrest Dr # 160, Thousand Oaks
(91360-5828)
PHONE...........................805 557-0930
Jay Abeywardena, *Vice Pres*
EMP: 65
SALES (corp-wide): 72.8B **Publicly Held**
SIC: 6021 National commercial banks
PA: Citigroup Inc.
  388 Greenwich St
  New York NY 10013
  212 559-1000

(P-9085)
CITIGROUP INC
300 E State St, Redlands (92373-5235)
PHONE...........................909 335-0547
EMP: 65
SALES (corp-wide): 72.8B **Publicly Held**
SIC: 6021 National commercial banks
PA: Citigroup Inc.
  388 Greenwich St
  New York NY 10013
  212 559-1000

(P-9086)
CITIGROUP INC
3996 Barranca Pkwy # 130, Irvine
(92606-8239)
PHONE...........................949 726-5124
EMP: 65
SALES (corp-wide): 90.7B **Publicly Held**
SIC: 6021
PA: Citigroup Inc.
  399 Park Ave
  New York NY 10013
  212 559-1000

(P-9087)
CITIGROUP INC
352 H St, Chula Vista (91910-5511)
PHONE...........................619 498-3158
EMP: 65
SALES (corp-wide): 72.8B **Publicly Held**
SIC: 6021 National commercial banks

HQ: Citibank, National Association
  701 E 60th St N
  Sioux Falls SD 57104
  605 331-2626

(P-9088)
CITY NATIONAL BANK (DH)
555 S Flower St Fl 21, Los Angeles
(90071-2303)
PHONE...........................310 888-6000
Russell Goldsmith, *CEO*
Gina Calipes, *President*
Iris Pyun, *President*
Christopher J Warmuth, *President*
Christopher J Carey, *CFO*
▲ EMP: 300 EST: 1968
SQ FT: 80,000
SALES: 1.8B
SALES (corp-wide): 21.4B **Privately Held**
SIC: 6021 6022 National commercial
  banks; state commercial banks
HQ: Rbc Usa Holdco Corporation
  3 World Financial Ctr
  New York NY 10281
  212 858-7200

(P-9089)
CITY NATIONAL BANK
Also Called: C N B Commercial Banking Ctr
3484 Central Ave, Riverside (92506-2156)
PHONE...........................951 276-8800
Bruce Wachtel, *Manager*
EMP: 50
SALES (corp-wide): 21.4B **Privately Held**
SIC: 6021 National commercial banks
HQ: City National Bank
  555 S Flower St Fl 21
  Los Angeles CA 90071
  310 888-6000

(P-9090)
CITY NATIONAL BANK
Also Called: City National Investments
225 Broadway Ste 500, San Diego
(92101-5029)
PHONE...........................619 645-6100
Michael Nunlee, *Manager*
EMP: 100
SALES (corp-wide): 21.4B **Privately Held**
SIC: 6021 National commercial banks
HQ: City National Bank
  555 S Flower St Fl 21
  Los Angeles CA 90071
  310 888-6000

(P-9091)
CITY NATIONAL BANK
Also Called: Residential Mortgage Ctr 39
2100 Park Pl Ste 150, El Segundo
(90245-4912)
P.O. Box 60938, Los Angeles (90060-0938)
PHONE...........................310 297-6606
J W Lewis, *Senior VP*
EMP: 145
SALES (corp-wide): 21.4B **Privately Held**
SIC: 6021 National commercial banks
HQ: City National Bank
  555 S Flower St Fl 21
  Los Angeles CA 90071
  310 888-6000

(P-9092)
COMERICA BANK
1442 N Main St, Walnut Creek
(94596-4605)
PHONE...........................925 941-1900
Christophere Coutelier, *Manager*
EMP: 67
SALES (corp-wide): 3.6B **Publicly Held**
SIC: 6021 National commercial banks
HQ: Comerica Bank
  1717 Main St
  Dallas TX 75201
  214 462-4000

(P-9093)
COMMUNITY WEST BANK
445 Pine Ave, Goleta (93117-3709)
PHONE...........................805 692-5821
Will Cunningham, *Officer*
Joseph Stronks, *Exec VP*
Paul S Ulrich, *Exec VP*
Jason Bietz, *Vice Pres*
Elizabeth Crandall, *Vice Pres*
EMP: 100

SALES (corp-wide): 45.2MM **Publicly Held**
SIC: **6021** National commercial banks
HQ: Community West Bank
5827 Hollister Ave
Goleta CA 93117
805 692-5821

(P-9094)
FB CORPORATION
1211 E Valley Blvd, Alhambra
(91801-5235)
PHONE..........................626 300-0880
Tim Wang, *Manager*
EMP: 218
SALES (corp-wide): 224.7MM **Privately Held**
WEB: www.firstbanks.com
SIC: **6021** National commercial banks
PA: Fb Corporation
135 N Meramec Ave
Saint Louis MO 63105
314 854-4600

(P-9095)
FIRST COMMUNITY BANCORP
5900 La Place Ct Ste 200, Carlsbad
(92008-8832)
PHONE..........................858 756-3023
Andrew Colker, *Principal*
EMP: 51 EST: 2018
SALES (est): 226.6K
SALES (corp-wide): 1.3B **Publicly Held**
SIC: **6021** National commercial banks
PA: Pacwest Bancorp
9701 Wilshire Blvd # 700
Beverly Hills CA 90212
310 887-8500

(P-9096)
FIRST NATIONAL BANK
6110 El Tordo, Rancho Santa Fe (92067)
PHONE..........................858 756-3023
Matthew P Wagner, *CEO*
Robert Borgman, *President*
Lynn M Hopkins, *CFO*
Sali Tice, *Vice Pres*
Steen Weber, *Vice Pres*
EMP: 262 EST: 1982
SQ FT: 7,000
SALES (est): 297.5K
SALES (corp-wide): 1.3B **Publicly Held**
SIC: **6021** National commercial banks; purchasers of accounts receivable & commercial paper; factors of commercial paper
PA: Pacwest Bancorp
9701 Wilshire Blvd # 700
Beverly Hills CA 90212
310 887-8500

(P-9097)
JPMORGAN CHASE BANK NAT ASSN
5095 Business Center Dr, Fairfield
(94534-1631)
PHONE..........................707 864-4700
Elana Thomas, *Manager*
Shailesh Regmi, *Site Mgr*
EMP: 150
SALES (corp-wide): 131.4B **Publicly Held**
SIC: **6021** National commercial banks
HQ: Jpmorgan Chase Bank, National Association
1111 Polaris Pkwy
Columbus OH 43240
614 436-3055

(P-9098)
JPMORGAN CHASE BANK NAT ASSN
100 S Vincent Ave Fl 1, West Covina
(91790-2902)
PHONE..........................626 919-3129
Larry Gomez, *Branch Mgr*
EMP: 89
SALES (corp-wide): 131.4B **Publicly Held**
SIC: **6021** National commercial banks
HQ: Jpmorgan Chase Bank, National Association
1111 Polaris Pkwy
Columbus OH 43240
614 436-3055

(P-9099)
JPMORGAN CHASE BANK NAT ASSN
Also Called: Financial Division
1100 Palm Ave, Imperial Beach
(91932-1619)
PHONE..........................619 424-8197
Roger Debock, *Principal*
EMP: 50
SALES (corp-wide): 131.4B **Publicly Held**
SIC: **6021** National commercial banks
HQ: Jpmorgan Chase Bank, National Association
1111 Polaris Pkwy
Columbus OH 43240
614 436-3055

(P-9100)
MERCHANTS BANK CALIFORNIA N A
1 Civic Plaza Dr Ste 100, Carson
(90745-7958)
P.O. Box 6008, Long Beach (90806-0008)
PHONE..........................310 549-4350
Joyce Yamasaki, *CEO*
Daniel K Roberts, *Principal*
EMP: 75
SQ FT: 5,551
SALES: 6.9MM **Privately Held**
WEB: www.merchantsbankca.com
SIC: **6021** National commercial banks

(P-9101)
MERCHANTS BANK OF COMMERCE (HQ)
Also Called: Redding Bank of Commerce
1951 Churn Creek Rd, Redding
(96002-0246)
PHONE..........................530 224-7355
Randall S Eslick, *President*
Kendra Groundwater, *President*
Brenda Truett, *President*
Linda J Miles, *CFO*
Patrick J Moty, *Ch Credit Ofcr*
EMP: 80
SQ FT: 10,000
SALES: 50.7MM
SALES (corp-wide): 56.7MM **Publicly Held**
WEB: www.rosevillebankofcommerce.com
SIC: **6021** National commercial banks
PA: Bank Of Commerce Holdings
1951 Churn Creek Rd
Redding CA 96002
530 722-3952

(P-9102)
MUFG UNION BANK FOUNDATION
445 S Figueroa St Ste 710, Los Angeles
(90071-1615)
PHONE..........................213 236-5000
Masashi Oka, *President*
John F Harrigan, *Ch of Bd*
Carol Brewer, *President*
Runa Kargupta, *Officer*
Anne Kupfer, *Officer*
EMP: 4200
SALES (est): 399.2MM **Privately Held**
SIC: **6021** National commercial banks

(P-9103)
MUFG UNION BANK NATIONAL ASSN (DH)
400 California St Fl 14, San Francisco
(94104-1302)
PHONE..........................415 705-7000
Norimichi Kanari, *President*
Kyota Omori, *Ch of Bd*
Mark W Midkiff, *Vice Chairman*
Timothy H Wennes, *Vice Chairman*
Patrick Nygren, *President*
▲ EMP: 1000 EST: 1864
SALES: 5.1B **Privately Held**
SIC: **6021** National commercial banks
HQ: Mufg Americas Holdings Corporation
1251 Ave Of The Americas
New York NY 10020
212 782-6800

(P-9104)
MUFG UNION BANK NATIONAL ASSN
120 S San Pedro St, Los Angeles
(90012-5300)
P.O. Box 3248 (90051-1248)
PHONE..........................213 972-5500
Yoshio Morita, *Branch Mgr*
Scott Hammargren, *Managing Dir*
Hue Duong, *Analyst*
EMP: 50
SQ FT: 60,299 **Privately Held**
SIC: **6021** National commercial banks
HQ: Mufg Union Bank, National Association
400 California St Fl 14
San Francisco CA 94104
415 705-7000

(P-9105)
MUFG UNION BANK NATIONAL ASSN
20 E Carrillo St, Santa Barbara
(93101-2707)
PHONE..........................805 564-6410
Steve Mihalic, *Vice Pres*
Hal Ashe, *Vice Pres*
Cyndi Hunter, *Vice Pres*
Joe Servi, *Vice Pres*
Linda Trejo, *Vice Pres*
EMP: 75 **Privately Held**
WEB: www.pacificcapitalbank.com
SIC: **6021 6022** National commercial banks; state commercial banks
HQ: Mufg Union Bank, National Association
400 California St Fl 14
San Francisco CA 94104
415 705-7000

(P-9106)
MUFG UNION BANK NATIONAL ASSN
Also Called: U B C 200
9460 Wilshire Blvd # 200, Beverly Hills
(90212-2732)
P.O. Box 1268 (90213-1268)
PHONE..........................310 550-6522
G Denton Folkes, *Branch Mgr*
EMP: 80 **Privately Held**
SIC: **6021** National commercial banks
HQ: Mufg Union Bank, National Association
400 California St Fl 14
San Francisco CA 94104
415 705-7000

(P-9107)
MUFG UNION BANK NATIONAL ASSN
900 S Main St, Los Angeles (90015-1730)
P.O. Box 2278 (90051-0278)
PHONE..........................213 312-4500
Michael Padula, *Sales/Mktg Mgr*
EMP: 82 **Privately Held**
SIC: **6021** National commercial banks
HQ: Mufg Union Bank, National Association
400 California St Fl 14
San Francisco CA 94104
415 705-7000

(P-9108)
MUFG UNION BANK NATIONAL ASSN
15800 S Western Ave, Gardena
(90247-3704)
PHONE..........................310 354-4700
Takeo Kittaka, *Branch Mgr*
EMP: 50 **Privately Held**
SIC: **6021** National commercial banks
HQ: Mufg Union Bank, National Association
400 California St Fl 14
San Francisco CA 94104
415 705-7000

(P-9109)
MUFG UNION BANK NATIONAL ASSN
460 Hegenberger Rd Fl 3, Oakland
(94621-1423)
PHONE..........................510 891-2495
Steve Nicholson, *Business Anlyst*
Charlie Donner, *Business Anlyst*
EMP: 100 **Privately Held**
SIC: **6021** National commercial banks

HQ: Mufg Union Bank, National Association
400 California St Fl 14
San Francisco CA 94104
415 705-7000

(P-9110)
NORTHERN TRUST COMPANY
2049 Century Park E # 3600, Los Angeles
(90067-3210)
PHONE..........................310 282-3800
James Dryden, *Branch Mgr*
Richard Blackman, *Vice Pres*
Gerald Gallagher, *Vice Pres*
Christopher Harrer, *Vice Pres*
Lynn Knox, *Vice Pres*
EMP: 50
SALES (corp-wide): 6.6B **Publicly Held**
SIC: **6021** National commercial banks
HQ: The Northern Trust Company
50 S La Salle St
Chicago IL 60603
312 630-6000

(P-9111)
NOVARE NAT SETTLEMENT SVC LLC
320 Commerce Ste 150, Irvine
(92602-1364)
PHONE..........................714 352-4088
Cathy McIndoo, *President*
Juli Silva, *Receptionist*
Darren Aplet, *Assistant*
EMP: 50
SALES (est): 1.4MM **Privately Held**
SIC: **6021** National commercial banks

(P-9112)
PACIFIC WESTERN BANK
Also Called: Rancho Santa Fe
6110 El Tordo, Rancho Santa Fe (92067)
PHONE..........................858 756-3023
EMP: 262
SALES (corp-wide): 1.3B **Publicly Held**
SIC: **6021 6153** National commercial banks; purchasers of accounts receivable & commercial paper; factors of commercial paper
HQ: Pacific Western Bank
9701 Wilshire Blvd # 700
Beverly Hills CA 90212
310 887-8500

(P-9113)
PACIFIC WESTERN BANK
5900 La Place Ct Ste 200, Carlsbad
(92008-8832)
PHONE..........................760 918-2469
Suzanne Brennan, *Manager*
AVI Demirdjian, *Vice Pres*
EMP: 52
SALES (corp-wide): 1.3B **Publicly Held**
WEB: www.pacificwesternbank.com
SIC: **6021** National commercial banks
HQ: Pacific Western Bank
9701 Wilshire Blvd # 700
Beverly Hills CA 90212
310 887-8500

(P-9114)
PACIFIC WESTERN BANK
900 Cantebury Pl Ste 300, Escondido
(92025)
PHONE..........................760 432-1100
Michael Perdue, *Branch Mgr*
EMP: 80
SALES (corp-wide): 1.3B **Publicly Held**
WEB: www.pacificwesternbank.com
SIC: **6021** National commercial banks
HQ: Pacific Western Bank
9701 Wilshire Blvd # 700
Beverly Hills CA 90212
310 887-8500

(P-9115)
PNC BANK NATIONAL ASSOCIATION
2 N Lake Ave Ste 440, Pasadena
(91101-4197)
PHONE..........................626 432-4500
Thomas Soltz, *Branch Mgr*
Jeffrey Cristol, *Vice Pres*
EMP: 60
SALES (corp-wide): 19.9B **Publicly Held**
WEB: www.pncfunds.com
SIC: **6021** National trust companies with deposits, commercial

PRODUCTS & SVCS

HQ: Pnc Bank, National Association
222 Delaware Ave
Wilmington DE 19801
877 762-2000

(P-9116)
PNC BANK NATIONAL ASSOCIATION
465 N Halstead St Ste 160, Pasadena
(91107-6018)
PHONE.................................626 351-2211
Dennis Hayashi, *Manager*
Robert Butler, *Manager*
EMP: 76
SALES (corp-wide): 19.9B **Publicly Held**
WEB: www.pncfunds.com
SIC: **6021** National trust companies with
deposits, commercial
HQ: Pnc Bank, National Association
222 Delaware Ave
Wilmington DE 19801
877 762-2000

(P-9117)
PORREY PINES BANK INC
Also Called: Western Alliance Bank
1951 Webster St, Oakland (94612-2909)
PHONE.................................510 899-7500
Larry Fountain, *Manager*
Dianne Williams, *Manager*
EMP: 380
SALES (est): 81.4MM
SALES (corp-wide): 1B **Publicly Held**
WEB: www.altaalliancebank.com
SIC: **6021** National commercial banks
PA: Western Alliance Bancorporation
1 E Wshington St Ste 1400
Phoenix AZ 85004
602 389-3500

(P-9118)
SILICON VALLEY BANK
15260 Ventura Blvd # 1800, Sherman Oaks
(91403-5350)
PHONE.................................818 382-2600
Mark Turk, *Branch Mgr*
EMP: 80
SALES (corp-wide): 2.7B **Publicly Held**
SIC: **6021** National commercial banks
HQ: Silicon Valley Bank
3003 Tasman Dr
Santa Clara CA 95054
408 654-7400

(P-9119)
SIX RIVERS NATIONAL BANK (HQ)
402 F St, Eureka (95501-1008)
PHONE.................................707 443-8400
Fax: 707 443-3631
EMP: 51
SALES: 46.3MM
SALES (corp-wide): 206.7MM **Publicly Held**
SIC: **6021**
PA: Trico Bancshares
63 Constitution Dr
Chico CA 95973
530 898-0300

(P-9120)
UMPQUA BANK
Also Called: Encino Branch
16501 Ventura Blvd, Encino (91436-2007)
PHONE.................................818 385-1362
Gil Dalmau, *President*
Brent McClure, *Vice Pres*
Karen Norman, *Vice Pres*
John Swanson, *Vice Pres*
Christopher Clark, *Administration*
EMP: 62
SALES (corp-wide): 1.3B **Publicly Held**
SIC: **6021** National commercial banks
HQ: Umpqua Bank
445 Se Main St
Roseburg OR 97470
541 440-3961

(P-9121)
US BANK NATIONAL ASSOCIATION
Also Called: US Bank
10021 Bloomfield St, Los Alamitos
(90720-2207)
PHONE.................................562 795-7520

Catherine Marker, *Office Mgr*
EMP: 50
SALES (corp-wide): 25.7B **Publicly Held**
SIC: **6021** National commercial banks
HQ: U.S. Bank National Association
425 Walnut St Fl 14
Cincinnati OH 45202
513 632-4234

(P-9122)
US BANK NATIONAL ASSOCIATION
Also Called: US Bank
1420 Kettner Blvd Ste 101, San Diego
(92101-2639)
PHONE.................................619 744-2140
Murray L Galinson, *Branch Mgr*
Stephanie Taylor, *Vice Pres*
EMP: 100
SALES (corp-wide): 25.7B **Publicly Held**
SIC: **6021** National commercial banks
HQ: U.S. Bank National Association
425 Walnut St Fl 14
Cincinnati OH 45202
513 632-4234

(P-9123)
WACHOVIA A DIVISION WELLS F
420 Montgomery St, San Francisco
(94104-1207)
PHONE.................................415 571-2832
John G Stumpf, *Principal*
John Ney, *Officer*
David Ferry, *Vice Pres*
Suzanne Harley, *Vice Pres*
Hiram Thompson, *Software Engr*
EMP: 576 EST: 2011
SALES (est): 258.3MM **Privately Held**
SIC: **6021** National commercial banks

(P-9124)
WELLS FARGO & COMPANY (PA)
420 Montgomery St Frnt, San Francisco
(94104-1205)
PHONE.................................866 249-3302
Charles W Scharf, *President*
Elizabeth A Duke, *Ch of Bd*
John R Shrewsberry, *CFO*
William M Daley, *Chairman*
Richard D Levy, *Exec VP*
▲ EMP: 184 EST: 1929
SQ FT: 300,000
SALES: 101B **Publicly Held**
SIC: **6021** National commercial banks

(P-9125)
WELLS FARGO BANK LTD
333 S Grand Ave Ste 500, Los Angeles
(90071-1569)
PHONE.................................213 253-6227
Randy Reyes, *Branch Mgr*
Theodore Craver, *Bd of Directors*
L Avila, *Vice Pres*
EMP: 79
SALES: 426.3MM
SALES (corp-wide): 101B **Publicly Held**
SIC: **6021** National commercial banks
HQ: Wfc Holdings, Llc
420 Montgomery St
San Francisco CA 94104
415 396-7392

(P-9126)
WELLS FARGO BANK NA
Also Called: Operations
333 S Hope St Ste D100, Los Angeles
(90071-3003)
PHONE.................................213 628-2251
Shaffi Poswal, *Branch Mgr*
EMP: 250
SALES (corp-wide): 101B **Publicly Held**
WEB: www.wellsfargo.com
SIC: **6021** National commercial banks
HQ: Wells Fargo Bank, National Association
101 N Phillips Ave
Sioux Falls SD 57104
605 575-6900

(P-9127)
WELLS FARGO BANK NATIONAL ASSN
10225 Riverside Dr, Toluca Lake
(91602-2501)
PHONE.................................818 766-7172
Marita Kesheshyn, *Manager*
EMP: 50
SALES (corp-wide): 101B **Publicly Held**
WEB: www.wellsfargo.com
SIC: **6021** National commercial banks
HQ: Wells Fargo Bank, National Association
101 N Phillips Ave
Sioux Falls SD 57104
605 575-6900

(P-9128)
WELLS FARGO BANK NATIONAL ASSN
120 Kearny St Ste 1750, San Francisco
(94108-4814)
PHONE.................................415 396-6267
Jean Arcos, *Manager*
EMP: 50
SALES (corp-wide): 101B **Publicly Held**
WEB: www.wellsfargo.com
SIC: **6021** National commercial banks
HQ: Wells Fargo Bank, National Association
101 N Phillips Ave
Sioux Falls SD 57104
605 575-6900

(P-9129)
WELLS FARGO BANK NATIONAL ASSN
1 Montgomery St Ste 200, San Francisco
(94104-4517)
P.O. Box 63005 (94163-0001)
PHONE.................................415 396-6161
Bob Besozzi, *Manager*
EMP: 60
SQ FT: 4,000
SALES (corp-wide): 101B **Publicly Held**
WEB: www.wellsfargo.com
SIC: **6021** National commercial banks
HQ: Wells Fargo Bank, National Association
101 N Phillips Ave
Sioux Falls SD 57104
605 575-6900

(P-9130)
WELLS FARGO BANK NATIONAL ASSN
1120 K St, Modesto (95354-2398)
PHONE.................................209 578-6810
Robert Moules, *Manager*
EMP: 59
SALES (corp-wide): 101B **Publicly Held**
WEB: www.wellsfargo.com
SIC: **6021** National commercial banks
HQ: Wells Fargo Bank, National Association
101 N Phillips Ave
Sioux Falls SD 57104
605 575-6900

(P-9131)
WELLS FARGO BANK NATIONAL ASSN
2170 Tully Rd, San Jose (95122-1345)
PHONE.................................408 998-3714
Crystal Nguyen, *Manager*
Lisa Vo, *Consultant*
EMP: 50
SALES (corp-wide): 101B **Publicly Held**
WEB: www.wellsfargo.com
SIC: **6021** National commercial banks
HQ: Wells Fargo Bank, National Association
101 N Phillips Ave
Sioux Falls SD 57104
605 575-6900

(P-9132)
WELLS FARGO BANK NATIONAL ASSN
4365 Executive Dr Fl 18, San Diego
(92121-2194)
PHONE.................................858 622-6958
James Cimino, *Manager*
Dennis Kim, *President*

Robert Gilbert, *Associate*
Gregory Hansen, *Associate*
EMP: 75
SALES (corp-wide): 101B **Publicly Held**
WEB: www.wellsfargo.com
SIC: **6021** National commercial banks
HQ: Wells Fargo Bank, National Association
101 N Phillips Ave
Sioux Falls SD 57104
605 575-6900

(P-9133)
WELLS FARGO BANK NATIONAL ASSN
901 Main St, NAPA (94559-3044)
PHONE.................................707 259-5552
Patty Belt, *Manager*
EMP: 70
SALES (corp-wide): 101B **Publicly Held**
WEB: www.wellsfargo.com
SIC: **6021** National commercial banks
HQ: Wells Fargo Bank, National Association
101 N Phillips Ave
Sioux Falls SD 57104
605 575-6900

(P-9134)
WELLS FARGO BANK NATIONAL ASSN
Merchant Paymnt A0347-023
1655 Grant St, Concord (94520-2600)
PHONE.................................925 746-3718
EMP: 60
SQ FT: 57,192
SALES (corp-wide): 97.7B **Publicly Held**
SIC: **6021**
HQ: Wells Fargo Bank, National Association
101 N Phillips Ave
Sioux Falls SD 57104
605 575-6900

(P-9135)
WELLS FARGO BANK NATIONAL ASSN
Also Called: Trade Services E2002-031
9000 Flair Dr Fl 3, El Monte (91731-2826)
PHONE.................................626 312-3006
Marilyn Benoit, *Manager*
EMP: 500
SALES (corp-wide): 101B **Publicly Held**
WEB: www.wellsfargo.com
SIC: **6021** National commercial banks
HQ: Wells Fargo Bank, National Association
101 N Phillips Ave
Sioux Falls SD 57104
605 575-6900

(P-9136)
WELLS FARGO BANK NATIONAL ASSN
7714 Girard Ave, La Jolla (92037-4483)
PHONE.................................858 454-0362
EMP: 525
SALES (corp-wide): 101B **Publicly Held**
WEB: www.wellsfargo.com
SIC: **6021** National commercial banks
HQ: Wells Fargo Bank, National Association
101 N Phillips Ave
Sioux Falls SD 57104
605 575-6900

(P-9137)
WELLS FARGO BANK NATIONAL ASSN
Also Called: Roseville Foothills and Jct
5007 Foothills Blvd, Roseville
(95747-6503)
PHONE.................................916 724-2982
Susan Adams, *Branch Mgr*
EMP: 85
SALES (corp-wide): 101B **Publicly Held**
SIC: **6021** National commercial banks
HQ: Wells Fargo Bank, National Association
101 N Phillips Ave
Sioux Falls SD 57104
605 575-6900

(P-9138)
WELLS FARGO BANK NATIONAL ASSN
60 W Hamilton Ave, Campbell (95008-0505)
PHONE..................................408 378-8155
Titi Vu, *Manager*
EMP: 50
SALES (corp-wide): 101B **Publicly Held**
WEB: www.wellsfargo.com
SIC: **6021** National commercial banks
HQ: Wells Fargo Bank, National Association
101 N Phillips Ave
Sioux Falls SD 57104
605 575-6900

(P-9139)
WELLS FARGO BANK NATIONAL ASSN
100 Spear St Ste 100 # 100, San Francisco (94105-1578)
PHONE..................................415 777-9497
Praneet Chahal, *Principal*
EMP: 319
SALES (corp-wide): 101B **Publicly Held**
SIC: **6021** National commercial banks
HQ: Wells Fargo Bank, National Association
101 N Phillips Ave
Sioux Falls SD 57104
605 575-6900

(P-9140)
WELLS FARGO BANK NATIONAL ASSN
1620 E Roseville Pkwy, Roseville (95661-3995)
PHONE..................................916 774-2249
Kathie Gedney, *Manager*
Dennis McKey, *Info Tech Dir*
Dennis A McKey, *Info Tech Mgr*
Nichelle Van Rossum, *Manager*
EMP: 300
SALES (corp-wide): 101B **Publicly Held**
WEB: www.wellsfargo.com
SIC: **6021** National commercial banks
HQ: Wells Fargo Bank, National Association
101 N Phillips Ave
Sioux Falls SD 57104
605 575-6900

(P-9141)
WELLS FARGO BANK NATIONAL ASSN
3440 Flair Dr, El Monte (91731-2883)
PHONE..................................626 573-6452
Lori Morgan, *Principal*
Joseph Ciancimino, *Vice Pres*
Rick Fisher, *Project Mgr*
Carl Herr, *VP Mktg*
EMP: 250
SALES (corp-wide): 101B **Publicly Held**
WEB: www.wellsfargo.com
SIC: **6021** National commercial banks
HQ: Wells Fargo Bank, National Association
101 N Phillips Ave
Sioux Falls SD 57104
605 575-6900

(P-9142)
WELLS FARGO BANK NATIONAL ASSN
Also Called: San Lorenzo 0119
16000 Hesperian Blvd, San Lorenzo (94580-2450)
PHONE..................................510 276-0875
Jan Miller, *Branch Mgr*
EMP: 50
SALES (corp-wide): 101B **Publicly Held**
WEB: www.wellsfargo.com
SIC: **6021** National commercial banks
HQ: Wells Fargo Bank, National Association
101 N Phillips Ave
Sioux Falls SD 57104
605 575-6900

(P-9143)
WELLS FARGO BANK NATIONAL ASSN
39265 Paseo Padre Pkwy, Fremont (94538-1611)
PHONE..................................510 792-3512
George Sezidarias, *Manager*
EMP: 59
SALES (corp-wide): 101B **Publicly Held**
WEB: www.wellsfargo.com
SIC: **6021** National commercial banks
HQ: Wells Fargo Bank, National Association
101 N Phillips Ave
Sioux Falls SD 57104
605 575-6900

(P-9144)
WELLS FARGO BANK NATIONAL ASSN
950 Southland Dr, Hayward (94545-1544)
P.O. Box 3367 (94540-3367)
PHONE..................................510 266-0595
Kay Maloy, *Manager*
EMP: 55
SALES (corp-wide): 101B **Publicly Held**
WEB: www.wellsfargo.com
SIC: **6021** National commercial banks
HQ: Wells Fargo Bank, National Association
101 N Phillips Ave
Sioux Falls SD 57104
605 575-6900

(P-9145)
WELLS FARGO BANK NATIONAL ASSN
2301 Watt Ave, Sacramento (95825-0666)
PHONE..................................916 440-4570
Scott Caddow, *Manager*
EMP: 50
SALES (corp-wide): 101B **Publicly Held**
WEB: www.wellsfargo.com
SIC: **6021** National commercial banks
HQ: Wells Fargo Bank, National Association
101 N Phillips Ave
Sioux Falls SD 57104
605 575-6900

(P-9146)
WELLS FARGO BANK NATIONAL ASSN
5798 Stoneridge Mall Rd, Pleasanton (94588-2862)
PHONE..................................925 463-1983
Richard Thornton, *Branch Mgr*
EMP: 84
SALES (corp-wide): 101B **Publicly Held**
SIC: **6021** National commercial banks
HQ: Wells Fargo Bank, National Association
101 N Phillips Ave
Sioux Falls SD 57104
605 575-6900

(P-9147)
WELLS FARGO BANK NATIONAL ASSN
28350 S Western Ave, Rancho Palos Verdes (90275-1499)
PHONE..................................310 831-0632
Sandy Walia, *Branch Mgr*
EMP: 60
SALES (corp-wide): 101B **Publicly Held**
WEB: www.wellsfargo.com
SIC: **6021** National commercial banks
HQ: Wells Fargo Bank, National Association
101 N Phillips Ave
Sioux Falls SD 57104
605 575-6900

(P-9148)
WELLS FARGO BANK NATIONAL ASSN
464 California St, San Francisco (94104-1204)
PHONE..................................415 222-1360
John D Baker II, *CEO*
Robert Deignan, *Vice Pres*
Hans Sitarz, *Vice Pres*
Bill Stash, *Vice Pres*
Richard Toomey, *Vice Pres*

EMP: 50
SALES (corp-wide): 101B **Publicly Held**
WEB: www.wellsfargo.com
SIC: **6021** National commercial banks
HQ: Wells Fargo Bank, National Association
101 N Phillips Ave
Sioux Falls SD 57104
605 575-6900

(P-9149)
WELLS FARGO BANK NATIONAL ASSN
455 Market, Fremont (94536)
PHONE..................................415 222-6834
Wyman Yuu, *Manager*
EMP: 250
SALES (corp-wide): 101B **Publicly Held**
WEB: www.wellsfargo.com
SIC: **6021** National commercial banks
HQ: Wells Fargo Bank, National Association
101 N Phillips Ave
Sioux Falls SD 57104
605 575-6900

(P-9150)
WELLS FARGO BANK NATIONAL ASSN
665 Marsh St, San Luis Obispo (93401-3930)
PHONE..................................805 541-0143
Mark Corella, *Branch Mgr*
EMP: 84
SALES (corp-wide): 101B **Publicly Held**
WEB: www.wellsfargo.com
SIC: **6021** National commercial banks
HQ: Wells Fargo Bank, National Association
101 N Phillips Ave
Sioux Falls SD 57104
605 575-6900

(P-9151)
WELLS FARGO BANK NATIONAL ASSN
420 Montgomery St Fl 6, San Francisco (94104-1207)
PHONE..................................415 394-4021
Paul Rettig, *Manager*
EMP: 1000
SALES (corp-wide): 101B **Publicly Held**
WEB: www.wellsfargo.com
SIC: **6021** National commercial banks
HQ: Wells Fargo Bank, National Association
101 N Phillips Ave
Sioux Falls SD 57104
605 575-6900

(P-9152)
WELLS FARGO BANK NATIONAL ASSN
2220 Mountain Blvd # 160, Oakland (94611-2950)
P.O. Box 1559 (94604-1559)
PHONE..................................510 530-3095
Ellen Thomas, *Manager*
EMP: 65
SALES (corp-wide): 101B **Publicly Held**
WEB: www.wellsfargo.com
SIC: **6021** National commercial banks
HQ: Wells Fargo Bank, National Association
101 N Phillips Ave
Sioux Falls SD 57104
605 575-6900

(P-9153)
WELLS FARGO BANK NATIONAL ASSN
18712 Gridley Rd, Cerritos (90703-5410)
PHONE..................................562 924-1616
Susan De Lazzer, *Sales/Mktg Mgr*
EMP: 50
SALES (corp-wide): 101B **Publicly Held**
WEB: www.wellsfargo.com
SIC: **6021** National commercial banks
HQ: Wells Fargo Bank, National Association
101 N Phillips Ave
Sioux Falls SD 57104
605 575-6900

(P-9154)
WELLS FARGO BANK NATIONAL ASSN
3440 Walnut Ave Fl 3, Fremont (94538-2210)
PHONE..................................510 745-5025
Yung Lew, *Division Mgr*
EMP: 300
SALES (corp-wide): 101B **Publicly Held**
WEB: www.wellsfargo.com
SIC: **6021** National commercial banks
HQ: Wells Fargo Bank, National Association
101 N Phillips Ave
Sioux Falls SD 57104
605 575-6900

(P-9155)
WELLS FARGO BANK NATIONAL ASSN
Wells Fargo Investments
433 N Camden Dr Ste 1200, Beverly Hills (90210-4426)
P.O. Box 20160, Long Beach (90801-3160)
PHONE..................................310 285-5817
Steve Mann, *Manager*
Keith Prendergast, *Loan Officer*
EMP: 200
SALES (corp-wide): 101B **Publicly Held**
WEB: www.wellsfargo.com
SIC: **6021** National commercial banks
HQ: Wells Fargo Bank, National Association
101 N Phillips Ave
Sioux Falls SD 57104
605 575-6900

(P-9156)
WFC HOLDINGS LLC (HQ)
420 Montgomery St, San Francisco (94104-1207)
PHONE..................................415 396-7392
Richard M Kovacevich, *Ch of Bd*
Larry Salvati, *Opers Staff*
William Sheehan, *Sales Staff*
EMP: 200 EST: 1998
SQ FT: 750,000
SALES (est): 1.7B
SALES (corp-wide): 101B **Publicly Held**
SIC: **6021** National commercial banks
PA: Wells Fargo & Company
420 Montgomery St Frnt
San Francisco CA 94104
866 249-3302

(P-9157)
ZIONS BANCORPORATION NAT ASSN
Also Called: California Bank & Trust
1130 S Baldwin Ave, Arcadia (91007-7508)
PHONE..................................626 445-5355
Sunny Han-Jeon, *Branch Mgr*
EMP: 70
SALES (corp-wide): 3B **Publicly Held**
SIC: **6021** National commercial banks
PA: N A Zions Bancorporation
1 S Main St Fl 11
Salt Lake City UT 84133
801 844-7637

(P-9158)
ZIONS BANCORPORATION NAT ASSN
Also Called: California Bank & Trust
1451 Solano Ave, Albany (94706-2146)
PHONE..................................415 524-1200
Fred Angeli, *Branch Mgr*
EMP: 58
SALES (corp-wide): 3B **Publicly Held**
SIC: **6021** National commercial banks
PA: N A Zions Bancorporation
1 S Main St Fl 11
Salt Lake City UT 84133
801 844-7637

(P-9159)
ZIONS BANCORPORATION NAT ASSN
Also Called: California Bank & Trust
9590 Foothill Blvd, Rancho Cucamonga (91730-3546)
PHONE..................................909 581-1680
Ruby Huey, *Manager*
EMP: 105

SALES (corp-wide): 3B **Publicly Held**
SIC: 6021 National commercial banks
PA: N A Zions Bancorporation
1 S Main St Fl 11
Salt Lake City UT 84133
801 844-7637

(P-9160)
ZIONS BANCORPORATION NAT ASSN
California Bank & Trust
11622 El Camino Real, San Diego
(92130-2049)
PHONE..................................858 793-7400
Andre Ellis, *President*
Andrew Fain, *President*
Rosemary Larkin, *President*
Angela Hamamura, *Treasurer*
Helena McArron, *Officer*
EMP: 50
SALES (corp-wide): 3B **Publicly Held**
SIC: 6021 National commercial banks
PA: N A Zions Bancorporation
1 S Main St Fl 11
Salt Lake City UT 84133
801 844-7637

(P-9161)
ZIONS BANCORPORATION NAT ASSN
Also Called: California Bank & Trust
6313 Mission Gorge Rd, San Diego
(92120-2502)
PHONE..................................619 521-5800
Burt Brigida, *Vice Pres*
EMP: 82
SALES (corp-wide): 3B **Publicly Held**
SIC: 6021 National commercial banks
PA: N A Zions Bancorporation
1 S Main St Fl 11
Salt Lake City UT 84133
801 844-7637

(P-9162)
ZIONS BANCORPORATION NAT ASSN
Also Called: California Bank & Trust
100 Crprate Pinte Ste 110, Culver City
(90230)
PHONE..................................310 258-9300
Jeff Watts, *Branch Mgr*
EMP: 149
SALES (corp-wide): 3B **Publicly Held**
WEB: www.calbt.com
SIC: 6021 National commercial banks
PA: N A Zions Bancorporation
1 S Main St Fl 11
Salt Lake City UT 84133
801 844-7637

6022 State Commercial Banks

(P-9163)
BANK OF HOPE
550 S Western Ave, Los Angeles
(90020-4208)
PHONE..................................213 389-5550
EMP: 50
SALES (corp-wide): 710.3MM **Publicly Held**
SIC: 6022 State commercial banks
HQ: Bank Of Hope
3200 Wilshire Blvd # 1400
Los Angeles CA 90010
213 639-1700

(P-9164)
BANK OF MARIN
Also Called: Northgate Branch
4460 Redwood Hwy Ste 1, San Rafael
(94903-1952)
PHONE..................................415 472-2265
Janet Hayward, *Manager*
EMP: 78 **Publicly Held**
WEB: www.bankofmarin.com
SIC: 6022 State trust companies accepting
deposits, commercial
HQ: Bank Of Marin
504 Redwood Blvd Ste 100
Novato CA 94947
415 763-4520

(P-9165)
BANK OF MARIN BANCORP (PA)
504 Redwood Blvd Ste 100, Novato
(94947-6923)
P.O. Box 2039 (94948-2039)
PHONE..................................415 763-4520
Russell A Colombo, *President*
Brian M Sobel, *Ch of Bd*
Megan Garner, *President*
Eddie Roslin, *President*
Carol Trueblood, *President*
EMP: 105
SALES: 105.2MM **Publicly Held**
SIC: 6022 State commercial banks

(P-9166)
BANK OF ORIENT (HQ)
100 Pine St Ste 600, San Francisco
(94111-5108)
P.O. Box 2489 (94126-2489)
PHONE..................................415 338-0668
Ernest L Go, *Ch of Bd*
Michael R Delucchi, *COO*
Andy Hou, *COO*
Carl Andersen, *CFO*
Mark K McDonald, *Exec VP*
EMP: 65
SQ FT: 20,000
SALES: 30.6MM
SALES (corp-wide): 39.8MM **Privately Held**
SIC: 6022 State trust companies accepting
deposits, commercial
PA: Orient Bancorporation
100 Pine St Ste 600
San Francisco CA 94111
415 567-1554

(P-9167)
BANK OF SIERRA (HQ)
90 N Main St, Porterville (93257-3712)
P.O. Box 1930 (93258-1930)
PHONE..................................559 782-4300
Kevin McPhaill, *President*
Morris Tharp, *Ch of Bd*
Kelli Blackburn, *President*
Karen S Nishimura, *President*
Dustin Oliver, *President*
EMP: 105
SQ FT: 37,000
SALES: 102.1MM
SALES (corp-wide): 123.2MM **Publicly Held**
WEB: www.bankofthesierra.com
SIC: 6022 State commercial banks
PA: Sierra Bancorp
86 N Main St
Porterville CA 93257
559 782-4900

(P-9168)
BANK OF STOCKTON (HQ)
301 E Miner Ave, Stockton (95202-2501)
P.O. Box 1110 (95201-3003)
PHONE..................................209 929-1600
Robert M Eberhardt, *President*
Kelly Christian, *President*
Douglass M Eberhardt, *President*
John Morrison, *President*
William Maxwell, *COO*
EMP: 180 EST: 1867
SQ FT: 15,000
SALES: 125.6MM
SALES (corp-wide): 81MM **Privately Held**
WEB: www.netbos.com
SIC: 6022 State trust companies accepting
deposits, commercial

(P-9169)
BANK OF THE WEST (HQ)
180 Montgomery St # 1400, San Francisco
(94104-4297)
PHONE..................................415 765-4800
J Michael Shepherd, *CEO*
Randy Arnold, *Partner*
Vanessa Midgley, *Shareholder*
Mir Ali, *President*
Nicole Auyang, *President*
▲ EMP: 1000 EST: 1874
SQ FT: 30,000
SALES: 3.1B
SALES (corp-wide): 2.7B **Privately Held**
SIC: 6022 State commercial banks

PA: Bnp Paribas
16 Boulevard Des Italiens
Paris 9e Arrondissement 75009
825 334-335

(P-9170)
BANNER BANK
1350 Rosecrans St, San Diego
(92106-2636)
PHONE..................................619 243-7900
Michael R Peters, *Branch Mgr*
Robert Cafaro, *Vice Pres*
Matt Towery, *Vice Pres*
EMP: 50 **Publicly Held**
SIC: 6022 State commercial banks
HQ: Banner Bank
10 S 1st Ave
Walla Walla WA 99362
800 272-9933

(P-9171)
BBVA USA
Also Called: Compass Bank
195 W Ontario Ave, Corona (92882-5276)
PHONE..................................951 279-7071
Eileen Blaga, *Branch Mgr*
Natalie Corente, *VP Bus Dvlpt*
EMP: 364
SALES (corp-wide): 1.4B **Privately Held**
SIC: 6022 State commercial banks
HQ: Bbva Usa
15 20th St S Ste 100
Birmingham AL 35233
205 297-1986

(P-9172)
BBVA USA
Also Called: Compass Bank
201 N Main St, Manteca (95336-4632)
PHONE..................................209 239-1381
Grace Henderson, *Branch Mgr*
EMP: 364
SALES (corp-wide): 1.4B **Privately Held**
WEB: www.guarantybank.com
SIC: 6022 State commercial banks
HQ: Bbva Usa
15 20th St S Ste 100
Birmingham AL 35233
205 297-1986

(P-9173)
BBVA USA
Also Called: Compass Bank
2427 W Hammer Ln, Stockton
(95209-2367)
PHONE..................................209 473-6925
Gabriel Riley, *Branch Mgr*
EMP: 364
SALES (corp-wide): 1.4B **Privately Held**
WEB: www.guarantybank.com
SIC: 6022 State commercial banks
HQ: Bbva Usa
15 20th St S Ste 100
Birmingham AL 35233
205 297-1986

(P-9174)
BBVA USA
Also Called: Compass Bank
2562 Pacific Ave, Stockton (95204-4438)
PHONE..................................209 939-3288
Brian Stemen, *Branch Mgr*
Debra Flint, *Manager*
EMP: 364
SALES (corp-wide): 1.4B **Privately Held**
WEB: www.guarantybank.com
SIC: 6022 State commercial banks
HQ: Bbva Usa
15 20th St S Ste 100
Birmingham AL 35233
205 297-1986

(P-9175)
BENEFICIAL STATE BANK (HQ)
Also Called: Onecalifornia Bank
1438 Webster St Ste 100, Oakland
(94612-3229)
P.O. Box 400, Ilwaco WA (98624-0400)
PHONE..................................510 550-8420
Kat Taylor, *CEO*
Randell Leach, *President*
Michael Fratarcangeli, *CFO*
Thu Ncuyen, *CFO*
Richard Fletcher, *Exec VP*
EMP: 57

SALES: 42.7MM **Privately Held**
SIC: 6022 State commercial banks

(P-9176)
BUSA SERVICING INC (DH)
Also Called: Banamex USA
2029 Century Park E # 4200, Los Angeles
(90067-2901)
PHONE..................................310 203-3400
Manuel Sanchez Lugo, *Ch of Bd*
Rebecca Macieira-Kaufmann, *CEO*
Roger Johnston, *Ch Credit Ofcr*
Gabriel De La Peza, *Exec VP*
Theodore Michaels, *Exec VP*
EMP: 200
SALES (est): 30.4MM
SALES (corp-wide): 72.8B **Publicly Held**
WEB: www.ccbusa.com
SIC: 6022 State commercial banks
HQ: Banamex Usa Bancorp
2029 Century Park E Fl 42
Los Angeles CA 90067
310 203-3440

(P-9177)
CATHAY BANK (HQ)
9650 Flair Dr, El Monte (91731-3005)
PHONE..................................626 279-3698
Dunson K Cheng, *Ch of Bd*
Heng W Chen, *CFO*
Florence Lee, *Assoc VP*
James R Brewer, *Exec VP*
Edward K Kim, *Exec VP*
▲ EMP: 125 EST: 1962
SALES: 456.2MM
SALES (corp-wide): 719.6MM **Publicly Held**
WEB: www.newasiabk.com
SIC: 6022 State trust companies accepting
deposits, commercial
PA: Cathay General Bancorp
777 N Broadway
Los Angeles CA 90012
213 625-4700

(P-9178)
CATHAY BANK
Also Called: Monterey Park Branch
250 S Atlantic Blvd, Monterey Park
(91754-2778)
PHONE..................................626 588-1911
Frank Chen, *Principal*
Joyce Tsao, *Officer*
EMP: 100
SALES (corp-wide): 719.6MM **Publicly Held**
WEB: www.newasiabk.com
SIC: 6022 6021 State commercial banks;
national commercial banks
HQ: Cathay Bank
9650 Flair Dr
El Monte CA 91731
626 279-3698

(P-9179)
CATHAY BANK
800 W 6th St Ste 200, Los Angeles
(90017-2705)
PHONE..................................213 896-0098
Wilson Tang, *Manager*
EMP: 100
SALES (corp-wide): 719.6MM **Publicly Held**
WEB: www.newasiabk.com
SIC: 6022 6082 State commercial banks;
foreign trade & international banking insti-
tutions
HQ: Cathay Bank
9650 Flair Dr
El Monte CA 91731
626 279-3698

(P-9180)
CATHAY BANK
General Bank Credit ADM Dept
4128 Temple City Blvd, Rosemead
(91770-1550)
P.O. Box 3302, Los Angeles (90078-3302)
PHONE..................................626 452-1582
Domenic Massei, *Manager*
EMP: 120
SALES (corp-wide): 719.6MM **Publicly Held**
WEB: www.newasiabk.com
SIC: 6022 State commercial banks

HQ: Cathay Bank
9650 Flair Dr
El Monte CA 91731
626 279-3698

(P-9181)
CENTRAL VALLEY CMNTY BANCORP (PA)
7100 N Fincl Dr Ste 101, Fresno (93720)
PHONE..................................559 298-1775
James M Ford, *President*
Daniel J Doyle, *Ch of Bd*
David A Kinross, *CFO*
Patrick J Carman, *Ch Credit Ofcr*
Karen Musson, *Bd of Directors*
EMP: 231 EST: 2000
SALES: 74.5MM **Publicly Held**
WEB: www.cvcb.com
SIC: 6022 State commercial banks

(P-9182)
CENTRAL VALLEY COMMUNITY BANK
120 N Floral St, Visalia (93291-6202)
PHONE..................................559 625-8733
Tobi Sumida, *COO*
EMP: 75
SALES (corp-wide): 74.5MM **Publicly Held**
SIC: 6022 State commercial banks
HQ: Central Valley Community Bank
600 Pollasky Ave
Clovis CA 93612
559 323-3384

(P-9183)
CENTRAL VALLEY COMMUNITY BANK
Also Called: Folsom Lake Bank
905 Sutter St Ste 100, Folsom (95630-2479)
PHONE..................................916 985-8700
EMP: 50
SALES (corp-wide): 74.5MM **Publicly Held**
SIC: 6022 State commercial banks
HQ: Central Valley Community Bank
600 Pollasky Ave
Clovis CA 93612
559 323-3384

(P-9184)
CENTRAL VALLEY COMMUNITY BANK (HQ)
600 Pollasky Ave, Clovis (93612-1838)
PHONE..................................559 323-3384
Daniel J Doyle, *CEO*
James M Ford, *President*
David A Kinross, *CFO*
Thomas L Sommer, *Ch Credit Ofcr*
James Kim, *Exec VP*
EMP: 117
SQ FT: 11,400
SALES: 48MM
SALES (corp-wide): 74.5MM **Publicly Held**
SIC: 6022 State commercial banks
PA: Central Valley Community Bancorp
7100 N Fincl Dr Ste 101
Fresno CA 93720
559 298-1775

(P-9185)
CENTRAL VALLEY COMMUNITY BANK
Clovis Community Bank RE Div
7100 N Fincl Dr Ste 101, Fresno (93720)
PHONE..................................559 298-1775
Jeffrey Pace, *Manager*
Ted Thome, *Site Mgr*
EMP: 230
SALES (corp-wide): 74.5MM **Publicly Held**
SIC: 6022 State commercial banks
HQ: Central Valley Community Bank
600 Pollasky Ave
Clovis CA 93612
559 323-3384

(P-9186)
CITIZENS BUSINESS BANK (HQ)
701 N Haven Ave Ste 350, Ontario (91764-4920)
P.O. Box 51000 (91761-1087)
PHONE..................................909 980-4030

Toll Free:..........................877 -
Christopher D Myers, *President*
Connie Fetcho, *President*
Barbara Lowry, *President*
David C Harvey, *COO*
E Allen Nicholson, *CFO*
▲ EMP: 150
SQ FT: 23,000
SALES: 329MM
SALES (corp-wide): 405.3MM **Publicly Held**
WEB: www.cbbank.com
SIC: 6022 State trust companies accepting deposits, commercial
PA: Cvb Financial Corp.
701 N Haven Ave Ste 350
Ontario CA 91764
909 980-4030

(P-9187)
CITIZENS BUSINESS BANK
1401 Dove St Ste 100, Newport Beach (92660-2425)
PHONE..................................949 440-5200
Christopher D Myers, *President*
EMP: 90
SALES (corp-wide): 405.3MM **Publicly Held**
SIC: 6022 State trust companies accepting deposits, commercial
HQ: Citizens Business Bank
701 N Haven Ave Ste 350
Ontario CA 91764
909 980-4030

(P-9188)
CITIZENS BUSINESS BANK
505 E Colorado Blvd, Pasadena (91101-2002)
P.O. Box 3938, Ontario (91761-0992)
PHONE..................................626 577-1700
EMP: 50
SALES (corp-wide): 405.3MM **Publicly Held**
SIC: 6022 6029 State trust companies accepting deposits, commercial; commercial banks
HQ: Citizens Business Bank
701 N Haven Ave Ste 350
Ontario CA 91764
909 980-4030

(P-9189)
CITIZENS BUSINESS BANK
4100 W Alameda Ave # 101, Burbank (91505-4153)
PHONE..................................818 843-0707
Edward J Mylett Jr, *Senior VP*
EMP: 52
SALES (corp-wide): 405.3MM **Publicly Held**
WEB: www.cbbank.com
SIC: 6022 State commercial banks
HQ: Citizens Business Bank
701 N Haven Ave Ste 350
Ontario CA 91764
909 980-4030

(P-9190)
CITIZENS BUSINESS BANK
Also Called: Downtown Business Fincl Ctr
1230 17th St, Bakersfield (93301-4609)
PHONE..................................661 281-0300
Bart Hill, *Branch Mgr*
John Ivy, *Vice Pres*
Cindy Trejo, *Vice Pres*
EMP: 98
SALES (corp-wide): 405.3MM **Publicly Held**
SIC: 6022 State trust companies accepting deposits, commercial
HQ: Citizens Business Bank
701 N Haven Ave Ste 350
Ontario CA 91764
909 980-4030

(P-9191)
EAST WEST BANK (HQ)
135 N Los Robles Ave # 1, Pasadena (91101-1758)
PHONE..................................626 768-6000
Dominic Ng, *Ch of Bd*
Donald S Chow, *President*
Betty Liu, *President*
Thomas J Tolda, *CFO*
Stephen Kwan, *Officer*

◆ EMP: 300
SQ FT: 18,000
SALES: 1.5B
SALES (corp-wide): 1.8B **Publicly Held**
WEB: www.eastwest.com
SIC: 6022 State commercial banks
PA: East West Bancorp, Inc.
135 N Los Robles Ave Fl 7
Pasadena CA 91101
626 768-6000

(P-9192)
EAST WEST BANK
555 Montgomery St Bsmt, San Francisco (94111-2516)
PHONE..................................415 391-8912
Michael Kay, *Branch Mgr*
Keith Kishiyama, *Vice Pres*
Emily Ong, *Vice Pres*
Yohance Clark, *Engineer*
Lisa WEI, *Engineer*
EMP: 200
SALES (corp-wide): 1.8B **Publicly Held**
WEB: www.ibankunited.com
SIC: 6022 State commercial banks
HQ: East West Bank
135 N Los Robles Ave # 1
Pasadena CA 91101
626 768-6000

(P-9193)
EAST WEST BANK
228 W Garvey Ave, Monterey Park (91754-1603)
PHONE..................................626 280-1688
John Lee, *Branch Mgr*
EMP: 61
SALES (corp-wide): 1.8B **Publicly Held**
WEB: www.eastwest.com
SIC: 6022 State commercial banks
HQ: East West Bank
135 N Los Robles Ave # 1
Pasadena CA 91101
626 768-6000

(P-9194)
EXCHANGE BANK
2 E Washington St, Petaluma (94952-3197)
PHONE..................................707 762-5555
Rick Mossy, *Branch Mgr*
EMP: 53
SALES (corp-wide): 106.6MM **Privately Held**
WEB: www.exchangebank.com
SIC: 6022 State trust companies accepting deposits, commercial
PA: Exchange Bank
545 4th St
Santa Rosa CA 95401
707 524-3000

(P-9195)
EXCHANGE BANK
6290 Commerce Blvd, Rohnert Park (94928-2166)
P.O. Box 1008 (94927-1008)
PHONE..................................707 584-7300
R Marraffino, *Manager*
EMP: 450
SQ FT: 2,500
SALES (corp-wide): 106.6MM **Privately Held**
WEB: www.exchangebank.com
SIC: 6022 State commercial banks
PA: Exchange Bank
545 4th St
Santa Rosa CA 95401
707 524-3000

(P-9196)
FARMERS MERCHANTS BNK LONG BCH (HQ)
Also Called: F&M Bank
302 Pine Ave, Long Beach (90802-2326)
P.O. Box 1370 (90801-1370)
PHONE..................................562 437-0011
W Henry Walker, *CEO*
Lamonte Lee, *President*
Joseph Meza, *President*
Larry Prible, *President*
Kenneth G Walker, *President*
▲ EMP: 130
SQ FT: 150,000

SALES: 265.7MM **Privately Held**
WEB: www.fmb.com
SIC: 6022 6029 State trust companies accepting deposits, commercial; commercial banks

(P-9197)
FARMERS MERCHANTS BNK LONG BCH
1695 Adolfo Lopez Dr, Seal Beach (90740-5620)
PHONE..................................562 430-4724
Leon Aiossa, *Manager*
EMP: 150 **Privately Held**
WEB: www.fmb.com
SIC: 6022 6029 State trust companies accepting deposits, commercial; commercial banks
HQ: Farmers & Merchants Bank Of Long Beach
302 Pine Ave
Long Beach CA 90802
562 437-0011

(P-9198)
FARMERS MRCHANTS BNK CENTL CAL
8799 Elk Grove Blvd, Elk Grove (95624-1742)
PHONE..................................916 394-3200
Patti Ruiz, *Manager*
EMP: 214
SALES (corp-wide): 148.6MM **Publicly Held**
WEB: www.fmbonline.com
SIC: 6022 6021 State commercial banks; national commercial banks
HQ: Farmers & Merchants Bank Of Central California
121 W Pine St
Lodi CA 95240
209 367-2300

(P-9199)
FIRST CHOICE BANK
888 W 6th St Ste 200, Los Angeles (90017-2728)
PHONE..................................213 617-0082
EMP: 65
SALES (corp-wide): 67.9MM **Publicly Held**
SIC: 6022 State commercial banks
HQ: First Choice Bank
17785 Center Court Dr N # 750
Cerritos CA 90703
562 345-9092

(P-9200)
FIRST CHOICE BANK (HQ)
17785 Center Court Dr N # 750, Cerritos (90703-9310)
PHONE..................................562 345-9092
Robert Franko, *Principal*
Phillip Thong, *Vice Chairman*
Sejal Hira, *President*
Gene May, *Ch Credit Ofcr*
Dayna Herron, *Officer*
EMP: 66
SQ FT: 6,000
SALES: 36.4MM
SALES (corp-wide): 67.9MM **Publicly Held**
WEB: www.firstchoicebankca.com
SIC: 6022 State trust companies accepting deposits, commercial
PA: First Choice Bancorp
17785 Center Court Dr N # 750
Cerritos CA 90703
562 345-9092

(P-9201)
FIRST NORTHERN BANK OF DIXON (HQ)
Also Called: First Northern Community
195 N 1st St, Dixon (95620-3025)
P.O. Box 547 (95620-0547)
PHONE..................................707 678-4422
Owen J Onsum, *President*
Alison Jewett, *President*
Jeremiah Z Smith, *COO*
Louise A Walker, *CFO*
T Joe Danelson, *Ch Credit Ofcr*
EMP: 59 EST: 1910
SQ FT: 14,000

P R O D U C T S   &   S V C S

SALES: 48.1MM **Publicly Held**
SIC: 6022 State trust companies accepting deposits, commercial

(P-9202)
FIRST REGIONAL BANCORP
1801 Century Park E # 800, Los Angeles (90067-2302)
PHONE..................................310 552-1776
H Anthony Gartshore, *President*
Gary M Horgan, *Ch of Bd*
Elizabeth Thompson, *CFO*
Lawrence J Sherman, *Vice Ch Bd*
Thomas E McCullough, *Admin Sec*
EMP: 288
SQ FT: 19,734
SALES (est): 46.1MM **Privately Held**
WEB: www.firstregional.com
SIC: 6022 State commercial banks

(P-9203)
FIRST REPUBLIC BANK
44 Montgomery St Ste 110, San Francisco (94104-4600)
PHONE..................................415 392-3888
Monica Brazil, *Manager*
Tony Valencia, *Store Mgr*
Eric Wilson, *Senior Engr*
Sergei Lubensky, *Director*
EMP: 127
SALES (corp-wide): 2.9B **Publicly Held**
WEB: www.firstrepublic.com
SIC: 6022 State commercial banks
PA: First Republic Bank
111 Pine St Fl 2
San Francisco CA 94111
415 392-1400

(P-9204)
FIRST REPUBLIC BANK
2550 Sand Hill Rd Ste 100, Menlo Park (94025-7095)
PHONE..................................650 233-8880
Gayle Nickel, *Branch Mgr*
EMP: 127
SALES (corp-wide): 2.9B **Publicly Held**
SIC: 6022 State commercial banks
PA: First Republic Bank
111 Pine St Fl 2
San Francisco CA 94111
415 392-1400

(P-9205)
FIRST REPUBLIC BANK
888 S Figueroa St Ste 100, Los Angeles (90017-5325)
PHONE..................................213 239-8883
Sev Araradian, *Branch Mgr*
EMP: 127
SALES (corp-wide): 2.9B **Publicly Held**
SIC: 6022 State commercial banks
PA: First Republic Bank
111 Pine St Fl 2
San Francisco CA 94111
415 392-1400

(P-9206)
FIRST REPUBLIC BANK
224 Brookwood Rd, Orinda (94563-3015)
PHONE..................................925 254-8993
Dina Zapanta, *Branch Mgr*
EMP: 127
SALES (corp-wide): 2.9B **Publicly Held**
SIC: 6022 State commercial banks
PA: First Republic Bank
111 Pine St Fl 2
San Francisco CA 94111
415 392-1400

(P-9207)
FIRST REPUBLIC BANK
1215 El Camino Real, Menlo Park (94025-4208)
PHONE..................................650 470-8888
Andrea Jefferson, *Manager*
EMP: 135
SALES (corp-wide): 2.9B **Publicly Held**
SIC: 6022 State commercial banks
PA: First Republic Bank
111 Pine St Fl 2
San Francisco CA 94111
415 392-1400

(P-9208)
FREMONT BANK (HQ)
39150 Fremont Blvd, Fremont (94538-1313)
P.O. Box 5101 (94537-5101)
PHONE..................................510 505-5226
Morris Hyman, *Ch of Bd*
Andy Mastorakis, *President*
Bradford L Anderson, *CEO*
Patti Greenup, *COO*
Ron Wagner, *CFO*
EMP: 250
SQ FT: 20,000
SALES: 195.2MM
SALES (corp-wide): 195.5MM **Privately Held**
WEB: www.fremontbank.com
SIC: 6022 State commercial banks
PA: Fremont Bancorporation
39150 Fremont Blvd
Fremont CA 94538
510 792-2300

(P-9209)
GREAT WESTERN BANCORP INC
706 S Hill St, Los Angeles (90014-2711)
PHONE..................................213 622-1895
James Tolich, *Branch Mgr*
EMP: 284
SALES (corp-wide): 555.4MM **Publicly Held**
SIC: 6022 State commercial banks
PA: Great Western Bancorp, Inc.
225 S Main Ave
Sioux Falls SD 57104
605 334-2548

(P-9210)
HANMI BANK (HQ)
3660 Wilshire Blvd Ph A, Los Angeles (90010-2387)
PHONE..................................213 382-2200
Joon H Lee, *Ch of Bd*
Susan Kim, *President*
Chong Guk Kum, *President*
Jenny Park, *President*
Sam Rukh, *President*
▲ **EMP:** 152 **EST:** 1981
SQ FT: 35,000
SALES: 242.1MM
SALES (corp-wide): 258.9MM **Publicly Held**
WEB: www.hanmi.com
SIC: 6022 State commercial banks
PA: Hanmi Financial Corporation
3660 Wlshire Blvd Pnthuse
Los Angeles CA 90010
213 382-2200

(P-9211)
HERITAGE BANK OF COMMERCE (HQ)
150 Almaden Blvd Lbby, San Jose (95113-2010)
PHONE..................................408 947-6900
Walter Kaczmarek, *CEO*
Keith Wilton, *President*
Michael Ong, *Ch Credit Ofcr*
John Angelesco, *Officer*
Lawrence D McGovern, *Officer*
EMP: 120
SQ FT: 36,000
SALES: 116.4MM
SALES (corp-wide): 139.4MM **Publicly Held**
WEB: www.heritagebankofcommerce.com
SIC: 6022 State trust companies accepting deposits, commercial
PA: Heritage Commerce Corp
150 Almaden Blvd Lbby
San Jose CA 95113
408 947-6900

(P-9212)
ISRAEL DISCOUNT BANK NEW YORK
Also Called: Downtown Los Angeles Branch
888 S Figueroa St Ste 550, Los Angeles (90017-5306)
PHONE..................................213 861-6440
Leon Recanati, *Principal*
EMP: 177
SALES (corp-wide): 2.2B **Privately Held**
SIC: 6022 State commercial banks
HQ: Israel Discount Bank Of New York
511 5th Ave
New York NY 10017
212 551-8500

(P-9213)
LOS ROBLES BANK
33 W Thousand Oaks Blvd, Thousand Oaks (91360-4416)
P.O. Box 1438 (91358-0438)
PHONE..................................805 373-6763
Fax: 805 379-2857
EMP: 52
SQ FT: 11,000
SALES (est): 5.3MM
SALES (corp-wide): 5.2B **Privately Held**
SIC: 6022
HQ: Mufg Americas Holdings Corporation
1251 Ave Of The Americas
New York NY 10020
212 782-6800

(P-9214)
MANUFACTURERS BANK (HQ)
515 S Figueroa St Fl 4, Los Angeles (90071-3301)
PHONE..................................213 489-6200
Mitsugu Serizawa, *CEO*
Koichi Miyata, *President*
Naresh Sheth, *President*
Karen Abajian, *Exec VP*
Adrian Danescu, *Exec VP*
▲ **EMP:** 164
SQ FT: 69,206
SALES: 88.9MM **Privately Held**
WEB: www.manubank.com
SIC: 6022 State commercial banks

(P-9215)
MECHANICS BANK
Crb Auto
18400 Von Karman Ave, Irvine (92612-1514)
PHONE..................................855 272-2886
Bill Katafias, *CEO*
Karen Ho, *Admin Asst*
Maryann Herring, *Regl Sales Mgr*
Paul Benjamin, *Manager*
Priscilla Colunga, *Manager*
EMP: 270
SALES (corp-wide): 48.7MM **Privately Held**
SIC: 6022 State commercial banks
HQ: The Mechanics Bank
1111 Civic Dr
Walnut Creek CA 94596
800 797-6324

(P-9216)
MECHANICS BANK
725 Alfred Nobel Dr, Hercules (94547-1897)
P.O. Box 5610 (94547-5610)
PHONE..................................510 741-7545
Alexey Bulankov, *Vice Pres*
Deepinder Sandhu, *Software Dev*
Chad Mallory, *Technology*
Marina Cotto, *Analyst*
EMP: 57
SQ FT: 69,184
SALES (corp-wide): 48.7MM **Privately Held**
SIC: 6022 State commercial banks
HQ: The Mechanics Bank
1111 Civic Dr
Walnut Creek CA 94596
800 797-6324

(P-9217)
MECHANICS BANK
301 Main St, Salinas (93901-2700)
PHONE..................................831 422-6642
Ida Chan, *Principal*
Steve Lawson, *Vice Pres*
Russell Mills, *Vice Pres*
Lisa Ostarello, *Broker*
EMP: 125
SALES (corp-wide): 48.7MM **Privately Held**
WEB: www.community-bnk.com
SIC: 6022 6163 6029 State commercial banks; loan brokers; commercial banks
HQ: The Mechanics Bank
1111 Civic Dr
Walnut Creek CA 94596
800 797-6324

(P-9218)
MUFG UNION BANK NATIONAL ASSN
1201 5th Ave, San Diego (92101-4214)
PHONE..................................619 230-4666
Ralph C Allen, *Branch Mgr*
Suzuko Burton, *Officer*
Robert Villarreal, *Exec VP*
Marguerite Boutelle, *Senior VP*
Kevin Barrie, *Vice Pres*
EMP: 62 **Privately Held**
SIC: 6022 State commercial banks
HQ: Mufg Union Bank, National Association
400 California St Fl 14
San Francisco CA 94104
415 705-7000

(P-9219)
ONEUNITED BANK
Also Called: Family Savings Bank
3683 Crenshaw Blvd, Los Angeles (90016-4890)
PHONE..................................323 295-3381
Kevin Cohee, *Ch of Bd*
EMP: 72
SALES (corp-wide): 27.4MM **Privately Held**
SIC: 6022 State commercial banks
PA: Oneunited Bank
100 Franklin St Ste 600
Boston MA 02110
617 457-4400

(P-9220)
OP BANCORP
1000 Wilshire Blvd # 500, Los Angeles (90017-2462)
PHONE..................................213 892-9999
Min J Kim, *President*
Brian Choi, *Ch of Bd*
Christine Y OH, *CFO*
EMP: 154 **EST:** 2016
SQ FT: 15,239
SALES: 59.4MM **Privately Held**
SIC: 6022 State commercial banks

(P-9221)
PACIFIC CAST BNKERS BANCSHARES (PA)
1676 N Calif Blvd Ste 300, Walnut Creek (94596-4185)
PHONE..................................415 399-1900
Steven A Brown, *President*
Michael Douhren, *CFO*
Nino Petroni, *Ch Credit Ofcr*
Tracy Holcomb, *Exec VP*
EMP: 65 **EST:** 1996
SQ FT: 16,000
SALES: 21.1MM **Privately Held**
WEB: www.pcbb.com
SIC: 6022 State commercial banks

(P-9222)
PACIFIC COAST BANKERS BANK
1676 N Calif Blvd Ste 300, Walnut Creek (94596-4185)
PHONE..................................415 399-1900
Steve Brown, *President*
Nino Petroni, *COO*
Eric Davis, *Senior VP*
Lavanya Chandrasekhar, *Vice Pres*
Helen Gee, *Analyst*
EMP: 60
SALES: 40.7MM
SALES (corp-wide): 21.1MM **Privately Held**
SIC: 6022 State commercial banks
PA: Pacific Coast Bankers' Bancshares
1676 N Calif Blvd Ste 300
Walnut Creek CA 94596
415 399-1900

(P-9223)
PACIFIC MERCANTILE BANK (HQ)
Also Called: Pmbc
949 S Coast Dr Ste 300, Costa Mesa (92626-7733)
PHONE..................................714 438-2500
Brad R Dinsmore, *President*
Steven Buster, *President*
Neil B Kornswiet, *President*
Thomas M Vertin, *President*
Robert E Sjogren, *COO*

▲ = Import ▼ = Export
◆ = Import/Export

EMP: 50
SALES: 53.9MM
SALES (corp-wide): 67.1MM **Publicly Held**
SIC: **6022** 6712 State trust companies accepting deposits, commercial; bank holding companies
PA: Pacific Mercantile Bancorp
   949 S Coast Dr Ste 105
   Costa Mesa CA 92626
   714 438-2500

(P-9224)
PACIFIC PREMIER BANK (HQ)
17901 Von Karman Ave, Irvine (92614-6297)
PHONE.................714 431-4000
Steven R Gardner, *President*
Jeff C Jones, *Ch of Bd*
Ronald J Nicolas Jr, *CFO*
Kent Smith, *CFO*
Donn Jakosky, *Ch Credit Ofcr*
EMP: 104
SQ FT: 36,159
SALES: 298.1MM **Publicly Held**
SIC: **6022** State commercial banks

(P-9225)
PACIFIC PREMIER BANK
333 S Grand Ave Ste 3560, Los Angeles (90071-3477)
PHONE.................213 626-0085
EMP: 78 **Publicly Held**
SIC: **6022** State trust companies accepting deposits, commercial
HQ: Pacific Premier Bank
   17901 Von Karman Ave
   Irvine CA 92614
   714 431-4000

(P-9226)
PACIFIC WESTERN BANK
818 W 7th St Ste 220, Los Angeles (90017-3449)
PHONE.................213 430-7000
EMP: 112
SALES (corp-wide): 1.3B **Publicly Held**
SIC: **6022** State commercial banks
HQ: Pacific Western Bank
   9701 Wilshire Blvd # 700
   Beverly Hills CA 90212
   310 887-8500

(P-9227)
PACIFIC WESTERN BANK
11150 W Olympic Blvd # 100, Los Angeles (90064-1817)
PHONE.................310 996-9100
Chris Bower, *Manager*
Todd Savitz, *Senior VP*
EMP: 50
SALES (corp-wide): 1.3B **Publicly Held**
WEB: www.pacificwesternbank.com
SIC: **6022** State commercial banks
HQ: Pacific Western Bank
   9701 Wilshire Blvd # 700
   Beverly Hills CA 90212
   310 887-8500

(P-9228)
PACIFIC WESTERN BANK
900 Canterbury Pl Ste 300, Escondido (92025-3846)
PHONE.................760 432-1350
Bruce Mills, *CFO*
Leticia Trujillo, *Assistant VP*
EMP: 108
SALES (corp-wide): 1.3B **Publicly Held**
WEB: www.pacificwesternbank.com
SIC: **6022** State commercial banks
HQ: Pacific Western Bank
   9701 Wilshire Blvd # 700
   Beverly Hills CA 90212
   310 887-8500

(P-9229)
PACIFIC WESTERN BANK
9955 Mission Gorge Rd, Santee (92071-3841)
PHONE.................619 562-6400
Bruce Ives, *Manager*
EMP: 60
SALES (corp-wide): 1.3B **Publicly Held**
WEB: www.pacificwesternbank.com
SIC: **6022** State trust companies accepting deposits, commercial

HQ: Pacific Western Bank
   9701 Wilshire Blvd # 700
   Beverly Hills CA 90212
   310 887-8500

(P-9230)
PACIFIC WESTERN BANK
12481 High Bluff Dr # 350, San Diego (92130-3585)
PHONE.................858 436-3500
Richard Casey, *Branch Mgr*
EMP: 53
SALES (corp-wide): 1.3B **Publicly Held**
SIC: **6022** State commercial banks
HQ: Pacific Western Bank
   9701 Wilshire Blvd # 700
   Beverly Hills CA 90212
   310 887-8500

(P-9231)
PACIFIC WESTERN BANK
Also Called: Los Padres Bank
610 Alamo Pintado Rd, Solvang (93463-2202)
PHONE.................805 688-6644
Craig Cerny, *President*
EMP: 189
SALES (corp-wide): 1.3B **Publicly Held**
SIC: **6022** State commercial banks
HQ: Pacific Western Bank
   9701 Wilshire Blvd # 700
   Beverly Hills CA 90212
   310 887-8500

(P-9232)
PREMIER COMMERCIAL BANCORP
2400 E Katella Ave # 125, Anaheim (92806-5920)
PHONE.................714 978-2400
Kenneth J Cosgrove, *Ch of Bd*
Ashokkumar Patel, *President*
Viktor R Uehlinger, *CFO*
Stephen W Pihl, *Exec VP*
David Plourde, *Exec VP*
EMP: 64
SALES: 22.3MM **Privately Held**
SIC: **6022** State commercial banks

(P-9233)
PROVIDENT SAVINGS BANK LLC
Also Called: Provident Bank
3756 Central Ave, Riverside (92506-2469)
PHONE.................951 686-6060
Craig Blunden, *Mng Member*
Robert G Schrader, *COO*
Donavon P Ternes, *CFO*
Donald L Blanchard, *Senior VP*
Lilian Brunner, *Senior VP*
EMP: 100
SALES: 45.5K **Privately Held**
SIC: **6022** State commercial banks

(P-9234)
RCB CORPORATION (PA)
Also Called: River City Bank
2485 Natomas Park Dr # 100, Sacramento (95833-2937)
P.O. Box 15247 (95851-0247)
PHONE.................916 567-2600
Stephen Fleming, *President*
Shawn Devlin, *Ch of Bd*
Anker Christensen, *CFO*
Jon Kelly, *Founder*
Karrie Blevins, *Exec VP*
EMP: 80
SQ FT: 34,000
SALES (est): 72MM **Privately Held**
SIC: **6022** State commercial banks

(P-9235)
RIVER CITY BANK (HQ)
2485 Natomas Park Dr # 100, Sacramento (95833-2975)
P.O. Box 15247 (95851-0247)
PHONE.................916 567-2600
Stephen A Fleming, *President*
Lynda Fagerberg, *President*
Camille Lasky, *President*
Anker Christensen, *CFO*
Ryan Gilbert, *Bd of Directors*
EMP: 80
SQ FT: 15,000

SALES: 71.1MM
SALES (corp-wide): 72MM **Privately Held**
WEB: www.rcbank.com
SIC: **6022** State commercial banks
PA: Rcb Corporation
   2485 Natomas Park Dr # 100
   Sacramento CA 95833
   916 567-2600

(P-9236)
SAEHAN BANK (PA)
3200 Wilshire Blvd # 700, Los Angeles (90010-1333)
PHONE.................213 368-7700
Dong IL Kim, *President*
Dong II Kim, *President*
EMP: 50
SQ FT: 12,000
SALES (est): 26.4MM **Privately Held**
SIC: **6022** State trust companies accepting deposits, commercial

(P-9237)
SAVINGS BANK MENDOCINO COUNTY (PA)
Also Called: SBMC
200 N School St, Ukiah (95482-4811)
P.O. Box 3600 (95482-3600)
PHONE.................707 462-6613
Charles B Mannon, *Ch of Bd*
Scott Yandell, *President*
Mark Driedger, *COO*
Bruce Little, *CFO*
Tara Hatton, *Officer*
EMP: 130 EST: 1903
SALES: 41.8MM **Privately Held**
WEB: www.savingsbank.com
SIC: **6022** State commercial banks

(P-9238)
SECURITY CALIFORNIA BANCORP
3403 10th St Ste 830, Riverside (92501-3666)
PHONE.................951 368-2265
James A Robinson, *CEO*
Jim Robinson, *Ch of Bd*
Thomas Ferrer, *CFO*
Dolly L Nugent, *Ch Credit Ofcr*
EMP: 63
SALES (est): 334.3K **Privately Held**
SIC: **6022** State commercial banks

(P-9239)
SIERRA BANCORP
7029 N Ingram Ave Ste 101, Fresno (93650-1091)
PHONE.................559 449-8145
Frank Oliver, *Principal*
EMP: 82
SALES (corp-wide): 123.2MM **Publicly Held**
SIC: **6022** State commercial banks
PA: Sierra Bancorp
   86 N Main St
   Porterville CA 93257
   559 782-4900

(P-9240)
STANDARD CHARTERED BANK
601 S Figueroa St # 2775, Los Angeles (90017-5877)
PHONE.................626 639-8000
Jim Mc Cabe, *CEO*
EMP: 225
SALES (corp-wide): 23.8B **Privately Held**
SIC: **6022** 6282 6029 State trust companies accepting deposits, commercial; investment advisory service; commercial banks
HQ: Standard Chartered Bank
   1 Basinghall Avenue
   London EC2V
   207 885-8888

(P-9241)
SUNWEST BANK (DH)
2050 Main St Fl 3, Irvine (92614-8255)
P.O. Box 1028, Tustin (92781-1028)
PHONE.................714 730-4441
Glenn Gray, *President*
Carson Lappetito, *President*
Wesley Thomas, *President*
Chris Walsh, *President*
Jason Raefski, *CFO*

EMP: 50
SQ FT: 30,000
SALES: 54.6MM **Privately Held**
SIC: **6022** State commercial banks

(P-9242)
SVB FINANCIAL GROUP (PA)
3003 Tasman Dr, Santa Clara (95054-1191)
PHONE.................408 654-7400
Roger F Dunbar, *Ch of Bd*
Greg W Becker, *President*
John China, *President*
Philip C Cox, *President*
Michael L Dreyer, *COO*
EMP: 102
SQ FT: 213,625
SALES: 2.7B **Publicly Held**
SIC: **6022** State commercial banks

(P-9243)
TORREY PINES BANK (HQ)
12220 El Camino Real # 200, San Diego (92130-2091)
PHONE.................858 523-4600
Fax: 858 755-0875
EMP: 103
SALES (est): 19.1MM
SALES (corp-wide): 554.9MM **Publicly Held**
WEB: www.torreypinesbank.com
SIC: **6022**
PA: Western Alliance Bancorporation
   1 E Wshington St Ste 1400
   Phoenix AZ 85004
   602 389-3500

(P-9244)
TRICO BANCSHARES
2844 F St, Eureka (95501-4423)
PHONE.................707 476-0981
EMP: 66
SALES (corp-wide): 277.5MM **Publicly Held**
SIC: **6022** State commercial banks
PA: Trico Bancshares
   63 Constitution Dr
   Chico CA 95973
   530 898-0300

(P-9245)
UMPQUA BANK
7777 Alvarado Rd Ste 515, La Mesa (91942-8306)
PHONE.................619 668-5159
EMP: 81
SALES (corp-wide): 1.2B **Publicly Held**
SIC: **6022**
HQ: Umpqua Bank
   445 Se Main St
   Roseburg OR 97470
   541 440-3961

(P-9246)
VALLEY REPUBLIC BANK
5000 California Ave # 110, Bakersfield (93309-0711)
PHONE.................661 371-2000
Geraud Smith, *President*
Ashley Brown, *President*
Stephen M Annis, *COO*
Garth A Corrigan, *CFO*
Cindy Talley, *Officer*
EMP: 85
SQ FT: 8,000
SALES: 23.2MM **Privately Held**
SIC: **6022** State commercial banks

(P-9247)
WESTERN ALLIANCE BANK
Also Called: Bridge Bank
55 Almaden Blvd Ste 200, San Jose (95113-1619)
PHONE.................408 423-8500
Lee Shodiss, *Vice Pres*
Tim R Bruckner, *Ch Credit Ofcr*
Sheetal Cordova, *Vice Pres*
EMP: 70
SALES (corp-wide): 1B **Publicly Held**
SIC: **6022** 8742 State commercial banks; management consulting services
HQ: Western Alliance Bank
   1 E Wshington St Ste 1400
   Phoenix AZ 85004

6029 Commercial Banks,

(P-9248)
BANC CALIFORNIA NATIONAL ASSN
10100 Santa Monica Blvd, Los Angeles (90067-4003)
PHONE....................310 286-0710
Richard Smith, *President*
Richard Herrin, *Exec VP*
EMP: 50
SALES (corp-wide): 446.7MM **Publicly Held**
SIC: 6029 Commercial banks
HQ: Banc Of California, National Association
3 Macarthur Pl
Santa Ana CA 92707
877 770-2262

(P-9249)
BANK OF TOKYO LTD
Also Called: Union Bank
445 S Figueroa St # 2700, Los Angeles (90071-1602)
PHONE....................213 488-3700
Jiro Ishicaka, *Branch Mgr*
Mary Bunnell, *Vice Pres*
Robin Gold, *Vice Pres*
Jeff Orsborn, *Vice Pres*
Maria Flores, *Administration*
EMP: 625 **Privately Held**
SIC: 6029 Commercial banks
PA: Mufg Bank, Ltd.
2-7-1, Marunouchi
Chiyoda-Ku TKY 100-0

(P-9250)
CALIFORNIA FIRST NATIONAL BANK
Also Called: University Lease
28 Executive Park Ste 200, Irvine (92614-4741)
P.O. Box 2509, Santa Ana (92707-0509)
PHONE....................949 255-0500
S Leslie Jewett, *President*
Glen T Tsuma, *Vice Chairman*
Yvonne Cattell, *CFO*
Darren Higuchi, *Vice Pres*
EMP: 80
SQ FT: 36,000
SALES: 28.5MM
SALES (corp-wide): 36.6MM **Publicly Held**
WEB: www.calfirstbancorp.com
SIC: 6029 Commercial banks
PA: California First National Bancorp
28 Executive Park Ste 200
Irvine CA 92614
949 255-0500

(P-9251)
COMMERCIAL FINANCE & L
12626 High Bluff Dr # 370, San Diego (92130-2074)
P.O. Box 2562, Del Mar (92014-1862)
PHONE....................858 866-8525
Vadim Garry Lyulkin, *President*
ARI Gold, *Vice Pres*
Dennis Kaminsky, *Vice Pres*
Dean G Lyulkin, *Principal*
William S Stern, *Principal*
EMP: 65
SALES (est): 24.7MM **Privately Held**
WEB: www.bankofcardiff.com
SIC: 6029 Commercial banks

(P-9252)
FIRST FOUNDATION INC
301 N Lake Ave Ste 100, Pasadena (91101-4108)
PHONE....................626 993-1300
Carol Golbranson, *Branch Mgr*
EMP: 156 **Publicly Held**
SIC: 6029 Commercial banks
PA: First Foundation Inc.
18101 Von Karman Ave # 7
Irvine CA 92612

(P-9253)
FIRST REPUBLIC BANK
750 Redwood Hwy Frontage # 1218, Mill Valley (94941-2483)
PHONE....................415 389-0880
Vince Franceschi, *Branch Mgr*
Linford Ian, *Vice Pres*
Yang Linda, *Vice Pres*
Andrew Huang, *Associate Dir*
Gordon Richard, *Managing Dir*
EMP: 135
SALES (corp-wide): 2.9B **Publicly Held**
SIC: 6029 Commercial banks
PA: First Republic Bank
111 Pine St Fl 2
San Francisco CA 94111
415 392-1400

(P-9254)
FIRST REPUBLIC BANK
101 Pine St, San Francisco (94111-5629)
PHONE....................415 392-1400
Jeffrey Schottenstein, *Managing Dir*
Justin Steingraber, *Director*
Dan Murphy, *Manager*
EMP: 80
SALES (corp-wide): 2.9B **Publicly Held**
SIC: 6029 Commercial banks
PA: First Republic Bank
111 Pine St Fl 2
San Francisco CA 94111
415 392-1400

(P-9255)
FIRST REPUBLIC BANK
1280 4th Ave, San Diego (92101-4294)
PHONE....................619 238-9088
EMP: 135
SALES (corp-wide): 2.9B **Publicly Held**
SIC: 6029 Commercial banks
PA: First Republic Bank
111 Pine St Fl 2
San Francisco CA 94111
415 392-1400

(P-9256)
FIRST REPUBLIC BANK
653 Irving St, San Francisco (94122-2401)
PHONE....................415 564-8881
EMP: 135
SALES (corp-wide): 2.9B **Publicly Held**
SIC: 6029 Commercial banks
PA: First Republic Bank
111 Pine St Fl 2
San Francisco CA 94111
415 392-1400

(P-9257)
FIRST REPUBLIC BANK
1355 Market St Ste 140, San Francisco (94103-1337)
PHONE....................415 487-0888
EMP: 135
SALES (corp-wide): 2.9B **Publicly Held**
SIC: 6029 Commercial banks
PA: First Republic Bank
111 Pine St Fl 2
San Francisco CA 94111
415 392-1400

(P-9258)
FIRST REPUBLIC BANK
405 Howard St Ste 110, San Francisco (94105-2665)
PHONE....................415 975-3877
EMP: 135
SALES (corp-wide): 2.9B **Publicly Held**
SIC: 6029 Commercial banks
PA: First Republic Bank
111 Pine St Fl 2
San Francisco CA 94111
415 392-1400

(P-9259)
FIRST REPUBLIC BANK
1888 Century Park E # 200, Los Angeles (90067-1706)
PHONE....................310 712-1888
Simon Clark, *Branch Mgr*
Paul Feinstein, *Managing Dir*
Jim Felton, *Credit Staff*
Spencer Haly, *Sr Associate*
Mary Deckebach, *Director*
EMP: 65
SALES (corp-wide): 2.9B **Publicly Held**
SIC: 6029 Commercial banks

PA: First Republic Bank
111 Pine St Fl 2
San Francisco CA 94111
415 392-1400

(P-9260)
FIRST REPUBLIC BANK (PA)
111 Pine St Fl 2, San Francisco (94111-5606)
PHONE....................415 392-1400
James H Herbert II, *Ch of Bd*
Hafize Gaye Erkan, *President*
Jason C Bender, *COO*
Michael J Roffler, *CFO*
Katherine August-Dewilde, *Vice Ch Bd*
EMP: 332
SALES: 2.9B **Publicly Held**
WEB: www.firstrepublic.com
SIC: 6029 Commercial banks

(P-9261)
HSBC BUSINESS CREDIT (USA)
Also Called: Hsbc Bank USA NA
660 S Figueroa St, Los Angeles (90017-3442)
PHONE....................213 553-8089
Celia Anderson-Hayes, *Manager*
EMP: 85
SQ FT: 4,000
SALES (corp-wide): 87.7B **Privately Held**
SIC: 6029 Commercial banks
HQ: Hsbc Business Credit (Usa) Inc
452 5th Ave Fl 4
New York NY 10018
800 511-1918

(P-9262)
HSBC FINANCE CORPORATION
1420 El Paseo De Saratoga, San Jose (95130-1633)
PHONE....................408 796-3600
EMP: 142
SALES (corp-wide): 87.7B **Privately Held**
SIC: 6029 Commercial banks
HQ: Hsbc Finance Corporation
1421 W Shure Dr Ste 100
Arlington Heights IL 60004
224 880-7000

(P-9263)
HSBC FINANCE CORPORATION
725 N Broadway, Los Angeles (90012-2819)
PHONE....................213 628-8167
Clarence Ho, *Branch Mgr*
EMP: 142
SALES (corp-wide): 87.7B **Privately Held**
SIC: 6029 Commercial banks
HQ: Hsbc Finance Corporation
1421 W Shure Dr Ste 100
Arlington Heights IL 60004
224 880-7000

(P-9264)
JPMORGAN CHASE BANK NAT ASSN
860 E Colorado Blvd, Pasadena (91101-2107)
PHONE....................626 795-5177
Vickie Davinski, *Branch Mgr*
David Chang, *Loan Officer*
EMP: 60
SQ FT: 74,640
SALES (corp-wide): 131.4B **Publicly Held**
SIC: 6029 Commercial banks
HQ: Jpmorgan Chase Bank, National Association
1111 Polaris Pkwy
Columbus OH 43240
614 436-3055

(P-9265)
JPMORGAN CHASE BANK NAT ASSN
Also Called: Washington Mutual
12051 Ventura Blvd, Studio City (91604-2609)
PHONE....................818 763-7343
Manny Abebi, *Branch Mgr*
EMP: 50
SALES (corp-wide): 131.4B **Publicly Held**
SIC: 6029 Commercial banks

HQ: Jpmorgan Chase Bank, National Association
1111 Polaris Pkwy
Columbus OH 43240
614 436-3055

(P-9266)
LUTHER BURBANK CORPORATION
20 Pacifica Ste 600, Irvine (92618-3389)
PHONE....................949 428-8043
EMP: 55 **Publicly Held**
SIC: 6029 Commercial banks
PA: Luther Burbank Corporation
520 3rd St Fl 4
Santa Rosa CA 95401

(P-9267)
MECHANICS BANK (DH)
1111 Civic Dr, Walnut Creek (94596-3895)
PHONE....................800 797-6324
John Decero, *President*
E Michael Downer, *Vice Chairman*
Suman Raj, *President*
Kenneth Russell, *President*
Nathan Duda, *CFO*
EMP: 110 **EST:** 1905
SQ FT: 77,000
SALES: 140.9MM
SALES (corp-wide): 48.7MM **Privately Held**
SIC: 6029 Commercial banks
HQ: Eb Acquisition Company Llc
200 Crescent Ct Ste 1350
Dallas TX 75201
214 871-5151

(P-9268)
MUFG BANK LTD
Also Called: Bank of Tokyo
777 S Figueroa St Ste 600, Los Angeles (90017-5806)
PHONE....................213 488-3700
Kim Amada, *Branch Mgr*
EMP: 100 **Privately Held**
SIC: 6029 Commercial banks
HQ: Mufg Bank, Ltd.
1251 Ave Of The Americas
New York NY 10020

(P-9269)
N A TOMATOBANK
901 S Baldwin Ave, Arcadia (91007-6704)
PHONE....................626 759-9200
Charles Fenton, *CEO*
Lichen Herman, *President*
EMP: 57
SALES: 18MM
SALES (corp-wide): 17MM **Privately Held**
SIC: 6029 Commercial banks
PA: Tfc Holding Company
18605 Gale Ave Ste 238
City Of Industry CA 91748
626 363-9708

(P-9270)
OPUS BANK
200 W Commonwealth Ave, Fullerton (92832-1811)
PHONE....................714 578-7500
EMP: 110 **Publicly Held**
SIC: 6029 Commercial banks
PA: Opus Bank
19900 Macarthur Blvd # 1200
Irvine CA 92612

(P-9271)
SEACOAST COMMERCE BANK (HQ)
11939 Rncho Brnrdo Rd Ste, San Diego (92128)
PHONE....................858 432-7000
Richard M Sanborn, *CEO*
Allan W Arendsee, *Ch of Bd*
David H Bartram, *COO*
Rahul Barot, *Officer*
Jay Jung, *Officer*
EMP: 60
SALES: 45.3MM **Privately Held**
WEB: www.seacoastcommercebank.com
SIC: 6029 Commercial banks

PA: Seacoast Commerce Banc Holdings
11939 Rancho Bernardo Rd
San Diego CA 92128
858 432-7000

(P-9272)
SILICON VALLEY BANK (HQ)
3003 Tasman Dr, Santa Clara
(95054-1191)
PHONE..........................408 654-7400
Greg Becker, *CEO*
Erin Platts, *President*
Michael Dreyer, *COO*
Cecilia Shea, *CFO*
Harry Kellogg, *Vice Ch Bd*
EMP: 592
SQ FT: 100,000
SALES: 1.8B
SALES (corp-wide): 2.7B **Publicly Held**
WEB: www.svbsecurities.com
SIC: 6029 Commercial banks
PA: Svb Financial Group
3003 Tasman Dr
Santa Clara CA 95054
408 654-7400

(P-9273)
TRI COUNTIES BANK (HQ)
63 Constitution Dr, Chico (95973-4937)
PHONE..........................530 898-0300
William J Casey, *Ch of Bd*
Suzanne Youngs, *Shareholder*
Alex A Vereschagin Jr, *Ch of Bd*
Richard P Smith, *President*
John S Fleshood, *COO*
EMP: 75
SALES: 230.4MM
SALES (corp-wide): 277.5MM **Publicly
Held**
WEB: www.tricountiesbank.com
SIC: 6029 6163 Commercial banks; loan
brokers
PA: Trico Bancshares
63 Constitution Dr
Chico CA 95973
530 898-0300

(P-9274)
TRI COUNTIES BANK
975 El Camino Real, South San Francisco
(94080-3203)
PHONE..........................650 583-8450
EMP: 184
SALES (corp-wide): 277.5MM **Publicly
Held**
SIC: 6029 Commercial banks
HQ: Tri Counties Bank
63 Constitution Dr
Chico CA 95973
530 898-0300

(P-9275)
TRI COUNTIES BANK
305 Railroad Ave Ste 1, Nevada City
(95959-2854)
PHONE..........................530 478-6001
Eileen Counts, *Opers Mgr*
EMP: 91
SALES (corp-wide): 277.5MM **Publicly
Held**
SIC: 6029 Commercial banks
HQ: Tri Counties Bank
63 Constitution Dr
Chico CA 95973
530 898-0300

(P-9276)
WESTERN ALLIANCE BANK
455 Market St Ste 1050, San Francisco
(94105-5409)
PHONE..........................415 230-4834
EMP: 70
SALES (corp-wide): 1B **Publicly Held**
SIC: 6029 Commercial banks
HQ: Western Alliance Bank
1 E Wshington St Ste 1400
Phoenix AZ 85004

(P-9277)
WESTERN ALLIANCE BANK
7545 Irvine Center Dr # 200, Irvine
(92618-2932)
PHONE..........................949 222-0855
EMP: 70

SALES (corp-wide): 1B **Publicly Held**
SIC: 6029 Commercial banks
HQ: Western Alliance Bank
1 E Wshington St Ste 1400
Phoenix AZ 85004

6035 Federal Savings Institutions

(P-9278)
CITIBANK FSB (HQ)
1 Sansome St, San Francisco
(94104-4448)
PHONE..........................415 627-6000
David A Brooks, *Ch of Bd*
Jay Compton, *President*
Edgar Ancona, *Treasurer*
Michael McCarthy, *Officer*
EMP: 300 **EST:** 1921
SQ FT: 20,000
SALES (est): 101.2MM
SALES (corp-wide): 72.8B **Publicly Held**
SIC: 6035 Federal savings banks
PA: Citigroup Inc.
388 Greenwich St
New York NY 10013
212 559-1000

(P-9279)
**EL DORADO SAVINGS BANK
(PA)**
4040 El Dorado Rd, Placerville
(95667-5269)
P.O. Box 1208 (95667-1208)
PHONE..........................530 622-1492
Thomas Meuser, *Ch of Bd*
George Cook Jr, *President*
Anne Wilson, *President*
William H Blucher, *CFO*
William Buechler, *CFO*
EMP: 55
SQ FT: 37,779
SALES: 58MM **Privately Held**
WEB: www.eldoradosavingsbank.com
SIC: 6035 Federal savings & loan associations

(P-9280)
**JPMORGAN CHASE BANK NAT
ASSN**
400 E Main St Fl 2, Stockton (95202-3002)
PHONE..........................209 460-2888
Robert T Barnum, *Manager*
EMP: 950
SALES (corp-wide): 131.4B **Publicly
Held**
SIC: 6035 6211 Federal savings banks;
security brokers & dealers
HQ: Jpmorgan Chase Bank, National Association
1111 Polaris Pkwy
Columbus OH 43240
614 436-3055

(P-9281)
ONEWEST BANK NA
3500 E 7th St, Long Beach (90804-5137)
PHONE..........................562 433-0971
Fax: 562 433-0975
EMP: 56
SALES (corp-wide): 876.3MM **Privately
Held**
SIC: 6035
HQ: Onewest Bank N.A.
888 E Walnut St
Pasadena CA 91103
626 535-4300

(P-9282)
PACIFIC STATE BANCORP
1899 W March Ln, Stockton (95207-6402)
PHONE..........................209 870-3214
Rick D Simas, *President*
Justin R Garner, *CFO*
Gary A Stewart, *Ch Credit Ofcr*
Justin Garner, *Vice Pres*
EMP: 89
SALES (est): 564.3K **Privately Held**
WEB: www.pacificstatebank.com
SIC: 6035 Savings institutions, federally
chartered

(P-9283)
PAN AMERICAN BANK FSB
18191 Von Karman Ave # 300, Irvine
(92612-7106)
PHONE..........................949 224-1917
Jim Vagim, *President*
EMP: 350
SQ FT: 20,000
SALES: 2MM
SALES (corp-wide): 20.5MM **Privately
Held**
WEB: www.panamerbank.com
SIC: 6035 Savings institutions, federally
chartered
PA: United Panam Financial Corp.
1071 Camelback St Ste 100
Newport Beach CA 92660
949 224-1226

(P-9284)
**PROVIDENT SAVINGS BANK
(HQ)**
6570 Magnolia Ave, Riverside
(92506-2410)
P.O. Box 59998 (92517-1998)
PHONE..........................951 782-6177
Craig G Blunden, *Ch of Bd*
Donavon Ternes, *President*
Lee Sunarto, *Treasurer*
David S Weiant,
Richard L Gale, *Senior VP*
EMP: 55
SALES: 68.5MM **Publicly Held**
WEB: www.myprovident.com
SIC: 6035 Federal savings & loan associations

(P-9285)
PROVIDENT SAVINGS BANK
Also Called: Provident Bank
6674 Brockton Ave, Riverside
(92506-3020)
PHONE..........................951 686-6060
Pam Cuthbertson, *Manager*
EMP: 100 **Publicly Held**
SIC: 6035 Federal savings & loan associations
HQ: Provident Savings Bank
6570 Magnolia Ave
Riverside CA 92506
951 782-6177

(P-9286)
TRACY BANCSHARES INC
1003 N Central Ave, Tracy (95376-3914)
PHONE..........................209 836-5111
Janis Mattos, *Branch Mgr*
John Strawn, *Vice Pres*
Shannon Richardson, *Assistant VP*
EMP: 51
SQ FT: 11,500
SALES (est): 4MM **Privately Held**
SIC: 6035 Savings institutions, federally
chartered

(P-9287)
UNIVERSAL BANK (PA)
3455 S Nogales St Fl 2, West Covina
(91792-5106)
PHONE..........................626 854-2818
Frank Chang, *President*
Dwayne Matsuda, *President*
Edgar Gatchlian, *Vice Pres*
Bobbe Sigler, *Director*
EMP: 53
SQ FT: 28,223
SALES: 13.4MM **Privately Held**
WEB: www.universalbank.com
SIC: 6035 Federal savings banks

6036 Savings Institutions, Except Federal

(P-9288)
EXCHANGE BANK (PA)
Also Called: Eb
545 4th St, Santa Rosa (95401-6323)
P.O. Box 403 (95402-0403)
PHONE..........................707 524-3000
Gary T Hartwick, *CEO*
Pam Maslak, *President*
Cyndi Perez, *President*
William R Schrader, *President*
Byron Webb, *President*

EMP: 135
SQ FT: 50,000
SALES: 106.6MM **Privately Held**
WEB: www.exchangebank.com
SIC: 6036 8741 6022 State savings
banks, not federally chartered; management services; state commercial banks

(P-9289)
**LUTHER BURBANK SAVINGS
(HQ)**
500 3rd St, Santa Rosa (95401-6321)
P.O. Box 1783 (95402-1783)
PHONE..........................707 578-9216
John Biggs, *President*
Victor S Trione, *Ch of Bd*
Ken Hense, *President*
Joanne Bell, *Vice Pres*
Jose Casillas, *Vice Pres*
EMP: 50
SQ FT: 11,000
SALES: 181.7MM **Publicly Held**
WEB: www.lutherburbanksavings.com
SIC: 6036 6035 Savings & loan associations, not federally chartered; federal savings & loan associations

(P-9290)
**MALAGA FINANCIAL
CORPORATION (PA)**
2514 Via Tejon, Palos Verdes Estates
(90274-1311)
PHONE..........................310 375-9000
Randy C Bowers, *President*
Jerry Donahue, *Ch of Bd*
Jasna Penich, *CFO*
Gayle Cdebaca, *Assoc VP*
Mel Hashimoto, *Vice Pres*
EMP: 88
SALES (est): 9.9MM **Privately Held**
SIC: 6036 State savings banks, not federally chartered

6061 Federal Credit Unions

(P-9291)
ALLIANCE CREDIT UNION (PA)
3315 Almaden Expy Ste 55, San Jose
(95118-1557)
P.O. Box 18460 (95158-8460)
PHONE..........................408 445-3386
Eileen M Lewis, *President*
Barbara Alumbaugh, *Bd of Directors*
Ram Misra, *Bd of Directors*
Larry Carter, *Vice Pres*
Sean Chambers, *Vice Pres*
EMP: 73 **EST:** 1952
SQ FT: 40,000
SALES: 13.4MM **Privately Held**
SIC: 6061 Federal credit unions

(P-9292)
**ALTAONE FEDERAL CREDIT
UNION (PA)**
Also Called: ALTA ONE FCU
701 S China Lake Blvd, Ridgecrest
(93555-5027)
P.O. Box 1209 (93556-1209)
PHONE..........................760 371-7000
Pamela Easley, *President*
Beverly Wagner, *President*
Bill Christensen, *Officer*
Brandon Iversen, *Officer*
Linda Fisher, *Office Mgr*
EMP: 114 **EST:** 1947
SQ FT: 33,000
SALES: 29.2MM **Privately Held**
WEB: www.altaone.net
SIC: 6061 Federal credit unions

(P-9293)
**ARROWHEAD CENTRAL CREDIT
UNION (PA)**
8686 Haven Ave, Rancho Cucamonga
(91730-9109)
P.O. Box 4100 (91729-4100)
PHONE..........................866 212-4333
Darin Woinarowicz, *CEO*
Raymond Mesler, *CFO*
Marie A Alonzo, *Chairman*
Doug Hallen, *Treasurer*
Susan Conjurski, *Exec VP*
EMP: 301 **EST:** 1949
SQ FT: 40,000

SALES: 42.5MM **Privately Held**
SIC: 6061 Federal credit unions

(P-9294)
BAY FEDERAL CREDIT UNION (PA)
3333 Clares St, Capitola (95010-2564)
PHONE..........................831 479-6000
Dennis Osmer, *Chairman*
H Duane Smith, *Vice Chairman*
Michael Leung, *Treasurer*
Manny Escarcega, *Assoc VP*
Ivonne J Guzman, *Admin Sec*
EMP: 160
SALES: 33MM **Privately Held**
WEB: www.bayfed.com
SIC: 6061 Federal credit unions

(P-9295)
CAL TECH EMPLYEES FDERAL CR UN (PA)
Also Called: CALTECH EFCU
528 Foothill Blvd, La Canada Flintridge (91011-3506)
P.O. Box 11001 (91012-6001)
PHONE..........................818 952-4444
Richard Harris, *Principal*
Stephen L Proia, *Ch of Bd*
Richard L Harris, *President*
Willis Chapman, *Vice Ch Bd*
Yuling LI, *Officer*
EMP: 84
SALES: 47.2MM **Privately Held**
WEB: www.caltech.edu
SIC: 6061 Federal credit unions

(P-9296)
CALIFORNIA COAST CREDIT UNION
5890 Pcf Ctr Blvd Frnt, San Diego (92121)
PHONE..........................858 495-1600
Alan Carithers, *Branch Mgr*
EMP: 145
SALES (corp-wide): 77.2MM **Privately Held**
SIC: 6061 Federal credit unions
PA: California Coast Credit Union
9201 Spectrum Center Blvd # 300
San Diego CA 92123
858 495-1600

(P-9297)
CALIFORNIA COAST CREDIT UNION
8131 Allison Ave, La Mesa (91942-5523)
P.O. Box 502080, San Diego (92150-2080)
PHONE..........................858 495-1600
Gail Lillie, *Branch Mgr*
EMP: 55
SALES (corp-wide): 77.2MM **Privately Held**
WEB: www.calcoastcu.org
SIC: 6061 Federal credit unions
PA: California Coast Credit Union
9201 Spectrum Center Blvd # 300
San Diego CA 92123
858 495-1600

(P-9298)
CALIFORNIA CREDIT UNION
11331 Camarillo St, North Hollywood (91602-1216)
PHONE..........................818 291-5434
Chuck Schafer, *Vice Pres*
EMP: 86
SALES (corp-wide): 104MM **Privately Held**
SIC: 6061 Federal credit unions
PA: The California Credit Union
701 N Brand Blvd Ste 100
Glendale CA 91203
818 291-6700

(P-9299)
CALIFORNIA CREDIT UNION
333 S Beaudry Ave Ste 215, Los Angeles (90017-5141)
PHONE..........................213 975-1254
Harvey Teresa, *Principal*
Ted Fujimoto, *Bd of Directors*
EMP: 51
SALES (corp-wide): 104MM **Privately Held**
SIC: 6061 Federal credit unions

PA: The California Credit Union
701 N Brand Blvd Ste 100
Glendale CA 91203
818 291-6700

(P-9300)
CALIFORNIA CREDIT UNION
3550 W Century Blvd # 103, Inglewood (90303-1242)
PHONE..........................310 671-1080
Shawn T Thompson, *Branch Mgr*
EMP: 86
SALES (corp-wide): 104MM **Privately Held**
SIC: 6061 Federal credit unions
PA: The California Credit Union
701 N Brand Blvd Ste 100
Glendale CA 91203
818 291-6700

(P-9301)
CHEVRON FEDERAL CREDIT UNION (PA)
500 12th St Ste 200, Oakland (94607-4084)
P.O. Box 2069 (94604-2069)
PHONE..........................888 884-4630
James Mooney, *President*
Heather Pender, *Officer*
Wanda Quinto, *Officer*
Neil Sawyer, *Vice Pres*
John Canavan, *Executive*
EMP: 54 **EST:** 1935
SQ FT: 25,663
SALES: 113.6MM **Privately Held**
SIC: 6061 Federal credit unions

(P-9302)
COAST CENTRAL CREDIT UNION (PA)
2650 Harrison Ave, Eureka (95501-3223)
PHONE..........................707 445-8801
Dean Christensen, *President*
Tom Noonan, *Treasurer*
Robert Taborski, *Officer*
Ed Christians, *Vice Pres*
Ches Meierding, *Vice Pres*
EMP: 150 **EST:** 1932
SQ FT: 17,000
SALES: 43.1MM **Privately Held**
WEB: www.coastccu.org
SIC: 6061 Federal credit unions

(P-9303)
CREDIT UNION SOUTHERN CAL (PA)
8028 Greenleaf Ave, Whittier (90602-2109)
P.O. Box 200 (90608-0200)
PHONE..........................562 698-8326
Dave Gunderson, *President*
Ed Fost, *COO*
Peter Putnam, *CFO*
Debbie Childs, *Exec VP*
▲ **EMP:** 52
SQ FT: 12,000
SALES: 50.6MM **Privately Held**
WEB: www.cusocal.com
SIC: 6061 Federal credit unions

(P-9304)
CREDIT UNION SOUTHERN CAL
8101 E Kaiser Blvd, Anaheim (92808-2243)
P.O. Box 27666 (92809-0122)
PHONE..........................562 698-8326
Dave Gunderson, *CEO*
EMP: 119
SALES (corp-wide): 50.6MM **Privately Held**
WEB: www.cusocal.com
SIC: 6061 Federal credit unions
PA: Credit Union Of Southern California
8028 Greenleaf Ave
Whittier CA 90602
562 698-8326

(P-9305)
EDUCATIONAL EMPLOYEES CR UN (PA)
2222 W Shaw Ave, Fresno (93711-3419)
PHONE..........................559 437-7700
Barbara Thomas, *Chairman*
Elizabeth Dooley, *President*
Rick Browning, *Treasurer*
Charles Ciapponi, *Officer*

Julie Mattern, *Vice Pres*
EMP: 110 **EST:** 1934
SQ FT: 44,000
SALES: 89.5MM **Privately Held**
SIC: 6061 Federal credit unions

(P-9306)
FINANCIAL PARTNERS CREDIT UN (PA)
7800 Imperial Hwy, Downey (90242-3457)
P.O. Box 7005 (90241-7005)
PHONE..........................562 904-3000
John Crites, *Ch of Bd*
Nader Moghaddam, *President*
Albert Hernandez, *COO*
Joe Brancucci, *Officer*
Mark Penn, *Officer*
EMP: 73
SQ FT: 32,000
SALES: 47MM **Privately Held**
WEB: www.fpcu.org
SIC: 6061 Federal credit unions

(P-9307)
FIREFIGHTERS FIRST CREDIT UN (PA)
815 Colorado Blvd, Los Angeles (90041-1720)
PHONE..........................323 254-1700
Dixie Abramian, *CEO*
Ronald Jackson, *Treasurer*
Ceasar Del Toro, *Officer*
Timothy Lewison, *Vice Pres*
Ceasar Deltoro, *Business Dir*
EMP: 138
SQ FT: 25,000
SALES: 46.2MM **Privately Held**
WEB: www.lafirecu.org
SIC: 6061 Federal credit unions

(P-9308)
FIRST CITY CREDIT UNION (PA)
717 W Temple St Ste 400, Los Angeles (90012-2632)
P.O. Box 86008 (90086-0008)
PHONE..........................213 482-3477
James D Likens, *Ch of Bd*
Cindy Sprankle, *President*
Steve Punch, *CEO*
Terry O'Steen, *COO*
Richard Reese, *CFO*
EMP: 105
SQ FT: 24,896
SALES: 20.9MM **Privately Held**
SIC: 6061 Federal credit unions

(P-9309)
FIRST ENTERTAINMENT CREDIT UN (PA)
6735 Forest Lawn Dr # 100, Los Angeles (90068-1055)
P.O. Box 100 (90078-0100)
PHONE..........................323 851-3673
Charles A Bruen, *President*
Lucy Wander-Perna, *Ch of Bd*
Lisa Landt, *CFO*
Irwin Jacobson, *Treasurer*
Kasha Reed, *Branch Mgr*
EMP: 80 **EST:** 1998
SQ FT: 57,000
SALES: 49MM **Privately Held**
SIC: 6061 Federal credit unions

(P-9310)
FIRST TECHNOLOGY FEDERAL CR UN (PA)
2702 Orchard Pkwy, San Jose (95134-2012)
PHONE..........................855 855-8805
Greg A Mitchell, *President*
Scott Jenner, *President*
Hank Sigmon, *CFO*
Monique Little,
Jay Franklin, *Vice Pres*
EMP: 100
SALES: 564.7MM **Privately Held**
WEB: www.1sttech.com
SIC: 6061 Federal credit unions

(P-9311)
FIRST TECHNOLOGY FEDERAL CR UN
1011 Sunset Blvd Ste 210, Rocklin (95765-3782)
PHONE..........................855 855-8805

Greg A Mitchell, *CEO*
Noel Magana, *Manager*
EMP: 211
SALES (corp-wide): 564.7MM **Privately Held**
SIC: 6061 Federal credit unions
PA: First Technology Federal Credit Union
2702 Orchard Pkwy
San Jose CA 95134
855 855-8805

(P-9312)
FIRST US COMMUNITY CREDIT UN (PA)
580 University Ave # 100, Sacramento (95825-6528)
PHONE..........................916 576-5700
Carol Hauck, *CEO*
Richard Cochran, *President*
Brian W Doyle, *Chairman*
Richard D Cochran, *Treasurer*
Richard Bender, *Admin Sec*
EMP: 72
SQ FT: 10,000
SALES: 11.9MM **Privately Held**
SIC: 6061 Federal credit unions

(P-9313)
FOOTHILL FEDERAL CREDIT UNION (PA)
30 S 1st Ave, Arcadia (91006-3604)
P.O. Box 660130 (91066-0130)
PHONE..........................626 445-0950
Brian Hall, *President*
Mike Abata, *Ch of Bd*
Fred Weiss, *Chairman*
Mike Allee, *Treasurer*
Rick Ashley, *Bd of Directors*
EMP: 50
SQ FT: 12,077
SALES: 14.5MM **Privately Held**
WEB: www.foothillfederalcreditunion.com
SIC: 6061 Federal credit unions

(P-9314)
FRONTWAVE CREDIT UNION (PA)
1278 Rocky Point Dr, Oceanside (92056-5867)
PHONE..........................760 430-7511
David L Davis, *CEO*
Michelle Denton, *CFO*
Carrie Foster, *CFO*
Todd Kern, *Chief Mktg Ofcr*
Nancy Harvey, *Officer*
EMP: 107
SQ FT: 22,000
SALES: 29.2MM **Privately Held**
WEB: www.pmcu.com
SIC: 6061 Federal credit unions

(P-9315)
HANIN FEDERAL CREDIT UNION (PA)
3700 Wilshire Blvd # 104, Los Angeles (90010-2902)
PHONE..........................213 368-9000
Howard Ree, *Chairman*
Ike Park, *Branch Mgr*
Kim Michael, *Technology*
EMP: 50
SQ FT: 2,190
SALES: 1.8MM **Privately Held**
WEB: www.haninfcu.org
SIC: 6061 Federal credit unions

(P-9316)
HERITAGE COMMUNITY CREDIT UN (PA)
10399 Old Placerville Rd, Sacramento (95827-2506)
P.O. Box 790, Rancho Cordova (95741-0790)
PHONE..........................916 364-1700
Judy Flores, *CEO*
Matt Harms, *CFO*
Brandon Ivie, *CFO*
Christine Haroldson, *Vice Pres*
Chad Suggs, *Vice Pres*
EMP: 50
SALES: 6.8MM **Privately Held**
SIC: 6061 Federal credit unions

(P-9317)
HERITAGE COMMUNITY CREDIT UN
10399 Old Clasaville Rd, Rancho Cordova (95670)
PHONE................................916 364-1700
Steve Pogemiller, *Branch Mgr*
EMP: 50
SALES (corp-wide): 6.8MM **Privately Held**
SIC: 6061 Federal credit unions
PA: Heritage Community Credit Union
10399 Old Placerville Rd
Sacramento CA 95827
916 364-1700

(P-9318)
KERN FEDERAL CREDIT UNION
1717 Truxtun Ave, Bakersfield (93301-5102)
PHONE................................661 327-9461
Brandon Ivie, *CEO*
Brenda O'Doherty, *President*
George Fuentes, *Loan Officer*
Ashley Morrison,
EMP: 65
SQ FT: 17,000
SALES: 9.1MM **Privately Held**
WEB: www.kernfcu.org
SIC: 6061 6163 Federal credit unions; loan brokers

(P-9319)
KERN MEMBER INSURANCE SERVICES
Also Called: Kern Federal Credit Union
1717 Truxtun Ave, Bakersfield (93301-5102)
P.O. Box 1667 (93302-1667)
PHONE................................661 327-9461
Deann Straub, *President*
Gloria Scales, *Vice Pres*
Susan Jones, *Principal*
EMP: 50
SALES: 7.8MM **Privately Held**
WEB: www.kernfederalcreditunion.com
SIC: 6061 Federal credit unions

(P-9320)
KERN SCHOOLS FEDERAL CREDIT UN (PA)
Also Called: KSFCU
11500 Bolthouse Dr, Bakersfield (93311-8822)
P.O. Box 9506 (93389-9506)
PHONE................................661 833-7900
Stephen P Renock IV, *President*
Neil Marshall, *CFO*
Scott Begin, *Bd of Directors*
Shelli Anglim, *Admin Sec*
Shari Butler, *Exec Sec*
EMP: 60
SQ FT: 18,000
SALES: 51.6MM **Privately Held**
WEB: www.ksfcu.com
SIC: 6061 Federal credit unions

(P-9321)
KINECTA FEDERAL CREDIT UNION (PA)
1440 Rosecrans Ave, Manhattan Beach (90266-3702)
PHONE................................310 643-5400
Keith Sultemeier, *CEO*
Randall G Dotemoto, *President*
Douglas C Wicks, *President*
Steve Lumm, *CEO*
Joseph E Whitaker, *COO*
EMP: 250
SQ FT: 80,000
SALES: 159.4MM **Privately Held**
SIC: 6061 Federal credit unions

(P-9322)
LOGIX FEDERAL CREDIT UNION (PA)
2340 N Hollywood Way, Burbank (91505-1124)
P.O. Box 10249 (91510-0249)
PHONE................................888 718-5328
Ana Fonseca, *CEO*
Dave Styler, *COO*
Sean Brown, *Officer*
Kara Buss, *Officer*
Ariel Cabrera, *Officer*

EMP: 210
SQ FT: 75,000
SALES: 220.4MM **Privately Held**
SIC: 6061 Federal credit unions

(P-9323)
LOS ANGELES FEDERAL CREDIT UN (PA)
300 S Glendale Ave # 100, Glendale (91205-1752)
PHONE................................818 242-8640
John T DEA, *CEO*
Richard Lie, *CFO*
Anthony Cuevas, *Senior VP*
Leta Cook, *Vice Pres*
Craig Stalnaker, *Vice Pres*
EMP: 100
SQ FT: 40,000
SALES: 34.8MM **Privately Held**
SIC: 6061 Federal credit unions

(P-9324)
MERCED SCHOOL EMPLOYEES F C U (PA)
Also Called: MSEFCU
1021 Olivewood Dr, Merced (95348-1218)
P.O. Box 1349 (95341-1349)
PHONE................................209 383-5550
Nancy Deavours, *President*
Jennifer Riedeman, *Admin Sec*
EMP: 52 **EST:** 1954
SQ FT: 16,500
SALES: 15MM **Privately Held**
WEB: www.mercedschoolcu.org
SIC: 6061 Federal credit unions

(P-9325)
MERIWEST CREDIT UNION (PA)
5615 Chesbro Ave Ste 100, San Jose (95123-3057)
P.O. Box 530953 (95153-5353)
PHONE................................408 363-3200
Toll Free:................................877 -
Julie A Kirsch, *Principal*
Steven G Johnson, *CEO*
Christopher Owen, *CEO*
Brian Hennessey, *CFO*
Hudson Lee, *CFO*
EMP: 130
SQ FT: 61,000
SALES: 54.4MM **Privately Held**
WEB: www.meriwest.com
SIC: 6061 Federal credit unions

(P-9326)
MISSION FEDERAL CREDIT UNION (PA)
5785 Oberlin Dr Ste 312, San Diego (92121-3752)
PHONE................................858 546-2184
Debra Schwartz, *CEO*
Jennifer Collins, *President*
Vince Nowicki, *President*
Charles Rion, *President*
Ronald Arauj, *CFO*
EMP: 550
SQ FT: 59,956
SALES: 83.4MM **Privately Held**
SIC: 6061 Federal credit unions

(P-9327)
MISSION FEDERAL SERVICES LLC (PA)
10325 Meanley Dr, San Diego (92131-3011)
P.O. Box 919023 (92191-9023)
PHONE................................858 524-2850
Debra Schwartz, *CEO*
Rose Hartley, *COO*
Peter Sainato, *CFO*
Gary M Devan, *Senior VP*
Richard Hartley, *Senior VP*
EMP: 150
SQ FT: 55,000
SALES: 111.3MM **Privately Held**
WEB: www.missionfcu.org
SIC: 6061 Federal credit unions

(P-9328)
MOCSE FEDERAL CREDIT UNION
3600 Coffee Rd, Modesto (95355-1164)
PHONE................................209 572-3600
Tracey Kerr, *President*
Charlie Rodgers, *CFO*

Justin Garcia, *Technical Staff*
EMP: 82
SQ FT: 20,000
SALES: 9MM **Privately Held**
WEB: www.mocse.org
SIC: 6061 6062 Federal credit unions; state credit unions

(P-9329)
MONTEREY CREDIT UNION (PA)
501 E Franklin St, Monterey (93940-3077)
P.O. Box 3288 (93942-3288)
PHONE................................831 647-1000
David Laredo, *Chairman*
Ed Brown, *Vice Chairman*
J Stewart Fuller, *CEO*
Penprase Jim, *CFO*
Bibi Lamere, *Officer*
EMP: 55
SQ FT: 10,000
SALES: 8.9MM **Privately Held**
SIC: 6061 Federal credit unions

(P-9330)
NAVY FEDERAL CREDIT UNION
2040 Harbison Dr, Vacaville (95687-3906)
PHONE................................888 842-6328
Patsy Vanouwerkerk, *Branch Mgr*
EMP: 122
SALES (corp-wide): 5.3B **Privately Held**
SIC: 6061 Federal credit unions
PA: Navy Federal Credit Union
820 Follin Ln Se
Vienna VA 22180
703 255-8000

(P-9331)
NOBLE CREDIT UNION (PA)
2580 W Shaw Ln Frnt, Fresno (93711-2776)
P.O. Box 8027 (93747-8027)
PHONE................................559 252-5000
Karen B Cobb, *Ch of Bd*
Doug Papagni, *Chairman*
Linzie Daniel, *Treasurer*
Mary Ann Rogozinski, *Treasurer*
Robert Vandergon, *Vice Ch Bd*
EMP: 50
SQ FT: 12,000
SALES: 29.4MM **Privately Held**
WEB: www.fresnocfcu.org
SIC: 6061 Federal credit unions

(P-9332)
ORANGE COUNTYS CREDIT UNION (PA)
1721 E Saint Andrew Pl, Santa Ana (92705-4934)
P.O. Box 11777 (92711-1777)
PHONE................................714 755-5900
Shruti S Miyashiro, *President*
Ryan Huff, *President*
Amanda Verive, *President*
Greg Krause, *CFO*
Dan Dillon, *Chairman*
EMP: 157
SALES: 53.2MM **Privately Held**
SIC: 6061 Federal credit unions

(P-9333)
PACIFIC SERVICE CREDIT UNION (PA)
3000 Clayton Rd, Concord (94519-2731)
P.O. Box 8191, Walnut Creek (94596-8191)
PHONE................................888 858-6878
Jenna Lampson, *President*
Lawrence Labonte, *CFO*
David Sena, *Chairman*
Vicki Turano, *Treasurer*
Lawrence D Labonte, *Senior VP*
EMP: 76
SQ FT: 23,689
SALES: 35MM **Privately Held**
SIC: 6061 Federal credit unions

(P-9334)
PATELCO CREDIT UNION
310 Hartz Ave, Danville (94526-3308)
PHONE................................925 785-9487
EMP: 85
SALES (corp-wide): 211.7MM **Privately Held**
SIC: 6061 Federal credit unions

PA: Patelco Credit Union
5050 Hopyard Rd
Pleasanton CA 94588
800 358-8228

(P-9335)
PATELCO CREDIT UNION (PA)
5050 Hopyard Rd, Pleasanton (94588-3353)
P.O. Box 8020 (94588-8601)
PHONE................................800 358-8228
Erin Mendez, *CEO*
Debra Chaw, *Vice Chairman*
Jesse Rivera, *Vice Chairman*
Sue Gruber, *CFO*
Richard Wada,
EMP: 250 **EST:** 1936
SQ FT: 36,000
SALES: 211.7MM **Privately Held**
WEB: www.patelco.org
SIC: 6061 Federal credit unions

(P-9336)
PRIORITY ONE CREDIT UNION (PA)
1631 Huntington Dr, South Pasadena (91030-4746)
PHONE................................323 682-1999
Diedra Brooks, *Ch of Bd*
Celinda Grande, *President*
Charles Wiggington Sr, *President*
Manuel Gatmaitan, *CFO*
Thomas Gathers Jr, *Treasurer*
EMP: 78
SQ FT: 2,000
SALES: 5.1MM **Privately Held**
SIC: 6061 Federal credit unions

(P-9337)
REDWOOD CREDIT UNION
1129 S Cloverdale Blvd A, Cloverdale (95425-4482)
PHONE................................800 479-7928
Negri Cynthia, *Vice Pres*
Fitzpatrick Melissa, *Analyst*
EMP: 77
SALES (corp-wide): 158.2MM **Privately Held**
SIC: 6061 Federal credit unions
PA: Redwood Credit Union
3033 Cleveland Ave # 100
Santa Rosa CA 95403
707 545-4000

(P-9338)
REDWOOD CREDIT UNION (PA)
3033 Cleveland Ave # 100, Santa Rosa (95403-2126)
P.O. Box 6104 (95406-0104)
PHONE................................707 545-4000
Brett Martinez, *President*
Dina Miller, *President*
Judy James, *Bd of Directors*
Jason Ehn, *Officer*
Shanti Knapp, *Officer*
EMP: 190
SQ FT: 20,000
SALES: 158.2MM **Privately Held**
WEB: www.redwoodcu.org
SIC: 6061 Federal credit unions

(P-9339)
REDWOOD CREDIT UNION
1390 Market St, San Francisco (94102-5402)
PHONE................................800 479-7928
EMP: 52
SALES (corp-wide): 158.2MM **Privately Held**
SIC: 6061 Federal credit unions
PA: Redwood Credit Union
3033 Cleveland Ave # 100
Santa Rosa CA 95403
707 545-4000

(P-9340)
SAFE AMERICA CREDIT UNION (PA)
6001 Gibraltar Dr, Pleasanton (94588-2707)
P.O. Box 11269 (94588-1269)
PHONE................................925 734-4111
Barry Roach, *CEO*
Chuck Dunbar, *CFO*
Frank Zampella, *Chairman*
Janice Cox, *Officer*

PRODUCTS & SVCS

Candy Davis, *Vice Pres*
EMP: 70
SQ FT: 27,000
SALES: 15.3MM **Privately Held**
WEB: www.safeamerica.com
SIC: 6061 Federal credit unions

(P-9341)
SAFE CREDIT UNION
Also Called: Financial Transaction
9055 Woodcreek Oaks Blvd # 150, Ro-
seville (95747-5159)
PHONE..........................916 979-7233
Serna Yong, *Branch Mgr*
EMP: 50
SALES (corp-wide): 91.9MM **Privately
Held**
SIC: 6061 Federal credit unions
PA: Safe Credit Union
2295 Iron Point Rd # 100
Folsom CA 95630
916 979-7233

(P-9342)
SAG- AFTRA FEDERAL
134 N Kenwood St, Burbank (91505-4201)
P.O. Box 11419 (91510-1419)
PHONE..........................818 562-3400
Randy Kahn, *Chairman*
Roger Runyan, *CEO*
Sid Henderson, *Exec VP*
Phillip Weiss, *Vice Pres*
Samuel Ketsoyan, *Loan Officer*
EMP: 52
SQ FT: 5,500
SALES: 9.7MM **Privately Held**
SIC: 6061 Federal credit unions

(P-9343)
SAN DIEGO COUNTY CREDIT
UNION (PA)
6545 Sequence Dr, San Diego
(92121-4363)
PHONE..........................877 732-2848
Irene Oberbauer, *President*
Theresa Halleck, *President*
Robert Marchand, *CFO*
Valerie Kwiatkowski, *Exec VP*
Heather Moshier, *Exec VP*
▲ **EMP:** 239 **EST:** 1938
SQ FT: 50,000
SALES: 210.8MM **Privately Held**
WEB: www.sdccu.net
SIC: 6061 Federal credit unions

(P-9344)
SAN FRANCISCO FEDERAL CR
UN (PA)
770 Golden Gate Ave Fl 1, San Francisco
(94102-3194)
PHONE..........................415 775-5377
William Wolverton, *CEO*
Luenna Kim, *Ch of Bd*
Todd Rydstrom, *Vice Chairman*
Steve Ho, *COO*
Jelena Ewart, *Treasurer*
▲ **EMP:** 250
SQ FT: 35,500
SALES: 37.9MM **Privately Held**
WEB: www.sffederalcu.org
SIC: 6061 Federal credit unions

(P-9345)
SAN MATEO CREDIT UNION (PA)
350 Convention Way # 300, Redwood City
(94063-1436)
P.O. Box 910 (94064-0910)
PHONE..........................650 363-1725
Berry Jolette, *President*
Amanda Lum, *Partner*
Magda Gonzalez, *Ch of Bd*
Robert Carter, *President*
Motley Snuth, *Treasurer*
▲ **EMP:** 55
SQ FT: 18,300
SALES: 49.2MM **Privately Held**
SIC: 6061 Federal credit unions

(P-9346)
SAN MATEO CREDIT UNION
1515 S El Camino Real # 100, San Mateo
(94402-3099)
PHONE..........................650 363-1725
Preston Monroe, *Principal*
Adela Balea, *Officer*
EMP: 191

SALES (est): 6.8MM
SALES (corp-wide): 49.2MM **Privately
Held**
SIC: 6061 Federal credit unions
PA: San Mateo Credit Union
350 Convention Way # 300
Redwood City CA 94063
650 363-1725

(P-9347)
SANTA CLARA CNTY FEDERAL
CR UN (PA)
1641 N 1st St Ste 245, San Jose
(95112-4519)
PHONE..........................408 282-0700
Mike Delmonico, *CEO*
Divine David, *Officer*
Joseph Bonacci, *Vice Pres*
Linda Elrod, *Vice Pres*
Michael Kadel, *Vice Pres*
EMP: 55 **EST:** 1950
SQ FT: 42,000
SALES: 24.5MM **Privately Held**
SIC: 6061 Federal credit unions

(P-9348)
SCE FEDERAL CREDIT UNION
(PA)
Also Called: SCE FCU
12701 Schabarum Ave, Baldwin Park
(91706-6807)
P.O. Box 8017, El Monte (91734-2317)
PHONE..........................626 960-6888
Dennis Huber, *CEO*
George Poitou, *COO*
Daniel Rader, *CFO*
Kitty Hunter-Warringt, *Officer*
David Vidaurri, *Branch Mgr*
EMP: 90 **EST:** 1952
SQ FT: 30,000
SALES: 32.7MM **Privately Held**
WEB: www.scefcu.org
SIC: 6061 Federal credit unions

(P-9349)
SCHOOLSFIRST FEDERAL
CREDIT UN (PA)
2115 N Broadway, Santa Ana
(92706-2613)
P.O. Box 11547 (92711-1547)
PHONE..........................714 258-4000
Bill Cheney, *President*
Cynthia Covarrubias, *Officer*
Adam Jacoby, *Officer*
Martha Monzon, *Exec VP*
Emilio Arenas, *Vice Pres*
EMP: 270
SALES: 497.6MM **Privately Held**
SIC: 6061 Federal credit unions

(P-9350)
SEA WEST CAST GARD FDRAL
CR UN (PA)
8750 Mountain Blvd, Oakland
(94605-4500)
P.O. Box 4949 (94605-6949)
PHONE..........................510 568-4100
Tom Doherty, *CEO*
EMP: 56 **EST:** 1959
SQ FT: 12,000
SALES: 9.9MM **Privately Held**
SIC: 6061 Federal credit unions

(P-9351)
SESLOC FEDERAL CREDIT
UNION (PA)
3855 Broad St, San Luis Obispo
(93401-7109)
P.O. Box 5360 (93403-5360)
PHONE..........................805 543-1816
Bertha Foxford, *President*
Andy Bechinsky, *Senior VP*
Micki Myall, *Vice Pres*
Travis Ruppe, *Corp Comm Staff*
Colleen Murphy, *Manager*
EMP: 77
SQ FT: 19,700
SALES: 28.6MM **Privately Held**
WEB: www.sesloc.com
SIC: 6061 Federal credit unions

(P-9352)
SIERRA CENTRAL CREDIT
UNION (PA)
1351 Harter Pkwy, Yuba City (95993-2604)
PHONE..........................530 671-3009
John Cassidy, *CEO*
Ron Sweeney, *Exec VP*
Rhonda Eliason, *Purchasing*
EMP: 90
SQ FT: 8,000
SALES: 38.1MM **Privately Held**
WEB: www.sierracentral.com
SIC: 6061 Federal credit unions

(P-9353)
SKYONE FEDERAL CREDIT
UNION (PA)
14600 Aviation Blvd, Hawthorne
(90250-6656)
PHONE..........................310 491-7500
Eileen C Rivera, *CEO*
Amy Chambers, *COO*
Shannon Doiron, *Chief Mktg Ofcr*
Anni Haroutunian, *Officer*
Armando Gonzalez, *Vice Pres*
EMP: 58
SQ FT: 40,000
SALES: 18.4MM **Privately Held**
SIC: 6061 Federal credit unions

(P-9354)
SPECTRUM CREDIT UNION
500 12th St Ste 200, Oakland
(94607-4084)
PHONE..........................510 251-6000
Jim Mooney, *CEO*
EMP: 200
SALES (est): 10.4MM **Privately Held**
SIC: 6061 Federal credit unions

(P-9355)
STANFORD FEDERAL CREDIT
UNION (PA)
Also Called: SFCU
1860 Embarcadero Rd # 200, Palo Alto
(94303-3320)
P.O. Box 10690 (94303-0843)
PHONE..........................650 725-1000
Jane S Duperrault, *Ch of Bd*
Tana Hutchison, *Treasurer*
Brian Thornton, *Vice Pres*
Jerry L Jobe, *Admin Sec*
Michael A Hindery, *Director*
EMP: 61
SALES: 84.9MM **Privately Held**
SIC: 6061 Federal credit unions

(P-9356)
STAR ONE CREDIT UNION (PA)
1306 Bordeaux Dr, Sunnyvale
(94089-1005)
P.O. Box 3643 (94088-3643)
PHONE..........................408 543-5202
Rick Heldebrant, *President*
Scott Dunlap, *Treasurer*
Maricela Avelar, *Officer*
Nya Munday, *Officer*
Elizabeth Rodriguez, *Officer*
EMP: 107
SQ FT: 25,000
SALES: 229.2MM **Privately Held**
SIC: 6061 Federal credit unions

(P-9357)
TELESIS COMMUNITY CREDIT
UNION (PA)
9301 Winnetka Ave, Chatsworth
(91311-6069)
PHONE..........................818 885-1226
Grace Mayo, *President*
Jean Faenza, *Exec VP*
EMP: 90
SQ FT: 17,000
SALES: 14.9MM **Privately Held**
SIC: 6061 6163 Federal credit unions;
loan brokers

(P-9358)
TRAVIS CREDIT UNION
1300 E Covell Blvd, Davis (95616-1300)
PHONE..........................707 449-4000
EMP: 500

SALES (corp-wide): 122.2MM **Privately
Held**
SIC: 6061 6062 Federal credit unions;
state credit unions
PA: Travis Credit Union
1 Travis Way
Vacaville CA 95687
707 449-4000

(P-9359)
TRAVIS CREDIT UNION
1796 Tuolumne St, Vallejo (94589-2619)
PHONE..........................800 877-8328
EMP: 500
SALES (corp-wide): 122.2MM **Privately
Held**
SIC: 6061 6022 6021 6029 Federal
credit unions; state commercial banks;
national commercial banks; commercial
banks
PA: Travis Credit Union
1 Travis Way
Vacaville CA 95687
707 449-4000

(P-9360)
TRAVIS CREDIT UNION
2095 Diamond Blvd Ste 115, Concord
(94520-5832)
PHONE..........................800 877-8328
Travis Credit, *Owner*
EMP: 500
SALES (corp-wide): 122.2MM **Privately
Held**
SIC: 6061 6062 Federal credit unions;
state credit unions
PA: Travis Credit Union
1 Travis Way
Vacaville CA 95687
707 449-4000

(P-9361)
TRAVIS CREDIT UNION
3263 Claremont Way, NAPA (94558-3313)
PHONE..........................800 877-8328
Marlene Myers, *Branch Mgr*
EMP: 500
SALES (corp-wide): 122.2MM **Privately
Held**
SIC: 6061 6022 6029 Federal credit
unions; state commercial banks; commer-
cial banks
PA: Travis Credit Union
1 Travis Way
Vacaville CA 95687
707 449-4000

(P-9362)
TRAVIS CREDIT UNION (PA)
1 Travis Way, Vacaville (95687-3276)
P.O. Box 2069 (95696-2069)
PHONE..........................707 449-4000
Patsy Vanouwerkerk, *CEO*
Damian Alarcon, *Officer*
Jessica Leal, *Officer*
John Caladim, *Vice Pres*
Marie Keen, *Vice Pres*
EMP: 300
SQ FT: 12,000
SALES: 122.2MM **Privately Held**
SIC: 6061 Federal credit unions

(P-9363)
TRAVIS CREDIT UNION
1515 K St, Sacramento (95814-4051)
PHONE..........................916 443-1446
EMP: 500
SALES (corp-wide): 122.2MM **Privately
Held**
SIC: 6061 Federal credit unions
PA: Travis Credit Union
1 Travis Way
Vacaville CA 95687
707 449-4000

(P-9364)
TRAVIS CREDIT UNION
1194 W Olive Ave, Merced (95348-1952)
PHONE..........................209 723-0732
Patsy Vanouwerkerk, *CEO*
EMP: 500
SALES (corp-wide): 122.2MM **Privately
Held**
SIC: 6061 Federal credit unions

PA: Travis Credit Union
1 Travis Way
Vacaville CA 95687
707 449-4000

(P-9365)
TRAVIS CREDIT UNION
11 Cernon St, Vacaville (95688-2803)
PHONE.............................707 449-4000
Phil Christiansen, *Manager*
EMP: 500
SALES (corp-wide): 122.2MM **Privately Held**
SIC: 6061 Federal credit unions
PA: Travis Credit Union
1 Travis Way
Vacaville CA 95687
707 449-4000

(P-9366)
TRAVIS CREDIT UNION
2570 N Texas St, Fairfield (94533-1606)
PHONE.............................707 449-4000
Gloria Niccoli, *Manager*
EMP: 500
SALES (corp-wide): 122.2MM **Privately Held**
SIC: 6061 Federal credit unions
PA: Travis Credit Union
1 Travis Way
Vacaville CA 95687
707 449-4000

(P-9367)
TRAVIS CREDIT UNION
1372 E Main St, Woodland (95776-3551)
PHONE.............................800 877-8328
Jason Braga, *Manager*
EMP: 500
SALES (corp-wide): 122.2MM **Privately Held**
SIC: 6061 6022 6021 6029 Federal credit unions; state commercial banks; national commercial banks; commercial banks
PA: Travis Credit Union
1 Travis Way
Vacaville CA 95687
707 449-4000

(P-9368)
TRAVIS CREDIT UNION
2020 Harbison Dr, Vacaville (95687-3910)
PHONE.............................707 449-4000
Cathy Redman, *Branch Mgr*
EMP: 500
SALES (corp-wide): 122.2MM **Privately Held**
SIC: 6061 Federal credit unions
PA: Travis Credit Union
1 Travis Way
Vacaville CA 95687
707 449-4000

(P-9369)
TUCOEMAS FEDERAL CREDIT UNION (PA)
5222 W Cypress Ave, Visalia (93277-8305)
P.O. Box 5011 (93278-5011)
PHONE.............................559 737-5900
Linda Reese, *President*
Mike Ryan, *CFO*
Susan Warkentin, *Vice Pres*
Elizabeth Legaspi, *Personnel*
EMP: 97
SALES: 8.5MM **Privately Held**
SIC: 6061 Federal credit unions

(P-9370)
TUCOEMAS FEDERAL CREDIT UNION
2300 W Whitendale Ave, Visalia (93277-6131)
P.O. Box 5011 (93278-5011)
PHONE.............................559 429-7094
John McHarry, *Manager*
EMP: 54
SQ FT: 19,413
SALES (corp-wide): 8.5MM **Privately Held**
SIC: 6061 Federal credit unions
PA: Tucoemas Federal Credit Union
5222 W Cypress Ave
Visalia CA 93277
559 737-5900

(P-9371)
UNCLE CREDIT UNION (PA)
2100 Las Positas Ct, Livermore (94551-7301)
PHONE.............................925 447-5001
Harold Roundtree, *CEO*
Jason Eder, *President*
Fidela Hernandez, *President*
Jim Ott, *President*
Wendy Zanotelli, *COO*
▲ **EMP:** 58
SQ FT: 17,000
SALES: 15.1MM **Privately Held**
WEB: www.unclecu.com
SIC: 6061 Federal credit unions

(P-9372)
UNIFY FINANCIAL FEDERAL CR UN (PA)
1899 Western Way Ste 100, Torrance (90501-1146)
P.O. Box 10018, Manhattan Beach (90267-7518)
PHONE.............................310 536-5000
Gordon M Howe, *CEO*
Tracey Ewert, *Officer*
Susan Osa, *Assoc VP*
Scott Johnson, *Vice Pres*
Vicki Lynes, *Vice Pres*
EMP: 80 **EST:** 1958
SALES: 125.5MM **Privately Held**
WEB: www.western.org
SIC: 6061 Federal credit unions

(P-9373)
UNITED SVCS AMER FEDERAL CR UN (PA)
Also Called: USA Federal Credit Union
9999 Willow Creek Rd, San Diego (92131-1117)
PHONE.............................858 831-8100
Martin Cassell, *President*
Jim Bedinger, *Vice Pres*
Ron Davis, *Vice Pres*
Shannon Roffe, *Production*
EMP: 90
SQ FT: 42,000
SALES (est): 21MM **Privately Held**
WEB: www.usafed.org
SIC: 6061 Federal credit unions

(P-9374)
UNIVERSITY CREDIT UNION
1500 S Sepulveda Blvd, Los Angeles (90025-3312)
PHONE.............................310 477-6628
Charles Bumbarger, *President*
Tristan Dion Chen, *Chief Mktg Ofcr*
Jose Ascencio, *Officer*
Wendy Kollwitz, *Officer*
Patrick Aragon, *Vice Pres*
EMP: 104
SALES: 18.7MM **Privately Held**
SIC: 6061 Federal credit unions

(P-9375)
USC CREDIT UNION
3720 S Flower St, Los Angeles (90089-4303)
PHONE.............................213 821-7100
Gary J Perez, *President*
Alex Johnson, *Officer*
Gary Perez, *Executive*
Valerie Ives, *Branch Mgr*
David Schauer-West, *Technology*
EMP: 56
SQ FT: 4,000
SALES: 24.1MM
SALES (corp-wide): 4.9B **Privately Held**
SIC: 6061 Federal credit unions
PA: University Of Southern California
3720 S Flower St Fl 3
Los Angeles CA 90089
213 740-7762

(P-9376)
VALLEY FIRST CREDIT UNION (PA)
1419 J St, Modesto (95354-1014)
P.O. Box 1411 (95353-1411)
PHONE.............................209 549-8511
Hank Barrett, *Exec Dir*
Fred Cruz, *CEO*
Dennis Barta, *CFO*
Gary Hall, *Treasurer*

Ken Karn, *Vice Pres*
EMP: 90
SALES: 18.9MM **Privately Held**
SIC: 6061 Federal credit unions

(P-9377)
VENTURA COUNTY CREDIT UNION (PA)
2575 Vista Del Mar Dr, Ventura (93001-3900)
PHONE.............................805 477-4000
Joseph Schroeder, *President*
Beverly Armendariz, *President*
Sean McCulloch, *President*
Linda Sim, *CFO*
Erica Abara, *Officer*
EMP: 84
SQ FT: 22,500
SALES: 33.2MM **Privately Held**
SIC: 6061 Federal credit unions

(P-9378)
XCEED FINANCIAL CREDIT UNION (PA)
888 N Nash St, El Segundo (90245-2826)
PHONE.............................800 932-8222
Teresa Freeborn, *President*
Todd Helmerson, *Officer*
Michael Stavrakis, *Vice Pres*
Holly Phan, *Prgrmr*
Marina Perez, *Programmer Anys*
EMP: 96
SQ FT: 30,000
SALES: 33.7MM **Privately Held**
WEB: www.xfcu.org
SIC: 6061 Federal credit unions

6062 State Credit Unions

(P-9379)
1ST UNITED SERVICES CREDIT UN (PA)
5901 Gibraltar Dr, Pleasanton (94588-2718)
P.O. Box 11746 (94588-1746)
PHONE.............................800 649-0193
Victor Quint, *President*
Shirley Sifuentes, *COO*
Victoria Pipkin, *CFO*
Steve Stone,
Sarah Leslie, *Officer*
▲ **EMP:** 60
SQ FT: 20,000
SALES: 37.5MM **Privately Held**
SIC: 6062 State credit unions

(P-9380)
ALTURA CREDIT UNION (PA)
2847 Campus Pkwy, Riverside (92507-0906)
PHONE.............................888 883-7228
Toll Free:.............................888 -
Mark Hawkins, *President*
Diana Wilcox, *CFO*
Blanca Sanchez, *Officer*
Patty Sanchez, *Officer*
Ron Woodbury, *Exec VP*
EMP: 59
SQ FT: 60,000
SALES: 48.3MM **Privately Held**
SIC: 6062 State credit unions, not federally chartered

(P-9381)
AMERICAN FIRST CREDIT UNION (PA)
700 N Harbor Blvd, La Habra (90631-4026)
PHONE.............................562 691-1112
Jon Shigematsu, *CFO*
Tam Nguyen, *Vice Pres*
Kyle Young, *Executive*
Brian Thompson,
EMP: 96 **EST:** 1956
SQ FT: 10,000
SALES: 25.4MM **Privately Held**
SIC: 6062 State credit unions

(P-9382)
AMERICAS CHRISTIAN CREDIT UN (PA)
Also Called: Accu
2100 E Route 66 Ste 100, Glendora (91740-4623)
PHONE.............................626 208-5400
Mendell Thompson, *President*
Lucinda Garcia, *Officer*
Naomi Paris, *Officer*
Nicolette Harms, *Senior VP*
Terri Snyder, *Senior VP*
EMP: 61 **EST:** 1958
SQ FT: 22,000
SALES: 15.2MM **Privately Held**
SIC: 6062 State credit unions, not federally chartered

(P-9383)
CALIFORNIA COAST CREDIT UNION (PA)
9201 Spectrum Center Blvd # 300, San Diego (92123-1407)
P.O. Box 502080 (92150-2080)
PHONE.............................858 495-1600
Marla Shepard, *CEO*
Ruth Peshkoff, *Ch of Bd*
Carol Walker, *Senior VP*
Rene McKee, *Vice Pres*
Charles Wallace, *Vice Pres*
EMP: 74
SALES: 77.2MM **Privately Held**
WEB: www.calcoastcu.com
SIC: 6062 6163 State credit unions, not federally chartered; loan brokers

(P-9384)
CALIFORNIA CREDIT UNION (PA)
701 N Brand Blvd Ste 100, Glendale (91203-4231)
P.O. Box 29100 (91209-9100)
PHONE.............................818 291-6700
Steve O'Connell, *CEO*
Danny Pak, *President*
Jason Pugh, *President*
Hudson Lee, *CFO*
Mark Lovewell, *CFO*
EMP: 120
SALES: 104MM **Privately Held**
WEB: www.californiacu.org
SIC: 6062 6061 State credit unions, not federally chartered; federal credit unions

(P-9385)
CHRISTIAN COMMUNITY CREDIT UN (PA)
255 N Lone Hill Ave, San Dimas (91773-2308)
P.O. Box 3012, Covina (91722-9012)
PHONE.............................626 915-7551
Marji Hughes, *CEO*
John T Walling, *President*
Michael Garcia, *Officer*
David Estridge, *Exec VP*
Scott J Reitsma, *Senior VP*
EMP: 70 **EST:** 1957
SQ FT: 24,000
SALES: 25MM **Privately Held**
WEB: www.christiancommunitycu.com
SIC: 6062 State credit unions, not federally chartered

(P-9386)
CHRISTIAN COMMUNITY CREDIT UN
101 S Barranca Ave, Covina (91723-2814)
PHONE.............................800 347-2228
EMP: 70
SQ FT: 17,286
SALES (corp-wide): 25MM **Privately Held**
SIC: 6062 State credit unions, not federally chartered
PA: Christian Community Credit Union
255 N Lone Hill Ave
San Dimas CA 91773
626 915-7551

P
R
O
D
U
C
T
S

&

S
V
C
S

(P-9387)
COASTHILLS CREDIT UNION (PA)
Also Called: CSCU
3880 Constellation Rd, Lompoc
(93436-1404)
P.O. Box 200 (93438-0200)
PHONE.................................805 733-7600
Jeff York, *President*
Cathy Cachu, *President*
Marty Chatham, *CFO*
Nathalie D Cohen, *Officer*
Faby Figueroa, *Officer*
EMP: 80
SQ FT: 30,000
SALES: 44.6MM **Privately Held**
WEB:
www.coasthillsfederalcreditunion.com
SIC: 6062 State credit unions, not federally
chartered

(P-9388)
COMMONWEALTH CENTRAL CREDIT UN (PA)
5890 Silver Creek Vly Rd, San Jose
(95138-1027)
P.O. Box 641690 (95164-1690)
PHONE.................................408 531-3100
Craig Weber, *CEO*
Michael F Filice, *Vice Chairman*
David Hook, *Vice Chairman*
Viktoria Earle, *CFO*
James Crawford, *Treasurer*
EMP: 69
SQ FT: 36,432
SALES: 18.6MM **Privately Held**
WEB: www.commonwealthccu.org
SIC: 6062 State credit unions

(P-9389)
EDUCATIONAL EMPLOYEES CR UN
1460 W 7th St, Hanford (93230-4938)
PHONE.................................559 587-4460
Dianne Mitchell, *Owner*
EMP: 50
SALES (corp-wide): 89.5MM **Privately Held**
SIC: 6062 6061 State credit unions, not
federally chartered; federal credit unions
PA: Educational Employees Credit Union
2222 W Shaw Ave
Fresno CA 93711
559 437-7700

(P-9390)
EDUCATIONAL EMPLOYEES CR UN
3488 W Shaw Ave, Fresno (93711-3216)
P.O. Box 5242 (93755-5242)
PHONE.................................559 896-0222
Bruce L Barnett, *President*
Seth Davis, *Security Mgr*
Jim Lowe, *Marketing Staff*
Rochelle Martin, *Director*
Jan Dipinto, *Manager*
EMP: 80
SQ FT: 17,939
SALES (corp-wide): 89.5MM **Privately Held**
SIC: 6062 State credit unions, not federally
chartered
PA: Educational Employees Credit Union
2222 W Shaw Ave
Fresno CA 93711
559 437-7700

(P-9391)
EL MONTE COMMUNITY CREDIT UN
11718 Ramona Blvd, El Monte
(91732-2310)
PHONE.................................626 444-0501
Evamarie Reta, *President*
EMP: 87
SQ FT: 3,405
SALES: 977K **Privately Held**
WEB: www.emcecu.org
SIC: 6062 State credit unions

(P-9392)
EVANGELICAL CHRISTIAN CR UN
955 W Imperial Hwy # 100, Brea
(92821-3814)
PHONE.................................714 671-5700
EMP: 157
SALES (corp-wide): 37.2MM **Privately Held**
SIC: 6062 6061
PA: Evangelical Christian Credit Union
955 W Imperial Hwy # 100
Brea CA 92821
714 671-5700

(P-9393)
EVANGELICAL CHRISTIAN CR UN (PA)
Also Called: ECCU
955 W Imperial Hwy # 100, Brea
(92821-3814)
P.O. Box 2400 (92822-2400)
PHONE.................................714 671-5700
Abel Pomar, *CEO*
Susan Rushing, *COO*
Gregory Talbott, *CFO*
Tom Honan, *Senior VP*
Patty Staples, *Senior VP*
EMP: 90
SQ FT: 125,000
SALES: 25.5MM **Privately Held**
WEB: www.ministrypartners.net
SIC: 6062 State credit unions, not federally
chartered

(P-9394)
GOLDEN 1 CREDIT UNION
1282 Stabler Ln Ste 640, Yuba City
(95993-2625)
PHONE.................................877 465-3361
Choni Weigman, *Manager*
EMP: 117
SALES (corp-wide): 378.9MM **Privately Held**
SIC: 6062 State credit unions
PA: Golden 1 Credit Union
8945 Cal Center Dr
Sacramento CA 95826
916 732-2900

(P-9395)
GOLDEN 1 CREDIT UNION (PA)
8945 Cal Center Dr, Sacramento
(95826-3239)
P.O. Box 15966 (95852-0966)
PHONE.................................916 732-2900
Teresa Halleck, *President*
Richard Alfaro, *Officer*
Johnathan Brennan, *Officer*
Paul Fausone, *Officer*
George Myers, *Officer*
EMP: 400 **EST:** 1933
SQ FT: 100,000
SALES: 378.9MM **Privately Held**
WEB: www.goldenone.com
SIC: 6062 State credit unions, not federally
chartered

(P-9396)
GOLDEN 1 CREDIT UNION
Also Called: Unknown
2942 Main St, Susanville (96130-4730)
PHONE.................................530 251-0205
EMP: 78
SALES (corp-wide): 378.9MM **Privately Held**
SIC: 6062 State credit unions
PA: Golden 1 Credit Union
8945 Cal Center Dr
Sacramento CA 95826
916 732-2900

(P-9397)
KEYPOINT CREDIT UNION (PA)
2805 Bowers Ave Ste 105, Santa Clara
(95051-0972)
PHONE.................................408 731-4100
T Bradford Canfield, *CEO*
Keith Stattenfield, *Vice Chairman*
Timothy M Kramer, *President*
John Herrick, *CFO*
Trent McIlhaney, *CFO*
EMP: 123
SQ FT: 60,715

SALES: 48.6MM **Privately Held**
WEB: www.keypointcu.com
SIC: 6062 State credit unions, not federally
chartered

(P-9398)
LOS ANGELES POLICE CREDIT UN (PA)
Also Called: L A P F C U
16150 Sherman Way, Van Nuys
(91406-3938)
P.O. Box 10188 (91410-0188)
PHONE.................................818 787-6520
Tyler E Izen, *Ch of Bd*
G Michael Padgett, *President*
Angelino Cayanan, *CFO*
Warren D Spayth, *Treasurer*
Joseph MA, *Officer*
EMP: 100
SQ FT: 30,000
SALES: 35.1MM **Privately Held**
WEB: www.lapfcu.org
SIC: 6062 6061 State credit unions, not
federally chartered; federal credit unions

(P-9399)
NORTHROP GRUMMAN FEDERAL CR UN (PA)
879 W 190th St Ste 800, Gardena
(90248-4205)
PHONE.................................310 808-4000
Stanley R Swenson Jr, *President*
Stephen Considine, *Vice Chairman*
Joe Demichele, *CFO*
Kathi Harper, *Chairman*
Georgetta A Wolff, *Vice Pres*
EMP: 60 **EST:** 1946
SALES: 39.3MM **Privately Held**
SIC: 6062 State credit unions

(P-9400)
NUVISION FINCL FEDERAL CR UN (PA)
7812 Edinger Ave Ste 100, Huntington
Beach (92647-3727)
P.O. Box 1220 (92647-1220)
PHONE.................................714 375-8000
Roger Ballard, *CEO*
John Afdem, *CFO*
Brian Hershfield, *CFO*
Robert Geraci, *Treasurer*
Chris Clausen, *Vice Pres*
EMP: 137
SALES: 71.2MM **Privately Held**
WEB: www.nuvision.coop
SIC: 6062 State credit unions, not federally
chartered

(P-9401)
PREMIER AMERICA CREDIT UNION (PA)
19867 Prairie St Lbby, Chatsworth
(91311-6532)
P.O. Box 2178 (91313-2178)
PHONE.................................818 772-4000
John M Merlo, *President*
Gary Holmen, *Vice Chairman*
Nancy Wheeler-Chandler, *Vice Chairman*
Brad Cunningham, *CFO*
James Anderson, *Chairman*
EMP: 135
SQ FT: 80,000
SALES: 86MM **Privately Held**
WEB: www.premier.org
SIC: 6062 6163 State credit unions, not
federally chartered; loan brokers

(P-9402)
PROVIDENT CREDIT UNION (PA)
303 Twin Dolphin Dr # 303, Redwood City
(94065-1419)
P.O. Box 8007 (94063-0907)
PHONE.................................650 508-0300
Maurice Schmid, *Chairman*
Ludelle Morrow, *President*
Jim Ernest, *CEO*
Claudia Jimenez, *Officer*
Edwin Macabebe, *Officer*
EMP: 130
SQ FT: 150,000
SALES: 73MM **Privately Held**
SIC: 6062 State credit unions, not federally
chartered

(P-9403)
SACRAMENTO CREDIT UNION (PA)
800 H St Ste 100, Sacramento
(95814-2686)
P.O. Box 2351 (95812-2351)
PHONE.................................916 444-6070
Toll Free:.................................888 -
Bhavnesh Makin, *CEO*
James Batson, *CFO*
Blake Cairney, *Vice Pres*
Megan Caldwell, *Vice Pres*
Ken Gladden, *Vice Pres*
EMP: 64
SQ FT: 39,138
SALES: 19.6MM **Privately Held**
WEB: www.sactocu.org
SIC: 6062 6163 State credit unions, not
federally chartered; loan brokers

(P-9404)
SAFE CREDIT UNION (PA)
2295 Iron Point Rd # 100, Folsom
(95630-8767)
PHONE.................................916 979-7233
Dave Roughton, *CEO*
James Allen, *President*
Kathern Gaskins, *Treasurer*
Damian Azimi, *Sr Corp Ofcr*
Samo Korosec, *Sr Corp Ofcr*
EMP: 160
SQ FT: 57,000
SALES: 91.9MM **Privately Held**
SIC: 6062 State credit unions, not federally
chartered

(P-9405)
SCHOOLS FINANCIAL CREDIT UNION (PA)
1485 Response Rd Ste 126, Sacramento
(95815-5261)
P.O. Box 526001 (95852-6001)
PHONE.................................916 569-5400
James P Jordan III, *President*
Tim Marriott, *CFO*
David Menker, *Vice Pres*
Jason Stiles, *Vice Pres*
Millard Baker, *Admin Mgr*
EMP: 150
SQ FT: 56,000
SALES: 60.9MM **Privately Held**
SIC: 6062 State credit unions, not federally
chartered

(P-9406)
SOUTHLAND CREDIT UNION (PA)
10701 Los Alamitos Blvd, Los Alamitos
(90720-2353)
P.O. Box 7022, Downey (90241-7022)
PHONE.................................562 862-6831
Ferris R Foster, *CEO*
Jose L Manzano, *Vice Chairman*
Rene Lejay, *COO*
Tom Lent, *CFO*
Bradley P Silcox, *Treasurer*
EMP: 60
SALES: 24.8MM **Privately Held**
WEB: www.southlandcreditunion.com
SIC: 6062 State credit unions, not federally
chartered

(P-9407)
SOUTHLAND CREDIT UNION
8545 Florence Ave, Downey (90240-4014)
PHONE.................................562 862-6831
Kathy Vitale, *Manager*
EMP: 55
SALES (corp-wide): 24.8MM **Privately Held**
WEB: www.southlandcreditunion.com
SIC: 6062 6141 State credit unions, not
federally chartered; personal credit institu-
tions
PA: Southland Credit Union
10701 Los Alamitos Blvd
Los Alamitos CA 90720
562 862-6831

(P-9408)
TECHNOLOGY CREDIT UNION
1562 S Bascom Ave, San Jose
(95125-6108)
PHONE.................................408 467-2382
Steve Donahue, *Branch Mgr*

EMP: 74
SALES (corp-wide): 97.7MM Privately Held
SIC: 6062 6061 State credit unions, not federally chartered; federal credit unions
PA: Technology Credit Union
2010 N 1st St Ste 200
San Jose CA 95131
408 451-9111

(P-9409)
TECHNOLOGY CREDIT UNION
43848 Pcf Commons Blvd, Fremont (94538-3804)
PHONE..................................408 467-2385
Steven Fisher, *Owner*
Debra Bowman, *Vice Pres*
EMP: 74
SALES (corp-wide): 97.7MM Privately Held
SIC: 6062 State credit unions, not federally chartered
PA: Technology Credit Union
2010 N 1st St Ste 200
San Jose CA 95131
408 451-9111

(P-9410)
TECHNOLOGY CREDIT UNION (PA)
2010 N 1st St Ste 200, San Jose (95131-2024)
P.O. Box 1409 (95109-1409)
PHONE 408 451-9111
Kenneth Burns, *President*
Wendy Cheney, *President*
Dean Davis, *President*
Emily Yuan, *President*
Barbara B Kamm, *CEO*
EMP: 133
SQ FT: 23,000
SALES: 97.7MM Privately Held
SIC: 6062 State credit unions, not federally chartered

(P-9411)
TECHNOLOGY CREDIT UNION
490 California Ave, Palo Alto (94306-1900)
PHONE..................................650 326-6445
Robert Hayes, *Branch Mgr*
EMP: 74
SALES (corp-wide): 97.7MM Privately Held
SIC: 6062 State credit unions, not federally chartered
PA: Technology Credit Union
2010 N 1st St Ste 200
San Jose CA 95131
408 451-9111

(P-9412)
WESCOM CENTRAL CREDIT UNION (PA)
123 S Marengo Ave, Pasadena (91101-2428)
P.O. Box 7058 (91109-7058)
PHONE..................................888 493-7266
Toll Free:.............................888 -
Darren Williams, *Principal*
Cindy Law, *Officer*
Bryan Tinoco, *Officer*
Kevin Vogt, *Officer*
Jonathon Allen, *Vice Pres*
EMP: 425
SQ FT: 90,000
SALES: 133.7MM Privately Held
WEB: www.wescom.org
SIC: 6062 State credit unions, not federally chartered

(P-9413)
WHEELHOUSE CREDIT UNION (PA)
9212 Balboa Ave, San Diego (92123-1514)
P.O. Box 719099 (92171-9099)
PHONE..................................619 297-4835
Stuart Camblin, *President*
John Stabler, *CFO*
Michael Glogowski, *Vice Pres*
Gloria Liberti, *Vice Pres*
Adele Sandberg, *Vice Pres*
EMP: 58
SQ FT: 20,000

SALES: 12.2MM Privately Held
WEB: www.sdmcu.com
SIC: 6062 State credit unions, not federally chartered

6081 Foreign Banks, Branches & Agencies

(P-9414)
HONG KONG & SHANGHAI BANKING
Also Called: Hong Kong Bank
770 Wilshire Blvd Ste 800, Los Angeles (90017-3719)
PHONE..................................213 626-2460
EMP: 60
SALES (corp-wide): 79.8B Privately Held
SIC: 6081
HQ: Hongkong And Shanghai Banking Corporation Limited, The
Hsbc Main Bldg
Central District HK
282 211-11

6082 Foreign Trade & Intl Banks

(P-9415)
PARIBAS ASSET MANAGEMENT INC
1 Front St Fl 23, San Francisco (94111-5325)
PHONE..................................415 772-1300
Francois Denis, *Principal*
William J La Herran, *Vice Pres*
EMP: 66
SALES (corp-wide): 2.7B Privately Held
WEB: www.bnpparibas.com
SIC: 6082 Foreign trade & international banking institutions
HQ: Paribas Asset Management, Inc.
787 7th Ave Fl 27
New York NY 10019
-

6091 Nondeposit Trust Facilities

(P-9416)
DEUTSCHE BANK NATIONAL TR CO
1761 E Saint Andrew Pl, Santa Ana (92705-4934)
PHONE..................................714 247-6054
F Jim Della Sala, *Principal*
David West, *Managing Dir*
EMP: 75
SALES (est): 9.2MM
SALES (corp-wide): 13.6B Privately Held
SIC: 6091 6021 Nondeposit trust facilities; national commercial banks
HQ: Deutsche Bank Trust Company Americas
60 Wall St Bsmt 1
New York NY 10005
212 250-2500

(P-9417)
SUNAMERICA INC (HQ)
1 Sun America Ctr Fl 38, Los Angeles (90067-6101)
PHONE..................................310 772-6000
Eli Broad, *Chairman*
Jay S Wintrob, *CEO*
James R Belardi, *Exec VP*
Jana Waring Greer, *Exec VP*
Michael J Akers, *Senior VP*
EMP: 1000 EST: 1957
SQ FT: 95,845
SALES (est): 2.1B
SALES (corp-wide): 47.3B Publicly Held
SIC: 6091 6311 6211 6282 Nondeposit trust facilities; life insurance carriers; mutual funds, selling by independent salesperson; brokers, security; dealers, security; manager of mutual funds, contract or fee basis; pension & retirement plan consultants; pension, health & welfare funds

---

PA: American International Group, Inc.
80 Pine St Fl 4
New York NY 10005
212 770-7000

6099 Functions Related To Deposit Banking, NEC

(P-9418)
ACCURATE SERVICES INC
Also Called: Accurate Express
3429 Glendale Blvd, Los Angeles (90039-1814)
PHONE..................................323 906-1000
Ester Fishman, *CEO*
EMP: 107
SQ FT: 2,475
SALES (est): 14.4MM Privately Held
SIC: 6099 Check clearing services

(P-9419)
ACE CASH EXPRESS INC
6302 Van Buren Blvd, Riverside (92503-2051)
PHONE..................................951 509-3506
Michael Mc Knight, *Branch Mgr*
EMP: 105
SALES (corp-wide): 2.6B Privately Held
WEB: www.acecashexpress.com
SIC: 6099 Check cashing agencies
HQ: Populus Financial Group, Inc
1231 Greenway Dr Ste 600
Irving TX 75038
972 550-5000

(P-9420)
ASCENDANTFX CAPITAL USA INC
3478 Buskirk Ave Ste 1000, Pleasant Hill (94523-4378)
PHONE..................................201 633-4667
Jason Mugford, *President*
Greg Allen, *Treasurer*
Bernard Beck, *Ch Credit Ofcr*
Dan Caputo, *Vice Pres*
Nabeel Siddiqui, *Principal*
EMP: 57
SALES (est): 7.2MM
SALES (corp-wide): 3.7MM Privately Held
SIC: 6099 Foreign currency exchange
PA: Ascendantfx Capital Inc
200 Bay St N Suite 1625
Toronto ON M5J 2
416 943-0123

(P-9421)
ASSOCIATED FOREIGN EXCH INC (HQ)
Also Called: Afex
21045 Califa St, Woodland Hills (91367-5104)
PHONE..................................888 307-2339
Jan Vlietstra, *CEO*
Irving Barr, *Ch of Bd*
Fred Kunik, *President*
Richard Verasamy, *CFO*
Guido Schulz, *Exec VP*
EMP: 57
SALES (est): 27.8MM Privately Held
WEB: www.afex.com
SIC: 6099 Foreign currency exchange

(P-9422)
ASSOCTED FGN EXCH HOLDINGS INC (PA)
21045 Califa St, Woodland Hills (91367-5104)
PHONE..................................818 386-2702
Irving Barr, *Chairman*
Fred Kunik, *President*
Jan Vliestra, *CEO*
EMP: 89
SALES: 58MM Privately Held
SIC: 6099 Foreign currency exchange

(P-9423)
AXOS CLEARING LLC (HQ)
4350 La Jolla Village Dr, San Diego (92122-1243)
PHONE..................................858 350-6200
Obert Hajdukovich, *President*
EMP: 637

SALES (est): 24.7MM
SALES (corp-wide): 647.6MM Publicly Held
SIC: 6099 Automated clearinghouses
PA: Axos Financial, Inc.
4350 La Jolla Village Dr
San Diego CA 92122
858 350-6200

(P-9424)
BLACKHAWK NETWORK INC (DH)
6220 Stoneridge Mall Rd, Pleasanton (94588-3260)
PHONE..................................925 226-9990
Talbott Roche, *President*
Tiana Lombardo, *Partner*
Jessica Madigan, *Partner*
Nicole Watkins, *Partner*
Mike Gionfriddo, *President*
EMP: 625 EST: 2005
SALES (est): 802.8MM
SALES (corp-wide): 178.4MM Privately Held
SIC: 6099 Electronic funds transfer network, including switching
HQ: Blackhawk Network Holdings, Inc.
6220 Stoneridge Mall Rd
Pleasanton CA 94588
925 226-9990

(P-9425)
BLACKHAWK NETWORK HOLDINGS INC (HQ)
6220 Stoneridge Mall Rd, Pleasanton (94588-3260)
PHONE..................................925 226-9990
Talbott Roche, *President*
Heather Blair, *Partner*
Nicole Watkins, *Partner*
Nick Samurkas, *COO*
Charles O Garner, *CFO*
EMP: 500
SQ FT: 149,000
SALES: 2.2B
SALES (corp-wide): 178.4MM Privately Held
WEB: www.safeway.com
SIC: 6099 Electronic funds transfer network, including switching
PA: Bhn Holdings, Inc.
6220 Stoneridge Mall Rd
Pleasanton CA 94588
925 226-9990

(P-9426)
COINBASE INC (PA)
Also Called: Blockr.io
548 Market St Ste 23008, San Francisco (94104-5401)
PHONE..................................415 275-2890
Brian David Armstrong, *CEO*
Emilie Choi, *President*
Brian Brooks,
Jeff Horowitz, *Officer*
Dan Yoo, *VP Business*
EMP: 76
SALES (est): 87.4MM Privately Held
SIC: 6099 Foreign currency exchange

(P-9427)
CONTINENTAL CURRENCY SVCS INC (HQ)
Also Called: Continental Ex Money Order Co
1108 E 17th St, Santa Ana (92701-2600)
PHONE..................................714 569-0300
Irving Barr, *Ch of Bd*
Fred Kunik, *President*
Silvia Posada, *Officer*
Frank Ochoa, *Sales Staff*
EMP: 50
SQ FT: 10,000
SALES (est): 11.7MM
SALES (corp-wide): 242.1MM Privately Held
SIC: 6099 Check cashing agencies
PA: Continental Currency Services, Inc.
1108 E 17th St
Santa Ana CA 92701
714 569-0300

(P-9428)
CONTINENTAL CURRENCY SVCS INC (PA)
Also Called: Cash It Here
1108 E 17th St, Santa Ana (92701-2600)
P.O. Box 10970 (92711-0970)
PHONE..................................714 569-0300
Fred Kunik, *President*
Irving Barr, *Ch of Bd*
Bradley Hauser, *COO*
David Wilder, *COO*
Dave Atwater, *Security Dir*
EMP: 80
SQ FT: 12,500
SALES (est): 242.1MM **Privately Held**
SIC: 6099 Check cashing agencies; electronic funds transfer network, including switching; money order issuance

(P-9429)
CONTINENTAL EXCH SOLUTIONS INC (HQ)
Also Called: Ria Financial Service
6565 Knott Ave, Buena Park (90620-1139)
PHONE..................................714 522-7044
Juan C Bianchi, *CEO*
Shawn D Fielder, *CFO*
Renie De Vera, *Project Mgr*
Hilda Hurtado, *Technology*
Armando Chavez, *Opers Staff*
EMP: 101
SALES: 539.7MM **Publicly Held**
SIC: 6099 Electronic funds transfer network, including switching

(P-9430)
CU COOPERATIVE SYSTEMS INC (PA)
Also Called: Co-Op Network
9692 Haven Ave, Rancho Cucamonga (91730-5891)
PHONE..................................909 948-2500
Todd Clark, *President*
Tom Sargent, *Ch of Bd*
John Bommarito, *Treasurer*
Matt Kardell, *Officer*
Shaun Gehman, *Senior VP*
▲ EMP: 285
SALES: 399.9MM **Privately Held**
SIC: 6099 Automated teller machine (ATM) network; electronic funds transfer network, including switching

(P-9431)
DEBISYS INC (PA)
Also Called: Emida Technologies
27442 Portola Pkwy # 150, Foothill Ranch (92610-2823)
PHONE..................................949 699-1401
Dennis Andrews, *CEO*
Jim Wodach, *CFO*
Ang L Pelaez, *Vice Pres*
Oscar Cortes, *Opers Mgr*
Shane Belovsky, *Director*
EMP: 80
SQ FT: 10,000
SALES (est): 59MM **Privately Held**
WEB: www.emida.net
SIC: 6099 Automated teller machine (ATM) network

(P-9432)
EDC SERVICE CORPORATION
415 N Vineyard Ave # 205, Ontario (91764-5493)
PHONE..................................909 390-4747
Stephen Bezuidenhout, *President*
Wendy Bezuidenhout, *Vice Pres*
EMP: 60
SQ FT: 8,500
SALES (est): 5.3MM **Privately Held**
SIC: 6099 Automated clearinghouses

(P-9433)
FCTI INC (PA)
11766 Wilshire Blvd # 1100, Los Angeles (90025-6561)
PHONE..................................310 405-0022
Jeff Wernecke, *President*
Robel Gugsa, *CEO*
Sean Burke, *Senior VP*
Jesus Carrillo, *Vice Pres*
Mata Christopher, *Vice Pres*
EMP: 72

SALES (est): 23MM **Privately Held**
WEB: www.fcti.net
SIC: 6099 Automated teller machine (ATM) network

(P-9434)
FINASTRA MERCHANT SERVICES INC (PA)
333 Bush St Fl 26, San Francisco (94104-2806)
PHONE..................................415 277-9900
Reuven Ben Menachem, *CEO*
Edward Ho, *President*
Bryan Schreiber, *Treasurer*
Mierzwa Dennis, *Vice Pres*
Dave Keenan, *Vice Pres*
EMP: 60
SQ FT: 14,000
SALES (est): 53.3MM **Privately Held**
WEB: www.bankserv.com
SIC: 6099 Electronic funds transfer network, including switching

(P-9435)
FIRST DATA HARDWARE SVCS INC
8875 Washington Blvd A, Roseville (95678-6214)
PHONE..................................916 632-7600
Dan Mandel, *Branch Mgr*
EMP: 325
SALES (corp-wide): 5.8B **Publicly Held**
SIC: 6099 Electronic funds transfer network, including switching
HQ: First Data Hardware Services Inc.
1169 Canton Rd
Marietta GA 30066

(P-9436)
FLAGSTAR BANCORP INC
949 S Coast Dr Ste 100, Costa Mesa (92626-7737)
PHONE..................................714 549-9100
Mark Cook, *Loan Officer*
Ann Heinz, *Loan Officer*
EMP: 172 **Publicly Held**
SIC: 6099 Check clearing services
PA: Flagstar Bancorp, Inc.
5151 Corporate Dr
Troy MI 48098

(P-9437)
G P M M MONEY CENTERS INC
Also Called: Dollar Smart
1460 Doris Ave, Oxnard (93030-8771)
P.O. Box 6963 (93031-6963)
PHONE..................................619 288-7607
Greg Palmer, *President*
Ryan Romero, *Business Mgr*
EMP: 50
SALES (est): 6.2MM **Privately Held**
SIC: 6099 Check cashing agencies

(P-9438)
GRANITE ESCROW SERVICES
439 N Canon Dr Ste 220, Beverly Hills (90210-3933)
PHONE..................................310 288-0110
Sue Nichols, *Branch Mgr*
Lisa Rietz, *Officer*
EMP: 59
SALES (corp-wide): 10MM **Privately Held**
SIC: 6099 Escrow institutions other than real estate
PA: Granite Escrow Services
450 Nwport Ctr Dr Ste 600
Newport Beach CA 92660
949 720-0110

(P-9439)
LENLYN LIMITED WHICH WILL DO B (HQ)
6151 W Century Blvd, Los Angeles (90045-5307)
P.O. Box 92192 (90009-2192)
PHONE..................................310 417-3432
Bharat Shah, *CEO*
Mark Garrett, *IT/INT Sup*
EMP: 75
SQ FT: 1,000

SALES (est): 17.8MM
SALES (corp-wide): 2.4MM **Privately Held**
WEB: www.iceplc.com
SIC: 6099 Foreign currency exchange

(P-9440)
MANIFLO MONEY EXCHANGE INC
1442 Highland Ave, National City (91950-4624)
PHONE..................................619 434-7200
Florino Agpaoa, *President*
Ferdinand Agpaoa, *President*
Rodel Agpaoa, *Vice Pres*
EMP: 65
SQ FT: 1,500
SALES (est): 12.7MM **Privately Held**
WEB: www.maniflo.com
SIC: 6099 Electronic funds transfer network, including switching

(P-9441)
SERFIN FUNDS TRANSFER (PA)
1000 S Fremont Ave A-O, Alhambra (91803-8800)
PHONE..................................626 457-3070
Richard Stevenson, *President*
EMP: 100
SALES (est): 9.3MM **Privately Held**
SIC: 6099 Electronic funds transfer network, including switching

(P-9442)
XOOM CORPORATION
425 Market St Ste 1200, San Francisco (94105-5404)
PHONE..................................415 777-4800
John Kunze, *President*
Ryno Blignaut, *CFO*
Christopher G Ferro, *Ch Credit Ofcr*
Julian King, *Senior VP*
Bobby Aitkenhead, *Vice Pres*
EMP: 190
SQ FT: 35,552
SALES: 159MM
SALES (corp-wide): 15.4B **Publicly Held**
SIC: 6099 Electronic funds transfer network, including switching
HQ: Paypal, Inc.
2211 N 1st St
San Jose CA 95131
877 981-2163

┌─────────────────────────┐
│ **6111 Federal Credit** │
│   **Agencies**   │
└─────────────────────────┘

(P-9443)
AGAMERICA FCB (PA)
3636 American River Dr # 100, Sacramento (95864-5952)
PHONE..................................651 282-8800
James D Kirk, *President*
David B Newlin, *CFO*
Roger J Cramer, *Ch Credit Ofcr*
Gregory J Buehne, *Senior VP*
Chris Doherty, *Vice Pres*
EMP: 85
SALES (est): 867K **Privately Held**
SIC: 6111 6163 Federal & federally sponsored credit agencies; loan brokers

(P-9444)
DEUTSCHE BANK NATIONAL TR CO (DH)
2000 Avenue Of The Stars, Los Angeles (90067-4700)
PHONE..................................213 620-8200
EMP: 52
SALES: 149.6MM
SALES (corp-wide): 13.6B **Privately Held**
SIC: 6111 National Consumer Cooperative Bank
HQ: Deutsche Bank Trust Company Americas
60 Wall St Bsmt 1
New York NY 10005
212 250-2500

(P-9445)
EDUCATIONAL CREDIT MGT CORP
Also Called: Ecmc-CA
P.O. Box 419045 (95741-9045)
PHONE..................................800 367-1590
EMP: 293
SALES (corp-wide): 391.9MM **Privately Held**
SIC: 6111 Federal & federally sponsored credit agencies
PA: Educational Credit Management Corporation
111 Washington Ave S # 1400
Minneapolis MN 55401
651 221-0566

(P-9446)
FEDERAL HM LN BNK SAN FRNCISCO (PA)
333 Bush St Ste 2700, San Francisco (94104-2806)
PHONE..................................415 616-1000
John F Luikart, *Ch of Bd*
Tamara L McInerney, *Shareholder*
Deb Eldridge, *President*
Gwen Hill, *President*
Jamie Leong, *President*
▲ EMP: 262 EST: 1932
SQ FT: 108,147
SALES: 2.5B **Privately Held**
WEB: www.fhlbsf.com
SIC: 6111 Federal & federally sponsored credit agencies

(P-9447)
FRESNO-MADERA FEDERAL LAND
305 N I St, Madera (93637-3062)
P.O. Box 13069, Fresno (93794-3069)
PHONE..................................559 674-2437
Rob Kratz, *Manager*
EMP: 58
SALES (corp-wide): 10.2MM **Privately Held**
SIC: 6111 Federal Land Banks
PA: Fresno-Madera Federal Land Bank Association
4635 W Spruce Ave
Fresno CA 93722
559 277-7000

(P-9448)
LAW SCHOOL FINANCIAL INC
Also Called: Law School Loans
175 S Lake Ave Unit 200, Pasadena (91101-2629)
PHONE..................................626 243-1800
Harrison A Barnes, *President*
Dennis Geselowitz, *CFO*
EMP: 190
SQ FT: 25,000
SALES (est): 15.5MM **Privately Held**
WEB: www.lawschoolloans.com
SIC: 6111 Student Loan Marketing Association

(P-9449)
LBS FINANCIAL CREDIT UNION
1401 Quail St Ste 130, Newport Beach (92660-2772)
PHONE..................................714 893-5111
Laurie Skinner, *Manager*
Jennifer Trejo, *Vice Pres*
Kevin Gleason, *Associate*
EMP: 55
SALES (corp-wide): 48MM **Privately Held**
SIC: 6111 6036 Federal & federally sponsored credit agencies; savings & loan associations, not federally chartered
PA: Lbs Financial Credit Union
5505 Garden Grove Blvd # 500
Westminster CA 92683
562 598-9007

(P-9450)
LBS FINANCIAL CREDIT UNION (PA)
5505 Garden Grove Blvd # 500, Westminster (92683-1894)
PHONE..................................562 598-9007
Jeffrey A Napper, *President*
Gene Allen, *Ch of Bd*
Sue White, *CFO*

Dug Woog, *Treasurer*
Susan Delanghe, *Vice Pres*
EMP: 120
SQ FT: 63,000
SALES: 48MM **Privately Held**
SIC: 6111 6163 Federal & federally sponsored credit agencies; loan brokers

(P-9451)
YOSEMITE FARM CREDIT ACA (PA)
806 W Monte Vista Ave, Turlock (95382-7242)
P.O. Box 3278 (95381-3278)
PHONE..................209 667-2366
Leonard Van Eldern, *President*
Tracy Sparks, *CFO*
EMP: 60
SQ FT: 9,000
SALES: 108.4MM **Privately Held**
WEB: www.yosemitefarmcredit.com
SIC: 6111 Federal Land Banks

6141 Personal Credit Institutions

(P-9452)
AMERICAN HONDA FINANCE CORP (DH)
Also Called: Honda Financial Services
20800 Madrona Ave, Torrance (90503-4915)
P.O. Box 2295 (90509-2295)
PHONE..................310 972-2239
Hideo Tamaka, *CEO*
John Weisickle, *CFO*
Stephan Smith, *Senior VP*
Debbie Lemire, *Admin Asst*
Jim Crane, *Administration*
EMP: 200 **EST:** 1980
SQ FT: 50,288
SALES: 2B **Privately Held**
WEB: www.americanhondafinancecorporation.com
SIC: 6141 Financing: automobiles, furniture, etc., not a deposit bank; automobile & consumer finance companies
HQ: American Honda Motor Co., Inc.
  1919 Torrance Blvd
  Torrance CA 90501
  310 783-2000

(P-9453)
AMERICAN HONDA FINANCE CORP
10801 Walker St Ste 140, Cypress (90630-5042)
PHONE..................714 816-8110
EMP: 72 **Privately Held**
SIC: 6141 Financing: automobiles, furniture, etc., not a deposit bank
HQ: American Honda Finance Corporation
  20800 Madrona Ave
  Torrance CA 90503
  310 972-2239

(P-9454)
BALBOA CAPITAL CORPORATION (PA)
575 Anton Blvd Fl 12, Costa Mesa (92626-7169)
PHONE..................949 756-0800
Patrick Byrne, *CEO*
Phil Silva, *President*
Robert Rasmussen, *COO*
James Grant, *Vice Pres*
Patrick Ontal, *Vice Pres*
EMP: 200
SQ FT: 24,000
SALES (est): 101.9MM **Privately Held**
WEB: www.balboacapital.com
SIC: 6141 Automobile & consumer finance companies

(P-9455)
CASHCALL INC
1 City Blvd W Ste 102, Orange (92868-3621)
P.O. Box 66007, Anaheim (92816-6007)
PHONE..................949 752-4600
John Paul Reddam, *CEO*
Ethan Taub, *Chief Mktg Ofcr*
Andrew Brown, *Officer*

Jeff Bates, *Vice Pres*
Steve Klopstock, *Vice Pres*
EMP: 1400
SALES (est): 359.3MM **Privately Held**
WEB: www.cashcall.com
SIC: 6141 Personal finance licensed loan companies, small

(P-9456)
CONSUMER PORTFOLIO SVCS INC
19500 Jamboree Rd, Irvine (92612-2411)
PHONE..................949 788-5695
Charles E Bradley Jr, *Manager*
Tim Leblanc, *Sales Mgr*
Corey Burton, *Marketing Staff*
Susan Rojas, *Supervisor*
EMP: 214 **Publicly Held**
WEB: www.consumerportfolio.com
SIC: 6141 Personal credit institutions
PA: Consumer Portfolio Services, Inc.
  3800 Howard Hughes Pkwy
  Las Vegas NV 89169

(P-9457)
CONSUMER PORTFOLIO SVCS INC
16355 Laguna Canyon Rd, Irvine (92618-3801)
P.O. Box 57071 (92619-7071)
PHONE..................949 753-6800
EMP: 78 **Publicly Held**
SIC: 6141 Financing: automobiles, furniture, etc., not a deposit bank
PA: Consumer Portfolio Services, Inc.
  3800 Howard Hughes Pkwy
  Las Vegas NV 89169

(P-9458)
ELEVATE CREDIT INC
11710 El Camino Real, San Diego (92130-2099)
PHONE..................817 928-1500
EMP: 112
SALES (corp-wide): 786.6MM **Publicly Held**
SIC: 6141 Licensed loan companies, small
PA: Elevate Credit, Inc.
  4150 Intl Plz Ste 300
  Fort Worth TX 76109
  817 928-1500

(P-9459)
FLURISH INC
Also Called: Lendup
1750 Broadway 300, Oakland (94612-2106)
PHONE..................855 253-6387
Sasha Orloff, *CEO*
Bill Donnelly, *CFO*
Kathleen Fitzpatrick, *Vice Pres*
Robert Novick, *Vice Pres*
Jacob Rosenberg, *Admin Sec*
EMP: 80
SALES: 12MM **Privately Held**
SIC: 6141 Consumer finance companies

(P-9460)
FORD MOTOR COMPANY
4900 Hopyard Rd Ste 220, Pleasanton (94588-3345)
PHONE..................925 351-6205
Craig Krisan, *Branch Mgr*
EMP: 63
SQ FT: 10,000
SALES (corp-wide): 160.3B **Publicly Held**
WEB: www.ford.com
SIC: 6141 Installment sales finance, other than banks
PA: Ford Motor Company
  1 American Rd
  Dearborn MI 48126
  313 322-3000

(P-9461)
GREEN DOT CORPORATION (PA)
3465 E Foothill Blvd # 100, Pasadena (91107-6072)
P.O. Box 5100 (91117-0100)
PHONE..................626 765-2000
Steven W Streit, *President*

William I Jacobs, *Ch of Bd*
Mary J Dent, *CEO*
Kuan Archer, *COO*
Mark L Shifke, *CFO*
EMP: 99 **EST:** 1999
SQ FT: 140,000
SALES: 1B **Publicly Held**
WEB: www.greendotcorp.com
SIC: 6141 7389 Personal credit institutions; credit card service

(P-9462)
HSBC FINANCE CORPORATION
931 Corporate Center Dr, Pomona (91768-2642)
PHONE..................909 623-3355
Mark Marks, *Principal*
EMP: 800
SALES (corp-wide): 87.7B **Privately Held**
WEB: www.household.com
SIC: 6141 7389 6351 6159 Consumer finance companies; credit card service; credit & other financial responsibility insurance; machinery & equipment finance leasing; mortgage bankers; life insurance carriers
HQ: Hsbc Finance Corporation
  1421 W Shure Dr Ste 100
  Arlington Heights IL 60004
  224 880-7000

(P-9463)
HYUNDAI CAPITAL AMERICA (DH)
Also Called: Hyundai Finance
3161 Michelson Dr # 1900, Irvine (92612-4418)
PHONE..................714 965-3000
Sam Sanghyuk Suh, *CEO*
Sukjoon Won, *President*
Jwa Jin Cho, *CEO*
Minsok Randy Park, *CFO*
Carol Moore, *Vice Pres*
EMP: 68
SQ FT: 60,000
SALES (est): 104MM **Privately Held**
SIC: 6141 Automobile loans, including insurance
HQ: Hyundai Motor America
  10550 Talbert Ave
  Fountain Valley CA 92708
  714 965-3000

(P-9464)
JMAC LENDING INC
2510 Redhill Ave, Santa Ana (92705-5542)
PHONE..................949 390-2688
MAI Christina Pham, *President*
Michael Falce, *Vice Pres*
Kathy Brookings, *Executive*
Bridgette Klein, *Executive*
EMP: 60
SALES: 24MM **Privately Held**
WEB: www.jmaclending.com
SIC: 6141 Financing: automobiles, furniture, etc., not a deposit bank

(P-9465)
LOAN NOW
3100 S Harbor Blvd # 180, Santa Ana (92704-6823)
PHONE..................714 352-2250
Art Fedich, *Vice Pres*
Brenda Vasquez, *Executive*
Lilian Tran, *Financial Analy*
EMP: 68 **EST:** 2016
SALES (est): 5.1MM **Privately Held**
SIC: 6141 Personal credit institutions

(P-9466)
LOBEL FINANCIAL CORPORATION (PA)
1150 N Magnolia Ave, Anaheim (92801-2605)
P.O. Box 3000 (92803-3000)
PHONE..................714 995-3333
Harvey Lobel, *CEO*
Gary Lobel, *Corp Secy*
David Lobel, *Vice Pres*
Murray Lobel, *Vice Pres*
Sean Stewart, *Technology*
EMP: 66 **EST:** 1979
SQ FT: 11,000
SALES (est): 33.9MM **Privately Held**
SIC: 6141 Automobile loans, including insurance

(P-9467)
MITSUBISHI MOTORS CR AMER INC (DH)
6400 Katella Ave, Cypress (90630-5208)
P.O. Box 6014 (90630-0014)
PHONE..................714 799-4730
Dan Booth, *President*
Hideyuki Kitamura, *Treasurer*
Charles Tredway, *Exec VP*
Ellen Gleberman, *Admin Sec*
Denise Rice, *Manager*
EMP: 394
SQ FT: 32,256
SALES (est): 32.4MM **Privately Held**
WEB: www.acvl.com
SIC: 6141 6159 Automobile loans, including insurance; truck finance leasing; finance leasing, vehicles: except automobiles & trucks
HQ: Mitsubishi Motors North America, Inc.
  6400 Katella Ave
  Cypress CA 90630
  714 799-4730

(P-9468)
MONTEREY FINANCIAL SVCS INC (PA)
4095 Avenida De La Plata, Oceanside (92056-5802)
P.O. Box 5199 (92052-5199)
PHONE..................760 639-3500
Robert Steinke, *President*
Kathi Steinke, *Vice Pres*
Kathyleen Steinke, *Vice Pres*
Chris Hughes, *Exec Dir*
Dustin Chung, *Engineer*
EMP: 110
SQ FT: 27,000
SALES: 12.9MM **Privately Held**
WEB: www.montereyfinancial.com
SIC: 6141 8721 7322 8742 Consumer finance companies; billing & bookkeeping service; collection agency, except real estate; financial consultant

(P-9469)
NATIONAL PLANNING CORPORATION
100 N Pacific Coast Hwy # 1800, El Segundo (90245-5612)
PHONE..................800 881-7174
John C Johnson, *President*
Caren Coleman, *Vice Pres*
Sarah Corce, *Vice Pres*
Jim Dafalco, *Vice Pres*
EMP: 150
SALES (est): 36.7MM **Privately Held**
SIC: 6141 Automobile & consumer finance companies

(P-9470)
NORTH AMERICAN ACCEPTANCE CORP
Also Called: An Open Check
3191 Red Hill Ave Ste 100, Costa Mesa (92626-3451)
PHONE..................714 868-3195
Marco J Rasic, *CEO*
Mary Clancey Rasic, *Vice Pres*
EMP: 123
SQ FT: 24,000
SALES (est): 16.6MM **Privately Held**
WEB: www.naacceptance.com
SIC: 6141 6719 Automobile & consumer finance companies; personal holding companies, except banks

(P-9471)
PAYOFF INC
Also Called: Happy Money
3200 Park Center Dr # 800, Costa Mesa (92626-1979)
PHONE..................949 430-0630
Scott Saunders, *CEO*
Christopher Hilliard, *Ch Credit Ofcr*
Adam Zarlengo,
Mark Dicamillo, *Vice Pres*
Eli Martinez, *Administration*
EMP: 89
SQ FT: 19,500
SALES (est): 24.4MM **Privately Held**
SIC: 6141 Personal credit institutions

(PA)=Parent Co (HQ)=Headquarters (DH)=Div Headquarters
✪ = New Business established in last 2 years

2019 Directory of California
Wholesalers and Services Companies

407

P R O D U C T S & S V C S

(P-9472)
TRADING FINANCIAL CREDIT LLC (PA)
Also Called: Trading Financial Capital
3055 Wilshire Blvd # 530, Los Angeles
(90010-1145)
PHONE..................213 375-3113
Daniel Joelson, *President*
EMP: 50
SQ FT: 9,000
SALES: 7.5MM **Privately Held**
SIC: 6141 Personal credit institutions

(P-9473)
WILSHIRE CONSUMER CREDIT
Also Called: 1800-R-Ado
4751 Wilshire Blvd, Los Angeles
(90010-3827)
P.O. Box 76809 (90076-0809)
PHONE..................323 692-8585
Ian Anderson, *President*
EMP: 50
SALES (est): 5.2MM **Privately Held**
SIC: 6141 Automobile & consumer finance
companies

6153 Credit Institutions, Short-Term Business

(P-9474)
AMERICAN MERCHANT CENTER INC
6819 Sepulveda Blvd # 311, Van Nuys
(91405-4463)
PHONE..................818 947-1700
Victor Olechno, *President*
Jeffrey Vaynberg, *Vice Pres*
Jenifer Nutzmann, *Sales Executive*
EMP: 70 **EST:** 1987
SQ FT: 5,000
SALES (est): 8.1MM **Privately Held**
WEB: www.americanmerchant.com
SIC: 6153 Credit card services, central
agency collection

(P-9475)
BANK AMERICA NATIONAL ASSN
400 National Way, Simi Valley
(93065-6414)
PHONE..................805 520-5100
Danette Samilton, *Vice Pres*
EMP: 100
SALES (corp-wide): 110.5B **Publicly Held**
SIC: 6153 Working capital financing
HQ: Bank Of America, National Association
100 S Tryon St
Charlotte NC 28202
704 386-5681

(P-9476)
BANKAMERICA FINANCIAL INC
Also Called: Bank of America
315 Montgomery St, San Francisco
(94104-1856)
PHONE..................415 622-3521
James A Dern, *President*
Lewis W Teel, *Ch of Bd*
Michael K Riley, *Treasurer*
Roberto Araniva, *Officer*
John Carson, *Senior VP*
EMP: 1700
SALES (est): 431.3K
SALES (corp-wide): 110.5B **Publicly Held**
SIC: 6153 6141 6282 Factors of commer-
cial paper; consumer finance companies;
investment advisory service
PA: Bank Of America Corporation
100 N Tryon St Ste 170
Charlotte NC 28202
704 386-5681

(P-9477)
BLUEVINE CAPITAL INC
401 Warren St Ste 300, Redwood City
(94063-1578)
PHONE..................888 216-9619
Eyal Lifshitz, *CEO*
Molly Orsborn, *Partner*
Brad Brodigan, *Ch Credit Ofcr*
Reydavid Julio, *Vice Pres*

Eric Mondloch, *Vice Pres*
EMP: 70
SALES (est): 851.4K **Privately Held**
SIC: 6153 Working capital financing

(P-9478)
COGENT FINANCIAL GROUP
5199 E Pacific Coast Hwy, Long Beach
(90804-3309)
PHONE..................562 985-1388
Theodore Schlegel, *CEO*
EMP: 60
SQ FT: 6,500
SALES (est): 6.6MM **Privately Held**
WEB: www.cogentfinancialgroup.com
SIC: 6153 Purchasers of accounts receiv-
able & commercial paper

(P-9479)
CONRAD ACCEPTANCE CORPORATION
Also Called: Conrad Credit
476 W Vermont Ave, Escondido
(92025-6529)
PHONE..................760 735-5000
Keith Richenbacher, *President*
William Huss, *CFO*
John Page, *Vice Pres*
Bob Pranik, *Admin Sec*
Ernie Recesetar, *Director*
EMP: 50
SQ FT: 6,000
SALES (est): 5.4MM
SALES (corp-wide): 22.3MM **Privately Held**
SIC: 6153 Purchasers of accounts receiv-
able & commercial paper
PA: Conrad Credit Corp.
476 W Vermont Ave
Escondido CA 92025
800 826-6723

(P-9480)
EAST LOS ANGELES COMMUNITY UN (PA)
Also Called: Telacu
5400 E Olympic Blvd Fl 3, Commerce
(90022-5147)
PHONE..................323 721-1655
David C Lizarraga, *Ch of Bd*
Paul Samuel, *CFO*
Michael D Lizarraga, *Exec VP*
Jay Bell, *Senior VP*
Jerry Barham, *Vice Pres*
EMP: 50 **EST:** 1968
SQ FT: 60,000
SALES: 17.7MM **Privately Held**
WEB: www.telacu.com
SIC: 6153 8322 6512 6514 Short-term
business credit; multi-service center; non-
residential building operators; dwelling
operators, except apartments

(P-9481)
ENCORE CAPITAL GROUP INC (PA)
3111 Cmino Del Rio N Ste, San Diego
(92108)
PHONE..................877 445-4581
Ashish Masih, *President*
Michael P Monaco, *Ch of Bd*
Paul Grinberg, *President*
Jonathan C Clark, *CFO*
Gregory L Call, *Officer*
EMP: 71 **EST:** 1990
SQ FT: 118,000
SALES: 1.3B **Publicly Held**
WEB: www.encorecapitalgroup.com
SIC: 6153 Purchasers of accounts receiv-
able & commercial paper

(P-9482)
FUNDING CIRCLE USA INC
Also Called: Endurance Lending Network
747 Front St Fl 4, San Francisco
(94111-1922)
PHONE..................855 385-5356
Sam Hodges, *Director*
Jerome Le Luel, *Officer*
Rohit Sharma, *Vice Pres*
Renee Nichols, *Office Mgr*
Damien Wilson, *Sr Software Eng*
EMP: 55 **EST:** 2014

SALES (est): 54.5MM
SALES (corp-wide): 182.2MM **Privately Held**
SIC: 6153 Working capital financing
HQ: Funding Circle Ltd
71 Queen Victoria Street
London EC4V

(P-9483)
GENERAL ELECTRIC COMPANY
3100 Zinfandel Dr Ste 255, Rancho Cor-
dova (95670-6391)
P.O. Box 4596, New York NY (10163-4596)
PHONE..................916 286-8020
EMP: 119
SALES (corp-wide): 121.6B **Publicly Held**
SIC: 6153 Short-term business credit
PA: General Electric Company
41 Farnsworth St
Boston MA 02210
617 443-3000

(P-9484)
HANA COMMERCIAL FINANCE INC
1000 Wilshire Blvd Fl 20, Los Angeles
(90017-5645)
PHONE..................213 240-1234
Suyong Kim, *CFO*
Sunnie Kim, *CEO*
Young Shim, *COO*
Suyoung Kim, *CFO*
EMP: 85 **EST:** 2016
SALES (est): 6.5MM **Privately Held**
SIC: 6153 Factoring services

(P-9485)
HYUNDAI MOTOR AMERICA (HQ)
10550 Talbert Ave, Fountain Valley
(92708-6032)
P.O. Box 20850 (92728-0850)
PHONE..................714 965-3000
Kyung SOO Lee, *President*
Brian Smith, *COO*
Youngil Ko, *CFO*
Angela Zepeda, *Chief Mktg Ofcr*
Jerry Flannery, *Exec VP*
◆ **EMP:** 454
SQ FT: 469,000
SALES (est): 368.3MM **Privately Held**
WEB: www.hmaservice.com
SIC: 6153 5511 6141 Short-term business
credit; automobiles, new & used; automo-
bile & consumer finance companies

(P-9486)
INPUT 1 LLC
6200 Canoga Ave Ste 400, Woodland Hills
(91367-2459)
PHONE..................818 340-0030
Todd Greenbaum, *Mng Member*
Suzie Williams, *Vice Pres*
Erika Gnacadja, *Software Engr*
Pavel Wolfson, *Software Engr*
Andrew Scatoloni, *Broker*
EMP: 110
SQ FT: 24,000
SALES: 18.9MM **Privately Held**
WEB: www.input1.com
SIC: 6153 7371 Short-term business
credit; computer software development &
applications; computer software develop-
ment

(P-9487)
MIDLAND CREDIT MANAGEMENT INC (HQ)
3111 Camino Del Rio N # 103, San Diego
(92108-5721)
P.O. Box 939069 (92193-9069)
PHONE..................877 240-2377
Kenneth A Vecchione, *CEO*
Carl Gregory, *President*
Christian Escalante, *Officer*
Anabel Levy, *Senior VP*
Robin Pruitt, *Senior VP*
EMP: 1800
SALES (est): 399.2MM
SALES (corp-wide): 1.3B **Publicly Held**
WEB: www.encorecapitalgroup.com
SIC: 6153 Short-term business credit

PA: Encore Capital Group, Inc.
3111 Cmino Del Rio N Ste
San Diego CA 92108
877 445-4581

(P-9488)
NATIONS CAPITAL GROUP LLC
Also Called: Nations Surgery Center
5353 Balboa Blvd Ste 300, Encino
(91316-2863)
PHONE..................818 793-2050
Fax: 818 793-2059
EMP: 50
SALES (corp-wide): 5.1MM **Privately Held**
SIC: 6153
PA: Nations Capital Group, Llc
5370 S Durango Dr
Las Vegas NV

(P-9489)
PLAYSPAN LLC
2900 Gordon Ave Ste 201, Santa Clara
(95051-0718)
P.O. Box 8999, San Francisco (94128-
8999)
PHONE..................408 617-9155
Alfred F Kelly Jr, *President*
Julie Whitehead, *CFO*
Lex Bayer, *General Mgr*
Andrew Magruder, *CTO*
Tony Weber, *Opers Staff*
EMP: 50
SQ FT: 3,500
SALES (est): 6.9MM **Publicly Held**
SIC: 6153 Credit card services, central
agency collection
PA: Visa Inc.
900 Metro Center Blvd
Foster City CA 94404

(P-9490)
PROSPER FUNDING LLC
101 2nd St Fl 15, San Francisco
(94105-3672)
PHONE..................415 593-5400
Stephan Vermut, *Principal*
EMP: 73
SALES (est): 682.6K
SALES (corp-wide): 104.3MM **Privately Held**
SIC: 6153 Working capital financing
PA: Prosper Marketplace, Inc.
221 Main St Fl 3
San Francisco CA 94105
415 593-5400

(P-9491)
RELIANT SERVICES GROUP LLC
Also Called: Reliant Funding Group
9540 Towne Centre Dr # 100, San Diego
(92121-1988)
PHONE..................877 850-0998
Adam Stettner,
Paul Norman, *CFO*
Steven Kietz, *Chief Mktg Ofcr*
Lindsay Patten, *VP Human Res*
EMP: 180
SALES (est): 5.5MM **Privately Held**
SIC: 6153 Working capital financing

(P-9492)
RIVIERA FINANCE OF TEXAS INC (PA)
220 Avenue I, Redondo Beach
(90277-5617)
PHONE..................310 540-3993
David B Clark, *President*
Kenneth J Wong, *CFO*
EMP: 200
SQ FT: 5,000
SALES (est): 16.2MM **Privately Held**
SIC: 6153 Factors of commercial paper

(P-9493)
SEQUOIA RESIDENTIAL FUNDING
1 Belvedere Pl Ste 330, Mill Valley
(94941-2493)
PHONE..................415 389-7373
George Bull, *CEO*
EMP: 90

SALES: 13.3MM **Publicly Held**
SIC: **6153** 7389 Working capital financing;
financial services
PA: Redwood Trust, Inc.
1 Belvedere Pl Ste 300
Mill Valley CA 94941

(P-9494)
VEROS CREDIT LLC (PA)
2333 N Broadway Ste 400, Santa Ana
(92706-1656)
P.O. Box 11914 (92711-1914)
PHONE..................................714 415-6185
Cyrus Bozorgi, *Mng Member*
EMP: 51
SALES (est): 15.1MM **Privately Held**
SIC: **6153** Working capital financing

(P-9495)
WELLS FARGO COML DIST FIN LLC
3100 Zinfandel Dr Ste 255, Rancho Cor-
dova (95670-6391)
PHONE..................................916 636-2020
EMP: 94
SALES (corp-wide): 101B **Publicly Held**
SIC: **6153** Mercantile financing
HQ: Wells Fargo Commercial Distribution
Finance, Llc
10 S Wacker Dr
Chicago IL 60606
847 747-6800

6159 Credit Institutions, Misc Business

(P-9496)
AMERICAN AGCREDIT FLCA (PA)
400 Aviation Blvd Ste 100, Santa Rosa
(95403-1181)
P.O. Box 1120 (95402-1120)
PHONE..................................707 545-1200
Ron Carli, *CEO*
Karen Carstens, *President*
Heidi Dahle, *President*
Byron Enix, *President*
Becky Steckel, *President*
EMP: 91
SQ FT: 26,000
SALES (est): 118.5MM
SALES (corp-wide): 130.4MM **Privately Held**
WEB: www.agloan.com
SIC: **6159** Agricultural credit institutions

(P-9497)
AMERICAN CAPITAL GROUP INC
Also Called: A C G
23382 Mill Creek Dr # 115, Laguna Hills
(92653-7932)
PHONE..................................949 271-5800
Carl Heaton, *President*
Carl J Heaton, *President*
Sam Maffey, *Portfolio Mgr*
David Salas, *Portfolio Mgr*
Nicholas Wood, *Accountant*
EMP: 64
SALES (est): 11.9MM **Privately Held**
WEB: www.acgcapital.com
SIC: **6159** Equipment & vehicle finance
leasing companies
PA: Nationwide Capital Holdings, Inc.
31726 Rncho Viejo Ste 111
San Juan Capistrano CA
949 271-5816

(P-9498)
ATEL CAPITAL GROUP (PA)
Also Called: Leasing Equipment
600 Montgomery St Fl 9, San Francisco
(94111-2711)
PHONE..................................800 543-2835
Dean L Cash, *CEO*
Paritosh K Choksi, *CFO*
Partichosh Choksi, *CFO*
Russell Wilder, *Ch Credit Ofcr*
Jonas Kriks, *Officer*
EMP: 80
SALES (est): 29.4MM **Privately Held**
SIC: **6159** Machinery & equipment finance
leasing

(P-9499)
BANC AMERICA LSG & CAPITL LLC (DH)
555 California St Fl 4, San Francisco
(94104-1506)
PHONE..................................415 765-7349
Eric Lundquist, *Managing Dir*
Daniel Monberg, *Vice Pres*
EMP: 150
SALES (est): 363.7MM
SALES (corp-wide): 110.5B **Publicly Held**
SIC: **6159** Machinery & equipment finance
leasing
HQ: Bank Of America, National Association
100 S Tryon St
Charlotte NC 28202
704 386-5681

(P-9500)
CAPNET FINANCIAL SERVICES INC (PA)
Also Called: Capital Network Funding Svcs
11901 Santa Monica Blvd, Los Angeles
(90025-2767)
PHONE..................................877 980-0558
John Armstrn, *CEO*
Blake Johnson, *President*
Michael Kromnick, *CFO*
Armita Dalal, *Controller*
EMP: 90
SQ FT: 23,000
SALES (est): 12MM **Privately Held**
WEB: www.capnetusa.com
SIC: **6159** Equipment & vehicle finance
leasing companies

(P-9501)
ELECTRONIC COMMERCE LLC
1 City Blvd W Ste 1850, Orange
(92868-3636)
PHONE..................................800 770-5520
Darnell Ponder, *Managing Prtnr*
EMP: 85
SQ FT: 7,000
SALES (est): 13.5MM **Privately Held**
SIC: **6159** Intermediate investment banks

(P-9502)
FUNDBOX INC
300 Montgomery St Ste 900, San Francisco
(94104-1921)
PHONE..................................415 509-1343
Eyal Shinar, *CEO*
Prashant Fuloria, *Officer*
Katie Silverman, *Admin Asst*
Rose Zhong, *VP Finance*
Sasha Dobrolioubov, *Business Mgr*
EMP: 150
SQ FT: 8,300
SALES: 300MM **Privately Held**
SIC: **6159** Small business investment com-
panies
PA: Fundbox Ltd
23 Yehuda Halevy
Tel Aviv-Jaffa
369 428-00

(P-9503)
GENERAL ELECTRIC COMPANY
2995 Red Hill Ave Ste 100, Costa Mesa
(92626-5984)
PHONE..................................714 434-4111
Teri Lo, *Manager*
EMP: 147
SALES (corp-wide): 121.6B **Publicly Held**
WEB: www.gecapital.com
SIC: **6159** Equipment & vehicle finance
leasing companies; machinery & equip-
ment finance leasing
PA: General Electric Company
41 Farnsworth St
Boston MA 02210
617 443-3000

(P-9504)
GENERAL ELECTRIC COMPANY
17901 Von Karman Ave # 600, Irvine
(92614-6297)
P.O. Box 4596, New York NY (10163-4596)
PHONE..................................949 838-3043
Mark Dawejko, *Branch Mgr*
EMP: 159

SALES (corp-wide): 121.6B **Publicly
Held**
WEB: www.gecapital.com
SIC: **6159** Equipment & vehicle finance
leasing companies
PA: General Electric Company
41 Farnsworth St
Boston MA 02210
617 443-3000

(P-9505)
INTERLINK
Also Called: Interlink Company The
10940 Wilshire Blvd, Los Angeles
(90024-3915)
PHONE..................................310 734-1499
Shezad Rokerya, *Director*
Dr Charles Kohlhaas, *Vice Chairman*
Jason P Caramanis, *Exec VP*
EMP: 103
SQ FT: 4,000
SALES (est): 8.6MM **Privately Held**
SIC: **6159** 8742 Intermediate investment
banks; banking & finance consultant

(P-9506)
MARWIT CAPITAL PARTNERS II LP (PA)
24 Corporate Plaza Dr # 100, Newport
Beach (92660-7966)
PHONE..................................949 861-3636
Mathew L Witte, *Partner*
Chris L Britt, *Partner*
Laurie Sey Mour, *Partner*
EMP: 315
SQ FT: 3,000
SALES (est): 28.8MM **Privately Held**
SIC: **6159** 5699 Small business invest-
ment companies; western apparel

(P-9507)
NATIONS FIRST CAPITAL LLC
Also Called: Go Capital
516 Gibson Dr Ste 160, Roseville
(95678-5792)
PHONE..................................855 396-3600
Evan Lang, *Mng Member*
Dan Summers,
EMP: 70
SALES (est): 14.3MM **Privately Held**
SIC: **6159** Equipment & vehicle finance
leasing companies

(P-9508)
NATIONWIDE FUNDING LLC
5520 Trabuco Rd Ste 100, Irvine
(92620-5700)
PHONE..................................949 679-3600
Evan Lang, *Mng Member*
Josh Splinter,
EMP: 50
SQ FT: 12,000
SALES (est): 9.4MM **Privately Held**
SIC: **6159** 7359 Machinery & equipment fi-
nance leasing; equipment rental & leasing

(P-9509)
PACIFIC CAPITAL COMPANIES LLC
11620 Wilshire Blvd, Los Angeles
(90025-1706)
PHONE..................................800 583-3015
Charles Anderson, *Managing Prtnr*
EMP: 150
SQ FT: 10,000
SALES (est): 17.8MM **Privately Held**
SIC: **6159** Automobile finance leasing

(P-9510)
TRINITY CAPITAL CORPORATION (DH)
475 Sansome St Fl 19, San Francisco
(94111-3112)
PHONE..................................415 956-5174
Don J McGrath, *CEO*
Jerry Newell, *President*
Christopher Kelly, *VP Bus Dvlpt*
Katherine Utsumi, *Marketing Staff*
EMP: 74
SQ FT: 19,232
SALES (est): 35MM
SALES (corp-wide): 2.7B **Privately Held**
WEB: www.trinitycapital.com
SIC: **6159** 8741 Machinery & equipment fi-
nance leasing; management services

SALES (corp-wide): 121.6B **Publicly
Held**
WEB: www.gecapital.com
SIC: **6159** Equipment & vehicle finance
leasing companies
PA: General Electric Company
41 Farnsworth St
Boston MA 02210
617 443-3000

HQ: Bank Of The West
180 Montgomery St # 1400
San Francisco CA 94104
415 765-4800

(P-9511)
WELLS FARGO CAPITAL FIN LLC (DH)
2450 Colo Ave Ste 3000w, Santa Monica
(90404)
PHONE..................................310 453-7300
Peter E Schwab,
Jeff Carbery, *Exec VP*
Michael Ackad, *Vice Pres*
Fahad Haroon, *Vice Pres*
Nichol Shuart, *Vice Pres*
EMP: 99
SALES (est): 36.5MM
SALES (corp-wide): 101B **Publicly Held**
WEB: www.wellsfargo.com
SIC: **6159** Loan institutions, general & in-
dustrial
HQ: Wells Fargo Bank, National Associa-
tion
101 N Phillips Ave
Sioux Falls SD 57104
605 575-6900

(P-9512)
WESTLAKE SERVICES LLC (PA)
Also Called: Westlake Financial Services
4751 Wilshire Blvd # 100, Los Angeles
(90010-3847)
P.O. Box 76809 (90076-0809)
PHONE..................................323 692-8800
Don Hankey, *Ch of Bd*
Ian Anderson, *President*
Ralph Ontiveros, *President*
James Vagim, *President*
Paul Kerwin, *CFO*
EMP: 169
SQ FT: 22,000
SALES (est): 40.4MM **Privately Held**
WEB: www.westlakefinancial.com
SIC: **6159** 6141 Automobile finance leas-
ing; personal credit institutions

6162 Mortgage Bankers & Loan Correspondents

(P-9513)
A D BILICH INC
Also Called: Preferred Financial
11 Crow Canyon Ct Ste 100, San Ramon
(94583-1981)
PHONE..................................925 820-5557
Tim Barnes, *President*
Anthony D Bilich, *Owner*
John Engstrom, *CFO*
Angela Bilich, *Admin Sec*
Dwight Domonkos, *Loan Officer*
EMP: 50
SQ FT: 4,000
SALES (est): 7.8MM **Privately Held**
WEB: www.preferredfinancial.com
SIC: **6162** Mortgage bankers

(P-9514)
AGIRE MORTGAGE CORPORATION
2125 E Katella Ave # 350, Anaheim
(92806-6072)
PHONE..................................714 564-5821
Robin Auerbach, *President*
EMP: 50
SALES (est): 5.1MM **Privately Held**
SIC: **6162** Mortgage bankers

(P-9515)
ALL CALIFORNIA MORTGAGE INC (PA)
17 E Sr Frncis Drke Bl200, Larkspur
(94939)
PHONE..................................415 925-5225
Bruce Fonarow, *President*
Robert Knoll, *Partner*
Chuck Scoma, *Partner*
Jeffrey Drawdy, *Vice Pres*
Kevin Mulcahy, *Branch Mgr*
EMP: 66
SQ FT: 4,600
SALES (est): 7.9MM **Privately Held**
SIC: **6162** Mortgage bankers & correspon-
dents

P
R
O
D
U
C
T
S

&

S
V
C
S

(P-9516)
AMBER FINANCIAL GROUP LLC (PA)
Also Called: Amber Mortgage
11415 W Bernardo Ct, San Diego
(92127-1639)
PHONE..................................858 487-7209
Trena Papageorge,
Julian Kozar,
EMP: 110
SQ FT: 8,000
SALES (est): 7.6MM **Privately Held**
SIC: 6162 Mortgage bankers

(P-9517)
AMERICAN FINANCIAL NETWORK INC (PA)
Also Called: Gateway Home Realty
10 Pointe Dr Ste 330, Brea (92821-7620)
PHONE..................................909 606-3905
John B Sherman, *President*
John R Sherman, *Vice Pres*
Yang Gao, *Technical Mgr*
Bryan Gilbert, *Sales Staff*
EMP: 200
SQ FT: 8,000
SALES (est): 183.5MM **Privately Held**
SIC: 6162 Mortgage bankers

(P-9518)
AMERICAN INTERBANC MRTG LLC
4 Park Plz Ste 650, Irvine (92614-2522)
PHONE..................................714 957-9430
Jiangping J He,
Michael Czerwinski, *Officer*
Mary Drummond, *Opers Mgr*
Pamela Halvo, *Underwriter*
EMP: 50 **EST:** 1998
SALES (est): 7.5MM **Privately Held**
WEB: www.eloans4u.com
SIC: 6162 6163 Mortgage bankers; loan
brokers
PA: Seashine Financial Llc
4 Park Plz Ste 650
Irvine CA 92614

(P-9519)
AMERICAN INTERNET MORTGAGE INC
Also Called: Aimloan.com, A Direct Lender
4121 Camino Del Rio S, San Diego
(92108-4103)
PHONE..................................888 411-4246
Vincent J Kasperick, *President*
Jill Lantz, *Manager*
EMP: 106 **EST:** 1998
SQ FT: 4,500
SALES: 63.6MM **Privately Held**
SIC: 6162 Mortgage bankers

(P-9520)
AMERICAN PACIFIC MORTGAGE CORP
300 Tamal Plz Ste 250, Corte Madera
(94925-1170)
PHONE..................................415 891-8706
Ryan Madden, *Branch Mgr*
Vince Breen, *Partner*
Bart Welles, *Vice Pres*
Foster Weeks, *Loan Officer*
Vicki Bahnasy, *Loan*
EMP: 50 **Privately Held**
SIC: 6162 Mortgage bankers & correspondents
PA: American Pacific Mortgage Corporation
3000 Lava Ridge Ct # 200
Roseville CA 95661

(P-9521)
AMERICAN PACIFIC MORTGAGE CORP (PA)
Also Called: Big Valley Mortgage
3000 Lava Ridge Ct # 200, Roseville
(95661-2800)
PHONE..................................916 960-1325
Kurt Reisig, *CEO*
Bill Lowman, *President*
David Mack, *COO*
Ralph Hints, *CFO*
David Butler, *Officer*
EMP: 120

SQ FT: 35,000
SALES (est): 417.6MM **Privately Held**
WEB: www.apmmortgage.com
SIC: 6162 Mortgage bankers

(P-9522)
AMERICAN TRANSPORT INC
Also Called: Bankers Diversified Mortgage
3910 Prospect Ave Ste A, Yorba Linda
(92886-1776)
PHONE..................................714 567-8000
David Hahnfeld, *President*
Diane G Hahnfeld, *Treasurer*
David N Hartman, *Vice Pres*
EMP: 60
SQ FT: 32,000
SALES (est): 4MM **Privately Held**
WEB: www.bankersdiversified.com
SIC: 6162 Mortgage brokers, using own
money

(P-9523)
AMERICASH
3080 Bristol St Ste 300, Costa Mesa
(92626-3059)
PHONE..................................714 994-7554
Paul Giangrande, *CEO*
Eric Harrington, *Vice Pres*
Michael Martin, *Vice Pres*
EMP: 50
SALES (est): 12.5MM **Privately Held**
WEB: www.americashloans.com
SIC: 6162 Mortgage bankers

(P-9524)
AMERIPATH MORTGAGE CORPORATION
6410 Oak Cyn Ste 200, Irvine
(92618-5215)
PHONE..................................949 753-9211
Paul B Akers, *President*
Kirk L Redding, *CEO*
Roger Stoll, *Bd of Directors*
Jo Beth Montoya, *Vice Pres*
EMP: 112
SQ FT: 22,286
SALES (est): 8.4MM **Privately Held**
WEB: www.amclend.com
SIC: 6162 Mortgage bankers

(P-9525)
ARCS COMMERCIAL MORTGAGE CO LP (DH)
26901 Agoura Rd Ste 200, Calabasas
(91301-5109)
PHONE..................................818 676-3274
Timothy White, *CEO*
EMP: 110
SQ FT: 15,000
SALES (est): 32.2MM
SALES (corp-wide): 19.9B **Publicly Held**
SIC: 6162 Mortgage bankers
HQ: Pnc Bank, National Association
222 Delaware Ave
Wilmington DE 19801
877 762-2000

(P-9526)
BAY EQUITY LLC (PA)
Also Called: Bay Equity Home Loans
28 Liberty Ship Way # 2800, Sausalito
(94965-3319)
PHONE..................................415 632-5150
Casey McGovern, *President*
Taraya Caple, *Officer*
Ryan Colbert, *Officer*
Adina Erridge, *Officer*
Robert Gullick, *Officer*
EMP: 53
SQ FT: 6,000
SALES (est): 24.7MM **Privately Held**
SIC: 6162 Mortgage bankers

(P-9527)
BEAR STEARNS COMPANIES LLC
Also Called: Bear Stern Residential Mrtg
1833 Alton Pkwy, Irvine (92606-4902)
PHONE..................................949 856-8300
Troy Gotscahall, *Branch Mgr*
EMP: 780
SALES (corp-wide): 131.4B **Publicly Held**
WEB: www.bearstearns.com
SIC: 6162 Mortgage bankers

HQ: Bear Stearns Companies Llc
383 Madison Ave
New York NY 10179
212 272-2000

(P-9528)
BERKSHIRE MORTGAGE FIN CORP
Also Called: Vauche Bank Berkshire Mortgage
7575 Irvine Center Dr # 200, Irvine
(92618-2987)
PHONE..................................949 754-6300
Jeff Day, *Manager*
EMP: 80
SALES (corp-wide): 13.6B **Privately Held**
SIC: 6162 Mortgage bankers
HQ: Berkshire Mortgage Finance Corporation
1 North Beacon St Fl 14
Allston MA 02134
617 523-0066

(P-9529)
BROKER SOLUTIONS INC
233 Milford Dr, Corona Del Mar
(92625-3118)
PHONE..................................800 450-2010
EMP: 82 **Privately Held**
SIC: 6162 Mortgage bankers & correspondents
PA: Broker Solutions, Inc.
14511 Myford Rd Ste 100
Tustin CA 92780

(P-9530)
BSNAP LLC
4 Hutton Centre Dr Fl 10, Santa Ana
(92707-8713)
PHONE..................................657 269-4410
EMP: 99
SALES (est): 2.4MM **Privately Held**
SIC: 6162

(P-9531)
CAL MUTUAL INC
2040 S Santa Cruz St # 115, Anaheim
(92805-6821)
PHONE..................................888 700-4650
Dennis Shane Dailey, *President*
EMP: 87
SALES (est): 484K **Privately Held**
SIC: 6162 6531 Mortgage bankers & correspondents; real estate agent, residential

(P-9532)
CALIBER HOME LOANS INC
6600 Koll Center Pkwy, Pleasanton
(94566-3256)
PHONE..................................925 417-3491
Tim Soldati, *Principal*
Karstin Hickerson, *Officer*
Wendy Werdmuller, *Loan*
Mary Story, *Consultant*
EMP: 76
SALES (corp-wide): 2.3B **Privately Held**
SIC: 6162 Mortgage bankers & correspondents
PA: Caliber Home Loans, Inc.
1525 S Belt Line Rd
Coppell TX 75019
800 401-6587

(P-9533)
CALIBER HOME LOANS INC
3700 Hilborn Rd Ste 700, Fairfield
(94534-7997)
PHONE..................................707 432-1000
Sanjiv Das, *Principal*
Jessica Nix, *Manager*
Heather Quinlan, *Manager*
Daun Sherr, *Accounts Exec*
EMP: 300
SALES (corp-wide): 2.3B **Privately Held**
SIC: 6162 Mortgage bankers & correspondents
PA: Caliber Home Loans, Inc.
1525 S Belt Line Rd
Coppell TX 75019
800 401-6587

(P-9534)
CALIBER HOME LOANS INC
1111 Chapala St, Santa Barbara
(93101-3158)
PHONE..................................805 883-6800
Sarah Chicone, *Receptionist*
EMP: 76
SALES (corp-wide): 2.3B **Privately Held**
SIC: 6162 6141 Loan correspondents;
personal credit institutions
PA: Caliber Home Loans, Inc.
1525 S Belt Line Rd
Coppell TX 75019
800 401-6587

(P-9535)
CAPITAL PLUS FINANCIAL CORP
909 W Laurel St Ste 250, San Diego
(92101-1224)
PHONE..................................619 744-1900
Frank Sharpe, *President*
Doug Lipar, *Vice Pres*
Evelyn Cervantes, *Opers Staff*
EMP: 50
SQ FT: 5,000
SALES (est): 5.2MM **Privately Held**
SIC: 6162 Mortgage brokers, using own
money

(P-9536)
CARRINGTON MRTG HOLDINGS LLC
1600 S Douglass Rd # 110, Anaheim
(92806-5948)
PHONE..................................888 267-0584
Phil Grassbaugh, *Vice Pres*
Steve Patton, *Exec VP*
Rick Sharga, *Exec VP*
Rob Petruska, *Senior VP*
Jeremy Drang, *Vice Pres*
EMP: 123
SQ FT: 192,000
SALES (est): 31.4MM
SALES (corp-wide): 39MM **Privately Held**
SIC: 6162 Mortgage bankers & correspondents
PA: Carrington Capital Management Llc
1700 E Putnam Ave Ste 501
Old Greenwich CT 06870
203 661-6186

(P-9537)
CENTURY FINANCE INCORPORATED
Also Called: Villagecraft Quality Furn
2461 Santa Monica Blvd, Santa Monica
(90404-2138)
PHONE..................................310 281-3081
RC Zarate, *President*
Franceisca Zarate, *CFO*
Ezzio Delpino, *Corp Secy*
EMP: 56
SALES (est): 4.5MM **Privately Held**
SIC: 6162 2514 Mortgage bankers & correspondents; metal household furniture

(P-9538)
CHAPEL FUNDING CORPORATION
26521 Rancho Pkwy S, Lake Forest
(92630-8329)
PHONE..................................949 580-1800
Nina Mitchel, *President*
EMP: 165
SALES (est): 10.4MM **Privately Held**
WEB: www.chapelfunding.com
SIC: 6162 Mortgage bankers & correspondents

(P-9539)
CITIGROUP INC
840 N Eckhoff St Ste 140, Orange
(92868-1054)
PHONE..................................714 938-0748
Michael B Zeller, *Sales & Mktg St*
Lori Anderson, *Vice Pres*
Michael Berardo, *Vice Pres*
Lina Bianco, *Vice Pres*
Bin Liu, *Vice Pres*
EMP: 100

▲ = Import ▼=Export
◆ =Import/Export

SALES (corp-wide): 72.8B **Publicly Held**
WEB: www.citigroup.com
SIC: **6162** 6163 Mortgage bankers & correspondents; loan brokers
PA: Citigroup Inc.
388 Greenwich St
New York NY 10013
212 559-1000

(P-9540)
COUNTRYWIDE CAPITAL MKTS LLC (DH)
4500 Park Granada, Calabasas (91302-1613)
PHONE.....................818 225-3000
Angelo R Mozilo, *Ch of Bd*
Stanfard L Kurland, *CFO*
Ron Kripalani, *Director*
EMP: 182
SALES (est): 44.2MM
SALES (corp-wide): 110.5B **Publicly Held**
SIC: **6162** Mortgage brokers, using own money
HQ: Countrywide Financial Corporation
4500 Park Granada
Calabasas CA 91302
818 225-3000

(P-9541)
COUNTRYWIDE FINANCIAL CORP (HQ)
4500 Park Granada, Calabasas (91302-1613)
P.O. Box 7137, Pasadena (91109-7137)
PHONE.....................818 225-3000
Angelo R Mozilo, *Ch of Bd*
David Sambol, *President*
Jack W Schakett, *COO*
Eric P Sieracki, *CFO*
David Kuhn, *Exec VP*
EMP: 1100
SQ FT: 225,000
SALES (est): 6.4B
SALES (corp-wide): 110.5B **Publicly Held**
WEB: www.countrywide.com
SIC: **6162** 6211 6361 6411 Mortgage bankers; brokers, security; dealers, security; title insurance; life insurance agents; loan brokers; real estate investors, except property operators
PA: Bank Of America Corporation
100 N Tryon St Ste 170
Charlotte NC 28202
704 386-5681

(P-9542)
COUNTRYWIDE HOME LOANS INC (DH)
225 W Hillcrest Dr, Thousand Oaks (91360-7883)
PHONE.....................818 225-3000
Michael Schloessmann, *Ch of Bd*
Angelo R Mozilo, *Ch of Bd*
David Sambol, *President*
Carlos M Garcia, *COO*
Thomas K McLaughlin, *CFO*
EMP: 700 EST: 1969
SQ FT: 220,000
SALES (est): 579.7MM
SALES (corp-wide): 110.5B **Publicly Held**
WEB: www.mycountrywide.com
SIC: **6162** Mortgage bankers
HQ: Countrywide Financial Corporation
4500 Park Granada
Calabasas CA 91302
818 225-3000

(P-9543)
COUNTRYWIDE HOME LOANS INC
801 N Brand Blvd Ste 750, Glendale (91203-3218)
PHONE.....................818 550-8700
Lynda Martinlawley, *Manager*
EMP: 150
SALES (corp-wide): 110.5B **Publicly Held**
WEB: www.mycountrywide.com
SIC: **6162** Mortgage bankers

HQ: Countrywide Home Loans, Inc.
225 W Hillcrest Dr
Thousand Oaks CA 91360
818 225-3000

(P-9544)
CRESTLINE FUNDING CORPORATION
18851 Pardeen Ave, San Diego (92108)
PHONE.....................949 863-8600
Scott M Brown, *President*
Brad Helman, *CFO*
Maddie Mullins, *Loan*
David Paulsen, *Loan*
EMP: 50
SQ FT: 18,500
SALES (est): 12.3MM **Privately Held**
WEB: www.crestlinewholesale.com
SIC: **6162** Mortgage bankers

(P-9545)
DECISION READY SOLUTIONS INC
400 Spectrum Center Dr # 2050, Irvine (92618-5024)
PHONE.....................949 400-1126
Ravi Ramanathan, *President*
Claudia Sanchez, *COO*
Tom Schmidt, *CFO*
Matthew Lichtner, *Exec VP*
Ranjeev Kumar, *Vice Pres*
EMP: 50 EST: 2011
SALES (est): 2.2MM **Privately Held**
SIC: **6162** 7371 7372 Mortgage bankers; computer software systems analysis & design, custom; business oriented computer software

(P-9546)
ECI CORPORATION A CORP NEV (PA)
Also Called: Coast Capital
4300 Stevens Creek Blvd # 275, San Jose (95129-1249)
PHONE.....................408 941-9268
Robert Genisman, *CEO*
Pete Cline, *President*
Robin Cline, *Treasurer*
David Belleville, *Vice Pres*
Nina Genisman, *Admin Sec*
EMP: 70
SQ FT: 9,000
SALES (est): 5.4MM **Privately Held**
WEB: www.eci-corp.com
SIC: **6162** Mortgage brokers, using own money

(P-9547)
EXECUTIVE FINANCIAL HM LN CORP
Also Called: Executive Home Loan
12501 Chandler Blvd, Valley Village (91607-1941)
PHONE.....................818 285-5626
Michael Nikravesh, *President*
Ron Fattal, *Vice Pres*
EMP: 50
SALES (est): 5MM **Privately Held**
SIC: **6162** Mortgage bankers & correspondents

(P-9548)
FINANCE AMERICA LLC (HQ)
1901 Main St Ste 150, Irvine (92614-0516)
PHONE.....................949 440-1000
Brian Libman,
Karen H Cornell,
Graham Fleming,
Arthur K Rice,
EMP: 186
SQ FT: 60,000
SALES (est): 150.1MM
SALES (corp-wide): 28.1MM **Privately Held**
WEB: www.closeasap.com
SIC: **6162** 6163 Mortgage bankers; loan brokers
PA: Lehman Brothers Holdings Inc.
277 Park Ave Fl 46
New York NY 10172
646 285-9000

(P-9549)
FINANCE AMERICA MORTGAGE LLC
13200 Crossroads Pkwy N, City of Industry (91746-3459)
PHONE.....................562 478-4664
Gabriel Garza, *Manager*
Ryan Kim, *Exec VP*
James Kim, *Regl Sales Mgr*
EMP: 252 **Privately Held**
SIC: **6162** Mortgage bankers
PA: Finance Of America Mortgage Llc
300 Welsh Rd Bldg 5
Horsham PA 19044

(P-9550)
FIRST CALIFORNIA MRTG CO II
1400 N Mcdowell Blvd # 300, Petaluma (94954-6553)
P.O. Box 11868, San Rafael (94912-1868)
PHONE.....................415 209-0910
Dennis M Hart, *Ch of Bd*
Christopher Hart, *President*
Elizabeth Armstrong, *Director*
EMP: 100
SALES (est): 12.8MM **Privately Held**
WEB: www.firstcal.net
SIC: **6162** Mortgage bankers & correspondents

(P-9551)
FIRST PRIORITY FINANCIAL INC
3700 Hilborn Rd Ste 700, Fairfield (94534-7997)
PHONE.....................707 432-1000
Timothy Kearns, *President*
David Soldati, *CFO*
Dennis Hughes, *Vice Pres*
Michael Soldati, *Vice Pres*
EMP: 300
SQ FT: 4,500
SALES (est): 1.6MM **Privately Held**
WEB: www.lendscape.com
SIC: **6162** Mortgage bankers & correspondents

(P-9552)
GOLDEN EMPIRE MORTGAGE INC
664 Shoppers Ln Ste A, Covina (91723-3536)
PHONE.....................626 967-3236
Joe Ewens, *Branch Mgr*
EMP: 72
SALES (corp-wide): 67.9MM **Privately Held**
SIC: **6162** Mortgage bankers & correspondents
PA: Golden Empire Mortgage, Inc.
1200 Discovery Dr Ste 300
Bakersfield CA 93309
661 328-1600

(P-9553)
GOLDEN EMPIRE MORTGAGE INC
Also Called: Gem Mortgage
420 Barstow Rd, Barstow (92311-2952)
PHONE.....................760 256-3593
Tim Silva, *Branch Mgr*
EMP: 60
SALES (corp-wide): 67.9MM **Privately Held**
SIC: **6162** Mortgage bankers & correspondents
PA: Golden Empire Mortgage, Inc.
1200 Discovery Dr Ste 300
Bakersfield CA 93309
661 328-1600

(P-9554)
GOLDEN EMPIRE MORTGAGE INC (PA)
1200 Discovery Dr Ste 300, Bakersfield (93309-7036)
PHONE.....................661 328-1600
John Copeland, *Manager*
EMP: 80
SALES (est): 67.9MM **Privately Held**
SIC: **6162** Mortgage bankers

(P-9555)
GOLDEN EMPIRE MORTGAGE INC (PA)
2130 Chester Ave, Bakersfield (93301-4471)
PHONE.....................661 328-1600
Howard Kootstra, *CEO*
Joe Ewens, *Exec VP*
Robert Satnick, *Exec VP*
Rebecca Wegman, *Exec VP*
John Thomas, *Vice Pres*
EMP: 100
SQ FT: 25,000
SALES (est): 50.8MM **Privately Held**
WEB: www.gemcorp.com
SIC: **6162** Mortgage bankers

(P-9556)
GUARANTEED RATE INC
1455 Frazee Rd Ste 500, San Diego (92108-4350)
PHONE.....................760 310-6008
Trent Annicharico, *Branch Mgr*
EMP: 129 **Privately Held**
SIC: **6162** Mortgage bankers
PA: Guaranteed Rate, Inc.
3940 N Ravenswood Ave
Chicago IL 60613

(P-9557)
GUILD MORTGAGE COMPANY
3626 Fair Oaks Blvd, Sacramento (95864-7200)
PHONE.....................916 486-6257
Mary Ann McGarry, *Branch Mgr*
EMP: 50
SALES (corp-wide): 1.2B **Privately Held**
SIC: **6162** Mortgage bankers & correspondents
PA: Guild Mortgage Company
5898 Copley Dr Fl 4
San Diego CA 92111
800 365-4441

(P-9558)
HCL FINANCE INC (PA)
Also Called: Home Community Lending
2560 Mission College Blvd, Santa Clara (95054-1217)
PHONE.....................408 845-9035
Hong Cheng, *President*
Nancy Cheng, *Vice Pres*
EMP: 107
SQ FT: 9,000
SALES (est): 7.6MM **Privately Held**
WEB: www.hclfinance.com
SIC: **6162** Mortgage bankers & correspondents

(P-9559)
HOME CAPITAL GROUP
948 N Grand Ave, Covina (91724-2045)
PHONE.....................626 331-4213
Raymond Mark Gonzales, *Partner*
Rick Starr, *Partner*
EMP: 68
SALES (est): 3.4MM **Privately Held**
SIC: **6162** Mortgage bankers & correspondents

(P-9560)
HOMEBRIDGE FINANCIAL SVCS INC
15301 Ventura Blvd, Sherman Oaks (91403-3102)
PHONE.....................818 981-0606
Douglas Rotella, *President*
EMP: 1700 **Privately Held**
SIC: **6162** Mortgage bankers & correspondents
PA: Homebridge Financial Services, Inc.
194 Wood Ave S Fl 9
Iselin NJ 08830

(P-9561)
HOMEQ SERVICING CORPORATION (DH)
4837 Watt Ave, North Highlands (95660-5108)
PHONE.....................916 339-6192
Arthur Lyon, *President*
Keith G Becher, *COO*
Mark K Metz, *Admin Sec*

EMP: 1000 EST: 1967
SALES (est): 79.4MM
SALES (corp-wide): 1B Publicly Held
WEB: www.homeq.com
SIC: 6162 6163 6111 6159 Mortgage
   bankers; agents, farm or business loan;
   Student Loan Marketing Association; au-
   tomobile finance leasing
HQ: Ocwen Loan Servicing, Llc
   1661 Worthington Rd # 100
   West Palm Beach FL 33409
   561 682-8000

(P-9562)
HSBC FINANCE CORPORATION
21801 Ventura Bouelvard, Woodland Hills
(91364)
PHONE.................................818 999-9175
EMP: 303
SALES (corp-wide): 87.7B Privately Held
WEB: www.household.com
SIC: 6162 Mortgage bankers
HQ: Hsbc Finance Corporation
   1421 W Shure Dr Ste 100
   Arlington Heights IL 60004
   224 880-7000

(P-9563)
IMPAC MORTGAGE CORP
19500 Jamboree Rd Ste 100, Irvine
(92612-2426)
PHONE.................................949 475-3600
Joseph R Tomkinson, President
EMP: 298
SALES (est): 62.6MM Publicly Held
SIC: 6162 Mortgage bankers
PA: Impac Mortgage Holdings, Inc.
   19500 Jamboree Rd Ste 100
   Irvine CA 92612

(P-9564)
INTERNATIONAL HOME MORTGAGE
13601 Whittier Blvd # 311, Whittier
(90605-1968)
PHONE.................................562 945-7753
Rick Arciniega, Manager
EMP: 75
SALES (est): 5.1MM Privately Held
SIC: 6162 Mortgage bankers & correspon-
   dents

(P-9565)
ISERVE RESIDENTIAL LENDING LLC
16745 W Bernardo Dr # 100, San Diego
(92127-1908)
PHONE.................................858 486-4169
Doug Wilson, Director
Angela Kidd, Officer
Karina Ponce, Officer
Robert Sanders, Area Mgr
Mauricio Ahumada, Branch Mgr
EMP: 100
SALES (est): 18.9MM Privately Held
SIC: 6162 Bond & mortgage companies

(P-9566)
JMJ FINANCIAL GROUP (PA)
26800 Aliso Viejo Pkwy # 200, Aliso Viejo
(92656-2625)
PHONE.................................949 340-6336
Virgil Kyle, President
Devin Langager, Partner
Thomas Kish, COO
Ryan Robertson, CFO
Alex Araoz, Branch Mgr
EMP: 50
SQ FT: 10,000
SALES: 500MM Privately Held
SIC: 6162 Mortgage bankers

(P-9567)
JUST MORTGAGE INC
8577 Haven Ave Ste 306, Rancho Cuca-
monga (91730-4850)
PHONE.................................562 908-5000
Eun H Choi, CEO
Sang H Jeung, President
Bryan Choi, Vice Pres
EMP: 118
SQ FT: 49,750
SALES (est): 15.9MM Privately Held
SIC: 6162 Mortgage bankers & correspon-
   dents

(P-9568)
KONDAUR CAPITAL CORPORATION (PA)
333 S Anita Dr Ste 400, Orange
(92868-3314)
PHONE.................................714 352-2038
John Kontouis, President
EMP: 150
SALES (est): 2.2MM Privately Held
SIC: 6162 Mortgage bankers

(P-9569)
LAKE COUNTY HOME LOANS
Also Called: Selzer Home Loans
350 E Gobbi St, Ukiah (95482-5511)
PHONE.................................707 462-4000
Richard Selzer, Owner
Elisa Moilanen, Admin Sec
EMP: 50
SALES (est): 4.4MM Privately Held
SIC: 6162 Mortgage bankers & correspon-
   dents

(P-9570)
LAND HOME FINANCIAL SVCS INC (PA)
1355 Willow Way Ste 250, Concord
(94520-8113)
PHONE.................................925 676-7038
Bradley Harold Waite, CEO
Angela Warren, President
David Waite, CFO
Jennie Davis, Officer
Tiffany Jamieson, Officer
EMP: 50
SQ FT: 6,000
SALES (est): 20.7MM Privately Held
SIC: 6162 Loan correspondents

(P-9571)
LENDUS LLC
3240 Stone Valley Rd W, Alamo
(94507-1555)
PHONE.................................925 295-9300
EMP: 720
SALES (est): 156.4K Privately Held
SIC: 6162 Mortgage bankers & correspon-
   dents

(P-9572)
LENDUSA LLC (PA)
Also Called: RPM Mortgage
3240 Stone Valley Rd W, Alamo
(94507-1555)
PHONE.................................925 295-9300
Kier Evergreen, Partner
Leah Gaona, Partner
Gary Scoma, Ch Credit Ofcr
Jeremy Ogata, Officer
Nick Rowson, Officer
EMP: 55
SALES (est): 54.5MM Privately Held
SIC: 6162 Mortgage bankers & correspon-
   dents

(P-9573)
LENOX FINANCIAL MORTGAGE CORP
Also Called: Weslend Financial
200 Sandpointe Ave # 800, Santa Ana
(92707-5783)
PHONE.................................949 428-5100
Wesley C Hoaglund, CEO
Robert Oconnor, Executive
Trinh Bui, Business Mgr
Louise Woods, Regl Sales Mgr
Cheryl Smith, Sales Mgr
EMP: 105
SALES (est): 51.4MM Privately Held
SIC: 6162 Mortgage bankers

(P-9574)
LEON CHIEN CORP
Also Called: RE Max 2000 Realty
17843 Colima Rd, City of Industry
(91748-1729)
PHONE.................................626 964-8302
Kuan Sung, CEO
EMP: 80
SALES (est): 8.5MM Privately Held
SIC: 6162 Mortgage bankers & correspon-
   dents

(P-9575)
LMB MORTGAGE SERVICES INC (HQ)
Also Called: Lowermybills
4859 W Slauson Ave # 405, Los Angeles
(90056-1290)
PHONE.................................310 348-6800
Steve Krenzer, CEO
Pat Gregory, CFO
Jeff Hughes, Vice Pres
Burr Hilsabeck, Executive
Melinda Catlett, Executive Asst
EMP: 150
SALES (est): 22MM
SALES (corp-wide): 1.7B Privately Held
SIC: 6162 Mortgage bankers
PA: Rock Holdings Inc.
   1090 Woodward Ave
   Detroit MI 48226
   313 373-7700

(P-9576)
LOANDEPOTCOM LLC
901 N Palm Canyon Dr, Palm Springs
(92262-4450)
PHONE.................................760 797-6000
Anthony Hsieh, Branch Mgr
EMP: 1029 Privately Held
SIC: 6162 Mortgage bankers
PA: Loandepot.Com, Llc
   26642 Towne Centre Dr
   Foothill Ranch CA 92610

(P-9577)
LOANDEPOTCOM LLC (PA)
Also Called: Customer Loan Depot
26642 Towne Centre Dr, Foothill Ranch
(92610-2808)
PHONE.................................888 337-6888
Anthony Hsieh, CEO
David Norris, President
Jon Frojen, CFO
David King, Chief Mktg Ofcr
David Rosenthal, Officer
EMP: 963
SALES (est): 1.3B Privately Held
WEB: www.loandepot.com
SIC: 6162 Mortgage bankers

(P-9578)
LONG BEACH INVESTMENT GROUP
Also Called: Dream Home & Investments Rlty
2041 Pacific Coast Hwy, Lomita
(90717-2685)
PHONE.................................562 595-7277
Henry Salazar, President
EMP: 50
SQ FT: 6,000
SALES (est): 2.7MM Privately Held
SIC: 6162 Mortgage bankers & correspon-
   dents

(P-9579)
MASON MCDUFFIE MORTGAGE CORP (PA)
2010 Crow Canyon Pl # 400, San Ramon
(94583-1344)
PHONE.................................925 242-4400
Marilyn Richardson, CEO
Jack Radin, CFO
Herb Tasker, Chairman
Carl Cardarelli, Officer
Bob Digrazia, Officer
EMP: 83
SALES (est): 6.2MM Privately Held
WEB: www.mmcdcorp.com
SIC: 6162 Mortgage bankers

(P-9580)
METRO HOME LOAN INC
Also Called: Metro City
15301 Ventura Blvd # 400, Sherman Oaks
(91403-3102)
PHONE.................................818 461-9840
Paul Whiley, Vice Pres
EMP: 99
SALES (est): 5MM Privately Held
SIC: 6162 Mortgage bankers & correspon-
   dents

(P-9581)
MISSION HILLS MORTGAGE CORP (HQ)
Also Called: Mission Hills Mortgage Bankers
18500 Von Karman Ave # 1100, Irvine
(92612-0546)
PHONE.................................714 972-3832
Jay Ledbetter, President
Brian Tilton, Vice Pres
EMP: 140
SQ FT: 27,000
SALES (est): 38.7MM
SALES (corp-wide): 132.1MM Privately
Held
WEB: www.mhmc.com
SIC: 6162 Mortgage bankers & correspon-
   dents
PA: Tarbell Financial Corporation
   1403 N Tustin Ave Ste 380
   Santa Ana CA 92705
   714 972-0988

(P-9582)
MORTGAGE CAPITAL ASSOC INC
11150 W Olympic Blvd # 1160, Los Angeles
(90064-1826)
PHONE.................................310 477-6877
Jay Steren, CEO
EMP: 54
SALES (est): 6.9MM Privately Held
WEB: www.100percentloan.com
SIC: 6162 Mortgage bankers & correspon-
   dents

(P-9583)
MORTGAGE CAPITAL PARTNERS INC
12400 Wilshire Blvd # 900, Los Angeles
(90025-1030)
PHONE.................................310 295-2900
Carolyn W Chang, President
David Anthony, President
Charles Glenn, Vice Pres
Trevor Lane, Vice Pres
Tamie Eagan, Loan
EMP: 80 EST: 2008
SALES (est): 11.2MM Privately Held
SIC: 6162 Mortgage bankers

(P-9584)
MOUNTAIN WEST FINANCIAL INC (PA)
Also Called: Mortgage Works Financial
1209 Nevada St Ste 200, Redlands
(92374-4581)
PHONE.................................909 793-1500
Gary H Martell Jr, President
Michael W Douglas, CFO
Brian Daily, Senior VP
EMP: 391
SQ FT: 4,729
SALES (est): 80.1MM Privately Held
WEB: www.mwfinc.com
SIC: 6162 Mortgage bankers

(P-9585)
OCMBC INC
Also Called: Ocmban
19000 Macarthur Blvd # 200, Irvine
(92612-1420)
PHONE.................................714 479-0999
Rabi H Aziz, CEO
Madelina L Colon, President
Hector Chaidez, Division Mgr
Sona Dominova, Accounts Exec
Mary Gutierrez, Underwriter
EMP: 70 EST: 2001
SQ FT: 12,500
SALES (est): 11.8MM Privately Held
WEB: www.helpufinance.com
SIC: 6162 Mortgage bankers

(P-9586)
ONEMAIN HOLDINGS INC
2401 Claribel Rd Ste C, Riverbank
(95367-9480)
PHONE.................................209 869-8030
Sean Craig, Branch Mgr
EMP: 91
SALES (corp-wide): 4.2B Publicly Held
SIC: 6162 Mortgage bankers & correspon-
   dents

PA: Onemain Holdings, Inc.
601 Nw 2nd St
Evansville IN 47708
812 424-8031

(P-9587)
ONEMAIN HOLDINGS INC
31712 Casino Dr Ste 6a, Lake Elsinore
(92530-4513)
PHONE...................................951 245-5029
EMP: 91
SALES (corp-wide): 4.2B **Publicly Held**
SIC: 6162 Mortgage bankers & correspondents
PA: Onemain Holdings, Inc.
601 Nw 2nd St
Evansville IN 47708
812 424-8031

(P-9588)
OPTIMA MORTGAGE CORPORATION
2081 Bus Ctr Dr Ste 230, Irvine (92612)
PHONE...................................714 389-4650
Mansour Sadeghi, *President*
Shiva Sadeghi, *Treasurer*
EMP: 55
SQ FT: 14,000
SALES: 5.1MM **Privately Held**
WEB: www.60minuteloan.com
SIC: 6162 Mortgage bankers

(P-9589)
OWNIT MORTGAGE SOLUTIONS INC
Also Called: Security Pacific Home Loans
4360 Park Terrace Dr # 100, Westlake Village (91361-5696)
PHONE...................................513 872-6922
Bill Dallas, *President*
Bruce Dickinson, *COO*
John Duhadway, *CFO*
John Du Hadway, *Vice Pres*
Brian Thompson, *VP Finance*
EMP: 500
SQ FT: 47,857
SALES (est): 33.4MM **Privately Held**
SIC: 6162 Mortgage bankers & correspondents; loan brokers

(P-9590)
PARAMOUNT EQUITY MORTGAGE LLC
22 Executive Park Ste 100, Irvine
(92614-2700)
PHONE...................................916 290-9999
Hayes Barnard, *President*
EMP: 150
SALES (corp-wide): 113.1MM **Privately Held**
SIC: 6162 Mortgage bankers
PA: Paramount Equity Mortgage, Llc
8781 Sierra College Blvd
Roseville CA 95661
916 290-9999

(P-9591)
PEOPLES CHOICE HOME (PA)
7515 Irvine Center Dr, Irvine (92618-2930)
PHONE...................................949 494-6167
Neil B Kornswiet, *CEO*
EMP: 55
SQ FT: 20,000
SALES (est): 16.9MM **Privately Held**
SIC: 6162 Mortgage companies, urban

(P-9592)
PLAZA HOME MORTGAGE INC (PA)
4820 Eastgate Mall # 100, San Diego
(92121-1993)
PHONE...................................858 346-1200
Kevin Parra, *President*
Marc Godt, *Officer*
James Cutri, *Exec VP*
Michael Fontaine, *Exec VP*
Michael Modell, *Senior VP*
EMP: 50 **EST:** 2000
SQ FT: 1,000
SALES (est): 172.2MM **Privately Held**
WEB: www.plazahomemortgages.com
SIC: 6162 Mortgage bankers

(P-9593)
PRIVATE NAT MRTG ACCPTANCE LLC (HQ)
Also Called: Pennymac
6101 Condor Dr, Agoura Hills (91301)
PHONE...................................818 224-7401
Jeff Grogin,
Steve Bailey, *Security Dir*
EMP: 800
SALES (est): 138.7MM
SALES (corp-wide): 1.1B **Publicly Held**
SIC: 6162 Mortgage bankers
PA: Pennymac Financial Services, Inc.
3043 Townsgate Rd
Westlake Village CA 91361
818 224-7442

(P-9594)
PROVIDENT FINCL HOLDINGS INC
9245 Laguna Springs Dr # 13, Elk Grove
(95758-7987)
PHONE...................................916 709-3257
Chris Opfer, *Branch Mgr*
EMP: 85 **Publicly Held**
SIC: 6162 Mortgage bankers & correspondents
PA: Provident Financial Holdings, Inc.
3756 Central Ave
Riverside CA 92506

(P-9595)
PROVIDENT FUNDING ASSOC LP (PA)
851 Traeger Ave Ste 100, San Bruno
(94066-3091)
P.O. Box 5914, Santa Rosa (95402-5914)
PHONE...................................650 652-1300
Doug Pica, *General Ptnr*
Lori Pica, *COO*
Chris Tauscher, *Treasurer*
Glenn Wertheim, *Exec VP*
Mike Jantz, *Vice Pres*
EMP: 50
SALES (est): 88.7MM **Privately Held**
SIC: 6162 Mortgage bankers

(P-9596)
PROVIDENT MRTG CPITL ASSOC INC
Also Called: P M C A
1633 Bayshore Hwy Ste 155, Burlingame
(94010-1515)
PHONE...................................650 652-1300
Craig Pica, *Ch of Bd*
Mark Lefanowicz, *CFO*
Michelle Blake, *Admin Sec*
John Kubiak, *CIO*
EMP: 600
SALES (est): 16.9MM **Privately Held**
SIC: 6162 Mortgage bankers

(P-9597)
QUALITY HOME LOANS
Also Called: Clear Credit Capital
27001 Agoura Rd Ste 200, Agoura Hills
(91301-5357)
PHONE...................................818 206-6600
Patrick Weaver, *President*
John T Gaiser, *President*
Randy Miller, *CFO*
Christopher Powell, *Vice Pres*
EMP: 220
SQ FT: 47,500
SALES: 18MM **Privately Held**
WEB: www.qualityhomeloans.com
SIC: 6162 Mortgage bankers & correspondents

(P-9598)
REAL ESTATE EQUITY EXCHANGE
Also Called: Unison
650 California St Fl 18, San Francisco
(94108-2722)
PHONE...................................415 992-4200
Thomas Stonholtz, *CEO*
EMP: 75
SALES (est): 279K **Privately Held**
SIC: 6162 Mortgage bankers & correspondents

(P-9599)
RESIDENTIAL BANCORP (PA)
22632 Goln Spgs Dr Ste 20, Diamond Bar
(91765)
PHONE...................................330 499-8333
Corey A Wood, *CEO*
William H James III, *President*
Michael J Luu, *CFO*
Tobias Hoy, *Exec VP*
Tom Wong, *Exec VP*
EMP: 57
SQ FT: 10,000
SALES (est): 10.8MM **Privately Held**
SIC: 6162 Mortgage bankers

(P-9600)
RUSHMORE LOAN MGT SVCS LLC (PA)
15480 Laguna Canyon Rd, Irvine
(92618-2132)
P.O. Box 514707, Los Angeles (90051-4707)
PHONE...................................949 727-4798
Terry Smith, *CEO*
Clayton Goff, *Vice Pres*
Sandy Hildreth, *Vice Pres*
Sheeba Mehdi, *Vice Pres*
David Powell, *Vice Pres*
EMP: 859
SQ FT: 3,000
SALES (est): 5.4MM **Privately Held**
SIC: 6162 Mortgage bankers & correspondents

(P-9601)
SEA BREEZE FINANCIAL SERVICES (PA)
Also Called: Sea Breeze Mortgage Services
18191 Von Karman Ave # 150, Irvine
(92612-7104)
P.O. Box 19079, Anaheim (92817-9079)
PHONE...................................949 223-9700
Leonard Hamilton, *President*
Curtis Green, *Executive*
Gary Pyke, *Sales Staff*
Jeff Whiteman, *Manager*
EMP: 50
SQ FT: 50,000
SALES (est): 9.2MM **Privately Held**
SIC: 6162 Mortgage bankers & correspondents

(P-9602)
SECURITY NAT MSTR HOLDG CO LLC (PA)
323 5th St, Eureka (95501-0305)
P.O. Box 1028 (95502-1028)
PHONE...................................707 442-2818
Robin P Arkley II, *CEO*
EMP: 140
SQ FT: 15,000
SALES (est): 48.3MM **Privately Held**
SIC: 6162 Mortgage bankers & correspondents

(P-9603)
SIERRA PACIFIC MORTGAGE CO INC
104 Traffic Way, Arroyo Grande
(93420-3450)
PHONE...................................805 489-6060
EMP: 88
SALES (corp-wide): 195.9MM **Privately Held**
SIC: 6162 Mortgage bankers
PA: Sierra Pacific Mortgage Company, Inc.
1180 Iron Point Rd # 200
Folsom CA 95630
916 932-1700

(P-9604)
SIERRA PACIFIC MORTGAGE CO INC (PA)
1180 Iron Point Rd # 200, Folsom
(95630-8321)
PHONE...................................916 932-1700
James Coffrini, *President*
Nicole Cervantes, *Officer*
Paul Hubbard, *Officer*
Adam Kain, *Officer*
Michelle Shaman, *Officer*
EMP: 580
SALES (est): 195.9MM **Privately Held**
WEB: www.premiumlending.com
SIC: 6162 Mortgage bankers

(P-9605)
SUN WEST MORTGAGE COMPANY INC (PA)
Also Called: Lowrates.com, 1st Liberty
6131 Orangethorpe Ave # 500, Buena Park
(90620-4903)
PHONE...................................800 453-7884
Pavan Agarwal, *CEO*
Hari S Agarwal, *President*
Sharda Agarwal, *Corp Secy*
Jim Trapinski, *Exec VP*
Anita Agarwal, *Vice Pres*
EMP: 57
SQ FT: 9,800
SALES (est): 27.8MM **Privately Held**
SIC: 6162 6163 Mortgage bankers; loan brokers

(P-9606)
US CREDIT BANCORP INC
851 20th St, Santa Monica (90403-2002)
P.O. Box 1727 (90406-1727)
PHONE...................................310 829-2112
Michel Rone, *President*
M Matsumote, *Corp Secy*
EMP: 85
SQ FT: 6,500
SALES: 45MM **Privately Held**
SIC: 6162 6799 Mortgage bankers; real estate investors, except property operators

(P-9607)
WALKER & DUNLOP INC
12100 Wilshire Blvd # 1500, Los Angeles
(90025-7129)
PHONE...................................301 215-5500
Willy Walker, *Manager*
EMP: 63 **Publicly Held**
SIC: 6162 6411 6531 Mortgage bankers; insurance agents, brokers & service; real estate agents & managers
PA: Walker & Dunlop, Inc.
7501 Wisconsin Ave 1200e
Bethesda MD 20814

(P-9608)
WELLS FARGO HOME MORTGAGE INC
3010 Lava Ridge Ct # 150, Roseville
(95661-3075)
PHONE...................................916 782-2221
Scott Nutter, *Manager*
Drew Collins, *Vice Pres*
EMP: 50
SALES (corp-wide): 101B **Publicly Held**
WEB: www.wfhm.com
SIC: 6162 Mortgage bankers & correspondents
HQ: Wells Fargo Home Mortgage Inc
1 Home Campus
Des Moines IA 50328
515 324-3707

(P-9609)
WELLS FARGO HOME MORTGAGE INC
5540 Fermi Ct Fl 2002, Carlsbad
(92008-7325)
PHONE...................................760 603-7000
Kathleen Vauthan, *Vice Pres*
Carolina McEnaney, *Marketing Mgr*
EMP: 400
SALES (corp-wide): 101B **Publicly Held**
WEB: www.wfhm.com
SIC: 6162 Mortgage bankers
HQ: Wells Fargo Home Mortgage Inc
1 Home Campus
Des Moines IA 50328
515 324-3707

(P-9610)
WOODSIDE GROUP INC
Also Called: Hillsborough
3509 Coffee Rd Ste D10, Modesto
(95355-1358)
PHONE...................................209 579-2030
Mike Golkin, *Manager*
EMP: 50
SALES (corp-wide): 143.4MM **Privately Held**
SIC: 6162 Mortgage bankers & correspondents

PA: Woodside Group, Llc
460 W 50 N Ste 200
Salt Lake City UT 84101
801 869-3950

6163 Loan Brokers

(P-9611)
5 ARCHES LLC
19800 Macarthur Blvd, Irvine (92612-2421)
PHONE....................................949 387-8092
Shawn Miller, *CEO*
Gene Clark, *President*
Steven Davis, *CFO*
Melissa Ninofranco, *Human Resources*
Cristina Diaz, *Manager*
EMP: 95
SALES (est): 486K **Publicly Held**
SIC: 6163 Loan brokers
PA: Redwood Trust, Inc.
1 Belvedere Pl Ste 300
Mill Valley CA 94941

(P-9612)
ACCESS TO LOANS FOR LEARNING
1230 Rosecrans Ave # 560, Manhattan Beach (90266-2477)
PHONE....................................310 979-4700
Chris Chapman, *President*
Charles Bull, *CEO*
EMP: 50
SALES: 61.8MM **Privately Held**
WEB: www.allstudentloan.org
SIC: 6163 Mortgage brokers arranging for loans, using money of others

(P-9613)
AMERICAN FUNDING
Also Called: American Realty
5369 Camden Ave Ste 240, San Jose (95124-5809)
PHONE....................................408 269-4238
Ali Haider, *CEO*
EMP: 60
SALES (est): 4.8MM **Privately Held**
WEB: www.americanfunding.com
SIC: 6163 6531 Mortgage brokers arranging for loans, using money of others; real estate agents & managers

(P-9614)
AMERICAN LIBERTY CAPITAL CORP
Also Called: American Liberty Funding
19000 Macarthur Blvd # 400, Irvine (92612-1438)
P.O. Box 10059, Newport Beach (92658-0059)
PHONE....................................949 623-0288
Christopher Chase, *President*
Mike R Chase, *Shareholder*
Chris Bull, *Admin Sec*
EMP: 105
SALES (est): 7.1MM **Privately Held**
SIC: 6163 Mortgage brokers arranging for loans, using money of others

(P-9615)
AMERIQUEST CAPITAL CORPORATION (PA)
1100 W Twn Cntry Rd R, Orange (92868-4600)
PHONE....................................714 564-0600
Aseem Mital, *President*
Aaron Ayala, *Director*
EMP: 400
SQ FT: 85,000
SALES (est): 532MM **Privately Held**
SIC: 6163 Mortgage brokers arranging for loans, using money of others

(P-9616)
CAL COAST FINANCIAL INC
39355 California St # 101, Fremont (94538-1447)
PHONE....................................510 683-9850
Roger Bakshi, *CEO*
EMP: 70
SALES (est): 3.1MM **Privately Held**
SIC: 6163 Mortgage brokers arranging for loans, using money of others

(P-9617)
CINTIVA FINANCIAL CORPORATION
10145 Pacific Hts 800, San Diego (92121-4242)
PHONE....................................877 246-8482
Richard A Myers, *President*
Niket Kulkarni, *Vice Pres*
Don Sarver, *Vice Pres*
EMP: 60
SQ FT: 12,500
SALES (est): 4MM **Privately Held**
WEB: www.cintiva.com
SIC: 6163 Mortgage brokers arranging for loans, using money of others

(P-9618)
CLEARPATH LENDING
15635 Alton Pkwy Ste 300, Irvine (92618-7332)
PHONE....................................949 502-3577
Amir Ali Omid, *CEO*
Mark Hoagland, *Officer*
Jorge Lopez, *Officer*
Lily Ali, *Loan Officer*
Jose Coutino, *Loan Officer*
EMP: 130 **EST:** 2012
SALES (est): 985.9K **Privately Held**
SIC: 6163 Mortgage brokers arranging for loans, using money of others

(P-9619)
CMG MORTGAGE INC (PA)
3160 Crow Canyon Rd # 400, San Ramon (94583-1382)
PHONE....................................619 554-1327
Christopher M George, *CEO*
Todd L Hempstead, *Senior VP*
Denise Tragale, *Vice Pres*
Harrison George, *Loan Officer*
Lori Millar, *Loan*
EMP: 349
SQ FT: 5,500
SALES (est): 99.3MM **Privately Held**
WEB: www.pacificguarantee.com
SIC: 6163 Mortgage brokers arranging for loans, using money of others

(P-9620)
COMMERCE HOME MORTGAGE INC (HQ)
Also Called: Bank of Commerce Mortgage
3130 Crow Canyon Pl # 400, San Ramon (94583-1140)
PHONE....................................925 830-1500
Scott Simonich, *President*
EMP: 60
SQ FT: 1,400
SALES (est): 2.5MM
SALES (corp-wide): 56.7MM **Publicly Held**
SIC: 6163 Mortgage brokers arranging for loans, using money of others
PA: Bank Of Commerce Holdings
1951 Churn Creek Rd
Redding CA 96002
530 722-3952

(P-9621)
E&S FINANCIAL GROUP INC
Also Called: Capital Mortgage Services
3140 Telegraph Rd Ste A, Ventura (93003-3238)
PHONE....................................805 644-1621
Jordan Eller, *President*
John Bartnicki, *Loan*
EMP: 70
SALES (est): 2.9MM **Privately Held**
SIC: 6163 Mortgage brokers arranging for loans, using money of others

(P-9622)
E-LOAN INC (DH)
6230 Stoneridge Mall Rd, Pleasanton (94588-3260)
PHONE....................................925 847-6200
Mark E Lefanowicz, *President*
EMP: 850
SQ FT: 118,000
SALES (est): 54.6MM
SALES (corp-wide): 2.6B **Publicly Held**
WEB: www.e-loan.com
SIC: 6163 6162 Mortgage brokers arranging for loans, using money of others; mortgage bankers & correspondents

HQ: Popular Finance Inc
326 Salud St El El Senorial Cond
Ponce PR 00716
787 844-2760

(P-9623)
EMERY FINANCIAL INC (PA)
Also Called: Wjbradley Mortgage Capital
625 Kings Rd, Newport Beach (92663-5711)
PHONE....................................949 219-0640
Bradford Sarvak, *President*
Jay Anderson, *Officer*
Mike Henderson, *Officer*
Matthew Sarvak, *Officer*
Peggy Suber, *Officer*
EMP: 60
SALES (est): 13.6MM **Privately Held**
WEB: www.emeryfinancial.com
SIC: 6163 Mortgage brokers arranging for loans, using money of others

(P-9624)
ESNA CORPORATION
44300 Lowtree Ave Ste 100, Lancaster (93534-4166)
PHONE....................................661 206-6010
Duane Faust, *President*
EMP: 50
SALES (est): 2.5MM **Privately Held**
SIC: 6163 Mortgage brokers arranging for loans, using money of others

(P-9625)
FIRST NATIONWIDE MORTGAGE CORP
18440 Bermuda St, Northridge (91326-3102)
PHONE....................................818 209-3134
EMP: 133
SALES (corp-wide): 72.8B **Publicly Held**
SIC: 6163 6162 Mortgage brokers arranging for loans, using money of others; mortgage bankers & correspondents
HQ: First Nationwide Mortgage Corporation
5280 Corporate Dr
Frederick MD 21703

(P-9626)
GETRIGHT VENTURES INC
3675 Rocky Shore Ct, Vallejo (94591-6349)
PHONE....................................510 402-4816
Joseph Pamplieda, *President*
Eddie E Bansag, *CFO*
EMP: 80
SALES (est): 3.4MM **Privately Held**
WEB: www.getrightrealty.com
SIC: 6163 Mortgage brokers arranging for loans, using money of others

(P-9627)
HARVEST SMALL BUSINESS FIN LLC
24422 Avenida De Carlota, Laguna Hills (92653)
PHONE....................................949 446-8683
David Scherer, *Mng Member*
Brian Crawford, *President*
Evan Mitnick, *CFO*
Todd Massas, *Officer*
Adam Seery, *Exec VP*
EMP: 51
SALES (est): 3.4MM **Privately Held**
SIC: 6163 Mortgage brokers arranging for loans, using money of others

(P-9628)
INTERNATIONAL CITY MRTG INC
2990 Inland Empire Blvd # 111, Ontario (91764-4899)
PHONE....................................909 944-7361
Diana Madrigal, *Manager*
EMP: 66
SALES (corp-wide): 4.1MM **Privately Held**
SIC: 6163 Mortgage brokers arranging for loans, using money of others
PA: International City Mortgage, Inc.
200 Sandpointe Ave # 650
Santa Ana CA 92707
714 637-6200

(P-9629)
IZT MORTGAGE INC (PA)
Also Called: Ameritech Mortgage
3011 Citrus Cir Ste 202, Walnut Creek (94598-2631)
P.O. Box 492239, Los Angeles (90049-8239)
PHONE....................................925 946-1858
Zoran Trajanovich, *CEO*
Irina Trajanovich, *President*
EMP: 50
SQ FT: 12,000
SALES (est): 10MM **Privately Held**
SIC: 6163 Mortgage brokers arranging for loans, using money of others

(P-9630)
KINGS PAWNSHOP
Also Called: Kings Jewelry and Loan
800 S Vermont Ave, Los Angeles (90005-1521)
PHONE....................................213 383-5555
Sam Shocket, *President*
EMP: 52
SQ FT: 11,000
SALES (est): 7.8MM **Privately Held**
WEB: www.kingspawn.com
SIC: 6163 5944 Loan brokers; jewelry stores

(P-9631)
LENDINGCLUB ASSET MGT LLC
71 Stevenson St Ste 300, San Francisco (94105-2985)
PHONE....................................415 632-5600
Carrie Dolan,
Russ Elmer, *Principal*
EMP: 293
SALES (est): 4.8MM **Publicly Held**
SIC: 6163 Loan brokers
PA: Lendingclub Corporation
595 Market St Fl 4
San Francisco CA 94105

(P-9632)
LIBERTY AMERICAN MORTGAGE CORP (PA)
193 Blue Ravine Rd # 240, Folsom (95630-4756)
PHONE....................................916 780-3000
Frank A Sousa, *President*
William Templeton, *Ch of Bd*
Dan Martinelli, *COO*
Jennifer Robinson, *CFO*
Patrick White, *Chairman*
EMP: 92
SQ FT: 18,000
SALES (est): 8MM **Privately Held**
WEB: www.libam.com
SIC: 6163 6162 Mortgage brokers arranging for loans, using money of others; mortgage bankers

(P-9633)
LMB OPCO LLC
Also Called: Lowermybills
12181 Bluff Creek Dr, Playa Vista (90094-2992)
PHONE....................................310 348-6800
Jeff Hughes, *CEO*
EMP: 320
SALES (est): 5.5MM **Privately Held**
SIC: 6163 7389 Mortgage brokers arranging for loans, using money of others; financial services

(P-9634)
M & A MORTGAGE INC
1600 N Broadway Ste 1020, Santa Ana (92706-3930)
PHONE....................................714 560-1970
EMP: 75
SALES: 25MM **Privately Held**
SIC: 6163

(P-9635)
MARK 1 MORTGAGE CORPORATION (PA)
1342 E Chapman Ave, Orange (92866-2219)
PHONE....................................714 752-5700
Mark D Prather, *President*
EMP: 50
SQ FT: 8,000

▲ = Import ▼=Export
◆ =Import/Export

SALES (est): 16.8MM **Privately Held**
SIC: 6163 Mortgage brokers arranging for loans, using money of others

(P-9636)
MERRILL LYNCH PIERCE FENNER
Also Called: Merrill Lynch Wealth MGT
800 E Colo Blvd Ste 400, Pasadena (91101)
PHONE.................................626 304-1596
Ken Park, *Advisor*
EMP: 100
SALES (corp-wide): 110.5B **Publicly Held**
SIC: 6163 6211 Loan brokers; bond dealers & brokers
HQ: Merrill Lynch, Pierce, Fenner & Smith Incorporated
111 8th Ave
New York NY 10011
800 637-7455

(P-9637)
MORTGAGE CORP AMERICA INC
Also Called: Mortgage Corp of America
2315 Kuehner Dr Ste 115, Simi Valley (93063-3960)
PHONE.................................805 582-2220
Bradley A Rice, *President*
Deena Monette, *Manager*
Christopher Bunce, *Real Est Agnt*
EMP: 60
SQ FT: 16,000
SALES (est): 5.1MM **Privately Held**
WEB: www.mcastar.com
SIC: 6163 Mortgage brokers arranging for loans, using money of others

(P-9638)
NATIONAL CREDIT INDUSTRIES INC
Also Called: Century 21
1100 Via Verde, San Dimas (91773-4401)
PHONE.................................626 967-4355
Oscar Rodriguez, *President*
Ashley Alvarez, *Admin Sec*
Mireya Ruiz, *Admin Sec*
Lucy Hollingsworth, *Sales Mgr*
Irma Ortega, *Sales Associate*
EMP: 90
SALES (est): 2MM **Privately Held**
SIC: 6163 Mortgage brokers arranging for loans, using money of others

(P-9639)
NEWWEST MORTGAGE COMPANY
Also Called: Newwest Funding
8255 Firestone Blvd # 101, Downey (90241-4800)
PHONE.................................562 861-8393
David Samak, *President*
Kendra Samak, *Treasurer*
EMP: 60
SQ FT: 5,000
SALES (est): 5.1MM **Privately Held**
SIC: 6163 Mortgage brokers arranging for loans, using money of others

(P-9640)
PACIFIC UNION INTL INC
135 W Napa St Ste 200, Sonoma (95476-6632)
PHONE.................................707 934-2300
Jill Silvas, *Branch Mgr*
Ashley Brown, *Broker*
Jeffrey Lokey, *Real Est Agnt*
Matt Sevenau, *Real Est Agnt*
EMP: 539 **Privately Held**
SIC: 6163 Loan agents
PA: Pacific Union International, Inc.
1 Letterman Dr Bldg C
San Francisco CA 94129

(P-9641)
PENNYMAC CORP
27001 Agoura Rd, Agoura Hills (91301-5339)
PHONE.................................818 878-8416
Stanford L Kurland, *President*
EMP: 203

SALES (est): 46.3MM **Privately Held**
SIC: 6163 Loan brokers
PA: Pennymac Mortgage Investment Trust
6101 Condor Dr
Moorpark CA 93021

(P-9642)
PINNACLE FUNDING GROUP INC
2092 Omega Rd Ste H, San Ramon (94583-1230)
PHONE.................................925 552-5302
William Howard Paul III, *President*
EMP: 50
SQ FT: 5,000
SALES (est): 3.2MM **Privately Held**
SIC: 6163 Mortgage brokers arranging for loans, using money of others

(P-9643)
PROSPER MARKETPLACE INC (PA)
221 Main St Fl 3, San Francisco (94105-1911)
PHONE.................................415 593-5400
David Kimball, *CEO*
EMP: 64
SALES: 104.3MM **Privately Held**
SIC: 6163 Loan brokers

(P-9644)
SAND CANYON CORPORATION (HQ)
7595 Irvine Center Dr # 100, Irvine (92618-2958)
P.O. Box 57080 (92619-7080)
PHONE.................................949 727-9425
Robert Dubrish, *President*
Dale M Sugimoto, *CEO*
Steve Nadon, *COO*
William O'Neill, *CFO*
EMP: 100
SQ FT: 140,000
SALES (est): 180.7MM
SALES (corp-wide): 3B **Publicly Held**
WEB: www.oomc.com
SIC: 6163 6162 Loan brokers; mortgage bankers & correspondents
PA: H&R Block, Inc.
1 H&R Block Way
Kansas City MO 64105
816 854-3000

(P-9645)
SOCIAL FINANCE INC (PA)
Also Called: Sofi
234 1st St, San Francisco (94105-2624)
PHONE.................................415 612-8229
Anthony Noto, *CEO*
Steve Freiberg, *CFO*
Joanne Bradford, *Chief Mktg Ofcr*
Robert Lavet, *Officer*
Ashish Jain, *Vice Pres*
EMP: 160
SQ FT: 20,000
SALES (est): 245.8MM **Privately Held**
SIC: 6163 Loan brokers

(P-9646)
SOCIAL FINANCE INC
375 Healdsburg Ave # 280, Healdsburg (95448-4151)
PHONE.................................707 473-9889
EMP: 637
SALES (corp-wide): 245.8MM **Privately Held**
SIC: 6163 Loan brokers
PA: Social Finance, Inc.
234 1st St
San Francisco CA 94105
415 612-8229

(P-9647)
TARBELL FINANCIAL CORPORATION (PA)
1403 N Tustin Ave Ste 380, Santa Ana (92705-8691)
PHONE.................................714 972-0988
Donald Tarbell, *CEO*
Tina Jimov, *President*
Jin Lee, *COO*
Ronald Tarbell, *CFO*
Elizabeth Tarbell, *Admin Sec*
EMP: 100

SQ FT: 60,000
SALES (est): 132.1MM **Privately Held**
SIC: 6163 6531 6099 Mortgage brokers arranging for loans, using money of others; real estate brokers & agents; escrow institutions other than real estate

---

6211 Security Brokers & Dealers

(P-9648)
ABM JANITORIAL SERVICES INC
Also Called: ABM Securities
3580 Wilshire Blvd # 1130, Los Angeles (90010-2501)
PHONE.................................213 384-0600
EMP: 1500
SALES (corp-wide): 6.4B **Publicly Held**
SIC: 6211 Security brokers & dealers
HQ: Abm Janitorial Services, Inc.
1111 Fannin St Ste 1500
Houston TX 77002
866 624-1520

(P-9649)
ADVENT SECURITIES INVESTMENTS (PA)
Also Called: Olympic Security
9631 Alondra Blvd Ste 202, Bellflower (90706-3674)
PHONE.................................562 920-5467
Cynthia Jocson, *President*
Eric Sera, *Treasurer*
EMP: 50
SQ FT: 5,000
SALES (est): 32.4MM **Privately Held**
SIC: 6211 5699 Security brokers & dealers; uniforms

(P-9650)
ANALYTIC US MARKET NEUTRAL OFF
555 W 5th St Fl 50, Los Angeles (90013-1066)
PHONE.................................213 688-3015
Harindra Desilva, *President*
EMP: 70
SALES (est): 6.9MM **Privately Held**
SIC: 6211 Investment firm, general brokerage

(P-9651)
B B & K FUND SERVICES INC
950 Tower Ln Ste 1900, Foster City (94404-2131)
PHONE.................................650 571-5800
Thomas Bailard, *CEO*
EMP: 50
SALES (est): 2.7MM
SALES (corp-wide): 4.5MM **Privately Held**
WEB: www.bailard.com
SIC: 6211 Security brokers & dealers
HQ: Bailard, Inc.
950 Tower Ln Ste 1900
Foster City CA 94404
650 571-5800

(P-9652)
BARCLAYS CAPITAL INC
Also Called: Lehman Brothers
10250 Santa Monica Blvd # 24, Los Angeles (90067-6482)
PHONE.................................310 481-4100
Barclay Perry, *Branch Mgr*
Sonya Del Crognale, *Financial Exec*
EMP: 60
SALES (corp-wide): 36.8B **Privately Held**
WEB: www.lehmanbrothers.com
SIC: 6211 Investment firm, general brokerage
HQ: Barclays Capital Inc.
745 7th Ave
New York NY 10019
212 526-7000

(P-9653)
BBAM US LP
Also Called: Bbam Arcft Holdings 139 Labuan
50 California St Fl 14, San Francisco (94111-4683)
PHONE.................................415 267-1600

Steve Vissis, *CEO*
EMP: 349
SALES (est): 18.1MM **Privately Held**
SIC: 6211 Investment bankers
HQ: Bbam Llc
50 California St Fl 14
San Francisco CA 94111
415 267-1600

(P-9654)
BLACKSTONE TECHNOLOGY GROUP (PA)
33 New Montgomery St # 850, San Francisco (94105-4539)
PHONE.................................415 837-1400
David Mysona, *CEO*
Casey Courneen, *President*
Giles Kesteloot, *President*
Patrick James, *COO*
Rakesh Agrawal, *Exec VP*
EMP: 100
SQ FT: 10,000
SALES (est): 135.3MM **Privately Held**
WEB: www.bstonetech.com
SIC: 6211 Security brokers & dealers

(P-9655)
BROADREACH CAPITL PARTNERS LLC (PA)
855 El Camino Real # 350, Palo Alto (94301-2305)
PHONE.................................650 331-2500
John A Foster, *Director*
Eli Khari,
Philip Flip F Maritz, *Director*
Craig G Vought, *Director*
EMP: 4010
SALES (est): 394.6MM **Privately Held**
WEB: www.broadreachcp.com
SIC: 6211 Investment firm, general brokerage

(P-9656)
BTIG LLC (PA)
Also Called: Baypoint Trading
600 Montgomery St Fl 6, San Francisco (94111-2708)
PHONE.................................415 248-2200
Scott Kovalik,
Brian Endres, *CFO*
Andrea Alfonso, *Vice Pres*
Christina Arsenault, *Vice Pres*
Camille Cordero, *Vice Pres*
EMP: 77
SALES (est): 104.5MM **Privately Held**
SIC: 6211 Investment firm, general brokerage

(P-9657)
CANTOR FITZGERALD L P
1925 Century Park E # 700, Los Angeles (90067-2718)
PHONE.................................310 282-6500
Bill Wright, *Manager*
Joseph Wind, *Executive*
Benjamin Finkelstein, *Managing Dir*
EMP: 100
SALES (corp-wide): 880.5MM **Privately Held**
SIC: 6211 Brokers, security
PA: Cantor Fitzgerald L P
499 Park Ave
New York NY 10022
212 938-5000

(P-9658)
CANYON PARTNERS INCORPORATED (HQ)
2000 Ave Of The Sts Fl 11, Los Angeles (90067)
PHONE.................................310 272-1000
Joshua S Friedman, *CEO*
Mitchell R Julis, *CEO*
John Simpson, *COO*
John Plaga, *CFO*
Robert Campion, *Vice Pres*
EMP: 57
SQ FT: 5,500
SALES (est): 24.6MM **Privately Held**
WEB: www.cjuf.com
SIC: 6211 Investment firm, general brokerage
PA: Canyon Partners, Llc
2000 Avenue Of The Stars # 11
Los Angeles CA 90067
310 272-1000

(P-9659)
CASEY SECURITIES INC (PA)
301 Pine St, San Francisco (94104-3301)
PHONE.............................415 544-5030
Richard Casey, *Ch of Bd*
George Gasparini, *President*
Kathleen Gallagher, *Vice Pres*
Scott Nelson, *Vice Pres*
EMP: 74 **EST:** 1976
SQ FT: 800
SALES (est): 7.6MM **Privately Held**
SIC: 6211 Brokers, security; stock brokers
& dealers

(P-9660)
CHARLES SCHWAB & CO INC (HQ)
211 Main St Fl 17, San Francisco
(94105-1901)
P.O. Box 636009, Littleton CO (80163-
6009)
PHONE.............................415 636-7000
Walt Bettinger, *CEO*
Tom D Seip, *Sr Exec VP*
Bernard Clark, *Exec VP*
Dawn G Lepore, *Exec VP*
Elizabeth G Sawi, *Exec VP*
EMP: 76
SQ FT: 295,000
SALES (est): 2.3B
SALES (corp-wide): 10.1B **Publicly Held**
WEB: www.schwab.com
SIC: 6211 Brokers, security; dealers, secu-
rity; investment firm, general brokerage
PA: The Charles Schwab Corporation
211 Main St Fl 17
San Francisco CA 94105
415 667-7000

(P-9661)
CHARLES SCHWAB CORPORATION (PA)
211 Main St Fl 17, San Francisco
(94105-1901)
PHONE.............................415 667-7000
Walter W Bettinger II, *President*
Charles R Schwab, *Ch of Bd*
Joseph R Martinetto, *COO*
Peter B Crawford, *CFO*
David R Garfield, *Exec VP*
EMP: 125 **EST:** 1986
SQ FT: 662,000
SALES: 10.1B **Publicly Held**
WEB: www.schwab.com
SIC: 6211 6091 6282 7389 Brokers, se-
curity; investment bankers; investment
firm, general brokerage; nondeposit trust
facilities; investment advice; investment
advisory service; financial services

(P-9662)
CHARLES SCHWAB CORPORATION
10770 Donner Pass Rd # 103, Truckee
(96161-4880)
PHONE.............................530 448-8038
EMP: 69
SALES (corp-wide): 10.1B **Publicly Held**
SIC: 6211 Stock brokers & dealers
PA: The Charles Schwab Corporation
211 Main St Fl 17
San Francisco CA 94105
415 667-7000

(P-9663)
CHARLES SCHWAB CORPORATION
826 Wilshire Blvd, Santa Monica
(90401-1810)
PHONE.............................310 752-9951
EMP: 69
SALES (corp-wide): 10.1B **Publicly Held**
SIC: 6211 Brokers, security
PA: The Charles Schwab Corporation
211 Main St Fl 17
San Francisco CA 94105
415 667-7000

(P-9664)
CHARLES SCHWAB CORPORATION
1900 Avenue Of The Stars # 101, Los Angeles (90067-4302)
PHONE.............................714 385-6000
Jane E Fry, *Branch Mgr*

EMP: 104
SALES (corp-wide): 10.1B **Publicly Held**
SIC: 6211 Security brokers & dealers
PA: The Charles Schwab Corporation
211 Main St Fl 17
San Francisco CA 94105
415 667-7000

(P-9665)
CHARLES SCHWAB CORPORATION
1400 Grant Ave Ste 101, Novato
(94945-3155)
PHONE.............................415 294-3503
Michael Dolan, *President*
EMP: 69
SALES (corp-wide): 10.1B **Publicly Held**
SIC: 6211 Security brokers & dealers
PA: The Charles Schwab Corporation
211 Main St Fl 17
San Francisco CA 94105
415 667-7000

(P-9666)
CHARLES SCHWAB CORPORATION
12481 High Bluff Dr # 100, San Diego
(92130-3583)
PHONE.............................858 523-2454
Greg Matthews, *Branch Mgr*
Dex Yudelson, *Associate*
EMP: 50
SALES (corp-wide): 10.1B **Publicly Held**
WEB: www.schwab.com
SIC: 6211 Brokers, security
PA: The Charles Schwab Corporation
211 Main St Fl 17
San Francisco CA 94105
415 667-7000

(P-9667)
CITIGROUP GLOBAL MARKETS INC
Also Called: Smith Barney
444 S Flower St Fl 35, Los Angeles
(90071-2980)
P.O. Box 30367 (90030-0367)
PHONE.............................213 486-8811
Bruce Brereton, *Branch Mgr*
Talonna Moore, *Officer*
EMP: 180
SALES (corp-wide): 72.8B **Publicly Held**
WEB: www.salomonsmithbarney.com
SIC: 6211 Stock brokers & dealers
HQ: Citigroup Global Markets Inc.
388 Greenwich St Fl 18
New York NY 10013
212 816-6000

(P-9668)
CITIGROUP GLOBAL MARKETS INC
Also Called: Salomon Smith Barney
2381 Rosecrans Ave # 115, El Segundo
(90245-4920)
PHONE.............................310 727-9533
Russ Bortonaro, *Branch Mgr*
EMP: 56
SALES (corp-wide): 72.8B **Publicly Held**
WEB: www.salomonsmithbarney.com
SIC: 6211 Security brokers & dealers
HQ: Citigroup Global Markets Inc.
388 Greenwich St Fl 18
New York NY 10013
212 816-6000

(P-9669)
CITIGROUP GLOBAL MARKETS INC
Also Called: Salomon Smith Barney
155 Cadillac Dr Fl 1, Sacramento
(95825-5499)
PHONE.............................916 567-2056
Mike Dellisant, *Manager*
EMP: 50
SALES (corp-wide): 72.8B **Publicly Held**
WEB: www.salomonsmithbarney.com
SIC: 6211 Security brokers & dealers
HQ: Citigroup Global Markets Inc.
388 Greenwich St Fl 18
New York NY 10013
212 816-6000

(P-9670)
CITIGROUP GLOBAL MARKETS INC
4350 La Jolla Village Dr, San Diego
(92122-1243)
PHONE.............................858 597-7777
Joe Capano, *Manager*
EMP: 71
SALES (corp-wide): 72.8B **Publicly Held**
WEB: www.salomonsmithbarney.com
SIC: 6211 Security brokers & dealers;
stock brokers & dealers
HQ: Citigroup Global Markets Inc.
388 Greenwich St Fl 18
New York NY 10013
212 816-6000

(P-9671)
CITIGROUP GLOBAL MARKETS INC
Also Called: Smith Barney
21250 Hawthorne Blvd # 650, Torrance
(90503-5506)
PHONE.............................310 540-9511
David Calomese, *Manager*
EMP: 50
SALES (corp-wide): 72.8B **Publicly Held**
WEB: www.salomonsmithbarney.com
SIC: 6211 Security brokers & dealers;
stock brokers & dealers
HQ: Citigroup Global Markets Inc.
388 Greenwich St Fl 18
New York NY 10013
212 816-6000

(P-9672)
CITIGROUP GLOBAL MARKETS INC
Also Called: Smith Barney
1901 Main St Ste 800, Irvine (92614-0515)
PHONE.............................949 955-7500
John Konop, *General Mgr*
EMP: 85
SALES (corp-wide): 72.8B **Publicly Held**
WEB: www.salomonsmithbarney.com
SIC: 6211 6221 Investment firm, general
brokerage; commodity contracts brokers,
dealers
HQ: Citigroup Global Markets Inc.
388 Greenwich St Fl 18
New York NY 10013
212 816-6000

(P-9673)
CITIGROUP GLOBAL MARKETS INC
Also Called: Smith Barney
1225 Prospect St, La Jolla (92037-3687)
PHONE.............................858 456-4900
Erik Kivmkrugh, *Office Mgr*
EMP: 72
SALES (corp-wide): 72.8B **Publicly Held**
WEB: www.salomonsmithbarney.com
SIC: 6211 Security brokers & dealers;
stock brokers & dealers
HQ: Citigroup Global Markets Inc.
388 Greenwich St Fl 18
New York NY 10013
212 816-6000

(P-9674)
CITIGROUP GLOBAL MARKETS INC
Also Called: Salomon Smith Barney
5250 N Palm Ave Ste 321, Fresno
(93704-2213)
PHONE.............................559 438-2542
Jeff Branch, *Sales/Mktg Mgr*
EMP: 50
SALES (corp-wide): 72.8B **Publicly Held**
WEB: www.salomonsmithbarney.com
SIC: 6211 8742 Security brokers & deal-
ers; stock brokers & dealers; financial
consultant
HQ: Citigroup Global Markets Inc.
388 Greenwich St Fl 18
New York NY 10013
212 816-6000

(P-9675)
CITIGROUP GLOBAL MARKETS INC
Also Called: Smith Barney
609 Deep Valley Dr # 400, Rllng HLS Est
(90274-3629)
P.O. Box 2809, Pls Vrds Pnsl (90274-8809)
PHONE.............................310 544-3600
Paul Tanzmen, *Manager*
EMP: 65
SALES (corp-wide): 72.8B **Publicly Held**
WEB: www.salomonsmithbarney.com
SIC: 6211 Stock brokers & dealers
HQ: Citigroup Global Markets Inc.
388 Greenwich St Fl 18
New York NY 10013
212 816-6000

(P-9676)
CITIGROUP GLOBAL MARKETS INC
456 W Foothill Blvd, Claremont
(91711-2711)
PHONE.............................909 625-0781
Tony Battaglia, *Manager*
EMP: 60
SALES (corp-wide): 72.8B **Publicly Held**
WEB: www.salomonsmithbarney.com
SIC: 6211 Stock brokers & dealers
HQ: Citigroup Global Markets Inc.
388 Greenwich St Fl 18
New York NY 10013
212 816-6000

(P-9677)
CITIGROUP GLOBAL MARKETS INC
Also Called: Smith Barneys
2775 Sand Hill Rd Ste 120, Menlo Park
(94025-7085)
PHONE.............................650 926-7600
Guy Dietrich, *Principal*
EMP: 103
SALES (corp-wide): 72.8B **Publicly Held**
WEB: www.salomonsmithbarney.com
SIC: 6211 Security brokers & dealers
HQ: Citigroup Global Markets Inc.
388 Greenwich St Fl 18
New York NY 10013
212 816-6000

(P-9678)
CITIGROUP INC
1 Sansome St Fl 27, San Francisco
(94104-4426)
PHONE.............................415 617-8524
Chuck Prince, *President*
EMP: 60
SALES (corp-wide): 72.8B **Publicly Held**
WEB: www.citigroup.com
SIC: 6211 Investment bankers
PA: Citigroup Inc.
388 Greenwich St
New York NY 10013
212 559-1000

(P-9679)
CITIMORTGAGE INC
6160 Stoneridge Mall Rd # 150, Pleasanton
(94588-3285)
PHONE.............................925 730-3800
Ernie Guzman, *Manager*
EMP: 50
SALES (corp-wide): 72.8B **Publicly Held**
SIC: 6211 Investment firm, general broker-
age
HQ: Citimortgage, Inc.
1000 Technology Dr
O Fallon MO 63368
636 261-2484

(P-9680)
COLDWELL BANKER AND ASSOCIATES (PA)
Also Called: Coldwell Banker Inland Brokers
23823 Clinton Keith Rd # 102, Wildomar
(92595-7734)
PHONE.............................951 304-2900
Raquel Wilks, *Manager*
Frieda Wyant, *Sales Associate*
Sara Araujo, *Mktg Coord*
Rene Ramirez, *Mktg Coord*
Andrea Childers, *Manager*
EMP: 60

SALES (est): 7.1MM **Privately Held**
SIC: 6211 Security brokers & dealers

(P-9681)
COUNTRYWIDE SECURITIES CORP
4500 Park Granada, Calabasas
(91302-1613)
P.O. Box 7137, Pasadena (91109-7137)
PHONE..................818 225-3000
Angelo Mozilo, *Ch of Bd*
Ranjit Kripalani, *President*
EMP: 275 EST: 1981
SALES (est): 41.7MM
SALES (corp-wide): 110.5B **Publicly Held**
SIC: 6211 Security brokers & dealers
HQ: Countrywide Capital Markets, Llc
4500 Park Granada
Calabasas CA 91302

(P-9682)
CREDIT SSSE SECURITIES USA LLC
10880 Wilshire Blvd, Los Angeles
(90024-4101)
PHONE..................213 253-2600
Reza Zafari, *Principal*
Thomas Davidov, *Admin Sec*
EMP: 75
SALES (corp-wide): 21B **Privately Held**
SIC: 6211 Investment bankers
HQ: Credit Suisse Securities (Usa) Llc
11 Madison Ave Bsmt 1b
New York NY 10010
212 325-2000

(P-9683)
CREDIT SUISSE (USA) INC
650 California St Fl 31, San Francisco
(94108-2612)
PHONE..................415 249-2100
Carey Timbrell, *Manager*
EMP: 100
SALES (corp-wide): 21B **Privately Held**
SIC: 6211 Investment bankers
HQ: Credit Suisse (Usa), Inc.
11 Madison Ave Frnt 1
New York NY 10010
212 325-2000

(P-9684)
CREDIT SUISSE (USA) INC
650 California St Fl 28, San Francisco
(94108-2609)
PHONE..................415 678-3940
Susan Winegar, *Manager*
EMP: 50
SALES (corp-wide): 21B **Privately Held**
SIC: 6211 Investment bankers
HQ: Credit Suisse (Usa), Inc.
11 Madison Ave Frnt 1
New York NY 10010
212 325-2000

(P-9685)
DA DAVIDSON & CO
Also Called: Crowell, Weedon & Co.
624 S Grand Ave Ste 2600, Los Angeles
(90017-3327)
PHONE..................213 620-1850
Andrew Crowell, *Vice Chairman*
James Cronk, *Opers Staff*
Don Crowell, *Director*
David Medina, *Advisor*
EMP: 310
SALES (corp-wide): 418.4MM **Privately Held**
SIC: 6211 Stock brokers & dealers
HQ: D.A. Davidson & Co.
8 3rd St N
Great Falls MT 59401
406 727-4200

(P-9686)
DEUTSCHE BANK TR CO AMERICAS
101 California St # 4500, San Francisco
(94111-5802)
PHONE..................415 617-4200
Edmond Hon, *Vice Pres*
EMP: 130
SQ FT: 3,600

SALES (corp-wide): 13.6B **Privately Held**
WEB: www.db.com
SIC: 6211 Investment bankers
HQ: Deutsche Bank Trust Company Americas
60 Wall St Bsmt 1
New York NY 10005
212 250-2500

(P-9687)
EMBASSADOR PRIVATE SECURITIES
1341 Evans Ave, San Francisco
(94124-1705)
PHONE..................415 822-8811
Rj Hongisto, *Director*
Rj Hingisto, *Director*
David Culot, *Manager*
EMP: 55
SQ FT: 4,500
SALES (est): 4.7MM **Privately Held**
SIC: 6211 Security brokers & dealers

(P-9688)
FIRST ALLIED SECURITIES INC (HQ)
655 W Broadway Fl 11, San Diego
(92101-8487)
P.O. Box 85549 (92186-5549)
PHONE..................619 702-9600
Adam Antoniades, *CEO*
Kelly Coulter, *President*
Kevin Keefe, *President*
Tiy O'Neal, *COO*
Gregg S Glaser, *CFO*
EMP: 75
SALES (est): 88.2MM **Privately Held**
SIC: 6211 Brokers, security; security brokers & dealers

(P-9689)
FOREX CAPITAL MARKETS LLC
201 Mission St Ste 290, San Francisco
(94105-1859)
PHONE..................415 343-4874
Chris Pelton, *Branch Mgr*
EMP: 95
SALES (corp-wide): 91.2MM **Privately Held**
SIC: 6211 Brokers, security
PA: Forex Capital Markets L.L.C.
55 Water St Fl 50
New York NY 10041
646 355-0839

(P-9690)
FRANKLIN TMPLETON INV SVCS LLC (DH)
Also Called: Franklin Templeton Investment
3344 Quality Dr, Rancho Cordova
(95670-7361)
P.O. Box 2258 (95741-2258)
PHONE..................916 463-1500
Charles B Johnson, *Ch of Bd*
Basil Fox, *President*
Greg Johnson, *President*
Robert Smith, *Senior VP*
May Tong, *Senior VP*
EMP: 1200
SQ FT: 40,000
SALES (est): 576.7MM
SALES (corp-wide): 5.7B **Publicly Held**
SIC: 6211 6282 Traders, security; investment advisory service

(P-9691)
FREMONT MUTUAL FUNDS INC
333 Market St Ste 2600, San Francisco
(94105-2127)
PHONE..................800 548-4539
David L Redo, *CEO*
Michael Kosich, *President*
Vincent P Kuhn, *Exec VP*
Albert Kirschbaum, *Senior VP*
Peter Landini, *Senior VP*
EMP: 55
SQ FT: 19,000
SALES (est): 4.8MM **Privately Held**
SIC: 6211 Mutual funds, selling by independent salesperson

(P-9692)
GI GP IV LLC (PA)
Also Called: GI Partners
188 The Embarcadero # 700, San Francisco (94105-1231)
PHONE..................415 688-4800
Richard Magnuson, *Mng Member*
Mike Stuppler, *Vice Pres*
Angela Zhang, *Vice Pres*
David Mace, *Managing Dir*
EMP: 50
SALES (est): 22.6MM **Privately Held**
SIC: 6211 6512 Investment bankers; commercial & industrial building operation

(P-9693)
GOLD PARENT LP
11111 Santa Monica Blvd, Los Angeles
(90025-3333)
PHONE..................310 954-0444
Jonathan D Sokoloff, *Principal*
EMP: 3400 EST: 2016
SALES (est): 107.2MM **Privately Held**
SIC: 6211 Investment bankers

(P-9694)
GOLDMAN SACHS & CO
Also Called: Goldman Sachs
555 California St # 4500, San Francisco
(94104-1675)
PHONE..................415 393-7500
Eff Martin, *Partner*
Guy Muzio, *Partner*
Cole Feinberg, *Vice Pres*
Donald Fortune, *Vice Pres*
Nils Hellmer, *Vice Pres*
EMP: 200
SALES (corp-wide): 36.6B **Publicly Held**
WEB: www.gs.com
SIC: 6211 6282 Investment bankers; investment advice
HQ: Goldman Sachs & Co. Llc
200 West St Bldg 200 # 200
New York NY 10282
212 346-5440

(P-9695)
GOLDMAN SACHS & CO
Also Called: Goldman Sachs
2121 Avenue Stars 2600, Los Angeles
(90067)
PHONE..................310 407-5700
John Mallory, *Branch Mgr*
Yoonie Lane, *Vice Pres*
Jason Silletti, *Vice Pres*
EMP: 120
SALES (corp-wide): 36.6B **Publicly Held**
WEB: www.gs.com
SIC: 6211 Investment bankers
HQ: Goldman Sachs & Co. Llc
200 West St Bldg 200 # 200
New York NY 10282
212 346-5440

(P-9696)
GORES GROUP LLC (PA)
9800 Wilshire Blvd, Beverly Hills
(90212-1804)
PHONE..................310 209-3010
Alec Gores, *CEO*
Joseph Page, *COO*
Dewey Turner III, *Senior VP*
Barrett Sprowl, *Vice Pres*
Cara Thomas, *Controller*
EMP: 60
SALES (est): 3.8B **Privately Held**
SIC: 6211 7372 5734 Investment firm, general brokerage; prepackaged software; computer software & accessories

(P-9697)
HILLTOP SECURITIES INC
8350 Wilshire Blvd, Beverly Hills
(90211-2327)
PHONE..................800 765-2200
Peter Cappos, *Branch Mgr*
EMP: 50
SALES (corp-wide): 1.6B **Publicly Held**
SIC: 6211 Investment bankers
HQ: Hilltop Securities Inc.
1201 Elm St Ste 3500
Dallas TX 75270
214 859-1800

(P-9698)
IMPERIAL CAPITAL GROUP LLC (PA)
2000 Ave Of The, Los Angeles (90067)
PHONE..................310 246-3700
Randall Wooster,
Lenny Bianco, *Senior VP*
James P Kenney, *Managing Dir*
Jonathan Glionna, *Financial Analy*
Jason Reese,
EMP: 70
SQ FT: 14,909
SALES (est): 10.4MM **Privately Held**
SIC: 6211 Stock brokers & dealers

(P-9699)
IMPERIAL CAPITAL LLC (PA)
10100 Santa Monica Blvd # 2400, Los Angeles (90067-4136)
PHONE..................310 246-3700
Randall Wooster, *CEO*
Tom Corcoran, *President*
Randall E Wooster, *CEO*
Mark Martis, *COO*
Harry Chung, *CFO*
EMP: 85
SALES (est): 33.2MM **Privately Held**
SIC: 6211 Investment bankers

(P-9700)
INTREPID INV BANKERS LLC
11755 Wilshire Blvd # 2200, Los Angeles
(90025-1567)
PHONE..................310 478-9000
Ed Bagdasarian, *CEO*
Steve Davis, *Managing Dir*
Gary Rabishaw, *Managing Dir*
Chris Park, *Director*
Kyle Berkman, *Associate*
EMP: 620
SALES (est): 130.4K **Privately Held**
SIC: 6211 Investment bankers
HQ: Mufg Americas Holdings Corporation
1251 Ave Of The Americas
New York NY 10020
212 782-6800

(P-9701)
INVESTMENT TECH GROUP INC
400 Crprate Pinte Ste 855, Culver City
(90230)
PHONE..................310 216-6777
EMP: 150
SALES (corp-wide): 634.8MM **Publicly Held**
SIC: 6211 7371
PA: Investment Technology Group, Inc.
1 Liberty Plz
New York NY 10282
212 588-4000

(P-9702)
JEFFERIES LLC
11100 Santa Monica Blvd # 12, Los Angeles
(90025-3387)
PHONE..................310 445-1199
Chris Kanoff, *Branch Mgr*
Cep Kifer, *Vice Pres*
Sarah Choi, *Associate*
EMP: 60
SALES (corp-wide): 4.7B **Publicly Held**
SIC: 6211 Brokers, security; dealers, security
HQ: Jefferies Llc
520 Madison Ave Fl 10
New York NY 10022
212 284-2300

(P-9703)
JMP SECURITIES LLC (DH)
600 Montgomery St # 1100, San Francisco
(94111-2713)
PHONE..................415 835-8900
Joseph A Jolson, *CEO*
Carter D Mack, *President*
Raymond S Jackson, *CFO*
Jason Butler, *Vice Pres*
Steven King, *Vice Pres*
EMP: 55
SALES (est): 63.1MM
SALES (corp-wide): 193.9MM **Publicly Held**
SIC: 6211 Investment bankers

HQ: Jmp Group Inc.
600 Montgomery St # 1100
San Francisco CA 94111
415 835-8900

(P-9704)
JP MORGAN SECURITIES LLC
Also Called: Bear Stearns
14061 Mercado Dr, Del Mar (92014-2949)
PHONE.............................310 201-2693
EMP: 85
SALES (corp-wide): 106.2B **Publicly Held**
SIC: 6211
HQ: J.P. Morgan Securities Llc
383 Madison Ave Fl 9
New York NY 10179
212 272-2000

(P-9705)
K A ASSOCIATES INC
1800 Avenue Of The Stars # 200, Los Angeles (90067-4204)
PHONE.............................310 556-2721
Richard Kayne, *CEO*
David Shladovsky, *Admin Sec*
EMP: 116
SALES: 1.3MM **Privately Held**
SIC: 6211 Security brokers & dealers

(P-9706)
LEAR CAPITAL INC
1990 S Bundy Dr Ste 600, Los Angeles (90025-5256)
PHONE.............................310 571-0190
John Ohanesian, *President*
Mary Boston, *Chief Mktg Ofcr*
David Wolfe, *Managing Dir*
Sandeep D'Souza, *Technology*
Katya Askar, *Sales Dir*
EMP: 72
SQ FT: 4,500
SALES (est): 324MM **Privately Held**
WEB: www.goldcentral.com
SIC: 6211 Mineral, oil & gas leasing & royalty dealers

(P-9707)
LEERINK PARTNERS LLC
255 California St Fl 12, San Francisco (94111-4923)
PHONE.............................800 778-1164
Jeffrey Leerink, *CEO*
Dereka Young, *Executive Asst*
EMP: 82 **Privately Held**
SIC: 6211 Brokers, security; investment bankers
PA: Leerink Partners Llc
1 Federal St Fl 37
Boston MA 02110

(P-9708)
LERETA LLC (PA)
1123 Park View Dr, Covina (91724-3748)
PHONE.............................626 543-1765
John Walsh, *CEO*
John Permejo, *President*
James V Micali, *COO*
Tyler Page, *CFO*
Chris Masten, *Exec VP*
EMP: 450
SQ FT: 40,000
SALES (est): 297.9MM **Privately Held**
SIC: 6211 6541 6361 Tax certificate dealers; title search companies; real estate title insurance

(P-9709)
M L STERN & CO LLC (DH)
8350 Wilshire Blvd Fl 1, Beverly Hills (90211-2324)
PHONE.............................323 658-4400
Milford L Stern,
Richard Dimino, *Vice Pres*
Stacy Stern, *Vice Pres*
Bill Pinkerton, *Branch Mgr*
Corey Falikoff, *Info Tech Mgr*
EMP: 117
SQ FT: 8,100
SALES (est): 44.1MM
SALES (corp-wide): 1.6B **Publicly Held**
SIC: 6211 Brokers, security

HQ: Hilltop Securities Holdings Llc
200 Crescent Ct Ste 1330
Dallas TX 75201
214 855-2177

(P-9710)
MAP ENERGY LLC
3000 El Camino Real, Palo Alto (94306-2100)
PHONE.............................650 324-9095
Jane Woodward,
EMP: 85
SALES (est): 2.6MM **Privately Held**
SIC: 6211 Security brokers & dealers

(P-9711)
MERLIN SECURITIES LLC
45 Fremont St Ste 3000, San Francisco (94105-2256)
PHONE.............................415 848-0269
Stephan P Vermut,
Robert Garrett, *Senior Partner*
Regina O'Neill,
EMP: 65
SALES (est): 9.3MM
SALES (corp-wide): 101B **Publicly Held**
SIC: 6211 Security brokers & dealers
HQ: Everen Capital Corporation
301 S College St
Charlotte NC 28202

(P-9712)
MERRILL LYNCH PIERCE FENNER
333 Middlefield Rd, Menlo Park (94025-3552)
PHONE.............................650 473-7888
Fax: 650 473-7800
EMP: 75
SALES (corp-wide): 95.1B **Publicly Held**
SIC: 6211
HQ: Merrill Lynch, Pierce, Fenner & Smith Incorporated
111 8th Ave
New York NY 10011
800 637-7455

(P-9713)
MERRILL LYNCH PIERCE FENNER
16830 Ventura Blvd # 601, Encino (91436-1707)
PHONE.............................818 528-7809
Paul Pepperman, *Manager*
Andrea Abeger, *Consultant*
EMP: 57
SALES (corp-wide): 110.5B **Publicly Held**
WEB: www.merlyn.com
SIC: 6211 8742 Security brokers & dealers; financial consultant
HQ: Merrill Lynch, Pierce, Fenner & Smith Incorporated
111 8th Ave
New York NY 10011
800 637-7455

(P-9714)
MERRILL LYNCH PIERCE FENNER
3075b Hansen Way, Palo Alto (94304-1000)
PHONE.............................650 842-2440
Huert Chang, *Branch Mgr*
EMP: 75
SALES (corp-wide): 110.5B **Publicly Held**
WEB: www.merlyn.com
SIC: 6211 Security brokers & dealers
HQ: Merrill Lynch, Pierce, Fenner & Smith Incorporated
111 8th Ave
New York NY 10011
800 637-7455

(P-9715)
MERRILL LYNCH PIERCE FENNER
730 Patricia Dr, San Luis Obispo (93405-1036)
PHONE.............................661 802-0764
Martin B Epperson, *Principal*
EMP: 50

SALES (corp-wide): 110.5B **Publicly Held**
SIC: 6211 Brokers, security
HQ: Merrill Lynch, Pierce, Fenner & Smith Incorporated
111 8th Ave
New York NY 10011
800 637-7455

(P-9716)
MERRILL LYNCH PIERCE FENNER
520 Newport Center Dr # 1900, Newport Beach (92660-8808)
PHONE.............................949 467-3760
David Gunta, *Branch Mgr*
Mark Beach, *Vice Pres*
Timothy Scudder, *Vice Pres*
Howard Leon, *Director*
EMP: 240
SALES (corp-wide): 110.5B **Publicly Held**
SIC: 6211 Security brokers & dealers
HQ: Merrill Lynch, Pierce, Fenner & Smith Incorporated
111 8th Ave
New York NY 10011
800 637-7455

(P-9717)
MERRILL LYNCH PIERCE FENNER
300 E Esplanade Dr, Oxnard (93036-1238)
PHONE.............................800 964-5182
James Hardy, *Branch Mgr*
EMP: 240
SALES (corp-wide): 110.5B **Publicly Held**
SIC: 6211 Security brokers & dealers
HQ: Merrill Lynch, Pierce, Fenner & Smith Incorporated
111 8th Ave
New York NY 10011
800 637-7455

(P-9718)
MERRILL LYNCH PIERCE FENNER
333 Middlefield Rd # 202, Menlo Park (94025-3552)
PHONE.............................650 473-7888
Deborah Germenis, *Branch Mgr*
Cory Goligoski, *Vice Pres*
Hilary Jones, *Manager*
EMP: 240
SALES (corp-wide): 110.5B **Publicly Held**
SIC: 6211 Security brokers & dealers
HQ: Merrill Lynch, Pierce, Fenner & Smith Incorporated
111 8th Ave
New York NY 10011
800 637-7455

(P-9719)
MERRILL LYNCH PIERCE FENNER
701 B St Ste 2350, San Diego (92101-8125)
PHONE.............................619 699-3700
Quinton Ellis, *Branch Mgr*
Nathan Labiak, *Finance*
Scott Breckenridge, *Analyst*
Robert Fleming, *Manager*
James Gilmore, *Manager*
EMP: 150
SALES (corp-wide): 110.5B **Publicly Held**
WEB: www.merlyn.com
SIC: 6211 8742 Security brokers & dealers; financial consultant
HQ: Merrill Lynch, Pierce, Fenner & Smith Incorporated
111 8th Ave
New York NY 10011
800 637-7455

(P-9720)
MERRILL LYNCH PIERCE FENNER
50 W San Fernando St # 16, San Jose (95113-2420)
PHONE.............................408 283-3000
Patricia Williams, *Manager*
Peter Verbica, *Advisor*

EMP: 50
SALES (corp-wide): 110.5B **Publicly Held**
WEB: www.merlyn.com
SIC: 6211 6282 Security brokers & dealers; investment advice
HQ: Merrill Lynch, Pierce, Fenner & Smith Incorporated
111 8th Ave
New York NY 10011
800 637-7455

(P-9721)
MERRILL LYNCH PIERCE FENNER
2049 Century Park E # 1100, Los Angeles (90067-3101)
PHONE.............................310 407-3900
Michael Rogers, *Branch Mgr*
EMP: 120
SALES (corp-wide): 110.5B **Publicly Held**
WEB: www.merlyn.com
SIC: 6211 Security brokers & dealers
HQ: Merrill Lynch, Pierce, Fenner & Smith Incorporated
111 8th Ave
New York NY 10011
800 637-7455

(P-9722)
MERRILL LYNCH PIERCE FENNER
1331 N Calif Blvd Ste 400, Walnut Creek (94596-4561)
PHONE.............................925 945-4800
Michael Dunn, *Branch Mgr*
Kelly Milligan, *Manager*
Lee Coburn, *Agent*
EMP: 85
SALES (corp-wide): 110.5B **Publicly Held**
WEB: www.merlyn.com
SIC: 6211 8742 Security brokers & dealers; financial consultant
HQ: Merrill Lynch, Pierce, Fenner & Smith Incorporated
111 8th Ave
New York NY 10011
800 637-7455

(P-9723)
MERRILL LYNCH PIERCE FENNER
101 California St Fl 24, San Francisco (94111-5898)
PHONE.............................415 274-7000
Jim Delancey, *Manager*
Christine Koh-Wong, *Vice Pres*
Randal Avey, *Manager*
David Moyne, *Manager*
EMP: 50
SALES (corp-wide): 110.5B **Publicly Held**
WEB: www.merlyn.com
SIC: 6211 6282 Stock brokers & dealers; investment advice
HQ: Merrill Lynch, Pierce, Fenner & Smith Incorporated
111 8th Ave
New York NY 10011
800 637-7455

(P-9724)
MERRILL LYNCH PIERCE FENNER
100 Spectrum Center Dr # 1100, Irvine (92618-4962)
P.O. Box 2550, Laguna Hills (92654-2550)
PHONE.............................949 859-2900
Pete Henvika, *Branch Mgr*
Jeffrey Dewees, *Advisor*
Jason Roxby, *Consultant*
Megan Stirrat, *Consultant*
EMP: 90
SALES (corp-wide): 110.5B **Publicly Held**
WEB: www.merlyn.com
SIC: 6211 Security brokers & dealers
HQ: Merrill Lynch, Pierce, Fenner & Smith Incorporated
111 8th Ave
New York NY 10011
800 637-7455

(P-9725)

MERRILL LYNCH PIERCE FENNER

7825 Fay Ave Ste 300, La Jolla
(92037-4255)
PHONE..........................858 456-3600
Paul Sullivan, *Manager*
Gary Wardein, *Manager*
EMP: 60
SALES (corp-wide): 110.5B **Publicly Held**
WEB: www.merlyn.com
SIC: 6211 Security brokers & dealers
HQ: Merrill Lynch, Pierce, Fenner & Smith
Incorporated
111 8th Ave
New York NY 10011
800 637-7455

(P-9726)

MIZUHO SECURITIES USA INC

3 Embarcadero Ctr # 1620, San Francisco
(94111-4049)
PHONE..........................415 268-5500
EMP: 53 **Privately Held**
SIC: 6211 Security brokers & dealers
HQ: Mizuho Securities Usa Llc
320 Park Ave Fl 12
New York NY 10022
212 282-3000

(P-9727)

MORGAN STANLEY

55 S Lake Ave Ste 800, Pasadena
(91101-2677)
PHONE..........................626 405-9313
Alan Whitman, *Branch Mgr*
EMP: 60
SALES (corp-wide): 50.1B **Publicly Held**
SIC: 6211 Stock brokers & dealers
PA: Morgan Stanley
1585 Broadway
New York NY 10036
212 761-4000

(P-9728)

MORGAN STANLEY

4350 La Jolla Village Dr # 1000, San Diego
(92122-1247)
PHONE..........................858 597-7777
Joe McDoval, *General Mgr*
EMP: 50
SALES (corp-wide): 50.1B **Publicly Held**
SIC: 6211 Security brokers & dealers
PA: Morgan Stanley
1585 Broadway
New York NY 10036
212 761-4000

(P-9729)

MORGAN STANLEY

1901 Main St Ste 700, Irvine (92614-0514)
PHONE..........................949 809-1200
EMP: 200
SALES (corp-wide): 50.1B **Publicly Held**
SIC: 6211 Security brokers & dealers
PA: Morgan Stanley
1585 Broadway
New York NY 10036
212 761-4000

(P-9730)

MORGAN STANLEY & CO LLC

407 Capitol Mall Ste 1900, Sacramento
(95814)
PHONE..........................916 444-8041
Henry Auwinger, *Branch Mgr*
EMP: 50
SALES (corp-wide): 50.1B **Publicly Held**
WEB: www.msvp.com
SIC: 6211 Stock brokers & dealers
HQ: Morgan Stanley & Co. Llc
1585 Broadway
New York NY 10036
212 761-4000

(P-9731)

MORGAN STANLEY & CO LLC

5250 N Palm Ave Ste 321, Fresno
(93704-2213)
PHONE..........................559 431-5900
Gregory Conner, *Manager*
Jeffrey Branch, *Branch Mgr*
Marlyn Milloy, *Manager*
EMP: 50

SALES (corp-wide): 50.1B **Publicly Held**
WEB: www.msvp.com
SIC: 6211 Security brokers & dealers
HQ: Morgan Stanley & Co. Llc
1585 Broadway
New York NY 10036
212 761-4000

(P-9732)

MORGAN STANLEY & CO LLC

2677 N Main St Fl 10, Santa Ana
(92705-6633)
P.O. Box 11998 (92711-1998)
PHONE..........................714 836-5181
Mark Albers, *Branch Mgr*
EMP: 60
SALES (corp-wide): 50.1B **Publicly Held**
WEB: www.msvp.com
SIC: 6211 Stock brokers & dealers
HQ: Morgan Stanley & Co. Llc
1585 Broadway
New York NY 10036
212 761-4000

(P-9733)

MORGAN STANLEY & CO LLC

101 W Broadway Ste 1800, San Diego
(92101-8298)
PHONE..........................619 236-1331
Eddie Dyer, *Branch Mgr*
EMP: 80
SQ FT: 13,000
SALES (corp-wide): 50.1B **Publicly Held**
WEB: www.msvp.com
SIC: 6211 Investment bankers
HQ: Morgan Stanley & Co. Llc
1585 Broadway
New York NY 10036
212 761-4000

(P-9734)

MORGAN STANLEY & CO LLC

9100 Ming Ave Ste 205, Bakersfield
(93311-1329)
PHONE..........................661 663-8100
Tom Woodward, *Manager*
EMP: 53
SALES (corp-wide): 50.1B **Publicly Held**
WEB: www.msvp.com
SIC: 6211 Brokers, security
HQ: Morgan Stanley & Co. Llc
1585 Broadway
New York NY 10036
212 761-4000

(P-9735)

MORGAN STANLEY & CO LLC

1999 Harrison St Ste 2200, Oakland
(94612-3559)
PHONE..........................510 839-8080
Renee Arst, *Manager*
EMP: 60
SALES (corp-wide): 50.1B **Publicly Held**
WEB: www.msvp.com
SIC: 6211 Security brokers & dealers
HQ: Morgan Stanley & Co. Llc
1585 Broadway
New York NY 10036
212 761-4000

(P-9736)

MORGAN STANLEY & CO LLC

216 Lorton Ave, Burlingame (94010-4204)
PHONE..........................650 340-6550
Jane Kelly, *Principal*
EMP: 75
SALES (corp-wide): 50.1B **Publicly Held**
WEB: www.msvp.com
SIC: 6211 Investment bankers
HQ: Morgan Stanley & Co. Llc
1585 Broadway
New York NY 10036
212 761-4000

(P-9737)

MORGAN STANLEY & CO LLC

1453 3rd St Ste 200, Santa Monica
(90401-3451)
P.O. Box 2310 (90407-2310)
PHONE..........................310 319-5200
Thomas Padden, *Manager*
EMP: 65
SALES (corp-wide): 50.1B **Publicly Held**
WEB: www.msvp.com
SIC: 6211 Investment bankers

HQ: Morgan Stanley & Co. Llc
1585 Broadway
New York NY 10036
212 761-4000

(P-9738)

MORGAN STANLEY & CO LLC

225 W Santa Clara St # 900, San Jose
(95113-1746)
PHONE..........................408 947-2200
William Svoboda, *Branch Mgr*
EMP: 60
SALES (corp-wide): 50.1B **Publicly Held**
WEB: www.msvp.com
SIC: 6211 Brokers, security
HQ: Morgan Stanley & Co. Llc
1585 Broadway
New York NY 10036
212 761-4000

(P-9739)

MORGAN STANLEY & CO LLC

9665 Wilshire Blvd # 600, Beverly Hills
(90212-2315)
PHONE..........................310 285-4800
Margaret Black, *Manager*
EMP: 160
SALES (corp-wide): 50.1B **Publicly Held**
WEB: www.msvp.com
SIC: 6211 Security brokers & dealers
HQ: Morgan Stanley & Co. Llc
1585 Broadway
New York NY 10036
212 761-4000

(P-9740)

MORGAN STANLEY & CO LLC

101 California St Fl 3, San Francisco
(94111-5890)
PHONE..........................415 693-6000
Renee Arst, *Manager*
EMP: 300
SALES (corp-wide): 50.1B **Publicly Held**
WEB: www.msvp.com
SIC: 6211 Brokers, security
HQ: Morgan Stanley & Co. Llc
1585 Broadway
New York NY 10036
212 761-4000

(P-9741)

MYERS CAPITAL PARTNERS LLC

790 S Oak Knoll Ave, Pasadena
(91106-4461)
PHONE..........................626 568-1398
William E Myers,
Kit McCoullogh,
EMP: 50
SALES (est): 7.6MM **Privately Held**
WEB: www.myerscapitalpartners.com
SIC: 6211 Investment firm, general brokerage

(P-9742)

NOMURA SECURITIES INTL INC

425 California St # 2600, San Francisco
(94104-2211)
PHONE..........................415 445-3831
John Denning, *Branch Mgr*
EMP: 340 **Privately Held**
SIC: 6211 Dealers, security
HQ: Nomura Securities International, Inc.
Worldwide Plaza 309 W 49t
New York NY 10019
212 667-9000

(P-9743)

PACIFIC GROWTH EQUITIES LLC

1 Bush St Fl 17, San Francisco
(94104-4425)
PHONE..........................415 274-6800
Thomas J Dietz, *CEO*
Kurtis Fechtmeyer, *Principal*
Richard Osgood,
EMP: 85
SQ FT: 34,000
SALES: 44MM **Privately Held**
WEB: www.pacgrow.com
SIC: 6211 Security brokers & dealers; investment bankers

(P-9744)

PACIFIC SELECT DISTRIBUTORS

Also Called: Pacific Mutual Distributors
700 Newport Center Dr # 4, Newport Beach
(92660-6307)
PHONE..........................949 219-3011
Gerald W Robinson, *President*
Edward R Byrd, *CFO*
Kathy R Gough, *Assoc VP*
Audrey L Milfs, *Admin Sec*
Thomas C Sutton, *Director*
EMP: 96
SQ FT: 300,000
SALES (est): 372K
SALES (corp-wide): 12.8B **Privately Held**
SIC: 6211 Brokers, security; dealers, security
HQ: Pacific Life Insurance Company
700 Newport Center Dr
Newport Beach CA 92660
949 219-3011

(P-9745)

PARKSIDE LENDING LLC

180 Redwood St Ste 250, San Francisco
(94102-3283)
PHONE..........................415 771-3700
Alan Sagatelyan,
Helen Matoesian, *Officer*
Bill Chudy, *Exec VP*
Barbara Fagundes, *Vice Pres*
Dee Albanese, *Executive*
EMP: 60
SQ FT: 5,097
SALES (est): 84.6MM **Privately Held**
WEB: www.parksidelending.com
SIC: 6211 Mortgages, buying & selling

(P-9746)

PLAZA HOME MORTGAGE INC

6420 Sequence Dr Ste 200, San Diego
(92121-4319)
PHONE..........................714 508-6406
Kevin Parra, *President*
EMP: 114
SALES (corp-wide): 172.2MM **Privately Held**
SIC: 6211 6162 Mortgages, buying & selling; loan correspondents
PA: Plaza Home Mortgage, Inc.
4820 Eastgate Mall # 100
San Diego CA 92121
858 346-1200

(P-9747)

RBC CAPITAL MARKETS LLC

9665 Wilshire Blvd Fl 4, Beverly Hills
(90212-2311)
PHONE..........................310 273-7600
Elliot Katz, *Branch Mgr*
Phil Hammitt, *Senior VP*
Maria Lupu, *Vice Pres*
Jay Marshall, *Vice Pres*
Mark Lininger, *Consultant*
EMP: 50
SALES (corp-wide): 21.4B **Privately Held**
WEB: www.hough.com
SIC: 6211 Investment bankers
HQ: Rbc Capital Markets, Llc
60 S 6th St Ste 700
Minneapolis MN 55402
612 371-2711

(P-9748)

REYES HOLDINGS LLC

Also Called: Crest Beverage
8870 Liquid Ct, San Diego (92121-2234)
PHONE..........................858 452-2300
Steve Souratas, *President*
Bobbie Keeling, *Analyst*
EMP: 300 **Privately Held**
SIC: 6211 Distributors, security
PA: Reyes Holdings, L.L.C.
6250 N River Rd Ste 9000
Rosemont IL 60018

(P-9749)

ROTH CAPITAL PARTNERS LLC (PA)

888 San Clemente Dr # 400, Newport
Beach (92660-6366)
PHONE..........................800 678-9147
Byron Roth, *CEO*

John Chambers, *Vice Ch Bd*
Warren Dunnavant II, *Vice Pres*
Daniel Friedman, *Vice Pres*
Sherry He, *Vice Pres*
EMP: 100
SQ FT: 52,000
SALES (est): 50.1MM **Privately Held**
WEB: www.rothcp.com
SIC: 6211 Investment bankers; brokers, security

(P-9750)
SHAMROCK PLUS INC
Also Called: Shamrock Center
4444 W Lakeside Dr Lbby, Burbank
(91505-4069)
PHONE..................................818 845-4444
Stanley Gold, *President*
EMP: 50
SQ FT: 12,000
SALES (est): 3.4MM
SALES (corp-wide): 16.3MM **Privately Held**
SIC: 6211 Brokers, security; investment bankers; investment certificate sales
HQ: Shamrock Holdings Of California, Inc.
4444 W Lakeside Dr Lbby
Burbank CA 91505
818 845-4444

(P-9751)
STANDARD PACIFIC CAPITAL LLC
101 California St Fl 36, San Francisco
(94111-5831)
PHONE..................................415 352-7100
Andrew Midler, *Managing Prtnr*
Jivko Moutafov, *Analyst*
Dan Martin,
EMP: 50
SQ FT: 9,000
SALES (est): 12.7MM **Privately Held**
SIC: 6211 Investment firm, general brokerage

(P-9752)
STOCKCROSS FINANCIAL SVCS INC (DH)
9464 Wilshire Blvd, Beverly Hills
(90212-2707)
PHONE..................................800 993-2015
Richard S Gebbia, *President*
Michael Jonathan Colombino, *CFO*
George H Kupper, *Admin Sec*
EMP: 50
SQ FT: 8,000
SALES (est): 20.3MM
SALES (corp-wide): 30MM **Publicly Held**
WEB: www.stockcross.com
SIC: 6211 Brokers, security; dealers, security
HQ: Muriel Siebert & Co., Inc.
15 Exchange Pl Ste 615
Jersey City NJ 07302
212 644-2400

(P-9753)
STONE & YOUNGBERG LLC (PA)
1 Ferry Plz, San Francisco (94111-4212)
PHONE..................................415 445-2300
Terry Maas, *Principal*
Kenneth E Williams, *President*
Mitchell H Gage, *CFO*
B Craig Hutson, *Senior VP*
Kevin R Montoya, *Senior VP*
EMP: 130
SQ FT: 19,034
SALES (est): 35.7MM **Privately Held**
WEB: www.syllc.com
SIC: 6211 6282 Bond dealers & brokers; investment advice

(P-9754)
TAKENAKA PARTNERS LLC (PA)
801 S Figueroa St Ste 620, Los Angeles
(90017-5556)
PHONE..................................213 593-4011
Yukuo Takenaka, *President*
Yoshiko Nakaoki, *CFO*
Yoshinobu Fukushima, *Exec VP*
Kris Fujita, *Vice Pres*
Ippei Suzuki, *Vice Pres*
EMP: 50
SQ FT: 5,183

SALES (est): 7.5MM **Privately Held**
WEB: www.takenakapartners.com
SIC: 6211 Investment bankers

(P-9755)
TANIMURA BROTHERS
81 Hitchcock Rd, Salinas (93908-9449)
PHONE..................................831 424-0841
Tom Tanimura, *Partner*
George Tanimura, *Partner*
John Tanimura, *Partner*
EMP: 70 **EST:** 1948
SALES (est): 9.9MM **Privately Held**
SIC: 6211 Investment firm, general brokerage

(P-9756)
TCW FUNDS MANAGEMENT INC
865 S Figueroa St # 2100, Los Angeles
(90017-2588)
PHONE..................................213 244-0000
Thomas Larkin, *Ch of Bd*
Marc I Stern, *President*
William E Sonnebron, *CFO*
Ernest O Ellison, *Officer*
Alvin R Albe Jr, *Exec VP*
EMP: 550
SALES (est): 31.8MM
SALES (corp-wide): 226.2MM **Privately Held**
SIC: 6211 Security brokers & dealers
PA: The Tcw Group Inc
865 S Figueroa St # 1800
Los Angeles CA 90017
213 244-0000

(P-9757)
THE CHARLES SCHWAB TRUST CO (HQ)
425 Market St Fl 7, San Francisco
(94105-5405)
PHONE..................................415 371-0518
James McCool, *CEO*
Nancy Larget, *Vice Pres*
Aaron Lafary, *Business Anlyst*
Steve Cartwright, *Manager*
EMP: 50
SALES (est): 35.7MM
SALES (corp-wide): 10.1B **Publicly Held**
SIC: 6211 Security brokers & dealers
PA: The Charles Schwab Corporation
211 Main St Fl 17
San Francisco CA 94105
415 667-7000

(P-9758)
THOMAS WEISEL PARTNERS LLC (DH)
1 Montgomery St Ste 3700, San Francisco
(94104-5537)
PHONE..................................415 364-2500
Thomas Weisel,
Michael Carr, *Vice Pres*
Joseph Corso, *Vice Pres*
Wilson Lam, *Vice Pres*
Chris Ohlweiler, *Vice Pres*
EMP: 300 **EST:** 1998
SALES (est): 67.7MM
SALES (corp-wide): 3.2B **Publicly Held**
WEB: www.tweisel.com
SIC: 6211 Investment bankers
HQ: Thomas Weisel Partners Group Inc.
1 Montgomery St Fl 36
San Francisco CA 94104
415 364-2500

(P-9759)
UBS FINANCIAL SERVICES INC
777 S Figueroa St # 5100, Los Angeles
(90017-5800)
P.O. Box 90051 (90009-0051)
PHONE..................................213 972-1511
Wes Jennison, *Manager*
EMP: 200
SALES (corp-wide): 29.6B **Privately Held**
SIC: 6211 Brokers, security
HQ: Ubs Financial Services Inc.
1285 Ave Of The Americas
New York NY 10019
212 713-2000

(P-9760)
UBS FINANCIAL SERVICES INC
131 S Rodeo Dr Ste 200, Beverly Hills
(90212-2428)
PHONE..................................310 274-8441

Randall Grossblatt, *Manager*
John Buchanan, *Vice Pres*
Lane Goldstein, *Vice Pres*
Fingleson Eri Mitchel, *Vice Pres*
Justin T Reese, *Vice Pres*
EMP: 100
SALES (corp-wide): 29.6B **Privately Held**
SIC: 6211 Bond dealers & brokers; brokers, security; stock brokers & dealers
HQ: Ubs Financial Services Inc.
1285 Ave Of The Americas
New York NY 10019
212 713-2000

(P-9761)
UBS FINANCIAL SERVICES INC
600 W Broadway Ste 2100, San Diego
(92101-3356)
PHONE..................................619 236-0460
David Jones, *Manager*
Christopher Hagopian, *Vice Pres*
Daniel Banks, *Manager*
James Peasley, *Advisor*
EMP: 130
SALES (corp-wide): 29.6B **Privately Held**
SIC: 6211 Dealers, security
HQ: Ubs Financial Services Inc.
1285 Ave Of The Americas
New York NY 10019
212 713-2000

(P-9762)
UBS FINANCIAL SERVICES INC
1 California St Ste 2000, San Francisco
(94111-5437)
PHONE..................................415 954-6700
Loren Neumann, *Branch Mgr*
Alexander Taft, *Vice Pres*
Robert Vallercorse, *Vice Pres*
EMP: 175
SALES (corp-wide): 29.6B **Privately Held**
SIC: 6211 Stock brokers & dealers
HQ: Ubs Financial Services Inc.
1285 Ave Of The Americas
New York NY 10019
212 713-2000

(P-9763)
UBS FINANCIAL SERVICES INC
888 San Clemente Dr # 300, Newport
Beach (92660-6366)
PHONE..................................949 760-5308
Don Dalis, *Branch Mgr*
Gianna Drake-Kerrison, *Vice Pres*
Bruce Tenenbaum, *Vice Pres*
Douglas Cosgrove, *Data Proc Dir*
Jon Dunavold, *Advisor*
EMP: 175
SALES (corp-wide): 29.6B **Privately Held**
SIC: 6211 Stock brokers & dealers
HQ: Ubs Financial Services Inc.
1285 Ave Of The Americas
New York NY 10019
212 713-2000

(P-9764)
UBS FINANCIAL SERVICES INC
1610 Arden Way Ste 200, Sacramento
(95815-4041)
PHONE..................................916 648-7200
Tom Qvustgaard, *Branch Mgr*
Eric P Schraeder, *Agent*
EMP: 50
SALES (corp-wide): 29.6B **Privately Held**
SIC: 6211 Security brokers & dealers
HQ: Ubs Financial Services Inc.
1285 Ave Of The Americas
New York NY 10019
212 713-2000

(P-9765)
UBS FINANCIAL SERVICES INC
555 California St # 4650, San Francisco
(94104-1789)
PHONE..................................415 398-6400
Tony Tarrab, *Vice Pres*
Karen Stinger, *Administration*
EMP: 100
SALES (corp-wide): 29.6B **Privately Held**
SIC: 6211 Investment bankers
HQ: Ubs Financial Services Inc.
1285 Ave Of The Americas
New York NY 10019
212 713-2000

(P-9766)
UBS SECURITIES LLC
555 California St # 4650, San Francisco
(94104-1789)
PHONE..................................415 352-5650
Kirt Engle, *Branch Mgr*
Jeffrey B Burke, *Vice Pres*
Angel K Chen, *Vice Pres*
Dean Meniktas, *Vice Pres*
EMP: 65
SALES (corp-wide): 29.6B **Privately Held**
SIC: 6211 Brokers, security; dealers, security
HQ: Ubs Securities Llc
677 Washington Blvd
Stamford CT 06901
-

(P-9767)
W R HAMBRECHT CO INC (PA)
Bay 3 Pier 1, San Francisco (94111)
PHONE..................................415 551-8600
William R Hambrecht, *Ch of Bd*
Jonathan Fayman, *CFO*
Clay Corbus, *Co-CEO*
EMP: 60 **EST:** 1998
SQ FT: 25,000
SALES (est): 21.4MM **Privately Held**
WEB: www.wrhambrecht.com
SIC: 6211 Investment bankers

(P-9768)
WADDELL & REED INC
695 Town Center Dr # 200, Costa Mesa
(92626-7128)
PHONE..................................714 437-7510
Daralee Barbera, *Director*
James Raines, *Bd of Directors*
Darci Kelley, *Manager*
Mark Larsen, *Manager*
William Knoke, *Advisor*
EMP: 65 **Publicly Held**
SIC: 6211 8742 Security brokers & dealers; financial consultant
HQ: Waddell & Reed, Inc.
6300 Lamar Ave
Shawnee Mission KS 66202
913 236-2000

(P-9769)
WEDBUSH SECURITIES INC (HQ)
1000 Wilshire Blvd # 800, Los Angeles
(90017-2466)
P.O. Box 30014 (90030-0014)
PHONE..................................213 688-8000
Edward W Wedbush, *President*
Robert Limmer, *Owner*
Peter Allman-Ward, *CFO*
Dan Billings, *CFO*
David Weaver, *CFO*
EMP: 300 **EST:** 1955
SQ FT: 100,000
SALES (est): 308MM
SALES (corp-wide): 318.4MM **Privately Held**
WEB: www.einvestmentbank.com
SIC: 6211 Brokers, security; stock brokers & dealers; bond dealers & brokers
PA: Wedbush, Inc.,
1000 Wilshire Blvd # 900
Los Angeles CA 90017
213 688-8080

(P-9770)
WELLS FARGO CLEARING SVCS LLC
Also Called: Wells Fargo Advisors
777 S Figueroa St # 4700, Los Angeles
(90017-5800)
PHONE..................................213 486-5200
Tom Barker, *Manager*
Howard Durlester, *Vice Pres*
EMP: 50
SALES (corp-wide): 101B **Publicly Held**
WEB: www.wachoviasec.com
SIC: 6211 8742 Stock brokers & dealers; financial consultant
HQ: Wells Fargo Clearing Services, Llc
1 N Jefferson Ave Fl 7
Saint Louis MO 63103
314 955-3000

▲ = Import ▼=Export
◆ =Import/Export

(P-9771)
WELLS FARGO CLEARING SVCS LLC
Also Called: Wells Fargo Advisors
555 California St # 2300, San Francisco
(94104-1598)
PHONE....................................415 291-1200
Kevin Kitchin, *Manager*
Gary Garabedian, *Vice Pres*
Harry Gong, *Vice Pres*
Derek Holtzinger, *Vice Pres*
Tony Rivera, *Vice Pres*
EMP: 115
SALES (corp-wide): 101B **Publicly Held**
WEB: www.wachoviasec.com
SIC: 6211 6282 Stock brokers & dealers;
  investment advice
HQ: Wells Fargo Clearing Services, Llc
  1 N Jefferson Ave Fl 7
  Saint Louis MO 63103
  314 955-3000

(P-9772)
WELLS FARGO CLEARING SVCS LLC
Also Called: Wells Fargo Advisors
888 Prospect St Ste 220, La Jolla
(92037-4261)
PHONE....................................858 456-7706
Bill Ryan, *Manager*
John Armstrong, *Vice Pres*
Sylvia Geffen, *Vice Pres*
Patrick Kearney, *Vice Pres*
Josh O'Brien, *Vice Pres*
EMP: 50
SALES (corp-wide): 101B **Publicly Held**
WEB: www.wachoviasec.com
SIC: 6211 Stock brokers & dealers
HQ: Wells Fargo Clearing Services, Llc
  1 N Jefferson Ave Fl 7
  Saint Louis MO 63103
  314 955-3000

(P-9773)
WELLS FARGO CLEARING SVCS LLC
Also Called: Wells Fargo Advisors
3020 Old Ranch Pkwy # 190, Seal Beach
(90740-2765)
PHONE....................................562 594-1220
EMP: 50
SALES (corp-wide): 97.7B **Publicly Held**
SIC: 6211
HQ: Wells Fargo Clearing Services, Llc
  1 N Jefferson Ave
  Saint Louis MO 63103
  314 955-3000

(P-9774)
WELLS FARGO CLEARING SVCS LLC
Also Called: Wells Fargo Advisors
5820 Canoga Ave Ste 100, Woodland Hills
(91367-6517)
PHONE....................................818 226-2222
Jeff Bouchard, *Manager*
Lary Bloom, *Vice Pres*
Thomas A Eisenstadt, *Vice Pres*
Shawn Hare, *Vice Pres*
Darin Miller, *Vice Pres*
EMP: 60
SALES (corp-wide): 101B **Publicly Held**
WEB: www.wachoviasec.com
SIC: 6211 Stock brokers & dealers
HQ: Wells Fargo Clearing Services, Llc
  1 N Jefferson Ave Fl 7
  Saint Louis MO 63103
  314 955-3000

(P-9775)
WINDJAMMER CAPITAL INVSTR III
Also Called: Westwind Equity Investors
610 Newport Center Dr # 1100, Newport
Beach (92660-6419)
PHONE....................................949 706-9989
Robert Bartholomew, *Chairman*
Matt Anderson, *Vice Pres*
J Derek Watson, *Principal*
Jeff Miehe,
Mike Wattles,
EMP: 724
SALES (est): 46.2MM **Privately Held**
SIC: 6211 Investment firm, general broker-
  age

(P-9776)
ZELL ASSOCIATES INC (PA)
Also Called: Investment Real Estate
1777 Hamilton Ave # 1250, San Jose
(95125-5418)
PHONE....................................408 978-1950
Sherman Zell, *President*
Sylvia Delpier, *Vice Pres*
Marie Jasinsky, *Director*
EMP: 72
SQ FT: 3,000
SALES (est): 15.3MM **Privately Held**
WEB: www.zell.com
SIC: 6211 6531 6552 Syndicate shares
  (real estate, entertainment, equip.) sales;
  real estate managers; real estate brokers
  & agents; subdividers & developers

6221 Commodity Contracts Brokers & Dealers

(P-9777)
APEX BULK COMMODITIES INC
14080 Slover Ave, Fontana (92337-7039)
PHONE....................................909 854-9991
Steve Gale, *Branch Mgr*
Derrick Wyatt, *Maintenance Dir*
EMP: 68
SALES (corp-wide): 74.9MM **Privately Held**
SIC: 6221 Commodity contracts brokers,
  dealers
PA: Apex Bulk Commodities, Inc.
  12531 Violet Rd Ste A
  Adelanto CA 92301
  760 246-6077

(P-9778)
GLOBAL FUTURES EXCH & TRDG CO
303 17th St, Santa Monica (90402-2223)
PHONE....................................818 996-0401
Kathy Hakimian, *President*
Francis Marcale, *Manager*
EMP: 80
SALES (est): 14.3MM **Privately Held**
WEB: www.gfetc.com
SIC: 6221 Commodity brokers, contracts

(P-9779)
MERRILL LYNCH PIERCE FENNER
145 S State College Blvd # 300, Brea
(92821-5844)
PHONE....................................714 257-4400
Robert Max, *Manager*
Stephanie Sheeks, *Director*
EMP: 69
SALES (corp-wide): 110.5B **Publicly Held**
WEB: www.merlyn.com
SIC: 6221 Commodity brokers, contracts;
  commodity dealers, contracts
HQ: Merrill Lynch, Pierce, Fenner & Smith
  Incorporated
  111 8th Ave
  New York NY 10011
  800 637-7455

(P-9780)
MERRILL LYNCH PIERCE FENNER
800 E Colo Blvd Ste 400, Pasadena
(91101)
PHONE....................................626 844-8500
Mark Mixon, *Manager*
Lawrence De Santis, *Advisor*
Steven Rice, *Advisor*
EMP: 80
SALES (corp-wide): 110.5B **Publicly Held**
WEB: www.merlyn.com
SIC: 6221 Commodity brokers, contracts;
  commodity dealers, contracts
HQ: Merrill Lynch, Pierce, Fenner & Smith
  Incorporated
  111 8th Ave
  New York NY 10011
  800 637-7455

6231 Security & Commodity Exchanges

(P-9781)
NYSE ARCA INC
115 Sansome St, San Francisco
(94104-3601)
PHONE....................................415 393-4000
Philip D Defeo, *CEO*
David Diamond, *CFO*
Paul N Koutoulas, *Exec VP*
Peter Armstrong, *Senior VP*
Hark Yip, *Senior VP*
EMP: 265 EST: 1882
SALES (est): 512.9K
SALES (corp-wide): 4.9B **Publicly Held**
SIC: 6231 Stock exchanges
HQ: Nyse Group, Inc.
  11 Wall St
  New York NY 10005
  212 656-3000

6282 Investment Advice

(P-9782)
ALLWORTH FINANCIAL LP
Also Called: Hanson McClain Advisors
135 Camino Dorado Ste 1, NAPA
(94558-7531)
PHONE....................................888 577-2489
EMP: 90 **Privately Held**
SIC: 6282 Investment advisory service
PA: Allworth Financial, L.P.
  8775 Folsom Blvd Ste 100
  Sacramento CA 95826

(P-9783)
AMERICAN ADVISORS GROUP (PA)
3800 W Chapman Ave Fl 3, Orange
(92868-1638)
PHONE....................................866 948-0003
Reza Jahangiri, *President*
Sean Baker, *Officer*
Richard Cornelsen, *Officer*
Mark Cooley, *Vice Pres*
Michelle Kaulback, *Vice Pres*
EMP: 50
SQ FT: 4,500
SALES (est): 24.1MM **Privately Held**
SIC: 6282 Futures advisory service

(P-9784)
AMERICAN CENTURY INV MGT INC
Also Called: American Century Investments
1665 Charleston Rd, Mountain View
(94043-1211)
PHONE....................................650 965-8300
EMP: 200
SALES (corp-wide): 704.8MM **Privately Held**
SIC: 6282 Investment advisory service
HQ: American Century Investment Man-
  agement, Inc.
  4500 Main St
  Kansas City MO 64111
  816 531-5575

(P-9785)
AMERICAN FINANCIAL NETWORK INC
8505 Florence Ave, Downey (90240-4014)
PHONE....................................562 861-1414
Alejandro Ascencio, *Branch Mgr*
EMP: 88
SALES (corp-wide): 183.5MM **Privately Held**
SIC: 6282 Investment advice
PA: American Financial Network, Inc.
  10 Pointe Dr Ste 330
  Brea CA 92821
  909 606-3905

(P-9786)
AMERICAN FINANCIAL NETWORK INC
14748 Pipeline Ave Ste A, Chino Hills
(91709-6024)
PHONE....................................909 287-7585

EMP: 53
SALES (corp-wide): 183.5MM **Privately Held**
SIC: 6282 Investment advice
PA: American Financial Network, Inc.
  10 Pointe Dr Ste 330
  Brea CA 92821
  909 606-3905

(P-9787)
AMERICAN FINANCIAL NETWORK INC
2125 Oak Grove Rd, Walnut Creek
(94598-2536)
PHONE....................................925 705-7710
EMP: 81
SALES (corp-wide): 99.2MM **Privately Held**
SIC: 6282
PA: American Financial Network, Inc.
  10 Pointe Dr Ste 330
  Brea CA 92821
  909 606-3905

(P-9788)
ANDERSON KAYNE CAPITAL
1800 Avenue Of The, Los Angeles (90067)
PHONE....................................800 231-7414
Richard Kayne, *Chairman*
Edward Cerny, *Managing Prtnr*
Robert Sinnott, *CEO*
Curt Biren, *Vice Pres*
Meegan T Motisi, *Vice Pres*
EMP: 300
SALES: 977.4K **Privately Held**
SIC: 6282 Investment advisory service

(P-9789)
ASSETMARK INC (HQ)
1655 Grant St Ste 1000, Concord
(94520-2789)
PHONE....................................925 521-1040
Charles Goldman, *President*
Jason Thomas, *CEO*
Myra Rothfeld, *Chief Mktg Ofcr*
Jerry Chafkin, *Ch Invest Ofcr*
John Koval, *Officer*
EMP: 50
SQ FT: 15,000
SALES (est): 39.2MM
SALES (corp-wide): 2.5B **Privately Held**
WEB: www.genworthwealth.com
SIC: 6282 Manager of mutual funds, con-
  tract or fee basis
PA: Huatai Securities Co., Ltd.
  No.228,Jiangdong Middle Rd.
  Nanjing 21000
  258 338-7793

(P-9790)
ASSETMARK FINCL HOLDINGS INC
1655 Grant St 10, Concord (94520-2600)
PHONE....................................925 521-2200
Charles Goldman, *President*
Xiaodan Liu, *Ch of Bd*
Carrie Hansen, *COO*
Gary Zyla, *CFO*
Michael Kim, *Officer*
EMP: 600
SALES: 363.6MM **Privately Held**
SIC: 6282 Investment advice

(P-9791)
AXA ADVISORS LLC
3435 Wilshire Blvd # 2500, Los Angeles
(90010-2011)
PHONE....................................213 251-1600
Yong Parks, *Manager*
Yujin OH, *Admin Asst*
Jenny Jung, *Info Tech Mgr*
Joseph Cho, *Advisor*
Kyuhyun Shin, *Consultant*
EMP: 90
SALES (corp-wide): 12B **Publicly Held**
WEB: www.axacs.com
SIC: 6282 Investment advisory service
HQ: Axa Advisors, Llc
  1290 Ave Of Amrcs Fl Cnc1
  New York NY 10104
  212 554-1234

(P-9792)
AYCO COMPANY LP
17885 Von Karman Ave # 300, Irvine
(92614-5225)
PHONE..................949 955-1544
Emmett Clancy, *Manager*
America Moua, *Data Proc Staff*
Krystle St Claire, *Personnel Assit*
Veronica Lay, *Opers Staff*
Hilda Parada, *Sales Executive*
EMP: 150
SALES (corp-wide): 36.6B Publicly Held
WEB: www.ayco.com
SIC: 6282 8742 Investment counselors; financial consultant
HQ: The Ayco Company L P
321 Broadway
Saratoga Springs NY 12866
518 886-4000

(P-9793)
B B & K HOLDINGS (PA)
Also Called: Bailard
950 Tower Ln Ste 1900, Foster City
(94404-2131)
PHONE..................650 571-5800
Thomas E Bailard, *Chairman*
Burney Sparks, *President*
Barbara Bailey, *Treasurer*
EMP: 50
SALES (est): 4.5MM Privately Held
SIC: 6282 Investment advisory service

(P-9794)
BAILARD INC (HQ)
950 Tower Ln Ste 1900, Foster City
(94404-2131)
PHONE..................650 571-5800
Thomas E Bailard, *Ch of Bd*
Henry Newhall, *President*
Burnice E Sparks Jr, *President*
Barbara Bailey, *CFO*
Preston Sargent, *Exec VP*
EMP: 50
SQ FT: 150,000
SALES (est): 11.2MM
SALES (corp-wide): 4.5MM Privately Held
WEB: www.bailard.com
SIC: 6282 Investment advisory service
PA: B B & K Holdings
950 Tower Ln Ste 1900
Foster City CA 94404
650 571-5800

(P-9795)
BAM ADVISOR SERVICES LLC
Also Called: Loring Ward
10 Almaden Blvd Fl 15, San Jose
(95113-2226)
PHONE..................800 366-7266
EMP: 60 Privately Held
SIC: 6282 Investment advisory service
PA: Bam Advisor Services, Llc
8182 Maryland Ave Ste 500
Saint Louis MO 63105

(P-9796)
**BLACKROCK GLOBAL
INVESTORS**
400 Howard St, San Francisco
(94105-2618)
PHONE..................415 670-2000
Patricia Dunn, *CEO*
Blake Grossman, *Principal*
Carter Lyons, *Principal*
EMP: 1100
SQ FT: 65,000
SALES (est): 119.1MM Publicly Held
SIC: 6282 Investment advisory service
PA: Blackrock, Inc.
55 E 52nd St
New York NY 10055

(P-9797)
BLX GROUP LLC
777 S Figueroa St # 3200, Los Angeles
(90017-5800)
PHONE..................213 612-2400
EMP: 60 EST: 2010
SQ FT: 13,000
SALES (est): 6.3MM Privately Held
SIC: 6282

(P-9798)
C2 FINANCIAL CORPORATION
3000 Citrus Cir Ste 118, Walnut Creek
(94598-2694)
PHONE..................925 938-1300
Star Darden, *Branch Mgr*
EMP: 162
SALES (corp-wide): 8.2MM Privately
Held
SIC: 6282 Investment advice
PA: C2 Financial Corporation
10509 Vista Sorrento Pkwy # 200
San Diego CA 92121
858 312-4900

(P-9799)
C2 FINANCIAL CORPORATION
978 Burlingame Ave, Clovis (93612-0464)
PHONE..................559 824-2300
EMP: 108
SALES (corp-wide): 8.2MM Privately
Held
SIC: 6282 Investment advice
PA: C2 Financial Corporation
10509 Vista Sorrento Pkwy
San Diego CA 92121
858 312-4900

(P-9800)
C2 FINANCIAL CORPORATION
703 Sunset Ct, San Diego (92109-7024)
PHONE..................858 220-2112
EMP: 216
SALES (corp-wide): 8.2MM Privately
Held
SIC: 6282 Investment advice
PA: C2 Financial Corporation
10509 Vista Sorrento Pkwy # 200
San Diego CA 92121
858 312-4900

(P-9801)
CALIBER CAPITAL GROUP LLC
5900 Katella Ave Ste A101, Cypress
(90630-5019)
PHONE..................714 507-1998
David Kim,
EMP: 2214
SALES (est): 101.5MM Privately Held
SIC: 6282 8111 Investment advice; legal
services

(P-9802)
CALLAN LLC (PA)
600 Montgomery St Ste 800, San Francisco
(94111-2710)
PHONE..................415 974-5060
Ronald D Peyton, *CEO*
Gregory C Allen, *President*
Karen Witham, *President*
Ronald Peyton, *CEO*
James Callahan, *Exec VP*
EMP: 120 EST: 1973
SQ FT: 43,000
SALES (est): 50.7MM Privately Held
WEB: www.callan.com
SIC: 6282 8742 Investment advisory service; banking & finance consultant

(P-9803)
**CAPITAL GROUP COMPANIES
INC**
11100 Santa Monica Blvd # 1500, Los Angeles (90025-3395)
PHONE..................310 996-6238
David Fisher, *Ch of Bd*
Gregory Johnson, *Vice Pres*
Will Thompson, *Vice Pres*
Dexter Williams, *Vice Pres*
Kathleen Dempsey, *General Mgr*
EMP: 260
SALES (corp-wide): 2.2B Privately Held
WEB: www.capgroup.org
SIC: 6282 6722 Manager of mutual funds,
contract or fee basis; management investment, open-end
PA: The Capital Group Companies Inc
333 S Hope St Fl 55
Los Angeles CA 90071
213 486-9200

(P-9804)
**CAPITAL GROUP COMPANIES
INC (PA)**
Also Called: Capital Group, The
333 S Hope St Fl 55, Los Angeles
(90071-3061)
PHONE..................213 486-9200
Philip De Toledo, *CEO*
Sandra Chuon, *President*
Mark Cuenca, *President*
Cindi Grossinger, *President*
Kevin Hogan, *President*
EMP: 800
SQ FT: 106,000
SALES (est): 2.2B Privately Held
WEB: www.capgroup.org
SIC: 6282 6091 6722 8741 Investment
advice; nondeposit trust facilities; mutual
fund sales, on own account; management
services

(P-9805)
**CAPITAL GROUP COMPANIES
INC**
1 Market Plz Ste 1800, San Francisco
(94105-1018)
PHONE..................213 486-1698
Chris Buchbinder, *Branch Mgr*
Stephanie Orr, *President*
Michael Dutton, *COO*
Toni Brown, *Vice Pres*
Damian Carroll, *Vice Pres*
EMP: 413
SALES (corp-wide): 2.2B Privately Held
WEB: www.capgroup.org
SIC: 6282 6722 Manager of mutual funds,
contract or fee basis; management investment, open-end
PA: The Capital Group Companies Inc
333 S Hope St Fl 55
Los Angeles CA 90071
213 486-9200

(P-9806)
**CAPITAL GROUP COMPANIES
INC**
Also Called: Capital Group Private Markets
M1, Irvine (92618)
PHONE..................949 975-5000
EMP: 478
SALES (corp-wide): 2.2B Privately Held
WEB: www.capgroup.org
SIC: 6282 6091 6722 8741 Investment
advice; nondeposit trust facilities; management investment, open-end; management
services
PA: The Capital Group Companies Inc
333 S Hope St Fl 55
Los Angeles CA 90071
213 486-9200

(P-9807)
**CAPITAL RESEARCH AND MGT
CO (HQ)**
333 S Hope St Fl 55, Los Angeles
(90071-3061)
PHONE..................213 486-9200
R Michael Shanahan, *Ch of Bd*
James F Rothenberg, *Ch of Bd*
Timothy Armour, *CEO*
Susi Silverman, *CFO*
Jonathan Knowles, *Exec VP*
EMP: 500
SALES (est): 1.1B
SALES (corp-wide): 2.2B Privately Held
SIC: 6282 Investment research; manager
of mutual funds, contract or fee basis
PA: The Capital Group Companies Inc
333 S Hope St Fl 55
Los Angeles CA 90071
213 486-9200

(P-9808)
**CAPITAL RESEARCH AND MGT
CO**
6455 Irvine Center Dr, Irvine (92618-4518)
P.O. Box 2205, Brea (92822-2205)
PHONE..................949 975-5000
Damien Jordan, *Branch Mgr*
Christine Mueller, *Facilities Mgr*
EMP: 75

SALES (corp-wide): 2.2B Privately Held
SIC: 6282 6211 6726 6722 Investment
research; manager of mutual funds, contract or fee basis; underwriters, security;
investment offices; management investment, open-end
HQ: Capital Research And Management
Company
333 S Hope St Fl 55
Los Angeles CA 90071
213 486-9200

(P-9809)
CHURCHILL MGT GROUP CORP
5900 Wilshire Blvd # 400, Los Angeles
(90036-5013)
PHONE..................877 937-7110
Fred A Fern, *President*
Brad Rodgers, *Assoc VP*
David TSE, *Exec VP*
Matthew Arber, *Vice Pres*
William Condon, *Vice Pres*
EMP: 50
SALES (est): 12.5MM Privately Held
WEB: www.churchillmanagement.com
SIC: 6282 Investment counselors

(P-9810)
**DEUTSCHE INV MGT AMERICAS
INC**
101 California St # 2400, San Francisco
(94111-5802)
PHONE..................415 648-9408
Victor L Hymes, *Director*
EMP: 50
SALES (corp-wide): 13.6B Privately Held
SIC: 6282 Investment advisory service
HQ: Deutsche Investment Management
Americas Inc.
345 Park Ave Uppr L-1
New York NY 10154
800 349-4281

(P-9811)
ENRICH FINANCIAL INC
18653 Ventura Blvd, Tarzana (91356-4103)
PHONE..................818 237-2100
Arian J Eghbali, *CEO*
Eliza Morris, *Accounts Exec*
EMP: 63
SALES (est): 494K Privately Held
SIC: 6282 Investment advice

(P-9812)
EP WEALTH ADVISORS LLC
250 Lafayette Cir, Lafayette (94549-7691)
PHONE..................925 283-2201
EMP: 57
SALES (corp-wide): 3.1MM Privately
Held
SIC: 6282 Investment advisory service
PA: Ep Wealth Advisors, Llc
21515 Hawthorne Blvd # 1200
Torrance CA 90503
310 543-4559

(P-9813)
**FIRST AMERICAN TRUST
COMPANY (HQ)**
5 First American Way, Santa Ana
(92707-5913)
P.O. Box 267 (92702-0267)
PHONE..................714 560-7856
Toll Free:..................877 -
Thomas M Kelley, *President*
Kelly Dudley, *COO*
Teri Pierce, *CFO*
Eric R McMullen, *Officer*
Darliene Evans, *Trust Officer*
EMP: 54
SQ FT: 34,625
SALES: 82MM Publicly Held
SIC: 6282 Investment advisory service

(P-9814)
FMR LLC
1995 University Ave, Berkeley
(94704-1058)
PHONE..................800 225-6447
EMP: 103
SALES (corp-wide): 15B Privately Held
SIC: 6282 Investment advisory service
PA: Fmr Llc
245 Summer St
Boston MA 02210
617 563-7000

(P-9815)
FMR LLC
1220 Rsville Pkwy Ste 100, Roseville (95678)
PHONE...................................916 784-3649
Dave Taylor, *Principal*
Caron Strop, *Vice Pres*
Timothy Averett, *Managing Dir*
Cory Lusher, *Managing Dir*
EMP: 103
SALES (corp-wide): 15B **Privately Held**
SIC: 6282 Investment advisory service
PA: Fmr Llc
245 Summer St
Boston MA 02210
617 563-7000

(P-9816)
FORWARD MANAGEMENT LLC
Also Called: Webster Investment Management
101 California St Fl 16, San Francisco (94111-6100)
P.O. Box 1345, Denver CO (80201-1345)
PHONE...................................415 869-6300
John Blaisdell, *CEO*
Jeffrey P Cusack, *President*
Robert S Naka, *Senior VP*
Marianne Carter, *Vice Pres*
Mark Guadagnini, *Vice Pres*
EMP: 100
SQ FT: 22,000
SALES (est): 23.1MM
SALES (corp-wide): 82.3MM **Privately Held**
WEB: www.sierraclubfund.com
SIC: 6282 Investment advisory service
PA: Salient Partners, L.P.
4265 San Felipe St Fl 8
Houston TX 77027
713 993-4675

(P-9817)
FRANKLIN ADVISERS INC (HQ)
1 Franklin Pkwy, San Mateo (94403-1906)
PHONE...................................650 312-2000
Charles B Johnson, *Ch of Bd*
EMP: 1700
SQ FT: 120,000
SALES (est): 115.1MM
SALES (corp-wide): 5.7B **Publicly Held**
WEB: www.frk.com
SIC: 6282 Investment advice
PA: Franklin Resources, Inc.
1 Franklin Pkwy
San Mateo CA 94403
650 312-2000

(P-9818)
FRANKLIN RESOURCES INC (PA)
1 Franklin Pkwy, San Mateo (94403-1906)
PHONE...................................650 312-2000
Gregory E Johnson, *Ch of Bd*
Jennifer M Johnson, *President*
Matthew Nicholls, *CFO*
Rupert H Johnson Jr, *Vice Ch Bd*
Craig S Tyle, *Exec VP*
EMP: 68
SALES: 5.7B **Publicly Held**
WEB: www.frk.com
SIC: 6282 6722 6726 Investment advice; management investment, open-end; management investment funds, closed-end

(P-9819)
FRANKLIN TEMPLETON SVCS LLC
1 Franklin Pkwy, San Mateo (94403-1906)
PHONE...................................650 312-3000
Martin L Flanagan, *President*
Charles B Johnson, *Ch of Bd*
EMP: 2500
SALES (est): 163MM
SALES (corp-wide): 5.7B **Publicly Held**
WEB: www.frk.com
SIC: 6282 Investment advice
PA: Franklin Resources, Inc.
1 Franklin Pkwy
San Mateo CA 94403
650 312-2000

(P-9820)
FRANKLIN TMPLETON INV SVCS LLC
3366 Quality Dr, Rancho Cordova (95670-7363)
PHONE...................................650 312-2000
Bavel Fox, *Branch Mgr*
EMP: 103
SALES (corp-wide): 5.7B **Publicly Held**
SIC: 6282 Investment advisory service
HQ: Franklin Templeton Investor Services, Llc
3344 Quality Dr
Rancho Cordova CA 95670
916 463-1500

(P-9821)
FRANKLIN TMPLETON INV SVCS LLC
5130 Hacienda Dr Fl 4, Dublin (94568-7598)
PHONE...................................925 875-2619
Priscilla Voyer, *Manager*
EMP: 200
SALES (corp-wide): 5.7B **Publicly Held**
SIC: 6282 Investment advisory service
HQ: Franklin Templeton Investor Services, Llc
3344 Quality Dr
Rancho Cordova CA 95670
916 463-1500

(P-9822)
FREMONT GROUP LLC (PA)
199 Fremont St Fl 19, San Francisco (94105-2261)
PHONE...................................415 284-8880
Deborah L Duncans,
David R Covin, *COO*
Sol Coffino, *Vice Pres*
Yotam Stanger, *Vice Pres*
Salexander Ramsay, *Managing Dir*
EMP: 50
SQ FT: 50,000
SALES (est): 38.9MM **Privately Held**
SIC: 6282 Investment advisory service

(P-9823)
FUND SERVICES ADVISORS INC
777 S Figueroa St # 3200, Los Angeles (90017-5800)
PHONE...................................213 612-2196
Mark Creger, *President*
EMP: 50
SQ FT: 2,000
SALES (est): 3.6MM **Privately Held**
WEB: www.bondlogistix.com
SIC: 6282 Investment advisory service

(P-9824)
HEARTHSTONE INC
24151 Ventura Blvd, Calabasas (91302-1449)
PHONE...................................818 385-0005
James Pugash, *CEO*
Anthony Botte, *Senior VP*
Mark Porath, *Manager*
EMP: 70
SALES (est): 11.8MM **Privately Held**
WEB: www.hearthadvisors.com
SIC: 6282 Investment advice

(P-9825)
HIGHMARK CAPITAL MANAGEMENT
350 California St Fl 22, San Francisco (94104-1435)
PHONE...................................800 582-4734
Earle Malm, *President*
Christian Anderson, *Vice Pres*
Dorothy Cooney, *Vice Pres*
Cori Farwell, *Vice Pres*
Richard Grise, *Vice Pres*
EMP: 93
SALES (est): 14.7MM **Privately Held**
SIC: 6282 Investment advisory service
HQ: Mufg Union Bank, National Association
400 California St Fl 14
San Francisco CA 94104
415 705-7000

(P-9826)
HOULIHAN LOKEY INC (PA)
10250 Constellation Blvd, Los Angeles (90067-6200)
PHONE...................................310 788-5200
Scott L Beiser, *CEO*
Scott J Adelson, *President*
David A Preiser, *President*
J Lindsey Alley, *CFO*
Deirdre Johnson, *Officer*
EMP: 300
SALES: 1B **Publicly Held**
WEB: www.hlhz.com
SIC: 6282 6211 Investment advice; security brokers & dealers; investment bankers

(P-9827)
JONES LANG LSALLE AMERICAS INC
2211 Michelson Dr, Irvine (92612-1384)
PHONE...................................949 296-3600
James Jasionowski, *Owner*
Timothy Johnson, *Director*
EMP: 161
SALES (corp-wide): 16.3B **Publicly Held**
SIC: 6282 Investment advice
HQ: Jones Lang Lasalle Americas, Inc.
200 E Randolph St # 4300
Chicago IL 60601
312 782-5800

(P-9828)
KAGAN CAPITAL MANAGEMENT INC
Also Called: Paul Kagan Associates
126 Clock Tower Pl, Carmel (93923-8791)
PHONE...................................831 624-1536
Paul Kagan, *President*
Norman Glaser, *Vice Pres*
EMP: 85
SQ FT: 18,000
SALES (est): 7.1MM **Privately Held**
SIC: 6282 Investment advisory service

(P-9829)
KRAVITZ INVESTMENT SVCS INC
16030 Ventura Blvd # 200, Encino (91436-2731)
PHONE...................................818 995-6100
Daniel Kravitz, *President*
EMP: 100
SALES (est): 226.6K **Privately Held**
SIC: 6282 Investment advice

(P-9830)
MARLIN EQUITY PARTNERS LLC (PA)
338 Pier Ave, Hermosa Beach (90254-3617)
PHONE...................................310 364-0100
David McGovern, *Mng Member*
Jason Connors, *Info Tech Mgr*
Joselyn Choi, *Accounting Mgr*
AZ Virji, *General Counsel*
Steve Johnson,
EMP: 80
SQ FT: 16,000
SALES (est): 1.8B **Privately Held**
WEB: www.marlinequity.com
SIC: 6282 3661 Investment advisory service; telephones & telephone apparatus; multiplex equipment, telephone & telegraph

(P-9831)
MERCER GLOBAL SECURITIES LLC
1801 E Cabrillo Blvd A, Santa Barbara (93108-2897)
PHONE...................................805 565-1681
Gene Dongieux Jr, *Mng Member*
Douglas Maxwell, *CFO*
Howard Rochestie,
Glen Wysel,
Sydney Martinez, *Associate*
EMP: 77 EST: 1995
SALES (est): 6.6MM **Privately Held**
SIC: 6282 Investment advisory service

(P-9832)
MORGAN STANLEY
800 Nwport Ctr Dr Ste 500, Newport Beach (92660)
P.O. Box 2000 (92658-8936)
PHONE...................................949 760-2440
Mark Zielinski, *Branch Mgr*
EMP: 60
SALES (corp-wide): 50.1B **Publicly Held**
SIC: 6282 6211 Investment advisory service; security brokers & dealers
PA: Morgan Stanley
1585 Broadway
New York NY 10036
212 761-4000

(P-9833)
NEWLAND REAL ESTATE GROUP LLC (HQ)
4790 Eastgate Mall # 150, San Diego (92121-2060)
PHONE...................................858 455-7503
Robert B McLeod, *President*
Tim Durie, *Vice Pres*
Douglas L Hageman, *Vice Pres*
Jim Henry, *Vice Pres*
Lynneah Hudson, *Vice Pres*
EMP: 51
SQ FT: 12,000
SALES (est): 86MM **Privately Held**
SIC: 6282 6552 Investment advice; subdividers & developers

(P-9834)
OAKTREE CAPITAL MANAGEMENT LP (DH)
333 S Grand Ave Ste 2800, Los Angeles (90071-1530)
PHONE...................................213 830-6300
Bruce Karsh, *President*
John Frank, *Director*
EMP: 120
SALES (est): 1.6B
SALES (corp-wide): 43B **Publicly Held**
WEB: www.oaktreecapital.com
SIC: 6282 6722 6211 Investment advisory service; management investment, open-end; security brokers & dealers

(P-9835)
ONE ROCK CAPITAL PARTNERS LLC
11601 Wilshire Blvd # 1960, Los Angeles (90025-1755)
PHONE...................................213 292-5870
Kimberly Reed, *Owner*
EMP: 91 **Privately Held**
SIC: 6282 Investment advice
PA: One Rock Capital Partners, Llc
30 Rockefeller Plz # 5400
New York NY 10112

(P-9836)
ONEMAIN HOLDINGS INC
2278 Foothill Blvd, La Verne (91750-2944)
PHONE...................................909 392-5578
EMP: 69
SALES (corp-wide): 4.2B **Publicly Held**
SIC: 6282 Investment advice
PA: Onemain Holdings, Inc.
601 Nw 2nd St
Evansville IN 47708
812 424-8031

(P-9837)
PAYDEN AND RYGEL (PA)
333 S Grand Ave Ste 3200, Los Angeles (90071-1552)
PHONE...................................213 625-1900
Joan Payden, *CEO*
Brad Hersh, *Treasurer*
Scott J Weiner, *Principal*
EMP: 140
SQ FT: 58,000
SALES (est): 86.8MM **Privately Held**
WEB: www.payden.com
SIC: 6282 6211 Investment counselors; security brokers & dealers

PRODUCTS & SVCS

(P-9838)
PERFORMANT TECHNOLOGIES INC
333 N Canyons Pkwy # 100, Livermore (94551-9478)
PHONE...............................925 960-4800
Lisa Im, *President*
Todd Ford, *Bd of Directors*
Brian Golson, *Bd of Directors*
William Hansen, *Bd of Directors*
Paula Chinchiolo, *Officer*
EMP: 350
SALES (est): 43.7MM **Publicly Held**
SIC: 6282 Investment advice
PA: Performant Financial Corporation
　　333 N Canyons Pkwy # 100
　　Livermore CA 94551

(P-9839)
PLAN MEMBER FINANCIAL CORP
Also Called: Planmember Services
6187 Carpinteria Ave, Carpinteria (93013-2805)
PHONE...............................800 874-6910
Jon Ziehl, *CEO*
Mike Kulesza, *Partner*
Kevin Twohy, *Partner*
Terrall Janeway, *COO*
EMP: 100
SQ FT: 6,000
SALES (est): 34MM **Privately Held**
WEB: www.planmemberfinancialcorporation.com
SIC: 6282 Investment counselors

(P-9840)
PREMIERE FINANCIAL
Also Called: Premiere Properties
6498 Willow Pl, Carlsbad (92011-4212)
PHONE...............................760 518-5034
Richard Luichi, *Owner*
EMP: 100 EST: 2013
SALES: 400K **Privately Held**
SIC: 6282 8742 Investment advice; financial consultant

(P-9841)
PRESIDIO WEALTH MANAGEMENT LLC
101 California St # 2400, San Francisco (94111-5802)
PHONE...............................415 449-2500
Brodie Cobb, *Managing Prtnr*
Michael Russo, *Managing Prtnr*
Lisa Bean, *Vice Pres*
Kelly Lawson, *Vice Pres*
Jeff Zlot, *Principal*
EMP: 50
SQ FT: 2,500
SALES (est): 4.2MM **Privately Held**
WEB: www.sncinvestment.com
SIC: 6282 Investment advisory service

(P-9842)
QUADION LLC
Also Called: Mar-Kell Seal
17651 Armstrong Ave, Irvine (92614-5727)
PHONE...............................714 546-0994
EMP: 1100 EST: 1945
SQ FT: 30,000
SALES (est): 110.7MM
SALES (corp-wide): 91.2B **Publicly Held**
SIC: 6282
HQ: Norwest Venture Capital Management, Inc.
　　80 S 8th St Ste 3600
　　Minneapolis MN 55402
　　612 215-1600

(P-9843)
RELATIONAL INVESTORS LLC
12400 High Bluff Dr Ste 6, San Diego (92130-3077)
PHONE...............................858 704-3333
David Batchelder, *Mng Member*
Ralph Whitworth,
EMP: 52
SALES (est): 21MM **Privately Held**
SIC: 6282 Investment advisory service

(P-9844)
RESEARCH AFFILIATES CAPITAL LP
620 Nwport Ctr Dr Ste 900, Newport Beach (92660)
PHONE...............................949 325-8700
Rob Arnott, *CEO*
Katrina F Sherrerd, *COO*
Adam Willis, *Senior VP*
Trevor Schuesler, *Vice Pres*
Jason Hsu, *CIO*
EMP: 82
SALES (est): 10.8MM **Privately Held**
SIC: 6282 Investment advisory service; futures advisory service; investment research

(P-9845)
RESEARCH AFFILIATES LLC
620 Nwport Ctr Dr Ste 900, Newport Beach (92660)
PHONE...............................949 325-8700
Rob Arnott, *CEO*
Katrina Sherrerd, *COO*
Asher Ailey, *Officer*
Jeffrey Smith, *Officer*
Jeff Wilson, *Senior VP*
EMP: 80
SALES (est): 22.8MM **Privately Held**
WEB: www.researchaffiliates.com
SIC: 6282 Investment counselors

(P-9846)
RNC CAPITAL MANAGEMENT LLC
Also Called: Rnc Genter Capital Management
11601 Wilshire Blvd Ph 25, Los Angeles (90025-1770)
PHONE...............................310 477-6543
Dan Genter,
EMP: 65
SQ FT: 20,000
SALES (est): 17.9MM **Privately Held**
WEB: www.rncgenter.com
SIC: 6282 Investment counselors

(P-9847)
S&P GLOBAL INC
1566 Moffett St, Salinas (93905-3342)
PHONE...............................831 393-6044
David Taggard, *President*
EMP: 149
SALES (corp-wide): 6.2B **Publicly Held**
WEB: www.mcgraw-hill.com
SIC: 6282 Investment advisory service
PA: S&P Global Inc.
　　55 Water St Fl 37
　　New York NY 10041
　　212 438-1000

(P-9848)
SAGEPOINT FINANCIAL INC
3723 Birch St Ste 9, Newport Beach (92660-2614)
PHONE...............................949 756-1462
Jeffrey M Auld, *CEO*
Rayna Elmendorf, *Manager*
Charles Curtin, *Advisor*
Patrick McCormick, *Agent*
EMP: 405 EST: 2010
SALES (est): 668.9K
SALES (corp-wide): 651.5MM **Privately Held**
SIC: 6282 Investment advisory service
HQ: Sagepoint Financial, Inc.
　　20 E Thomas Rd Ste 2000
　　Phoenix AZ 85012

(P-9849)
STANDARD POORS FINCL SVCS LLC
1 California St Fl 31, San Francisco (94111-5401)
PHONE...............................415 371-5000
Steve Zimmerman, *Manager*
EMP: 50
SALES (corp-wide): 6.2B **Publicly Held**
WEB: www.mcgraw-hill.com
SIC: 6282 Investment advisory service
HQ: Standard & Poor's Financial Services Llc
　　55 Water St Fl 49
　　New York NY 10041
　　212 438-2000

(P-9850)
TCW GROUP INC (PA)
865 S Figueroa St # 1800, Los Angeles (90017-2543)
PHONE...............................213 244-0000
David Lippman, *President*
David S Devito, *COO*
Richard M Villa, *CFO*
Meredith S Jackson, *Exec VP*
Heather Conforto Beatty, *Senior VP*
EMP: 450
SALES (est): 226.2MM **Privately Held**
SIC: 6282 6211 Investment advisory service; security brokers & dealers

(P-9851)
TPG SIXTH STREET PARTNERS LLC
345 California St Ste 330, San Francisco (94104-2606)
PHONE...............................415 743-1500
Alan Waxman,
Mahesh Khambete, *Partner*
Karen Lau, *Vice Pres*
EMP: 125
SALES (est): 3.3MM **Privately Held**
SIC: 6282 Investment advisory service

(P-9852)
TRANSAMERICA CBO I INC
600 Montgomery St Fl 16, San Francisco (94111-2718)
PHONE...............................415 983-4000
EMP: 64
SALES (est): 2.2MM **Privately Held**
SIC: 6282
HQ: Transamerica Corporation
　　4333 Edgewood Rd Ne
　　Cedar Rapids IA 52499
　　319 398-8511

(P-9853)
UNITED CPITL FNCL ADVISERS LLC
620 Nwport Ctr Dr Ste 500, Newport Beach (92660)
PHONE...............................949 999-8500
EMP: 77 EST: 2009
SALES (est): 17.2MM **Privately Held**
SIC: 6282 8742

(P-9854)
WELLS CAPITAL MANAGEMENT INC (DH)
525 Market St Fl 10, San Francisco (94105-2718)
PHONE...............................415 396-8000
Kirk Heartman, *President*
Marissa Buckley, *Vice Pres*
Lucia Cronin, *Vice Pres*
Rona Jaffe, *Vice Pres*
Gilbert Southwell, *Vice Pres*
EMP: 50
SQ FT: 20,000
SALES (est): 91.8MM
SALES (corp-wide): 101B **Publicly Held**
WEB: www.hawaiicaptives.com
SIC: 6282 Investment advisory service
HQ: Wells Fargo Bank, National Association
　　101 N Phillips Ave
　　Sioux Falls SD 57104
　　605 575-6900

(P-9855)
WENTWORTH HAUSER & VIOLICH INC
301 Battery St Fl 4, San Francisco (94111-3237)
PHONE...............................415 981-6911
Steve Rhone, *CEO*
Judith Stevens, *President*
Earl Bell, *CFO*
Phillip Fox, *Exec VP*
George Springman, *CIO*
EMP: 78 EST: 1937
SQ FT: 14,000
SALES (est): 23MM **Privately Held**
WEB: www.lntyee.com
SIC: 6282 Investment advisory service
PA: Laird Norton Investment Management, Inc.
　　801 2nd Ave Ste 1300
　　Seattle WA 98104

(P-9856)
WETHERBY ASSET MANAGEMENT
580 California St Fl 8, San Francisco (94104-1029)
PHONE...............................415 399-9159
Debra L Wetherby, *President*
Tom Ngo, *Partner*
Christopher Hauswirth, *Shareholder*
Joseph Khamsehpour, *Shareholder*
Chris Hauswirth, *COO*
EMP: 55
SALES (est): 17.3MM **Privately Held**
WEB: www.wetherby.com
SIC: 6282 Investment advisory service

(P-9857)
WINDSTAR CAPITAL ADVISORS
10940 Wilshire Blvd # 2300, Los Angeles (90024-3916)
PHONE...............................310 505-3720
Jack Risko, *President*
EMP: 208
SALES (est): 12.5MM **Privately Held**
SIC: 6282 4213 Investment advice; heavy hauling

6289 Security & Commodity Svcs, NEC

(P-9858)
ACCELERIZE INC
204 Riverside Ave, Newport Beach (92663-4011)
PHONE...............................949 515-2166
Brian S Ross, *Manager*
EMP: 61 **Publicly Held**
SIC: 6289 Financial reporting
PA: Accelerize Inc.
　　2601 Ocean Park Blvd # 310
　　Santa Monica CA 90405

(P-9859)
AMERICAN FUNDS SERVICE COMPANY
Also Called: Emerging Markets Growth Fund
6455 Irvine Center Dr, Irvine (92618-4518)
P.O. Box 6007, Indianapolis IN (46206-6007)
PHONE...............................949 975-5000
Josie Cortez, *Branch Mgr*
EMP: 50
SALES (corp-wide): 2.2B **Privately Held**
WEB: www.cganywhere.net
SIC: 6289 6282 Security transfer agents; investment advice
HQ: American Funds Service Company
　　6455 Irvine Center Dr
　　Irvine CA 92618
　　949 975-5000

6311 Life Insurance Carriers

(P-9860)
AMERICAN GEN LF INSUR CO DEL
Also Called: AIG
1 Montgomery St Fl 25, San Francisco (94104-4558)
PHONE...............................415 836-2700
Gordon Knight, *President*
Craig Crowder, *President*
Linda Sproule, *President*
Linda Jiao, *Tech/Comp Coord*
Mark P Foletti, *Production*
EMP: 300
SALES (corp-wide): 47.3B **Publicly Held**
WEB: www.aiglifeinsurancecompany.com
SIC: 6311 Life insurance
HQ: American General Life Insurance Company Of Delaware
　　2727 Allen Pkwy Ste A
　　Houston TX 77019
　　713 522-1111

(P-9861)
ASSOCIATED INDEMNITY CORP
1465 N Mcdowell Blvd # 100, Petaluma
(94954-6516)
P.O. Box 970, O Fallon MO (63366-0970)
PHONE..................................415 899-2000
D Andrew Torrance, *Chairman*
Jill E Paterson, *CFO*
Linda E Wright, *Treasurer*
Cynthia L Pevehouse, *Senior VP*
EMP: 2498
SQ FT: 240,000
SALES (est): 48.9MM
SALES (corp-wide): 24.9B **Privately Held**
WEB: www.firemansfund.com
SIC: 6311 6321 6331 6351 Life insurance carriers; accident insurance carriers; fire, marine & casualty insurance & carriers; surety insurance
HQ: Fireman's Fund Insurance Company
1465 N Mcdowell Blvd # 100
Petaluma CA 94954
415 899-2000

(P-9862)
AXA ADVISORS LLC
701 B St Ste 1500, San Diego
(92101-8170)
PHONE..................................619 239-0018
EMP: 80 **Publicly Held**
SIC: 6311 6321 6411 6282
HQ: Axa Advisors, Llc
1290 Ave Of Amrcs Fl Cnc1
New York NY 10104
212 554-1234

(P-9863)
BEST LIFE AND HEALTH INSUR CO
17701 Mitchell N, Irvine (92614-6028)
P.O. Box 19721 (92623-9721)
PHONE..................................949 253-4080
Donald R Lawrenz, *Ch of Bd*
Alfred Stoefell, *Shareholder*
Edith Christensen, *Executive Asst*
Nancy Mashhoud, *Accountant*
Marie Pacheco, *VP Opers*
EMP: 60
SQ FT: 22,000
SALES (est): 31MM
SALES (corp-wide): 12.3MM **Privately Held**
SIC: 6311 6324 Life insurance carriers; hospital & medical service plans
PA: Pension Administrators Inc
17701 Mitchell N
Irvine CA 92614
949 253-4080

(P-9864)
BUILDERS & TRADESMENS INSUR
6610 Sierra College Blvd, Rocklin
(95677-4306)
PHONE..................................916 772-9200
Norbert Hohlbein, *Principal*
Matt Horton, *Assoc VP*
Angela Jorgensen, *Sales Staff*
EMP: 61
SALES (est): 34.8MM **Privately Held**
WEB: www.btisonline.com
SIC: 6311 Life insurance

(P-9865)
CENTURY-NATIONAL INSURANCE CO (HQ)
16650 Sherman Way Ste 200, Van Nuys
(91406-3782)
PHONE..................................818 760-0880
Weldon Wilson, *CEO*
Michael Mahoney, *President*
Judy Osborn, *CFO*
Marie Balicki, *Admin Sec*
Mary Wagner, *Admin Sec*
EMP: 260
SQ FT: 41,000
SALES: 51.9MM **Publicly Held**
SIC: 6311 Life insurance carriers

(P-9866)
EQUITABLE VARIABLE LF INSUR CO
701 B St Ste 1500, San Diego
(92101-8170)
PHONE..................................619 239-0018

Jamie Smith, *Manager*
Brian Bickford, *Vice Pres*
Michael Dooher, *Agent*
EMP: 65
SALES (est): 7.5MM **Privately Held**
SIC: 6311 Life insurance

(P-9867)
FARMERS GROUP INC
Also Called: Farmers Insurance
700 S Flower St Ste 2800, Los Angeles
(90017-4215)
PHONE..................................213 615-2500
Agie Lerner, *Legal Staff*
Ana Sanchez, *Office Mgr*
Vanessa Jackson, *Project Mgr*
Jill Hageman, *Marketing Staff*
EMP: 60
SALES (corp-wide): 48.2B **Privately Held**
WEB: www.farmers.com
SIC: 6311 6799 Life insurance carriers; real estate investors, except property operators
HQ: Farmers Group, Inc.
6301 Owensmouth Ave
Woodland Hills CA 91367
323 932-3200

(P-9868)
GOLDEN STATE MUTL LF INSUR CO (PA)
1999 W Adams Blvd, Los Angeles
(90018-3500)
P.O. Box 26894, San Francisco (94126-6894)
PHONE..................................713 526-4361
Larkin Teasley, *President*
EMP: 100 **EST:** 1925
SQ FT: 57,000
SALES (est): 38.9MM **Privately Held**
SIC: 6311 Mutual association life insurance; life insurance carriers; life reinsurance

(P-9869)
JOHN ALDEN LIFE INSURANCE CO
20950 Warner Center Ln A, Woodland Hills
(91367-6560)
PHONE..................................818 595-7600
Thomas Christenson, *Branch Mgr*
EMP: 65
SALES (corp-wide): 8B **Publicly Held**
WEB: www.jalden.com
SIC: 6311 Life insurance
HQ: Alden John Life Insurance Company
501 W Michigan St
Milwaukee WI 53203
414 271-3011

(P-9870)
MASSACHUSETTS MUTL LF INSUR CO
Also Called: Massmutual
8383 Wilshire Blvd # 600, Beverly Hills
(90211-2425)
PHONE..................................323 965-6339
Grant D Fraser, *Branch Mgr*
David Streit, *Sales Staff*
Harvey Warren, *Author*
Kaleem Ansari, *Associate*
EMP: 60
SALES (corp-wide): 254.5B **Privately Held**
WEB: www.massmutual.com
SIC: 6311 Life insurance
PA: Massachusetts Mutual Life Insurance Company
1295 State St
Springfield MA 01111
413 788-8411

(P-9871)
NEW FIRST FINCL RESOURCES LLC
100 Spectrum Center Dr # 400, Irvine
(92618-4966)
PHONE..................................949 223-2160
Richard Roberts,
Eric Woith, *Marketing Mgr*
EMP: 212
SALES (est): 7.2MM **Privately Held**
SIC: 6311 Life insurance

(P-9872)
NEW YORK LIFE INSURANCE CO
191 Sand Creek Rd Ste 200, Brentwood
(94513-2220)
PHONE..................................925 809-7020
Dan Torres, *Branch Mgr*
EMP: 93
SALES (corp-wide): 13.3B **Privately Held**
SIC: 6311 Life insurance
PA: New York Life Insurance Company
51 Madison Ave Bsmt 1b
New York NY 10010
212 576-7000

(P-9873)
NEW YORK LIFE INSURANCE CO
675 Placentia Ave Ste 250, Brea
(92821-6171)
PHONE..................................714 255-5100
Michael V Ceci, *Branch Mgr*
Darren Durrill, *Vice Pres*
Hadi Hassan, *Advisor*
Vicente Mesa, *Advisor*
Julia Hsiao, *Agent*
EMP: 58
SALES (corp-wide): 13.3B **Privately Held**
WEB: www.newyorklife.com
SIC: 6311 Life insurance
PA: New York Life Insurance Company
51 Madison Ave Bsmt 1b
New York NY 10010
212 576-7000

(P-9874)
NEW YORK LIFE INSURANCE CO
3757 State St Ste 310, Santa Barbara
(93105-3133)
PHONE..................................805 898-7625
Mona Vargas, *Branch Mgr*
Dale Jones, *Manager*
EMP: 58
SALES (corp-wide): 13.3B **Privately Held**
WEB: www.newyorklife.com
SIC: 6311 Life insurance
PA: New York Life Insurance Company
51 Madison Ave Bsmt 1b
New York NY 10010
212 576-7000

(P-9875)
NEW YORK LIFE INSURANCE CO
801 N Brand Blvd, Glendale (91203-1237)
PHONE..................................818 662-7500
Tigran Basmadkian, *Managing Prtnr*
Scott R Alexander, *Sales Associate*
Carl Crawford, *Advisor*
Eszylfie Taylor, *Advisor*
EMP: 58
SALES (corp-wide): 13.3B **Privately Held**
WEB: www.newyorklife.com
SIC: 6311 Life insurance
PA: New York Life Insurance Company
51 Madison Ave Bsmt 1b
New York NY 10010
212 576-7000

(P-9876)
NEW YORK LIFE INSURANCE CO
1731 Tech Dr Ste 400, San Jose (95110)
PHONE..................................408 392-9782
Victor Vuong, *Partner*
John Lawless, *Advisor*
Ryan MAI, *Advisor*
Elizabeth Siregar, *Advisor*
Estelita Tanedo, *Advisor*
EMP: 100
SALES (corp-wide): 13.3B **Privately Held**
WEB: www.newyorklife.com
SIC: 6311 Life insurance
PA: New York Life Insurance Company
51 Madison Ave Bsmt 1b
New York NY 10010
212 576-7000

(P-9877)
NEW YORK LIFE INSURANCE CO
4204 Riverwalk Pkwy # 200, Riverside
(92505-3391)
PHONE..................................951 354-2094
Tim Crumbaker, *Branch Mgr*
Michael J O'Neill, *Sales Associate*
Jeff Czerwinski, *Advisor*
Michael Koury, *Advisor*
EMP: 75
SALES (corp-wide): 13.3B **Privately Held**
WEB: www.newyorklife.com
SIC: 6311 Life insurance
PA: New York Life Insurance Company
51 Madison Ave Bsmt 1b
New York NY 10010
212 576-7000

(P-9878)
NEW YORK LIFE INSURANCE CO
2020 Main St Ste 1200, Irvine
(92614-8235)
PHONE..................................949 797-2400
Christopher Prudhomme, *Owner*
Monzur A Mollah, *Sales Associate*
Scott Ziegelmeier, *Sales Associate*
Timothy Carter, *Agent*
Uday C Shah, *Agent*
EMP: 70
SALES (corp-wide): 13.3B **Privately Held**
WEB: www.newyorklife.com
SIC: 6311 Life insurance
PA: New York Life Insurance Company
51 Madison Ave Bsmt 1b
New York NY 10010
212 576-7000

(P-9879)
NEW YORK LIFE INSURANCE CO
2999 Douglas Blvd Ste 350, Roseville
(95661-3839)
PHONE..................................916 774-6200
Mark Ham, *Manager*
Rick Skinner, *Administration*
Rick Stivers, *Sales Executive*
Denise Ash, *Sales Associate*
Stephen Milano, *Advisor*
EMP: 100
SALES (corp-wide): 13.3B **Privately Held**
WEB: www.newyorklife.com
SIC: 6311 Life insurance
PA: New York Life Insurance Company
51 Madison Ave Bsmt 1b
New York NY 10010
212 576-7000

(P-9880)
NEW YORK LIFE INSURANCE CO
4365 Executive Dr Ste 800, San Diego
(92121-2130)
PHONE..................................858 623-8600
Antonio Montalvo, *Branch Mgr*
Michael Cole, *Advisor*
Trevor Isaacs, *Agent*
EMP: 140
SALES (corp-wide): 13.3B **Privately Held**
WEB: www.newyorklife.com
SIC: 6311 Life insurance
PA: New York Life Insurance Company
51 Madison Ave Bsmt 1b
New York NY 10010
212 576-7000

(P-9881)
NEW YORK LIFE INSURANCE CO
2633 Camino Ramon Ste 525, San Ramon
(94583-2174)
PHONE..................................415 999-9576
John Walker, *Manager*
Derek Chu, *Producer*
EMP: 58
SALES (corp-wide): 13.3B **Privately Held**
WEB: www.newyorklife.com
SIC: 6311 Life insurance
PA: New York Life Insurance Company
51 Madison Ave Bsmt 1b
New York NY 10010
212 576-7000

PRODUCTS & SVCS

(P-9882)
NEW YORK LIFE INSURANCE CO
300 E Esplanade Dr # 2050, Oxnard (93036-0267)
PHONE.................................805 656-4598
Ashwani Kumarrana, *Principal*
Judy Sun, *Advisor*
EMP: 50
SALES (corp-wide): 13.3B **Privately Held**
WEB: www.newyorklife.com
SIC: **6311** Life insurance
PA: New York Life Insurance Company
51 Madison Ave Bsmt 1b
New York NY 10010
212 576-7000

(P-9883)
NEW YORK LIFE INSURANCE CO
6300 Wilshire Blvd # 1900, Los Angeles (90048-5221)
PHONE.................................323 782-3000
Jerry M Fish, *Managing Prtnr*
Anthony Conde, *Research*
Wayne Bragg, *Marketing Mgr*
Charles J Altmann, *Sales Associate*
Tessa Ingel, *Sales Associate*
EMP: 50
SALES (corp-wide): 13.3B **Privately Held**
WEB: www.newyorklife.com
SIC: **6311** Life insurance
PA: New York Life Insurance Company
51 Madison Ave Bsmt 1b
New York NY 10010
212 576-7000

(P-9884)
NEW YORK LIFE INSURANCE CO
140 Via Verde Ste 200, San Dimas (91773-5117)
PHONE.................................909 305-6500
Eddie Chao, *Manager*
Betty Shubin, *Admin Mgr*
Edwin S Ige, *Broker*
EMP: 100
SALES (corp-wide): 13.3B **Privately Held**
WEB: www.newyorklife.com
SIC: **6311** Life insurance
PA: New York Life Insurance Company
51 Madison Ave Bsmt 1b
New York NY 10010
212 576-7000

(P-9885)
PACIFIC LIFE & ANNUITY COMPANY
700 Newport Center Dr, Newport Beach (92660-6307)
P.O. Box 9000 (92658-9030)
PHONE.................................949 219-3011
James Morris, *President*
Khanh T Tran, *CFO*
Audrey L Milfs, *Vice Pres*
Brian Klemens, *Controller*
Christina Q He, *Assistant VP*
EMP: 650
SQ FT: 125,000
SALES (est): 203.9MM
SALES (corp-wide): 12.8B **Privately Held**
SIC: **6311 6411** Life insurance carriers; insurance agents, brokers & service
HQ: Pacific Life Insurance Company
700 Newport Center Dr
Newport Beach CA 92660
949 219-3011

(P-9886)
PATRA CORPORATION (PA)
1107 Inv Blvd Ste 100, El Dorado Hills (95762)
PHONE.................................415 595-9987
Dan Easterlin, *President*
Bob Murphy, *Officer*
Tony LI, *CTO*
Jessica Casteel, *Director*
EMP: 133 EST: 2007
SALES (est): 80.1MM **Privately Held**
SIC: **6311** Life insurance

(P-9887)
PRINCIPAL FINANCIAL GROUP INC
1350 E Spruce Ave Ste 100, Fresno (93720-3373)
PHONE.................................559 261-2000
William E Griffith, *Manager*
Rodney Thornton, *General Mgr*
Melissa Bradley-Sperlin, *Sales Associate*
Tony Palermo, *Advisor*
Geoffrey T Barry, *Agent*
EMP: 80 **Publicly Held**
SIC: **6311** Life insurance
PA: Principal Financial Group, Inc.
711 High St
Des Moines IA 50392

(P-9888)
SUNAMERICA LIFE INSURANCE CO (DH)
1 Sun America Ctr Fl 36, Los Angeles (90067-6104)
PHONE.................................310 772-6000
Jay Wintrob, *President*
N S Gillis, *CFO*
Scott L Robinson, *CFO*
Mark A Zaeske, *Treasurer*
Mike Libby, *Vice Pres*
EMP: 69 EST: 1890
SQ FT: 75,000
SALES (est): 2.6B
SALES (corp-wide): 47.3B **Publicly Held**
WEB: www.sunamericaproduce.com
SIC: **6311** Life insurance
HQ: Safg Retirement Services, Inc.
1 Sun America Ctr Fl 36
Los Angeles CA 90067
310 772-6000

(P-9889)
TRANSAMERICA FINANCE CORP
1731 W Medical Center Dr, Anaheim (92801-1837)
PHONE.................................714 778-5100
Jim Karsch, *Manager*
EMP: 65
SALES (corp-wide): 16.5B **Privately Held**
SIC: **6311 6512** Life insurance; commercial & industrial building operation
HQ: Transamerica Finance Corporation
600 Montgomery St Fl 16
San Francisco CA 94111
415 983-4000

(P-9890)
TRUCK UNDERWRITERS ASSOCIATION
Farmers Insurance
6303 Owensmouth Ave Fl 1, Woodland Hills (91367-2200)
PHONE.................................323 932-3200
Jane Franklin, *Vice Pres*
Kelly Chu, *Project Mgr*
John Katona, *Technology*
Harry Kim, *Manager*
Steven M Shibel, *Manager*
EMP: 900
SQ FT: 275,000
SALES (corp-wide): 48.2B **Privately Held**
SIC: **6311 6331 6321** Life insurance; fire, marine & casualty insurance; accident & health insurance
HQ: Truck Underwriters Association
4680 Wilshire Blvd
Los Angeles CA 90010
323 932-3200

(P-9891)
ULTRALINK LLC
535 Anton Blvd Ste 200, Costa Mesa (92626-7680)
PHONE.................................714 427-5500
Tony Ton, *Owner*
Vince Sheeran, *CEO*
Jack Baumann, *COO*
Dan Lieber, *Chairman*
Jeff Graves, *Vice Ch Bd*
EMP: 120
SALES (est): 31.4MM **Privately Held**
SIC: **6311** Life insurance carriers

(P-9892)
WILLIS INSURANCE SVCS CAL INC
4250 Executive Sq Ste 250, La Jolla (92037-9104)
PHONE.................................858 678-2000
Jack Yelverton, *Branch Mgr*
EMP: 50 **Privately Held**
SIC: **6311** Life insurance
HQ: Willis Insurance Services Of California, Inc.
525 Market St Ste 3400
San Francisco CA 94105
415 955-0100

(P-9893)
ZENITH INSURANCE COMPANY
4460 Rosewood Dr Ste 300, Pleasanton (94588-3086)
P.O. Box 8002 (94588-8602)
PHONE.................................925 460-0600
Jon Lindsay, *Manager*
Brad Nichols, *Vice Pres*
Christina Walburn, *Sales Staff*
Mike Choi, *Manager*
Karen Williams, *Underwriter*
EMP: 90
SALES (corp-wide): 17.7B **Privately Held**
SIC: **6311 6321 6324 6331** Life insurance; accident & health insurance; hospital & medical service plans; fire, marine & casualty insurance
HQ: Zenith Insurance Company
21255 Califa St
Woodland Hills CA 91367
818 713-1000

6321 Accident & Health Insurance

(P-9894)
21ST CENTURY LF & HLTH CO INC (PA)
Also Called: Lifecare Assurance Company
21600 Oxnard St Ste 1500, Woodland Hills (91367-4972)
P.O. Box 4243 (91365-4243)
PHONE.................................818 887-4436
James M Glickman, *President*
Pamela Corbally, *President*
Paul Weber, *President*
Alan S Hughes, *CEO*
Daniel J Di Sipio, *CFO*
EMP: 246
SQ FT: 50,000
SALES (est): 167.8MM **Privately Held**
WEB: www.lifecareassurance.com
SIC: **6321** Health insurance carriers

(P-9895)
ALLIANZ REINSURANCE AMER INC
Also Called: San Francisco Reinsurance Co
1465 N Mcdowell Blvd, Petaluma (94954-6516)
PHONE.................................415 899-2000
Joe Beneducci, *President*
Vicki Kottmann, *Director*
EMP: 70
SQ FT: 240,000
SALES: 248.9MM
SALES (corp-wide): 24.9B **Privately Held**
WEB: www.firemansfund.com
SIC: **6321** Reinsurance carriers, accident & health
HQ: Fireman's Fund Insurance Company
1465 N Mcdowell Blvd # 100
Petaluma CA 94954
415 899-2000

(P-9896)
ALTAMED HEALTH SERVICES CORP
535 S 2nd Ave, Covina (91723-3013)
PHONE.................................626 214-1480
Robert Young, *Owner*
EMP: 69
SALES (corp-wide): 677.8MM **Privately Held**
SIC: **6321** Accident & health insurance carriers

PA: Altamed Health Services Corporation
2040 Camfield Ave
Commerce CA 90040
323 725-8751

(P-9897)
ANTHEM INC
1101 Anacapa St Ste 300, Santa Barbara (93101-2048)
PHONE.................................805 560-3520
EMP: 334
SALES (corp-wide): 92.1B **Publicly Held**
SIC: **6321 6324** Health insurance carriers; dental insurance
PA: Anthem, Inc.
220 Virginia Ave
Indianapolis IN 46204
317 488-6000

(P-9898)
AON BENFIELD FAC INC
199 Fremont St Fl 15, San Francisco (94105-2299)
PHONE.................................415 486-6900
Matt Davis, *Manager*
EMP: 200
SALES (corp-wide): 10.7B **Privately Held**
SIC: **6321 6311** Reinsurance carriers, accident & health; life insurance
HQ: Aon Benfield Fac Inc.
200 E Randolph St Fl 15
Chicago IL 60601
312 381-5300

(P-9899)
AUTO CLUB ENTERPRISES (PA)
3333 Fairview Rd Msa451, Costa Mesa (92626-1610)
P.O. Box 25001, Santa Ana (92799-5001)
PHONE.................................714 850-5111
Robert T Bouttier, *CEO*
Thomas Mc Kernon, *President*
Robert Bouttier, *COO*
John F Boyle, *Treasurer*
Filomena Andre, *Vice Pres*
EMP: 1200
SQ FT: 700,000
SALES (est): 3.4B **Privately Held**
WEB: www.aaa-newmexico.com
SIC: **6321** Accident & health insurance

(P-9900)
AUTO CLUB ENTERPRISES
8761 Santa Monica Blvd, West Hollywood (90069-4538)
PHONE.................................310 914-8500
Bob Szhwab, *Manager*
EMP: 444
SALES (corp-wide): 3.4B **Privately Held**
WEB: www.aaa-newmexico.com
SIC: **6321** Accident & health insurance
PA: Auto Club Enterprises
3333 Fairview Rd Msa451
Costa Mesa CA 92626
714 850-5111

(P-9901)
B C LIFE & HEALTH INSURANCE CO
21555 Oxnard St, Woodland Hills (91367-4943)
PHONE.................................818 703-2345
David Helwig, *President*
Kenneth C Zurek, *CFO*
Nicholas L Becker, *Principal*
Thomas Geiser, *Admin Sec*
Stacy Borsuk, *Director*
EMP: 66
SALES (est): 18.7MM **Privately Held**
SIC: **6321** Indemnity plans health insurance, except medical service

(P-9902)
CAREMORE MEDICAL GROUP INC
12900 Park Plz Ste 150, Lakewood (90805)
PHONE.................................562 622-2900
John Short, *Director*
Josie Rivera, *Principal*
EMP: 300 EST: 2011
SALES (est): 45.6MM
SALES (corp-wide): 92.1B **Publicly Held**
SIC: **6321** Health insurance carriers

▲ = Import ▼=Export
◆ =Import/Export

PA: Anthem, Inc.
220 Virginia Ave
Indianapolis IN 46204
317 488-6000

(P-9903)
COUNTY OF KINGS
330 Campus Dr, Hanford (93230-4375)
PHONE.....................559 584-1411
Kathy Mittlighder, *Director*
EMP: 110 **Privately Held**
SIC: 6321 9431 Accident & health insurance;
PA: County Of Kings
1400 W Lacey Blvd
Hanford CA 93230
559 582-0326

(P-9904)
DOCTORS COMPANY FOUNDATION
185 Greenwood Rd, NAPA (94558-7540)
PHONE.....................800 421-2368
Richard E Anderson, *CEO*
Dave McHale, *Officer*
Shannon McBride, *Analyst*
EMP: 755 EST: 2014
SALES (est): 329.7MM **Privately Held**
SIC: 6321 Health insurance carriers

(P-9905)
E D D 2100
Also Called: Disability Insurance
3127 Transworld Dr # 150, Stockton (95206-4988)
P.O. Box 1928 (95201-1928)
PHONE.....................209 941-6501
Judy Cruz, *Office Mgr*
Marcy Pruitt, *Managing Prtnr*
EMP: 92 EST: 1940
SALES (est): 16.8MM **Privately Held**
SIC: 6321 Disability health insurance

(P-9906)
HEALTHPOCKET INC
444 Castro St Ste 710, Mountain View (94041-2080)
PHONE.....................800 984-8015
Bruce Telkamp, *CEO*
Sheldon Wang, *President*
Regis Haegler, *Finance*
Julia Bringans, *Director*
EMP: 98
SALES (est): 28.1MM
SALES (corp-wide): 351.1MM **Publicly Held**
SIC: 6321 Health insurance carriers
PA: Health Insurance Innovations, Inc.
15438 N Florida Ave # 201
Tampa FL 33613
813 397-1187

(P-9907)
INLAND EMPIRE HEALTH PLAN (PA)
Also Called: Iehp
10801 6th St Ste 120, Rancho Cucamonga (91730-5987)
P.O. Box 1400 (91729-1400)
PHONE.....................909 890-2000
Jarrod McNaughton, *CEO*
Chet Uma, *CFO*
Bob Buster, *Chairman*
Sue Arcidiacono, *Chief Mktg Ofcr*
EMP: 850
SQ FT: 72,000
SALES (est): 1B **Privately Held**
WEB: www.iehp.org
SIC: 6321 6324 Health insurance carriers; health maintenance organization (HMO), insurance only

(P-9908)
KAISER FUNDATION HLTH PLAN INC (PA)
1 Kaiser Plz, Oakland (94612-3610)
PHONE.....................510 271-5800
Bernard J Tyson, *Ch of Bd*
Gregory A Adams, *President*
Dave Underriner, *President*
Laura Gallardo, *COO*
Wendy Watson, *COO*
EMP: 450 EST: 1955
SQ FT: 90,000

SALES (est): 76.5B **Privately Held**
WEB: www.kaiser.com
SIC: 6321 Accident & health insurance

(P-9909)
KINGS VIEW WORK EXPERIENCE CTR
703 I St, Los Banos (93635-4308)
PHONE.....................209 826-8118
David Toliver, *Administration*
Irma Torrez, *Manager*
EMP: 50
SALES (est): 5MM **Privately Held**
SIC: 6321 7641 Disability health insurance; furniture repair & maintenance

(P-9910)
LIFECARE ASSURANCE COMPANY
21600 Oxnard St Fl 16, Woodland Hills (91367-4976)
P.O. Box 4243 (91365-4243)
PHONE.....................818 887-4436
James Glickman, *President*
Alan S Hughes, *COO*
Daniel J Disipio, *CFO*
Peter Diffley, *Vice Pres*
Gwen D Franklin, *Vice Pres*
EMP: 246
SQ FT: 35,000
SALES: 326.9MM
SALES (corp-wide): 167.8MM **Privately Held**
WEB: www.lifecareassurance.com
SIC: 6321 6411 6311 Accident & health insurance; insurance agents, brokers & service; life insurance
PA: 21st Century Life And Health Company, Inc.
21600 Oxnard St Ste 1500
Woodland Hills CA 91367
818 887-4436

(P-9911)
MOLINA HEALTHCARE OF CALIFORNI
200 Oceangate Ste 100, Long Beach (90802-4317)
PHONE.....................562 435-3666
Richard Chambers, *CEO*
J Mario Molina, *Ch of Bd*
John Kotal, *President*
Terry Bayer, *COO*
Dr James Howatt, *Officer*
EMP: 2800
SALES (est): 329.7MM
SALES (corp-wide): 18.8B **Publicly Held**
SIC: 6321 8011 Health insurance carriers; clinic, operated by physicians
PA: Molina Healthcare, Inc.
200 Oceangate Ste 100
Long Beach CA 90802
562 435-3666

(P-9912)
SANTA BARBARA SAN LUIS OBISPO
Also Called: Cencal Health
4050 Calle Real, Santa Barbara (93110-3413)
PHONE.....................800 421-2560
Robert Freeman, *CEO*
Sherry Clark, *Executive Asst*
Ileana Villarreal,
EMP: 140
SALES (est): 64.8MM **Privately Held**
SIC: 6321 Accident & health insurance

(P-9913)
SANTE HEALTH SYSTEM INC (PA)
Also Called: Sante Community Physicians
7370 N Palm Ave Ste 101, Fresno (93711-5782)
P.O. Box 1507 (93716-1507)
PHONE.....................559 228-5400
Mateo F Desoto, *CEO*
Scott Wells, *President*
Janine Stephenson, *Chief Mktg Ofcr*
Chris Cheney, *Officer*
Debbie Keena, *Vice Pres*
EMP: 76
SQ FT: 20,000

SALES (est): 154.9MM **Privately Held**
SIC: 6321 7371 Accident & health insurance; computer software development & applications

(P-9914)
STATE COMPENSATION INSUR FUND
2901 N Ventura Rd Ste 100, Oxnard (93036-1126)
PHONE.....................888 782-8338
Martin Goldman, *Manager*
EMP: 400
SALES (corp-wide): 1.3B **Privately Held**
WEB: www.scif.com
SIC: 6321 9651 Disability health insurance; insurance commission, government;
PA: State Compensation Insurance Fund
333 Bush St Fl 8
San Francisco CA 94104
888 782-8338

(P-9915)
WESTERN HEALTH ADVANTAGE
2349 Gateway Oaks Dr # 100, Sacramento (95833-4244)
PHONE.....................916 567-1950
Garry Maisel, *President*
Rita Ruecker, *Treasurer*
David Walker, *Admin Asst*
Mark Budge, *Administration*
Bruce Qin, *Software Dev*
EMP: 100
SQ FT: 25,000
SALES: 726MM **Privately Held**
WEB: www.westernhealth.com
SIC: 6321 Health insurance carriers

6324 Hospital & Medical Svc Plans Carriers

(P-9916)
AETNA HEALTH CALIFORNIA INC
1 Embarcadero Ctr 300, San Francisco (94111-3628)
PHONE.....................415 645-8200
Sue Hallett, *Branch Mgr*
Marisa Lin, *Manager*
Saeeda Shaikh, *Manager*
Christy Leong, *Consultant*
EMP: 80
SALES (corp-wide): 194.5B **Publicly Held**
SIC: 6324 Health maintenance organization (HMO), insurance only
HQ: Aetna Health Of California, Inc.
515 S Flower St
Los Angeles CA 90071
925 543-9223

(P-9917)
AETNA HEALTH CALIFORNIA INC (DH)
515 S Flower St, Los Angeles (90071-2201)
PHONE.....................925 543-9223
John Brian Ternan, *CEO*
Rick M Jelinek, *Exec VP*
Pamela M Lemon, *Vice Pres*
Louise McCleery, *Vice Pres*
Johnetta Semper, *Vice Pres*
EMP: 198
SALES (est): 289.1MM
SALES (corp-wide): 194.5B **Publicly Held**
SIC: 6324 Health maintenance organization (HMO), insurance only

(P-9918)
AGILON HEALTH INC
1 World Trade Ctr, Long Beach (90831-0002)
PHONE.....................562 256-3800
Ron Kuerbide, *CEO*
Patricia Parker, *President*
Ted Halkias, *CFO*
EMP: 100
SQ FT: 12,000
SALES: 300MM **Privately Held**
SIC: 6324 Health maintenance organization (HMO), insurance only

(P-9919)
ALAMEDA ALLIANCE FOR HEALTH
1240 S Loop Rd, Alameda (94502-7084)
PHONE.....................510 747-4555
Ingrid Lamirault, *CEO*
Roberta Robertson, *Executive Asst*
Pandiyarajan Subburaman, *Info Tech Mgr*
Kathy Gordon, *Business Anlyst*
Jasdeep Joga, *Business Anlyst*
EMP: 135
SQ FT: 50,000
SALES (est): 116.9MM **Privately Held**
WEB: www.alamedaalliance.com
SIC: 6324 Health maintenance organization (HMO), insurance only

(P-9920)
ALIGNMENT HEALTH PLAN
Also Called: Citizens Choice Health Plan
1100 W Town & Country, Orange (92868-4600)
PHONE.....................323 728-7232
Chuck Weber, *President*
Elizabeth Tejada, *COO*
Charlotte Leblanc,
EMP: 90
SALES (est): 49.6MM **Privately Held**
WEB: www.mycchp.com
SIC: 6324 Health maintenance organization (HMO), insurance only
PA: Alignment Healthcare, Usa Llc
1100 W Town And Country R
Orange CA 92868
844 310-2247

(P-9921)
ANTHEM INC
4236 Silverado Dr, Thousand Oaks (91360-6854)
PHONE.....................805 231-0994
EMP: 441
SALES (corp-wide): 92.1B **Publicly Held**
SIC: 6324 Hospital & medical service plans
PA: Anthem, Inc.
220 Virginia Ave
Indianapolis IN 46204
317 488-6000

(P-9922)
ANTHEM INC
4553 La Tienda Rd, Westlake Village (91362-3800)
PHONE.....................562 622-2869
Angela Canton, *Vice Pres*
Dina Jimenez, *Program Mgr*
Nancy Margolis, *Admin Sec*
Michael Voll, *Marketing Staff*
Jonathon Eastman, *Director*
EMP: 585
SALES (corp-wide): 92.1B **Publicly Held**
SIC: 6324 Hospital & medical service plans
PA: Anthem, Inc.
220 Virginia Ave
Indianapolis IN 46204
317 488-6000

(P-9923)
BLUE CROSS & BLUE SHIELD MICH
6300 Wilshire Blvd # 970, Los Angeles (90048-5204)
PHONE.....................323 782-3046
Kenneth August, *Branch Mgr*
EMP: 203
SALES (corp-wide): 8B **Privately Held**
SIC: 6324 Hospital & medical service plans
PA: Blue Cross Blue Shield Of Michigan Mutual Insurance Company
600 E Lafayette Blvd
Detroit MI 48226
313 225-9000

(P-9924)
BLUE CROSS OF CALIFORNIA (DH)
4553 La Tienda Rd, Westlake Village (91362-3800)
PHONE.....................805 557-6050
Mark Morgan, *President*
Kenneth C Zurek, *CFO*
Thomas C Geiser, *Admin Sec*
EMP: 133
SQ FT: 427,104

PRODUCTS & SVCS

SALES (est): 190.6MM
SALES (corp-wide): 92.1B **Publicly Held**
SIC: 6324 6411 Health maintenance organization (HMO), insurance only; insurance agents, brokers & service

(P-9925)
CALIFORNIA PHYSICIANS SERVICE
2020 17th St, Bakersfield (93301-4252)
PHONE..............................661 631-2277
Ricard Maiatico, *Owner*
EMP: 126
SALES (corp-wide): 17.6B **Privately Held**
WEB: www.blueshieldcafoundation.org
SIC: 6324 6321 Hospital & medical service plans; accident & health insurance
PA: California Physicians' Service
　　50 Beale St Bsmt 2
　　San Francisco CA 94105
　　415 229-5000

(P-9926)
CALIFORNIA PHYSICIANS SERVICE
Also Called: Blue Sheild of California
2066 Camel Ln Apt 24, Walnut Creek (94596-5955)
PHONE..............................925 927-7419
John Durst, *Branch Mgr*
Maggie Pedroza, *Analyst*
EMP: 232
SALES (corp-wide): 17.6B **Privately Held**
WEB: www.blueshieldcafoundation.org
SIC: 6324 Hospital & medical service plans
PA: California Physicians' Service
　　50 Beale St Bsmt 2
　　San Francisco CA 94105
　　415 229-5000

(P-9927)
CALIFORNIA PHYSICIANS SERVICE (PA)
Also Called: Blue Shield of California
50 Beale St Bsmt 2, San Francisco (94105-1819)
P.O. Box 272540, Chico (95927-2540)
PHONE..............................415 229-5000
Paul Markovich, *President*
Bruce Bodoken, *Ch of Bd*
Karen Vigil, *CEO*
Heidi Kunz, *CFO*
Eric Book, *Chief Mktg Ofcr*
EMP: 900 EST: 1939
SQ FT: 120,000
SALES: 17.6B **Privately Held**
WEB: www.blueshieldcafoundation.org
SIC: 6324 Hospital & medical service plans

(P-9928)
CALIFORNIA PHYSICIANS SERVICE
4700 Bechelli Ln, Redding (96002-3506)
PHONE..............................530 351-6115
EMP: 158
SALES (corp-wide): 17.6B **Privately Held**
SIC: 6324 Hospital & medical service plans
PA: California Physicians' Service
　　50 Beale St Bsmt 2
　　San Francisco CA 94105
　　415 229-5000

(P-9929)
CALIFORNIA PHYSICIANS SERVICE
Also Called: Blue Shield of California
4203 Town Center Blvd, El Dorado Hills (95762-7100)
P.O. Box 7168, San Francisco (94120-7168)
PHONE..............................916 350-7800
Eric Lam, *Director*
Steve Maguire, *Project Mgr*
Patti Castro, *Manager*
Maria Leone, *Manager*
Trent Thomas, *Manager*
EMP: 260
SALES (corp-wide): 17.6B **Privately Held**
WEB: www.blueshieldcafoundation.org
SIC: 6324 6321 Hospital & medical service plans; accident & health insurance
PA: California Physicians' Service
　　50 Beale St Bsmt 2
　　San Francisco CA 94105
　　415 229-5000

(P-9930)
CALIFORNIA PHYSICIANS SERVICE
Also Called: Blue Shield of California
100 N Pacific Coast Hwy # 2000, El Segundo (90245-4359)
PHONE..............................310 744-2668
Aubrey Chernick, *Branch Mgr*
EMP: 126
SALES (corp-wide): 17.6B **Privately Held**
WEB: www.blueshieldcafoundation.org
SIC: 6324 Hospital & medical service plans
PA: California Physicians' Service
　　50 Beale St Bsmt 2
　　San Francisco CA 94105
　　415 229-5000

(P-9931)
CALIFORNIA PHYSICIANS SERVICE
Also Called: Blue Shield of California
6300 Canoga Ave Ste A, Woodland Hills (91367-8000)
PHONE..............................818 598-8000
John Headberg, *Branch Mgr*
EMP: 400
SALES (corp-wide): 17.6B **Privately Held**
WEB: www.blueshieldcafoundation.org
SIC: 6324 Hospital & medical service plans
PA: California Physicians' Service
　　50 Beale St Bsmt 2
　　San Francisco CA 94105
　　415 229-5000

(P-9932)
CENTENE CHWP
1699 W Main St, El Centro (92243-5421)
PHONE..............................760 482-5593
EMP: 145
SALES (est): 10.7MM **Publicly Held**
SIC: 6324 Health maintenance organization (HMO), insurance only
PA: Centene Corporation
　　7700 Forsyth Blvd Ste 800
　　Saint Louis MO 63105

(P-9933)
CENTENE CORPORATION
7755 Center Ave, Huntington Beach (92647-3007)
PHONE..............................714 934-3373
EMP: 84 **Publicly Held**
SIC: 6324 Health maintenance organization (HMO), insurance only
PA: Centene Corporation
　　7700 Forsyth Blvd Ste 800
　　Saint Louis MO 63105

(P-9934)
CENTENE CORPORATION
550 Main St, Placerville (95667-5643)
PHONE..............................530 626-5773
EMP: 99 **Publicly Held**
SIC: 6324 Hospital & medical service plans
PA: Centene Corporation
　　7700 Forsyth Blvd Ste 800
　　Saint Louis MO 63105

(P-9935)
CENTENE CORPORATION
12033 Foundation Pl, Gold River (95670-4502)
PHONE..............................314 505-6689
EMP: 125 **Publicly Held**
SIC: 6324 Hospital & medical service plans
PA: Centene Corporation
　　7700 Forsyth Blvd Ste 800
　　Saint Louis MO 63105

(P-9936)
CENTER FOR ELDERS INDEPENDENCE
Also Called: C E I
510 17th St Ste 400, Oakland (94612-1570)
PHONE..............................510 433-1150
Peter Szutu, *President*
EMP: 225 EST: 1981
SALES: 65.4MM **Privately Held**
WEB: www.cei.elders.org
SIC: 6324 Hospital & medical service plans

(P-9937)
CHOC HEALTH ALLIANCE
1120 W La Veta Ave # 450, Orange (92868-4224)
PHONE..............................714 565-5100
Roger Austin, *CEO*
EMP: 65
SALES (est): 19.3MM
SALES (corp-wide): 194.5B **Publicly Held**
WEB: www.chochealthalliance.com
SIC: 6324 Hospital & medical service plans
HQ: Anderson Schaller Inc
　　4500 E Cotton Center Blvd
　　Phoenix AZ 85040
　　602 659-1123

(P-9938)
CIGNA HEALTHCARE CAL INC
1 Front St Ste 1700, San Francisco (94111-5392)
PHONE..............................415 374-2500
William Burke, *Branch Mgr*
Marlene Matsuoka, *Vice Pres*
Candace Boss, *Business Mgr*
Justin France, *Regl Sales Mgr*
Jessica Beasecker, *Sales Staff*
EMP: 226
SALES (corp-wide): 141.6B **Publicly Held**
SIC: 6324 Health maintenance organization (HMO), insurance only
HQ: Cigna Healthcare Of California, Inc.
　　400 N Brand Blvd Ste 400 # 400
　　Glendale CA 91203
　　818 500-6262

(P-9939)
CIGNA HEALTHCARE CAL INC (DH)
400 N Brand Blvd Ste 400 # 400, Glendale (91203-2357)
P.O. Box 188045, Chattanooga TN (37422-8045)
PHONE..............................818 500-6262
Leroy Volberding, *President*
Bobby Federico, *Executive*
Nancy Ho, *Business Dir*
David Yeager, *Controller*
Susan Ewers, *Director*
EMP: 400
SQ FT: 110,000
SALES (est): 301.6MM
SALES (corp-wide): 141.6B **Publicly Held**
SIC: 6324 Health maintenance organization (HMO), insurance only
HQ: Healthsource, Inc.
　　2 College Park Dr
　　Hooksett NH 03106
　　603 268-7000

(P-9940)
CIGNA HEALTHCARE CAL INC
2801 Townsgate Rd Ste 121, Thousand Oaks (91361-3029)
PHONE..............................805 230-8300
Peter Albert, *Director*
EMP: 233
SALES (corp-wide): 141.6B **Publicly Held**
SIC: 6324 Group hospitalization plans
HQ: Cigna Healthcare Of California, Inc.
　　400 N Brand Blvd Ste 400 # 400
　　Glendale CA 91203
　　818 500-6262

(P-9941)
CIGNA HEALTHCARE CAL INC
5300 W Tulare Ave Ste 100, Visalia (93277-3700)
PHONE..............................559 738-2000
Rich Keena, *Vice Pres*
Raemee Anderson, *Cust Mgr*
Vicki Clements, *Director*
Elsa Quintanilla, *Associate*
EMP: 500
SALES (corp-wide): 141.6B **Publicly Held**
SIC: 6324 Health maintenance organization (HMO), insurance only
HQ: Cigna Healthcare Of California, Inc.
　　400 N Brand Blvd Ste 400 # 400
　　Glendale CA 91203
　　818 500-6262

(P-9942)
COUNTY OF LOS ANGELES
Also Called: Community Health Plan
1000 S Fremont Ave Unit 4, Alhambra (91803-8859)
PHONE..............................626 299-5300
Dave Beck, *Director*
EMP: 140 **Privately Held**
WEB: www.co.la.ca.us
SIC: 6324 9431 Hospital & medical service plans; mental health agency administration, government
PA: County Of Los Angeles
　　500 W Temple St Ste 437
　　Los Angeles CA 90012
　　213 974-1101

(P-9943)
DELTA DENTAL OF CALIFORNIA
1450 Frazee Rd Ste 200, San Diego (92108-4341)
P.O. Box 261391 (92196-1391)
PHONE..............................619 683-2549
Delta California, *Branch Mgr*
EMP: 259
SALES (corp-wide): 5.8B **Privately Held**
SIC: 6324 Dental insurance
PA: Delta Dental Of California
　　560 Mission St Ste 1300
　　San Francisco CA 94105
　　415 972-8300

(P-9944)
DELTA DENTAL OF CALIFORNIA (PA)
560 Mission St Ste 1300, San Francisco (94105-0938)
PHONE..............................415 972-8300
Mike Castro, *President*
Nilesh Patel, *COO*
Alicia Weber, *Acting CFO*
Mike Hankinson, *Exec VP*
Charles Lamont, *Exec VP*
EMP: 487
SQ FT: 241,000
SALES: 5.8B **Privately Held**
WEB: www.deltadentalca.com
SIC: 6324 Dental insurance

(P-9945)
DELTA DENTAL OF CALIFORNIA
Also Called: Delta Dental Plan
11155 International Dr, Sacramento (95826)
PHONE..............................916 853-7373
Tony Barth, *Branch Mgr*
Darlene E Gillespie, *Officer*
Perry Htay, *Administration*
Gunasekaran Ekambaram, *Prgrmr*
Leeja Pillai, *Prgrmr*
EMP: 1000
SALES (corp-wide): 5.8B **Privately Held**
WEB: www.deltadentalca.com
SIC: 6324 Dental insurance
PA: Delta Dental Of California
　　560 Mission St Ste 1300
　　San Francisco CA 94105
　　415 972-8300

(P-9946)
HEALDSBURG DIST HOSP REHAB SVC
1540 Healdsburg Ave, Healdsburg (95448-3253)
PHONE..............................707 433-9150
Stacy Smithson, *Manager*
EMP: 100
SALES (est): 20.1MM **Privately Held**
WEB: www.healdsburghospital.com
SIC: 6324 Hospital & medical service plans

(P-9947)
HEALTH NET LLC (HQ)
21650 Oxnard St Fl 25, Woodland Hills (91367-7829)
PHONE..............................818 676-6000
Jay M Gellert, *President*
Rich Hall, *Officer*
Juanell Hefner, *Officer*
Angelee F Bouchard, *Senior VP*
Jody Giordano, *Vice Pres*
EMP: 250
SQ FT: 115,488

▲ = Import ▼=Export
◆ =Import/Export

SALES (est): 1.7B **Publicly Held**
SIC: **6324** 6311 Hospital & medical service plans; life insurance carriers

(P-9948)
HEALTH NET CALIFORNIA INC
101 N Brand Blvd Ste 1500, Glendale (91203-2659)
PHONE..................................818 543-9037
Kevin J Walker, *Manager*
EMP: 128 **Publicly Held**
SIC: **6324** Hospital & medical service plans
HQ: Health Net Of California, Inc.
   7700 Forsyth Blvd
   Saint Louis MO 63105
   818 676-6775

(P-9949)
HEALTH NET CALIFORNIA INC
155 Grand Ave Lbby, Oakland (94612-3758)
PHONE..................................510 465-9600
Eric Johnson, *Manager*
Susan Sall, *Manager*
EMP: 450 **Publicly Held**
SIC: **6324** 6321 Hospital & medical service plans; accident & health insurance
HQ: Health Net Of California, Inc.
   7700 Forsyth Blvd
   Saint Louis MO 63105
   818 676-6775

(P-9950)
HEALTH NET CALIFORNIA INC
Also Called: Fhpa
12033 Foundation Pl, Gold River (95670-4502)
PHONE..................................916 935-3520
Jeffery Slynn, *Vice Pres*
Dorothy Tucker, *Executive Asst*
Isaias Pena, *Administration*
Jim Wheeler, *Database Admin*
Capcap Roubart, *Analyst*
EMP: 300 **Publicly Held**
SIC: **6324** Hospital & medical service plans
HQ: Health Net Of California, Inc.
   7700 Forsyth Blvd
   Saint Louis MO 63105
   818 676-6775

(P-9951)
HEALTH NET FEDERAL SVCS LLC (DH)
2025 Aerojet Rd, Rancho Cordova (95742-6418)
P.O. Box 2890 (95741-2890)
PHONE..................................916 935-5000
Thomas F Carrato, *President*
Molly Tuttle, *Technology*
Nithya Rajaraman, *Analyst*
Garrett Grinder, *Director*
EMP: 700
SQ FT: 100,000
SALES (est): 1.2B **Publicly Held**
SIC: **6324** Hospital & medical service plans
HQ: Health Net Of California, Inc.
   7700 Forsyth Blvd
   Saint Louis MO 63105
   818 676-6775

(P-9952)
HEALTH PLAN OF SAN JOAQUIN
7751 S Manthey Rd, French Camp (95231-9802)
PHONE..................................209 942-6300
Amy Shinn, *CEO*
EMP: 120
SALES (est): 96.5MM **Privately Held**
SIC: **6324** Health maintenance organization (HMO), insurance only

(P-9953)
HEALTHNET CALIFORNIA INC
Also Called: Healthnet Seniority Plus
1661 Golden Rain Rd, Seal Beach (90740-4907)
PHONE..................................562 598-4043
Terry Anguiano Redd, *District Mgr*
EMP: 75
SALES (est): 6MM **Privately Held**
WEB: www.healthnetcalifornia.com
SIC: **6324** Health maintenance organization (HMO), insurance only

(P-9954)
INLAND EMPIRE HEALTH PLAN
805 W 2nd St Ste C, San Bernardino (92410-3255)
P.O. Box 1800, Rancho Cucamonga (91729-1800)
PHONE..................................866 228-4347
EMP: 428 **Privately Held**
SIC: **6324** 8742 Health maintenance organization (HMO), insurance only; hospital & health services consultant
PA: Inland Empire Health Plan
   10801 6th St Ste 120
   Rancho Cucamonga CA 91730

(P-9955)
INTER-VALLEY HEALTH PLAN INC
300 S Park Ave Ste 300 # 300, Pomona (91766-1546)
P.O. Box 6002 (91769-6002)
PHONE..................................909 623-6333
Ronald Bolding, *CEO*
Paul Biberkraut, *CFO*
Michael Nelson, *CFO*
Robin Davis, *Vice Pres*
Patricia Jacobson, *Vice Pres*
EMP: 70
SQ FT: 54,700
SALES: 271.1MM **Privately Held**
WEB: www.ivhp.com
SIC: **6324** 8011 Hospital & medical service plans; offices & clinics of medical doctors

(P-9956)
KAISER FOUNDATION HOSPITALS
Also Called: Kaiser Foundation Health Plan
30116 Eigenbrodt Way, Union City (94587-1225)
PHONE..................................510 675-5777
Colleen McKeown, *Manager*
EMP: 99
SALES (corp-wide): 76.5B **Privately Held**
SIC: **6324** Hospital & medical service plans
HQ: Kaiser Foundation Hospitals Inc
   1 Kaiser Plz
   Oakland CA 94612
   510 271-6611

(P-9957)
KAISER FOUNDATION HOSPITALS
Also Called: Kaiser Foundation Health Plan
2350 Geary Blvd Fl 2, San Francisco (94115-3305)
PHONE..................................415 833-2616
Reva Kopel, *Principal*
Lyle Shlager, *Gastroenterlgy*
Mary Donati, *Internal Med*
Alfredo Lopez, *Oncology*
Kavneet Alag, *Senior Mgr*
EMP: 85
SALES (corp-wide): 76.5B **Privately Held**
SIC: **6324** Hospital & medical service plans
HQ: Kaiser Foundation Hospitals Inc
   1 Kaiser Plz
   Oakland CA 94612
   510 271-6611

(P-9958)
KAISER FOUNDATION HOSPITALS
Also Called: Kaiser Foundation Health Plan
393 E Walnut St, Pasadena (91188-0002)
PHONE..................................626 405-5000
David Lamm, *Branch Mgr*
Stephen Derose, *Research*
Javier Gomez, *Property Mgr*
EMP: 50
SALES (corp-wide): 76.5B **Privately Held**
WEB: www.kaiser.com
SIC: **6324** Hospital & medical service plans
HQ: Kaiser Foundation Hospitals Inc
   1 Kaiser Plz
   Oakland CA 94612
   510 271-6611

(P-9959)
KAISER FOUNDATION HOSPITALS
Also Called: Kaiser Foundation Health Plan
1761 Broadway St Ste 210, Vallejo (94589-2227)
PHONE..................................707 645-2720
Cynthia Chandler, *Director*
Schieree Harmon, *Admin Mgr*
Gail Fahey,
EMP: 75
SALES (corp-wide): 76.5B **Privately Held**
WEB: www.kaiser.com
SIC: **6324** Hospital & medical service plans
HQ: Kaiser Foundation Hospitals Inc
   1 Kaiser Plz
   Oakland CA 94612
   510 271-6611

(P-9960)
KAISER FOUNDATION HOSPITALS
Also Called: Kaiser Foundation Health Plan
820 Las Gallinas Ave, San Rafael (94903-3410)
PHONE..................................415 444-3522
Bob Johnson, *Branch Mgr*
John M Maas, *Psychologist*
EMP: 100
SALES (corp-wide): 76.5B **Privately Held**
WEB: www.kaiser.com
SIC: **6324** Hospital & medical service plans
HQ: Kaiser Foundation Hospitals Inc
   1 Kaiser Plz
   Oakland CA 94612
   510 271-6611

(P-9961)
KAISER FOUNDATION HOSPITALS
Also Called: Kaiser Foundation Health Plan
1550 W Manchester Ave, Los Angeles (90047-5424)
PHONE..................................800 954-8000
EMP: 85
SALES (corp-wide): 76.5B **Privately Held**
SIC: **6324** Hospital & medical service plans
HQ: Kaiser Foundation Hospitals Inc
   1 Kaiser Plz
   Oakland CA 94612
   510 271-6611

(P-9962)
KAISER FOUNDATION HOSPITALS
Also Called: Kaiser Foundation Health Plan
255 W Macarthur Blvd, Oakland (94611-5641)
PHONE..................................510 752-7864
Albert Carver, *Branch Mgr*
EMP: 85
SALES (corp-wide): 76.5B **Privately Held**
SIC: **6324** Hospital & medical service plans
HQ: Kaiser Foundation Hospitals Inc
   1 Kaiser Plz
   Oakland CA 94612
   510 271-6611

(P-9963)
KAISER FOUNDATION HOSPITALS
Also Called: Kaiser Foundation Health Plan
4785 N 1st St, Fresno (93726-0513)
PHONE..................................559 448-4555
EMP: 85
SALES (corp-wide): 76.5B **Privately Held**
SIC: **6324** Hospital & medical service plans
HQ: Kaiser Foundation Hospitals Inc
   1 Kaiser Plz
   Oakland CA 94612
   510 271-6611

(P-9964)
KAISER FOUNDATION HOSPITALS
Also Called: Kaiser Foundation Health Plan
10305 Promenade Pkwy, Elk Grove (95757-9400)
PHONE..................................916 544-6000
EMP: 85
SALES (corp-wide): 76.5B **Privately Held**
SIC: **6324** Hospital & medical service plans

HQ: Kaiser Foundation Hospitals Inc
   1 Kaiser Plz
   Oakland CA 94612
   510 271-6611

(P-9965)
KAISER FOUNDATION HOSPITALS
Also Called: Kaiser Foundation Health Plan
14011 Park Ave, Victorville (92392-2413)
PHONE..................................888 750-0036
EMP: 85
SALES (corp-wide): 76.5B **Privately Held**
SIC: **6324** Hospital & medical service plans
HQ: Kaiser Foundation Hospitals Inc
   1 Kaiser Plz
   Oakland CA 94612
   510 271-6611

(P-9966)
KAISER FOUNDATION HOSPITALS
Also Called: Kaiser Foundation Health Plan
17140 Bernardo Center Dr, San Diego (92128-2093)
PHONE..................................619 528-5000
David Kvancz, *Branch Mgr*
EMP: 85
SALES (corp-wide): 76.5B **Privately Held**
SIC: **6324** Hospital & medical service plans
HQ: Kaiser Foundation Hospitals Inc
   1 Kaiser Plz
   Oakland CA 94612
   510 271-6611

(P-9967)
KAISER FOUNDATION HOSPITALS
Also Called: Kaiser Foundation Health Plan
5893 Copley Dr, San Diego (92111-7906)
PHONE..................................619 528-5000
Justin Wu, *Surgeon*
EMP: 85
SALES (corp-wide): 76.5B **Privately Held**
SIC: **6324** Hospital & medical service plans
HQ: Kaiser Foundation Hospitals Inc
   1 Kaiser Plz
   Oakland CA 94612
   510 271-6611

(P-9968)
KAISER FOUNDATION HOSPITALS
Also Called: Kaiser Foundation Health Plan
27309 Madison Ave, Temecula (92590-5685)
PHONE..................................866 984-7483
David Kvancz, *Vice Pres*
Kevin Mielke, *Family Practiti*
EMP: 85
SALES (corp-wide): 76.5B **Privately Held**
SIC: **6324** Hospital & medical service plans
HQ: Kaiser Foundation Hospitals Inc
   1 Kaiser Plz
   Oakland CA 94612
   510 271-6611

(P-9969)
KAISER FOUNDATION HOSPITALS
Also Called: Kaiser Foundation Health Plan
11001 Sepulveda Blvd, Mission Hills (91345-1413)
PHONE..................................888 778-5000
EMP: 85
SALES (corp-wide): 76.5B **Privately Held**
SIC: **6324** Hospital & medical service plans
HQ: Kaiser Foundation Hospitals Inc
   1 Kaiser Plz
   Oakland CA 94612
   510 271-6611

(P-9970)
KAISER FOUNDATION HOSPITALS
Also Called: Kaiser Foundation Health Plan
8001 Ventura Canyon Ave, Panorama City (91402-6312)
PHONE..................................818 375-2028
Teresa Park, *Branch Mgr*
EMP: 85
SALES (corp-wide): 76.5B **Privately Held**
SIC: **6324** Hospital & medical service plans

P
R
O
D
U
C
T
S

&

S
V
C
S

HQ: Kaiser Foundation Hospitals Inc
1 Kaiser Plz
Oakland CA 94612
510 271-6611

(P-9971)
KAISER FOUNDATION HOSPITALS
Also Called: Kaiser Foundation Health Plan
27303 Sleepy Hollow Ave S, Hayward
(94545-4203)
PHONE...............510 454-1000
EMP: 85
SALES (corp-wide): 15.7B **Privately Held**
SIC: 6324
HQ: Kaiser Foundation Hospitals Inc
1 Kaiser Plz
Oakland CA 94612
510 271-6611

(P-9972)
KAISER FOUNDATION HOSPITALS
Also Called: Kaiser Foundation Health Plan
5620 Mesmer Ave, Los Angeles
(90230-6315)
PHONE...............800 954-8000
EMP: 85
SALES (corp-wide): 76.5B **Privately Held**
SIC: 6324 Hospital & medical service plans
HQ: Kaiser Foundation Hospitals Inc
1 Kaiser Plz
Oakland CA 94612
510 271-6611

(P-9973)
KAISER FOUNDATION HOSPITALS
Also Called: Vaxaville Medical Offices
1 Quality Dr, Vacaville (95688-9494)
PHONE...............707 624-4000
Murty Savitala, Principal
EMP: 50
SALES (corp-wide): 76.5B **Privately Held**
WEB: www.kaiserpermanente.org
SIC: 6324 Hospital & medical service plans
HQ: Kaiser Foundation Hospitals Inc
1 Kaiser Plz
Oakland CA 94612
510 271-6611

(P-9974)
KAISER FOUNDATION HOSPITALS
Also Called: Kaiser Foundation Health Plan
1011 S East St Fl 1, Anaheim
(92805-5749)
PHONE...............714 284-6634
Ruth Ann Ferreria, Manager
EMP: 100
SQ FT: 63,920
SALES (corp-wide): 76.5B **Privately Held**
WEB: www.kaiser.com
SIC: 6324 Hospital & medical service plans
HQ: Kaiser Foundation Hospitals Inc
1 Kaiser Plz
Oakland CA 94612
510 271-6611

(P-9975)
KAISER FOUNDATION HOSPITALS
Also Called: Kaiser Foundation Health Plan
220 E Hacienda Ave, Campbell
(95008-6617)
PHONE...............408 871-6500
Joyce Snowbarger, Manager
Kathie Latz, Human Resources
Inna Spier, Med Doctor
Shan Zhu, Med Doctor
EMP: 100
SALES (corp-wide): 76.5B **Privately Held**
WEB: www.kaiser.com
SIC: 6324 8062 Hospital & medical service plans; general medical & surgical hospitals
HQ: Kaiser Foundation Hospitals Inc
1 Kaiser Plz
Oakland CA 94612
510 271-6611

(P-9976)
KAISER FOUNDATION HOSPITALS
Also Called: Kaiser Foundation Health Plan
25 N Via Monte, Walnut Creek
(94598-2510)
PHONE...............925 926-3000
Phil Newbold, Principal
Virginia Martinez, Executive Asst
Tim Donald, Technical Mgr
Oscar Miranda, IT/INT Sup
George Panagiotopoulos, IT/INT Sup
EMP: 70
SQ FT: 79,360
SALES (corp-wide): 76.5B **Privately Held**
WEB: www.kaiser.com
SIC: 6324 Hospital & medical service plans
HQ: Kaiser Foundation Hospitals Inc
1 Kaiser Plz
Oakland CA 94612
510 271-6611

(P-9977)
KAISER FOUNDATION HOSPITALS
Also Called: Kaiser Foundation Health Plan
2071 Herndon Ave, Clovis (93611-6101)
PHONE...............559 324-5100
Angela H Kuo, Med Doctor
Brian Guthrie, Pediatrics
EMP: 99
SQ FT: 67,465
SALES (corp-wide): 76.5B **Privately Held**
WEB: www.kaiser.com
SIC: 6324 Hospital & medical service plans
HQ: Kaiser Foundation Hospitals Inc
1 Kaiser Plz
Oakland CA 94612
510 271-6611

(P-9978)
KAISER FOUNDATION HOSPITALS
Also Called: Kaiser Foundation Health Plan
21263 Erwin St, Woodland Hills
(91367-3715)
PHONE...............888 515-3500
EMP: 99
SALES (corp-wide): 76.5B **Privately Held**
WEB: www.kaiser.com
SIC: 6324 Hospital & medical service plans
HQ: Kaiser Foundation Hospitals Inc
1 Kaiser Plz
Oakland CA 94612
510 271-6611

(P-9979)
KAISER FOUNDATION HOSPITALS
Also Called: Kaiser Foundation Health Plan
1840 Sierra Gardens Dr, Roseville
(95661-2912)
PHONE...............916 784-4050
Don Vu, Principal
EMP: 99
SQ FT: 102,150
SALES (corp-wide): 76.5B **Privately Held**
WEB: www.kaiser.com
SIC: 6324 Hospital & medical service plans
HQ: Kaiser Foundation Hospitals Inc
1 Kaiser Plz
Oakland CA 94612
510 271-6611

(P-9980)
KAISER FOUNDATION HOSPITALS
Also Called: Kaiser Foundation Health Plan
40595 Westlake Dr, Oakhurst
(93644-9024)
PHONE...............559 658-8388
CHI Ly, Principal
EMP: 99
SALES (corp-wide): 76.5B **Privately Held**
WEB: www.kaiser.com
SIC: 6324 Hospital & medical service plans
HQ: Kaiser Foundation Hospitals Inc
1 Kaiser Plz
Oakland CA 94612
510 271-6611

(P-9981)
KAISER FOUNDATION HOSPITALS
Also Called: Kaiser Foundation Health Plan
2295 S Vineyard Ave, Ontario
(91761-7925)
PHONE...............888 750-0036
Arlene Freeman, Manager
EMP: 99
SALES (corp-wide): 76.5B **Privately Held**
WEB: www.kaiser.com
SIC: 6324 Hospital & medical service plans
HQ: Kaiser Foundation Hospitals Inc
1 Kaiser Plz
Oakland CA 94612
510 271-6611

(P-9982)
KAISER FOUNDATION HOSPITALS
Also Called: Kaiser Foundation Health Plan
42575 Washington St, Palm Desert
(92211-8850)
PHONE...............760 360-1475
EMP: 99
SALES (corp-wide): 76.5B **Privately Held**
WEB: www.kaiser.com
SIC: 6324 Hospital & medical service plans
HQ: Kaiser Foundation Hospitals Inc
1 Kaiser Plz
Oakland CA 94612
510 271-6611

(P-9983)
KAISER FOUNDATION HOSPITALS
Also Called: Kaiser Foundation Health Plan
888 S Hill Rd, Ventura (93003-8400)
PHONE...............888 515-3500
Michael Steinbaum, Manager
EMP: 99
SALES (corp-wide): 76.5B **Privately Held**
WEB: www.kaiser.com
SIC: 6324 Hospital & medical service plans
HQ: Kaiser Foundation Hospitals Inc
1 Kaiser Plz
Oakland CA 94612
510 271-6611

(P-9984)
KAISER FOUNDATION HOSPITALS
Also Called: Kaiser Foundation Health Plan
3401 S Harbor Blvd, Santa Ana
(92704-7933)
PHONE...............888 988-2800
Linh Kamikawa, Principal
EMP: 99
SALES (corp-wide): 76.5B **Privately Held**
WEB: www.kaiser.com
SIC: 6324 Hospital & medical service plans
HQ: Kaiser Foundation Hospitals Inc
1 Kaiser Plz
Oakland CA 94612
510 271-6611

(P-9985)
KAISER FOUNDATION HOSPITALS
Also Called: Kaiser Foundation Health Plan
1717 Date Pike, San Bernardino (92404)
PHONE...............888 750-0036
Jim Morrison, Manager
EMP: 99
SQ FT: 18,253
SALES (corp-wide): 76.5B **Privately Held**
WEB: www.kaiser.com
SIC: 6324 Hospital & medical service plans
HQ: Kaiser Foundation Hospitals Inc
1 Kaiser Plz
Oakland CA 94612
510 271-6611

(P-9986)
KAISER FOUNDATION HOSPITALS
Also Called: Kaiser Foundation Health Plan
11911 Central Ave, Chino (91710-1906)
PHONE...............888 750-0036
Ken Lee, Principal
EMP: 99
SALES (corp-wide): 76.5B **Privately Held**
WEB: www.kaiser.com
SIC: 6324 Hospital & medical service plans

HQ: Kaiser Foundation Hospitals Inc
1 Kaiser Plz
Oakland CA 94612
510 271-6611

(P-9987)
KAISER FOUNDATION HOSPITALS
Also Called: Kaiser Foundation Health Plan
395 Hickey Blvd, Daly City (94015-2770)
PHONE...............650 301-5860
Arthur Chin, Principal
Jennifer Chang, Emerg Med Spec
Natasha Brasic, Diag Radio
Samuel N Fallejo,
EMP: 99
SALES (corp-wide): 76.5B **Privately Held**
WEB: www.kaiser.com
SIC: 6324 Hospital & medical service plans
HQ: Kaiser Foundation Hospitals Inc
1 Kaiser Plz
Oakland CA 94612
510 271-6611

(P-9988)
KAISER FOUNDATION HOSPITALS
Also Called: Kaiser Foundation Health Plan
3553 Whipple Rd, Union City (94587-1507)
PHONE...............510 675-2170
Mani Kammula, Principal
EMP: 99
SALES (corp-wide): 76.5B **Privately Held**
WEB: www.kaiser.com
SIC: 6324 Hospital & medical service plans
HQ: Kaiser Foundation Hospitals Inc
1 Kaiser Plz
Oakland CA 94612
510 271-6611

(P-9989)
KAISER FOUNDATION HOSPITALS
Also Called: Kaiser Foundation Health Plan
2417 Naglee Rd, Tracy (95304-7324)
PHONE...............209 832-6339
EMP: 84
SALES (corp-wide): 76.5B **Privately Held**
WEB: www.kaiser.com
SIC: 6324 Hospital & medical service plans
HQ: Kaiser Foundation Hospitals Inc
1 Kaiser Plz
Oakland CA 94612
510 271-6611

(P-9990)
KAISER FOUNDATION HOSPITALS
Also Called: Kaiser Foundation Health Plan
901 El Camino Real, San Bruno
(94066-3009)
PHONE...............650 742-2100
Allen Wu, Principal
EMP: 99
SALES (corp-wide): 76.5B **Privately Held**
WEB: www.kaiser.com
SIC: 6324 Hospital & medical service plans
HQ: Kaiser Foundation Hospitals Inc
1 Kaiser Plz
Oakland CA 94612
510 271-6611

(P-9991)
KAISER FOUNDATION HOSPITALS
Also Called: Kaiser Foundation Health Plan
3554 Round Barn Blvd, Santa Rosa
(95403-0929)
PHONE...............707 571-3835
Jay Kelley, Manager
EMP: 99
SALES (corp-wide): 76.5B **Privately Held**
WEB: www.kaiser.com
SIC: 6324 Hospital & medical service plans
HQ: Kaiser Foundation Hospitals Inc
1 Kaiser Plz
Oakland CA 94612
510 271-6611

(P-9992)
KAISER FOUNDATION HOSPITALS
Also Called: Kaiser Foundation Health Plan
3925 Old Redwood Hwy, Santa Rosa
(95403-1719)
PHONE................................707 393-4033
Clay Wheeler, *Principal*
EMP: 99
SALES (corp-wide): 76.5B **Privately Held**
WEB: www.kaiser.com
SIC: 6324 Hospital & medical service plans
HQ: Kaiser Foundation Hospitals Inc
  1 Kaiser Plz
  Oakland CA 94612
  510 271-6611

(P-9993)
KAISER FOUNDATION HOSPITALS
Also Called: Kaiser Foundation Health Plan
1320 Standiford Ave, Modesto
(95350-0726)
PHONE................................855 268-4096
Anita Vohra, *Principal*
EMP: 99
SALES (corp-wide): 76.5B **Privately Held**
WEB: www.kaiser.com
SIC: 6324 Hospital & medical service plans
HQ: Kaiser Foundation Hospitals Inc
  1 Kaiser Plz
  Oakland CA 94612
  510 271-6611

(P-9994)
KAISER FOUNDATION HOSPITALS
Also Called: Kaiser Foundation Health Plan
5900 State Farm Dr # 100, Rohnert Park
(94928-2149)
PHONE................................707 206-3000
Noel Smith, *Branch Mgr*
Judith Heiler, *Family Practiti*
Michael Maggioncalda, *Family Practiti*
EMP: 85
SALES (corp-wide): 76.5B **Privately Held**
WEB: www.kaiser.com
SIC: 6324 Hospital & medical service plans
HQ: Kaiser Foundation Hospitals Inc
  1 Kaiser Plz
  Oakland CA 94612
  510 271-6611

(P-9995)
KAISER FOUNDATION HOSPITALS
Also Called: Kaiser Foundation Health Plan
2417 Central Ave, Alameda (94501-4515)
PHONE................................510 752-1190
Michael Gorin, *Branch Mgr*
EMP: 99
SALES (corp-wide): 76.5B **Privately Held**
WEB: www.kaiser.com
SIC: 6324 Hospital & medical service plans
HQ: Kaiser Foundation Hospitals Inc
  1 Kaiser Plz
  Oakland CA 94612
  510 271-6611

(P-9996)
KAISER FOUNDATION HOSPITALS
Also Called: Kaiser Foundation Health Plan
969 Broadway, Oakland (94607-4017)
PHONE................................510 251-0121
Mary Sage, *Branch Mgr*
EMP: 99
SALES (corp-wide): 76.5B **Privately Held**
WEB: www.kaiser.com
SIC: 6324 Hospital & medical service plans
HQ: Kaiser Foundation Hospitals Inc
  1 Kaiser Plz
  Oakland CA 94612
  510 271-6611

(P-9997)
KAISER FOUNDATION HOSPITALS
Also Called: Kaiser Foundation Health Plan
9333 Rosecrans Ave, Bellflower
(90706-2141)
PHONE................................562 461-3084
Arlene M Dolorico MD, *Manager*
EMP: 99

SALES (corp-wide): 76.5B **Privately Held**
WEB: www.kaiser.com
SIC: 6324 Hospital & medical service plans
HQ: Kaiser Foundation Hospitals Inc
  1 Kaiser Plz
  Oakland CA 94612
  510 271-6611

(P-9998)
KAISER FOUNDATION HOSPITALS
Also Called: Kaiser Foundation Health Plan
2651 Highland Ave, Selma (93662-3392)
PHONE................................559 898-6000
Hong-Hanh Ton-Nu, *Principal*
EMP: 99
SQ FT: 37,081
SALES (corp-wide): 76.5B **Privately Held**
WEB: www.kaiser.com
SIC: 6324 Hospital & medical service plans
HQ: Kaiser Foundation Hospitals Inc
  1 Kaiser Plz
  Oakland CA 94612
  510 271-6611

(P-9999)
KAISER FOUNDATION HOSPITALS
Also Called: Kaiser Foundation Health Plan
4201 W Chapman Ave, Orange
(92868-1505)
PHONE................................714 748-7622
Doug Gustason, *Branch Mgr*
EMP: 99
SALES (corp-wide): 76.5B **Privately Held**
WEB: www.kaiser.com
SIC: 6324 Hospital & medical service plans
HQ: Kaiser Foundation Hospitals Inc
  1 Kaiser Plz
  Oakland CA 94612
  510 271-6611

(P-10000)
KAISER FOUNDATION HOSPITALS
Also Called: Kaiser Foundation Health Plan
1717 E Vista Chino Ste B2, Palm Springs
(92262-3569)
PHONE................................866 370-1942
Ed McMahon, *Principal*
EMP: 99
SALES (corp-wide): 76.5B **Privately Held**
WEB: www.kaiser.com
SIC: 6324 Hospital & medical service plans
HQ: Kaiser Foundation Hospitals Inc
  1 Kaiser Plz
  Oakland CA 94612
  510 271-6611

(P-10001)
KAISER FOUNDATION HOSPITALS
Also Called: Kaiser Foundation Health Plan
20790 Madrona Ave, Torrance
(90503-3777)
PHONE................................800 780-1230
Shirley Oka, *Principal*
EMP: 99
SALES (corp-wide): 76.5B **Privately Held**
WEB: www.kaiser.com
SIC: 6324 Hospital & medical service plans
HQ: Kaiser Foundation Hospitals Inc
  1 Kaiser Plz
  Oakland CA 94612
  510 271-6611

(P-10002)
KAISER FOUNDATION HOSPITALS
Also Called: Kaiser Foundation Health Plan
365 E Hillcrest Dr, Thousand Oaks
(91360-5820)
PHONE................................888 515-3500
Beverly Torres, *Branch Mgr*
EMP: 72
SALES (corp-wide): 76.5B **Privately Held**
WEB: www.kaiser.com
SIC: 6324 Hospital & medical service plans
HQ: Kaiser Foundation Hospitals Inc
  1 Kaiser Plz
  Oakland CA 94612
  510 271-6611

(P-10003)
KAISER FOUNDATION HOSPITALS
Also Called: Kaiser Foundation Health Plan
3900 Alamo St, Simi Valley (93063-2111)
PHONE................................888 515-3500
Nami Kim, *Principal*
EMP: 99
SALES (corp-wide): 76.5B **Privately Held**
WEB: www.kaiser.com
SIC: 6324 Hospital & medical service plans
HQ: Kaiser Foundation Hospitals Inc
  1 Kaiser Plz
  Oakland CA 94612
  510 271-6611

(P-10004)
KAISER FOUNDATION HOSPITALS
Also Called: Kaiser Foundation Health Plan
30400 Camino Capistrano, San Juan
Capistrano (92675-1300)
PHONE................................888 988-2800
Patrick Roth, *Branch Mgr*
EMP: 99
SALES (corp-wide): 76.5B **Privately Held**
WEB: www.kaiser.com
SIC: 6324 Hospital & medical service plans
HQ: Kaiser Foundation Hospitals Inc
  1 Kaiser Plz
  Oakland CA 94612
  510 271-6611

(P-10005)
KAISER FOUNDATION HOSPITALS
Also Called: Kaiser Foundation Health Plan
9961 Sierra Ave, Fontana (92335-6720)
P.O. Box None (92335)
PHONE................................909 427-3910
Gerald Mc Call, *Branch Mgr*
Vikas Mehta, *Med Doctor*
EMP: 99
SALES (corp-wide): 76.5B **Privately Held**
WEB: www.kaiser.com
SIC: 6324 Hospital & medical service plans
HQ: Kaiser Foundation Hospitals Inc
  1 Kaiser Plz
  Oakland CA 94612
  510 271-6611

(P-10006)
KAISER FOUNDATION HOSPITALS
Also Called: Kaiser Foundation Health Plan
12200 Bellflower Blvd, Downey
(90242-2804)
PHONE................................562 622-4190
Jim Harrington, *Branch Mgr*
EMP: 99
SALES (corp-wide): 76.5B **Privately Held**
WEB: www.kaiser.com
SIC: 6324 Hospital & medical service plans
HQ: Kaiser Foundation Hospitals Inc
  1 Kaiser Plz
  Oakland CA 94612
  510 271-6611

(P-10007)
KAISER FOUNDATION HOSPITALS
Also Called: Kaiser Foundation Health Plan
5755 Cottle Rd, San Jose (95123-3640)
PHONE................................408 972-3376
Donald D Mordecai, *Branch Mgr*
Kathleen Bonal, *Psychologist*
Kavitha Raja, *Neurology*
EMP: 99
SALES (corp-wide): 76.5B **Privately Held**
WEB: www.kaiser.com
SIC: 6324 8011 6321 Hospital & medical
service plans; offices & clinics of medical
doctors; accident & health insurance
HQ: Kaiser Foundation Hospitals Inc
  1 Kaiser Plz
  Oakland CA 94612
  510 271-6611

(P-10008)
KAISER FOUNDATION HOSPITALS
Also Called: Kaiser Foundation Health Plan
11666 Sherman Way, North Hollywood
(91605-5831)
PHONE................................818 503-7082
Charles Ford, *Manager*
EMP: 53
SALES (corp-wide): 76.5B **Privately Held**
WEB: www.kaiser.com
SIC: 6324 Hospital & medical service plans
HQ: Kaiser Foundation Hospitals Inc
  1 Kaiser Plz
  Oakland CA 94612
  510 271-6611

(P-10009)
KAISER FOUNDATION HOSPITALS
Also Called: Kaiser Foundation Health Plan
1625 I St, Modesto (95354-1121)
P.O. Box 577680 (95357-7680)
PHONE................................209 557-1000
Larry Stump, *Director*
EMP: 60
SALES (corp-wide): 76.5B **Privately Held**
WEB: www.kaiser.com
SIC: 6324 Health maintenance organiza-
tion (HMO), insurance only
HQ: Kaiser Foundation Hospitals Inc
  1 Kaiser Plz
  Oakland CA 94612
  510 271-6611

(P-10010)
KAISER FOUNDATION HOSPITALS
Also Called: Kaiser Foundation Health Plan
200 N Lewis St Fl 1, Orange (92868-1538)
PHONE................................888 988-2800
Harriet Brown, *Director*
James De Fontes III, *Anesthesiology*
EMP: 60
SALES (corp-wide): 76.5B **Privately Held**
WEB: www.kaiser.com
SIC: 6324 8011 Hospital & medical service
plans; clinic, operated by physicians
HQ: Kaiser Foundation Hospitals Inc
  1 Kaiser Plz
  Oakland CA 94612
  510 271-6611

(P-10011)
KAISER FUNDATION HLTH PLAN INC
3801 Howe St, Oakland (94611-5312)
PHONE................................510 752-7644
EMP: 85
SALES (corp-wide): 76.5B **Privately Held**
SIC: 6324 Health maintenance organiza-
tion (HMO), insurance only
PA: Kaiser Foundation Health Plan, Inc.
  1 Kaiser Plz
  Oakland CA 94612
  510 271-5800

(P-10012)
KAISER FUNDATION HLTH PLAN INC
4460 Hacienda Dr, Pleasanton
(94588-2761)
PHONE................................510 271-5800
Linsey Dicks, *Manager*
Sudha Sharma, *Exec Dir*
Fred Miller, *Administration*
Ilana Soyferman, *Info Tech Mgr*
Amarjit Hothi, *Technology*
EMP: 100
SALES (corp-wide): 76.5B **Privately Held**
WEB: www.kaiser.com
SIC: 6324 Health maintenance organiza-
tion (HMO), insurance only
PA: Kaiser Foundation Health Plan, Inc.
  1 Kaiser Plz
  Oakland CA 94612
  510 271-5800

(P-10013)
KAISER FUNDATION HLTH PLAN INC
1950 Franklin St Fl 3, Oakland
(94612-5190)
PHONE................................510 987-2255

PRODUCTS & SVCS

Jean Nudellman, *Manager*
EMP: 70
SALES (corp-wide): 76.5B **Privately Held**
WEB: www.kaiser.com
SIC: 6324 Health maintenance organization (HMO), insurance only
PA: Kaiser Foundation Health Plan, Inc.
  1 Kaiser Plz
  Oakland CA 94612
  510 271-5800

(P-10014)
LIBERTY DENTAL PLAN CAL INC
340 Commerce Ste 100, Irvine
(92602-1358)
PHONE..................949 223-0007
Amir Hossein Neshat, *Principal*
Randy Brecher, *Vice Pres*
Terry Allen, *General Mgr*
John McCarthy, *General Mgr*
Anita Garcia, *Network Mgr*
EMP: 300
SALES (est): 194.5MM **Privately Held**
SIC: 6324 Dental insurance

(P-10015)
LIBERTY DENTAL PLAN NEVADA INC
340 Commerce, Irvine (92602-1334)
PHONE..................888 703-6999
Amir Neshat, *President*
EMP: 54
SALES (est): 7.1MM **Privately Held**
SIC: 6324 Dental insurance

(P-10016)
LOCAL INITIATIVE HEALTH AUTHOR
Also Called: L.A. Care Health Plan
1055 W 7th St Fl 10, Los Angeles
(90017-2750)
PHONE..................213 694-1250
John Baackes, *CEO*
Cindy Doorn, *Partner*
Dino Kasdagly, *COO*
Marie Montgomery, *CFO*
Tim Reilly, *CFO*
EMP: 900
SALES (est): 329.7MM **Privately Held**
SIC: 6324 Health maintenance organization (HMO), insurance only

(P-10017)
MANAGED HEALTH NETWORK
7755 Center Ave Ste 700, Huntington
Beach (92647-9126)
PHONE..................714 934-5519
Carol McLean, *Branch Mgr*
Brian Staller, *Director*
Dewitt Whitehurst, *Manager*
EMP: 580 **Publicly Held**
SIC: 6324 Hospital & medical service plans
HQ: Managed Health Network
  2370 Kerner Blvd
  San Rafael CA 94901
  415 460-8168

(P-10018)
MANAGED HEALTH NETWORK (DH)
2370 Kerner Blvd, San Rafael
(94901-5613)
P.O. Box 10207 (94912-0207)
PHONE..................415 460-8168
Jeffrey Bairstow, *CEO*
Jerry Coil, *President*
Steven Sell, *President*
Linda Brisbane, *COO*
Jonathan Wormhoudt, *COO*
EMP: 500
SQ FT: 97,314
SALES (est): 195.5MM **Publicly Held**
SIC: 6324 8099 8093 8011 Hospital & medical service plans; health maintenance organization (HMO), insurance only; medical services organization; specialty outpatient clinics; offices & clinics of medical doctors
HQ: Health Net, Llc
  21650 Oxnard St Fl 25
  Woodland Hills CA 91367
  818 676-6000

(P-10019)
MOLINA HEALTHCARE INC
1500 Hughes Way, Long Beach
(90810-1870)
PHONE..................310 221-3031
Sathiyaraj Thangavel, *Info Tech Mgr*
EMP: 272
SALES (corp-wide): 18.8B **Publicly Held**
SIC: 6324 6321 Hospital & medical service plans; accident & health insurance
PA: Molina Healthcare, Inc.
  200 Oceangate Ste 100
  Long Beach CA 90802
  562 435-3666

(P-10020)
ON LOK SENIOR HEALTH SERVICES (PA)
Also Called: On Lok Lifeways
1333 Bush St, San Francisco
(94109-5691)
PHONE..................415 292-8888
Robert Edmondson, *CEO*
Grace LI, *COO*
Sue Wong, *CFO*
Niewiarowski Chris, *Technology*
Eileen Kunz, *Director*
EMP: 570
SQ FT: 40,000
SALES: 120.9MM **Privately Held**
SIC: 6324 8082 Health maintenance organization (HMO), insurance only; home health care services

(P-10021)
ON LOK SENIOR HEALTH SERVICES
Also Called: On Lok Life Ways
3683 Peralta Blvd, Fremont (94536-3708)
PHONE..................510 249-2700
Janice Fujii, *Manager*
EMP: 50
SALES (corp-wide): 120.9MM **Privately Held**
SIC: 6324 8082 Health maintenance organization (HMO), insurance only; home health care services
PA: On Lok Senior Health Services
  1333 Bush St
  San Francisco CA 94109
  415 292-8888

(P-10022)
OPTUMRX INC
Also Called: Prescription Solutions
2858 Loker Ave E Ste 100, Carlsbad
(92010-6673)
P.O. Box 509075, San Diego (92150-9075)
PHONE..................760 804-2399
Sean O'Rourke, *Manager*
Erin Grant, *Administration*
EMP: 400
SALES (corp-wide): 226.2B **Publicly Held**
SIC: 6324 Hospital & medical service plans
HQ: Optumrx, Inc.
  2300 Main St
  Irvine CA 92614

(P-10023)
OPTUMRX INC (DH)
Also Called: Prescription Solutions
2300 Main St, Irvine (92614-6223)
P.O. Box 509075, San Diego (92150-9075)
PHONE..................714 825-3600
Mark Thierer, *CEO*
Timothy Wicks, *President*
Jeff Park, *COO*
Jeffrey Grosklags, *CFO*
David Oberg, *Vice Pres*
EMP: 300
SALES (est): 22.2B
SALES (corp-wide): 226.2B **Publicly Held**
SIC: 6324 6321 Hospital & medical service plans; accident & health insurance
HQ: United Healthcare Services Inc.
  9900 Bren Rd E Ste 300w
  Minnetonka MN 55343
  952 936-1300

(P-10024)
PACIFICARE DENTAL
3110 W Lake Center Dr, Santa Ana
(92704-6917)
PHONE..................661 631-8613
Jerry Vaccaro, *President*
EMP: 195 **EST:** 1972
SQ FT: 5,000
SALES (est): 54.8MM
SALES (corp-wide): 226.2B **Publicly Held**
SIC: 6324 Dental insurance
HQ: Pacificare Health Plan Administrators, Inc.
  3120 W Lake Center Dr
  Santa Ana CA 92704
  714 825-5200

(P-10025)
PACIFICARE HEALTH PLAN ADMIN (DH)
3120 W Lake Center Dr, Santa Ana
(92704-6917)
P.O. Box 25186 (92799-5186)
PHONE..................714 825-5200
David Reed, *Ch of Bd*
Coy F Baugh, *Treasurer*
Debra Lord, *Project Mgr*
Marilyn Drysch, *VP Finance*
EMP: 400 **EST:** 1975
SQ FT: 220,000
SALES: 12.2B
SALES (corp-wide): 226.2B **Publicly Held**
SIC: 6324 Group hospitalization plans

(P-10026)
PACIFICARE HEALTH SYSTEMS LLC (HQ)
5995 Plaza Dr, Cypress (90630-5028)
PHONE..................714 952-1121
Howard Phanstiel, *CEO*
Paul Bihm, *Vice Pres*
Joy Higa, *Vice Pres*
Paul Drago, *Executive*
Nikkie Pool, *Executive Asst*
EMP: 550
SQ FT: 104,000
SALES (est): 12.6B
SALES (corp-wide): 226.2B **Publicly Held**
WEB: www.pacificare.com
SIC: 6324 Health maintenance organization (HMO), insurance only
PA: Unitedhealth Group Incorporated
  9900 Bren Rd E Ste 300w
  Minnetonka MN 55343
  952 936-1300

(P-10027)
PACIFICDENTAL BENEFITS INC (PA)
2300 Clayton Rd Ste 1000, Concord
(94520-2168)
PHONE..................925 363-6000
John Gaebel, *President*
Randy Breacher, *CFO*
Nilesh Patel, *Vice Pres*
EMP: 145
SQ FT: 18,530
SALES (est): 40.5MM **Privately Held**
SIC: 6324 6321 Dental insurance; accident & health insurance

(P-10028)
PARTNERSHIP HEALTH PLAN CAL
4665 Business Center Dr, Fairfield
(94534-1675)
PHONE..................707 863-4100
Jack Horn, *CEO*
Liz Gibboney, *COO*
Gary Erickson, *CFO*
Lisa Malvo, *Associate Dir*
Jennifer Bush, *Executive Asst*
EMP: 290
SQ FT: 75,000
SALES (est): 231.9MM **Privately Held**
SIC: 6324 Health maintenance organization (HMO), insurance only

(P-10029)
PERMANENTE KAISER INTL (HQ)
Also Called: Kp International
1 Kaiser Plz, Oakland (94612-3610)
PHONE..................510 271-5910
Bernard J Tyson, *CEO*
Raymond J Baxter, *CEO*
Bill Marsh, *COO*
Kathy Lancaster, *CFO*
Megan Gannaway, *Officer*
EMP: 146
SALES (est): 822MM
SALES (corp-wide): 76.5B **Privately Held**
SIC: 6324 Hospital & medical service plans
PA: Kaiser Foundation Health Plan, Inc.
  1 Kaiser Plz
  Oakland CA 94612
  510 271-5800

(P-10030)
PERMANENTE MEDICAL GROUP INC
220 Oyster Point Blvd, South San Francisco (94080-1911)
PHONE..................650 827-6500
Milan Patel, *Branch Mgr*
EMP: 70
SALES (corp-wide): 76.5B **Privately Held**
SIC: 6324 Hospital & medical service plans
HQ: The Permanente Medical Group Inc
  1950 Franklin St Fl 18th
  Oakland CA 94612
  866 858-2226

(P-10031)
PERMANENTE MEDICAL GROUP INC
900 Veterans Blvd Ste 400, Redwood City
(94063-1742)
PHONE..................650 598-2852
Diana Patino, *Principal*
EMP: 70
SALES (corp-wide): 76.5B **Privately Held**
SIC: 6324 Hospital & medical service plans
HQ: The Permanente Medical Group Inc
  1950 Franklin St Fl 18th
  Oakland CA 94612
  866 858-2226

(P-10032)
PERMANENTE MEDICAL GROUP INC
1725 Eastshore Hwy, Berkeley
(94710-1703)
PHONE..................510 559-5119
Susan Yee, *Administration*
EMP: 58
SALES (corp-wide): 76.5B **Privately Held**
WEB: www.permanente.net
SIC: 6324 Hospital & medical service plans
HQ: The Permanente Medical Group Inc
  1950 Franklin St Fl 18th
  Oakland CA 94612
  866 858-2226

(P-10033)
PERMANENTE MEDICAL GROUP INC
2238 Geary Blvd, San Francisco
(94115-3416)
PHONE..................415 833-2000
Philip R Madvig MD Physn, *Principal*
Gregory V Mandrussow, *Emerg Med Spec*
Leah Klinger, *Med Doctor*
Yulan Liao, *Med Doctor*
Dee Marie Munoz, *Pharmacist*
EMP: 140
SALES (corp-wide): 76.5B **Privately Held**
WEB: www.permanente.net
SIC: 6324 Hospital & medical service plans
HQ: The Permanente Medical Group Inc
  1950 Franklin St Fl 18th
  Oakland CA 94612
  866 858-2226

(P-10034)
PERMANENTE MEDICAL GROUP INC
3555 Whipple Rd, Union City (94587-1507)
PHONE..................510 675-4010
Deana Medinas, *Director*
EMP: 100

SALES (corp-wide): 76.5B **Privately Held**
WEB: www.permanente.net
SIC: **6324** Hospital & medical service plans
HQ: The Permanente Medical Group Inc
1950 Franklin St Fl 18th
Oakland CA 94612
866 858-2226

(P-10035)
PERMANENTE MEDICAL GROUP INC
Also Called: Kaiser Prmnnte Modesto Med Ctr
4601 Dale Rd, Modesto (95356-9718)
PHONE..............................209 735-5000
Jennifer A Beard, *Principal*
Hesham Attaya, *Surgeon*
Amardeep S Deol, *Obstetrician*
Naresh A Patel, *Hematology*
Cynthia Lan, *Internal Med*
EMP: 63
SALES (corp-wide): 76.5B **Privately Held**
SIC: **6324** Hospital & medical service plans
HQ: The Permanente Medical Group Inc
1950 Franklin St Fl 18th
Oakland CA 94612
866 858-2226

(P-10036)
PHYSICIAN ASSOC SAN GABRIEL
199 S Los Robles Ave, Pasadena (91101-2452)
PHONE..............................626 817-8300
Barton Wald MD, *President*
Theresa David, *COO*
EMP: 210
SALES (est): 65.1MM **Privately Held**
WEB: www.physicianassoc.com
SIC: **6324** Health maintenance organization (HMO), insurance only

(P-10037)
PRIVATE MEDICAL-CARE INC
12898 Towne Center Dr, Cerritos (90703-8546)
PHONE..............................562 924-8311
Robert Elliott, *President*
EMP: 154
SALES (est): 40.4MM
SALES (corp-wide): 5.8B **Privately Held**
WEB: www.deltadentalca.org
SIC: **6324** Dental insurance
PA: Delta Dental Of California
560 Mission St Ste 1300
San Francisco CA 94105
415 972-8300

(P-10038)
PRUDENTIAL INSUR CO OF AMER
180 Montgomery St # 1900, San Francisco (94104-4205)
PHONE..............................415 486-3050
Tom Rhee, *Manager*
EMP: 97
SALES (corp-wide): 62.9B **Publicly Held**
SIC: **6324 6321 6311 6411** Health maintenance organization (HMO), insurance only; accident & health insurance; life insurance; insurance agents
HQ: The Prudential Insurance Company Of America
751 Broad St
Newark NJ 07102
973 802-6000

(P-10039)
REW INC
973 Higuera St Ste A, San Luis Obispo (93401-3614)
PHONE..............................805 541-1308
Robert Wacker, *CEO*
Sarah Robertson, *Admin Asst*
EMP: 63
SALES: 950K **Privately Held**
SIC: **6324** Hospital & medical service plans

(P-10040)
SAFEGUARD HEALTH ENTPS INC (HQ)
95 Enterprise Ste 100, Aliso Viejo (92656-2605)
PHONE..............................800 880-1800
Steven J Baileys DDS, *Ch of Bd*

James E Buncher, *President*
Stephen J Baker, *COO*
Dennis L Gates, *CFO*
Ronald I Brendzel, *Senior VP*
EMP: 355
SQ FT: 68,000
SALES (est): 88.3MM
SALES (corp-wide): 67.9B **Publicly Held**
SIC: **6324** Dental insurance
PA: Metlife, Inc.
200 Park Ave
New York NY 10166
212 578-9500

(P-10041)
SCAN CALIFORNIA MANAGEMENT CO
3800 Kilroy Airport Way, Long Beach (90806-2494)
PHONE..............................562 989-5100
Chris Wing, *CEO*
EMP: 966
SALES (est): 1.1MM
SALES (corp-wide): 2.8B **Privately Held**
SIC: **6324** Hospital & medical service plans
PA: Scan Group
3800 Kilroy Arprt Way # 100
Long Beach CA 90806
562 308-2733

(P-10042)
SCAN GROUP (PA)
3800 Kilroy Arprt Way # 100, Long Beach (90806-2494)
PHONE..............................562 308-2733
Chris Wing, *CEO*
Vinod Mohan, *CFO*
Lisa N Davis, *Vice Pres*
Eve Gelb, *Vice Pres*
Kathryn Qin, *Vice Pres*
EMP: 306
SALES (est): 2.8B **Privately Held**
SIC: **6324** Hospital & medical service plans

(P-10043)
SECOND OPINION MED GRP INC
2876 Sycamore Dr Ste 305, Simi Valley (93065-1550)
PHONE..............................805 496-4315
Rajeswari Ananda, *Principal*
Punita Khanna, *Vice Pres*
EMP: 99
SQ FT: 1,500
SALES (est): 13.1MM **Privately Held**
SIC: **6324** Hospital & medical service plans

(P-10044)
SENIOR CARE (PA)
Also Called: Scan Health Plan
3800 Kilroy Airport Way, Long Beach (90806-2494)
P.O. Box 22616 (90801-5616)
PHONE..............................562 989-5100
David Schmidt, *CEO*
Jennie Hansen, *Bd of Directors*
Rebecca Learner, *Senior VP*
Virginia Havai, *Vice Pres*
Roger Lapp, *Vice Pres*
EMP: 857
SQ FT: 119,219
SALES (est): 329.7MM **Privately Held**
WEB: www.scanhealthplan.com
SIC: **6324** Health maintenance organization (HMO), insurance only

(P-10045)
SENIOR CARE
Also Called: Independence At Home Iah
2501 Cherry Ave Ste 380, Long Beach (90755-2050)
PHONE..............................562 492-9878
Kit Donaldson, *Branch Mgr*
EMP: 55
SALES (est): 4.6MM
SALES (corp-wide): 329.7MM **Privately Held**
WEB: www.scanhealthplan.com
SIC: **6324** Health maintenance organization (HMO), insurance only
PA: Senior Care Action Network Foundation
3800 Kilroy Airport Way
Long Beach CA 90806
562 989-5100

(P-10046)
SHARP HEALTH PLAN
8520 Tech Way Ste 200, San Diego (92123-1450)
PHONE..............................858 499-8300
Melissa Hayden-Cook, *President*
Leslie Pels-Beck, *COO*
Rita Datko, *CFO*
Michael Byrd, *Vice Pres*
Dr Cary Shames, *Vice Pres*
EMP: 98
SALES: 322.6MM
SALES (corp-wide): 3.4B **Privately Held**
SIC: **6324** Health maintenance organization (HMO), insurance only
PA: Sharp Healthcare
8695 Spectrum Center Blvd
San Diego CA 92123
858 499-4000

(P-10047)
SIERRA HEALTH SERVICES LLC
2423 W March Ln Ste 100, Stockton (95207-8250)
P.O. Box 7096 (95267-0096)
PHONE..............................209 956-7725
Earl Ohgman, *Mng Member*
Cindy Birmingham,
Candice Almonte, *Director*
Gianelli Buensuceso CPC, *Director*
Zandra Padilla, *Director*
EMP: 50
SALES (est): 25.8MM **Privately Held**
SIC: **6324 8011** Hospital & medical service plans; specialized medical practitioners, except internal; physicians' office, including specialists

(P-10048)
SOUTHERN CAL PRMNNTE MED GROUP
13652 Cantara St, Panorama City (91402-5423)
PHONE..............................800 272-3500
Arthur Phelps, *Branch Mgr*
Earle Johnson, *Officer*
Mario K Ngan, *Pathologist*
Ramamohan RAO, *Obstetrician*
Lauren E Krieger, *Osteopathy*
EMP: 70
SALES (corp-wide): 3.5B **Privately Held**
SIC: **6324** Hospital & medical service plans
PA: Southern California Permanente Medical Group
393 Walnut Dr
Pasadena CA 91107
626 405-5704

(P-10049)
SOUTHERN CAL PRMNNTE MED GROUP
Also Called: Kaiser Foundation Health Plan
5855 Copley Dr Ste 250, San Diego (92111-7908)
PHONE..............................858 974-1000
Tom Cooper, *Manager*
Travis Van Ness, *Admin Asst*
Eugene Rhee, *Urology*
Dan McDermott, *Podiatrist*
EMP: 75
SQ FT: 89,984
SALES (corp-wide): 3.5B **Privately Held**
WEB: www.kaiser.com
SIC: **6324** Health maintenance organization (HMO), insurance only
PA: Southern California Permanente Medical Group
393 Walnut Dr
Pasadena CA 91107
626 405-5704

(P-10050)
SOUTHERN CAL PRMNNTE MED GROUP
10800 Magnolia Ave, Riverside (92505-3043)
PHONE..............................866 984-7483
Jeffrey A Weisz, *Principal*
EMP: 266
SALES (corp-wide): 3.5B **Privately Held**
SIC: **6324** Hospital & medical service plans

PA: Southern California Permanente Medical Group
393 Walnut Dr
Pasadena CA 91107
626 405-5704

(P-10051)
SOUTHERN CAL PRMNNTE MED GROUP
1511 W Garvey Ave N, West Covina (91790-2138)
PHONE..............................626 960-4844
Jarvis Ngati, *Psychiatry*
Christine Um, *Psychiatry*
Charina Tubon, *Nurse*
EMP: 70
SALES (corp-wide): 3.5B **Privately Held**
SIC: **6324** Hospital & medical service plans
PA: Southern California Permanente Medical Group
393 Walnut Dr
Pasadena CA 91107
626 405-5704

(P-10052)
SOUTHERN CAL PRMNNTE MED GROUP
Also Called: Tustin Executive Center
17542 17th St Ste 300, Tustin (92780-1960)
PHONE..............................714 734-4500
Adamma Agufoh, *Director*
EMP: 70
SALES (corp-wide): 3.5B **Privately Held**
SIC: **6324** Hospital & medical service plans
PA: Southern California Permanente Medical Group
393 Walnut Dr
Pasadena CA 91107
626 405-5704

(P-10053)
SOUTHERN CAL PRMNNTE MED GROUP (PA)
Also Called: Kaiser Permanente
393 Walnut Dr, Pasadena (91107)
PHONE..............................626 405-5704
Bernard J Tyson, *Principal*
Kathryn Beiser, *Vice Pres*
Vanessa M Benavides, *Vice Pres*
Diana Atkinson, *Project Mgr*
Pam Asbill, *Analyst*
EMP: 60 EST: 1981
SQ FT: 600,000
SALES (est): 3.5B **Privately Held**
SIC: **6324** Health maintenance organization (HMO), insurance only

(P-10054)
SOUTHERN CAL PRMNNTE MED GROUP
Also Called: S C P M G
1255 W Arrow Hwy, San Dimas (91773-2340)
PHONE..............................909 394-2505
EMP: 50
SALES (corp-wide): 3.5B **Privately Held**
WEB: www.permanente.net
SIC: **6324** Hospital & medical service plans
PA: Southern California Permanente Medical Group
393 Walnut Dr
Pasadena CA 91107
626 405-5704

(P-10055)
SOUTHERN CAL PRMNNTE MED GROUP
6860 Avenida Encinas, Carlsbad (92011-3201)
PHONE..............................619 528-5000
Walter Borschel, *Administration*
Dorothy Honda,
EMP: 532
SALES (corp-wide): 3.5B **Privately Held**
SIC: **6324** Hospital & medical service plans
PA: Southern California Permanente Medical Group
393 Walnut Dr
Pasadena CA 91107
626 405-5704

P
R
O
D
U
C
T
S

&

S
V
C
S

(P-10056)
SOUTHERN CAL PRMNNTE MED GROUP
Also Called: Kaiser Permanente
9353 Imprl Hwy Grdn Med, Downey (90242)
PHONE..................562 657-2200
Elizabeth Norheim, *Orthopedist*
Yawen Wang, *Neurology*
Ted Leem, *Otolaryngology*
Nikki Du, *Pharmacist*
Kyle Goldberg, *Director*
EMP: 4341
SALES (corp-wide): 3.5B **Privately Held**
SIC: 6324 Hospital & medical service plans
PA: Southern California Permanente Medical Group
393 Walnut Dr
Pasadena CA 91107
626 405-5704

(P-10057)
SUPERIOR VISION SERVICES INC (PA)
Also Called: Versant Health
11090 White Rock Rd, Rancho Cordova (95670-6082)
PHONE..................800 507-3800
Kirk Rothrock, *CEO*
Jonathan Bicknell, *CFO*
Brian Silverberg, *CFO*
Kimberley Hess, *Senior VP*
Stephanie Lucas, *Senior VP*
EMP: 70
SQ FT: 12,000
SALES (est): 33.7MM **Privately Held**
WEB: www.superiorvision.com
SIC: 6324 Hospital & medical service plans

(P-10058)
UHC OF CALIFORNIA (DH)
Also Called: Pacificare of California
5995 Plaza Dr, Cypress (90630-5028)
PHONE..................714 952-1121
Brad A Bowlus, *Principal*
Michael Montevideo, *Treasurer*
Lisa Espinosa, *Branch Mgr*
Joseph S Konowiecki, *Admin Sec*
Melanie Zierer, *Technology*
EMP: 800
SALES (est): 257.3MM
SALES (corp-wide): 226.2B **Publicly Held**
WEB: www.rxsol.com
SIC: 6324 8732 Health maintenance organization (HMO), insurance only; commercial nonphysical research

(P-10059)
UNITED BEHAVIORAL HEALTH
Also Called: Pacificare
2300 Clayton Rd Ste 1000, Concord (94520-2168)
PHONE..................925 246-1343
Fred Dodson, *Branch Mgr*
Michael Ponce, *Technician*
EMP: 150
SALES (corp-wide): 226.2B **Publicly Held**
WEB: www.unitedbehavioralhealth.com
SIC: 6324 Health maintenance organization (HMO), insurance only
HQ: United Behavioral Health
425 Market St Fl 18
San Francisco CA 94105
415 547-1403

(P-10060)
UNITEDHEALTH GROUP INC
Also Called: Pacificare Health Systems
7891 Moonmist Cir, Huntington Beach (92648-5434)
PHONE..................714 969-9050
Andrew Hall, *Branch Mgr*
Vinod Burugupalli, *Director*
Scott Schulz, *Director*
EMP: 300
SALES (corp-wide): 226.2B **Publicly Held**
WEB: www.unitedhealthgroup.com
SIC: 6324 Health maintenance organization (HMO), insurance only
PA: Unitedhealth Group Incorporated
9900 Bren Rd E Ste 300w
Minnetonka MN 55343
952 936-1300

(P-10061)
UNITEDHEALTH GROUP INC
Also Called: Pacificare Health Systems
5701 Katella Ave, Cypress (90630-5006)
PHONE..................952 936-1300
Mike Wallace, *Branch Mgr*
Audrey Palmer, *Administration*
Debbie Navarro, *Info Tech Dir*
Gaurav Jain, *Info Tech Mgr*
Frank Mesa, *Info Tech Mgr*
EMP: 100
SALES (corp-wide): 226.2B **Publicly Held**
WEB: www.unitedhealthgroup.com
SIC: 6324 Health maintenance organization (HMO), insurance only
PA: Unitedhealth Group Incorporated
9900 Bren Rd E Ste 300w
Minnetonka MN 55343
952 936-1300

(P-10062)
UNITEDHEALTH GROUP INC
2080 E 20th St, Chico (95928-7702)
PHONE..................530 879-8251
Rhonda Work, *Project Mgr*
Shannon Cloud, *Opers Spvr*
Mark Franks, *Opers Staff*
Denise Crawford, *Manager*
Wendy Pugliano, *Manager*
EMP: 270
SALES (corp-wide): 226.2B **Publicly Held**
SIC: 6324 Health maintenance organization (HMO), insurance only
PA: Unitedhealth Group Incorporated
9900 Bren Rd E Ste 300w
Minnetonka MN 55343
952 936-1300

(P-10063)
VISION SERVICE PLAN (PA)
Also Called: C V S Optical Lab Div
3333 Quality Dr, Rancho Cordova (95670-9757)
PHONE..................916 851-5000
James Robinson Lynch, *CEO*
▲ EMP: 1600
SQ FT: 300,000
SALES (est): 4.4B **Privately Held**
WEB: www.vsp.com
SIC: 6324 5048 Hospital & medical service plans; ophthalmic goods

(P-10064)
VSP HOLDING COMPANY INC
3333 Quality Dr, Rancho Cordova (95670-7985)
PHONE..................916 851-5000
James Robinson Lynch, *CEO*
EMP: 52
SALES (est): 22.9MM **Privately Held**
SIC: 6324 Hospital & medical service plans

6331 Fire, Marine & Casualty Insurance

(P-10065)
AAA TRAVEL
1650 S Delaware St, San Mateo (94402-2623)
PHONE..................650 572-5600
Monica Iskander, *Manager*
EMP: 50
SALES (est): 3.8MM **Privately Held**
SIC: 6331 Automobile insurance

(P-10066)
ALLIANZ GLOBL RISKS US INSUR (DH)
Also Called: Allianz Insurance Company
2350 W Empire Ave, Burbank (91504-3350)
P.O. Box 7780 (91510-7780)
PHONE..................818 260-7500
Hugh Burgess, *CEO*
Paul Yun, *President*
Randy Renn, *CFO*
Arthur Moossmann, *Officer*
Joel Kim, *Administration*
EMP: 175
SQ FT: 20,000

SALES (est): 564.4MM
SALES (corp-wide): 24.9B **Privately Held**
SIC: 6331 Property damage insurance; fire, marine & casualty insurance & carriers; workers' compensation insurance
HQ: Fireman's Fund Insurance Company
1465 N Mcdowell Blvd # 100
Petaluma CA 94954
415 899-2000

(P-10067)
ALLIANZ GLOBL RISKS US INSUR
Also Called: Allianz Insurance Company
1465 N Mcdowell Blvd, Petaluma (94954-6516)
PHONE..................415 899-3758
Lori Oaks, *Manager*
EMP: 400
SALES (corp-wide): 24.9B **Privately Held**
SIC: 6331 Fire, marine & casualty insurance
HQ: Allianz Global Risks Us Insurance Company
2350 W Empire Ave
Burbank CA 91504
818 260-7500

(P-10068)
ALLIANZ UNDERWRITERS INSUR CO
Also Called: Allianz Globl Corp & Specialty
2350 W Empire Ave Ste 200, Burbank (91504-3350)
PHONE..................818 260-7500
Paul Yun, *Vice Pres*
EMP: 86
SALES (est): 42.1MM
SALES (corp-wide): 24.9B **Privately Held**
WEB: www.azoa.com
SIC: 6331 Fire, marine & casualty insurance
PA: Allianz Se
Koniginstr. 28
Munchen 80802
893 800-0

(P-10069)
ALLSTATE INSURANCE COMPANY
21950 Copley Dr Ste 130, Diamond Bar (91765-4461)
PHONE..................909 612-5504
Rick Finney, *Manager*
EMP: 1005 **Publicly Held**
SIC: 6331 6351 Fire, marine & casualty insurance: stock; automobile insurance; property damage insurance; mortgage guarantee insurance
HQ: Allstate Insurance Company
2775 Sanders Rd
Northbrook IL 60062
847 402-5000

(P-10070)
AMERICAN AUTOMOBILE ASSCTN
Also Called: Csaa Insurance AAA
1501 Farmers Ln, Santa Rosa (95405-7525)
P.O. Box 2906 (95405-0906)
PHONE..................707 566-4000
Al Holcomb, *Branch Mgr*
EMP: 125
SALES (corp-wide): 907.9MM **Privately Held**
WEB: www.californiastateautomobileassociation.c
SIC: 6331 4724 6311 Automobile insurance; tourist agency arranging transport, lodging & car rental; life insurance
PA: American Automobile Association Of Northern California, Nevada & Utah
1900 Powell St Ste 1200
Emeryville CA 94608
800 922-8228

(P-10071)
AMERICAN AUTOMOBILE ASSOCIATIO
Also Called: Csaa Travel Agency
1277 Treat Blvd Ste 1000, Walnut Creek (94597-8863)
PHONE..................510 596-3669
Tim Condon, *CEO*

Clay Creasy, *CFO*
EMP: 400
SALES (est): 16.2MM **Privately Held**
SIC: 6331 8699 Automobile insurance; automobile owners' association

(P-10072)
AMERICAN HOME ASSURANCE CO
777 S Figueroa St Ste 300, Los Angeles (90017-5801)
PHONE..................213 689-3500
Lynn Schwertner, *Branch Mgr*
EMP: 300
SALES (corp-wide): 47.3B **Publicly Held**
WEB: www.americanhomeassuranceco.com
SIC: 6331 7371 Fire, marine & casualty insurance; custom computer programming services
HQ: American Home Assurance Co Inc
70 Pine St Fl 1
New York NY 10005
212 770-7000

(P-10073)
AMERICAN INSURANCE COMPANY INC
1465 N Mcdowell Blvd, Petaluma (94954-6516)
PHONE..................415 899-2000
Mike Larocco, *President*
Heidi Townzen, *Human Res Mgr*
EMP: 4400
SALES (est): 329.7MM
SALES (corp-wide): 24.9B **Privately Held**
SIC: 6331 Fire, marine & casualty insurance
PA: Allianz Se
Koniginstr. 28
Munchen 80802
893 800-0

(P-10074)
ARROWHEAD GEN INSUR AGCY INC (DH)
701 B St Ste 2100, San Diego (92101-8197)
PHONE..................619 881-8600
Chris L Walker, *CEO*
Peter C Arrowsmith, *General Ptnr*
Steve Boyd, *President*
Wendy Castelo, *President*
Robert T Kingsley, *President*
EMP: 240
SQ FT: 74,000
SALES (est): 222.3MM
SALES (corp-wide): 2B **Publicly Held**
SIC: 6331 6411 Automobile insurance; insurance agents, brokers & service
HQ: Arrowhead Management Company
701 B St Ste 2100
San Diego CA 92101
619 881-8733

(P-10075)
CA STE ATOM ASSOC INTR-INS BUR
Also Called: Via Magazine
150 Van Ness Ave, San Francisco (94102-5200)
PHONE..................415 565-2012
Kent Evans, *Branch Mgr*
Carey Powell, *Engineer*
Elaine L Wong, *Sales Staff*
EMP: 2000
SALES (corp-wide): 907.9MM **Privately Held**
WEB: www.viamagazine.com
SIC: 6331 2721 Automobile insurance; property damage insurance; magazines: publishing & printing
HQ: California State Automobile Association Inter-Insurance Bureau
1276 S California Blvd
Walnut Creek CA 94596
925 287-7600

(P-10076)
CALIFORNIA AUTOMOBILE INSUR CO (HQ)
Also Called: Cai Company
555 W Imperial Hwy, Brea (92821-4802)
P.O. Box 1150 (92822-1150)
PHONE..................714 232-8669

George Joseph, *President*
Leo Lam, *CFO*
EMP: 800
SQ FT: 80,000
SALES (est): 610.6MM
SALES (corp-wide): 3.3B **Publicly Held**
WEB: www.californiaautoinsurance-company.com
SIC: 6331 Automobile insurance
PA: Mercury General Corporation
4484 Wilshire Blvd
Los Angeles CA 90010
323 937-1060

(P-10077)
CALIFORNIA CAPITAL INSUR CO (PA)
Also Called: Capital Insurance Group
2300 Garden Rd, Monterey (93940-5326)
P.O. Box 3110 (93942-3110)
PHONE.....................831 233-5500
L Arnold Chatterton, *President*
Andrew Doll, *COO*
Davis Tyndall, *CFO*
Walter Benett, *Vice Pres*
John Halberstadt, *Vice Pres*
EMP: 142
SQ FT: 50,000
SALES: 200.7MM **Privately Held**
SIC: 6331 Fire, marine & casualty insurance & carriers; automobile insurance

(P-10078)
CALIFORNIA CASUALTY MGT CO (HQ)
Also Called: California Casualty
1875 S Grant St Ste 800, San Mateo (94402-7030)
PHONE.....................650 574-4000
Carl B Brown, *Ch of Bd*
Manik Peddada, *President*
Joseph L Volponi, *President*
Michael Ray, *CFO*
James R Englese, *Senior VP*
▲ **EMP:** 135
SALES: 121.8MM
SALES (corp-wide): 239.8MM **Privately Held**
SIC: 6331 8741 Reciprocal interinsurance exchanges: fire, marine, casualty; management services
PA: California Casualty Indemnity Exchange
1900 Almeda De Las Pulgas
San Mateo CA 94403
650 574-4000

(P-10079)
CALIFORNIA STATE AUTOMOBILE (HQ)
Also Called: Triple A
1276 S California Blvd, Walnut Creek (94596-5123)
P.O. Box 22221, Oakland (94623-2221)
PHONE.....................925 287-7600
James R Pouliot, *CEO*
Carrie Tabor, *Human Resources*
Michele Salmon, *Marketing Staff*
Trina Elkins, *Sales Staff*
Cristi Knudsen, *Database Market*
EMP: 1600
SQ FT: 400,000
SALES (est): 880.6MM
SALES (corp-wide): 907.9MM **Privately Held**
WEB: www.viamagazine.com
SIC: 6331 Automobile insurance
PA: American Automobile Association Of Northern California, Nevada & Utah
1900 Powell St Ste 1200
Emeryville CA 94608
800 922-8228

(P-10080)
CALIFORNIA STATE AUTOMOBILE
Also Called: AAA
510a Veterans Blvd, Redwood City (94063-1122)
PHONE.....................650 572-5600
Rita Timewell, *Manager*
EMP: 100

SALES (corp-wide): 907.9MM **Privately Held**
WEB: www.viamagazine.com
SIC: 6331 6411 Automobile insurance; property & casualty insurance agent
HQ: California State Automobile Association Inter-Insurance Bureau
1276 S California Blvd
Walnut Creek CA 94596
925 287-7600

(P-10081)
CALIFRNIA CSLTY INDEMNITY EXCH (PA)
1900 Almeda De Las Pulgas, San Mateo (94403-1222)
PHONE.....................650 574-4000
Thomas R Brown, *Chairman*
Mike Ray, *CFO*
Ian Small, *Vice Pres*
Yvette Jones, *Analyst*
Beth Nagy, *Marketing Mgr*
EMP: 130 **EST:** 1914
SQ FT: 90,000
SALES: 239.8MM **Privately Held**
SIC: 6331 Workers' compensation insurance; automobile insurance; property damage insurance; fire, marine & casualty insurance & carriers

(P-10082)
COMMERCIAL CARRIERS INSUR AGCY
4 Centerpointe Dr Ste 300, La Palma (90623-1074)
PHONE.....................562 404-4900
Charles J Escalante, *President*
Henry H Escalante, *Ch of Bd*
Shannon S Walker, *Treasurer*
Helen M Escalante, *Admin Sec*
EMP: 221
SQ FT: 16,000
SALES (est): 49.4MM **Privately Held**
WEB: www.cciainsurance.com
SIC: 6331 Fire, marine & casualty insurance
HQ: Meadowbrook, Inc.
26255 American Dr
Southfield MI 48034
248 358-1100

(P-10083)
COMPWEST INSURANCE COMPANY
100 Pringle Ave Ste 515, Walnut Creek (94596-3558)
PHONE.....................415 593-5100
William J Mudge, *President*
Patrick Persse, *CFO*
Gene J Simpson, *Vice Pres*
Cyndi Kroop, *Regional Mgr*
Grace Hastings, *Administration*
EMP: 140
SALES (est): 51.2MM **Privately Held**
SIC: 6331 Reciprocal interinsurance exchanges: fire, marine, casualty

(P-10084)
FACTORY MUTUAL INSURANCE CO
Also Called: FM Global
1333 N Calif Blvd Ste 200, Walnut Creek (94596-4559)
PHONE.....................925 934-2200
Andrew Scanlon, *Branch Mgr*
Monique Modelo, *Admin Mgr*
Harry Yonemoto, *Technical Staff*
Becklin Davis, *Engineer*
Kevin Paynter, *Engineer*
EMP: 109
SALES (corp-wide): 4B **Privately Held**
SIC: 6331 6411 Property damage insurance; insurance agents, brokers & service
PA: Factory Mutual Insurance Co
270 Central Ave
Johnston RI 02919
401 275-3000

(P-10085)
FACTORY MUTUAL INSURANCE CO
Also Called: FM Global
6320 Canoga Ave Ste 1100, Woodland Hills (91367-2578)
P.O. Box 9270, Van Nuys (91409-9270)
PHONE.....................818 227-2200
Angie Benitez, *Admin Asst*
John Labanieh, *Engineer*
Jeffrey Tenn, *Sales Staff*
Sham Ganguli, *Assistant VP*
EMP: 100
SALES (corp-wide): 4B **Privately Held**
SIC: 6331 Property damage insurance
PA: Factory Mutual Insurance Co
270 Central Ave
Johnston RI 02919
401 275-3000

(P-10086)
FARMERS GROUP INC (HQ)
Also Called: Farmers Insurance
6301 Owensmouth Ave, Woodland Hills (91367-2216)
P.O. Box 2450, Grand Rapids MI (49501-2450)
PHONE.....................323 932-3200
Jeff Dailey, *CEO*
Tony Desantis, *President*
Steve McAnena, *President*
Mhayse Samalya, *President*
Scott Lindquist, *CFO*
▲ **EMP:** 2100 **EST:** 1927
SALES (est): 11B
SALES (corp-wide): 48.2B **Privately Held**
WEB: www.farmers.com
SIC: 6331 Automobile insurance; reciprocal interinsurance exchanges: fire, marine, casualty
PA: Zurich Insurance Group Ag
C/O Zurich Versicherungs-Gesellschaft Ag
ZUrich ZH 8002
446 252-525

(P-10087)
FIREMANS FUND INSURANCE CO (HQ)
1465 N Mcdowell Blvd # 100, Petaluma (94954-6516)
PHONE.....................415 899-2000
Gary Bhojwani, *Ch of Bd*
Antonio Derossi, *COO*
Kevin Walker, *CFO*
Robyn Hahn, *Chief Mktg Ofcr*
Christian Kortebein, *Senior VP*
EMP: 2242 **EST:** 1864
SQ FT: 240,000
SALES (est): 2.4B
SALES (corp-wide): 24.9B **Privately Held**
WEB: www.firemansfund.com
SIC: 6331 6351 6321 Fire, marine & casualty insurance & carriers; property damage insurance; fire, marine & casualty insurance: stock; workers' compensation insurance; surety insurance; credit & other financial responsibility insurance; liability insurance; reinsurance carriers, accident & health
PA: Allianz Se
Koniginstr. 28
Munchen 80802
893 800-0

(P-10088)
FIREMANS FUND INSURANCE CO
9275 Sky Park Ct, San Diego (92123-4386)
P.O. Box 85920 (92186-5920)
PHONE.....................858 492-3019
Kelly Rauch, *Principal*
EMP: 131
SALES (corp-wide): 24.9B **Privately Held**
WEB: www.firemansfund.com
SIC: 6331 Property damage insurance
HQ: Fireman's Fund Insurance Company
1465 N Mcdowell Blvd # 100
Petaluma CA 94954
415 899-2000

(P-10089)
FIREMANS FUND INSURANCE CO
2350 W Empire Ave Ste 200, Burbank (91504-3350)
PHONE.....................818 953-6533
Karmyn Downs, *Manager*
EMP: 206
SALES (corp-wide): 24.9B **Privately Held**
WEB: www.firemansfund.com
SIC: 6331 Property damage insurance
HQ: Fireman's Fund Insurance Company
1465 N Mcdowell Blvd # 100
Petaluma CA 94954
415 899-2000

(P-10090)
FRANK GATES SERVICE COMPANY
2400 E Katella Ave # 650, Anaheim (92806-5974)
PHONE.....................800 994-4611
Gary Graham, *Manager*
Nancy Neely, *Accountant*
EMP: 60
SALES (corp-wide): 97.3MM **Privately Held**
WEB: www.fgsc.com
SIC: 6331 Workers' compensation insurance
HQ: The Frank Gates Service Company
5000 Bradenton Ave # 100
Dublin OH 43017
614 793-8000

(P-10091)
GLENN E PORTER
3955 Coffee Rd, Bakersfield (93308-5024)
PHONE.....................661 615-1500
Glenn E Porter, *Principal*
Glenn Porter, *Principal*
EMP: 50
SALES (est): 4.6MM **Privately Held**
SIC: 6331 Property damage insurance

(P-10092)
GOLDEN EAGLE INSURANCE CORP (DH)
525 B St Ste 1300, San Diego (92101-4421)
P.O. Box 85826 (92186-5826)
PHONE.....................619 744-6000
J Paul Condrin III, *CEO*
Frank J Kotarba, *President*
Cynthia Weston, *Business Anlyst*
Stephen Henningsen, *Analyst*
Nate Chance, *Manager*
EMP: 250 **EST:** 1997
SALES (est): 96.7MM
SALES (corp-wide): 38.3B **Privately Held**
SIC: 6331 Property damage insurance
HQ: Liberty Mutual Insurance Company
175 Berkeley St
Boston MA 02116
617 357-9500

(P-10093)
GREAT AMERICAN INSURANCE CO
5750 Wilshire Blvd 360, Los Angeles (90036-3697)
PHONE.....................323 937-8600
Bob Nagaishi, *Branch Mgr*
EMP: 100 **Publicly Held**
SIC: 6331 Fire, marine & casualty insurance
HQ: Great American Insurance Company
301 E 4th St Fl 24
Cincinnati OH 45202
513 369-5000

(P-10094)
GREAT AMERICAN INSURANCE CO
725 S Figueroa St # 3400, Los Angeles (90017-5434)
PHONE.....................213 430-4300
Thom Smith, *Division Pres*
Kirby Harness, *Vice Pres*
Rocio Garcia, *Division Mgr*
Alvin Esguerra, *Administration*
Russell Olson, *Business Anlyst*
EMP: 142 **Publicly Held**
SIC: 6331 Fire, marine & casualty insurance

HQ: Great American Insurance Company
301 E 4th St Fl 24
Cincinnati OH 45202
513 369-5000

(P-10095)
HARTFORD CASUALTY INSURANCE CO
101 Montgomery St # 2700, San Francisco (94104-4179)
PHONE...............................415 836-4800
William Reynolds, *Manager*
Debra Robertson, *Executive*
Martin Rebolledo, *Admin Mgr*
Imee Mendoza, *Executive Asst*
Laura Bongiorno, *Regl Sales Mgr*
EMP: 600 **Publicly Held**
SIC: **6331** Fire, marine & casualty insurance; mutual; property damage insurance
HQ: Hartford Casualty Insurance Company
1 Hartford Plz
Hartford CT 06155
860 547-5000

(P-10096)
HERITAGE INDEMNITY COMPANY
23 Pasteur, Irvine (92618-3816)
PHONE...............................303 987-5500
Adam Pope, *President*
EMP: 80
SALES (est): 5.2MM
SALES (corp-wide): 250MM **Privately Held**
SIC: **6331** Automobile insurance
HQ: Amtrust Financial Services, Inc.
59 Maiden Ln Fl 43
New York NY 10038

(P-10097)
ICW GROUP HOLDINGS INC (PA)
15025 Innovation Dr, San Diego (92128-3455)
P.O. Box 85563 (92186-5563)
PHONE...............................858 350-2400
Kevin M Prior, *CEO*
Ernest Rady, *Ch of Bd*
Sariborz Rostamian, *Treasurer*
Todd Hartline, *Vice Pres*
Paul Zamora, *Vice Pres*
EMP: 60 EST: 1974
SQ FT: 160,000
SALES (est): 328MM **Privately Held**
SIC: **6331** 6411 Fire, marine & casualty insurance & carriers; insurance brokers

(P-10098)
INSURANCE COMPANY OF WEST (HQ)
Also Called: I C W
15025 Innovation Dr, San Diego (92128-3455)
P.O. Box 85563 (92186-5563)
PHONE...............................858 350-2400
Kevin Prior, *President*
Ernest Rady, *Ch of Bd*
H Michael Freet, *Treasurer*
Todd Hartline, *Vice Pres*
EMP: 135
SQ FT: 150,000
SALES (est): 328MM **Privately Held**
SIC: **6331** Property damage insurance
PA: Icw Group Holdings, Inc.
15025 Innovation Dr
San Diego CA 92128
858 350-2400

(P-10099)
KRAMER-WILSON COMPANY INC (PA)
Also Called: Century National
6345 Balboa Blvd Ste 190, Encino (91316-1515)
P.O. Box 3999, North Hollywood (91609-0599)
PHONE...............................818 760-0880
Weldon Wilson, *CEO*
Kevin Wilson, *President*
Daniel Sherrin, *CFO*
Mary Ann Wagner, *Admin Sec*
EMP: 240
SQ FT: 41,000

SALES (est): 257.2MM **Privately Held**
WEB: www.cnico.com
SIC: **6331** Fire, marine & casualty insurance & carriers

(P-10100)
LIBERTY MUTUAL INSURANCE CO
21515 Hawthorne Blvd # 550, Torrance (90503-6528)
PHONE...............................310 316-9428
Lynnean Chisom, *Branch Mgr*
Gabriel De, *Personnel*
EMP: 110
SALES (corp-wide): 38.3B **Privately Held**
SIC: **6331** Fire, marine & casualty insurance
HQ: Liberty Mutual Insurance Company
175 Berkeley St
Boston MA 02116
617 357-9500

(P-10101)
LIBERTY MUTUAL INSURANCE CO
101 Mission St Ste 740, San Francisco (94105-1737)
PHONE...............................415 957-1175
Gary Countryman, *Ch of Bd*
EMP: 150
SALES (corp-wide): 38.3B **Privately Held**
WEB: www.libertymutual.com
SIC: **6331** Fire, marine & casualty insurance
HQ: Liberty Mutual Insurance Company
175 Berkeley St
Boston MA 02116
617 357-9500

(P-10102)
LIBERTY MUTUAL INSURANCE CO
13405 Folsom Blvd Ste 200, Folsom (95630-4738)
PHONE...............................916 294-9518
Charles Frazier, *Principal*
EMP: 107
SALES (corp-wide): 38.3B **Privately Held**
SIC: **6331** Fire, marine & casualty insurance
HQ: Liberty Mutual Insurance Company
175 Berkeley St
Boston MA 02116
617 357-9500

(P-10103)
LIBERTY MUTUAL INSURANCE CO
3633 Inland Empire Blvd # 280, Ontario (91764-4946)
P.O. Box 51486 (91761-0086)
PHONE...............................909 476-6688
Candi Peterson, *Sales/Mktg Mgr*
Andrew Jones, *Manager*
EMP: 100
SALES (corp-wide): 38.3B **Privately Held**
WEB: www.libertymutual.com
SIC: **6331** 6311 Fire, marine & casualty insurance; life insurance carriers
HQ: Liberty Mutual Insurance Company
175 Berkeley St
Boston MA 02116
617 357-9500

(P-10104)
LIBERTY MUTUAL INSURANCE CO
790 The City Dr S Ste 200, Orange (92868-4941)
P.O. Box 11020 (92856-8120)
PHONE...............................714 937-1400
Linda Vanauran, *Manager*
Eric Cady, *Project Mgr*
EMP: 200
SALES (corp-wide): 38.3B **Privately Held**
WEB: www.libertymutual.com
SIC: **6331** 6311 Fire, marine & casualty insurance; life insurance
HQ: Liberty Mutual Insurance Company
175 Berkeley St
Boston MA 02116
617 357-9500

(P-10105)
LIBERTY MUTUAL INSURANCE CO
20500 Belshaw Ave, Carson (90746-3506)
P.O. Box 212, Hingham MA (02043-0212)
PHONE...............................781 740-1920
Ronald Anderson, *Manager*
EMP: 155
SALES (corp-wide): 38.3B **Privately Held**
WEB: www.libertymutual.com
SIC: **6331** 6311 Fire, marine & casualty insurance; life insurance carriers
HQ: Liberty Mutual Insurance Company
175 Berkeley St
Boston MA 02116
617 357-9500

(P-10106)
LIBERTY MUTUAL INSURANCE CO
1750 Howe Ave Ste 450, Sacramento (95825-3368)
PHONE...............................916 564-1792
Natalie Dougherty, *Manager*
EMP: 340
SALES (corp-wide): 38.3B **Privately Held**
WEB: www.libertymutual.com
SIC: **6331** Fire, marine & casualty insurance
HQ: Liberty Mutual Insurance Company
175 Berkeley St
Boston MA 02116
617 357-9500

(P-10107)
MERCURY CASUALTY COMPANY (HQ)
Also Called: M C C
555 W Imperial Hwy, Brea (92821-4802)
P.O. Box 54600, Los Angeles (90054-0600)
PHONE...............................323 937-1060
Gabriel Tirador, *CEO*
George Joseph, *CEO*
EMP: 600 EST: 1962
SALES (est): 3.2B
SALES (corp-wide): 3.3B **Publicly Held**
SIC: **6331** 6351 Automobile insurance; warranty insurance, home
PA: Mercury General Corporation
4484 Wilshire Blvd
Los Angeles CA 90010
323 937-1060

(P-10108)
MERCURY GENERAL CORPORATION (PA)
4484 Wilshire Blvd, Los Angeles (90010-3710)
P.O. Box 36662 (90036-0662)
PHONE...............................323 937-1060
Gabriel Tirador, *President*
Theodore R Stalick, *CFO*
Joshua Little, *Bd of Directors*
Martha Marcon, *Bd of Directors*
Christopher Graves, *Officer*
EMP: 87 EST: 1961
SQ FT: 41,000
SALES: 3.3B **Publicly Held**
WEB: www.mercuryinsurance.com
SIC: **6331** 6411 Automobile insurance; property damage insurance; fire, marine & casualty insurance & carriers; insurance agents, brokers & service

(P-10109)
MERCURY INSURANCE COMPANY
555 W Imperial Hwy, Brea (92821-4839)
P.O. Box 1150 (92822-1150)
PHONE...............................714 671-6700
Gave Tirador, *President*
Toni Chavez, *Marketing Staff*
Kim Burton, *Manager*
John Rivera, *Manager*
EMP: 89
SALES (corp-wide): 3.3B **Publicly Held**
WEB: www.coveryourhome.com
SIC: **6331** 6411 Fire, marine & casualty insurance; insurance agents, brokers & service
HQ: Mercury Insurance Company
4484 Wilshire Blvd
Los Angeles CA 90010
323 937-1060

(P-10110)
MERCURY INSURANCE COMPANY
Also Called: Mercury Insurance Group
104 Woodmere Rd, Folsom (95630-4705)
PHONE...............................916 353-4859
Beverly Ramm, *Vice Pres*
EMP: 89
SALES (corp-wide): 3.3B **Publicly Held**
WEB: www.coveryourhome.com
SIC: **6331** 6411 Fire, marine & casualty insurance; insurance claim processing, except medical
HQ: Mercury Insurance Company
4484 Wilshire Blvd
Los Angeles CA 90010
323 937-1060

(P-10111)
MERCURY INSURANCE COMPANY
Also Called: Mercury Insurance Broker
1433 Santa Monica Blvd, Santa Monica (90404-1709)
PHONE...............................310 451-4943
Ken Donaldson, *Owner*
EMP: 89
SALES (corp-wide): 3.3B **Publicly Held**
WEB: www.coveryourhome.com
SIC: **6331** 6411 Fire, marine & casualty insurance; insurance agents, brokers & service
HQ: Mercury Insurance Company
4484 Wilshire Blvd
Los Angeles CA 90010
323 937-1060

(P-10112)
MERCURY INSURANCE COMPANY
1700 Greenbriar Ln, Brea (92821-5971)
PHONE...............................714 255-5000
Ken Kitzmiller, *Branch Mgr*
EMP: 96
SALES (corp-wide): 3.3B **Publicly Held**
SIC: **6331** Fire, marine & casualty insurance
HQ: Mercury Insurance Company
4484 Wilshire Blvd
Los Angeles CA 90010
323 937-1060

(P-10113)
MERCURY INSURANCE COMPANY (HQ)
4484 Wilshire Blvd, Los Angeles (90010-3710)
P.O. Box 54600 (90054-0600)
PHONE...............................323 937-1060
Gabe Tirador, *CEO*
Ted Stalick, *CFO*
George Joseph, *Chairman*
Victor Joseph, *Vice Pres*
Judith Walters, *Vice Pres*
EMP: 160
SQ FT: 40,809
SALES (est): 3.5B
SALES (corp-wide): 3.3B **Publicly Held**
WEB: www.coveryourhome.com
SIC: **6331** Fire, marine & casualty insurance
PA: Mercury General Corporation
4484 Wilshire Blvd
Los Angeles CA 90010
323 937-1060

(P-10114)
MERCURY INSURANCE COMPANY
9635 Gran Rdge Dr Ste 200, San Diego (92123)
P.O. Box 82167 (92138-2167)
PHONE...............................858 694-4100
Randy Petro, *Manager*
EMP: 100
SALES (corp-wide): 3.3B **Publicly Held**
WEB: www.coveryourhome.com
SIC: **6331** 6399 Fire, marine & casualty insurance; warranty insurance, automobile
HQ: Mercury Insurance Company
4484 Wilshire Blvd
Los Angeles CA 90010
323 937-1060

▲ = Import ▼=Export
◆ =Import/Export

(P-10115)
MERCURY INSURANCE COMPANY
27200 Tourney Rd Ste 400, Valencia (91355-4997)
PHONE..............................661 291-6470
David Levy, *Manager*
EMP: 89
SALES (corp-wide): 3.3B **Publicly Held**
SIC: 6331 Fire, marine & casualty insurance
HQ: Mercury Insurance Company
4484 Wilshire Blvd
Los Angeles CA 90010
323 937-1060

(P-10116)
MERCURY INSURANCE SERVICES LLC
4484 Wilshire Blvd, Los Angeles (90010-3710)
PHONE..............................323 937-1060
Gabriel Tirador, *CEO*
EMP: 4000
SALES: 2.7B
SALES (corp-wide): 3.3B **Publicly Held**
SIC: 6331 Property damage insurance
HQ: Mercury Casualty Company
555 W Imperial Hwy
Brea CA 92821
323 937-1060

(P-10117)
METROMILE INC (PA)
690 Folsom St Ste 200, San Francisco (94107-1397)
PHONE..............................888 244-1702
Dan Preston, *CEO*
Carrie Dolan, *CFO*
Bhanu Pullela, *Chief Mktg Ofcr*
Debra Jack, *Vice Pres*
Paw Andersen, *CTO*
EMP: 80
SALES (est): 123.5MM **Privately Held**
SIC: 6331 Automobile insurance

(P-10118)
MID CENTURY INSURANCE COMPANY
6303 Owensmouth Ave, Woodland Hills (91367-2264)
PHONE..............................323 932-7116
Ron Coble, *Senior VP*
Bob Woudstra, *President*
EMP: 250
SALES (est): 74.5MM
SALES (corp-wide): 48.2B **Privately Held**
SIC: 6331 6351 Automobile insurance; fidelity insurance
HQ: Farmers Insurance Exchange
6301 Owensmouth Ave
Woodland Hills CA 91367
323 932-3200

(P-10119)
PALOMAR HOLDINGS INC
7979 Ivanhoe Ave Ste 500, La Jolla (92037-4513)
PHONE..............................619 567-5290
Mac Armstrong, *CEO*
James Ryan Clark, *Ch of Bd*
Heath A Fisher, *President*
Jon Christianson, *COO*
T Christopher Uchida, *CFO*
EMP: 63
SQ FT: 14,700
SALES: 72.9MM **Privately Held**
SIC: 6331 Fire, marine & casualty insurance

(P-10120)
PROGRESSIVE CORPORATION
Also Called: Progressive Insurance
2470 Via Mariposa, San Dimas (91773-4420)
PHONE..............................626 232-1540
Aaron Cavazos, *Branch Mgr*
EMP: 83
SALES (corp-wide): 31.9B **Publicly Held**
SIC: 6331 Fire, marine & casualty insurance
PA: The Progressive Corporation
6300 Wilson Mills Rd
Mayfield Village OH 44143
440 461-5000

(P-10121)
PROGRESSIVE CORPORATION
Also Called: Progressive Insurance
150 N Hill Dr Ste 9, Brisbane (94005-1023)
PHONE..............................440 461-5000
EMP: 83
SALES (corp-wide): 31.9B **Publicly Held**
SIC: 6331 Fire, marine & casualty insurance
PA: The Progressive Corporation
6300 Wilson Mills Rd
Mayfield Village OH 44143
440 461-5000

(P-10122)
REPUBLIC INDEMNITY CO AMER
100 Pine St Fl 14, San Francisco (94111-5116)
P.O. Box 7878 (94120-7878)
PHONE..............................415 981-3200
Darryl Yim, *Vice Pres*
EMP: 100 **Publicly Held**
SIC: 6331 Workers' compensation insurance
HQ: Republic Indemnity Company Of America
15821 Ventura Blvd # 370
Encino CA 91436
818 990-9860

(P-10123)
REPUBLIC INDEMNITY CO AMER (DH)
15821 Ventura Blvd # 370, Encino (91436-2936)
P.O. Box 20036 (91416-0036)
PHONE..............................818 990-9860
Dwayne Marioni, *CEO*
Marion Chappel, *Senior VP*
Craig Borstelmann, *Vice Pres*
David Kairo, *Info Tech Dir*
Anu Ponto, *Analyst*
EMP: 129
SQ FT: 70,000
SALES: 810.4MM **Publicly Held**
SIC: 6331 Workers' compensation insurance
HQ: Pennsylvania Company Inc
1 E 4th St
Cincinnati OH 45202
513 579-2121

(P-10124)
REPUBLIC INDEMNITY COMPANY CAL
Also Called: RICA
15821 Ventura Blvd # 370, Encino (91436-2936)
P.O. Box 20036 (91416-0036)
PHONE..............................818 990-9860
Dwayne T Marioni, *President*
Shila Euper, *Admin Sec*
EMP: 127
SALES (est): 13.5MM **Publicly Held**
SIC: 6331 Fire, marine & casualty insurance
HQ: Republic Indemnity Company Of America
15821 Ventura Blvd # 370
Encino CA 91436
818 990-9860

(P-10125)
RESIDENCE MUTUAL INSURANCE CO
2172 Dupont Dr Ste 220, Irvine (92612-1359)
PHONE..............................949 724-9402
Joe Crail, *President*
Michael Hardy, *CFO*
Carmen Estrada, *Manager*
EMP: 65
SQ FT: 35,000
SALES: 27.1MM **Privately Held**
SIC: 6331 Property damage insurance

(P-10126)
RICHARD J MENDOZA INC
501 2nd St Ste 330, San Francisco (94107-4131)
PHONE..............................415 644-0180
Jeff Pallesen, *President*
Todd George, *Officer*
EMP: 95 **EST**: 2001

SALES (est): 12.4MM
SALES (corp-wide): 418MM **Publicly Held**
SIC: 6331 Fire, marine & casualty insurance
PA: Nv5 Global, Inc.
200 S Park Rd Ste 350
Hollywood FL 33021
954 495-2112

(P-10127)
ROYAL SPECIALTY UNDWRT INC
Also Called: Rsui Group
15303 Ventura Blvd # 500, Sherman Oaks (91403-3110)
PHONE..............................818 922-6700
Christine Chinen, *Administration*
Melanie Stevenson, *Vice Pres*
Allison Thoburn, *Vice Pres*
Myra Caagbay, *Administration*
Vaylor Trucks, *Engineer*
EMP: 75
SALES (corp-wide): 6.8B **Publicly Held**
SIC: 6331 6411 Fire, marine & casualty insurance; insurance agents, brokers & service
HQ: Royal Specialty Underwriting, Inc.
945 E Paces Ferry Rd Ne # 189
Atlanta GA 30326
404 231-2366

(P-10128)
SEQUOIA INSURANCE COMPANY (DH)
31 Upper Ragsdale Dr, Monterey (93940-5771)
P.O. Box 1510 (93942-1510)
PHONE..............................831 655-9612
Thomas G Moylan, *President*
EMP: 60
SALES (est): 31.5MM
SALES (corp-wide): 250MM **Privately Held**
WEB: www.sequoiains.com
SIC: 6331 Fire, marine & casualty insurance & carriers; property damage insurance

(P-10129)
STATE COMPENSATION INSUR FUND (PA)
Also Called: STATE FUND
333 Bush St Fl 8, San Francisco (94104-2806)
P.O. Box 8192, Pleasanton (94588-8792)
PHONE..............................888 782-8338
Vernon Steiner, *President*
Hilda Padua, *President*
Rick Law, *COO*
Beatriz Sanchez, *COO*
Peter Guastamachio, *CFO*
EMP: 75
SQ FT: 80,000
SALES: 1.3B **Privately Held**
WEB: www.scif.com
SIC: 6331 Workers' compensation insurance

(P-10130)
STATE COMPENSATION INSUR FUND
Also Called: Santa Ana District Office
1750 E 4th St Fl 3, Santa Ana (92705-3929)
PHONE..............................714 565-5000
Liz Glidden, *Manager*
Matthew Day, *Legal Staff*
Dina Camiolo, *Manager*
Gonzalo Deguzman, *Clerk*
EMP: 270
SALES (corp-wide): 1.3B **Privately Held**
WEB: www.scif.com
SIC: 6331 9651 Workers' compensation insurance; insurance commission, government;
PA: State Compensation Insurance Fund
333 Bush St Fl 8
San Francisco CA 94104
888 782-8338

(P-10131)
STATE COMPENSATION INSUR FUND
Also Called: Bakersfield District Office
9801 Camino Media Ste 101, Bakersfield (93311-1312)
P.O. Box 21810 (93390-1810)
PHONE..............................661 664-4000
Robert Kean, *Manager*
Mike La Deaux, *Executive*
EMP: 190
SALES (corp-wide): 1.3B **Privately Held**
WEB: www.scif.com
SIC: 6331 9651 Workers' compensation insurance; insurance commission, government;
PA: State Compensation Insurance Fund
333 Bush St Fl 8
San Francisco CA 94104
888 782-8338

(P-10132)
STATE COMPENSATION INSUR FUND
Also Called: Oakland District Office
2955 Peralta Oaks Ct, Oakland (94605-5319)
PHONE..............................510 577-3000
EMP: 200
SALES (corp-wide): 1.5B **Privately Held**
SIC: 6331 9651 6321
PA: State Compensation Insurance Fund
333 Bush St Fl 8
San Francisco CA 94104
888 782-8338

(P-10133)
STATE COMPENSATION INSUR FUND
Also Called: San Jose District Office
333 W San Carlos St # 950, San Jose (95110-2726)
PHONE..............................888 782-8338
Jerry Madden, *Manager*
EMP: 210
SALES (corp-wide): 1.3B **Privately Held**
WEB: www.scif.com
SIC: 6331 9651 Workers' compensation insurance; insurance commission, government;
PA: State Compensation Insurance Fund
333 Bush St Fl 8
San Francisco CA 94104
888 782-8338

(P-10134)
STATE COMPENSATION INSUR FUND
Also Called: Redding District Office
364 Knollcrest Dr, Redding (96002-0175)
P.O. Box 496049 (96049-6049)
PHONE..............................888 782-8338
Michael Labeaux, *Manager*
David Olsen, *Analyst*
EMP: 170
SALES (corp-wide): 1.3B **Privately Held**
WEB: www.scif.com
SIC: 6331 9651 Workers' compensation insurance; regulation, miscellaneous commercial sectors;
PA: State Compensation Insurance Fund
333 Bush St Fl 8
San Francisco CA 94104
888 782-8338

(P-10135)
STATE COMPENSATION INSUR FUND
Also Called: San Diego District Office
10105 Pacific Hgts Blvd, San Diego (92121-4249)
PHONE..............................888 782-8338
Lisa Middleton, *Manager*
EMP: 350
SALES (corp-wide): 1.3B **Privately Held**
WEB: www.scif.com
SIC: 6331 9651 Workers' compensation insurance; insurance commission, government;
PA: State Compensation Insurance Fund
333 Bush St Fl 8
San Francisco CA 94104
888 782-8338

(P-10136)
STATE COMPENSATION INSUR FUND
Also Called: Fresno District Office
10 E Rver Pk Pl E Ste 110, Fresno (93720)
PHONE....................................559 433-2700
John Putnam, *District Mgr*
Monica Segura, *Underwriter*
EMP: 270
SALES (corp-wide): 1.3B **Privately Held**
WEB: www.scif.com
SIC: 6331 9651 Workers' compensation
insurance; insurance commission, government;
PA: State Compensation Insurance Fund
333 Bush St Fl 8
San Francisco CA 94104
888 782-8338

(P-10137)
STATE COMPENSATION INSUR FUND
Also Called: State Fund Office
655 N Central Ave Ste 200, Glendale
(91203-1424)
P.O. Box 92503, Los Angeles (90009-2503)
PHONE....................................213 576-7335
Linda Hoban, *Manager*
Mario Escalante, *Technology*
William Poncelet, *Auditor*
Yvette Montano-Anda, *Manager*
EMP: 185
SALES (corp-wide): 1.3B **Privately Held**
WEB: www.scif.com
SIC: 6331 9651 Workers' compensation
insurance; insurance commission, government;
PA: State Compensation Insurance Fund
333 Bush St Fl 8
San Francisco CA 94104
888 782-8338

(P-10138)
STATE COMPENSATION INSUR FUND
655 N Central Ave Ste 200, Glendale
(91203-1424)
P.O. Box 92503, Los Angeles (90009-2503)
PHONE....................................323 266-5551
EMP: 185
SALES (corp-wide): 1.3B **Privately Held**
WEB: www.scif.com
SIC: 6331 9651 Workers' compensation
insurance; insurance commission, government;
PA: State Compensation Insurance Fund
333 Bush St Fl 8
San Francisco CA 94104
888 782-8338

(P-10139)
STATE COMPENSATION INSUR FUND
Also Called: Stockton District Office
3247 W March Ln Ste 110, Stockton
(95219-2363)
PHONE....................................888 782-8338
Tom Clark, *Manager*
Belinda Walker, *Manager*
EMP: 200
SALES (corp-wide): 1.3B **Privately Held**
WEB: www.scif.com
SIC: 6331 9651 6411 Workers' compensation insurance; insurance commission, government; ; insurance agents, brokers & service
PA: State Compensation Insurance Fund
333 Bush St Fl 8
San Francisco CA 94104
888 782-8338

(P-10140)
STATE COMPENSATION INSUR FUND
Also Called: Los Angeles District Office
655 N Central Ave Ste 200, Glendale
(91203-1424)
P.O. Box 65005, Fresno (93650-5005)
PHONE....................................888 782-8338
Linda Hoban, *Manager*
Michael Banks, *Information Mgr*
Beatriz Sanchez, *Opers Mgr*
EMP: 185

SALES (corp-wide): 1.3B **Privately Held**
WEB: www.scif.com
SIC: 6331 9651 6321 Workers' compensation insurance; insurance commission, government; ; accident & health insurance
PA: State Compensation Insurance Fund
333 Bush St Fl 8
San Francisco CA 94104
888 782-8338

(P-10141)
STATE COMPENSATION INSUR FUND
Also Called: Sacramento District Office
2275 Gateway Oaks Dr, Sacramento
(95833-3224)
PHONE....................................916 924-5100
Gary Dunlap, *Manager*
EMP: 325
SALES (corp-wide): 1.3B **Privately Held**
WEB: www.scif.com
SIC: 6331 9651 Workers' compensation insurance; insurance commission, government;
PA: State Compensation Insurance Fund
333 Bush St Fl 8
San Francisco CA 94104
888 782-8338

(P-10142)
STATE COMPENSATION INSUR FUND
Also Called: Eureka District Office
800 W Harris St Ste 37, Eureka
(95503-3929)
PHONE....................................707 443-9721
Steve Mackey, *Branch Mgr*
Arlene David, *Technology*
EMP: 55
SALES (corp-wide): 1.3B **Privately Held**
WEB: www.scif.com
SIC: 6331 9651 Workers' compensation insurance; insurance commission, government;
PA: State Compensation Insurance Fund
333 Bush St Fl 8
San Francisco CA 94104
888 782-8338

(P-10143)
STATE COMPENSATION INSUR FUND
Also Called: Riverside District Office
6301 Day St, Riverside (92507-0902)
PHONE....................................888 782-8338
Barbara Katzka, *Manager*
Leslie Martinez, *Executive*
Gil D Santos, *Chief Engr*
Beverly Rosas, *Counsel*
Laurie Coughenour, *Manager*
EMP: 250
SALES (corp-wide): 1.3B **Privately Held**
WEB: www.scif.com
SIC: 6331 9651 Workers' compensation insurance; insurance commission, government;
PA: State Compensation Insurance Fund
333 Bush St Fl 8
San Francisco CA 94104
888 782-8338

(P-10144)
STATE COMPENSATION INSUR FUND
5880 Owens Dr, Pleasanton (94588-3900)
PHONE....................................925 523-5000
Patricia Smith, *Manager*
Joan Quintanilla, *Regional Mgr*
Bill Serrao, *Info Tech Mgr*
Bhargav Patel, *Software Dev*
Madhavi Alluri, *Programmer Anys*
EMP: 185
SALES (corp-wide): 1.3B **Privately Held**
WEB: www.scif.com
SIC: 6331 9441 Workers' compensation insurance; administration of social & manpower programs;
PA: State Compensation Insurance Fund
333 Bush St Fl 8
San Francisco CA 94104
888 782-8338

(P-10145)
STATE COMPENSATION INSUR FUND
5890 Owens Dr, Pleasanton (94588-3900)
PHONE....................................888 782-8338
Alicia Reyes, *Principal*
Murali Krishna, *Programmer Anys*
Michelle Albert, *Legal Staff*
Michelle Kawaguchi, *Manager*
EMP: 185
SALES (corp-wide): 1.3B **Privately Held**
SIC: 6331 Workers' compensation insurance
PA: State Compensation Insurance Fund
333 Bush St Fl 8
San Francisco CA 94104
888 782-8338

(P-10146)
STATE COMPENSATION INSUR FUND
Also Called: Los Angles Dst Off Policy Svcs
900 Corporate Center Dr, Monterey Park
(91754-7620)
P.O. Box 65005, Fresno (93650-5005)
PHONE....................................323 266-5000
Joe Codron, *Officer*
Jerri Shaul, *Broker*
Jose Altamirano, *Opers Staff*
Shweta Singhal, *Sr Project Mgr*
Kingsley Uba, *Manager*
EMP: 150
SALES (corp-wide): 1.3B **Privately Held**
WEB: www.scif.com
SIC: 6331 9651 Workers' compensation insurance; insurance commission, government;
PA: State Compensation Insurance Fund
333 Bush St Fl 8
San Francisco CA 94104
888 782-8338

(P-10147)
TRISTAR INSURANCE GROUP INC (PA)
Also Called: Tristart Risk Management
100 Oceangate Ste 700, Long Beach
(90802-4368)
PHONE....................................562 495-6600
Thomas J Veale, *President*
Denise J Cotter, *CFO*
Joseph McLaughlin, *Senior VP*
Mary Ann Lubeskie, *Vice Pres*
Pamela Sheffield, *Branch Mgr*
EMP: 700
SQ FT: 9,000
SALES (est): 363.2MM **Privately Held**
SIC: 6331 8741 Workers' compensation insurance; management services

(P-10148)
WAWANESA GENERAL INSURANCE CO
Also Called: Wawansea General Insurance
9050 Friars Rd Ste 200, San Diego
(92108-5800)
P.O. Box 82867 (92138-2867)
PHONE....................................619 285-6020
Jeff Goy, *CEO*
Larry Smith, *CFO*
Angie Cantillon, *Vice Pres*
Leo Morales, *Marketing Mgr*
Rebecca Greene, *General Counsel*
EMP: 500
SALES (est): 302.9MM
SALES (corp-wide): 2.8B **Privately Held**
SIC: 6331 Automobile insurance; property damage insurance
PA: Wawanesa Mutual Insurance Company, The
191 Broadway Suite 900
Winnipeg MB R3C 3
204 985-3923

(P-10149)
WESTERN GENERAL HOLDING CO (PA)
5230 Las Virgenes Rd # 100, Calabasas
(91302-3448)
PHONE....................................818 880-9070
Robert M Ehrlich, *Ch of Bd*
Daniel Mallut, *President*
Marlene Kushner, *Admin Sec*
EMP: 240 **EST:** 1999
SQ FT: 51,000

SALES (est): 98.7MM **Privately Held**
SIC: 6331 Fire, marine & casualty insurance

(P-10150)
WESTERN GENERAL INSURANCE CO
5230 Las Virgenes Rd, Calabasas
(91302-3448)
PHONE....................................818 880-9070
Robert M Ehrlich, *Ch of Bd*
Denise M Tyson, *COO*
John Albanese, *CFO*
Daniel Mallut, *Exec VP*
Marleen Kushner, *Admin Sec*
EMP: 165
SQ FT: 51,000
SALES (est): 65.3MM
SALES (corp-wide): 98.7MM **Privately Held**
SIC: 6331 Automobile insurance
PA: Western General Holding Co
5230 Las Virgenes Rd # 100
Calabasas CA 91302
818 880-9070

(P-10151)
WORKERS COMPENSATION (PA)
Also Called: WCIRB
1221 Broadway Ste 900, Oakland
(94612-1995)
PHONE....................................888 229-2472
William Mudge, *President*
Brenda Keys, *Senior VP*
Timothy Benjamin, *Vice Pres*
EMP: 207
SQ FT: 31,000
SALES: 38.5MM **Privately Held**
SIC: 6331 Workers' compensation insurance

(P-10152)
WORKMENS AUTO INSURANCE CO
714 W Olympic Blvd # 800, Los Angeles
(90015-1440)
PHONE....................................213 742-8700
Jeanette Shammas, *Ch of Bd*
Nicholas J Lannotti, *President*
Denise M Tyson, *President*
EMP: 100
SALES (est): 67.3MM **Privately Held**
SIC: 6331 Fire, marine & casualty insurance

(P-10153)
ZENITH INSURANCE COMPANY (DH)
Also Called: Zenith A Fairfax Company, The
21255 Califa St, Woodland Hills
(91367-5021)
P.O. Box 9055, Van Nuys (91409-9055)
PHONE....................................818 713-1000
Stanley R Zax, *Ch of Bd*
Jack D Miller, *President*
Scott Perrotty, *President*
Kari Van Gundy, *CFO*
Paul Ramont, *Exec VP*
EMP: 400 **EST:** 1950
SQ FT: 120,000
SALES (est): 1B
SALES (corp-wide): 17.7B **Privately Held**
SIC: 6331 Workers' compensation insurance; automobile insurance; agricultural insurance; property damage insurance
HQ: Zenith National Insurance Corp.
21255 Califa St
Woodland Hills CA 91367
818 713-1000

(P-10154)
ZENITH INSURANCE COMPANY
7676 Hazard Center Dr # 1200, San Diego
(92108-4517)
PHONE....................................619 299-6252
Brian Anderson, *Manager*
Steve Adams, *Vice Pres*
Hector Lopez, *HR Admin*
Arlene Schroeder, *Sales Executive*
Amy Trexler, *Nurse*
EMP: 53
SALES (corp-wide): 17.7B **Privately Held**
SIC: 6331 6211 Workers' compensation insurance; underwriters, security

HQ: Zenith Insurance Company
21255 Califa St
Woodland Hills CA 91367
818 713-1000

(P-10155)
ZURICH AMERICAN INSURANCE CO
777 S Figueroa St Ste 400, Los Angeles
(90017-5802)
PHONE.................................213 270-0600
EMP: 53
SALES (corp-wide): 48.2B Privately Held
SIC: 6331 Fire, marine & casualty insurance
HQ: Zurich American Insurance Company
1299 Zurich Way
Schaumburg IL 60196
800 987-3373

(P-10156)
ZURICH AMERICAN INSURANCE CO
525 Market St Ste 2900, San Francisco
(94105-2737)
PHONE.................................415 538-7100
Bill Dougherty, Marketing Staff
Saul Partida, Facilities Mgr
Leah Kimball, Manager
EMP: 200
SALES (corp-wide): 48.2B Privately Held
WEB: www.zurichna.com
SIC: 6331 Fire, marine & casualty insurance
HQ: Zurich American Insurance Company
1299 Zurich Way
Schaumburg IL 60196
800 987-3373

6351 Surety Insurance Carriers

(P-10157)
AIA HOLDINGS INC (PA)
Also Called: Associated Bond
26560 Agoura Rd Ste 100, Calabasas
(91302-2015)
PHONE.................................818 222-4999
Brian N Nairin, President
Robert Kersnick, COO
Mark Francis, CFO
Norman Konvitz, Exec VP
Fred Mitterhoff, Exec VP
EMP: 51
SQ FT: 8,000
SALES (est): 23.1MM Privately Held
WEB: www.aiasurety.com
SIC: 6351 Fidelity or surety bonding

(P-10158)
AMERICAN CONTRS INDEMNITY CO (DH)
Also Called: HCC Surety Group
801 S Figueroa St Ste 700, Los Angeles
(90017-2523)
PHONE.................................213 330-1309
Adam S Pessin, President
Paul A Yasilli, Vice Pres
Azniv Tashdjian, Info Tech Mgr
Jeff Ball, Commercial
EMP: 150
SALES: 160MM Privately Held
WEB: www.hccsurety.com
SIC: 6351 Surety insurance bonding

(P-10159)
AXIOM HOME WARRANTY LLC
2015 Manhattan B, Redondo Beach
(90278)
PHONE.................................844 562-9466
EMP: 190
SALES (est): 104.1K
SALES (corp-wide): 17.4MM Privately Held
SIC: 6351 Warranty insurance, home
PA: Wedgewood Inc.
2015 Manhattan Beach Blvd # 100
Redondo Beach CA 90278
310 640-3070

(P-10160)
BETA HEALTHCARE GROUP (PA)
1443 Danville Blvd, Alamo (94507-1911)
PHONE.................................925 838-6070
Tom Wander, CEO
Michael Willard, CFO
April Johnson, Vice Pres
Andrea Raub, Vice Pres
Deborah Verdream, Human Res Dir
EMP: 60
SQ FT: 10,000
SALES (est): 38.6MM Privately Held
SIC: 6351 6411 Liability insurance; insurance agents, brokers & service

(P-10161)
CAP-MPT (PA)
333 S Hope St Fl 8, Los Angeles
(90071-3001)
PHONE.................................213 473-8600
Jim Weidner, CEO
Michael Wormley MD, Ch of Bd
John Donaldson, CFO
Nancy Brusegaard Johnson, Senior VP
Thomas Andre, Vice Pres
EMP: 140
SALES (est): 63.2MM Privately Held
SIC: 6351 Liability insurance

(P-10162)
DEVELOPERS SURETY INDEMNITY CO (DH)
Also Called: Insco Dico Group, The
17771 Cowan Ste 100, Irvine (92614-6044)
P.O. Box 19725 (92623-9725)
PHONE.................................949 263-3300
Walter Crowell, President
Harry C Crowell, Ch of Bd
David Rhodes, Exec VP
Jodi Traeger, Info Tech Mgr
EMP: 70
SQ FT: 25,000
SALES (est): 48.7MM
SALES (corp-wide): 250MM Privately Held
SIC: 6351 Fidelity or surety bonding

(P-10163)
DOCTORS COMPANY INSURANCE SVCS
185 Greenwood Rd, NAPA (94558-7540)
P.O. Box 2900 (94558-0900)
PHONE.................................707 226-0100
Manuel F Puebla, Ch of Bd
Jack Meyer, President
EMP: 300
SALES (est): 58.9MM
SALES (corp-wide): 700.4MM Privately Held
WEB:
www.residentialsavingsmortgage.com
SIC: 6351 6331 Liability insurance; fire, marine & casualty insurance
PA: The Doctors' Company An Interinsurance Exchange
185 Greenwood Rd
Napa CA 94558
707 226-0100

(P-10164)
INDEMNITY COMPANY CALIFORNIA (DH)
17771 Cowan Ste 100, Irvine (92614-6044)
P.O. Box 19725 (92623-9725)
PHONE.................................949 263-3300
Harry C Crowell, Chairman
Fern Haberman, CFO
Sam Zaza, CFO
Walter A Crowell, Admin Sec
EMP: 71
SQ FT: 50,000
SALES (est): 9.2MM
SALES (corp-wide): 250MM Privately Held
SIC: 6351 Fidelity or surety bonding

(P-10165)
NATIONAL SURETY CORPORATION
1465 N Mcdowell Blvd # 100, Petaluma
(94954-6516)
PHONE.................................415 899-2000
Lori D Fouche, CEO
EMP: 1000

SALES (est): 142.8MM
SALES (corp-wide): 24.9B Privately Held
SIC: 6351 Surety insurance
HQ: Fireman's Fund Insurance Company
1465 N Mcdowell Blvd # 100
Petaluma CA 94954
415 899-2000

(P-10166)
NMI HOLDINGS INC
2100 Powell St Fl 12th, Emeryville
(94608-1894)
PHONE.................................855 530-6642
Bradley M Shuster, Ch of Bd
Claudia J Merkle, President
Adam Pollitzer, CFO
Steven Scheid, Bd of Directors
William J Leatherberry,
EMP: 299 EST: 2011
SQ FT: 47,000
SALES: 275MM Privately Held
SIC: 6351 Mortgage guarantee insurance

(P-10167)
XL SPECIALTY INSURANCE CORP
1340 Treat Blvd, Walnut Creek
(94597-2101)
P.O. Box 8098 (94596)
PHONE.................................925 942-6142
Jim Bily, Assistant VP
EMP: 70
SALES (corp-wide): 1MM Privately Held
SIC: 6351 Surety insurance
HQ: Xl Specialty Insurance Company
10 N Martingale Rd # 220
Schaumburg IL 60173
847 517-2990

6361 Title Insurance

(P-10168)
CALIFORNIA TITLE CO NTHRN CAL
1955 Hunts Ln Ste 102, San Bernardino
(92408-3344)
PHONE.................................909 825-8800
Jim Sollami, Manager
EMP: 103 Privately Held
WEB: www.octitle.com
SIC: 6361 Title insurance
HQ: California Title Company Of Northern California
1551 N Tustin Ave Ste 300
Santa Ana CA 92705
714 558-2836

(P-10169)
CALIFORNIA TITLE COMPANY
2365 Northside Dr Ste 250, San Diego
(92108-2719)
PHONE.................................619 516-5227
Jim Waterman, President
Chuck Bishop, Assistant
EMP: 65
SALES (est): 8.3MM
SALES (corp-wide): 4.3MM Privately Held
SIC: 6361 Title insurance
PA: California Title Company
28202 Cabot Rd Ste 625
Laguna Niguel CA 92677
949 582-8709

(P-10170)
CHICAGO TITLE AND TRUST CO
535 N Brnd Blvrd Fl 3 Flr 3, Glendale
(91203)
PHONE.................................818 548-0222
Mike Bossard, Principal
Kevin Lail, Officer
Daryl Savidis, Officer
Edwin Ditlow, Vice Pres
EMP: 50
SALES (corp-wide): 7.5B Publicly Held
SIC: 6361 Real estate title insurance
HQ: Chicago Title And Trust Company
10 S La Salle St Ste 3100
Chicago IL 60603
312 223-2000

(P-10171)
CHICAGO TITLE COMPANY
675 N 1st St Ste 400, San Jose
(95112-5111)
PHONE.................................408 292-4212
Randy Couurk, Owner
Ray Marine, Exec VP
Madeline G M Lovejoy, Vice Pres
EMP: 114 EST: 2010
SALES (est): 305.7K Privately Held
SIC: 6361 Real estate title insurance

(P-10172)
CHICAGO TITLE COMPANY
701 B St Ste 1120, San Diego
(92101-8103)
PHONE.................................619 230-6340
Madeline Lovejoy, Principal
Joe Goodman, Principal
Madeline G M Lovejoy, Principal
EMP: 107 EST: 1984
SQ FT: 2,650
SALES (est): 25.4MM Privately Held
SIC: 6361 Title insurance

(P-10173)
CHICAGO TITLE COMPANY
725 S Figueroa St Ste 200, Los Angeles
(90017-5403)
PHONE.................................213 488-4375
Cheryl Yanez, President
Deborah Nickerson, Human Resources
Madeline Lovejoy, Assistant VP
Maria Leal, Supervisor
EMP: 70
SALES (est): 22.4MM
SALES (corp-wide): 7.5B Publicly Held
SIC: 6361 Title insurance
PA: Fidelity National Financial, Inc.
601 Riverside Ave Fl 4
Jacksonville FL 32204
904 854-8100

(P-10174)
CHICAGO TITLE COMPANY
7330 N Palm Ave Ste 101, Fresno
(93711-5768)
PHONE.................................559 451-3700
Mark Barsotti, Vice Pres
Lisa Williams, Agent
EMP: 60 EST: 1989
SQ FT: 10,000
SALES (est): 4.5MM Privately Held
SIC: 6361 Real estate title insurance

(P-10175)
CHICAGO TITLE INSURANCE CO
105 Lake Forest Way, Folsom
(95630-4708)
PHONE.................................916 985-0300
Steve Siqueiros, Manager
EMP: 50
SALES (corp-wide): 7.5B Publicly Held
SIC: 6361 Real estate title insurance
HQ: Chicago Title Insurance Company
4050 Calle Real
Santa Barbara CA 93110

(P-10176)
CHICAGO TITLE INSURANCE CO
925 Highland Pointe Dr # 340, Roseville
(95678-5423)
PHONE.................................916 783-7195
Patty Harris, Vice Pres
Kristen Gomes, Officer
Laura Morales, Officer
Joann Perez, Officer
Alisha Wood, Officer
EMP: 293
SALES (corp-wide): 7.5B Publicly Held
SIC: 6361 Real estate title insurance
HQ: Chicago Title Insurance Company
601 Riverside Ave
Jacksonville FL 32204

(P-10177)
CHICAGO TITLE INSURANCE CO (HQ)
4050 Calle Real, Santa Barbara
(93110-3413)
PHONE.................................805 565-6900
William Halvorsen, President
A Larry Sisk, Treasurer
Peter G Leemputte, Vice Pres

P R O D U C T S & S V C S

EMP: 150
SQ FT: 44,637
SALES (est): 769.8MM
SALES (corp-wide): 7.5B **Publicly Held**
SIC: 6361 Real estate title insurance
PA: Fidelity National Financial, Inc.
601 Riverside Ave Fl 4
Jacksonville FL 32204
904 854-8100

(P-10178)
CHICAGO TITLE INSURANCE CO
120 N Floral St, Visalia (93291-6202)
P.O. Box 1191 (93279-1191)
PHONE.....................559 733-3814
Scott Collins, *President*
EMP: 64
SALES (corp-wide): 7.5B **Publicly Held**
SIC: 6361 Real estate title insurance
HQ: Chicago Title Insurance Company
4050 Calle Real
Santa Barbara CA 93110

(P-10179)
COMMONWEALTH LAND TITLE CO
6 Executive Cir Ste 100, Irvine
(92614-6732)
PHONE.....................949 460-4500
Carl Brown, *CEO*
EMP: 100
SALES (corp-wide): 7.5B **Publicly Held**
WEB: www.laurabarnetthomes.com
SIC: 6361 Title insurance
HQ: Commonwealth Land Title Insurance
Company
201 Cncourse Blvd Ste 200
Glen Allen VA 23059
904 854-8100

(P-10180)
CORINTHIAN TITLE COMPANY INC
5030 Camino De La Siesta, San Diego
(92108-3116)
PHONE.....................619 299-4800
Robert J Romano, *Co-CEO*
Michael Godwin, *COO*
Larry Vinti, *CFO*
Robert Romano, *Co-CEO*
Doris Darlek, *Officer*
EMP: 70
SQ FT: 6,000
SALES (est): 12.1MM **Privately Held**
SIC: 6361 Title insurance

(P-10181)
EQUITY TITLE COMPANY (DH)
801 N Brand Blvd Ste 400, Glendale
(91203-3261)
PHONE.....................818 291-4400
Jim Cossell, *President*
Margaret Good, *Officer*
Kevin Razban, *Officer*
Dindo De, *Vice Pres*
Neil Gulley, *Vice Pres*
EMP: 80 EST: 1979
SALES (est): 35.5MM **Publicly Held**
SIC: 6361 Real estate title insurance

(P-10182)
FEDELITY NATIONAL TITLE CO ORG
5000 Van Nuys Blvd 500, Sherman Oaks
(91403-1793)
PHONE.....................818 758-6849
Richard Stine, *Principal*
Sheila Isham, *Officer*
Tamara Ortiz, *Vice Pres*
Renny Harris, *Sales Executive*
Tracy Montoya, *Sales Staff*
EMP: 99 EST: 2010
SALES (est): 16.1MM **Privately Held**
SIC: 6361 Title insurance

(P-10183)
FIDELITY NAT HM WARRANTY CO
1850 Gateway Blvd Ste 400, Concord
(94520-8446)
PHONE.....................925 356-0194
Bill Jensen, *Manager*
EMP: 150

SALES (corp-wide): 7.5B **Publicly Held**
WEB: www.fnhw.com
SIC: 6361 Title insurance
HQ: Fidelity National Home Warranty Company
2950 Buskirk Ave Ste 201
Walnut Creek CA

(P-10184)
FIRST AMERICAN FINANCIAL CORP (PA)
1 First American Way, Santa Ana
(92707-5913)
PHONE.....................714 250-3000
Parker S Kennedy, *Ch of Bd*
George Livermore, *President*
Kathy Vian, *President*
Dennis J Gilmore, *CEO*
Mark E Seaton, *CFO*
EMP: 146
SQ FT: 490,000
SALES: 5.7B **Publicly Held**
SIC: 6361 6351 Title insurance; surety insurance

(P-10185)
FIRST AMERICAN MORTGAGE SVCS
3 First American Way, Santa Ana
(92707-5913)
PHONE.....................714 250-4210
Wes Mee, *President*
Jeanie Matten, *Senior VP*
Margarita Mejia, *Supervisor*
EMP: 350
SALES (est): 134.2MM **Privately Held**
SIC: 6361 Title insurance

(P-10186)
FIRST AMERICAN TITLE INSUR CO (HQ)
1 First American Way, Santa Ana
(92707-5913)
P.O. Box 267 (92702-0267)
PHONE.....................800 854-3643
Dennis J Gilmore, *CEO*
Kurt Pfotenhauer, *Vice Chairman*
Kevin Wall, *President*
Curt Caspersen, *COO*
Curt G Johnson, *Vice Ch Bd*
EMP: 146
SALES (est): 2.8B **Publicly Held**
WEB: www.fatc.com
SIC: 6361 Real estate title insurance

(P-10187)
FIRST AMERICAN TITLE INSUR CO
411 Ivy St, San Diego (92101-2108)
PHONE.....................619 238-1776
Steve Mustin, *Manager*
Larry Buster, *Accounts Mgr*
Michael Murphy, *Representative*
EMP: 160
SQ FT: 14,911 **Publicly Held**
WEB: www.fatc.com
SIC: 6361 6541 6531 Real estate title insurance; title abstract offices; real estate agents & managers
HQ: First American Title Insurance Company
1 First American Way
Santa Ana CA 92707
800 854-3643

(P-10188)
FIRST AMERICAN TITLE INSUR CO
1855 W Rdlands Blvd 100, Redlands
(92373)
PHONE.....................909 889-0311
Dan Williams, *Manager*
Jeff Bright, *Manager*
EMP: 140 **Publicly Held**
WEB: www.fatc.com
SIC: 6361 6541 Real estate title insurance; title abstract offices
HQ: First American Title Insurance Company
1 First American Way
Santa Ana CA 92707
800 854-3643

(P-10189)
FIRST AMERICAN TITLE INSUR CO (HQ)
330 Soquel Ave, Santa Cruz (95062-2300)
PHONE.....................714 250-3109
James Boxdell, *Vice Pres*
Brad Wimmer, *Officer*
Gregg Christiansen, *Software Dev*
Eric Nils Bergkvist, *Analyst*
Tim Young, *Manager*
EMP: 3000
SQ FT: 98,000
SALES (est): 498.7MM **Publicly Held**
WEB: www.fatcola.com
SIC: 6361 Real estate title insurance

(P-10190)
FIRST AMERICAN TITLE INSUR CO
899 Pacific St, San Luis Obispo
(93401-3635)
P.O. Box 1147 (93406-1147)
PHONE.....................805 543-8900
Kevin Irot, *Director*
Lisa Blasquez, *Officer*
EMP: 50 **Publicly Held**
WEB: www.fatc.com
SIC: 6361 Real estate title insurance
HQ: First American Title Insurance Company
1 First American Way
Santa Ana CA 92707
800 854-3643

(P-10191)
FIRST AMERICAN TITLE INSUR CO
Also Called: First American Casualty Insur
9 First American Way, Santa Ana
(92707-5913)
PHONE.....................714 800-3000
Raymond Rai, *Branch Mgr*
EMP: 180 **Publicly Held**
WEB: www.fatc.com
SIC: 6361 Real estate title insurance
HQ: First American Title Insurance Company
1 First American Way
Santa Ana CA 92707
800 854-3643

(P-10192)
FIRST AMERICAN TITLE INSUR CO
Also Called: First Amercn Lenders Advantage
1855 Gateway Blvd Ste 700, Concord
(94520-8455)
PHONE.....................925 798-2800
Tom Schlesinger, *Manager*
Jim Welch, *Vice Pres*
EMP: 70 **Publicly Held**
WEB: www.fatc.com
SIC: 6361 6541 Real estate title insurance; title & trust companies
HQ: First American Title Insurance Company
1 First American Way
Santa Ana CA 92707
800 854-3643

(P-10193)
FIRST AMERICAN TITLE INSUR CO
First American Mortgage Svcs
3 First American Way, Santa Ana
(92707-5913)
PHONE.....................714 250-4000
Pat McLaughlin, *Branch Mgr*
Mike Williams, *President*
Brian Lobuts, *Vice Pres*
Rhonda Gaffney, *Opers Staff*
Carolyn Comer, *Manager*
EMP: 534 **Publicly Held**
SIC: 6361 6541 6531 Real estate title insurance; title abstract offices; real estate agents & managers
HQ: First American Title Insurance Company
1 First American Way
Santa Ana CA 92707
800 854-3643

(P-10194)
FRONTIER TITLE CO (PA)
1499 Oliver Rd, Fairfield (94534-3492)
PHONE.....................707 427-5400
Leonard Gianno, *President*
Jeff Olson, *Exec VP*
Mark Gamba, *Manager*
EMP: 50
SQ FT: 10,000
SALES (est): 8.8MM **Privately Held**
WEB: www.frontiertitleco.com
SIC: 6361 Title insurance

(P-10195)
LAWYERS TITLE COMPANY
4542 Ruffner St Ste 200, San Diego
(92111-2239)
PHONE.....................858 650-3900
John Wall, *Branch Mgr*
Dee D Burland, *Officer*
Janelle Ramirez, *Opers Staff*
Josh White, *Manager*
EMP: 80
SQ FT: 1,800
SALES (corp-wide): 7.5B **Publicly Held**
SIC: 6361 Real estate title insurance
HQ: Lawyers Title Company
7530 N Glenoaks Blvd
Burbank CA 91504
818 767-0425

(P-10196)
LAWYERS TITLE COMPANY (HQ)
7530 N Glenoaks Blvd, Burbank
(91504-1052)
PHONE.....................818 767-0425
Edward Zerwekh, *CEO*
Phil Rodriguez, *Officer*
Edward Beierle, *Senior VP*
Steve Bauer, *Vice Pres*
Mark Quandt, *Vice Pres*
EMP: 50
SQ FT: 20,000
SALES (est): 107MM
SALES (corp-wide): 7.5B **Publicly Held**
SIC: 6361 6531 Real estate title insurance; escrow agent; real estate
PA: Fidelity National Financial, Inc.
601 Riverside Ave Fl 4
Jacksonville FL 32204
904 854-8100

(P-10197)
LAWYERS TITLE INSURANCE CORP
18551 Von Karman Ave # 100, Irvine
(92612-1552)
PHONE.....................949 223-5575
Dan Williams, *Branch Mgr*
EMP: 70
SALES (corp-wide): 7.5B **Publicly Held**
WEB: www.diamondtitleco.com
SIC: 6361 6541 Real estate title insurance; title & trust companies
HQ: Lawyers Title Insurance Corporation
601 Riverside Ave
Jacksonville FL 32204
888 866-3684

(P-10198)
NORTH AMERICAN TITLE CO INC
Also Called: N A T C
6612 Owens Dr 100, Pleasanton
(94588-3334)
PHONE.....................925 399-3000
Jim White, *Manager*
EMP: 60
SQ FT: 32,000
SALES (corp-wide): 20.5B **Publicly Held**
WEB: www.natic.com
SIC: 6361 Real estate title insurance
HQ: North American Title Company, Inc.
1855 Gateway Blvd Ste 600
Concord CA 94520
925 935-5599

(P-10199)
OLD REPUBLIC TITLE COMPANY
101 N Brand Blvd Ste 1400, Glendale
(91203-2691)
PHONE.....................818 240-1936
Merv Morris, *President*
Janice Aurelio, *Officer*

Katie Catlow, *Officer*
Joann Cheng, *Officer*
Kelli Dentone, *Officer*
EMP: 641 **EST:** 1967
SQ FT: 25,000
SALES (est): 260.8MM
SALES (corp-wide): 6B **Publicly Held**
WEB: www.oldrepublictitle.com
SIC: 6361 Title insurance
HQ: Old Republic Title Holding Company, Inc.
275 Battery St Ste 1500
San Francisco CA 94111
415 421-3500

(P-10200)
OLD REPUBLIC TITLE COMPANY
584 S Main St, Salinas (93901-3347)
PHONE....................831 757-8051
Ron Peterson, *President*
EMP: 50
SALES (corp-wide): 6B **Publicly Held**
WEB: www.ortc.com
SIC: 6361 Real estate title insurance
HQ: Old Republic Title Company
275 Battery St Ste 1500
San Francisco CA 94111
415 421-3500

(P-10201)
STEWART TITLE CALIFORNIA INC (DH)
7676 Hazard Center Dr # 1400, San Diego (92108-4516)
PHONE....................619 692-1600
Steve Vivanco, *President*
Gregg Unrath, *Treasurer*
Deborah Britza, *Officer*
Brian Glaze, *Vice Pres*
EMP: 140
SQ FT: 44,000
SALES (est): 142.5MM
SALES (corp-wide): 1.9B **Publicly Held**
WEB: www.stewarttitleco.com
SIC: 6361 Guarantee of titles
HQ: Stewart Title Company
1360 Post Oak Blvd # 100
Houston TX 77056
713 625-8100

(P-10202)
STEWART TITLE CALIFORNIA INC
525 N Brand Blvd Ste 200, Glendale (91203-3993)
PHONE....................818 502-2700
James Reynolds, *Division Pres*
Sandra Kuhlman, *Vice Pres*
Tamara Ortiz, *Vice Pres*
Lynette Sosa, *Asst Controller*
Marcia Packota, *Marketing Staff*
EMP: 125
SALES (corp-wide): 1.9B **Publicly Held**
SIC: 6361 Real estate title insurance
HQ: Stewart Title Of California, Inc.
7676 Hazard Center Dr # 1400
San Diego CA 92108
619 692-1600

(P-10203)
TICOR TITLE COMPANY CALIFORNIA
4210 Riverwalk Pkwy # 200, Riverside (92505-3313)
PHONE....................951 509-0211
Anthony Andre, *Branch Mgr*
EMP: 50
SALES (corp-wide): 7.5B **Publicly Held**
SIC: 6361 Real estate title insurance
HQ: Ticor Title Company Of California
1500 Quail St Ste 300
Newport Beach CA 92660
714 289-7100

(P-10204)
TICOR TITLE INSURANCE COMPANY (DH)
131 N El Molino Ave, Pasadena (91101-1873)
PHONE....................616 302-3121
John Rau, *Ch of Bd*
Gust Totlis, *CFO*
Peter Leemputte, *Treasurer*
Paul T Sands Jr, *Exec VP*

Bryan Willis, *Vice Pres*
EMP: 146
SQ FT: 44,637
SALES (est): 252.1MM
SALES (corp-wide): 7.5B **Publicly Held**
WEB: www.ticortitleindy.com
SIC: 6361 Real estate title insurance
HQ: Chicago Title And Trust Company
10 S La Salle St Ste 3100
Chicago IL 60603
312 223-2000

(P-10205)
WFG NATIONAL TITLE INSUR CO (PA)
Also Called: Alliance Title
700 N Brand Blvd Ste 1100, Glendale (91203-1208)
PHONE....................818 476-4000
Jeffrey Fox, *CEO*
Brandon Baker, *President*
Roberto Olivera, *President*
Chris White, *President*
James Lokay, *CFO*
EMP: 300 **EST:** 1980
SQ FT: 15,000
SALES (est): 142MM **Privately Held**
WEB: www.investorstitle.com
SIC: 6361 Title insurance

6371 Pension, Health & Welfare Funds

(P-10206)
ALAMEDA COUNTY EMPLOYEES RETIR
Also Called: Acera
475 14th St Ste 1000, Oakland (94612-1916)
PHONE....................510 628-3000
Charles Conrad, *General Mgr*
Catherine Walker, *CEO*
Elizabeth Rogers, *Bd of Directors*
Darryl Walker, *Trustee*
Betty TSE, *Ch Invest Ofcr*
EMP: 70
SALES (est): 44.6MM **Privately Held**
WEB: www.acera.org
SIC: 6371 Pension funds

(P-10207)
ASSOCTED THIRD PTY ADMNSTRTORS
2831 Camino Del Rio S, San Diego (92108-3802)
PHONE....................619 358-8140
EMP: 200
SALES (corp-wide): 482.8MM **Privately Held**
SIC: 6371
PA: Associated Third Party Administrators Inc
222 N Sepulveda Blvd # 2000
El Segundo CA 90245
-

(P-10208)
CAL SOUTHERN UNITED FOOD
Also Called: U F C Pension Trust Fund
6425 Katella Ave, Cypress (90630-5246)
P.O. Box 6010 (90630-0010)
PHONE....................714 220-2297
P Thompson, *Administration*
William Smith, *Analyst*
Dawn Fujihara, *Bookkeeper*
Carol Antonucci, *Human Res Mgr*
Patricia Mathieu, *Director*
EMP: 240 **EST:** 1957
SQ FT: 36,000
SALES (est): 97.4MM **Privately Held**
WEB: www.scufcwfunds.com
SIC: 6371 Pension funds

(P-10209)
CALIFOR STATE TEACH RETIRE SYS (DH)
Also Called: Cal Strs
100 Waterfront Pl, West Sacramento (95605-2807)
P.O. Box 15275, Sacramento (95851-0275)
PHONE....................800 228-5453
James D Mosman, *CEO*
Dana Dillon, *Ch of Bd*

Sharon Hendricks, *Ch of Bd*
Todd Golterman, *Technology*
EMP: 129
SQ FT: 100,000
SALES (est): 444.7MM **Privately Held**
WEB: www.calstrs.com
SIC: 6371 9441 Pension, health & welfare funds; administration of social & manpower programs;

(P-10210)
CALIFORNIA GOVRNMNT OPR AGNCY
Also Called: Califrnia Tchers Rtirement Sys
7667 Folsom Blvd Fl 3, Sacramento (95826-2618)
PHONE....................800 228-5453
James D Mosman, *Director*
EMP: 535 **Privately Held**
SIC: 6371 Pension, health & welfare funds
HQ: California Government Operations Agency
915 Capitol Mall Ste 200
Sacramento CA 95814
-

(P-10211)
CALIFORNIA PUBLIC EMPLYEES RET
Also Called: Calpers Investment Office
400 P St Ste 1204, Sacramento (95814-5346)
PHONE....................916 795-3000
Fred Buenrostro, *Manager*
Laurel Aagaard, *Human Res Mgr*
EMP: 150 **Privately Held**
WEB: www.calpers.net
SIC: 6371 9441 Pension funds; administration of social & manpower programs;
HQ: California Public Employees' Retirement System
400 Q St
Sacramento CA 95811
-

(P-10212)
CALIFORNIA PUBLIC EMPLYEES RET (DH)
400 Q St, Sacramento (95811-6201)
P.O. Box 942706 (94229-2706)
PHONE....................916 795-3000
Anne Stausboll, *CEO*
Kathie Vaughn, *Officer*
Robert D Walton, *Officer*
Terri Westbrook, *Officer*
Gloria Moore Andrews, *Exec VP*
EMP: 1600
SALES (est): 1.2B **Privately Held**
WEB: www.calpers.net
SIC: 6371 9441 Pension funds; administration of social & manpower programs;

(P-10213)
CHELBAY SCHULER & CHELBAY (PA)
Also Called: United Administrative Services
6800 Santa Teresa Blvd # 100, San Jose (95119-1238)
P.O. Box 5057 (95150-5057)
PHONE....................408 288-4400
Robert J Bradley, *President*
Sharon Crist, *Vice Pres*
Brea Geesaman, *Manager*
Alice Espinoza, *Supervisor*
EMP: 100
SQ FT: 35,000
SALES (est): 46.6MM **Privately Held**
WEB: www.chelbayins.com
SIC: 6371 Pension funds

(P-10214)
COUNTY OF LOS ANGELES
Also Called: Public Social Services
27233 Camp Plenty Rd, Canyon Country (91351-2634)
PHONE....................661 298-3406
Hilda Ochoa, *Manager*
Kyle Fortson, *Officer*
EMP: 60 **Privately Held**
WEB: www.co.la.ca.us
SIC: 6371 Union welfare, benefit & health funds

PA: County Of Los Angeles
500 W Temple St Ste 437
Los Angeles CA 90012
213 974-1101

(P-10215)
COUNTY OF SHASTA
Also Called: Shasta County Calworks
1400 California St, Redding (96001-1004)
PHONE....................530 225-5000
Linda Parks, *Manager*
EMP: 90 **Privately Held**
WEB: www.rsdnmp.org
SIC: 6371 8748 Union welfare, benefit & health funds; employee programs administration
PA: County Of Shasta
1450 Court St Ste 308a
Redding CA 96001
530 225-5561

(P-10216)
EMPLOYEE BENEFITS SECURITY ADM
Also Called: Los Angeles Regional Office
1055 E Colo Blvd Ste 200, Pasadena (91106)
PHONE....................626 229-1000
EMP: 55 **Publicly Held**
SIC: 6371
HQ: Employee Benefits Security Administration
200 Constitution Ave Nw
Washington DC 20210
202 219-8233

(P-10217)
LIPMAN INSUR ADMNISTRATORS INC (PA)
39420 Liberty St Ste 260, Fremont (94538-2297)
P.O. Box 5820 (94537-5820)
PHONE....................510 796-4676
Frederic J Lipman, *President*
Janet Sylvester, *CFO*
Margaret Epstein, *Admin Sec*
EMP: 60
SQ FT: 14,000
SALES (est): 42.9MM **Privately Held**
SIC: 6371 Union welfare, benefit & health funds

(P-10218)
LOS ANGELES CNTY EMP RETIREMNT (PA)
Also Called: LACERA
300 N Lake Ave Ste 720, Pasadena (91101-5674)
P.O. Box 7060 (91109-7060)
PHONE....................626 564-6000
Gregg Rademather, *CEO*
Vivian Gray, *Trustee*
Jonathan Grabel, *Ch Invest Ofcr*
Robert Santos, *Officer*
Christopher J Wagner, *Sr Invest Ofcr*
EMP: 340
SQ FT: 85,000
SALES: 2B **Privately Held**
SIC: 6371 Pension funds

(P-10219)
MOTION PCTURE HLTH WLFARE FUND
11365 Ventura Blvd # 300, Studio City (91604-3148)
P.O. Box 1999 (91614-0999)
PHONE....................818 769-0007
Thomas Zimmerman, *Exec Dir*
Theodre Friesen, *CFO*
Long Voong, *IT/INT Sup*
EMP: 215
SQ FT: 27,715
SALES (est): 20.9MM **Privately Held**
SIC: 6371 Union welfare, benefit & health funds

(P-10220)
MOTION PICTURE INDUSTRY PLANS
11365 Ventura Blvd # 300, Studio City (91604-3148)
PHONE....................818 769-0007
David Wescoe, *CEO*
Chuck Killian, *CFO*
Victor Delgado, *Administration*

Joel Manfredo, *CIO*
Patrick Carmona, *Info Tech Dir*
EMP: 150
SQ FT: 12,500
SALES (est): 85.9MM **Privately Held**
SIC: 6371 Pension, health & welfare funds

(P-10221)
NORCO FIRE DEPARTMENT
3902 Hillside Ave, Norco (92860-1515)
PHONE....................951 737-8097
Ron Larson, *President*
EMP: 700
SALES (est): 245.4K **Privately Held**
SIC: 6371 Union funds

(P-10222)
PRODUCER -WRITERS GUILD
2900 W Alameda Ave # 1100, Burbank
(91505-4267)
PHONE....................818 846-1015
Jim Hedges, *Administration*
Rocco Calabrese, *Administration*
Alan Weidlich, *CIO*
Bob Chen, *Network Mgr*
Sero Eskandaryan, *Web Dvlpr*
EMP: 70
SQ FT: 30,000
SALES (est): 39.9MM **Privately Held**
WEB: www.wgaplans.org
SIC: 6371 Pension funds; pensions

(P-10223)
PUBLIC EMPLOYEES
RETIREMENT
Also Called: Calpers
400 Q St, Sacramento (95811-6201)
PHONE....................916 795-3400
Russell Fong, *Branch Mgr*
Kelly Brown, *Administration*
Mike Pieracci, *Software Engr*
Charles Carrasco, *Business Anlyst*
Eric Asai, *IT/INT Sup*
EMP: 331 **Privately Held**
SIC: 6371 9441 Pension funds; adminis-
tration of social & manpower programs;
HQ: California Public Employees' Retire-
ment System
400 Q St
Sacramento CA 95811

(P-10224)
SCREEN ACTORS GUILD -
AMERICAN
Also Called: Screen Actors Guild-Producers
3601 W Olive Ave Fl 2, Burbank
(91505-4662)
P.O. Box 7830 (91510-7830)
PHONE....................818 954-9400
Terence Young, *Admin Dir*
Amanda Bernard, *Exec Dir*
Sherry Donnelly, *Accountant*
Francis Zaragoza, *Accountant*
Gene Kalpakian, *Controller*
EMP: 184
SALES (corp-wide): 59.7MM **Privately
Held**
SIC: 6371 6411 Pensions; pension & re-
tirement plan consultants
PA: Screen Actors Guild - American Feder-
ation Of Television And Radio Artists
5757 Wilshire Blvd Fl 7
Los Angeles CA 90036
415 391-7510

(P-10225)
UNITED ADMINISTRATIVE
SERVICES
6800 Santa Teresa Blvd # 100, San Jose
(95119-1239)
PHONE....................408 288-4400
David Andresen, *President*
Sharon Crist, *Vice Pres*
EMP: 107
SQ FT: 35,000
SALES (est): 11.7MM
SALES (corp-wide): 46.6MM **Privately
Held**
WEB: www.eebenefitplans.com
SIC: 6371 Pension funds; union welfare,
benefit & health funds
PA: Chelbay, Schuler & Chelbay
6800 Santa Teresa Blvd # 100
San Jose CA 95119
408 288-4400

(P-10226)
WOODMONT REALTY ADVISORS
INC
1050 Ralston Ave, Belmont (94002-2240)
PHONE....................650 592-3960
Ronald V Granville, *CEO*
Howard Friedman, *President*
Caryn Kali, *CFO*
Sarah Davison, *Property Mgr*
Greg Perez, *Property Mgr*
EMP: 70
SQ FT: 10,000
SALES (est): 15.8MM **Privately Held**
WEB: www.wres.com
SIC: 6371 Pension funds
PA: Woodmont Real Estate Services, L.P.
1050 Ralston Ave
Belmont CA 94002

6399 Insurance Carriers, NEC

(P-10227)
AMERICAN INTL GROUP INC
Also Called: Sun America
777 S Figueroa St # 1800, Los Angeles
(90017-5800)
PHONE....................213 689-3500
Gregg Piltch, *President*
Douglas Dowling, *Vice Pres*
Landon O'Hara, *Vice Pres*
Cara Hilton, *Technology*
Ali Seyed-Kazemi, *Technology*
EMP: 300
SALES (corp-wide): 47.3B **Publicly Held**
SIC: 6399 Deposit insurance
PA: American International Group, Inc.
80 Pine St Fl 4
New York NY 10005
212 770-7000

(P-10228)
CALIFRNIA INSUR GUARANTEE
ASSN
Also Called: C I G A
101 N Brand Blvd Ste 600, Glendale
(91203-2653)
P.O. Box 29066 (91209-9066)
PHONE....................818 844-4300
Lawrence E Mulryan, *Director*
Elizabeth Hunter, *Treasurer*
Dena Williams, *Officer*
Wayne Wilson, *Exec Dir*
Devo Heller, *Info Tech Dir*
EMP: 110 **EST:** 1969
SALES (est): 72.2MM **Privately Held**
WEB: www.caiga.org
SIC: 6399 Health insurance for pets

(P-10229)
FEDERAL DEPOSIT INSURANCE
CORP
1333 S Mayflower Ave # 450, Monrovia
(91016-4066)
PHONE....................626 359-7152
Donald Powell, *Manager*
EMP: 123
SALES (corp-wide): 11.6B **Privately Held**
WEB: www.fdic.gov
SIC: 6399 9311 Federal Deposit Insurance
Corporation (FDIC); finance, taxation &
monetary policy;
PA: Federal Deposit Insurance Corporation
550 17th St Nw
Washington DC 20429
877 275-3342

(P-10230)
FEDERAL DEPOSIT INSURANCE
CORP
Also Called: FDIC-San Frncisco Regional Off
25 Jessie St Ste 2300, San Francisco
(94105-2780)
PHONE....................415 546-0160
Stan Ivie, *Branch Mgr*
Pat Sloan, *Vice Pres*
George Masa, *Principal*
Martin Briseno, *Admin Asst*
Lloyd Miller, *IT/INT Sup*
EMP: 150
SQ FT: 127,215

SALES (corp-wide): 11.6B **Privately Held**
WEB: www.fdic.gov
SIC: 6399 9311 Federal Deposit Insurance
Corporation (FDIC); finance, taxation &
monetary policy
PA: Federal Deposit Insurance Corporation
550 17th St Nw
Washington DC 20429
877 275-3342

(P-10231)
FEDERAL DEPOSIT INSURANCE
CORP
Also Called: FDIC
5150 W Goldleaf Cir # 405, Los Angeles
(90056-1662)
PHONE....................323 545-9260
EMP: 123
SALES (corp-wide): 11.6B **Privately Held**
WEB: www.fdic.gov
SIC: 6399 9311 Federal Deposit Insurance
Corporation (FDIC);
PA: Federal Deposit Insurance Corporation
550 17th St Nw
Washington DC 20429
877 275-3342

(P-10232)
FEDERAL DEPOSIT INSURANCE
CORP
Also Called: F D I C
1532 Eureka Rd Ste 102, Roseville
(95661-3054)
PHONE....................916 789-8580
Andrea Davis, *Manager*
EMP: 123
SALES (corp-wide): 11.6B **Privately Held**
WEB: www.fdic.gov
SIC: 6399 9311 Federal Deposit Insurance
Corporation (FDIC); finance, taxation &
monetary policy;
PA: Federal Deposit Insurance Corporation
550 17th St Nw
Washington DC 20429
877 275-3342

(P-10233)
KANOPY INSURANCE CENTER
LLC
545 N Mountain Ave # 205, Upland
(91786-5055)
PHONE....................877 513-2434
Ryan McClintock, *CEO*
EMP: 140 **EST:** 2013
SQ FT: 1,700
SALES: 650K **Privately Held**
SIC: 6399 6311 6351 Warranty insurance,
automobile; life insurance; warranty insur-
ance, home

(P-10234)
LISI INC
2677 N Main St Ste 350, Santa Ana
(92705-6750)
PHONE....................714 460-5153
Philip Lebherz, *Branch Mgr*
Ryan Esway, *Sales Staff*
Kay Jacobson, *Underwriter*
EMP: 71
SALES (corp-wide): 100.3MM **Privately
Held**
SIC: 6399 Deposit insurance
PA: Lisi, Inc.
1600 W Hillsdale Blvd # 202
San Mateo CA 94402
650 348-4131

(P-10235)
ROBERT W BAIRD & CO INC
360 Sierra College Dr # 200, Grass Valley
(95945-5088)
PHONE....................530 271-3000
Jonathan H Lee, *Director*
Preston Daniells, *Advisor*
EMP: 848
SALES (est): 1.8MM
SALES (corp-wide): 312.7MM **Privately
Held**
SIC: 6399 Deposit insurance
PA: Baird Holding Company
777 E Wisconsin Ave
Milwaukee WI 53202
414 765-3500

(P-10236)
SQUARETRADE INC (DH)
600 Harrison St Ste 400, San Francisco
(94107-1370)
PHONE....................415 541-1000
Ahmedulla Khaishgi, *President*
Mark Etnyre, *CFO*
Steve Abernethy, *Chairman*
Vince Tseng, *Officer*
EMP: 146
SQ FT: 54,000
SALES (est): 1.1B **Publicly Held**
WEB: www.squaretrade.com
SIC: 6399 Warranty insurance, product;
except automobile
HQ: Allstate Non Insurance Holdings Inc
2775 Sanders Rd Ste D
Northbrook IL 60062
847 402-5000

(P-10237)
TOPA INSURANCE COMPANY
(HQ)
1800 Ave Of Stars # 1200, Los Angeles
(90067-4200)
PHONE....................310 201-0451
John E Anderson, *Ch of Bd*
Harris Hur, *President*
Noshirwan Marfatia, *President*
Dan Sherrin, *CFO*
Harry W Degner, *Vice Ch Bd*
EMP: 79
SALES (est): 45MM
SALES (corp-wide): 433.6MM **Privately
Held**
WEB: www.mcnabbins.com
SIC: 6399 Warranty insurance, product;
except automobile
PA: Topa Equities, Ltd.
1800 Ave Of The
Los Angeles CA 90067
310 203-9199

6411 Insurance Agents, Brokers & Svc

(P-10238)
21ST CENTURY INSURANCE
COMPANY (DH)
6301 Owensmouth Ave, Woodland Hills
(91367-2216)
PHONE....................877 310-5687
Glenn A Pfeil, *CEO*
Richard R Andre, *Senior VP*
Michael J Cassanego, *Senior VP*
Dean E Stark, *Senior VP*
Barbary Baer, *Principal*
EMP: 1800
SQ FT: 412,000
SALES (est): 800.6MM
SALES (corp-wide): 48.2B **Privately Held**
SIC: 6411 Fire insurance underwriters' lab-
oratories
HQ: 21st Century North America Insurance
Company
3 Beaver Valley Rd
Wilmington DE 19803
877 310-5687

(P-10239)
ABD INSURANCE & FINCL SVCS
INC (PA)
3 Waters Park Dr Ste 100, San Mateo
(94403-1162)
PHONE....................650 488-8565
Brian M Hetherington, *CEO*
Kurt De Grosz, *President*
Carolyn Locke, *President*
Helen Yu, *COO*
Michael F McCloskey, *CFO*
EMP: 72 **EST:** 2009
SQ FT: 14,000
SALES (est): 61.6MM
SALES (corp-wide): 58MM **Privately
Held**
SIC: 6411 Insurance brokers

(P-10240)
ACE FINANCIAL SERVICES INC
Also Called: Ace Property & Casualty
39300 Civic Center Dr # 290, Fremont
(94538-2338)
PHONE....................510 790-4600

Angela Argiros, *Principal*
EMP: 70
SALES (corp-wide): 32.7B **Privately Held**
WEB: www.ace-ina.com
SIC: 6411 6331 Insurance agents, brokers
& service; fire, marine & casualty insurance
HQ: Chubb Insurance Company
11133 Ave Of The Americas
New York NY 10019
212 642-7800

(P-10241)
ACE USA
39300 Civic Center Dr # 290, Fremont
(94538-2337)
PHONE...................................510 790-4695
EMP: 65
SALES (est): 3.8MM
SALES (corp-wide): 17.2B **Privately Held**
SIC: 6411
HQ: Ace Usa, Inc.
436 Walnut St
Philadelphia PA 19106
215 923-5352

(P-10242)
ADMINSURE INC
3380 Shelby St, Ontario (91764-5566)
PHONE...................................909 718-1200
Alithia Vargas-Flores, *President*
EMP: 130
SQ FT: 30,000
SALES (est): 1.6MM **Privately Held**
WEB: www.colenandlee.com
SIC: 6411 Insurance agents

(P-10243)
ADRIANAS INSURANCE SVCS
INC (PA)
9445 Charles Smith Ave, Rancho Cucamonga (91730-5546)
PHONE...................................909 291-4040
Leon Fregoso, *President*
EMP: 54
SALES (est): 71.5MM **Privately Held**
SIC: 6411 Insurance agents

(P-10244)
AIG DIRECT INSURANCE SVCS
INC
9640 Gran Rdge Dr Ste 200, San Diego
(92123)
PHONE...................................858 309-3000
Ron Harris, *CEO*
Laura Huffman, *Exec VP*
Patty Karstein, *Vice Pres*
Kevin Wilshusen, *Vice Pres*
EMP: 275
SQ FT: 24,000
SALES (est): 91.5MM
SALES (corp-wide): 47.3B **Publicly Held**
WEB: www.matrixdirect.com
SIC: 6411 Insurance agents
HQ: American General Life Insurance Company
2727 Allen Pkwy Ste A
Houston TX 77019
713 522-1111

(P-10245)
ALL MOTORISTS INSURANCE
AGENCY
Also Called: W G Warranty and Insur Svcs
5230 Las Virgenes Rd # 100, Calabasas
(91302-3448)
PHONE...................................818 880-9070
Robert M Ehrlich, *President*
Patsy Brents, *Treasurer*
Daniel Mallut, *Exec VP*
Marleen F Kushner, *Admin Sec*
EMP: 250
SQ FT: 51,000
SALES (est): 33.4MM
SALES (corp-wide): 98.7MM **Privately**
Held
WEB: www.westerngeneral.com
SIC: 6411 Insurance agents, brokers &
service
PA: Western General Holding Co
5230 Las Virgenes Rd # 100
Calabasas CA 91302
818 880-9070

(P-10246)
ALLSTATE RESEARCH AND PLG
CTR
4200 Bohannon Dr Ste 200, Menlo Park
(94025-1019)
PHONE...................................650 833-6200
Peggy Brinkmann, *Director*
EMP: 90
SALES (est): 9.5MM **Publicly Held**
SIC: 6411 Insurance agents, brokers &
service
PA: The Allstate Corporation
2775 Sanders Rd
Northbrook IL 60062

(P-10247)
AMERICAN AUTOMOBILE
Also Called: Csaa Travel Agency
3055 Oak Rd, Walnut Creek (94597-2098)
PHONE...................................925 279-2300
John Wu, *Principal*
EMP: 67
SALES (corp-wide): 907.9MM **Privately**
Held
WEB: www.californiastateautomobileassociation.c
SIC: 6411 7549 Insurance agents, brokers
& service; inspection & diagnostic service,
automotive
PA: American Automobile Association Of
Northern California, Nevada & Utah
1900 Powell St Ste 1200
Emeryville CA 94608
800 922-8228

(P-10248)
AMERICAN FIDELITY
ASSURANCE CO
3649 W Beechwood Ave # 103, Fresno
(93711-0693)
PHONE...................................559 230-2107
Amanda Dillon, *Branch Mgr*
EMP: 99 **Privately Held**
SIC: 6411 Insurance agents
HQ: American Fidelity Assurance Company
9000 Cameron Pkwy
Oklahoma City OK 73114
405 523-2000

(P-10249)
AMERICAN GENERAL LIFE
INSUR
455 Hickey Blvd Ste 500, Daly City
(94015-2631)
PHONE...................................650 994-6679
Yuriy Kushnir, *Sales Staff*
Roger Relph, *Administration*
EMP: 80
SALES (corp-wide): 47.3B **Publicly Held**
WEB: www.dejonghfinancial.com
SIC: 6411 6311 Insurance agents, brokers
& service; life insurance
HQ: American General Life Insurance
1 Franklin Sq
Springfield IL 62703
217 528-2011

(P-10250)
AMERICAN INTL GROUP INC
Also Called: AIG Private Client Group
9350 Waxie Way Ste 300, San Diego
(92123-1052)
PHONE...................................619 682-4058
Jack Devlin, *Manager*
Alex Posadas, *Executive*
Sue Johnson, *Program Mgr*
Angela Thomas, *Technician*
Bradley R McGowan, *Finance Mgr*
EMP: 150
SALES (corp-wide): 47.3B **Publicly Held**
WEB: www.aiglifeinsurancecompany.com
SIC: 6411 Insurance agents, brokers &
service
PA: American International Group, Inc.
80 Pine St Fl 4
New York NY 10005
212 770-7000

(P-10251)
AMERICAN SPECIALTY HEALTH
INC (PA)
10221 Wateridge Cir # 201, San Diego
(92121-2702)
PHONE...................................858 754-2000

George Devries III, *CEO*
Kim Dugan, *CFO*
William Komer Jr, *Treasurer*
Doug Metz, *Officer*
Kirk Hartman, *Assoc VP*
EMP: 146
SALES: 424MM **Privately Held**
SIC: 6411 8082 Insurance information &
consulting services; home health care
services

(P-10252)
AMERICAS FLOOD SERVICES
INC
3350 Country Club Dr # 201, Cameron Park
(95682-8657)
P.O. Box 913112, Denver CO (80291-3112)
PHONE...................................916 636-9460
John F Gibson, *President*
EMP: 100
SQ FT: 5,000
SALES (est): 10.7MM
SALES (corp-wide): 161.5MM **Privately**
Held
SIC: 6411 6331 Insurance agents; fire,
marine & casualty insurance
PA: The Bruce Seibels Group Inc
1501 Lady St
Columbia SC 29201
803 748-2000

(P-10253)
AMICA MUTUAL INSURANCE
COMPANY
3200 Park Center Dr # 650, Costa Mesa
(92626-7163)
PHONE...................................877 972-6422
Robert Mc Girr, *Principal*
Peter Gearon, *Manager*
Dominique Cothran, *Accounts Mgr*
Laurie Leehan, *Contractor*
Michele Bray, *Representative*
EMP: 60
SALES (corp-wide): 2B **Privately Held**
WEB: www.amica.com
SIC: 6411 Insurance agents, brokers &
service
PA: Amica Mutual Insurance Company
100 Amica Way
Lincoln RI 02865
800 992-6422

(P-10254)
AMWINS INSURANCE BRKG
CAL LLC (HQ)
21550 Oxnard St Ste 1100, Woodland Hills
(91367-7106)
PHONE...................................818 772-1774
Michael Steven Decarlo,
George Maggay, *President*
Jones Kristin, *Vice Pres*
Scott Strickland, *Vice Pres*
Garrett Hayes, *Info Tech Dir*
EMP: 60 **EST:** 1981
SQ FT: 16,000
SALES (est): 20.6MM
SALES (corp-wide): 773MM **Privately**
Held
SIC: 6411 Insurance brokers
PA: Amwins Group, Inc.
4725 Piedmont Row Dr # 600
Charlotte NC 28210
704 749-2700

(P-10255)
ANCHOR GENERAL INSURANCE
AGCY
10256 Meanley Dr, San Diego
(92131-3009)
P.O. Box 509020 (92150-9020)
PHONE...................................858 527-3600
Abdulla Badani, *President*
EMP: 203
SALES (est): 56.1MM **Privately Held**
SIC: 6411 Insurance agents

(P-10256)
ANDREINI & COMPANY (PA)
220 W 20th Ave, San Mateo (94403-1339)
PHONE...................................650 573-1111
Michael J Colzani, *CEO*
Craig Oden, *Managing Prtnr*
Jeff Tebow, *Managing Prtnr*
John Andreini, *President*
Henry Chen, *CFO*

EMP: 95
SQ FT: 30,000
SALES (est): 80.9MM **Privately Held**
WEB: www.andreini.com
SIC: 6411 Insurance brokers; insurance
agents

(P-10257)
ANKA BEHAVIORAL HEALTH
INC
Also Called: Phoenix Home Lf Mutl Insur Co
2100 State St, Hemet (92543-7623)
PHONE...................................951 929-2744
Don Cox, *Administration*
EMP: 156
SALES (corp-wide): 40.4MM **Privately**
Held
SIC: 6411 8051 Property & casualty insurance agent; mental retardation hospital
PA: Anka Behavioral Health, Incorporated
3840 Buskirk Ave Ste 300
Pleasant Hill CA 94523
925 825-4700

(P-10258)
AON CONSULTING INC
707 Wilshire Blvd # 2500, Los Angeles
(90017-3534)
PHONE...................................818 506-4300
Richard Schumacher, *Manager*
EMP: 60
SQ FT: 18,000
SALES (corp-wide): 10.7B **Privately Held**
WEB: www.radford.com
SIC: 6411 7361 Insurance brokers; employment agencies
HQ: Aon Consulting, Inc.
200 E Randolph St Ll3
Chicago IL 60601

(P-10259)
AON CONSULTING INC
3461 Fair Oaks Blvd, Sacramento
(95864-5702)
PHONE...................................800 558-0655
Kelly McMillan, *Branch Mgr*
EMP: 61
SALES (corp-wide): 10.7B **Privately Held**
SIC: 6411 Insurance brokers
HQ: Aon Consulting, Inc.
200 E Randolph St Ll3
Chicago IL 60601

(P-10260)
AON CONSULTING INC
21900 Burbank Blvd # 101, Woodland Hills
(91367-6469)
PHONE...................................562 345-4700
EMP: 61
SALES (corp-wide): 10.7B **Privately Held**
SIC: 6411 Insurance brokers
HQ: Aon Consulting, Inc.
200 E Randolph St Ll3
Chicago IL 60601

(P-10261)
AON CONSULTING INC
851 Van Ness Ave Fl 2, San Francisco
(94109-7876)
PHONE...................................800 283-1667
EMP: 61
SALES (corp-wide): 10.7B **Privately Held**
SIC: 6411 Insurance brokers
HQ: Aon Consulting, Inc.
200 E Randolph St Ll3
Chicago IL 60601

(P-10262)
AON CONSULTING INC
160 Via Verde Ste 200, San Dimas
(91773-5121)
PHONE...................................800 815-1823
EMP: 61
SALES (corp-wide): 10.7B **Privately Held**
SIC: 6411 Insurance brokers
HQ: Aon Consulting, Inc.
200 E Randolph St Ll3
Chicago IL 60601

P
R
O
D
U
C
T
S
&
S
V
C
S

(P-10263)
AON CONSULTING INC
199 Fremont St Fl 11, San Francisco
(94105-2291)
PHONE..............................415 486-6226
Matt Davis, *Manager*
EMP: 250
SALES (corp-wide): 10.7B **Privately Held**
SIC: 6411 Insurance brokers
HQ: Aon Consulting, Inc.
   200 E Randolph St Ll3
   Chicago IL 60601
   -

(P-10264)
AON CONSULTING INC
5000 E Spring St Ste 100, Long Beach
(90815-5217)
PHONE..............................562 496-2888
EMP: 68
SALES (corp-wide): 10.7B **Privately Held**
SIC: 6411 Insurance brokers
HQ: Aon Consulting, Inc.
   200 E Randolph St Ll3
   Chicago IL 60601

(P-10265)
AON CONSULTING INC
255 S Lake Ave Ste 900, Pasadena
(91101-3001)
PHONE..............................626 683-5200
Joan Miles, *CEO*
EMP: 68
SALES (corp-wide): 10.7B **Privately Held**
SIC: 6411 Insurance brokers
HQ: Aon Consulting, Inc.
   200 E Randolph St Ll3
   Chicago IL 60601

(P-10266)
AON CONSULTING & INSUR SVCS
199 Fremont St Fl 14, San Francisco
(94105-2253)
PHONE..............................415 486-7500
Judy Vukovich, *Senior VP*
EMP: 85
SALES (est): 19.2MM
SALES (corp-wide): 10.7B **Privately Held**
WEB: www.radford.com
SIC: 6411 8742 Insurance brokers; med-
   ical insurance claim processing, contract
   or fee basis; management consulting
   services
HQ: Aon Consulting, Inc.
   200 E Randolph St Ll3
   Chicago IL 60601

(P-10267)
AON RISK SVCS COMPANIES INC
707 Wilshire Blvd # 2600, Los Angeles
(90017-3501)
PHONE..............................213 630-3200
Eric Stocker, *Branch Mgr*
EMP: 71
SALES (corp-wide): 10.7B **Privately Held**
WEB: www.ecomponline.com
SIC: 6411 Insurance brokers
HQ: Aon Risk Services Companies, Inc.
   200 E Randolph St Fl 14
   Chicago IL 60601

(P-10268)
APFELD & NEAL INSURANCE SVCS
11022 Winners Cir Ste 100, Los Alamitos
(90720-2869)
PHONE..............................714 821-7041
Jay Apfeld, *Partner*
Gary Neal, *Partner*
EMP: 50
SQ FT: 7,000
SALES (est): 3.9MM **Privately Held**
SIC: 6411 Insurance agents

(P-10269)
APOLLO AGENCIES INC (PA)
Also Called: Ais, Associated Insurance Svc
700 W 1st St Ste 2, Tustin (92780-2948)
PHONE..............................714 832-2100

Michael A Jacobs, *President*
Thomas Crandell, *Treasurer*
EMP: 72
SQ FT: 6,000
SALES (est): 9.2MM **Privately Held**
WEB: www.apolloinsurance.net
SIC: 6411 Insurance agents

(P-10270)
APPLIED UNDERWRITERS INC
950 Tower Ln Ste 1400, Foster City
(94404-2128)
P.O. Box 281900, San Francisco (94128-
1900)
PHONE..............................415 656-5000
Ellen Gardiner, *Vice Pres*
Katy Van Horn, *Executive Asst*
EMP: 50
SALES (corp-wide): 343.2MM **Privately
Held**
WEB: www.applieduw.com
SIC: 6411 Insurance agents, brokers &
   service
PA: Applied Underwriters, Inc.
   10805 Old Mill Rd
   Omaha NE 68154
   402 342-4900

(P-10271)
ARROWHEAD MANAGEMENT COMPANY (DH)
701 B St Ste 2100, San Diego
(92101-8197)
PHONE..............................619 881-8733
Patrick Kilkenny, *Ch of Bd*
Marianne Harmon, *Corp Secy*
Sergio Castro, *Analyst*
EMP: 71
SALES (est): 243.3MM
SALES (corp-wide): 2B **Publicly Held**
WEB: www.arrowheadgrp.com
SIC: 6411 8741 Insurance agents, brokers
   & service; administrative management
HQ: Arrowhead General Insurance Agency,
   Inc.
   701 B St Ste 2100
   San Diego CA 92101
   800 669-1889

(P-10272)
ARROYO INSURANCE SERVICES INC (PA)
440 E Huntington Dr # 100, Arcadia
(91006-3750)
P.O. Box 661840 (91066-1840)
PHONE..............................626 799-9532
Robert J Knauf, *President*
Richard Beedle, *Corp Secy*
James Armitage, *Vice Pres*
Jim Simands, *Vice Pres*
Kerry Vogel, *Accountant*
EMP: 52
SQ FT: 3,500
SALES (est): 38.8MM **Privately Held**
SIC: 6411 Insurance brokers

(P-10273)
ARTHUR J GALLAGHER & CO
Also Called: Gallagher Bassett
18201 Von Karman Ave # 200, Irvine
(92612-1069)
PHONE..............................949 349-9800
Yvonne Norte, *Manager*
Amber Seggie, *President*
Jennie Kauke, *Vice Pres*
Brendon Pollis, *Producer*
EMP: 50
SALES (corp-wide): 6.9B **Publicly Held**
SIC: 6411 Insurance agents, brokers &
   service
PA: Arthur J. Gallagher & Co.
   2850 Golf Rd Ste 1000
   Rolling Meadows IL 60008
   630 773-3800

(P-10274)
ARTHUR J GALLAGHER & CO
Also Called: Kemper Insurance
505 N Brand Blvd Ste 600, Glendale
(91203-3944)
PHONE..............................818 539-2300
Scott Firestone, *Branch Mgr*
Jason Coughlin, *President*
Shannon Kearney, *President*
Dane Lupe, *President*
Jayne S Mazziotti, *President*

EMP: 200
SALES (corp-wide): 6.9B **Publicly Held**
WEB: www.ajg.com
SIC: 6411 Insurance agents, brokers &
   service
PA: Arthur J. Gallagher & Co.
   2850 Golf Rd Ste 1000
   Rolling Meadows IL 60008
   630 773-3800

(P-10275)
ARTHUR J GALLAGHER & CO
500 N Santa Fe St, Visalia (93292-5065)
PHONE..............................559 733-1181
Kelly Ventura, *Accounts Exec*
EMP: 90
SALES (corp-wide): 6.9B **Publicly Held**
SIC: 6411 Insurance agents
PA: Arthur J. Gallagher & Co.
   2850 Golf Rd Ste 1000
   Rolling Meadows IL 60008
   630 773-3800

(P-10276)
ARTHUR J GALLAGHER & CO
1825 Chicago Ave Ste 240, Riverside
(92507-2374)
PHONE..............................800 217-9800
EMP: 55
SALES (corp-wide): 6.9B **Publicly Held**
SIC: 6411 Insurance agents, brokers &
   service
PA: Arthur J. Gallagher & Co.
   2850 Golf Rd Ste 1000
   Rolling Meadows IL 60008
   630 773-3800

(P-10277)
ARTHUR J GALLAGHER & CO
Also Called: Gallagher Construction Svcs
1 Market Spear Tower, San Francisco
(94105)
PHONE..............................415 546-9300
Douglas B Bowring, *President*
Nichole Salzman, *President*
James F Buckley III, *Senior VP*
Jeff Lane, *Vice Pres*
John Stein, *Exec Dir*
EMP: 200
SQ FT: 20,000
SALES (corp-wide): 6.9B **Publicly Held**
WEB: www.ajg.com
SIC: 6411 Insurance agents, brokers &
   service
PA: Arthur J. Gallagher & Co.
   2850 Golf Rd Ste 1000
   Rolling Meadows IL 60008
   630 773-3800

(P-10278)
ARTHUR J GALLAGHER & CO
7910 N Ingram Ave Ste 201, Fresno
(93711-5828)
PHONE..............................559 436-0833
Mahlon Buck, *Manager*
Alison Berry, *President*
EMP: 55
SALES (corp-wide): 6.9B **Publicly Held**
WEB: www.ajg.com
SIC: 6411 Insurance agents, brokers &
   service
PA: Arthur J. Gallagher & Co.
   2850 Golf Rd Ste 1000
   Rolling Meadows IL 60008
   630 773-3800

(P-10279)
ARTHUR J GALLAGHER & CO
Also Called: Kemper Insurance
3697 Mt Diablo Blvd # 300, Lafayette
(94549-3747)
PHONE..............................925 299-1112
Douglas Bowring, *Branch Mgr*
Gina Endrina, *Client Mgr*
Monica Kozak, *Client Mgr*
EMP: 50
SALES (corp-wide): 6.9B **Publicly Held**
WEB: www.ajg.com
SIC: 6411 Insurance agents, brokers &
   service
PA: Arthur J. Gallagher & Co.
   2850 Golf Rd Ste 1000
   Rolling Meadows IL 60008
   630 773-3800

(P-10280)
ASSOCIATED PENSION CONS INC (PA)
2035 Forest Ave, Chico (95928-7620)
P.O. Box 1282 (95927-1282)
PHONE..............................530 343-4233
Matt Blofsky, *President*
Marc Roberts, *Treasurer*
Linda Madsen, *Vice Pres*
Gloria Anderson, *Admin Asst*
John Olsen, *VP Opers*
EMP: 51
SQ FT: 20,000
SALES (est): 6.6MM **Privately Held**
SIC: 6411 Pension & retirement plan con-
   sultants

(P-10281)
ASSURANT INC
2677 N Main St Ste 600, Santa Ana
(92705-6629)
PHONE..............................714 571-3900
Eric Juarez, *Branch Mgr*
EMP: 300
SALES (corp-wide): 8B **Publicly Held**
WEB: www.us.fortis.com
SIC: 6411 Insurance agents
PA: Assurant, Inc.
   28 Liberty St Fl 41
   New York NY 10005
   212 859-7000

(P-10282)
ASSUREDPARTNERS INC
1455 Response Rd Ste 260, Sacramento
(95815-5263)
PHONE..............................916 443-0200
EMP: 56 **Privately Held**
SIC: 6411 Insurance agents
PA: Assuredpartners, Inc.
   200 Colonial Center Pkwy
   Lake Mary FL 32746

(P-10283)
ATHENS INSURANCE SERVICE INC
Also Called: Athens Administrators
2552 Stanwell Dr Ste 100, Concord
(94520-4851)
P.O. Box 4029 (94524-4029)
PHONE..............................925 826-1000
James C Jenkins, *Ch of Bd*
James R Jenkins, *President*
Jodi Ellington, *CFO*
EMP: 250
SALES (est): 56.8MM **Privately Held**
SIC: 6411 Insurance claim adjusters, not
   employed by insurance company

(P-10284)
ATLAS GENERAL INSUR SVCS LLC
4365 Executive Dr Ste 400, San Diego
(92121-2136)
PHONE..............................858 529-6700
William Trzos,
Greg Mosher, *President*
Robbie Bartolo, *Analyst*
Joanne Montillano, *Underwriter*
EMP: 153
SALES: 27MM **Privately Held**
SIC: 6411 Insurance agents

(P-10285)
AUTO INS SPCIALISTS-LONG BEACH
Also Called: Ais - Auto Insur Specialists
5000 E Spring St Ste 100, Long Beach
(90815-5217)
PHONE..............................562 496-2888
James F Caird, *President*
EMP: 60
SALES (est): 5.2MM
SALES (corp-wide): 3.3B **Publicly Held**
SIC: 6411 6331 Insurance agents, brokers
   & service; fire, marine & casualty insur-
   ance
HQ: Auto Insurance Specialists, Llc
   17785 Center Court Dr N # 110
   Cerritos CA 90703
   562 345-6247

(P-10286)
AUTO INSURANCE SPECIALISTS LLC (DH)
17785 Center Court Dr N # 110, Cerritos (90703-8573)
PHONE..................562 345-6247
Mark Ribisi, *CEO*
Chris Bremer, *CFO*
Jerry Baker, *Vice Pres*
Mark Casas, *Vice Pres*
Lani Elkin, *Vice Pres*
EMP: 210
SQ FT: 45,000
SALES (est): 97.5MM
SALES (corp-wide): 3.3B **Publicly Held**
SIC: 6411 Insurance brokers

(P-10287)
AUTOMOBILE CLUB SOUTHERN CAL
Also Called: AAA - Auto CLB Southern Cal
6787 Carnelian St Ste A, Rancho Cuca-monga (91701-4564)
PHONE..................909 477-8600
EMP: 256
SALES (corp-wide): 7.2B **Privately Held**
SIC: 6411 Insurance agents, brokers & service
PA: Automobile Club Of Southern California
2601 S Figueroa St
Los Angeles CA 90007
213 741-3686

(P-10288)
AUTOMOBILE CLUB SOUTHERN CAL (PA)
Also Called: A A A Automobile Club So Cal
2601 S Figueroa St, Los Angeles (90007-3294)
P.O. Box 25001, Santa Ana (92799-5001)
PHONE..................213 741-3686
Robert T Bouttier, *Principal*
Zoo Babies, *President*
Peter R McDonald, *Senior VP*
Jayne Bradford, *Vice Pres*
Phil Bybee, *Vice Pres*
EMP: 150
SQ FT: 425,000
SALES (est): 7.2B **Privately Held**
SIC: 6411 8699 Insurance agents; auto-mobile owners' association

(P-10289)
AUTOMOBILE CLUB SOUTHERN CAL
33323 Fairview R Ste Msa, Costa Mesa (92626)
PHONE..................213 741-3686
EMP: 254
SALES (corp-wide): 7.2B **Privately Held**
SIC: 6411 Insurance agents
PA: Automobile Club Of Southern California
2601 S Figueroa St
Los Angeles CA 90007
213 741-3686

(P-10290)
AUTOMOBILE CLUB SOUTHERN CAL
Also Called: AAA Auto Club
3333 Fairview Rd, Costa Mesa (92626-1698)
PHONE..................714 885-1343
Becky Martinez, *Branch Mgr*
Goutham Nellutla, *Mng Officer*
Carmel Urquhart, *Recruiter*
Heather Billotti, *Senior Buyer*
Valerie Granados, *Sales Staff*
EMP: 200
SALES (corp-wide): 7.2B **Privately Held**
SIC: 6411 Insurance agents, brokers & service
PA: Automobile Club Of Southern California
2601 S Figueroa St
Los Angeles CA 90007
213 741-3686

(P-10291)
AUTOMOBILE CLUB SOUTHERN CAL
10540 Fthill Blvd Ste 100, Rancho Cuca-monga (91730)
PHONE..................909 980-0233
Alice Holguin, *Branch Mgr*

Grace Curtis, *Office Mgr*
EMP: 108
SALES (corp-wide): 7.2B **Privately Held**
SIC: 6411 Insurance agents, brokers & service
PA: Automobile Club Of Southern California
2601 S Figueroa St
Los Angeles CA 90007
213 741-3686

(P-10292)
AUTOMOBILE CLUB SOUTHERN CAL
2666 Del Mar Heights Rd, Del Mar (92014-3100)
PHONE..................858 481-7181
Tom McKernan, *Manager*
EMP: 108
SALES (corp-wide): 7.2B **Privately Held**
SIC: 6411 Insurance agents, brokers & service
PA: Automobile Club Of Southern California
2601 S Figueroa St
Los Angeles CA 90007
213 741-3686

(P-10293)
AXA EQUITABLE LIFE INSUR CO
Also Called: Equitable Life Assurance
3777 La Jolla Village Dr, San Diego (92122-1080)
PHONE..................858 552-1234
Alen Farwell, *Manager*
EMP: 70
SALES (corp-wide): 12B **Publicly Held**
WEB: www.equitable.com
SIC: 6411 Insurance agents, brokers & service
HQ: Axa Equitable Life Insurance Company
1290 Avenue Of The Americ
New York NY 10104
212 554-1234

(P-10294)
BARRY MCPHERSON INC
1932 E Deere Ave Ste 240, Santa Ana (92705-5716)
PHONE..................425 343-5000
Kenneth B McPherson, *President*
EMP: 240
SALES (est): 26MM **Privately Held**
SIC: 6411 Insurance agents, brokers & service

(P-10295)
BENEFIT & RISK MANAGEMENT SVCS
80 Iron Point Cir Ste 200, Folsom (95630-8593)
P.O. Box 2140 (95763-2140)
PHONE..................916 467-1200
Matthew Allen Schafer, *CEO*
Luke Schafer, *Vice Pres*
Paul Schafer, *Vice Pres*
Igor Pilichev, *CIO*
William Hardison, *Info Tech Dir*
EMP: 130
SQ FT: 15,000
SALES (est): 38.9MM **Privately Held**
WEB: www.brms-online.com
SIC: 6411 Insurance information & consult-ing services

(P-10296)
BENETECH INC (PA)
3841 N Freeway Blvd # 185, Sacramento (95834-1948)
P.O. Box 348570 (95834-8570)
PHONE..................916 484-6811
Robert L Brandon, *President*
Wes Jones, *CFO*
James Casalegno, *Senior VP*
Betsy G Beaumon, *Vice Pres*
Chris Blazek, *Vice Pres*
EMP: 60 **EST:** 1974
SQ FT: 20,000
SALES (est): 24.5MM **Privately Held**
SIC: 6411 Pension & retirement plan con-sultants

(P-10297)
BENETECH INC
4420 Auburn Blvd Fl 2, Sacramento (95841-4146)
P.O. Box 348570 (95834-8570)
PHONE..................916 484-6811

Kelly Roberts, *Manager*
Janet Chapman, *Manager*
EMP: 50
SALES (corp-wide): 24.5MM **Privately Held**
SIC: 6411 Pension & retirement plan con-sultants
PA: Benetech, Inc
3841 N Freeway Blvd # 185
Sacramento CA 95834
916 484-6811

(P-10298)
BERKSHIRE HATHAWAY HOMESTATES (HQ)
1 California St Ste 600, San Francisco (94111-5403)
P.O. Box 881716 (94188-1716)
PHONE..................415 433-1650
Louis B Rovens, *President*
Sargent Michael, *Commercial*
Michael Pisani, *Supervisor*
EMP: 180 **EST:** 1998
SQ FT: 51,000
SALES (est): 157.1MM
SALES (corp-wide): 225.3B **Publicly Held**
WEB: www.acpac.com
SIC: 6411 Insurance claim processing, ex-cept medical
PA: Berkshire Hathaway Inc.
3555 Farnam St Ste 1140
Omaha NE 68131
402 346-1400

(P-10299)
BERKSHIRE HATHAWAY HOMESTATES
2020 Camino Del Rio N, San Diego (92108-1541)
PHONE..................619 686-8424
Michael Millwood, *Manager*
EMP: 70
SALES (corp-wide): 225.3B **Publicly Held**
WEB: www.acpac.com
SIC: 6411 Insurance claim processing, ex-cept medical
HQ: Berkshire Hathaway Homestates
1 California St Ste 600
San Francisco CA 94111
415 433-1650

(P-10300)
BICKMORE AND ASSOCIATES INC (DH)
Also Called: Bickmore Risk Svcs Consulting
1750 Creekside Oaks Dr # 200, Sacra-mento (95833-3648)
PHONE..................916 244-1100
Greg L Trout, *CEO*
John Alltop, *President*
L Robert Kramer, *President*
Jeffrey C Grubbs, *COO*
Kailey Adams, *Admin Asst*
EMP: 70
SQ FT: 25,500
SALES (est): 43.4MM
SALES (corp-wide): 97.3MM **Privately Held**
WEB: www.brsrisk.com
SIC: 6411 Insurance information & consult-ing services
HQ: York Risk Services Group, Inc.
1 Upper Pond Rd Ste 4
Parsippany NJ 07054
973 404-1200

(P-10301)
BILL WILSON CENTER (PA)
3490 The Alameda, Santa Clara (95050-4333)
PHONE..................408 243-0222
Sparky Harlan, *CEO*
Kirsten Mc Keraghan, *Program Mgr*
Judy Whittier, *Commissioner*
Tesla Fuentes, *Case Mgr*
EMP: 72
SQ FT: 19,000
SALES: 16.5MM **Privately Held**
SIC: 6411 Insurance agents, brokers & service

(P-10302)
BUILDERS & TRADESMENS
6610 Sierra College Blvd, Rocklin (95677-4306)
PHONE..................916 772-9200
Norbert Hohlbein, *President*
Jeff Erickson, *Vice Pres*
Lisa Erickson, *Vice Pres*
Jeff Hohlbein, *Vice Pres*
Paul Hohlbein, *Vice Pres*
EMP: 75
SQ FT: 15,000
SALES (est): 56.4MM
SALES (corp-wide): 250MM **Privately Held**
WEB: www.btisinc.com
SIC: 6411 Insurance brokers; fire insur-ance underwriters' laboratories
HQ: Amtrust Financial Services, Inc.
59 Maiden Ln Fl 43
New York NY 10038

(P-10303)
C M A ALLIANCE
Also Called: Cornerstone Marketing Alliance
16542 Ventura Blvd # 210, Encino (91436-2005)
PHONE..................818 981-0800
Steve Pato, *Owner*
EMP: 50 **EST:** 2001
SALES (est): 3.7MM **Privately Held**
WEB: www.cma-la.com
SIC: 6411 Insurance agents, brokers & service

(P-10304)
CA STE ATOM ASSOC INTR-INS BUR
Also Called: AAA
900 Miramonte Ave, Mountain View (94040-2457)
P.O. Box 391840 (94039-1840)
PHONE..................650 623-3200
Jerry Hall, *Branch Mgr*
Henry Wong, *Sales Staff*
Rosa Rodriguez, *Agent*
EMP: 60
SQ FT: 15,414
SALES (corp-wide): 907.9MM **Privately Held**
WEB: www.viamagazine.com
SIC: 6411 Insurance claim processing, ex-cept medical
HQ: California State Automobile Associa-tion Inter-Insurance Bureau
1276 S California Blvd
Walnut Creek CA 94596
925 287-7600

(P-10305)
CABRILLO GEN INSUR AGCY INC
7071 Convoy Ct Ste 201, San Diego (92111-1023)
P.O. Box 17425 (92177-7425)
PHONE..................858 244-0550
Robert Jester, *President*
Micheal McNitt, *Vice Pres*
EMP: 88 **EST:** 2005
SALES (est): 11.9MM **Privately Held**
SIC: 6411 Insurance agents, brokers & service

(P-10306)
CAESAR AND SEIDER INSUR SVCS (PA)
Also Called: Talbot Insurance & Fincl Svcs
40 E Alamar Ave Ste 4, Santa Barbara (93105-3400)
P.O. Box 3310 (93130-3310)
PHONE..................805 682-2571
Thomas Caesar, *President*
Ray Seider, *Vice Pres*
EMP: 52 **EST:** 1954
SQ FT: 2,400
SALES (est): 7.3MM **Privately Held**
SIC: 6411 Insurance brokers

(P-10307)
CALIFORNIA CLINICAL TRIALS
3828 Delmas Ter 2, Culver City (90232-2713)
PHONE..................310 945-1780
Murry Rosenthal, *CEO*

PRODUCTS & SVCS

EMP: 200 **EST:** 1989
SALES (est): 16.3MM **Privately Held**
SIC: 6411 8731 Research services, insurance; commercial physical research

(P-10308)
CALIFORNIA FAIR PLAN ASSN
3435 Wilshire Blvd # 1200, Los Angeles (90010-1911)
PHONE......................213 487-0111
Stuart M Wilkinson, *President*
Amar Bains, *Technology*
Tessa Thomas, *Technology*
Raul Paez, *Supervisor*
EMP: 80
SALES (est): 17.7MM **Privately Held**
WEB: www.cfpnet.com
SIC: 6411 Insurance agents

(P-10309)
CALIFORNIA HEALTHCARE
Also Called: C.H.M.B.
700 La Terraza Blvd # 200, Escondido (92025-3868)
PHONE......................760 520-1333
Bob Svendsen, *CEO*
Chris Thibodeau, *CFO*
Vicki Brown, *Vice Pres*
Donna Forster, *Vice Pres*
Martha Pinal, *Vice Pres*
EMP: 135
SQ FT: 16,000
SALES (est): 52.2MM **Privately Held**
WEB: www.chmb.com
SIC: 6411 Medical insurance claim processing, contract or fee basis

(P-10310)
CALIFRNIA PHYSCN REIMBURSEMENT
1321 Butte St Apt 202, Redding (96001-1065)
PHONE......................530 241-0473
Jane Rehberg, *President*
EMP: 73
SALES (est): 9.9MM **Privately Held**
WEB: www.cprbilling.com
SIC: 6411 Medical insurance claim processing, contract or fee basis

(P-10311)
CAMICO MUTUAL INSURANCE CO (PA)
1800 Gateway Dr Ste 300, San Mateo (94404-4072)
PHONE......................650 378-6874
Ricardo R Rosario, *President*
Robert P Evans, *Ch of Bd*
Jay H Stewart, *CFO*
Rachel Ehrlich, *Officer*
Judith Frederiksen, *Vice Pres*
EMP: 80
SQ FT: 22,000
SALES: 32.4MM **Privately Held**
SIC: 6411 Professional standards services, insurance

(P-10312)
CANNON COCHRAN MGT SVCS INC
Also Called: Ccmsi
18881 Von Karman Ave # 380, Irvine (92612-6580)
PHONE......................949 474-6500
William Hougland, *Manager*
Andy Hougland, *Branch Mgr*
EMP: 59 **Privately Held**
SIC: 6411 Insurance agents
HQ: Cannon Cochran Management Services, Inc.
　　2 E Main St Towne Ctr
　　Danville IL 61832
　　217 446-1089

(P-10313)
CARNEGIE AGENCY INC
2101 Corp Cntr Dr Ste 150, Newbury Park (91320-1436)
PHONE......................805 445-1470
John Smith, *President*
Chuck Smith, *Vice Pres*
EMP: 50
SQ FT: 40,000

SALES (est): 7.8MM **Privately Held**
WEB: www.cgia.com
SIC: 6411 Insurance agents, brokers & service

(P-10314)
CARTEL MARKETING INC
Also Called: Insure Express Insurance Svc
5230 Las Virgenes Rd # 250, Calabasas (91302-3448)
PHONE......................818 483-1130
Robert M Humphreys, *Ch of Bd*
Jack Edelstein, *President*
William Russell, *CFO*
Michael Neustadt, *Officer*
Sean Willis, *Exec VP*
EMP: 102
SQ FT: 14,000
SALES (est): 23.6MM
SALES (corp-wide): 41.5MM **Privately Held**
WEB: www.cartel.net
SIC: 6411 Insurance agents & brokers
HQ: Expresslink, Inc.
　　16501 Ventura Blvd # 300
　　Encino CA 91436
　　818 788-5555

(P-10315)
CHARLES M KAMIYA AND SONS INC
Also Called: Kamiya, Kenneth M Insurance
373 Van Ness Ave Ste 200, Torrance (90501-6239)
PHONE......................310 781-2066
Kenneth Kamiya, *President*
Edward Kamiya, *Vice Pres*
EMP: 54
SALES (est): 7.5MM **Privately Held**
WEB: www.kamiyainsurance.com
SIC: 6411 Insurance agents

(P-10316)
CHOIC ADMINI INSUR SERVI
Also Called: California Choice
721 S Parker St Ste 200, Orange (92868-4772)
PHONE......................714 542-4200
Michael Close, *President*
Raymond D Godeke, *Vice Pres*
Macpherson Ta Reis, *Vice Pres*
Steve Van Wart, *Vice Pres*
John M Word, *Vice Pres*
EMP: 500
SALES (est): 94.6MM **Privately Held**
WEB: www.wordup.com
SIC: 6411 Insurance agents

(P-10317)
CHUBB US HOLDING INC
455 Market St Ste 500, San Francisco (94105-2539)
PHONE......................415 547-4400
Steve Meyers, *Branch Mgr*
Bruce Jervis, *Exec VP*
Shannon Newman, *Human Res Dir*
Brian E Witzmann, *Manager*
EMP: 68
SALES (corp-wide): 32.7B **Privately Held**
WEB: www.ace.bm
SIC: 6411 Property & casualty insurance agent
HQ: Chubb Us Holding Inc.
　　1601 Chestnut St
　　Philadelphia PA 19192

(P-10318)
CHUBB US HOLDING INC
Also Called: Inamar
3131 Camino Del Rio N, San Diego (92108-5701)
PHONE......................619 563-2400
Linda Andres, *Manager*
EMP: 212
SALES (corp-wide): 32.7B **Privately Held**
WEB: www.ace.bm
SIC: 6411 Insurance agents, brokers & service
HQ: Chubb Us Holding Inc.
　　1601 Chestnut St
　　Philadelphia PA 19192

(P-10319)
CHUBB US HOLDING INC
9200 Oakdale Ave, Chatsworth (91311-6500)
P.O. Box 3500, Woodland Hills (91365-3500)
PHONE......................818 428-3600
James Perry, *Branch Mgr*
Sean Drury, *Supervisor*
EMP: 150
SALES (corp-wide): 32.7B **Privately Held**
WEB: www.ace.bm
SIC: 6411 Property & casualty insurance agent; patrol services, insurance
HQ: Chubb Us Holding Inc.
　　1601 Chestnut St
　　Philadelphia PA 19192

(P-10320)
CLAIMS MANAGEMENT INC
1101 Crksde Rdge Dr 100, Roseville (95678)
P.O. Box 619079 (95661-9079)
PHONE......................916 631-1250
Kathy Peterson, *President*
Virginia Marsh, *Master*
Mardis Devore, *Manager*
EMP: 130
SQ FT: 23,000
SALES (est): 21.2MM **Privately Held**
WEB: www.claimsmanagement.com
SIC: 6411 Insurance claim adjusters, not employed by insurance company

(P-10321)
CNA FINANCIAL CORPORATION
Also Called: CNA Insurance
1800 E Imperial Hwy # 200, Brea (92821-6062)
P.O. Box 6500 (92822-6500)
PHONE......................714 255-2200
John C Magee III, *Branch Mgr*
EMP: 200
SALES (corp-wide): 14B **Publicly Held**
SIC: 6411 6331 Insurance agents, brokers & service; fire, marine & casualty insurance
HQ: Cna Financial Corporation
　　151 N Franklin St Ste 700
　　Chicago IL 60606
　　312 822-5000

(P-10322)
CNA SURETY CORPORATION
1455 Frazee Rd Ste 801, San Diego (92108-4309)
PHONE......................619 682-3550
Ron Fawcett, *Manager*
Jennifer Purdon, *Research Analys*
EMP: 71
SALES (corp-wide): 14B **Publicly Held**
SIC: 6411 Insurance agents, brokers & service
HQ: Cna Surety Corporation
　　333 S Wabash Ave Ste 41s
　　Chicago IL 60604
　　312 822-5000

(P-10323)
COASTAL SELECT INSURANCE CO
4820 Busineca Ctr Dr 20, Fairfield (94534)
PHONE......................707 863-3700
Kevin Nish, *President*
Karen Padovese, *COO*
EMP: 50 **EST:** 1996
SALES (est): 4.9MM **Privately Held**
WEB: www.pacificselectproperty.com
SIC: 6411 Insurance agents, brokers & service
PA: Geovera Holdings, Inc.
　　4820 Busineca Ctr Dr 20
　　Fairfield CA 94534

(P-10324)
COLDWELL BANKER
580 El Camino Real, San Carlos (94070-2412)
PHONE......................650 596-5400
EMP: 80 **EST:** 2011
SALES (est): 5.7MM **Privately Held**
SIC: 6411

(P-10325)
COLLECTIVEHEALTH INC
Also Called: Collective Health
85 Bluxome St, San Francisco (94107-1605)
PHONE......................650 376-3804
Ali Diab, *CEO*
Ken Hahn, *CFO*
Susan Dybbs, *Vice Pres*
Keely Anson, *Executive Asst*
Andrew Bennett, *Executive Asst*
EMP: 410 **EST:** 2013
SQ FT: 6,000
SALES (est): 3.9MM **Privately Held**
SIC: 6411 7379 7372 Medical insurance claim processing, contract or fee basis; ; business oriented computer software

(P-10326)
COMMERCE WEST INSURANCE CO
6130 Stoneridge Mall Rd # 400, Pleasanton (94588-3279)
P.O. Box 8006 (94588-8606)
PHONE......................925 730-6400
Jerald Fels, *President*
Michael Vrban, *CFO*
George Jeffers, *Applctn Conslt*
EMP: 60
SQ FT: 23,000
SALES: 113MM
SALES (corp-wide): 200.2K **Privately Held**
WEB: www.commercewest.net
SIC: 6411 Insurance agents, brokers & service
HQ: The Commerce Insurance Company
　　211 Main St
　　Webster MA 01570
　　508 943-9000

(P-10327)
COMPASS REAL ESTATE LLC
Also Called: Leslie Thompson
204 Via San Remo, Newport Beach (92663-5512)
PHONE......................949 945-8176
Leslie Thompson, *Manager*
EMP: 372
SALES (corp-wide): 36.1MM **Privately Held**
SIC: 6411 Real estate insurance agents
PA: Compass Real Estate, Llc
　　90 5th Ave Fl 3
　　New York NY 10011
　　212 913-9058

(P-10328)
CONEXIS BNEFT ADMINSTRATORS LP (HQ)
721 S Parker St Ste 300, Orange (92868-4732)
PHONE......................714 835-5006
Michael Close, *President*
Steve Huynh, *Vice Pres*
John Ball, *Director*
EMP: 120
SQ FT: 57,000
SALES (est): 233.9MM
SALES (corp-wide): 383.5MM **Privately Held**
SIC: 6411 Insurance information & consulting services
PA: Word & Brown, Insurance Administrators, Inc.
　　721 S Parker St Ste 300
　　Orange CA 92868
　　714 835-5006

(P-10329)
CONFIE SEGUROS INC (HQ)
Also Called: Freeway Insurance
7711 Center Ave Ste 200, Huntington Beach (92647-9124)
PHONE......................714 252-2500
Joseph Waked, *CEO*
Mordy Rothberg, *President*
Valeria Rico, *COO*
Robert Trebing, *CFO*
Kyle Garst, *Vice Pres*
EMP: 146
SALES (est): 969.3MM
SALES (corp-wide): 948.8MM **Privately Held**
SIC: 6411 Insurance brokers

PA: Confie Seguros California, Inc.
7711 Center Ave Ste 200
Huntington Beach CA 92647
714 252-2649

(P-10330)
CONFIE SEGUROS HOLDINGS II CO (PA)
7711 Center Ave Ste 200, Huntington Beach (92647-9124)
PHONE..................714 252-2649
Robert Trebing, *CFO*
Ryan Raddatz, *Director*
EMP: 160
SALES (est): 96.5MM **Privately Held**
SIC: 6411 Insurance agents, brokers & service

(P-10331)
CORVEL CORPORATION
10750 4th St Ste 100, Rancho Cucamonga (91730-0980)
PHONE..................909 257-3700
Lorie Gonzalez, *Branch Mgr*
Debra Anderson, *Supervisor*
EMP: 114
SALES (corp-wide): 595.7MM **Publicly Held**
WEB: www.corvel.com
SIC: 6411 Insurance agents, brokers & service
PA: Corvel Corporation
2010 Main St Ste 600
Irvine CA 92614
949 851-1473

(P-10332)
CORVEL ENTERPRISE COMP INC
2010 Main St Ste 600, Irvine (92614-7272)
PHONE..................949 851-1473
Daniel J Starck, *CEO*
EMP: 99
SALES: 950K **Privately Held**
SIC: 6411 Insurance agents, brokers & service

(P-10333)
CREST FINANCIAL CORPORATION (DH)
12641 166th St, Cerritos (90703-2101)
P.O. Box 3190 (90703-3190)
PHONE..................562 733-6500
Susan Scurti, *President*
Shannon S Walker, *CFO*
Michael Costello, *Senior VP*
Walter E Erker, *Vice Pres*
EMP: 62
SQ FT: 15,000
SALES (est): 31.9MM **Privately Held**
SIC: 6411 7311 Insurance agents; insurance information & consulting services; insurance adjusters; insurance agents & brokers; advertising agencies

(P-10334)
CSAA INSURANCE EXCHANGE (PA)
3055 Oak Rd, Walnut Creek (94597-2098)
P.O. Box 23392, Oakland (94623-0392)
PHONE..................800 922-8228
Paula Downey, *President*
Greg Meyer, *COO*
Marie Andel, *Officer*
Michael Zukerman, *Officer*
Linda Goldstein, *Exec VP*
EMP: 95
SALES (est): 2.8B **Privately Held**
SIC: 6411 Insurance agents

(P-10335)
CSAC EXCESS INSURANCE AUTH
75 Iron Point Cir Ste 200, Folsom (95630-8813)
PHONE..................916 850-7300
Michael Fleming, *CEO*
Christine Kerns, *Vice Pres*
Patty Kopec, *Vice Pres*
Paul Moore, *Vice Pres*
Natalee Kolenski, *Admin Asst*
EMP: 60
SQ FT: 13,613

SALES (est): 10.5MM **Privately Held**
WEB: www.csac-eia.org
SIC: 6411 Insurance agents

(P-10336)
CUSTOMZED SVCS ADMNSTRTORS INC
Also Called: Global Care Travel
4181 Ruffin Rd Ste 150, San Diego (92123-1876)
P.O. Box 939057 (92193-9057)
PHONE..................858 810-2004
Christopher Carnicelli, *CEO*
John Martini, *CFO*
Linda Barger, *Principal*
Roberta Cremeans, *Asst Controller*
Christopher Zentner, *Director*
EMP: 140
SQ FT: 11,000
SALES (est): 50.3MM
SALES (corp-wide): 3.7B **Privately Held**
WEB: www.csatravelprotection.com
SIC: 6411 4724 Insurance agents; travel agencies
HQ: Generali Global Assistance, Inc.
4330 East West Hwy # 1000
Bethesda MD 20814
240 330-1000

(P-10337)
CYBER POLICY
1 California St Ste 1100, San Francisco (94111-5412)
PHONE..................877 626-9991
Keith Moore, *CEO*
EMP: 103
SALES: 10MM **Privately Held**
SIC: 6411 Insurance agents, brokers & service

(P-10338)
DEL AMO INSURANCE SERVICES
910 Lomita Blvd Ste E, Harbor City (90710-2200)
P.O. Box 910 (90710-0910)
PHONE..................310 534-3444
David Blunt, *President*
EMP: 60
SALES (est): 10.7MM **Privately Held**
SIC: 6411 Insurance agents & brokers

(P-10339)
DENTISTS INSURANCE COMPANY (HQ)
Also Called: Tdic
1201 K St Ste 1600, Sacramento (95814-3925)
P.O. Box 1582 (95812-1582)
PHONE..................916 443-4567
Mark Soeth, *President*
Cindy Hartwell, *Analyst*
Melanie Duval, *Director*
Dora Earls, *Director*
Rose Faletoese, *Underwriter*
EMP: 118 EST: 1979
SQ FT: 12,000
SALES (est): 21.2MM
SALES (corp-wide): 21.4MM **Privately Held**
WEB: www.thedentists.com
SIC: 6411 Insurance agents, brokers & service
PA: California Dental Association Inc
1201 K St Fl 14
Sacramento CA 95814
916 443-0505

(P-10340)
DIBUDUO DFENDIS INSUR BRKS LLC (PA)
6873 N West Ave, Fresno (93711-4308)
P.O. Box 5479 (93755-5479)
PHONE..................559 432-0222
Matt Defendis, *Partner*
Mike De Fendis, *Partner*
Tony Canizales, *Vice Pres*
Debra Duckering, *Vice Pres*
Jon McNally, *Info Tech Dir*
EMP: 93 EST: 1960
SQ FT: 22,000
SALES (est): 53MM **Privately Held**
WEB: www.dibu.com
SIC: 6411 Insurance agents

(P-10341)
DMA CLAIMS INC (PA)
Also Called: Dma Claims Services
330 N Brand Blvd Ste 230, Glendale (91203-2380)
P.O. Box 26004 (91222-6004)
PHONE..................323 342-6800
Thomas J Reitze, *President*
Duke Snider, *Manager*
Tom Walsh, *Agent*
EMP: 74
SQ FT: 20,000
SALES (est): 109.4MM **Privately Held**
WEB: www.davidmorse.com
SIC: 6411 Insurance claim adjusters, not employed by insurance company; insurance adjusters

(P-10342)
DMA CLAIMS INC
7188 Via Carmela, San Jose (95139-1125)
PHONE..................800 649-7602
Mark Rost, *Principal*
EMP: 62
SALES (corp-wide): 109.4MM **Privately Held**
SIC: 6411 Insurance adjusters
PA: Dma Claims, Inc.
330 N Brand Blvd Ste 230
Glendale CA 91203
323 342-6800

(P-10343)
DMA CLAIMS INC
Also Called: David Morse & Assoc.
330 N Brand Blvd Ste 230, Glendale (91203-2380)
PHONE..................323 342-6800
Dan Mara, *Branch Mgr*
EMP: 62
SALES (corp-wide): 109.4MM **Privately Held**
SIC: 6411 Insurance adjusters
PA: Dma Claims, Inc.
330 N Brand Blvd Ste 230
Glendale CA 91203
323 342-6800

(P-10344)
DOCTORS MANAGEMENT COMPANY (HQ)
185 Greenwood Rd, NAPA (94558-6270)
P.O. Box 2900 (94558-0900)
PHONE..................707 226-0100
Richard E Anderson, *CEO*
Eugene M Bullis, *CFO*
Kenneth R Chrisman, *Exec VP*
William J Gallagher, *Senior VP*
Michael Yacob, *Principal*
EMP: 200
SQ FT: 72,000
SALES (est): 232.2MM
SALES (corp-wide): 700.4MM **Privately Held**
SIC: 6411 Insurance information & consulting services; insurance claim processing, except medical
PA: The Doctors' Company An Interinsurance Exchange
185 Greenwood Rd
Napa CA 94558
707 226-0100

(P-10345)
EDGEWOOD PARTNERS INSUR CTR
1390 Willow Pass Rd # 800, Concord (94520-7924)
PHONE..................415 356-3900
EMP: 105
SALES (corp-wide): 42.7MM **Privately Held**
SIC: 6411 8742 Insurance brokers; property & casualty insurance agent; management consulting services
HQ: Edgewood Partners Insurance Center
425 California St # 2400
San Francisco CA 94104

(P-10346)
EDGEWOOD PARTNERS INSUR CTR (HQ)
Also Called: Epic Insurance
425 California St # 2400, San Francisco (94104-2102)
P.O. Box 5900, San Mateo (94402-5900)
PHONE..................415 356-3900
Peter Garvey, *CEO*
Stephen Adkins, *Officer*
Chris Duncan, *Officer*
Daniel J Crawford, *Exec VP*
Philip V Moyles Jr, *Exec VP*
EMP: 65
SQ FT: 18,897
SALES (est): 370.5MM
SALES (corp-wide): 42.7MM **Privately Held**
WEB: www.edgewoodins.com
SIC: 6411 Insurance brokers
PA: Epic Holdings Inc.
1390 Willow Pass Rd # 800
Concord CA 94520
650 295-4600

(P-10347)
EDGEWOOD PRTNERS INSUR CTR INC
1010 B St Ste 423, San Rafael (94901-2921)
PHONE..................415 456-4323
Todd Sishman, *Branch Mgr*
EMP: 85
SALES (corp-wide): 42.7MM **Privately Held**
SIC: 6411 Insurance brokers
HQ: Edgewood Partners Insurance Center
425 California St # 2400
San Francisco CA 94104

(P-10348)
EHEALTHINSURANCE SERVICES INC (HQ)
2625 Augustine Dr Ste 201, Santa Clara (95054-2956)
PHONE..................650 584-2700
Ellen O Tausche, *Principal*
Rob Lapstuen, *President*
Bill Shaughnessy, *President*
Jiang Wu, *President*
Samuel C Gibbs III, *Senior VP*
EMP: 100
SALES (est): 86.7MM
SALES (corp-wide): 251.4MM **Publicly Held**
WEB: www.anysure.com
SIC: 6411 Insurance agents, brokers & service
PA: Ehealth, Inc.
440 E Middlefield Rd
Mountain View CA 94043
650 584-2700

(P-10349)
ESURANCE INSURANCE SVCS INC (HQ)
Also Called: PNC
650 Davis St, San Francisco (94111-1981)
PHONE..................415 875-4500
Gary C Tolman, *CEO*
Jonathan Adkisson, *CFO*
Alan Gellman, *Chief Mktg Ofcr*
Eric Brandt, *Officer*
Nancy Abraham, *Vice Pres*
EMP: 140
SQ FT: 10,000
SALES (est): 373MM **Publicly Held**
SIC: 6411 Insurance agents

(P-10350)
EVIDERA ARCHIMEDES INC
450 Sansome St Ste 650, San Francisco (94111-3380)
PHONE..................415 490-0400
Jon Williams, *President*
Lynn Okamoto, *Senior VP*
Josh Adler, *Vice Pres*
Denis Getsios, *Vice Pres*
C Andy Schuetz, *Director*
EMP: 60

PRODUCTS & SVCS

SALES (est): 12.4MM
SALES (corp-wide): 1.1B **Privately Held**
WEB: www.archimedesmodel.com
SIC: 6411 Insurance information & consulting services
HQ: Evidera, Inc.
7101 Wscnsin Ave Ste 1400
Bethesda MD 20814

(P-10351)
FARMERS GROUP INC
Also Called: Farmers Insurance
13950 Ramona Ave, Chino (91710-5427)
PHONE.....................909 839-2020
Mike Dyer, *Branch Mgr*
EMP: 82
SALES (corp-wide): 48.2B **Privately Held**
WEB: www.farmers.com
SIC: 6411 4226 4225 Insurance agents, brokers & service; special warehousing & storage; general warehousing & storage
HQ: Farmers Group, Inc.
6301 Owensmouth Ave
Woodland Hills CA 91367
323 932-3200

(P-10352)
FARMERS GROUP INC
Also Called: Farmers Insurance
429 Llewellyn Ave, Campbell (95008-1948)
PHONE.....................408 557-1100
William Garrity, *Manager*
EMP: 50
SALES (corp-wide): 48.2B **Privately Held**
WEB: www.farmers.com
SIC: 6411 Insurance agents, brokers & service
HQ: Farmers Group, Inc.
6301 Owensmouth Ave
Woodland Hills CA 91367
323 932-3200

(P-10353)
FARMERS GROUP INC
Also Called: Farmers Insurance
550 S Hill St Ste 1309, Los Angeles (90013-2292)
PHONE.....................818 249-3000
Leo Denlea Jr, *President*
EMP: 88
SALES (corp-wide): 48.2B **Privately Held**
WEB: www.farmers.com
SIC: 6411 Insurance agents, brokers & service
HQ: Farmers Group, Inc.
6301 Owensmouth Ave
Woodland Hills CA 91367
323 932-3200

(P-10354)
FARMERS GROUP INC
Also Called: Farmers Insurance
6518 Antelope Rd, Citrus Heights (95621-1077)
PHONE.....................916 727-4600
Bruce Bailey, *Manager*
EMP: 75
SALES (corp-wide): 48.2B **Privately Held**
WEB: www.farmers.com
SIC: 6411 Insurance agents, brokers & service
HQ: Farmers Group, Inc.
6301 Owensmouth Ave
Woodland Hills CA 91367
323 932-3200

(P-10355)
FARMERS GROUP INC
Also Called: Farmers Insurance
6303 Owensmouth Ave Fl 1, Woodland Hills (91367-2200)
PHONE.....................805 583-7400
EMP: 900
SALES (corp-wide): 74.2B **Privately Held**
SIC: 6411
HQ: Farmers Group, Inc.
6301 Owensmouth Ave
Woodland Hills CA 91367
323 932-3200

(P-10356)
FARMERS INSURANCE EXCHANGE (DH)
6301 Owensmouth Ave, Woodland Hills (91367-2216)
PHONE.....................323 932-3200
Jeff Pailey, *CEO*
Ron Myhan, *CFO*
Thomas Noh, *CFO*
Melissa Joye, *Officer*
Anthony La Rosa, *Engineer*
EMP: 3000
SQ FT: 210,000
SALES (est): 1.8B
SALES (corp-wide): 48.2B **Privately Held**
SIC: 6411 Insurance agents, brokers & service
HQ: Farmers Group, Inc.
6301 Owensmouth Ave
Woodland Hills CA 91367
323 932-3200

(P-10357)
FARMERS INSURANCE EXCHANGE
411 E Pine St Ste A, Exeter (93221-1800)
PHONE.....................559 594-4149
Sammy Harrell, *Branch Mgr*
EMP: 326
SALES (corp-wide): 48.2B **Privately Held**
SIC: 6411 Insurance agents, brokers & service
HQ: Farmers Insurance Exchange
6301 Owensmouth Ave
Woodland Hills CA 91367
323 932-3200

(P-10358)
FARMERS INSURANCE FED CRED UNI (PA)
4601 Wilshire Blvd # 110, Los Angeles (90010-3880)
P.O. Box 36911 (90036-0911)
PHONE.....................323 209-6000
Mark Herter, *CEO*
Sandy Medeiros, *President*
Laszlo Haredy, *Chairman*
Sylvia Diaz, *Officer*
Brian Leonard, *Officer*
EMP: 70
SQ FT: 12,000
SALES: 48.7MM **Privately Held**
WEB: www.figfederalcu.com
SIC: 6411 Insurance agents, brokers & service

(P-10359)
FCE BENEFIT ADMINISTRATORS INC (PA)
1528 S El Camino Real # 307, San Mateo (94402-3060)
PHONE.....................650 341-0306
Gary Beckman, *President*
Donald Shackelford, *Assoc VP*
Isaac Domenech, *Exec VP*
Tom Leon, *Exec VP*
Steve Porter, *Exec VP*
EMP: 150
SQ FT: 10,000
SALES (est): 36MM **Privately Held**
WEB: www.fcebenefit.com
SIC: 6411 Insurance agents

(P-10360)
FEDERAL INSURANCE COMPANY
21820 Burbank Blvd # 330, Woodland Hills (91367-6476)
P.O. Box 4208 (91365)
PHONE.....................818 596-6100
Walter Guzzo, *Branch Mgr*
EMP: 80
SQ FT: 1,000
SALES (corp-wide): 32.7B **Privately Held**
WEB: www.federalinsurancecompany.com
SIC: 6411 Insurance agents, brokers & service
HQ: Federal Insurance Company
202 N Illinois St # 2600
Indianapolis IN 46204
908 903-2000

(P-10361)
FEDERAL INSURANCE COMPANY
Also Called: Chubb
275 Battery St Fl 12, San Francisco (94111-3305)
PHONE.....................415 273-6300
Cliston Thomas, *Manager*
Tyler Bausom, *Underwriter*
EMP: 100
SALES (corp-wide): 32.7B **Privately Held**
WEB: www.federalinsurancecompany.com
SIC: 6411 Insurance agents, brokers & service
HQ: Federal Insurance Company
202 N Illinois St # 2600
Indianapolis IN 46204
908 903-2000

(P-10362)
FIDELITY NATIONAL FINCL INC
1300 Dove St Ste 310, Newport Beach (92660-2417)
PHONE.....................949 622-5000
Rob Vavrock, *Branch Mgr*
Licette Woods, *Officer*
Jim John, *Exec VP*
Debby Boyd, *Vice Pres*
Jaime Hong, *Vice Pres*
EMP: 80
SALES (corp-wide): 7.5B **Publicly Held**
SIC: 6411 Insurance agents, brokers & service
PA: Fidelity National Financial, Inc.
601 Riverside Ave Fl 4
Jacksonville FL 32204
904 854-8100

(P-10363)
FINANCIAL PACIFIC INSURANCE CO
3850 Atherton Rd, Rocklin (95765-3700)
PHONE.....................916 630-5000
Robert C Goodell, *Principal*
EMP: 81
SALES (est): 192.5K **Publicly Held**
SIC: 6411 Insurance agents, brokers & service
HQ: Financial Pacific Insurance Group, Inc
3880 Atherton Rd
Rocklin CA 95765

(P-10364)
FIRE INSURANCE EXCHANGE (PA)
4680 Wilshire Blvd, Los Angeles (90010-3807)
PHONE.....................323 932-3200
Martin Feinstein, *President*
John Harrington, *President*
Ron Myhan, *Treasurer*
Deborah Aldredge, *Officer*
Doren Hohl, *Admin Sec*
EMP: 2300
SALES: 1B **Privately Held**
SIC: 6411 Insurance agents, brokers & service

(P-10365)
FMC FINANCIAL GROUP (PA)
4675 Macarthur Ct # 1250, Newport Beach (92660-8803)
PHONE.....................949 225-9369
James Chapel, *Owner*
▲ **EMP:** 75
SALES (est): 36.8MM **Privately Held**
WEB: www.fmcfg.com
SIC: 6411 Insurance agents & brokers

(P-10366)
FREEWAY INSURANCE (PA)
Also Called: South Coast Auto Insurance
7711 Center Ave Ste 200, Huntington Beach (92647-9124)
PHONE.....................714 252-2500
Elias Assaf, *President*
Norm Hudson, *COO*
John Klaeb, *Vice Pres*
EMP: 120
SQ FT: 20,000
SALES (est): 115.5MM **Privately Held**
WEB: www.seguroahora.com
SIC: 6411 Insurance agents

(P-10367)
G J SULLIVAN CO INC
725 S Figueroa St # 1900, Los Angeles (90017-5496)
PHONE.....................213 626-1000
Gerald J Sullivan, *President*
Steve Fetchet, *Vice Pres*
Lois Massa, *Vice Pres*
Ray Chen, *Analyst*
Barbara Reilly, *Human Res Mgr*
EMP: 60
SALES (est): 19.5MM
SALES (corp-wide): 86.8MM **Privately Held**
WEB: www.gjs.com
SIC: 6411 Insurance brokers
HQ: Gerald J. Sullivan & Associates, Inc.
Insurance Brokers
800 W 6th St Ste 1800
Los Angeles CA
213 626-1000

(P-10368)
GEICO CORPORATION
2033 Arden Way Ste C, Sacramento (95825-2210)
PHONE.....................707 448-7172
Vincent Harris, *Branch Mgr*
EMP: 147
SALES (corp-wide): 225.3B **Publicly Held**
SIC: 6411 Insurance agents, brokers & service
HQ: Geico Corporation
5260 Western Ave
Chevy Chase MD 20815
301 986-3000

(P-10369)
GEICO GENERAL INSURANCE CO
14111 Danielson St, Poway (92064-6886)
PHONE.....................858 848-8200
Elizabeth Shew, *Principal*
EMP: 378
SALES (corp-wide): 225.3B **Publicly Held**
SIC: 6411 Insurance agents, brokers & service
HQ: Geico General Insurance Company
1 Geico Plz
Washington DC 20076

(P-10370)
GEOVERA SPECIALTY INSURANCE CO
1455 Oliver Rd, Fairfield (94534-3472)
PHONE.....................707 863-3700
Karen Padovese, *President*
Kevin Nish, *President*
Lori Gomez, *Vice Pres*
Catherine Sparks, *Info Tech Mgr*
Steve Wynn, *Senior Engr*
EMP: 60
SALES (est): 8.3MM **Privately Held**
WEB: www.homeinsurer.com
SIC: 6411 Insurance brokers
PA: Geovera Holdings, Inc.
4820 Businecä Ctr Dr 20
Fairfield CA 94534

(P-10371)
GGIS INSURANCE SERVICES INC
Also Called: Guardian General Insur Svcs
600 N Brand Blvd Ste 300, Glendale (91203-4207)
PHONE.....................818 553-2110
EMP: 135
SALES (est): 12.7MM **Privately Held**
WEB: www.guardiangeneral.com
SIC: 6411

(P-10372)
GOOD DEAL INSURANCE SERVICES
2140 S Hacienda Blvd A, Hacienda Heights (91745-7200)
PHONE.....................626 275-6795
Chung Hwei Chang, *President*
EMP: 70
SQ FT: 4,000

SALES (est): 7.6MM **Privately Held**
SIC: 6411 Insurance agents

(P-10373)
GROSSLIGHT INSURANCE INC
1333 Westwood Blvd, Los Angeles (90024-4949)
PHONE..................310 473-9611
Joan Schiewe, *CEO*
Steven Schiewe, *President*
Linda Flanagan, *General Mgr*
Anthony Moreno, *VP Sales*
EMP: 60
SQ FT: 15,000
SALES (est): 14.7MM
SALES (corp-wide): 16.5MM **Privately Held**
WEB: www.grosslight.com
SIC: 6411 Insurance agents
PA: Pcf Insurance Services Of The West, Llc
6200 Canoga Ave Ste 325
Woodland Hills CA 91367
818 703-8057

(P-10374)
GS LEVINE INSURANCE SVCS INC
10505 Sorrento Valley Rd # 200, San Diego (92121-1619)
PHONE..................858 481-8692
Gary S Levine, *CEO*
Ross Afsahi, *President*
Dick Avakian, *COO*
EMP: 62
SQ FT: 17,000
SALES (est): 11MM
SALES (corp-wide): 6.9B **Publicly Held**
WEB: www.gslevineins.com
SIC: 6411 Insurance brokers
PA: Arthur J. Gallagher & Co.
2850 Golf Rd Ste 1000
Rolling Meadows IL 60008
630 773-3800

(P-10375)
HAMILTON BRWART INSUR AGCY LLC
1282 W Arrow Hwy, Upland (91786-5040)
P.O. Box 1949 (91785-1949)
PHONE..................909 920-3250
Hamilton Brewart,
Derek Brewart,
EMP: 67
SQ FT: 12,000
SALES (est): 12.3MM **Privately Held**
WEB: www.hamiltonbrewart.com
SIC: 6411 Insurance agents; insurance brokers

(P-10376)
HARTFORD FIRE INSURANCE CO
12009 Foundation Pl # 100, Gold River (95670-4534)
PHONE..................916 294-1000
John Buckalew, *Manager*
Robert Hughes, *Vice Pres*
EMP: 300 **Publicly Held**
WEB:
www.hartfordinvestmentscanada.com
SIC: 6411 Insurance agents, brokers & service
HQ: Hartford Fire Insurance Company
1 Hartford Plz
Hartford CT 06115
860 547-5000

(P-10377)
HARTFORD FIRE INSURANCE CO
777 S Figueroa St Ste 700, Los Angeles (90017-5861)
PHONE..................213 452-5179
Rich Long, *Sales Staff*
EMP: 212 **Publicly Held**
WEB:
www.hartfordinvestmentscanada.com
SIC: 6411 Insurance agents, brokers & service
HQ: Hartford Fire Insurance Company
1 Hartford Plz
Hartford CT 06115
860 547-5000

(P-10378)
HEALTH COMP ADMINISTRATORS (PA)
621 Santa Fe Ave, Fresno (93721-2724)
P.O. Box 45018 (93718-5018)
PHONE..................559 499-2450
Phillip Musson, *President*
Michael Bouskos, *Vice Pres*
Mike Bouskos, *Vice Pres*
Yer Xiong, *Accountant*
Karrish Reznicek, *Train & Dev Mgr*
EMP: 185
SALES (est): 30.8MM **Privately Held**
SIC: 6411 Medical insurance claim processing, contract or fee basis

(P-10379)
HEALTHCOMP
Also Called: Healthcomp Administrators
621 Santa Fe Ave, Fresno (93721-2724)
P.O. Box 45018 (93718-5018)
PHONE..................559 499-2450
Phillip Musson, *CEO*
Michael Bouskos, *CFO*
Monique Bouskos, *Vice Pres*
Kelly Ferreira, *Vice Pres*
Charles Johnson, *Vice Pres*
EMP: 260
SQ FT: 50,000
SALES (est): 58.9MM **Privately Held**
WEB: www.healthcomp.com
SIC: 6411 Medical insurance claim processing, contract or fee basis

(P-10380)
HEALTHMARKETS INC
3152 Red Hill Ave Ste 200, Costa Mesa (92626-3418)
PHONE..................949 486-0600
Matthew Small, *Manager*
Matt Small, *Manager*
EMP: 54
SALES (corp-wide): 933.1MM **Privately Held**
SIC: 6411 Insurance agents, brokers & service
PA: Healthmarkets, Inc.
9151 Blvd 256
North Richland Hills TX 76180
817 255-3100

(P-10381)
HEALTHSMART MANAGEMENT SERVICE
10855 Bus Ctr Dr Ste C, Cypress (90630)
P.O. Box 6300 (90630-0063)
PHONE..................714 947-8600
Carol Houchins, *President*
EMP: 90
SALES (est): 16.4MM **Privately Held**
WEB: www.healthsmartmso.com
SIC: 6411 8741 8721 Medical insurance claim processing, contract or fee basis; hospital management; business management; billing & bookkeeping service

(P-10382)
HEFFERNAN INSURANCE BROKERS
Also Called: Heffernan Group
180 Howard St Ste 200, San Francisco (94105-1663)
PHONE..................800 829-9996
Jeffrey Hamlin, *Branch Mgr*
Janice Berthold, *Vice Pres*
Marc Paletta, *Vice Pres*
Patricia Bustillos, *Admin Asst*
John Peterson, *CTO*
EMP: 50
SALES (corp-wide): 193.2MM **Privately Held**
WEB: www.heffgroup.com
SIC: 6411 Insurance brokers
PA: Heffernan Insurance Brokers
1350 Carlback Ave
Walnut Creek CA 94596
925 934-8500

(P-10383)
HUB INTRNTIONAL INSUR SVCS INC
3636 American River Dr # 200, Sacramento (95864-5952)
PHONE..................916 974-7800
Sergey Vorobets, *Producer*

Michelle Robinson, *Asst Mgr*
Sharon Davis, *Accounts Mgr*
Sandi Pullen, *Accounts Mgr*
EMP: 90 **Privately Held**
SIC: 6411 Insurance agents; insurance brokers
HQ: Hub International Insurance Services Inc.
3390 University Ave # 300
Riverside CA 92501
951 788-8500

(P-10384)
HUB INTRNTIONAL INSUR SVCS INC
Also Called: Der Manouel Insurance Group
548 W Cromwell Ave # 101, Fresno (93711-5714)
PHONE..................559 447-4600
Lyn Fauntleroy, *Partner*
Maria Hustedde, *Admin Asst*
Britt Gosswiller, *Broker*
Karen Edie, *Personnel*
Karen Keyes, *Personnel*
EMP: 71 **Privately Held**
SIC: 6411 Insurance agents
HQ: Hub International Insurance Services Inc.
3390 University Ave # 300
Riverside CA 92501
951 788-8500

(P-10385)
HUB INTRNTIONAL INSUR SVCS INC
40 E Alamar Ave, Santa Barbara (93105-3469)
PHONE..................805 682-2571
Darren Tesars, *Manager*
Raymond Seider, *Vice Pres*
Josh Stichter, *Vice Pres*
Beth Mitchell, *Broker*
Blanca Vega, *Accounts Mgr*
EMP: 52 **Privately Held**
SIC: 6411 Insurance agents, brokers & service
HQ: Hub International Insurance Services Inc.
3390 University Ave # 300
Riverside CA 92501
951 788-8500

(P-10386)
INSURANCE SERVICES AMERCN LLC
300 E Esplanade Dr # 2100, Oxnard (93036-1238)
PHONE..................805 981-2220
Stanley Braun,
Nancy Braun,
Myrtle Solomon,
EMP: 70
SALES (est): 4.2MM **Privately Held**
SIC: 6411 Insurance agents & brokers

(P-10387)
INTEGRO USA INC
115 N El Molino Ave, Pasadena (91101-1804)
PHONE..................626 795-9000
Steve Titus, *General Mgr*
EMP: 50
SALES (corp-wide): 329MM **Privately Held**
SIC: 6411 Insurance agents
HQ: Integro Usa Inc.
1 State St Fl 9
New York NY 10004
212 295-8000

(P-10388)
INTERCARE SPECIALTY RISK INS (PA)
Also Called: Isr Holdings
130 Diamond Creek Pl # 2, Roseville (95747-5197)
PHONE..................916 757-1200
Kevin Hamm, *President*
EMP: 54 **EST:** 2008
SALES (est): 9.9MM **Privately Held**
SIC: 6411 Property & casualty insurance agent

(P-10389)
INTERNTNAL PRNSRANCE ASSOC LLC
504 Redwood Blvd Ste 240e, Novato (94947-6925)
PHONE..................415 223-5548
David M Hofele, *Mng Member*
Minnie Kyotani, *Director*
EMP: 50
SALES (est): 7.5MM **Privately Held**
SIC: 6411 Insurance brokers

(P-10390)
INTERWEST INSURANCE SVCS LLC (PA)
Also Called: Kemper Insurance
8950 Cal Center Dr # 200, Sacramento (95826-3259)
PHONE..................916 488-3100
Tom Williams, *Chairman*
Thomas Williams, *President*
Keith Schuler, *CEO*
Nancy Luttenbacher, *COO*
Donald Pollard, *CFO*
EMP: 173
SQ FT: 20,000
SALES (est): 206MM **Privately Held**
WEB: www.infosourcecafe.com
SIC: 6411 Insurance brokers

(P-10391)
INTERWEST INSURANCE SVCS LLC
5 Sierra Gate Plz Fl 2nd, Roseville (95678-6637)
PHONE..................916 784-1008
EMP: 60
SALES (corp-wide): 206MM **Privately Held**
SIC: 6411 Insurance agents
PA: Interwest Insurance Services, Llc
8950 Cal Center Dr # 200
Sacramento CA 95826
916 488-3100

(P-10392)
INTERWEST INSURANCE SVCS LLC
Also Called: Lindo Hanna & Abbott
1357 E Lassen Ave Ste 100, Chico (95973-7824)
P.O. Box 8110 (95927-8110)
PHONE..................530 895-1010
Keith Shuler, *CEO*
EMP: 70
SALES (corp-wide): 206MM **Privately Held**
WEB: www.infosourcecafe.com
SIC: 6411 Insurance agents, brokers & service
PA: Interwest Insurance Services, Llc
8950 Cal Center Dr # 200
Sacramento CA 95826
916 488-3100

(P-10393)
INVESMART INC
55 Almaden Blvd Ste 800, San Jose (95113-1612)
PHONE..................408 961-2800
Kent Buckles, *CEO*
EMP: 55
SALES (est): 59MM **Privately Held**
WEB: www.stancorpfinancial.com
SIC: 6411 Pension & retirement plan consultants
HQ: Stancorp Financial Group, Inc.
1100 Sw 6th Ave
Portland OR 97204
971 321-7000

(P-10394)
JAMES C JENKINS INSUR SVC INC
Also Called: Athens Insurance
1390 Willow Pass Rd, Concord (94520-5200)
PHONE..................925 798-3334
John Hahn, *CEO*
Peter Garvey, *President*
Karman Chan, *CFO*
Janet McClain, *Exec VP*
Jason Del Grande, *Vice Pres*
EMP: 125 **EST:** 1977
SQ FT: 30,000

SALES (est): 37.2MM
SALES (corp-wide): 42.7MM **Privately Held**
SIC: 6411 Insurance brokers
HQ: Edgewood Partners Insurance Center
425 California St # 2400
San Francisco CA 94104

(P-10395)
JAMES G PARKER INSURANCE ASSOC (PA)
Also Called: Bacome Insurance Agency
1753 E Fir Ave, Fresno (93720-3840)
P.O. Box 3947 (93650-3947)
PHONE..................................559 222-7722
James G Parker, *President*
Janice W Parker, *Treasurer*
Leroy Berrett, *Vice Pres*
Jon Parker, *Vice Pres*
Gerald Thompson, *Vice Pres*
EMP: 70
SQ FT: 13,000
SALES (est): 80.5MM **Privately Held**
SIC: 6411 Insurance agents

(P-10396)
JANET HILTON
Also Called: Allstate
990 W 190th St Ste 300, Torrance
(90502-4461)
P.O. Box 660636, Dallas TX (75266-0636)
PHONE..................................310 851-7200
Janet Hilton, *Principal*
Jeanette Forni, *Sales Mgr*
EMP: 100
SALES (est): 4.9MM **Privately Held**
SIC: 6411 Insurance agents, brokers & service

(P-10397)
JOHN HANCOCK LIFE INSUR CO USA (DH)
865 S Figueroa St # 3320, Los Angeles
(90017-2543)
PHONE..................................213 689-0813
Emeritus D'Alessandro, *CEO*
William Horan, *Managing Prtnr*
David F D'Alessandro, *President*
Ross Fryer, *President*
Gregory P Winn, *Treasurer*
▲ EMP: 2000 EST: 1862
SQ FT: 3,600,000
SALES (est): 3B
SALES (corp-wide): 29.5B **Privately Held**
WEB: www.jhcases.com
SIC: 6411 6351 6371 6321 Insurance agents & brokers; mortgage guarantee insurance; pensions; accident insurance carriers; health insurance carriers
HQ: John Hancock Financial Services, Inc.
200 Clarendon St
Boston MA 02116
617 572-6000

(P-10398)
KASPICK & CO LLC (DH)
203 Redwood Shores Pkwy # 300, Redwood City (94065-6121)
PHONE..................................650 585-4100
Lindy Sherwood, *Managing Dir*
Corinne Bruand, *Trust Officer*
Kris Hecht, *Administration*
EMP: 60
SALES (est): 19.3MM
SALES (corp-wide): 30.3B **Privately Held**
WEB: www.kaspick.com
SIC: 6411 Insurance agents, brokers & service
HQ: Teachers Insurance And Annuity Association-College Retirement Equities Fund
730 3rd Ave Ste 2a
New York NY 10017
212 490-9000

(P-10399)
KEENAN & ASSOCIATES
1791 Broadway St Ste 200, Redwood City
(94063-2487)
P.O. Box 2707, Torrance (90509-2707)
PHONE..................................650 306-0616
Jessica Blakiston, *Manager*
EMP: 55 **Privately Held**
SIC: 6411 Insurance claim adjusters, not employed by insurance company

HQ: Keenan & Associates
2355 Crenshaw Blvd # 200
Torrance CA 90501
310 212-3344

(P-10400)
KEENAN & ASSOCIATES (HQ)
2355 Crenshaw Blvd # 200, Torrance
(90501-3395)
P.O. Box 4328 (90510-4328)
PHONE..................................310 212-3344
John Keenan, *Ch of Bd*
Sean Smith, *CEO*
Davis Seres, *COO*
Henry Loubet, *Senior VP*
Art Choi, *Vice Pres*
EMP: 339
SQ FT: 80,000
SALES (est): 432.5MM **Privately Held**
WEB: www.keenanhealthcare.com
SIC: 6411 Insurance brokers

(P-10401)
KEENAN & ASSOCIATES
626 H St, Eureka (95501-1026)
PHONE..................................707 268-1616
Kay Byrnes, *Manager*
EMP: 55 **Privately Held**
SIC: 6411 Insurance information & consulting services
HQ: Keenan & Associates
2355 Crenshaw Blvd # 200
Torrance CA 90501
310 212-3344

(P-10402)
KEENAN & ASSOCIATES
3550 Vine St Ste 200, Riverside
(92507-4175)
P.O. Box 79991 (92513-1991)
PHONE..................................951 788-0330
Karleen Smartiss, *Manager*
EMP: 65 **Privately Held**
WEB: www.keenanhealthcare.com
SIC: 6411 6371 Insurance brokers; pension, health & welfare funds
HQ: Keenan & Associates
2355 Crenshaw Blvd # 200
Torrance CA 90501
310 212-3344

(P-10403)
KEENAN & ASSOCIATES
2868 Prospect Park Dr # 600, Rancho Cordova (95670-6020)
PHONE..................................916 858-2981
Nancy Conner, *Manager*
Denise Keener, *Supervisor*
EMP: 70 **Privately Held**
WEB: www.keenanhealthcare.com
SIC: 6411 Insurance information & consulting services
HQ: Keenan & Associates
2355 Crenshaw Blvd # 200
Torrance CA 90501
310 212-3344

(P-10404)
KEENAN & ASSOCIATES
1740 Tech Dr Ste 300, San Jose (95110)
PHONE..................................408 441-0754
Mickey Armstrong, *Manager*
EMP: 50 **Privately Held**
WEB: www.keenanhealthcare.com
SIC: 6411 Insurance brokers
HQ: Keenan & Associates
2355 Crenshaw Blvd # 200
Torrance CA 90501
310 212-3344

(P-10405)
KEENAN & ASSOCIATES
901 Calle Amanecer # 200, San Clemente
(92673-4211)
PHONE..................................949 940-1760
Steve Gedestad, *Principal*
EMP: 55 **Privately Held**
WEB: www.keenanhealthcare.com
SIC: 6411 Insurance brokers
HQ: Keenan & Associates
2355 Crenshaw Blvd # 200
Torrance CA 90501
310 212-3344

(P-10406)
KONING & ASSOCIATES INC (PA)
1631 Willow St Ste 220, San Jose
(95125-5108)
PHONE..................................408 265-3800
Chris Koning, *President*
EMP: 50
SALES: 6MM **Privately Held**
WEB: www.koningassociates.com
SIC: 6411 7389 Insurance claim adjusters, not employed by insurance company; inspection & investigation services, insurance;

(P-10407)
KORAM INSURANCE CENTER INC
3807 Wilshire Blvd # 400, Los Angeles
(90010-3104)
PHONE..................................323 660-1000
Edward Haan, *CEO*
James D Hahn, *Ch of Bd*
Edward M Hahn, *President*
EMP: 58 EST: 1974
SQ FT: 3,300
SALES (est): 5.8MM **Privately Held**
WEB: www.koraminsurance.com
SIC: 6411 Insurance agents

(P-10408)
LEAVITT GROUP ENTERPRISES INC
785 E Washington Blvd # 4, Crescent City
(95531-8343)
PHONE..................................707 465-6508
Debbie Koehlerschmidt, *Branch Mgr*
EMP: 130
SALES (corp-wide): 211MM **Privately Held**
SIC: 6411 Insurance agents
PA: Leavitt Group Enterprises Inc
216 S 200 W
Cedar City UT 84720
435 586-1555

(P-10409)
LISI INC (PA)
1600 W Hillsdale Blvd # 202, San Mateo
(94402-3766)
PHONE..................................650 348-4131
Philip Lebherz, *Ch of Bd*
Becky Patel, *CEO*
Ken Doyle, *Senior VP*
Kevin Timone, *Senior VP*
Tamara Henderson, *Vice Pres*
EMP: 60
SQ FT: 18,000
SALES (est): 100.3MM **Privately Held**
WEB: www.lisibroker.com
SIC: 6411 Insurance agents

(P-10410)
LOCKTON COMPANIES LLC-PACIFI (HQ)
Also Called: Lockton Insurance Brokers
777 S Figueroa St # 5200, Los Angeles
(90017-5800)
PHONE..................................213 689-0500
Timothy J Noonan, *President*
Nate Mundy, *Senior VP*
Robert L Johnson, *Vice Pres*
Julie Law, *Vice Pres*
Tony Murray, *Vice Pres*
EMP: 350
SQ FT: 72,300
SALES (est): 178.7MM
SALES (corp-wide): 1.8B **Privately Held**
SIC: 6411 Insurance brokers
PA: Lockton, Inc.
444 W 47th St Ste 900
Kansas City MO 64112
816 960-9000

(P-10411)
LOEWS CORPORATION
4000 Coronado Bay Rd, Coronado
(92118-3290)
PHONE..................................619 424-4000
Kathleen Cochran, *General Mgr*
Scott Munday, *Supervisor*
EMP: 400

SALES (corp-wide): 14B **Publicly Held**
WEB: www.loews.com
SIC: 6411 Insurance agents, brokers & service
PA: Loews Corporation
667 Madison Ave Fl 7
New York NY 10065
212 521-2000

(P-10412)
MANAGED CARE SYSTEMS KERN CNTY
Also Called: MCS
5251 Office Park Dr # 405, Bakersfield
(93309-0404)
PHONE..................................661 716-7100
Bob Severs, *CEO*
EMP: 80
SALES (est): 8.2MM **Privately Held**
SIC: 6411 7363 Medical insurance claim processing, contract or fee basis; medical help service

(P-10413)
MARKEL CORP
Also Called: Associated Intl Insur Co
21600 Oxnard St Ste 900, Woodland Hills
(91367-7834)
PHONE..................................818 595-0600
Anthony Markel, *President*
Andrew Barnard, *CEO*
Steven Markel, *Vice Ch Bd*
James Morales, *Underwriter*
EMP: 272
SQ FT: 32,000
SALES (est): 29.7MM
SALES (corp-wide): 6.8B **Publicly Held**
SIC: 6411 Insurance agents, brokers & service
HQ: Markel North America, Inc
4521 Highwoods Pkwy
Glen Allen VA 23060
804 747-0136

(P-10414)
MARKEL WEST INC
21600 Oxnard St Ste 400, Woodland Hills
(91367-4800)
PHONE..................................818 595-0600
Anthony Markel, *President*
EMP: 50
SALES (est): 5.2MM
SALES (corp-wide): 6.8B **Publicly Held**
WEB: www.markelcorp.com
SIC: 6411 Insurance agents, brokers & service
PA: Markel Corporation
4521 Highwoods Pkwy
Glen Allen VA 23060
804 747-0136

(P-10415)
MAROEVICH OSHEA & COGHLAN
Also Called: M O C Insurance Services
44 Montgomery St Ste 1700, San Francisco
(94104-4704)
PHONE..................................415 957-0600
Van Maroevich, *CEO*
Gerald Clifford, *CFO*
Jerry Clifford, *CFO*
Steve Elkins, *Exec VP*
Peter Brown, *Senior VP*
EMP: 60
SQ FT: 10,000
SALES (est): 17.6MM **Privately Held**
WEB: www.mocins.com
SIC: 6411 Insurance brokers

(P-10416)
MARSH & MCLENNAN AGENCY LLC
1 Polaris Way Ste 300, Aliso Viejo
(92656-5358)
PHONE..................................949 544-8460
Joe Tapias, *Branch Mgr*
Drew Lambert, *Executive*
EMP: 86
SALES (corp-wide): 14.9B **Publicly Held**
WEB: www.barneyandbarney.com
SIC: 6411 Insurance brokers; life insurance agents
HQ: Marsh & Mclennan Agency Llc
360 Hamilton Ave Ste 930
White Plains NY 10601

(P-10417)
MARSH & MCLENNAN AGENCY LLC
201 California St Ste 900, San Francisco (94101-5011)
PHONE...............................415 243-4160
Paul Hering, *CEO*
Scott Reynolds, *Vice Pres*
Yelena Delaquize, *Client Mgr*
EMP: 86
SALES (corp-wide): 14.9B **Publicly Held**
SIC: 6411 Insurance brokers; life insurance agents
HQ: Marsh & Mclennan Agency Llc
360 Hamilton Ave Ste 930
White Plains NY 10601
-

(P-10418)
MARSH & MCLENNAN AGENCY LLC
9171 Towne Centre Dr # 500, San Diego (92122-1234)
PHONE...............................858 457-3414
Paul Hering, *Branch Mgr*
Pj Jacquelin, *Partner*
Peter Epstine, *Vice Pres*
Jennifer Balestrieri, *Executive*
Victor Botello, *Executive*
EMP: 200
SALES (corp-wide): 14.9B **Publicly Held**
SIC: 6411 Insurance brokers; life insurance agents
HQ: Marsh & Mclennan Agency Llc
360 Hamilton Ave Ste 930
White Plains NY 10601

(P-10419)
MARSH & MCLENNAN COMPANIES INC
777 S Figueroa St # 2200, Los Angeles (90017-5820)
PHONE...............................213 346-5555
Kris Davis, *Branch Mgr*
Kathleen Habermann, *Vice Pres*
John Heatherton, *Vice Pres*
Laura L Johnson, *Vice Pres*
Patricia Osmena, *Vice Pres*
EMP: 80
SALES (corp-wide): 14.9B **Publicly Held**
WEB: www.seabury.com
SIC: 6411 Insurance brokers
PA: Marsh & Mclennan Companies, Inc.
1166 Avenue Of The Americ
New York NY 10036
212 345-5000

(P-10420)
MARSH USA INC
345 California St # 1300, San Francisco (94104-2606)
PHONE...............................415 743-8000
Mike Kelley, *Office Mgr*
Mike Kelly, *Officer*
Becky Anderson, *Vice Pres*
Yvonne Cho, *Vice Pres*
Austin Neff, *Vice Pres*
EMP: 64
SALES (corp-wide): 14.9B **Publicly Held**
WEB: www.marsh.com
SIC: 6411 Insurance brokers
HQ: Marsh Usa Inc.
1166 Ave Of The Americas
New York NY 10036
212 345-6000

(P-10421)
MARSH USA INC
1735 Tech Dr Ste 790, San Jose (95110)
PHONE...............................408 467-5600
Andrew Haaser, *Manager*
EMP: 62
SALES (corp-wide): 14.9B **Publicly Held**
SIC: 6411 Insurance brokers
HQ: Marsh Usa Inc.
1166 Ave Of The Americas
New York NY 10036
212 345-6000

(P-10422)
MAXSON YOUNG ASSOC INC
180 Montgomery St # 2100, San Francisco (94104-4231)
PHONE...............................415 228-6400

Vernon Chalfant, *CEO*
EMP: 120
SALES (est): 12.2MM **Privately Held**
SIC: 6411 Insurance adjusters

(P-10423)
MC GRAW COMMERCIAL INSUR SVC
Also Called: McGraw Insurance Services
8185 E Kaiser Blvd, Anaheim (92808-2214)
PHONE...............................714 939-9875
Vivian Tafolla, *Principal*
EMP: 51
SALES (est): 3.2MM
SALES (corp-wide): 60.6MM **Privately Held**
SIC: 6411 Insurance agents, brokers & service
PA: Mc Graw Commercial Insurance Service, Inc
3601 Haven Ave
Menlo Park CA

(P-10424)
MEDICAL EYE SERVICES INC
345 Baker St, Costa Mesa (92626-4518)
P.O. Box 25209, Santa Ana (92799-5209)
PHONE...............................714 619-4660
Aspasia Shappet, *President*
Felix Cruz, *Manager*
David Grenell, *Manager*
Rodney Mattos, *Manager*
Sanny Vuu, *Assistant*
EMP: 100
SQ FT: 12,000
SALES (est): 24.6MM **Privately Held**
SIC: 6411 Insurance claim processing, except medical
PA: The Eye Care Network Of California Inc
345 Baker St
Costa Mesa CA 92626

(P-10425)
MEDICAL INSURANCE EXCHANGE CAL
6250 Claremont Ave, Oakland (94618-1324)
PHONE...............................510 596-4935
Dr Bradford Cohn, *President*
Dr William Donald, *Vice Chairman*
Linda Matson, *Vice Pres*
Dr Conrad Anderson, *Admin Sec*
Fred Stafford, *Technician*
EMP: 74
SQ FT: 13,000
SALES (est): 13MM **Privately Held**
WEB: www.miec.com
SIC: 6411 Loss prevention services, insurance

(P-10426)
METROPOLITAN LIFE INSUR CO
Also Called: MetLife
425 Market St Ste 960, San Francisco (94105-2423)
PHONE...............................415 536-1065
Henry Loubouet, *Director*
Chris Rothering, *Analyst*
Christina Gwe Hong, *Counsel*
EMP: 375
SALES (corp-wide): 67.9B **Publicly Held**
SIC: 6411 Insurance agents & brokers
HQ: Metropolitan Life Insurance Company (Inc)
1095 Ave Of The Americas
New York NY 10036
908 253-1000

(P-10427)
MICHAEL MAGUIRE & ASSOCIATES
611 Anton Blvd Ste 900, Costa Mesa (92626-7684)
PHONE...............................714 435-7500
Michael Maguire, *Owner*
EMP: 50
SALES (est): 4.2MM **Privately Held**
SIC: 6411 8111 Insurance agents, brokers & service; general practice attorney, lawyer

(P-10428)
MITCHELL BUCKMAN INC (PA)
Also Called: Kemper Insurance
500 N Santa Fe St, Visalia (93292-5065)
P.O. Box 629 (93279-0629)
PHONE...............................559 733-1181
EMP: 80
SQ FT: 16,000
SALES (est): 50.1MM **Privately Held**
WEB: www.bminc.com
SIC: 6411

(P-10429)
MOMENTOUS INSURANCE BRKG INC
5990 Sepulvda Blvd # 550, Van Nuys (91411-2536)
PHONE...............................818 933-2700
Diane Brinson Schiele, *President*
Erin Gaston, *Senior VP*
David Oliver, *Senior VP*
Michelle Boyer, *Principal*
Carla Cave, *Principal*
EMP: 78
SALES (est): 30.9MM **Privately Held**
SIC: 6411 Insurance agents; insurance brokers

(P-10430)
MORGAN KLEPPE & NASH
Also Called: Mkni
501 N Church St, Visalia (93291-5004)
P.O. Box 1390 (93279-1390)
PHONE...............................559 732-3436
Keith Kleppe, *Partner*
Gerry Folmer, *Partner*
EMP: 58
SQ FT: 2,500
SALES (est): 22MM **Privately Held**
WEB: www.morgankleppenash.com
SIC: 6411 Insurance agents, brokers & service

(P-10431)
MORRIS GRRITANO INSUR AGCY INC
1122 Laurel Ln, San Luis Obispo (93401-5895)
P.O. Box 1189 (93406-1189)
PHONE...............................805 543-6887
Brendan Morris, *CEO*
David Morgan, *Shareholder*
Kelly Morgan, *Shareholder*
Kerry Pollock, *Shareholder*
John Pullock, *Shareholder*
EMP: 85
SQ FT: 14,000
SALES (est): 25.5MM **Privately Held**
WEB: www.morrisgarritano.com
SIC: 6411 Insurance agents, brokers & service; insurance brokers

(P-10432)
NATIONAL GENERAL INSURANCE CO
Also Called: GMAC Insurance
3633 Inland Empire Blvd # 700, Ontario (91764-4922)
PHONE...............................909 944-8085
Steven Wright, *Manager*
EMP: 86 **Publicly Held**
SIC: 6411 Insurance agents, brokers & service
HQ: National General Insurance Company
5757 Phantom Dr Ste 200
Hazelwood MO 63042
314 493-8000

(P-10433)
NATIONAL RTREMENT PARTNERS INC (PA)
34700 Pacific Coast Hwy, Capistrano Beach (92624-1351)
PHONE...............................949 488-8726
William R Chetney, *CEO*
Timothy O'Brien, *President*
Robert France, *COO*
Lawrence Craig Smith, *Officer*
Richard Darian, *Exec VP*
EMP: 53
SALES (est): 15.3MM **Privately Held**
WEB: www.n-r-p.com
SIC: 6411 Pension & retirement plan consultants

(P-10434)
NETWORKED INSURANCE AGENTS LLC
Also Called: Direct Access Insurance Svcs
443 Crown Point Cir Ste A, Grass Valley (95945-9557)
PHONE...............................800 682-8476
George Biancardi, *President*
Kelly McRae, *CFO*
Larry Oslie, *Exec VP*
Phyllis Hayes, *Vice Pres*
Patti Leonard, *Vice Pres*
EMP: 110
SQ FT: 15,000
SALES (est): 39.6MM
SALES (corp-wide): 773MM **Privately Held**
WEB: www.nia-ins.com
SIC: 6411 Insurance agents
PA: Amwins Group, Inc.
4725 Piedmont Row Dr # 600
Charlotte NC 28210
704 749-2700

(P-10435)
NEW ALLIANCE INSURANCE BROKERS
3700 Santa Fe Ave Ste 300, Long Beach (90810-2171)
PHONE...............................424 205-6700
Marcello Povolo, *President*
EMP: 50
SALES: 25MM **Privately Held**
SIC: 6411 Insurance agents

(P-10436)
NEW YORK LIFE INSURANCE CO
1300 S El Cmno Real 400, San Mateo (94402)
PHONE...............................650 571-1220
K B Sareen, *Manager*
Hai Vu, *Technology*
Zachary E Whitman, *Sales Associate*
EMP: 400
SALES (corp-wide): 13.3B **Privately Held**
WEB: www.newyorklife.com
SIC: 6411 Insurance agents & brokers
PA: New York Life Insurance Company
51 Madison Ave Bsmt 1b
New York NY 10010
212 576-7000

(P-10437)
NEW YORK LIFE INSURANCE CO
205 E Rver Pk Cir Ste 250, Fresno (93720)
PHONE...............................559 447-3900
Bert Moosios, *Agent*
Robert L Lim, *Sales Associate*
Kat McGeee, *Director*
Roy McKenney, *Manager*
Frederick Rich, *Advisor*
EMP: 58
SALES (corp-wide): 13.3B **Privately Held**
WEB: www.newyorklife.com
SIC: 6411 Insurance agents & brokers
PA: New York Life Insurance Company
51 Madison Ave Bsmt 1b
New York NY 10010
212 576-7000

(P-10438)
NEW YORK LIFE INSURANCE CO
425 Market St Fl 16, San Francisco (94105-2498)
PHONE...............................415 393-6060
Kevin Choi, *Manager*
Shao Chang, *Advisor*
Marife Tenoyan, *Agent*
EMP: 50
SALES (corp-wide): 13.3B **Privately Held**
WEB: www.newyorklife.com
SIC: 6411 Insurance agents & brokers
PA: New York Life Insurance Company
51 Madison Ave Bsmt 1b
New York NY 10010
212 576-7000

(P-10439)
NEW YORK LIFE INSURANCE CO
7112 N Fresno St Ste 100, Fresno
(93720-2949)
PHONE................................559 447-3900
Janz Myderup, *Branch Mgr*
Russell K Auyeung, *Sales Associate*
William A Dotson, *Sales Associate*
Richard S Elia, *Sales Associate*
Robert A Jones, *Sales Associate*
EMP: 100
SALES (corp-wide): 13.3B **Privately Held**
WEB: www.newyorklife.com
SIC: 6411 Insurance agents & brokers
PA: New York Life Insurance Company
51 Madison Ave Bsmt 1b
New York NY 10010
212 576-7000

(P-10440)
NNA INSURANCE SERVICES
9350 De Soto Ave, Chatsworth
(91311-4926)
P.O. Box 2402 (91313-2402)
PHONE................................818 739-4071
Milton G Valera, *Ch of Bd*
Thomas A Heymann, *CEO*
Robert A Clarke, *CFO*
Deborah M Thaw, *Exec VP*
Deborah Valera, *Vice Pres*
▲ EMP: 204
SQ FT: 55,000
SALES (est): 40.4MM **Privately Held**
WEB: www.nationalnotary.com
SIC: 6411 Insurance agents, brokers & service

(P-10441)
NORCAL MUTUAL INSURANCE CO (PA)
575 Market St Fl 10, San Francisco
(94105-2885)
PHONE................................415 397-9703
Theodore Scott Diener, *CEO*
Jim Sunsari, *President*
Jaan Sidorov, *Bd of Directors*
Christoph Dugre, *Assoc VP*
Lucy Sam, *Assoc VP*
EMP: 285
SALES (est): 336.4MM **Privately Held**
SIC: 6411 6331 Insurance agents; fire, marine & casualty insurance

(P-10442)
NORTHWEST INSURANCE AGENCY
Also Called: Bondi-Nderson Assoc Insur Brks
418 B St Ste 100, Santa Rosa
(95401-8500)
PHONE................................707 573-1300
Mary Feli, *President*
EMP: 55
SALES (est): 5.2MM **Privately Held**
SIC: 6411 Insurance brokers

(P-10443)
NORTHWESTERN MUTL FINCL NETWRK (PA)
4225 Executive Sq # 1250, La Jolla
(92037-9122)
PHONE................................619 234-3111
Garrett J Bleakley, *Owner*
Candace Berkman, *CTO*
Ann Williamsen, *Representative*
EMP: 120
SALES (est): 25MM **Privately Held**
SIC: 6411 Insurance agents, brokers & service

(P-10444)
OLD REPUBLIC CONTRACTORS INS
225 S Lake Ave Ste 900, Pasadena
(91101-3011)
PHONE................................626 683-5200
Joan Miles, *CEO*
Arthina James, *Vice Pres*
Crystal McMillan, *Vice Pres*
Kevin Peters, *Vice Pres*
Chris Phillips, *Vice Pres*
EMP: 91

SALES (est): 19.4MM
SALES (corp-wide): 6B **Publicly Held**
SIC: 6411 Insurance agents, brokers & service
HQ: Old Republic General Insurance Group, Inc.
307 N Michigan Ave # 1418
Chicago IL 60601

(P-10445)
OLD REPUBLIC HM PROTECTION INC
2 Annabel Ln Ste 112, San Ramon
(94583-1377)
P.O. Box 5017 (94583-0917)
PHONE................................925 866-1500
Gwen M Gallagher, *President*
Ed Adams, *Vice Pres*
Pj Cochran, *Vice Pres*
Lorna Mello, *Vice Pres*
Gail Stevens, *Vice Pres*
EMP: 305
SQ FT: 39,500
SALES (est): 98.5MM
SALES (corp-wide): 6B **Publicly Held**
WEB: www.orhp.com
SIC: 6411 Insurance agents, brokers & service
PA: Old Republic International Corporation
307 N Michigan Ave
Chicago IL 60601
312 346-8100

(P-10446)
OMEGA INSURANCE SERVICES
Also Called: Word and Brown
721 S Parker St Ste 300, Orange
(92868-4732)
PHONE................................714 973-0311
D P Thomas, *CEO*
Clinton Gee, *CFO*
Jeffrey Compangano, *Vice Pres*
David Duker, *Vice Pres*
Jeff Hecht, *Vice Pres*
EMP: 50
SQ FT: 2,500
SALES (est): 17.3MM **Privately Held**
SIC: 6411 Insurance brokers

(P-10447)
OWEN & COMPANY
1455 Response Rd Ste 260, Sacramento
(95815-5263)
PHONE................................916 993-2700
Jere Owen, *President*
John Owen, *Treasurer*
Michael Fitzgerald, *Producer*
Coreen Hoffman, *Sales Staff*
Helen Merrell, *Manager*
EMP: 57
SQ FT: 4,741
SALES (est): 13.5MM **Privately Held**
SIC: 6411 8111 Insurance brokers; legal services

(P-10448)
PACIFIC COMPENSATION INSUR CO
1 Baxter Way Ste 170, Westlake Village
(91362-3819)
P.O. Box 5034, Thousand Oaks (91359-5034)
PHONE................................818 575-8500
Marc E Schmittlein, *President*
Todd Hines, *Vice Pres*
Kris Mathis, *Vice Pres*
Teresa Smiley, *Vice Pres*
Shawn Wright, *Vice Pres*
EMP: 150
SALES (est): 74.8MM **Privately Held**
WEB: www.edicwc.com
SIC: 6411 Insurance agents, brokers & service
HQ: Pacific Compensation Corporation
1 Baxter Way Ste 170
Westlake Village CA 91362

(P-10449)
PACIFIC INDEMNITY COMPANY
Also Called: Chubb
555 S Flower St Ste 300, Los Angeles
(90071-2427)
PHONE................................213 622-2334
John Fennigan, *President*

Melinda Kefalas, *Admin Asst*
Dale Pringle, *Manager*
Maribel Arias, *Assistant VP*
Alan Leach, *Assistant VP*
EMP: 300
SALES (est): 62.9MM
SALES (corp-wide): 32.7B **Privately Held**
WEB: www.chubb.com
SIC: 6411 6331 6351 Insurance agents, brokers & service; fire, marine & casualty insurance: mutual; surety insurance
HQ: Ina Chubb Holdings Inc
436 Walnut St
Philadelphia PA 19106
215 640-1000

(P-10450)
PACIFIC PIONEER INSUR GROUP (PA)
Also Called: Pacific Pioneer Insur Group
6363 Katella Ave, Cypress (90630-5205)
PHONE................................714 228-7888
Lin W Lan, *Founder*
Danni Hernandez, *Branch Mgr*
Laurie Eusebio, *Marketing Staff*
Sonia Morris, *Assistant*
Colleen Eng, *Underwriter*
EMP: 104
SQ FT: 32,000
SALES (est): 17.5MM **Privately Held**
SIC: 6411 Insurance agents

(P-10451)
PACIFIC SPECIALTY INSURANCE CO
2200 Geng Rd Ste 200, Palo Alto
(94303-3358)
P.O. Box 40, Anaheim (92815-0040)
PHONE................................800 303-5000
Timothy Joel Summers, *CEO*
John Mc Graw, *Shareholder*
Ann Mc Graw-Morrical, *Shareholder*
John Chu, *President*
Mike Mc Graw, *President*
EMP: 50
SQ FT: 20,000
SALES (est): 17MM **Privately Held**
WEB: www.pacificspecialty.com
SIC: 6411 Insurance agents
PA: Western Service Contract Corp.
2200 Geng Rd Ste 200
Palo Alto CA

(P-10452)
PEGASUS RISK MANAGEMENT INC (PA)
Also Called: Status Medical Management
642 Galaxy Way, Modesto (95356-9606)
P.O. Box 5038 (95352-5038)
PHONE................................209 574-2800
Ray Simon, *President*
Paula Towe, *Vice Pres*
EMP: 70
SQ FT: 10,000
SALES (est): 24.4MM **Privately Held**
WEB: www.statusmedical.com
SIC: 6411 Insurance claim processing, except medical

(P-10453)
PERR & KNIGHT INC (PA)
401 Wilshire Blvd Ste 300, Santa Monica
(90401-1454)
PHONE................................310 230-9339
Timothy B Perr, *CEO*
Courtney Hughes, *Manager*
EMP: 93
SQ FT: 10,098
SALES (est): 46.1MM **Privately Held**
SIC: 6411 Loss prevention services, insurance; research services, insurance; reporting services, insurance

(P-10454)
PLANPRESCRIBER INC
440 E Middlefield Rd, Mountain View
(94043-4006)
PHONE................................650 584-2700
Bruce A Telkamp, *CEO*
EMP: 258
SALES (est): 74.6MM
SALES (corp-wide): 251.4MM **Publicly Held**
SIC: 6411 Insurance agents, brokers & service

PA: Ehealth, Inc.
440 E Middlefield Rd
Mountain View CA 94043
650 584-2700

(P-10455)
POLISEEK AIS INSUR SLTIONS INC
17785 Center Court Dr N # 250, Cerritos
(90703-8573)
PHONE................................866 480-7335
Mark Ribisi, *President*
Chris Bremer, *CFO*
Lani Elkin, *VP Opers*
Romayne Levee, *VP Mktg*
Mark Casas, *VP Sales*
EMP: 70
SALES (est): 8.6MM
SALES (corp-wide): 3.3B **Publicly Held**
SIC: 6411 Insurance agents, brokers & service
HQ: Ais Management, Llc
17785 Center Court Dr N # 250
Cerritos CA 90703

(P-10456)
POLYCOMP ADMINISTRATIVE SVCS
3000 Lava Ridge Ct # 130, Roseville
(95661-2802)
PHONE................................916 773-3480
Pamela Constantino, *Systems Mgr*
EMP: 50
SQ FT: 4,500
SALES (corp-wide): 32.3MM **Privately Held**
WEB: www.polycomp.net
SIC: 6411 Pension & retirement plan consultants
PA: Polycomp Administrative Services Inc
16030 Ventura Blvd # 200
Encino CA 91436
818 716-0111

(P-10457)
PRECEPT INC (DH)
Also Called: Precept Group The
130 Theory Ste 200, Irvine (92617-3065)
PHONE................................949 955-1430
Wade R Olson, *President*
Steve Williams, *President*
Steve Zarate, *COO*
Christopher H Coulter, *Chief Mktg Ofcr*
Karen Reid, *Officer*
EMP: 90
SQ FT: 32,000
SALES (est): 41.4MM
SALES (corp-wide): 13B **Publicly Held**
WEB: www.preceptgroup.com
SIC: 6411 Insurance brokers

(P-10458)
PREFERRED EMPLOYERS INSUR CO
9797 Aero Dr Ste 200, San Diego
(92123-1898)
P.O. Box 85478 (92186-5478)
PHONE................................619 688-3900
Linda R Smith, *President*
Eric Hansen, *Vice Pres*
Kimberly Erickson, *Human Res Mgr*
Scot Wright, *Production*
Mark Beaulieu, *Marketing Staff*
EMP: 70
SALES (est): 17MM
SALES (corp-wide): 7.6B **Publicly Held**
WEB: www.preferredworkcomp.com
SIC: 6411 Insurance information & consulting services
PA: W. R. Berkley Corporation
475 Steamboat Rd Fl 1
Greenwich CT 06830
203 629-3000

(P-10459)
PREMIER DEALER SERVICES INC
9449 Balboa Ave Ste 300, San Diego
(92123-4395)
PHONE................................858 810-1700
John R Topits, *President*
Lisle Greenweller, *COO*
Kurt Wolery, *Senior VP*
A Kurt Wolery, *Admin Sec*

EMP: 100
SALES (est): 26.5MM **Privately Held**
WEB: www.pdsadm.com
SIC: 6411 Insurance agents, brokers & service

(P-10460)
PRIMERICA FINANCIAL SVCS INC
27470 Jefferson Ave 5a, Temecula (92590-2693)
PHONE.............................951 695-4325
Mary Simeta, *Manager*
EMP: 70 **Publicly Held**
SIC: 6411 Insurance agents & brokers
HQ: Primerica Financial Services, Inc.
3120 Breckinridge Blvd
Duluth GA 30099
800 544-5445

(P-10461)
PRIMERICA LIFE INSURANCE CO
260 Sheridan Ave Ste B42, Palo Alto (94306-2046)
PHONE.............................650 323-2554
Omonike Wesipuryear, *Branch Mgr*
EMP: 121 **Publicly Held**
SIC: 6411 Insurance agents & brokers
HQ: Primerica Life Insurance Company
1 Primerica Pkwy
Duluth GA 30099
770 381-1000

(P-10462)
PRIMERICA LIFE INSURANCE CO
41307 12th St W Ste 200, Palmdale (93551-1455)
PHONE.............................661 947-9070
Belia Rosales, *Branch Mgr*
EMP: 126 **Publicly Held**
SIC: 6411 Insurance agents & brokers
HQ: Primerica Life Insurance Company
1 Primerica Pkwy
Duluth GA 30099
770 381-1000

(P-10463)
PRIMERICA LIFE INSURANCE CO
175 N Cawston Ave, Hemet (92545-5277)
PHONE.............................951 652-6190
EMP: 126 **Publicly Held**
SIC: 6411 6799 Insurance agents & brokers; investors
HQ: Primerica Life Insurance Company
1 Primerica Pkwy
Duluth GA 30099
770 381-1000

(P-10464)
PRINCIPAL FINANCIAL GROUP INC
500 N Brand Blvd Ste 1800, Glendale (91203-3305)
PHONE.............................818 243-7141
Jim Rhodes, *Branch Mgr*
Jennifer T Love, *Sales Associate*
Cfa K J Wolf, *Sales Associate*
EMP: 80 **Publicly Held**
SIC: 6411 Insurance agents, brokers & service
PA: Principal Financial Group, Inc.
711 High St
Des Moines IA 50392
-

(P-10465)
PROFESSIONAL INSUR ASSOC INC (PA)
Also Called: Professsional Insurance
1100 Industrial Rd Ste 3, San Carlos (94070-4131)
P.O. Box 1266 (94070-1266)
PHONE.............................650 592-7333
Paula Hammack, *President*
Devan Hammack, *Assoc VP*
Paul Hammack, *Vice Pres*
Lisa Colville, *Admin Asst*
Anne Johnson, *Administration*
EMP: 50
SQ FT: 9,000

SALES (est): 61MM **Privately Held**
WEB: www.piainc.com
SIC: 6411 Insurance agents; insurance brokers

(P-10466)
PROPERTYPLUS INSUR AGCY INC
21820 Burbank Blvd # 130, Woodland Hills (91367-6476)
PHONE.............................818 432-2640
EMP: 745
SALES (est): 81.7K
SALES (corp-wide): 31.9B **Publicly Held**
SIC: 6411 Real estate insurance agents
HQ: Arx Holding Corp.
1 Asi Way N
Saint Petersburg FL 33702
727 821-8765

(P-10467)
PRUDENTIAL INSUR CO OF AMER
3333 Michelson Dr Ste 820, Irvine (92612-0655)
PHONE.............................949 440-5300
Jay Skolnick, *Manager*
EMP: 50
SALES (corp-wide): 62.9B **Publicly Held**
SIC: 6411 Insurance agents, brokers & service
HQ: The Prudential Insurance Company Of America
751 Broad St
Newark NJ 07102
973 802-6000

(P-10468)
PRUDENTIAL INSUR CO OF AMER
101 California St Fl 40, San Francisco (94111-6127)
PHONE.............................415 398-7310
Micheal Jamieson, *Manager*
Miki Sakata, *Vice Pres*
Michael Tagliaferro, *Vice Pres*
Jocelyn Friel, *Director*
Kenji Tamaoki, *Director*
EMP: 80
SALES (corp-wide): 62.9B **Publicly Held**
SIC: 6411 Insurance agents, brokers & service
HQ: The Prudential Insurance Company Of America
751 Broad St
Newark NJ 07102
973 802-6000

(P-10469)
PRUDENTIAL INSUR CO OF AMER
15303 Ventura Blvd # 1550, Sherman Oaks (91403-6624)
PHONE.............................818 990-2122
Craig Biggf, *Manager*
Walt Danheiser, *Representative*
EMP: 50
SALES (corp-wide): 62.9B **Publicly Held**
SIC: 6411 Insurance agents, brokers & service
HQ: The Prudential Insurance Company Of America
751 Broad St
Newark NJ 07102
973 802-6000

(P-10470)
PRUDENTIAL INSUR CO OF AMER
5990 Sepulvda Blvd # 300, Van Nuys (91411-2500)
PHONE.............................818 901-0028
EMP: 60
SALES (corp-wide): 41.4B **Publicly Held**
SIC: 6411
HQ: The Prudential Insurance Company Of America
751 Broad St
Newark NJ 07102
973 802-6000

(P-10471)
QUALIFIED BENEFITS INC
21021 Ventura Blvd # 100, Woodland Hills (91364-2200)
PHONE.............................818 594-4900
Greg Taylor, *President*
Angelo Mazzone, *Admin Sec*
EMP: 50
SQ FT: 11,500
SALES (est): 7.3MM **Privately Held**
WEB: www.qben.com
SIC: 6411 Pension & retirement plan consultants
PA: Qbi, Llc
21031 Ventura Blvd # 1200
Woodland Hills CA 91364

(P-10472)
QUALITY CLAIMS MANAGEMENT CORP
2763 Camino Del Rio S, San Diego (92108-3708)
PHONE.............................619 450-8600
Ronald Reitz, *President*
Robyn Markow, *Assoc VP*
Thomas Holthus, *Admin Sec*
Brian Reschke, *Business Anlyst*
Amy Carpenter, *Project Mgr*
EMP: 60
SQ FT: 8,000
SALES (est): 12.9MM **Privately Held**
WEB: www.qualityclaims.com
SIC: 6411 Insurance claim adjusters, not employed by insurance company

(P-10473)
R MC CLOSKEY INSURANCE AGENCY
Also Called: Tax and Financial Group
4001 Macarthur Blvd # 300, Newport Beach (92660-2505)
PHONE.............................949 223-8100
Richard Mc Closkey, *President*
Art Veyna, *Partner*
Brian McNulty, *Managing Prtnr*
Paul Thomas, *Managing Prtnr*
Christine Bond, *COO*
EMP: 120
SQ FT: 15,000
SALES (est): 38.7MM **Privately Held**
WEB: www.tfgroup.com
SIC: 6411 Insurance agents; life insurance agents

(P-10474)
RAMKADE INSURANCE SERVICES
Also Called: Time Financial Services
21550 Oxnard St Ste 500, Woodland Hills (91367-7111)
PHONE.............................818 444-1340
Kate Kinkade, *President*
Patrick Ramsey, *Vice Pres*
EMP: 60
SALES (est): 7.5MM
SALES (corp-wide): 72.8B **Publicly Held**
WEB: www.timefin.com
SIC: 6411 Insurance agents
HQ: Citi Investor Services, Inc.
105 Eisenhower Pkwy Ste 2
Roseland NJ 07068

(P-10475)
RAMSELL PUBLIC HEALTH RX LLC
200 Webster St Ste 300, Oakland (94607-4108)
PHONE.............................510 587-2600
Eric A Flowers,
Thomas Laker,
EMP: 51
SQ FT: 1,500
SALES (est): 3.8MM
SALES (corp-wide): 10.8MM **Privately Held**
SIC: 6411 Medical insurance claim processing, contract or fee basis
PA: Ramsell Corporation
200 Webster St Ste 200 # 200
Oakland CA 94607
510 587-2659

(P-10476)
REHAB WEST INC
277 Rancheros Dr Ste 190, San Marcos (92069-2982)
PHONE.............................619 518-3710
Sharon Douglas, *CEO*
Carol Holub, *CFO*
Carol Clark, *Admin Asst*
Sandra Ashlock, *Nurse*
Jessica Koski, *Nurse*
EMP: 50
SQ FT: 3,000
SALES: 5.5MM **Privately Held**
WEB: www.rehabwest.com
SIC: 6411 Medical insurance claim processing, contract or fee basis

(P-10477)
RON FILICE ENTERPRISES INC
Also Called: Filice Insurance Agency
738 N 1st St Ste 202, San Jose (95112-6371)
PHONE.............................408 294-0477
Ron Filice, *President*
Silvia G Lucero, *Officer*
Chris Lazio, *Exec VP*
Chuck Batchelder, *Vice Pres*
Mike Chavez, *Vice Pres*
EMP: 50
SQ FT: 3,000
SALES (est): 14.9MM **Privately Held**
SIC: 6411 Insurance agents

(P-10478)
RSI INSURANCE BROKERS INC (DH)
4000 Westerly Pl Ste 110, Newport Beach (92660-2347)
PHONE.............................714 546-6616
Barry Rabune, *President*
Ben Thomas, *Vice Pres*
Linda Miller, *Manager*
Aaron Fawcett, *Agent*
EMP: 50
SALES (est): 9.5MM
SALES (corp-wide): 711.8MM **Privately Held**
WEB: www.rsiinsurancebrokers.com
SIC: 6411 Insurance brokers
HQ: Acrisure, Llc
5664 Prairie Creek Dr Se
Caledonia MI 49316
800 748-0351

(P-10479)
RUTLEDGE CLAIMS MANAGEMENT INC
14286 Danielson St # 103, Poway (92064-8819)
PHONE.............................858 883-2000
Thomas W Rutledge, *CEO*
Aubrey Gilmore, *COO*
EMP: 100
SALES (est): 16.4MM **Privately Held**
SIC: 6411 Insurance information & consulting services

(P-10480)
SAFE-GUARD PRODUCTS INTL LLC
18100 Von Karman Ave # 150, Irvine (92612-0174)
PHONE.............................800 742-7896
Randy Barkowitz, *Branch Mgr*
EMP: 96 **Privately Held**
SIC: 6411 Property & casualty insurance agent
PA: Safe-Guard Products International Llc
2 Concourse Pkwy Ste 500
Atlanta GA 30328

(P-10481)
SAFECO INSURANCE COMPANY AMER
330 N Brand Blvd Ste 680, Glendale (91203-2385)
PHONE.............................818 956-4250
Don Chambers, *Manager*
EMP: 160
SALES (corp-wide): 38.3B **Privately Held**
SIC: 6411 Insurance agents, brokers & service

HQ: Safeco Insurance Company Of America
1001 4th Ave Ste 800
Seattle WA 98185
206 545-5000

(P-10482)
SCC ESA DEPT OF RISK MGMT
Also Called: ESA Risk Management
2310 N 1st St Ste 202, San Jose
(95131-1040)
PHONE..................408 441-4207
EMP: 65
SALES (est): 2.8MM **Privately Held**
WEB: www.esariskmanagement.com
SIC: **6411**

(P-10483)
SCHIRMER FIRE PROTECTION ENG
Also Called: AON
707 Wilshire Blvd # 2600, Los Angeles
(90017-3501)
PHONE..................213 630-2020
Jacqueline Bychowski, *Office Mgr*
Mark Rochholz, *COO*
EMP: 99
SALES (corp-wide): 237.5MM **Privately Held**
SIC: **6411** Insurance brokers
HQ: Schirmer Fire Protection Engineering
Corporation
200 E Randolph St
Chicago IL 60601

(P-10484)
SCOTTISH AMERICAN INSURANCE (PA)
Also Called: Yates & Associates
2002 E Mcfadden Ave # 100, Santa Ana
(92705-4766)
PHONE..................714 550-5050
Paul A Thomson, *CEO*
Carl Ledbetter, *President*
James M Yates, *President*
Bob Mestayer, *Vice Pres*
Bradley Chadwick, *Executive*
EMP: 69
SQ FT: 14,300
SALES (est): 17.2MM **Privately Held**
WEB: www.yates-assoc.com
SIC: **6411** Insurance brokers

(P-10485)
SEDGWICK CLAIMS MGT SVCS INC
1410 Rocky Ridge Dr Ste 3, Roseville
(95661-2811)
P.O. Box 619066 (95661)
PHONE..................916 771-2900
David Banta, *Principal*
EMP: 348
SALES (corp-wide): 97.3MM **Privately Held**
SIC: **6411** Insurance claim adjusters, not
employed by insurance company
PA: Sedgwick Claims Management Services, Inc.
8125 Sedgwick Way
Memphis TN 38125
901 415-7400

(P-10486)
SEDGWICK CLAIMS MGT SVCS INC
3280 E Foothill Blvd # 350, Pasadena
(91107-3103)
P.O. Box 14435, Lexington KY (40512-4435)
PHONE..................626 568-1415
Barbara Jones, *Principal*
Monica Soto, *Executive*
Josh Trunk, *Litigation*
Patrick Neylan, *Assistant VP*
Marialuisa Dapuetto, *Supervisor*
EMP: 70
SALES (corp-wide): 97.3MM **Privately Held**
SIC: **6411** Insurance claim adjusters, not
employed by insurance company

(P-10487)
SEDGWICK CLAIMS MGT SVCS INC
24025 Park Sorrento # 200, Calabasas
(91302-4018)
P.O. Box 9830 (91372-0830)
PHONE..................818 591-9444
John Gernert, *Manager*
Shawn Johnson, *Vice Pres*
Jeff Loeffelman, *Business Dir*
Debbie Buckhouse,
EMP: 200
SALES (corp-wide): 97.3MM **Privately Held**
WEB: www.sedgwickcms.com
SIC: **6411** Insurance claim adjusters, not
employed by insurance company
PA: Sedgwick Claims Management Services, Inc.
8125 Sedgwick Way
Memphis TN 38125
901 415-7400

(P-10488)
SEDGWICK CLAIMS MGT SVCS INC
2101 Webster St, Oakland (94612-3011)
PHONE..................510 302-3000
Athanasios Soha, *Branch Mgr*
David Hocutt, *President*
Joyce Crain, *Admin Asst*
Garry Hageman, *Technology*
Terra White, *Manager*
EMP: 70
SALES (corp-wide): 97.3MM **Privately Held**
WEB: www.sedgwickcms.com
SIC: **6411** Insurance claim adjusters, not
employed by insurance company
PA: Sedgwick Claims Management Services, Inc.
8125 Sedgwick Way
Memphis TN 38125
901 415-7400

(P-10489)
SEDGWICK CLAIMS MGT SVCS INC
1851 Heritage Ln, Sacramento
(95815-4926)
PHONE..................916 568-7394
EMP: 70
SALES (corp-wide): 97.3MM **Privately Held**
SIC: **6411** Insurance claim adjusters, not
employed by insurance company
PA: Sedgwick Claims Management Services, Inc.
8125 Sedgwick Way
Memphis TN 38125
901 415-7400

(P-10490)
SEDGWICK CMS HOLDINGS INC
3633 Inland Empire Blvd, Ontario
(91764-4922)
PHONE..................909 477-5500
Kim Pech, *Branch Mgr*
Malcolm Dodge, *Vice Pres*
Katrina Zitnik, *Vice Pres*
Robin Azevedo, *VP Bus Dvlpt*
Rick Miller, *Opers Staff*
EMP: 1133
SALES (corp-wide): 12.2B **Privately Held**
SIC: **6411** Insurance claim adjusters, not
employed by insurance company
PA: Sedgwick Cms Holdings, Inc.
1100 Ridgeway Loop Rd # 200
Memphis TN 38120
901 415-7400

(P-10491)
SELECTQUOTE INSURANCE SERVICES (PA)
595 Market St Fl 10, San Francisco
(94105-2899)
PHONE..................415 543-7338
Charan J Singh, *President*
Tom Grant, *Vice Chairman*

Robert Edwards, *COO*
Steven H Gerber, *Vice Pres*
Paul Gregory, *Vice Pres*
EMP: 200
SALES (est): 259.7MM **Privately Held**
WEB: www.selectquote.com
SIC: **6411** Life insurance agents

(P-10492)
SEQUOIA INSURANCE COMPANY
P.O. Box 1510, Monterey (93942-1510)
PHONE..................916 933-9524
EMP: 72 **Publicly Held**
SIC: **6411**
HQ: Sequoia Insurance Company
31 Upper Ragsdale Dr
Monterey CA 93940
831 655-9612

(P-10493)
SHAW & PETERSEN INSURANCE INC
Also Called: Harbor's Insurance
1313 5th St, Eureka (95501-0660)
PHONE..................707 443-0845
Maurice O Shaw Sr, *President*
Maurice O Shaw Jr, *Corp Secy*
EMP: 50
SQ FT: 3,000
SALES (est): 8.8MM **Privately Held**
WEB: www.shawandpetersen.com
SIC: **6411** Insurance agents

(P-10494)
SIGNATURE RESOURCES INSURANCE
Also Called: John Hancock
19900 Macarthur Blvd # 920, Irvine
(92612-8417)
PHONE..................949 930-2400
Gary Kaltenbach, *Owner*
Nina Manning, *Office Mgr*
William Barnett,
Susan Oleary,
Michael S Keith, *Manager*
EMP: 60
SQ FT: 1,800
SALES (est): 10.2MM **Privately Held**
WEB: www.signatureresources.net
SIC: **6411** Insurance agents & brokers

(P-10495)
SKYLES INSURANCE AGENCY
9840 Business Park Dr, Sacramento
(95827-1745)
PHONE..................916 361-9585
Theron Skyles, *Partner*
EMP: 50
SALES (est): 6.6MM **Privately Held**
SIC: **6411** Insurance agents

(P-10496)
SPECIALTY RISK SERVICES INC
1 Pointe Dr Ste 220, Brea (92821-7631)
P.O. Box 7007, La Habra (90632-7007)
PHONE..................714 674-1000
Sharon Bartholomew, *Principal*
EMP: 87
SALES (corp-wide): 97.3MM **Privately Held**
SIC: **6411** Insurance agents, brokers &
service
HQ: Specialty Risk Services, Inc.
100 Corporate Dr Ste 211
Windsor CT 06095

(P-10497)
SPECIALTY RISK SERVICES INC
6140 Stoneridge Mall Rd # 245, Pleasanton
(94588-3233)
PHONE..................877 809-9478
Eric Hansen, *Principal*
EMP: 117
SALES (corp-wide): 97.3MM **Privately Held**
WEB: www.srsconnect.com
SIC: **6411** Insurance claim processing, except medical; loss prevention services, insurance
HQ: Specialty Risk Services, Inc.
100 Corporate Dr Ste 211
Windsor CT 06095

(P-10498)
STATE FARM FIRE AND CSLTY CO
Also Called: State Farm Insurance
5127 W Walnut Ave, Visalia (93277-3472)
PHONE..................559 625-4330
Patrick Salazar, *Manager*
Elaine R Rider, *Agent*
EMP: 63
SALES (corp-wide): 39.5B **Privately Held**
WEB: www.statefarm.net
SIC: **6411** Insurance agents & brokers
HQ: State Farm Fire And Casualty Company
Three State Frm Plz S H-4
Bloomington IL 61710
309 766-2311

(P-10499)
STATE FARM FIRE AND CSLTY CO
Also Called: State Farm Insurance
6400 State Farm Dr, Rohnert Park (94928)
PHONE..................707 588-6011
Glen Dorsett, *Manager*
EMP: 500
SALES (corp-wide): 39.5B **Privately Held**
WEB: www.statefarm.net
SIC: **6411** Insurance agents & brokers
HQ: State Farm Fire And Casualty Company
Three State Frm Plz S H-4
Bloomington IL 61710
309 766-2311

(P-10500)
STATE FARM MUTL AUTO INSUR CO
Also Called: State Farm Insurance
12122 S Halldale Ave # 200, Los Angeles
(90047-5320)
PHONE..................309 766-2311
Sang H Pyo, *Principal*
Stephan Buckley, *Manager*
Bernard Gandara, *Manager*
Maria Gonzalez, *Manager*
Roy D McKinney, *Manager*
EMP: 326
SALES (corp-wide): 39.5B **Privately Held**
WEB: www.statefarm.com
SIC: **6411** Insurance agents & brokers
PA: State Farm Mutual Automobile Insurance Company
1 State Farm Plz
Bloomington IL 61710
309 766-2311

(P-10501)
STATE FARM MUTL AUTO INSUR CO
Also Called: State Farm Insurance
16656 Ventura Blvd # 203, Encino
(91436-1918)
PHONE..................818 849-5126
Laetania Richardson, *Manager*
EMP: 71
SALES (corp-wide): 39.5B **Privately Held**
SIC: **6411** Insurance agents & brokers
PA: State Farm Mutual Automobile Insurance Company
1 State Farm Plz
Bloomington IL 61710
309 766-2311

(P-10502)
STATE FARM MUTL AUTO INSUR CO
Also Called: State Farm Insurance
30125 Agoura Rd Ste 200, Agoura Hills
(91301-4322)
PHONE..................818 597-4300
Dennis Pitta, *Branch Mgr*
Robert Downes, *Manager*
Susan L Erkfritz, *Manager*
Frejeanne Scott, *Manager*
EMP: 72
SALES (corp-wide): 39.5B **Privately Held**
WEB: www.statefarm.com
SIC: **6411** Insurance agents & brokers
PA: State Farm Mutual Automobile Insurance Company
1 State Farm Plz
Bloomington IL 61710
309 766-2311

(P-10503)
STATE FARM MUTL AUTO INSUR CO
Also Called: State Farm Insurance
1558 Fitzgerald Dr, Pinole (94564-2229)
PHONE....................510 222-1102
Donald L Greco, *Owner*
EMP: 72
SALES (corp-wide): 39.5B **Privately Held**
WEB: www.statefarm.com
SIC: 6411 Insurance agents & brokers
PA: State Farm Mutual Automobile Insur-
ance Company
1 State Farm Plz
Bloomington IL 61710
309 766-2311

(P-10504)
STATE FARM MUTL AUTO INSUR CO
Also Called: State Farm Insurance
1705 E 10th St Apt 201, Long Beach
(90813-6347)
PHONE....................310 632-9810
Phil Davis, *Manager*
Don Catalina, *Principal*
Brad Garofalo, *Manager*
EMP: 72
SALES (corp-wide): 39.5B **Privately Held**
WEB: www.statefarm.com
SIC: 6411 Insurance agents & brokers
PA: State Farm Mutual Automobile Insur-
ance Company
1 State Farm Plz
Bloomington IL 61710
309 766-2311

(P-10505)
STATE FARM MUTL AUTO INSUR CO
Also Called: State Farm Insurance
17122 Slover Ave Ste 106, Fontana
(92337-7588)
PHONE....................909 349-2050
Lenita Graves, *Manager*
Ken Williams, *Broker*
John T Diehl, *Manager*
EMP: 72
SALES (corp-wide): 39.5B **Privately Held**
WEB: www.statefarm.com
SIC: 6411 Insurance agents & brokers
PA: State Farm Mutual Automobile Insur-
ance Company
1 State Farm Plz
Bloomington IL 61710
309 766-2311

(P-10506)
STATE FARM MUTL AUTO INSUR CO
Also Called: State Farm Insurance
2019 24th St, Bakersfield (93301-3814)
PHONE....................661 324-4077
Roger Hess, *Branch Mgr*
Jake Harless, *Manager*
Luis Ogas, *Manager*
EMP: 72
SALES (corp-wide): 39.5B **Privately Held**
WEB: www.statefarm.com
SIC: 6411 Insurance agents & brokers
PA: State Farm Mutual Automobile Insur-
ance Company
1 State Farm Plz
Bloomington IL 61710
309 766-2311

(P-10507)
STATE FARM MUTL AUTO INSUR CO
Also Called: State Farm Insurance
2555 Flores St Ste 175, San Mateo
(94403-2343)
PHONE....................650 345-3571
Jake Bursalyan, *Manager*
Alice Hu, *Manager*
EMP: 72
SALES (corp-wide): 39.5B **Privately Held**
WEB: www.statefarm.com
SIC: 6411 Insurance agents & brokers
PA: State Farm Mutual Automobile Insur-
ance Company
1 State Farm Plz
Bloomington IL 61710
309 766-2311

(P-10508)
STATE FARM MUTL AUTO INSUR CO
Also Called: State Farm Insurance
900 Old River Rd 400, Bakersfield
(93311-9501)
PHONE....................309 766-2311
Mike Memoly, *Owner*
Liz Schneider-Smith, *Recruiter*
Edward Austin, *Manager*
Ted Bowersox, *Manager*
EMP: 72
SALES (corp-wide): 39.5B **Privately Held**
WEB: www.statefarm.com
SIC: 6411 Insurance agents & brokers
PA: State Farm Mutual Automobile Insur-
ance Company
1 State Farm Plz
Bloomington IL 61710
309 766-2311

(P-10509)
STATE FARM MUTL AUTO INSUR CO
Also Called: State Farm Insurance
40315 Junction Dr Ste A, Oakhurst
(93644-9159)
PHONE....................559 683-3467
Marilyn Rigg, *Branch Mgr*
EMP: 72
SALES (corp-wide): 39.5B **Privately Held**
WEB: www.statefarm.com
SIC: 6411 Insurance agents & brokers
PA: State Farm Mutual Automobile Insur-
ance Company
1 State Farm Plz
Bloomington IL 61710
309 766-2311

(P-10510)
STATE FARM MUTL AUTO INSUR CO
Also Called: State Farm Insurance
5345 Fallbrook Ave, Woodland Hills
(91367-6112)
PHONE....................818 887-1060
Gary Hoover, *Manager*
Vic Nader, *Agent*
EMP: 72
SALES (corp-wide): 39.5B **Privately Held**
WEB: www.statefarm.com
SIC: 6411 Insurance agents & brokers
PA: State Farm Mutual Automobile Insur-
ance Company
1 State Farm Plz
Bloomington IL 61710
309 766-2311

(P-10511)
STATE FARM MUTL AUTO INSUR CO
Also Called: State Farm Insurance
845 Via De La Paz Ste 12, Pacific Pal-
isades (90272-3627)
PHONE....................310 454-0349
Vince Gurino, *Manager*
EMP: 72
SALES (corp-wide): 39.5B **Privately Held**
WEB: www.statefarm.com
SIC: 6411 Insurance agents & brokers
PA: State Farm Mutual Automobile Insur-
ance Company
1 State Farm Plz
Bloomington IL 61710
309 766-2311

(P-10512)
STATE FARM MUTL AUTO INSUR CO
Also Called: State Farm Insurance
8040 W 3rd St, Los Angeles (90048-4307)
PHONE....................323 852-6868
Daniel Williams, *Manager*
EMP: 72
SALES (corp-wide): 39.5B **Privately Held**
WEB: www.statefarm.com
SIC: 6411 Insurance agents & brokers
PA: State Farm Mutual Automobile Insur-
ance Company
1 State Farm Plz
Bloomington IL 61710
309 766-2311

(P-10513)
STATE FARM MUTL AUTO INSUR CO
Also Called: State Farm Insurance
4600 Ashe Rd Ste 308, Bakersfield
(93313-2040)
PHONE....................661 664-9663
Keith Stonebraker, *Branch Mgr*
EMP: 72
SALES (corp-wide): 39.5B **Privately Held**
WEB: www.statefarm.com
SIC: 6411 Insurance agents & brokers
PA: State Farm Mutual Automobile Insur-
ance Company
1 State Farm Plz
Bloomington IL 61710
309 766-2311

(P-10514)
STRATEGIC FINANCIAL GROUP
18191 Von Karman Ave # 100, Irvine
(92612-7103)
PHONE....................949 622-7200
Shawn Mackey, *Principal*
EMP: 50
SALES (est): 3.6MM **Privately Held**
SIC: 6411 Insurance agents

(P-10515)
SUN COAST GEN INSUR AGCY INC
23042 Mill Creek Dr, Laguna Hills
(92653-1214)
P.O. Box 30750 (92654-0750)
PHONE....................949 768-1132
Jeffrey Yeskin, *CEO*
David Yeskin, *President*
Larua Gibson, *CFO*
Scott Boren, *Chief Mktg Ofcr*
Rosie Garcia, *Technology*
EMP: 55
SQ FT: 13,000
SALES (est): 12.4MM **Privately Held**
WEB: www.suncoastinsurance.com
SIC: 6411 Insurance agents

(P-10516)
SUNLAND INSURANCE AGENCY
4961 E Kings Canyon Rd, Fresno
(93727-3812)
P.O. Box 779, Clovis (93613-0779)
PHONE....................559 251-7861
Michael Denman, *Owner*
EMP: 765
SALES (est): 166.4K
SALES (corp-wide): 3.3B **Publicly Held**
SIC: 6411 Insurance agents
HQ: Mercury Insurance Company
4484 Wilshire Blvd
Los Angeles CA 90010
323 937-1060

(P-10517)
SURECO HLTH LF INSUR AGCY INC
201 E Sndpint Dr Ste 600, Santa Ana
(92707)
PHONE....................866 235-5515
Marc Steven Bablot, *CEO*
EMP: 75
SALES: 12MM **Privately Held**
SIC: 6411 Insurance agents, brokers &
service

(P-10518)
SURVIVAL INSURANCE INC
Also Called: Survival Insurance Brkg A Cal
2550 N Hollywood Way # 120, Burbank
(91505-1055)
PHONE....................818 565-1584
Richard Acunto, *Ch of Bd*
Susan Mithoff, *Vice Pres*
EMP: 240
SQ FT: 10,000
SALES (est): 22.7MM **Privately Held**
SIC: 6411 Insurance brokers

(P-10519)
TBG INSURANCE SERVICES CORP
100 N Pacific Coast Hwy # 50, El Segundo
(90245-4359)
PHONE....................310 203-8770
Michael R Shute, *CEO*
Michael Glickman, *CFO*

EMP: 260
SALES (est): 45.7MM
SALES (corp-wide): 62.9B **Publicly Held**
SIC: 6411 8111 Insurance agents, brokers
& service; legal services
PA: Prudential Financial, Inc.
751 Broad St
Newark NJ 07102
973 802-6000

(P-10520)
THOITS INSURANCE SERVICE INC
444 Castro St Ste 200, Mountain View
(94041-2051)
PHONE....................408 792-5400
EMP: 67
SQ FT: 16,250
SALES: 14.3MM **Privately Held**
WEB: www.thoits-insurance.com
SIC: 6411 Insurance agents

(P-10521)
TOKIO MARINE MANAGEMENT INC
800 E Colorado Blvd Ste 8, Pasadena
(91101-2103)
P.O. Box 7127 (91109-7127)
PHONE....................626 568-7600
Kaz Takashima, *Manager*
EMP: 250 **Privately Held**
SIC: 6411 6331 6321 Insurance brokers;
fire, marine & casualty insurance; acci-
dent & health insurance
HQ: Tokio Marine Management, Inc.
1221 Park Ave Ste 1500
New York NY 10128
212 297-6600

(P-10522)
TRAVELERS INDEMNITY COMPANY
Also Called: Travelers Insurance
21688 Gateway Center Dr # 300, Diamond
Bar (91765-2451)
P.O. Box 660055, Dallas TX (75266-0055)
PHONE....................909 612-3000
Annet Ball, *Manager*
Remy Dayrit, *Manager*
Anna Soliman, *Underwriter*
EMP: 200
SALES (corp-wide): 30.2B **Publicly Held**
WEB: www.travelers.com
SIC: 6411 6331 Insurance agents, brokers
& service; fire, marine & casualty insur-
ance
HQ: The Travelers Indemnity Company
1 Tower Sq
Hartford CT 06183
860 277-0111

(P-10523)
TRAVELERS PROPERTY CSLTY CORP
Also Called: Travelers Insurance
401 Lennon Ln, Walnut Creek
(94598-2508)
P.O. Box 13089, Sacramento (95813-3089)
PHONE....................925 945-4000
Julie Weisert, *Branch Mgr*
EMP: 300
SALES (corp-wide): 30.2B **Publicly Held**
WEB: www.travelerspc.com
SIC: 6411 Insurance agents, brokers &
service
HQ: Travelers Property Casualty Corp.
1 Tower Sq 8ms
Hartford CT 06183

(P-10524)
TRI-AD ACTUARIES INC
221 W Crest St Ste 300, Escondido
(92025-1737)
PHONE....................760 743-7555
Curtis Hamilton, *CEO*
Robert Krier, *CFO*
Thad Hamilton, *Vice Pres*
Judy Simons, *Vice Pres*
EMP: 117
SQ FT: 17,500

SALES (est): 40.5MM **Privately Held**
WEB: www.tri-ad.com
SIC: **6411** 8742 Pension & retirement plan consultants; human resource consulting services

(P-10525)
TRISTAR RISK MANAGEMENT
203 N Golden Circle Dr # 200, Santa Ana (92705-4011)
PHONE..................714 543-0700
Thomas Veale, *Branch Mgr*
EMP: 69
SALES (corp-wide): 363.2MM **Privately Held**
WEB: www.tristarrisk.com
SIC: **6411** 8742 Inspection & investigation services, insurance; management consulting services
HQ: Tristar Risk Management
100 Oceangate Ste 700
Long Beach CA 90802
562 495-6600

(P-10526)
UNIFAX INSURANCE SYSTEMS INC
26050 Mureau Rd Fl 2, Calabasas (91302-3174)
PHONE..................818 591-9800
Erwin Cheldin, *President*
Lester Aaron, *Treasurer*
Cary Cheldin, *Exec VP*
Michael Odmark, *Supervisor*
EMP: 80
SQ FT: 50,000
SALES (est): 8.8MM
SALES (corp-wide): 33.6MM **Publicly Held**
WEB: www.crusaderinsurance.com
SIC: **6411** Insurance brokers
PA: Unico American Corporation
26050 Mureau Rd Fl 2
Calabasas CA 91302
818 591-9800

(P-10527)
UNITED CHINESE AMERICAN GENERA (PA)
Also Called: Uca General Insurance
6363 Katella Ave, Cypress (90630-5205)
PHONE..................714 228-7800
Robert Lan, *President*
Lin Lan, *Shareholder*
Ping Chen, *Corp Secy*
EMP: 58
SQ FT: 20,000
SALES (est): 10.1MM **Privately Held**
WEB: www.ucageneral.com
SIC: **6411** Insurance agents

(P-10528)
UNITED INSURANCE COMPANY
5601 E Slauson Ave # 105, Commerce (90040-2997)
PHONE..................323 869-9381
Norman Petrousian, *District Mgr*
EMP: 50
SALES (est): 5.2MM **Privately Held**
SIC: **6411** Insurance agents, brokers & service

(P-10529)
UNITED STATES FIRE INSUR CO
Also Called: Crum & Forster
777 S Figueroa St # 1500, Los Angeles (90017-5810)
PHONE..................213 797-3100
Mark Owens, *Manager*
Wilton Nunes, *Executive*
EMP: 53
SALES (corp-wide): 17.7B **Privately Held**
SIC: **6411** Insurance agents
HQ: United States Fire Insurance Company
305 Madison Ave
Morristown NJ 07960
973 490-6600

(P-10530)
UNUM LIFE INSURANCE CO AMER
Also Called: Unumprovident
655 N Central Ave, Glendale (91203-1422)
PHONE..................818 291-4739
Vicki Riggs, *Branch Mgr*

EMP: 195 **Publicly Held**
SIC: **6411** Insurance agents, brokers & service
HQ: Unum Life Insurance Company Of America
2211 Congress St
Portland ME 04122
207 575-2211

(P-10531)
USI INSURANCE SERVICES NAT
1350 Treat Blvd Ste 550, Walnut Creek (94597-7999)
PHONE..................925 988-1700
Brian Heatherington, *Director*
EMP: 70 **Privately Held**
SIC: **6411** Insurance agents, brokers & service
HQ: Usi Insurance Services National, Inc.
150 N Michigan Ave # 3900
Chicago IL 60601
866 294-2571

(P-10532)
USI INSURANCE SERVICES NAT INC
1039a N Mcdowell Blvd, Petaluma (94954-1173)
PHONE..................707 769-2900
Wayne Shira, *Manager*
EMP: 80 **Privately Held**
SIC: **6411** Insurance agents, brokers & service
HQ: Usi Insurance Services National, Inc.
150 N Michigan Ave # 3900
Chicago IL 60601
866 294-2571

(P-10533)
USI INSURANCE SERVICES NAT INC
5200 N Palm Ave Ste 114, Fresno (93704-2225)
PHONE..................559 666-2001
Debra Powers, *Branch Mgr*
EMP: 70 **Privately Held**
SIC: **6411** Insurance agents, brokers & service
HQ: Usi Insurance Services National, Inc.
150 N Michigan Ave # 3900
Chicago IL 60601
866 294-2571

(P-10534)
USI INSURANCE SERVICES NAT INC
777 S Figueroa St # 2100, Los Angeles (90017-5800)
PHONE..................213 253-6700
Alan Boring, *Director*
EMP: 123 **Privately Held**
SIC: **6411** Insurance agents, brokers & service
HQ: Usi Insurance Services National, Inc.
150 N Michigan Ave # 3900
Chicago IL 60601
866 294-2571

(P-10535)
USI INSURANCE SERVICES NAT INC
10940 White Rock Rd, Rancho Cordova (95670-6182)
PHONE..................916 589-8000
Donna Flores, *Branch Mgr*
EMP: 210 **Privately Held**
SIC: **6411** Insurance agents, brokers & service
HQ: Usi Insurance Services National, Inc.
150 N Michigan Ave # 3900
Chicago IL 60601
866 294-2571

(P-10536)
USI INSURANCE SERVICES NAT INC
201 Mission St Ste 1100, San Francisco (94105-8100)
PHONE..................628 201-9001
Samuel Jones, *Branch Mgr*
EMP: 200 **Privately Held**
SIC: **6411** Insurance agents, brokers & service

HQ: Usi Insurance Services National, Inc.
150 N Michigan Ave # 3900
Chicago IL 60601
866 294-2571

(P-10537)
USI OF SOUTHERN CALIFORNIA INS
21700 Oxnard St Ste 1200, Woodland Hills (91367-7578)
PHONE..................818 251-3000
Mike Rastigue, *President*
Mark Goldberg, *Vice Pres*
Bernadette Jackson, *Vice Pres*
Alexander Ross, *Vice Pres*
EMP: 50
SQ FT: 15,000
SALES (est): 10.4MM **Privately Held**
WEB: www.usicondo.com
SIC: **6411** Insurance agents; life insurance agents
HQ: Usi Service Corporation
100 Summit Lake Dr # 400
Valhalla NY 10595

(P-10538)
USI SOUTH COAST
Also Called: Kemper Insurance
29a Technology Dr 200, Irvine (92618-2302)
PHONE..................949 790-9200
Randy Joe Hartman, *Vice Pres*
John Hayden, *Exec VP*
Armando Castro, *Vice Pres*
Greg Tamanaha, *Vice Pres*
Brian Cutick, *Architect*
EMP: 60
SQ FT: 5,000
SALES (est): 6.8MM **Privately Held**
SIC: **6411** 7513 Insurance agents, brokers & service; property & casualty insurance agent; truck rental & leasing, no drivers

(P-10539)
VALUEOPTIONS OF CALIFORNIA
Also Called: Value Options-V B H
5665 Plaza Dr Ste 400, Cypress (90630-5037)
PHONE..................800 228-1286
Juan Molina, *VP Opers*
Steve Rockowitz, *Ch of Bd*
Jolene Myrter, *CFO*
EMP: 200
SALES (est): 19.8MM
SALES (corp-wide): 482.1MM **Privately Held**
WEB: www.fhchealthsystems.com
SIC: **6411** 6321 Insurance agents, brokers & service; accident & health insurance
PA: Fhc Health Systems, Inc
240 Corporate Blvd # 212
Norfolk VA 23502
757 459-5100

(P-10540)
VAN BEURDEN INSURANCE SVCS INC (PA)
Also Called: Kemper Insurance
1600 Draper St, Kingsburg (93631-1911)
P.O. Box 67 (93631-0067)
PHONE..................559 634-7125
William J Van Beurden, *President*
Chris V Beurden, *Vice Pres*
Brian Loven, *Vice Pres*
Chris Van Beurden, *Vice Pres*
Glenda Claytor, *Technician*
EMP: 67
SQ FT: 20,000
SALES (est): 29.6MM **Privately Held**
WEB: www.vanbeurden.com
SIC: **6411** Insurance agents & brokers

(P-10541)
VEBA ADMINISTRATORS INC
Also Called: Benefit Planning
4640 Admiralty Way Fl 9, Marina Del Rey (90292-6630)
PHONE..................310 577-1444
Guy Hocker, *President*
Richard Caplan, *Vice Pres*
Anthony Delfino, *Vice Pres*
Richard Kaplan, *Vice Pres*
EMP: 50

HQ: Usi Insurance Services National, Inc.
150 N Michigan Ave # 3900
Chicago IL 60601
866 294-2571

SALES (est): 7.3MM **Privately Held**
WEB: www.benplaninc.com
SIC: **6411** 6141 Pension & retirement plan consultants; financing: automobiles, furniture, etc., not a deposit bank

(P-10542)
VELAPOINT LLC
16802 Aston, Irvine (92606-4835)
PHONE..................877 434-1904
Kyal Moody, *Branch Mgr*
EMP: 77
SALES (corp-wide): 11.7MM **Privately Held**
SIC: **6411** Insurance agents, brokers & service
PA: Velapoint Llc
1100 Nw Compton Dr # 200
Beaverton OR 97006
503 608-3947

(P-10543)
W BROWN & ASSC PROPERTY & CSU
19000 Macarthur Blvd, Irvine (92612-1438)
PHONE..................949 851-2060
Scott Brown, *President*
EMP: 60
SALES (est): 34.2MM **Privately Held**
SIC: **6411** Insurance agents

(P-10544)
WARNER PACIFIC INSUR SVCS INC (PA)
32110 Agoura Rd, Westlake Village (91361-4026)
PHONE..................408 298-4049
John H Nelson, *CEO*
Debbie Adrian, *Vice Pres*
David Nelson, *Vice Pres*
Jennifer Morrison, *Sales Executive*
Cris Tummler, *Director*
EMP: 115
SQ FT: 10,000
SALES (est): 119.1MM **Privately Held**
SIC: **6411** Insurance brokers

(P-10545)
WESCOM HOLDINGS LLC (HQ)
123 S Marengo Ave, Pasadena (91101-2428)
PHONE..................888 493-7266
Darren Williams, *CEO*
Debbie Shepherd, *Branch Mgr*
Jorge Hernandez, *Loan*
EMP: 82
SALES (est): 3.2MM
SALES (corp-wide): 133.7MM **Privately Held**
SIC: **6411** 6211 7371 Insurance agents, brokers & service; investment firm, general brokerage; computer software development & applications
PA: Wescom Central Credit Union
123 S Marengo Ave
Pasadena CA 91101
888 493-7266

(P-10546)
WESTERN MUTUAL INSURANCE CO (PA)
2172 Dupont Dr Ste 220, Irvine (92612-1359)
P.O. Box 19626 (92623-9626)
PHONE..................949 724-9402
Joe Crail, *President*
Dan Greulich, *Vice Pres*
Joshua Sanders, *Technical Mgr*
Yuli Kasdjono, *Accountant*
Carmen Estrada, *Manager*
EMP: 68
SQ FT: 13,000
SALES (est): 24.3MM **Privately Held**
WEB: www.insureourhome.com
SIC: **6411** Insurance agents, brokers & service

(P-10547)
WESTERN UNITED INSURANCE CO
Also Called: Csaa Insur Group Walnut Creek
3349 Michelson Dr Ste 100, Irvine (92612-0688)
P.O. Box 24523, Oakland (94623-1523)
PHONE..................800 959-9842

James B Schallert, *President*
EMP: 165
SQ FT: 50,000
SALES (est): 27.2MM
SALES (corp-wide): 907.9MM **Privately Held**
WEB: www.californiastateautomobileassociation.c
SIC: 6411 Insurance agents
PA: American Automobile Association Of Northern California, Nevada & Utah
1900 Powell St Ste 1200
Emeryville CA 94608
800 922-8228

(P-10548)
WESTWOOD INSURANCE AGENCY (DH)
8407 Fllbrook Ave Ste 200, Canoga Park (91304)
PHONE................818 990-9715
John Flynn, *President*
Mark Nettleton, *Vice Pres*
EMP: 89
SQ FT: 17,765
SALES (est): 17.5MM **Publicly Held**
WEB: www.westwoodinsurance.com
SIC: 6411 Insurance agents
HQ: National General Lender Services, Inc.
210 Interstate N Pkwy
Atlanta GA 30339
770 690-8400

(P-10549)
WILSHIRE INSURANCE COMPANY
Also Called: Accidental Fire & Casualty
1206 W Avenue J Ste 100, Lancaster (93534-2953)
P.O. Box 7006 (93539-7006)
PHONE................661 940-7300
Stephen Stephano, *President*
Deborah Wrinkle, *Executive*
EMP: 50
SALES (est): 8MM **Privately Held**
SIC: 6411 Insurance agents

(P-10550)
WINTERTHUR U S HOLDINGS INC
888 S Figueroa St Ste 570, Los Angeles (90017-5449)
PHONE................213 228-0281
Ken McClelland, *Branch Mgr*
EMP: 240 **Privately Held**
SIC: 6411 6311 6331 Property & casualty insurance agent; life insurance; fire, marine & casualty insurance
HQ: Winterthur U. S. Holdings Inc
1 General Dr
Sun Prairie WI 53596
608 837-4440

(P-10551)
WINTON IRLAND STROM GREEN INSU (PA)
Also Called: Winton-Ireland, Strom and Gr
627 E Canal Dr, Turlock (95380-4022)
P.O. Box 3277 (95381-3277)
PHONE................209 667-0995
Michael Ireland, *President*
Jeff Quinn, *Vice Pres*
EMP: 88
SQ FT: 10,000
SALES (est): 20.6MM **Privately Held**
WEB: www.wintonireland.com
SIC: 6411 Insurance brokers

(P-10552)
WM MICHAEL STEMLER INC (PA)
Also Called: DELTA HEALTH SYSTEMS
3244 Brookside Rd Ste 200, Stockton (95219-2384)
P.O. Box 1227 (95201-1227)
PHONE................209 948-8483
William M Stemler, *CEO*
Richard Roge, *President*
Patti Silva, *Exec VP*
Nilam Panchal, *VP Finance*
EMP: 110
SQ FT: 30,100

SALES: 22.1MM **Privately Held**
WEB: www.deltahealthsystems.com
SIC: 6411 Medical insurance claim processing, contract or fee basis

(P-10553)
WM MICHAEL STEMLER INC
7110 N Fresno St Ste 350, Fresno (93720-2933)
PHONE................559 228-4144
Robert Maes, *Branch Mgr*
EMP: 150
SALES (corp-wide): 22.1MM **Privately Held**
SIC: 6411 Medical insurance claim processing, contract or fee basis
PA: Wm. Michael Stemler, Incorporated
3244 Brookside Rd Ste 200
Stockton CA 95219
209 948-8483

(P-10554)
WOOD GUTMANN BOGART INSUR BRKG
Also Called: W G B
15901 Red Hill Ave # 100, Tustin (92780-7318)
PHONE................714 505-7000
Kevin S Bogart, *CEO*
Christopher Vargas, *Assoc VP*
Bill Holdren, *Exec VP*
Nikki Brown, *Vice Pres*
Elena Viera, *Vice Pres*
EMP: 93
SALES (est): 30.5MM **Privately Held**
WEB: www.wgbib.com
SIC: 6411 Insurance agents

(P-10555)
WOODRUFF-SAWYER & CO (PA)
50 California St Fl 12, San Francisco (94111-4646)
PHONE................415 391-2141
Charles Rosson, *CEO*
Zac Overbay, *COO*
Kristine Furrer, *Senior VP*
Stephen Gaitley, *Senior VP*
Charles Shoemaker, *Senior VP*
EMP: 240
SQ FT: 54,000
SALES (est): 233.3MM **Privately Held**
SIC: 6411 Insurance brokers

(P-10556)
WORLDWIDE HOLDINGS INC (PA)
725 S Figueroa St # 1900, Los Angeles (90017-5496)
PHONE................213 236-4500
Donald R Davis, *Chairman*
Davis D Moore, *President*
Daniel Colacurcio, *Exec VP*
David Gorin, *Executive*
Leslie Shaw, *Administration*
EMP: 85
SQ FT: 23,000
SALES (est): 86.8MM **Privately Held**
WEB: www.wwfi.com
SIC: 6411 Insurance agents, brokers & service

(P-10557)
WORXSITEHR INSUR SOLUTIONS INC
5000 Parkway Calabasas # 302, Calabasas (91302-1400)
PHONE................877 479-3591
EMP: 60
SQ FT: 2,500
SALES (est): 4.7MM **Privately Held**
SIC: 6411 7371

┌─────────────────────────┐
│ **6512 Operators Of** │
│ **Nonresidential Bldgs** │
└─────────────────────────┘

(P-10558)
5 DIAMOND PROTECTION INC
2901 W Macarthur Blvd, Santa Ana (92704-6910)
PHONE................949 466-1367
Mohammad Sayed, *President*
Troy Sims, *Director*
EMP: 99

SALES: 200K **Privately Held**
SIC: 6512 Nonresidential building operators

(P-10559)
6500 HLLISTER AVE PARTNERS LLC
6500 Hollister Ave, Goleta (93117-3011)
PHONE................805 722-1362
Rob Ramirez, *Manager*
EMP: 100
SALES (est): 2MM **Privately Held**
SIC: 6512 Commercial & industrial building operation

(P-10560)
AAT TORREY RESERVE 6 LLC
11455 El Cmino Real Ste 2, San Diego (92130)
PHONE................858 350-2600
John Chamberlain, *Principal*
Wade Lange, *Vice Pres*
EMP: 60
SALES (est): 1.3MM
SALES (corp-wide): 28.9MM **Privately Held**
SIC: 6512 Nonresidential building operators
PA: American Assets, Inc.
11455 El Cmno Rl Ste 140
San Diego CA 92130
858 350-2600

(P-10561)
ABBEY-PROPERTIES LLC (PA)
12447 Lewis St Ste 203, Garden Grove (92840-6601)
PHONE................562 435-2100
Donald G Abbey,
EMP: 75
SQ FT: 276,000
SALES (est): 5.1MM **Privately Held**
WEB: www.theabbeyco.com
SIC: 6512 Commercial & industrial building operation

(P-10562)
ALEXANDER PROPERTIES COMPANY
2600 Camino Ramon Ste 201, San Ramon (94583-5000)
P.O. Box 640 (94583-0640)
PHONE................925 866-0100
John T Waterhouse, *CEO*
Alexander Mehran, *Principal*
EMP: 50
SALES (est): 2.7MM **Privately Held**
SIC: 6512 Commercial & industrial building operation

(P-10563)
ALISAM OXNARD OPERATING
Also Called: Water Drops Express Carwash
212 26th St Ste 246, Santa Monica (90402-2524)
PHONE................310 877-7179
Bob Bandabi, *Mng Member*
Sam Siam, *Mng Member*
EMP: 116
SALES: 32MM **Privately Held**
SIC: 6512 Nonresidential building operators

(P-10564)
ALLIED SWISS LIMITED
Also Called: Allied Swift
2636 Vista Pacific Dr, Oceanside (92056-3514)
PHONE................760 941-1702
Wade Prescott, *Partner*
Bruce Damon, *Ltd Ptnr*
Robert Hively, *Ltd Ptnr*
Bonnie Prescott, *Ltd Ptnr*
Chip Prescott, *Ltd Ptnr*
EMP: 112
SQ FT: 21,000
SALES (est): 6.6MM **Privately Held**
WEB: www.alliedswiss.net
SIC: 6512 Commercial & industrial building operation

(P-10565)
ALPINE VILLAGE
Also Called: Alpine Inn Restaurant
833 Torrance Blvd Ste 1a, Torrance (90502-1733)
PHONE................310 327-4384
Ursula Wilson, *CEO*
EMP: 250
SALES (est): 15.5MM **Privately Held**
WEB: www.alpinevillage.net
SIC: 6512 Commercial & industrial building operation

(P-10566)
AMERICARE HLTH RETIREMENT INC
Also Called: Silvergate San Marcos
1550 Security Pl Ofc, San Marcos (92078-4063)
PHONE................760 744-4484
Melba Dunn, *Administration*
EMP: 100
SQ FT: 51,071
SALES (corp-wide): 11.8MM **Privately Held**
WEB: www.americarehr.com
SIC: 6512 8051 Nonresidential building operators; skilled nursing care facilities
PA: Americare Health & Retirement, Inc.
140 Lomas Santa Fe Dr # 103
Solana Beach CA 92075
858 792-0696

(P-10567)
ANTELOPE VALLEY MALL
1233 W Rancho Vista Blvd # 405, Palmdale (93551-3947)
PHONE................661 266-9150
Greg Lenners, *General Mgr*
George D Zamias Developer, *Partner*
EMP: 70
SALES (est): 3.6MM **Privately Held**
WEB: www.av-mall.com
SIC: 6512 Shopping center, property operation only

(P-10568)
APPLIED COMPANIES RE LLC
28020 Avenue Stanford, Valencia (91355-1105)
P.O. Box 802078, Santa Clarita (91380-2078)
PHONE................661 257-0090
Mary Elizabeth Klinger, *CEO*
Joseph Klinger, *Vice Pres*
EMP: 50
SALES (est): 158.4K **Privately Held**
SIC: 6512 Nonresidential building operators

(P-10569)
ARDEN REALTY INC (HQ)
11601 Wilshire Blvd Fl 5, Los Angeles (90025-1995)
PHONE................310 966-2600
Joaquin De Monet, *CEO*
Robert Peddicord, *COO*
Kevin Early, *CFO*
David A Swartz, *Senior VP*
Michael Lynch, *CIO*
EMP: 68
SALES (est): 15.6MM
SALES (corp-wide): 121.6B **Publicly Held**
WEB: www.ardenrealty.com
SIC: 6512 Commercial & industrial building operation
PA: General Electric Company
41 Farnsworth St
Boston MA 02210
617 443-3000

(P-10570)
ARE- MARYLAND NO 31 LLC
385 E Colo Blvd Ste 299, Pasadena (91101)
PHONE................626 578-0777
Lawrence Diamond, *Exec VP*
Sam Barton, *Exec Dir*
Scott Loftin, *Exec Dir*
EMP: 50
SALES (est): 574.7K **Privately Held**
SIC: 6512 Nonresidential building operators

(P-10571)
BAY WEST SHWPLACE INVSTORS LLC (PA)
Also Called: Sheplace Design Center
2 Henry Adams St Ste 450, San Francisco (94103-5000)
PHONE................................415 490-5800
Tim Threadway, *Chairman*
EMP: 60 **EST:** 1983
SALES (est): 5MM **Privately Held**
SIC: 6512 5712 Commercial & industrial building operation; furniture stores

(P-10572)
BPR PROPERTIES BERKELEY LLC
953 Industrial Ave # 100, Palo Alto (94303-4923)
PHONE................................650 424-1400
Bhupendra B Patel,
Shashank Parasnis, *Info Tech Dir*
Lynne Reelfs, *Manager*
Teresa Ilagan, *Accounts Mgr*
EMP: 130
SALES (est): 12.2MM **Privately Held**
SIC: 6512 Nonresidential building operators

(P-10573)
BRIDGE HOUSING ACQUISITION
1 Hawthorne St Ste 400, San Francisco (94105-3909)
PHONE................................415 989-1111
Carol Gilante, *President*
Lydia Tan, *Vice Pres*
EMP: 80
SALES: 937.8K **Privately Held**
SIC: 6512 Nonresidential building operators

(P-10574)
BUILDING SERVICES/SYSTEM INC
2575 Stanwell Dr, Concord (94520-4888)
PHONE................................925 688-1234
Sam Martinovich, *Principal*
Sam Mardinovich, *Principal*
EMP: 99
SALES (est): 5.5MM **Privately Held**
SIC: 6512 Commercial & industrial building operation

(P-10575)
CASDEN BUILDERS LLC
9090 Wilshire Blvd Fl 3, Beverly Hills (90211-1851)
PHONE................................310 274-5553
Robert Hilderbrand,
Marilley Joe, *Project Mgr*
Mike Murray, *Superintendent*
EMP: 50
SALES (est): 1.6MM **Privately Held**
SIC: 6512 Nonresidential building operators

(P-10576)
CB RICHARD ELLIS STRTGC PRTNRS
515 S Flower St, Los Angeles (90071-2201)
PHONE................................213 683-4200
Richard Ellis,
Ken Raven, *Finance*
EMP: 100
SALES (est): 3.8MM
SALES (corp-wide): 21.3B **Publicly Held**
WEB: www.cbrichardellis.com
SIC: 6512 Nonresidential building operators
PA: Cbre Group, Inc.
400 S Hope St Ste 25
Los Angeles CA 90071
213 613-3333

(P-10577)
CESAR CHAVEZ STUDENT CENTER
Also Called: Snackademic
1650 Holloway Ave Rm C134, San Francisco (94132-1722)
PHONE................................415 338-7362
Guy Dalpe, *Exec Dir*
EMP: 130

SALES: 5MM **Privately Held**
SIC: 6512 Nonresidential building operators

(P-10578)
CITY OF ANAHEIM
Also Called: Anaheim Arena
2695 E Katella Ave, Anaheim (92806-5904)
PHONE................................714 704-2400
Tim Ryan, *Manager*
EMP: 450 **Privately Held**
WEB: www.anaheim.net
SIC: 6512 7941 Nonresidential building operators; sports field or stadium operator, promoting sports events
PA: City Of Anaheim
200 S Anaheim Blvd
Anaheim CA 92805
714 765-5162

(P-10579)
CITY OF FAIRFIELD
Also Called: Fairfield Community Center
1000 Webster St, Fairfield (94533-4883)
PHONE................................707 428-7435
Karin McMillan, *Mayor*
EMP: 150 **Privately Held**
WEB: www.fairfieldpoa.com
SIC: 6512 Auditorium & hall operation
PA: City Of Fairfield
1000 Webster St
Fairfield CA 94533
707 428-7569

(P-10580)
DAVID D BOHANNON ORGANIZATION (PA)
Also Called: San Lorenzo Village Shopg Ctr
60 31st Ave, San Mateo (94403-3404)
PHONE................................650 345-8222
David D Bohannon II, *President*
Scott Bohannon, *Senior VP*
Ernest Lotti Jr, *Vice Pres*
Frances E Nelson, *Director*
EMP: 61
SQ FT: 5,000
SALES (est): 7MM **Privately Held**
SIC: 6512 6552 Commercial & industrial building operation; subdividers & developers

(P-10581)
DESERT HOT SPRINGS REAL PROPER
Also Called: Desert Hot Springs Spa Hotel
10805 Palm Dr, Desert Hot Springs (92240-2511)
PHONE................................760 329-6000
Lynn Byrnes, *CEO*
EMP: 85 **EST:** 1988
SQ FT: 44,070
SALES (est): 903.6K **Privately Held**
SIC: 6512 Nonresidential building operators

(P-10582)
DESERT SPRINGS HOTEL
10805 Palm Dr, Desert Hot Springs (92240-2511)
PHONE................................760 251-3399
Lynn Byrnes, *President*
EMP: 50
SALES (est): 1.6MM **Privately Held**
SIC: 6512 Nonresidential building operators

(P-10583)
DONAHUE SCHRIBER RLTY GROUP LP (PA)
Also Called: Ds Lakeshore LP
200 Baker St Ste 100, Costa Mesa (92626-4551)
PHONE................................714 545-1400
Patrick S Donahue, *CEO*
Lawrence P Casey, *President*
Lisa L Hirose, *Exec VP*
Mark L Whitfield, *Exec VP*
Warren Adair, *Vice Pres*
EMP: 100
SQ FT: 44,805
SALES (est): 23.6MM **Privately Held**
WEB: www.donahueschriber.com
SIC: 6512 Shopping center, property operation only

(P-10584)
DONAHUE SCHRIBER RLTY GROUP LP
5082 N Palm Ave, Fresno (93704-2231)
PHONE................................714 545-1400
Elizabeth Schreiber, *Manager*
Melody Alcantara, *Administration*
Stacy Cashman, *Administration*
Ramona Vidales, *Administration*
Rex Santiago, *Analyst*
EMP: 57
SALES (corp-wide): 23.6MM **Privately Held**
SIC: 6512 Shopping center, property operation only
PA: Donahue Schriber Realty Group, L.P.
200 Baker St Ste 100
Costa Mesa CA 92626
714 545-1400

(P-10585)
DONAHUE SCHRIBER RLTY GROUP LP
8020 E Santa Ana Cyn Rd, Anaheim (92808-1110)
PHONE................................714 283-3535
Patrick S Donahue, *Branch Mgr*
EMP: 57
SALES (corp-wide): 23.6MM **Privately Held**
SIC: 6512 Shopping center, property operation only
PA: Donahue Schriber Realty Group, L.P.
200 Baker St Ste 100
Costa Mesa CA 92626
714 545-1400

(P-10586)
DONAHUE SCHRIBER RLTY GROUP LP
12925 El Camino Real J22, San Diego (92130-1891)
PHONE................................858 793-5757
Pat Snow, *Branch Mgr*
Tim Sullivan, *Property Mgr*
EMP: 57
SALES (corp-wide): 23.6MM **Privately Held**
WEB: www.donahueschriber.com
SIC: 6512 Shopping center, property operation only
PA: Donahue Schriber Realty Group, L.P.
200 Baker St Ste 100
Costa Mesa CA 92626
714 545-1400

(P-10587)
ENTREPRENEURIAL CAPITAL CORP
4100 Nwport Pl Dr Ste 400, Newport Beach (92660)
PHONE................................949 809-3900
John K Abel, *Principal*
EMP: 240
SALES (corp-wide): 33.2MM **Privately Held**
SIC: 6512 Commercial & industrial building operation
PA: Entrepreneurial Capital Corporation
4100 Newport Place Dr # 400
Newport Beach CA 92660
949 809-3900

(P-10588)
ESKATON (PA)
5105 Manzanita Ave Ste D, Carmichael (95608-0523)
PHONE................................916 334-0296
Todd Murch, *CEO*
Trevor Hammond, *COO*
William Pace, *CFO*
Sheri Peifer, *Officer*
Jesse Adams, *Exec Dir*
EMP: 1400
SQ FT: 27,000
SALES: 142MM **Privately Held**
SIC: 6512 8051 Commercial & industrial building operation; convalescent home with continuous nursing care

(P-10589)
FLORDO OAKLEY HALL
Also Called: FLOR DO OAKLEY CLUB
520 2nd St, Oakley (94561-2158)
P.O. Box 466 (94561-0466)
PHONE................................925 625-4076
Joe Peisoto, *President*
Sam Billeci, *Treasurer*
Emidio Fonseca, *Treasurer*
David Alves, *Trustee*
Jose Peisoto, *Director*
EMP: 170
SQ FT: 5,000
SALES: 132.6K **Privately Held**
SIC: 6512 Auditorium & hall operation

(P-10590)
FOREST CITY RENTAL PRPTS CORP
Oasis Fd Crt Antelope Vly Mall
1233 W Avenue P Ste 900, Palmdale (93551-3950)
PHONE................................661 266-9150
Brian Gardner, *Manager*
EMP: 80
SALES (corp-wide): 633.8MM **Privately Held**
SIC: 6512 Shopping center, property operation only; commercial & industrial building operation
HQ: Forest City Properties, Llc
127 Public Sq Ste 3100
Cleveland OH 44114
216 621-6060

(P-10591)
FRATERNAL ORDER EAGLES 1582
Also Called: Eagles Hall
124 Vernon St, Roseville (95678-2631)
P.O. Box 766 (95678-0766)
PHONE................................916 782-2694
Charles Chase, *Admin Sec*
EMP: 120
SALES: 22.9K **Privately Held**
SIC: 6512 8641 Nonresidential building operators; civic social & fraternal associations

(P-10592)
FRED H LUNDBLADE JR
Also Called: Lundblade Builders
939 Koster St Ste B, Eureka (95501-0106)
PHONE................................707 442-8049
Fred H Lundblade, *Owner*
EMP: 58
SALES (est): 2.5MM **Privately Held**
SIC: 6512 6513 1521 1541 Nonresidential building operators; apartment building operators; single-family housing construction; industrial buildings & warehouses

(P-10593)
FREEDOM PROPERTIES-HEMET LLC
Also Called: Village The
27122b Paseo Espada B, San Juan Capistrano (92675-5706)
PHONE................................949 489-0430
Cheryl L Roskamp, *Mng Member*
Ms Cheryl L Roskamp, *Mng Member*
EMP: 250 **EST:** 1999
SALES (est): 2.7MM **Privately Held**
SIC: 6512 Nonresidential building operators

(P-10594)
FREMONT PROPERTIES INC
199 Fremont St Ste 1900, San Francisco (94105-2245)
PHONE................................415 284-8500
Allen Dachs, *CEO*
David Wall, *Exec VP*
Christopher Quiett, *Vice Pres*
Gry Faber, *Principal*
Suzanne Gagan, *Principal*
EMP: 50
SALES (est): 3.1MM
SALES (corp-wide): 18MM **Privately Held**
SIC: 6512 Nonresidential building operators

PA: Fremont Investors, Inc.
199 Fremont St Fl 19
San Francisco CA 94105
415 284-8500

(P-10595)
G B & P CITRUS CO INC (PA)
1601 E Olympic Blvd # 111, Los Angeles
(90021-1936)
PHONE.................................213 312-1380
Sam Perricone, *President*
Henry Beyer, *Vice Pres*
Paul Golub, *Admin Sec*
EMP: 98 EST: 1970
SALES (est): 5.3MM **Privately Held**
SIC: 6512 5148 2037 Commercial & industrial building operation; fruits; fruit juices

(P-10596)
GEHR DEVELOPMENT CORPORATION (HQ)
7400 E Slauson Ave, Commerce
(90040-3308)
PHONE.................................323 728-5558
David Lifschitz, *CFO*
Alfred Somekh, *President*
EMP: 70
SALES (est): 5.1MM
SALES (corp-wide): 84.8MM **Privately Held**
WEB: www.gehr.com
SIC: 6512 6513 Commercial & industrial building operation; apartment building operators
PA: The Gehr Group Inc
7400 E Slauson Ave
Commerce CA 90040
323 728-5558

(P-10597)
GIRARDI AND KEEFE
1126 Wilshire Blvd, Los Angeles
(90017-1904)
PHONE.................................213 489-5330
Thomas Girardi, *Partner*
Bob Keefe, *Partner*
John A Girardi, *Partner*
EMP: 100
SQ FT: 21,000
SALES (est): 3.3MM **Privately Held**
SIC: 6512 Commercial & industrial building operation

(P-10598)
GLENDALE ASSOCIATES LTD
Also Called: Apple Store Glendale Galleria
100 W Broadway Ste 100 # 100, Glendale
(91210-1230)
PHONE.................................818 246-6737
Properties Knickerbocker, *Principal*
Knickerbocker Properties, *Partner*
EMP: 100
SALES (est): 6.1MM **Privately Held**
SIC: 6512 Shopping center, property operation only

(P-10599)
GONGS MARKET OF SANGER INC (PA)
Also Called: Gong's Ventures
1825 Academy Ave, Sanger (93657-3798)
PHONE.................................559 875-5576
William Gong, *President*
Bessie Gong Ohashi, *Corp Secy*
Thomas Gong, *Vice Pres*
EMP: 50
SQ FT: 35,000
SALES (est): 4.7MM **Privately Held**
SIC: 6512 Property operation, retail establishment

(P-10600)
GREENTREE PROPERTY MGT INC
1 Bush St Fl 9, San Francisco
(94104-4415)
PHONE.................................415 347-8600
Yat Pang Au, *President*
Eric Lakin, *Sr Project Mgr*
Jay Pedde, *Director*
Marissa Rodriguez, *Case Mgr*
Greg Goglin, *Manager*
EMP: 50 EST: 2011

SALES (est): 3.5MM **Privately Held**
SIC: 6512 Property operation, retail establishment

(P-10601)
GROSSMONT SHOPPING CENTER CO
Also Called: Grossmont Center Management
5500 Grsmnt Ctr Dr # 213, La Mesa
(91942-3016)
PHONE.................................619 465-2900
Thomas J Magee, *President*
EMP: 57 EST: 1960
SQ FT: 3,000
SALES (est): 5.4MM **Privately Held**
SIC: 6512 Shopping center, property operation only

(P-10602)
GUMBINER SAVETT INC CPA
Also Called: Gumbiner, Savett, Finkel, Fing
1723 Cloverfield Blvd, Santa Monica
(90404-4017)
PHONE.................................310 828-9798
Louis Savett, *Ch of Bd*
Charles Gumbiner, *President*
Gary Finkel, *Exec VP*
Rodney Fingleson, *Vice Pres*
Gilbert Greene, *Vice Pres*
EMP: 90
SQ FT: 25,000
SALES (est): 11.5MM **Privately Held**
WEB: www.gscpa.com
SIC: 6512 Nonresidential building operators

(P-10603)
H D S I MANAGMENT
3460 S Broadway, Los Angeles
(90007-4409)
PHONE.................................323 231-1104
Noel Sweitzer, *Partner*
EMP: 50
SALES (est): 1.9MM **Privately Held**
SIC: 6512 Nonresidential building operators

(P-10604)
HAILWOOD INC
Also Called: Chase Bros Dairy
5755 Valentine Rd Ste 203, Ventura
(93003-7460)
P.O. Box 1272, Oxnard (93032-1272)
PHONE.................................805 487-4981
Glywn S Chase Jr, *President*
Miriam Wille, *Corp Secy*
H M Chase, *Vice Pres*
EMP: 75
SQ FT: 1,600,000
SALES (est): 3.8MM **Privately Held**
SIC: 6512 5143 5451 2024 Commercial & industrial building operation; dairy products, except dried or canned; dairy products stores; ice cream & frozen desserts

(P-10605)
HALSTEAD PARTNERSHIP
Also Called: Sundt Construction
2850 Gateway Oaks Dr # 450, Sacramento
(95833-4347)
PHONE.................................916 830-8000
John Wald, *Managing Prtnr*
EMP: 60
SALES (est): 7.3MM **Privately Held**
SIC: 6512 Nonresidential building operators

(P-10606)
HARDAGE HOSPITALITY LLC
Also Called: Chase Suite Hotel Newark
39150 Cedar Blvd, Newark (94560-5024)
PHONE.................................510 795-1200
Bill Marzonie, *Branch Mgr*
EMP: 50
SQ FT: 100,978 **Privately Held**
SIC: 6512 Nonresidential building operators
PA: Hardage Hospitality, Llc
12555 High Bluff Dr # 330
San Diego CA 92130

(P-10607)
HEALTH CARE WORKERS UNION (PA)
Also Called: Local 250 Health Care Wkrs Un
560 Thomas L Berkley Way, Oakland
(94612-1602)
PHONE.................................510 251-1250
Sal Rosselli, *President*
Sarah Steck, *Opers Mgr*
EMP: 200
SQ FT: 25,777
SALES (est): 8.3MM **Privately Held**
SIC: 6512 8631 Commercial & industrial building operation; labor unions & similar labor organizations

(P-10608)
HUDSON TCHMART CMMERCE CTR LLC
5201 Great America Pkwy, Santa Clara
(95054-1122)
PHONE.................................408 451-4440
Mark Lammas, *COO*
Wendy Contreras, *Exec Sec*
EMP: 99 EST: 2015
SQ FT: 284,440
SALES (est): 1.2MM **Publicly Held**
SIC: 6512 Commercial & industrial building operation
PA: Hudson Pacific Properties, Inc.
11601 Wilshire Blvd Fl 6
Los Angeles CA 90025

(P-10609)
HYDROX PROPERTIES XII LLC
3170 Hilltop Mall Rd, Richmond
(94806-1921)
PHONE.................................510 262-7200
Mechanics Bank, *Principal*
EMP: 69 EST: 2011
SALES (est): 3.3MM **Privately Held**
SIC: 6512 Nonresidential building operators

(P-10610)
ICW VALENCIA LLC
11455 El Camino Real, San Diego
(92130-2088)
PHONE.................................858 350-2600
John Chamberlain, *Principal*
EMP: 65
SALES (est): 1.4MM
SALES (corp-wide): 28.9MM **Privately Held**
SIC: 6512 Nonresidential building operators
PA: American Assets, Inc.
11455 El Cmno Rl Ste 140
San Diego CA 92130
858 350-2600

(P-10611)
INTEX RECREATION CORP
1665 Hughes Way, Long Beach
(90810-1835)
PHONE.................................310 549-5400
Kwai Kenny, *Exec Dir*
Phil Mimaki, *Creative Dir*
Carlos Bartra, *Engineer*
EMP: 102
SALES (corp-wide): 171.8MM **Privately Held**
SIC: 6512 Nonresidential building operators
PA: Intex Recreation Corp
4001 Via Oro Ave Ste 210
Long Beach CA 90810
310 549-5400

(P-10612)
INVITATION HOMES INC
465 N Halstead St Ste 150, Pasadena
(91107-6017)
PHONE.................................805 372-2900
Luke Kochniuk, *Branch Mgr*
Steve Ratts, *Superintendent*
EMP: 80
SALES (corp-wide): 1.7B **Publicly Held**
SIC: 6512 Nonresidential building operators
PA: Invitation Homes Inc.
1717 Main St Ste 2000
Dallas TX 75201
972 421-3600

(P-10613)
JAMESON PROPERTIES CO INC
3530 Wilshire Blvd # 600, Los Angeles
(90010-2328)
PHONE.................................213 487-3770
Eric Kim, *General Mgr*
David Lee, *President*
Scott Burrin, *Managing Dir*
EMP: 50
SQ FT: 4,000
SALES: 159.1K **Privately Held**
WEB: www.jamisonservices.com
SIC: 6512 Commercial & industrial building operation

(P-10614)
JOHNSON SERVICE GROUP INC
950 S Bascom Ave, San Jose
(95128-3536)
PHONE.................................408 728-9510
EMP: 850
SALES (corp-wide): 138.2MM **Privately Held**
SIC: 6512 Commercial & industrial building operation
PA: Johnson Service Group, Inc.
1 E Oakhill Dr Ste 200
Westmont IL 60559
630 655-3500

(P-10615)
LAGUNA COUNTRY MART LTD INC
Also Called: Lumberyard Plaza Mall
12410 Santa Monica Blvd, Los Angeles
(90025-2522)
PHONE.................................310 826-5635
Michael Koss, *President*
EMP: 50
SALES (est): 2.6MM **Privately Held**
SIC: 6512 Shopping center, property operation only

(P-10616)
LOS ANGELES CONVEN AND EXH
Also Called: Los Angeles Dept Convetion Tou
1201 S Figueroa St, Los Angeles
(90015-1308)
PHONE.................................213 741-1151
Brad Gessner, *General Mgr*
Annie Bebber, *President*
Carisa Norton, *Vice Pres*
Nancy Walker, *Vice Pres*
Thomas Drew, *Manager*
EMP: 288
SQ FT: 867,000
SALES: 21.5MM **Privately Held**
WEB: www.laconventioninn.com
SIC: 6512 Commercial & industrial building operation; property operation, auditoriums & theaters

(P-10617)
MACERICH COMPANY
Also Called: Stonewood Ctr Mall Office
251 Stonewood St, Downey (90241-3935)
PHONE.................................562 861-9233
Charlie Hallums, *Manager*
EMP: 50
SALES (corp-wide): 960.3MM **Publicly Held**
WEB: www.macerich.com
SIC: 6512 Shopping center, property operation only
PA: Macerich Company
401 Wilshire Blvd Ste 700
Santa Monica CA 90401
310 394-6000

(P-10618)
MALIBU CONFERENCE CENTER INC
327 Latigo Canyon Rd, Malibu
(90265-2708)
PHONE.................................818 889-6440
Glen Gerson, *President*
EMP: 500
SALES: 35.6MM **Privately Held**
WEB: www.trainingsites.com
SIC: 6512 Commercial & industrial building operation

(P-10619)
MCCLELLAN FACILITIES SVCS LLC
3140 Peacekeeper Way, McClellan (95652-2508)
PHONE..............................916 965-7100
Larry Kelley, *President*
Frank Meyers, *Vice Pres*
EMP: 52
SALES (est): 2.4MM **Privately Held**
SIC: 6512 Property operation, retail establishment

(P-10620)
MFW PARTNERS
1120 Silverado St, La Jolla (92037-4524)
PHONE..............................858 454-8857
Leah Hurwitz, *Managing Prtnr*
Esther Belinski, *Partner*
Anita Tobias, *Partner*
Evie Weinstock, *Partner*
EMP: 50
SALES (est): 2.2MM **Privately Held**
SIC: 6512 Nonresidential building operators

(P-10621)
MILLS CORPORATION
Also Called: Ontario Mills Shopping Center
1 Mills Cir Ste 1 # 1, Ontario (91764-5215)
PHONE..............................909 484-8300
Laurence Siegel, *Branch Mgr*
EMP: 60 **Privately Held**
WEB: www.millscorp.com
SIC: 6512 Shopping center, property operation only
HQ: The Mills Corporation
5425 Wisconsin Ave # 300
Chevy Chase MD 20815
301 968-6000

(P-10622)
MILWOOD HEALTHCARE INC
Also Called: MAYWOOD ACRES HEALTHCARE
2641 S C St, Oxnard (93033-4502)
PHONE..............................626 274-4345
Alger Brion, *CEO*
Christian Canga, *Records Dir*
Shirley Realica, *Food Svc Dir*
Tami Le, *Hlthcr Dir*
Gloria Olguin, *Director*
EMP: 97
SQ FT: 10,000
SALES: 7.6MM **Privately Held**
SIC: 6512 Nonresidential building operators

(P-10623)
MULLER-ING-GATEWAY LLC
23521 Paseo De Valencia # 200, Laguna Hills (92653-3107)
PHONE..............................951 687-2900
Jon Muller, *President*
EMP: 80
SALES (est): 1.4MM **Privately Held**
SIC: 6512 Commercial & industrial building operation

(P-10624)
MUTH DEVELOPMENT CO INC
Also Called: Orco Block
11100 Beach Blvd, Stanton (90680-3219)
PHONE..............................714 527-2239
Richard Muth, *President*
Dwayne Gleason, *Vice Pres*
Lynn Muth, *Vice Pres*
Tom Ruggeri, *Controller*
EMP: 80
SALES (est): 4.5MM **Privately Held**
SIC: 6512 Nonresidential building operators

(P-10625)
N G A ASSOCIATES
205 W Alvarado St, Fallbrook (92028-2025)
PHONE..............................760 726-4015
EMP: 50
SALES (est): 948.2K **Privately Held**
SIC: 6512

(P-10626)
NEDERLANDER OF CALIFORNIA INC
6233 Hollywood Blvd Fl 2, Los Angeles (90028-5310)
PHONE..............................323 468-1700
James M Nederlander, *Chairman*
Robert Nederlander, *President*
EMP: 50 EST: 1975
SQ FT: 2,500
SALES (est): 3.5MM **Privately Held**
WEB: www.greektheatrela.com
SIC: 6512 7922 Theater building, ownership & operation; theatrical producers & services

(P-10627)
NEVINS-ADAMS PROPERTIES INC (PA)
Also Called: Nevins Adams Properties
920 Garden St Ste A, Santa Barbara (93101-7465)
PHONE..............................805 963-2884
Henry Nevins, *President*
David Adams, *Chairman*
EMP: 250
SALES (est): 9.2MM **Privately Held**
WEB: www.nevinsadams.com
SIC: 6512 Commercial & industrial building operation

(P-10628)
NORTHRIDGE 07 A LLC
12411 Ventura Blvd, Studio City (91604-2407)
PHONE..............................818 505-6777
Cathy Reynolds,
Alan Fox,
EMP: 80
SALES (est): 4.3MM **Privately Held**
SIC: 6512 Commercial & industrial building operation

(P-10629)
OATES BUZZ ENTERPRISES
Also Called: Folsom Manlove Venture
555 Capitol Mall Ste 900, Sacramento (95814-4606)
PHONE..............................916 381-3600
Marvin L Oates, *Partner*
Carl Best, *Partner*
EMP: 100
SALES (est): 5.3MM **Privately Held**
SIC: 6512 6552 6531 Nonresidential building operators; subdividers & developers; real estate agents & managers

(P-10630)
OLEN COMMERCIAL REALTY CORP
Also Called: Olen Residential Realty
7 Corporate Plaza Dr, Newport Beach (92660-7904)
PHONE..............................949 644-6536
Igor M Olenicoff, *President*
Andrei Olenicoff, *Corp Secy*
EMP: 400 EST: 1974
SQ FT: 44,000
SALES (est): 25.5MM **Privately Held**
SIC: 6512 Commercial & industrial building operation

(P-10631)
OLTMANS INVESTMENT COMPANY
Also Called: Oltmans Property Management
10005 Mission Mill Rd, Whittier (90601-1739)
P.O. Box 985 (90608-0985)
PHONE..............................562 948-4242
J O Oltmans II, *President*
Basil C Johnson, *Managing Prtnr*
Robert Roy, *Managing Prtnr*
Gregory V Grupp, *Controller*
EMP: 50
SQ FT: 56,000
SALES (est): 3.2MM **Privately Held**
SIC: 6512 6552 Commercial & industrial building operation; subdividers & developers

(P-10632)
ONE TOWN CENTER ASSOCIATES LLC
3315 Fairview Rd, Costa Mesa (92626-1610)
PHONE..............................714 435-2100
Stan Taeder, *Director*
Debbie Alcock, *Treasurer*
Karen Graham, *Associate Dir*
EMP: 50
SALES (est): 155K **Privately Held**
SIC: 6512 Commercial & industrial building operation

(P-10633)
PACIFIC EAGLE HOLDINGS CORP
353 Sacramento St Ste 360, San Francisco (94111-3688)
PHONE..............................415 398-2473
Michael Simons, *Exec VP*
EMP: 87 **Privately Held**
SIC: 6512 6531 Commercial & industrial building operation; real estate managers
PA: Pacific Eagle Holdings Corporation
353 Sacramento St # 1788
San Francisco CA 94111

(P-10634)
PIER 39 LIMITED PARTNERSHIP (PA)
Beach Embarcadero Level 3, San Francisco (94133)
PHONE..............................415 705-5500
Robert A Moor, *General Ptnr*
Molly M South, *Partner*
Paul Frentsos, *Exec VP*
Howard Pickett, *Exec VP*
Lysa Lewin, *Vice Pres*
EMP: 200 EST: 1968
SQ FT: 200,000
SALES: 40MM **Privately Held**
SIC: 6512 Commercial & industrial building operation

(P-10635)
PROPERTY INSIGHT
202 E Airport Dr Ste 210, San Bernardino (92408-3429)
PHONE..............................909 876-6505
Frank Trujillo, *Principal*
Karen Schwartz, *Vice Pres*
EMP: 200
SALES (est): 64.1MM
SALES (corp-wide): 7.5B **Publicly Held**
SIC: 6512 Nonresidential building operators
PA: Fidelity National Financial, Inc.
601 Riverside Ave Fl 4
Jacksonville FL 32204
904 854-8100

(P-10636)
PVCC INC (PA)
Also Called: Pacific View Companies
8100 La Mesa Blvd Ste 101, La Mesa (91942-6498)
PHONE..............................619 463-4040
Charles I Feurzeig, *President*
Robert Teal, *CFO*
Charles R Swimmer, *Corp Secy*
James M Houck, *Vice Pres*
Robert Houck, *Vice Pres*
EMP: 62
SQ FT: 1,400
SALES (est): 5.8MM **Privately Held**
WEB: www.pacificviewcompanies.com
SIC: 6512 6513 Shopping center, property operation only; apartment building operators

(P-10637)
RP REALTY PARTNERS LLC
990 W 8th St Ste 600, Los Angeles (90017-2831)
PHONE..............................310 207-6990
Stuart Ruben, *Director*
Howard Aminoff, *Exec VP*
Yashaar Amin, *Vice Pres*
Annie Lippman, *Executive Asst*
Sarah Stern, *Accounting Mgr*
EMP: 50

SALES (est): 4.4MM **Privately Held**
SIC: 6512 Commercial & industrial building operation

(P-10638)
RPI CARLSBAD LP
Also Called: Shoppes At Carlsbad, The
2525 El Camino Real # 100, Carlsbad (92008-1204)
PHONE..............................760 729-6183
Andrew Silberfein, *President*
EMP: 128
SALES (est): 203.8K
SALES (corp-wide): 43B **Publicly Held**
SIC: 6512 Commercial & industrial building operation
HQ: Rouse Properties, Llc
1114 Ave Of The Americas
New York NY 10036
212 608-5108

(P-10639)
SAN DEGO CNVNTION CTR CORP INC (PA)
111 W Harbor Dr, San Diego (92101-7822)
PHONE..............................619 525-5000
Carol Wallace, *President*
Karen Totaro, *COO*
Roosevelt Carter, *Officer*
Andy Mikschl, *Vice Pres*
Jamie Bohnemann, *Executive Asst*
EMP: 68
SALES (est): 91.1MM **Privately Held**
SIC: 6512 Nonresidential building operators

(P-10640)
SAN DIEGO THEATRES INC
Also Called: CIVIC THEATRE
1100 3rd Ave, San Diego (92101-4113)
P.O. Box 124920 (92112-4920)
PHONE..............................619 615-4000
Donald M Telford, *CEO*
EMP: 200
SALES: 8MM **Privately Held**
WEB: www.sandiegotheatres.org
SIC: 6512 Theater building, ownership & operation

(P-10641)
SANTA MONICA CITY OF
Also Called: Civic Auditorium
1855 Main St, Santa Monica (90401-3209)
PHONE..............................310 458-8551
Carole Curtin, *Manager*
EMP: 50 **Privately Held**
WEB: www.santamonicapd.org
SIC: 6512 9111 Auditorium & hall operation; mayors' offices
PA: City Of Santa Monica
1685 Main St
Santa Monica CA 90401
310 458-8411

(P-10642)
SFI 2365 IRON POINT LLC
260 California St # 1100, San Francisco (94111-4396)
PHONE..............................415 395-9701
Christopher Peatross, *President*
EMP: 50 EST: 2016
SALES (est): 695.4K **Privately Held**
SIC: 6512 Nonresidential building operators

(P-10643)
SFI CARLSBAD LLC
260 California St # 1100, San Francisco (94111-4396)
PHONE..............................415 395-9701
Christopher Peatross,
EMP: 50 EST: 2015
SALES (est): 695.4K **Privately Held**
SIC: 6512 Nonresidential building operators

(P-10644)
SHENYANG ZHONG YI TIN-PLATING
Also Called: Professional Services Company
843 Clay St, San Francisco (94108-1614)
PHONE..............................415 788-2280
Ku Hing Pong, *Principal*
EMP: 130
SQ FT: 250

SALES (est): 3.6MM **Privately Held**
SIC: **6512** 5023 Nonresidential building operators; home furnishings

(P-10645)
SHOPPING CENTER MGT CORP
660 Stanford Shopping Ctr, Palo Alto (94304-1400)
PHONE..............................650 617-8234
David B Longbine, *President*
EMP: 54
SALES (est): 2MM **Privately Held**
SIC: **6512** Shopping center, property operation only

(P-10646)
SHORENSTEIN COMPANY LLC
235 Montgomery St Fl 15, San Francisco (94104-3102)
PHONE..............................415 772-7000
Douglas Shorenstein,
James Pierre, *Exec VP*
Julie Burdick, *Vice Pres*
James Collins, *Vice Pres*
Gina McFarland, *Vice Pres*
EMP: 50
SALES (est): 4.3MM **Privately Held**
SIC: **6512** Commercial & industrial building operation

(P-10647)
SHORENSTEIN PROPERTIES LLC (PA)
235 Montgomery St Fl 16, San Francisco (94104-3104)
PHONE..............................415 772-7000
Douglas W Shorenstein, *CEO*
Glenn A Shannon, *President*
D Drew Dowsett, *Senior VP*
Katie McGettigan, *Senior VP*
Bob Deitchman, *Vice Pres*
EMP: 125
SQ FT: 20,000
SALES (est): 50MM **Privately Held**
SIC: **6512** Commercial & industrial building operation

(P-10648)
SIERRA VISTA 16 A LLC
12411 Ventura Blvd, Studio City (91604-2407)
PHONE..............................818 505-6777
Cathy Reynolds, *Vice Pres*
Kristina Sheldon, *Supervisor*
EMP: 50
SALES (est): 632.2K **Privately Held**
SIC: **6512** Shopping center, community (100,000 - 300,000 sq ft)

(P-10649)
SIGNATURE SERVICES
4425 Jamboree Rd Ste 250, Newport Beach (92660-3002)
PHONE..............................949 851-9391
Vanessa Sanchez, *Principal*
Chad Horning, *President*
Lupe Mendoza, *Controller*
EMP: 75
SALES (est): 7.8MM **Privately Held**
SIC: **6512** Commercial & industrial building operation

(P-10650)
SMG HOLDINGS INC
225 E Broadway 312, Glendale (91205-1008)
P.O. Box 572559, Tarzana (91357-2559)
PHONE..............................310 432-2893
EMP: 69
SALES (corp-wide): 23.7B **Privately Held**
SIC: **6512** Nonresidential building operators
HQ: Smg Holdings, Llc
300 Cnshohckn State Rd # 450
Conshohocken PA 19428

(P-10651)
SMG HOLDINGS INC
Also Called: S M G
747 Howard St, San Francisco (94103-3118)
PHONE..............................650 738-8737
Allan Crawford, *Finance*
EMP: 110

SALES (corp-wide): 23.7B **Privately Held**
WEB: www.smgworld.com
SIC: **6512** 5812 8742 8741 Auditorium & hall operation; eating places; management consulting services; management services
HQ: Smg Holdings, Llc
300 Cnshohckn State Rd # 450
Conshohocken PA 19428

(P-10652)
SMG HOLDINGS LLC
Also Called: Long Beach Convention Center
300 E Ocean Blvd, Long Beach (90802-4825)
PHONE..............................562 499-7611
Charles Beirne, *General Mgr*
Louis Forgione, *Manager*
EMP: 69
SALES (corp-wide): 23.7B **Privately Held**
WEB: www.smgworld.com
SIC: **6512** Nonresidential building operators
HQ: Smg Holdings, Llc
300 Cnshohckn State Rd # 450
Conshohocken PA 19428

(P-10653)
SOLARI ENTERPRISES INC
1507 W Yale Ave, Orange (92867-3447)
PHONE..............................714 282-2520
Johrita Solari, *President*
Mary Oliver, *Regional Mgr*
Kara Cappeluti, *Office Mgr*
Cappeluti Matt, *Info Tech Dir*
Dalila Franco, *Personnel Assit*
EMP: 140
SQ FT: 8,400
SALES (est): 17.5MM **Privately Held**
SIC: **6512** Property operation, retail establishment

(P-10654)
SOTOYOME MEDICAL BUILDING LLC
Also Called: Redwood Regional Medical Group
990 Sonoma Ave Ste 15, Santa Rosa (95404-4813)
PHONE..............................707 525-4000
Harold Phillips,
Sharon Debenedetti, *COO*
EMP: 80
SQ FT: 27,000
SALES (est): 9.8MM **Privately Held**
SIC: **6512** Commercial & industrial building operation

(P-10655)
SOUTH COAST PLAZA LLC (PA)
Also Called: South Coast Plaza Village
3333 Bristol St Ofc, Costa Mesa (92626-1811)
PHONE..............................714 546-0110
N R Segerstrom, *Mng Member*
Debra Downing, *Exec Dir*
David Grant, *General Mgr*
Rebecca Chien, *Admin Sec*
Elizabeth Papp, *Admin Asst*
EMP: 55
SQ FT: 8,000
SALES (est): 20.7MM **Privately Held**
WEB: www.blackstarrfrost.com
SIC: **6512** Shopping center, property operation only

(P-10656)
SOUTH COAST PLAZA LLC
Also Called: South Coast Plaza Mall
3333 Bristol St Ofc, Costa Mesa (92626-1811)
PHONE..............................714 435-2000
David Grant, *Manager*
EMP: 60
SALES (corp-wide): 20.7MM **Privately Held**
WEB: www.blackstarrfrost.com
SIC: **6512** Shopping center, property operation only
PA: South Coast Plaza, Llc
3333 Bristol St Ofc
Costa Mesa CA 92626
714 546-0110

(P-10657)
SOUTHTOWN INDUSTRIAL PARK
Also Called: Neff Construction
1701 S Bon View Ave 104, Ontario (91761-4412)
PHONE..............................909 947-3768
Kenneth L Neff, *President*
EMP: 50
SALES (est): 2.1MM **Privately Held**
SIC: **6512** Nonresidential building operators

(P-10658)
SPECTACOR MANAGEMENT GROUP
300 E Ocean Blvd, Long Beach (90802-4825)
PHONE..............................562 436-3636
Charlie Beirne, *General Mgr*
Mohnie Mangat, *Opers Staff*
EMP: 439
SQ FT: 4,000
SALES (est): 13.6MM **Privately Held**
SIC: **6512** Nonresidential building operators

(P-10659)
STARCITY PROPERTIES INC
1020 Kearny St, San Francisco (94133-4526)
PHONE..............................415 918-2224
Jon Dishotsky, *CEO*
Jesse Suarez, *CFO*
EMP: 58 EST: 2016
SALES (est): 170.5K **Privately Held**
SIC: **6512** Nonresidential building operators

(P-10660)
SUNAMERICA HSNG FND 1071
1 Sun America Ctr Fl 36, Los Angeles (90067-6104)
PHONE..............................310 772-6000
Eric Geisler, *CFO*
EMP: 110
SALES (est): 3.2MM **Privately Held**
SIC: **6512** 6513 Nonresidential building operators; apartment building operators

(P-10661)
TARIFF BUILDING ASSOCIATES LP (PA)
222 Kearny St Ste 200, San Francisco (94108-4537)
PHONE..............................415 397-5572
Michael Depatie, *CEO*
Cheryl Lovelace, *Vice Pres*
Michael Thibodeau, *Info Tech Dir*
Cesar Herrera, *Project Mgr*
EMP: 60 EST: 1998
SALES (est): 1.3MM **Privately Held**
SIC: **6512** 6513 Property operation, retail establishment; residential hotel operation

(P-10662)
TEGTMEIER ASSOCIATES INC
6701 Clark Rd, Paradise (95969-2833)
PHONE..............................530 872-7700
John Tegemeier, *President*
EMP: 58
SQ FT: 24,000
SALES (corp-wide): 3.3MM **Privately Held**
SIC: **6512** 7841 5049 Theater building, ownership & operation; video disk/tape rental to the general public; theatrical equipment & supplies
PA: Tegtmeier Associates Inc.
14 Mansion Ct
Menlo Park CA 94025
650 847-1639

(P-10663)
TOM HOM INVESTMENT CORP
7660 Fay Ave Ste H, La Jolla (92037-4843)
P.O. Box 6950, San Diego (92166-0950)
PHONE..............................858 456-5000
Tom Hom, *President*
William Newbern, *President*
Les Harvey, *CFO*
EMP: 100
SQ FT: 2,000

SALES (est): 3.2MM **Privately Held**
SIC: **6512** Nonresidential building operators

(P-10664)
TOPA MANAGEMENT COMPANY (PA)
1800 Avenue Of The Stars # 1400, Los Angeles (90067-4220)
PHONE..............................310 203-9199
James Brooks, *CEO*
Jim Brooks, *President*
Jeanne Gettemy-Lazar, *CFO*
Darren Bell, *Vice Pres*
Paul Gienger, *Vice Pres*
EMP: 158
SALES (est): 14MM **Privately Held**
WEB: www.topamanagement.com
SIC: **6512** Commercial & industrial building operation

(P-10665)
TRIAD PROPERTIES
995 Riverside St, Ventura (93001-1636)
PHONE..............................805 648-5008
Denise Wise, *Principal*
John Polanskey, *Ch of Bd*
Jim White, *Ch of Bd*
Joe Nocella, *CFO*
Edward L Moses, *Principal*
EMP: 60
SALES: 451.8K **Privately Held**
SIC: **6512** Nonresidential building operators

(P-10666)
UNIVERSITY BUSINESS CTR ASSOC
5425 Hollister Ave # 160, Santa Barbara (93111-3341)
PHONE..............................601 354-3555
David H Hoster II, *CEO*
EMP: 80
SALES (est): 2.2MM
SALES (corp-wide): 300.3MM **Publicly Held**
SIC: **6512** Commercial & industrial building operation
PA: Eastgroup Properties, Inc.
400 W Parkway Pl Ste 100
Ridgeland MS 39157
601 354-3555

(P-10667)
US PROPERTY GROUP INC
Also Called: Manchester Center
1901 E Shields Ave # 203, Fresno (93726-5313)
PHONE..............................559 227-1901
Kevin Mahieu, *Manager*
Paula Jesme, *Finance*
Sandra Cortez, *Marketing Staff*
Morrel Bagunu, *Manager*
EMP: 50
SALES (est): 4MM **Privately Held**
WEB: www.manchester-center.com
SIC: **6512** Shopping center, property operation only

(P-10668)
VALLEY PROPERTIES INC
10324 Balboa Blvd Lbby, Granada Hills (91344-7363)
PHONE..............................818 360-3430
Peter J McKinnon, *President*
EMP: 90
SALES (est): 3.5MM **Privately Held**
SIC: **6512** Nonresidential building operators

(P-10669)
VIRGA INVESTMENT PROPERTY
430 S George Wash Blvd, Yuba City (95993-9154)
PHONE..............................530 755-4409
Larry S Virga, *Owner*
EMP: 143
SALES: 300K **Privately Held**
SIC: **6512** Nonresidential building operators

PRODUCTS & SVCS

(P-10670)
**WEST SIDE REHAB
CORPORATION**
1755 Kings Way, Los Angeles (90069)
PHONE................................323 231-4174
Dean Foley, *President*
EMP: 200
SQ FT: 1,500
SALES (est): 4.8MM **Privately Held**
SIC: 6512 Commercial & industrial building
operation

(P-10671)
WEST VILLE PALM DESERT
Also Called: Palm Desert Town Center
72840 Highway 111 Ste 115, Palm Desert
(92260-3345)
PHONE................................760 346-2121
Norie Bowlan, *Manager*
EMP: 50
SQ FT: 373,000
SALES (est): 3.1MM **Privately Held**
SIC: 6512 Shopping center, property oper-
ation only

(P-10672)
WESTFIELD LLC (DH)
2049 Century Park E # 4000, Los Angeles
(90067-3101)
PHONE................................813 926-4600
Peter Lowy, *CEO*
Mark Stefanel, *CFO*
Fransz De Zilva, *Network Mgr*
Ramond Chan, *Business Anlyst*
Kevin Kang, *Project Mgr*
EMP: 400
SQ FT: 120,000
SALES (est): 173.1MM **Privately Held**
WEB: www.westfieldamerica.com
SIC: 6512 Shopping center, property oper-
ation only
HQ: Westfield America, Inc.
2049 Century Park E Fl 41
Los Angeles CA 90067
310 478-4456

(P-10673)
WESTFIELD AMERICA INC (HQ)
2049 Century Park E Fl 41, Los Angeles
(90067-3101)
PHONE................................310 478-4456
Peter S Lowy, *CEO*
Mark A Stefanek, *CFO*
Charles Delana, *Exec VP*
Elizabeth Westman, *Senior VP*
Brian Kumfer, *Vice Pres*
EMP: 200 **EST:** 1924
SALES (est): 164.1MM **Privately Held**
WEB: www.westfieldamerica.com
SIC: 6512 Shopping center, property oper-
ation only

(P-10674)
**WESTFIELD AMERICA LTD
PARTNR**
2049 Century Park E # 4100, Los Angeles
(90067-3101)
PHONE................................310 277-3898
John Widdup, *CEO*
Beth Campbell, *Exec VP*
David Balasa, *Vice Pres*
Steven Goodman, *Vice Pres*
Larry Green, *Vice Pres*
EMP: 500
SALES (est): 8.9MM **Privately Held**
SIC: 6512 Shopping center, property oper-
ation only
HQ: Westfield, Llc
2049 Century Park E # 4000
Los Angeles CA 90067
-

(P-10675)
**WESTLAKE DEVELOPMENT
GROUP LLC (PA)**
520 S El Camino Real # 900, San Mateo
(94402-1722)
PHONE................................650 579-1010
T M Chang, *Mng Member*
William H C Chang,
EMP: 75
SQ FT: 80,000

SALES (est): 12.4MM **Privately Held**
WEB: www.westlake-global.com
SIC: 6512 6513 6531 Shopping center,
property operation only; commercial & industrial building operation; apartment
building operators; retirement hotel operation; real estate agents & managers

6513 Operators Of
Apartment Buildings

(P-10676)
10632 BOLSA AVENUE LP
Also Called: SYCAMORE COURT APT
500 Nwport Ctr Dr Ste 200, Newport Beach
(92660)
P.O. Box 13326 (92658-5093)
PHONE................................949 673-1221
Shawn Boyd, *Principal*
EMP: 62 **EST:** 2017
SALES (est): 633.4K **Privately Held**
SIC: 6513 Apartment building operators

(P-10677)
1658 CAMDEN LLC
12147 Riverside Dr, North Hollywood
(91607-3832)
PHONE................................818 769-1944
F Samuel Malik,
EMP: 50
SALES (est): 1.7MM **Privately Held**
SIC: 6513 Apartment building operators

(P-10678)
**2ND FLOOR MAIN STREET
CONCEPTS**
126 Main St Ste 201, Huntington Beach
(92648-8132)
PHONE................................714 969-9000
EMP: 50
SALES (est): 1.1MM **Privately Held**
SIC: 6513 Apartment building operators

(P-10679)
7410 WOODMAN AVENUE LLC
Also Called: Kaufman Properties
22837 Ventura Blvd # 201, Woodland Hills
(91364-1224)
PHONE................................805 496-4336
Mark Kaufman,
Elizabeth Kirby, *Director*
EMP: 100
SALES (est): 4.1MM **Privately Held**
SIC: 6513 Apartment building operators

(P-10680)
A COMMUNITY OF FRIENDS
3701 Wilshire Blvd # 700, Los Angeles
(90010-2813)
PHONE................................213 480-0809
Dora Leong Gallo, *CEO*
Maggie Ip, *Accounting Mgr*
Jose Torres, *Sr Project Mgr*
Michelle Thomson, *Case Mgr*
Dennis Bullock, *Manager*
EMP: 60
SQ FT: 5,800
SALES: 9MM **Privately Held**
WEB: www.acof.org
SIC: 6513 Apartment building operators

(P-10681)
AAH HUDSON LP
Also Called: Hudson Gardens
1255 N Hudson Ave, Pasadena
(91104-2868)
PHONE................................626 794-9179
Victoria Miranda, *Comms Mgr*
Ellen Guccione, *Exec VP*
EMP: 3400
SALES: 200K **Publicly Held**
SIC: 6513 Apartment building operators
PA: Apartment Investment & Management
Company
4582 S Ulster St Ste 1100
Denver CO 80237

(P-10682)
**ALDERSLY RETIREMENT
CENTER**
Also Called: ALDERSLY RETIREMENT
COMMUNITY
326 Mission Ave, San Rafael (94901-3425)
PHONE................................415 453-9271
Joanne Maxwell, *Administration*
Tracey Brown, *Nursing Dir*
EMP: 75 **EST:** 1921
SQ FT: 3,000
SALES: 1.9MM **Privately Held**
WEB: www.aldersly.com
SIC: 6513 Retirement hotel operation

(P-10683)
**ALL HALLOWS PRESERVATION
LP**
Also Called: All Hallows Garden Apartments
54 Navy Rd, San Francisco (94124-2825)
PHONE................................415 285-3909
Leeann Morein, *Senior VP*
George Buchanan, *Partner*
EMP: 3900
SALES: 950K **Publicly Held**
SIC: 6513 Apartment building operators
HQ: Aimco Properties, L.P.
4582 S Ulster St Ste 1100
Denver CO 80237

(P-10684)
ALTENHEIM INC
1720 Macarthur Blvd, Oakland
(94602-1766)
PHONE................................510 530-4013
Cathy Hoopaugh, *Director*
EMP: 64 **EST:** 1890
SALES: 310.5K **Privately Held**
SIC: 6513 8051 Retirement hotel opera-
tion; skilled nursing care facilities; ex-
tended care facility

(P-10685)
**AMERICAN BAPTIST HOMES OF
WEST**
Also Called: American Baptist Homes of West
460 E Fern Ave, Redlands (92373-6040)
PHONE................................909 335-3077
Mildred Makamure, *Manager*
EMP: 200
SALES (corp-wide): 21.8MM **Privately
Held**
SIC: 6513 Retirement hotel operation
HQ: American Baptist Homes Of The West
6120 Stoneridge Mall Rd # 300
Pleasanton CA 94588
925 924-7100

(P-10686)
AR PRESERVATION LP
201 Eddy St, San Francisco (94102-2715)
PHONE................................415 776-2151
Donald Falk, *Principal*
EMP: 99
SALES (est): 2.2MM **Privately Held**
SIC: 6513 Apartment building operators

(P-10687)
ASPEN APTS I
165 Eddy St, San Francisco (94102)
PHONE................................415 673-5879
EMP: 99
SALES (est): 3.4MM **Privately Held**
SIC: 6513

(P-10688)
**ASPEN GROVE APARTMENTS
LLC**
450 E 8th St, Gilroy (95020-6650)
PHONE................................408 848-6400
Linda Mandolini, *Mng Member*
Kit Fong, *General Mgr*
EMP: 99
SALES (est): 1.6MM **Privately Held**
SIC: 6513 Apartment building operators

(P-10689)
ATRIA SENIOR LIVING INC
Also Called: Montego Heights Lodge
1400 Montego, Walnut Creek
(94598-2950)
PHONE................................925 938-6611
Kathy Moore, *Manager*
Shari Boswell, *Business Dir*

Gina Dibattista, *Business Dir*
Melissa Dunn, *Business Dir*
Debby Kirchner, *Business Dir*
EMP: 55
SALES (corp-wide): 3.7B **Publicly Held**
WEB: www.atriacom.com
SIC: 6513 Retirement hotel operation
HQ: Atria Senior Living Inc.
300 E Market St Ste 100
Louisville KY 40202

(P-10690)
ATRIA SENIOR LIVING INC
Also Called: Atria Grand Oaks
22032 Arrowhead Ln, Lake Forest
(92630-2301)
PHONE................................805 370-5400
Evan Granucci, *Branch Mgr*
EMP: 70
SALES (corp-wide): 3.7B **Publicly Held**
SIC: 6513 Retirement hotel operation
HQ: Atria Senior Living .Inc.
300 E Market St Ste 100
Louisville KY 40202

(P-10691)
BAYVIEW PRESERVATION LP
5 Commer Ct, San Francisco (94124-2713)
PHONE................................415 285-7344
Leeann Morein, *Senior VP*
Jennifer Hardee, *Partner*
David Robertson, *Partner*
EMP: 3900 **EST:** 2008
SALES (est): 31MM **Publicly Held**
SIC: 6513 Apartment building operators
HQ: Aimco Properties, L.P.
4582 S Ulster St Ste 1100
Denver CO 80237

(P-10692)
BEAR CREEK MANOR
2929 M St, Merced (95348-3215)
PHONE................................209 723-4674
H Davidson, *Principal*
EMP: 50
SALES (est): 1.1MM **Privately Held**
SIC: 6513 Apartment building operators

(P-10693)
BELMONT VILLAGE LP
Also Called: Belmont Village of Sunnyvale
1039 E El Camino Real, Sunnyvale
(94087-7719)
PHONE................................408 720-8498
Dorothy Passarella, *Manager*
EMP: 60
SALES (corp-wide): 41.3MM **Privately
Held**
SIC: 6513 Retirement hotel operation
PA: Belmont Village, L.P.
7660 Woodway Dr Ste 400
Houston TX 77063
713 463-1700

(P-10694)
BELMONT VILLAGE LP
455 E Angeleno Ave, Burbank
(91501-3077)
PHONE................................818 972-2405
Mary Jane Rodriguez, *Manager*
Clint Strickland, *Exec Dir*
Leslie Brown, *Human Res Dir*
Jime Laylo, *QC Dir*
Michelle Scuillon, *Hlthcr Dir*
EMP: 60
SALES (corp-wide): 41.3MM **Privately
Held**
SIC: 6513 Retirement hotel operation
PA: Belmont Village, L.P.
7660 Woodway Dr Ste 400
Houston TX 77063
713 463-1700

(P-10695)
BELMONT VILLAGE LP
5701 Crestridge Rd, Rancho Palos Verdes
(90275-4962)
PHONE................................310 377-9977
Judith Uy-Dillaruz, *Manager*
EMP: 60
SALES (corp-wide): 41.3MM **Privately
Held**
SIC: 6513 Retirement hotel operation

PA: Belmont Village, L.P.
7660 Woodway Dr Ste 400
Houston TX 77063
713 463-1700

(P-10696)
BELMONT VILLAGE LP
Also Called: Belmont Village of Hollywood
2051 N Highland Ave, Los Angeles
(90068-1373)
PHONE...................323 874-7711
Kevin Ward, *Manager*
EMP: 50
SQ FT: 96,800
SALES (corp-wide): 41.3MM **Privately Held**
SIC: 6513 Retirement hotel operation
PA: Belmont Village, L.P.
7660 Woodway Dr Ste 400
Houston TX 77063
713 463-1700

(P-10697)
BIRTCHER/AETNA LAGUNA HILLS
Also Called: Wellington, The
24903 Moulton Pkwy Ofc, Laguna Hills
(92653-6403)
PHONE...................949 458-2311
Scott Mc Nutt, *Vice Pres*
EMP: 100
SQ FT: 292,000
SALES (est): 6.3MM **Privately Held**
SIC: 6513 Retirement hotel operation

(P-10698)
BRADDOCK & LOGAN INC
Also Called: Mission Pines Apts
3600 Pine St Apt 3600 # 3600, Martinez
(94553-8505)
PHONE...................925 229-1747
Russell Schaadt, *General Mgr*
Lorraine Guerra, *Manager*
EMP: 62
SALES (est): 1.6MM **Privately Held**
SIC: 6513 Apartment hotel operation

(P-10699)
BROOKDALE BREA
285 W Central Ave, Brea (92821-3374)
PHONE...................714 706-9968
Chuck Uceusa, *Exec Dir*
EMP: 50
SALES (est): 316.9K **Privately Held**
SIC: 6513 Retirement hotel operation

(P-10700)
BROOKDALE SENIOR LIVING COMMUN
Also Called: Wynwood At The Palms
25585 Van Leuven St, Loma Linda
(92354-2442)
PHONE...................909 796-5421
David Tamo, *Manager*
EMP: 60
SALES (corp-wide): 4.5B **Publicly Held**
WEB: www.assisted.com
SIC: 6513 Retirement hotel operation
HQ: Brookdale Senior Living Communities,
Inc.
6737 W Wa St Ste 2300
Milwaukee WI 53214
414 918-5000

(P-10701)
BROWNING APARTMENTS
1104 Browning Blvd, Los Angeles
(90037-1662)
PHONE...................213 252-8847
Tina Booth, *Manager*
EMP: 50
SALES: 55.4K **Privately Held**
SIC: 6513 Apartment building operators

(P-10702)
CAL SOUTHERN PRESBT HOMES
Also Called: Regents Point
19191 Harvard Ave Ofc, Irvine
(92612-8624)
PHONE...................949 854-9500
Melinda Forney, *Manager*
Veronica Reyes, *Human Res Dir*
EMP: 175

SALES (corp-wide): 101.5MM **Privately Held**
WEB: www.scths.com
SIC: 6513 8052 8051 Retirement hotel operation; intermediate care facilities; skilled nursing care facilities
PA: Southern California Presbyterian Homes
516 Burchett St
Glendale CA 91203
818 247-0420

(P-10703)
CAL SOUTHERN PRESBT HOMES (PA)
516 Burchett St, Glendale (91203-1014)
PHONE...................818 247-0420
John H Cochrane, *CEO*
Gerald W Dingivan, *CEO*
Ruben Grigorians, *Treasurer*
Stacey McGarvin, *Food Svc Dir*
EMP: 55 EST: 1955
SQ FT: 11,000
SALES: 101.5MM **Privately Held**
WEB: www.scths.com
SIC: 6513 Retirement hotel operation

(P-10704)
CAL SOUTHERN PRESBT HOMES
Also Called: Windsor Manor
1230 E Windsor Rd Ofc, Glendale
(91205-2674)
PHONE...................818 244-7219
Marc Herrera, *Branch Mgr*
EMP: 110
SQ FT: 139,840
SALES (corp-wide): 101.5MM **Privately Held**
WEB: www.scths.com
SIC: 6513 Retirement hotel operation
PA: Southern California Presbyterian Homes
516 Burchett St
Glendale CA 91203
818 247-0420

(P-10705)
CAL SOUTHERN PRESBT HOMES
Also Called: PARK PASEO
516 Burchett St, Glendale (91203-1014)
PHONE...................818 247-0420
Gerald W Dingivan, *President*
Greg Bearce, *Vice Pres*
Dewayne McMullin, *Principal*
EMP: 55
SALES: 410K **Privately Held**
WEB: www.parkpaseo.com
SIC: 6513 Retirement hotel operation

(P-10706)
CAL SOUTHERN PRESBT HOMES
Also Called: Royal Oaks
1763 Royal Oaks Dr Ofc, Duarte
(91010-1989)
PHONE...................626 357-1632
Tina Heaney, *Manager*
EMP: 161
SALES (corp-wide): 101.5MM **Privately Held**
WEB: www.scths.com
SIC: 6513 Retirement hotel operation
PA: Southern California Presbyterian Homes
516 Burchett St
Glendale CA 91203
818 247-0420

(P-10707)
CALIFORNIA ODD FELLOWS (PA)
Also Called: Meadows of NAPA Valley
1800 Atrium Pkwy, NAPA (94559-4837)
PHONE...................707 257-7885
Wayne Panchesson, *Exec Dir*
Rina Famularcano, *Nursing Dir*
EMP: 100
SQ FT: 219,000
SALES (est): 1.5MM **Privately Held**
WEB: www.meadowsofnapavalley.org
SIC: 6513 8051 8322 Retirement hotel operation; convalescent home with continuous nursing care; old age assistance

(P-10708)
CALIFORNIA ODD FELLOWS
Also Called: Meadows Nappa Valley Care Ctr
1800 Atrium Pkwy, NAPA (94559-4837)
PHONE...................707 257-7885
Wyane Panchesson, *Administration*
EMP: 65
SQ FT: 30,000
SALES (corp-wide): 1.5MM **Privately Held**
WEB: www.meadowsofnapavalley.org
SIC: 6513 8051 Apartment building operators; skilled nursing care facilities
PA: California Odd Fellows Housing Of Napa, Incorporated
1800 Atrium Pkwy
Napa CA 94559
707 257-7885

(P-10709)
CASA SANDOVAL LLC
1200 Russell Way, Hayward (94541-7708)
PHONE...................510 727-1700
Wai Tsin Chang, *
EMP: 90
SQ FT: 215,000
SALES (est): 8.8MM **Privately Held**
WEB: www.casasandoval.com
SIC: 6513 Retirement hotel operation

(P-10710)
CHARLES & CYNTHIA EBERLY INC
Also Called: The Eberly Company
8383 Wilshire Blvd # 906, Beverly Hills
(90211-2425)
PHONE...................323 937-6468
Charles Eberly, *President*
Cynthia Eberly, *Vice Pres*
Cynthia A Eberly, *Vice Pres*
Charles Edwards, *Marketing Staff*
John Ene, *Supervisor*
EMP: 90
SALES (est): 7.4MM **Privately Held**
WEB: www.eberlyco.com
SIC: 6513 Apartment building operators

(P-10711)
CLASSIC PARK LANE PARTNERSHIP
Also Called: Park Lane A Classic Residenc
200 Glenwood Cir Ofc, Monterey
(93940-6773)
PHONE...................831 373-0101
Steve Brudnick, *Exec Dir*
Park Lane Investment, *Partner*
Jim Cox, *Director*
EMP: 83
SQ FT: 190,000
SALES (est): 3.1MM **Privately Held**
SIC: 6513 8361 Retirement hotel operation; home for the aged

(P-10712)
COMMERCIAL PROPERTY MANAGEMENT (PA)
3251 W 6th St Ste 109, Los Angeles
(90020-5018)
PHONE...................213 739-2000
David Soufer, *President*
Daniel Azadegan, *Analyst*
EMP: 64
SQ FT: 4,500
SALES (est): 4MM **Privately Held**
WEB: www.cpmusa.com
SIC: 6513 Apartment building operators

(P-10713)
CREATIVE HOUSING & SVCS LLC
605 E Huntington Dr # 207, Monrovia
(91016-6352)
PHONE...................626 403-5454
George Mercer, *Director*
Scott Darrel, *Chairman*
Sylvia Karl, *Vice Pres*
EMP: 105
SQ FT: 6,000
SALES: 1.1MM **Privately Held**
WEB: www.chmshousing.org
SIC: 6513 Apartment building operators

(P-10714)
DOMINICAN OAKS CORPORATION
3400 Paul Sweet Rd Ofc, Santa Cruz
(95065-1559)
PHONE...................831 462-6257
Patience Beck, *Manager*
Brenda Bouch, *Executive*
Brenda Barber, *Human Res Dir*
Debra Ruoghty, *Sales Mgr*
Eric Botkin, *Director*
EMP: 80
SALES: 11MM **Privately Held**
WEB: www.dominicanoaks.com
SIC: 6513 Retirement hotel operation

(P-10715)
E J WILLIAMS PROPERTY MGT
5637 N Pershing Ave Ste D, Stockton
(95207-4943)
P.O. Box 7185 (95267-0185)
PHONE...................209 473-4022
Ej Williams, *Principal*
EMP: 60
SALES (est): 360.6K **Privately Held**
SIC: 6513 Apartment building operators

(P-10716)
EAH ELENA GARDENS LP
Also Called: EAH HOUSING
1902 Lakewood Dr, San Jose
(95132-1409)
PHONE...................415 295-8840
Cindy McAnally, *Principal*
EMP: 278
SALES: 3MM
SALES (corp-wide): 38.5MM **Privately Held**
WEB: www.centennialvillage.com
SIC: 6513 Apartment building operators
PA: Eah Inc.
22 Pelican Way
San Rafael CA 94901
415 258-1800

(P-10717)
EAST BAY ASIAN LOCAL DEV CORP
1825 San Pablo Ave # 200, Oakland
(94612-1517)
PHONE...................510 267-1917
Jeremy Liu, *Exec Dir*
Judy Graboyes, *Associate Dir*
Joshua Simon, *Exec Dir*
Anne Robertson, *Executive Asst*
Kyle Lee, *Software Dev*
EMP: 109
SQ FT: 78,000
SALES: 18MM **Privately Held**
WEB: www.ebaldc.org
SIC: 6513 Apartment building operators

(P-10718)
EDGEWOOD PROPERTIES (PA)
3096 Sandstone Rd, Alamo (94507-1617)
PHONE...................925 838-2847
Jim Darst, *Partner*
Jim Rafton, *Partner*
EMP: 80
SQ FT: 600
SALES (est): 2.9MM **Privately Held**
SIC: 6513 Apartment building operators

(P-10719)
EMERITUS CORPORATION
Also Called: Villa Del Rey Retirement Inn
1351 E Washington Ave, Escondido
(92027-1934)
PHONE...................760 741-3055
Pam Judkins, *Branch Mgr*
EMP: 50
SQ FT: 60,000
SALES (corp-wide): 4.5B **Publicly Held**
WEB: www.emeraldestatesslc.com
SIC: 6513 Retirement hotel operation
HQ: Emeritus Corporation
3131 Elliott Ave Ste 500
Milwaukee WI 53214

(P-10720)
EMERITUS CORPORATION
Also Called: Emeritus At Casa Glendale
426 Piedmont Ave, Glendale (91206-3448)
PHONE...................818 246-7457

PRODUCTS & SVCS

David Wilkens, *Branch Mgr*
EMP: 50
SALES (corp-wide): 4.5B **Publicly Held**
SIC: 6513 Retirement hotel operation
HQ: Emeritus Corporation
3131 Elliott Ave Ste 500
Milwaukee WI 53214

(P-10721)
EMERITUS CORPORATION
Also Called: Creston Village
1919 Creston Rd Ofc, Paso Robles
(93446-4475)
PHONE..................805 239-1313
Tonya Hogue, *Director*
EMP: 50
SALES (corp-wide): 4.5B **Publicly Held**
WEB: www.emeraldestatesslc.com
SIC: 6513 Retirement hotel operation
HQ: Emeritus Corporation
3131 Elliott Ave Ste 500
Milwaukee WI 53214

(P-10722)
ENCORE SENIOR LIVING III LLC
Also Called: Encore Senior Vlg At Riverside
6280 Clay St, Riverside (92509-6005)
PHONE..................951 360-1616
Barbara Reece, *Director*
EMP: 50 **Privately Held**
WEB: www.retirementinn.com
SIC: 6513 Retirement hotel operation
PA: Encore Senior Living Iii, Llc
400 Locust St Ste 820
Des Moines IA 50309

(P-10723)
ESSEX PROPERTY TRUST INC
(PA)
1100 Park Pl Ste 200, San Mateo
(94403-7107)
PHONE..................650 655-7800
Michael J Schall, *President*
Michael T Dance, *CFO*
Keith R Guericke, *Vice Ch Bd*
Irving Lyons, *Bd of Directors*
Thomas Robinson, *Bd of Directors*
EMP: 83
SQ FT: 39,600
SALES: 1.4B **Privately Held**
SIC: 6513 Apartment building operators

(P-10724)
FAIRWOOD ASSOCIATES APTS
Also Called: Fairwood Apartments
8893 Fair Oaks Blvd Ofc, Carmichael
(95608-2672)
PHONE..................916 944-0152
Leeann Morein, *Principal*
Arthur F Evans, *Partner*
The National Housing Partnersh, *Partner*
Jennifer Hardee, *Principal*
Joanette Stiron, *Manager*
EMP: 99
SALES: 500K **Publicly Held**
WEB: www.fairwoodapartments.com
SIC: 6513 Apartment building operators
PA: Apartment Investment & Management
Company
4582 S Ulster St Ste 1100
Denver CO 80237

(P-10725)
FATHERS OF ST CHARLES
Also Called: Villa Sclabrini Retirement Ctr
10631 Vinedale St, Sun Valley
(91352-2825)
PHONE..................818 768-6500
Ermete Nazzani, *Director*
Father E Nazzini, *Bd of Directors*
EMP: 188
SQ FT: 90,000
SALES: 5MM **Privately Held**
SIC: 6513 8051 Retirement hotel opera-
tion; skilled nursing care facilities

(P-10726)
FENTON SCRIPPS LANDING LLC
Also Called: H.G. Fenton Company
9970 Erma Rd, San Diego (92131-2425)
PHONE..................858 586-0206
Michael Neal, *Mng Member*

EMP: 99
SALES (est): 1.9MM **Privately Held**
SIC: 6513 Apartment building operators

(P-10727)
FIFTY PENINSULA PARTNERS
Also Called: Sterling Court
850 N El Camino Real Ofc, San Mateo
(94401-3787)
PHONE..................650 344-8200
S St Charles, *Exec Dir*
Sarah St Charles, *Exec Dir*
Sarah Stcharles, *Exec Dir*
Joanne Coughlin, *Mktg Dir*
Ely Ramos, *Food Svc Dir*
EMP: 55
SALES (est): 4.8MM **Privately Held**
SIC: 6513 Retirement hotel operation

(P-10728)
FOREMOST HEALTHCARE
CENTERS
Also Called: Health Care Developers
17581 Sultana St, Hesperia (92345-6552)
PHONE..................760 244-5579
Leonard Crites, *Owner*
Barbara Bandringa, *Owner*
EMP: 60
SALES (est): 1.7MM **Privately Held**
SIC: 6513 Apartment building operators

(P-10729)
FRONT PORCH COMMUNITIES
849 Coast Blvd, La Jolla (92037-4223)
PHONE..................858 454-2151
Justin Weber, *Exec Dir*
David Weidert, *Exec Dir*
EMP: 100
SALES (corp-wide): 165.1MM **Privately**
Held
SIC: 6513 8052 8361 Retirement hotel
operation; intermediate care facilities; res-
idential care
PA: Front Porch Communities And Services
- Casa De Manana, Llc
800 N Brand Blvd Fl 19
Glendale CA 91203
818 729-8100

(P-10730)
FRONT PORCH COMMUNITIES
Also Called: Wesley Palms
2567 2nd Ave Unit 312, San Diego
(92103-6579)
PHONE..................858 274-4110
Ben Gefke, *Manager*
Debbie Helmer, *Vice Pres*
Lani Thiel, *Manager*
EMP: 330
SALES (corp-wide): 165.1MM **Privately**
Held
SIC: 6513 Retirement hotel operation
PA: Front Porch Communities And Services
- Casa De Manana, Llc
800 N Brand Blvd Fl 19
Glendale CA 91203
818 729-8100

(P-10731)
FSQ RIO LAS PALMAS
BUSINESS TR
877 E March Ln Apt 378, Stockton
(95207-5880)
PHONE..................209 957-4711
Sam Ogden, *Exec Dir*
EMP: 54
SALES (est): 2.6MM **Publicly Held**
WEB: www.fivestarqualitycare.com
SIC: 6513 Retirement hotel operation
PA: Five Star Senior Living Inc.
400 Centre St
Newton MA 02458

(P-10732)
GABLES OF OJAI LLC
701 N Montgomery St, Ojai (93023-1844)
PHONE..................805 646-1446
Sue Collingsworth, *Director*
EMP: 56
SALES (est): 2.7MM
SALES (corp-wide): 10.5MM **Privately**
Held
WEB: www.gablesofojai.com
SIC: 6513 Retirement hotel operation

PA: The Parsons Group Inc
1 N Calle Chavez Ste 200
Santa Barbara CA 93101
805 564-3341

(P-10733)
GERSON BAKER & ASSOCIATES
Also Called: Westlake Village Apartments
333 Park Plaza Dr Ofc, Daly City
(94015-1538)
PHONE..................650 756-0959
Gerson Baker, *Owner*
EMP: 100
SQ FT: 5,000
SALES (est): 6.5MM **Privately Held**
WEB: www.westlakevillageapts.com
SIC: 6513 Apartment hotel operation

(P-10734)
GK MANAGEMENT CO INC
Also Called: Studio Royale
3975 Overland Ave, Culver City
(90232-3722)
PHONE..................310 836-1812
Karen Longo, *Manager*
EMP: 60
SALES (corp-wide): 26.4MM **Privately**
Held
WEB: www.gkind.com
SIC: 6513 Apartment building operators
PA: Gk Management Co., Inc.
5150 Overland Ave
Culver City CA 90230
310 204-2050

(P-10735)
HARVEST FACILITY HOLDINGS
LP
Also Called: Mission Cmmons Rtrment Rs-
dence
10 Terracina Blvd Ofc, Redlands
(92373-4800)
PHONE..................909 793-8691
John Degoucvia, *Manager*
EMP: 80 **Privately Held**
WEB: www.holidaytouch.com
SIC: 6513 Retirement hotel operation
HQ: Harvest Facility Holdings Lp
5885 Meadows Rd Ste 500
Lake Oswego OR 97035
503 370-7070

(P-10736)
HG FENTON COMPANY
7577 Mission Valley Rd # 200, San Diego
(92108-4432)
PHONE..................619 400-0120
Mike Neal, *CEO*
Henry Hunte, *Principal*
EMP: 84
SALES (est): 14.4MM **Privately Held**
SIC: 6513 6519 Apartment building opera-
tors; real property lessors

(P-10737)
HIGNELL INCORPORATED
Also Called: Sierra Manor Apts
1836 Laburnum Ave, Chico (95926-2375)
PHONE..................530 345-1965
Becky Nelson, *Branch Mgr*
EMP: 80
SALES (corp-wide): 41.1MM **Privately**
Held
SIC: 6513 Apartment building operators
PA: Hignell, Incorporated
1750 Humboldt Rd
Chico CA 95928
530 894-0404

(P-10738)
INGLEWOOD MEADOWS KBS
LP
1 S Locust St, Inglewood (90301-1808)
PHONE..................310 820-4888
Thomas Safran, *Partner*
EMP: 90
SALES: 1,000K **Privately Held**
SIC: 6513 Apartment building operators

(P-10739)
INTEGRAL SENIOR LIVING LLC
(PA)
2333 State St Ste 300, Carlsbad
(92008-1691)
PHONE..................760 547-2863

Sue Farrow,
Terry Ervin, *President*
Allison Singler, *Sales Staff*
Tracee Degrande,
Suzanne Foley,
EMP: 148
SALES (est): 70.1MM **Privately Held**
SIC: 6513 Retirement hotel operation

(P-10740)
INVESTORS MGT TR RE GROUP
INC (PA)
Also Called: I M T
15303 Ventura Blvd # 200, Sherman Oaks
(91403-3110)
PHONE..................818 784-4700
John M Tesoriero, *President*
Frank Hutter, *CFO*
Scott Burns, *Vice Pres*
Joseph Elhabr, *Vice Pres*
Christopher Hill, *Vice Pres*
EMP: 50
SQ FT: 8,000
SALES (est): 18.3MM **Privately Held**
SIC: 6513 Apartment building operators

(P-10741)
IRVINE APT COMMUNITIES LP
(HQ)
Also Called: I A C
110 Innovation Dr, Irvine (92617-3040)
PHONE..................949 720-5600
Raymond Watson, *Vice Chairman*
Mike Ellis, *Exec VP*
EMP: 200
SQ FT: 8,316
SALES (est): 61.5MM
SALES (corp-wide): 2B **Privately Held**
WEB: www.rental-living.com
SIC: 6513 6552 6798 Apartment building
operators; subdividers & developers; real
estate investment trusts
PA: The Irvine Company Llc
550 Newport Center Dr # 160
Newport Beach CA 92660
949 720-2000

(P-10742)
JEWISH SENIOR LIVING GROUP
302 Silver Ave, San Francisco
(94112-1510)
PHONE..................415 562-2600
Daniel Ruth, *President*
Olga Strashnaya, *Info Tech Mgr*
Ken Diep, *Engineer*
Terrence Scott, *Controller*
Pat Navarro, *Human Resources*
EMP: 60
SALES: 8.4MM **Privately Held**
SIC: 6513 Retirement hotel operation

(P-10743)
JOHN COLLINS CO INC
5155 Cedarwood Rd Mgr, Bonita
(91902-1942)
PHONE..................818 227-2190
EMP: 97
SALES (corp-wide): 1.7MM **Privately**
Held
SIC: 6513 Apartment building operators
PA: The John Collins Co Inc
5135 N Harbor Dr
San Diego CA

(P-10744)
JOHN STEWART COMPANY
Also Called: Meadow Glen Apartments
2451 Meadowview Rd, Sacramento
(95832-1467)
PHONE..................415 345-4400
David Lawler, *Manager*
Elyssa Newberry, *Director*
EMP: 200
SALES (corp-wide): 122MM **Privately**
Held
SIC: 6513 Apartment building operators
PA: John Stewart Company
1388 Sutter St Ste 1100
San Francisco CA 94109
415 345-4400

(P-10745)
JONES & JONES MGT GROUP INC
8220 Topanga Canyon Blvd, Canoga Park (91304-3844)
P.O. Box 6550, Woodland Hills (91365-6550)
PHONE..................................818 594-0019
John D Jones, *President*
Helen Jones, *CEO*
Margaret Jones Dry, *Vice Pres*
Connie Wilgus, *Vice Pres*
Leonisha Tolbert, *Manager*
EMP: 142
SALES (est): 11.5MM **Privately Held**
SIC: 6513 Apartment building operators

(P-10746)
JP ALLEN INC
150 E Angeleno Ave, Burbank (91502-1911)
PHONE..................................818 841-4770
Mark Crigler, *President*
Rich Reid, *Finance Dir*
EMP: 300
SQ FT: 100,000
SALES (est): 4MM **Privately Held**
SIC: 6513 7011 Apartment building operators; hotel, franchised

(P-10747)
KISCO SENIOR LIVING LLC
Also Called: Drake Terrace
275 Los Ranchitos Rd, San Rafael (94903-3673)
PHONE..................................415 491-1935
EMP: 95
SALES (corp-wide): 138.2MM **Privately Held**
SIC: 6513 Retirement hotel operation
PA: Senior Kisco Living Llc
5790 Fleet St Ste 300
Carlsbad CA 92008
760 804-5900

(P-10748)
KISCO SENIOR LIVING LLC
1731 W Medical Center Dr, Anaheim (92801-1837)
PHONE..................................714 872-9785
Carol Bush, *Director*
EMP: 72
SALES (corp-wide): 138.2MM **Privately Held**
SIC: 6513 Retirement hotel operation
PA: Senior Kisco Living Llc
5790 Fleet St Ste 300
Carlsbad CA 92008
760 804-5900

(P-10749)
KISCO SENIOR LIVING LLC
Also Called: KRC Santa Margarita
21952 Buena Suerte, Rcho STA Marg (92688-3903)
PHONE..................................949 888-2250
Rick Lansford, *Branch Mgr*
EMP: 100
SALES (corp-wide): 138.2MM **Privately Held**
WEB: www.kiscosl.com
SIC: 6513 Retirement hotel operation
PA: Senior Kisco Living Llc
5790 Fleet St Ste 300
Carlsbad CA 92008
760 804-5900

(P-10750)
KISCO SENIOR LIVING LLC
1100 E Spruce Ave Ofc, Fresno (93720-3314)
PHONE..................................559 449-8070
EMP: 55
SALES (corp-wide): 138.2MM **Privately Held**
WEB: www.kiscosl.com
SIC: 6513 Retirement hotel operation
PA: Senior Kisco Living Llc
5790 Fleet St Ste 300
Carlsbad CA 92008
760 804-5900

(P-10751)
KISCO SENIOR LIVING LLC
Also Called: Oak View Snoma Hlls Apartments
1350 Oak View Cir, Rohnert Park (94928-6411)
PHONE..................................707 585-1800
Kim Healis, *Branch Mgr*
EMP: 66
SALES (corp-wide): 138.2MM **Privately Held**
WEB: www.kiscosl.com
SIC: 6513 Retirement hotel operation
PA: Senior Kisco Living Llc
5790 Fleet St Ste 300
Carlsbad CA 92008
760 804-5900

(P-10752)
KISCO SENIOR LIVING LLC
Also Called: KRC Los Altos
1174 Los Altos Ave Ofc, Los Altos (94022-1059)
PHONE..................................650 948-7337
Felora Lotfi, *Branch Mgr*
EMP: 50
SALES (corp-wide): 138.2MM **Privately Held**
WEB: www.kiscosl.com
SIC: 6513 Retirement hotel operation
PA: Senior Kisco Living Llc
5790 Fleet St Ste 300
Carlsbad CA 92008
760 804-5900

(P-10753)
LA SALLE APARTMENTS
Also Called: La Salle Preservation
30 Whitfield Ct Ste 1, San Francisco (94124-2840)
PHONE..................................415 647-0607
Leeann Morein, *Principal*
Jennifer Hardee, *Principal*
EMP: 99 **EST:** 2008
SALES (est): 2.5MM **Privately Held**
SIC: 6513 Apartment building operators

(P-10754)
LASSLEY ENTERPRISES INC
Also Called: Western Homes
1289 E Shaw Ave, Fresno (93710-7801)
P.O. Box 26988 (93729-6988)
PHONE..................................559 226-4300
Larry Lassley, *President*
Floyd Lassley, *President*
Terry Graham, *Corp Secy*
Lorraine Lassley, *Vice Pres*
EMP: 50
SQ FT: 4,000
SALES (est): 1.7MM **Privately Held**
SIC: 6513 Apartment building operators

(P-10755)
LEGACY PARTNERS HOLLYWOOD
1600 Vine St, Los Angeles (90028-8818)
PHONE..................................949 930-7706
Tim O'Brien, *Partner*
Brandon Tran, *Web Dvlpr*
Andrew Koly, *Mktg Dir*
Richard West, *Accounts Exec*
EMP: 91
SALES (est): 2.1MM **Privately Held**
SIC: 6513 Apartment building operators

(P-10756)
LEISURE CARE INC
Also Called: Norlyn Builders Newport Beach
1455 Superior Ave, Newport Beach (92663-6127)
PHONE..................................949 645-6833
Connie Marvick, *Administration*
Newport Beach Plaza Retirement, *General Ptnr*
M David Green, *Ltd Ptnr*
Jerome Pastor, *Ltd Ptnr*
Chuck Lytle, *CEO*
EMP: 60
SQ FT: 90,000
SALES (est): 4MM **Privately Held**
SIC: 6513 Retirement hotel operation

(P-10757)
LINCOLN MARINERS ASSOC LTD
Also Called: Mariners Cove Apartments
4392 W Point Loma Blvd, San Diego (92107-1128)
PHONE..................................619 225-1473
Leeann Morein, *Principal*
Jennifer Hardee, *Principal*
EMP: 99
SALES (est): 3.3MM **Privately Held**
WEB: www.marinerscoveapartments.com
SIC: 6513 Apartment building operators

(P-10758)
LIVERMORE SNIOR LVING ASSOC LP
Also Called: Leisure Care
900 E Stanley Blvd # 383, Livermore (94550-4089)
PHONE..................................925 371-2300
Mike Palmer, *General Mgr*
EMP: 50
SALES (est): 4.2MM **Privately Held**
SIC: 6513 Retirement hotel operation

(P-10759)
LIVING OPPORTUNITIES MGT CO
6900 Seville Ave, Huntington Park (90255-4970)
PHONE..................................323 589-5956
Karla Gomez, *Director*
EMP: 209
SALES (corp-wide): 11MM **Privately Held**
SIC: 6513 Apartment building operators
PA: Living Opportunities Management Co
3787 Worsham Ave
Long Beach CA 90808
562 595-7567

(P-10760)
LONGWOOD MANAGEMENT CORP
Also Called: California Villa
6728 Sepulveda Blvd, Van Nuys (91411-1248)
PHONE..................................818 781-6348
Jackie Beltran, *Administration*
EMP: 50
SALES (corp-wide): 170MM **Privately Held**
SIC: 6513 8361 Retirement hotel operation; residential care
PA: Longwood Management Corp.
4032 Wilshire Blvd Fl 6
Los Angeles CA 90010
213 389-6900

(P-10761)
LONGWOOD MANAGEMENT CORP
Also Called: Woodland Park Retirement Hotel
895 E Pasadena St, Pomona (91767-4930)
PHONE..................................818 884-7100
Susan Weisbarth, *Manager*
EMP: 68
SQ FT: 66,332
SALES (corp-wide): 170MM **Privately Held**
SIC: 6513 Retirement hotel operation
PA: Longwood Management Corp.
4032 Wilshire Blvd Fl 6
Los Angeles CA 90010
213 389-6900

(P-10762)
LONGWOOD MANAGEMENT INC
Also Called: Huntington Rsdntial Rtrment Ht
20920 Earl St Ofc, Torrance (90503-4357)
PHONE..................................310 370-5828
Heather Argeta, *Administration*
Chiqui Olalia, *Administration*
EMP: 65
SALES (est): 2.1MM **Privately Held**
WEB: www.longwoodmanagement.com
SIC: 6513 Retirement hotel operation

(P-10763)
LOS ANGELES SENIOR CITIZEN
Also Called: PICO WOOSTER SENIOR HOUSING
1425 S Wooster St, Los Angeles (90035-3456)
PHONE..................................310 271-9670
Anne Friedrich, *President*
EMP: 55
SALES: 656.4K **Privately Held**
SIC: 6513 Retirement hotel operation

(P-10764)
M&M ASSEET MANAGEMENT GNL
2936 W El Segundo Blvd, Gardena (90249-1558)
PHONE..................................310 769-6669
Ram K Mittal, *Principal*
Lillian Mittal, *Exec VP*
Evelyn Revellame, *Controller*
EMP: 99
SALES (est): 2.1MM **Privately Held**
SIC: 6513 Apartment building operators

(P-10765)
MARINA CITY CLUB LP A CALI
4333 Admiralty Way, Marina Del Rey (90292-5469)
PHONE..................................310 822-0611
J H Snyder, *Partner*
Lewis Geyser, *Partner*
Lon Snyder, *Partner*
Milton Swimmer, *Partner*
Eileen Mc Carthy, *Sales Dir*
EMP: 125 **EST:** 1969
SQ FT: 10,000
SALES (est): 7.6MM **Privately Held**
WEB: www.marinacityclub.com
SIC: 6513 7997 4493 Apartment building operators; membership sports & recreation clubs; marinas

(P-10766)
MAYER ASSOCIATES
9090 Wilshire Blvd Fl 3, Beverly Hills (90211-1851)
PHONE..................................310 274-5553
Alan I Casden, *Partner*
Alan Casden, *Partner*
EMP: 100
SALES (est): 2MM **Privately Held**
SIC: 6513 Apartment building operators

(P-10767)
MBK REAL ESTATE LTD A CALFOR
100 Lockewood Ln, Scotts Valley (95066-3900)
PHONE..................................831 438-7533
Kit Siemer, *Exec Dir*
EMP: 80 **Privately Held**
SIC: 6513 Retirement hotel operation
HQ: Mbk Real Estate Ltd., A California Limited Partnership
4 Park Plz Ste 1700
Irvine CA 92614
949 789-8300

(P-10768)
MBK REAL ESTATE LTD A CALIFOR
Also Called: Ocean House Retirement Inn
2107 Ocean Ave Ofc, Santa Monica (90405-2282)
PHONE..................................310 399-3227
Lesley Henriksen, *Exec Dir*
EMP: 50 **Privately Held**
SIC: 6513 Retirement hotel operation
HQ: Mbk Real Estate Ltd., A California Limited Partnership
4 Park Plz Ste 1700
Irvine CA 92614
949 789-8300

(P-10769)
MERCY HSING CALIFORNIA XXXIV
Also Called: Edith Witt Senior Community
66 9th St, San Francisco (94103-1427)
PHONE..................................415 503-0816
Abelle Cochico, *Manager*
Teresa Walorski, *Administration*
EMP: 99

SALES: 84.9K **Privately Held**
SIC: 6513 Apartment building operators

(P-10770)
MERRILL GARDENS LLC
350 Locust Dr Apt L215, Vallejo
(94591-4226)
PHONE..............................707 553-2698
Frank Cook, *Branch Mgr*
EMP: 62 **Privately Held**
SIC: 6513 Retirement hotel operation
PA: Merrill Gardens L.L.C.
1938 Frview Ave E Ste 300
Seattle WA 98102

(P-10771)
MERRILL GARDENS LLC
4855 Snyder Ln Apt 152, Rohnert Park
(94928-4863)
PHONE..............................707 585-7878
Jason Englehorn, *Branch Mgr*
EMP: 62 **Privately Held**
SIC: 6513 Retirement hotel operation
PA: Merrill Gardens L.L.C.
1938 Frview Ave E Ste 300
Seattle WA 98102

(P-10772)
MERRILL GARDENS LLC
Also Called: Merrill Gardens At Bankers HI
2567 2nd Ave, San Diego (92103-6503)
PHONE..............................619 961-4990
Nancy Robinson, *President*
EMP: 63 **Privately Held**
SIC: 6513 Retirement hotel operation
PA: Merrill Gardens L.L.C.
1938 Frview Ave E Ste 300
Seattle WA 98102

(P-10773)
MERRILL GARDENS LLC
17200 Goldenwest St # 101, Huntington
Beach (92647-9510)
PHONE..............................714 842-6569
Caroline Contreras, *Corp Comm Staff*
Claudia Lopez, *Nursing Dir*
EMP: 52 **Privately Held**
SIC: 6513 Retirement hotel operation
PA: Merrill Gardens L.L.C.
1938 Frview Ave E Ste 300
Seattle WA 98102

(P-10774)
MERRILL GARDENS LLC
2115 Winchester Blvd, Campbell
(95008-3443)
PHONE..............................408 370-6431
EMP: 52 **Privately Held**
SIC: 6513 Retirement hotel operation
PA: Merrill Gardens L.L.C.
1938 Frview Ave E Ste 300
Seattle WA 98102

(P-10775)
MERRILL GARDENS LLC
1220 Suey Rd Bldg A, Santa Maria
(93454-2687)
PHONE..............................805 310-4102
Ole Vonfrausing-Borch,
Stephen Start,
EMP: 70
SALES (est): 4.6MM **Privately Held**
SIC: 6513 Retirement hotel operation

(P-10776)
MERRILL GARDENS LLC
800 Oregon St, Sonoma (95476-6445)
PHONE..............................707 996-7101
Sunny Notimoh, *Manager*
EMP: 63 **Privately Held**
SIC: 6513 Retirement hotel operation
PA: Merrill Gardens L.L.C.
1938 Frview Ave E Ste 300
Seattle WA 98102

(P-10777)
MERRILL GARDENS LLC
430 N Union Rd, Manteca (95337-4367)
PHONE..............................209 823-0164
Travis Barnett, *Manager*

EMP: 63 **Privately Held**
SIC: 6513 Retirement hotel operation
PA: Merrill Gardens L.L.C.
1938 Frview Ave E Ste 300
Seattle WA 98102
-

(P-10778)
MERRILL GARDENS LLC
Also Called: Merrill Gardns At Chateau Whit
13250 Philadelphia St Ofc, Whittier
(90601-4319)
PHONE..............................562 693-0505
Suzie Magpayo, *Manager*
EMP: 60 **Privately Held**
SIC: 6513 Retirement hotel operation
PA: Merrill Gardens L.L.C.
1938 Frview Ave E Ste 300
Seattle WA 98102

(P-10779)
**MID-PENINSULA TYRELLA
CORP (PA)**
658 Bair Island Rd # 300, Redwood City
(94063)
PHONE..............................650 299-8000
Fran Wagstaff, *Exec Dir*
EMP: 65
SALES: 286.1K **Privately Held**
SIC: 6513 Apartment building operators

(P-10780)
MONARK LP
2804 W El Segundo Blvd, Gardena
(90249-1551)
PHONE..............................310 769-6669
Evelyn Revellame, *CFO*
EMP: 99
SALES (est): 1.9MM **Privately Held**
SIC: 6513 Apartment building operators

(P-10781)
MONROE RESIDENCE CLUB
Also Called: Kenmore Residence Club
1570 Sutter St, San Francisco
(94109-5307)
PHONE..............................415 771-9119
Irene Lieberman, *Owner*
EMP: 75
SQ FT: 1,000
SALES (est): 2.2MM **Privately Held**
WEB: www.monroeresidenceclub.com
SIC: 6513 Residential hotel operation

(P-10782)
**MONTE VISTA RETIREMENT
LODGE**
Also Called: Monte Vista Village
2211 Massachusetts Ave, Lemon Grove
(91945-3616)
PHONE..............................619 465-1331
Sidney Goodman, *Partner*
John Goodman, *Partner*
Donna Hanson, *Partner*
Amos Heilicher, *Partner*
Daniel Heilicher, *Partner*
EMP: 90
SALES (est): 5.6MM **Privately Held**
WEB: www.montevistalodge.com
SIC: 6513 Retirement hotel operation

(P-10783)
**MP SHORELINE ASSOC LTD
PARTNR**
Also Called: Shorebreeze Apartments
460 N Shoreline Blvd, Mountain View
(94043-4661)
PHONE..............................650 966-1327
Matt Franklin, *President*
EMP: 50
SALES: 2.7MM
SALES (corp-wide): 41.9K **Privately Held**
SIC: 6513 Apartment building operators
PA: Stanford Mid-Peninsula Urban Coalition
303 Vintage Park Dr # 250
Foster City CA 94404
650 356-2900

(P-10784)
MT VIEW APARTMENTS LLC
3170 Crow Canyon Pl # 165, San Ramon
(94583-1347)
P.O. Box 308 (94583-0308)
PHONE..............................925 866-8429

Dennis Fuller,
EMP: 60
SALES (est): 2.9MM **Privately Held**
SIC: 6513 Apartment building operators

(P-10785)
**NORMAND/WLSHIRE RTRMENT
HT INC**
Also Called: CALIFORNIA HEALTHCARE
AND REHA
6700 Sepulveda Blvd, Van Nuys
(91411-1248)
PHONE..............................818 373-5429
Jerry Catama, *Administration*
EMP: 99
SALES: 21.5MM **Privately Held**
SIC: 6513 8059 Retirement hotel opera-
tion; convalescent home

(P-10786)
NORTHGATE TERRACE APTS
1290 Northgate Dr Apt 48, Yuba City
(95991-1565)
PHONE..............................530 671-2026
Dennis McLear, *President*
EMP: 100
SALES (est): 2MM **Privately Held**
SIC: 6513 Apartment hotel operation

(P-10787)
OAK CREEK APARTMENTS
Also Called: Gerson Bakar & Associates
1600 Sand Hill Rd, Palo Alto (94304-2047)
PHONE..............................650 327-1600
Gerson Bakar, *Partner*
A S Wilsey, *General Ptnr*
EMP: 50 **EST:** 1968
SQ FT: 300,000
SALES (est): 3.6MM
SALES (corp-wide): 42.5MM **Privately
Held**
WEB: www.oakcreekapts.com
SIC: 6513 Apartment hotel operation
PA: Jalson Co., Inc.
201 Filbert St Ste 700
San Francisco CA 94133
415 391-1313

(P-10788)
**OCONNER WOODS A
CALIFORNIA**
3400 Wagner Heights Rd, Stockton
(95209-4843)
PHONE..............................209 956-3400
Scot Sinclair, *President*
EMP: 100
SQ FT: 3,000
SALES (est): 3.6MM
SALES (corp-wide): 24.6MM **Privately
Held**
SIC: 6513 Retirement hotel operation
PA: St. Joseph's Regional Housing Corpo-
ration
3400 Wagner Heights Rd
Stockton CA 95209
209 956-3400

(P-10789)
**OCONNOR WOODS HOUSING
CORP**
3400 Wagner Heights Rd, Stockton
(95209-4843)
PHONE..............................209 956-3400
Edward G Schoeder, *President*
Scot Sinclair, *Exec Dir*
Dawn Shimel, *Director*
Kimberly Baumgarten, *Manager*
EMP: 100
SALES: 29.1MM
SALES (corp-wide): 24.6MM **Privately
Held**
WEB: www.oconnorwoods.org
SIC: 6513 Retirement hotel operation
PA: St. Joseph's Regional Housing Corpo-
ration
3400 Wagner Heights Rd
Stockton CA 95209
209 956-3400

(P-10790)
**OLIVE GROVE RETIREMENT
RESORT**
7858 California Ave, Riverside
(92504-2599)
PHONE..............................951 687-2241

Kendall Jamison, *Director*
EMP: 65 **EST:** 1982
SQ FT: 170,000
SALES (est): 3.7MM **Privately Held**
WEB: www.olivegrove.com
SIC: 6513 Retirement hotel operation

(P-10791)
PAHC APARTMENTS INC
2595 E Byshore Rd Ste 200, Palo Alto
(94303)
PHONE..............................650 321-9709
Marlene Prentergast, *President*
EMP: 50
SALES: 3.3MM **Privately Held**
SIC: 6513 Apartment building operators

(P-10792)
PANORAMA PARK APTS
401 W Columbus St Apt 64, Bakersfield
(93301-5819)
PHONE..............................661 325-4047
Latanya Gordon, *Manager*
Leeann Morein, *Partner*
EMP: 99
SALES (est): 2.4MM **Privately Held**
SIC: 6513 Apartment building operators

(P-10793)
PARK NEWPORT LTD (PA)
Also Called: Park Newport Apartments
1 Park Newport, Newport Beach
(92660-5004)
PHONE..............................949 644-1900
Gerson Bakar, *Owner*
Craig Capelouto, *Manager*
EMP: 75 **EST:** 1970
SQ FT: 10,000
SALES (est): 4.2MM **Privately Held**
WEB: www.parknewport.com
SIC: 6513 Apartment building operators

(P-10794)
PARKWAY APARTMENTS LLC
3170 Crow Canyon Pl # 165, San Ramon
(94583-1347)
PHONE..............................925 866-8429
Dennis Fuller, *Owner*
EMP: 50
SALES (est): 1.2MM **Privately Held**
SIC: 6513 Apartment building operators

(P-10795)
PARSONS GROUP INC (PA)
Also Called: Urban Group, The
1 N Calle Chavez Ste 200, Santa Barbara
(93101)
PHONE..............................805 564-3341
Robert Parsons, *President*
Alyce Parsons, *COO*
EMP: 100
SALES (est): 10.5MM **Privately Held**
WEB: www.parsonsgroupinc.com
SIC: 6513 Apartment building operators

(P-10796)
**PASEO VLG HSING PARTNERS
LP**
1115 N Citron St, Anaheim (92801-2328)
PHONE..............................714 991-9172
Jim Brooks, *Controller*
Tesa Doleman,
EMP: 50
SALES (est): 1.8MM **Privately Held**
SIC: 6513 Apartment building operators

(P-10797)
**PINOLE ASSISTED LIVING
CMNTY**
Also Called: PINOLE SENIOR VILLAGE
2850 Estates Ave, Pinole (94564-1416)
PHONE..............................510 758-1122
Tim McDonough, *President*
Melody Martini, *Vice Pres*
Debra Savoie, *Exec Dir*
EMP: 54
SALES: 4.1MM **Privately Held**
SIC: 6513 Retirement hotel operation

(P-10798)
**PIONEER TOWERS RHF
PARTNERS LP**
515 P St Ofc, Sacramento (95814-6310)
PHONE..............................916 443-6548
Laverne R Joseph, *Managing Prtnr*

Deborah Stouff, *Principal*
EMP: 50
SALES: 2.6MM **Privately Held**
SIC: 6513 Apartment building operators

(P-10799)
PLB MANAGEMENT LLC
Also Called: Park Labrea Management
6200 W 3rd St, Los Angeles (90036-3157)
PHONE.................................323 549-5400
Dan James,
Greg Holihan,
EMP: 50
SALES (est): 3.4MM **Privately Held**
WEB: www.parklabrea.com
SIC: 6513 Apartment building operators

(P-10800)
PLUMMER VLG PRESERVATION LP
15450 Plummer St, North Hills
(91343-2141)
PHONE.................................818 891-0646
Leeann Morein, *Partner*
Leeann Moreinm, *Partner*
EMP: 99
SALES: 950K **Publicly Held**
SIC: 6513 Apartment building operators
HQ: Aimco Properties, L.P.
4582 S Ulster St Ste 1100
Denver CO 80237

(P-10801)
PROVIDENT GROUP CROWN PNTE LLC
Also Called: Crown Pointe Retirement
737 Magnolia Ave Ofc, Corona
(92879-7005)
PHONE.................................951 737-7482
Steve Hicks, *Mng Member*
Kathy Franco,
Debra Lockwood,
EMP: 56
SALES (est): 3.2MM **Privately Held**
SIC: 6513 Retirement hotel operation

(P-10802)
R & B REALTY GROUP
Also Called: Oakwood Garden Apts
3600 Barham Blvd, Los Angeles
(90068-1106)
PHONE.................................323 851-3450
Tal Amquest, *Manager*
EMP: 100
SALES (corp-wide): 124.3MM **Privately Held**
SIC: 6513 Apartment building operators
PA: Oakwood Worldwide (Us) Lp
2222 Corinth Ave
Los Angeles CA 90064
800 888-0808

(P-10803)
R & B REALTY GROUP
Also Called: Oakwood Apartments
22122 Victory Blvd, Woodland Hills
(91367-1937)
PHONE.................................818 710-5400
William Frill, *Manager*
EMP: 80
SALES (corp-wide): 124.3MM **Privately Held**
SIC: 6513 Apartment building operators
PA: Oakwood Worldwide (Us) Lp
2222 Corinth Ave
Los Angeles CA 90064
800 888-0808

(P-10804)
R & B REALTY GROUP
Also Called: Oakwood Apts
4111 Via Marina, Marina Del Rey
(90292-5302)
PHONE.................................310 751-4545
Heather Hermann, *Manager*
EMP: 55
SALES (corp-wide): 124.3MM **Privately Held**
SIC: 6513 Apartment building operators
PA: Oakwood Worldwide (Us) Lp
2222 Corinth Ave
Los Angeles CA 90064
800 888-0808

(P-10805)
RAHF IV CASA PANORAMA LP
14555 Osborne St, Panorama City
(91402-1820)
PHONE.................................216 621-6060
EMP: 50
SALES (est): 498.2K **Privately Held**
SIC: 6513 Apartment building operators

(P-10806)
RAHF IV GROVE LP
227 W H St, Ontario (91762-2717)
PHONE.................................216 621-6060
Angelo Pimpas, *Principal*
EMP: 50
SALES (est): 498.2K **Privately Held**
SIC: 6513 Apartment building operators

(P-10807)
RANCE KING PROPERTIES INC (PA)
Also Called: R K Properties
3737 E Broadway, Long Beach
(90803-6104)
PHONE.................................562 240-1000
William Rance King Jr, *President*
Steve King, *Vice Pres*
Steven King, *Vice Pres*
Heather Fitzgerald, *Property Mgr*
EMP: 104
SQ FT: 5,000
SALES (est): 16.3MM **Privately Held**
WEB: www.rkprop.com
SIC: 6513 Apartment building operators

(P-10808)
REGENCY HILL ASSOCIATES
Also Called: La Mirage
6560 Ambrosia Dr, San Diego
(92124-3133)
PHONE.................................619 281-5200
David Nethercut, *President*
EMP: 58
SQ FT: 3,000
SALES (est): 3.2MM **Privately Held**
SIC: 6513 Apartment building operators

(P-10809)
RICK WEISS NEW HOPE APARTMENTS
1637 Appian Way, Santa Monica
(90401-3249)
PHONE.................................310 395-1026
Reint Alberts, *Manager*
EMP: 50
SALES: 707K **Privately Held**
SIC: 6513 Apartment building operators

(P-10810)
SAN DIMAS RETIREMENT CENTER (PA)
Also Called: Longwood Management
834 W Arrow Hwy, San Dimas
(91773-2418)
PHONE.................................909 599-8441
Frankie Ramirez, *Administration*
EMP: 70
SALES (est): 3.4MM **Privately Held**
SIC: 6513 8059 Retirement hotel operation; personal care home, with health care

(P-10811)
SATELLITE FIRST COMMUNITIES LP (PA)
1835 Alcatraz Ave, Berkeley (94703-2714)
PHONE.................................510 647-0700
Susan Friedland, *Exec Dir*
EMP: 54
SALES (est): 732.1K **Privately Held**
SIC: 6513 Apartment building operators

(P-10812)
SHOREVIEW PRESERVATION LP
35 Lillian Ct, San Francisco (94124-2822)
PHONE.................................415 647-6922
George Buchanan, *Partner*
EMP: 99
SALES: 950K **Publicly Held**
SIC: 6513 Apartment building operators
HQ: Aimco Properties, L.P.
4582 S Ulster St Ste 1100
Denver CO 80237

(P-10813)
SIGN OF DOVE
Also Called: Sunrise Retirement Villa
707 Sunrise Ave Ofc, Roseville
(95661-4531)
PHONE.................................916 786-3277
Debbie Norman, *Manager*
EMP: 60 **Privately Held**
WEB: www.signdove.com
SIC: 6513 Retirement hotel operation
PA: Sign Of The Dove
22900 Ventura Blvd # 200
Woodland Hills CA

(P-10814)
SILVERADO ORCHARDS (PA)
Also Called: Management Associates
601 Pope St Ofc, Saint Helena
(94574-1275)
P.O. Box 102 (94574-0102)
PHONE.................................707 963-1461
Alan Baldwin, *General Ptnr*
L Meade Baldwin, *General Ptnr*
EMP: 100 **EST:** 1975
SQ FT: 80,000
SALES (est): 4.9MM **Privately Held**
WEB: www.silveradoorchards.com
SIC: 6513 Retirement hotel operation

(P-10815)
SNAPDRAGON PLACE 1 LP
702 County Square Dr, Ventura
(93003-5450)
PHONE.................................805 659-3791
Nancy Conk, *Partner*
EMP: 86
SALES (est): 3.2MM **Privately Held**
SIC: 6513 Apartment building operators

(P-10816)
SOUTH BAY VLLA PRESERVATION LP
13111 S San Pedro St, Los Angeles
(90061-2760)
PHONE.................................310 516-7325
Leeann Morein, *Vice Pres*
EMP: 99
SALES: 950K **Publicly Held**
SIC: 6513 Apartment building operators
HQ: Aimco Properties, L.P.
4582 S Ulster St Ste 1100
Denver CO 80237

(P-10817)
SPRUCE GROVE INC (PA)
3719 S Plaza Dr, Santa Ana (92704-7463)
PHONE.................................714 546-4255
Jim Carter, *Principal*
Sheri Zirschky, *Regional Mgr*
Keith Landers, *Project Mgr*
Dale Godges, *Controller*
Julie Chapman, *Payroll Mgr*
EMP: 75
SALES (est): 11.4MM **Privately Held**
SIC: 6513 1522 Apartment hotel operation; apartment building construction

(P-10818)
ST JSEPHS REGIONAL HSING CORP (PA)
3400 Wagner Heights Rd, Stockton
(95209-4843)
PHONE.................................209 956-3400
Edward G Schroeder, *President*
EMP: 300
SALES: 24.6MM **Privately Held**
SIC: 6513 8741 8052 Apartment building operators; hospital management; nursing & personal care facility management; intermediate care facilities

(P-10819)
STEADFAST MANAGEMENT CO INC
Also Called: Flanders Pointe Apts
15520 Tustin Village Way, Tustin
(92780-4211)
PHONE.................................714 542-2229
EMP: 105
SALES (corp-wide): 58.7MM **Privately Held**
SIC: 6513 6531 Apartment building operators; real estate managers

PA: Steadfast Management Company, Inc.
18100 Von Karman Ave
Irvine CA 92612
949 748-3000

(P-10820)
STERLING-ASE LTD PARTNERSHIP
Also Called: Sterling Inn
17738 Francesca Rd, Victorville
(92395-5105)
PHONE.................................760 951-9507
Aaron Koelsch, *Managing Prtnr*
Bill Ziprick, *Ltd Ptnr*
EMP: 125
SQ FT: 98,000
SALES (est): 5.3MM **Privately Held**
SIC: 6513 Retirement hotel operation

(P-10821)
STONESFAIR FINANCIAL CORP
577 Airport Blvd Ste 700, Burlingame
(94010-2024)
PHONE.................................650 347-0442
Karl E Bakhtiari, *President*
Maryann Fair, *Director*
Emily Henry, *Asst Mgr*
EMP: 60
SALES (est): 936.2K **Privately Held**
WEB: www.stonesfairfinancial.com
SIC: 6513 6514 Apartment building operators; residential building, four or fewer units: operation

(P-10822)
SUMMERVILLE SENIOR LIVING INC
10615 Jordan Rd, Whittier (90603-2932)
PHONE.................................562 943-3724
Granger Cobb, *CEO*
EMP: 51
SALES (corp-wide): 4.5B **Publicly Held**
SIC: 6513 Apartment building operators
HQ: Summerville Senior Living, Inc.
3131 Elliott Ave Ste 500
Seattle WA 98121
206 298-2909

(P-10823)
SUMMERVILLE SENIOR LIVING INC
20801 Devonshire St, Chatsworth
(91311-3216)
PHONE.................................818 341-2552
Ram Nemani, *Owner*
EMP: 51
SALES (corp-wide): 4.5B **Publicly Held**
SIC: 6513 Retirement hotel operation
HQ: Summerville Senior Living, Inc.
3131 Elliott Ave Ste 500
Seattle WA 98121
206 298-2909

(P-10824)
SUNRISE RETIREMENT VILLA
707 Sunrise Ave Ofc, Roseville
(95661-4531)
PHONE.................................916 786-3277
Ed Latin, *General Ptnr*
Mike Klein, *General Ptnr*
EMP: 60
SQ FT: 180,000
SALES (est): 2.4MM **Privately Held**
SIC: 6513 Apartment building operators

(P-10825)
TANTRA LAKE PARTNERS LP
18802 Bardeen Ave, Irvine (92612-1521)
PHONE.................................949 756-5959
Sares Regis Holdings, *General Ptnr*
EMP: 120 **EST:** 1998
SALES (est): 3.6MM **Privately Held**
SIC: 6513 Apartment building operators

(P-10826)
TERRACINA MEADOWS APTS
4500 Tynebourne St F105, Sacramento
(95834-2556)
PHONE.................................916 419-0925
Gary Benn, *COO*
Tarna Sadler, *Manager*
EMP: 50
SALES (est): 1.3MM **Privately Held**
SIC: 6513 Apartment building operators

PRODUCTS & SVCS

(P-10827)
THE PINES LTD
1423 E Washington Ave, El Cajon
(92019-2559)
PHONE................................619 447-1880
Helen Sue, *Partner*
Tim Sliger, *General Mgr*
EMP: 111
SALES (est): 4.1MM **Privately Held**
SIC: 6513 Apartment building operators

(P-10828)
TOPANGA VILLAS COMPANY
Also Called: Warner Villa
5807 Topanga Canyon Blvd, Woodland Hills
(91367-4626)
PHONE................................818 884-8017
Catherine Hayes, *Partner*
Universal Properties, *Partner*
EMP: 100
SALES (est): 4.4MM **Privately Held**
SIC: 6513 Apartment building operators

(P-10829)
TPG REFLECTIONS II LLC
Also Called: Tpg/Calstrs
444 S Flower St Ste 600, Los Angeles
(90071-2907)
PHONE................................213 613-1900
James A Thomas,
Michael McGrath, *Manager*
EMP: 99
SALES: 950K **Privately Held**
SIC: 6513 Apartment building operators

(P-10830)
TREES APARTMENTS LLC
7030 Eigleberry St, Gilroy (95020-6465)
PHONE................................408 848-6400
Linda Mandolini, *President*
EMP: 99
SALES (est): 1.3MM **Privately Held**
SIC: 6513 Apartment building operators

(P-10831)
TUOLUMNE CITY INV GRP II LP
Also Called: Tuolumne Cy Senior Apartments
18402 Tuolumne Rd Apt 31, Tuolumne
(95379-9719)
PHONE................................209 928-1567
Rod Moore, *Principal*
EMP: 50
SALES (est): 872.6K **Privately Held**
SIC: 6513 Apartment building operators

(P-10832)
TURK & EDDY ASSOCIATES LP
201 Eddy St, San Francisco (94102-2715)
PHONE................................415 474-6524
Donald Falk, *Exec Dir*
EMP: 65
SALES (est): 883.8K **Privately Held**
SIC: 6513 Apartment building operators

(P-10833)
VASONA MANAGEMENT INC
Also Called: Marina Breeze
13949 Doolittle Dr, San Leandro
(94577-5548)
PHONE................................510 352-8728
Willie Johnson, *Principal*
EMP: 273
SALES (corp-wide): 37.3MM **Privately
Held**
SIC: 6513 Apartment building operators
PA: Vasona Management, Inc.
    18 E Main St
    Los Gatos CA 95030
    408 354-4200

(P-10834)
VENTAGE SENIOR HOUSING
Also Called: Avalon At Newport
4000 Hilaria Way, Newport Beach
(92663-3610)
PHONE................................949 631-3555
Mary Heilgeist, *Exec Dir*
Barbara Briscoe, *Exec Dir*
EMP: 50
SQ FT: 41,704
SALES (est): 1.8MM **Privately Held**
SIC: 6513 Retirement hotel operation

(P-10835)
**VILLA PASEO SENIOR
RESIDENCES**
Also Called: Villa Paseo Palms
2818 Ramada Dr, Paso Robles
(93446-3981)
PHONE................................805 227-4588
Jim Brooks, *Controller*
Tesa Doleman,
EMP: 99
SALES: 950K **Privately Held**
SIC: 6513 Apartment building operators

(P-10836)
VILLA SERRA CORPORATION
1320 Padre Dr Apt 103, Salinas
(93901-2162)
PHONE................................831 754-5532
Chuck Major, *Vice Pres*
EMP: 65
SQ FT: 160,000
SALES (est): 4.5MM **Privately Held**
SIC: 6513 8361 Retirement hotel opera-
tion; geriatric residential care

(P-10837)
VILLAGE GLEN APARTMENTS
633 S Pasadena Ave Apt 45, Glendora
(91740-6804)
PHONE................................626 963-4575
Julie Flores, *Manager*
EMP: 98
SALES (est): 1.5MM **Privately Held**
SIC: 6513 Apartment building operators

(P-10838)
**VINTAGE SENIOR HOUSING
LLC**
Also Called: Vintage Simi Hills
5300 E Los Angeles Ave, Simi Valley
(93063-4136)
PHONE................................805 583-3500
John Peter,
EMP: 317
SALES (corp-wide): 23.3MM **Privately
Held**
SIC: 6513 Retirement hotel operation
PA: Senior Vintage Housing Llc
    23 Corporate Plaza Dr # 190
    Newport Beach CA 92660
    949 719-4080

(P-10839)
VINTAGE SENIOR LIVING CORP
27783 Center Dr, Mission Viejo
(92692-3603)
PHONE................................949 364-6210
EMP: 75
SALES (est): 503.9K **Privately Held**
SIC: 6513 Retirement hotel operation

(P-10840)
**VINTAGE SENIOR
MANAGEMENT INC**
91 Napa Rd, Sonoma (95476-7691)
PHONE................................707 595-0009
EMP: 1161 **Privately Held**
SIC: 6513 Retirement hotel operation
PA: Senior Vintage Management Inc
    23 Corporate Plaza Dr # 190
    Newport Beach CA 92660

(P-10841)
VIVA GROUP INC
Also Called: Rent.com
11766 Wilshire Blvd # 300, Los Angeles
(90025-6570)
PHONE................................310 449-6400
Bill McKnight, *General Mgr*
Gretchen Humbert, *CFO*
Alain Avakian, *CTO*
Rosemary Ledesma, *Software Engr*
Roxanne Argana, *Accounts Exec*
EMP: 100
SALES (est): 6.8MM **Privately Held**
SIC: 6513 7375 Apartment building opera-
tors; information retrieval services

(P-10842)
WAMC COMPANY INC (PA)
Also Called: Cal West Enterprises
7420 Clairemont Mesa Blvd, San Diego
(92111-1546)
PHONE................................858 454-2753

Peter Valenti, *President*
James Bashor, *Principal*
EMP: 85
SALES (est): 1.9MM **Privately Held**
SIC: 6513 Apartment building operators

(P-10843)
**WILLIAM WARREN PROPERTIES
INC**
201 Wilshire Blvd Ste 102, Santa Monica
(90401-1220)
PHONE................................310 454-1500
William Hobin, *President*
EMP: 100
SALES (est): 6.2MM
SALES (corp-wide): 33.9MM **Privately
Held**
SIC: 6513 Apartment building operators
PA: The William Warren Group Inc
    201 Wilshire Blvd Ste 102
    Santa Monica CA 90401
    310 451-2130

(P-10844)
**WILLMARK CMMNTIES UNIV
VLG INC (PA)**
9948 Hibert St Ste 210, San Diego
(92131-1034)
PHONE................................858 271-0582
Mark Schmidt, *President*
EMP: 78
SQ FT: 2,000
SALES (est): 5.3MM **Privately Held**
SIC: 6513 1522 Apartment building opera-
tors; multi-family dwellings, new construc-
tion; condominium construction

(P-10845)
WILLOW GLEN VILLA A
1660 Gaton Dr, San Jose (95125-4534)
PHONE................................408 266-1660
EMP: 70
SQ FT: 146,000
SALES: 3MM **Privately Held**
SIC: 6513

(P-10846)
WINDHAM AT SAINT AGNES
1100 E Spruce Ave Ofc, Fresno
(93720-3314)
PHONE................................559 449-8070
Sue Hefty, *Vice Pres*
Transamerica Realty Investment, *Owner*
EMP: 66
SQ FT: 200,000
SALES (est): 3.6MM **Privately Held**
SIC: 6513 Retirement hotel operation

(P-10847)
WINNRESIDENTIAL LTD PARTNR
Also Called: Hci
255 Washington Rd, Chowchilla
(93610-1909)
PHONE................................559 665-9600
EMP: 266
SALES (corp-wide): 6.9MM **Privately
Held**
SIC: 6513 Apartment building operators
PA: Winnresidential Limited Partnership
    6 Faneuil Hall Market Pl
    Boston MA 02109
    617 742-4500

(P-10848)
**WOODLAND RESIDENTIAL
SERVICES**
Also Called: Wrs
1381 E Gum Ave, Woodland (95776-4275)
PHONE................................530 419-0059
Parm Kajley, *CEO*
Jack Kenealy, *Vice Pres*
EMP: 66
SALES (est): 3.2MM **Privately Held**
SIC: 6513 Apartment building operators

(P-10849)
WOODSPEAR PROPERTIES (PA)
810 Los Vallecitos Blvd # 214, San Marcos
(92069-1451)
PHONE................................760 761-4340
Steven Spierer, *Partner*
John A Woodward, *Partner*
Debbie Ware, *Admin Asst*
Libby Pecson, *Accounting Mgr*
Jennifer Crone, *Bookkeeper*

EMP: 50
SQ FT: 7,200
SALES (est): 4.7MM **Privately Held**
WEB: www.woodspearproperties.com
SIC: 6513 6512 Apartment building opera-
tors; nonresidential building operators

**6514 Operators Of
Dwellings, Except**

(P-10850)
**ACTION PROPERTY
MANAGEMENT INC (PA)**
2603 Main St Ste 500, Irvine (92614-4261)
PHONE................................949 450-0202
Matthew Holbrook, *CEO*
Virginia Meade, *Regional Mgr*
Patrick Anderson, *General Mgr*
Amanda Barry, *General Mgr*
Cyndi Bolander, *General Mgr*
EMP: 90
SQ FT: 18,000
SALES (est): 86.9MM
SALES (corp-wide): 95.6MM **Privately
Held**
SIC: 6514 8641 Residential building, four
or fewer units: operation; homeowners'
association

(P-10851)
**BAY AREA COMMUNITY SVCS
INC**
Also Called: Woodroe Place
22505 Woodroe Ave, Hayward
(94541-3410)
PHONE................................510 537-1688
Dan Pratt, *Exec Dir*
EMP: 180
SALES (corp-wide): 1MM **Privately Held**
SIC: 6514 Dwelling operators, except
apartments
PA: Bay Area Community Services, Inc.
    390 40th St
    Oakland CA 94609
    510 613-0330

(P-10852)
EAH INC (PA)
Also Called: Eah Housing
22 Pelican Way, San Rafael (94901-5545)
PHONE................................415 258-1800
Laura Hall, *President*
Cathy Macy, *CFO*
Alvin Bonnett, *Senior VP*
Karen Belanger, *Vice Pres*
Michael Farrel, *Vice Pres*
EMP: 70 **EST:** 1968
SQ FT: 30,000
SALES: 38.5MM **Privately Held**
WEB: www.centennialvillage.com
SIC: 6514 Residential building, four or
fewer units: operation

(P-10853)
HOME PORT INC
5030 Union Ave, San Jose (95124-5432)
PHONE................................408 377-4134
Peter Villareal, *Manager*
EMP: 99
SALES: 234.5K
SALES (corp-wide): 41.9K **Privately Held**
SIC: 6514 6513 Residential building, four
or fewer units: operation; apartment build-
ing operators
PA: Stanford Mid-Peninsula Urban Coalition
    303 Vintage Park Dr # 250
    Foster City CA 94404
    650 356-2900

(P-10854)
MENLO GATEWAY INC
Also Called: MIDPEN HOUSING
303 Vintage Park Dr # 250, Foster City
(94404-1166)
PHONE................................650 356-2900
Mark Battey, *Chairman*
Peter Villareal, *Principal*
Luina Palchak, *Manager*
EMP: 99
SALES: 31.1MM
SALES (corp-wide): 41.9K **Privately Held**
SIC: 6514 6513 Residential building, four
or fewer units: operation; apartment build-
ing operators

▲ = Import ▼=Export
◆ =Import/Export

PA: Stanford Mid-Peninsula Urban Coalition
303 Vintage Park Dr # 250
Foster City CA 94404
650 356-2900

(P-10855)
MERRILL GARDENS
Also Called: Country Suites By Carlson
2860 Country Dr Ofc, Fremont
(94536-5338)
PHONE.................................510 790-1645
Dan Bodily, *Owner*
EMP: 65
SALES (est): 1.5MM **Privately Held**
SIC: 6514 Dwelling operators, except
apartments

(P-10856)
MIDPEN RESIDENT SERVICES CORP
303 Vintage Park Dr # 250, Foster City
(94404-1166)
PHONE.................................650 356-2965
Fran Wagstaff, *President*
Lory Candelf, *Vice Pres*
EMP: 300
SALES: 6.6MM
SALES (corp-wide): 41.9K **Privately Held**
SIC: 6514 6513 Residential building, four
or fewer units: operation; apartment build-
ing operators
PA: Stanford Mid-Peninsula Urban Coalition
303 Vintage Park Dr # 250
Foster City CA 94404
650 356-2900

(P-10857)
MP MORSE COURT ASSOCIATES
Also Called: Morse Court Apartments
825 Morse Ave, Sunnyvale (94085-3070)
PHONE.................................408 734-9442
Matthew O Franklin, *Partner*
Luina Palchak, *Manager*
EMP: 99
SALES: 70K
SALES (corp-wide): 41.9K **Privately Held**
SIC: 6514 6513 Residential building, four
or fewer units: operation; apartment build-
ing operators
PA: Stanford Mid-Peninsula Urban Coalition
303 Vintage Park Dr # 250
Foster City CA 94404
650 356-2900

(P-10858)
PROFESSIONAL COMMUNITY MGT CAL
Also Called: Pcm
27051 Towne Centre Dr # 200, Foothill
Ranch (92610-2819)
PHONE.................................949 768-7261
Jeffrey Olson, *CEO*
EMP: 80
SALES (corp-wide): 55MM **Privately Held**
WEB: www.pcm-ca.com
SIC: 6514 Dwelling operators, except
apartments
PA: Professional Community Management
Of California
27051 Towne Centre Dr # 200
Foothill Ranch CA 92610
800 369-7260

(P-10859)
SARATOGA COURT INC
Also Called: MID PENN HOUSING
18855 Cox Ave, Saratoga (95070-4159)
PHONE.................................408 866-1392
Matthew Franklin, *President*
EMP: 99
SALES: 441.6K
SALES (corp-wide): 41.9K **Privately Held**
SIC: 6514 6513 Residential building, four
or fewer units: operation; apartment build-
ing operators
PA: Stanford Mid-Peninsula Urban Coalition
303 Vintage Park Dr # 250
Foster City CA 94404
650 356-2900

(P-10860)
VIVENTE 1 INC
Also Called: MIDPEN HOUSING
2400 Enborg Ln, San Jose (95128-2641)
PHONE.................................408 279-2706
Matthew O Franklin, *President*
EMP: 99
SALES: 446.8K
SALES (corp-wide): 41.9K **Privately Held**
SIC: 6514 6513 Residential building, four
or fewer units: operation; apartment build-
ing operators
PA: Stanford Mid-Peninsula Urban Coalition
303 Vintage Park Dr # 250
Foster City CA 94404
650 356-2900

(P-10861)
VIVENTE 2 INC
5347 Dent Ave, San Jose (95118-2900)
PHONE.................................408 279-2706
Matthew O Franklin, *President*
Peter Villareal, *Manager*
EMP: 99
SALES: 568.6K
SALES (corp-wide): 41.9K **Privately Held**
SIC: 6514 6513 Residential building, four
or fewer units: operation; apartment build-
ing operators
PA: Stanford Mid-Peninsula Urban Coalition
303 Vintage Park Dr # 250
Foster City CA 94404
650 356-2900

6515 Operators of Residential Mobile Home

(P-10862)
BARBACCIA PROPERTIES
Also Called: Villa Theresa Mobile Home Park
165 Blossom Hill Rd, San Jose
(95123-5938)
PHONE.................................408 225-1010
Cy Barbaccia, *Partner*
Eva Antonio, *Partner*
Lena Barbaccia, *Partner*
Lou Barbaccia, *Partner*
EMP: 80
SQ FT: 5,000
SALES: 7MM **Privately Held**
SIC: 6515 7999 Mobile home site opera-
tors; golf driving range

(P-10863)
MOBILE HM COMMUNITIES OF AMER (PA)
1122 Willow St Ste 200, San Jose
(95125-3103)
PHONE.................................408 279-5200
G Jeffery Moore, *President*
Ron Zraick, *Corp Secy*
Rudy Steadler, *Vice Pres*
EMP: 150
SALES (est): 7.9MM **Privately Held**
SIC: 6515 Mobile home site operators

(P-10864)
R C ROBERTS & CO (PA)
Also Called: Sands Rv Resort
801 A St, San Rafael (94901-3010)
PHONE.................................415 456-8600
Barbel Roberts,
Niels Roberts,
Scott Roberts,
EMP: 216 EST: 1977
SQ FT: 3,000
SALES (est): 11MM **Privately Held**
SIC: 6515 7011 6531 Mobile home site
operators; resort hotel; real estate agents
& managers

(P-10865)
WATERHOUSE MANAGEMENT CORP
500 Giuseppe Ct Ste 2, Roseville
(95678-6305)
PHONE.................................916 772-4918
Kenneth Watershouse, *President*
EMP: 150
SQ FT: 10,000
SALES (est): 10MM **Privately Held**
SIC: 6515 Mobile home site operators

6519 Lessors Of Real Estate, NEC

(P-10866)
711 HOPE LP
3470 Wilshire Blvd # 700, Los Angeles
(90010-2207)
PHONE.................................213 365-5000
Pat Birgham, *Partner*
EMP: 250
SALES (est): 12.3MM **Privately Held**
SIC: 6519 6512 Real property lessors;
commercial & industrial building operation

(P-10867)
A G PACEMAN INC
1100 Industrial Rd Ste 11, San Carlos
(94070-4131)
PHONE.................................650 592-7282
Darrell W Leong, *President*
Anna Leong, *Treasurer*
EMP: 55
SQ FT: 30,000
SALES (est): 2.6MM **Privately Held**
SIC: 6519 Real property lessors

(P-10868)
AB/SW 70 S LAKE OWNER LLC
70 S Lake Ave, Pasadena (91101-4703)
PHONE.................................650 571-2200
Nancy Chau, *Vice Pres*
EMP: 50
SALES (est): 468.4K **Privately Held**
SIC: 6519 Real property lessors

(P-10869)
CALIFORNIA PARKING COMPANY (PA)
Also Called: Dnj Parking
768 Sansome St, San Francisco
(94111-1704)
P.O. Box 2882 (94126-2882)
PHONE.................................415 781-4896
Richard Puccinelli, *President*
Ron Britz, *Vice Pres*
Ronald Britz, *Vice Pres*
Robert Puccinelli, *Vice Pres*
EMP: 90
SQ FT: 1,300
SALES (est): 4.8MM **Privately Held**
WEB: www.californiaparking.com
SIC: 6519 6512 7521 Real property
lessors; nonresidential building operators;
parking lots

(P-10870)
COLTON REAL ESTATE GROUP (PA)
Also Called: Mvp Partners
515 Cabrillo Park Dr # 305, Santa Ana
(92701-5016)
PHONE.................................949 475-4200
Dave Colton, *President*
John Mc Clintock, *CFO*
John McClintock, *Vice Pres*
Nancy Dang, *Administration*
Joe Campion, *Facilities Dir*
EMP: 55
SQ FT: 7,000
SALES (est): 7.1MM **Privately Held**
SIC: 6519 Real property lessors

(P-10871)
EASTLAND TOWER PARTNERSHIP
Also Called: Eastland Executive Office
1932 E Garvey Ave S, West Covina
(91791-1910)
PHONE.................................626 858-2000
Ziad Alahassen, *Partner*
EMP: 50
SALES (est): 2MM **Privately Held**
SIC: 6519 Real property lessors

(P-10872)
ELEVATE PROPERTY SERVICES LP
19700 Fairchild Ste 150, Irvine
(92612-2500)
PHONE.................................562 219-2101
Andrew Layland, *Principal*
Kerrigan Capital LLC, *General Ptnr*
EMP: 50

SALES (est): 2.5MM **Privately Held**
SIC: 6519 Real property lessors

(P-10873)
EVERETT MALL 01 LLC
12411 Ventura Blvd, Studio City
(91604-2407)
PHONE.................................818 505-6777
Alan Fox,
Eric Diamond, *COO*
EMP: 50
SALES (est): 1.1MM **Privately Held**
SIC: 6519 Real property lessors

(P-10874)
FREMONT REALTY CAPITAL LP
199 Fremont St Fl 19, San Francisco
(94105-2255)
PHONE.................................415 284-8665
Claude J Zinngrabe Jr, *Managing Prtnr*
Victor Kwok, *CFO*
Josh Dobies, *Vice Pres*
Brett Nissenberg, *Vice Pres*
David Peranich, *Vice Pres*
EMP: 73
SQ FT: 100,000
SALES (est): 3.4MM
SALES (corp-wide): 38.9MM **Privately Held**
WEB: www.fremontrealtycapital.com
SIC: 6519 8742 Real property lessors;
real estate consultant
PA: Fremont Group, L.L.C.
199 Fremont St Fl 19
San Francisco CA 94105
415 284-8880

(P-10875)
IC BP III HOLDINGS XV LLC
1 Sansome St Fl 15, San Francisco
(94104-4448)
PHONE.................................415 273-4250
Ray Kim, *Principal*
Mark Bailey,
EMP: 50 EST: 2015
SALES (est): 1MM **Privately Held**
SIC: 6519 7389 Sub-lessors of real estate;

(P-10876)
LAACO LTD (PA)
Also Called: Storage West
431 W 7th St, Los Angeles (90014-1601)
PHONE.................................213 622-1254
Karen L Hathaway, *President*
Bryan J Cusworth, *CFO*
John K Hathaway, *Vice Pres*
Steven K Hathaway, *Vice Pres*
Marcy Segura, *Admin Asst*
EMP: 125
SQ FT: 100,000
SALES (est): 22.6MM **Privately Held**
SIC: 6519 7997 7011 5812 Real property
lessors; yacht club; membership; hotels;
resort hotel; eating places

(P-10877)
LYON REALTY
4340 Golden Center Dr A, Placerville
(95667-6280)
PHONE.................................530 295-4444
Michael Levedahl, *CFO*
Mary Meyer, *Broker*
Cathy Harrington, *Marketing Staff*
EMP: 124 **Privately Held**
SIC: 6519 6531 Real property lessors;
real estate brokers & agents
PA: Lyon Realty
2280 Del Paso Rd Ste 100
Sacramento CA 95834

(P-10878)
MAXIMUS REAL ESTATE PARTNERS
1 Maritime Plz Ste 1900, San Francisco
(94111-3509)
PHONE.................................415 584-4832
Robert Rosania, *CEO*
Seth Mallen, *Treasurer*
Ramon Godinez, *Director*
Jessica Wiley, *Manager*
EMP: 100
SALES (est): 1.3MM **Privately Held**
SIC: 6519 Sub-lessors of real estate

(P-10879)
MT EDEN NURSERY CO INC (PA)
2124 Bering Dr, San Jose (95131-2013)
PHONE..........................408 213-5777
Yoshimi Shibata, *President*
Lori Librero, *Sales Staff*
EMP: 50
SALES (est): 2.8MM **Privately Held**
SIC: 6519 Farm land leasing

(P-10880)
OCEAN VIEW MANOR LP
Also Called: Ocean View Manor Apartments
3533 Empleo St, San Luis Obispo
(93401-7334)
PHONE..........................805 781-3088
John Fowler, *CEO*
EMP: 70 EST: 2016
SQ FT: 10,000
SALES (est): 587.4K **Privately Held**
SIC: 6519 Real property lessors

(P-10881)
PACIFIC EQUITIES CAPTL
Also Called: V G Pacific Equities
1640 S Sepulveda Blvd # 308, Los Angeles
(90025-7510)
P.O. Box 25991 (90025-0991)
PHONE..........................310 477-5300
David S Rosen, *President*
Jennifer Rider, *Partner*
Hunter Nickell, *Vice Pres*
Richard Steiner, *Vice Pres*
Laura Flynn, *Executive*
EMP: 75
SALES (est): 4.7MM **Privately Held**
WEB: www.pacificequities.net
SIC: 6519 Landholding office

(P-10882)
PACIFIC YGNACIO CORPORATION
201 California St Ste 500, San Francisco
(94111-5028)
PHONE..........................925 939-3275
Robin Andrews, *Manager*
EMP: 61 EST: 1998
SQ FT: 105,495
SALES (est): 1.7MM **Privately Held**
WEB: www.paceagle.com
SIC: 6519 Real property lessors
PA: Pacific Eagle Holdings Corporation
353 Sacramento St # 1788
San Francisco CA 94111

(P-10883)
PLDA INC
2570 N 1st St 218, San Jose (95131-1035)
PHONE..........................408 273-4528
Jean-Yves Brena, *President*
Jerry Ardizzone, *Vice Pres*
Francesca Spigarelli, *Admin Mgr*
Gael Paul, *CTO*
EMP: 55
SALES (est): 1.8MM **Privately Held**
WEB: www.plda.com
SIC: 6519 Real property lessors

6531 Real Estate Agents & Managers

(P-10884)
1370 REALTY CORP
14545 Friar St Ste 101, Van Nuys
(91411-2357)
PHONE..........................818 817-0092
Kambiz Merabi, *President*
EMP: 180
SQ FT: 16,400
SALES: 4.9MM **Privately Held**
SIC: 6531 Real estate agents & managers

(P-10885)
1524 ABBOT KINNEY LLC
1746 Abbot Kinney Blvd, Venice
(90291-4839)
PHONE..........................310 907-6517
Tami Pardee, *Mng Member*
Brian Buxton, *Client Mgr*
EMP: 60 EST: 2015
SALES (est): 1.5MM **Privately Held**
SIC: 6531 Real estate agent, commercial

(P-10886)
1755 EFM 1 LLC
1755 Kings Way, Los Angeles (90069)
PHONE..........................323 231-4174
Tim English,
Timothy English,
EMP: 70
SALES (est): 1.8MM **Privately Held**
SIC: 6531 6513 Rental agent, real estate;
apartment building operators

(P-10887)
2300 WEST EL SECUNDO LP
11916 Eucalyptus Ave, Hawthorne
(90250-2820)
PHONE..........................310 769-6669
Evelyn Revellame, *Controller*
EMP: 99
SALES (est): 2.1MM **Privately Held**
SIC: 6531 Real estate managers

(P-10888)
A F GILMORE COMPANY
6301 W 3rd St, Los Angeles (90036-3154)
P.O. Box 480314 (90048-1314)
PHONE..........................323 939-1191
Henry Hilty Jr, *President*
Ernest Mauritson, *Vice Pres*
Leonora Wojciechowska, *Executive Asst*
EMP: 55 EST: 1915
SALES (est): 7.7MM **Privately Held**
SIC: 6531 Real estate managers

(P-10889)
A G SPANOS MANAGEMENT INC
10100 Trinity Pkwy Fl 5, Stockton
(95219-7242)
P.O. Box 7126 (95267-0126)
PHONE..........................209 478-7954
Alexander G Spanos, *President*
Jeremiah T Murphy, *CFO*
George Spanos, *Corp Secy*
EMP: 50
SQ FT: 5,000
SALES (est): 1.7MM **Privately Held**
SIC: 6531 Real estate managers
PA: A.G. Spanos Companies
10100 Trinity Pkwy Fl 5
Stockton CA 95219

(P-10890)
ABODE COMMUNITIES
1149 S Hill St Fl 7, Los Angeles
(90015-2219)
PHONE..........................213 629-2702
Robin Hughes, *President*
Rick Saperstein, *CFO*
Kenneth Krug, *Chairman*
Sandra Kulli, *Chairman*
Gio Aliano, *Vice Pres*
▲ EMP: 150
SQ FT: 10,094
SALES: 6.3MM **Privately Held**
SIC: 6531 8712 8711 Housing authority
operator; architectural services; engineer-
ing services

(P-10891)
ACTUAL REALITY PICTURES INC
Also Called: The Residence
16030 Ventura Blvd # 380, Encino
(91436-2778)
PHONE..........................818 325-8800
Rj Cutler, *President*
EMP: 50
SALES (est): 1.8MM **Privately Held**
SIC: 6531 Real estate agent, residential

(P-10892)
ADAMS & BARNES INC
Also Called: Century 21
433 W Foothill Blvd, Monrovia
(91016-2025)
PHONE..........................626 358-1858
Lou Jean Barnes, *President*
Andrew Barnes, *Treasurer*
Thomas E Adams, *Vice Pres*
Stone Bradley, *Sales Staff*
EMP: 50
SALES (est): 3.9MM **Privately Held**
WEB: www.c21ab.com
SIC: 6531 Real estate agent, residential

(P-10893)
AFFORDABLE HSING KEY PARTNERS
815 W Ocean Ave, Lompoc (93436-6526)
PHONE..........................805 736-3423
Fred Lamont, *Exec Dir*
Mark Manion, *Agent*
EMP: 86
SALES (est): 2MM **Privately Held**
SIC: 6531 Housing authority operator

(P-10894)
AGUA CALIENTE DEVELOPMENT AUTH
5401 Dinah Shore Dr, Palm Springs
(92264-5970)
PHONE..........................760 699-6800
Richard M Milanovich, *Chairman*
EMP: 99
SALES (est): 6MM
SALES (corp-wide): 202.5MM **Privately Held**
SIC: 6531 Real estate leasing & rentals
PA: Agua Caliente Band Of Cahuilla Indi-
ans
5401 Dinah Shore Dr
Palm Springs CA 92264
760 699-6800

(P-10895)
ALAIN PINEL REALTORS
Junipero Between 5 & 6 # 56, Carmel
(93921)
PHONE..........................831 622-1040
Ron Kirendole, *Manager*
EMP: 65
SALES (est): 2.6MM **Privately Held**
SIC: 6531 Real estate brokers & agents

(P-10896)
ALAIN PINEL REALTORS INC
2001 Union St Ste 200, San Francisco
(94123-4135)
PHONE..........................415 814-6690
Paul Hulme, *CEO*
CRS Faught, *Vice Pres*
Mary Gebhardt, *Vice Pres*
Mark Bonn, *Managing Dir*
Elena Elsoukov, *Accountant*
EMP: 62
SALES (corp-wide): 11.8MM **Privately Held**
SIC: 6531 Real estate brokers & agents
PA: Alain Pinel Realtors, Inc.
12772 Sartga Snyvl Rd # 1000
Saratoga CA 95070
408 741-1111

(P-10897)
ALAIN PINEL REALTORS INC
626 Tamalpais Dr, Corte Madera
(94925-1633)
PHONE..........................415 755-1111
Steve Dickason, *Vice Pres*
Beth Brody, *Sales Staff*
Cecile Hawkins, *Sales Staff*
EMP: 62
SALES (corp-wide): 11.8MM **Privately Held**
SIC: 6531 Real estate brokers & agents
PA: Alain Pinel Realtors, Inc.
12772 Sartga Snyvl Rd # 1000
Saratoga CA 95070
408 741-1111

(P-10898)
ALAIN PINEL REALTORS INC
520 S El Camino Real # 100, San Mateo
(94402-1714)
PHONE..........................650 548-1111
Ron Gable, *Manager*
Aimee Kevorkian, *Executive Asst*
Gregory Terry, *Info Tech Mgr*
Anna Wong, *Broker*
Robin Wrigley, *Broker*
EMP: 70
SALES (corp-wide): 11.8MM **Privately Held**
SIC: 6531 Real estate brokers & agents
PA: Alain Pinel Realtors, Inc.
12772 Sartga Snyvl Rd # 1000
Saratoga CA 95070
408 741-1111

(P-10899)
ALAIN PINEL REALTORS INC
750 University Ave # 150, Los Gatos
(95032-7697)
PHONE..........................408 358-1111
Jeff Barnett, *Manager*
Mikala Caune, *Sales Staff*
Theresa Balandra, *Senior Mgr*
Alex Bouja, *Real Est Agnt*
Sandhya Murthy, *Real Est Agnt*
EMP: 55
SALES (corp-wide): 11.8MM **Privately Held**
SIC: 6531 Real estate brokers & agents
PA: Alain Pinel Realtors, Inc.
12772 Sartga Snyvl Rd # 1000
Saratoga CA 95070
408 741-1111

(P-10900)
ALAIN PINEL REALTORS INC
2911 Cleveland Ave, Santa Rosa
(95403-2715)
PHONE..........................707 636-3800
Dennis Park, *Branch Mgr*
EMP: 51
SALES (corp-wide): 11.8MM **Privately Held**
SIC: 6531 Real estate brokers & agents
PA: Alain Pinel Realtors, Inc.
12772 Sartga Snyvl Rd # 1000
Saratoga CA 95070
408 741-1111

(P-10901)
ALAIN PINEL REALTORS INC
900 Main St Ste 101, Pleasanton
(94566-6073)
PHONE..........................925 251-1111
Carol Rodoni, *Owner*
EMP: 62
SALES (corp-wide): 11.8MM **Privately Held**
SIC: 6531 Real estate brokers & agents
PA: Alain Pinel Realtors, Inc.
12772 Sartga Snyvl Rd # 1000
Saratoga CA 95070
408 741-1111

(P-10902)
ALAIN PINEL REALTORS INC
1440 Chapin Ave Ste 200, Burlingame
(94010-4011)
PHONE..........................650 375-1111
Janice Woods, *Branch Mgr*
Naomi Gable, *Sales Staff*
Susie Montgelas, *Sales Staff*
EMP: 62
SALES (corp-wide): 11.8MM **Privately Held**
SIC: 6531 Real estate brokers & agents
PA: Alain Pinel Realtors, Inc.
12772 Sartga Snyvl Rd # 1000
Saratoga CA 95070
408 741-1111

(P-10903)
ALAIN PINEL REALTORS INC
578 University Ave, Palo Alto (94301-1901)
PHONE..........................650 323-1111
Robert Gerlach, *Manager*
EMP: 120
SALES (corp-wide): 11.8MM **Privately Held**
SIC: 6531 Real estate brokers & agents
PA: Alain Pinel Realtors, Inc.
12772 Sartga Snyvl Rd # 1000
Saratoga CA 95070
408 741-1111

(P-10904)
ALAIN PINEL REALTORS INC
167 S San Antonio Rd # 1, Los Altos
(94022-3055)
PHONE..........................650 941-1111
Gary Wheeler, *Manager*
Jeff Stricker, *Broker*
Crystle Borrego, *Sales Associate*
EMP: 100
SALES (corp-wide): 11.8MM **Privately Held**
SIC: 6531 Real estate brokers & agents
PA: Alain Pinel Realtors, Inc.
12772 Sartga Snyvl Rd # 1000
Saratoga CA 95070
408 741-1111

(P-10905)
ALAIN PINEL REALTORS INC
1550 El Camino Real # 100, Menlo Park (94025-4117)
PHONE....................650 462-1111
Mary Gebhardt, *Manager*
EMP: 80
SALES (corp-wide): 11.8MM **Privately Held**
SIC: 6531 Real estate brokers & agents
PA: Alain Pinel Realtors, Inc.
12772 Sartga Snyvl Rd # 1000
Saratoga CA 95070
408 741-1111

(P-10906)
ALAMEDA PRODUCE MARKET LLC
761 Terminal St Ste 2, Los Angeles (90021-1111)
PHONE....................213 221-3400
Richard Meruelo,
Miguel Echemendia, *Vice Pres*
EMP: 80 **EST:** 1997
SQ FT: 22,000
SALES (est): 4.6MM **Privately Held**
SIC: 6531 Real estate agent, commercial

(P-10907)
ALLIANCE BAY FUNDING INC
37600 Central Ct Ste 264, Newark (94560-3440)
PHONE....................510 742-6600
Dawar Lodin, *President*
EMP: 90
SALES (est): 4.7MM **Privately Held**
SIC: 6531 Real estate agents & managers

(P-10908)
ALLIANT ASSET MGT CO LLC (PA)
21600 Oxnard St Ste 1200, Woodland Hills (91367-4949)
PHONE....................818 668-2805
Shawn Horwitz, *Mng Member*
Hammad Graham, *Vice Pres*
Brett Flanders, *Analyst*
Scott Koticks,
Matthew Breiner, *Sr Project Mgr*
EMP: 81
SQ FT: 19,816
SALES (est): 20.3MM **Privately Held**
SIC: 6531 Broker of manufactured homes, on site

(P-10909)
ALLMARK INC (PA)
10070 Arrow Rte, Rancho Cucamonga (91730-4194)
PHONE....................909 989-7556
Wayne Slavitt, *CEO*
Michael Krcelic, *President*
Pat Price, *CFO*
Steve Strebel, *CFO*
Michael Payne, *Treasurer*
EMP: 65
SQ FT: 3,167
SALES (est): 9.1MM **Privately Held**
WEB: www.allmarkproperties.com
SIC: 6531 Real estate managers

(P-10910)
ALTERA REAL ESTATE
33522 Niguel Rd Ste 200, Dana Point (92629-4009)
PHONE....................949 547-7351
Matt Brabeck, *Principal*
EMP: 356 **EST:** 2008
SALES (est): 6.5MM **Privately Held**
SIC: 6531 Buying agent, real estate

(P-10911)
ALTON MANAGEMENT CORPORATION (PA)
7532 Macarthur Blvd, Oakland (94605-2938)
PHONE....................510 663-0177
Alfred Reynolds, *CEO*
Arnold Raynolds, *President*
William R Hutton, *Vice Pres*
Latisha Woods, *Administration*
Santos Lam, *Controller*
EMP: 85
SQ FT: 5,000
SALES (est): 7.2MM **Privately Held**
WEB: www.altoncorp.com
SIC: 6531 Real estate managers

(P-10912)
AMARIK PROPERTIES INC (PA)
Also Called: A P I Property Management
1400 Bristol St N Ste 220, Newport Beach (92660-2965)
PHONE....................714 505-5200
Richard Hauer, *President*
Margie Tabrizi, *VP Opers*
EMP: 75
SALES (est): 5.6MM **Privately Held**
SIC: 6531 Real estate managers

(P-10913)
AMERICAN MARKETING SYSTEMS INC
Also Called: Amsi Real Estate Services
2800 Van Ness Ave, San Francisco (94109-1426)
PHONE....................800 747-7784
Zoya Lee Smithton, *Director*
Robb Fleischer, *Director*
EMP: 75
SQ FT: 8,000
SALES (est): 20MM **Privately Held**
WEB: www.amsisf.com
SIC: 6531 Real estate brokers & agents

(P-10914)
AMERICAN REALTY CENTRE INC
120 S Glendale Ave, Glendale (91205-1195)
PHONE....................323 666-6111
Peter P Chorebanian, *President*
EMP: 55
SQ FT: 1,961
SALES (est): 3.2MM **Privately Held**
WEB: www.americanrealtycentre.com
SIC: 6531 Real estate agent, residential

(P-10915)
APPRAISER LOFT LLC
3027 Townsgate Rd Ste 140, Westlake Village (91361-5871)
PHONE....................858 832-8334
Aman Makka, *Mng Member*
EMP: 50 **EST:** 2007
SQ FT: 20,000
SALES (est): 2.6MM **Privately Held**
SIC: 6531 Appraiser, real estate

(P-10916)
ARCADIA MANAGEMENT SERVICE CO
5185 Cherry Ave Ste 10, San Jose (95118-3783)
P.O. Box 5368 (95150-5368)
PHONE....................408 286-4440
Michael Fletcher, *President*
EMP: 50
SALES (est): 3.1MM **Privately Held**
SIC: 6531 Cooperative apartment manager

(P-10917)
AREA HOUSING AUTHORITY (PA)
1400 W Hillcrest Dr, Newbury Park (91320-2721)
PHONE....................805 480-9991
Douglas A Tapking, *Exec Dir*
George McGehee, *General Mgr*
Alexandria Banks, *Executive Asst*
Dennise Avila, *Info Tech Mgr*
EMP: 50
SQ FT: 24,000
SALES (est): 38.8MM **Privately Held**
WEB: www.ahacv.org
SIC: 6531 Housing authority operator

(P-10918)
ARGENT MANAGEMENT CO LLC
2392 Morse Ave, Irvine (92614-6234)
PHONE....................949 777-4070
Rosemarie Dyvig, *Mng Member*
Frank Faye, *CFO*
Joe Garcia, *Vice Pres*
Tara Sheehan, *Vice Pres*
Steve Elieff,
EMP: 72
SALES (est): 8.5MM **Privately Held**
SIC: 6531 Rental agent, real estate

(P-10919)
ARGON ENTERPRISES INC
Also Called: Pacific Properties Realty
13658 Hawthorne Blvd, Hawthorne (90250-5824)
PHONE....................310 349-8777
Armando Gonzalez, *President*
EMP: 92
SQ FT: 5,000
SALES (est): 2.9MM **Privately Held**
SIC: 6531 Multiple listing service, real estate

(P-10920)
ARROYO & COATES INC
425 California St # 2000, San Francisco (94104-2102)
PHONE....................415 445-7800
Tom Coates, *Ch of Bd*
Brad Colton, *President*
Pedro Arroyo, *Corp Secy*
EMP: 60
SQ FT: 7,500
SALES (est): 3.3MM **Privately Held**
WEB: www.acventures.com
SIC: 6531 Real estate brokers & agents

(P-10921)
ASSOCIATED REALTORS
27411 Viana, Mission Viejo (92692-3211)
PHONE....................949 813-1888
Heleen Chaban, *Partner*
Helene Chaban, *Partner*
Edward Coury, *Partner*
EMP: 80 **EST:** 1976
SQ FT: 5,000
SALES (est): 5MM **Privately Held**
WEB: www.ocrelocate.com
SIC: 6531 Real estate brokers & agents

(P-10922)
ASTRO REALTY INC
Also Called: Century 21
11305 183rd St, Cerritos (90703-5434)
PHONE....................562 924-3381
Louis Rosencrance, *President*
EMP: 65
SALES (est): 2MM **Privately Held**
SIC: 6531 Real estate agent, residential

(P-10923)
ATLAS HOSPITALITY GROUP
1901 Main St Ste 175, Irvine (92614-0517)
PHONE....................949 622-3400
Alan Reay, *President*
S Shah, *Vice Pres*
EMP: 90
SALES (est): 1.2MM **Privately Held**
WEB: www.atlashospitality.com
SIC: 6531 Real estate agent, commercial

(P-10924)
AUCHANTE INC
Also Called: Remax VIP
6730 Florence Ave, Bell Gardens (90201-4946)
PHONE....................562 231-1880
Eliazar Felix, *President*
Maria Felix, *Vice Pres*
EMP: 75
SQ FT: 15,000
SALES (est): 2.9MM **Privately Held**
SIC: 6531 Real estate agent, residential

(P-10925)
AUCTIONCOM INC
1 Mauchly Ste 27, Irvine (92618-2305)
PHONE....................800 499-6199
Jeffrey Frieden, *CEO*
Jake Seid, *President*
James Corum, *COO*
Tim Morse, *CFO*
Virginia Pierce, *CFO*
EMP: 200
SQ FT: 18,000
SALES (est): 14.2MM **Privately Held**
WEB: WWW.AUCTION.COM
SIC: 6531 Auction, real estate

(P-10926)
AUCTIONCOM LLC
Also Called: Ten-X
3050 S Del St Ste 201, San Mateo (94403)
PHONE....................949 609-5376
EMP: 163 **Privately Held**
SIC: 6531 Real estate agents & managers

PA: Auction.Com, Llc
1 Mauchly
Irvine CA 92618
-

(P-10927)
AUCTIONCOM LLC
Also Called: Ten-X
3501 Jamboree Rd Ste 5000, Newport Beach (92660-2959)
PHONE....................949 609-5376
EMP: 81 **Privately Held**
SIC: 6531 Real estate brokers & agents
PA: Auction.Com, Llc
1 Mauchly
Irvine CA 92618

(P-10928)
AUCTIONCOM LLC (PA)
1 Mauchly, Irvine (92618-2305)
PHONE....................949 859-2777
Monte J M Koch, *CEO*
Jeffrey Frieden, *CEO*
Min Alexander, *COO*
Jim Corum, *COO*
Daniel Culler, *COO*
EMP: 83
SALES (est): 170.7MM **Privately Held**
SIC: 6531 Real estate agents & managers

(P-10929)
AVALONBAY COMMUNITIES INC
Also Called: Avalon At Penasquitos Hills
2050 Main St Ste 1200, Irvine (92614-8280)
PHONE....................949 955-6200
Chris Payne, *Vice Pres*
EMP: 50
SALES (corp-wide): 2.2B **Publicly Held**
WEB: www.avalonbay.com
SIC: 6531 Real estate managers
PA: Avalonbay Communities, Inc.
671 N Glebe Rd Ste 800
Arlington VA 22203
703 329-6300

(P-10930)
AVANTRA REAL ESTATE SERVICES
Also Called: Avantra Financial
148 E Fthill Blvd Ste 100, Arcadia (91006)
PHONE....................626 357-7028
Robert B Doeppel, *CEO*
Vicky Hansen, *President*
Debbie Bello, *Treasurer*
Gina Olivares, *Admin Sec*
EMP: 50
SQ FT: 1,800
SALES: 35MM **Privately Held**
WEB: www.avantrahomes.com
SIC: 6531 Real estate brokers & agents

(P-10931)
B F MANAGEMENT
117 N Fuller Ave, Los Angeles (90036-2811)
PHONE....................323 931-7776
Chaim Freeman, *Owner*
EMP: 70
SQ FT: 1,000
SALES (est): 990K **Privately Held**
SIC: 6531 Real estate agents & managers

(P-10932)
BARCELON ASSOCIATES MGT CORP
590 Lennon Ln Ste 110, Walnut Creek (94598-5923)
PHONE....................925 627-7000
Mark Barcelon, *CEO*
Sandy Barcelon, *Co-CEO*
Sean Barcelon, *Director*
Barry Cammer, *Director*
Ryan Geer, *Manager*
EMP: 250
SQ FT: 3,000
SALES (est): 2.8MM **Privately Held**
WEB: www.barcelon.com
SIC: 6531 Real estate managers

P
R
O
D
U
C
T
S
&
S
V
C
S

(P-10933)
BAYCO FINANCIAL CORPORATION (PA)
24050 Madison St Ste 101, Torrance
(90505-6016)
PHONE..................................310 378-8181
Brenda McKenneth, *President*
Robert Cohen, *Ch of Bd*
Sheri Pfau, *Treasurer*
Mary Colin, *Vice Pres*
Karen Botchin, *Manager*
EMP: 53
SALES (est): 2MM **Privately Held**
SIC: 6531 Real estate managers

(P-10934)
BEETHOVEN HOLDINGS INC
Also Called: Keller William Realty
400 E Main St Ste 110, Visalia
(93291-6320)
PHONE..................................559 733-4100
Albert Meggers, *Principal*
Daisy Aldaco, *Real Est Agnt*
Kimberly Hogue, *Real Est Agnt*
Lynne Kendrick, *Real Est Agnt*
Rudy Martinez, *Real Est Agnt*
EMP: 250 **EST:** 2007
SALES (est): 12.2MM **Privately Held**
SIC: 6531 Real estate agent, residential

(P-10935)
BEITLER & ASSOCIATES INC (PA)
Also Called: Beitler Commercial Realty Svcs
825 S Barrington Ave, Los Angeles
(90049-6759)
PHONE..................................310 820-2955
Barry Beitler, *CEO*
Robert H Sargent, *CFO*
Robert Sargent, *CFO*
Tony Dorn, *Exec VP*
Willa Fields, *Exec VP*
EMP: 120 **EST:** 1980
SQ FT: 13,000
SALES (est): 10.3MM **Privately Held**
WEB: www.beitler.com
SIC: 6531 Real estate agent, commercial

(P-10936)
BERKELEY 75 HSING PARTNERS LP
1936 University Ave # 130, Berkeley
(94704-1054)
PHONE..................................510 705-1488
Jim Brooks, *Controller*
EMP: 50 **EST:** 2014
SALES (est): 1.7MM **Privately Held**
SIC: 6531 Real estate agents & managers

(P-10937)
BERKSHIRE HATTAWAY HOME SERVCS
Also Called: Mulhearn Group
16404 Colima Rd, Hacienda Heights
(91745-5502)
PHONE..................................626 913-2808
Bruce Mulhearn, *President*
James Liao, *Admin Sec*
Alex Vidaurrazaga, *Broker*
Carlos Brito, *Real Est Agnt*
Linda Haslim, *Real Est Agnt*
EMP: 75
SALES (est): 3MM **Privately Held**
SIC: 6531 Real estate agent, residential

(P-10938)
BERRO MANAGEMENT
3950 Parmnt Blvd Ste 115, Lakewood
(90712)
PHONE..................................562 432-3444
Jack Berro, *President*
EMP: 52
SQ FT: 2,000
SALES (est): 2.9MM **Privately Held**
SIC: 6531 Real estate managers

(P-10939)
BETTER HOMES AND GARDENS MASON
5887 Lone Tree Way Ste A, Antioch
(94531-8625)
PHONE..................................925 776-2740
Melody Royal, *Manager*
Melissa Case, *Real Est Agnt*

Julie Georgiou, *Real Est Agnt*
EMP: 60 **EST:** 2010
SALES (est): 1.3MM **Privately Held**
SIC: 6531 Real estate agent, residential

(P-10940)
BEVERLYWOOD REALTY INC
2800 S Robertson Blvd, Los Angeles
(90034-2406)
PHONE..................................310 836-8322
Stanley Shapiro, *President*
EMP: 50
SALES (est): 1.8MM **Privately Held**
WEB: www.beverlywoodha.com
SIC: 6531 Real estate brokers & agents

(P-10941)
BIOMED REALTY TRUST INC
7677 Gateway Blvd Ste 100, Newark
(94560-1190)
PHONE..................................510 505-0932
EMP: 56
SALES (corp-wide): 674.6MM **Privately Held**
SIC: 6531 Real estate brokers & agents
PA: Biomed Realty Trust, Inc.
   17190 Bernardo Center Dr
   San Diego CA 92128
   858 485-9840

(P-10942)
BLACK KNGHT RE DATA SLTONS LLC (DH)
Also Called: Black Knight Data & Analytics
121 Theory Ste 100, Irvine (92617-3209)
PHONE..................................626 808-9000
Anthony Jabbour, *CEO*
EMP: 4200
SALES (est): 599.3K
SALES (corp-wide): 1.1B **Publicly Held**
SIC: 6531 Real estate listing services
HQ: Black Knight Financial Services, Inc.
   601 Riverside Ave
   Jacksonville FL 32204
   904 854-5100

(P-10943)
BLACKROCK HOLDCO 2 INC
Also Called: Metrick Property Management
50 California St Ste 200, San Francisco
(94111-4605)
PHONE..................................415 678-2000
Ron Zuzack, *Director*
EMP: 80 **Publicly Held**
WEB: www.blackrock.com
SIC: 6531 Real estate managers
HQ: Blackrock Holdco 2, Inc.
   40 E 52nd St
   New York NY 10022
   212 754-5300

(P-10944)
BLAYNE PACELLI
12345 Ventura Blvd Ste A, Studio City
(91604-2511)
PHONE..................................310 383-6281
Blayne Joseph Pacelli, *Owner*
EMP: 85
SALES (est): 1.3MM **Privately Held**
SIC: 6531 Real estate brokers & agents

(P-10945)
BMR 21 ERIE ST LLC
17190 Bernardo Center Dr, San Diego
(92128-7030)
PHONE..................................858 485-9840
Alan D Gold, *CEO*
EMP: 71
SALES (est): 404.8K
SALES (corp-wide): 674.6MM **Privately Held**
SIC: 6531 Real estate brokers & agents
HQ: Biomed Realty, L.P.
   17190 Bernardo Center Dr
   San Diego CA 92128
   858 485-9840

(P-10946)
BNC REAL ESTATE (PA)
Also Called: Nussbaum, Barry Company
990 Highland Dr Ste 203, Solana Beach
(92075-2427)
PHONE..................................858 481-3000
Barry Nussbaum, *President*
Richard Gelbart, *Senior VP*
EMP: 300

SQ FT: 900
SALES (est): 16.3MM **Privately Held**
WEB: www.bncrealestate.com
SIC: 6531 Real estate managers; real estate investors, except property operators

(P-10947)
BPAZ HOLDINGS 2 LLC
1 Sansome St Ste 1500, San Francisco
(94104-4449)
PHONE..................................972 354-6250
Matt Novak,
EMP: 50
SALES (est): 620.3K
SALES (corp-wide): 1MM **Privately Held**
SIC: 6531 Real estate agents & managers
PA: Bkly Ptn Crps Idst Ptshp Llc
   1 Sansome St Ste 1500
   San Francisco CA 94104
   972 354-6250

(P-10948)
BROSAMER & WALL LLC
1777 Oakland Blvd Ste 300, Walnut Creek
(94596-4063)
PHONE..................................925 932-7900
Charles Wall, *Mng Member*
Cynthia Lundquist, *Controller*
Robert Brosamer,
EMP: 50
SALES (est): 8.8MM **Privately Held**
SIC: 6531 8711 Rental agent, real estate; construction & civil engineering

(P-10949)
BRUNSWICK CORNER PARTNERSHIP
Also Called: Ray Stone
550 Howe Ave Ste 200, Sacramento
(95825-8339)
PHONE..................................916 649-7500
J Todd Stone, *Partner*
EMP: 50
SALES (est): 2.3MM **Privately Held**
SIC: 6531 Real estate agents & managers

(P-10950)
BUCHANAN STREET PARTNERS LP
3501 Jamboree Rd Ste 4200, Newport Beach (92660-2958)
PHONE..................................949 721-1414
Robert Brunswick, *CEO*
Timothy Ballard, *COO*
James Gill, *Vice Pres*
Kimberly Kanen, *Vice Pres*
Eric Snyder, *Principal*
EMP: 85
SALES (est): 4MM **Privately Held**
SIC: 6531 Real estate agents & managers

(P-10951)
BURKSHIRE HAS A WAY HOME SERVC
Also Called: Prudential
16810 Ventura Blvd Fl 1, Encino
(91436-1778)
PHONE..................................818 501-4800
Kathy King, *Manager*
William T Taylor, *Asst Mgr*
EMP: 70 **EST:** 2000
SALES (est): 3MM **Privately Held**
WEB: www.homes2estates.net
SIC: 6531 Real estate agent, residential

(P-10952)
BURLEIGH POINT LTD (DH)
Also Called: Billabong U S A
5600 Argosy Ave Ste 100, Huntington Beach (92649-1063)
PHONE..................................949 428-3200
McNeil Seymour Fiske Jr, *CEO*
Paul Naude, *President*
Neil Fiske, *CEO*
Jeff Streader, *COO*
Tom Gumpert, *Vice Pres*
◆ **EMP:** 198
SQ FT: 80,000
SALES (est): 47.2MM
SALES (corp-wide): 43B **Publicly Held**
SIC: 6531 6513 Real estate agent, residential; residential hotel operation

(P-10953)
BUZZ OATES MANAGEMENT SERVICES
555 Capitol Mall Ste 900, Sacramento
(95814-4606)
PHONE..................................916 381-3843
Phil Oates, *Chairman*
Larry Allbaugh, *President*
Mike Stodden, *CFO*
Kimberly Chambers, *Vice Pres*
EMP: 50
SQ FT: 8,630
SALES (est): 5.2MM **Privately Held**
SIC: 6531 Real estate agent, commercial

(P-10954)
C B COAST NEWPORT PROPERTIES
Also Called: Coldwell Bnkr Rsdntial
840 Nwport Ctr Dr Ste 100, Newport Beach
(92660)
PHONE..................................949 644-1600
Daniel F Bibb, *President*
Tom Queen, *Senior VP*
Gary Legrand, *VP Finance*
Cristi Ulrich, *Associate*
EMP: 100
SQ FT: 7,300
SALES (est): 3.8MM **Publicly Held**
WEB: www.cbestates.com
SIC: 6531 Real estate agent, residential; selling agent, real estate
HQ: Coldwell Banker Residential Real Estate
   27271 Las Ramblas
   Mission Viejo CA 92691
   949 367-1800

(P-10955)
C C CONNECTION INC
Also Called: Re/Maxcc
2950 Buskirk Ave Ste 140, Walnut Creek
(94597-7773)
PHONE..................................925 937-0100
Robert Decker, *President*
Debbie Carter, *Treasurer*
Andrea Cannedy, *Opers Staff*
Kim McIntosh, *Real Est Agnt*
EMP: 57
SQ FT: 4,200
SALES (est): 2.9MM **Privately Held**
WEB: www.re-pro.com
SIC: 6531 Real estate agent, residential

(P-10956)
C-21 SUPER STARS
Also Called: 21st Century Super Stars.
22342 Avenida Empresa, Rcho STA Marg
(92688-2140)
PHONE..................................949 389-1600
Phillip Romero, *Owner*
EMP: 90
SALES (est): 1.6MM **Privately Held**
SIC: 6531 Real estate agent, residential

(P-10957)
C21 PEAK
Also Called: Prellis Mortgage Company
11011 Balboa Blvd, Granada Hills
(91344-5008)
PHONE..................................818 363-1717
Ron Prechtl, *President*
Kathy Prechtl, *CFO*
Shannon Greene, *Info Tech Mgr*
Eric Oneil, *Maintence Staff*
Sarah McNeeley, *Maint Spvr*
EMP: 136
SQ FT: 7,400
SALES (est): 7.8MM **Privately Held**
WEB: www.c21allmoves.com
SIC: 6531 8741 Real estate agent, residential; management services

(P-10958)
CALDWELL BANKER INC
Also Called: Coldwell Banker
40 Main St Ste E100, Vista (92083-5831)
PHONE..................................760 941-6888
Susan Anderson, *Office Mgr*
Jim Morrow, *President*
Cat Adair, *Sales Associate*
Travis Robbins, *Consultant*
Debi Vail, *Real Est Agnt*
EMP: 80

SALES (est): 3.2MM **Privately Held**
SIC: 6531 Real estate agent, residential

(P-10959)
CALDWELL REALTY
14831 Whittier Blvd # 102, Whittier
(90605-1747)
PHONE....................................562 907-5655
Donald Caldwell, *Owner*
EMP: 60
SALES (est): 1.9MM **Privately Held**
SIC: 6531 Real estate agent, residential

(P-10960)
CALIFORNIA GOLDEN REALTY
26752 Calaroga Ave, Hayward
(94545-3505)
PHONE....................................408 822-6000
Renu Bhardwaj, *Principal*
Igor Feoktistov, *Administration*
Mike Powers, *Software Engr*
Cornelia Nyman, *Marketing Mgr*
Petra Bernhard, *Marketing Staff*
EMP: 804
SALES (est): 34.7MM **Privately Held**
SIC: 6531 Real estate brokers & agents

(P-10961)
CANTAMAR PROPERTY MGT INC
Also Called: Meruelo Enterprises
9550 Firestone Blvd # 105, Downey
(90241-5560)
PHONE....................................562 862-4470
Alex Meruelo, *President*
EMP: 50
SALES (est): 3.4MM **Privately Held**
SIC: 6531 Real estate managers

(P-10962)
CARITAS MANAGEMENT CORPORATION
1358 Valencia St, San Francisco
(94110-3715)
PHONE....................................415 647-7191
Robert Zerrilla, *President*
EMP: 55
SQ FT: 3,000
SALES (est): 4.9MM
SALES (corp-wide): 7.9MM **Privately Held**
SIC: 6531 Real estate managers
PA: Mission Housing Development Corporation
474 Valencia St Ste 280
San Francisco CA 94103
415 864-6432

(P-10963)
CARLTON SENIOR LIVING
Also Called: Carlton Plaza of San Leandro
1000 E 14th St, San Leandro (94577-3787)
PHONE....................................510 636-0660
Harry Darrett, *Manager*
EMP: 65
SQ FT: 96,676
SALES (corp-wide): 29.6MM **Privately Held**
SIC: 6531 Real estate agents & managers
PA: Senior Carlton Living Inc
4005 Port Chicago Hwy # 120
Concord CA 94520
925 338-2434

(P-10964)
CARLTON SENIOR LIVING INC
6915 Elk Grove Blvd, Elk Grove
(95758-5526)
PHONE....................................916 714-2404
Kimberly Carlton, *Branch Mgr*
EMP: 50
SALES (corp-wide): 29.6MM **Privately Held**
SIC: 6531 Real estate managers
PA: Senior Carlton Living Inc
4005 Port Chicago Hwy # 120
Concord CA 94520
925 338-2434

(P-10965)
CARMEL PARTNERS INC (PA)
1000 Sansome St Fl 1, San Francisco
(94111-1342)
PHONE....................................415 273-2900
Ron Zeff, *CEO*
Quinn R Barton III, *Managing Prtnr*

Dan Garibaldi, *Managing Prtnr*
Mike Lahorgue, *President*
Dennis Markus, *CFO*
EMP: 120
SALES (est): 69MM **Privately Held**
WEB: www.carmelpartners.net
SIC: 6531 6519 Real estate agents & managers; real property lessors

(P-10966)
CARUSO MGT LTD A CAL LTD PRTNR
Also Called: Commons At Calabasas, The
101 The Grove Dr, Los Angeles
(90036-6221)
PHONE....................................323 900-8100
Rick Caruso, *Partner*
Peter Hayden, *President*
Carol Pacheco, *President*
Jackie Levy, *Exec VP*
Matt Middlebrook, *Exec VP*
EMP: 100
SALES (est): 14.5MM **Privately Held**
SIC: 6531 Rental agent, real estate

(P-10967)
CASBN INVESTMENT INC
Also Called: RE Max Westlake Investments
345 Gellert Blvd Ste A, Daly City
(94015-2617)
PHONE....................................650 991-2800
Francis Ng, *President*
EMP: 60
SALES (est): 4.3MM **Privately Held**
SIC: 6531 6163 Real estate agent, residential; mortgage brokers arranging for loans, using money of others

(P-10968)
CASSIDY TRLY PROP MGT SN FRNCS
201 California St Ste 800, San Francisco
(94111-5002)
PHONE....................................415 781-8100
EMP: 69 EST: 2010
SALES (est): 14MM
SALES (corp-wide): 5.7B **Privately Held**
SIC: 6531
HQ: Cushman & Wakefield, Inc.
225 W Wacker Dr Ste 3000
Chicago IL 60606
312 424-8000

(P-10969)
CB C&C PROPERTIES/COMM DI INC
2120 Churn Creek Rd, Redding
(96002-0738)
PHONE....................................530 221-7551
Steve Craft, *President*
EMP: 70
SALES (est): 1.4MM **Privately Held**
SIC: 6531 Real estate agent, residential

(P-10970)
CB RICHARD ELLIS RE SVCS LLC
Also Called: Cbre Valuation and Advisory
355 S Grand Ave Ste 2700, Los Angeles
(90071-1596)
PHONE....................................213 613-3333
Cicily Dostalek, *Branch Mgr*
James Millon, *Exec VP*
Nicole Bise, *Vice Pres*
Tim Gifford, *Vice Pres*
Spencer Merkord, *Vice Pres*
EMP: 80
SALES (corp-wide): 21.3B **Publicly Held**
WEB: www.insigniafinancial.com
SIC: 6531 Real estate agent, commercial
HQ: Cb Richard Ellis Real Estate Services, Llc
200 Park Ave Fl 19
New York NY 10166
212 984-8000

(P-10971)
CBABR INC (PA)
Also Called: Coldwell Banker
31620 Rr Cyn Rd Ste A, Canyon Lake
(92587-9476)
PHONE....................................951 640-7056
Budge Huskey, *CEO*
EMP: 73
SQ FT: 4,000

SALES (est): 3.7MM **Privately Held**
WEB: www.margaretmccoy.com
SIC: 6531 Real estate agent, residential

(P-10972)
CBRE INC
500 Capitol Mall Ste 2400, Sacramento
(95814-4752)
PHONE....................................916 446-6800
David Brennan, *Exec Dir*
Natalia Cornacchioli, *Admin Asst*
Alan Quicho, *Graphic Designe*
Anthony Burnett, *Asst Broker*
Kristy Gilger, *Manager*
EMP: 100
SALES (corp-wide): 21.3B **Publicly Held**
SIC: 6531 Real estate agent, commercial
HQ: Cbre, Inc.
400 S Hope St Ste 25
Los Angeles CA 90071
213 613-3333

(P-10973)
CBRE INC (HQ)
Also Called: CB Richard Ellis
400 S Hope St Ste 25, Los Angeles
(90071-2800)
PHONE....................................213 613-3333
Bob Sulentic, *President*
Jamie Dennison, *Partner*
Camille Julmy, *Vice Chairman*
Thomas Monahan, *Vice Chairman*
Aron Will, *Vice Chairman*
▲ EMP: 150
SALES (est): 1.7B
SALES (corp-wide): 21.3B **Publicly Held**
SIC: 6531 6726 Real estate agent, commercial; real estate managers; appraiser, real estate; investment offices
PA: Cbre Group, Inc.
400 S Hope St Ste 25
Los Angeles CA 90071
213 613-3333

(P-10974)
CBRE INC
2125 E Katella Ave # 100, Anaheim
(92806-6072)
P.O. Box 9410 (92812-7410)
PHONE....................................714 939-2100
Jeff Moore, *Branch Mgr*
Dan Powers, *Vice Pres*
EMP: 200
SALES (corp-wide): 21.3B **Publicly Held**
SIC: 6531 8742 Real estate agent, commercial; management consulting services
HQ: Cbre, Inc.
400 S Hope St Ste 25
Los Angeles CA 90071
213 613-3333

(P-10975)
CBRE INC
4900 Rivergrade Rd A110, Baldwin Park
(91706-1401)
PHONE....................................626 814-7900
Shashi Panat, *Manager*
EMP: 300
SALES (corp-wide): 21.3B **Publicly Held**
SIC: 6531 Real estate agent, commercial
HQ: Cbre, Inc.
400 S Hope St Ste 25
Los Angeles CA 90071
213 613-3333

(P-10976)
CBRE INC
15303 Ventura Blvd # 200, Van Nuys
(91403-3110)
PHONE....................................818 907-4600
Don Hudson, *Manager*
EMP: 60
SQ FT: 11,000
SALES (corp-wide): 21.3B **Publicly Held**
SIC: 6531 Real estate agent, commercial
HQ: Cbre, Inc.
400 S Hope St Ste 25
Los Angeles CA 90071
213 613-3333

(P-10977)
CBRE INC
225 W Santa Clara St # 1050, San Jose
(95113-1723)
PHONE....................................408 453-7400
Mark Schmidt, *Manager*

Scott Prosser, *Vice Pres*
EMP: 100
SALES (corp-wide): 21.3B **Publicly Held**
SIC: 6531 Real estate agent, commercial
HQ: Cbre, Inc.
400 S Hope St Ste 25
Los Angeles CA 90071
213 613-3333

(P-10978)
CBRE INC
2221 Rosecrans Ave # 101, El Segundo
(90245-4935)
PHONE....................................310 363-4900
Myles Helm, *Director*
Tanquary Grafton, *Exec VP*
Dean Haney, *Vice Pres*
Ben Knight, *Vice Pres*
EMP: 175
SALES (corp-wide): 21.3B **Publicly Held**
SIC: 6531 Real estate agent, commercial
HQ: Cbre, Inc.
400 S Hope St Ste 25
Los Angeles CA 90071
213 613-3333

(P-10979)
CBRE INC
234 S Brand Blvd Ste 800, Glendale
(91204-1362)
PHONE....................................818 502-6700
David Josker, *Director*
EMP: 85
SALES (corp-wide): 21.3B **Publicly Held**
SIC: 6531 Real estate agent, commercial
HQ: Cbre, Inc.
400 S Hope St Ste 25
Los Angeles CA 90071
213 613-3333

(P-10980)
CBRE INC
Also Called: Cbre Capstone
1840 Century Park E # 900, Los Angeles
(90067-2110)
PHONE....................................310 550-2500
Jim Kruse, *Director*
Rocky Binswanger, *Vice Pres*
Lynda Boyer, *Vice Pres*
Anthony Gatti, *Vice Pres*
Dean Zander, *Vice Pres*
EMP: 90
SALES (corp-wide): 21.3B **Publicly Held**
SIC: 6531 Real estate agent, commercial
HQ: Cbre, Inc.
400 S Hope St Ste 25
Los Angeles CA 90071
213 613-3333

(P-10981)
CBRE INC
4365 Executive Dr # 1600, San Diego
(92121-2101)
PHONE....................................858 546-4600
John Frager, *Sales/Mktg Dir*
EMP: 160
SALES (corp-wide): 21.3B **Publicly Held**
SIC: 6531 Real estate agent, commercial
HQ: Cbre, Inc.
400 S Hope St Ste 25
Los Angeles CA 90071
213 613-3333

(P-10982)
CBRE INC
4141 Inland Empire Blvd # 100, Ontario
(91764-5025)
PHONE....................................909 418-2000
Joe Cesta, *Director*
Cray Carlson, *Senior VP*
Eric Chen, *Vice Pres*
Dan Dela Paz, *Vice Pres*
Erik Wanland, *Vice Pres*
EMP: 100
SALES (corp-wide): 21.3B **Publicly Held**
SIC: 6531 Real estate agent, commercial
HQ: Cbre, Inc.
400 S Hope St Ste 25
Los Angeles CA 90071
213 613-3333

P R O D U C T S   &   S V C S

(P-10983)
CBRE GLOBAL INVESTORS LLC (DH)
Also Called: Global Innovation Partner
601 S Figueroa St Ste 49, Los Angeles
(90017-5253)
PHONE.....................213 683-4200
Ritson Ferguson, CEO
Charles Leitner, CEO
Maurice Voskuilen, CFO
Jane Hufnagel, Managing Dir
Deanna Thomas, Office Mgr
EMP: 150
SALES (est): 96.4MM
SALES (corp-wide): 21.3B Publicly Held
WEB: www.cbreglobalindestors.com
SIC: 6531 Real estate agent, commercial
HQ: Cbre, Inc.
    400 S Hope St Ste 25
    Los Angeles CA 90071
    213 613-3333

(P-10984)
CBRE GROUP INC (PA)
400 S Hope St Ste 25, Los Angeles
(90071-2800)
PHONE.....................213 613-3333
Robert E Sulentic, President
William F Concannon, CEO
Michael J Lafitte, CEO
Daniel G Queenan, CEO
Kevin Aussef, COO
EMP: 250
SALES: 21.3B Publicly Held
WEB: www.cbrichardellis.com
SIC: 6531 6162 8742 Real estate agent,
commercial; real estate managers; ap-
praiser, real estate; mortgage bankers;
real estate consultant

(P-10985)
CBSRR INC
Also Called: Coldwell Banker Sky Ridge Rlty
27206 Hwy 189, Blue Jay (92317)
P.O. Box 189, Lake Arrowhead (92352-
0189)
PHONE.....................909 336-2131
Steve Keefe, President
Stephen Keefe, President
Jamie Keefe, Vice Pres
John Lorenz, Associate
EMP: 62
SALES (est): 4.8MM Privately Held
WEB: www.cbskyridge.com
SIC: 6531 Real estate agent, residential

(P-10986)
CEDAR MANAGEMENT LLC
Also Called: Cedar Signature
3233 Dnald Douglas Loop S, Santa Monica
(90405-3235)
P.O. Box 7484 (90406-7484)
PHONE.....................310 396-3100
Adam Pasori,
EMP: 80
SQ FT: 10,000
SALES (est): 3.8MM Privately Held
SIC: 6531 Real estate managers

(P-10987)
CENTURY 21
301 Dickson Hill Rd Ste A, Fairfield
(94533-7203)
PHONE.....................707 429-2121
Linda Green, President
EMP: 50
SALES (est): 1.3MM Privately Held
SIC: 6531 Real estate agent, residential

(P-10988)
CENTURY 21 A BETTER SVC RLTY
8077 2nd St Fl Fl, Downey (90241)
PHONE.....................562 287-0230
David Sarinana, President
Nelson Sanchez, Vice Pres
EMP: 99
SALES (est): 2.1MM Privately Held
SIC: 6531 Real estate agent, residential

(P-10989)
CENTURY 21 A BETTER SVC RLTY
5831 Firestone Blvd Ste J, South Gate
(90280-3718)
PHONE.....................562 806-1000
David Sarinana, President
Blanca Sarinana, Vice Pres
EMP: 97
SQ FT: 4,000
SALES (est): 3.7MM Privately Held
WEB: www.c21abetterservice.com
SIC: 6531 Real estate agents & managers

(P-10990)
CENTURY 21 ABLE INC
3202 Governor Dr Ste 100, San Diego
(92122-2939)
PHONE.....................858 450-2100
Tom Kumz, President
Monica Jaraba, Officer
EMP: 56
SALES (est): 1.7MM Privately Held
SIC: 6531 Real estate agent, residential

(P-10991)
CENTURY 21 ALPHA LLC
1630 W Campbell Ave Ste 1, Campbell
(95008-1500)
P.O. Box 1221, San Martin (95046-1221)
PHONE.....................408 369-2000
Ed Zimbrick, Mng Member
EMP: 89
SALES (est): 2.6MM Privately Held
WEB: www.century21alpha.com
SIC: 6531 Real estate agent, residential

(P-10992)
CENTURY 21 AMBER REALTY INC
21024 Wood Ave Apt A, Torrance
(90503-4143)
PHONE.....................310 625-4363
David Sheerin, President
EMP: 80
SALES (est): 3.5MM Privately Held
WEB: www.c21amber.com
SIC: 6531 Real estate agent, residential

(P-10993)
CENTURY 21 BEVERLYWOOD REALTY
2800 S Robertson Blvd, Los Angeles
(90034-2489)
PHONE.....................310 836-8321
Stanley Shaprio, President
Jerald Shapiro, Vice Pres
Sheryl Shaprio, Vice Pres
EMP: 55
SALES (est): 2.2MM Privately Held
SIC: 6531 7389 Real estate agent, resi-
dential; notary publics

(P-10994)
CENTURY 21 CREST
4005 Foothill Blvd, La Crescenta
(91214-1623)
PHONE.....................818 248-9100
Ray Mirzakhanian, Owner
EMP: 66
SALES (est): 1.1MM Privately Held
SIC: 6531 Real estate agent, residential
PA: E.A.M. Enterprises Inc.
    4005 Foothill Blvd
    La Crescenta CA 91214

(P-10995)
CENTURY 21 DSTNCTIVE PRPTS INC
Also Called: Century 21 Green Gable RE
1450 Ary Ln Ste A, Dixon (95620-4413)
PHONE.....................707 678-9211
Linda Green, President
EMP: 92
SQ FT: 2,200
SALES: 485K Privately Held
SIC: 6531 Real estate agent, residential

(P-10996)
CENTURY 21 EXCELLENCE
5207 Rosemead Blvd Ste 1, Pico Rivera
(90660-2734)
PHONE.....................562 948-4553
Manuel Davila, Partner

Mike Oycque, Partner
EMP: 50
SQ FT: 5,100
SALES (est): 2.6MM Privately Held
SIC: 6531 Real estate agent, residential

(P-10997)
CENTURY 21 EXCLUSIVE REALTORS
22831 Hawthorne Blvd, Torrance
(90505-3615)
PHONE.....................310 373-5252
EMP: 130 EST: 1998
SALES (est): 2.6MM Privately Held
SIC: 6531

(P-10998)
CENTURY 21 GOLDEN REALTY (PA)
482 N Rosemead Blvd, Pasadena
(91107-3000)
PHONE.....................626 797-6680
Carol Gharossian, Administration
Patrick Mc Ginley, Executive
Katheryn Henry, Director
EMP: 60
SALES (est): 3.2MM Privately Held
SIC: 6531 Real estate agent, residential

(P-10999)
CENTURY 21 HALEY & ASSOCIATES
699 Wshington Blvd Ste B5, Roseville
(95678)
PHONE.....................916 782-1500
James Haley, President
EMP: 72
SQ FT: 1,400
SALES: 1.9MM Privately Held
SIC: 6531 Real estate agent, residential

(P-11000)
CENTURY 21 HOME REALTORS (PA)
4110 Edison Ave Ste 210, Chino
(91710-8410)
PHONE.....................909 591-0158
Derek Wood, President
Amy Gaona, Office Admin
Candida Echeverria, Broker
EMP: 100
SQ FT: 11,000
SALES (est): 6MM Privately Held
SIC: 6531 Real estate agent, residential;
escrow agent, real estate

(P-11001)
CENTURY 21 HOME REALTORS
Also Called: Century 21 King Realtors
8338 Day Creek Blvd # 101, Rancho Cuca-
monga (91739-9366)
P.O. Box 3424 (91729-3424)
PHONE.....................909 980-8000
Julio Cardenas, Manager
Carlos Tovar, Real Est Agnt
EMP: 90 Privately Held
SIC: 6531 Real estate agent, residential
PA: Century 21 Home Realtors
    4110 Edison Ave Ste 210
    Chino CA 91710

(P-11002)
CENTURY 21 LANDMARK PROPERTIES
1650 Ximeno Ave Ste 120, Long Beach
(90804-2179)
PHONE.....................562 422-0911
Fax: 562 428-1842
EMP: 50 EST: 1960
SALES (est): 2.3MM Privately Held
SIC: 6531

(P-11003)
CENTURY 21 LES RYAN REALTY
1057 College Ave Ofc Ste, Santa Rosa
(95404-4128)
PHONE.....................707 577-7777
Pat Provost, Partner
EMP: 75
SALES (corp-wide): 2.3MM Privately
Held
WEB: www.c21lesryan.com
SIC: 6531 Real estate agent, residential

PA: Century 21 Les Ryan Realty
    495 E Perkins St Ste A
    Ukiah CA

(P-11004)
CENTURY 21 LUDECKE INC (PA)
34 E Foothill Blvd, Arcadia (91006-2305)
PHONE.....................626 445-0123
Michael W Ludecke, President
EMP: 100
SALES (est): 5.5MM Privately Held
WEB: www.c21ludecke.com
SIC: 6531 Real estate agent, residential

(P-11005)
CENTURY 21 MASTERS
480 W Rowland St Ste B, Covina
(91723-2964)
PHONE.....................626 732-6184
Jody Fox, Branch Mgr
EMP: 52
SALES (corp-wide): 7.4MM Privately
Held
SIC: 6531 Real estate agent, residential
PA: Century 21 Masters
    1169 Fairway Dr Ste 100
    Walnut CA 91789
    909 595-6697

(P-11006)
CENTURY 21 SHOWCASE INC
7835 Church St, Highland (92346-4380)
PHONE.....................909 936-9334
Jeff Stoffel, President
EMP: 60
SALES (est): 2.9MM Privately Held
WEB: www.century21showcase.com
SIC: 6531 Real estate agent, residential

(P-11007)
CENTURY ADANALIAN & VASQUEZ
Also Called: Century 21
1415 W Shaw Ave, Fresno (93711-3608)
PHONE.....................559 244-6000
Bill Adanalian, President
Greg Vasquez, Vice Pres
Percy Saucedo, Office Mgr
EMP: 62
SQ FT: 4,250
SALES (est): 3.5MM Privately Held
SIC: 6531 Real estate agent, residential

(P-11008)
CENTURY PROPERTIES OWNERS ASSN
Also Called: Century, The
1 W Century Dr, Los Angeles (90067-3401)
PHONE.....................310 272-8580
EMP: 50
SALES (est): 4.7MM Privately Held
SIC: 6531 Real estate agent, residential

(P-11009)
CH MARKET CENTER INC
Also Called: Keller Williams Realty
4200 Chino Health Ste 325, Chino Hills
(91709)
PHONE.....................909 628-9100
Nick Lanza, President
David Porchas, President
Suzi Moret, Principal
EMP: 75
SALES (est): 3.8MM Privately Held
SIC: 6531 Real estate agent, residential

(P-11010)
CHARLES DUNN CO INC
Also Called: Charles Dunn Raltor State Svcs
800 W 6th St Ste 800 # 800, Los Angeles
(90017-2741)
PHONE.....................213 481-1800
Walter J Conn, President
Richard C Dunn, President
Eleanor B Dunn, Vice Pres
Joseph Dunn, Admin Sec
Kristin L Tonkin, Manager
EMP: 200
SALES (est): 4.6MM Privately Held
SIC: 6531 Real estate brokers & agents

(P-11011)
CHARLES DUNN RE SVCS INC (PA)
800 W 6th St Ste 600, Los Angeles (90017-2709)
PHONE..............................213 270-6200
Walter Conn, *CEO*
Patrick Conn, *President*
EMP: 86
SQ FT: 30,000
SALES (est): 7.8MM **Privately Held**
WEB: www.charlesdunn.com
SIC: 6531 Real estate brokers & agents; real estate managers

(P-11012)
CHARTER REALTY GROUP INC (PA)
12400 Wilshire Blvd, Los Angeles (90025-1019)
PHONE..............................310 826-3174
Arnold L Porath, *President*
David Meltzer, *Vice Pres*
EMP: 80
SQ FT: 3,200
SALES (est): 8.5MM **Privately Held**
SIC: 6531 Rental agent, real estate

(P-11013)
CHILD DEVELOPMENT INCORPORATED
17341 Jacquelyn Ln, Huntington Beach (92647-5713)
PHONE..............................714 842-4064
EMP: 311
SALES (corp-wide): 28MM **Privately Held**
SIC: 6531 Real estate agents & managers
PA: Child Development Incorporated
350 Woodview Ave
Morgan Hill CA 95037
408 556-7300

(P-11014)
CHRISTIAN AND WAKEFIELD (PA)
Also Called: Burnham Real Estate
110 W A St Ste 900, San Diego (92101-3705)
P.O. Box 122910 (92112-2910)
PHONE..............................619 236-1555
Stath Karras, *President*
Mike Philbin, *Senior VP*
Jon Walz, *Senior VP*
EMP: 53
SQ FT: 22,000
SALES (est): 5.4MM **Privately Held**
SIC: 6531 Real estate brokers & agents

(P-11015)
CHRISTIAN CHURCH HOMES
Also Called: Westlake Christian Terrace - E
251 28th St, Oakland (94611-6063)
PHONE..............................510 893-2998
John Jordan, *Branch Mgr*
EMP: 259
SALES (corp-wide): 13.5MM **Privately Held**
SIC: 6531 Real estate agents & managers
PA: Christian Church Homes
303 Hegenberger Rd # 201
Oakland CA 94621
510 632-6712

(P-11016)
CHRISTOPHER RANSOM LLC
1300 Clay St, Oakland (94612-1425)
P.O. Box 268 (94604-0268)
PHONE..............................510 345-9144
Christopher Ransom Jr, *Mng Member*
EMP: 76
SALES: 15MM **Privately Held**
SIC: 6531 Real estate agents & managers

(P-11017)
CITIVEST INC
4340 Von Karman Ave # 110, Newport Beach (92660-1201)
PHONE..............................949 474-0440
Dana Haynes, *President*
Johnathan Loevenguth, *CFO*
Larry Weese, *Exec VP*
Allen Gambrell, *Project Mgr*
Michael Mossman, *Project Mgr*
EMP: 90

SQ FT: 4,000
SALES (est): 10.4MM **Privately Held**
WEB: www.citivestinc.com
SIC: 6531 Real estate managers

(P-11018)
CLEARCAPITALCOM INC
10266 Truckee Airport Rd, Truckee (96161-3310)
PHONE..............................530 550-2500
Duane Andrews, *CEO*
Becky Andrews, *Bd of Directors*
Johnson Russell, *Officer*
Kenon Chen, *Exec VP*
Beth Buell, *Vice Pres*
EMP: 100
SALES (corp-wide): 68.6MM **Privately Held**
SIC: 6531 Appraiser, real estate
PA: Clearcapital.Com, Inc.
300 E 2nd St Ste 1405
Reno NV 89501
775 470-5656

(P-11019)
CLEARCAPITALCOM INC
1410 Rocky Ridge Dr # 250, Roseville (95661-2811)
PHONE..............................530 582-5011
Duane Andrews, *CEO*
Ron Rowan, *CFO*
Sheila Ryan, *Officer*
Simon Blackburn, *Exec VP*
Larry Robinson, *CTO*
EMP: 100
SALES (corp-wide): 76.2MM **Privately Held**
SIC: 6531 Real estate agents & managers
PA: Clearcapital.Com, Inc.
300 E 2nd St Ste 1405
Reno NV 89501
775 470-5656

(P-11020)
COAST TO COAST REALTY
Also Called: Century 21
18879 Brasilia Dr, Porter Ranch (91326-1919)
PHONE..............................818 360-2609
Debbie Abeyesinhe, *Owner*
EMP: 80
SALES (est): 2MM **Privately Held**
WEB: www.debbisellsthevalley.com
SIC: 6531 Real estate agent, residential

(P-11021)
COASTAL ALLIANCE HOLDINGS INC
Also Called: Coldwell Banker Coastl Aliance
1650 Ximeno Ave Ste 120, Long Beach (90804-2179)
PHONE..............................562 370-1000
Jack Irvin, *President*
EMP: 140
SALES (est): 6.6MM **Privately Held**
SIC: 6531 Real estate agent, residential

(P-11022)
COASTSIDE SENIOR HOUSING LIMIT
925 Main St, Half Moon Bay (94019-2379)
PHONE..............................415 355-7100
Jane Graf,
EMP: 50
SALES: 549K **Privately Held**
SIC: 6531 Real estate leasing & rentals

(P-11023)
COLDWELL BANKER
730 Alhambra Blvd Ste 150, Sacramento (95816-3885)
PHONE..............................916 447-5900
Michael Lippi, *Manager*
Patti McNulty-Langdon, *Sales Associate*
Michael Onstead, *Director*
Wendi Reinl, *Manager*
Laura Steed, *Manager*
EMP: 60
SALES (est): 2.6MM **Privately Held**
SIC: 6531 Real estate agent, residential

(P-11024)
COLDWELL BANKER
9332 Fuerte Dr, La Mesa (91941-4199)
PHONE..............................619 460-6600
Rick Hoffman, *President*

Steve Wilson, *Manager*
Kay Lemenager, *Real Est Agnt*
EMP: 88
SQ FT: 4,000
SALES (est): 3.6MM **Privately Held**
SIC: 6531 Real estate agent, residential

(P-11025)
COLDWELL BANKER
740 Garden View Ct # 100, Encinitas (92024-2474)
PHONE..............................760 753-5616
Jeff Hayes, *Manager*
Brian Axford, *Sales Associate*
EMP: 75
SALES (est): 3.4MM **Privately Held**
SIC: 6531 Real estate agent, residential

(P-11026)
COLDWELL BANKER
1377 El Camino Real, Menlo Park (94025-4210)
PHONE..............................650 324-4456
Chris Rafmussen, *Manager*
Regan Byers-Cinelli, *Asst Broker*
Julie Ray, *Broker*
Glenn Bartkowiak, *Real Est Agnt*
Kelly Griggs, *Real Est Agnt*
EMP: 80
SALES (est): 320.7K **Privately Held**
SIC: 6531 Real estate agent, residential

(P-11027)
COLDWELL BANKER
248 Main St Ste 200, Half Moon Bay (94019-7120)
PHONE..............................650 726-1100
Greg Cowen, *Partner*
Stella Johnson, *Partner*
William Mahar, *Principal*
Rose Serdy, *Principal*
EMP: 50
SALES (est): 2.4MM **Privately Held**
SIC: 6531 Real estate agent, residential

(P-11028)
COLDWELL BANKER AMARAL & ASSOC
3775 Main St Ste E, Oakley (94561-5793)
PHONE..............................925 439-7400
Arron Manwos, *Owner*
EMP: 65
SALES (est): 1.5MM **Privately Held**
SIC: 6531 Real estate agent, residential

(P-11029)
COLDWELL BANKER HOME SOURCE
15500 W Sand St Ste 2, Victorville (92392-2931)
PHONE..............................760 684-8100
Jason Lamoreaux, *Owner*
Chris Lamoreaux, *Owner*
EMP: 60
SALES (est): 1MM **Privately Held**
SIC: 6531 Real estate agent, residential

(P-11030)
COLDWELL BANKER PREMIER PRPTS
1498 E Valley Rd, Santa Barbara (93108-1241)
PHONE..............................805 565-2200
Chuck Farish, *President*
Sally Hanseth, *Sales Associate*
Edna Sizlo, *Director*
Gina Meyers, *Real Est Agnt*
William Turner, *Real Est Agnt*
EMP: 70 **EST:** 1998
SALES (est): 1.7MM **Privately Held**
WEB: www.betsyzwick.com
SIC: 6531 Real estate agent, residential

(P-11031)
COLDWELL BANKER PROF GROUP
2860 Zanker Rd Ste 204, San Jose (95134-2120)
PHONE..............................408 383-1044
Kathy Low, *Principal*
EMP: 90
SALES (est): 3MM **Privately Held**
WEB: www.kathylow.com
SIC: 6531 Real estate agent, residential

(P-11032)
COLDWELL BANKER PROPERTY SHOP
727 W Ojai Ave, Ojai (93023-3726)
PHONE..............................805 646-7288
Dennis Guernsey, *President*
Larry Wilde Od, *Owner*
EMP: 60
SALES (est): 3.2MM **Privately Held**
WEB: www.ojaicoldwell.com
SIC: 6531 Real estate agent, residential

(P-11033)
COLDWELL BANKER RE CORP
15490 Ventura Blvd # 100, Sherman Oaks (91403-3033)
PHONE..............................818 995-2424
Bill Dalton, *Branch Mgr*
Erna Braun, *Executive*
Connie Harrison, *Broker*
Yolanda Thunderwolf, *Broker*
Lauren Tizabi, *Broker*
EMP: 60 **Publicly Held**
SIC: 6531 Real estate agent, residential
HQ: Coldwell Banker Real Estate Corporation
175 Park Ave
Madison NJ 07940
973 407-2000

(P-11034)
COLDWELL BANKER RE CORP
1000 Sunset Dr Ste 190, Roseville (95678)
PHONE..............................408 981-7200
Maxine Feil, *Manager*
EMP: 50 **Publicly Held**
WEB: www.coldwellbanker.com
SIC: 6531 Real estate agent, residential
HQ: Coldwell Banker Real Estate Corporation
175 Park Ave
Madison NJ 07940
973 407-2000

(P-11035)
COLDWELL BANKER RE CORP
300 E State St, Redlands (92373-5235)
PHONE..............................909 792-4147
Sheila Cannon, *Owner*
EMP: 50 **Publicly Held**
WEB: www.coldwellbanker.com
SIC: 6531 Real estate agent, residential
HQ: Coldwell Banker Real Estate Corporation
175 Park Ave
Madison NJ 07940
973 407-2000

(P-11036)
COLDWELL BANKER RE LLC
1712 Meridian Ave Ste C, San Jose (95125-5587)
PHONE..............................408 723-3300
James Nichols, *Mng Member*
Ronaldo Dela Vega, *Sales Associate*
Stephanie Golden, *Sales Staff*
Dana Mitchell, *Sales Staff*
Joe Brown, *Manager*
EMP: 75
SALES (est): 39.7MM **Publicly Held**
SIC: 6531 Real estate agent, residential
PA: Realogy Holdings Corp.
175 Park Ave
Madison NJ 07940

(P-11037)
COLDWELL BANKER RESIDENTIAL (DH)
27742 Vista Del Lago # 1, Mission Viejo (92692-1119)
PHONE..............................949 837-5700
Robert M Becker, *President*
Carol Ryniewicz, *Asst Broker*
Linda A Priest, *Asst Treas*
Matthew Kaae, *Broker*
Patty McQuail, *Broker*
EMP: 75
SALES (est): 14.3MM **Publicly Held**
WEB: www.mdeedy.com
SIC: 6531 Real estate agent, residential

(P-11038)
COLDWELL BANKER RESIDENTIAL RE (DH)
27271 Las Ramblas, Mission Viejo (92691-8041)
PHONE..................949 367-1800
Robert Becker, *President*
Jan Palya, *Sales Staff*
EMP: 410
SQ FT: 6,000
SALES (est): 77.4MM **Publicly Held**
WEB: www.cbestates.com
SIC: 6531 Real estate agent, residential

(P-11039)
COLDWELL BANKER RESIDENTIAL RE
15 E Foothill Blvd, Arcadia (91006-2399)
PHONE..................626 445-5500
Jack Cooley, *Principal*
EMP: 63
SALES (est): 3MM **Privately Held**
SIC: 6531 Real estate agent, residential

(P-11040)
COLDWELL BANKER TOWN & COUNTRY
345 E Rowland St, Covina (91723-3153)
PHONE..................626 966-3688
Norman Cox, *Manager*
EMP: 70
SQ FT: 7,000
SALES (est): 3.5MM **Privately Held**
WEB: www.cbtcsocal.com
SIC: 6531 Real estate agent, residential

(P-11041)
COLDWELL BANKERS RESIDENTIAL
21060 Redwood Rd Ste 100, Castro Valley (94546-5931)
PHONE..................510 583-5400
Nelly Jagroop, *Manager*
Gregory Ricchini, *Broker*
Jose Cervantes, *Sales Associate*
Richard Dibona, *Consultant*
Leslie Drury, *Real Est Agnt*
EMP: 90
SALES (corp-wide): 1.4MM **Privately Held**
WEB: www.laurarivera.com
SIC: 6531 Real estate agent, residential
PA: Coldwell Bankers Residential
604 Lindero Canyon Rd
Agoura Hills CA 91377
818 575-2660

(P-11042)
COLDWELL BANKERS RESIDENTIAL (PA)
604 Lindero Canyon Rd, Agoura Hills (91377-5455)
PHONE..................818 575-2660
Irma Haldane, *Manager*
Brian Barber, *CFO*
Mike James, *Vice Pres*
Anthony Papillo, *Executive*
Randy Paller, *Admin Sec*
EMP: 52
SALES (est): 1.4MM **Privately Held**
WEB: www.sharonberman.com
SIC: 6531 Real estate agent, residential

(P-11043)
COLDWELL BNKR RESIDENTIAL BRKG
181 2nd Ave Ste 100, San Mateo (94401-3830)
PHONE..................650 558-6800
EMP: 52 **Publicly Held**
SIC: 6531 Real estate agent, residential
HQ: Coldwell Banker Residential Brokerage
1855 Gateway Blvd Ste 750
Concord CA 94520
925 275-3000

(P-11044)
COLDWELL BNKR RESIDENTIAL BRKG
500 Auburn Folsom Rd # 300, Auburn (95603-5645)
PHONE..................530 823-7653
Randi Greene, *Principal*
EMP: 52 **Publicly Held**

SIC: 6531 Real estate agent, residential
HQ: Coldwell Banker Residential Brokerage
1855 Gateway Blvd Ste 750
Concord CA 94520
925 275-3000

(P-11045)
COLDWELL BNKR RESIDENTIAL BRKG (DH)
Also Called: Valley of California, Inc.
1855 Gateway Blvd Ste 750, Concord (94520-3290)
PHONE..................925 275-3000
Bruce G Zipf, *CEO*
Avram Goldman, *President*
Melissa Huntsman, *Research*
Eric Peterson, *Analyst*
Melanie Snow, *Broker*
EMP: 100
SALES (est): 18.1MM **Publicly Held**
WEB: www.cbnorcal.com
SIC: 6531 Real estate agent, residential

(P-11046)
COLDWELL BNKR RESIDENTIAL BRKG
1427 Chapin Ave, Burlingame (94010-4002)
PHONE..................650 558-4200
Rachel Ni, *Branch Mgr*
Stephan Marshall, *Asst Broker*
Joanne Huh, *Sales Associate*
James Koh, *Sales Associate*
EMP: 52 **Publicly Held**
SIC: 6531 Real estate agent, residential
HQ: Coldwell Banker Residential Brokerage
1855 Gateway Blvd Ste 750
Concord CA 94520
925 275-3000

(P-11047)
COLDWELL BNKR RESIDENTIAL BRKG
2140 41st Ave Ste 100, Capitola (95010-2067)
PHONE..................831 462-9000
Spencer Hays, *Branch Mgr*
Keith Jackson, *Broker*
EMP: 52 **Publicly Held**
SIC: 6531 Real estate agent, residential
HQ: Coldwell Banker Residential Brokerage
1855 Gateway Blvd Ste 750
Concord CA 94520
925 275-3000

(P-11048)
COLDWELL BNKR RESIDENTIAL BRKG
166 N Canon Dr Ste 200, Beverly Hills (90210-5304)
PHONE..................310 273-3113
Betty Graham, *Manager*
Roni Heller, *Broker*
Andrew Sacks, *Sales Associate*
Michael Sahakian, *Marketing Staff*
Monica De Brik, *Real Est Agnt*
EMP: 74 **Publicly Held**
WEB: www.bonnieo.com
SIC: 6531 Real estate agent, residential
HQ: Coldwell Banker Residential Brokerage Company
27271 Las Ramblas
Mission Viejo CA 92691

(P-11049)
COLDWELL BNKR RESIDENTIAL BRKG
1390 Noriega St, San Francisco (94122-4495)
PHONE..................415 447-8800
Mark Best, *Branch Mgr*
Nina Style, *Real Est Agnt*
Tara Burke, *Associate*
EMP: 52 **Publicly Held**
WEB: www.markbest.com
SIC: 6531 Real estate agent, residential
HQ: Coldwell Banker Residential Brokerage
1855 Gateway Blvd Ste 750
Concord CA 94520
925 275-3000

(P-11050)
COLDWELL BNKR RESIDENTIAL BRKG
1081 N Palm Canyon Dr, Palm Springs (92262-4419)
PHONE..................760 325-4500
Thomas Ogle, *Branch Mgr*
Cena Rasmussen, *Asst Broker*
Tricia Giroud, *Real Est Agnt*
Hilda Horvat, *Real Est Agnt*
Raymond Sosa, *Associate*
EMP: 74 **Publicly Held**
WEB: www.bonnieo.com
SIC: 6531 Real estate agent, residential
HQ: Coldwell Banker Residential Brokerage Company
27271 Las Ramblas
Mission Viejo CA 92691
-

(P-11051)
COLDWELL BNKR RESIDENTIAL BRKG
5034 Sunrise Blvd, Fair Oaks (95628-4945)
PHONE..................916 966-8200
Donna Kopp, *Principal*
Mary Grebitus, *Asst Broker*
Derek Jones, *Sales Associate*
EMP: 52 **Publicly Held**
WEB: www.kathyfox.com
SIC: 6531 Real estate agent, residential
HQ: Coldwell Banker Residential Brokerage
1855 Gateway Blvd Ste 750
Concord CA 94520
925 275-3000

(P-11052)
COLDWELL BNKR RESIDENTIAL BRKG
21580 Yorba Linda Blvd, Yorba Linda (92887-3748)
PHONE..................714 832-0020
Tom Iovenitti, *President*
Scott Day, *Consultant*
Daniel Swoish, *Real Est Agnt*
EMP: 50
SALES (est): 1.5MM **Privately Held**
SIC: 6531 Real estate agent, residential

(P-11053)
COLDWELL BNKR RESIDENTIAL BRKG
23647 Calabasas Rd, Calabasas (91302-1502)
PHONE..................818 222-0023
Bill Dalton, *Manager*
Denice Rice, *Broker*
Heidi Adams, *Sales Associate*
Larry Keller, *Sales Associate*
Patricia Mardell, *Sales Associate*
EMP: 100 **Publicly Held**
WEB: www.bonnieo.com
SIC: 6531 Real estate agent, residential
HQ: Coldwell Banker Residential Brokerage Company
27271 Las Ramblas
Mission Viejo CA 92691

(P-11054)
COLDWELL BNKR RESIDENTIAL BRKG
72605 Highway 111 Ste B2, Palm Desert (92260-3392)
PHONE..................760 776-9898
Ron Gerlich, *Manager*
Elizabeth Arcaro, *Associate*
EMP: 100 **Publicly Held**
WEB: www.bonnieo.com
SIC: 6531 Real estate agent, residential
HQ: Coldwell Banker Residential Brokerage Company
27271 Las Ramblas
Mission Viejo CA 92691

(P-11055)
COLDWELL BNKR RESIDENTIAL BRKG
45000 Club Dr, Indian Wells (92210-8856)
PHONE..................760 771-5454
Diane Busch, *Manager*
Pamla Abramson, *Sales Associate*

James Davis, *Sales Associate*
Vicki Rodehaver, *Senior Mgr*
Nadine Elliott, *Real Est Agnt*
EMP: 74 **Publicly Held**
WEB: www.bonnieo.com
SIC: 6531 Real estate agent, residential
HQ: Coldwell Banker Residential Brokerage Company
27271 Las Ramblas
Mission Viejo CA 92691

(P-11056)
COLDWELL BNKR RESIDENTIAL BRKG
410 Sims Rd, Santa Cruz (95060-1326)
PHONE..................831 420-2628
Prakash Desai, *Broker*
Paul Grisanti, *Broker*
Michael Adari, *Sales Associate*
EMP: 59 **Privately Held**
SIC: 6531 Real estate agent, residential
PA: Coldwell Banker Residential Brokerage
3 Parkway North Blvd # 400
Deerfield IL 60015

(P-11057)
COLDWELL BNKR RESIDENTIAL BRKG
3340 Walnut Ave Ste 110, Fremont (94538-2215)
PHONE..................510 608-7600
Diane Petek, *Asst Broker*
Marina Saucedo, *Asst Broker*
Alex Cyriac, *Broker*
Peter Liu, *Real Est Agnt*
Michele McKay, *Real Est Agnt*
EMP: 52 **Publicly Held**
SIC: 6531 Real estate agent, residential
HQ: Coldwell Banker Residential Brokerage
1855 Gateway Blvd Ste 750
Concord CA 94520
925 275-3000

(P-11058)
COLDWELL BNKR RSDENTIAL RE LLC
410 N Santa Cruz Ave, Los Gatos (95030-5321)
PHONE..................408 355-1500
Karen Trolan, *Manager*
Elizabeth Winegar-Howard, *Broker*
Wendy Chen-Shen, *Sales Associate*
John Heringer, *Sales Associate*
David Propach, *Sales Staff*
EMP: 100 **Publicly Held**
SIC: 6531 Real estate agent, residential
HQ: Coldwell Banker Residential Real Estate Llc
6285 Barfield Rd Ste 100
Atlanta GA 30328
404 705-1500

(P-11059)
COLDWELL BNKR RSDNTIAL RE SVCS
4370 Town Center Blvd # 270, El Dorado Hills (95762-7140)
PHONE..................916 933-1155
Maxine Feil, *Branch Mgr*
Kathy Burk, *Sales Staff*
Larkin Bullard, *Real Est Agnt*
EMP: 65 **Publicly Held**
SIC: 6531 Real estate agent, residential
HQ: Coldwell Banker Residential Real Estate Services, Inc.
27742 Vista Del Lago # 1
Mission Viejo CA 92692
949 837-5700

(P-11060)
COLDWER BANKER PREVIEWS
Also Called: Coldwell Banker
9069 W Sunset Blvd # 100, West Hollywood (90069)
PHONE..................310 278-9470
Fran Hughes, *Manager*
Tony Papillo, *Branch Mgr*
SOO Kim, *Broker*
Anthony Papillo, *Sales Executive*
Paul Chang, *Sales Associate*
EMP: 120
SALES (est): 2.8MM **Privately Held**
SIC: 6531 Real estate agent, residential

▲ = Import ▼=Export
◆ =Import/Export

(P-11061)
COLLEGE PARK REALTY INC (PA)
Also Called: Re/Max
10791 Los Alamitos Blvd, Los Alamitos (90720-2309)
PHONE..............................562 594-6753
Barry Binder, *President*
Betty Binder, *Treasurer*
Carol Treadway, *Vice Pres*
Cary Hairabedian, *Executive*
Josh Jones, *Info Tech Dir*
EMP: 146
SQ FT: 5,000
SALES (est): 9MM **Privately Held**
WEB: www.joannmurphy.com
SIC: 6531 Real estate agent, residential

(P-11062)
COLLEGE PARK REALTY INC
Also Called: Remax College Park Realty
2610 Los Coyotes Diagonal, Long Beach (90815-1355)
PHONE..............................562 982-0300
Marian Edwards, *Principal*
EMP: 50
SALES (est): 1.8MM
SALES (corp-wide): 9MM **Privately Held**
WEB: www.joannmurphy.com
SIC: 6531 Real estate agent, residential
PA: College Park Realty Inc
    10791 Los Alamitos Blvd
    Los Alamitos CA 90720
    562 594-6753

(P-11063)
COLLIERS INTERNATIONAL
101 2nd St Ste 1100, San Francisco (94105-3652)
PHONE..............................415 788-3100
Herbert Damner Jr, *Partner*
Tony Crossley, *Exec VP*
James Sobel, *Vice Pres*
Alan Collenette, *Managing Dir*
Scott Harper, *Director*
EMP: 65
SALES (est): 6.7MM
SALES (corp-wide): 2.8B **Privately Held**
SIC: 6531 Real estate brokers & agents
HQ: Colliers International New England, Llc
    160 Federal St Fl 11
    Boston MA 02110
    617 330-8000

(P-11064)
COLLIERS INTL PRPERTY CONS INC
4660 La Jolla Village Dr # 100, San Diego (92122-4601)
PHONE..............................858 455-1515
Tony Albin Senior, *Vice Pres*
Mike Erwin, *Exec VP*
Derek Applbaum, *Vice Pres*
Richard Lebert, *Vice Pres*
Evan McDonald, *Vice Pres*
EMP: 50
SALES (corp-wide): 2.8B **Privately Held**
SIC: 6531 Real estate agent, commercial
HQ: Colliers International Property Consultants Inc.
    601 Union St Ste 3320
    Seattle WA 98101
    206 695-4200

(P-11065)
COLLIERS INTL PRPERTY CONS INC
301 University Ave # 100, Sacramento (95825-5537)
PHONE..............................916 929-5999
Randy Dixon, *Manager*
EMP: 100
SALES (corp-wide): 2.8B **Privately Held**
SIC: 6531 Real estate agent, commercial
HQ: Colliers International Property Consultants Inc.
    601 Union St Ste 3320
    Seattle WA 98101
    206 695-4200

(P-11066)
COLLIERS PARRISH INTL INC
Also Called: Colliers Investment Services
225 W Santa Clara St, San Jose (95113-1723)
PHONE..............................408 282-3800
Mike Burke, *Manager*
Marne Michaels, *Senior VP*
Matt Arya, *Vice Pres*
Susan Gregory, *Vice Pres*
Terry Healy, *Vice Pres*
EMP: 70
SALES (corp-wide): 20.6MM **Privately Held**
WEB: www.terraceaustin.com
SIC: 6531 Real estate agent, commercial
PA: Parrish Colliers International Inc
    1 Almaden Blvd Ste 300
    San Jose CA 95113

(P-11067)
COLLIERS PARRISH INTL INC
1850 Mt Diablo Blvd # 200, Walnut Creek (94596-4476)
PHONE..............................925 279-1050
Edward Delbeccaro, *Manager*
Henry Englehardt, *Vice Pres*
Kevin Van Voorhis, *Planning*
Terri Durkovic, *Opers Mgr*
EMP: 51
SALES (corp-wide): 20.6MM **Privately Held**
WEB: www.terraceaustin.com
SIC: 6531 Real estate brokers & agents
PA: Parrish Colliers International Inc
    1 Almaden Blvd Ste 300
    San Jose CA 95113

(P-11068)
COLONY MANAGEMENT INC
Also Called: Colony Advisors
1999 Ave Of The, Los Angeles (90067)
PHONE..............................310 282-8820
Thomas A Barrack, *CEO*
Mark Hedstrom, *CFO*
EMP: 75
SQ FT: 15,000
SALES (est): 4.7MM **Privately Held**
WEB: www.colonyinc.com
SIC: 6531 Real estate brokers & agents
PA: Colony Capital, Llc
    2450 Broadway Ste 600
    Santa Monica CA 90404

(P-11069)
COMPASS REAL ESTATE LLC
617 Saxony Pl Ste 101, Encinitas (92024-2797)
PHONE..............................760 979-5609
Heather Olson, *Branch Mgr*
EMP: 558
SALES (corp-wide): 36.1MM **Privately Held**
SIC: 6531 Real estate brokers & agents
PA: Compass Real Estate, Llc
    90 5th Ave Fl 3
    New York NY 10011
    212 913-9058

(P-11070)
CONAM MANAGEMENT CORPORATION (PA)
3990 Ruffin Rd Ste 100, San Diego (92123-4805)
PHONE..............................858 614-7200
J Bradley Forrester, *CEO*
Robert Svatos, *CFO*
Daniel J Epstein, *Chairman*
Julie Brawn-Whiteside, *Exec VP*
Frazier Crawford, *Exec VP*
EMP: 142
SQ FT: 45,634
SALES (est): 22.8MM **Privately Held**
SIC: 6531 Real estate managers

(P-11071)
CONTINENTAL 155 5TH CORP
2041 Rosecrans Ave # 200, El Segundo (90245-4707)
PHONE..............................310 640-1520
Richard C Lundquist, *President*
Marcia Helfer, *Vice Pres*
EMP: 50

SALES (est): 1.4MM
SALES (corp-wide): 34.4MM **Privately Held**
WEB: www.continentaldevelopment.com
SIC: 6531 Real estate agent, commercial
PA: Continental Development Corporation
    2041 Rosecrans Ave # 200
    El Segundo CA 90245
    310 640-1520

(P-11072)
COOK REALTY INC
Also Called: Cook Realty Sales
4305 Freeport Blvd, Sacramento (95822-2045)
PHONE..............................916 451-6702
Frank Cook, *President*
Barbara Cook, *Corp Secy*
Trey Bonetti, *Vice Pres*
Lindsay Filby, *Office Mgr*
Mark Warmack, *Office Mgr*
EMP: 106
SALES (est): 5.7MM **Privately Held**
WEB: www.cookrealty.net
SIC: 6531 Real estate agent, residential; real estate brokers & agents

(P-11073)
CORE REALTY HOLDINGS MGT INC
Also Called: Crh Management
1600 Dove St Ste 450, Newport Beach (92660-2447)
PHONE..............................949 863-1031
Dougless Morehead, *CEO*
Marc Raskulinecz, *Senior VP*
Larry Goswiller, *Vice Pres*
Justin Morehead, *Vice Pres*
Erin Khamis, *Training Dir*
EMP: 99
SALES (est): 4.9MM **Privately Held**
SIC: 6531 Real estate managers

(P-11074)
CORELOGIC INC
201 Spear St Fl 4, San Francisco (94105-1669)
PHONE..............................714 250-6400
EMP: 50
SALES (corp-wide): 1.8B **Publicly Held**
SIC: 6531
PA: Corelogic, Inc.
    40 Pacifica Ste 900
    Irvine CA 92618
    949 214-1000

(P-11075)
CORELOGIC INC
40 Pacifica Ste 900, Irvine (92618-7487)
PHONE..............................714 250-6400
EMP: 50
SALES (corp-wide): 1.8B **Publicly Held**
SIC: 6531
PA: Corelogic, Inc.
    40 Pacifica Ste 900
    Irvine CA 92618
    949 214-1000

(P-11076)
CORINTHIAN REALTY LLC
3902 Smith St, Union City (94587-2616)
PHONE..............................510 487-8653
EMP: 60
SALES (est): 2.5MM **Privately Held**
SIC: 6531

(P-11077)
CORLAND COMPANIES (PA)
Also Called: Carlson
17542 17th St Ste 420, Tustin (92780-7928)
P.O. Box 807 (92781-0807)
PHONE..............................714 573-7780
Chis Hide, *President*
EMP: 60
SALES (est): 4.6MM **Privately Held**
SIC: 6531 Real estate managers

(P-11078)
CORONADO FINANCIAL CORP
Also Called: Prudential
940 Eastlake Pkwy, Chula Vista (91914-3558)
PHONE..............................619 946-1900
Corey Shepard, *President*
Jolene Shepard, *Treasurer*

EMP: 50
SQ FT: 10,000
SALES (est): 3.5MM **Privately Held**
SIC: 6531 Real estate agent, residential

(P-11079)
COSTAR GROUP INC
8910 University Center Ln # 300, San Diego (92122-1029)
PHONE..............................858 458-4900
Todd Thelen, *Manager*
Laura Blumenauer, *Executive*
Nigel Davidson, *Research*
Jonelle Lenz, *Research*
Shannon Turner, *Research*
EMP: 230
SALES (corp-wide): 1.1B **Publicly Held**
WEB: www.costar.com
SIC: 6531 Real estate agent, commercial
PA: Costar Group, Inc.
    1331 L St Nw Ste 2
    Washington DC 20005
    202 346-6500

(P-11080)
COVELO INDIAN COMMUNITY CENTER
Also Called: C I C C
Hwy 162, Covelo (95428)
PHONE..............................707 983-8478
Otis Botherton, *Administration*
EMP: 100
SALES (est): 3MM **Privately Held**
SIC: 6531 Real estate agents & managers

(P-11081)
CROCKER GROUP LLC
1101 E Orangewood Ave, Anaheim (92805-6827)
PHONE..............................714 221-5621
Peter Barker, *Principal*
EMP: 75
SALES (est): 1.2MM **Privately Held**
SIC: 6531 Real estate agent, residential

(P-11082)
CUSHMAN & WAKEFIELD INC
Also Called: Terranomics
1350 Bayshore Hwy Ste 900, Burlingame (94010-1818)
PHONE..............................650 347-3700
Sheryl Simpson, *Branch Mgr*
John Brackett, *Partner*
Tom Christian, *Partner*
Staci E Cole, *Partner*
Jamie D'Alessandro, *Partner*
EMP: 50
SALES (corp-wide): 8.2B **Privately Held**
SIC: 6531 8742 Real estate leasing & rentals; real estate consultant
HQ: Cushman & Wakefield, Inc.
    225 W Wacker Dr Ste 3000
    Chicago IL 60606
    312 424-8000

(P-11083)
CUSHMAN & WAKEFIELD CAL INC (DH)
1 Maritime Plz Ste 900, San Francisco (94111-3412)
PHONE..............................408 275-6730
Joseph Stettinius Jr, *CEO*
Randy Borron, *President*
Robert Rudin, *Exec VP*
Robert Mangino, *Associate Dir*
Edward Grammens, *Exec Dir*
EMP: 110
SQ FT: 26,500
SALES (est): 310.7MM
SALES (corp-wide): 8.2B **Privately Held**
WEB: www.cushwake-nb.com
SIC: 6531 Real estate brokers & agents; real estate agent, commercial; real estate managers; appraiser, real estate
HQ: Cushman & Wakefield, Inc.
    225 W Wacker Dr Ste 3000
    Chicago IL 60606
    312 424-8000

(P-11084)
CUSHMAN & WAKEFIELD CAL INC
18111 Von Karman Ave # 1000, Irvine (92612-7101)
PHONE..............................949 474-4004

PRODUCTS & SVCS

Dee Shipley, *Sales/Mktg Mgr*
EMP: 50
SALES (corp-wide): 8.2B **Privately Held**
WEB: www.cushwake-nb.com
SIC: 6531 Real estate agent, commercial
HQ: Cushman & Wakefield Of California,
Inc.
1 Maritime Plz Ste 900
San Francisco CA 94111
408 275-6730

(P-11085)
CWS APARTMENT HOMES LLC
(PA)
Also Called: Cws Capital Partners
14 Corporate Plaza Dr # 210, Newport
Beach (92660-7928)
PHONE..................................949 640-4200
Gary Carmell,
Steven J Sherwood,
EMP: 450 **EST:** 1998
SQ FT: 5,000
SALES (est): 30.3MM **Privately Held**
WEB: www.cwsapartments.com
SIC: 6531 Rental agent, real estate

(P-11086)
DAVID LYNG & ASSOCIATES INC
Also Called: America Drean Realty
1041 41st Ave Ste A, Santa Cruz
(95062-4466)
PHONE..................................831 429-5700
Don Berig, *Owner*
EMP: 85
SALES (corp-wide): 7.5MM **Privately
Held**
SIC: 6531 Real estate agent, residential
PA: David Lyng & Associates Inc
1041 41st Ave
Santa Cruz CA 95062
831 476-0100

(P-11087)
DAYMARK REALTY ADVISORS
INC
Also Called: Daymark Properties Realty
750 B St Ste 2620, San Diego
(92101-8172)
PHONE..................................714 975-2999
Todd A Mikles, *CEO*
EMP: 400 **EST:** 2010
SALES (est): 20.6MM **Privately Held**
SIC: 6531 Real estate brokers & agents

(P-11088)
DEAN GOODMAN INC
10833 Valley View St # 240, Cypress
(90630-5046)
PHONE..................................714 229-8999
Candice H Miller, *President*
Amber Henson, *Admin Mgr*
Ray Pelaez, *Dean*
Adriana Soto, *Dean*
Mon Guadagno, *Manager*
EMP: 55
SALES (est): 4.8MM **Privately Held**
WEB: www.goodmandean.com
SIC: 6531 Appraiser, real estate

(P-11089)
DENOVA HOME SALES INC
Also Called: Denova Homes
1500 Willow Pass Ct, Concord
(94520-1009)
PHONE..................................925 852-0545
David Sanson, *President*
Lori Sanson, *Vice Pres*
Michael Evans, *Planning*
Peter Giles, *Project Mgr*
Cindi Jefferies, *Purchasing*
EMP: 84
SQ FT: 1,850
SALES (est): 9.3MM **Privately Held**
WEB: www.denovahomes.com
SIC: 6531 Real estate brokers & agents

(P-11090)
DESERT RESORT
MANAGEMENT
42635 Melanie Pl Ste 103, Palm Desert
(92211-9113)
PHONE..................................760 831-0172
Mark Dodge, *President*
EMP: 52
SQ FT: 11,000

SALES (est): 5.3MM **Privately Held**
SIC: 6531 Condominium manager; real estate managers

(P-11091)
DIABLO REALTY INC
Also Called: Pacific Mortgage Resources
975 Ygnacio Valley Rd, Walnut Creek
(94596-3825)
PHONE..................................925 933-9300
Linda Jean Anderson, *President*
Moses Guillory, *Corp Secy*
EMP: 50
SQ FT: 7,000
SALES (est): 3.5MM **Privately Held**
WEB: www.diablorealty.com
SIC: 6531 6163 Real estate brokers &
agents; mortgage brokers arranging for
loans, using money of others

(P-11092)
DIAMOND RIDGE
CORPORATION
Also Called: Re/Max
121 S Mountain Ave, Upland (91786-6257)
PHONE..................................909 949-0605
Jennifer Lynn Puglisi, *CEO*
Laura Aldridge, *Broker*
Sonja Coffee, *Broker*
Jose Garcia, *Broker*
Melvin Munguia, *Broker*
EMP: 165
SALES (est): 8.4MM **Privately Held**
SIC: 6531 Real estate agent, residential

(P-11093)
DIEZ & LEIS RE GROUP INC
Also Called: Prudential Norcal Realty
5120 Manzanita Ave # 120, Carmichael
(95608-0558)
PHONE..................................916 487-4287
Ron Leis, *President*
EMP: 60
SQ FT: 10,000
SALES (est): 3MM
SALES (corp-wide): 62.9B **Publicly Held**
SIC: 6531 Real estate agent, residential
HQ: Brer Affiliates Llc
18500 Von Karman Ave # 400
Irvine CA 92612
949 794-7900

(P-11094)
DILBECK INC (PA)
Also Called: Dilbeck Realtors
1030 Foothill Blvd, La Canada
(91011-3285)
PHONE..................................818 790-6774
Mark Dilbeck, *Ch of Bd*
Lynn Kornmann, *CFO*
Sean Baroni, *Vice Pres*
Bruce Dilbeck, *Admin Sec*
Don Valantine, *Sales Executive*
EMP: 70
SQ FT: 9,000
SALES (est): 7.3MM **Privately Held**
WEB: www.lacanadarealestate.com
SIC: 6531 Real estate agent, commercial;
real estate managers

(P-11095)
DILBECK INC
2943 Foothill Blvd, La Crescenta
(91214-3412)
PHONE..................................818 248-2248
Susan Lindsey, *Branch Mgr*
EMP: 80
SALES (corp-wide): 7.3MM **Privately
Held**
WEB: www.lacanadarealestate.com
SIC: 6531 Real estate agent, commercial
PA: Dilbeck Inc.
1030 Foothill Blvd
La Canada CA 91011
818 790-6774

(P-11096)
DILBECK INC
Also Called: Dilbeck Realtors
850 Hampshire Rd Ste A, Westlake Village
(91361-2800)
PHONE..................................805 379-1880
Chuck Lech, *Branch Mgr*
Kerri Dunton, *Real Est Agnt*
Charone Gilmore, *Real Est Agnt*
Judi Irwin, *Real Est Agnt*

Diane R Kane, *Real Est Agnt*
EMP: 50
SALES (corp-wide): 7.3MM **Privately
Held**
WEB: www.lacanadarealestate.com
SIC: 6531 Real estate agent, commercial;
real estate managers
PA: Dilbeck Inc.
1030 Foothill Blvd
La Canada CA 91011
818 790-6774

(P-11097)
DILBECK INC
Also Called: Dilbeck Realtors
225 E Colorado Blvd, Pasadena
(91101-1903)
PHONE..................................626 584-0101
Ray Hayes, *Manager*
EMP: 60
SALES (corp-wide): 7.3MM **Privately
Held**
WEB: www.lacanadarealestate.com
SIC: 6531 Real estate agent, commercial
PA: Dilbeck Inc.
1030 Foothill Blvd
La Canada CA 91011
818 790-6774

(P-11098)
DONAHUE SCHRBER RLTY
GROUP INC (PA)
200 Baker St Ste 100, Costa Mesa
(92626-4551)
PHONE..................................714 545-1400
Thomas Schriber, *Ch of Bd*
Patrick S Donahue, *President*
Larry Casey, *CFO*
EMP: 80
SQ FT: 20,000
SALES (est): 11.3MM **Privately Held**
WEB: www.montebellotowncenter.com
SIC: 6531 Real estate agent, commercial

(P-11099)
DOUG ARNOLD REAL ESTATE
INC (PA)
Also Called: Coldwell Banker
505 2nd St, Davis (95616-4618)
PHONE..................................530 758-3080
Doug Arnold, *President*
J David Taoramino, *Treasurer*
EMP: 50
SQ FT: 7,000
SALES (est): 4.4MM **Privately Held**
WEB: www.coldwellbankerdougarnold.com
SIC: 6531 Real estate agent, residential

(P-11100)
DOUGLAS ELLIMAN REAL
ESTATE
150 El Camino Dr Fl 1, Beverly Hills
(90212-2734)
PHONE..................................310 595-3888
Collin Keanan, *General Mgr*
Stephen Kotler, *President*
EMP: 50
SALES (est): 548.5K **Privately Held**
SIC: 6531 Real estate brokers & agents

(P-11101)
DOUGLAS EMMETT REALTY
FUND 199
808 Wilshire Blvd Ste 200, Santa Monica
(90401-1889)
PHONE..................................310 255-7700
Dan Emmett, *Principal*
EMP: 60
SALES (est): 1.4MM
SALES (corp-wide): 881.3MM **Privately
Held**
SIC: 6531 Real estate brokers & agents
PA: Douglas Emmett, Inc.
1299 Ocean Ave Ste 1000
Santa Monica CA 90401
310 255-7700

(P-11102)
DPPM INC
Also Called: Zephyr Real Estate
4040 24th St, San Francisco (94114-3716)
PHONE..................................415 695-7707
Fax: 415 695-1106
EMP: 80

SALES (corp-wide): 16.4MM **Privately
Held**
SIC: 6531
PA: Dppm, Inc.
850 7th St
San Francisco CA 94127
415 348-1212

(P-11103)
DREAM HOME ESTATES INC
2901 W Coast Hwy Ste 200, Newport
Beach (92663-4045)
PHONE..................................949 415-4646
David Prewitt, *CEO*
EMP: 50
SALES (est): 1MM **Privately Held**
SIC: 6531 6799 8742 Selling agent, real
estate; real estate investors, except prop-
erty operators; real estate consultant

(P-11104)
DUNLAP PROPERTY GROUP
INC
801 E Chapman Ave Ste 233, Fullerton
(92831-3847)
P.O. Box 4308 (92834-4308)
PHONE..................................714 879-0111
Paul Dunlap, *President*
EMP: 55
SALES (est): 2.5MM **Privately Held**
SIC: 6531 Appraiser, real estate

(P-11105)
E-N REALTY II
Also Called: Century 21 E
1081 Grand Ave, Diamond Bar
(91765-2210)
PHONE..................................909 597-1736
John Newe, *President*
EMP: 50
SALES (est): 2.1MM **Privately Held**
SIC: 6531 Real estate agent, residential

(P-11106)
EAM ENTERPRISES INC (PA)
Also Called: Crest R E O & Relocation
4005 Foothill Blvd, La Crescenta
(91214-1623)
PHONE..................................818 248-9100
Razmik Mirzakhanian, *CEO*
EMP: 270
SQ FT: 5,000
SALES (est): 15.4MM **Privately Held**
SIC: 6531 Real estate agent, residential

(P-11107)
EAPPRAISEIT LLC (PA)
12395 First American Way, Poway
(92064-6897)
PHONE..................................800 281-6200
Anthony Merlo,
Devid Feildman, *Principal*
Diane Swanson, *Director*
Frank V McMahon, *Manager*
EMP: 65
SALES (est): 4.6MM **Privately Held**
WEB: www.eappraiseit.com
SIC: 6531 Appraiser, real estate

(P-11108)
EAST CRSON II HSING
PRTNERS LP
401 W Carson St, Carson (90745-2616)
PHONE..................................310 522-9606
Jim Brooks, *Controller*
EMP: 99
SALES (est): 1.8MM **Privately Held**
SIC: 6531 Real estate agents & managers

(P-11109)
EAST HALL INVESTORS INC
Also Called: Keller Williams Realtors
11601 Blocker Dr Ste 200, Auburn
(95603-4650)
PHONE..................................530 328-1900
Daryl Rogers, *President*
Ralph Carpenter, *Branch Mgr*
Shane Cheng, *Real Est Agnt*
Jim Cope, *Real Est Agnt*
Frank Enderle, *Real Est Agnt*
EMP: 80
SALES (est): 1.7MM **Privately Held**
SIC: 6531 Real estate agent, residential

(P-11110)
EDEN HOUSING MANAGEMENT INC (PA)
22645 Grand St, Hayward (94541-5031)
PHONE..............................510 582-1460
Linda Mandolini, *President*
Jan Peters, *COO*
Tony MA, *CFO*
Tracy Griffin, *Human Res Mgr*
Brian Gordon, *Property Mgr*
EMP: 50
SALES: 7MM **Privately Held**
SIC: 6531 Real estate managers

(P-11111)
EGOMOTION CORP (PA)
Also Called: Zeus Living
321 11th St, San Francisco (94103-4313)
PHONE..............................415 849-4662
Kulveer Taggar, *CEO*
Srinivas Panguluri, *COO*
Joseph Wong, *CTO*
Sara Katz, *Human Resources*
EMP: 50
SALES (est): 4MM **Privately Held**
SIC: 6531 6514 6513 Real estate leasing & rentals; dwelling operators, except apartments; apartment building operators

(P-11112)
ELIZABETH LARSON
3736 Jackson St, San Francisco (94118-1609)
PHONE..............................415 409-7300
Elizabeth Larson, *Owner*
EMP: 60
SALES (est): 1.3MM **Privately Held**
WEB: www.elarsonphoto.com
SIC: 6531 Auction, real estate

(P-11113)
EMPIRE ESTATES INC
Also Called: Prudential
10750 Civic Center Dr # 100, Rancho Cucamonga (91730-3891)
PHONE..............................909 980-3100
Kim Senecal, *President*
EMP: 100
SQ FT: 4,500
SALES (est): 6.6MM **Privately Held**
WEB: www.kimsenecal.com
SIC: 6531 Real estate agent, residential

(P-11114)
EMPIRE REALTY ASSOCIATES INC
380 Diablo Rd, Danville (94526-3468)
PHONE..............................925 217-5000
Judi Keenholtz, *CEO*
Brian Moggan, *General Mgr*
Don Morton, *Real Est Agnt*
Kasie Robertson, *Real Est Agnt*
Lindsey Sindayen, *Real Est Agnt*
EMP: 60
SALES (est): 5.5MM **Privately Held**
WEB: www.empirera.com
SIC: 6531 Real estate agent, residential
PA: Pacific Union International, Inc.
1 Letterman Dr Bldg C
San Francisco CA 94129

(P-11115)
ERA REALTY CENTER
49 Placerville Dr, Placerville (95667-3901)
PHONE..............................530 295-2900
Dan Jacuzzi, *Owner*
EMP: 60
SALES (est): 2MM **Privately Held**
SIC: 6531 Real estate agent, residential

(P-11116)
ESSEX PROPERTIES LLC
18012 Sky Park Cir # 200, Irvine (92614-6671)
PHONE..............................949 798-8100
Jim Niger, *President*
Burrel D Magnusson, *Chairman*
Linda Webber, *Vice Pres*
Susan Longshore, *Marketing Staff*
EMP: 75
SALES (est): 6.3MM **Privately Held**
SIC: 6531 Real estate agent, commercial

(P-11117)
ETHAN CONRAD PROPERTIES INC (PA)
1300 National Dr Ste 100, Sacramento (95834-1981)
PHONE..............................916 779-1000
Ethan Conrad, *President*
Kenneth Miller, *CFO*
Chase Burke, *Vice Pres*
Marissa Todd, *Executive Asst*
Ryan Healy, *Project Mgr*
EMP: 53
SQ FT: 45,063
SALES: 45MM **Privately Held**
WEB: www.ethanconradprop.com
SIC: 6531 Real estate agents & managers

(P-11118)
EVANS/SIPES INC (PA)
Also Called: Re/Max
5720 Ralston St Ste 100, Ventura (93003-7845)
PHONE..............................805 644-1242
Glenn Sipes, *President*
Jerry Beebe, *CFO*
Michael Sipes, *Vice Pres*
Editha Colitti, *Office Mgr*
Harold Powell, *Broker*
EMP: 250
SQ FT: 35,000
SALES (est): 19MM **Privately Held**
WEB: www.cynthialoughman.com
SIC: 6531 Real estate agent, residential

(P-11119)
EVOQ PROPERTIES INC
1318 E 7th St Ste 200, Los Angeles (90021-1128)
PHONE..............................213 988-8890
Martin Caveroy, *CEO*
John Charles Maddux, *President*
Andrew Murray, *CFO*
Miguel Enrique Echemendia, *Officer*
Lynn Beckemeyer, *Exec VP*
EMP: 82
SALES (est): 6.4MM **Privately Held**
WEB: www.meruelomaddux.com
SIC: 6531 Real estate agent, commercial; real estate agent, residential

(P-11120)
EXCELLNCE OF INLAND EMPIRE INC
Also Called: Century 21
9568 Archibald Ave # 110, Rancho Cucamonga (91730-5744)
PHONE..............................909 758-4311
Ramiro Majia, *President*
Luis Oliver, *CFO*
EMP: 106
SQ FT: 8,874
SALES: 3.5MM **Privately Held**
SIC: 6531 7389 Real estate agent, residential; brokers' services

(P-11121)
EXPREAL INC
Also Called: Century 21 Experience
7168 Archibald Ave # 100, Alta Loma (91701-5061)
PHONE..............................909 373-4400
Peter Gottuso, *Vice Pres*
Lynne Garretson, *Real Est Agnt*
EMP: 99
SALES: 950K **Privately Held**
SIC: 6531 Real estate agent, residential

(P-11122)
F M TARBELL CO
18295 Collier Ave, Lake Elsinore (92530-2755)
PHONE..............................951 471-5333
Carol Rounsley, *Manager*
EMP: 70
SALES (corp-wide): 132.1MM **Privately Held**
SIC: 6531 Real estate agent, commercial
HQ: F. M. Tarbell Co
1403 N Tustin Ave Ste 380
Santa Ana CA 92705
714 972-0988

(P-11123)
F M TARBELL CO
Also Called: Tarbel Realtors
39028 Winchester Rd # 101, Murrieta (92563-3505)
PHONE..............................951 677-3565
Joe McAllen, *General Mgr*
EMP: 80
SALES (corp-wide): 132.1MM **Privately Held**
SIC: 6531 Real estate agent, commercial
HQ: F. M. Tarbell Co
1403 N Tustin Ave Ste 380
Santa Ana CA 92705
714 972-0988

(P-11124)
F M TARBELL CO
Also Called: Tarbell Realtors
321 S State College Blvd, Anaheim (92806-4118)
PHONE..............................714 772-8990
Fax: 714 772-3801
EMP: 55
SALES (corp-wide): 134.2MM **Privately Held**
SIC: 6531
HQ: F. M. Tarbell Co
1403 N Tustin Ave Ste 380
Santa Ana CA 92705
714 972-0988

(P-11125)
F M TARBELL CO
Also Called: Tarbell Realtors
6396 E Santa Ana Cyn Rd, Anaheim (92807-2365)
PHONE..............................714 637-7240
Mercedes Sedano, *Manager*
EMP: 50
SALES (corp-wide): 132.1MM **Privately Held**
WEB: www.tarbell.com
SIC: 6531 Real estate brokers & agents
HQ: F. M. Tarbell Co
1403 N Tustin Ave Ste 380
Santa Ana CA 92705
714 972-0988

(P-11126)
F M TARBELL CO (HQ)
Also Called: Tarbell Realtors
1403 N Tustin Ave Ste 380, Santa Ana (92705-8691)
PHONE..............................714 972-0988
Tina Jimov, *President*
Donald M Tarbell, *CEO*
Eva De Fuente, *Real Est Agnt*
EMP: 110
SQ FT: 60,000
SALES (est): 26.5MM
SALES (corp-wide): 132.1MM **Privately Held**
WEB: www.tarbell.com
SIC: 6531 Real estate agent, residential
PA: Tarbell Financial Corporation
1403 N Tustin Ave Ste 380
Santa Ana CA 92705
714 972-0988

(P-11127)
F M TARBELL CO
Also Called: Tarbell Realtors
315 Magnolia Ave, Corona (92879-3300)
PHONE..............................951 280-6040
Danny Vallejo, *Manager*
EMP: 190
SALES (corp-wide): 132.1MM **Privately Held**
WEB: www.tarbell.com
SIC: 6531 Real estate brokers & agents
HQ: F. M. Tarbell Co
1403 N Tustin Ave Ste 380
Santa Ana CA 92705
714 972-0988

(P-11128)
F M TARBELL CO
Also Called: Tarbell Realtors
25201 La Paz Rd, Laguna Hills (92653-5118)
PHONE..............................949 830-6030
Dianne Montgomery, *Manager*
EMP: 62
SQ FT: 10,325

SALES (corp-wide): 132.1MM **Privately Held**
WEB: www.tarbell.com
SIC: 6531 Real estate agent, commercial
HQ: F. M. Tarbell Co
1403 N Tustin Ave Ste 380
Santa Ana CA 92705
714 972-0988

(P-11129)
F M TARBELL CO
Also Called: Tarbell Realtors
27701 Scott Rd Ste 103, Menifee (92584-9434)
PHONE..............................951 301-5932
Kathy Ranier, *Manager*
EMP: 60
SALES (corp-wide): 132.1MM **Privately Held**
WEB: www.tarbell.com
SIC: 6531 Real estate brokers & agents
HQ: F. M. Tarbell Co
1403 N Tustin Ave Ste 380
Santa Ana CA 92705
714 972-0988

(P-11130)
F M TARBELL CO
Also Called: Tarbell Realtors
31685 Temecula Pkwy Ste B, Temecula (92592-2872)
PHONE..............................951 303-0307
West Ives, *Manager*
EMP: 135
SALES (corp-wide): 132.1MM **Privately Held**
WEB: www.tarbell.com
SIC: 6531 Real estate brokers & agents
HQ: F. M. Tarbell Co
1403 N Tustin Ave Ste 380
Santa Ana CA 92705
714 972-0988

(P-11131)
F M TARBELL CO
Also Called: Tarbell Realtors
4040 Barranca Pkwy # 220, Irvine (92604-4766)
PHONE..............................949 559-8451
Sheila Mayers, *Manager*
EMP: 72
SALES (corp-wide): 132.1MM **Privately Held**
WEB: www.tarbell.com
SIC: 6531 Real estate agent, residential
HQ: F. M. Tarbell Co
1403 N Tustin Ave Ste 380
Santa Ana CA 92705
714 972-0988

(P-11132)
F M TARBELL CO
2409 S Vineyard Ave Ste A, Ontario (91761-6401)
PHONE..............................951 270-1022
Nancy Foster, *Branch Mgr*
George Ibarra, *Real Est Agnt*
EMP: 70
SALES (corp-wide): 132.1MM **Privately Held**
SIC: 6531 Real estate brokers & agents
HQ: F. M. Tarbell Co
1403 N Tustin Ave Ste 380
Santa Ana CA 92705
714 972-0988

(P-11133)
F M TARBELL CO
Also Called: Tarbell Realtors
73700 El Paseo, Palm Desert (92260-4380)
PHONE..............................760 346-7405
Dan Trevino, *Branch Mgr*
EMP: 50
SALES (corp-wide): 132.1MM **Privately Held**
WEB: www.tarbell.com
SIC: 6531 Real estate brokers & agents
HQ: F. M. Tarbell Co
1403 N Tustin Ave Ste 380
Santa Ana CA 92705
714 972-0988

PRODUCTS & SVCS

(P-11134)
F M TARBELL CO
Also Called: Tarbell Realtors
1365 E 19th St Ste A, Upland
(91784-4201)
PHONE...................................909 982-8881
Bill Velto, *Manager*
Clement Lai, *Real Est Agnt*
EMP: 102
SALES (corp-wide): 132.1MM **Privately Held**
WEB: www.tarbell.com
SIC: 6531 Real estate brokers & agents
HQ: F. M. Tarbell Co
    1403 N Tustin Ave Ste 380
    Santa Ana CA 92705
    714 972-0988

(P-11135)
FAR WEST MANAGEMENT CORP (PA)
17941 Mitchell S Ste A, Irvine
(92614-6832)
P.O. Box 11976, Santa Ana (92711-1976)
PHONE...................................949 863-1757
Richard W Silver, *CEO*
Richard Franklin, *Corp Secy*
EMP: 53
SQ FT: 13,000
SALES (est): 6.6MM **Privately Held**
SIC: 6531 Condominium manager

(P-11136)
FELSON COMPANIES INC
1290 B St Ste 210, Hayward (94541-2996)
PHONE...................................510 538-1150
Joseph Felson, *President*
Joseph Lee Felson, *President*
Elliot Felson, *Corp Secy*
Victor Richard Felson, *Vice Pres*
EMP: 90
SQ FT: 4,000
SALES (est): 8.3MM **Privately Held**
SIC: 6531 Real estate managers

(P-11137)
FILLMORE MARKETPLACE LP
Also Called: Fillmore Marketplace I
1223 Webster St, San Francisco
(94115-5021)
PHONE...................................415 921-6514
Jim Brooks, *Controller*
EMP: 50
SALES (est): 1.1MM **Privately Held**
SIC: 6531 Real estate agents & managers

(P-11138)
FIRST & LA REALTY CORP (PA)
Also Called: Century 21 Hill Top Realtors
1301 E Los Angeles Ave, Simi Valley
(93065-2882)
PHONE...................................805 581-0021
Robert Connlee, *President*
Pat Connlee, *Treasurer*
Susan Hill, *Admin Sec*
EMP: 67
SQ FT: 2,600
SALES (est): 3.7MM **Privately Held**
WEB: www.patconlee.com
SIC: 6531 Real estate agent, residential

(P-11139)
FIRST AMERCN PROF RE SVCS INC (PA)
200 Commerce, Irvine (92602-5000)
PHONE...................................714 250-1400
Larry Davidson, *President*
Jerry Bumbaugh, *CFO*
Mickey Allee, *Exec VP*
Scott Klein, *Vice Pres*
Kim Bellows, *Physician Asst*
EMP: 240
SQ FT: 28,000
SALES (est): 10MM **Privately Held**
WEB: www.firstamsms.com
SIC: 6531 Real estate agents & managers

(P-11140)
FIRST AMERICAN TEAM REALTY INC (PA)
Also Called: Best Financial, The
2501 Cherry Ave Ste 100, Signal Hill
(90755-2039)
PHONE...................................562 427-7765
Steve S Vong, *President*

Ron Jimenez, *Manager*
EMP: 170
SQ FT: 3,300
SALES (est): 8.8MM **Privately Held**
WEB: www.firstamericanteam.com
SIC: 6531 Real estate agent, residential

(P-11141)
FIRST FAMILY HOMES
Also Called: Century 21
12027 Paramount Blvd, Downey
(90242-2307)
PHONE...................................562 862-7373
William C Park, *President*
Soomi Park, *Corp Secy*
EMP: 50
SALES (est): 2.2MM **Privately Held**
WEB: www.century21prorealty.com
SIC: 6531 6798 Real estate agent, residential; real estate investment trusts

(P-11142)
FIRST MARIN REALTY INC
145 Lomita Dr, Mill Valley (94941-1403)
PHONE...................................415 383-9393
Douglas B Engel, *President*
Bruce Engel, *Ch of Bd*
Marcine Engel, *Vice Pres*
Brigetta Engle, *Vice Pres*
EMP: 60
SQ FT: 10,000
SALES: 3MM **Privately Held**
WEB: www.firstmarin.net
SIC: 6531 Real estate agent, residential

(P-11143)
FIRST TEAM RE - ORANGE CNTY
74855 Country Club Dr, Palm Desert
(92260-1961)
PHONE...................................760 340-9911
Todd Banks, *Branch Mgr*
Edborg Cherie, *Controller*
EMP: 64
SALES (corp-wide): 82.5MM **Privately Held**
SIC: 6531 Real estate agent, residential; real estate brokers & agents
PA: First Team Real Estate - Orange
    County
    108 Pacifica Ste 300
    Irvine CA 92618
    888 236-1943

(P-11144)
FIRST TEAM RE - ORANGE CNTY
18180 Yorba Linda Blvd # 501, Yorba Linda
(92886-3901)
PHONE...................................714 223-2143
EMP: 100
SALES (corp-wide): 63.6MM **Privately Held**
SIC: 6531
PA: First Team Real Estate - Orange
    County
    108 Pacifica Ste 300
    Irvine CA 92618
    888 236-1943

(P-11145)
FIRST TEAM RE - ORANGE CNTY
12501 Seal Beach Blvd # 100, Seal Beach
(90740-2763)
PHONE...................................562 596-9911
Judy Sharp, *Manager*
Dave Pedneault, *Sales Mgr*
Karl Heim,
Stacy Ryan, *Manager*
David Chalfant, *Real Est Agnt*
EMP: 150
SALES (corp-wide): 82.5MM **Privately Held**
WEB: www.coastcitiesescrow.com
SIC: 6531 Real estate agent, residential; real estate brokers & agents
PA: First Team Real Estate - Orange
    County
    108 Pacifica Ste 300
    Irvine CA 92618
    888 236-1943

(P-11146)
FIRST TEAM RE - ORANGE CNTY
4 Corporate Plaza Dr # 100, Newport
Beach (92660-7906)
PHONE...................................949 759-5747
Jennifer Berman, *Office Mgr*
Kristin Ajer, *Real Est Agnt*
Ilene Aldrich, *Real Est Agnt*
Margaret Brien, *Real Est Agnt*
Susan Chotkevys, *Real Est Agnt*
EMP: 55
SALES (corp-wide): 82.5MM **Privately Held**
WEB: www.coastcitiesescrow.com
SIC: 6531 Real estate brokers & agents
PA: First Team Real Estate - Orange
    County
    108 Pacifica Ste 300
    Irvine CA 92618
    888 236-1943

(P-11147)
FIRST TEAM RE - ORANGE CNTY (PA)
Also Called: First Team Walk-In Realty
108 Pacifica Ste 300, Irvine (92618-7435)
PHONE...................................888 236-1943
Cameron Merage, *CEO*
Michele Harrington, *COO*
Michelle Williams Harringto, *Vice Pres*
Carlos Aguirre, *Info Tech Dir*
Mike Leong, *Technical Staff*
EMP: 160 EST: 1976
SQ FT: 8,000
SALES (est): 82.5MM **Privately Held**
WEB: www.coastcitiesescrow.com
SIC: 6531 Real estate agent, residential

(P-11148)
FIRST TEAM RE - ORANGE CNTY
Also Called: First State
20100 Brookhurst St, Huntington Beach
(92646-4938)
PHONE...................................714 965-2244
Wally Malesh, *Manager*
Gwen J Miller, *Real Est Agnt*
Christina Moreno, *Real Est Agnt*
Tamzi R Richardson, *Real Est Agnt*
Joe G Sire, *Real Est Agnt*
EMP: 100
SALES (corp-wide): 82.5MM **Privately Held**
WEB: www.coastcitiesescrow.com
SIC: 6531 Real estate brokers & agents
PA: First Team Real Estate - Orange
    County
    108 Pacifica Ste 300
    Irvine CA 92618
    888 236-1943

(P-11149)
FIRST TEAM RE - ORANGE CNTY
42 64th Pl, Long Beach (90803-5676)
PHONE...................................562 346-5088
EMP: 78
SALES (corp-wide): 82.5MM **Privately Held**
SIC: 6531 Real estate agent, residential
PA: First Team Real Estate - Orange
    County
    108 Pacifica Ste 300
    Irvine CA 92618
    888 236-1943

(P-11150)
FIRST TEAM RE - ORANGE CNTY
32451 Golden Lantern # 210, Laguna
Niguel (92677-5344)
PHONE...................................949 240-7979
Mark Kojac, *General Mgr*
Alejandra Kutzner, *Sales Staff*
Beau Beardslee, *Real Est Agnt*
Jacqueline Chase, *Real Est Agnt*
Colleen Crane, *Real Est Agnt*
EMP: 140
SALES (corp-wide): 82.5MM **Privately Held**
WEB: www.coastcitiesescrow.com
SIC: 6531 Real estate brokers & agents

PA: First Team Real Estate - Orange
    County
    108 Pacifica Ste 300
    Irvine CA 92618
    888 236-1943

(P-11151)
FIRST TEAM RE - ORANGE CNTY
Also Called: 1st Team Real Estate
17240 17th St, Tustin (92780-1940)
PHONE...................................714 544-5456
Michael Hampton, *Manager*
Rochelle McKeehan, *Administration*
Scott Gruszczynski, *Controller*
Steve Roberts, *Broker*
Jessica Griffith, *Nurse*
EMP: 137
SALES (corp-wide): 82.5MM **Privately Held**
WEB: www.coastcitiesescrow.com
SIC: 6531 Real estate brokers & agents
PA: First Team Real Estate - Orange
    County
    108 Pacifica Ste 300
    Irvine CA 92618
    888 236-1943

(P-11152)
FIRST TEAM RE - ORANGE CNTY
8028 E Santa Ana Cyn Rd, Anaheim
(92808-1108)
PHONE...................................714 974-9191
Anna Bennet, *Manager*
Sandra Meucci, *Office Admin*
Alexander Thompson, *Broker*
Anna Bennett, *Real Est Agnt*
Bruce Brown, *Real Est Agnt*
EMP: 63
SALES (corp-wide): 82.5MM **Privately Held**
WEB: www.coastcitiesescrow.com
SIC: 6531 Real estate brokers & agents
PA: First Team Real Estate - Orange
    County
    108 Pacifica Ste 300
    Irvine CA 92618
    888 236-1943

(P-11153)
FIRST TEAM RE - ORANGE CNTY
26711 Aliso Creek Rd # 200, Aliso Viejo
(92656-4820)
PHONE...................................949 389-0004
Michele Williams, *Branch Mgr*
EMP: 150
SALES (corp-wide): 82.5MM **Privately Held**
WEB: www.bhsi.com
SIC: 6531 Real estate agents & managers
PA: First Team Real Estate - Orange
    County
    108 Pacifica Ste 300
    Irvine CA 92618
    888 236-1943

(P-11154)
FIRSTSERVICE RESIDENTIAL (HQ)
Also Called: Merit Property Management Inc
15241 Laguna Canyon Rd, Irvine
(92618-3146)
PHONE...................................949 448-6000
Bob Cardoza, *President*
Katie Ward, *Principal*
Dawn Suskin, *Exec Dir*
Beth Farrell, *General Mgr*
Laurie Kendrick, *General Mgr*
EMP: 200
SQ FT: 21,000
SALES (est): 39MM
SALES (corp-wide): 1.9B **Privately Held**
SIC: 6531 Real estate managers
PA: Firstservice Corporation
    1140 Bay St Suite 4000
    Toronto ON M5S 2
    416 960-9500

▲ = Import ▼=Export
◆ =Import/Export

(P-11155)
FIRSTSRVICE RSIDENTIAL CAL INC (DH)
195 N Euclid Ave, Upland (91786-6055)
P.O. Box 1510 (91785-1510)
PHONE....................909 981-4131
Glennon Gray, *President*
James Gray, *Vice Pres*
Kathy Johnston, *Division Mgr*
Tad Creasey, *Property Mgr*
Deborah Maglasang, *Property Mgr*
EMP: 69
SQ FT: 16,000
SALES (est): 7.5MM
SALES (corp-wide): 1.9B **Privately Held**
WEB: www.euclidmanagement.com
SIC: 6531 Real estate managers

(P-11156)
FKC PARTNERS A CAL LTD PARTNR
Also Called: Fkc Properties
180 N Rverview Dr Ste 100, Anaheim (92808)
PHONE....................714 528-9864
Paul Kramer,
EMP: 50
SALES (est): 2.4MM **Privately Held**
SIC: 6531 Real estate brokers & agents

(P-11157)
FLYNN PROPERTIES INC
225 Bush St Ste 1470, San Francisco (94104-4226)
PHONE....................415 835-0225
Greg Flynn, *President*
Carol Foster, *CFO*
Ronald Bellamy, *Officer*
Sara Botwood-Guest, *Vice Pres*
Toto Haba, *Vice Pres*
EMP: 50
SALES (est): 4.8MM **Privately Held**
SIC: 6531 Real estate agent, commercial

(P-11158)
FPI MANAGEMENT INC (PA)
800 Iron Point Rd, Folsom (95630-9004)
PHONE....................916 357-5300
Dennis Treadaway, *President*
Ken Hunt, *Shareholder*
Gary Quattrin, *Shareholder*
David Divine, *Vice Pres*
Tracie Freeman, *Vice Pres*
EMP: 50
SQ FT: 18,000
SALES (est): 98.4MM **Privately Held**
WEB: www.fpimgt.com
SIC: 6531 Real estate managers

(P-11159)
FRANK HOWARD ALLEN FINCL CORP
Also Called: Frank Howard Allen Real Estate
1016 Irwin St, San Rafael (94901-3320)
PHONE....................415 456-3000
Fred Angeli, *Manager*
EMP: 55 **Publicly Held**
WEB: www.fhallen.com
SIC: 6531 Real estate agent, residential
HQ: Frank Howard Allen Financial Corporation
1013 2nd St
Novato CA
415 897-4444

(P-11160)
FRED LEEDS PROPERTIES
3860 Crenshaw Blvd # 201, Los Angeles (90008-1816)
PHONE....................310 826-2466
Fred Leeds, *President*
Rayna Faumuina, *Administration*
EMP: 50
SQ FT: 3,000
SALES (est): 3.1MM **Privately Held**
WEB: www.fredleedsproperties.com
SIC: 6531 Real estate agents & managers

(P-11161)
FUSION REAL ESTATE NETWORK INC
1300 National Dr Ste 170, Sacramento (95834-1991)
PHONE....................916 448-3174
Gwen Scott, *President*

James Becker, *Vice Pres*
Helen Whitelaw, *Vice Pres*
EMP: 90
SQ FT: 4,400
SALES (est): 5.2MM **Privately Held**
SIC: 6531 Real estate brokers & agents

(P-11162)
G M A C-ONE SOURCE REALTY
898 Jackman St, El Cajon (92020-3057)
PHONE....................619 405-6231
Greg Seaman, *Owner*
EMP: 56
SALES (est): 2.2MM **Privately Held**
SIC: 6531 Real estate agents & managers

(P-11163)
GEMMM CORP
587 W Los Angeles Ave, Moorpark (93021-1709)
PHONE....................805 267-2700
Dave Ward, *Branch Mgr*
EMP: 59
SALES (corp-wide): 8.5MM **Privately Held**
SIC: 6531 Real estate brokers & agents
PA: Gemmm Corp
2860 E Thousand Oaks Blvd
Thousand Oaks CA 91362
805 496-0555

(P-11164)
GEMMM CORP
2211 Memory Ln, Westlake Village (91361-5524)
PHONE....................818 522-0740
Chris Doernes, *Branch Mgr*
EMP: 59
SALES (corp-wide): 8.5MM **Privately Held**
SIC: 6531 Real estate brokers & agents
PA: Gemmm Corp
2860 E Thousand Oaks Blvd
Thousand Oaks CA 91362
805 496-0555

(P-11165)
GEMMM CORP (PA)
Also Called: Prudential
2860 E Thousand Oaks Blvd, Thousand Oaks (91362-3201)
PHONE....................805 496-0555
Robert L Majorino, *President*
Anthony Principe, *CFO*
Robert Hamilton, *Vice Pres*
Lynn Gilbert, *Admin Sec*
Nancy Eke, *Sales Executive*
EMP: 100
SQ FT: 12,500
SALES (est): 8.5MM **Privately Held**
WEB: www.prucalhomes.com
SIC: 6531 Real estate agent, residential

(P-11166)
GIC REAL ESTATE INC (HQ)
1 Bush St Ste 1100, San Francisco (94104-4417)
PHONE....................415 229-1800
Adam Gallistel, *CEO*
EMP: 60
SQ FT: 10,000
SALES (est): 15.5MM **Privately Held**
SIC: 6531 6799 Real estate managers; real estate investors, except property operators

(P-11167)
GK MANAGEMENT CO INC (PA)
5150 Overland Ave, Culver City (90230-4914)
PHONE....................310 204-2050
Carole Glodney, *CEO*
Jona Goldrich, *Vice Pres*
Cecy Avilla, *Regional Mgr*
Perla Lagman, *Accountant*
Janice Baran, *Manager*
EMP: 150
SALES (est): 25.2MM
SALES (corp-wide): 26.4MM **Privately Held**
WEB: www.gkind.com
SIC: 6531 Real estate managers

(P-11168)
GK MANAGEMENT CO INC
Also Called: Coronado Royale
299 Prospect Pl, Coronado (92118-1967)
PHONE....................619 437-1777
Rudy Littlefield, *Manager*
EMP: 50
SALES (corp-wide): 26.4MM **Privately Held**
WEB: www.gkind.com
SIC: 6531 6513 Real estate managers; retirement hotel operation
PA: Gk Management Co., Inc.
5150 Overland Ave
Culver City CA 90230
310 204-2050

(P-11169)
GK MANAGEMENT CO INC
Also Called: Kittridge Gardens
6540 Wilbur Ave, Reseda (91335-5927)
PHONE....................818 705-8834
Jane Pouchino, *Manager*
EMP: 80
SALES (corp-wide): 26.4MM **Privately Held**
WEB: www.gkind.com
SIC: 6531 6513 Real estate managers; apartment building operators
PA: Gk Management Co., Inc.
5150 Overland Ave
Culver City CA 90230
310 204-2050

(P-11170)
GLENBOROUGH LLC (PA)
400 S El Camino Real # 1100, San Mateo (94402-1706)
PHONE....................650 343-9300
Andrew Batinovich, *CEO*
Terri Garnick, *Senior VP*
EMP: 60
SALES: 7MM **Privately Held**
SIC: 6531 Real estate managers

(P-11171)
GOLD COUNTRY MANAGEMENT INC
1825 Bell St Ste 100, Sacramento (95825-1020)
PHONE....................916 929-3003
James Gately, *President*
EMP: 70 **EST:** 1993
SALES (est): 2.8MM **Privately Held**
SIC: 6531 Real estate managers

(P-11172)
GOLDEN RAIN FOUNDATION (PA)
Also Called: Rossmoor
1001 Golden Rain Rd, Walnut Creek (94595-2441)
P.O. Box 2070 (94595-0070)
PHONE....................925 988-7700
Stephen Adams, *CEO*
Rick Chakoff, *CFO*
Steve Adams, *Executive*
Tess Haskett, *Finance*
Lucy Limon, *Opers Staff*
EMP: 53
SQ FT: 5,000
SALES (est): 23.8MM **Privately Held**
WEB: www.rossmoornews.com
SIC: 6531 8011 2711 7997 Real estate managers; offices & clinics of medical doctors; newspapers; golf club, membership

(P-11173)
GOODMAN NORTH AMERICA LLC
18201 Von Karman Ave, Irvine (92612-1000)
PHONE....................949 407-0100
Brandon Birtcher, *CEO*
Dan Grable, *COO*
Shannon Hondl, *Officer*
Anthony Alexander, *Associate Dir*
Charles Crossland, *Managing Dir*
EMP: 100
SALES (est): 10.2MM **Privately Held**
SIC: 6531 6552 1542 Real estate managers; land subdividers & developers, commercial; commercial & office building, new construction

(P-11174)
GRAND PACIFIC RESORTS INC (PA)
5900 Pasteur Ct Ste 200, Carlsbad (92008-7336)
P.O. Box 4068 (92018-4068)
PHONE....................760 431-8500
Timothy J Stripe, *CEO*
Crystal Gonzalez, *COO*
David Brown, *Vice Pres*
Jeff Farr, *Vice Pres*
Shelli Herman, *Admin Mgr*
EMP: 250
SQ FT: 22,000
SALES (est): 166.9MM **Privately Held**
WEB: www.grandpacificresorts.com
SIC: 6531 7011 Time-sharing real estate sales, leasing & rentals; hotels & motels

(P-11175)
GREENBRIAR MANAGEMENT COMPANY
Also Called: Greenbriar Homes Community
43160 Osgood Rd, Fremont (94539-5608)
PHONE....................510 497-8200
Gilbert M Meyer, *CEO*
Carol Meyer, *Vice Pres*
EMP: 100
SQ FT: 16,932
SALES (est): 6.2MM **Privately Held**
SIC: 6531 Cooperative apartment manager

(P-11176)
GREGA BROOKE SRA
18501 Riverside Dr, Sonoma (95476-4509)
P.O. Box 268 (95476-0268)
PHONE....................707 938-3362
Grega Brooke, *Principal*
EMP: 50
SALES (est): 1.3MM **Privately Held**
SIC: 6531 Appraiser, real estate

(P-11177)
GREYSTAR MANAGEMENT SVCS LP
6320 Canoga Ave Ste 1512, Woodland Hills (91367-2526)
PHONE....................818 596-2180
Grace White, *Owner*
EMP: 311 **Privately Held**
SIC: 6531 Real estate brokers & agents
PA: Greystar Management Services, L.P.
750 Bering Dr Ste 300
Houston TX 77057

(P-11178)
GREYSTAR MANAGEMENT SVCS LP
620 Nwport Ctr Dr Fl 15 Flr 15, Newport Beach (92660)
PHONE....................949 705-0010
Kevin Kaverna, *Director*
Jennifer Jackson, *Regional Mgr*
Richard Paschke, *Regional Mgr*
Christopher Harraka, *Analyst*
Kevin Kaberna, *Director*
EMP: 656 **Privately Held**
SIC: 6531 Real estate managers
PA: Greystar Management Services, L.P.
750 Bering Dr Ste 300
Houston TX 77057

(P-11179)
GRISWORLD REAL ESTATE MGT (PA)
5703 Oberlin Dr Ste 300, San Diego (92121-1743)
PHONE....................858 597-6100
Robert Griswold, *President*
Ted Smith, *Principal*
EMP: 65
SQ FT: 3,000
SALES (est): 3.1MM **Privately Held**
WEB: www.griswoldremgmt.com
SIC: 6531 8111 Real estate managers; legal services

(P-11180)
GRUBB CO INC
1960 Mountain Blvd, Oakland (94611-2894)
PHONE....................510 339-0400

(PA)=Parent Co (HQ)=Headquarters (DH)=Div Headquarters
✪ = New Business established in last 2 years

2019 Directory of California
Wholesalers and Services Companies

481

PRODUCTS & SVCS

D J Grubb Jr, *President*
Laura Castillo, *Office Mgr*
Sherry Benninger, *Asst Broker*
Julie Gardner, *Broker*
Judith Glass, *Broker*
EMP: 53
SQ FT: 2,800
SALES (est): 5.3MM **Privately Held**
WEB: www.grubbco.com
SIC: 6531 Real estate agent, commercial

(P-11181)
GRUPE COMPANY (PA)
3255 W March Ln Ste 400, Stockton
(95219-2352)
P.O. Box 7576 (95267-0576)
PHONE..................................209 473-6000
Frank A Passadore, *President*
Greenlaw Grupe Jr, *Ch of Bd*
Mark Fischer, *CFO*
Chris Conklin, *Vice Pres*
Maurice Liu, *Vice Pres*
EMP: 60 **EST:** 1960
SQ FT: 7,000
SALES (est): 86.7MM **Privately Held**
WEB: www.grupe.com
SIC: 6531 1542 Real estate agent, resi-
dential; real estate brokers & agents;
commercial & office building, new con-
struction

(P-11182)
GUARANTEE REAL ESTATE
756 W Shaw Ave Ste 105, Fresno
(93704-2223)
PHONE..................................559 650-6030
Sandy Darling, *Vice Pres*
Reginia Teter, *President*
J Scott Leonard, *CEO*
Phyllis N Strom, *Principal*
Reedley Guarantee, *Admin Asst*
EMP: 50
SALES (est): 2.5MM **Privately Held**
SIC: 6531 Real estate brokers & agents

(P-11183)
**GUARANTEE REAL ESTATE
CORP**
180 W Bullard Ave Ste 101, Clovis
(93612-0998)
PHONE..................................559 321-6040
Kyle Chaney, *Branch Mgr*
EMP: 51
SALES (corp-wide): 225.3B **Publicly
Held**
SIC: 6531 Real estate brokers & agents
HQ: Guarantee Real Estate Corporation
3 E River Park Pl E
Fresno CA 93720
559 650-6000

(P-11184)
HANNAKNAPP REALTY INC
Also Called: Century 21
15311 Bear Valley Rd # 1, Hesperia
(92345-0833)
PHONE..................................760 244-8557
Hannelore Hannaknapp, *President*
Charles Knapp, *Owner*
EMP: 50
SALES (est): 2.5MM **Privately Held**
SIC: 6531 Real estate agent, residential

(P-11185)
HARMONY ESCROW INC
17100 Gillette Ave, Irvine (92614-5603)
PHONE..................................949 474-1134
Rande Johnsen, *President*
Ann Rell, *Assistant*
EMP: 60
SALES: 950K **Privately Held**
SIC: 6531 Real estate brokers & agents

(P-11186)
HARTWIG REALTY INC (PA)
Also Called: Coldwell Banker Hartwig Co
43912 20th St W, Lancaster (93534-5221)
PHONE..................................661 948-8424
Burl W Patterson, *President*
Conrad Engelhardt, *Vice Pres*
EMP: 89
SQ FT: 20,000
SALES (est): 5.3MM **Privately Held**
WEB: www.landinfonow.com
SIC: 6531 Real estate agent, residential

(P-11187)
HDSI MANAGEMENT INC (PA)
3460 S Broadway, Los Angeles
(90007-4409)
PHONE..................................323 231-1104
Noel L Sweitzer, *President*
EMP: 65
SQ FT: 5,500
SALES (est): 5.7MM **Privately Held**
SIC: 6531 Real estate managers

(P-11188)
HE INC
Also Called: Hastings Enterprises
3 E 3rd Ave, San Mateo (94401-4279)
PHONE..................................650 794-1128
Newlin Hastings, *President*
Brian Beckham, *Vice Pres*
EMP: 56
SQ FT: 2,500
SALES: 7MM **Privately Held**
WEB: www.hastingsenterprises.net
SIC: 6531 6552 Real estate agent, com-
mercial; land subdividers & developers,
commercial

(P-11189)
HELM MANAGEMENT CO (PA)
Also Called: Helm, The
4668 Nebo Dr Ste A, La Mesa
(91941-5200)
PHONE..................................619 589-6222
Tom Hensley, *President*
Jack Noy, *Sr Project Mgr*
EMP: 90
SQ FT: 1,176
SALES (est): 9.6MM **Privately Held**
WEB: www.helmmanagement.com
SIC: 6531 Real estate managers; time-
sharing real estate sales, leasing &
rentals; rental agent, real estate; condo-
minium manager

(P-11190)
HINES INTERESTS LTD PARTNR
1 Hacker Way Bldg 10, Menlo Park
(94025-1456)
PHONE..................................650 518-6139
Melissa Perla, *Senior Mgr*
EMP: 170
SALES (corp-wide): 1.7B **Privately Held**
SIC: 6531 Real estate agent, commercial
PA: Hines Interests Limited Partnership
2800 Post Oak Blvd # 4800
Houston TX 77056
713 621-8000

(P-11191)
**HMS AGRICULTURAL
CORPORATION**
46247 Arabia St, Indio (92201-5840)
P.O. Box 1787 (92202-1787)
PHONE..................................760 347-2335
Ole Fogh-Andersen, *President*
Earline Taylor, *Treasurer*
Linden Anderson, *Vice Pres*
Henry Bastidas, *Vice Pres*
EMP: 70 **EST:** 1975
SQ FT: 1,600
SALES (est): 4.5MM **Privately Held**
SIC: 6531 Real estate managers

(P-11192)
HOUSE SEVEN GABLES RE INC
19440 Goldenwest St, Huntington Beach
(92648-2116)
PHONE..................................714 500-3300
Terry Reay, *Manager*
EMP: 90
SALES (corp-wide): 23.1MM **Privately
Held**
SIC: 6531 Real estate agent, residential
PA: House Of Seven Gables Real Estate,
Inc.
12651 Newport Ave
Tustin CA 92780
714 731-3777

(P-11193)
HOUSE SEVEN GABLES RE INC
Also Called: AMC
16872 Bolsa Chica St # 100, Huntington
Beach (92649-3509)
PHONE..................................714 754-6262
Kelli Ludden, *CFO*
EMP: 71

SALES (corp-wide): 23.1MM **Privately
Held**
SIC: 6531 Real estate agents & managers
PA: House Of Seven Gables Real Estate,
Inc.
12651 Newport Ave
Tustin CA 92780
714 731-3777

(P-11194)
HOUSE SEVEN GABLES RE INC
Also Called: Cole, Norman Anne
5753 E Santa Ana Canyon P, Anaheim
(92807-3230)
PHONE..................................714 282-0306
Kelli Ludden, *CFO*
EMP: 71
SALES (corp-wide): 23.1MM **Privately
Held**
WEB: www.sevengables.com
SIC: 6531 Real estate brokers & agents
PA: House Of Seven Gables Real Estate,
Inc.
12651 Newport Ave
Tustin CA 92780
714 731-3777

(P-11195)
**HOUSING ATHRTY OF THE CNTY
OF**
2160 41st Ave, Capitola (95010-2040)
PHONE..................................831 454-9455
Jennifer Panetta, *Exec Dir*
Beth Ahlgren, *Analyst*
Mark Failor, *Property Mgr*
EMP: 65
SALES: 58MM **Privately Held**
SIC: 6531 Real estate managers

(P-11196)
HUNT ENTERPRISES INC
Also Called: Shibui Apartments
2270 Sepulveda Blvd # 50, Torrance
(90501-5304)
PHONE..................................310 325-1496
EMP: 113
SQ FT: 53,813
SALES (corp-wide): 13.1MM **Privately
Held**
SIC: 6531 Real estate leasing & rentals
PA: Hunt Enterprises, Inc.
4416 W 154th St
Lawndale CA 90260
310 675-3555

(P-11197)
HUNTER REALTY INC
Also Called: Prudential
2605 S Miller St Ste 101, Santa Maria
(93455-1774)
PHONE..................................805 346-8688
David Cabot, *President*
EMP: 155
SALES (est): 5.6MM **Privately Held**
SIC: 6531 8742 Real estate agent, resi-
dential; real estate consultant

(P-11198)
**HYATT VACATION OWNERSHIP
INC**
9615 Brighton Way M180, Beverly Hills
(90210-5140)
PHONE..................................310 285-0990
John Burlingame, *Exec VP*
EMP: 80
SALES (est): 1.3MM **Privately Held**
SIC: 6531 Real estate leasing & rentals

(P-11199)
I D PROPERTY CORPORATION
Also Called: Property I D
1001 Wilshire Blvd # 100, Los Angeles
(90017-2821)
PHONE..................................213 625-0100
Carlos Siderman, *President*
John Cote, *President*
Victor Marquez, *Executive*
Alex Lopez, *Accounting Mgr*
Dave Dominge, *Sales Executive*
EMP: 120
SALES (est): 11.6MM **Privately Held**
SIC: 6531 8742 Real estate listing serv-
ices; real estate consultant

(P-11200)
IC BP III HOLDINGS XII LLC
1 Sansome St Ste 1500, San Francisco
(94104-4449)
PHONE..................................415 549-5054
Aaron Snegg, *Manager*
EMP: 60
SALES (est): 2.5MM **Privately Held**
SIC: 6531 Real estate leasing & rentals

(P-11201)
IDS REAL ESTATE GROUP (PA)
Also Called: I S D
515 S Figueroa St Fl 16, Los Angeles
(90071-3301)
PHONE..................................213 627-9937
Murad M Siam, *CEO*
David G Mgrubllan, *President*
Mickey Siam, *COO*
Jeff Newman, *CFO*
Patrick D Spillane, *Senior VP*
EMP: 60
SQ FT: 20,000
SALES (est): 19.1MM **Privately Held**
SIC: 6531 Real estate agent, commercial;
real estate managers

(P-11202)
INLAND EMPIRE RE SOLUTIONS
Also Called: Remax Legends
8794 19th St, Alta Loma (91701-4608)
P.O. Box 129, Rancho Cucamonga (91739-
0129)
PHONE..................................909 476-1000
EMP: 76
SQ FT: 5,600
SALES: 4MM **Privately Held**
SIC: 6531

(P-11203)
**INMAN SPINOSA & BUCHAN
INC**
Also Called: Landmark Realty Center
28901 S Wstn Ave Ste 139, Rancho Palos
Verdes (90275)
PHONE..................................310 519-1080
Gordon Inman, *President*
Nancy Inman, *Treasurer*
Donna Buchan, *Vice Pres*
Robert Ashfield, *Real Est Agnt*
EMP: 58 **EST:** 1976
SALES (est): 3.4MM **Privately Held**
WEB: www.salsorrentino.com
SIC: 6531 6163 Real estate brokers &
agents; mortgage brokers arranging for
loans, using money of others

(P-11204)
**INTERNET ESCROW SERVICES
INC**
180 Montgomery St Ste 650, San Francisco
(94104-4208)
PHONE..................................888 511-8600
Robert Barrie, *CEO*
Neil Katz, *CFO*
Jackson Elsegood, *General Mgr*
EMP: 69 **EST:** 1999
SALES: 7.5MM **Privately Held**
WEB: www.internetescrowservices.com
SIC: 6531 Escrow agent, real estate
PA: Freelancer Limited
L 20 World Sq 680 George St
Sydney NSW 2000

(P-11205)
**INTERO REAL ESTATE
SERVICES**
7652 Monterey St, Gilroy (95020-5216)
PHONE..................................408 848-8400
Kathie Kingston, *President*
Shauntel Gullatt, *Sales Staff*
Ricardo Arteaga, *Real Est Agnt*
Demetrick Caballero, *Real Est Agnt*
EMP: 62
SALES (est): 2.2MM **Privately Held**
SIC: 6531 Real estate agent, residential

(P-11206)
INTERO REAL ESTATE SVCS INC
12900 Saratoga Ave, Saratoga
(95070-4668)
PHONE..................................408 741-1600
Tom Tagnoli, *General Mgr*
Bryan Robertson, *Branch Mgr*

Lydia Wang, *Branch Mgr*
Kate Gable, *Marketing Mgr*
Laurie Hansen, *Sales Associate*
EMP: 81
SALES (corp-wide): 225.3B **Publicly Held**
SIC: 6531 Real estate brokers & agents
HQ: Intero Real Estate Services, Inc.
10275 N De Anza Blvd
Cupertino CA 95014
408 342-3000

(P-11207)
INTERO REAL ESTATE SVCS INC
8255 Firestone Blvd # 200, Downey (90241-4877)
PHONE...............................562 861-7242
Oscar Mendoza, *Principal*
EMP: 81
SALES (corp-wide): 225.3B **Publicly Held**
SIC: 6531 Real estate agent, commercial
HQ: Intero Real Estate Services, Inc.
10275 N De Anza Blvd
Cupertino CA 95014
408 342-3000

(P-11208)
INTERO REAL ESTATE SVCS INC
32145 Alvarado Niles Rd # 101, Union City (94587-2930)
PHONE...............................510 489-8989
Joey Anudon, *Branch Mgr*
EMP: 81
SALES (corp-wide): 225.3B **Publicly Held**
SIC: 6531 Real estate agent, commercial; real estate brokers & agents
HQ: Intero Real Estate Services, Inc.
10275 N De Anza Blvd
Cupertino CA 95014
408 342-3000

(P-11209)
INTERO REAL ESTATE SVCS INC
5890 Silver Creek Vly Rd, San Jose (95138-1027)
PHONE...............................408 574-5000
Robert Cruz, *Manager*
EMP: 150
SALES (corp-wide): 225.3B **Publicly Held**
SIC: 6531 6519 Real estate agent, residential; real property lessors
HQ: Intero Real Estate Services, Inc.
10275 N De Anza Blvd
Cupertino CA 95014
408 342-3000

(P-11210)
INTERO REAL ESTATE SVCS INC
Also Called: Intero Silicon Valley
1900 Camden Ave, San Jose (95124-2942)
PHONE...............................408 558-3600
Terry Meyer, *COO*
Raunak Gulshan, *Manager*
Saurabh Malhotra, *Manager*
EMP: 50
SALES (est): 1.9MM **Privately Held**
SIC: 6531 7389 Real estate agent, residential; office facilities & secretarial service rental

(P-11211)
INVESERVE CORPORATION
123 S Chapel Ave, Alhambra (91801-3951)
PHONE...............................626 458-3435
Norman Chang, *President*
Amy Chang, *Vice Pres*
Michael Fang, *Advisor*
EMP: 80
SQ FT: 1,000
SALES (est): 7.2MM **Privately Held**
WEB: www.inveserve.com
SIC: 6531 Real estate agent, commercial; real estate managers

(P-11212)
INZUNZA REAL ESTATE INC
Also Called: Entrepreneur Preferred
25310 Madison Ave Ste 101, Murrieta (92562-8908)
PHONE...............................951 544-8801
Jorge Inzunza, *President*
EMP: 60

SALES (est): 129.9K **Privately Held**
SIC: 6531 Real estate brokers & agents

(P-11213)
IVY REALTY
611 S Wilton Pl, Los Angeles (90005-3220)
PHONE...............................213 386-8888
J D Kym, *CEO*
Christina Lee, *Mktg Dir*
Janet Lee, *Mktg Dir*
Joana Chang, *Real Est Agnt*
Grace Kim, *Real Est Agnt*
EMP: 50
SALES (est): 1.8MM **Privately Held**
WEB: www.ivyrealty.com
SIC: 6531 Real estate brokers & agents

(P-11214)
J & P FINANCIAL INC (PA)
Also Called: Realty Executives
330 W Felicita Ave Ste E1, Escondido (92025-6534)
PHONE...............................760 738-9000
Joe W Cobb Jr, *President*
Paula Cobb, *Vice Pres*
EMP: 50
SQ FT: 5,370
SALES (est): 2.6MM **Privately Held**
SIC: 6531 Real estate agent, residential

(P-11215)
J BARON INC
Also Called: Re/Max
5299 Alton Pkwy, Irvine (92604-8604)
PHONE...............................949 451-1200
Tom Baron, *President*
Max Nejad, *Broker*
Katy Obrejan, *Broker*
Andy Tseng, *Broker*
Max Vargas, *Broker*
EMP: 96
SALES (est): 6MM **Privately Held**
SIC: 6531 Real estate agent, residential

(P-11216)
J H SYNDER CO LLC
5757 Wilshire Blvd Ph 30, Los Angeles (90036-3690)
PHONE...............................323 857-5546
Jerome Snyder, *Managing Prtnr*
Joseph Irvine, *Vice Pres*
Patrick Irvine, *Vice Pres*
Dan Schneider, *Vice Pres*
Mary Schwei, *Executive*
EMP: 60
SALES (est): 4.6MM **Privately Held**
SIC: 6531 Buying agent, real estate

(P-11217)
JALMAR PROPERTIES INC (PA)
12121 Wilshire Blvd # 1120, Los Angeles (90025-1164)
PHONE...............................310 207-8481
James H Donell, *President*
Stephen J Donell, *President*
Todd Donell, *Vice Pres*
EMP: 50
SALES (est): 4.5MM **Privately Held**
SIC: 6531 6799 6552 Real estate managers; real estate investors, except property operators; subdividers & developers

(P-11218)
JAMBOREE REALTY CORP (PA)
Also Called: Jamboree Management
22982 Mill Creek Dr, Laguna Hills (92653-1214)
PHONE...............................949 380-0300
Fred G Sparks, *President*
Richard M Tucker, *CEO*
Kathleen Tucker, *Treasurer*
Terri Boykin, *Admin Asst*
Lori Guay, *Accounting Mgr*
EMP: 120
SALES (est): 17.5MM **Privately Held**
SIC: 6531 Real estate agents & managers

(P-11219)
JB PARTNERS GROUP INC
18375 Ventura Blvd, Tarzana (91356-4218)
PHONE...............................818 668-8201
Robert E Hart, *Principal*
EMP: 117

SALES (est): 3.9MM
SALES (corp-wide): 18.5MM **Privately Held**
SIC: 6531 Real estate leasing & rentals
PA: The Laramar Group L L C
222 S Riverside Plz
Chicago IL 60606
312 669-1200

(P-11220)
JMS REALTORS LTD (PA)
Also Called: Realty Concepts
575 E Alluvial Ave # 101, Fresno (93720-2822)
PHONE...............................559 490-1500
John M Shamshoian, *CEO*
Judy Kubale, *Executive Asst*
Lisa Fazio, *Broker*
Deanna Spellman, *Broker*
Stephanie Jimenez, *Sales Mgr*
EMP: 172 EST: 1991
SALES (est): 16.2MM **Privately Held**
SIC: 6531 7389 Selling agent, real estate; brokers, contract services

(P-11221)
JOE CANPAGNA
Also Called: Prudential
2830 Shelter Island Dr, San Diego (92106-2733)
PHONE...............................619 222-0555
Joe Canpagna, *Manager*
EMP: 90 EST: 1998
SALES (est): 2MM **Privately Held**
WEB: www.bythewood.com
SIC: 6531 Real estate agent, residential

(P-11222)
JOHN G SHIPLEY
Also Called: Century 21
100 W Valencia Mesa Dr # 201, Fullerton (92835-3765)
PHONE...............................714 626-2000
John G Shipley, *Owner*
EMP: 90
SALES (est): 4MM **Privately Held**
WEB: www.c21discovery.com
SIC: 6531 Real estate agent, residential

(P-11223)
JOHN STEWART COMPANY
191 Heritage Ln, Dixon (95620-4873)
PHONE...............................707 676-5660
EMP: 73
SALES (corp-wide): 122MM **Privately Held**
SIC: 6531 Real estate managers
PA: John Stewart Company
1388 Sutter St Ste 1100
San Francisco CA 94109
415 345-4400

(P-11224)
JOHN STEWART COMPANY
888 S Figueroa St Ste 700, Los Angeles (90017-5320)
PHONE...............................213 787-2700
Monica Salirdano, *Branch Mgr*
Richard Himmelberger, *Regional Mgr*
EMP: 50
SALES (corp-wide): 122MM **Privately Held**
SIC: 6531 6513 Real estate managers; apartment building operators
PA: John Stewart Company
1388 Sutter St Ste 1100
San Francisco CA 94109
415 345-4400

(P-11225)
JOHN STEWART COMPANY (PA)
1388 Sutter St Ste 1100, San Francisco (94109-5454)
PHONE...............................415 345-4400
John K Stewart, *Chairman*
Jack D Gardner, *CEO*
Noah Schwartz, *COO*
Michael Smith-Heimer, *CFO*
Dan Levine, *Senior VP*
EMP: 80
SQ FT: 15,000
SALES (est): 122MM **Privately Held**
WEB: www.jsco.net
SIC: 6531 6552 6726 Real estate managers; subdividers & developers; investors syndicates

(P-11226)
JONES LANG LASALLE INC
4444 Mkt St Ste 1100, San Francisco (94111)
PHONE...............................415 395-4900
Chris Albrow, *Manager*
Johanna Metz, *General Mgr*
Michelle Thomas, *Property Mgr*
Hugh Reina, *Manager*
EMP: 200
SALES (corp-wide): 16.3B **Publicly Held**
WEB: www.joneslanglasalle.com
SIC: 6531 Real estate agent, commercial
PA: Jones Lang Lasalle Incorporated
200 E Randolph St # 4300
Chicago IL 60601
312 782-5800

(P-11227)
KELLER WILLIAMS REALTY
Also Called: Keller Williams Realtors
39 Calle De Los Ositos, Carmel Valley (93924-9711)
PHONE...............................831 622-6200
Bert Aronson, *Principal*
Nancy Erfan, *Principal*
Jenifer A Jacobs, *Real Est Agnt*
EMP: 60
SALES (est): 1.6MM **Privately Held**
SIC: 6531 Real estate agent, residential

(P-11228)
KELLER WILLIAMS REALTY
Also Called: Keller Williams Realtors
100 N Citrus Ave, Covina (91723-2022)
PHONE...............................626 384-2803
John Hollander, *Principal*
EMP: 70 EST: 2015
SALES (est): 166.3K **Privately Held**
SIC: 6531 6519 Real estate agent, residential; real property lessors

(P-11229)
KELLER WILLIAMS REALTY
Also Called: Keller Williams Realtors
23670 Hawthorne Blvd # 100, Torrance (90505-5968)
PHONE...............................310 375-3511
Linda Hayden, *Business Mgr*
Melinda Biezonsky, *Real Est Agnt*
Betty Fogg, *Real Est Agnt*
Jamie Pagliano, *Real Est Agnt*
Joseph Potts, *Real Est Agnt*
EMP: 300
SALES (est): 8.8MM **Privately Held**
SIC: 6531 Real estate agent, residential

(P-11230)
KELLER WILLIAMS REALTY
Also Called: Keller Williams Realtors
12530 Hesperia Rd Ste 110, Victorville (92395-5848)
PHONE...............................760 951-5242
Brad Bodell, *Owner*
EMP: 99
SALES (est): 2.7MM **Privately Held**
SIC: 6531 Real estate agent, residential

(P-11231)
KELLER WILLIAMS REALTY
Also Called: Keller Williams Realtors
7898 Mission Grove Pkwy S # 102, Riverside (92508-5053)
PHONE...............................951 215-0787
Daniel Bell, *Principal*
Kimberly Campbell, *Real Est Agnt*
Debbie Galaviz, *Real Est Agnt*
Sue Miskelly, *Real Est Agnt*
Joanna Wiley, *Real Est Agnt*
EMP: 50
SALES: 950K **Privately Held**
SIC: 6531 Real estate agent, residential

(P-11232)
KELLER WILLIAMS REALTY INC
Also Called: Keller Williams Realtors
400 E Main St, Visalia (93291-6315)
PHONE...............................559 733-4100
Jillian Bos, *Branch Mgr*
EMP: 100
SALES (corp-wide): 74.3MM **Privately Held**
SIC: 6531 Real estate agent, residential

PRODUCTS & SVCS

PA: Keller Williams Realty, Inc.
1221 S Mopac Expy Ste 400
Austin TX 78746
512 327-3070

(P-11233)
KELLER WLLAMS RLTY BVRLY HILLS
439 N Canon Dr Ste 300, Beverly Hills (90210-3909)
PHONE...................310 432-6400
Paul Morris, *Principal*
EMP: 90
SALES (est): 4.8MM **Privately Held**
SIC: 6531 Real estate agent, residential

(P-11234)
KENNEDY-WILSON INC (PA)
151 El Camino Dr, Beverly Hills (90212-2704)
PHONE...................310 887-6400
William McMorrow, *Ch of Bd*
Justin Enbody, *CFO*
Matt Windisch, *Exec VP*
Scott Gordon, *Senior VP*
Tracy Allen, *Vice Pres*
EMP: 103
SALES (est): 41.6MM **Privately Held**
SIC: 6531 6799 Auction, real estate; real estate investors, except property operators

(P-11235)
KENNETH P SLAUGHT INC
200 E Carrillo St Ste 200 # 200, Santa Barbara (93101-2144)
PHONE...................805 962-8989
Kenneth P Slaught, *President*
EMP: 50
SALES (est): 1.4MM **Privately Held**
SIC: 6531 Real estate brokers & agents

(P-11236)
KENNY PABST
248 Redondo Ave, Long Beach (90803-5952)
PHONE...................562 439-2147
George Pabst, *Owner*
EMP: 50
SALES (est): 1.3MM **Privately Held**
SIC: 6531 Real estate managers

(P-11237)
KEYSTONE PCF PROPERTY MGT INC (PA)
Also Called: Reflections and Enclave Hoa
16775 Von Karman Ave # 100, Irvine (92606-4966)
PHONE...................949 833-2600
Cary Treff, *President*
Denise Bergstrom, *COO*
Jared Jones, *CFO*
Gerry Kay, *CFO*
Jaime Chandler, *Vice Pres*
EMP: 56
SALES (est): 9.5MM **Privately Held**
WEB: www.canyonview.net
SIC: 6531 Real estate managers

(P-11238)
KIDDER MATHEWS LLC
12230 El Camino Real # 400, San Diego (92130-2090)
PHONE...................858 509-1200
Mickey Morera, *Manager*
EMP: 102
SALES (corp-wide): 97MM **Privately Held**
SIC: 6531 6519 Real estate agent, commercial; real property lessors
PA: Kidder Mathews Inc.
601 Union St Ste 4720
Seattle WA 98101
206 296-9600

(P-11239)
KING MONSTER INC
Also Called: Realty One Group Solution
27451 Tourney Rd Ste 140, Valencia (91355-6306)
PHONE...................661 253-3000
Rich Szerman, *President*
Barabara Westover, *Treasurer*
Jean Szerman, *Vice Pres*
Patrick Raach, *Admin Sec*
EMP: 68

SQ FT: 5,000
SALES: 500K **Privately Held**
WEB: www.silvercreekrealty.com
SIC: 6531 Real estate agent, residential

(P-11240)
KOLL MANAGEMENT SERVICES INC
4343 Von Karman Ave, Newport Beach (92660-2099)
PHONE...................949 833-3030
Donald M Koll, *Ch of Bd*
EMP: 2400
SALES (est): 28.4MM **Privately Held**
SIC: 6531 8741 Real estate managers; management services

(P-11241)
LA CIENEGA ASSOCIATES
Also Called: Beverly Center
8500 Beverly Blvd Ste 501, Los Angeles (90048-6277)
PHONE...................310 854-0071
Laurel Crary-Globus, *General Mgr*
Sheldon Gordon, *Partner*
A Alfred Taubman, *Partner*
EMP: 75
SQ FT: 2,500
SALES (est): 5.7MM **Privately Held**
SIC: 6531 6512 Real estate brokers & agents; auditorium & hall operation

(P-11242)
LAGUNA WOODS VILLAGE
24351 El Toro Rd, Laguna Woods (92637-4901)
P.O. Box 2220, Laguna Hills (92654-2220)
PHONE...................949 597-4267
Milton John, *Director*
Russ Disbro, *Director*
EMP: 1000
SALES: 13.8K **Privately Held**
SIC: 6531 Real estate agents & managers

(P-11243)
LAPHAM COMPANY INC
Also Called: Lapham Company Management
4844 Telegraph Ave, Oakland (94609-2010)
PHONE...................510 531-6000
Jon Shahoian, *President*
Jon M Shahoian, *President*
Tsegab Assefa, *Vice Pres*
Menna Tesfatsion, *Vice Pres*
Jim Sweetman, *Controller*
EMP: 85 EST: 1947
SQ FT: 10,500
SALES (est): 8.2MM **Privately Held**
WEB: www.laphamcompany.com
SIC: 6531 Real estate agent, residential; real estate managers

(P-11244)
LARRY BLAIR REALTOR
2488 Junipero Serra Blvd, Daly City (94015-1633)
PHONE...................650 991-5267
Larry Blair, *Principal*
EMP: 50
SALES (est): 989.1K **Privately Held**
SIC: 6531 Real estate brokers & agents

(P-11245)
LBA REALTY LLC (PA)
3347 Michelson Dr Ste 200, Irvine (92612-0687)
PHONE...................949 833-0400
Philip A Belling, *Mng Member*
Jeff Badertscher, *Vice Pres*
Tim Brosnan, *Vice Pres*
Michael Coppola, *Vice Pres*
Scott Landsittel, *Vice Pres*
EMP: 50
SALES (est): 28.8MM **Privately Held**
SIC: 6531 Real estate agent, commercial

(P-11246)
LEE & ASSOC COMM REAL EST SVCS
Also Called: Lee & Associates Coml RE Svcs
3535 Inland Empire Blvd, Ontario (91764-4908)
PHONE...................909 989-7771
Donald Kazanjian, *President*
Vincent Anthony, *Vice Pres*
Michael Chavez, *Vice Pres*

Douglas Earnhart, *Vice Pres*
Paul Earnhart, *Vice Pres*
EMP: 50
SALES (est): 4.7MM **Privately Held**
WEB: www.lee-assoc.com
SIC: 6531 8742 Real estate agent, commercial; real estate consultant

(P-11247)
LEE & ASSOCIATES COML RE SVCS (PA)
7700 Irvine Center Dr # 600, Irvine (92618-2923)
PHONE...................949 727-1200
John Matus, *Vice Pres*
Russ Johnson, *President*
Guy La Ferrara, *Corp Secy*
Mike Baker, *Vice Pres*
Thomas Gioia, *Director*
EMP: 50
SQ FT: 8,500
SALES (est): 3.3MM **Privately Held**
SIC: 6531 Real estate agent, commercial

(P-11248)
LEE & ASSOCIATES REALTY GROUP
Also Called: LEE& Associates
100 Bayview Cir Ste 600, Newport Beach (92660-2982)
PHONE...................949 724-1000
Steve Jehorek, *President*
EMP: 50
SQ FT: 8,600
SALES (est): 3.9MM **Privately Held**
SIC: 6531 Real estate agent, commercial

(P-11249)
LEROY DURBIN
Also Called: Century 21
14620 Lakewood Blvd, Bellflower (90706-2860)
PHONE...................562 531-2001
Alex Lurchin, *Owner*
Leroy Durbin, *Owner*
EMP: 85
SALES (est): 2.1MM **Privately Held**
SIC: 6531 Real estate agent, residential

(P-11250)
LION CREEK SENIOR HOUSING PART
Also Called: Lion Creek Crossing V
6710 Lion Way, Oakland (94621-3370)
PHONE...................510 878-9120
Jim Brooks, *Controller*
Tesa Doleman,
EMP: 99
SALES (est): 2.6MM **Privately Held**
SIC: 6531 Real estate agents & managers

(P-11251)
LOIS LAUER REALTY
Also Called: Century 21
1998 Orange Tree Ln, Redlands (92374-2841)
PHONE...................909 748-7000
David Coy, *President*
Lawn Brian, *CEO*
Ann Bryan, *Treasurer*
Brenda Davis, *Bd of Directors*
Shirley Harrington, *Vice Pres*
EMP: 250
SQ FT: 17,000
SALES (est): 14MM **Privately Held**
WEB: www.loislauer.com
SIC: 6531 Real estate agent, residential

(P-11252)
LONG DRAGON REALTY CO INC
Also Called: Long Dragon Financial Service
2633 S Baldwin Ave, Arcadia (91007-8325)
PHONE...................626 309-7999
Renee Ho, *CEO*
Robert Ho, *President*
George Ho, *Treasurer*
John S Lee, *Real Est Agnt*
WEI Tang, *Real Est Agnt*
EMP: 120
SQ FT: 5,000

SALES (est): 6.7MM **Privately Held**
WEB: www.longdragonrealty.com
SIC: 6531 6163 6799 Real estate brokers & agents; mortgage brokers arranging for loans, using money of others; real estate investors, except property operators

(P-11253)
LOS OSOS MANAGEMENT CO INC (PA)
3130 W Main St Ste A, Visalia (93291-5765)
P.O. Box 7508 (93290-7508)
PHONE...................559 733-4328
Robert Lee, *CFO*
Pat Kong, *President*
Frank Lee, *Director*
Fred Lee, *Director*
EMP: 85 EST: 1976
SQ FT: 2,000
SALES (est): 4.9MM **Privately Held**
SIC: 6531 8741 Real estate managers; management services

(P-11254)
LOU BOZIGIAN
5900 Alleppo Ln, Palmdale (93551-2825)
PHONE...................661 948-4737
Lou Bozigian, *President*
EMP: 60
SALES (est): 1.8MM **Privately Held**
WEB: www.coldwellbanker-bozigian.com
SIC: 6531 8742 Real estate brokers & agents; real estate consultant

(P-11255)
LOWE ENTERPRISES INC
11777 San Vicente Blvd # 900, Los Angeles (90049-6615)
PHONE...................310 820-6661
EMP: 221
SALES (corp-wide): 865.7MM **Privately Held**
SIC: 6531 Real estate managers
PA: Lowe Enterprises, Inc.
11777 San Vicente Blvd # 900
Los Angeles CA 90049
310 820-6661

(P-11256)
LOYDA YU REAL ESTATE INC
860 Kuhn Dr Ste 200, Chula Vista (91914-4517)
PHONE...................619 475-7777
Loyda Calvano, *President*
EMP: 60
SALES (est): 212.6K **Privately Held**
SIC: 6531 Real estate agent, residential

(P-11257)
LRES CORPORATION (PA)
765 The City Dr S Ste 300, Orange (92868-6916)
PHONE...................714 520-5737
Roger Beane, *President*
Mark R Johnson, *President*
Paul Abbamonto, *COO*
Susheel Mantha, *CFO*
Richard Cimino, *Senior VP*
EMP: 91
SQ FT: 11,000
SALES: 27MM **Privately Held**
WEB: www.lrescorp.com
SIC: 6531 Real estate managers

(P-11258)
LYON REAL ESTATE
150 Natoma Station Dr # 300, Folsom (95630-7965)
PHONE...................916 355-7000
Michael Lyon, *CFO*
Annette Black, *Partner*
Hengi Manouchehri, *Executive*
Carol Kellog, *Office Mgr*
Jessica Reagan, *Office Admin*
EMP: 75
SALES (est): 2.3MM **Privately Held**
SIC: 6531 Real estate agent, residential; real estate brokers & agents

(P-11259)
LYON REALTY
8814 Madison Ave, Fair Oaks (95628-3908)
PHONE...................916 962-0111
Nicholas Kellogg, *Real Estate*

Patty Crawford, *Real Est Agnt*
Patricia C Nelson, *Real Est Agnt*
EMP: 218 Privately Held
SIC: 6531 Selling agent, real estate
PA: Lyon Realty
2280 Del Paso Rd Ste 100
Sacramento CA 95834

(P-11260)
LYON REALTY (PA)
2280 Del Paso Rd Ste 100, Sacramento
(95834-9701)
PHONE..........................916 574-8800
Patrick Shey, *President*
Rod Bouvia, *Broker*
Joann Kaleel, *Broker*
Tim Pierce, *Sales Associate*
Pamela Crawford, *Real Est Agnt*
EMP: 900
SALES (est): 19.6MM **Privately Held**
SIC: 6531 6519 Real estate agent, residential; real property lessors

(P-11261)
M & S ACQUISITION
CORPORATION (PA)
707 Wilshire Blvd # 5200, Los Angeles
(90017-3501)
PHONE..........................213 385-1515
Mark Santarsiero, *CFO*
Robert Kerslake, *Ch of Bd*
Paul Craig, *CFO*
Merle Atkins, *Exec VP*
John Spude, *Exec VP*
EMP: 115
SALES (est): 11.7MM **Privately Held**
SIC: 6531 8742 Appraiser, real estate; management consulting services

(P-11262)
M S E ENTERPRISES INC (PA)
Also Called: Marshall S Ezralow & Assoc
23622 Calabasas Rd # 200, Calabasas
(91302-1549)
PHONE..........................818 223-3500
Marshall S Ezralow, *President*
EMP: 90
SALES (est): 3.6MM **Privately Held**
WEB: www.ezralow.com
SIC: 6531 Real estate managers

(P-11263)
MACDONALD HOUSING
PARTNERS LP
Also Called: Trinity Plaza
350 Macdonald Ave Ste 100, Richmond
(94801-3097)
PHONE..........................510 620-0865
Jim Brooks, *Controller*
Tesa Doleman, *Manager*
EMP: 50 EST: 2009
SALES (est): 1.2MM **Privately Held**
SIC: 6531 Real estate agents & managers

(P-11264)
MACERICH COMPANY
10800 W Pico Blvd Ste 312, Los Angeles
(90064-2187)
PHONE..........................310 474-5940
Ken Raffensberger, *Manager*
EMP: 52
SALES (corp-wide): 960.3MM **Publicly Held**
SIC: 6531 Real estate agent, commercial
PA: Macerich Company
401 Wilshire Blvd Ste 700
Santa Monica CA 90401
310 394-6000

(P-11265)
MAJESTY ONE PROPERTIES
INC
6249 Quartz St, Rancho Cucamonga
(91701-3437)
PHONE..........................909 980-8000
Julio Cardenas, *President*
EMP: 130
SALES (est): 3.7MM **Privately Held**
SIC: 6531 Real estate agents & managers

(P-11266)
MALIBU REALTY INC
Also Called: Malibu Realty Property MGT
22809 Pacific Coast Hwy, Malibu
(90265-5873)
PHONE..........................310 457-5124
Eugene Calvin Barginear, *President*
Barbara Barginear, *CFO*
Jill Barginear-Getz, *Admin Sec*
EMP: 50
SALES (est): 4.4MM **Privately Held**
WEB: www.caroldarrow.com
SIC: 6531 Real estate brokers & agents

(P-11267)
MANGOLD PROPERTY
MANAGEMENT
575 Calle Principal, Monterey
(93940-2811)
PHONE..........................831 372-1338
Thomas Mangold, *Owner*
EMP: 65
SQ FT: 13,000
SALES (est): 5.7MM **Privately Held**
WEB: www.mangoldproperties.com
SIC: 6531 Real estate managers

(P-11268)
MARCUS & MILLICHAP INC (PA)
23975 Park Sorrento # 400, Calabasas
(91302-4014)
PHONE..........................818 212-2250
Hessam Nadji, *President*
Mitchell R Labar, *COO*
Martin E Louie, *CFO*
George Shaheen, *Bd of Directors*
Chad Atwood, *Vice Pres*
EMP: 64
SQ FT: 24,028
SALES: 814.8MM **Publicly Held**
SIC: 6531 Buying agent, real estate

(P-11269)
MARCUS & MILLICHAP CAPITL
CORP
23975 Park Sorrento # 400, Calabasas
(91302-4014)
PHONE..........................818 212-2250
George Marcus, *President*
David Shillingtonas, *President*
Michael Shaffner, *Assoc VP*
Dean Giannakopoulos, *Senior VP*
Danny Abergel, *Vice Pres*
EMP: 50
SALES (est): 3.1MM
SALES (corp-wide): 814.8MM **Publicly Held**
SIC: 6531 Real estate agent, commercial
HQ: Marcus & Millichap Real Estate Investment Services, Inc.
23975 Park Sorrento # 400
Calabasas CA 91302

(P-11270)
MARCUS & MILLICHAP REAL
ESTATE
Also Called: Ponderosa Mobile Estates
750 Battery St Fl 5, San Francisco
(94111-1531)
PHONE..........................415 391-9220
Jeffrey M Mishkin, *Sales Mgr*
Jeff Mishkin, *Manager*
EMP: 50
SALES (corp-wide): 70.9MM **Privately Held**
SIC: 6531 8742 Real estate brokers & agents; real estate consultant
HQ: Marcus & Millichap Real Estate Investment Services Of Indiana, Inc.
2626 Hanover St
Palo Alto CA 94304
650 494-1400

(P-11271)
MARCUS MILLICHAP CORP RE
SVCS (HQ)
2626 Hanover St, Palo Alto (94304-1132)
PHONE..........................650 391-1700
William Millichap, *Ch of Bd*
EMP: 60
SQ FT: 12,509

SALES (est): 3MM
SALES (corp-wide): 70.9MM **Privately Held**
SIC: 6531 Real estate brokers & agents
PA: The Marcus & Millichap Company
777 California Ave
Palo Alto CA 94304
650 494-1400

(P-11272)
MARCUS MILLICHAP REIS NEV
INC
23975 Park Sorrento # 400, Calabasas
(91302-4015)
PHONE..........................650 494-1400
George M Marcus, *Owner*
EMP: 70
SALES (est): 4.4MM
SALES (corp-wide): 814.8MM **Publicly Held**
SIC: 6531 Buying agent, real estate
PA: Marcus & Millichap, Inc.
23975 Park Sorrento # 400
Calabasas CA 91302
818 212-2250

(P-11273)
MARCUS MLLCHAP RE INV
SVCS INC (HQ)
Also Called: Instititonal Property Advisors
23975 Park Sorrento # 400, Calabasas
(91302-4015)
PHONE..........................818 212-2250
William Millichap, *President*
Richard Matricaria, *Exec VP*
JD Parker, *Exec VP*
Richard Katzenstein, *Vice Pres*
Tyler Theobald, *Vice Pres*
EMP: 50
SALES (est): 13.1MM
SALES (corp-wide): 814.8MM **Publicly Held**
SIC: 6531 Real estate agents & managers
PA: Marcus & Millichap, Inc.
23975 Park Sorrento # 400
Calabasas CA 91302
818 212-2250

(P-11274)
MARRAKESH MANAGEMENT
CORP
47000 Marrakesh Dr, Palm Desert
(92260-5805)
PHONE..........................760 568-2688
Barbara Valdivia, *Controller*
Dan Cooper, *Exec VP*
EMP: 50
SQ FT: 5,000
SALES: 704.3K **Privately Held**
WEB: www.marrakeshcountryclub.com
SIC: 6531 Real estate managers

(P-11275)
MASON-MCDUFFIE REAL
ESTATE INC
Also Called: Prudential
2095 Rose St Ste 100, Berkeley
(94709-1997)
PHONE..........................510 705-8611
Phina Chrisentery, *Manager*
Ellen Lynch, *Sales Associate*
EMP: 70
SALES (corp-wide): 33.1MM **Privately Held**
WEB: www.mohrparkneighbors.com
SIC: 6531 Real estate agent, residential
PA: Mason-Mcduffie Real Estate, Inc.
1555 Riviera Ave Ste E
Walnut Creek CA 94596
925 924-4600

(P-11276)
MASON-MCDUFFIE REAL
ESTATE INC
Also Called: Prudential
2051 Mt Diablo Blvd, Walnut Creek
(94596-4301)
PHONE..........................925 932-1000
Steve Curtis, *Manager*
EMP: 78
SALES (corp-wide): 33.1MM **Privately Held**
WEB: www.mohrparkneighbors.com
SIC: 6531 Real estate agent, residential

PA: Mason-Mcduffie Real Estate, Inc.
1555 Riviera Ave Ste E
Walnut Creek CA 94596
925 924-4600

(P-11277)
MASON-MCDUFFIE REAL
ESTATE INC
Also Called: Prudential
5887 Lone Tree Way Ste A, Antioch
(94531-8625)
PHONE..........................925 776-2740
Melody Royal, *Manager*
EMP: 52
SALES (corp-wide): 33.1MM **Privately Held**
WEB: www.mohrparkneighbors.com
SIC: 6531 Real estate agent, residential
PA: Mason-Mcduffie Real Estate, Inc.
1555 Riviera Ave Ste E
Walnut Creek CA 94596
925 924-4600

(P-11278)
MASON-MCDUFFIE REAL
ESTATE INC
21060 Redwood Rd Ste 100, Castro Valley
(94546-5931)
PHONE..........................510 886-7511
Gretchen Pearson, *Manager*
EMP: 50
SALES (corp-wide): 33.1MM **Privately Held**
WEB: www.mohrparkneighbors.com
SIC: 6531 Real estate agent, residential
PA: Mason-Mcduffie Real Estate, Inc.
1555 Riviera Ave Ste E
Walnut Creek CA 94596
925 924-4600

(P-11279)
MASON-MCDUFFIE REAL
ESTATE INC
Also Called: Predentials
3320 Grand Ave, Oakland (94610-2737)
PHONE..........................510 834-2010
Amberson McCulloch, *Manager*
Ernest Villafranca, *Real Est Agnt*
EMP: 80
SALES (corp-wide): 33.1MM **Privately Held**
WEB: www.mohrparkneighbors.com
SIC: 6531 Real estate agent, commercial
PA: Mason-Mcduffie Real Estate, Inc.
1555 Riviera Ave Ste E
Walnut Creek CA 94596
925 924-4600

(P-11280)
MASON-MCDUFFIE REAL
ESTATE INC
Also Called: Dutra Realty
5950 Stoneridge Dr, Pleasanton
(94588-2706)
PHONE..........................925 734-5000
Frank Cannella, *Manager*
EMP: 80
SALES (corp-wide): 33.1MM **Privately Held**
WEB: www.mohrparkneighbors.com
SIC: 6531 Real estate agent, residential
PA: Mason-Mcduffie Real Estate, Inc.
1555 Riviera Ave Ste E
Walnut Creek CA 94596
925 924-4600

(P-11281)
MATTHEWS RETAIL GROUP INC
Also Called: Matthews Real Estate Inv Svcs
841 Apollo St Ste 150, El Segundo
(90245-4724)
PHONE..........................866 889-0550
Kyle B Matthews, *President*
Chad Kurz, *Managing Prtnr*
Radoslav Zlatkov, *CFO*
Redoslav Zlatkov, *CFO*
David Harrington, *Exec VP*
EMP: 59
SALES (est): 2.1MM **Privately Held**
SIC: 6531 7389 Real estate agent, commercial; financial services

(P-11282)
MAX SOMMERS REAL ESTATE
615 Esplanade Unit 312, Redondo Beach (90277-4135)
PHONE..................310 560-1499
Max Sommers, *Owner*
EMP: 75
SALES (est): 1.5MM **Privately Held**
SIC: 6531 Real estate brokers & agents

(P-11283)
MBK REAL ESTATE COMPANIES
Also Called: MBK Laguna
4 Park Plz Ste 1700, Irvine (92614-2559)
PHONE..................949 789-8300
Kain Matsumoto, *Chairman*
Kent Crandall, *CFO*
Edward Stokx, *CFO*
Vijay Pandurangadu, *Vice Pres*
Yoshitaka Suzuki, *Vice Pres*
EMP: 50
SALES (est): 7.2MM **Privately Held**
WEB: www.mitsui.co.jp
SIC: 6531 Real estate agents & managers
PA: Mitsui & Co., Ltd.
1-1-3, Marunouchi
Chiyoda-Ku TKY 100-0

(P-11284)
MBK REAL ESTATE LTD A CALFOR (HQ)
4 Park Plz Ste 1700, Irvine (92614-2559)
PHONE..................949 789-8300
Stefan Markowitz, *General Ptnr*
Kent Crandall, *CFO*
Jonathan Evans, *Analyst*
Clarence Curtis, *Senior Mgr*
EMP: 58
SALES (est): 9.6MM **Privately Held**
SIC: 6531 Real estate managers; auction, real estate

(P-11285)
MCM PARTNERS INC
Also Called: Prudential
6111 Johnson Ct Ste 110, Pleasanton (94588-3373)
PHONE..................925 463-9500
Janet P Cristano, *President*
EMP: 65
SALES (est): 2.5MM **Privately Held**
SIC: 6531 Real estate agent, residential

(P-11286)
MCMILLIN RE & MRTG CO INC
320 E H St, Chula Vista (91910-7483)
PHONE..................619 422-4500
Amrian Adan, *Manager*
EMP: 60
SALES (corp-wide): 3.8MM **Privately Held**
SIC: 6531 Buying agent, real estate
PA: Mcmillin Real Estate & Mortgage Company, Inc.
4210 Bonita Rd Ste B
Bonita CA

(P-11287)
MELISSA BRADLEY RE INC
3249 Browns Valley Rd, NAPA (94558-5424)
PHONE..................707 258-3900
Carol Adler, *Branch Mgr*
EMP: 51
SALES (corp-wide): 8.9MM **Privately Held**
SIC: 6531 Real estate agent, residential
PA: Melissa Bradley Real Estate, Inc.
55 Broadway Blvd
Fairfax CA

(P-11288)
MELISSA BRADLEY RE INC
1401 4th St, Santa Rosa (95404-4015)
PHONE..................707 536-0888
Robert Bradley, *Branch Mgr*
EMP: 51
SALES (corp-wide): 8.9MM **Privately Held**
SIC: 6531 Real estate brokers & agents

PA: Melissa Bradley Real Estate, Inc.
55 Broadway Blvd
Fairfax CA

(P-11289)
MELISSA BRADLEY RE INC
1690 Tiburon Blvd, Belvedere Tiburon (94920-2543)
PHONE..................415 435-2705
Arlene Manalo, *Branch Mgr*
EMP: 51
SALES (corp-wide): 8.9MM **Privately Held**
SIC: 6531 Real estate agent, residential
PA: Melissa Bradley Real Estate, Inc.
55 Broadway Blvd
Fairfax CA

(P-11290)
MELISSA BRADLEY RE INC
1701 Novato Blvd Ste 100, Novato (94947-3002)
PHONE..................415 209-1000
Julie Mello, *Branch Mgr*
Kirtis Donaldson, *Real Est Agnt*
Pamela S English, *Real Est Agnt*
EMP: 100
SALES (corp-wide): 8.9MM **Privately Held**
SIC: 6531 Real estate agent, residential
PA: Melissa Bradley Real Estate, Inc.
55 Broadway Blvd
Fairfax CA

(P-11291)
MEMCO HOLDINGS INC
10390 Santa Monica Blvd # 210, Los Angeles (90025-5058)
PHONE..................310 277-0057
Mitchell Stein, *President*
EMP: 130
SALES (est): 3.6MM **Privately Held**
SIC: 6531 Real estate managers

(P-11292)
MERCY HOUSING CALIFORNIA XXVI
Also Called: Mercy Housing Calif Xxv
2512 River Plaza Dr, Sacramento (95833-3677)
PHONE..................916 414-4400
Greg Sparks, *General Ptnr*
EMP: 60
SALES (est): 1.7MM
SALES (corp-wide): 429MM **Privately Held**
SIC: 6531 Real estate agents & managers
HQ: Mercy Housing California Xxv, A California Limited Partnership
1256 Market St
San Francisco CA 94102

(P-11293)
MERIDIAN MANAGEMENT GROUP
1145 Bush St, San Francisco (94109-5919)
PHONE..................415 434-9700
Randall Chapman, *President*
Gil Dowd, *Vice Pres*
Russell Flynn, *Vice Pres*
James R Wilson, *Admin Sec*
Sharon Lui, *Human Res Dir*
EMP: 160
SQ FT: 6,200
SALES (est): 15.3MM **Privately Held**
WEB: www.mmgroup.com
SIC: 6531 Real estate managers

(P-11294)
MERRILL GARDENS LLC
799 Yellowstone Dr, Vacaville (95687-3449)
PHONE..................707 447-7496
Holly Sullins, *Branch Mgr*
EMP: 60 **Privately Held**
SIC: 6531 Real estate agents & managers
PA: Merrill Gardens L.L.C.
1938 Frview Ave E Ste 300
Seattle WA 98102

(P-11295)
MESA MANAGEMENT INC
1451 Quail St Ste 201, Newport Beach (92660-2741)
P.O. Box 2990 (92658-9018)
PHONE..................949 851-0995
Steve Mensinger, *President*
Robert Lucas, *Vice Pres*
EMP: 70
SQ FT: 5,000
SALES (est): 9.9MM **Privately Held**
WEB: www.mesamanagement.net
SIC: 6531 Real estate managers

(P-11296)
MGR SERVICES INC
1425 W Foothill Blvd # 300, Upland (91786-8007)
PHONE..................909 981-4466
Michael Rademaker, *President*
Tony Hermosillo, *Manager*
EMP: 73
SQ FT: 13,000
SALES (est): 5.7MM **Privately Held**
WEB: www.mgrservices.com
SIC: 6531 Selling agent, real estate; real estate managers

(P-11297)
MODULAR SYSTEMS INC
Also Called: MSI
800 Garden St Ste K, Santa Barbara (93101-1596)
PHONE..................805 963-9350
Antonio R Romasanta, *President*
Angie Schultz, *Admin Sec*
EMP: 52
SQ FT: 6,000
SALES (est): 2.7MM **Privately Held**
SIC: 6531 8742 Real estate managers; management consulting services

(P-11298)
MOONSTONE MANAGEMENT CORP (PA)
Also Called: Moonstone Hotel Properties
2905 Burton Dr, Cambria (93428-4001)
PHONE..................805 927-4200
Dirk Winter, *President*
Matthew Holder, *CIO*
Griffin Moore, *Asst Controller*
John Hughes, *Financial Analy*
Sunshine Rimelen, *Controller*
EMP: 175
SQ FT: 5,000
SALES (est): 14.1MM **Privately Held**
SIC: 6531 Real estate managers

(P-11299)
MOSS & COMPANY INC (PA)
15300 Ventura Blvd # 418, Sherman Oaks (91403-3140)
PHONE..................310 453-0911
Cindy Gray, *President*
Don Shields, *COO*
Chris Gray, *Exec VP*
Henriette Saffron, *Vice Pres*
David S Stairs, *Business Dir*
EMP: 94
SQ FT: 10,000
SALES (est): 12.6MM **Privately Held**
SIC: 6531 Real estate managers

(P-11300)
MOUNTAIN HIGH RESORT ASSOC LLC
24512 Highway 2, Wrightwood (92397)
P.O. Box 3010 (92397-3010)
PHONE..................760 249-5808
Karl Kapuscinski,
John McColly, *VP Sales*
Joseph Stocking, *Marketing Mgr*
Michelle Roy,
EMP: 900
SALES (est): 48.3MM **Privately Held**
SIC: 6531 Real estate managers

(P-11301)
MOUNTAIN-PACIFIC FINANCIAL (PA)
Also Called: Re/Max
1010 Prospect St Ste 300, La Jolla (92037-4109)
PHONE..................858 456-8420
Geoffrey Mountain, *President*

Noah O Connell, *Broker*
Russ Craig, *Broker*
Lisa Hall, *Broker*
Heather Caden, *Real Est Agnt*
EMP: 70
SQ FT: 7,500
SALES (est): 3.8MM **Privately Held**
WEB: www.distinctivepropertiesrealestate.com
SIC: 6531 Real estate agent, residential

(P-11302)
MOVE INC
8428 Calvin Ave, Northridge (91324-4212)
PHONE..................818 701-0012
Dan Laudo, *Branch Mgr*
EMP: 126
SALES (corp-wide): 10B **Publicly Held**
SIC: 6531 Real estate listing services
HQ: Move, Inc.
3315 Scott Blvd Ste 250
Santa Clara CA 95054
408 558-7100

(P-11303)
MOVE INC (HQ)
Also Called: Realsuite SM
3315 Scott Blvd Ste 250, Santa Clara (95054-3139)
PHONE..................408 558-7100
Steven H Berkowitz, *CEO*
Sunil Mehrotra, *President*
Eric Thorkilsen, *President*
Bryan Charap, *CFO*
Rachel C Glaser, *CFO*
EMP: 500
SQ FT: 32,405
SALES (est): 183.9MM
SALES (corp-wide): 10B **Publicly Held**
WEB: www.homestore.com
SIC: 6531 Real estate listing services; multiple listing service, real estate
PA: News Corporation
1211 Avenue Of The Americ
New York NY 10036
212 416-3400

(P-11304)
MOVE CO
30700 Russell Ranch Rd # 100, Westlake Village (91362-9501)
PHONE..................805 557-2300
EMP: 110
SALES (est): 7.8MM **Privately Held**
SIC: 6531 Real estate agent, commercial

(P-11305)
MOVOTO LLC
1900 S Norfolk St Ste 222, San Mateo (94403-1172)
PHONE..................888 766-8686
Shiro Takeuchi, *CEO*
Mark Brandemuehl, *COO*
EMP: 51
SALES (est): 1.2MM **Privately Held**
SIC: 6531 Real estate agent, residential

(P-11306)
MP TICE OAKS ASSOCIATES A CA
Also Called: Tice Oaks Apartments
2150 Valley Blvd, Walnut Creek (94595)
PHONE..................650 356-2976
Matthew O Franklin, *Partner*
EMP: 99
SALES: 600K **Privately Held**
SIC: 6531 Real estate agents & managers

(P-11307)
MULHEARN REALTORS INC
Also Called: Tifanny Mulhearn Realtors
11306 183rd St Ste 101, Cerritos (90703-5408)
PHONE..................562 860-2443
Bruce Mulhearn, *Branch Mgr*
EMP: 70
SALES (corp-wide): 15MM **Privately Held**
WEB: www.prucarealty.com
SIC: 6531 Real estate agent, residential
PA: Mulhearn Realtors, Inc.
18000 Studebaker Rd # 205
Cerritos CA 90703
562 860-2625

(P-11308)
MURCOR INC
Also Called: Pcv Murcor Real Estate Svcs
740 Corp Ctr Dr, Pomona (91768)
PHONE..................909 623-4001
Keith D Murray, *President*
Cindy Nasser, *COO*
Tim Scherf, *COO*
Jon Deuren, *CFO*
Richard J Barkley, *Exec VP*
EMP: 225
SALES (est): 17.8MM **Privately Held**
SIC: 6531 Appraiser, real estate

(P-11309)
NELSON SHELTON & ASSOCIATES
Also Called: Nelson, Shelton, & Associates
355 N Canon Dr, Beverly Hills
(90210-4704)
PHONE..................310 271-2229
Mark Shelton, *Vice Pres*
Elsa Nelson, *Vice Pres*
EMP: 200
SALES (est): 7.2MM **Privately Held**
WEB: www.jeffmarkell.com
SIC: 6531 Real estate agent, residential

(P-11310)
NEVIN LEVY LLP A PARTNERSHIP
50 California St Ste 1500, San Francisco
(94111-4612)
PHONE..................415 800-5770
Nathan Diehl, *Vice Chairman*
EMP: 63
SQ FT: 4,000
SALES (est): 1.6MM **Privately Held**
SIC: 6531 Buying agent, real estate

(P-11311)
NEW HOME PROFESSIONALS
Also Called: Estate Investment Group
6500 Dublin Blvd Ste 201, Dublin
(94568-3152)
P.O. Box 2398 (94568-0239)
PHONE..................925 556-1555
Jay Lange, *President*
EMP: 150 **EST:** 1984
SALES (est): 6.1MM **Privately Held**
SIC: 6531 Real estate agents & managers

(P-11312)
NEWMARK & COMPANY RE INC
Also Called: Newmark Grubb Knight Frank
4675 Macarthur Ct # 1600, Newport Beach
(92660-1875)
PHONE..................949 608-2000
Oliver Fleener, *Vice Pres*
EMP: 96
SALES (corp-wide): 2B **Publicly Held**
SIC: 6531 Real estate brokers & agents
HQ: Newmark & Company Real Estate, Inc.
125 Park Ave
New York NY 10017
212 372-2000

(P-11313)
NEWPORT PACIFIC CAPITAL CO INC (PA)
17300 Red Hill Ave # 280, Irvine
(92614-5656)
PHONE..................949 852-5575
Michael Sullivan, *CEO*
Clarke Fairbrother, *President*
Steve Binder, *CFO*
Maria Horton, *Regional Mgr*
Celeste Taylor, *Executive Asst*
EMP: 150
SQ FT: 3,100
SALES (est): 18MM **Privately Held**
SIC: 6531 Rental agent, real estate; broker
of manufactured homes, on site

(P-11314)
NIJJAR REALTY INC (PA)
4900 Santa Anita Ave 2b, El Monte
(91731-1498)
P.O. Box 6085 (91734-2085)
PHONE..................626 575-0062
Daljit Kler, *Principal*
Mike Nijjar, *President*
Swaranjit S Nijjar, *CEO*
Peter Nijjar, *Treasurer*
EMP: 75

SQ FT: 2,000
SALES (est): 7.5MM **Privately Held**
SIC: 6531 Real estate brokers & agents;
real estate agent, commercial; real estate
agent, residential

(P-11315)
NMMS TWIN PEAKS LLC
Also Called: PBR Twin Peaks
5850 Canoga Ave Ste 650, Woodland Hills
(91367-6573)
PHONE..................818 710-6100
Sandra Kist,
Sanford Siegal,
EMP: 100
SALES (est): 4.9MM **Privately Held**
SIC: 6531 Real estate agent, commercial

(P-11316)
NMS PROPERTIES INC
1430 5th St Ste 101, Santa Monica
(90401-4423)
PHONE..................310 475-7600
Naum Shekhter, *CEO*
Margot Shekhter, *President*
Dino Ciarmoli, *Exec VP*
Scott Walter, *Exec VP*
EMP: 95
SALES (est): 13.9MM **Privately Held**
SIC: 6531 Real estate managers

(P-11317)
NNJ SERVICES INC
9610 Waples St, San Diego (92121-2955)
PHONE..................858 550-7900
Lelnor Hugus, *CEO*
Mike Packard, *President*
EMP: 250
SALES (est): 5.5MM **Privately Held**
WEB: www.nnj.com
SIC: 6531 Real estate agents & managers

(P-11318)
NOBLE TOWER PRESERVATION LP
1515 Lakeside Dr, Oakland (94612-4558)
PHONE..................510 444-5228
Larry Lipton, *Principal*
Tesa Doleman, *Manager*
EMP: 99
SALES (est): 3.7MM **Privately Held**
SIC: 6531 Real estate agents & managers

(P-11319)
NORCAL GOLD INC
Also Called: Re/Max
2340 E Bidwell St, Folsom (95630-3455)
PHONE..................916 984-8778
Michael Kooken, *Manager*
Patsy Barab, *COO*
Thomas Bilotta, *Broker*
Deborah Colman, *Broker*
Sara Crouch, *Broker*
EMP: 50
SALES (corp-wide): 21.7MM **Privately
Held**
SIC: 6531 Real estate agent, residential
PA: Norcal Gold, Inc.
5200 Sunrise Blvd Ste 5
Fair Oaks CA 95628
916 218-6700

(P-11320)
NORTHGATE TER CMNTY PARTNER LP
550 24th St, Oakland (94612-1757)
PHONE..................510 465-9346
Fax: 510 465-0604
EMP: 50
SQ FT: 49,846
SALES (est): 1.8MM **Privately Held**
SIC: 6531

(P-11321)
NOURMAND & ASSOCIATES
421 N Beverly Dr Ste 200, Beverly Hills
(90210-4643)
PHONE..................310 274-4000
Saeed Nourmand, *President*
Myra Nourmand, *Agent*
Brendan Brown, *Real Est Agnt*
Nevada Solis, *Real Est Agnt*
EMP: 50
SALES (est): 2.3MM **Privately Held**
WEB: www.andreabest.net
SIC: 6531 Real estate agent, residential

(P-11322)
NRT COMMERCIAL UTAH LLC
Also Called: Coldwell Banker
42 S Pasadena Ave, (91105-1943)
PHONE..................626 449-5222
Dale Williamson, *Manager*
EMP: 100 **Publicly Held**
WEB: www.nrtinc.com
SIC: 6531 Real estate agent, residential
HQ: Nrt Commercial Utah Llc
175 Park Ave
Madison NJ 07940

(P-11323)
NSW REAL ESTATE HOLDINGS LLC
99 S Hill Dr Ste A, Brisbane (94005-1282)
PHONE..................415 467-7600
Richard F Leao, *President*
EMP: 90
SALES (est): 8.4MM **Privately Held**
SIC: 6531 Real estate brokers & agents

(P-11324)
NUTEC ENTERPRISES INC
Also Called: Prudential
24200 Magic Mountain Pkwy # 105, Valencia (91355-4887)
PHONE..................661 287-3200
Roxanna Ramey, *President*
Mark Jenkins, *Vice Pres*
EMP: 94
SQ FT: 5,000
SALES (est): 3.5MM **Privately Held**
WEB: www.scvfinehomes.com
SIC: 6531 Real estate agent, residential

(P-11325)
OMNINET TWIN TOWERS GP LLC
9420 Wilshire Blvd # 400, Beverly Hills
(90212-3151)
PHONE..................310 300-4100
Jacquie Felan,
EMP: 50 **EST:** 2012
SALES (est): 1.7MM **Privately Held**
SIC: 6531 Real estate agents & managers

(P-11326)
OMNINET TWIN TOWERS LP
9420 Wilshire Blvd # 400, Beverly Hills
(90212-3151)
PHONE..................310 300-4110
Andrea Constantini, *Manager*
EMP: 50
SQ FT: 215,000
SALES (est): 2.7MM **Privately Held**
SIC: 6531 Fiduciary, real estate

(P-11327)
ON CENTRAL REALTY INC
1648 Colorado Blvd, Los Angeles (90041)
PHONE..................323 543-8500
Vazrik Bonyadi, *Branch Mgr*
EMP: 355 **Privately Held**
SIC: 6531 6519 Real estate brokers &
agents; real property lessors
PA: On Central Realty, Inc.
1625 W Glenoaks Blvd
Glendale CA 91201

(P-11328)
OPENDOOR LABS INC (PA)
1 Post St Fl 11, San Francisco
(94104-5215)
PHONE..................415 510-7213
Eric Wu, *CEO*
JD Ross, *President*
Gautam Gupta, *COO*
Jason Child, *CFO*
Keith Rabois, *Chairman*
EMP: 59
SALES (est): 49.2MM **Privately Held**
SIC: 6531 Buying agent, real estate; selling agent, real estate; rental agent, real
estate

(P-11329)
OPENDOOR LABS INC
Also Called: Opendoor Property
8880 Cal Center Dr # 400, Sacramento
(95826-3222)
PHONE..................888 352-7075
EMP: 82
SALES (corp-wide): 49.2MM **Privately
Held**
SIC: 6531 Buying agent, real estate; rental
agent, real estate; selling agent, real estate
PA: Opendoor Labs Inc.
1 Post St Fl 11
San Francisco CA 94104
415 510-7213

(P-11330)
OPENDOOR LABS INC
Also Called: Opendoor Property
11801 Pierce St Ste 200, Riverside
(92505-4400)
PHONE..................888 352-7075
EMP: 82
SALES (corp-wide): 49.2MM **Privately
Held**
SIC: 6531 Buying agent, real estate; rental
agent, real estate; selling agent, real estate
PA: Opendoor Labs Inc.
1 Post St Fl 11
San Francisco CA 94104
415 510-7213

(P-11331)
ORCHARD HOLDINGS GROUP INC
1 Venture Ste 300, Irvine (92618-7416)
PHONE..................949 502-8300
James Saccacio, *President*
Larry Spencer, *Vice Pres*
Bud Reynolds, *Admin Sec*
EMP: 160
SQ FT: 1,300
SALES (est): 7.6MM **Privately Held**
SIC: 6531 Real estate agents & managers

(P-11332)
PACIFIC CITIES MANAGEMENT INC (PA)
Also Called: Westcal Management
6056 Rutland Dr Ste 1, Carmichael
(95608-0514)
P.O. Box 417127, Sacramento (95841-
7127)
PHONE..................916 348-1188
Michael Force, *President*
EMP: 55
SQ FT: 2,600
SALES (est): 4.2MM **Privately Held**
SIC: 6531 Real estate managers

(P-11333)
PACIFIC HOUSING MANAGEMENT (PA)
945 Katella St, Laguna Beach
(92651-3705)
PHONE..................714 508-1777
Richard Hall, *President*
EMP: 60
SALES (est): 3.6MM **Privately Held**
WEB: www.sharonmichael.com
SIC: 6531 Real estate managers

(P-11334)
PACIFIC MEDICAL BUILDINGS LP
Also Called: P M B
3394 Carmel Mountain Rd # 200, San
Diego (92121-1073)
PHONE..................858 794-1900
Jeffrey L Rush MD, *Mng Member*
Stephen King, *Vice Pres*
Elizabeth A Powell,
Robert A Rosenthal,
Mark Toothacre,
EMP: 55
SQ FT: 5,000
SALES (est): 7MM **Privately Held**
SIC: 6531 Real estate managers

(P-11335)
PACIFIC MONARCH RESORTS INC
7 Grenada St, Laguna Niguel (92677-4825)
PHONE..................................949 228-1396
EMP: 72
SALES (corp-wide): 18.3MM Privately Held
SIC: 6531 Real estate agents & managers
PA: Pacific Monarch Resorts, Inc.
    4000 Macarthur Blvd # 600
    Newport Beach CA 92660
    949 609-2400

(P-11336)
PACIFIC MONARCH RESORTS INC (PA)
Also Called: Vacation Interval Realty
4000 Macarthur Blvd # 600, Newport Beach (92660-2517)
PHONE..................................949 609-2400
Mark D Post, CEO
Richard Muller, President
Nick Baldwin, Vice Pres
Pete Mitchell, VP Sales
Carlton Post, Director
EMP: 100
SQ FT: 20,000
SALES (est): 18.3MM Privately Held
SIC: 6531 7011 Time-sharing real estate sales, leasing & rentals; vacation lodges

(P-11337)
PACIFIC RIM REALTY GROUP
740 Lucille Ct, Moorpark (93021-1241)
P.O. Box 364 (93020-0364)
PHONE..................................805 553-9562
Stuart Groten, President
EMP: 50
SALES: 950K Privately Held
SIC: 6531 Real estate brokers & agents

(P-11338)
PACIFIC UNION CO
1550 Tiburon Blvd Ste U, Belvedere (94920-2516)
PHONE..................................415 789-8686
Kathleen Brady, Real Est Agnt
EMP: 66
SALES (corp-wide): 65MM Privately Held
SIC: 6531 Real estate brokers & agents
PA: Pacific Union Co.
    1699 Van Ness Ave 2
    San Francisco CA 94109
    415 929-7100

(P-11339)
PACIFIC UNION CO
1699 Van Ness Ave, San Francisco (94109-3608)
PHONE..................................415 474-6600
Linda Harrison, Manager
EMP: 65
SALES (corp-wide): 65MM Privately Held
WEB: www.sfcommercial.com
SIC: 6531 6552 Real estate brokers & agents; subdividers & developers
PA: Pacific Union Co.
    1699 Van Ness Ave 2
    San Francisco CA 94109
    415 929-7100

(P-11340)
PACIFIC UNION INTL INC
23 Ross Cmn, Ross (94957-9900)
PHONE..................................415 461-8686
Don Leisey, Manager
EMP: 270 Privately Held
SIC: 6531 Real estate brokers & agents
PA: Pacific Union International, Inc.
    1 Letterman Dr Bldg C
    San Francisco CA 94129

(P-11341)
PACIFIC UNION INTL INC
1900 Mountain Blvd # 102, Oakland (94611-2800)
PHONE..................................510 338-1379
Wendy Kandasamy, Partner
Nino Gaetano, Broker
Ted Weber, Broker

Betty Wong, Broker
Kathleen Foster, Assistant
EMP: 270 Privately Held
SIC: 6531 Real estate brokers & agents
PA: Pacific Union International, Inc.
    1 Letterman Dr Bldg C
    San Francisco CA 94129

(P-11342)
PACIFIC UNION RE GROUP (DH)
1699 Van Ness Ave 2, San Francisco (94109-3608)
PHONE..................................415 929-7100
Sandy Shaffer, President
EMP: 80
SQ FT: 700
SALES (est): 11.2MM
SALES (corp-wide): 1.6MM Privately Held
WEB: www.bayarea-newhomes.com
SIC: 6531 6163 8741 Real estate agent, commercial; mortgage brokers arranging for loans, using money of others; financial management for business

(P-11343)
PACIFIC UNION RESIDENTAL BRKG
1900 Mountain Blvd # 102, Oakland (94611-2800)
PHONE..................................510 339-6460
Pamela Hoffman, President
EMP: 72
SALES (est): 2.5MM
SALES (corp-wide): 1.6MM Privately Held
WEB: www.bayarea-newhomes.com
SIC: 6531 Real estate agent, residential
HQ: Pacific Union Real Estate Group Ltd
    1699 Van Ness Ave 2
    San Francisco CA 94109
    415 929-7100

(P-11344)
PACIFICA HOTEL COMPANY (HQ)
39 Argonaut, Aliso Viejo (92656-4152)
PHONE..................................805 957-0095
Matthew D Marquis, CEO
Mike Barnard, President
Dale J Marquis, CEO
Todd Moreau, Vice Pres
Jorge Sanchez, Technology
EMP: 50
SQ FT: 12,500
SALES (est): 58.9MM
SALES (corp-wide): 59.1MM Privately Held
WEB: www.cottage-inn.com
SIC: 6531 7011 Real estate brokers & agents; real estate managers; hotels & motels
PA: Invest West Financial Corp
    1933 Cliff Dr Ste 1
    Santa Barbara CA 93109
    805 957-0095

(P-11345)
PALADIN REALTY PARTNERS LLC (PA)
10880 Wilshire Blvd # 1400, Los Angeles (90024-4119)
PHONE..................................310 914-2410
James R Worms,
John S Gerson,
Michael B Lenard,
EMP: 50
SALES (est): 3.1MM Privately Held
SIC: 6531 Real estate agent, commercial

(P-11346)
PANATTONI DEVELOPMENT CO INC (PA)
2442 Dupont Dr, Irvine (92612-1523)
PHONE..................................916 381-1561
Carl Panattoni, Chairman
Whitfield Hamilton, Partner
Rob Riner, Partner
Dudley Mitchell, President
Greg Thurman, President
EMP: 90
SALES (est): 33.5MM Privately Held
SIC: 6531 Real estate agent, commercial

(P-11347)
PARAGON REAL ESTATE GROUP
350 Rhode Island St, San Francisco (94103-5182)
PHONE..................................415 323-4066
Jeff Salgado, Principal
Fanny Lam, Vice Pres
Sonia Roll, Vice Pres
Dierk Herbermann, General Mgr
Kitt Flood, Broker
EMP: 59
SALES (corp-wide): 3.2MM Privately Held
SIC: 6531 Real estate agent, residential
PA: Paragon Real Estate Group Of San Francisco, Inc.
    1400 Van Ness Ave
    San Francisco CA 94109
    415 292-2384

(P-11348)
PARAMUNT CONTRS DEVELOPERS INC
Also Called: Tops Auto Parks
6464 W Sunset Blvd # 700, Los Angeles (90028-8001)
PHONE..................................323 464-7050
Brad Folb, President
Brian Folb, Exec VP
EMP: 50 EST: 1949
SQ FT: 102,000
SALES (est): 4.9MM Privately Held
WEB: www.folbart.com
SIC: 6531 1541 1521 Real estate managers; industrial buildings & warehouses; single-family housing construction

(P-11349)
PARK REGENCY INC
10146 Balboa Blvd, Granada Hills (91344-7408)
PHONE..................................818 363-6116
Joseph Alexander, President
Patrick Pace, CFO
Ken Engeron, Vice Pres
Kenneth Engeron, Vice Pres
Melody Cutler, Info Tech Mgr
EMP: 70
SQ FT: 4,500
SALES (est): 4.5MM Privately Held
WEB: www.parkregency.com
SIC: 6531 Real estate agent, residential; real estate agent, commercial

(P-11350)
PARMA MANAGEMENT CO INC
6390 Greenwich Dr Ste 150, San Diego (92122-5958)
P.O. Box 22209 (92192-2209)
PHONE..................................858 457-4999
Leon Parma, President
David Kressin, Vice Pres
Michael Parma, Vice Pres
EMP: 50 EST: 2000
SALES (est): 4.7MM Privately Held
SIC: 6531 Real estate agents & managers

(P-11351)
PARWOOD PRESERVATION LP
Also Called: Northpointe Apartment Homes
5441 N Paramount Blvd, Long Beach (90805-5128)
PHONE..................................562 531-7880
Larry Lipton, Partner
EMP: 99
SALES (est): 4MM Privately Held
SIC: 6531 Real estate agents & managers

(P-11352)
PASSCO COMPANIES LLC (PA)
2050 Main St Ste 650, Irvine (92614-8265)
PHONE..................................949 442-1000
William O Passo,
William H Winn, President
Thomas B Jahncke, Senior VP
Tom Jahncke, Senior VP
Jeff Olshan, Vice Pres
EMP: 63
SALES (est): 20.9MM Privately Held
WEB: www.passco.com
SIC: 6531 Real estate brokers & agents

(P-11353)
PATHSTONE FAMILY OFFICE LLC
Also Called: Pathstone Federal Street
1900 Avenue Of The, Los Angeles (90067)
PHONE..................................888 750-7284
Steve Braverman, Principal
EMP: 109
SALES (corp-wide): 387.9K Privately Held
SIC: 6531 Appraiser, real estate
PA: Pathstone Family Office, Llc
    10 Sterling Blvd Ste 402
    Englewood NJ 07631
    888 750-7284

(P-11354)
PAUL CALVO AND COMPANY
1619 W Garvey Ave N # 201, West Covina (91790-2144)
PHONE..................................626 814-8000
Paul Calvo, Owner
EMP: 50
SALES (est): 3MM Privately Held
WEB: www.calvogroup.com
SIC: 6531 Real estate agent, commercial; real estate managers

(P-11355)
PCS PROPERTY MANAGMENT LLC
11859 Wilshire Blvd # 600, Los Angeles (90025-6616)
PHONE..................................310 231-1000
Michael Ross, Branch Mgr
EMP: 136 Privately Held
SIC: 6531 Real estate managers
PA: Pcs Property Managment Llc
    4500 Woodman Ave Ofc
    Sherman Oaks CA 91423

(P-11356)
PEARSON REALTY (PA)
7480 N Palm Ave Ste 101, Fresno (93711-5501)
PHONE..................................559 432-6200
John Stewart, CEO
Doug Collins, Vice Pres
Matt McEwen, Vice Pres
Mel Lubisich, Broker
Stanley Kjar, Sales Mgr
EMP: 65
SQ FT: 12,000
SALES (est): 5.4MM Privately Held
WEB: www.pearsonfarms.com
SIC: 6531 Real estate agent, residential; appraiser, real estate

(P-11357)
PICKFORD REALTY INC
Also Called: Prudential
1015 Nipomo St Ste 100, San Luis Obispo (93401-3890)
PHONE..................................805 782-6000
Eric Pinpker, Branch Mgr
EMP: 51
SALES (corp-wide): 2.1MM Privately Held
SIC: 6531 Real estate agent, residential
HQ: Pickford Realty, Inc.
    12544 High Bluff Dr # 420
    San Diego CA 92130
    888 995-7575

(P-11358)
PINNACLE ESTATE PROPERTIES (PA)
Also Called: Pinnacle Escrow Company
9137 Reseda Blvd, Northridge (91324-3039)
PHONE..................................818 993-4707
Dana Potter, President
Jimmy Stewart, Broker
Matthew Black, Marketing Staff
Philip Fernandes, Sales Staff
Cheryl Howard, Consultant
EMP: 120
SQ FT: 13,000
SALES (est): 12.6MM Privately Held
WEB: www.billparent.com
SIC: 6531 Real estate agent, commercial; escrow agent, real estate

(P-11359)
PITTS & BACHMANN REALTORS INC
1436 State St, Santa Barbara
(93101-2512)
PHONE..........................805 963-1391
Patty Tunnicliffe, *Manager*
EMP: 70
SALES (corp-wide): 4.4MM **Privately Held**
WEB: www.bridgetmurphyhomes.com
SIC: 6531 Real estate agents & managers
PA: Pitts & Bachmann Realtors Inc
    1165 Coast Village Rd K
    Santa Barbara CA 93108
    805 682-6415

(P-11360)
PK NEVADA LLC
1317 5th Fl 2, Santa Monica
(90401-1470)
PHONE..........................310 255-0025
Kenneth Pressberg,
EMP: 50
SALES (est): 1.9MM **Privately Held**
WEB: www.pknevada.com
SIC: 6531 Real estate agents & managers

(P-11361)
PLAZA MANOR PRESERVATION LP
Also Called: Summer Crest Apartments
2615 E Plaza Blvd, National City
(91950-4017)
PHONE..........................619 475-2125
Larry Lipton, *Principal*
Las Palmas Foundation, *Partner*
Michael Herrington, *Partner*
EMP: 1828
SALES (est): 34.4MM **Privately Held**
SIC: 6531 Real estate agents & managers

(P-11362)
POMONA HOUSING PARTNERS LP
Also Called: Pomona Intergenerational
1731 W Holt Ave, Pomona (91768-3347)
PHONE..........................909 622-1010
Jim Brooks, *Controller*
Tesa Doleman,
Donise Jackson, *Manager*
EMP: 50 **EST:** 2014
SALES (est): 2MM **Privately Held**
SIC: 6531 Real estate agents & managers

(P-11363)
POWERHOUSE REALTY INC
Also Called: Century 21 Powerhouse Realty
3452 E Florence Ave, Huntington Park
(90255-5835)
PHONE..........................323 562-7777
Francisco Granadeno, *President*
Andrea Fernando, *Vice Pres*
EMP: 70
SALES (est): 4MM **Privately Held**
WEB: www.powerhouserealty.com
SIC: 6531 Real estate agent, residential

(P-11364)
PPM REAL ESTATE INC
3575 San Pablo Dam Rd, El Sobrante
(94803-7205)
P.O. Box 20621 (94820-0621)
PHONE..........................510 758-5636
Raymond D Smith, *President*
Ray Smith, *President*
EMP: 75
SALES (est): 3.1MM **Privately Held**
WEB: www.samuelchu.com
SIC: 6531 Real estate agent, residential

(P-11365)
PREFERRED BROKERS INC (PA)
Also Called: Coldwell Banker
9100 Ming Ave Ste 100, Bakersfield
(93311-1329)
PHONE..........................661 836-2345
John Mackessey, *President*
EMP: 70
SQ FT: 8,000
SALES (est): 4.9MM **Privately Held**
WEB: www.lesliewalters.com
SIC: 6531 Real estate agent, residential

(P-11366)
PREMIER VALLEY INC A CAL CORP (PA)
Also Called: Century 21
1414 E F St Bldg A, Oakdale (95361-9251)
PHONE..........................209 847-6111
John Melo, *CEO*
Larry Matos, *Vice Pres*
Roel Mandac, *Broker*
Ed Gookin, *Property Mgr*
Sonja Herndon, *Property Mgr*
EMP: 57
SQ FT: 5,522
SALES (est): 6.9MM **Privately Held**
SIC: 6531 8742 Real estate agent, residential; real estate consultant

(P-11367)
PRESCOTT COMPANIES (PA)
5950 La Place Ct Ste 200, Carlsbad
(92008-8852)
PHONE..........................760 634-4700
Gloria Todisco, *President*
EMP: 110
SQ FT: 11,000
SALES (est): 11MM **Privately Held**
SIC: 6531 Real estate managers

(P-11368)
PRITCHETT RAPF AND ASSOCIATES
23732 Malibu Rd, Malibu (90265-4603)
PHONE..........................310 456-6771
Jim Rapf, *Partner*
Jack Pritchett, *Partner*
Lisa Yuhasz, *Office Mgr*
Matt Rapf, *Asst Broker*
Shelly Yrigoyen, *Marketing Mgr*
EMP: 62
SALES (est): 4.2MM **Privately Held**
SIC: 6531 Rental agent, real estate

(P-11369)
PRO GROUP INC
Also Called: Keller Williams Realtors
4160 Temescal Canyon Rd # 500, Corona
(92883-4642)
PHONE..........................951 271-3000
James Brown, *President*
Jim Brown, *President*
Joseph Regan, *CFO*
David Clark, *Vice Pres*
Lucien Kalefe, *Agent*
EMP: 195
SQ FT: 18,000
SALES (est): 6MM **Privately Held**
SIC: 6531 Real estate agent, residential

(P-11370)
PROFESSIONAL COMMUNITY MGT CAL (PA)
Also Called: P C M
27051 Towne Centre Dr # 200, Foothill
Ranch (92610-2819)
PHONE..........................800 369-7260
Donny Disbro, *CEO*
Russ Disbro, *Senior VP*
Susan Finley, *Vice Pres*
Michelle Thomson, *Vice Pres*
EMP: 50
SQ FT: 12,000
SALES (est): 55MM **Privately Held**
WEB: www.pcm-ca.com
SIC: 6531 Real estate managers

(P-11371)
PROFESSIONAL COMMUNITY MGT CAL
Also Called: Sun Lakes Country Club
850 Country Club Dr, Banning
(92220-5306)
PHONE..........................951 845-2191
Mike Bennett, *Manager*
EMP: 50
SALES (corp-wide): 55MM **Privately Held**
WEB: www.pcm-ca.com
SIC: 6531 Real estate managers
PA: Professional Community Management
    Of California
    27051 Towne Centre Dr # 200
    Foothill Ranch CA 92610
    800 369-7260

(P-11372)
PROFESSIONAL COMMUNITY MGT CAL
Also Called: Pcm
24351 El Toro Rd, Laguna Woods
(92637-4901)
PHONE..........................949 206-0580
Milt Johns, *Manager*
EMP: 134
SALES (corp-wide): 55MM **Privately Held**
WEB: www.pcm-ca.com
SIC: 6531 Real estate managers
PA: Professional Community Management
    Of California
    27051 Towne Centre Dr # 200
    Foothill Ranch CA 92610
    800 369-7260

(P-11373)
PROFESSIONAL COMMUNITY MGT CAL
Also Called: Leisure World Resales
23522 Paseo De Valencia, Laguna Hills
(92653)
P.O. Box 2220 (92654-2220)
PHONE..........................949 597-4200
Gabrielle Velten, *Manager*
EMP: 134
SALES (corp-wide): 55MM **Privately Held**
WEB: www.pcm-ca.com
SIC: 6531 Real estate managers
PA: Professional Community Management
    Of California
    27051 Towne Centre Dr # 200
    Foothill Ranch CA 92610
    800 369-7260

(P-11374)
PROLAND PROPERTY MANAGMENT LLC (PA)
Also Called: Hollingshead Management
2510 W 7th St Fl 2, Los Angeles
(90057-3802)
PHONE..........................213 738-8175
Ronald Gregg,
James Harris,
EMP: 80
SQ FT: 5,000
SALES (est): 5.8MM **Privately Held**
SIC: 6531 Real estate managers

(P-11375)
PROMETHEUS RE GROUP INC (PA)
1900 S Norfolk St Ste 150, San Mateo
(94403-1161)
PHONE..........................650 931-3400
Sanford N Diller, *CEO*
Bill Levia, *CFO*
Jackie Safier, *Exec VP*
John Ghio, *Vice Pres*
Justin Halada, *Vice Pres*
EMP: 140
SALES (est): 45.5MM **Privately Held**
WEB: www.prometheusreg.com
SIC: 6531 6552 Real estate managers;
    land subdividers & developers, commercial; land subdividers & developers, residential

(P-11376)
PROPERTY MANAGEMENT ASSOC INC (PA)
Also Called: Capital Commercial Property
6011 Bristol Pkwy, Culver City
(90230-6601)
PHONE..........................323 295-2000
Thomas Spear, *President*
Patrick Lacey, *COO*
Joshua Fein, *CFO*
Steve Merz, *Portfolio Mgr*
Mitra Jafarpour, *Property Mgr*
EMP: 130
SQ FT: 6,500
SALES (est): 13MM **Privately Held**
WEB: www.wemanageproperties.com
SIC: 6531 Real estate managers

(P-11377)
PROPERTY MANAGEMENT CONS (PA)
11717 Bernardo Plaza Ct # 220, San Diego
(92128-2412)
PHONE..........................858 485-9811
Richard L Grant, *Principal*
Bonnie Grant, *Treasurer*
Gregory Grant, *Principal*
Vivian Worley, *Administration*
Dimo Deliivanov, *Manager*
EMP: 50 **EST:** 1980
SALES (est): 4.3MM **Privately Held**
SIC: 6531 Real estate managers

(P-11378)
PRUDENTIAL 24 HOUR REAL ESTATE
8635 Florence Ave Ste 101, Downey
(90240-4045)
PHONE..........................562 861-7257
Mel Berdelis, *Owner*
EMP: 80
SALES (est): 2.9MM **Privately Held**
WEB: www.prudential24hours.com
SIC: 6531 Real estate brokers & agents

(P-11379)
PRUDENTIAL AMRCN RLTY A CAL LP
9003 Reseda Blvd Ste 105, Northridge
(91324-3942)
PHONE..........................818 993-8900
John Maquar, *Partner*
EMP: 50
SALES (est): 2.4MM
SALES (corp-wide): 225.3B **Publicly Held**
WEB: www.patrussell4re.com
SIC: 6531 Real estate agent, residential
PA: Berkshire Hathaway Inc.
    3555 Farnam St Ste 1140
    Omaha NE 68131
    402 346-1400

(P-11380)
PRUDENTIAL CA REALTY
39275 Mssion Blvd Ste 103, Fremont
(94539)
PHONE..........................510 487-6088
William L Salgado, *President*
Grace Pinacate, *Admin Sec*
EMP: 58
SALES (est): 2.2MM **Privately Held**
WEB: www.kensmithrealty.com
SIC: 6531 Real estate agent, residential

(P-11381)
PRUDENTIAL CALIFORNIA REALTY
677 Portola Dr, San Francisco
(94127-1207)
PHONE..........................415 664-9400
Steven Spears, *President*
EMP: 90
SALES (est): 4.1MM **Privately Held**
WEB: www.propertyinsanfrancisco.com
SIC: 6531 Real estate agent, residential

(P-11382)
PRUDENTIAL CALIFORNIA REALTY
976 Main St Ste A, Ramona (92065-1970)
PHONE..........................858 487-3520
Jon Cook, *President*
Leeann Iacino, *COO*
EMP: 81
SQ FT: 1,200
SALES (est): 3.8MM **Privately Held**
WEB: www.wattshername.com
SIC: 6531 Real estate agent, residential

(P-11383)
PRUDENTIAL REALTY CORP
1430 Taraval St, San Francisco
(94116-2346)
PHONE..........................415 566-9800
Sam Cadelinia, *President*
Wayne MA, *CTO*
Frank Mack, *Broker*
EMP: 66
SALES (est): 2.6MM **Privately Held**
SIC: 6531 Real estate agent, residential

PRODUCTS & SVCS

(P-11384)
PS BUSINESS PARKS LP
701 Western Ave, Glendale (91201-2349)
PHONE..........................818 244-8080
Maria Hawthorne, *Partner*
Safu Rana, *Manager*
EMP: 99
SALES (est): 6.1MM
SALES (corp-wide): 413.5MM **Publicly Held**
SIC: 6531 Real estate agent, commercial
PA: Ps Business Parks, Inc.
       701 Western Ave
       Glendale CA 91201
       818 244-8080

(P-11385)
QAL AFFILIATE INC
Also Called: Century 21 Golden Hills
2680 S White Rd Ste 150, San Jose
(95148-2079)
PHONE..........................408 238-5111
Bob Fernandez, *President*
EMP: 50
SQ FT: 7,000
SALES (est): 2.6MM **Privately Held**
WEB: www.c21goldenhills.com
SIC: 6531 Real estate agent, residential

(P-11386)
R & B REALTY GROUP LP
Also Called: Oakwood Worldwide
1 World Trade Ctr # 2400, Long Beach
(90831-0002)
PHONE..........................310 478-1021
Howard F Ruby, *Partner*
EMP: 1500
SALES (est): 52.4MM **Privately Held**
SIC: 6531 Buying agent, real estate

(P-11387)
RAINBOW REALTY CORPORATION
Also Called: Century 21
24221 Paseo De Valencia, Laguna Woods
(92637-3112)
PHONE..........................949 770-9626
Frank J Hill, *President*
EMP: 55 **EST:** 1978
SALES (est): 3.4MM **Privately Held**
WEB: www.lizhead.net
SIC: 6531 Real estate agent, residential

(P-11388)
RAM COMMERCIAL ENTERPRISES INC
Also Called: Homepointe Property Management
5896 S Land Park Dr, Sacramento
(95822-3311)
P.O. Box 221660 (95822-8660)
PHONE..........................916 429-1205
Robert Machado, *President*
Cheryl Colburn, *Property Mgr*
Alexandra Goldthwaite, *Property Mgr*
Shannon Reece, *Property Mgr*
Michelle Wight, *Property Mgr*
EMP: 50
SALES (est): 4.7MM **Privately Held**
WEB: www.homepointe.com
SIC: 6531 Real estate managers

(P-11389)
RAMSEY REAL ESTATE GROUP
13714 Boquita Dr, Del Mar (92014-3410)
P.O. Box 1530, Beverly Hills (90213-1530)
PHONE..........................800 685-7734
Jeffrey T Ramsey, *CEO*
EMP: 50
SALES (est): 208.6K **Privately Held**
SIC: 6531 Real estate brokers & agents

(P-11390)
RAMSEY-SHILLING RESIDENTIAL RE
3360 Barham Blvd, Los Angeles
(90068-1473)
PHONE..........................323 851-5512
Michael Alley, *Owner*
Darrielle Ehrheart, *Real Est Agnt*
EMP: 75
SALES (est): 1.7MM **Privately Held**
SIC: 6531 Real estate agent, residential

(P-11391)
RANCHO MISSION VIEJO LLC (PA)
Also Called: Ladera Ranch
28811 Ortega Hwy, San Juan Capistrano
(92675-2023)
P.O. Box 9 (92693-0009)
PHONE..........................949 240-3363
Anthony R Moiso, *Principal*
Gilbert G Aguirre, *Exec VP*
Michael Balsamo, *Senior VP*
Richard Broming, *Senior VP*
Gregory S Edwards, *Senior VP*
EMP: 60
SQ FT: 42,000
SALES (est): 11.4MM **Privately Held**
WEB: www.ranchomissionviejo.com
SIC: 6531 Real estate managers; escrow agent, real estate

(P-11392)
RE MAX ALL CITIES LK ARROWHEAD
28200 Highway 189, Lake Arrowhead
(92352-9700)
PHONE..........................909 337-6111
Kelli Todd, *President*
EMP: 50
SALES (est): 1.1MM **Privately Held**
SIC: 6531 Real estate agent, residential

(P-11393)
RE MAX PARKSIDE REAL ESTATE
Also Called: RCA Properties
711 12th St, Paso Robles (93446-2206)
PHONE..........................805 239-3310
Peter Dankin, *President*
Kaye D Rickerd, *Real Est Agnt*
Canet Cynthia, *Associate*
EMP: 60
SALES (est): 4.2MM **Privately Held**
WEB: www.janstemperbrown.com
SIC: 6531 Real estate agent, residential

(P-11394)
RE/MAX
201 New Stine Rd Ste 300, Bakersfield
(93309-2680)
PHONE..........................661 616-4040
Debra L Craig, *Owner*
EMP: 50
SALES (est): 1.3MM **Privately Held**
SIC: 6531 Real estate agent, residential

(P-11395)
RE/MAX LLC
Also Called: Remax Champions Real Estate
1071 E 16th St, Upland (91784-9148)
PHONE..........................303 770-5531
None G Brmgr, *Branch Mgr*
EMP: 50
SALES (corp-wide): 212.6MM **Publicly Held**
SIC: 6531 Real estate agent, residential
HQ: Re/Max, Llc
       5075 S Syracuse St
       Denver CO 80237
       303 770-5531

(P-11396)
RE/MAX BEACH CITIES REALTY MAR
400 S Sepulveda Blvd # 100, Manhattan
Beach (90266-6814)
PHONE..........................310 376-2225
Robert Kenneth Todd, *Owner*
Patricia Hedstrom, *Executive*
Leslie Klein, *Broker*
Sloane Sanders, *Broker*
Jennifer Riddle, *Opers Staff*
EMP: 150
SQ FT: 15,000
SALES (est): 5.7MM **Privately Held**
SIC: 6531 Real estate agent, residential

(P-11397)
RE/MAX MAGIC
11420 Ming Ave Ste 530, Bakersfield
(93311-1369)
PHONE..........................661 616-4040
Debbie Banducci, *Owner*
EMP: 50
SALES (est): 546K **Privately Held**
SIC: 6531 Real estate agent, residential

(P-11398)
RE/MAX OF VALENCIA INC (PA)
25101 The Old Rd, Santa Clarita
(91381-2206)
PHONE..........................661 255-2650
John O'Hare, *President*
John Ohare, *President*
Alice O'Hare, *Vice Pres*
Robin Castagnola, *Controller*
Kristi Davalos, *Broker*
EMP: 125
SQ FT: 10,000
SALES (est): 7.5MM **Privately Held**
WEB: www.kathybost.com
SIC: 6531 8742 Real estate agent, residential; escrow agent, real estate; real estate consultant

(P-11399)
RE/MAX PLOS VRDES RLTY / EXCES
Also Called: Remax Estate Properties
450 Silver Spur Rd, Rancho Palos Verdes
(90275-3573)
PHONE..........................310 541-5224
Kevin Mullen, *Manager*
Davor Sunjara, *Administration*
Jeff Kashanchi, *Info Tech Mgr*
Kristen Hernandez, *Training Dir*
Jay Deai, *Property Mgr*
EMP: 50
SALES (corp-wide): 8.8MM **Privately Held**
WEB: www.realestatebymichele.com
SIC: 6531 Real estate agent, residential
PA: Re/Max Palos Verdes Realty/Exces
       63 Malaga Cove Plz
       Palos Verdes Estates CA 90274
       310 378-9494

(P-11400)
REAL ESTATE AMERICA INC
2000 Powell St Ste 100, Emeryville
(94608-1774)
P.O. Box 494846, Port Charlotte FL
(33949-4846)
PHONE..........................510 594-3100
Kareem K Macarthur, *President*
EMP: 55 **Privately Held**
SIC: 6531 Real estate brokers & agents
PA: Real Estate America, Inc.
       10120 S Estrn Ave Ste 200
       Henderson NV 89052

(P-11401)
REAL ESTATE CALIFORNIA DEPT
Also Called: Property Management
3737 Main St Ofc, Riverside (92501-3338)
PHONE..........................951 715-0130
Bobie Sanchez, *Manager*
EMP: 100 **Privately Held**
SIC: 6531 9532 Real estate brokers & agents; urban & community development;
HQ: California Department Of Real Estate
       2201 Broadway Lowr
       Sacramento CA
       -

(P-11402)
REAL PROPERTY SYSTEMS INC
1443 E Washington Blvd, Pasadena
(91104-2650)
PHONE..........................760 243-1143
Michael Palmer, *President*
EMP: 250
SALES (est): 6.2MM **Privately Held**
WEB: www.realpropertysystems.com
SIC: 6531 Real estate agents & managers

(P-11403)
REALOGY HOLDINGS CORP
Also Called: Artisan Sotheby's Intl. Realty
3554 Round Barn Blvd, Santa Rosa
(95403-0929)
PHONE..........................707 284-1111
Eric Drew, *Branch Mgr*
Rosemarie Corrigan, *Sales Staff*
EMP: 485 **Publicly Held**
SIC: 6531 Real estate agent, residential
PA: Realogy Holdings Corp.
       175 Park Ave
       Madison NJ 07940
       -

(P-11404)
REALTOR SFR GREEN
4090 Mission Blvd, San Diego
(92109-5043)
PHONE..........................858 488-4090
Brian Barber, *General Mgr*
EMP: 50 **EST:** 2011
SALES (est): 1.1MM **Privately Held**
SIC: 6531 Real estate brokers & agents

(P-11405)
REALTY EXECUTIVES
26650 The Old Rd Ste 300, Valencia
(91381-0754)
PHONE..........................661 286-8600
Jim Tanner, *President*
David Loyd, *Vice Pres*
Tiffany Bennett, *Broker*
Ken Putt, *Broker*
John Carris, *Real Est Agnt*
EMP: 150
SALES (est): 4.9MM **Privately Held**
SIC: 6531 Real estate agent, residential

(P-11406)
REALTY ONE GROUP INC
19322 Jesse Ln, Riverside (92508-5072)
PHONE..........................951 565-8105
EMP: 55
SALES (corp-wide): 26.7MM **Privately Held**
SIC: 6531 Real estate agent, residential
PA: Realty One Group, Inc.
       7545 Irvine Center Dr # 250
       Irvine CA 92618
       949 596-4300

(P-11407)
REDFIN CORPORATION
655 Montgomery St # 1430, San Francisco
(94111-2631)
PHONE..........................206 340-8794
Glenn Kelman, *Branch Mgr*
Serena Jiang, *Engineer*
Sasai Zhang, *Buyer*
Steve Moses, *Manager*
Keith Thomas, *Manager*
EMP: 465
SALES (corp-wide): 486.9MM **Publicly Held**
SIC: 6531 Real estate brokers & agents
PA: Redfin Corporation
       1099 Stewart St Ste 600
       Seattle WA 98101
       206 576-8333

(P-11408)
REFERRAL REALTY INC
1601 S De Anza Blvd # 150, Cupertino
(95014-5358)
PHONE..........................408 996-8100
Morise Nahouraii, *President*
Madeline Stevenson, *Admin Asst*
Lisa Leung, *Broker*
Tom Cooper, *Agent*
EMP: 55
SQ FT: 5,800
SALES (est): 3.2MM **Privately Held**
WEB: www.referralrealty.com
SIC: 6531 Real estate brokers & agents

(P-11409)
REGENCY PARK SENIOR LIVING INC
Also Called: Regency Park El Molino
245 S El Molino Ave, Pasadena
(91101-2996)
PHONE..........................626 578-0460
Emil Fish, *President*
EMP: 81
SALES (corp-wide): 10.2MM **Privately Held**
SIC: 6531 Real estate agents & managers
PA: Regency Park Senior Living, Inc.
       150 S Los Robles Ave # 480
       Pasadena CA 91101
       626 773-8800

(P-11410)
REGISTRY MONITORING INS SRVCS
Also Called: Rmis
5388 Sterling Center Dr, Westlake Village
(91361-4688)
PHONE..........................800 400-4924

Marvin Landon, *Chairman*
Hayden Landon, *President*
Kelsey Nagelmann, *Executive Asst*
Matthew Mandery, *Software Dev*
John McKinney, *Software Dev*
EMP: 115
SALES (est): 17.2MM **Privately Held**
WEB: www.registrymonitoring.com
SIC: 6531 6411 Real estate agents & managers; insurance information & consulting services

(P-11411)
RELS LLC
Also Called: Rels Valuation
40 Pacifica Ste 900, Irvine (92618-7487)
PHONE..............................949 214-1000
Frank D Martell, *COO*
EMP: 1300
SALES (est): 584.1K
SALES (corp-wide): 1.7B **Publicly Held**
WEB: www.rels.com
SIC: 6531 7323 Appraiser, real estate; commercial (mercantile) credit reporting bureau
PA: Corelogic, Inc.
40 Pacifica Ste 900
Irvine CA 92618
949 214-1000

(P-11412)
REMAX ACTIVE REALTY
Also Called: Remax Active Teal State
4056 Decoto Rd, Fremont (94555-3201)
PHONE..............................510 505-1660
Fay Louis, *Owner*
Alcutse Aninao, *Real Est Agnt*
Jamie Chan, *Associate*
Qin Frank, *Associate*
EMP: 50 **EST:** 2001
SALES (est): 2MM **Privately Held**
SIC: 6531 Real estate agent, residential

(P-11413)
REMAX ALL STARS REALTY
765 N Main St, Corona (92880-1440)
PHONE..............................951 739-4000
Bret Meckes, *Owner*
Brian Bucsit, *Associate*
EMP: 64
SALES (est): 2.1MM **Privately Held**
SIC: 6531 Real estate agent, residential

(P-11414)
REMAX GOLD
Also Called: Re/Max
3620 Fair Oaks Blvd # 300, Sacramento (95864-7263)
PHONE..............................916 609-2800
Pam Porter, *General Mgr*
Jaci Wallace, *Manager*
Wanda Christensen, *Real Est Agnt*
Victoria Leas, *Real Est Agnt*
Ted Russert, *Real Est Agnt*
EMP: 85
SALES (est): 2.6MM **Privately Held**
SIC: 6531 7389 Real estate agent, residential; brokers, business: buying & selling business enterprises

(P-11415)
REMAX METRO INC
Also Called: Re/Max
150 Paularino Ave Ste 125, Costa Mesa (92626-3318)
PHONE..............................714 557-2544
Joseph Brodrick, *President*
EMP: 60
SALES (est): 2.3MM **Privately Held**
SIC: 6531 Real estate agent, residential

(P-11416)
REMAX OLSON
Also Called: Re/Max
30699 Russell Ranch Rd, Westlake Village (91362-7315)
PHONE..............................805 267-4929
Todd Olson, *Owner*
Keith Myers, *President*
Barbara Zieger, *Controller*
EMP: 70
SALES (est): 3.4MM **Privately Held**
WEB: www.joedecarlo.com
SIC: 6531 Real estate agent, residential

(P-11417)
RETIREMENT HOUSING FOUNDATION (PA)
911 N Studebaker Rd # 100, Long Beach (90815-4980)
PHONE..............................562 257-5100
Laverne R Joseph, *CEO*
Raymond East, *Ch of Bd*
Christina E Potter, *Vice Chairman*
Darryl M Sexton, *Vice Chairman*
Frank G Jahrling, *Treasurer*
EMP: 65
SALES: 39.7MM **Privately Held**
WEB: www.bixbyknollstowers.com
SIC: 6531 Real estate agents & managers

(P-11418)
RETIREMENT HOUSING FOUNDATION
Also Called: Plymouth Square
1319 N Madison St Ofc, Stockton (95202-1001)
PHONE..............................209 466-4341
Gary Wiemers, *Administration*
EMP: 100
SALES (corp-wide): 39.7MM **Privately Held**
WEB: www.bixbyknollstowers.com
SIC: 6531 Real estate agents & managers
PA: Retirement Housing Foundation Inc
911 N Studebaker Rd # 100
Long Beach CA 90815
562 257-5100

(P-11419)
RICHARD REALTY GROUP INC
Also Called: Realty Group San Diego
2792 Gateway Rd Ste 103, Carlsbad (92009-1749)
PHONE..............................760 603-8377
Bill Richard, *CEO*
Jan Richard, *CFO*
Janis Richard, *Vice Pres*
Daylene Grose, *Agent*
EMP: 60 **EST:** 2009
SALES (est): 3.5MM **Privately Held**
SIC: 6531 Real estate agent, residential

(P-11420)
RIPHAGEN & BULLERDICK INC
Also Called: Re/Max
5925 Ball Rd, Cypress (90630-3245)
PHONE..............................714 763-2100
Gary Riphagen, *President*
Gerry Bullerdick, *Treasurer*
Kerry Louis, *Manager*
EMP: 50
SQ FT: 2,600
SALES (est): 4MM **Privately Held**
WEB: www.remaxtiffany.com
SIC: 6531 Real estate agent, residential

(P-11421)
RODEO REALTY INC
15300 Ventura Blvd # 500, Sherman Oaks (91403-3144)
PHONE..............................818 986-7300
Jason Katzman, *Branch Mgr*
Kenny Nelson, *Graphic Designe*
Tim Egan, *Marketing Staff*
EMP: 76
SALES (corp-wide): 72.3MM **Privately Held**
SIC: 6531 Real estate brokers & agents
PA: Rodeo Realty, Inc.
9171 Wilshire Blvd # 321
Beverly Hills CA 90210
818 349-9997

(P-11422)
RODEO REALTY INC
11940 San Vicente Blvd, Los Angeles (90049-5004)
PHONE..............................310 873-0100
Simon Pozi, *Manager*
Peter Maurice, *Director*
Jennifer Meyers, *Real Est Agnt*
Ashley Novak, *Real Est Agnt*
EMP: 68
SALES (corp-wide): 72.3MM **Privately Held**
SIC: 6531 Real estate agent, residential

(P-11423)
RODEO REALTY INC
Also Called: Paramount Properties Encino BR
17501 Ventura Blvd, Encino (91316-3836)
PHONE..............................818 285-3700
Syd Leibovitch, *President*
EMP: 76
SALES (est): 2.3MM
SALES (corp-wide): 72.3MM **Privately Held**
SIC: 6531 Real estate brokers & agents
PA: Rodeo Realty, Inc.
9171 Wilshire Blvd # 321
Beverly Hills CA 90210
818 349-9997

(P-11424)
RODEO REALTY INC
12345 Ventura Blvd Ste A, Studio City (91604-2511)
PHONE..............................818 308-8273
Sib Leibovitch, *President*
EMP: 80
SALES (corp-wide): 72.3MM **Privately Held**
SIC: 6531 Real estate brokers & agents
PA: Rodeo Realty, Inc.
9171 Wilshire Blvd # 321
Beverly Hills CA 90210
818 349-9997

(P-11425)
RODEO REALTY INC (PA)
Also Called: Paramount Properties
9171 Wilshire Blvd # 321, Beverly Hills (90210-5562)
PHONE..............................818 349-9997
Sydney Leibovitch, *CEO*
EMP: 76
SQ FT: 5,000
SALES (est): 72.3MM **Privately Held**
WEB: www.jennifer4homes.com
SIC: 6531 Real estate agent, residential

(P-11426)
RODEO REALTY INC
9338 Reseda Blvd Ste 102, Northridge (91324-2986)
PHONE..............................818 349-9997
Teresa Todd, *Branch Mgr*
EMP: 100
SALES (corp-wide): 72.3MM **Privately Held**
WEB: www.jennifer4homes.com
SIC: 6531 Real estate brokers & agents
PA: Rodeo Realty, Inc.
9171 Wilshire Blvd # 321
Beverly Hills CA 90210
818 349-9997

(P-11427)
RODEO REALTY INC
23901 Calabasas Rd # 1050, Calabasas (91302-3379)
PHONE..............................818 657-4609
Lu Duffy, *Branch Mgr*
EMP: 76
SALES (corp-wide): 72.3MM **Privately Held**
SIC: 6531 6519 6162 6141 Real estate brokers & agents; real property lessors; loan correspondents; personal credit institutions
PA: Rodeo Realty, Inc.
9171 Wilshire Blvd # 321
Beverly Hills CA 90210
818 349-9997

(P-11428)
RODEO REALTY INC
Also Called: Paramount Properties
21031 Ventura Blvd # 100, Woodland Hills (91364-2208)
PHONE..............................818 999-2030
Demetra Kalizki, *Manager*
EMP: 100
SALES (corp-wide): 72.3MM **Privately Held**
WEB: www.jennifer4homes.com
SIC: 6531 Real estate brokers & agents

PA: Rodeo Realty, Inc.
9171 Wilshire Blvd # 321
Beverly Hills CA 90210
818 349-9997

(P-11429)
RONALD L WOLFE & ASSOC INC
Also Called: Wolfe & Associates
173 Chapel St, Santa Barbara (93111-2333)
PHONE..............................805 964-6770
Ronald L Wolfe, *President*
Kerry Bentz, *Portfolio Mgr*
Christopher Popp, *Supervisor*
EMP: 50 **EST:** 1971
SQ FT: 5,000
SALES (est): 5MM **Privately Held**
WEB: www.rlwa.com
SIC: 6531 Real estate managers

(P-11430)
ROSANO PARTNERS
3530 Wilshire Blvd # 1750, Los Angeles (90010-2339)
PHONE..............................213 802-0300
Sagiv Rosano, *CEO*
EMP: 50
SALES (est): 4.3MM **Privately Held**
WEB: www.rosanopartners.com
SIC: 6531 Real estate agent, commercial

(P-11431)
RSC ASSOCIATES INC (PA)
3120 Cohasset Rd Ste 5, Chico (95973-0978)
PHONE..............................530 893-8228
Steven Baddely, *CEO*
Richard Gillaspie, *President*
Laura Carter, *CFO*
Cynthia Bryan, *Admin Sec*
EMP: 122
SQ FT: 3,000
SALES (est): 10.6MM **Privately Held**
SIC: 6531 Real estate managers

(P-11432)
RVTLZATION ANAHEIM II PARTNERS
1515 S Calle Del Mar, Anaheim (92802-2607)
PHONE..............................714 520-4041
EMP: 75 **EST:** 2014
SALES (est): 1.7MM **Privately Held**
SIC: 6531

(P-11433)
S & P COMPANY (PA)
100 Shoreline Hwy B395, Mill Valley (94941-6608)
PHONE..............................415 332-0550
Bernard Orsi, *CEO*
▼ **EMP:** 52 **EST:** 1932
SQ FT: 5,000
SALES (est): 3.5MM **Privately Held**
SIC: 6531 Real estate agents & managers

(P-11434)
S D PROPERTY MANAGEMENT INC
Also Called: Four Seasons Landscaping
14937 Delano St, Van Nuys (91411-2123)
PHONE..............................323 658-7990
Steve Darrison, *President*
EMP: 60
SQ FT: 1,150
SALES (est): 3.1MM **Privately Held**
SIC: 6531 Real estate managers

(P-11435)
S P R E INC
Also Called: Security Pacific RE Brkg
3223 Blume Dr, Richmond (94806-5782)
PHONE..............................510 222-8340
Jack Burns Sr, *President*
Betty Couzens, *Corp Secy*
Ray De Gennaro, *Vice Pres*
EMP: 100
SQ FT: 16,000
SALES (est): 5.2MM **Privately Held**
WEB: www.spre.com
SIC: 6531 Real estate brokers & agents

(P-11436)
S&J STADTLER INC
Also Called: Remax Accord
5980 Stoneridge Dr # 122, Pleasanton
(94588-4518)
PHONE..................................925 847-8900
Jerry Stadtler, *Owner*
EMP: 330
SALES (corp-wide): 21.8MM **Privately Held**
SIC: 6531 Real estate agent, residential
PA: S&J Stadtler Inc
313 Sycamore Valley Rd W
Danville CA 94526
925 838-4100

(P-11437)
SAN DIEGO MORTGAGE & RE
9461 Grsmnt Smt Dr Ste D, La Mesa
(91941-4165)
PHONE..................................619 334-7779
Mark Revetta, *President*
EMP: 50
SALES: 25MM **Privately Held**
SIC: 6531 Real estate brokers & agents

(P-11438)
SANTA ROSA & SONOMA CO REAL ES
1057 College Ave, Santa Rosa
(95404-4128)
PHONE..................................707 524-1124
EMP: 50
SALES (est): 2MM **Privately Held**
SIC: 6531

(P-11439)
SATELLITE MANAGEMENT CO (PA)
Also Called: Ccts
1010 E Chestnut Ave, Santa Ana
(92701-6497)
PHONE..................................714 558-2411
Ronald Jensen, *CEO*
Mary E Conzelman, *Vice Pres*
Helen M Jensen, *Vice Pres*
EMP: 121
SQ FT: 800
SALES (est): 24.2MM **Privately Held**
WEB: www.satellitemanagement.com
SIC: 6531 Real estate managers

(P-11440)
SCHWEIZER RENA
Also Called: White House Properties
15720 Ventura Blvd # 100, Encino
(91436-2914)
PHONE..................................818 501-7100
Marty William, *Owner*
Rena Schweizer, *Owner*
EMP: 60
SALES (est): 1.4MM **Privately Held**
WEB: www.realwinds.com
SIC: 6531 Real estate agent, residential

(P-11441)
SCOTT PLACE ASSOCIATES
60 31st Ave, San Mateo (94403-3404)
PHONE..................................650 345-8222
David Bohannon, *General Ptnr*
David D Bohannon, *General Ptnr*
EMP: 60
SALES (est): 2MM **Privately Held**
SIC: 6531 Real estate managers

(P-11442)
SEC PAC INC
Also Called: Security Pacific Real Estate
1555 Riviera Ave Ste E, Walnut Creek
(94596-7321)
PHONE..................................925 938-9200
Allan Hibbard, *President*
Michael R Clancy, *Executive*
Richard J Clancy, *Principal*
EMP: 60
SQ FT: 10,000
SALES (est): 2.8MM **Privately Held**
WEB: www.soldbymarian.com
SIC: 6531 Real estate agent, residential

(P-11443)
SECURITY PACIFIC RE BRKG
292 Violet Rd, Hercules (94547-1027)
PHONE..................................510 245-9901
Jack Burns Sr, *President*

Bill Prather, *Manager*
EMP: 90
SALES (est): 1.8MM **Privately Held**
WEB: www.billprather.com
SIC: 6531 Real estate brokers & agents

(P-11444)
SERVICE CORP INTERNATIONAL
Also Called: SCI
3500 Pacific View Dr, Corona Del Mar
(92625-1112)
PHONE..................................949 644-2700
Ruby Louis, *Branch Mgr*
EMP: 65
SALES (corp-wide): 3.1B **Publicly Held**
WEB: www.sci-corp.com
SIC: 6531 7261 Cemetery management service; crematory
PA: Service Corporation International
1929 Allen Pkwy
Houston TX 77019
713 522-5141

(P-11445)
SFT REALTY GALWAY DOWNS LLC
Also Called: Kentina
38801 Los Porralitos, Temecula (92592)
P.O. Box 4404 Jeremie Dr
PHONE..................................951 232-1880
Kenneth C Smith, *Mng Member*
EMP: 70 EST: 2013
SQ FT: 2,000
SALES: 400K **Privately Held**
SIC: 6531 Real estate agents & managers

(P-11446)
SHE MANAGES PROPERTIES INC (PA)
9340 Hazard Way Ste B2, San Diego
(92123-1228)
PHONE..................................619 291-6300
Karen Martinez, *President*
Jorge Martinez, *Corp Secy*
EMP: 65
SQ FT: 1,700
SALES (est): 10.2MM **Privately Held**
WEB: www.shemanages.com
SIC: 6531 Real estate managers

(P-11447)
SHEA HOMES ARIZONA LTD PARTNR
655 Brea Canyon Rd, Walnut
(91789-3078)
PHONE..................................909 594-9500
EMP: 55
SALES (est): 92.7K
SALES (corp-wide): 2.2B **Privately Held**
SIC: 6531 Real estate agents & managers
HQ: Shea Homes Limited Partnership, A
California Limited Partnership
655 Brea Canyon Rd
Walnut CA 91789

(P-11448)
SHEA PROPERTIES MGT CO INC
130 Vantis Dr Ste 200, Aliso Viejo
(92656-2691)
P.O. Box 62814, Irvine (92602-6093)
PHONE..................................949 389-7000
Colm Macken, *CEO*
EMP: 347
SQ FT: 48,000
SALES (est): 26.9MM
SALES (corp-wide): 2.2B **Privately Held**
SIC: 6531 Rental agent, real estate
PA: J. F. Shea Co., Inc.
655 Brea Canyon Rd
Walnut CA 91789
909 594-9500

(P-11449)
SHII LLC
Also Called: Frontier Communities
2151 E Cnvntn Ctr Way # 222, Ontario
(91764-5429)
PHONE..................................909 354-8000
James Previti, *Mng Member*
Mark Hicks, *VP Sales*
Ed Hunter, *Sales Staff*
EMP: 50

SALES (est): 4.4MM **Privately Held**
SIC: 6531 Real estate brokers & agents

(P-11450)
SKYHILL FINANCIAL INC
5772 Bolsa Ave Ste 100, Huntington Beach
(92649-1134)
PHONE..................................714 657-3938
Rosanne Covy, *President*
Angela Hess, *COO*
Tyrone Helton, *Technology*
Bryan Palomares, *Assistant VP*
EMP: 60
SALES (est): 3.6MM **Privately Held**
SIC: 6531 8741 Real estate managers; administrative management

(P-11451)
SMITH & SONS INVESTMENT CO
735 Ohms Way, Costa Mesa (92627-4305)
PHONE..................................949 646-9648
Walker Smith III, *President*
Kim S Lazarus, *Treasurer*
Clarke Smith, *Vice Pres*
EMP: 50
SQ FT: 4,700
SALES (est): 2.6MM **Privately Held**
SIC: 6531 Real estate agent, commercial; real estate managers

(P-11452)
SMITH COLEMAN INC
Also Called: Century 21
707 N La Brea Ave, Inglewood
(90302-2203)
PHONE..................................310 671-8271
Ellis Smith, *President*
EMP: 50
SALES (est): 3.1MM **Privately Held**
WEB: www.joeltaylorrealestate.com
SIC: 6531 Real estate agent, residential

(P-11453)
SNOWCREEK PROPERTY MANAGEMENT
Also Called: Snow Creek Resort
1254 Old Mammoth Rd, Mammoth Lakes
(93546)
P.O. Box 1647 (93546-1647)
PHONE..................................760 934-3333
Linda Dempsey, *Owner*
Brent Cook, *Controller*
Jodi Melton, *Broker*
John Morris, *Opers Staff*
Allison Page, *Real Est Agnt*
EMP: 50
SALES (est): 2.5MM **Privately Held**
WEB: www.snowcreekresort.com
SIC: 6531 Time-sharing real estate sales, leasing & rentals

(P-11454)
SOLA IMPACT FUND II LP
9221 Kalmia St, Los Angeles (90002-2600)
PHONE..................................323 306-4648
Martin Muoto, *Partner*
EMP: 50
SALES (corp-wide): 62.8MM **Privately Held**
SIC: 6531 Housing authority operator
PA: Sola Impact Fund Ii, Lp
8629 S Vermont Ave
Los Angeles CA 90044
323 306-4648

(P-11455)
SOLA IMPACT FUND II LP
1401 E 52nd St, Los Angeles (90011-4964)
PHONE..................................323 306-4648
Martin Muoto, *General Ptnr*
EMP: 50
SALES (corp-wide): 62.8MM **Privately Held**
SIC: 6531 Housing authority operator
PA: Sola Impact Fund Ii, Lp
8629 S Vermont Ave
Los Angeles CA 90044
323 306-4648

(P-11456)
SOLA IMPACT FUND II LP
1639 E 92nd St, Los Angeles (90002-2373)
PHONE..................................323 306-4648
Martin Muoto, *General Ptnr*
EMP: 50

SALES (corp-wide): 62.8MM **Privately Held**
SIC: 6531 Housing authority operator
PA: Sola Impact Fund Ii, Lp
8629 S Vermont Ave
Los Angeles CA 90044
323 306-4648

(P-11457)
SOLA IMPACT FUND II LP
629 E 48th St, Los Angeles (90011-4049)
PHONE..................................323 306-4648
Martin A Muoto, *General Ptnr*
EMP: 50
SALES (corp-wide): 62.8MM **Privately Held**
SIC: 6531 Housing authority operator
PA: Sola Impact Fund Ii, Lp
8629 S Vermont Ave
Los Angeles CA 90044
323 306-4648

(P-11458)
SOLA IMPACT FUND II LP
11809 Robin St, Los Angeles (90059-2840)
PHONE..................................323 306-4648
Martin A Muoto, *General Ptnr*
EMP: 50
SALES (corp-wide): 62.8MM **Privately Held**
SIC: 6531 Real estate leasing & rentals
PA: Sola Impact Fund Ii, Lp
8629 S Vermont Ave
Los Angeles CA 90044
323 306-4648

(P-11459)
SOLANO GATEWAY REALTY INC (PA)
2420 Martin Rd Ste 100, Fairfield
(94534-8610)
PHONE..................................707 422-1725
Stephen C Spencer, *President*
Bev Dorsett, *Vice Pres*
Cathy Spencer, *Real Est Agnt*
EMP: 100
SALES (est): 5.2MM **Privately Held**
WEB: www.pamsigel.com
SIC: 6531 Real estate agent, residential

(P-11460)
SOLANO PACIFIC CORPORATION
Also Called: Coldwell Banker Solano Pacific
900 1st St, Benicia (94510-3218)
PHONE..................................707 745-6000
Richard A Bortolazzo, *CEO*
Joseph Banuat, *President*
Mercedes De Luca, *IT Executive*
EMP: 100
SQ FT: 5,000
SALES (est): 3.3MM **Privately Held**
SIC: 6531 Real estate agent, residential

(P-11461)
SOTHEBYS INTL RLTY INC
23405 Pacific Coast Hwy, Malibu
(90265-4824)
PHONE..................................310 456-6431
Michael Novotny, *General Mgr*
EMP: 50 **Publicly Held**
SIC: 6531 Real estate brokers & agents
HQ: Sotheby's International Realty, Inc.
38 E 61st St
New York NY 10065
212 606-7660

(P-11462)
SOUTH COUNTY HOUSING CORP (PA)
16500 Monterey St Ste 120, Morgan Hill
(95037-5193)
P.O. Box 4112, San Jose (95150-4112)
PHONE..................................510 582-1460
Dennis Lalor, *CEO*
John Cesare, *CFO*
Nestor Nu A EZ, *Finance*
EMP: 50
SQ FT: 13,000
SALES: 856.9K **Privately Held**
WEB: www.scounty.com
SIC: 6531 Real estate agent, residential

(P-11463)
SPUS7 125 CAMBRIDGEPARK LP
515 S Flower St Ste 3100, Los Angeles (90071-2233)
PHONE...................................213 683-4200
EMP: 135 **EST:** 2014
SALES (est): 1.9MM
SALES (corp-wide): 21.3B **Publicly Held**
SIC: 6531 Real estate agent, commercial
HQ: Cbre Global Investors, Llc
601 S Figueroa St Ste 49
Los Angeles CA 90017
213 683-4200

(P-11464)
SPUS7 150 CAMBRIDGEPARK LP
515 S Flower St Ste 3100, Los Angeles (90071-2233)
PHONE...................................213 683-4200
EMP: 180
SALES (est): 2.7MM
SALES (corp-wide): 21.3B **Publicly Held**
SIC: 6531 Real estate agent, commercial
HQ: Cbre Global Investors, Llc
601 S Figueroa St Ste 49
Los Angeles CA 90017
213 683-4200

(P-11465)
STAR REAL ESTATE SOUTH COUNTY
26711 Aliso Creek Rd 200a, Aliso Viejo (92656-4822)
PHONE...................................949 389-0004
Michelle Williams, *President*
Dave Barlet, *Real Est Agnt*
EMP: 250 **EST:** 1976
SALES (est): 7.7MM **Privately Held**
SIC: 6531 6519 Real estate agent, residential; escrow agent, real estate; mine property leasing

(P-11466)
STARPOINT PROPERTY MGT LLC
Also Called: Vision Realty Managements
450 N Roxbury Dr Ste 1050, Beverly Hills (90210-4235)
PHONE...................................310 247-0550
Paul Daneshrad,
Sheila Dameshrad,
Michael Farahnik,
EMP: 110
SALES (est): 8.8MM **Privately Held**
SIC: 6531 Real estate agents & managers

(P-11467)
STEVE ROBERSON
Also Called: Century 21
7825 Florence Ave, Downey (90240-3850)
PHONE...................................562 927-2626
Steve Roberson, *Owner*
EMP: 65 **EST:** 1977
SQ FT: 4,000
SALES (est): 2.9MM **Privately Held**
SIC: 6531 Real estate agent, residential

(P-11468)
STONESFAIR MANAGEMENT LLC (PA)
577 Airport Blvd Ste 700, Burlingame (94010-2024)
PHONE...................................650 401-3810
Karl E Bakhtiari,
Maryann Fair, *Vice Pres*
Andy Leong, *Controller*
Wilme Ng, *Human Resources*
Karl Bakhtiari,
EMP: 60
SALES (est): 7.1MM **Privately Held**
SIC: 6531 Real estate managers

(P-11469)
STRATEGIC PROPERTY MANAGEMENT
2055 3rd Ave Ste 200, San Diego (92101-2058)
PHONE...................................619 295-2211
Don Clausson, *Principal*
Strauss Randy, *CFO*
Matthew Daniel, *Controller*
EMP: 75

SALES (est): 7.8MM **Privately Held**
WEB: www.stratprop.com
SIC: 6531 Real estate managers

(P-11470)
SUNNY HILLS-PALLADIUM LLC (PA)
2500 E Foothill Blvd 50, West Covina (91791)
PHONE...................................626 304-0310
Donald Lam,
Tim Pappas, *Director*
EMP: 50
SALES (est): 5.3MM **Privately Held**
SIC: 6531 6282 Real estate brokers & agents; manager of mutual funds, contract or fee basis

(P-11471)
SVN INTERNATIONAL CORP
Also Called: Sperry Van Ness
11999 San Vicente Blvd # 215, Los Angeles (90049-5131)
PHONE...................................310 979-0800
David Rich, *Senior VP*
Kanna Sunkara, *Advisor*
EMP: 55 **Privately Held**
WEB: www.kittywallaceteam.com
SIC: 6531 Real estate agent, commercial
PA: Svn International Corp.
745 Atlantic Ave Fl 8
Boston MA 02111

(P-11472)
T ROYAL MANAGEMENT (PA)
7419 N Cedar Ave Ste 102, Fresno (93720-3640)
PHONE...................................559 447-9887
David Michael Thomas, *CEO*
James Ganson, *Shareholder*
EMP: 55
SQ FT: 5,000
SALES (est): 3.2MM **Privately Held**
WEB: www.royaltmanagement.com
SIC: 6531 Real estate managers

(P-11473)
TAHOE SEASONS RESORT TIME INTE
3901 Saddle Rd, South Lake Tahoe (96150-8707)
P.O. Box 16300 (96151-6300)
PHONE...................................530 541-6700
Michael Presley, *General Mgr*
EMP: 123
SALES (est): 10.5MM **Privately Held**
WEB: www.tahoeseasons.com
SIC: 6531 7011 5813 5812 Time-sharing real estate sales, leasing & rentals; hotels & motels; drinking places; eating places

(P-11474)
TARBELL FINANCIAL CORPORATION
1440 Industrial Park Ave, Redlands (92374-4517)
PHONE...................................909 335-0750
Maria Luevano, *Branch Mgr*
EMP: 60
SALES (corp-wide): 132.1MM **Privately Held**
SIC: 6531 Real estate agent, residential
PA: Tarbell Financial Corporation
1403 N Tustin Ave Ste 380
Santa Ana CA 92705
714 972-0988

(P-11475)
TEAM SPIRIT REALTY INC
6301 Beach Blvd Ste 225, Buena Park (90621-4031)
PHONE...................................714 562-0404
Edward Son, *President*
EMP: 50
SALES (est): 1.2MM **Privately Held**
SIC: 6531 Real estate brokers & agents

(P-11476)
TEN-X LLC
1301 Shoreway Rd Ste 425, Belmont (94002-4154)
PHONE...................................800 793-6107
Monte J M Koch, *Branch Mgr*
EMP: 285 **Privately Held**

SIC: 6531 Real estate brokers & agents
PA: Auction.Com, Llc
1 Mauchly
Irvine CA 92618

(P-11477)
TENDERLOIN HOUSING CLINIC INC (PA)
126 Hyde St, San Francisco (94102-3606)
PHONE...................................415 771-9850
Randall Shaw, *President*
Ovid Morgan, *Property Mgr*
Danny Smith, *Asst Director*
Tyrone Anderson, *Case Mgr*
Reina Cristales, *Case Mgr*
EMP: 250
SALES (est): 40.3MM **Privately Held**
WEB: www.thclinic.org
SIC: 6531 8111 Real estate agents & managers; legal services

(P-11478)
TERRA COASTAL PROPERTIES INC
Also Called: Prudential Malibu Realty
23405 Pacific Coast Hwy, Malibu (90265-4824)
PHONE...................................310 457-2534
Michael Novotny, *CEO*
EMP: 50
SALES (est): 2.4MM **Privately Held**
SIC: 6531 Real estate brokers & agents

(P-11479)
TERRA VISTA MANAGEMENT INC
Also Called: Terra Vista Management
2211 Pacific Beach Dr, San Diego (92109-5626)
PHONE...................................858 581-4200
Micheal Gelfand, *Branch Mgr*
EMP: 120
SALES (corp-wide): 13MM **Privately Held**
SIC: 6531 7033 4225 4226 Real estate managers; trailer parks & campsites; general warehousing & storage; special warehousing & storage; nonresidential building operators
PA: Vista Terra Management Inc
6310 San Vicente Blvd # 506
Los Angeles CA 90048
323 954-5900

(P-11480)
TERRY MEYER
Also Called: Coldwell Banker Residential RE
1712 Meridian Ave Ste C, San Jose (95125-5587)
PHONE...................................408 723-3300
EMP: 61
SALES (est): 1.7MM **Privately Held**
SIC: 6531

(P-11481)
THIRD & MISSION ASSOCIATES LLC
Also Called: Paramount
680 Mission St, San Francisco (94105-4000)
PHONE...................................415 341-8457
Jim Brooks, *Controller*
Tesa Doleman,
EMP: 50
SALES (est): 2.3MM **Privately Held**
SIC: 6531 Real estate managers

(P-11482)
THOMAS J HOBAN (PA)
Also Called: Hoban Management
215 W Lexington Ave, El Cajon (92020-4411)
PHONE...................................619 442-1665
Thomas J Hoban, *Owner*
Jacqueline Conger, *Executive Asst*
Debra Teich, *Property Mgr*
Arturo Gonzalez, *Maint Spvr*
Thomas J Castonguay,
EMP: 50
SQ FT: 1,700
SALES (est): 11.9MM **Privately Held**
WEB: www.hoban-management.com
SIC: 6531 Real estate brokers & agents; real estate managers

(P-11483)
THOMAS M OBINSON JR
7480 N Palm Ave Ste 101, Fresno (93711-5501)
PHONE...................................559 432-6200
Thomas Robinson, *Owner*
EMP: 55
SALES (est): 1.1MM **Privately Held**
SIC: 6531 Real estate agent, commercial

(P-11484)
TOPA BERKELEY LTD
1800 Avenue Of The Stars, Los Angeles (90067-4201)
PHONE...................................310 203-9199
John Anderson, *Owner*
EMP: 100
SALES (est): 2.8MM **Privately Held**
SIC: 6531 Real estate managers

(P-11485)
TRANSPACIFIC MANAGEMENT SVC
15661 Red Hill Ave # 205, Tustin (92780-7328)
PHONE...................................714 285-2626
William Sasser, *President*
Sherrie Fitchen, *Exec VP*
Michelle Pate, *Vice Pres*
EMP: 55
SALES (est): 5.4MM **Privately Held**
WEB: www.transpacinc.com
SIC: 6531 Real estate agents & managers

(P-11486)
TRANSWESTERN CORP POINTE LLC
600 Crprate Pinte Ste 250, Culver City (90230)
PHONE...................................310 642-1001
Dave Rock,
EMP: 99
SALES: 950K **Privately Held**
SIC: 6531 Real estate agent, commercial

(P-11487)
TRG INC
Also Called: Rosenthal Group, The
1350 Abbot Kinney Blvd # 101, Venice (90291-3893)
P.O. Box 837 (90294-0837)
PHONE...................................310 396-6750
R J Rosenthal, *President*
EMP: 100
SALES (est): 3.3MM **Privately Held**
WEB: www.trgnational.com
SIC: 6531 Real estate agents & managers

(P-11488)
TRILOGY REALTY GROUP INC
2025 N Mantle Ln, Santa Ana (92705-7614)
PHONE...................................937 206-0725
Garrett J Hilseth, *CEO*
EMP: 100 **EST:** 2014
SALES (est): 1.9MM **Privately Held**
SIC: 6531 Real estate brokers & agents

(P-11489)
TRIMONT LAND COMPANY (DH)
Also Called: Northstar-At-Tahoe
5001 Northstar Dr, Truckee (96161-4236)
P.O. Box 129 (96160-0129)
PHONE...................................530 562-1010
Robert A Katz, *CEO*
Michael Barkin, *CFO*
▲ **EMP:** 300
SALES (est): 19.4MM **Publicly Held**
SIC: 6531 7011 Real estate managers; ski lodge; resort hotel

(P-11490)
TROOP REAL ESTATE INC
4165 E Thousand Oaks Blvd # 100, Westlake Village (91362-3814)
PHONE...................................805 402-3028
Jeff Rosenblum, *Branch Mgr*
Patti Hepple, *Executive*
Samantha Kirkpatrick, *Broker*
Sharon Phelps, *Asst Mgr*
Maryann Baum, *Real Est Agnt*
EMP: 56

(PA)=Parent Co (HQ)=Headquarters (DH)=Div Headquarters
✪ = New Business established in last 2 years

2019 Directory of California
Wholesalers and Services Companies

493

PRODUCTS & SVCS

SALES (corp-wide): 16MM **Privately Held**

SIC: **6531** Real estate agent, residential; real estate brokers & agents

PA: Troop Real Estate, Inc.
3200 E Los Angeles Ave # 18
Simi Valley CA 93065
805 581-3200

(P-11491)
TROOP REAL ESTATE INC (PA)
3200 E Los Angeles Ave # 18, Simi Valley (93065-3971)
PHONE.................................805 581-3200
Brian C Troop, *CEO*
Robert C Swanson, *Broker*
Kenneth W Grech, *Mktg Dir*
Jon Palacios, *Sales Associate*
Kelly Estes, *Sales Staff*
EMP: 95
SQ FT: 10,000
SALES (est): 16MM **Privately Held**
WEB: www.scottpetto.com
SIC: **6531** Real estate agent, residential; real estate brokers & agents

(P-11492)
TRZ HOLDINGS II INC
Also Called: Brookfield Properties
725 S Figueroa St # 1850, Los Angeles (90017-5524)
PHONE.................................213 955-7170
Tim Callahan, *Manager*
EMP: 280
SALES (corp-wide): 43B **Publicly Held**
SIC: **6531 6552** Real estate managers; subdividers & developers
HQ: Trz Holdings Ii Llc
3 World Financial Ctr
New York NY 10281
212 693-8150

(P-11493)
UNITED CALIFORNIA REALTY INC
12829 Bear Valley Rd, Victorville (92392-9786)
PHONE.................................760 949-4040
Bob Gates, *President*
C V Tirone, *President*
Philip Tirone, *Corp Secy*
EMP: 65
SQ FT: 3,600
SALES (est): 3.2MM **Privately Held**
WEB: www.ucrproperties.com
SIC: **6531** Real estate agent, commercial

(P-11494)
UNIVERSE HOLDINGS DEV CO LLC
350 S Beverly Dr Ste 210, Beverly Hills (90212-4816)
PHONE.................................310 785-0077
Henry Manoucheri,
EMP: 50
SQ FT: 1,100
SALES (est): 1.9MM **Privately Held**
SIC: **6531** Real estate agents & managers

(P-11495)
US REAL ESTATE SERVICES INC
Also Called: Res.net
25520 Commercentre Dr # 1, Lake Forest (92630-8884)
PHONE.................................949 598-9920
Keith Guenther, *CEO*
Michael Bull, *CFO*
Gregory Metz, *Treasurer*
Garrett Mays, *Vice Pres*
Tiffany Malm-Ruiz, *Director*
EMP: 90
SQ FT: 37,000
SALES (est): 12.7MM **Privately Held**
WEB: www.usres.com
SIC: **6531** Real estate managers

(P-11496)
USA MULTIFAMILY MANAGEMENT
3200 Douglas Blvd Ste 200, Roseville (95661-4238)
PHONE.................................916 773-6060
Karen McCurdy, *President*
EMP: 130
SQ FT: 5,020

SALES (est): 758.8K
SALES (corp-wide): 1.1MM **Privately Held**
WEB: www.usapropfund.com
SIC: **6531** Real estate managers
PA: Usa Properties Fund, Inc.
3200 Douglas Blvd Ste 200
Roseville CA 95661
916 773-6060

(P-11497)
V TROTH INC
Also Called: Berkshire Hathaway
1801 W Avenue K Ste 101, Lancaster (93534-5999)
P.O. Box 2024 (93539-2024)
PHONE.................................661 948-4646
Debra K Anderson, *President*
Donald L Anderson, *Vice Pres*
Mark A Troth, *Admin Sec*
Mark Troth, *Real Est Agnt*
EMP: 75
SALES (est): 4.8MM **Privately Held**
SIC: **6531 8742** Real estate agent, residential; real estate consultant

(P-11498)
VALUATION CONCEPTS LLC
Also Called: Appraisal Trend
16350 Ventura Blvd D140, Encino (91436-5300)
PHONE.................................818 812-6233
Kendrick Jackson,
EMP: 90 EST: 2010
SQ FT: 500
SALES (est): 1.9MM **Privately Held**
SIC: **6531** Appraiser, real estate

(P-11499)
VELOCITY COMMERCIAL CAPITL LLC
30699 Russell Ranch Rd, Westlake Village (91362-7315)
PHONE.................................818 532-3700
Christopher D Farrar,
Mark Szczepaniak, *CFO*
David Bilandzija, *Officer*
Joseph Cowell, *Senior VP*
Jason Haye, *Vice Pres*
EMP: 50
SQ FT: 15,000
SALES (est): 10MM **Privately Held**
WEB: www.velocitycommercial.com
SIC: **6531** Real estate agent, commercial

(P-11500)
VILLAGEWAY MANAGEMENT INC
Also Called: Villageway Property Manage-
23041 Ave De La Carlta # 270, Laguna Hills (92653-1545)
PHONE.................................949 450-1515
Janet Walley, *President*
Melanie Young, *Marketing Staff*
EMP: 70 EST: 1969
SQ FT: 14,000
SALES (est): 5.9MM **Privately Held**
WEB: www.villageway.com
SIC: **6531** Real estate managers

(P-11501)
VISTA ANGLINA HSING PRTNRS LP
418 E Edgeware Rd, Los Angeles (90026-5693)
PHONE.................................213 482-4718
Tesa Doleman,
Jim Brooks, *Controller*
EMP: 50 EST: 2013
SALES (est): 1.9MM **Privately Held**
SIC: **6531** Real estate agents & managers

(P-11502)
VISTA VALENCIA GROUP INC
Also Called: Coldwell Banker
25545 Via Paladar, Valencia (91355-3153)
PHONE.................................661 255-4600
Carol James, *CEO*
Roy Medows, *Bd of Directors*
Joan Byrd, *General Mgr*
Greg Handy, *General Mgr*
Michael Houlette, *Webmaster*
EMP: 50

SALES (est): 3MM **Privately Held**
WEB: www.cbvista.com
SIC: **6531** Real estate agent, residential

(P-11503)
VOIT REAL ESTATE SERVICES LP
101 Shipyard Way Ste A, Newport Beach (92663-4447)
PHONE.................................949 644-8648
Bob Voit, *Managing Prtnr*
EMP: 130
SALES (est): 6.9MM **Privately Held**
WEB: www.voitco.com
SIC: **6531** Real estate agent; commercial

(P-11504)
WALTER E MCGUIRE RE INC
360 Primrose Rd, Burlingame (94010-4005)
PHONE.................................650 348-0222
Charles Moore, *President*
Reg Grady, *Sales Associate*
EMP: 180
SALES (est): 3.4MM
SALES (corp-wide): 20.4MM **Privately Held**
WEB: www.mcguire.com
SIC: **6531** Real estate brokers & agents
PA: Walter E. Mcguire Real Estate, Inc.
2001 Lombard St
San Francisco CA 94123
415 929-1500

(P-11505)
WALTER E MCGUIRE RE INC (PA)
2001 Lombard St, San Francisco (94123-2808)
PHONE.................................415 929-1500
Charles Moore, *CEO*
Robin Dustan, *Partner*
Alex Buehlmann, *COO*
Ron Lathouwers, *CFO*
Carlos Rivas, *Administration*
EMP: 262 EST: 1919
SQ FT: 10,000
SALES (est): 20.4MM **Privately Held**
WEB: www.mcguire.com
SIC: **6531** Real estate agent, residential

(P-11506)
WALTER E MCGUIRE RE INC
Also Called: Raymond Brown Company
17 Bluxome St, San Francisco (94107-1605)
PHONE.................................415 296-0123
Aldo Congi, *Manager*
Kristen Thompson, *Real Est Agnt*
EMP: 50
SALES (est): 1.5MM
SALES (corp-wide): 20.4MM **Privately Held**
WEB: www.mcguire.com
SIC: **6531** Real estate agent, residential
PA: Walter E. Mcguire Real Estate, Inc.
2001 Lombard St
San Francisco CA 94123
415 929-1500

(P-11507)
WATERMARK RTRMENT CMMNTIES INC
3890 Nobel Dr, San Diego (92122-5786)
PHONE.................................858 597-8000
Barbara Wilkinson, *Manager*
EMP: 75 **Privately Held**
SIC: **6531** Real estate managers
HQ: Watermark Retirement Communities, Inc.
2020 W Rudasill Rd
Tucson AZ 85704
520 797-4000

(P-11508)
WELK RESORT GROUP INC (PA)
Also Called: Welk Resort Center
300 Rancheros Dr Ste 450, San Marcos (92069-2969)
PHONE.................................760 652-4913
Larry Welk, *CEO*
Jennifer Robinson, *Treasurer*
Gary Fritzinger, *Officer*
Eric Burd, *Vice Pres*
Trina Miller, *Vice Pres*

EMP: 50
SALES (est): 104.7MM **Privately Held**
WEB: www.welksandiego.com
SIC: **6531 6552 7992 7011** Time-sharing real estate sales, leasing & rentals; subdividers & developers; public golf courses; hotels & motels; eating places; tour operators

(P-11509)
WELLS & BENNETT REALTORS (PA)
1451 Leimert Blvd, Oakland (94602-1896)
PHONE.................................510 531-7000
Barton W Bennett, *Owner*
Jeannine Nelson, *Manager*
Tracy Lee L Butler, *Real Est Agnt*
EMP: 65
SQ FT: 5,000
SALES (est): 3.1MM **Privately Held**
WEB: www.wellsandbennett.com
SIC: **6531 6512** Real estate agent, commercial; real estate managers; nonresidential building operators; commercial & industrial building operation

(P-11510)
WELLTOWER INC
144 W D St Ste 202, Encinitas (92024-3572)
PHONE.................................760 436-4122
Roland Vanloan, *Director*
EMP: 405
SALES (corp-wide): 4.7B **Publicly Held**
SIC: **6531** Buying agent, real estate
PA: Welltower Inc.
4500 Dorr St
Toledo OH 43615
419 247-2800

(P-11511)
WESTCOE REALTORS INC
Also Called: Westcoe Escrow Division
7191 Magnolia Ave, Riverside (92504-3805)
PHONE.................................951 784-2500
Rich Simonin, *Manager*
Richard Simonin, *Vice Pres*
Scott Hooks, *Broker*
Samantha Dollahite, *Mktg Coord*
EMP: 65
SQ FT: 11,200
SALES (est): 4.3MM **Privately Held**
WEB: www.louanneludwig.com
SIC: **6531** Real estate agent, residential

(P-11512)
WESTERN AMERICA PROPERTIES LLC
111 N Sepulveda Blvd # 330, Manhattan Beach (90266-6813)
P.O. Box 1597 (90267-1597)
PHONE.................................310 374-4381
James Perley,
EMP: 89
SALES (est): 2.7MM **Privately Held**
SIC: **6531** Real estate agent, commercial

(P-11513)
WESTERN NATIONAL SECURITIES (PA)
8 Executive Cir, Irvine (92614-6746)
P.O. Box 19528 (92623-9528)
PHONE.................................949 862-6200
Michael K Hayde, *CEO*
James Gilly, *President*
Jerry Lapointe, *Principal*
Charlotte Alvarado, *Admin Asst*
Nick Meach, *Manager*
EMP: 120 EST: 1981
SQ FT: 35,000
SALES (est): 18.8MM **Privately Held**
WEB: www.jpi.com
SIC: **6531** Real estate managers

(P-11514)
WESTLAKE REALTY GROUP INC (PA)
520 S El Camino Real # 900, San Mateo (94402-1722)
PHONE.................................650 579-1010
M Gary Wong, *President*
EMP: 66
SALES: 5MM **Privately Held**
SIC: **6531** Real estate agents & managers

(P-11515)
WESTMINSTER HOUSING PARTENERS
Also Called: Windsor Court/Stratford Place
8140 13th St, Westminster (92683-4794)
PHONE................714 891-3000
Jim Brooks, *Controller*
Tesa Doleman,
EMP: 50
SALES (est): 2.1MM **Privately Held**
SIC: 6531 Real estate agents & managers

(P-11516)
WHEATLAND SCHOOL DISTRICT
Also Called: Realty World
100 Wheatland Park Dr, Wheatland
(95692-9286)
PHONE................530 633-3135
Justin Guzman, *President*
EMP: 85
SALES (corp-wide): 22.1MM **Privately Held**
SIC: 6531 Real estate agent, residential
PA: Wheatland School District
    111 Main St
    Wheatland CA 95692
    530 633-3130

(P-11517)
WILLIAM L LYON & ASSOC INC
Also Called: Lyon & Associates Realtors
2801 J St, Sacramento (95816-4315)
PHONE................916 447-7878
Laure Woodgundlach, *Manager*
Elizabeth Weintraub, *Property Mgr*
Debra Davis, *Manager*
John Meuser, *Manager*
Daniel De Back, *Real Est Agnt*
EMP: 55
SALES (est): 1.6MM
SALES (corp-wide): 98.4MM **Privately Held**
WEB: www.lyonre.com
SIC: 6531 Real estate agent, residential
PA: L Lyon William & Associates Inc
    3640 American River Dr
    Sacramento CA 95864
    916 978-4200

(P-11518)
WILLIAM L LYON & ASSOC INC
Also Called: Lyon Realtors
8814 Madison Ave, Fair Oaks
(95628-3908)
PHONE................916 535-0356
Clay Sigg, *Manager*
EMP: 70
SALES (est): 2.1MM
SALES (corp-wide): 98.4MM **Privately Held**
WEB: www.lyonre.com
SIC: 6531 Real estate brokers & agents
PA: L Lyon William & Associates Inc
    3640 American River Dr
    Sacramento CA 95864
    916 978-4200

(P-11519)
WILLIAMS KELLER REALTY
Also Called: Keller Williams Realtors
7005 Boardwalk Dr, Granite Bay
(95746-9203)
PHONE................916 774-6700
William Hall, *President*
Paul Boudier, *Web Proj Mgr*
Boudier Paul, *Network Mgr*
EMP: 60
SALES (est): 2.2MM **Privately Held**
SIC: 6531 Real estate managers

(P-11520)
WILLIS ALLEN REAL ESTATE (PA)
1131 Wall St, La Jolla (92037-4579)
P.O. Box 1887 (92038-1887)
PHONE................858 459-4033
Andrew E Nelson, *President*
Jane Granados, *Officer*
Kate Maciver, *Risk Mgmt Dir*
Bob Wendt, *Branch Mgr*
Jazmin Gardner, *Admin Asst*
EMP: 50
SQ FT: 6,000
SALES (est): 5.1MM **Privately Held**
SIC: 6531 Real estate agent, residential

(P-11521)
WILLIS ALLEN REAL ESTATE
6024 Pasco Delicias, Rancho Santa Fe
(92067)
P.O. Box 107 (92067-0107)
PHONE................858 756-2444
Gary Wheeler, *Manager*
EMP: 50
SALES (corp-wide): 5.1MM **Privately Held**
SIC: 6531 Real estate agent, residential
PA: Willis Allen Real Estate
    1131 Wall St
    La Jolla CA 92037
    858 459-4033

(P-11522)
WILLOW GLEN HSING PARTNERS LP
465 Willow Glen Way # 100, San Jose
(95125-6513)
PHONE................408 267-7252
Jim Brooks, *Controller*
Tesa Doleman,
EMP: 50 EST: 2014
SALES (est): 1.1MM **Privately Held**
SIC: 6531 Real estate brokers & agents

(P-11523)
WILMARK MANAGEMENT SERVICES (PA)
Also Called: Wilmark Development
9948 Hibert St Ste 210, San Diego
(92131-1034)
PHONE................858 271-0583
Mark S Schmidt, *President*
EMP: 65
SALES (est): 3.2MM **Privately Held**
SIC: 6531 Real estate managers

(P-11524)
WINDERMERE REAL ESTATE EAST
71691 Highway 111, Rancho Mirage
(92270-4441)
PHONE................760 568-2568
Bob Deville, *Principal*
Eric Forsberg, *Technology*
Catherine Cripe, *Asst Broker*
Judy Cieslikowski, *Broker*
Rocio Flores, *Broker*
EMP: 67
SALES (corp-wide): 13.5MM **Privately Held**
SIC: 6531 Real estate brokers & agents
PA: Windermere Real Estate East Inc
    14405 Se 36th St Ste 100
    Bellevue WA 98006
    425 643-5500

(P-11525)
YORBA PROPERTIES CORP
Also Called: Re/Max
20459 Yorba Linda Blvd, Yorba Linda
(92886-3043)
PHONE................714 777-5112
Gerry Bullerdick, *President*
Cari Suttle, *Broker*
Kelly Poole, *Real Est Agnt*
EMP: 75
SQ FT: 6,000
SALES (est): 3.4MM **Privately Held**
WEB: www.eastlakevillage.net
SIC: 6163 Real estate agent, residential; mortgage brokers arranging for loans, using money of others

(P-11526)
YOUNG REALTORS
Also Called: Joan Young Co Realtors
971 S Westlake Blvd # 100, Westlake Village (91361-3115)
PHONE................805 497-0947
Fax: 805 494-8986
EMP: 53
SALES (est): 1.5MM **Privately Held**
SIC: 6531

(P-11527)
Z & M ASSOCIATES INC
Also Called: Referral Realty Cupertino
1601 S Danza Blvd Ste 150, Cupertino
(95014)
PHONE................408 996-8100
Moise Nahouraii, *President*

EMP: 85
SALES (est): 2.7MM **Privately Held**
SIC: 6531 Real estate agent, residential

(P-11528)
ZENITH HEALTH CARE
Also Called: Regency Park
245 S El Molino Ave, Pasadena
(91101-2905)
PHONE................626 578-0460
Sandy Wooters, *Administration*
Nancy Oconnor, *Administration*
EMP: 70
SALES (est): 2MM **Privately Held**
WEB: www.zenithadm.com
SIC: 6531 Real estate agents & managers

(P-11529)
ZEPHYR PARTNERS RE-LLC
700 2nd St, Encinitas (92024-4459)
PHONE................858 558-3650
Brad Termini,
Ryan Herrell, *Vice Pres*
Dean Loisel, *Vice Pres*
Jim McMenamin, *Vice Pres*
Heidi Blair, *Executive Asst*
EMP: 50
SALES (est): 4MM **Privately Held**
SIC: 6531 Real estate agents & managers

6541 Title Abstract Offices

(P-11530)
CALIFORNIA TITLE COMPANY (PA)
28202 Cabot Rd Ste 625, Laguna Niguel
(92677-1261)
PHONE................949 582-8709
Dave Erb, *President*
Jim Waterman, *President*
Christina Hattem, *CFO*
Manny Manuel, *Officer*
David Skarman, *Vice Pres*
EMP: 65
SALES (est): 4.3MM **Privately Held**
SIC: 6541 Title abstract offices

(P-11531)
CHICAGO TITLE & ESCROW
316 W Mission Ave Ste 110, Escondido
(92025-1731)
PHONE................760 746-3882
Joanne Lockard, *President*
Joann Lockard, *President*
Anne Radstinner, *Vice Pres*
EMP: 50
SALES (est): 16MM
SALES (corp-wide): 7.5B **Publicly Held**
WEB: www.fntg.com
SIC: 6541 Title & trust companies
PA: Fidelity National Financial, Inc.
    601 Riverside Ave Fl 4
    Jacksonville FL 32204
    904 854-8100

(P-11532)
CHICAGO TITLE INSURANCE CO
3127 Transworld Dr # 103, Stockton
(95206-4988)
P.O. Box 7638 (95267-0638)
PHONE................209 952-5500
Lisa Westfall, *Branch Mgr*
Tabo Ogata, *Officer*
Alyssa Schenker, *Sales Executive*
EMP: 60
SALES (corp-wide): 7.5B **Publicly Held**
SIC: 6541 6361 6099 Title & trust companies; title insurance; escrow institutions other than real estate
HQ: Chicago Title Insurance Company
    4050 Calle Real
    Santa Barbara CA 93110

(P-11533)
FIRST AMERICAN TITLE INSUR CO
1001 Galaxy Way Ste 101, Concord
(94520-5736)
PHONE................925 356-7000
Connie Pickett, *Manager*
EMP: 80 **Publicly Held**
WEB: www.fatc.com

SIC: 6541 Title abstract offices
HQ: First American Title Insurance Company
    1 First American Way
    Santa Ana CA 92707
    800 854-3643

(P-11534)
ORANGE CAST TITLE SOUTHERN CAL
2461 W La Palma Ave Fl 1, Anaheim
(92801-2670)
PHONE................714 822-3211
Barbara Kooey, *Manager*
EMP: 100 **Privately Held**
SIC: 6541 Title abstract offices
PA: Orange Coast Title Company
    1551 N Tustin Ave Ste 300
    Santa Ana CA 92705

(P-11535)
PACIFIC COAST TITLE COMPANY
200 W Glenoaks Blvd # 100, Glendale
(91202-3621)
PHONE................818 244-5273
Brian Lenox, *Branch Mgr*
EMP: 73
SALES (corp-wide): 67.1MM **Privately Held**
SIC: 6541 Title & trust companies
PA: Pacific Coast Title Company
    1111 E Katella Ave # 120
    Orange CA 92867
    714 744-4317

(P-11536)
TITLE RECORDS INC
8926 Sunland Blvd, Sun Valley
(91352-2843)
PHONE................818 767-9610
Brad Westover, *President*
Timothy Morgan, *Ch of Bd*
Kenneth Sean Pratt, *President*
EMP: 63
SQ FT: 88,000
SALES (est): 1.9MM **Privately Held**
SIC: 6541 Title search companies

6552 Land Subdividers & Developers

(P-11537)
A M S PARTNERSHIP (PA)
Also Called: La Mancha Development
1517 S Sepulveda Blvd, Los Angeles
(90025-3311)
PHONE................310 312-6698
Marvin B Levine, *Partner*
Samuel Bachner, *Partner*
EMP: 60
SQ FT: 2,500
SALES (est): 7.7MM **Privately Held**
SIC: 6552 6512 Subdividers & developers; commercial & industrial building operation

(P-11538)
ALLEN DEVELOPMENT PARTNERS LLC (PA)
125 Sbridge 100, Visalia (93291)
PHONE................559 732-5425
Richard S Allen,
Kevin Noell,
EMP: 60
SALES (est): 4.5MM **Privately Held**
SIC: 6552 Subdividers & developers

(P-11539)
AMCAL COMMUNITIES INC
30141 Agoura Rd Ste 100, Agoura Hills
(91301-2020)
PHONE................818 706-0694
Percival Vaz, *President*
EMP: 50
SALES (est): 4.4MM **Privately Held**
SIC: 6552 Land subdividers & developers, residential

PRODUCTS & SVCS

(P-11540)
AMERICAN NWLAND COMMUNITIES LP (PA)
9820 Towne Centre Dr # 100, San Diego (92121-1912)
PHONE..............................858 455-7503
Ladonna K Monsees, *CEO*
Vicki R Mullins, *CFO*
Noel Webb, *CFO*
Keith Hurand, *Senior VP*
Alan Bauer, *Vice Pres*
EMP: 50
SQ FT: 12,000
SALES (est): 123.3MM **Privately Held**
SIC: 6552 Land subdividers & developers, commercial

(P-11541)
ANNABEL INVESTMENT COMPANY
Also Called: Sunset Development Company
2600 Camino Ramon Ste 201, San Ramon (94583-5000)
P.O. Box 640 (94583-0640)
PHONE..............................925 866-0100
Alexander Mehran, *Partner*
EMP: 100
SQ FT: 1,000,000
SALES (est): 5.9MM **Privately Held**
SIC: 6552 Subdividers & developers

(P-11542)
BEARD LAND & INVESTMENT CO (PA)
530 11th St, Modesto (95354-3518)
P.O. Box 1113 (95353-1113)
PHONE..............................209 524-4631
Ron Jackson, *CEO*
Tom L Nielsen, *Treasurer*
Kori Brown, *Admin Asst*
EMP: 137 EST: 1926
SQ FT: 14,374
SALES (est): 9MM **Privately Held**
SIC: 6552 4011 Subdividers & developers; interurban railways

(P-11543)
BEVERLY HILLS COUNTRY CLUB
3084 Motor Ave, Los Angeles (90064-4746)
PHONE..............................310 836-4400
Gene Axelrod, *Partner*
EMP: 130
SQ FT: 100,000
SALES (est): 15.6MM **Privately Held**
WEB: www.beverlyhillscc.com
SIC: 6552 6531 7997 Subdividers & developers; real estate agents & managers; membership sports & recreation clubs

(P-11544)
BOSTON PROPERTIES LTD PARTNR
4 Embarcadero Ctr Lbby 1, San Francisco (94111-5906)
PHONE..............................415 772-0700
Robert Pester, *Manager*
EMP: 61
SALES (corp-wide): 2.7B **Publicly Held**
SIC: 6552 6531 Land subdividers & developers, commercial; real estate agents & managers
HQ: Boston Properties Limited Partnership
800 Boylston St Ste 1900
Boston MA 02199
617 236-3300

(P-11545)
BRADDOCK & LOGAN GROUP II LP
4155 Blackhawk Plaza Cir # 201, Danville (94506-4903)
PHONE..............................925 736-4000
Joseph Raphel, *Managing Prtnr*
EMP: 200
SALES (est): 8.5MM **Privately Held**
SIC: 6552 Subdividers & developers

(P-11546)
BRIDGE HOUSING CORPORATION (PA)
600 California St Fl 9, San Francisco (94108-2706)
PHONE..............................415 989-1111
Cynthia Parker, *President*
Susan Johnson, *Exec VP*
Kimberly McKay, *Exec VP*
Lydia Tan, *Exec VP*
▲ EMP: 90
SQ FT: 12,000
SALES: 30.6MM **Privately Held**
SIC: 6552 Land subdividers & developers, residential

(P-11547)
BROOKFELD BAY AREA HLDINGS LLC
Also Called: Brookfield Homes
500 La Gonda Way Ste 100, Danville (94526-1747)
PHONE..............................925 743-8000
John J J Ryan,
Hillary Brown, *Administration*
Joseph Yoon, *Project Mgr*
April Battle, *Finance*
Debbie Aufdenkamp, *Sales Mgr*
EMP: 60
SALES (est): 14.2MM **Privately Held**
SIC: 6552 Land subdividers & developers, residential

(P-11548)
BURBANK HOUSING DEV CORP
790 Sonoma Ave, Santa Rosa (95404-4713)
PHONE..............................707 526-9782
David W Spilman, *CEO*
Charles A Cornell, *President*
John Lowry, *President*
Stuart W Martin, *Treasurer*
Julie Heredia, *Executive*
EMP: 156
SQ FT: 9,850
SALES: 9.1MM **Privately Held**
SIC: 6552 Land subdividers & developers, residential

(P-11549)
CABRILLO ECONOMIC DEV CORP (PA)
702 County Square Dr # 200, Ventura (93003-5450)
PHONE..............................805 659-3791
Rodney Femandez, *CEO*
Eileen Panter, *Pastor*
Joseph Eldred, *Manager*
Juana Toma, *Asst Mgr*
EMP: 72
SQ FT: 22,000
SALES (est): 13MM **Privately Held**
SIC: 6552 Subdividers & developers

(P-11550)
CAREER DEV INST FOR EXCPTNL
1470 Marsh Way, Riverside (92501-1962)
PHONE..............................951 337-3678
Alan Schwerdt, *Principal*
EMP: 50 EST: 2015
SALES: 807.9K **Privately Held**
SIC: 6552 Subdividers & developers

(P-11551)
CARLTON SENIOR LIVING INC
Also Called: Chateau Pleasant Hill 2
2770 Pleasant Hill Rd Ofc, Concord (94523-2086)
PHONE..............................925 935-1660
Linda Jackson, *Manager*
EMP: 65
SALES (corp-wide): 29.6MM **Privately Held**
SIC: 6552 Subdividers & developers
PA: Senior Carlton Living Inc
4005 Port Chicago Hwy # 120
Concord CA 94520
925 338-2434

(P-11552)
CASDEN COMPANY LLC
9606 Santa Monica Blvd # 3, Beverly Hills (90210-4420)
PHONE..............................310 274-5553
Alan I Casden,
Alan Casden,
Robert Decker, *Director*
EMP: 100
SQ FT: 40,000
SALES (est): 8.9MM **Privately Held**
SIC: 6552 Land subdividers & developers, residential

(P-11553)
COLRICH COMMUNITIES INC
444 W Beech St Ste 300, San Diego (92101-2942)
PHONE..............................858 350-7672
Richard Gabriel, *Ch of Bd*
Colin Seid, *President*
Maggie Lucas, *Admin Sec*
EMP: 60
SALES (est): 8.1MM **Privately Held**
SIC: 6552 Subdividers & developers

(P-11554)
COMSTOCK CROSSER ASSOC DEV INC
Also Called: Comstock Homes
321 12th St Ste 200, Manhattan Beach (90266-5354)
PHONE..............................310 546-5781
David Lauletta, *CEO*
Gary L Lyter, *CFO*
Dan Crosser, *Vice Pres*
Eric Winquist, *Finance Mgr*
Danielle Bishop, *Purch Agent*
EMP: 50
SQ FT: 7,000
SALES (est): 14.2MM **Privately Held**
WEB: www.comstock-homes.com
SIC: 6552 Land subdividers & developers, residential

(P-11555)
COUNTY OF YUBA
Also Called: Yuba County Planning Dept
915 8th St Ste 123, Marysville (95901-5273)
PHONE..............................530 749-5470
Kevin Mallen, *Branch Mgr*
EMP: 80 **Privately Held**
SIC: 6552 Subdividers & developers
PA: County Of Yuba
915 8th St Ste 109
Marysville CA 95901
530 749-7575

(P-11556)
DANCO COMMUNITIES
5251 Ericson Way Ste A, Arcata (95521-9274)
PHONE..............................707 822-9000
Dan Johnson, *CEO*
Kathryn Hungerford, *Executive Asst*
EMP: 99
SALES (est): 1.3MM **Privately Held**
SIC: 6552 Subdividers & developers

(P-11557)
DAVIDSON COMMUNITIES LLC (PA)
Also Called: Davidson Builders
1302 Camino Del Mar, Del Mar (92014-2508)
PHONE..............................858 259-8500
William A Davidson,
Jerry L Leaming,
EMP: 50
SQ FT: 14,000
SALES (est): 13.1MM **Privately Held**
WEB: www.davidsoncommunities.com
SIC: 6552 Subdividers & developers

(P-11558)
DIABLO GRANDE LTD PARTNERSHIP
9521 Morton Davis Dr, Patterson (95363-8610)
PHONE..............................209 892-7421
Donald Panoz, *Ltd Ptnr*
Jay Morton Davis, *Ltd Ptnr*
EMP: 100
SQ FT: 18,000

SALES (est): 6.7MM
SALES (corp-wide): 111.5MM **Privately Held**
WEB: www.diablograride.com
SIC: 6552 7011 7992 5812 Subdividers & developers; resort hotel; public golf courses; eating places
HQ: Elan Chateau Resorts Llc
100 Rue Charlemagne Dr
Braselton GA 30517

(P-11559)
DYA ASSOC
8335 W Sunset Blvd # 320, Los Angeles (90069-1538)
PHONE..............................323 364-4270
David Yashar, *Principal*
EMP: 60 EST: 2015
SALES (est): 1.9MM **Privately Held**
SIC: 6552 Subdividers & developers

(P-11560)
EDAW INC (HQ)
300 California St Fl 5, San Francisco (94104-1411)
PHONE..............................415 955-2800
Joseph E Brown, *CEO*
Jason Prior, *President*
Dana Waymire, *CFO*
Vaughan Davies, *Principal*
Jason Bowen, *Controller*
EMP: 120
SQ FT: 18,072
SALES (est): 115MM
SALES (corp-wide): 20.1B **Publicly Held**
WEB: www.edaw.com
SIC: 6552 0781 Subdividers & developers; landscape architects
PA: Aecom
1999 Avenue Of The Stars # 2600
Los Angeles CA 90067
213 593-8000

(P-11561)
EUREKA REALTY PARTNERS INC (PA)
Also Called: Craig Realty Group
4100 Macarthur Blvd # 200, Newport Beach (92660-2064)
PHONE..............................949 224-4100
Steven L Craig, *CEO*
Rino Larosa, *Vice Pres*
Lori Smith, *Vice Pres*
Sally Terando, *Vice Pres*
Linda Alexander, *Executive*
EMP: 280
SQ FT: 15,000
SALES (est): 39MM **Privately Held**
WEB: www.craigrealtygroup.com
SIC: 6552 Land subdividers & developers, commercial

(P-11562)
FC METROPOLITAN LOFTS INC
Also Called: Forrest City Development
949 S Hope St Ste 100, Los Angeles (90015-1455)
PHONE..............................213 488-0010
Kevin Ratner, *President*
Ronald A Ratner, *President*
EMP: 80
SALES (est): 4.8MM **Privately Held**
SIC: 6552 Subdividers & developers

(P-11563)
FOOTHILL ESTATES INC
400 Griffin St, Salinas (93901-4344)
PHONE..............................831 422-7819
Frederick A Jensen, *President*
E A Jensen, *Agent*
EMP: 90
SALES (est): 4.7MM **Privately Held**
WEB: www.foothillestates.com
SIC: 6552 Land subdividers & developers, residential

(P-11564)
GOLDRICH & KEST INDUSTRIES LLC (PA)
5150 Overland Ave, Culver City (90230-4914)
P.O. Box 3623 (90231-3623)
PHONE..............................310 204-2050
Warren Breslow,
EMP: 750

SQ FT: 5,000
SALES (est): 295.2MM **Privately Held**
SIC: 6552 Subdividers & developers

(P-11565)
GOLDRICHKEST (PA)
5150 Overland Ave, Culver City
(90230-4914)
P.O. Box 3623 (90231-3623)
PHONE..................310 204-2050
Jona Goldrich, *President*
Sol Kest, *Vice Pres*
EMP: 250
SQ FT: 5,000
SALES (est): 30.3MM **Privately Held**
SIC: 6552 Land subdividers & developers,
commercial

(P-11566)
GROUPE DEVELOPMENT ASSOCIATES
Also Called: Brook Side Development
3255 W March Ln Fl 4, Stockton
(95219-2304)
P.O. Box 7576 (95267-0576)
PHONE..................209 473-6000
Fritz Grupe, *Chairman*
EMP: 100
SQ FT: 500
SALES (est): 4MM **Privately Held**
SIC: 6552 Land subdividers & developers,
commercial; land subdividers & develop-
ers, residential

(P-11567)
HINES GS PROPERTIES INC
101 California St # 1000, San Francisco
(94111-5802)
PHONE..................415 982-6200
James B Buie, *Exec VP*
EMP: 50
SQ FT: 7,000
SALES (corp-wide): 1.7B **Privately Held**
SIC: 6552 Subdividers & developers
HQ: Hines Gs Properties, Inc.
2800 Post Oak Blvd
Houston TX 77056
713 621-8000

(P-11568)
KEITH DEVELOPMENT CORPORATION
2777 Cleveland Ave # 109, Santa Rosa
(95403-2763)
PHONE..................707 528-8703
Joseph P Keith, *President*
Frank Denney, *Vice Pres*
Chris Coles, *Admin Sec*
EMP: 50
SQ FT: 2,000
SALES: 17MM **Privately Held**
SIC: 6552 1521 Land subdividers & devel-
opers, residential; new construction, sin-
gle-family houses

(P-11569)
KING VENTURES
285 Bridge St, San Luis Obispo
(93401-5510)
PHONE..................805 544-4444
John E King, *Owner*
Ben Neuman, *Business Mgr*
EMP: 126
SQ FT: 10,000
SALES (est): 9.4MM **Privately Held**
WEB: www.kingventures.net
SIC: 6552 6512 Land subdividers & devel-
opers, commercial; land subdividers & de-
velopers, residential; commercial &
industrial building operation

(P-11570)
LAND SERVICES LANDSCAPE CONTRS
901 Brown Rd, Fremont (94539-7089)
PHONE..................510 656-8101
John Ahner, *President*
Kari E Wood, *Office Mgr*
EMP: 80
SQ FT: 11,000
SALES (est): 9.5MM **Privately Held**
SIC: 6552 Subdividers & developers

(P-11571)
LODI DEVELOPMENT INC
Also Called: Anderson Homes
1420 S Mills Ave Ste E, Lodi (95242-4291)
P.O. Box 1237 (95241-1237)
PHONE..................209 367-7600
Larry W Anderson, *President*
Bob Dolliver Sr, *COO*
Craig Barton, *CFO*
EMP: 50
SQ FT: 5,000
SALES (est): 3.3MM **Privately Held**
WEB: www.lodidevelopment.com
SIC: 6552 Land subdividers & developers,
commercial

(P-11572)
LOWE ENTERPRISES INC
11777 San Vincente Blvd S, Los Angeles
(90049)
PHONE..................310 820-6661
Bob Lowe, *President*
Bill Wethe, *CFO*
Peter S Morgan, *Senior VP*
EMP: 100
SQ FT: 15,000
SALES (est): 4.5MM
SALES (corp-wide): 865.7MM **Privately Held**
SIC: 6552 Land subdividers & developers,
commercial
HQ: Lowe Development Corporation-Re-
serve Manager
11777 San Vicente Blvd
Los Angeles CA 90049
310 820-6661

(P-11573)
LOWE ENTERPRISES RE GROUP
Also Called: Lowe Enterprises Coml Group
11777 San Vicente Blvd # 900, Los Angeles
(90049-5011)
PHONE..................310 820-6661
Bob Lowe, *President*
Michael Mansager, *Vice Pres*
EMP: 90 **EST:** 1994
SQ FT: 10,000
SALES (est): 3.6MM
SALES (corp-wide): 865.7MM **Privately Held**
WEB: www.loweenterprises.com
SIC: 6552 6531 Land subdividers & devel-
opers, commercial; real estate managers
PA: Lowe Enterprises, Inc.
11777 San Vicente Blvd # 900
Los Angeles CA 90049
310 820-6661

(P-11574)
M H PODELL COMPANY (PA)
Also Called: Nicholas A Stevens
22 Battery St Ste 404, Burlingame (94010)
PHONE..................415 296-8800
Michael Podell, *President*
EMP: 51
SALES (est): 7.7MM **Privately Held**
WEB: www.mhpodell.com
SIC: 6552 6513 Subdividers & developers;
apartment building operators

(P-11575)
M TIMM DEVELOPMENT INC (PA)
233 E Carrillo St Ste D, Santa Barbara
(93101-2186)
PHONE..................805 963-0358
Milan Timm, *President*
Matt Easter, *Vice Pres*
EMP: 110
SQ FT: 3,400
SALES (est): 21.2MM **Privately Held**
WEB: www.mtimm.com
SIC: 6552 Land subdividers & developers,
commercial; land subdividers & develop-
ers, residential

(P-11576)
MAKAR PROPERTIES LLC (PA)
Also Called: Makallon La Jolla Properties
4100 Macarthur Blvd # 150, Newport Beach
(92660-2063)
P.O. Box 7080 (92658-7080)
PHONE..................949 255-1100
Paul P Makarechian, *CEO*

Peter Ciaccia, *President*
Douglas Kiel, *COO*
Ben Mearig, *Vice Pres*
Tony Daly, *Business Dir*
EMP: 1200
SALES (est): 54.5MM **Privately Held**
SIC: 6552 Land subdividers & devel-
opers, commercial; commercial & office
building, new construction

(P-11577)
MEANY WILSON L P
4 Embarcadero Ctr # 3330, San Francisco
(94111-4184)
PHONE..................415 905-5300
Thomas P Sullivan, *Partner*
EMP: 50
SQ FT: 22,000
SALES (est): 7MM **Privately Held**
WEB: www.wmspartners.com
SIC: 6552 6531 Land subdividers & devel-
opers, commercial; real estate agents &
managers

(P-11578)
MEYER PROPERTIES CORP (PA)
4320 Von Karman Ave, Newport Beach
(92660-2004)
PHONE..................949 862-0500
Robert E Meyer, *President*
EMP: 53
SQ FT: 5,200
SALES (est): 7.5MM **Privately Held**
WEB: www.meyerprop.com
SIC: 6552 6512 Land subdividers & devel-
opers, commercial; nonresidential build-
ing operators

(P-11579)
MIDPEN HOUSING CORPORATION
303 Vintage Park Dr # 250, Foster City
(94404-1166)
PHONE..................650 356-2900
Mark Battey, *CEO*
Matthew O Franklin, *President*
Pam Prasad, *Administration*
EMP: 300
SQ FT: 20,000
SALES (est): 22.3MM **Privately Held**
SIC: 6552 Land subdividers & developers,
residential

(P-11580)
MORELAND PCF SNOQUALMIE LLC
5060 California Ave # 1150, Bakersfield
(93309-0728)
PHONE..................661 322-1081
Terry L Moreland, *Ch of Bd*
Tammy Fleming, *President*
EMP: 150
SQ FT: 3,000
SALES (est): 11.1MM **Privately Held**
SIC: 6552 6512 Land subdividers & devel-
opers, commercial; commercial & indus-
trial building operation

(P-11581)
MOUNTAIN RETREAT INCORPORATED
111 Deerwood Rd Ste 100, San Ramon
(94583-4445)
P.O. Box 178 (94583-0178)
PHONE..................925 838-7780
EMP: 100 **EST:** 1976
SQ FT: 8,000
SALES (est): 5.7MM **Privately Held**
SIC: 6552 6531

(P-11582)
NATIONAL CMNTY RENAISSANCE CAL (PA)
9421 Haven Ave, Rancho Cucamonga
(91730-5886)
PHONE..................909 483-2444
Steven J Pontell, *CEO*
Sebastiano Sterpa, *Chairman*
John Seymour, *Vice Pres*
Doretta Bryan, *Admin Sec*
Sarah Walker, *Planning*
EMP: 100
SALES: 53.3K **Privately Held**
SIC: 6552 Subdividers & developers

(P-11583)
NEHEMIAH PROGRESSIVE HOUSING D
424 N 7th St Ste 250, Sacramento
(95811-0210)
PHONE..................916 231-1999
Scott Syphax, *CEO*
Walt Mc Daniel, *CFO*
EMP: 60
SQ FT: 1,500
SALES (est): 316.5K **Privately Held**
WEB: www.nehemiahcorp.org
SIC: 6552 Land subdividers & developers,
residential
PA: Nehemiah Corporation Of America
640 Bercut Dr Ste A
Sacramento CA 95811

(P-11584)
NEWLAND GROUP INC (PA)
Also Called: Newland Northwest
4790 Eastgate Mall # 150, San Diego
(92121-2060)
PHONE..................858 455-7503
Robert B Mc Leod, *President*
Ladonna Monsees, *President*
Teri Slavik-Tsuyuki, *Vice Pres*
Malee Tobias, *Vice Pres*
Fran Elgas, *Office Mgr*
EMP: 50
SQ FT: 40,000
SALES (est): 18.5MM **Privately Held**
SIC: 6552 Subdividers & developers

(P-11585)
NW MANOR COMMUNITY PARTNERS LP
17782 Sky Park Cir, Irvine (92614-6404)
PHONE..................714 662-5565
Anand Kannan, *Partner*
Brian Brooks, *General Ptnr*
Perry Harenda, *General Ptnr*
Karen Buckland, *Project Mgr*
Caitlin Marroquin, *Project Mgr*
EMP: 85
SQ FT: 25,000
SALES (est): 3MM **Privately Held**
SIC: 6552 Subdividers & developers

(P-11586)
O & S HOLDINGS LLC
11611 San Vicente Blvd, Los Angeles
(90049-5106)
PHONE..................310 207-8600
Gary Safady,
Paul Orfalea,
EMP: 50
SALES: 2MM **Privately Held**
WEB: www.osholdings.com
SIC: 6552 Land subdividers & developers,
commercial

(P-11587)
OCEAN COLONY PARTNERS LLC
Also Called: Half Moon Bay Golf Links
2450 Cabrillo Hwy S # 200, Half Moon Bay
(94019-2266)
PHONE..................650 726-5764
William E Barrett, *Partner*
Bill Murray, *Pub Rel Staff*
Zac Casey, *Manager*
EMP: 175
SQ FT: 6,000
SALES (est): 27.5MM **Privately Held**
SIC: 6552 7992 7389 Subdividers & de-
velopers; public golf courses; telephone
services

(P-11588)
OLIVERMCMILLAN LLC (DH)
733 8th Ave, San Diego (92101-6407)
PHONE..................619 321-1111
Morgan Dene Oliver, *CEO*
Michael O'Hanlon, *COO*
Bill Persky, *CFO*
Erick Klafter, *General Mgr*
Rhoda Banuelos, *Executive Asst*
EMP: 51
SQ FT: 19,900

PRODUCTS & SVCS

SALES (est): 74.5MM
SALES (corp-wide): 1.6MM **Privately Held**
WEB: www.olivermcmillan.com
SIC: 6552 Land subdividers & developers, commercial; land subdividers & developers, residential
HQ: Brookfield Residential Properties Inc
4906 Richard Rd Sw
Calgary AB T3E 6
403 231-8900

(P-11589)
OLSON URBAN HOUSING LLC
Also Called: Olson Company, The
3010 Old Ranch Pkwy # 100, Seal Beach (90740-2750)
PHONE...................................562 596-4770
Steve Olson,
William E Holford, *President*
Todd J Olson, *President*
Stephen E Olson, *CEO*
Scott Laurie, *COO*
EMP: 60
SALES (est): 10.1MM **Privately Held**
SIC: 6552 Subdividers & developers

(P-11590)
PACIFIC UNION HOMES INC (PA)
675 Hartz Ave Ste 300, Danville (94526-3859)
PHONE...................................925 314-3800
Jeffrey W Abramson, *President*
Todd Deutscher, *CFO*
Matt Tunney, *Vice Pres*
Tammy Reyes, *Admin Sec*
EMP: 75
SALES (est): 11.9MM **Privately Held**
WEB: www.pacificunionhomes.com
SIC: 6552 Subdividers & developers

(P-11591)
PARDEE HOMES (DH)
177 E Colo Blvd Ste 550, Pasadena (91105)
PHONE...................................310 955-3100
Peter M Orser, *CEO*
Michael V McGee, *President*
Jon Lash, *COO*
William Bryan, *Treasurer*
Angela Courtney, *Sales Staff*
EMP: 53
SQ FT: 35,000
SALES (est): 28.7MM
SALES (corp-wide): 3.2B **Publicly Held**
WEB: www.pardeehomes.com
SIC: 6552 1531 Subdividers & developers; operative builders

(P-11592)
PBP HOTEL LLC
Also Called: Double Tree Club Ht San Diego
1515 Hotel Cir S, San Diego (92108-3409)
PHONE...................................619 881-6900
Bu Patel,
Sunil Madhav,
John Murphy, *Mng Member*
EMP: 60
SQ FT: 6,000
SALES (est): 8.6MM
SALES (corp-wide): 74.2MM **Privately Held**
WEB: www.doubletreeclubsd.com
SIC: 6552 7011 Land subdividers & developers, commercial; hotels & motels
PA: Tarsadia Hotels
620 Newport Center Dr # 1400
Newport Beach CA 92660
949 610-8000

(P-11593)
PDC CAPITAL GROUP LLC
250 Fischer Ave, Costa Mesa (92626-4515)
PHONE...................................866 500-8550
Emilio Francisco, *CEO*
Joseph N Fransciso, *Admin Sec*
Wilkin Acedera, *CTO*
EMP: 52
SQ FT: 25,000
SALES (est): 50MM **Privately Held**
SIC: 6552 Subdividers & developers

(P-11594)
PUBLIC INVESTMENT CORPORATION
4340 Eucalyptus Ave, Chino (91710-9705)
PHONE...................................310 451-5227
EMP: 199
SALES (corp-wide): 13.9MM **Privately Held**
SIC: 6552 Subdividers & developers
PA: Public Investment Corporation
1207 W Magnolia Blvd C
Burbank CA 91506
310 451-5227

(P-11595)
R F R CORPORATION
Also Called: Biltwell Roofing
3310 Verdugo Rd, Los Angeles (90065-2845)
PHONE...................................800 346-7663
Bruce Radenbaugh, *President*
Steven Radenbaugh, *Vice Pres*
EMP: 92
SQ FT: 1,000
SALES (est): 8.8MM **Privately Held**
WEB: www.biltwell.com
SIC: 6552 Subdividers & developers

(P-11596)
ROCKEFELLER GROUP DEV CORP
4 Park Plz Ste 840, Irvine (92614-3504)
PHONE...................................949 468-1800
Kevin Hackett, *President*
Tom McCormick, *Vice Pres*
EMP: 81
SALES (est): 6.6MM **Privately Held**
SIC: 6552 Land subdividers & developers, commercial
HQ: Rockefeller Group Development Corporation
1221 Ave Of Americas 17th Flr 17
New York NY 10020
212 282-2100

(P-11597)
RWR HOMES INC (PA)
1014 S Westlake Blvd # 14, Westlake Village (91361-3108)
PHONE...................................805 413-1792
R William Rheinschild, *President*
EMP: 65
SQ FT: 3,800
SALES (est): 8MM **Privately Held**
SIC: 6552 Subdividers & developers

(P-11598)
S P THOMAS CO OF NORTHERN CAL (PA)
1201 Plumber Way Ste 112, Roseville (95678-3565)
PHONE...................................916 786-2040
Stephen P Thomas, *President*
Grace Thomas, *Corp Secy*
Richard Smith, *Vice Pres*
EMP: 57
SQ FT: 2,000
SALES: 500K **Privately Held**
SIC: 6552 Land subdividers & developers, commercial

(P-11599)
SEECON BUILT HOMES INC
4021 Port Chicago Hwy, Concord (94520-1134)
P.O. Box 4113 (94524-4113)
PHONE...................................925 671-7711
Albert Seeno Jr, *President*
EMP: 80
SQ FT: 16,000
SALES (est): 6MM **Privately Held**
SIC: 6552 1542 1521 Land subdividers & developers, commercial; land subdividers & developers, residential; nonresidential construction; single-family housing construction

(P-11600)
SHAPELL INDUSTRIES LLC (HQ)
Also Called: S & S Construction Co
8383 Wilshire Blvd # 700, Beverly Hills (90211-2425)
PHONE...................................323 655-7330
Nathan Shapell, *CEO*

Margaret F Leong, *CFO*
David Shapell, *Exec VP*
Max Webb, *Senior VP*
Karie Mowery, *Regional Mgr*
EMP: 100
SQ FT: 25,000
SALES: 84.6MM
SALES (corp-wide): 7.1B **Publicly Held**
WEB: www.shapell.com
SIC: 6552 6514 1522 Land subdividers & developers, residential; residential building, four or fewer units: operation; residential construction
PA: Toll Brothers, Inc.
250 Gibralter Rd
Horsham PA 19044
215 938-8000

(P-11601)
SHERWOOD DEVELOPMENT COMPANY (PA)
2300 Norfield Ct, Thousand Oaks (91361-5354)
PHONE...................................805 496-1833
David H Murdock, *CEO*
Justin Murdock Jr, *Partner*
EMP: 50
SQ FT: 2,000
SALES (est): 10.7MM **Privately Held**
WEB: www.sherwoodcc.com
SIC: 6552 7992 7991 5813 Subdividers & developers; public golf courses; physical fitness facilities; drinking places; eating places

(P-11602)
SIERRA PACIFIC DEVELOPMENT
1470 W Herndon Ave # 100, Fresno (93711-0552)
PHONE...................................559 256-1300
Paul Owhadi, *President*
EMP: 70
SQ FT: 14,000
SALES (est): 5.4MM **Privately Held**
SIC: 6552 Land subdividers & developers, commercial; land subdividers & developers, residential

(P-11603)
SIGNATURE PROPERTIES INC
4670 Willow Rd Ste 200, Pleasanton (94588-8588)
PHONE...................................925 463-1122
Mike Ghielmetti, *President*
Farren Crabtree, *Project Mgr*
EMP: 75
SQ FT: 24,000
SALES (est): 4.4MM **Privately Held**
SIC: 6552 Subdividers & developers

(P-11604)
SM 10000 PROPERTY LLC
Also Called: Michelle Pasternak
10000 Santa Monica Blvd, Los Angeles (90067-7000)
PHONE...................................305 374-5700
Roman Speron, *CEO*
EMP: 55
SALES (est): 1MM **Privately Held**
SIC: 6552 Subdividers & developers

(P-11605)
STEELWAVE INC (PA)
999 Baker Way Ste 200, San Mateo (94404-5047)
PHONE...................................650 571-2200
Barry S Diraimondo, *CEO*
C Preston Butcher, *President*
Meghan Fauss, *President*
Rick Wada, *Senior VP*
Melodie Borg, *Vice Pres*
EMP: 175 **EST:** 2004
SALES (est): 392.5MM **Privately Held**
WEB: www.legacypartners.com
SIC: 6552 8741 6531 6512 Land subdividers & developers, commercial; land subdividers & developers, residential; financial management for business; real estate agents & managers; nonresidential building operators

(P-11606)
STEELWAVE INC
3335 Susan St Ste 100, Costa Mesa (92626-1647)
PHONE...................................949 863-0390

Erik Hansen, *Senior VP*
EMP: 170
SALES (corp-wide): 392.5MM **Privately Held**
WEB: www.legacypartners.com
SIC: 6552 Land subdividers & developers, commercial; land subdividers & developers, residential
PA: Steelwave, Inc.
999 Baker Way Ste 200
San Mateo CA 94404
650 571-2200

(P-11607)
STEELWAVE LLC
999 Baker Way Ste 200, San Mateo (94404-5047)
PHONE...................................650 571-2200
Preston Butcher, *Mng Member*
Debra Smith, *COO*
McClure Charles, *Vice Pres*
Aaron Dwinell, *Vice Pres*
Michael Navarro, *Vice Pres*
EMP: 1200
SALES (est): 54.4MM **Privately Held**
SIC: 6552 8741 6531 Land subdividers & developers, commercial; financial management for business; real estate agents & managers

(P-11608)
SUNDANCE FINANCIAL INC
2505 Congress St Ste 220, San Diego (92110-2847)
PHONE...................................619 298-9877
Russ R Richard, *President*
Jason Khoury, *Vice Pres*
Noel F Khoury, *Admin Sec*
EMP: 50 **EST:** 1971
SALES (est): 2.8MM **Privately Held**
WEB: www.legacybldg.com
SIC: 6552 Subdividers & developers

(P-11609)
SUNRISE DESERT PARTNERS
Also Called: Toscana
300 Eagle Cir, Palm Desert (92211)
PHONE...................................760 404-1280
Mike Van, *Branch Mgr*
EMP: 100
SALES (corp-wide): 36.8MM **Privately Held**
WEB: www.indianridgecc.com
SIC: 6552 Land subdividers & developers, commercial; land subdividers & developers, residential
PA: Sunrise Desert Partners, A California Limited Partnership
300 Eagle Dance Cir
Palm Desert CA 92211
760 772-7227

(P-11610)
SUNRISE DESERT PARTNERS (PA)
Also Called: Sunrise Company
300 Eagle Dance Cir, Palm Desert (92211-7440)
PHONE...................................760 772-7227
William Bone, *Partner*
Julie Bloom, *Vice Pres*
Keith Gaw, *Supervisor*
Delfino Rivera, *Asst Supt*
EMP: 200
SQ FT: 6,000
SALES (est): 36.8MM **Privately Held**
WEB: www.indianridgecc.com
SIC: 6552 Land subdividers & developers, commercial; land subdividers & developers, residential

(P-11611)
TAHOE LAKE PARTNERS LLC
855 Bordeaux Way Ste 200, NAPA (94558-7585)
P.O. Box 2490 (94558-0523)
PHONE...................................707 255-9890
Tim Wilkens,
EMP: 68
SALES (est): 5.5MM **Privately Held**
SIC: 6552 Land subdividers & developers, commercial

(P-11612)
TAYLOR MORRISON CALIFORNIA LLC
100 Spectrum Center Dr # 1450, Irvine (92618-4984)
PHONE..............................949 341-1200
Stephen J Wethor, *Mng Member*
Jyll Fuhler, *Consultant*
EMP: 181
SALES (est): 5.8MM
SALES (corp-wide): 4.2B **Publicly Held**
SIC: 6552 Land subdividers & developers, residential
HQ: Taylor Morrison Home li Corporation
4900 N Scottsdale Rd # 2000
Scottsdale AZ 85251
480 840-8100

(P-11613)
TD DESERT DEV LTD PARTNR (HQ)
Also Called: Rancho La Quinta Country Club
81570 Carboneras, La Quinta (92253-8219)
PHONE..............................760 777-1001
Nolan Sparks, *Vice Pres*
Marc McAlpine, *Senior VP*
EMP: 150
SALES (est): 55.1MM
SALES (corp-wide): 5.9B **Privately Held**
WEB: www.rancholaquinta.com
SIC: 6552 Land subdividers & developers, residential
PA: Drummond Company, Inc.
1000 Urban Center Dr # 300
Vestavia AL 35242
205 945-6500

(P-11614)
TELACU INDUSTRIES INC (HQ)
5400 E Olympic Blvd # 300, Commerce (90022-5187)
PHONE..............................323 721-1655
David Lizarraga, *CEO*
Michael D Lizarraga, *President*
Lauren L Rraga, *Vice Pres*
Priscilla L Rraga, *Vice Pres*
Humberto Veloso, *General Mgr*
EMP: 50 **EST:** 1975
SQ FT: 17,000
SALES: 195.4K
SALES (corp-wide): 17.7MM **Privately Held**
SIC: 6552 6162 Subdividers & developers; loan correspondents
PA: East Los Angeles Community Union Inc
5400 E Olympic Blvd Fl 3
Commerce CA 90022
323 721-1655

(P-11615)
TOSCANA LAND LLC
300 Eagle Dance Cir, Palm Desert (92211-7440)
PHONE..............................760 772-7200
Toscana Land LP, *General Ptnr*
Phillip Smith, *President*
EMP: 100
SALES (est): 5.2MM **Privately Held**
SIC: 6552 Subdividers & developers

(P-11616)
TOWBES GROUP INC (PA)
21 E Victoria St Ste 200, Santa Barbara (93101-2605)
P.O. Box 20130 (93120-0130)
PHONE..............................805 962-2121
Michael Towbes, *CEO*
Craig Zimmerman, *President*
R D R Deaver, *CFO*
Michelle Konoske, *CFO*
Robert Skinner, *Exec VP*
EMP: 98
SQ FT: 7,250
SALES (est): 22.8MM **Privately Held**
SIC: 6552 6512 1542 Subdividers & developers; nonresidential building operators; nonresidential construction

(P-11617)
UNITED DEVELOPMENT GROUP INC
2805 Dickens St Ste 103, San Diego (92106-2764)
PHONE..............................858 244-0900

William Ayyad, *President*
Kit Sparks, *CFO*
Andrew Garza, *Asst Controller*
Darla Rasmussen, *Manager*
EMP: 50
SQ FT: 3,000
SALES (est): 7.8MM **Privately Held**
SIC: 6552 Land subdividers & developers, commercial

(P-11618)
UNIWELL CORPORATION
2233 Ventura St, Fresno (93721-2915)
PHONE..............................559 268-1000
Steve Klein, *Manager*
EMP: 90
SALES (corp-wide): 28.3MM **Privately Held**
WEB: www.uniwell.com
SIC: 6552 Subdividers & developers
PA: Uniwell Corporation
21172 Figueroa St
Carson CA 90745
310 782-8888

(P-11619)
USA PROPERTIES FUND INC (PA)
3200 Douglas Blvd Ste 200, Roseville (95661-4238)
PHONE..............................916 773-6060
Geoffrey C Brown, *President*
Kristen Hawkins, *Treasurer*
Steven Gall, *Exec VP*
Edward R Herzog, *Exec VP*
Michael McCleery, *Senior VP*
EMP: 75
SQ FT: 10,500
SALES: 1.1MM **Privately Held**
WEB: www.usapropfund.com
SIC: 6552 6531 Subdividers & developers; real estate agents & managers

(P-11620)
VOIT DEVELOPMENT MANAGER INC
Also Called: Voit Commercial Brokerage
2020 Main St Ste 100, Irvine (92614-8218)
PHONE..............................949 851-5110
Fax: 949 261-9092
EMP: 57
SALES (corp-wide): 25.4MM **Privately Held**
SIC: 6552 6531
PA: Voit Development Manager, Inc.
101 Shipyard Way Ste M
Newport Beach CA 92663
949 644-8648

(P-11621)
WATT PROPERTIES INC (PA)
Also Called: Watt Commercial Properties
2716 Ocean Park Blvd # 2025, Santa Monica (90405-5207)
PHONE..............................310 314-2430
Janet Watt Van Huisen, *Ch of Bd*
Jim Maginn, *Managing Prtnr*
Susan Rorison, *President*
James Maginn, *CEO*
Melanie Rush, *CFO*
EMP: 78
SQ FT: 8,700
SALES (est): 17.7MM **Privately Held**
WEB: www.wattcommercial.com
SIC: 6552 6512 6531 Land subdividers & developers, commercial; shopping center, property operation only; real estate managers

(P-11622)
WESTFIELD AMERICA LTD PARTNR
2049 Century Park E Fl 41, Los Angeles (90067-3101)
PHONE..............................310 478-4456
Peter Lowy, *Partner*
EMP: 99
SQ FT: 81,909
SALES (est): 5.8MM **Privately Held**
SIC: 6552 Land subdividers & developers, commercial

6553 Cemetery Subdividers & Developers

(P-11623)
ALDERWOODS (DELAWARE) INC
Also Called: Lakewood Memorial Pk & Fnrl HM
900 Santa Fe Ave, Hughson (95326-9240)
PHONE..............................209 883-0411
Robin Warn, *Admin Mgr*
EMP: 50
SALES (corp-wide): 3.1B **Publicly Held**
WEB: www.memorialparkfuneral.com
SIC: 6553 7261 Cemeteries, real estate operation; funeral home
HQ: Alderwoods (Delaware), Inc.
1929 Allen Pkwy
Houston TX 77019

(P-11624)
CHAPEL OF CHIMES (DH)
Also Called: Alameda Chapel of The Chimes
32992 Mission Blvd, Hayward (94544-8277)
PHONE..............................510 471-3363
Andy Bryant, *President*
Gordon Swallow, *Treasurer*
David Madden, *Manager*
Lisa Rogers, *Manager*
EMP: 71
SQ FT: 10,000
SALES (est): 29.9MM
SALES (corp-wide): 51.8MM **Publicly Held**
WEB: www.bailingyuan.com
SIC: 6553 7261 Cemeteries, real estate operation; mausoleum operation; funeral home; crematory
HQ: Skylawn
32992 Mission Blvd
Hayward CA 94544
510 471-3363

(P-11625)
CHAPEL OF CHIMES
Also Called: Skylawn Memorial Park
100 Lifemark Rd, Redwood City (94062-4592)
P.O. Box 5070, San Mateo (94402-0070)
PHONE..............................650 349-4411
Rich McGown, *General Mgr*
EMP: 80
SALES (corp-wide): 51.8MM **Publicly Held**
WEB: www.bailingyuan.com
SIC: 6553 7261 Cemeteries, real estate operation; crematory
HQ: Chapel Of The Chimes
32992 Mission Blvd
Hayward CA 94544
510 471-3363

(P-11626)
FOREST LAWN MEMORIAL-PARK ASSN
Also Called: Forest Lawn Memorial & Mortuar
4471 Lincoln Ave, Cypress (90630-2507)
P.O. Box 1151, Glendale (91209-1151)
PHONE..............................714 828-3131
Don Gras, *Branch Mgr*
EMP: 80
SALES (corp-wide): 129.4MM **Privately Held**
SIC: 6553 7261 Cemeteries, real estate operation; funeral service & crematories
PA: Forest Lawn Memorial-Park Association
1712 S Glendale Ave
Glendale CA 91205
323 254-3131

(P-11627)
FOREST LAWN MEMORIAL-PARK ASSN
Also Called: Hollywood Hills
6300 Forest Lawn Dr, Los Angeles (90068-1096)
PHONE..............................323 254-7251
Wilma Joanis, *Branch Mgr*
EMP: 100

SALES (corp-wide): 129.4MM **Privately Held**
SIC: 6553 7261 Cemeteries, real estate operation; funeral service & crematory
PA: Forest Lawn Memorial-Park Association
1712 S Glendale Ave
Glendale CA 91205
323 254-3131

(P-11628)
FOREST LAWN MEMORIAL-PARK ASSN
1500 E San Antonio Dr, Long Beach (90807-1233)
PHONE..............................562 424-1631
Kim Evans, *Manager*
EMP: 60
SALES (corp-wide): 129.4MM **Privately Held**
SIC: 6553 7261 Cemeteries, real estate operation; crematory
PA: Forest Lawn Memorial-Park Association
1712 S Glendale Ave
Glendale CA 91205
323 254-3131

(P-11629)
HANIL DEVELOPMENT INC
Also Called: Aroma Wilshire Center
3680 Wilshire Blvd B01, Los Angeles (90010-2708)
PHONE..............................213 387-0111
Yeong Ik Kweon, *CEO*
Hyun Shin, *CFO*
Kee June Huh, *Vice Pres*
Sung Moon, *Executive*
Jae Whang, *Executive*
EMP: 50
SALES (est): 2.8MM **Privately Held**
WEB: www.aromaresort.com
SIC: 6553 Real property subdividers & developers, cemetery lots only

(P-11630)
LAKEWOOD MEM PK FNRL SVCS INC
Also Called: Lakewood Memorial Pk & Fnrl HM
900 Santa Fe Ave, Hughson (95326-9240)
PHONE..............................209 883-4465
Robin Warn, *President*
EMP: 50 **EST:** 1988
SALES (est): 2.2MM **Privately Held**
SIC: 6553 7261 Cemeteries, real estate operation; funeral home

(P-11631)
OAKDALE MEMORIAL PARK (PA)
1401 S Grand Ave, Glendora (91740-5406)
PHONE..............................626 335-0281
Genny Delgado, *Manager*
EMP: 75 **EST:** 1890
SQ FT: 10,000
SALES (est): 8.9MM **Privately Held**
SIC: 6553 Cemeteries, real estate operation

(P-11632)
ROMAN CATHOLIC ARCHDIOCESE OF
Also Called: Holy Cross Cemetery
1500 Old Mission Rd, Daly City (94014)
PHONE..............................650 756-2060
Kathy Atkinson, *Director*
EMP: 55
SALES (corp-wide): 77.1MM **Privately Held**
WEB: www.strita.edu
SIC: 6553 Cemetery association
PA: The Roman Catholic Archdiocese Of San Francisco
1 Peter Yorke Way 1 # 1
San Francisco CA 94109
415 614-5500

(P-11633)
ROMAN CTHLIC BISHP OF SAN JOSE
Also Called: Gate of Heaven Cemetery
22555 Cristo Rey Dr, Los Altos (94024-7424)
PHONE..............................833 304-0763

P R O D U C T S & S V C S

April Ouellette, *Principal*
Denise Fullerton, *Director*
EMP: 1035
SALES (corp-wide): 57.7MM **Privately Held**
SIC: 6553 Cemeteries, real estate operation
PA: The Roman Catholic Bishop Of San Jose
1150 N 1st St Ste 100
San Jose CA 95112
408 983-0100

(P-11634)
ROSE HILLS COMPANY (HQ)
Also Called: Rose Hills Mem Pk & Mortuary
3888 Workman Mill Rd, Whittier
(90601-1626)
PHONE..................562 699-0921
Dennis Poulson, *Ch of Bd*
Kenton Woods, *President*
Shawn Aylesworth, *Vice Pres*
Ophelia Camero, *Vice Pres*
Mary Guzman, *Vice Pres*
EMP: 595
SQ FT: 143,950
SALES (est): 177.7MM **Privately Held**
WEB: www.rosehill.com
SIC: 6553 Real property subdividers & developers, cemetery lots only
PA: Rose Hills Holdings Corp.
3888 Workman Mill Rd
Whittier CA 90601
562 699-0921

(P-11635)
ROSE HILLS HOLDINGS CORP (PA)
Also Called: Rose Hills Mem Pk & Mortuary
3888 Workman Mill Rd, Whittier
(90601-1626)
PHONE..................562 699-0921
Pat Monroe, *CEO*
Nick Clark, *Marketing Staff*
Ivette Gonzalez, *Advisor*
EMP: 500
SQ FT: 143,950
SALES (est): 177.7MM **Privately Held**
SIC: 6553 Cemetery subdividers & developers

(P-11636)
SERVICE CORP INTERNATIONAL
Also Called: SCI
1999 S El Camino Real, Oceanside
(92054-5754)
PHONE..................760 754-6600
Debra Allen, *General Mgr*
Debra Kurtz, *General Mgr*
EMP: 80
SALES (corp-wide): 3.1B **Publicly Held**
WEB: www.sci-corp.com
SIC: 6553 7261 Cemetery association; funeral service & crematories
PA: Service Corporation International
1929 Allen Pkwy
Houston TX 77019
713 522-5141

6712 Offices Of Bank Holding Co's

(P-11637)
BANAMEX USA BANCORP (DH)
2029 Century Park E Fl 42, Los Angeles
(90067-2901)
PHONE..................310 203-3440
Salvador Villar Jr, *President*
Francisco Moreno Sr, *Vice Pres*
EMP: 210
SALES (est): 66.7MM
SALES (corp-wide): 72.8B **Publicly Held**
SIC: 6712 6029 6022 Bank holding companies; commercial banks; state commercial banks

(P-11638)
GRANDPOINT CAPITAL INC
333 S Grand Ave Ste 4250, Los Angeles
(90071-1587)
PHONE..................213 542-4410
Don M Griffith, *CEO*
Deborah M Marsten, *Vice Chairman*

Deborah A Marsten, *COO*
Jerro Otsuki, *CFO*
Deborah Marsten, *Bd of Directors*
EMP: 181 **Privately Held**
SIC: 6712 Bank holding companies

(P-11639)
MISSION VALLEY BANCORP
9116 Sunland Blvd, Sun Valley
(91352-2052)
PHONE..................818 394-2300
Tamara Gurney, *CEO*
Carrie Burrell, *Vice Pres*
EMP: 53
SALES: 1,000K **Privately Held**
WEB: www.missionvalleybank.com
SIC: 6712 Bank holding companies

6719 Offices Of Holding Co's, NEC

(P-11640)
ABA HOLDINGS LLC
4777 Ruffner St, San Diego (92111-1519)
PHONE..................858 565-4131
Steven B Andrade,
James C Hunt, *Treasurer*
Robin Callaway, *Executive*
Jaimi Lomas, *General Mgr*
Richard Gleichauf, *VP Finance*
EMP: 200 **Privately Held**
SIC: 6719 Investment holding companies, except banks

(P-11641)
ABBEY MANAGEMENT COMPANY LLC
330 Golden Shore Ste 300, Long Beach
(90802-4283)
PHONE..................562 243-2100
Donald Abbey, *Mng Member*
Kevin Dillard, *Treasurer*
Dennis Loput Jr, *Admin Sec*
EMP: 60 **Privately Held**
SIC: 6719 Investment holding companies, except banks

(P-11642)
AF SOFTWARE HOLDINGS INC
1825 S Grant St Ste 900, San Mateo
(94402-2675)
PHONE..................888 317-3395
Bernadette Nixon, *CEO*
Carlton Baab, *CFO*
Kamil Chaudhary, *Admin Sec*
EMP: 349 **Privately Held**
SIC: 6719 Investment holding companies, except banks

(P-11643)
AF SOFTWARE PARENT INC
1825 S Grant St Ste 900, San Mateo
(94402-2675)
PHONE..................888 317-3395
Bernadette Nixon, *CEO*
Carlton Baab, *CFO*
Kamil Chaudhary, *Admin Sec*
EMP: 349 **Privately Held**
SIC: 6719 Investment holding companies, except banks

(P-11644)
AMBULNZ CO LLC
1151 S Boyle Ave, Los Angeles
(90023-2109)
PHONE..................877 311-5555
Michael Witkowski, *Principal*
Stan Vashovsky, *Principal*
EMP: 99 **Privately Held**
SIC: 6719 Holding companies

(P-11645)
ARCH BAY HOLDINGS LLC
327 W Maple Ave, Monrovia (91016-3331)
PHONE..................949 679-2400
EMP: 60 **EST:** 2008 **Privately Held**
SIC: 6719

(P-11646)
BAVARIA HOLDINGS INC
1 Letterman Dr Bldg C, San Francisco
(94129-2402)
PHONE..................415 418-2900
Dipanjan Deb, *President*

Tom Ludwig, *COO*
Chris Adams, *Vice Pres*
My Le Nguyen, *Vice Pres*
Eugene Mesgar, *Vice Pres*
EMP: 615
SALES (corp-wide): 1.5B **Privately Held**
SIC: 6719 Investment holding companies, except banks
HQ: Francisco Partners, L.P.
1 Letterman Dr Bldg C
San Francisco CA 94129
415 418-2900

(P-11647)
BPAZ HOLDINGS 18 LLC
1 Sansome St Fl 15, San Francisco
(94104-4448)
P.O. Box 2689 (94126-2689)
PHONE..................972 354-6250
Rob Saidi, *Mng Member*
EMP: 60 **Privately Held**
SIC: 6719 Holding companies

(P-11648)
BPAZ HOLDINGS 6 LLC
1 Sansome St Ste 1500, San Francisco
(94104-4449)
PHONE..................415 295-8080
Rob Saidi, *Vice Pres*
EMP: 80 **Privately Held**
SIC: 6719 Holding companies

(P-11649)
BRIDGE GROUP HH INC
5090 Shoreham Pl Ste 209, San Diego
(92122-5935)
PHONE..................858 455-5000
Jason Murray, *CEO*
EMP: 126 **Privately Held**
SIC: 6719 Investment holding companies, except banks

(P-11650)
CCC PROPERTY HOLDINGS LLC
Also Called: Contractors Cargo Company
500 S Alameda St, Compton (90221-3801)
P.O. Box 5290 (90224-5290)
PHONE..................310 609-1957
Gerald Wheeler, *Ch of Bd*
Carla Ann Wheeler, *CFO*
Jerry Wheeler, *Chairman*
Gerald J Wheeler, *Principal*
Kim Dorio, *Admin Sec*
EMP: 121 **EST:** 2009
SQ FT: 18,000 **Privately Held**
SIC: 6719 Investment holding companies, except banks

(P-11651)
CLEARBALANCE HOLDINGS LLC
3636 Nobel Dr Ste 250, San Diego
(92122-1042)
PHONE..................858 535-0870
Mitch Patridge, *CEO*
EMP: 50 **Privately Held**
SIC: 6719 Investment holding companies, except banks

(P-11652)
COADNA HOLDINGS INC
1020 Stewart Dr, Sunnyvale (94085-3914)
PHONE..................408 736-1100
Jim Yuan, *President*
Irene Yum, *CFO*
Oliver Lu, *Officer*
Tom LI, *Senior VP*
EMP: 80 **EST:** 2000
SALES (corp-wide): 1.3B **Publicly Held**
SIC: 6719 3661 Investment holding companies, except banks; fiber optics communications equipment
PA: Ii-Vi Incorporated
375 Saxonburg Blvd
Saxonburg PA 16056
724 352-4455

(P-11653)
CONCRETE HOLDING CO CAL INC
15821 Ventura Blvd # 475, Encino
(91436-2915)
PHONE..................818 788-4228
Don Unmacht, *Principal*

Dominique Bidet, *Vice Pres*
EMP: 293
SQ FT: 4,000
SALES (corp-wide): 484.9MM **Privately Held**
SIC: 6719 Investment holding companies, except banks
HQ: National Cement Company, Inc.
15821 Ventura Blvd # 475
Encino CA 91436
818 728-5200

(P-11654)
CONDOR TRADING LP
600 Montgomery St Fl 6, San Francisco
(94111-2708)
PHONE..................415 248-2200
Scott Kovalik, *CEO*
Brian Endres, *CFO*
Yojna Verma, *Senior VP*
EMP: 560 **Privately Held**
SIC: 6719 Investment holding companies, except banks

(P-11655)
CSU HOLDING COMPANY
531 Stone Rd, Benicia (94510-1113)
PHONE..................707 746-0353
Jochen Michalski, *President*
EMP: 50 **EST:** 2002 **Privately Held**
SIC: 6719 Investment holding companies, except banks

(P-11656)
DELIMEX HOLDINGS INC
7878 Airway Rd, San Diego (92154-8305)
PHONE..................619 210-2700
Neil Harrison, *President*
Dori Reap, *CEO*
Christopher J Puma, *Vice Pres*
John B Puma, *Vice Pres*
Greggory R Surabian, *Vice Pres*
▲ **EMP:** 550
SQ FT: 86,917
SALES (corp-wide): 26.2B **Publicly Held**
WEB: www.delimex.com
SIC: 6719 Personal holding companies, except banks
HQ: H J Heinz Finance Company
1 Ppg Pl Ste 3100
Pittsburgh PA 15222
412 456-5700

(P-11657)
DPR HOLDINGS LLC
Also Called: Massnexus
4804 Laurel Canyon Blvd, Studio City
(91607-3717)
PHONE..................323 761-9829
Anthony Dickson, *Mng Member*
Mark Burton, *COO*
Chris Burns, *CFO*
EMP: 50 **EST:** 2011 **Privately Held**
SIC: 6719 Investment holding companies, except banks

(P-11658)
EM EAGLE PURCHASER LLC (PA)
4420 Rosewood Dr Ste 500, Pleasanton
(94588-3059)
PHONE..................855 224-8572
EMP: 1480
SALES (est): 41.6MM **Privately Held**
SIC: 6719 Investment holding companies, except banks

(P-11659)
FINE CHEMICALS HOLDINGS CORP
Hwy 50 Hzel Ave Bldg 0501, Rancho Cordova (95741)
P.O. Box 1718 (95741-1718)
PHONE..................916 357-6880
Fraser Preston, *President*
John Sobchak, *CFO*
Michael Gallagher, *Corp Secy*
EMP: 450 **Privately Held**
SIC: 6719 Investment holding companies, except banks

(P-11660)
FORTRESS HOLDING GROUP LLC
5500 E Santa Ana Canyon R, Anaheim (92807-3139)
PHONE...............................714 202-8710
Loise Perez, *Chairman*
Adam Forbs, *President*
EMP: 90 Privately Held
SIC: 6719 Investment holding companies, except banks

(P-11661)
GAF HOLDINGS INC
1300 E Mineral King Ave, Visalia (93292-6913)
P.O. Box 1431 (93279-1431)
PHONE...............................559 734-3333
Don Groppetti, *President*
EMP: 300 EST: 1999 Privately Held
SIC: 6719 Personal holding companies, except banks

(P-11662)
GBP PARENT CORP (HQ)
2321 Rosecrans Ave # 3255, El Segundo (90245-4985)
PHONE...............................424 254-9774
EMP: 587
SALES (corp-wide): 50.2MM Privately Held
SIC: 6719 Investment holding companies, except banks
PA: Pacific Avenue Capital Partners, Llc
2321 Rosecrans Ave # 3255
El Segundo CA 90245
424 254-9774

(P-11663)
GCM HOLDING CORPORATION
1350 Atlantic St, Union City (94587-2004)
PHONE...............................510 475-0404
Seamus Meagher, *President*
EMP: 300 Privately Held
SIC: 6719 8711 3444 3541 Investment holding companies, except banks; machine tool design; sheet metalwork; machine tools, metal cutting type

(P-11664)
GEOVERA HOLDINGS INC (PA)
4820 Busineca Ctr Dr 20, Fairfield (94534)
PHONE...............................707 863-3700
Kevin M Nish, *President*
Frank Albertson, *Vice Pres*
Darrell Gray, *Vice Pres*
Frank Lazzeroni, *Vice Pres*
Rich Runyan, *Vice Pres*
EMP: 65 Privately Held
SIC: 6719 Investment holding companies, except banks

(P-11665)
GGC ADMINISTRATION LLC
Also Called: Golden Gate Capital
1 Embarcadero Ctr Fl 39, San Francisco (94111-3714)
PHONE...............................415 983-2700
Stephan Scholl, *President*
EMP: 8590 Privately Held
SIC: 6719 Personal holding companies, except banks

(P-11666)
GLOBAL HOLDINGS INC
1230 Rosecrans Ave # 660, Manhattan Beach (90266-2477)
PHONE...............................818 905-6000
Sam Solakyan, *CEO*
EMP: 150 Privately Held
SIC: 6719 Investment holding companies, except banks

(P-11667)
GORES NORMENT HOLDINGS INC
10877 Wilshire Blvd # 1805, Los Angeles (90024-4341)
PHONE...............................310 209-3010
Alex Gores, *Principal*
EMP: 246
SALES (corp-wide): 3.8B Privately Held
SIC: 6719 Investment holding companies, except banks

PA: The Gores Group Llc
9800 Wilshire Blvd
Beverly Hills CA 90212
310 209-3010

(P-11668)
GREENCYCLE US HOLDING INC
4686 Mercury St, San Diego (92111-2428)
PHONE...............................858 677-0884
Hernan De La Vega, *CEO*
Marco Rudolph, *Exec VP*
Hendrick Dillinger, *Vice Pres*
Katya Leitner, *Vice Pres*
EMP: 80
SALES: 18MM
SALES (corp-wide): 355.8K Privately Held
SIC: 6719 4953 Investment holding companies, except banks; recycling, waste materials
HQ: Greencycle Umweltmanagement Gmbh
Stiftsbergstr. 1
Neckarsulm 74172
713 230-7731

(P-11669)
GS FOODS GROUP
11755 Wilshire Blvd # 14, Los Angeles (90025-1506)
PHONE...............................310 806-9780
Sean Leer, *CEO*
EMP: 427 Privately Held
SIC: 6719 Investment holding companies, except banks

(P-11670)
HEALTHFUSION HOLDINGS INC (HQ)
100 N Rios Ave, Solana Beach (92075-1238)
PHONE...............................858 523-2120
Seth M Flam, *President*
Jonathan Flam, *CFO*
Jordan Adams, *Business Mgr*
Justin Berg, *Manager*
EMP: 54 EST: 2000
SALES (est): 18.5MM
SALES (corp-wide): 529.1MM Publicly Held
WEB: www.healthfusion.com
SIC: 6719 Investment holding companies, except banks
PA: Nextgen Healthcare, Inc.
18111 Von Karman Ave # 8
Irvine CA 92612
949 255-2600

(P-11671)
HONOLUA BAY HOLDINGS LLC
Also Called: Quartz Hill Post Acute
2120 Benton Dr, Redding (96003-2151)
PHONE...............................530 243-6317
Dan Gill, *Mng Member*
Kevin Galbasini,
Cameron Rosenhan,
EMP: 50 Privately Held
SIC: 6719 Holding companies

(P-11672)
HORIBA AMERICAS HOLDING INC (HQ)
9755 Research Dr, Irvine (92618-4626)
PHONE...............................949 250-4811
Juichi Saito, *CEO*
Pattie Jones, *Controller*
EMP: 1055 EST: 2017
SALES (est): 79.8MM Privately Held
SIC: 6719 Personal holding companies, except banks

(P-11673)
IF HOLDING INC (PA)
Also Called: Initiative Food Company
1912 Industrial Way, Sanger (93657-9508)
PHONE...............................559 875-3354
John Ypma, *President*
John P Mulvaney, *Vice Pres*
David F Markle, *Admin Sec*
EMP: 130
SQ FT: 200,094 Privately Held
WEB: www.initfoods.com
SIC: 6719 Investment holding companies, except banks

(P-11674)
INDUSTRIAL GRWTH PARTNERS V LP
101 Mission St Ste 1500, San Francisco (94105-1731)
PHONE...............................415 882-4550
Michael Beaumont, *Mng Member*
EMP: 200 Privately Held
SIC: 6719 Investment holding companies, except banks

(P-11675)
J BRAND HOLDINGS LLC
1318 E 7th St Ste 260, Los Angeles (90021-1131)
PHONE...............................212 228-8181
Jeffrey Rudes,
Kimberly Briskey, *Planning*
Adriana Arellano, *Production*
Alison Lee, *Associate*
Thai Nguyen, *Associate*
EMP: 60 Privately Held
SIC: 6719 Investment holding companies, except banks
PA: Fast Retailing Co., Ltd.
9-7-1, Akasaka
Minato-Ku TKY 107-0

(P-11676)
MAFAB INC (PA)
1925 Century Park E # 650, Los Angeles (90067-2752)
PHONE...............................714 893-0551
Ronald B Grey, *President*
Ronald Grey, *President*
EMP: 60
SQ FT: 3,600
SALES (est): 14.4MM Privately Held
SIC: 6719 Personal holding companies, except banks

(P-11677)
MILESTONE TOPCO INC (HQ)
901 Mariners Island Blvd, San Mateo (94404-1592)
PHONE...............................650 376-2300
Steve Lucas, *CEO*
EMP: 949
SALES (corp-wide): 9B Publicly Held
SIC: 6719 Investment holding companies, except banks
PA: Adobe Inc.
345 Park Ave
San Jose CA 95110
408 536-6000

(P-11678)
MISSION ENERGY HOLDING COMPANY
2600 Michelson Dr # 1700, Irvine (92612-1550)
PHONE...............................949 752-5588
Mark C Clarke, *CEO*
Thomas R McDaniel, *President*
W James Scilacci, *CFO*
EMP: 1890
SALES (corp-wide): 12.6B Publicly Held
WEB: www.edison.com
SIC: 6719 Personal holding companies, except banks
HQ: Edison Mission Group Inc.
2244 Walnut Grove Ave
Rosemead CA 91770
626 302-2222

(P-11679)
MLIM HOLDINGS LLC
350 Camino De La Reina, San Diego (92108-3003)
PHONE...............................619 299-3131
Douglas Manchester, *Chairman*
John Lynch, *CEO*
EMP: 768 Privately Held
SIC: 6719 Investment holding companies, except banks

(P-11680)
N2 ACQUISITION COMPANY INC
Also Called: N2 Imaging Systems
14440 Myford Rd, Irvine (92606-1001)
PHONE...............................714 942-3563
Tony Bacarella, *CEO*
Timothy Boyle, *CFO*
EMP: 92 Privately Held

SIC: 6719 Investment holding companies, except banks

(P-11681)
NOVOZYMES US INC
1445 Drew Ave, Davis (95618-4880)
PHONE...............................530 757-8100
Ejner Bech Jensen, *CEO*
Glen Medwin, *President*
EMP: 675 EST: 2000
SALES (corp-wide): 20.1B Privately Held
SIC: 6719 Investment holding companies, except banks
HQ: Novozymes A/S
Krogshovej 36
BagsvArd 2880
444 600-00

(P-11682)
NRP HOLDING CO INC (PA)
1 Mauchly, Irvine (92618-2305)
PHONE...............................949 583-1000
Jeffrey P Frieden, *President*
Ali Haralson, *Exec VP*
Ken Rivkin, *Exec VP*
Robert Friedman, *Vice Pres*
Robert D Friedman, *Vice Pres*
EMP: 200
SQ FT: 40,000
SALES (est): 50.2MM Privately Held
SIC: 6719 Investment holding companies, except banks

(P-11683)
PARIS BLUES INC (PA)
2397 Miguel Miranda Ave, Duarte (91010-3319)
PHONE...............................310 605-2000
Jose Quant, *President*
EMP: 95 Privately Held
SIC: 6719 Personal holding companies, except banks

(P-11684)
PARPRO HOLDINGS CO LTD
9355 Airway Rd Ste 4, San Diego (92154-7931)
PHONE...............................619 498-9004
Matthew Dharm, *Officer*
Dan Torres, *Buyer*
Subhash Aghera, *Prdtn Mgr*
EMP: 250 Privately Held
SIC: 6719 Investment holding companies, except banks
PA: Parpro Corporation
No. 67-1, Dongyuan Rd., Zhongli Industrial Park
Taoyuan City TAY

(P-11685)
PHOTO HOLDINGS LLC
2800 Bridge Pkwy, Redwood City (94065-1192)
PHONE...............................650 610-5200
Ryan O'Hara, *President*
EMP: 1934 Privately Held
SIC: 6719 Investment holding companies, except banks

(P-11686)
PLANT HOLDINGS INC (HQ)
42555 Rio Nedo, Temecula (92590-3726)
PHONE...............................951 719-2100
Gino Bonanotte, *CEO*
EMP: 400
SALES (corp-wide): 7.3B Publicly Held
SIC: 6719 3661 Investment holding companies, except banks; telephone station equipment & parts, wire
PA: Motorola Solutions, Inc.
500 W Monroe St Ste 4400
Chicago IL 60661
847 576-5000

(P-11687)
PLATINUM GROUP COMPANIES INC (PA)
Also Called: Top Finance Company
22560 La Quilla Dr, Chatsworth (91311-1221)
P.O. Box 280518, Northridge (91328-0518)
PHONE...............................818 721-3800
David Mandel, *CEO*
Sandy To, *Treasurer*
Larry Leonidas, *Info Tech Dir*

Netzel Robert, *Info Tech Mgr*
Marilyn Vateri, *Finance*
EMP: 125
SQ FT: 20,000
SALES (est): 39.6MM **Privately Held**
SIC: 6719 Personal holding companies, except banks

(P-11688)
PROJECT BOAT HOLDINGS LLC
360 N Crescent Dr Bldg S, Beverly Hills (90210-2529)
PHONE......................310 712-1850
Tom Gores,
Tom T Gores,
Johnny O Lopez,
EMP: 3174 **Privately Held**
SIC: 6719 Investment holding companies, except banks
PA: Platinum Equity, Llc
360 N Crescent Dr Bldg S
Beverly Hills CA 90210

(P-11689)
PROJECT SKYLINE INTERMEDIATE H
360 N Crescent Dr Bldg S, Beverly Hills (90210-2529)
PHONE......................310 712-1850
Tom Gores, *President*
EMP: 2020 **Privately Held**
SIC: 6719 Investment holding companies, except banks

(P-11690)
RIVER ROCK EQUIPMENT LLC
216 Kenroy Ln, Roseville (95678-4202)
PHONE......................916 791-1609
Warren Holt,
James Castle, *CFO*
James Wagner, *Controller*
Bob Lettek,
EMP: 100
SQ FT: 2,500
SALES: 1MM **Privately Held**
SIC: 6719 Investment holding companies, except banks

(P-11691)
SAN FRANCISCO FORTY NINERS
4949 Mrie P Debartolo Way, Santa Clara (95054-1156)
PHONE......................408 562-4949
John York, *Owner*
Les Schmidt, *COO*
EMP: 90 **EST:** 1977
SALES: 3.9MM **Privately Held**
SIC: 6719 Investment holding companies, except banks

(P-11692)
SHARESPOST INC
555 Montgomery St # 1400, San Francisco (94111-2541)
PHONE......................800 279-7754
Greg Brogger, *CEO*
Ericka McKiernan, *CFO*
EMP: 70 **Privately Held**
SIC: 6719 Investment holding companies, except banks

(P-11693)
SKEFFINGTON ENTERPRISES INC
2200 S Yale St, Santa Ana (92704-4404)
PHONE......................714 540-1700
William J Skeffington, *President*
John Skeffington, *CFO*
EMP: 100
SQ FT: 180,000
SALES: 32.1MM **Privately Held**
SIC: 6719 Personal holding companies, except banks

(P-11694)
SPR OP CO INC
70 W Ohio Ave Ste H, Richmond (94804-2033)
PHONE......................510 232-5030
Matt Guelfi, *President*
Richard Olson, *CFO*
Matthew Guelfi, *Vice Pres*
Michael Guelfi, *Vice Pres*

Marc Caposino, *Creative Dir*
EMP: 150 **EST:** 1975
SQ FT: 105,000 **Privately Held**
WEB: www.hartmann-studios.com
SIC: 6719 Investment holding companies, except banks

(P-11695)
STANTEC HOLDINGS DEL III INC
Also Called: Stantec Oil and Gas
5500 Ming Ave Ste 300, Bakersfield (93309-4627)
PHONE......................661 396-3770
Robert Gomes, *President*
Ysmael Suarez, *Engineer*
EMP: 182
SALES (est): 40.4MM
SALES (corp-wide): 3.2B **Privately Held**
SIC: 6719 Investment holding companies, except banks
PA: Stantec Inc
10220 103 Ave Nw Suite 400
Edmonton AB T5J 0
780 917-7000

(P-11696)
STURGEON SERVICES INTL INC (PA)
Also Called: Sturgeon & Son
3511 Gilmore Ave, Bakersfield (93308-6205)
P.O. Box 2840 (93303-2840)
PHONE......................661 322-4408
Paul H Sturgeon, *President*
Oliver Sturgeon, *Ch of Bd*
Joe D'Angelo, *CFO*
Gina Blankenship, *Vice Pres*
EMP: 50
SQ FT: 5,000
SALES (est): 182.8MM **Privately Held**
SIC: 6719 Personal holding companies, except banks

(P-11697)
TOKAI INTL HOLDINGS INC (PA)
2055 S Haven Ave, Ontario (91761-0736)
PHONE......................909 930-5000
Felix M Hon, *CEO*
EMP: 50
SALES (est): 11.3MM **Privately Held**
SIC: 6719 Investment holding companies, except banks

(P-11698)
TRADESHIFT HOLDINGS INC (HQ)
221 Main St Ste 250, San Francisco (94105-1907)
PHONE......................800 381-3585
Christian Lanng, *CEO*
Jigish Avalani, *President*
Jeppe Rindom, *CFO*
Peter Van Pruissen, *CFO*
Evan Osheroff, *Vice Pres*
EMP: 80 **EST:** 2011
SALES (est): 40.8MM
SALES (corp-wide): 34.7MM **Privately Held**
SIC: 6719 Investment holding companies, except banks

(P-11699)
TRANSAMERICA INTL HOLDINGS
600 Montgomery St Fl 16, San Francisco (94111-2718)
PHONE......................415 983-4000
EMP: 220 **Privately Held**
SIC: 6719
HQ: Transamerica Corporation
4333 Edgewood Rd Ne
Cedar Rapids IA 52499
319 398-8511

(P-11700)
TRESTLES HOLDINGS LLC
Also Called: Oaks Post Acute, The
450 Hayes Ln, Petaluma (94952-4010)
PHONE......................707 778-8686
Stephanie Walsh, *Principal*
Kevin Galbasini, *Principal*
Dan Gill, *Principal*
Cameron Rosenhan, *Principal*
EMP: 88 **Privately Held**
SIC: 6719 Holding companies

(P-11701)
TREX PARTNERS LLC
10455 Pacific Center Ct, San Diego (92121-4339)
PHONE......................858 646-5300
Kenneth Tang,
Doug Bletcher, *Info Tech Dir*
Tod Barrett, *Webmaster*
EMP: 200 **Privately Held**
SIC: 6719 Investment holding companies, except banks

(P-11702)
UTBLO INC
11061 Los Alamitos Blvd, Los Alamitos (90720-3201)
PHONE......................562 493-3664
Wendi Rothman, *President*
EMP: 120
SQ FT: 12,000
SALES (corp-wide): 5.8B **Publicly Held**
WEB: www.lovinoven.com
SIC: 6719 Personal holding companies, except banks
HQ: Treehouse Private Brands, Inc.
2021 Spring Rd Ste 600
Oak Brook IL 60523

(P-11703)
VISIONARY INTEGRATION (PA)
Also Called: VIP
80 Iron Point Cir Ste 100, Folsom (95630-8592)
PHONE......................916 985-9625
Jonna A Ward, *President*
EMP: 95
SQ FT: 9,000
SALES (est): 99.2MM **Privately Held**
SIC: 6719 Personal holding companies, except banks

(P-11704)
WCCO HOLDINGS INC
6913 W Acco St, Montebello (90640-5403)
PHONE......................800 421-6150
Kevin Curtis, *President*
Joe Laws, *COO*
Norman Fujitaki, *CFO*
Michael A Curtis, *Exec VP*
Darlene Ramirez, *Senior Buyer*
◆ **EMP:** 280
SQ FT: 175,000
SALES: 90MM **Privately Held**
WEB: www.wilburcurtis.com
SIC: 6719 3589 Investment holding companies, except banks; coffee brewing equipment

(P-11705)
YF ART HOLDINGS GP LLC
9130 W Sunset Blvd, Los Angeles (90069-3110)
PHONE......................678 441-1400
Fred Boehler, *President*
EMP: 10600 **Privately Held**
SIC: 6719 Investment holding companies, except banks

6722 Management Investment Offices

(P-11706)
ABSOLUTE RETURN PORTFOLIO
700 Newport Center Dr, Newport Beach (92660-6307)
P.O. Box 9000 (92658-9030)
PHONE......................800 800-7646
EMP: 2079
SALES (est): 44.2MM
SALES (corp-wide): 12.8B **Privately Held**
SIC: 6722 Money market mutual funds
HQ: Pacific Life Fund Advisors Llc
700 Newport Center Dr
Newport Beach CA 92660

(P-11707)
ADVANCED COMMERCIAL CORPORATIO
5900 Pasteur Ct Ste 200, Carlsbad (92008-7336)
P.O. Box 4068 (92018-4068)
PHONE......................760 431-8500
Tim Stripe, *CEO*
David Brown, *President*
Cheryl Cunningham, *COO*
Angie Greenig, *Technology*
EMP: 110
SALES (est): 12.2MM **Privately Held**
WEB: www.vacation-resales.com
SIC: 6722 Management investment, open-end

(P-11708)
ALLIANCEBERNSTEIN LP
1999 Ave Of The Sts 215, Los Angeles (90067)
PHONE......................310 286-6000
Alan D Croll, *Branch Mgr*
Susannah Emami, *Vice Pres*
Peter Scholze, *Vice Pres*
Scott Wendelin, *Vice Pres*
EMP: 60
SALES (corp-wide): 1MM **Privately Held**
WEB: www.bernstein.com
SIC: 6722 Money market mutual funds
HQ: Alliancebernstein L.P.
1345 Avenue Of The Americ
New York NY 10105
212 969-1000

(P-11709)
AMCAP FUND INC
333 S Hope St Ste Levb, Los Angeles (90071-3003)
PHONE......................213 486-9200
Marry Clemeson, *President*
Mary C Hall, *Treasurer*
Gordon Crawford, *Senior VP*
Paul G Haaga Jr, *Senior VP*
Walter Stern, *Principal*
EMP: 300
SQ FT: 2,000
SALES: 723.1MM **Privately Held**
SIC: 6722 Mutual fund sales, on own account

(P-11710)
AMERICAN FUNDS DISTRS INC (DH)
333 S Hope St Ste Levb, Los Angeles (90071-3003)
PHONE......................213 486-9200
Michael Johnston, *Ch of Bd*
Larry Clemmensen, *Ch of Bd*
J Kelly Webb, *Treasurer*
Robert Hartig, *Vice Pres*
Brendan Mahoney, *Vice Pres*
EMP: 116
SQ FT: 6,000
SALES: 1B
SALES (corp-wide): 2.2B **Privately Held**
SIC: 6722 Mutual fund sales, on own account; money market mutual funds
HQ: Capital Research And Management Company
333 S Hope St Fl 55
Los Angeles CA 90071
213 486-9200

(P-11711)
AMERICAN MUTUAL FUND INC
333 S Hope St Fl 51, Los Angeles (90071-1420)
PHONE......................213 486-9200
Jonathan B Lovelace Jr, *Ch of Bd*
James K Dunton, *Ch of Bd*
Robert G O'Donnell, *President*
Mary C Hall, *Treasurer*
Mary Hall, *Treasurer*
EMP: 200 **EST:** 1949
SQ FT: 5,000
SALES: 1.3B **Privately Held**
SIC: 6722 Money market mutual funds

(P-11712)
ARES MANAGEMENT CORPORATION (PA)
2000 Avenue Of The Stars # 12, Los Angeles (90067-4733)
PHONE......................310 201-4100

Michael J Arougheti, *President*
R Kipp Deveer, *Partner*
Antony P Ressler, *Ch of Bd*
Michael R McFerran, *COO*
Michael D Weiner, *Partner*
EMP: 89
SALES: 958.4MM **Publicly Held**
SIC: 6722 Management investment, open-end

(P-11713)
ARES MANAGEMENT LLC (HQ)
2000 Avenue Of The Stars # 12, Los Angeles (90067-4733)
PHONE....................310 201-4100
Antony Ressler, *President*
Greg Margolies, *Senior Partner*
Sunny Parmar, *Officer*
Alexander Morgan, *Assoc VP*
Seth Brufsky, *Vice Pres*
EMP: 60
SALES (est): 926.5MM
SALES (corp-wide): 958.4MM **Publicly Held**
SIC: 6722 Management investment, open-end
PA: Ares Management Corporation
2000 Avenue Of The Stars # 12
Los Angeles CA 90067
310 201-4100

(P-11714)
ARES MANAGEMENT LLC
1999 Ave Of Stars Fl 37, Los Angeles (90067-4650)
PHONE....................310 201-4100
Tony Ressler, *Branch Mgr*
EMP: 170
SALES (corp-wide): 958.4MM **Publicly Held**
SIC: 6722 Management investment, open-end
HQ: Ares Management Llc
2000 Avenue Of The Stars # 12
Los Angeles CA 90067
310 201-4100

(P-11715)
AURORA RESURGENCE FUND LP
10877 Wilshire Blvd # 2100, Los Angeles (90024-4341)
PHONE....................310 551-0101
Steven D Smith, *Managing Prtnr*
Anthony Disimone, *Partner*
Matt Homme, *Partner*
Peter Leibman, *Partner*
Ryan McCarthy, *Partner*
EMP: 700
SALES (est): 47.2MM **Privately Held**
SIC: 6722 Money market mutual funds

(P-11716)
BAY GROVE CAPITAL GROUP LLC (PA)
801 Montgomery St Fl 5, San Francisco (94133-5151)
PHONE....................415 229-7953
Kevin Marchetti,
Adam Forste, *Managing Prtnr*
Kristina Hentschel, *Executive*
Michael Billings,
Geoff Colla,
EMP: 50
SALES (est): 53.6MM **Privately Held**
SIC: 6722 Management investment, open-end

(P-11717)
BLACKROCK FUNDS III
400 Howard St, San Francisco (94105-2618)
PHONE....................415 597-2000
Mike Sobel, *Principal*
Sathish Balakrishnan, *Vice Pres*
Craig Dehner, *Vice Pres*
David Kirkbride, *Vice Pres*
Darien Lum, *Vice Pres*
EMP: 56
SALES (est): 25.9MM **Privately Held**
SIC: 6722 Management investment, open-end

(P-11718)
BLACKROCK INSTNL TR NAT ASSN (HQ)
Also Called: Ishares
400 Howard St, San Francisco (94105-2618)
PHONE....................415 597-2000
Laurence D Fink, *CEO*
Robert S Kapito, *President*
James Parsons, *President*
EMP: 600
SQ FT: 65,000
SALES: 1.5B **Publicly Held**
SIC: 6722 Money market mutual funds

(P-11719)
BRANDES INV PARTNERS INC (PA)
11988 Charmaine Way Ste 6, San Diego (92131)
P.O. Box 919048 (92191-9048)
PHONE....................858 755-0239
Charles H Brandes, *Ch of Bd*
Christopher Garrett, *Partner*
Brent V Woods, *CEO*
Leah Brock, *Vice Pres*
Matt Brundage, *Vice Pres*
EMP: 121
SQ FT: 27,000
SALES (est): 119.9MM **Privately Held**
WEB: www.brandes.com
SIC: 6722 Money market mutual funds

(P-11720)
BROADRACH CPITL PRTNERS FUND I
248 Homer Ave, Palo Alto (94301-2722)
PHONE....................650 331-2500
EMP: 987
SALES (est): 20.2MM
SALES (corp-wide): 394.6MM **Privately Held**
SIC: 6722 Money market mutual funds
PA: Broadreach Capital Partners Llc
855 El Camino Real # 350
Palo Alto CA 94301
650 331-2500

(P-11721)
COLFIN ESH FUNDING LLC
2450 Broadway Fl 6, Santa Monica (90404-3570)
PHONE....................310 282-8820
EMP: 239
SALES (est): 693.9K
SALES (corp-wide): 2.6B **Publicly Held**
SIC: 6722 Management investment, open-end
PA: Colony Capital, Inc.
515 S Flower St Fl 44
Los Angeles CA 90071
310 282-8820

(P-11722)
DODGE & COX
555 California St # 4000, San Francisco (94104-1538)
PHONE....................415 981-1710
Dana M Emery, *CEO*
John A Gunn, *Chairman*
Marian Z Baldauf, *Treasurer*
John Loll, *Treasurer*
C Bryan Cameron, *Senior VP*
EMP: 195 **EST:** 1930
SQ FT: 45,000
SALES (est): 268.2MM **Privately Held**
WEB: www.dodgeandcox.com
SIC: 6722 Money market mutual funds

(P-11723)
ENCORE FUND LP
555 California St # 2975, San Francisco (94104-1503)
PHONE....................415 676-4000
Jeff Skelton, *President*
John Dowd, *Vice Pres*
Steve Colamarino, *Managing Dir*
Nitin Motwani, *Managing Dir*
Bill Powers, *Admin Mgr*
EMP: 70
SALES (est): 4.1MM **Privately Held**
SIC: 6722 Management investment, open-end

(P-11724)
FARALLON CAPITAL PARTNERS LP (PA)
1 Maritime Plz Ste 2100, San Francisco (94111-3528)
PHONE....................415 421-2132
Chun R Ding, *Mng Member*
Jim Swerkes, *Managing Prtnr*
Colby Clark, *Managing Dir*
Steve Heath, *Managing Dir*
Michael Linn, *Managing Dir*
EMP: 105
SQ FT: 8,000
SALES (est): 26.1MM **Privately Held**
SIC: 6722 Management investment, open-end

(P-11725)
FORTRESS INVESTMENT GROUP LLC
10250 Constellation Blvd # 2300, Los Angeles (90067-6200)
PHONE....................310 228-3030
Ian Schnider, *Director*
EMP: 74 **Privately Held**
SIC: 6722 Management investment, open-end
HQ: Fortress Investment Group Llc
1345 Avenue Of The Americ
New York NY 10105
212 798-6100

(P-11726)
FORTRESS INVESTMENT GROUP LLC
42 Florida St Flr, San Francisco (94103)
PHONE....................415 284-7400
Avner Husen, *Managing Dir*
EMP: 74 **Privately Held**
SIC: 6722 Management investment, open-end
HQ: Fortress Investment Group Llc
1345 Avenue Of The Americ
New York NY 10105
212 798-6100

(P-11727)
FTV MANAGEMENT COMPANY LP
Also Called: Financial Technology Ventures
555 California St # 2900, San Francisco (94104-1503)
PHONE....................415 291-8164
Liron Gitig, *Partner*
Karen Derr Gilbert, *Partner*
David Haynes, *Partner*
Adam Hallquist, *Vice Pres*
Robert Kaufman, *Vice Pres*
EMP: 148
SALES (est): 39.7MM **Privately Held**
SIC: 6722 Money market mutual funds

(P-11728)
HALL CAPITAL PARTNERS LLC (PA)
1 Maritime Plz Fl 5, San Francisco (94111-3408)
PHONE....................415 288-0544
Kathryn A Hall, *CEO*
John W Buoymaster, *President*
William Powers, *COO*
EMP: 90
SQ FT: 6,000
SALES (est): 45.3MM **Privately Held**
WEB: www.offithall.com
SIC: 6722 Management investment, open-end

(P-11729)
KAYNE ANDERSON RUDNI
1800 Avenue Of The Stars # 200, Los Angeles (90067-4204)
PHONE....................310 229-9260
Stephen Rigali,
Sheryl Sadis, *CFO*
Judith Ridder, *Officer*
Spuds Powell, *Vice Pres*
Joyce Hill, *Office Admin*
EMP: 60
SQ FT: 20,000
SALES (est): 13.7MM **Publicly Held**
WEB: www.kayne.com
SIC: 6722 Management investment, open-end

HQ: Virtus Partners, Inc.
755 Main St
Hartford CT 06103

(P-11730)
MACFARLANE PARTNERS LLC (PA)
201 Spear St Ste 1000, San Francisco (94105-1667)
PHONE....................415 356-2500
Victor B Macfarlane, *Ch of Bd*
Gregory M Vilkin, *President*
Susan A Kreusch, *CFO*
Katharine Ryan-Weiss, *Vice Pres*
David Dressler, *Principal*
EMP: 53
SQ FT: 14,000
SALES (est): 18.3MM **Privately Held**
SIC: 6722 Management investment, open-end

(P-11731)
MCMILLIN MANAGEMENT SVCS LP (HQ)
Also Called: McMillin Homes
2750 Womble Rd Ste 102, San Diego (92106-6114)
P.O. Box 85104 (92186-5104)
PHONE....................619 477-4117
Scott McMillin, *General Ptnr*
Mark McMillin, *Partner*
EMP: 224
SALES (est): 34.8MM
SALES (corp-wide): 50MM **Privately Held**
WEB: www.mcmillin.com
SIC: 6722 8611 Management investment, open-end; business associations
PA: Mcmillin Companies, Llc
2750 Womble Rd Ste 102
San Diego CA 92106
619 477-4117

(P-11732)
OAKTREE HOLDINGS INC
333 S Grand Ave Ste 2800, Los Angeles (90071-1530)
PHONE....................213 830-6300
EMP: 767 **EST:** 2014
SALES (est): 168.1K **Privately Held**
SIC: 6722 Management investment, open-end
PA: Oaktree Capital Group Holdings, L.P.
333 S Grand Ave Fl 28
Los Angeles CA 90071

(P-11733)
OAKTREE REAL ESTATE OPPORTUNIT
333 S Grand Ave Fl 28, Los Angeles (90071-3492)
PHONE....................213 830-6300
EMP: 767 **EST:** 2014
SALES (est): 19.1MM **Privately Held**
SIC: 6722 Management investment, open-end
PA: Oaktree Capital Group Holdings, L.P.
333 S Grand Ave Fl 28
Los Angeles CA 90071

(P-11734)
OAKTREE STRATEGIC INCOME LLC
333 S Grand Ave Fl 28, Los Angeles (90071-3492)
PHONE....................213 830-6300
EMP: 1534 **EST:** 2015
SALES (est): 52.6MM **Privately Held**
SIC: 6722 Management investment, open-end
PA: Oaktree Capital Group Holdings, L.P.
333 S Grand Ave Fl 28
Los Angeles CA 90071

(P-11735)
OCM REAL ESTATE OPPORTUNITIES
333 S Grand Ave Fl 28, Los Angeles (90071-3492)
PHONE....................213 830-6300
EMP: 1023 **EST:** 2014

SALES (est): 271.6K **Privately Held**
SIC: 6722 Management investment, open-end
PA: Oaktree Capital Group Holdings, L.P.
   333 S Grand Ave Fl 28
   Los Angeles CA 90071

(P-11736)
ORANGE COUNTY EMPLOYEES RETIR
2223 S Wellington Ave, Santa Ana (92701)
PHONE...................................714 558-6200
Raymond Fleming, *CEO*
Molly Murphy, *CIO*
Robert Kinsler, *Info Tech Mgr*
Tarek Turaigi, *Investment Ofcr*
David Beeson, *Analyst*
EMP: 51
SALES (est): 6.9MM **Privately Held**
WEB: www.ocers.org
SIC: 6722 8111 Management investment, open-end; legal services

(P-11737)
PACIFIC INVESTMENT MGT CO LLC (DH)
Also Called: Pimco
650 Newport Center Dr, Newport Beach (92660-6392)
P.O. Box 6430 (92658-6430)
PHONE...................................949 720-6000
Emmanuel Roman, *CEO*
Jay Jacobs, *President*
Robin Shanahan, *COO*
Peter Strelow, *COO*
John Lane, *CFO*
EMP: 240
SQ FT: 25,000
SALES (est): 671.3MM
SALES (corp-wide): 24.9B **Privately Held**
SIC: 6722 Management investment, open-end
HQ: Allianz Asset Management Of America Llc
   650 Newport Center Dr
   Newport Beach CA 92660
   949 219-2200

(P-11738)
PIMCO FUNDS DISTRIBUTION CO
840 Nwport Ctr Dr Ste 100, Newport Beach (92660)
PHONE...................................949 720-4761
Bill Gross, *CEO*
EMP: 300
SALES (est): 12.1MM **Privately Held**
SIC: 6722 Money market mutual funds

(P-11739)
PW FUND B LP
7585 Longe St, Stockton (95206-4940)
PHONE...................................916 379-3852
EMP: 80
SALES (est): 117.1K **Privately Held**
SIC: 6722 Money market mutual funds

(P-11740)
R & S INVESTMENTS LLC
1 Bush St Fl 9, San Francisco (94104-4415)
PHONE...................................415 591-2700
G Randy Hecht, *Mng Member*
John Casconi, *President*
Matthew Fessler, *President*
Jason Muntner, *President*
Laura Beall, *Executive Asst*
EMP: 100
SALES (est): 21.8MM
SALES (corp-wide): 413.4MM **Publicly Held**
WEB: www.rsinvestments.com
SIC: 6722 Management investment, open-end
HQ: Victory Capital Management Inc.
   4900 Tiedeman Rd Fl 4
   Brooklyn OH 44144

(P-11741)
STAMOS CAPITAL PARTNERS LP
2498 Sand Hill Rd, Menlo Park (94025-6940)
PHONE...................................650 233-5000
Peter Stamos, *CEO*
Allie Lui, *Executive Asst*
Adam Afshar, *Technology*
Karina Leal, *Finance*
Jared Kanover, *General Counsel*
EMP: 55
SALES (est): 9MM **Privately Held**
SIC: 6722 Management investment, open-end

(P-11742)
SUNAMERICA INVESTMENTS INC
1 Sun America Ctr Fl 38, Los Angeles (90067-6101)
PHONE...................................310 772-6000
EMP: 200
SALES (est): 7.2MM
SALES (corp-wide): 52.3B **Publicly Held**
SIC: 6722
HQ: Sunamerica Inc.
   1 Sun America Ctr Fl 38
   Los Angeles CA 90067
   310 772-6000

(P-11743)
US SMALL CPITL VALUE PORTFOLIO
1299 Ocean Ave Ste 150, Santa Monica (90401-1002)
PHONE...................................310 395-8005
David Booth, *President*
EMP: 70
SALES (est): 5.5MM **Privately Held**
SIC: 6722 Money market mutual funds

(P-11744)
VANTAGEPOINT VENTURE PARTNERS
1001 Bayhill Dr Ste 300, San Bruno (94066-3061)
PHONE...................................650 866-3100
Alan E Salzman, *Partner*
EMP: 56
SALES (est): 5.2MM
SALES (corp-wide): 4.7MM **Privately Held**
SIC: 6722 Mutual fund sales, on own account
PA: Vantagepoint Capital Partners
   1111 Bayhill Dr Ste 220
   San Bruno CA 94066
   650 866-3100

(P-11745)
VIHARAS GROUP INC
1919 W Artesia Blvd, Compton (90220-5397)
PHONE...................................310 537-6700
Ashok Patel, *President*
EMP: 75 EST: 2007
SALES (est): 4.8MM **Privately Held**
SIC: 6722 Management investment, open-end

(P-11746)
WELLS FARGO INTL BOND CIT
525 Market St Fl 10, San Francisco (94105-2718)
PHONE...................................415 396-4943
Gary Schlossberg, *Vice Pres*
Warren Baker, *Portfolio Mgr*
Alison Shimada, *Analyst*
EMP: 197
SALES (est): 13.5MM
SALES (corp-wide): 101B **Publicly Held**
SIC: 6722 Money market mutual funds
HQ: Wells Capital Management Incorporated
   525 Market St Fl 10
   San Francisco CA 94105
   415 396-8000

(P-11747)
WESTERN ASSET CORE PLUS
385 E Colorado Blvd, Pasadena (91101-1923)
PHONE...................................626 844-9400
Larry Clark, *Principal*

EMP: 97
SALES (est): 251.6K
SALES (corp-wide): 2.9B **Publicly Held**
SIC: 6722 Money market mutual funds
HQ: Western Asset Management Company, Llc
   385 E Colorado Blvd # 250
   Pasadena CA 91101
   626 844-9265

(P-11748)
WESTERN ASSET MGT CO LLC (HQ)
385 E Colorado Blvd # 250, Pasadena (91101-1929)
PHONE...................................626 844-9265
James W Hirschmann III, *CEO*
Travis M Carr, *COO*
Jody Hiramoto, *Officer*
Andrew Kang, *Officer*
Steve Sibley, *Vice Pres*
▲ EMP: 50
SQ FT: 55,000
SALES (est): 221.1MM
SALES (corp-wide): 2.9B **Publicly Held**
SIC: 6722 Management investment, open-end
PA: Legg Mason Inc
   100 International Dr
   Baltimore MD 21202
   410 539-0000

(P-11749)
ZILLIONAIRE EMPRESS DANIELLE B
8549 Wilshire Blvd # 817, Beverly Hills (90211-3104)
PHONE...................................310 461-9923
EMP: 1000
SQ FT: 300
SALES (est): 44.6MM **Privately Held**
SIC: 6722

6726 Unit Investment Trusts, Face-Amount Certificate Offices

(P-11750)
ASIA PACIFIC CAPITAL
345 Suth Fgroa St Ste 100, Los Angeles (90071)
PHONE...................................213 628-8800
Eddy Chao, *CEO*
EMP: 85
SALES (est): 6.4MM **Privately Held**
WEB: www.apccusa.com
SIC: 6726 Investment offices

(P-11751)
CENTURY PK CAPITL PARTNERS LLC (PA)
2101 Rosecrans Ave # 4275, El Segundo (90245-4749)
PHONE...................................310 867-2210
Martin A Sarafa,
Guy Zaczepinski, *Partner*
Charles W Roellig, *Managing Prtnr*
Martin Sarafa, *Managing Prtnr*
Paul J Wolf, *Managing Prtnr*
EMP: 160
SALES (est): 65.8MM **Privately Held**
WEB: www.cpclp.com
SIC: 6726 3569 3086 3448 Management investment funds, closed-end; firefighting apparatus & related equipment; carpet & rug cushions, foamed plastic; ramps: prefabricated metal

(P-11752)
GLOBAL REACH 18 INC (PA)
10100 Santa Monica Blvd # 900, Los Angeles (90067-4003)
PHONE...................................310 203-5850
Haim Saban, *CEO*
Adam Chesnoff, *President*
Fred Gluckman, *CFO*
Joel Andryc, *Ch Credit Ofcr*
Philip Han, *Exec VP*
EMP: 51

SALES (est): 55.4MM **Privately Held**
WEB: www.saban.com
SIC: 6726 6531 6799 Investment offices; real estate agents & managers; investors

(P-11753)
HAWAII PARENT CORP
600 Montgomery St Fl 32, San Francisco (94111-2807)
PHONE...................................415 263-3660
Orlando Bravo, *Partner*
EMP: 495 EST: 2013
SALES (est): 18.1MM **Privately Held**
SIC: 6726 Investment offices

(P-11754)
INTERNATIONAL INDUS PK INC
5440 Morehouse Dr # 4000, San Diego (92121-1798)
PHONE...................................858 623-9000
David Wick, *Vice Pres*
Lindsay Arobone, *Administration*
EMP: 99
SALES (est): 8.5MM **Privately Held**
SIC: 6726 Investment offices

(P-11755)
J ALEXANDER INVESTMENTS INC (PA)
Also Called: Investment Banking
922 S Barrington Ave A, Los Angeles (90049-5554)
PHONE...................................213 687-8400
James Alexander, *President*
EMP: 70
SQ FT: 4,500
SALES (est): 10.1MM **Privately Held**
WEB: www.investmentbanking.com
SIC: 6726 Investment offices

(P-11756)
PARALLAX CAPITAL PARTNERS LLC (PA)
23332 Mill Creek Dr # 155, Laguna Hills (92653-1679)
PHONE...................................949 296-4800
James Hale,
Lisa Hale,
Michael Hale,
William Koneval,
Scott Lencz,
EMP: 131
SALES (est): 18.3MM **Privately Held**
WEB: www.parallaxcap.com
SIC: 6726 Investment offices

(P-11757)
RIMROCK HIGH INCOME PLUS FUND
100 Innovation Dr Ste 200, Irvine (92617-3207)
PHONE...................................949 381-7800
Paul C Westhead, *CEO*
Barbara Crowell, *CFO*
Jeff Bemis, *Senior VP*
EMP: 50
SALES (est): 357.9K **Privately Held**
WEB: www.rimrockcapital.com
SIC: 6726 Management investment funds, closed-end

(P-11758)
SILVER LAKE PARTNERS LP (PA)
2775 Sand Hill Rd Ste 100, Menlo Park (94025-7085)
PHONE...................................650 233-8120
Jim Davidson, *Partner*
Yolande Jun, *Partner*
Shawn O'Neill, *Partner*
Thomas Conneely, *Vice Pres*
Geoffrey Oltmans, *Managing Dir*
EMP: 70
SALES (est): 64.1MM **Privately Held**
SIC: 6726 Investment offices

(P-11759)
SILVER LAKE PARTNERS II LP
10080 N Wolfe Dr Sw3190, Cupertino (95014-2544)
PHONE...................................408 454-4732
Andy Wagner, *Branch Mgr*
EMP: 97

▲ = Import ▼=Export
◆ =Import/Export

SALES (corp-wide): 307.9MM **Privately Held**
SIC: **6726** Investment offices
PA: Silver Lake Partners Ii, L.P.
   2775 Sand Hill Rd Ste 100
   Menlo Park CA 94025
   650 233-8120

(P-11760)
SILVER LAKE PARTNERS II LP
Also Called: Silver Lake Financial
1 Market Plz, San Francisco (94105-1101)
PHONE.........................415 293-4355
Roger Whittlin, *Manager*
EMP: 243
SALES (corp-wide): 307.9MM **Privately Held**
SIC: **6726** Investment offices
PA: Silver Lake Partners Ii, L.P.
   2775 Sand Hill Rd Ste 100
   Menlo Park CA 94025
   650 233-8120

(P-11761)
SPUS7 235 PINE LP
235 Pine St Ste 125, San Francisco (94104-2706)
PHONE.........................231 683-4200
Pamela Craig, *General Ptnr*
Ming Lee, *General Ptnr*
EMP: 99
SQ FT: 25,000
SALES (est): 6.5MM **Privately Held**
SIC: **6726** Investment offices

(P-11762)
SPUS7 MIAMI ACC LP
515 S Flower St Ste 3100, Los Angeles (90071-2233)
PHONE.........................213 683-4200
Mark Zikakis, *Principal*
Pamela Craig, *Partner*
EMP: 50 EST: 2014
SQ FT: 25,000
SALES (est): 5.8MM **Privately Held**
SIC: **6726** Investment offices

(P-11763)
VECTOR TALENT II LLC
1 Market St Ste 2300, San Francisco (94105-1414)
PHONE.........................415 293-5000
Alex Slusky, *President*
EMP: 736
SALES (est): 49.9MM **Privately Held**
SIC: **6726** Investment offices

6732 Education, Religious & Charitable Trusts

(P-11764)
CALIFORNIA CMNTY FOUNDATION (PA)
221 S Figueroa St Ste 400, Los Angeles (90012-3760)
PHONE.........................213 413-4130
Antonia Hernandez, *President*
Tom Unterman, *Ch of Bd*
Steve Cobb, *CFO*
Peter Dunn, *Vice Pres*
Karen Illig, *Headmaster*
EMP: 60
SQ FT: 16,000
SALES (est): 16.2MM **Privately Held**
WEB: www.ccf-la.org
SIC: **6732** Charitable trust management

(P-11765)
CALIFORNIA MARITIME ACDMY
200 Maritime Academy Dr, Vallejo (94590-8181)
PHONE.........................707 654-1000
Tom Cropper, *CEO*
Beverly Byl, *Vice Pres*
Ken Toet, *Controller*
EMP: 200
SALES: 1.8MM **Privately Held**
WEB: www.maritime-education.com
SIC: **6732** Educational trust management

(P-11766)
CALWORKS PARTNR CONFERENCE
5151 Murphy Canyon Rd # 220, San Diego (92123-4440)
PHONE.........................858 292-2900
Pat Rickard, *President*
EMP: 50
SALES (est): 6.2MM **Privately Held**
SIC: **6732** Educational trust management

(P-11767)
COMMUNITY PARTNERS INTL
2560 9th St Ste 315b, Berkeley (94710-2567)
PHONE.........................510 225-9676
Si Thura, *Exec Dir*
EMP: 117
SALES: 10.4MM **Privately Held**
SIC: **6732** Trusts: educational, religious, etc.

(P-11768)
HENRY J KAISER FMLY FOUNDATION (PA)
185 Berry St Ste 2000, San Francisco (94107-1704)
PHONE.........................650 854-9400
Drew Altman, *President*
Aaron Desautels, *Officer*
Trina Scott, *Officer*
Diane Rowland, *Exec VP*
Koonal Gandhi, *Senior VP*
EMP: 135 EST: 1948
SQ FT: 185,000
SALES (est): 26.3MM **Privately Held**
SIC: **6732** Trusts: educational, religious, etc.

(P-11769)
KRISHNAMURTI FOUNDATION AMER (PA)
134 Besant Rd, Ojai (93023-2305)
P.O. Box 1560 (93024-1560)
PHONE.........................805 646-2726
Jaap Sluijter, *Exec Dir*
Holly Johnson, *Program Mgr*
Gopal Krishnamurthy, *Program Dir*
EMP: 65
SQ FT: 10,000
SALES (est): 4.9MM **Privately Held**
WEB: www.oakgroveschool.org
SIC: **6732** Educational trust management; charitable trust management

(P-11770)
OAKLAND PUBLIC EDUCATION FUND
520 3rd St Ste 109, Oakland (94607-3503)
P.O. Box 71005 (94612-7105)
PHONE.........................510 221-6968
Robert Spencer, *President*
Brian Stanley, *Exec Dir*
Bridget Daly, *Executive Asst*
Sarah Price, *Admin Asst*
Helen Vance, *Accountant*
EMP: 95 EST: 2003
SALES: 30.3MM **Privately Held**
SIC: **6732** Trusts: educational, religious, etc.

(P-11771)
PERVERTED JSTICE FUNDATION INC
703 Pier Ave Ste B154, Hermosa Beach (90254-3960)
PHONE.........................310 910-9380
Xavier Von Erck, *President*
Dennis Kerr, *CFO*
EMP: 200
SALES (est): 105.6K **Privately Held**
SIC: **6732** Trusts: educational, religious, etc.

(P-11772)
UCLA FOUNDATION
10920 Wilshire Blvd # 200, Los Angeles (90024-6502)
PHONE.........................310 794-3193
Peter Hayashida, *Exec Dir*
Peter L Evans, *COO*
Neal Axelrod, *Treasurer*
Yael APT, *Associate Dir*
Linda Seo, *Associate Dir*

EMP: 317
SALES: 691.9MM **Privately Held**
SIC: **6732** Educational trust management

(P-11773)
UCR BOTANY AND PLANT SCIENCES
3401 Watkins Dr, Riverside (92507-4633)
PHONE.........................951 827-5133
Michael Roose, *Principal*
EMP: 99
SALES (est): 6.2MM **Privately Held**
SIC: **6732** Trusts: educational, religious, etc.

(P-11774)
US GREEN BUILDING COUNCIL -
Also Called: US GREEN BUILDING COUN-CIL INLA
2879 Breezy Meadow Ln, Corona (92883-5915)
P.O. Box 2181, Redlands (92373-0721)
PHONE.........................818 621-4880
Jennifer Ward, *CEO*
EMP: 99
SALES: 48.5K **Privately Held**
SIC: **6732** Trusts: educational, religious, etc.

6733 Trusts Except Educational, Religious & Charitable

(P-11775)
2100 TRUST LLC (PA)
625 N Grand Ave, Santa Ana (92701-4347)
PHONE.........................877 469-7344
Erek J Delorenzi, *Principal*
Thomas Halligan, *Director*
Linda Knudtson, *Manager*
Josh Moore, *Manager*
Joshua Cain, *Editor*
EMP: 200
SALES (est): 2.5B **Privately Held**
SIC: **6733** Trusts

(P-11776)
ANNENBERG FOUNDATION TRUST (PA)
37977 Bob Hope Dr, Rancho Mirage (92270-2008)
PHONE.........................760 202-2222
Geoffrey Cowan, *President*
Wallis Annenberg, *CEO*
Debbi Hinton, *CFO*
Lauren Bon, *Trustee*
Diane Deshong, *Trustee*
EMP: 60
SALES: 26.8MM **Privately Held**
SIC: **6733** Trusts

(P-11777)
CAPITAL GUARDIAN TRUST COMPANY (HQ)
333 S Hope St Fl 52, Los Angeles (90071-3061)
PHONE.........................213 486-9200
Richard C Barker, *Ch of Bd*
Robert Ronus, *President*
Bill Flumenbaum, *Vice Pres*
Ralph Heckert, *Vice Pres*
Thomas Hogh, *Vice Pres*
EMP: 100
SQ FT: 6,000
SALES (est): 47MM
SALES (corp-wide): 2.2B **Privately Held**
SIC: **6733** Trusts, except educational, religious, charity: management
PA: The Capital Group Companies Inc
   333 S Hope St Fl 55
   Los Angeles CA 90071
   213 486-9200

(P-11778)
CARPENTER FNDS ADMNSTRTIVE OFF
265 Hegenberger Rd # 100, Oakland (94621-1443)
PHONE.........................510 633-0333
David Lee, *CEO*
Maria Gonzalez, *Controller*
EMP: 79 EST: 1953

SQ FT: 60,956
SALES: 15MM **Privately Held**
WEB: www.carpenterfunds.com
SIC: **6733** Trusts, except educational, religious, charity: management

(P-11779)
CHRISTMAS BONUS FUND OF THE PL
501 Shatto Pl Fl 5, Los Angeles (90020-1730)
PHONE.........................213 385-6161
Milton D Johnson, *Administration*
Mike Ayre, *Ch of Bd*
E A Norris, *Ch of Bd*
Allen Jones Jr, *Co-COB*
Raymond Forman, *Trustee*
EMP: 60
SQ FT: 70,000
SALES: 4.7MM **Privately Held**
SIC: **6733** Trusts, except educational, religious, charity: management

(P-11780)
CONSUMER LOAN UNDERLYING
71 Stevenson St Ste 1000, San Francisco (94105-2967)
PHONE.........................415 767-4105
EMP: 115
SALES (est): 76.6K **Publicly Held**
SIC: **6733** Trusts
PA: Lendingclub Corporation
   595 Market St Fl 4
   San Francisco CA 94105

(P-11781)
DEFINED CONTRIBUTION TRUST FUN
Also Called: SOUTHERN CALIFORNIA PIPE TRADE
501 Shatto Pl Ste 500, Los Angeles (90020-1730)
PHONE.........................213 385-6161
Milton D Johnson, *CEO*
Mike Ayre, *Ch of Bd*
Raymond Forman, *Trustee*
Charles La Bouff, *Admin Sec*
EMP: 60
SQ FT: 70,000
SALES: 75.2MM **Privately Held**
SIC: **6733** Trusts, except educational, religious, charity: management

(P-11782)
DEUTSCHE BANK NATIONAL TR CO
1761 E Saint Andrew Pl, Santa Ana (92705-4934)
PHONE.........................714 247-6000
Gary Vaughn, *Manager*
Joseph Campbell, *Sales Staff*
EMP: 53
SALES (corp-wide): 13.6B **Privately Held**
SIC: **6733** 6111 Trusts; banks for cooperatives
HQ: Deutsche Bank National Trust Co
   2000 Avenue Of The Stars
   Los Angeles CA 90067
   213 620-8200

(P-11783)
DEVEREUX FOUNDATION
Also Called: Devereux Center In California
El Colegio Rd, Goleta (93117)
PHONE.........................805 968-2525
Amy Evans, *Director*
Mr David Weisman, *Human Res Dir*
EMP: 350
SALES (corp-wide): 460.5MM **Privately Held**
SIC: **6733** 8361 8031 Trusts; group foster home; offices & clinics of osteopathic physicians
PA: Devereux Foundation
   444 Devereux Dr
   Villanova PA 19085
   610 520-3000

(P-11784)
ESSEX PROPERTY TRUST INC
Also Called: Huxley Apartments, The
1234 Larrabee St, West Hollywood (90069-2004)
PHONE.........................323 461-9346

Mike Shall, *CEO*
EMP: 50
SALES (corp-wide): 1.4B **Privately Held**
SIC: 6733 Trusts
PA: Essex Property Trust, Inc.
1100 Park Pl Ste 200
San Mateo CA 94403
650 655-7800

(P-11785)
FIRST NATIONAL BANK (PA)
401 W A St Ste 200, San Diego
(92101-7917)
PHONE..................................619 233-5588
Mike Perdue, *President*
EMP: 75
SALES (est): 56.2MM **Privately Held**
SIC: 6733 Trusts

(P-11786)
IMMIGRATION VOICE
3561 Homestead Rd 375, Santa Clara
(95051-5161)
PHONE..................................408 204-2200
Aman Kapoor, *Owner*
Dheeraj Kohli, *VP Opers*
Gaurav Gupta, *Manager*
EMP: 99
SALES: 136.3K **Privately Held**
SIC: 6733 Trusts

(P-11787)
IMPAC SECURED ASSETS CORP
19500 Jamboree Rd, Irvine (92612-2411)
PHONE..................................949 475-3600
Ronald Martin Morrison, *Administration*
EMP: 92
SALES (est): 123.6K **Publicly Held**
SIC: 6733 Trusts
HQ: Impac Funding Corporation
19500 Jamboree Rd
Irvine CA 92612

(P-11788)
IRON WORKERS LOCAL 433
Also Called: California Field Ironwrkrs
252 Hillcrest Ave, San Bernardino
(92408-2120)
PHONE..................................909 884-5500
Fax: 909 885-0047
EMP: 50
SALES (est): 1.5MM **Privately Held**
SIC: 6733

(P-11789)
IRONWRKER EMPLYEES BENEFT CORP
Also Called: Ironworkers Union
131 N El Molino Ave # 330, Pasadena
(91101-1873)
PHONE..................................626 792-7337
Dick Zampa, *President*
Glen Cline, *Exec Dir*
Rise Spiegel, *Exec Dir*
EMP: 65
SQ FT: 19,000
SALES (est): 10.9MM **Privately Held**
SIC: 6733 Trusts, except educational, religious, charity: management; vacation funds for employees

(P-11790)
J D RUSH COMPANY INC (HQ)
5900 E Lerdo Hwy, Shafter (93263-4023)
PHONE..................................661 392-1900
James Varner, *CEO*
Paul Sahey, *Corp Secy*
Teri Seely, *Vice Pres*
Lisa Tatum, *Vice Pres*
Danny Seely, *VP Mfg*
◆ **EMP:** 105
SQ FT: 3,000
SALES (est): 99.9MM
SALES (corp-wide): 111MM **Privately Held**
SIC: 6733 Private estate, personal investment & vacation fund trusts
PA: Varner Family Limited Partnership
5900 E Lerdo Hwy
Shafter CA 93263
661 399-1163

(P-11791)
KAISER FOUNDATION HOSPITALS
Also Called: Otay Mesa Medical Offices
4650 Palm Ave, San Diego (92154-8404)
PHONE..................................619 662-5107
EMP: 454
SALES (corp-wide): 76.5B **Privately Held**
SIC: 6733 Trusts
HQ: Kaiser Foundation Hospitals Inc
1 Kaiser Plz
Oakland CA 94612
510 271-6611

(P-11792)
KAISER FOUNDATION HOSPITALS
Also Called: Kaiser Permanente
4647 Zion Ave, San Diego (92120-2507)
PHONE..................................619 528-5888
Kathy Roper, *Manager*
Charles Columbus, *Vice Pres*
Jeff Johnson, *Exec Dir*
Han Lin, *Internal Med*
Minh V Le, *Emerg Med Spec*
EMP: 3000
SALES (corp-wide): 76.5B **Privately Held**
WEB: www.kaiserpermanente.org
SIC: 6733 8062 Trusts; general medical & surgical hospitals
HQ: Kaiser Foundation Hospitals Inc
1 Kaiser Plz
Oakland CA 94612
510 271-6611

(P-11793)
KAISER FOUNDATION HOSPITALS
Also Called: Martinez Medical Offices
200 Muir Rd, Martinez (94553-4672)
PHONE..................................925 372-1000
Bryan Fong, *Principal*
Pablo Baker, *Chief Engr*
Sandra Seier, *Family Practiti*
Rama Yarlagadda, *Internal Med*
Lisa Kendrick, *Manager*
EMP: 200
SALES (corp-wide): 76.5B **Privately Held**
WEB: www.kaiserpermanente.org
SIC: 6733 8011 Trusts; general & family practice, physician/surgeon
HQ: Kaiser Foundation Hospitals Inc
1 Kaiser Plz
Oakland CA 94612
510 271-6611

(P-11794)
KAISER FOUNDATION HOSPITALS
Also Called: Kaiser Permanente
5119 Pomona Blvd, Los Angeles
(90022-1711)
PHONE..................................323 881-5516
Judy Nantes, *Manager*
EMP: 50
SALES (corp-wide): 76.5B **Privately Held**
WEB: www.kaiserpermanente.org
SIC: 6733 Trusts
HQ: Kaiser Foundation Hospitals Inc
1 Kaiser Plz
Oakland CA 94612
510 271-6611

(P-11795)
KAISER FOUNDATION HOSPITALS
Also Called: Moreno Valley Heacock Med Offs
12815 Heacock St, Moreno Valley
(92553-2836)
PHONE..................................951 601-6174
Mark Ituah, *Principal*
EMP: 50
SALES (corp-wide): 76.5B **Privately Held**
WEB: www.kaiserpermanente.org
SIC: 6733 Trusts
HQ: Kaiser Foundation Hospitals Inc
1 Kaiser Plz
Oakland CA 94612
510 271-6611

(P-11796)
KAISER FOUNDATION HOSPITALS
Also Called: Kaiser Permanente
3285 Claremont Way, NAPA (94558-3313)
PHONE..................................707 258-2500
Debby Bacon, *Branch Mgr*
Julie Winter, *Med Doctor*
EMP: 200
SALES (corp-wide): 76.5B **Privately Held**
WEB: www.kaiserpermanente.org
SIC: 6733 8093 8062 Trusts, except educational, religious, charity: management; specialty outpatient clinics; general medical & surgical hospitals
HQ: Kaiser Foundation Hospitals Inc
1 Kaiser Plz
Oakland CA 94612
510 271-6611

(P-11797)
KAISER FOUNDATION HOSPITALS
Also Called: Kaiser Permanente
789 E Cooley Dr, Colton (92324-4007)
PHONE..................................909 427-5521
Barry A Wolfman, *Principal*
Vinod Dasika, *Family Practiti*
Patricia G McGhee, *Family Practiti*
EMP: 793
SQ FT: 23,088
SALES (corp-wide): 76.5B **Privately Held**
WEB: www.kaiserpermanente.org
SIC: 6733 Trusts
HQ: Kaiser Foundation Hospitals Inc
1 Kaiser Plz
Oakland CA 94612
510 271-6611

(P-11798)
KAISER FOUNDATION HOSPITALS
Also Called: Corona Medical Offices
182 Granite St, Corona (92879-1288)
PHONE..................................866 984-7483
Randy Florence, *Branch Mgr*
EMP: 793
SALES (corp-wide): 76.5B **Privately Held**
SIC: 6733 8011 Trusts; internal medicine practitioners; general & family practice, physician/surgeon
HQ: Kaiser Foundation Hospitals Inc
1 Kaiser Plz
Oakland CA 94612
510 271-6611

(P-11799)
KAISER FOUNDATION HOSPITALS
Also Called: Orange County-Irvine Med Ctr
6640 Alton Pkwy, Irvine (92618-3734)
PHONE..................................949 932-5000
George Disalvo, *Branch Mgr*
Tony D Fang, *Surgeon*
Gail F Mattson-Gates, *Surgeon*
Peter S Paik, *Surgeon*
Shahed Ghanimati, *Obstetrician*
EMP: 379
SALES (corp-wide): 76.5B **Privately Held**
SIC: 6733 Trusts
HQ: Kaiser Foundation Hospitals Inc
1 Kaiser Plz
Oakland CA 94612
510 271-6611

(P-11800)
MANAGEMENT TRUST ASSN INC
100 E Thousand Oaks Blvd, Thousand
Oaks (91360-5713)
PHONE..................................805 496-5514
EMP: 116 **Privately Held**
SIC: 6733 Trusts
PA: The Management Trust Association Inc
15661 Red Hill Ave # 201
Tustin CA 92780

(P-11801)
MANAGEMENT TRUST ASSN INC
9815 Carroll Canyon Rd, San Diego
(92131-1123)
PHONE..................................858 547-4373

Diane Houston, *Branch Mgr*
EMP: 116 **Privately Held**
SIC: 6733 Trusts
PA: The Management Trust Association Inc
15661 Red Hill Ave # 201
Tustin CA 92780

(P-11802)
MANAGEMENT TRUST ASSN INC
4160 Temescal Canyon Rd # 202, Corona
(92883-4625)
PHONE..................................951 694-1758
EMP: 116 **Privately Held**
SIC: 6733 Trusts
PA: The Management Trust Association Inc
15661 Red Hill Ave # 201
Tustin CA 92780

(P-11803)
MANAGEMENT TRUST ASSN INC (PA)
Also Called: Management Trust, The
15661 Red Hill Ave # 201, Tustin
(92780-7300)
PHONE..................................714 285-2626
William B Sasser, *CEO*
EMP: 58
SALES: 135MM **Privately Held**
SIC: 6733 Trusts

(P-11804)
MTC FINANCIAL INC
Also Called: Trustee Corps
17100 Gillette Ave, Irvine (92614-5603)
PHONE..................................949 252-8300
Fax: 949 634-1011
EMP: 50 **EST:** 1992
SALES (est): 4.7MM **Privately Held**
SIC: 6733

(P-11805)
NORTHERN CAL RET CLKS-EMP FUND
190 N Wiget Ln Ste 110, Walnut Creek
(94598-2476)
PHONE..................................925 746-7530
Jeff Chapman, *Administration*
EMP: 120
SQ FT: 11,000
SALES (est): 4.2MM **Privately Held**
SIC: 6733 Vacation funds for employees

(P-11806)
OPERATING ENGINEERS FUNDS INC (PA)
100 Corson St Ste 222, Pasadena
(91103-3892)
P.O. Box 7063 (91109-7063)
PHONE..................................866 400-5200
Mike Roddy, *CEO*
Matt Erieg, *COO*
Chuck Killian, *CFO*
Klairissa Sikorski, *Admin Asst*
Paul Egge, *CIO*
EMP: 135
SQ FT: 84,600
SALES (est): 47.2MM **Privately Held**
WEB: www.oefunds.com
SIC: 6733 Trusts, except educational, religious, charity: management

(P-11807)
PIMCO MORTGAGE INCOME TR INC
650 Newport Center Dr, Newport Beach
(92660-6310)
PHONE..................................949 720-6000
Casey Newell, *CEO*
Jason Mandinach, *President*
John Lane, *CFO*
EMP: 284
SALES (est): 3.4MM
SALES (corp-wide): 24.9B **Privately Held**
SIC: 6733 Trusts
HQ: Pacific Investment Management Company Llc
650 Newport Center Dr
Newport Beach CA 92660
949 720-6000

(P-11808)
**PMT CRDIT RISK TRNSF TR
2015-1**
3043 Townsgate Rd, Westlake Village
(91361-3027)
PHONE..................................818 224-7028
EMP: 81
SALES (est): 76.6K **Privately Held**
SIC: 6733 Trusts
PA: Pennymac Mortgage Investment Trust
6101 Condor Dr
Moorpark CA 93021

(P-11809)
**PMT CRDIT RISK TRNSF TR
2015-2**
3043 Townsgate Rd, Westlake Village
(91361-3027)
PHONE..................................818 224-7442
EMP: 239
SALES (est): 76.6K **Privately Held**
SIC: 6733 Trusts
PA: Pennymac Mortgage Investment Trust
6101 Condor Dr
Moorpark CA 93021

(P-11810)
PNMAC GMSR ISSUER TRUST
3043 Townsgate Rd, Westlake Village
(91361-3027)
PHONE..................................818 746-2271
EMP: 1067
SALES (est): 84.3K
SALES (corp-wide): 1.1B **Publicly Held**
SIC: 6733 Trusts
PA: Pennymac Financial Services, Inc.
3043 Townsgate Rd
Westlake Village CA 91361
818 224-7442

(P-11811)
PROVIDENCE HEALTH SYSTEM
Also Called: Little Co Mary Hosp Pavilion
4320 Maricopa St, Torrance (90503-4314)
PHONE..................................310 543-5900
Mary Ann Young, *Manager*
EMP: 200
SALES (corp-wide): 15.2B **Privately Held**
WEB: www.lcmhs.org
SIC: 6733 8069 8051 Trusts; specialty
hospitals, except psychiatric; skilled nurs-
ing care facilities
HQ: Providence Health System-Southern
California
1801 Lind Ave Sw
Renton WA 98057
425 525-3355

(P-11812)
PROVIDENCE HEALTH SYSTEM
3551 Voyager St Ste 201, Torrance
(90503-1674)
PHONE..................................310 370-5895
EMP: 200
SALES (corp-wide): 17.6B **Privately Held**
SIC: 6733
HQ: Providence Health System-Southern
California
1801 Lind Ave Sw
Renton WA 98057
425 525-3355

(P-11813)
PROVIDENCE HEALTH SYSTEM
511 S Buena Vista St, Burbank
(91505-4809)
PHONE..................................818 846-8141
EMP: 200
SALES (corp-wide): 15.2B **Privately Held**
WEB: www.lcmhs.org
SIC: 6733 Trusts
HQ: Providence Health System-Southern
California
1801 Lind Ave Sw
Renton WA 98057
425 525-3355

(P-11814)
QUALITY LOAN SERVICE CORP
2763 Camino Del Rio S, San Diego
(92108-3708)
PHONE..................................619 645-7711
Kevin R McCarthy, *CEO*

Dave Owen, *COO*
Adriana Banuelos, *Trustee*
Courtney Pybas, *Officer*
Victoria Logan, *Vice Pres*
EMP: 384
SALES (est): 30.7MM **Privately Held**
WEB: www.qualityloan.com
SIC: 6733 Trusts, except educational, reli-
gious, charity: management

(P-11815)
**SHOPCORE PROPERTIES LP
(DH)**
10920 Via Frontera # 220, San Diego
(92127-1734)
PHONE..................................858 613-1800
Luke Petherbridge, *Partner*
Sharon Filbig, *Executive Asst*
Robert Kamenec, *Financial Analy*
Jessica Chiang, *Analyst*
Jane Ashkin, *Accountant*
EMP: 60
SALES (est): 105.5MM **Privately Held**
SIC: 6733 Trusts

(P-11816)
**SOHNEN BARRY AS CO
TRUSTEE**
8945 Eice Rd, Santa Fe Springs (90670)
PHONE..................................562 946-3531
Barry Sohnen, *President*
EMP: 50
SALES (est): 1.3MM **Privately Held**
SIC: 6733 Trusts

(P-11817)
**SOUTHERN CAL PIPE TRADES
ADM (PA)**
Also Called: Southern Cal Pipe Trades ADM
501 Shatto Pl Ste 500, Los Angeles
(90020-1730)
PHONE..................................213 385-6161
Milton D Johnson, *President*
Steven Kwan, *Administration*
Armine Hovhanessian, *Manager*
EMP: 70
SQ FT: 70,000
SALES (est): 23.7MM **Privately Held**
WEB: www.marinavillage.net
SIC: 6733 6513 Trusts, except educa-
tional, religious, charity: management; re-
tirement hotel operation

(P-11818)
**TCW VALUE ADDED LTD
PARTNR**
865 S Figueroa St, Los Angeles
(90017-2543)
PHONE..................................213 244-0000
EMP: 53
SALES (est): 5MM
SALES (corp-wide): 226.2MM **Privately
Held**
SIC: 6733 Private estate, personal invest-
ment & vacation fund trusts
HQ: Tcw Asset Management Company Llc
865 S Figueroa St # 2100
Los Angeles CA 90017
213 244-0000

(P-11819)
**UFCW & EMPLOYERS TRUST
LLC (PA)**
1000 Burnett Ave Ste 110, Concord
(94520-2000)
PHONE..................................800 552-2400
Jody Osterweil, *Administration*
Trent Broadhead, *Recruiter*
EMP: 110
SQ FT: 57,600
SALES (est): 584.1MM **Privately Held**
SIC: 6733 Trusts

(P-11820)
**VACATION AND HOLIDAY
BENEFIT F**
501 Shatto Pl Fl 5, Los Angeles
(90020-1730)
PHONE..................................213 385-6161
Milton D Johnson, *Administration*
Mike Ayre, *Ch of Bd*
E A Norris, *Ch of Bd*
Allen Jones Jr, *Co-COB*
Raymond Forman, *Trustee*
EMP: 60

SQ FT: 70,000
SALES (est): 3MM **Privately Held**
SIC: 6733 Trusts, except educational, reli-
gious, charity: management

(P-11821)
**VARNER FAMILY LTD
PARTNERSHIP (PA)**
5900 E Lerdo Hwy, Shafter (93263-4023)
PHONE..................................661 399-1163
James Varner, *General Ptnr*
EMP: 80
SALES (est): 111MM **Privately Held**
SIC: 6733 Private estate, personal invest-
ment & vacation fund trusts

(P-11822)
**WATTS HEALTH FOUNDATION
INC**
Also Called: Watts Health Center
10300 Compton Ave, Los Angeles
(90002-3628)
PHONE..................................323 357-6688
Clyde W Oden, *Manager*
Marlene Lopez, *Pediatrics*
Renee Katz,
EMP: 450
SALES (corp-wide): 31.9MM **Privately
Held**
WEB: www.sonnytran.com
SIC: 6733 8322 8011 Trusts; individual &
family services; offices & clinics of med-
ical doctors
HQ: Watts Health Foundation, Inc.
3405 W Imperial Hwy # 304
Inglewood CA 90303
310 424-2220

**6794 Patent Owners &
Lessors**

(P-11823)
**ADVANCED FRESH CONCEPTS
CORP (PA)**
Also Called: A F C
19205 S Laurel Park Rd, Rancho
Dominguez (90220-6032)
PHONE..................................310 604-3630
Ryuji Ishii, *CEO*
Jeff Seiler, *Vice Pres*
Jeffery Seiler, *Vice Pres*
Frederick Tam, *Asst Controller*
Masahiko Tajima, *Director*
◆ EMP: 52
SQ FT: 60,000
SALES (est): 34MM **Privately Held**
WEB: www.afcsushi.com
SIC: 6794 2032 2092 5141 Patent own-
ers & lessors; Chinese foods: packaged
in cans, jars, etc.; fresh or frozen pack-
aged fish; food brokers

(P-11824)
BGRS RELOCATION INC (DH)
Also Called: Brookfield Relocation Inc.
3333 Michelson Dr # 1000, Irvine
(92612-0625)
PHONE..................................949 794-7900
Brian McEleney, *President*
▲ EMP: 100
SALES (est): 93.9MM
SALES (corp-wide): 43B **Publicly Held**
WEB: www.randalgoodson.net
SIC: 6794 Franchises, selling or licensing
HQ: Brer Services Inc
16260 N 71st St
Scottsdale AZ 85254
949 794-7900

(P-11825)
BRER AFFILIATES LLC (DH)
Also Called: Prudential RE Affiliates Inc
18500 Von Karman Ave # 400, Irvine
(92612-0504)
PHONE..................................949 794-7900
John Vanderwall, *Ch of Bd*
Patti Ray, *Senior VP*
Gary Kooba, *Broker*
EMP: 208
SQ FT: 55,500

SALES (est): 120.1MM
SALES (corp-wide): 62.9B **Publicly Held**
WEB: www.preacanada.com
SIC: 6794 6531 Franchises, selling or li-
censing; real estate agents & managers
HQ: The Prudential Insurance Company Of
America
751 Broad St
Newark NJ 07102
973 802-6000

(P-11826)
DOLBY LABS LICENSING CORP
100 Potrero Ave, San Francisco
(94103-4886)
PHONE..................................415 558-0200
Ray Dolby, *Chairman*
N William Jasper Jr, *President*
Eric Cohen, *Vice Pres*
John Couling, *Vice Pres*
Jeffrey Eid, *Vice Pres*
EMP: 125
SQ FT: 50,000
SALES (est): 22.5MM
SALES (corp-wide): 1.1B **Publicly Held**
WEB: www.dolby.net
SIC: 6794 Patent buying, licensing, leasing
PA: Dolby Laboratories, Inc.
1275 Market St
San Francisco CA 94103
415 558-0200

(P-11827)
**EL POLLO LOCO HOLDINGS
INC (PA)**
3535 Harbor Blvd Ste 100, Costa Mesa
(92626-1494)
PHONE..................................714 599-5000
Stephen J Sather, *President*
Michael G Maselli, *Ch of Bd*
Laurance Roberts, *CFO*
Edward Valle, *Chief Mktg Ofcr*
Jason Weintraub,
EMP: 164
SQ FT: 29,880
SALES: 435.8MM **Publicly Held**
SIC: 6794 5812 Franchises, selling or li-
censing; Mexican restaurant

(P-11828)
LICENSALE INC
900 Bush St Apt 205, San Francisco
(94109-6379)
PHONE..................................604 681-6888
Benjamin Arazy, *President*
Mingsheng Qiu, *CFO*
EMP: 100
SALES: 25MM **Privately Held**
SIC: 6794 8748 Patent buying, licensing,
leasing; business consulting

(P-11829)
ORIGINAL PETES PIZZA INC
2001 J St, Sacramento (95811-3119)
PHONE..................................916 442-6770
Steve Presson, *President*
David Edmiston, *Vice Pres*
EMP: 50
SALES (est): 3.6MM **Privately Held**
SIC: 6794 5812 Franchises, selling or li-
censing; eating places

(P-11830)
**QUALCOMM INTERNATIONAL
INC (HQ)**
5775 Morehouse Dr, San Diego
(92121-1714)
PHONE..................................858 587-1121
Steve Altman, *President*
Derek Aberle, *Exec VP*
John Becker, *Buyer*
EMP: 4000
SALES (est): 429.4MM
SALES (corp-wide): 24.2B **Publicly Held**
SIC: 6794 Patent buying, licensing, leasing
PA: Qualcomm Incorporated
5775 Morehouse Dr
San Diego CA 92121
858 587-1121

(P-11831)
**RELIGIOUS TECHNOLOGY
CENTER**
Also Called: RTC
1710 Ivar Ave Ste 1100, Los Angeles
(90028-5575)
PHONE....................323 663-3258
Warren McShane, *President*
Barbara Griffin, *Treasurer*
Laurisse Stuckenbrock, *Admin Sec*
EMP: 67
SQ FT: 1,200
SALES (est): 10.9MM **Privately Held**
WEB: www.rtc.org
SIC: 6794 8661 Copyright buying & licensing; religious organizations

(P-11832)
**RISK MANAGEMENT
SOLUTIONS INC (DH)**
7575 Gateway Blvd Ste 300, Newark
(94560-1196)
PHONE....................510 505-2500
Karen White, *CEO*
Karl Armani, *Senior VP*
Auguste Boissonnade, *Vice Pres*
Karen Clarke, *Vice Pres*
Andrew Coburn, *Vice Pres*
EMP: 140
SALES (est): 200.1MM **Privately Held**
SIC: 6794 6411 Patent owners & lessors; insurance information & consulting services
HQ: Dmgi Land & Property Europe Ltd
5-7 Abbey Court
Exeter
844 844-9966

(P-11833)
RPX CORPORATION (HQ)
1 Market Plz Towes, San Francisco
(94105-1101)
PHONE....................866 779-7641
Dan McCurdy, *CEO*
Robert H Heath, *CFO*
Jon Knight, *Exec VP*
Mallun Yen, *Exec VP*
Martin E Roberts, *Senior VP*
EMP: 60
SQ FT: 67,000
SALES: 330.4MM
SALES (corp-wide): 8.5MM **Privately Held**
SIC: 6794 8741 Patent owners & lessors; business management

(P-11834)
TENSILICA INC (HQ)
3393 Octavius Dr, Santa Clara
(95054-3004)
P.O. Box 202769, Dallas TX (75320-2769)
PHONE....................408 986-8000
Jack Guedj, *President*
Chris Carney, *CFO*
Keith Van Sickle, *CFO*
Ashish Dixia, *Senior VP*
Beatrice Fu, *Senior VP*
EMP: 80
SQ FT: 20,000
SALES (est): 19.5MM
SALES (corp-wide): 2.1B **Publicly Held**
WEB: www.tensilica.com
SIC: 6794 9621 Patent owners & lessors; licensing agencies
PA: Cadence Design Systems, Inc.
2655 Seely Ave Bldg 5
San Jose CA 95134
408 943-1234

(P-11835)
TIVO CORPORATION (PA)
2160 Gold St, San Jose (95002-3700)
PHONE....................408 519-9100
David Shull, *President*
Michael Hawkey, *Senior VP*
Matt Milne, *Risk Mgmt Dir*
EMP: 65 EST: 1997
SQ FT: 127,000
SALES: 695.8MM **Publicly Held**
SIC: 6794 7374 Patent owners & lessors; computer graphics service

(P-11836)
**UNIVERSAL STDIOS LICENSING
LLC**
100 Universal City Plz, Universal City
(91608-1002)
PHONE....................818 695-1273
Sheetal Madadi, *Manager*
Mike Metz, *Executive*
Gabriela Kornzweig, *Admin Sec*
Evan Langweiler, *Manager*
EMP: 150
SALES (est): 4MM
SALES (corp-wide): 94.5B **Publicly Held**
SIC: 6794 Copyright buying & licensing
HQ: Nbcuniversal Media, Llc
30 Rockefeller Plz Fl 2
New York NY 10112
212 664-4444

(P-11837)
**VIACOM CONSUMER
PRODUCTS INC**
5555 Melrose Ave, Los Angeles
(90038-3989)
PHONE....................323 956-5634
Andrea Hein, *President*
Charles Phillips, *Vice Chairman*
Mike Goldman, *Senior VP*
Terry Helton, *Senior VP*
Dawn Abel, *Vice Pres*
EMP: 50 EST: 1991
SALES (est): 5.8MM
SALES (corp-wide): 12.9B **Publicly Held**
WEB: www.viacom.com
SIC: 6794 Patent buying, licensing, leasing
HQ: Paramount Pictures Corporation
5555 Melrose Ave
Los Angeles CA 90038
323 956-5000

(P-11838)
**WONDERLAND MUSIC
COMPANY INC**
500 S Buena Vista St, Burbank
(91521-0001)
PHONE....................818 840-1671
Chris Montan, *Principal*
EMP: 55
SALES (est): 3.8MM
SALES (corp-wide): 90.2B **Publicly Held**
SIC: 6794 Patent owners & lessors
HQ: Disney Enterprises, Inc.
500 S Buena Vista St
Burbank CA 91521
818 560-1000

(P-11839)
WSM INVESTMENTS LLC
Also Called: Topco Sales
3990b Heritage Oak Ct, Simi Valley
(93063-6716)
PHONE....................818 332-4600
Scott Tucker, *CEO*
Martin Tucker, *Ch of Bd*
Autumn O'Bryan, *COO*
Michael Siegel, *COO*
Louie Astorga, *Director*
▲ EMP: 145 EST: 2009
SQ FT: 150,000
SALES (est): 20.1MM
SALES (corp-wide): 15.1MM **Privately Held**
WEB: www.topco-sales.com
SIC: 6794 5122 5099 4731 Performance rights, publishing & licensing; cosmetics; novelties, durable; freight forwarding
PA: Lover Health Science And Technology Incorporated Co., Ltd.
No.1208, Taihu Ave., Economic Development Zone
Changxing County 31310
572 612-1028

**6798 Real Estate Investment
Trusts**

(P-11840)
**AMERICAN ASSETS TRUST INC
(PA)**
11455 El Cmino Real Ste 2, San Diego
(92130)
PHONE....................858 350-2600
Ernest S Rady, *Ch of Bd*

Jerry Gammieri, *Vice Pres*
EMP: 53
SALES: 330.8MM **Privately Held**
SIC: 6798 Real estate investment trusts

(P-11841)
AMERICAN HOMES TRUST
450 Camino Hermoso, San Marcos
(92078-8905)
PHONE....................619 694-7821
Jesse Bookheim, *Owner*
EMP: 100
SQ FT: 23,000
SALES: 2MM **Privately Held**
SIC: 6798 Real estate investment trusts

(P-11842)
AMERICAN REALTY ADVISORS
515 S Flower St Ste 4900, Los Angeles
(90071-2220)
PHONE....................818 545-1152
Stanley Iezman, *President*
Gregory A Blomstrand, *Principal*
Scott Darling, *Principal*
EMP: 58
SALES (est): 3.4MM **Privately Held**
SIC: 6798 Real estate investment trusts

(P-11843)
AMH PORTFOLIO ONE LLC
Also Called: Beazer Pre-Owned Rental Homes
30601 Agoura Rd Ste 200, Agoura Hills
(91301-2148)
PHONE....................480 921-4600
David P Singelyn, *CEO*
EMP: 108 EST: 2014
SALES (est): 57MM
SALES (corp-wide): 1B **Publicly Held**
SIC: 6798 Realty investment trusts
PA: American Homes 4 Rent
30601 Agoura Rd Ste 200
Agoura Hills CA 91301
805 413-5300

(P-11844)
ANCHOR LOANS LP
Also Called: Anchor Nationwide Loans
5230 Las Virgenes Rd # 105, Calabasas
(91302-3447)
PHONE....................310 395-0010
Stephen Pollack, *CEO*
Bryan Thompson, *CFO*
Matt Ediger, *Vice Pres*
Betsy Castorena, *Admin Asst*
Zaw Htet, *Web Dvlpr*
EMP: 200
SALES (est): 213.3K **Privately Held**
SIC: 6798 Real estate investment trusts

(P-11845)
BIOMED REALTY LP (HQ)
17190 Bernardo Center Dr, San Diego
(92128-7030)
PHONE....................858 485-9840
Alan D Gold, *Principal*
Denis Sullivan, *Ch Invest Ofcr*
John Bonanno, *Vice Pres*
Angela Merculief, *Director*
EMP: 50
SQ FT: 61,286
SALES: 674.6MM **Privately Held**
WEB: www.biomedrealty.com
SIC: 6798 6531 Real estate investment trusts; real estate brokers & agents
PA: Biomed Realty Trust, Inc.
17190 Bernardo Center Dr
San Diego CA 92128
858 485-9840

(P-11846)
**BROOKFIELD DTLA FUND
OFFICE**
355 S Grand Ave Ste 3300, Los Angeles
(90071-1592)
PHONE....................213 626-3300
Dennis Friedrich, *Branch Mgr*
EMP: 70
SALES (corp-wide): 43B **Publicly Held**
SIC: 6798 Real estate investment trusts
HQ: Brookfield Dtla Fund Office Trust Inc.
4 Wrld Fncl Ctr Fl 15
New York NY 10281
212 417-7064

(P-11847)
CANYON VIEW CAPITAL INC
331 Soquel Ave Ste 100, Santa Cruz
(95062-2330)
PHONE....................831 480-6335
Robert J Davidson, *CEO*
Jandro Parducho, *Principal*
Alison Ruday, *Principal*
EMP: 80
SALES: 60MM **Privately Held**
SIC: 6798 Real estate investment trusts

(P-11848)
COLONY CAPITAL INC (PA)
515 S Flower St Fl 44, Los Angeles
(90071-2201)
PHONE....................310 282-8820
Thomas J Barrack Jr, *Ch of Bd*
Mark M Hedstrom, *CEO*
Darren J Tangen, *CFO*
Douglas Crocker, *Bd of Directors*
Nancy Curtin, *Bd of Directors*
EMP: 50
SALES: 2.6B **Publicly Held**
SIC: 6798 Real estate investment trusts

(P-11849)
**CORE REALTY HOLDINGS LLC
(PA)**
1600 Dove St Ste 450, Newport Beach
(92660-2447)
PHONE....................949 863-1031
Doug Morehead, *Mng Member*
Jonathan Harmer, *CFO*
William Russ Colvin, *Chm Emeritus*
Gary Davi, *CIO*
Erin Khamis, *Training Dir*
EMP: 53
SALES (est): 31.4MM **Privately Held**
WEB: www.corerealtyholdings.com
SIC: 6798 Realty investment trusts

(P-11850)
DALLAS UNION HOTEL INC
Also Called: Sheraton
150 Corson St, Pasadena (91103-3839)
PHONE....................626 356-1000
Leo Majich, *President*
Rona Bevando, *Treasurer*
Jeff Ford, *Vice Pres*
EMP: 170
SALES (est): 4.4MM
SALES (corp-wide): 47.2MM **Privately Held**
WEB: www.sheratongranddfw.com
SIC: 6798 Real estate investment trusts
PA: Operating Engineers Funds Inc
100 Corson St Ste 222
Pasadena CA 91103
866 400-5200

(P-11851)
**DIGITAL REALTY TRUST LP
(HQ)**
4 Embarcadero Ctr # 3200, San Francisco
(94111-4188)
PHONE....................415 738-6500
A William Stein, *CEO*
Digital Realty Trust, *General Ptnr*
Jarrett B Appleby, *COO*
Andrew P Power, *CFO*
EMP: 1345
SALES: 3B **Privately Held**
SIC: 6798 Real estate investment trusts
PA: Digital Realty Trust, Inc.
4 Embarcadero Ctr # 3200
San Francisco CA 94111
415 738-6500

(P-11852)
EQUINIX INC (PA)
1 Lagoon Dr Ste 400, Redwood City
(94065-1564)
PHONE....................650 598-6000
Charles Meyers, *President*
Peter F Van Camp, *Ch of Bd*
Keith D Taylor, *CFO*
Karl Strohmeyer, *Ch Credit Ofcr*
Brandi Galvin Morandi,
EMP: 220
SALES: 5B **Publicly Held**
WEB: www.equinix.com
SIC: 6798 7374 Real estate investment trusts; computer processing services

(P-11853)
ESSEX PROPERTY TRUST INC
8795 Folsom Blvd Ste 101, Sacramento
(95826-3720)
PHONE.................................916 381-0345
Laurie Bernhard, *Branch Mgr*
EMP: 70
SALES (corp-wide): 1.4B **Privately Held**
WEB: www.breproperties.com
SIC: 6798 Real estate investment trusts
PA: Essex Property Trust, Inc.
1100 Park Pl Ste 200
San Mateo CA 94403
650 655-7800

(P-11854)
GR HARDESTER LLC
21088 Calistoga Rd, Middletown
(95461-9300)
P.O. Box 308 (95461-0308)
PHONE.................................707 987-2325
Ross Hardester,
Walter Hardester,
EMP: 127 EST: 1999
SALES (est): 5.2MM **Privately Held**
SIC: 6798 Real estate investment trusts

(P-11855)
HEALTHPEAK PROPERTIES INC (PA)
1920 Main St Ste 1200, Irvine
(92614-7230)
PHONE.................................949 407-0700
Thomas M Herzog, *CEO*
Brian G Cartwright, *Ch of Bd*
Thomas M Klaritch, *COO*
Peter A Scott, *CFO*
David B Henry, *Bd of Directors*
EMP: 65
SALES: 1.8B **Publicly Held**
WEB: www.hcpi.com
SIC: 6798 Real estate investment trusts

(P-11856)
HUDSON PACIFIC PROPERTIES INC (PA)
11601 Wilshire Blvd Fl 6, Los Angeles
(90025-0509)
PHONE.................................310 445-5700
Victor J Coleman, *Ch of Bd*
Mark T Lammas, *COO*
Latoya Ross, *Treasurer*
Richard Fried, *Bd of Directors*
Jonathan Glaser, *Bd of Directors*
EMP: 55
SALES: 728.4MM **Publicly Held**
SIC: 6798 Real estate investment trusts

(P-11857)
IMPAC MORTGAGE HOLDINGS INC (PA)
19500 Jamboree Rd Ste 100, Irvine
(92612-2426)
PHONE.................................949 475-3600
Joseph R Tomkinson, *Ch of Bd*
William S Ashmore, *President*
George A Mangiaracina, *President*
Brian Kuelbs, *CFO*
Todd R Taylor, *CFO*
EMP: 564
SQ FT: 210,000
SALES: 105MM **Publicly Held**
SIC: 6798 Real estate investment trusts

(P-11858)
IRVINE EASTGATE OFFICE II LLC
Also Called: Irvine Company Office Property
550 Newport Center Dr, Newport Beach
(92660-7011)
P.O. Box 2460 (92658-8960)
PHONE.................................949 720-2000
Pam Van Nort, *Vice Pres*
Penny Gross, *Vice Chairman*
EMP: 3000
SQ FT: 3,000
SALES (est): 331.5MM **Privately Held**
SIC: 6798 Real estate investment trusts

(P-11859)
JONES LANG LA SALLE
515 S Flower St Fl 13, Los Angeles
(90071-2201)
PHONE.................................213 239-6000
Peter Belisle, *General Mgr*

Maureen Hawley, *Sr Associate*
EMP: 80 EST: 2011
SALES (est): 6.1MM **Privately Held**
SIC: 6798 Real estate investment trusts

(P-11860)
KILROY REALTY CORPORATION (PA)
12200 W Olympic Blvd # 200, Los Angeles
(90064-1044)
PHONE.................................310 481-8400
John Kilroy, *Ch of Bd*
Jeffrey Hawken, *COO*
Tyler Rose, *CFO*
Angelica Cunningham, *Exec VP*
Stephen Rosetta, *Exec VP*
EMP: 93
SQ FT: 150,832
SALES: 747.3MM **Publicly Held**
WEB: www.kilroyrealty.com
SIC: 6798 Real estate investment trusts

(P-11861)
LBA REALTY FUND III - III LLC
3347 Michelson Dr Ste 200, Irvine
(92612-0687)
PHONE.................................949 833-0400
Perry Schonfeld, *Principal*
Aileen Chiang, *Accountant*
EMP: 99
SALES (est): 4.4MM **Privately Held**
SIC: 6798 Real estate investment trusts

(P-11862)
LBA RLTY FUND I-COMPANY IV LLC
3347 Michelson Dr Ste 950, Irvine
(92612-1692)
PHONE.................................949 955-9321
Michael Memoly,
EMP: 99
SALES (est): 7MM **Privately Held**
SIC: 6798 Real estate investment trusts

(P-11863)
MACERICH COMPANY (PA)
401 Wilshire Blvd Ste 700, Santa Monica
(90401-1452)
PHONE.................................310 394-6000
Thomas E O'Hern, *CEO*
Steven R Hash, *Ch of Bd*
Edward C Coppola, *President*
Scott W Kingsmore, *CFO*
Ann C Menard,
EMP: 80 EST: 1965
SALES: 960.3MM **Publicly Held**
WEB: www.macerich.com
SIC: 6798 Real estate investment trusts

(P-11864)
MAGUIRE PROPERTIES TWR 17 LLC
1733 Ocean Ave Fl 4, Santa Monica
(90401-3223)
PHONE.................................310 857-1100
Martin Griffiths,
EMP: 99
SALES (est): 4.5MM **Privately Held**
SIC: 6798 Real estate investment trusts

(P-11865)
MERABI & SONS LLC
14545 Friar St Ste 101, Van Nuys
(91411-2357)
PHONE.................................818 817-0006
Kambiz Merabi, *Managing Dir*
EMP: 135
SQ FT: 15,000
SALES: 1.5MM **Privately Held**
WEB: www.merabiandsons.com
SIC: 6798 Real estate investment trusts

(P-11866)
MERIDIAN INDUSTRIAL TRUST
455 Market St Ste 1700, San Francisco
(94105-2456)
PHONE.................................415 281-3900
Allen J Anderson, *CEO*
Milton K Reeder, *President*
Dennis D Higgs, *Senior VP*
EMP: 60
SALES: 66.1MM **Privately Held**
SIC: 6798 Real estate investment trusts

(P-11867)
MYRA INVESTMENT AND DEV CORP
47 W 6th St, Tracy (95376-4109)
PHONE.................................209 834-2343
Abdul Siddiqi, *President*
EMP: 55
SQ FT: 2,500
SALES (est): 3.1MM **Privately Held**
SIC: 6798 Realty investment trusts

(P-11868)
ONE EMBARCADERO CENTER VENTURE
4 Embarcadero Ctr Ste 1, San Francisco
(94111-4106)
PHONE.................................415 772-0700
Bob Pester, *Regional Mgr*
EMP: 70
SALES (est): 4.1MM
SALES (corp-wide): 2.7B **Publicly Held**
SIC: 6798 Real estate investment trusts
HQ: Boston Properties Limited Partnership
800 Boylston St Ste 1900
Boston MA 02199
617 236-3300

(P-11869)
PACIFICA COMPANIES LLC (PA)
1775 Hancock St Ste 200, San Diego
(92110-2036)
PHONE.................................619 296-9000
Deepak Israni, *President*
Ashok Israni, *Chairman*
EMP: 57
SALES (est): 442.6MM **Privately Held**
SIC: 6798 6512 Real estate investment
trusts; nonresidential building operators

(P-11870)
PMT ISSUER TRUST - FMSR
3043 Townsgate Rd, Westlake Village
(91361-3027)
PHONE.................................818 224-7028
EMP: 239 EST: 2018
SALES (est): 91.4K **Privately Held**
SIC: 6798 Real estate investment trusts
PA: Pennymac Mortgage Investment Trust
6101 Condor Dr
Moorpark CA 93021

(P-11871)
PRIME ADMINISTRATION LLC
Also Called: Prime Group
357 S Curson Ave, Los Angeles
(90036-5201)
P.O. Box 360859 (90036-1359)
PHONE.................................323 549-7155
Daniel H James, *Chairman*
John C Atwater, *CEO*
Kris Bloom, *Exec VP*
Luke Pfaffinger, *Vice Pres*
Chris Scroggin, *Vice Pres*
EMP: 522
SALES (est): 81.4MM **Privately Held**
SIC: 6798 Real estate investment trusts

(P-11872)
PROLOGIS INC (PA)
Bay 1 Pier 1, San Francisco (94111)
PHONE.................................415 394-9000
Hamid R Moghadam, *Ch of Bd*
Edward S Nekritz,
Sander Breugelmans, *Vice Pres*
Simon Cox, *Vice Pres*
Pete Crovo, *Vice Pres*
EMP: 460
SALES: 2.8B **Publicly Held**
WEB: www.amb.com
SIC: 6798 Real estate investment trusts

(P-11873)
PROLOGIS LP (HQ)
Bay 1 Pier 1, San Francisco (94111)
PHONE.................................415 394-9000
Hamid R Moghadam, *Ch of Bd*
Thomas S Olinger, *CFO*
Lori A Palazzolo,
EMP: 452
SALES: 2.8B **Publicly Held**
WEB: www.amb.com
SIC: 6798 6799 Real estate investment
trusts; real estate investors, except prop-
erty operators

PA: Prologis, Inc.
Bay 1 Pier 1
San Francisco CA 94111
415 394-9000

(P-11874)
PS BUSINESS PARKS INC (PA)
701 Western Ave, Glendale (91201-2349)
PHONE.................................818 244-8080
Joseph D Russell Jr, *CEO*
Ronald L Havner Jr, *Ch of Bd*
Maria R Hawthorne, *President*
John W Petersen, *COO*
Jeffrey D Hedges, *CFO*
◆ EMP: 77
SALES: 413.5MM **Publicly Held**
WEB: www.psbusinessparks.com
SIC: 6798 Real estate investment trusts

(P-11875)
QUAIL HILL INVESTMENTS INC
Also Called: Remax Value Properties
1124 Meridian Ave, San Jose (95125-4329)
PHONE.................................408 978-9000
EMP: 110
SALES (est): 5.9MM **Privately Held**
WEB: www.colleenanddennisb.com
SIC: 6798

(P-11876)
SCI REAL ESTATE INVSTMENTS LLC
11620 Wilshire Blvd Fl 9, Los Angeles
(90025-6820)
PHONE.................................310 361-8588
Marc J Paul,
James McCubbin,
Robert A Robotti,
EMP: 60
SQ FT: 10,000
SALES (est): 6.5MM **Privately Held**
SIC: 6798 Real estate investment trusts

(P-11877)
T C W REALTY FUND VI
Also Called: C B Richard Ellis Investors
515 S Flower St Fl 31, Los Angeles
(90071-2201)
PHONE.................................213 683-4200
Bob Zerbst, *CEO*
Debra Tonemah, *Partner*
Trust C West, *Trustee*
Kenneth Rapp, *Exec VP*
CAM Stanton, *Vice Pres*
EMP: 150
SQ FT: 24,000
SALES (est): 9.5MM **Privately Held**
SIC: 6798 Realty investment trusts

(P-11878)
TORREY AAT POINT LLC
11455 El Camino Real, San Diego
(92130-2088)
PHONE.................................858 350-2600
Ernest Rady, *CEO*
Robert Barton, *CFO*
EMP: 80
SALES (est): 4.4MM **Privately Held**
SIC: 6798 Real estate investment trusts

(P-11879)
US ADVISOR LLC
600 Trancas St, NAPA (94558-3083)
PHONE.................................707 253-9953
Kevin Fitzgerald, *Mng Member*
Kathaleen Scanlon,
EMP: 73
SQ FT: 3,200
SALES (est): 3.6MM **Privately Held**
SIC: 6798 Real estate investment trusts

(P-11880)
WESTCOAST PERFORMANCE PDTS USA
Also Called: Zantos Living Trust
3100 E Coronado St, Anaheim
(92806-1914)
PHONE.................................714 630-4411
Robert Zantos, *President*
EMP: 70
SALES (corp-wide): 5.6MM **Privately Held**
WEB: www.westcoastinc.com
SIC: 6798 Real estate investment trusts

P R O D U C T S & S V C S

PA: Westcoast Performance Products
(Usa) Inc
3100 E Coronado St
Anaheim CA
714 630-4411

(P-11881)
WESTERN ASSET MRTG CAPITL CORP
385 E Colorado Blvd, Pasadena
(91101-1923)
PHONE..................626 844-9400
Jennifer W Murphy, *President*
James W Hirschmann III, *Ch of Bd*
Elliott Neumayer, *COO*
Lisa Meyer, *CFO*
Steven Perzyna, *CFO*
EMP: 821
SALES: 49.7MM **Privately Held**
SIC: 6798 Real estate investment trusts

6799 Investors, NEC

(P-11882)
500 STARTUPS MANAGEMENT CO LLC
Also Called: Spacer.com
444 Castro St Ste 1200, Mountain View
(94041-2050)
PHONE..................650 743-4738
Dave McClure, *Mng Member*
Khailee Ng, *Managing Prtnr*
Bedy Yang, *Managing Prtnr*
Aman Verjee, *COO*
Javier Glanz, *VP Business*
EMP: 120
SALES (est): 11.4MM **Privately Held**
SIC: 6799 Investors
HQ: Spacer.Com.Au Pty Ltd
Level 3
Pyrmont NSW 2009

(P-11883)
ABS CAPITAL PARTNERS III LP
101 California St Fl 24, San Francisco
(94111-5898)
PHONE..................415 617-2800
John Mallon, *Branch Mgr*
EMP: 100 **Privately Held**
SIC: 6799 Investors
PA: Abs Capital Partners Iii, L.P.
400 E Pratt St Ste 910
Baltimore MD 21202

(P-11884)
ADG CORPORATION
1871 Market St, San Francisco
(94103-1112)
PHONE..................415 864-4090
David Levy, *President*
Gerald K Dowd, *Admin Sec*
EMP: 50 EST: 1977
SALES (est): 2.4MM **Privately Held**
WEB: www.adg.vn
SIC: 6799 Venture capital companies

(P-11885)
ADMIRALTY PARTNERS INC
1170 Somera Rd, Los Angeles
(90077-2628)
PHONE..................310 471-3772
Jon Kutler, *President*
Sara Kutler, *Administration*
EMP: 51
SALES (est): 1.8MM **Privately Held**
WEB: www.admiraltypartners.com
SIC: 6799 3675 Real estate investors, except property operators; electronic capacitors

(P-11886)
ATRIUM CAPITAL CORP
3000 Sand Hill Rd 2-130, Menlo Park
(94025-7142)
P.O. Box 307 (94026-0307)
PHONE..................650 233-7878
Russell B Pyne, *Managing Dir*
Andy Baumbusch, *Principal*
Kelli Ahn, *Marketing Staff*
EMP: 1505

SALES (est): 94.6MM **Privately Held**
WEB: www.atriumcapital.com
SIC: 6799 Investors

(P-11887)
BARCLAYS CAPITAL INC
155 Linfield Dr, Menlo Park (94025-3764)
PHONE..................650 289-6000
Stu Francis, *Branch Mgr*
Laurence Braham, *Managing Dir*
EMP: 70
SALES (corp-wide): 36.8B **Privately Held**
WEB: www.lehmanbrothers.com
SIC: 6799 Investors
HQ: Barclays Capital Inc.
745 7th Ave
New York NY 10019
212 526-7000

(P-11888)
BERTRAM CAPITAL MANAGEMENT LLC
950 Tower Ln Ste 1000, Foster City
(94404-4244)
PHONE..................650 358-5000
Jeff Drazan, *Partner*
Ryan Craig, *Partner*
David Hellier, *Partner*
Jared Ruger, *Partner*
Ingrid Swenson, *Partner*
EMP: 261
SALES (est): 46.8MM **Privately Held**
SIC: 6799 Venture capital companies

(P-11889)
BIRTCHER ANDRSON INVESTORS LLC
31910 Del Obispo St # 100, San Juan
Capistrano (92675-3182)
PHONE..................949 545-0526
Robert M Anderson,
EMP: 50
SALES (est): 2.4MM **Privately Held**
SIC: 6799 Investors

(P-11890)
BROADREACH CAPITL PARTNERS LLC
6430 W Sunset Blvd # 504, Los Angeles
(90028-7901)
PHONE..................310 691-5760
Andre Ramillon, *Branch Mgr*
EMP: 1645
SALES (corp-wide): 394.6MM **Privately Held**
SIC: 6799 Investors
PA: Broadreach Capital Partners Llc
855 El Camino Real # 350
Palo Alto CA 94301
650 331-2500

(P-11891)
BROADREACH CAPITL PARTNERS LLC
235 Montgomery St # 1018, San Francisco
(94104-2902)
PHONE..................415 354-4640
John A Foster, *Branch Mgr*
EMP: 1316
SALES (corp-wide): 394.6MM **Privately Held**
SIC: 6799 Investors
PA: Broadreach Capital Partners Llc
855 El Camino Real # 350
Palo Alto CA 94301
650 331-2500

(P-11892)
BUCHANAN FUND I LLC
620 Nwport Ctr Dr Ste 850, Newport Beach
(92660)
PHONE..................949 721-1414
Timothy Ballard, *Mng Member*
Matt Olson, *Commercial*
EMP: 75
SQ FT: 5,400
SALES (est): 3.5MM **Privately Held**
SIC: 6799 Real estate investors, except property operators

(P-11893)
BY-THE-BAY INVESTMENTS INC
37000 Fremont Blvd, Fremont
(94536-3604)
PHONE..................510 793-2581

Javier Samaniego, *Branch Mgr*
EMP: 292 **Privately Held**
SIC: 6799 Investors
PA: By-The-Bay Investments, Inc.
360 Kiely Blvd Ste 270
San Jose CA 95129

(P-11894)
CALL TO ACTION LLC (PA)
11601 Wilshire Blvd Fl 23, Los Angeles
(90025-1759)
PHONE..................310 996-7200
Colin Sapire, *Mng Member*
Richard Kam, *Marketing Mgr*
Lenny Sands,
▲ EMP: 100
SQ FT: 9,500
SALES (est): 38.3MM **Privately Held**
SIC: 6799 Investors

(P-11895)
CANESSA INVESTMENTS N V
9434 Cherokee Ln, Beverly Hills
(90210-1704)
PHONE..................310 273-8543
Allen Martin, *Manager*
EMP: 50
SALES (est): 2.7MM **Privately Held**
SIC: 6799 Investors

(P-11896)
CAPITAL BRANDS DIST LLC
11601 Wilshire Blvd Fl 23, Los Angeles
(90025-1759)
PHONE..................310 996-7200
Lenny Sands,
EMP: 70
SALES (est): 123.5K
SALES (corp-wide): 9.4MM **Privately Held**
SIC: 6799 Investors
PA: Capital Brands Holdings Inc.
11601 Wilshire Blvd Fl 23
Los Angeles CA 90025
310 996-7200

(P-11897)
CARFINANCE CAPITAL LLC
7525 Irvine Center Dr # 250, Irvine
(92618-3066)
P.O. Box 57053 (92619-7053)
PHONE..................888 227-9555
Dennis Morris,
Michael Ritter,
EMP: 540
SALES (est): 1.4MM **Privately Held**
SIC: 6799 6141 Investors; financing: automobiles, furniture, etc., not a deposit bank
PA: Flagship Credit Acceptance Llc
3 Christy Dr Ste 203
Chadds Ford PA 19317

(P-11898)
CASTER FAMILY ENTERPRISES INC
4607 Mission Gorge Pl, San Diego
(92120-4132)
PHONE..................619 287-8893
Terrence R Caster, *President*
Barbara Caster, *Vice Pres*
Fran Ching, *Executive*
Gregory Brown, *CTO*
James Poole, *Info Tech Dir*
EMP: 125 EST: 1973
SQ FT: 250,000
SALES (est): 12.9MM **Privately Held**
WEB: www.castergrp.com
SIC: 6799 6512 6531 Real estate investors, except property operators; commercial & industrial building operation; real estate agents & managers

(P-11899)
CB RICHARD ELLIS STRATEGIC PAR
515 S Flower St Ste 3100, Los Angeles
(90071-2233)
PHONE..................213 614-6862
Vance Maddocks, *Principal*
Graham D Dent, *Analyst*
EMP: 62
SALES (est): 3.9MM **Privately Held**
SIC: 6799 Investors

(P-11900)
CCCC GROWTH FUND LLC
899 El Centro St, South Pasadena
(91030-3101)
PHONE..................626 441-8770
Carl L Herrmann Jr, *Mng Member*
EMP: 61
SQ FT: 10,000
SALES (est): 5.2MM **Privately Held**
SIC: 6799 6411 Investors; insurance agents, brokers & service

(P-11901)
CLEARLAKE CAPITAL GROUP LP (PA)
233 Wilshire Blvd Ste 800, Santa Monica
(90401-1207)
PHONE..................310 400-8800
Behdad Eghbali, *Partner*
Jose Feliciano, *Partner*
Fred Ebrahemi, *General Counsel*
EMP: 258
SALES (est): 927.5MM **Privately Held**
SIC: 6799 Commodity investors

(P-11902)
CLEARVIEW CAPITAL LLC
12100 Wilshire Blvd # 800, Los Angeles
(90025-7140)
PHONE..................310 806-9555
Larry Simon, *Branch Mgr*
EMP: 879
SALES (corp-wide): 310.1MM **Privately Held**
SIC: 6799 Venture capital companies
PA: Clearview Capital, Llc
1010 Washington Blvd # 1
Stamford CT 06901
203 698-2777

(P-11903)
CORRIDOR CAPITAL LLC (PA)
12400 Walsh Ave Ste 645, Los Angeles
(90066)
PHONE..................310 442-7000
Craig L Enenstein, *CEO*
Jessamyn Davis, *CFO*
Edward A Monnier, *Managing Dir*
Glenn Garbutt, *Planning*
Cameron Reilly,
EMP: 126
SALES (est): 54.4MM **Privately Held**
SIC: 6799 Venture capital companies

(P-11904)
CRESTMONT CAPITAL LLC
2030 Main St, Irvine (92614-7219)
PHONE..................800 949-0401
Gregory Keleshian,
EMP: 250
SALES (est): 6MM **Privately Held**
SIC: 6799 Investors

(P-11905)
CVF CAPITAL PARTNERS INC
Also Called: Central Valley Fund, The
1590 Drew Ave Ste 110, Davis
(95618-7849)
PHONE..................530 757-7004
Jose C Blanco, *CEO*
Edward McNulty, *President*
Chris Carleson, *Vice Pres*
EMP: 150
SALES (est): 6.9MM **Privately Held**
SIC: 6799 Investors

(P-11906)
D E SHAW VALENCE LLC
2735 Sand Hill Rd Ste 105, Menlo Park
(94025-7126)
PHONE..................650 926-9460
Michael Lee, *Branch Mgr*
EMP: 197 **Privately Held**
SIC: 6799 Investors
PA: D. E. Shaw Valence, L.L.C.
120 W 45th St Fl 39
New York NY 10036

(P-11907)
DAVIDON FIVE STAR CORP
Also Called: Davidon Homes
1600 S Main St Ste 150, Walnut Creek
(94596-5341)
PHONE..................925 945-8000

Donald Chaiken, *Owner*
John Albini, *Vice Pres*
EMP: 80
SALES (est): 5MM **Privately Held**
SIC: 6799 Real estate investors, except property operators

(P-11908)
EASIA GOLF INVESTMENT LLC
84000 Terra Lago Pkwy, Indio
(92203-9706)
PHONE..........................760 775-2000
Jon Lee, *General Mgr*
EMP: 60
SALES (est): 42MM **Privately Held**
SIC: 6799 Investors

(P-11909)
EMP III INC
Also Called: Duarte Manor
1755 Mrtn Lthr Kng Jr Blv, Los Angeles
(90058-1522)
PHONE..........................323 231-4174
Ernie Piltil, *President*
Tim English, *CEO*
Scott Mason, *Vice Pres*
EMP: 80
SALES (est): 5.9MM **Privately Held**
SIC: 6799 Real estate investors, except property operators

(P-11910)
ENCORE CNSMR CAPITL FUND II LP (PA)
111 Pine St Ste 1825, San Francisco
(94111-5626)
PHONE..........................415 296-9850
Gary Smith, *CEO*
Kate Wallman, *Vice Pres*
Shannon Horn, *Admin Asst*
Nichole Novak, *Associate*
EMP: 88
SALES (est): 10MM **Privately Held**
SIC: 6799 Venture capital companies

(P-11911)
END-TIME MESSAGE & SUPPORT
855 W 125th St, Los Angeles (90044-3811)
PHONE..........................323 756-6252
Alvin Labostrie, *Vice Pres*
EMP: 50
SALES (est): 2.1MM **Privately Held**
SIC: 6799 Real estate investors, except property operators

(P-11912)
ENGINEERED FOREST PRODUCTS LLC
Also Called: Future Homes International
1340 Bollinger Cyn, Moraga (94556-2742)
P.O. Box 6092 (94570-6092)
PHONE..........................925 376-0881
Gregory L Koepf,
Greg Koepf, *President*
Anne-Marie Koepf, *Admin Sec*
EMP: 100
SQ FT: 5,000
SALES: 100K **Privately Held**
SIC: 6799 Venture capital companies

(P-11913)
FRANCISCO PARTNERS MGT LP (PA)
1 Letterman Dr Ste 410, San Francisco
(94129-1495)
PHONE..........................415 418-2900
Dipanjan Deb, *Partner*
Benjamin Ball, *Partner*
Neil Garfinkel, *Partner*
David Golob, *Partner*
Duncan James, *Partner*
EMP: 50
SQ FT: 15,000
SALES (est): 1.5B **Privately Held**
WEB: www.franciscopartners.com
SIC: 6799 7372 Venture capital companies; application computer software

(P-11914)
GAMUT CONSTRUCTION COMPANY INC
9340 Santa Anita Ave # 105, Rancho Cucamonga (91730-6149)
PHONE..........................909 948-0500

Mark Scarlatelli, *President*
Mark Scalatelli, *President*
Michelynn Scalatelli, *Corp Secy*
James White, *Vice Pres*
EMP: 75
SQ FT: 2,500
SALES (est): 4.8MM **Privately Held**
SIC: 6799 1521 Real estate investors, except property operators; general remodeling, single-family houses

(P-11915)
GENSTAR CAPITAL LP
4 Embarcadero Ctr # 1500, San Francisco
(94111-4106)
PHONE..........................415 834-2350
Jean-Pierre L Conte, *Partner*
Richard F Hoskins, *Partner*
Richard D Paterson, *Partner*
EMP: 560
SALES (est): 31.4MM **Privately Held**
SIC: 6799 Investors

(P-11916)
GOLDEN INTERNATIONAL
424 S Los Angeles St # 2, Los Angeles
(90013-1470)
PHONE..........................213 628-1388
GI Hanbae, *Branch Mgr*
EMP: 2968
SALES (corp-wide): 153.5MM **Privately Held**
SIC: 6799 Investors
PA: Golden International
36720 Palmdale Rd
Rancho Mirage CA 92270
760 568-1912

(P-11917)
GREEN EQUITY INVESTORS III L P
11111 Santa Monica Blvd # 2000, Los Angeles (90025-3333)
PHONE..........................310 954-0444
Jonathan D Sokoloff, *Partner*
Leonald G LP, *General Ptnr*
◆ **EMP:** 1115
SQ FT: 15,000
SALES (est): 39.8MM **Privately Held**
SIC: 6799 Investors

(P-11918)
GREEN EQUITY INVESTORS IV LP (PA)
11111 Santa Monica Blvd, Los Angeles
(90025-3333)
PHONE..........................310 954-0444
Jonathan D Sokoloff, *Mng Member*
Lily W Chang, *Controller*
EMP: 15000
SALES (est): 270.5MM **Privately Held**
SIC: 6799 Investors

(P-11919)
GSA DES PLAINES LLC
10100 Santa Monica Blvd # 2600, Los Angeles (90067-4003)
PHONE..........................310 557-5100
Daniel Goldstone, *Mng Member*
Adam Chesnoff,
EMP: 70
SQ FT: 100
SALES (est): 118.3K **Privately Held**
SIC: 6799 Real estate investors, except property operators

(P-11920)
HARVARD GRAND INV INC A CAL
2 Civic Plaza Dr, Carson (90745-2231)
PHONE..........................310 513-7560
Chang Hun Lee, *President*
Kathy Choy, *Controller*
EMP: 99 **EST:** 2007
SALES: 950K **Privately Held**
SIC: 6799 Investors

(P-11921)
HERCULES CAPITAL INC (PA)
400 Hamilton Ave Ste 310, Palo Alto
(94301-1805)
PHONE..........................650 289-3060
Scott Bluestein, *President*
Robert P Badavas, *Ch of Bd*
Harry Feuerstein, *COO*

David Lund, *CFO*
Seth Meyer, *CFO*
EMP: 67
SQ FT: 14,500
SALES: 207.7MM **Publicly Held**
WEB: www.herculestech.com
SIC: 6799 Venture capital companies

(P-11922)
IDEALAB HOLDINGS LLC (PA)
130 W Union St, Pasadena (91103-3628)
PHONE..........................626 585-6900
Bill Gross, *CEO*
Marcia Goodstein, *President*
Craig Chrisney, *CFO*
Allen Morgan, *Bd of Directors*
Kristen Ding, *Vice Pres*
EMP: 626 **EST:** 1996
SALES (est): 152.9MM **Privately Held**
WEB: www.idealab.com
SIC: 6799 5045 5734 Venture capital companies; computer software; computer software & accessories

(P-11923)
INCUBE LABS LLC (PA)
2051 Ringwood Ave, San Jose
(95131-1703)
PHONE..........................408 457-3700
Mir Imran, *CEO*
Angela Murch, *Assoc VP*
Mir Hashim, *Vice Pres*
Phil Morgan, *Vice Pres*
Ben Tranchina, *Vice Pres*
EMP: 100
SQ FT: 24,000
SALES (est): 3.1MM **Privately Held**
SIC: 6799 Venture capital companies

(P-11924)
JH CAPITAL PARTNERS LP
451 Jackson St, San Francisco
(94111-1615)
PHONE..........................415 364-0300
John Hansen, *Partner*
EMP: 50
SALES (est): 1.7MM **Privately Held**
SIC: 6799 Venture capital companies

(P-11925)
KLEINER PRKINS CFELD BYERS LLC (PA)
Also Called: Kpcb
2750 Sand Hill Rd, Menlo Park
(94025-7020)
PHONE..........................650 233-2750
Mamoon Hamid, *General Ptnr*
William Hearst III, *General Ptnr*
Tom Jermoluk, *General Ptnr*
Bill Joy, *General Ptnr*
Noah Knauf, *General Ptnr*
EMP: 163 **EST:** 1984
SQ FT: 11,000
SALES (est): 39.2MM **Privately Held**
WEB: www.kpcb.com
SIC: 6799 3691 Venture capital companies; storage batteries

(P-11926)
KLEINPARTNERS CAPITAL CORP
400 Continental Blvd # 600, El Segundo
(90245-5076)
PHONE..........................310 426-2055
Edward McMahon, *President*
Greg Klein, *Chairman*
EMP: 405
SALES (est): 13.6MM **Privately Held**
SIC: 6799 Investors

(P-11927)
KM FRESNO INVESTORS LLC
6222 Wilshire Blvd # 650, Los Angeles
(90048-5123)
PHONE..........................323 556-6600
David J Nagel, *President*
EMP: 50
SQ FT: 152,117
SALES (est): 2.8MM **Privately Held**
SIC: 6799 6531 Investors; real estate managers

(P-11928)
KOHLBERG KRAVIS ROBERTS CO LP
Also Called: K K R
2800 Sand Hill Rd Ste 200, Menlo Park
(94025-7080)
PHONE..........................650 233-6560
Michael Michelson, *Manager*
Lisa McKenzie, *Executive Asst*
Ed Ruiz, *Technology*
Maura McCabe, *Manager*
EMP: 55 **Publicly Held**
WEB: www.kkr.com
SIC: 6799 Venture capital companies
HQ: Kohlberg Kravis Roberts & Co. L.P.
9 W 57th St Ste 4200
New York NY 10019
212 750-8300

(P-11929)
LIGHTHOUSE CAPITAL FUNDING
Also Called: Light House Group, The
15332 Antioch St Ste 540, Pacific Palisades
(90272-3603)
PHONE..........................310 230-8335
Gary Leshgold, *President*
Jennifer Napier, *VP Mktg*
Michelle Madden, *Marketing Staff*
Oliver Babcock, *Associate*
EMP: 50
SALES (est): 5.1MM **Privately Held**
WEB: www.lighthousecapitalfunding.net
SIC: 6799 Venture capital companies

(P-11930)
M & H REALTY PARTNERS LP
353 Sacramento St Fl 21, San Francisco
(94111-3620)
PHONE..........................415 693-9000
Peter Merlone, *Managing Prtnr*
EMP: 70
SALES (est): 4.2MM **Privately Held**
SIC: 6799 Real estate investors, except property operators

(P-11931)
MARINE HOLDING US CORP
6000 Condor Dr, Moorpark (93021-2601)
PHONE..........................805 529-2000
Francois Mirallie, *President*
Joel Silva, *CFO*
Mark Cortell, *Vice Pres*
Anita Cox, *Asst Treas*
Elisa Mojica, *Asst Sec*
EMP: 650
SALES (est): 17.1MM
SALES (corp-wide): 2.4B **Publicly Held**
SIC: 6799 Investors
HQ: Zodiac Pool Solutions Llc
2882 Whiptail Loop # 100
Carlsbad CA 92010
760 599-9600

(P-11932)
MARLIN EQUITY PARTNERS III LP (PA)
338 Pier Ave, Hermosa Beach
(90254-3617)
PHONE..........................310 364-0100
David McGovern, *Mng Member*
George Kase,
Peter Spasov,
Nick Kaiser, *Mng Member*
EMP: 230
SALES (est): 15.7MM **Privately Held**
SIC: 6799 Venture capital companies

(P-11933)
MATSUSHITA INTERNATIONAL CORP (PA)
1141 Via Callejon, San Clemente
(92673-6230)
PHONE..........................949 498-1000
Hiroyuki Matsushita, *President*
EMP: 80
SALES (est): 22.8MM **Privately Held**
SIC: 6799 3711 3714 Real estate investors, except property operators; automobile assembly, including specialty automobiles; motor vehicle parts & accessories

(P-11934)
MCMILLIN COMPANIES LLC (PA)
Also Called: McMillin Homes
2750 Womble Rd Ste 102, San Diego (92106-6114)
PHONE.................................619 477-4117
Scott McMillin, *CEO*
Mark D McMillin, *President*
Robin Lewis, *Vice Pres*
Lucelia Rios, *Accountant*
EMP: 80 **EST:** 1998
SALES: 50MM **Privately Held**
WEB: www.mcmillinrealty.com
SIC: 6799 Real estate investors, except property operators

(P-11935)
MSD CAPITAL LP
100 Wilshire Blvd # 1450, Santa Monica (90401-1110)
PHONE.................................310 458-3600
John Sauter, *Manager*
EMP: 52
SALES (corp-wide): 34.4MM **Privately Held**
SIC: 6799 Venture capital companies; real estate investors, except property operators; security speculators for own account
PA: Msd Capital L.P.
645 5th Ave Fl 21
New York NY 10022
212 303-1650

(P-11936)
N S B N INVESTMENTS LLC
9454 Wilshire Blvd Fl 4, Beverly Hills (90212-2907)
PHONE.................................310 273-2501
Ken Miles,
Maris Bredt, *Admin Asst*
Joey Frou, *Info Tech Mgr*
William Esensten,
William D Esensten,
EMP: 75
SALES (est): 3.7MM **Privately Held**
WEB: www.nsbn.com
SIC: 6799 Investors

(P-11937)
NEW CIVIC COMPANY LTD
870 Market St Ste 1168, San Francisco (94102-2916)
PHONE.................................415 986-1668
Zhonggen LI, *President*
Jun Chen, *Vice Pres*
EMP: 164
SALES (est): 9.5MM **Privately Held**
SIC: 6799 Investors

(P-11938)
NNN REALTY INVESTORS LLC
19700 Fairchild Ste 300, Irvine (92612-2515)
PHONE.................................714 667-8252
Jeffrey T Hanson, *President*
Michael Van Dusen, *Senior VP*
Fred D Cochran, *Vice Pres*
Todd A Mikles,
EMP: 458 **EST:** 1998
SQ FT: 18,800
SALES (est): 128.5K **Privately Held**
SIC: 6799 6531 Investors; real estate managers

(P-11939)
NORWEST VENTURE PARTNERS VI LP
525 University Ave # 800, Palo Alto (94301-1922)
PHONE.................................650 289-2243
EMP: 60
SALES (est): 2.3MM
SALES (corp-wide): 101B **Publicly Held**
SIC: 6799 Venture capital companies
PA: Wells Fargo & Company
420 Montgomery St Frnt
San Francisco CA 94104
866 249-3302

(P-11940)
NRLL LLC
Also Called: Land Disposition Company
1 Mauchly, Irvine (92618-2305)
PHONE.................................949 768-7777
Robert D Friedman,
Jeffrey Friedman,
EMP: 50
SQ FT: 18,000
SALES (est): 4MM
SALES (corp-wide): 47.1MM **Privately Held**
WEB: www.landdisposition.com
SIC: 6799 Real estate investors, except property operators
PA: Nrp Holding Co., Inc.
1 Mauchly
Irvine CA 92618
949 583-1000

(P-11941)
NUMERO UNO MARKET
4373 S Vermont Ave, Los Angeles (90037-2411)
PHONE.................................323 231-9403
Philip Lopez, *President*
EMP: 80
SALES (corp-wide): 30MM **Privately Held**
SIC: 6799 Investors
PA: Numero Uno Market
701 E Jefferson Blvd
Los Angeles CA 90011
323 846-5842

(P-11942)
NUMERO UNO MARKET
9127 S Figueroa St, Los Angeles (90003-3905)
PHONE.................................213 381-1734
EMP: 80
SALES (corp-wide): 30MM **Privately Held**
SIC: 6799 Investors
PA: Numero Uno Market
701 E Jefferson Blvd
Los Angeles CA 90011
323 846-5842

(P-11943)
NUTRITION PARENT LLC
1950 University Ave # 350, East Palo Alto (94303-2250)
PHONE.................................650 321-4910
Rich Lawson, *Principal*
EMP: 1398
SALES (est): 41.2MM **Privately Held**
SIC: 6799 Investors

(P-11944)
OTTS ASIA
Also Called: Newshire Investment
10015 Baring Cross St, Los Angeles (90044-4511)
PHONE.................................562 259-3447
Asia Otts, *Owner*
Devon Moorer, *Owner*
EMP: 80
SALES (est): 1.5MM **Privately Held**
SIC: 6799 Investors

(P-11945)
P-WAVE HOLDINGS LLC
10877 Wilshire Blvd, Los Angeles (90024-4341)
PHONE.................................310 209-3010
Alec Gores,
EMP: 2179 **EST:** 2012
SALES (est): 38.1MM **Privately Held**
SIC: 6799 Investors

(P-11946)
PARTHENON CAPITAL LLC
4 Embarcadero Ctr # 2500, San Francisco (94111-4106)
PHONE.................................415 913-3900
Robert Hood, *Principal*
Eli Berlin, *Vice Pres*
Lesly Schlender, *Research*
EMP: 1041
SALES (corp-wide): 219.1MM **Privately Held**
WEB: www.parthenoncapital.com
SIC: 6799 Venture capital companies
PA: Parthenon Capital, Llc
1 Federal St Fl 21
Boston MA 02110
617 960-4000

(P-11947)
PEDESTAL CAPITAL II LLC
13111 Sycamore Dr, Norwalk (90650-8339)
PHONE.................................562 863-5555

Rui Zhao, *Principal*
Adam Stanchina, *Principal*
EMP: 80
SALES (est): 3.5MM **Privately Held**
SIC: 6799 Investors

(P-11948)
PLUG & PLAY LLC
370 Convention Way, Redwood City (94063-1405)
PHONE.................................650 722-2195
Saeed Amidi, *Branch Mgr*
EMP: 70
SALES (corp-wide): 20MM **Privately Held**
SIC: 6799 7389 Investors; office facilities & secretarial service rental
PA: Plug & Play, Llc
440 N Wolfe Rd
Sunnyvale CA 94085
408 524-1400

(P-11949)
POULIN CORPORATION (PA)
Also Called: Liberty Ambulance
111 S Mahan St, Ridgecrest (93555-5430)
PHONE.................................760 375-6531
Cheryl Poulin, *President*
Brandalyn Sonnenberg, *Corp Secy*
EMP: 75
SALES (est): 7.6MM **Privately Held**
SIC: 6799 Real estate investors, except property operators

(P-11950)
PYRAMID PEAK CORPORATION
450 Nwport Ctr Dr Ste 650, Newport Beach (92660)
PHONE.................................949 769-8600
Cindy Ragsdale, *President*
Cindy Brown, *COO*
EMP: 70
SALES (est): 7.9MM **Privately Held**
SIC: 6799 Investors

(P-11951)
R H O CAPITAL PARTNERS INC
525 University Ave # 1350, Palo Alto (94301-1934)
PHONE.................................650 463-0300
Mark Leschley, *Principal*
Joshua Ruch, *Partner*
EMP: 50
SALES (est): 3.3MM **Privately Held**
SIC: 6799 Venture capital companies

(P-11952)
REGENT LP (PA)
9720 Wilshire Blvd, Beverly Hills (90212-2021)
PHONE.................................310 299-4100
Michael A Reinstein, *CEO*
Roxanna Sassanian, *CFO*
EMP: 85
SALES (est): 38.3MM **Privately Held**
SIC: 6799 Investors

(P-11953)
ROLL PROPERTIES INTL INC
Also Called: Paramout Farms
13646 Highway 33, Lost Hills (93249-9719)
PHONE.................................661 797-6500
Bill Bowers, *Manager*
Patty Mendez, *Export Mgr*
EMP: 121
SALES (corp-wide): 27.2MM **Privately Held**
WEB: www.roll.com
SIC: 6799 Real estate investors, except property operators
PA: Roll Properties International, Inc.
11444 W Olympic Blvd # 10
Los Angeles CA 90064
310 966-5700

(P-11954)
RUSTIC CANYON GROUP LLC
Also Called: Rustic Canyon Partners
201 Santa Monica Blvd # 500, Santa Monica (90401-2213)
PHONE.................................310 998-8000
Nate Redmond, *Managing Prtnr*
Mike Shundoff, *Administration*
David Kirkland, *Analyst*
John Babcock,
Lee Bailey,

EMP: 75
SALES (est): 6.5MM **Privately Held**
WEB: www.rusticanyon.com
SIC: 6799 Venture capital companies

(P-11955)
SEQUOIA CAPITAL OPERATIONS LLC
2800 Sand Hill Rd Ste 100, Menlo Park (94025-7079)
PHONE.................................650 854-3927
Donald Valentine, *General Ptnr*
Doug Leone, *General Ptnr*
Tom McMurray, *General Ptnr*
Bryan Schreier, *General Ptnr*
Thomas Stephenson, *General Ptnr*
EMP: 89
SQ FT: 6,000
SALES (est): 46.7MM **Privately Held**
WEB: www.sequoiacap.com
SIC: 6799 Venture capital companies

(P-11956)
STEELPOINT CAPITAL PARTNERS LP
2081 Faraday Ave, Carlsbad (92008-7230)
PHONE.................................858 764-8700
James A Caccavo, *General Ptnr*
Adam Dell, *General Ptnr*
Scott Tierney, *General Ptnr*
Jim Sullivan, *Partner*
EMP: 80
SALES (est): 8MM
SALES (corp-wide): 24.7MM **Privately Held**
SIC: 6799 Investors
PA: Moore Capital Management, Lp
11 Times Sq Ste 36
New York NY 10036
212 782-7000

(P-11957)
SUNSTONE HOTEL INVESTORS LLC (PA)
200 Spectrum Dr Fl 21, Irvine (92618)
PHONE.................................949 330-4000
Ken Cruse, *CEO*
Robert A Alter, *Ch of Bd*
Jon D Kline, *President*
David Sloan, *President*
Bryan Giglia, *CFO*
EMP: 56
SALES (est): 51.9MM **Privately Held**
WEB: www.sunstonehotels.com
SIC: 6799 7011 Real estate investors, except property operators; hotels & motels

(P-11958)
TANO CAPITAL LLC
1 Franklin Pkwy, San Mateo (94403-1906)
PHONE.................................650 212-0330
Chuck Johnson, *Founder*
Terry Robacker, *COO*
Candace Lyche, *Officer*
Peter Dabrowski, *Managing Dir*
Kamran Siddiqui, *General Mgr*
EMP: 50
SALES (est): 4.8MM **Privately Held**
SIC: 6799 Investors

(P-11959)
TC PROPERTY MGT A CALIFORNI
1224 Cottonwood St Ofc, Woodland (95695-4349)
PHONE.................................530 666-5799
Ted Caldwell, *President*
EMP: 80 **EST:** 1982
SALES (est): 4.1MM **Privately Held**
SIC: 6799 6531 Real estate investors, except property operators; real estate managers

(P-11960)
TCG CAPITAL MANAGEMENT LP
1733 Ocean Ave Ste 300, Santa Monica (90401-3265)
PHONE.................................310 633-2900
Peter Chernin, *CEO*
EMP: 135
SALES (est): 2.4MM **Privately Held**
SIC: 6799 Investors

▲ = Import ▼=Export
◆ =Import/Export

(P-11961)
TCMI INC (PA)
Also Called: Technology Crossover Ventures
250 Middlefield Rd, Menlo Park
(94025-3560)
PHONE..............................650 614-8200
Nari Ansari, *Principal*
Ric Fenton, *General Ptnr*
Jay Hoag, *President*
Richard Kimball, *CEO*
Nicholas Crowne, *Vice Pres*
EMP: 50 EST: 1995
SQ FT: 2,700
SALES (est): 25.3MM **Privately Held**
WEB: www.tcv.com
SIC: 6799 Venture capital companies

(P-11962)
**TENNENBAUM CAPITL
PARTNERS LLC (HQ)**
Also Called: T C P
2951 28th St Ste 1000, Santa Monica
(90405-2993)
PHONE..............................310 566-1000
Lee Landrum, *Managing Prtnr*
Michael Leitner, *Managing Prtnr*
Howard Levkowitz, *Managing Prtnr*
Philip Tseng, *Managing Prtnr*
Rajneesh Vig, *Managing Prtnr*
EMP: 67
SQ FT: 15,850
SALES (est): 175.9MM **Publicly Held**
SIC: 6799 Venture capital companies

(P-11963)
THOMA BRAVO LLC
600 Montgomery St Fl 32, San Francisco
(94111-2807)
PHONE..............................415 263-3660
Seth Boro, *Branch Mgr*
Brian Jaffee, *Vice Pres*
Peter Stefanski, *Vice Pres*
Lea Brookes, *Consultant*
Andy Lueke, *Associate*
EMP: 497 **Privately Held**
SIC: 6799 Venture capital companies
PA: Thoma Bravo, Llc
150 N Riverside Plz # 2800
Chicago IL 60606

(P-11964)
ULTIMATE CREATIONS LLC
516 W Shaw Ave Ste 200, Fresno
(93704-2515)
PHONE..............................559 221-4936
Duwayne Turner,
EMP: 51
SALES (est): 1.2MM **Privately Held**
SIC: 6799 8742 Investors; real estate consultant

(P-11965)
**VANTAGEPOINT CAPITAL
PARTNERS (PA)**
1111 Bayhill Dr Ste 220, San Bruno
(94066-3198)
PHONE..............................650 866-3100
Alan E Salzman, *Partner*
James Marver, *Partner*
EMP: 70
SALES (est): 4.7MM **Privately Held**
SIC: 6799 Venture capital companies

(P-11966)
**VANTAGEPOINT MANAGEMENT
INC (PA)**
Also Called: Vantagepoint Capital Partners
1111 Bayhill Dr Ste 220, San Bruno
(94066-3198)
PHONE..............................650 866-3100
Alan E Salzman, *CEO*
Harold Friedman, *CFO*
Tom Bevilacqua, *Managing Dir*
Neil Wolff, *Managing Dir*
James D Marver, *Admin Sec*
EMP: 65
SQ FT: 21,166
SALES (est): 14.4MM **Privately Held**
SIC: 6799 Venture capital companies

(P-11967)
WEDGEWOOD INC (PA)
2015 Manhattan Beach Blvd # 100, Redondo Beach (90278-1226)
PHONE..............................310 640-3070
Gregory L Geiser, *CEO*
Eric Borgeson, *Owner*
Bruce H McLain, *Partner*
Jim Henry, *Vice Chairman*
Steve Meilicke, *CFO*
EMP: 77
SQ FT: 3,200
SALES (est): 17.4MM **Privately Held**
SIC: 6799 Real estate investors, except property operators

(P-11968)
WESTAR CAPITAL ASSOC II LLC
949 S Coast Dr, Costa Mesa (92626-7737)
PHONE..............................714 481-5160
George Argyros, *Branch Mgr*
EMP: 1184
SALES (corp-wide): 110.4MM **Privately Held**
SIC: 6799 Investors
PA: Westar Capital Associates Ii, Llc
949 S Coast Dr Ste 170
Costa Mesa CA 92626
714 481-5160

(P-11969)
WESTCORE DELTA LLC
Also Called: Westcore Croydon
4350 La Jolla Village Dr # 900, San Diego
(92122-1246)
P.O. Box 844405, Los Angeles (90084-4405)
PHONE..............................858 625-4100
Don Ankeny, *CEO*
Marc Brutten, *Ch of Bd*
EMP: 60
SQ FT: 14,000
SALES (est): 6MM **Privately Held**
SIC: 6799 Real estate investors, except property operators

(P-11970)
**WESTPORT CAPITAL
PARTNERS LLC**
2121 Rosecrans Ave # 4325, El Segundo
(90245-4744)
PHONE..............................310 294-1234
Russel S Bernard, *Branch Mgr*
Harry Ramnath, *Technology*
EMP: 53 **Privately Held**
SIC: 6799 Investors
PA: Westport Capital Partners Llc
40 Danbury Rd
Wilton CT 06897

7011 Hotels, Motels & Tourist Courts

(P-11972)
1000 AGUAJITO OP CO LLC
Also Called: Hilton Garden Inn Monterey
1000 Aguajito Rd, Monterey (93940-4801)
PHONE..............................831 373-6141
Jayson Zimmer, *General Mgr*
EMP: 77
SALES (est): 3.2MM **Privately Held**
SIC: 7011 Hotels & motels

(P-11973)
**120 SOUTH LOS ANGELES
STREET H**
Also Called: Kyoto Grand Hotel
120 S Los Angeles St, Los Angeles
(90012-3724)
PHONE..............................213 629-1200
Shannon King,

(P-11971)
WNC HOUSING LP
17782 Sky Park Cir, Irvine (92614-6404)
PHONE..............................714 662-5565
Willfred Cooper, *President*
Tom Riha, *CFO*
EMP: 50
SALES (est): 4.4MM **Privately Held**
SIC: 6799 Real estate investors, except property operators

Joseph Kuhn,
EMP: 99
SALES (est): 4.3MM **Privately Held**
SIC: 7011 Hotels

(P-11974)
1260 BB PROPERTY LLC
Also Called: Four Ssons Rsort Santa Barbara
1260 Channel Dr, Santa Barbara
(93108-2805)
PHONE..............................805 969-2261
Isadore Sharp, *Chairman*
J Allen Smith, *President*
Karen Earp, *General Mgr*
Graham Crossley, *Finance Dir*
Diane Kildun, *Human Res Dir*
EMP: 500 EST: 1986
SALES (est): 36.9MM **Privately Held**
SIC: 7011 Hotels

(P-11975)
15TH & L INVESTORS LLC
1121 15th St, Sacramento (95814-4011)
PHONE..............................916 267-6805
Anthony R Giannoni, *Mng Member*
Shelly Moranville, *Mng Member*
EMP: 55
SALES (est): 2.8MM **Privately Held**
SIC: 7011 Hotel, franchised

(P-11976)
1651 TIBURON HOTEL LLC
Also Called: Lodge At Tiburon
1651 Tiburon Blvd, Belvedere Tiburon
(94920-2511)
PHONE..............................401 946-4600
James Procaccianti,
EMP: 80
SALES (est): 324.3K **Privately Held**
SIC: 7011 Hotels

(P-11977)
1835 COLUMBIA STREET LP
Also Called: Porto Vista Hotel
1835 Columbia St, San Diego
(92101-2505)
PHONE..............................619 564-3993
Moe Siry, *Partner*
Arnold Ming, *Finance*
Dave Threet, *Sales Staff*
Tom McMahan, *Director*
EMP: 80 EST: 1992
SALES: 5MM **Privately Held**
SIC: 7011 Hotels

(P-11978)
23627 CALABASAS ROAD LLC
Also Called: Anza A Calabasas Hotel, The
23627 Calabasas Rd, Calabasas
(91302-1502)
PHONE..............................818 222-5300
Mona Rigdon, *Principal*
James McCrimmon, *Principal*
EMP: 65
SALES (est): 696.6K **Privately Held**
SIC: 7011 Hotels

(P-11979)
417 STOCKTON ST LLC
1180 S Beverly Dr Ste 508, Los Angeles
(90035-1157)
PHONE..............................323 327-9656
Jim Ciki, *Finance*
EMP: 60
SALES (est): 429.7K **Privately Held**
SIC: 7011 Hotels & motels

(P-11980)
425 NORTH POINT STREET LLC
Also Called: Tuscan Inn
101 California St Ste 950, San Francisco
(94111-5826)
PHONE..............................800 648-4626
Jan Misch,
EMP: 99
SALES (est): 5.6MM **Privately Held**
SIC: 7011 Hotels

(P-11981)
**4290 EL CAMINO PROPERTIES
LP**
Also Called: Cabana Hotel
4290 El Camino Real, Palo Alto
(94306-4404)
PHONE..............................650 857-0787
Bhupendra B Patel, *Owner*

Elias Samonte, *Director*
EMP: 146
SALES (est): 5.2MM **Privately Held**
SIC: 7011 Hotels

(P-11982)
48123 CA INVESTORS LLC
Also Called: Ventana Inn & Spa
48123 Highway 1, Big Sur (93920-9538)
PHONE..............................831 667-2331
Kent L Colwell, *Mng Member*
Bruce Card, *Engineer*
EMP: 152
SALES (est): 11.6MM **Privately Held**
WEB: www.ventanainn.com
SIC: 7011 5812 Bed & breakfast inn; eating places

(P-11983)
495 GEARY LLC
Also Called: Clift Hotels
495 Geary St, San Francisco (94102-1222)
PHONE..............................415 775-4700
Mary Coller, *Controller*
EMP: 220
SALES (est): 2.3MM **Privately Held**
SIC: 7011 Hotels
HQ: Morgans Hotel Group Co. Llc
475 10th Ave Fl 11
New York NY 10018
212 277-4100

(P-11984)
51ST ST & 8TH AVE CORP
Also Called: Loews Coronado Bay Resort
4000 Coronado Bay Rd, Coronado
(92118-3290)
PHONE..............................619 424-4000
Johnathan M Tish, *Principal*
Barbara Vale, *Executive*
Brigitte Lundrigan, *Exec Dir*
Sarah Moran, *Pub Rel Dir*
Roy Craft, *Marketing Staff*
▲ EMP: 550
SALES (est): 33.6MM **Privately Held**
SIC: 7011 Hotels

(P-11985)
**550 FLOWER ST OPERATIONS
LLC**
Also Called: Standard Hotel, The
550 S Flower St, Los Angeles
(90071-2501)
PHONE..............................213 892-8080
Andre Balaz,
Laurent Fraticelli, *Manager*
EMP: 200
SQ FT: 172,197
SALES (est): 6MM **Privately Held**
WEB: www.standardhotel.com
SIC: 7011 5813 5812 Hotels; drinking places; eating places

(P-11986)
5TH AVENUE PARTNERS LLC
1047 5th Ave, San Diego (92101-5101)
PHONE..............................619 515-3000
Stephen Rebeil,
EMP: 300
SALES (est): 3.4MM **Privately Held**
SIC: 7011 Hotels

(P-11987)
6417 SELMA HOTEL LLC
Also Called: Dream Hollywood
6417 Selma Ave, Los Angeles
(90028-7310)
PHONE..............................323 844-6417
Richard Heyman, *Mng Member*
Danny Benaderet, *Sales Staff*
Andrea Schneider, *Director*
EMP: 250
SALES: 6.8MM **Privately Held**
SIC: 7011 Hotels

(P-11988)
8110 AERO HOLDING LLC
Also Called: Sheraton
8110 Aero Dr, San Diego (92123-1715)
PHONE..............................858 277-8888
Lucy Burni, *Mng Member*
Nabih Geha, *Principal*
EMP: 210

PRODUCTS & SVCS

SALES (est): 10.5MM **Privately Held**
WEB: www.sheratonfourpointshotel.com
SIC: 7011 5813 5812 Hotels & motels;
drinking places; eating places

(P-11989)
901 WEST OLYMPIC BLVD LP
Also Called: Courtyard & Residence Inn La
901 W Olympic Blvd, Los Angeles
(90015-1327)
PHONE...................................347 992-5707
Greg Steinhauer, *Partner*
Homer Williams, *Partner*
EMP: 110
SQ FT: 286,000
SALES (est): 11.5MM **Privately Held**
SIC: 7011 Hotels & motels

(P-11990)
A J ESPRIT
Also Called: Comfort Inn
5102 N Harbor Dr, San Diego
(92106-2356)
PHONE...................................619 223-8171
A J Esprit, *Manager*
EMP: 50
SALES (est): 1.1MM **Privately Held**
WEB: www.comfortinnattheharbor.com
SIC: 7011 Hotels & motels

(P-11991)
ACCOR BUS & LEISURE N AMER LLC
Also Called: Hotel Sofitel
223 Twin Dolphin Dr, Redwood City
(94065-1414)
PHONE...................................650 598-9000
John Hutar, *Manager*
Gabriela Salazar, *Regional Mgr*
Ron Ram, *Engineer*
Rex Umbay, *Engineer*
EMP: 200
SALES (corp-wide): 1.1B **Privately Held**
SIC: 7011 Hotels & motels
HQ: Accor Business And Leisure North
America, Llc
3470 Nw 82nd Ave Ste 600
Doral FL 33122

(P-11992)
ACCOR CORP
Also Called: Sofitel Los Angeles
8555 Beverly Blvd, Los Angeles
(90048-3303)
PHONE...................................310 278-5444
Gunter Zweimuller, *Manager*
Eric McCauley, *Receiver*
Vincent Lelay, *Vice Pres*
Stephane Lombard, *Vice Pres*
David Hamerman, *Security Dir*
EMP: 200
SQ FT: 380,000
SALES (est): 7.9MM
SALES (corp-wide): 1.1B **Privately Held**
SIC: 7011 5812 Hotels; eating places
PA: Accor
82 Rue Henry Farman
Issy-Les-Moulineaux 92130
146 429-193

(P-11993)
ACCOR SERVICES US LLC
101 Wilshire Blvd, Santa Monica
(90401-1106)
PHONE...................................310 319-3122
Karl Buchta, *General Mgr*
Walter Moerbe, *Controller*
EMP: 275
SALES (corp-wide): 1.1B **Privately Held**
SIC: 7011 Hotels
HQ: Accor Services Us Llc
950 Mason St
San Francisco CA 94108
415 772-5000

(P-11994)
ACCOR SERVICES US LLC (HQ)
Also Called: Fairmont Hotel
950 Mason St, San Francisco
(94108-6000)
PHONE...................................415 772-5000
April Schizley, *Manager*
Laura Chapman, *Associate Dir*
Josh Miller, *General Mgr*
April Sheesley, *Executive Asst*

Emiko Shibuya, *Technology*
EMP: 1000
SQ FT: 2,100
SALES (est): 258.2MM
SALES (corp-wide): 1.1B **Privately Held**
SIC: 7011 Hotels
PA: Accor
82 Rue Henry Farman
Issy-Les-Moulineaux 92130
146 429-193

(P-11995)
AGUA CLNTE BAND CHILLA INDIANS
Also Called: Agua Caliente Casino & Resort
32250 Bob Hope Dr, Rancho Mirage
(92270-2704)
PHONE...................................760 321-2000
Ken Kettler, *Branch Mgr*
Frank Charolla, *CFO*
Art Huizar, *Business Anlyst*
David McCarthy, *Business Anlyst*
Susan Wells, *Engineer*
EMP: 1000
SALES (corp-wide): 202.5MM **Privately Held**
WEB: www.hotwatercasino.com
SIC: 7011 Casino hotel
PA: Agua Caliente Band Of Cahuilla Indi-
ans
5401 Dinah Shore Dr
Palm Springs CA 92264
760 699-6800

(P-11996)
AGUA CLNTE BAND CHILLA INDIANS
Also Called: Spa Resort Casino
401 E Amado Rd, Palm Springs
(92262-6403)
PHONE...................................800 854-1279
Ramona Grinager, *Principal*
Savannah Cook, *Manager*
Vicki Chavez, *Supervisor*
EMP: 1000
SALES (corp-wide): 202.5MM **Privately Held**
SIC: 7011 7991 Casino hotel; spas
PA: Agua Caliente Band Of Cahuilla Indi-
ans
5401 Dinah Shore Dr
Palm Springs CA 92264
760 699-6800

(P-11997)
AL ANWA USA INCORPORATED
Also Called: Marina International Hotel
4200 Admiralty Way, Marina Del Rey
(90292-5422)
PHONE...................................310 301-2000
Mohammed Khan, *Manager*
EMP: 120
SALES (corp-wide): 2.7MM **Privately Held**
WEB: www.marinaintlhotel.com
SIC: 7011 Hotels
PA: Al Anwa Usa Incorporated
2200 Nw 50th St Ste 240
Oklahoma City OK

(P-11998)
ALADDIN SONORA MOTOR INN
14260 Mono Way, Sonora (95370-8654)
PHONE...................................209 533-4971
David E Kalash, *Owner*
EMP: 50
SALES (est): 1.1MM **Privately Held**
WEB: www.aladdininn.com
SIC: 7011 5812 Motor inn; eating places

(P-11999)
ALBION RIVER INN INCORPORATED
3790 N Highway 1, Albion (95410-9781)
P.O. Box 100 (95410-0100)
PHONE...................................707 937-1919
Peter Wells, *President*
Flurry Healy, *Vice Pres*
EMP: 65
SQ FT: 15,000
SALES (est): 3.5MM **Privately Held**
WEB: www.albionriverinn.com
SIC: 7011 Inns

(P-12000)
ALLIANCE RVRSIDE HSPTALITY LLC
Also Called: Courtyard By Mrriott Riverside
21520 Yorba Linda Blvd, Yorba Linda
(92887-3762)
PHONE...................................949 229-3168
Chiangsun Wang, *Mng Member*
EMP: 50
SALES: 3.8MM **Privately Held**
SIC: 7011 Hotels & motels

(P-12001)
ALOFT ONTARIO-RANCHO CUCAMONGA
Also Called: Ihr Grnbuck Rncho Ccmnga
Ventr
10480 4th St, Rancho Cucamonga
(91730-5893)
PHONE...................................909 484-2018
Cristina Riveroll, *Owner*
Yani Duran, *Director*
EMP: 55
SALES (est): 3MM **Privately Held**
SIC: 7011 Hotels

(P-12002)
ALPINE MEADOWS SKI AREA
Also Called: Alpine Meadows Ski Resort
2600 Alpine Meadows Rd, Alpine Meadows
(96146-9854)
PHONE...................................530 583-4232
John Cumming, *President*
Rick D Vaux, *CFO*
Nick Badami, *Admin Sec*
Jessica Richitelli, *Manager*
▲ EMP: 50
SQ FT: 30,000
SALES (est): 5MM **Privately Held**
WEB: www.skialpine.com
SIC: 7011 Ski lodge; resort hotel
HQ: The Squaw Valley Development Com-
pany
1960 Squaw Valley Rd
Olympic Valley CA 96146
530 452-6985

(P-12003)
AMERICAN PROPERTY MANAGEMENT
Also Called: Pleasanton Hilton Hotel
7050 Johnson Dr, Pleasanton
(94588-3328)
PHONE...................................925 463-8000
Han-Ching Lin, *President*
Hui-Ying Chou, *Vice Pres*
EMP: 190
SQ FT: 191,112
SALES (est): 9.1MM **Privately Held**
SIC: 7011 5813 5812 Hotels & motels;
drinking places; eating places

(P-12004)
AMERICAN PRPRTY-MNAGEMENT CORP
Also Called: U. S. Grant Hotel
326 Broadway, San Diego (92101-4812)
PHONE...................................619 232-3121
John Gallegon, *Manager*
EMP: 200
SALES (corp-wide): 183MM **Privately Held**
WEB: www.americanpropertymanagement-
corp.com
SIC: 7011 Hotels & motels
PA: American Property-Management Cor-
poration
8910 University Center Ln # 100
San Diego CA 92122
858 964-5500

(P-12005)
AMGREEN-KARENA HT PARTNR LTD (PA)
Also Called: Radisson Inn
5743 Corsa Ave Ste 200, Westlake Village
(91362-7312)
PHONE...................................818 707-9494
Jerald Greenstein, *Partner*
Joe Amorosa, *Partner*
EMP: 93
SALES (est): 3.6MM **Privately Held**
SIC: 7011 Hotels & motels

(P-12006)
ANAHEIM CA LLC
Also Called: Doubltree Ht Anhim-Orange Cnty
100 The City Dr S, Orange (92868-3204)
PHONE...................................714 634-4500
Denise Pflum, *Manager*
EMP: 65
SALES (est): 6.1MM **Privately Held**
SIC: 7011 Hotels & motels

(P-12007)
ANAHEIM HOTEL LLC
Also Called: Sheraton Pk Ht At Anheim Rsort
1855 S Harbor Blvd, Anaheim
(92802-3509)
PHONE...................................714 750-1811
Russ Cox, *Manager*
EMP: 200
SALES (est): 2.7MM **Privately Held**
SIC: 7011 Hotels & motels
PA: Anaheim Hotel, Llc
575 E Parkcntr Blvd 500
Boise ID 83706
-

(P-12008)
ANAHEIM PARK HOTEL
Also Called: Wyndham Hotels & Resorts
222 W Houston Ave, Fullerton
(92832-3453)
PHONE...................................714 992-1700
Fred Menoufi, *Partner*
Abdul El Mekligiange, *General Mgr*
EMP: 101
SQ FT: 174,123
SALES (est): 1.4MM **Privately Held**
SIC: 7011 YWCA/YWHA hotel; hotels

(P-12009)
ANAHEIM PARK INN AND CAMELOT
1520 S Harbor Blvd, Anaheim
(92802-2312)
PHONE...................................714 635-7275
Suren Badalian, *Owner*
EMP: 75
SALES (est): 1.9MM **Privately Held**
WEB: www.bei-hotels.com
SIC: 7011 Hotels & motels

(P-12010)
ANAHEIM PLAZA HOTEL INC
Also Called: Anaheim Plaza Hotel & Suites
1700 S Harbor Blvd, Anaheim
(92802-2316)
PHONE...................................714 772-5900
Saroj Patel, *CEO*
EMP: 150
SQ FT: 5,600
SALES (est): 4.5MM **Privately Held**
WEB: www.anaheimplazahotel.com
SIC: 7011 5812 5813 Motels; eating
places; drinking places

(P-12011)
APIC HOTELS GROUP LLC (HQ)
Also Called: Haiyi Hotels Worldwide
5 Thomas Mellon Cir # 305, San Francisco
(94134-2501)
PHONE...................................415 692-1502
Jennifer Zhang,
Wilson Chen,
EMP: 200
SQ FT: 100,000
SALES (est): 1.3MM **Privately Held**
SIC: 7011 Resort hotel; resort hotel, fran-
chised

(P-12012)
APPLE EGHT HOSPITALITY MGT INC
Also Called: Courtyard Cypress
5865 Katella Ave, Cypress (90630-5008)
PHONE...................................714 827-1010
Gary Liss, *Branch Mgr*
EMP: 59 **Privately Held**
WEB: www.dimdev.com
SIC: 7011 Hotel, franchised
HQ: Apple Eight Hospitality Management,
Inc.
814 E Main St
Richmond VA 23219

(P-12013)
APPLE HOSPITALITY REIT INC
Also Called: Hilton Garden Inn Sacramento
2540 Venture Oaks Way, Sacramento
(95833-3200)
PHONE................................916 568-5400
Jeff Irving, *General Mgr*
EMP: 55 EST: 2007
SALES (est): 674.2K **Privately Held**
SIC: 7011 Hotels & motels

(P-12014)
APPLE INNS INC
Also Called: Marina Inn
68 Monarch Bay Dr, San Leandro
(94577-6427)
PHONE................................510 895-1311
Audrey Velasquez, *Branch Mgr*
Peter Schultz, *President*
David Miller, *Vice Pres*
EMP: 50
SALES (est): 2.9MM **Privately Held**
WEB: www.sanleandromarinainn.com
SIC: 7011 Motels

(P-12015)
APPLE NINE HOSPITALITY MGT
Also Called: Courtyard San Diego Central
8651 Spectrum Center Blvd, San Diego
(92123-1489)
PHONE................................858 573-0700
Matthew Spencer, *General Mgr*
David Buckley, *President*
Alex Wiley, *COO*
EMP: 87
SALES (est): 1.8MM **Privately Held**
SIC: 7011 Hotels & motels

(P-12016)
ARAMARK SERVICES INC
800 Asilomar Blvd, Pacific Grove
(93950-3704)
P.O. Box 537 (93950-0537)
PHONE................................831 372-8016
Enos Esquivel, *Director*
Valerie Connell, *Vice Pres*
Sanj Kharbanda, *Vice Pres*
Brandi Hardy, *Executive*
Aileen Laracuente, *Executive*
EMP: 210 **Publicly Held**
SIC: 7011 Hotels
HQ: Aramark Services, Inc.
2400 Market St Ste 600
Philadelphia PA 19103
215 238-3000

(P-12017)
ARETE HOTELS LLC
2229 Den Helder Dr, Modesto
(95356-0729)
PHONE................................209 602-7952
Kimberly Ali, *CEO*
Heather Houser, *Accountant*
EMP: 74
SALES (est): 280.3K **Privately Held**
SIC: 7011 Resort hotel

(P-12018)
ARGONAUT HOTEL
495 Jefferson St, San Francisco
(94109-1314)
PHONE................................415 563-0800
Micheal Ditatie, *CEO*
EMP: 175
SALES (est): 6.7MM **Privately Held**
SIC: 7011 Resort hotel; hotels

(P-12019)
ART PICCADILLY SHAW LLC
Also Called: Piccadilly Inn Airport
5115 E Mckinley Ave, Fresno (93727-2033)
PHONE................................559 375-7760
Kathy Bell, *Branch Mgr*
EMP: 100
SALES (corp-wide): 8.9MM **Privately Held**
SIC: 7011 5813 5812 Hotels; drinking places; eating places
PA: Art Piccadilly Shaw Llc
2305 W Shaw Ave
Fresno CA 93711
559 348-5520

(P-12020)
ART PICCADILLY SHAW LLC
Piccadilly Inn-University
4961 N Cedar Ave, Fresno (93726-1062)
PHONE................................559 224-4200
Theresa Cross, *Branch Mgr*
EMP: 120
SALES (corp-wide): 8.9MM **Privately Held**
SIC: 7011 Motels
PA: Art Piccadilly Shaw Llc
2305 W Shaw Ave
Fresno CA 93711
559 348-5520

(P-12021)
ASCOT HOTEL LP
Also Called: Hotel Angeleno
170 N Church Ln, Los Angeles
(90049-2044)
PHONE................................310 476-6411
Mark Beccaria, *Partner*
Jackie Vargas, *Sales Mgr*
Dean Yamashita, *Sales Staff*
Scott Gordon, *Manager*
Jennifer Raney, *Manager*
EMP: 125 EST: 2008
SALES: 16.5MM **Privately Held**
SIC: 7011 Hotels

(P-12022)
ASHFORD TRS NICKEL LLC (PA)
Also Called: Walnut Creek Embassy Suites
1345 Treat Blvd, Walnut Creek
(94597-2173)
PHONE................................925 934-2500
Montgomery J Bennett,
EMP: 80
SALES (est): 4.2MM **Privately Held**
SIC: 7011 7389 Hotels & motels; office facilities & secretarial service rental

(P-12023)
ATASCADERO HOTEL PARTNERS LLC
Also Called: Springhill Suites
900 El Camino Real, Atascadero
(93422-1424)
PHONE................................805 462-3500
Elizabeth Eberly, *Accounting Mgr*
EMP: 52
SALES (est): 251.7K **Privately Held**
SIC: 7011 Hotels & motels

(P-12024)
ATRIUM FINANCE I LP
Also Called: Holiday Inn
300 J St, Sacramento (95814-2210)
PHONE................................916 446-0100
Liz Tavernese, *General Ptnr*
Elizabeth Tavernese, *General Mgr*
EMP: 150 EST: 2005
SALES (est): 6.2MM **Privately Held**
SIC: 7011 Hotels & motels
HQ: Atrium Hospitality Lp
12735 Morris Road Ext # 400
Alpharetta GA 30004
678 762-0005

(P-12025)
ATRIUM PLAZA LLC
Also Called: San Mateo Marriott
1770 S Amphlett Blvd, San Mateo
(94402-2708)
PHONE................................650 653-6000
Ron Anderhan,
Mario Urroz, *Info Tech Mgr*
Parwinder Kaur, *Finance*
Kathy Nicholl, *Human Res Dir*
Sam Sattavorn, *Purch Dir*
EMP: 208
SALES (est): 4.9MM **Privately Held**
SIC: 7011 Hotels

(P-12026)
AVIARA FSRC ASSOCIATES LIMITED
7100 Aviara Resort Dr, Carlsbad
(92011-4908)
PHONE................................760 603-6800
Robert Cima, *General Mgr*
Aviara Resort Club, *General Ptnr*
Hef IV LLC, *General Ptnr*
EMP: 1200

SALES (est): 12.6MM **Publicly Held**
SIC: 7011 Resort hotel
HQ: Aviara Resort Associates Limited Partnership, A California Limited Partnership
7100 Aviara Resort Dr
Carlsbad CA 92011
760 448-1234

(P-12027)
AVIARA RESORT ASSOCIATES (HQ)
Also Called: Park Hyatt Aviara
7100 Aviara Resort Dr, Carlsbad
(92011-4908)
PHONE................................760 448-1234
Maritz Wolff, *General Ptnr*
▲ EMP: 100
SALES (est): 17.6MM **Publicly Held**
SIC: 7011 Hotels & motels

(P-12028)
AWH BURBANK HOTEL LLC
Also Called: Marriott Burbank
2500 N Hollywood Way, Burbank
(91505-1019)
PHONE................................813 843-6000
William Deforrest, *CEO*
Chad Cooley, *Vice Pres*
Russell Flicker, *Vice Pres*
Bernard Michael, *Vice Pres*
Jonathan Rosenfeld, *Vice Pres*
EMP: 176 EST: 2014
SALES (est): 7.6MM **Privately Held**
SIC: 7011 Hotels

(P-12029)
AYRES - PASO ROBLES LP
Also Called: Allegretto Vineyard Resort
2700 Buena Vista Dr, Paso Robles
(93446-9530)
PHONE................................714 850-0409
EMP: 120
SALES (est): 830.1K **Privately Held**
SIC: 7011 Hotels

(P-12030)
AYRES GROUP (PA)
355 Bristol St, Costa Mesa (92626-7922)
PHONE................................714 540-6060
Bruce F Ayres, *CEO*
EMP: 58
SALES (est): 61MM **Privately Held**
SIC: 7011 8741 1531 Hotels; management services; operative builders

(P-12031)
B H R OPERATIONS LLC
Also Called: Crown Plaza
777 Bellew Dr, Milpitas (95035-7900)
PHONE................................408 321-9500
Roy Escobar, *Mng Member*
Winnie Kwok, *General Mgr*
EMP: 100
SQ FT: 250,000
SALES (est): 1.8MM **Privately Held**
WEB: www.bristolhotels.com
SIC: 7011 Motel, franchised
HQ: Bristol Hotel & Resorts Inc.
3 Ravinia Dr Ste 100
Atlanta GA 30346

(P-12032)
B S A PARTNERS
Also Called: Residence Inn By Marriott
14419 Firestone Blvd, La Mirada
(90638-5912)
PHONE................................714 523-2800
Jim Gilbert, *General Mgr*
William Swank, *General Ptnr*
William E Swank Jr, *General Ptnr*
EMP: 80
SQ FT: 102,943
SALES (est): 3.7MM **Privately Held**
SIC: 7011 Hotels & motels

(P-12033)
BADALIAN ENTERPRISES INC
Also Called: Park Inn
1540 S Harbor Blvd, Anaheim
(92802-2312)
PHONE................................714 635-4082
Ernest Badalian, *President*
Bonny Harutunian, *Treasurer*
Greg Badalian, *Vice Pres*

Suren Badalian, *Vice Pres*
Patricia Coomb, *Sales Staff*
EMP: 90
SQ FT: 55,000
SALES (est): 5.5MM **Privately Held**
SIC: 7011 Hotels & motels

(P-12034)
BALDWIN HOSPITALITY LLC
Also Called: Courtyard By Marriott
14635 Baldwin Ave, Baldwin Park (91706)
PHONE................................626 962-6000
Lina Mita, *Branch Mgr*
Kathy Vicario, *Executive*
Henry Zamora, *General Mgr*
EMP: 80
SQ FT: 148,187
SALES (corp-wide): 4.4MM **Privately Held**
SIC: 7011 Hotels & motels
PA: Baldwin Hospitality Llc
411 E Huntington Dr # 305
Arcadia CA 91006
626 446-2988

(P-12035)
BANEY CORPORATION
Also Called: Oxford Suites Chico
2035 Business Ln, Chico (95928-7628)
PHONE................................530 899-9090
Chris Coder, *Manager*
Catalino Aranda, *Engineer*
Gennero Filice, *Manager*
EMP: 52 **Privately Held**
WEB: www.oxfordsuites.com
SIC: 7011 Resort hotel; hotels
PA: Baney Corporation
475 Ne Bellevue Dr # 210
Bend OR 97701

(P-12036)
BARONA RESORT & CASINO
1932 Wildcat Canyon Rd, Lakeside
(92040-1553)
PHONE................................619 443-2300
Dean Allen, *Senior VP*
Nick Dillon, *Exec VP*
Troy Simpson, *Exec VP*
Linda Jordan, *Senior VP*
Jeffty Connelly, *Vice Pres*
EMP: 3500
SALES (est): 96MM **Privately Held**
WEB: www.barona.com
SIC: 7011 Resort hotel

(P-12037)
BARTELL HOTELS
Also Called: Hilton San Diego Airport/Hrbr
1960 Harbor Island Dr, San Diego
(92101-1013)
PHONE................................619 291-6700
Luis Barrios, *General Mgr*
EMP: 100
SALES (corp-wide): 57.8MM **Privately Held**
SIC: 7011 Hotels
PA: Bartell Hotels
4875 N Harbor Dr
San Diego CA 92106
619 224-1556

(P-12038)
BARTELL HOTELS
Also Called: Humphreys Half Moon Inn
2303 Shelter Island Dr, San Diego
(92106-3109)
PHONE................................619 224-3411
Sergio Davies, *Manager*
EMP: 200
SALES (corp-wide): 57.8MM **Privately Held**
WEB: www.holinnbayside.com
SIC: 7011 5812 5813 Motels; eating places; cocktail lounge
PA: Bartell Hotels
4875 N Harbor Dr
San Diego CA 92106
619 224-1556

(P-12039)
BARTELL HOTELS
1710 W Mission Bay Dr, San Diego
(92109-7810)
PHONE................................619 222-6440
Kevin Konopasek, *General Mgr*

PRODUCTS & SVCS

EMP: 200
SALES (corp-wide): 57.8MM **Privately Held**
WEB: www.holinnbayside.com
SIC: 7011 4493 5812 Hotels; marinas; eating places
PA: Bartell Hotels
4875 N Harbor Dr
San Diego CA 92106
619 224-1556

(P-12040)
BARTELL HOTELS
Also Called: Pacific Terrace
610 Diamond St, San Diego (92109-2444)
PHONE..............................858 581-3500
Bob Kingery, *Branch Mgr*
EMP: 50
SALES (corp-wide): 57.8MM **Privately Held**
SIC: 7011 Hotels
PA: Bartell Hotels
4875 N Harbor Dr
San Diego CA 92106
619 224-1556

(P-12041)
BARTELL HOTELS
Also Called: Best Western Island Palms
2051 Shelter Island Dr, San Diego (92106-3105)
PHONE..............................619 222-0561
Jim Finnegan, *Manager*
EMP: 70
SQ FT: 56,500
SALES (corp-wide): 57.8MM **Privately Held**
WEB: www.holinnbayside.com
SIC: 7011 Hotels & motels
PA: Bartell Hotels
4875 N Harbor Dr
San Diego CA 92106
619 224-1556

(P-12042)
BARTELL HOTELS
Also Called: Sheraton
3299 Holiday Ct, La Jolla (92037-1830)
PHONE..............................858 453-5500
Craig Reber, *Owner*
EMP: 81
SQ FT: 68,159
SALES (corp-wide): 57.8MM **Privately Held**
WEB: www.holinnbayside.com
SIC: 7011 5812 Hotels & motels; eating places
PA: Bartell Hotels
4875 N Harbor Dr
San Diego CA 92106
619 224-1556

(P-12043)
BASSLAKE LLC
39255 Marina Dr, Bass Lake (93604)
PHONE..............................559 642-3121
Kyu Sun Choe, *Principal*
Sun Wha Choe, *Principal*
EMP: 99
SALES (est): 1MM **Privately Held**
SIC: 7011 Resort hotel

(P-12044)
BAVARIAN LION COMPANY CAL (PA)
Also Called: Flamingo Resort Hotel
2777 4th St, Santa Rosa (95405-4795)
PHONE..............................707 545-8530
Pierre Ehret, *President*
EMP: 200 EST: 1976
SQ FT: 32,000
SALES (est): 16.9MM **Privately Held**
WEB: www.flamingohotel.com
SIC: 7011 7991 Resort hotel; health club

(P-12045)
BAY CLUB HOTEL AND MARINA A C
Also Called: The Bay Club Hotel and Marina
2131 Shelter Island Dr, San Diego (92106-3106)
PHONE..............................619 224-8888
Frank Hope, *Partner*
Bob Collins, *Partner*
Chuck Hope, *Partner*
Ed Malone, *Partner*

EMP: 55
SQ FT: 200,000
SALES (est): 5.4MM **Privately Held**
WEB: www.bayclubhotel.com
SIC: 7011 6512 5812 5813 Resort hotel; lessors of piers, docks, associated buildings & facilities; American restaurant; bars & lounges

(P-12046)
BAYVIEW PROPERTIES INC (PA)
Also Called: Best Western, The Beach Resort
2600 Sand Dunes Dr, Monterey (93940-3838)
PHONE..............................831 394-3321
Theodore Richter, *President*
EMP: 99
SALES (est): 6.3MM **Privately Held**
WEB: www.montereybeachhotel.com
SIC: 7011 Hotels & motels

(P-12047)
BAYVIEW PROPERTIES INC
Also Called: Best Western
2600 Sand Dunes Dr, Monterey (93940-3838)
PHONE..............................831 655-7650
Allison Nord, *Manager*
EMP: 65
SALES (corp-wide): 6.3MM **Privately Held**
WEB: www.montereybeachhotel.com
SIC: 7011 Hotels & motels
PA: Bayview Properties, Inc.
2600 Sand Dunes Dr
Monterey CA 93940
831 394-3321

(P-12048)
BAYVIEW PROPERTIES INC
Also Called: Carmel Mission Inn
3665 Rio Rd, Carmel (93923-8609)
PHONE..............................831 624-1841
John Elford, *Manager*
EMP: 65
SQ FT: 40,000
SALES (corp-wide): 6.3MM **Privately Held**
WEB: www.montereybeachhotel.com
SIC: 7011 Motel, franchised
PA: Bayview Properties, Inc.
2600 Sand Dunes Dr
Monterey CA 93940
831 394-3321

(P-12049)
BEACH MOTEL PARTNERS LTD
Also Called: Harbor View Inn
28 W Cabrillo Blvd, Santa Barbara (93101-3504)
PHONE..............................800 755-0222
Antonio R Romasanta, *Partner*
Birgit Romasanta, *Partner*
Junior Zermeno, *Manager*
EMP: 60 EST: 1983
SQ FT: 40,000
SALES (est): 6.4MM **Privately Held**
SIC: 7011 Motels

(P-12050)
BEAR RIVER CASINO
Also Called: Bear River Casino Hotel
11 Bear Paws Way, Loleta (95551-9684)
PHONE..............................707 733-9644
John McGinnis, *Executive Asst*
Jesse Orr, *CTO*
Nicole Dees, *Accounting Mgr*
Wendy Bates, *Human Res Dir*
Kyle Hudson, *Cust Mgr*
EMP: 286 **Privately Held**
SIC: 7011 Casino hotel
PA: Bear River Casino
27 Bear River Dr
Loleta CA 95551

(P-12051)
BEHRINGER HARVARD WILSHIRE BLV
Also Called: Hotel Palomar
10740 Wilshire Blvd, Los Angeles (90024-4493)
PHONE..............................310 475-8711
Ravi Sikand, *Partner*
EMP: 99

SALES (est): 8.4MM **Privately Held**
SIC: 7011 6531 Hotels; real estate agents & managers

(P-12052)
BELMONT CORPORATION
Also Called: Best Western
901 Park Ave, South Lake Tahoe (96150-6938)
PHONE..............................530 542-1101
Wilson Williford, *President*
EMP: 60
SALES (est): 3.7MM **Privately Held**
WEB: www.stationhouseinn.com
SIC: 7011 5012 Hotels & motels; automobiles & other motor vehicles

(P-12053)
BELVEDERE HOTEL PARTNERSHIP
Also Called: Peninsula Beverly Hill's
9882 Santa Monica Blvd, Beverly Hills (90212-1605)
PHONE..............................310 551-2888
Ali Kasikci, *Manager*
EMP: 442
SALES (corp-wide): 16.9MM **Privately Held**
WEB: www.patandmelody.com
SIC: 7011 6512 5813 5812 Hotels; non-residential building operators; drinking places; eating places
PA: The Belvedere Hotel Partnership
421 N Beverly Dr Ste 350
Beverly Hills CA 90210

(P-12054)
BELVEDERE PARTNERSHIP
Also Called: Peninsula Beverly Hills, The
9882 Santa Monica Blvd, Beverly Hills (90212-1605)
PHONE..............................310 551-2888
Robert Zarnegan, *President*
David Retumalta, *Payroll Mgr*
Darlene Adams, *Sales Staff*
Leila Abdelghani, *Director*
▲ EMP: 400
SALES (est): 25.3MM **Privately Held**
SIC: 7011 Bed & breakfast inn; hotels

(P-12055)
BERESFORD CORPORATION
Also Called: Beresford Arms, The
635 Sutter St, San Francisco (94102-1017)
PHONE..............................415 673-9900
Richard Osborn, *Branch Mgr*
EMP: 75
SALES (corp-wide): 6.4MM **Privately Held**
WEB: www.beresford.com
SIC: 7011 Hotels
PA: Beresford Corporation
582 Market St Ste 912
San Francisco CA 94104
415 981-7386

(P-12056)
BEST WESTERN BAYSHORE INN
3500 Broadway, Eureka (95503-3810)
PHONE..............................707 268-8005
Mark Watson, *President*
Emily Manfredonia, *General Mgr*
EMP: 50
SALES (est): 2.5MM **Privately Held**
WEB: www.bwbayshoreinn.com
SIC: 7011 Hotels & motels

(P-12057)
BEST WESTERN HILLTOP INN
2300 Hilltop Dr, Redding (96002-0508)
PHONE..............................530 221-6100
Ed Rullman,
Steve Gaines, *General Ptnr*
Steven Wahrlich, *General Ptnr*
Tracy Wahrlich, *General Ptnr*
EMP: 50
SQ FT: 10,000
SALES (est): 3.1MM **Privately Held**
WEB: www.thehilltopinn.com
SIC: 7011 5812 5813 Hotels & motels; eating places; drinking places

(P-12058)
BEST WESTERN HOTEL TOMO
1800 Sutter St, San Francisco (94115-3220)
PHONE..............................415 921-4000
Sean Salera, *CFO*
EMP: 50 EST: 2007
SALES (est): 1MM
SALES (corp-wide): 4.3MM **Privately Held**
SIC: 7011 Hotels & motels
PA: Khp Iii Sf Sutter Llc
1800 Sutter St
San Francisco CA 94115
415 921-4000

(P-12059)
BEST WESTERN INTERNATIONAL INC
805 S Kaweah Ave, Exeter (93221-9361)
PHONE..............................559 592-8118
Neil Patel, *Manager*
EMP: 80
SALES (corp-wide): 141.8MM **Privately Held**
SIC: 7011 Hotels & motels
PA: Best Western International, Inc.
6201 N 24th Pkwy
Phoenix AZ 85016
602 957-4200

(P-12060)
BEST WESTERN PLUS-HERITAGE INN
Also Called: Holiday Inn
111 E March Ln, Stockton (95207-5854)
PHONE..............................209 474-3301
Ganatra Vasant, *Mng Member*
EMP: 50
SALES (est): 1.4MM **Privately Held**
SIC: 7011 Hotels & motels

(P-12061)
BEST WESTERN STOVALLS INN
Also Called: Best Western Park Place
1544 S Harbor Blvd, Anaheim (92802-2312)
PHONE..............................714 776-4800
Lilian Wright, *General Mgr*
EMP: 50
SALES (est): 1.3MM
SALES (corp-wide): 11.3MM **Privately Held**
WEB: www.anaheiminn.com
SIC: 7011 Hotels & motels
PA: Best Western Stovalls Inn
1110 W Katella Ave
Anaheim CA 92802
714 956-4430

(P-12062)
BEST WESTERN STOVALLS INN (PA)
1110 W Katella Ave, Anaheim (92802-2805)
PHONE..............................714 956-4430
James Stovall, *Partner*
Bill O'Connell, *Partner*
Minta Pettis-Stovall, *Partner*
Robert Stovall, *Partner*
Patty Smith, *Sales Mgr*
EMP: 220
SQ FT: 4,800
SALES (est): 11.3MM **Privately Held**
WEB: www.anaheiminn.com
SIC: 7011 Hotels & motels

(P-12063)
BESTON DEVELOPMENT
Also Called: Bristol, The
1055 1st Ave, San Diego (92101-4808)
PHONE..............................619 232-6315
EMP: 60
SALES: 2MM **Privately Held**
WEB: www.bristolhotelsandiego.com
SIC: 7011

(P-12064)
BEVERLY BLVD LEASECO LLC
Also Called: Sofitel Luxury Hotels
8555 Beverly Blvd, Los Angeles (90048-3303)
PHONE..............................310 278-5444
Pierre-Louis Renou,
David Hamerman, *Security Dir*

Mark Wilkinson, *General Mgr*
Robert-Jan Woltering, *General Mgr*
Lucet Angeles, *Project Mgr*
EMP: 100
SALES (est): 7.8MM
SALES (corp-wide): 1.1B **Privately Held**
SIC: 7011 Hotels & motels
PA: Accor
82 Rue Henry Farman
Issy-Les-Moulineaux 92130
146 429-193

(P-12065)
BEVERLY HILLS LUXURY HOTEL LLC
1801 Century Park E # 1200, Los Angeles (90067-2334)
PHONE.................................310 274-9999
Kenneth Bordewick, *Mng Member*
Bharath Bangalore, *Finance*
Remy Papazian, *Sales Staff*
Mercedes Lucero, *Director*
EMP: 450
SALES (est): 22.3MM **Privately Held**
SIC: 7011 Resort hotel; hotels

(P-12066)
BEVERLY SUNSTONE HILLS LLC
Also Called: Residence Inn By Marriott
1177 S Beverly Dr, Los Angeles (90035-1119)
PHONE.................................310 228-4100
Robert Alter, *CEO*
EMP: 60
SALES (est): 1.5MM **Privately Held**
SIC: 7011 Hotels & motels

(P-12067)
BH PARTN A CALIF LIMIT PARTNE (PA)
Also Called: Bahia Resort Hotels
998 W Mission Bay Dr, San Diego (92109-7803)
PHONE.................................858 539-7635
Anne L Evans, *General Ptnr*
William L Evans, *Partner*
Alyssa Stewart, *Executive Asst*
Christina Remmling, *CTO*
Oliver Mendoza, *Network Enginr*
EMP: 300
SALES (est): 56MM **Privately Held**
WEB: www.missionbayresorts.com
SIC: 7011 6531 5812 Resort hotel; real estate managers; real estate leasing & rentals; eating places

(P-12068)
BH PARTN A CALIF LIMIT PARTNE
Also Called: The Lodge At Torrey Pines
11480 N Torrey Pines Rd A, La Jolla (92037-1045)
PHONE.................................858 453-4420
Luis Badios, *Manager*
Dan Fullen, *General Mgr*
Stephanie Chavez, *Executive Asst*
Dan Ferbal, *Human Res Dir*
Giovanni Dominguez, *Purch Mgr*
EMP: 100
SALES (corp-wide): 56MM **Privately Held**
WEB: www.missionbayresorts.com
SIC: 7011 5813 5812 Resort hotel; drinking places; eating places
PA: Bh Partnership, A Califoria Limited Partnership
998 W Mission Bay Dr
San Diego CA 92109
858 539-7635

(P-12069)
BHR TRS TAHOE LLC
Also Called: Ritz-Carlton Lake Tahoe, The
13031 Ritz Carlton, Truckee (96161)
PHONE.................................530 562-3045
Chris Stevens, *Asst Mgr*
EMP: 248
SALES (est): 464.5K
SALES (corp-wide): 431.4MM **Privately Held**
SIC: 7011 Resort hotel
PA: Braemar Hotels & Resorts Inc.
14185 Dallas Pkwy # 1100
Dallas TX 75254
972 490-9600

(P-12070)
BICYCLE CASINO LP
Also Called: Bicycle Hotel and Casino
888 Bicycle Casino Dr, Bell Gardens (90201-7617)
PHONE.................................562 806-4646
Hashem Minaiy, *General Ptnr*
Jovani Rivera, *Manager*
EMP: 1500 **EST:** 1984
SALES (est): 13.1MM **Privately Held**
SIC: 7011 Casino hotel

(P-12071)
BIG RIVER LTD-DESIGN
Also Called: Big River Lodge
44850 Comptche Ukiah Rd, Mendocino (95460-9007)
P.O. Box 487 (95460-0487)
PHONE.................................707 937-5615
Jeff Stanford, *Co-Owner*
Joan Stanford, *Co-Owner*
EMP: 70
SQ FT: 40,000
SALES (est): 3.6MM **Privately Held**
WEB: www.stanfordinn.com
SIC: 7011 5551 5941 5261 Resort hotel; canoes; kayaks; bicycle & bicycle parts; surfing equipment & supplies; nursery stock, seeds & bulbs; antiques; bathing suits; marine apparel

(P-12072)
BILTMORE HOTEL
2151 Laurelwood Rd, Santa Clara (95054-2796)
PHONE.................................408 988-8411
Dafney Kang, *Owner*
Barbara Ratcliffe, *General Mgr*
EMP: 110
SALES (est): 2.2MM **Privately Held**
SIC: 7011 Resort hotel

(P-12073)
BISHOP PAIUTE GAMING CORP
Also Called: Paiute Palace Casino
2742 N Sierra Hwy, Bishop (93514-2218)
PHONE.................................760 872-6005
Gloriana Bailey, *President*
EMP: 150
SALES (est): 8MM **Privately Held**
WEB: www.paiutepalace.com
SIC: 7011 Casino hotel

(P-12074)
BLACK MEADOW LANDING
156100 Black Meadow Rd, Parker Dam (92267)
P.O. Box 98 (92267-0098)
PHONE.................................760 663-4901
George H Field Jr, *Owner*
EMP: 55
SQ FT: 100,000
SALES (est): 1.6MM **Privately Held**
WEB: www.blackmeadowlanding.com
SIC: 7011 7033 5411 5812 Motels; recreational vehicle parks; grocery stores, independent; restaurant, family: independent

(P-12075)
BLUE DEVILS LESSEE LLC
Also Called: Le Merdien Dlfina Santa Monica
530 Pico Blvd, Santa Monica (90405-1223)
PHONE.................................310 399-9344
Jon Bortz, *Ch of Bd*
Eric Williams, *Sales Mgr*
Raymond Martz, *Sales Mgr*
EMP: 170
SALES (est): 21.6MM **Privately Held**
SIC: 7011 Hotels

(P-12076)
BLUE LAKE CASINO
777 Casino Way Blue Lk Blue Lake, Blue Lake (95525)
P.O. Box 1128 (95525-1128)
PHONE.................................707 668-5101
Eric Ramos, *President*
EMP: 50
SALES (est): 5MM **Privately Held**
SIC: 7011 Casino hotel

(P-12077)
BODEGA BAY ASSOCIATES
Also Called: Bodega Bay Lodge
1100 Alma St Ste 106, Menlo Park (94025-3344)
PHONE.................................650 330-8888
Ellis J Alden,
EMP: 95
SALES: 6.2MM **Privately Held**
SIC: 7011 Motels

(P-12078)
BOREAL RIDGE CORPORATION
Also Called: Boreal Ski Area
19749 Boreal Ridge Rd, Soda Springs (95728)
P.O. Box 39, Truckee (96160-0039)
PHONE.................................530 426-1012
John Cumming, *President*
Jodi Churich, *Vice Pres*
EMP: 110
SQ FT: 10,000
SALES (est): 11.5MM
SALES (corp-wide): 96MM **Privately Held**
WEB: www.powdr.com
SIC: 7011 7999 Ski lodge; hotels; ski rental concession
PA: Powdr Corp.
1794 Olympic Pkwy Ste 210
Park City UT 84098
435 658-5500

(P-12079)
BOYKIN MGT CO LTD LBLTY CO
Also Called: Hampton Inn
3888 Greenwood St, San Diego (92110-4412)
PHONE.................................619 299-6633
Tom Whelan, *Principal*
EMP: 50
SALES (corp-wide): 38.6MM **Privately Held**
WEB: www.wangyufei.com
SIC: 7011 Hotels & motels
PA: Boykin Management Company Limited Liability Company
8015 W Kenton Cir Ste 220
Huntersville NC 28078
704 896-2880

(P-12080)
BOYKIN MGT CO LTD LBLTY CO
Also Called: Radisson Inn
200 Marina Blvd, Berkeley (94710-1608)
PHONE.................................510 548-7920
Neil Pasan, *Manager*
EMP: 300
SALES (corp-wide): 38.6MM **Privately Held**
WEB: www.wangyufei.com
SIC: 7011 5812 5813 Hotels & motels; eating places; drinking places
PA: Boykin Management Company Limited Liability Company
8015 W Kenton Cir Ste 220
Huntersville NC 28078
704 896-2880

(P-12081)
BRAEMAR PARTNERSHIP
Also Called: Catamaran Resort Hotel
3999 Mission Blvd, San Diego (92109-6959)
PHONE.................................858 488-1081
Robert Gleason, *CFO*
The Trust of W D Evans, *Partner*
Anne L Evans, *Managing Prtnr*
Chavez Rocio, *Human Res Mgr*
Victoria Hartwell, *Manager*
EMP: 350
SALES (est): 16.2MM **Privately Held**
WEB: www.catamaranresort.com
SIC: 7011 5812 5813 Resort hotel; American restaurant; cocktail lounge

(P-12082)
BRE DIAMOND HOTEL LLC
Also Called: Ritz-Carlton Halfmoon Bay
1 Miramontes Point Rd, Half Moon Bay (94019-2376)
PHONE.................................650 712-7000
John Berndt, *Manager*
David Bartlett, *Vice Pres*
EMP: 118

SALES (corp-wide): 5.6MM **Privately Held**
WEB: www.shci.com
SIC: 7011 Hotels & motels
HQ: Bre Diamond Hotel Llc
200 W Madison St Ste 1700
Chicago IL 60606
312 658-5000

(P-12083)
BRE SELECT HOTELS OPER LLC
Also Called: Hilton
30 Ranch Dr, Milpitas (95035-5103)
PHONE.................................408 719-1313
Greg Juceam, *Exec VP*
Tabitha Christensen, *Manager*
EMP: 52 **EST:** 2013
SALES (est): 228.8K **Privately Held**
SIC: 7011 Hotels & motels

(P-12084)
BRE/JAPANTOWN OWNER LLC
Also Called: Hotel Kabuki
1625 Post St, San Francisco (94115-3603)
PHONE.................................415 922-3200
Craig Walterman, *General Mgr*
EMP: 100
SALES (est): 2.4MM **Privately Held**
SIC: 7011 Hotels

(P-12085)
BRIDGE BAY RESORT & MARINA
10300 Bridge Bay Rd, Redding (96003-9419)
PHONE.................................530 275-3021
Howard Weinberg,
EMP: 75
SALES (est): 5.3MM
SALES (corp-wide): 8.4MM **Privately Held**
WEB: www.sevencrown.com
SIC: 7011 Resort hotel
PA: Peloria Marinas Llc
2550 Via Tejon Ste 2b
Palos Verdes Estates CA 90274
310 363-7775

(P-12086)
BRIDGE PARTNERS INC (PA)
1850 Mt Diablo Blvd, Walnut Creek (94596-4428)
PHONE.................................925 256-9448
Steve Klein, *President*
Ken Beall, *CFO*
Julie Gutzwiller, *CFO*
Stephen Emery, *Managing Dir*
Velina A Barnes, *Manager*
EMP: 62
SQ FT: 2,000
SALES (est): 4MM **Privately Held**
WEB: www.bridgepartners.com
SIC: 7011 6513 6514 8742 Hotels & motels; apartment building operators; dwelling operators, except apartments; real estate consultant

(P-12087)
BRIGHT BRISTOL STREET LLC
Also Called: Crowne Plaza Costa Mesa
3131 Bristol St, Costa Mesa (92626-3037)
PHONE.................................714 557-3000
Nermin Khalil, *General Mgr*
Tom Van Winkle, *General Mgr*
Benjamin Shih, *Project Mgr*
Jillian Clary, *Sales Mgr*
Giovanna Castellanos, *Sales Staff*
EMP: 85
SALES (est): 404.1K **Privately Held**
SIC: 7011 Hotels & motels

(P-12088)
BRILLIANCE INVESTMENT LLC
Also Called: Days Inn
8350 Edes Ave, Oakland (94621-1307)
PHONE.................................510 568-1880
Amit Motawala, *Mng Member*
EMP: 55
SQ FT: 70,000
SALES (est): 2.2MM **Privately Held**
SIC: 7011 5812 5813 Hotels & motels; restaurant, family: independent; bars & lounges

P
R
O
D
U
C
T
S

&

S
V
C
S

(P-12089)
BRISAM LAX (DE) LLC
Also Called: Holiday Inn
9901 S La Cienega Blvd, Los Angeles
(90045-5915)
PHONE....................310 649-5151
Steve Hostetter, General Mgr
David Romero, Sales Mgr
Joyce Camou, Sales Staff
Joann Endow, Sales Staff
Rodolfo Gutierrez, Director
EMP: 95
SALES (est): 4.1MM Privately Held
SIC: 7011 Hotels & motels

(P-12090)
BRISTOL HOTEL
1055 1st Ave, San Diego (92101-4808)
PHONE....................619 232-6141
Eric Horodas, Owner
Lupe Veliz, Admin Asst
EMP: 90
SQ FT: 56,000
SALES (est): 4.6MM Privately Held
WEB: www.bristol.polhotels.com
SIC: 7011 5812 5813 Hotels; eating
places; bars & lounges

(P-12091)
BROADMOOR HOTEL (PA)
Also Called: The Broadmoore
1499 Sutter St, San Francisco
(94109-5417)
PHONE....................415 776-7034
Irene Lieberman, President
◆ EMP: 220
SALES (est): 9.6MM Privately Held
WEB: www.granadasf.com
SIC: 7011 Resort hotel

(P-12092)
BROADMOOR HOTEL
Gaylord Suites
1465 65th St Apt 274, Emeryville
(94608-1168)
PHONE....................415 673-8445
Tony Daviduskis, Branch Mgr
Cassie Hernandez, Director
EMP: 75
SQ FT: 85,619
SALES (est): 1MM
SALES (corp-wide): 9.6MM Privately
Held
WEB: www.granadasf.com
SIC: 7011 6513 Resort hotel; apartment
hotel operation
PA: Broadmoor Hotel
1499 Sutter St
San Francisco CA 94109
415 776-7034

(P-12093)
BROADMOOR HOTEL
Also Called: Granada Hotel
1000 Sutter St, San Francisco
(94109-5818)
PHONE....................415 673-2511
Tony Daviduskis, Manager
EMP: 70
SALES (est): 1.2MM
SALES (corp-wide): 9.6MM Privately
Held
WEB: www.granadasf.com
SIC: 7011 Resort hotel
PA: Broadmoor Hotel
1499 Sutter St
San Francisco CA 94109
415 776-7034

(P-12094)
**BROOKFIELD DTLA FUND
OFFICE**
Also Called: Westin Pasadena, The
191 N Los Robles Ave, Pasadena
(91101-1707)
PHONE....................626 792-2727
Jonathan Litvack, General Mgr
Beatrice Hsu, Vice Pres
EMP: 70
SALES (corp-wide): 43B Publicly Held
WEB: www.maguireproperties.com
SIC: 7011 5812 5813 7299 Hotels & mo-
tels; American restaurant; bars & lounges;
banquet hall facilities

HQ: Brookfield Dtla Fund Office Trust Inc.
4 Wrld Fncl Ctr Fl 15
New York NY 10281
212 417-7064

(P-12095)
BROOKTRAILS LODGE LLC
24675 Birch St, Willits (95490-8476)
P.O. Box 297 (95490-0297)
PHONE....................707 459-1596
Robert S Gitlin, Manager
EMP: 54
SQ FT: 87,120
SALES (est): 1MM Privately Held
SIC: 7011 Tourist camps, cabins, cottages
& courts

(P-12096)
BSHH II LLC
Also Called: Bre El Segundo Property Owner
475 N Pacific Coast Hwy, El Segundo
(90245-4446)
PHONE....................310 356-4587
Glenn Alba, Branch Mgr
EMP: 50
SALES (corp-wide): 1.8MM Privately
Held
SIC: 7011 Hotels & motels
PA: Bshh Ii Llc
525 N Pacific Coast Hwy
El Segundo CA 90245
310 356-4577

(P-12097)
**BURTON-WAY HOUSE LTD A
CA**
Also Called: Four Seasons Hotel
2 Dole Dr, Westlake Village (91362-7300)
PHONE....................805 214-8075
Robert Cohen, Branch Mgr
EMP: 205
SALES (corp-wide): 31.1MM Privately
Held
SIC: 7011 Hotels
PA: Burton Way Hotels, Ltd., A California
Limited Partnership
2029 Century Park E # 2200
Los Angeles CA 90067
310 552-6623

(P-12098)
**BURTON-WAY HOUSE LTD A
CA**
Also Called: Four Seasons Hotel
300 S Doheny Dr, Los Angeles
(90048-3704)
PHONE....................310 273-2222
Mehdi Efpekari, General Mgr
EMP: 225
SALES (corp-wide): 31.1MM Privately
Held
SIC: 7011 5812 Hotels; eating places
PA: Burton Way Hotels, Ltd., A California
Limited Partnership
2029 Century Park E # 2200
Los Angeles CA 90067
310 552-6623

(P-12099)
**BURTON-WAY HOUSE LTD A
CA (PA)**
Also Called: Four Seasons Hotel
2029 Century Park E # 2200, Los Angeles
(90067-2901)
PHONE....................310 552-6623
Robert Cohen, General Ptnr
Joseph Cohen, Partner
EMP: 50
SALES (est): 31.1MM Privately Held
SIC: 7011 Hotels

(P-12100)
BY THE BLUE SEA LLC
Also Called: Shutters On The Beach
1 Pico Blvd, Santa Monica (90405-1063)
PHONE....................310 458-0030
Tim Dubois, President
Klaus Mennekes, Vice Pres
Leslie McCammon, Sales Staff
Ruben Hernandez, Manager
EMP: 350
SALES (est): 22.4MM Privately Held
SIC: 7011 Hotels

(P-12101)
C N L HOTEL DEL PARTNERS LP
1500 Orange Ave, San Diego (92118-2918)
PHONE....................619 522-8299
Todd Shallan, Partner
EMP: 1100
SALES (est): 6.8MM Privately Held
SIC: 7011 Hotels

(P-12102)
C W HOTELS LTD
Also Called: JW Marriott Le Merigot
1740 Ocean Ave, Santa Monica
(90401-3214)
PHONE....................310 395-9700
Damien Hirsch, General Mgr
EMP: 150
SALES (corp-wide): 5.1MM Privately
Held
SIC: 7011 Hotels & motels
PA: C W Hotels Ltd
740 Centre View Blvd
Crestview Hills KY 41017
859 578-1000

(P-12103)
**CACHE CREEK CASINO
RESORT**
14455 State Highway 16, Brooks
(95606-9707)
P.O. Box 65 (95606-0065)
PHONE....................530 796-3118
Wendy Carter, Vice Pres
Bill Harland, Vice Pres
Mark Longshore Vice Pres
Ron Vargas, Executive
Tavis Feese, Info Tech Mgr
EMP: 200
SALES (est): 111.6MM Privately Held
SIC: 7011 Casino hotel
PA: Yocha Dehe Wintun Nation
18960 County Rd 75 A
Brooks CA 95606
530 796-3400

(P-12104)
CALHOT ILLINIOS LLC
Also Called: Ramada Inn
5250 W El Segundo Blvd, Hawthorne
(90250-4142)
PHONE....................310 536-9800
Fred Groth, General Mgr
Kairey Choi, Manager
EMP: 160
SALES (est): 3.1MM Privately Held
SIC: 7011 5812 Hotels & motels; eating
places

(P-12105)
CALIFORNIA BISTRO AT FO
Also Called: Four Seasons Resort Aviara
7100 Aviara Resort Dr, Carlsbad
(92011-4908)
PHONE....................760 603-3700
Vince Parotta, President
EMP: 51
SALES (est): 2.2MM Privately Held
SIC: 7011 Resort hotel

(P-12106)
**CALIFORNIA CLUB LUCKY
LADY**
Also Called: Lucky Lady Card Room
5526 El Cajon Blvd, San Diego
(92115-3623)
PHONE....................619 287-6690
Stanley Penn, Owner
EMP: 50
SQ FT: 7,000
SALES: 500K Privately Held
WEB: www.calicasinos.net
SIC: 7011 Casino hotel

(P-12107)
**CALIFORNIA COMMERCE CLUB
INC**
Also Called: Commerce Casino
6131 Telegraph Rd, Commerce
(90040-2501)
PHONE....................323 721-2100
Haig Papaian, CEO
Dante Oliveto, CFO
Harvey Ross, Vice Pres
Andrew Schneiderman, Vice Pres
Ralph Wong, Vice Pres

EMP: 2600
SQ FT: 350,000
SALES (est): 105.9MM Privately Held
WEB: www.commercecasino.com
SIC: 7011 5812 Casino hotel; eating
places

(P-12108)
CAMINO REAL GROUP LLC
Also Called: Hilton
840 E El Camino Real, Mountain View
(94040-2808)
PHONE....................650 964-1700
Garrett Ritter, Manager
EMP: 50
SALES (est): 3.5MM Privately Held
SIC: 7011 Hotels & motels

(P-12109)
**CAMPBELL HHG HOTEL DEV
LLP**
Also Called: Courtyard By Marriott San Jose
655 Creekside Way, Campbell
(95008-0636)
PHONE....................408 626-9590
Brian Fox, Managing Prtnr
EMP: 50
SALES (est): 2.1MM Privately Held
SIC: 7011 7389 Hotels & motels; office fa-
cilities & secretarial service rental

(P-12110)
**CANDLEBERRY PROPERTIES
LP**
Also Called: AC Hotel Beverly Hills
6399 Wilshire Blvd, Los Angeles
(90048-5703)
PHONE....................323 852-7000
Jack Nourafshan, Managing Prtnr
EMP: 50 EST: 1994
SQ FT: 100,000
SALES: 31.2K Privately Held
SIC: 7011 Hotels & motels

(P-12111)
CANOGA HOTEL CORPORATION
Also Called: Hilton Wdlnd Hlls / Los Angles
6360 Canoga Ave, Woodland Hills
(91367-2501)
PHONE....................818 595-1000
James Evans, CFO
Debra Chica, Sales Staff
EMP: 200
SALES (est): 4.3MM Privately Held
SIC: 7011 Hotels & motels

(P-12112)
CANTERBURY HOTEL CORP
Also Called: Wyndham Canterbury At
750 Sutter St, San Francisco (94109-6417)
PHONE....................415 345-3200
Dean Lehr, President
Jacqueline W Lehr, Ch of Bd
Frederick T Smith, Treasurer
Jon Lehr, Vice Pres
EMP: 110
SQ FT: 98,410
SALES (est): 3.5MM Privately Held
WEB: www.canterbury-hotel.com
SIC: 7011 5812 6531 Hotels; eating
places; time-sharing real estate sales,
leasing & rentals

(P-12113)
CAPITOL REGENCY LLC
Also Called: Hyatt Regency Sacramento
1209 L St, Sacramento (95814-3936)
PHONE....................916 443-1234
Randy Verrue,
Stephanie Schreiber, Opers Staff
Brenda Miller, Sales Executive
EMP: 360
SALES (est): 22.6MM Privately Held
SIC: 7011 Hotels & motels

(P-12114)
**CARLTON HOTEL PROPERTIES
LP**
1075 Sutter St, San Francisco
(94109-5866)
PHONE....................415 673-0242
Diane Feinstein, Partner
Richard Blum, Partner
Eileen Gartland, Partner
EMP: 55

SQ FT: 76,000
SALES (est): 3.8MM **Privately Held**
SIC: 7011 5812 Hotels; eating places

(P-12115)
CARMEL VALLEY RANCH
Also Called: Carmel Valley Ranch Hotel
1 Old Ranch Rd, Carmel (93923-8579)
PHONE...................831 625-9500
Thomas Becker, *General Mgr*
Cv Ranch, *General Ptnr*
David Hunter, *Engineer*
Luke Barnett, *Food Svc Dir*
Kristin Bobb, *Director*
EMP: 250 **EST:** 1993
SALES (est): 23MM **Privately Held**
SIC: 7011 7997 6552 Resort hotel; tennis
club, membership; golf club, membership;
subdividers & developers

(P-12116)
CARMEL VLY MRTG BORROWER LLC
Also Called: Carmel Valley Resort
1 Old Ranch Rd, Carmel (93923-8551)
PHONE...................831 625-9500
Laura Bell, *Principal*
EMP: 99
SALES (est): 1.5MM **Privately Held**
SIC: 7011 Resort hotel

(P-12117)
CARNEROS INN LLC
Also Called: Poumtjack Hotels
4048 Sonoma Hwy, NAPA (94559-9745)
PHONE...................707 299-4880
Keith Rogal, *CEO*
Nick Monroe, *CFO*
Frederick Fennikoh, *General Mgr*
Randy Valdez, *General Mgr*
Jonathan Vail, *Info Tech Mgr*
EMP: 350
SQ FT: 50,000
SALES (est): 22.1MM **Privately Held**
SIC: 7011 Resort hotel; hotels

(P-12118)
CARPENTERS SOUTHWEST ADM CORP (PA)
533 S Fremont Ave, Los Angeles
(90071-1712)
P.O. Box 17969 (90017-0969)
PHONE...................213 386-8590
Douglas McCarron, *CEO*
Rod Webber, *Info Tech Mgr*
Sandra Maloney, *Project Mgr*
Nina Gutierrez, *Controller*
Betty Becerra, *Manager*
EMP: 70
SQ FT: 25,000
SALES (est): 49.6MM **Privately Held**
SIC: 7011 Hotels & motels

(P-12119)
CARPINTERIA MOTOR INN INC
Also Called: Best Western
4558 Carpinteria Ave, Carpinteria
(93013-1863)
PHONE...................805 684-0473
Kevin Sweniak, *General Mgr*
EMP: 50
SALES (est): 1.9MM **Privately Held**
SIC: 7011 Hotels & motels

(P-12120)
CARSON OPERATING COMPANY LLC
Also Called: Doubletree By Hilton Carson
2 Civic Plaza Dr, Carson (90745-2231)
PHONE...................310 830-9200
Greg Guthrie, *General Mgr*
Leroy Russell, *Controller*
EMP: 90 **EST:** 2015
SALES (est): 2.1MM **Privately Held**
SIC: 7011 Hotels & motels

(P-12121)
CASA MADRONA HOTEL AND SPA LLC
801 Bridgeway, Sausalito (94965-2186)
PHONE...................415 332-0502
John Warren Mays,
Brian Kelley, *Controller*
Jeremy Gaunt, *Human Res Mgr*
Darren Oliver, *Marketing Staff*

Steven Raucher, *Manager*
EMP: 55
SQ FT: 18,000
SALES (est): 4.1MM **Privately Held**
WEB: www.casamadrona.com
SIC: 7011 5812 Hotels; eating places
PA: Olympus Real Estate Corp
5080 Spectrum Dr
Addison TX 75001

(P-12122)
CASA MUNRAS HOTEL LLC
700 Munras Ave, Monterey (93940-3110)
PHONE...................831 375-2411
Karl K Hoagland III,
EMP: 82
SALES: 950K **Privately Held**
SIC: 7011 Hotels

(P-12123)
CASTLBLACK PISMO BCH OWNER LLC
Also Called: Hilton Garden Inn Pismo
601 James Way, Pismo Beach
(93449-3502)
PHONE...................805 773-6020
Gordon Jackson, *Manager*
Laura Benner, *Vice Pres*
EMP: 50
SALES (est): 1.4MM
SALES (corp-wide): 18.7MM **Privately Held**
SIC: 7011 Hotels & motels
PA: Castleblack Owner Holdings, Llc
399 Park Ave Fl 18
New York NY 10022
212 547-2609

(P-12124)
CASTLEHILL PROPERTIES INC (PA)
Also Called: Residnce Inn By Mrrott Stckton
3240 W March Ln, Stockton (95219-2341)
PHONE...................209 472-9800
Jeff Carpenter, *General Mgr*
Eric Pipitone, *Manager*
EMP: 52 **EST:** 1997
SALES (est): 4.8MM **Privately Held**
SIC: 7011 Hotels & motels

(P-12125)
CAVALIER INN INC
Also Called: Cavalier Oceanfront Resort
9415 Hearst Dr, San Simeon (93452-9724)
PHONE...................805 927-4688
Mona Rigdon, *Principal*
Barb Hanchett, *CFO*
Michael Hanchett, *Principal*
Lu Fletcher, *Exec Dir*
EMP: 80
SALES (est): 599.6K **Privately Held**
SIC: 7011 Inns

(P-12126)
CAVALIER INN INCORPORATED
Also Called: Best Western
250 San Simeon Ave Ste 4c, San Simeon
(93452-9715)
PHONE...................805 927-6444
Michael R Hanchett, *President*
Barbara J Hanchett, *CFO*
EMP: 90
SALES (est): 4.8MM **Privately Held**
WEB: www.cavalierresort.com
SIC: 7011 Hotels & motels

(P-12127)
CAVALLO POINT LLC (PA)
601 Murray Cir, Sausalito (94965)
PHONE...................415 339-4700
Peter Heinmann, *Partner*
Lonny Watne, *Branch Mgr*
Brendan Carlin, *General Mgr*
Jackie Alcantara, *Sales Mgr*
Kalyana Krishnamoorthy, *Director*
EMP: 80 **EST:** 2007
SALES (est): 11MM **Privately Held**
SIC: 7011 Hotels

(P-12128)
CB-1 HOTEL
Also Called: Four Seasons Hotel
757 Market St, San Francisco
(94103-2001)
PHONE...................415 633-3788

Douglas Housley, *General Mgr*
Tara Forkum, *Sales Staff*
EMP: 99
SQ FT: 59,300
SALES (est): 6.8MM **Privately Held**
SIC: 7011 Hotels

(P-12129)
CDC SAN FRANCISCO LLC
Also Called: Intercontinental San Francisco
888 Howard St, San Francisco
(94103-3011)
PHONE...................415 616-6512
Peter Koehler,
EMP: 99 **EST:** 2007
SALES: 950K **Privately Held**
SIC: 7011 Hotels

(P-12130)
CELEBRITY CASINOS INC
Also Called: Crystal Casino & Hotel
123 E Artesia Blvd, Compton (90220-4921)
PHONE...................310 631-3838
Mark A Kelegian, *President*
Haig Kelegian Jr, *CEO*
EMP: 400
SQ FT: 190,000
SALES (est): 17.5MM **Privately Held**
SIC: 7011 Casino hotel

(P-12131)
CENTURY NATIONAL PROPERTIES (PA)
Also Called: Daytona Surfise
12200 Sylvan St Ste 250, North Hollywood
(91606-3229)
PHONE...................818 760-0880
Weldon Wilson, *President*
Judith Osborne, *Treasurer*
Marie Balicki, *Admin Sec*
EMP: 61
SQ FT: 92,000
SALES (est): 3.7MM **Privately Held**
SIC: 7011 Hotels & motels

(P-12132)
CENTURY WILSHIRE INC
Also Called: Century Wilshire Hotel
9400 Culver Blvd, Culver City
(90232-2617)
PHONE...................310 558-9400
Theodora Mallick, *President*
Monika Mallick, *Corp Secy*
Seth Horowitz, *Vice Pres*
Maya Mallick, *Principal*
Virginie Rogers, *Controller*
EMP: 70
SQ FT: 38,000
SALES (est): 5.5MM **Privately Held**
WEB: www.centurywilshirehotel.com
SIC: 7011 Resort hotel; hotels

(P-12133)
CH CUPERTINO OWNER LLC
Also Called: Cypress Hotel
10050 S De Anza Blvd, Cupertino
(95014-2128)
PHONE...................408 253-8900
David Hayes, *Marketing Staff*
EMP: 130
SALES (est): 8MM **Privately Held**
WEB: www.thecypresshotel.com
SIC: 7011 Hotels

(P-12134)
CHAMINADE LTD
Also Called: Chaminade At Santa Cruz
1 Chaminade Ln, Santa Cruz (95065-1524)
PHONE...................831 475-5600
Tom O'Shea, *General Mgr*
James Birpo, *General Ptnr*
James Greggs, *General Ptnr*
Don Murchanson, *General Ptnr*
Paula Hamilton, *Planning*
EMP: 200 **EST:** 1979
SQ FT: 12,000
SALES: 10.3MM **Privately Held**
SIC: 7011 Resort hotel

(P-12135)
CHAMPION INVESTMENT CORP (PA)
12809 Oakfield Way, Poway (92064-1520)
PHONE...................917 712-7807
Chia-Sheng Hou, *President*
Pi-Lien Hou, *Treasurer*

EMP: 100
SALES (est): 1MM **Privately Held**
SIC: 7011 Hotels & motels

(P-12136)
CHAMSON MANAGEMENT INC
Also Called: Doubletree Hotel
7 Hutton Centre Dr, Santa Ana
(92707-5753)
PHONE...................714 751-2400
Jung-Hsiung Chiu, *President*
Magaly Marquez, *Accounting Mgr*
Corina Calderon, *Sales Mgr*
EMP: 90
SALES (est): 4.2MM **Privately Held**
SIC: 7011 Hotels & motels

(P-12137)
CHATEAU LA JOLLA INN
233 Prospect St, La Jolla (92037-4600)
PHONE...................858 459-4451
Toll Free:...................888 -
Robert Collins, *Partner*
Jeff Fee, *Partner*
EMP: 50 **EST:** 1978
SQ FT: 40,000
SALES (est): 3.9MM **Privately Held**
WEB: www.chateaulajollainn.com
SIC: 7011 Inns

(P-12138)
CHESAPEAKE LODGING TRUST
Also Called: Le Meridian Hotel
333 Battery St Lbby, San Francisco
(94111-3234)
PHONE...................415 296-2900
Joel Myers, *Director*
Joel Ellis, *Director*
Zachary Starke, *Director*
Michael Cochran, *Manager*
Fabrina Pena-Guzman, *Manager*
EMP: 87
SALES (est): 9.8MM **Privately Held**
SIC: 7011 7021 Hotels; lodging house, ex-
cept organization

(P-12139)
CHINA PEAK MOUNTAIN RESORT LLC
59265 Hwy 168, Lakeshore (93634)
P.O. Box 236 (93634-0236)
PHONE...................559 233-2500
Tim Cohee, *CEO*
Rich Bailey, *Manager*
Roger Myers, *Manager*
EMP: 74
SALES (est): 7.4MM **Privately Held**
SIC: 7011 Resort hotel

(P-12140)
CHIRAG HOSPITALITY INC
Also Called: Super 8 Motel
2440 Lombard St, San Francisco
(94123-2604)
PHONE...................415 922-0244
Chirag Patel, *CEO*
Mishan Giri, *Manager*
EMP: 78
SALES (est): 159.9K **Privately Held**
SIC: 7011 Hotels & motels

(P-12141)
CHOA HOPE LLC
Also Called: Sioux City Ht & Conference Ctr
515 W Washington Ave, Escondido
(92025-1628)
PHONE...................712 277-4101
Peter Parsons, *General Mgr*
EMP: 50
SALES (est): 1.9MM **Privately Held**
SIC: 7011 Hotels

(P-12142)
CHOICE HOTELS INTL INC
Also Called: Econo Lodge Inn & Suites
20688 Tracy Ave, Buttonwillow
(93206-9782)
PHONE...................661 764-5207
Gary Paradis, *General Mgr*
EMP: 98
SALES (corp-wide): 1B **Publicly Held**
SIC: 7011 Hotels & motels
PA: Choice Hotels International, Inc.
1 Choice Hotels Cir
Rockville MD 20850
301 592-5000

PRODUCTS & SVCS

(P-12143)
CHSP TRS FISHERMAN WHARF LLC
Also Called: Hyatt Fisherman's Wharf
555 N Point St, San Francisco (94133-1311)
PHONE...............................415 563-1234
James Francis, *President*
EMP: 180
SALES (est): 2MM
SALES (corp-wide): 2.7B **Publicly Held**
SIC: 7011 5813 5812 Hotels & motels; bars & lounges; eating places
HQ: Chesapeake Lodging Trust
4300 Wilson Blvd Ste 625
Arlington VA 22203

(P-12144)
CHSP TRS LOS ANGELES LLC
Also Called: Hilton Checkers Los Angeles
535 S Grand Ave, Los Angeles (90071-2601)
PHONE...............................213 624-0000
Eddie Andre, *Principal*
Paul Chambers, *Engineer*
EMP: 88
SALES (est): 2.5MM
SALES (corp-wide): 52.2MM **Privately Held**
SIC: 7011 Hotels & motels
PA: Crestline Hotels & Resorts, Llc
3950 University Dr # 301
Fairfax VA 22030
571 529-6100

(P-12145)
CHUKCHANSI GOLD RESORT CASINO
711 Lucky Ln, Coarsegold (93614-8206)
PHONE...............................866 794-6946
Richard Williams, *Owner*
Chanel Wright, *Officer*
Elaine McFarland, *Social Dir*
Tim Bos, *Security Dir*
BJ Martin, *General Mgr*
EMP: 1400
SQ FT: 489,000
SALES (est): 43.7MM **Privately Held**
SIC: 7011 Casino hotel

(P-12146)
CIM GROUP LP (PA)
Also Called: Commercial Inv MGT Group
4700 Wilshire Blvd Ste 1, Los Angeles (90010-3854)
PHONE...............................323 860-4900
Avraham Shemesch, *Partner*
Eric P Rubenfeld, *Partner*
Dmitry Gordeychev, *Assoc VP*
John Walton, *Assoc VP*
Garett Bjorkman, *Vice Pres*
EMP: 81
SALES (est): 199.5MM **Privately Held**
WEB: www.cimgroup.com
SIC: 7011 6798 6552 Hotels & motels; real estate investment trusts; land subdividers & developers, commercial

(P-12147)
CIM/OAKLAND CITY CENTER LLC
Also Called: City Center Grill
1001 Broadway, Oakland (94607-4019)
PHONE...............................510 451-4000
John Mazzoni, *Manager*
Avraham Shemesh, *Principal*
Keith Montgomery, *Controller*
EMP: 99
SALES (est): 8.1MM **Privately Held**
SIC: 7011 Hotels & motels

(P-12148)
CITRUS NORTH VENTURE
6591 Collins Dr Ste E11, Moorpark (93021-1493)
PHONE...............................256 428-2000
Marc Pierguidi, *Admin Sec*
EMP: 99
SALES (est): 273.9K **Privately Held**
SIC: 7011 Hotel, franchised

(P-12149)
CITY OF SAN JOSE
Also Called: Dolce Hayes Mansion
200 Edenvale Ave, San Jose (95136-3309)
PHONE...............................408 226-6765
Cedric Fasbender, *General Mgr*
Shelley Domondon, *Executive Asst*
EMP: 140 **Privately Held**
WEB: www.csjfinance.org
SIC: 7011 Hotels
PA: City Of San Jose
200 E Santa Clara St
San Jose CA 95113
408 535-3500

(P-12150)
CLAREMONT HT PRPTS LTD PARTNR
Also Called: Claremont Hotel Club & Spa
41 Tunnel Rd, Berkeley (94705-2429)
PHONE...............................510 843-3000
Len Czarnecki, *Mng Member*
Michael Coughlin, *Finance Dir*
Brandy Jones, *Sales Staff*
Denise Strasburg, *Manager*
EMP: 550
SALES (est): 17.9MM
SALES (corp-wide): 1.1B **Privately Held**
SIC: 7011 Resort hotel; hotels
HQ: Accor Services Us Llc
950 Mason St
San Francisco CA 94108
415 772-5000

(P-12151)
CLAREMONT STAR LP
Also Called: Doubletree Hotel
555 W Foothill Blvd, Claremont (91711-3478)
PHONE...............................909 482-0124
Harry Wu, *Partner*
Shawn Chen, *Partner*
Tiffany Wu, *General Mgr*
Tom Abercrombie, *Chief Engr*
▲ **EMP:** 50
SALES (est): 3.8MM **Privately Held**
SIC: 7011 Hotels & motels

(P-12152)
CLARION HOTEL SAN JOSE AIRPORT
1355 N 4th St, San Jose (95112-4783)
PHONE...............................408 453-5340
Ajay Shingal,
Ram Garg,
Mira Shingal,
EMP: 90
SALES (est): 3.1MM **Privately Held**
SIC: 7011 Hotels

(P-12153)
CLASSIC RIVERDALE INC
Also Called: Hyatt Hotel
200 Glenwood Cir, Monterey (93940-6741)
PHONE...............................831 373-0101
Matt Madison, *Partner*
EMP: 81
SALES (corp-wide): 79.7MM **Privately Held**
WEB: www.hyattclassic.com
SIC: 7011 Hotels & motels
PA: Classic Riverdale, Inc.
200 W Madison St Ste 3700
Chicago IL 60606
312 803-8800

(P-12154)
CLASSIC RSDENCE MGT LTD PARTNR
Also Called: Hyatt Hotel
200 Glenwood Cir Ofc, Monterey (93940-6773)
PHONE...............................831 373-0101
Deann Daniel, *Exec Dir*
EMP: 100
SQ FT: 196,000
SALES (est): 3.8MM **Privately Held**
SIC: 7011 8322 Hotels & motels; senior citizens' center or association

(P-12155)
CLOCKTOWER INN
Also Called: Ramada Clock Tower Inn
181 E Santa Clara St, Ventura (93001-2715)
PHONE...............................805 652-0141
S Patel, *President*
Bahgat Tadros, *Asst Treas*
EMP: 65
SQ FT: 29,000
SALES (est): 3.3MM **Privately Held**
SIC: 7011 Hotels

(P-12156)
CLUB ONE CASINO INC
1033 Van Ness Ave, Fresno (93721-2006)
PHONE...............................559 497-3000
Kyle R Kirkland, *President*
George Sarantos, *President*
Jeremy Newman, *Mktg Dir*
EMP: 325
SQ FT: 25,000
SALES (est): 14.6MM **Privately Held**
WEB: www.clubonecasino.com
SIC: 7011 Casino hotel

(P-12157)
CLUB QUARTERS SAN FRANCISCO
424 Clay St, San Francisco (94111-3207)
PHONE...............................415 268-3606
Sanj Rai, *Manager*
Joeann La Madrid, *Sales Executive*
EMP: 99
SALES (est): 3.1MM **Privately Held**
SIC: 7011 Hotels

(P-12158)
CNCML A CALIFORNIA LTD PARTNR
Also Called: Plumpjack The
1920 Squaw Valley Rd, Olympic Valley (96146)
P.O. Box 2407 (96146-2407)
PHONE...............................530 583-1578
Hilary Newsom, *President*
Jeremy Scherer, *Vice Pres*
Milham D Wakin, *Vice Pres*
Steve Lamb, *General Mgr*
Rob McCormick, *Sales Staff*
EMP: 100 **EST:** 1975
SQ FT: 20,000
SALES (est): 5.8MM **Privately Held**
SIC: 7011 5812 Resort hotel; eating places

(P-12159)
CNI THL OPS LLC
Also Called: Sheraton Hotel San Jose
1801 Barber Ln, Milpitas (95035-7419)
P.O. Box 93, San Jose (95103-0093)
PHONE...............................408 943-0600
Keon Marvasti, *Manager*
EMP: 98
SQ FT: 148,435
SALES (corp-wide): 135.3MM **Privately Held**
WEB: www.hicrystallake.com
SIC: 7011 Hotels & motels
PA: Cni Thl Ops, Llc
515 S Flower St Fl 44
Los Angeles CA

(P-12160)
CNI THL PROPCO FE LLC
Also Called: Four Points Bakersfield
5101 California Ave, Bakersfield (93309-1623)
PHONE...............................661 325-9700
Keon Marvasti,
EMP: 80
SALES (est): 599.6K **Privately Held**
SIC: 7011 Hotels & motels

(P-12161)
COLONY PALMS HOTEL LLC
572 N Indian Canyon Dr, Palm Springs (92262-6030)
PHONE...............................760 969-1800
Al Wertheimer, *Owner*
Ashley Ross, *Principal*
EMP: 70 **EST:** 2011
SALES (est): 2.3MM **Privately Held**
SIC: 7011 Resort hotel; hotels

(P-12162)
COLUMBIA HOSPITALITY INC
Also Called: Inns of Monterey
652 Cannery Row, Monterey (93940-1021)
PHONE...............................831 646-8900
Randy Bernard, *Manager*
EMP: 120
SALES (corp-wide): 86MM **Privately Held**
WEB: www.coastalhotel.com
SIC: 7011 5813 5812 Hotels; drinking places; eating places
PA: Columbia Hospitality Inc
2200 Alaskan Way Ste 200
Seattle WA 98121
206 441-6666

(P-12163)
COLUMBIA HOSPITALITY INC
Also Called: Hotel Pacific
300 Pacific St, Monterey (93940-2418)
PHONE...............................831 373-5700
Randy Venard, *Manager*
Fady Hanna, *General Mgr*
EMP: 55
SALES (corp-wide): 86MM **Privately Held**
WEB: www.coastalhotel.com
SIC: 7011 Hotels
PA: Columbia Hospitality Inc
2200 Alaskan Way Ste 200
Seattle WA 98121
206 441-6666

(P-12164)
COLUMBIA HOSPITALITY INC
Also Called: Victorian Inn
487 Foam St, Monterey (93940-1409)
PHONE...............................831 373-8000
Patrick Mallone, *Manager*
EMP: 50
SALES (corp-wide): 86MM **Privately Held**
WEB: www.coastalhotel.com
SIC: 7011 Hotels
PA: Columbia Hospitality Inc
2200 Alaskan Way Ste 200
Seattle WA 98121
206 441-6666

(P-12165)
COLUMBIA WOODLAKE LLC
500 Leisure Ln, Sacramento (95815-4207)
PHONE...............................206 728-9063
Alex Washburn, *President*
Leigh Noble, *CFO*
EMP: 90
SALES (est): 1.2MM **Privately Held**
SIC: 7011 Resort hotel

(P-12166)
COMFORT CALIFORNIA INC
Also Called: Comfort Inn
2775 Van Ness Ave, San Francisco (94109-1423)
PHONE...............................415 928-5000
Todd Symynuk, *Branch Mgr*
EMP: 50
SALES (corp-wide): 189.8MM **Privately Held**
WEB: www.clarionanaheim.com
SIC: 7011 Hotels & motels
HQ: Comfort California, Inc.
10750 Columbia Pike # 300
Silver Spring MD 20901
301 592-3800

(P-12167)
COMFORT CALIFORNIA INC
Also Called: Clarion Hotel
616 W Convention Way, Anaheim (92802-3401)
PHONE...............................714 750-3131
Mike Thomas, *Branch Mgr*
Cathy Dutton, *Sales Dir*
EMP: 83
SALES (corp-wide): 189.8MM **Privately Held**
WEB: www.clarionanaheim.com
SIC: 7011 Hotels & motels
HQ: Comfort California, Inc.
10750 Columbia Pike # 300
Silver Spring MD 20901
301 592-3800

(P-12168)
COMFORT SUITES
Also Called: Comfort Inn
121 E Grand Ave, South San Francisco
(94080-4800)
PHONE..................................650 589-7100
David R Lane, *CFO*
Steven Nokes, *Partner*
Lani Zachary, *Sales Staff*
EMP: 100
SQ FT: 5,000
SALES (est): 3.1MM **Privately Held**
SIC: 7011 Hotels & motels

(P-12169)
CONCORD HOTEL LLC
Also Called: Crowne Plaza Concord
45 John Glenn Dr, Concord (94520-5604)
PHONE..................................925 521-3751
Dave Warner,
Aaron Olson, *General Mgr*
EMP: 95
SALES: 8MM **Privately Held**
SIC: 7011 Hotels & motels

(P-12170)
CONESTOGA HOTEL
Also Called: Holiday Inn
1240 S Walnut St, Anaheim (92802-2241)
PHONE..................................714 535-0300
Kevin Clayton, *General Mgr*
Mark Nunneley, *CFO*
Tom Van Winkle, *General Mgr*
▲ **EMP:** 90
SQ FT: 150,000
SALES (est): 2.2MM **Privately Held**
WEB: www.conestogahotel.com
SIC: 7011 5812 5813 Hotels & motels;
American restaurant; drinking places

(P-12171)
COUNTRY INN &SUITE BY CARLSON
231 N Vineyard Ave, Ontario (91764-4427)
PHONE..................................909 937-6000
Peter Bhakta, *Owner*
EMP: 50
SALES (est): 639.5K **Privately Held**
SIC: 7011 Hotels & motels

(P-12172)
COUNTRYSIDE INN-CORONA LP
Also Called: Ayres Hotel Laguna Woods
24341 El Toro Rd, Laguna Woods
(92637-4901)
PHONE..................................949 588-0131
Vince Neale, *Manager*
EMP: 60
SALES (corp-wide): 33.8MM **Privately Held**
WEB: www.ayreshotelgroup.com
SIC: 7011 Resort hotel
PA: Countryside Inn-Corona, L.P.
1900 Frontage Rd
Corona CA 92882
714 540-6060

(P-12173)
COUNTRYSIDE INN-CORONA LP
Also Called: Countryside Suites By Ayres
325 Bristol St, Costa Mesa (92626-5998)
PHONE..................................714 549-0300
Steve Winning, *General Mgr*
EMP: 100
SALES (corp-wide): 33.8MM **Privately Held**
WEB: www.ayreshotelgroup.com
SIC: 7011 5813 5812 Hotels; drinking places; eating places
PA: Countryside Inn-Corona, L.P.
1900 Frontage Rd
Corona CA 92882
714 540-6060

(P-12174)
COURTYARD BY MARRIOTT
595 Hotel Cir S, San Diego (92108-3403)
PHONE..................................619 291-5720
Veronica Butler, *Director*
Tracey Palmberg, *Sales Executive*
EMP: 60
SALES (est): 3MM **Privately Held**
SIC: 7011 Hotels & motels

(P-12175)
COURTYARD BY MARRIOTT
1605 Calle Joaquin, San Luis Obispo
(93405-7214)
PHONE..................................805 786-4200
James Flagg,
EMP: 55
SALES (est): 2.2MM **Privately Held**
SIC: 7011 Hotels & motels

(P-12176)
COURTYARD BY MARRIOTT
2500 Larkspur Landing Cir, Larkspur
(94939-1831)
PHONE..................................415 925-1800
Sam Pahlazan, *Principal*
Sam Pahlavan, *General Mgr*
EMP: 80
SALES (est): 1.9MM **Privately Held**
SIC: 7011 Hotels & motels

(P-12177)
COURTYARD BY MARRIOTT
1905 S Azusa Ave, Hacienda Heights
(91745-6850)
PHONE..................................626 965-1700
Michael Sweany, *Principal*
Maritza Mejia, *General Mgr*
EMP: 80
SALES (est): 2MM **Privately Held**
SIC: 7011 Hotels & motels

(P-12178)
COURTYARD BY MARRIOTT/LAX
6161 W Century Blvd, Los Angeles
(90045-5310)
PHONE..................................310 981-2350
Patricia Marks, *Finance*
EMP: 63
SALES (est): 861.7K **Privately Held**
SIC: 7011 Hotels & motels

(P-12179)
COURTYARD MANAGEMENT CORP
Also Called: Courtyard By Marriott
21101 Ventura Blvd, Woodland Hills
(91364-2104)
PHONE..................................818 999-2200
J Willard Marriott, *Principal*
EMP: 55
SALES (corp-wide): 20.7B **Publicly Held**
SIC: 7011 Hotels & motels
HQ: Courtyard Management Corporation
10400 Fernwood Rd
Bethesda MD 20817

(P-12180)
COURTYARD MANAGEMENT CORP
Also Called: Courtyard By Marriott Irvine
7955 Irvine Center Dr, Irvine (92618-3207)
PHONE..................................949 453-1033
Audun Poulsen, *General Mgr*
EMP: 70
SALES (corp-wide): 20.7B **Publicly Held**
SIC: 7011 Hotels & motels
HQ: Courtyard Management Corporation
10400 Fernwood Rd
Bethesda MD 20817

(P-12181)
COURTYARD MANAGEMENT CORP
Also Called: Courtyard By Marriott
2250 Contra Costa Blvd, Pleasant Hill
(94523-3744)
PHONE..................................925 691-1444
Trace Moviel, *Branch Mgr*
EMP: 50
SALES (corp-wide): 20.7B **Publicly Held**
SIC: 7011 Hotels & motels
HQ: Courtyard Management Corporation
10400 Fernwood Rd
Bethesda MD 20817

(P-12182)
COURTYARD MANAGEMENT CORP
Also Called: Courtyard By Marriott
10683 White Rock Rd, Rancho Cordova
(95670-6002)
PHONE..................................916 638-3800
John Lister, *Branch Mgr*
EMP: 50
SALES (corp-wide): 20.7B **Publicly Held**
SIC: 7011 Hotels & motels
HQ: Courtyard Management Corporation
10400 Fernwood Rd
Bethesda MD 20817

(P-12183)
COURTYARD MANAGEMENT CORP
Also Called: Courtyard By Marriott
2000 E Mariposa Ave, El Segundo
(90245-5027)
PHONE..................................310 322-0700
Steve Vandesteeg, *Manager*
EMP: 167
SALES (corp-wide): 20.7B **Publicly Held**
SIC: 7011 Hotels & motels
HQ: Courtyard Management Corporation
10400 Fernwood Rd
Bethesda MD 20817

(P-12184)
COURTYARD OXNARD
600 E Esplanade Dr, Oxnard (93036-2403)
PHONE..................................805 988-3600
Patricia Tewes, *General Mgr*
Maria Zavala, *Executive*
EMP: 80
SALES (est): 128.1K **Privately Held**
SIC: 7011 Hotels & motels

(P-12185)
COURTYARD-CENTRAL
Also Called: Courtyard By Marriott San Dieg
8651 Spectrum Center Blvd, San Diego
(92123-1489)
PHONE..................................858 573-0700
Brnet Andrus, *President*
Sherry Chester, *General Mgr*
EMP: 70
SALES (est): 2.9MM **Privately Held**
WEB: www.cy-kearnymesa.com
SIC: 7011 7389 Hotels & motels; office facilities & secretarial service rental

(P-12186)
CPH MONARCH HOTEL LLC
Also Called: St Regis Resort Monarch Beach
1 Monarch Beach Resort, Dana Point
(92629-4085)
PHONE..................................949 234-3200
Paul Makarechian, *President*
EMP: 1100
SQ FT: 300,000
SALES (est): 56.1MM
SALES (corp-wide): 46.5MM **Privately Held**
SIC: 7011 Resort hotel
PA: Washington Real Estate Holdings Llc
600 University St # 2820
Seattle WA 98101
206 613-5300

(P-12187)
CREEDENCE LESSEE LLC
Also Called: Hotel Zoe
425 N Point St, San Francisco
(94133-1405)
PHONE..................................415 561-1100
Emily Chung, *Director*
EMP: 99
SALES (est): 864.5K **Privately Held**
SIC: 7011 Hotels
PA: Pebblebrook Hotel Trust
7315 Wscnsin Ave Ste 1100
Bethesda MD 20814

(P-12188)
CRESTLINE HOTELS & RESORTS INC
Also Called: Kyoto Grand Hotel and Gardens
120 S Los Angeles St 11, Los Angeles
(90012-3724)
PHONE..................................213 629-1200
Richard Gaines, *General Mgr*
Joe Kuhn, *General Mgr*
Phyllis Navarrete, *Human Res Dir*
Jeannette Garcia, *Human Resources*
Samuel Reece, *Opers Staff*
EMP: 250
SALES (est): 4.3MM
SALES (corp-wide): 52.2MM **Privately Held**
SIC: 7011 5812 5813 Hotels; restaurant, family: independent; drinking places
PA: Crestline Hotels & Resorts, Llc
3950 University Dr # 301
Fairfax VA 22030
571 529-6100

(P-12189)
CRESTLINE HOTELS & RESORTS LLC
Also Called: Renaissance Palm Springs Hotel
888 E Tahquitz Canyon Way, Palm Springs
(92262-6708)
PHONE..................................760 322-6000
Eric Hill, *Controller*
EMP: 200
SALES (corp-wide): 52.2MM **Privately Held**
WEB: www.crestlinehotels.com
SIC: 7011 Hotels & motels
PA: Crestline Hotels & Resorts, Llc
3950 University Dr # 301
Fairfax VA 22030
571 529-6100

(P-12190)
CROWN PLAZA SD
Also Called: Islands Restaurant & Lounge
2270 Hotel Cir N, San Diego (92108-2810)
PHONE..................................619 297-1101
Anna Cooper, *Manager*
EMP: 60
SALES (est): 2.4MM **Privately Held**
WEB: www.islandssushi.com
SIC: 7011 5812 Hotels & motels; eating places

(P-12191)
CROWNE PLAZA LAX LLC
5985 W Century Blvd, Los Angeles
(90045-5477)
PHONE..................................310 258-1321
Paul Gibbs, *General Mgr*
EMP: 250
SALES (est): 7.1MM **Privately Held**
WEB: www.crowneplaza.com
SIC: 7011 Hotels
HQ: Intercontinental Hotels Group Resources, Inc.
3 Ravinia Dr Ste 100
Atlanta GA 30346
770 604-5000

(P-12192)
CTC GROUP INC (DH)
Also Called: Doubletree Hotel
21333 Hawthorne Blvd, Torrance
(90503-5602)
PHONE..................................310 540-0500
John Huang, *CEO*
EMP: 145
SALES (est): 17MM
SALES (corp-wide): 2.7B **Publicly Held**
WEB: www.hiltontorrance.com
SIC: 7011 Hotels & motels

(P-12193)
CUPERTINO LESSEE LLC
Also Called: Juniper Hotel
10050 S De Anza Blvd, Cupertino
(95014-2128)
PHONE..................................908 253-8900
Peggy Chen, *General Mgr*
EMP: 120
SALES: 19.5MM
SALES (corp-wide): 2.7B **Publicly Held**
SIC: 7011 5812 Hotels; American restaurant

PA: Park Hotels & Resorts Inc.
1775 Tysons Blvd Fl 7
Tysons VA 22102
571 302-5757

(P-12194)
CUSTOM HOTEL LLC
8639 Lincoln Blvd, Los Angeles
(90045-3503)
PHONE.................................310 645-0400
Alisa Matthews, *General Mgr*
Jerry Peck, *Controller*
EMP: 100
SALES (est): 3.6MM
SALES (corp-wide): 231.8MM **Privately Held**
SIC: 7011 Hotels & motels
PA: Joie De Vivre Hospitality, Llc
1750 Geary Blvd
San Francisco CA 94115
415 835-0300

(P-12195)
CUSTOM HOUSE HOTEL LP
Also Called: Portola Hotel & Spa
2 Portola Plz, Monterey (93940-2419)
PHONE.................................831 649-4511
Dan Pollock,
EMP: 91
SALES (est): 10.7MM **Privately Held**
SIC: 7011 Bed & breakfast inn; hotels

(P-12196)
CWGP LIMITED PARTNERSHIP
Also Called: Marriott
1740 Ocean Ave, Santa Monica
(90401-3214)
PHONE.................................310 395-9700
Kai Beumer, *General Mgr*
Sig K Otloff, *General Mgr*
EMP: 100
SALES (est): 5.1MM **Privately Held**
WEB: www.lemerigotbeachhotel.com
SIC: 7011 Hotels & motels
PA: C W Hotels Ltd
740 Centre View Blvd
Crestview Hills KY 41017
859 578-1100

(P-12197)
CY GASLAMP LLC
Also Called: Courtyard San Diego Gaslamp
453 6th Ave, San Diego (92101-7007)
PHONE.................................619 544-1004
Tim Billing, *General Mgr*
Ana Dervi, *Accounts Mgr*
EMP: 65
SALES (est): 1MM **Privately Held**
SIC: 7011 Hotels & motels

(P-12198)
CY SAC OPERATOR LLC
Also Called: Courtyard Sacramento-Midtown
4422 Y St, Sacramento (95817-2220)
PHONE.................................916 455-6800
Colleen Jimenez,
Roshan Bhakta,
EMP: 67
SALES: 4.9MM **Privately Held**
SIC: 7011 Hotels & motels

(P-12199)
D & W LLC
Also Called: Ramada Inn
3501 Rindge Ln, Redondo Beach
(90278-1420)
PHONE.................................310 345-0075
Paul Ding,
Jane Ding,
Jenny Wu,
EMP: 55
SQ FT: 80,000
SALES (est): 859.8K **Privately Held**
SIC: 7011 Hotels & motels

(P-12200)
DARENSBURG ROGHAIR & RENIER
Also Called: Quailty Inn of Barstow
1520 E Main St, Barstow (92311-3230)
PHONE.................................760 256-6891
Charles Darensburg, *Partner*
EMP: 50
SALES (est): 1.2MM **Privately Held**
SIC: 7011 5812 Motel, franchised; American restaurant

(P-12201)
DAVIDSON HOTEL PARTNERS LP
Also Called: Agoura Hills Renaissance Hotel
30100 Agoura Rd, Agoura Hills
(91301-2004)
PHONE.................................818 707-1220
Larry Mills, *Partner*
EMP: 120 **Privately Held**
SIC: 7011 Hotels & motels
PA: Davidson Hotel Partners, L.P
1 Ravinia Dr Ste 1600
Atlanta GA 30346

(P-12202)
DAWN RANCH LODGE & RD HSE REST
16467 Hwy 116, Guerneville (95446-8328)
P.O. Box 45 (95446-0045)
PHONE.................................707 869-0656
Michael Clark, *President*
EMP: 65 EST: 1905
SQ FT: 23,226
SALES (est): 2.1MM **Privately Held**
SIC: 7011 5813 5812 Resort hotel; bar (drinking places); eating places

(P-12203)
DAYS INN BAKERSFIELD
Also Called: Regency Inn
818 Real Rd, Bakersfield (93309-1002)
PHONE.................................661 324-6666
Robert King, *President*
EMP: 135
SQ FT: 40,000
SALES (est): 1.5MM **Privately Held**
SIC: 7011 5812 5813 7933 Hotels & motels; eating places; cocktail lounge; bowling centers

(P-12204)
DCP JL TRITON SF LLC
Also Called: Hotel Triton
342 Grant Ave, San Francisco
(94108-3607)
PHONE.................................844 808-0290
F Matthew Dinapoli,
Ben Lawson, *General Mgr*
EMP: 50
SALES (est): 184.9K **Privately Held**
SIC: 7011 Hotels

(P-12205)
DESTINATION RESIDENCES LLC
Also Called: Shadow Mnt Rsort/Rcqut CL Tns
45750 San Luis Rey Ave, Palm Desert
(92260-4728)
PHONE.................................760 346-4647
Sindy Calhoun, *Manager*
EMP: 50
SALES (corp-wide): 865.7MM **Privately Held**
WEB: www.destinationhotels.com
SIC: 7011 5699 6531 Resort hotel; sports apparel; condominium manager
HQ: Destination Residences Llc
10333 E Dry Creek Rd
Englewood CO 80112
303 799-3830

(P-12206)
DIAMOND INTL INVESTMENT LLC
3737 N Blackstone Ave, Fresno
(93726-5307)
PHONE.................................559 226-2200
Betty Qi,
Alvin Cachaper, *Manager*
EMP: 63 EST: 2015
SALES (est): 1.1MM **Privately Held**
SIC: 7011 Hotel, franchised

(P-12207)
DIAMOND MOUNTAIN CASINO
900 Skyline Dr, Susanville (96130-6071)
PHONE.................................530 252-1100
Campbell Jamieson, *Manager*
Matthew Wolcott, *COO*
Jill Ault, *Officer*
Ted Cutler, *Exec Dir*
Bob Nay, *Security Dir*
EMP: 135
SQ FT: 24,000
SALES (est): 9.7MM **Privately Held**
WEB: www.diamondmountaincasino.com
SIC: 7011 Casino hotel

(P-12208)
DIAMOND RESORTS LLC
Also Called: Palm Canyon Resort & Spa
2800 S Palm Canyon Dr, Palm Springs
(92264-9337)
PHONE.................................760 866-1800
Allison Wickerham, *Mng Member*
Lila Carrabus, *Chief Mktg Ofcr*
Carl Ellis, *Principal*
Todd Connelly, *General Mgr*
Kate Anderson, *Pub Rel Dir*
EMP: 100 EST: 2004
SALES: 300K **Privately Held**
WEB: www.palmcanyonresort.org
SIC: 7011 5812 7991 Resort hotel; American restaurant; spas

(P-12209)
DIAMONDROCK SAN DEGO TNANT LLC
Also Called: Westin San Diego
400 W Broadway, San Diego (92101-3504)
PHONE.................................619 239-4500
John Beaton,
Pamela Ford Green, *Accounting Mgr*
Deidre Bengston, *Sales Staff*
Khoa Hoang, *Manager*
Faul Lotz, *Manager*
EMP: 300
SQ FT: 337,717
SALES (est): 9.2MM
SALES (corp-wide): 863.7MM **Publicly Held**
SIC: 7011 Hotels & motels
HQ: Diamondrock Hospitality Limited Partnership
3 Bethesda Metro Ctr
Bethesda MD 20814

(P-12210)
DIMENSION DEVELOPMENT TWO LLC
Also Called: Sheraton
11611 Bernardo Plaza Ct, San Diego
(92128-2408)
PHONE.................................858 485-9250
Douglas R Korn, *Branch Mgr*
EMP: 60
SALES (corp-wide): 57.6MM **Privately Held**
WEB: www.dimdev.com
SIC: 7011 Hotels & motels
PA: Dimension Development Two, Llc
769 Highway 494
Natchitoches LA 71457
318 352-9519

(P-12211)
DISNEY ENTERPRISES INC
1150 W Magic Way, Anaheim (92802-2247)
PHONE.................................714 778-6600
Michael D Eisner, *President*
Kelli Bazen, *Executive*
Weita Jimmy, *Executive*
Gregory J Deems, *Meeting Planner*
Deborah Hahn, *Sales Staff*
EMP: 3500
SALES (corp-wide): 90.2B **Publicly Held**
SIC: 7011 Resort hotel
HQ: Disney Enterprises, Inc.
500 S Buena Vista St
Burbank CA 91521
818 560-1000

(P-12212)
DISNEY ENTERPRISES INC
1717 S Disneyland Dr, Anaheim
(92802-2308)
PHONE.................................714 999-0990
Samantha Muntz, *Principal*
EMP: 300
SALES (corp-wide): 90.2B **Publicly Held**
SIC: 7011 5813 5812 Resort hotel; drinking places; eating places
HQ: Disney Enterprises, Inc.
500 S Buena Vista St
Burbank CA 91521
818 560-1000

(P-12213)
DISNEYLAND INTERNATIONAL
1580 S Disneyland Dr, Anaheim
(92802-2294)
PHONE.................................714 956-6746
EMP: 300
SALES (corp-wide): 90.2B **Publicly Held**
SIC: 7011 Resort hotel
HQ: Disneyland International
1313 S Harbor Blvd
Anaheim CA 92802
714 781-4565

(P-12214)
DJONT OPERATIONS LLC
Also Called: Embassy Suites
150 Anza Blvd, Burlingame (94010-1924)
PHONE.................................650 342-4600
Ernie Catanzaro, *General Mgr*
EMP: 51
SALES (corp-wide): 1.7B **Privately Held**
SIC: 7011 Hotels & motels
HQ: Djont Operations, L.L.C.
125 E Houston St
San Antonio TX 78205

(P-12215)
DJONT/CMB SSF LEASING LLC
Also Called: Embassy Sites-So San Francisco
250 Gateway Blvd, South San Francisco
(94080-7018)
PHONE.................................650 589-3400
Rudy Ortiz, *General Mgr*
Dee Bradford, *Executive*
EMP: 60
SALES (est): 348.4K
SALES (corp-wide): 1.7B **Privately Held**
SIC: 7011 Hotels & motels
HQ: Rangers Sub I, Llc
3 Bethesda Metro Ctr # 1000
Bethesda MD 20814

(P-12216)
DKN HOTEL LLC (PA)
42 Corporate Park Ste 200, Irvine
(92606-3104)
PHONE.................................714 427-4320
Kiran Patel, *CEO*
Nilesh Patel, *Co-Owner*
John Jorgensen, *Vice Pres*
Bhalesh Gandhi, *Controller*
Rita Lopez, *Hum Res Coord*
EMP: 290
SQ FT: 4,000
SALES (est): 41.5MM **Privately Held**
WEB: www.dknhotels.com
SIC: 7011 Hotels & motels

(P-12217)
DKN HOTEL LLC
Also Called: Holiday Inn
1240 S Walnut St, Anaheim (92802-2241)
PHONE.................................714 535-0300
Niral Munshaw, *Branch Mgr*
EMP: 88
SALES (corp-wide): 41.5MM **Privately Held**
WEB: www.dknhotels.com
SIC: 7011 Hotels & motels
PA: Dkn Hotel, Llc
42 Corporate Park Ste 200
Irvine CA 92606
714 427-4320

(P-12218)
DNC PRKS RESORTS AT TENAYA INC (DH)
Also Called: Tenaya Lodge
1122 Highway 41, Fish Camp (93623)
P.O. Box 159 (93623-0159)
PHONE.................................877 247-9241
Kevin T Kelly, *President*
Thomas Barney, *Vice Pres*
Ron Burnheimer, *Controller*
EMP: 77
SALES (est): 6.9MM
SALES (corp-wide): 3B **Privately Held**
SIC: 7011 Resort hotel; hotels

(P-12219)
DNC PRKS RSRTS AT YOSEMITE INC
Also Called: Yosemite Concession Services
9001 Village Dr, Yosemite Ntpk (95389)
PHONE..................................209 372-1001
Dan Jensen, *President*
Paul Jensen, *Vice Pres*
Paul Jeppson, *Vice Pres*
Dan Lyle, *Director*
Alison Grove, *Manager*
EMP: 1100
SALES (est): 50MM
SALES (corp-wide): 3B **Privately Held**
SIC: 7011 5399 5812 5947 Resort hotel; vacation lodges; country general stores; eating places; snack shop; gift shop; gasoline service stations; tours, conducted
HQ: Delaware North Companies Parks & Resorts, Inc.
250 Delaware Ave Ste 100
Buffalo NY 14202

(P-12220)
DODGE RIDGE CORPORATION
Also Called: Dodge Ridge Winter Sports Area
1 Dodge Ridge Rd, Pinecrest (95364)
P.O. Box 1188 (95364-0188)
PHONE..................................209 536-5300
Jason Reed, *CFO*
Erin Jensen, *Human Resources*
Smith Jason, *Opers Staff*
Kenneth Hurst, *Manager*
EMP: 350
SQ FT: 10,000
SALES (est): 13.9MM **Privately Held**
WEB: www.dodgeridge.com
SIC: 7011 7033 Ski lodge; campgrounds

(P-12221)
DOLCE INTERNATIONAL / NAPA LLC
1600 Atlas Peak Rd, NAPA (94558-1425)
PHONE..................................707 257-0200
Steven A Rudnitsky, *President*
EMP: 484
SALES (est): 2.4MM
SALES (corp-wide): 1.8B **Publicly Held**
SIC: 7011 Hotels & motels
HQ: Dolce International Holdings, Inc.
22 Sylvan Way
Parsippany NJ 07054
201 307-8700

(P-12222)
DOLPHIN BAY HT & RESIDENCE INC
Also Called: Dolphin Bay Hotel & Residences
2727 Shell Beach Rd, Shell Beach (93449-1602)
PHONE..................................805 773-4300
Richard J Loughead Jr, *CEO*
Christina Stieb, *Marketing Staff*
EMP: 90
SALES (est): 5MM **Privately Held**
SIC: 7011 Hostels; hotels

(P-12223)
DOLPHINS COVE RESORT LTD
Also Called: Worldmark By Wyndham
465 W Orangewood Ave, Anaheim (92802-4759)
PHONE..................................714 980-0830
Jennifer Eaton, *Principal*
EMP: 90
SALES (est): 3.3MM **Privately Held**
SIC: 7011 6531 Resort hotel; time-sharing real estate sales, leasing & rentals

(P-12224)
DOMINION INTERNATIONAL INC
Also Called: Hampton Inn
2305 Longport Ct, Elk Grove (95758-7127)
PHONE..................................916 683-9545
Perry Ferrera, *General Mgr*
EMP: 100
SALES (est): 2.9MM **Privately Held**
SIC: 7011 Hotels & motels

(P-12225)
DONALD T STERLING CORPORATION
Also Called: Beverly Hills Plaza Hotel
10300 Wilshire Blvd, Los Angeles (90024-4772)
PHONE..................................310 275-5575
Zair Caceres, *Branch Mgr*
EMP: 80
SALES (corp-wide): 8.5MM **Privately Held**
SIC: 7011 Hotels
PA: Donald T. Sterling Corporation
9441 Wilshire Blvd Ph
Beverly Hills CA 90212
310 278-8000

(P-12226)
DOUBLETREE BY HILTON HOTEL
1985 E Grand Ave, El Segundo (90245-5015)
PHONE..................................310 322-0999
Jordan Austin, *General Mgr*
Mark Lewis, *Vice Pres*
Dave Schrader, *Principal*
EMP: 110 **EST:** 2011
SALES (est): 893.4K **Privately Held**
SIC: 7011 Hotels

(P-12227)
DOUBLETREE BY HILTON HOTEL
1515 Hotel Cir S, San Diego (92108-3409)
PHONE..................................619 881-6900
Victor Ravago, *Manager*
Evette Betancourt, *Accounting Mgr*
Shari Stauder, *Director*
Anakaren Felix, *Manager*
EMP: 70 **EST:** 2015
SALES (est): 707K **Privately Held**
SIC: 7011 Hotels & motels

(P-12228)
DOUBLETREE BY HILTON SAN JOSE
Also Called: San Jose Lessee LLC
2050 Gateway Pl, San Jose (95110-1047)
PHONE..................................408 453-4000
Missoon Kong, *General Mgr*
Rowan Tejada, *Finance*
EMP: 99
SALES (est): 877.3K
SALES (corp-wide): 2.7B **Publicly Held**
SIC: 7011 Hotels & motels
HQ: Park Us Lessee Holdings Inc.
1600 Tysons Blvd Ste 1000
Mc Lean VA 22102
703 883-1052

(P-12229)
DOUBLETREE HOTEL
888 Montebello Blvd, Rosemead (91770-4303)
PHONE..................................323 722-8800
Ying Ning Huang, *Partner*
Katy Huang, *Executive*
EMP: 100
SQ FT: 110,000
SALES (est): 4.7MM **Privately Held**
SIC: 7011 Hotels & motels

(P-12230)
DOUBLTREE SUITES BY HILTON LLC
Also Called: Doubletree Hotel
2085 S Harbor Blvd, Anaheim (92802-3513)
PHONE..................................714 750-3000
Amrit K Patel,
Subhabrata Roy, *General Mgr*
Christopher Neilson, *Technology*
William R O'Connell,
Shirish H Patel,
EMP: 175
SALES (est): 10.5MM **Privately Held**
WEB: www.orangewood.net
SIC: 7011 5812 Hotels & motels; American restaurant

(P-12231)
DT ONTRIO HT PRTNERS LSSEE LLC
Also Called: Doubletree By Hilton Ontario
222 N Vineyard Ave, Ontario (91764-4428)
PHONE..................................909 937-0900
Bassam Shahin, *President*
Raffi Ararxian, *Finance*
EMP: 255
SALES (est): 472K **Privately Held**
SIC: 7011 Hotels

(P-12232)
DTRS SANTA MONICA LLC
Also Called: Loews Santa Monica Beach Hotel
1700 Ocean Ave, Santa Monica (90401-3214)
PHONE..................................310 458-6700
Paul Leclerc, *General Mgr*
John Thaeker, *Regional VP*
Tanya Bolton, *Human Res Dir*
Sierra Trujillo, *Natl Sales Mgr*
Sarah Best, *Sales Dir*
EMP: 300
SQ FT: 300,000
SALES (est): 18.8MM **Privately Held**
SIC: 7011 Resort hotel; hotels

(P-12233)
DTRS ST FRANCIS LLC
Also Called: Westin St. Francis, The
335 Powell St, San Francisco (94102-1804)
PHONE..................................415 397-7000
Marc Swerdlow, *President*
Mark Zettl, *COO*
EMP: 1000
SALES (est): 20.8MM
SALES (corp-wide): 48.9MM **Privately Held**
WEB: www.westinstfrancis.com
SIC: 7011 Hotels
HQ: Ultima Hospitality, L.L.C.
30 S Wacker Dr Ste 3600
Chicago IL 60606
312 948-4500

(P-12234)
E H SUMMIT INC (PA)
Also Called: Luxe Sunset Boulevard Hotel
11461 W Sunset Blvd, Los Angeles (90049-2031)
PHONE..................................310 476-6571
Efrem Harkhan, *CEO*
Julie Sevilla, *Marketing Staff*
Jana Adamova, *Sales Staff*
EMP: 130
SALES (est): 13.9MM **Privately Held**
SIC: 7011 Hotels

(P-12235)
E H SUMMIT INC
360 N Rodeo Dr, Beverly Hills (90210-5177)
PHONE..................................310 273-0300
Efrem Harkhan, *President*
EMP: 65
SALES (est): 595.7K **Privately Held**
SIC: 7011 Hotels
PA: E. H. Summit, Inc.
11461 W Sunset Blvd
Los Angeles CA 90049

(P-12236)
EAST PALO ALTO HOTEL DEV INC
Also Called: Four Seasons Hotel Silicon Vly
2050 University Ave, East Palo Alto (94303-2248)
PHONE..................................650 566-1200
Tracy Mercer, *General Mgr*
EMP: 210
SALES (est): 9.1MM **Privately Held**
SIC: 7011 7389 Resort hotel; office facilities & secretarial service rental

(P-12237)
EASUN INC
2001 Point West Way, Sacramento (95815-4702)
PHONE..................................916 929-8855
Benjamin Shih, *Director*
EMP: 250

SALES: 20MM **Privately Held**
SIC: 7011 Hotels & motels

(P-12238)
ECONOMY INN
1243 E Main St, Barstow (92311-2408)
PHONE..................................760 256-5601
Mike Patel, *Owner*
EMP: 50
SALES (est): 960.4K **Privately Held**
WEB: www.elliott.com
SIC: 7011 Motels

(P-12239)
EDWARD THOMAS COMPANIES
Also Called: Jolly Roger Inn
640 W Katella Ave, Anaheim (92802-3411)
PHONE..................................714 782-7500
Fred Kokash, *Branch Mgr*
Alex Patel, *General Mgr*
EMP: 100
SALES (corp-wide): 3.6MM **Privately Held**
WEB: www.jollyrogerhotel.com
SIC: 7011 5812 Motels; eating places
PA: The Edward Thomas Companies
9950 Santa Monica Blvd
Beverly Hills CA 90212
310 859-9366

(P-12240)
EDWARD THOMAS HOSPITALITY CORP
Also Called: Shutters On The Beach
1 Pico Blvd, Santa Monica (90405-1063)
PHONE..................................310 458-0030
Klaus Mennekes, *Branch Mgr*
EMP: 350
SALES (corp-wide): 15.3MM **Privately Held**
WEB: www.shuttersonthebeach.com
SIC: 7011 5812 7991 5813 Hotels; eating places; physical fitness facilities; drinking places
PA: The Edward Thomas Hospitality Corp
9950 Santa Monica Blvd
Beverly Hills CA 90212
310 859-9366

(P-12241)
EHT ESAN LLC
Also Called: Embassy Suites Anaheim North
3100 E Frontera St, Anaheim (92806-2820)
PHONE..................................714 632-1221
Howard Wu, *Principal*
Louisa Yeung, *Principal*
EMP: 75
SALES (est): 705.8K **Privately Held**
SIC: 7011 Hotels & motels

(P-12242)
EL CORDOVA HOTEL
Also Called: Pacific Terrace Inn
1351 Orange Ave, Coronado (92118-2916)
PHONE..................................619 435-4131
Mark Francois, *General Mgr*
Robert Mc Ginnis, *Partner*
Robert Bottomley, *Manager*
Alex Hernandez, *Manager*
Zanete Millar, *Manager*
EMP: 100
SQ FT: 20,000
SALES (est): 3.8MM **Privately Held**
WEB: www.elcordovahotel.com
SIC: 7011 Resort hotel; motels

(P-12243)
EL DORADO ENTERPRISES INC
Also Called: Hustler Casino
1000 W Redondo Beach Blvd, Gardena (90247-4192)
PHONE..................................310 719-9800
Larry C Flynt, *CEO*
Tom Candy, *General Mgr*
John Villarama, *Graphic Designe*
Kenneth Schoenhofen, *Director*
Patee McGuire, *Manager*
EMP: 760
SALES (est): 31.1MM **Privately Held**
WEB: www.hustlergaming.com
SIC: 7011 Casino hotel

(P-12244)
EL RANCHO MOTEL INC
Also Called: Best Wstn El Rancho Inn Suites
1100 El Camino Real, Millbrae
(94030-2098)
PHONE....................650 588-8500
John C Wilms, *President*
Paul Wilms, *Vice Pres*
Michael Brogdon, *General Mgr*
Jenny Wong, *Receptionist*
EMP: 168
SQ FT: 23,958
SALES (est): 7.1MM **Privately Held**
WEB: www.elranchoinn.com
SIC: 7011 5812 5813 7991 Hotels & motels; eating places; drinking places; physical fitness facilities

(P-12245)
ELIZABETHAN INN ASSOCIATES LP
Also Called: The Sterling Hotel
1935 Wright St Apt 231, Sacramento
(95825-1191)
PHONE....................916 448-1300
Sandra Wasserman, *Partner*
EMP: 90
SQ FT: 15,000
SALES (est): 1.4MM **Privately Held**
WEB: www.sterlinghotel.com
SIC: 7011 5812 7299 Hotels; ethnic food restaurants; banquet hall facilities

(P-12246)
ELK VALLEY CASINO INC
2500 Howland Hill Rd, Crescent City
(95531-9241)
PHONE....................707 464-1020
Dale Miller, *Ch of Bd*
Lawanda Quinnell, *Vice Pres*
Larry Johnson, *General Mgr*
John Green, *Software Engr*
Kerri Vue, *Human Resources*
EMP: 125 EST: 1995
SQ FT: 35,000
SALES (est): 5.8MM **Privately Held**
WEB: www.elkvalleycasino.com
SIC: 7011 Casino hotel

(P-12247)
EMBARCADERO INN ASSOCIATES
Also Called: Hotel Griffon
155 Steuart St, San Francisco
(94105-1206)
PHONE....................415 495-2100
Edward Marinucci, *General Ptnr*
Pacific Union Investment Corpo, *General Ptnr*
EMP: 125
SALES (est): 5MM **Privately Held**
WEB: www.hotelgriffon.com
SIC: 7011 5812 Hotels; family restaurants

(P-12248)
EMBASSY SUITES MANAGEMENT LLC
4550 La Jolla Village Dr, San Diego
(92122-1248)
PHONE....................858 453-0400
EMP: 102 EST: 2007
SALES (est): 955.1K **Privately Held**
SIC: 7011 Hotels & motels

(P-12249)
EMERIK HOTEL CORP
Also Called: Luxe City Center
1020 S Figueroa St, Los Angeles
(90015-1305)
PHONE....................213 748-1291
Emerson Glazer, *President*
Art Malmgren, *CFO*
John Kelly, *Vice Pres*
James Jones, *Admin Sec*
Shannon Colbert, *Sales Staff*
EMP: 90
SALES: 8MM **Privately Held**
WEB: www.hicitycenter.com
SIC: 7011 5813 5812 Hotels; bar (drinking places); American restaurant

(P-12250)
ENCINA PEPPER TREE JOINT VENTR (PA)
Also Called: Best Western
3850 State St, Santa Barbara
(93105-3112)
PHONE....................805 687-5511
Jeanette Webber, *Managing Prtnr*
David Potter, *Partner*
Camille Shaar, *Partner*
Pamela Webber, *Partner*
Clark Chivaun, *General Mgr*
EMP: 70
SQ FT: 100,000
SALES (est): 12.9MM **Privately Held**
WEB: www.sbhotels.com
SIC: 7011 Hotels & motels

(P-12251)
EQUISTAR IRVINE COMPANY LLC
Also Called: Hilton Irvine
18800 Macarthur Blvd, Irvine (92612-1410)
PHONE....................949 833-3331
Meristar Mezzanine Borrower, *Manager*
EMP: 99
SALES (est): 5.2MM **Privately Held**
SIC: 7011 Hotels & motels

(P-12252)
ERGS AIM HOTEL REALTY LLC
Also Called: Embassy Suites Anaheim Orange
400 N State College Blvd, Orange
(92868-1708)
PHONE....................714 938-1111
Eric Pyland, *Business Mgr*
John Rogers, *CEO*
EMP: 75
SQ FT: 50,000
SALES (est): 2.1MM **Privately Held**
SIC: 7011 Hotels & motels

(P-12253)
ERGS AIM HOTEL REALTY LLC
Also Called: Doubletree Suites Doheny
34402 Pacific Coast Hwy, Dana Point
(92624-1211)
PHONE....................949 661-1100
Brian Nordahl,
Louisa Yeung, *Administration*
EMP: 54 EST: 2017
SALES (est): 212.6K **Privately Held**
SIC: 7011 Hotels & motels

(P-12254)
ESA P PRTFOLIO OPER LESSEE LLC
Also Called: Extended Stay America
4881 Birch St, Newport Beach
(92660-2112)
PHONE....................949 851-2711
William Arter, *Branch Mgr*
Russ Herbel, *Manager*
EMP: 50
SALES (corp-wide): 1.2B **Publicly Held**
WEB: www.weddingbells.net
SIC: 7011 Hotels & motels
HQ: Esa P Portfolio Operating Lessee, Llc
11525 N Community House R
Charlotte NC 28277
980 345-1600

(P-12255)
ESA P PRTFOLIO OPER LESSEE LLC
Also Called: Extended Stay America
1635 W Katella Ave, Orange (92867-3412)
PHONE....................714 639-8608
Leilani Reynolds, *Branch Mgr*
EMP: 73
SALES (corp-wide): 1.2B **Publicly Held**
WEB: www.weddingbells.net
SIC: 7011 Hotels & motels
HQ: Esa P Portfolio Operating Lessee, Llc
11525 N Community House R
Charlotte NC 28277
980 345-1600

(P-12256)
ET WHITEHALL SEASCAPE LLC
Also Called: Hotel Casa Del Mar
1910 Ocean Way, Santa Monica
(90405-1083)
PHONE....................310 581-5533

Edward Slatkin,
Thomas Slatkin,
EMP: 202
SQ FT: 200,000
SALES (est): 12.2MM **Privately Held**
WEB: www.hotelcasadelmar.com
SIC: 7011 5812 Hotels; eating places

(P-12257)
EUROPEAN HOTL INVSTRS OF CA
Also Called: Doubletree Hotel
1985 E Grandave, El Segundo (90245)
PHONE....................310 322-0999
Tim River, *Manager*
EMP: 50
SALES (est): 1.7MM
SALES (corp-wide): 6.7MM **Privately Held**
SIC: 7011 Hotels & motels
PA: European Hotel Investors I I, A California Limited Partnership
2532 Dupont Dr
Irvine CA 92612
949 474-7368

(P-12258)
EUROPEAN HOTL INVSTRS OF CA (PA)
Also Called: O H I
2532 Dupont Dr, Irvine (92612-1524)
PHONE....................949 474-7368
Timothy R Busch, *General Ptnr*
T R Busch Realty Corp, *Partner*
EMP: 80
SQ FT: 9,000
SALES (est): 6.7MM **Privately Held**
SIC: 7011 Hotels & motels

(P-12259)
EVERGREEN DSTNTION HLDINGS LLC
Also Called: Evergreen Lodge
33160 Evergreen Rd, Groveland
(95321-9772)
PHONE....................209 379-2606
Brian Anderluh,
Joe Juszkiewicz, *General Mgr*
Donna West, *Financial Exec*
Teri Marshall, *Sales Dir*
Tara Stetz, *Sales Staff*
EMP: 75 EST: 1975
SQ FT: 6,000
SALES (est): 4.9MM **Privately Held**
SIC: 7011 5812 Resort hotel; eating places

(P-12260)
EXECUTIVE INN INC
Also Called: Ramada Inn
1217 Wildwood Ave, Sunnyvale
(94089-2701)
PHONE....................408 245-5330
Roger Chang, *President*
Jeffry S C Chang, *President*
Jeff Shannon, *General Mgr*
David C M Chang, *Admin Sec*
EMP: 97
SQ FT: 15,400
SALES (est): 4.7MM **Privately Held**
SIC: 7011 Hotels & motels

(P-12261)
FARGO COLONIAL LLC
Also Called: Grande Colonial
910 Prospect St, La Jolla (92037-4144)
PHONE....................858 454-2181
Roger Joseph,
Jose Virissimo, *Chief Engr*
EMP: 63
SQ FT: 46,480
SALES (est): 9.6MM **Privately Held**
WEB: www.thegrandecolonial.com
SIC: 7011 5812 Hotels; eating places

(P-12262)
FC EL SEGUNDO LLC
Also Called: Cambria El Segundo Lax
199 Continental Blvd, El Segundo
(90245-4525)
PHONE....................702 439-7945
Milton B Patipa, *Senior VP*
EMP: 75
SQ FT: 86,106

SALES (est): 341.8K **Privately Held**
SIC: 7011 Hotels

(P-12263)
FEDERTED INDANS GRTON RNCHERIA
Graton Resort & Casino
630 Park Ct, Rohnert Park (94928-7906)
PHONE....................707 588-7100
Greg Sarris, *Branch Mgr*
EMP: 822 **Privately Held**
SIC: 7011 Casino hotel
PA: Federated Indians Of Graton Rancheria
6400 Redwood Dr Ste 300
Rohnert Park CA 94928
619 917-9566

(P-12264)
FERRADO GARDEN COURT LLC
520 Cowper St Ste 100, Palo Alto
(94301-1826)
PHONE....................650 543-2224
Ferrado Inmuebles SL, *Mng Member*
Barbara Gross,
EMP: 60
SQ FT: 63,620
SALES (est): 1MM **Privately Held**
WEB: www.gardencourt.com
SIC: 7011 Hotels

(P-12265)
FESS PRKER-RED LION GEN PARTNR
Also Called: Doubletree Hotel
633 E Cabrillo Blvd, Santa Barbara
(93103-3611)
PHONE....................805 564-4333
Fess Parker, *Partner*
EMP: 325
SALES (est): 14.8MM **Privately Held**
SIC: 7011 Hotels & motels

(P-12266)
FIRST HOTELS INTERNATIONAL INC
Also Called: Radisson Inn
295 N E St, San Bernardino (92401-1507)
P.O. Box 1805 (92402-1805)
PHONE....................909 884-9364
James Deskus, *General Mgr*
Cindy Gardner, *Treasurer*
Choqchet Koski, *Controller*
Ivan Verheijen, *Manager*
EMP: 140
SALES (est): 2.9MM **Privately Held**
SIC: 7011 Hotels & motels

(P-12267)
FITNESS RIDGE MALIBU LLC
Also Called: Biggest Lser Ftnes Rdge Malibu
277 Latigo Canyon Rd, Malibu
(90265-2707)
PHONE....................818 874-1300
EMP: 56
SALES (est): 1.2MM **Privately Held**
SIC: 7011 7991

(P-12268)
FJS INC
Also Called: Anabella Hotel The
888 S Disneyland Dr # 400, Anaheim
(92802-1847)
PHONE....................714 905-1050
Francis J Sparolini, *CEO*
C Y Chan, *President*
Rachel Moorhead, *Admin Sec*
EMP: 118
SALES (est): 9MM **Privately Held**
WEB: www.anabellahotel.com
SIC: 7011 Resort hotel

(P-12269)
FLORENCE VILLA HOTEL
Also Called: The Villa Florence Hotel
225 Powell St, San Francisco
(94102-2205)
PHONE....................415 397-7700
Steve Miller, *General Mgr*
April Otton, *Sales Mgr*
EMP: 200
SALES (est): 505.2MM **Privately Held**
WEB: www.villaflorence.com
SIC: 7011 5812 Hotels; eating places

PA: Pebblebrook Hotel Trust
7315 Wscnsin Ave Ste 1100
Bethesda MD 20814

(P-12270)
FLORENCE VILLA HOTEL LLC
225 Powell St, San Francisco
(94102-2205)
PHONE..........................415 397-7700
Sue Hefty,
Marit Davey,
EMP: 99
SALES (est): 1.2MM **Privately Held**
SIC: 7011 Hotels

(P-12271)
FORCE-OAKLEAF LP
Also Called: Courtyard By Marriott
6333 Bristol Pkwy, Culver City
(90230-6904)
PHONE..........................310 484-7000
Andy Eklov, *Partner*
EMP: 66
SQ FT: 167,792
SALES (est): 1.9MM **Privately Held**
SIC: 7011 Hotels & motels

(P-12272)
**FORGE-VIDOVICH MOTEL
LIMITED**
Also Called: Cupertino Inn
10889 N De Anza Blvd, Cupertino
(95014-0439)
PHONE..........................408 996-7700
John Vidovich, *General Ptnr*
Stephen J Vidovich, *General Ptnr*
Marguerite Lambert, *Manager*
EMP: 60
SQ FT: 8,323
SALES (est): 4.3MM **Privately Held**
WEB: www.cupertinoinn.com
SIC: 7011 Hotels

(P-12273)
FORTUNA ENTERPRISES LP
Also Called: Hilton
5711 W Century Blvd, Los Angeles
(90045-5672)
PHONE..........................310 410-4000
Henry H Hsu, *Partner*
Christine Hsu, *Partner*
David Hsu, *Partner*
Myra Hayes, *Asst Sec*
EMP: 450
SQ FT: 2,700
SALES (est): 32.7MM **Privately Held**
SIC: 7011 5812 5813 Hotels & motels;
eating places; bar (drinking places)
HQ: Universal Fortuna Investment, Inc
5711 W Century Blvd # 1628
Los Angeles CA 90045

(P-12274)
**FOUNDERS MANAGEMENT II
CORP**
Also Called: Crowne Plaza Hotel
1221 Chess Dr, Foster City (94404-1173)
PHONE..........................650 570-5700
Solomon Tsai, *Managing Dir*
Scott Castle, *General Mgr*
Deena Castle, *Sales Dir*
▲ EMP: 275
SQ FT: 280,000
SALES (est): 14MM **Privately Held**
SIC: 7011 5812 5813 Hotels & motels;
eating places; bar (drinking places)

(P-12275)
FOUNTAINGROVE INN LLC
Also Called: Fountngrove Inn Conference Ctr
101 Fountaingrove Pkwy, Santa Rosa
(95403-1777)
P.O. Box 12277 (95406-2277)
PHONE..........................707 578-6101
Robert Miller,
Ceclie Kraus, *Director*
EMP: 100
SQ FT: 79,200
SALES (est): 7.7MM **Privately Held**
WEB: www.fountaingroveinn.com
SIC: 7011 5812 Resort hotel; eating
places

(P-12276)
FOUR POINTS BY SHERATON
9750 Airport Blvd, Los Angeles
(90045-5404)
PHONE..........................310 645-4600
Jonh Vickers, *President*
EMP: 57
SALES (est): 2.7MM **Privately Held**
SIC: 7011 Hotels & motels

(P-12277)
**FOUR POINTS SAN JOSE
DOWNTOWN**
211 S 1st St, San Jose (95113-2702)
PHONE..........................408 282-8800
Randy Zimmerman, *General Mgr*
EMP: 50
SALES (est): 1.1MM **Privately Held**
SIC: 7011 Resort hotel; hotels

(P-12278)
FOUR SEASONS HOTEL INC
Also Called: Four Ssons Hotel-San Francisco
735 Market St Fl 6, San Francisco
(94103-2034)
PHONE..........................415 633-3441
Stan Bromley, *Branch Mgr*
EMP: 515
SALES (corp-wide): 1.9MM **Privately
Held**
SIC: 7011 Hotels
HQ: Four Seasons Hotels Limited
1165 Leslie St
North York ON M3C 2
416 449-1750

(P-12279)
FOUR SEASONS HOTEL INC
2050 University Ave, East Palo Alto
(94303-2248)
PHONE..........................650 566-1200
Robert Whitfield, *Manager*
Florian Riedel, *General Mgr*
Marvin Wong, *Finance*
Cassie Conching, *Manager*
EMP: 515
SALES (corp-wide): 1.9MM **Privately
Held**
SIC: 7011 Hotels
HQ: Four Seasons Hotels Limited
1165 Leslie St
North York ON M3C 2
416 449-1750

(P-12280)
FOUR SISTERS INNS
Also Called: 1906 Lodge
1060 Adella Ave, Coronado (92118-2908)
PHONE..........................619 437-1900
Susan Nelson, *General Mgr*
EMP: 154
SALES (corp-wide): 25MM **Privately
Held**
SIC: 7011 Motels
PA: Four Sisters Inns
460 Alma St Ste 100
Monterey CA 93940
831 649-0908

(P-12281)
FPL LLC
Also Called: Wyndham Garden Pierpont Inn
550 San Jon Rd, Ventura (93001-3745)
PHONE..........................805 643-6144
EMP: 55
SALES (est): 968.1K **Privately Held**
SIC: 7011

(P-12282)
FREMONT MARRIOTT
46100 Landing Pkwy, Fremont
(94538-6437)
PHONE..........................510 413-3700
John Ault, *General Mgr*
EMP: 130
SALES (est): 567.6K **Privately Held**
SIC: 7011 Hotels

(P-12283)
FRENCH REDWOOD INC
Also Called: Hotel Sfitel San Francisco Bay
223 Twin Dolphin Dr, Redwood City
(94065-1414)
PHONE..........................650 598-9000
EMP: 228

SALES (est): 7.7MM
SALES (corp-wide): 1B **Privately Held**
WEB: www.hbsaward.com
SIC: 7011 5813 5812
PA: Accor
82 Rue Henry Farman
Issy Les Moulineaux 92130
146 429-193

(P-12284)
FRESNO AIRPORT HOTELS LLC
Also Called: Wyndham Garden Fresno Airport
5090 E Clinton Way, Fresno (93727-1506)
PHONE..........................559 252-3611
Rohit Kumar, *President*
Leslie Beninga, *Director*
EMP: 65
SALES (est): 2.2MM **Privately Held**
SIC: 7011 Hotels

(P-12285)
FRESNO HOTEL PARTNERS LP
Also Called: Ramada Inn
324 E Shaw Ave, Fresno (93710-7610)
PHONE..........................559 224-4040
Arianna Navarro, *Sales Staff*
EMP: 60
SALES (est): 2.3MM **Privately Held**
SIC: 7011 7991 5812 7999 Hotels & mo-
tels; physical fitness facilities; eating
places; swimming pool, non-membership

(P-12286)
G5 GLOBAL PARTNERS IX LLC
Also Called: Ramada Plz Ht San Dego/ Ht Cir
2151 Hotel Cir S, San Diego (92108-3314)
PHONE..........................619 291-6500
EMP: 75
SALES (est): 950K **Privately Held**
SIC: 7011

(P-12287)
**GALLERIA PARK ASSOCIATES
LLC**
Also Called: Galleria Park Hotel
191 Sutter St, San Francisco (94104-4501)
PHONE..........................415 781-3060
James Lim, *General Mgr*
Fred De Stefano, *Exec VP*
Paul Frentsos, *Mng Member*
EMP: 68
SQ FT: 109,673
SALES (est): 8.5MM **Privately Held**
WEB: www.galleriapark.com
SIC: 7011 6512 5813 5812 Hotels; non-
residential building operators; drinking
places; eating places

(P-12288)
GARDEN COURT HOTEL
520 Cowper St Ste 100, Palo Alto
(94301-1826)
PHONE..........................650 322-9000
Norman Rosenblatt, *General Ptnr*
Irwin G Kasle, *General Ptnr*
Nan Rosenblatt, *General Ptnr*
Sanford H Webster, *General Ptnr*
EMP: 90
SQ FT: 67,000
SALES (est): 6.9MM **Privately Held**
SIC: 7011 5812 Hotels; eating places

(P-12289)
**GASLAMP HOTEL
MANAGEMENT INC**
202 Island Ave, San Diego (92101-6826)
PHONE..........................619 234-0977
Dana Blasi, *President*
EMP: 168
SALES (est): 3.5MM **Privately Held**
SIC: 7011 8741 Resort hotel; hotel or
motel management

(P-12290)
**GCCFC 2005-GG5 Y ST LTD
PARTNR**
Also Called: Courtyard By Marriott S
4422 Y St, Sacramento (95817-2220)
PHONE..........................916 455-6800
Ken Brewer, *General Mgr*
Beth Gamble, *Controller*
EMP: 70
SALES: 950K **Privately Held**
SIC: 7011 Hotels & motels

(P-12291)
GEARY DARLING LESSEE INC
Also Called: Marker Hotel, The
501 Geary St, San Francisco (94102-1640)
PHONE..........................415 292-0100
Alfred L Young, *CEO*
EMP: 150
SQ FT: 20,000
SALES (est): 378.9MM **Privately Held**
WEB: www.monaco-sf.com
SIC: 7011 7991 5813 5812 Hotels; physi-
cal fitness facilities; drinking places; eat-
ing places; banquet hall facilities
PA: Pebblebrook Hotel Trust
7315 Wscnsin Ave Ste 1100
Bethesda MD 20814

(P-12292)
GENTRY ASSOCIATES LLC
Also Called: Park Manor Suites
525 Spruce St, San Diego (92103-5814)
PHONE..........................619 291-0999
Elizabeth Willis, *Mng Member*
EMP: 80
SALES (est): 3.8MM **Privately Held**
WEB: www.parkmanorsuites.com
SIC: 7011 5812 6531 Resort hotel; eating
places; time-sharing real estate sales,
leasing & rentals

(P-12293)
GEORGIAN HOTEL
1415 Ocean Ave, Santa Monica
(90401-2101)
PHONE..........................310 395-9945
Richard Dodrill,
EMP: 55
SQ FT: 40,000
SALES (est): 4.8MM **Privately Held**
WEB: www.georgianhotel.com
SIC: 7011 5812 Hotels; American restau-
rant

(P-12294)
GGWH LLC
Also Called: Holiday Inn
9440 Santa Monica Blvd # 610, Beverly
Hills (90210-4653)
PHONE..........................310 786-1700
Emerson Glazer,
Ericka Glazer,
EMP: 55
SALES (est): 1MM **Privately Held**
SIC: 7011 5812 5813 Hotels & motels;
eating places; drinking places

(P-12295)
GHG PROPERTIES LLC
Also Called: Whittier Grand Hotel
7320 Greenleaf Ave, Whittier (90602-1620)
PHONE..........................562 945-8511
Grace Hu,
Joseph Fan, *Manager*
EMP: 80
SALES (est): 322.5K **Privately Held**
SIC: 7011 Hotels & motels

(P-12296)
**GLACIER HOUSE FRANCHISEE
LLC**
Also Called: Holiday Inn
12960 Day St, Moreno Valley (92553-7000)
PHONE..........................951 455-3644
Dominique Freeman, *Principal*
EMP: 50
SALES (est): 277.3K **Privately Held**
SIC: 7011 Hotels & motels

(P-12297)
**GOLDEN DOOR PROPERTIES
LLC**
777 Deer Springs Rd, San Marcos
(92069-9757)
PHONE..........................760 744-5777
Joanne Conway, *Mng Member*
Kathy Van Ness, *Officer*
Melanie Flynn, *Technology*
Trish Donovan, *Accountant*
Cecelia Mahan, *Auditor*
EMP: 139
SQ FT: 50,000
SALES (est): 13.9MM **Privately Held**
SIC: 7011 Hotels & motels

PRODUCTS & SVCS

(P-12298)
GOLDEN HOTEL LLC
Also Called: Radisson Suites Anaheim
7762 Beach Blvd, Buena Park
(90620-1935)
PHONE.....................714 739-5600
Hieu M Bui,
Rod Hertz, *General Mgr*
EMP: 65
SALES: 980K **Privately Held**
SIC: 7011 Hotels & motels

(P-12299)
GOLDEN HOTELS LTD PARTNERSHIP
Also Called: Atrium Hotel
18700 Macarthur Blvd, Irvine (92612-1409)
PHONE.....................949 833-2770
Mike Wang, *Partner*
Pacific Coast Realty Services, *General Ptnr*
John Wang, *Partner*
Roshni Patel, *Sales Mgr*
Frederick Pina, *Manager*
EMP: 140
SQ FT: 120,000
SALES (est): 7.1MM **Privately Held**
WEB: www.atriumhotel.com
SIC: 7011 Resort hotel; hotels

(P-12300)
GOLDEN WEST HOTEL PARTNERSHIP (PA)
724 Rincon Dr, Aptos (95003)
PHONE.....................619 233-7594
Jeraldine Wolff, *Partner*
Ann Platt, *Partner*
Sarah Platt, *Partner*
Shearn H Platt, *Partner*
Allan Rudick, *Partner*
EMP: 60
SQ FT: 90,000
SALES (est): 3.1MM **Privately Held**
SIC: 7011 Hotels

(P-12301)
GOLDENPARK LLC
Also Called: Norwalk Marriott Hotel
16209 Paramount Blvd # 214, Paramount
(90723-5461)
PHONE.....................562 863-5555
Dae In Kim,
Jane N Kim,
EMP: 100
SQ FT: 138,944
SALES (est): 4.7MM **Privately Held**
SIC: 7011 Hotel, franchised

(P-12302)
GOLETA HHG HOTEL DEV LP
Also Called: Hilton Garden Inn Santa
6878 Hollister Ave, Goleta (93117-3017)
PHONE.....................805 562-5996
Yuly Rivera, *Admin Asst*
Patricia Santini, *Officer*
EMP: 60
SQ FT: 95,678
SALES (est): 225.9K **Privately Held**
SIC: 7011 Hotels & motels

(P-12303)
GOODRICH LAX A CAL LTD PARTNR
Also Called: Quality Hotel Airport
310 W Longden Ave, Arcadia (91007-8235)
PHONE.....................626 254-9988
Xi Min Yuan, *Partner*
Parminder Sangha, *Principal*
EMP: 80
SALES: 4MM **Privately Held**
SIC: 7011 Hotels & motels

(P-12304)
GRAND DEL MAR RESORT LP
5300 Grand Del Mar Ct, San Diego
(92130-4901)
PHONE.....................858 314-2000
Tom Voss, *Partner*
Edward Castillo, *Info Tech Mgr*
Akash Chakravarty, *Director*
Shawn Cox, *Director*
Eugenia Carson-Schwob, *Manager*
EMP: 570
SALES (est): 33MM **Privately Held**
SIC: 7011 Resort hotel; hotels

(P-12305)
GRAND PACIFIC CARLSBAD HT LP
Also Called: Sheraton Carlsbad Resort & Spa
5480 Grand Pacific Dr, Carlsbad
(92008-4723)
PHONE.....................760 827-2400
Tim Shinkle, *CFO*
John Wehner, *Engineer*
Janina Kershaw, *Controller*
Erin Lindquist, *Human Res Dir*
Stephanie Gonzalez, *Hum Res Coord*
EMP: 272
SALES (est): 17.5MM **Privately Held**
SIC: 7011 Hotels & motels

(P-12306)
GRAND PACIFIC RESORTS SVCS LP
5900 Pasteur Ct Ste 200, Carlsbad
(92008-7336)
PHONE.....................760 431-8500
Timothy Stripe, *Partner*
David Brown, *Partner*
Sherrie McIntosh, *Manager*
EMP: 120
SQ FT: 22,000
SALES (est): 5.6MM **Privately Held**
SIC: 7011 Resort hotel

(P-12307)
GRANLIBAKKEN MANAGEMENT CO LTD
Also Called: Granlibakken Ski Racquet Resort
725 Granlibakken Rd, Tahoe City (96145)
P.O. Box 6329 (96145-6329)
PHONE.....................800 543-3221
Willem G C Parson, *President*
Norma Parson, *Treasurer*
EMP: 60
SALES: 7MM **Privately Held**
WEB: www.granlibakken.com
SIC: 7011 Resort hotel

(P-12308)
GRANVILLE HOTEL CORP
13111 Sycamore Dr, Norwalk (90650-8339)
PHONE.....................562 863-5555
Lawrence Lui, *President*
James Evans, *CFO*
Anthony Carter, *Vice Pres*
EMP: 115
SALES (est): 1.2MM **Privately Held**
WEB: www.sheratonuptown.com
SIC: 7011 Hotel, franchised

(P-12309)
GREAT WESTERN HOTELS CORP
Also Called: Heritage Inn
1050 N Norma St, Ridgecrest
(93555-3151)
PHONE.....................760 446-6543
Victoria Moore, *Manager*
EMP: 50
SALES (corp-wide): 11.8MM **Privately Held**
WEB: www.danapointmarinainn.com
SIC: 7011 Hotels
PA: Great Western Hotels Corp
401 W Imperial Hwy
La Habra CA

(P-12310)
GREEN TREE CAPITAL LP
Also Called: Green Tree Inn
14173 Green Tree Blvd, Victorville
(92395-4343)
PHONE.....................760 245-3461
Cathy Davis, *General Mgr*
Philip Elghanian,
EMP: 55
SQ FT: 52,647
SALES (est): 1.2MM **Privately Held**
SIC: 7011 Hotels & motels

(P-12311)
GREENS GROUP INC
9289 Research Dr, Irvine (92618-4286)
PHONE.....................949 829-4902
Ashutosh Kadakia, *CFO*
EMP: 145
SQ FT: 2,526

SALES (est): 654.9K **Privately Held**
SIC: 7011 Resort hotel, franchised

(P-12312)
GREENWOOD HOLDINGS LLC
Also Called: Four Points San Diego-Seaworld
3888 Greenwood St, San Diego
(92110-4412)
PHONE.....................619 299-6633
Imad T Mansour, *President*
EMP: 69
SALES: 5MM **Privately Held**
SIC: 7011 Hotels & motels

(P-12313)
GRINGTEAM INC
Also Called: Doubletree Hotel
14455 Penasquitos Dr, San Diego
(92129-1603)
PHONE.....................858 485-4145
Russ Tanakaya, *General Mgr*
EMP: 140
SALES (corp-wide): 2.7B **Publicly Held**
WEB: www.dtwarrenplace.com
SIC: 7011 Hotels & motels
HQ: Gringteam Inc
21725 Gateway Center Dr
Diamond Bar CA 91765

(P-12314)
GRINGTEAM INC
Also Called: Doubletree Hotel
2050 Gateway Pl, San Jose (95110-1011)
PHONE.....................408 453-4000
David Costain, *General Mgr*
EMP: 350
SALES (corp-wide): 2.7B **Publicly Held**
WEB: www.dtwarrenplace.com
SIC: 7011 5812 Hotels & motels; eating places
HQ: Gringteam Inc
21725 Gateway Center Dr
Diamond Bar CA 91765
-

(P-12315)
GRINGTEAM INC
Also Called: Doubltree By Hilton Ht Bkrsfeld
3100 Camino Del Rio Ct, Bakersfield
(93308-6245)
PHONE.....................661 426-7919
Robert Balmer, *Manager*
EMP: 234
SALES (corp-wide): 2.7B **Publicly Held**
WEB: www.doralpalmsprings.com
SIC: 7011 7299 Hotels; banquet hall facilities
HQ: Gringteam Inc
21725 Gateway Center Dr
Diamond Bar CA 91765
-

(P-12316)
GRINGTEAM INC
Also Called: Doubletree Hotel
201 E Macarthur Blvd, Santa Ana
(92707-5776)
PHONE.....................714 825-3333
Marsha Hansen, *General Mgr*
EMP: 182
SALES (corp-wide): 2.7B **Publicly Held**
WEB: www.dtwarrenplace.com
SIC: 7011 Hotels & motels
HQ: Gringteam Inc
21725 Gateway Center Dr
Diamond Bar CA 91765
-

(P-12317)
GRINGTEAM INC
Also Called: Doubletree Hotel
2001 Point West Way, Sacramento
(95815-4702)
PHONE.....................916 929-8855
Chris Mellini, *Manager*
EMP: 350
SALES (corp-wide): 2.7B **Publicly Held**
WEB: www.dtwarrenplace.com
SIC: 7011 5812 5813 7991 Hotels & motels; eating places; bar (drinking places); physical fitness facilities
HQ: Gringteam Inc
21725 Gateway Center Dr
Diamond Bar CA 91765

(P-12318)
GRINGTEAM INC
Also Called: Doubletree Hotel
1150 9th St Frnt, Modesto (95354-0823)
PHONE.....................209 526-6000
Cindy Power, *Manager*
EMP: 270
SALES (corp-wide): 2.7B **Publicly Held**
WEB: www.dtwarrenplace.com
SIC: 7011 5813 Hotels & motels; drinking places
HQ: Gringteam Inc
21725 Gateway Center Dr
Diamond Bar CA 91765

(P-12319)
GRINGTEAM INC
Also Called: Doubletree By Hilton
7450 Hazard Center Dr, San Diego
(92108-4539)
PHONE.....................619 297-5466
Karima Zaki, *Manager*
EMP: 300
SALES (corp-wide): 2.7B **Publicly Held**
WEB: www.doralpalmsprings.com
SIC: 7011 5812 Hotels & motels; eating places
HQ: Gringteam Inc
21725 Gateway Center Dr
Diamond Bar CA 91765

(P-12320)
GRINGTEAM INC
Also Called: Doubletree Hotel
835 Airport Blvd, Burlingame (94010-1922)
PHONE.....................650 344-5500
Liza Normandy, *Branch Mgr*
Romeo Arellano, *Info Tech Dir*
EMP: 175
SALES (corp-wide): 2.7B **Publicly Held**
WEB: www.doralpalmsprings.com
SIC: 7011 6512 5813 5812 Hotels & motels; nonresidential building operators; drinking places; eating places
HQ: Gringteam Inc
21725 Gateway Center Dr
Diamond Bar CA 91765

(P-12321)
GRINGTEAM INC
Also Called: Doubletree Hotel
34402 Pacific Coast Hwy, Dana Point
(92624-1211)
PHONE.....................949 661-1100
Mike Peludo, *Manager*
EMP: 80
SALES (corp-wide): 2.7B **Publicly Held**
WEB: www.doralpalmsprings.com
SIC: 7011 Hotels & motels
HQ: Gringteam Inc
21725 Gateway Center Dr
Diamond Bar CA 91765

(P-12322)
GROSVENOR PROPERTIES LTD
Also Called: Best Western
380 S Airport Blvd, South San Francisco
(94080-6704)
PHONE.....................650 873-3200
Jim McGuire, *Manager*
Jim Mc Guire, *Technical Staff*
David Huddleston, *Opers Mgr*
EMP: 160
SALES (corp-wide): 41.5MM **Privately Held**
WEB: www.grosvenorsfo.com
SIC: 7011 5813 5812 7299 Hotels & motels; drinking places; eating places; banquet hall facilities
PA: Grosvenor Properties Ltd.
222 Front St Fl 7
San Francisco CA 94111
415 421-5940

(P-12323)
GROSVENOR VISALIA ASSOCIATES
Also Called: Holiday Inn
9000 W Airport Dr, Visalia (93277-9511)
PHONE.....................559 651-5000
Robert K Werbe, *General Ptnr*
Dave Maxey, *Controller*

EMP: 52
SQ FT: 163,415
SALES (est): 3.9MM **Privately Held**
SIC: 7011 Hotels & motels

(P-12324)
GUESTY INC
340 S Lemon Ave, Walnut (91789-2706)
PHONE....................................415 244-0277
Amiad Soto, *CEO*
EMP: 109
SALES (est): 605K **Privately Held**
SIC: 7011 7371 Vacation lodges; computer software development & applications

(P-12325)
H C T INC
Also Called: Hyatt Regency Mission Bay Spa
1441 Quivira Rd, San Diego (92109-7805)
PHONE....................................619 224-1234
Mohsen Kaleghi, *President*
Mark S Hoplamazian, *President*
Heather Podmenik, *Director*
Joann Hatfield, *Manager*
EMP: 300
SALES (est): 17.6MM
SALES (corp-wide): 2.7B **Publicly Held**
SIC: 7011 4491 5813 5812 Hotels & motels; marine terminals; piers, incl. buildings & facilities: operation & maintenance; drinking places; eating places
HQ: Chesapeake Lodging Trust
4300 Wilson Blvd Ste 625
Arlington VA 22203

(P-12326)
H D G ASSOCIATES
Also Called: Hotel Marmonte
1111 E Cabrillo Blvd, Santa Barbara (93103-3701)
PHONE....................................805 963-0744
Ruth Grande, *President*
EMP: 125
SQ FT: 150,000
SALES (est): 3MM
SALES (corp-wide): 4.4B **Publicly Held**
WEB: www.hotelmarmonte.com
SIC: 7011 Hotels
HQ: Hyatt Corporation
150 N Riverside Plz
Chicago IL 60606
312 750-1234

(P-12327)
H2 HOTEL LLC
Also Called: Comfort Suites
219 Healdsburg Ave, Healdsburg (95448-4103)
PHONE....................................707 431-2202
David Huish,
John Huish,
Scott Huish,
Shane Huish,
EMP: 80
SALES (est): 1.8MM **Privately Held**
SIC: 7011 Hotel, franchised

(P-12328)
HALF MOON BAY LODGE
Also Called: Best Wstn Half Moon Bay Lodge
2400 Cabrillo Hwy S, Half Moon Bay (94019-2253)
PHONE....................................650 726-9000
Keith Wesstlmann, *Manager*
EMP: 50
SALES (est): 2.4MM **Privately Held**
SIC: 7011 Hotels & motels

(P-12329)
HAMPSTEAD LAFAYETTE HOTEL LLC
Also Called: Innsuites Hotels
2223 El Cajon Blvd, San Diego (92104-1103)
PHONE....................................619 296-2101
James Green, *Manager*
EMP: 50
SALES (est): 1.2MM
SALES (corp-wide): 1.1MM **Privately Held**
WEB: www.lafayettehotelsd.com
SIC: 7011 Resort hotel; hotels

PA: Lafayette Hampstead Hotel Llc
2223 El Cajon Blvd
San Diego CA 92104
619 296-2101

(P-12330)
HAMPTON INN NORCO CORONA NORTH
1530 Hamner Ave, Norco (92860-2939)
PHONE....................................951 279-1111
Mahendra B Desai, *Executive Asst*
EMP: 80
SALES (est): 2MM **Privately Held**
SIC: 7011 Hotels & motels

(P-12331)
HANDLERY HOTELS INC
Also Called: Handlery Union Square Hotel
351 Geary St, San Francisco (94102-1801)
PHONE....................................415 781-7800
John Handlery, *Manager*
EMP: 150
SALES (corp-wide): 31.4MM **Privately Held**
WEB: www.handlery.com
SIC: 7011 Resort hotel
PA: Handlery Hotels, Inc.
180 Geary St Ste 700
San Francisco CA 94108
415 781-4550

(P-12332)
HANDLERY HOTELS INC
950 Hotel Cir N, San Diego (92108-2995)
PHONE....................................415 781-4550
John Martin, *Manager*
EMP: 150
SALES (corp-wide): 31.4MM **Privately Held**
WEB: www.handlery.com
SIC: 7011 5941 5812 5947 Hotels; golf goods & equipment; eating places; gift, novelty & souvenir shop; drinking places
PA: Handlery Hotels, Inc.
180 Geary St Ste 700
San Francisco CA 94108
415 781-4550

(P-12333)
HANFORD HOTELS LLC
17542 17th St Ste 450, Tustin (92780-1964)
PHONE....................................714 210-0400
Donald E Sodaro, *Mng Member*
William A Caine Jr,
EMP: 189
SQ FT: 5,000
SALES (est): 2.8MM **Privately Held**
WEB: www.hanfordhotels.com
SIC: 7011 Hotels & motels

(P-12334)
HARBOR ISLAND HOTEL GROUP LP
Also Called: Four Points Sheraton Ventura
1050 Schooner Dr, Ventura (93001-4273)
PHONE....................................805 658-1212
Joseph Fan, *Managing Prtnr*
EMP: 80
SALES (est): 9MM **Privately Held**
SIC: 7011 Hotels & motels

(P-12335)
HARBOR SUITES LLC
Also Called: Hampton Inn
11747 Harbor Blvd, Garden Grove (92840-2701)
PHONE....................................714 703-8800
David Womack, *Principal*
Navin Dimond, *Principal*
Amy Kotal, *Principal*
EMP: 50
SALES (est): 184.9K **Privately Held**
SIC: 7011 Hotels & motels

(P-12336)
HARBOR VIEW HOTEL VENTURES LLC
Also Called: Doubletree Ht San Diego Dwntwn
1646 Front St, San Diego (92101-2920)
PHONE....................................619 239-6800
Michael Gallegos, *Mng Member*
Rita Baca, *General Mgr*
Joanie Clapper, *Sales Mgr*

Patricia Gallegos, *Sales Mgr*
Nichole Carino, *Sales Staff*
EMP: 100
SALES (est): 6.4MM **Privately Held**
SIC: 7011 Hotels & motels

(P-12337)
HARBOR VIEW HOTELS INC
Also Called: Hilton San Francisco
600 Airport Blvd, Burlingame (94010-1920)
PHONE....................................650 340-8500
James Evans, *CFO*
EMP: 99
SALES (est): 6MM **Privately Held**
WEB: www.sheratonsfo.com
SIC: 7011 Hotels & motels

(P-12338)
HARDAGE HOSPITALITY LLC (PA)
12555 High Bluff Dr # 330, San Diego (92130-3005)
PHONE....................................858 314-7910
Samuel A Hardage, *Chairman*
Marybeth Smith, *Senior VP*
Mark Rousseau, *Vice Pres*
Beth A Chaney, *Executive Asst*
Keith Hindenlang, *VP Accounting*
EMP: 81
SALES (est): 7.6MM **Privately Held**
SIC: 7011 Hotels

(P-12339)
HAVASU LANDING CASINO (PA)
1 Main St, Needles (92363-9216)
PHONE....................................760 858-5380
EMP: 72
SALES: 3.9MM **Privately Held**
SIC: 7011 Casino hotel

(P-12340)
HAWAIIAN GARDENS CASINO
11871 Carson St, Hawaiian Gardens (90716-1127)
PHONE....................................562 860-5887
David Moskowitz, *CEO*
Irving Moskowitz, *President*
EMP: 1000
SALES (est): 41.4MM **Privately Held**
WEB: www.hgcasino.com
SIC: 7011 Casino hotel

(P-12341)
HAWAIIAN HOTELS & RESORTS INC
2830 Borchard Rd, Newbury Park (91320-3810)
PHONE....................................805 480-0052
Edward J Hogan, *President*
EMP: 100
SALES (est): 3.8MM
SALES (corp-wide): 7.2B **Privately Held**
WEB: www.hawaiihotels.com
SIC: 7011 Resort hotel; hotels
HQ: Pleasant Holidays, Llc
2404 Townsgate Rd
Westlake Village CA 91361

(P-12342)
HAYES MANSION CONFERENCE CTR
200 Edenvale Ave, San Jose (95136-3309)
PHONE....................................408 226-3200
Vickie Leong, *Principal*
Edward Robledo, *Manager*
EMP: 140
SALES (est): 4.6MM **Privately Held**
WEB: www.hayesmansion.com
SIC: 7011 Hotels

(P-12343)
HAZENS INVESTMENT LLC
Also Called: Sheraton
6101 W Century Blvd, Los Angeles (90045-5310)
PHONE....................................310 642-1111
Curtiss Allen, *COO*
Mario Mora, *Exec VP*
Juana Padilla, *Vice Pres*
Greg Yanez, *Business Mgr*
Agustin Ortega, *Marketing Staff*
EMP: 395

SALES (est): 34MM **Privately Held**
WEB: www.edgemastery.com
SIC: 7011 Hotels & motels

(P-12344)
HCAL LLC
Also Called: Harrahs Resort Southern Cal
777 S Resort Dr, Valley Center (92082)
PHONE....................................760 751-3100
EMP: 220
SALES (est): 931.7K
SALES (corp-wide): 8.3B **Publicly Held**
SIC: 7011 Casino hotel
PA: Caesars Entertainment Corporation
1 Caesars Palace Dr
Las Vegas NV 89109
702 407-6000

(P-12345)
HEI HOSPITALITY LLC
Also Called: Marriott
21850 Oxnard St, Woodland Hills (91367-3631)
PHONE....................................818 887-4800
Clay Andrews, *Manager*
EMP: 167
SALES (corp-wide): 250.3MM **Privately Held**
SIC: 7011 Hotels & motels
PA: Hei Hospitality, Llc
101 Merritt 7
Norwalk CT 06851
203 849-8844

(P-12346)
HEI LONG BEACH LLC
Also Called: Hilton Hotels
701 W Ocean Blvd, Long Beach (90831-3100)
PHONE....................................562 983-3400
Clark Christopher, *Principal*
HEI Hospitality Fund Holdings,
EMP: 125
SALES (est): 4.5MM
SALES (corp-wide): 250.3MM **Privately Held**
SIC: 7011 Hotels & motels
PA: Hei Hospitality, Llc
101 Merritt 7
Norwalk CT 06851
203 849-8844

(P-12347)
HEI MISSION VALLEY LP
Also Called: San Diego Mission Vly Hilton
901 Camino Del Rio S, San Diego (92108-3515)
PHONE....................................619 299-2729
Dan Weber, *General Ptnr*
EMP: 220
SQ FT: 219,000
SALES (est): 3.6MM **Privately Held**
SIC: 7011 Hotels & motels

(P-12348)
HHC TRS PORTSMOUTH LLC
Also Called: Renaissance Palm Springs
888 E Tahquitz Canyon Way, Palm Springs (92262-6708)
PHONE....................................760 322-6000
David Kimichik,
EMP: 95 EST: 2003
SALES (est): 2.1MM **Privately Held**
SIC: 7011 Hotels & motels

(P-12349)
HHLP SAN DIEGO LESSEE LLC
Also Called: Marriott
530 Broadway, San Diego (92101-5206)
PHONE....................................619 446-3000
Ashish Parikh, *Manager*
EMP: 90
SQ FT: 1,000,000
SALES (est): 3.7MM **Privately Held**
SIC: 7011 Hotels & motels

(P-12350)
HI ANAHEIM LLC
100 W Katella Ave, Anaheim (92802-3602)
PHONE....................................714 533-1500
Ajesh Patel,
EMP: 60
SALES (est): 205.3K **Privately Held**
SIC: 7011 Hotels

(P-12351)
HI FRESNO HOSPITALITY LLC
Also Called: Radisson Ht Frsno Cnfrence Ctr
1055 Van Ness Ave, Fresno (93721-2006)
PHONE........................559 233-6650
Mukesh Shah, *Mng Member*
EMP: 70
SALES: 4MM **Privately Held**
SIC: 7011 Hotels & motels

(P-12352)
HIGHLANDS INN INC
Also Called: Hyatt Carmel Highlands
120 Highland Dr, Carmel (93923-9607)
P.O. Box 1700 (93921-1700)
PHONE........................831 620-1234
Mel Bettcher, *Managing Dir*
Paul C Reed, *CEO*
EMP: 225
SALES (est): 4.2MM **Privately Held**
SIC: 7011 7389 Hotels & motels; time-
share condominium exchange

(P-12353)
**HIGHLANDS INN INVESTORS II
LP**
Also Called: Hyatt Hotel
120 Highland Dr, Carmel (93923-9607)
PHONE........................831 624-3801
Ulrich Samietz, *General Mgr*
Highlands Inn Investors, *Ltd Ptnr*
Sheryl Haley, *Manager*
EMP: 260
SALES (est): 7.6MM **Privately Held**
SIC: 7011 5812 5813 5947 Hotels & mo-
tels; American restaurant; drinking places;
gift, novelty & souvenir shop

(P-12354)
HILTON EL SEGUNDO LLC
Also Called: Hiltonm Grdn Inn Lax El Sgundo
2100 E Mariposa Ave, El Segundo
(90245-5002)
PHONE........................310 726-0100
Brianna Akins,
EMP: 60 EST: 2013
SALES (est): 2.3MM **Privately Held**
SIC: 7011 Hotels & motels

(P-12355)
HILTON GARDEN IN SAN MATEO
Also Called: Hilton Garden Hotel
2000 Bridgepointe Pkwy, Foster City
(94404-1586)
PHONE........................650 522-9000
Derrick Hudson, *Manager*
EMP: 60
SALES (corp-wide): 3.6MM **Privately
Held**
SIC: 7011 Hotels & motels
PA: Hilton Garden In San Mateo
2000 Bridgepointe Pkwy
Foster City CA 94404
650 522-9000

(P-12356)
HILTON GARDEN INN
510 Lewelling Blvd, San Leandro
(94579-1803)
PHONE........................510 346-5533
Burt Knewson, *Manager*
EMP: 80
SALES (est): 2.8MM **Privately Held**
SIC: 7011 Hotels & motels

(P-12357)
HILTON GARDEN INNS MGT LLC
6450 Carlsbad Blvd, Carlsbad
(92011-1058)
PHONE........................760 476-0800
Robert Moore, *General Mgr*
EMP: 116
SALES (corp-wide): 8.9B **Publicly Held**
WEB: www.esirvine.com
SIC: 7011 Hotels & motels
HQ: Hilton Garden Inns Management Llc
7930 Jones Branch Dr
Mc Lean VA 22102
703 883-1000

(P-12358)
HILTON GARDEN INNS MGT LLC
2100 E Mariposa Ave, El Segundo
(90245-5002)
PHONE........................310 726-0100

Barbara Bejan, *Manager*
EMP: 67
SQ FT: 87,198
SALES (corp-wide): 8.9B **Publicly Held**
SIC: 7011 Hotels & motels
HQ: Hilton Garden Inns Management Llc
7930 Jones Branch Dr
Mc Lean VA 22102
703 883-1000

(P-12359)
HILTON GARDEN INNS MGT LLC
2801 Constitution Dr Fl 2, Livermore
(94551-7613)
PHONE........................925 292-2000
Joan Baldon, *Manager*
EMP: 50
SALES (corp-wide): 8.9B **Publicly Held**
SIC: 7011 Hotels & motels
HQ: Hilton Garden Inns Management Llc
7930 Jones Branch Dr
Mc Lean VA 22102
703 883-1000

(P-12360)
**HILTON LOS ANGLES
UNIVERSAL CY**
555 Universal Hollywood Dr, Universal City
(91608-1001)
PHONE........................818 506-2500
Juan Aquinde, *General Mgr*
Matthew La Vine, *Managing Dir*
▲ EMP: 380
SALES (est): 15.2MM **Privately Held**
SIC: 7011 Hotels

(P-12361)
**HILTON RESORT PALM
SPRINGS**
400 E Tahquitz Canyon Way, Palm Springs
(92262-6605)
PHONE........................760 320-6868
Aftab Dada, *General Mgr*
EMP: 200
SALES (est): 8.1MM **Privately Held**
WEB: www.hiltonpalmsprings.com
SIC: 7011 Hotels

(P-12362)
**HILTON SAN FRANCISCO FINCL
DST**
750 Kearny St, San Francisco
(94108-1860)
PHONE........................415 433-6600
Randall King, *Principal*
J San Miguel, *Asst Director*
EMP: 52
SALES (est): 3.7MM **Privately Held**
WEB: www.sanfranciscohiltonhotel.com
SIC: 7011 Hotels & motels

(P-12363)
HILTON UNIVERSAL HOTEL
555 Universal Hollywood Dr, Universal City
(91608-1001)
PHONE........................818 506-2500
Michelle Szeto, *Principal*
EMP: 99
SALES (est): 1.3MM
SALES (corp-wide): 14.1MM **Privately
Held**
SIC: 7011 Hotels & motels
HQ: Sun Hill Properties, Inc.
555 Universal Hollywood Dr
Universal City CA 91608
818 506-2500

(P-12364)
**HILTON WOODLAND HILLS &
TOWERS**
6360 Canoga Ave, Woodland Hills
(91367-2501)
PHONE........................818 595-1000
Ed Debries, *General Mgr*
Conoga Hotel Corporation, *Partner*
▲ EMP: 200
SALES (est): 6.8MM **Privately Held**
SIC: 7011 5813 5812 Hotels & motels;
drinking places; eating places

(P-12365)
HISTORIC MISSION INN CORP
Also Called: Mission Inn Hotel and Spa, The
3649 Mission Inn Ave, Riverside
(92501-3364)
P.O. Box 1433 (92502-1433)
PHONE........................951 784-0300
Duane R Roberts, *President*
Diana Rosure, *Vice Pres*
Shannon Walters, *Vice Pres*
Richard Shippee, *Admin Sec*
Robert Galvin, *Info Tech Dir*
EMP: 460
SALES (est): 33.2MM **Privately Held**
WEB: www.missioninn.com
SIC: 7011 7991 Resort hotel; spas
PA: Entrepreneurial Capital Corporation
4100 Newport Place Dr # 400
Newport Beach CA 92660
949 809-3900

(P-12366)
**HISTORICAL PROPERTIES INC
(PA)**
Also Called: Horton Grand Hotel
311 Island Ave, San Diego (92101-6923)
PHONE........................619 230-8417
Doris J Rose, *President*
Santiago Ojeda, *CEO*
Maria Overton, *Controller*
Jennifer Nauta, *Sales Staff*
EMP: 96
SQ FT: 60,000
SALES (est): 8.6MM **Privately Held**
WEB: www.hortongrand.com
SIC: 7011 Hotels

(P-12367)
HIT PORTFOLIO I NTC TRS LP
Also Called: Residence Inn La Lax El Segndo
2135 E El Segundo Blvd, El Segundo
(90245-4503)
PHONE........................310 333-0888
EMP: 50
SALES (corp-wide): 606MM **Privately
Held**
SIC: 7011 Hotels & motels
HQ: Hit Portfolio I Ntc Trs, Lp
3950 University Dr # 301
Fairfax VA 22030
571 529-6078

(P-12368)
HIT PORTFOLIO II NTC TRS LP
Also Called: Courtyard San Diego Carlsbad
5835 Owens Ave, Carlsbad (92008-6562)
PHONE........................760 431-9399
Minda Zoloth, *Branch Mgr*
EMP: 50
SALES (corp-wide): 606MM **Privately
Held**
SIC: 7011 Hotels & motels
HQ: Hit Portfolio Ii Ntc Trs, Lp
106 York Rd
Jenkintown PA

(P-12369)
HIT PORTFOLIO II TRS LLC
Also Called: Anaheim/Orange Hilton Suites
400 N State College Blvd, Orange
(92868-1708)
PHONE........................714 938-1111
John Ault, *Manager*
EMP: 120
SALES (corp-wide): 2.7B **Publicly Held**
WEB: www.hiltondirect.com
SIC: 7011 5812 Hotels & motels; eating
places
HQ: Hit Portfolio Ii Trs, Llc
7930 Jones Branch Dr
Mc Lean VA 22102
703 883-1000

(P-12370)
HMBL LLC
Also Called: Holiday Inn
8400 W Sunset Blvd Ste 3a, West Holly-
wood (90069-1934)
PHONE........................323 656-8090
Robert Jackson, *Mng Member*
Glen Grush,
Joel Leebove,
David Rose,
EMP: 125
SQ FT: 1,500

SALES (est): 2.4MM **Privately Held**
SIC: 7011 Hotels & motels

(P-12371)
HOLIDAY GARDEN SF CORP
Also Called: Residence In Anaheim
1700 S Clementine St, Anaheim
(92802-2902)
PHONE........................714 533-3555
Hai-Ni Chen, *President*
EMP: 50 EST: 1997
SALES: 7MM **Privately Held**
SIC: 7011 Hotels & motels

(P-12372)
HOLIDAY GARDEN WC CORP
Also Called: Holiday Inn Ex Walnut Creek
2730 N Main St, Walnut Creek
(94597-2732)
PHONE........................925 932-3332
Justin Saylor, *General Mgr*
Candice Kelly, *Marketing Staff*
EMP: 50
SALES (est): 232.5K **Privately Held**
SIC: 7011 Hotels & motels

(P-12373)
**HOLIDAY INN & SUITES
ANNAHEIM**
1240 S Walnut St, Anaheim (92802-2241)
PHONE........................714 535-0300
Eva Huang, *Principal*
Tom Van Winkle, *General Mgr*
EMP: 75
SALES (est): 1.2MM **Privately Held**
SIC: 7011 Hotels & motels

(P-12374)
**HOLIDAY INN EXPRESS
MERCED**
730 Motel Dr, Merced (95341-5151)
PHONE........................209 383-0333
Kainth Brothers, *Principal*
EMP: 100
SALES (est): 1.7MM **Privately Held**
SIC: 7011 Hotels & motels

(P-12375)
**HOLIDAY INN HOTEL
TORRANCE**
19800 S Vermont Ave, Torrance
(90502-1138)
PHONE........................310 781-9100
David Britton, *General Mgr*
EMP: 130
SQ FT: 95,000
SALES (est): 9.9MM **Privately Held**
SIC: 7011 Hotels & motels

(P-12376)
**HOLIDAY INN RNCHO
BERNARDO LLC**
17065 W Bernardo Dr, San Diego
(92127-1495)
PHONE........................858 485-6530
Hsuan Jau Lin,
Yon Huang,
EMP: 55
SALES (est): 2.9MM **Privately Held**
SIC: 7011 Hotels & motels

(P-12377)
HOLLYWOOD STANDARD LLC
Also Called: Standard The
8300 W Sunset Blvd, Los Angeles
(90069-1516)
PHONE........................323 822-3111
Andre Balazs,
Paul Green, *Engineer*
Ian Innocent, *Purch Mgr*
Edward Farwick, *Sales Staff*
Sid Mehra, *Director*
EMP: 170 EST: 1996
SALES (est): 6.7MM **Privately Held**
SIC: 7011 Hotels

(P-12378)
HOME AWAY INC
54432 Road 432, Bass Lake (93604)
P.O. Box 149 (93604-0149)
PHONE........................559 642-3121
Kyusun Choe, *President*
Sun Choe, *Admin Sec*
EMP: 65

▲ = Import ▼=Export
◆ =Import/Export

SALES (est): 3.6MM **Privately Held**
SIC: **7011** Hotels & motels

(P-12379)
HOMEWOOD SUITES MANAGEMENT LLC
1103 Embarcadero, Oakland (94606-5122)
PHONE.............................510 663-2700
Jason Oliveras, *Manager*
EMP: 50
SALES (corp-wide): 8.9B **Publicly Held**
WEB: www.esirvine.com
SIC: **7011** Hotels & motels
HQ: Homewood Suites Management Llc
7930 Jones Branch Dr
Mc Lean VA 22102
703 883-1000

(P-12380)
HOMEWOOD VILLAGE RESORTS LLC
Also Called: Homewood Mountain Resort
5145 W Lake Blvd, Homewood (96141)
PHONE.............................530 525-2992
Todd Chapman, *CEO*
EMP: 50
SALES (est): 1.9MM **Privately Held**
SIC: **7011** Ski lodge

(P-12381)
HONEYMOON REAL ESTATE LP
Also Called: Avalon Hotel
9400 W Olympic Blvd, Beverly Hills
(90212-4552)
PHONE.............................310 277-5221
Brad Korzen, *Partner*
EMP: 90
SQ FT: 400,000
SALES (est): 5.5MM **Privately Held**
WEB: www.avalonhotel.com
SIC: **7011** Hotels

(P-12382)
HONG KONG & SHANGHAI HOTELS
Also Called: The Peninsula Beverly Hills
9882 Santa Monica Blvd, Beverly Hills
(90212-1605)
PHONE.............................310 551-2888
Ali Kasikci, *Branch Mgr*
EMP: 75 **Privately Held**
WEB: www.hshgroup.com
SIC: **7011** Hotels
PA: Hongkong And Shanghai Hotels, Limited, The
8/F St George's Bldg
Central District HK

(P-12383)
HOSPITALITY VENTURES MGT LLC
Also Called: Embassy Suites
101 Mcinnis Pkwy, San Rafael
(94903-2773)
PHONE.............................415 499-9222
Rudy Otriz, *Manager*
EMP: 65
SALES (corp-wide): 37.3MM **Privately Held**
WEB: www.esirvine.com
SIC: **7011** 5812 5813 Hotels & motels; eating places; drinking places
PA: Hospitality Ventures Management, Llc.
990 Hammond Dr Ste 325
Atlanta GA 30328
404 467-9299

(P-12384)
HOST HOTELS & RESORTS INC
Also Called: Marriott Fisherman's Wharf
1250 Columbus Ave, San Francisco
(94133-1327)
PHONE.............................415 775-7555
Michael Promos, *Branch Mgr*
EMP: 170
SALES (corp-wide): 5.5B **Publicly Held**
SIC: **7011** Hotels & motels
PA: Host Hotels & Resorts, Inc.
6903 Rockledge Dr # 1500
Bethesda MD 20817
240 744-1000

(P-12385)
HOST HOTELS & RESORTS INC
1 Market Pl, San Diego (92101-7714)
PHONE.............................619 232-1234
Ted Kanatas, *Manager*
EMP: 170
SALES (est): 5.5B **Publicly Held**
WEB: www.hyatt.com
SIC: **7011** Hotels & motels
PA: Host Hotels & Resorts, Inc.
6903 Rockledge Dr # 1500
Bethesda MD 20817
240 744-1000

(P-12386)
HOST HOTELS & RESORTS LP
Also Called: Newport Bch Marriott Ht & Spa
900 Newport Center Dr, Newport Beach
(92660-6206)
PHONE.............................949 640-4000
Paul Cahill, *General Mgr*
Scott Baril, *Vice Pres*
John Fishell, *Vice Pres*
Tom Hennessey, *Vice Pres*
Len Lisewsky, *Vice Pres*
EMP: 100
SALES (corp-wide): 5.5B **Publicly Held**
WEB: www.scmarriott.com
SIC: **7011** 5813 5812 Hotels & motels; drinking places; eating places
HQ: Host Hotels & Resorts, L.P.
6903 Rockledge Dr # 1500
Bethesda MD 20817
240 744-1000

(P-12387)
HOST HOTELS & RESORTS LP
Also Called: Marriott
8757 Rio San Diego Dr, San Diego
(92108-1620)
PHONE.............................619 692-3800
Dan Stenz, *Branch Mgr*
EMP: 66
SALES (corp-wide): 5.5B **Publicly Held**
WEB: www.scmarriott.com
SIC: **7011** Hotels & motels
HQ: Host Hotels & Resorts, L.P.
6903 Rockledge Dr # 1500
Bethesda MD 20817
240 744-1000

(P-12388)
HOST HOTELS & RESORTS LP
Also Called: Hyatt Rgncy San Frncisco Arprt
1333 Bayshore Hwy, Burlingame
(94010-1804)
PHONE.............................650 347-1234
Keith Butz, *Manager*
EMP: 64
SALES (corp-wide): 5.5B **Publicly Held**
WEB: www.scmarriott.com
SIC: **7011** Hotels & motels
HQ: Host Hotels & Resorts, L.P.
6903 Rockledge Dr # 1500
Bethesda MD 20817
240 744-1000

(P-12389)
HOST HOTELS & RESORTS LP
Also Called: JW Marriott Desert
74855 Country Club Dr, Palm Desert
(92260-1961)
PHONE.............................760 341-2211
Ken Forths, *Manager*
Lisa Kajtor, *Manager*
EMP: 64
SALES (corp-wide): 5.5B **Publicly Held**
WEB: www.scmarriott.com
SIC: **7011** Hotels & motels
HQ: Host Hotels & Resorts, L.P.
6903 Rockledge Dr # 1500
Bethesda MD 20817
240 744-1000

(P-12390)
HOST HOTELS & RESORTS LP
Also Called: Sheraton San Diego Ht & Marina
1380 Harbor Island Dr, San Diego
(92101-1007)
PHONE.............................619 291-2900
Joe Terzi, *Branch Mgr*
EMP: 66
SALES (corp-wide): 5.5B **Publicly Held**
WEB: www.scmarriott.com
SIC: **7011** Hotels & motels

(P-12391)
HOST HOTELS & RESORTS LP
Also Called: San Francisco Marriott Marquis
55 4th St, San Francisco (94103-3156)
PHONE.............................415 896-1600
Dan Kellher, *Manager*
Dan Kelleher, *President*
Sara Gomez, *Director*
EMP: 66
SALES (corp-wide): 5.5B **Publicly Held**
WEB: www.scmarriott.com
SIC: **7011** 5813 5812 Hotels & motels; drinking places; eating places
HQ: Host Hotels & Resorts, L.P.
6903 Rockledge Dr # 1500
Bethesda MD 20817
240 744-1000

(P-12392)
HOST HOTELS & RESORTS LP
1800 Old Bayshore Hwy, Burlingame
(94010-1203)
PHONE.............................650 692-9100
EMP: 66
SALES (corp-wide): 5.5B **Publicly Held**
WEB: www.scmarriott.com
SIC: **7011** Hotels & motels
HQ: Host Hotels & Resorts, L.P.
6903 Rockledge Dr # 1500
Bethesda MD 20817
240 744-1000

(P-12393)
HOST HOTELS & RESORTS LP
Also Called: Ritz-Carlton Ht Marina Del Rey
4375 Admiralty Way, Venice (90292-5434)
PHONE.............................310 823-1700
Robert Thomas, *Branch Mgr*
EMP: 66
SALES (corp-wide): 5.5B **Publicly Held**
WEB: www.scmarriott.com
SIC: **7011** Hotels & motels
HQ: Host Hotels & Resorts, L.P.
6903 Rockledge Dr # 1500
Bethesda MD 20817
240 744-1000

(P-12394)
HOST HOTELS & RESORTS LP
Also Called: Costa Mesa Marriott Suites
500 Anton Blvd, Costa Mesa (92626-1911)
PHONE.............................714 957-1100
Ronda Richardson, *General Mgr*
EMP: 66
SALES (corp-wide): 5.5B **Publicly Held**
WEB: www.scmarriott.com
SIC: **7011** 5813 5812 Hotels & motels; drinking places; eating places
HQ: Host Hotels & Resorts, L.P.
6903 Rockledge Dr # 1500
Bethesda MD 20817
240 744-1000

(P-12395)
HOST HOTELS & RESORTS LP
Also Called: Marriott
500 Bayview Cir, Newport Beach
(92660-2933)
PHONE.............................949 854-4500
Pam Ryan, *Manager*
EMP: 66
SALES (corp-wide): 5.5B **Publicly Held**
WEB: www.scmarriott.com
SIC: **7011** 7389 Hotels & motels; office facilities & secretarial service rental
HQ: Host Hotels & Resorts, L.P.
6903 Rockledge Dr # 1500
Bethesda MD 20817
240 744-1000

(P-12396)
HOST HOTELS & RESORTS LP
Also Called: Westin Los Angeles Airport
5400 W Century Blvd, Los Angeles
(90045-5975)
PHONE.............................310 216-5858
Kimbell John, *CEO*
EMP: 66
SALES (corp-wide): 5.5B **Publicly Held**
WEB: www.scmarriott.com
SIC: **7011** Hotels & motels

HQ: Host Hotels & Resorts, L.P.
6903 Rockledge Dr # 1500
Bethesda MD 20817
240 744-1000

(P-12397)
HOST HOTELS & RESORTS LP
Also Called: Marriott
1400 Park View Ave, Manhattan Beach
(90266-3714)
PHONE.............................310 546-7511
William Newton, *Director*
Suzanne Largoza, *Technology*
EMP: 62
SALES (corp-wide): 5.5B **Publicly Held**
WEB: www.scmarriott.com
SIC: **7011** 7997 Hotels & motels; golf club, membership
HQ: Host Hotels & Resorts, L.P.
6903 Rockledge Dr # 1500
Bethesda MD 20817
240 744-1000

(P-12398)
HOST HOTELS & RESORTS LP
Also Called: Marriott
4100 Admiralty Way, Marina Del Rey
(90292-6207)
PHONE.............................310 301-3000
Susan Reardon, *Manager*
Janet Luna, *Director*
EMP: 66
SALES (corp-wide): 5.5B **Publicly Held**
WEB: www.scmarriott.com
SIC: **7011** 5812 7389 Hotels & motels; eating places; office facilities & secretarial service rental
HQ: Host Hotels & Resorts, L.P.
6903 Rockledge Dr # 1500
Bethesda MD 20817
240 744-1000

(P-12399)
HOST INTERNATIONAL INC
Also Called: Marriott
1661 Airport Blvd Ste 3e, San Jose
(95110-1216)
PHONE.............................408 294-1702
Fax: 408 294-4260
EMP: 180
SALES (corp-wide): 9.4MM **Privately Held**
SIC: **7011**
HQ: Host International, Inc.
6905 Rockledge Dr Fl 1
Bethesda MD 20817
240 694-4100

(P-12400)
HOST INTERNATIONAL INC
3835 N Harbor Dr, San Diego
(92101-1073)
PHONE.............................619 231-5100
Cynthia Lias, *Branch Mgr*
EMP: 193
SALES (corp-wide): 863.3K **Privately Held**
SIC: **7011** Hotels
HQ: Host International, Inc.
6905 Rockledge Dr Fl 1
Bethesda MD 20817
240 694-4100

(P-12401)
HOTEL ADVENTURES LLC
17662 Irvine Blvd Ste 4, Tustin
(92780-3132)
PHONE.............................714 730-7717
Brad Perrin, *Mng Member*
EMP: 75
SALES (est): 2.8MM **Privately Held**
SIC: **7011** Hotels

(P-12402)
HOTEL CIRCLE INN & SUITES
2201 Hotel Cir S, San Diego (92108-3315)
PHONE.............................619 851-6800
Fred Sandoval, *Manager*
EMP: 50
SQ FT: 70,000
SALES (est): 3.2MM **Privately Held**
SIC: **7011** Motels

P

R

O

D

U

C

T

S

&

S

V

C

S

(P-12403)
HOTEL CIRCLE PROPERTY LLC
Also Called: Town and Country Hotel
500 Hotel Cir N, San Diego (92108-3005)
PHONE...................................619 291-7131
April Shute, *Mng Member*
Reuben Medina, *Opers Staff*
EMP: 500
SQ FT: 1,132,560
SALES (est): 6.8MM **Privately Held**
SIC: 7011 Resort hotel

(P-12404)
HOTEL DEL CORONADO LP
1500 Orange Ave, Coronado (92118-2986)
PHONE...................................619 522-8011
Brian Miller, *Partner*
EMP: 51
SALES (est): 10MM **Privately Held**
SIC: 7011 Hotels

(P-12405)
HOTEL DIAMOND
220 W 4th St, Chico (95928-5315)
PHONE...................................530 893-3100
Wayne Cook, *Owner*
Sandy Teague, *VP Finance*
EMP: 50
SQ FT: 19,800
SALES (est): 1.6MM **Privately Held**
SIC: 7011 Hotels

(P-12406)
HOTEL DURANT A LTD PARTNERSHIP
Also Called: Henry's Pub
2600 Durant Ave, Berkeley (94704-1711)
PHONE...................................510 845-8981
Stephen Wahrlich, *General Ptnr*
Thunderbird Investors, *General Ptnr*
Tracy W Wahrlich Jr, *General Ptnr*
EMP: 84
SQ FT: 57,730
SALES (est): 4.5MM **Privately Held**
WEB: www.hoteldurant.com
SIC: 7011 5812 5813 6512 Hotels; American restaurant; bar (drinking places); nonresidential building operators

(P-12407)
HOTEL HEALDSBURG (PA)
25 Matheson St, Healdsburg (95448-4107)
PHONE...................................707 431-2800
Aziz Zhari, *Manager*
Most Rev Aziz Zhari, *Manager*
EMP: 62
SQ FT: 57,500
SALES (est): 7.5MM **Privately Held**
WEB: www.hotelhealdsburg.com
SIC: 7011 Hotels

(P-12408)
HOTEL HEALDSBURG
317 Healdsburg Ave, Healdsburg (95448-4105)
PHONE...................................707 922-5399
Charlie Palmer, *Branch Mgr*
EMP: 60
SALES (corp-wide): 7.5MM **Privately Held**
SIC: 7011 Inns
PA: Hotel Healdsburg
25 Matheson St
Healdsburg CA 95448
707 431-2800

(P-12409)
HOTEL LA JOLLA
7955 La Jolla Shores Dr, La Jolla (92037-3301)
PHONE...................................858 459-0261
Juliana Bancraft, *President*
Juan Cruz, *Chief Engr*
Lora Hepp, *Finance Dir*
EMP: 82
SALES (est): 4.5MM **Privately Held**
WEB: www.hotellajolla.com
SIC: 7011 Resort hotel; hotels

(P-12410)
HOTEL MAC RESTAURANT INC
50 Washington Ave, Richmond (94801-3945)
PHONE...................................510 233-0576
William Burnett, *President*

EMP: 50 **EST:** 1978
SQ FT: 4,000
SALES (est): 3.4MM **Privately Held**
WEB: www.hotelmac.net
SIC: 7011 5812 5813 Hotels & motels; eating places; bar (drinking places)

(P-12411)
HOTEL NAPA II OPCO LP
Also Called: Homewood Suites
4755 Business Center Dr, Fairfield (94534-1916)
PHONE...................................707 863-0300
Raymond Schulte, *Managing Prtnr*
EMP: 50 **EST:** 2016
SALES (est): 223.7K **Privately Held**
SIC: 7011 Hotels & motels

(P-12412)
HOTEL NIKKO SAN FRANCISCO INC
222 Mason St, San Francisco (94102-2115)
PHONE...................................415 394-1111
Vincent Rafanan, *CFO*
Anna Marie Presutti, *Vice Pres*
David Ng, *Info Tech Dir*
Julio Canel, *Opers Staff*
Emmanuel Sakellarios, *Opers Staff*
EMP: 260
SQ FT: 540,000
SALES (est): 23.2MM **Privately Held**
WEB: www.hotelnikkosf.com
SIC: 7011 5812 5813 7991 Resort hotel; eating places; bar (drinking places); health club; banquet hall facilities
HQ: Okura Nikko Hotel Management Co., Ltd.
2-4-11, Higashishinagawa
Shinagawa-Ku TKY 140-0

(P-12413)
HOTEL TONIGHT INC (PA)
901 Market St Ste 310, San Francisco (94103-1752)
PHONE...................................800 208-2949
Sam Shank, *CEO*
Tony Grimminck, *CFO*
Kelly Russell, *Office Mgr*
Alfred Chung, *Info Tech Dir*
Chas Lemley, *Software Dev*
EMP: 56
SALES (est): 18MM **Privately Held**
SIC: 7011 Hotels

(P-12414)
HOTEL WHITCOMB
1231 Market St, San Francisco (94103-1405)
PHONE...................................415 626-8000
Thomas Chan, *Controller*
Meng Zhang, *Sales Mgr*
Khaled AMR, *Marketing Staff*
Beth Augustine, *Sales Staff*
EMP: 99 **EST:** 1988
SALES (est): 4.4MM **Privately Held**
SIC: 7011 Hotels

(P-12415)
HOWARD JOHN
Also Called: Chick-Fil-A
7681 Carson Blvd, Long Beach (90808-2367)
PHONE...................................562 425-4232
John Howard, *Owner*
EMP: 70
SALES (est): 1.2MM **Privately Held**
SIC: 7011 Hotels & motels

(P-12416)
HOWARD JOHNSON (PA)
1380 S Harbor Blvd, Anaheim (92802-2310)
PHONE...................................714 776-6120
James P Edmondson, *President*
Jonathan Whitehead, *Info Tech Dir*
Jeri Stoddard, *Manager*
EMP: 125 **EST:** 1968
SQ FT: 200
SALES (est): 7.5MM **Privately Held**
SIC: 7011 Hotels & motels

(P-12417)
HPT TRS IHG-2 INC
Also Called: Candlewood Suites
481 El Camino Real, Santa Clara (95050-4300)
PHONE...................................408 241-9305
Liz Olson, *Owner*
EMP: 74 **Publicly Held**
SIC: 7011 Hotels
HQ: Hpt Trs Ihg-2, Inc.
255 Washington St Ste 300
Newton MA 02458
617 964-8389

(P-12418)
HPT TRS IHG-2 INC
Also Called: Holiday Inn
1915 S Manchester Ave, Anaheim (92802-3802)
PHONE...................................714 748-7777
Sven Grunder, *General Mgr*
EMP: 100
SQ FT: 3,540 **Publicly Held**
WEB: www.sixcontinenthotels.com
SIC: 7011 Hotels & motels
HQ: Hpt Trs Ihg-2, Inc.
255 Washington St Ste 300
Newton MA 02458
617 964-8389

(P-12419)
HPT TRS IHG-2 INC
Also Called: Crowne Plaza
5985 W Century Blvd, Los Angeles (90045-5477)
PHONE...................................310 642-7500
Michael Payton, *Manager*
EMP: 100 **Publicly Held**
WEB: www.sixcontinenthotels.com
SIC: 7011 Hotels & motels
HQ: Hpt Trs Ihg-2, Inc.
255 Washington St Ste 300
Newton MA 02458
617 964-8389

(P-12420)
HPT TRS IHG-2 INC
Also Called: Crowne Plaza
300 N Harbor Dr, Redondo Beach (90277-2552)
PHONE...................................310 318-8888
Paul Gibbs, *Branch Mgr*
EMP: 300 **Publicly Held**
WEB: www.sixcontinenthotels.com
SIC: 7011 Hotels & motels
HQ: Hpt Trs Ihg-2, Inc.
255 Washington St Ste 300
Newton MA 02458
617 964-8389

(P-12421)
HPT TRS IHG-2 INC
Also Called: Staybridge Suites
900 Hamlin Ct, Sunnyvale (94089-1401)
PHONE...................................408 745-1515
Tina Messenger, *Branch Mgr*
EMP: 50 **Publicly Held**
WEB: www.hptreit.com
SIC: 7011 Hotels & motels
HQ: Hpt Trs Ihg-2, Inc.
255 Washington St Ste 300
Newton MA 02458
617 964-8389

(P-12422)
HST LESSEE BOSTON LLC
Also Called: Sheraton
1380 Harbor Island Dr, San Diego (92101-1007)
PHONE...................................619 692-2255
Joe Tursey, *General Mgr*
EMP: 60
SALES (corp-wide): 20.7B **Publicly Held**
SIC: 7011 Hotels & motels
HQ: Hst Lessee Boston Llc
39 Dalton St
Boston MA 02199
617 236-2000

(P-12423)
HST LESSEE SAN DIEGO LP
Also Called: Sheraton San Diego Ht & Marina
1380 Harbor Island Dr, San Diego (92101-1007)
PHONE...................................619 291-2900
Joe Tursey, *Principal*

Donna Bruns, *Manager*
EMP: 426
SQ FT: 75,000
SALES (est): 31.1MM
SALES (corp-wide): 5.5B **Publicly Held**
WEB: www.sheratonsandiegohotelandma-rina.com
SIC: 7011 5812 5947 5813 Hotels & motels; eating places; gift, novelty & souvenir shop; drinking places; marinas
PA: Host Hotels & Resorts, Inc.
6903 Rockledge Dr # 1500
Bethesda MD 20817
240 744-1000

(P-12424)
HUMNIT HOTEL AT LAX LLC
Also Called: Concourse Hotel At
6225 W Century Blvd, Los Angeles (90045-5311)
PHONE...................................424 702-1234
Jina Luman, *Principal*
EMP: 99 **EST:** 2013
SQ FT: 49,500
SALES (est): 2.9MM **Privately Held**
SIC: 7011 Hotels

(P-12425)
HUNTINGTON HOTEL COMPANY
Also Called: Inn At Rancho Santa Fe, The
5951 Linea Del Cielo, Rancho Santa Fe (92067)
PHONE...................................858 756-1131
Scott Jenkins, *CEO*
Jerome Strack, *General Mgr*
Michelle Yanagi, *General Mgr*
Kathy Reese, *Sales Dir*
Debbie Grenowich, *Director*
EMP: 88
SQ FT: 5,000
SALES (est): 7.5MM **Privately Held**
SIC: 7011 5812 Resort hotel; eating places

(P-12426)
HUOYEN INTERNATIONAL INC
Also Called: Hotel Fullerton Anaheim, The
1500 S Raymond Ave, Fullerton (92831-5236)
PHONE...................................714 635-9000
Hsi Jung Yang, *President*
EMP: 90
SQ FT: 144,698
SALES (est): 4.3MM **Privately Held**
SIC: 7011 Hotel, franchised

(P-12427)
HUSKIES LESSEE LLC
Also Called: Sir Francis Drake Hotel
450 Powell St, San Francisco (94102-1504)
PHONE...................................415 392-7755
John Price, *General Mgr*
EMP: 375
SALES (est): 32MM **Privately Held**
SIC: 7011 Hotels

(P-12428)
HYATT COPORATION AS AGENT OF B
7100 Aviara Resort Dr, Carlsbad (92011-4908)
PHONE...................................760 603-6851
Byron Peacock,
EMP: 58
SALES (est): 5.8MM **Privately Held**
SIC: 7011 Resort hotel

(P-12429)
HYATT CORPORATION
Also Called: Hyatt Hotel
8401 W Sunset Blvd, Los Angeles (90069-1909)
PHONE...................................323 656-1234
Tim Flodin, *Manager*
Scott Allen, *General Mgr*
Scott Mason, *General Mgr*
Dena Roady, *General Mgr*
Natalie Heffner, *Executive Asst*
EMP: 165
SALES (corp-wide): 4.4B **Publicly Held**
WEB: www.hyatt.com
SIC: 7011 5812 5813 Hotels & motels; restaurant, family: independent; bar (drinking places)

▲ = Import ▼=Export
◆ =Import/Export

HQ: Hyatt Corporation
150 N Riverside Plz
Chicago IL 60606
312 750-1234

(P-12430)
HYATT CORPORATION
4001 Northstar Dr, Truckee (96161-4250)
PHONE....................................530 562-3900
Beryl Guyon, *Branch Mgr*
EMP: 316
SALES (corp-wide): 4.4B **Publicly Held**
SIC: 7011 Vacation lodges
HQ: Hyatt Corporation
150 N Riverside Plz
Chicago IL 60606
312 750-1234

(P-12431)
HYATT CORPORATION
Also Called: Hyatt Los Angeles Airport
6225 W Century Blvd, Los Angeles
(90045-5311)
PHONE..............................312 750-1234
Donald J Henderson, *Manager*
Christine Haddad, *Marketing Staff*
EMP: 500
SALES (corp-wide): 4.4B **Publicly Held**
SIC: 7011 5812 5813 Hotels; restaurant,
family; chain; bar (drinking places)
HQ: Hyatt Corporation
150 N Riverside Plz
Chicago IL 60606
312 750-1234

(P-12432)
HYATT CORPORATION
3500 Market St, Riverside (92501-2841)
PHONE....................................909 240-9526
Bonnie Gardner, *General Mgr*
EMP: 316
SALES (corp-wide): 4.4B **Publicly Held**
SIC: 7011 Hotels
HQ: Hyatt Corporation
150 N Riverside Plz
Chicago IL 60606
312 750-1234

(P-12433)
HYATT CORPORATION
Also Called: Grand Hyatt San Francisco
345 Stockton St, San Francisco
(94108-4606)
PHONE....................................415 848-6050
Steve Trent, *Manager*
Jordan Meisner, *Vice Pres*
Sara Frey, *Human Res Mgr*
Michael Scherbert, *Sales Dir*
Prianka Malhotra, *Sales Staff*
EMP: 500
SALES (corp-wide): 4.4B **Publicly Held**
WEB: www.hyatt.com
SIC: 7011 5813 5812 6512 Hotels & mo-
tels; drinking places; eating places; non-
residential building operators
HQ: Hyatt Corporation
150 N Riverside Plz
Chicago IL 60606
312 750-1234

(P-12434)
HYATT CORPORATION
Also Called: Hyatt Hotel
50 Drumm St, San Francisco (94111)
PHONE....................................415 788-1234
Matthew Adams, *Manager*
EMP: 900
SALES (corp-wide): 4.4B **Publicly Held**
WEB: www.hyatt.com
SIC: 7011 5812 5813 Hotels & motels;
eating places; bar (drinking places)
HQ: Hyatt Corporation
150 N Riverside Plz
Chicago IL 60606
312 750-1234

(P-12435)
HYATT CORPORATION
Also Called: Hyatt House San Ramon
2323 San Ramon Vly Blvd, San Ramon
(94583-1607)
PHONE....................................925 743-1882
Pam Callahan, *Branch Mgr*
Kerry Knudson, *General Mgr*
EMP: 317

SALES (corp-wide): 4.4B **Publicly Held**
SIC: 7011 Hotels
HQ: Hyatt Corporation
150 N Riverside Plz
Chicago IL 60606
312 750-1234

(P-12436)
HYATT CORPORATION
Also Called: Hyatt Hotel
200 S Pine Ave, Long Beach (90802-4537)
PHONE....................................562 432-0161
Steve Smith, *Manager*
Takang Tashi, *General Mgr*
Henry Swindler, *Director*
Timothy Wai, *Manager*
EMP: 500
SALES (corp-wide): 4.4B **Publicly Held**
WEB: www.hyatt.com
SIC: 7011 7299 Hotels & motels; banquet
hall facilities
HQ: Hyatt Corporation
150 N Riverside Plz
Chicago IL 60606
312 750-1234

(P-12437)
HYATT CORPORATION
Also Called: Hyatt Regency Orange County
11999 Harbor Blvd, Garden Grove
(92840-2703)
PHONE....................................714 750-1234
Kevin Kennedy, *Manager*
Kevin Kim, *Tech/Comp Coord*
Glen Wilson, *Engineer*
EMP: 300
SALES (corp-wide): 4.4B **Publicly Held**
WEB: www.hyatt.com
SIC: 7011 Hotels & motels
HQ: Hyatt Corporation
150 N Riverside Plz
Chicago IL 60606
312 750-1234

(P-12438)
HYATT CORPORATION
Also Called: Hyatt Regency Monterey
1 Old Golf Course Rd, Monterey
(93940-4908)
PHONE....................................831 372-1234
Michael Koffler, *Manager*
Neal Matsumoto, *Controller*
EMP: 420
SALES (corp-wide): 4.4B **Publicly Held**
WEB: www.hyatt.com
SIC: 7011 Hotels & motels
HQ: Hyatt Corporation
150 N Riverside Plz
Chicago IL 60606
312 750-1234

(P-12439)
HYATT CORPORATION
Also Called: Hyatt Hotel
17900 Jamboree Rd, Irvine (92614-6211)
PHONE....................................949 975-1234
Rod T Schinnerer, *General Mgr*
EMP: 450
SALES (corp-wide): 4.4B **Publicly Held**
WEB: www.hyatt.com
SIC: 7011 7992 7991 5813 Hotels & mo-
tels; public golf courses; physical fitness
facilities; drinking places; eating places
HQ: Hyatt Corporation
150 N Riverside Plz
Chicago IL 60606
312 750-1234

(P-12440)
HYATT CORPORATION
Also Called: Hyatt Grand Champion Resort
44600 Indian Wells Ln, Indian Wells
(92210-8707)
PHONE....................................760 341-1000
Allan Farwell, *Manager*
Tom Netting, *Vice Pres*
Natalie Maupin, *Comms Mgr*
Sandy Martinez, *Planning*
Bob Colson, *Chf Purch Ofc*
EMP: 500
SALES (corp-wide): 4.4B **Publicly Held**
WEB: www.hyatt.com
SIC: 7011 5813 5812 Hotels; drinking
places; eating places

HQ: Hyatt Corporation
150 N Riverside Plz
Chicago IL 60606
312 750-1234

(P-12441)
HYATT CORPORATION
Also Called: Hyatt Hotel
1107 Jamboree Rd, Newport Beach
(92660-6219)
PHONE....................................949 729-1234
Ruth Benjamin, *General Mgr*
Paul Lu, *General Mgr*
Martha Collins, *Sales Associate*
Onie Carreon, *Manager*
EMP: 300
SALES (corp-wide): 4.4B **Publicly Held**
WEB: www.hyatt.com
SIC: 7011 5813 5812 Hotels & motels;
drinking places; eating places
HQ: Hyatt Corporation
150 N Riverside Plz
Chicago IL 60606
312 750-1234

(P-12442)
HYATT CORPORATION
55 E Brokaw Rd, San Jose (95112-4202)
PHONE....................................408 453-3006
Frank Palacios, *Principal*
EMP: 314
SALES (corp-wide): 4.4B **Publicly Held**
SIC: 7011 8741 Hotels; hotel or motel
management
HQ: Hyatt Corporation
150 N Riverside Plz
Chicago IL 60606
312 750-1234

(P-12443)
HYATT CORPORATION
Also Called: Hyatt Regency San Francisco Ht
5 Embarcadero Ctr, San Francisco
(94111-4800)
PHONE....................................415 788-1234
Jerry Simmons, *General Mgr*
Harish Chand, *Admin Sec*
Dominic Beecham, *Opers Staff*
Judy Cronkhite, *Sales Dir*
Manuel Cristerna, *Sales Mgr*
EMP: 600
SALES (corp-wide): 4.4B **Publicly Held**
WEB: www.hyatt.com
SIC: 7011 5812 5813 Hotels & motels;
eating places; drinking places
HQ: Hyatt Corporation
150 N Riverside Plz
Chicago IL 60606
312 750-1234

(P-12444)
HYATT CORPORATION
Also Called: Andaz Sandiego
600 F St, San Diego (92101-6310)
PHONE....................................619 849-1234
Rusty Middleton, *Branch Mgr*
EMP: 200
SALES (corp-wide): 4.4B **Publicly Held**
SIC: 7011 Resort hotel
HQ: Hyatt Corporation
150 N Riverside Plz
Chicago IL 60606
312 750-1234

(P-12445)
HYATT EQUITIES LLC
Also Called: Hyatt Hotel
1740 N 1st St, San Jose (95112)
PHONE....................................408 993-1234
Manou Mobesesahi, *Branch Mgr*
EMP: 253
SALES (corp-wide): 4.4B **Publicly Held**
SIC: 7011 Hotels & motels
HQ: Hyatt Equities, L.L.C.
71 S Wacker Dr Fl 14
Chicago IL 60606
312 750-1234

(P-12446)
**HYATT HOTELS MANAGEMENT
CORP**
24500 Town Center Dr, Valencia
(91355-1322)
PHONE....................................661 799-1234
Chris Aldiere, *Manager*
EMP: 140

SALES (corp-wide): 4.4B **Publicly Held**
WEB: www.hyattvacations.com
SIC: 7011 7299 5812 Hotels & motels;
banquet hall facilities; caterers
HQ: Hyatt Hotels Management Corporation
71 S Wacker Dr Ste 1000
Chicago IL 60606
312 750-1234

(P-12447)
**HYATT HOTELS MANAGEMENT
CORP**
Also Called: Regency Caterers By Hyatt
3777 Lajolla Village Dr, San Diego (92122)
PHONE....................................858 552-1234
Chris Alteri, *Manager*
EMP: 485
SALES (corp-wide): 4.4B **Publicly Held**
WEB: www.hyattvacations.com
SIC: 7011 5812 5813 Hotels & motels;
caterers; drinking places
HQ: Hyatt Hotels Management Corporation
71 S Wacker Dr Ste 1000
Chicago IL 60606
312 750-1234

(P-12448)
**HYATT HOTELS MANAGEMENT
CORP**
285 N Palm Canyon Dr, Palm Springs
(92262-5525)
PHONE....................................760 322-9000
Dania Duke, *Manager*
EMP: 200
SALES (corp-wide): 4.4B **Publicly Held**
WEB: www.hyattvacations.com
SIC: 7011 7299 5812 Hotels & motels;
banquet hall facilities; caterers
HQ: Hyatt Hotels Management Corporation
71 S Wacker Dr Ste 1000
Chicago IL 60606
312 750-1234

(P-12449)
**HYATT HOTELS MANAGEMENT
CORP**
4219 El Camino Real, Palo Alto
(94306-4405)
PHONE....................................650 352-1234
Colleen Kareti, *General Mgr*
EMP: 365
SALES (corp-wide): 4.4B **Publicly Held**
WEB: www.hyattvacations.com
SIC: 7011 5813 5812 Hotels & motels;
drinking places; eating places
HQ: Hyatt Hotels Management Corporation
71 S Wacker Dr Ste 1000
Chicago IL 60606
312 750-1234

(P-12450)
**HYATT HOTELS MANAGEMENT
CORP**
1 Old Golf Course Rd, Monterey
(93940-4908)
PHONE....................................831 372-1234
EMP: 500
SQ FT: 10,000
SALES (corp-wide): 4.4B **Publicly Held**
WEB: www.hyattvacations.com
SIC: 7011 Hotels & motels
HQ: Hyatt Hotels Management Corporation
71 S Wacker Dr Ste 1000
Chicago IL 60606
312 750-1234

(P-12451)
HYATT REGENCY SANTA CLARA
5101 Great America Pkwy, Santa Clara
(95054-1118)
PHONE....................................408 200-1234
Peter Reice, *General Mgr*
EMP: 68
SALES (est): 6.3MM **Privately Held**
SIC: 7011 Hotels & motels

(P-12452)
I CYPRESS COMPANY (PA)
Also Called: Pebble Beach Company
1700 17 Mile Dr, Pebble Beach (93953)
P.O. Box 1418 (93953-1418)
PHONE....................................831 647-7500
Bill Perocchi, *CEO*
Clint Eastwood, *Partner*
Cody Plott, *President*

David Heuck, *CFO*
Mark Stilwell, *Exec VP*
EMP: 60
SALES (est): 149.4MM **Privately Held**
SIC: 7011 Resort hotel

(P-12453)
IA LODGING NAPA SOLANO TRS LLC
Also Called: NAPA Valley Marriott
3425 Solano Ave, NAPA (94558-2709)
PHONE..............................707 253-8600
Amanda Hawkins-Vogel, *General Mgr*
EMP: 210
SQ FT: 200,000
SALES (est): 561.9K **Publicly Held**
SIC: 7011 Resort hotel, franchised
PA: Xenia Hotels & Resorts, Inc.
200 S Orange Ave Ste 2700
Orlando FL 32801

(P-12454)
IHG MANAGEMENT (MARYLAND) LLC
Also Called: Crown Plaza Los Angeles
5985 W Century Blvd, Los Angeles
(90045-5477)
PHONE..............................310 642-7500
William Block, *Finance Dir*
EMP: 250
SQ FT: 14,000
SALES: 30MM **Privately Held**
SIC: 7011 Hotels & motels

(P-12455)
IHMS (SF) LLC
Also Called: Campton Place, A Taj Hotel
340 Stockton St, San Francisco
(94108-4609)
PHONE..............................415 781-5555
Sanjay Jain,
Raghav Desai, *Vice Pres*
Dinesh Bhatt, *General Mgr*
Rakesh Kant, *General Mgr*
Juanita Santos, *General Mgr*
EMP: 150
SALES (est): 8.8MM
SALES (corp-wide): 372.5MM **Privately Held**
SIC: 7011 Hotels
HQ: International Hotel Management Services Inc.
2 E 61st St
New York NY 10065

(P-12456)
INDIAN WELLS RESORT HOTEL
76661 Us Highway 111, Indian Wells
(92210-8972)
PHONE..............................760 345-6466
Brad Weimer, *President*
EMP: 50
SQ FT: 240,000
SALES (est): 3.6MM **Privately Held**
WEB: www.indianwellsresort.com
SIC: 7011 5812 Resort hotel; eating places

(P-12457)
INDIGO HOSPITALITY MANAGEMENT
Also Called: Indigo Hotels
1817 N Sepulveda Blvd, Manhattan Beach
(90266-2901)
PHONE..............................310 787-7795
B C Patel, *President*
Barrett Patel, *Director*
EMP: 50 **EST:** 1992
SALES (est): 1.1MM **Privately Held**
WEB: www.indigohotels.com
SIC: 7011 Hotels

(P-12458)
INN AT SCOTTS VALLEY LLC
Also Called: Hilton Santa Cruz/Scotts Vly
6001 La Madrona Dr, Scotts Valley
(95060-1057)
PHONE..............................831 440-1000
Rich Higdon, *Mng Member*
EMP: 70
SQ FT: 130,000
SALES (est): 2.8MM **Privately Held**
SIC: 7011 Hotels & motels

(P-12459)
INNCAL INCORPORATED (PA)
1919 Grand Canal Blvd B5, Stockton
(95207-8114)
PHONE..............................209 473-4667
Carl W Thompson Jr, *President*
Francine Thompson, *Vice Pres*
Norma Agulo, *Controller*
EMP: 90
SQ FT: 6,300
SALES (est): 3.8MM **Privately Held**
WEB: www.inncal.com
SIC: 7011 Hotels & motels

(P-12460)
INTERCONTINENTAL HOTELS
888 Howard St, San Francisco
(94103-3011)
PHONE..............................415 616-6500
Peter Koehler, *General Mgr*
EMP: 150 **Privately Held**
WEB: www.southforkhotel.com
SIC: 7011 Hotels
HQ: Intercontinental Hotels Of San Francisco, Inc.
3 Ravinia Dr Ste 100
Atlanta GA 30346

(P-12461)
INTERCONTINENTAL HOTELS GROUP
Also Called: Crowne Plaza
17941 Von Karman Ave, Irvine
(92614-6253)
PHONE..............................949 863-1999
Jim Alexander, *Owner*
EMP: 180 **Privately Held**
WEB: www.hptreit.com
SIC: 7011 Hotels & motels
HQ: Intercontinental Hotels Group Resources, Inc.
3 Ravinia Dr Ste 100
Atlanta GA 30346
770 604-5000

(P-12462)
INTERCONTINENTAL HOTELS GROUP
Also Called: Hotel Indigo San Diego
509 9th Ave, San Diego (92101-7213)
PHONE..............................619 727-4000
Raul Lopez, *General Mgr*
EMP: 60 **Privately Held**
SIC: 7011 Hotels
HQ: Intercontinental Hotels Group Resources, Inc.
3 Ravinia Dr Ste 100
Atlanta GA 30346
770 604-5000

(P-12463)
INTERCONTINENTAL HOTELS GROUP
Also Called: Holiday Inn
50 8th St, San Francisco (94103-1409)
PHONE..............................415 626-6103
Gino Lazzara, *General Mgr*
EMP: 160 **Privately Held**
SIC: 7011 5813 5812 6512 Hotels & motels; drinking places; eating places; non-residential building operators
HQ: Intercontinental Hotels Group Resources, Inc.
3 Ravinia Dr Ste 100
Atlanta GA 30346
770 604-5000

(P-12464)
INTERCONTINENTAL HOTELS GROUP
Also Called: Holiday Inn
19800 S Vermont Ave, Torrance
(90502-1126)
PHONE..............................310 781-9100
David Britton, *General Mgr*
EMP: 74 **Privately Held**
SIC: 7011 Hotels & motels
HQ: Intercontinental Hotels Group Resources, Inc.
3 Ravinia Dr Ste 100
Atlanta GA 30346
770 604-5000

(P-12465)
INTERCONTINENTAL HOTELS GROUP
Also Called: San Francisco Marriott Un Sq
480 Sutter St, San Francisco (94108-3901)
PHONE..............................415 398-8900
John Simonich, *Branch Mgr*
EMP: 210 **Privately Held**
WEB: www.southforkhotel.com
SIC: 7011 Hotels
HQ: Intercontinental Hotels Group Resources, Inc.
3 Ravinia Dr Ste 100
Atlanta GA 30346
770 604-5000

(P-12466)
INTERCONTINENTAL HOTELS GROUP
Also Called: Holiday Inn
495 Bay St, San Francisco (94133-1860)
PHONE..............................415 771-9000
Sheila Martin, *General Mgr*
EMP: 252 **Privately Held**
WEB: www.sixcontinenthotels.com
SIC: 7011 8741 Hotels & motels; hotel or motel management
HQ: Intercontinental Hotels Group Resources, Inc.
3 Ravinia Dr Ste 100
Atlanta GA 30346
770 604-5000

(P-12467)
INTERCONTINENTAL HOTELS GROUP
Also Called: Holiday Inn
5650 Calle Real, Goleta (93117-2319)
PHONE..............................805 964-6241
Gary Opdahl, *General Mgr*
EMP: 65 **Privately Held**
WEB: www.sixcontinenthotels.com
SIC: 7011 Hotels & motels
HQ: Intercontinental Hotels Group Resources, Inc.
3 Ravinia Dr Ste 100
Atlanta GA 30346
770 604-5000

(P-12468)
INTERCONTINENTAL HOTELS GROUP
Also Called: Holiday Inn
550 N Point St, San Francisco
(94133-1312)
PHONE..............................415 409-4600
Mike Cunningham, *Manager*
EMP: 50 **Privately Held**
WEB: www.southforkhotel.com
SIC: 7011 Hotels & motels
HQ: Intercontinental Hotels Group Resources, Inc.
3 Ravinia Dr Ste 100
Atlanta GA 30346
770 604-5000

(P-12469)
INTERCONTINENTAL HOTELS GROUP
Also Called: Crowne Plaza Irvine-Orange Cou
17941 Von Karman Ave, Irvine
(92614-6253)
PHONE..............................949 863-1999
Martin Driskel, *Opers-Prdtn-Mfg*
EMP: 100 **Privately Held**
WEB: www.southforkhotel.com
SIC: 7011 5813 5812 Hotels & motels; drinking places; eating places
HQ: Intercontinental Hotels Group Resources, Inc.
3 Ravinia Dr Ste 100
Atlanta GA 30346
770 604-5000

(P-12470)
INTERCONTINENTAL HOTELS GROUP
2280 S Haven Ave, Ontario (91761-0739)
PHONE..............................909 930-5555
Lori Whiting, *Manager*
EMP: 122 **Privately Held**
WEB: www.southforkhotel.com
SIC: 7011 Hotels

HQ: Intercontinental Hotels Group Resources, Inc.
3 Ravinia Dr Ste 100
Atlanta GA 30346
770 604-5000

(P-12471)
INTERSTATE HOTELS RESORTS INC
Also Called: Sheraton
2500 Mason St, San Francisco
(94133-1450)
PHONE..............................415 362-5500
David Gievens, *Manager*
EMP: 250 **Privately Held**
WEB: www.sheratonokc.com
SIC: 7011 Hotels & motels
HQ: Interstate Hotels & Resorts, Inc.
2011 Crystal Dr Ste 1100
Arlington VA 22202
703 387-3100

(P-12472)
INTERSTATE HOTELS RESORTS INC
Also Called: Marriott Los Angeles Downtown
333 S Figueroa St, Los Angeles
(90071-1001)
PHONE..............................213 617-1133
Guenet Kelelatchew, *Director*
EMP: 220
SQ FT: 143,000 **Privately Held**
WEB: www.sheratonokc.com
SIC: 7011 8741 Hotels; hotel or motel management
HQ: Interstate Hotels & Resorts, Inc.
2011 Crystal Dr Ste 1100
Arlington VA 22202
703 387-3100

(P-12473)
INTERSTATE HOTELS RESORTS INC
Also Called: Hilton Garden Inn Carlsbad Bch
6450 Carlsbad Blvd, Carlsbad
(92011-1058)
PHONE..............................760 476-0800
Bob Moore, *Manager*
EMP: 70 **Privately Held**
WEB: www.sheratonokc.com
SIC: 7011 Hotels & motels
HQ: Interstate Hotels & Resorts, Inc.
2011 Crystal Dr Ste 1100
Arlington VA 22202
703 387-3100

(P-12474)
INTERSTATE HOTELS RESORTS INC
Also Called: Westin Bonaventure Ht & Suites
404 S Figueroa St 418a, Los Angeles
(90071-1710)
PHONE..............................213 624-1000
Peter Zen, *President*
Mike Estes, *Purch Mgr*
EMP: 500 **Privately Held**
WEB: www.sheratonokc.com
SIC: 7011 Hotels & motels
HQ: Interstate Hotels & Resorts, Inc.
2011 Crystal Dr Ste 1100
Arlington VA 22202
703 387-3100

(P-12475)
INTERSTATE HOTELS RESORTS INC
Also Called: Radisson Inn
32083 Alvarado Niles Rd, Union City
(94587-2942)
PHONE..............................510 489-2200
Peter San, *General Mgr*
EMP: 140 **Privately Held**
WEB: www.sheratonokc.com
SIC: 7011 5812 5813 Hotels & motels; eating places; bar (drinking places)
HQ: Interstate Hotels & Resorts, Inc.
2011 Crystal Dr Ste 1100
Arlington VA 22202
703 387-3100

▲ = Import ▼=Export
◆ =Import/Export

(P-12476)
INTERSTATE HOTELS RESORTS INC
Also Called: Hilton Sacramento Arden West
2200 Harvard St, Sacramento
(95815-3306)
PHONE.................................916 922-4700
Howard Harris, *General Mgr*
EMP: 200 Privately Held
WEB: www.sheratonokc.com
SIC: 7011 5812 5813 5947 Hotels & motels; eating places; drinking places; gift, novelty & souvenir shop
HQ: Interstate Hotels & Resorts, Inc.
2011 Crystal Dr Ste 1100
Arlington VA 22202
703 387-3100

(P-12477)
INTERSTATE HOTELS RESORTS INC
Also Called: Hilton
18800 Macarthur Blvd, Irvine (92612-1410)
PHONE.................................949 833-9999
Ted Holmquist, *General Mgr*
Dori Familiant, *General Mgr*
EMP: 185 Privately Held
WEB: www.sheratonokc.com
SIC: 7011 Hotels & motels
HQ: Interstate Hotels & Resorts, Inc.
2011 Crystal Dr Ste 1100
Arlington VA 22202
703 387-3100

(P-12478)
IRP LAX HOTEL LLC
Also Called: Four Points by Sheraton LAX
9750 Airport Blvd, Los Angeles
(90045-5404)
PHONE.................................310 645-4600
Phil Baxter,
EMP: 240
SQ FT: 337,720
SALES (est): 7.5MM
SALES (corp-wide): 20.1B Publicly Held
SIC: 7011 Hotels & motels
HQ: Tishman Hotel Corporation
666 5th Ave Fl 38
New York NY 10103

(P-12479)
ISLAND HOSPITALITY MGT LLC
Residence Inn By Marriott
750 Lakeway Dr, Sunnyvale (94085-4011)
PHONE.................................408 720-1000
Hugo Hernandez, *Branch Mgr*
EMP: 50
SALES (corp-wide): 764.3MM Privately Held
WEB: www.napleshamptoninn.com
SIC: 7011 Hotels & motels
PA: Island Hospitality Management, Llc
222 Lakeview Ave Ste 200
West Palm Beach FL 33401

(P-12480)
ISLAND HOSPITALITY MGT LLC
Also Called: Residence Inn By Marriott
2000 Winward Way, San Mateo
(94404-2472)
PHONE.................................650 574-4700
Omar Paredes, *Branch Mgr*
EMP: 60
SALES (corp-wide): 764.3MM Privately Held
WEB: www.napleshamptoninn.com
SIC: 7011 Hotels & motels
PA: Island Hospitality Management, Llc
222 Lakeview Ave Ste 200
West Palm Beach FL 33401

(P-12481)
ISLAND HOSPITALITY MGT LLC
Residence Inn By Marriott
1080 Stewart Dr, Sunnyvale (94085-3917)
PHONE.................................408 720-8893
Kort Gursu, *Manager*
EMP: 59
SALES (corp-wide): 764.3MM Privately Held
WEB: www.napleshamptoninn.com
SIC: 7011 Hotels & motels

PA: Island Hospitality Management, Llc
222 Lakeview Ave Ste 200
West Palm Beach FL 33401

(P-12482)
ISLAND HOSPITALITY MGT LLC
Also Called: Residence Inn By Marriott
2025 Convention Ctr Way, Ontario
(91764-4450)
PHONE.................................909 937-6788
Frank Palacios, *Branch Mgr*
EMP: 50
SALES (corp-wide): 764.3MM Privately Held
WEB: www.napleshamptoninn.com
SIC: 7011 Hotels & motels
PA: Island Hospitality Management, Llc
222 Lakeview Ave Ste 200
West Palm Beach FL 33401

(P-12483)
ISLAND HOSPITALITY MGT LLC
Also Called: Summerfield Suites By Hyatt
400 Concourse Dr, Belmont (94002-4125)
PHONE.................................650 591-8600
Trinity Nguyen, *Branch Mgr*
Denise Eldrich, *General Mgr*
Alvin Magcale, *General Mgr*
EMP: 80
SALES (corp-wide): 764.3MM Privately Held
WEB: www.napleshamptoninn.com
SIC: 7011 Hotels & motels
PA: Island Hospitality Management, Llc
222 Lakeview Ave Ste 200
West Palm Beach FL 33401

(P-12484)
J5TH LLC
Also Called: Residence Inn By Mariott
356 6th Ave, San Diego (92101-7186)
PHONE.................................619 487-1200
Rajan Hansji, *Mng Member*
Sajan Hansji,
Dilip Kanji,
EMP: 55
SALES (est): 2.7MM Privately Held
SIC: 7011 7389 Hotels & motels; office facilities & secretarial service rental

(P-12485)
JACK PARKER CORP
Also Called: Le Parker Meridien Palm Sprng
4200 E Palm Canyon Dr, Palm Springs
(92264-5230)
PHONE.................................760 770-5000
Adam Glick, *President*
Brandon McCurley, *General Mgr*
▲ **EMP: 177**
SALES (est): 5MM Privately Held
SIC: 7011 Hotels

(P-12486)
JC RESORTS INN
17550 Bernardo Oaks Dr, San Diego
(92128-2112)
PHONE.................................858 487-0700
Katherine Colachis, *Owner*
EMP: 80
SALES (est): 1.1MM Privately Held
SIC: 7011 Resort hotel

(P-12487)
JCK HOTELS LLC
Also Called: Holiday Inn
9888 Mira Mesa Blvd, San Diego
(92131-1025)
PHONE.................................858 635-5566
Brad Housewoorth,
Judy Fang,
George Liu,
Gloria Liu,
EMP: 55
SQ FT: 4,800
SALES (est): 2.8MM Privately Held
WEB: www.mmpcusa.com
SIC: 7011 Hotels & motels

(P-12488)
JHC INVESTMENT INC
Also Called: Dt Club Hotel Santa Ana
7 Hutton Centre Dr, Santa Ana
(92707-5753)
PHONE.................................714 751-2400
Jung-Hsiung Chiu, *President*
EMP: 70 EST: 1993
SQ FT: 85,000
SALES (est): 2.4MM Privately Held
SIC: 7011 Hotels

(P-12489)
JJ GRAND HOTEL
620 S Harvard Blvd, Los Angeles
(90005-2510)
PHONE.................................213 383-3000
James Lee, *President*
Kuija Kim, *President*
EMP: 60
SALES (est): 1.4MM Privately Held
WEB: www.jjgrandhotel.com
SIC: 7011 Resort hotel; hotels

(P-12490)
JOIE DE VIVRE HOSPITALITY LLC (PA)
1750 Geary Blvd, San Francisco
(94115-3715)
PHONE.................................415 835-0300
Stephen T Conley Jr, *CEO*
Dan Korn, *Vice Pres*
Robin Donovan, *General Mgr*
Suzie Yang, *General Mgr*
Rachel Carlton, *Executive Asst*
EMP: 50
SALES: 231.8MM Privately Held
WEB: www.hotelbijou.com
SIC: 7011 Hotels

(P-12491)
JOIE DE VIVRE HOSPITALITY INC
Also Called: Wild Palms Hotel & Bar
910 E Fremont Ave, Sunnyvale
(94087-3702)
PHONE.................................408 738-0500
Steven C Y Chen, *President*
EMP: 51
SQ FT: 80,000
SALES: 4.8MM Privately Held
SIC: 7011 Hotels

(P-12492)
JP ALLEN EXTENDED STAY
Also Called: Holiday Inn
150 E Angeleno Ave, Burbank
(91502-1911)
PHONE.................................818 841-4770
Chris Haven, *Manager*
EMP: 50
SALES (est): 2.3MM
SALES (corp-wide): 5.1MM Privately Held
SIC: 7011 Hotels & motels
PA: Jp Allen Extended Stay
450 Pioneer Dr
Glendale CA 91203
818 956-0202

(P-12493)
JP ALLEN EXTENDED STAY (PA)
Also Called: Days Inn
450 Pioneer Dr, Glendale (91203-1713)
PHONE.................................818 956-0202
Joe Perry, *Owner*
EMP: 126
SQ FT: 4,000
SALES (est): 5.1MM Privately Held
SIC: 7011 Hotels & motels

(P-12494)
JS HOSPITALITY GROUP LLC
Also Called: Courtyard Oxnard Ventura
600 E Esplanade Dr, Oxnard (93036-2403)
PHONE.................................805 988-3600
Joseph Fan,
EMP: 100
SALES (est): 4.5MM Privately Held
SIC: 7011 Hotels & motels

(P-12495)
JWMCC LIMITED PARTNERSHIP
Also Called: Hyatt Hotel
2151 Avenue Of The Stars, Los Angeles
(90067-5004)
PHONE.................................310 277-1234
Ulrich Samietz, *General Mgr*
▲ **EMP: 353**
SQ FT: 4,600
SALES (est): 5MM Privately Held
SIC: 7011 5812 Hotels & motels; eating places

(P-12496)
K3 DEV LLC
Also Called: AC Hotel San Jose Sunnyvale
CU
725 S Fair Oaks Ave, Sunnyvale
(94086-7915)
PHONE.................................408 733-7950
Mayur Patel, *Principal*
Mona Rigdon, *Principal*
EMP: 80
SALES (est): 1.7MM Privately Held
SIC: 7011 Hotels

(P-12497)
KAIDAN HOSPITALITY LP
Also Called: Red Lion Hotel Redding
1830 Hilltop Dr, Redding (96002-0212)
PHONE.................................530 221-8700
EMP: 66
SALES (est): 3.6MM Privately Held
WEB: www.westcoasthotels.com
SIC: 7011 Hotels & motels

(P-12498)
KALPANA LLC (PA)
620 Newport Center Dr # 1600, Newport
Beach (92660-8016)
PHONE.................................949 610-8200
Mayur Patel, *Principal*
Padmesh Patel, *Mng Member*
Padmesh M Patel, *Mng Member*
EMP: 300
SALES (est): 6.7MM Privately Held
SIC: 7011 Hotels & motels

(P-12499)
KALPANA LLC
Also Called: San Dego Mission Vly Hilton Ht
901 Camino Del Rio S, San Diego
(92108-3515)
PHONE.................................619 543-9000
Jack Giacomini, *General Mgr*
EMP: 250
SALES (est): 3.4MM
SALES (corp-wide): 6.7MM Privately Held
WEB: www.doralpalmsprings.com
SIC: 7011 5812 7299 Hotels & motels; eating places; banquet hall facilities
PA: Kalpana, Llc
620 Newport Center Dr # 1600
Newport Beach CA 92660
949 610-8200

(P-12500)
KANG FAMILY PARTNERS LLC
Also Called: Santa Ynez Valley Marriott
555 Mcmurray Rd, Buellton (93427-9559)
PHONE.................................805 688-1000
Daphne Kang, *Mng Member*
Karla Azahar, *General Mgr*
Jesus Gomez, *Sales Staff*
Wanda Macpherson, *Sales Staff*
Jack Von Schlichting, *Manager*
EMP: 110
SALES: 6MM Privately Held
WEB: www.santaynezhotels.com
SIC: 7011 Hotel, franchised; hotels

(P-12501)
KAVA HOLDINGS INC (DH)
Also Called: Hotel Bel-Air
701 Stone Canyon Rd, Los Angeles
(90077-2909)
PHONE.................................310 472-1211
Hj Suharafadzil, *President*
Helen Smith, *President*
Christopher Cowdary, *CEO*
Franois Delahaye, *COO*
Eugenio Pirri, *Vice Pres*
EMP: 200
SQ FT: 30,000

SALES (est): 24.6MM
SALES (corp-wide): 507.9MM **Privately Held**
WEB: www.hotelbelair.com
SIC: 7011 Resort hotel; hotels
HQ: Dorchester Group Limited
57 Berkeley Square
London W1J 6
207 629-4848

(P-12502)
KEN REAL ESTATE LEASE LTD
Also Called: Anaheim Majestic Garden Hotel
900 S Disneyland Dr, Anaheim
(92802-1844)
PHONE....................714 778-1700
Shigeru Sato, *President*
Bruno Nocco, *Chief Engr*
Andrew Dang, *Controller*
EMP: 99
SALES (est): 8.4MM **Privately Held**
SIC: 7011 Resort hotel

(P-12503)
KESARI HOSPITALITY LLC
445 Hotel Cir S, San Diego (92108-3402)
PHONE....................619 298-1291
Kalpesh Kalthia, *Mng Member*
EMP: 72 EST: 2015
SQ FT: 18,774
SALES (est): 250.8K **Privately Held**
SIC: 7011 Resort hotel, franchised

(P-12504)
KEY INN LTD A CAL LTD PARTNR
Also Called: Key Inn & Suites
1611 El Camino Real, Tustin (92780-5203)
PHONE....................714 832-3220
Ed Pankey, *Partner*
Peter Pankey, *Partner*
Rocio Castillo, *Manager*
EMP: 50
SALES (est): 3.5MM **Privately Held**
WEB: www.keyinntustin.com
SIC: 7011 Motels

(P-12505)
KHANNA ENTPS - II LTD PARTNR
Also Called: Crowne Plz Scramento Northeast
5321 Date Ave, Sacramento (95841-2512)
PHONE....................916 338-5800
Ravi Khanna, *Partner*
Anil Khanna, *Partner*
Ashwin Khanna, *Partner*
Rajesh Khanna, *Partner*
Parveen Chand, *Director*
EMP: 114
SALES (est): 7.2MM **Privately Held**
WEB: www.sacnortheast.com
SIC: 7011 Hotels & motels

(P-12506)
KHATRI INC
Also Called: Khatri Properties
1608 Sunrise Ave Ste 6, Modesto
(95350-4678)
PHONE....................209 576-1481
Anil Khatri, *Manager*
EMP: 50
SQ FT: 10,662
SALES (corp-wide): 5.8MM **Privately Held**
SIC: 7011 Hotels & motels
PA: Khatri, Inc.
20700 Manter Rd
Castro Valley CA 94552
510 886-7909

(P-12507)
KHP II SAN DIEGO HOTEL LLC (PA)
Also Called: Palomar San Diego
1047 5th Ave, San Diego (92101-5101)
PHONE....................619 515-3000
Nikki Leondakis, *Mng Member*
Mark Van Cooney,
EMP: 100
SALES: 8.6MM **Privately Held**
SIC: 7011 Hotels

(P-12508)
KHP III GOLETA LLC
Also Called: Goodland
5650 Calle Real, Goleta (93117-2319)
PHONE....................805 964-6241
Wesley Lau, *Accounting Mgr*
Danielle Santilli, *Associate Dir*
Robert Cole, *General Mgr*
Ernesto Rubio, *Engineer*
Miguel Serrano, *Engineer*
EMP: 99 EST: 2016
SALES (est): 893.5K **Privately Held**
SIC: 7011 5812 Resort hotel; American restaurant

(P-12509)
KIMPTON HOTEL & REST GROUP LLC
Also Called: Serrano Hotel
405 Taylor St, San Francisco (94102-1701)
PHONE....................415 885-2500
John Turner, *General Mgr*
Benjamin Malmquist, *General Mgr*
Sarah Mendoza, *Asst Controller*
Maricar Miller, *Finance*
Liezel Custodio, *Human Res Mgr*
EMP: 100 **Privately Held**
WEB: www.kuletos.com
SIC: 7011 7299 Hotels; banquet hall facilities
HQ: Kimpton Hotel & Restaurant Group Llc
222 Kearny St Ste 200
San Francisco CA 94108
415 397-5572

(P-12510)
KIMPTON HOTEL & REST GROUP LLC (HQ)
222 Kearny St Ste 200, San Francisco
(94108-4537)
PHONE....................415 397-5572
Mike Depatie, *CEO*
Mike Defrino, *COO*
Niki Leondakis, *COO*
Ben Rowe, *CFO*
Joe Long, *Exec VP*
EMP: 100
SALES (est): 469.2MM **Privately Held**
WEB: www.kuletos.com
SIC: 7011 8741 6794 Hotels; hotel or motel management; franchises, selling or licensing

(P-12511)
KIMPTON HOTEL & REST GROUP LLC
Also Called: Tuscan Inn
425 N Point St, San Francisco
(94133-1405)
PHONE....................415 561-1100
Jan Misch, *Manager*
EMP: 85 **Privately Held**
WEB: www.kuletos.com
SIC: 7011 7299 5813 Hotels; banquet hall facilities; drinking places
HQ: Kimpton Hotel & Restaurant Group Llc
222 Kearny St Ste 200
San Francisco CA 94108
415 397-5572

(P-12512)
KIMPTON HOTEL & REST GROUP LLC
Also Called: Pescatore
2455 Mason St, San Francisco
(94133-1401)
PHONE....................415 561-1111
Leon Calahan, *Manager*
EMP: 74 **Privately Held**
WEB: www.kuletos.com
SIC: 7011 Hotels
HQ: Kimpton Hotel & Restaurant Group Llc
222 Kearny St Ste 200
San Francisco CA 94108
415 397-5572

(P-12513)
KIMPTON HOTEL & REST GROUP LLC
Also Called: Hotel Moneco
501 Geary St, San Francisco (94102-1640)
PHONE....................415 292-0100
Jimmy Hord, *Manager*
EMP: 88 **Privately Held**
WEB: www.kuletos.com

SIC: 7011 5812 Hotels; eating places
HQ: Kimpton Hotel & Restaurant Group Llc
222 Kearny St Ste 200
San Francisco CA 94108
415 397-5572

(P-12514)
KINGLEDON INC
Also Called: Ventura Beach Marriott Hotel
2055 Harbor Blvd, Ventura (93001-3707)
PHONE....................805 643-6000
Chaohui Liu, *CEO*
Kathy Stanford, *Human Res Dir*
EMP: 150 EST: 2013
SALES (est): 3.1MM **Privately Held**
SIC: 7011 Hotels

(P-12515)
KINGS INN HOTEL SAN DIEGO
Also Called: Kings Inn Hotel & Grille
1333 Hotel Cir S, San Diego (92108-3491)
PHONE....................619 297-2231
C Andro Petersen, *President*
Wilson Kenyetta, *Sales Staff*
David Parrent, *Sales Staff*
EMP: 70
SALES (est): 5.2MM **Privately Held**
SIC: 7011 Resort hotel; hotels

(P-12516)
KINTETSU ENTERPRISES CO AMER (HQ)
Also Called: Kintetsu Enterprises Co Amer
21241 S Wstn Ave Ste 100, Torrance
(90501)
PHONE....................310 782-9300
Hisao Hiro, *President*
EMP: 200
SALES (est): 14MM **Privately Held**
WEB: www.miyakola.com
SIC: 7011 6512 Hotel, franchised; nonresidential building operators

(P-12517)
KINTETSU ENTERPRISES CO AMER
328 E 1st St, Los Angeles (90012-3902)
PHONE....................213 617-2000
Akimasa Yoneda, *Branch Mgr*
EMP: 80 **Privately Held**
WEB: www.miyakola.com
SIC: 7011 Hotels
HQ: Kintetsu Enterprises Company Of America
21241 S Wstn Ave Ste 100
Torrance CA 90501
310 782-9300

(P-12518)
KITTRIDGE HOTELS & RESORTS LLC
Also Called: Hard Rock Hotel Palm Springs
150 S Indian Canyon Dr, Palm Springs
(92262-6604)
PHONE....................760 325-9676
Stan Kantowski,
Heidi Walker, *Manager*
EMP: 64
SALES (est): 3MM **Privately Held**
WEB: www.hotelzoso.com
SIC: 7011 Hotels

(P-12519)
KMS FISHERMANS WHARF LP
Also Called: Tuscan Inn
425 N Point St, San Francisco
(94133-1405)
PHONE....................415 561-1100
Laura Meith, *Director*
Jan Misch, *Partner*
EMP: 110
SQ FT: 97,724
SALES (est): 3.2MM **Privately Held**
WEB: www.tuscaninn.com
SIC: 7011 Hotel, franchised

(P-12520)
KNOTTS BERRY FARM LLC
Also Called: Knott's Berry Farm Hotel
7675 Crescent Ave, Buena Park
(90620-3947)
PHONE....................714 995-1111
Stan Dlander, *Manager*
Kate Mendez, *Director*
EMP: 230

SALES (corp-wide): 1.3B **Publicly Held**
WEB: www.knotts.com
SIC: 7011 Resort hotel
HQ: Berry Knott's Farm Llc
8039 Beach Blvd
Buena Park CA 90620
714 827-1776

(P-12521)
KSL RESORTS HOTEL DEL CORONADO
1500 Orange Ave, Coronado (92118-2918)
PHONE....................619 435-6611
Bob Antes, *Principal*
EMP: 82
SALES (est): 2.1MM
SALES (corp-wide): 8.9B **Publicly Held**
SIC: 7011 Hotels
HQ: Hilton Supply Management Llc
7930 Jones Branch Dr # 400
Mc Lean VA 22102
703 883-1000

(P-12522)
KUMAR HOTELS INC
Also Called: Holiday Inn
545 N Humboldt Ave, Willows
(95988-3502)
PHONE....................530 934-8900
Pawan Kumar, *President*
EMP: 150
SALES (est): 4.6MM **Privately Held**
SIC: 7011 Hotels & motels

(P-12523)
L & O ALISO VIEJO LLC
Also Called: Renaissance Hotel Clubsport
50 Enterprise, Aliso Viejo (92656-6026)
PHONE....................949 643-6700
Ed Tomlin, *General Mgr*
Marnie Harvey, *Opers Dir*
Damon Durante, *Sales Staff*
EMP: 55
SALES (est): 4.7MM **Privately Held**
SIC: 7011 Hotels & motels

(P-12524)
L & S INVESTMENT CO INC
Also Called: Best Western
14173 Green Tree Blvd, Victorville
(92395-4343)
PHONE....................760 245-3461
Walter Schroeder, *Ch of Bd*
EMP: 100
SQ FT: 120,000
SALES (est): 1.6MM **Privately Held**
SIC: 7011 Hotels & motels

(P-12525)
L-O CORONADO HOTEL INC
1500 Orange Ave, Coronado (92118-2918)
PHONE....................619 435-6611
Tod Shallon, *President*
Jeff Senior, *VP Mktg*
EMP: 1350 EST: 1886
SALES (est): 7.2MM **Privately Held**
WEB: www.shopsatthedel.com
SIC: 7011 5812 5941 5813 Resort hotel; eating places; tennis goods & equipment; cocktail lounge

(P-12526)
L-O SOMA HOTEL INC
Also Called: Argent Hotel, The
50 3rd St, San Francisco (94103-3106)
PHONE....................415 974-6400
Charles S Peck, *President*
Peter A Del Franco, *Exec VP*
Ronald A Silva, *Exec VP*
EMP: 420
SALES: 8.7MM
SALES (corp-wide): 865.7MM **Privately Held**
WEB: www.destinationhotels.com
SIC: 7011 5812 Hotels; eating places
HQ: Destination Residences Llc
10333 E Dry Creek Rd
Englewood CO 80112
303 799-3830

(P-12527)
LA HOTEL VENTURE LLC
Also Called: Los Angeles Marriott Downtown
333 S Figueroa St, Los Angeles
(90071-1001)
PHONE....................213 617-1133

HEI Huang,
Libby Zarrahy, *Chief Mktg Ofcr*
Carl Sprayberry, *General Mgr*
Conant Elisa Ann, *Sales Staff*
Lavon Minor, *Sales Staff*
EMP: 400
SALES (est): 12.7MM **Privately Held**
SIC: 7011 Hotels

(P-12528)
LA JOLLA BCH & TENNIS CLB INC
Also Called: Shores Restaurant
8110 Camino Del Oro, La Jolla
(92037-3108)
PHONE....................858 459-8271
John Cambel, *Manager*
EMP: 155
SALES (corp-wide): 28.2MM **Privately Held**
WEB: www.ljbtc.com
SIC: 7011 5812 5813 7299 Resort hotel; restaurant, family: independent; cocktail lounge; banquet hall facilities
PA: La Jolla Beach & Tennis Club, Inc.
2000 Spindrift Dr
La Jolla CA 92037
858 454-7126

(P-12529)
LA JOLLA COVE HOTEL & MOTEL
Also Called: La Jolla Cove Motel
1155 Coast Blvd, La Jolla (92037-3627)
P.O. Box 1067 (92038-1067)
PHONE....................858 459-2621
Helen Jackman, *Vice Pres*
EMP: 78 EST: 1959
SQ FT: 78,000
SALES (est): 4.8MM **Privately Held**
WEB: www.lajollacove.com
SIC: 7011 Hotels

(P-12530)
LA POSTA CASINO
Also Called: La Posta Band Mission Indians
777 Crestwood Rd, Boulevard (91905)
PHONE....................619 824-4100
Dwendolyn Prada, *President*
James Hill, *Corp Secy*
EMP: 140
SQ FT: 20,000
SALES (est): 3.3MM **Privately Held**
SIC: 7011 Casino hotel

(P-12531)
LAFAYETTE PARK HOTEL CORP (PA)
1100 Alma St Ste 106, Menlo Park
(94025-3344)
PHONE....................650 330-8888
Ellis J Alden, *President*
Katherine H Alden, *President*
EMP: 500
SQ FT: 2,500
SALES (est): 9.2MM **Privately Held**
WEB: www.lafayetteparkhotel.com
SIC: 7011 Hotels

(P-12532)
LAGUNA HILLS HOTEL DEV VENTR
Also Called: Holiday Inn
25205 La Paz Rd, Laguna Hills
(92653-5105)
PHONE....................949 586-5000
June Chen, *Partner*
Clement Chen, *President*
EMP: 100
SQ FT: 102,241
SALES (est): 2.4MM **Privately Held**
WEB: www.holidayinngreaterlosangeles.com
SIC: 7011 5812 7299 Hotels & motels; eating places; banquet hall facilities

(P-12533)
LAKE ARRWHEAD RSORT OPRTOR INC (HQ)
Also Called: Marriott
27984 Hwy 189, Lake Arrowhead (92352)
PHONE....................909 336-1511
Carmen Rodriguez, *CEO*
Veronique Williams, *Administration*
EMP: 115

SALES (est): 11.8MM
SALES (corp-wide): 20.7B **Publicly Held**
WEB: www.laresort.com
SIC: 7011 5813 5812 Resort hotel; drinking places; eating places
PA: Marriott International, Inc.
10400 Fernwood Rd
Bethesda MD 20817
301 380-3000

(P-12534)
LAKE NATOMA LODGING LP
Also Called: Lake Natoma Inn
702 Gold Lake Dr, Folsom (95630-2559)
PHONE....................916 351-1500
Robert Leach, *Partner*
Rick Fenstermaker, *General Ptnr*
Elizabeth Kuwabara, *Manager*
EMP: 80
SQ FT: 82,000
SALES (est): 5.3MM **Privately Held**
WEB: www.lakenatomainn.com
SIC: 7011 Hotel, franchised; hotels

(P-12535)
LAMP LITER ASSOCIATES
Also Called: Lamp Liter Inn
3130 W Main St Ste A, Visalia
(93291-5765)
P.O. Box 7508 (93290-7508)
PHONE....................559 733-4328
Robert Lee, *General Mgr*
EMP: 75
SQ FT: 100,000
SALES (est): 3.3MM **Privately Held**
WEB: www.lampliter.net
SIC: 7011 5812 5813 Motels; eating places; cocktail lounge

(P-12536)
LANDMARK HOTELS LLC
Also Called: Landmark Princess
312 Broadway St Ste 204, Laguna Beach
(92651-4335)
PHONE....................949 640-5040
Richard Packard, *President*
EMP: 150
SALES (est): 12.9MM **Privately Held**
SIC: 7011 Hotels

(P-12537)
LANGHAM HOTELS PACIFIC CORP
Also Called: Langham Hotels International
1401 S Oak Knoll Ave, Pasadena
(91106-4508)
PHONE....................617 451-1900
Ka Shui Lo, *President*
Brett Butcher, *Vice Pres*
Ron Pellerine, *General Mgr*
Andy Hobbs, *Engineer*
Surachit Vongtanaanek, *Engineer*
EMP: 55
SALES (est): 6.4MM **Privately Held**
SIC: 7011 Hotels; resort hotel

(P-12538)
LARKSPUR HSPTALITY DEV MGT LLC
Also Called: Hilton Garden Inn San
670 Gateway Blvd, South San Francisco
(94080-7014)
PHONE....................650 872-1515
Brian Fox, *General Mgr*
EMP: 100 **Privately Held**
SIC: 7011 Hotels & motels
PA: Larkspur Hospitality Development And Management Company, Llc
125 E Sir F Drake Blvd
Larkspur CA 94939

(P-12539)
LAV HOTEL CORP
Also Called: Whaling Bar & Grill
1132 Prospect St, La Jolla (92037-4533)
PHONE....................858 454-0771
Harry Collins, *President*
W M Allen Sr, *Bd of Directors*
W M Allen Jr, *Vice Pres*
Elvia Carrillo, *Facilities Dir*
EMP: 250
SQ FT: 1,000
SALES (est): 13MM **Privately Held**
WEB: www.lavalencia.com
SIC: 7011 Hotels

(P-12540)
LAX HOSPITALITY LP
Also Called: Radisson Inn
6225 W Century Blvd, Los Angeles
(90045-5311)
PHONE....................310 670-9000
Sushli Israni, *Principal*
EMP: 200
SQ FT: 26,000
SALES (est): 11MM **Privately Held**
SIC: 7011 Hotels & motels

(P-12541)
LAX HOTEL VENTURES LLC
Also Called: Four Points Sheraton Lax
9750 Airport Blvd, Los Angeles
(90045-5404)
PHONE....................310 645-4600
EMP: 50
SALES (est): 950K **Privately Held**
SIC: 7011

(P-12542)
LAX PLAZA HOTEL
6333 Bristol Pkwy, Culver City
(90230-6904)
PHONE....................310 902-2202
Lindsay Butcher, *General Mgr*
EMP: 120
SALES (est): 1MM **Privately Held**
WEB: www.laxplazahotel.com
SIC: 7011 5812 5813 Hotels & motels; eating places; bars & lounges

(P-12543)
LB FUNDING LLC
Also Called: Hilton Hotel Long Beach
701 W Ocean Blvd, Long Beach
(90831-3100)
PHONE....................562 983-3400
John Murphy,
EMP: 97 EST: 2013
SALES (est): 4.5MM **Privately Held**
SIC: 7011 Hotels & motels

(P-12544)
LC TRS INC
Also Called: La Costa Resort & Spa
2100 Costa Del Mar Rd, Carlsbad
(92009-6823)
PHONE....................760 438-9111
Mike Shannon, *President*
Scott Dalecio, *Vice Pres*
EMP: 872
SQ FT: 5,000
SALES (est): 61.1MM **Privately Held**
SIC: 7011 5812 Resort hotel; eating places

(P-12545)
LE MONTROSE HOTEL
Also Called: Le Montrose Suite Hotel
900 Hammond St Apt 434, West Hollywood
(90069-4443)
PHONE....................310 855-1115
John Douponce, *Managing Prtnr*
Arlene Figueroa, *Manager*
EMP: 69
SQ FT: 1,000
SALES (est): 3.9MM **Privately Held**
WEB: www.lemontrose.com
SIC: 7011 Hotels

(P-12546)
LEE-VICTORVILLE HOTEL CORP
Also Called: Green Tree Inn
14173 Green Tree Blvd, Victorville
(92395-4343)
PHONE....................760 245-3461
Walter M Schroeder, *President*
EMP: 105
SQ FT: 380,000
SALES (est): 5.4MM **Privately Held**
SIC: 7011 Bed & breakfast inn

(P-12547)
LEISURE SPORTS INC
Also Called: Renaissance Clubsport
2805 Jones Rd, Walnut Creek
(94597-7848)
PHONE....................925 938-3058
Brian Amador, *General Mgr*
Gani Mabilangan, *Facilities Dir*
Charli Martucci, *Director*
Annie Wong, *Director*
Jennifer Grimes, *Manager*

EMP: 330
SALES (corp-wide): 68.8MM **Privately Held**
WEB: www.leisuresportsinc.com
SIC: 7011 Hotels & motels
PA: Leisure Sports, Inc.
4670 Willow Rd Ste 100
Pleasanton CA 94588
925 600-1966

(P-12548)
LH INDIAN WELLS OPERATING LLC
4500 Indian Wells Ln, Indian Wells (92210)
PHONE....................760 341-2200
Bob Low, *Principal*
EMP: 220
SALES (est): 4.2MM **Privately Held**
SIC: 7011 7991 Resort hotels; spas
PA: Lh Indian Wells Holding, Llc
11777 San Vicente Blvd
Los Angeles CA 90049

(P-12549)
LH UNIVERSAL OPERATING LLC
Also Called: Sheraton Universal Hotel
333 Unversal Hollywood Dr, Universal City
(91608-1001)
PHONE....................818 980-1212
Robert Lowe,
Sean Waldron, *Security Dir*
Virginia Clark, *General Mgr*
Alex Sorour, *General Mgr*
Dai Vondran, *General Mgr*
EMP: 280
SALES: 30MM **Privately Held**
SIC: 7011 Hotels & motels; hotels

(P-12550)
LHO MSSION BAY RSIE LESSEE INC
Also Called: Hilton
1775 E Mission Bay Dr, San Diego
(92109-6801)
PHONE....................619 276-4010
Greg Fracassa, *Mng Member*
EMP: 360
SALES (est): 18.1MM **Privately Held**
SIC: 7011 5812 5947 Hotels & motels; eating places; gift, novelty & souvenir shop

(P-12551)
LHO SANTA CRUZ ONE LESSE INC
Also Called: Chaminade of Santa Cruz
1 Chaminade Ln, Santa Cruz (95065-1524)
PHONE....................831 475-5600
Alfred L Young Jr, *CEO*
EMP: 193
SQ FT: 50,000
SALES (est): 487.6MM **Privately Held**
SIC: 7011 Resort hotel
PA: Pebblebrook Hotel Trust
7315 Wscnsin Ave Ste 1100
Bethesda MD 20814

(P-12552)
LHOBERGE LESSEE INC
Also Called: L'Auberge Del Mar
1540 Camino Del Mar, Del Mar
(92014-2411)
PHONE....................858 259-1515
Jamie Sabatier, *CEO*
Charles Peck, *President*
Dennis Fischer, *Vice Pres*
EMP: 250
SQ FT: 84,312
SALES (est): 16.7MM **Privately Held**
WEB: www.laubergedelmar.com
SIC: 7011 Resort hotel

(P-12553)
LIBERTY STATION HHG HOTEL LP
Also Called: Courtyard By Marr San Diego Ai
2592 Laning Rd, San Diego (92106-6418)
PHONE....................619 221-1900
Kevin Keefer, *Partner*
EMP: 60
SALES (est): 3.1MM **Privately Held**
SIC: 7011 Hotels & motels

(P-12554)
LIBERTY STATION HHG HOTEL LP
Also Called: Homewood Suites Libery Station
2576 Laning Rd, San Diego (92106-6418)
PHONE..................................619 222-0500
Rick Brown, *General Mgr*
Kevin Keefer, *Partner*
EMP: 50
SALES (est): 2.5MM **Privately Held**
SIC: 7011 Hotels & motels

(P-12555)
LINCOLN PLAZA HOTEL INC
123 S Lincoln Ave, Monterey Park
(91755-2914)
PHONE..................................626 571-8818
Thira Ratanapreukskul, *President*
William H Roach, *Corp Secy*
EMP: 60
SQ FT: 95,600
SALES (est): 2.6MM **Privately Held**
WEB: www.lincolnplazahotel.net
SIC: 7011 Hotels

(P-12556)
LIONSGATE HT & CONFERENCE CTR
3410 Westover St, McClellan (95652-1005)
PHONE..................................916 643-6222
Lary Kelly, *President*
Laura Kennedy, *COO*
EMP: 90
SALES: 5MM **Privately Held**
SIC: 7011 Hotels

(P-12557)
LITTLE RIVER INN INC
Also Called: Little River Inn and Golf Crse
7901 N Highway 1, Little River
(95456-9527)
P.O. Box B (95456-0430)
PHONE..................................707 937-5942
Charles D Hervilla, *CEO*
Susan Mc Kinney, *Vice Pres*
Cally Dym, *General Mgr*
Dan Sirkin, *Manager*
Terry Stratton, *Superintendent*
EMP: 100
SQ FT: 3,000
SALES (est): 8.1MM **Privately Held**
WEB: www.littleriverinn.com
SIC: 7011 5812 Bed & breakfast inn; American restaurant

(P-12558)
LLC WOODWARD WEST
28400 Stallion Springs Dr, Tehachapi
(93561-5266)
PHONE..................................661 822-7900
Debbie Williams,
Darlene Olson, *Bookkeeper*
Richie Velasquez, *Mktg Dir*
Jake Kinney, *Director*
Karen Mathews, *Director*
EMP: 143
SALES (est): 2.2MM **Privately Held**
WEB: www.woodwardwest.com
SIC: 7011 Vacation lodges

(P-12559)
LODGEWORKS LP
1230 1st St, NAPA (94559-2930)
PHONE..................................707 690-9800
Michael Collins, *Branch Mgr*
EMP: 60
SALES (est): 205.3K
SALES (corp-wide): 42.1MM **Privately Held**
SIC: 7011 Hotels & motels
PA: Lodgeworks, L.P.
8100 E 22nd St N Bldg 500
Wichita KS 67226
316 681-5100

(P-12560)
LOEWS HOLLYWOOD HOTEL LLC
1755 N Highland Ave, Hollywood
(90028-4403)
PHONE..................................323 450-2235
Jonathan Tisch, *Ch of Bd*
Michael Hu, *Treasurer*
Gary Belvedere, *Vice Pres*
Randy Tribolet, *Admin Sec*

Albert Fattal, *Info Tech Dir*
EMP: 375 **EST:** 2012
SALES (est): 15MM
SALES (corp-wide): 14B **Publicly Held**
SIC: 7011 Hotels
PA: Loews Corporation
667 Madison Ave Fl 7
New York NY 10065
212 521-2000

(P-12561)
LONE CYPRESS COMPANY LLC
US Open At Pebble Beach
17 Mile Dr, Pebble Beach (93953)
P.O. Box 567 (93953-0567)
PHONE..................................831 624-3811
Robert Lapso, *Branch Mgr*
EMP: 1500
SALES (corp-wide): 378.4MM **Privately Held**
WEB: www.pebblebeach.com
SIC: 7011 7992 5813 5812 Resort hotel; public golf courses; drinking places; eating places
PA: Pebble Beach Resort Co Dba Lone Cypress Shop
2700 17 Mile Dr
Pebble Beach CA 93953
831 647-7500

(P-12562)
LONG BEACH GOLDEN SAILS INC
Also Called: Best Western Golden Sails Ht
23545 Crenshaw Blvd # 100, Torrance
(90505-5218)
PHONE..................................562 596-1631
Luis Vasquez, *President*
Ruben Garza, *Vice Pres*
Vicki Arreguin, *Sales Staff*
▲ **EMP:** 100
SQ FT: 150,000
SALES (est): 5.9MM **Privately Held**
WEB: www.goldensailshotel.com
SIC: 7011 5812 5813 Hotels & motels; restaurant, family: independent; bar (drinking places)
PA: Abp Hotel, Llc
2200 W Valley Blvd
Alhambra CA 91803
562 596-1631

(P-12563)
LONG POINT DEVELOPMENT LLC
Also Called: Terranea Resort
100 Terranea Way, Rancho Palos Verdes
(90275-1013)
PHONE..................................310 265-2800
Terri Haack, *Mng Member*
Agnelo Fernandes, *Vice Pres*
Jennifer Yang, *Executive Asst*
Wagner Jeffery, *CTO*
Kevin McKee, *VP Finance*
EMP: 1000 **EST:** 2004
SALES (est): 65.4MM **Privately Held**
SIC: 7011 Resort hotel

(P-12564)
LOWE ENTERPRISES INC (PA)
Also Called: Lei AG Seattle
11777 San Vicente Blvd # 900, Los Angeles
(90049-5084)
PHONE..................................310 820-6661
Robert J Lowe, *President*
Sara Bravo, *President*
James Sabatier, *President*
Rick Swagerty, *President*
Terri Haack, *Exec VP*
EMP: 125
SQ FT: 20,000
SALES (est): 865.7MM **Privately Held**
WEB: www.ccpavilion.com
SIC: 7011 6552 Hotels & motels; subdividers & developers

(P-12565)
LQ MANAGEMENT LLC
Also Called: La Quinta Inn
5249 W Century Blvd, Los Angeles
(90045-5917)
PHONE..................................310 645-2200
Ryan Thayer, *Branch Mgr*
EMP: 63 **Publicly Held**
WEB: www.neubayern.net
SIC: 7011 Hotels & motels

HQ: Lq Management L.L.C.
909 Hidden Rdg Ste 600
Irving TX 75038
214 492-6600

(P-12566)
LQR PROPERTY LLC
Also Called: La Quinta Resort & Club
49499 Eisenhower Dr, La Quinta
(92253-2722)
PHONE..................................760 564-4111
Katherine Stoker, *Opers Staff*
Candace Bengtson, *Asst Director*
Andrew Ferraro, *Asst Director*
EMP: 91
SALES (est): 10.2MM **Privately Held**
SIC: 7011 7999 Hotels & motels; golf driving range

(P-12567)
LUCKY CHANCES INC
Also Called: Lucky Chances Casino
1700 Hillside Blvd, Colma (94014-2801)
PHONE..................................650 758-2237
Rommel R Medina, *CEO*
Ruell Medina, *President*
Chrystal Lee, *HR Admin*
Ralph Baude, *Manager*
Dustin Chase, *Manager*
EMP: 650
SALES (est): 23.2MM **Privately Held**
SIC: 7011 Casino hotel

(P-12568)
M&C HOTEL INTERESTS INC
Also Called: Sheraton
530 Pico Blvd, Santa Monica (90405-1223)
PHONE..................................310 399-9344
Lisa Nagahori, *Branch Mgr*
EMP: 55 **Privately Held**
WEB: www.richfield.com
SIC: 7011 Hotels & motels
HQ: M&C Hotel Interests, Inc.
6560 Greenwood Plaza Blvd # 300
Greenwood Village CO 80111

(P-12569)
M4DEV LLC
Also Called: Hilton Garden Inn
2137 Pacific Hwy Ste A, San Diego
(92101-8472)
PHONE..................................619 696-6300
Mayur Patel,
Ryan Turnello, *Finance*
EMP: 100 **EST:** 2016
SALES (est): 63.5K **Privately Held**
SIC: 7011 Hotels & motels

(P-12570)
M6 DEV LLC
Also Called: Springhill Suites
1801 S Harbor Blvd, Anaheim
(92802-3509)
PHONE..................................714 533-2101
Mona Rigdon, *Principal*
Mayur Patel, *Principal*
EMP: 50
SALES (est): 198.4K **Privately Held**
SIC: 7011 Hotels & motels

(P-12571)
MADRONA MNR WINE CNTRY INN
1001 Westside Rd, Healdsburg
(95448-9434)
PHONE..................................707 433-4231
William R Konrad, *President*
Hesterly Jason, *Facilities Dir*
Gertrude V Konrad,
Arielle Larson, *Director*
EMP: 55 **EST:** 1983
SQ FT: 1,800
SALES (est): 4.1MM **Privately Held**
WEB: www.madronamanor.com
SIC: 7011 5812 Bed & breakfast inn; Italian restaurant; Chinese restaurant; French restaurant; American restaurant

(P-12572)
MAJESTIC INDUSTRY HILLS LLC
Also Called: Pacific Plms Conference Resort
1 Industry Hills Pkwy, City of Industry
(91744-5160)
PHONE..................................626 810-4455

Scott Huntsman, *Branch Mgr*
John Semcken, *Principal*
EMP: 360
SALES (est): 4.6MM
SALES (corp-wide): 32MM **Privately Held**
SIC: 7011 7999 7389 7299 Resort hotel; tennis courts, outdoor/indoor: non-membership; convention & show services; banquet hall facilities
PA: Majestic Industry Hills, Llc
1 Industry Hills Pkwy
City Of Industry CA 91744
562 692-9581

(P-12573)
MAKAR ANAHEIM LLC
Also Called: Hilton
777 W Convention Way, Anaheim
(92802-3425)
PHONE..................................714 740-4431
Paul Makarechian,
Shaun Robinson, *General Mgr*
Laurie Calaunan, *Sales Staff*
Molly Tomita, *Sales Staff*
Lauren Nelson, *Director*
EMP: 1200
SQ FT: 1,000,000
SALES (est): 41.8MM **Privately Held**
SIC: 7011 Hotels & motels

(P-12574)
MAMMOTH MOUNTAIN SKI AREA LLC (DH)
Also Called: Mammoth Mountain Inn
10001 Minaret Rd, Mammoth Lakes
(93546)
P.O. Box 24 (93546-0024)
PHONE..................................760 934-2571
Rusty Gregory, *President*
David Cummings, *Partner*
Dick Flotho, *Officer*
Bruce Burton, *Vice Pres*
Tammy Innocenti, *Vice Pres*
EMP: 347
SQ FT: 140,000
SALES (est): 137.9MM
SALES (corp-wide): 129.4MM **Privately Held**
WEB: www.mammothmotocross.com
SIC: 7011 5812 Ski lodge; resort hotel; eating places
HQ: Hawk Guarantor, Llc
100 Saint Paul St Ste 800
Denver CO 80206
720 284-6400

(P-12575)
MANAS HOSPITALITY LLC
Also Called: Holiday Inn
445 Hotel Cir S, San Diego (92108-3402)
PHONE..................................619 298-1291
Rajesh Chollera,
Hitesh Kalthia,
EMP: 50
SQ FT: 63,424
SALES (est): 816.3K **Privately Held**
SIC: 7011 Hotels & motels

(P-12576)
MANCHESTER GRAND RESORTS LP
Also Called: Manchster Grnd Hyatt San Diego
1 Market Pl Fl 33, San Diego (92101-7714)
PHONE..................................619 232-1234
Mark S Hoplamazian, *CEO*
Douglas F Manchester, *Partner*
Gebhard F Rainer, *CFO*
Alexander Bremer, *Officer*
H Charles Floyd, *Exec VP*
EMP: 810
SALES (est): 28.7MM
SALES (corp-wide): 5.5B **Publicly Held**
WEB: www.hyatt.com
SIC: 7011 Hotel, franchised
PA: Host Hotels & Resorts, Inc.
6903 Rockledge Dr # 1500
Bethesda MD 20817
240 744-1000

(P-12577)
MARINE CORPS UNITED STATES
Also Called: Camp Pendleton Billeting Fund
A St Bldg 1341, Camp Pendleton (92055)
PHONE..................................760 430-4709

Monique Ramirez, *Director*
Jeanette Naputi, *Accounting Mgr*
EMP: 50 **Publicly Held**
WEB: www.usmc.mil
SIC: 7011 Hotels & motels
HQ: United States Marine Corps
Pentagon Rm 4b544
Washington DC 20380

(P-12578)
MARRIOT COURTYARD
Also Called: Courtyard By Marriott
580 Beach St, San Francisco (94133-1128)
PHONE..................415 775-1103
James Edmondson, *Owner*
EMP: 50 **EST:** 1995
SALES (est): 1.9MM **Privately Held**
SIC: 7011 Hotels & motels

(P-12579)
MARRIOTT GRAND RESIDENCE
1001 Heavenly Village Way, South Lake Tahoe (96150-6983)
PHONE...............530 542-8400
Steve Weitz, *President*
Marriot International, *Owner*
EMP: 320
SALES (est): 6.9MM **Privately Held**
SIC: 7011 Hotels & motels

(P-12580)
MARRIOTT INTERNATIONAL INC
5835 Owens Ave, Carlsbad (92008-6562)
PHONE...............760 431-9399
Alicia Clements, *Branch Mgr*
EMP: 173
SALES (corp-wide): 20.7B **Publicly Held**
SIC: 7011 Hotels & motels
PA: Marriott International, Inc.
10400 Fernwood Rd
Bethesda MD 20817
301 380-3000

(P-12581)
MARRIOTT INTERNATIONAL INC
4381 Myra Ave, Cypress (90630-4131)
PHONE...............714 209-6586
EMP: 175
SALES (corp-wide): 20.7B **Publicly Held**
SIC: 7011 Hotels & motels
PA: Marriott International, Inc.
10400 Fernwood Rd
Bethesda MD 20817
301 380-3000

(P-12582)
MARRIOTT INTERNATIONAL INC
11966 El Camino Real, San Diego (92130-2592)
PHONE...............858 523-1700
Michael Woldowski, *Branch Mgr*
Cassandra Scantlebury, *Supervisor*
Tyler Ward, *Supervisor*
EMP: 167
SALES (corp-wide): 20.7B **Publicly Held**
SIC: 7011 5812 Hotels & motels; American restaurant
PA: Marriott International, Inc.
10400 Fernwood Rd
Bethesda MD 20817
301 380-3000

(P-12583)
MARRIOTT INTERNATIONAL INC
5855 W Century Blvd, Los Angeles (90045-5614)
PHONE...............310 641-5700
Jim Burns, *General Mgr*
Nate Siehr, *Vice Pres*
Todd Castor, *Surgery Dir*
Kim N Chieppa, *Principal*
Rich Forbes, *General Mgr*
EMP: 900
SALES (corp-wide): 20.7B **Publicly Held**
SIC: 7011 7389 6513 Hotels & motels; office facilities & secretarial service rental; residential hotel operation

PA: Marriott International, Inc.
10400 Fernwood Rd
Bethesda MD 20817
301 380-3000

(P-12584)
MARRIOTT INTERNATIONAL INC
299 2nd St, San Francisco (94105-3123)
PHONE...............415 947-0700
Lance Rohf, *Manager*
Benjamin Brown, *Opers Mgr*
EMP: 100
SALES (corp-wide): 20.7B **Publicly Held**
SIC: 7011 6531 5812 5813 Hotels & motels; real estate managers; eating places; drinking places
PA: Marriott International, Inc.
10400 Fernwood Rd
Bethesda MD 20817
301 380-3000

(P-12585)
MARRIOTT INTERNATIONAL INC
Also Called: Springhill Suites
900 Bayfront Ct, San Diego (92101-3007)
PHONE...............619 831-0225
Mike Murphy, *General Mgr*
EMP: 100
SALES (corp-wide): 20.7B **Publicly Held**
SIC: 7011 Hotels & motels
PA: Marriott International, Inc.
10400 Fernwood Rd
Bethesda MD 20817
301 380-3000

(P-12586)
MARRIOTT INTERNATIONAL INC
46100 Landing Pkwy, Fremont (94538-6437)
PHONE...............510 413-3700
Orlando Carrasquillo, *Manager*
Yolanda Serranto, *Human Res Dir*
EMP: 200
SALES (corp-wide): 20.7B **Publicly Held**
SIC: 7011 7389 Hotels & motels; office facilities & secretarial service rental
PA: Marriott International, Inc.
10400 Fernwood Rd
Bethesda MD 20817
301 380-3000

(P-12587)
MARRIOTT INTERNATIONAL INC
18000 Von Karman Ave, Irvine (92612-1004)
PHONE...............949 724-3606
Satinder Palpa, *Branch Mgr*
Bobby Shoemaker, *Planning*
Oscar Gamero, *Purchasing*
Ray Leon, *Manager*
Yugo Takahashi, *Manager*
EMP: 500
SALES (corp-wide): 20.7B **Publicly Held**
SIC: 7011 7389 Hotels & motels; office facilities & secretarial service rental
PA: Marriott International, Inc.
10400 Fernwood Rd
Bethesda MD 20817
301 380-3000

(P-12588)
MARRIOTT INTERNATIONAL INC
4240 La Jolla Village Dr, La Jolla (92037-1407)
PHONE...............858 587-1414
Paul Corsinita, *Manager*
Dan Kaplan, *General Mgr*
Adela Pastrana, *Admin Sec*
Eddie Huerta, *Finance*
Adele Steingrubey, *Finance*
EMP: 337
SALES (corp-wide): 20.7B **Publicly Held**
SIC: 7011 Hotels & motels
PA: Marriott International, Inc.
10400 Fernwood Rd
Bethesda MD 20817
301 380-3000

(P-12589)
MARRIOTT INTERNATIONAL INC
350 Calle Principal, Monterey (93940-2416)
PHONE...............831 649-4234
Rene Boskoff, *Branch Mgr*
Andrew Leavitt, *Engineer*
EMP: 225
SALES (corp-wide): 20.7B **Publicly Held**
SIC: 7011 5813 5812 Hotels; bar (drinking places); grills (eating places)
PA: Marriott International, Inc.
10400 Fernwood Rd
Bethesda MD 20817
301 380-3000

(P-12590)
MARRIOTT INTERNATIONAL INC
4700 Airport Plaza Dr, Long Beach (90815-1252)
PHONE...............562 425-5210
Miran Ahmed, *Branch Mgr*
Shannon Cattron, *Manager*
EMP: 210
SALES (corp-wide): 20.7B **Publicly Held**
SIC: 7011 Hotels & motels
PA: Marriott International, Inc.
10400 Fernwood Rd
Bethesda MD 20817
301 380-3000

(P-12591)
MARRIOTT INTERNATIONAL INC
14400 Aviation Blvd, Hawthorne (90250-6654)
PHONE...............310 725-9696
David Laatz, *Branch Mgr*
EMP: 167
SALES (corp-wide): 20.7B **Publicly Held**
SIC: 7011 Hotels & motels
PA: Marriott International, Inc.
10400 Fernwood Rd
Bethesda MD 20817
301 380-3000

(P-12592)
MARRIOTT INTERNATIONAL INC
39802 Cedar Blvd, Newark (94560-5340)
PHONE...............510 657-4600
Scott Crunk, *Manager*
EMP: 167
SALES (corp-wide): 20.7B **Publicly Held**
SIC: 7011 Hotels & motels
PA: Marriott International, Inc.
10400 Fernwood Rd
Bethesda MD 20817
301 380-3000

(P-12593)
MARRIOTT INTERNATIONAL INC
1325 Broadway, Sonoma (95476-7505)
PHONE...............707 935-6600
Dave Dolquist, *General Mgr*
EMP: 200
SQ FT: 1,500
SALES (corp-wide): 20.7B **Publicly Held**
SIC: 7011 Hotels & motels
PA: Marriott International, Inc.
10400 Fernwood Rd
Bethesda MD 20817
301 380-3000

(P-12594)
MARRIOTT INTERNATIONAL INC
3130 S Harbor Blvd # 500, Santa Ana (92704-6829)
PHONE...............714 545-5261
Wynne Prima, *Branch Mgr*
Ruth Rain, *Opers Mgr*
EMP: 167
SALES (corp-wide): 20.7B **Publicly Held**
SIC: 7011 Hotels & motels
PA: Marriott International, Inc.
10400 Fernwood Rd
Bethesda MD 20817
301 380-3000

(P-12595)
MARRIOTT INTERNATIONAL INC
900 W Olympic Blvd, Los Angeles (90015-1338)
PHONE...............213 284-3862
Dawn Frederick, *Executive*
Rich Stade, *Executive*
Kimberly Bailey, *Manager*
EMP: 167
SALES (corp-wide): 20.7B **Publicly Held**
SIC: 7011 Hotels & motels
PA: Marriott International, Inc.
10400 Fernwood Rd
Bethesda MD 20817
301 380-3000

(P-12596)
MARRIOTT INTERNATIONAL INC
1800 Old Bayshore Hwy, Burlingame (94010-1203)
PHONE...............650 692-9100
Stan Moore, *Manager*
Cliff Clark, *General Mgr*
Raphael Santiago, *Human Res Dir*
EMP: 167
SALES (corp-wide): 20.7B **Publicly Held**
SIC: 7011 7389 Hotels & motels; office facilities & secretarial service rental
PA: Marriott International, Inc.
10400 Fernwood Rd
Bethesda MD 20817
301 380-3000

(P-12597)
MARRIOTT INTERNATIONAL INC
Also Called: Residence Inn By Marriott
900 Bayfront Ct, San Diego (92101-3007)
PHONE...............619 831-0224
Evangelina Alaniz, *Accountant*
EMP: 99 **EST:** 2016
SALES (est): 533.8K **Privately Held**
SIC: 7011 Hotels & motels

(P-12598)
MARRIOTT RSRTS HSPITALITY CORP
1091 Pinehurst Ln, Palm Desert (92260-1636)
PHONE...............760 779-1200
Glenn Knorr, *Engineer*
Kristen Kennedy, *Manager*
EMP: 53 **Publicly Held**
SIC: 7011 Hotels & motels
HQ: Marriott Resorts Hospitality Corporation
6649 W Wood Blvd Ste 500
Orlando FL 32821
407 206-6000

(P-12599)
MARRIOTTS NEWPORT COAST VILLA
23000 Newport Coast Dr, Newport Beach (92657-2100)
PHONE...............949 464-6000
Eric Penningroth, *Owner*
EMP: 56
SALES (est): 4.5MM **Privately Held**
SIC: 7011 Resort hotel

(P-12600)
MARRIOTTS SHADOW RIDGE
9003 Shadow Ridge Rd, Palm Desert (92211-2057)
PHONE...............760 674-2600
John Faulk, *Owner*
EMP: 81
SALES (est): 7.5MM **Privately Held**
SIC: 7011 Resort hotel

(P-12601)
MARTIN RESORTS INC (PA)
1201 Palm St, San Luis Obispo (93408-3115)
P.O. Box 12060 (93406-2060)
PHONE...............805 545-7900
Noreen Martin, *CEO*
Margaret Johnson, *COO*
Roger Philips, *CFO*
Laura Sherlock, *Vice Pres*
Erica Fryburger, *General Mgr*
EMP: 252
SQ FT: 7,000

PRODUCTS & SVCS

SALES (est): 13.9MM **Privately Held**
WEB: www.pismo.com
SIC: 7011 Resort hotel

(P-12602)
MASON STREET OPCO LLC
Also Called: Fairmont San Francisco
950 Mason St, San Francisco
(94108-6000)
PHONE..............................415 772-5000
Seung Geon Kim, *President*
Kary Clark, *Human Res Mgr*
Daniel Kramer, *Asst Sec*
EMP: 850
SQ FT: 750,000
SALES: 112MM
SALES (corp-wide): 1.1B **Privately Held**
SIC: 7011 Hotels
HQ: Accor Services Us Llc
   950 Mason St
   San Francisco CA 94108
   415 772-5000

(P-12603)
MAYFAIR HOTEL
1430 Amherst Ave Apt 5, Los Angeles
(90025-0358)
PHONE..............................213 484-9789
Tung Shui Ng, *President*
EMP: 60
SQ FT: 228,800
SALES (est): 3.8MM **Privately Held**
WEB: www.mayfairla.com
SIC: 7011 Hotels

(P-12604)
MBIPCH LLC
Also Called: Malibu Beach Inn
22211 Pacific Coast Hwy, Malibu
(90265-5028)
PHONE..............................310 456-6444
Richard Sherman, *CEO*
Jill Jennings, *General Mgr*
Zia Katayoon, *Opers Staff*
Scott Margot, *Marketing Staff*
VA Der Woude Pauli, *Manager*
EMP: 52
SALES (est): 3.3MM **Privately Held**
SIC: 7011 Resort hotel

(P-12605)
MBP LAND LLC
Also Called: Courtyard Marriott Mission Vly
595 Hotel Cir S, San Diego (92108-3403)
PHONE..............................619 291-5720
John Blem, *Mng Member*
Evan Hitter, *General Mgr*
EMP: 56
SALES: 750K
SALES (corp-wide): 179.2MM **Privately
Held**
SIC: 7011 Hotels & motels
PA: Evolution Hospitality, Llc
   1211 Puerta Del Sol # 170
   San Clemente CA 92673
   949 325-1350

(P-12606)
**MCCLELLAN HOSPITALITY
SVCS LLC**
3140 Peacekeeper Way, McClellan
(95652-2508)
PHONE..............................916 965-7100
Larry Kelley,
Douglas Hart,
EMP: 75
SALES (est): 1.2MM **Privately Held**
SIC: 7011 5812 Hotels & motels; caterers

(P-12607)
**MENDOCINO HOTEL & RESORT
CORP**
Also Called: Mendocino Hotel & Grdn Suites
45080 Main St, Mendocino (95460)
PHONE..............................707 937-0511
Thomas Clark Kravis, *Owner*
Carlos Pena, *Executive*
Juan C Pena, *Executive*
Dan Clark, *Info Tech Mgr*
Cindy Rhinehart, *Data Proc Staff*
EMP: 80
SQ FT: 12,500

SALES (est): 3.2MM **Privately Held**
WEB: www.mendocinohotel.com
SIC: 7011 5812 5813 7299 Hotels; eating
places; bars & lounges; banquet hall facilities

(P-12608)
MERCHANT VALLEY CORP
Also Called: Best Wstn Plus Clnga Inn Sites
1786 Jayne Ave, Coalinga (93210-9249)
PHONE..............................916 410-2021
Sareena Merchant, *Principal*
Mike Merchant, *Principal*
EMP: 50
SALES (est): 494K **Privately Held**
SIC: 7011 Hotels & motels

(P-12609)
**MERISTAR SAN PEDRO HILTON
LLC**
Also Called: Hilton Port Los Angls-San Pdro
2800 Via Cabrillo Marina, San Pedro
(90731-7223)
PHONE..............................310 514-3344
Paul Whetsell, *Mng Member*
Jeff Milnes, *CEO*
John Emery, *CFO*
EMP: 176
SALES (est): 1.7MM **Privately Held**
WEB: www.sheratonokc.com
SIC: 7011 Hotels & motels
HQ: Interstate Hotels & Resorts, Inc.
   2011 Crystal Dr Ste 1100
   Arlington VA 22202
   703 387-3100

(P-12610)
MERITAGE RESORT LLC
Also Called: Meritage Resort and Spa, The
875 Bordeaux Way, NAPA (94558-7524)
PHONE..............................707 251-1900
Timothy R Busch, *President*
Michael M Palmer, *General Mgr*
Rashann Flores, *Hum Res Coord*
Tami Pacho, *Human Res Mgr*
Sonya Lake, *Regl Sales Mgr*
EMP: 350
SALES (est): 17MM **Privately Held**
SIC: 7011 Hotels

(P-12611)
MERRITT HOSPITALITY LLC
Also Called: Hilton
701 W Ocean Blvd, Long Beach
(90831-3100)
PHONE..............................562 983-3400
Grace Sun, *Sales Mgr*
EMP: 250
SALES (corp-wide): 250.3MM **Privately
Held**
SIC: 7011 7991 5813 5812 Hotels & mo-
tels; physical fitness facilities; drinking
places; eating places
HQ: Merritt Hospitality, Llc
   101 Merritt 7 Ste 14
   Norwalk CT 06851
   203 849-8844

(P-12612)
MERRITT HOSPITALITY LLC
Also Called: Marriott
2701 Nutwood Ave, Fullerton (92831-5400)
PHONE..............................714 738-7800
Tom Beebon, *Manager*
EMP: 125
SALES (corp-wide): 250.3MM **Privately
Held**
SIC: 7011 7991 5813 5812 Hotels & mo-
tels; physical fitness facilities; drinking
places; eating places
HQ: Merritt Hospitality, Llc
   101 Merritt 7 Ste 14
   Norwalk CT 06851
   203 849-8844

(P-12613)
MESA PROPERTIES GP
25 Mauchly Ste 305, Irvine (92618-2331)
PHONE..............................949 857-1905
John Jourard, *Sales Mgr*
EMP: 60
SALES (est): 1.9MM **Privately Held**
SIC: 7011 Hotels

(P-12614)
METROPOLIS HOTEL MGT LLC
Also Called: Hotel Indigo Los Angles Dwntwn
899 Francisco St, Los Angeles
(90017-2534)
PHONE..............................213 683-4855
Raymond Vermolen, *General Mgr*
EMP: 120
SALES: 25MM **Privately Held**
SIC: 7011 Hotels
HQ: Inter-Continental Hotels Corporation
   3 Ravinia Dr Ste 100
   Atlanta GA 30346
   770 604-5000

(P-12615)
MHRP RESORT INC
Also Called: Mountain High Ski Resort
24510 Highway 2, Wrightwood (92397)
P.O. Box 3010 (92397-3010)
PHONE..............................760 249-5808
Russel S Bernard, *President*
W Gregory Geiger, *Vice Pres*
Kenneth Liang, *Vice Pres*
Marc Porosoff, *Vice Pres*
Chris Castillo, *Technology*
EMP: 100
SALES (est): 6MM **Privately Held**
WEB: www.mountainhighskiresort.com
SIC: 7011 Ski lodge

(P-12616)
MIKADO HOTELS INC
Also Called: Mikado Best Western Hotel
12600 Riverside Dr, North Hollywood
(91607-3411)
PHONE..............................818 763-9141
Jerome Frick, *CEO*
Edmond Petrossian, *President*
Diran Yahyayan, *Vice Pres*
EMP: 50
SQ FT: 71,500
SALES (est): 2.1MM **Privately Held**
SIC: 7011 5812 5813 Hotel, franchised;
restaurant, lunch counter; cocktail lounge

(P-12617)
MILE POST PROPERTIES LLC
Also Called: La Quinta Inn
1050 Van Ness Ave, San Francisco
(94109-6934)
PHONE..............................415 673-4711
Fred Reed, *General Mgr*
EMP: 100
SQ FT: 100,000
SALES (est): 1.5MM **Privately Held**
SIC: 7011 Hotels & motels

(P-12618)
MILLBRAE WCP HOTEL II LLC
Also Called: Aloft Sfo
401 E Millbrae Ave, Millbrae (94030-3111)
PHONE..............................650 443-5500
Marc Swerdlow, *President*
Mark Zettl, *COO*
EMP: 50
SQ FT: 288,000
SALES (est): 4MM
SALES (corp-wide): 48.9MM **Privately
Held**
SIC: 7011 Hotels & motels
HQ: Ultima Hospitality, L.L.C.
   30 S Wacker Dr Ste 3600
   Chicago IL 60606
   312 948-4500

(P-12619)
MISSION RANCH INC
26270 Dolores St, Carmel (93923-9215)
PHONE..............................831 624-6436
Roy Kaufman, *President*
Howard Bernstein, *Treasurer*
Clint Eastwood, *Director*
EMP: 50
SALES (est): 3.5MM **Privately Held**
SIC: 7011 7999 Resort hotel; tennis club,
non-membership

(P-12620)
**MISSION STUART HT
PARTNERS LLC**
Also Called: Hotel Vitale
8 Mission St, San Francisco (94105-1227)
PHONE..............................415 278-3700
Fax: 415 278-3750
EMP: 200

SALES (est): 10.8MM **Privately Held**
WEB: www.hotelvitale.com
SIC: 7011

(P-12621)
**MISSION VALLEY HT OPERATOR
INC**
595 Hotel Cir S, San Diego (92108-3403)
PHONE..............................619 291-5720
Michael Medzigian, *President*
George Gudgeon, *Treasurer*
EMP: 75
SALES (est): 1.2MM **Privately Held**
SIC: 7011 Hotel, franchised
PA: Carey Watermark Investors Incorpo-
rated
   50 Rockefeller Plz
   New York NY 10020

(P-12622)
MIYAKO HOTELS
328 E 1st St Ste 510, Los Angeles
(90012-3902)
PHONE..............................213 617-2000
Akimasa Yoneda, *President*
EMP: 56
SALES (est): 2.3MM **Privately Held**
SIC: 7011 Hotel, franchised; hotels

(P-12623)
MODESTO HOSPITALITY LLC
Also Called: Doubltree By Hilton Ht Modesto
1150 9th St, Modesto (95354-0823)
PHONE..............................209 526-6000
EMP: 180
SALES (est): 424.9K **Privately Held**
SIC: 7011 Hotels & motels

(P-12624)
**MODESTO HOSPITALITY
LESSEE LLC**
Also Called: Doubletree Hotel Modesto
1150 9th St Ste C, Modesto (95354-0857)
PHONE..............................209 526-6000
EMP: 99
SALES: 950K **Privately Held**
SIC: 7011

(P-12625)
MONO WIND CASINO
Also Called: Big Sandy Rancheria
37302 Rancheria Ln, Auberry
(93602-9423)
P.O. Box 1060 (93602-1060)
PHONE..............................559 855-4350
Connie Lewis, *Principal*
Elizabeth D Kipp, *Principal*
EMP: 100
SALES (est): 6.6MM **Privately Held**
WEB: www.monowindcasino.com
SIC: 7011 5812 Casino hotel; restaurant,
family; independent

(P-12626)
**MONTAGE HOTELS & RESORTS
LLC**
Also Called: Montage Beverly Hills
225 N Canon Dr, Beverly Hills
(90210-5301)
PHONE..............................310 499-4199
Alan Fuerstman, *Branch Mgr*
EMP: 450
SALES (est): 1MM
SALES (corp-wide): 117.9MM **Privately
Held**
SIC: 7011 7991 Hotels; spas
PA: Montage Hotels & Resorts, Llc
   3 Ada Ste 100
   Irvine CA 92618
   949 715-5002

(P-12627)
**MONTAGE HOTELS & RESORTS
LLC (PA)**
Also Called: Montage Laguna Beach
3 Ada Ste 100, Irvine (92618-2322)
P.O. Box 52031, Phoenix AZ (85072-2031)
PHONE..............................949 715-5002
Alan Fuerstman, *Mng Member*
Jason Herthel, *President*
Donald Johnson-Kidder, *President*
Iqbal Bashir, *Vice Pres*
James D Bermingham, *Vice Pres*
EMP: 1770

SQ FT: 586,000
SALES (est): 117.9MM **Privately Held**
WEB: www.montagehotels.com
SIC: 7011 Hotels

(P-12628)
MONTCLAIR HOTELS MB LLC
Also Called: Holiday Inn
1050 Burnett Ave, Concord (94520-5713)
PHONE................................925 687-5500
Stephanie Mullen, *General Mgr*
EMP: 75
SALES (est): 965.6K **Privately Held**
WEB: www.montclairhotels.com
SIC: 7011 Hotels & motels
PA: Montclair Hotels Mb, Llc
6600 Mannheim Rd
Rosemont IL 60018

(P-12629)
MONTECITO SEQUOIA INC
Also Called: Montecito Sequoia Lodge
8000 Generals Hwy, Kings Canyon Nationa
(93633)
P.O. Box 858, Kcnp (93633-0858)
PHONE................................559 565-3388
Virginia C Barnes, *President*
EMP: 61 **EST:** 1960
SALES (est): 2.2MM **Privately Held**
SIC: 7011 Resort hotel

(P-12630)
MONTEREY PLAZA HT LTD PARTNR
Also Called: Monterey Plaza Hotel & Spa
400 Cannery Row, Monterey (93940-7501)
PHONE................................800 334-3999
John V Narigi, *General Ptnr*
EMP: 360
SALES (est): 24.5MM **Privately Held**
WEB: www.montereyplazahotel.com
SIC: 7011 Resort hotel; hotels

(P-12631)
MORGANS HOTEL GROUP MGT LLC
Also Called: Miramar Hotel
1555 S Jameson Ln, Santa Barbara
(93108)
PHONE................................805 969-2203
Philip Dailey, *General Mgr*
EMP: 130 **Privately Held**
WEB: www.mondrianhotel.com
SIC: 7011 Hotels
HQ: Morgans Hotel Group Management Llc
475 10th Ave Fl 11
New York NY 10018

(P-12632)
MORGANS HOTEL GROUP MGT LLC
Also Called: Mondrian Hotel
8440 W Sunset Blvd, Los Angeles
(90069-1912)
PHONE................................323 650-8999
David Weidlich, *General Mgr*
Norbert Relecker, *General Mgr*
EMP: 200 **Privately Held**
WEB: www.mondrianhotel.com
SIC: 7011 5813 5812 Hotels; drinking
places; eating places
HQ: Morgans Hotel Group Management Llc
475 10th Ave Fl 11
New York NY 10018

(P-12633)
MORGANS HOTEL GROUP MGT LLC
Also Called: Clift Hotel Four Season
495 Geary St, San Francisco (94102-1222)
PHONE................................415 775-4700
Alexandra Walterstiel, *General Mgr*
EMP: 200
SQ FT: 271,387 **Privately Held**
WEB: www.mondrianhotel.com
SIC: 7011 5812 7991 5813 Hotels; eating
places; physical fitness facilities; drinking
places
HQ: Morgans Hotel Group Management Llc
475 10th Ave Fl 11
New York NY 10018

(P-12634)
MOTEL 6 OPERATING LP
5101 W Century Blvd, Inglewood
(90304-1223)
PHONE................................310 419-1234
Amad Serhat, *Manager*
Ray Sitzhugh, *General Mgr*
EMP: 53
SQ FT: 112,875
SALES (corp-wide): 643.4MM **Privately Held**
WEB: www.motel6.com
SIC: 7011 Hotels & motels
HQ: Motel 6 Operating L.P.
4001 Intl Pkwy Ste 500
Carrollton TX 75007
972 360-9000

(P-12635)
MOUNTAIN SPRINGS KIRKWOOD LLC
1501 Kirkwood Meadows Dr, Kirkwood
(95646)
PHONE................................209 258-6000
Charles E Cobb Jr, *Mng Member*
Tobin T Cobb
Bud D Klein,
EMP: 200
SALES (est): 2MM **Privately Held**
SIC: 7011 Ski lodge; resort hotel

(P-12636)
MSR HOTELS & RESORTS INC
Also Called: Embassy Suites- Santa Clara
2885 Lakeside Dr, Santa Clara
(95054-2805)
PHONE................................408 496-6400
Teri Owens, *Branch Mgr*
EMP: 80
SALES (corp-wide): 50.1B **Publicly Held**
SIC: 7011 Hotels & motels
HQ: Msr Hotels & Resorts, Inc.
450 S Orange Ave
Orlando FL 32801
407 650-1000

(P-12637)
NAPA ES LEASING LLC
Also Called: Embassy Suites
1075 California Blvd, NAPA (94559-1061)
PHONE................................707 253-9540
Reynaldo Zertuche, *General Mgr*
EMP: 117
SALES (est): 475.9K
SALES (corp-wide): 1.7B **Privately Held**
SIC: 7011 Hotels & motels
HQ: Rangers Sub I, Llc
3 Bethesda Metro Ctr # 1000
Bethesda MD 20814

(P-12638)
NAPA VALLEY LODGE LP
Also Called: Bodega Bay Lodge
103 Coast Highway 1, Bodega Bay
(94923-9723)
PHONE................................707 875-3525
Ellis Alden, *Owner*
EMP: 60
SALES (corp-wide): 4.7MM **Privately Held**
WEB: www.napavalleylodge.com
SIC: 7011 Vacation lodges
PA: Napa Valley Lodge L.P.
2230 Madison St
Yountville CA 94599
707 944-2468

(P-12639)
NARVEN ENTERPRISES INC
Also Called: Holiday Inn
1430 7th Ave Ste B, San Diego
(92101-2815)
PHONE................................619 239-2261
Behram Baxter, *President*
EMP: 75
SQ FT: 6,000
SALES (est): 5.6MM **Privately Held**
SIC: 7011 Hotels & motels

(P-12640)
NATIONAL HOSPITALITY LLC
Also Called: Royal Scandinavian Inn
400 Alisal Rd, Solvang (93463-3741)
P.O. Box 30 (93464-0030)
PHONE................................805 688-8000

Cynthia Elwood, *Mng Member*
EMP: 80
SQ FT: 65,000
SALES (est): 1.7MM **Privately Held**
WEB: www.royalscandinavianinn.com
SIC: 7011 5812 7299 5813 Inns; eating
places; banquet hall facilities; cocktail
lounge

(P-12641)
NEW FIGUEROA HOTEL INC
1000 S Hope St Apt 201, Los Angeles
(90015-1492)
PHONE................................213 627-8971
Uno Thimansson, *President*
Elyse Omori, *Vice Pres*
EMP: 70
SQ FT: 200,000
SALES (est): 5.8MM **Privately Held**
SIC: 7011 5812 5813 Resort hotel; eating
places; bars & lounges

(P-12642)
NEWARK COURTYARD BY MARRIOTT
34905 Newark Blvd, Newark (94560-1215)
PHONE................................510 792-5200
Melody Lanthorn, *Manager*
EMP: 60
SALES (est): 1.7MM **Privately Held**
SIC: 7011 Hotels & motels

(P-12643)
NEWPORT HOSPITALITY GROUP INC
Also Called: Holiday Inn
801 Truxtun Ave, Bakersfield (93301-4726)
PHONE................................661 323-1900
Eric Iokal, *Manager*
EMP: 200
SALES (est): 2.2MM
SALES (corp-wide): 97.9MM **Privately Held**
WEB: www.newport-hospitality.com
SIC: 7011 Hotels & motels
PA: Newport Hospitality Group Inc
1048 Irvine Ave Ste 365
Newport Beach CA
949 706-7002

(P-12644)
NEWPORT HOTEL CAPITAL LLC
Also Called: Hotel Menage
1221 S Harbor Blvd, Anaheim
(92805-6004)
PHONE................................714 758-0900
Rob Kaulfonic, *Vice Pres*
EMP: 123
SALES (est): 5.3MM **Privately Held**
SIC: 7011 5813 5812 Hotels; drinking
places; eating places

(P-12645)
NHCA INC
Also Called: Crowne Plz Los Angeles Hbr Ht
2330 Grand Ave, Long Beach
(90815-1761)
PHONE................................310 519-8200
SM Nasarudin, *CEO*
Ramon Torres, *Engineer*
EMP: 151
SALES (est): 9.2MM **Privately Held**
WEB: www.sheratonlaharbor.com
SIC: 7011 Hotels

(P-12646)
NICKS COVE INC
23240 Ca 1, Marshall (94940)
PHONE................................415 663-1033
Ruth Gibson, *Owner*
Nicks Cove, *President*
Katrina Garrett, *Opers Mgr*
Alison Bottner, *Manager*
Erikka Newton, *Manager*
EMP: 70
SQ FT: 1,000
SALES (est): 1.5MM **Privately Held**
SIC: 7011 Hotels; bed & breakfast inn

(P-12647)
NOB HILL PROPERTIES INC
Also Called: Big Four Restaurant
1075 California St, San Francisco
(94108-2281)
PHONE................................415 474-5400
John Cope, *President*

Newton Cope Sr, *Ch of Bd*
Newton Cope Jr, *Vice Pres*
EMP: 280
SALES (est): 17.6MM **Privately Held**
WEB: www.nobhillspa.com
SIC: 7011 5812 Hotels; eating places

(P-12648)
NOBLE AEW VINEYARD CREEK LLC
Also Called: Hyatt Vineyard Creek Ht & Spa
170 Railroad St, Santa Rosa (95401-6266)
PHONE................................707 284-1234
Josephine Redrico, *Principal*
EMP: 99
SALES (est): 950K **Privately Held**
SIC: 7011 Hotels & motels

(P-12649)
NOBLE/UTAH LONG BEACH LLC
Also Called: Westin Long Beach Hotel, The
333 E Ocean Blvd, Long Beach
(90802-4827)
PHONE................................562 436-3000
Mitesh B Shah, *Mng Member*
EMP: 250
SQ FT: 51,000
SALES (est): 8.5MM
SALES (corp-wide): 35.2MM **Privately Held**
SIC: 7011 Hotels & motels
PA: Noble Investment Group Llc
2000 Monarch Towe 3424
Atlanta GA 30326
404 262-9660

(P-12650)
NOIRO WEST LLC
Also Called: Sheraton Suites San Diego
701 A St, San Diego (92101-4611)
PHONE................................619 819-6620
Richard M Kelleher,
EMP: 200
SQ FT: 99,999
SALES (est): 8.2MM **Privately Held**
SIC: 7011 Hotels & motels

(P-12651)
NORTHERN QUEEN INC
Also Called: Northern Queen Inn
400 Railroad Ave, Nevada City
(95959-2868)
PHONE................................530 265-4492
Roy J Ramey, *President*
Jacqueline Ramey, *Corp Secy*
Colleen Flores, *Vice Pres*
Diane Mansfield, *Systems Mgr*
EMP: 65
SQ FT: 32,000
SALES (est): 2MM **Privately Held**
SIC: 7011 6552 Motels; subdividers & de-
velopers

(P-12652)
NORTHWEST HOTEL CORPORATION (PA)
Also Called: Howard Johnson
1380 S Harbor Blvd, Anaheim
(92802-2310)
PHONE................................714 776-6120
James P Edmondson, *President*
Jonathan Whitehead, *General Mgr*
EMP: 62
SQ FT: 50,000
SALES (est): 7MM **Privately Held**
SIC: 7011 Hotels & motels

(P-12653)
NPL ANAHEIM INVESTMENTS LLC
Also Called: Homewood Suites Anaheim Re-
sort
2010 S Harbor Blvd, Anaheim
(92802-3514)
PHONE................................714 750-2010
Curtis Olson, *President*
Matthew Kaufman, *Corp Secy*
Ajesh Patel, *Vice Pres*
EMP: 68 **EST:** 2013
SQ FT: 165,000
SALES (est): 355.1K **Privately Held**
SIC: 7011 Hotels & motels

PRODUCTS & SVCS

(P-12654)
NREA-TRC 711 LLC
Also Called: Sheraton Downtown Los Angeles
711 S Hope St, Los Angeles　(90017-3803)
PHONE...................................213 488-3500
EMP: 200
SQ FT: 470,000
SALES (est): 10.5MM　Privately Held
SIC: 7011　Hotels & motels

(P-12655)
OAK CREEK　LP
Also Called: Holiday Inn
21725 Gateway Center Dr, Diamond Bar
(91765-2400)
PHONE...................................909 860-5440
Billy Mendez, Partner
Sammi Wang, Principal
EMP: 60
SALES (est): 2.9MM　Privately Held
SIC: 7011　Hotels & motels

(P-12656)
OAK VALLEY HOTEL LLC
2270 Hotel Cir N, San Diego (92108-2810)
PHONE...................................619 297-1101
Benjamin Shih,
EMP: 99
SALES (est): 675.5K　Privately Held
SIC: 7011　Hotels

(P-12657)
OAKLAND RENAISSANCE ASSOCIATES
Also Called: Marriott
1001 Broadway, Oakland　(94607-4019)
PHONE...................................510 451-4000
Steven Williams, Director
Keith Montgomery, Controller
EMP: 80
SALES (est): 612K　Privately Held
SIC: 7011　Hotels & motels

(P-12658)
OAKLAND RENAISSANCE ASSOCIATES
Also Called: Oakland Mrriott Hotels Resorts
1001 Broadway, Oakland　(94607-4019)
PHONE...................................510 451-4000
EMP: 380
SALES (corp-wide): 7.1MM　Privately Held
SIC: 7011　Hotels
PA: Oakland Renaissance Associates
388 9th St Ste 222
Oakland CA 94607
510 238-3400

(P-12659)
OCEAN AVENUE LLC
Also Called: Fairmont Miramar Hotel
101 Wilshire Blvd, Santa Monica
(90401-1106)
PHONE...................................310 576-7777
Ellis O'Connor, Mng Member
Ariana Port-Sonenshine, Sales Staff
An K Verbeeck, Director
Stephanie Berman, Manager
Andres Fernandez, Manager
EMP: 275
SQ FT: 209,000
SALES (est): 20.2MM
SALES (corp-wide): 1.1B　Privately Held
SIC: 7011　7299 Hotels; banquet hall facilities
HQ: Accor Services Us Llc
950 Mason St
San Francisco CA 94108
415 772-5000

(P-12660)
OCEAN HOLIDAY LP
Also Called: Holiday Inn
1401 Carmelo Dr, Oceanside　(92054-1012)
PHONE...................................760 231-7000
Joseph Fan, Partner
EMP: 55
SALES (est): 1.1MM　Privately Held
SIC: 7011　Hotels & motels

(P-12661)
OCEAN PARK HOTELS　INC
Also Called: Hilton
1000 Aguajito Rd, Monterey (93940-4801)
PHONE...................................831 373-6141

Cherie Davis, General Mgr
EMP: 115
SALES (corp-wide): 13.5MM　Privately Held
WEB: www.ophot.com
SIC: 7011　5813　8741 Hotels & motels; drinking places; hotel or motel management
PA: Ocean Park Hotels, Inc.
9777 Blue Larkspur Ln # 102
Monterey CA 93940
805 544-0812

(P-12662)
OCEAN PARK HOTELS　INC
Also Called: Hilton
27710 The Old Rd, Valencia　(91355-1036)
PHONE...................................661 284-3200
Angela Peterson, Branch Mgr
EMP: 60
SALES (corp-wide): 13.5MM　Privately Held
WEB: www.ophot.com
SIC: 7011　Hotels & motels
PA: Ocean Park Hotels, Inc.
9777 Blue Larkspur Ln # 102
Monterey CA 93940
805 544-0812

(P-12663)
OCEAN PARK HOTELS MMEX LLC
Also Called: Holiday Inn
27513 Wayne Mills Pl, Valencia
(91355-4980)
PHONE...................................661 284-2101
James Flagg,
EMP: 50
SQ FT: 5,322
SALES (est): 2.1MM　Privately Held
SIC: 7011　Hotels & motels

(P-12664)
OCEANS ELEVEN CASINO
121 Brooks St, Oceanside (92054-3424)
PHONE...................................760 439-6988
Mark Kelegian, Managing Prtnr
Rachel Kinney, Admin Asst
Carlos Lopez, Facilities Dir
Zaven Esmaili, Manager
Sandy Zook, Manager
EMP: 367 EST: 1996
SQ FT: 30,000
SALES (est): 15.9MM　Privately Held
WEB: www.oceans11.com
SIC: 7011　Casino hotel

(P-12665)
OHI RESORT HOTELS　LLC
Also Called: Wyndham Anaheim Garden Grove
12021 Harbor Blvd, Garden Grove
(92840-4001)
PHONE...................................714 867-5555
Jeremy Yujuico, Principal
Donna Coins, Sales Staff
EMP: 98
SALES (est): 5.2MM　Privately Held
SIC: 7011　Hotels

(P-12666)
OJAI VALLEY INN GOLF COURSE
Also Called: Ojai Valley Spa
905 Country Club Rd, Ojai　(93023-3789)
PHONE...................................805 646-2420
Thad Hyland, Director
Doug Bowman, Info Tech Mgr
Vanessa Jimenez, Human Res Mgr
Hannah Hathaway, Marketing Mgr
Brenda Alcazar, Manager
EMP: 600
SALES (est): 8.5MM　Privately Held
WEB: www.ojaivalleyspa.com
SIC: 7011　7992　5941 Resort hotel; public golf courses; sporting goods & bicycle shops

(P-12667)
OLD TOWN FMLY HOSPITALITY CORP
Also Called: Fiesta De Reyes
4962 Concannon Ct, San Diego
(92130-2723)
PHONE...................................619 246-8010

Chuck Ross, President
EMP: 240 EST: 2009
SQ FT: 1,600
SALES: 16MM　Privately Held
SIC: 7011　5812 Hotels; eating places

(P-12668)
OLS HOTELS & RESORTS　LLC (PA)
16000 Ventura Blvd # 1010, Encino
(91436-2744)
PHONE...................................818 905-8280
John Fitts, Principal
Martti Mannaoja, CFO
Roger Vasey, Exec VP
Sarie Mannoja, Vice Pres
Russ Abell, General Mgr
EMP: 2045
SQ FT: 9,500
SALES (est): 60.6MM　Privately Held
WEB: www.outriggerlodging.com
SIC: 7011　Hotels & motels

(P-12669)
OLS HOTELS & RESORTS　LLC
Also Called: Marriott
14635 Bldwin Pk Towne Ctr, Baldwin Park
(91706-5548)
PHONE...................................626 962-6000
Peter Ehienberg, Manager
Jiyu Liang, Human Res Dir
Vecario Kathy, Marketing Staff
EMP: 509
SALES (est): 4.7MM
SALES (corp-wide): 60.6MM　Privately Held
WEB: www.outriggerlodging.com
SIC: 7011　Hotels & motels
PA: Ols Hotels & Resorts, Llc
16000 Ventura Blvd # 1010
Encino CA 91436
818 905-8280

(P-12670)
OLS HOTELS & RESORTS　LP
Also Called: Le Parc Suite Hotel
733 W Knoll Dr, West Hollywood
(90069-5207)
PHONE...................................310 855-1115
Sam Ebeid, CEO
Martti Mannoja, Exec VP
Kealii Alexander, Vice Pres
Barry Podob, Sales Dir
Jennifer Hagenbuch, Sales Staff
EMP: 105
SALES (corp-wide): 60.6MM　Privately Held
WEB: www.outriggerlodging.com
SIC: 7011　8741 Hotels; hotel or motel management
PA: Ols Hotels & Resorts, Llc
16000 Ventura Blvd # 1010
Encino CA 91436
818 905-8280

(P-12671)
OMNI HOTELS CORPORATION
41000 Bob Hope Dr, Rancho Mirage
(92270-4416)
PHONE...................................760 568-2727
EMP: 256
SALES (corp-wide): 1.2B　Privately Held
SIC: 7011　Hotels & motels
HQ: Omni Hotels Corporation
4001 Maple Ave Ste 500
Dallas TX 75219
972 871-5600

(P-12672)
OMNI HOTELS CORPORATION
675 L St, San Diego (92101-7022)
PHONE...................................619 231-6664
Ed Netzhammer, Manager
Michele Nash, Finance
Chris Kramer, Director
Jennifer Aello, Manager
Julie Larsen, Manager
EMP: 300
SALES (corp-wide): 1.2B　Privately Held
WEB: www.omnihotels.com
SIC: 7011　Hotels & motels
HQ: Omni Hotels Corporation
4001 Maple Ave Ste 500
Dallas TX 75219
972 871-5600

(P-12673)
OMNI HOTELS CORPORATION
500 California St, San Francisco
(94104-1001)
PHONE...................................415 677-9494
Michael Casey, Branch Mgr
Kelsey Angel, Sales Staff
Brett Howard, Sales Staff
Molly Nettleship, Sales Staff
Adam Pickett, Manager
EMP: 264
SALES (corp-wide): 1.2B　Privately Held
WEB: www.omnihotels.com
SIC: 7011　Hotels & motels
HQ: Omni Hotels Corporation
4001 Maple Ave Ste 500
Dallas TX 75219
972 871-5600

(P-12674)
OMNI HOTELS CORPORATION
251 S Olive St Fl 1, Los Angeles
(90012-3002)
PHONE...................................213 617-3300
Bob Greeney, General Mgr
Kathy Faulk, General Mgr
Mark Schwabenbauer, General Mgr
Carolyn Harber, Info Tech Mgr
EMP: 250
SALES (corp-wide): 1.2B　Privately Held
WEB: www.omnihotels.com
SIC: 7011　Hotels & motels
HQ: Omni Hotels Corporation
4001 Maple Ave Ste 500
Dallas TX 75219
972 871-5600

(P-12675)
OMNI LA COSTA RESORT & SPA LLC
Also Called: Audrey's Boutique
2100 Costa Del Mar Rd, Carlsbad
(92009-6823)
PHONE...................................760 438-9111
Cydney Bruno, Manager
EMP: 50
SALES (corp-wide): 3.1MM　Privately Held
SIC: 7011　Hotels & motels
PA: Omni La Costa Resort & Spa, Llc
2100 Costa Del Mar Rd
Carlsbad CA 92009
760 438-9111

(P-12676)
ONE NOB HILL ASSOCIATES LLC
Also Called: Intercontinental Mark Hopkins
999 California St, San Francisco
(94108-2250)
PHONE...................................415 392-3434
Mary Ann Gonzales, General Mgr
EMP: 86
SALES (est): 2.3MM　Privately Held
SIC: 7011　Hotels & motels

(P-12677)
ONTARIO AIRPORT HOTEL CORP
Also Called: Hilton
4949 Great America Pkwy, Santa Clara
(95054-1216)
PHONE...................................408 562-6709
James Evans, CFO
Gary Hauck, Engineer
Patricia Veron, Human Res Mgr
Karen Mathews, Rector
▲ EMP: 127
SQ FT: 169,768
SALES (est): 9.3MM　Privately Held
WEB: www.hiltonsantaclara.com
SIC: 7011　Hotels & motels

(P-12678)
ORCHARD INTERNATIONAL GROUP (PA)
Also Called: Orchard Hotel
665 Bush St, San Francisco (94108-3510)
PHONE...................................415 362-8878
S C Huang, President
Robert Huang, CEO
EMP: 100
SQ FT: 60,000
SALES: 12.4MM　Privately Held
SIC: 7011　Hotels

(P-12679)
OTB ACQUISITION LLC
Also Called: Sierra Vista Extended Stay
770 S Brea Blvd Ste 227, Brea
(92821-5399)
PHONE..............................520 458-0540
EMP: 119 **Privately Held**
SIC: 7011 Hotels & motels
PA: Otb Acquisition Llc
2201 W Royal Ln Ste 240
Irving TX 75063

(P-12680)
OUTRIGGER HOTELS HAWAII
Also Called: Marina International Hotel
4200 Admiralty Way, Venice (90292-5422)
PHONE..............................310 301-2000
Mohammed Khan, *General Mgr*
EMP: 80
SALES (corp-wide): 143.6MM **Privately
Held**
WEB: www.outriggerhawaii.com
SIC: 7011 6531 Hotels; real estate managers
PA: Outrigger Hotels Hawaii
2375 Kuhio Ave Fl 4
Honolulu HI 96815
808 921-6510

(P-12681)
OUTRIGGER HOTELS HAWAII
Grafton On Sunset, The
8462 W Sunset Blvd, West Hollywood
(90069-1912)
PHONE..............................323 491-9015
Kevin Briggs, *Branch Mgr*
Leota Rhaburn, *Sales Mgr*
Carlos Marroquin, *Manager*
EMP: 98
SALES (corp-wide): 143.6MM **Privately
Held**
WEB: www.outriggerhawaii.com
SIC: 7011 Hotels
PA: Outrigger Hotels Hawaii
2375 Kuhio Ave Fl 4
Honolulu HI 96815
808 921-6510

(P-12682)
OVIS LLC
Also Called: Ojai Valley Inn & Spa
905 Country Club Rd, Ojai (93023-3734)
PHONE..............................805 646-5511
Toll Free:..............................888
Stephen Crown, *Mng Member*
Charif Zahrane, *Info Tech Dir*
Tammy Barbey, *Engineer*
Ken Link, *Engineer*
Brian Skaggs, *Engineer*
EMP: 600
SALES (est): 43.5MM **Privately Held**
WEB: www.ojairesort.com
SIC: 7011 5813 5812 Resort hotel; drinking places; eating places

(P-12683)
OXFORD PALACE HOTEL
745 S Oxford Ave, Los Angeles
(90005-2909)
PHONE..............................213 382-7756
Bowhan Kim, *Principal*
Don W Chang, *Principal*
Bora Park, *Sales Dir*
EMP: 96
SALES (est): 5.6MM **Privately Held**
WEB: www.oxfordhotel.com
SIC: 7011 5812 Resort hotel; Korean
restaurant

(P-12684)
OXNARD BEACH HOTEL LP
350 E Port Hueneme Rd, Port Hueneme
(93041-3209)
PHONE..............................805 488-6560
Joseph Fan, *Partner*
EMP: 50 **EST:** 2012
SALES (est): 1.1MM **Privately Held**
SIC: 7011 Hotels

(P-12685)
PACIFIC BEACH HOUSE LLC
(PA)
Also Called: Beach House Ht - Half Moon Bay
4100 Cabrillo Hwy N, Half Moon Bay
(94019-5219)
P.O. Box 129 (94019-0129)
PHONE..............................650 712-0220
Dana Daho, *General Mgr*
Charlotte Papedis, *General Mgr*
EMP: 95 **EST:** 1997
SQ FT: 5,007
SALES (est): 4.5MM **Privately Held**
SIC: 7011 7999 Hotels; bathing beach,
non-membership

(P-12686)
PACIFIC CAMBRIA INC
Also Called: Cambria Pines Lodge
2905 Burton Dr, Cambria (93428-4001)
PHONE..............................805 927-6114
Dirk Winter, *President*
Teri O'Rourke, *Sales Mgr*
Rebecca Ramos, *Marketing Staff*
Bram Winter, *Manager*
EMP: 90
SQ FT: 70,000
SALES (est): 5.8MM **Privately Held**
WEB: www.cambriapineslodge.com
SIC: 7011 5812 5813 Hotels; resort hotel;
restaurant, family: independent; bar
(drinking places)

(P-12687)
PACIFIC CITY HOTEL LLC
Also Called: Pasea Hotel & Spa
21080 Pacific Coast Hwy, Huntington
Beach (92648-5305)
PHONE..............................714 698-6100
Joe Leinacker, *General Mgr*
Lynette Dodd, *Asst Controller*
Giovanni Prada, *Marketing Staff*
EMP: 300
SALES: 2.8MM **Privately Held**
SIC: 7011 Resort hotel; hotels

(P-12688)
PACIFIC GROVE ASLMAR OPER
CORP
Also Called: Asilomar Conference Center
800 Asilomar Blvd, Pacific Grove
(93950-3704)
PHONE..............................831 372-8016
Fax: 831 372-7227
EMP: 250
SQ FT: 20,000
SALES: 13.2MM **Privately Held**
SIC: 7011

(P-12689)
PACIFIC HOTEL DEV VENTR LP
Also Called: Sheraton Palo Alto
625 El Camino Real, Palo Alto
(94301-2301)
PHONE..............................650 347-8260
Clement Chen, *Vice Pres*
EMP: 200
SALES (est): 7.7MM **Privately Held**
SIC: 7011 Hotels & motels

(P-12690)
PACIFIC HOTEL MANAGEMENT
LLC (PA)
Also Called: Clement Chen & Associates
400 S El Camino Real # 200, San Mateo
(94402-1731)
PHONE..............................650 347-8260
Clement Chen III, *Property Mgr*
Jose Mancia, *Executive*
Jerry Regester, *Executive*
Kress Fischer, *Exec Dir*
Nicole Harris, *General Mgr*
EMP: 850 **EST:** 1964
SQ FT: 5,175
SALES (est): 32MM **Privately Held**
WEB: www.pacifichotelmanagement.com
SIC: 7011 6552 Hotels & motels; subdividers & developers

(P-12691)
PACIFIC HOTEL MANAGEMENT
LLC
Also Called: Sheraton
1603 Powell St, Emeryville (94608-2436)
PHONE..............................510 547-7888

Michelle Sims, *Owner*
Veerayuth Phumsaythong, *Officer*
Naruechon Suksompong, *Officer*
Lokesh Menaria, *Executive*
Sunit Sukosit, *Executive*
EMP: 122
SALES (est): 3.9MM
SALES (corp-wide): 32MM **Privately
Held**
SIC: 7011 Hotels & motels
PA: Pacific Hotel Management, Llc
400 S El Camino Real # 200
San Mateo CA 94402
650 347-8260

(P-12692)
PACIFIC HOTEL MANAGEMENT
LLC
Also Called: Courtyard By Marriott
3150 Garrity Way, Richmond (94806-1983)
PHONE..............................510 262-0700
Curt Newport, *Branch Mgr*
EMP: 122
SALES (est): 3.4MM
SALES (corp-wide): 32MM **Privately
Held**
WEB: www.pacifichotelmanagement.com
SIC: 7011 7389 Hotels & motels; office facilities & secretarial service rental
PA: Pacific Hotel Management, Llc
400 S El Camino Real # 200
San Mateo CA 94402
650 347-8260

(P-12693)
PACIFIC HOTEL MANAGEMENT
LLC
Also Called: Sheraton
625 El Camino Real, Palo Alto
(94301-2301)
PHONE..............................650 328-2800
Jim Rebosio, *General Mgr*
Annie Tepe, *Social Dir*
Sagir Ahmed, *Controller*
Grace Wang, *Sales Mgr*
Cathy Faber, *Sales Staff*
EMP: 300
SALES (est): 5.5MM
SALES (corp-wide): 32MM **Privately
Held**
SIC: 7011 Hotels & motels
PA: Pacific Hotel Management, Llc
400 S El Camino Real # 200
San Mateo CA 94402
650 347-8260

(P-12694)
PACIFIC HOTEL MANAGEMENT
INC
Also Called: Radison Hotel Newport Beach
4545 Macarthur Blvd, Newport Beach
(92660-2022)
PHONE..............................949 608-1091
Ron Mavaddat, *President*
EMP: 140
SALES: 15MM **Privately Held**
SIC: 7011 Hotels & motels

(P-12695)
PACIFIC HUNTINGTON HOTEL
CORP
Also Called: Langham Huntington Hotel &
Spa
1401 S Oak Knoll Ave, Pasadena
(91106-4508)
PHONE..............................626 568-3900
Ying Shek Lo, *President*
Haruko Murphy, *Office Mgr*
Claudia Child, *Credit Mgr*
Alice Baumstark, *Sales Staff*
EMP: 600
SQ FT: 21,193
SALES (est): 1MM **Privately Held**
SIC: 7011 Resort hotel
PA: Langham Hotels International Limited
33/F Great Eagle Ctr
Wan Chai HK

(P-12696)
PACIFIC SNOW VALLEY
RESORT LLC
Also Called: Holiday Inn Resort At Lodge
40650 Village Dr, Big Bear Lake
(92315-2164)
PHONE..............................909 866-3121
Dennis Montes, *General Mgr*
EMP: 60 **Privately Held**
SIC: 7011 7299 5812 5813 Vacation
lodges; banquet hall facilities; eating
places; drinking places
PA: Pacific Snow Valley Resort Llc
1427 W Valley Blvd # 201
Alhambra CA 91803

(P-12697)
PACIFICA HIORANGE LP
Also Called: Hampton Inn
2720 Hotel Ter, Santa Ana (92705-5602)
PHONE..............................714 556-3838
Russell Fraser, *General Ptnr*
Arlene Kostock, *CFO*
EMP: 80 **EST:** 2012
SALES (est): 3.4MM **Privately Held**
SIC: 7011 Hotels & motels

(P-12698)
PACIFICA HOSTS INC
Also Called: Radisson Inn
6225 W Century Blvd, Los Angeles
(90045-5311)
PHONE..............................310 670-9000
Ashok Israni, *President*
EMP: 249
SALES (corp-wide): 113.2MM **Privately
Held**
SIC: 7011 6552 5813 5812 Hotels & motels; subdividers & developers; drinking
places; eating places
PA: Pacifica Hosts, Inc.
1775 Hancock St Ste 200
San Diego CA 92110
619 296-9000

(P-12699)
PACIFICA HOSTS INC
700 16th St, Sacramento (95814-2002)
PHONE..............................619 296-9000
EMP: 114
SALES (corp-wide): 113.2MM **Privately
Held**
SIC: 7011 Hotels & motels
PA: Pacifica Hosts, Inc.
1775 Hancock St Ste 200
San Diego CA 92110
619 296-9000

(P-12700)
PACIFICA HOTEL &
CONFERENCE CE
Also Called: Radisson Hotel La Westside
6161 W Centinela Ave, Culver City
(90230-6306)
PHONE..............................310 649-1776
Jim Collins, *General Ptnr*
Robert Leonard, *Partner*
EMP: 190
SALES (est): 4.4MM **Privately Held**
SIC: 7011 6512 5812 7389 Hotels & motels; commercial & industrial building operation; eating places; convention & show
services

(P-12701)
PACIFICA HOTEL COMPANY
Also Called: Shelter Point Hotel & Marina
1551 Shelter Island Dr, San Diego
(92106-3102)
PHONE..............................619 221-8000
Henric Larsen, *General Mgr*
Allison Doerfler, *General Mgr*
EMP: 200
SALES (corp-wide): 59.1MM **Privately
Held**
WEB: www.cottage-inn.com
SIC: 7011 4493 Hotels; marinas
HQ: Pacifica Hotel Company
39 Argonaut
Aliso Viejo CA 92656
805 957-0095

(P-12702)
PACIFICA HOTEL COMPANY
Also Called: Best Western Half Moon Bay
2400 Cabrillo Hwy S, Half Moon Bay
(94019-2253)
PHONE..................................650 726-9000
Curt Picillo, *Manager*
EMP: 50
SALES (corp-wide): 59.1MM **Privately Held**
WEB: www.cottage-inn.com
SIC: 7011 Hotels & motels
HQ: Pacifica Hotel Company
39 Argonaut
Aliso Viejo CA 92656
805 957-0095

(P-12703)
PACIFICA SAN JOSE LP
Also Called: Wyndham San Jose
1775 Hancock St Ste 100, San Diego
(92110-2035)
PHONE..................................619 296-9000
Ashok Israni, *Partner*
Deepak Israni, *Partner*
Sushil Israni, *Partner*
EMP: 175
SALES: 12MM **Privately Held**
SIC: 7011 Hotels & motels

(P-12704)
PACKARD REALTY INC
Also Called: Holiday Inn
9901 S La Cienega Blvd, Los Angeles
(90045-5915)
PHONE..................................310 649-5151
Tommy Spencer, *General Mgr*
EMP: 85
SALES (est): 1.5MM **Privately Held**
WEB: www.hilax.com
SIC: 7011 Hotels & motels
PA: Packard Realty Inc.
9555 Chesapeake Dr # 202
San Diego CA 92123

(P-12705)
PALA CASINO SPA & RESORT
11154 Highway 76, Pala (92059-2904)
PHONE..................................760 510-5100
Toll Free:..................................877
Robert Smith, *Ch of Bd*
Bill Bembenek, *CEO*
Shauna Anton, *CFO*
Michael Crenshaw, *Vice Pres*
Linda Jackson, *Executive*
EMP: 1800 EST: 2000
SQ FT: 140,000
SALES (est): 88.1MM **Privately Held**
WEB: www.palacasino.com
SIC: 7011 Casino hotel

(P-12706)
**PALA MESA LIMITED
PARTNERSHIP**
Also Called: Pala Mesa Resort
2001 Old Highway 395, Fallbrook
(92028-9771)
PHONE..................................760 728-5881
Kevin Poorbaugh, *Managing Prtnr*
Amy Krausnick, *Asst Controller*
Mark Mittlehauser, *Sales Staff*
Mirilen Archuleta, *Director*
Leslie Herbach, *Manager*
EMP: 225
SALES (est): 8.9MM **Privately Held**
WEB: www.palamesa.com
SIC: 7011 7992 Resort hotel; public golf
courses

(P-12707)
PALMDALE RESORT INC
Also Called: Holiday Inn
38630 5th St W, Palmdale (93551-4208)
PHONE..................................661 947-8055
Toni Vilopas, *Owner*
EMP: 50
SQ FT: 71,394
SALES (est): 2.6MM **Privately Held**
WEB: www.hipalmdale.com
SIC: 7011 Hotels & motels

(P-12708)
PALMETTO HOSPITALITY
Also Called: Hilton Garden Inn Palo Alto
4216 El Camino Real, Palo Alto
(94306-4404)
PHONE..................................650 843-0795
Jason Boehm, *Vice Pres*
EMP: 50
SALES (est): 482.3K **Privately Held**
SIC: 7011 Hotels & motels

(P-12709)
**PAN PCFIC HTELS RSRTS AMER
INC**
Also Called: Pan Pacific San Diego
400 W Broadway, San Diego (92101-3504)
PHONE..................................619 239-4500
Jim Hollister, *General Mgr*
Alice Cota, *Sales Staff*
EMP: 330
SALES (corp-wide): 16.2MM **Privately Held**
SIC: 7011 5812 Hotels; eating places
PA: Pan Pacific Hotels And Resorts Amer-
ica Inc.
500 Post St Ste 800
San Francisco CA 94102
415 732-7747

(P-12710)
PARADISE LESSEE INC
Also Called: Paradise Point Resort & Spa
1404 Vacation Rd, San Diego
(92109-7905)
PHONE..................................858 274-4630
Alfred L Young, *CEO*
EMP: 328
SALES (est): 828.6MM **Privately Held**
WEB: www.paradisepoint.com
SIC: 7011 Resort hotel
PA: Pebblebrook Hotel Trust
7315 Wscnsin Ave Ste 1100
Bethesda MD 20814

(P-12711)
PARK HOTELS & RESORTS INC
Also Called: Hilton
633 E Cabrillo Blvd, Santa Barbara
(93103-3611)
PHONE..................................805 564-4333
Dean Feldmeier, *Manager*
John Blomstrand, *Security Dir*
Maria Lanza, *Human Res Dir*
EMP: 300
SALES (corp-wide): 2.7B **Publicly Held**
WEB: www.esirvine.com
SIC: 7011 Hotels & motels
PA: Park Hotels & Resorts Inc.
1775 Tysons Blvd Fl 7
Tysons VA 22102
571 302-5757

(P-12712)
PARK HOTELS & RESORTS INC
Also Called: Embassy Suites
901 E Calaveras Blvd, Milpitas
(95035-5419)
PHONE..................................408 942-0400
Bonnie Benson, *Manager*
Tara Weber, *CTO*
Brian Contildes, *Chief Engr*
Evangelina Sarracino, *Mktg Dir*
Anastasia Beals, *Marketing Staff*
EMP: 65
SALES (corp-wide): 2.7B **Publicly Held**
WEB: www.esirvine.com
SIC: 7011 5813 5812 Hotels & motels;
drinking places; eating places
PA: Park Hotels & Resorts Inc.
1775 Tysons Blvd Fl 7
Tysons VA 22102
571 302-5757

(P-12713)
PARK HOTELS & RESORTS INC
Also Called: Embassy Suites Brea
900 E Birch St, Brea (92821-5812)
PHONE..................................714 990-6000
Jay Badillo, *Branch Mgr*
EMP: 60
SALES (corp-wide): 2.7B **Publicly Held**
SIC: 7011 Hotels & motels

(P-12714)
PARK HOTELS & RESORTS INC
Also Called: Hilton
1775 E Mission Bay Dr, San Diego
(92109-6801)
PHONE..................................619 276-4010
Patrick Duffy, *Director*
Carlos Nava, *Purch Dir*
Donna Daniel, *Marketing Mgr*
Shawn McAteer, *Director*
Jenny Miller, *Manager*
EMP: 360
SALES (corp-wide): 2.7B **Publicly Held**
SIC: 7011 5812 5947 Hotels & motels;
eating places; gift, novelty & souvenir
shop
PA: Park Hotels & Resorts Inc.
1775 Tysons Blvd Fl 7
Tysons VA 22102
571 302-5757

(P-12715)
PARK HOTELS & RESORTS INC
Also Called: San Francisco Hilton & Towers
333 Ofarrell St, San Francisco
(94102-2116)
PHONE..................................415 771-1400
Holger B Gantz, *Manager*
Rowan Tejada, *Finance*
Leann Katayama, *Director*
Vincent Venenciano, *Director*
Carmen Cruz, *Manager*
EMP: 330
SALES (corp-wide): 2.7B **Publicly Held**
WEB: www.esirvine.com
SIC: 7011 5812 7299 Hotels; eating
places; banquet hall facilities
PA: Park Hotels & Resorts Inc.
1775 Tysons Blvd Fl 7
Tysons VA 22102
571 302-5757

(P-12716)
PARK HOTELS & RESORTS INC
Also Called: Hilton
1 Hegenberger Rd, Oakland (94621-1405)
P.O. Box 2549 (94614-0549)
PHONE..................................510 635-5000
Mark Clement, *General Mgr*
Lillian Virdure, *Telecom Exec*
EMP: 114
SALES (corp-wide): 2.7B **Publicly Held**
WEB: www.esirvine.com
SIC: 7011 5813 5812 Hotels & motels;
drinking places; eating places
PA: Park Hotels & Resorts Inc.
1775 Tysons Blvd Fl 7
Tysons VA 22102
571 302-5757

(P-12717)
PARK HOTELS & RESORTS INC
Also Called: Hilton
10950 N Torrey Pines Rd, La Jolla
(92037-1006)
PHONE..................................858 450-4569
Patrick Duffy, *Manager*
EMP: 50
SALES (corp-wide): 2.7B **Publicly Held**
WEB: www.esirvine.com
SIC: 7011 5813 5812 Hotels & motels;
drinking places; eating places
PA: Park Hotels & Resorts Inc.
1775 Tysons Blvd Fl 7
Tysons VA 22102
571 302-5757

(P-12718)
PARK HOTELS & RESORTS INC
Also Called: Embassy Suites
1075 California Blvd, NAPA (94559-1061)
PHONE..................................707 253-9540
Reynaldo Zertuche, *Manager*
EMP: 80
SQ FT: 83,251
SALES (corp-wide): 2.7B **Publicly Held**
WEB: www.esirvine.com
SIC: 7011 Hotels & motels

(P-12719)
PARK HOTELS & RESORTS INC
Also Called: Hilton Hotels
700 N Haven Ave, Ontario (91764-4902)
PHONE..................................909 980-3420
Christopher J Nassetta, *Branch Mgr*
EMP: 116
SALES (corp-wide): 2.7B **Publicly Held**
SIC: 7011 Hotels & motels
PA: Park Hotels & Resorts Inc.
1775 Tysons Blvd Fl 7
Tysons VA 22102
571 302-5757

(P-12720)
PARK HOTELS & RESORTS INC
Also Called: Hilton
168 S Los Robles Ave, Pasadena
(91101-2430)
PHONE..................................626 577-1000
Todd Iacono, *Manager*
EMP: 248
SALES (corp-wide): 2.7B **Publicly Held**
WEB: www.esirvine.com
SIC: 7011 5812 7389 7299 Hotels & mo-
tels; eating places; hotel & motel reserva-
tion service; banquet hall facilities;
drinking places
PA: Park Hotels & Resorts Inc.
1775 Tysons Blvd Fl 7
Tysons VA 22102
571 302-5757

(P-12721)
PARK HOTELS & RESORTS INC
55 Cyril Magnin St, San Francisco
(94102-2812)
PHONE..................................415 392-8000
Steve Cowan, *General Mgr*
EMP: 500
SALES (corp-wide): 2.7B **Publicly Held**
SIC: 7011 5812 Hotels; American restau-
rant
PA: Park Hotels & Resorts Inc.
1775 Tysons Blvd Fl 7
Tysons VA 22102
571 302-5757

(P-12722)
PARK HOTELS & RESORTS INC
Also Called: Embassy Suites
1211 E Garvey St, Covina (91724-3666)
PHONE..................................626 915-3441
Seig Heglund, *Manager*
EMP: 75
SALES (corp-wide): 2.7B **Publicly Held**
WEB: www.esirvine.com
SIC: 7011 7991 7359 7299 Hotels & mo-
tels; physical fitness facilities; equipment
rental & leasing; banquet hall facilities
PA: Park Hotels & Resorts Inc.
1775 Tysons Blvd Fl 7
Tysons VA 22102
571 302-5757

(P-12723)
PARK HOTELS & RESORTS INC
Also Called: Hilton
9876 Wilshire Blvd, Beverly Hills
(90210-3115)
PHONE..................................310 415-3340
Beverly Hilton, *Principal*
EMP: 113
SALES (corp-wide): 2.7B **Publicly Held**
WEB: www.esirvine.com
SIC: 7011 Hotels & motels
PA: Park Hotels & Resorts Inc.
1775 Tysons Blvd Fl 7
Tysons VA 22102
571 302-5757

(P-12724)
PARK HOTELS & RESORTS INC
Also Called: Hilton
4130 Lake Tahoe Blvd, South Lake Tahoe
(96150-6965)
PHONE..................................530 543-2126
John Steinbach, *Manager*
EMP: 250

SALES (corp-wide): 2.7B **Publicly Held**
WEB: www.esirvine.com
SIC: **7011** Hotels & motels
PA: Park Hotels & Resorts Inc.
1775 Tysons Blvd Fl 7
Tysons VA 22102
571 302-5757

(P-12725)
PARK HOTELS & RESORTS INC
Also Called: Embassy Suites
150 Anza Blvd, Burlingame (94010-1924)
PHONE..................................650 342-4600
Christopher Beckman, *General Mgr*
EMP: 130
SALES (corp-wide): 2.7B **Publicly Held**
WEB: www.esirvine.com
SIC: **7011** 5812 Hotels & motels;
drinking places; eating places
PA: Park Hotels & Resorts Inc.
1775 Tysons Blvd Fl 7
Tysons VA 22102
571 302-5757

(P-12726)
PARK HOTELS & RESORTS INC
Also Called: Embassy Suites
211 E Huntington Dr, Arcadia (91006-3745)
PHONE..................................626 445-8525
Stig Hedlund, *Manager*
EMP: 116
SALES (corp-wide): 2.7B **Publicly Held**
WEB: www.esirvine.com
SIC: **7011** Hotels & motels
PA: Park Hotels & Resorts Inc.
1775 Tysons Blvd Fl 7
Tysons VA 22102
571 302-5757

(P-12727)
PARK HOTELS & RESORTS INC
Also Called: Embassy Suites
8425 Firestone Blvd, Downey
(90241-3843)
PHONE..................................562 861-1900
Stig Hedlund, *Branch Mgr*
EMP: 100
SALES (corp-wide): 2.7B **Publicly Held**
WEB: www.esirvine.com
SIC: **7011** 5813 5812 Hotels & motels;
drinking places; eating places
PA: Park Hotels & Resorts Inc.
1775 Tysons Blvd Fl 7
Tysons VA 22102
571 302-5757

(P-12728)
PARK HOTELS & RESORTS INC
Also Called: Embassy Suites
7762 Beach Blvd, Buena Park
(90620-1935)
PHONE..................................714 739-5600
Juergen Oswald, *General Mgr*
EMP: 65
SALES (corp-wide): 2.7B **Publicly Held**
WEB: www.esirvine.com
SIC: **7011** Hotels & motels
PA: Park Hotels & Resorts Inc.
1775 Tysons Blvd Fl 7
Tysons VA 22102
571 302-5757

(P-12729)
PARK HOTELS & RESORTS INC
Also Called: Hilton
700 N Haven Ave, Ontario (91764-4902)
PHONE..................................909 980-0400
Robert Smith, *Branch Mgr*
EMP: 116
SALES (corp-wide): 2.7B **Publicly Held**
WEB: www.esirvine.com
SIC: **7011** 5813 5812 Hotels & motels;
drinking places; eating places
PA: Park Hotels & Resorts Inc.
1775 Tysons Blvd Fl 7
Tysons VA 22102
571 302-5757

(P-12730)
PARK HOTELS & RESORTS INC
Also Called: Hilton
225 W Valley Blvd, San Gabriel
(91776-3743)
PHONE..................................626 270-2700
Charles Noh, *Manager*
EMP: 116

SALES (corp-wide): 2.7B **Publicly Held**
WEB: www.esirvine.com
SIC: **7011** Hotels & motels
PA: Park Hotels & Resorts Inc.
1775 Tysons Blvd Fl 7
Tysons VA 22102
571 302-5757

(P-12731)
PARK HOTELS & RESORTS INC
Also Called: Embassy Suites
2120 Main St, Irvine (92614-6219)
PHONE..................................949 553-8332
Mari Hnatt, *Manager*
EMP: 114
SALES (corp-wide): 2.7B **Publicly Held**
WEB: www.esirvine.com
SIC: **7011** Hotels & motels
PA: Park Hotels & Resorts Inc.
1775 Tysons Blvd Fl 7
Tysons VA 22102
571 302-5757

(P-12732)
PARK HOTELS & RESORTS INC
Also Called: Hilton
3050 Bristol St, Costa Mesa (92626-3036)
PHONE..................................714 540-7000
Shaun Robinson, *General Mgr*
Scott Bruno, *Manager*
EMP: 307
SALES (corp-wide): 2.7B **Publicly Held**
WEB: www.esirvine.com
SIC: **7011** 5812 7299 Hotels & motels;
eating places; banquet hall facilities
PA: Park Hotels & Resorts Inc.
1775 Tysons Blvd Fl 7
Tysons VA 22102
571 302-5757

(P-12733)
PARK HOTELS & RESORTS INC
Also Called: Hilton
5711 W Century Blvd, Los Angeles
(90045-5672)
PHONE..................................310 410-4000
David Villarrubia, *General Mgr*
EMP: 116
SALES (corp-wide): 2.7B **Publicly Held**
WEB: www.esirvine.com
SIC: **7011** 5812 Hotels & motels; eating
places
PA: Park Hotels & Resorts Inc.
1775 Tysons Blvd Fl 7
Tysons VA 22102
571 302-5757

(P-12734)
PARK HOTELS & RESORTS INC
Also Called: Embassy Suites
3100 E Frontera St, Anaheim (92806-2820)
PHONE..................................714 632-1221
Margo Gilbert, *Manager*
EMP: 65
SALES (corp-wide): 2.7B **Publicly Held**
WEB: www.esirvine.com
SIC: **7011** 8741 6794 Hotels & motels;
hotel or motel management; franchises,
selling or licensing
PA: Park Hotels & Resorts Inc.
1775 Tysons Blvd Fl 7
Tysons VA 22102
571 302-5757

(P-12735)
PARK HOTELS & RESORTS INC
Also Called: Embassy Suites
250 Gateway Blvd, South San Francisco
(94080-7018)
PHONE..................................650 589-3400
Rudy Ortiz, *General Mgr*
EMP: 65
SALES (corp-wide): 2.7B **Publicly Held**
WEB: www.esirvine.com
SIC: **7011** Hotels & motels
PA: Park Hotels & Resorts Inc.
1775 Tysons Blvd Fl 7
Tysons VA 22102
571 302-5757

(P-12736)
PARK HOTELS & RESORTS INC
Also Called: Embassy Suites
901 Ski Run Blvd, South Lake Tahoe
(96150-8569)
PHONE..................................530 541-6122

Verla Younker, *Manager*
Phil Moulton, *Principal*
EMP: 50
SALES (corp-wide): 2.7B **Publicly Held**
WEB: www.esirvine.com
SIC: **7011** Hotels & motels
PA: Park Hotels & Resorts Inc.
1775 Tysons Blvd Fl 7
Tysons VA 22102
571 302-5757

(P-12737)
PARK INN BY RADISSON
3737 N Blackstone Ave, Fresno
(93726-5307)
PHONE..................................559 226-2200
Betty Qi, *Owner*
EMP: 75
SALES (est): 1.3MM **Privately Held**
SIC: **7011** Hotels & motels

(P-12738)
PARK INN BY READISSON FRESNO
Also Called: Park Central Hotel Fresno
3737 N Blackstone Ave, Fresno
(93726-5307)
PHONE..................................559 226-2200
Lori Lascola, *General Mgr*
EMP: 62 EST: 2011
SALES (est): 2.8MM **Privately Held**
SIC: **7011** Hotels & motels

(P-12739)
PARK PLAZA HOTEL
150 Hegenberger Rd, Oakland
(94521-1422)
PHONE..................................510 635-5300
Tracy W Wahrlich Jr, *President*
Carl T Doughty, *General Ptnr*
Bert Taprizi, *General Ptnr*
Stephen Wahrlich, *General Ptnr*
EMP: 50
SALES (est): 1.4MM **Privately Held**
WEB: www.parkplazaoakland.com
SIC: **7011** Hotel, franchised

(P-12740)
PASADENA HOTEL DEV VENTR LP
Also Called: Sheraton Pasadena
303 Cordova St, Pasadena (91101-2426)
PHONE..................................626 449-4000
Ray Serafin, *Principal*
David Iwane, *Principal*
Ikeda Harry, *Engineer*
Kathleen Blackman, *Sales Mgr*
Susan Dunn, *Sales Mgr*
EMP: 99
SALES (est): 6MM **Privately Held**
SIC: **7011** Hotels & motels

(P-12741)
PASADENA RBLES ACQUISITION LLC
168 S Los Robles Ave, Pasadena
(91101-2430)
PHONE..................................626 577-1000
Vince Cuce, *Officer*
Cheree Goodall, *Office Mgr*
EMP: 99 EST: 2015
SQ FT: 85,000
SALES (est): 441.1K **Privately Held**
SIC: **7011** Hotels & motels

(P-12742)
PASKENTA BAND NOMLAKI INDIANS
Also Called: Rolling Hills Casino
2655 Everett Freeman Way, Corning
(96021-9000)
P.O. Box 709 (96021-0709)
PHONE..................................530 528-3500
Everett Freeman, *Chairman*
Jeff Realander, *COO*
Gary Poynor, *CFO*
Joshua Morris, *IT/INT Sup*
Jeremy Olson, *Purch Mgr*
EMP: 493
SALES (est): 14.9MM **Privately Held**
WEB: www.paskenta.org
SIC: **7011** Casino hotel

(P-12743)
PASO ROBLES INN LLC
Also Called: Paso Robles Hotel
1103 Spring St, Paso Robles (93446-2598)
PHONE..................................805 238-2660
Paul Wallace, *General Mgr*
Tom Martin, *Owner*
Kim Eady, *Partner*
Andrew Litton, *Partner*
Ken Litton, *Partner*
EMP: 52
SALES (est): 2.5MM **Privately Held**
WEB: www.pasoroblesinn.com
SIC: **7011** 5812 5813 Hotels; restaurant,
family: independent; cocktail lounge

(P-12744)
PAUMA BAND OF MISSION INDIANS
Casino Pauma
777 Pauma Reservation Rd, Pauma Valley
(92061)
P.O. Box 1067 (92061-1067)
PHONE..................................760 742-2177
Richard Darder, *CEO*
EMP: 500 **Privately Held**
WEB: www.casinopauma.com
SIC: **7011** Casino hotel
PA: Pauma Band Of Mission Indians
1010 Pauma Reservation Rd
Pauma Valley CA 92061
760 742-1289

(P-12745)
PEACOCK STES RESORT LTD PARTNR
1745 S Anaheim Blvd, Anaheim
(92805-6518)
PHONE..................................714 535-8255
Sheldon Ginsburg, *General Ptnr*
Shell Development Corporation-, *General
Ptnr*
Perry Snyderman, *General Ptnr*
EMP: 60
SQ FT: 75,000
SALES (est): 2.3MM **Privately Held**
WEB: www.peacocksuitesresort.com
SIC: **7011** 6531 Resort hotel; hotels; time-
sharing real estate sales, leasing &
rentals

(P-12746)
PECHANGA DEVELOPMENT CORP
Also Called: Pechanga Resort & Casino
45000 Pechanga Pkwy, Temecula
(92592-5810)
P.O. Box 9041 (92589-9041)
PHONE..................................951 695-4655
Patrick Murphy, *CEO*
Oda Becerra, *Partner*
Jerry Konchar, *CFO*
Christina McMenamin, *Treasurer*
Edith Atwood, *Vice Pres*
◆ EMP: 4000
SALES (est): 206.1MM **Privately Held**
WEB: www.pechangarv.com
SIC: **7011** 7929 7999 Casino hotel; enter-
tainment service; gambling establishment

(P-12747)
PEEKAY INVESTMENTS PRPTS LLC
Also Called: Clarion Hotel
901 N China Lake Blvd, Ridgecrest
(93555-3160)
PHONE..................................714 403-1923
Valerie Keval, *Branch Mgr*
Belen Garza, *Manager*
EMP: 50
SALES (corp-wide): 1.3MM **Privately
Held**
SIC: **7011** Hotels & motels
PA: Peekay Investments Properties Llc
977 Huntington Way
Perris CA 92571
714 404-2201

(P-12748)
PEPPER TREE INN
Also Called: Rodeway Inn
645 N Lake Blvd, Tahoe City (96145)
P.O. Box 29 (96145-0029)
PHONE..................................530 583-3711
Thomas Brown, *Manager*

EMP: 65
SQ FT: 18,609
SALES (corp-wide): 4MM **Privately Held**
WEB: www.pismosands.com
SIC: 7011 Hotels & motels
PA: Pepper Tree Inn
998 Hilmar St
Santa Clara CA

(P-12749)
PEPPERMILL CASINOS INC
4021 Port Chicago Hwy, Concord
(94520-1122)
PHONE...............................925 671-7711
Ronald Rives, *Manager*
Deverie Hogan, *Manager*
EMP: 200 **Privately Held**
WEB: www.thepeppermillcasinonv.com
SIC: 7011 7999 Casino hotel; gambling
establishment
PA: Peppermill Casinos, Inc.
90 W Grove St Ste 600
Reno NV 89509

(P-12750)
PHF II BURBANK LLC
Also Called: Burbank Airport Mariott Hotel
2500 N Hollywood Way, Burbank
(91505-1019)
PHONE...............................818 843-6000
Linda Davey, *Mng Member*
Jose Pahati, *Controller*
EMP: 220
SALES (est): 10MM **Privately Held**
SIC: 7011 Hotels & motels

(P-12751)
PHF RUBY LLC
Also Called: Marriott Vacatlon Club Pulse
2620 Jones St, San Francisco
(94133-1306)
PHONE...............................415 885-4700
Jose L Torres,
Anthony Kai Chiu Ceng,
EMP: 118
SALES (est): 6.8MM **Privately Held**
SIC: 7011 Hotel, franchised

(P-12752)
PICCADILLY HOSPITALITY LLC
Also Called: Piccadilly Inn Shaw
2305 W Shaw Ave, Fresno (93711-3411)
PHONE...............................559 348-5520
Mu-Pien Chien, *President*
Gene Chien, *Vice Pres*
EMP: 50 EST: 2012
SALES (est): 1.4MM **Privately Held**
SIC: 7011 Resort hotel; hotels

(P-12753)
PIER PONT HOTEL LP
550 San Jon Rd, Ventura (93001-3745)
PHONE...............................805 643-6144
EMP: 50
SALES (est): 692.9K **Privately Held**
SIC: 7011

(P-12754)
PIERPONT INN INC
Also Called: Central Coast Management
550 San Jon Rd, Ventura (93001-3754)
P.O. Box 335, Grover Beach (93483-0335)
PHONE...............................805 643-0245
Subhash Patel, *President*
Mauline Patel, *Vice Pres*
EMP: 50 EST: 1956
SALES (est): 2.1MM **Privately Held**
WEB: www.pierpontinn.com
SIC: 7011 5812 Bed & breakfast inn;
drive-in restaurant

(P-12755)
PINE & POWELL PARTNERS LLC
Also Called: Stanford Court Hotel
905 California St, San Francisco
(94108-2201)
PHONE...............................415 989-3500
Naveen Kakarla,
Rose Rivera, *Administration*
Bryan Terris, *Engineer*
Luz Chatman, *Marketing Mgr*
Michael Baier,
EMP: 99

SQ FT: 287,000
SALES (est): 301.3K **Privately Held**
SIC: 7011 Hotels & motels

(P-12756)
PINNACLE 1617 LLC
Also Called: Four Points By Sheraton
1617 1st Ave, San Diego (92101-3003)
PHONE...............................619 239-9600
Bharat Lall, *Mng Member*
Sue Depascale,
Hema Lall,
Nabih Geha, *Manager*
EMP: 50 EST: 2011
SALES (est): 4.1MM **Privately Held**
SIC: 7011 Hotels & motels

(P-12757)
PINNACLE RVRSIDE HSPITALITY LP
Also Called: Riverside Marriott
3400 Market St, Riverside (92501-2826)
PHONE...............................951 784-8000
Dr Bharat Lall, *General Ptnr*
EMP: 190
SALES (est): 7.9MM **Privately Held**
SIC: 7011 Hotels

(P-12758)
PIONEER SQUARE HOTEL COMPANY
1940 Fillmore St, San Francisco
(94115-2745)
PHONE...............................415 346-2323
Bart Seidler, *President*
EMP: 50
SALES (est): 1.5MM **Privately Held**
SIC: 7011 Hotels

(P-12759)
PISMO COAST VILLAGE INC
165 S Dolliver St, Pismo Beach
(93449-2999)
PHONE...............................805 773-1811
Jay Jamison, *CEO*
Ronald Nunlist, *President*
Wayne Hardesty, *CFO*
Terris Hughes, *Exec VP*
Dwight Plumley, *Vice Pres*
EMP: 60
SALES: 8.4MM **Privately Held**
WEB: www.pismocoastvillage.com
SIC: 7011 Resort hotel

(P-12760)
PLAYA PROPER JV LLC
Also Called: Custom Hotel
8639 Lincoln Blvd, Los Angeles
(90045-3503)
PHONE...............................310 645-0400
Brad Korzen, *CEO*
Bryan De Lowe, *President*
Jeffrey Cruz, *Finance*
EMP: 80
SALES (est): 10.1MM **Privately Held**
SIC: 7011 Hotels

(P-12761)
PLEASANT CANYON HOTEL INC
Also Called: Residence Inn By Marriott
11920 Dublin Canyon Rd, Pleasanton
(94588-2818)
PHONE...............................925 847-0535
James Evans, *CFO*
EMP: 50 EST: 1996
SQ FT: 98,496
SALES (est): 3.4MM **Privately Held**
SIC: 7011 Hotels & motels

(P-12762)
PLEASANTON PROJECT OWNER LLC
Also Called: Marriott
11950 Dublin Canyon Rd, Pleasanton
(94588-2818)
PHONE...............................925 847-7592
Dianna Teves, *General Mgr*
Takako Smith, *Finance Dir*
EMP: 60
SALES: 16MM **Privately Held**
SIC: 7011 Hotels & motels

(P-12763)
PONTE VINEYARD INN
35001 Rancho Cal Rd, Temecula
(92591-4008)
PHONE...............................951 587-6688
Sarah Martinez, *General Mgr*
EMP: 75 EST: 2012
SALES (est): 413.6K **Privately Held**
SIC: 7011 Hotels

(P-12764)
PORTFOLIO HOTELS & RESORTS LLC
Also Called: Casa Munras Garden Hotel
700 Munras Ave, Monterey (93940-3110)
PHONE...............................831 375-2411
Meredith Wood, *Principal*
EMP: 50
SALES (est): 751.9K **Privately Held**
SIC: 7011 Hotels
PA: Portfolio Hotels & Resorts, Llc
601 Oakmont Ln Ste 420
Westmont IL 60559

(P-12765)
PORTOFINO HOTEL PARTNERS LP
Also Called: Hotel Portofino
260 Portofino Way, Redondo Beach
(90277-2033)
PHONE...............................310 379-8481
Glenn Bishop, *Principal*
Rick Galeano, *Chief Engr*
Christina Gallegos, *Controller*
Yvette Antoniou, *Sales Staff*
Luann Uszler, *Sales Staff*
EMP: 151
SALES (est): 11.1MM **Privately Held**
WEB: www.hotelportofino.com
SIC: 7011 Hotels

(P-12766)
PORTOFINO INN & SUITES ANAHEIM
1831 S Harbor Blvd, Anaheim
(92802-3509)
PHONE...............................714 782-7600
Jennifer Reihl, *Director*
Ricardo De La Torre, *Chief Engr*
Matthew Lacy, *Controller*
EMP: 727
SALES (est): 20.3MM
SALES (corp-wide): 74.2MM **Privately Held**
SIC: 7011 Inns
PA: Tarsadia Hotels
620 Newport Center Dr # 1400
Newport Beach CA 92660
949 610-8000

(P-12767)
POSADA ROYALE HOTEL & SUITES
1775 Madera Rd, Simi Valley (93065-3049)
PHONE...............................805 584-6300
Larry Rogers, *Partner*
Peter Zegers, *Partner*
EMP: 50
SQ FT: 55,000
SALES (est): 3.4MM **Privately Held**
WEB: www.posadaroyale.com
SIC: 7011 5812 7389 7299 Hotels; American restaurant; convention & show services; banquet hall facilities

(P-12768)
POST STREET RENAISSANCE
Also Called: Prescott Hotel, The
545 Post St, San Francisco (94102-1228)
PHONE...............................415 563-0303
John Dern, *President*
EMP: 300
SALES (est): 14.1MM **Privately Held**
WEB: www.prescotthotel.com
SIC: 7011 Resort hotel; hotels
HQ: Kimpton Hotel & Restaurant Group Llc
222 Kearny St Ste 200
San Francisco CA 94108
415 397-5572

(P-12769)
PR RANCHO HOTEL LLC
11260 Point East Dr, Rancho Cordova
(95742-6232)
PHONE...............................916 638-4141
Viorica Sanchevici, *Principal*
Guneet Bajwa, *Principal*
EMP: 53
SALES (est): 459K **Privately Held**
SIC: 7011 Hotels

(P-12770)
PRESIDIO HOTEL GROUP LLC (PA)
1011 10th St, Sacramento (95814-3501)
PHONE...............................707 429-6000
Sushil Patel, *Mng Member*
Dipti Lala, *Controller*
Edward Delorme, *Mng Member*
EMP: 225
SQ FT: 2,100
SALES (est): 4.5MM **Privately Held**
SIC: 7011 Hotels & motels

(P-12771)
PRESIDIO HOTEL GROUP LLC
Also Called: Fairfield Inn
10713 White Rock Rd, Rancho Cordova
(95670-6031)
PHONE...............................916 631-7500
Sushil Patel, *Branch Mgr*
EMP: 74
SALES (corp-wide): 4.5MM **Privately Held**
SIC: 7011 Hotels & motels
PA: Presidio Hotel Group, Llc
1011 10th St
Sacramento CA 95814
707 429-6000

(P-12772)
PROFICIENT LLC
Also Called: Crowne Plz Los Angeles Hbr Ht
601 S Palos Verdes St, San Pedro
(90731-3329)
PHONE...............................310 519-8200
Joyce Wang, *Principal*
EMP: 99
SALES (est): 3.2MM **Privately Held**
SIC: 7011 Hotels & motels

(P-12773)
PRUTEL JOINT VENTURE
Also Called: Ritz-Carlton Laguna Niguel
1 Ritz Carlton Dr, Dana Point (92629-4205)
PHONE...............................949 240-2000
W B Johnson, *Partner*
Prudential Realty, *Partner*
Paul Patterson, *CFO*
Madelyn Abbot, *Vice Pres*
EMP: 700
SALES (est): 28.3MM **Privately Held**
SIC: 7011 Hotels & motels

(P-12774)
PT GAMING LLC
235 Oregon St, El Segundo (90245-4215)
PHONE...............................323 260-5060
Patrick Tierney, *Mng Member*
Jamie Breen, *Controller*
Rita Radics, *Human Res Mgr*
Gina Schiazzano, *Personnel Assit*
Kirk Blackinton, *Senior Mgr*
EMP: 700
SQ FT: 7,000
SALES (est): 17.5MM **Privately Held**
SIC: 7011 Casino hotel

(P-12775)
PYRAMID ADVISORS LTD PARTNR
Also Called: Marriott
11950 Dublin Canyon Rd, Pleasanton
(94588-2818)
PHONE...............................925 847-6000
Norval Nelson, *General Mgr*
EMP: 70
SALES (corp-wide): 150.9MM **Privately Held**
SIC: 7011 Hotels & motels
PA: Pyramid Advisors Limited Partnership
1 Post Office Sq
Boston MA 02109
617 202-2033

▲ = Import ▼=Export
◆ =Import/Export

(P-12776)
Q S H PROPERTIES INC
Also Called: Quality Inn
2701 Hotel Ter, Santa Ana (92705-5603)
PHONE..........................714 957-9200
Vahi M Melkonian, *President*
Cheng Wu, *Manager*
EMP: 52
SALES (est): 3.2MM Privately Held
SIC: 7011 Hotels & motels

(P-12777)
Q S SAN LUIS OBISPO LP
Also Called: Quality Inn
1631 Monterey St, San Luis Obispo
(93401-2929)
PHONE..........................805 541-5001
George Newland, *Partner*
Harold Parker, *General Ptnr*
Robert Warmington, *General Ptnr*
Angela Kimball, *Sales Staff*
Christopher Houston, *Accounts Mgr*
EMP: 50
SALES (est): 2.5MM Privately Held
SIC: 7011 Hotels & motels

(P-12778)
QUAIL LODGE INC
Also Called: Covey, The
8205 Valley Greens Dr, Carmel
(93923-9513)
PHONE..........................831 624-1581
Clement Kwok, *CEO*
William Lawson Little, *Vice Pres*
Michael Ochs, *Chief Engr*
EMP: 250
SQ FT: 20,000
SALES (est): 25.3MM Privately Held
WEB: www.quaillodge.com
SIC: 7011 7997 7389 5941 Resort hotel;
golf club, membership; convention &
show services; golf goods & equipment;
eating places; subdividers & developers

(P-12779)
QUEENSBAY HOTEL LLC (PA)
444 W Ocean Blvd, Long Beach
(90802-4518)
PHONE..........................562 628-0625
Kambiz Babaoff, *Mng Member*
Michael Moskowitz
EMP: 102
SALES (est): 2.5MM Privately Held
SIC: 7011 Hotels & motels

(P-12780)
QUEENSBAY HOTEL LLC
Also Called: Hotel Maya
700 Queensway Dr, Long Beach
(90802-6343)
PHONE..........................562 481-3910
Cherie Davis, *Manager*
EMP: 100
SALES (est): 6.3MM
SALES (corp-wide): 2.5MM Privately
Held
SIC: 7011 Hotels
PA: Queensbay Hotel, Llc
444 W Ocean Blvd
Long Beach CA 90802
562 628-0625

(P-12781)
R & K INTERESTS INC (PA)
Also Called: Investor's Property Services
15707 Rockfield Blvd # 225, Irvine
(92618-2829)
PHONE..........................949 900-6160
Robert C Warren III, *President*
Kyle C Warren, *Senior VP*
David Crain, *Vice Pres*
Patricia Sheehan, *Vice Pres*
Joan Jacks, *Director*
EMP: 200
SQ FT: 8,000
SALES (est): 5.5MM Privately Held
SIC: 7011 Hotels & motels

(P-12782)
R C HOTELS INC
Also Called: Hotel On Huntington Beach
7667 Center Ave, Huntington Beach
(92647-3073)
PHONE..........................714 891-0123
Toll Free:..........................877 -
Shu Chin Kou, *President*

Christopher Deguzman, *Sales Staff*
EMP: 60
SQ FT: 114,012
SALES (est): 3.3MM Privately Held
SIC: 7011 Resort hotel; hotels

(P-12783)
R P S RESORT CORP
1600 N Indian Canyon Dr, Palm Springs
(92262-4602)
PHONE..........................760 327-8311
Douglas McCarron, *President*
EMP: 250
SALES (est): 2.1MM
SALES (corp-wide): 49.6MM Privately
Held
WEB: www.psriv.com
SIC: 7011 Resort hotel
HQ: The San Bernardino Hilton
285 E Hospitality Ln
San Bernardino CA 92408
909 889-0133

(P-12784)
RADISSON HOTEL AT USC
Also Called: Radisson Inn
3540 S Figueroa St, Los Angeles
(90007-4313)
PHONE..........................213 748-4141
EMP: 120 EST: 1977
SALES (est): 587.4K Privately Held
SIC: 7011

(P-12785)
RADISSON HOTEL SANTA MARIA
3455 Skyway Dr, Santa Maria
(93455-2501)
PHONE..........................805 928-8000
Ryan Swack, *Principal*
EMP: 60
SQ FT: 60,000
SALES (est): 3MM Privately Held
SIC: 7011 5812 Hotels & motels; eating
places

(P-12786)
RADISSON HT FISHERMANS WHARF
250 Beach St, San Francisco
(94133-1291)
PHONE..........................415 392-6700
John Sevilla, *General Mgr*
EMP: 100
SALES (est): 4.2MM Privately Held
SIC: 7011 Hotels & motels

(P-12787)
RADLAX GATEWAY HOTEL LLC
Also Called: Radisson Inn
6225 W Century Blvd, Los Angeles
(90045-5311)
PHONE..........................310 670-9000
Peter Dumon, *Mng Member*
EMP: 300
SALES (est): 9.6MM Privately Held
SIC: 7011 Hotels & motels
PA: Portfolio Hotels & Resorts, Llc
601 Oakmont Ln Ste 420
Westmont IL 60559

(P-12788)
RAFFLES LRMITAGE BEVERLY HILLS
Also Called: L'Ermitage Hotel
9291 Burton Way, Beverly Hills
(90210-3709)
PHONE..........................310 278-3344
Jack Naderkhani, *General Mgr*
Kirsten Appel, *Mng Member*
Stephanie Yesenofski, *Director*
EMP: 249
SALES (est): 11MM
SALES (corp-wide): 1.1B Privately Held
SIC: 7011 5813 5812 Hotels; drinking
places; eating places
HQ: Raffles International Limited
250 North Bridge Road
Singapore 17910

(P-12789)
RALEIGH ENTERPRISES INC (PA)
Also Called: Raleigh Holdings
5300 Melrose Ave Fl 4, Los Angeles
(90038-5114)
PHONE..........................310 899-8900
Kristen J Raleigh, *CEO*
George I Rosenthal, *Ch of Bd*
Mark Rosenthal, *President*
Phyllis Alexander, *Administration*
Yolanda Montellano, *Opers Staff*
EMP: 130
SQ FT: 20,000
SALES (est): 43.7MM Privately Held
WEB: www.raleighenterprises.com
SIC: 7011 Hotels & motels

(P-12790)
RAMADA PLAZA HT ANAHEIM RESORT
515 W Katella Ave, Anaheim (92802-3609)
PHONE..........................714 991-6868
Stephen Hsu, *Owner*
EMP: 200 EST: 1998
SALES (est): 3.3MM Privately Held
SIC: 7011 Hotels

(P-12791)
RANCHO BERNARDO PARTNERS LTD
Also Called: Radisson Inn
11520 W Bernardo Ct, San Diego
(92127-1602)
P.O. Box 1538, San Marcos (92079-1538)
PHONE..........................858 451-6600
Jonathan Jacobs, *Managing Prtnr*
EMP: 60
SQ FT: 87,214
SALES (est): 3.9MM Privately Held
SIC: 7011 Hotels & motels

(P-12792)
RANCHO LEONERO RESORT
5671 Palmer Way Ste E, Carlsbad
(92010-7256)
PHONE..........................760 438-2905
Genie Ireland, *Owner*
John Ireland, *Partner*
EMP: 50
SALES (est): 1.7MM Privately Held
SIC: 7011 Resort hotel

(P-12793)
RANCHO VALENCIA RESORT
5921 Valencia Cir, Rancho Santa Fe
(92067-9520)
P.O. Box 9126 (92067-4126)
PHONE..........................858 756-1123
Jeffrey Essakow, *Mng Member*
Mark Blevins, *Finance*
Gabriel Duran, *Payroll Mgr*
Stacy Jacobs, *Opers Staff*
Oz Soykok, *Opers Staff*
EMP: 300
SALES (est): 24.8MM Privately Held
WEB: www.ranchovalencia.com
SIC: 7011 Resort hotel; hotels

(P-12794)
RECP CY OXNARD LLC
Also Called: Courtyard By Marriott Oxnard
600 E Esplanade Dr, Oxnard (93036-2403)
PHONE..........................805 604-7527
Mary Reece, *Principal*
Recp III Cal West Hotels LLC, *Mng Member*
Patrick Mullin, *Manager*
EMP: 70
SQ FT: 103,000
SALES (est): 3.3MM Privately Held
SIC: 7011 Hotels & motels

(P-12795)
RECP RI OXNARD LLC
Also Called: Residnce Inn By Mrriott Oxnard
2101 W Vineyard Ave, Oxnard
(93036-2268)
PHONE..........................805 278-2200
Doug Pflaumer, *Manager*
Millicent Bennett, *Principal*
Recp III Cal West Hotels LLC, *Mng Member*
EMP: 150
SQ FT: 103,000
SALES (est): 4.3MM Privately Held
SIC: 7011 Hotels & motels

(P-12796)
RECP/WNDSOR SCRAMENTO VENTR LP
Also Called: Windsor Capital Holet Group
4422 Y St, Sacramento (95817-2220)
PHONE..........................916 455-6800
Mike Cryan, *CEO*
Recp Windsor Rim Sacramento GP,
General Ptnr
EMP: 72
SALES (est): 1.9MM Privately Held
SIC: 7011 Hotels

(P-12797)
RED EARTH CASINO
3089 Norm Niver Rd, Thermal
(92274-6550)
PHONE..........................760 395-1200
Andrew Miranda, *General Mgr*
Nigel White, *Owner*
EMP: 150
SQ FT: 15,000
SALES (est): 7.5MM Privately Held
SIC: 7011 Casino hotel

(P-12798)
REDDING RANCHERIA (PA)
2000 Redding Rancheria Rd, Redding
(96001-5528)
PHONE..........................530 225-8979
Tracy Edward, *CEO*
Christi Hines, *CFO*
Tamra Olson, *CFO*
Dani Hayward, *Manager*
EMP: 60
SQ FT: 16,360
SALES (est): 36.5MM Privately Held
WEB: www.redding-rancheria.com
SIC: 7011 Hotels & motels

(P-12799)
REICHERT LENGFELD LTD PARTNR
Also Called: RI Properties
725 Folger Ave, Albany (94710-2809)
PHONE..........................510 845-1077
Diana R Meyer, *Partner*
Herbert R Meyer, *General Ptnr*
EMP: 90
SQ FT: 1,500
SALES (est): 3.5MM Privately Held
SIC: 7011 Hotels & motels

(P-12800)
REMINGTON HOTEL CORPORATION
Also Called: Palm Springs Renaissance
888 E Tahquitz Canyon Way, Palm Springs
(92262-6708)
PHONE..........................760 322-6000
EMP: 85 Privately Held
SIC: 7011 Hotels & motels
PA: Remington Hotel Corporation
14185 Dallas Pkwy # 1150
Dallas TX 75254

(P-12801)
REMINGTON HOTEL CORPORATION
Also Called: Holiday Inn
1150 S Beverly Dr, Los Angeles
(90035-1120)
PHONE..........................310 553-6561
Jack Jones, *Branch Mgr*
EMP: 59 Privately Held
WEB: www.remingtonhotels.com
SIC: 7011 Hotels & motels
PA: Remington Hotel Corporation
14185 Dallas Pkwy # 1150
Dallas TX 75254

(P-12802)
RENAISSANCE HOTEL HOLDINGS INC
1325 Broadway, Sonoma (95476-7505)
PHONE..........................707 935-6600
Dave Dalquist, *General Mgr*
Rick Eldridge, *Finance*
Gina Thayer, *Manager*
EMP: 99
SALES (est): 1.4MM Privately Held
SIC: 7011 Hotels & motels

(P-12803)
RENAISSANCE HOTEL MGT CO LLC
Also Called: Marriott
9620 Airport Blvd, Los Angeles
(90045-5402)
PHONE....................310 337-2800
Gregory Lehman, *Manager*
Jenny Ulch, *Finance*
EMP: 300
SALES (corp-wide): 20.7B **Publicly Held**
SIC: 7011 5813 5812 7389 Hotels & motels; drinking places; eating places; office facilities & secretarial service rental
HQ: Renaissance Hotel Operating Company
10400 Fernwood Rd
Bethesda MD 20817

(P-12804)
RENAISSANCE HOTEL MGT CO LLC
Also Called: Renaissance Indian Wells
44400 Indian Wells Ln, Indian Wells
(92210-8708)
PHONE....................760 773-4444
Tom Tabler, *Principal*
EMP: 600
SALES (corp-wide): 20.7B **Publicly Held**
WEB: www.renaissancehotel.com
SIC: 7011 Hotels & motels
HQ: Renaissance Hotel Operating Company
10400 Fernwood Rd
Bethesda MD 20817

(P-12805)
RENAISSANCE HOTEL MGT CO LLC
Also Called: Marriott
905 California St, San Francisco
(94108-2201)
PHONE....................415 989-3500
Bill Love, *Branch Mgr*
Urmilla Amin,
EMP: 167
SALES (corp-wide): 20.7B **Publicly Held**
SIC: 7011 Hotels & motels
HQ: Renaissance Hotel Operating Company
10400 Fernwood Rd
Bethesda MD 20817
-

(P-12806)
RENAISSNCE ESMRALDA RESORT SPA
44400 Indian Wells Ln, Indian Wells
(92210-8708)
PHONE....................760 773-4444
John Kalinski, *Principal*
Terry Venema, *Engineer*
EMP: 70
SALES (est): 5.1MM **Privately Held**
SIC: 7011 Hotels & motels

(P-12807)
RENESON HOTELS INC (PA)
Also Called: Carriage Inn
2700 Junipero Serra Blvd, Daly City
(94015-1634)
PHONE....................650 449-5353
Alrene Flynn, *Chairman*
Garrett Grialou, *President*
Doug Sherer, *CFO*
Diane Grialou, *Admin Sec*
▲ **EMP:** 100
SALES (est): 28.6MM **Privately Held**
WEB: www.renesonhotels.com
SIC: 7011 Hotels & motels

(P-12808)
RENESON HOTELS INC
Also Called: Hotel Britton
112 7th St, San Francisco (94103-2809)
PHONE....................415 621-7001
Norman Onaga, *General Mgr*
EMP: 150
SALES (corp-wide): 28.6MM **Privately Held**
WEB: www.renesonhotels.com
SIC: 7011 Hotels

PA: Reneson Hotels, Inc.
2700 Junipero Serra Blvd
Daly City CA 94015
650 449-5353

(P-12809)
RESERVATION RANCH (PA)
356 Sarina Rd N, Smith River (95567)
P.O. Box 75 (95567-0075)
PHONE....................707 487-3516
Henry L Westbrook III, *Partner*
EMP: 160
SQ FT: 2,000
SALES (est): 5MM **Privately Held**
WEB: www.reservationranch.com
SIC: 7011 0241 Hotels & motels; dairy heifer replacement farm

(P-12810)
RESIDENCE INN BY MARRIOTT
5322 N Diana St, Fresno (93710-6700)
PHONE....................559 222-8900
Juliee May, *Manager*
EMP: 80
SALES (est): 2.3MM **Privately Held**
SIC: 7011 Hotels & motels

(P-12811)
RESIDENCE INN BY MARRIOTT
1700 S Clementine St, Anaheim
(92802-2909)
PHONE....................714 533-3555
Rosa Cook, *General Mgr*
Hai-Ni Chen, *COO*
EMP: 80
SALES (est): 1.3MM **Privately Held**
SIC: 7011 Hotels & motels

(P-12812)
RESIDENCE INN BY MARRIOTT
700 W Kimberly Ave, Placentia
(92870-6329)
PHONE....................714 996-0555
Paulette Lombrodi, *Principal*
Nancy Medrano, *Manager*
EMP: 80
SALES (est): 1.9MM **Privately Held**
SIC: 7011 Hotels & motels

(P-12813)
RESIDENCE INN BY MARRIOTT
11002 Rancho Carmel Dr, San Diego
(92128-4288)
PHONE....................858 673-1900
Casey Grieme, *Manager*
EMP: 80
SALES (est): 1.9MM **Privately Held**
SIC: 7011 Hotels & motels

(P-12814)
RESIDENCE INN BY MARRIOTT LLC
5852 Stadium St, San Diego (92122-3305)
PHONE....................858 587-1770
Joe Kuhn, *Manager*
James Burkel, *Engineer*
EMP: 89
SALES (corp-wide): 20.7B **Publicly Held**
SIC: 7011 Hotels & motels
HQ: Residence Inn By Marriott, Llc
10400 Fernwood Rd
Bethesda MD 20817
301 380-3000

(P-12815)
RESIDENCE INN BY MARRIOTT LLC
38305 Cook St, Palm Desert (92211-1794)
PHONE....................760 776-0050
Michael Gerano, *Branch Mgr*
EMP: 167
SALES (corp-wide): 20.7B **Publicly Held**
SIC: 7011 Hotels & motels
HQ: Residence Inn By Marriott, Llc
10400 Fernwood Rd
Bethesda MD 20817
301 380-3000

(P-12816)
RESIDENCE INN BY MARRIOTT LLC
2135 E El Segundo Blvd, El Segundo
(90245-4503)
PHONE....................310 333-0888
Ray Cruickshanks, *Manager*

EMP: 167
SALES (corp-wide): 20.7B **Publicly Held**
SIC: 7011 Hotels & motels
HQ: Residence Inn By Marriott, Llc
10400 Fernwood Rd
Bethesda MD 20817
301 380-3000

(P-12817)
RESIDENCE INN BY MARRIOTT LLC
5400 Kearny Mesa Rd, San Diego
(92111-1394)
PHONE....................858 278-2100
Doug Former, *Branch Mgr*
Shirley Walker, *President*
Jonathan Correll, *General Mgr*
EMP: 167
SALES (corp-wide): 20.7B **Publicly Held**
SIC: 7011 Hotels & motels
HQ: Residence Inn By Marriott, Llc
10400 Fernwood Rd
Bethesda MD 20817
301 380-3000

(P-12818)
RESIDENCE INN BY MARRIOTT LLC
2025 Convention Ctr Way, Ontario
(91764-4450)
PHONE....................909 937-6788
Frank Palacios, *General Mgr*
Carlos Mendoza, *General Mgr*
EMP: 167
SALES (corp-wide): 20.7B **Publicly Held**
SIC: 7011 Hotels & motels
HQ: Residence Inn By Marriott, Llc
10400 Fernwood Rd
Bethesda MD 20817
301 380-3000

(P-12819)
RESIDENCE INN BY MARRIOTT LLC
1015 Montecito Dr, Corona (92879-1760)
PHONE....................951 371-0107
Fred Kokash, *Branch Mgr*
EMP: 167
SALES (corp-wide): 20.7B **Publicly Held**
SIC: 7011 Hotels & motels
HQ: Residence Inn By Marriott, Llc
10400 Fernwood Rd
Bethesda MD 20817
301 380-3000

(P-12820)
RESIDENCE INN BY MARRIOTT LLC
4111 E Willow St, Long Beach
(90815-1740)
PHONE....................562 595-0909
Lucas Fiamengo, *Manager*
Juan Ochoa, *Chief Engr*
EMP: 167
SALES (corp-wide): 20.7B **Publicly Held**
SIC: 7011 Hotels & motels
HQ: Residence Inn By Marriott, Llc
10400 Fernwood Rd
Bethesda MD 20817
301 380-3000

(P-12821)
RESIDENCE INN BY MARRIOTT LLC
700 Ellinwood Way, Pleasant Hill
(94523-4700)
PHONE....................925 689-1010
Trish Snowden, *Principal*
EMP: 167
SALES (corp-wide): 20.7B **Publicly Held**
SIC: 7011 Hotels & motels
HQ: Residence Inn By Marriott, Llc
10400 Fernwood Rd
Bethesda MD 20817
301 380-3000

(P-12822)
RESIDNCE INN BY MRRIOTT IRVINE
10 Morgan, Irvine (92618-2003)
PHONE....................949 380-3000
Camillo Bruce, *Manager*
Oscar Garcia, *Opers Mgr*
EMP: 80

SALES (est): 2.1MM **Privately Held**
SIC: 7011 Hotels & motels

(P-12823)
RESORT AT PELICAN HILL LLC
22701 Pelican Hill Rd S, Newport Coast
(92657-2008)
PHONE....................949 467-6800
Elia Gutierrez, *Director*
Monique Sagapolutele, *Officer*
Tim La Duke, *Executive*
Jon Martin, *General Mgr*
Hania Martin, *Admin Asst*
EMP: 187 **EST:** 2006
SALES (est): 23.4MM **Privately Held**
SIC: 7011 Resort hotel

(P-12824)
RIO VISTA DEVELOPMENT COMPANY (PA)
Also Called: Holiday Inn
4222 Vineland Ave, North Hollywood
(91602-3318)
PHONE....................818 980-8000
Scott A Mills, *Principal*
Scott Mills, *General Mgr*
Khondaker Bashar, *Controller*
Elizabeth Jacobs, *Human Res Dir*
Rhocelli Pascual, *Marketing Mgr*
EMP: 135
SQ FT: 100,000
SALES (est): 13.5MM **Privately Held**
WEB: www.beverlygarland.com
SIC: 7011 Hotels & motels

(P-12825)
RITZ-CARLTON HOTEL COMPANY LLC
690 Market St, San Francisco
(94104-5101)
PHONE....................415 781-9000
John Fitzgerald, *Branch Mgr*
EMP: 343
SALES (corp-wide): 20.7B **Publicly Held**
SIC: 7011 Hotels & motels
HQ: The Ritz-Carlton Hotel Company Llc
10400 Fernwood Rd
Bethesda MD 20817
301 380-3000

(P-12826)
RITZ-CARLTON HOTEL COMPANY LLC
Also Called: Ritz Carlton
68900 Frank Sinatra Dr, Rancho Mirage
(92270-5300)
PHONE....................760 321-8282
EMP: 349
SALES (corp-wide): 20.7B **Publicly Held**
SIC: 7011 Hotels & motels
HQ: The Ritz-Carlton Hotel Company Llc
10400 Fernwood Rd
Bethesda MD 20817
301 380-3000

(P-12827)
RITZ-CARLTON HOTEL COMPANY LLC
1 Ritz Carlton Dr, Dana Point (92629-4206)
PHONE....................949 240-5020
Janinie Vanderoy, *Branch Mgr*
Lisa Holladay, *Vice Pres*
Samantha Boone, *Executive*
Cristiano Buono, *General Mgr*
Mike Kass, *General Mgr*
EMP: 348
SALES (corp-wide): 20.7B **Publicly Held**
SIC: 7011 Hotels & motels
HQ: The Ritz-Carlton Hotel Company Llc
10400 Fernwood Rd
Bethesda MD 20817
301 380-3000

(P-12828)
RITZ-CARLTON HOTEL COMPANY LLC
8301 Hollister Ave, Santa Barbara
(93117-2474)
PHONE....................805 968-0100
EMP: 650
SALES (corp-wide): 20.7B **Publicly Held**
SIC: 7011 Hotels & motels

HQ: The Ritz-Carlton Hotel Company Llc
10400 Fernwood Rd
Bethesda MD 20817
301 380-3000

(P-12829)
RITZ-CARLTON HOTEL COMPANY LLC
Also Called: Ritz-Carlton San Francisco
600 Stockton St, San Francisco
(94108-2386)
PHONE...............................415 773-6168
Edward Madey, *Manager*
Jo-Anne Hill, *President*
Nickolas Tice, *General Mgr*
Tyler Crist, *Info Tech Dir*
Mwanza Major, *Director*
EMP: 500
SALES (corp-wide): 20.7B **Publicly Held**
WEB: www.ritz-carlton.com
SIC: 7011 Hotels & motels
HQ: The Ritz-Carlton Hotel Company Llc
10400 Fernwood Rd
Bethesda MD 20817
301 380-3000

(P-12830)
RITZ-CARLTON HOTEL COMPANY LLC
Also Called: Ritz Carlton Rancho Mirage
68900 Frank Sinatra Dr, Rancho Mirage
(92270-5300)
PHONE...............................760 321-8282
James H Palllin Jr, *Manager*
EMP: 313
SALES (corp-wide): 20.7B **Publicly Held**
WEB: www.ritz-carlton.com
SIC: 7011 Hotels & motels
HQ: The Ritz-Carlton Hotel Company Llc
10400 Fernwood Rd
Bethesda MD 20817
301 380-3000

(P-12831)
RITZ-CARLTON MARINA DEL REY
4375 Admiralty Way, Marina Del Rey
(90292-5434)
PHONE...............................310 823-1700
Robert Thomas, *Principal*
Don Quimby, *Manager*
EMP: 81
SALES (est): 5.3MM **Privately Held**
SIC: 7011 Hotels & motels

(P-12832)
RIVER ROCK ENTERTAINMENT AUTH
Also Called: River Rock Casino
3250 Highway 128, Geyserville
(95441-8908)
P.O. Box 607 (95441-0607)
PHONE...............................707 857-2777
David Fendrick, *CEO*
Joseph R Callahan, *CFO*
Yola Bawlec, *Exec Sec*
EMP: 616
SALES (est): 14.1MM **Privately Held**
SIC: 7011 Casino hotel

(P-12833)
RIVIERA REINCARNATE LLC
Also Called: Palm Sprng Riviera Resorts Spa
1600 N Indian Canyon Dr, Palm Springs
(92262-4602)
PHONE...............................760 327-8311
Jim Manion,
EMP: 78
SALES (est): 10.1MM **Privately Held**
SIC: 7011 Resort hotel

(P-12834)
RLJ HGN EMERYVILLE LESSEE LP
Also Called: Hilton Garden Inn Emeryville
1800 Powell St, Emeryville (94608-1808)
PHONE...............................510 658-9300
EMP: 99
SQ FT: 89,000
SALES (est): 559.6K **Privately Held**
SIC: 7011 Hotels & motels

(P-12835)
RLJHGN EMERYVILLE LESSEE LP
Also Called: Hilton
1800 Powell St, Emeryville (94608-1808)
PHONE...............................510 658-9300
Mark Burden, *CEO*
Jeff Virgil, *CFO*
EMP: 120
SQ FT: 476
SALES (est): 5.5MM **Privately Held**
SIC: 7011 Hotels & motels

(P-12836)
RMS FOUNDATION INC
Also Called: Queen Mary Hotel
1126 Queens Hwy, Long Beach
(90802-6331)
PHONE...............................562 435-3511
Joseph F Prevratil, *President*
Jazmin Loya, *Hum Res Coord*
Christopher Wilmoth, *Marketing Staff*
Lea Quiambao, *Sales Staff*
Karen Sellers, *Sales Staff*
EMP: 650
SQ FT: 750,000
SALES (est): 29.7MM **Privately Held**
WEB: www.queenmary.com
SIC: 7011 Hotels & motels
PA: City Of Long Beach
411 W Ocean Blvd
Long Beach CA 90802
562 570-6450

(P-12837)
ROOSEVELT HOTEL LLC
Also Called: Hollywood Roosevelt Hotel
7000 Hollywood Blvd, Los Angeles
(90028-6003)
PHONE...............................323 466-7000
Goodwin Gaw, *Mng Member*
Timothy Suh, *Accounting Mgr*
Michelle Soliman, *Asst Controller*
Colleen Jimenez, *Controller*
Maselina Taulanga, *Purch Mgr*
EMP: 200
SALES (est): 16.8MM **Privately Held**
WEB: www.hollywoodroosevelt.com
SIC: 7011 5813 5812 Hotels; drinking places; eating places

(P-12838)
ROPPONGI-TAHOE LP A CALIFORNI
Also Called: Lake Tahoe Resort Hotel
4130 Lake Tahoe Blvd, South Lake Tahoe
(96150-6965)
PHONE...............................530 544-5400
Kunihiro Nakayabu, *Managing Prtnr*
Masaru Saito, *Managing Prtnr*
Joseph McDaniel, *Controller*
Bill Cottrill, *Marketing Staff*
EMP: 200
SALES (est): 12MM **Privately Held**
WEB: www.embassytahoe.com
SIC: 7011 Resort hotel; hotels

(P-12839)
ROSANNA INC
Also Called: Avenue of Arts Wyndham Hotel
3350 Avenue Of The Arts, Costa Mesa
(92626-1913)
PHONE...............................714 751-5100
Nick Price, *General Mgr*
Rachael Moorhead, *President*
Paul Sanford, *CEO*
Rosanna Chan, *Principal*
Tony Birge, *Chief Engr*
EMP: 151
SALES (est): 9.4MM **Privately Held**
SIC: 7011 5812 Hotels; food bars; caterers

(P-12840)
ROSCOE REAL ESTATE LTD PARTNR
Also Called: Elkor Properties
1819 Ocean Ave, Santa Monica
(90401-3215)
PHONE...............................310 260-7500
Vincent Piro, *General Mgr*
Elkor Trio LL LLC, *General Ptnr*
EMP: 80

SALES (est): 3.7MM **Privately Held**
WEB: www.viceroysantamonica.com
SIC: 7011 7389 Hotels; hotel & motel reservation service

(P-12841)
ROSEVILLE TOWNE PLACE SUITES
10569 Fairway Dr, Roseville (95678-3570)
PHONE...............................916 782-2232
Gary Tharaldson, *Principal*
Lynda Abrams, *Principal*
EMP: 99
SALES (est): 1.5MM **Privately Held**
SIC: 7011 Hotel, franchised

(P-12842)
ROYAL GORGE NORDIC SKI RESORT (PA)
Also Called: Royal Gorge Crss Cntry Ski Rst
9411 Hillside Rd, Soda Springs (95728)
PHONE...............................530 426-3871
John Slouber, *President*
Frances Wiesel, *Admin Sec*
EMP: 150 EST: 1971
SQ FT: 50,000
SALES (est): 3.7MM **Privately Held**
SIC: 7011 Resort hotel

(P-12843)
ROYAL HOSPITALITY INCORPORATED
Also Called: Ramada Inn
5550 Kearny Mesa Rd, San Diego
(92111-1304)
PHONE...............................858 278-0800
Maurice Coreia, *President*
EMP: 60
SQ FT: 63,000
SALES (est): 4.6MM **Privately Held**
WEB: www.ramadasandiego.com
SIC: 7011 Hotels & motels

(P-12844)
RP SCS WSD HOTEL LLC
Also Called: W San Diego Hotel
421 W B St, San Diego (92101-3501)
PHONE...............................619 398-3020
Michael O'Donohue, *General Mgr*
Maria Veronica Rodriguez, *Finance Dir*
EMP: 60
SALES (est): 4.9MM **Privately Held**
SIC: 7011 Hotel, franchised

(P-12845)
RP/KINETIC PARC 55 OWNER LLC
Also Called: Parc 55 Hotel
55 Cyril Magnin St, San Francisco
(94102-2812)
PHONE...............................415 392-8000
Steve Barick,
Joeann Lamadrid, *President*
Peter Beheda, *Senior VP*
Gary Gutierrez, *Vice Pres*
Rob Gauthier, *General Mgr*
EMP: 450
SALES (est): 21.1MM **Privately Held**
SALES (corp-wide): 6.8B **Publicly Held**
WEB: www.parc55hotel.com
SIC: 7011 Hotels
PA: The Blackstone Group Inc
345 Park Ave Ste 1100
New York NY 10154
212 583-5000

(P-12846)
RPC OLD TOWN AVENUE OWNER LLC
Also Called: Fairfield Inn
3900 Old Town Ave, San Diego
(92110-2904)
PHONE...............................619 299-7400
Evan Hitter, *Director*
Amber Wilson, *Executive*
EMP: 55
SALES (est): 1.3MM **Privately Held**
SIC: 7011 Hotels & motels

(P-12847)
RPC OLD TOWN JEFFERSON
Also Called: San Diego Old Town
2435 Jefferson St, San Diego
(92110-3026)
PHONE...............................619 725-4221

Budd Barmeyer, *General Mgr*
Amberly Edmond, *Sales Staff*
Evan Hitter, *Director*
EMP: 60
SQ FT: 5,000
SALES (est): 4.5MM **Privately Held**
WEB: www.sunstonehotels.com
SIC: 7011 Hotel, franchised

(P-12848)
RPD HOTELS 18 LLC (PA)
Also Called: Vagabond Inns
2361 Rosecrans Ave # 150, El Segundo
(90245-7906)
PHONE...............................213 746-1531
Juan Sanchez Llaca, *President*
Don Johnson,
Stewart Rubin,
EMP: 800
SALES (est): 26MM **Privately Held**
SIC: 7011 Motels

(P-12849)
RT PASAD HOTEL PARTNERS LP
Also Called: Courtyard By Marriott
180 N Fair Oaks Ave, Pasadena
(91103-3614)
PHONE...............................626 403-7600
Timothy Bristol, *General Mgr*
Luis Guzman, *Plant Mgr*
EMP: 140
SQ FT: 165,342
SALES (est): 7.2MM **Privately Held**
SIC: 7011 Hotels & motels

(P-12850)
RT SAN DIEGO LLC
Also Called: Residence Inn San Diego
5400 Kearny Mesa Rd, San Diego
(92111-1303)
PHONE...............................858 278-2100
Allan V Rose, *General Mgr*
Adam Lutz, *General Mgr*
Lily Ann Marten,
EMP: 50
SALES (est): 8.3MM **Privately Held**
SIC: 7011 Hotel, franchised

(P-12851)
RT SD-DENVER LP
Also Called: Residnc By Mria San Dego Cntl
5400 Kearny Mesa Rd, San Diego
(92111-1303)
PHONE...............................858 278-2100
J Correll, *General Mgr*
Jonathan Correll, *General Mgr*
EMP: 50
SALES (est): 131.9K **Privately Held**
SIC: 7011 Hotels & motels

(P-12852)
RUBICON B HACIENDA LLC
Also Called: Fairfield Inn
525 N Pacific Coast Hwy, El Segundo
(90245-4496)
PHONE...............................424 290-5000
Marc Gordon,
EMP: 56
SALES (est): 841.9K **Privately Held**
SIC: 7011 Hotels & motels

(P-12853)
RUBICON B HACIENDA LLC
Also Called: Aloft El Sgnd-Los Angles Arprt
475 N Pacific Coast Hwy, El Segundo
(90245-4446)
PHONE...............................424 290-5555
Ped Prembaph, *General Mgr*
Marc Gordon,
EMP: 87
SALES (est): 495.5K **Privately Held**
SIC: 7011 Hotels & motels

(P-12854)
RUFFIN HOTEL CORP OF CAL
Also Called: Long Beach Marriott
4700 Airport Plaza Dr, Long Beach
(90815-1252)
PHONE...............................562 425-5210
Phillip G Ruffin, *President*
Jennifer Robinson, *Director*
EMP: 260

P R O D U C T S & S V C S

SALES (est): 13.8MM **Privately Held**
WEB: www.lbmarriott.com
SIC: **7011** 5812 5813 Hotels; eating places; coffee shop; drinking places

(P-12855)
RYDE HOTEL LLC
Also Called: Ryde Motel
14340 State Highway 160, Walnut Grove (95690-9742)
PHONE...................................916 776-1318
Toll Free:..................................888 -
Janice G Leroy,
EMP: 50 EST: 1997
SALES (est): 1.5MM **Privately Held**
WEB: www.rydehotel.com
SIC: **7011** 5812 Hotels; eating places

(P-12856)
S R H H INC
Also Called: Radisson Inn
1085 E El Camino Real, Sunnyvale (94087-3755)
PHONE...................................408 247-0800
Donald Bramer, *President*
Gaylon Patterson, *Treasurer*
John Branagh, *Admin Sec*
EMP: 50
SQ FT: 150,000
SALES (est): 1.3MM **Privately Held**
SIC: **7011** 5812 5813 Hotels & motels; American restaurant; cocktail lounge

(P-12857)
S W K PROPERTIES LLC
Also Called: Holiday Inn
2726 S Grand Ave Lbby, Santa Ana (92705-5404)
PHONE...................................714 481-6300
Rod Hurt, *Manager*
Barbara Smith, *Info Tech Mgr*
Frank Atayde, *Manager*
EMP: 66
SALES (est): 2.6MM
SALES (corp-wide): 3.4MM **Privately Held**
SIC: **7011** Hotels & motels
PA: S W K Properties Llc
3807 Wilshire Blvd # 1226
Los Angeles CA 90010
213 383-9204

(P-12858)
S W K PROPERTIES LLC (PA)
Also Called: Sheraton Ontario Airport Hotel
3807 Wilshire Blvd # 1226, Los Angeles (90010-3101)
PHONE...................................213 383-9204
Eric Cha,
EMP: 199
SQ FT: 3,000
SALES (est): 3.4MM **Privately Held**
SIC: **7011** Hotels & motels

(P-12859)
SACRAMENTO HOTEL PARTNERS LLC
100 Capitol Mall, Sacramento (95814-3244)
PHONE...................................916 326-5000
Vishwa Nand, *Manager*
EMP: 90
SALES (corp-wide): 7MM **Privately Held**
WEB: www.essacramento.com
SIC: **7011** Hotels & motels
PA: Sacramento Hotel Partners, Llc
100 Saratoga Ave Ste 300
Santa Clara CA 95051
408 249-2500

(P-12860)
SACRAMENTO HOTEL PARTNERS LLC (PA)
100 Saratoga Ave Ste 300, Santa Clara (95051-7337)
PHONE...................................408 249-2500
John Kehriotis,
EMP: 79
SALES (est): 7MM **Privately Held**
WEB: www.essacramento.com
SIC: **7011** Hotels & motels

(P-12861)
SACRAMNTO FORTY NINER TRVL PLZ
Also Called: Sacramento 49er
2828 El Centro Rd, Sacramento (95833-9602)
PHONE...................................916 927-4774
Tristen Griffith, *President*
Terrace Rust, *Vice Pres*
Matthew Hiibel, *Manager*
Paul Millette, *Manager*
EMP: 125 EST: 1976
SQ FT: 27,000
SALES (est): 7.8MM **Privately Held**
WEB: www.sacramento49er.com
SIC: **7011** 5331 5812 5541 Motels; variety stores; restaurant, family: independent; truck stops

(P-12862)
SAGA SEAL CO LTD
Also Called: Pacific Inn, The
600 Marina Dr, Seal Beach (90740-6123)
PHONE...................................562 493-7501
Steve Bader, *President*
Gene Sugita, *General Mgr*
EMP: 80
SQ FT: 33,597
SALES (est): 4.3MM **Privately Held**
SIC: **7011** Hotels

(P-12863)
SAGE HOSPITALITY RESOURCES LLC
Also Called: Courtyard By Marriott
700 W Huntington Dr, Monrovia (91016-3104)
PHONE...................................626 357-5211
Dennis Hollingdrake, *Manager*
EMP: 100
SALES (corp-wide): 336.9MM **Privately Held**
WEB: www.21chotel.com
SIC: **7011** Hotels & motels
PA: Sage Hospitality Resources L.L.C.
1575 Welton St Ste 300
Denver CO 80202
303 595-7200

(P-12864)
SAGE HOSPITALITY RESOURCES LLC
Also Called: Homewood Suites Hilton Sfo
2000 Shoreline Ct, Brisbane (94005-1802)
PHONE...................................650 589-1600
Gina Merz, *Branch Mgr*
EMP: 67
SALES (corp-wide): 336.9MM **Privately Held**
WEB: www.21chotel.com
SIC: **7011** Hotels & motels
PA: Sage Hospitality Resources L.L.C.
1575 Welton St Ste 300
Denver CO 80202
303 595-7200

(P-12865)
SAJAHTERA INC
Also Called: Beverly Hills Hotel
9641 Sunset Blvd, Beverly Hills (90210-2938)
PHONE...................................310 276-2251
Junaidi Masri, *President*
Mark Kirk, *Engineer*
Porfirio Caamal, *Accounting Mgr*
Ana Martinez, *Credit Mgr*
Linda Gee, *Accountant*
EMP: 600
SQ FT: 10,758
SALES (est): 44.2MM
SALES (corp-wide): 507.9MM **Privately Held**
WEB: www.sajahtera.com
SIC: **7011** Resort hotel; hotels
HQ: Dorchester Group Limited
57 Berkeley Square
London W1J 6
207 629-4848

(P-12866)
SALT LAKE HOTEL ASSOCIATES LP (PA)
222 Kearny St Ste 200, San Francisco (94108-4537)
PHONE...................................415 397-5572

Tom Lataur, *President*
Paula Harris, *Vice Pres*
Ted Hirschberger, *Vice Pres*
EMP: 111 EST: 1997
SALES (est): 3.5MM **Privately Held**
SIC: **7011** Hotels

(P-12867)
SAN BERNARDINO HILTON (HQ)
285 E Hospitality Ln, San Bernardino (92408-3411)
PHONE...................................909 889-0133
Douglas McCarron, *President*
Morgan McPherson, *Exec Dir*
Ronald Schoen, *Admin Sec*
EMP: 152
SALES (est): 27.6MM
SALES (corp-wide): 49.6MM **Privately Held**
WEB: www.web66.com
SIC: **7011** 6512 5812 Hotels & motels; commercial & industrial building operation; eating places
PA: Carpenters Southwest Administrative Corporation
533 S Fremont Ave
Los Angeles CA 90071
213 386-8590

(P-12868)
SAN DEGO MRROTT MARQUIS MARINA
333 W Harbor Dr, San Diego (92101-7709)
PHONE...................................301 380-3000
Ray Warren, *Principal*
Michele Elstrom, *Executive*
Traci Russell, *Executive*
Anna Shaw, *Executive*
Erikk Hilgert, *General Mgr*
EMP: 50
SALES (est): 4.1MM **Privately Held**
SIC: **7011** Resort hotel

(P-12869)
SAN DIEGO FARAH PARTNERS
Also Called: Holiday Inn
1430 7th Ave Ste B, San Diego (92101-2815)
PHONE...................................619 239-2261
Berham Baxter, *General Ptnr*
EMP: 50
SQ FT: 99,999
SALES (est): 2.1MM **Privately Held**
SIC: **7011** Hotels & motels

(P-12870)
SAN DIEGO HOTEL COMPANY LLC
Also Called: Marriott San Dego Gslamp Qrter
660 K St, San Diego (92101-7036)
PHONE...................................619 696-0234
James Evans, *CFO*
Dennis Darabie, *Director*
EMP: 135
SALES (est): 6.2MM **Privately Held**
WEB: www.sheratonuptown.com
SIC: **7011** Hotels

(P-12871)
SAN DIEGO HOTEL LEASE LLC
Also Called: Courtyard By Marriott
530 Broadway, San Diego (92101-5206)
PHONE...................................619 446-3000
J W Marriott, *Chairman*
Arne M Sorenson, *CEO*
Carl T Berquist, *Exec VP*
Allina Boohoff, *Mng Member*
EMP: 200
SQ FT: 126,742
SALES (est): 6MM **Privately Held**
SIC: **7011** Hotels & motels

(P-12872)
SAN DIEGO LESSEE LLC
Also Called: Doubletree By Hilton
7450 Hazard Center Dr, San Diego (92108-4539)
PHONE...................................619 297-5466
Owen Wilcox,
Kevin J Jacobs, *CFO*
Sean Dell'orto, *Treasurer*
Kristin Campbell, *Exec VP*
Joseph Berger, *Senior VP*
EMP: 140

SALES: 20.3MM
SALES (corp-wide): 2.7B **Publicly Held**
SIC: **7011** Hotels & motels
PA: Park Hotels & Resorts Inc.
1775 Tysons Blvd Fl 7
Tysons VA 22102
571 302-5757

(P-12873)
SAN FRANCISCO HOTEL ASSOCIATES
Also Called: Masa's
650 Bush St, San Francisco (94108-3509)
PHONE...................................415 392-4666
Michael Lennon, *Partner*
EMP: 80
SQ FT: 46,067
SALES (est): 1.8MM **Privately Held**
WEB: www.vintagecourt.com
SIC: **7011** 5812 Hotels; French restaurant

(P-12874)
SAN FRANCISCO HOTEL GROUP LLC
Also Called: Loews Regency San Francisco
222 Sansome St, San Francisco (94104-2703)
PHONE...................................415 276-9888
Yue-Tin Chang, *President*
Jonathan Tisch, *Chairman*
Tracy Lee, *Controller*
EMP: 183
SALES (est): 7.1MM
SALES (corp-wide): 14B **Publicly Held**
SIC: **7011** Resort hotel
HQ: Loews Hotels Holding Corporation
667 Madison Ave
New York NY 10065
212 521-2000

(P-12875)
SAN JOSE AIRPORT GARDEN HOTEL
1740 N 1st St, San Jose (95112-4508)
PHONE...................................408 793-3300
EMP: 99
SALES (est): 2.2MM **Privately Held**
SIC: **7011**

(P-12876)
SAN JOSE AIRPORT HOTEL LLC
Also Called: Holiday Inn
1740 N 1st St, San Jose (95112)
PHONE...................................408 793-3939
Manou Mobedshahi, *Mng Member*
Harry Engineer,
EMP: 230
SALES (est): 6.2MM **Privately Held**
SIC: **7011** Hotels & motels

(P-12877)
SAN JOSE FAIRMONT LESSEE LLC
170 S Market St Lbby, San Jose (95113-2361)
PHONE...................................408 998-1900
Cirilo Custodio,
Alberto Mansilla, *Purch Mgr*
EMP: 500
SALES: 69MM
SALES (corp-wide): 1.1B **Privately Held**
WEB: www.cp.ca
SIC: **7011** 5812 5813 Resort hotel; ethnic food restaurants; cocktail lounge
PA: Accor
82 Rue Henry Farman
Issy-Les-Moulineaux 92130
146 429-193

(P-12878)
SAN MARCOS CATERERS INC
Also Called: Quails Inn Motel
1025 La Bonita Dr, San Marcos (92078-5220)
PHONE...................................760 744-0120
Gordon N Frazar, *President*
Ronald Frazar, *Corp Secy*
Dodi Holiday, *General Mgr*
EMP: 60 EST: 1962
SALES (est): 4.3MM **Privately Held**
WEB: www.lakesanmarcosresort.com
SIC: **7011** 5812 Motels; caterers

(P-12879)
SAN PSQUAL BAND MSSION INDIANS
Also Called: Valley View Casino
16300 Nyemii Pass Rd, Valley Center
(92082-6769)
P.O. Box 2379 (92082-2379)
PHONE....................................760 291-5500
Toll Free:..........................866 -
Bruce Howards, *General Mgr*
Don Haig, *President*
Edward Gutierrez, *Supervisor*
EMP: 500 **Privately Held**
WEB: www.sanpasqualindians.org
SIC: 7011 Casino hotel
PA: San Pasqual Band Of Mission Indians
16400 Kumeyaay Way
Valley Center CA 92082

(P-12880)
SAN PSQUAL CSINO DEV GROUP INC
Also Called: Valley View Casino
16300 Nyemii Pass Rd, Valley Center
(92082-6769)
PHONE....................................760 291-5500
Joe Navarro, *President*
Michael Gorczynski, *Treasurer*
Al Cope, *Vice Pres*
Howard Silver, *Vice Pres*
Michael Caputto, *Security Dir*
EMP: 50
SQ FT: 62,000
SALES (est): 5MM **Privately Held**
SIC: 7011 Casino hotel
PA: San Pasqual Band Of Mission Indians
16400 Kumeyaay Way
Valley Center CA 92082

(P-12881)
SAN RAFAEL HILLCREST LLC
Also Called: Four Points San Rafael
1010 Northgate Dr, San Rafael
(94903-2502)
PHONE....................................415 479-8800
Beth Gamble,
EMP: 51
SQ FT: 50,000
SALES (est): 474.1K **Privately Held**
SIC: 7011 Hotels & motels

(P-12882)
SANDM SAN DEGO MRRIOTT DEL MAR
11966 El Camino Real, San Diego
(92130-2592)
PHONE....................................858 523-1700
Jenessa Schaniel, *Principal*
John Peart, *General Mgr*
EMP: 1000
SALES (est): 870.1K **Privately Held**
SIC: 7011 Hotels

(P-12883)
SANDWICH SPOT (PA)
1630 18th St, Sacramento (95811-6702)
PHONE....................................916 492-2613
Tom Heally, *Principal*
EMP: 61
SALES (est): 8.4MM **Privately Held**
SIC: 7011 Bed & breakfast inn

(P-12884)
SANTA CLARA TENANT CORP
Also Called: Embassy Suites- Santa Clara
2885 Lakeside Dr, Santa Clara
(95054-2805)
PHONE....................................408 496-6400
T Owens, *General Mgr*
Teri Owens, *General Mgr*
EMP: 90
SALES (est): 4MM
SALES (corp-wide): 1.4B **Privately Held**
SIC: 7011 Hotels & motels
PA: Ashford Hospitality Trust Inc
14185 Dallas Pkwy # 1100
Dallas TX 75254
972 490-9600

(P-12885)
SANTA CRUZ HOTEL ASSOCIATES
Also Called: West Coast Santa Cruz Hotel
175 W Cliff Dr, Santa Cruz (95060-5438)
PHONE....................................831 426-4330
Brian Corbell, *President*
EMP: 150
SALES (est): 2.4MM **Privately Held**
SIC: 7011 Resort hotel

(P-12886)
SANTA MARIA HOTEL CORP
Also Called: Holiday Inn
2100 N Broadway, Santa Maria
(93454-1140)
PHONE....................................805 928-6000
Lawrence Lui, *President*
EMP: 88
SALES (est): 4.6MM **Privately Held**
SIC: 7011 5812 7389 Hotels & motels;
eating places; convention & show services

(P-12887)
SANTA MONICA HOTEL OWNER LLC
Also Called: Doubletree Suites By Hilton SA
1707 4th St, Santa Monica (90401-3301)
PHONE....................................310 395-3332
EMP: 135
SALES (est): 3.8MM **Privately Held**
SIC: 7011 Hotels & motels

(P-12888)
SANTA MONICA HSR LTD PARTNR
Also Called: Doubletree Hotel
1707 4th St, Santa Monica (90401-3301)
PHONE....................................310 395-3332
Shashi Poudyal, *Manager*
EMP: 160
SALES (est): 4.5MM **Privately Held**
WEB: www.doubletreesantamonica.com
SIC: 7011 5812 Hotels & motels; eating places

(P-12889)
SANTA MONICA PROPER JV LLC
700 Wilshire Blvd, Santa Monica
(90401-1708)
PHONE....................................310 620-9990
Brad Korzen, *CEO*
EMP: 250
SALES (est): 51.2MM **Privately Held**
SIC: 7011 Hotels

(P-12890)
SANTANA ROW HOTEL PARTNERS LP
355 Santana Row Ste 1010, San Jose
(95128-2050)
PHONE....................................408 551-0010
Bonnie Best, *General Mgr*
EMP: 200 **Privately Held**
SIC: 7011 Hotels
PA: Santana Row Hotel Partners Lp
4400 Post Oak Pkwy Ste 16
Houston TX 77027

(P-12891)
SARATOGA CAPITAL INC
Also Called: Hotel De Anza
233 W Santa Clara St, San Jose
(95113-1710)
PHONE....................................408 286-1000
Alison McAennon, *Manager*
EMP: 65
SALES (corp-wide): 19.7MM **Privately Held**
WEB: www.saratogacapital.net
SIC: 7011 Hotels & motels
HQ: Saratoga Capital, Inc.
485 Alberto Way Ste 200
Los Gatos CA 95032
408 298-8600

(P-12892)
SAVE QUEEN LLC
429 Shoreline Village Dr I, Long Beach
(90802-8136)
PHONE....................................562 435-3511

Sean Meddock, *Mng Member*
Sonja West, *Accounts Mgr*
EMP: 500 EST: 2007
SALES (est): 15.9MM **Privately Held**
SIC: 7011 Hotels

(P-12893)
SC HARP EL SEGUNDO LLC
1985 E Grand Ave, El Segundo
(90245-5015)
PHONE....................................310 322-0999
Dave Harvey, *Mng Member*
EMP: 84
SALES (est): 950K **Privately Held**
SIC: 7011 Hotels & motels

(P-12894)
SD HOTEL CIRCLE LLC
Also Called: Homewood Suites San Diego Hote
2201 Hotel Cir S, San Diego (92108-3315)
PHONE....................................619 881-6800
Mayur Patel, *Principal*
Louisa Yeung, *Administration*
EMP: 75
SALES (est): 256.8K **Privately Held**
SIC: 7011 Hotels & motels

(P-12895)
SD STADIUM HOTEL LLC
Also Called: Hilton Garded
3805 Murphy Canyon Rd, San Diego
(92123-4404)
PHONE....................................858 278-9300
Mayur Patel,
Michael Mc Cullough, *Info Tech Dir*
Mark Avenido, *Chief Engr*
Leeling Kirven, *Sales Staff*
EMP: 100
SALES (est): 2.8MM **Privately Held**
WEB: www.hioldtownhotel.com
SIC: 7011 Hotels & motels

(P-12896)
SE SAN DIEGO HOTEL LLC
1047 5th Ave, San Diego (92101-5101)
PHONE....................................619 515-3000
Ador Bustamante, *Director*
Amy Cannon, *Counsel*
EMP: 51
SALES (est): 4.5MM **Privately Held**
SIC: 7011 Resort hotel

(P-12897)
SEACLIFF INN INC
Also Called: Best Western
7500 Old Dominion Ct, Aptos (95003-3807)
PHONE....................................831 661-4671
Frank Giuliani, *President*
T J Scott, *Treasurer*
Norm BEI, *Vice Pres*
Coleen Giuliani, *Admin Sec*
Gustavo Heredia, *Maintence Staff*
EMP: 90
SQ FT: 60,000
SALES (est): 5.6MM **Privately Held**
WEB: www.seacliffinn.com
SIC: 7011 Hotels & motels

(P-12898)
SEASCAPE RESORT LTD A CALIF
Also Called: Sanderlings
19 Seascape Vlg, Aptos (95003-6102)
PHONE....................................831 662-7120
Mark Holcomb, *General Ptnr*
EMP: 300
SQ FT: 45,000
SALES (est): 8MM **Privately Held**
WEB: www.seascaperesort.com
SIC: 7011 Resort hotel

(P-12899)
SEASIDE LAGUNA INN & SUITES
1661 S Coast Hwy, Laguna Beach
(92651-3228)
PHONE....................................949 494-9717
Tino Farjad, *General Mgr*
EMP: 51
SQ FT: 27,500
SALES (est): 925.4K **Privately Held**
WEB: www.seacliffmotel.com
SIC: 7011 Hotels; motels

(P-12900)
SECOND STREET CORPORATION
Also Called: Huntley Hotel Santa Monica Bch
1111 2nd St, Santa Monica (90403-5003)
PHONE....................................310 394-5454
Sohrab Sassounian, *President*
Dora Levy, *Shareholder*
Marschinda Felix, *COO*
Helal M El-Sherif, *CFO*
Shiva Aghaipour, *Vice Pres*
EMP: 250
SQ FT: 185,000
SALES (est): 17MM **Privately Held**
SIC: 7011 5812 Hotels; eating places

(P-12901)
SELECT HOTELS GROUP LLC
Also Called: Hyatt Pl Fremont/Silicon Vly
3101 W Warren Ave, Fremont
(94538-6428)
PHONE....................................510 623-6000
John McEngee, *Manager*
EMP: 50
SALES (corp-wide): 4.4B **Publicly Held**
WEB: www.amerisuites.com
SIC: 7011 Hotels & motels
HQ: Select Hotels Group, L.L.C.
71 S Wacker Dr
Chicago IL 60606
312 750-1234

(P-12902)
SELECT HOTELS GROUP LLC
Also Called: Hyatt House Rancho Cordova
11260 Point East Dr, Rancho Cordova
(95742-6232)
PHONE....................................916 638-4141
Brett Tmekei, *General Mgr*
EMP: 50
SALES (corp-wide): 4.4B **Publicly Held**
WEB: www.hallmarksuites.com
SIC: 7011 Hotels
HQ: Select Hotels Group, L.L.C.
71 S Wacker Dr
Chicago IL 60606
312 750-1234

(P-12903)
SELVI-VIDOVICH LP
Also Called: Grand Hotel The
865 W El Camino Real, Sunnyvale
(94087-1154)
PHONE....................................408 720-8500
John Vidovich, *Managing Prtnr*
Al Selvi, *Partner*
EMP: 70
SQ FT: 90,805
SALES (est): 3.8MM **Privately Held**
WEB: www.thegrandhotel.com
SIC: 7011 Hotels

(P-12904)
SERVICE HOSPITALITY LLC
1050 Burnett Ave, Concord (94520-5713)
PHONE....................................925 566-8820
Maryann Rhoe,
EMP: 70
SALES (est): 443.3K **Privately Held**
SIC: 7011 Seasonal hotel

(P-12905)
SETHI MANAGEMENT INC
183 Calle Magdalena # 101, Encinitas
(92024-3793)
PHONE....................................760 652-4010
J P Sethi, *President*
Ganisha Sethi, *COO*
Gilbert Preciado, *Controller*
EMP: 99
SALES (est): 3.2MM **Privately Held**
SIC: 7011 Hotels & motels

(P-12906)
SEVEN RESORTS INC (PA)
9771 Irvine Center Dr, Irvine (92618-4343)
PHONE....................................949 588-7100
David A Ohanesian, *President*
Jacqueline S Anderson, *Treasurer*
Lynda L Ohanesian-Druan, *Admin Sec*
EMP: 394
SALES (est): 10.7MM **Privately Held**
WEB: www.sevencrown.com
SIC: 7011 Resort hotel

PRODUCTS & SVCS

(P-12907)
SEVEN SEAS ASSOCIATES LLC
Also Called: Seven Seas Best Western
411 Hotel Cir S, San Diego (92108-3402)
PHONE..................................619 291-1300
Joe Toczylowski,
Eisler Family Trust,
Orwitz Family Trust,
Zolt Family Trust,
EMP: 108
SQ FT: 101,000
SALES (est): 8.7MM Privately Held
WEB: www.bw7seas.com
SIC: 7011 Motels

(P-12908)
SFD PARTNERS LLC
Also Called: Sir Francis Drake Hotel
450 Powell St, San Francisco
(94102-1504)
PHONE..................................415 392-7755
John Price, General Mgr
EMP: 350
SALES (est): 2.8MM Privately Held
WEB: www.sirfrancisdrake.com
SIC: 7011 5812 5813 7389 Hotels; eating
places; drinking places; hotel & motel
reservation service

(P-12909)
**SHAMROCK-HOSTMARK PALM
DESRT**
74700 Highway 111, Palm Desert
(92260-3806)
PHONE..................................760 340-6600
Bob Cataldo,
Gerri Lynch,
EMP: 87
SALES (est): 3.1MM Privately Held
SIC: 7011 Hotels & motels

(P-12910)
SHC BURBANK II LLC
Also Called: Marriott
2500 N Hollywood Way, Burbank
(91505-1019)
PHONE..................................818 843-6000
EMP: 210
SALES (est): 10.7MM Privately Held
SIC: 7011

(P-12911)
SHELL VACATIONS LLC
Also Called: Donatello
501 Post St, San Francisco (94102-1228)
PHONE..................................415 441-7100
Alan Hompkins, Principal
EMP: 60 Publicly Held
SIC: 7011 6531 Resort hotel; time-sharing
real estate sales, leasing & rentals
HQ: Shell Vacations L.L.C.
40 Skokie Blvd Ste 350
Northbrook IL 60062

(P-12912)
SHEN ZHEN NEW WORLD II LLC
Also Called: Sheraton Universal Hotel
333 Unversal Hollywood Dr, Universal City
(91608-1001)
PHONE..................................818 980-1212
Ming Yu,
EMP: 99
SALES (est): 3.2MM Privately Held
SIC: 7011 Hotels & motels

(P-12913)
**SHERATON HTL SAN DIEGO
MSN VLY**
Also Called: Sheraton San Diego Mission Vly
1433 Camino Del Rio S, San Diego
(92108-3521)
PHONE..................................619 321-4602
Cynthia Adams Carlin, Administration
Kheam Taing, General Mgr
Yazmin Gutierrez, Controller
Brooke Vandenbrink, Controller
Alicia Ernenwein, Human Res Dir
EMP: 100
SALES (est): 2.7MM Privately Held
SIC: 7011 Hotels & motels

(P-12914)
SHERATON LLC
2500 Mason St, San Francisco
(94133-1450)
PHONE..................................415 362-5500
Jim Sega, Manager
EMP: 300
SALES (corp-wide): 20.7B Publicly Held
SIC: 7011 Hotels & motels
HQ: The Sheraton Llc
1111 Westchester Ave
White Plains NY 10604
800 328-6242

(P-12915)
SHERATON LLC
6101 W Century Blvd, Los Angeles
(90045-5310)
PHONE..................................310 642-1111
Michael Washington, General Mgr
EMP: 500
SALES (corp-wide): 20.7B Publicly Held
SIC: 7011 5813 5812 Hotels & motels;
drinking places; eating places
HQ: The Sheraton Llc
1111 Westchester Ave
White Plains NY 10604
800 328-6242

(P-12916)
SHERATON LLC
1230 J St 13th, Sacramento (95814-2907)
PHONE..................................916 447-1700
Gunter Stannius, Manager
EMP: 328
SALES (corp-wide): 20.7B Publicly Held
WEB: www.sheraton.com
SIC: 7011 Hotels & motels
HQ: The Sheraton Llc
1111 Westchester Ave
White Plains NY 10604
800 328-6242

(P-12917)
SHERATON LLC
11960 Foothill Blvd, Rancho Cucamonga
(91739-9370)
PHONE..................................909 204-6100
EMP: 328
SALES (corp-wide): 20.7B Publicly Held
SIC: 7011 Hotels & motels
HQ: The Sheraton Llc
1111 Westchester Ave
White Plains NY 10604
800 328-6242

(P-12918)
SHERATON LLC
5990 Stoneridge Mall Rd, Pleasanton
(94588-3229)
PHONE..................................925 463-3330
Marilyn Milligan, Manager
EMP: 328
SALES (corp-wide): 20.7B Publicly Held
SIC: 7011 Hotels & motels
HQ: The Sheraton Llc
1111 Westchester Ave
White Plains NY 10604
800 328-6242

(P-12919)
SHERATON REDDING HOTEL
Also Called: Sheraton Redding At The Sundia
820 Sundial Bridge Dr, Redding
(96001-0978)
PHONE..................................530 364-2800
Marjorie Culley, General Mgr
EMP: 100
SALES (est): 35.8K Privately Held
SIC: 7011 Hotels

(P-12920)
**SHERTON GRDN GROVE
ANHEIM S HT**
12221 Harbor Blvd, Garden Grove
(92840-4005)
PHONE..................................714 703-8400
Ronnie Lam, Owner
EMP: 80
SALES (est): 2.1MM Privately Held
SIC: 7011 Resort hotel

(P-12921)
**SHERWOOD VALLEY
RANCHERIA**
Also Called: Sherwood Vlley Rnchria Casino
100 Kawi Pl, Willits (95490-4674)
PHONE..................................707 459-7330
Kani Neves, Manager
EMP: 60 Privately Held
SIC: 7011 Casino hotel
PA: Sherwood Valley Rancheria
190 Sherwood Hill Dr
Willits CA 95490
707 459-9690

(P-12922)
SHORE HOTEL
1515 Ocean Ave, Santa Monica
(90401-2118)
PHONE..................................310 458-1515
Julie Ward, Principal
Steve Farzam, COO
Gerry Peck, General Mgr
Roger Grajeda, Engineer
Laura Martinez, Human Res Dir
EMP: 56 EST: 2011
SALES (est): 3.8MM Privately Held
SIC: 7011 Resort hotel; hotels

(P-12923)
**SHRI SIDHI VINAYAKA HOTEL
INC**
Also Called: Hilton
500 Leisure Ln, Sacramento (95815-4207)
PHONE..................................855 922-5252
Vinod Kumar Sharma, CEO
EMP: 197
SALES (est): 5.4MM Privately Held
SIC: 7011 Hotels & motels

(P-12924)
SIDJON CORPORATION
Also Called: Livermore Casino
3571 1st St, Livermore (94551-4901)
PHONE..................................925 606-6135
Sidney Ahn, CEO
Kristen Salisbury, Director
EMP: 100 EST: 2007
SQ FT: 15,000
SALES (est): 3.5MM Privately Held
SIC: 7011 Casino hotel

(P-12925)
SIERRA AT TAHO SKI RESORTS
1111 Sierra At Tahoe Rd, Twin Bridges
(95735-9505)
PHONE..................................530 659-7519
John Rice, President
George Gillette, President
EMP: 50 EST: 1996
SALES (est): 1.9MM Privately Held
SIC: 7011 Resort hotel, franchised

(P-12926)
SILICON VALLEY HWANG LLC
Also Called: Radisson Plaza Hotel Inn
1471 N 4th St, San Jose (95112-4716)
PHONE..................................408 452-0200
John Simpson, Principal
EMP: 150
SQ FT: 112,218
SALES (est): 2.2MM Privately Held
SIC: 7011 Hotels & motels

(P-12927)
**SILVERADO RSORT SVCS
GROUP LLC**
1600 Atlas Peak Rd, NAPA (94558-1425)
PHONE..................................707 257-0200
Tim Wall, Mng Member
Olivia Devlin, Marketing Staff
Roger Kent,
Johnny Miller,
EMP: 450
SALES (est): 26MM Privately Held
SIC: 7011 Resort hotel

(P-12928)
SIMI WEST INC
Also Called: Grand Vista Hotel
999 Enchanted Way, Simi Valley
(93065-1998)
PHONE..................................760 346-5502
Leo Cook, Ch of Bd
Marcia Foulks, General Mgr
Paul Gale, Chief Engr

Lea Foulks, Sales Staff
Tawny Byron, Manager
EMP: 120
SALES (est): 1.7MM Privately Held
SIC: 7011 Hotels & motels

(P-12929)
SINCLAIR COMPANIES
Also Called: Westgate Hotel
1055 2nd Ave, San Diego (92101-4811)
PHONE..................................619 238-1818
Richard Cox, Branch Mgr
Ronaldo Santiago, Sales Staff
EMP: 160
SALES (corp-wide): 3.9B Privately Held
SIC: 7011 Hotels
PA: The Sinclair Companies
550 E South Temple
Salt Lake City UT 84102
801 524-2700

(P-12930)
**SISKIYOU DEVELOPMENT
COMPANY**
Also Called: HI Lo Motel
88 S Weed Blvd, Edgewood (96094-2607)
PHONE..................................530 938-2731
Shawn Zanni, Manager
EMP: 65
SALES (corp-wide): 14.2MM Privately
Held
WEB: www.sisdevco.com
SIC: 7011 Motels
PA: Siskiyou Development Company Inc
79 S Weed Blvd Ste 2
Weed CA 96094
530 938-2904

(P-12931)
SITA RAM LLC
Also Called: Best Western Amador Inn
200 S State Highway 49, Jackson
(95642-2548)
PHONE..................................209 223-0211
Kumar Sharma,
Puwan Kumar,
EMP: 100
SQ FT: 8,000
SALES (est): 3.1MM Privately Held
WEB: www.sitaram.com
SIC: 7011 5812 5813 7991 Hotels & mo-
tels; eating places; bar (drinking places);
physical fitness facilities

(P-12932)
SIX CONTINENTS HOTELS INC
Also Called: Holiday Inn
19901 Prairie Ave, Torrance (90503-1687)
PHONE..................................310 371-8525
John Bvell, Manager
EMP: 97 Privately Held
SIC: 7011 Hotels & motels
HQ: Six Continents Hotels, Inc.
3 Ravinia Dr Ste 100
Atlanta GA 30346
770 604-2000

(P-12933)
SIX CONTINENTS HOTELS INC
Also Called: Holiday Inn
8244 Orion Ave, Van Nuys (91406-1344)
PHONE..................................818 989-5010
Bob Yeager, General Mgr
EMP: 70 Privately Held
SIC: 7011 5812 Hotels & motels; restau-
rant, family; chain; box lunch stand
HQ: Six Continents Hotels, Inc.
3 Ravinia Dr Ste 100
Atlanta GA 30346
770 604-2000

(P-12934)
SIX CONTINENTS HOTELS INC
Also Called: Holiday Inn
1020 S Figueroa St, Los Angeles
(90015-1305)
PHONE..................................213 748-1291
Emerson Glazer, President
EMP: 100 Privately Held
WEB: www.sixcontinenthotels.com
SIC: 7011 5812 5813 Hotels & motels;
eating places; bar (drinking places)
HQ: Six Continents Hotels, Inc.
3 Ravinia Dr Ste 100
Atlanta GA 30346
770 604-2000

(P-12935)
SIX CONTINENTS HOTELS INC
Also Called: Holiday Inn
19800 S Vermont Ave, Torrance (90502-1126)
PHONE..............................310 781-9100
David Britton, *General Mgr*
EMP: 140 **Privately Held**
WEB: www.sixcontinenthotels.com
SIC: 7011 Hotels & motels
HQ: Six Continents Hotels, Inc.
3 Ravinia Dr Ste 100
Atlanta GA 30346
770 604-2000

(P-12936)
SIX CONTINENTS HOTELS INC
Also Called: Holiday Inn
1355 N Harbor Dr, San Diego (92101-3321)
PHONE..............................619 232-3861
Tony Lovoy, *General Mgr*
EMP: 75 **Privately Held**
WEB: www.sixcontinenthotels.com
SIC: 7011 Hotels & motels
HQ: Six Continents Hotels, Inc.
3 Ravinia Dr Ste 100
Atlanta GA 30346
770 604-2000

(P-12937)
SIX CONTINENTS HOTELS INC
Also Called: Crown Plaza
11950 Dublin Canyon Rd # 609, Pleasanton (94588-2818)
PHONE..............................925 847-6000
Cathy Ryle, *Manager*
EMP: 75 **Privately Held**
WEB: www.sixcontinenthotels.com
SIC: 7011 Hotels & motels
HQ: Six Continents Hotels, Inc.
3 Ravinia Dr Ste 100
Atlanta GA 30346
770 604-2000

(P-12938)
SIX CONTINENTS HOTELS INC
Also Called: Staybridge Suites
1110 A St, San Diego (92101-4732)
PHONE..............................619 795-4000
Chris Jones, *Manager*
EMP: 97 **Privately Held**
WEB: www.sixcontinenthotels.com
SIC: 7011 Hotels & motels
HQ: Six Continents Hotels, Inc.
3 Ravinia Dr Ste 100
Atlanta GA 30346
770 604-2000

(P-12939)
SIX CONTINENTS HOTELS INC
Also Called: Holiday Inn
700 National City Blvd, National City (91950-1124)
PHONE..............................619 474-2800
Larry Oneal, *General Mgr*
EMP: 80 **Privately Held**
WEB: www.sixcontinenthotels.com
SIC: 7011 Hotels & motels
HQ: Six Continents Hotels, Inc.
3 Ravinia Dr Ste 100
Atlanta GA 30346
770 604-2000

(P-12940)
SKY COURT USA INC
Also Called: Hyatt Westlake Plaza Hotel
880 S Westlake Blvd, Westlake Village (91361-2905)
PHONE..............................805 497-9991
Tetsuo Nishida, *President*
EMP: 180
SALES (est): 2.3MM **Privately Held**
SIC: 7011 Hotels & motels

(P-12941)
SMITH RIVER LUCKY 7 CASINO
350 N Indian Rd, Smith River (95567-9474)
PHONE..............................707 487-7777
Terry Westrick, *Partner*
EMP: 70 **EST:** 1997
SALES (est): 5.2MM **Privately Held**
SIC: 7011 Casino hotel

(P-12942)
SMOKE TREE INC
Also Called: Smoke Tree Ranch
1850 Smoke Tree Ln, Palm Springs (92264-1602)
PHONE..............................760 327-1221
Lisa Bell, *Manager*
Dana Fosberg, *Human Res Dir*
Brad Poncher, *Manager*
EMP: 85 **EST:** 1945
SALES (est): 5.7MM **Privately Held**
WEB: www.smoketreeinc.com
SIC: 7011 Resort hotel

(P-12943)
SNOW SUMMIT SKI CORPORATION (PA)
880 Summit Blvd, Big Bear Lake (92315)
P.O. Box 77 (92315-0077)
PHONE..............................909 866-5766
Richard C Kun, *President*
Wade Reeser, *COO*
Robert Tarras, *CFO*
Alan Macquoid, *Treasurer*
Robert Law, *Vice Pres*
EMP: 150
SQ FT: 10,000
SALES (est): 70.3MM **Privately Held**
WEB: www.bearmtn.com
SIC: 7011 5812 Ski lodge; American restaurant

(P-12944)
SONOMA HOTEL OPERATOR INC
Also Called: Fairmont Snoma Mission Inn Spa
100 Boyes Blvd, Sonoma (95476-3678)
P.O. Box 1447 (95476-1447)
PHONE..............................707 938-9000
Rick Corcoran, *General Mgr*
Michele Kelley, *Sales Mgr*
Michelle Gilman-Jasen, *Marketing Staff*
Alice Fay, *Sales Staff*
Amy Landreville, *Sales Staff*
EMP: 101
SALES (corp-wide): 1.1B **Privately Held**
WEB: www.cp.ca
SIC: 7011 Hotels
HQ: Sonoma Hotel Operator, Inc.
50 Rockefeller Plz
New York NY 10020

(P-12945)
SONOMA HOTEL PARTNERS LP
Also Called: Sheraton Sonoma Cnty Petaluma
745 Baywood Dr, Petaluma (94954-5388)
PHONE..............................707 283-2888
Scott Satterfield, *General Mgr*
Michael Trillo, *Sales Staff*
Sharon Gilsenan, *Director*
Yi Cheng, *Assistant*
EMP: 95 **EST:** 1999
SQ FT: 134,732
SALES (est): 6.5MM **Privately Held**
SIC: 7011 Hotels & motels; hotels

(P-12946)
SOULDRIVER LESSEE INC
Also Called: Hotel Solamar
435 6th Ave, San Diego (92101-7007)
PHONE..............................619 819-9500
Maria Streedy, *President*
Shannon Foster, *General Mgr*
Salvador Rojas, *Chief Engr*
Nina Leung, *Finance*
Edward Podolske, *Accountant*
EMP: 80
SALES (est): 6.8MM **Privately Held**
SIC: 7011 Hotels

(P-12947)
SOUTH COAST WESTIN HOTEL CO
Also Called: Starwood Hotels & Resorts
686 Anton Blvd, Costa Mesa (92626-1920)
PHONE..............................714 540-2500
Steve Heyer, *CEO*
Bob Jenness, *Vice Pres*
Mike Hall, *Managing Dir*
EMP: 99

SALES (est): 6.7MM
SALES (corp-wide): 20.7B **Publicly Held**
SIC: 7011 5812 Hotels & motels; eating places
HQ: Starwood Hotels & Resorts Worldwide, Llc
1 Star Pt
Stamford CT 06902
203 964-6000

(P-12948)
SOUTHBOURNE INC
Also Called: Campton Place Hotel
340 Stockton St, San Francisco (94108-4609)
PHONE..............................415 781-5555
Reymond Dixon, *Director*
Maria Conlon, *Administration*
EMP: 131
SALES (est): 5.4MM **Privately Held**
WEB: www.camptonplace.com
SIC: 7011 Hotels
PA: Taj Hotels
Nandafata Aral Korpana
Wardha MH

(P-12949)
SPA RESORT CASINO (PA)
401 E Amado Rd, Palm Springs (92262-6403)
PHONE..............................888 999-1995
Kato Moy, *General Mgr*
Agvahgue Eahilla Indian, *Owner*
Duke Stacy, *Food Svc Dir*
Frank Charolla, *Manager*
EMP: 1000
SALES (est): 24.7MM **Privately Held**
SIC: 7011 Resort hotel; casino hotel

(P-12950)
SPECTRUM HOTEL GROUP LLC
Also Called: Double Three Htlirvinespectrum
90 Pacifica, Irvine (92618-3312)
PHONE..............................949 471-8888
Timothy R Busch,
EMP: 100
SALES (est): 5.6MM **Privately Held**
SIC: 7011 7991 5812 Hotels & motels; physical fitness facilities; eating places

(P-12951)
SPECTRUM HOTEL GROUP LLC
Also Called: Doubletree Hotel
90 Pacifica, Irvine (92618-3312)
PHONE..............................949 471-8888
Tim Busch, *President*
EMP: 100
SALES (est): 3MM **Privately Held**
WEB: www.doubletreeirvinespectrum.com
SIC: 7011 7991 5812 Hotels & motels; physical fitness facilities; eating places

(P-12952)
SPF CAPITAL REAL ESTATE LLC
Also Called: Crown Plaza La Harbor Hotel
601 S Palos Verdes St, San Pedro (90731-3329)
PHONE..............................310 519-8200
Tiegang Yin, *Principal*
Tim Yin, *Principal*
EMP: 99 **EST:** 2017
SALES (est): 651.4K **Privately Held**
SIC: 7011 Hotels

(P-12953)
SPIRE CONCESSIONS LLC
Also Called: Marriott Burbank
2500 N Hollywood Way, Burbank (91505-1019)
PHONE..............................818 843-6000
William Deforrest, *CEO*
William Keating, *President*
Chad Cooley, *Vice Pres*
Russell Flicker, *Vice Pres*
Bernard Michael, *Vice Pres*
EMP: 80
SALES (est): 2.1MM **Privately Held**
SIC: 7011 Hotels

(P-12954)
SPORTSMENS LODGE HOTEL LLC
12825 Ventura Blvd, Studio City (91604-2397)
PHONE..............................818 769-4700

Mark Harlig,
Stephen Chavez, *General Mgr*
Dagmara Pawelczyk, *Accounting Mgr*
Michael Dunkel, *Controller*
Tiffany Flowers, *Controller*
EMP: 120 **EST:** 1962
SQ FT: 100,000
SALES (est): 5.9MM **Privately Held**
WEB: www.slhotel.com
SIC: 7011 5812 5813 Hotels; American restaurant; cocktail lounge

(P-12955)
SQUAW CREEK ASSOCIATES LLC
Also Called: Resort At Squaw Creek
400 Squaw Creek Rd, Alpine Meadows (96146-9778)
P.O. Box 3333, Olympic Valley (96146-3333)
PHONE..............................530 581-6624
Andrea Baltzegar,
Andre Priemer, *General Mgr*
Terry Ozanich, *Controller*
Claudia Martinello, *Manager*
Connor Pearson, *Supervisor*
EMP: 600 **EST:** 1990
SALES (est): 34.9MM **Privately Held**
WEB: www.squawcreek.com
SIC: 7011 Resort hotel

(P-12956)
SQUAW VALLEY DEVELOPMENT CO (HQ)
Also Called: Squaw Valley Ski
1960 Squaw Valley Rd, Olympic Valley (96146)
P.O. Box 2007 (96146-2007)
PHONE..............................530 452-6985
Andrew D Wirth, *CEO*
Lori Pommerenck, *Treasurer*
Brittany Clelan, *Vice Pres*
Ronnie Whitelaw, *Chief Engr*
Dee Byrne, *Director*
EMP: 88
SALES (est): 33.2MM **Privately Held**
SIC: 7011 5812 5813 7929 Hostels; ski lodge; eating places; bar (drinking places); entertainment service

(P-12957)
SQUAW VALLEY SKI CORPORATION (DH)
1960 Squaw Valley Rd, Olympic Valley (96146)
P.O. Box 2007 (96146-2007)
PHONE..............................530 583-6985
Alexander C Cushing, *Ch of Bd*
Steve La Grandeur, *President*
Mike Livak, *President*
Nancy R Wendt, *President*
Andy Wirth, *President*
EMP: 96
SQ FT: 200,000
SALES (est): 28.1MM **Privately Held**
SIC: 7011 Resort hotel
HQ: The Squaw Valley Development Company
1960 Squaw Valley Rd
Olympic Valley CA 96146
530 452-6985

(P-12958)
SS HERITAGE INN ONTARIO LLC
3595 E Guasti Rd, Ontario (91761-3705)
PHONE..............................909 937-5000
Aimee Fyke, *Mng Member*
EMP: 99
SALES (est): 597K **Privately Held**
SIC: 7011 Inns

(P-12959)
STANDARD HOLLYWOOD LESSEE LLC
Also Called: Standard Hollywood, The
8300 W Sunset Blvd, Los Angeles (90069-1516)
PHONE..............................323 822-3102
B Reichelt, *Finance*
Kim Wattsman, *General Mgr*
Brian Reichelt, *Finance*
EMP: 200
SALES (est): 16MM **Privately Held**
SIC: 7011 Hotels

(P-12960)
STANFORD HOTELS CORPORATION
Also Called: Hilton Santa Clara
4949 Great America Pkwy, Santa Clara
(95054-1216)
PHONE..................408 330-0001
Peter Dolton, *Manager*
EMP: 195 **Privately Held**
SIC: 7011 Hotels
PA: Stanford Hotels Corporation
433 California St Ste 700
San Francisco CA 94104

(P-12961)
STANFORD HOTELS CORPORATION (PA)
433 California St Ste 700, San Francisco
(94104-2011)
PHONE..................415 398-3333
Lawrence Lui, *President*
James Evans, *CFO*
◆ EMP: 50
SQ FT: 12,000
SALES (est): 32.1MM **Privately Held**
WEB: www.sheratonuptown.com
SIC: 7011 Hotels

(P-12962)
STANFORD PARK HOTEL
100 El Camino Real, Menlo Park
(94025-5292)
PHONE..................650 322-1234
Ellis Alden, *Partner*
Western Lodging Flume Corpor, *Partner*
EMP: 212
SQ FT: 122,000
SALES (est): 11.7MM **Privately Held**
WEB: www.stanfordparkhotel.com
SIC: 7011 5813 5812 Resort hotel; drinking places; eating places

(P-12963)
STARLIGHT MANAGEMENT GROUP
Also Called: Wyndham Garden San Jose Arprt
1355 N 4th St, San Jose (95112-4714)
PHONE..................408 334-7456
Ajay Shingal, *Vice Pres*
Genna Polonia, *General Mgr*
Jaya Shingal, *Director*
EMP: 99
SALES (est): 3.6MM **Privately Held**
SIC: 7011 Hotels

(P-12964)
STARWOOD HOTEL
Also Called: Starwood Hotels & Resorts
5990 Green Valley Cir, Culver City
(90230-6907)
PHONE..................310 641-7740
Ian Gee, *Mng Member*
EMP: 60
SALES (est): 3.2MM
SALES (corp-wide): 20.7B **Publicly Held**
SIC: 7011 Hotels & motels
HQ: Starwood Hotels & Resorts Worldwide, Llc
1 Star Pt
Stamford CT 06902
203 964-6000

(P-12965)
STARWOOD HOTELS & RESORTS
10480 4th St, Rancho Cucamonga
(91730-5893)
PHONE..................909 484-2018
Sharon Richards, *Manager*
EMP: 195
SALES (corp-wide): 20.7B **Publicly Held**
SIC: 7011 Hotels & motels
HQ: Starwood Hotels & Resorts Worldwide, Llc
1 Star Pt
Stamford CT 06902
203 964-6000

(P-12966)
STARWOOD HOTELS & RESORTS
401 E Millbrae Ave, Millbrae (94030-3111)
PHONE..................650 692-6363
Tim Lucher, *Branch Mgr*
EMP: 99
SALES (corp-wide): 20.7B **Publicly Held**
SIC: 7011 Hotels & motels
HQ: Starwood Hotels & Resorts Worldwide, Llc
1 Star Pt
Stamford CT 06902
203 964-6000

(P-12967)
STARWOOD HOTELS & RESORTS
125 3rd St, San Francisco (94103-3107)
PHONE..................415 284-4000
Elias Assaly, *Manager*
EMP: 195
SALES (corp-wide): 31.2MM **Privately Held**
SIC: 7011 Hotels & motels
HQ: Qatar Investment Authority
Ooredoo Building West Bay Area, Diplomatic Street
Doha

(P-12968)
STARWOOD HOTELS & RESORTS
910 Broadway Cir, San Diego
(92101-6114)
PHONE..................619 239-2200
Doug Korn, *General Mgr*
EMP: 250
SALES (corp-wide): 20.7B **Publicly Held**
SIC: 7011 7991 6512 5812 Hotels & motels; physical fitness facilities; nonresidential building operators; eating places
HQ: Starwood Hotels & Resorts Worldwide, Llc
1 Star Pt
Stamford CT 06902
203 964-6000

(P-12969)
STARWOOD HTLS & RSRTS WRLDWDE
335 Powell St, San Francisco
(94102-1804)
PHONE..................415 397-7000
Joe Burger, *Manager*
EMP: 300
SALES (corp-wide): 20.7B **Publicly Held**
SIC: 7011 5812 Hotels & motels; eating places
HQ: Starwood Hotels & Resorts Worldwide, Llc
1 Star Pt
Stamford CT 06902
203 964-6000

(P-12970)
STARWOOD HTLS & RSRTS WRLDWDE
930 Hilgard Ave, Los Angeles
(90024-3033)
PHONE..................310 208-8765
Parita Burmee, *Branch Mgr*
EMP: 185
SALES (corp-wide): 20.7B **Publicly Held**
SIC: 7011 Hotels & motels
HQ: Starwood Hotels & Resorts Worldwide, Llc
1 Star Pt
Stamford CT 06902
203 964-6000

(P-12971)
STARWOOD HTLS & RSRTS WRLDWDE
181 3rd St, San Francisco (94103-3107)
PHONE..................415 777-5300
Toni Knorr, *General Mgr*
EMP: 100
SALES (corp-wide): 20.7B **Publicly Held**
SIC: 7011 Hotels & motels

(P-12972)
STARWOOD HTLS & RSRTS WRLDWDE
404 S Figueroa St, Los Angeles
(90071-1710)
PHONE..................213 624-1000
Bryan Fitzgerald, *Manager*
EMP: 810
SALES (corp-wide): 20.7B **Publicly Held**
SIC: 7011 Hotels & motels
HQ: Starwood Hotels & Resorts Worldwide, Llc
1 Star Pt
Stamford CT 06902
203 964-6000

(P-12973)
STARWOOD HTLS & RSRTS WRLDWDE
1010 Northgate Dr, San Rafael
(94903-2502)
PHONE..................415 479-8800
Susan Bell, *General Mgr*
EMP: 140
SALES (corp-wide): 20.7B **Publicly Held**
SIC: 7011 5812 Hotels; eating places
HQ: Starwood Hotels & Resorts Worldwide, Llc
1 Star Pt
Stamford CT 06902
203 964-6000

(P-12974)
STARWOOD HTLS & RSRTS WRLDWDE
71333 Dinah Shore Dr, Rancho Mirage
(92270-1501)
PHONE..................760 328-5955
Ken Pilgrim, *Manager*
Dawn O'Flannery-Cleveland, *Sales Staff*
EMP: 486
SALES (corp-wide): 20.7B **Publicly Held**
SIC: 7011 Hotels & motels
HQ: Starwood Hotels & Resorts Worldwide, Llc
1 Star Pt
Stamford CT 06902
203 964-6000

(P-12975)
STARWOOD HTLS & RSRTS WRLDWDE
2 New Montgomery St, San Francisco
(94105-3402)
PHONE..................415 512-1111
T Staramelino, *Business Mgr*
EMP: 195
SALES (corp-wide): 20.7B **Publicly Held**
SIC: 7011 Hotels & motels
HQ: Starwood Hotels & Resorts Worldwide, Llc
1 Star Pt
Stamford CT 06902
203 964-6000

(P-12976)
STARWOOD HTLS & RSRTS WRLDWDE
6250 Hollywood Blvd, Los Angeles
(90028-5325)
PHONE..................323 798-1300
Leon Young, *General Mgr*
EMP: 195
SALES (corp-wide): 20.7B **Publicly Held**
SIC: 7011 Hotels & motels
HQ: Starwood Hotels & Resorts Worldwide, Llc
1 Star Pt
Stamford CT 06902
203 964-6000

(P-12977)
STARWOOD HTLS & RSRTS WRLDWDE
601 W Mckinley Ave, Pomona
(91768-1635)
PHONE..................909 622-2220
John Gilbert, *General Mgr*
Michele Reyner, *Sales Staff*
EMP: 195
SALES (corp-wide): 20.7B **Publicly Held**
SIC: 7011 Hotels & motels
HQ: Starwood Hotels & Resorts Worldwide, Llc
1 Star Pt
Stamford CT 06902
203 964-6000

(P-12978)
STARWOOD HTLS & RSRTS WRLDWDE
1617 1st Ave, San Diego (92101-3003)
PHONE..................619 239-9600
Gary Comeaux, *General Mgr*
EMP: 60
SALES (corp-wide): 20.7B **Publicly Held**
SIC: 7011 Hotels & motels
HQ: Starwood Hotels & Resorts Worldwide, Llc
1 Star Pt
Stamford CT 06902
203 964-6000

(P-12979)
STOCKBRIDGE/SBE HOLDINGS LLC
5900 Wilshire Blvd # 3100, Los Angeles
(90036-5013)
PHONE..................323 655-8000
Sam Nazarian, *CEO*
EMP: 3000
SALES (est): 61MM **Privately Held**
SIC: 7011 Hotels; casino hotel

(P-12980)
STOCKTON HOTEL LTD
Also Called: Stockton Hilton Hotel
2323 Grand Canal Blvd, Stockton
(95207-6554)
PHONE..................209 957-9090
Robert Hong, *General Mgr*
Edward Hazard, *General Ptnr*
Claude Viergutz, *General Mgr*
Lilly McIntyre, *Controller*
EMP: 130
SALES (est): 206K **Privately Held**
SIC: 7011 Hotel, franchised

(P-12981)
STONEBRIDGE MCWHINNEY LLC
Also Called: Hampton Inn
11747 Harbor Blvd, Garden Grove
(92840-2701)
PHONE..................714 703-8800
Thomas Long, *Manager*
EMP: 50
SALES (corp-wide): 8.8MM **Privately Held**
WEB: www.sleepinnpueblo.com
SIC: 7011 Hotels & motels
PA: Stonebridge Mcwhinney Llc
9100 E Panorama Dr # 300
Englewood CO 80112
303 785-3100

(P-12982)
STRESS RELIEF SERVICES
12603 Mariposa Rd, Victorville
(92395-6004)
PHONE..................760 241-7472
Nicole Williams, *Owner*
EMP: 60
SALES (est): 1.8MM **Privately Held**
SIC: 7011 Hotels

(P-12983)
SUGAR BOWL CORPORATION
629 Sugar Bowl Rd, Norden (95724)
P.O. Box 5 (95724-0005)
PHONE..................530 426-9000
Nancy Bechtle, *Ch of Bd*
Warren Haellman, *Shareholder*
Robert H Kautz, *President*
Bonny Bavetta, *CFO*
Dan Kingsley, *Treasurer*
▲ EMP: 100
SQ FT: 30,000
SALES (est): 9.4MM **Privately Held**
SIC: 7011 Resort hotel

(P-12984)
SUN HILL PROPERTIES INC (HQ)
Also Called: Hilton Los Angls/Nversal Cy Ht
555 Unversal Hollywood Dr, Universal City
(91608-1001)
PHONE.................................818 506-2500
Denn Hu, *Ch of Bd*
Michelle Szeto, *Controller*
Vicente Jaramillo, *VP Human Res*
▲ EMP: 350
SALES (est): 17.3MM
SALES (corp-wide): 14.1MM **Privately Held**
WEB: www.sfbayleasing.com
SIC: 7011 Hotels & motels
PA: Universal Paragon Corporation
150 Executive Park Blvd # 4000
San Francisco CA 94134
415 468-6676

(P-12985)
SUNNYSIDE RESORT
1850 W Lake Blvd, Tahoe City (96145)
P.O. Box 5969 (96145-5969)
PHONE.................................530 583-7200
Sandy Saxton, *President*
J Robert Thibaut, *Vice Pres*
Don Edelstein, *Manager*
EMP: 75
SALES (est): 3.6MM **Privately Held**
WEB: www.sunnysideresort.com
SIC: 7011 5812 5813 Resort hotel; American restaurant; bar (drinking places)

(P-12986)
SUNNYVALE SOF-X OWNER L P
Also Called: Sheraton Hotel Sunnyvale
1100 N Mathilda Ave, Sunnyvale
(94089-1206)
PHONE.................................408 542-8264
Nick Antonopoulos, *Principal*
Anita Evans, *Principal*
EMP: 50
SQ FT: 120,000
SALES (est): 477.4K **Privately Held**
SIC: 7011 Hotels & motels; hotels

(P-12987)
SUNSET TOWER HOTEL LLC
8358 W Sunset Blvd, Los Angeles
(90069-1516)
PHONE.................................323 654-7100
E Peter Krulewitch, *Mng Member*
Jeffrey Klein, *Mng Member*
EMP: 52
SALES (est): 5.8MM **Privately Held**
SIC: 7011 Resort hotel; hotels

(P-12988)
SUNSHINE MIDTOWN LLC
Also Called: Radisson Hotel Phoenix Cy Ctr
631 W Katella Ave, Anaheim (92802-3410)
PHONE.................................602 604-4900
Nick Thompson, *General Mgr*
EMP: 50
SALES (est): 1.7MM **Privately Held**
SIC: 7011 7299 Hotels; banquet hall facilities

(P-12989)
SUNSTONE CENTER CRT LESSEE INC
200 Spectrum Center Dr # 21, Irvine
(92618-5003)
PHONE.................................949 382-4000
John V Arabia, *CFO*
Lindsay Monge, *Vice Pres*
EMP: 160
SALES (est): 2.2MM
SALES (corp-wide): 1.1B **Publicly Held**
SIC: 7011 5812 5813 Hotels; eating places; drinking places
HQ: Sunstone Hotel Trs Lessee, Inc.
120 Vantis Dr Ste 350
Aliso Viejo CA 92656

(P-12990)
SUNSTONE DURANTE LLC
Also Called: Hilton San Diego/Del Mar
15575 Jimmy Durante Blvd, Del Mar
(92014-1901)
PHONE.................................858 792-5200
Scott Sloan, *Mng Member*

Damien Proctor, *Principal*
EMP: 250
SALES (est): 10.1MM **Privately Held**
SIC: 7011 Hotels & motels

(P-12991)
SUNSTONE HOTEL INVESTORS LLC
Also Called: Holiday Inn
14299 Firestone Blvd, La Mirada
(90638-5523)
PHONE.................................714 739-8500
Dalla Rodriguez, *Manager*
EMP: 122
SALES (corp-wide): 51.9MM **Privately Held**
WEB: www.sunstonehotels.com
SIC: 7011 6512 5812 Hotels & motels; nonresidential building operators; eating places
PA: Sunstone Hotel Investors, L.L.C.
200 Spectrum Dr Fl 21
Irvine CA 92618
949 330-4000

(P-12992)
SUNSTONE HOTEL INVESTORS LLC
Also Called: Embassy Suites
39375 5th St W, Palmdale (93551-3886)
PHONE.................................661 267-6587
Randy Keller, *Manager*
EMP: 122
SALES (corp-wide): 51.9MM **Privately Held**
SIC: 7011 Hotels & motels
PA: Sunstone Hotel Investors, L.L.C.
200 Spectrum Dr Fl 21
Irvine CA 92618
949 330-4000

(P-12993)
SUNSTONE HOTEL INVESTORS LLC
2 Civic Plaza Dr, Carson (90745-2231)
PHONE.................................310 830-9200
John Schulv, *General Mgr*
EMP: 75
SALES (corp-wide): 51.9MM **Privately Held**
WEB: www.sunstonehotels.com
SIC: 7011 7991 5812 Hotels; physical fitness facilities; eating places
PA: Sunstone Hotel Investors, L.L.C.
200 Spectrum Dr Fl 21
Irvine CA 92618
949 330-4000

(P-12994)
SUNSTONE HOTEL INVESTORS LLC
Also Called: Holiday Inn
1617 1st Ave Ste 16, San Diego
(92101-3003)
PHONE.................................619 239-6171
John Ault, *Manager*
EMP: 65
SALES (corp-wide): 51.9MM **Privately Held**
WEB: www.sunstonehotels.com
SIC: 7011 5812 Hotels & motels; eating places
PA: Sunstone Hotel Investors, L.L.C.
200 Spectrum Dr Fl 21
Irvine CA 92618
949 330-4000

(P-12995)
SUNSTONE HOTEL INVESTORS LLC
Also Called: Marriott
3425 Solano Ave, NAPA (94558-2709)
PHONE.................................707 253-8600
Micheal George, *Opers-Prdtn-Mfg*
EMP: 100
SALES (corp-wide): 51.9MM **Privately Held**
WEB: www.sunstonehotels.com
SIC: 7011 Hotels & motels
PA: Sunstone Hotel Investors, L.L.C.
200 Spectrum Dr Fl 21
Irvine CA 92618
949 330-4000

(P-12996)
SUNSTONE HOTEL INVESTORS LLC
Also Called: Hawthorn Suites
1752 S Clementine St, Anaheim
(92802-2902)
PHONE.................................714 635-5000
Warren Nocon, *Branch Mgr*
EMP: 122
SALES (corp-wide): 51.9MM **Privately Held**
WEB: www.sunstonehotels.com
SIC: 7011 Hotels & motels
PA: Sunstone Hotel Investors, L.L.C.
200 Spectrum Dr Fl 21
Irvine CA 92618
949 330-4000

(P-12997)
SUNSTONE HOTEL INVESTORS LLC
Also Called: Embassy Suites
9801 Airport Blvd, Los Angeles
(90045-5407)
PHONE.................................310 215-1000
Phil Campaneli, *Manager*
EMP: 150
SALES (corp-wide): 51.9MM **Privately Held**
WEB: www.sunstonehotels.com
SIC: 7011 Hotels & motels
PA: Sunstone Hotel Investors, L.L.C.
200 Spectrum Dr Fl 21
Irvine CA 92618
949 330-4000

(P-12998)
SUNSTONE HOTEL INVESTORS LLC
6161 W Century Blvd, Los Angeles
(90045-5310)
PHONE.................................310 649-1400
Connie White, *Mng Member*
Suthikiati Chirathvat, *President*
EMP: 122
SALES (corp-wide): 51.9MM **Privately Held**
WEB: www.sunstonehotels.com
SIC: 7011 Hotels & motels
PA: Sunstone Hotel Investors, L.L.C.
200 Spectrum Dr Fl 21
Irvine CA 92618
949 330-4000

(P-12999)
SUNSTONE HOTEL MANAGEMENT INC
Also Called: Marriott
3400 Market St, Riverside (92501-2826)
PHONE.................................951 784-8000
Tom Donahue, *Manager*
EMP: 200
SALES (corp-wide): 37.6MM **Privately Held**
WEB: www.sunstoneshopper.com
SIC: 7011 Hotels & motels
PA: Sunstone Hotel Management Inc
120 Vantis Dr Ste 350
Aliso Viejo CA 92656

(P-13000)
SUNSTONE HOTEL PROPERTIES INC
Also Called: Residence Inn By Marriott
1177 S Beverly Dr, Los Angeles
(90035-1119)
PHONE.................................310 228-4100
Tom Beedon, *General Mgr*
EMP: 79 **Privately Held**
WEB: www.sunstonehotelproperties.com
SIC: 7011 Hotels & motels
HQ: Sunstone Hotel Properties Inc
120 Vantis Dr Ste 350
Aliso Viejo CA 92656

(P-13001)
SUNSTONE HOTEL PROPERTIES INC
Also Called: Residence Inn By Marriott
1700 N Sepulveda Blvd, Manhattan Beach
(90266-5015)
PHONE.................................310 546-7627

Sandi Rae Kraft, *Branch Mgr*
EMP: 79 **Privately Held**
WEB: www.sunstonehotelproperties.com
SIC: 7011 Hotels & motels
HQ: Sunstone Hotel Properties Inc
120 Vantis Dr Ste 350
Aliso Viejo CA 92656

(P-13002)
SUNSTONE HOTEL PROPERTIES INC (DH)
Also Called: Hampton Inn
120 Vantis Dr Ste 350, Aliso Viejo
(92656-2686)
PHONE.................................949 330-4000
Arthur Buser, *President*
EMP: 120
SALES (est): 111.8MM **Privately Held**
WEB: www.sunstonehotelproperties.com
SIC: 7011 Hotels & motels
HQ: Interstate Hotels & Resorts, Inc.
4501 Fairfax Dr Ste 500
Arlington VA 22202
703 387-3100

(P-13003)
SUNSTONE OCEAN LESSEE INC
200 Spectrum Center Dr # 2100, Irvine
(92618-5009)
PHONE.................................949 382-4000
John V Arabia, *CFO*
Lindsay Monge, *Treasurer*
Juan Lomeli, *Info Tech Mgr*
EMP: 275
SQ FT: 302,000
SALES (est): 5.7MM
SALES (corp-wide): 1.1B **Publicly Held**
SIC: 7011 Hotels & motels
HQ: Sunstone Hotel Trs Lessee, Inc.
120 Vantis Dr Ste 350
Aliso Viejo CA 92656

(P-13004)
SUNSTONE TOP GUN LLC
Also Called: Embassy Stes San Dego-La Jolla
4550 La Jolla Village Dr, San Diego
(92122-1248)
PHONE.................................858 453-0400
Sunstone Holdco,
EMP: 100
SALES (est): 2.7MM
SALES (corp-wide): 1.1B **Publicly Held**
SIC: 7011 Hotels & motels
HQ: Sunstone Hotel Partnership, Llc
120 Vantis Dr Ste 350
Aliso Viejo CA 92656

(P-13005)
SUNSTONE TOP GUN LESSEE INC
Also Called: Embassy Suites By Hilton San
4550 La Jolla Village Dr, San Diego
(92122-1248)
PHONE.................................949 330-4000
Kenneth E Cruse, *CEO*
John V Arabia, *CFO*
Lindsay Monge, *Treasurer*
EMP: 150 EST: 2006
SALES (est): 202.8K
SALES (corp-wide): 1.1B **Publicly Held**
SIC: 7011 Hotels & motels
HQ: Sunstone Hotel Trs Lessee, Inc.
120 Vantis Dr Ste 350
Aliso Viejo CA 92656

(P-13006)
SVI LAX LLC
Also Called: Residence Inn By Marriot Lax/C
5933 W Century Blvd, Los Angeles
(90045-5471)
PHONE.................................310 281-0300
Robert A Alter,
EMP: 60
SQ FT: 213,000
SALES: 12MM **Privately Held**
SIC: 7011 Hotels & motels

(P-13007)
SWISS HOTEL GROUP INC
18 W Spain St, Sonoma (95476-5601)
PHONE..................................707 938-2884
Henry Marioni, *President*
EMP: 60 EST: 1929
SQ FT: 6,350
SALES: 2.3MM **Privately Held**
WEB: www.swisshotelsonoma.com
SIC: 7011 5813 5812 Hotels; bar (drink-
ing places); steak restaurant

(P-13008)
SWVP DEL MAR HOTEL LLC
Also Called: DoubleTree by Hilton
11915 El Camino Real, San Diego
(92130-2539)
PHONE..................................858 481-5900
Tom Donahue, *Manager*
EMP: 120 EST: 2015
SALES (est): 5.3MM **Privately Held**
SIC: 7011 Hotel, franchised

(P-13009)
SWVP WESTLAKE LLC
Also Called: Hyatt Westlake
880 S Westlake Blvd, Westlake Village
(91361-2905)
PHONE..................................805 557-1234
David Coonan, *General Mgr*
EMP: 250
SALES (corp-wide): 3.6MM **Privately
Held**
WEB: www.hyatt.com
SIC: 7011 Motels
PA: Swvp Westlake Llc
12790 El Camino Real
San Diego CA 92130
858 480-2900

(P-13010)
**SYCAMORE MINERAL SPRING
RESORT**
1215 Avila Beach Dr, San Luis Obispo
(93405-8048)
PHONE..................................805 595-7302
Russell Kiessig, *President*
John King, *President*
Steve Gregory, *Vice Pres*
Charles Yates, *Vice Pres*
EMP: 65 EST: 1975
SQ FT: 36,150
SALES (est): 2.9MM **Privately Held**
WEB: www.smsr.com
SIC: 7011 7991 Resort hotel; spas

(P-13011)
SYDELL HOTELS LLC
Also Called: Line Hotel, The
3515 Wilshire Blvd, Los Angeles
(90010-2301)
PHONE..................................213 381-7411
Doug Elpern,
Sierra Pontak, *Office Mgr*
Nahal Khatami,
Stephanie Saik, *Human Res Dir*
William Retana, *Security Mgr*
EMP: 130
SALES (est): 11.3MM
SALES (corp-wide): 22.9MM **Privately
Held**
SIC: 7011 Resort hotel
PA: Sydell Group Llc
30 W 26th St Fl 12
New York NY 10010
646 810-0208

(P-13012)
T I C HOTELS INC
Also Called: Best Western Bayside Inn
555 W Ash St, San Diego (92101-3414)
PHONE..................................619 238-7577
Tracey Wicken, *General Mgr*
EMP: 55 **Privately Held**
WEB: www.tichotels.com
SIC: 7011 Hotels & motels
HQ: T I C Hotels Inc
1811 State St Ste C
Santa Barbara CA

(P-13013)
T I C HOTELS INC
Also Called: Shorecliff Properties
2555 Price St, Pismo Beach (93449-2111)
PHONE..................................805 773-4671

Edward Brown, *Systems Mgr*
Barbara Parra, *General Mgr*
Karen Fyfe, *Human Res Dir*
EMP: 100 **Privately Held**
WEB: www.tichotels.com
SIC: 7011 5812 5813 Hotels & motels;
eating places; bar (drinking places)
HQ: T I C Hotels Inc
1811 State St Ste C
Santa Barbara CA

(P-13014)
T M MIAN & ASSOCIATES INC
Also Called: Hilton Garden Inn Calabasas
24150 Park Sorrento, Calabasas
(91302-4101)
PHONE..................................818 591-2300
Shawn Nicoles, *General Mgr*
EMP: 69
SALES (corp-wide): 14.9MM **Privately
Held**
SIC: 7011 Hotels & motels
PA: T. M. Mian & Associates, Inc.
1055 Regal Row
Dallas TX 75247
972 960-2024

(P-13015)
T M MIAN & ASSOCIATES INC
Also Called: Hilton
2000 Solar Dr, Oxnard (93036-2694)
PHONE..................................805 983-8600
T M Mian, *Partner*
EMP: 56
SALES (corp-wide): 14.9MM **Privately
Held**
SIC: 7011 Hotels & motels
PA: T. M. Mian & Associates, Inc.
1055 Regal Row
Dallas TX 75247
972 960-2024

(P-13016)
T-12 THREE LLC
Also Called: Hard Rock Hotel
207 5th Ave, San Diego (92101-6908)
PHONE..................................619 702-3000
Nilesh Madhav, *Mng Member*
Brent Takeymia, *Info Tech Mgr*
Mark Andrews, *Engineer*
Burt Sharpe, *Chief Engr*
Josh Carr, *Finance*
EMP: 356
SALES (est): 23.9MM **Privately Held**
SIC: 7011 Hotels

(P-13017)
TABLE MOUNTAIN CASINO
8184 Table Mountain Rd, Friant (93626)
P.O. Box 445 (93626-0445)
PHONE..................................559 822-7777
Frances Dandy, *Senior VP*
Troy Benne, *CFO*
Brian Rankin, *Technical Staff*
Rick Peterson, *Engineer*
Mark Solomon, *Human Res Dir*
EMP: 1000
SQ FT: 30,000
SALES (est): 51.4MM **Privately Held**
WEB: www.tmcasino.com
SIC: 7011 Casino hotel

(P-13018)
**TACHI PALACE HOTEL &
CASINO**
17225 Jersey Ave, Lemoore (93245-9760)
PHONE..................................559 924-7751
Tachi Yokut, *Owner*
Santa Yokut, *Owner*
Richard Laudale, *CFO*
Willie Barrios, *General Mgr*
Anita Baga, *Human Res Dir*
EMP: 1500
SALES (est): 59.5MM **Privately Held**
SIC: 7011 Casino hotel

(P-13019)
TAHOE BEACH & SKI CLUB
3601 Lake Tahoe Blvd, South Lake Tahoe
(96150-8915)
PHONE..................................530 541-6220
Roy Fraser, *President*
Tamara Hollingsworth, *Manager*
EMP: 60

SALES (est): 2.9MM **Privately Held**
WEB: www.tahoebeachandski.com
SIC: 7011 6513 Resort hotel; apartment
hotel operation

(P-13020)
TERRE DU SOLEIL LTD
Also Called: Auberge Du Soleil
180 Rutherford Hill Rd, Rutherford (94573)
P.O. Box B (94573-0902)
PHONE..................................707 963-1211
George Goeggel, *General Ptnr*
Robert Harmon, *General Ptnr*
Bradley Reynolds, *General Ptnr*
Claude Rouas, *General Ptnr*
Kevin Krueger, *Engineer*
EMP: 125
SQ FT: 20,000
SALES (est): 18.2MM **Privately Held**
WEB: www.aubergedusoleil.com
SIC: 7011 5812 Resort hotel; French
restaurant

(P-13021)
**TESI INVESTMENT COMPANY
LLC**
Also Called: Best Western Pasada At Harbor
5005 N Harbor Dr, San Diego
(92106-2307)
PHONE..................................619 224-3254
Jorge Mendoza, *Mng Member*
Octavio Terrazas Jr, *President*
EMP: 60
SQ FT: 9,825
SALES: 1.8MM **Privately Held**
SIC: 7011 Hotels & motels

(P-13022)
**THOMAS EDWARD COMPANIES
(PA)**
9950 Santa Monica Blvd, Beverly Hills
(90212-1607)
PHONE..................................310 859-9366
Edward Slatkin, *Partner*
Thomas Slatkin, *Partner*
Jon Andera, *Vice Pres*
Fran Fkuebler, *Office Mgr*
Fran Kuebler, *Office Mgr*
EMP: 116
SQ FT: 1,000
SALES (est): 3.6MM **Privately Held**
WEB: www.jollyrogerhotel.com
SIC: 7011 Hotels & motels

(P-13023)
TIBURON HOSPITALITY LLC
Also Called: Super 8 Motel
901 Real Rd, Bakersfield (93309-1003)
PHONE..................................661 322-1012
Mark Grotewohl, *Partner*
Tiburon Capital LLC, *Partner*
▲ EMP: 150
SQ FT: 1,600
SALES: 6.4MM **Privately Held**
SIC: 7011 Hotels & motels

(P-13024)
TIBURON HOTEL LLC
Also Called: Lodge At Tiburon, The
1651 Tiburon Blvd, Belvedere Tiburon
(94920-2511)
PHONE..................................415 435-5996
Mike Schuminsky, *Mng Member*
EMP: 77
SALES (est): 4.3MM **Privately Held**
SIC: 7011 7389 Hotels; office facilities &
secretarial service rental

(P-13025)
TIC HOTELS INC
Also Called: Tic Worldwide
555 W Ash St, San Diego (92101-3414)
PHONE..................................619 238-7577
M Gardacio, *Vice Pres*
Suzy Briggs, *Corp Secy*
T I C Hotels,
EMP: 50
SALES (est): 1MM **Privately Held**
SIC: 7011 Resort hotel

(P-13026)
TIC WORLD-WIDE CORP
Also Called: Best Western
555 W Ash St, San Diego (92101-3414)
PHONE..................................619 233-7500
Mamo Takeuchi, *President*

EMP: 55
SQ FT: 67,381
SALES (est): 3.7MM **Privately Held**
WEB: www.baysideinn.com
SIC: 7011 Hotels & motels

(P-13027)
TIDES CENTER
124 Turk St, San Francisco (94102-3926)
PHONE..................................415 359-9401
EMP: 178 **Privately Held**
SIC: 7011 Hotels & motels
PA: The Tides Center
The Prsdio 1014 Trney Ave
San Francisco CA 94129

(P-13028)
**TODAYS HOTEL CORPORATION
(PA)**
Also Called: Holiday Inn
1500 Van Ness Ave, San Francisco
(94109-4606)
PHONE..................................415 441-4000
Ming Nin Zen, *President*
EMP: 106
SALES (est): 50.4MM **Privately Held**
WEB: www.goldengatewayhotel.com
SIC: 7011 Hotels & motels

(P-13029)
TODAYS VI LLC
Also Called: Amerisuites
4760 Mills Cir, Ontario (91764-5223)
PHONE..................................909 980-2200
Peter Zen,
Paul Zen,
EMP: 60
SALES (est): 1.3MM **Privately Held**
SIC: 7011 Hotels & motels

(P-13030)
TORRES-MARTINEZ
Also Called: Red Earth Casino
3089 Norm Niver Rd, Thermal
(92274-6550)
PHONE..................................760 395-1200
David Seufert, *Branch Mgr*
EMP: 150 **Privately Held**
SIC: 7011 Casino hotel
PA: Torres-Martinez Desert Cahuilla Indians
66725 Martinez Rd
Thermal CA 92274
760 397-0300

(P-13031)
TOWNEPLACE SUITES
Also Called: TownePlace Suites By Marriott
700 E Campbell Ave, Campbell
(95008-2104)
PHONE..................................408 370-4510
Elece Otten, *Owner*
EMP: 80
SALES (est): 1.7MM **Privately Held**
SIC: 7011 Hotel, franchised

(P-13032)
TPG LA COMMERCE LLC
Also Called: Doubletree By Hilton La - Com
5757 Telegraph Rd, Commerce
(90040-1513)
PHONE..................................401 946-4600
Elizabeth Procaccianti,
Michelle Joyal, *Administration*
EMP: 100
SALES (est): 961.1K **Privately Held**
SIC: 7011 Hotels & motels

(P-13033)
TR BIG SUR MANAGEMENT LLC
48123 Highway 1, Big Sur (93920-9538)
PHONE..................................831 667-4212
Thomas Becker, *Director*
EMP: 50
SALES (est): 203.4K
SALES (corp-wide): 4.4B **Publicly Held**
SIC: 7011 Resort hotel
PA: Hyatt Hotels Corporation
150 N Riverside Plz Fl 8
Chicago IL 60606
312 750-1234

(P-13034)
TR WARNER CENTER LP
Also Called: Warner Center Marriott Hotel
21850 Oxnard St, Woodland Hills
(91367-3631)
PHONE..............................818 887-4800
Clay Andrews, *Mng Member*
EMP: 300
SQ FT: 500,000
SALES (est): 10.2MM **Privately Held**
SIC: 7011 Hotels

(P-13035)
TRADEWINDS LODGE (PA)
Also Called: Cliff House Restaurant
400 S Main St, Fort Bragg (95437-4806)
PHONE..............................707 964-4761
Dominic Affinito, *Partner*
EMP: 100
SQ FT: 19,000
SALES (est): 5MM **Privately Held**
SIC: 7011 5812 5813 6512 Motels;
restaurant, family: independent; seafood
restaurants; bars & lounges; commercial
& industrial building operation; land subdi-
viders & developers, commercial; land
subdividers & developers, residential

(P-13036)
TRADEWINDS PARTNERSHIP
Also Called: Tradewinds Lodge Partnership
2920 Arden Way Ste F1, Sacramento
(95825-1393)
PHONE..............................916 333-5239
Michelle V Affinito, *Partner*
Michelle Affinito, *CFO*
EMP: 60
SALES: 950K **Privately Held**
SIC: 7011 1531 Hotels & motels; operative
builders

(P-13037)
TRCF REDONDO LLC
Also Called: Homewood Suites Redondo
2430 Marine Ave, Redondo Beach
(90278-1103)
PHONE..............................310 536-1209
Brad Wagstaff, *Manager*
EMP: 50
SALES (est): 184.9K **Privately Held**
SIC: 7011 Hotels & motels

(P-13038)
TREVI PARTNERS A CALIF LP
Also Called: Tollhouse Hotel
140 S Santa Cruz Ave, Los Gatos
(95030-6702)
PHONE..............................408 395-7070
Marie Tallman, *Manager*
Jim Gerney, *General Mgr*
EMP: 88 **Privately Held**
WEB: www.marinholidayinnexpress.com
SIC: 7011 5812 Hotels; eating places
HQ: Trevi Partners, A Calif. L.P.
6680 Regional St
Dublin CA 94568
925 828-7750

(P-13039)
TREVI PARTNERS A CALIF LP (HQ)
Also Called: Holiday Inn
6680 Regional St, Dublin (94568-2916)
PHONE..............................925 828-7750
Micheal McDavid, *General Mgr*
EMP: 68
SALES (est): 17.4MM **Privately Held**
WEB: www.marinholidayinnexpress.com
SIC: 7011 Hotels & motels

(P-13040)
TREVI PARTNERS A CALIF LP
Also Called: Best Wstn Carmel Mission Inn
3665 Rio Rd, Carmel (93923-8609)
PHONE..............................831 624-1841
Jose Cortega, *Manager*
EMP: 76 **Privately Held**
WEB: www.marinholidayinnexpress.com
SIC: 7011 Hotels & motels
HQ: Trevi Partners, A Calif. L.P.
6680 Regional St
Dublin CA 94568
925 828-7750

(P-13041)
TREVI PARTNERS A CALIF LP (PA)
5955 Coronado Ln, Pleasanton
(94588-8518)
PHONE..............................925 225-4000
Michael Madden, *Partner*
EMP: 120
SALES (est): 17.4MM **Privately Held**
SIC: 7011 Hotels & motels

(P-13042)
TRI-STAR CCW MANAGEMENT L P
Also Called: Doubletree Hotel-Lax
1985 E Grand Ave, El Segundo
(90245-5015)
PHONE..............................310 322-0999
Harry Wu, *Partner*
Norman Chang, *Partner*
Shau An Chen, *Partner*
▲ **EMP:** 99
SALES (est): 2.1MM **Privately Held**
SIC: 7011 Hotels & motels

(P-13043)
TRIGILD INTERNATIONAL INC
Also Called: Ramada Inn
2151 Hotel Cir S, San Diego (92108-3314)
PHONE..............................619 295-6886
Charlie Holiday, *Manager*
EMP: 80
SALES (corp-wide): 20.6MM **Privately
Held**
WEB: www.trigild.com
SIC: 7011 Hotels & motels
PA: Trigild International, Inc.
3323 Carmel Mountain Rd # 2
San Diego CA 92121
858 720-6700

(P-13044)
TUCSON HOTELS LP
Also Called: Holiday Inn
1800 Powell St, Oakland (94608-1808)
PHONE..............................510 658-9300
Pat Goss, *Manager*
EMP: 300 **Privately Held**
WEB:
www.embassysuitesoutdoorworld.com
SIC: 7011 5813 5812 7991 Hotels & mo-
tels; motels; drinking places; eating
places; physical fitness facilities
PA: Tucson Hotels Lp
2711 Centerville Rd # 400
Wilmington DE 19808

(P-13045)
TUCSON HOTELS LP
Also Called: Holiday Inn
300 J St, Sacramento (95814-2210)
PHONE..............................916 446-0100
Liz Tavernese, *Manager*
Natalie Fo, *Sales Staff*
Cathleen Dao, *Manager*
EMP: 165 **Privately Held**
WEB: www.holidayinnportland.com
SIC: 7011 5812 5813 Hotels & motels;
restaurant, family: independent; bar
(drinking places)
PA: Tucson Hotels Lp
2711 Centerville Rd # 400
Wilmington DE 19808

(P-13046)
TUCSON HOTELS LP
Also Called: Holiday Inn
300 J St, Sacramento (95814-2210)
PHONE..............................916 446-0100
Liz Tavernese, *Manager*
EMP: 153 **Privately Held**
SIC: 7011 Hotels & motels
PA: Tucson Hotels Lp
2711 Centerville Rd # 400
Wilmington DE 19808

(P-13047)
TUCSON HOTELS LP
Also Called: Embassy Stes Monterey Bay Htl
1441 Canyon Del Rey Blvd, Seaside
(93955-4729)
PHONE 831 393-1115

Rick Weichert, *Manager*
Greg Keebler, *General Mgr*
EMP: 156 **Privately Held**
WEB: www.holidayinnportland.com
SIC: 7011 5813 5812 Hotels & motels;
drinking places; eating places
PA: Tucson Hotels Lp
2711 Centerville Rd # 400
Wilmington DE 19808

(P-13048)
TWDC ENTERPRISES 18 CORP
Also Called: Disneyland
1598 S Harbor Blvd, Anaheim (92802)
PHONE..............................714 781-4278
Ed Greier, *Branch Mgr*
EMP: 170
SALES (corp-wide): 90.2B **Publicly Held**
SIC: 7011 Resort hotel
HQ: Twdc Enterprises 18 Corp.
500 S Buena Vista St
Burbank CA 91521

(P-13049)
TYME MAIDU TRIBE-BERRY CREEK
Also Called: Gold Country Casino
4020 Olive Hwy, Oroville (95966-5527)
PHONE..............................530 538-4560
Jim E Tribal, *CEO*
Jeff Fields, *Officer*
Grant Townsend, *Vice Pres*
Debra A Tribal, *Vice Pres*
Ed White, *General Mgr*
EMP: 519
SALES (est): 32.9MM **Privately Held**
WEB: www.goldcountrycasino.com
SIC: 7011 Casino hotel

(P-13050)
UKA LLC
Also Called: Tarsadia Hotels
620 Newport Center Dr # 1400, Newport
Beach (92660-8025)
PHONE..............................949 610-8000
B U Patel, *Mng Member*
Pushpa Patel,
EMP: 50
SQ FT: 12,000
SALES (est): 466.2K **Privately Held**
SIC: 7011 Hotels

(P-13051)
UNITED AUBURN INDIAN COMMUNITY
Also Called: Thunder Valley Casino
1200 Athens Ave, Lincoln (95648-9328)
PHONE..............................916 408-7777
Scott Garawitz, *Branch Mgr*
Michael Kuhn, *President*
Nancy Yang, *President*
Sean Dunne, *Officer*
John Comeau, *Vice Pres*
EMP: 1227 **Privately Held**
WEB: www.thundervalleyresort.com
SIC: 7011 Casino hotel
PA: United Auburn Indian Community
10720 Indian Hill Rd
Auburn CA 95603

(P-13052)
UNIVERSAL PARAGON CORPORATION (PA)
150 Executive Park Blvd # 4000, San Fran-
cisco (94134-3319)
PHONE..............................415 468-6676
Denn Hu, *Ch of Bd*
EMP: 370
SQ FT: 200,000
SALES (est): 14.1MM **Privately Held**
WEB: www.sfbayleasing.com
SIC: 7011 6512 6552 Hotels & motels;
commercial & industrial building opera-
tion; land subdividers & developers, resi-
dential; land subdividers & developers,
commercial

(P-13053)
UNIWELL CORPORATION
Also Called: Holiday Inn
7000 Beach Blvd, Buena Park
(90620-1832)
PHONE..............................714 522-7000
Tracy Myer, *Branch Mgr*
Elaine Chan, *Principal*
Teddy Katuari, *Principal*
EMP: 150
SALES (corp-wide): 28.3MM **Privately
Held**
WEB: www.uniwell.com
SIC: 7011 5813 5812 Hotels & motels;
drinking places; eating places
PA: Uniwell Corporation
21172 Figueroa St
Carson CA 90745
310 782-8888

(P-13054)
UNIWELL FRESNO HOTEL LLC
Also Called: Doubletree By Hilton Fresno
2233 Ventura St, Fresno (93721-2915)
PHONE..............................559 268-1000
Steve Klein,
Kristine Bacon, *Manager*
Kris Doyle, *Manager*
EMP: 100
SALES (est): 8.4MM **Privately Held**
SIC: 7011 Hotels & motels

(P-13055)
UPHAM HOTEL
1404 De La Vina St # 93101, Santa Bar-
bara (93101-3057)
PHONE..............................805 962-0058
Carl Johnson, *Owner*
Janice Winn, *Manager*
EMP: 50
SALES (est): 1.3MM **Privately Held**
WEB: www.uphamhotel.com
SIC: 7011 Resort hotel

(P-13056)
URBAN COMMONS QUEENSWAY LLC
Also Called: Queen Mary, The
1126 Queens Hwy, Long Beach
(90802-6331)
PHONE..............................562 499-1611
Christopher Otamias,
EMP: 900 **EST:** 2016
SALES (est): 1.3MM **Privately Held**
SIC: 7011 Hotels

(P-13057)
US GRANT HOTEL VENTURES LLC
326 Broadway, San Diego (92101-4800)
PHONE..............................619 744-2007
Daniel Tucker,
EMP: 80
SQ FT: 99,999
SALES (est): 7.2MM **Privately Held**
SIC: 7011 Resort hotel; hotels

(P-13058)
US HOTEL AND RESORT MGT INC
Also Called: Regency Inn
2544 Newport Blvd, Costa Mesa
(92627-1331)
PHONE..............................949 650-2988
Peggy Chen, *Manager*
EMP: 83
SALES (corp-wide): 25.5MM **Privately
Held**
WEB: www.regency-mgmt.com
SIC: 7011 Resort hotel
HQ: U.S. Hotel And Resort Management,
Inc.
3211 W Sencore Dr
Sioux Falls SD 57107
605 334-2371

(P-13059)
VALADON HOTEL LLC
Also Called: Petit Ermitage
8822 Cynthia St, West Hollywood
(90069-4502)
PHONE..............................310 854-1114
Stefan Ashkenazy,
Nicolas Black, *General Mgr*
Jeannette Campos, *Finance*

Renee Gonzales, *Controller*
Laura Martinez, *Human Res Dir*
EMP: 80
SQ FT: 40,000
SALES (est): 7.5MM **Privately Held**
WEB: www.valadonhotel.com
SIC: 7011 Hotels

(P-13060)
VAN NESS HOTEL INC
1050 Van Ness Ave, San Francisco
(94109-6934)
PHONE..................415 673-4711
John M Scheurer, *President*
EMP: 90
SALES (est): 2.4MM **Privately Held**
SIC: 7011 Hotels

(P-13061)
VENTU PARK LLC
Also Called: Palm Garden Hotel
495 N Ventu Park Rd, Thousand Oaks
(91320-2707)
PHONE..................805 716-4200
Bob Zonitch, *Principal*
Michael Garik, *Principal*
Dave Warner, *Principal*
Nicole Schram, *Manager*
EMP: 70
SALES: 4MM **Privately Held**
SIC: 7011 Hotels

(P-13062)
**VENTURA HSPTALITY
PARTNERS LLC**
Also Called: Crowne Plaza Ventura Beach
450 Harbor Blvd, Ventura (93001-2708)
PHONE..................805 648-2100
David Storm,
Liam Thorpe, *Sales Staff*
Jodi Wagner, *Director*
Lorenzo Isaac, *Supervisor*
EMP: 140
SQ FT: 143,000
SALES: 10MM **Privately Held**
SIC: 7011 Hotels & motels

(P-13063)
VERASA MANAGEMENT LLC
1314 Mckinstry St, NAPA (94559-1900)
PHONE..................707 257-1800
Stewart Andersen, *Mng Member*
EMP: 94 **EST:** 2010
SALES (est): 3MM **Privately Held**
SIC: 7011 Hotels

(P-13064)
**VICTORVLLE TRSURE
HOLDINGS LLC**
Also Called: Holiday Inn
15494 Palmdale Rd, Victorville
(92392-2408)
PHONE..................760 245-6565
Benjamin Gonzales, *General Mgr*
Jane Battle, *Supervisor*
EMP: 75
SALES (est): 875.6K **Privately Held**
SIC: 7011 5812 Hotels & motels; Ameri-
can restaurant

(P-13065)
VILLAGIO INN & SPA LLC
6481 Washington St, Yountville
(94599-1331)
PHONE..................707 944-8877
Kerry Egan,
Jonathan Stephens, *Executive*
Melissa Mackey, *Info Tech Mgr*
Dave Bottarini, *Engineer*
Sean Dempsey, *Opers Dir*
▲ **EMP:** 147
SALES (est): 8.8MM
SALES (corp-wide): 9.8MM **Privately
Held**
WEB: www.villagio.com
SIC: 7011 Hotels
PA: The Vintage Inn
6541 Washington St
Yountville CA 94599
707 944-1112

(P-13066)
VINTNERS INN
4350 Barnes Rd, Santa Rosa
(95403-1514)
PHONE..................707 575-7350

Donald Carano,
EMP: 100
SQ FT: 30,670
SALES: 3.9MM **Privately Held**
WEB: www.vintnersinn.com
SIC: 7011 Motels; inns

(P-13067)
VISCAMAR LLC
Also Called: Presidian Hotel
300 S Court St, Visalia (93291-6214)
PHONE..................559 636-1111
H Drake Leddy,
EMP: 91
SQ FT: 134,055
SALES (est): 2.5MM **Privately Held**
SIC: 7011 Hotels

(P-13068)
VWI CONCORD LLC
Also Called: Hilton Concord
1970 Diamond Blvd, Concord
(94520-5718)
PHONE..................925 827-2000
Jack Hlavac, *General Mgr*
Jim Dunbar, *Officer*
EMP: 130
SALES (est): 9.1MM **Privately Held**
SIC: 7011 Hotels & motels

(P-13069)
W LOS ANGELES
Also Called: Westwood Marquis Hotel &
Grdns
930 Hilgard Ave, Los Angeles
(90024-3033)
P.O. Box 14029, Scottsdale AZ (85267-
4029)
PHONE..................310 208-8765
George I Rosenthal, *President*
Mark Rosenthal, *COO*
Anil Sharma, *CFO*
EMP: 330
SALES (est): 11MM
SALES (corp-wide): 43.7MM **Privately
Held**
WEB: www.raleighenterprises.com
SIC: 7011 Resort hotel; hotels
PA: Raleigh Enterprises, Inc.
5300 Melrose Ave Fl 4
Los Angeles CA 90038
310 899-8900

(P-13070)
W-BEL AGE LLC
1020 N San Vicente Blvd, West Hollywood
(90069-3802)
PHONE..................310 854-1111
Laura Bell, *Principal*
EMP: 99
SALES (est): 875.8K **Privately Held**
SIC: 7011 Hotels & motels

(P-13071)
W-EMERALD LLC
Also Called: Westin San Diego
400 W Broadway, San Diego (92101-3504)
PHONE..................619 239-4500
John Beaton, *General Mgr*
EMP: 230
SQ FT: 99,999
SALES (est): 4.5MM **Privately Held**
SIC: 7011 Hotels & motels

(P-13072)
**W2005 NEW CNTURY HT
PRTFLIO LP**
Also Called: Sheraton Hotel Sunnyvale
1100 N Mathilda Ave, Sunnyvale
(94089-1206)
PHONE..................408 745-6000
Epenesa Pakola, *Manager*
EMP: 53 **Privately Held**
WEB: www.hicrystallake.com
SIC: 7011 Hotels & motels
PA: W2005 New Century Hotel Portfolio,
L.P.
6011 Connection Dr
Irving TX 75039

(P-13073)
W2005 WYN HOTELS LP
Also Called: Doubletree Hotel
5757 Telegraph Rd, Commerce
(90040-1513)
PHONE..................323 887-8100
Steve Barick, *COO*
Bill Wuepper, *Manager*
EMP: 81 **EST:** 1991
SALES (est): 3.8MM **Privately Held**
SIC: 7011 Hotels & motels

(P-13074)
**WALTERS FAMILY
PARTNERSHIP**
Also Called: Hilton Resort In Palm Spring
400 E Tahquitz Canyon Way, Palm Springs
(92262-6605)
PHONE..................760 320-6868
Lance Walters, *Partner*
EMP: 150
SQ FT: 200,000
SALES (est): 7.1MM **Privately Held**
SIC: 7011 5813 5812 Hotels & motels;
drinking places; eating places

(P-13075)
**WARWICK CALIFORNIA
CORPORATION**
Also Called: Warwick Hotel San Francisco
490 Geary St, San Francisco (94102-1223)
PHONE..................415 992-3809
Richard Chiu, *President*
Joseph Tung, *Vice Pres*
EMP: 60
SQ FT: 23,386
SALES (est): 2.6MM
SALES (corp-wide): 355.8K **Privately
Held**
WEB: www.warwicksf.com
SIC: 7011 7299 Hotels; banquet hall facili-
ties
PA: Warwick Holdings Sa
Rue Eugene Ruppert 6
Luxembourg

(P-13076)
WASHINGTON INN LLC
Also Called: Holiday Inn
737 Washington Blvd, Marina Del Rey
(90292-5542)
PHONE..................310 821-4455
John Mathews,
Doug Pflumer, *General Mgr*
EMP: 80
SALES (est): 1.8MM **Privately Held**
SIC: 7011 Hotels & motels

(P-13077)
WATERFALL RESORT
5951 Encina Rd Ste 207, Goleta
(93117-6252)
P.O. Box 6440, Ketchikan AK (99901-1440)
PHONE..................805 879-3780
Chuck Beard, *Director*
EMP: 100
SALES (est): 1.5MM **Privately Held**
WEB: www.waterfallresort.com
SIC: 7011 Seasonal hotel

(P-13078)
WATERFRONT HOTEL LLC
Also Called: Hilton
21100 Pacific Coast Hwy, Huntington Beach
(92648-5307)
PHONE..................714 845-8000
John Gilbert, *Manager*
EMP: 298 **Privately Held**
WEB: www.waterfrontresort.com
SIC: 7011 5813 5812 7299 Hotels & mo-
tels; drinking places; eating places; ban-
quet hall facilities
PA: The Waterfront Hotel Llc
660 Newport Center Dr
Newport Beach CA
-

(P-13079)
**WATERFRONT PLAZA HOTEL
LLC**
10 Washington St, Oakland (94607-3751)
PHONE..................510 836-3800
Clyde R Gibb, *General Ptnr*
Thunderbird Investors, *General Ptnr*

EMP: 65 **EST:** 1964
SALES (est): 4.2MM **Privately Held**
SIC: 7011 Resort hotel; hotels

(P-13080)
WCO HOTELS INC (DH)
Also Called: Disneyland Hotel
1150 W Magic Way, Anaheim (92802-2247)
PHONE..................323 636-3251
Tony Bruno, *President*
Cynthia Harriss, *Principal*
Hidel Amemiya, *VP Opers*
EMP: 57
SALES (est): 58.7MM
SALES (corp-wide): 90.2B **Publicly Held**
SIC: 7011 5812 Resort hotel; eating
places

(P-13081)
**WELCOME GROUP
MANAGEMENT LLC**
Also Called: Marriott
300 S Court St, Visalia (93291-6214)
PHONE..................310 378-6666
Amarjit Shokeen,
Sheri A O'Hara, *Executive*
EMP: 97
SQ FT: 3,224
SALES (est): 115.2K **Privately Held**
SIC: 7011 Hotels & motels

(P-13082)
WELK GROUP INC (PA)
Also Called: Welk Music Group
8860 Lawrence Welk Dr, Escondido
(92026-6403)
PHONE..................760 749-3000
Jon Fredricks, *President*
Marc L Luzzatto, *COO*
Kaethe Brandt, *Executive Asst*
Brian Thompson, *Technology*
Lois Webster, *Director*
EMP: 345
SQ FT: 6,200
SALES (est): 100.2MM **Privately Held**
SIC: 7011 5099 Resort hotel; compact
discs; tapes & cassettes, prerecorded

(P-13083)
**WEST HOTEL PARTNERS LP
(PA)**
Also Called: Hilton San Jose and Towers
11828 La Grange Ave 200, Los Angeles
(90025-5212)
PHONE..................310 477-3593
Lewis Wolff, *General Ptnr*
Philip Dinapoli, *Partner*
EMP: 246
SQ FT: 3,000
SALES (est): 7.7MM **Privately Held**
WEB: www.firstconf.com
SIC: 7011 5812 5813 7299 Hotels & mo-
tels; eating places; drinking places; ban-
quet hall facilities

(P-13084)
WEST HOTEL PARTNERS LP
Also Called: Hilton
300 Almaden Blvd, San Jose (95110-2703)
PHONE..................408 947-4450
John Southwell, *Branch Mgr*
EMP: 200
SALES (est): 6.6MM
SALES (corp-wide): 7.7MM **Privately
Held**
WEB: www.firstconf.com
SIC: 7011 7371 6512 5813 Hotels & mo-
tels; custom computer programming serv-
ices; nonresidential building operators;
drinking places; eating places
PA: West Hotel Partners, L.P.
11828 La Grange Ave 200
Los Angeles CA 90025
310 477-3593

(P-13085)
WEST INN & SUITES LLC
4970 Avenida Encinas, Carlsbad
(92008-4343)
PHONE..................760 448-4500
Debbie Vought,
Veronica Garcia, *Administration*
Sylvia Battle, *Director*
Nicholas Seistrup, *Manager*
Sherrina Watson, *Supervisor*
EMP: 80

SALES (est): 3.9MM **Privately Held**
WEB: www.westinnandsuites.com
SIC: 7011 Inns; hotels

(P-13086)
WEST SAN CRLOS HT PARTNERS LLC
Also Called: Hyatt Place San Jose Hotel
282 Almaden Blvd, San Jose (95113-2003)
PHONE..............................408 998-0400
F Matthew Dinapoli,
Tina Castaneda, *Administration*
EMP: 65
SALES: 1B **Privately Held**
SIC: 7011 Hotels & motels

(P-13087)
WESTGROUP SAN DIEGO ASSOCIATES
Also Called: Paradise Point Resort
1404 Vacation Rd, San Diego (92109-7905)
PHONE..............................858 274-4630
David Feeney, *Partner*
EMP: 500
SALES (est): 18.4MM **Privately Held**
SIC: 7011 Resort hotel

(P-13088)
WESTIN DESERT WILLOW
75 Willow Ridge, Palm Desert (92260-0305)
PHONE..............................760 636-7003
Jim Moran, *General Mgr*
Warren Jerome, *Opers Staff*
EMP: 75
SALES (est): 2.9MM **Privately Held**
SIC: 7011 Hotels & motels

(P-13089)
WESTLAKE PROPERTIES INC
Also Called: Westlake Village Inn
31943 Agoura Rd, Westlake Village (91361-4427)
PHONE..............................818 889-0230
John Notter, *Principal*
Maria H Solorzano, *Sales Dir*
Elizabeth Villavicencio, *Manager*
EMP: 150
SALES (est): 8.7MM **Privately Held**
WEB: www.westlakevillageinn.com
SIC: 7011 Resort hotel

(P-13090)
WESTLAND HOTEL CORPORATION
Also Called: Best Western Stockton Inn
4219 E Waterloo Rd, Stockton (95215-2304)
PHONE..............................209 931-3131
Champ Patel, *Manager*
EMP: 50 **Privately Held**
SIC: 7011 Hotels & motels
PA: Westland Hotel Corporation
8885 Rio San Diego Dr
San Diego CA

(P-13091)
WESTPOST BERKELEY LLC
Also Called: Doubletree By Hilton Brky Mrna
200 Marina Blvd, Berkeley (94710-1608)
PHONE..............................510 548-7920
Moez Mangalgi, *Mng Member*
EMP: 99
SALES (est): 5.4MM **Privately Held**
SIC: 7011 Hotels & motels

(P-13092)
WESTWARD HOSPITALITY MGT
200 Marina Blvd, Berkeley (94710-1608)
PHONE..............................510 548-7920
Patrick Birmingham, *Principal*
Rafael Fernandez, *Principal*
EMP: 99
SALES: 15MM **Privately Held**
SIC: 7011 Hotels & motels

(P-13093)
WHATEVER IT TAKES INC
Also Called: Desert Hot Springs Spa Hotel
10805 Palm Dr, Desert Hot Springs (92240-2511)
PHONE..............................760 329-6000
Michael Bickford, *President*

EMP: 50
SQ FT: 50,000
SALES (est): 2.8MM **Privately Held**
SIC: 7011 5812 Resort hotel; eating places

(P-13094)
WHB CORPORATION
Also Called: Millennium Biltmore Hotel
506 S Grand Ave, Los Angeles (90071-2602)
PHONE..............................213 624-1011
John Demola, *Branch Mgr*
Daniel Desbaillets, *COO*
Colin Wang, *Vice Pres*
Sandra Avalos, *Executive*
Maselina Hansen, *Executive*
EMP: 630 **Privately Held**
SIC: 7011 5812 5813 Hotels; eating places; drinking places
HQ: Whb Corporation
7600 E Orchard Rd 230s
Greenwood Village CO 80111
303 779-2000

(P-13095)
WHGCA LLC
Also Called: Hilton Sacramento Arden West
2200 Harvard St, Sacramento (95815-3306)
PHONE..............................916 922-4700
Alex Vargas, *Controller*
EMP: 231
SALES (est): 6.8MM
SALES (corp-wide): 74.1MM **Privately Held**
SIC: 7011 Hotels & motels
HQ: Westminster Hospitality Inc
5847 San Felipe St # 4650
Houston TX 77057
713 782-9100

(P-13096)
WIN RIVER HOTEL CORPORATION
Also Called: Hilton
5050 Bechelli Ln, Redding (96002-3539)
PHONE..............................530 226-5111
Glen Howard, *President*
EMP: 50
SALES (est): 2.6MM
SALES (corp-wide): 36.5MM **Privately Held**
SIC: 7011 Hotels & motels
PA: Redding Rancheria
2000 Redding Rancheria Rd
Redding CA 96001
530 225-8979

(P-13097)
WIN TIME LTD (PA)
Also Called: Holiday Inn
9335 Kearny Mesa Rd, San Diego (92126-4502)
PHONE..............................858 695-2300
Herman Lin, *General Ptnr*
Chue-Huang Chiu, *Partner*
Yi-Ho Huang, *Partner*
EMP: 250
SQ FT: 100,000
SALES (est): 17.6MM **Privately Held**
SIC: 7011 Hotels & motels

(P-13098)
WIN-RIVER RESORT & CASINO
2100 Redding Rancheria Rd, Redding (96001-5530)
PHONE..............................530 243-3377
Redding Rancheria Tribe, *Owner*
Christi Ross, *CFO*
Esteban Pizano, *Vice Pres*
Gary Hayward, *General Mgr*
Kim Kinyln, *General Mgr*
EMP: 310
SQ FT: 3,000
SALES (est): 12.3MM **Privately Held**
SIC: 7011 Casino hotel

(P-13099)
WINDSOR CAPITAL GROUP INC
Also Called: Residence Inn By Marriott
2101 W Vineyard Ave, Oxnard (93036-2268)
PHONE..............................805 988-0627
Doug Pflaumer, *Branch Mgr*
EMP: 100

SALES (corp-wide): 159.7MM **Privately Held**
WEB: www.snowbirdpackage.com
SIC: 7011 Hotels & motels
PA: Windsor Capital Group, Inc.
3250 Ocean Park Blvd # 350
Santa Monica CA 90405
310 566-1100

(P-13100)
WINDSOR CAPITAL GROUP INC
Also Called: Pacific Suites Hotel
3250 Ocean Park Blvd # 350, Santa Monica (90405-3257)
PHONE..............................310 566-1100
Michael D Cryan, *Manager*
Kevin D Phipps, *General Mgr*
EMP: 78
SALES (corp-wide): 159.7MM **Privately Held**
WEB: www.snowbirdpackage.com
SIC: 7011 Hotels
PA: Windsor Capital Group, Inc.
3250 Ocean Park Blvd # 350
Santa Monica CA 90405
310 566-1100

(P-13101)
WINDSOR CAPITAL GROUP INC
Also Called: Embassy Suites Arcadia
3250 Ocean Park Blvd # 350, Santa Monica (90405-3257)
PHONE..............................310 566-1100
EMP: 78
SALES (corp-wide): 159.7MM **Privately Held**
WEB: www.snowbirdpackage.com
SIC: 7011 Hotels & motels
PA: Windsor Capital Group, Inc.
3250 Ocean Park Blvd # 350
Santa Monica CA 90405
310 566-1100

(P-13102)
WINDSOR CAPITAL GROUP INC
Also Called: Embassy Suites Lompoc
3250 Ocean Park Blvd # 350, Santa Monica (90405-3257)
PHONE..............................209 577-3825
EMP: 78
SALES (corp-wide): 159.7MM **Privately Held**
WEB: www.snowbirdpackage.com
SIC: 7011 Hotels & motels
PA: Windsor Capital Group, Inc.
3250 Ocean Park Blvd # 350
Santa Monica CA 90405
310 566-1100

(P-13103)
WINDSOR CAPITAL GROUP INC
Also Called: Marriott
3250 Ocean Park Blvd # 350, Santa Monica (90405-3257)
PHONE..............................209 577-3825
Shawn Williams, *Manager*
EMP: 78
SALES (corp-wide): 159.7MM **Privately Held**
WEB: www.snowbirdpackage.com
SIC: 7011 Hotels & motels
PA: Windsor Capital Group, Inc.
3250 Ocean Park Blvd # 350
Santa Monica CA 90405
310 566-1100

(P-13104)
WINDSOR CAPITAL GROUP INC
Also Called: Embassy Suites
900 E Birch St, Brea (92821-5812)
PHONE..............................714 990-6000
Regina Samy, *Manager*
EMP: 74
SQ FT: 48,164
SALES (corp-wide): 159.7MM **Privately Held**
SIC: 7011 Hotels & motels
PA: Windsor Capital Group, Inc.
3250 Ocean Park Blvd # 350
Santa Monica CA 90405
310 566-1100

(P-13105)
WINDSOR CAPITAL GROUP INC
Also Called: Embassy Suites
29345 Rancho California, Temecula (92591-5201)
PHONE..............................951 676-5656
Tom Demott, *General Mgr*
EMP: 75
SALES (corp-wide): 159.7MM **Privately Held**
SIC: 7011 Hotels & motels
PA: Windsor Capital Group, Inc.
3250 Ocean Park Blvd # 350
Santa Monica CA 90405
310 566-1100

(P-13106)
WINDSOR CAPITAL GROUP INC
3250 Ocean Park Blvd # 350, Santa Monica (90405-3257)
PHONE..............................310 566-1100
EMP: 78
SALES (corp-wide): 159.7MM **Privately Held**
WEB: www.snowbirdpackage.com
SIC: 7011 Hotels
PA: Windsor Capital Group, Inc.
3250 Ocean Park Blvd # 350
Santa Monica CA 90405
310 566-1100

(P-13107)
WINDSOR CAPITAL GROUP INC
Also Called: Embassy Suites El Paso
3250 Ocean Park Blvd # 350, Santa Monica (90405-3257)
PHONE..............................310 566-1100
EMP: 78
SALES (corp-wide): 159.7MM **Privately Held**
WEB: www.snowbirdpackage.com
SIC: 7011 Hotels & motels
PA: Windsor Capital Group, Inc.
3250 Ocean Park Blvd # 350
Santa Monica CA 90405
310 566-1100

(P-13108)
WINDSOR CAPITAL GROUP INC
Also Called: Embassy Suites
1325 E Dyer Rd, Santa Ana (92705-5615)
PHONE..............................714 241-3800
Samuel Sansone, *Manager*
Tom Pugh, *General Mgr*
EMP: 87
SALES (corp-wide): 159.7MM **Privately Held**
SIC: 7011 5813 5812 Hotels & motels; drinking places; eating places
PA: Windsor Capital Group, Inc.
3250 Ocean Park Blvd # 350
Santa Monica CA 90405
310 566-1100

(P-13109)
WINDSOR CAPITAL GROUP INC
Also Called: Marriott
1510 University Ave, Riverside (92507-4468)
PHONE..............................951 276-1200
Jim Larson, *General Mgr*
EMP: 68
SALES (corp-wide): 159.7MM **Privately Held**
WEB: www.snowbirdpackage.com
SIC: 7011 Hotels & motels
PA: Windsor Capital Group, Inc.
3250 Ocean Park Blvd # 350
Santa Monica CA 90405
310 566-1100

(P-13110)
WJ NEWPORT LLC
Also Called: Marriott
4500 Macarthur Blvd, Newport Beach (92660-2010)
PHONE..............................949 476-2001
Wenjing Yang,
EMP: 190
SALES: 27.5MM **Privately Held**
SIC: 7011 5812 7389 Resort hotel; family restaurants;

(P-13111)
WMK SACRAMENTO LLC
Also Called: Doubltree By Hilton Scrmento Ht
2001 Point West Way, Sacramento
(95815-4702)
PHONE..........................916 929-8855
Ken Leone, *General Mgr*
EMP: 250
SALES: 17MM **Privately Held**
SIC: 7011 Hotel, franchised

(P-13112)
WOODBINE LGACY/PLAYA OWNER LLC
Also Called: Doubletree By Hilton Los Angel
6161 W Centinela Ave, Culver City
(90230-6306)
PHONE..........................678 292-4962
Lakeisha Walker, *Principal*
EMP: 75
SALES (est): 1.1MM **Privately Held**
SIC: 7011 Hotels & motels

(P-13113)
WOODFIN SUITE HOTELS LLC
Also Called: Chase Suite and Woodfin Hotels
12555 High Bluff Dr # 330, San Diego
(92130-3005)
PHONE..........................858 314-7910
Sam Hardage, *CEO*
Richard Meza, *CFO*
EMP: 780
SQ FT: 10,000
SALES (est): 29.2MM **Privately Held**
SIC: 7011 Hotels

(P-13114)
WORLD MARK OF OCEANSIDE
Also Called: World Mark By Trend West
1301 Carmelo Dr, Oceanside (92054-1089)
PHONE..........................760 721-0890
Gene Hensley, *President*
EMP: 52
SALES (est): 2MM **Privately Held**
SIC: 7011 Resort hotel

(P-13115)
WORLD TRADE CTR HT ASSOC LTD
Also Called: Long Beach Hilton, The
701 W Ocean Blvd, Long Beach
(90831-3100)
PHONE..........................562 983-3400
Steve Holloway, *Controller*
Greater Los Angeles Trade Cent, *General Ptnr*
Matsushita International Corpo, *Ltd Ptnr*
EMP: 250
SALES (est): 6.6MM **Privately Held**
SIC: 7011 7991 5813 5812 Hotels & motels; physical fitness facilities; drinking places; eating places

(P-13116)
WS HDM LLC
Also Called: Hilton San Diego/Del Mar
15575 Jimmy Durante Blvd, Del Mar
(92014-1901)
PHONE..........................858 792-5200
Al Hatfield, *Partner*
Scott Sloan, *General Mgr*
Kaylee Meyer, *Finance Dir*
EMP: 99 EST: 2012
SQ FT: 240,000
SALES (est): 2.6MM **Privately Held**
SIC: 7011 Hotels & motels

(P-13117)
WS MMV HOTEL LLC
Also Called: San Diego Marriott Mission Vly
8757 Rio San Diego Dr, San Diego
(92108-1620)
PHONE..........................619 692-3800
EMP: 99 EST: 2016
SALES (est): 331.4K **Privately Held**
SIC: 7011 Hotels & motels

(P-13118)
WW LBV INC
Also Called: Radisson Inn
30100 Agoura Rd, Agoura Hills
(91301-2004)
PHONE..........................818 707-1220
Clay Andrews, *General Mgr*
EMP: 103

SALES (corp-wide): 74.1MM **Privately Held**
SIC: 7011 6022 5812 5813 Hotels & motels; state commercial banks; caterers; drinking places
PA: Ww Lbv Inc.
2000 Hotel Plaza Blvd
Lake Buena Vista FL 32830
407 828-2424

(P-13119)
WW SAN DIEGO HARBOR ISLAND LLC
Also Called: Hilton
1960 Harbor Island Dr, San Diego
(92101-1013)
PHONE..........................619 291-6700
Shahid Kayani, *General Mgr*
Maria E Pace, *Human Res Mgr*
Pam Richardson, *Human Res Mgr*
Sandy Gallo, *Marketing Mgr*
EMP: 120
SALES: 11.5MM
SALES (corp-wide): 74.1MM **Privately Held**
WEB: www.hiltonharborisland.com
SIC: 7011 Hotels & motels
PA: Ww Lbv Inc.
2000 Hotel Plaza Blvd
Lake Buena Vista FL 32830
407 828-2424

(P-13120)
WYNDHAM INTERNATIONAL INC
222 W Houston Ave, Fullerton
(92832-3453)
PHONE..........................714 992-1700
EMP: 102 **Publicly Held**
WEB: www.wyndham.com
SIC: 7011 Hotel, franchised
HQ: Wyndham International, Inc
22 Sylvan Way
Parsippany NJ 07054
973 753-6000

(P-13121)
WYNDHAM INTERNATIONAL INC
888 E Tahquitz Canyon Way, Palm Springs
(92262-6708)
PHONE..........................760 322-6000
Jennie Hui, *Branch Mgr*
EMP: 102 **Publicly Held**
WEB: www.wyndham.com
SIC: 7011 Hotel, franchised
HQ: Wyndham International, Inc
22 Sylvan Way
Parsippany NJ 07054
973 753-6000

(P-13122)
WYNDHAM INTERNATIONAL INC
Also Called: Wyndham San Dego At Emrald Plz
400 W Broadway, San Diego (92101-3504)
PHONE..........................619 239-4500
John Beaton, *Branch Mgr*
Genna Polonia, *General Mgr*
Marilola Felix, *Sales Staff*
EMP: 102 **Publicly Held**
WEB: www.wyndham.com
SIC: 7011 Hotel, franchised
HQ: Wyndham International, Inc
22 Sylvan Way
Parsippany NJ 07054
973 753-6000

(P-13123)
WYNDHAM INTERNATIONAL INC
Also Called: Wyndham Hotels & Resorts
1 Old Ranch Rd, Carmel (93923-8551)
PHONE..........................831 625-9500
Henry Dunwall, *Owner*
EMP: 102 **Publicly Held**
WEB: www.wyndham.com
SIC: 7011 Hotels & motels
HQ: Wyndham International, Inc
22 Sylvan Way
Parsippany NJ 07054
973 753-6000

(P-13124)
WYNDHAM INTERNATIONAL INC
Also Called: Wyndham Garden Hotel
5757 Telegraph Rd, Commerce
(90040-1513)
PHONE..........................323 887-4331
Swiet Lana Cahill, *Manager*
EMP: 85 **Publicly Held**
WEB: www.wyndham.com
SIC: 7011 5812 Hotels; eating places
HQ: Wyndham International, Inc
22 Sylvan Way
Parsippany NJ 07054
973 753-6000

(P-13125)
WYNDHAM INTERNATIONAL INC
3350 Ave Of The Arts, Costa Mesa
(92626-1913)
PHONE..........................714 751-5100
Thomas Smalley, *General Mgr*
EMP: 100 **Publicly Held**
WEB: www.wyndham.com
SIC: 7011 5812 5813 Hotels; eating places; drinking places
HQ: Wyndham International, Inc
22 Sylvan Way
Parsippany NJ 07054
973 753-6000

(P-13126)
WYNDHAM INTERNATIONAL INC
Also Called: Wyndham Hotels & Resorts
400 Concourse Dr, Belmont (94002-4125)
PHONE..........................650 591-8600
Sylvia Chu, *Manager*
EMP: 50 **Publicly Held**
WEB: www.wyndham.com
SIC: 7011 Hotels
HQ: Wyndham International, Inc
22 Sylvan Way
Parsippany NJ 07054
973 753-6000

(P-13127)
WYNDHAM INTERNATIONAL INC
Also Called: Wyndham Hotels & Resorts
1350 N 1st St, San Jose (95112-4709)
PHONE..........................408 451-3050
Gary Hageman, *Branch Mgr*
Christine R Hopkins, *Comms Dir*
Madina Moore, *Director*
EMP: 140 **Publicly Held**
WEB: www.wyndham.com
SIC: 7011 5813 5812 Hotels; drinking places; eating places
HQ: Wyndham International, Inc
22 Sylvan Way
Parsippany NJ 07054
973 753-6000

(P-13128)
XANTERRA PARKS & RESORTS INC
Also Called: Furnace Creek Ranch & Inn
Hwy 190, Death Valley (92328)
P.O. Box 187 (92328-0187)
PHONE..........................760 786-2345
Dominie Lenz, *Branch Mgr*
EMP: 215
SALES (corp-wide): 388MM **Privately Held**
WEB: www.amfac.com
SIC: 7011 Resort hotel
HQ: Parks Xanterra & Resorts Inc
6312 S Fiddlers Green Cir
Greenwood Village CO 80111
303 600-3400

(P-13129)
XLD GROUP LLC
Also Called: Torrance Marriott Hotel
3635 Fashion Way, Torrance (90503-4809)
PHONE..........................310 316-3636
Pam Ryan, *General Mgr*
Herbert Smith, *Accountant*
Jon Jackson, *Director*
Francis Martin, *Manager*
EMP: 66
SALES (est): 4.2MM
SALES (corp-wide): 3.5MM **Privately Held**
WEB: www.scmarriott.com
SIC: 7011 7389 Hotels; office facilities & secretarial service rental

PA: Xld Group, Llc
500 Sansome St Ste 502
San Francisco CA

(P-13130)
YHB LONG BEACH LLC
Also Called: Holiday Inn
2640 N Lakewood Blvd, Long Beach
(90815-1715)
PHONE..........................562 597-4401
Traycee Mayer, *Principal*
Kim Mooyon, *General Mgr*
Yvette Almeida, *Manager*
EMP: 90
SALES (est): 6.1MM **Privately Held**
WEB: www.hilongbeach.com
SIC: 7011 Hotels & motels

(P-13131)
YHB SAN FRANCISCO LLC
Also Called: Pickwick Hotel The
85 5th St, San Francisco (94103-1812)
PHONE..........................415 421-7500
Fred Kleisner, *CEO*
John Valerio, *Director*
EMP: 65
SALES (est): 3.7MM **Privately Held**
WEB: www.thepickwickhotel.com
SIC: 7011 Hotels

(P-13132)
YOSEMITE MANAGEMENT GROUP LLC (PA)
Also Called: Bryce Canyon Resorts
11128 Hwy 140, El Portal (95318)
P.O. Box 650 (95318-0650)
PHONE..........................209 379-2817
Gerald Fischer,
Kevin Shelton, *Vice Pres*
Charles Fischer,
Christina Fischer,
Karane Fischer,
EMP: 75
SALES (est): 7MM **Privately Held**
WEB: www.yosemite-motels.com
SIC: 7011 Hotels & motels

(P-13133)
ZHG INC
Also Called: Monterey Beach Hotel
2600 Sand Dunes Dr, Monterey
(93940-3838)
PHONE..........................831 394-3321
Theodore Richter, *President*
EMP: 85
SQ FT: 4,996
SALES (est): 2.6MM **Privately Held**
SIC: 7011 Hotels

(P-13134)
ZKS REAL ESTATE PARTNERS LLC
Also Called: Marriott
2355 N Main St, Walnut Creek
(94596-3547)
PHONE..........................925 934-2000
James Kerrigan, *Manager*
Julie Johnson, *Marketing Staff*
EMP: 50
SALES (est): 2.5MM **Privately Held**
WEB: www.zks.com
SIC: 7011 Hotels & motels
PA: Zks Real Estate Partners Llc
1330 Arnold Dr Ste 142
Martinez CA 94553

7021 Rooming & Boarding Houses

(P-13135)
AISHA ACADEMY
706 S Pershing Ave, Stockton
(95203-3243)
P.O. Box 4638, Inglewood (90309-4638)
PHONE..........................310 908-1962
Kelvin Williams, *Exec Dir*
Krystal Williams, *CFO*
EMP: 99
SQ FT: 139,800
SALES: 4.5K **Privately Held**
SIC: 7021 Rooming & boarding houses

▲ = Import ▼=Export
◆ =Import/Export

(P-13136)
CAL POLY CORPORATION
Also Called: Housing Services
Cal Poly Bldg 31, San Luis Obispo (93407)
PHONE.................................805 756-1587
Alan Pepe, *Manager*
EMP: 70
SALES (corp-wide): 46.7MM **Privately Held**
WEB: www.calpolyarts.org
SIC: 7021 Dormitory, commercially operated
PA: Cal Poly Corporation
1 Grand Ave Bldg 15
San Luis Obispo CA 93407
805 756-1131

(P-13137)
CROCODILE BAY LODGE
Also Called: Lynch Creek Medical Management
731 Southpoint Blvd, Petaluma
(94954-1495)
PHONE.................................707 559-7990
Robert T Williams, *Consultant*
John F Galloway, *Exec VP*
David Kanski, *Director*
Tara Harrell, *Manager*
Robert T Willaims, *Consultant*
▼ **EMP:** 192
SQ FT: 2,500
SALES (est): 3.3MM **Privately Held**
WEB: www.crocodilebay.com
SIC: 7021 4724 Lodging house, except organization; travel agencies

(P-13138)
INTERNATIONAL HOUSE
Also Called: INTERNATIONAL HOUSE AT U C BER
2299 Piedmont Ave Ste 535, Berkeley
(94720-2392)
PHONE.................................510 642-9490
Robert M Berdahl, *Ch of Bd*
Joseph Lurie, *Exec Dir*
Nancy Sayavong, *Instructor*
Larnie Macasieb, *Director*
Hector Nolla, *Manager*
EMP: 162
SQ FT: 100,000
SALES: 16.6MM **Privately Held**
SIC: 7021 Rooming & boarding houses

(P-13139)
PACIFIC LABOR SERVICES INC
5690 Cypress Rd, Oxnard (93033-8509)
P.O. Box 824, Buellton (93427-0824)
PHONE.................................805 488-4625
EMP: 50
SQ FT: 62,000
SALES: 1.1MM **Privately Held**
WEB: www.pacificlaborsourceinc.com
SIC: 7021 7363 7361

7032 Sporting & Recreational Camps

(P-13140)
ADVENTRES RLLING CROSS-COUNTRY
Also Called: Adventures Cross-Country
242 Redwd Hwy Frntge 1, Mill Valley
(94941-6613)
PHONE.................................415 332-5075
Scott A Von Eschen, *President*
Eben Coenen, *Director*
Lisa Halsted, *Director*
EMP: 133
SQ FT: 2,500
SALES (est): 3.7MM **Privately Held**
WEB: www.adventurescrosscountry.com
SIC: 7032 Summer camp, except day & sports instructional

(P-13141)
ALISAL PROPERTIES (PA)
Also Called: Alisal Guest Ranch
1054 Alisal Rd, Solvang (93463-3033)
PHONE.................................805 688-6411
Palmer Jackson, *President*
Susanne Powell, *Corp Secy*
Walter D Seemann, *Bd of Directors*
Joan Y Jackson, *Vice Pres*
Joan Jackson, *Vice Pres*

EMP: 160
SQ FT: 10,000
SALES (est): 24.6MM **Privately Held**
WEB: www.alisal.com
SIC: 7032 7997 Sporting camps; golf club, membership

(P-13142)
ALLIANCE RDWODS CNFRNCE GRUNDS
6250 Bohemian Hwy, Occidental
(95465-9105)
PHONE.................................707 874-3507
James Blake, *Exec Dir*
Sharon Akers, *Admin Sec*
Kevin Chandler, *Human Resources*
Jon Maves, *Pastor*
Abby Abrahams, *Manager*
EMP: 65
SQ FT: 1,392
SALES (est): 3.6MM **Privately Held**
WEB: www.allianceredwoods.com
SIC: 7032 Recreational camps; youth camps; Bible camp

(P-13143)
BEACHSPORTS INC
600 N Catalina Ave, Redondo Beach
(90277-2134)
PHONE.................................310 372-2202
Jack Tingley, *President*
EMP: 50
SALES: 436.3K **Privately Held**
SIC: 7032 Summer camp, except day & sports instructional

(P-13144)
BIG LGUE DREAMS CONSULTING LLC
33700 Date Palm Dr, Cathedral City
(92234-4731)
PHONE.................................760 324-5600
Steve Navarro, *Vice Pres*
EMP: 118
SALES (corp-wide): 45.7MM **Privately Held**
SIC: 7032 Recreational camps
PA: Big League Dreams Consulting, Llc
16333 Fairfield Ranch Rd
Chino Hills CA 91709
909 287-1700

(P-13145)
CALIFORNIA DEPT FISH WILDLIFE
Also Called: Sacramento Valley Region 2
1701 Nimbus Rd Ste A, Gold River
(95670-4503)
PHONE.................................916 358-2900
Tina Bartlett, *Manager*
EMP: 200 **Privately Held**
WEB: www.caltaxidermy.com
SIC: 7032 7999 9512 Hunting camp; fishing lakes & piers, operation;
HQ: California Department Of Fish And Wildlife
1416 9th St Fl 12
Sacramento CA 95814

(P-13146)
CITY OF LOS ANGELES
Also Called: Parks & Recreation Dept
3200 Canyon Dr, Los Angeles
(90068-2422)
PHONE.................................323 467-7193
Kathrynn Penny, *Director*
EMP: 50 **Privately Held**
WEB: www.lacity.org
SIC: 7032 9512 7999 Sporting & recreational camps; recreational program administration, government; ; recreation center
PA: City Of Los Angeles
200 N Spring St Ste 303
Los Angeles CA 90012
213 978-0600

(P-13147)
EASTER SEALS INC
Also Called: Camp Harmon Easter Seal Soc
16403 Highway 9, Boulder Creek
(95006-9696)
PHONE.................................831 338-3383
Jennifer Whalen, *Manager*

EMP: 60
SALES (corp-wide): 73MM **Privately Held**
WEB: www.eastersealsinc.com
SIC: 7032 7033 Sporting & recreational camps; trailer parks & campsites
PA: Easter Seals, Inc.
141 W Jackson Blvd 1400a
Chicago IL 60604
312 726-6200

(P-13148)
GUIDED DISCOVERIES INC
Also Called: Desert Sun Science Center, The
26800 Saunders Meadows Rd, Idyllwild
(92549)
P.O. Box 3399 (92549-3399)
PHONE.................................951 659-6062
Allen Tiso, *Director*
EMP: 50
SALES (est): 1MM
SALES (corp-wide): 17.1MM **Privately Held**
SIC: 7032 8299 Sporting & recreational camps; educational services
PA: Guided Discoveries, Inc.
27282 Calle Arroyo
San Juan Capistrano CA 92675
800 645-1423

(P-13149)
HUME LAKE CHRISTIAN CAMPS INC
64144 Hume Lake Rd Ofc, Miramonte
(93628-9600)
PHONE.................................559 305-7770
Genie Coe, *Accountant*
Aubrie Wright, *Executive Asst*
Michelle Wilcox, *Administration*
Rob McInteer, *Technical Staff*
Angie Clark, *Opers-Prdtn-Mfg*
EMP: 78
SALES (corp-wide): 12.6MM **Privately Held**
SIC: 7032 Bible camp
PA: Hume Lake Christian Camps Inc
5545 E Hedges Ave
Fresno CA 93727
559 251-6055

(P-13150)
MAMMOTH MOUNTAIN LAKE CORP
10001 Minaret Rd, Mammoth Lakes
(93546)
P.O. Box 24 (93546-0024)
PHONE.................................760 934-2571
Alan Gregory, *CEO*
Bill Cockroft, *Vice Pres*
Tom Hodges, *Vice Pres*
Rusty Gregory, *Principal*
Sergio Moreno, *Division Mgr*
EMP: 450
SALES (est): 3.2MM
SALES (corp-wide): 129.4MM **Privately Held**
SIC: 7032 Sporting & recreational camps
HQ: Mammoth Mountain Ski Area, Llc
10001 Minaret Rd
Mammoth Lakes CA 93546
760 934-2571

(P-13151)
MOUNT HERMON ASSOCIATION INC (PA)
Also Called: Christian Conference Grounds
37 Conference Dr, Mount Hermon (95041)
PHONE.................................831 335-4466
Roger E Williams, *Exec Dir*
Jeremy Bentley, *Vice Pres*
Jon Wilcox, *Executive*
Ron Demolar, *Associate Dir*
Kerry Phibbs, *Associate Dir*
EMP: 100
SQ FT: 10,000
SALES (est): 12.6MM **Privately Held**
WEB: www.mhcamps.org
SIC: 7032 5942 Bible camp; books, religious

(P-13152)
SILVER SPUR CHRISTIAN CAMP
17301 Silver Spur Dr, Tuolumne
(95379-9638)
PHONE.................................209 928-4248
Stephen Johnson, *Director*

Marie Johnson, *Administration*
Kristen Hughes, *Relations*
EMP: 60
SALES (est): 2MM **Privately Held**
WEB: www.silverspur.com
SIC: 7032 7011 Recreational camps; hotels & motels

(P-13153)
UNITED CMPS CNFRENCES RETREATS (PA)
Also Called: UCCR
1304 Sthpint Blvd Ste 200, Petaluma
(94954)
PHONE.................................707 762-3220
Mike Carr, *President*
Matthew Compton-Clark, *COO*
Tina Heck, *Director*
EMP: 98
SQ FT: 1,700
SALES: 2.5MM **Privately Held**
WEB: www.uccr.org
SIC: 7032 Recreational camps; youth camps

(P-13154)
WESTMINSTER WOODS CAMP & CONFE
6510 Bohemian Hwy, Occidental
(95465-9101)
PHONE.................................707 874-2426
Sheila Denton, *Principal*
Tony Fry, *Supervisor*
EMP: 50
SALES (est): 187.5K **Privately Held**
SIC: 7032 Sporting & recreational camps

(P-13155)
WINNARAINBOW INC (PA)
Also Called: CAMP WINNARAINBOW
1301 Henry St, Berkeley (94709-1928)
P.O. Box 1359, Laytonville (95454-1359)
PHONE.................................510 525-4304
Jahanara Romney, *Director*
Dr Larry Brilliant, *Treasurer*
Hugh Romney, *Co-Director*
EMP: 50
SALES: 1.5MM **Privately Held**
WEB: www.wavygravy.net
SIC: 7032 Summer camp, except day & sports instructional

7033 Trailer Parks & Camp Sites

(P-13156)
BURLINGAME INDUSTRIES INC (PA)
Also Called: Eagle Roofing Products
3546 N Riverside Ave, Rialto (92377-3878)
PHONE.................................909 355-7000
Robert C Burlingame, *Ch of Bd*
Kevin C Burlingame, *President*
Rich Jones, *CFO*
Seamus P Burlingame, *Exec VP*
William L Robinson, *Admin Sec*
EMP: 100 **EST:** 1989
SQ FT: 100,000
SALES (est): 81.5MM **Privately Held**
SIC: 7033 0971 3559 3259 Campgrounds; hunting preserve; tile making machines; roofing tile, clay; asphalt felts & coatings

(P-13157)
BURLINGAME INDUSTRIES INC
Also Called: Resort Campground Intl
277 Lytle Creek Rd, Lytle Creek
(92358-9751)
PHONE.................................909 887-7038
Bob Boyter, *Manager*
EMP: 103
SALES (corp-wide): 81.5MM **Privately Held**
SIC: 7033 Campgrounds; campsite
PA: Burlingame Industries, Incorporated
3546 N Riverside Ave
Rialto CA 92377
909 355-7000

(P-13158)
CALIFORNIA LAND MGT SVCS CORP
Also Called: Calif Land Management
2165 Fallen Leaf Rd, South Lake Tahoe (96150)
PHONE.............................530 544-5994
Gayle Ellis, *General Mgr*
EMP: 50
SALES (corp-wide): 12.7MM **Privately Held**
WEB: www.clm-services.com
SIC: 7033 Trailer parks & campsites
PA: California Land Management Services Corporation
675 Gilman St
Palo Alto CA 94301
650 322-1181

(P-13159)
COLORADO RIVER ADVENTURES INC (PA)
Also Called: Yuma Lakes Resort
2715 Parker Dam Rd, Earp (92242-9712)
P.O. Box 1088, Parker AZ (85344-1088)
PHONE.............................760 663-3737
Phil Younis, *President*
Debbie Crook, *Office Mgr*
Randy Wright, *Research*
Joaquin Vences, *Art Dir*
EMP: 112
SQ FT: 6,500
SALES (est): 5.5MM **Privately Held**
WEB: www.coloradoriveradventures.com
SIC: 7033 8641 7032 Campgrounds; social club, membership; recreational camps

(P-13160)
COUNTY OF SAN MATEO
Also Called: Parks Department
455 County Ctr Fl 4, Redwood City (94063-9728)
PHONE.............................650 363-4020
Eduardo Castillo, *Analyst*
David Holland, *Exec Dir*
Cecily Harris, *General Mgr*
EMP: 55 **Privately Held**
WEB: www.ci.sanmateo.ca.us
SIC: 7033 9199 Trailer park;
PA: County Of San Mateo
400 County Ctr
Redwood City CA 94063
650 363-4123

(P-13161)
DE ANZA CAMPLAND LLC (PA)
2211 Pacific Beach Dr, San Diego (92109-5626)
PHONE.............................858 581-4200
Alvin Collins, *Principal*
EMP: 60
SALES (est): 1.7MM **Privately Held**
SIC: 7033 Trailer park

(P-13162)
EL CAPITAN CANYON LLC
11560 Calle Real, Santa Barbara (93117-9789)
PHONE.............................805 685-3887
Roger Himovitz, *Mng Member*
Kate Maclean, *Controller*
Terri Bowman, *Sales Staff*
Kendra Summers, *Sales Staff*
Bob Cochran, *Director*
EMP: 62
SALES (est): 4.7MM **Privately Held**
WEB: www.elcapitanranch.com
SIC: 7033 Campgrounds

(P-13163)
EMERALD BROOK LLC
Also Called: Emerald Desert Rv Resort
76000 Frank Sinatra Dr, Palm Desert (92211-5031)
PHONE.............................760 345-4770
Neil Brandom,
EMP: 50
SQ FT: 8,000
SALES (est): 1.7MM **Privately Held**
WEB: www.emeralddesert.com
SIC: 7033 7997 Recreational vehicle parks; golf club, membership

(P-13164)
SAN FRNCSCO NORTH/PETALUMA KOA
20 Rainsville Rd, Petaluma (94952-8121)
PHONE.............................707 763-1492
William Wood, *President*
Judith Wood, *Corp Secy*
EMP: 50
SQ FT: 2,000
SALES (est): 2.3MM **Privately Held**
WEB: www.petalumakoakampground.com
SIC: 7033 4119 Campgrounds; sightseeing bus

(P-13165)
THOUSAND TRAILS INC
Also Called: N A C O
31191 Hardin Flat Rd, Groveland (95321-9716)
PHONE.............................209 962-0100
John Kimbrough, *Manager*
EMP: 50 **Publicly Held**
WEB: www.indianpt.com
SIC: 7033 Campgrounds
HQ: Thousand Trails, Inc.
2325 Highway 90
Gautier MS 39553
228 497-3594

(P-13166)
TRAILER PARK INC
4300 Soquel Dr Spc 90, Soquel (95073-2140)
PHONE.............................831 462-3271
Mark Kalemos, *Principal*
EMP: 96 **Privately Held**
SIC: 7033 Trailer park
PA: Trailer Park, Inc.
6922 Hollywood Blvd Fl 12
Los Angeles CA 90028
-

7041 Membership-Basis Hotels

(P-13167)
AIRBNB INC (PA)
888 Brannan St, San Francisco (94103-4928)
PHONE.............................415 800-5959
Brian Chesky, *CEO*
Greg Greeley, *President*
Belinda Johnson, *COO*
Joe Gebbia,
Nathan Blecharczyk, *Officer*
EMP: 1032 **EST:** 2008
SALES (est): 274.6MM **Privately Held**
SIC: 7041 Residence club, organization

(P-13168)
ASSOCIATED STUDENTS INC
333 S Twin Oaks Valley Rd, San Marcos (92096-0001)
PHONE.............................760 750-4990
Susana Figueroa, *President*
Laura Poggi, *Exec Dir*
EMP: 50 **EST:** 1991
SALES (est): 1.3MM **Privately Held**
SIC: 7041 Boarding house, fraternity & sorority

(P-13169)
BERKELEY STUDENT COOP INC
2424 Ridge Rd, Berkeley (94709-1212)
PHONE.............................510 848-1936
Janette E Stokley, *Exec Dir*
Palmer Buchholz, *President*
Marjorie Greene, *CFO*
Twyla Parks, *Human Res Mgr*
Alfred Twu, *Corp Comm Staff*
EMP: 100
SQ FT: 18,000
SALES (est): 12.3MM **Privately Held**
WEB: www.usca.org
SIC: 7041 Boarding house, organization

(P-13170)
CITY OF SUNNYVALE
Also Called: Housing Division
456 W Olive Ave, Sunnyvale (94086-7661)
P.O. Box 3707 (94088-3707)
PHONE.............................408 730-7451
Gary Luebbers, *Principal*
EMP: 99 **Privately Held**

SIC: 7041 Rooming houses
PA: City Of Sunnyvale
456 W Olive Ave
Sunnyvale CA 94086
408 730-7415

(P-13171)
GAMMA PHI BETA SORORITY INC
Also Called: Delta PHI Chapter
890 Camino Pescadero, Goleta (93117-4768)
PHONE.............................805 968-4221
Amber Setrakain, *President*
EMP: 90
SALES: 280.7K **Privately Held**
WEB: www.gammaphibetaucsb.com
SIC: 7041 8641 7011 Membership-basis organization hotels; university club; hotels & motels

(P-13172)
HEART CONSCIOUSNESS CHURCH (PA)
Also Called: Harbin Hot Springs
18424 Harbin Springs Rd, Middletown (95461-9687)
P.O. Box 782 (95461-0782)
PHONE.............................707 987-2477
Robert F Hartley, *President*
Suzie Lecavalier, *Treasurer*
Julie Adams, *Vice Pres*
Sajjad Mahmud, *Vice Pres*
EMP: 110
SQ FT: 4,000
SALES: 4.8MM **Privately Held**
WEB: www.harbinhotsprings.com
SIC: 7041 Membership-basis organization hotels

(P-13173)
NATIONAL COMMUNITY RENAISSANCE (PA)
9421 Haven Ave, Rancho Cucamonga (91730-5886)
PHONE.............................909 483-2444
Steve Pontell, *President*
Tracy Thomas, *CFO*
Ciriaco Pinedo, *Exec VP*
Michael M Ruane, *Exec VP*
Doretta Bryan, *Vice Pres*
EMP: 51 **EST:** 1997
SALES: 5.6MM **Privately Held**
SIC: 7041 Lodging house, organization

(P-13174)
NAVY EXCHANGE SERVICE COMMAND
Also Called: Navy Bachelor Quarters
1395 Hussey Rd, Ridgecrest (93555)
PHONE.............................760 939-8681
Mike Biddlingmeier, *Branch Mgr*
EMP: 95 **Publicly Held**
WEB: www.navy-nex.com
SIC: 7041 Lodging house, organization
HQ: Navy Exchange Service Command
3280 Virginia Beach Blvd
Virginia Beach VA 23452
757 631-3696

(P-13175)
PHI DELTA THETA INC
17740 Halsted St, Northridge (91325-2025)
P.O. Box 34082, Granada Hills (91394-4082)
PHONE.............................818 885-9940
Jason McKnight, *President*
Bryan Guerrero, *Treasurer*
Evan Perez, *Principal*
EMP: 50
SALES (est): 809.2K **Privately Held**
WEB: www.redarc.com
SIC: 7041 8641 Fraternities & sororities; fraternal associations

(P-13176)
SIGMA KAPPA SORORITY
2409 Warring St, Berkeley (94704-2593)
PHONE.............................510 540-9142
Donna Jollymour, *President*
EMP: 80
SALES: 868.4K **Privately Held**
SIC: 7041 Sorority residential house

7211 Power Laundries, Family & Commercial

(P-13177)
AMERICAN ETC INC
Also Called: Royal Laundry
1140 San Mateo Ave, South San Francisco (94080-6602)
PHONE.............................650 873-5353
Kenn T Edwards, *CEO*
Don Luckenbach, *President*
Marilou Bilbao, *Administration*
Martha A Guzman, *Controller*
Maddie Alvarez, *Director*
EMP: 325
SQ FT: 70,000
SALES (est): 21.1MM **Privately Held**
SIC: 7211 Power laundries, family & commercial

(P-13178)
ANITSA INC
Also Called: Valet Services
6032 Shull St, Bell Gardens (90201-6237)
PHONE.............................213 237-0533
Margo Minisiam, *President*
Gary Von, *Executive*
Joe Brancatelli, *Chief Engr*
Marilyn Enriquez, *Accounting Mgr*
EMP: 135
SQ FT: 65,000
SALES (est): 7.1MM **Privately Held**
WEB: www.anitsa.com
SIC: 7211 8742 Power laundries, family & commercial; industry specialist consultants

(P-13179)
BRAUN LINEN SERVICE INC
A-1 Pomona Linen
396 La Mesa St, Pomona (91766-2129)
P.O. Box 317 (91769-0317)
PHONE.............................909 623-2678
Jim Moore, *Manager*
EMP: 100
SALES (corp-wide): 10.1MM **Privately Held**
SIC: 7211 7213 5947 Power laundries, family & commercial; linen supply; gifts & novelties
PA: Braun Linen Service, Inc.
16514 Garfield Ave
Paramount CA 90723
909 623-2678

(P-13180)
DEL MAR FRENCH LAUNDRY
508 Del Monte Ave, Monterey (93940-2405)
P.O. Box 1141 (93942-1141)
PHONE.............................831 375-9597
Cedo Godspodnetich, *President*
Cynthia Godspodnetich, *Admin Sec*
EMP: 50
SQ FT: 12,150
SALES: 1MM **Privately Held**
SIC: 7211 Power laundries, family & commercial

(P-13181)
MONTEREY BAY ACADAMY LAUNDRY
Also Called: Campus Laundry
675 Beach Dr, Watsonville (95076-1904)
PHONE.............................831 728-1481
Tim Kuprock, *Principal*
Jay Ketelsen, *General Mgr*
Jay Ketelson, *Manager*
EMP: 70
SALES (est): 1.7MM **Privately Held**
SIC: 7211 7213 Power laundries, family & commercial; linen supply

(P-13182)
RADIANT SERVICES CORP (PA)
651 W Knox St, Gardena (90248-4409)
PHONE.............................310 327-6300
Mina Keywanfar, *CEO*
Shahrokh Keywanfar, *President*
Jamshid Beroukhim, *Vice Pres*
Nelson Zager, *Vice Pres*
Ester Manuel, *Controller*
EMP: 235

SALES (est): 15.5MM **Privately Held**
WEB: www.radiantservices.com
SIC: **7211** 7216 Power laundries, family &
commercial; drycleaning plants, except
rugs

(P-13183)
ROYAL AIRLINE LINEN INC
125 N Ash Ave, Inglewood (90301-1648)
PHONE...............................310 677-9885
Kathleen Cunningham, *CEO*
EMP: 100
SQ FT: 12,800
SALES (est): 5.8MM **Privately Held**
SIC: **7211** Laundry collecting & distributing
outlet

(P-13184)
YUEN YEE LAUNDRY &
CLEANERS
Also Called: Yee Yuen Linen Service
2575 S Normandie Ave, Los Angeles
(90007-1598)
PHONE...............................323 734-7205
Deborah Morikawa, *President*
Luis Lee, *Corp Secy*
Cynthia Louie, *Vice Pres*
EMP: 80
SQ FT: 20,000
SALES (est): 4.6MM **Privately Held**
WEB: www.yeeyuenlinen.com
SIC: **7211** Laundry collecting & distributing
outlet

7212 Garment Pressing &
Cleaners' Agents

(P-13185)
JOSEPH DIPUZO
Also Called: Superclean America
601 E Tahquitz Canyon Way # 120, Palm
Springs (92262-6700)
P.O. Box 3006 (92263-3006)
PHONE...............................760 325-1200
Joseph Dipuzo, *Owner*
EMP: 50
SALES (est): 701.6K **Privately Held**
SIC: **7212** Laundry & drycleaner agents

7213 Linen Sply

(P-13186)
ALSCO INC
1009 Factory St, Richmond (94801-2166)
PHONE...............................510 237-9634
EMP: 84
SALES (corp-wide): 658.7MM **Privately
Held**
SIC: **7213**
PA: Alsco Inc.
505 E South Temple
Salt Lake City UT 84102
801 328-8831

(P-13187)
ALSCO INC
900 N Highland Ave, Los Angeles
(90038-2413)
PHONE...............................323 465-5111
Mike Keller, *Branch Mgr*
EMP: 180
SALES (corp-wide): 922.9MM **Privately
Held**
WEB: www.amlinen.com
SIC: **7213** Uniform supply
PA: Alsco Inc.
505 E 200 S Ste 101
Salt Lake City UT 84102
801 328-8831

(P-13188)
ALSCO INC
2215 Palma Dr, Ventura (93003-6437)
PHONE...............................805 650-6578
John Mc Carty, *Branch Mgr*
EMP: 85
SALES (corp-wide): 922.9MM **Privately
Held**
SIC: **7213** 5087 Uniform supply; laundry
equipment & supplies

PA: Alsco Inc.
505 E 200 S Ste 101
Salt Lake City UT 84102
801 328-8831

(P-13189)
ALSCO INC
705 W Grape St, San Diego (92101-2212)
P.O. Box 122671 (92112-2671)
PHONE...............................619 234-7291
Mike Scacco, *Branch Mgr*
Roberta Carleton, *Office Mgr*
Shaun Davis, *Regl Sales Mgr*
EMP: 110
SALES (corp-wide): 922.9MM **Privately
Held**
WEB: www.amlinen.com
SIC: **7213** Uniform supply
PA: Alsco Inc.
505 E 200 S Ste 101
Salt Lake City UT 84102
801 328-8831

(P-13190)
ALSCO INC
1575 Indiana St, San Francisco
(94107-3529)
PHONE...............................415 648-9266
Jonathan Silver, *Branch Mgr*
Nick Axsom, *General Mgr*
Jyoti Dhami, *Office Mgr*
David Torres, *Chief Engr*
EMP: 100
SALES (corp-wide): 922.9MM **Privately
Held**
WEB: www.amlinen.com
SIC: **7213** Uniform supply
PA: Alsco Inc.
505 E 200 S Ste 101
Salt Lake City UT 84102
801 328-8831

(P-13191)
ALSCO INC
1750 S Zeyn St, Anaheim (92802-2904)
P.O. Box 25068 (92825-5068)
PHONE...............................714 774-4165
Scott Norris, *Manager*
EMP: 100
SQ FT: 16,008
SALES (corp-wide): 922.9MM **Privately
Held**
SIC: **7213** 7218 Uniform supply; industrial
launderers
PA: Alsco Inc.
505 E 200 S Ste 101
Salt Lake City UT 84102
801 328-8831

(P-13192)
ALSCO INC
3311 Industrial Dr, Santa Rosa
(95403-2094)
PHONE...............................707 523-3311
Denny Bunch, *General Mgr*
EMP: 100
SQ FT: 36,448
SALES (corp-wide): 922.9MM **Privately
Held**
WEB: www.amlinen.com
SIC: **7213** Uniform supply
PA: Alsco Inc.
505 E 200 S Ste 101
Salt Lake City UT 84102
801 328-8831

(P-13193)
ALSCO INC
2275 Junction Ave, San Jose (95131-1211)
PHONE...............................408 279-2345
Paul Johnson, *Manager*
EMP: 110
SQ FT: 53,760
SALES (corp-wide): 922.9MM **Privately
Held**
WEB: www.amlinen.com
SIC: **7213** 7218 Uniform supply; industrial
launderers
PA: Alsco Inc.
505 E 200 S Ste 101
Salt Lake City UT 84102
801 328-8831

(P-13194)
ALSCO INC
3391 Lanatt St, Sacramento (95819-1917)
PHONE...............................916 454-5545
Michael Hollemdeck, *Branch Mgr*
Michael Hollenbeck, *Site Mgr*
EMP: 100
SALES (corp-wide): 922.9MM **Privately
Held**
WEB: www.amlinen.com
SIC: **7213** Uniform supply
PA: Alsco Inc.
505 E 200 S Ste 101
Salt Lake City UT 84102
801 328-8831

(P-13195)
AMERICAN TEXTILE MAINT CO
Also Called: Medico Professional Linen Svc
1705 Hooper Ave, Los Angeles
(90021-3111)
P.O. Box 4928, Long Beach (90804-0928)
PHONE...............................213 749-4433
Kenny Immazumi, *Manager*
EMP: 50
SALES (corp-wide): 197.6MM **Privately
Held**
WEB: www.amtextile.net
SIC: **7213** Uniform supply
PA: American Textile Maintenance Com-
pany
1667 W Washington Blvd
Los Angeles CA 90007
323 731-3132

(P-13196)
AMERICAN TEXTILE MAINT CO
Also Called: Republic Uniform
3001 E Anaheim St, Long Beach
(90804-3810)
PHONE...............................562 438-7656
Lawrence Pallan, *Manager*
EMP: 75
SALES (corp-wide): 197.6MM **Privately
Held**
WEB: www.amtextile.net
SIC: **7213** Linen supply
PA: American Textile Maintenance Com-
pany
1667 W Washington Blvd
Los Angeles CA 90007
323 731-3132

(P-13197)
AMERICAN TEXTILE MAINT CO
Also Called: Republic Master Chefs Textile
3001 E Anaheim St, Long Beach
(90804-3810)
PHONE...............................562 438-1126
Lawrence Pallan, *Branch Mgr*
EMP: 86
SALES (corp-wide): 197.6MM **Privately
Held**
SIC: **7213** Linen supply
PA: American Textile Maintenance Com-
pany
1667 W Washington Blvd
Los Angeles CA 90007
323 731-3132

(P-13198)
AMERICAN TEXTILE MAINT CO
Also Called: Master-Chef's Linen Rental
1664 W Washington Blvd, Los Angeles
(90007-1115)
PHONE...............................323 735-1661
Bob Brill, *Branch Mgr*
EMP: 130
SALES (corp-wide): 197.6MM **Privately
Held**
WEB: www.amtextile.net
SIC: **7213** Towel supply; uniform supply
PA: American Textile Maintenance Com-
pany
1667 W Washington Blvd
Los Angeles CA 90007
323 731-3132

(P-13199)
AMERIPRIDE SERVICES INC
109 Calle Propano Ste C, Paso Robles
(93446-5950)
PHONE...............................805 239-9449
Matt Wenzel, *Branch Mgr*
Keith Jones, *Site Mgr*
EMP: 100 **Publicly Held**

WEB: www.ameripride.com
SIC: **7213** Uniform supply
HQ: Ameripride Services, Inc.
10801 Wayzata Blvd # 100
Minnetonka MN 55305
800 750-4628

(P-13200)
AMERIPRIDE SERVICES INC
3750 Eastside Rd, Redding (96001-3807)
PHONE...............................530 242-0564
J Oldham, *Branch Mgr*
EMP: 50 **Publicly Held**
SIC: **7213** Uniform supply
HQ: Ameripride Services, Inc.
10801 Wayzata Blvd # 100
Minnetonka MN 55305
800 750-4628

(P-13201)
AMERIPRIDE SERVICES INC
Also Called: Ameripride Unifom Svcs
335 Washington St, Bakersfield
(93307-2719)
PHONE...............................661 324-7941
EMP: 110
SQ FT: 34,000 **Publicly Held**
SIC: **7213** 7218
HQ: Ameripride Services, Inc.
10801 Wayzata Blvd # 100
Minnetonka MN 55305
800 750-4628

(P-13202)
AMERIPRIDE SERVICES INC
4206 S B St, Stockton (95206-3990)
PHONE...............................209 982-0020
Walter Locke, *Branch Mgr*
EMP: 50 **Publicly Held**
WEB: www.ameripride.com
SIC: **7213** 7218 Uniform supply; industrial
launderers
HQ: Ameripride Services, Inc.
10801 Wayzata Blvd # 100
Minnetonka MN 55305
800 750-4628

(P-13203)
AMERIPRIDE SERVICES INC
2230 W Chapman Ave, Orange
(92868-2316)
PHONE...............................714 385-8991
Frank Saldana, *Branch Mgr*
EMP: 50 **Publicly Held**
WEB: www.ameripride.com
SIC: **7213** 7218 Uniform supply; industrial
launderers
HQ: Ameripride Services, Inc.
10801 Wayzata Blvd # 100
Minnetonka MN 55305
800 750-4628

(P-13204)
AMERIPRIDE SERVICES INC
3701 Collins Ave Ste 5b, Richmond
(94806-2079)
PHONE...............................800 748-6178
John Galletta, *Manager*
EMP: 50 **Publicly Held**
WEB: www.ameripride.com
SIC: **7213** 7218 Uniform supply; industrial
launderers
HQ: Ameripride Services, Inc.
10801 Wayzata Blvd # 100
Minnetonka MN 55305
800 750-4628

(P-13205)
AMERIPRIDE SERVICES INC
1356 Dayton St Ste R, Salinas
(93901-4427)
PHONE...............................800 882-5326
Jason Saathoff, *President*
EMP: 50 **Publicly Held**
WEB: www.ameripride.com
SIC: **7213** 7218 Uniform supply; industrial
launderers
HQ: Ameripride Services, Inc.
10801 Wayzata Blvd # 100
Minnetonka MN 55305
800 750-4628

PRODUCTS & SVCS

(P-13206)
ARAMARK UNF & CAREER AP LLC
855 Mckendrie St, San Jose (95126-1295)
P.O. Box 28383 (95159-8383)
PHONE..................408 243-9824
Brett Borba, *Manager*
Mike Duncanson, *Merchandising*
EMP: 100 Publicly Held
WEB: www.aramark-uniform.com
SIC: 7213 7218 Uniform supply; industrial launderers
HQ: Aramark Uniform & Career Apparel, Llc
115 N First St Ste 203
Burbank CA 91502
818 973-3700

(P-13207)
ARAMARK UNF & CAREER AP LLC
15525 Garfield Ave, Paramount (90723-4033)
P.O. Box 1799 (90723-1799)
PHONE..................323 774-4216
Dave Canzani, *Owner*
EMP: 71 Publicly Held
WEB: www.aramark-uniform.com
SIC: 7213 Uniform supply
HQ: Aramark Uniform & Career Apparel, Llc
115 N First St Ste 203
Burbank CA 91502
818 973-3700

(P-13208)
ARAMARK UNF & CAREER AP LLC
3333 N Sabre Dr, Fresno (93727-7816)
P.O. Box 1289, Clovis (93613-1289)
PHONE..................559 291-6631
Anthony Mollica, *Sales/Mktg Mgr*
Janis Hill, *Info Tech Mgr*
Nancy Christian, *Purch Agent*
EMP: 200
SQ FT: 130,449 Publicly Held
WEB: www.aramark-uniform.com
SIC: 7213 Uniform supply
HQ: Aramark Uniform & Career Apparel, Llc
115 N First St Ste 203
Burbank CA 91502
818 973-3700

(P-13209)
ARAMARK UNF & CAREER AP LLC
5665 Eastgage Dr, San Diego (92121)
PHONE..................858 550-5200
EMP: 196 Publicly Held
WEB: www.aramark-uniform.com
SIC: 7213 Linen supply
HQ: Aramark Uniform & Career Apparel, Llc
115 N First St Ste 203
Burbank CA 91502
818 973-3700

(P-13210)
ARAMARK UNF & CAREER AP LLC
440 Carolina St, San Francisco (94107-2304)
PHONE..................415 244-8332
Deborah Hupp, *Manager*
EMP: 250 Publicly Held
WEB: www.aramark-uniform.com
SIC: 7213 Uniform supply
HQ: Aramark Uniform & Career Apparel, Llc
115 N First St Ste 203
Burbank CA 91502
818 973-3700

(P-13211)
BRAUN LINEN SERVICE INC (PA)
Also Called: A-1 Pomona Linen
16514 Garfield Ave, Paramount (90723-5304)
P.O. Box 348 (90723-0348)
PHONE..................909 623-2678
Richard A Cornwell, *CEO*
William S Cornwell, *Vice Pres*
EMP: 125 EST: 1985
SQ FT: 28,000
SALES (est): 10.1MM Privately Held
SIC: 7213 Towel supply; table cover supply

(P-13212)
CAL SOUTHERN SERVICES
Also Called: Socal Uniform Rental
419 Mcgroarty St, San Gabriel (91776-2302)
PHONE..................626 281-5942
EMP: 99
SALES (est): 3.1MM Privately Held
SIC: 7213

(P-13213)
CALIFORNIA LINEN SERVICES INC
40 E California Blvd, Pasadena (91105-3203)
PHONE..................626 564-4576
Brian O'Neil, *President*
Myrna Pulido, *Executive*
Kelly Huizinga, *Office Mgr*
Mary Hilliard, *Sales Mgr*
EMP: 60
SALES (est): 2.3MM Privately Held
SIC: 7213 Uniform supply

(P-13214)
CINTAS CORPORATION
3201 Dnville Blvd Ste 285, Alamo (94507)
PHONE..................925 743-1745
EMP: 54
SALES (corp-wide): 6.8B Publicly Held
SIC: 7213 5999 5912 5699 Uniform supply; alarm & safety equipment stores; drug stores & proprietary stores; uniforms & work clothing
PA: Cintas Corporation
6800 Cintas Blvd
Cincinnati OH 45262
513 459-1200

(P-13215)
CINTAS CORPORATION NO 3
2829 Workman Mill Rd, Whittier (90601-1549)
PHONE..................562 692-8741
Bryce Littlejohn, *General Mgr*
Edward Cadena, *Manager*
EMP: 100
SALES (corp-wide): 6.8B Publicly Held
WEB: www.cintas-corp.com
SIC: 7213 7218 Uniform supply; industrial launderers
HQ: Cintas Corporation No 3
6800 Cintas Blvd
Mason OH 45040

(P-13216)
CINTAS CORPORATION NO 3
7735 Paramount Blvd, Pico Rivera (90660-4308)
PHONE..................562 368-3200
Robert Choonover, *Manager*
Steve Mildner, *Sales Dir*
Frank Ruiz, *Sales Staff*
Rebecca Romero, *Manager*
EMP: 150
SQ FT: 63,910
SALES (corp-wide): 6.8B Publicly Held
WEB: www.cintas-corp.com
SIC: 7213 Uniform supply
HQ: Cintas Corporation No 3
6800 Cintas Blvd
Mason OH 45040

(P-13217)
CINTAS CORPORATION NO 3
2150 Proforma Ave, Ontario (91761-8518)
PHONE..................909 930-9096
Jim Ewald, *President*
EMP: 150
SQ FT: 49,705
SALES (corp-wide): 6.8B Publicly Held
SIC: 7213 Uniform supply
HQ: Cintas Corporation No 3
6800 Cintas Blvd
Mason OH 45040

(P-13218)
CINTAS CORPORATION NO 3
28334 Industry Dr, Valencia (91355-4103)
PHONE..................661 310-7400
Eric Curtis, *Branch Mgr*
Jason Fujiki, *Manager*
EMP: 94

SALES (corp-wide): 6.8B Publicly Held
WEB: www.cintas-corp.com
SIC: 7213 Uniform supply
HQ: Cintas Corporation No 3
6800 Cintas Blvd
Mason OH 45040

(P-13219)
CITY TOWEL & DUST SERVICE INC
Also Called: Sunset Linen Service
3016 Dutton Ave, Santa Rosa (95407-7886)
PHONE..................707 542-0391
Michael Erwin, *President*
EMP: 50
SQ FT: 5,000
SALES (est): 3.3MM Privately Held
SIC: 7213 7211 Uniform supply; linen supply, non-clothing; laundry collecting & distributing outlet

(P-13220)
COMPLETE LINEN SVC
Also Called: Complete Linen Services
290 S Maple Ave, South San Francisco (94080-6304)
PHONE..................650 873-1221
Steve Bruni, *President*
Patrice Bruni, *Treasurer*
Colin Morf, *Vice Pres*
Kathy Lobos, *Admin Asst*
EMP: 100
SQ FT: 14,000
SALES (est): 7.2MM Privately Held
WEB: www.completelinen.com
SIC: 7213 Linen supply

(P-13221)
FOASBERG LAUNDRY & CLRS INC (PA)
Also Called: Crdn of Southern La County
640 E Wardlow Rd, Long Beach (90807-4624)
P.O. Box 17965 (90807-7965)
PHONE..................562 426-7345
James W Foasberg, *CEO*
Richard Foasberg, *Vice Pres*
EMP: 55
SQ FT: 40,000
SALES (est): 4.2MM Privately Held
SIC: 7213 7216 7211 7218 Uniform supply; drycleaning collecting & distributing agency; laundry collecting & distributing outlet; industrial launderers

(P-13222)
GBS LINENS INC (PA)
Also Called: GBS Party Linens
305 N Muller St, Anaheim (92801-5445)
PHONE..................714 778-6448
Pravin Mody, *President*
Ameer P Mody, *Vice Pres*
Sudha Mody, *Vice Pres*
Sujata Mody, *Admin Sec*
EMP: 100
SQ FT: 57,000
SALES (est): 12.3MM Privately Held
WEB: www.gbslinens.com
SIC: 7213 2392 7211 5023 Linen supply; household furnishings; power laundries, family & commercial; home furnishings; textile mill waste & remnant processing

(P-13223)
LA TAVOLA LLC (PA)
2655 Napa Valley Corp Dr, NAPA (94558)
PHONE..................707 257-3358
Betsy Stone, *President*
Sara Cilloni, *Sales Associate*
Danielle Sanchez, *Merchandising*
Whitney Werts, *Sales Staff*
Deva Moore, *Accounts Mgr*
EMP: 99
SALES (est): 4.6MM Privately Held
SIC: 7213 Linen supply

(P-13224)
MISSION LINEN SUPPLY
Also Called: Mission Linen & Uniform Svc
2727 Industry St, Oceanside (92054-4810)
PHONE..................760 757-9099
Graig Rogers, *Principal*
Lupe Avalos, *Admin Sec*
EMP: 108

SALES (corp-wide): 180.2MM Privately Held
WEB: www.missions.com
SIC: 7213 7218 Uniform supply; industrial launderers
PA: Mission Linen Supply
717 E Yanonali St
Santa Barbara CA 93103
805 730-3620

(P-13225)
MISSION LINEN SUPPLY
Mission Linen & Uniform Svc
399 Errol St, Morro Bay (93442-1896)
PHONE..................805 772-4451
Josh Offil, *General Mgr*
EMP: 50
SALES (corp-wide): 180.2MM Privately Held
WEB: www.missions.com
SIC: 7213 Uniform supply
PA: Mission Linen Supply
717 E Yanonali St
Santa Barbara CA 93103
805 730-3620

(P-13226)
MISSION LINEN SUPPLY
Also Called: Mission Linen & Uniform Svc
7520 Reese Rd, Sacramento (95828-3707)
PHONE..................916 423-3179
Peppy Secaile, *Manager*
Irving Dungca, *Area Mgr*
Kristi Bell, *Office Mgr*
Sanchez Patricia, *Buyer*
Harlin Scott, *Mfg Staff*
EMP: 125
SALES (corp-wide): 180.2MM Privately Held
WEB: www.missions.com
SIC: 7213 7218 Uniform supply; industrial launderers
PA: Mission Linen Supply
717 E Yanonali St
Santa Barbara CA 93103
805 730-3620

(P-13227)
MISSION LINEN SUPPLY
Also Called: Mission Linen & Uniform Svc
315 Kern St, Salinas (93905-2595)
PHONE..................831 424-1707
Mark Rogers, *Manager*
Mark Sanchez, *General Mgr*
EMP: 59
SALES (corp-wide): 180.2MM Privately Held
WEB: www.missions.com
SIC: 7213 Uniform supply
PA: Mission Linen Supply
717 E Yanonali St
Santa Barbara CA 93103
805 730-3620

(P-13228)
MISSION LINEN SUPPLY
Also Called: Mission Linen Supply & Svcs
1401 Summer St, Eureka (95501-2246)
PHONE..................707 443-8681
Jack Anderson, *General Mgr*
EMP: 58
SALES (corp-wide): 180.2MM Privately Held
WEB: www.missions.com
SIC: 7213 Uniform supply
PA: Mission Linen Supply
717 E Yanonali St
Santa Barbara CA 93103
805 730-3620

(P-13229)
MISSION LINEN SUPPLY
Also Called: Mission Linen & Uniform Svc
2555 S Orange Ave, Fresno (93725-1398)
PHONE..................559 268-0647
Allen Gregory, *Manager*
Lupe Guizar, *Representative*
EMP: 75
SALES (corp-wide): 180.2MM Privately Held
WEB: www.missions.com
SIC: 7213 Uniform supply
PA: Mission Linen Supply
717 E Yanonali St
Santa Barbara CA 93103
805 730-3620

(P-13230)
MISSION LINEN SUPPLY
Also Called: Mission Linen & Uniform Svc
505 Maulhardt Ave, Oxnard (93030-7925)
PHONE....................................805 485-6794
Matthew Aguelli, *Manager*
Nina Zinn, *General Mgr*
Jennifer Strong, *Office Mgr*
EMP: 55
SALES (corp-wide): 180.2MM **Privately Held**
WEB: www.missions.com
SIC: 7213 Towel supply
PA: Mission Linen Supply
717 E Yanonali St
Santa Barbara CA 93103
805 730-3620

(P-13231)
MISSION LINEN SUPPLY
Also Called: Mission Linen & Uniform Svc
550 Florida St, San Francisco
(94110-1960)
PHONE....................................510 429-7305
Ken Eggers, *Manager*
EMP: 120
SALES (corp-wide): 180.2MM **Privately Held**
WEB: www.missions.com
SIC: 7213 7218 Linen supply, non-clothing; linen supply, clothing; industrial launderers
PA: Mission Linen Supply
717 E Yanonali St
Santa Barbara CA 93103
805 730-3620

(P-13232)
MISSION LINEN SUPPLY
Also Called: Mission Linen & Uniform Svc
712 E Montecito St, Santa Barbara
(93103-3295)
PHONE....................................805 962-7687
Curtos Lopez, *Manager*
Sean Fallon, *Area Mgr*
Chris Phelps, *General Mgr*
Rebecca Hillan, *Office Mgr*
Viet Pham, *Chief Engr*
EMP: 50
SALES (corp-wide): 180.2MM **Privately Held**
WEB: www.missions.com
SIC: 7213 Uniform supply
PA: Mission Linen Supply
717 E Yanonali St
Santa Barbara CA 93103
805 730-3620

(P-13233)
MISSION LINEN SUPPLY
Also Called: Mission Linen & Uniform Svc
1340 W 7th St, Chico (95928-4907)
PHONE....................................530 342-4110
Nick Katzenstein, *Manager*
David Simcox, *Area Mgr*
EMP: 50
SALES (corp-wide): 180.2MM **Privately Held**
WEB: www.missions.com
SIC: 7213 5699 Uniform supply; uniforms & work clothing
PA: Mission Linen Supply
717 E Yanonali St
Santa Barbara CA 93103
805 730-3620

(P-13234)
MISSION LINEN SUPPLY
Also Called: Mission Linen & Uniform Svc
602 S Western Ave, Santa Maria
(93458-5496)
PHONE....................................805 922-3579
Bill Bently, *General Mgr*
EMP: 80
SALES (corp-wide): 180.2MM **Privately Held**
WEB: www.missions.com
SIC: 7213 Uniform supply
PA: Mission Linen Supply
717 E Yanonali St
Santa Barbara CA 93103
805 730-3620

(P-13235)
MISSION LINEN SUPPLY
Also Called: Mission Linen & Uniform Svc
5400 Alton Way, Chino (91710-7601)
PHONE....................................909 393-5589
Mike Keller, *Manager*
EMP: 400
SALES (corp-wide): 180.2MM **Privately Held**
WEB: www.missions.com
SIC: 7213 7218 Linen supply, non-clothing; linen supply, clothing; industrial launderers
PA: Mission Linen Supply
717 E Yanonali St
Santa Barbara CA 93103
805 730-3620

(P-13236)
MORGAN SERVICES INC
Also Called: Morgan Linen Service
905 Yale St, Los Angeles (90012-1724)
PHONE....................................213 485-9666
Mark Smith, *Branch Mgr*
Michelle Valenzuela, *Admin Asst*
Christopher Dugan, *Sales Staff*
EMP: 100
SQ FT: 51,339
SALES (corp-wide): 38.6MM **Privately Held**
WEB: www.morganservices.com
SIC: 7213 7218 Linen supply; industrial launderers
PA: Morgan Services, Inc.
323 N Michigan Ave
Chicago IL 60601
312 346-3181

(P-13237)
PARK CLEANERS INC (PA)
Also Called: Park Uniform Rentals
419 Mcgroarty St, San Gabriel
(91776-2302)
PHONE....................................626 281-5942
James L Brittain, *President*
Ted Doll, *Vice Pres*
Theodore W Doll, *Vice Pres*
EMP: 75
SQ FT: 7,000
SALES (est): 2.4MM **Privately Held**
SIC: 7213 7216 Uniform supply; cleaning & dyeing, except rugs

(P-13238)
PRUDENTIAL OVERALL SUPPLY
Also Called: Store 17
5300 Gabbert Rd, Moorpark (93021-1772)
P.O. Box 11210, Santa Ana (92711-1210)
PHONE....................................805 529-0833
Mark Stanton, *Manager*
Diane Ortega, *General Mgr*
Kelli Cather, *Office Mgr*
Michelle Singleterry, *Admin Sec*
Mary J Nirenberg, *Admin Asst*
EMP: 56
SALES (corp-wide): 158.2MM **Privately Held**
WEB: www.pos-clean.com
SIC: 7213 5087 7218 Uniform supply; janitors' supplies; wiping towel supply
PA: Prudential Overall Supply
1661 Alton Pkwy
Irvine CA 92606
949 250-4855

(P-13239)
RFID CORPORATION
701 Willow Pass Rd Ste 10, Pittsburg
(94565-1803)
PHONE....................................925 473-9978
John Burskens, *Plant Mgr*
EMP: 190 **Publicly Held**
SIC: 7213 Uniform supply
HQ: Rfid Corporation
1901 S Meyers Rd Ste 630
Oakbrook Terrace IL 60181
678 823-4100

(P-13240)
RFID TEXTILE SERVICES INC
300 E Commercial St, Pomona
(91767-5506)
PHONE....................................909 623-5135
Albert Cunningham, *General Mgr*
EMP: 65 **Publicly Held**
SIC: 7213 Uniform supply

HQ: Rfid Textile Services, Inc.
1105 Lakewood Pkwy # 210
Alpharetta GA 30009
678 823-4100

(P-13241)
RICHARD K NEWMAN AND ASSOC INC (PA)
Also Called: Sparkle Uniform & Linen Svc
121 Monterey St, Bakersfield (93305-3406)
PHONE....................................661 634-1130
Jeffrey C Newman Sr, *Ch of Bd*
Jeffrey C Newman Jr, *President*
Mike Daniel, *COO*
Jeff Newman Jr, *Executive*
Alison Daniel, *Office Mgr*
EMP: 50
SQ FT: 26,000
SALES (est): 7.6MM **Privately Held**
WEB: www.sparklerental.com
SIC: 7213 7216 Linen supply, non-clothing; uniform supply; drycleaning collecting & distributing agency

(P-13242)
SYNERGY HEALTH NORTH AMER INC
2240 E Artesia Blvd, Long Beach
(90805-1739)
PHONE....................................562 428-5858
Gary Metz, *Manager*
EMP: 72 **Privately Held**
SIC: 7213 Linen supply
HQ: Synergy Health North America, Inc.
3903 Northdale Blvd 100e
Tampa FL 33624
813 891-9550

(P-13243)
UNIFIRST CORPORATION
4630 Beloit Dr Ste 40, Sacramento
(95838-2449)
PHONE....................................916 929-3766
Jerald Satterlfield, *Branch Mgr*
EMP: 50
SALES (corp-wide): 1.8B **Publicly Held**
SIC: 7213 5949 5699 Uniform supply; needlework goods & supplies; uniforms
PA: Unifirst Corporation
68 Jonspin Rd
Wilmington MA 01887
978 658-8888

7215 Coin Operated Laundries & Cleaning

(P-13244)
ALL VALLEY WASHER SERVICE INC
15008 Delano St, Van Nuys (91411-2016)
PHONE....................................818 787-1100
Ron Feinstein, *President*
Billy Feinstein, *Treasurer*
Robert Feinstein, *Vice Pres*
Trini Valenzuela, *Marketing Staff*
Jocelyn Perez, *Sales Staff*
EMP: 70
SQ FT: 11,000
SALES (est): 9.2MM **Privately Held**
WEB: www.allvalleywasher.com
SIC: 7215 6531 7359 5087 Laundry, coin-operated; real estate agents & managers; appliance rental; laundry equipment & supplies

(P-13245)
AUTOMATIC LEASING INC
Also Called: Master Rent
260 Fulton St, Fresno (93721-3127)
PHONE....................................559 233-2444
Peter Pierre III, *President*
EMP: 421
SALES (corp-wide): 10.1MM **Privately Held**
WEB: www.alcoservices.com
SIC: 7215 7514 Coin-operated laundries & cleaning; passenger car rental
PA: Automatic Leasing, Inc.
445 S Figueroa St
Los Angeles CA
213 746-4117

(P-13246)
CLEAN KING LAUNDRY SYSTEMS INC
15431 Chatsworth St, Mission Hills
(91345-1905)
P.O. Box 8689, Northridge (91327-8689)
PHONE....................................818 363-5500
Brian Merkel, *President*
EMP: 50
SALES (est): 1.5MM **Privately Held**
SIC: 7215 Coin-operated laundries & cleaning

(P-13247)
COINMACH CORPORATION (PA)
Also Called: Reliable Co
3628 San Fernando Rd, Glendale
(91204-2944)
PHONE....................................818 637-4300
EMP: 80
SQ FT: 22,000
SALES (est): 4.6MM **Privately Held**
SIC: 7215 7211 5087

(P-13248)
CSC SERVICEWORKS HOLDINGS INC
Also Called: Kwik Wash Laundries
32910 Alvarado Niles Rd # 150, Union City
(94587-3103)
PHONE....................................510 429-0900
Mike Hagen, *Manager*
EMP: 150
SALES (corp-wide): 361.2MM **Privately Held**
SIC: 7215 Laundry, coin-operated
PA: Csc Serviceworks Holdings, Inc.
303 Sunnyside Blvd # 70
Plainview NY 11803
516 349-8555

(P-13249)
OCEANSIDE LAUNDRY LLC
Also Called: Campus Laundry
675 Beach Dr, Watsonville (95076-1904)
PHONE....................................831 722-4358
Gregory Anderson, *President*
EMP: 100
SALES (est): 8.1MM **Privately Held**
SIC: 7215 Coin-operated laundries & cleaning

(P-13250)
PRO-WASH INC
9117 S Main St, Los Angeles (90003-3722)
PHONE....................................323 756-6000
Steve Koo, *President*
EMP: 70
SQ FT: 20,000
SALES (est): 3.1MM **Privately Held**
WEB: www.prowashconsulting.com
SIC: 7215 Laundry, coin-operated

(P-13251)
PWS HOLDINGS LLC
6500 Flotilla St, Commerce (90040-1714)
PHONE....................................323 721-8832
Morton Pollack, *Mng Member*
Jose Franco, *Sales Associate*
Eric Steinberg,
EMP: 125
SALES (est): 1.7MM **Privately Held**
WEB: www.pwsholdings.com
SIC: 7215 Coin-operated laundries & cleaning

(P-13252)
WASH MLTFMILY LDRY SYSTEMS LLC (PA)
100 N Pacific Coast Hwy, El Segundo
(90245-4359)
PHONE....................................310 643-8491
Jim Gimeson, *CEO*
Arthur J Long, *CFO*
Andres De Armas, *Risk Mgmt Dir*
Ross Van Horne, *Exec Dir*
Donn Eckardt, *Manager*
EMP: 150
SQ FT: 130,000
SALES (est): 52.5MM **Privately Held**
WEB: www.weblaundry.com
SIC: 7215 Laundry, coin-operated

P R O D U C T S & S V C S

7216 Dry Cleaning Plants, Except Rug Cleaning

(P-13253)
CAMARO CLEANERS CORP (PA)
1515 Wedgewood Dr, Hillsborough
(94010-7343)
PHONE..................................650 343-4296
Modesto Gomez, *CEO*
EMP: 85
SQ FT: 20,000
SALES (est): 543.4K **Privately Held**
SIC: 7216 Drycleaning plants, except rugs

(P-13254)
COIT SERVICES INC
1297 Logan Ave, Costa Mesa
(92626-4004)
PHONE..................................949 760-0760
John Comer, *Branch Mgr*
Jan Carney, *President*
EMP: 50
SALES (corp-wide): 46.7MM **Privately Held**
SIC: 7216 7217 Drycleaning plants, except rugs; carpet & upholstery cleaning
PA: Coit Services, Inc.
897 Hinckley Rd
Burlingame CA 94010
650 697-5471

(P-13255)
CUSTOM COMMERCIAL DRY CLRS INC (PA)
Also Called: Frsteam By Custom Commercial
3201 Investment Blvd, Hayward
(94545-3813)
PHONE..................................510 723-1000
Courtney Nicholas, *CEO*
Jim Nicholas, *President*
Ryan Meekma, *Vice Pres*
Holly Murry, *Vice Pres*
Shane Tolman, *Sales Staff*
EMP: 50
SALES (est): 4.4MM **Privately Held**
SIC: 7216 Cleaning & dyeing, except rugs

(P-13256)
INTER-CITY CLEANERS
438 S Airport Blvd, South San Francisco
(94080-6908)
PHONE..................................650 875-9200
Hans Gelfand, *Co-Owner*
Vera Gelfand, *Co-Owner*
EMP: 68
SQ FT: 9,000
SALES (est): 4.6MM **Privately Held**
WEB: www.intercitycleaners.com
SIC: 7216 7219 Cleaning & dyeing, except rugs; laundry, except power & coin-operated

(P-13257)
PICO CLEANER INC (PA)
9150 W Pico Blvd, Los Angeles
(90035-1320)
PHONE..................................310 274-2431
Sharam Jahanbani, *CEO*
Simon Djahanbani, *President*
EMP: 80
SQ FT: 10,000
SALES (est): 5.6MM **Privately Held**
WEB: www.picocleaners.com
SIC: 7216 Cleaning & dyeing, except rugs; curtain cleaning & repair

(P-13258)
SANTA BARBARA FABRICARE INC
Also Called: Ablitt's Fine Cleaners
14 W Gutierrez St, Santa Barbara
(93101-3423)
PHONE..................................805 963-6677
Neil Ablitt, *President*
R Neil Ablitt, *President*
Sue Ablitt, *Vice Pres*
Sean Nguyen, *General Mgr*
EMP: 50
SQ FT: 12,500
SALES (est): 3MM **Privately Held**
SIC: 7216 7211 7212 Cleaning & dyeing, except rugs; power laundries, family & commercial; valet apparel service

(P-13259)
SHADKOR INC
Also Called: Milt & Michael Master Dry Clrs
4021 W Alameda Ave, Burbank
(91505-4335)
PHONE..................................818 953-4627
Thomas Agha, *President*
Milton Shortkoff, *Corp Secy*
EMP: 60
SQ FT: 4,345
SALES (est): 3.2MM **Privately Held**
SIC: 7216 Cleaning & dyeing, except rugs

(P-13260)
STERLING WESTWOOD INC
Also Called: Sterling Dry Cleaners
3405 Overland Ave, Los Angeles
(90034-5405)
PHONE..................................310 287-2431
Harry Gershenson, *Manager*
EMP: 55
SALES (corp-wide): 2.1MM **Privately Held**
SIC: 7216 Drycleaning plants, except rugs
PA: Sterling Westwood Inc
1600 Westwood Blvd
Los Angeles CA 90024
310 474-8525

(P-13261)
VALETOR INC
Also Called: Hollyway Cleaners
8359 Santa Monica Blvd, Los Angeles
(90069-4312)
PHONE..................................323 654-1271
Fatehali Amersi, *President*
EMP: 50
SQ FT: 4,000
SALES (est): 1.8MM **Privately Held**
SIC: 7216 7215 Cleaning & dyeing, except rugs; laundry, coin-operated

7217 Carpet & Upholstery Cleaning

(P-13262)
BONDED INC (PA)
Also Called: Bonded Carpet
7831 Ostrow St, San Diego (92111-3602)
P.O. Box 23910 (92193-3910)
PHONE..................................858 576-8400
Mitch Adler, *President*
Betty Wrona, *CFO*
Sherri Adler, *Vice Pres*
Melissa Ameida, *Administration*
Jacquelyn Clark, *Administration*
EMP: 82
SQ FT: 16,500
SALES (est): 7.6MM **Privately Held**
WEB: www.bondedcarpet.com
SIC: 7217 5023 Carpet & furniture cleaning on location; home furnishings; fireplace equipment & accessories

(P-13263)
C & S DRAPERIES INC
Also Called: Coit Restoration Services
4210 Kiernan Ave, Modesto (95356-9758)
PHONE..................................209 466-5371
Pete Bakker, *CEO*
Helen Bakker, *CEO*
EMP: 150
SQ FT: 50,000
SALES (est): 9.4MM **Privately Held**
SIC: 7217 Carpet & furniture cleaning on location; carpet & rug cleaning plant; carpet & rug cleaning & repairing plant

(P-13264)
CARPET SOLUTIONS
28126 Peacock Ridge Dr # 115, Rancho Palos Verdes (90275-7108)
PHONE..................................310 886-3800
Yenling Huan, *Owner*
EMP: 50
SALES (est): 1.3MM **Privately Held**
SIC: 7217 1752 Carpet & upholstery cleaning; carpet laying

(P-13265)
CHROMA SYSTEMS
Also Called: Southcoast Dyeing & Finishing
3201 S Susan St, Santa Ana (92704-6838)
PHONE..................................714 557-8480

Peer Vinther, *Partner*
Monterey Carpets, *Partner*
Camelot Carpet Mills, *Partner*
EMP: 100
SQ FT: 200,000
SALES (est): 3.3MM **Privately Held**
SIC: 7217 2273 Carpet & rug dyeing plant; carpets & rugs

(P-13266)
COLT SERVICES INC
Also Called: Stanley Steemer Carpet Cleaner
9655 Via Excelencia, San Diego
(92126-4555)
PHONE..................................858 271-9910
Toll Free:..................................888 -
Steven R Thompson, *President*
EMP: 100
SQ FT: 33,000
SALES (est): 9MM **Privately Held**
SIC: 7217 Carpet & furniture cleaning on location

(P-13267)
DESIGNERS LLC (PA)
Also Called: Nex Systems
235 Frank West Cir, Stockton
(95206-4045)
PHONE..................................209 982-0600
Keith Bewley,
Doug Mc Kee, *CFO*
Steven Azevedo,
EMP: 60
SQ FT: 8,000
SALES (est): 5.7MM **Privately Held**
WEB: www.nexsystems.com
SIC: 7217 Carpet & furniture cleaning on location

(P-13268)
EXPRESS CONTRACTORS INC
11625 Industry Ave, Fontana (92337-6931)
P.O. Box 310279 (92331-0279)
PHONE..................................951 360-6500
Amaer Alhamwi, *President*
EMP: 100
SQ FT: 10,000
SALES (est): 9.7MM **Privately Held**
SIC: 7217 1752 1721 1743 Carpet & rug cleaning & repairing plant; carpet & rug cleaning plant; carpet & rug dyeing plant; carpet laying; painting & paper hanging; terrazzo, tile, marble, mosaic work

(P-13269)
J&M KEYSTONE INC
2709 Via Orange Way Ste A, Spring Valley
(91978-1708)
PHONE..................................619 466-9876
Ronald D Martin, *CEO*
Dale Whittle, *Corp Secy*
James Bronson, *Vice Pres*
EMP: 60
SQ FT: 9,100
SALES: 14MM **Privately Held**
WEB: www.jmkeystone.com
SIC: 7217 1542 1799 8744 Carpet & furniture cleaning on location; commercial & office buildings, renovation & repair; steam cleaning of building exteriors; ; air duct cleaning; floor waxing; repairing fire damage, single-family houses

(P-13270)
STANLEY STEEMER OF LOS ANGLES (PA)
841 W Foothill Blvd, Azusa (91702-2815)
PHONE..................................626 791-9400
Kevin Pucci, *President*
Jeff Pucci, *Vice Pres*
EMP: 62
SQ FT: 100,000
SALES (est): 7MM **Privately Held**
SIC: 7217 1799 Carpet & furniture cleaning on location; post-disaster renovations

7218 Industrial Launderers

(P-13271)
AMERICAN TEXTILE MAINT CO
2201 E Carson St, Long Beach
(90807-3043)
PHONE..................................562 424-1607
Steve Jones, *Manager*

EMP: 180
SALES (corp-wide): 197.6MM **Privately Held**
WEB: www.amtextile.net
SIC: 7218 7213 Industrial launderers; uniform supply
PA: American Textile Maintenance Company
1667 W Washington Blvd
Los Angeles CA 90007
323 731-3132

(P-13272)
AMERIPRIDE SERVICES INC
Also Called: Ameripride Uniform Services
1050 W Whites Bridge Ave, Fresno
(93706-1328)
PHONE..................................559 266-0627
Matt Wencel, *Manager*
Carl Anderson, *Sales Executive*
EMP: 100 **Publicly Held**
WEB: www.ameripride.com
SIC: 7218 7213 Radiation protective garment supply; linen supply
HQ: Ameripride Services, Inc.
10801 Wayzata Blvd # 100
Minnetonka MN 55305
800 750-4628

(P-13273)
ARAMARK UNF & CAREER AP LLC
1617 Jim Way, Modesto (95358-5703)
PHONE..................................209 368-9785
Manny Martinez, *General Mgr*
Greg Moyers, *Accounts Exec*
EMP: 60 **Publicly Held**
WEB: www.aramark-uniform.com
SIC: 7218 Industrial launderers
HQ: Aramark Uniform & Career Apparel, Llc
115 N First St Ste 203
Burbank CA 91502
818 973-3700

(P-13274)
ARAMARK UNF & CAREER AP LLC
115 N First St, Burbank (91502-1856)
P.O. Box 7891 (91510-7891)
PHONE..................................818 973-3700
John Vegas, *District Mgr*
David Michaelson, *Controller*
Alma Magana, *Opers Staff*
Jon Slayton, *Opers Staff*
Darris Thomas, *Production*
EMP: 62 **Publicly Held**
SIC: 7218 Industrial launderers
HQ: Aramark Uniform & Career Apparel, Llc
115 N First St Ste 203
Burbank CA 91502
818 973-3700

(P-13275)
ARAMARK UNF & CAREER AP LLC
1419 National Dr, Sacramento
(95834-1946)
P.O. Box 340910 (95834-0910)
PHONE..................................916 286-4100
Jeff Black, *Manager*
EMP: 300 **Publicly Held**
WEB: www.aramark-uniform.com
SIC: 7218 7213 Industrial launderers; uniform supply
HQ: Aramark Uniform & Career Apparel, Llc
115 N First St Ste 203
Burbank CA 91502
818 973-3700

(P-13276)
ARAMARK UNF & CAREER AP LLC (DH)
115 N First St Ste 203, Burbank
(91502-1857)
P.O. Box 101179, Pasadena (91189-0005)
PHONE..................................818 973-3700
Mike Fadden, *Mng Member*
Caralee Brown, *Vice Pres*
Dan Craig, *Vice Pres*
Ryan Flaherty, *Vice Pres*
Dave Henry, *Vice Pres*
EMP: 250
SQ FT: 63,000

SALES (est): 767.6MM **Publicly Held**
WEB: www.aramark-uniform.com
SIC: **7218** Industrial uniform supply;
treated equipment supply: mats, rugs,
mops, cloths, etc.; wiping towel supply
HQ: Aramark Uniform & Career Apparel
Group, Inc.
1101 Market St Ste 45
Philadelphia PA 19107
215 238-3000

(P-13277)
ARAMARK UNF & CAREER AP LLC
755 Butte St, Redding (96001-0928)
PHONE..............................530 241-6433
Michael Brodeur, *Manager*
EMP: 70 **Publicly Held**
WEB: www.aramark-uniform.com
SIC: **7218** 7213 Industrial launderers; uni-
form supply
HQ: Aramark Uniform & Career Apparel, Llc
115 N First St Ste 203
Burbank CA 91502
818 973-3700

(P-13278)
ARAMARK UNF & CAREER AP LLC
330 Chestnut St, Oakland (94607-2528)
PHONE..............................510 835-9285
Art Wake, *Branch Mgr*
Sue Harding, *Executive*
EMP: 200
SQ FT: 10,000 **Publicly Held**
WEB: www.aramark-uniform.com
SIC: **7218** Wiping towel supply
HQ: Aramark Uniform & Career Apparel, Llc
115 N First St Ste 203
Burbank CA 91502
818 973-3700

(P-13279)
ARAMARK UNF & CAREER AP LLC
4422 Dunham St, Los Angeles
(90023-4113)
PHONE..............................323 266-0555
Alice Stewart, *General Mgr*
Boris Mezhebovsky, *Administration*
EMP: 230 **Publicly Held**
WEB: www.aramark-uniform.com
SIC: **7218** Industrial launderers
HQ: Aramark Uniform & Career Apparel, Llc
115 N First St Ste 203
Burbank CA 91502
818 973-3700

(P-13280)
ARAMARK UNF & CAREER AP LLC
3101 W Adams St, Santa Ana
(92704-5807)
P.O. Box 20378, Fountain Valley (92728-
0378)
PHONE..............................714 545-4877
Mark Papapendorf, *Manager*
Jose Deleon, *District Mgr*
Jerry Robinson, *Technology*
EMP: 80
SQ FT: 15,317 **Publicly Held**
WEB: www.aramark-uniform.com
SIC: **7218** 7213 Industrial launderers; uni-
form supply
HQ: Aramark Uniform & Career Apparel, Llc
115 N First St Ste 203
Burbank CA 91502
818 973-3700

(P-13281)
ARAMARK UNF & CAREER AP LLC
31148 San Antonio St, Hayward
(94544-7906)
P.O. Box 5034 (94540)
PHONE..............................510 487-1855
Dave Tyquiengco, *Manager*
EMP: 70 **Publicly Held**
WEB: www.aramark-uniform.com
SIC: **7218** Industrial uniform supply;
treated equipment supply: mats, rugs,
mops, cloths, etc.; wiping towel supply

HQ: Aramark Uniform & Career Apparel, Llc
115 N First St Ste 203
Burbank CA 91502
818 973-3700

(P-13282)
ARAMARK UNF & CAREER AP LLC
5000 Forni Dr, Concord (94520-1223)
P.O. Box 5826 (94524-0826)
PHONE..............................925 827-3782
Ray Rhode, *Manager*
Khonethai Delossantos, *Office Mgr*
EMP: 69 **Publicly Held**
WEB: www.aramark-uniform.com
SIC: **7218** 7213 Industrial launderers; uni-
form supply
HQ: Aramark Uniform & Career Apparel, Llc
115 N First St Ste 203
Burbank CA 91502
818 973-3700

(P-13283)
ARAMARK UNF & CAREER AP LLC
1135 Hall Ave, Riverside (92509-1870)
P.O. Box 33470 (92519-0470)
PHONE..............................951 274-9622
Gene West, *Manager*
EMP: 100 **Publicly Held**
WEB: www.aramark-uniform.com
SIC: **7218** 7213 Industrial launderers; uni-
form supply
HQ: Aramark Uniform & Career Apparel, Llc
115 N First St Ste 203
Burbank CA 91502
818 973-3700

(P-13284)
ARAMARK UNF & CAREER AP LLC
15372 Cobalt St, Sylmar (91342-2729)
PHONE..............................818 364-8272
Brad Drummond, *Principal*
EMP: 63 **Publicly Held**
SIC: **7218** Industrial launderers
HQ: Aramark Uniform & Career Apparel, Llc
115 N First St Ste 203
Burbank CA 91502
818 973-3700

(P-13285)
ARAMARK UNF & CAREER AP LLC
440 N Canal St, South San Francisco
(94080-4603)
PHONE..............................650 244-9332
David Techlingco, *Manager*
EMP: 70 **Publicly Held**
WEB: www.aramark-uniform.com
SIC: **7218** Industrial launderers
HQ: Aramark Uniform & Career Apparel, Llc
115 N First St Ste 203
Burbank CA 91502
818 973-3700

(P-13286)
ARAMARK UNIFORM SERVICES
1419 National Dr, Sacramento
(95834-1946)
PHONE..............................916 286-4100
Gary Koolhof, *Principal*
Bill Ledbetter, *Purch Agent*
EMP: 99
SALES (est): 6.1MM **Publicly Held**
SIC: **7218** Industrial launderers
PA: Aramark
1101 Mkt St Aramark Twr Aramark
Tower
Philadelphia PA 19107

(P-13287)
BOWSMITH INC (PA)
131 2nd St, Exeter (93221-1947)
P.O. Box 428 (93221-0428)
PHONE..............................559 592-9485
Allan L Smith, *CEO*
Kenneth Berg, *Vice Pres*
Tonnie Garnett, *Purch Mgr*
Ricky Garnett, *Safety Mgr*
Victor Gonzales, *Safety Mgr*
EMP: 75 EST: 1974
SQ FT: 14,400

SALES (est): 8.4MM **Privately Held**
WEB: www.bowsmith.com
SIC: **7218** 4971 Industrial equipment laun-
derers; irrigation systems

(P-13288)
CINTAS CORPORATION NO 2
2188 Del Franco St Ste 70, San Jose
(95131-1583)
PHONE..............................408 292-6700
Scott Douglas Farmer, *Branch Mgr*
Erika Klein, *Training Spec*
Arrika Garcia, *Plant Mgr*
Cynthia Manning, *Sales Staff*
Nick Kramer, *Manager*
EMP: 88
SALES (corp-wide): 6.8B **Publicly Held**
WEB: www.cintas-corp.com
SIC: **7218** Industrial uniform supply
HQ: Cintas Corporation No. 2
6800 Cintas Blvd
Mason OH 45040
-

(P-13289)
CINTAS CORPORATION NO 3
5500 Young St, Bakersfield (93311-9648)
PHONE..............................661 282-4300
EMP: 79
SALES (corp-wide): 6.8B **Publicly Held**
SIC: **7218** Industrial uniform supply
HQ: Cintas Corporation No. 3
6800 Cintas Blvd
Mason OH 45040
-

(P-13290)
CINTAS CORPORATION NO 3
675 32nd St, San Diego (92102-3301)
PHONE..............................619 239-1001
Kevin Nolan, *Branch Mgr*
EMP: 150
SQ FT: 7,000
SALES (corp-wide): 6.8B **Publicly Held**
WEB: www.cintas-corp.com
SIC: **7218** 7213 Industrial uniform supply;
uniform supply
HQ: Cintas Corporation No. 3
6800 Cintas Blvd
Mason OH 45040
-

(P-13291)
CINTAS CORPORATION NO 3
20929 Cabot Blvd, Hayward (94545-1155)
PHONE..............................510 352-6330
Stephen Dee, *Branch Mgr*
EMP: 79
SALES (corp-wide): 6.8B **Publicly Held**
WEB: www.cintas-corp.com
SIC: **7218** Industrial uniform supply
HQ: Cintas Corporation No. 3
6800 Cintas Blvd
Mason OH 45040
-

(P-13292)
CINTAS CORPORATION NO 3
20100 S Susana Rd, Compton
(90221-5722)
PHONE..............................310 725-2850
Bryce Littlejohn, *Branch Mgr*
EMP: 79
SALES (corp-wide): 6.8B **Publicly Held**
SIC: **7218** Industrial uniform supply
HQ: Cintas Corporation No. 3
6800 Cintas Blvd
Mason OH 45040
-

(P-13293)
CINTAS CORPORATION NO 3
1231 National Dr, Sacramento
(95834-1902)
PHONE..............................916 419-8519
Doyle Denny, *Manager*
EMP: 150
SALES (corp-wide): 6.8B **Publicly Held**
WEB: www.cintas-corp.com
SIC: **7218** Industrial uniform supply
HQ: Cintas Corporation No. 3
6800 Cintas Blvd
Mason OH 45040
-

(P-13294)
CINTAS CORPORATION NO 3
1851 S Wineville Ave, Ontario
(91761-3667)
PHONE..............................909 390-4912
Adrian Sandoval, *Manager*
EMP: 79
SALES (corp-wide): 6.8B **Publicly Held**
WEB: www.cintas-corp.com
SIC: **7218** Industrial launderers
HQ: Cintas Corporation No. 3
6800 Cintas Blvd
Mason OH 45040

(P-13295)
CINTAS CORPORATION NO 3
220 Demeter St, East Palo Alto
(94303-1303)
PHONE..............................650 589-4300
EMP: 79
SALES (corp-wide): 6.8B **Publicly Held**
SIC: **7218** Industrial uniform supply
HQ: Cintas Corporation No. 3
6800 Cintas Blvd
Mason OH 45040
-

(P-13296)
G&K SERVICES LLC
5900 Alder Ave, Sacramento (95828-1110)
PHONE..............................916 381-5500
Rich Pland, *Branch Mgr*
EMP: 80
SALES (corp-wide): 6.8B **Publicly Held**
WEB: www.gkservices.com
SIC: **7218** 5699 7213 Industrial uniform
supply; uniforms; uniform supply
HQ: G&K Services, Llc
6800 Cintas Blvd
Mason OH 45040
952 912-5500

(P-13297)
G&K SERVICES LLC
1229 California Ave, Pittsburg
(94565-4112)
PHONE..............................925 427-4401
Scott Hartesty, *Branch Mgr*
EMP: 50
SQ FT: 40,202
SALES (corp-wide): 6.8B **Publicly Held**
WEB: www.gkservices.com
SIC: **7218** 7213 Industrial uniform supply;
uniform supply
HQ: G&K Services, Llc
6800 Cintas Blvd
Mason OH 45040
952 912-5500

(P-13298)
GARMENT INDUSTRY LAUNDRY
710 W 58th St, Los Angeles (90037-4034)
PHONE..............................323 752-8335
Lyle Dean Foreman, *President*
Bjarne Schmidt, *Vice Pres*
EMP: 200
SQ FT: 30,000
SALES (est): 6.2MM **Privately Held**
SIC: **7218** 7211 Industrial launderers;
power laundries, family & commercial

(P-13299)
INTERNATIONAL GARMENT FINISHER
Also Called: I G F
2144 W Gaylord St, Long Beach
(90813-1034)
PHONE..............................562 983-7400
Richard Kim, *President*
EMP: 100
SALES (est): 3.4MM **Privately Held**
WEB: www.igf.com
SIC: **7218** Industrial launderers

(P-13300)
MISSION LINEN SUPPLY
Also Called: Mission Linen & Uniform Svc
435 W Market St, Salinas (93901-1498)
PHONE..............................831 424-1753
Bill McCreary, *Manager*
EMP: 150

SALES (corp-wide): 180.2MM **Privately Held**
WEB: www.missions.com
SIC: 7218 7213 Industrial uniform supply; linen supply
PA: Mission Linen Supply
717 E Yanonali St
Santa Barbara CA 93103
805 730-3620

(P-13301)
MISSION LINEN SUPPLY
Also Called: Mission Linen & Uniform Svc
7524 Reese Rd, Sacramento (95828-3707)
PHONE....................916 423-3135
Ed Morrow, *Manager*
EMP: 150
SALES (corp-wide): 180.2MM **Privately Held**
WEB: www.missions.com
SIC: 7218 7213 Industrial launderers; uniform supply
PA: Mission Linen Supply
717 E Yanonali St
Santa Barbara CA 93103
805 730-3620

(P-13302)
PRUDENTIAL OVERALL SUPPLY
6920 Bandini Blvd, Commerce (90040-3382)
PHONE....................323 724-4888
Mark Albertson, *Manager*
Jennifer Shearer, *Sales Staff*
EMP: 100
SQ FT: 40,000
SALES (corp-wide): 158.2MM **Privately Held**
WEB: www.pos-clean.com
SIC: 7218 7213 5087 Industrial launderers; uniform supply; janitors' supplies
PA: Prudential Overall Supply
1661 Alton Pkwy
Irvine CA 92606
949 250-4855

(P-13303)
PRUDENTIAL OVERALL SUPPLY (PA)
1661 Alton Pkwy, Irvine (92606-4877)
P.O. Box 11210, Santa Ana (92711-1210)
PHONE....................949 250-4855
Dan Clark, *CEO*
Thomas C Watts, *President*
Donald C Lahn, *Vice Ch Bd*
Stefan Schurter, *Executive*
Donny Pyne, *District Mgr*
▲ **EMP:** 95
SQ FT: 20,000
SALES: 158.2MM **Privately Held**
WEB: www.pos-clean.com
SIC: 7218 Wiping towel supply

(P-13304)
PRUDENTIAL OVERALL SUPPLY
Also Called: Prudential Dust Control
6997 Jurupa Ave, Riverside (92504-1009)
PHONE....................951 687-0440
Jay Boyer, *General Mgr*
EMP: 127
SALES (corp-wide): 158.2MM **Privately Held**
WEB: www.pos-clean.com
SIC: 7218 Industrial launderers
PA: Prudential Overall Supply
1661 Alton Pkwy
Irvine CA 92606
949 250-4855

(P-13305)
PRUDENTIAL OVERALL SUPPLY
2485 Ash St, Vista (92081-8424)
PHONE....................760 727-7163
Jason Thaffin, *Branch Mgr*
EMP: 95
SQ FT: 38,476
SALES (corp-wide): 158.2MM **Privately Held**
WEB: www.pos-clean.com
SIC: 7218 7213 5699 Industrial launderers; uniform supply; uniforms & work clothing
PA: Prudential Overall Supply
1661 Alton Pkwy
Irvine CA 92606
949 250-4855

(P-13306)
PRUDENTIAL OVERALL SUPPLY
Also Called: Prudential Cleanroom Services
1437 N Milpitas Blvd, Milpitas (95035-3154)
PHONE....................408 719-0886
Tim Bleigh, *Manager*
Tim N Bleigh, *Manager*
EMP: 99
SQ FT: 30,201
SALES (corp-wide): 158.2MM **Privately Held**
WEB: www.pos-clean.com
SIC: 7218 Wiping towel supply
PA: Prudential Overall Supply
1661 Alton Pkwy
Irvine CA 92606
949 250-4855

(P-13307)
PRUDENTIAL OVERALL SUPPLY
Also Called: Prudential Cleanroom Services
6948 Bandini Blvd, Commerce (90040-3326)
PHONE....................323 722-0636
Chris Wealch, *General Mgr*
Gary Oien, *Business Mgr*
Sandra Sepulveda, *Plant Supt*
Gina Torres, *Manager*
EMP: 65
SQ FT: 21,925
SALES (corp-wide): 158.2MM **Privately Held**
WEB: www.pos-clean.com
SIC: 7218 7213 7349 Industrial launderers; uniform supply; cleaning service, industrial or commercial
PA: Prudential Overall Supply
1661 Alton Pkwy
Irvine CA 92606
949 250-4855

(P-13308)
PRUDENTIAL OVERALL SUPPLY
1260 E North Ave, Fresno (93725-1930)
PHONE....................559 264-8231
Rick Ponce, *Branch Mgr*
Mark Willis, *General Mgr*
Michael Brown, *VP Sales*
Rudy Robles, *Manager*
EMP: 80
SQ FT: 42,704
SALES (corp-wide): 158.2MM **Privately Held**
WEB: www.pos-clean.com
SIC: 7218 7213 Industrial launderers; linen supply
PA: Prudential Overall Supply
1661 Alton Pkwy
Irvine CA 92606
949 250-4855

(P-13309)
RFID TEXTILE SERVICES INC
1575 N Case St, Orange (92867-3635)
PHONE....................714 998-6109
Alicia Silva, *Branch Mgr*
EMP: 194 **Publicly Held**
SIC: 7218 7213 Industrial launderers; uniform supply
HQ: Rfid Textile Services, Inc.
1105 Lakewood Pkwy # 210
Alpharetta GA 30009
678 823-4100

(P-13310)
RFID TEXTILE SERVICES INC
8190 Murray Ave, Gilroy (95020-4605)
PHONE....................408 840-7504
John Beurskens, *Manager*
EMP: 89 **Publicly Held**
SIC: 7218 7213 Industrial launderers; linen supply
HQ: Rfid Textile Services, Inc.
1105 Lakewood Pkwy # 210
Alpharetta GA 30009
678 823-4100

(P-13311)
SPECIALIZED LAUNDRY SVCS INC
Also Called: 1st Class Laundry Services
33485 Western Ave, Union City (94587-3201)
PHONE....................510 487-8297
Jefferey Lee Schlagel, *CEO*

EMP: 165
SQ FT: 24,000
SALES: 7.3MM **Privately Held**
SIC: 7218 Industrial launderers

(P-13312)
STONE BLUE INC
Also Called: Pink Diamonds
2501 E 28th St, Vernon (90058-1429)
PHONE....................323 277-0008
Judy OH, *President*
EMP: 100
SQ FT: 70,000
SALES (est): 3.3MM **Privately Held**
SIC: 7218 Industrial clothing launderers

(P-13313)
UNIFIRST CORPORATION
819 N Hunter St, Stockton (95202-1706)
PHONE....................209 941-8364
Peter Bernadicou, *Principal*
EMP: 50
SALES (corp-wide): 1.8B **Publicly Held**
WEB: www.unifirst.com
SIC: 7218 7213 Industrial uniform supply; uniform supply
PA: Unifirst Corporation
68 Jonspin Rd
Wilmington MA 01887
978 658-8888

(P-13314)
UNIFIRST CORPORATION
4041 Market St, San Diego (92102-4593)
PHONE....................619 263-6116
Jesse Sandoval, *Manager*
EMP: 60
SQ FT: 22,685
SALES (corp-wide): 1.8B **Publicly Held**
WEB: www.unifirst.com
SIC: 7218 7213 Industrial uniform supply; work clothing supply; radiation protective garment supply; uniform supply
PA: Unifirst Corporation
68 Jonspin Rd
Wilmington MA 01887
978 658-8888

(P-13315)
UNIFIRST CORPORATION
700 Etiwanda Ave Ste C, Ontario (91761-8608)
PHONE....................909 390-8670
Jeff Martin, *Manager*
EMP: 130
SALES (corp-wide): 1.8B **Publicly Held**
WEB: www.unifirst.com
SIC: 7218 7213 Industrial uniform supply; work clothing supply; radiation protective garment supply; uniform supply
PA: Unifirst Corporation
68 Jonspin Rd
Wilmington MA 01887
978 658-8888

(P-13316)
UNIFIRST CORPORATION
2016 Zanker Rd, San Jose (95131-2110)
PHONE....................408 297-8101
EMP: 60
SALES (corp-wide): 1.8B **Publicly Held**
SIC: 7218 Radiation protective garment supply
PA: Unifirst Corporation
68 Jonspin Rd
Wilmington MA 01887
978 658-8888

(P-13317)
WORKRITE UNIFORM COMPANY INC (DH)
1701 Lombard St Ste 200, Oxnard (93030-8235)
PHONE....................805 483-0175
Philip C Williamson, *CEO*
Keith Suddaby, *President*
Mark Adler, *Vice Pres*
Beth Bohan, *Executive*
Jim Vochoska, *Executive*
EMP: 385 **EST:** 1968
SALES (est): 26.4MM
SALES (corp-wide): 13.8MM **Publicly Held**
SIC: 7218 Flame & heat resistant clothing supply

HQ: Williamson-Dickie Manufacturing Company, Llc
509 W Vickery Blvd
Fort Worth TX 76104
817 336-7201

```
7219 Laundry & Garment
Svcs, NEC
```

(P-13318)
ARAMARK SERVICES INC
1405 E 58th Pl, Los Angeles (90001-1207)
PHONE....................323 587-7661
Barry Eastill, *Manager*
David Radmilovich, *Director*
EMP: 100
SQ FT: 22,000 **Publicly Held**
SIC: 7219 7218 Laundry, except power & coin-operated; industrial launderers
HQ: Aramark Services, Inc.
2400 Market St Ste 600
Philadelphia PA 19103
215 238-3000

(P-13319)
CM LAUNDRY LLC
14919 S Figueroa St, Gardena (90248-1720)
PHONE....................310 436-6170
Luis Rodriguez,
Anthony Millar,
Ernesto Munoz, *Mng Member*
EMP: 100
SQ FT: 26,500
SALES (est): 4.9MM **Privately Held**
SIC: 7219 Laundry, except power & coin-operated

(P-13320)
DY-DEE SERVICE PASADENA INC
Also Called: California Linen Service
40 E California Blvd, Pasadena (91105-3203)
PHONE....................626 792-6183
Brian O'Neil, *President*
Andrew Oneil, *General Mgr*
Mary Hilliard, *Sales Mgr*
EMP: 60
SQ FT: 15,000
SALES (est): 4.2MM **Privately Held**
WEB: www.calinen.com
SIC: 7219 7213 Diaper service; linen supply, non-clothing

(P-13321)
DYDEE SERVICE OF PASEDENA
Also Called: California Linen
40 E California Blvd, Pasadena (91105-3203)
PHONE....................626 240-0115
Bryan O'Nell, *Owner*
EMP: 100 **EST:** 1938
SALES: 8MM **Privately Held**
SIC: 7219 Diaper service

(P-13322)
JOB OPTIONS INCORPORATED
1110 S Washington Ave, San Bernardino (92408-2244)
PHONE....................909 890-4612
EMP: 820
SQ FT: 35,800 **Privately Held**
WEB: www.joboptionsinc.org
SIC: 7219 Fur garment cleaning, repairing & storage
PA: Job Options, Incorporated
3465 Camino Dl Rio S 30
San Diego CA 92108

(P-13323)
KL CUTTING SERVICE INC
2250 Maple Ave, Los Angeles (90011-1190)
PHONE....................213 742-9001
Alex Palomino, *General Mgr*
Mark Feldman, *President*
EMP: 164 **EST:** 1997
SQ FT: 78,200
SALES (est): 7.8MM **Privately Held**
SIC: 7219 Garment making, alteration & repair

(P-13324)
PENINOU FRENCH LDRY & CLRS INC (PA)
101 S Maple Ave, South San Francisco (94080-6303)
PHONE...................800 392-2532
Todd Edwards, *CEO*
EMP: 90
SQ FT: 25,000
SALES (est): 6.2MM **Privately Held**
WEB: www.peninou.com
SIC: 7219 7216 French hand laundry; drycleaning collecting & distributing agency

(P-13325)
STAR LAUNDRY SERVICES INC
Also Called: Star Services
3410 Main St, San Diego (92113-3803)
PHONE...................619 572-1009
Abraham Yang, *President*
Suddeth Jeff, *Payroll Mgr*
EMP: 80
SALES (est): 1.6MM **Privately Held**
SIC: 7219 Laundry, except power & coin-operated

(P-13326)
T POINTS INC
350 W Mrtn Lthr King Jr, Los Angeles (90037-4529)
PHONE...................323 846-9176
EMP: 50
SALES (est): 695.8K **Privately Held**
SIC: 7219

7221 Photographic Studios, Portrait

(P-13327)
BAY PHOTO INC
2959 Park Ave Ste A, Soquel (95073-2863)
PHONE...................831 475-6090
Larry Abitbol, *Principal*
Lawrence Christina, *Admin Asst*
EMP: 138
SALES (corp-wide): 33MM **Privately Held**
SIC: 7221 Photographer, still or video
PA: Bay Photo, Inc.
920 Disc Dr
Scotts Valley CA
831 475-6686

(P-13328)
LIFETOUCH INC
7916 Alta Sunrise Ln, Citrus Heights (95610-7904)
PHONE...................916 535-7733
Chris Rousso, *Branch Mgr*
EMP: 80
SALES (corp-wide): 1.9B **Privately Held**
WEB: www.lifetouch.com
SIC: 7221 Photographer, still or video
HQ: Lifetouch Inc.
11000 Viking Dr
Eden Prairie MN 55344
952 826-4000

(P-13329)
LIFETOUCH NAT SCHL STUDIOS INC
30351 Huntwood Ave, Hayward (94544-7015)
PHONE...................510 293-1818
John Capistrant, *Manager*
EMP: 50
SALES (corp-wide): 1.9B **Privately Held**
SIC: 7221 School photographer
HQ: Lifetouch National School Studios Inc.
11000 Viking Dr Ste 300
Eden Prairie MN 55344
952 826-4000

(P-13330)
LIFETOUCH PORTRAIT STUDIOS INC
9770 Carroll Centre Rd C, San Diego (92126-6504)
PHONE...................858 693-9197
Kim Clark, *Manager*
EMP: 50
SQ FT: 1,200

SALES (corp-wide): 1.9B **Privately Held**
WEB: www.jcpportraits.com
SIC: 7221 Photographer, still or video; school photographer
HQ: Lifetouch Portrait Studios Inc.
11000 Viking Dr
Eden Prairie MN 55344
952 826-4335

7231 Beauty Shops

(P-13331)
ALEXANDERS GRAND SALON
Also Called: Alexander's Grand Salon & Spa
5579 E Santa Ana Cyn Rd, Anaheim (92807-3143)
PHONE...................714 282-6438
Fax: 714 282-6446
EMP: 65
SALES (est): 1.3MM **Privately Held**
SIC: 7231

(P-13332)
ALLEN EDWARDS BEAUTY SALON (PA)
Also Called: Edwards, Allen Beauty Salon
16101 Ventura Blvd # 155, Encino (91436-2500)
PHONE...................818 981-7711
Paul Canter, *President*
Allen Edwards, *Admin Sec*
EMP: 100
SALES (est): 1.1MM **Privately Held**
SIC: 7231 Beauty shops

(P-13333)
BEAUTY BARRAGE LLC
4340 Von Karman Ave # 200, Newport Beach (92660-1201)
PHONE...................949 771-3399
Sonia Summers, *CEO*
Heather Forcari, *Vice Pres*
Rebekah Von Der Hellen, *Vice Pres*
Brady Heyborne, *Vice Pres*
Alissa Spencer, *Vice Pres*
EMP: 220
SALES (est): 42.1K **Privately Held**
SIC: 7231 8742 Beauty shops; marketing consulting services

(P-13334)
BEAUTY BAZAR INC
Also Called: La Belle Days Spas and Salons
36 Stanford Shopping Ctr, Palo Alto (94304-1423)
PHONE...................650 326-8522
Vella Schner, *Owner*
EMP: 80
SALES (corp-wide): 3.6MM **Privately Held**
WEB: www.labelledayspas.com
SIC: 7231 5999 Cosmetology & personal hygiene salons; toiletries, cosmetics & perfumes
PA: Beauty Bazar Inc
36 Stanford Shopping Ctr
Palo Alto CA

(P-13335)
BEAUTY RECOGNIZED LP
224 Via Rodeo Dr, Beverly Hills (90210-5142)
PHONE...................310 278-7646
Jose Eber,
EMP: 70
SALES (est): 909.8K **Privately Held**
SIC: 7231 Unisex hair salons

(P-13336)
CLASS ACT HAIR & NAIL SALON
2795 Bechelli Ln, Redding (96002-1924)
PHONE...................530 223-3442
EMP: 69
SALES (est): 598.4K **Privately Held**
SIC: 7231

(P-13337)
DAGER CORPORATION (PA)
Also Called: Supercuts
8004 Flsom Hydre Aburn Rd, Folsom (95630)
PHONE...................916 989-4229
Glenn R James, *President*

EMP: 100
SALES (est): 1.9MM **Privately Held**
SIC: 7231 Unisex hair salons

(P-13338)
DIANAS MEXICAN FOOD PDTS INC
Also Called: Diana's Beauty Salon
5841 S Figueroa St, Los Angeles (90003-1061)
PHONE...................323 758-4845
EMP: 76
SALES (corp-wide): 76.4MM **Privately Held**
SIC: 7231 Beauty shops
PA: Diana's Mexican Food Products, Inc.
16330 Pioneer Blvd
Norwalk CA 90650
562 926-5802

(P-13339)
DUKE FINANCIAL CO INC
100 N Rancho Santa Fe Rd # 117, San Marcos (92069-1280)
PHONE...................858 694-1215
Ted Nelson, *President*
Craig Bingham, *VP Finance*
EMP: 184
SALES (est): 2.6MM **Privately Held**
SIC: 7231 6282 Hairdressers; investment advisory service

(P-13340)
EMPOWEREDEXPANSIONS CORP (PA)
Also Called: Expansive Collections
714 Westbourne Dr, West Hollywood (90069-5104)
PHONE...................310 492-5988
Gerard Quiroga, *President*
EMP: 55
SALES (est): 2.9MM **Privately Held**
SIC: 7231 7389 6794 Manicurist, pedicurist; ; franchises, selling or licensing

(P-13341)
ESALONCOM LLC
1910 E Maple Ave, El Segundo (90245-3411)
PHONE...................866 550-2424
Francisco Gimenec,
Aaron Chan, *President*
Graham Jones, *COO*
Lani Kuramoto, *Vice Pres*
Allen Branson, *Software Dev*
EMP: 52
SALES (est): 4.9MM **Privately Held**
SIC: 7231 Unisex hair salons

(P-13342)
FABULOUS & COMPANY LLC
19553 Enadia Way, Reseda (91335-3620)
PHONE...................818 261-7242
Maya Riley,
EMP: 50
SALES (est): 133.3K **Privately Held**
SIC: 7231 Beauty shops

(P-13343)
FEDERICO BEAUTY INSTITUTE
1515 Sports Dr Ste 100, Sacramento (95834-1905)
PHONE...................916 929-4242
Jeremy Frederico, *President*
EMP: 50
SALES (est): 1.2MM **Privately Held**
SIC: 7231 Beauty schools

(P-13344)
FERGUSON SALON MANAGEMENT
2946 State St Ste F, Carlsbad (92008-2336)
P.O. Box 2804 (92018-2804)
PHONE...................760 434-4141
Elizabeth Ferguson, *President*
EMP: 50
SQ FT: 1,000
SALES (est): 966K **Privately Held**
SIC: 7231 Hairdressers

(P-13345)
FERGUSON SALON MANAGEMENT INC
1104 Knowles Ave, Carlsbad (92008-1459)
P.O. Box 2804 (92018-2804)
PHONE...................760 434-5008
Elizabeth Ferguson, *President*
Marvin Ferguson, *CFO*
EMP: 50
SALES (est): 2MM **Privately Held**
SIC: 7231 7241 Beauty shops; barber shops

(P-13346)
FLORIDA BEAUTY FLORA INC
6205 Ventura Blvd, Ventura (93003-7226)
PHONE...................805 642-1633
Ronen Koubi, *Branch Mgr*
EMP: 108
SALES (corp-wide): 55.9MM **Privately Held**
SIC: 7231 Beauty shops
PA: Florida Beauty Flora, Inc.
3400 Nw 74th Ave Ste 1
Miami FL 33122
305 503-1200

(P-13347)
GATES OF SPAIN WIBEL
2545 Mission St, Pasadena (91108-1691)
PHONE...................626 441-3078
William J Bell, *President*
Susan Bell, *Co-Owner*
Vicki Lanzarotta, *Admin Sec*
EMP: 50 **EST:** 1959
SALES (est): 1MM **Privately Held**
SIC: 7231 Cosmetology & personal hygiene salons

(P-13348)
GF CARNEROS TENANT LLC
Also Called: Carneros Resort and Spa
4048 Sonoma Hwy, NAPA (94559-9745)
PHONE...................707 299-4900
Monda Rigdon,
Mimi Vandyk, *Sales Mgr*
Robert Heiser,
Zion Curiel, *Director*
EMP: 50
SALES (est): 639.7K **Privately Held**
SIC: 7231 Cosmetology & personal hygiene salons

(P-13349)
HAIR FASHION INC
Also Called: Cristophe Salon
348 N Beverly Dr, Beverly Hills (90210-4701)
PHONE...................310 274-0851
Cristopher Schatteman, *President*
Cristophe Schatteman, *President*
EMP: 80
SQ FT: 7,000
SALES (est): 2.4MM **Privately Held**
WEB: www.cristophesalon.com
SIC: 7231 Unisex hair salons

(P-13350)
HOSHALL CORPORATION
Also Called: Hoshall Designer Group
6608 Folsom Auburn Rd # 4, Folsom (95630-2147)
PHONE...................916 987-1995
William C Hoshall, *President*
EMP: 50 **EST:** 1964
SALES (est): 1.3MM **Privately Held**
WEB: www.hoshallssalonandspa.com
SIC: 7231 5621 5999 Manicurist, pedicurist; ready-to-wear apparel, women's; cosmetics

(P-13351)
JOSEPH COZZA SALON INC (PA)
77 Maiden Ln Fl 2, San Francisco (94108-5417)
PHONE...................415 433-3030
Joseph Bisazza, *President*
Joseph Cozza, *Corp Secy*
▲ **EMP:** 60
SALES (est): 2.5MM **Privately Held**
WEB: www.josephcozzasalon.com
SIC: 7231 Unisex hair salons

(P-13352)
MINILUXE INC
11965 San Vicente Blvd, Los Angeles
(90049-5003)
PHONE.........................424 442-1630
EMP: 65
SALES (corp-wide): 15MM Privately
Held
SIC: 7231 Manicurist, pedicurist
PA: Miniluxe, Inc.
　1 Faneuil Hall Sq Fl 7
　Boston MA 02109
　617 684-2731

(P-13353)
**ORGANIC & SUSTAINABLE
BUTY INC**
5933 Bowcroft St, Los Angeles
(90016-4301)
PHONE.........................310 815-8201
Jessica Iclisoy, President
Arthur Iclisoy, Managing Dir
EMP: 50
SALES (est): 1.9MM Privately Held
SIC: 7231 2844 Beauty shops; hair prepa-
rations, including shampoos; suntan lo-
tions & oils; face creams or lotions

(P-13354)
PILGRIM PLACE IN CLAREMONT
Also Called: Pilgrim Place Beauty Salon
721 Harrison Ave, Claremont (91711-4539)
PHONE.........................909 621-9581
Will Cunitz, Sales/Mktg Dir
EMP: 180
SALES (corp-wide): 19.5MM Privately
Held
WEB: www.pilgrimplace.org
SIC: 7231 Beauty shops
PA: Pilgrim Place In Claremont
　625 Mayflower Rd
　Claremont CA 91711
　909 399-5500

(P-13355)
PLATINUM STRANDS SALON
3443 E Chapman Ave, Orange
(92869-3812)
PHONE.........................714 532-2633
Donald Anderson, Owner
Sam Ardalan, Owner
Thomas Penna, Manager
EMP: 65
SALES (est): 818.2K Privately Held
SIC: 7231 Hairdressers

(P-13356)
REGIS CORPORATION
Also Called: Vidal Sassoon Salon
9403 Santa Monica Blvd, Beverly Hills
(90210-4604)
PHONE.........................310 274-8791
EMP: 50
SALES (corp-wide): 1.7B Publicly Held
SIC: 7231
PA: Regis Corporation
　7201 Metro Blvd
　Edina MN 55439
　952 947-7777

(P-13357)
**ROBERT CROMEANS SALON
(PA)**
410 A St, San Diego (92101-4202)
PHONE.........................858 270-9975
Robert Cromeans, Owner
EMP: 50
SQ FT: 3,300
SALES (est): 1MM Privately Held
WEB: www.robertcromeans.com
SIC: 7231 Hairdressers

(P-13358)
SALON LUJON INC
216 N Harbor Blvd, Fullerton (92832-3604)
PHONE.........................714 738-1882
Rale Whitesell, Manager
Lulu Poore, Admin Sec
EMP: 60
SQ FT: 3,000
SALES (est): 1.4MM Privately Held
SIC: 7231 7991 Unisex hair salons; spas

(P-13359)
SALON-SALON
1700 Mchenry Ave Ste 29, Modesto
(95350-4340)
PHONE.........................209 571-3500
Norma Foster Maddy, Partner
Chris Johnson, Partner
EMP: 55
SQ FT: 10,500
SALES (est): 1.7MM Privately Held
SIC: 7231 5621 5999 Hairdressers; bou-
tiques; hair care products

(P-13360)
**SUPERCUTS ADMNISTRATIVE
OFFICE (PA)**
7750 El Cmino Real Ste 2g, Carlsbad
(92009)
PHONE.........................760 753-5543
Robert Jerome, Owner
EMP: 240
SQ FT: 750
SALES: 6MM Privately Held
SIC: 7231 Unisex hair salons

(P-13361)
**TONI & GUY HAIRDRESSING
(PA)**
1177 Newport Center Dr, Newport Beach
(92660-6950)
PHONE.........................949 721-1666
Frank Chirico, Partner
Olivia Price, Manager
EMP: 50
SALES (est): 1.5MM Privately Held
SIC: 7231 Hairdressers

(P-13362)
TRILOGY SQUAW SPA LLC
Also Called: Trilogy Day Spa
451 Manhattan Beach Blvd, Manhattan
Beach (90266-5345)
PHONE.........................310 760-0044
Shandra Shaw,
Ratna Goravani, Director
EMP: 50
SALES (est): 1.3MM Privately Held
SIC: 7231 Facial salons

(P-13363)
ULTA BEAUTY INC
11485 Carmel Mountain Rd, San Diego
(92128-4618)
PHONE.........................858 376-4574
EMP: 203
SALES (corp-wide): 6.7B Publicly Held
SIC: 7231 Beauty shops
PA: Ulta Beauty, Inc.
　1000 Remington Blvd # 120
　Bolingbrook IL 60440
　630 410-4800

(P-13364)
**ULTA SALON COSMT
FRAGRANCE INC**
9000 Ming Ave, Bakersfield (93311-1318)
PHONE.........................661 664-1402
EMP: 155
SALES (corp-wide): 6.7B Publicly Held
SIC: 7231 5999 Beauty shops; toiletries,
cosmetics & perfumes
HQ: Ulta Salon, Cosmetics & Fragrance,
Inc.
　1000 Remington Blvd # 120
　Bolingbrook IL 60440
　630 410-4800

7241 Barber Shops

(P-13365)
CUTTING EDGE PROTECTION I
381 Crosby St, Altadena (91001-5569)
PHONE.........................949 307-1596
Anthony Beaty, President
Greg Hammond, Vice Pres
EMP: 50
SALES (est): 335.8K Privately Held
WEB: www.tmbhollywood.com
SIC: 7241 Barber shops

(P-13366)
HAIRCUTTERS
1230 W Imperial Hwy Ste A, La Habra
(90631-6961)
PHONE.........................562 690-2217
EMP: 92
SALES (corp-wide): 14.9MM Privately
Held
SIC: 7241 7231
PA: The Haircutters
　5160 Van Nuys Blvd
　Sherman Oaks CA
　818 716-5319

**7251 Shoe Repair &
Shoeshine Parlors**

(P-13367)
NAFTA SHOES INC
14632 Nelson Ave, City of Industry
(91744-4346)
PHONE.........................626 369-9681
Ralph Chen, President
Angel Chen, Vice Pres
EMP: 100
SQ FT: 40,000
SALES (est): 2.3MM Privately Held
WEB: www.naftashoehospital.com
SIC: 7251 3144 3143 5139 Shoe repair
shop; women's footwear, except athletic;
men's footwear, except athletic; shoes

**7261 Funeral Svcs &
Crematories**

(P-13368)
**CYPRESS FUNERAL SERVICES
INC**
Also Called: Cypress Lawn Funeral Home
1370 El Camino Real, Colma (94014-3239)
PHONE.........................650 550-8808
Kenneth E Varner, President
EMP: 150
SALES (est): 5.1MM Privately Held
SIC: 7261 Funeral home

(P-13369)
DESERT VIEW FUNERAL HOME
11478 Amargosa Rd, Victorville
(92392-8125)
PHONE.........................760 244-0007
Jim Larkin, CEO
Terry Harmon, Vice Pres
EMP: 50
SALES (est): 1.1MM Privately Held
SIC: 7261 Funeral home

(P-13370)
F R A LP
1702 Fairhaven Ave, Santa Ana
(92705-6821)
PHONE.........................714 633-1442
Fred Forgy Jr, Partner
Jack Stanley, Partner
EMP: 70 EST: 1911
SQ FT: 12,000
SALES (est): 2.2MM Privately Held
SIC: 7261 6512 6553 5999 Crematory;
commercial & industrial building opera-
tion; mausoleum operation; gravestones,
finished; flowers, fresh

(P-13371)
**LIGHT HSE MEMORIALS
RECEPTIONS (PA)**
Also Called: White and Day
5310 Torrance Blvd, Torrance
(90503-4012)
PHONE.........................310 792-7599
John Kirk, CEO
Ronald F Day, President
Pamela Day, Treasurer
EMP: 75
SQ FT: 6,121
SALES (est): 5.6MM Privately Held
WEB: www.ricemortuary.com
SIC: 7261 Funeral home

(P-13372)
**NEPTUNE MANAGEMENT
CORPORATION**
4065 Mowry Ave, Fremont (94538-1339)
PHONE.........................510 797-2269
EMP: 67 Privately Held
SIC: 7261 Funeral service & crematories
PA: Neptune Management Corporation
　100 Nw 70th Ave Ste 200
　Plantation FL 33317

(P-13373)
**NEPTUNE MANAGEMENT
CORPORATION**
9650 Fairway Dr 120, Roseville
(95678-3537)
PHONE.........................916 771-5300
EMP: 67 Privately Held
SIC: 7261 Funeral home
PA: Neptune Management Corporation
　100 Nw 70th Ave Ste 200
　Plantation FL 33317

(P-13374)
PIERCE BROTHERS (DH)
Also Called: SCI
10621 Victory Blvd, North Hollywood
(91606-3918)
PHONE.........................818 763-9121
Oliver Yeo, Manager
R L Waltrip, Ch of Bd
David Anderson, President
Curtis Briggs, Vice Pres
Ray Gipson, Vice Pres
EMP: 80 EST: 1902
SQ FT: 10,000
SALES (est): 8.5MM
SALES (corp-wide): 3.1B Publicly Held
SIC: 7261 6553 Crematory; cemeteries,
real estate operation
HQ: Sci Funeral Services Of New York, Inc.
　1929 Allen Pkwy
　Houston TX 77019
　713 522-5141

(P-13375)
**ROMAN CATH ARCH OF LOS
ANGELS**
Also Called: Holy Cross Cemetary & Ma-
soleum
5835 W Slauson Ave, Culver City
(90230-6505)
PHONE.........................310 836-5500
Maria Arascor, Manager
EMP: 50
SALES (corp-wide): 539.2MM Privately
Held
WEB: www.smes.com
SIC: 7261 6553 Funeral service & crema-
tories; cemetery subdividers & developers
PA: The Roman Catholic Archbishop Of Los
Angeles
　3424 Wilshire Blvd
　Los Angeles CA 90010
　213 637-7000

(P-13376)
**ROMAN CATH ARCH OF LOS
ANGELS**
Also Called: Calvary Cemetery
199 N Hope Ave, Santa Barbara
(93110-1609)
PHONE.........................805 687-8811
Gwen Hueston, Branch Mgr
EMP: 611
SALES (corp-wide): 539.2MM Privately
Held
SIC: 7261 6553 Funeral service & crema-
tories; cemetery subdividers & developers
PA: The Roman Catholic Archbishop Of Los
Angeles
　3424 Wilshire Blvd
　Los Angeles CA 90010
　213 637-7000

(P-13377)
ROSE HILLS MORTUARY INC
Also Called: Rose Hills Co
3888 Workman Mill Rd, Whittier
(90601-1626)
P.O. Box 110 (90608-0110)
PHONE.........................562 699-0921
Dennis Poulsen, Ch of Bd

Bruce Lazenby, *Exec Dir*
Ophelia Camero, *Administration*
Jin Chon, *Administration*
Neil Barnhard, *Info Tech Dir*
EMP: 850
SQ FT: 230,000
SALES (est): 15.1MM **Privately Held**
SIC: 7261 6553 Funeral home; cemetery subdividers & developers

(P-13378)
SAN DIEGO CEMETERY ASSN
Also Called: El Camino Mem Pk & Mortuary
5600 Carroll Canyon Rd, San Diego
(92121-1702)
PHONE..................................858 453-2121
Adrienne Trousdale, *President*
Paul Hickman, *Treasurer*
Betty Flake, *Admin Sec*
EMP: 60
SQ FT: 10,000
SALES (est): 2.8MM **Privately Held**
SIC: 7261 6553 Funeral service & crematories; cemetery subdividers & developers

(P-13379)
SINAI TEMPLE
Also Called: Mt Sinai Mem Pk & Mortuary
5950 Forest Lawn Dr, Los Angeles
(90068-1010)
PHONE..................................323 469-6000
Len Lawrence, *Manager*
Stephen Bookbinder, *Planning*
Kimber Sax, *Sales Mgr*
Frank Gilbert, *Facilities Mgr*
Eric Shani, *Manager*
EMP: 125
SQ FT: 22,633
SALES (corp-wide): 23.3MM **Privately Held**
WEB: www.mt-sinai.com
SIC: 7261 6553 Funeral home; cemeteries, real estate operation
PA: Temple Sinai
10400 Wilshire Blvd
Los Angeles CA 90024
310 475-6401

(P-13380)
STEWART ENTERPRISES INC
Also Called: El Camino Mem Pk & Mortuary
5600 Carroll Canyon Rd, San Diego
(92121-1702)
PHONE..................................858 453-2121
Virginia McCuyston, *Manager*
EMP: 50
SALES (corp-wide): 3.1B **Publicly Held**
WEB: www.stewartenterprises.com
SIC: 7261 Funeral service & crematories
HQ: Stewart Enterprises, Inc.
1333 S Clearview Pkwy
New Orleans LA 70121
504 729-1400

(P-13381)
TEMPLE ISRAEL OF HOLLYWOOD (PA)
Also Called: Hillside Mem Pk & Mortuary
7300 Hollywood Blvd, Los Angeles
(90046-2999)
PHONE..................................323 876-8330
Steve Sloan, *President*
David Cremin, *Treasurer*
Renee Mochkatel, *Vice Pres*
Jane Zuckerman, *Exec Dir*
Nancy Ortenberg, *Admin Sec*
EMP: 83
SQ FT: 15,000
SALES (est): 8.7MM **Privately Held**
SIC: 7261 8299 Funeral service & crematories; religious school

7291 Tax Return Preparation Svcs

(P-13382)
AHG INC
340 S Lemon Ave 6633, Walnut
(91789-2706)
PHONE..................................703 596-0111
Sanzar Kakar, *Officer*
EMP: 300

SALES: 7.5MM **Privately Held**
SIC: 7291 8721 Tax return preparation services; accounting, auditing & bookkeeping; payroll accounting service

(P-13383)
ANDERSEN TAX LLC
400 Suth Hope St Ste 2000, Los Angeles
(90071)
PHONE..................................213 593-2300
Kurt Brune, *Managing Dir*
EMP: 152
SALES (corp-wide): 43MM **Privately Held**
SIC: 7291 Tax return preparation services
PA: Andersen Tax Llc
100 1st St Ste 1600
San Francisco CA 94105
415 764-2700

(P-13384)
COMMONWEALTH EQUITY SVCS LLP
Also Called: Commonwealth Financial Network
20 Corporate Park Ste 150, Irvine
(92606-5183)
PHONE..................................949 336-6440
Karen Caporaso, *Principal*
EMP: 55
SALES (corp-wide): 233.7MM **Privately Held**
SIC: 7291 Tax return preparation services
PA: Commonwealth Equity Services, Llc
29 Sawyer Rd Ste 2
Waltham MA 02453
781 736-7980

(P-13385)
EDGE FINANCIAL INC
10100 Santa Monica Blvd, Los Angeles
(90067-4003)
PHONE..................................323 857-5809
Light Silver, *President*
EMP: 50
SQ FT: 3,500
SALES (est): 1MM **Privately Held**
WEB: www.stopirsdebt.com
SIC: 7291 7389 Tax return preparation services; legal & tax services

(P-13386)
EXACTAX INC (PA)
1100 E Orangethorpe Ave # 100, Anaheim
(92801-5168)
P.O. Box 61048 (92803-6148)
PHONE..................................714 284-4802
Kevin Love, *President*
Franklin Pang, *Shareholder*
Richard Johnson, *Treasurer*
Michael Leonetti, *Vice Pres*
Bob Lynch, *Vice Pres*
EMP: 74
SQ FT: 18,000
SALES (est): 2.5MM **Privately Held**
WEB: www.exactax.com
SIC: 7291 7371 Tax return preparation services; computer software development

(P-13387)
H & R BLOCK INC
401 N Broadway Ste B, Santa Maria
(93454-4121)
PHONE..................................805 349-9266
Bill Norris, *Branch Mgr*
EMP: 70
SALES (corp-wide): 3B **Publicly Held**
WEB: www.hrblock.com
SIC: 7291 Tax return preparation services
PA: H&R Block, Inc.
1 H&R Block Way
Kansas City MO 64105
816 854-3000

(P-13388)
H & R BLOCK INC
4300 Sonoma Blvd Ste 600, Vallejo
(94589-2211)
PHONE..................................707 643-1856
Vince Largo, *Manager*
EMP: 200
SALES (corp-wide): 3B **Publicly Held**
WEB: www.hrblock.com
SIC: 7291 Tax return preparation services

PA: H&R Block, Inc.
1 H&R Block Way
Kansas City MO 64105
816 854-3000

(P-13389)
H&R BLOCK INC
Also Called: H & R Block
1745 Van Ness Ave, San Francisco
(94109-3620)
PHONE..................................415 441-2666
Sharon Williams, *Manager*
EMP: 50
SALES (corp-wide): 3B **Publicly Held**
WEB: www.hrblock.com
SIC: 7291 Tax return preparation services
PA: H&R Block, Inc.
1 H&R Block Way
Kansas City MO 64105
816 854-3000

(P-13390)
HATFIELD INC
Also Called: Visor
5 3rd St Ste 525, San Francisco
(94103-3216)
PHONE..................................415 802-8635
Gernot Zacke, *Director*
EMP: 50
SALES (est): 150.4K **Privately Held**
SIC: 7291 Tax return preparation services

(P-13391)
J B LAQUINDANUM & ASSOCIATES
2608 Springs Rd, Vallejo (94591-5713)
PHONE..................................707 648-0501
J B Laquindanum, *Owner*
EMP: 50
SQ FT: 9,156
SALES (est): 527.6K **Privately Held**
SIC: 7291 Tax return preparation services

(P-13392)
OPTIMA TAX RELIEF LLC
3100 S Harbor Blvd # 250, Santa Ana
(92704-6823)
PHONE..................................714 361-4636
Jesse Torres,
Jarrod Bassin, *Vice Pres*
Mick Cotten, *IT/INT Sup*
John Premysler, *Finance Mgr*
Harry Langenberg,
EMP: 180
SQ FT: 30,000
SALES (est): 13.1MM **Privately Held**
WEB: www.optimataxrelief.com
SIC: 7291 Tax return preparation services

(P-13393)
TAX CREDIT CO LLC
6255 W Sunset Blvd # 2200, Los Angeles
(90028-7403)
PHONE..................................323 927-0752
Brandon Edwards, *CEO*
Larae Pieroni, *Senior VP*
Ben Floor, *Sr Associate*
EMP: 125
SALES (est): 99.9K **Privately Held**
SIC: 7291 Tax return preparation services

7299 Miscellaneous Personal Svcs, NEC

(P-13394)
1NTEGER LLC
1437 7th St Ste 400, Santa Monica
(90401-2635)
PHONE..................................424 320-2977
Joan Manning, *Principal*
EMP: 50
SALES (est): 310.5K **Privately Held**
SIC: 7299 Information services, consumer

(P-13395)
A-1 EVENT & PARTY RENTALS
Also Called: A1 Event & Party Rentals
251 E Front St, Covina (91723-1613)
PHONE..................................626 967-0500
Chet Fortney, *President*
Rene Martinez, *Vice Pres*
Steven Martinez, *Traffic Dir*
EMP: 55
SQ FT: 40,000

SALES (est): 3.4MM **Privately Held**
SIC: 7299 7359 Party planning service; party supplies rental services

(P-13396)
AMERICOR FUNDING INC
18200 Von Karman Ave # 600, Irvine
(92612-7146)
PHONE..................................866 333-8686
Banir Ganatra, *CEO*
EMP: 170
SALES (est): 388.2K **Privately Held**
SIC: 7299 Debt counseling or adjustment service, individuals

(P-13397)
APPLE VLLEY/ VCTRVLLE CNSRTIUM
14955 Dale Evans Pkwy, Apple Valley
(92307-3061)
PHONE..................................760 240-7000
Keneth J Henderson, *Exec Dir*
EMP: 65
SALES (est): 470.8K **Privately Held**
SIC: 7299 Information services, consumer

(P-13398)
AT YOUR HOME FAMILYCARE
6540 Lusk Blvd Ste C266, San Diego
(92121-2783)
PHONE..................................858 625-0406
Laurie Edwards-Tate, *President*
EMP: 200
SQ FT: 2,000
SALES (est): 5.4MM **Privately Held**
WEB: www.atyourhomefamilycare.com
SIC: 7299 8082 Babysitting bureau; home health care services

(P-13399)
BANQUET FACILITIES
Also Called: Indian Hills Golf Club
6000 Camino Real, Riverside
(92509-5310)
PHONE..................................951 360-2081
John De Zoetez, *Manager*
EMP: 50
SALES (est): 391.3K **Privately Held**
SIC: 7299 Banquet hall facilities

(P-13400)
BELCAMPO GROUP INC
Also Called: Belcampo Meat
329 N Phillipe Ln, Yreka (96097-9413)
PHONE..................................530 842-5200
Anya Sernald, *President*
EMP: 70
SALES (corp-wide): 16.5MM **Privately Held**
SIC: 7299 5421 Butcher service, processing only; meat markets, including freezer provisioners
PA: Belcampo Group, Inc.
65 Webster St
Oakland CA 94607
510 250-7810

(P-13401)
BEST VALET PARKING CORPORATION
12792 Valley View St # 201, Garden Grove
(92845-2510)
PHONE..................................800 708-2538
Michael Raemer, *President*
Aran Shelly, *General Mgr*
EMP: 100
SQ FT: 650
SALES (est): 5MM **Privately Held**
SIC: 7299 Valet parking

(P-13402)
BUCKINGHAM PROPERTY MANAGEMENT
Also Called: Coventry Cove Apartments
12609 Moffatt Ln, Fresno (93730-9704)
PHONE..................................559 322-1105
Cher Cha, *Principal*
Nora Barrera, *Area Mgr*
Katie Miller, *Manager*
EMP: 94
SALES (corp-wide): 13MM **Privately Held**
SIC: 7299 Apartment locating service

PRODUCTS & SVCS

PA: Buckingham Property Management Inc
601 W Shaw Ave Ste A
Clovis CA 93612
559 452-8250

(P-13403)
CALIFORNIA SUN CENTERS INC
8265 Sierra College Blvd, Roseville
(95661-9403)
PHONE................................916 789-9767
Michael Blore, *CEO*
EMP: 80
SALES (est): 1MM **Privately Held**
SIC: 7299 5651 Tanning salon; family
clothing stores

(P-13404)
CALLSOURCE INC (PA)
Also Called: Call Source
5601 Lindero Canyon Rd # 200, Westlake
Village (91362-6493)
PHONE................................818 673-4700
Jerry Feldman, *CEO*
Pogo Parr, *President*
Tim Gomoll, *Vice Pres*
Tim Tran, *Project Mgr*
Raine Wolf, *Project Mgr*
▲ **EMP:** 200
SQ FT: 7,600
SALES (est): 19MM **Privately Held**
WEB: www.rentline.com
SIC: 7299 7389 Information services, con-
sumer; telephone services

(P-13405)
CATTLEMENS
Also Called: Cattlemens Restaurant
2882 Kitty Hawk Rd, Livermore
(94551-7666)
PHONE................................925 447-1224
Jackie Gibson, *General Mgr*
EMP: 70
SALES (corp-wide): 19.5MM **Privately
Held**
WEB: www.beststeakinthewest.com
SIC: 7299 5812 Banquet hall facilities;
American restaurant
PA: Cattlemens
250 Dutton Ave
Santa Rosa CA 95407
707 528-1040

(P-13406)
CHOURA VENUE SERVICES
Also Called: Choura Vnue Svcs At Carson Ctr
4101 E Willow St, Long Beach
(90815-1740)
PHONE................................562 426-0555
James Choura, *CEO*
Devin Wright, *Director*
EMP: 99
SALES (est): 6.7MM **Privately Held**
SIC: 7299 5812 Information services, con-
sumer; caterers

(P-13407)
CINTAS CORPORATION NO 2
18050 Central Ave, Carson (90746-4006)
PHONE................................310 635-8713
Cluadia Sanchez, *Manager*
EMP: 69
SALES (corp-wide): 6.8B **Publicly Held**
WEB: www.cintas-corp.com
SIC: 7299 Personal appearance services
HQ: Cintas Corporation No. 2
6800 Cintas Blvd
Mason OH 45040

(P-13408)
CINTAS CORPORATION NO 3
777 139th Ave, San Leandro (94578-3218)
PHONE................................510 352-6330
Brian Delbecq, *General Mgr*
EMP: 50
SQ FT: 25,000
SALES (corp-wide): 6.8B **Publicly Held**
WEB: www.cintas-corp.com
SIC: 7299 2326 Clothing rental services;
men's & boys' work clothing
HQ: Cintas Corporation No. 3
6800 Cintas Blvd
Mason OH 45040

(P-13409)
CLASSMATES MEDIA CORPORATION
21301 Burbank Blvd, Woodland Hills
(91367-6679)
PHONE................................818 287-3600
Mark R Goldston, *Ch of Bd*
Paul J Pucino, *CFO*
Frederic A Randall Jr, *Exec VP*
Frederic Randall, *Exec VP*
Sally McKenzie, *Vice Pres*
EMP: 346
SALES (est): 4.7MM **Publicly Held**
WEB: www.classmatesmedia.com
SIC: 7299 7389 Personal document & in-
formation services; advertising, promo-
tional & trade show services
HQ: United Online, Inc.
21255 Burbank Blvd # 400
Woodland Hills CA 91367
818 287-3000

(P-13410)
CLUTTER INC (PA)
3526 Hayden Ave, Culver City
(90232-2413)
PHONE................................800 805-4023
ARI Mir, *CEO*
Elana Siegel, *Officer*
Nathan Blake, *Project Mgr*
EMP: 142
SALES (est): 31.4MM **Privately Held**
SIC: 7299 4212 Personal item care & stor-
age services; moving services

(P-13411)
CONDUIT LNGAGE SPECIALISTS INC
22720 Ventura Blvd # 100, Woodland Hills
(91364-1305)
PHONE................................859 299-3178
Art Mathews, *Branch Mgr*
EMP: 85
SALES (corp-wide): 8.2MM **Privately
Held**
SIC: 7299 Personal appearance services
PA: Conduit Language Specialists, Inc.
110 Augusta Way
Paris KY 40361
818 389-4333

(P-13412)
CONSUMER CR CNSLING SVC SAN FR (PA)
Also Called: Credit Counselor of California
1655 Grant St Ste 1300, Concord
(94520-2789)
PHONE................................888 456-2227
Rico Delgadillo, *CEO*
EMP: 60 **EST:** 1969
SQ FT: 14,000
SALES (est): 4MM **Privately Held**
WEB: www.cccssf.org
SIC: 7299 Debt counseling or adjustment
service, individuals

(P-13413)
CORINTHIAN INTL PRKG SVCS INC
Also Called: Corinthian Parking Services
19925 Stevens Creek Blvd B, Cupertino
(95014-2300)
PHONE................................408 867-7275
Douglas E Knapp, *CEO*
Todd Fedde, *Vice Pres*
Kyle Baldasano, *Director*
Jonathan Covey, *Manager*
Laura Gomes, *Manager*
EMP: 500
SQ FT: 6,000
SALES (est): 18.5MM **Privately Held**
WEB: www.corinthianparking.com
SIC: 7299 7521 4119 Valet parking; park-
ing garage; limousine rental, with driver

(P-13414)
CORPORATE SOUL LLC
433 Hudson St, Healdsburg (95448-4461)
P.O. Box 2371 (95448-2371)
PHONE................................707 431-7781
Michele Boudreaux, *Mng Member*
EMP: 270
SQ FT: 2,000

SALES (est): 4.2MM **Privately Held**
WEB: www.corporatesoul.net
SIC: 7299 Massage parlor

(P-13415)
CP OPCO LLC (HQ)
Also Called: Classic Party Rentals
901 W Hillcrest Blvd A, Inglewood
(90301-2101)
PHONE................................310 966-4900
EMP: 2300
SALES (est): 154.7MM **Privately Held**
SALES (corp-wide): 1.9MM **Privately
Held**
SIC: 7299

(P-13416)
CRYSTAL VALET PARKING INC
4477 Hollywood Blvd 209, Los Angeles
(90027-6006)
P.O. Box 27386 (90027-0386)
PHONE................................323 663-7275
Greg Gee, *President*
EMP: 70
SALES (est): 1.1MM **Privately Held**
SIC: 7299 Valet parking

(P-13417)
DANERICA ENTERPRISES INC
Also Called: Tax Resolution Services, Co
23901 Calabasas Rd # 1068, Calabasas
(91302-3305)
PHONE................................818 774-1813
Michael Rozbruch, *CEO*
R Brian Compton, *President*
Natalie Yildiz, *Controller*
Stephanie Riley, *Human Res Mgr*
Michael Castaneda, *Manager*
EMP: 100 **EST:** 1998
SQ FT: 15,000
SALES (est): 4.7MM **Privately Held**
WEB: www.taxresolution.com
SIC: 7299 Personal financial services

(P-13418)
DEBTMERICA LLC
Also Called: Debtmerica Relief
3100 S Harbor Blvd # 250, Santa Ana
(92704-6823)
PHONE................................714 389-4200
Jesse Torres,
Harry Langenberg,
Tony Gaeta, *Consultant*
Marrietta Kelly, *Consultant*
EMP: 65
SQ FT: 15,000
SALES (est): 5MM **Privately Held**
WEB: www.debtmerica.com
SIC: 7299 Debt counseling or adjustment
service, individuals

(P-13419)
DESTINATION RESIDENCES LLC
Also Called: Tesancia La Jlla Ht Spa Resort
9700 N Torrey Pines Rd, La Jolla
(92037-1102)
PHONE................................858 550-1000
Charlie Peck, *President*
Kim Ponsoll, *Sales Mgr*
Kevin Steinbuch, *Sales Mgr*
Lulu G Parks, *Director*
Summer Shoemaker, *Director*
EMP: 256
SALES (corp-wide): 865.7MM **Privately
Held**
WEB: www.destinationhotels.com
SIC: 7299 7389 7991 7011 Banquet hall
facilities; convention & show services;
spas; hotels
HQ: Destination Residences Llc
10333 E Dry Creek Rd
Englewood CO 80112
303 799-3830

(P-13420)
DROISYS INC
46540 Fremont Blvd # 516, Fremont
(94538-6487)
PHONE................................407 610-0916
EMP: 87
SALES (corp-wide): 28.4MM **Privately
Held**
SIC: 7299 Information services, consumer

PA: Droisys Inc.
46540 Fremont Blvd # 516
Fremont CA 94538
408 874-8333

(P-13421)
EHARMONY INC (HQ)
Also Called: Eharmony.com
10900 Wilshire Blvd Fl 17, Los Angeles
(90024-6522)
P.O. Box 241810 (90024-9610)
PHONE................................424 258-1199
Grant Langston, *CEO*
Galen Buckwalter, *Vice Pres*
Steve Carter, *Vice Pres*
Erickson Dan, *Vice Pres*
Miguel Garcia, *Administration*
EMP: 119
SQ FT: 6,000
SALES (est): 15.6MM
SALES (corp-wide): 4.5B **Privately Held**
WEB: www.eharmony.com
SIC: 7299 Dating service
PA: Prosiebensat.1 Media Se
Medienallee 7
Unterfohring 85774
899 507-10

(P-13422)
EMPYR INCORPORATED
8910 University Center Ln # 400, San
Diego (92122-1025)
PHONE................................888 664-5669
Jon Carder, *President*
Frank Asaro, *CFO*
Jarrod Cuzens, *Principal*
Jason Bausewein, *Sr Software Eng*
Mike Stevenson, *Web Proj Mgr*
EMP: 65
SALES (est): 4.5MM
SALES (corp-wide): 60.1B **Publicly Held**
SIC: 7299 Tax refund discounting
PA: Sysco Corporation
1390 Enclave Pkwy
Houston TX 77077
281 584-1390

(P-13423)
EVEREST WTRPRFING RSTRTION INC
1270 Missouri St, San Francisco
(94107-3310)
PHONE................................415 282-9800
Keith Goldstein, *President*
Mark Murray, *Vice Pres*
Andrina Howell, *Administration*
Tenzin Dechen, *Opers-Prdtn-Mfg*
Kenneth Bettencourt, *Opers Staff*
EMP: 64
SQ FT: 5,000
SALES (est): 4.9MM **Privately Held**
WEB: www.everestsf.com
SIC: 7299 Home improvement & renova-
tion contractor agency

(P-13424)
FREEDOM FINANCIAL NETWORK LLC (PA)
Also Called: Freedom Debt Relief
1875 S Grant St Ste 400, San Mateo
(94402-2676)
PHONE................................650 393-6619
Bradford Stroh,
Rich Ransom, *CFO*
Megan Hanley, *Chief Mktg Ofcr*
Gregory Estrada, *Vice Pres*
Kevin Gallegos, *Vice Pres*
EMP: 85
SQ FT: 20,000
SALES (est): 22.9MM **Privately Held**
WEB: www.freedomfinancialnetwork.com
SIC: 7299 Debt counseling or adjustment
service, individuals

(P-13425)
GALKOS CONSTRUCTION INC (PA)
15262 Pipeline Ln, Huntington Beach
(92649-1136)
PHONE................................714 373-8545
Frank E Gialketsis, *President*
Lonnie Gailketsis, *Vice Pres*
EMP: 54

SALES (est): 9.6MM **Privately Held**
WEB: www.galkos.com
SIC: **7299** Home improvement & renovation contractor agency

(P-13426)
GLEN IVY HOT SPRINGS
1001 Brea Mall, Brea (92821-5721)
PHONE..................................714 990-2090
Jen Breakey, *Manager*
EMP: 190
SALES (corp-wide): 12.2MM **Privately Held**
SIC: **7299** 7991 5812 5699 Massage parlor; spas; cafe; bathing suits; toiletries, cosmetics & perfumes
PA: Glen Ivy Hot Springs
25000 Glen Ivy Rd
Corona CA 92883
951 277-3529

(P-13427)
HANDYMAN CONNECTION
1740 W Katella Ave Ste G, Orange (92867-3434)
PHONE..................................714 288-0077
Rich Panitz, *President*
Linda Panitz, *Vice Pres*
EMP: 50
SQ FT: 1,000
SALES (est): 1.5MM **Privately Held**
WEB: www.omnigen.com
SIC: **7299** Handyman service

(P-13428)
HOMETOWN BUFFET INC
Also Called: Hometown Buffet 261
11471 South St, Cerritos (90703-6600)
PHONE..................................562 402-8307
Mary Woods, *General Mgr*
EMP: 51
SALES (corp-wide): 674.1MM **Privately Held**
WEB: www.hometownbuffet.com
SIC: **7299** Banquet hall facilities
HQ: Hometown Buffet Inc.
120 Chula Vis
San Antonio TX 78232

(P-13429)
IDEAL PRODUCTS LLC
14724 Ventura Blvd Fl 200, Sherman Oaks (91403-3514)
PHONE..................................818 217-2574
Mark Bess, *Mng Member*
Craig Shandler,
Michael Badar, *Mng Member*
EMP: 50
SALES (est): 2MM **Privately Held**
WEB: www.idealproduct.com
SIC: **7299** Information services, consumer

(P-13430)
IMPACT DESTINATIONS & EVENTS
Also Called: Impact Events
1005 Market St Unit 402, San Francisco (94103-1627)
PHONE..................................415 766-4170
Dan Houdek, *President*
EMP: 50
SALES (est): 254.9K **Privately Held**
SIC: **7299** Party planning service

(P-13431)
INFORMATION & REFERRAL FED LOS
Also Called: 211 La County
526 W Las Tunas Dr, San Gabriel (91776-1111)
P.O. Box 726 (91778-0726)
PHONE..................................626 350-1841
Maribel Marin, *CEO*
Amy Latzer, *COO*
Laura Nelson, *CFO*
Alana Hitchcock, *Executive Asst*
Victor Rivas, *Project Mgr*
EMP: 100
SQ FT: 23,000
SALES (est): 8.8MM **Privately Held**
WEB: www.211-la.net
SIC: **7299** Information services, consumer

(P-13432)
INTERNATIONAL MISSING PERSONS
609 S Broder St, Anaheim (92804-3232)
P.O. Box 2542 (92814-0542)
PHONE..................................714 827-1947
EMP: 55
SALES: 4.3MM **Privately Held**
SIC: **7299**

(P-13433)
JENNY CRAIG INC (PA)
5770 Fleet St, Carlsbad (92008-4700)
PHONE..................................760 696-4000
Monty Sharma, *CEO*
Patricia Larchet, *Ch of Bd*
Jim Kelly, *CFO*
Leesa Eichberger, *Chief Mktg Ofcr*
Alan V Dobies, *Vice Pres*
EMP: 220
SQ FT: 75,000
SALES (est): 129.5MM **Privately Held**
WEB: www.jennycraig.com
SIC: **7299** 6794 5149 5499 Diet center, without medical staff; franchises, selling or licensing; diet foods; dietetic foods

(P-13434)
JENNY CRAIG WGHT LOSS CTRS INC (HQ)
5770 Fleet St, Carlsbad (92008-4700)
PHONE..................................760 696-4000
Dana Fiser, *President*
Kent Kreh, *Ch of Bd*
Patti Larchet, *President*
Jenny Craig, *CEO*
James Kelly, *CFO*
EMP: 130
SQ FT: 50,000
SALES (est): 67.8MM
SALES (corp-wide): 129.5MM **Privately Held**
SIC: **7299** 7991 Diet center, without medical staff; weight reducing clubs
PA: Jenny Craig, Inc.
5770 Fleet St
Carlsbad CA 92008
760 696-4000

(P-13435)
JN PROJECTS INC
Also Called: Hellosign
333 Brannan St, San Francisco (94107-1810)
PHONE..................................415 766-0273
Joseph H Walla, *CEO*
MAI Ton, *Vice Pres*
Jack Dauer, *Executive*
Desmond Weindorf, *Software Engr*
Alex Confer, *Technology*
EMP: 100
SALES (est): 2.3MM **Publicly Held**
SIC: **7299** Personal document & information services
PA: Dropbox, Inc.
1800 Owens St Ste 200
San Francisco CA 94158

(P-13436)
LIBERTY DEBT RELIEF LLC
333 City Blvd W Fl 17, Orange (92868-5905)
PHONE..................................800 756-8447
Omar Chouche, *CEO*
Aaron Bauer, *Mng Member*
EMP: 65
SALES (est): 697.9K **Privately Held**
SIC: **7299** Debt counseling or adjustment service, individuals

(P-13437)
MASSAGE PLACE
2516 Overland Ave, Los Angeles (90064-3333)
PHONE..................................310 204-3004
Michael Marylander, *Branch Mgr*
EMP: 200
SALES (corp-wide): 2.6MM **Privately Held**
SIC: **7299** Massage parlor
PA: The Massage Place
245 Main St
Venice CA 90291
310 399-5566

(P-13438)
MASTROIANNI FAMILY ENTPS LTD
Also Called: Jay's Catering
10581 Garden Grove Blvd, Garden Grove (92843-1128)
PHONE..................................310 952-1700
Jay Mastroiannis, *President*
EMP: 78
SALES (corp-wide): 34.9MM **Privately Held**
WEB: www.jayscatering.com
SIC: **7299** Banquet hall facilities
PA: Mastroianni Family Enterprises Ltd.
10581 Garden Grove Blvd
Garden Grove CA 92843
714 636-6045

(P-13439)
MICHAAEL S HENSLEY
Also Called: Hensly Event Resources
180 W Hill Pl, Brisbane (94005-1216)
PHONE..................................650 692-7007
Michael Hensley, *President*
Susan Kidwell, *General Mgr*
Javier Guardado, *Manager*
Arnie Kelber, *Accounts Mgr*
Joe Dempsey, *Consultant*
EMP: 120
SALES (est): 801.1K **Privately Held**
SIC: **7299** 5947 Party planning service; party favors

(P-13440)
MOUNTASIA OF SANTA CLARITA
Also Called: Mountasia Family Fun Center
21516 Golden Triangle Rd, Santa Clarita (91350-2612)
PHONE..................................661 253-4386
Michael Fleming, *Partner*
David Fleming, *Partner*
Michael A Fleming, *Partner*
EMP: 60
SALES (est): 1.7MM **Privately Held**
SIC: **7299** 7999 Party planning service; skating rink operation services

(P-13441)
MOVE SALES INC (DH)
Also Called: Homestore Apartments & Rentals
3315 Scott Blvd Ste 250, Santa Clara (95054-3139)
PHONE..................................805 557-2300
Steve Berkowitz, *CEO*
Maria Pietrosorte, *President*
Debbie Neuberger, *Senior VP*
Arul Daniel, *Vice Pres*
Larry Peterson, *Vice Pres*
EMP: 75
SALES (est): 12.3MM
SALES (corp-wide): 10B **Publicly Held**
SIC: **7299** Apartment locating service
HQ: Move, Inc.
3315 Scott Blvd Ste 250
Santa Clara CA 95054
408 558-7100

(P-13442)
ONE CALL PLUMBER GOLETA
140 Nectarine Ave Apt 4, Goleta (93117-3359)
PHONE..................................805 284-0441
One Call Plumber Goleta, *Owner*
EMP: 99
SALES: 0 **Privately Held**
SIC: **7299** Handyman service

(P-13443)
PACIFIC EVENT PRODUCTIONS INC (PA)
Also Called: Pep Creations
6989 Corte Santa Fe, San Diego (92121-3260)
PHONE..................................858 458-9908
Lawrence J Toll, *CEO*
George Duff, *President*
Joanne Mera, *Admin Sec*
Greg May, *Info Tech Mgr*
Cecilia Forsyth, *Sales Staff*
EMP: 250
SQ FT: 30,000
SALES (est): 15MM **Privately Held**
WEB: www.pacificevents.com
SIC: **7299** Party planning service

(P-13444)
PALMDALE WOMANS CLUB
2141 E Avenue Q, Palmdale (93550-4040)
P.O. Box 901825 (93590-1825)
PHONE..................................661 266-3008
Shirley Haning, *President*
Helen Cleveland, *President*
Jackie Lawslo, *President*
EMP: 52
SQ FT: 3,215
SALES: 24.1K **Privately Held**
WEB: www.palmdalewomansclub.com
SIC: **7299** 8699 Personal appearance services; charitable organization

(P-13445)
PALO ALTO HILLS GOLF AN
3000 Alexis Dr, Palo Alto (94304-1303)
PHONE..................................650 948-1800
Padmanabhan Srinagesh, *CEO*
Dirk Zander, *General Mgr*
Marian Paragas, *Controller*
Kamron Memor, *Food Svc Dir*
Cassie Harris, *Director*
EMP: 75
SQ FT: 25,000
SALES (est): 7.7MM **Privately Held**
WEB: www.pahgcc.com
SIC: **7299** 7997 Banquet hall facilities; golf club, membership

(P-13446)
PARTY PANTRY GARDEN ROOM
12777 Knott St, Garden Grove (92841-3903)
PHONE..................................714 899-0626
Lisa Waddell, *Owner*
EMP: 50 EST: 1971
SALES (est): 705.2K **Privately Held**
SIC: **7299** Banquet hall facilities

(P-13447)
PLAN-IT INTERACTIVE INC (PA)
150 W Industrial Way, Benicia (94510-1016)
PHONE..................................707 752-6010
Skip Smith, *CEO*
Louis Smith, *President*
EMP: 50
SQ FT: 24,000
SALES (est): 4.1MM **Privately Held**
WEB: www.interactivegame.com
SIC: **7299** Party planning service

(P-13448)
PPS PARKING INC
1800 E Garry Ave Ste 107, Santa Ana (92705-5803)
P.O. Box 16635, Irvine (92623-6635)
PHONE..................................949 223-8707
Steve Paliska, *President*
Stephen Paliska, *COO*
EMP: 506
SQ FT: 5,000
SALES (est): 9.2MM **Privately Held**
SIC: **7299** 8748 Valet parking; business consulting

(P-13449)
PRAETORIAN USA
Also Called: Praetorian Event Services
925 Lakeville St 129, Petaluma (94952-3329)
PHONE..................................707 780-8020
Kathy J Kingman, *President*
EMP: 99
SALES: 200K **Privately Held**
SIC: **7299** 7389 Party planning service;

(P-13450)
PREMIER RESIDENTIAL SVCS LLC
43100 Cook St Ste 101, Palm Desert (92211-3124)
P.O. Box 13250 (92255-3250)
PHONE..................................760 773-4081
Daniel Loera, *Mng Member*
Cindy Voyles, *Manager*
EMP: 60
SALES (est): 213.2K **Privately Held**
SIC: **7299** Miscellaneous personal service

(P-13451)
RAINCROSS HOSPITALITY CORP (PA)
Also Called: Riverside Aditorium Events Ctr
3637 5th St, Riverside (92501-2816)
PHONE................................951 346-4700
Edward Weggeland, *President*
Debbie Guthrie, *Senior VP*
Mark Lewis, *Security Dir*
Marcy Hernandez, *Office Mgr*
Oscar Ornelas, *Engineer*
EMP: 56
SQ FT: 1,500
SALES (est): 5.6MM **Privately Held**
SIC: 7299 Banquet hall facilities; party planning service

(P-13452)
RETREAT & CONFERENCE CENTER
Also Called: De Lasalle Institute
4401 Redwood Rd, NAPA (94558-9708)
PHONE................................707 252-3810
Linda Bausch, *Director*
EMP: 50 **EST:** 2001
SALES (est): 471.9K **Privately Held**
SIC: 7299 8661 Wedding chapel, privately operated; community church

(P-13453)
SERVIZ INC
15303 Ventura Blvd # 1600, Sherman Oaks (91403-3133)
PHONE................................818 381-4826
Zorik Gordon, *CEO*
Michael Klien, *President*
Max Dichter, *Vice Pres*
Garry Galinsky, *CTO*
Jeremy Burgess, *Software Engr*
EMP: 70
SQ FT: 8,000
SALES (est): 10.8MM **Privately Held**
SIC: 7299 Home improvement & renovation contractor agency

(P-13454)
SLC OPERATING LTD PARTNERSHIP
Also Called: Sheraton Universal Hotel
333 Unversal Hollywood Dr, North Hollywood (91608-1001)
PHONE................................818 980-1212
Silvio Campos, *Branch Mgr*
EMP: 350
SALES (corp-wide): 20.7B **Publicly Held**
SIC: 7299 7011 6512 5813 Banquet hall facilities; hotels; nonresidential building operators; drinking places; eating places
HQ: Slc Operating Limited Partnership
　　2231 E Camelback Rd # 400
　　Phoenix AZ 85016

(P-13455)
SOIREE VALET PARKING SERVICE
1470 Howard St, San Francisco (94103-2523)
PHONE................................415 284-9700
Jamie Dyos, *President*
Katie Dyos, *Business Dir*
Calvin Lun, *Opers Mgr*
EMP: 150
SQ FT: 3,000
SALES: 2.8MM **Privately Held**
WEB: www.soireevalet.com
SIC: 7299 7521 Valet parking; automobile parking

(P-13456)
TRUECAR INC
1401 Ocean Ave Ste 300, Santa Monica (90401-2163)
PHONE................................800 200-2000
EMP: 95
SALES (corp-wide): 353.5MM **Publicly Held**
SIC: 7299 5012 Information services, consumer; automotive brokers
PA: Truecar, Inc.
　　120 Broadway Ste 200
　　Santa Monica CA 90401
　　800 200-2000

(P-13457)
USA VALET PARKING LLC
980 9th St Ste 1620, Sacramento (95814-2719)
PHONE................................916 792-1055
Steven Baver, *Mng Member*
EMP: 50
SALES: 126.9K **Privately Held**
SIC: 7299 7521 Valet parking; outdoor parking services

(P-13458)
VISAGE IMAGING INC
12625 High Bluff Dr # 205, San Diego (92130-2053)
PHONE................................858 345-4410
Sam Hupert, *CEO*
Brad Levin, *General Mgr*
Jay Namboothiri, *Engineer*
EMP: 75
SQ FT: 1,200
SALES: 3MM **Privately Held**
SIC: 7299 7379 Personal document & information services; computer related consulting services
PA: Pro Medicus Limited
　　450 Swan St
　　Richmond VIC 3121

(P-13459)
WATERCOURSE WAY
Also Called: Water Course Way
165 Channing Ave, Palo Alto (94301-2409)
PHONE................................650 462-2000
John Roberts, *Partner*
Watercourse Way, *Partner*
EMP: 120
SALES (est): 3.8MM **Privately Held**
WEB: www.watercourseway.com
SIC: 7299 Massage parlor

(P-13460)
WEDGEWOOD HSPITALITY GROUP INC
43385 Business Park Dr, Temecula (92590-3688)
PHONE................................951 491-8110
Daniel Bylund, *CFO*
Jeff Tucci, *Vice Pres*
EMP: 50
SQ FT: 5,000
SALES (est): 192K **Privately Held**
SIC: 7299 Banquet hall facilities

(P-13461)
WESTERN COSTUME LEASING
11041 Vanowen St, North Hollywood (91605-6314)
PHONE................................818 760-0900
Eddie Marks, *President*
Kristin Holbak, *Executive Asst*
EMP: 60
SQ FT: 150,000
SALES (est): 1.1MM
SALES (corp-wide): 6.5MM **Privately Held**
WEB: www.westerncostume.com
SIC: 7299 Costume rental
HQ: Western Costume Co.
　　11041 Vanowen St
　　North Hollywood CA 91605
　　818 760-0900

(P-13462)
Z VALET INC
Also Called: Z Valet & Shuttle Service
4221 Wilshire Blvd 170-11, Los Angeles (90010-3519)
PHONE................................323 954-3700
Daniel Ziv, *President*
EMP: 225
SQ FT: 1,500
SALES (est): 5.2MM **Privately Held**
WEB: www.zvalet.com
SIC: 7299 7363 8748 Valet parking; chauffeur service; business consulting

---

7311 Advertising Agencies

(P-13463)
180LA LLC
12555 W Jefferson Blvd # 200, Los Angeles (90066-7047)
PHONE................................310 382-1400
Michael Allen, *Mng Member*
Cooper Olson, *Creative Dir*
Erin Bremmer, *Project Mgr*
Jason Lau, *Buyer*
Natasha Wellesley, *Production*
EMP: 110
SQ FT: 13,000
SALES: 24.4MM
SALES (corp-wide): 15.2B **Publicly Held**
WEB: www.180la.com
SIC: 7311 Advertising consultant
HQ: Tbwa Worldwide Inc.
　　488 Madison Ave
　　New York NY 10022

(P-13464)
72ANDSUNNY LLC
12101 Bluff Creek Dr, Playa Vista (90094-2627)
PHONE................................310 215-9009
John Boiler,
Sedef Onar, *Officer*
Glenn Cole,
Matt Jarvis,
Robert Nakata,
EMP: 126
SALES (est): 41.7MM **Privately Held**
SIC: 7311 Advertising agencies

(P-13465)
A S I CORPORATION
Also Called: Bridgford Foods
1308 N Patt St, Anaheim (92801-2551)
PHONE................................714 526-5533
Allan L Bridgford, *Chairman*
Robert E Schulze, *President*
Raymond F Lancy, *Vice Pres*
William L Bridgford, *Admin Sec*
▲ **EMP:** 200
SQ FT: 95,000
SALES (est): 13.8MM
SALES (corp-wide): 174.2MM **Publicly Held**
WEB: www.bridgford.com
SIC: 7311 2711 Advertising consultant; newspapers
HQ: Bridgford Foods Corporation
　　1308 N Patt St
　　Anaheim CA 92801
　　714 526-5533

(P-13466)
AAAZA INC
3250 Wilshire Blvd # 1901, Los Angeles (90010-1609)
PHONE................................213 380-8333
Zan Ng, *CEO*
Jeanine Kim, *Shareholder*
Peter Huang, *President*
EMP: 60
SQ FT: 3,000
SALES (est): 9.8MM **Privately Held**
WEB: www.aaaza.com
SIC: 7311 Advertising consultant

(P-13467)
ADARA INC (PA)
1070 E Meadow Cir, Palo Alto (94303-4230)
PHONE................................408 876-6360
Layton Han, *CEO*
Elizabeth Harz, *President*
Frank Teruel, *COO*
Arnold Gee, *Officer*
Cecilia Hayes, *Officer*
EMP: 80 **EST:** 2005
SALES (est): 25.5MM **Privately Held**
SIC: 7311 Advertising consultant

(P-13468)
ADLINK CABLE ADVERTISING LLC
11150 Santa Monica Blvd # 100, Los Angeles (90025-3380)
PHONE................................310 477-3994
Bob McCauley,
EMP: 120
SALES (est): 12MM **Privately Held**
WEB: www.adlink.com
SIC: 7311 Advertising consultant

(P-13469)
AIRPUSH INC
11400 W Olympic Blvd, Los Angeles (90064-1550)
PHONE................................877 944-2490
Asher Delug, *CEO*
David K Awamoto, *President*
Inman Breaux, *COO*
Matt Shaw, *Officer*
David Kawamoto, *Senior VP*
EMP: 140
SALES (est): 16.6MM **Privately Held**
SIC: 7311 Advertising agencies

(P-13470)
ALCONE MARKETING GROUP INC (HQ)
Also Called: Jeep Gear
4 Studebaker, Irvine (92618-2012)
PHONE................................949 595-5322
William Hahn, *CEO*
Sean Conciatore, *Ch Credit Ofcr*
Bill Hahn, *Principal*
▲ **EMP:** 100
SQ FT: 90,000
SALES (est): 22.1MM
SALES (corp-wide): 15.2B **Publicly Held**
WEB: www.alconemarketing.com
SIC: 7311 Advertising consultant
PA: Omnicom Group Inc.
　　437 Madison Ave
　　New York NY 10022
　　212 415-3600

(P-13471)
AMOBEE INC (DH)
901 Marshall St 200, Redwood City (94063-2026)
PHONE................................650 353-4399
Kim Perell, *CEO*
Craig Foster, *CFO*
Steve Hoffman, *CFO*
Gabi Schindler, *Chief Mktg Ofcr*
Chad Bronstein, *Officer*
EMP: 148
SALES (est): 69.5MM
SALES (corp-wide): 13MM **Privately Held**
WEB: www.amobee.com
SIC: 7311 Advertising agencies

(P-13472)
AVIA TECH LLC
7220 Trade St Ste 300, San Diego (92121-2334)
PHONE................................858 777-5000
Dwight Gould, *CEO*
Cheryl Gould,
EMP: 56
SQ FT: 8,000
SALES (est): 9.2MM **Privately Held**
SIC: 7311 Advertising agencies

(P-13473)
AYZENBERG GROUP INC
49 E Walnut St, Pasadena (91103-3832)
PHONE................................626 584-4070
Eric Ayzenberg, *President*
Chris Younger, *Partner*
Matt Bretz, *Vice Pres*
Bill Buckley, *Vice Pres*
Joey Jones, *Vice Pres*
▲ **EMP:** 65
SQ FT: 10,000
SALES (est): 19.4MM **Privately Held**
WEB: www.ayzenberg.com
SIC: 7311 7336 Advertising consultant; commercial art & graphic design

(P-13474)
BARRETT SF
250 Sutter St Ste 200, San Francisco (94108-4451)
PHONE................................415 986-2960
Abby John, *CEO*
Todd Eisner, *Creative Dir*
Michael Reardon, *Accounting Mgr*
Nash Rachel, *Finance*
Charlotte Dugoni, *Producer*
EMP: 50

SALES (est): 1.5MM **Privately Held**
SIC: 7311 Advertising agencies

(P-13475)
BASIS WORLDWIDE
1557 7th St, Santa Monica (90401-2605)
PHONE..........................424 261-2354
Joe Dipietro, *CEO*
EMP: 50
SALES (est): 1.1MM **Privately Held**
SIC: 7311 Advertising consultant

(P-13476)
BATTERY MARKETING INC
Also Called: Battery Agency
6515 W Sunset Blvd # 200, Hollywood
(90028-7261)
PHONE..........................323 467-7267
Anson Sowby, *CEO*
Steve Orenstein, *CFO*
Philip Khosid, *Officer*
Mackenzie Busch, *Production*
Maximilian Kislevitz, *Director*
EMP: 52
SALES (est): 3.7MM **Privately Held**
SIC: 7311 Advertising consultant

(P-13477)
BBDO WORLDWIDE INC
600 California St Fl 8, San Francisco
(94108-2726)
PHONE..........................415 808-6200
Linda D Merrick, *Senior VP*
Melissa Miller, *Vice Pres*
Linda Domercq, *Controller*
Amanda D'Aloise, *Manager*
EMP: 60
SALES (corp-wide): 15.2B **Publicly Held**
WEB: www.bbdo.com
SIC: 7311 Advertising consultant
HQ: Bbdo Worldwide Inc.
1285 Ave Of The Amer
New York NY 10019
212 459-5000

(P-13478)
BDS MARKETING LLC (DH)
10 Holland, Irvine (92618-2504)
PHONE..........................800 234-4237
Ken Kress, *CEO*
Scott McDaniel, *President*
Tracy Neff, *COO*
Randy Schrock, *Senior VP*
Eric Wartman, *Vice Pres*
EMP: 120
SALES (corp-wide): 255.7MM **Privately Held**
WEB: www.bdsmarketing.com
SIC: 7311 8743 8732 Advertising consultant; promotion service; commercial non-physical research
HQ: Bds Solutions Group, Llc
10 Holland
Irvine CA 92618
949 472-6700

(P-13479)
BUTLER SHINE STERN PRTNERS LLC
Also Called: Bssp
20 Liberty Ship Way, Sausalito
(94965-3312)
PHONE..........................415 331-6049
Greg Stern,
Dennis Moore, *CFO*
Matthew Curry, *Officer*
Don Luu, *Opers Staff*
John Butler,
EMP: 139
SALES (est): 44.1MM **Privately Held**
SIC: 7311 Advertising consultant

(P-13480)
CADREON LLC
600 Battery St, San Francisco
(94111-1817)
PHONE..........................415 262-5900
Ian Johnson, *General Mgr*
Karin Mihkels, *Senior VP*
Matt Bayer, *Vice Pres*
Jason Chambers, *Vice Pres*
John George, *Vice Pres*
EMP: 120
SALES (corp-wide): 9.7B **Publicly Held**
SIC: 7311 Advertising consultant

HQ: Cadreon, Llc
100 W 33rd St Fl 8
New York NY 10001

(P-13481)
CASANOVA PNDRILL PBLICIDAD INC (PA)
275 Mccormick Ave Ste 1a, Costa Mesa
(92626-3325)
PHONE..........................949 474-5001
Daniel Nance, *President*
Laura Marella, *Vice Pres*
Jean Malley Vega, *Vice Pres*
Jose Molina, *Executive*
Jonathan Lackey, *Creative Dir*
EMP: 55
SQ FT: 12,000
SALES (est): 10.4MM **Privately Held**
WEB: www.casanova.com
SIC: 7311 Advertising agencies

(P-13482)
CREATIVE CHANNEL SERVICES LLC (HQ)
Also Called: C C S
6601 Center Dr W Ste 400, Los Angeles
(90045-1577)
PHONE..........................310 482-6500
Andy Restivo, *CEO*
Michael Butler, *CFO*
Hanoz Gandhi, *Exec VP*
George Plumb, *Exec VP*
Will Pipkin, *Regional Mgr*
EMP: 76
SALES (est): 34.1MM
SALES (corp-wide): 15.2B **Publicly Held**
WEB: www.creativechannel.com
SIC: 7311 Advertising agencies
PA: Omnicom Group Inc.
437 Madison Ave
New York NY 10022
212 415-3600

(P-13483)
CREW CREATIVE ADVERTISING LLC
7966 Beverly Blvd, Los Angeles
(90048-4511)
PHONE..........................310 451-3225
Damon Wolf, *Mng Member*
John Cain, *COO*
Jennifer Cain,
Charles Reimers,
Maria Reimers,
EMP: 165
SQ FT: 65,000
SALES (est): 11.1MM **Privately Held**
WEB: www.crewcreative.com
SIC: 7311 Advertising agencies

(P-13484)
D AUGUSTINE & ASSOCIATES
Also Called: Augustine Ideas
3017 Douglas Blvd Ste 200, Roseville
(95661-3837)
PHONE..........................916 774-9600
Debra Augustine, *CEO*
Robert Nelson, *COO*
Beth Harris, *Business Dir*
Samantha Burns, *Graphic Designe*
Jeff Emmerling, *Graphic Designe*
EMP: 52
SALES (est): 9.7MM **Privately Held**
SIC: 7311 Advertising consultant

(P-13485)
DAILEY & ASSOCIATES
8687 Melrose Ave Ste G300, West Hollywood (90069-5701)
PHONE..........................323 490-3847
Jean Grabow, *CEO*
Michelle Wong, *President*
William Waldner, *Treasurer*
Michael Perdigao, *Exec VP*
Rob Greenwald, *Vice Pres*
EMP: 82 EST: 1964
SALES (est): 14.9MM **Privately Held**
WEB: www.daileyads.com
SIC: 7311 Advertising consultant

(P-13486)
DAVID & GOLIATH LLC
909 N Pacific Coast Hwy # 700, El Segundo (90245-2724)
PHONE..........................310 445-5200
Yumi Prentice, *President*
Wells Davis, *Officer*
Bobby Pearce, *Officer*
EMP: 200
SQ FT: 1,000
SALES (est): 33.5MM **Privately Held**
WEB: www.dngla.com
SIC: 7311 Advertising consultant
PA: Innocean Worldwide Inc.
308 Gangnam-Daero, Gangnam-Gu
Seoul 06253

(P-13487)
DAVISELEN ADVERTISING INC (PA)
865 S Figueroa St # 1200, Los Angeles
(90017-2543)
PHONE..........................213 688-7000
Mark Davis, *CEO*
Stan Kaplan, *Partner*
Jim Kelly, *Partner*
Malu Santamaria, *Partner*
Robert Elen, *President*
EMP: 172 EST: 1915
SQ FT: 32,000
SALES (est): 27.7MM **Privately Held**
WEB: www.daviselen.com
SIC: 7311 Advertising agencies

(P-13488)
DAVISELEN ADVERTISING INC
420 Stevens Ave Ste 240, Solana Beach
(92075-2079)
PHONE..........................858 847-0789
Jim Kelly, *Branch Mgr*
EMP: 61
SALES (corp-wide): 27.7MM **Privately Held**
SIC: 7311 Advertising consultant
PA: Daviselen Advertising, Inc.
865 S Figueroa St # 1200
Los Angeles CA 90017
213 688-7000

(P-13489)
DDB WORLDWIDE
340 Main St, Venice (90291-2524)
PHONE..........................310 907-1500
Nick Bishop, *Manager*
Joanne Howes, *Partner*
EMP: 175
SALES (corp-wide): 15.2B **Publicly Held**
SIC: 7311 Advertising agencies
HQ: Ddb Worldwide Communications
Group, Inc.
437 Madison Ave Fl 11
New York NY 10022
212 415-2000

(P-13490)
DDB WORLDWIDE
600 California St Fl 7, San Francisco
(94108-2731)
PHONE..........................415 732-3600
Mary Moudry, *President*
Ryan De Leon, *Administration*
EMP: 160
SALES (corp-wide): 15.2B **Publicly Held**
SIC: 7311 Advertising consultant
HQ: Ddb Worldwide Communications
Group, Inc.
437 Madison Ave Fl 11
New York NY 10022
212 415-2000

(P-13491)
DEDICATED MEDIA INC (PA)
909 N Pacific Coast Hwy # 320, El Segundo (90245-2734)
PHONE..........................310 524-9400
Scott Yamano, *CEO*
Chris Berman, *COO*
Ryan Becker, *Vice Pres*
Brian Malone, *Vice Pres*
EMP: 53
SQ FT: 45,000
SALES (est): 15.3MM **Privately Held**
WEB: www.dedicatedla.com
SIC: 7311 Advertising consultant

(P-13492)
DEFY MEDIA LLC
8750 Wilshire Blvd # 200, Beverly Hills
(90211-2703)
PHONE..........................310 360-4141
Keith Richman,
Matt Ryan, *Sales Staff*
EMP: 99
SALES (est): 2.5MM **Privately Held**
SIC: 7311 Advertising agencies

(P-13493)
DELPHI PRODUCTIONS INC (PA)
Also Called: Group Delphi
950 W Tower Ave, Alameda (94501-5049)
PHONE..........................510 748-7494
Justin Hersh, *President*
Pete Bowes, *CFO*
Darlene Lee, *Bd of Directors*
Kyle Wood, *Senior VP*
Tony Erpelding, *Vice Pres*
EMP: 142
SQ FT: 148,000
SALES (est): 48.9MM **Privately Held**
WEB: www.delphiproductions.com
SIC: 7311 Advertising agencies

(P-13494)
DEUTSCH LA INC
5454 Beethoven St, Los Angeles
(90066-7017)
PHONE..........................310 862-3000
Mike Sheldon, *CEO*
Guto Araki, *Exec VP*
Dana Commandatore, *Exec VP*
Walter Smith, *Exec VP*
Lauren Tetuan, *Exec VP*
EMP: 100 EST: 1995
SALES (est): 25.2MM
SALES (corp-wide): 9.7B **Publicly Held**
SIC: 7311 Advertising agencies
PA: The Interpublic Group Of Companies
Inc
909 3rd Ave
New York NY 10022
212 704-1200

(P-13495)
DGWB INC
Also Called: Dgwb Advg & Communications
217 N Main St Ste 200, Santa Ana
(92701-4843)
PHONE..........................714 881-2300
Mike Wiseman, *CEO*
Mike Weisman, *Partner*
Dean Heacock, *CFO*
Annie Liu, *Executive*
Danika Petersen, *Executive*
EMP: 70
SALES (est): 21.2MM **Privately Held**
SIC: 7311 Advertising consultant

(P-13496)
DGWB VENTURES LLC
Also Called: Advertising
217 N Main St Ste 200, Santa Ana
(92701-4843)
P.O. Box 11863 (92711-1863)
PHONE..........................714 881-2308
Mike Weisman,
Madeline Dossin,
John Gothold,
Mike Shudak,
EMP: 95
SQ FT: 25,839
SALES (est): 916.2K **Privately Held**
SIC: 7311 Advertising consultant

(P-13497)
DIGITAL OPERATIVE INC
404 Camino Del, San Diego (92110)
PHONE..........................310 630-0072
William D Cook, *Principal*
Sagar Bhatt, *Software Dev*
Craig Brugh, *Software Dev*
Christian Carlson, *Software Dev*
Danny Ginn, *Software Dev*
EMP: 50
SALES (est): 5.1MM
SALES (corp-wide): 22.3MM **Privately Held**
SIC: 7311 Advertising agencies
PA: Trans Cosmos America, Inc.
879 W 190th St Ste 410
Gardena CA 90248
310 630-0072

(P-13498)
DIRECT PARTNERS INC (HQ)
12777 W Jefferson Blvd # 120, Los Angeles
(90066-7038)
PHONE............................310 482-4200
Tom Harrison, *President*
Tom Parr, *CFO*
Barry Wagner, *Admin Sec*
EMP: 52
SQ FT: 31,000
SALES (est): 11.1MM
SALES (corp-wide): 15.2B **Publicly Held**
WEB: www.directpartners.com
SIC: 7311 Advertising consultant
PA: Omnicom Group Inc.
　　437 Madison Ave
　　New York NY 10022
　　212 415-3600

(P-13499)
DOREMUS & COMPANY
55 Union St Fl 3, San Francisco
(94111-1244)
PHONE............................415 273-7800
Garrett Lawrence, *Manager*
EMP: 50
SALES (corp-wide): 15.2B **Publicly Held**
WEB: www.doremus.com
SIC: 7311 7319 Advertising consultant;
sky writing
HQ: Doremus & Company
　　200 Varick St Fl 11
　　New York NY 10014
　　212 366-3000

(P-13500)
ELANCE INC (HQ)
2625 Augustine Dr Ste 601, Santa Clara
(95054-2956)
PHONE............................650 316-7500
Stephane Kasriel, *President*
Brian Kinion, *CFO*
Efstratios Karamanlakis, *Vice Pres*
Anthony Massarweh, *Program Mgr*
Ed Heyer, *Business Mgr*
EMP: 148
SQ FT: 20,000
SALES (est): 47MM
SALES (corp-wide): 253.3MM **Publicly
Held**
WEB: www.elance.com
SIC: 7311 Advertising consultant
PA: Upwork Inc.
　　2625 Augustine Dr Ste 601
　　Santa Clara CA 95054
　　650 316-7500

(P-13501)
ELEVEN INC
Also Called: Eleven Communications
500 Sansome St Ste 100, San Francisco
(94111-3213)
PHONE............................415 707-1111
Courtney Buechert, *CEO*
Ted Bluey, *Partner*
Michael Borosky, *Partner*
Alison Fowler, *Partner*
Jarett Hausske, *Partner*
EMP: 120
SALES: 22MM **Privately Held**
WEB: www.eleveninc.com
SIC: 7311 Advertising agencies

(P-13502)
**EPICENTRO ADVERTISING
MKTG SVC**
2370 Qume Dr Ste B, San Jose
(95131-1842)
PHONE............................408 453-0353
Maria Schabbing, *Owner*
EMP: 50
SALES (est): 5.1MM **Privately Held**
SIC: 7311 Advertising consultant

(P-13503)
EQAL INC
5250 Lankershim Blvd # 720, North Holly-
wood (91601-3188)
PHONE............................818 276-6300
Miles Beckett, *CEO*
Greg Goodfried, *President*
Robert Weiss, *COO*
Tyler Rubin, *CFO*
EMP: 147

SALES (est): 11.7MM
SALES (corp-wide): 1.2B **Publicly Held**
SIC: 7311 Advertising consultant
HQ: Everyday Health, Inc.
　　345 Hudson St Rm 1600
　　New York NY 10014
　　646 728-9500

(P-13504)
EVANS HARDY & YOUNG INC
Also Called: Ehy
829 De La Vina St Ste 100, Santa Barbara
(93101-3285)
PHONE............................805 963-5841
Jim L Evans, *President*
Sue Andrews, *CFO*
Dennis Hardy, *Exec VP*
Donald Deluccio, *Vice Pres*
Malena Cruz, *Controller*
EMP: 50
SQ FT: 5,000
SALES (est): 11.9MM **Privately Held**
WEB: www.ehy.com
SIC: 7311 Advertising consultant

(P-13505)
**EVOLVE MEDIA HOLDINGS LLC
(PA)**
Also Called: Springboard
5140 W Goldleaf Cir G100, Los Angeles
(90056-1666)
PHONE............................310 449-1890
Aaron Broder, *CEO*
Brian Fitzgerald, *President*
Michael Kumin, *CEO*
Geoff Schiller, *Officer*
Walder Amaya, *Senior VP*
EMP: 225
SALES (est): 27.3MM **Privately Held**
SIC: 7311 8742 Advertising agencies;
management consulting services; market-
ing consulting services

(P-13506)
**EXPONENTIAL INTERACTIVE
INC (HQ)**
5858 Horton St Ste 300, Emeryville
(94608-2183)
PHONE............................510 250-5500
Dilip Dasilva, *President*
Tim Brown, *Officer*
Philip Buxton, *Officer*
Amritpal Bedi, *Vice Pres*
Harris Bernstein, *Vice Pres*
EMP: 90 EST: 2000
SALES (est): 23.1MM **Privately Held**
WEB: www.tribalfusion.com
SIC: 7311 Advertising consultant
PA: Exponential Interactive Uk Limited
　　C/O Thomas Alexander & Company L
　　London
　　203 411-7401

(P-13507)
FCB WORLDWIDE INC
Also Called: Draftfcb
1160 Battery St Ste 250, San Francisco
(94111-1216)
PHONE............................415 820-8545
Ian Beavis, *Branch Mgr*
Ken Copen, *Prdtn Dir*
EMP: 524
SALES (corp-wide): 9.7B **Publicly Held**
SIC: 7311 Advertising agencies
HQ: Fcb Worldwide, Inc.
　　100 W 33rd St Fl 5
　　New York NY 10001
　　212 885-3000

(P-13508)
FORTY FOUR GROUP LLC
Also Called: Origaudio
17391 Mount Cliffwood Cir, Fountain Valley
(92708-4102)
PHONE............................949 407-6360
Michael Szymczak,
Jason Lucash,
▲ EMP: 58
SQ FT: 2,000
SALES (est): 535.9K **Privately Held**
SIC: 7311 Advertising agencies

(P-13509)
FULLSCREEN INC (HQ)
12180 Millennium Ste 100, Playa Vista
(90094-2951)
PHONE............................310 202-3333
George Strompolos, *CEO*
Whit Richards, *CFO*
Michael Wann, *Officer*
David Ho, *Exec VP*
Randy Ahn, *Vice Pres*
EMP: 81 EST: 2011
SALES (est): 50.1MM
SALES (corp-wide): 2.1MM **Privately
Held**
SIC: 7311 Advertising agencies
PA: Otter Media Holdings, Llc
　　12180 Millennium Ste 200
　　Playa Vista CA 90094
　　310 202-3333

(P-13510)
**GIANT CREATIVE STRATEGY
LLC**
1700 Montgomery St # 485, San Francisco
(94111-1025)
PHONE............................415 655-5200
Steven Gold, *CEO*
Larry Caringi, *President*
Adam Gelling, *President*
Jeff Nemy, *CFO*
Eric Steckelman, *Officer*
EMP: 150
SQ FT: 24,000
SALES (est): 36MM
SALES (corp-wide): 288.9MM **Privately
Held**
WEB: www.giantagency.com
SIC: 7311 Advertising agencies
PA: Huntsworth Plc
　　8th Floor Holborn Gate
　　London WC2A
　　203 861-3999

(P-13511)
GL NEMIROW INC
Also Called: Terry Hines & Assoc
2550 N Hollywood Way, Burbank
(91505-1055)
PHONE............................818 562-9433
Grant W Nemirow, *President*
Ralph Terracciano, *CFO*
Ralph Terraciano, *CFO*
Norm Hayes, *IT/INT Sup*
Kevin Kerr, *Art Dir*
EMP: 97
SALES (est): 14MM **Privately Held**
WEB: www.thatrailers.com
SIC: 7311 Advertising agencies

(P-13512)
**GOODBY SLVERSTEIN
PARTNERS INC**
Also Called: Goodby Silverstein & Partners
720 California St, San Francisco
(94108-2440)
PHONE............................415 392-0669
Rich Silverstein, *CEO*
Margaret Coles, *Partner*
Brian McPherson, *Managing Prtnr*
Robert Riccardi, *Managing Prtnr*
Derek Robson, *Managing Prtnr*
EMP: 200
SQ FT: 60,000
SALES (est): 52.3MM
SALES (corp-wide): 15.2B **Publicly Held**
WEB: www.omnicomgroup.com
SIC: 7311 Advertising consultant
PA: Omnicom Group Inc.
　　437 Madison Ave
　　New York NY 10022
　　212 415-3600

(P-13513)
GREYSTRIPE INCORPORATED
30699 Russell Ranch Rd # 250, Westlake
Village (91362-7315)
PHONE............................415 644-1702
Michael Chang, *CEO*
Kurt Hawks, *COO*
Erica Chriss, *Senior VP*
Alvaro Bravo, *Vice Pres*
Andy Choi, *CTO*
EMP: 136
SALES (est): 3.1MM **Publicly Held**
SIC: 7311 Advertising agencies

HQ: Conversant, Llc
　　30699 Russell Ranch Rd # 250
　　Westlake Village CA 91362
　　818 575-4500

(P-13514)
**GRIZZARD CMMNCATIONS
GROUP INC**
2 N Lake Ave, Pasadena (91101-1858)
PHONE............................818 543-1315
Philip Stolberg, *Branch Mgr*
EMP: 55
SALES (corp-wide): 15.2B **Publicly Held**
SIC: 7311 Advertising agencies
HQ: Grizzard Communications Group, Inc.
　　3500 Lenox Rd Ne Ste 1900
　　Atlanta GA 30326
　　404 522-8330

(P-13515)
HAVAS EDGE LLC (PA)
2386 Faraday Ave Ste 200, Carlsbad
(92008-7223)
PHONE............................760 929-0041
Steve Netzley, *CEO*
Greg Johnson, *COO*
Eric Bush, *CFO*
Neil Nguyen, *Officer*
Abed Abusaleh, *Exec VP*
EMP: 53
SALES (est): 22.4MM **Privately Held**
WEB: www.eurorscg-drtv.com
SIC: 7311 Advertising agencies

(P-13516)
HOBBS HERDER ADVERTISING
Also Called: Hobbs/Herder Training
419 Main St, Huntington Beach
(92648-5199)
PHONE............................800 999-6090
Greg Herder, *Ch of Bd*
John Surge, *President*
EMP: 85
SQ FT: 18,500
SALES (est): 12.7MM **Privately Held**
WEB: www.hobbsherder.com
SIC: 7311 Advertising consultant

(P-13517)
HORIZON MEDIA INC
1888 Century Park E # 700, Los Angeles
(90067-1702)
PHONE............................310 282-0909
Zach Rosenberg, *Branch Mgr*
EMP: 300
SALES (corp-wide): 119MM **Privately
Held**
SIC: 7311 Advertising agencies
PA: Horizon Media, Inc.
　　75 Varick St Ste 1404
　　New York NY 10013
　　212 220-5000

(P-13518)
HORN GROUP INC
101 Montgomery St Fl 15, San Francisco
(94104-4147)
PHONE............................415 905-4000
Sabrina Horn, *President*
Todd Cadley, *Exec VP*
Katie Neuman, *Senior VP*
Smita Topolski, *Vice Pres*
Brian Sinderson, *Managing Dir*
EMP: 50
SQ FT: 13,000
SALES (est): 340K **Privately Held**
WEB: www.horngroup.com
SIC: 7311 Advertising agencies

(P-13519)
HVSF TRANSITION LLC
Also Called: Heat
1100 Sansome St, San Francisco
(94111-1205)
PHONE............................415 477-1999
John Elder, *President*
EMP: 60
SQ FT: 12,000
SALES (est): 11.5MM
SALES (corp-wide): 5.5B **Privately Held**
WEB: www.sfheat.com
SIC: 7311 Advertising consultant
HQ: Deloitte Consulting Llp
　　30 Rockefeller Plz
　　New York NY 10112
　　212 492-4000

(P-13520)
I MEAN IT CREATIVE INC
1643 Buckingham Rd, Los Angeles
(90019-5904)
PHONE.....................310 287-1000
Emrah Yucel, *President*
EMP: 50
SALES (est): 6.2MM **Privately Held**
SIC: 7311 Advertising agencies

(P-13521)
ICON MEDIA DIRECT INC (PA)
5910 Lemona Ave, Van Nuys (91411-3006)
PHONE.....................818 995-6400
Nancy Lazkani, *CEO*
Seth Klein, *COO*
Minnie Dimesa, *Vice Pres*
Jeff Lazkani, *Vice Pres*
Gordon Kwong, *Executive*
EMP: 90
SQ FT: 16,445
SALES (est): 18.6MM **Privately Held**
WEB: www.iconmediadirect.com
SIC: 7311 Advertising agencies

(P-13522)
ICONIC COLLECTIVE LLC ✪
4136 Del Rey Ave Ste 601, Marina Del Rey
(90292-5604)
PHONE.....................877 930-0409
Wesley Rick Rabe,
EMP: 75 EST: 2019
SALES (est): 2.5MM **Privately Held**
SIC: 7311 8742 7812 7336 Advertising
agencies; marketing consulting services;
television film production; graphic arts &
related design

(P-13523)
IGNITE HEALTH LLC (PA)
7535 Irvine Center Dr # 200, Irvine
(92618-2962)
PHONE.....................949 861-3200
Matt Brown, *President*
Brian Lefkowitz, *Officer*
Alison Ward, *Accounting Mgr*
Richard E Fair,
Fabio Gratton,
EMP: 116
SQ FT: 15,000
SALES (est): 12.5MM **Privately Held**
WEB: www.ignitehealth.com
SIC: 7311 Advertising consultant

(P-13524)
**INNOCEAN WRLDWIDE
AMERICAS LLC (HQ)**
180 5th St Ste 200, Huntington Beach
(92648-7107)
PHONE.....................714 861-5200
Yun Jong Beak, *CFO*
Tim Blett, *COO*
Eddie Austin, *Vice Pres*
Ben Gogley, *Vice Pres*
Barney Goldberg, *Vice Pres*
EMP: 75
SALES (est): 36.5MM **Privately Held**
WEB: www.worldmarketinggroup.com
SIC: 7311 Advertising consultant

(P-13525)
**INTER/MEDIA TIME BUYING
CORP (PA)**
Also Called: Inter/Media Advertising
22120 Clarendon St # 300, Woodland Hills
(91367-6315)
PHONE.....................818 995-1455
Robert B Yallen, *President*
James Christensen, *Vice Pres*
Malena Cruz, *Vice Pres*
Grant Rosenquist, *Vice Pres*
Jackie Rivera, *Executive*
EMP: 50
SQ FT: 12,000
SALES (est): 21MM **Privately Held**
WEB: www.intermedia-advertising.com
SIC: 7311 Advertising agencies

(P-13526)
**INTERACTIVE MEDIA HOLDINGS
(DH)**
Also Called: Viant
2722 Michelson Dr Ste 100, Irvine
(92612-8905)
PHONE.....................949 861-8888

Timothy C Vanderhook, *President*
Larry Madden, *CFO*
Roy Luna, *Exec VP*
Bill Schild, *Exec VP*
Varoujan Bedirian, *Senior VP*
EMP: 77
SALES (est): 19.3MM
SALES (corp-wide): 3.1B **Publicly Held**
SIC: 7311 7313 Advertising agencies;
newspaper advertising representative
HQ: Ti Gotham Inc.
225 Liberty St
New York NY 10281
212 522-1212

(P-13527)
**INTERTREND
COMMUNICATIONS INC**
228 E Broadway, Long Beach
(90802-4840)
PHONE.....................562 733-1888
Julia Huang, *CEO*
Susanna Jue, *General Mgr*
Stacy Liu, *Executive Asst*
Flo Kuraoka, *Administration*
Linda Palacios, *Planning*
▲ **EMP:** 70
SQ FT: 10,000
SALES (est): 15.8MM **Privately Held**
WEB: www.intertrend.com
SIC: 7311 Advertising consultant

(P-13528)
ISEARCH MEDIA LLC
1710 S Amphlett Blvd # 320, San Mateo
(94402-2703)
PHONE.....................415 358-0882
Maury Domengeaux, *CEO*
Scott Rayden, *President*
Charles Hentrich, *CTO*
EMP: 56
SALES (est): 282.8K
SALES (corp-wide): 5.9MM **Privately
Held**
SIC: 7311 Advertising agencies
HQ: 3q Digital, Inc.
155 Bovet Rd Ste 480
San Mateo CA 94402
650 539-4124

(P-13529)
IW GROUP (PA)
6300 Wilshire Blvd # 2150, Los Angeles
(90048-5232)
PHONE.....................310 289-5500
Bill Imada, *CEO*
Nita Song, *President*
EMP: 54
SQ FT: 7,500
SALES (est): 17.7MM **Privately Held**
WEB: www.iwgroupinc.com
SIC: 7311 8743 Advertising consultant;
public relations services

(P-13530)
**J WALTER THOMPSON USA
LLC**
303 2nd St, San Francisco (94107-1366)
PHONE.....................415 268-5555
Greg Rowan, *Branch Mgr*
EMP: 66
SALES (corp-wide): 20B **Privately Held**
SIC: 7311 Advertising agencies
HQ: J. Walter Thompson U.S.A., Llc
466 Lexington Ave Fl 2
New York NY 10017
212 210-7000

(P-13531)
**JACK MORTON WORLDWIDE
INC**
1840 Century Park E # 1800, Los Angeles
(90067-2119)
PHONE.....................310 967-2400
Gemma Roskam, *Principal*
EMP: 53
SALES (corp-wide): 9.7B **Publicly Held**
SIC: 7311 7812 Advertising consultant;
audio-visual program production
HQ: Jack Morton Worldwide Inc.
500 Harrison Ave Ste 5r
Boston MA 02118
617 585-7000

(P-13532)
KERN ORGANIZATION INC
Also Called: Kern Direct Marketing
20955 Warner Center Ln, Woodland Hills
(91367-6511)
PHONE.....................818 703-8775
Russell Kern, *President*
Zeke Ibarbia, *CFO*
Steven Orenstein, *CFO*
David Azulay, *Senior VP*
Tom Mackendrick, *Vice Pres*
EMP: 80
SQ FT: 11,350
SALES (est): 23.7MM
SALES (corp-wide): 15.2B **Publicly Held**
WEB: www.thekernorg.com
SIC: 7311 Advertising consultant
PA: Omnicom Group Inc.
437 Madison Ave
New York NY 10022
212 415-3600

(P-13533)
KOVEL/FULLER LLC
9925 Jefferson Blvd, Culver City
(90232-3505)
PHONE.....................310 841-4444
John Fuller, *President*
J Reilly, *Vice Pres*
Leila Reynolds, *Vice Pres*
Kristin Bruno, *VP Business*
Lee Kovel, *Creative Dir*
EMP: 55
SQ FT: 40,000
SALES (est): 12.8MM **Privately Held**
WEB: www.kovelfuller.com
SIC: 7311 Advertising consultant

(P-13534)
LOCAL CORPORATION (PA)
Also Called: Local.com
7555 Irvine Center Dr, Irvine (92618-2930)
P.O. Box 50700 (92619-0700)
PHONE.....................949 784-0800
Frederick G Thiel, *Ch of Bd*
Kenneth S Cragun, *CFO*
Scott Reinke, *Officer*
Erick Herring, *Senior VP*
Paula Brici, *Sr Associate*
EMP: 59
SQ FT: 34,612
SALES (est): 83.1MM **Publicly Held**
SIC: 7311 Advertising agencies

(P-13535)
LOS DEFENSORES INC
20101 Hamilton Ave # 300, Torrance
(90502-1351)
PHONE.....................310 519-4050
Mary Ann Walker, *President*
Amir Tamjidi, *Info Tech Mgr*
Yolanda Moreno, *Accountant*
EMP: 50
SQ FT: 3,000
SALES (est): 3.7MM **Privately Held**
SIC: 7311 8111 Advertising agencies; gen-
eral practice attorney, lawyer

(P-13536)
LOWCOM LLC
818 W 7th St Ste 700, Los Angeles
(90017-3430)
PHONE.....................213 408-0080
Lawrence Ng,
Fred Hsu,
EMP: 150
SALES (est): 9MM **Privately Held**
WEB: www.lowermybills.com
SIC: 7311 Advertising agencies

(P-13537)
MACHINTEL CORPORATION
4225 Executive Sq Ste 955, La Jolla
(92037-9152)
PHONE.....................617 517-3090
Mark Choudhari, *Ch of Bd*
Pravin Thombare, *Research Analys*
Ruchi Choudhari, *Director*
EMP: 60 EST: 2010
SALES (est): 3.1MM **Privately Held**
SIC: 7311 Advertising agencies

(P-13538)
**MCCANN WORLD GROUP INC
(PA)**
Also Called: Universal McCann
653 Front St, San Francisco (94111-1913)
PHONE.....................415 262-5500
Daryl Lee, *CEO*
Sarah Personette, *President*
Jim Baller, *Vice Pres*
Nicole Dowswell, *Vice Pres*
EMP: 68 EST: 2009
SALES (est): 15.3MM **Privately Held**
SIC: 7311 Advertising consultant

(P-13539)
**MCCANN-ERICKSON
CORPORATION (HQ)**
135 Main St Fl 21, San Francisco
(94105-1812)
PHONE.....................415 348-5600
Don Hov, *CFO*
Nancy Tynan, *Senior VP*
Neena Koyen, *Vice Pres*
Nicole Bourboulis, *Executive Asst*
James Brennan, *Director*
EMP: 100
SQ FT: 37,000
SALES (est): 14.9MM
SALES (corp-wide): 9.7B **Publicly Held**
SIC: 7311 Advertising agencies
PA: The Interpublic Group Of Companies
Inc
909 3rd Ave
New York NY 10022
212 704-1200

(P-13540)
MEA DIGITAL WORX LLC
Also Called: Piston Agency
530 B St Ste 1900, San Diego
(92101-4472)
PHONE.....................619 238-8923
Michael Chaney, *CEO*
John Hartman, *President*
Andrew Resnick, *CFO*
Mark Burr, *Vice Pres*
Alex Chernyak, *VP Bus Dvlpt*
EMP: 50
SALES (est): 9.6MM **Privately Held**
WEB: www.meadigital.com
SIC: 7311 8742 Advertising consultant;
marketing consulting services

(P-13541)
**MEDIABRANDS WORLDWIDE
INC**
5700 Wilshire Blvd # 400, Los Angeles
(90036-3659)
PHONE.....................323 370-8000
Murray Grondin, *Vice Pres*
Melinda Frye, *Supervisor*
EMP: 300
SALES (corp-wide): 9.7B **Publicly Held**
WEB: www.wimc.com
SIC: 7311 Advertising agencies
HQ: Mediabrands Worldwide, Inc.
653 Front St
San Francisco CA 94111
212 605-7000

(P-13542)
MEDIAPLEX INC (DH)
30699 Russell Ranch Rd # 250, Westlake
Village (91362-7315)
PHONE.....................818 575-4500
Gregory R Raifman, *Ch of Bd*
Costa John, *COO*
Francis P Patchel, *CFO*
Ruiqing Jiang, *CTO*
Mark Joseph, *CTO*
EMP: 100
SALES (est): 5.8MM **Publicly Held**
WEB: www.mediaplex.com
SIC: 7311 Advertising agencies
HQ: Conversant, Llc
30699 Russell Ranch Rd # 250
Westlake Village CA 91362
818 575-4500

(P-13543)
MEKANISM INC (PA)
640 2nd St Fl 3, San Francisco
(94107-4066)
PHONE.....................415 908-4000
Jason Harris, *CEO*

Pete Caban, *CEO*
Michael Zlatoper, *COO*
Eric Cosper, *Creative Dir*
Matt Stafford, *Creative Dir*
EMP: 50
SALES (est): 13.2MM **Privately Held**
WEB: www.mekanism.com
SIC: 7311 Advertising agencies

(P-13544)
MENDELSOHN/ZIEN ADVG LLC
11901 Santa Monica Blvd # 618, Los Angeles (90025-2767)
PHONE..........................310 444-1990
Richard Zien,
Jordin Mendelsohn,
EMP: 75 **EST:** 1982
SQ FT: 7,000
SALES (est): 8.3MM **Privately Held**
WEB: www.mzad.com
SIC: 7311 Advertising agencies
PA: Hakuhodo Incorporated
5-3-1, Akasaka
Minato-Ku TKY 107-0

(P-13545)
MERINGCARSON HOLDINGS (PA)
1700 I St Ste 210, Sacramento (95811-3018)
PHONE..........................916 441-0571
David Mering, *CEO*
Colm Conn, *Senior Partner*
Lori Bartle, *President*
Lorie Brewster, *CFO*
Greg Carson, *Ch Credit Ofcr*
EMP: 85
SQ FT: 11,000
SALES (est): 25.1MM **Privately Held**
WEB: www.meringcarson.com
SIC: 7311 Advertising consultant

(P-13546)
METRO ONE TELECOM INC
4900 Rivergrade Rd B210, Irwindale (91706-1401)
PHONE..........................626 337-8100
Gary Brent, *Manager*
EMP: 150
SALES (corp-wide): 44.7MM **Publicly Held**
WEB: www.metro1.com
SIC: 7311 7389 Advertising agencies; telephone services
PA: Metro One Telecommunications, Inc.
1331 Nw Lovejoy St # 900
Portland OR 97209
503 643-9500

(P-13547)
MUTESIX GROUP INC
Also Called: Mutesix, An Iprospect Company
6080 Center Dr Ste 900, Los Angeles (90045-9226)
PHONE..........................310 215-3467
Steve Weiss, *CEO*
Daniel Rutberg, *President*
EMP: 120
SALES (est): 6.6MM **Privately Held**
SIC: 7311 Advertising agencies
HQ: Dentsu Aegis London Limited
10 Triton Street
London NW1 3
207 430-6000

(P-13548)
MYPOINTSCOM LLC (HQ)
Also Called: My Points.com
44 Montgomery St Ste 1050, San Francisco (94104-4621)
PHONE..........................415 615-1100
Jeff Goldstein, *CFO*
Mark Harrington, *Exec VP*
Edward Zinser, *Exec VP*
Mv Krishnamurthy, *Senior VP*
Tripti Thakur, *Vice Pres*
EMP: 60
SALES (est): 10.8MM
SALES (corp-wide): 53.9MM **Privately Held**
WEB: www.mypoints.com
SIC: 7311 Advertising agencies

PA: Prodege, Llc
100 N Pacific Coast Hwy # 800
El Segundo CA 90245
310 294-9599

(P-13549)
NEXSTAR DIGITAL LLC
12777 W Jefferson Blvd, Los Angeles (90066-7048)
PHONE..........................310 971-9300
Morgan Harris, *Branch Mgr*
EMP: 100
SALES (corp-wide): 2.7B **Publicly Held**
SIC: 7311 Advertising agencies
HQ: Nexstar Digital, Llc
545 E John Carpenter Fwy
Irving TX 75062
972 373-8800

(P-13550)
NEXTROLL INC (PA)
2300 Harrison St Fl 2, San Francisco (94110-2013)
PHONE..........................877 723-7655
Toby Gabriner, *CEO*
Robin Bordoli, *President*
Peter Krivkovich, *COO*
Aaron Bell,
Mee Patrick, *Vice Pres*
EMP: 110
SALES (est): 40.3MM **Privately Held**
SIC: 7311 Advertising consultant

(P-13551)
OGILVY & MATHER WORLDWIDE INC
2425 Olympic Blvd 2200w, Santa Monica (90404-4095)
PHONE..........................310 280-2200
Hugh Branigan, *Branch Mgr*
EMP: 75
SALES (corp-wide): 20B **Privately Held**
SIC: 7311 Advertising consultant
HQ: Ogilvy & Mather Worldwide, Inc.
636 11th Ave
New York NY 10036
212 237-4000

(P-13552)
OMELET LLC (PA)
3540 Hayden Ave, Culver City (90232-2413)
PHONE..........................213 427-6400
Thas Naseemuddeen, *CEO*
Naj Allana, *CFO*
Don Kurz, *Chairman*
Ryan Fey, *Officer*
Sarah Ceglarski, *Exec Dir*
EMP: 65
SQ FT: 7,500
SALES (est): 12.4MM **Privately Held**
SIC: 7311 Advertising consultant

(P-13553)
ONE PLANET OPS INC (PA)
Also Called: Buyerlink
1820 Bonanza St Ste 200, Walnut Creek (94596-4376)
PHONE..........................925 983-2800
Payam Zamani, *CEO*
David Wittenkamp, *CFO*
David Greene, *Vice Pres*
Tom Kelley, *Vice Pres*
John Lambertus, *Vice Pres*
EMP: 121
SALES (est): 38.3MM **Privately Held**
WEB: www.reply.com
SIC: 7311 Advertising agencies

(P-13554)
OPENX TECHNOLOGIES INC (DH)
888 E Walnut St Fl 2, Pasadena (91101-1897)
PHONE..........................855 673-6948
Tim Cadogan, *CEO*
Peter Klibowitz, *Partner*
Len Mendoza, *Partner*
Wendy Myotsang, *Partner*
John Gentry, *President*
▲ **EMP:** 103
SALES (est): 67.7MM **Privately Held**
SIC: 7311 Advertising agencies

(P-13555)
ORGANIC HOLDINGS INC
Also Called: Organic On
600 California St Fl 8, San Francisco (94108-2726)
PHONE..........................415 581-5300
Jonathan Nelson, *CEO*
EMP: 350
SALES (est): 24MM **Privately Held**
SIC: 7311 7374 8742 7375 Advertising consultant; computer graphics service; management consulting services; information retrieval services

(P-13556)
OVERSEENET (PA)
550 S Hope St Ste 200, Los Angeles (90071-2672)
PHONE..........................213 408-0080
Debra Domeyer, *CEO*
Lawrence Ng, *President*
Dwayne Walker, *President*
Elizabeth Murray, *CFO*
Gene Chuang, *CTO*
EMP: 170
SQ FT: 54,000
SALES (est): 20.6MM **Privately Held**
WEB: www.oversee.net
SIC: 7311 Advertising agencies

(P-13557)
PEREIRA & ODELL LLC (PA)
215 2nd St Ste 100, San Francisco (94105-3141)
PHONE..........................415 284-9916
Nancy Daum, *CFO*
Andrew O'Dell, *CEO*
Jaime Robinson, *Officer*
Joshua F Brandau, *Vice Pres*
Colin Spooner, *Vice Pres*
EMP: 95
SALES (est): 21.8MM **Privately Held**
WEB: www.pereiraodell.com
SIC: 7311 Advertising consultant

(P-13558)
PHELPS GROUP
12121 W Bluff Dr Ste 200, Playa Vista (90094)
PHONE..........................310 752-4400
Jose Lozano, *CEO*
Ed Chambliss, *Managing Prtnr*
Glenn Schieke, *COO*
Robert Berry, *CFO*
Myles Watling, *CFO*
EMP: 50 **EST:** 1981
SQ FT: 17,000
SALES (est): 21MM **Privately Held**
WEB: www.phelpsgroup.com
SIC: 7311 Advertising consultant

(P-13559)
PORTER CRISPIN & LLC BOGUSKY
2110 Colorado Ave Ste 200, Santa Monica (90404-3763)
PHONE..........................305 859-2070
Ryan Skubic, *Manager*
EMP: 125
SALES (corp-wide): 1.4B **Publicly Held**
SIC: 7311 Advertising consultant
HQ: Crispin Porter & Bogusky Llc
3390 Mary St Ste 300
Boulder CO 80301
305 859-2070

(P-13560)
POSTAER RUBIN AND ASSOCIATES (PA)
Also Called: R P Direct
2525 Colorado Ave Ste 100, Santa Monica (90404-5576)
PHONE..........................310 394-4000
Willam C Hagelstein, *CEO*
Gerrold R Rubin, *Ch of Bd*
Vincent Mancuso, *CFO*
Larry Postaer, *Exec VP*
Dennis Remsing, *Exec VP*
EMP: 148
SQ FT: 130,000
SALES (est): 61.3MM **Privately Held**
SIC: 7311 Advertising consultant

(P-13561)
PUBMATIC INC (PA)
305 Main St Fl 1, Redwood City (94063-1729)
PHONE..........................650 351-9162
Rajeev Goel, *CEO*
Steve Pantelick, *CFO*
Larry Harris, *Chief Mktg Ofcr*
Terri Walter, *Chief Mktg Ofcr*
Shrirang Bapat, *Vice Pres*
EMP: 86
SQ FT: 4,000
SALES (est): 63.5MM **Privately Held**
SIC: 7311 Advertising agencies

(P-13562)
Q1MEDIA INC
300 Continental Blvd # 615, El Segundo (90245-5046)
PHONE..........................512 388-2300
Phil Banfield, *Branch Mgr*
EMP: 62
SALES (corp-wide): 11.4MM **Privately Held**
SIC: 7311 Advertising agencies
PA: Q1media, Inc.
8240 N Mopac Expy Ste 250
Austin TX 78759
512 388-2300

(P-13563)
QUAD/GRAPHICS INC
Also Called: Sacramento Div
1201 Shore St, West Sacramento (95691-3510)
PHONE..........................916 371-9500
Dan Coffee, *Administration*
Bob Boone, *Opers Mgr*
Linda Myers, *Production*
EMP: 250
SALES (corp-wide): 4.1B **Publicly Held**
WEB: www.vertisinc.com
SIC: 7311 2759 2752 Advertising agencies; commercial printing; commercial printing, lithographic
PA: Quad/Graphics Inc.
N61w23044 Harrys Way
Sussex WI 53089
414 566-6000

(P-13564)
QUIGLY-SIMPSON HEPPELWHITE INC
Also Called: Quigley-Simpson La
11601 Wilshire Blvd Fl 7, Los Angeles (90025-0509)
PHONE..........................310 996-5800
Kathryn Browne, *CFO*
Gerald Bagg, *Ch of Bd*
Renee Hill Young, *Ch of Bd*
Duryea Ruffins, *President*
Alissa Stakgold, *President*
EMP: 150
SQ FT: 10,500
SALES (est): 39.4MM **Privately Held**
WEB: www.quigleysimpson.com
SIC: 7311 7319 Advertising agencies; media buying service

(P-13565)
RAPP WORLDWIDE INC
12777 W Jefferson Blvd, Los Angeles (90066-7048)
PHONE..........................310 563-7200
Collins Rapp, *Branch Mgr*
EMP: 100
SALES (corp-wide): 15.2B **Publicly Held**
SIC: 7311 Advertising consultant
HQ: Rapp Worldwide Inc.
437 Madison Ave
New York NY 10022

(P-13566)
REACHLOCAL INC (HQ)
21700 Oxnard St Ste 1600, Woodland Hills (91367-7586)
PHONE..........................818 274-0260
Sharon T Rowlands, *CEO*
Jonathan Greer, *Partner*
Katie McCullin, *Partner*
Michael Kline, *COO*
Ross G Landsbaum, *CFO*
EMP: 148
SQ FT: 38,592

SALES: 382.6MM
SALES (corp-wide): 2.9B **Publicly Held**
SIC: 7311 7375 Advertising consultant;
on-line data base information retrieval
PA: Gannett Co., Inc.
7950 Jones Branch Dr
Mc Lean VA 22102
703 854-6000

(P-13567)
RED INTERACTIVE AGENCY LLC (PA)
3420 Ocean Park Blvd # 3080, Santa Monica (90405-3325)
PHONE...................310 399-4242
Brian Lovell, *CEO*
Donny Makower, *President*
Derek Van Den Bosch, *COO*
Derek Bosch, *COO*
Vance Dubberly, *Vice Pres*
EMP: 100
SALES (est): 15.3MM **Privately Held**
SIC: 7311 Advertising consultant

(P-13568)
RESCUE AGENCY PUB BENEFT LLC (PA)
2437 Morena Blvd, San Diego (92110-4152)
PHONE...................619 231-7555
Kristin Carroll, *CEO*
Jeffrey Jordan, *President*
Dennis Triplett, *COO*
Mayo Djakaria, *Officer*
Michelle Bellon, *Vice Pres*
EMP: 70
SALES (est): 6MM **Privately Held**
SIC: 7311 8732 Advertising agencies; sociological research

(P-13569)
RICHARDS GROUP INC
Also Called: Metro Pcs
888 S Figueroa St # 1400, Los Angeles (90017-5449)
PHONE...................214 891-5700
Gene Howe, *Owner*
EMP: 175
SALES (corp-wide): 104.4MM **Privately Held**
SIC: 7311 Advertising agencies
PA: The Richards Group Inc
2801 N Cntl Expy Ste 100
Dallas TX 75204
214 891-5700

(P-13570)
ROSEMONT MEDIA LLC
1010 Turquoise St Ste 201, San Diego (92109-1266)
PHONE...................858 200-0044
Mike Lubisich, *Mng Member*
Michael Lubisich, *CFO*
Michel Corinne, *Opers Staff*
Sarah Bryce,
Courtney Humes,
EMP: 50
SALES (est): 1.2MM **Privately Held**
WEB: www.rosemontmedia.com
SIC: 7311 8742 Advertising consultant;
marketing consulting services

(P-13571)
RUBICON PROJECT INC (PA)
12181 Bluff Creek Dr Fl 4, Los Angeles (90094-3234)
PHONE...................310 207-0272
Michael G Barrett, *President*
David L Day, *CFO*
Blima Tuller, *Officer*
Matthew Breedlove, *Vice Pres*
Mark Bulleri, *Vice Pres*
EMP: 148
SQ FT: 47,000
SALES: 124.6MM **Publicly Held**
SIC: 7311 Advertising agencies

(P-13572)
RUNYON SALTZMAN INC
Also Called: Rse
2020 L St Ste 100, Sacramento (95811-4260)
PHONE...................916 446-9900
Christopher Holben, *President*
Estelle Saltzman, *Ch of Bd*
Paul McClure, *Vice Pres*

Scott Rose, *Vice Pres*
Steve Fong, *Creative Dir*
EMP: 65
SQ FT: 14,000
SALES: 39MM **Privately Held**
WEB: www.rs-e.com
SIC: 7311 8743 Advertising consultant;
public relations & publicity

(P-13573)
RW LYNCH CO INC (PA)
2333 San Ramon Valley Blv, San Ramon (94583-4429)
P.O. Box 5159 (94583-5159)
PHONE...................925 837-3877
Randall W Lynch, *CEO*
Brian Lynch, *President*
Stephen Grazzini, *CFO*
Ed Holtz, *Business Mgr*
EMP: 77
SQ FT: 19,000
SALES (est): 17.8MM **Privately Held**
WEB: www.lawonline.com
SIC: 7311 Advertising consultant

(P-13574)
SAATCHI & SAATCHI N AMER INC
Team One Advertising
13031 W Jefferson Blvd, Los Angeles (90094-7000)
PHONE...................310 437-2500
Amanda Taft, *President*
Patty Schiappa, *Officer*
Magan Felitto, *Executive*
Craig Crawford, *Creative Dir*
Elizabeth Brownsen, *Exec Dir*
EMP: 250
SALES (corp-wide): 22.3MM **Privately Held**
WEB: www.saatchila.com
SIC: 7311 Advertising agencies
HQ: Saatchi & Saatchi North America, Inc.
1675 Broadway
New York NY 10019
212 463-2000

(P-13575)
SCDRG INC
473 S Carnegie Dr, San Bernardino (92408-4207)
PHONE...................818 874-0830
Richard Seiglery, *President*
Richard Seigler, *President*
Mark Seigler, *Creative Dir*
EMP: 66
SQ FT: 10,000
SALES: 7MM **Privately Held**
SIC: 7311 Advertising consultant

(P-13576)
SCORPION DESIGN LLC
27750 Entertainment Dr, Valencia (91355-1091)
PHONE...................661 702-0100
Rustin Kretz, *CEO*
Megan Bennett, *Manager*
EMP: 565
SQ FT: 100,000
SALES (est): 98.4MM **Privately Held**
WEB: www.scorpiondesign.com
SIC: 7311 Advertising agencies

(P-13577)
SEARCH AGENCY INC (PA)
801 N Brand Blvd Ste 1020, Glendale (91203-1279)
PHONE...................310 582-5700
David Hughes, *CEO*
Peter Harington, *CFO*
David Otto Rahmel, *Exec VP*
Matt Kain, *Risk Mgmt Dir*
EMP: 90
SALES (est): 17.1MM **Privately Held**
SIC: 7311 Advertising agencies

(P-13578)
SHARETHIS INC (PA)
3000 El Camino Real 5-150, Palo Alto (94306-2121)
PHONE...................650 641-0191
Dana Hayes Jr, *CEO*
Tim Schigel, *Ch of Bd*
Matt Gallatin, *CFO*
Paul Lentz, *Senior VP*
Jeff Hochberg, *Vice Pres*

EMP: 50 **EST:** 2004
SALES (est): 11.9MM **Privately Held**
SIC: 7311 7313 7372 Advertising consultant; electronic media advertising representatives; prepackaged software

(P-13579)
SIERRA WEATHERIZATION CO INC
43 E Main St Ste B, Los Gatos (95030-6907)
PHONE...................408 354-1900
Peter Hofmann, *President*
Amy Diffenderfer, *Corp Secy*
EMP: 99
SALES (est): 12MM **Privately Held**
SIC: 7311 Advertising agencies

(P-13580)
SRAX INC (PA)
Also Called: SOCIAL REALITY
456 Seaton St, Los Angeles (90013-2235)
PHONE...................323 694-9800
Christopher Miglino, *Ch of Bd*
Molly Young, *Managing Prtnr*
Kristoffer Nelson, *COO*
Michael Malone, *CFO*
Randy Ferrell, *Exec VP*
EMP: 60
SALES: 9.8MM **Publicly Held**
SIC: 7311 Advertising agencies

(P-13581)
STEEL HOUSE INC
3644 Eastham Dr, Culver City (90232-2411)
PHONE...................310 773-3331
Mark Douglas, *CEO*
Rory Mitchell, *Ch Credit Ofcr*
Vin Bhardwaj, *Vice Pres*
Lindsey Breeden, *Vice Pres*
Robert Cornell, *Vice Pres*
EMP: 160 **EST:** 2009
SALES (est): 10.9MM **Privately Held**
SIC: 7311 Advertising agencies

(P-13582)
SUISSA MILLER ADVERTISING LLC
8687 Melrose Ave, West Hollywood (90069-5701)
PHONE...................310 392-9666
David Suissa,
Bruce Miller,
EMP: 100
SQ FT: 40,000
SALES (est): 5.4MM **Privately Held**
SIC: 7311 Advertising agencies

(P-13583)
SWIRL INC
Also Called: Swirl McGarrybowen
101 Montgomery St Ste 200, San Francisco (94129-1732)
PHONE...................415 276-8300
Martin Lauber, *Chairman*
Matt Hofherr, *Partner*
Ryan Lindholm, *President*
Wayne Esplana, *CFO*
Tasha McVeigh, *Officer*
EMP: 60
SQ FT: 10,000
SALES (est): 695.2K **Privately Held**
WEB: www.swirl.net
SIC: 7311 Advertising agencies
HQ: Dentsu Mcgarry Bowen Llc
601 W 26th St Rm 1150
New York NY 10001
212 598-2900

(P-13584)
TAPJOY INC (PA)
353 Sacramento St Ste 600, San Francisco (94111-3604)
PHONE...................415 766-6900
Steve Wadsworth, *President*
Zachary Drake, *Partner*
Matthew Service, *COO*
Al Wood, *CFO*
George Garrick, *Chairman*
EMP: 54 **EST:** 2007
SALES (est): 15.9MM **Privately Held**
SIC: 7311 Advertising agencies

(P-13585)
TBWA WORLDWIDE INC
Also Called: Media Arts Lab
1017 16th St Apt C, Santa Monica (90403-4330)
PHONE...................310 305-4400
Larry Kelly, *Owner*
Beth Keamy, *Associate Dir*
Dana Franklin, *Software Dev*
Greg Lizanich, *Opers Staff*
Keane Julia, *Producer*
EMP: 133
SALES (corp-wide): 15.2B **Publicly Held**
SIC: 7311 Advertising consultant
HQ: Tbwa Worldwide Inc.
488 Madison Ave
New York NY 10022

(P-13586)
TMP WORLDWIDE ADVERTISING & CO
330 N Brand Blvd Ste 1050, Glendale (91203-2875)
PHONE...................818 539-2000
Gretchen Edwards, *Vice Pres*
Wendy De Haas, *Manager*
EMP: 74
SALES (corp-wide): 296.3MM **Privately Held**
SIC: 7311 Advertising agencies
HQ: Tmp Worldwide Advertising & Communications, Llc
125 Broad St Fl 10
New York NY 10004

(P-13587)
TODDA MERGER SUB INC
Also Called: Petrol Advertising
443 N Varney St, Burbank (91502-1733)
PHONE...................323 644-3720
EMP: 70
SALES (est): 1.4MM
SALES (corp-wide): 8.1MM **Privately Held**
SIC: 7311 Advertising consultant
PA: Toadman Interactive Ab (Publ)
Sveavagen 20
Stockholm 111 5
708 887-252

(P-13588)
TRAILER PARK INC
6922 Hollywood Blvd # 1200, Los Angeles (90028-6132)
PHONE...................310 845-8400
Joel Johnston, *President*
EMP: 60 **Privately Held**
SIC: 7311 7812 Advertising agencies; motion picture & video production
PA: Trailer Park, Inc.
6922 Hollywood Blvd Fl 12
Los Angeles CA 90028

(P-13589)
TRAILER PARK INC (PA)
6922 Hollywood Blvd Fl 12, Los Angeles (90028-6132)
P.O. Box 2950 (90078-2950)
PHONE...................310 845-3000
Tim Nett, *President*
Matt Brubaker, *CEO*
Ali Aleisawi, *COO*
Howard Moggs, *Senior VP*
Benedict Coulter, *Vice Pres*
EMP: 100
SQ FT: 8,000
SALES (est): 36.4MM **Privately Held**
SIC: 7311 Advertising agencies

(P-13590)
UE AUTHORITY CO
Also Called: Underground Elephant
225 Broadway Ste 2200, San Diego (92101-5011)
PHONE...................800 466-4178
Jason Kulpa, *President*
William Huff, *CFO*
Michael Norman, *Chief Mktg Ofcr*
Taryn Lomas, *Officer*
Lauren Alexander, *Exec VP*
EMP: 100

P R O D U C T S & S V C S

SALES (est): 25MM **Privately Held**
SIC: 7311 7371 Advertising consultant;
computer software development

(P-13591)
US INTERACTIVE DELAWARE
1270 Oakmead Pkwy Ste 318, Sunnyvale
(94085-4044)
PHONE...................................408 863-7500
Sunil Mathur, *Branch Mgr*
EMP: 139 **Privately Held**
SIC: 7311 Advertising consultant
PA: U.S. Interactive Corp Delaware
1270 Oakmead Pkwy Ste 318
Sunnyvale CA 94085

(P-13592)
**VALASSIS COMMUNICATIONS
INC**
1575 Corporate Dr, Costa Mesa
(92626-1467)
PHONE...................................714 751-4006
Steve Scott, *Manager*
EMP: 52 **Privately Held**
WEB: www.valassis.com
SIC: 7311 Advertising agencies
HQ: Valassis Communications, Inc.
19975 Victor Pkwy
Livonia MI 48152
734 591-3000

(P-13593)
**VENABLES/BELL & PARTNERS
LLC**
Also Called: Vbp Orange
201 Post St Fl 2, San Francisco
(94108-5027)
PHONE...................................415 288-3300
Paul Venables, *Mng Member*
Will McGinness, *Creative Dir*
Justin Moore, *Creative Dir*
Erich Pfeifer, *Creative Dir*
Anne-Louise Pettersson, *Office Mgr*
EMP: 190
SQ FT: 30,000
SALES (est): 54.8MM **Privately Held**
WEB: www.venablesbell.com
SIC: 7311 Advertising consultant

(P-13594)
**VERTICAL SEARCH WORKS
INC**
1808 Aston Ave Ste 170, Carlsbad
(92008-7367)
PHONE...................................212 967-9502
EMP: 60
SALES (corp-wide): 12.3MM **Privately
Held**
SIC: 7311
PA: Vertical Search Works, Inc.
336 W 37th St Rm 100
New York NY
212 967-9502

(P-13595)
VISIONAIRE GROUP INC
Also Called: Tvgla
400 Crprate Pinte Ste 700, Culver City
(90230)
PHONE...................................310 823-1800
Dimitry Ioffe, *CEO*
Bryan Pettigrew, *President*
Long Tran, *Creative Dir*
Quixari Ruffin, *Info Tech Mgr*
Andrew Kan, *Web Dvlpr*
EMP: 52 **EST:** 2007
SALES (est): 10.9MM **Privately Held**
SIC: 7311 Advertising consultant

(P-13596)
VITRO LLC
2305 Historic Decatur Rd # 205, San Diego
(92106-6073)
PHONE...................................619 234-0408
Tom Sullivan, *President*
EMP: 90
SALES (est): 14.8MM **Privately Held**
SIC: 7311 Advertising consultant

(P-13597)
VITROROBERTSON LLC
2305 Historic Decatur Rd, San Diego
(92106-6050)
PHONE...................................619 234-0408

John Vitro, *Principal*
Tom Sullivan, *President*
Alan Bonine, *Exec VP*
Chelsie Earl, *Executive*
Marissa Walsh, *Executive*
EMP: 89
SQ FT: 12,000
SALES (est): 17.3MM
SALES (corp-wide): 1.4B **Publicly Held**
WEB: www.vitrorobertson.com
SIC: 7311 Advertising consultant
PA: Mdc Partners Inc.
745 5th Ave Fl 19
New York NY 10151
646 429-1800

(P-13598)
WALKER ADVERTISING LLC
20101 Hamilton Ave # 300, Torrance
(90502-1351)
PHONE...................................310 519-4050
Mary Ann Walker, *CEO*
Amir Tamjidi, *Info Tech Mgr*
Josephine Nguyen, *Software Dev*
Lesly Frausto, *Technology*
Myrna Yin, *Technology*
EMP: 50
SALES (est): 14.1MM **Privately Held**
WEB: www.walkeradvertising.com
SIC: 7311 Advertising consultant

(P-13599)
WONDERFUL AGENCY
11444 W Olympic Blvd # 210, Los Angeles
(90064-1559)
PHONE...................................310 966-8600
Stewart A Resnick, *CEO*
EMP: 1613
SALES (est): 144.9K
SALES (corp-wide): 1.5B **Privately Held**
SIC: 7311 Advertising consultant
PA: The Wonderful Company Llc
11444 W Olympic Blvd # 210
Los Angeles CA 90064
310 966-5700

(P-13600)
YOUNG & RUBICAM INC
Also Called: Y & R
303 2nd St Ste N300, San Francisco
(94107-3638)
PHONE...................................415 882-0600
Michael Reese, *Branch Mgr*
John Rynehart, *Director*
EMP: 120
SALES (corp-wide): 20B **Privately Held**
SIC: 7311 Advertising consultant
HQ: Young & Rubicam Llc
3 Columbus Cir
New York NY 10019
212 210-3000

(P-13601)
YUB INC
520 Logue Ave, Mountain View
(94043-4049)
PHONE...................................650 265-7316
Alastair Rampell, *President*
Edward Lim, *CTO*
EMP: 177
SQ FT: 5,000
SALES (est): 7.3MM **Publicly Held**
SIC: 7311 7374 Advertising agencies;
computer time-sharing
PA: Quotient Technology Inc.
400 Logue Ave
Mountain View CA 94043
-

(P-13602)
YUME INC (DH)
601 Montgomery St # 1600, San Francisco
(94111-2603)
PHONE...................................650 591-9400
Ted Hastings, *President*
Dan Slivjanovski, *COO*
Ed Reginelli, *CFO*
Frank Barbieri, *Officer*
Michael Hudes, *Officer*
EMP: 59 **EST:** 2004
SQ FT: 20,400
SALES (est): 160.4MM
SALES (corp-wide): 60MM **Privately
Held**
SIC: 7311 Advertising consultant

(P-13603)
Z57 INC (DH)
10045 Mesa Rim Rd, San Diego
(92121-2913)
PHONE...................................858 623-5577
Steve Weber, *President*
Cynthia Sener, *Vice Pres*
Logan Gibbs, *Marketing Staff*
Eric Mir, *Marketing Staff*
Bria Phillips, *Marketing Staff*
EMP: 55
SALES (est): 8.4MM
SALES (corp-wide): 3B **Privately Held**
WEB: www.z57.com
SIC: 7311 Advertising agencies
HQ: Constellation Homebuilder Systems
Inc.
888 S Dsnyland Dr Ste 430
Tustin CA 92780
714 768-6100

(P-13604)
ZEETOGROUP LLC
Also Called: Zeeto Media
925 B St Fl 5, San Diego (92101-4697)
PHONE...................................888 771-9194
Matthew Marcin, *Mng Member*
Stephan Goss, *CEO*
Shayne Cardwell, *Vice Pres*
Jezer Balangcod, *Accounting Mgr*
Greg Kuchcik, *Human Res Dir*
EMP: 55 **EST:** 2007
SALES (est): 17.2MM **Privately Held**
SIC: 7311 Advertising agencies

(P-13605)
ZVENTS INC
199 Fremont St Fl 4, San Francisco
(94105-6634)
PHONE...................................408 376-7346
Ethan Stock, *President*
EMP: 50
SALES (est): 6.1MM **Privately Held**
WEB: www.zvents.com
SIC: 7311 Advertising agencies

**7312 Outdoor Advertising
Svcs**

(P-13606)
BAMKO INC
11620 Wilshire Blvd # 610, Los Angeles
(90025-1267)
PHONE...................................310 470-5859
▲ **EMP:** 150
SALES (est): 33.2MM **Privately Held**
WEB: www.bamko.net
SIC: 7312 7311

(P-13607)
MOBPARTNER INC
4151 Mddlfield Rd Ste 100, San Francisco
(94103)
PHONE...................................650 300-6388
Jamel Agaoua, *CEO*
EMP: 60
SALES (est): 3MM
SALES (corp-wide): 2.1MM **Privately
Held**
SIC: 7312 Outdoor advertising services
PA: Mobpartner
Mobpartner Bemob S
Paris 1er Arrondissement 75001
158 393-400

(P-13608)
OUTFRONT MEDIA INC
2635 N 1st St Ste 236, San Jose
(95134-2054)
PHONE...................................408 457-0111
EMP: 153
SALES (corp-wide): 1.6B **Publicly Held**
SIC: 7312 Outdoor advertising services
PA: Outfront Media Inc.
405 Lexington Ave Fl 17
New York NY 10174
212 297-6400

(P-13609)
OUTFRONT MEDIA LLC
1695 Eastshore Hwy, Berkeley
(94710-1733)
PHONE...................................510 527-3350
Rob Scheling, *Branch Mgr*

Matt Molina, *Sales Mgr*
EMP: 100
SQ FT: 13,068
SALES (corp-wide): 1.6B **Publicly Held**
SIC: 7312 Outdoor advertising services
HQ: Outfront Media Llc
405 Lexington Ave Fl 14
New York NY 10174
212 297-6400

(P-13610)
VOLTA CHARGING LLC
155 De Haro St, San Francisco
(94103-5121)
PHONE...................................415 735-5169
Scott Mercer, *CEO*
Chris Wendel, *President*
Debra Crow, *CFO*
Dr Abdellah Cherkaoui, *Senior VP*
Jon Michaels, *Senior VP*
EMP: 70
SQ FT: 8,250
SALES (est): 710.2K
SALES (corp-wide): 7.5MM **Privately
Held**
SIC: 7312 7694 Outdoor advertising serv-
ices; electric motor repair
PA: Volta Industries Llc
144 King St
San Francisco CA 94107
917 838-3590

**7313 Radio, TV & Publishers
Adv Reps**

(P-13611)
AD RESULTS MEDIA LLC
111 C St, Encinitas (92024-3514)
PHONE...................................858 480-5223
Kurt Kaufer, *Manager*
EMP: 56
SALES (corp-wide): 157.9MM **Privately
Held**
SIC: 7313 Electronic media advertising
representatives
PA: Ad Results Media, Llc
320 Westcott St Ste 101
Houston TX 77007
713 783-1800

(P-13612)
APPSFLYER LTD
111 New Montgomery St, San Francisco
(94105-3605)
PHONE...................................415 636-9430
Armando Osuna, *Partner*
Sha Liang, *Partner*
Vrushali Khatav, *President*
Sunil Bhagwan, *Vice Pres*
Hagar Brockman, *Creative Dir*
EMP: 80
SALES (est): 2.1MM **Privately Held**
SIC: 7313 Electronic media advertising
representatives

(P-13613)
ATTN INC
729 Seward St, Los Angeles (90038-3503)
PHONE...................................323 413-2878
Jarrett Moreno, *CEO*
Matthew Segel, *President*
Hannah Johnson, *Executive Asst*
EMP: 200
SQ FT: 100,000
SALES (est): 1.6MM **Privately Held**
SIC: 7313 Radio, television, publisher rep-
resentatives

(P-13614)
BEACHBODY LLC (PA)
Also Called: Product Partners
3301 Exposition Blvd Fl 3, Santa Monica
(90404-5082)
PHONE...................................310 883-9000
Carl Daikeler, *CEO*
Sue Collyns, *CFO*
Jon Congdon, *Chief Mktg Ofcr*
Brad Ramberg, *Exec VP*
Rose Pulver, *Comms Mgr*
▲ **EMP:** 500
SALES (est): 146.1MM **Privately Held**
SIC: 7313 7999 Electronic media advertis-
ing representatives; physical fitness in-
struction

(P-13615)
BREITBART NEWS NETWORK LLC
Also Called: Bnn
149 S Barrington Ste 735, Los Angeles (90049)
PHONE....................424 371-0585
Laurence Solov, *Mng Member*
Ana Barrera, *CFO*
Eric Rasnic, *Sales Staff*
Neil Munro, *Manager*
EMP: 60
SALES (est): 225.8K **Privately Held**
SIC: 7313 Electronic media advertising representatives

(P-13616)
BRITE MEDIA LLC
Also Called: Brite Promotions
16027 Ventura Blvd # 210, Encino (91436-2876)
PHONE....................818 826-5790
Greg Martin, *Branch Mgr*
EMP: 105
SALES (corp-wide): 20.8MM **Privately Held**
SIC: 7313 Electronic media advertising representatives
PA: Brite Media Llc
    350 Frank Ogawa Plz
    Oakland CA 94612
    877 479-7777

(P-13617)
CANVAS WORLDWIDE LLC
12015 Bluff Creek Dr, Los Angeles (90094-2930)
PHONE....................424 303-4300
Kaya Lobaczewski, *President*
Jason Croddy, *Vice Pres*
Brian Diamond, *Vice Pres*
Steve Gibson, *Vice Pres*
Matt Lawler, *Vice Pres*
EMP: 250
SALES (est): 49.5K **Privately Held**
SIC: 7313 Electronic media advertising representatives

(P-13618)
CURTCO PUBLISHING LLC (PA)
Also Called: Worth Magazine
29160 Heathercliff Rd # 1, Malibu (90265-6310)
PHONE....................310 589-7700
-Td Captital,
Weston Persido,
EMP: 80
SQ FT: 7,680
SALES (est): 3.4MM **Privately Held**
WEB: www.worth.com
SIC: 7313 Printed media advertising representatives

(P-13619)
DAILY JOURNAL CORPORATION
915 E 1st St, Los Angeles (90012-4042)
PHONE....................213 229-5500
Tu To, *Controller*
EMP: 50
SALES (corp-wide): 40.7MM **Publicly Held**
WEB: www.dailyjournal.com
SIC: 7313 Newspaper advertising representative
PA: Daily Journal Corporation
    915 E 1st St
    Los Angeles CA 90012
    213 229-5300

(P-13620)
DANIEL J EDELMAN INC
Also Called: Edelman Public Relations
201 Baldwin Ave, San Mateo (94401-3914)
PHONE....................650 762-2800
Bob Angus, *Branch Mgr*
Nicole Dorsa, *Vice Pres*
Ben Laws, *Vice Pres*
Mike Heymsfield, *Executive*
Colleen Kuhn, *Executive*
EMP: 100
SALES (corp-wide): 441.1MM **Privately Held**
SIC: 7313 8743 Electronic media advertising representatives; public relations & publicity

HQ: Daniel J. Edelman, Inc.
    200 E Randolph St Fl 63
    Chicago IL 60601
    312 240-3000

(P-13621)
DANIEL J EDELMAN INC
Also Called: Edelman Public Relations
5900 Wilshire Blvd # 2400, Los Angeles (90036-5022)
PHONE....................323 857-9100
EMP: 53
SALES (corp-wide): 790.4MM **Privately Held**
SIC: 7313 8743
HQ: Daniel J. Edelman, Inc.
    200 E Randolph St Fl 63
    Chicago IL 60601
    312 240-3000

(P-13622)
DEMAND ONE MEDIA LLC (PA)
Also Called: DEMAND MEDIA
1655 26th St, Santa Monica (90404-4016)
PHONE....................310 656-6253
James R Quandt, *Ch of Bd*
Jill Angel, *Senior VP*
Michele Calhoun, *Senior VP*
Andrea Stanford, *Senior VP*
Kevin McLain, *Vice Pres*
EMP: 148
SQ FT: 52,000
SALES: 155MM **Publicly Held**
WEB: www.demandmedia.com
SIC: 7313 7336 7371 Electronic media advertising representatives; creative services to advertisers, except writers; computer software development & applications

(P-13623)
EDMUNDSCOM INC (HQ)
2401 Colorado Ave, Santa Monica (90404-3585)
PHONE....................310 309-6300
Peter Steinlauf, *Ch of Bd*
Seth Berkowitz, *President*
AVI Steinlauf, *CEO*
Allen Ollis, *CFO*
Ken Levin, *Exec VP*
▲ EMP: 550 EST: 1966
SALES: 212MM **Privately Held**
WEB: www.edmunds.com
SIC: 7313 Electronic media advertising representatives

(P-13624)
EL CLASIFICADO (PA)
11205 Imperial Hwy, Norwalk (90650-2229)
PHONE....................323 837-4095
Martha C Dela Torre, *President*
Gil Garcia, *CFO*
EMP: 96
SALES (est): 12.4MM **Privately Held**
SIC: 7313 Newspaper advertising representative

(P-13625)
GHOST MANAGEMENT GROUP LLC
41 Discovery, Irvine (92618-3150)
PHONE....................949 870-1400
Justin Hartfield, *CEO*
Doug Francis, *President*
Albert Lopez, *CFO*
Amyra Finamore, *Marketing Staff*
Chris Beals, *General Counsel*
EMP: 175
SQ FT: 44,820
SALES: 40MM **Privately Held**
SIC: 7313 7371 Electronic media advertising representatives; computer software development & applications; custom computer programming services

(P-13626)
JAYLANEENTERTAINMENT CORP
585 Fernando Dr, Novato (94945-3333)
PHONE....................707 820-2773
EMP: 65 EST: 2016
SALES (est): 941.1K **Privately Held**
SIC: 7313

(P-13627)
LIVEUNIVERSE INC
9255 W Sunset Blvd # 1010, West Hollywood (90069-3309)
PHONE....................310 492-2200
Bradley D Greenspan, *CEO*
Toan Nguyen, *CTO*
EMP: 60
SQ FT: 10,137
SALES (est): 3.2MM **Privately Held**
SIC: 7313 Electronic media advertising representatives

(P-13628)
NAPASTYLE INC (PA)
360 Industrial Ct Ste A, NAPA (94558)
PHONE....................707 251-5100
Renee Thomas Jacobs, *President*
▲ EMP: 50
SALES (est): 6.6MM **Privately Held**
SIC: 7313 Radio, television, publisher representatives

(P-13629)
OBSCURA DIGITAL INCORPORATED
14 Louisiana St, San Francisco (94107-4383)
PHONE....................415 227-9979
Chris Lejeune, *CEO*
David Shulman, *CFO*
Kimber Sterling, *Vice Pres*
Chris Dadzitis, *Technician*
Travis Threlkel, *Systems Staff*
▲ EMP: 50
SQ FT: 40,000
SALES (est): 8.2MM
SALES (corp-wide): 1.6B **Publicly Held**
WEB: www.obscuradigital.com
SIC: 7313 Electronic media advertising representatives; printed media advertising representatives
PA: The Madison Square Garden Company
    2 Penn Plz Fl 15
    New York NY 10121
    212 465-6000

(P-13630)
PAC-12 ENTEPRISES LLC
360 3rd St Ste 300, San Francisco (94107-2163)
PHONE....................415 580-4200
Lydia Murphy Stevens, *President*
David Aufhauser, *President*
Jamie Zaninovich, *COO*
Ron McQuate, *CFO*
Lydia Murphy-Stephans, *Exec VP*
EMP: 120
SQ FT: 11,000
SALES (est): 355.6MM **Privately Held**
WEB: www.pac-10.org
SIC: 7313 Electronic media advertising representatives

(P-13631)
PENSKE MEDIA CORPORATION (PA)
11175 Santa Monica Blvd, Los Angeles (90025-3330)
PHONE....................310 321-5000
Jay Penske, *COO*
George Grobar, *COO*
Judith R Margolin, *Vice Pres*
Sarlina See,
Alex Bahamaca, *Manager*
EMP: 100
SALES (est): 40.8MM **Privately Held**
SIC: 7313 4899 Electronic media advertising representatives; data communication services

(P-13632)
QW MEDIA INTERNATIONAL LLC
620 Newport Center Dr # 11, Newport Beach (92660-6420)
PHONE....................949 200-4616
Marianne Moy, *Chairman*
Drian Hirabayashi, *Vice Pres*
Brian Hirabayashi, *Principal*
▲ EMP: 50
SALES: 2MM **Privately Held**
SIC: 7313 Printed media advertising representatives

(P-13633)
SHED MEDIA US INC
3800 Barham Blvd Ste 410, Los Angeles (90068-1042)
PHONE....................323 904-4680
Nick Emmerson, *President*
Dan Peirson, *Vice Pres*
Josh Mills, *Admin Sec*
Diem Pham, *Personnel Assit*
Jeremy Finn, *Producer*
EMP: 55
SALES (est): 9.8MM **Privately Held**
SIC: 7313 Electronic media advertising representatives

(P-13634)
STUDIO 71 LP
Also Called: Collective Digital Studio, LLC
8383 Wilshire Blvd Ste 10, Beverly Hills (90211-2425)
PHONE....................323 370-1500
Reza Isad,
Matthew Brannen, *Partner*
John Carle, *Vice Pres*
Dana Shayegan, *Vice Pres*
Gerry Sigala, *Opers Staff*
EMP: 150 EST: 2011
SQ FT: 15,000
SALES: 60MM
SALES (corp-wide): 4.5B **Privately Held**
SIC: 7313 Electronic media advertising representatives
PA: Prosiebensat.1 Media Se
    Medienallee 7
    Unterfohring 85774
    899 507-10

(P-13635)
THOUGHTFUL MEDIA GROUP INC
Also Called: Thoughtful Asia Limited
14724 Ventura Blvd # 1110, Sherman Oaks (91403-3511)
PHONE....................818 465-7500
Jak C Severson, *President*
Dan Thorman, *CFO*
Timothy Kwok, *Exec VP*
Christopher Davidson, *Senior VP*
Bani Tan, *Vice Pres*
EMP: 70
SALES (est): 4.4MM **Privately Held**
SIC: 7313 Electronic media advertising representatives

(P-13636)
TI GOTHAM INC
2 Embarcadero Ctr # 1900, San Francisco (94111-3823)
PHONE....................415 982-5000
Tim Richards, *Manager*
EMP: 60
SALES (corp-wide): 3.1B **Publicly Held**
SIC: 7313 Magazine advertising representative
HQ: Ti Gotham Inc.
    225 Liberty St
    New York NY 10281
    212 522-1212

(P-13637)
TI GOTHAM INC
Time Magazine
11766 Wilshire Blvd # 1700, Los Angeles (90025-6538)
PHONE....................310 268-7200
Sally Masters, *Branch Mgr*
Amir Toubia, *Associate Dir*
Aaron Anderson, *Exec Dir*
EMP: 200
SALES (corp-wide): 3.1B **Publicly Held**
SIC: 7313 Magazine advertising representative
HQ: Ti Gotham Inc.
    225 Liberty St
    New York NY 10281
    212 522-1212

(P-13638)
TRAVELZOO USA INC
800 W El Camino Re, Mountain View (94040)
PHONE....................650 316-6956
Chris Loughlin, *CEO*
Ralph Bartel, *President*
Wayne Lee, *CFO*
Scott Loomis, *Software Dev*

P R O D U C T S & S V C S

Hamid Vossoughi, *Software Engr*
EMP: 81
SALES (est): 17.8MM
SALES (corp-wide): 111.3MM **Publicly Held**
WEB: www.travelzoo.com
SIC: 7313 Electronic media advertising representatives
PA: Travelzoo
   590 Madison Ave Rm 3700
   New York NY 10022
   212 484-4900

(P-13639)
ULTRADOT MEDIA
9908 Bell Ranch Dr, Santa Fe Springs (90670-2972)
PHONE..........................562 906-0737
Bill Shears, *President*
EMP: 75
SALES (est): 3.7MM **Privately Held**
WEB: www.ultradotmedia.com
SIC: 7313 7336 Printed media advertising representatives; commercial art & graphic design

(P-13640)
WALDBERG INC
Also Called: Refinery, The
14455 Ventura Blvd Fl 3, Sherman Oaks (91423-2687)
PHONE..........................818 843-0004
Adam Waldman, *CEO*
Brad Hochberg, *President*
Seth Ward, *Graphic Designe*
Jeff Lyman CPA, *Controller*
Alexa Lareau, *Production*
EMP: 100
SQ FT: 5,000
SALES (est): 5.4MM **Privately Held**
SIC: 7313 Electronic media advertising representatives; printed media advertising representatives

(P-13641)
WGA WEST INC
7000 W 3rd St, Los Angeles (90048-4321)
PHONE..........................323 782-4512
Chris Keyser, *President*
Danielle Forbes, *Counsel*
EMP: 100 **EST:** 1954
SALES (est): 3.9MM **Privately Held**
SIC: 7313 Electronic media advertising representatives

7319 Advertising, NEC

(P-13642)
ADVERTISING CONSULTANTS INC (PA)
Also Called: American Crclation Innovations
330 Golden Shore Ste 410, Long Beach (90802-4271)
PHONE..........................310 233-2750
Keith Somers, *President*
John G Walsh, *COO*
Kent Brown, *CFO*
Robert Somers, *Chairman*
EMP: 160 **EST:** 1966
SQ FT: 60,000
SALES (est): 19.1MM **Privately Held**
WEB: www.acicirculation.com
SIC: 7319 Distribution of advertising material or sample services

(P-13643)
AEGIS SOFTWARE INC
Also Called: Destination Webcam
5580 La Jolla Blvd # 436, La Jolla (92037-7651)
PHONE..........................858 551-1652
Alan Edwards, *President*
EMP: 50
SALES (est): 3MM **Privately Held**
WEB: www.ecodb.com
SIC: 7319 Media buying service

(P-13644)
BAY AREA NEWS GROUP E BAY LLC (HQ)
6270 Houston Pl Ste A, Dublin (94568-3161)
PHONE..........................925 302-1683
William D Singleton,

Michael Tully,
EMP: 60
SALES (est): 9.4MM
SALES (corp-wide): 22.1MM **Privately Held**
SIC: 7319 Media buying service
PA: California Newspapers Partnership
   4 N 2nd St Ste 800
   San Jose CA 95113
   408 920-5333

(P-13645)
CARAT
85 2nd St Fl 6, San Francisco (94105-3464)
PHONE..........................415 541-2700
A S Bracone, *Branch Mgr*
Alyssa Cooper, *Vice Pres*
Elissa Melendez, *Associate Dir*
Helen Wright, *Planning*
Danielle Mercer, *Finance*
EMP: 67
SALES (est): 6MM
SALES (corp-wide): 13.4MM **Privately Held**
SIC: 7319 Media buying service
PA: Carat
   150 E 42nd St Fl 13
   New York NY 10017
   212 591-9100

(P-13646)
CARAT N AMER DNTSU AGEIS NTWRK
5800 Bristol Pkwy Fl 5, Culver City (90230-6696)
PHONE..........................310 255-1000
John Barnes, *Branch Mgr*
Chimere Soltis, *Sr Associate*
Helen Calderon, *Supervisor*
EMP: 135 **Privately Held**
SIC: 7319 7313 Media buying service; printed media advertising representatives
HQ: Carat North America Dentsu Aegeis Network
   150 E 42nd St Fl 14
   New York NY 10017
   212 591-9100

(P-13647)
CBS INTERACTIVE INC
2900 W Alameda Ave, Burbank (91505-4220)
PHONE..........................415 344-1813
EMP: 127
SALES (corp-wide): 25.9B **Publicly Held**
SIC: 7319 Distribution of advertising material or sample services
HQ: Cbs Interactive Inc.
   235 2nd St
   San Francisco CA 94105

(P-13648)
CBS INTERACTIVE INC (DH)
Also Called: Cbsi
235 2nd St, San Francisco (94105-3124)
PHONE..........................415 344-2000
Jarl Mohn, *Ch of Bd*
Barry Briggs, *President*
Jim Lanzone, *President*
Joseph Gillespie, *Exec VP*
Domenico Dimeglio, *Vice Pres*
EMP: 600
SQ FT: 283,000
SALES (est): 267.1MM
SALES (corp-wide): 25.9B **Publicly Held**
WEB: www.mysimon.com
SIC: 7319 7375 4832 Distribution of advertising material or sample services; on-line data base information retrieval; radio broadcasting stations
HQ: Cbs Corporation
   51 W 52nd St Bsmt 1
   New York NY 10019
   212 975-4321

(P-13649)
CIE DIGITAL LABS LLC (PA)
Also Called: Choice Internet
19900 Macarthur Blvd # 1000, Irvine (92612-8415)
PHONE..........................949 381-6200
Anderee Berengian, *CEO*
Alvin Fong, *Officer*
Frances Lliles, *Office Mgr*

David Ho, *Prgrmr*
Evelyn Lee, *Human Res Dir*
EMP: 55
SQ FT: 13,500
SALES (est): 9.5MM **Privately Held**
SIC: 7319 Display advertising service

(P-13650)
FASTCLICK INC
Also Called: Fastclick.com
530 E Montecito St, Santa Barbara (93103-3252)
PHONE..........................805 689-9839
Kurt A Johnson, *President*
Fred Krupica, *CFO*
James Aviani, *CTO*
EMP: 87
SQ FT: 14,900
SALES (est): 4.8MM **Publicly Held**
WEB: www.fastclick.com
SIC: 7319 Circular & handbill distribution; coupon distribution
HQ: Conversant, Llc
   30699 Russell Ranch Rd # 250
   Westlake Village CA 91362
   818 575-4500

(P-13651)
GILS DISTRIBUTING SERVICE
Also Called: Great Western Distributing Svc
718 E 8th St, Los Angeles (90021-1802)
PHONE..........................213 627-0539
Feleciano Gil, *President*
Gloria Gil, *Corp Secy*
Fidel Gil, *Vice Pres*
EMP: 112
SQ FT: 5,000
SALES (est): 5.4MM **Privately Held**
SIC: 7319 4215 Circular & handbill distribution; courier services, except by air

(P-13652)
IMAGE OPTIONS
80 Icon, Foothill Ranch (92610-3000)
PHONE..........................949 586-7665
Tim Bennett, *CEO*
Brian Hite, *President*
Dave Bales, *COO*
Dave Brewer, *Vice Pres*
Joseph Im, *Vice Pres*
EMP: 101
SQ FT: 22,000
SALES (est): 21.8MM **Privately Held**
SIC: 7319 7336 Display advertising service; commercial art & graphic design; art design services

(P-13653)
KSL MEDIA INC
15910 Ventura Blvd # 900, Encino (91436-2802)
PHONE..........................212 468-3395
Kalman Liebowitz, *Ch of Bd*
Hank Cohen, *President*
Russell Meisels, *CFO*
EMP: 130
SQ FT: 13,000
SALES (est): 365.9MM **Privately Held**
WEB: www.kslmedia.com
SIC: 7319 Media buying service

(P-13654)
LEGGETT & PLATT INCORPORATED
Beeline Group
31023 Huntwood Ave, Hayward (94544-7007)
PHONE..........................510 487-8063
Fax: 510 441-1782
EMP: 100
SALES (corp-wide): 3.7B **Publicly Held**
SIC: 7319
PA: Leggett & Platt, Incorporated
   1 Leggett Rd
   Carthage MO 64836
   417 358-8131

(P-13655)
MEDIABRANDS WORLDWIDE INC (HQ)
Also Called: Rapport Worldwide
653 Front St, San Francisco (94111-1913)
PHONE..........................212 605-7000
Jim Elms, *CEO*
Peter Mears, *President*
Caroline Bivens, *COO*

Katherine Kilebrew, *COO*
Chris Sahota, *CFO*
▲ **EMP:** 550
SQ FT: 75,000
SALES (est): 178.9MM
SALES (corp-wide): 9.7B **Publicly Held**
WEB: www.wimc.com
SIC: 7319 7311 Media buying service; advertising consultant
PA: The Interpublic Group Of Companies Inc
   909 3rd Ave
   New York NY 10022
   212 704-1200

(P-13656)
NATIONAL CBLE CMMNICATIONS LLC
Also Called: Nca,
11150 Santa Monica Blvd # 900, Los Angeles (90025-3380)
PHONE..........................310 231-0745
Dori Wilde, *Manager*
EMP: 75
SALES (corp-wide): 94.5B **Publicly Held**
SIC: 7319 1799 7313 Transit advertising services; cable splicing service; radio, television, publisher representatives
HQ: National Cable Communications Llc
   405 Lexington Ave Fl 6
   New York NY 10174
   212 548-3300

(P-13657)
ND SYSTEMS INC
5750 Hellyer Ave, San Jose (95138-1000)
PHONE..........................408 776-0085
Jim Ciardella, *CFO*
Trina Ciraulo, *COO*
Jonah Post, *Technical Mgr*
Yang Zheng, *Engineer*
EMP: 75
SALES (est): 4.5MM **Privately Held**
WEB: www.nationaldisplay.com
SIC: 7319 Display advertising service

(P-13658)
PALISADES MEDIA GROUP INC (PA)
Also Called: Palisades Interactive
1601 Cloverf Blvd 6000n, Santa Monica (90404-4178)
PHONE..........................310 564-5400
Roger Schaffner, *Ch of Bd*
Rhona Dass, *Senior VP*
Genevieve Wiersema, *Vice Pres*
EMP: 58
SQ FT: 13,000
SALES (est): 18MM **Privately Held**
WEB: www.palisadesmedia.com
SIC: 7319 Media buying service

(P-13659)
PINTEREST INC
808 Brannan St, San Francisco (94103-4904)
PHONE..........................415 400-4645
Ben Silbermann, *Branch Mgr*
EMP: 131
SALES (corp-wide): 755.9MM **Publicly Held**
SIC: 7319 Display advertising service
PA: Pinterest, Inc.
   808 Brannan St
   San Francisco CA 94103
   415 617-5585

(P-13660)
QUOTIENT TECHNOLOGY INC (PA)
400 Logue Ave, Mountain View (94043-4019)
PHONE..........................650 605-4600
Steven R Boal, *Ch of Bd*
Alex DEA, *Partner*
Kate Mueller, *Partner*
Chad Summe, *COO*
Ronald J Fior, *CFO*
EMP: 144
SQ FT: 91,000
SALES: 386.9MM **Publicly Held**
SIC: 7319 Coupon distribution

(P-13661)
REVENUE FRONTIER LLC
Also Called: Media Design Group
6922 Hollywood Blvd 2, Los Angeles
(90028-6117)
PHONE....................................310 584-9200
Greg Thomas, *CEO*
Ross McConnell, *President*
Patrick Romagnano, *COO*
Michael Marrone, *Vice Pres*
Mike Scott, *Director*
EMP: 55
SALES (est): 7.5MM **Privately Held**
WEB: www.revenuefrontier.com
SIC: 7319 Media buying service

(P-13662)
SMALL BUSINESS ADVERTISING INC
24009 Ventura Blvd # 245, Calabasas
(91302-1418)
PHONE....................................818 262-8923
Stephen Tackett, *President*
EMP: 50
SALES (est): 765.5K **Privately Held**
SIC: 7319 8742 Advertising; marketing
consulting services

(P-13663)
TURN INC (DH)
901 Marshall St Ste 200, Redwood City
(94063-2026)
PHONE....................................650 353-4399
Kim Perrell, *CEO*
Maureen Cullen, *Senior Partner*
Maureen Lee, *Senior Partner*
Alexander Knudsen, *Partner*
Bill Demas, *President*
EMP: 116
SQ FT: 14,000
SALES (est): 47.8MM
SALES (corp-wide): 13MM **Privately Held**
WEB: www.turn.com
SIC: 7319 Display advertising service

(P-13664)
US INTERNATIONAL MEDIA LLC (PA)
Also Called: US Outdoor
3415 S Sepulveda Blvd # 800, Los Angeles
(90034-6060)
PHONE....................................310 482-6700
Dennis Holt, *CEO*
Sixto Castillo, *Exec VP*
Sherry Catchpole, *Exec VP*
DOT Dilorenzo, *Exec VP*
Doug Livingston, *Exec VP*
EMP: 93
SQ FT: 5,000
SALES (est): 22MM **Privately Held**
WEB: www.usintlmedia.com
SIC: 7319 Media buying service

(P-13665)
VIANT TECHNOLOGY LLC (DH)
Also Called: Viant US
2722 Michelson Dr Ste 100, Irvine
(92612-8905)
PHONE....................................949 861-8888
Timothy Vanderhook, *CEO*
Christopher Vanderhook, *COO*
Lawerence Madden, *CFO*
Brian Bell, *Vice Pres*
Adam Paz, *Vice Pres*
EMP: 200
SALES (est): 51.9MM
SALES (corp-wide): 3.1B **Publicly Held**
SIC: 7319 Display advertising service
HQ: Ti Gotham Inc.
225 Liberty St
New York NY 10281
212 522-1212

(P-13666)
WEST COAST COUPON INC
9400 Oso Ave, Chatsworth (91311-6020)
PHONE....................................818 341-2400
Mark Fischer, *President*
Doug Rewers, *Vice Pres*
EMP: 50
SQ FT: 30,000

SALES (est): 8.3MM **Privately Held**
SIC: 7319 2731 5961 Coupon distribution; books: publishing & printing; computer software, mail order

(P-13667)
ZAMBEZI LLC
10441 Jefferson Blvd, Culver City
(90232-3512)
PHONE....................................310 450-6800
Jean Freeman, *Mng Member*
Chad Markham, *Info Tech Dir*
James Freeman,
Erickson Ilog,
Gavin Lester,
EMP: 65
SALES (est): 4.1MM **Privately Held**
SIC: 7319 7389 Advertising; advertising,
promotional & trade show services

7322 Adjustment & Collection Svcs

(P-13668)
ACCOUNT CONTROL TECHNOLOGY INC
5500 Ming Ave Ste 185, Bakersfield
(93309-4623)
PHONE....................................661 395-5702
Sam Shawwa, *Manager*
EMP: 50 **Privately Held**
WEB: www.accountcontrol.com
SIC: 7322 Collection agency, except real
estate
HQ: Account Control Technology Inc.
21700 Oxnard St Ste 1860
Woodland Hills CA 91367

(P-13669)
ARS NATIONAL SERVICES INC (PA)
201 W Grand Ave, Escondido
(92025-2603)
P.O. Box 463023 (92046-3023)
PHONE....................................800 456-5053
Jason Howerton, *President*
John Howerton, *Chairman*
Jim Beck, *Vice Pres*
Robert Lord, *VP Bus Dvlpt*
Kathy Howerton, *Admin Sec*
EMP: 150
SQ FT: 33,000
SALES (est): 32.8MM **Privately Held**
WEB: www.arsnational.com
SIC: 7322 Collection agency, except real
estate

(P-13670)
ATTORNEY RECOVERY SYSTEMS INC (PA)
18757 Burbank Blvd # 300, Tarzana
(91356-3375)
PHONE....................................818 774-1420
Gene Bloom, *President*
Debbie Delgado, *Manager*
EMP: 70
SALES (est): 5.7MM **Privately Held**
WEB: www.legalcollection.com
SIC: 7322 8111 Collection agency, except
real estate; legal services

(P-13671)
CAINE & WEINER COMPANY INC (PA)
5805 Sepulvda Blvd # 400, Van Nuys
(91411-2546)
P.O. Box 55848, Sherman Oaks (91413-
0848)
PHONE....................................818 226-6000
Greg A Cohen, *President*
Brad Schaffer, *Senior VP*
John Handley, *Vice Pres*
Rick Luther, *Vice Pres*
Steve Simon, *Vice Pres*
EMP: 90
SQ FT: 14,400
SALES (est): 22.4MM **Privately Held**
WEB: www.caine-weiner.com
SIC: 7322 Collection agency, except real
estate

(P-13672)
CALIFORNIA BUSINESS BUREAU INC (PA)
Also Called: Medical Billing Services
1711 S Mountain Ave, Monrovia
(91016-4256)
P.O. Box 5010 (91017-7110)
PHONE....................................626 303-1515
Michael J Sigal, *President*
Kathy Tree, *Information Mgr*
EMP: 132 EST: 1973
SQ FT: 24,000
SALES (est): 11MM
SALES (corp-wide): 16.3MM **Privately Held**
WEB: www.cbbinc.com
SIC: 7322 Collection agency, except real
estate

(P-13673)
CB ASSOCIATES INC
11659 Haynes St, North Hollywood
(91606-2530)
PHONE....................................424 777-8214
Candie Fernandez, *President*
Branden Fernandez, *COO*
Daniel Pettway Jr, *CFO*
EMP: 50
SALES (est): 1.7MM **Privately Held**
SIC: 7322 Collection agency, except real
estate

(P-13674)
CBSJ FINANCIAL CORPORATION
1735 N 1st St Ste 250, San Jose
(95112-4531)
PHONE....................................408 792-4600
Bertha Martin, *President*
EMP: 100 EST: 1983
SALES (est): 4.4MM **Privately Held**
WEB: www.cbsj.com
SIC: 7322 Collection agency, except real
estate

(P-13675)
CMRE FINANCIAL SERVICES INC
3075 E Imperial Hwy # 200, Brea
(92821-6753)
PHONE....................................714 528-3200
Jack C Nixon, *CEO*
Sandy Lawrence, *President*
Andrea Parr, *Corp Secy*
John Nixon, *Exec VP*
Patrick Nixon, *Vice Pres*
EMP: 450 EST: 2000
SQ FT: 35,000
SALES (est): 40.1MM **Privately Held**
WEB: www.cmrefsi.com
SIC: 7322 Collection agency, except real
estate

(P-13676)
COLLECTECH SYSTEMS INC (DH)
2290 Agate Ct 1a, Simi Valley
(93065-1935)
PHONE....................................818 597-7500
Steve Kent, *Exec VP*
EMP: 175
SQ FT: 19,376
SALES (est): 9.6MM **Privately Held**
SIC: 7322 Collection agency, except real
estate
HQ: Intellirisk Management Corporation
335 Madison Ave Fl 27
New York NY 10017
646 274-3030

(P-13677)
COLLECTION TECHNOLOGY INC
Also Called: C T I
10801 6th St Ste 200, Rancho Cucamonga
(91730-5904)
P.O. Box 2200 (91729-2200)
PHONE....................................800 743-4284
Chris Van Dellen, *CEO*
Paul Van Dellen, *President*
EMP: 100
SALES (est): 5.9MM **Privately Held**
WEB: www.collectiontechnology.com
SIC: 7322 Collection agency, except real
estate

(P-13678)
CONRAD CREDIT CORPORATION
476 W Vermont Ave, Escondido
(92025-6529)
P.O. Box 770 (92033-0770)
PHONE....................................760 735-5000
Keith Richenbacher, *President*
John Page, *Vice Pres*
Bob Pranik, *Admin Sec*
EMP: 50
SQ FT: 6,000
SALES (est): 5.9MM
SALES (corp-wide): 22.3MM **Privately Held**
SIC: 7322 Collection agency, except real
estate
PA: Conrad Credit Corp.
476 W Vermont Ave
Escondido CA 92025
800 826-6723

(P-13679)
CREDIT BUREAU NAPA COUNTY INC
Also Called: Chase Receivables
1247 Broadway, Sonoma (95476-7503)
PHONE....................................707 940-3000
Fred Merrill, *Chairman*
Andrew Heinricher, *Manager*
EMP: 145
SQ FT: 1,357
SALES (est): 12.2MM **Privately Held**
WEB: www.chaserec.com
SIC: 7322 Collection agency, except real
estate

(P-13680)
EGS FINANCIAL CARE INC (DH)
5 Park Plz Ste 1100, Irvine (92614-8502)
PHONE....................................877 217-4423
Jay King, *President*
Steven Winokur, *CFO*
Derek Rains, *Vice Pres*
Joshua Gindin, *Admin Sec*
Marieta San Pedro, *Technology*
▲ EMP: 300 EST: 1966
SALES (est): 239.6MM
SALES (corp-wide): 6.6B **Privately Held**
SIC: 7322 Collection agency, except real
estate

(P-13681)
FCI LENDER SERVICES INC
Also Called: F C I
8180 E Kaiser Blvd, Anaheim
(92808-2277)
PHONE....................................800 931-2424
Michael W Griffith, *President*
EMP: 105
SQ FT: 19,000
SALES (est): 24.3MM **Privately Held**
WEB: www.trustfci.com
SIC: 7322 Adjustment & collection services

(P-13682)
FINANCIAL CREDIT NETWORK INC (PA)
1300 W Main St, Visalia (93291-5825)
P.O. Box 3084 (93278-3084)
PHONE....................................559 733-7550
Alicia Sundstrom, *President*
Kris Davisson, *Vice Pres*
Jeanie Weber, *IT/INT Sup*
EMP: 51
SQ FT: 11,000
SALES (est): 6.6MM **Privately Held**
WEB: www.fcnetwork.com
SIC: 7322 Collection agency, except real
estate

(P-13683)
GRANT & WEBER (PA)
Also Called: Grant & Weber Travel
26610 Agoura Rd Ste 209, Calabasas
(91302-2975)
P.O. Box 8669 (91372-8669)
PHONE....................................818 878-7700
Jimi Bingham, *CEO*
Kim Mehr, *Vice Pres*
Mary Kempski, *CIO*
Janette Velardi, *Controller*
Bob Layton, *Sales Staff*
▲ EMP: 84
SQ FT: 30,000

SALES (est): 27.8MM **Privately Held**
WEB: www.grantweber.com
SIC: 7322 Collection agency, except real estate

(P-13684)
H P SEARS CO INC
Also Called: HP Sears Co.
2000 18th St, Bakersfield (93301-4292)
P.O. Box 2307 (93303-2307)
PHONE..............................661 325-5981
James P Sears, *President*
Chris Thompson, *General Mgr*
Adreanna Morales, *Accounts Exec*
EMP: 60
SALES (est): 2.6MM **Privately Held**
SIC: 7322 Collection agency, except real estate

(P-13685)
H&H RESOLUTION LLC
151 Bernal Rd Ste 6, San Jose (95119-1306)
PHONE..............................408 362-2293
Daniel Oditt, *Mng Member*
EMP: 100
SALES (est): 1MM **Privately Held**
SIC: 7322 Collection agency, except real estate

(P-13686)
INTELLIRISK MANAGEMENT CORP
31229 Cedar Valley Dr, Westlake Village (91362-4036)
PHONE..............................818 575-5400
Jim Pond, *Branch Mgr*
EMP: 50 **Privately Held**
SIC: 7322 Adjustment & collection services
HQ: Intellirisk Management Corporation
335 Madison Ave Fl 27
New York NY 10017
646 274-3030

(P-13687)
J & L COLLECTIONS SERVICES INC
Also Called: J&L Teamworks
8220 Longleaf Dr 400, Elk Grove (95758-1322)
PHONE..............................800 481-6006
Donald R Johnsen, *President*
Kenneth M Lamont, *CFO*
Jay Dittman, *Vice Pres*
Sean M Escobar, *Vice Pres*
James W Hughes, *Vice Pres*
EMP: 85
SALES: 6.5MM
SALES (corp-wide): 27.6MM **Privately Held**
SIC: 7322 Collection agency, except real estate
PA: Uscb, Inc.
355 S Grand Ave Ste 3200
Los Angeles CA 90071
213 985-2111

(P-13688)
JJ MAC INTYRE CO INC (PA)
4160 Temescal Canyon Rd, Corona (92883-4625)
P.O. Box 78150 (92877-0138)
PHONE..............................951 898-4300
Scott M Hall, *CEO*
Kenneth A Lee, *President*
EMP: 115
SQ FT: 28,254
SALES (est): 7.5MM **Privately Held**
WEB: www.jjmac.com
SIC: 7322 Collection agency, except real estate

(P-13689)
KINGS CREDIT SERVICES
96 Shaw Ave Ste 221, Clovis (93612-3842)
PHONE..............................559 322-2550
Randall Burchfield, *Owner*
Vicki Callahan, *Vice Pres*
Jeffrey Adams, *Director*
EMP: 55
SALES (est): 2.3MM **Privately Held**
SIC: 7322 Collection agency, except real estate

(P-13690)
NATIONAL COMMERCIAL SERVICES
6644 Valjean Ave Ste 100, Van Nuys (91406-5816)
PHONE..............................818 701-4400
Zoran Jovanoski, *President*
Zoran Jovanovski, *President*
Natalie Mansour, *Vice Pres*
Darlene Martinez, *Legal Staff*
Frank Russo, *Manager*
EMP: 52
SQ FT: 4,500
SALES: 1.2MM **Privately Held**
WEB: www.ncslegalservices.com
SIC: 7322 Collection agency, except real estate

(P-13691)
OPTIO SOLUTIONS LLC
Also Called: Qualia Collection Services
1444 N Mcdowell Blvd, Petaluma (94954-6515)
PHONE..............................800 360-2827
Chris Schumacher, *CEO*
Ray Stawiarski, *Manager*
EMP: 200 **EST:** 2007
SALES: 11.7MM **Privately Held**
SIC: 7322 Collection agency, except real estate

(P-13692)
PCI COLLECTIONS INC
Also Called: P C I & Associates
402 W Broadway Fl 4, San Diego (92101-3554)
P.O. Box 3206, Gardena (90247-1406)
PHONE..............................619 595-3114
Emanuel Theodore Davis, *CEO*
Donna Tusack, *Human Res Mgr*
Jahan Jamshidi, *Director*
EMP: 262
SALES (est): 10.8MM **Privately Held**
SIC: 7322 Collection agency, except real estate

(P-13693)
PERFORMANT RECOVERY INC
Also Called: DCS
17080 S Harlan Rd, Lathrop (95330-8739)
PHONE..............................209 858-3500
James Tracey, *Principal*
Celeste Vargas, *Consultant*
Carol Winston, *Supervisor*
EMP: 200 **Publicly Held**
SIC: 7322 Collection agency, except real estate
HQ: Performant Recovery, Inc.
333 N Canyons Pkwy # 100
Livermore CA 94551
209 858-3994

(P-13694)
PERFORMANT RECOVERY INC (HQ)
333 N Canyons Pkwy # 100, Livermore (94551-9478)
PHONE..............................209 858-3994
Lisa Im, *CEO*
Hakan Orvell, *CFO*
Bruce Calvin, *Admin Sec*
EMP: 118
SQ FT: 31,000
SALES (est): 53.6MM **Publicly Held**
SIC: 7322 8742 7371 Collection agency, except real estate; financial consultant; custom computer programming services

(P-13695)
PROFESSIONAL BUREAU OF COLLECT
9675 Elk Grove Florin Rd, Elk Grove (95624-2225)
PHONE..............................916 685-3399
Travis Justus, *Branch Mgr*
EMP: 115 **Privately Held**
SIC: 7322 Collection agency, except real estate
PA: Professional Bureau Of Collections Of Maryland, Inc.
5295 Dtc Pkwy
Greenwood Village CO 80111

(P-13696)
QUADRAMED CORPORATION
Also Called: Corona Rgional Med Ctr Bus Off
800 S Main St, Corona (92882-3420)
PHONE..............................951 736-6290
John Caldrone, *CEO*
EMP: 810
SALES (corp-wide): 3B **Privately Held**
WEB: www.quadramed.com
SIC: 7322 Collection agency, except real estate
HQ: Quadramed Corporation
2300 Corp Park Dr Ste 400
Herndon VA 20171
703 709-2300

(P-13697)
QUALIFIED BLLING CLLCTIONS LLC
Also Called: Q B C
4601 Wilshire Blvd Fl 3, Los Angeles (90010-3884)
PHONE..............................323 556-3470
Thomas Baker, *COO*
Peter Yeh, *COO*
Tom Baker, *Vice Pres*
Edith Marquez, *Human Res Dir*
Jack Chao, *Relations*
EMP: 200 **EST:** 1982
SALES (est): 3.4MM **Privately Held**
SIC: 7322 Collection agency, except real estate

(P-13698)
RM GALICIA INC
Also Called: Progressive Management Systems
1521 W Cameron Ave # 100, West Covina (91790-2738)
P.O. Box 2220 (91793-2220)
PHONE..............................626 813-6200
Timothy Chase Banta, *CEO*
Carol Ryan, *Exec VP*
Bill Gutierrez, *Vice Pres*
EMP: 125 **EST:** 1978
SQ FT: 20,000
SALES (est): 15.7MM **Privately Held**
WEB: www.pmscollects.com
SIC: 7322 Collection agency, except real estate

(P-13699)
SANTA CLARA COUNTY OF
Also Called: Revenue, Dept of
1555 Berger Dr Fl 1, San Jose (95112-2716)
P.O. Box 1897 (95109-1897)
PHONE..............................408 282-3200
Robert McGrath, *Branch Mgr*
Ed Bagsik,
EMP: 15 **Privately Held**
WEB: www.countyairports.org
SIC: 7322 9311 Adjustment & collection services; taxation department, government;
PA: County Of Santa Clara
3180 Newberry Dr Ste 150
San Jose CA 95118
408 299-5105

(P-13700)
SEQUOIA CONCEPTS INC
Also Called: Sequoia Financial Services
28632 Roadside Dr Ste 110, Agoura Hills (91301-6074)
PHONE..............................818 409-6000
Roy Duplessis, *President*
Denise Duplessis, *Vice Pres*
Roy Deplessis II, *Admin Sec*
EMP: 75
SQ FT: 9,100
SALES (est): 8.5MM **Privately Held**
WEB: www.sequoiafinancial.com
SIC: 7322 Collection agency, except real estate

(P-13701)
UNIVERSAL ACCOUNTS INC
690 E Green St Ste 300, Pasadena (91101-2121)
PHONE..............................626 356-7900
Lon Yatman, *President*
Esther Yatman, *Exec VP*
Weng Tang, *Manager*
Weng L Tang, *Agent*
EMP: 60

SQ FT: 14,000
SALES (est): 5.1MM **Privately Held**
WEB: www.fhs-unifi.com
SIC: 7322 Collection agency, except real estate

(P-13702)
USCB INC
3535 Wilshire Blvd # 700, Los Angeles (90010)
PHONE..............................213 387-6181
Rose Erin, *Manager*
Nelly Ruben, *Human Res Dir*
EMP: 75
SALES (corp-wide): 27.6MM **Privately Held**
WEB: www.uscbinc.com
SIC: 7322 Collection agency, except real estate
PA: Uscb, Inc.
355 S Grand Ave Ste 3200
Los Angeles CA 90071
213 985-2111

(P-13703)
USCB INC (PA)
Also Called: Uscb America
355 S Grand Ave Ste 3200, Los Angeles (90071-1591)
PHONE..............................213 985-2111
Albert Cadena, *Sales Executive*
Melvin F Shaw, *President*
John McCrosky, *CFO*
Pedro Guijarro, *Assoc VP*
Thomas Isgrigg, *Exec VP*
EMP: 213
SQ FT: 34,000
SALES (est): 27.6MM **Privately Held**
WEB: www.uscbinc.com
SIC: 7322 8741 Collection agency, except real estate; management services

(P-13704)
VENGROFF WILLIAMS & ASSOC INC
2099 S State College Blvd # 300, Anaheim (92806-6149)
PHONE..............................714 889-6200
Robert Sherman, *Branch Mgr*
Joseph Torba, *President*
EMP: 213
SALES (corp-wide): 18.8MM **Privately Held**
SIC: 7322 Collection agency, except real estate
PA: Vengroff, Williams & Associates, Inc.
2211 Fruitville Rd
Sarasota FL 34237
941 363-5200

7323 Credit Reporting Svcs

(P-13705)
A-CHECK AMERICA INC (PA)
Also Called: A-Check America, Member Act 1
1501 Research Park Dr, Riverside (92507-2114)
PHONE..............................951 750-1501
Janice B Howroyd, *CEO*
Carlos Lacambra, *President*
Michael Hoyal, *CFO*
Don Shimizu, *Exec VP*
Gregg Hassler, *Vice Pres*
▲ **EMP:** 170 **EST:** 1978
SQ FT: 30,000
SALES (est): 31.3MM **Privately Held**
WEB: www.acheckamerica.com
SIC: 7323 7375 Credit reporting services; information retrieval services

(P-13706)
ACEVA TECHNOLOGIES INC
1810 Gateway Dr Ste 360, San Mateo (94404-4063)
PHONE..............................650 227-5500
Sundeep Jain, *Principal*
EMP: 200
SALES (est): 6.8MM
SALES (corp-wide): 8.4B **Publicly Held**
WEB: www.aceva.com
SIC: 7323 Credit clearinghouse

HQ: Fis Data Systems Inc.
200 Campus Dr
Collegeville PA 19426
484 582-2000

(P-13707)
CLAIMREMEDI INC
2235 Mercury Way Ste 107, Santa Rosa
(95407-5472)
PHONE..................................707 827-1274
H Peter Bowhall, *CEO*
Bob Bleyhl, *Exec VP*
EMP: 60
SALES: 7.5MM
SALES (corp-wide): 24MM **Privately Held**
SIC: 7323 Credit clearinghouse
PA: Esolutions, Inc.
8215 W 108th Ter
Overland Park KS 66210
866 633-4726

(P-13708)
CORELOGIC INC
Also Called: Corelogic Info Solutions
11010 White Rock Rd, Rancho Cordova
(95670-6361)
PHONE..................................916 431-2146
Christine Christian, *Branch Mgr*
David Hamilton, *Sr Project Mgr*
Patricia Bales, *Supervisor*
EMP: 95
SALES (corp-wide): 1.7B **Publicly Held**
SIC: 7323 Credit reporting services
PA: Corelogic, Inc.
40 Pacifica Ste 900
Irvine CA 92618
949 214-1000

(P-13709)
CORELOGIC CREDCO LLC (HQ)
40 Pacifica Ste 900, Irvine (92618-7487)
PHONE..................................949 214-1000
Frank Martel, *President*
Jim Balas, *CFO*
Barry Sando, *Managing Dir*
Ranga Potluri, *Info Tech Mgr*
Agustus Bautista, *Network Mgr*
EMP: 220 EST: 2005
SALES (est): 9.4MM
SALES (corp-wide): 1.7B **Publicly Held**
WEB: www.facredco.com
SIC: 7323 8748 Credit bureau & agency;
business consulting
PA: Corelogic, Inc.
40 Pacifica Ste 900
Irvine CA 92618
949 214-1000

(P-13710)
DUN & BRADSTREET INC
Also Called: D&B
1 Embarcadero Ctr # 2060, San Francisco
(94111-3757)
PHONE..................................925 216-2493
Shannon Myatt, *Sales Staff*
Terry Mintz, *Executive*
Timothy Denney, *Marketing Staff*
Michael Langner, *Director*
Laura Powers, *Director*
EMP: 76
SALES (corp-wide): 1.7B **Privately Held**
SIC: 7323 Commercial (mercantile) credit
reporting bureau
HQ: Dun & Bradstreet, Inc
103 John F Kennedy Pkwy
Short Hills NJ 07078
973 921-5500

(P-13711)
EXPERIAN CORPORATION
475 Anton Blvd, Santa Ana (92704)
PHONE..................................714 830-7000
Rick Cortese, *CEO*
Margaret B Smith, *President*
Deborah Zuccarini, *President*
Scot Thomas, *CEO*
Peg Smith, *Vice Pres*
EMP: 5059
SQ FT: 323,000
SALES (est): 98.4MM
SALES (corp-wide): 4.6B **Privately Held**
SIC: 7323 Credit bureau & agency; com-
mercial (mercantile) credit reporting bu-
reau

HQ: Experian Na Unlimited
Landmark House
Nottingham NOTTS

(P-13712)
EXPERIAN INFO SOLUTIONS INC (DH)
475 Anton Blvd, Costa Mesa (92626-7037)
P.O. Box 5001 (92628-5001)
PHONE..................................714 830-7000
Chris Callero, *CEO*
Stan Oliai, *Exec VP*
Stephen Burnside, *Senior VP*
Faith Gaudino, *Vice Pres*
Darryl Gibson, *Vice Pres*
EMP: 3700
SQ FT: 323,000
SALES (est): 1.4B
SALES (corp-wide): 4.6B **Privately Held**
WEB: www.experian.com
SIC: 7323 Credit bureau & agency; com-
mercial (mercantile) credit reporting bu-
reau
HQ: Experian Holdings, Inc.
475 Anton Blvd
Costa Mesa CA 92626
714 830-7000

(P-13713)
EXPERIAN INFO SOLUTIONS INC
Also Called: Experian Marketing
841 Apollo St Ste 200, El Segundo
(90245-4722)
PHONE..................................310 343-6700
Dana Shupe, *Branch Mgr*
EMP: 110
SALES (corp-wide): 4.6B **Privately Held**
SIC: 7323 Credit reporting services
HQ: Experian Information Solutions, Inc.
475 Anton Blvd
Costa Mesa CA 92626
714 830-7000

(P-13714)
EXPERIAN INFO SOLUTIONS INC
18500 Von Karman Ave # 400, Irvine
(92612-0511)
PHONE..................................949 567-3731
Ed Ojdana, *President*
Rosemary Kotanjian, *Vice Pres*
Michael Nguyen, *Vice Pres*
Adrianna Quintero, *Vice Pres*
Jeff Schwarzer, *Vice Pres*
EMP: 200
SALES (corp-wide): 4.6B **Privately Held**
WEB: www.experian.com
SIC: 7323 Commercial (mercantile) credit
reporting bureau
HQ: Experian Information Solutions, Inc.
475 Anton Blvd
Costa Mesa CA 92626
714 830-7000

(P-13715)
INFORMATIVE RESEARCH (PA)
13030 Euclid St Ste 209, Garden Grove
(92843-1334)
P.O. Box 2379 (92842-2379)
PHONE..................................714 638-2855
Randy Buckner, *CEO*
Sean Buckner, *President*
Patrick Buckner, *Vice Pres*
Dan Gilbreth, *Vice Pres*
Patrick Kelly, *Vice Pres*
EMP: 50 EST: 1946
SALES (est): 10.5MM **Privately Held**
WEB: www.informativeresearch.com
SIC: 7323 Credit reporting services

(P-13716)
MORTGAGE FAX INC
18685 Main St Ste 101, Huntington Beach
(92648-1719)
PHONE..................................714 899-2656
Joanne Ahmadi, *President*
EMP: 65
SQ FT: 8,500
SALES (est): 4.4MM **Privately Held**
WEB: www.mortgagefaxinc.com
SIC: 7323 Credit bureau & agency

┌─────────────────────────────┐
│ **7331 Direct Mail Advertising** │
│ **Svcs** │
└─────────────────────────────┘

(P-13717)
ADVANTAGE MAILING LLC (PA)
Also Called: Advantage Mailing Service
1600 N Kraemer Blvd, Anaheim
(92806-1410)
P.O. Box 66013 (92816-6013)
PHONE..................................714 538-3881
Tom Ling, *President*
Thomas C Ling, *President*
Brett Noss, *CFO*
Cara Cohan, *Vice Pres*
Diane Denish, *Sales Mgr*
EMP: 180
SQ FT: 60,000
SALES (est): 50.1MM **Privately Held**
WEB: www.advmailing.com
SIC: 7331 Mailing service

(P-13718)
ALL DIRECT MAIL SERVICES INC
Also Called: Mr Mailer
5091 4th St, Baldwin Park (91706-2173)
PHONE..................................818 833-7773
Dennis Zetting, *CEO*
Doug Zetting, *President*
Theresa Elkins, *Vice Pres*
Shirley Stephens, *Admin Sec*
EMP: 102
SQ FT: 50,000
SALES (est): 6.9MM **Privately Held**
WEB: www.admsi.com
SIC: 7331 Mailing service

(P-13719)
AST SPORTSWEAR INC
P.O. Box 17219 (92817-7219)
PHONE..................................714 223-2030
EMP: 424 **Privately Held**
SIC: 7331 Mailing service
PA: Ast Sportswear, Inc.
2701 E Imperial Hwy
Brea CA 92821

(P-13720)
BUSINESS SERVICES NETWORK
1275 Fairfax Ave Ste 103, San Francisco
(94124-1759)
PHONE..................................415 282-8161
Harry Yue, *President*
Carlos Lamar, *Vice Pres*
EMP: 72
SQ FT: 31,120
SALES (est): 7.9MM **Privately Held**
WEB: www.bsnc.com
SIC: 7331 2752 7374 Mailing service;
commercial printing, offset; data process-
ing service

(P-13721)
DATABASE MARKETING GROUP INC
5 Peters Canyon Rd # 150, Irvine
(92606-1793)
PHONE..................................714 727-0800
John A Engstrom, *President*
Sharon M Engstrom, *Vice Pres*
Sharon Engstrom, *Vice Pres*
Scott Humphrey, *Business Dir*
Robert Jansen, *Administration*
EMP: 300
SQ FT: 12,000
SALES (est): 32MM **Privately Held**
WEB: www.dbmgroup.com
SIC: 7331 8742 Mailing service; marketing
consulting services

(P-13722)
FINANCIAL STATEMENT SVCS INC (PA)
Also Called: Fssi
3300 S Fairview St, Santa Ana
(92704-7004)
PHONE..................................714 436-3326
Jennifer Dietz, *CEO*
Henry Perez, *COO*
Karen Elsbury, *CFO*
Dick O'Neil, *Vice Pres*

Jon Dietz, *Admin Sec*
EMP: 144
SQ FT: 167,000
SALES: 19.2MM **Privately Held**
WEB: www.fssi-ca.com
SIC: 7331 7374 2759 Mailing service;
data processing & preparation; laser print-
ing

(P-13723)
HARTE-HANKS DIRECT MAIL/CALIFO
2337 W Commonwealth Ave, Fullerton
(92833-2997)
PHONE..................................714 738-5478
Larry Franklin, *Ch of Bd*
Richard Hockhouser, *President*
Donald R Crews, *Vice Pres*
EMP: 85
SQ FT: 65,000
SALES (est): 3.8MM
SALES (corp-wide): 284.6MM **Publicly Held**
SIC: 7331 Direct mail advertising services
PA: Harte Hanks, Inc.
9601 Mcallister Fwy # 610
San Antonio TX 78216
210 829-9000

(P-13724)
INFOGROUP INC
951 Mariners Island Blvd # 130, San Mateo
(94404-1558)
PHONE..................................650 389-0700
Fax: 650 389-0707
EMP: 75
SALES (corp-wide): 151.6MM **Privately Held**
SIC: 7331 2741
PA: Infogroup Inc.
1020 E 1st St
Papillion NE 68046
402 836-4500

(P-13725)
IRON MOUNTAIN FULFILLMENT (HQ)
Also Called: Iron Mountain Assurance Corp
565 Sinclair Frontage Rd, Milpitas
(95035-5413)
PHONE..................................408 945-1600
Mike Smith, *President*
EMP: 50
SALES (est): 17.4MM
SALES (corp-wide): 4.2B **Publicly Held**
WEB: www.comac.com
SIC: 7331 Direct mail advertising services
PA: Iron Mountain Incorporated
1 Federal St Fl 7
Boston MA 02110
617 535-4766

(P-13726)
K/P LLC
13947 Washington Ave, San Leandro
(94578-3220)
PHONE..................................510 614-7800
Rich De Senglau, *Branch Mgr*
EMP: 50
SALES (corp-wide): 107.8MM **Privately Held**
WEB: www.kpcorporation.com
SIC: 7331 Direct mail advertising services
PA: Kp Llc
13951 Washington Ave
San Leandro CA 94578
510 346-0729

(P-13727)
KP LLC
Also Called: Hunter Advertising Mail Co
13951 Washington Ave, San Leandro
(94578-3220)
PHONE..................................510 346-0729
Rich De Senglau, *President*
EMP: 140
SALES (corp-wide): 107.8MM **Privately Held**
WEB: www.kpcorporation.com
SIC: 7331 Direct mail advertising services
PA: Kp Llc
13951 Washington Ave
San Leandro CA 94578
510 346-0729

PRODUCTS & SVCS

(P-13728)
M M DIRECT MARKETING INC
14271 Corporate Dr, Garden Grove
(92843-5000)
PHONE.................................714 265-4100
Godfred P Otueye, *President*
EMP: 300
SALES (est): 8.7MM
SALES (corp-wide): 49.5MM **Privately Held**
WEB: www.moneymailer.com
SIC: 7331 6794 Mailing service; franchises, selling or licensing
PA: Money Mailer, Llc
  6261 Katella Ave Ste 200
  Cypress CA 90630
  714 889-3800

(P-13729)
MAILMARK ENTERPRISES LLC
8587 Canoga Ave, Canoga Park
(91304-2609)
PHONE.................................818 407-0660
Barry Silver,
EMP: 50
SQ FT: 15,500
SALES (est): 5.3MM **Privately Held**
WEB: www.mailmark.com
SIC: 7331 Mailing service

(P-13730)
MERCURY MAILING SYSTEMS INC
2727 Exposition Blvd, Los Angeles
(90018-4119)
PHONE.................................323 730-0307
Paul Hood, *President*
Cynthia Garcia, *VP Sales*
EMP: 70
SQ FT: 20,000
SALES (est): 3.3MM **Privately Held**
SIC: 7331 Mailing service

(P-13731)
MONEY MAILER LLC (PA)
Also Called: Mm Advertising
6261 Katella Ave Ste 200, Cypress
(90630-5249)
PHONE.................................714 889-3800
Gary Mulloy,
Mike Hisket,
Dennis Jenkins,
John Patinella,
Chris Rimlinger,
EMP: 250
SQ FT: 60,000
SALES (est): 49.5MM **Privately Held**
WEB: www.moneymailer.com
SIC: 7331 6794 Direct mail advertising services; franchises, selling or licensing

(P-13732)
MOPAR ENTERPRISES
Also Called: West Coast Mailing & Dist
1710 Dornoch Ct Ste A, San Diego
(92154-7235)
PHONE.................................858 492-1123
EMP: 60
SQ FT: 49,278
SALES (est): 4.3MM **Privately Held**
SIC: 7331

(P-13733)
MRT INC
19781 Pauling, Foothill Ranch
(92610-2606)
PHONE.................................949 348-2292
Rick Theder, *President*
Tracy Vanevery, *Admin Sec*
EMP: 50
SQ FT: 18,000
SALES (est): 7.5MM **Privately Held**
WEB: www.impactorder.com
SIC: 7331 Direct mail advertising services

(P-13734)
PENSION ADMINISTRATORS INC (PA)
Also Called: Beneficial Administration
17701 Mitchell N, Irvine (92614-6028)
PHONE.................................949 253-4080
Donald R Lawrenz, *President*
John Der Schraaf, *Treasurer*
Paul Peatross, *Vice Pres*
EMP: 105

SALES (est): 12.3MM **Privately Held**
SIC: 7331 6311 Mailing service; life insurance

(P-13735)
POMONA COLLEGE
333 N College Way, Claremont
(91711-4429)
PHONE.................................909 621-8000
David W Oxtoby, *President*
EMP: 102
SALES (corp-wide): 193.4MM **Privately Held**
SIC: 7331 8221 Addressing service; college, except junior
PA: Pomona College
  550 N College Ave
  Claremont CA 91711
  909 621-8135

(P-13736)
PREMIER MAILING INC
Also Called: Premier Mailing Services
14522 Garfield Ave, Paramount
(90723-3426)
PHONE.................................562 408-2134
Ramon Arribeno, *President*
EMP: 50 **EST:** 1999
SQ FT: 5,200
SALES (est): 7.6MM **Privately Held**
SIC: 7331 Mailing service

(P-13737)
R R DONNELLEY & SONS COMPANY
Also Called: RR Donnelley
18915 S Laurel Park Rd, Rancho Dominguez (90220-6005)
PHONE.................................310 784-8485
Kelly Martinez, *Vice Pres*
EMP: 50
SALES (corp-wide): 6.8B **Publicly Held**
SIC: 7331 Mailing service
PA: R. R. Donnelley & Sons Company
  35 W Wacker Dr
  Chicago IL 60601
  312 326-8000

(P-13738)
REAL ESTATE IMAGE INC
Also Called: Advanced Image Direct
1415 S Acacia Ave, Fullerton (92831-5317)
PHONE.................................714 502-3900
Ty McMillin, *President*
Hugo Solorio, *Vice Pres*
Perry Wilson, *VP Sales*
Bob Kitajima, *Maintence Staff*
Debbie Trump, *Manager*
EMP: 200
SQ FT: 136,000
SALES (est): 29MM **Privately Held**
WEB: www.advancedimagedirect.com
SIC: 7331 2752 Direct mail advertising services; commercial printing, lithographic

(P-13739)
SPECTRUM INFORMATION SVCS LLC (PA)
16 Technology Dr Ste 107, Irvine
(92618-2323)
PHONE.................................949 752-7070
Curtis Pilon, *President*
Jim Bradford, *CFO*
Glenn O Dell, *Vice Pres*
Leslie MAI, *Office Mgr*
EMP: 70
SQ FT: 142,000
SALES (est): 10MM **Privately Held**
SIC: 7331 7375 4731 Mailing service; information retrieval services; shipping documents preparation

(P-13740)
STAMPSCOM INC (PA)
1990 E Grand Ave, El Segundo
(90245-5013)
PHONE.................................310 482-5800
Kenneth T McBride, *Ch of Bd*
Kyle Huebner, *President*
Jeff Carberry, *CFO*
Bradford Jones, *Bd of Directors*
Sebastian Buerba, *Chief Mktg Ofcr*
EMP: 147 **EST:** 1996
SQ FT: 99,600

SALES: 586.9MM **Publicly Held**
WEB: www.stamps.com
SIC: 7331 5961 4813 Mailing service; catalog & mail-order houses;

(P-13741)
T G T ENTERPRISES INC
Also Called: Anderson Direct Marketing
12650 Danielson Ct, Poway (92064-6822)
PHONE.................................858 413-0300
Ted Tietge, *CEO*
Randy Dale, *President*
Vicky Ruegsegger, *Officer*
Scott Hopkins, *Exec VP*
Mimi Flowers, *Vice Pres*
EMP: 130
SQ FT: 77,000
SALES (est): 31.8MM **Privately Held**
WEB: www.andersondirectmail.com
SIC: 7331 2759 Mailing service; commercial printing

(P-13742)
TOWNE INC
Also Called: Towne Advertising
3441 W Macarthur Blvd, Santa Ana
(92704-6805)
PHONE.................................714 540-3095
Tarek Elkomi, *Branch Mgr*
EMP: 100
SALES (corp-wide): 20MM **Privately Held**
SIC: 7331 7311 Mailing service; advertising agencies
PA: Towne, Inc.
  3441 W Macarthur Blvd
  Santa Ana CA 92704
  714 540-3095

(P-13743)
TRANSMRCAN MLING FLFLLMENT INC
355 State Pl, Escondido (92029-1359)
PHONE.................................760 745-5343
Paul Barron, *CEO*
Heather Benjamin, *Vice Pres*
Eleanor Monica, *Vice Pres*
Patty Benitez, *Accounts Mgr*
EMP: 100
SALES (est): 16.8MM **Privately Held**
WEB: www.transamericanmailing.com
SIC: 7331 Mailing service

(P-13744)
VALASSIS DIRECT MAIL INC
6955 Mowry Ave, Newark (94560-4924)
PHONE.................................510 505-6500
Debra Robinson, *Manager*
EMP: 100 **Privately Held**
WEB: www.advo.com
SIC: 7331 Mailing service
HQ: Valassis Direct Mail, Inc.
  235 Great Pond Dr
  Windsor CT 06095
  800 437-0479

7334 Photocopying & Duplicating Svcs

(P-13745)
ABI ATTORNEYS SERVICE INC (PA)
Also Called: ABI VIP Attorney Service
2015 W Park Ave, Redlands (92373-6271)
P.O. Box 9240 (92375-2440)
PHONE.................................909 793-0613
Alice J Benge, *President*
Chuck Benge, *Corp Secy*
EMP: 80
SQ FT: 7,500
SALES (est): 6.1MM **Privately Held**
WEB: www.abivip.com
SIC: 7334 Photocopying & duplicating services

(P-13746)
AMERICAN LEGAL COPY-OR LLC
98 Battery St Ste 220, San Francisco
(94111-5509)
PHONE.................................415 777-4449
Kevin Brooks, *Manager*
EMP: 100 **Privately Held**

WEB: www.alcweb.com
SIC: 7334 Photocopying & duplicating services
PA: American Legal Copy-Or, Llc
  1001 4th Ave Ste 300
  Seattle WA 98154

(P-13747)
AMERICAN REPROGRAPHICS CO LLC
Also Called: Ford Graphics
934 Venice Blvd, Los Angeles
(90015-3230)
PHONE.................................213 745-3145
Juan Carlos, *Principal*
Bruce Newton, *Accounts Exec*
EMP: 100
SALES (corp-wide): 400.7MM **Publicly Held**
WEB: www.e-arc.com
SIC: 7334 7336 7374 Blueprinting service; commercial art & graphic design; computer graphics service
HQ: American Reprographics Company, L.L.C.
  1981 N Broadway Ste 385
  Walnut Creek CA 94596
  925 949-5100

(P-13748)
AMERICAN REPROGRAPHICS CO LLC
Also Called: Brownie's Digital Imaging
1322 V St, Sacramento (95818-1418)
PHONE.................................916 443-1322
Jack Anderson, *Manager*
EMP: 80
SALES (corp-wide): 400.7MM **Publicly Held**
WEB: www.e-arc.com
SIC: 7334 Blueprinting service
HQ: American Reprographics Company, L.L.C.
  1981 N Broadway Ste 385
  Walnut Creek CA 94596
  925 949-5100

(P-13749)
AMERICAN REPROGRAPHICS CO LLC
Also Called: ARC Imaging Resources
616 Monterey Pass Rd, Monterey Park
(91754-2419)
PHONE.................................626 289-5021
Doug Elffers, *Mng Member*
EMP: 52
SALES (corp-wide): 400.7MM **Publicly Held**
WEB: www.e-arc.com
SIC: 7334 Photocopying & duplicating services
HQ: American Reprographics Company, L.L.C.
  1981 N Broadway Ste 385
  Walnut Creek CA 94596
  925 949-5100

(P-13750)
AMERICAN REPROGRAPHICS CO LLC
San Jose Blueprint
821 Martin Ave, Santa Clara (95050-2903)
PHONE.................................408 295-5770
Norma Mathews, *Human Res Mgr*
EMP: 90
SALES (corp-wide): 400.7MM **Publicly Held**
WEB: www.e-arc.com
SIC: 7334 Blueprinting service
HQ: American Reprographics Company, L.L.C.
  1981 N Broadway Ste 385
  Walnut Creek CA 94596
  925 949-5100

(P-13751)
AMERICAN REPROGRAPHICS CO LLC
Also Called: Consolidated Reprographics
345 Clinton St, Costa Mesa (92626-6011)
PHONE.................................714 751-2680
Erick Hazell, *Vice Pres*
EMP: 150
SQ FT: 42,000

SALES (corp-wide): 400.7MM **Publicly Held**
WEB: www.e-arc.com
SIC: 7334 Blueprinting service
HQ: American Reprographics Company, L.L.C.
1981 N Broadway Ste 385
Walnut Creek CA 94596
925 949-5100

(P-13752)
AMERICAN REPROGRAPHICS CO LLC
Also Called: Ocb Riverside
4295 Main St, Riverside (92501-3822)
PHONE...................................951 686-0530
Jesse De La Cruz, *General Mgr*
EMP: 75
SALES (corp-wide): 400.7MM **Publicly Held**
WEB: www.ocbinc.com
SIC: 7334 Photocopying & duplicating services
HQ: American Reprographics Company, L.L.C.
1981 N Broadway Ste 385
Walnut Creek CA 94596
925 949-5100

(P-13753)
ARC DOCUMENT SOLUTIONS INC
655 N Central Ave, Glendale (91203-1422)
PHONE...................................818 242-6555
Michael Cohanzard, *CEO*
Lisa Beaty, *Manager*
EMP: 120
SALES (corp-wide): 400.7MM **Publicly Held**
SIC: 7334 Blueprinting service
PA: Arc Document Solutions, Inc.
12657 Alcosta Blvd # 200
San Ramon CA 94583
925 949-5100

(P-13754)
ARC DOCUMENT SOLUTIONS INC
1207 John Reed Ct Ste A, City of Industry (91745-2421)
PHONE...................................626 333-7005
Steve Ostrander, *Manager*
EMP: 92
SALES (corp-wide): 400.7MM **Publicly Held**
SIC: 7334 Photocopying & duplicating services
PA: Arc Document Solutions, Inc.
12657 Alcosta Blvd # 200
San Ramon CA 94583
925 949-5100

(P-13755)
ARC DOCUMENT SOLUTIONS INC
American Reprographics Company
945 Bryant St Ste 1000, San Francisco (94103-4523)
PHONE...................................415 495-8700
Soren Goodman, *General Mgr*
Suri Suriyakumar, *CEO*
EMP: 50
SALES (corp-wide): 400.7MM **Publicly Held**
WEB: www.e-arc.com
SIC: 7334 Blueprinting service
PA: Arc Document Solutions, Inc.
12657 Alcosta Blvd # 200
San Ramon CA 94583
925 949-5100

(P-13756)
ARC DOCUMENT SOLUTIONS INC
Also Called: Reliable Graphics
15019 Califa St, Van Nuys (91411-3003)
PHONE...................................818 908-0222
Danny Mesa, *Branch Mgr*
EMP: 120
SQ FT: 15,727
SALES (corp-wide): 400.7MM **Publicly Held**
SIC: 7334 Blueprinting service

PA: Arc Document Solutions, Inc.
12657 Alcosta Blvd # 200
San Ramon CA 94583
925 949-5100

(P-13757)
ASSOCTED REPRODUCTION SVCS INC
Also Called: ARS
13925 Whittier Blvd, Whittier (90605-2037)
PHONE...................................562 696-1181
John A Antonelli, *CEO*
John W Antonelli, *President*
Marsha Antonelli, *Vice Pres*
Ron Weingarten, *Info Tech Mgr*
Angelica Gonzalez, *Accountant*
EMP: 160
SQ FT: 25,000
SALES (est): 14.6MM **Privately Held**
WEB: www.arslegal.com
SIC: 7334 Photocopying & duplicating services

(P-13758)
CAPITOL LLC (PA)
Also Called: Capitol Dgtal Dcment Solutions
615 Las Tunas Dr Ste L, Arcadia (91007-8470)
PHONE...................................626 445-0402
Lucas Marcus, *Mng Member*
John E Stacey,
EMP: 300
SALES (est): 17.9MM **Privately Held**
WEB: www.capitolusa.com
SIC: 7334 Photocopying & duplicating services

(P-13759)
CRISP ENTERPRISES INC (PA)
Also Called: C2 Imaging
3180 Pullman St, Costa Mesa (92626-3323)
PHONE...................................714 668-5955
Gary Crisp, *CEO*
William Govaars II, *Shareholder*
Arthur Gregory Lundeen III, *Shareholder*
Barry Malkin, *COO*
Julie Crisp, *Exec VP*
EMP: 60
SQ FT: 28,000
SALES (est): 26.7MM **Privately Held**
WEB: www.c2repro.com
SIC: 7334 Blueprinting service

(P-13760)
FEDEX OFFICE & PRINT SVCS INC
2799 E Thousand Oaks Blvd, Thousand Oaks (91362-3257)
PHONE...................................805 379-1552
EMP: 50
SALES (corp-wide): 69.6B **Publicly Held**
WEB: www.kinkos.com
SIC: 7334 Photocopying & duplicating services
HQ: Fedex Office And Print Services, Inc.
7900 Legacy Dr
Plano TX 75024
800 463-3339

(P-13761)
FEDEX OFFICE & PRINT SVCS INC
13488 Maxella Ave, Marina Del Rey (90292-4300)
PHONE...................................310 827-2297
EMP: 50
SALES (corp-wide): 69.6B **Publicly Held**
WEB: www.kinkos.com
SIC: 7334 Photocopying & duplicating services
HQ: Fedex Office And Print Services, Inc.
7900 Legacy Dr
Plano TX 75024
800 463-3339

(P-13762)
FEDEX OFFICE & PRINT SVCS INC
800 Wilshire Blvd, Los Angeles (90017-2604)
P.O. Box Shire Blvd (90017)
PHONE...................................213 892-1700
Lenore Samela, *Sales Staff*
Joseph Villa, *Sales Staff*

EMP: 50
SALES (corp-wide): 69.6B **Publicly Held**
WEB: www.kinkos.com
SIC: 7334 Photocopying & duplicating services
HQ: Fedex Office And Print Services, Inc.
7900 Legacy Dr
Plano TX 75024
800 463-3339

(P-13763)
KNOX SERVICES LLC (PA)
1522 Brookhollow Dr Ste 3, Santa Ana (92705-5412)
PHONE...................................714 479-1650
Stephen L Knox,
Terry Ashman,
Steven L Bubel,
Robert C Porambo,
EMP: 70
SQ FT: 5,200
SALES (est): 4.5MM **Privately Held**
SIC: 7334 Photocopying & duplicating services

(P-13764)
LASR INC
Also Called: First Reprographic
1517 Beverly Blvd, Los Angeles (90026-5704)
P.O. Box 749469 (90074-9469)
PHONE...................................877 591-9979
Martin Kayondo, *President*
Rick Matsumoto, *Opers Mgr*
EMP: 120
SALES (est): 728K **Privately Held**
SIC: 7334 Photocopying & duplicating services

(P-13765)
OPTISOURCE TECHNOLOGIES INC
1855 W Katella Ave # 170, Orange (92867-3441)
PHONE...................................714 288-0825
Trang Nguyen, *President*
David Nguyen, *President*
EMP: 50 EST: 1997
SQ FT: 5,500
SALES: 2.1MM **Privately Held**
WEB: www.optisource.com
SIC: 7334 Blueprinting service

(P-13766)
SECOND IMAGE NATIONAL LLC (PA)
170 E Arrow Hwy, San Dimas (91773-3336)
P.O. Box 52969, Houston TX (77052-2969)
PHONE...................................800 229-7477
Norman Fogwell, *CEO*
EMP: 145
SQ FT: 25,500
SALES (est): 23.7MM **Privately Held**
WEB: www.secondimage.net
SIC: 7334 Photocopying & duplicating services

(P-13767)
UCLA COPY SERVICES
555 Westwood Plz Ste B, Los Angeles (90095-8351)
PHONE...................................310 794-6371
James Muh, *Director*
Alex Caro, *Admin Asst*
David Aberbush, *Director*
Bill Lundy, *Manager*
Alice Ovanesian, *Manager*
EMP: 50
SALES (est): 3.4MM **Privately Held**
SIC: 7334 2759 Photocopying & duplicating services; commercial printing

(P-13768)
V A ANDERSON ENTERPRISES INC
2680 Bishop Dr Ste 140, San Ramon (94583-4453)
PHONE...................................925 866-6150
Fax: 925 866-6664
EMP: 73
SALES (corp-wide): 8.3MM **Privately Held**
SIC: 7334

EMP: 50
SALES (corp-wide): 69.6B **Publicly Held**
WEB: www.kinkos.com
SIC: 7334 Photocopying & duplicating services
HQ: Fedex Office And Print Services, Inc.
7900 Legacy Dr
Plano TX 75024
800 463-3339

PA: V. A. Anderson Enterprises, Inc.
400 Atlas St
Brea CA 92821
714 990-6100

7335 Commercial Photography

(P-13769)
BRANDED ENTRMT NETWRK INC (PA)
15250 Ventura Blvd # 300, Sherman Oaks (91403-3201)
PHONE...................................310 342-1500
Gary Shenk, *CEO*
Joe Schick, *CFO*
Kristin Glushon, *Exec VP*
Ted Sheffield, *Exec VP*
Jim Mitchell, *Senior VP*
EMP: 233
SALES (est): 97.3MM **Privately Held**
WEB: www.corbis.com
SIC: 7335 Commercial photography

(P-13770)
GETTY IMAGES INC
Also Called: Gettyone Image Bank
6300 Wilshire Blvd # 1600, Los Angeles (90048-5227)
PHONE...................................323 202-4200
Anne Marion, *Branch Mgr*
Pancho Bernasconi, *Vice Pres*
Joel Andritsch, *IT/INT Sup*
Bruce Bennett, *Director*
Amy Lehfeldt, *Director*
EMP: 100
SALES (corp-wide): 278.6MM **Privately Held**
WEB: www.getty-images.com
SIC: 7335 Commercial photography
PA: Getty Images, Inc.
605 5th Ave S Ste 400
Seattle WA 98104
206 925-5000

(P-13771)
PRIMARY COLOR SYSTEMS CORP
401 Coral Cir, El Segundo (90245-4622)
PHONE...................................310 841-0250
Ed Phillips, *Branch Mgr*
EMP: 130
SALES (corp-wide): 61MM **Privately Held**
SIC: 7335 7384 Photographic studio, commercial; photofinishing laboratory
PA: Primary Color Systems Corporation
11130 Holder St
Cypress CA 90630
949 660-7080

7336 Commercial Art & Graphic Design

(P-13772)
BLT & ASSOCIATES INC
6430 W Sunset Blvd # 800, Los Angeles (90028-7911)
PHONE...................................323 860-4000
Clive Baillie, *President*
Mike Eller, *Creative Dir*
Alison Roberto, *Director*
Billy Stanek, *Editor*
Amy Bennett, *Accounts Exec*
EMP: 170
SQ FT: 15,000
SALES (est): 20.2MM **Privately Held**
WEB: www.bltomato.com
SIC: 7336 Graphic arts & related design

(P-13773)
CHAMPION SIGNS INCORPORATED
7835 Wilkerson Ct, San Diego (92111-3606)
PHONE...................................858 751-2900
Ron Johnson, *President*
EMP: 50
SQ FT: 8,000
SALES (est): 3.2MM **Privately Held**
WEB: www.championsigns.net
SIC: 7336 Silk screen design

(P-13774)
CINNABAR
4571 Electronics Pl, Los Angeles
(90039-1007)
PHONE...............................818 842-8190
Jonathan Katz, *President*
EMP: 200
SQ FT: 60,000
SALES (est): 19.6MM **Privately Held**
SIC: 7336 3999 7819 Graphic arts & related design; theatrical scenery; sound (effects & music production), motion picture; visual effects production

(P-13775)
CINNABAR CALIFORNIA INC
4571 Electronics Pl, Los Angeles
(90039-1007)
PHONE...............................818 842-8190
Jonathan Katz, *Chairman*
Basil Katz, *CEO*
Leslie Crawford, *Vice Pres*
Kip Katz, *Vice Pres*
Jeff Crocker, *Project Mgr*
EMP: 60
SQ FT: 55,271
SALES (est): 16.7MM **Privately Held**
SIC: 7336 8712 1796 Art design services; architectural services; installing building equipment

(P-13776)
CONSOLIDATED DESIGN WEST INC
Also Called: Cdw
1345 S Lewis St, Anaheim (92805-6431)
PHONE...............................714 999-1476
Victor John Perrillo, *CEO*
Michael Brown, *Vice Pres*
Rick Gaulden, *Sales Executive*
Melissa Saldana, *Sales Executive*
Matt Propeck, *Sales Mgr*
▲ EMP: 80
SQ FT: 7,500
SALES (est): 17.1MM **Privately Held**
SIC: 7336 2754 Package design; commercial printing, gravure

(P-13777)
CONTINENTAL GRAPHICS CORP (HQ)
Also Called: Continental Data Graphics
4060 N Lakewood Blvd, Long Beach
(90808-1700)
PHONE...............................714 503-4200
David Malmo, *CEO*
James Mills, *CFO*
Michael Parven, *Exec VP*
John Aitchison, *Program Mgr*
Liza Gernert, *Executive Asst*
EMP: 200
SQ FT: 45,000
SALES (est): 57.5MM
SALES (corp-wide): 101.1B **Publicly Held**
WEB: www.cdgnow.com
SIC: 7336 8741 8711 8999 Commercial art & graphic design; management services; engineering services; technical writing
PA: The Boeing Company
    100 N Riverside Plz
    Chicago IL 60606
    312 544-2000

(P-13778)
COUNTY OF LOS ANGELES
Also Called: Gateway
1 Gateway Plz, Los Angeles (90012-3745)
P.O. Box 90012 (90009-0012)
PHONE...............................213 922-6210
Roger Snoball, *Owner*
EMP: 1000 **Privately Held**
WEB: www.co.la.ca.us
SIC: 7336 9621 Commercial art & graphic design; transportation department: government, non-operating;
PA: County Of Los Angeles
    500 W Temple St Ste 437
    Los Angeles CA 90012
    213 974-1101

(P-13779)
CUSTOMLINE PROFESSIONAL
567 S Melrose St, Placentia (92870-6305)
PHONE...............................714 996-1333
Dan Mattox, *President*
EMP: 300
SQ FT: 60,000
SALES (est): 26.1MM **Privately Held**
WEB: www.customlinescreenprint.com
SIC: 7336 Silk screen design

(P-13780)
DANDREA GRAPHIC CORPORTION
Also Called: D'Andrea Graphics
6100 Gateway Dr, Cypress (90630-4840)
PHONE...............................310 642-0260
David D'Andrea, *CEO*
Patrick Salter, *Info Tech Mgr*
Bonnie Crowder, *Project Mgr*
Hannah McDaniel, *Project Mgr*
▲ EMP: 80
SQ FT: 25,000
SALES (est): 17.8MM **Privately Held**
SIC: 7336 Graphic arts & related design

(P-13781)
DESTINATION MOON LP
Also Called: Turner Dockworth
615 Battery St Fl 6, San Francisco
(94111-1808)
PHONE...............................415 675-7777
David Turner, *CEO*
Bruce Duckworth, *COO*
Jamie McCathie, *Creative Dir*
Sarah Moffat, *Creative Dir*
Joanne Chan, *General Mgr*
EMP: 70
SQ FT: 5,600
SALES (est): 8MM **Privately Held**
SIC: 7336 Graphic arts & related design

(P-13782)
DSH WEST INC
Also Called: Dsh Graphics
5455 Camino De Bryant, Yorba Linda
(92887-4209)
PHONE...............................714 692-8777
Ron Herrera, *President*
Donna Herrera, *President*
EMP: 75
SALES (est): 7.8MM **Privately Held**
SIC: 7336 Creative services to advertisers, except writers; graphic arts & related design

(P-13783)
FINAL FILM
Also Called: Flash Point Graphix
3620 W Valhalla Dr, Burbank (91505-1127)
PHONE...............................323 467-0700
Thomas L Saliba, *Ch of Bd*
Guy S Claudy, *President*
Gregory D Davidiian, *CEO*
Raymond Hebrank, *CFO*
Ron Dejesus, *Vice Pres*
EMP: 62
SQ FT: 20,000
SALES (est): 10MM **Privately Held**
WEB: www.finalfilm.com
SIC: 7336 Graphic arts & related design

(P-13784)
FROG DESIGN INC (DH)
1130 Howard St, San Francisco
(94103-3914)
PHONE...............................415 442-4804
Doreen Lorenzo, *CEO*
Toshi Mogi, *President*
Andy Zimmerman, *President*
Craig Ayers, *CFO*
Alec Cooper, *Vice Pres*
▲ EMP: 100
SALES (est): 31.6MM
SALES (corp-wide): 1.1B **Privately Held**
WEB: www.frogdesign.com
SIC: 7336 Graphic arts & related design

(P-13785)
GEL PAK LLC
31398 Huntwood Ave, Hayward
(94544-7818)
PHONE...............................510 576-2220
Jeanne Beacham, *Principal*
Mike Tran, *Engineer*
Ginger Demello, *Prdtn Mgr*

Roger Scoffone, *Sales Staff*
EMP: 75
SALES (est): 217.5K
SALES (corp-wide): 25.8MM **Privately Held**
SIC: 7336 Package design
PA: Delphon Industries, Llc
    31398 Huntwood Ave
    Hayward CA 94544
    510 576-2220

(P-13786)
HARDING MKTG CMMUNICATIONS INC (PA)
Also Called: Harding & Associates
377 S Daniel Way, San Jose (95128-5120)
PHONE...............................408 345-4545
James F Harding, *CEO*
Maria Richard, *CFO*
EMP: 70
SQ FT: 10,000
SALES (est): 11MM **Privately Held**
WEB: www.hardingmarketing.com
SIC: 7336 Graphic arts & related design

(P-13787)
IDEO LP (PA)
780 High St, Palo Alto (94301-2420)
PHONE...............................650 289-3400
Sandy Speicher, *CEO*
Kim Powers, *Executive Asst*
Nicole Olano, *IT/INT Sup*
Eric Williamsen, *Technology*
Matt Adams, *Engineer*
EMP: 135
SALES (est): 40MM **Privately Held**
WEB: www.ideo.com
SIC: 7336 7389 8711 Commercial art & graphic design; design, commercial & industrial; engineering services

(P-13788)
LANDOR ASSOCIATES INTL LTD (DH)
1001 Front St, San Francisco (94111-1467)
PHONE...............................415 365-1700
Lois Jacobs, *CEO*
Cheryl Giovannoni, *President*
Gabriel Miller, *President*
Ran Wadleigh, *CFO*
Craig Branigan, *Chairman*
EMP: 200
SQ FT: 44,000
SALES (est): 27.8MM
SALES (corp-wide): 20B **Privately Held**
SIC: 7336 Graphic arts & related design
HQ: Young & Rubicam Llc
    3 Columbus Cir
    New York NY 10019
    212 210-3000

(P-13789)
LATERAL DESIGNS INC
Also Called: Logo Design Pros
639 Front St Fl 3, San Francisco
(94111-1970)
PHONE...............................415 847-6618
Cliff Kaplan, *President*
Csaba Menyhart, *CFO*
EMP: 100
SALES (est): 5MM **Privately Held**
SIC: 7336 Graphic arts & related design

(P-13790)
MARKET TECH MEDIA CORPORATION
27220 Turnberry Ln # 190, Valencia
(91355-1018)
PHONE...............................661 257-4745
Thomas Rice, *President*
Vance Kirby, *COO*
Richard Van Slyke, *Manager*
EMP: 100
SQ FT: 54,000
SALES (est): 7.9MM **Privately Held**
WEB: www.addcart.com
SIC: 7336 7311 Graphic arts & related design; advertising agencies

(P-13791)
MIRUM INC
Also Called: Digitaria
350 10th Ave Ste 1200, San Diego
(92101-8702)
PHONE...............................619 237-5552

Daniel Khabie, *CEO*
Doug Hecht, *President*
Gary Correia, *CFO*
Tom Siebert, *Vice Pres*
Jason Garrett, *VP Bus Dvlpt*
EMP: 200
SQ FT: 4,000
SALES (est): 27.2MM
SALES (corp-wide): 20B **Privately Held**
WEB: www.digitaria.com
SIC: 7336 Graphic arts & related design
HQ: J. Walter Thompson U.S.A., Llc
    466 Lexington Ave Fl 2
    New York NY 10017
    212 210-7000

(P-13792)
MOTION THEORY INC
Also Called: Mirada
444 W Ocean Blvd Ste 1400, Long Beach
(90802-4522)
PHONE...............................310 396-9433
Andrew Merkin,
Janell Perez, *CFO*
Hector Ramirez, *Technology*
Sascha Flick, *Mktg Dir*
Matthew Cullen,
EMP: 110
SQ FT: 25,000
SALES: 27MM **Privately Held**
WEB: www.motiontheory.com
SIC: 7336 7371 7812 Graphic arts & related design; computer software development & applications; motion picture production

(P-13793)
MOTIVATIONAL SYSTEMS INC (PA)
2200 Cleveland Ave, National City
(91950-6412)
PHONE...............................619 474-8246
Robert D Yound, *CEO*
Joe Jordan, *Treasurer*
Bob Charette, *Vice Pres*
David Cowan, *Vice Pres*
Anne Devlin, *Vice Pres*
EMP: 100 EST: 1975
SQ FT: 50,000
SALES (est): 28.1MM **Privately Held**
WEB: www.motivationalsystems.com
SIC: 7336 3993 Graphic arts & related design; signs & advertising specialties

(P-13794)
ONE K STUDIOS LLC
Also Called: 1k Studios
3400 W Olive Ave Ste 300, Burbank
(91505-5408)
PHONE...............................818 531-3800
Matt Kennedy,
Steve Klinenberg,
Mitchell Rubinstein,
Jayson Won,
EMP: 50
SQ FT: 25,000
SALES (est): 5.7MM **Privately Held**
WEB: www.one-k.com
SIC: 7336 Commercial art & graphic design

(P-13795)
PROLOGUE FILMS (PA)
Also Called: Title Boy
534 Victoria Ave, Venice (90291-4833)
PHONE...............................310 589-9090
Kyle Cooper, *President*
Lisa Bolan, *Creative Dir*
EMP: 50
SALES (est): 4.8MM **Privately Held**
SIC: 7336 Graphic arts & related design

(P-13796)
PULP STUDIO INCORPORATED
Also Called: CGB
2100 W 139th St, Gardena (90249-2412)
P.O. Box 16231, Beverly Hills (90209-2231)
PHONE...............................310 815-4999
Bernard Lax, *CEO*
Lynda N Lax, *President*
Oscar Ramirez, *Vice Pres*
Kirk Johnson, *Exec Dir*
Henry Marquis, *Technician*
◆ EMP: 60
SQ FT: 36,000

SALES (est): 18.9MM **Privately Held**
WEB: www.pulpstudio.com
SIC: 7336 3229 Commercial art & graphic design; glass furnishings & accessories

(P-13797)
REFINERY AV LLC
14455 Ventura Blvd Fl 3, Sherman Oaks (91423-2687)
PHONE..................................818 843-0004
Adam Waldman, *Mng Member*
EMP: 50 **EST:** 2013
SALES (est): 82.2K **Privately Held**
SIC: 7336 Graphic arts & related design

(P-13798)
RYOT CORP
11995 Bluff Creek Dr, Playa Vista (90094-2929)
PHONE..................................323 356-1787
Bryn Mooser, *CEO*
Ricky Baba, *Creative Dir*
Katie Katz, *Project Mgr*
Tarik Benbrahim, *Producer*
Eric Day, *Producer*
EMP: 100
SALES (est): 1MM **Privately Held**
SIC: 7336 7371 Still film producer; computer software development & applications

(P-13799)
SCREENWORKS LLC
Also Called: Screenworks Nep
1900 Compton Ave Ste 101, Corona (92881-7261)
PHONE..................................951 279-8877
Kevin Rabbitt, *CEO*
Kevin Hoyle, *Vice Pres*
Cheri Navarro, *Administration*
Sam Artinger, *Opers Staff*
Amy Segawa, *Sales Staff*
▲ **EMP:** 74 **EST:** 2012
SALES (est): 488K
SALES (corp-wide): 119.2MM **Privately Held**
SIC: 7336 Graphic arts & related design
HQ: Nep Supershooters, Lp
2 Beta Dr
Pittsburgh PA 15238
412 826-1414

(P-13800)
TECH FLEX PACKAGE
12624 Daphne Ave, Hawthorne (90250-3310)
PHONE..................................323 241-1800
Neil Kinney, *President*
▲ **EMP:** 50
SALES (est): 2MM **Privately Held**
SIC: 7336 Package design

(P-13801)
THE DESIGNORY INC (HQ)
211 E Ocean Blvd Ste 100, Long Beach (90802-4850)
PHONE..................................562 624-0200
Paul Hosea, *CEO*
Matt Radigan, *CFO*
Joel Fuller, *Exec VP*
Carol Fukunaga, *Creative Dir*
Candy Ho, *Creative Dir*
EMP: 115
SALES (est): 12.4MM
SALES (corp-wide): 15.2B **Publicly Held**
WEB: www.designory.com
SIC: 7336 Graphic arts & related design
PA: Omnicom Group Inc.
437 Madison Ave
New York NY 10022
212 415-3600

7338 Secretarial & Court Reporting Svcs

(P-13802)
ATKINSON-BAKER INC (PA)
500 N Brand Blvd Fl 3, Glendale (91203-1945)
P.O. Box 29054 (91209-9054)
PHONE..................................818 551-7300
Alan Atkinson Baker, *CEO*
Adrienne Macdonald, *Vice Pres*
Karyn Polak, *Director*

Dan Clemente, *Manager*
Cynthia Salinas, *Manager*
EMP: 173
SQ FT: 23,000
SALES: 36MM **Privately Held**
WEB: www.atkinsonbaker.com
SIC: 7338 Court reporting service

(P-13803)
HUTCHINGS COURT REPORTERS LLC (PA)
400 N Tustin Ave Ste 301, Santa Ana (92705-3852)
PHONE..................................702 314-7200
Ali Rizvi, *CEO*
Linda Shaw, *Managing Prtnr*
Seth Hertin, *COO*
Madison Seward, *Exec VP*
Ty Clutterbuck, *Principal*
EMP: 50 **EST:** 1953
SQ FT: 6,800
SALES (est): 25.8MM **Privately Held**
WEB: www.hutchings.com
SIC: 7338 Court reporting service

(P-13804)
RETT INC
Also Called: Canedy Court Reporting
402 W Broadway Ste 400, San Diego (92101-3554)
PHONE..................................619 231-0403
Vicki Canedy, *President*
Blake Canedy, *CEO*
EMP: 100
SQ FT: 1,500
SALES: 2MM **Privately Held**
SIC: 7338 Court reporting service

(P-13805)
SOFTSCRIPT INC
2215 Campus Dr, El Segundo (90245-0001)
PHONE..................................310 451-2110
Howard Wisnicki, *CEO*
Carla Rigdon, *Vice Pres*
Alexander Edwards, *Engineer*
Eugene Scala, *Human Res Dir*
Alyson Richards, *Personnel*
EMP: 1200
SALES (est): 49.5MM **Privately Held**
WEB: www.softscript.com
SIC: 7338 Secretarial & typing service

(P-13806)
VERITXT/CLFORNIA REPORTING LLC
20 Corporate Park, Irvine (92606-5139)
PHONE..................................714 432-1711
John Olsen,
Una Elias, *President*
Paul Hilts, *Executive*
EMP: 50
SALES (est): 4.4MM
SALES (corp-wide): 74.3MM **Privately Held**
WEB: www.jilio.com
SIC: 7338 Court reporting service
HQ: Veritext, Llc
290 W Mount Pleasant Ave
Livingston NJ 07039
973 410-4040

7342 Disinfecting & Pest Control Svcs

(P-13807)
A-ABLE INC (PA)
Also Called: Fume-A-Pest & Termite Control
17801 Ventura Blvd, Encino (91316-3616)
PHONE..................................323 658-5779
Michael Herson, *President*
Jack Herson, *Vice Pres*
EMP: 65 **EST:** 1971
SQ FT: 9,026
SALES (est): 4.2MM **Privately Held**
SIC: 7342 1799 Pest control in structures; termite control; steam cleaning of building exteriors

(P-13808)
ABLE EXTERMINATORS INC
68 N Sunset Ave, San Jose (95116-2036)
P.O. Box 5339 (95150-5339)
PHONE..................................408 251-6500

Don Petree, *Vice Pres*
Shawna Petree, *Vice Pres*
Benjamin Harmssen, *Broker*
William Senter, *Real Est Agnt*
EMP: 51
SQ FT: 4,000
SALES (est): 4.3MM **Privately Held**
WEB: www.ablexterm.com
SIC: 7342 Termite control; exterminating & fumigating

(P-13809)
CARTWRIGHT TERMITE & PEST CTRL
51360 Calle Guatemala, La Quinta (92253-2916)
P.O. Box 658 (92247-0658)
PHONE..................................760 771-6091
Fax: 760 771-4881
EMP: 50
SALES (est): 2.6MM **Privately Held**
SIC: 7342

(P-13810)
CATS USA INC
Also Called: Cats U S A Pest Control
5683 Whitnall Hwy, North Hollywood (91601-2213)
P.O. Box 151 (91603-0151)
PHONE..................................818 506-1000
Hirotaka Otomo, *Ch of Bd*
EMP: 100
SQ FT: 3,900
SALES (est): 7MM **Privately Held**
SIC: 7342 Pest control in structures
HQ: Cats, Inc.
15-13, Nampeidaicho
Shibuya-Ku TKY 150-0

(P-13811)
CLARK PEST CTRL STOCKTON INC (HQ)
555 N Guild Ave, Lodi (95240-0809)
P.O. Box 1480 (95241-1480)
PHONE..................................209 368-7152
Gary Rollins, *CEO*
EMP: 70
SQ FT: 2,500
SALES: 108.2MM
SALES (corp-wide): 1.8B **Publicly Held**
SIC: 7342 Exterminating & fumigating; pest control in structures; termite control
PA: Rollins, Inc.
2170 Piedmont Rd Ne
Atlanta GA 30324
404 888-2000

(P-13812)
CLARK PEST CTRL STOCKTON INC
480 E Service Rd, Modesto (95358-9491)
PHONE..................................209 524-6384
Ron Fair, *Manager*
EMP: 60
SALES (corp-wide): 1.8B **Publicly Held**
SIC: 7342 Pest control in structures
HQ: Clark Pest Control Of Stockton, Inc.
555 N Guild Ave
Lodi CA 95240
209 368-7152

(P-13813)
CLARK PEST CTRL STOCKTON INC
5822 Roseville Rd, Sacramento (95842-3071)
PHONE..................................916 925-7000
Steven Adams, *Manager*
EMP: 100
SQ FT: 3,100
SALES (corp-wide): 1.8B **Publicly Held**
SIC: 7342 Exterminating & fumigating; pest control in structures
HQ: Clark Pest Control Of Stockton, Inc.
555 N Guild Ave
Lodi CA 95240
209 368-7152

(P-13814)
CLARK PEST CTRL STOCKTON INC
811 U Banks, Vacaville (95688)
PHONE..................................707 446-9748
Ron Gardner, *Manager*

EMP: 50
SQ FT: 1,300
SALES (corp-wide): 1.8B **Publicly Held**
SIC: 7342 Pest control in structures
HQ: Clark Pest Control Of Stockton, Inc.
555 N Guild Ave
Lodi CA 95240
209 368-7152

(P-13815)
CLARK PEST CTRL STOCKTON INC
4816 Clowes St, Stockton (95210-3506)
P.O. Box 1480, Lodi (95241-1480)
PHONE..................................209 474-3204
Joe Dinubilo, *Manager*
EMP: 50
SALES (corp-wide): 1.8B **Publicly Held**
SIC: 7342 Pest control in structures
HQ: Clark Pest Control Of Stockton, Inc.
555 N Guild Ave
Lodi CA 95240
209 368-7152

(P-13816)
CLARK PEST CTRL STOCKTON INC
2313 Research Dr, Livermore (94550-3824)
PHONE..................................925 449-6203
Dave Erichsen, *Manager*
EMP: 60
SALES (corp-wide): 1.8B **Publicly Held**
SIC: 7342 Pest control in structures
HQ: Clark Pest Control Of Stockton, Inc.
555 N Guild Ave
Lodi CA 95240
209 368-7152

(P-13817)
CLARK PEST CTRL STOCKTON INC
11285 White Rock Rd, Rancho Cordova (95742-6504)
PHONE..................................916 635-7770
Robert Golubski, *Manager*
EMP: 50
SALES (corp-wide): 1.8B **Publicly Held**
SIC: 7342 Pest control in structures
HQ: Clark Pest Control Of Stockton, Inc.
555 N Guild Ave
Lodi CA 95240
209 368-7152

(P-13818)
CLEANRITE INC
5430 Florin Perkins Rd, Sacramento (95826-4835)
PHONE..................................916 381-1321
Eric Martin, *Branch Mgr*
EMP: 71
SALES (corp-wide): 12.5MM **Privately Held**
SIC: 7342 7217 Disinfecting services; carpet & upholstery cleaning
PA: Cleanrite, Inc.
1200 W East Ave
Chico CA 95926
530 891-0333

(P-13819)
CORKYS PEST CONTROL INC
909 Rancheros Dr, San Marcos (92069-3028)
PHONE..................................760 432-8801
Corky Mizer, *President*
▲ **EMP:** 60
SQ FT: 5,000
SALES (est): 6.6MM **Privately Held**
SIC: 7342 0782 2879 5211 Pest control in structures; lawn & garden services; insecticides & pesticides; insulation material, building; landscape services; handyman service

(P-13820)
CRANE ACQUISITION INC
Also Called: Crane Pest Control
2700 Geary Blvd, San Francisco (94118-3406)
PHONE..................................415 922-1666
Harold Stein, *President*
Harry J Cynkus, *Treasurer*
Peter Davidson, *Vice Pres*
Eugene Iarocci, *Admin Sec*

PRODUCTS & SVCS

EMP: 86
SQ FT: 6,000
SALES (est): 7.1MM
SALES (corp-wide): 1.8B **Publicly Held**
WEB: www.cranepestcontrol.com
SIC: 7342 Exterminating & fumigating; pest control services
PA: Rollins, Inc.
2170 Piedmont Rd Ne
Atlanta GA 30324
404 888-2000

(P-13821)
ECOLA SERVICES INC
15314 Devonshire St Ste F, Mission Hills (91345-2773)
PHONE....................818 920-7301
Susan Fries, *President*
Dennis McClure, *Regional Mgr*
Angie Gutierrez, *Cust Mgr*
EMP: 52
SQ FT: 10,000
SALES (est): 4.6MM **Privately Held**
WEB: www.ecolatermite.com
SIC: 7342 Termite control; pest control services

(P-13822)
HOMEGUARD INCORPORATED (PA)
Also Called: Redrocks Fumigation
510 Madera Ave, San Jose (95112-2918)
PHONE....................408 993-1900
James Steffenson Jr, *President*
Jim Hessling, *Treasurer*
Stacy Rife, *Admin Asst*
Casey Clay, *Manager*
Jasmine Ocanas, *Manager*
EMP: 56
SQ FT: 6,000
SALES (est): 12.3MM **Privately Held**
SIC: 7342 Termite control

(P-13823)
LLOYD PEST CONTROL CO
19161 Newhall St, North Palm Springs (92258)
P.O. Box 580490 (92258-0490)
PHONE....................951 232-9687
EMP: 55
SALES (corp-wide): 16.5MM **Privately Held**
SIC: 7342 Pest control in structures
PA: The Lloyd Pest Control Co
935 Sherman St
San Diego CA 92110
619 298-9865

(P-13824)
LLOYD PEST CONTROL CO
566 E Dyer Rd, Santa Ana (92707-3737)
PHONE....................714 979-6021
Mike Magnuson, *Manager*
EMP: 50
SALES (corp-wide): 16.5MM **Privately Held**
SIC: 7342 Pest control in structures; termite control
PA: The Lloyd Pest Control Co
935 Sherman St
San Diego CA 92110
619 298-9865

(P-13825)
MCCLENAHAN PEST CONTROL INC
1 Arastradero Rd, Portola Valley (94028-8012)
PHONE....................650 326-8781
James M Mc Clenahan, *President*
EMP: 50
SALES (est): 1.6MM **Privately Held**
SIC: 7342 Pest control in structures

(P-13826)
OCONNOR PEST CONTROL VISALIA
1728 W Prospect Ave, Visalia (93291-2628)
PHONE....................559 366-4853
EMP: 100
SALES (est): 1MM **Privately Held**
SIC: 7342 Pest control in structures

(P-13827)
ROLLINS INC
5830 E Shields Ave, Fresno (93727-8071)
PHONE....................559 292-8222
EMP: 66
SALES (corp-wide): 1.8B **Publicly Held**
SIC: 7342 Exterminating & fumigating
PA: Rollins, Inc.
2170 Piedmont Rd Ne
Atlanta GA 30324
404 888-2000

(P-13828)
STATEWIDE PEST CONTROL CO INC (PA)
Also Called: Stanley Pest Control
2555 Loma Ave, South El Monte (91733-1417)
PHONE....................626 443-2847
Kevin Harness, *President*
Steven Carrillo, *Office Mgr*
Burdene Peterson, *Admin Sec*
Tim Cadwallader, *Manager*
Brandon Ledford, *Manager*
EMP: 106 **EST:** 1945
SQ FT: 5,000
SALES (est): 14.2MM **Privately Held**
WEB: www.stanleypest.com
SIC: 7342 Pest control in structures

(P-13829)
TERMINIX INTL CO LTD PARTNR
3055 N California St, Burbank (91504-2005)
PHONE....................818 972-2037
Tarvis Braun, *Manager*
EMP: 50
SALES (corp-wide): 1.9B **Publicly Held**
SIC: 7342 Pest control services
HQ: The Terminix International Company Limited Partnership
150 Peabody Pl
Memphis TN 38103
901 766-1400

(P-13830)
TERMINIX INTL CO LTD PARTNR
6678 Owens Dr Ste 100, Pleasanton (94588-3324)
PHONE....................925 460-5063
Robert Castillo, *Sales/Mktg Mgr*
EMP: 70
SALES (corp-wide): 1.9B **Publicly Held**
SIC: 7342 Pest control services
HQ: The Terminix International Company Limited Partnership
150 Peabody Pl
Memphis TN 38103
901 766-1400

(P-13831)
TERMINIX INTL CO LTD PARTNR
649 S Waterman Ave Ste A, San Bernardino (92408-2365)
PHONE....................909 332-2479
Rodney Prince, *Principal*
EMP: 50
SALES (corp-wide): 1.9B **Publicly Held**
SIC: 7342 Pest control services
HQ: The Terminix International Company Limited Partnership
150 Peabody Pl
Memphis TN 38103
901 766-1400

(P-13832)
TERMINIX INTL CO LTD PARTNR
21113 Superior St, Chatsworth (91311-4309)
PHONE....................818 361-1191
Kyle Quinn, *Manager*
Keith Poindexter, *Branch Mgr*
Darren Moen, *Sales Executive*
EMP: 56
SALES (corp-wide): 1.9B **Publicly Held**
SIC: 7342 Pest control services
HQ: The Terminix International Company Limited Partnership
150 Peabody Pl
Memphis TN 38103
901 766-1400

(P-13833)
WESTERN EXTERMINATOR COMPANY
3333 W Temple St, Los Angeles (90026-4523)
PHONE....................310 274-9244
Paul Trammell, *Manager*
Rebecca Barraza, *Administration*
EMP: 85
SQ FT: 10,264
SALES (corp-wide): 3.1B **Privately Held**
WEB: www.west-ext.com
SIC: 7342 Exterminating & fumigating
HQ: Western Exterminator Company
305 N Crescent Way
Anaheim CA 92801
714 517-9000

(P-13834)
WESTERN EXTERMINATOR COMPANY
1985 W Wardlow Rd, Long Beach (90810-2037)
PHONE....................310 835-3513
Sandi Quintana, *Manager*
EMP: 50
SALES (corp-wide): 3.1B **Privately Held**
WEB: www.west-ext.com
SIC: 7342 Pest control in structures
HQ: Western Exterminator Company
305 N Crescent Way
Anaheim CA 92801
714 517-9000

(P-13835)
WESTERN EXTERMINATOR COMPANY
Also Called: Target Specialty Products
15415 Marquardt Ave, Santa Fe Springs (90670-5711)
P.O. Box 3408 (90670-1408)
PHONE....................562 802-2238
Rich Records, *Manager*
Brayden Henrie, *Sales Staff*
EMP: 100
SALES (corp-wide): 3.1B **Privately Held**
WEB: www.west-ext.com
SIC: 7342 Exterminating & fumigating
HQ: Western Exterminator Company
305 N Crescent Way
Anaheim CA 92801
714 517-9000

(P-13836)
YOUR WAY FUMIGATION INC
41880 Kalmia St Ste 170, Murrieta (92562-8838)
PHONE....................951 699-9116
Jose Manuel Aguilar, *President*
EMP: 90
SALES (est): 8.4MM **Privately Held**
SIC: 7342 Exterminating & fumigating

7349 Building Cleaning & Maintenance Svcs, NEC

(P-13837)
A1 BUILDING MANAGEMENT INC
2461 E Orangethorpe Ave # 200, Fullerton (92831-5302)
PHONE....................714 447-3800
Trent Pollack, *President*
EMP: 125
SALES (est): 1.8MM **Privately Held**
SIC: 7349 Building maintenance services

(P-13838)
ABM ELCTRCAL LTG SOLUTIONS INC
6940 Koll Center Pkwy # 100, Pleasanton (94566-3100)
PHONE....................408 399-3030
EMP: 65
SALES (corp-wide): 6.4B **Publicly Held**
SIC: 7349 Lighting maintenance service
HQ: Abm Electrical & Lighting Solutions, Inc.
14201 Franklin Ave
Tustin CA 92780
866 226-2838

(P-13839)
ABM ELCTRCAL LTG SOLUTIONS INC (DH)
14201 Franklin Ave, Tustin (92780-7008)
PHONE....................866 226-2838
Henrick C Slipsager, *CEO*
James S Lusk, *Exec VP*
Tracy K Price, *Exec VP*
Jennifer Atkins, *Executive*
Scott Tapia, *Sales Staff*
EMP: 100
SQ FT: 4,803
SALES (est): 515.9K
SALES (corp-wide): 6.4B **Publicly Held**
WEB: www.sundownlighting.com
SIC: 7349 Lighting maintenance service
HQ: Abm Facility Solutions Group, Llc
1201 Louisiana St
Houston TX 77002
832 214-5500

(P-13840)
ABM FACILITY SERVICES INC (DH)
Also Called: ABM Engineering
1266 14th St Ste 103, Oakland (94607-2247)
PHONE....................510 251-0381
Mike Latham, *CEO*
J E Benton III, *President*
Cornel Sneekes, *Exec VP*
George Sundby, *Senior VP*
George Toole, *Engineer*
EMP: 100
SALES (est): 57.7MM
SALES (corp-wide): 6.4B **Publicly Held**
SIC: 7349 Janitorial service, contract basis

(P-13841)
ABM INDUSTRIES INCORPORATED
5300 S Eastrn Ave Ste 110, Los Angeles (90040)
PHONE....................323 720-4020
Anthony Bernard, *Executive*
Clint Dart, *General Mgr*
Paula Davis, *VP Human Res*
EMP: 50
SALES (corp-wide): 6.4B **Publicly Held**
SIC: 7349 Janitorial service, contract basis
PA: Abm Industries Incorporated
1 Liberty Plz Fl 7
New York NY 10006
212 297-0200

(P-13842)
ABM JANITORIAL SERVICES INC
1335 N Plaza Dr Ste C, Visalia (93291-8838)
PHONE....................559 651-1612
Tony Bautista, *Branch Mgr*
EMP: 90
SALES (corp-wide): 6.4B **Publicly Held**
SIC: 7349 Janitorial service, contract basis
HQ: Abm Janitorial Services, Inc.
1111 Fannin St Ste 1500
Houston TX 77002
866 624-1520

(P-13843)
ABM JANITORIAL SERVICES INC
6671 Owens Dr, Pleasanton (94588-3335)
PHONE....................925 924-0270
Greg Bu Puis, *Manager*
EMP: 267
SALES (corp-wide): 6.4B **Publicly Held**
SIC: 7349 Janitorial service, contract basis
HQ: Abm Janitorial Services, Inc.
1111 Fannin St Ste 1500
Houston TX 77002
866 624-1520

(P-13844)
ABM JANITORIAL SERVICES INC
830 Riverside Pkwy Ste 40, West Sacramento (95605-1505)
PHONE....................916 374-1739
Sean Petone, *Manager*
Alfredo Perez, *Opers Mgr*
EMP: 320

SALES (corp-wide): 6.4B **Publicly Held**
SIC: **7349** Janitorial service, contract basis
HQ: Abm Janitorial Services, Inc.
   1111 Fannin St Ste 1500
   Houston TX 77002
   866 624-1520

(P-13845)
ABM JANITORIAL SERVICES INC
11955 Jack Benny Dr # 104, Rancho Cuca-
monga (91739-9230)
PHONE..................................909 987-3700
WEB: www.advancemaintenance.com
Linda Mason, *District Mgr*
EMP: 105
SALES (corp-wide): 6.4B **Publicly Held**
SIC: **7349** Janitorial service, contract basis
HQ: Abm Janitorial Services, Inc.
   1111 Fannin St Ste 1500
   Houston TX 77002
   866 624-1520

(P-13846)
ABM JANITORIAL SERVICES INC
2385 Arch Airport Rd # 100, Stockton
(95206-4403)
PHONE..................................209 983-3923
Tony McGrat, *Manager*
EMP: 105
SALES (corp-wide): 6.4B **Publicly Held**
SIC: **7349** Janitorial service, contract basis
HQ: Abm Janitorial Services, Inc.
   1111 Fannin St Ste 1500
   Houston TX 77002
   866 624-1520

(P-13847)
ACCELERATED ENVMTL SVCS INC
23601 Taft Hwy, Bakersfield (93311)
P.O. Box 398, Taft (93268-0398)
PHONE..................................661 765-4003
John E Neumann, *President*
EMP: 100
SQ FT: 25,440
SALES (est): 4.2MM **Privately Held**
SIC: **7349** Cleaning service, industrial or
commercial

(P-13848)
ACCENT SERVICE COMPANY INC
2001 Lemnos Dr, Costa Mesa
(92626-3535)
P.O. Box 9495, Newport Beach (92658-
9495)
PHONE..................................877 611-0131
Dan Yasui, *President*
EMP: 99
SQ FT: 200
SALES: 6MM **Privately Held**
WEB: www.accentsc.com
SIC: **7349** Building maintenance services

(P-13849)
ACME BUILDING MAINTENANCE CO (DH)
941 Catherine St, Alviso (95002)
PHONE..................................408 263-5911
Richard Sanchez, *President*
Henry Sanchez, *Ch of Bd*
Solomon Wong, *Treasurer*
EMP: 80
SQ FT: 8,000
SALES (est): 25.1MM
SALES (corp-wide): 6.4B **Publicly Held**
SIC: **7349** Janitorial service, contract
basis; building component cleaning serv-
ice
HQ: Gca Services Group, Inc.
   1350 Euclid Ave Ste 1500
   Cleveland OH 44115
   800 422-8760

(P-13850)
ADHEI ENTERPRISES INC
Also Called: Knudtson Building Maint Svc
4627 Lemona Ave, Sherman Oaks
(91403-2428)
PHONE..................................818 788-7680
Jacqueline Campbell, *President*
Dayna Campbell, *Sales Staff*
EMP: 50 EST: 1962

SALES (est): 1.2MM **Privately Held**
SIC: **7349** Janitorial service, contract basis

(P-13851)
ADVANCE BUILDING MAINTENANCE
9601 Wilshire Blvd Gl25, Beverly Hills
(90210-5217)
PHONE..................................310 247-0077
Forrest I Nolin, *President*
EMP: 500
SALES (est): 9.8MM **Privately Held**
WEB: www.advancemaintenance.com
SIC: **7349** Janitorial service, contract basis

(P-13852)
ADVANCED CLNROOM MCRCLEAN CORP
Also Called: A C M
3250 S Susan St Ste A, Santa Ana
(92704-6807)
PHONE..................................714 751-1152
Janet Ford, *CEO*
David Agostine, *COO*
Brian Enright, *General Mgr*
Norma Lopez, *Accountant*
Daniel Brandt, *Manager*
▲ EMP: 200
SQ FT: 3,500
SALES (est): 8.8MM **Privately Held**
WEB: www.advcleanroom.com
SIC: **7349** **8734** Cleaning service, indus-
trial or commercial; testing laboratories

(P-13853)
AESTHETIC MAINTENANCE CORP
Also Called: AMC
1625 Palo Alto St Ste 301, Los Angeles
(90026)
PHONE..................................213 353-1525
Curtiss Pierose. *President*
EMP: 50
SQ FT: 1,000
SALES (est): 1.9MM **Privately Held**
SIC: **7349** Janitorial service, contract basis

(P-13854)
ALL CARE INDUSTRIES INC
16747 1/2 Parkside Ave, Cerritos
(90703-1840)
PHONE..................................562 623-4009
Christopher Kim, *President*
Charles Lee, *Vice Pres*
EMP: 100
SALES: 1.7MM **Privately Held**
SIC: **7349** Janitorial service, contract basis

(P-13855)
ALL CONTROL CLEANING INC
124 N Aviador St Ste 1, Camarillo
(93010-8321)
P.O. Box 341, Newbury Park (91319-0341)
PHONE..................................805 987-4210
Lee Parrilla, *President*
Syeda Parrilla, *Admin Sec*
EMP: 52
SQ FT: 5,000
SALES (est): 1.5MM **Privately Held**
SIC: **7349** Building maintenance services

(P-13856)
ALLSTAR COMMERCIAL CLEANING
8583 Aero Dr Apt 1039, San Diego
(92123-1719)
PHONE..................................858 715-0500
Michael Paul McCarthy, *CEO*
Adam Bolio, *Co-Owner*
EMP: 50
SALES (est): 1MM **Privately Held**
SIC: **7349** Janitorial service, contract basis

(P-13857)
AMERI-KLEEN
Also Called: Ameri-Kleen Building Services
313 W Beach St, Watsonville (95076-4508)
P.O. Box 2167 (95077-2167)
PHONE..................................831 722-8888
Marisol Tavera, *Branch Mgr*
EMP: 450 **Privately Held**
SIC: **7349** Building maintenance services

PA: Ameri-Kleen
   119 W Beach St
   Watsonville CA 95076

(P-13858)
AMERI-KLEEN
Also Called: Ameri-Kleen Building Services
1023 E Grand Ave, Arroyo Grande
(93420-2504)
PHONE..................................805 546-0706
Dan Erpenbach, *Branch Mgr*
EMP: 250 **Privately Held**
SIC: **7349** Janitorial service, contract basis
PA: Ameri-Kleen
   119 W Beach St
   Watsonville CA 95076

(P-13859)
AMERICAN BLDG MAINT CO OF ILL
44870 Osgood Rd, Fremont (94539-6101)
PHONE..................................510 573-1618
EMP: 50
SALES (corp-wide): 6.4B **Publicly Held**
SIC: **7349** Building maintenance services
HQ: American Building Maintenance Co Of
   Illinois, Inc
   420 Taylor St 200
   San Francisco CA 94102
   415 351-4386

(P-13860)
AMERICAN BLDG MAINT CO-WEST (HQ)
75 Broadway Ste 111, San Francisco
(94111-1423)
PHONE..................................415 733-4000
Henrik Slipsager, *President*
Douglas Bowlus, *Treasurer*
Harry H Kahn, *Admin Sec*
EMP: 150
SALES (est): 27.6MM
SALES (corp-wide): 6.4B **Publicly Held**
SIC: **7349** Janitorial service, contract basis
PA: Abm Industries Incorporated
   1 Liberty Plz Fl 7
   New York NY 10006
   212 297-0200

(P-13861)
AMERICAN BUILDING MAINT CO NY
101 California St, San Francisco
(94111-5802)
PHONE..................................415 733-4000
Henrik Slipsager, *President*
Douglas Bowlus, *Treasurer*
Scott Salmirs, *Exec VP*
EMP: 4530
SALES (est): 31.7MM
SALES (corp-wide): 6.4B **Publicly Held**
SIC: **7349** Janitorial service, contract basis
PA: Abm Industries Incorporated
   1 Liberty Plz Fl 7
   New York NY 10006
   212 297-0200

(P-13862)
AMERICAN BUILDING SERVICE INC
4578 Crow Canyon Pl, Castro Valley
(94552-4804)
P.O. Box 32, San Leandro (94577-0003)
PHONE..................................510 483-5120
Rui Donaldo Teixeira Canha, *President*
EMP: 100
SALES (est): 3.2MM **Privately Held**
SIC: **7349** Janitorial service, contract basis

(P-13863)
AMERICAN SERVICES AND PRODUCTS
Also Called: American Janitor Services
949 Camino Dos Rios, Thousand Oaks
(91360-2360)
PHONE..................................805 375-2858
Dorothy Clemen, *President*
Mel Clemen, *Vice Pres*
Ron Clemen, *Admin Sec*
EMP: 60
SQ FT: 800

SALES: 1.2MM **Privately Held**
WEB: www.greenstoyotadirect.com
SIC: **7349** Janitorial service, contract basis

(P-13864)
ANDOVER MAINTENANCE INC
Also Called: Specialty Services
45 La Porte St, Arcadia (91006-2826)
PHONE..................................626 254-1651
Daniel Tellez, *President*
Peter Richards, *Vice Pres*
Bob Daly, *Opers Mgr*
EMP: 73
SQ FT: 3,500
SALES (est): 3MM **Privately Held**
SIC: **7349** Janitorial service, contract basis

(P-13865)
AQUACLEAN JANITORIAL
9403 Compass Point Dr S, San Diego
(92126-5536)
P.O. Box 722557 (92172-2557)
PHONE..................................858 537-9090
Amir B Chaudri, *President*
EMP: 65
SALES (est): 947.8K **Privately Held**
SIC: **7349** Janitorial service, contract basis

(P-13866)
ARAMARK FACILITY SERVICES LLC
941 W 35th St, Los Angeles (90007)
PHONE..................................213 740-8968
Ron Cote, *Manager*
EMP: 200 **Publicly Held**
SIC: **7349** Janitorial service, contract basis
HQ: Aramark Facility Services, Llc
   2400 Market St 209
   Philadelphia PA 19103
   215 238-3000

(P-13867)
ARAMARK FACILITY SERVICES LLC
5301 Bolsa Ave Bldg 10, Huntington Beach
(92647-2048)
PHONE..................................714 372-0683
Christopher Olsen-Bates, *Manager*
EMP: 50 **Publicly Held**
SIC: **7349** Janitorial service, contract
basis; building maintenance, except repairs
HQ: Aramark Facility Services, Llc
   2400 Market St 209
   Philadelphia PA 19103
   215 238-3000

(P-13868)
AVALON BUILDING MAINTENANCE (PA)
3148 E La Palma Ave Ste A, Anaheim
(92806-2805)
PHONE..................................714 693-2407
Steve J Healis, *CEO*
Tom Poston, *CFO*
Tom Devlin, *Admin Sec*
EMP: 220
SQ FT: 5,000
SALES (est): 8.5MM **Privately Held**
WEB: www.avaloncorona.com
SIC: **7349** Building maintenance services

(P-13869)
BERGENSONS PROPERTY SVCS INC
Also Called: Solve All Facility Services
3605 Ocean Ranch Blvd # 200, Oceanside
(92056-2695)
PHONE..................................760 631-5111
Mark M Minasian, *CEO*
Kris McDevitt, *President*
Aram Minasian, *President*
James Henley, *Exec VP*
Graham Powers, *Vice Pres*
EMP: 2000
SQ FT: 2,000
SALES (est): 52.1MM **Privately Held**
WEB: www.bergensons.com
SIC: **7349** Building maintenance, except
repairs; janitorial service, contract basis

(P-13870)
BILLING SERVICES PLUS DBA APEX
70 Dorman Ave, San Francisco (94124-1809)
PHONE...................415 604-3515
Gina Gregori, *Principal*
EMP: 99
SQ FT: 300
SALES (est): 470.9K **Privately Held**
SIC: 7349 Building & office cleaning services; building cleaning service

(P-13871)
BISSELL BROTHERS JANITORIAL
Also Called: Bissell Bros Bldg Maint Servic
3207 Luyung Dr, Rancho Cordova (95742-6862)
PHONE...................916 635-1852
David Bissell, *CEO*
EMP: 80
SQ FT: 2,400
SALES (est): 2.3MM **Privately Held**
WEB: www.cleaningcrew.com
SIC: 7349 Janitorial service, contract basis

(P-13872)
BRITEWORKS INC
620 N Commercial Ave, Covina (91723-1309)
PHONE...................626 337-0099
Anita Ron, *President*
Gracie Corona, *Office Mgr*
EMP: 75
SQ FT: 4,800
SALES (est): 2.8MM **Privately Held**
WEB: www.briteworks.com
SIC: 7349 Janitorial service, contract basis

(P-13873)
C E B M INC
3100 E Cedar St Ste 17, Ontario (91761-7695)
PHONE...................909 975-4440
William Dazalla, *President*
Robert Dazalla, *Vice Pres*
EMP: 50
SQ FT: 2,000
SALES (est): 1.2MM **Privately Held**
WEB: www.cebm.net
SIC: 7349 Janitorial service, contract basis

(P-13874)
CALDERON BUILDING MAINTENANCE
3822 Sherman St, San Diego (92110-4322)
P.O. Box 3550 (92163-1550)
PHONE...................619 269-5940
Andres J Calderon, *President*
Maria Calderon, *Admin Sec*
EMP: 90
SALES (est): 2.2MM **Privately Held**
WEB: www.calderoninc.com
SIC: 7349 Janitorial service, contract basis

(P-13875)
CALICO BUILDING SERVICES INC
15550 Rockfield Blvd C, Irvine (92618-2791)
PHONE...................949 380-8707
Ron Strand, *President*
Orlando Fernandez, *Vice Pres*
Christopher Guidry, *Vice Pres*
Thomas Miquelon, *Vice Pres*
Marisa Personius, *Executive Asst*
EMP: 185
SQ FT: 1,700
SALES (est): 9MM **Privately Held**
WEB: www.calicoweb.com
SIC: 7349 Janitorial service, contract basis

(P-13876)
CARRASCO HELEO
Also Called: Building Cleaning Systems
2510 N Grand Ave Ste 102, Santa Ana (92705-8753)
PHONE...................714 639-1759
Heleo Carrasco, *President*
EMP: 130
SALES (est): 4.5MM **Privately Held**
WEB: www.buildingcleaningsystems.com
SIC: 7349 Janitorial service, contract basis

(P-13877)
CITY OF LOS ANGELES
Also Called: General Services
3330 W 36th St, Los Angeles (90018-3610)
PHONE...................213 847-2799
Melody McCormick, *Branch Mgr*
EMP: 60 **Privately Held**
WEB: www.lacity.org
SIC: 7349 9611 Building maintenance services; administration of general economic programs;
PA: City Of Los Angeles
200 N Spring St Ste 303
Los Angeles CA 90012
213 978-0600

(P-13878)
CITY OF PALMDALE
Also Called: Public Works Dept
39101 3rd St E, Palmdale (93550-3209)
PHONE...................661 267-5338
Gene Trevail, *Superintendent*
Michael Gass, *Manager*
EMP: 135 **Privately Held**
SIC: 7349 9111 Building maintenance services; mayors' offices
PA: City Of Palmdale
38300 Sierra Hwy
Palmdale CA 93550
661 267-5115

(P-13879)
CITY OF PASADENA
Also Called: Mayor Office
117 E Colorado Blvd, Pasadena (91105-1938)
PHONE...................626 744-4311
Bill Bogaard, *Mayor*
EMP: 70 **Privately Held**
WEB: www.cityofpasadena.net
SIC: 7349 9111 Building maintenance services; mayors' offices
PA: City Of Pasadena
100 N Garfield Ave
Pasadena CA 91101
626 744-4386

(P-13880)
CITY OF SALINAS
426 Work St, Salinas (93901-4308)
PHONE...................831 758-7233
Denise Estrada, *Director*
EMP: 89 **Privately Held**
WEB: www.co.monterey.ca.us
SIC: 7349 9224 Building maintenance services; fire department, not including volunteer
PA: City Of Salinas
200 Lincoln Ave
Salinas CA 93901
831 758-7489

(P-13881)
CITY OF SAN MATEO
Also Called: Corporate Yard
1949 Pacific Blvd, San Mateo (94403-1430)
PHONE...................650 522-7300
Vernon Ficklind, *Manager*
EMP: 60 **Privately Held**
WEB: www.cityarts-sm.org
SIC: 7349 9111 Building maintenance services; mayors' offices
PA: City Of San Mateo
330 W 20th Ave
San Mateo CA 94403
650 522-7000

(P-13882)
CJ MODEL HOME MAINTENANCE INC
240 Spring St, Pleasanton (94566-6626)
P.O. Box 5547 (94566-1547)
PHONE...................925 485-3280
Carrie Wevill, *President*
Richard Wevill, *Admin Sec*
EMP: 70
SQ FT: 2,200
SALES (est): 4.5MM **Privately Held**
WEB: www.cjsmodelhome.com
SIC: 7349 Building component cleaning service

(P-13883)
CLEAN-A-RAMA MAINT SVC LLC
526 Columbus Ave Fl 2, San Francisco (94133-2802)
PHONE...................415 495-5298
Giuseppe Marchini,
Marcello Sebastiani,
EMP: 60
SQ FT: 800
SALES (est): 1.3MM **Privately Held**
SIC: 7349 Janitorial service, contract basis

(P-13884)
COAST TO COAST WATER DAMAGE
Also Called: Coast To Coast Restoration
10881 La Tuna Canyon Rd, Sun Valley (91352-2010)
PHONE...................818 255-3323
Hayko Aldzhikyan, *President*
Marina Demirchyan, *Vice Pres*
EMP: 50
SQ FT: 9,000
SALES (est): 1.4MM **Privately Held**
WEB: www.c2crestoration.com
SIC: 7349 Building maintenance services

(P-13885)
COASTAL BUILDING SERVICES INC
718 N Hariton St, Orange (92868-1314)
PHONE...................714 775-2855
Hipolito G Arias, *CEO*
Brett Dunstan, *CFO*
Marina Pohl, *Office Mgr*
Lupe Godinez, *Admin Sec*
Dalila Baltazar, *Administration*
EMP: 300
SQ FT: 5,300
SALES (est): 8.9MM **Privately Held**
WEB: www.coastalbuildingservice.com
SIC: 7349 Janitorial service, contract basis

(P-13886)
COBB WATERBLASTING INC
Also Called: Cobb Property Services
1145 W Shelley Ct, Orange (92868-1200)
PHONE...................714 769-2622
Mark Cobb, *President*
Dorothy Cobb, *Vice Pres*
William Roche, *Admin Sec*
EMP: 82 EST: 1989
SALES (est): 2.5MM **Privately Held**
SIC: 7349 Building cleaning service

(P-13887)
COME LAND MAINT SVC CO INC
1419 N San Fernando Blvd # 250, Burbank (91504-4185)
PHONE...................818 567-2455
Grace H Lee, *President*
William Lee, *Admin Sec*
EMP: 513
SQ FT: 12,750
SALES (est): 8.7MM
SALES (corp-wide): 4MM **Privately Held**
SIC: 7349 Janitorial service, contract basis
PA: Come Land, Inc.
1419 N San Fernando Blvd # 250
Burbank CA 91504
818 567-2455

(P-13888)
COMMON AREA MAINT SVCS INC (PA)
Also Called: CAM Services
5664 Selmaraine Dr, Culver City (90230-6120)
PHONE...................310 390-3552
Jim Swindle, *CEO*
David A Herrera, *President*
Sidney Young, *Principal*
Brooke Cowdrey, *Accounts Exec*
EMP: 87
SQ FT: 4,000
SALES (est): 13.4MM **Privately Held**
WEB: www.camservices.com
SIC: 7349 Building maintenance, except repairs

(P-13889)
CONSOLIDATED CLEANING SERVICES
6353 Westover Dr, Oakland (94611-1603)
PHONE...................510 663-2585
Joanne King, *President*
Michael Herling, *COO*
EMP: 100
SQ FT: 7,500
SALES (est): 3.4MM **Privately Held**
SIC: 7349 Building maintenance, except repairs; janitorial service, contract basis

(P-13890)
CONTRACT SERVICES GROUP INC
Also Called: Celex Solutions
480 Capricorn St, Brea (92821-3203)
P.O. Box 8815 (92822-5815)
PHONE...................714 582-1800
John Pearce, *CEO*
Casey Pearce, *President*
EMP: 250
SALES (est): 9.6MM **Privately Held**
SIC: 7349 Janitorial service, contract basis

(P-13891)
CONTRLLED CNTMINATION SVCS LLC
Also Called: Controlled Contamination Svcs
11696 Sorrento Valley Rd # 200, San Diego (92121-1043)
PHONE...................888 263-9886
Christopher Zines, *Mng Member*
Kelly Lacey, *Area Mgr*
Dan Sexton, *Business Mgr*
Erica Sheely, *Hum Res Coord*
Sharon Vizcaya, *HR Admin*
EMP: 140
SALES (est): 8.8MM **Privately Held**
SIC: 7349 Cleaning service, industrial or commercial

(P-13892)
CONTROLLED CONTAMINATION SVCS
Also Called: CCS
23595 Cabot Blvd Ste 115, Hayward (94545-1681)
PHONE...................510 728-1106
Brian Thaler, *Manager*
Hector Famania, *Opers Mgr*
EMP: 66
SALES (est): 1.9MM **Privately Held**
SIC: 7349 Cleaning service, industrial or commercial

(P-13893)
CORPORATE BUILDING SVCS INC
3325 Wilshire Blvd # 1240, Los Angeles (90010-1728)
PHONE...................213 252-0999
Bruce Kim, *President*
Cindy Kim, *Admin Sec*
EMP: 200
SQ FT: 2,000
SALES: 3.5MM **Privately Held**
SIC: 7349 Janitorial service, contract basis

(P-13894)
CORPORATION SERVICE COMPANY
Also Called: Prentice Hall Legal Fincl Svcs
2710 Gateway Oaks Dr, Sacramento (95833-3505)
PHONE...................302 636-5400
EMP: 100
SQ FT: 12,000
SALES (corp-wide): 394.6MM **Privately Held**
WEB: www.incspot.com
SIC: 7349 Building maintenance services
PA: Corporation Service Company Inc
251 Little Falls Dr
Wilmington DE 19808
302 636-5400

(P-13895)
COSTLESS MAINTENANCE SVCS CO
Also Called: Cmsc
3254 19th St, San Francisco (94110-1917)
PHONE...................415 550-8819
Marlene Samson, *President*
Norma Edar, *CFO*
Guillermo Guzman, *Vice Pres*
EMP: 55
SALES: 1.8MM **Privately Held**
SIC: 7349 Janitorial service, contract basis

(P-13896)
COUNTY OF CONTRA COSTA
Also Called: General Services
2099 Arnold Industrial Wa, Concord
(94520-5321)
PHONE..................................925 646-5877
Jerry Redic, *Manager*
EMP: 100 Privately Held
SIC: 7349 9199 Building maintenance services; general government administration;
PA: County Of Contra Costa
625 Court St Ste 100
Martinez CA 94553
925 957-5280

(P-13897)
COUNTY OF EL DORADO
El Dorado Cnty Bldg & Grounds
3000 Fairlane Ct Ste 2, Placerville
(95667-4100)
PHONE..................................530 621-5845
Bruce Pease, *Manager*
EMP: 76 Privately Held
WEB: www.filmtahoe.com
SIC: 7349 9111 Building maintenance services; executive offices
PA: County Of El Dorado
330 Fair Ln
Placerville CA 95667
530 621-5830

(P-13898)
COUNTY OF SACRAMENTO
Also Called: Airfield Maintenance
7207 Earhart Dr, Sacramento (95837-1104)
PHONE..................................916 874-0746
Terry Sutton, *Branch Mgr*
EMP: 80 Privately Held
WEB: www.sna.com
SIC: 7349 9311 Building maintenance services;
PA: County Of Sacramento
700 H St Ste 7650
Sacramento CA 95814
916 874-5544

(P-13899)
CREATIVE MAINTENANCE SYSTEMS
1340 Reynolds Ave Ste 111, Irvine
(92614-5503)
PHONE..................................949 852-2871
Bill Koop, *President*
Christina Alexander, *Vice Pres*
EMP: 100
SQ FT: 2,000
SALES (est): 2.3MM Privately Held
SIC: 7349 Building cleaning service

(P-13900)
CROSSROADS FACILITY SVCS INC
9300 Tech Center Dr # 100, Sacramento
(95826-2565)
PHONE..................................916 568-5230
David Deleonardis, *President*
Bill Walters, *Corp Secy*
EMP: 57
SQ FT: 5,700
SALES (est): 1MM Privately Held
SIC: 7349 1752 0781 Janitorial service, contract basis; wood floor installation & refinishing; landscape services

(P-13901)
CROWN BUILDING MAINTENANCE CO
1832 Tribute Rd Ste H, Sacramento
(95815-4309)
PHONE..................................916 920-9556
Jeff Marquis, *Principal*
EMP: 1110
SALES (corp-wide): 300.6MM Privately Held
SIC: 7349 1623 Janitorial service, contract basis; water, sewer & utility lines
PA: Crown Building Maintenance Co.
868 Folsom St
San Francisco CA 94107
415 981-8070

(P-13902)
CROWN BUILDING MAINTENANCE CO
Also Called: Able Building Maintenance
3300 W Macarthur Blvd, Santa Ana
(92704-6804)
PHONE..................................714 434-9494
Robert Hughes, *CEO*
EMP: 50
SALES (corp-wide): 300.6MM Privately Held
SIC: 7349 Janitorial service, contract basis
PA: Crown Building Maintenance Co.
868 Folsom St
San Francisco CA 94107
415 981-8070

(P-13903)
CROWN BUILDING MAINTENANCE CO
235 Pine St Ste 600, San Francisco
(94104-2745)
PHONE..................................303 680-3713
Dan Jaster, *Branch Mgr*
EMP: 493
SALES (corp-wide): 300.6MM Privately Held
SIC: 7349 8711 Janitorial service, contract basis; engineering services
PA: Crown Building Maintenance Co.
868 Folsom St
San Francisco CA 94107
415 981-8070

(P-13904)
CROWN BUILDING MAINTENANCE CO
5482 Complex St Ste 108, San Diego
(92123-1125)
PHONE..................................858 560-5785
Dan Jaster, *Branch Mgr*
EMP: 247
SALES (corp-wide): 300.6MM Privately Held
SIC: 7349 8711 Janitorial service, contract basis; engineering services
PA: Crown Building Maintenance Co.
868 Folsom St
San Francisco CA 94107
415 981-8070

(P-13905)
CROWN BUILDING MAINTENANCE CO
Also Called: Able Building Maintenance
2601 S Figueroa St # 299, Los Angeles
(90007-3254)
PHONE..................................213 765-7800
Brian Pagac, *Principal*
EMP: 50
SALES (corp-wide): 300.6MM Privately Held
WEB: www.ableserve.com
SIC: 7349 8711 Janitorial service, contract basis; engineering services
PA: Crown Building Maintenance Co.
868 Folsom St
San Francisco CA 94107
415 981-8070

(P-13906)
CROWN ENERGY SERVICES INC
Also Called: Able Engineering Services
2601 S Figueroa St Fl 1, Los Angeles
(90007-3254)
PHONE..................................213 765-7800
Ed Figueroa, *Manager*
EMP: 800 Privately Held
SIC: 7349 Janitorial service, contract basis
PA: Crown Energy Services, Inc.
868 Folsom St
San Francisco CA 94107

(P-13907)
CROWN FACILITY SOLUTIONS
3617 W Macarthur Blvd, Santa Ana
(92704-6847)
PHONE..................................657 266-0821
Brent Shears, *President*
EMP: 50
SQ FT: 1,950

SALES: 1.2MM **Privately Held**
SIC: 7349 Building maintenance, except repairs; janitorial service, contract basis

(P-13908)
CULVER-MELIN ENTERPRISES
Also Called: ServiceMaster
2150 Wardrobe Ave, Merced (95341-6400)
P.O. Box 2192 (95344-0192)
PHONE..................................209 726-9182
David Melin, *President*
EMP: 70
SALES (est): 2.7MM Privately Held
SIC: 7349 Building maintenance services

(P-13909)
CUSHMAN & WAKEFIELD INC
800 W El Camino Real, Mountain View
(94040-2567)
PHONE..................................408 664-5403
EMP: 131
SALES (corp-wide): 8.2B Privately Held
SIC: 7349 Janitorial service, contract basis
HQ: Cushman & Wakefield, Inc.
225 W Wacker Dr Ste 3000
Chicago IL 60606
312 424-8000

(P-13910)
D S P SERVICE INC
Also Called: D S P Janitorial Service
23762 Foley St Ste 3, Hayward
(94545-1662)
PHONE..................................510 782-2200
Don Wallace, *President*
Dawn Wallace, *Corp Secy*
Gloria Wallace, *Vice Pres*
EMP: 50
SQ FT: 2,000
SALES: 1MM Privately Held
WEB: www.dspjanitorial.com
SIC: 7349 Janitorial service, contract basis

(P-13911)
DAN LOFGREN
Also Called: Central Cleaning Co
7707 Forsythia Ct, Pleasanton
(94588-4818)
PHONE..................................925 846-6632
Dan Lofgren, *Owner*
EMP: 60
SALES: 1.5MM Privately Held
SIC: 7349 Building maintenance services

(P-13912)
DANLIL ENTERPRISE INC
Also Called: Sterling Building Services
1440 S State College Blvd, Anaheim
(92806-5724)
PHONE..................................714 776-7705
Dan Rubio, *President*
EMP: 75
SQ FT: 2,000
SALES: 2.5MM Privately Held
WEB: www.jabezbs.com
SIC: 7349 Janitorial service, contract basis

(P-13913)
DAVE CALHOUN AND ASSOC LLC
2575 Stanwell Dr Ste 100, Concord
(94520-4838)
PHONE..................................925 688-1234
Sam Martinovich, *CEO*
Dave Calhoun, *President*
Salvador Gurule, *Vice Pres*
Missy Calhoun, *Administration*
Eric Brown, *Accounts Mgr*
EMP: 195
SALES (est): 8.6MM Privately Held
WEB: www.bsminc.com
SIC: 7349 Building cleaning service

(P-13914)
DMS FACILITY SERVICES INC
Also Called: D M S
3137 Skyway Ct, Fremont (94539-5910)
PHONE..................................510 656-9400
Loren Dotts, *Manager*
EMP: 800
SALES (corp-wide): 60.6MM Privately Held
WEB: www.dms-services.com
SIC: 7349 0782 Building maintenance, except repairs; lawn & garden services

PA: Dms - Facility Services, Inc.
1040 Arroyo Dr
South Pasadena CA 91030
626 305-8500

(P-13915)
DYNAMIC MAINTENANCE SVCS INC
837 Arnold Dr Ste 220, Martinez
(94553-6534)
PHONE..................................925 228-7434
Arturo Ramos, *President*
Susan K Moore, *CFO*
Violet Ramos, *Corp Secy*
Maria L Ramos, *Vice Pres*
Pablo Juarez, *General Mgr*
EMP: 52 EST: 2006
SQ FT: 536
SALES: 1.8MM Privately Held
SIC: 7349 Janitorial service, contract basis

(P-13916)
EBM JANITORIAL SERVICES INC
Also Called: Excellent Building Maintenance
5260 Bonsai Ave Ste E, Moorpark
(93021-1768)
P.O. Box 204, Newbury Park (91319-0204)
PHONE..................................805 523-3700
Matt Mullen, *President*
EMP: 70
SALES (est): 1.3MM Privately Held
SIC: 7349 Janitorial service, contract basis

(P-13917)
ELITE CRAFTSMAN (PA)
Also Called: Stockmar Industrial
2763 Saint Louis Ave, Long Beach
(90755-2025)
P.O. Box 90458 (90809-0458)
PHONE..................................562 989-3511
William C Stockmar, *President*
George N Negrete, *Vice Pres*
Linda Pierson, *Admin Sec*
Linda S Pierson, *Admin Sec*
EMP: 130 EST: 1972
SQ FT: 10,000
SALES (est): 8.7MM Privately Held
SIC: 7349 Building maintenance services

(P-13918)
ELITE MAINTENANCE SERVICES INC
7770 Regents Rd Ste 113, San Diego
(92122-1967)
PHONE..................................619 516-7000
Heidi Anderson, *President*
EMP: 55
SALES (est): 1MM Privately Held
SIC: 7349 Building cleaning service

(P-13919)
EMPIRE BUILDING SERVICES INC
1570 E Edinger Ave Ste D, Santa Ana
(92705-4909)
P.O. Box 26, Tustin (92781-0026)
PHONE..................................714 836-7700
Suzanne De Rossett, *President*
Rebecca Ewald, *Executive*
Lily Martinez, *Admin Asst*
Rebecca Johnson, *Representative*
Mario Guevara, *Supervisor*
EMP: 80
SALES (est): 3.7MM Privately Held
SIC: 7349 Building cleaning service; janitorial service, contract basis

(P-13920)
ENVIRONMENT CONTROL
3065 N Sunnyside Ave # 101, Fresno
(93727-1344)
PHONE..................................559 456-9791
Dick Johns, *Partner*
Kit Seals, *Partner*
EMP: 50
SALES (est): 1.2MM Privately Held
SIC: 7349 Janitorial service, contract basis

(P-13921)
EVERGREEN CLEANING SYSTEMS INC
3325 Wilshire Blvd # 622, Los Angeles
(90010-1747)
PHONE..................................213 386-3260
John Lee, *President*

EMP: 50
SALES (est): 1.3MM **Privately Held**
SIC: 7349 Janitorial service, contract basis

(P-13922)
EXCEL BUILDING SERVICES LLC
1061 Serpentine Ln Ste H, Pleasanton (94566-4793)
PHONE...................925 474-1080
Jennifer Fabrique, *CEO*
Jack Fabrique, *President*
Steve Sui, *CFO*
Scott Henley, *Exec VP*
Cindy Sui, *Accountant*
EMP: 1300 EST: 1998
SQ FT: 5,000
SALES (est): 50.7MM **Privately Held**
SIC: 7349 Janitorial service, contract basis

(P-13923)
FACILITY MASTERS INC (PA)
1604 Kerley Dr, San Jose (95112-4815)
PHONE...................408 436-9090
Ramsin Bitmansour, *CEO*
James Machado, *President*
Osvaldo Almeida, *Vice Pres*
EMP: 345
SQ FT: 7,000
SALES (est): 13.8MM **Privately Held**
SIC: 7349 Janitorial service, contract basis

(P-13924)
FAME SYSTEMS INC
301 Hearst Dr, Oxnard (93030-5158)
PHONE...................805 485-0808
Sal Mejia, *President*
Jesus Mejia, *Vice Pres*
EMP: 50
SALES: 2.5MM **Privately Held**
WEB: www.famesystems.com
SIC: 7349 Janitorial service, contract basis

(P-13925)
FIELDS CONSTRUCTION SERVICES
Also Called: Fields Win Clg Win Protection
5715 Southfront Rd Ste B1, Livermore (94551-7807)
PHONE...................925 294-8183
Daniel Fields, *President*
EMP: 60
SALES (est): 1.5MM **Privately Held**
SIC: 7349 1799 Cleaning service, industrial or commercial; coating, caulking & weather, water & fireproofing

(P-13926)
FLAIR BUILDING SERVICES INC
Also Called: Flair Building Maintenance
3470 Edward Ave, Santa Clara (95054-2130)
PHONE...................408 987-4040
Oscar Pena, *President*
Shirely McEvoy, *Treasurer*
EMP: 90
SQ FT: 2,400
SALES: 3.7MM **Privately Held**
SIC: 7349 Window cleaning

(P-13927)
FLUOR FACILITY & PLANT SVCS
124 Blossom Hill Rd Ste H, San Jose (95123-2397)
PHONE...................408 256-1333
Brett Heckel, *Finance Mgr*
EMP: 250
SALES (corp-wide): 19.1B **Publicly Held**
SIC: 7349 Building maintenance services
HQ: Fluor Facility & Plant Services, Inc
3 Polaris Way
Aliso Viejo CA
949 349-2000

(P-13928)
FLUOR INDUSTRIAL SERVICES INC
1 Enterprise, Aliso Viejo (92656-2606)
PHONE...................949 439-2000
▲ EMP: 1000 EST: 1986
SALES (est): 6.9MM
SALES (corp-wide): 19.1B **Publicly Held**
SIC: 7349 Building maintenance services

HQ: Fluor Enterprises, Inc.
6700 Las Colinas Blvd
Irving TX 75039
469 398-7000

(P-13929)
FOUNTAIN VALLEY SCHOOL DST
Also Called: South Valley School District
17330 Mount Herrmann St, Fountain Valley (92708-4104)
PHONE...................714 668-5882
Joe Hastie, *Maint Spvr*
Mark Johnson, *Superintendent*
EMP: 75
SALES (corp-wide): 71.1MM **Privately Held**
SIC: 7349 Building maintenance services
PA: Fountain Valley School District
10055 Slater Ave
Fountain Valley CA 92708
714 668-5886

(P-13930)
FREMONT UNIFIED SCHOOL DST
43772 S Grimmer Blvd, Fremont (94538-6308)
PHONE...................510 657-0761
Toby Black, *Manager*
Susan Gauthier, *Clerk*
EMP: 228
SALES (corp-wide): 250MM **Privately Held**
SIC: 7349 Building maintenance services
PA: Fremont Unified School District
4210 Technology Dr
Fremont CA 94538
510 657-2350

(P-13931)
FRESNO UNIFIED SCHOOL DISTRICT
Also Called: Maintenance Department
4600 N Brawley Ave, Fresno (93722-3921)
PHONE...................559 457-3074
Ron Tessada, *Director*
EMP: 170
SALES (corp-wide): 616.1MM **Privately Held**
WEB: www.fresno.k12.ca.us
SIC: 7349 Building maintenance services
PA: Fresno Unified School District
2309 Tulare St
Fresno CA 93721
559 457-3000

(P-13932)
GALAXY BUILDING SYSTEMS INC
23978 Craftsman Rd, Calabasas (91302-1437)
PHONE...................818 340-6557
Gerald C Baggett, *President*
EMP: 150 EST: 1968
SALES (est): 3.2MM **Privately Held**
WEB: www.galaxyservicesca.com
SIC: 7349 Janitorial service, contract basis

(P-13933)
GAMBOA SERVICE INC
Also Called: Corporate Image Maintenance
2116 S Wright St, Santa Ana (92705-5314)
PHONE...................714 966-5325
Gilbert Gamboa, *President*
EMP: 55
SQ FT: 2,800
SALES (est): 2MM **Privately Held**
SIC: 7349 Janitorial service, contract basis

(P-13934)
GENERAL SERVICES CAL DEPT
9645 Butterfield Way # 1503, Sacramento (95827-1501)
P.O. Box 277376 (95827-7376)
PHONE...................916 845-4942
Jeff Henninger, *Director*
EMP: 120 **Privately Held**
WEB: www.4c.net
SIC: 7349 9199 Building maintenance services; general government administration;

HQ: California Department Of General Services
707 3rd St
West Sacramento CA 95605
-

(P-13935)
GENERAL SERVICES CAL DEPT
1304 O St Ste 301, Sacramento (95814-5906)
PHONE...................916 445-4566
Fred Lucy, *Principal*
EMP: 2000 **Privately Held**
WEB: www.4c.net
SIC: 7349 9199 Building maintenance services; general government administration;
HQ: California Department Of General Services
707 3rd St
West Sacramento CA 95605
-

(P-13936)
GENERAL SERVICES CAL DEPT
Also Called: Building and Property MGT BR
300 S Spring St Ste 1726, Los Angeles (90013-1256)
PHONE...................213 897-2241
Christopher Robles, *Regional Mgr*
EMP: 65 **Privately Held**
WEB: www.4c.net
SIC: 7349 9199 Building maintenance services; general government administration;
HQ: California Department Of General Services
707 3rd St
West Sacramento CA 95605
-

(P-13937)
GHOSSAIN & TRUELOCK ENTPS INC
Also Called: Custom Service Systems
783 Palmyrita Ave Ste A, Riverside (92507-1817)
P.O. Box 5596 (92517-5596)
PHONE...................951 781-9345
Kenneth Truelock, *President*
David L Truelock, *CEO*
Robert K Ghossain, *Bd of Directors*
Bob Ghossain, *Manager*
Maria Carnero, *Accounts Mgr*
EMP: 80
SALES (est): 2.7MM **Privately Held**
WEB: www.cssclean.com
SIC: 7349 Janitorial service, contract basis

(P-13938)
GLEN ALPINE BUILDING SVCS INC
24685 Oneil Ave, Hayward (94544-1627)
P.O. Box 738 (94543-0738)
PHONE...................510 582-7400
Janice Lynn Slade, *President*
EMP: 60
SALES: 1.8MM **Privately Held**
SIC: 7349 Janitorial service, contract basis

(P-13939)
GLENN BUILDING SERVICES INC
1148 N Lake Ave Apt 1, Pasadena (91104-3729)
PHONE...................626 398-8000
Christopher Garcia, *President*
Yvonne Pico, *Vice Pres*
EMP: 85
SALES: 600K **Privately Held**
SIC: 7349 Janitorial service, contract basis

(P-13940)
GLOBAL BUILDING SERVICES INC (PA)
27433 Tourney Rd Ste 280, Valencia (91355-5619)
PHONE...................800 675-6643
Julio Belloso, *President*
EMP: 585
SALES (est): 29.9MM **Privately Held**
WEB: www.globalbuildingservices.com
SIC: 7349 Janitorial service, contract basis

(P-13941)
GMI BUILDING SERVICES INC
8001 Vickers St, San Diego (92111-1917)
PHONE...................858 279-6262
Larry Abrams, *President*
Barry Williamson, *CFO*
Dorothy Sorensen, *Human Res Mgr*
Joe Schmidt, *Manager*
EMP: 225
SQ FT: 15,000
SALES (est): 9.6MM **Privately Held**
SIC: 7349 5087 Janitorial service, contract basis; janitors' supplies

(P-13942)
GMS JANITORIAL SERVICES INC
8690 Aero Dr Ste 115, San Diego (92123-1757)
PHONE...................858 569-6009
Rene Gonzalez, *President*
EMP: 66
SALES (est): 1.7MM **Privately Held**
SIC: 7349 Janitorial service, contract basis

(P-13943)
GREEN GUARD SERVICES INC
611 Rock Springs Rd, Escondido (92025-1622)
PHONE...................619 488-1065
Nathan Leathers, *CEO*
Adam Willis, *General Mgr*
EMP: 58
SALES (est): 748.1K **Privately Held**
SIC: 7349 Janitorial service, contract basis

(P-13944)
H U S D MAINTENANCE OPERATION
24400 Amador St, Hayward (94544-1302)
PHONE...................510 784-2666
Joseph Zanini, *Director*
EMP: 80
SALES (est): 1.2MM **Privately Held**
SIC: 7349 Building maintenance services

(P-13945)
HARBOR BUILDING SERVICES
2701 Plaza Del Amo # 706, Torrance (90503-7314)
PHONE...................310 320-2966
Peter Lescord, *Owner*
EMP: 86
SQ FT: 3,000
SALES (est): 2.7MM **Privately Held**
SIC: 7349 Janitorial service, contract basis

(P-13946)
HARPERS MODEL HOME MAINTENANCE
Also Called: Harper's Model Homes Services
1949 5th St Ste 108, Davis (95616-4026)
P.O. Box 4590, El Dorado Hills (95762-0021)
PHONE...................916 335-0282
Karen L Harper, *President*
Karen Harper, *President*
Garay Harper, *Admin Sec*
EMP: 70
SQ FT: 1,600
SALES (est): 1.8MM **Privately Held**
SIC: 7349 Building cleaning service

(P-13947)
HAYNES BUILDING SERVICE LLC
16027 Arrow Hwy Ste I, Baldwin Park (91706-2064)
PHONE...................626 359-6100
John P Scharler, *President*
Michael Franco, *Vice Pres*
EMP: 175
SQ FT: 20,000
SALES (est): 5.3MM **Privately Held**
WEB: www.haynesservices.com
SIC: 7349 Janitorial service, contract basis

(P-13948)
HUNTER EASTERDAY CORPORATION
1475 N Hundley St, Anaheim (92806-1323)
PHONE...................714 238-3400
Sam Easterday, *CEO*
Manny Jones, *President*

Joanne Easterday, *CFO*
Gilbert Anzaldua, *Vice Pres*
EMP: 135
SQ FT: 4,400
SALES (est): 4.2MM **Privately Held**
WEB: www.ebmcorp.com
SIC: 7349 5087 Janitorial service, contract basis; building maintenance, except repairs; janitors' supplies

(P-13949)
HYDROCHEM LLC
Also Called: Hydro Chem Industrial Services
901 Loveridge Rd 592, Pittsburg
(94565-2811)
P.O. Box 1859 (94565-0859)
PHONE....................925 432-1749
Jodi White, *Manager*
EMP: 65
SALES (corp-wide): 607.5MM **Privately Held**
WEB: www.hydrochem.com
SIC: 7349 Cleaning service, industrial or commercial
HQ: Hydrochem Llc
900 Georgia Ave
Deer Park TX 77536
713 393-5600

(P-13950)
IMPEC GROUP INC (PA)
3350 Scott Blvd Bldg 8, Santa Clara
(95054-3108)
PHONE....................408 330-9350
Raffy Espiritu, *President*
Christina Hudnall, *Senior VP*
Carly Tortorelli, *Senior VP*
Christine Chen, *Vice Pres*
Jason Fang, *Admin Mgr*
EMP: 53 **EST:** 1991
SQ FT: 5,000
SALES (est): 15.9MM **Privately Held**
WEB: www.cleaninnovation.com
SIC: 7349 Janitorial service, contract basis

(P-13951)
INNOVATIONS BUILDING SVCS LLC
402 S Orange Ave Apt D, Monterey Park
(91755-7554)
PHONE....................323 787-6068
Helbert Daniel Torres, *Principal*
EMP: 100
SALES (est): 1.1MM **Privately Held**
SIC: 7349 Janitorial service, contract basis

(P-13952)
INTEGRATED CLG SOLUTIONS INC
Also Called: I C S
3043 Mission St, San Francisco
(94110-4501)
PHONE....................415 821-6757
Nicholas Mettler, *President*
Edith Cuares, *Human Res Mgr*
Michael Henriques, *Opers Mgr*
EMP: 50
SQ FT: 2,500
SALES: 8MM **Privately Held**
WEB: www.nomoredirt.com
SIC: 7349 Janitorial service, contract basis

(P-13953)
INTEGRITY MANAGEMENT SVCS INC
141 W Dana St Ste 100, Nipomo
(93444-9152)
P.O. Box 976 (93444-0976)
PHONE....................805 238-0905
Raul Torres, *President*
EMP: 200
SALES (est): 6.1MM **Privately Held**
SIC: 7349 Janitorial service, contract basis

(P-13954)
ISS FACILITY SERVICES INC
Also Called: Loma Cleaning Service
40563 Encyclopedia Cir, Fremont
(94538-2469)
PHONE....................650 593-9774
Peter Beck, *Vice Pres*
EMP: 300
SALES (corp-wide): 11.2B **Privately Held**
SIC: 7349 Janitorial service, contract basis

HQ: Iss Facility Services, Inc.
1017 Central Pkwy N # 100
San Antonio TX 78232
-

(P-13955)
JABEZ BUILDING SERVICES INC
2094 Orange Ave, Costa Mesa
(92627-2101)
PHONE....................714 776-7705
Daniel Rubio, *President*
Mary Rubio, *Vice Pres*
EMP: 60
SALES (est): 1.4MM **Privately Held**
SIC: 7349 Janitorial service, contract basis

(P-13956)
JAN PRO CLG SYSTEMS STHERN CAL
2401 E Katella Ave # 525, Anaheim
(92806-5939)
PHONE....................714 220-0500
Dave Rhodes, *Manager*
EMP: 50
SALES (est): 683.1K
SALES (corp-wide): 526K **Privately Held**
SIC: 7349 5087 Building maintenance services; service establishment equipment
PA: Jan Pro Cleaning Systems Of Southern California
3875 Hopyard Rd Ste 194
Pleasanton CA 94588
714 220-0500

(P-13957)
JANITORIAL EQUIPMENT SVCS INC
Also Called: King Janitorial Equipment Svcs
11752 Garden Grove Blvd # 100, Garden Grove (92843-1423)
PHONE....................951 205-8937
Javier Brito, *CFO*
EMP: 55
SALES: 950K **Privately Held**
SIC: 7349 Building maintenance services

(P-13958)
K & P JANITORIAL SERVICES
412 S Pacific Coast Hwy # 200, Redondo Beach (90277-3712)
PHONE....................310 540-8878
Kelly Lynch, *President*
EMP: 100
SALES (est): 3.2MM **Privately Held**
SIC: 7349 Janitorial service, contract basis

(P-13959)
KBM FCLITY SLTONS HOLDINGS LLC
Also Called: Kbm Building Services
7976 Engineer Rd Ste 200, San Diego
(92111-1935)
PHONE....................858 467-0202
Brian Snow, *CEO*
Susan Cologna, *CFO*
Rene Tuthscher, *Vice Pres*
Shaun Gordon, *Director*
Robert Kennedy III, *Director*
EMP: 500
SQ FT: 10,000
SALES (est): 19.3MM
SALES (corp-wide): 25.9MM **Privately Held**
SIC: 7349 Janitorial service, contract basis
PA: Pristine Environments Inc
7925 Jones Branch Dr LI330
Mc Lean VA 22102
703 245-4751

(P-13960)
KM INDUSTRIAL INC
2375 W Esther St, Long Beach
(90813-1029)
PHONE....................562 786-6200
Will Colon, *CEO*
Rich Bartel, *President*
EMP: 128
SALES (est): 6.7MM
SALES (corp-wide): 2.9B **Privately Held**
SIC: 7349 Cleaning service, industrial or commercial

HQ: K2 Industrial Services, Inc.
3838 N Sam Houston Pkwy E
Houston TX 77032
850 477-6437

(P-13961)
LANDMARK SERVICES INC
410 N Fairview St, Santa Ana
(92703-3412)
PHONE....................714 547-6308
Dan Rogers, *President*
EMP: 60
SQ FT: 130,000
SALES: 4MM **Privately Held**
SIC: 7349 Janitorial service, contract basis

(P-13962)
LEES MAINTENANCE SERVICE INC
14740 Keswick St, Van Nuys (91405-1205)
PHONE....................818 988-6644
Tyrone P Ingram, *President*
EMP: 275 **EST:** 1961
SQ FT: 3,000
SALES (est): 10.2MM **Privately Held**
WEB: www.leesmaint.com
SIC: 7349 5087 Janitorial service, contract basis; laundry & dry cleaning equipment & supplies

(P-13963)
LEWIS & TAYLOR LLC
Also Called: Lewis & Taylor Bldg Svc Contrs
440 Bryant St, San Francisco
(94107-1303)
PHONE....................415 781-3496
Michael L Milstein, *President*
Howard Sturdevant, *Accounting Mgr*
Mayela Ortiz, *Human Res Mgr*
Juan Vargas, *Opers Staff*
EMP: 150
SQ FT: 4,000
SALES: 6.4MM **Privately Held**
WEB: www.lewistaylor.com
SIC: 7349 Building maintenance, except repairs; janitorial service, contract basis; window cleaning; chemical cleaning services

(P-13964)
LIFE CYCLE ENGINEERING INC
2535 Camino Del Rio S # 250, San Diego
(92108-3754)
PHONE....................619 785-5990
John Spencer, *Manager*
Thomas Hekman, *Program Mgr*
Adam B Duncan, *Engineer*
EMP: 80
SALES (corp-wide): 91.1MM **Privately Held**
WEB: www.lcesd.com
SIC: 7349 Building maintenance, except repairs
PA: Life Cycle Engineering, Inc.
4360 Corporate Rd Ste 100
North Charleston SC 29405
843 744-7110

(P-13965)
LITTLE GIANT BLDG MAINT INC
15 Brooks Pl, Pacifica (94044-4403)
PHONE....................415 508-0282
David Dellanini, *President*
EMP: 230
SALES (corp-wide): 9.2MM **Privately Held**
SIC: 7349 7217 Window cleaning; carpet & upholstery cleaning
PA: Little Giant Building Maintenance, Inc.
1485 Bay Shore Blvd # 117
San Francisco CA 94124
415 508-0282

(P-13966)
LODI UNIFIED SCHOOL DISTRICT
Also Called: Maintenance & Operations
1305 E Vine St, Lodi (95240-3179)
PHONE....................209 331-7181
Mike Matranga, *Manager*
EMP: 65
SALES (corp-wide): 360.5MM **Privately Held**
WEB: www.lodiusd.net
SIC: 7349 Building maintenance services

PA: Lodi Unified School District
1305 E Vine St
Lodi CA 95240
209 331-7000

(P-13967)
LONG BEACH UNIFIED SCHOOL DST
Also Called: Maintenance
2425 Webster Ave, Long Beach
(90810-3204)
PHONE....................562 997-7550
Joe Rasch, *Director*
Clifton Christopher, *Education*
Huot Daro, *Education*
EMP: 200
SALES (corp-wide): 865.3MM **Privately Held**
WEB: www.lbusd.k12.ca.us
SIC: 7349 School custodian, contract basis
PA: Long Beach Unified School District
1515 Hughes Way
Long Beach CA 90810
562 997-8000

(P-13968)
LOS ANGELES UNIFIED SCHOOL DST
Also Called: Maintenance Dept
17729 S Figueroa St, Gardena
(90248-4237)
PHONE....................310 808-1500
Roger Finstad, *Director*
EMP: 50
SALES (corp-wide): 4B **Privately Held**
WEB: www.lausd.k12.ca.us
SIC: 7349 School custodian, contract basis
PA: Los Angeles Unified School District
333 S Beaudry Ave Ste 209
Los Angeles CA 90017
213 241-1000

(P-13969)
LUXERA INC
39300 Civic Center Dr # 145, Fremont
(94538-5397)
PHONE....................510 456-7690
Leonard Simon Livschitz, *CEO*
EMP: 50 **EST:** 2010
SALES (est): 1MM **Privately Held**
SIC: 7349 Lighting maintenance service

(P-13970)
M-N-Z JANITORIAL SERVICES INC
2109 W Burbank Blvd, Burbank
(91506-1231)
PHONE....................323 851-4115
Marc De Mauregne, *Exec VP*
Dennis Krebs, *Shareholder*
Zorina Russell Kroop, *President*
Gene Figueroa, *Project Mgr*
EMP: 110
SQ FT: 1,000
SALES (est): 2.9MM **Privately Held**
WEB: www.mnz.com
SIC: 7349 1799 Building maintenance, except repairs; construction site cleanup

(P-13971)
MAINTENANCE SERVICE FOR THE CY
Also Called: Public Works Superintendent
1616 Fortmann Way, Alameda
(94501-1274)
PHONE....................510 865-3778
Lance Bryant, *Superintendent*
EMP: 51
SALES (est): 1MM **Privately Held**
SIC: 7349 Building maintenance services

(P-13972)
MAINTENANCE STAFF INC
122 W 8th St, Long Beach (90813-4371)
PHONE....................562 493-3982
Vivian M Frahm, *President*
EMP: 2600
SALES (est): 18MM **Privately Held**
WEB: www.maintenancestaff.com
SIC: 7349 Janitorial service, contract basis

(P-13973)
MARK GARCIA
Also Called: All In One Complete Bldg Svcs
5131 Ellsworth Rd Ste B, Vacaville
(95688-9483)
P.O. Box 2383 (95696-2383)
PHONE..........................707 446-4529
Mark Garcia, *Owner*
EMP: 60
SQ FT: 4,000
SALES: 250K **Privately Held**
SIC: 7349 1799 1521 Janitorial service,
contract basis; cleaning new buildings
after construction; cleaning building exte-
riors; repairing fire damage, single-family
houses

(P-13974)
MASTER CLEAN USA INC
Also Called: Janitorial
5511 Ekwill St Ste D, Santa Barbara
(93111-2361)
P.O. Box 8032, Goleta (93118-8032)
PHONE..........................805 681-0950
Jessica Sanchez Hoseler, *CEO*
EMP: 50
SALES (est): 1.8MM **Privately Held**
SIC: 7349 7389 1799 Maid services, con-
tract or fee basis; ; construction site
cleanup

(P-13975)
MAXIM SERVICES LTD INC
2470 Estand Way, Pleasant Hill
(94523-3912)
PHONE..........................925 969-1907
Gregory Higgins, *President*
EMP: 60
SQ FT: 800
SALES (est): 1.7MM **Privately Held**
SIC: 7349 Janitorial service, contract basis

(P-13976)
MCKOWSKIS MAINT SYSTEMS INC
10979 San Dego Mission Rd, San Diego
(92108-2431)
PHONE..........................619 269-4600
James R McElwee, *President*
Paulina Zamora, *Officer*
Paulina Suarez, *Maintence Staff*
EMP: 55 **EST:** 1979
SQ FT: 7,000
SALES (est): 5MM **Privately Held**
WEB: www.mckowskis.com
SIC: 7349 Janitorial service, contract basis

(P-13977)
MERCHANTS BUILDING MAINT CO
1639 E Edinger Ave Ste C, Santa Ana
(92705-5013)
PHONE..........................714 973-9272
George Rodriguez, *Branch Mgr*
EMP: 300
SALES (corp-wide): 128.1MM **Privately Held**
WEB: www.mbmonline.com
SIC: 7349 Building maintenance, except
repairs
PA: Merchants Building Maintenance Com-
pany
1190 Monterey Pass Rd
Monterey Park CA 91754
323 881-6701

(P-13978)
MERCHANTS BUILDING MAINT CO (PA)
1190 Monterey Pass Rd, Monterey Park
(91754-3615)
PHONE..........................323 881-6701
Theodore Haas, *CEO*
David Haas, *President*
Karen T Haas, *Treasurer*
Krista M Haas, *Vice Pres*
Cesar Prado, *Branch Mgr*
EMP: 96
SQ FT: 8,000
SALES (est): 128.1MM **Privately Held**
WEB: www.mbmonline.com
SIC: 7349 Janitorial service, contract basis

(P-13979)
MERCHANTS BUILDING MAINT CO
9555 Dist Ave 102, San Diego (92121)
PHONE..........................858 455-0163
Eric Ruiz, *Manager*
EMP: 380
SALES (corp-wide): 128.1MM **Privately Held**
WEB: www.mbmonline.com
SIC: 7349 Janitorial service, contract basis
PA: Merchants Building Maintenance Com-
pany
1190 Monterey Pass Rd
Monterey Park CA 91754
323 881-6701

(P-13980)
MERCHANTS BUILDING MAINT CO
1995 W Holt Ave, Pomona (91768-3352)
PHONE..........................909 622-8260
Angel Meza, *Branch Mgr*
EMP: 220
SALES (corp-wide): 128.1MM **Privately Held**
WEB: www.mbmonline.com
SIC: 7349 7381 Janitorial service, contract
basis; security guard service
PA: Merchants Building Maintenance Com-
pany
1190 Monterey Pass Rd
Monterey Park CA 91754
323 881-6701

(P-13981)
MERCHANTS BUILDING MAINT CO
606 Monterey Paca Rd 20 Ste 202, Mon-
terey Park (91754)
PHONE..........................323 881-8902
Michael Anthony Palma,
Wallace Reid, *Vice Pres*
EMP: 130
SALES (corp-wide): 128.1MM **Privately Held**
WEB: www.mbmonline.com
SIC: 7349 7381 Janitorial service, contract
basis; detective & armored car services
PA: Merchants Building Maintenance Com-
pany
1190 Monterey Pass Rd
Monterey Park CA 91754
323 881-6701

(P-13982)
MIDA INDUSTRIES INC
6101 Obispo Ave, Long Beach
(90805-3799)
PHONE..........................562 616-1020
Michael T Drake, *President*
John Durfee, *President*
Dawit Kidane, *CFO*
John Valencia, *Vice Pres*
EMP: 250
SQ FT: 10,000
SALES (est): 14.9MM **Privately Held**
WEB: www.midaindustries.com
SIC: 7349 1799 Janitorial service, contract
basis; asbestos removal & encapsulation

(P-13983)
MINTIE CORPORATION (PA)
Also Called: Mintie Technologies
1114 N San Fernando Rd, Los Angeles
(90065-1126)
PHONE..........................323 225-4111
Kevin J Mintie, *CEO*
James M Mintie, *Exec VP*
Ambar Torres, *Admin Asst*
Jim Bieritz, *Director*
EMP: 80 **EST:** 1940
SQ FT: 8,000
SALES (est): 14MM **Privately Held**
WEB: www.mintie.com
SIC: 7349 Building cleaning service; air
duct cleaning

(P-13984)
MISSION LINEN SUPPLY
6590 Central Ave, Newark (94560-3933)
PHONE..........................510 996-3416
EMP: 87

SALES (corp-wide): 180.2MM **Privately Held**
SIC: 7349 7213 7211 Janitorial service,
contract basis; linen supply; power laundries, family & commercial
PA: Mission Linen Supply
717 E Yanonali St
Santa Barbara CA 93103
805 730-3620

(P-13985)
MOLLY MAID
24412 Muirlands Blvd A, Lake Forest
(92630-3900)
PHONE..........................949 367-8000
Stephen Schatan, *Owner*
EMP: 50
SQ FT: 2,000
SALES (est): 1MM **Privately Held**
SIC: 7349 7363 7299 Maid services, con-
tract or fee basis; domestic help service;
handyman service

(P-13986)
MONTEBELLO UNIFIED SCHOOL
Also Called: Maintenance & Operation Dept
500 Hendricks St Fl 2, Montebello
(90640-1566)
PHONE..........................323 887-2140
Virgil Downs, *Principal*
EMP: 100
SALES (corp-wide): 296.9MM **Privately Held**
SIC: 7349 Building maintenance services
PA: Montebello Unified School District Pro-
tective League
123 S Montebello Blvd
Montebello CA 90640
323 887-7900

(P-13987)
MORENO & ASSOCIATES INC
1260 Birchwood Dr, Sunnyvale
(94089-2205)
PHONE..........................408 924-0353
Ernie Moreno, *President*
Paul Lima, *Vice Pres*
Alfredo Cortez, *Opers Spvr*
Apreza Felix, *Opers Spvr*
Patti Swigart,
EMP: 60
SQ FT: 1,100
SALES (est): 2.9MM **Privately Held**
WEB: www.morenoclean.com
SIC: 7349 Janitorial service, contract basis

(P-13988)
NEALS JANITORIAL SERVICE
1588 Calco Creek Dr, San Jose
(95124-4372)
PHONE..........................408 271-9944
Ralph B Neal, *Owner*
EMP: 50
SQ FT: 3,000
SALES (est): 996.4K **Privately Held**
SIC: 7349 Janitorial service, contract
basis; window cleaning

(P-13989)
NEXSENTIO INC
1346 Ridder Park Dr, San Jose
(95131-2313)
PHONE..........................408 392-9249
Danielle Bunel, *President*
Rene Velazquez, *Vice Pres*
EMP: 77 **EST:** 2006
SALES (est): 2.4MM **Privately Held**
SIC: 7349 7299 Janitorial service, contract
basis; handyman service

(P-13990)
NMS MANAGEMENT INC
155 W 35th St Ste A, National City
(91950-7922)
PHONE..........................619 425-0440
David Guaderrama, *President*
Sophia Guaderrama, *Exec VP*
EMP: 75
SQ FT: 8,300
SALES: 3MM **Privately Held**
SIC: 7349 0781 Building maintenance, ex-
cept repairs; janitorial service, contract
basis; landscape services

(P-13991)
NO MORE DIRT INC
1699 Valencia St, San Francisco
(94110-5012)
PHONE..........................415 821-6757
Nicholas D Mettler, *President*
Jonathan Mack, *Accounts Mgr*
EMP: 150
SALES (est): 4.1MM **Privately Held**
SIC: 7349 Janitorial service, contract basis

(P-13992)
NORTH COAST CLEANING SERVICES
211 7th St, Eureka (95501-1701)
P.O. Box 177 (95502-0177)
PHONE..........................707 269-0838
Dave Toor, *President*
Charles Powell, *President*
EMP: 50
SALES (est): 1.4MM **Privately Held**
SIC: 7349 Janitorial service, contract basis

(P-13993)
NORTH STAR BUILDING MAINT INC
2828 Cochran St Ste 214, Simi Valley
(93065-2780)
PHONE..........................805 518-0417
Glenn Rose, *President*
Jamie Rose, *Vice Pres*
Michael Paisley, *VP Sales*
EMP: 60
SQ FT: 800
SALES: 1MM **Privately Held**
SIC: 7349 Janitorial service, contract basis

(P-13994)
OAKLAND UNIFIED SCHOOL DST
Also Called: Facilities Management
955 High St, Oakland (94601-4404)
PHONE..........................510 535-2717
Timothy White, *Asst Supt*
Maxine Jasper, *Office Mgr*
Vaughn Hovanessian, *Teacher*
Colland Jang, *Manager*
EMP: 150
SALES (corp-wide): 677MM **Privately Held**
WEB: www.ousd.k12.ca.us
SIC: 7349 Building maintenance services
PA: Oakland Unified School District
1000 Broadway Ste 300
Oakland CA 94607
510 434-7790

(P-13995)
ONE SILVER SERVE INC
Also Called: SERVPRO Encino/Sherman
Oaks
17835 Ventura Blvd # 108, Encino
(91316-3634)
PHONE..........................818 995-6444
Alan Reed, *CEO*
EMP: 50
SALES (est): 1.7MM **Privately Held**
SIC: 7349 Building maintenance services

(P-13996)
OPTIMA BUILDING SERVICES MAINT
210 Mountain View Ave, Santa Rosa
(95407-8203)
PHONE..........................707 586-6640
Adolfo Mendoza, *President*
EMP: 100
SALES (est): 2.3MM **Privately Held**
SIC: 7349 Building cleaning service

(P-13997)
PACIFIC BUILDING MAINT INC
Also Called: Servicmster Clean By Integrity
130 Garden St Bldg 2b1, Santa Barbara
(93101-1832)
PHONE..........................805 969-5221
Jennifer Evans, *Principal*
EMP: 57
SALES (corp-wide): 7.2MM **Privately Held**
SIC: 7349 Building maintenance services
PA: Pacific Building Maintenance, Inc.
1601 Ives Ave Ste E
Oxnard CA 93033
805 642-0214

(P-13998)

PACIFIC CLEANING SERVICE INC

3334 Pacific Coast Hwy # 205, Corona Del Mar (92625-2328)
PHONE...................949 829-8790
Jeff Murray, *President*
Chris Bello, *Associate*
EMP: 50
SQ FT: 1,500
SALES (est): 2.2MM **Privately Held**
WEB: www.pacificwindow.com
SIC: 7349 Window cleaning

(P-13999)

PANAMA-BUENA VISTA UN SCHL DST

Also Called: District Office East
5901 Schirra Ct, Bakersfield (93313-2161)
PHONE...................661 397-2205
Diane McConnell, *President*
EMP: 160
SALES (corp-wide): 214.5MM **Privately Held**
SIC: 7349 Building maintenance services
PA: Panama-Buena Vista Union School District
4200 Ashe Rd
Bakersfield CA 93313
661 831-8331

(P-14000)

PARADISE BUILDING SERVICES

9664 Hermosa Ave, Rancho Cucamonga (91730-5812)
PHONE...................909 399-0707
Chris Clifton, *President*
Susan Cutshaw, *Vice Pres*
EMP: 115
SQ FT: 5,500
SALES (est): 3MM **Privately Held**
SIC: 7349 Janitorial service, contract basis

(P-14001)

PARAGON COML BLDG MAINT INC

6731 32nd St Ste J, North Highlands (95660-3042)
PHONE...................916 334-8801
Dwayne Willis, *President*
EMP: 80
SALES (est): 2.2MM **Privately Held**
SIC: 7349 Janitorial service, contract basis

(P-14002)

PBM MAINTENANCE CORP

Also Called: Professional Building Maint
8523 Lankershim Blvd, Sun Valley (91352-3127)
PHONE...................818 771-1100
Fernando Real, *CEO*
David Lorin, *President*
▲ **EMP:** 400
SQ FT: 40,000
SALES (est): 9MM **Privately Held**
WEB: www.pbmco.net
SIC: 7349 1799 Janitorial service, contract basis; steam cleaning of building exteriors

(P-14003)

PBMS INC

Also Called: Premier Building Maint Svcs
1909 Wilshire Blvd, Los Angeles (90057-3604)
PHONE...................213 386-2552
Bryant S Kim, *President*
Kim Bryant, *Owner*
EMP: 100
SQ FT: 1,400
SALES (est): 3.3MM **Privately Held**
SIC: 7349 Janitorial service, contract basis

(P-14004)

PEERLESS BUILDING MAINT INC

4665 Mountain Lakes Blvd, Redding (96003-1450)
PHONE...................530 222-6369
Jan Pauline Tuttle, *CEO*
Terry Tuttle, *President*
EMP: 100
SQ FT: 8,000
SALES: 3MM **Privately Held**
SIC: 7349 Janitorial service, contract basis

(P-14005)

PEERLESS MAINTENANCE SERVICE

1100 S Euclid St, La Habra (90631-6807)
P.O. Box 3900 (90632-3900)
PHONE...................714 871-3380
Linda Gabriel, *President*
David Gabriel, *Corp Secy*
Ralph Dergazarian, *Vice Pres*
Deanne Derg, *Manager*
Nasser Badawi, *Supervisor*
EMP: 300
SQ FT: 2,000
SALES (est): 9.3MM **Privately Held**
WEB: www.peerlesssvc.com
SIC: 7349 Janitorial service, contract basis

(P-14006)

PEGASUS BUILDING SVCS CO INC

7966 Arjons Dr Ste A, San Diego (92126-6361)
PHONE...................858 444-2290
Jeffery Baker, *Manager*
Lynda Scott, *Vice Pres*
Victoria Lee, *District Mgr*
Irma Rehberg, *Opers-Prdtn-Mfg*
EMP: 105
SALES (corp-wide): 17.3MM **Privately Held**
SIC: 7349 Janitorial service, contract basis
PA: Pegasus Building Services Company, Inc.
7966 Arjons Dr Ste A
San Diego CA 92126
858 444-2290

(P-14007)

PEGASUS BUILDING SVCS CO INC (PA)

7966 Arjons Dr Ste A, San Diego (92126-6361)
PHONE...................858 444-2290
Judith Becker, *President*
Laura Cortez, *Regional Mgr*
Betty Hernandez, *District Mgr*
Mark Tarin, *VP Opers*
Santiago Hernandez, *Opers Mgr*
EMP: 245
SQ FT: 12,800
SALES (est): 17.3MM **Privately Held**
SIC: 7349 Janitorial service, contract basis

(P-14008)

PERFORMANCE BUILDING SERVICES

Also Called: Performance Cleanroom Services
22642 Lambert St Ste 409, Lake Forest (92630-1645)
PHONE...................949 364-4364
James Chriss, *President*
Robert Lynch, *Vice Pres*
Ron Matthews, *Vice Pres*
Ramiro Teodoro, *Accounts Mgr*
EMP: 104
SALES: 5MM **Privately Held**
WEB: www.performance-now.com
SIC: 7349 7699 Janitorial service, contract basis; cleaning services

(P-14009)

PLATINUM CLG INDIANAPOLIS LLC

1522 2nd St, Santa Monica (90401-2303)
PHONE...................310 584-8000
William Hertz,
EMP: 460 **EST:** 2008
SALES (est): 12.2MM **Privately Held**
SIC: 7349 Building & office cleaning services

(P-14010)

PLATINUM FACILITIES SERVICES

1530 Oakland Rd Ste 120, San Jose (95112-1241)
PHONE...................408 998-9004
Roger K Daniels, *President*
Sherry Jackson, *Finance Mgr*
EMP: 150
SALES (est): 4.4MM **Privately Held**
SIC: 7349 Janitorial service, contract basis

(P-14011)

POLARIS BUILDING MAINTENANCE

2580 Wyandotte St Ste E, Mountain View (94043-2366)
PHONE...................650 964-9400
Frank Schwarb, *President*
Roger Gomez, *Vice Pres*
EMP: 80
SQ FT: 2,700
SALES (est): 3.4MM **Privately Held**
SIC: 7349 Janitorial service, contract basis; building maintenance, except repairs

(P-14012)

PONDEROSA BUILDERS INC

Also Called: United Building Services
3300 W Macarthur Blvd, Santa Ana (92704-6804)
PHONE...................714 434-9494
Robert Hughes, *President*
EMP: 800
SQ FT: 10,000
SALES (est): 11.4MM **Privately Held**
WEB: www.ubservices.com
SIC: 7349 Janitorial service, contract basis; window cleaning

(P-14013)

PREMIER FLOOR CARE INC (PA)

390 Carrol Ct Ste C, Brentwood (94513-7376)
PHONE...................925 679-4901
Cedric Moore, *President*
EMP: 105
SALES (est): 2.5MM **Privately Held**
SIC: 7349 3589 Janitorial service, contract basis; commercial cleaning equipment

(P-14014)

PRIORITY BUILDING SERVICES LLC

7313 Carroll Rd Ste G, San Diego (92121-2319)
PHONE...................858 695-1326
Simon Rocha, *Branch Mgr*
EMP: 310 **Privately Held**
SIC: 7349 Janitorial service, contract basis
PA: Priority Building Services Llc
521 Mercury Ln
Brea CA 92821

(P-14015)

PRIORITY BUILDING SERVICES LLC (PA)

Also Called: Priority Landscape Services
521 Mercury Ln, Brea (92821-4831)
PHONE...................714 255-2940
Simon Rocha, *President*
David Kraushaar, *Sales Mgr*
Scott Nankervis,
Sergio Alvarez, *Manager*
EMP: 65
SQ FT: 6,000
SALES (est): 24.1MM **Privately Held**
WEB: www.prioritybuildingservices.com
SIC: 7349 Janitorial service, contract basis

(P-14016)

PRO BUILDING MAINTENANCE INC

149 N Maple St Ste H, Corona (92880-1773)
PHONE...................951 279-3386
Carl Hoff, *CEO*
Christina L Hoff, *Principal*
Jackie Troglia, *Representative*
EMP: 120
SQ FT: 1,600
SALES: 7.5MM **Privately Held**
SIC: 7349 Janitorial service, contract basis

(P-14017)

PROFESSIONAL JANITORIAL SVC

234 Eucalyptus Dr B, El Segundo (90245-3820)
P.O. Box 646 (90245-0646)
PHONE...................310 410-1452
Michael Mc Grath, *President*
EMP: 50

SALES (est): 600.5K **Privately Held**
SIC: 7349 Janitorial service, contract basis

(P-14018)

PROFESSIONAL MAINT SYSTEMS INC

Also Called: Professional Maint Systems
4912 Naples St, San Diego (92110-3820)
P.O. Box 80038 (92138-0038)
PHONE...................619 276-1150
Karen Berry, *CEO*
Peter Alicea, *District Mgr*
Hector Romero, *Opers Mgr*
Cesar Diaz, *Opers Staff*
Phil Senescall, *Director*
EMP: 925
SQ FT: 9,000
SALES (est): 32.1MM **Privately Held**
WEB: www.pmsjanitorial.com
SIC: 7349 Janitorial service, contract basis

(P-14019)

PROPERTY MAINTENANCE COMPANY (PA)

Also Called: Dkd Property Management
255 W Julian St Ste 301, San Jose (95110-2406)
PHONE...................408 297-7849
Sue Williams, *President*
EMP: 115 **EST:** 1979
SQ FT: 6,000
SALES (est): 2.3MM **Privately Held**
SIC: 7349 Building maintenance, except repairs

(P-14020)

PROTEC ASSOCIATION SERVICES (PA)

Also Called: Protec Building Services
10180 Willow Creek Rd, San Diego (92131-1636)
PHONE...................858 569-1080
J David Rauch, *President*
Scot Clark, *Shareholder*
Russ Piccoli, *Shareholder*
Libbey Rauch, *Shareholder*
George Vanoofbree, *Shareholder*
EMP: 140
SQ FT: 12,500
SALES (est): 26.7MM **Privately Held**
SIC: 7349 Building maintenance services

(P-14021)

QUALITY COAST INCORPORATED

2462 Main St Ste H, Chula Vista (91911-4671)
PHONE...................619 443-9192
Consuelo Rosengreen, *President*
Richard Rosengreen, *Treasurer*
EMP: 50
SALES (est): 1.7MM **Privately Held**
WEB: www.qualitycoast.com
SIC: 7349 Janitorial service, contract basis

(P-14022)

RAINBOW - BRITE INDUS SVCS LLC

463 E Salmon River Dr, Fresno (93730-0860)
PHONE...................559 925-2580
Diana Tutson-Snowden, *CEO*
EMP: 100
SALES (est): 3.5MM **Privately Held**
SIC: 7349 Janitorial service, contract basis
PA: Santa Rosa Indian Community Of The Santa Rosa Rancheria
16835 Alkali Dr
Lemoore CA 93245
559 924-1278

(P-14023)

RANSCAPES INC

30 Hughes St Ste 209, Irvine (92618-1916)
P.O. Box 50580 (92619-0580)
PHONE...................866 883-9297
Ran Tomaino, *President*
Susan Tomaino, *Corp Secy*
EMP: 50
SQ FT: 2,000
SALES (est): 2.8MM **Privately Held**
WEB: www.ranscapes.com
SIC: 7349 Janitorial service, contract basis

(P-14024)
REDWOOD BUILDING MAINT CO
1364 N Mcdowell Blvd B, Petaluma
(94954-1116)
P.O. Box 750985 (94975-0985)
PHONE....................707 782-9100
Robert Stanley, *Owner*
EMP: 75
SQ FT: 2,000
SALES (est): 2.1MM **Privately Held**
WEB: www.rbmco.com
SIC: 7349 Janitorial service, contract basis

(P-14025)
RESOURCE COLLECTION INC
Also Called: Command Guard Services
3771 W 242nd St Ste 205, Torrance
(90505-6566)
PHONE....................310 219-3272
Martin Benom, *Ch of Bd*
Steven Jacobson, *Corp Secy*
Paula Benom, *Vice Pres*
Marilyn Jacobson, *Vice Pres*
EMP: 1400
SQ FT: 15,000
SALES (est): 16.4MM **Privately Held**
WEB: www.resourcecollection.com
SIC: 7349 7381 0782 3564 Air duct
cleaning; guard services; lawn & garden
services; air cleaning systems

(P-14026)
**REYNOLDS CLEANING
SERVICES INC**
544 Lakemead Way, Emerald Hills
(94062-3919)
PHONE....................650 599-0202
James R Reynolds Jr, *President*
EMP: 110
SALES: 3.2MM **Privately Held**
WEB: www.reynoldscleaning.com
SIC: 7349 Janitorial service, contract basis

(P-14027)
**RHINO BUILDING SERVICES
INC**
6650 Flanders Dr Ste K, San Diego
(92121-3908)
PHONE....................858 455-1440
Cody Sears, *President*
EMP: 120
SQ FT: 110
SALES (est): 3.6MM **Privately Held**
WEB: www.rhinoliningsindustrial.com
SIC: 7349 Janitorial service, contract basis

(P-14028)
**RNA ANN ARBOR
INCORPORATED**
508 S Smith Ave Ste A202, Corona
(92882-7605)
PHONE....................877 762-7511
EMP: 66
SALES (corp-wide): 18.4MM **Privately
Held**
SIC: 7349 Janitorial service, contract basis
PA: R.N.A. Of Ann Arbor, Incorporated
717 W Ellsworth Rd
Ann Arbor MI 48108
877 762-7511

(P-14029)
**ROGAN BUILDING SERVICES
INC**
1531 7th St, Riverside (92507-4454)
P.O. Box 5787 (92517-5787)
PHONE....................951 248-1261
Byron Lee Rogan, *President*
Anne Rogan, *Admin Sec*
EMP: 50
SQ FT: 5,000
SALES (est): 1.6MM **Privately Held**
SIC: 7349 Building maintenance, except
repairs; janitorial service, contract basis

(P-14030)
**ROY JORGENSEN ASSOCIATES
INC**
19001 S Western Ave, Torrance
(90501-1106)
PHONE....................310 468-2478
Mark Thomas, *Principal*
EMP: 65

SALES (corp-wide): 108.2MM **Privately
Held**
SIC: 7349 Building maintenance services
PA: Roy Jorgensen Associates, Inc.
3735 Buckeystown Pike
Buckeystown MD 21717
281 723-2099

(P-14031)
ROYAL CREST BUILDING MAINT
8601 Roland St Ste E, Buena Park
(90621-4809)
P.O. Box 391 (90621-0391)
PHONE....................714 562-5034
Robert Young, *President*
Carry Young, *Vice Pres*
Shaun Black, *Manager*
EMP: 50
SQ FT: 2,400
SALES (est): 1.6MM **Privately Held**
SIC: 7349 Janitorial service, contract basis

(P-14032)
RUBICON ENTERPRISES INC
Also Called: RUBICON PROGRAMS
2500 Bissell Ave, Richmond (94804-1815)
PHONE....................510 235-1516
Richard Aubry PHD, *Exec Dir*
Jonathan Bash, *Comms Mgr*
EMP: 220
SALES: 4.3MM **Privately Held**
SIC: 7349 8322 8331 Building mainte-
nance services; social service center; job
training & vocational rehabilitation serv-
ices

(P-14033)
**RUBICON PROGRAMS
INCORPORATED (PA)**
2500 Bissell Ave, Richmond (94804-1815)
PHONE....................510 235-1516
Jane Fischberg, *President*
Larry Brunink, *Officer*
Delia Cantu, *Office Mgr*
Adrienne Kimball, *Admin Sec*
Hallie Friedman, *Administration*
EMP: 75 EST: 1973
SQ FT: 14,500
SALES: 15.9MM **Privately Held**
SIC: 7349 8322 8331 Building mainte-
nance services; social service center; job
training & vocational rehabilitation serv-
ices

(P-14034)
RUIZ JANITORIAL CO INC
446 Heller St, Redwood City (94063-2207)
PHONE....................650 222-2078
Guadalupe Ruiz, *President*
EMP: 50
SALES: 1.5MM **Privately Held**
SIC: 7349 Janitorial service, contract basis

(P-14035)
S J GENERAL BUILDING MAINT
919 Berryessa Rd Ste 10, San Jose
(95133-1087)
PHONE....................408 392-0800
Armando Lamas, *President*
EMP: 60
SALES (est): 2.9MM **Privately Held**
SIC: 7349 Janitorial service, contract basis

(P-14036)
**SAN BERNARDINO CITY UNF
SCHOOL**
Also Called: Building Services
956 W 9th St, San Bernardino
(92411-2844)
PHONE....................909 388-6100
Bob Leon, *Director*
EMP: 220
SALES (corp-wide): 712MM **Privately
Held**
WEB: www.sbcusd.k12.ca.us
SIC: 7349 8741 8211 Building mainte-
nance services; management services;
elementary & secondary schools
PA: San Bernardino City Unified School
District
777 N F St
San Bernardino CA 92410
909 381-1100

(P-14037)
**SANTA CLARA VALLEY
CORPORATION**
Also Called: Swenson Developers and Contrs
715 N 1st St Ste 27, San Jose
(95112-6309)
PHONE....................408 947-1100
Case Swenson, *President*
Lisa Swenson, *Admin Sec*
Heather Solis, *Project Mgr*
Kevin Young, *Project Mgr*
Aaron Gallaty, *Sales Staff*
EMP: 85
SQ FT: 1,200
SALES (est): 3.9MM **Privately Held**
SIC: 7349 0782 7623 7699 Building
maintenance, except repairs; janitorial
service, contract basis; lawn services; re-
frigeration service & repair; elevators: in-
spection, service & repair

(P-14038)
**SBM MANAGEMENT SERVICES
LP**
5241 Arnold Ave, McClellan (95652-1025)
PHONE....................866 855-2211
Charles Somers, *CEO*
Ken Silva, *CFO*
Donald Tracy, *Exec VP*
Don Tracy, *Principal*
Ronald Alvarado, *Administration*
EMP: 300
SALES (est): 79.7MM **Privately Held**
SIC: 7349 Janitorial service, contract basis

(P-14039)
SBM SITE SERVICES LLC (PA)
Also Called: S B M
5241 Arnold Ave, McClellan (95652-1025)
PHONE....................916 922-7600
Charles Somers, *Mng Member*
Melissa Croteau, *Regional Mgr*
Darin Morino, *Regional Mgr*
Dave Sweet, *Regional Mgr*
Kerry Dwyer, *Area Mgr*
EMP: 5500
SQ FT: 25,000
SALES (est): 98.4MM **Privately Held**
SIC: 7349 Building maintenance services

(P-14040)
SBRM INC (PA)
Also Called: Servicmster Cmplete Rstoration
2342 Meyers Ave, Escondido (92029-1008)
PHONE....................760 480-0208
Barbara Robert, *President*
Mike Gamez, *Admin Sec*
EMP: 70
SQ FT: 20,000
SALES (est): 11MM **Privately Held**
WEB: www.smsos.com
SIC: 7349 1521 Building maintenance
services; repairing fire damage, single-
family houses

(P-14041)
SCV FACILITIES SERVICES
1907 W 75th St, Los Angeles (90047-2325)
PHONE....................310 803-4588
Samuel Valdez, *Owner*
EMP: 72
SALES: 1.6MM **Privately Held**
SIC: 7349 7389 Janitorial service, contract
basis; cleaning service, industrial or com-
mercial;

(P-14042)
SEAFUS CORPORATION
Also Called: ServiceMaster
1365 Lowrie Ave, South San Francisco
(94080-6403)
PHONE....................415 584-6100
David Decker, *President*
Beth Decker, *CFO*
EMP: 50
SQ FT: 4,500
SALES: 1,000K **Privately Held**
SIC: 7349 7217 Building maintenance
services; carpet & upholstery cleaning

(P-14043)
SERVI-TEK INC
Also Called: Servi-Tek Janitorial Services
3970 Sorrento Valley Blvd, San Diego
(92121-1416)
PHONE....................858 638-7735
Bryan McMinn,
Maria Zarzosa, *QC Mgr*
Eric S Friz,
Kurt G Lester,
Bryan D McMinn,
EMP: 300
SQ FT: 2,000
SALES (est): 10.2MM **Privately Held**
WEB: www.servitek.com
SIC: 7349 Janitorial service, contract basis

(P-14044)
SERVICE BY MEDALLION
Also Called: Medallion Cnstr Clean-Up
411 Clyde Ave, Mountain View
(94043-2209)
PHONE....................650 625-1010
Roland H Strick, *CEO*
Elias Nacif, *Vice Pres*
Roland F Strick, *Vice Pres*
Trino Cardenas, *District Mgr*
Maria E Strick, *Admin Sec*
EMP: 490 EST: 1978
SQ FT: 7,000
SALES (est): 25.7MM **Privately Held**
WEB: www.servicebymedallion.com
SIC: 7349 Janitorial service, contract basis

(P-14045)
**SERVICEMASTER COMPANY
LLC**
1003 Hi Point St, Los Angeles
(90035-2607)
PHONE....................760 298-7001
Samuel Druhora, *Branch Mgr*
EMP: 85
SALES (corp-wide): 1.9B **Publicly Held**
SIC: 7349 Building maintenance services
HQ: The Servicemaster Company Llc
150 Peabody Pl Ste 103
Memphis TN 38103
901 597-1400

(P-14046)
**SERVICEMASTER COMPANY
LLC**
216 N Clara St, Santa Ana (92703-3518)
PHONE....................714 245-1465
Gregg Gills, *Manager*
EMP: 200
SALES (corp-wide): 1.9B **Publicly Held**
WEB: www.servicemaster.com
SIC: 7349 Building maintenance services
HQ: The Servicemaster Company Llc
150 Peabody Pl Ste 103
Memphis TN 38103
901 597-1400

(P-14047)
SERVICO BUILDING MAINT CO
13732b Carmel Ave, Glen Ellen (95442)
P.O. Box 25 (95442-0025)
PHONE....................707 935-1224
Gary D'Acquisto, *Owner*
EMP: 100
SQ FT: 800
SALES (est): 2MM **Privately Held**
SIC: 7349 7217 Janitorial service, contract
basis; window cleaning; carpet & furniture
cleaning on location

(P-14048)
SERVPRO OF MENDOCINO
3001 S State St Ste 5, Ukiah (95482-6966)
PHONE....................707 462-3848
Doug Bridges, *Principal*
EMP: 50
SALES (est): 430.6K **Privately Held**
SIC: 7349 Building maintenance services

(P-14049)
SFUSD BUILDING GROUND
834 Toland St, San Francisco
(94124-1314)
PHONE....................415 695-5508
John Bitoff, *Director*
EMP: 100
SALES (est): 3.5MM **Privately Held**
SIC: 7349 Building maintenance services

(P-14050)
SIGNATURE BUILDING MAINT INC
4005 Clipper Ct, Fremont (94538-6540)
P.O. Box 110340, Campbell (95011-0340)
PHONE..................................408 377-8066
Anna Murphy, *President*
Jeff Lolyd, *CFO*
Patrick Murphy, *General Mgr*
Tony Reyes, *Admin Sec*
Joe Megill, *Opers Mgr*
EMP: 80 EST: 1999
SALES (est): 3.5MM **Privately Held**
WEB: www.signaturefacilities.com
SIC: 7349 Building cleaning service

(P-14051)
SIGNIFICANT CLEANING SVCS LLC
148 E Virginia St Ste 1, San Jose
(95112-5881)
PHONE..................................408 559-5959
Larry Lovaglia,
Jeff Davidson, *Branch Mgr*
Eduardo Cardoza, *Opers Mgr*
Juan Baron, *Manager*
John Ornales, *Manager*
EMP: 105 EST: 1988
SALES: 4.1MM **Privately Held**
WEB: www.significantcleaning.com
SIC: 7349 Cleaning service, industrial or commercial

(P-14052)
SITE CREW INC
3185 Airway Ave Ste G, Costa Mesa
(92626-4601)
PHONE..................................714 668-0100
Tina Manavi, *CEO*
EMP: 300
SQ FT: 2,160
SALES (est): 8MM **Privately Held**
WEB: www.sitecrewinc.com
SIC: 7349 Janitorial service, contract basis

(P-14053)
SKYLSTAD-SCHOELEN CO INC
Also Called: ServiceMaster
3130 Skyway Dr Ste 701, Santa Maria
(93455-1800)
PHONE..................................805 349-0503
Jeffrey Hopson, *CEO*
EMP: 80
SALES (est): 2.2MM **Privately Held**
SIC: 7349 Building maintenance services

(P-14054)
SO CAL LAND MAINTENANCE INC
2965 E Coronado St, Anaheim
(92806-2502)
PHONE..................................714 231-1454
Stephen Guise, *Principal*
EMP: 72 EST: 2011
SALES (est): 958.1K **Privately Held**
SIC: 7349 Building maintenance services

(P-14055)
SOUTHERN CAL MAID SVC CRPT CLG
14909 Crenshaw Blvd # 209, Gardena
(90249-3665)
P.O. Box 1653 (90249-0653)
PHONE..................................310 675-0585
Rueben Trejo, *President*
Art Rivas, *Nursing Dir*
EMP: 98
SALES (est): 1.8MM **Privately Held**
SIC: 7349 7217 Maid services, contract or fee basis; carpet & furniture cleaning on location

(P-14056)
SPENCER BUILDING MAINTENANCE
10457 Old Placerville Rd, Sacramento
(95827-2508)
PHONE..................................916 922-1900
Aaron D Spencer, *President*
Jose Yanez, *Opers Staff*
Gordon Platt, *Accounts Mgr*
EMP: 307
SQ FT: 5,000

SALES (est): 10.9MM **Privately Held**
WEB: www.spencerservices.com
SIC: 7349 Janitorial service, contract basis

(P-14057)
STAR BRITE BUILDING MAINT
2688 Dawson Ave, Long Beach
(90755-2020)
PHONE..................................562 988-2829
Eric E Jenderko, *President*
EMP: 329 EST: 1989
SALES: 500K **Privately Held**
SIC: 7349 Janitorial service, contract basis

(P-14058)
STEVE AND BETH CHAPUT
Also Called: Molly Maid
1025 Sentinel Dr Ste 103, La Verne
(91750-3281)
PHONE..................................909 596-9994
Steve Chaput, *Partner*
Beth Chaput, *Partner*
EMP: 50
SALES (est): 1MM **Privately Held**
SIC: 7349 Maid services, contract or fee basis

(P-14059)
SUMMIT BUILDING SERVICES INC
1128 Willow Pass Ct, Concord
(94520-1006)
PHONE..................................925 827-9500
Matt Colchico, *Owner*
Seth Pitzer, *Office Mgr*
EMP: 100
SALES (est): 2.5MM **Privately Held**
SIC: 7349 Janitorial service, contract basis

(P-14060)
SUNSET BUILDING MAINTANCE INC
Also Called: Sunset Building Maintenance
1920 Lafayette St Ste E, Santa Clara
(95050-3956)
PHONE..................................408 727-3408
Marisela Del Rio, *President*
EMP: 50
SQ FT: 1,000
SALES (est): 1.2MM **Privately Held**
SIC: 7349 Janitorial service, contract basis

(P-14061)
SUPERIOR ENVMTL SVCS INC
Also Called: SES
6383 Lake Arrowhead Dr, San Diego
(92119-3534)
P.O. Box 19784 (92159-0784)
PHONE..................................619 462-7079
Kevin Tullgren, *President*
Jared Dunn, *Regional Mgr*
Danny Sawyer, *Regional Mgr*
EMP: 50
SQ FT: 2,000
SALES: 1MM **Privately Held**
SIC: 7349 Cleaning service, industrial or commercial

(P-14062)
SWAYZERS INCORPORATED
Also Called: Swayzer A-1 Sanitizing
1663 E Del Amo Blvd, Carson
(90746-2937)
P.O. Box 4365 (90749-4365)
PHONE..................................323 979-7223
Samuel Swayzer, *President*
Regina Swayzer, *Vice Pres*
EMP: 60
SALES (est): 1.7MM **Privately Held**
SIC: 7349 Building cleaning service

(P-14063)
THOREAU JANITORIAL SVCS INC
Also Called: Thoreau Services Nationwide
5120 W Goldleaf Cir # 10, Los Angeles
(90056-1292)
PHONE..................................310 822-8017
Nicki Frank, *President*
Dan Firestone, *Shareholder*
Robert Firestone, *Shareholder*
EMP: 150
SQ FT: 1,300
SALES (est): 5.3MM **Privately Held**
SIC: 7349 Building cleaning service

(P-14064)
TIM HOFER INC
Also Called: Environment Control
148 N Akers St, Visalia (93291-5121)
P.O. Box 6445 (93290-6445)
PHONE..................................559 732-6676
Timothy Hofer, *President*
Suzanne Hofer, *Admin Sec*
EMP: 103
SQ FT: 5,700
SALES: 2.6MM **Privately Held**
SIC: 7349 Janitorial service, contract basis

(P-14065)
TOTAL QUALITY MAINTENANCE INC
895 Commercial St, Palo Alto
(94303-4906)
PHONE..................................650 846-4700
Peter Vesanovic, *President*
Dee Vesanovic, *Admin Sec*
EMP: 180
SQ FT: 2,000
SALES (est): 5.8MM **Privately Held**
SIC: 7349 Janitorial service, contract basis

(P-14066)
TRINITY BUILDING SERVICES
430 N Canal St Ste 2, South San Francisco
(94080-4665)
PHONE..................................650 873-2121
Mike A Boschetto, *President*
EMP: 275
SALES (est): 9.5MM **Privately Held**
WEB: www.trinityservices.com
SIC: 7349 Janitorial service, contract basis

(P-14067)
TSCM CORPORATION
17791 Jamestown Ln, Huntington Beach
(92647-7134)
PHONE..................................714 841-1988
Margaret Pappano, *President*
Frank Pappano, *Vice Pres*
Frank J Pappano, *Vice Pres*
Jacki Wun, *Office Mgr*
Mendez Carlos, *Opers Staff*
EMP: 55
SALES: 4.7MM **Privately Held**
WEB: www.tscmcorp.com
SIC: 7349 1799 Building maintenance services; steam cleaning of building exteriors

(P-14068)
TUTTLE FAMILY ENTERPRISES INC
Also Called: Peerless Building Maint Co
21020 Superior St, Chatsworth
(91311-4321)
PHONE..................................818 534-2566
Tim Tuttle, *CEO*
EMP: 350 EST: 1948
SALES (est): 10.7MM **Privately Held**
SIC: 7349 Building maintenance, except repairs

(P-14069)
ULTIMATE MAINTENANCE SVCS INC
4237 Redondo Beach Blvd, Lawndale
(90260-3341)
PHONE..................................310 542-1474
Paul Marmol, *President*
EMP: 50
SALES (est): 2.2MM **Privately Held**
WEB:
www.ultimatemaintenanceservices.com
SIC: 7349 Janitorial service, contract basis

(P-14070)
UNISERVE FACILITIES SVCS CORP (PA)
Also Called: Union Building Maintenance
2363 S Atlantic Blvd, Commerce
(90040-1256)
PHONE..................................213 533-1000
Sam M Hwang, *Ch of Bd*
Eugene Hwang, *Marketing Staff*
James Jeon, *Accounts Exec*
EMP: 1150
SQ FT: 5,000
SALES (est): 8.5MM **Privately Held**
SIC: 7349 Janitorial service, contract basis

(P-14071)
UNISERVE FACILITIES SVCS CORP
1200 Getty Center Dr, Los Angeles
(90049-1657)
PHONE..................................310 440-6747
F Jackson, *Opers Staff*
EMP: 620
SALES (corp-wide): 8.5MM **Privately Held**
SIC: 7349 Janitorial service, contract basis
PA: Uniserve Facilities Services Corporation
2363 S Atlantic Blvd
Commerce CA 90040
213 533-1000

(P-14072)
UNITED BUILDING MAINT INC
8211 Sierra College Blvd, Roseville
(95661-9404)
PHONE..................................916 772-8101
Valerie Lynne Sherman, *CEO*
Paula Fischer, *Vice Pres*
EMP: 225
SQ FT: 2,500
SALES: 4.3MM **Privately Held**
SIC: 7349 Janitorial service, contract basis

(P-14073)
UNIVERSAL BLDG SVCS & SUP CO (PA)
3120 Pierce St, Richmond (94804-5996)
PHONE..................................510 527-1078
Grace Brusseau, *CEO*
Leonard Brusseau, *President*
Mia Tripodi, *Administration*
Rita Vitaliano, *Manager*
EMP: 250 EST: 1963
SQ FT: 20,000
SALES (est): 34.4MM **Privately Held**
WEB: www.ubsco.com
SIC: 7349 5087 5169 Janitorial service, contract basis; janitors' supplies; chemicals & allied products

(P-14074)
UNIVERSAL BLDG SVCS & SUP CO
421 N Buchanan Cir, Pacheco
(94553-5142)
PHONE..................................925 934-5533
Frank Batra, *Controller*
EMP: 125
SALES (corp-wide): 34.4MM **Privately Held**
WEB: www.ubsco.com
SIC: 7349 Janitorial service, contract basis
PA: Universal Building Services And Supply Co.
3120 Pierce St
Richmond CA 94804
510 527-1078

(P-14075)
UNIVERSAL BLDG SVCS & SUP CO
430 Roberson Ln, San Jose (95112-1125)
PHONE..................................408 995-5111
Su Miles, *Branch Mgr*
EMP: 125
SALES (corp-wide): 34.4MM **Privately Held**
WEB: www.ubsco.com
SIC: 7349 Janitorial service, contract basis
PA: Universal Building Services And Supply Co.
3120 Pierce St
Richmond CA 94804
510 527-1078

(P-14076)
UNIVERSAL BUILDING MAINT LLC (DH)
1551 N Tustin Ave Ste 650, Santa Ana
(92705-8664)
PHONE..................................714 619-9700
Mark Olivas, *President*
Scott Savoie, *CFO*
EMP: 656
SALES (est): 156.1K
SALES (corp-wide): 5.2B **Privately Held**
SIC: 7349 Janitorial service, contract basis

HQ: Universal Services Of America, Lp
1551 N Tustin Ave Fl 6
Santa Ana CA 92705
714 619-9700

(P-14077)
UNIVERSAL SITE SERVICES INC
3174 Luyung Dr Ste 3, Rancho Cordova
(95742-6576)
PHONE....................................916 635-1122
EMP: 56
SALES (corp-wide): 6.7MM **Privately Held**
SIC: 7349 4959 0782 Building maintenance, except repairs; road, airport &
parking lot maintenance services; lawn
services
PA: Universal Site Services, Inc.
760 E Capitol Ave
Milpitas CA 95035
800 647-9337

(P-14078)
UNIVERSAL SITE SERVICES INC (PA)
760 E Capitol Ave, Milpitas (95035-6812)
PHONE....................................800 647-9337
Gina Vella, *President*
Joseph Vella, *Vice Pres*
Ricardo Alimorong, *Regional Mgr*
Carlos Iturralde, *Regional Mgr*
Gabriel Mariscal, *Regl Sales Mgr*
EMP: 54
SQ FT: 20,000
SALES: 6.7MM **Privately Held**
WEB: www.universalsweeping.com
SIC: 7349 4959 0782 Building mainte-
nance, except repairs; road, airport &
parking lot maintenance services; lawn
services

(P-14079)
US METRO GROUP INC
Also Called: Metro Building Maintenance
605 S Wilton Pl, Los Angeles (90005-3220)
PHONE....................................213 382-6435
Charles Kim, *CEO*
Jennifer Park, *CFO*
Marilynn Salomon, *CFO*
Philip Gregg, *General Mgr*
Thereza Han, *Business Mgr*
EMP: 800
SQ FT: 40,000
SALES (est): 37.8MM **Privately Held**
SIC: 7349 Janitorial service, contract basis

(P-14080)
VARSITY CONTRACTORS INC
24155 Laguna Hills Mall, Laguna Hills
(92653-3667)
PHONE....................................949 586-8283
EMP: 67
SALES (corp-wide): 543.1MM **Privately Held**
SIC: 7349 Janitorial service, contract basis
HQ: Varsity Contractors, Inc.
1055 S 3600 W Ste 101
Salt Lake City UT 84104
208 232-8598

(P-14081)
WARD ENTERPRISES
2679 Buhach Rd, Atwater (95301-2504)
P.O. Box 413 (95301-0413)
PHONE....................................209 358-0445
Waverly Pryor, *Partner*
Dennis Williams, *Partner*
EMP: 358
SQ FT: 5,284
SALES: 941K **Privately Held**
SIC: 7349 7217 5999 Janitorial service,
contract basis; maid services, contract or
fee basis; carpet & furniture cleaning on
location; cleaning equipment & supplies

(P-14082)
WEST COAST MAINTENANCE INC
16312 S Main St, Gardena (90248-2822)
PHONE....................................310 324-2511
Christopher Mehl, *President*
Maribel Guzman, *Opers Staff*
Mari Guzman, *Director*
EMP: 65

SALES: 840K **Privately Held**
WEB: www.westcoastmaintenance.com
SIC: 7349 Window cleaning

(P-14083)
WURMS JANITORIAL SERVICE INC
544 Bateman Cir, Corona (92880-2011)
PHONE....................................951 582-0003
Larry Stewart, *President*
Pam Costa, *Vice Pres*
EMP: 80
SALES: 1.4MM **Privately Held**
SIC: 7349 Janitorial service, contract basis

(P-14084)
ZWS/ABS JOINT VENTURE LLC
39899 Balentine Dr # 200, Newark
(94560-5355)
P.O. Box 1485 (94560-6485)
PHONE....................................510 461-1433
Shavila Singh, *Mng Member*
EMP: 60
SALES: 2MM **Privately Held**
SIC: 7349 Building maintenance services

7352 Medical Eqpt Rental & Leasing

(P-14085)
APRIA HEALTHCARE LLC
2150 Trabajo Dr Ste B, Oxnard
(93030-8800)
PHONE....................................805 278-6700
Tammy Martin, *Manager*
EMP: 115 **Privately Held**
WEB: www.apria.com
SIC: 7352 5999 7359 5047 Medical
equipment rental; medical apparatus &
supplies; equipment rental & leasing;
medical & hospital equipment
HQ: Apria Healthcare Llc
26220 Enterprise Ct
Lake Forest CA 92630
949 639-2000

(P-14086)
APRIA HEALTHCARE LLC
10090 Willow Creek Rd, San Diego
(92131-1623)
PHONE....................................858 653-6800
Bruce Bowman, *Branch Mgr*
EMP: 89 **Privately Held**
WEB: www.apria.com
SIC: 7352 Medical equipment rental
HQ: Apria Healthcare Llc
26220 Enterprise Ct
Lake Forest CA 92630
949 639-2000

(P-14087)
APRIA HEALTHCARE LLC
1931 Lundy Ave, San Jose (95131-1847)
PHONE....................................949 639-2163
Josepf Ware, *Manager*
EMP: 55 **Privately Held**
WEB: www.apria.com
SIC: 7352 5999 Medical equipment rental;
medical apparatus & supplies
HQ: Apria Healthcare Llc
26220 Enterprise Ct
Lake Forest CA 92630
949 639-2000

(P-14088)
APRIA HEALTHCARE LLC
3636 N Laughlin Rd # 190, Santa Rosa
(95403-1063)
PHONE....................................707 543-0979
Jennifier Lasiter, *Principal*
EMP: 53 **Privately Held**
WEB: www.apria.com
SIC: 7352 Medical equipment rental
HQ: Apria Healthcare Llc
26220 Enterprise Ct
Lake Forest CA 92630
949 639-2000

(P-14089)
OPTION ONE HOME MED EQP INC
1220 Research Dr Ste A, Redlands
(92374-4563)
P.O. Box 40700, Mesa AZ (85274-0700)
PHONE....................................909 478-5413
David Scheven, *CEO*
EMP: 117
SQ FT: 36,000
SALES (est): 11.9MM **Privately Held**
WEB: www.lifecaresoln.com
SIC: 7352 5999 Medical equipment rental;
medical apparatus & supplies

(P-14090)
RAC & ASSOCIATES
Also Called: Special Care
9541 Ridgehaven Ct, San Diego
(92123-1624)
PHONE....................................858 694-5800
Terry Racciato, *President*
Joseph Racciato, *Vice Pres*
Gregory Racciato, *Project Mgr*
EMP: 60
SQ FT: 15,000
SALES (est): 7MM **Privately Held**
SIC: 7352 Medical equipment rental

(P-14091)
WOUNDCO HOLDINGS INC
10877 Wilshire Blvd, Los Angeles
(90024-4341)
PHONE....................................310 551-0101
Timothy J Hart, *CEO*
EMP: 500
SALES (est): 20MM **Privately Held**
SIC: 7352 Medical equipment rental

7353 Heavy Construction Eqpt Rental & Leasing

(P-14092)
AMERICAN CRANE RENTAL INC
17800 Comconex Rd, Manteca
(95336-8121)
P.O. Box 308, Escalon (95320-0308)
PHONE....................................209 838-8815
Keith Powell, *CEO*
Denise Powell, *CFO*
Everett Powell, *Vice Pres*
Gary Rich, *Accounting Mgr*
Pam Reynolds, *Sales Staff*
EMP: 65
SALES (est): 6.5MM **Privately Held**
SIC: 7353 Cranes & aerial lift equipment,
rental or leasing

(P-14093)
BIGRENTZ INC
Also Called: Bigrentz.com
1063 Mcgaw Ave Ste 200, Irvine
(92614-5553)
PHONE....................................855 999-5438
Scott Cannon, *CEO*
Dallas Imbimbo, *Ch of Bd*
Neda Imbimbo, *CFO*
Stephen Jesson, *Exec VP*
Nicholas Kovacevich, *Vice Pres*
EMP: 75
SQ FT: 15,852
SALES (est): 28.4MM **Privately Held**
SIC: 7353 Earth moving equipment, rental
or leasing

(P-14094)
D&D EQUIPMENT RENTAL LLC
2596 Mission St Ste 201, San Marino
(91108-1678)
PHONE....................................562 903-9333
Gary Darnell,
John Allaire,
EMP: 50
SALES (est): 6MM **Privately Held**
WEB: www.ddrental.com
SIC: 7353 Earth moving equipment, rental
or leasing

(P-14095)
EXTERRAN INC
3449 Santa Anita Ave, El Monte
(91731-2424)
PHONE....................................626 455-0739
EMP: 51

SALES (corp-wide): 3.1B **Publicly Held**
SIC: 7353
HQ: Exterran, Inc.
16666 Northchase Dr
Houston TX 77060
281 836-7000

(P-14096)
GALENA EQUIPMENT RENTAL LLC
Also Called: Biggie Crane and Ritting
10700 Bigge St, San Leandro
(94577-1032)
PHONE....................................510 638-8100
Brock Settlemier,
Reid Settlemeier,
Weston Settlemier,
EMP: 50
SALES (est): 8.6MM **Privately Held**
SIC: 7353 Cranes & aerial lift equipment,
rental or leasing

(P-14097)
HARBOR INDUSTRIAL SERVICES
211 N Marine Ave, Wilmington
(90744-5724)
PHONE....................................310 522-1193
W Michael Hawk, *President*
Kent Phillips, *CFO*
Steve Hessenauer, *VP Bus Dvlpt*
▲ EMP: 80 EST: 1993
SALES (est): 9.6MM **Privately Held**
WEB: www.harborindustrial.com
SIC: 7353 Cranes & aerial lift equipment,
rental or leasing

(P-14098)
HAWTHORNE MACHINERY CO (PA)
Also Called: Hawthorne Cat
16945 Camino San Bernardo, San Diego
(92127-2499)
PHONE....................................858 674-7000
Tee K Ness, *President*
David Ness, *COO*
Bob Price, *Exec VP*
Robert Price, *Exec VP*
Liza Mamea, *Branch Mgr*
◆ EMP: 200 EST: 1941
SQ FT: 130,000
SALES (est): 195.6MM **Privately Held**
SIC: 7353 7699 5082 7359 Heavy con-
struction equipment rental; construction
equipment repair; construction & mining
machinery; equipment rental & leasing

(P-14099)
HAWTHORNE MACHINERY CO (HQ)
Also Called: Caterpillar Authorized Dealer
16945 Camino San Bernardo, San Diego
(92127-2499)
PHONE....................................858 674-7000
Tee K Ness, *CEO*
Bob Price, *Exec VP*
Paul Hawthorne, *Vice Pres*
Mike Johnson, *Vice Pres*
Steve Sager, *Vice Pres*
EMP: 100
SQ FT: 130,000
SALES (est): 14.9MM
SALES (corp-wide): 195.6MM **Privately Held**
WEB: www.hawthornelift.com
SIC: 7353 5084 Heavy construction equip-
ment rental; industrial machinery & equip-
ment
PA: Hawthorne Machinery Co.
16945 Camino San Bernardo
San Diego CA 92127
858 674-7000

(P-14100)
JOHN M PHILLIPS LLC (PA)
Also Called: John M Phillips Oil Field Eqp
2755 Dawson Ave, Signal Hill
(90755-2021)
PHONE....................................562 595-7363
Nancy Freeze,
Becky Curry, *Office Mgr*
Kelly Freeze,
John Greenwell,
Michael Greenwell,
◆ EMP: 55

SQ FT: 3,000
SALES: 8.1MM **Privately Held**
WEB: www.johnmphillips.com
SIC: 7353 5084 Oil field equipment, rental
or leasing; oil well machinery, equipment
& supplies

(P-14101)
LLC BREWER CRANE
Also Called: Brewer Crane & Rigging
12570 Highway 67 Bldg 10, Lakeside
(92040-1159)
PHONE..................................619 390-8252
Brent S Brewer, *President*
Brent K Garcia, *CFO*
Rolynda Brewer, *Officer*
Teresa Lombardo, *Administration*
Andre Silva, *Foreman/Supr*
EMP: 72 **EST:** 1997
SQ FT: 2,500
SALES: 24MM **Privately Held**
WEB: www.brewercrane.com
SIC: 7353 Cranes & aerial lift equipment,
rental or leasing

(P-14102)
M T M & M INC
Also Called: Pick-A-Part
3333 Peck Rd, Monrovia (91016-5001)
PHONE..................................626 445-2922
Thomas Hutton, *President*
EMP: 100
SQ FT: 1,100
SALES (est): 7.5MM
SALES (corp-wide): 11.8B **Publicly Held**
WEB: www.pickapart.com
SIC: 7353 5093 Heavy construction equip-
ment rental; scrap & waste materials
HQ: Pick-Your-Part Auto Wrecking
1235 S Beach Blvd
Anaheim CA 92804
800 962-2277

(P-14103)
MARCO CRANE & RIGGING CO
10168 Channel Rd, Lakeside (92040-1704)
PHONE..................................619 938-8080
George Wheeler, *Sales/Mktg Mgr*
EMP: 70
SALES (corp-wide): 27.8MM **Privately
Held**
WEB: www.marcocrane.com
SIC: 7353 Cranes & aerial lift equipment,
rental or leasing
PA: Marco Crane & Rigging Co.
221 S 35th Ave
Phoenix AZ 85009
602 272-2671

(P-14104)
MAXIM CRANE WORKS LP
2373 S Mariposa Rd, Stockton
(95205-7811)
PHONE..................................209 464-7635
Darrel Sudduth, *Manager*
Victor Slater, *Sales Staff*
EMP: 150
SALES (corp-wide): 253.6MM **Privately
Held**
WEB: www.maximcrane.com
SIC: 7353 Cranes & aerial lift equipment,
rental or leasing
HQ: Maxim Crane Works, L.P.
1225 Wash Pike Ste 100
Bridgeville PA 15017
412 504-0200

(P-14105)
**NATIONAL BUSINESS GROUP
INC (PA)**
Also Called: National Tube & Steel
15319 Chatsworth St, Mission Hills
(91345-2040)
PHONE..................................818 221-6000
James Mooneyham, *President*
EMP: 85
SQ FT: 24,000
SALES (est): 123.3MM **Privately Held**
WEB: www.fence-rental.com
SIC: 7353 5039 7359 3496 Earth moving
equipment, rental or leasing; wire fence,
gates & accessories; garage facility & tool
rental; fencing, made from purchased
wire; utility trailer rental

(P-14106)
NOBLE RENTS INC
8314 Slauson Ave, Pico Rivera
(90660-4323)
PHONE..................................855 767-4424
Nabil Kassam, *CEO*
Suzy Taherian, *Corp Secy*
EMP: 65 **EST:** 2011
SQ FT: 62,766
SALES: 13.4MM **Privately Held**
SIC: 7353 Heavy construction equipment
rental

(P-14107)
NORTHWEST EXCAVATING INC
18201 Napa St, Northridge (91325-3374)
PHONE..................................818 349-5861
Susan Groff, *CEO*
Robbie Groff, *Vice Pres*
Jane Sotto, *Controller*
EMP: 72
SQ FT: 2,500
SALES (est): 14.2MM **Privately Held**
WEB: www.nwexc.com
SIC: 7353 1794 Heavy construction equip-
ment rental; excavation & grading, build-
ing construction

(P-14108)
**OFFSHORE CRANE & SERVICE
CO (PA)**
Also Called: T & T Truck & Crane Service
1375 N Olive St Ste A, Ventura
(93001-1375)
P.O. Box 1748 (93002-1748)
PHONE..................................805 648-3348
Earl G Holder, *CEO*
Tim Holder, *President*
Kimberly A Loft, *Treasurer*
Shawn Paul, *Vice Pres*
Christine Bowen, *Office Mgr*
EMP: 52 **EST:** 1970
SQ FT: 11,000
SALES (est): 14.2MM **Privately Held**
SIC: 7353 4212 Cranes & aerial lift equip-
ment, rental or leasing; truck rental with
drivers

(P-14109)
PEED EQUIPMENT COMPANY
43466 Business Park Dr, Temecula
(92590-5526)
PHONE..................................951 657-0900
Carolyn Peed, *President*
Michael Peed, *Treasurer*
David Peed, *Admin Sec*
EMP: 50
SQ FT: 17,000
SALES (est): 13.4MM **Privately Held**
SIC: 7353 7699 Heavy construction equip-
ment rental; construction equipment re-
pair

(P-14110)
RALPH D MITZEL INC
Also Called: Mitzel Company
1520 N Fairview St, Santa Ana
(92706-3111)
PHONE..................................714 554-4745
Ralph D Mitzel Jr, *President*
Bill Stehle, *CFO*
Arlene Mitzel, *Corp Secy*
John K Mitzel, *Vice Pres*
EMP: 100
SQ FT: 1,000
SALES (est): 13.2MM **Privately Held**
SIC: 7353 1794 Heavy construction equip-
ment rental; excavation & grading, build-
ing construction

(P-14111)
**RDO CONSTRUCTION
EQUIPMENT CO**
Also Called: John Deere Authorized Dealer
10108 Riverford Rd, Lakeside
(92040-2740)
PHONE..................................619 443-3758
Ron Offets, *President*
Christopher Scott, *General Mgr*
EMP: 60
SQ FT: 2,200

SALES (est): 13.2MM **Privately Held**
WEB: www.bbrental.com
SIC: 7353 5082 Heavy construction equipment rental; general construction machinery & equipment

(P-14112)
RJ ALLEN INC
10392 Stanford Ave, Garden Grove
(92840-6301)
PHONE..................................714 539-1022
Andrew Allen, *President*
Ron Markham, *Vice Pres*
Shannon Wood, *Office Mgr*
Rd Martinez, *Project Mgr*
Shawn Ellis, *Plant Mgr*
EMP: 65
SQ FT: 20,000
SALES (est): 16.8MM **Privately Held**
WEB: www.rjalleninc.com
SIC: 7353 Heavy construction equipment
rental

(P-14113)
**SAVALA EQUIPMENT COMPANY
INC (PA)**
Also Called: Savala Equipment Rentals
16402 Construction Cir E, Irvine
(92606-4408)
PHONE..................................949 552-1859
Sean Savala, *President*
Scott Damon, *VP Sales*
EMP: 60
SQ FT: 3,200
SALES (est): 16.4MM **Privately Held**
WEB: www.savala.com
SIC: 7353 Cranes & aerial lift equipment,
rental or leasing

(P-14114)
SHEEDY DRAYAGE CO (PA)
1215 Michigan St, San Francisco
(94107-3518)
P.O. Box 77004 (94107-0004)
PHONE..................................415 648-7171
Don Russell, *Chairman*
Richard Battaini, *President*
Michael A Battaini, *CEO*
Peter Hogan, *Corp Secy*
▲ **EMP:** 80 **EST:** 1925
SQ FT: 25,000
SALES (est): 24.9MM **Privately Held**
WEB: www.sheedycrane.com
SIC: 7353 Cranes & aerial lift equipment,
rental or leasing

(P-14115)
TONY R CRISALLI INC
3468 Campbell St, Riverside (92509-1029)
PHONE..................................951 727-0110
Tony R Crisalli, *President*
EMP: 50
SALES (est): 5.2MM **Privately Held**
SIC: 7353 Heavy construction equipment
rental

(P-14116)
**WASTE MGT COLLECTN
RECYCL INC**
1800 S Grand Ave, Santa Ana
(92705-4800)
PHONE..................................714 637-3010
Lee Hicks, *Principal*
Greg Ong, *Analyst*
Sissy Rivas, *Cust Mgr*
EMP: 350
SALES (est): 118.9MM
SALES (corp-wide): 14.9B **Publicly Held**
SIC: 7353 4953 Heavy construction equip-
ment rental; refuse collection & disposal
services
PA: Waste Management, Inc.
1001 Fannin St Ste 4000
Houston TX 77002
713 512-6200

(P-14117)
**WESTERN ENERGY SERVICES
CORP**
3430 Getty St, Bakersfield (93308-5248)
PHONE..................................403 984-5916
Alex Rn Macausland, *CEO*
Jeffrey K Bowers, *Vice Pres*
EMP: 200

SALES (est): 3MM **Privately Held**
SIC: 7353 Oil well drilling equipment, rental
or leasing

(P-14118)
**WESTERN PCF CRANE & EQP
LLC (DH)**
8600 Calabash Ave, Fontana (92335-3018)
PHONE..................................562 286-6618
Robert G Johnson, *President*
Robert G Jonhson, *President*
Ken Pugh, *Branch Mgr*
Randy Defosse, *General Mgr*
Matthew Mader, *Sales Staff*
EMP: 63
SQ FT: 45,000
SALES (est): 15.1MM
SALES (corp-wide): 181.8MM **Privately
Held**
SIC: 7353 Cranes & aerial lift equipment,
rental or leasing
HQ: Mi-Jack Products Inc.
3111 167th St
Hazel Crest IL 60429
708 596-5200

```
7359 Equipment Rental &
Leasing, NEC
```

(P-14119)
(A) TOOL SHED INC (PA)
Also Called: A Tool Shed Equipment Rentals
3700 Soquel Ave, Santa Cruz
(95062-1774)
PHONE..................................831 477-7133
Robert Pedersen, *President*
Bruce Harmon, *General Mgr*
Bonnie Pedersen, *Admin Sec*
EMP: 72
SQ FT: 2,500
SALES (est): 24.4MM **Privately Held**
WEB: www.atoolshed.com
SIC: 7359 Tool rental

(P-14120)
A-THRONE CO INC
1850 E 33rd St, Long Beach (90807-5208)
PHONE..................................562 981-1197
Michael L Rice, *President*
EMP: 55
SALES (est): 8.4MM **Privately Held**
WEB: www.athrone.com
SIC: 7359 1799 Portable toilet rental;
fence construction

(P-14121)
**ADVANCED TEST EQUIPMENT
CORP**
Also Called: Advanced Test Eqp Rentals
10401 Roselle St, San Diego (92121-1523)
PHONE..................................858 558-6500
James P Berg, *CEO*
Jill E Berg, *President*
Gabriel Alcala, *Technical Staff*
Chris Reed, *Business Mgr*
Michael Marcum, *Human Res Dir*
EMP: 60
SQ FT: 25,000
SALES (est): 19.3MM **Privately Held**
WEB: www.atecorp.com
SIC: 7359 Equipment rental & leasing

(P-14122)
AFTER-PARTY2 INC
2310 E Imperial Hwy, El Segundo
(90245-2813)
PHONE..................................310 535-3660
Michael Stern, *Manager*
EMP: 59 **Publicly Held**
SIC: 7359 Tent & tarpaulin rental
HQ: After-Party2, Inc.
901 W Hillcrest Blvd
Inglewood CA 90301
310 202-0011

(P-14123)
AIR LEASE CORPORATION (PA)
2000 Avenue Of The Stars 1000n, Los An-
geles (90067-4734)
PHONE..................................310 553-0555
John L Plueger, *President*
Steven F Udvar-Hazy, *Ch of Bd*
Pablo Chavez, *President*
Kenneth Coursey, *President*

Heidi Hyun, *President*
EMP: 74
SALES: 1.6B **Publicly Held**
SIC: 7359 7389 Aircraft rental; aircraft & industrial truck rental services; financial services

(P-14124)
AJAX PORTABLE SERVICES
Also Called: Waste Management
11240 Commercial Pkwy, Castroville (95012-3206)
PHONE..................................831 384-5000
David Steiner, *President*
Adam Mallory, *Business Anlyst*
Sam Ottosen, *Opers Mgr*
Damian Schmitt, *Opers Staff*
Robert Welborn, *Sales Staff*
EMP: 50
SALES (est): 5.3MM **Privately Held**
SIC: 7359 Portable toilet rental

(P-14125)
ALG INC
215 S Highway 101 Ste 111, Solana Beach (92075-1844)
PHONE..................................858 945-1312
Andrea Gilbert, *Principal*
EMP: 112 EST: 2010
SALES (est): 138.8K
SALES (corp-wide): 353.5MM **Publicly Held**
SIC: 7359 Aircraft rental
PA: Truecar, Inc.
120 Broadway Ste 200
Santa Monica CA 90401
800 200-2000

(P-14126)
ALTA EQUIPMENT LEASING COMPANY
50 California St Fl 24, San Francisco (94111-4624)
PHONE..................................415 875-1000
Michael J Sangiacomo, *President*
Archie L Humphrey, *COO*
Mark Lomele, *CFO*
EMP: 55
SALES (est): 3.5MM
SALES (corp-wide): 1.4B **Privately Held**
WEB: www.norcalwastesystemsofbutte-county.com
SIC: 7359 Equipment rental & leasing
PA: Recology Inc.
50 California St Ste 2400
San Francisco CA 94111
415 875-1000

(P-14127)
AMADA CAPITAL CORPORATION
7025 Firestone Blvd, Buena Park (90621-1869)
PHONE..................................714 739-2111
Mike Guerin, *President*
David Kehrli, *Vice Pres*
EMP: 100
SQ FT: 103,000
SALES (est): 13.5MM **Privately Held**
SIC: 7359 Equipment rental & leasing
HQ: Amada North America, Inc
7025 Firestone Blvd
Buena Park CA 90621

(P-14128)
ANDY GUMP INC
11551 Hart St, North Hollywood (91605-6204)
PHONE..................................818 255-0650
Gary Wood, *Manager*
Thomas Field, *Sales Mgr*
EMP: 70
SALES (est): 2.4MM
SALES (corp-wide): 21.6MM **Privately Held**
WEB: www.andygump.com
SIC: 7359 Portable toilet rental
PA: Andy Gump, Inc.
26410 Summit Cir
Santa Clarita CA 91350
661 251-7721

(P-14129)
ARENA STUART RENTALS INC
454 S Abbott Ave, Milpitas (95035-5258)
PHONE..................................408 856-3232
Michael Berman, *President*
EMP: 150
SALES (est): 1.7MM **Privately Held**
SIC: 7359 5947 Party supplies rental services; party favors

(P-14130)
BA LEASING & CAPITAL CORP (DH)
555 California St Fl 4, San Francisco (94104-1506)
PHONE..................................415 765-1804
Richard Harris, *President*
K Thomas Rose, *COO*
Rod Hurd, *Treasurer*
Oliver James Warner, *Vice Pres*
EMP: 130 EST: 1955
SALES (est): 6.3MM
SALES (corp-wide): 110.5B **Publicly Held**
SIC: 7359 Equipment rental & leasing
HQ: Banc Of America Leasing & Capital, Llc
555 California St Fl 4
San Francisco CA 94104
415 765-7349

(P-14131)
BAY CITIES CRANE & RIGGING INC (PA)
Also Called: Bragg Crane & Rigging
457 Parr Blvd, Richmond (94801-1133)
PHONE..................................510 232-7222
Marilynn Bragg, *President*
Mary Ann Pool, *Corp Secy*
John Anderson, *Executive*
Frank Dillon, *Branch Mgr*
Karen Daniels, *CIO*
EMP: 50 EST: 1970
SQ FT: 10,000
SALES (est): 6.4MM **Privately Held**
WEB: www.braggnorcal.com
SIC: 7359 7353 Equipment rental & leasing; cranes & aerial lift equipment, rental or leasing

(P-14132)
BBAM ARCFT HOLDINGS 137 LABUAN
50 California St Fl 14, San Francisco (94111-4683)
PHONE..................................415 267-1600
Steve Zissis, *CEO*
EMP: 100
SALES (est): 9.5MM **Privately Held**
SIC: 7359 Aircraft rental

(P-14133)
BRIGHT EVENT RENTALS LLC (PA)
Also Called: Wine Country Party & Events
1640 W 190th St, Torrance (90501-1113)
PHONE..................................310 202-0011
Michael Bjornstad, *Mng Member*
Christine Pease, *Accounting Mgr*
Gama Sanchez, *Opers Staff*
Paul Conway, *Director*
Tanya Kaplan, *Director*
▲ **EMP:** 240
SALES (est): 76.2MM **Privately Held**
SIC: 7359 Party supplies rental services

(P-14134)
BRIGHT EVENT RENTALS LLC
Also Called: Event Rentals San Diego
7069 Consolidated Way, San Diego (92121-2688)
PHONE..................................858 496-9700
EMP: 510
SALES (corp-wide): 76.2MM **Privately Held**
SIC: 7359 Party supplies rental services
PA: Bright Event Rentals, Llc
1640 W 190th St
Torrance CA 90501
310 202-0011

(P-14135)
BRIGHT EVENT RENTALS LLC
22674 Broadway Ste A, Sonoma (95476-8217)
PHONE..................................310 202-0011
Matt Wiltshire, *Manager*
EMP: 150
SALES (corp-wide): 76.2MM **Privately Held**
SIC: 7359 Party supplies rental services
PA: Bright Event Rentals, Llc
1640 W 190th St
Torrance CA 90501
310 202-0011

(P-14136)
BROOK FURNITURE RENTAL INC
Also Called: Brook Furniture Clearance Ctr
30985 Santana St, Hayward (94544-7029)
PHONE..................................510 487-4440
Robert W Crawford, *Owner*
EMP: 50
SALES (corp-wide): 86.6MM **Privately Held**
WEB: www.bfr.com
SIC: 7359 Furniture rental
HQ: Brook Furniture Rental, Inc.
100 N Field Dr Ste 220
Lake Forest IL 60045
847 810-4000

(P-14137)
CAI INTERNATIONAL INC (PA)
1 Market Plz Ste 900, San Francisco (94105-1101)
PHONE..................................415 788-0100
Victor M Garcia, *President*
David G Remington, *Ch of Bd*
Timothy B Page, *CFO*
Daniel J Hallahan, *Senior VP*
Camille G Cutino, *Vice Pres*
▼ **EMP:** 104
SALES: 432.1MM **Publicly Held**
WEB: www.capps.com
SIC: 7359 Shipping container leasing

(P-14138)
CAL WEST GENERAL ENGRG INC
5480 Baltimore Dr Ste 215, La Mesa (91942-2066)
PHONE..................................619 469-5811
Ronald E Provience, *CEO*
Frank A Passiglia, *President*
EMP: 50
SQ FT: 2,000
SALES (est): 4.6MM **Privately Held**
SIC: 7359 Equipment rental & leasing

(P-14139)
CENTRAL VALLEY PARTY SUPPLY
Also Called: Grand Events
3250 Dale Rd Ste I, Modesto (95356-0578)
PHONE..................................209 569-0399
Ray Pogue, *Principal*
EMP: 50
SQ FT: 37,000
SALES (est): 3.7MM **Privately Held**
WEB: www.grand-events.com
SIC: 7359 Party supplies rental services

(P-14140)
CHOURA EVENTS
540 Hawaii Ave, Torrance (90503-5148)
PHONE..................................310 320-6200
James Ryan Choura, *CEO*
Jim Sala, *Vice Pres*
Jeff Ginter, *Opers Staff*
EMP: 80 EST: 2014
SALES: 8MM **Privately Held**
SIC: 7359 Party supplies rental services

(P-14141)
COMPASS GROUP USA INC
Also Called: Canteen Vending
12640 Knott St, Garden Grove (92841-3902)
PHONE..................................714 899-2520
Ron Wanamaker, *Vice Pres*
Ralph Cuiccio, *Regional Dir*
Mike Pulsipher, *Manager*
EMP: 125

SALES (corp-wide): 29.6B **Privately Held**
WEB: www.compass-usa.com
SIC: 7359 7699 5962 Vending machine rental; vending machine repair; merchandising machine operators
HQ: Compass Group Usa, Inc.
2400 Yorkmont Rd
Charlotte NC 28217
704 328-4000

(P-14142)
CONCORD JET SERVICE INC
3000 Oak Rd Ste 200, Walnut Creek (94597-4506)
P.O. Box 907, Concord (94522-0907)
PHONE..................................925 825-2980
Kenneth Hoffman, *President*
Goy Fuller, *Principal*
EMP: 50
SALES (est): 4.6MM **Privately Held**
SIC: 7359 Aircraft rental

(P-14143)
CORT BUSINESS SERVICES CORP
14350 Grfield Ave Ste 500, Paramount (90723)
PHONE..................................562 582-1515
Pat Bockenstette, *Branch Mgr*
EMP: 70
SALES (corp-wide): 225.3B **Publicly Held**
SIC: 7359 Furniture rental
HQ: Cort Business Services Corporation
15000 Conference
Chantilly VA 20151
703 968-8500

(P-14144)
CP OPCO LLC
Also Called: Classic Party Rentals
22674 Broadway A, Sonoma (95476-8217)
PHONE..................................707 253-2332
EMP: 59
SALES (corp-wide): 1.9MM **Privately Held**
SIC: 7359
HQ: Cp Opco, Llc
901 W Hillcrest Blvd A
Inglewood CA 90301
310 966-4900

(P-14145)
CP OPCO LLC
Also Called: Classic Party Rentals
7069 Cnsld Way Ste 300, San Diego (92121)
PHONE..................................858 496-9700
EMP: 100
SALES (corp-wide): 1.9MM **Privately Held**
SIC: 7359
HQ: Cp Opco, Llc
901 W Hillcrest Blvd A
Inglewood CA 90301
310 966-4900

(P-14146)
CP OPCO LLC
Also Called: Classic Party Rentals
333 S Grand Ave Ste 4070, Los Angeles (90071-1544)
PHONE..................................209 524-1966
EMP: 59
SALES (corp-wide): 1.9MM **Privately Held**
SIC: 7359
HQ: Cp Opco, Llc
901 W Hillcrest Blvd A
Inglewood CA 90301
310 966-4900

(P-14147)
CP OPCO LLC
Also Called: Classic Party Rentals
11766 Wilshire Blvd # 380, Los Angeles (90025-6538)
PHONE..................................310 966-4900
EMP: 59
SALES (corp-wide): 1.9MM **Privately Held**
SIC: 7359
HQ: Cp Opco, Llc
901 W Hillcrest Blvd A
Inglewood CA 90301
310 966-4900

(P-14148)
CP OPCO LLC
Also Called: Classic Party Rentals
22674 Broadway A, Sonoma (95476-8217)
PHONE..............................650 652-0300
Fax: 650 697-9090
EMP: 59
SALES (corp-wide): 1.9MM **Privately
Held**
SIC: 7359
HQ: Cp Opco, Llc
　901 W Hillcrest Blvd A
　Inglewood CA 90301
　310 966-4900

(P-14149)
CP OPCO LLC
Also Called: Classic Party Rentals
1120 Mark Ave, Carpinteria (93013-2918)
PHONE..............................805 566-3566
Fax: 805 566-3599
EMP: 59
SALES (corp-wide): 1.9MM **Privately
Held**
SIC: 7359
HQ: Cp Opco, Llc
　901 W Hillcrest Blvd A
　Inglewood CA 90301
　310 966-4900

(P-14150)
CP OPCO LLC
Also Called: Classic Party Rentals
3101 S Harbor Blvd, Santa Ana
(92704-6826)
PHONE..............................714 540-6111
EMP: 100
SALES (corp-wide): 1.9MM **Privately
Held**
SIC: 7359
HQ: Cp Opco, Llc
　901 W Hillcrest Blvd A
　Inglewood CA 90301
　310 966-4900

(P-14151)
CWF INC
Also Called: A-1 Party Rentals
251 E Front St, Covina (91723-1613)
PHONE..............................626 967-0500
Chet Fortney, *President*
Angela Barrera, *Project Mgr*
▲ EMP: 51
SALES: 950K **Privately Held**
SIC: 7359 Party supplies rental services

(P-14152)
DIAMOND ENVIRONMENTAL SVCS LP
807 E Mission Rd, San Marcos
(92069-3002)
PHONE..............................760 744-7191
Eric De Jong,
Amanda Lamar, *Administration*
Renee Coles, *Sales Staff*
Viviana Valdez, *Sales Staff*
Belina Ybarra, *Cust Mgr*
EMP: 100 EST: 1997
SQ FT: 2,000
SALES (est): 20.9MM **Privately Held**
SIC: 7359 Portable toilet rental

(P-14153)
DISPATCH TRANSPORTATION LLC
Also Called: Dispatch Commodity Trucking
14032 Santa Ana Ave, Fontana
(92337-7035)
PHONE..............................909 355-5531
Bruce Degler,
Kim Pugmire,
EMP: 150
SQ FT: 3,500
SALES (est): 20.9MM **Privately Held**
WEB: www.proloaders.com
SIC: 7359 Equipment rental & leasing

(P-14154)
EAGLE HIGH REACH EQUIPMENT LLC
14241 Alondra Blvd, La Mirada
(90638-5501)
PHONE..............................619 265-2637
John Benjamin,
Al Deluca, *Technology*

Mary J Ray, *VP Human Res*
EMP: 70
SQ FT: 22,000
SALES (est): 4MM **Privately Held**
SIC: 7359 7353 5084 Equipment rental &
leasing; cranes & aerial lift equipment,
rental or leasing; materials handling ma-
chinery

(P-14155)
EL CAMINO RENTAL
1833 Oceanside Blvd Ste D, Oceanside
(92054-3456)
PHONE..............................760 722-7368
Bill Mahalic, *Owner*
Ted Donnelly, *General Mgr*
EMP: 50
SALES (est): 3.3MM **Privately Held**
WEB: www.elcaminorental.com
SIC: 7359 Party supplies rental services

(P-14156)
ELECTRO RENT CORPORATION (HQ)
Also Called: Rush Computer Rentals
8511 Fllbrook Ave Ste 200, West Hills
(91304)
P.O. Box 605, Newbury Park (91319-0605)
PHONE..............................818 786-2525
Michael Clark, *CEO*
Jay Geldmacher, *President*
Allen Sciarillo, *CFO*
Jim Platner, *Vice Pres*
Ilona M McDermott, *Info Tech Mgr*
EMP: 148 EST: 1965
SALES (est): 122.9MM **Privately Held**
SIC: 7359 7377 5065 5045 Electronic
equipment rental, except computers;
computer rental & leasing; electronic
parts & equipment; computers & acces-
sories, personal & home entertainment
PA: Elecor Intermediate Holding Ii Corpora-
tion
　360 N Crescent Dr
　Beverly Hills CA 90210
　310 712-1850

(P-14157)
EZ ACCEPTANCE INC
7651 Ronson Rd, San Diego (92111-1511)
PHONE..............................858 278-8351
Ronald Zagami, *President*
Mike Toomey, *Vice Pres*
EMP: 140
SALES (est): 4.2MM **Privately Held**
SIC: 7359 Equipment rental & leasing

(P-14158)
FENIX MARINE SERVICES LTD
614 Terminal Way, San Pedro
(90731-7453)
PHONE..............................310 548-8877
Sean Pierce, *President*
◆ EMP: 130 EST: 1978
SQ FT: 2,500
SALES (est): 35.7MM **Privately Held**
WEB: www.eaglemarineservices.com
SIC: 7359 Shipping container leasing
PA: P5 Infrastructure Llc
　6263 N Scottsdale Rd
　Scottsdale AZ 85250
　206 696-3648

(P-14159)
FIFTH & SUNSET ENTERPRISES LLC
Also Called: 5th & Sunset Productions
12322 Exposition Blvd, Los Angeles
(90064-1014)
PHONE..............................310 979-0212
Bruce E Kramer, *President*
EMP: 85
SQ FT: 19,000
SALES: 12.5MM **Privately Held**
SIC: 7359 7335 Equipment rental & leas-
ing; still & slide file production

(P-14160)
FINNCO SERVICES INCORPORATED
8241 Beech Ave, Fontana (92335-3210)
PHONE..............................909 355-0707
Matthew Finnerty, *Vice Pres*
Cynthia Finnerty, *CFO*
EMP: 52

SALES (est): 269.5K **Privately Held**
SIC: 7359 7699 Equipment rental & leasing; elevators: inspection, service & repair

(P-14161)
FREEMAN AUDIO VISUAL LLC
901 E South St, Anaheim (92805-5347)
PHONE..............................714 254-3400
Gabriele Buonacorsi, *Branch Mgr*
EMP: 200
SALES (corp-wide): 3.5B **Privately Held**
WEB: www.avwtelav.com
SIC: 7359 Audio-visual equipment & sup-
ply rental
HQ: Freeman Audio Visual, Llc
　1600 Viceroy Dr Ste 100
　Dallas TX 75235
　214 445-1000

(P-14162)
HANA FINANCIAL INC (PA)
1000 Wilshire Blvd Fl 20, Los Angeles
(90017-5645)
PHONE..............................213 240-1234
Sunnie S Kim, *CEO*
Kyle Kang, *Officer*
Michelle Yue, *Officer*
Young Shim, *Senior VP*
Kevin Thomas, *Senior VP*
▲ EMP: 85
SQ FT: 24,000
SALES (est): 15.1MM **Privately Held**
SIC: 7359 6153 6159 Equipment rental &
leasing; factoring services; small business
investment companies

(P-14163)
HERC RENTALS INC
Also Called: Herc Rentals 9741
5500 Commerce Blvd, Rohnert Park
(94928-1607)
PHONE..............................707 586-6491
Mark Hobson, *Regional Mgr*
Michael Tischbern, *General Mgr*
Kathy Fagan, *Manager*
EMP: 58
SALES (corp-wide): 1.9B **Publicly Held**
SIC: 7359 Equipment rental & leasing
HQ: Herc Rentals Inc.
　27500 Rverview Ctr Bldg 7
　Bonita Springs FL 34134
　800 654-6659

(P-14164)
HERC RENTALS INC
Also Called: Herc Rentals 9638
22422 S Alameda St, Carson (90810-1903)
PHONE..............................310 233-5000
Brian Dorte, *Manager*
EMP: 50
SQ FT: 19,494
SALES (corp-wide): 1.9B **Publicly Held**
WEB: www.hertzequip.com
SIC: 7359 Equipment rental & leasing
HQ: Herc Rentals Inc.
　27500 Rverview Ctr Bldg 7
　Bonita Springs FL 34134
　800 654-6659

(P-14165)
HERC RENTALS INC
Also Called: Herc Rentals 9643
6315 Snow Rd, Bakersfield (93308-9531)
PHONE..............................661 392-3661
Matt Hudnall, *Branch Mgr*
EMP: 225
SALES (corp-wide): 1.9B **Publicly Held**
SIC: 7359 Equipment rental & leasing
HQ: Herc Rentals Inc.
　27500 Rverview Ctr Bldg 7
　Bonita Springs FL 34134
　800 654-6659

(P-14166)
HERC RENTALS INC
Also Called: Herc Rentals 9748
5251 Industrial Way, Benicia (94510-1034)
PHONE..............................707 747-4444
John Moyer, *Manager*
EMP: 50
SALES (corp-wide): 1.9B **Publicly Held**
SIC: 7359 Equipment rental & leasing
HQ: Herc Rentals Inc.
　27500 Rverview Ctr Bldg 7
　Bonita Springs FL 34134
　800 654-6659

(P-14167)
HERC RENTALS INC
Also Called: Herc Rentals Prosolutions
7727 Oakport St, Oakland (94621-2026)
PHONE..............................510 633-2040
Ted Oshea, *Manager*
EMP: 225
SALES (corp-wide): 1.9B **Publicly Held**
SIC: 7359 Equipment rental & leasing
HQ: Herc Rentals Inc.
　27500 Rverview Ctr Bldg 7
　Bonita Springs FL 34134
　800 654-6659

(P-14168)
HOLZMUELLER CORPORATION
Also Called: Holzmueller Productions
1000 25th St, San Francisco (94107-3509)
PHONE..............................415 826-8383
Richard P Gentschel, *President*
Carol Gentschel, *Vice Pres*
Dave Tier, *Foreman/Supr*
Michael Hamlin, *Sales Mgr*
Jim Schelstrate, *Manager*
EMP: 50
SQ FT: 30,000
SALES (est): 6.9MM **Privately Held**
WEB: www.holzmueller.com
SIC: 7359 5719 1731 Sound & lighting
equipment rental; lighting fixtures; electri-
cal work

(P-14169)
HUB CONSTRUCTION SPC INC (PA)
Also Called: Hub Construction Sups & Eqp
379 S I St, San Bernardino (92410-2409)
PHONE..............................909 889-0161
Robert T Gogo, *President*
Bernice Gogo, *Corp Secy*
Casey Lester, *Technology*
Dean Beatty, *Purch Agent*
Louie Hernandez, *Sales Associate*
EMP: 50
SQ FT: 25,000
SALES (est): 39MM
SALES (corp-wide): 35.1MM **Privately
Held**
SIC: 7359 5082 Equipment rental & leas-
ing; construction & mining machinery

(P-14170)
IMPERIAL MRIDIAN COMPANIES INC
Also Called: Imca Capital
11901 Santa Monica Blvd # 338, Los Ange-
les (90025-2767)
PHONE..............................310 447-3460
Blake B Johnson, *President*
Emma Cabildo, *CFO*
EMP: 85
SQ FT: 10,200
SALES: 10MM **Privately Held**
SIC: 7359 Equipment rental & leasing

(P-14171)
J M EQUIPMENT COMPANY INC (PA)
Also Called: John Deere Authorized Dealer
321 Spreckels Ave, Manteca (95336-6007)
PHONE..............................209 522-3271
Ray Azevedo, *CEO*
Dave Baiocchi, *President*
Ed Henriquez, *President*
Vincent C Victorine, *CFO*
Audie Burgan, *Vice Pres*
EMP: 80
SQ FT: 7,000
SALES (est): 42.2MM **Privately Held**
WEB: www.jmequipment.com
SIC: 7359 5084 5999 Equipment rental &
leasing; materials handling machinery;
farm equipment & supplies; farm machin-
ery; farm tractors

(P-14172)
JALUX AMERICAS INC (HQ)
390 N Pcf Csthwy Ste 2000, El Segundo
(90245)
PHONE..............................310 524-1000
Osamu Yamaguchi, *Principal*
Shinichi Matsuyama, *President*
Yu Katahira, *Treasurer*
Naohiko Habuki, *Corp Secy*
Hidebumi Mori, *Exec VP*

P
R
O
D
U
C
T
S
&
S
V
C
S

◆ **EMP:** 50
SQ FT: 15,000
SALES: 22.6MM **Privately Held**
WEB: www.jaluxam.com
SIC: 7359 5088 5199 Aircraft rental; office
machine rental, except computers; aircraft
equipment & supplies; variety store mer-
chandise

(P-14173)
JC PARTY RENTALS INC
11562 Vanowen St, North Hollywood
(91605-6229)
PHONE..........................818 765-4819
Delmy Chavarria, *CEO*
Jose Urquilla, *President*
EMP: 52
SQ FT: 6,600
SALES: 653K **Privately Held**
SIC: 7359 Party supplies rental services

(P-14174)
JULES AND ASSOCIATES INC
515 S Figueroa St # 1900, Los Angeles
(90071-3336)
PHONE..........................213 362-5600
Jules Buenabenta, *President*
Michael Behar, *Senior VP*
Scott Monroe, *Senior VP*
Patrick Tully, *Executive*
Shane Westover, *Executive*
EMP: 51
SQ FT: 15,000
SALES (est): 140MM **Privately Held**
WEB: www.julesandassociates.com
SIC: 7359 Equipment rental & leasing

(P-14175)
KING EQUIPMENT LLC
1690 Ashley Way, Colton (92324-4000)
PHONE..........................909 986-5300
Ernie Quijada,
Sydney Reitz, *General Mgr*
Jenna Madaris, *Admin Asst*
Casey Wheeler, *Admin Asst*
Ronnie Kozna, *Info Tech Mgr*
EMP: 73
SALES (est): 23.3MM **Privately Held**
SIC: 7359 Equipment rental & leasing

(P-14176)
L A PARTY RENTS INC
13520 Saticoy St, Van Nuys (91402-6428)
PHONE..........................818 989-4300
Gerome Nehus, *CEO*
Kevin Dwyer, *Vice Pres*
Jerry Nehus, *CIO*
Jon Eckel, *Webmaster*
Rekha Sood, *Data Proc Staff*
EMP: 100
SALES (est): 11.3MM **Privately Held**
WEB: www.lapartyrents.com
SIC: 7359 Party supplies rental services

(P-14177)
LOUNGE 22 LLC (PA)
211 N Brand Blvd, Glendale (91203-2609)
PHONE..........................818 502-0700
Armen S Gharabegian,
Armen Gharabegian,
EMP: 70
SALES (est): 3.7MM **Privately Held**
WEB: www.lounge22.com
SIC: 7359 5712 Furniture rental; furniture
stores

(P-14178)
**MACQURIE ARCFT LSG SVCS
US INC**
2 Embarcadero Ctr Ste 200, San Francisco
(94111-3801)
PHONE..........................415 829-6600
John R Willingham, *CEO*
Harry Forsythe, *Exec VP*
Lea Banducci, *Vice Pres*
Nora Bergman, *Vice Pres*
Bruce Hogarth, *Vice Pres*
EMP: 60
SALES (est): 11.2MM **Privately Held**
SIC: 7359 Aircraft rental
PA: Macquarie Airfinance (No 2) Limited
South Bank House
Dublin 4

(P-14179)
MCGRATH RENTCORP
Adler Tank Rentals
5700 Las Positas Rd, Livermore
(94551-7806)
PHONE..........................925 606-9200
Steve Adler, *Principal*
EMP: 94
SALES (corp-wide): 498.3MM **Publicly
Held**
SIC: 7359 Equipment rental & leasing
PA: Mcgrath Rentcorp
5700 Las Positas Rd
Livermore CA 94551
925 606-9200

(P-14180)
MEETING SERVICES INC
Also Called: MSI Production Services
1125 Joshua Way, Vista (92081-7840)
PHONE..........................858 348-0100
John Brinkman, *CEO*
Ray Lucy, *Shareholder*
Suzanne Carlson, *Executive*
Greg Hurst, *Executive*
Rob Wisley, *Department Mgr*
EMP: 90
SALES: 12.7MM **Privately Held**
WEB: www.msiprod.com
SIC: 7359 7629 5049 Audio-visual equip-
ment & supply rental; electrical equipment
repair, high voltage; theatrical equipment
& supplies

(P-14181)
**MICROFINANCIAL
INCORPORATED**
2801 Townsgate Rd, Westlake Village
(91361-3003)
PHONE..........................805 367-8900
Richard Latour, *CEO*
EMP: 139
SALES (corp-wide): 62.5MM **Privately
Held**
SIC: 7359 Business machine & electronic
equipment rental services
HQ: Microfinancial Incorporated
1600 District Ave Ste 200
Burlington MA 01803
781 994-4800

(P-14182)
MICROLEASE INC (DH)
6060 Sepulveda Blvd, Van Nuys
(91411-2512)
PHONE..........................866 520-0200
Gordon Curwen, *Vice Pres*
Michael E Clark, *CEO*
EMP: 85
SQ FT: 20,000
SALES (est): 51.9MM
SALES (corp-wide): 122.9MM **Privately
Held**
WEB: www.microlease.com
SIC: 7359 Rental store, general
HQ: Microlease Limited
Unit 1 Waverley Industrial Estate
Harrow MIDDX HA1 4
208 420-0200

(P-14183)
**NATIONAL CNSTR RENTALS INC
(HQ)**
15319 Chatsworth St, Mission Hills
(91345-2040)
PHONE..........................818 221-6000
James R Mooneyham, *President*
W Robert Mooneyham, *President*
Ron Abbatepaolo, *Regional Mgr*
Rod Dizon, *Administration*
Stephanie Doan, *Accountant*
◆ **EMP:** 85
SQ FT: 23,000
SALES (est): 135.1MM
SALES (corp-wide): 123.3MM **Privately
Held**
WEB: www.rentnational.com
SIC: 7359 Equipment rental & leasing
PA: The National Business Group Inc
15319 Chatsworth St
Mission Hills CA 91345
818 221-6000

(P-14184)
OES EQUIPMENT LLC (PA)
37421 Centralmont Pl, Fremont
(94536-6536)
PHONE..........................510 284-1900
Peter Nosler,
Doug Woods,
EMP: 53
SQ FT: 20,000
SALES (est): 26.8MM **Privately Held**
SIC: 7359 Equipment rental & leasing

(P-14185)
OHANA PARTNERS INC (PA)
Also Called: Stuart Rental Company
454 S Abbott Ave, Milpitas (95035-5258)
PHONE..........................408 856-3232
Michael Berman, *CEO*
Andrew Sutton, *Vice Pres*
R Andrew Sutton, *Vice Pres*
Clara Ayala, *Controller*
Juan Rodriguez, *Production*
▲ **EMP:** 66
SALES: 15MM **Privately Held**
WEB: www.stuartrental.com
SIC: 7359 5947 Party supplies rental serv-
ices; tent & tarpaulin rental; gifts & novel-
ties

(P-14186)
P J J ENTERPRISES INC
1250 Delevan Dr, San Diego (92102-2437)
PHONE..........................619 232-6136
John Lenore, *President*
Dorothy Lenore, *Treasurer*
Roger Carey, *Director*
EMP: 70 EST: 1966
SQ FT: 20,000
SALES (est): 2.7MM
SALES (corp-wide): 173.8MM **Privately
Held**
WEB: www.johnlenore.com
SIC: 7359 Rental store, general
PA: Lenore John & Co
1250 Delevan Dr
San Diego CA 92102
619 232-6136

(P-14187)
PANAVISION INC (PA)
Also Called: Panavision Group
6101 Variel Ave, Woodland Hills
(91367-3722)
PHONE..........................818 316-1000
Ronald O Perelman, *Ch of Bd*
William C Bevins, *President*
Kimberly Snyder, *CEO*
Ross Landsbaum, *COO*
John Suh, *CFO*
▲ **EMP:** 440
SQ FT: 150,000
SALES (est): 150.2MM **Privately Held**
WEB: www.panastore.com
SIC: 7359 3861 3648 5063 Equipment
rental & leasing; cameras & related equip-
ment; stage lighting equipment; lighting
fixtures

(P-14188)
PARKMERCED INVESTORS LLC
3711 19th Ave, San Francisco
(94132-2641)
PHONE..........................877 243-5544
Bruce Ward,
Chris Bricker, *General Mgr*
Gayle Mustanich, *Accountant*
EMP: 50
SALES (est): 8.7MM **Privately Held**
SIC: 7359 Lawn & garden equipment
rental

(P-14189)
PDQ ENTERPRISES INC
11037 Penrose Ave, Los Angeles (91331)
PHONE..........................818 504-4900
EMP: 52
SALES (corp-wide): 23.4MM **Privately
Held**
SIC: 7359 Equipment rental & leasing
PA: Pdq Enterprises, Inc.
10826 Shoemaker Ave
Santa Fe Springs CA 90670
562 944-3206

(P-14190)
PICO RENTS INC
Also Called: Pico Party Rents
13414 S Figueroa St, Los Angeles
(90061-1144)
PHONE..........................310 275-9431
William Edwards Jr, *President*
Darren G Edwards, *Admin Sec*
EMP: 60
SQ FT: 24,500
SALES (est): 8MM **Privately Held**
WEB: www.picopartyrents.com
SIC: 7359 Party supplies rental services

(P-14191)
PINAMAR LLC
Also Called: Special Events
6909 Las Positas Rd Ste D, Livermore
(94551-5113)
PHONE..........................925 243-8979
Weston Cook,
Jose Lazo, *Production*
EMP: 60
SALES (est): 6.6MM **Privately Held**
WEB: www.pinamar.com
SIC: 7359 Party supplies rental services

(P-14192)
QUIXOTE STUDIOS LLC (PA)
Also Called: Quixote Production Vehicles
1011 N Fuller Ave, West Hollywood
(90046-6651)
PHONE..........................323 851-5030
Jordan T Kitaen, *Mng Member*
Rachel Karsh, *Executive Asst*
Erin Leahy, *Admin Asst*
Michael Matus, *Info Tech Mgr*
Michael Sundstrom, *Accounting Mgr*
EMP: 50
SQ FT: 32,000
SALES (est): 23.3MM **Privately Held**
WEB: www.quixotestudios.com
SIC: 7359 Sound & lighting equipment
rental

(P-14193)
R & D LEASING INC
Also Called: Blare's Air & Ground Services
19101 Kent Ave, Lemoore (93245-9137)
PHONE..........................559 924-1276
Roger Hewett, *President*
Diana Hewett, *Principal*
EMP: 67
SALES (est): 4MM **Privately Held**
SIC: 7359 Equipment rental & leasing

(P-14194)
**RAPHAELS PARTY RENTALS
INC (PA)**
8606 Miramar Rd, San Diego
(92126-4326)
PHONE..........................858 444-1692
Raphael Silverman, *President*
Phillip Silverman, *Vice Pres*
David Gonzales, *General Mgr*
Kitty Silverman, *Admin Sec*
Gary Armstead, *Project Mgr*
EMP: 175
SQ FT: 60,000
SALES (est): 14MM **Privately Held**
WEB: www.raphaels.com
SIC: 7359 Party supplies rental services

(P-14195)
S & S RENT-A-FENCE INC
Also Called: S & S Construction Services
4511 Rowland Ave, El Monte (91731-1123)
P.O. Box 367, Glendora (91740-0367)
PHONE..........................818 896-7710
Sergio Diez, *CEO*
Steve Lakie, *Principal*
Steven R Parsell, *Principal*
EMP: 60 EST: 1978
SQ FT: 1,800
SALES (est): 5MM **Privately Held**
WEB: www.sandsrentafence.com
SIC: 7359 Portable toilet rental

(P-14196)
SEACASTLE INC
4000 Executive Pkwy # 240, San Ramon
(94583-4257)
PHONE..........................925 480-3000
Kathleen Francis, *Vice Pres*
EMP: 65 **Privately Held**
SIC: 7359 Equipment rental & leasing

PA: Seacastle, Inc
123 Tice Blvd
Woodcliff Lake NJ 07677

(P-14197)
SHOWROOM INTERIORS LLC
Also Called: Vesta Luxury Home Staging
4900 E 50th St, Vernon (90058-2734)
PHONE..............................323 348-1551
Julianne Buckner, *Mng Member*
EMP: 105
SALES (est): 5MM **Privately Held**
SIC: 7359 Furniture rental
PA: Showroom, Inc
4900 E 50th St
Vernon CA 90058
323 348-1551

(P-14198)
SIERRA EQUIPMENT LEASING INC
Also Called: Sierra Mountain Express
1140 Suncast Ln, El Dorado Hills
(95762-9313)
PHONE..............................925 676-7300
Murray Zwicker, *President*
Carol Zwicker, *Treasurer*
EMP: 50
SALES (est): 10.1MM **Privately Held**
SIC: 7359 Industrial truck rental

(P-14199)
SOLA RENTALS INC
8629 S Vermont Ave, Los Angeles
(90044-4868)
PHONE..............................323 306-4648
John Lusk, *President*
Alexis Lujan, *Principal*
Martin Muoto, *Principal*
Ashley Allen, *Sales Staff*
Thomas Lofton, *Manager*
EMP: 50
SALES (est): 378K **Privately Held**
SIC: 7359 Equipment rental & leasing

(P-14200)
SR BRAY LLC
Also Called: Power Plus
2750 N Perris Blvd, Perris (92571-3234)
PHONE..............................951 436-2920
Tony Maldonado, *Manager*
EMP: 50 **Privately Held**
SIC: 7359 Equipment rental & leasing
PA: S.R. Bray Llc
1210 N Red Gum St
Anaheim CA 92806

(P-14201)
TEXTAINER EQUIPMENT MGT US LTD (DH)
650 California St Fl 16, San Francisco
(94108-2720)
PHONE..............................415 434-0551
Ernest Furtado, *CFO*
Robert Pedersen, *Exec VP*
Ilia Dini, *Administration*
EMP: 55
SQ FT: 15,000
SALES (est): 11.7MM **Privately Held**
WEB: www.textainer.com
SIC: 7359 Shipping container leasing
HQ: Textainer Group Holdings Ltd
650 California St Fl 16
San Francisco CA 94108
415 434-0551

(P-14202)
TEXTANER EQP INCOME FUND II LP
650 California St Fl 16, San Francisco
(94108-2720)
PHONE..............................415 434-0551
Ernest J Furtado, *CFO*
EMP: 80
SQ FT: 15,000
SALES (est): 2.6MM **Privately Held**
SIC: 7359 Shipping container leasing

(P-14203)
TOWN & COUNTRY EVENT RENTALS (PA)
Also Called: Tacer
7725 Airport Bus Pkwy, Van Nuys (91406)
PHONE..............................818 908-4211
Richard Loguercio, *CEO*
Sherry Stimatz, *Branch Mgr*
Wayne Tay, *Branch Mgr*
David Searcy, *General Mgr*
Camille Conroy, *Office Mgr*
▲ **EMP:** 400
SQ FT: 1,100
SALES (est): 28MM **Privately Held**
WEB:
www.townandcountryeventrentals.com
SIC: 7359 Party supplies rental services

(P-14204)
UNITED RENTALS NORTH AMER INC
2911 E Fremont St, Stockton (95205-3913)
P.O. Box 8810 (95208-0810)
PHONE..............................209 948-9500
Joe Doran, *Manager*
EMP: 61
SALES (corp-wide): 8B **Publicly Held**
WEB: www.ur.com
SIC: 7359 Equipment rental & leasing
HQ: United Rentals (North America), Inc.
100 Frederick St 700
Stamford CT 06902
203 622-3131

(P-14205)
UNITED RENTALS NORTH AMER INC
3455 San Gbriel Rver Pkwy, Pico Rivera
(90660-1450)
PHONE..............................562 695-0748
Donnie Richardson, *Manager*
Erica Gomez, *Executive*
Andy Hamrock, *Manager*
Jami McDermott, *Manager*
EMP: 125
SALES (corp-wide): 8B **Publicly Held**
WEB: www.unitedrentals.com
SIC: 7359 Rental store, general
HQ: United Rentals (North America), Inc.
100 Frederick St 700
Stamford CT 06902
203 622-3131

(P-14206)
UNITED SITE SERVICES CAL INC (PA)
242 Live Oak Ave, Irwindale (91706-1311)
PHONE..............................626 462-9110
Debbi Thornton, *Manager*
EMP: 90
SQ FT: 2,400
SALES (est): 3.9MM **Privately Held**
WEB: www.americanclassicsanitation.com
SIC: 7359 Portable toilet rental

(P-14207)
UNITED SITE SERVICES CAL INC
3408 Hillcap Ave, San Jose (95136-1306)
PHONE..............................408 295-2263
Frank Youngblood, *President*
Terence P Moriarty, *CFO*
Jim Youngblood, *Exec VP*
Dan Youngblood, *Vice Pres*
Liza Escobar, *Sales Staff*
EMP: 200
SALES (est): 26.2MM
SALES (corp-wide): 239.7MM **Privately Held**
WEB: www.acmeandsons.com
SIC: 7359 Portable toilet rental
PA: United Site Services, Inc.
118 Flanders Rd
Westborough MA 01581
508 594-2655

(P-14208)
VCI EVENT TECHNOLOGY INC
Also Called: Videocam
1261 S Simpson Cir, Anaheim
(92806-5530)
PHONE..............................714 772-2002
Toll Free:............................888 -
Evan H Goldschlag, *President*
Kirk Rhinehart, *Vice Pres*
▲ **EMP:** 166

SALES (est): 20MM **Privately Held**
WEB: www.videocam.net
SIC: 7359 Audio-visual equipment & supply rental

(P-14209)
WESTERN OILFIELDS SUPPLY CO (PA)
Also Called: Rain For Rent
3404 State Rd, Bakersfield (93308-4538)
P.O. Box 2248 (93303-2248)
PHONE..............................661 399-9124
Robert Lake, *CEO*
Maston Cunningham, *CFO*
Chris Lake, *Vice Pres*
Aurora Garza, *Exec Dir*
Keith Adams, *Branch Mgr*
▲ **EMP:** 150 **EST:** 1934
SQ FT: 57,000
SALES (est): 54.2MM **Privately Held**
WEB: www.rainforrent.com
SIC: 7359 3523 5083 Equipment rental & leasing; farm machinery & equipment; irrigation equipment

(P-14210)
WESTERN PRECOOLING SYSTEMS
761 Commercial Ave, Oxnard
(93030-7233)
PHONE..............................805 486-6371
Don Dearmond, *Branch Mgr*
EMP: 60
SALES (corp-wide): 62.3MM **Privately Held**
WEB: www.wpsox.com
SIC: 7359 Equipment rental & leasing
PA: Western Precooling Systems
43990 Fremont Blvd
Fremont CA 94538
510 656-2220

(P-14211)
WOW PARTY RENTAL INC
14575 Firestone Blvd, La Mirada
(90638-5914)
PHONE..............................714 367-3380
Kevin Rahimi, *President*
Rodrigo Rodrigues, *Vice Pres*
EMP: 52
SQ FT: 22,000
SALES (est): 1.5MM **Privately Held**
SIC: 7359 Party supplies rental services

7361 Employment Agencies

(P-14212)
24-HOUR MED STAFFING SVCS LLC
21700 Copley Dr Ste 270, Diamond Bar
(91765-5489)
PHONE..............................909 895-8960
Erlinda R Stone,
Carlo Tan, *Accountant*
EMP: 110
SALES (est): 4.4MM **Privately Held**
SIC: 7361 Employment agencies

(P-14213)
40 HRS INC
Also Called: 40 Hours Staffing
1669 Flanigan Dr, San Jose (95121-1682)
PHONE..............................408 414-0158
Bryan Phan, *President*
Danny Tran, *Cust Mgr*
Van Ngo, *Accounts Mgr*
EMP: 1000
SQ FT: 3,000
SALES (est): 31.7MM **Privately Held**
SIC: 7361 Executive placement

(P-14214)
A S A P PROFESSIONAL SERVICES
Also Called: ASAP Professional Services
3301 Loreto Dr, San Ramon (94583-3033)
P.O. Box 1224 (94583-6224)
PHONE..............................800 303-2727
Pam Sullivan, *President*
William Sullivan, *Vice Pres*
EMP: 80
SQ FT: 2,500

SALES (est): 4.3MM **Privately Held**
WEB: www.asapps.com
SIC: 7361 Employment agencies

(P-14215)
A-STAR STAFFING INC
3636 Camino Del Rio N # 102, San Diego
(92108-1722)
PHONE..............................619 574-7600
Diana M Barnes, *President*
Daniel R Barnes, *Admin Sec*
EMP: 165 **EST:** 1999
SQ FT: 2,400
SALES (est): 7.6MM **Privately Held**
WEB: www.astarstaffing.com
SIC: 7361 7363 Executive placement; placement agencies; help supply services; temporary help service

(P-14216)
AB CLOSING CORPORATION
Also Called: Kavaliro
1304 Southpoint Blvd, Petaluma
(94954-7464)
PHONE..............................707 766-1777
Jane E Hynes, *Branch Mgr*
EMP: 71 **Privately Held**
SIC: 7361 Executive placement
PA: A.B. Closing Corporation
12001 Res Pkwy Ste 344
Orlando FL 32826

(P-14217)
ABSO
101 Creekside Ridge Ct # 2, Roseville
(95678-3595)
PHONE..............................800 943-2589
William Greenblatt, *CEO*
Bradley Landin, *Vice Pres*
Natalie Voros, *Principal*
Nathan Wakefield, *Finance*
EMP: 135
SQ FT: 19,000
SALES (est): 5.8MM
SALES (corp-wide): 36.6MM **Privately Held**
WEB: www.absolutehire.com
SIC: 7361 Executive placement
PA: Sterling Infosystems, Inc.
1 State St Fl 24
New York NY 10004
800 899-2272

(P-14218)
ACCELON INC
2410 Camino Ramon Ste 194, San Ramon
(94583-4328)
PHONE..............................925 216-5735
Aizad Kamal, *CEO*
Unsa Kazmi Kamal, *CFO*
Manjiri Vilekar, *Exec Dir*
EMP: 50
SQ FT: 1,500
SALES (est): 1.9MM **Privately Held**
SIC: 7361 8742 Placement agencies; labor contractors (employment agency); construction project management consultant; business consultant

(P-14219)
ACCESS NURSES INC
5935 Cornerstone Ct W, San Diego
(92121-3737)
PHONE..............................858 458-4400
Alan Braynin, *CEO*
EMP: 100 **EST:** 2001
SQ FT: 20,000
SALES (est): 4.8MM **Privately Held**
WEB: www.accessnurses.com
SIC: 7361 Nurses' registry

(P-14220)
ACCOUNTABLE HEALTH STAFF INC
Also Called: Hrn Services
7777 Greenback Ln Ste 205, Citrus Heights
(95610-5800)
PHONE..............................916 286-7667
Tina Wilson, *Branch Mgr*
EMP: 357
SALES (corp-wide): 132.5MM **Privately Held**
SIC: 7361 Employment agencies

PA: Accountable Healthcare Staffing, Inc.
999 W Yamato Rd Ste 210
Boca Raton FL 33431
561 235-7810

(P-14221)
ACT 1 GROUP INC (PA)
Also Called: Actone Executive Search
1999 W 190th St, Torrance (90504-6202)
P.O. Box 2886 (90509-2886)
PHONE..............................310 532-1529
Janice B Howroyd, *CEO*
Carlton Bryant, *COO*
Jeff Kornreich, *CFO*
Jean Barrick, *Vice Pres*
Michael Hoyal, *Vice Pres*
EMP: 90
SQ FT: 18,026
SALES (est): 200.6MM **Privately Held**
WEB: www.act-1.com
SIC: 7361 8741 Employment agencies;
administrative management

(P-14222)
ALL HEALTH SERVICES CORP (PA)
206 W 8th St, Hanford (93230-4532)
PHONE..............................559 583-9101
Dave Matthews, *President*
Brenda Matthews, *CFO*
Michael Ross, *Vice Pres*
Jeremy Matthews, *Admin Sec*
Anna Herrera, *Opers Mgr*
EMP: 65
SALES: 9MM **Privately Held**
WEB: www.allhs.net
SIC: 7361 Employment agencies

(P-14223)
ALL IN ONE INC
Also Called: Act 1 Personnel Services
1999 W 190th St, Torrance (90504-6202)
P.O. Box 29048, Glendale (91209-9048)
PHONE..............................310 538-3374
Janice B Howroyd, *President*
Michael A Hoyal, *CFO*
Zia Islam, *Vice Pres*
Tina Bryant, *Admin Sec*
Mireya Arenas, *Administration*
EMP: 120
SALES (est): 13.6MM **Privately Held**
SIC: 7361 Employment agencies

(P-14224)
ALOIS LLC
Also Called: Alois Staffing
548 Market St Ste 47970, San Francisco
(94104-5401)
PHONE..............................215 297-4492
Farhad Wadia, *CEO*
Kinjal Desai, *COO*
Akanksha Mishra, *Tech Recruiter*
John Thomas,
EMP: 150
SALES: 20MM **Privately Held**
SIC: 7361 7389 Employment agencies;

(P-14225)
AMN HEALTHCARE SERVICES INC (PA)
12400 High Bluff Dr, San Diego
(92130-3077)
PHONE..............................866 871-8519
Susan R Salka, *President*
Douglas D Wheat, *Ch of Bd*
Ralph S Henderson, *President*
Brian M Scott, *CFO*
Cole Edmonson, *Officer*
EMP: 148
SQ FT: 175,672
SALES: 2.1B **Publicly Held**
WEB: www.amnhealthcare.com
SIC: 7361 Employment agencies

(P-14226)
ASGN INCORPORATED (PA)
26745 Malibu Hills Rd, Calabasas
(91301-5355)
PHONE..............................818 878-7900
Theodore S Hanson, *President*
Jeremy M Jones, *Ch of Bd*
William Brock, *Bd of Directors*
Jennifer Hankes Painter,
James L Brill, *Officer*
EMP: 148
SQ FT: 37,200

SALES: 3.4B **Publicly Held**
WEB: www.onassignment.com
SIC: 7361 7363 Employment agencies;
temporary help service

(P-14227)
ASSISTED HOME RECOVERY INC (PA)
Also Called: Assisted Home Care
8550 Balboa Blvd Lbby, Northridge
(91325-5808)
PHONE..............................818 894-8117
Elaine S Donley, *President*
Bill Donley, *Ch of Bd*
EMP: 110
SQ FT: 4,000
SALES (est): 10.3MM **Privately Held**
WEB: www.assistedca.com
SIC: 7361 Nurses' registry

(P-14228)
AVALON STAFFING LLC
550 Harvest Park Dr Ste B, Brentwood
(94513-4058)
PHONE..............................925 626-7138
Carisa Zink, *Mng Member*
Kristen Siebe, *Human Res Mgr*
John Zink, *Mng Member*
EMP: 70 **EST:** 2012
SQ FT: 1,500
SALES: 12MM **Privately Held**
SIC: 7361 Executive placement

(P-14229)
AYALA CORPORATION
Also Called: Ayala Farms
21510 S Chteau Fresno Ave, Riverdale
(93656-9673)
P.O. Box 187 (93656-0187)
PHONE..............................559 867-5700
Piedad Ayala, *President*
EMP: 150
SQ FT: 2,000
SALES (est): 9.2MM **Privately Held**
SIC: 7361 Labor contractors (employment
agency)

(P-14230)
B & R FARM LABOR CONTRACTOR
422 Mockingbird Ln, Fillmore (93015-1673)
P.O. Box 366 (93016-0366)
PHONE..............................805 524-1346
Birtha Delara, *Owner*
EMP: 200
SALES (est): 7MM **Privately Held**
SIC: 7361 0761 Labor contractors (em-
ployment agency); farm labor contractors

(P-14231)
BARONHR LLC
13085 Central Ave Ste 4, Chino
(91710-4184)
PHONE..............................909 517-3800
EMP: 119
SALES (corp-wide): 60.6MM **Privately
Held**
SIC: 7361 Employment agencies
PA: Baronhr, Llc
8101 E Kaiser Blvd
Anaheim CA 92808
714 860-7800

(P-14232)
BARRETT BUSINESS SERVICES INC
862 E Hospitality Ln, San Bernardino
(92408-3530)
PHONE..............................909 890-3633
EMP: 5002
SALES (corp-wide): 940.7MM **Publicly
Held**
SIC: 7361 Employment agencies
PA: Barrett Business Services Inc
8100 Ne Parkway Dr # 200
Vancouver WA 98662
360 828-0700

(P-14233)
BAY AREA TECHWORKERS (PA)
2000 Crow Canyon Pl # 150, San Ramon
(94583-4633)
PHONE..............................925 359-2200
Don Peed, *CEO*
Mark Thompson, *CFO*

HB Drake, *Vice Pres*
Rob Olsen, *Vice Pres*
Steve Powers, *Vice Pres*
EMP: 64
SQ FT: 8,609
SALES (est): 44.7MM **Privately Held**
WEB: www.techworkers.com
SIC: 7361 Placement agencies

(P-14234)
BOILING POINT REST SCA INC
13668 Valley Blvd Unit C2, City of Industry
(91746-2572)
PHONE..............................626 551-5181
CHI How Chou, *Chairman*
Michael Lin, *Vice Pres*
EMP: 300
SALES: 9.2MM **Privately Held**
SIC: 7361 5812 Employment agencies;
Chinese restaurant

(P-14235)
BULMARO CASTRO CONTRACTORS
Also Called: Bc Contractors
349 Belden St, Gonzales (93926)
P.O. Box 779 (93926-0779)
PHONE..............................831 675-2927
Bulmaro Castro, *President*
EMP: 200
SQ FT: 1,500
SALES: 3.5MM **Privately Held**
SIC: 7361 0761 Labor contractors (em-
ployment agency); farm labor contractors

(P-14236)
BUSINESS CONNECTIONS
Also Called: California Search Services
332 Pine St, Red Bluff (96080-3312)
PHONE..............................530 527-6229
Lynne Moule, *Owner*
EMP: 92
SALES (est): 3.8MM **Privately Held**
SIC: 7361 7363 Employment agencies;
temporary help service

(P-14237)
BUTLER AMERICA HOLDINGS INC (PA)
3820 State St Ste B, Santa Barbara
(93105-3182)
PHONE..............................805 880-1978
Robert Olson, *CEO*
Stephen Morrison, *CFO*
Shannon P Sorensen, *Director*
EMP: 1600 **EST:** 2014
SALES (est): 51.9MM **Privately Held**
SIC: 7361 Employment agencies

(P-14238)
BUTLER INTERNATIONAL INC (PA)
3820 State St Ste A, Santa Barbara
(93105-3182)
PHONE..............................805 882-2200
Edward M Kopko, *Ch of Bd*
Mark Koscinski, *CFO*
James J Beckley, *Senior VP*
Chris Hamel, *Vice Pres*
Jim Heun, *Vice Pres*
EMP: 200
SALES (est): 85.1MM **Privately Held**
WEB: www.butler.com
SIC: 7361 8742 Employment agencies;
management consulting services

(P-14239)
CALIFORNIA DEPT REHABILITATION
Also Called: San Francisco District Office
301 Howard St Ste 900, San Francisco
(94105-6606)
PHONE..............................415 904-7100
Theresa Woo, *Administration*
EMP: 60 **Privately Held**
WEB: www.carehab.org
SIC: 7361 9431 Employment agencies;
HQ: California Department Of Rehabilita-
tion
721 Capitol Mall Fl 6
Sacramento CA 95814

(P-14240)
CAMPOS DMETRIO FRM LABOR CONTR
Also Called: Campos Dmetrio Frm Labor
Contr
117 W Main St Ste 19, Woodland
(95695-2988)
P.O. Box 1288 (95776-1288)
PHONE..............................530 662-4143
Demetrio Campos, *President*
EMP: 100
SQ FT: 650
SALES (est): 4.4MM **Privately Held**
SIC: 7361 0761 Labor contractors (em-
ployment agency); farm labor contractors

(P-14241)
CANOGA PARK WORKSOURCE CENTER
Also Called: Arbor Employment & Training
21010 Vanowen St, Canoga Park
(91303-2804)
PHONE..............................818 596-4448
Gabe Ross, *President*
EMP: 50
SALES (est): 2MM **Privately Held**
SIC: 7361 Employment agencies

(P-14242)
CARE PLUS NORTH OF SAN DIEGO
2337 Eastridge Loop, Chula Vista
(91915-1111)
PHONE..............................619 421-0807
George Khoury, *Owner*
EMP: 67
SALES (est): 4MM **Privately Held**
WEB: www.careplusinternational.com
SIC: 7361 Nurses' registry

(P-14243)
CAREER GROUP INC (PA)
Also Called: Fourthfloor Fashion Talent
10100 Santa Monica Blvd # 900, Los Ange-
les (90067-4138)
PHONE..............................310 277-8188
Michael B Levine, *CEO*
Susan Levine, *President*
Scott H Pick, *CFO*
Emily Levine, *Vice Pres*
Kelly Rosenberg, *Vice Pres*
EMP: 2100 **EST:** 1980
SQ FT: 11,986
SALES (est): 96.7MM **Privately Held**
SIC: 7361 Executive placement

(P-14244)
CENTURY HLTH STAFFING SVCS INC
1701 Westwind Dr Ste 101, Bakersfield
(93301-3045)
PHONE..............................661 322-0606
Richard Ochieng, *President*
Lissa Harris-Soto, *Vice Pres*
Lissa Soto, *Opers Staff*
EMP: 213
SQ FT: 2,000
SALES (est): 226.4K **Privately Held**
SIC: 7361 Nurses' registry

(P-14245)
CERTIFIED NURSING REGISTRY INC
2707 E Valley Blvd # 309, West Covina
(91792-3198)
PHONE..............................626 912-1877
Maria Cristina C Sy, *President*
Wilson Sy, *Vice Pres*
EMP: 125
SQ FT: 2,000
SALES (est): 2.7MM **Privately Held**
SIC: 7361 Nurses' registry

(P-14246)
CLC INCORPORATED (PA)
3001 Lava Ridge Ct # 250, Roseville
(95661-2838)
PHONE..............................916 789-7600
Brad Barron, *President*
Duncan Hay, *Vice Pres*
Paul Heimburg, *Software Engr*
Corey Ball, *Technology*
David Jewett, *VP Finance*
EMP: 50

SQ FT: 20,000
SALES (est): 10MM **Privately Held**
WEB: www.clclegalplans.com
SIC: 7361 Employment agencies

(P-14247)
CLOUDSTAFF LLC (PA)
Also Called: 1st Class Event Services
1165 E San Antonio Dr D, Long Beach
(90807-2374)
PHONE................888 551-5339
Patrick Allen,
EMP: 81
SALES (est): 4.5MM **Privately Held**
SIC: 7361 Employment agencies

(P-14248)
COAST PERSONNEL SERVICES INC (PA)
2295 De La Cruz Blvd, Santa Clara
(95050-3020)
P.O. Box 328 (95052-0328)
PHONE................408 653-2100
Larry K Bunker, *CEO*
Michael Avidano, *Vice Pres*
Larry Broun, *Vice Pres*
Tonya King, *Recruiter*
EMP: 1895
SQ FT: 7,500
SALES (est): 42.7MM **Privately Held**
WEB: www.coastjobs.com
SIC: 7361 Employment agencies

(P-14249)
CODE AMERICA INC
Also Called: Stat Registry Service
235 E Broadway Ste 960, Long Beach
(90802-7802)
PHONE................562 502-7365
Julius Irumundomon, *President*
EMP: 80
SQ FT: 700
SALES: 1MM **Privately Held**
SIC: 7361 Employment agencies

(P-14250)
CONTEMPORARY SERVICES CORP (PA)
Also Called: C S C
17101 Superior St, Northridge
(91325-1961)
PHONE................818 885-5150
Damon Zumwalt, *CEO*
Jim Granger, *President*
Tony Braxton, *Security Dir*
Billy Barrett, *Branch Mgr*
Frank Moreau, *Branch Mgr*
▲ **EMP:** 148 EST: 1967
SQ FT: 20,000
SALES (est): 302.9MM **Privately Held**
WEB: www.csc-usa.com
SIC: 7361 Employment agencies

(P-14251)
CONTINUING LF COMMUNITIES LLC (PA)
Also Called: La Costa Glen
1940 Levante St, Carlsbad (92009-5174)
PHONE................760 704-6400
Richard D Aschenbrenner, *Mng Member*
E Justin Wilson III, *CEO*
Ryan Currie, *Vice Pres*
Darolyn Jorgensen, *Exec Dir*
Jo Baugh, *Executive Asst*
EMP: 84
SALES (est): 19.9MM **Privately Held**
SIC: 7361 Employment agencies

(P-14252)
COVENANT INDUSTRIES INC
Also Called: People Onesource
110 Pine Ave Ste 910, Long Beach
(90802-9447)
P.O. Box 7045, La Puente (91744-7045)
PHONE................951 808-3708
Statney Lattin, *CEO*
Joseph Randle El, *President*
Anna Roque, *Admin Sec*
EMP: 75
SQ FT: 2,500
SALES (est): 4.7MM **Privately Held**
WEB: www.covenantindustries.net
SIC: 7361 Employment agencies

(P-14253)
CREATIVE CIRCLE LLC (DH)
5900 Wilshire Blvd # 1100, Los Angeles
(90036-5036)
PHONE................323 930-2333
Lawrence Serf, *Mng Member*
Steve Pagnozzi, *Vice Pres*
Andrea Clayton, *VP Bus Dvlpt*
Jena Lepkowski, *Executive*
Kyle Pressley, *Executive*
EMP: 70
SALES (est): 21.9MM
SALES (corp-wide): 3.4B **Publicly Held**
SIC: 7361 Executive placement
HQ: Mscp V Cc Parent, Llc
5900 Wilshire Blvd # 1100
Los Angeles CA 90036
323 634-0156

(P-14254)
CROSS COUNTRY HEALTHCARE INC
1700 Iowa Ave Ste 210, Riverside
(92507-2403)
PHONE................951 786-7683
EMP: 144
SALES (corp-wide): 816.4MM **Publicly Held**
SIC: 7361 Employment agencies
PA: Cross Country Healthcare, Inc.
5201 Congress Ave Ste 100
Boca Raton FL 33487
561 998-2232

(P-14255)
CROSSROADS DIVERSFD SVCS INC
7011 Sylvan Rd Ste A, Citrus Heights
(95610-3800)
PHONE................916 676-2540
Danny Marquez, *Principal*
EMP: 79
SALES (corp-wide): 10.4MM **Privately Held**
SIC: 7361 Executive placement
PA: Crossroads Diversified Services, Inc.
9300 Tech Center Dr # 100
Sacramento CA 95826
916 457-1900

(P-14256)
CTPARTNERS EXEC SEARCH INC
8001 Irvine Center Dr, Irvine (92618-2938)
PHONE................949 754-2821
Robin Caldwell, *Branch Mgr*
EMP: 86
SALES (corp-wide): 159.1MM **Privately Held**
SIC: 7361 Executive placement
PA: Ctpartners Executive Search Inc.
1166 Avenue Of The Amrcs
New York NY 10036
212 588-3500

(P-14257)
CVPARTNERS INC (HQ)
655 Montgomery St # 1200, San Francisco
(94111-2635)
PHONE................415 543-8600
Kent Gray, *President*
Michal Krasnopolski, *IT/INT Sup*
EMP: 161
SALES (est): 5.8MM
SALES (corp-wide): 156.9MM **Privately Held**
SIC: 7361 Employment agencies
PA: Addison Professional Financial Search Llc
125 S Wacker Dr Fl 27
Chicago IL 60606
312 424-0300

(P-14258)
CYBERCODERS INC
Also Called: Cyberscientific
6591 Irvine Center Dr # 200, Irvine
(92618-2129)
PHONE................949 885-5151
Heidi Golledge, *CEO*
Linda Chea, *Partner*
Matt Miller, *COO*
Kc Brotherton, *Vice Pres*
Eric Coe, *Vice Pres*
EMP: 140

SALES (est): 17.2MM
SALES (corp-wide): 3.4B **Publicly Held**
WEB: www.cyberscientific.com
SIC: 7361 Executive placement
PA: Asgn Incorporated
26745 Malibu Hills Rd
Calabasas CA 91301
818 878-7900

(P-14259)
DELTA-T GROUP INC
4420 Hotel Circle Ct # 205, San Diego
(92108-3423)
PHONE................619 543-0556
EMP: 280 **Privately Held**
SIC: 7361 Employment agencies
PA: Delta-T Group, Inc.
950 E Haverford Rd # 200
Bryn Mawr PA 19010

(P-14260)
DIAMONDPEO LLC
27442 Calle Arroyo Ste A, San Juan Capistrano (92675-6753)
PHONE................714 728-5186
Veronica Lake,
EMP: 180
SALES (est): 500K **Privately Held**
SIC: 7361 Employment agencies

(P-14261)
DIVERSITY BUS SOLUTIONS INC
2515 S Euclid Ave, Ontario (91762-6620)
PHONE................909 395-0243
Sandy Tribby, *CEO*
EMP: 200 EST: 2011
SALES (est): 1.3MM **Privately Held**
SIC: 7361 Employment agencies

(P-14262)
DUNHILL WORLDWIDE
Also Called: Dunhill Staffing
101 California St, San Francisco
(94111-5802)
PHONE................415 814-6006
Jeff Goldman, *CEO*
EMP: 1258 EST: 2012
SQ FT: 50,000
SALES (est): 14.6MM **Privately Held**
SIC: 7361 Executive placement

(P-14263)
DURAN HUMAN CAPITAL PARTNERS
300 Orchard Cy Dr Ste 142, Campbell
(95008)
PHONE................408 540-0070
James Duran, *President*
EMP: 50
SALES (est): 2.9MM **Privately Held**
SIC: 7361 Executive placement

(P-14264)
DYNAMIC STAFFING INC (PA)
920 Reserve Dr Ste 150, Roseville
(95678-1382)
PHONE................916 773-3900
Michael J Reale, *President*
Keri J Case, *COO*
Steve Saucedo, *CFO*
Caesar Artolozaga, *Director*
EMP: 150
SQ FT: 2,768
SALES (est): 9.8MM **Privately Held**
SIC: 7361 Employment agencies

(P-14265)
E Z STAFFING INC (PA)
801 N Brand Blvd Ste 1120, Glendale
(91203-3239)
PHONE................818 845-2500
Abraham F Abirafeh, *President*
EMP: 298
SQ FT: 3,000
SALES (est): 13.1MM **Privately Held**
SIC: 7361 Nurses' registry

(P-14266)
EAGLE RESOURCES INC
516 W Boone St, Santa Maria
(93458-5614)
P.O. Box 6510 (93456-6510)
PHONE................805 922-0000
Guadalupe Castillo, *President*
Daniel Castillo Jr, *Vice Pres*

EMP: 100
SQ FT: 3,600
SALES: 4.2MM **Privately Held**
SIC: 7361 Labor contractors (employment agency)

(P-14267)
EASTRDGE PRSONNEL OF LAS VEGAS
530 Davis St, San Francisco (94111-1902)
PHONE................415 248-2567
EMP: 65
SALES (corp-wide): 9.1MM **Privately Held**
SIC: 7361 Employment agencies
PA: Eastridge Personnel Of Las Vegas Inc
2355 Northside Dr Ste 120
San Diego CA 92108
619 260-2000

(P-14268)
EASTRDGE PRSONNEL OF LAS VEGAS (PA)
Also Called: Eastridge Infotech
2355 Northside Dr Ste 120, San Diego
(92108-2714)
PHONE................619 260-2000
Robert Svet, *President*
Rio Wagner, *Tech Recruiter*
Marina Amaral, *Manager*
Armando Ruiz, *Accounts Mgr*
EMP: 50
SALES (est): 9.1MM **Privately Held**
WEB: www.eastridge-infotech.com
SIC: 7361 Employment agencies

(P-14269)
ELITE NURSING SERVICES INC
1915 W Orangewood Ave # 110, Orange
(92868-2084)
PHONE................714 919-7898
Lee Hadfield, *President*
EMP: 50
SQ FT: 2,000
SALES: 2.3MM **Privately Held**
SIC: 7361 Nurses' registry

(P-14270)
ELITECARE MEDICAL STAFFING LLC
761 E Locust Ave Ste 103, Fresno
(93720-3023)
PHONE................559 438-7700
Steve Poggi,
Stacey Green, *Opers Mgr*
EMP: 60
SALES (est): 4MM **Privately Held**
SIC: 7361 Nurses' registry

(P-14271)
ELVIRA SANDOVAL
Also Called: Sandoval Labor Contractor
2154 Hill Rd, Williams (95987-5123)
P.O. Box 81 (95987-0081)
PHONE................530 473-5718
Elvira Sandoval, *Owner*
EMP: 170
SALES (est): 7.6MM **Privately Held**
SIC: 7361 Employment agencies

(P-14272)
EMPLOYBRIDGE LLC (HQ)
Also Called: Select Staffing
301 Mentor Dr 210, Santa Barbara
(93111-3339)
PHONE................805 882-2200
Thomas A Bickes, *President*
Fred R Herbert, *President*
Julie Mellin, *President*
Steve Mills, *President*
Paul J Sorensen, *President*
EMP: 148
SALES (est): 447.6MM
SALES (corp-wide): 574.9MM **Privately Held**
WEB: www.selectpersonnel.com
SIC: 7361 Employment agencies
PA: Employbridge Holding Company
1040 Crown Pointe Pkwy
Atlanta GA 30338
770 671-1900

(P-14273)
EMPLOYMENT DEV CAL DEPT
Also Called: Workforce Resource Center
1410 S Broadway Ste E, Santa Maria
(93454-6971)
PHONE..................................805 614-1550
Judy Kelley, *Branch Mgr*
EMP: 100 **Privately Held**
WEB: www.mpic.org
SIC: 7361 9441 8331 7338 Employment
agencies; administration of social & man-
power programs; ; job training & voca-
tional rehabilitation services; secretarial &
court reporting
HQ: California Department Of Employment
Development
888 Suth Fgroa St Ste 200
Los Angeles CA 90017
916 654-8210

(P-14274)
EMPLOYMENT DEV CAL DEPT
Also Called: Edd Payroll Services
751 N St Fl 6, Sacramento (95814-4763)
P.O. Box 826880 (94280-0001)
PHONE..................................916 654-7867
Tina Campbell, *Chief*
EMP: 1000 **Privately Held**
WEB: www.mpic.org
SIC: 7361 9441 Employment agencies;
administration of social & manpower pro-
grams;
HQ: California Department Of Employment
Development
888 Suth Fgroa St Ste 200
Sacramento CA 90017
916 654-8210

(P-14275)
EMPLOYNET INC
838 S Main St Ste B, Salinas (93901-2408)
PHONE..................................831 233-9999
EMP: 1330
SALES (corp-wide): 33.7MM **Privately
Held**
SIC: 7361 Employment agencies
PA: Employnet, Inc.
2555 Garden Rd Ste H
Monterey CA 93940
866 527-4473

(P-14276)
**EPLICA CORPORATE SERVICES
INC**
2375 Northside Dr Ste 360, San Diego
(92108-2713)
PHONE..................................619 282-1400
Adam Svet, *CEO*
Mary Merkel, *Accounting Mgr*
EMP: 800 **EST:** 2010
SALES (est): 1MM
SALES (corp-wide): 179.5MM **Privately
Held**
SIC: 7361 Employment agencies
PA: Eplica, Inc.
2355 Northside Dr Ste 120
San Diego CA 92108
619 260-2000

(P-14277)
ESPARZA ENTERPRISES INC
3851 Fruitvale Ave A, Bakersfield
(93308-5111)
PHONE..................................661 831-0002
Irene Borland, *Manager*
EMP: 55
SALES (corp-wide): 98.4MM **Privately
Held**
WEB: www.esparzaenterprises.com
SIC: 7361 Labor contractors (employment
agency)
PA: Esparza Enterprises, Inc.
3851 Fruitvale Ave
Bakersfield CA 93308
661 831-0002

(P-14278)
ESPARZA ENTERPRISES INC
51335 Harrison St Ste 112, Coachella
(92236-1528)
PHONE..................................760 398-0349
Manuel Padilla, *Manager*
EMP: 680

SALES (corp-wide): 90.9MM **Privately
Held**
SIC: 7361 Labor contractors (employment
agency)
PA: Esparza Enterprises, Inc.
3851 Fruitvale Ave
Bakersfield CA 93308
661 831-0002

(P-14279)
ESPARZA ENTERPRISES INC
222 S Union Ave, Bakersfield (93307-3325)
PHONE..................................661 631-0347
EMP: 453
SALES (corp-wide): 90.9MM **Privately
Held**
SIC: 7361 Labor contractors (employment
agency)
PA: Esparza Enterprises, Inc.
3851 Fruitvale Ave
Bakersfield CA 93308
661 831-0002

(P-14280)
**EXECUTIVE PERSONNEL
SERVICES**
17842 Irvine Blvd Ste 236, Tustin
(92780-3244)
PHONE..................................714 310-9506
Mario Mendoza, *President*
Alinne Espinoza, *Vice Pres*
EMP: 300
SQ FT: 980
SALES (est): 179.3K **Privately Held**
SIC: 7361 Employment agencies

(P-14281)
**EXPRESS PERSONNEL
SERVICES**
870 W Onstott Frontage Rd E, Yuba City
(95991-3500)
PHONE..................................530 671-9202
Tina Williams, *President*
Tom Williams, *Vice Pres*
EMP: 60
SALES (est): 1.8MM **Privately Held**
SIC: 7361 Employment agencies

(P-14282)
FINEZI INC
31080 Blvd Ste 212, Union City (94587)
PHONE..................................510 790-4768
Madhu Puttur, *President*
Joyson Dsouza, *Tech Recruiter*
Manjunath Hebbar, *Recruiter*
Vignesh Pai, *Recruiter*
Anand Subramanya, *Recruiter*
EMP: 90
SALES (est): 4.9MM **Privately Held**
SIC: 7361 8742 Executive placement;
management consulting services

(P-14283)
FIRST CALL NURSING SVCS INC
1313 N Milpitas Blvd # 154, Milpitas
(95035-3180)
PHONE..................................408 262-1533
Franklin Camillo, *CEO*
Celina Salazar-Camillo, *President*
Celina Camillo, *General Mgr*
EMP: 180
SALES (est): 10.9MM **Privately Held**
WEB: www.firstcallnursingservices.com
SIC: 7361 Nurses' registry

(P-14284)
FLEXCARE LLC
Also Called: Flexcare Medical Staffing
990 Reserve Dr Ste 200, Roseville
(95678-1391)
PHONE..................................866 564-3589
Nate Porter, *Mng Member*
EMP: 1000
SALES (est): 451.8K **Privately Held**
SIC: 7361 Employment agencies

(P-14285)
FOWLER LABOR SERVICE INC
633 W Fresno St, Fowler (93625-9697)
PHONE..................................559 834-3723
Fax: 559 834-5949
EMP: 300
SQ FT: 3,250
SALES (est): 8.8MM **Privately Held**
SIC: 7361 0783

(P-14286)
FUENTES FARMS AG INC
2346 Glen Ave, Merced (95340-4059)
PHONE..................................209 722-7201
Edward Fuentes, *President*
EMP: 500
SALES (est): 12.4MM **Privately Held**
SIC: 7361 7363 0761 Labor contractors
(employment agency); help supply serv-
ices; farm labor contractors

(P-14287)
GARICH INC (PA)
Also Called: The Tristaff Group
6050 Santo Rd Ste 200, San Diego
(92124-6102)
PHONE..................................858 453-1331
Gary O Van Eik, *President*
Chris Papike, *Vice Pres*
Richard N Papike, *Vice Pres*
Thomas Tanner, *Vice Pres*
Kanani Masterson, *Managing Dir*
EMP: 295
SALES (est): 26.4MM **Privately Held**
SIC: 7361 8742 Employment agencies;
management consulting services

(P-14288)
GARICH INC
Also Called: Tristaff Group
504 E Alvarado St Ste 201, Fallbrook
(92028-2364)
PHONE..................................951 302-4750
Trevor Nevis, *Manager*
EMP: 521
SALES (corp-wide): 26.4MM **Privately
Held**
SIC: 7361 Employment agencies
PA: Garich Inc
6050 Santo Rd Ste 200
San Diego CA 92124
858 453-1331

(P-14289)
GENUENT USA LLC
2240 Douglas Blvd Ste 100, Roseville
(95661-3874)
PHONE..................................916 772-3700
Greg Abel, *Manager*
Michael Allen, *Director*
Angela Stark, *Manager*
EMP: 68
SALES (corp-wide): 12MM **Privately
Held**
SIC: 7361 Employment agencies
HQ: Genuent Usa, Llc
1400 Post Oak Blvd # 200
Houston TX 77056
713 547-4444

(P-14290)
GIGSURF INC
217 Dore St, San Francisco (94103-4307)
PHONE..................................415 894-2445
Nathan Goldfus, *CEO*
EMP: 450
SALES (est): 1.5MM **Privately Held**
SIC: 7361 Employment agencies

(P-14291)
GLOBAL HORIZONS INC
Also Called: Domestic Horizons
468 N Camden Dr Ste 200, Beverly Hills
(90210-4507)
PHONE..................................310 234-8475
Mordechai Orian, *President*
Robert Rutt, *CFO*
EMP: 400
SALES (est): 14.6MM **Privately Held**
WEB: www.gmpusa.com
SIC: 7361 Labor contractors (employment
agency)

(P-14292)
GLOBAL NURSES ONLINE INC
5301 Beethoven St Ste 200, Los Angeles
(90066-7052)
PHONE..................................310 306-2760
Dorika Mamboleo, *President*
Dorika Beckett, *President*
EMP: 100
SALES (est): 5.1MM **Privately Held**
WEB: www.globalnursesonline.com
SIC: 7361 Nurses' registry

(P-14293)
GO-STAFF INC
9878 Complex Dr, Oceanside (92054)
PHONE..................................760 730-8520
EMP: 1472
SALES (corp-wide): 43.6MM **Privately
Held**
SIC: 7361 Executive placement
PA: Go-Staff, Inc.
8798 Complex Dr
San Diego CA 92123
858 292-8562

(P-14294)
GO-STAFF INC
240 W Lincoln Ave, Anaheim (92805-2903)
PHONE..................................657 242-9350
EMP: 981
SALES (corp-wide): 43.6MM **Privately
Held**
SIC: 7361 Executive placement
PA: Go-Staff, Inc.
8798 Complex Dr
San Diego CA 92123
858 292-8562

(P-14295)
**GRANITE SOLUTIONS GROUPE
INC**
235 Montgomery St Ste 430, San Francisco
(94104-2907)
P.O. Box 3399, Diamond Springs (95619-
3399)
PHONE..................................415 963-3999
Daniel Hector L'Abbe, *CEO*
Ann Bauer, *Officer*
John Henning, *Executive*
Michael Lacson, *Executive Asst*
Andrew Johnson, *Recruiter*
EMP: 209
SQ FT: 3,582
SALES (est): 9.9MM **Privately Held**
WEB: www.granitesolutionsgroup.com
SIC: 7361 8742 Executive placement;
management consulting services

(P-14296)
GROWERS COMPANY INC
21570 Potter Rd, Salinas (93908-9727)
P.O. Box 6217 (93912-6217)
PHONE..................................831 424-3850
Jesse Garcia, *Director*
EMP: 100
SALES (corp-wide): 20MM **Privately
Held**
WEB: www.thegrowerscompany.com
SIC: 7361 Labor contractors (employment
agency)
PA: The Growers Company Inc
15834 S Avenue G
Somerton AZ 85350
928 627-8080

(P-14297)
HARDESTY LLC (PA)
19800 Macar Boule Ste 820, Irvine (92612)
PHONE..................................949 407-6625
Karl Hardesty, *CEO*
Natl Arthur Cohen, *Partner*
Dan Corredor, *Partner*
Skip D'Orazio, *Partner*
Tim De Cou, *Managing Prtnr*
EMP: 50
SQ FT: 5,000
SALES: 6MM **Privately Held**
SIC: 7361 Executive placement

(P-14298)
**HARVEST TECHNICAL SERVICE
INC**
1839 Ygnacio Valley Rd # 390, Walnut
Creek (94598-3214)
PHONE..................................925 937-4874
Judy Fick, *President*
Chris Fick, *Admin Sec*
Carla Adcock, *HR Admin*
Jen Lindsey, *Recruiter*
EMP: 150 **EST:** 1997
SQ FT: 1,000
SALES (est): 8.6MM **Privately Held**
WEB: www.harvtech.com
SIC: 7361 Executive placement

(P-14299)

HOLISTIC APPROACH INC

Also Called: Holistic Approach HM Hlth Care
4505 Precissi Ln Ste B, Stockton
(95207-6240)
PHONE 209 956-7050
Alice Sepulveda, *President*
Julian Sepulveda, *CFO*
Sylvia Sanchez, *Admin Sec*
EMP: 80
SQ FT: 6,000
SALES (est): 3.6MM **Privately Held**
SIC: 7361 8082 Nurses' registry; home
health care services

(P-14300)

HOWARD FISCHER ASSOCIATES INC

10020 N De Anza Blvd # 101, Cupertino
(95014-2213)
PHONE 408 374-0580
Howard Fisher, *President*
Eric Ferst, *Consultant*
EMP: 50 **EST:** 1977
SALES (est): 1.5MM **Privately Held**
SIC: 7361 Executive placement

(P-14301)

HOWROYD-WRIGHT EMPLYMNT AGCY (HQ)

Also Called: Apple One Employment
327 W Broadway, Glendale (91204-1301)
PHONE 818 240-8688
Janice Bryant Howroyd, *CEO*
Bernard Howroyd, *President*
Michael Hoyal, *CFO*
Brett Howroyd, *Vice Pres*
Heather Pierpoint, *Area Mgr*
EMP: 175
SQ FT: 27,000
SALES (est): 110.4MM
SALES (corp-wide): 200.6MM **Privately Held**
WEB: www.appleone.com
SIC: 7361 Labor contractors (employment
agency); executive placement
PA: The Act 1 Group Inc
1999 W 190th St
Torrance CA 90504
310 532-1529

(P-14302)

HOWROYD-WRIGHT EMPLYMNT AGCY

Also Called: Appleone Employment Services
325 W Broadway, Glendale (91204-1301)
PHONE 818 240-8688
Marie Rounsavell, *Manager*
Rachel Borowski, *President*
Brooke Mauldin, *Executive*
Jill Apperson, *Branch Mgr*
Leigh Borreson, *Branch Mgr*
EMP: 120
SALES (corp-wide): 200.6MM **Privately Held**
WEB: www.appleone.com
SIC: 7361 Labor contractors (employment
agency)
HQ: Howroyd-Wright Employment Agency,
Inc.
327 W Broadway
Glendale CA 91204
818 240-8688

(P-14303)

HYRIAN LLC

2355 Westwood Blvd, Los Angeles
(90064-2109)
PHONE 212 590-2567
Daniel Solmons,
Jason Berkowitz,
EMP: 110
SQ FT: 15,000
SALES (est): 3.9MM **Privately Held**
SIC: 7361 Executive placement

(P-14304)

IBFTECH INC

Also Called: Image Business Forms
343 Main St, El Segundo (90245-3814)
PHONE 424 217-8010
John Koch, *President*
Patricia Padilla, *Human Res Mgr*
Stephen Takahashi, *Recruiter*
EMP: 100

SQ FT: 4,000
SALES (est): 83.5MM **Privately Held**
WEB: www.chiptonross.com
SIC: 7361 Executive placement

(P-14305)

IDC TECHNOLOGIES INC (PA)

920 Hillview Ct Ste 250, Milpitas
(95035-4560)
PHONE 408 376-0212
Prateek Gattani, *CEO*
Yogen Malvia, *CFO*
Galvin Jha, *Vice Pres*
Prashant Kalyani, *Executive*
Mohammad Nadeem, *Executive*
EMP: 67
SQ FT: 4,000
SALES (est): 41.2MM **Privately Held**
SIC: 7361 Placement agencies

(P-14306)

IMPACT LOGISTICS

1155 S Milliken Ave Ste I, Ontario
(91761-8158)
PHONE 909 937-9035
David Hamilton, *Principal*
EMP: 50
SALES (est): 1.7MM **Privately Held**
WEB: www.impactlogistics.com
SIC: 7361 Labor contractors (employment
agency)

(P-14307)

IMPACT SOLUTIONS LLC

3604 Ocean Ranch Blvd, Oceanside
(92056-2669)
PHONE 760 231-0450
Toby Copeland,
EMP: 50
SQ FT: 3,000
SALES (est): 3.1MM **Privately Held**
SIC: 7361 Executive placement

(P-14308)

INCLINE INCORPORATED

Also Called: Hireforces
560 S Winchester Blvd # 500, San Jose
(95128-2560)
PHONE 408 454-1140
Ray Ghamous, *President*
Chris Kniffin, *Sales Staff*
EMP: 120
SALES (est): 4.4MM **Privately Held**
WEB: www.inclineinc.com
SIC: 7361 Labor contractors (employment
agency)

(P-14309)

INDOSYS CORPORATION

3315 San Felipe Rd Ste 37, San Jose
(95135-2000)
PHONE 408 705-1953
Sunil Kumar Bagai, *President*
Naina Bagai, *Vice Pres*
EMP: 140
SALES: 2.4MM **Privately Held**
WEB: www.indosys.com
SIC: 7361 Placement agencies

(P-14310)

INNOVTIVE SCNTFIC SLUTIONS INC

Also Called: Innovative Staffing Resources
17581 Irvine Blvd Ste 202, Tustin
(92780-3124)
PHONE 714 508-8620
Arlene Key Auster, *CEO*
Keith A Fiscus, *COO*
EMP: 120
SQ FT: 1,518
SALES: 7MM **Privately Held**
WEB: www.innstaff.com
SIC: 7361 Executive placement

(P-14311)

INTERNET BOOKING AGENCYCOM INC

Also Called: Santa For Hire.com
232 Via Eboli, Newport Beach
(92663-4604)
PHONE 949 673-7707
Robert Mindte, *CEO*
Felicia Mindte, *COO*
EMP: 500
SQ FT: 1,700

SALES (est): 16MM **Privately Held**
WEB: www.hireasanta.com
SIC: 7361 7922 Employment agencies;
theatrical producers & services

(P-14312)

INTERNTIONAL LONGSHORE WHSE UN

Also Called: Ilwu Local 46
Bldng 608 Port Heneme Hbr, Port Huen-
eme (93041)
P.O. Box 100 (93044-0100)
PHONE 805 488-2944
Larry Carlton, *Manager*
EMP: 100
SALES (corp-wide): 7.8MM **Privately Held**
WEB: www.ilwu10.org
SIC: 7361 4491 Labor contractors (em-
ployment agency); marine cargo handling
PA: International Longshore & Warehouse
Union
1188 Franklin St Fl 4
San Francisco CA 94109
415 775-0533

(P-14313)

IQTALENT PARTNERS LLC

171 Main St Ste 284, Los Altos
(94022-2912)
PHONE 888 501-4787
Tomislav Milic, *Mng Member*
Christopher Murdock,
EMP: 55
SALES (est): 256.3K **Privately Held**
SIC: 7361 Executive placement

(P-14314)

IRVINE TECHNOLOGY CORPORATION

17900 Von Karman Ave # 100, Irvine
(92614-6246)
PHONE 714 445-2624
Nicole McMackin, *President*
Kevin Orlando, *CFO*
Janet Thornby, *Vice Pres*
Michael Rose, *Admin Sec*
Phillip Degiuli, *Senior Mgr*
EMP: 160 **EST:** 2000
SQ FT: 8,000
SALES (est): 33.6MM **Privately Held**
WEB: www.irvinetechcorp.com
SIC: 7361 Executive placement

(P-14315)

JACKIE HOOFRING

Also Called: Avalon Staffing
3390 Auto Mall Dr, Westlake Village
(91362-3629)
PHONE 818 961-7272
Jackie Hoofring, *Owner*
EMP: 50
SQ FT: 200
SALES: 1MM **Privately Held**
SIC: 7361 Employment agencies

(P-14316)

JOSEPHINES PROF STAFFING (PA)

Also Called: Josephine's Personnel Services
2158 Ringwood Ave, San Jose
(95131-1720)
PHONE 408 943-0111
Josephine Hughes, *President*
Victoria Picard, *Administration*
EMP: 250
SQ FT: 4,000
SALES (est): 13.1MM **Privately Held**
WEB: www.jps-inc.com
SIC: 7361 8742 8721 7363 Placement
agencies; management consulting serv-
ices; accounting, auditing & bookkeeping;
help supply services

(P-14317)

KFORCE INC

4510 Executive Dr Ste 325, San Diego
(92121-3069)
PHONE 858 550-1645
Maryland Kaforey, *Manager*
Kathleen Mulvaney, *Tech Recruiter*
EMP: 66
SALES (corp-wide): 1.4B **Publicly Held**
WEB: www.kforce.com
SIC: 7361 Employment agencies

PA: Kforce Inc.
1001 E Palm Ave
Tampa FL 33605
813 552-5000

(P-14318)

KIMCO STAFFING SERVICES INC

3415 S Sepulveda Blvd # 1100, Los Ange-
les (90034-7090)
PHONE 310 622-1616
EMP: 595
SALES (corp-wide): 113.7MM **Privately Held**
SIC: 7361 Placement agencies
PA: Kimco Staffing Services, Inc.
17872 Cowan
Irvine CA 92614
949 331-1199

(P-14319)

KINETICOM INC (PA)

8885 Rio San Diego Dr # 210, San Diego
(92108-1626)
PHONE 619 330-3100
Michael Wager, *CEO*
Casey Marquand, *CFO*
Blair Bode, *Vice Pres*
William Coyman, *Vice Pres*
Michael Steadman, *Vice Pres*
EMP: 79
SQ FT: 6,000
SALES (est): 30.9MM **Privately Held**
WEB: www.kineticom.com
SIC: 7361 Executive placement

(P-14320)

L&T STAFFING INC (PA)

Also Called: Staffing Solutions
950 W 17th St Ste E, Santa Ana
(92706-3573)
PHONE 714 558-1821
Fortino Rivera, *CEO*
Lucia Montellano, *CFO*
EMP: 380
SQ FT: 1,500
SALES: 7MM **Privately Held**
SIC: 7361 Executive placement

(P-14321)

LA JOLLA NURSES HOME CARE

2223 Avenida De La Playa, La Jolla
(92037-3200)
PHONE 858 454-9339
Brittany Solerno, *Director*
Martin Murphy, *Treasurer*
Sonia Cantor, *Personnel*
Billie Davis, *VP Opers*
EMP: 240
SALES (est): 2.2MM
SALES (corp-wide): 6.5MM **Privately Held**
WEB: www.carehealthservices.com
SIC: 7361 8742 8082 Nurses' registry;
management consulting services; home
health care services
PA: Care Health Services, Inc
2290 10th Ave N Ste 304
Lake Worth FL 33461
561 433-8800

(P-14322)

LABOR FNDERS OF THE PALM BCHES

Also Called: Labor Finders Staffing
4325 N Blackstone Ave, Fresno
(93726-1902)
PHONE 559 221-2023
David Fritz, *Manager*
EMP: 60
SALES (corp-wide): 2.9MM **Privately Held**
SIC: 7361 Employment agencies
PA: Labor Finders Of The Palm Beaches
Inc
1401 S Military Trl H-1
West Palm Beach FL 33415
561 439-0605

(P-14323)

LAUREL LABOR SERVICES INC

727 Richmind Ct, Santa Maria
(93455-7133)
P.O. Box 5792 (93456-5792)
PHONE 805 928-0113
Lucy Laurel, *President*

EMP: 99
SQ FT: 950
SALES (est): 4.5MM **Privately Held**
SIC: 7361 Employment agencies

(P-14324)
LEADSTACK INC
1390 Market St Ste 200, San Francisco (94102-5404)
PHONE 628 200-3063
Kazi Ahmed, *CEO*
EMP: 64
SALES (est): 2.1MM **Privately Held**
SIC: 7361 Employment agencies

(P-14325)
LIBRARY ASSOCIATES LLC
Also Called: Lac Group
3110 N San Fernando Blvd, Burbank (91504-2503)
PHONE 626 529-6786
EMP: 262
SALES (corp-wide): 20MM **Privately Held**
SIC: 7361 Employment agencies
PA: Library Associates, Llc
　　2029 Century Park E # 438
　　Los Angeles CA 90067
　　323 852-1083

(P-14326)
LOAN ADMINISTRATION NETWRK INC
Also Called: Lani
18952 Macarthur Blvd # 315, Irvine (92612-1401)
PHONE 949 752-5246
Charlene Nichols, *President*
Catherine Anderson, *Vice Pres*
Mila Fernandez, *Accounting Mgr*
EMP: 100
SQ FT: 4,000
SALES (est): 5.4MM **Privately Held**
WEB: www.lani.com
SIC: 7361 8742 Employment agencies; financial consultant; training & development consultant; banking & finance consultant

(P-14327)
LONG BEACH UNIFIED SCHOOL DST
Also Called: Long Bch Unfied Schl Dst Lbusd
999 Atlantic Ave Fl 3, Long Beach (90813-4514)
PHONE 562 491-1281
Ramon Curiel, *Branch Mgr*
EMP: 657
SALES (corp-wide): 865.3MM **Privately Held**
SIC: 7361 Employment agencies
PA: Long Beach Unified School District
　　1515 Hughes Way
　　Long Beach CA 90810
　　562 997-8000

(P-14328)
LUIS ESPARZA SERVICES INC
183 Hwy 33, Maricopa (93252)
PHONE 661 766-2344
Luis Esparza, *President*
EMP: 500
SALES (est): 7MM **Privately Held**
SIC: 7361 8631 Labor contractors (employment agency); labor unions & similar labor organizations

(P-14329)
MAGANA LABOR SERVICES INC
2896 W Telegraph Rd, Fillmore (93015-9666)
PHONE 805 524-0446
Juvenal Magana, *Owner*
Miguel Magana, *Human Res Dir*
EMP: 200
SALES (est): 9.9MM **Privately Held**
SIC: 7361 8631 Labor contractors (employment agency); labor unions & similar labor organizations

(P-14330)
MATRIX RESOURCES INC
1 Embarcadero Ctr Ste 500, San Francisco (94111-3610)
PHONE 415 644-0642
EMP: 147
SALES (corp-wide): 186.5MM **Privately Held**
WEB: www.matrixresources.com
SIC: 7361 Employment agencies
PA: Matrix Resources, Inc.
　　400 Perimeter Center Ter
　　Atlanta GA 30346
　　770 677-2400

(P-14331)
MEGA FARM LABOR SERVICES INC
110 S Montclair St # 103, Bakersfield (93309-3118)
P.O. Box 744, Delano (93216-0744)
PHONE 661 229-8077
Belen Casimiro, *President*
EMP: 151
SALES (est): 4.4MM **Privately Held**
SIC: 7361 Labor contractors (employment agency)

(P-14332)
MHS CUSTOMER SERVICE INC
7586 Trade St Ste C, San Diego (92121-2427)
PHONE 858 695-2151
Don T Fryer, *President*
Theresa Phebes, *Vice Pres*
EMP: 75
SQ FT: 8,600
SALES (est): 6.3MM **Privately Held**
SIC: 7361 1542 1531 7299 Labor contractors (employment agency); nonresidential construction; operative builders; handyman service

(P-14333)
MID VALLEY LABOR SERVICES INC
19358 Avenue 18 1/2, Madera (93637-9709)
P.O. Box 899 (93639-0899)
PHONE 559 661-6390
Samuel Mascarenas, *President*
Ben Mascarenas, *CFO*
EMP: 500
SQ FT: 2,132
SALES: 27MM **Privately Held**
WEB: www.midvalleybirthingservices.com
SIC: 7361 Labor contractors (employment agency)

(P-14334)
MYA SYSTEMS INC
27 Maiden Ln Ste 300, San Francisco (94108-5431)
PHONE 877 679-0952
Eyal Grayevsky, *CEO*
Braydan Young, *President*
James Maddox, *CTO*
Jill Johnson, *Manager*
EMP: 50
SQ FT: 1,500
SALES (est): 547.7K **Privately Held**
SIC: 7361 Placement agencies

(P-14335)
NETPOLARITY INC
900 E Campbell Ave, Campbell (95008-2366)
PHONE 408 971-1100
Haixia Zhang, *CEO*
David Chuang, *President*
Cathleen Lariviere, *General Mgr*
Cesar Baltodano, *Tech Recruiter*
Alexander Chiang, *Tech Recruiter*
EMP: 500
SQ FT: 5,000
SALES (est): 44.2MM **Privately Held**
WEB: www.netpolarity.com
SIC: 7361 Placement agencies

(P-14336)
NETSOURCE INC
5955 Geary Blvd, San Francisco (94121-2006)
P.O. Box 590665 (94159-0665)
PHONE 415 831-3681

Lana Bondar, *President*
Riva Bondar, *Treasurer*
Eren Bondar, *Controller*
EMP: 55
SALES: 6MM **Privately Held**
WEB: www.netsourceweb.com
SIC: 7361 Executive placement

(P-14337)
NORTHWEST STAFFING RESOURCES
Also Called: Resource Staffing Group
701 University Ave # 120, Sacramento (95825-6700)
PHONE 916 960-2668
Windy Richard, *Manager*
EMP: 1883
SALES (corp-wide): 163.5MM **Privately Held**
WEB: www.nwstaffing.com
SIC: 7361 7363 Labor contractors (employment agency); temporary help service
PA: Northwest Staffing Resources, Inc.
　　851 Sw 6th Ave Ste 300
　　Portland OR 97204
　　503 323-9190

(P-14338)
NOVATIME TECHNOLOGY INC (HQ)
9680 Haven Ave Ste 200, Rancho Cucamonga (91730-5342)
PHONE 909 895-8100
Frank Su, *President*
Ian Sexton, *Senior VP*
Gil Sidhom, *Vice Pres*
Michael Manago, *Technology*
Ruben Sanchez, *Technical Staff*
▲ **EMP:** 60
SQ FT: 6,000
SALES: 18.8MM
SALES (corp-wide): 19.8MM **Privately Held**
WEB: www.novatime.com
SIC: 7361 Executive placement
PA: Ascentis Corporation
　　11995 Singletree Ln # 400
　　Eden Prairie MN 55344
　　800 229-2713

(P-14339)
NPH MEDICAL SERVICES
Also Called: Nurses & Prof Hlth Care
555 Flying V St Ste 5, Chico (95928-7698)
PHONE 530 899-2255
SIS Gilmore, *President*
Jim Gilmore, *Vice Pres*
EMP: 76
SALES (est): 80K **Privately Held**
SIC: 7361 Nurses' registry

(P-14340)
NURSE PROVIDERS INC
Also Called: Nursing Registry
355 Gellert Blvd Ste 110, Daly City (94015-2668)
PHONE 650 992-8559
Sherri Burke, *President*
EMP: 800
SQ FT: 1,400
SALES (est): 19.3MM **Privately Held**
SIC: 7361 Nurses' registry

(P-14341)
NURSEFINDERS LLC (HQ)
12400 High Bluff Dr, San Diego (92130-3077)
P.O. Box 919024 (92191-9024)
PHONE 858 314-7427
Susan Salka, *CEO*
Ralph S Henderson, *President*
Denise L Jackson, *Senior VP*
EMP: 110
SQ FT: 22,000
SALES (est): 101.7MM
SALES (corp-wide): 2.1B **Publicly Held**
WEB: www.nursefinders.com
SIC: 7361 8082 7363 8049 Placement agencies; home health care services; help supply services; temporary help service; nurses, registered & practical
PA: Amn Healthcare Services, Inc.
　　12400 High Bluff Dr
　　San Diego CA 92130
　　866 871-8519

(P-14342)
NURSES INTERNET STAFFING SVCS (PA)
6055 E Wash Blvd Ste 409, Commerce (90040-2425)
PHONE 323 720-9900
Sonny Park, *President*
Sue Park, *CFO*
Andrew J Song, *Director*
EMP: 120
SALES (est): 5.7MM **Privately Held**
WEB: www.nursesinternet.com
SIC: 7361 Nurses' registry

(P-14343)
OFFICEWORKS INC
300 Frank H Ste 269, Oakland (94612)
PHONE 510 444-2161
EMP: 96
SALES (corp-wide): 18.8MM **Privately Held**
SIC: 7361 Employment agencies
PA: Officeworks, Inc.
　　3200 E Guasti Rd Ste 100
　　Ontario CA 91761
　　909 606-4100

(P-14344)
OFFICEWORKS INC
11801 Pierce St Fl 2, Riverside (92505-4400)
PHONE 951 784-2534
EMP: 96
SALES (corp-wide): 18.8MM **Privately Held**
SIC: 7361 Employment agencies
PA: Officeworks, Inc.
　　3200 E Guasti Rd Ste 100
　　Ontario CA 91761
　　909 606-4100

(P-14345)
ONLINE TECHNICAL SERVICES INC (PA)
1901 S Bascom Ave Ste 840, Campbell (95008-2210)
PHONE 408 378-1100
Hans Lemcke, *Ch of Bd*
Brenton Hanlon, *Director*
Jim Piazza, *Director*
EMP: 50
SQ FT: 1,000
SALES (est): 2.4MM **Privately Held**
WEB: www.onlinetechnical.com
SIC: 7361 Placement agencies

(P-14346)
ORANGE COUNTY ONE STOP CENTER
Also Called: Coastal Community College
5405 Grdn Rd Blvd Ste 100, Westminster (92683)
PHONE 714 241-4900
Lois Wilkerson, *Director*
EMP: 55
SALES (est): 1.9MM **Privately Held**
WEB: www.coastalcommunitycollege.com
SIC: 7361 8742 Employment agencies; human resource consulting services

(P-14347)
P & P AGRILABOR
Highway 101 Floretta Rd, Chualar (93925)
PHONE 831 679-2307
P Concepcion Baclig, *Owner*
Purisima Concepcion Baclig, *Owner*
EMP: 80
SALES (est): 2.1MM **Privately Held**
SIC: 7361 Labor contractors (employment agency)

(P-14348)
PACIFIC GTWY WRKFRCE PRTNR INC
4811 Arprt Plz Dr Ste 200, Long Beach (90815)
PHONE 562 570-3700
Nick Schultz, *Exec Dir*
EMP: 50
SALES (est): 1.3MM **Privately Held**
SIC: 7361 Labor contractors (employment agency)

(P-14349)
PACIFIC RIM RESOURCES SRCH
14148 Brookhurst St, Garden Grove
(92843-4656)
PHONE...................714 638-0307
Trang Diem Tran, *CEO*
EMP: 200
SALES (est): 7.4MM **Privately Held**
WEB: www.prresources.net
SIC: 7361 Executive placement

(P-14350)
PARADIGM STAFFING SOLUTIONS
1970 Broadway Ste 615, Oakland
(94612-2218)
PHONE...................510 663-7860
Fax: 510 663-7866
EMP: 50
SALES (est): 2.3MM **Privately Held**
WEB: www.parastaffing.com
SIC: 7361

(P-14351)
PDS TECH INC
1798 Tech Dr Ste 130, San Jose (95110)
PHONE...................408 916-4848
EMP: 1231
SALES (corp-wide): 26.6MM **Privately Held**
SIC: 7361 Employment agencies
HQ: Pds Tech, Inc.
300 E John Carpenter Fwy # 700
Irving TX 75062
214 647-9600

(P-14352)
PDS TECH INC
3100 S Harbor Blvd # 135, Santa Ana
(92704-6823)
PHONE...................214 647-9600
Dj Englert, *Manager*
EMP: 82
SALES (corp-wide): 26.6MM **Privately Held**
WEB: www.pdstech.com
SIC: 7361 Employment agencies
HQ: Pds Tech, Inc.
300 E John Carpenter Fwy # 700
Irving TX 75062
214 647-9600

(P-14353)
PEMER PACKING CO INC
20260 Spence Rd, Salinas (93908-9507)
P.O. Box 4783 (93912-4783)
PHONE...................831 758-8586
Pedro Mercado, *President*
EMP: 800
SQ FT: 3,000
SALES (est): 36.1MM **Privately Held**
SIC: 7361 Labor contractors (employment agency)

(P-14354)
PEOPLE SCIENCE INC
951 Mariners Island Blvd, San Mateo
(94404-1558)
PHONE...................888 924-1004
Christine Nichlos, *CEO*
EMP: 50
SALES (corp-wide): 3.2MM **Privately Held**
SIC: 7361 Executive placement
PA: People Science Inc
595 Shrewsbury Ave # 102
Shrewsbury NJ 07702
888 924-1004

(P-14355)
PEOPLES CHOICE STAFFING INC
4218 Green River Rd # 101, Corona
(92880-1634)
PHONE...................951 735-0550
Denise Peoples, *President*
Wendell Peoples, *COO*
EMP: 100
SALES (est): 14.5MM **Privately Held**
WEB: www.peopleschoicestaffing.com
SIC: 7361 Placement agencies

(P-14356)
PEOPLEWARE TECHNICAL RESOURCES
302 W Grand Ave Ste 4, El Segundo
(90245-5108)
PHONE...................310 640-2406
Sheryl Rooker, *President*
Jeff Thaler, *CFO*
EMP: 60
SQ FT: 3,000
SALES (est): 2.7MM **Privately Held**
WEB: www.peoplewareinc.com
SIC: 7361 7363 Executive placement;
help supply services

(P-14357)
PLUS GROUP INC
Also Called: Jobs Plus
2551 Sn Rmn Vlly Blvd 2, San Ramon
(94583)
PHONE...................925 831-8551
Patrick O'Donnell, *Branch Mgr*
Kelly Karmer, *Recruiter*
EMP: 100 **Privately Held**
WEB: www.tpgstaffing.com
SIC: 7361 7363 Temporary help service;
executive placement
PA: The Plus Group Inc
7425 Janes Ave Ste 201
Woodridge IL 60517

(P-14358)
PRECISE FIT LIMITED ONE LLC
Also Called: Pfitech
17011 Beach Blvd Ste 900, Huntington
Beach (92647-5998)
PHONE...................310 824-1800
Richard Hernandez,
Meredith Kurtz, *Regional Mgr*
Thomas Justus, *Admin Sec*
Tony Galindo, *CTO*
Brandon Asire, *Comp Tech*
EMP: 380
SQ FT: 10,000
SALES: 20.5MM **Privately Held**
SIC: 7361 Employment agencies

(P-14359)
PREFERRED HLTHCARE RGISTRY INC
4909 Murphy Canyon Rd # 310, San Diego
(92123-4349)
P.O. Box 17860 (92177-7860)
PHONE...................800 787-6787
Melanie Reiten, *President*
Rebecca Edwards Diata, *Vice Pres*
EMP: 170
SQ FT: 2,100
SALES (est): 8.7MM **Privately Held**
WEB: www.preferredregistry.com
SIC: 7361 7363 Employment agencies;
temporary help service

(P-14360)
PREMIER HEALTHCARE SVCS LLC (HQ)
Also Called: Phs Staffing
3030 Old Ranch Pkwy # 100, Seal Beach
(90740-2752)
PHONE...................626 204-7930
Anthony H Strange, *CEO*
Melissa Awe, *Recruiter*
Clare Ryan, *Nurse*
Kelly Johnson, *Mng Member*
Masharne Townsend, *Manager*
EMP: 200
SALES (est): 26.2MM
SALES (corp-wide): 430.9MM **Privately Held**
WEB: www.phs-staffing.com
SIC: 7361 Nurses' registry
PA: Aveanna Healthcare, Llc
400 Interstate North Pkwy
Atlanta GA 30339
770 441-1580

(P-14361)
PREMIER INSITE GROUP INC
111 W Ocean Blvd Ste 400, Long Beach
(90802-4633)
PHONE...................562 741-5018
Jose Castellanos, *President*
Juan Calderon, *Treasurer*
Sandra Picos, *Exec Dir*

EMP: 99
SQ FT: 1,628
SALES (est): 2MM **Privately Held**
SIC: 7361 Labor contractors (employment
agency)

(P-14362)
PREMIER NURSING SERVICES INC (PA)
444 W Ocean Blvd Ste 1050, Long Beach
(90802-8129)
PHONE...................562 437-4313
Issam Osman, *President*
Nancy Bauguess, *Admin Sec*
Othman Omar, *Project Mgr*
EMP: 800
SQ FT: 2,000
SALES (est): 40.2MM **Privately Held**
WEB: www.premiernursing.com
SIC: 7361 Nurses' registry

(P-14363)
PRIVATE INDUSTRY CNCL SLNO CTY (PA)
Also Called: Workforce Dev Bd Solano Cnty
500 Chadbourne Rd, Fairfield
(94534-9656)
PHONE...................707 864-3370
Heather Henry, *Exec Dir*
Taffy Della-Cioppa, *Principal*
Robert Bloom, *Exec Dir*
EMP: 50
SALES (est): 4.2MM **Privately Held**
WEB: www.solanowib.org
SIC: 7361 8331 Employment agencies;
job training & vocational rehabilitation
services

(P-14364)
PROFESSNAL CREER PLACEMENTSCOM
1990 N Calif Blvd Fl 8, Walnut Creek
(94596-3742)
PHONE...................415 615-0688
Martin Shmagin, *CEO*
Cindy Fassler, *Vice Pres*
Cindy Sassler, *Vice Pres*
Elissa Wolf, *Director*
EMP: 50 EST: 2013
SQ FT: 1,459
SALES (est): 1.5MM **Privately Held**
SIC: 7361 Executive placement

(P-14365)
PROFESSNAL RGISTRY NETWRK CORP
20132 Canyon Dr, Yorba Linda
(92886-6058)
PHONE...................714 394-4071
George Makridis, *President*
EMP: 105
SALES (est): 6.3MM **Privately Held**
WEB: www.prncorp.net
SIC: 7361 Registries

(P-14366)
PROFILE OF SANTA CRUZ
Also Called: Experience Unlimited
2045 40th Ave Ste B, Capitola
(95010-2549)
PHONE...................831 479-0393
Lance Vera, *Exec Dir*
EMP: 70
SALES (est): 1.6MM **Privately Held**
WEB: www.santacruzprofile.org
SIC: 7361 Placement agencies

(P-14367)
PROPATH INC
17891 Cartwright Rd # 100, Irvine
(92614-4255)
PHONE...................949 341-8000
Doug Wooley, *Principal*
EMP: 50
SALES (est): 1.4MM **Privately Held**
SIC: 7361 Labor contractors (employment
agency)

(P-14368)
PROVEN SOLUTIONS INC
11150 Santa Monica Blvd # 1060, Los An-
geles (90025-1575)
PHONE...................310 933-4544
EMP: 51 **Privately Held**
SIC: 7361 Employment agencies

PA: Proven Solutions, Inc.
9444 Waples St Ste 440
San Diego CA 92121

(P-14369)
PS NATIONAL INC
Also Called: Professional Staffing
17645 Chatsworth St, Granada Hills
(91344-5602)
PHONE...................818 366-1300
Lee Leatherman, *President*
Ruth Leatherman, *Vice Pres*
EMP: 300 EST: 1977
SQ FT: 4,000
SALES (est): 12.7MM **Privately Held**
SIC: 7361 7363 Nurses' registry; help sup-
ply services

(P-14370)
PSINAPSE TECHNOLOGY LTD
1063 Serpentine Ln Ste A, Pleasanton
(94566-4808)
PHONE...................925 225-0400
Sylvia Luneau, *President*
Kesha Boyd, *Admin Asst*
Julia Barnes, *Manager*
EMP: 90
SQ FT: 4,000
SALES (est): 3.7MM **Privately Held**
WEB: www.psinapse.com
SIC: 7361 Placement agencies

(P-14371)
PTS ADVANCE
2860 Michelle Ste 150, Irvine (92606-1010)
PHONE...................949 268-4000
June Stein, *President*
Randy Nodalo, *Vice Pres*
David Stein, *Vice Pres*
Ronald Stein, *Vice Pres*
Russell Stein, *Vice Pres*
EMP: 220
SQ FT: 4,950
SALES: 30.6MM **Privately Held**
WEB: www.ptsstaffing.com
SIC: 7361 Employment agencies

(P-14372)
R N PRIORITY NURSING SERVICE
P.O. Box 234216 (92023-4216)
PHONE...................760 635-7776
Nancy Fournier, *Owner*
EMP: 60
SALES: 700K **Privately Held**
SIC: 7361 Nurses' registry

(P-14373)
RAMCO ENTERPRISES LP
325 Plaza Dr Ste 1, Santa Maria
(93454-6929)
PHONE...................805 922-9888
EMP: 991
SALES (corp-wide): 85MM **Privately Held**
SIC: 7361 Executive placement
PA: Ramco Enterprises, L.P.
710 La Guardia St
Salinas CA 93905
831 758-5272

(P-14374)
RAMCO ENTERPRISES LP
585 Auto Center Dr, Watsonville
(95076-3764)
PHONE...................831 722-3370
EMP: 743
SALES (corp-wide): 85MM **Privately Held**
SIC: 7361 Employment agencies
PA: Ramco Enterprises, L.P.
710 La Guardia St
Salinas CA 93905
831 758-5272

(P-14375)
RANDSTAD NORTH AMERICA INC
106 E 7th St, Hanford (93230-4642)
PHONE...................559 582-2700
Fawn Perryman, *Branch Mgr*
EMP: 104
SALES (corp-wide): 27.2B **Privately Held**
WEB: www.placementpros.com
SIC: 7361 Employment agencies

P
R
O
D
U
C
T
S
&
S
V
C
S

HQ: Randstad North America, Inc.
3625 Cumberland Blvd Se
Atlanta GA 30339
770 937-7000

(P-14376)
RANDSTAD NORTH AMERICA INC
27 Maiden Ln Ste 202, San Francisco
(94108-5440)
PHONE..................................415 397-3384
Mark Rivard, *Branch Mgr*
Jessica Zucker, *President*
EMP: 177
SALES (corp-wide): 27.2B **Privately Held**
WEB: www.placementpros.com
SIC: 7361 Employment agencies
HQ: Randstad North America, Inc.
3625 Cumberland Blvd Se
Atlanta GA 30339
770 937-7000

(P-14377)
RANDSTAD PROFESSIONALS US LLC
Also Called: Randstad Finance & Accounting
111 Anza Blvd Ste 202, Burlingame
(94010-1932)
PHONE..................................650 343-5111
Shannon Guzzetta, *Branch Mgr*
Anna Santiago, *HR Admin*
EMP: 235
SALES (corp-wide): 27.2B **Privately Held**
SIC: 7361 Executive placement
HQ: Randstad Professionals Us, Llc
150 Presidential Way Fl 4
Woburn MA 01801

(P-14378)
RANDSTAD TECHNOLOGIES LLC
8880 Rio San Diego Dr # 107, San Diego
(92108-1634)
PHONE..................................619 798-7300
Charity Cescolini, *Branch Mgr*
EMP: 64
SALES (corp-wide): 27.2B **Privately Held**
SIC: 7361 Employment agencies
HQ: Randstad Technologies, Llc
150 Presidential Way # 300
Woburn MA 01801
781 938-1910

(P-14379)
RCSN INC
10221 Slater Ave Ste 214, Fountain Valley
(92708-4751)
PHONE..................................714 965-0244
Catherin Long, *CEO*
Ann Lee, *CFO*
EMP: 150
SQ FT: 400
SALES (est): 4.1MM **Privately Held**
SIC: 7361 Executive placement

(P-14380)
READYLINK INC
72030 Metroplex Dr, Thousand Palms
(92276)
PHONE..................................760 343-7000
Daniel Caliendo, *Principal*
EMP: 99
SALES (est): 4MM **Privately Held**
SIC: 7361 Employment agencies

(P-14381)
READYLINK HEALTHCARE
72030 Metroplex Dr, Thousand Palms
(92276)
P.O. Box 1047 (92276-1047)
PHONE..................................760 343-7000
Barry L Treash, *President*
Sheri Price, *Manager*
EMP: 85
SALES (est): 8MM **Privately Held**
WEB: www.readylinkhealthcare.com
SIC: 7361 Labor contractors (employment agency)

(P-14382)
REAL TIME STAFFING SERVICES
Also Called: Select Staffing
301 Mentor Dr 210, Santa Barbara
(93111-3339)
PHONE..................................805 882-2200
Steve Sorensen, *Principal*
Judy Pacheco, *Branch Mgr*
Virginia Pabloff, *Sales Staff*
Stephen Sorensen, *Manager*
EMP: 99
SALES: 950K **Privately Held**
SIC: 7361 Employment agencies

(P-14383)
REDLANDS EMPLOYMENT SERVICES
Also Called: Redlands Staffing Services
4295 Jurupa St Ste 110, Ontario
(91761-1429)
PHONE..................................951 688-0083
Matt Tahlmeyer, *President*
EMP: 366 **Privately Held**
SIC: 7361 Placement agencies
PA: Redlands Employment Services Inc
499 W State St
Redlands CA 92373

(P-14384)
RELIABLE NURSING SOLUTIONS
16057 Kamana Rd Ste B, Apple Valley
(92307-0841)
PHONE..................................760 946-9191
Carol Grigsby, *President*
EMP: 85
SQ FT: 1,200
SALES (est): 2.7MM **Privately Held**
WEB: www.reliablenursing.com
SIC: 7361 Placement agencies

(P-14385)
RENTERIA SANTIAGO J FARM LABO
137 W Kern Ave, Mc Farland (93250-1348)
PHONE..................................661 792-0052
Santiago J Renteria, *Owner*
EMP: 150
SQ FT: 768
SALES (est): 6MM **Privately Held**
SIC: 7361 Labor contractors (employment agency)

(P-14386)
RESOURCES CONNECTION LLC (HQ)
Also Called: Resources Global Professionals
17101 Armstrong Ave # 100, Irvine
(92614-5742)
PHONE..................................714 430-6400
Donald B Murray, *Ch of Bd*
Susan Hicks, *Managing Prtnr*
Kate W Duchene, *President*
Herbert M Mueller, *CFO*
Tanja Cebula, *Exec VP*
EMP: 60 **EST:** 1999
SQ FT: 16,366
SALES: 583.4MM **Publicly Held**
WEB: www.resourcesconnection.com
SIC: 7361 8742 Executive placement; management consulting services

(P-14387)
RESPONSE 1 MEDICAL STAFFING
1101 Inv Blvd Ste 140, El Dorado Hills
(95762)
PHONE..................................916 932-0430
Cheree Love, *CEO*
Gordon Helm, *Shareholder*
Gary Slavit, *Shareholder*
Lajuan Knorr, *CFO*
Jody Dunbar, *Controller*
EMP: 150
SQ FT: 3,000
SALES: 12MM **Privately Held**
WEB: www.response1.com
SIC: 7361 Nurses' registry

(P-14388)
RIVIERA PARTNERS LLC (PA)
141 10th St, San Francisco (94103-2604)
PHONE..................................877 748-4372
Will Hunsinger, *COO*
Donald Hayden, *Vice Pres*
Marisette Pomales, *Executive Asst*
Christine Williams, *Executive Asst*
Ali Behnam,
EMP: 53
SALES (est): 8.4MM **Privately Held**
SIC: 7361 Executive placement

(P-14389)
ROBERT HALF INTERNATIONAL INC
Also Called: Officeteam
10 Almaden Blvd Ste 900, San Jose
(95113-2268)
PHONE..................................408 961-2975
Catrina Simbe, *Branch Mgr*
Kari Harris, *Credit Mgr*
Kim Davis, *Manager*
Dave McConnell, *Manager*
Daniel Powers, *Accounts Exec*
EMP: 92
SALES (corp-wide): 5.8B **Publicly Held**
SIC: 7361 Placement agencies
PA: Robert Half International Inc.
2884 Sand Hill Rd Ste 200
Menlo Park CA 94025
650 234-6000

(P-14390)
ROBERT HALF INTERNATIONAL INC
4 Lower Ragsdale Dr # 101, Monterey
(93940-7835)
PHONE..................................831 241-9042
Gabby Ayala, *Manager*
EMP: 94
SALES (corp-wide): 5.8B **Publicly Held**
SIC: 7361 Placement agencies
PA: Robert Half International Inc.
2884 Sand Hill Rd Ste 200
Menlo Park CA 94025
650 234-6000

(P-14391)
ROBERT HALF INTERNATIONAL INC
3000 Oak Rd, Walnut Creek (94597-2092)
PHONE..................................925 930-7766
Heath Harris, *Branch Mgr*
Hillary Hernandez, *Human Resources*
EMP: 92
SALES (corp-wide): 5.8B **Publicly Held**
SIC: 7361 Placement agencies
PA: Robert Half International Inc.
2884 Sand Hill Rd Ste 200
Menlo Park CA 94025
650 234-6000

(P-14392)
ROBERT HALF INTERNATIONAL INC
2280 Market St Ste 220, Riverside
(92501-2120)
PHONE..................................951 779-9081
Jason Buchbinder, *Manager*
EMP: 92
SALES (corp-wide): 5.8B **Publicly Held**
SIC: 7361 Placement agencies
PA: Robert Half International Inc.
2884 Sand Hill Rd Ste 200
Menlo Park CA 94025
650 234-6000

(P-14393)
ROBERT HALF INTERNATIONAL INC
Accountemps
10 Almaden Blvd Ste 900, San Jose
(95113-2268)
PHONE..................................408 293-8611
Monique Cruz, *Principal*
EMP: 50
SALES (corp-wide): 5.8B **Publicly Held**
WEB: www.rhii.com
SIC: 7361 Employment agencies
PA: Robert Half International Inc.
2884 Sand Hill Rd Ste 200
Menlo Park CA 94025
650 234-6000

(P-14394)
ROBERT HALF INTERNATIONAL INC
Also Called: Creative Group, The
P.O. Box 743295 (90074-3295)
PHONE..................................800 356-1994
EMP: 53
SALES (corp-wide): 5.8B **Publicly Held**
SIC: 7361 Employment agencies
PA: Robert Half International Inc.
2884 Sand Hill Rd Ste 200
Menlo Park CA 94025
650 234-6000

(P-14395)
ROBERT HALF INTERNATIONAL INC
4225 Executive Sq Ste 300, La Jolla
(92037-9212)
PHONE..................................888 744-9202
Paige Thomas, *Manager*
EMP: 92
SALES (corp-wide): 5.8B **Publicly Held**
WEB: www.rhii.com
SIC: 7361 Employment agencies
PA: Robert Half International Inc.
2884 Sand Hill Rd Ste 200
Menlo Park CA 94025
650 234-6000

(P-14396)
ROBERT HALF INTERNATIONAL INC
Also Called: Accountemps
50 California St Ste 1000, San Francisco
(94111-4613)
PHONE..................................415 434-1900
Katy Gigqere, *Branch Mgr*
EMP: 140
SALES (corp-wide): 5.8B **Publicly Held**
WEB: www.rhii.com
SIC: 7361 7363 Executive placement; help supply services
PA: Robert Half International Inc.
2884 Sand Hill Rd Ste 200
Menlo Park CA 94025
650 234-6000

(P-14397)
ROBERT HALF INTERNATIONAL INC
Accountemps
1850 Gateway Dr Ste 200, San Mateo
(94404-4061)
PHONE..................................650 574-8200
Stephanie Vinske, *Branch Mgr*
EMP: 50
SALES (corp-wide): 5.8B **Publicly Held**
SIC: 7361 Employment agencies
PA: Robert Half International Inc.
2884 Sand Hill Rd Ste 200
Menlo Park CA 94025
650 234-6000

(P-14398)
ROBERT HALF INTERNATIONAL INC
Also Called: Accountemps
2884 Sand Hill Rd Ste 200, Menlo Park
(94025-7059)
PHONE..................................650 234-6000
Paul Gentzkow, *President*
EMP: 99
SALES (corp-wide): 5.8B **Publicly Held**
WEB: www.rhii.com
SIC: 7361 Placement agencies
PA: Robert Half International Inc.
2884 Sand Hill Rd Ste 200
Menlo Park CA 94025
650 234-6000

(P-14399)
ROBERT HALF INTERNATIONAL INC
Also Called: Creative Group, The
2884 Sand Hill Rd Ste 200, Menlo Park
(94025-7059)
PHONE..................................650 234-6000
Paul Gentzkow, *President*
EMP: 100
SALES (corp-wide): 5.8B **Publicly Held**
WEB: www.rhii.com
SIC: 7361 7363 Placement agencies; temporary help service

PA: Robert Half International Inc.
2884 Sand Hill Rd Ste 200
Menlo Park CA 94025
650 234-6000

(P-14400)
ROBERT HALF INTERNATIONAL INC
Also Called: Office Team
2884 Sand Hill Rd Ste 200, Menlo Park
(94025-7059)
PHONE..................650 234-6000
Chris Hoffmann, *President*
EMP: 92
SALES (corp-wide): 5.8B **Publicly Held**
SIC: 7361 Employment agencies
PA: Robert Half International Inc.
2884 Sand Hill Rd Ste 200
Menlo Park CA 94025
650 234-6000

(P-14401)
ROBERT HALF INTERNATIONAL INC
Also Called: Officeteam
18200 Von Karman Ave # 800, Irvine
(92612-7158)
PHONE..................949 476-3199
Heather Kwon, *Office Mgr*
EMP: 92
SALES (corp-wide): 5.8B **Publicly Held**
SIC: 7361 8721 Placement agencies; ship crew agency; auditing services
PA: Robert Half International Inc.
2884 Sand Hill Rd Ste 200
Menlo Park CA 94025
650 234-6000

(P-14402)
ROBERT HALF INTERNATIONAL INC
790 E Colo Blvd Ste 650, Pasadena
(91101)
PHONE..................626 463-2037
Tania Hablian, *Branch Mgr*
EMP: 92
SALES (corp-wide): 5.8B **Publicly Held**
WEB: www.rhii.com
SIC: 7361 7363 Placement agencies; temporary help service
PA: Robert Half International Inc.
2884 Sand Hill Rd Ste 200
Menlo Park CA 94025
650 234-6000

(P-14403)
ROBERT HALF INTERNATIONAL INC
3600 W Byshore Rd Ste 103, Palo Alto
(94303)
PHONE..................650 812-9790
Christina Marinovich, *Principal*
EMP: 92
SALES (corp-wide): 5.8B **Publicly Held**
SIC: 7361 Placement agencies
PA: Robert Half International Inc.
2884 Sand Hill Rd Ste 200
Menlo Park CA 94025
650 234-6000

(P-14404)
ROBERT HALF INTERNATIONAL INC
Also Called: Office Team
2613 Camino Ramon, San Ramon
(94583-4289)
PHONE..................925 913-1000
Max Messner, *Manager*
EMP: 50
SALES (corp-wide): 5.8B **Publicly Held**
WEB: www.rhii.com
SIC: 7361 7363 Placement agencies; temporary help service
PA: Robert Half International Inc.
2884 Sand Hill Rd Ste 200
Menlo Park CA 94025
650 234-6000

(P-14405)
ROBERT HALF MGT RESOURCES
1999 Harrison St Ste 1100, Oakland
(94612-4708)
PHONE..................510 271-0910
Samantha Snyder, *Manager*

EMP: 50
SALES (est): 1.9MM **Privately Held**
SIC: 7361 Employment agencies

(P-14406)
ROBERT QUINTERO LABOR CONTG
1827 S Bardo St, Visalia (93277-4848)
PHONE..................559 732-6954
EMP: 50
SALES: 1MM **Privately Held**
SIC: 7361

(P-14407)
ROBERTAS LABOR CONTRACTING
137 Main St, Soledad (93960-3023)
P.O. Box I (93960-0860)
PHONE..................831 678-8176
Roberta Urquidez, *Owner*
EMP: 300
SALES (est): 9.2MM **Privately Held**
SIC: 7361 Labor contractors (employment agency)

(P-14408)
ROY CARRINGTON INC
Also Called: Human Resource Solutions
2460 Ceres Ave, Chico (95926-1057)
PHONE..................530 893-2100
Roy Carrington, *President*
EMP: 75
SALES: 1MM **Privately Held**
SIC: 7361 8721 Employment agencies; accounting, auditing & bookkeeping

(P-14409)
SAGE GROUP
33 Falmouth St, San Francisco
(94107-1046)
PHONE..................415 512-8200
Cara France, *CEO*
Chris Yelton, *President*
Sandy Minella, *Vice Pres*
EMP: 100 **EST:** 2016
SALES (est): 1.3MM
SALES (corp-wide): 68MM **Privately Held**
SIC: 7361 Employment agencies
PA: 24 Seven, Llc
41 Madison Ave Fl 37
New York NY 10010
212 966-4426

(P-14410)
SANDOVAL BROTHERS INC
36503 Mile End Rd, Soledad (93960-9689)
P.O. Box 1183 (93960-1183)
PHONE..................831 678-1465
Antonio Sandoval, *President*
EMP: 60 **EST:** 1997
SALES (est): 3.9MM **Privately Held**
SIC: 7361 Labor contractors (employment agency)

(P-14411)
SANTA ANA CITY OF
1000 E Santa Ana Blvd # 108, Santa Ana
(92701-3900)
PHONE..................714 565-2600
Gus Chamoro, *Manager*
Sylvia Robles, *Vice Pres*
Vincent Sarmiento, *Council Mbr*
EMP: 50 **Privately Held**
SIC: 7361 9111 Employment agencies; mayors' offices
PA: City Of Santa Ana
20 Civic Center Plz Fl 8
Santa Ana CA 92701
714 647-5400

(P-14412)
SANTA CLARA VLY JOB CAREER CTR
725 E Main St Ste 101, Santa Paula
(93060-2748)
PHONE..................805 933-8300
Art Hernandez, *Director*
EMP: 60
SALES (est): 1.3MM **Privately Held**
SIC: 7361 Employment agencies

(P-14413)
SCOTTS LABOR LEASING CO INC
Also Called: Scott's Glass Service
22560 Lucerne St, Carson (90745-4303)
P.O. Box 3683, Long Beach (90803-0683)
PHONE..................310 835-8388
Tom Scott, *President*
Cheri Scott, *Admin Sec*
David Mendoza, *Terminal Mgr*
John Severs, *Terminal Mgr*
Paul Legg, *Manager*
EMP: 80
SQ FT: 1,000
SALES: 1.5MM **Privately Held**
SIC: 7361 Employment agencies

(P-14414)
SE SCHER CORPORATION
Also Called: Acrobat Staffing
2525 Camino Del Rio S, San Diego
(92108-3717)
PHONE..................858 546-8300
Marc Caplan, *Branch Mgr*
Jessica Cox, *Assistant*
EMP: 918
SALES (corp-wide): 19.8MM **Privately Held**
SIC: 7361 Executive placement
PA: S.E. Scher Corporation
303 Hegenberger Rd # 300
Oakland CA 94621
415 431-8826

(P-14415)
SE SCHER CORPORATION
Also Called: Acrobat Staffing
6731 Five Star Blvd Ste C, Rocklin
(95677-2680)
PHONE..................916 632-1363
Steve Scher, *CEO*
EMP: 459
SALES (corp-wide): 19.8MM **Privately Held**
SIC: 7361 Employment agencies
PA: S.E. Scher Corporation
303 Hegenberger Rd # 300
Oakland CA 94621
415 431-8826

(P-14416)
SECURE NURSING SERVICE INC
3333 Wilshire Blvd # 625, Los Angeles
(90010-4106)
PHONE..................213 736-6771
Haesook Kim, *President*
Linda West, *Info Tech Dir*
EMP: 350 **EST:** 2001
SQ FT: 2,500
SALES (est): 6.5MM **Privately Held**
WEB: www.securenursing.com
SIC: 7361 Nurses' registry

(P-14417)
SEEDIF INC
215 Hockney Ave, Mountain View
(94041-1684)
PHONE..................408 930-3446
Shannon Nguyen, *President*
EMP: 50
SQ FT: 2,000
SALES: 3MM **Privately Held**
SIC: 7361 Employment agencies

(P-14418)
SELECT TEMPORARIES LLC (DH)
Also Called: Select Personnel Services
3820 State St, Santa Barbara
(93105-3182)
PHONE..................805 882-2200
Thomas A Bickes, *President*
Stephen Biersmith, *President*
Mark McComb, *COO*
Shawn W Poole, *CFO*
Gregory Netland, *Bd of Directors*
▲ **EMP:** 90
SQ FT: 30,000
SALES (est): 65.5MM
SALES (corp-wide): 574.9MM **Privately Held**
SIC: 7361 Employment agencies

HQ: Employment Solutions Management, Inc.
1040 Crown Pointe Pkwy
Atlanta GA 30338
770 671-1900

(P-14419)
SHARF WOODWARD & ASSOCIATES
5900 Sepulvda Blvd # 104, Van Nuys
(91411-2511)
PHONE..................818 989-2200
Bernard Sharf, *Co-President*
EMP: 90
SALES: 10MM **Privately Held**
WEB: www.swjobs.com
SIC: 7361 Executive placement

(P-14420)
SIRACUSA ENTERPRISES INC
Also Called: Quality Temp Staffing
17737 Chtswrth St Ste 200, Granada Hills
(91344-5628)
PHONE..................818 831-1130
Joe Alas, *President*
Marie Alas, *Vice Pres*
EMP: 70
SALES: 3.7MM **Privately Held**
SIC: 7361 Employment agencies

(P-14421)
SNELLING EMPLOYMENT LLC
2203 Harvbor Bay Pkwy, Alameda (94502)
PHONE..................510 769-4400
Michelle Berkovich, *Manager*
EMP: 100
SALES (corp-wide): 4.1B **Privately Held**
SIC: 7361 7363 Labor contractors (employment agency); temporary help service
HQ: Snelling Employment, Llc
12801 N Cntl Expy Ste 600
Dallas TX 75243

(P-14422)
SOCAL SERVICES INC
Also Called: Tsg
6336 Greenwich Dr Ste 100, San Diego
(92122-5922)
PHONE..................858 453-1331
Rich Papike, *President*
Gary Van Eik, *CEO*
Richard Papike, *CFO*
Richard J Kail, *Officer*
EMP: 250
SQ FT: 3,000
SALES (est): 15MM **Privately Held**
WEB: www.socalservices.com
SIC: 7361 7363 Employment agencies; temporary help service; office help supply service

(P-14423)
SOLEMNITY PERSONNEL
2008 Camfiled Ave, Commerce (90040)
PHONE..................323 718-3979
Peter Diaz, *Principal*
EMP: 50
SALES (est): 751.5K **Privately Held**
SIC: 7361 Employment agencies

(P-14424)
SPEC PERSONNEL LLC
Also Called: Spectra
1900 La Fytte St Unit 125, Santa Clara
(95050)
PHONE..................408 727-8000
Andrew Bergen, *Branch Mgr*
EMP: 150
SALES (corp-wide): 41.9MM **Privately Held**
SIC: 7361 Employment agencies
PA: Spec Personnel, Llc
4625 Creekstone Dr # 130
Durham NC 27703
203 254-9935

(P-14425)
SPECIAL EVENTS STAFFING
1015 N Lake Ave Ste 205, Pasadena
(91104-4575)
PHONE..................626 296-6771
Frank Barnes, *CEO*
EMP: 626
SQ FT: 900

PRODUCTS & SVCS

SALES: 3.3MM **Privately Held**
SIC: 7361 Employment agencies

(P-14426)
STAFF ASSISTANCE INC (PA)
72 Moody Ct Ste 100, Thousand Oaks
(91360-7426)
PHONE..............................818 894-7879
Bill Donley, *Ch of Bd*
Elaine S Donley, *President*
EMP: 300
SQ FT: 800
SALES: 3.8MM **Privately Held**
SIC: 7361 Nurses' registry

(P-14427)
STAFF ASSISTANCE INC
Also Called: Assisted Home Care
72 Moody Ct Ste 100, Thousand Oaks
(91360-7426)
PHONE..............................805 371-9980
Elaine Thinney, *Branch Mgr*
Sheila Masters, *Assistant*
EMP: 300 **Privately Held**
SIC: 7361 8082 Nurses' registry; home
health care services
PA: Staff Assistance Inc
72 Moody Ct Ste 100
Thousand Oaks CA 91360

(P-14428)
STAFFCHEX INC
20537 Devonshire St, Chatsworth
(91311-3208)
PHONE..............................818 709-6100
Steven Zingerman, *Principal*
EMP: 838
SALES (corp-wide): 65.2MM **Privately
Held**
SIC: 7361 Employment agencies
PA: Staffchex, Inc.
790 The City Dr S Ste 180
Orange CA 92868
714 912-7500

(P-14429)
STAFFING SOLUTIONS INC
Also Called: Balance Staffing
2142 Bering Dr, San Jose (95131-2013)
PHONE..............................408 980-9000
John Moss, *CEO*
Robert Feinstein, *President*
Genet Araya, *Engineer*
Sigurdsson Nick, *Controller*
Lazara Casalla-Prieto, *Recruiter*
EMP: 80 **EST:** 1997
SQ FT: 4,000
SALES (est): 8.7MM **Privately Held**
SIC: 7361 7363 Employment agencies;
help supply services

(P-14430)
STAR H-R
1822 Jefferson St, NAPA (94559-1618)
PHONE..............................707 265-9911
EMP: 1145
SALES (corp-wide): 46.7MM **Privately
Held**
SIC: 7361 Executive placement
PA: Star H-R
3820 Cypress Dr Ste 2
Petaluma CA 94954
707 762-4447

(P-14431)
STAR H-R
105 E 1st St, Cloverdale (95425-3701)
PHONE..............................707 894-4404
EMP: 867
SALES (corp-wide): 46.7MM **Privately
Held**
SIC: 7361 Employment agencies
PA: Star H-R
3820 Cypress Dr Ste 2
Petaluma CA 94954
707 762-4447

(P-14432)
T W R FRAMING
1661 Railroad St, Corona (92880-2503)
PHONE..............................951 279-2000
Tom Rhodes, *Owner*
Debbie Diter, *Controller*
Amy Strommer, *Director*
EMP: 100

SALES (est): 3.1MM **Privately Held**
WEB: www.twrframing.com
SIC: 7361 Labor contractors (employment
agency)

(P-14433)
TALENT SPACE INC
1650 The Alameda, San Jose
(95126-2307)
PHONE..............................408 330-1900
Lisa Flores, *President*
Dora Kaszper, *Partner*
Debbie Minardi, *Partner*
Nick Kumar, *Recruiter*
Christina Boardman, *Art Dir*
EMP: 80
SALES: 15MM **Privately Held**
SIC: 7361 Placement agencies

(P-14434)
TEAM-ONE EMPLYMENT SPCLSTS LLC
Also Called: Team One
2999 Overland Ave Ste 212, Los Angeles
(90064-4243)
PHONE..............................310 481-4480
Frank Moran,
EMP: 3281
SQ FT: 4,500
SALES: 35MM **Privately Held**
SIC: 7361 Placement agencies

(P-14435)
TECHNICAL TEMPS INC
Also Called: TTI
1096 Pecten Ct, Milpitas (95035-6805)
P.O. Box 610190, San Jose (95161-0190)
PHONE..............................408 956-8256
Judith Kalune, *President*
EMP: 100
SQ FT: 1,000
SALES (est): 4.1MM **Privately Held**
WEB: www.technicaltemps.com
SIC: 7361 Executive placement

(P-14436)
TEG STAFFING INC
Also Called: Eastridge Workforce Solutions
2355 Northside Dr Ste 200, San Diego
(92108-2706)
PHONE..............................619 260-2000
Adam Svet, *CEO*
Seth Stein, *President*
Jason Svet, *President*
Brandon Stanford, *CFO*
Erin Medina,
EMP: 1600
SALES (est): 17.9MM
SALES (corp-wide): 179.5MM **Privately
Held**
SIC: 7361 Employment agencies
PA: Eplica, Inc.
2355 Northside Dr Ste 120
San Diego CA 92108
619 260-2000

(P-14437)
TETRA TECH EXECUTIVE SVCS INC
3475 E Foothill Blvd, Pasadena
(91107-6024)
PHONE..............................626 470-2400
Sam Box, *Principal*
EMP: 162
SALES (est): 5.9MM
SALES (corp-wide): 2.9B **Publicly Held**
WEB: www.tetratech.com
SIC: 7361 Employment agencies
PA: Tetra Tech, Inc.
3475 E Foothill Blvd
Pasadena CA 91107
626 351-4664

(P-14438)
THOR GROUP INC (PA)
318 Avenue I Ste 167, Redondo Beach
(90277-5601)
PHONE..............................310 727-1777
Terry Thormodsgaard, *President*
EMP: 50
SALES (est): 2.4MM **Privately Held**
SIC: 7361 Placement agencies

(P-14439)
TLC SERVICES GROUP INC (PA)
Also Called: Trueblue Skilled Trade Group
1600 E 4th St Ste 340, Santa Ana
(92701-5194)
PHONE..............................714 541-5415
Mark Curtiss, *President*
Paul C Driskell, *Ch of Bd*
Liset Santacruz, *Manager*
Kevin Guthrie, *Accounts Mgr*
EMP: 84
SQ FT: 5,000
SALES (est): 3.3MM **Privately Held**
SIC: 7361 7363 Labor contractors (em-
ployment agency); temporary help service

(P-14440)
TOTAL MANAGEMENT SVCS AMER INC
Also Called: Tms America
21151 S Wstn Ave Ste 139, Torrance
(90501)
PHONE..............................310 328-0867
Pakaco Shimakage, *President*
EMP: 50
SALES: 1MM **Privately Held**
SIC: 7361 Executive placement

(P-14441)
TOTAL PROFESSIONAL NETWORK
Also Called: Core Medstaff
3946 Wilshire Blvd, Los Angeles
(90010-3303)
PHONE..............................213 382-5550
Elizabeth Ann Poe, *President*
Therese Nery, *Vice Pres*
EMP: 100
SALES (est): 4.9MM **Privately Held**
WEB: www.coremedstaff.com
SIC: 7361 Nurses' registry

(P-14442)
TREELINE STAFFING
100 Broadway, San Francisco
(94111-1430)
PHONE..............................415 819-7195
Boaz Mariles, *Principal*
EMP: 50
SALES (est): 636.4K **Privately Held**
SIC: 7361 Employment agencies

(P-14443)
TRINET GROUP INC (PA)
1 Park Pl Ste 600, Dublin (94568-7983)
PHONE..............................510 352-5000
Burton M Goldfield, *President*
Richard Beckert, *CFO*
Samantha Wellington,
Barrett Boston, *Senior VP*
Edward Griese, *Senior VP*
EMP: 120
SALES: 3.5B **Publicly Held**
WEB: www.trinet.com
SIC: 7361 8721 Employment agencies;
accounting, auditing & bookkeeping

(P-14444)
UAW-LBOR EMPLYMENT TRNING CORP
Also Called: One Stop Program
3965 S Vermont Ave, Los Angeles
(90037-1937)
PHONE..............................323 730-7900
Audrey Holmes, *Branch Mgr*
EMP: 125
SALES (corp-wide): 9.3MM **Privately
Held**
SIC: 7361 Employment agencies
PA: Uaw-Labor Employment And Training
Corporation
11010 Artesia Blvd # 100
Cerritos CA 90703
562 989-7700

(P-14445)
UAW-LBOR EMPLYMENT TRNING CORP (PA)
Also Called: LABOR EMPLOYMENT &
TRAINING
11010 Artesia Blvd # 100, Cerritos
(90703-2551)
PHONE..............................562 989-7700
Bruce Lee, *Chairman*
Robert Nelson, *President*

Phillip Tan, *CFO*
Marika Letkova, *Technology*
Arthur Guerrero, *Manager*
EMP: 155
SQ FT: 9,000
SALES: 9.3MM **Privately Held**
SIC: 7361 8331 Employment agencies;
work experience center

(P-14446)
UNITED TEMP SERVICES INC
694 Albanese Cir, San Jose (95111-1001)
PHONE..............................408 472-4309
EMP: 100
SALES: 1.5MM **Privately Held**
SIC: 7361 7363

(P-14447)
VACO SAN DIEGO LLC
4250 Executive Sq Ste 750, La Jolla
(92037-9105)
PHONE..............................858 642-0000
Brandy Sloatermen, *Mng Member*
Todd Sweat, *CFO*
Jerry Bostelman,
Jay Hollaman,
Brian Waller,
EMP: 58
SALES: 12.4MM **Privately Held**
SIC: 7361 Executive placement

(P-14448)
VALIDUS GROUP INC
Also Called: Ahr Professionals
1 Orchard Ste 210, Lake Forest
(92630-8314)
PHONE..............................949 457-7606
Brian Demeo, *CEO*
EMP: 75
SALES (est): 3.2MM **Privately Held**
SIC: 7361 Placement agencies

(P-14449)
VALLEY HEALTH CARE SYSTEMS INC
Also Called: Valley Healthcare Staffing
1300 National Dr Ste 140, Sacramento
(95834-1981)
PHONE..............................916 505-4112
Sejal Shah, *CEO*
Jason Beck, *President*
Wright Philip, *Administration*
Steve Swan, *CTO*
Lisa Baker, *Finance*
EMP: 150
SQ FT: 5,000
SALES (est): 11.4MM
SALES (corp-wide): 27.3MM **Privately
Held**
SIC: 7361 Nurses' registry
PA: Totalmed Staffing Inc.
221 W College Ave
Appleton WI 54911
920 968-8708

(P-14450)
VALLEY LABOR SERVICE INC
39678 Road 84, Dinuba (93618-9588)
P.O. Box 775 (93618-0775)
PHONE..............................559 591-5591
Jane Hobbs, *President*
Salvador Romero, *Vice Pres*
EMP: 100
SQ FT: 1,100
SALES (est): 5MM **Privately Held**
SIC: 7361 Labor contractors (employment
agency)

(P-14451)
VOTUM STAFFING INC
515 W Whittier Blvd, Montebello
(90640-5233)
PHONE..............................310 499-4902
Giuseppe Veneziano, *CEO*
EMP: 450
SALES (est): 14.1MM **Privately Held**
SIC: 7361 Employment agencies

(P-14452)
WEST VALLEY ENGINEERING INC
3875 Hopyard Rd Ste 130, Pleasanton
(94588-8505)
PHONE..............................925 416-9707
Mike Williams, *Branch Mgr*
EMP: 70

SALES (corp-wide): 49.5MM **Privately Held**
SIC: 7361 Employment agencies
PA: West Valley Engineering, Inc.
   390 Potrero Ave
   Sunnyvale CA 94085
   408 735-1420

(P-14453)
WMBE PAYROLLING INC
Also Called: Target Cw
9475 Chesapeake Dr Ste A, San Diego
(92123-1337)
PHONE..............................858 810-3000
Samer Khouli, *CEO*
Courtney Hyma, *Executive Asst*
Robyn ISE, *CTO*
Joyce Jordan, *Technical Staff*
Loni Botticelli, *Business Mgr*
EMP: 130
SALES: 250.2MM **Privately Held**
SIC: 7361 Placement agencies

(P-14454)
WOLT COM INC
Also Called: Woltcom
2300 Tech Pkwy Ste 8, Hollister (95023)
PHONE..............................940 271-4703
Less Than, *Branch Mgr*
EMP: 383
SALES (corp-wide): 10.3MM **Privately Held**
SIC: 7361 Employment agencies
PA: Wolt Com Inc
   2300 Tech Pkwy Ste 8
   Hollister CA 95023
   831 638-4900

(P-14455)
WONOLO INC
535 Mission St Fl 14, San Francisco
(94105-3253)
PHONE..............................415 766-7692
Yong Kim, *CEO*
Asher Brustein, *COO*
Minnie Fong, *Top Exec*
Beatrice Pang, *Vice Pres*
Jeremy Burton, *CTO*
EMP: 85 EST: 2014
SQ FT: 7,500
SALES (est): 1.4MM **Privately Held**
SIC: 7361 Labor contractors (employment agency)

(P-14456)
WORKFORCE ENTERPRISES WFE INC
800 N Haven Ave Ste 330, Ontario
(91764-4976)
PHONE..............................909 718-8915
Andrew Hernandez, *President*
EMP: 50
SALES (est): 87.8K **Privately Held**
SIC: 7361 Employment agencies

(P-14457)
XL STAFFING INC
Also Called: Excell Staffing & SEC Svcs
450 Fletcher Pkwy Ste 204, El Cajon
(92020-2520)
PHONE..............................619 579-0442
William Mackey, *President*
EMP: 200
SQ FT: 1,100
SALES (est): 10.6MM **Privately Held**
SIC: 7361 7381 Placement agencies; security guard service

(P-14458)
YANG C PARK
Also Called: Cal Facilities Management Co
3703 Payne Ave, San Jose (95117-3413)
P.O. Box 9306 (95157-0306)
PHONE..............................408 260-8066
Toll Free:..............................888
Yang C Park, *Owner*
EMP: 100
SALES (est): 4.4MM **Privately Held**
SIC: 7361 7349 Labor contractors (employment agency); building maintenance services

(P-14459)
YOUR EXECUTIVE SOLUTIONS
9054 Slauson Ave, Pico Rivera
(90660-4521)
PHONE..............................562 388-4150
Gani Gjonbalaj, *CEO*
EMP: 650
SQ FT: 2,000
SALES (est): 8.6MM **Privately Held**
SIC: 7361 Employment agencies

(P-14460)
ZENITH TALENT CORPORATION
3315 San Felipe Rd Ste 37, San Jose
(95135-2000)
PHONE..............................844 467-2300
Sunil Bagai, *CEO*
Naina Bagai, *Vice Pres*
Sameer Singh, *Executive*
Raja Ganesh, *Technology*
Taskeen Khan, *Technology*
EMP: 240
SALES: 9MM **Privately Held**
SIC: 7361 Executive placement

(P-14461)
ZOE HOLDING COMPANY INC
2143 Hurley Way, Sacramento
(95825-3253)
PHONE..............................916 646-3100
Ryan Johnson, *Branch Mgr*
Adrian Chacon, *Recruiter*
Nick Dungan, *Recruiter*
Bonnie Anderson, *Manager*
Michael Jurczak, *Accounts Mgr*
EMP: 131
SALES (corp-wide): 62.1MM **Privately Held**
SIC: 7361 Employment agencies
PA: Zoe Holding Company, Inc.
   7025 N Scottsdale Rd # 200
   Scottsdale AZ 85253
   602 508-1883

7363 Help Supply Svcs

(P-14462)
A P R INC
Also Called: Alpha Professional Resources
100 E Thsnd Oaks Blvd, Thousand Oaks
(91360)
PHONE..............................805 379-3400
Salvador Ramirez, *President*
Cliff Goodwin, *CFO*
Rick Ramirez, *Vice Pres*
Leslie Major, *Technology*
Imran Khan, *Technical Staff*
EMP: 125
SQ FT: 1,100
SALES: 6.3MM **Privately Held**
WEB: www.alphaprofessionals.com
SIC: 7363 7361 Temporary help service; employment agencies

(P-14463)
AARDVARK STAFFING INC
3017 Douglas Blvd Fl 3, Roseville
(95661-3848)
PHONE..............................916 774-7115
Laura O'Boyle, *Principal*
EMP: 50
SALES: 2.5MM **Privately Held**
SIC: 7363 Help supply services

(P-14464)
ADVANCE STAFFING INC
2060 Walsh Ave Ste 101, Santa Clara
(95050-2568)
P.O. Box 391447, Mountain View (94039-1447)
PHONE..............................408 205-6154
Jose Badillo, *President*
EMP: 300
SQ FT: 1,043
SALES: 9MM **Privately Held**
SIC: 7363 Temporary help service

(P-14465)
ADVANCED MEDICAL REVIEWS LLC
600 Crprate Pinte Ste 300, Culver City
(90230)
PHONE..............................310 575-0900
Barak Mevorak, *CEO*

EMP: 61
SQ FT: 10,000
SALES (est): 4.2MM **Privately Held**
WEB: www.advancedmedicalreviews.com
SIC: 7363 Medical help service
PA: Examworks Group, Inc.
   3280 Peachtree Rd Ne
   Atlanta GA 30305
   -

(P-14466)
ADVANTAGE WORKFORCE SVCS LLC
39 Stillman St, San Francisco
(94107-1309)
PHONE..............................415 212-6464
Sumir Meghani,
EMP: 125
SALES (est): 882.6K **Privately Held**
SIC: 7363 Temporary help service

(P-14467)
AFFILIATED TEMPORARY HELP
4359 Florence Ave, Bell (90201-3525)
P.O. Box 124 (90201-0124)
PHONE..............................323 771-1383
John G Carbett, *President*
Ron Thomas, *Vice Pres*
EMP: 400
SQ FT: 1,100
SALES (est): 9.9MM **Privately Held**
SIC: 7363 8322 Temporary help service; individual & family services

(P-14468)
AGOSTINI AND ASSOCIATES INC
Also Called: Agostini Health Care Staffing
1470 Civic Ct Ste 1760, Concord
(94520-7949)
P.O. Box 6337, Moraga (94570-6337)
PHONE..............................925 691-7300
Linda Hughes Agostini, *President*
Jules Agostini, *Corp Secy*
Bobbie Vicioso, *Director*
EMP: 50
SQ FT: 1,300
SALES (est): 2MM **Privately Held**
SIC: 7363 Medical help service

(P-14469)
ALLEGIS GROUP INC
1 Waters Park Dr, San Mateo (94403-1157)
PHONE..............................650 425-6950
EMP: 158
SALES (corp-wide): 13.4B **Privately Held**
SIC: 7363 Temporary help service
PA: Allegis Group, Inc.
   7301 Parkway Dr
   Hanover MD 21076
   410 579-3000

(P-14470)
ALTECH SERVICES INC
400 Continental Blvd Fl 6, El Segundo
(90245-5074)
PHONE..............................888 725-8324
EMP: 320 **Privately Held**
SIC: 7363 7361 Help supply services; labor contractors (employment agency)
PA: Altech Services, Inc.
   695 Rte 46 W Ste 301b
   Fairfield NJ 07004

(P-14471)
AMERICAN EAGLE SERVICES INC
1320 Arrow Hwy, La Verne (91750-5218)
PHONE..............................574 859-2055
Jeni Bartolotti, *President*
John Bartolotti, *Vice Pres*
EMP: 70
SQ FT: 1,100
SALES: 3.7MM **Privately Held**
SIC: 7363 7513 Temporary help service; truck rental & leasing, no drivers

(P-14472)
ANDERSON ASSOCIATES STAFFING (PA)
8200 Wilshire Blvd # 200, Beverly Hills
(90211-2328)
PHONE..............................323 930-3170
Tom Anderson, *President*

EMP: 200 EST: 1997
SALES (est): 5.6MM **Privately Held**
WEB: www.andersonstaff.com
SIC: 7363 Temporary help service

(P-14473)
ARCADIA SERVICES INC
4340 Redwood Hwy Ste 123, San Rafael
(94903-2104)
PHONE..............................248 352-7530
John E Elliott II, *Branch Mgr*
EMP: 51
SALES (corp-wide): 126.6MM **Privately Held**
SIC: 7363 8082 Medical help service; home health care services
PA: Arcadia Services, Inc.
   20750 Civic Center Dr # 100
   Southfield MI 48076
   248 352-7530

(P-14474)
ASCENT SERVICES GROUP INC
1001 Galaxy Way Ste 408, Concord
(94520-5758)
PHONE..............................925 627-4900
Joseph Nordlinger, *President*
Richard Lawrence, *CFO*
W Todd Peterson, *CFO*
Sudhir Sahu, *Chairman*
Max Levine, *Exec VP*
EMP: 450
SQ FT: 7,000
SALES (est): 48.1MM **Privately Held**
WEB: www.itascent.com
SIC: 7363 7379 Help supply services; computer related consulting services

(P-14475)
ASRC INDUSTRIAL SERVICES LLC (HQ)
2300 Clayton Rd Ste 1050, Concord
(94520-2100)
PHONE..............................707 644-7455
Brent Renfrew, *President*
Steve Ennis, *COO*
Alyssa Kidder, *Controller*
Claudia Blaine, *Human Res Dir*
Albert Curiel, *Manager*
EMP: 143
SALES (est): 758.6MM
SALES (corp-wide): 2.9B **Privately Held**
SIC: 7363 Industrial help service
PA: Arctic Slope Regional Corporation
   3900 C St Ste 801
   Anchorage AK 99503
   907 339-6000

(P-14476)
ATRIA SENIOR LIVING INC
100 Sterling Ct Ofc, Roseville
(95661-3753)
PHONE..............................916 786-7200
Leslie Elowson, *Administration*
EMP: 72
SALES (corp-wide): 3.7B **Publicly Held**
WEB: www.atriacom.com
SIC: 7363 Temporary help service
HQ: Atria Senior Living Inc.
   300 E Market St Ste 100
   Louisville KY 40202

(P-14477)
AYA HEALTHCARE INC (PA)
5930 Cornerstone Ct W # 300, San Diego
(92121-3741)
PHONE..............................858 458-4410
Alan Braynin, *President*
Dan Walter, *Vice Pres*
Kelly Correy, *General Mgr*
Joe McConville, *Business Anlyst*
Vincent Pham, *Business Anlyst*
EMP: 119
SQ FT: 20,000
SALES (est): 103.9MM **Privately Held**
SIC: 7363 8049 Temporary help service; nurses, registered & practical

(P-14478)
B2B STAFFING SERVICES INC
Also Called: B2b Payroll Services
4501 Cerritos Ave Ste 201, Cypress
(90630)
PHONE..............................714 243-4104
Brian Wigdor, *President*

Bruce Underwood, *CFO*
EMP: 300
SALES (est): 11.4MM **Privately Held**
SIC: 7363 Temporary help service

(P-14479)
BANYAN SOLUTIONS INC
Also Called: Banyon Transcription
2809 Blue Oak Ct, Brentwood
(94513-4617)
PHONE..................................650 766-9338
Jyoti Challi, *President*
EMP: 63
SALES (est): 1.7MM **Privately Held**
SIC: 7363 7389 Medical help service;

(P-14480)
BEHAVIORAL INTERVENTION ASSN
Also Called: B I A
2354 Powell St A, Emeryville (94608-1738)
PHONE..................................510 652-7445
Hilary Stubblefield, *Exec Dir*
Fred Baldi, *COO*
Deanne Detmers, *Program Dir*
Hilary S Baldi, *Director*
EMP: 50
SALES: 4.3MM **Privately Held**
WEB: www.bia4autism.org
SIC: 7363 Domestic help service

(P-14481)
BUTLER SERVICE GROUP INC (HQ)
3820 State St Ste A, Santa Barbara
(93105-3182)
PHONE..................................201 891-5312
Edward M Kopko, *President*
Michael C Hellriegel, *CFO*
R Scott Silver Hill, *Senior VP*
EMP: 100
SQ FT: 82,000
SALES (est): 31.2MM
SALES (corp-wide): 85.1MM **Privately Held**
SIC: 7363 8711 8748 3661 Engineering help service; engineering services; communications consulting; telephone & telegraph apparatus; general automotive repair shops
PA: Butler International, Inc.
3820 State St Ste A
Santa Barbara CA 93105
805 882-2200

(P-14482)
CALIFORNIA SCHL EMPLOYEES ASSN
4600 Santa Anita Ave, El Monte
(91731-1320)
PHONE..................................626 258-3300
Michael Leon, *Branch Mgr*
EMP: 295
SQ FT: 8,286
SALES (corp-wide): 65.6MM **Privately Held**
SIC: 7363 Help supply services
PA: California School Employees' Association
2045 Lundy Ave
San Jose CA 95131
408 473-1000

(P-14483)
CANON RECRUITING GROUP LLC
26531 Summit Cir, Santa Clarita
(91350-3049)
PHONE..................................661 252-7400
Laurie Grayem, *CEO*
Tim Grayem, *President*
EMP: 400
SQ FT: 7,500
SALES (est): 22MM **Privately Held**
SIC: 7363 7361 Office help supply service; executive placement

(P-14484)
CARDINAL POINT CAPTAINS INC
5005 Texas St Ste 104, San Diego
(92108-3722)
PHONE..................................760 438-7361
Jordan E Cousino, *CEO*
David Sadler, *Vice Pres*

Heather Jenkins, *Accountant*
Pasquale Derosa, *Manager*
Gene Garcia, *Consultant*
EMP: 56
SQ FT: 2,633
SALES (est): 1.1MM **Privately Held**
SIC: 7363 3812 Boat crew service; search & navigation equipment

(P-14485)
CARE MEDICAL TRNSP INC
Also Called: Care Ambulance
9770 Candida St, San Diego (92126-4536)
PHONE..................................858 653-4520
Kelvin Carlisle, *President*
EMP: 190
SQ FT: 14,000
SALES (est): 10.6MM **Privately Held**
SIC: 7363 Medical help service

(P-14486)
CHILDCARE CAREERS LLC
2000 Sierra Point Pkwy # 702, Brisbane
(94005-1874)
PHONE..................................650 372-0211
Jason Jones,
Damla Akbay, *Opers Staff*
Sabah Raza, *Opers Staff*
Pauline Ferguson, *Marketing Staff*
Jessica Guttenbeil, *Supervisor*
EMP: 1000 **EST:** 2010
SQ FT: 6,300
SALES (est): 8.3MM **Privately Held**
SIC: 7363 7361 Temporary help service; teachers' agency

(P-14487)
CLEARPATH MANAGEMENT GROUP INC (PA)
1215 W Center St Ste 102, Manteca
(95337-4280)
PHONE..................................209 239-8700
Renee Fink, *CEO*
Judy Gnade, *CFO*
Jason Posel, *Senior VP*
EMP: 286
SQ FT: 3,171
SALES (est): 16.3MM **Privately Held**
SIC: 7363 Temporary help service

(P-14488)
CLEARPATH WORKFORCE MGT INC
1215 W Center St Ste 102, Manteca
(95337-4280)
PHONE..................................209 239-8700
Renee Fink, *CEO*
Judy Gnade, *CFO*
Jason Posel, *Senior VP*
Sue Ortiz, *Vice Pres*
EMP: 275
SQ FT: 3,171
SALES: 28.8MM
SALES (corp-wide): 16.3MM **Privately Held**
SIC: 7363 Temporary help service
PA: Clearpath Management Group, Inc.
1215 W Center St Ste 102
Manteca CA 95337
209 239-8700

(P-14489)
CLP RESOURCES INC
1485 Bay Shore Blvd # 138, San Francisco
(94124-3002)
PHONE..................................415 508-0910
Richard Webb, *Branch Mgr*
Toby Karlitz, *Manager*
EMP: 50
SALES (corp-wide): 2.5B **Publicly Held**
SIC: 7363 Temporary help service
HQ: Clp Resources, Inc.
1015 A St
Tacoma WA 98402
775 321-8000

(P-14490)
CLP RESOURCES INC
1260 N Dutton Ave, Santa Rosa
(95401-4659)
PHONE..................................707 569-0200
Dan Rosiak, *Branch Mgr*
EMP: 50
SALES (corp-wide): 2.5B **Publicly Held**
SIC: 7363 Temporary help service

HQ: Clp Resources, Inc.
1015 A St
Tacoma WA 98402
775 321-8000

(P-14491)
CLP RESOURCES INC
1000 Sunrise Ave Ste 8a, Roseville
(95661-5471)
PHONE..................................916 788-0300
EMP: 60
SALES (corp-wide): 2.1B **Publicly Held**
SIC: 7363
HQ: Clp Resources, Inc.
1015 A St
Tacoma WA 98402
775 321-8000

(P-14492)
CLP RESOURCES INC
570 El Cmino Real Ste 170, Redwood City
(94063)
PHONE..................................650 261-2100
Vince Vargas, *Director*
EMP: 200
SALES (corp-wide): 2.5B **Publicly Held**
SIC: 7363 Temporary help service
HQ: Clp Resources, Inc.
1015 A St
Tacoma WA 98402
775 321-8000

(P-14493)
CLP RESOURCES INC
4460 Redwood Hwy Ste 14, San Rafael
(94903-1953)
PHONE..................................415 446-7000
EMP: 50
SALES (corp-wide): 2.1B **Publicly Held**
SIC: 7363
HQ: Clp Resources, Inc.
1015 A St
Tacoma WA 98402
775 321-8000

(P-14494)
CLP RESOURCES INC
741 E Ball Rd Ste 100, Anaheim
(92805-5952)
PHONE..................................714 300-0510
Brian Rogers, *Manager*
EMP: 100
SALES (corp-wide): 2.5B **Publicly Held**
SIC: 7363 Temporary help service
HQ: Clp Resources, Inc.
1015 A St
Tacoma WA 98402
775 321-8000

(P-14495)
CLP RESOURCES INC
Also Called: Contractors Labor Pool of La
111 N First St Ste 100, Burbank
(91502-1851)
PHONE..................................818 260-9190
Guan Santos, *Manager*
EMP: 85
SALES (corp-wide): 2.5B **Publicly Held**
SIC: 7363 7361 Temporary help service; employment agencies
HQ: Clp Resources, Inc.
1015 A St
Tacoma WA 98402
775 321-8000

(P-14496)
COMPUTERIZED MANAGEMENT
40 W Cochran St, Simi Valley
(93065-6251)
P.O. Box 190 (93062-0190)
PHONE..................................805 522-5999
Daryl Favale, *Owner*
Dale Fazvale, *President*
Thomas Brajkovich, *Info Tech Mgr*
EMP: 60
SALES (est): 1.2MM **Privately Held**
WEB: www.cmsmanagement.net
SIC: 7363 8721 Medical help service; billing & bookkeeping service

(P-14497)
CPE PEO INC
9200 W Sunset Blvd, West Hollywood
(90069-3502)
PHONE..................................310 385-1000
Lee C Samson, *CEO*

Jay Cober, *President*
Grace Drulius, *CFO*
Harold Walt, *CFO*
Larry Feigen, *Vice Ch Bd*
EMP: 90
SQ FT: 11,000
SALES (est): 2.8MM **Privately Held**
SIC: 7363 Employee leasing service

(P-14498)
CPM LTD INC (PA)
Also Called: Manpower
1855 1st Ave Ste 300, San Diego
(92101-2668)
PHONE..................................619 237-9900
Philip Blair, *President*
Tony Evenson, *CFO*
Catherine Blair, *Treasurer*
Bridget Beattie, *Exec VP*
Mara Swan, *Exec VP*
EMP: 1400 **EST:** 1977
SALES (est): 72.4MM **Privately Held**
WEB: www.manpower-sd.com
SIC: 7363 Manpower pools

(P-14499)
CRAFT RESOURCES INC
220 S Pcifc Cst Hwy 112, Redondo Beach
(90277)
P.O. Box 7000 (90277-8710)
PHONE..................................310 937-3744
Stephen A Lawrence, *President*
EMP: 150
SQ FT: 2,000
SALES (est): 5.1MM **Privately Held**
WEB: www.craft-resources.com
SIC: 7363 7361 Industrial help service; employment agencies

(P-14500)
CULINARY SERVICES AMERICA INC
Also Called: Culinary Staffing Service
6363 Wilshire Blvd # 305, Los Angeles
(90048-5701)
PHONE..................................323 965-7582
Randy Hopp, *President*
David Crego, *Recruiter*
EMP: 50
SQ FT: 1,200
SALES (est): 2.1MM **Privately Held**
SIC: 7363 7361 Temporary help service; employment agencies

(P-14501)
CW HEALTHCARE INC
2884 Wakefield Dr, Belmont (94002-2935)
PHONE..................................510 636-9000
Russell Jones, *President*
EMP: 50
SQ FT: 900
SALES (est): 1.3MM **Privately Held**
WEB: www.cwhealthcare.com
SIC: 7363 Medical help service

(P-14502)
DISCHARGE RESOURCE GROUP
Also Called: DRG Health Care Staffing
400 Oyster Point Blvd # 440, South San
Francisco (94080-1979)
PHONE..................................650 877-8111
Lawrence Hix, *CEO*
Marsha Hix, *Treasurer*
Lorie Descala, *Exec Dir*
Lucinda Ip, *Info Tech Mgr*
Georgia Abelardo, *Accounting Mgr*
EMP: 250
SQ FT: 2,000
SALES (est): 12.3MM **Privately Held**
WEB: www.drgstaffing.com
SIC: 7363 7361 Temporary help service; medical help service; employment agencies

(P-14503)
EPLICA INC (PA)
Also Called: Eastridge ADM Staffing
2355 Northside Dr Ste 120, San Diego
(92108-2714)
PHONE..................................619 260-2000
Robert Svet, *President*
EMP: 175 **EST:** 1971
SQ FT: 15,000

SALES (est): 179.5MM **Privately Held**
WEB: www.hr-solutions.com
SIC: **7363** 7361 Temporary help service;
employment agencies

(P-14504)
FAMILY SVC AGCY SAN FRANCISCO (PA)
Also Called: Felton Institute
1500 Franklin St, San Francisco
(94109-4523)
PHONE..................................415 474-7310
Albert Gilbert III, *President*
Yohana Quiroz, *COO*
Marvin L Davis, *CFO*
Liz Dalmacio, *Vice Pres*
Ed Fowler, *Program Mgr*
EMP: 70
SQ FT: 14,000
SALES: 19MM **Privately Held**
SIC: **7363** Help supply services

(P-14505)
FERNANDES & SONS GEN CONTRS
2110 S Bascom Ave Ste 201, Campbell
(95008-3288)
PHONE..................................408 626-9090
Larry Fernandes, *President*
Mike Fernandes, *Vice Pres*
EMP: 55
SALES (est): 4.8MM **Privately Held**
SIC: **7363** 8299 Medical help service; educational services

(P-14506)
FREEDOM STAFF LEASING INC
3142 Pacific Coast Hwy, Torrance
(90505-6746)
P.O. Box 1689, Wilmington (90748-1689)
PHONE..................................310 834-6621
Lofton Ryan Burris, *President*
EMP: 300
SQ FT: 1,000
SALES (est): 6.2MM **Privately Held**
WEB: www.freedompeo.com
SIC: **7363** Employee leasing service

(P-14507)
G R HELM INC
Also Called: Helm Technical Services
5050 Robert J Mathews Pkw, El Dorado
Hills (95762-5756)
P.O. Box 1975, Placerville (95667-1975)
PHONE..................................916 933-9697
Gordon Helm, *President*
EMP: 85
SQ FT: 1,050
SALES (est): 3.4MM **Privately Held**
WEB: www.helmtech.com
SIC: **7363** 7371 Labor resource services; computer software development

(P-14508)
GENESIS HOME HEALTH INC
1687 Erringer Rd Ste 202, Simi Valley
(93065-6509)
PHONE..................................805 520-7100
EMP: 50
SALES (est): 2.9MM **Privately Held**
SIC: **7363** 7361

(P-14509)
GET HEAL INC
528 Palisades Dr Ste 176, Pacific Palisades
(90272-2844)
PHONE..................................310 528-4957
EMP: 71
SALES (corp-wide): 11MM **Privately Held**
SIC: **7363** Medical help service
PA: Get Heal, Inc.
1880 Century Park E # 711
Los Angeles CA 90067
310 528-4957

(P-14510)
GOODWILL OF SILICON VALLEY (PA)
1080 N 7th St, San Jose (95112-4425)
PHONE..................................408 998-5774
Michael E Fox, *CEO*
Julie Coy, *CEO*
Frank Kent, *CEO*
Christopher King, *COO*
Christopher Baker, *CFO*

▲ EMP: 100
SQ FT: 180,000
SALES (est): 46.5MM **Privately Held**
SIC: **7363** 5932 Help supply services; used merchandise stores

(P-14511)
HOST HEALTHCARE INC
4225 Executive Sq # 1500, La Jolla
(92037-1487)
PHONE..................................858 999-3579
Adam Francis, *CEO*
William Bulger, *CFO*
Ilia Belkin, *Recruiter*
Tim Goelze, *Recruiter*
Hunter Hopkins, *Recruiter*
EMP: 525 EST: 2012
SQ FT: 1,400
SALES (est): 2.3MM **Privately Held**
SIC: **7363** Help supply services

(P-14512)
I N C BUILDERS INC
Also Called: Acme Staffing
1560 Ocotillo Dr Ste L, El Centro
(92243-4237)
PHONE..................................760 352-4200
Rebecca Deal, *Manager*
EMP: 350
SALES (corp-wide): 8.3MM **Privately Held**
SIC: **7363** Help supply services
PA: I N C Builders, Inc.
550 E 32nd St Ste 5a
Yuma AZ 85365
928 344-8367

(P-14513)
IASCO (PA)
1833 Castenada Dr, Burlingame
(94010-5716)
PHONE..................................707 252-3522
Robert J Walters, *President*
K T Jack, *Ch of Bd*
Camille King, *Treasurer*
John R Lee, *Exec VP*
Brenda Freeman, *Human Res Dir*
EMP: 275 EST: 1959
SALES (est): 7.7MM **Privately Held**
WEB: www.iasco.com
SIC: **7363** Pilot service, aviation

(P-14514)
INFINITY NURSES CARE INC
39159 Paseo Padre Pkwy # 111, Fremont
(94538-1608)
PHONE..................................510 713-8892
Angeles Santos, *President*
Richard Santos, *Vice Pres*
EMP: 100
SQ FT: 1,500
SALES: 15K **Privately Held**
SIC: **7363** 8082 Medical help service; home health care services

(P-14515)
INFINITY STAFFING SERVICE
710 Kirkpatric Ct Ste B, Hollister
(95023-2808)
PHONE..................................831 638-0360
Ramiro Rodriguez, *President*
Trisha Tafoya, *Business Mgr*
Esequiel Arrizon, *Sales Executive*
John Blackmouth, *Manager*
EMP: 260
SALES (est): 1.1MM **Privately Held**
SIC: **7363** Temporary help service

(P-14516)
INTERACTIVE MED SPECIALISTS
252 Waterside Cir, San Rafael
(94903-2795)
PHONE..................................415 472-4204
Jaleh Ebrahimi, *President*
Oranous Ebrahimi, *Treasurer*
Ghazaleh Ebrahimi, *Vice Pres*
Oranus Ebrahimi, *Vice Pres*
EMP: 70
SALES (est): 2.8MM **Privately Held**
WEB: www.imsspecialists.com
SIC: **7363** Medical help service

(P-14517)
INTERIM HLTHCARE NTHRN CAL INC (PA)
1647 Court St, Redding (96001-1737)
PHONE..................................530 221-1300
Robert Seawright, *President*
Renee Rand, *Admin Sec*
EMP: 350
SQ FT: 4,000
SALES (est): 12MM **Privately Held**
SIC: **7363** Temporary help service

(P-14518)
JOHN PAUL USA (PA)
575 Market St Ste 3050, San Francisco
(94105-5847)
PHONE..................................415 905-6088
David Amsellem, *CEO*
Amber Treshnell, *CEO*
Kim Barber, *Vice Pres*
Paul McKnight, *Admin Sec*
Steve Sim, *Accounting Mgr*
EMP: 103
SALES (est): 28.4MM **Privately Held**
WEB: www.lesconcierges.com
SIC: **7363** Help supply services

(P-14519)
JUNE GROUP LLC
Also Called: Qualstaff Resources
9444 Waples St Ste 100, San Diego
(92121-2940)
PHONE..................................858 450-4290
R Scott Silver-Hill, *Mng Member*
Janet Alvarez, *Recruiter*
Amber Boytis-Barriga, *Recruiter*
Kristy Hernandez, *Recruiter*
Jesse Lafferty, *Recruiter*
EMP: 100
SQ FT: 4,200
SALES (est): 4.1MM **Privately Held**
SIC: **7363** Temporary help service

(P-14520)
KAMPS COMPANY
1262 Dupont Ct, Manteca (95336-6003)
PHONE..................................209 823-8924
John Paul, *President*
John Kamps, *Shareholder*
EMP: 160
SQ FT: 3,000
SALES (est): 3MM **Privately Held**
SIC: **7363** Employee leasing service
PA: Kamps Propane, Inc.
1262 Dupont Ct
Manteca CA 95336

(P-14521)
KENSINGTON AGENCY INC
Also Called: Kensington Nursing Agency
8469 La Mesa Blvd, La Mesa
(91942-5335)
PHONE..................................619 280-6993
David Keyte, *General Mgr*
Deaydre Pulliam, *COO*
Deaydre L Pulliam, *Administration*
EMP: 50
SQ FT: 1,000
SALES (est): 3.2MM **Privately Held**
SIC: **7363** Temporary help service

(P-14522)
LANDMARK EVENT STAFFING
1965 Adams Ave, San Leandro
(94577-1005)
PHONE..................................510 632-9000
Peter Kranske, *Branch Mgr*
EMP: 1603 **Privately Held**
SIC: **7363** Help supply services
PA: Landmark Event Staffing Services, Inc.
4131 Harbor Walk Dr
Fort Collins CO 80525

(P-14523)
M K TECHNICAL SERVICES INC
4349 San Felipe Rd, San Jose
(95135-1507)
PHONE..................................408 528-0401
Margie Menz King, *President*
Johnie Staggs, *Administration*
EMP: 50
SQ FT: 1,000
SALES: 5MM **Privately Held**
SIC: **7363** Temporary help service

(P-14524)
MARATHON STAFFING SOLUTIONS
2950 Beacon Blvd Ste 45, West Sacramento (95691-5031)
PHONE..................................978 649-6230
Chris Panagiotopoulos, *Principal*
Suzanne Deshler, *Principal*
Athena Panagiotakos, *Principal*
EMP: 99
SALES (est): 734.6K **Privately Held**
SIC: **7363** Help supply services

(P-14525)
MAXIM HEALTHCARE SERVICES INC
631 River Oaks Pkwy, San Jose
(95134-1907)
PHONE..................................408 914-7478
EMP: 216
SALES (corp-wide): 1.5B **Privately Held**
SIC: **7363** Medical help service
PA: Maxim Healthcare Services, Inc.
7227 Lee Deforest Dr
Columbia MD 21046
410 910-1500

(P-14526)
MAXIM HEALTHCARE SERVICES INC
3580 Wilshire Blvd # 1000, Los Angeles
(90010-2544)
PHONE..................................866 465-5678
EMP: 144
SALES (corp-wide): 1.5B **Privately Held**
SIC: **7363** Medical help service
PA: Maxim Healthcare Services, Inc.
7227 Lee Deforest Dr
Columbia MD 21046
410 910-1500

(P-14527)
MAXIM HEALTHCARE SERVICES INC
Also Called: Riverside Companion Services
1845 Bus Ctr Dr Ste 112, San Bernardino
(92408)
PHONE..................................951 684-4148
Elijah Hall, *Manager*
Jeanette Garzon, *Accounts Mgr*
EMP: 304
SALES (corp-wide): 1.5B **Privately Held**
WEB: www.maximstaffing.com
SIC: **7363** Medical help service
PA: Maxim Healthcare Services, Inc.
7227 Lee Deforest Dr
Columbia MD 21046
410 910-1500

(P-14528)
ME AND ME INC
Also Called: Employee Solutions
14536 Roscoe Blvd Ste 112, Van Nuys
(91402-4103)
P.O. Box 801795, Santa Clarita (91380-1795)
PHONE..................................818 891-0197
Michael E Socha, *President*
EMP: 76
SALES: 2MM **Privately Held**
SIC: **7363** Medical help service

(P-14529)
MED STAFFING LLC
1860 Mowry Ave Ste 302, Fremont
(94538-1730)
PHONE..................................510 795-0114
Ramesh C Karipineni MD, *President*
Karen Parsons, *Opers Mgr*
EMP: 50
SALES (est): 750K **Privately Held**
SIC: **7363** Help supply services

(P-14530)
MEDICAL HOME SPECIALISTS INC
Also Called: Medical HM Care Professionals
2115 Churn Creek Rd, Redding
(96002-0732)
PHONE..................................530 226-5577
Kathy A McKillop, *CEO*
Elaine Flores, *COO*
EMP: 160
SQ FT: 1,600

SALES (est): 7.9MM **Privately Held**
WEB: www.medicalhomecarepros.com
SIC: 7363 Medical help service

(P-14531)
MEDICAL MANAGEMENT CONS INC (PA)
Also Called: MMC
8150 Beverly Blvd, Los Angeles
(90048-4513)
PHONE...................................310 659-3835
Mashi Rahmani, *President*
Chris Platt, *Human Res Mgr*
Andrew Amador, *Human Resources*
Walter Aguilar, *Accounts Mgr*
Rachel Miskofski, *Consultant*
EMP: 50
SQ FT: 21,000
SALES (est): 71.4MM **Privately Held**
WEB: www.mmchr.com
SIC: 7363 8742 8748 8721 Help supply services; hospital & health services consultant; employee programs administration; payroll accounting service

(P-14532)
MEDICAL SUPPORT SERVICES
6660 W Sunset Blvd Ste J, Los Angeles
(90028-7161)
PHONE...................................323 860-7994
Raynoldo Fernandez, *President*
EMP: 100
SQ FT: 1,000
SALES (est): 2.5MM **Privately Held**
WEB: www.mssregistryinc.com
SIC: 7363 7361 Medical help service; employment agencies

(P-14533)
MEDISCAN DIAGNOSTIC SVCS LLC
Also Called: Mediscan Staffing Services
21050 Califa St Ste 100, Woodland Hills
(91367-5103)
PHONE...................................818 758-4224
Val Serebryany, *President*
EMP: 100
SALES (est): 2.9MM
SALES (corp-wide): 816.4MM **Publicly Held**
WEB: www.mediscan.net
SIC: 7363 Medical help service
HQ: Mediscan Nursing Staffing, Llc
21050 Califa St Ste 100
Woodland Hills CA 91367
818 758-8680

(P-14534)
MERRITT HAWKINS & ASSOC LLC (HQ)
12400 High Bluff Dr, San Diego
(92130-3077)
PHONE...................................858 792-0711
Susan Salka Fka Nowakowski, *CEO*
Brian Scott, *CFO*
Brian M Scott, *CFO*
John Dillon, *Treasurer*
Denise Jackson, *Vice Pres*
EMP: 120
SQ FT: 96,000
SALES (est): 13.4MM
SALES (corp-wide): 2.1B **Publicly Held**
WEB: www.mhagroup.com
SIC: 7363 Medical help service
PA: Amn Healthcare Services, Inc.
12400 High Bluff Dr
San Diego CA 92130
866 871-8519

(P-14535)
MGA HEALTHCARE CALIFORNIA INC
879 W 190th St Ste 700, Gardena
(90248-4227)
PHONE...................................310 324-5591
David T Zowine, *President*
EMP: 50
SQ FT: 1,111
SALES (est): 2.5MM **Privately Held**
SIC: 7363 Temporary help service

(P-14536)
MSS NURSES REGISTRY INC
Also Called: Medical Support Services
6660 W Sunset Blvd Ste J, Los Angeles
(90028-7161)
PHONE...................................323 467-5717
Reynaldo Fernandez, *President*
Teresita Fernandez, *Principal*
EMP: 99
SALES (est): 1.8MM **Privately Held**
SIC: 7363 Temporary help service

(P-14537)
NATIONAL BUILDER SERVICES INC
3835 E Thousand Oaks Blvd R, Westlake Village (91362-3637)
PHONE...................................714 634-7800
Joseph M Wiseman, *President*
EMP: 100
SQ FT: 1,700
SALES (est): 3.2MM **Privately Held**
WEB: www.tti-nbs.com
SIC: 7363 Employee leasing service

(P-14538)
NEW DAY STAFFING INC
5920 Friars Rd Ste 104, San Diego
(92108-1077)
PHONE...................................619 481-5400
Julie Laurice, *President*
EMP: 150
SALES (est): 3.4MM **Privately Held**
SIC: 7363 Temporary help service

(P-14539)
NEW MEDISCAN II LLC
Also Called: Mediscan Staffing Services
21050 Califa St 100, Woodland Hills
(91367-5103)
PHONE...................................866 758-4224
Val Serebryany, *President*
EMP: 100
SQ FT: 7,500
SALES (est): 2.9MM
SALES (corp-wide): 816.4MM **Publicly Held**
WEB: www.mediscan.net
SIC: 7363 Medical help service
HQ: Mediscan Nursing Staffing, Llc
21050 Califa St Ste 100
Woodland Hills CA 91367
818 758-8680

(P-14540)
PEOPLEREADY INC
1405 Carmelo Dr 5112, Oceanside (92054)
PHONE...................................760 433-4980
Frank Guttierez, *Manager*
EMP: 50
SALES (corp-wide): 2.5B **Publicly Held**
SIC: 7363 Temporary help service
HQ: Peopleready, Inc.
1015 A St Unit A
Tacoma WA 98402
253 383-9101

(P-14541)
PERSONNEL PLUS INC (PA)
12052 Imperial Hwy # 200, Norwalk
(90650-3090)
P.O. Box 817 (90651-0817)
PHONE...................................562 712-5490
Kim Walia, *CEO*
Sue Failla, *Senior VP*
EMP: 155
SQ FT: 5,000
SALES (est): 4.9MM **Privately Held**
WEB: www.ppitemps.com
SIC: 7363 7361 Temporary help service; employment agencies

(P-14542)
PERSONNEL PREFERENCE INC
150 Boles St Ste A, Weed (96094-2586)
PHONE...................................530 938-3909
Jill Tillinghast, *President*
EMP: 150
SALES (est): 5.7MM **Privately Held**
SIC: 7363 7361 Temporary help service; employment agencies

(P-14543)
PHARMACY TEMPS INC
Also Called: Nor-Cal Medical Temps
2125 Paradise Dr, Belvedere Tiburon
(94920-1939)
P.O. Box 736 (94920-0736)
PHONE...................................415 459-5211
Kristina Glaves, *President*
EMP: 50
SALES: 700K **Privately Held**
SIC: 7363 Temporary help service

(P-14544)
PHOENIX ENGINEERING CO INC
Also Called: Phoenix Personnel
550 E Carson Plaza Dr # 112, Carson
(90746-7353)
P.O. Box 66395, Los Angeles (90066-0395)
PHONE...................................310 532-1134
Silvia Lugo, *President*
EMP: 100
SQ FT: 1,700
SALES (est): 5.5MM **Privately Held**
WEB: www.phoenix-engineering.com
SIC: 7363 7361 Office help supply service; employment agencies

(P-14545)
PLANT MAINTENANCE INC
Also Called: Temporary Plant Cleaners
1330 Arnold Dr Ste 147, Martinez
(94553-6538)
P.O. Box 48 (94553-0115)
PHONE...................................925 228-3285
Tim Hollz, *President*
Kenneth B Johnson, *Vice Pres*
EMP: 150 EST: 1996
SQ FT: 2,800
SALES: 2.3MM
SALES (corp-wide): 75MM **Privately Held**
WEB: www.montmech.com
SIC: 7363 Industrial help service
PA: Monterey Mechanical Co.
8275 San Leandro St
Oakland CA 94621
510 632-3173

(P-14546)
PLATINUM EMPIRE GROUP INC
Also Called: Platinum Healthcare Staffing
3521 Lomita Blvd Ste 202b, Torrance
(90505-5040)
P.O. Box 10338 (90505-1238)
PHONE...................................310 821-5888
Arun Mahtani, *President*
Naveen Yadav, *Technical Staff*
Aaron Quiboloy, *Human Res Mgr*
Maluh Silvano, *Manager*
EMP: 120
SQ FT: 400
SALES (est): 1.5MM **Privately Held**
WEB: www.platinumhealthcarestaffing.com
SIC: 7363 Temporary help service

(P-14547)
PROCEL TEMPORARY SERVICES INC
222 W 6th St Ste 370, San Pedro
(90731-3348)
PHONE...................................310 372-0560
Marilyn Stephens, *President*
David Trejo, *Accountant*
EMP: 500
SQ FT: 4,600
SALES (est): 22.2MM **Privately Held**
SIC: 7363 Temporary help service

(P-14548)
QUEST DISCOVERY SERVICES INC
700 E Bonita Ave, Pomona (91767-1906)
PHONE...................................310 769-5557
Tina Hicks, *Manager*
EMP: 57
SALES (corp-wide): 11.9MM **Privately Held**
SIC: 7363 7334 Help supply services; photocopying & duplicating services
PA: Quest Discovery Services, Inc.
981 Ridder Park Dr
San Jose CA 95131
408 441-7000

(P-14549)
QUEST DISCOVERY SERVICES INC
4600 Roseville Rd Ste 200, North Highlands (95660-5197)
PHONE...................................916 483-7030
Cindy Romero, *Principal*
EMP: 57
SALES (corp-wide): 11.9MM **Privately Held**
SIC: 7363 Help supply services
PA: Quest Discovery Services, Inc.
981 Ridder Park Dr
San Jose CA 95131
408 441-7000

(P-14550)
R L KLEIN & ASSOCIATES
3553 Atlantic Ave Ste A, Long Beach
(90807-5605)
PHONE...................................562 427-5577
Bob Klein, *Owner*
EMP: 60
SQ FT: 2,100
SALES: 1,000K **Privately Held**
SIC: 7363 Temporary help service

(P-14551)
RANDSTAD NORTH AMERICA INC
7014 N Cedar Ave, Fresno (93720-3300)
PHONE...................................559 297-0054
Tammy Wallace, *Branch Mgr*
EMP: 200
SALES (corp-wide): 27.2B **Privately Held**
SIC: 7363 Temporary help service
HQ: Randstad North America, Inc.
3625 Cumberland Blvd Se
Atlanta GA 30339
770 937-7000

(P-14552)
RANDSTAD NORTH AMERICA INC
1110 W Visalia Rd Ste 116, Exeter
(93221-1481)
PHONE...................................559 592-6700
Wendy Attaway, *Manager*
EMP: 254
SALES (corp-wide): 27.2B **Privately Held**
WEB: www.placementpros.com
SIC: 7363 Temporary help service
HQ: Randstad North America, Inc.
3625 Cumberland Blvd Se
Atlanta GA 30339
770 937-7000

(P-14553)
REAL TIME INFORMATION SVCS INC
Also Called: Real-Time Staffing Services
191 W Shaw Ave Ste 106, Fresno
(93704-2826)
PHONE...................................559 222-6456
Aijaz Ahmed, *CEO*
Eric Metler, *Engineer*
EMP: 50
SALES (est): 2.5MM **Privately Held**
WEB: www.realtimeca.com
SIC: 7363 Temporary help service

(P-14554)
REDWOOD HEALTHCARE STAFFING
600 B St Ste 1570, San Diego
(92101-4560)
PHONE...................................619 238-4180
Genevieve Lavin, *President*
EMP: 60 **Privately Held**
SIC: 7363 Temporary help service
PA: Redwood Healthcare Staffing
1015 Gayley Ave
Los Angeles CA 90024

(P-14555)
REGISTRY NETWORK INC (PA)
1207 Carlsbad Village Dr X, Carlsbad
(92008-1958)
PHONE...................................760 966-3700
John Fusco, *President*
Eric Frehe, *COO*
Laura Moeller, *Vice Pres*
EMP: 190

SQ FT: 500
SALES (est): 5MM Privately Held
WEB: www.registrynetwork.net
SIC: 7363 7361 Medical help service; nurses' registry

(P-14556)
RELIABLE HEALTH CARE SVCS INC
5705 Sepulveda Blvd, Culver City (90230-6406)
PHONE..................................310 397-2229
William A Benbassat, President
EMP: 50
SALES (est): 2.7MM Privately Held
WEB: www.reliablehealthcare.com
SIC: 7363 Temporary help service

(P-14557)
REMEDYTEMP INC (DH)
Also Called: Remedy Intelligent Staffing
101 Enterprise Ste 100, Aliso Viejo (92656-2604)
PHONE..................................949 425-7600
David Stephen Sorensen, CEO
Jeff R Mitchell, CFO
Richard Hulme, Exec VP
John Neff, Controller
Brandyn Jacob, Accounts Exec
EMP: 143
SQ FT: 51,000
SALES (est): 57MM
SALES (corp-wide): 574.9MM Privately Held
WEB: www.remedystaff.com
SIC: 7363 7361 Temporary help service; employment agencies

(P-14558)
RNCMBA INC
Also Called: Interim Services
4801 Truxtun Ave, Bakersfield (93309-0605)
PHONE..................................661 395-1700
Darlyn Baker, President
Chuck Baker, Vice Pres
Sue Smith, Office Mgr
Ann Devries, Manager
EMP: 125
SQ FT: 5,000
SALES (est): 5.4MM Privately Held
SIC: 7363 Temporary help service

(P-14559)
ROBERT A HALL
Also Called: Straight Edge
9769 Dawn Way, Windsor (95492-8879)
PHONE..................................707 837-8564
Robert Hall, President
Leslie Hall, CFO
Leslie A Hall, Manager
EMP: 60
SALES: 442.1K Privately Held
SIC: 7363 Manpower pools

(P-14560)
ROBERT HALF INTERNATIONAL INC (PA)
2884 Sand Hill Rd Ste 200, Menlo Park (94025-7059)
PHONE..................................650 234-6000
Harold M Messmer Jr, Ch of Bd
Paul F Gentzkow, President
Ben Hirsh, President
Joshua Howarth, President
Pablo Markelis, President
▲ EMP: 100
SALES: 5.8B Publicly Held
WEB: www.rhii.com
SIC: 7363 7361 8748 8721 Temporary help service; placement agencies; business consulting; auditing services

(P-14561)
ROTH STAFFING COMPANIES LP (PA)
Also Called: Ultimate Staffing Services
450 N State College Blvd, Orange (92868-1708)
PHONE..................................714 939-8600
Adam Roth, CEO
Frank Hyson, VP Finance
Veronica Meglio, Credit Staff
Bradley Chowen, Accountant
Renee Norwalk, Accountant

◆ EMP: 80
SALES: 344.4MM Privately Held
WEB: www.ultimatestaffing.com
SIC: 7363 Help supply services

(P-14562)
RX PRO HEALTH LLC
12400 High Bluff Dr, San Diego (92130-3077)
PHONE..................................858 369-4050
Susan R Salka, CEO
EMP: 1800
SQ FT: 175,000
SALES (est): 113.2K
SALES (corp-wide): 2.1B Publicly Held
WEB: www.amnhealthcare.com
SIC: 7363 Medical help service
PA: Amn Healthcare Services, Inc.
12400 High Bluff Dr
San Diego CA 92130
866 871-8519

(P-14563)
SAGE STAFFING CONSULTANTS INC (PA)
27441 Tourney Rd Ste 150, Valencia (91355-5312)
PHONE..................................661 254-4026
Laura Kincaid, CEO
Greg Kincaid, President
EMP: 200
SQ FT: 5,000
SALES (est): 9.1MM Privately Held
WEB: www.sagestaffing.com
SIC: 7363 Temporary help service

(P-14564)
SE SCHER CORPORATION
1585 The Alameda, San Jose (95126-2310)
PHONE..................................408 844-0772
William Friedeberg, President
Griffin Long, Manager
EMP: 612
SALES (corp-wide): 19.8MM Privately Held
SIC: 7363 Help supply services
PA: S.E. Scher Corporation
303 Hegenberger Rd # 300
Oakland CA 94621
415 431-8826

(P-14565)
SFN GROUP INC
114 Pacifica Ste 210, Irvine (92618-3320)
PHONE..................................949 727-8500
Tammy Hawkins, Manager
EMP: 75
SALES (corp-wide): 27.2B Privately Held
SIC: 7363 Temporary help service
HQ: Sfn Group, Inc.
2050 Spectrum Blvd
Fort Lauderdale FL 33309
954 308-7600

(P-14566)
SFN GROUP INC
Also Called: Spherion Staffing Group
3050 Bictor Ave Ste A, Redding (96002)
PHONE..................................530 222-3434
Sheryl Lakowski, Branch Mgr
EMP: 150
SALES (corp-wide): 27.2B Privately Held
SIC: 7363 Temporary help service
HQ: Sfn Group, Inc.
2050 Spectrum Blvd
Fort Lauderdale FL 33309
954 308-7600

(P-14567)
SPECTRUM PROF STAFFING INC
13520 Evening Creek Dr N # 300, San Diego (92128-8105)
PHONE..................................800 644-1150
Raymond Lucia, President
Bella Tarasov, Accounting Mgr
EMP: 200
SALES (est): 4.5MM Privately Held
SIC: 7363 Employee leasing service

(P-14568)
STAFF TODAY INCORPORATED
212 E Rowland St 313, Covina (91723-3146)
PHONE..................................800 928-5561
Paul Mwangi, President
EMP: 150
SALES (est): 770.2K Privately Held
SIC: 7363 7361 Temporary help service; employment agencies

(P-14569)
STAR H-R (PA)
Also Called: Star Staffing
3820 Cypress Dr Ste 2, Petaluma (94954-6964)
PHONE..................................707 762-4447
Carla Shevchuk, President
Lisa A Rogelstad, Vice Pres
Alan Fernandez, Recruiter
Jennifer Kraus, Recruiter
EMP: 58
SALES (est): 46.7MM Privately Held
SIC: 7363 Temporary help service

(P-14570)
SURGICAL STAFF INC
Surgical Staff, The
1523 G St, Sacramento (95814-1618)
PHONE..................................916 444-4424
Maryann Lesbirel, Manager
EMP: 200
SALES (corp-wide): 6.6MM Privately Held
WEB: www.mcnealtech.com
SIC: 7363 7361 Temporary help service; employment agencies
PA: Surgical Staff, Inc.
120 Saint Matthews Ave C
San Mateo CA 94401
650 558-3942

(P-14571)
TAD PGS INC
10805 Holder St Ste 250, Cypress (90630-5142)
PHONE..................................571 451-2428
Wendy Harkins, CFO
EMP: 99
SALES (corp-wide): 27.3B Privately Held
SIC: 7363 Temporary help service
HQ: Tad Pgs, Inc.
1001 3rd Ave W Ste 460
Bradenton FL 34205
941 746-4434

(P-14572)
TEGP INC
2375 Northside Dr Ste 360, San Diego (92108-2713)
PHONE..................................619 584-3408
Michael Santos, President
EMP: 1500
SALES (est): 27.3MM
SALES (corp-wide): 179.5MM Privately Held
SIC: 7363 Temporary help service
PA: Eplica, Inc.
2355 Northside Dr Ste 120
San Diego CA 92108
619 260-2000

(P-14573)
TEMP UNLIMITED LLC
11306 183rd St Ste 301, Cerritos (90703-5440)
P.O. Box 661358, Arcadia (91066-1358)
PHONE..................................562 860-3340
Carol Forrest, President
Greg Forrest, Vice Pres
EMP: 80 EST: 2001
SALES (est): 2.7MM Privately Held
SIC: 7363 Temporary help service

(P-14574)
TRANSFORCE INC
965 E Yosemite Ave Ste 7, Manteca (95336-5943)
PHONE..................................209 952-2573
EMP: 50
SALES (est): 2.7MM Privately Held
SIC: 7363

(P-14575)
TRUEBLUE INC
Also Called: Labor Ready
1362 Colusa Hwy, Yuba City (95993-9001)
PHONE..................................530 755-3291
Carol Pate, Manager
EMP: 125
SALES (corp-wide): 2.5B Publicly Held
WEB: www.laborready.com
SIC: 7363 Temporary help service
PA: Trueblue, Inc.
1015 A St
Tacoma WA 98402
253 383-9101

(P-14576)
TRUEBLUE INC
Also Called: Labor Ready
123 E Carrillo St, Santa Barbara (93101-2110)
PHONE..................................805 963-5370
Adam Lockhart, Manager
EMP: 50
SALES (corp-wide): 2.5B Publicly Held
WEB: www.laborready.com
SIC: 7363 Temporary help service
PA: Trueblue, Inc.
1015 A St
Tacoma WA 98402
253 383-9101

(P-14577)
TWO ROADS PROF RESOURCES INC
5122 Bolsa Ave Ste 112, Huntington Beach (92649-1050)
PHONE..................................714 901-3804
Tammy Gottschalk, President
Chris Hoff, Vice Pres
Michele Hoff, Vice Pres
Barry Vince, Vice Pres
Jackie Farber, Tech Recruiter
EMP: 110
SQ FT: 4,000
SALES (est): 5.6MM Privately Held
WEB: www.2roads.com
SIC: 7363 Temporary help service

(P-14578)
UNITED STATES DEPT OF NAVY
Also Called: Manpower
32444 Echo Ln Fl 3, San Diego (92147-5100)
PHONE..................................619 524-1069
EMP: 175 Publicly Held
SIC: 7363 Manpower pools
HQ: United States Department Of The Navy
1200 Navy Pentagon
Washington DC 20350

(P-14579)
USA STAFFING INC
505 Higuera St, San Luis Obispo (93401-6107)
PHONE..................................805 269-2677
Susan Elson, Principal
EMP: 75
SALES (est): 107.8K Privately Held
SIC: 7363 Temporary help service

(P-14580)
VACAVILLE CONDOLESCENT AND REH
585 Nut Tree Ct, Vacaville (95687-3353)
PHONE..................................707 449-8000
Joseph M Niccoli Jr, President
EMP: 150
SALES (est): 666.8K Privately Held
SIC: 7363 Medical help service

(P-14581)
VANPIKE INC (PA)
6336 Greenwich Dr Ste 100, San Diego (92122-5922)
PHONE..................................858 453-1331
Gary Van Eik, President
Richard Papike, Vice Pres
Jason Van Eik, Manager
EMP: 60
SQ FT: 9,000
SALES: 26MM Privately Held
WEB: www.tristaff.com
SIC: 7363 7361 Temporary help service; executive placement

PRODUCTS & SVCS

(P-14582)
VOLT MANAGEMENT CORP
Also Called: Volt Workforce Solutions
19191 S Vt Ave Ste 950, Torrance
(90502-1098)
PHONE..............................310 316-8523
Rhona Driggs, *Branch Mgr*
EMP: 130
SALES (corp-wide): 1B **Publicly Held**
SIC: 7363 Help supply services
HQ: Volt Management Corp.
    50 Charles Lindbergh Blvd # 206
    Uniondale NY 11553

(P-14583)
VOLT MANAGEMENT CORP
Also Called: Volt Temporary Services
2411 N Glassell St, Orange (92865-2717)
PHONE..............................714 921-7460
Rhona Driggs, *Branch Mgr*
EMP: 300
SALES (corp-wide): 1B **Publicly Held**
SIC: 7363 7373 Help supply services;
computer integrated systems design
HQ: Volt Management Corp.
    50 Charles Lindbergh Blvd # 206
    Uniondale NY 11553

(P-14584)
VOLT MANAGEMENT CORP
Also Called: Volt Workforce Solutions
1400 N Harbor Blvd # 103, Fullerton
(92835-4126)
PHONE..............................714 879-9330
Scott Giroux, *Branch Mgr*
EMP: 175
SQ FT: 11,000
SALES (corp-wide): 1B **Publicly Held**
SIC: 7363 Engineering help service
HQ: Volt Management Corp.
    50 Charles Lindbergh Blvd # 206
    Uniondale NY 11553

(P-14585)
VOLT MANAGEMENT CORP
Also Called: Volt Workforce Solutions
7676 Hazard Center Dr # 1000, San Diego
(92108-4503)
PHONE..............................858 576-3140
Rhona Driggs, *Branch Mgr*
EMP: 130
SALES (corp-wide): 1B **Publicly Held**
SIC: 7363 Help supply services
HQ: Volt Management Corp.
    50 Charles Lindbergh Blvd # 206
    Uniondale NY 11553

(P-14586)
VOLT MANAGEMENT CORP
Also Called: Volt Workforce Solutions
7676 Hazard Center Dr # 1000, San Diego
(92108-4503)
PHONE..............................858 578-0920
Rhona Driggs, *Branch Mgr*
EMP: 130
SALES (corp-wide): 1B **Publicly Held**
SIC: 7363 Temporary help service
HQ: Volt Management Corp.
    50 Charles Lindbergh Blvd # 206
    Uniondale NY 11553

(P-14587)
VOLT MANAGEMENT CORP
Also Called: Volt Workforce Solutions
7330 N Palm Ave Ste 105, Fresno
(93711-5768)
PHONE..............................559 435-1255
Scott Giroux, *Branch Mgr*
EMP: 130
SALES (corp-wide): 1B **Publicly Held**
SIC: 7363 7361 Temporary help service;
employment agencies
HQ: Volt Management Corp.
    50 Charles Lindbergh Blvd # 206
    Uniondale NY 11553

(P-14588)
VOLT MANAGEMENT CORP
Also Called: Volt Workforce Solutions
2401 N Glassell St, Orange (92865-2705)
P.O. Box 3708 (92857-0708)
PHONE..............................714 921-8800
Scott Giroux, *Branch Mgr*
EMP: 130
SALES (corp-wide): 1B **Publicly Held**
SIC: 7363 Help supply services
HQ: Volt Management Corp.
    50 Charles Lindbergh Blvd # 206
    Uniondale NY 11553

(P-14589)
VOLT MANAGEMENT CORP
Also Called: Volt Workforce Solutions
1544 Eureka Rd Ste 150, Roseville
(95661-3093)
PHONE..............................916 923-0454
Tim Chapman, *Branch Mgr*
EMP: 56
SALES (corp-wide): 1B **Publicly Held**
WEB: www.volt.com
SIC: 7363 Help supply services
HQ: Volt Management Corp.
    50 Charles Lindbergh Blvd # 206
    Uniondale NY 11553

(P-14590)
VOLT MANAGEMENT CORP
Also Called: Volt Workforce Solutions
1650 Iowa Ave Ste 140, Riverside
(92507-2432)
PHONE..............................951 789-8133
Scott Giroux, *Branch Mgr*
EMP: 56
SALES (corp-wide): 1B **Publicly Held**
WEB: www.volt.com
SIC: 7363 Help supply services
HQ: Volt Management Corp.
    50 Charles Lindbergh Blvd # 206
    Uniondale NY 11553

(P-14591)
VOLT MANAGEMENT CORP
Also Called: Volt Workforce Solutions
3558 Deer Park Dr 2, Stockton
(95219-2350)
PHONE..............................209 952-5627
Scott Giroux, *Branch Mgr*
EMP: 130
SALES (corp-wide): 1B **Publicly Held**
SIC: 7363 Help supply services
HQ: Volt Management Corp.
    50 Charles Lindbergh Blvd # 206
    Uniondale NY 11553

(P-14592)
VOLT MANAGEMENT CORP
Also Called: Volt Workforce Solutions
1701 Solar Dr Ste 145, Oxnard
(93030-0137)
PHONE..............................805 485-0506
Scott Giroux, *Branch Mgr*
EMP: 130
SALES (corp-wide): 1B **Publicly Held**
SIC: 7363 Help supply services
HQ: Volt Management Corp.
    50 Charles Lindbergh Blvd # 206
    Uniondale NY 11553

(P-14593)
WANNAJOB INC
Also Called: Construction Temps
2710 Saint Louis Ave, Signal Hill
(90755-2026)
PHONE..............................562 426-5272
William Davis,
EMP: 75
SQ FT: 300
SALES (est): 2.4MM **Privately Held**
SIC: 7363 7361 Temporary help service;
employment agencies

(P-14594)
WEAVE INCORPORATED (PA)
Also Called: Weave
1900 K St Ste 200, Sacramento
(95811-4187)
PHONE..............................916 448-2321
Beth Hassett, *Exec Dir*
Garry Maisel, *Ch of Bd*
Gina Roberson, *Officer*
Priya Batra, *Principal*
Neil Forester, *Principal*
EMP: 95
SALES: 5.9MM **Privately Held**
WEB: www.weaveinc.org
SIC: 7363 8322 Domestic help service; in-
dividual & family services

(P-14595)
**WEST VALLEY ENGINEERING
INC (PA)**
Also Called: West Valley Staffing Group
390 Potrero Ave, Sunnyvale (94085-4116)
PHONE..............................408 735-1420
Michael F Williams, *President*
Teresa Kossayian, *CFO*
Ann M Fisher, *Director*
Vanessa Carpio, *Manager*
Jereme Sischka, *Accounts Mgr*
EMP: 72
SALES (est): 49.5MM **Privately Held**
SIC: 7363 Temporary help service

(P-14596)
WIGHTMAN ENTERPRISES INC
Also Called: Csl Solutions
8017 Sacramento St, Fair Oaks
(95628-7526)
PHONE..............................916 961-2959
Michelle Wightman, *President*
EMP: 60
SQ FT: 1,176
SALES (est): 2.3MM **Privately Held**
WEB: www.cslweb.com
SIC: 7363 Employee leasing service

(P-14597)
WORK FORCE SERVICES INC
Also Called: Work Force Staffing
300 Truxtun Ave, Bakersfield (93301-5314)
PHONE..............................661 327-5019
Brooks Whitehead, *President*
Brenda Bynum, *Accounting Dir*
EMP: 250
SQ FT: 1,600
SALES (est): 9.8MM **Privately Held**
WEB: www.workforcestaffing1.com
SIC: 7363 Temporary help service

(P-14598)
ZB REHAB STAFFING INC
Also Called: Thera Home Care
650 El Camino Real Ste O, Redwood City
(94063-1345)
PHONE..............................650 396-2207
Greg McCarthy, *CEO*
EMP: 75
SALES: 2.5MM **Privately Held**
SIC: 7363 Help supply services

7371 Custom Computer Programming Svcs

(P-14599)
**22ND CENTURY
TECHNOLOGIES INC**
6203 San Ignacio Ave, San Jose
(95119-1371)
PHONE..............................866 537-9191
Satvinder Singh, *President*
EMP: 129
SALES (corp-wide): 89.9MM **Privately
Held**
SIC: 7371 Computer software systems
analysis & design, custom
PA: 22nd Century Technologies Inc.
    220 Davidson Ave Ste 100b
    Somerset NJ 08873
    732 537-9191

(P-14600)
2807 DEV LLC
2188 Edinburg Ave, Cardiff (92007)
PHONE..............................510 319-7820
George Green, *CEO*
EMP: 53
SALES (est): 808.2K **Privately Held**
SIC: 7371 Computer software develop-
ment & applications

(P-14601)
314E CORPORATION (PA)
6701 Koll Center Pkwy # 340, Pleasanton
(94566-8061)
PHONE..............................510 371-6736
Abhishek Begerhotta, *President*
Matthew Rusch, *Assoc VP*
Mikael Ambrozik, *Graphic Designe*
Thuc Huynh, *Business Mgr*
Eileen Cung, *Human Res Mgr*
EMP: 157
SQ FT: 10,078
SALES (est): 14.3MM **Privately Held**
WEB: www.314e.com
SIC: 7371 Computer software develop-
ment & applications

(P-14602)
3DNA CORP (PA)
Also Called: Nationbuilder
520 S Grand Ave Fl 2, Los Angeles
(90071-2600)
PHONE..............................213 394-4623
Jim H Gilliam, *President*
Toni Cowan-Brown, *Vice Pres*
Hilary DOE, *Vice Pres*
Laura Harris, *Vice Pres*
Jon Bratsis, *VP Bus Dvlpt*
EMP: 100
SALES (est): 11MM **Privately Held**
SIC: 7371 Computer software develop-
ment

(P-14603)
3K TECHNOLOGIES LLC
1114 Cadillac Ct, Milpitas (95035-3058)
PHONE..............................408 716-5900
Sireesha Chittabbathini,
Krishna Chittabbathini,
EMP: 105
SQ FT: 2,000
SALES: 13.8MM **Privately Held**
SIC: 7371 Custom computer programming
services

(P-14604)
4D INC
95 S Market St Ste 240, San Jose
(95113-2311)
PHONE..............................408 557-4600
Laurent Ribardiere, *CEO*
Phillipe Berthault, *CFO*
Doris Beaulieu, *Admin Sec*
Jean Laguerre, *QA Dir*
Add Komoncharoensir, *Technical Staff*
EMP: 101
SALES (est): 11MM
SALES (corp-wide): 937.3K **Privately
Held**
WEB: www.4d.com
SIC: 7371 7372 Computer software devel-
opment & applications; prepackaged soft-
ware
HQ: 4d
    Entree 4 Parc Des Erables
    Le Pecq 78230
    130 539-200

(P-14605)
5 NINE GROUP INC
Also Called: Franklin Data
1125 Lindero Canyon Rd, Westlake Village
(91362-5474)
PHONE..............................805 880-2948
Matthew Blake, *Exec VP*
Henry Dicker, *Officer*
John Aben, *Exec VP*
EMP: 250
SQ FT: 14,000
SALES: 48MM **Privately Held**
SIC: 7371 Custom computer programming
services

(P-14606)
6WIND USA INC
2445 Augustine Dr Ste 150, Santa Clara
(95054-3032)
PHONE..............................408 816-1366
Eric Carmes, *President*
Keith Broach, *Vice Pres*
Hojae Yoon, *Technical Mgr*
Charlie Ashton, *VP Mktg*
Kiran Iyengar, *Sales Staff*
EMP: 88

SALES (est): 283.5K **Privately Held**
SIC: **7371** Computer software development

(P-14607)
A MOBILE DEVELOPMENT
4500 Great America Pkwy, Santa Clara
(95054-1283)
PHONE....................................415 350-4532
John Adams, *Owner*
EMP: 150
SALES: 20MM **Privately Held**
SIC: **7371** 4119 Computer software development & applications; local rental transportation

(P-14608)
AARKI INC (PA)
530 Lakeside Dr Ste 260, Sunnyvale
(94085-4064)
PHONE....................................408 382-1180
Sid Bhatt, *President*
Weed Owen, *Vice Pres*
Cherrie Pua, *Executive*
Chinita Reyes, *Executive*
Sergey Yengoyan, *Sr Software Eng*
EMP: 50
SALES (est): 18.7MM **Privately Held**
SIC: **7371** 5199 Computer software development; advertising specialties

(P-14609)
ABACUS DATA SYSTEMS INC (HQ)
Also Called: Abacusnext
9171 Towne Centre Dr # 200, San Diego
(92122-1267)
PHONE....................................858 452-4280
Alessandra Lezama, *CEO*
EMP: 80
SQ FT: 10,000
SALES (est): 39.8MM **Privately Held**
SIC: **7371** 7374 Computer software systems analysis & design, custom; data processing & preparation; computer processing services; computer time-sharing
PA: Providence Strategic Growth Fund
50 Kennedy Plz Fl 18
Providence RI 02903
401 751-1700

(P-14610)
ABACUS SERVICE CORPORATION
1725 23rd St, Sacramento (95816-7100)
PHONE....................................916 288-8948
Michelle Reuter, *Branch Mgr*
EMP: 300
SALES (corp-wide): 42.1MM **Privately Held**
SIC: **7371** Custom computer programming services
PA: Abacus Service Corporation
25925 Telg Rd Ste 206
Southfield MI
248 324-9200

(P-14611)
ABBYY USA SOFTWARE HOUSE INC (DH)
890 Hillview Ct Ste 300, Milpitas
(95035-4574)
PHONE....................................408 457-9777
Ding Yuan Tang, *CEO*
Arthur Whipple, *President*
Sheryl Lodolce, *CFO*
Simon Jones, *Vice Pres*
Torsten Malchow, *Vice Pres*
EMP: 105
SQ FT: 31,000
SALES: 37MM
SALES (corp-wide): 355.8K **Privately Held**
SIC: **7371** Computer software development
HQ: Abbyy Software Limited

226 806-35

(P-14612)
ABZOOBA INC
1551 Mccarthy Blvd # 204, Milpitas
(95035-7437)
PHONE....................................650 453-8760
Vivek Vipul, *CEO*
Riti Chowdhury, *Executive*
Koel Dutta, *Executive*
Partha Das, *Project Mgr*
Saurav Nag, *Project Mgr*
EMP: 121 EST: 2010
SALES (est): 293.6K **Privately Held**
SIC: **7371** Computer software development

(P-14613)
ACCESS SYSTEMS AMERICAS INC
3965 Freedom Cir Ste 200, Santa Clara
(95054-1293)
PHONE....................................408 400-3000
Kiyo Oishi, *CEO*
Jeanne Seeley, *CFO*
Neale Foster, *Vice Pres*
Michael Kelley, *Vice Pres*
Sawako Takemoto, *Vice Pres*
EMP: 518
SQ FT: 71,000
SALES (est): 35.1MM **Privately Held**
WEB: www.palmsource.com
SIC: **7371** 7372 Computer software development; software programming applications; prepackaged software
PA: Access Co.,Ltd.
3, Kandaneribeicho
Chiyoda-Ku TKY 101-0

(P-14614)
ACHIEVO CORPORATION (PA)
1400 Terra Bella Ave E, Mountain View
(94043-3062)
PHONE....................................925 498-8864
Sandy Wai-Yan Chau, *CEO*
Robert P Lee, *President*
Bernard Mathaisel, *COO*
Julio Leung, *CFO*
Darryl Quan, *CFO*
EMP: 66
SALES (est): 57.8MM **Privately Held**
WEB: www.achievo.com
SIC: **7371** Custom computer programming services

(P-14615)
ACTIVISION BLIZZARD INC
3420 Ocean Park Blvd # 2000, Santa Monica (90405-3304)
PHONE....................................310 581-4700
EMP: 140
SALES (corp-wide): 7.5B **Publicly Held**
WEB: www.blizzard.com
SIC: **7371** Computer software development
PA: Activision Blizzard, Inc.
3100 Ocean Park Blvd
Santa Monica CA 90405
310 255-2000

(P-14616)
ADAPTAMED LLC
6699 Alvarado Rd Ste 2301, San Diego
(92120-5241)
PHONE....................................877 478-7773
Aparna Reddy,
EMP: 120
SALES (est): 1.6MM **Privately Held**
SIC: **7371** Computer software development

(P-14617)
ADCOLONY INC
11400 W Olympic Blvd # 1200, Los Angeles (90064-1583)
PHONE....................................650 625-1262
William Kassoy, *CEO*
Steve Lyons, *Vice Pres*
Matt Barash, *VP Bus Dvlpt*
Brandon Chau, *Creative Dir*
Eric Treworgy, *Sr Software Eng*
EMP: 100
SALES (est): 20.6MM
SALES (corp-wide): 5.7MM **Privately Held**
SIC: **7371** Computer software development

PA: Adcolony Holdings Us, Inc.
1875 S Grant St Ste 800
San Mateo CA 94402
650 625-1262

(P-14618)
ADDEPAR INC (PA)
303 Bryant St, Mountain View
(94041-1552)
PHONE....................................855 464-6268
Eric Poirier, *CEO*
Don Nilsson,
Daniel Bayer, *Senior VP*
Derek Brown, *Vice Pres*
Sally Buchanan, *Vice Pres*
EMP: 85
SALES (est): 20.1MM **Privately Held**
SIC: **7371** Computer software development

(P-14619)
ADLER DEV LLC
Also Called: Software Dev Technical Support
2554 Front St Apt 3, San Diego
(92103-6532)
PHONE....................................707 229-3162
Anthony Thomas, *Mng Member*
EMP: 60
SALES: 7MM **Privately Held**
SIC: **7371** Computer software development & applications

(P-14620)
ADVANCED SOFTWARE DESIGN INC
Also Called: Advanced Software Dynamics
1371 Oakland Blvd Ste 100, Walnut Creek
(94596-8407)
PHONE....................................925 975-0691
Manu Chatterjee, *CEO*
Sonali Singh, *President*
Shikha Chatterjee, *VP Opers*
EMP: 59
SQ FT: 1,200
SALES: 9MM **Privately Held**
WEB: www.asdglobal.com
SIC: **7371** 7373 8711 8742 Computer software development; computer integrated systems design; engineering services; management consulting services

(P-14621)
ADVENT SOFTWARE INC (HQ)
Also Called: SS&c Advent
600 Townsend St Fl 5, San Francisco
(94103-4945)
PHONE....................................415 543-7696
David Peter Hess Jr, *President*
Stephanie Dimarco, *Ch of Bd*
James Cox, *CFO*
Todd Gottula, *Exec VP*
Chris Momsen, *Exec VP*
EMP: 146
SQ FT: 158,264
SALES (est): 163.7MM
SALES (corp-wide): 3.4B **Publicly Held**
WEB: www.advent.com
SIC: **7371** 7373 7372 6722 Custom computer programming services; computer integrated systems design; systems software development services; computer systems analysis & design; prepackaged software; management investment, open-end
PA: Ss&C Technologies Holdings, Inc.
80 Lamberton Rd
Windsor CT 06095
860 298-4500

(P-14622)
AERA TECHNOLOGY INC (PA)
707 California St, Mountain View
(94041-2005)
PHONE....................................408 524-2222
Ram Mohan, *President*
Valerie Preston, *Partner*
Travis Adlman, *CFO*
Tony Wessels, *Chief Mktg Ofcr*
Shariq Mansoor, *Officer*
EMP: 56
SALES (est): 15.7MM **Privately Held**
WEB: www.fusionops.com
SIC: **7371** Computer software development

(P-14623)
AESTIVA SOFTWARE INC
3551 Voyager St Ste 201, Torrance
(90503-1674)
PHONE....................................310 697-0338
David M Silverberg, *President*
Eric Villicana, *Vice Pres*
EMP: 50
SALES (est): 3.9MM **Privately Held**
SIC: **7371** Computer software development

(P-14624)
AFTERSHOCK LA STUDIOS INC
3633 Lenawee Ave Ste 100, Los Angeles
(90016-4310)
PHONE....................................650 450-9660
EMP: 60 EST: 2016
SALES (est): 891.1K **Privately Held**
SIC: **7371**

(P-14625)
ALLDRAGON INTERNATIONAL INC
4285 Payne Ave 10028, San Jose
(95117-3324)
PHONE....................................408 410-6248
Tom Gong, *CEO*
Connie Kang, *President*
EMP: 50
SALES: 150K **Privately Held**
SIC: **7371** Computer software development & applications

(P-14626)
ALLIANCE INFORMATION TECHNOLOG (PA)
Also Called: Allianceit
7041 Koll Center Pkwy # 140, Pleasanton
(94566-3196)
PHONE....................................925 462-9787
Purushothama Polkampalli, *President*
Nihanth Krishna, *Opers Mgr*
EMP: 55
SQ FT: 2,000
SALES (est): 6.7MM **Privately Held**
SIC: **7371** 8748 7379 7372 Computer software development; systems engineering consultant, ex. computer or professional; data processing consultant; prepackaged software

(P-14627)
ALOGENT HOLDINGS INC
5868 Owens Ave Ste 200, Carlsbad
(92008-5517)
PHONE....................................760 410-9000
EMP: 80
SALES (corp-wide): 11.2MM **Privately Held**
SIC: **7371** Computer software development
PA: Alogent Holdings, Inc.
350 Technology Pkwy # 200
Norcross GA 30092
770 752-6400

(P-14628)
ALPHA NET CONSULTING LLC
3080 Olcott St Ste C235, Santa Clara
(95054-3281)
PHONE....................................408 330-0896
Gurderpinder Dhillon,
Naveen Grover, *Programmer Anys*
Surjit Bedi,
EMP: 85
SQ FT: 1,500
SALES: 18.6MM **Privately Held**
WEB: www.anetcorp.com
SIC: **7371** Custom computer programming services

(P-14629)
ALPHA SOFT SUPPORT LLC
8605 Santa Monica Blvd, West Hollywood
(90069-4109)
PHONE....................................857 219-5505
Kim Johnny, *CEO*
EMP: 51
SALES: 8MM **Privately Held**
SIC: **7371** Computer software development & applications

(P-14630)
ALPHABET INC (PA)
1600 Amphitheatre Pkwy, Mountain View
(94043-1351)
PHONE....................................650 253-0000
Larry Page, *CEO*
John L Hennessy, *Ch of Bd*
Sergey Brin, *President*
Ruth M Porat, *CFO*
EMP: 69 EST: 1998
SALES: 136.8B **Publicly Held**
SIC: 7371 Computer software develop-
ment & applications

(P-14631)
AMBER HOLDINGS INC
150 California St, San Francisco
(94111-4500)
PHONE....................................415 765-6500
Robert F Smith, *President*
Brian N Sheth, *Vice Pres*
Imran Shaikh, *Info Tech Dir*
EMP: 1010
SALES (est): 22.5MM
SALES (corp-wide): 5B **Privately Held**
SIC: 7371 Computer software develop-
ment; computer software development &
applications
HQ: Vista Equity Partners Fund Iii, L.P.
4 Embarcadero Ctr # 2000
San Francisco CA 94111

(P-14632)
AMDOCS INC
Innovis
1104 Investment Blvd, El Dorado Hills
(95762-5710)
PHONE....................................916 934-7000
Michael Saeger, *Manager*
Rachel Laufer, *Analyst*
Gabe Monarrez, *Analyst*
Cindy Knecht, *Director*
Diane Connolly, *Manager*
EMP: 336 **Privately Held**
WEB: www.amdocs.com
SIC: 7371 7389 7374 Computer software
systems analysis & design, custom; com-
puter software development; software
programming applications; financial serv-
ices; data processing & preparation
HQ: Amdocs, Inc.
1390 Tmberlake Manor Pkwy
Chesterfield MO 63017
314 212-7000

(P-14633)
AMDOCS BCS INC
1104 Investment Blvd, El Dorado Hills
(95762-5710)
PHONE....................................916 934-7000
EMP: 336
SALES (est): 557.9K
SALES (corp-wide): 3.5B **Privately Held**
SIC: 7371 7389 7374
HQ: Amdocs, Inc.
1390 Timberlake Manor Pkw
Chesterfield MO 63017
314 212-7000

(P-14634)
AMP TECHNOLOGIES LLC
445 Melrose Ct, San Ramon (94582-5103)
PHONE....................................877 442-2824
Neel Naicker, *CEO*
Arvind Sathyamoorthy, *CTO*
EMP: 140
SALES (est): 8.6MM **Privately Held**
SIC: 7371 Computer software develop-
ment & applications

(P-14635)
AMPLIFY EDUCATION INC
1032 Irving St Ste 445, San Francisco
(94122-2216)
PHONE....................................562 209-7875
EMP: 82
SALES (corp-wide): 243.4MM **Privately
Held**
SIC: 7371 Computer software develop-
ment
PA: Amplify Education, Inc.
55 Washington St Ste 800
Brooklyn NY 11201
212 213-8177

(P-14636)
AMZN MOBILE LLC
525 Market St Fl 19, San Francisco
(94105-2728)
PHONE....................................925 348-4580
EMP: 500
SALES (est): 7.8MM **Publicly Held**
SIC: 7371 Software programming applica-
tions
PA: Amazon.Com, Inc.
410 Terry Ave N
Seattle WA 98109

(P-14637)
ANAND SOFTWARE INC
4719 Quail Lakes Dr, Stockton
(95207-5267)
PHONE....................................209 287-1708
EMP: 99
SALES: 3MM **Privately Held**
SIC: 7371 7373

(P-14638)
ANIMOTO LLC
333 Kearny St Fl 6, San Francisco
(94108-3269)
PHONE....................................415 987-3139
Bradley C Jefferson, *CEO*
Russell G Keefe, *CFO*
EMP: 60
SQ FT: 15,000
SALES (est): 5.3MM **Privately Held**
SIC: 7371 Computer software develop-
ment

(P-14639)
**ANJANA SOFTWARE
SOLUTIONS INC**
1445 E Los Angeles Ave 301t, Simi Valley
(93065-2862)
PHONE....................................805 583-0121
Saravana Kumarasamy, *President*
Kritik A Govindan, *Treasurer*
Venkatesh Ramachandran, *Vice Pres*
▲ EMP: 75 EST: 2000
SQ FT: 3,000
SALES: 15.9MM **Privately Held**
SIC: 7371 Computer software develop-
ment
PA: Anjana Software Solutions Private Lim-
ited
Module No. 306, Nsic Software Tech-
nology Park
Chennai TN 60003

(P-14640)
ANNIE APP INC (DH)
23 Geary St Ste 3, San Francisco
(94108-5751)
PHONE....................................844 277-2664
Bertrand Schmitt, *CEO*
Marshall Nu, *COO*
Sujan Jain, *CFO*
Natasha Kehimkar,
Ted Krantz, *Officer*
EMP: 69
SALES (est): 54.9MM
SALES (corp-wide): 177.3K **Privately
Held**
SIC: 7371 Computer software develop-
ment; computer software development &
applications
HQ: Shanghai Qingtian Automatic Control
Complete Set Equipment Co., Ltd.
Rm 3539,Building 24,No.2,Xincheng
Road,Pudong New Dist.
Shanghai 20130
216 248-8355

(P-14641)
ANOMALI INCORPORATED
808 Winslow St, Redwood City
(94063-1608)
PHONE....................................408 800-4050
Hugh Njemanze, *CEO*
Drew Hamer, *CFO*
Dan Barahona, *Chief Mktg Ofcr*
Colby Derodeff, *Officer*
Sunil Nagdev, *Officer*
EMP: 100
SALES (est): 5.3MM **Privately Held**
SIC: 7371 Computer software develop-
ment

(P-14642)
APIGEE CORPORATION
1600 Amphitheatre Pkwy, Mountain View
(94043-1351)
PHONE....................................408 343-7300
Chet Kapoor, *CEO*
Tim Wan, *CFO*
Eric Cross, *Vice Pres*
Srinivasulu Grandhi, *Vice Pres*
Aashima Gupta, *Vice Pres*
EMP: 374
SQ FT: 41,000
SALES: 92MM
SALES (corp-wide): 136.8B **Publicly
Held**
WEB: www.sonoasystems.com
SIC: 7371 Computer software develop-
ment & applications
HQ: Google Llc
1600 Amphitheatre Pkwy
Mountain View CA 94043
650 253-0000

(P-14643)
APPERY LLC
1340 Treat Blvd Ste 375, Walnut Creek
(94597-7590)
PHONE....................................925 602-5504
Lynne Walter, *CFO*
Dimitry Binunsky, *Vice Pres*
EMP: 60
SQ FT: 7,200
SALES: 2MM **Privately Held**
SIC: 7371 Computer software develop-
ment & applications

(P-14644)
**APPLIED COMPUTER
SOLUTIONS (HQ)**
Also Called: ACS
15461 Springdale St, Huntington Beach
(92649-1335)
PHONE....................................714 861-2200
Sandy Davis, *President*
Warren Barnes, *CFO*
Darell Ruehle, *Executive*
Lina Asmar, *Office Mgr*
Daniel Hernandez, *Admin Asst*
EMP: 70
SQ FT: 60,000
SALES (est): 68.2MM
SALES (corp-wide): 1.3B **Privately Held**
WEB: www.acs-g.com
SIC: 7371 Custom computer programming
services; computer software development
PA: Pivot Technology Solutions Inc
55 Renfrew Dr Suite 200
Markham ON L3R 8
416 360-4777

(P-14645)
**APPLIED ENGINEERING MGT
CORP**
Also Called: Aem Corporation
760 Paseo Camarillo # 101, Camarillo
(93010-6000)
P.O. Box 1263 (93011-1263)
PHONE....................................805 484-1909
Anne Morgan, *Branch Mgr*
Sharon Demonsabert, *President*
Dave Brady, *Assoc VP*
Michele Saenz, *Assoc VP*
Manpreet Mudahar, *Associate Dir*
EMP: 250
SALES (est): 20.1MM
SALES (corp-wide): 47MM **Privately
Held**
WEB: www.aemcorp.com
SIC: 7371 Computer software develop-
ment
PA: Virginia Aem Corporation
13880 Dulles Corner Ln # 300
Herndon VA 20171
703 464-7030

(P-14646)
APPTIVO INC
34364 Eucalyptus Ter, Fremont
(94555-1983)
PHONE....................................650 906-1034
Bastin S Gerald, *CEO*
Kumar Devarakonda, *Vice Pres*
Randy Jacobs, *Manager*
Sunil Kumar Manthena, *Manager*
Todd Miner, *Manager*
EMP: 200 EST: 2009

SALES (est): 96.6K **Privately Held**
SIC: 7371 7389 Computer software development;

(P-14647)
ARABLE CORPORATION
530 University Ave, Palo Alto (94301-1900)
PHONE....................................650 331-1401
Ary Sarkar, *CEO*
EMP: 70
SALES: 4.5MM **Privately Held**
SIC: 7371 Computer software develop-
ment

(P-14648)
ARCSOFT INC (PA)
46605 Fremont Blvd, Fremont
(94538-6410)
PHONE....................................510 440-9901
Michael Deng, *President*
David Nagel, *Ch of Bd*
Todd Peters, *President*
Robert Mjaseth, *COO*
Hui Deng, *Officer*
▲ EMP: 59
SQ FT: 26,000
SALES (est): 60.3MM **Privately Held**
WEB: www.arcsoft.com
SIC: 7371 5734 Computer software devel-
opment; computer & software stores

(P-14649)
ARCTOUCH LLC
1001 Front St, San Francisco (94111-1424)
PHONE....................................415 944-2000
Eric Shapiro, *CEO*
Jeremy Stephan, *Partner*
Adam Fingerman, *Officer*
Paulo Michels, *Engineer*
Ross Buffington, *Opers Staff*
EMP: 200
SALES (est): 20.2MM
SALES (corp-wide): 20B **Privately Held**
SIC: 7371 Computer software develop-
ment & applications
HQ: Grey Global Group Llc
200 5th Ave Bsmt B
New York NY 10010
212 546-2000

(P-14650)
ARCULES INC
17875 Von Karman Ave # 450, Irvine
(92614-6212)
PHONE....................................949 439-0053
Andreas Pettersson, *CEO*
EMP: 70
SALES (est): 660K **Privately Held**
SIC: 7371 Software programming applica-
tions

(P-14651)
ARENA SOLUTIONS INC (PA)
989 E Hillsdale Blvd # 250, Foster City
(94404-4201)
PHONE....................................650 513-3500
Craig Livingston, *CEO*
Jan Russo, *President*
Ken Bozzini, *CFO*
Andrea Pitts, *Vice Pres*
Philip McMahon, *Surgery Dir*
▲ EMP: 65 EST: 2000
SALES (est): 19.6MM **Privately Held**
WEB: www.arenasolutions.com
SIC: 7371 Computer software develop-
ment

(P-14652)
ARIA SYSTEMS INC (PA)
100 Pine St Ste 2450, San Francisco
(94111-5230)
PHONE....................................415 852-7250
Tom Dibble, *President*
Bob Feghali, *Partner*
Peter Worth, *Officer*
Michael Breslin, *Vice Pres*
Janice Kennealy, *Vice Pres*
▼ EMP: 74
SALES (est): 36.7MM **Privately Held**
WEB: www.ariasystems.com
SIC: 7371 Computer software develop-
ment & applications

(P-14653)
ARICENT NA INC (DH)
Also Called: Altran
3979 Freedom Cir Ste 950, Santa Clara
(95054-1294)
PHONE..............................408 324-1800
Dominique Cerutti, *CEO*
EMP: 60
SALES (est): 4.3MM
SALES (corp-wide): 1.1B **Privately Held**
WEB: www.tforceinc.com
SIC: 7371 Computer software develop-
ment & applications
HQ: Altran Usa Holdings, Inc.
451 D St
Boston MA 02210
617 449-9790

(P-14654)
ARICENT US INC (DH)
Also Called: Aricent Technologies
3979 Freedom Cir Ste 950, Santa Clara
(95054-1294)
PHONE..............................408 329-7400
Frank Kern, *CEO*
Doreen Lorenzo, *President*
David Freedman, *CFO*
EMP: 50
SALES (est): 108.3MM
SALES (corp-wide): 1.1B **Privately Held**
WEB: www.emuzed.com
SIC: 7371 Computer software develop-
ment
HQ: Altran Usa Holdings, Inc.
451 D St
Boston MA 02210
617 449-9790

(P-14655)
ARTIZEN INCORPORATED
101 Golf Course Dr # 300, Rohnert Park
(94928-1718)
PHONE..............................650 261-9400
Parker Painter, *President*
EMP: 150
SQ FT: 2,200
SALES (est): 11.9MM **Privately Held**
SIC: 7371 Computer software develop-
ment & applications

(P-14656)
ASCENDIFY CORPORATION
221 Main St Ste 1350, San Francisco
(94105-1943)
PHONE..............................415 528-5503
Matt Hendrickson, *CEO*
Jason Ball, *Vice Pres*
Kelly King, *Vice Pres*
Derek Mercer, *Vice Pres*
Lauren Smith, *Vice Pres*
EMP: 50
SALES (est): 260K **Privately Held**
SIC: 7371 Computer software develop-
ment

(P-14657)
ASHUNYA INC
642 N Eckhoff St, Orange (92868-1004)
PHONE..............................714 385-1900
Melanie Merchant, *Principal*
EMP: 88
SALES (est): 7.8MM **Privately Held**
SIC: 7371 7372 7373 Computer software
development & applications; application
computer software; office computer automation systems integration; turnkey
vendors, computer systems; value-added
resellers, computer systems

(P-14658)
**ATLAS DATABASE SOFTWARE
CORP (PA)**
Also Called: Atlas Development
26679 Agoura Rd Ste 200, Calabasas
(91302-3812)
PHONE..............................818 340-7080
Robert D Atlas, *CEO*
Steven Atlas, *Vice Pres*
Robert M Clymer, *Vice Pres*
Lisa Conley, *Vice Pres*
Michelle Del Guercio, *Vice Pres*
EMP: 89
SQ FT: 15,000

SALES (est): 33.8MM **Privately Held**
WEB: www.atlasdev.com
SIC: 7371 Custom computer programming
services

(P-14659)
ATLAZ INC
10721 Fair Oaks Blvd, Fair Oaks
(95628-7212)
PHONE..............................415 671-6142
EMP: 70 **EST:** 2015
SALES (est): 1.2MM **Privately Held**
SIC: 7371

(P-14660)
ATRENTA INC (HQ)
690 E Middlefield Rd, Mountain View
(94043-4010)
PHONE..............................408 453-3333
Ajoy K Bose, *President*
Bert Clement, *COO*
Douglas Aitelli, *Vice Pres*
Mike Fazeli, *Vice Pres*
Mike Gianfagna, *Vice Pres*
EMP: 70
SQ FT: 8,000
SALES (est): 35.8MM
SALES (corp-wide): 3.1B **Publicly Held**
WEB: www.atrenta.com
SIC: 7371 Computer software develop-
ment
PA: Synopsys, Inc.
690 E Middlefield Rd
Mountain View CA 94043
650 584-5000

(P-14661)
AUDITBOARD INC (PA)
12800 Center Court Dr S # 100, Cerritos
(90703-9363)
PHONE..............................877 769-5444
Daniel Kim, *Vice Pres*
Karen Gift, *CFO*
EMP: 50
SQ FT: 10,000
SALES (est): 6.9MM **Privately Held**
SIC: 7371 Computer software develop-
ment

(P-14662)
AUTONOMIC LLC (PA)
745 Emerson St, Palo Alto (94301-2411)
PHONE..............................650 823-1806
Gavin Sherry,
Julie Davies, *COO*
Amy Wengler, *CFO*
EMP: 66 **EST:** 2016
SQ FT: 8,700
SALES (est): 5MM **Privately Held**
SIC: 7371 Software programming applica-
tions

(P-14663)
AVENUESOCIAL INC
440 N Wolfe Rd, Sunnyvale (94085-3869)
PHONE..............................510 275-4485
Salman Ghaznavi, *President*
Usman Ghaznavi, *COO*
Freddie Forrester, *Analyst*
EMP: 135
SQ FT: 1,000
SALES (est): 3MM **Privately Held**
SIC: 7371 Software programming applica-
tions

(P-14664)
**AWAREPOINT CORPORATION
(PA)**
Also Called: Aware Point
600 W Broadway Ste 250, San Diego
(92101-3357)
PHONE..............................858 345-5000
Tim Roche, *CEO*
EMP: 58
SALES (est): 15.3MM **Privately Held**
WEB: www.awarepoint.com
SIC: 7371 Software programming applica-
tions

(P-14665)
AXCIENT INC (HQ)
1161 San Antonio Rd, Mountain View
(94043-1028)
PHONE..............................650 314-7300
Matt Nachtrab, *CEO*
John Finegan, *CFO*

John Heslin, *CFO*
Jeff Cummings, *Officer*
Ben Nowacky, *Senior VP*
EMP: 59
SALES (est): 31.6MM
SALES (corp-wide): 6.6MM **Privately
Held**
WEB: www.axcient.com
SIC: 7371 Software programming applica-
tions
PA: Axcient Holdings, Llc
1161 San Antonio Rd
Mountain View CA 94043
650 314-7300

(P-14666)
AZUMIO INC (PA)
230 California Ave # 212, Palo Alto
(94306-1637)
PHONE..............................719 310-3774
Bojan Bostjancic, *President*
Jennifer Grenz, *Vice Pres*
Jasmine Duong, *Marketing Staff*
Maggie Ball, *Manager*
EMP: 103
SALES (est): 5.9MM **Privately Held**
SIC: 7371 Computer software develop-
ment

(P-14667)
B JACQUELINE AND ASSOC INC
Also Called: J B A
1192 N Lake Ave, Pasadena (91104-3739)
PHONE..............................626 844-1400
Jacqueline Buickians, *President*
Gary Buickians, *Admin Sec*
Taylor Pavain, *Accounts Exec*
EMP: 300
SQ FT: 4,000
SALES (est): 16.8MM **Privately Held**
SIC: 7371 7379 Computer software devel-
opment & applications; computer related
consulting services

(P-14668)
BAAZ INC
Also Called: Baaz Global
1 Hallidie Plz Ste 200, San Francisco
(94102-2931)
PHONE..............................408 621-6912
Ghanssan Salaneh, *CEO*
Michael Eisen, *Controller*
EMP: 75 **EST:** 2015
SALES (est): 144.5K
SALES (corp-wide): 4.7MM **Privately
Held**
SIC: 7371 Computer software develop-
ment & applications
PA: Rubix Global Holding, Inc.
1 Hallidie Plz Ste 200
San Francisco CA 94102
415 988-2606

(P-14669)
BABYFIRST AMERICAS LLC
10390 Santa Monica Blvd, Los Angeles
(90025-5058)
PHONE..............................310 442-9853
Guy Oranim, *CEO*
Sharon Rechter, *President*
Karl Knipliy, *CFO*
EMP: 75
SALES: 13MM **Privately Held**
SIC: 7371 Computer software develop-
ment & applications
PA: Bftv, Llc
10390 Santa Monica Blvd # 310
Los Angeles CA 90025
310 442-9853

(P-14670)
BAJA LIFE ONLINE PARTNERS
P.O. Box 4917 (92652-4917)
PHONE..............................949 376-4619
Erik Cutter, *Partner*
EMP: 50
SALES (est): 1.8MM **Privately Held**
WEB: www.bajalife.com
SIC: 7371 4724 Custom computer pro-
gramming services; travel agencies

(P-14671)
BAKBONE SOFTWARE INC (DH)
9540 Towne Centre Dr # 100, San Diego
(92121-1989)
PHONE..............................858 450-9009

Michael S Dell, *CEO*
Stephen J Felice, *President*
Roy Hogsed, *Senior VP*
Kenneth Horner, *Senior VP*
Brian Tgladden, *Senior VP*
EMP: 72
SQ FT: 22,600
SALES (est): 21.9MM
SALES (corp-wide): 1.5B **Privately Held**
WEB: www.bakbone.com
SIC: 7371 7375 Computer software sys-
tems analysis & design, custom; informa-
tion retrieval services
HQ: Quest Software, Inc.
4 Polaris Way
Aliso Viejo CA 92656
949 754-8000

(P-14672)
BASTILLE NETWORKS INC
499 Lake Ave, Santa Cruz (95062-3938)
PHONE..............................800 530-3341
Chris Risley, *CEO*
EMP: 50
SALES (est): 1MM **Privately Held**
SIC: 7371 Computer software develop-
ment

(P-14673)
BEA SYSTEMS INC (HQ)
2315 N 1st St, San Jose (95131-1010)
PHONE..............................650 506-7000
Alfred S Chuang, *Ch of Bd*
Alan Button, *Partner*
Ted Kimes, *President*
Mark T Carges, *Exec VP*
Richard Geraffo, *Exec VP*
EMP: 1000
SQ FT: 236,000
SALES (est): 189.9MM
SALES (corp-wide): 39.5B **Publicly Held**
WEB: www.beasys.com
SIC: 7371 7372 Computer software devel-
opment; prepackaged software
PA: Oracle Corporation
500 Oracle Pkwy
Redwood City CA 94065
650 506-7000

(P-14674)
**BENTLEY SYSTEMS
INCORPORATED**
1600 Riviera Ave Ste 300, Walnut Creek
(94596-3570)
PHONE..............................925 933-2525
EMP: 80
SALES (corp-wide): 854.3MM **Privately
Held**
SIC: 7371 8711
PA: Bentley Systems, Incorporated
685 Stockton Dr
Exton PA 19341
610 458-5000

(P-14675)
BIOCLINCA (PA)
Also Called: Synarc's
7707 Gateway Blvd Fl 3, Newark
(94560-1160)
PHONE..............................415 817-8900
Claus Christiansen, *CEO*
Harry K Genant, *Chairman*
Aaron Timm, *Vice Pres*
John Leonard, *Administration*
Arkady Gliner, *Sr Software Eng*
EMP: 153 **EST:** 1998
SQ FT: 40,000
SALES (est): 56.5MM **Privately Held**
WEB: www.synarc.com
SIC: 7371 Computer software develop-
ment & applications

(P-14676)
BIRD RIDES INC (PA)
406 Broadway Ste 369, Santa Monica
(90401-2314)
PHONE..............................866 205-2442
Travis Vanderzanden, *CEO*
Dennis Cinelli, *Vice Pres*
Yibo Ling, *Vice Pres*
EMP: 66
SALES (est): 53.7MM **Privately Held**
SIC: 7371 Computer software develop-
ment & applications

P
R
O
D
U
C
T
S

&

S
V
C
S

(P-14677)
BIRST INC
45 Fremont St Ste 1800, San Francisco
(94105-2219)
PHONE...................................415 766-4800
Jay Larson, *CEO*
Samuel Wolff, *CFO*
Carl Tsukahara, *Chief Mktg Ofcr*
Brad Peters, *Officer*
Paul Staelin, *Officer*
EMP: 300
SQ FT: 36,171
SALES (est): 60.7MM
SALES (corp-wide): 3.1B **Privately Held**
SIC: 7371 Computer software development
PA: Infor, Inc.
641 Ave Of The Americas # 4
New York NY 10011
646 336-1700

(P-14678)
BITALIGN INC
Also Called: Grio
201 Post St Fl 11, San Francisco
(94108-5083)
PHONE...................................415 395-9525
Douglas Kadlecek, *CEO*
Bradley Johnson, *CFO*
Colin Spooner, *Business Dir*
Vladimir Chernis, *Software Dev*
Sean Delaney, *Software Dev*
EMP: 60 **EST:** 2006
SQ FT: 6,000
SALES: 10.2MM **Privately Held**
SIC: 7371 Computer software development & applications

(P-14679)
BITFONE CORPORATION (PA)
32451 Golden Lantern # 301, Laguna
Niguel (92677-5344)
PHONE...................................949 234-7000
Gene Wang, *President*
Hang Michael Xu, *CFO*
Harri Okkonen, *Senior VP*
Chris Cassapakis, *Vice Pres*
Carla Fitzgerald, *Vice Pres*
EMP: 50 **EST:** 2000
SQ FT: 11,000
SALES (est): 4.3MM **Privately Held**
WEB: www.bitfone.com
SIC: 7371 Computer software development

(P-14680)
BITGLASS INC (PA)
675 Campbell Tech Pkwy # 225, Campbell
(95008-5095)
PHONE...................................408 337-0190
Rich Campagna, *Officer*
Jon Peppler, *Vice Pres*
Benjamin Rice, *Vice Pres*
Andrew Urushima, *Vice Pres*
Anoop Bhattacharjya, *Admin Sec*
EMP: 67
SQ FT: 10,000
SALES (est): 11.8MM **Privately Held**
SIC: 7371 Computer software development

(P-14681)
BITTORRENT INC
612 Howard St Ste 400, San Francisco
(94105-3944)
PHONE...................................408 641-4219
Aseem Mohanty, *President*
Jeremy Johnson, *Officer*
Chris Verzello, *Vice Pres*
Sergey Kranin, *Engineer*
Dorothy An, *General Counsel*
EMP: 50
SALES: 2MM **Privately Held**
SIC: 7371 Computer software development & applications

(P-14682)
BLACKLINE INC (PA)
21300 Victory Blvd Fl 12, Woodland Hills
(91367-7734)
PHONE...................................818 223-9008
Therese Tucker, *CEO*
John Brennan, *Ch of Bd*
Marc Huffman, *COO*
Mark Partin, *CFO*
Andres Botero, *Chief Mktg Ofcr*

EMP: 52
SQ FT: 89,000
SALES: 227.7MM **Publicly Held**
SIC: 7371 Computer software systems analysis & design, custom

(P-14683)
BLUEBEAM INC (PA)
443 S Raymond Ave, Pasadena
(91105-2630)
PHONE...................................626 788-4100
Jon Elliott, *CEO*
Richard Lee, *President*
Jim Atkinson, *Officer*
Warren Pereira, *Info Tech Dir*
William Sullivan, *Software Engr*
EMP: 200
SALES (est): 40.4MM **Privately Held**
WEB: www.bluebeam.com
SIC: 7371 Computer software development

(P-14684)
BLUFOCUS INC
2233 N Ontario St Ste 100, Burbank
(91504-4500)
PHONE...................................818 294-7695
Paulette E Pantoja, *CEO*
Jake Ramirez, *Business Dir*
Paul Chang, *Office Mgr*
David Roesner, *Project Mgr*
Amy Carlos, *Opers Mgr*
EMP: 60
SQ FT: 7,000
SALES (est): 5.9MM **Privately Held**
WEB: www.blufocus.com
SIC: 7371 8748 7379 Software programming applications; systems analysis & engineering consulting services; computer related consulting services

(P-14685)
BPO MANAGEMENT SERVICES INC (PA)
8175 E Kaiser Blvd 100, Anaheim
(92808-2214)
PHONE...................................714 972-2670
Patrick A Dolan, *Ch of Bd*
James Cortens, *President*
Donald W Rutherford, *CFO*
Koushik Dutta, *CTO*
Marc Maraccini, *Sales Staff*
EMP: 73
SQ FT: 5,871
SALES: 28.1MM **Privately Held**
SIC: 7371 Computer software development

(P-14686)
BRACKET GLOBAL LLC
88 Stevenson St, San Francisco
(94105-2707)
PHONE...................................415 293-1340
Kristen Dellaroca, *Branch Mgr*
Mania Shahvekilian, *Manager*
EMP: 100 **Privately Held**
SIC: 7371 8748 Computer software development; telecommunications consultant
HQ: Bracket Global Llc
575 E Swedesford Rd # 200
Wayne PA 19087
610 225-5900

(P-14687)
BRIENCE INC (DH)
Also Called: A Development Stage Company
128 Spear St Fl 3, San Francisco
(94105-5147)
PHONE...................................415 974-5300
Roderick McGeary, *Ch of Bd*
James Drumright, *COO*
Stephen E Recht, *CFO*
Keyur Patel, *Officer*
Mark Losh, *Senior VP*
EMP: 90
SQ FT: 15,000
SALES (est): 11MM
SALES (corp-wide): 306.2MM **Privately Held**
WEB: www.brience.com
SIC: 7371 Computer software development & applications

(P-14688)
BRIGHTEDGE TECHNOLOGIES INC (PA)
989 E Hillsdale Blvd, Foster City
(94404-2113)
PHONE...................................800 578-8023
Jim Yu, *President*
Jeffrey Bakus, *Vice Pres*
Joshua Crossman, *Vice Pres*
Barrett Foster, *Vice Pres*
Albert Gouyet, *Vice Pres*
EMP: 134
SALES (est): 93.8MM **Privately Held**
SIC: 7371 5045 Computer software development; computers, peripherals & software

(P-14689)
BRIGHTERION INC
123 Mission St Ste 1700, San Francisco
(94105-5133)
PHONE...................................415 986-5600
Akli Adjaoute, *CEO*
EMP: 62
SALES (est): 5.3MM
SALES (corp-wide): 14.9B **Publicly Held**
WEB: www.brighterion.com
SIC: 7371 Computer software development
PA: Mastercard Incorporated
2000 Purchase St
Purchase NY 10577
914 249-2000

(P-14690)
BRILLIO LLC
5201 Great America Pkwy # 100, Santa
Clara (95054-1157)
PHONE...................................800 317-0575
Praveen Joshi, *Sr Software Eng*
Dippi Das, *Technical Mgr*
Chaitali Mallick, *Human Res Dir*
EMP: 1034
SALES (corp-wide): 120MM **Privately Held**
SIC: 7371 7372 Computer software development; prepackaged software
PA: Brillio, Llc
399 Thornall St Ste 1
Edison NJ 08837
800 317-0575

(P-14691)
BRISTLECONE INCORPORATED
10 Almaden Blvd Ste 600, San Jose
(95113-2226)
PHONE...................................650 386-4000
Irfan A Khan, *President*
Rajesh Raghuvanshi, *Partner*
Naresh Hingorani, *Vice Pres*
Kulashekar Raghavan, *Vice Pres*
Bhaskar Ramanasundaram, *Vice Pres*
EMP: 1300 **EST:** 1998
SQ FT: 10,000
SALES (est): 88.5MM
SALES (corp-wide): 7.4B **Privately Held**
WEB: www.bcone.com
SIC: 7371 8742 Software programming applications; management consulting services
PA: Mahindra And Mahindra Limited
Mahindra Towers, 5th Floor, Dr. G .M.
Bosale Marg,
Mumbai MH 40001
222 490-1441

(P-14692)
BROADSOFT CONTACT CENTER INC
930 Hamlin Ct, Sunnyvale (94089-1401)
PHONE...................................408 338-0900
Prem Uppaluru, *CEO*
Arnab Mishra, *President*
Mike Shannahan, *CFO*
Gaya Vukkadala, *Senior VP*
Mukesh Sundaram, *CTO*
EMP: 50
SQ FT: 15,000
SALES (est): 6.9MM
SALES (corp-wide): 51.9B **Publicly Held**
SIC: 7371 8742 Computer software systems analysis & design, custom; management information systems consultant

HQ: Broadsoft, Inc.
9737 Washingtonian Blvd # 350
Gaithersburg MD 20878
301 977-9440

(P-14693)
BUILDINGMINDS INC
1200 Seaport Blvd, Redwood City
(94063-5537)
PHONE...................................973 397-6510
Thomas Sparno, *Principal*
EMP: 50
SALES: 5MM **Privately Held**
SIC: 7371 Computer software development & applications

(P-14694)
BULLUP INC
4365 Via Scorpresa, San Diego (92124)
PHONE...................................566 997-2543
Xiangyu Sun, *CEO*
EMP: 50
SALES (est): 772K **Privately Held**
SIC: 7371 Computer software development & applications

(P-14695)
BY WIND INC
Also Called: Blue Harbor
15 Enterprise Ste 520, Aliso Viejo
(92656-2656)
PHONE...................................949 385-6219
Jeffrey Danford, *CEO*
Jennifer Heil, *President*
Dan Charest, *Director*
EMP: 52
SQ FT: 4,500
SALES: 5MM **Privately Held**
SIC: 7371 6163 Computer software development; loan brokers

(P-14696)
BYND LLC
100 Montgomery St # 1102, San Francisco
(94104-4331)
PHONE...................................415 944-2293
Nicholas Rappolt, *CEO*
Matthew Iliffe, *Partner*
Patrick Reynolds, *Partner*
James Williams, *Finance*
Philip Cotty, *Director*
EMP: 100 **EST:** 2004
SALES (est): 467.4K
SALES (corp-wide): 342.1MM **Privately Held**
SIC: 7371 Computer software development & applications
PA: Next Fifteen Communications Group
Plc
75 Bermondsey Street
London SE1 3
207 908-6444

(P-14697)
BYTEDANCE INC
3000 El Camino Real 2-400, Palo Alto
(94306-2112)
PHONE...................................844 523-3993
Tian Zhao, *President*
EMP: 75
SALES: 36MM **Privately Held**
SIC: 7371 Computer software development & applications

(P-14698)
CADENT TECH INC (HQ)
4 N 2nd St Ste 1100, San Jose
(95113-1308)
PHONE...................................408 642-6400
Nick Troiano, *CEO*
Stephanie Mitchko-Beale, *COO*
Jonathan Batt, *CFO*
EMP: 55
SQ FT: 10,000
SALES (est): 10.7MM **Privately Held**
SIC: 7371 Computer software development & applications

(P-14699)
CAKE CORPORATION
Also Called: Sysco Labs
1528 S El Cmino Real Ste, San Mateo
(94402)
PHONE...................................650 215-7777
Mani Kulasooriya, *CEO*
Brian Beach, *Senior VP*

Shanil Fernando, *Vice Pres*
Paul Kelaita, *Vice Pres*
Jim O'Connor, *Vice Pres*
▲ EMP: 100 EST: 2010
SALES (est): 1.7MM
SALES (corp-wide): 60.1B **Publicly Held**
SIC: 7371 Computer software development & applications
PA: Sysco Corporation
   1390 Enclave Pkwy
   Houston TX 77077
   281 584-1390

(P-14700)
CALLFIRE INC
1410 2nd St Ste 200, Santa Monica
(90401-3349)
PHONE.....................213 221-2289
Michel Veys, *Principal*
Tridivesh Kidambi, *CFO*
Vijesh Mehta, *Corp Secy*
Marc Ladin, *Chief Mktg Ofcr*
Mike Collard, *Vice Pres*
EMP: 61
SALES (est): 13MM **Privately Held**
WEB: www.skyyconsulting.com
SIC: 7371 Computer software development

(P-14701)
CALLIDUS SOFTWARE INC (HQ)
Also Called: Calliduscloud
4140 Dublin Blvd Ste 400, Dublin
(94568-7757)
PHONE.....................925 251-2200
Leslie Stretch, *President*
Roxanne Oulman, *CFO*
Andres Botero, *Chief Mktg Ofcr*
Mary Ainsworth,
Matthew Kenneally, *Vice Pres*
EMP: 148
SQ FT: 109,000
SALES: 253MM
SALES (corp-wide): 28.2B **Privately Held**
WEB: www.callidussoftware.com
SIC: 7371 7372 Custom computer programming services; business oriented computer software
PA: Sap Se
   Dietmar-Hopp-Allee 16
   Walldorf 69190
   622 774-7474

(P-14702)
CAMPAIGN MONITOR USA INC
123 Mission St Fl 26, San Francisco
(94105-5140)
PHONE.....................888 533-8098
Alex Bard, *CEO*
EMP: 100 EST: 2014
SALES (est): 1.4MM **Privately Held**
SIC: 7371 Computer software development
HQ: Campaign Monitor Pty Ltd
   L 38 201-5 Elizabeth St
   Sydney NSW 2000

(P-14703)
CAPE CLEAR SOFTWARE INC
Also Called: Capeconnect
900 E Hamilton Ave # 100, Campbell
(95008-0664)
PHONE.....................408 879-7365
Annrai O'Toole, *CEO*
David Clark, *Vice Pres*
James Pasley, *CTO*
EMP: 85 EST: 1999
SALES (est): 2.6MM **Privately Held**
WEB: www.capeclear.com
SIC: 7371 Computer software development

(P-14704)
CARBONFIVE INCORPORATED
Also Called: Carbon Five
585 Howard St Fl 2, San Francisco
(94105-4677)
PHONE.....................415 546-0500
Don Thompson, *COO*
David Hendee, *Partner*
Mike Wynholds, *CEO*
Alex Cruikshank, *General Mgr*
Katie Armstrong, *Office Mgr*
EMP: 62

SALES (est): 7.6MM **Privately Held**
WEB: www.carbonfive.com
SIC: 7371 Computer software development

(P-14705)
CASK TECHNOLOGIES LLC (PA)
9350 Waxie Way Ste 210, San Diego
(92123-1005)
P.O. Box 80337 (92138-0337)
PHONE.....................888 418-7067
Elizabeth Guezzale,
Vanessa Dover, *Officer*
Lynwood Metts, *Vice Pres*
Kate Ehrle, *Business Dir*
Michael Lemon, *General Mgr*
EMP: 56
SALES: 46.2MM **Privately Held**
SIC: 7371 7379 8742 8748 Computer software development & applications; computer related consulting services; management consulting services; business consulting; engineering services

(P-14706)
CATAPHORA INC (PA)
3425 Edison Way, Menlo Park
(94025-1813)
P.O. Box 2007 (94026-2007)
PHONE.....................650 622-9840
Elizabeth B Charnock, *President*
EMP: 60
SQ FT: 25,000
SALES (est): 11.3MM **Privately Held**
WEB: www.cataphora.com
SIC: 7371 Computer software development

(P-14707)
CENTRIFY CORPORATION (PA)
3300 Tannery Way, Santa Clara
(95054-2828)
PHONE.....................669 444-5200
Tom Kemp, *President*
Mark Oldemeyer, *CFO*
Warren Smith, *Vice Pres*
Gary Taggart, *Vice Pres*
Fuad Madhani, *Administration*
EMP: 148
SQ FT: 8,300
SALES (est): 99.6MM **Privately Held**
WEB: www.centrify.com
SIC: 7371 Computer software development

(P-14708)
CHASE CREDIT SYSTEMS INC
300 E Magnolia Blvd # 502, Burbank
(91502-1145)
PHONE.....................818 762-6262
Perry Cohan, *President*
Ben Cohan, *Vice Pres*
EMP: 95
SALES (est): 3.9MM
SALES (corp-wide): 5.8B **Publicly Held**
SIC: 7371 Computer software systems analysis & design, custom
PA: Fiserv, Inc.
   255 Fiserv Dr
   Brookfield WI 53045
   262 879-5000

(P-14709)
CHELSIO COMMUNICATIONS INC
209 N Fair Oaks Ave, Sunnyvale
(94085-4423)
PHONE.....................408 962-3600
Kianoosh Naghshineh, *President*
William Delaney, *CFO*
Danny Gur, *Vice Pres*
Mehdi Mohtashemi, *Vice Pres*
Kun Taek Yim, *Vice Pres*
EMP: 130
SQ FT: 20,000
SALES (est): 19.5MM **Privately Held**
WEB: www.chelsio.com
SIC: 7371 Computer software systems analysis & design, custom
PA: Chelsio Communications Private Limited
   2 Floor, Uniworth Plaza,
   Bengaluru KA 56002

(P-14710)
CHEQUE GUARD INC
512 S Verdugo Dr, Burbank (91502-2344)
PHONE.....................818 563-9335
Emil Ramzy, *President*
Alfred Ramzi, *CEO*
Louris Khalaf, *COO*
EMP: 54 EST: 2002
SQ FT: 6,000
SALES: 1.6MM **Privately Held**
SIC: 7371 2893 Computer software development; printing ink

(P-14711)
CHROME RIVER TECHNOLOGIES INC (PA)
5757 Wilshire Blvd # 270, Los Angeles
(90036-5814)
PHONE.....................323 857-5800
Alan Richeimer, *President*
Matt Gahr, *Officer*
Julie Norquist Roy, *Officer*
Aviva Kram, *Vice Pres*
Jim Whitmore, *Vice Pres*
EMP: 70
SALES (est): 45.9MM **Privately Held**
SIC: 7371 Computer software development

(P-14712)
CIMATRON GIBBS LLC
Also Called: Gibbs & Associates
323 Science Dr, Moorpark (93021-2092)
PHONE.....................805 523-0004
Bill Gibbs, *Owner*
Sabrina Hayes, *Administration*
Andy Heffner, *Engineer*
Bruce King, *Engineer*
William F Gibbs,
EMP: 61
SQ FT: 22,500
SALES (est): 7.8MM **Publicly Held**
WEB: www.gibbsnc.com
SIC: 7371 Computer software development
PA: 3d Systems Corporation
   333 Three D Systems Cir
   Rock Hill SC 29730

(P-14713)
CLARIS INTERNATIONAL INC (HQ)
Also Called: Filemaker, Inc.
5201 Patrick Henry Dr, Santa Clara
(95054-1164)
PHONE.....................408 987-7000
Dominique Philippe Goupil, *President*
Bill Epling, *CFO*
Chung Le, *Vice Pres*
Scott Lewis, *Vice Pres*
Ann Monroe, *Vice Pres*
EMP: 230
SQ FT: 128,000
SALES: 95.4MM
SALES (corp-wide): 260.1B **Publicly Held**
WEB: www.filemaker.com
SIC: 7371 Computer software development & applications
PA: Apple Inc.
   1 Apple Park Way
   Cupertino CA 95014
   408 996-1010

(P-14714)
CLICK LABS INC
315 Montgomery St Fl 8, San Francisco
(94104-1803)
PHONE.....................415 658-5227
Samar Singla, *CEO*
Sarah Terrazas, *Vice Pres*
Singh Manpreet, *Executive*
Rubal Singh, *Manager*
EMP: 501
SALES (est): 14.9MM **Privately Held**
SIC: 7371 Computer software development

(P-14715)
CLINAPPS INC
9530 Towne Centre Dr # 120, San Diego
(92121-1981)
PHONE.....................858 866-0228
Timothy W Elliott, *President*

Michelle Elliott, *Vice Pres*
Terri Fisher, *Vice Pres*
Danny Pacheco, *Technology*
Tom Alvarez, *Manager*
EMP: 57
SQ FT: 7,000
SALES (est): 2.8MM **Privately Held**
SIC: 7371 Computer software development
HQ: Bracket Global Llc
   575 E Swedesford Rd # 200
   Wayne PA 19087
   610 225-5900

(P-14716)
CLOUDERA INC (PA)
395 Page Mill Rd Ste 300, Palo Alto
(94306-2066)
PHONE.....................650 362-0488
Martin Cole, *CEO*
Mike Kaleta, *Partner*
Jim Frankola, *CFO*
Eric Driscoll, *Vice Pres*
Angus Klein, *Vice Pres*
EMP: 148
SQ FT: 225,000
SALES: 479.9MM **Publicly Held**
SIC: 7371 Computer software development

(P-14717)
CLOUDPEOPLE GLOBAL
2485 Notre Dame Blvd, Chico
(95928-7161)
PHONE.....................530 591-7028
Sean Worthington, *President*
EMP: 50
SALES (est): 772K **Privately Held**
SIC: 7371 Computer software development & applications

(P-14718)
CLOUDVIRGA INC
5291 California Ave # 300, Irvine
(92617-3221)
PHONE.....................949 662-2944
Dan Sogorka, *CEO*
Michael Carney, *Director*
Patti Cook, *Director*
William Dallas, *Director*
Steven Shafran, *Director*
EMP: 80
SALES (est): 124.5K **Privately Held**
SIC: 7371 Computer software development & applications

(P-14719)
COGNITIVECLOUDS SOFTWARE INC
5433 Ontario Cmn, Fremont (94555-2930)
PHONE.....................415 234-3611
Prasanna Gopinath, *Principal*
EMP: 70
SALES (est): 1.1MM **Privately Held**
SIC: 7371 Computer software development & applications

(P-14720)
COMMISSION JUNCTION LLC (DH)
530 E Montecito St, Santa Barbara
(93103-3252)
PHONE.....................805 730-8000
James R Zarley, *CEO*
Kerri Pollard, *President*
Jeffrey A Pullen, *President*
Jim Buckley, *CFO*
Lex Sisney, *Chairman*
EMP: 52
SQ FT: 16,000
SALES (est): 15.5MM **Publicly Held**
WEB: www.cj.com
SIC: 7371 Computer software development & applications
HQ: Conversant, Llc
   30699 Russell Ranch Rd # 250
   Westlake Village CA 91362
   818 575-4500

(P-14721)
COMPULAW LLC
200 Crprate Pinte Ste 400, Culver City
(90230)
PHONE.....................310 553-3355
David Kalmick, *Mng Member*
Michael Armstrong,

PRODUCTS & SVCS

Stephanie Hall,
Lois Kalmick,
Alex Manners,
EMP: 50
SQ FT: 15,000
SALES (est): 2.4MM
SALES (corp-wide): 5.1B **Publicly Held**
WEB: www.compulaw.com
SIC: 7371 Computer software development; computer software development & applications; software programming applications
HQ: Aderant Holdings, Inc.
500 Northridge Rd Ste 800
Atlanta GA 30350

(P-14722)
COMPUTER PROC UNLIMITED INC
Also Called: Cpu Medical Management Systems
9235 Activity Rd Ste 104, San Diego (92126-4440)
PHONE..........................858 530-0875
Michael Stringer, *President*
Brian Castle, *CFO*
Doug Allem, *Treasurer*
Jean Campbell, *Senior VP*
Herald Bing, *Vice Pres*
EMP: 65
SQ FT: 11,250
SALES (est): 7.1MM
SALES (corp-wide): 214.3B **Publicly Held**
WEB: www.cpumms.com
SIC: 7371 5045 Computer software systems analysis & design, custom; computer peripheral equipment
PA: Mckesson Corporation
6555 State Highway 161
Irving TX 75039
972 446-4800

(P-14723)
COMPUTER RESOURCES GROUP INC
275 Battery St Ste 800, San Francisco (94111-3364)
PHONE..........................415 398-3535
Richard D Green, *Ch of Bd*
Allen Prestegard, *President*
EMP: 250
SQ FT: 12,000
SALES (est): 8.1MM **Privately Held**
SIC: 7371 7379 Custom computer programming services; computer related consulting services

(P-14724)
COMPUTER TASK GROUP INC
2033 Gateway Pl Fl 5, San Jose (95110-3709)
PHONE..........................408 573-6070
Randolph A Marks, *Branch Mgr*
EMP: 230
SALES (corp-wide): 358.7MM **Publicly Held**
SIC: 7371 Custom computer programming services
PA: Computer Task Group, Incorporated
800 Delaware Ave
Buffalo NY 14209
716 882-8000

(P-14725)
COMPUTER TASK GROUP INC
Also Called: Ctg
101 Metro Dr Ste 530, San Jose (95110-1341)
PHONE..........................800 992-5350
Larry Comstock, *Sales/Mktg Mgr*
EMP: 300
SALES (corp-wide): 358.7MM **Publicly Held**
WEB: www.ctg.com
SIC: 7371 7373 Custom computer programming services; computer systems analysis & design
PA: Computer Task Group, Incorporated
800 Delaware Ave
Buffalo NY 14209
716 882-8000

(P-14726)
COMPUTRITION INC (HQ)
8521 Fllbrook Ave Ste 100, Canoga Park (91304)
PHONE..........................818 961-3999
Scott Saklad, *President*
Kim C Goldberg, *Vice Pres*
Alina Freger, *IT/INT Sup*
Dominic Mittelholzer, *Sales Staff*
Yamilet Salazar,
EMP: 60
SQ FT: 16,763
SALES (est): 13.3MM
SALES (corp-wide): 3B **Privately Held**
WEB: www.computrition.com
SIC: 7371 7372 Computer software development; prepackaged software
PA: Constellation Software Inc
20 Adelaide St E Suite 1200
Toronto ON M5C 2
416 861-2279

(P-14727)
COMPVUE INC
440 N Wolfe Rd, Sunnyvale (94085-3869)
PHONE..........................408 892-9909
Rakesh Gupta, *CEO*
Velu P Padmanabhan, *Technology*
EMP: 70
SALES: 981.7K **Privately Held**
SIC: 7371 Computer software development

(P-14728)
CONCERRO INC (DH)
9276 Scranton Rd Ste 400, San Diego (92121-7714)
PHONE..........................858 882-8500
Graham Barnes, *CEO*
Cindy Watson, *COO*
Derrick Clackenbush, *CFO*
EMP: 50
SQ FT: 16,000
SALES (est): 5.1MM **Privately Held**
SIC: 7371 Computer software development
HQ: Api Healthcare Corporation
1550 Innovation Way
Hartford WI 53027
262 673-6815

(P-14729)
CONNOTATE TECHNOLOGIES INC
2601 Main St Ste 830, Irvine (92614-5219)
PHONE..........................949 270-1916
Keith Cooper, *CEO*
EMP: 50
SALES (corp-wide): 10MM **Privately Held**
SIC: 7371 Computer software writing services
PA: Connotate Technologies Inc.
317 George St Ste 320
New Brunswick NJ 08901
732 296-8844

(P-14730)
CORDIAL EXPERIENCE INC
402 W Broadway Ste 700, San Diego (92101-8572)
PHONE..........................619 793-9787
Jeremy Swift, *CEO*
Stephanie Robotham, *Chief Mktg Ofcr*
Shea Stringert, *VP Sales*
EMP: 70 **EST:** 2014
SALES (est): 542.3K **Privately Held**
SIC: 7371 Computer software systems analysis & design, custom

(P-14731)
CORELATION INC
2305 Historic Decatur Rd # 300, San Diego (92106-6073)
PHONE..........................619 876-5074
John F Landis, *CEO*
Theresa Benavidez, *CEO*
Hal Barnabas, *CFO*
Harold Barnabas, *CFO*
Kyle Young, *Admin Asst*
EMP: 200
SALES (est): 27.2MM **Privately Held**
SIC: 7371 Computer software development

(P-14732)
CORELYNX INC
11501 Dublin Blvd Ste 200, Dublin (94568-2827)
PHONE..........................877 267-3599
Manash Chaudhuri, *CEO*
EMP: 103
SQ FT: 500
SALES (est): 3MM **Privately Held**
SIC: 7371 Computer software development

(P-14733)
COREOS LLC
101 New Montgomery St # 5, San Francisco (94105-3624)
PHONE..........................888 733-4281
Alexander Polvi, *CEO*
Sarvesh Jagannivas, *Vice Pres*
Mike Saparov, *Vice Pres*
Brandon Philips, *CTO*
Melissa Smolensky, *Marketing Staff*
EMP: 52
SALES (est): 7.9MM
SALES (corp-wide): 79.5B **Publicly Held**
SIC: 7371 Computer software development
HQ: Red Hat, Inc.
100 E Davie St
Raleigh NC 27601
-

(P-14734)
CORETECHS STAFFING INC
50 Woodside Plz Ste 604, Redwood City (94061-2500)
PHONE..........................650 363-7960
Andrew Adelman, *President*
Randall Stratton, *Principal*
EMP: 55
SALES (est): 5.7MM **Privately Held**
SIC: 7371 Computer software systems analysis & design, custom

(P-14735)
CORPTAX LLC
21550 Oxnard St Ste 700, Woodland Hills (91367-7170)
PHONE..........................818 316-2400
Corey Caudill, *Technology*
Dale S Deobler, *Technology*
Justin Stull, *Technical Staff*
Olga Guler, *QC Mgr*
Ellen Snelling, *Marketing Staff*
EMP: 60 **Privately Held**
SIC: 7371 Computer software development
PA: Corptax, Llc
2100 E Lake Cook Rd # 800
Buffalo Grove IL 60089

(P-14736)
COUNTY OF LOS ANGELES
Also Called: Internal Services
1100 N Eastern Ave, Los Angeles (90063-3200)
PHONE..........................562 940-4324
David Wesolik, *General Mgr*
EMP: 2000 **Privately Held**
SIC: 7371 Computer software development & applications
PA: County Of Los Angeles
500 W Temple St Ste 437
Los Angeles CA 90012
213 974-1101

(P-14737)
COURSERA INC (PA)
381 E Evelyn Ave, Mountain View (94041-1530)
PHONE..........................650 963-9884
Jeff Maggioncalda, *CEO*
Lila Ibrahim, *COO*
John Madigan, *CFO*
Charlotte Crawford, *Admin Sec*
Julia Kostyukova, *Software Engr*
EMP: 53
SALES (est): 21.3MM **Privately Held**
SIC: 7371 Computer software development & applications

(P-14738)
COVEO SOFTWARE CORP
415 Mission St Fl 37, San Francisco (94105-2533)
PHONE..........................800 635-5476
Louis Tetu, *CEO*
Laurent Simoneau, *President*
Benoit Hogue, *CEO*
John Lavigueur, *CFO*
Mark Floisand, *Officer*
EMP: 64
SQ FT: 2,000
SALES (est): 349.8K
SALES (corp-wide): 14.4MM **Privately Held**
SIC: 7371 8748 Computer software development; business consulting
PA: Coveo Solutions Inc
3175 Ch Des Quatre-Bourgeois Bureau 200
Quebec QC G1W 2
418 263-1111

(P-14739)
COVERITY LLC (HQ)
185 Berry St Ste 6500, San Francisco (94107-1728)
PHONE..........................415 321-5200
Anthony Bettencourt, *President*
Jennifer Johnson, *Chief Mktg Ofcr*
Dave Peterson, *Chief Mktg Ofcr*
Bill Balicki, *Vice Pres*
John E Calonico Jr, *Vice Pres*
EMP: 80
SALES (est): 25.8MM
SALES (corp-wide): 3.1B **Publicly Held**
WEB: www.coverity.com
SIC: 7371 7372 Custom computer programming services; computer software development; software programming applications; prepackaged software
PA: Synopsys, Inc.
690 E Middlefield Rd
Mountain View CA 94043
650 584-5000

(P-14740)
CREATIVEBUG LLC
835 Market St Ste 700, San Francisco (94103-1906)
PHONE..........................415 325-5926
Ursula Morgan, *CEO*
Julie Roehm, *Opers Staff*
EMP: 95
SALES (est): 13.5MM
SALES (corp-wide): 2.7B **Privately Held**
SIC: 7371 Computer software development & applications
HQ: Jo-Ann Stores, Llc
5555 Darrow Rd
Hudson OH 44236
330 656-2600

(P-14741)
CRESCENT STAFFING INC (PA)
Also Called: Crescent Solutions
17871 Mitchell N Ste 100, Irvine (92614-6050)
PHONE..........................949 724-0304
Brian Fischbein, *CEO*
Nico Andino McGraw, *Business Mgr*
EMP: 195
SALES (est): 31.2MM **Privately Held**
WEB: www.crescent-enterprise.com
SIC: 7371 8748 7379 Computer software development; business consulting; computer related consulting services

(P-14742)
CROSSCAP MEDIA SERVICES INC (PA)
311 California St Ste 320, San Francisco (94104-2605)
PHONE..........................415 217-8860
Kenneth Craig Bushert, *President*
EMP: 72 **EST:** 2010
SALES (est): 5.9MM **Privately Held**
SIC: 7371 Computer software development; computer software development & applications

(P-14743)
CROSSLINK PROF TAX SLTIONS LLC (PA)
16916 S Harlan Rd, Lathrop (95330-8737)
P.O. Box 611, Tracy (95378-0611)
PHONE.............................800 345-4337
Leroy E Petz, *President*
Reynold F Sbrilli, *CEO*
Stephanie Tesfazghi, *CFO*
Reynold Sbrilli, *Officer*
Dan Higgins, *Admin Sec*
EMP: 93 **EST:** 1974
SALES (est): 20.7MM **Privately Held**
WEB: www.petzent.com
SIC: 7371 Software programming applications; computer software development & applications; computer software development

(P-14744)
CSC COVANSYS CORPORATION
34740 Tuxedo Cmn, Fremont (94555-2746)
PHONE.............................510 304-3430
Chris Pensy, *Manager*
EMP: 150
SALES (corp-wide): 20.7B **Publicly Held**
SIC: 7371 Custom computer programming services
HQ: Csc Covansys Corporation
3170 Fairview Park Dr
Falls Church VA 22042
703 876-1000

(P-14745)
CSS HOLDINGS INC
Also Called: Live Pos
7486 La Jolla Blvd, La Jolla (92037-5029)
PHONE.............................888 884-9224
Liad Biton, *CEO*
Sammy Kahen, *President*
EMP: 70
SQ FT: 5,000
SALES: 5.8MM **Privately Held**
SIC: 7371 7379 Computer software development; computer related consulting services

(P-14746)
CU DIRECT CORPORATION (PA)
Also Called: Cudc
2855 E Guasti Rd Ste 500, Ontario (91761-1253)
P.O. Box 51482 (91761-0082)
PHONE.............................909 481-2300
Antony Boutelle, *President*
Craig S Montesanti, *CFO*
Keith Sultemeier, *Chairman*
Erin Mendez, *Treasurer*
Jerry Neemann, *Officer*
EMP: 175
SQ FT: 30,000
SALES: 60MM **Privately Held**
SIC: 7371 Computer software development

(P-14747)
CYBERDEFENDER CORPORATION
617 W 7th St Fl 10, Los Angeles (90017-3879)
PHONE.............................323 449-0774
Kevin Harris, *CEO*
Igor Barash, *COO*
Sarah B Hicks, *Senior VP*
Steven R Okun, *Senior VP*
EMP: 379
SALES (est): 23.7MM **Privately Held**
WEB: www.networkdynamics.com
SIC: 7371 7372 Custom computer programming services; prepackaged software

(P-14748)
DAQRI LLC (PA)
1201 W 5th St Ste T800, Los Angeles (90017-1452)
P.O. Box 15548, Long Beach (90815-0548)
PHONE.............................213 375-8830
Roy Ashok, *CEO*
Brass Rob, *CFO*
Brian Selzer, *Vice Pres*
Troy West, *VP Bus Dvlpt*
Adrian Stannard, *Principal*
EMP: 79 **EST:** 2007

SALES (est): 47.8MM **Privately Held**
SIC: 7371 Computer software development

(P-14749)
DASSAULT SYSTEMES AMERICAS
6320 Canoga Ave Fl 3, Woodland Hills (91367-2573)
PHONE.............................818 999-2500
Kendall Pond, *President*
Ron Mazdra, *Engineer*
Eric Brayton, *Consultant*
EMP: 133
SALES (corp-wide): 1.8B **Privately Held**
SIC: 7371 Computer software development
HQ: Dassault Systemes Americas Corp.
175 Wyman St
Waltham MA 02451
781 810-3000

(P-14750)
DATABRICKS INC (PA)
160 Spear St Fl 13, San Francisco (94105-1546)
PHONE.............................415 494-7672
Ali Ghodsi, *CEO*
Brian Dirking, *Partner*
Mark Lobree, *Partner*
Dave Conte, *CFO*
Amy Reichanadter, *CFO*
EMP: 55
SQ FT: 18,000
SALES (est): 18.5MM **Privately Held**
SIC: 7371 Computer software systems analysis & design, custom

(P-14751)
DATAMEER INC (PA)
535 Mission St Ste 2602, San Francisco (94105-3260)
PHONE.............................650 286-9100
Stefan Groschupf, *CEO*
George Shahid, *CFO*
Steve Dille, *Chief Mktg Ofcr*
Lance Walter, *Chief Mktg Ofcr*
Kenneth Jakobsen, *Officer*
EMP: 52
SALES (est): 15.5MM **Privately Held**
SIC: 7371 Computer software development

(P-14752)
DATASTAX INC (PA)
3975 Freedom Cir Ste 400, Santa Clara (95054-1258)
PHONE.............................650 389-6000
Billy Bosworth, *CEO*
Robert O'Donovan, *CFO*
Karl Van Den Bergh, *Chief Mktg Ofcr*
Steve Rowland, *Exec VP*
Martin Van Ryswyk, *Exec VP*
EMP: 126 **EST:** 2011
SALES (est): 113.8MM **Privately Held**
SIC: 7371 Computer software development

(P-14753)
DAYBREAK GAME COMPANY LLC
15051 Avenue Of Science, San Diego (92128-3430)
PHONE.............................858 239-0500
John Smedley,
Richard Lawrence, *CTO*
Holly Chu, *Project Mgr*
Gary Bjornsson, *Technical Staff*
Geoff Goldberg, *Technical Staff*
▲ **EMP:** 450
SALES (est): 85.8MM **Privately Held**
SIC: 7371 Computer software development

(P-14754)
DAZ SYSTEMS LLC (DH)
800 Crprate Pinte Ste 100, Culver City (90230)
PHONE.............................310 640-1300
Walt Zipperman, *CEO*
Deborah Arnold, *President*
David Binkley, *COO*
Sriram Natarajan, *Technical Staff*
Lisa Savage, *Human Resources*
EMP: 56
SQ FT: 2,600

SALES (est): 44.1MM **Privately Held**
SIC: 7371 7372 Computer software development & applications; prepackaged software
HQ: Accenture Llp
161 N Clark St Ste 1100
Chicago IL 60601
312 693-0161

(P-14755)
DCM TECHNOLOGIES INC
Also Called: D C M Data Systems
39150 Paseo Padre Pkwy # 303, Fremont (94538-1698)
PHONE.............................510 791-2182
Janakiram Kaki, *Vice Pres*
Ashok Choudhury, *Executive*
Avnish Yadav, *Technology*
Sunil Alexander, *Director*
EMP: 100
SALES (est): 11MM **Privately Held**
WEB: www.dcmds.com
SIC: 7371 Computer software systems analysis & design, custom
PA: Baap Technologies India Private Limited
No. 7
Coimbatore TN
-

(P-14756)
DEALERSOCKET INC (PA)
100 Avenida La Pata, San Clemente (92673-6304)
P.O. Box 74866 (92673-0163)
PHONE.............................949 900-0300
Sejal Pietrzak, *President*
Jose Arcilla, *COO*
Cameron Darby, *COO*
Gary Ito, *CFO*
Matthew Redden, *Vice Pres*
EMP: 60
SALES (est): 104.3MM **Privately Held**
WEB: www.firesocket.com
SIC: 7371 Computer software systems analysis & design, custom

(P-14757)
DEMANDTEC LLC
1 Franklin Pkwy Bldg 910, San Mateo (94403-1906)
PHONE.............................914 499-1900
Daniel R Fishback, *President*
William R Phelps, *COO*
Mark A Culhane, *CFO*
Michael A Bromme, *Senior VP*
EMP: 340
SQ FT: 82,000
SALES (est): 605.4K
SALES (corp-wide): 79.5B **Publicly Held**
WEB: www.demandtec.com
SIC: 7371 Computer software development
PA: International Business Machines Corporation
1 New Orchard Rd Ste 1 # 1
Armonk NY 10504
914 499-1900

(P-14758)
DENA CORP
185 Berry St Ste 3000, San Francisco (94107-1799)
PHONE.............................415 375-3170
Shintaro Asako, *Principal*
Hiroaki Tokuda, *Asst Controller*
Kaiser Ng, *Finance*
EMP: 99 **EST:** 2014
SALES (est): 7.4MM **Privately Held**
SIC: 7371 Computer software development & applications

(P-14759)
DENKEN SOLUTIONS INC
9170 Irvine Center Dr # 200, Irvine (92618-4614)
PHONE.............................949 630-5263
Rajendra Maddula, *Director*
Eddie Gallardo, *CEO*
Anna Zufi, *Executive*
Gopi Denken, *Technology*
Vasu Kalathur, *Human Res Mgr*
EMP: 120 **EST:** 2013
SQ FT: 4,000

SALES (est): 17.3MM **Privately Held**
SIC: 7371 8742 8748 Computer software systems analysis & design, custom; computer software development & applications; management consulting services; business consulting; systems analysis & engineering consulting services

(P-14760)
DEVICE ANYWHERE
777 Mariners Isl Blvd # 250, San Mateo (94404-5008)
PHONE.............................650 655-6400
EMP: 68
SALES (est): 4.2MM **Privately Held**
SIC: 7371

(P-14761)
DEWMOBILE USA INC
2901 Tasman Dr Ste 107, Santa Clara (95054-1137)
PHONE.............................408 550-2818
Shangpin Chang, *CTO*
EMP: 50
SALES (est): 1.5MM **Privately Held**
SIC: 7371 Computer software development & applications

(P-14762)
DFUSION SOFTWARE INC
Also Called: Total Immersion
5900 Wilshire Blvd # 2550, Los Angeles (90036-5013)
PHONE.............................323 617-5577
Didier Lesteven, *CEO*
Bruno Uzzan, *Principal*
EMP: 50
SQ FT: 3,000
SALES (est): 3.9MM **Privately Held**
WEB: www.t-immersion.com
SIC: 7371 Computer software development

(P-14763)
DHAP DIGITAL INC
235 Montgomery St # 1320, San Francisco (94104-2902)
PHONE.............................415 962-4900
Philip Dzilvelis, *President*
Arikko Howell, *Principal*
EMP: 50 **EST:** 1997
SQ FT: 12,000
SALES: 5MM **Privately Held**
WEB: www.dhap.com
SIC: 7371 Computer software systems analysis & design, custom

(P-14764)
DIGITAL GUARDIAN INC
2101 Tasman Dr Ste 210, Santa Clara (95054-1020)
PHONE.............................408 716-4200
Chris Denaro, *Manager*
EMP: 348
SALES (corp-wide): 81.2MM **Privately Held**
SIC: 7371 Computer software development & applications
PA: Digital Guardian, Inc.
275 Wyman St Ste 250
Waltham MA 02451
781 788-8180

(P-14765)
DIGITE INC
21060 Homestead Rd # 220, Cupertino (95014-0204)
PHONE.............................408 418-3834
Suhas S Patil, *Ch of Bd*
Sridhar Auynam, *CEO*
Raghunath Basavanahalli, *Senior VP*
Sudipta Lahiri, *Senior VP*
Mahesh Singh, *Senior VP*
EMP: 150
SQ FT: 1,400
SALES (est): 6.9MM **Privately Held**
WEB: www.digite.com
SIC: 7371 Computer software development

(P-14766)
DISNEY INTERACTIVE STUDIOS INC
601 Circle Seven Dr, Glendale (91201-2332)
PHONE.............................818 560-1000

P R O D U C T S & S V C S

Peter Casciani, *Manager*
EMP: 120
SALES (corp-wide): 90.2B **Publicly Held**
SIC: 7371 Computer software development
HQ: Disney Interactive Studios, Inc.
500 S Buena Vista St
Burbank CA 91521
818 560-1000

(P-14767)
DISNEY INTERACTIVE STUDIOS INC
681 W Buena Vista St, Burbank
(91521-0001)
PHONE..........................818 553-5000
Gram Hoper, *Branch Mgr*
EMP: 120
SALES (corp-wide): 90.2B **Publicly Held**
SIC: 7371 Computer software development
HQ: Disney Interactive Studios, Inc.
500 S Buena Vista St
Burbank CA 91521
818 560-1000

(P-14768)
DOCKER INC (PA)
144 Townsend St Ste 100, San Francisco
(94107-1915)
PHONE..........................800 764-4847
Steve Singh, *CEO*
Gary Gilbert, *Partner*
Dan Guzman, *Partner*
Dan Powers, *Partner*
Eric Bardin, *CFO*
EMP: 55
SALES (est): 20.4MM **Privately Held**
SIC: 7371 Computer software development

(P-14769)
DOLPHIN IMAGING SYSTEMS LLC
9200 Oakdale Ave Ste 500, Chatsworth
(91311-6556)
PHONE..........................818 435-1368
Chester H Wang,
EMP: 50
SALES (est): 5.7MM
SALES (corp-wide): 5.5B **Publicly Held**
WEB: www.dolphinimaging.com
SIC: 7371 Computer software development
HQ: Patterson Dental Supply, Inc.
1031 Mendota Heights Rd
Saint Paul MN 55120
651 686-1600

(P-14770)
DORADO SOFTWARE INC
Also Called: Visiworks Software
4805 Golden Foothill Pkwy, El Dorado Hills
(95762-9651)
PHONE..........................916 673-1100
Timothy Sebring, *President*
Edward Kurzenski, *Vice Pres*
Roger Hosier, *CTO*
Brandon Norgaard, *Software Engr*
Joseph Sikich, *Software Engr*
EMP: 80
SALES (est): 13MM **Privately Held**
WEB: www.doradosoftware.com
SIC: 7371 Computer software development

(P-14771)
DP TECHNOLOGY CORP (PA)
Also Called: Esprit
1150 Avenida Acaso, Camarillo
(93012-8719)
PHONE..........................805 388-6000
Daniel Frayssinet, *CEO*
Paul Ricard, *President*
Simone Petruzzi, *Prgrmr*
Peter Kapas, *Technology*
Drew Peer, *Technology*
EMP: 60
SQ FT: 12,000
SALES (est): 18.4MM **Privately Held**
WEB: www.dptechnology.com
SIC: 7371 7373 7372 Computer software development; computer integrated systems design; prepackaged software

(P-14772)
DTEX SYSTEMS INC
3055 Olin Ave Ste 2000, San Jose
(95128-2069)
PHONE..........................408 418-3786
Christy Wyatt, *CEO*
Bahman Mahbod, *COO*
Debbie Tuck, *CFO*
Steve Holton, *Officer*
Steve Hewitt, *Vice Pres*
EMP: 50
SALES (est): 4.9MM **Privately Held**
SIC: 7371 Computer software development

(P-14773)
E Z DATA INC (HQ)
251 S Lake Ave Ste 200, Pasadena
(91101-3075)
PHONE..........................626 585-3505
Dale Okuno, *President*
EMP: 51
SALES (est): 5.9MM
SALES (corp-wide): 497.8MM **Publicly Held**
WEB: www.ez-data.com
SIC: 7371 Computer software development
PA: Ebix, Inc.
1 Ebix Way
Duluth GA 30097
678 281-2020

(P-14774)
ECONOSOFT INC
2375 Zanker Rd Ste 250, San Jose
(95131-1143)
PHONE..........................408 442-3663
Chander Shaiker, *President*
Sandeep Dogra, *Manager*
EMP: 72 **EST:** 2000
SALES (est): 3MM
SALES (corp-wide): 19.8MM **Privately Held**
SIC: 7371 Computer software systems analysis & design, custom
PA: Ace Technologies, Inc.
2375 Zanker Rd Ste 250
San Jose CA 95131
408 324-1203

(P-14775)
EFRONT FINANCIAL SOLUTIONS INC
135 Main St Ste 1330, San Francisco
(94105-1843)
PHONE..........................415 653-3239
Tarek Chouman, *CEO*
Matthew Bagley, *CFO*
Thibaut De Laval, *Chief Mktg Ofcr*
Sevgi Eason, *Vice Pres*
Alan Erickson, *Vice Pres*
EMP: 88
SALES (est): 1.3MM **Privately Held**
SIC: 7371 Computer software development & applications

(P-14776)
EGNYTE INC (PA)
1350 W Middlefield Rd, Mountain View
(94043-3061)
PHONE..........................650 968-4018
Vineet Jain, *President*
Jase Eskildsen, *Partner*
Kevin Patterson, *Partner*
Ben Rice, *President*
Benjamin Rice, *President*
EMP: 97 **EST:** 2008
SALES (est): 44.1MM **Privately Held**
SIC: 7371 Computer software development

(P-14777)
EHEALTHINSURANCE SERVICES INC
Also Called: Ehealth Insurance.com
11919 Foundation Pl # 100, Gold River
(95670-4537)
PHONE..........................916 608-6101
Robert Hurley, *Branch Mgr*
EMP: 120

SALES (corp-wide): 251.4MM **Publicly Held**
WEB: www.anysure.com
SIC: 7371 Computer software development
HQ: Ehealthinsurance Services, Inc.
2625 Augustine Dr Ste 201
Santa Clara CA 95054
650 584-2700

(P-14778)
EINFOCHIPS INC (HQ)
2025 Gateway Pl Ste 270, San Jose
(95110-1007)
PHONE..........................408 496-1882
Pratul Shroff, *CEO*
Sribash Dey, *Exec VP*
Vilesh Shah, *Program Mgr*
Amit Gajjar, *Sr Software Eng*
Dipesh Patel, *Sr Software Eng*
EMP: 52
SQ FT: 6,178
SALES (est): 23.9MM
SALES (corp-wide): 29.6B **Publicly Held**
SIC: 7371 7373 Computer software development; systems software development services; computer systems analysis & design; computer-aided system services; computer-aided design (CAD) systems service
PA: Arrow Electronics, Inc.
9201 E Dry Creek Rd
Centennial CO 80112
303 824-4000

(P-14779)
EINSTEIN INDUSTRIES INC
Also Called: Einstein Dental
6825 Flanders Dr, San Diego (92121-2905)
PHONE..........................858 459-1182
Robert C Silkey, *President*
Dean Hecker, *CFO*
Michael Hurley, *Vice Pres*
Robert Silkey, *Vice Pres*
Ted Ricasa, *Executive*
EMP: 180
SALES (est): 26.7MM **Privately Held**
WEB: www.einsteindental.com
SIC: 7371 8742 8322 Computer software development; marketing consulting services; referral service for personal & social problems

(P-14780)
ELASTIC PROJECTS INC
Also Called: Abstract
255 Golden Gate Ave, San Francisco
(94102-3709)
PHONE..........................415 857-1593
Josh Brewer, *CEO*
Kevin Smith, *CTO*
EMP: 100 **EST:** 2016
SQ FT: 8,000
SALES (est): 112.5K **Privately Held**
SIC: 7371 Computer software systems analysis & design, custom

(P-14781)
ELASTICSEARCH INC (HQ)
800 W El Cmino Real Ste 3, Mountain View
(94040)
PHONE..........................650 458-2620
Shay Banon, *CEO*
Lawrence Au, *Partner*
Janesh Moorjani, *CFO*
Nick White, *CFO*
Scott Fingerhut, *Vice Pres*
EMP: 70
SQ FT: 30,000
SALES (est): 19.6MM
SALES (corp-wide): 159.9MM **Privately Held**
SIC: 7371 Computer software development
PA: Elastic N.V.
Keizersgracht 281
Amsterdam
202 044-507

(P-14782)
ELLATION INC (PA)
Also Called: Crunchyroll
835 Market St Ste 700, San Francisco
(94103-1906)
PHONE..........................415 796-3560
Tom Pickett, *CEO*

Terry LI, *Vice Pres*
SAE Song, *Vice Pres*
Jason Hubbard, *Info Tech Mgr*
Brandon Lee, *Software Engr*
EMP: 70
SALES (est): 34.3MM **Privately Held**
SIC: 7371 5932 Computer software development & applications; used merchandise stores

(P-14783)
EMBARCADERO SYSTEMS CORP
1601 Harbor Bay Pkwy # 120, Alameda
(94502-3028)
PHONE..........................510 749-7400
Christopher R Redlich Jr, *Chairman*
Richard Beedenbender, *President*
John Sullivan, *Admin Sec*
Richard Robinson, *Administration*
EMP: 140
SQ FT: 27,000
SALES (est): 11.9MM **Privately Held**
WEB: www.esystem.com
SIC: 7371 Computer software development

(P-14784)
EMBRANE INC
2350 Mission College Blvd # 703, Santa Clara (95054-1556)
PHONE..........................408 550-2700
Bill Burns, *President*
Marco Di Benedetto, *CTO*
EMP: 50
SQ FT: 7,300
SALES (est): 5.3MM **Privately Held**
SIC: 7371 Computer software development

(P-14785)
EMETER CORPORATION
4000 E 3rd Ave Ste 400, Foster City
(94404-4827)
PHONE..........................650 227-7770
Lisa Caswell, *President*
Guido Frantzen, *CFO*
Shannon Amerman, *Vice Pres*
Chris King, *Risk Mgmt Dir*
Larsh Johnson, *CTO*
EMP: 130
SQ FT: 30,000
SALES (est): 18.1MM
SALES (corp-wide): 95B **Privately Held**
WEB: www.emeter.com
SIC: 7371 Computer software development
HQ: Siemens Industry, Inc.
1000 Deerfield Pkwy
Buffalo Grove IL 60089
847 215-1000

(P-14786)
ENGINEERAI CORP
6300 Arizona Cir, Los Angeles
(90045-1202)
PHONE..........................650 721-1158
Sachin Dev Duggal, *CEO*
Varghese Cherian, *COO*
EMP: 50
SALES (est): 20MM **Privately Held**
SIC: 7371 Computer software development & applications

(P-14787)
ENVIANCE INC (HQ)
5857 Owens Ave Ste 102, Carlsbad
(92008-5507)
PHONE..........................760 496-0200
Amy Stelling, *CEO*
David McCurdy, *COO*
Jeffrey Pownell, *CFO*
Ben Archibald, *Vice Pres*
Will Dunlap, *Vice Pres*
EMP: 73
SQ FT: 10,000
SALES (est): 30.4MM **Privately Held**
WEB: www.enviance.com
SIC: 7371 7374 Custom computer programming services; data processing & preparation

(P-14788)
ENVOY INC
410 Townsend St Ste 410 # 410, San Francisco (94107-1581)
PHONE.................................415 787-7871
Laurentiu Gadea, *CEO*
Hollie Wegman, *VP Mktg*
EMP: 100 **EST:** 2013
SALES (est): 1.6K **Privately Held**
SIC: 7371 Computer software development & applications

(P-14789)
EPITEC INC
515 Olive Ave, Vista (92083-3439)
PHONE.................................760 650-2515
William Grivas, *President*
EMP: 900
SALES (corp-wide): 67MM **Privately Held**
SIC: 7371 Computer software systems analysis & design, custom
PA: Epitec, Inc.
24800 Denso Dr Ste 150
Southfield MI 48033
248 353-6800

(P-14790)
EPITOME ENTERPRISES LLC
821 Mary Pl, Claremont (91711-2273)
PHONE.................................909 625-4728
EMP: 60
SALES (est): 1.8MM **Privately Held**
WEB: www.epitomeenterprises.com
SIC: 7371

(P-14791)
EQUATOR LLC (HQ)
Also Called: Equator Business Solutions
6060 Center Dr Ste 500, Los Angeles (90045-8857)
PHONE.................................310 469-9500
Chris Saitta, *CEO*
Robert McKinley, *President*
John Vella, *Officer*
Paul Lin, *Administration*
Amit Aggarwal, *Info Tech Dir*
EMP: 200
SALES: 45.4MM
SALES (corp-wide): 177.9K **Privately Held**
SIC: 7371 Computer software development & applications

(P-14792)
ERP INTEGRATED SOLUTIONS INC
1501 Hughes Way Ste 320, Long Beach (90810-1880)
PHONE.................................562 425-7800
Joseph Cabrera, *President*
Doug Cole, *Vice Pres*
Masaya Taya, *Managing Dir*
Anthony Raimo, *CTO*
EMP: 100
SQ FT: 5,000
SALES (est): 3.9MM **Privately Held**
WEB: www.erp-is.com
SIC: 7371 Computer software development

(P-14793)
ESCALATE INC (DH)
Also Called: Escalate Retail
10680 Treena St Ste 170, San Diego (92131-2443)
PHONE.................................858 457-3888
Stewart M Bloom, *CEO*
Mike Larkin, *CFO*
Richard Harmatiuk, *Vice Pres*
EMP: 290
SQ FT: 59,000
SALES (est): 27.2MM
SALES (corp-wide): 482.9MM **Privately Held**
SIC: 7371 7373 5045 Custom computer programming services; computer integrated systems design; computers, peripherals & software

(P-14794)
ESSENTIAL PRODUCTS INC
380 Portage Ave, Palo Alto (94306-2244)
PHONE.................................650 300-0000
Andrew E Rubin, *CEO*
Niccolo De Masi, *President*

Meena Srinivasan, *CFO*
Matt Hershenson, *Co-Founder*
Erika Ortiz, *Research*
EMP: 82
SALES (est): 8.8MM **Privately Held**
SIC: 7371 Computer software systems analysis & design, custom

(P-14795)
ESTUATE INC
830 Hillview Ct Ste 280, Milpitas (95035-4564)
PHONE.................................408 946-0002
Prakash Balebail, *President*
Nagaraja Kini, *CFO*
Subbarao Satyavolu, *Vice Pres*
Vijayalaxmi Nayakodi, *Executive*
Gopal K Vasudeva, *Administration*
EMP: 67
SQ FT: 2,558
SALES (est): 12.3MM **Privately Held**
SIC: 7371 Computer software development

(P-14796)
ETRIGUE CORPORATION
6399 San Ignacio Ave # 200, San Jose (95119-1215)
PHONE.................................408 490-2900
Jeffrey A Holmes, *CEO*
EMP: 50
SQ FT: 43,000
SALES (est): 3.7MM **Privately Held**
SIC: 7371 Computer software development

(P-14797)
EVEG INC
16540 Aston, Irvine (92606-4805)
PHONE.................................844 221-3359
Peter Krish, *Mng Member*
EMP: 50
SALES (est): 215.9K **Privately Held**
SIC: 7371 Computer software development & applications

(P-14798)
EVEREST CONSULTING GROUP INC
39650 Mission Blvd, Fremont (94539-3000)
PHONE.................................510 494-8440
Raj Kamalanathan, *Manager*
EMP: 85
SALES (corp-wide): 22.2MM **Privately Held**
WEB: www.everestconsulting.net
SIC: 7371 Computer software development
PA: Everest Consulting Group Inc.
3840 Park Ave Ste 203
Edison NJ 08820
732 548-2700

(P-14799)
EVERGENT TECHNOLOGIES INC (PA)
1250 Borregas Ave, Sunnyvale (94089-1309)
PHONE.................................408 718-5453
Vijay Sajja, *CEO*
Craig Barberich, *Vice Pres*
Ashok Bhaskar, *Vice Pres*
Bruce Lampert, *Vice Pres*
Sameer Kumar, *Admin Sec*
EMP: 292
SQ FT: 2,000
SALES: 5MM **Privately Held**
SIC: 7371 Computer software development

(P-14800)
EVERNOTE CORPORATION (PA)
Also Called: Skitch
305 Walnut St, Redwood City (94063-1731)
PHONE.................................650 216-7700
Chris O'Neill, *CEO*
Linda Kozlowski, *COO*
Jeff Shotts, *CFO*
Hitoshi Hokamura, *Chairman*
Bethany Brodsky, *Vice Pres*
▲ **EMP:** 134 **EST:** 2004
SALES (est): 113.5MM **Privately Held**
SIC: 7371 Software programming applications

(P-14801)
EVIDENTIO INC (HQ)
7901 Stoneridge Dr # 150, Pleasanton (94588-3677)
PHONE.................................855 933-1337
Mark McLaughlin, *CEO*
EMP: 85
SQ FT: 5,000
SALES: 8MM
SALES (corp-wide): 2.9B **Publicly Held**
SIC: 7371 Computer software systems analysis & design, custom; computer software development & applications
PA: Palo Alto Networks Inc.
3000 Tannery Way
Santa Clara CA 95054
408 753-4000

(P-14802)
EVISIONS INC (PA)
440 Exchange Ste 200, Irvine (92602-1390)
PHONE.................................949 833-1384
Joe Potenza, *President*
Penny Dobbs, *CFO*
Marianne D Jones, *Treasurer*
Michael Downhower, *Info Tech Dir*
Brian Stevens, *Sales Staff*
EMP: 56
SQ FT: 15,000
SALES (est): 16.8MM **Privately Held**
SIC: 7371 Computer software development

(P-14803)
EVOX PRODUCTIONS LLC (PA)
2363 E Pacifica Pl 305, Compton (90220-6212)
PHONE.................................310 605-1400
David Falstrup,
Carol Falstrup, *CFO*
Jeff Mancino, *CFO*
Peter Avildsen, *Chief Mktg Ofcr*
Chris Williams, *Vice Pres*
EMP: 58
SQ FT: 37,500
SALES (est): 11.4MM **Privately Held**
SIC: 7371 7335 Custom computer programming services; commercial photography

(P-14804)
EXIGEN (USA) INC (PA)
Also Called: Exigen Group
345 California St Fl 22, San Francisco (94104-2606)
PHONE.................................415 402-2600
Greg Shenkman, *CEO*
Alec Miloslavsky, *Ch of Bd*
Alex Kolt, *President*
Fazi Zand, *Vice Pres*
Sal Gerardo, *Principal*
EMP: 550
SQ FT: 26,000
SALES (est): 49.2MM **Privately Held**
WEB: www.exigengroup.com
SIC: 7371 Computer software development

(P-14805)
EXTREME NETWORKS INC
3585 Monroe St, Santa Clara (95051-7774)
PHONE.................................630 288-3665
Robert A Perry, *Branch Mgr*
Eddie Curran, *Sales Mgr*
Jake Howering, *Marketing Staff*
Chris Lavoie, *Director*
Juan Canela, *Manager*
EMP: 51 **Publicly Held**
SIC: 7371 Computer software development
PA: Extreme Networks, Inc.
6480 Via Del Oro
San Jose CA 95119

(P-14806)
FAMOUS SOFTWARE LLC (PA)
8080 N Palm Ave Ste 210, Fresno (93711-5797)
PHONE.................................559 438-3600
Kirk Parrish, *Human Res Mgr*
Brandon Roberts, *Technology*
Nick Calderon, *Sr Consultant*
Carolyn Craft, *Manager*

Tony Fazio, *Manager*
EMP: 60
SQ FT: 8,300
SALES: 10MM **Privately Held**
WEB: www.famoussoftware.com
SIC: 7371 7372 Computer software development; business oriented computer software

(P-14807)
FASTLY INC (PA)
475 Brannan St Ste 300, San Francisco (94107-5420)
P.O. Box 78266 (94107-8266)
PHONE.................................844 432-7859
Artur Bergman, *CEO*
Adriel Lares, *CFO*
Wolfgang Maasberg, *Exec VP*
Paul Luongo, *Senior VP*
Christopher Kennedy, *Vice Pres*
EMP: 110
SQ FT: 71,343
SALES: 144.5MM **Publicly Held**
SIC: 7371 Computer software development; computer software development & applications

(P-14808)
FCS SOFTWARE SOLUTIONS LIMITED
2375 Zanker Rd Ste 250, San Jose (95131-1143)
PHONE.................................408 324-1203
Dalip Kumar, *President*
Janak Sharma, *Director*
EMP: 99
SALES (est): 8.6MM **Privately Held**
SIC: 7371 Computer software development
PA: Fcs Software Solutions Limited
Plot No 83 Fcs House
Noida UP 20130

(P-14809)
FINANCIAL INFORMATION NETWORK
Also Called: F I N
6656 Valjean Ave, Van Nuys (91406-5816)
P.O. Box 7954 (91409-7954)
PHONE.................................818 782-0331
Jerry Sears, *President*
Alan Shepoiser, *CFO*
Rick Grogan, *Marketing Staff*
Heather Lundberg, *Sales Staff*
Heather Stryzinski, *Sales Staff*
EMP: 60
SQ FT: 6,000
SALES (est): 6.8MM **Privately Held**
WEB: www.fingps.com
SIC: 7371 7372 Custom computer programming services; prepackaged software

(P-14810)
FINANCIALFORCECOM INC (DH)
595 Market St Ste 2700, San Francisco (94105-2840)
PHONE.................................866 743-2220
Tod Nielsen, *President*
Joe Fuca, *President*
Nancy Skversky, *President*
Gordy Brooks, *CFO*
Jeremy Roche, *Founder*
EMP: 88
SALES (est): 90.5MM
SALES (corp-wide): 2.6MM **Privately Held**
SIC: 7371 Computer software development
HQ: Unit4 N.V.
Papendorpseweg 100
Utrecht 3528
184 444-444

(P-14811)
FLICKR INC
390 Fremont St, San Francisco (94105-2316)
PHONE.................................650 265-0396
Don Makaskill, *CEO*
Eric Willis, *President*
EMP: 50

SALES (est): 50.7K **Privately Held**
SIC: 7371 Custom computer programming
services; computer software development
& applications

(P-14812)
FLO HEALTH INC
541 Jefferson Ave Ste 100, Redwood City
(94063-1700)
PHONE............................510 303-9307
Maxim Scrobov, *CEO*
EMP: 78
SALES (corp-wide): 500K **Privately Held**
SIC: 7371 Computer software develop-
ment & applications
PA: Flo Health, Inc.
1013 Centre Rd Ste 403b
Wilmington DE 19805
302 498-8369

(P-14813)
FLUID INC (DH)
1611 Telegraph Ave # 400, Oakland
(94612-2150)
PHONE............................877 343-3240
Vanessa Cartwright, *CEO*
Tamir Scheinok, *COO*
Stephanie Wiseman, *Vice Pres*
Natalia Anguiano, *Office Mgr*
Alexander Palmo, *Sr Software Eng*
EMP: 61
SQ FT: 7,000
SALES (est): 18.5MM
SALES (corp-wide): 73.2MM **Privately
Held**
SIC: 7371 Computer software develop-
ment
HQ: Astound Commerce Corporation
1111 Bayhill Dr Ste 425
San Bruno CA 94066
800 591-4710

(P-14814)
FMG SUITE LLC (PA)
12395 World Trade Dr # 200, San Diego
(92128-3743)
PHONE............................888 364-1260
Craig Faulkner, *CEO*
Scott White, *COO*
Russ Clark, *CFO*
Chris Paley, *Vice Pres*
Cathy Sigismonti, *Vice Pres*
EMP: 50
SQ FT: 10,000
SALES: 3MM **Privately Held**
SIC: 7371 Computer software develop-
ment

(P-14815)
FNC INC
40 Pacifica Ste 900, Irvine (92618-7487)
PHONE............................714 866-1099
Neil Olsen, *Officer*
Christopher Floyd, *Administration*
EMP: 52
SALES (corp-wide): 52.7MM **Privately
Held**
SIC: 7371 Custom computer programming
services
PA: Fnc, Inc.
1214 Office Park Dr
Oxford MS 38655
662 236-2020

(P-14816)
FOCUS 360 INC
27721 La Paz Rd Ste B, Laguna Niguel
(92677-3949)
PHONE............................949 234-0008
Steven G Ormonde, *President*
Brent C Chase, *Vice Pres*
Michael Colwell, *Sales Associate*
EMP: 54
SQ FT: 18,300
SALES (est): 5.2MM **Privately Held**
WEB: www.focus360.com
SIC: 7371 Computer software develop-
ment

(P-14817)
**FORESCOUT TECHNOLOGIES
INC (PA)**
190 W Tasman Dr, San Jose (95134-1700)
PHONE............................408 213-3191
Michael Decesare, *President*
Theresia Gouw, *Ch of Bd*

Christopher Harms, *CFO*
David G Dewalt, *Vice Ch Bd*
Jason Pishotti, *Officer*
EMP: 148
SQ FT: 95,950
SALES: 297.6MM **Publicly Held**
WEB: www.forescout.com
SIC: 7371 Computer software develop-
ment

(P-14818)
**FORMULA ONE SYSTEMS INC
(HQ)**
2850 E 29th St, Long Beach (90806-2313)
PHONE............................562 424-7899
Patrick McMahon, *President*
EMP: 77
SQ FT: 23,000
SALES: 8MM
SALES (corp-wide): 32.9MM **Privately
Held**
WEB: www.acom.com
SIC: 7371 Computer software develop-
ment
PA: Acom Solutions, Inc.
2850 E 29th St
Long Beach CA 90806
562 424-7899

(P-14819)
FRONT PORCH INC (PA)
905 Mono Way, Sonora (95370-5206)
PHONE............................209 288-5500
Zach Britton, *CEO*
Zachary Britton, *President*
Cheri Oteri, *CEO*
Robert Hohne Jr, *CFO*
Ned Sudduth, *Vice Pres*
EMP: 60
SQ FT: 1,022
SALES (est): 10.1MM **Privately Held**
WEB: www.adfirst.com
SIC: 7371 Computer software develop-
ment

(P-14820)
**FRONTECH N FUJITSU AMER
INC**
2933 Bunker Hill Ln # 101, Santa Clara
(95054-1124)
PHONE............................408 982-3697
John Mullerworth, *Manager*
EMP: 100 **Privately Held**
WEB: www.fjicl.com
SIC: 7371 Computer software develop-
ment
HQ: Fujitsu Frontech North America, Inc.
27121 Towne Centre Dr # 100
Foothill Ranch CA 92610

(P-14821)
FUEL CYCLE INC (PA)
11859 Wilshire Blvd Fl 4, Los Angeles
(90025-6600)
PHONE............................323 556-5400
Bahram Nour-Omid, *CEO*
Ramesh Pidikiti, *President*
Steve Howe, *COO*
Menaka Gopinath, *Vice Pres*
EMP: 60
SQ FT: 15,000
SALES (est): 9.6MM **Privately Held**
SIC: 7371 Computer software develop-
ment

(P-14822)
FUJITSU GLOVIA INC (HQ)
200 Continental Blvd Fl 3, El Segundo
(90245-4510)
PHONE............................310 563-7000
Chikara Ono, *CEO*
Masahiro Cho, *CFO*
Jim Errington, *Exec VP*
James Gorham, *Vice Pres*
EMP: 150
SQ FT: 53,000
SALES (est): 46.7MM **Privately Held**
SIC: 7371 7372 Computer software devel-
opment; prepackaged software

(P-14823)
FUSIONONE INC
55 Almaden Blvd Ste 500, San Jose
(95113-1612)
PHONE............................408 282-1200

Mike Mulica, *CEO*
Rick Onyon, *Ch of Bd*
Ed Battle, *CFO*
Jay Burrell, *Exec VP*
Alexander Tsarkov, *Vice Pres*
EMP: 90
SQ FT: 13,000
SALES (est): 3.9MM
SALES (corp-wide): 325.8MM **Publicly
Held**
WEB: www.fusionone.com
SIC: 7371 Custom computer programming
services
PA: Synchronoss Technologies, Inc.
200 Crossing Blvd Fl 8
Bridgewater NJ 08807
866 620-3940

(P-14824)
**FUTURENET TECHNOLOGIES
CORP**
1320 Valley Vista Dr # 202, Diamond Bar
(91765-3956)
PHONE............................909 396-4000
Tom Liu, *President*
Jenny Liu, *Manager*
EMP: 123
SQ FT: 9,650
SALES (est): 8.7MM **Privately Held**
WEB: www.futurenet-tech.com
SIC: 7371 Computer software develop-
ment

(P-14825)
G2 DIRECT AND DIGITAL
Also Called: Grey Direct-E Marketing
612 Howard St Ste 400, San Francisco
(94105-3944)
PHONE............................415 421-1000
Felicia Montgomery, *Branch Mgr*
EMP: 50
SALES (corp-wide): 20B **Privately Held**
WEB: www.greydirect.com
SIC: 7371 Custom computer programming
services
HQ: G2 Direct And Digital
777 3rd Ave Ste 37
New York NY 10017
212 537-3700

(P-14826)
GAINSIGHT INC
400 Concar Dr 3, San Mateo (94402-2681)
PHONE............................888 623-8562
Nick Mehta, *CEO*
Igor Beckerman, *CFO*
Dan Steinman, *Ch Credit Ofcr*
Carol Mahoney,
Allison Pickens, *Officer*
EMP: 430
SALES (est): 3.9MM **Privately Held**
SIC: 7371 Computer software develop-
ment; computer software development &
applications

(P-14827)
**GEHRY TECHNOLOGIES INC
(HQ)**
12181 Bluff Creek Dr # 200, Playa Vista
(90094-2992)
PHONE............................310 862-1200
Meaghan Lloyd, *CEO*
Michael Lin, *CFO*
James Porter, *Managing Dir*
Dhruba Kalita, *CIO*
Dennis Sheldon, *CTO*
EMP: 50
SQ FT: 2,000
SALES (est): 14.5MM
SALES (corp-wide): 3.1B **Publicly Held**
WEB: www.foga.com
SIC: 7371 Computer software develop-
ment & applications
PA: Trimble Inc.
935 Stewart Dr
Sunnyvale CA 94085
408 481-8000

(P-14828)
GENEX (HQ)
800 Corporate Pointe # 100, Culver City
(90230-7667)
PHONE............................424 672-9500
Walter Schild, *CEO*
Gretchen Humbert, *CFO*
EMP: 130

SQ FT: 12,000
SALES (est): 10.4MM
SALES (corp-wide): 3.1B **Publicly Held**
WEB: www.genex.com
SIC: 7371 7379 4813 Computer software
development & applications; computer re-
lated consulting services;
PA: Meredith Corporation
1716 Locust St
Des Moines IA 50309
515 284-3000

(P-14829)
GENIUM INC
585 Broadway St, Redwood City
(94063-3122)
PHONE............................415 935-3593
Alexander Ledovskiy, *CEO*
Alex Iceman, *Exec Dir*
EMP: 50 **EST:** 2015
SQ FT: 40,000
SALES: 4MM **Privately Held**
SIC: 7371 Computer software develop-
ment

(P-14830)
GIGSTER INC
301 Howard St Ste 2100, San Francisco
(94105-6616)
PHONE............................941 888-4447
Chris Keene, *CEO*
Judy Kopa, *CFO*
Jennifer Dimas, *Chief Mktg Ofcr*
Marque Teegardin, *Officer*
May Sermonia, *Office Mgr*
EMP: 200
SALES (est): 185.4K **Privately Held**
SIC: 7371 Computer software develop-
ment & applications

(P-14831)
GIGYA INC (HQ)
2513 E Char Rd Ste 200, Mountain View
(94043)
PHONE............................650 353-7230
Patrick Salyer, *CEO*
Rooly Elieverov, *President*
Jean-Francois Hervy, *CFO*
Troy Abraham, *Vice Pres*
Derrick Arakaki, *Vice Pres*
EMP: 84
SQ FT: 16,000
SALES (est): 39.7MM
SALES (corp-wide): 28.2B **Privately Held**
WEB: www.gigya-inc.com
SIC: 7371 Computer software develop-
ment & applications
PA: Sap Se
Dietmar-Hopp-Allee 16
Walldorf 69190
622 774-7474

(P-14832)
GINGERIO INC
116 New Montgomery St # 5, San Fran-
cisco (94105-3607)
PHONE............................408 455-0574
Russell Gla, *CEO*
Michelle Patruno, *Office Mgr*
EMP: 62 **EST:** 2011
SALES (est): 5.5MM **Privately Held**
SIC: 7371 Custom computer programming
services
SIC: 7371 Computer software develop-
ment & applications

(P-14833)
**GLOBAL SERVICE RESOURCES
INC**
Also Called: Computerworks Technologies
711 S Victory Blvd, Burbank (91502-2426)
P.O. Box 4057 (91503-4057)
PHONE............................800 679-7658
Nick Sefayan, *President*
Val Casagrande, *Recruiter*
▲ **EMP:** 80
SQ FT: 7,000
SALES (est): 5MM **Privately Held**
WEB: www.cwservice.com
SIC: 7371 7363 Computer software devel-
opment; labor resource services; em-
ployee leasing service; engineering help
service; medical help service

(P-14834)
GLOBAL TOUCHPOINTS INC
3005 Douglas Blvd Ste 108, Roseville
(95661-4267)
PHONE..............................916 878-5954
Naren Kini, *CEO*
Udayan Chanda, *President*
Sandhya Shenoy, *Treasurer*
Seema Chanda, *Admin Sec*
EMP: 94
SQ FT: 2,174
SALES: 15MM **Privately Held**
SIC: 7371 7373 Computer software development; computer software development & applications; computer systems analysis & design; systems integration services

(P-14835)
GLOBALLOGIC INC (PA)
1741 Tech Dr Ste 400, San Jose (95110)
PHONE..............................408 273-8900
Shashank Samant, *CEO*
Jim Dellamore, *COO*
Scott Brubaker, *CFO*
Charles Wayne Grubbs, *CFO*
Wayne Grubbs, *CFO*
EMP: 213
SALES (est): 652.7MM **Privately Held**
WEB: www.globallogic.com
SIC: 7371 7373 7379 Computer software development; systems engineering, computer related; computer related consulting services

(P-14836)
GLOVIA INC
2250 E Imperial Hwy # 200, El Segundo
(90245-3508)
PHONE..............................310 563-7000
Howard Goldman, *Controller*
EMP: 200
SALES (est): 9MM **Privately Held**
SIC: 7371 Computer software development

(P-14837)
GLU MOBILE INC (PA)
875 Howard St Ste 100, San Francisco
(94103-3032)
PHONE..............................415 800-6100
Nick Earl, *President*
Niccolo De Masi, *Ch of Bd*
Eric R Ludwig, *COO*
Eric Ball, *Bd of Directors*
Lance Smith, *Bd of Directors*
EMP: 128
SQ FT: 57,000
SALES: 366.5MM **Publicly Held**
WEB: www.glu.com
SIC: 7371 3944 Computer software development & applications; computer software writing services; computer code authors; electronic games & toys

(P-14838)
GOOD SPORTS PLUS LTD
Also Called: ARC
370 Amapola Ave Ste 208, Torrance
(90501-7241)
PHONE..............................310 671-4400
Brad Lupien, *President*
Gary Lipsky, *President*
Elmer Axume, *COO*
Kitty Cohen, *Vice Pres*
EMP: 300
SQ FT: 3,500
SALES (est): 9.9MM **Privately Held**
SIC: 7371 7997 Custom computer programming services; outdoor field clubs

(P-14839)
GOOD TECHNOLOGY CORPORATION (HQ)
3001 Bishop Dr Ste 400, San Ramon
(94583-5005)
PHONE..............................408 352-9102
Christy Wyatt, *President*
Ronald J Fior, *CFO*
Barry Schuler, *Bd of Directors*
Lynn Lucas, *Chief Mktg Ofcr*
Cherylyn Chin, *Senior VP*
EMP: 160 EST: 2014
SQ FT: 80,000

SALES (est): 144.3MM
SALES (corp-wide): 904MM **Privately Held**
WEB: www.good.com
SIC: 7371 7382 Computer software development; custom computer programming services; protective devices, security
PA: Blackberry Limited
2200 University Ave E
Waterloo ON N2K 0
519 888-7465

(P-14840)
GOOGLE LLC (HQ)
1600 Amphitheatre Pkwy, Mountain View
(94043-1351)
P.O. Box 2050 (94042-2050)
PHONE..............................650 253-0000
Thomas Kurian, *CEO*
Laura Driussi, *Partner*
Obadiah Greenberg, *Partner*
Francisco Irao, *Partner*
Scott Beaumont, *President*
▲ EMP: 250 EST: 1998
SQ FT: 4,800,000
SALES (est): 35.2B
SALES (corp-wide): 136.8B **Publicly Held**
WEB: www.google.com
SIC: 7371 7375 Computer software development & applications; data base information retrieval
PA: Alphabet Inc.
1600 Amphitheatre Pkwy
Mountain View CA 94043
650 253-0000

(P-14841)
GRACENOTE INC (DH)
2000 Powell St Ste 1500, Emeryville
(94608-1820)
PHONE..............................510 428-7200
Stephen White, *President*
Eric Allen, *Senior VP*
Tal Ball, *Senior VP*
Desmond Cussen, *Senior VP*
Brian Hamilton, *Senior VP*
EMP: 99
SALES (est): 68.9MM
SALES (corp-wide): 6.5B **Privately Held**
WEB: www.gracenote.com
SIC: 7371 Software programming applications

(P-14842)
GRAND INTELLIGENCE LLC
2880 Zanker Rd Ste 203, San Jose
(95134-2122)
PHONE..............................408 954-7368
Marylyn Lin, *Mng Member*
Dongyan Wang, *COO*
EMP: 100 EST: 2012
SALES: 10MM **Privately Held**
SIC: 7371 Computer software development

(P-14843)
GRAPPA SOFTWARE INC
1470 Civic Ct Ste 309, Concord
(94520-5230)
PHONE..............................925 818-4760
Mark Fedin, *CEO*
Elena Florova, *Vice Pres*
EMP: 52
SALES: 11.5MM **Privately Held**
SIC: 7371 Computer software development

(P-14844)
GREE INTERNATIONAL INC
275 Battery St Ste 1700, San Francisco
(94111-3369)
PHONE..............................415 409-5200
Naoki Aoyagi, *CEO*
Neil Haldar, *President*
Andrew Sheppard, *COO*
Shanti Bergel, *Senior VP*
Takeshi Nakano, *Director*
EMP: 250
SALES (est): 31.4MM **Privately Held**
SIC: 7371 Computer software development & applications; computer software systems analysis & design, custom; software programming applications

PA: Gree, Inc.
6-10-1, Roppongi
Minato-Ku TKY 106-0
-

(P-14845)
GREE INTERNATIONAL ENTRMT INC
185 Berry St Ste 590, San Francisco
(94107-9105)
PHONE..............................415 409-5200
Andrew Sheppard, *CEO*
Ryotaro Shima, *COO*
Shanti Bergel, *Senior VP*
Yoshikazu Tanaka, *Director*
EMP: 220 EST: 2016
SALES (est): 3.3MM **Privately Held**
SIC: 7371 Computer software development & applications
PA: Gree, Inc.
6-10-1, Roppongi
Minato-Ku TKY 106-0
-

(P-14846)
GROUP AVANTICA INC
Also Called: Avantica Technologies
2680 Bayshore Pkwy # 416, Mountain View
(94043-1022)
PHONE..............................650 248-9678
Mario Chaves, *CEO*
Luis C Chaves, *President*
EMP: 260
SALES (est): 17.3MM **Privately Held**
WEB: www.avantica.net
SIC: 7371 Computer software development

(P-14847)
GT NEXUS INC (HQ)
1111 Broadway 5f, Oakland (94607-4139)
PHONE..............................510 808-2222
Sean Feeney, *CEO*
Guy Rey-Herme, *COO*
Andreas Stinnes, *Exec VP*
John Urban, *Exec VP*
Vynessa Alexander, *Vice Pres*
EMP: 74
SALES (est): 18.1MM
SALES (corp-wide): 3.1B **Privately Held**
WEB: www.gtnexus.com
SIC: 7371 Computer software development
PA: Infor, Inc.
641 Ave Of The Americas # 4
New York NY 10011
646 336-1700

(P-14848)
GTXCEL INC
2855 Telg Ave Ste 600, Berkeley (94705)
PHONE..............................800 609-8994
Becky Zehr, *Vice Pres*
Peter Stilson, *President*
EMP: 80
SQ FT: 10,000
SALES: 10MM **Privately Held**
SIC: 7371 Computer software development

(P-14849)
GUIDEBOOK INC (PA)
340 Bryant St Ste 400, San Francisco
(94107-1442)
PHONE..............................650 319-7233
Jeff Lewis, *CEO*
Vadim Dolt, *President*
Chris Hart, *CFO*
Pete Banks, *Vice Pres*
Wayne Morris, *Vice Pres*
EMP: 90
SQ FT: 6,500
SALES: 12MM **Privately Held**
SIC: 7371 Computer software development

(P-14850)
H & R ACCOUNTS INC
Also Called: Avadyne Health
3131 Cmino Del Rio N Ste, San Diego
(92108)
PHONE..............................619 819-8844
Linda Hevern, *Branch Mgr*
Tom Conway, *CFO*
EMP: 65

SALES (corp-wide): 29.6MM **Privately Held**
SIC: 7371 Computer software development
PA: H & R Accounts, Inc.
5320 22nd Ave
Moline IL 61265
309 736-2255

(P-14851)
HEAT WAVES LLC
Also Called: Heat Software
4087 Rivoli, Newport Beach (92660-9026)
PHONE..............................323 753-8441
Andrews Mitchell,
EMP: 135 EST: 2018
SALES (est): 2.1MM **Privately Held**
SIC: 7371 Computer software development & applications

(P-14852)
HEWLETT PACKARD
3000 Hanover St, Palo Alto (94304-1185)
PHONE..............................650 857-1501
EMP: 1835
SALES (est): 98.4MM **Privately Held**
SIC: 7371

(P-14853)
HGGC LLC (PA)
1950 University Ave # 350, East Palo Alto
(94303-2250)
PHONE..............................650 321-4910
Rich Lawson, *Mng Member*
Les Brown, *CFO*
Lee Story, *Senior VP*
Neil White, *Senior VP*
Bill Conrad, *Vice Pres*
EMP: 253
SALES (est): 132.9MM **Privately Held**
SIC: 7371 Computer software development & applications

(P-14854)
HIGH FIDELITY INC
185 Clara St Ste 100, San Francisco
(94107-4505)
PHONE..............................415 862-4434
Philip Rosedale, *CEO*
Tom Schofield, *COO*
Irena Heiberger, *CFO*
Ashleigh Harris, *Officer*
Brad Hefta-Gaub, *Officer*
EMP: 70 EST: 2013
SALES (est): 585.7K **Privately Held**
SIC: 7371 Computer software development & applications

(P-14855)
HONEYBOOK INC
539 Bryant St Ste 200, San Francisco
(94107-1269)
PHONE..............................770 403-9234
Oz Eliyahu, *CEO*
John Kramer, *COO*
Maya Wolkoon, *General Mgr*
Elad Gelman, *Software Engr*
Preet Kaur, *Accountant*
EMP: 55
SALES: 1MM **Privately Held**
SIC: 7371 Computer software development

(P-14856)
HOUZZ INC (PA)
285 Hamilton Ave Fl 4, Palo Alto
(94301-2540)
PHONE..............................650 326-3000
ADI Tatarko, *CEO*
Alon Cohen, *President*
Richard Wong, *CFO*
David Fisch, *Vice Pres*
Liza Hausman, *Vice Pres*
▼ EMP: 99
SALES (est): 50.8MM **Privately Held**
SIC: 7371 Computer software development

(P-14857)
HTEC GROUP INC (PA)
535 Mission St Fl 14, San Francisco
(94105-3253)
PHONE..............................650 949-4880
Aleksandar Cabrilo, *President*
Jamie Fox, *Vice Pres*
Jeffrey Landres, *Vice Pres*

Renee Logoluso, *Vice Pres*
Gail Rackliffe, *Vice Pres*
EMP: 99
SALES: 5MM **Privately Held**
SIC: 7371 Custom computer programming services

(P-14858)
HUMANITYCOM INC
50 Osgood Pl Ste 330, San Francisco (94133-4644)
PHONE...............................415 230-0108
Chris Amani, *CEO*
David Charron, *President*
Jack Robinson, *Vice Pres*
Andrej Luneski, *VP Engrg*
Dautovic Kristina, *Engineer*
EMP: 50
SALES: 2.5MM **Privately Held**
SIC: 7371 Computer software development

(P-14859)
HVANTAGE TECHNOLOGIES INC
6700 Fllbrook Ave Ste 222, West Hills (91307)
PHONE...............................818 661-6301
Krishna Baderia, *CEO*
EMP: 80
SALES (est): 1.3MM **Privately Held**
SIC: 7371 8748 7372 7373 Computer software development & applications; systems engineering consultant, ex. computer or professional; application computer software; business oriented computer software; systems engineering, computer related

(P-14860)
HYLAND SOFTWARE INC
2355 Main St Ste 100, Irvine (92614-4290)
PHONE...............................949 242-3100
Lloyd Warman, *Principal*
EMP: 60
SALES (corp-wide): 461.8MM **Privately Held**
WEB: www.onbase.com
SIC: 7371 Computer software development
HQ: Hyland Software, Inc.
28500 Clemens Rd
Westlake OH 44145

(P-14861)
HYPERGRID INC (PA)
201 San Antonio Cir # 245, Mountain View (94040-1275)
PHONE...............................650 316-5524
Manoj Nair, *CEO*
Bob Taccini, *CFO*
David Weier, *Senior VP*
Said Syed, *Vice Pres*
John Kim, *Principal*
EMP: 64
SALES (est): 20MM **Privately Held**
SIC: 7371 5045 Computer software development; computers, peripherals & software

(P-14862)
HYUNDAI ATVER TLMTICS AMER INC
10550 Talbert Ave Fl 2, Fountain Valley (92708-6032)
PHONE...............................949 381-6000
SOO Dong Park, *CEO*
Ui Chul Shi, *CFO*
Dennis Kelly, *Software Dev*
Chau Pham, *Senior Engr*
Phr-CA S Kim, *Human Res Mgr*
EMP: 56
SALES (est): 7.7MM **Privately Held**
SIC: 7371 Computer software systems analysis & design, custom; computer software development & applications; software programming applications

(P-14863)
IBASET FEDERAL SERVICES LLC (PA)
27442 Portola Pkwy # 300, Foothill Ranch (92610-2823)
PHONE...............................949 598-5200
Ladeira Poonian, *Chairman*
Vic Sial, *President*

Naveen Poonian, *COO*
Scott Baril, *Vice Pres*
Louis Columbus, *Vice Pres*
EMP: 75
SQ FT: 30,000
SALES (est): 43.4MM **Privately Held**
SIC: 7371 Computer software development

(P-14864)
IC COMPLIANCE LLC (PA)
Also Called: Talentwave
1065 E Hillsdale Blvd # 300, Foster City (94404-1613)
PHONE...............................650 378-4150
Teresa Creech, *CEO*
Jim Hanrahan, *CFO*
Jennifer Spicher, *Exec VP*
Fred Fuentes, *Principal*
Brian Benitez, *Program Mgr*
EMP: 2500
SQ FT: 5,100
SALES (est): 232.5MM **Privately Held**
WEB: www.gotoicon.com
SIC: 7371 8721 Computer software development & applications; payroll accounting service

(P-14865)
ICE DATA SERVICES INC
CMS Bondedge
2901 28th St Ste 300, Santa Monica (90405-2972)
PHONE...............................310 664-2500
Andrew Hausman, *Manager*
Kundu Gangadharan, *Manager*
EMP: 75
SALES (corp-wide): 4.9B **Publicly Held**
WEB: www.interactivedata.com
SIC: 7371 7372 Computer software development; prepackaged software
HQ: Ice Data Services, Inc.
32 Crosby Dr Ste 100
Bedford MA 01730

(P-14866)
ILLUMIO INC
920 De Guigne Dr, Sunnyvale (94085-3900)
PHONE...............................669 800-5000
Andrew Rubin, *CEO*
Anup Singh, *CFO*
Bobby Guhasarkar, *Chief Mktg Ofcr*
Jim Yares, *Senior VP*
Emily Couey, *Vice Pres*
EMP: 140 **EST:** 2012
SALES (est): 8MM **Privately Held**
SIC: 7371 Computer software systems analysis & design, custom

(P-14867)
IMPERVA INC (HQ)
3400 Bridge Pkwy Ste 200, Redwood City (94065-1195)
PHONE...............................650 345-9000
Christopher S Hylen, *President*
Tina Shaw, *Partner*
Jim Dildine, *CFO*
Mike Burns, *Treasurer*
Tram PHI, *Senior VP*
EMP: 148
SQ FT: 82,000
SALES: 321.7MM
SALES (corp-wide): 32.8MM **Privately Held**
WEB: www.imperva.com
SIC: 7371 Computer software development

(P-14868)
INDUS CORPORATION
1275 Columbus Ave, San Francisco (94133-1301)
PHONE...............................415 202-1830
EMP: 60
SALES (corp-wide): 2.5B **Publicly Held**
SIC: 7371 7372 7373 7379
HQ: Indus Corporation
1515 Wilson Blvd Ste 1100
Arlington VA 22209
703 506-6700

(P-14869)
INFLUXDATA INC
799 Market St Ste 400, San Francisco (94103-2001)
PHONE...............................415 295-1901
Jim Walsh, *Senior VP*
Will Paulus, *VP Sales*
EMP: 105
SALES (est): 145.4K **Privately Held**
SIC: 7371 Computer software development

(P-14870)
INITEK SOFT SOLUTIONS LLC
43674 Ellsworth St, Fremont (94539-5858)
PHONE...............................209 309-0263
Christopher Wood, *CEO*
EMP: 66
SALES: 8MM **Privately Held**
SIC: 7371 Computer software development & applications

(P-14871)
INNOPATH SOFTWARE INC (PA)
333 W El Camino Real # 290, Sunnyvale (94087-8128)
P.O. Box 2454, Cupertino (95015-2454)
PHONE...............................408 962-9200
John Fazio, *President*
Naresh Bansal, *Vice Pres*
Adrian Chan, *Vice Pres*
Mark Fazio, *Vice Pres*
Eric King, *Vice Pres*
EMP: 100
SALES (est): 17MM **Privately Held**
WEB: www.innopath.com
SIC: 7371 Computer software development

(P-14872)
INNOVASYSTEMS INTL LLC
850 Beech St Unit 1006, San Diego (92101-2895)
PHONE...............................619 955-5890
Noah Dicenso, *Sr Software Eng*
William Antilla, *Software Engr*
Tanya Mestechkina, *Software Engr*
Tim Burns, *Business Anlyst*
Monique Perry, *Project Mgr*
EMP: 79
SALES (corp-wide): 56.6MM **Privately Held**
SIC: 7371 Custom computer programming services
PA: Innovasystems International Llc
2385 Northside Dr Ste 300
San Diego CA 92108
619 756-6500

(P-14873)
INNOVASYSTEMS INTL LLC (PA)
2385 Northside Dr Ste 300, San Diego (92108-2716)
PHONE...............................619 756-6500
Lynn Hutton, *Mng Member*
Mary Gilmore, *Vice Pres*
Anthony Campbell, *Sr Software Eng*
James Kilty, *CTO*
Ian Chase, *Info Tech Mgr*
EMP: 99
SALES (est): 56.6MM **Privately Held**
WEB: www.innovasi.com
SIC: 7371 7373 7379 7376 Computer software systems analysis & design, custom; computer integrated systems design; computer related maintenance services; computer facilities management

(P-14874)
INSPIRA INC
4125 Blackford Ave # 255, San Jose (95117-1711)
PHONE...............................408 247-9500
Ravindra Gudapati, *President*
EMP: 60
SQ FT: 2,908
SALES: 3MM **Privately Held**
SIC: 7371 Software programming applications

(P-14875)
INSTABUG INC
855 El Camino Real, Palo Alto (94301-2305)
PHONE...............................650 422-9555
Moataz Soliman, *CTO*

EMP: 65
SALES (est): 949K **Privately Held**
SIC: 7371 Computer software development & applications

(P-14876)
INSTANT SYSTEMS INC
Also Called: Instantsys
447 King Ave, Fremont (94536-1516)
PHONE...............................510 657-8100
Vipin K Chawla, *President*
Uzay Takaoglu, *Vice Pres*
Navnit Saurabh, *Marketing Staff*
Mamta Chawla, *Director*
▲ **EMP:** 90
SALES (est): 3.8MM **Privately Held**
WEB: www.instantsys.com
SIC: 7371 7372 Custom computer programming services; computer software development & applications; business oriented computer software

(P-14877)
INSTART LOGIC INC (PA)
Also Called: Instart Labs
450 Lambert Ave, Palo Alto (94306-2219)
PHONE...............................888 418-5044
Sumit Dhawan, *CEO*
Mark Templeton, *Ch of Bd*
Manav Ratan Mital, *CEO*
Jony Hartono, *CFO*
Peter Blum, *Vice Pres*
EMP: 95
SALES (est): 27.4MM **Privately Held**
SIC: 7371 Computer software development; computer software development & applications

(P-14878)
INSTILL CORPORATION
777 Mariners Island Blvd # 400, San Mateo (94404-5008)
PHONE...............................650 645-2600
Robert Bonavito, *CEO*
Michael Devries, *President*
Michael R Peckham, *CFO*
Shermann Min, *Officer*
William Yaglou, *Vice Pres*
EMP: 115
SQ FT: 28,427
SALES (est): 7.4MM **Privately Held**
WEB: www.instill.com
SIC: 7371 Computer software development

(P-14879)
INTAPP INC (DH)
200 Portage Ave, Palo Alto (94306-2242)
PHONE...............................650 852-0400
John Hall, *CEO*
Stuart Douglass, *President*
Daniel Harsell, *President*
Kelvyn Stirk, *President*
Dan Tacone, *President*
EMP: 200
SALES: 100MM
SALES (corp-wide): 107.4MM **Privately Held**
WEB: www.intapp.com
SIC: 7371 7372 Computer software development & applications; business oriented computer software

(P-14880)
INTELLISWIFT SOFTWARE INC (PA)
Also Called: Magagnini
39600 Balentine Dr # 200, Newark (94560-5304)
PHONE...............................510 490-9240
Parag Patel, *CEO*
Keyur Karnik, *Vice Pres*
Bhaskar RAO, *Vice Pres*
Shannon Fox, *Executive*
Bob Patel, *Principal*
EMP: 225
SQ FT: 5,200
SALES (est): 67.7MM **Privately Held**
WEB: www.intelliswift.com
SIC: 7371 Custom computer programming services

(P-14881)
INTELLISYNC CORPORATION (HQ)
313 Fairchild Dr, Mountain View (94043-2215)
PHONE..............650 625-2185
Woodson Hobbs, *President*
Clyde Foster, *COO*
David Eichler, *CFO*
Robert Gerber, *Chief Mktg Ofcr*
Blair Hankins, *Technology*
EMP: 55
SQ FT: 33,821
SALES (est): 22MM
SALES (corp-wide): 25.8B **Privately Held**
SIC: 7371 7372 Computer software development; prepackaged software
PA: Nokia Oyj
Karakaari 7
Espoo 02610
104 488-000

(P-14882)
INTERANA INC
100 Redwood Shores Pkwy, Redwood City (94065-1155)
PHONE..............650 569-1122
Greg Smirin, *CEO*
Mark Larosa, *Vice Pres*
Mark Rubin, *Vice Pres*
Denise Mills, *Executive Asst*
Viknes Balasubramanee, *Software Engr*
EMP: 70
SQ FT: 18,000
SALES (est): 3.5MM **Privately Held**
SIC: 7371 Computer software development & applications

(P-14883)
INTERCOM INC
55 2nd St Ste 400, San Francisco (94105-4560)
PHONE..............831 920-7088
Eoghan McCabe, *CEO*
Des Traynor, *Officer*
Ciaran Lee, *CTO*
Christine Sotelo-Dag, *Marketing Staff*
Sara Yin, *Marketing Staff*
EMP: 300
SALES (est): 35.6MM **Privately Held**
SIC: 7371 Computer software development

(P-14884)
INTERNATIONAL BUS MCHS CORP
Also Called: IBM
555 Bailey Ave, San Jose (95141-1003)
PHONE..............408 463-2000
Lou Gerstner, *Manager*
Kevin Foster, *Partner*
Peter Whitney, *Executive*
Henry Chiu, *Software Dev*
Steve Selvaggio, *Software Engr*
EMP: 1500
SALES (corp-wide): 79.5B **Publicly Held**
WEB: www.ibm.com
SIC: 7371 7372 5961 Computer software development; prepackaged software; catalog & mail-order houses
PA: International Business Machines Corporation
1 New Orchard Rd Ste 1 # 1
Armonk NY 10504
914 499-1900

(P-14885)
INTERNET BLUEPRINT INC
Also Called: Bidmail
1177 Warner Ave, Tustin (92780-6458)
PHONE..............714 673-6000
Daniel Stapleton, *President*
Peter Amaraphornkul, *Info Tech Dir*
EMP: 50
SALES (est): 4.9MM **Privately Held**
SIC: 7371 Computer software development & applications

(P-14886)
INTERTRUST TECHNOLOGIES CORP (HQ)
920 Stewart Dr, Sunnyvale (94085-3921)
PHONE..............408 616-1600
Talal G Shamoon, *CEO*
David P Maher, *Exec VP*

Gilles Boccon Gibod, *Senior VP*
Jeff McDow, *Senior VP*
Bill Rainey, *Senior VP*
EMP: 161
SQ FT: 58,000
SALES (est): 23.7MM
SALES (corp-wide): 6.6MM **Privately Held**
SIC: 7371 Computer software development; computer software development & applications
PA: Fidelio Acquisition Company, Llc
550 Madison Ave Fl 33
New York NY 10022
212 833-8000

(P-14887)
IPTOR SUPPLY CHAIN SYSTEMS USA (DH)
Also Called: I B S
915 Highland Pointe Dr # 250, Roseville (95678-5421)
PHONE..............916 542-2820
Doug Braun, *CEO*
Christian Paulsson, *COO*
Fredrik Sandelin, *CFO*
David Rode, *Vice Pres*
Hiten Varia, *Vice Pres*
EMP: 153
SQ FT: 55,000
SALES (est): 25.9MM
SALES (corp-wide): 54.3MM **Privately Held**
WEB: www.ibsus.com
SIC: 7371 5045 Computer software development; computer software
HQ: Iptor Supply Chain Systems Ab
Hemvarnsgatan 11
Solna 171 5
862 723-00

(P-14888)
IRISE (PA)
2381 Rosecrans Ave # 100, El Segundo (90245-7903)
PHONE..............800 556-0399
Emmet B Keeffe III, *CEO*
Maurice Martin, *President*
Lionel Etrillard, *CFO*
Mitch Bishop, *Chief Mktg Ofcr*
Stephen Brickley, *Exec VP*
▲ EMP: 94
SALES (est): 38.5MM **Privately Held**
SIC: 7371 Computer software development

(P-14889)
IRONCLAD INC
325 5th St, San Francisco (94107-1040)
PHONE..............818 404-2777
Jason Boehmig, *CEO*
Wyeth Goodenough, *Ch Credit Ofcr*
Joyce Solano, *Chief Mktg Ofcr*
EMP: 59
SALES (est): 65.9K **Privately Held**
SIC: 7371 Computer software development & applications

(P-14890)
ISAAC FAIR CORPORATION
Also Called: Mindwave Software
3661 Valley Centre Dr, San Diego (92130-3321)
PHONE..............858 369-8000
Steve Gutschow, *Principal*
Dawn Davis, *Info Tech Mgr*
Robert Cunningham, *Opers Staff*
Joanna Rees,
Carol Byrne, *Director*
EMP: 88
SALES (corp-wide): 1B **Publicly Held**
WEB: www.fairisaac.com
SIC: 7371 Computer software development
PA: Fair Isaac Corporation
181 Metro Dr Ste 700
San Jose CA 95110
408 535-1500

(P-14891)
ISCS INC
100 Great Oaks Blvd # 100, San Jose (95119-1462)
PHONE..............408 362-3000
Andy J Scurto, *President*
Myron Meier, *President*

Andy Scurto, *President*
Tim Shelton, *CFO*
Doug Moore, *CTO*
EMP: 201
SQ FT: 11,000
SALES (est): 24.9MM
SALES (corp-wide): 719.5MM **Publicly Held**
SIC: 7371 Software programming applications
PA: Guidewire Software, Inc.
2850 S Del St Ste 400
San Mateo CA 94403
650 357-9100

(P-14892)
ISHERIFF INC
555 Twin Dolphin Dr # 135, Redwood City (94065-2139)
PHONE..............650 412-4300
Paul Lipman, *CEO*
Jon Botter, *President*
Eric Jenny, *CFO*
Marcus Smith, *CFO*
James Socas, *Chairman*
EMP: 235
SALES (est): 21.6MM **Privately Held**
SIC: 7371 Software programming applications
PA: Mimecast Uk Limited
Floor 4 1 Finsbury Avenue
London

(P-14893)
JIANGSU JUWANG INFO TECH CO (PA)
195 Recino St, Fremont (94539-3835)
PHONE..............510 967-3729
Song Han, *Owner*
EMP: 70
SALES (est): 2.2MM **Privately Held**
SIC: 7371 Computer software development & applications

(P-14894)
JIFF INC (HQ)
150 Spear St Ste 400, San Francisco (94105-1535)
PHONE..............415 829-1400
Mike Leonard, *Exec VP*
Matt Kirchstein, *Sr Software Eng*
Lucas Mercado, *Engineer*
Masooma Badar, *Controller*
Mackenzie Kassis, *Marketing Staff*
EMP: 400 EST: 2011
SALES (est): 6.4MM **Publicly Held**
SIC: 7371 Computer software development

(P-14895)
JUMPSHOT INC
333 Bryant St Ste 240, San Francisco (94107-1443)
PHONE..............415 212-9250
Deren Baker, *CEO*
Marcus Blatch, *Vice Pres*
Hong Tsui, *Vice Pres*
Michael Perlman, *Risk Mgmt Dir*
Chris Wasik, *Controller*
EMP: 85
SALES (est): 188.1K **Privately Held**
SIC: 7371 Computer software development & applications

(P-14896)
JUMPSTART GAMES INC
500 W 190th St Ste 300, Gardena (90248-4269)
PHONE..............424 645-4311
David Lord, *CEO*
James Czulewicz, *Admin Sec*
EMP: 59
SALES: 12.5MM **Privately Held**
SIC: 7371 5734 Computer software systems analysis & design, custom; computer software development; software, computer games
HQ: Netdragon Websoft Holdings Limited
Rm 2201-5&11 20/F Harbour Ctr
Wan Chai HK

(P-14897)
KABAM INC (HQ)
575 Market St Ste 2450, San Francisco (94105-2896)
PHONE..............604 256-0054
Seungwon Lee, *President*
Nick Earl, *President*
Jangwon Seo, *CFO*
Paxton R Cooper, *Senior VP*
Doug Inamine, *Senior VP*
EMP: 92 EST: 2006
SALES (est): 112.7MM
SALES (corp-wide): 1B **Privately Held**
SIC: 7371 Computer software development & applications; computer software development
PA: Netmarble Corporation
20/F G-Valley Biz Plaza
Seoul 08379
821 588-5180

(P-14898)
KALLIDUS INC
Also Called: Skava
425 Market St Ste 2200, San Francisco (94105-2434)
PHONE..............877 554-2176
Arish Ali, *President*
Khurram Khan, *Officer*
Phil Spade, *Assoc VP*
Gretchen Jones, *Executive Asst*
Loganayaki Kuppusamy, *Web Dvlpr*
EMP: 100
SALES (est): 4.2MM
SALES (corp-wide): 10.3B **Privately Held**
WEB: www.skava.com
SIC: 7371 Computer software development
PA: Infosys Limited
Plot No. 44 & 97a, Electronics City,
Bengaluru KA 56010
802 852-0261

(P-14899)
KAZEON SYSTEMS INC
2841 Mission College Blvd, Santa Clara (95054-1838)
PHONE..............650 641-8100
Fax: 650 641-8195
EMP: 80
SQ FT: 24,000
SALES (est): 3.9MM **Privately Held**
WEB: www.kazeon.com
SIC: 7371 7379

(P-14900)
KEEP TRUCKIN INC (PA)
55 Hawthorne St Ste 400, San Francisco (94105-3910)
PHONE..............855 434-3564
Obaid Khan, *President*
Shoaib Makani, *CEO*
Patrick Gibbs, *Opers Staff*
Rahul Chhabria, *Marketing Staff*
Rachel Eastwood, *Marketing Staff*
EMP: 50
SALES: 80MM **Privately Held**
SIC: 7371 Computer software development & applications

(P-14901)
KNOWLEDGE HOLDINGS INC (PA)
Also Called: Knowledge Adventure
2377 Crenshaw Blvd # 302, Torrance (90501-3331)
PHONE..............310 533-3400
David Lord, *President*
Thomas Swalla, *President*
Scott Brogi, *CFO*
William J Kennedy, *Vice Pres*
EMP: 70
SQ FT: 19,000
SALES (est): 5.2MM **Privately Held**
SIC: 7371 Computer software development

(P-14902)
KOFAX INC (PA)
15211 Laguna Canyon Rd, Irvine (92618-3146)
PHONE..............949 783-1000
Reynolds C Bish, *CEO*
Jamie Arnold, *CFO*
Cort Townsend, *CFO*
Kathleen Delaney, *Chief Mktg Ofcr*

Chris Huff, *Officer*
▼ **EMP:** 500
SQ FT: 100,000
SALES (est): 559.1MM **Privately Held**
SIC: 7371 3577 Computer software development; input/output equipment, computer

(P-14903)
KONG INC
251 Post St Ste 200, San Francisco
(94108-5021)
PHONE.................................415 754-9283
Augusto Marietti, *CEO*
Morgan Davies, *VP Bus Dvlpt*
EMP: 50 **EST:** 2009
SALES (est): 534K **Privately Held**
SIC: 7371 Computer software development & applications

(P-14904)
KRG TECHNOLOGIES INC
Also Called: K R G
25000 Ave Stnford Ste 243, Valencia
(91355)
PHONE.................................661 257-9967
Muthuramalingam Umapathi, *President*
Hemalatha Rajagopala, *Owner*
Balamurugan Subbiah, *Chairman*
Nivethan Niv, *Executive*
Hari Prasath, *Executive*
EMP: 600
SQ FT: 780
SALES: 68.4MM **Privately Held**
WEB: www.krgtech.com
SIC: 7371 Computer software development & applications

(P-14905)
KUGGA INC
1841 Sunnyvale Ave, Walnut Creek
(94597-1811)
PHONE.................................925 639-0721
Yifan Ren, *CEO*
EMP: 60
SALES (est): 891.1K **Privately Held**
SIC: 7371 Computer software development & applications

(P-14906)
KUTIR CORPORATION
3237 Nathan Ct, Fremont (94539-5026)
PHONE.................................510 402-4526
Gerry Ignatius, *President*
Ranjine Ramachandran, *CFO*
Prathiba Kalyan, *Vice Pres*
G L Kluttz, *Vice Pres*
Bhanu Morampudi, *Vice Pres*
EMP: 50
SALES (est): 6MM **Privately Held**
WEB: www.kutirtech.com
SIC: 7371 Computer software development

(P-14907)
LANGUAGE WEAVER INC
Also Called: Sdl
6060 Center Dr Ste 150, Los Angeles
(90045-8808)
PHONE.................................310 437-7300
Mark Tapling, *CEO*
Daniel Marcu, *COO*
Kevin Knight, *Vice Pres*
Kirti Vashee, *Vice Pres*
Amos Kariuki, *Software Dev*
EMP: 55
SQ FT: 6,000
SALES (est): 7MM **Privately Held**
WEB: www.languageweaver.com
SIC: 7371 Computer software development
PA: Sdl Plc
New Globe House
Maidenhead BERKS SL6 4
-

(P-14908)
LAXMI GROUP INC
Also Called: Importers Software
4699 Old Ironsides Dr # 100, Santa Clara
(95054-1824)
PHONE.................................408 329-7733
Gopal RAO, *President*
Shankar Ram, *Principal*
EMP: 60
SQ FT: 2,900

SALES: 6.4MM **Privately Held**
WEB: www.laxmigroup.com
SIC: 7371 Computer software development; help supply services

(P-14909)
LEANTAAS INC
471 El Cmino Real Ste 230, Santa Clara
(95050)
PHONE.................................650 409-3501
Mohan Giridharadas, *CEO*
Lloyd Martin, *CFO*
Michael Concordia, *Vice Pres*
Kelly Brambila, *Office Admin*
Phoebe Maio, *Software Engr*
EMP: 90
SQ FT: 500
SALES (est): 972K **Privately Held**
SIC: 7371 Computer software development

(P-14910)
LEVER INC
155 5th St 6, San Francisco (94103-2919)
PHONE.................................415 458-2731
Sarah Nahm, *CEO*
Justin Roberts, *Vice Pres*
Kelly Del Curto, *Executive*
Nathaniel Smith, *CTO*
Rachael Stedman, *Engineer*
EMP: 100 **EST:** 2014
SALES: 10MM **Privately Held**
SIC: 7371 Computer software development & applications

(P-14911)
LIGHTBEND INC
625 Market St Ste 1000, San Francisco
(94105-3312)
PHONE.................................877 989-7372
Mark Brewer, *President*
Steve Bean, *CFO*
Martin Odersky, *Chairman*
Kathleen Hayes, *Vice Pres*
Derek Henninger, *Vice Pres*
EMP: 72
SALES (est): 10MM **Privately Held**
SIC: 7371 Computer software development

(P-14912)
LIMINEX INC
Also Called: Goguardian
200 N Supulveda Blvd Ste, Hermosa Beach
(90254)
PHONE.................................424 529-6960
Advait Shinde, *CEO*
EMP: 145 **EST:** 2014
SQ FT: 16,000
SALES: 28MM **Privately Held**
SIC: 7371 7389 Computer software development; computer software development & applications;

(P-14913)
LINDEN RESEARCH INC
Also Called: Linden Lab
945 Battery St, San Francisco
(94111-1305)
PHONE.................................415 243-9000
Ebbe Altberg, *CEO*
Bob Komin, *COO*
Malcolm Dunne, *CFO*
John Zdanowski, *CFO*
Scott Butler, *Officer*
EMP: 330
SALES (est): 50.8MM **Privately Held**
WEB: www.lindenlab.com
SIC: 7371 Computer software development

(P-14914)
LOCATION LABS INC
2100 Powell St Fl 14, Emeryville
(94608-1826)
PHONE.................................510 601-7012
Egor Ioppe, *CEO*
Tasso Roumeliotis, *President*
Joel Grossman, *COO*
Chris Phillips, *Sr Software Eng*
Anthony Fregoso, *QA Dir*
EMP: 72
SALES (est): 3.5MM **Privately Held**
WEB: www.wavemarket.com
SIC: 7371 Computer software development

(P-14915)
**LOCKHEED MARTIN ORINCON
CORP (HQ)**
10325 Meanley Dr, San Diego
(92131-3011)
PHONE.................................858 455-5530
Daniel Alspach, *Ch of Bd*
EMP: 200
SQ FT: 41,000
SALES (est): 49.3MM **Publicly Held**
SIC: 7371 8731 Computer software development & applications; commercial physical research

(P-14916)
LOGILITY INC
4885 Greencraig Ln 200, San Diego
(92123-1664)
PHONE.................................858 565-4238
EMP: 55
SALES (corp-wide): 108.7MM **Publicly Held**
SIC: 7371 7372 Computer software development & applications; prepackaged software
HQ: Logility, Inc.
470 E Paces Ferry Rd Ne
Atlanta GA 30305
800 762-5207

(P-14917)
**LOGIX DEVELOPMENT
CORPORATION**
473 Post St, Camarillo (93010-8553)
PHONE.................................888 505-6449
David K Howington, *CEO*
Pauline Malysko, *President*
Anne Howington, *Vice Pres*
Nikki Mitchell, *Controller*
EMP: 83
SALES (est): 5.2MM **Privately Held**
WEB: www.pop3.com
SIC: 7371 Computer software development

(P-14918)
LOGLOGIC INC
110 Rose Orchard Way, San Jose
(95134-1358)
PHONE.................................408 215-5900
Guy Churchward, *CEO*
Joseph Consul, *CFO*
EMP: 170
SALES (est): 11MM
SALES (corp-wide): 885.6MM **Privately Held**
WEB: www.loglogic.com
SIC: 7371 Computer software development
HQ: Tibco Software Inc.
3307 Hillview Ave
Palo Alto CA 94304
-

(P-14919)
LOOP MEDIA INC
3900 W Alameda Ave # 1200, Burbank
(91505-4317)
PHONE.................................650 704-7409
Jon Niermann, *CEO*
Pete Mackenzie, *President*
Aaron Burcell, *COO*
Justis KAO, *Officer*
Liam McCallum, *Officer*
EMP: 60
SALES (est): 22.5MM **Privately Held**
SIC: 7371 7389 Computer software development & applications;

(P-14920)
LUCID VR INC
4500 Great America Pkwy, Santa Clara
(95054-1283)
PHONE.................................408 391-0506
Han Jin, *CEO*
Adam Rowell, *CTO*
EMP: 79 **EST:** 2015
SALES (est): 323.3K **Privately Held**
SIC: 7371 Computer software development

(P-14921)
LUCIDEUS INC
3260 Hillview Ave, Palo Alto (94304-1220)
PHONE.................................650 843-0988

Saket Modi, *CEO*
EMP: 200 **EST:** 2018
SALES (est): 50.7K **Privately Held**
SIC: 7371 Computer software development & applications

(P-14922)
MACHINE ZONE INC (PA)
Also Called: Epic War
1050 Page Mill Rd, Palo Alto (94304-1019)
PHONE.................................650 320-1678
Kristen Dumont, *CEO*
Tony Koinov, *President*
Eric Brown, *CFO*
Dan Nash, *CFO*
Tory Valenzuela, *Officer*
EMP: 89
SALES (est): 110.1MM **Privately Held**
SIC: 7371 Computer software development

(P-14923)
**MAGMA DESIGN AUTOMATION
INC (HQ)**
1650 Tech Dr Ste 100, San Jose (95110)
PHONE.................................408 565-7500
Rajeev Madhavan, *CEO*
Noriaki Kikuchi, *President*
Peter S Teshima, *CFO*
Saiyed Atiq Raza, *Bd of Directors*
Gregory C Walker, *Senior VP*
▲ **EMP:** 410
SQ FT: 106,854
SALES (est): 34MM
SALES (corp-wide): 3.1B **Publicly Held**
WEB: www.magma-da.com
SIC: 7371 7373 Computer software development; computer integrated systems design
PA: Synopsys, Inc.
690 E Middlefield Rd
Mountain View CA 94043
650 584-5000

(P-14924)
MAGNUS TECH SOLUTIONS INC
5205 Prospect Rd Ste 135, San Jose
(95129-5034)
PHONE.................................408 963-0808
Anurag Pal, *CEO*
Frank Henry, *Business Mgr*
Prabha Kanchan, *Recruiter*
Brad Wilson, *Sales Mgr*
EMP: 100
SALES (est): 4.6MM **Privately Held**
SIC: 7371 Computer software development

(P-14925)
MAINTECH INCORPORATED
2401 N Glassell St, Orange (92865-2705)
P.O. Box 13500 (92857-8500)
PHONE.................................714 921-8000
Tony Donato, *Vice Pres*
William D'Alessio, *Vice Pres*
Eric Duterte, *Network Enginr*
Craig Saffell, *Network Enginr*
Dwayne Paoner, *Network Tech*
EMP: 200
SQ FT: 1,200
SALES (corp-wide): 1.2MM **Privately Held**
SIC: 7371 3577 Computer software systems analysis & design, custom; computer peripheral equipment
HQ: Maintech, Incorporated
14 Commerce Dr Fl 2
Cranford NJ 07016
973 330-3200

(P-14926)
**MALWAREBYTES
CORPORATION**
3979 Freedom Cir Fl 12, Santa Clara
(95054-1256)
PHONE.................................408 852-4336
Marcin Kleczynski, *CEO*
Steve Smith, *Partner*
Rj Singh, *President*
Thomas R Fox, *CFO*
Mark Harris, *CFO*
EMP: 600
SALES (est): 12.8MM **Privately Held**
SIC: 7371 Software programming applications

(P-14927)
MAPR TECHNOLOGIES INC (PA)
Also Called: Mapr Data Technologies
4555 Great America Pkwy # 201, Santa
Clara (95054-1244)
PHONE.....................408 914-2390
John Schroeder, *CEO*
Daniel K Atler, *CFO*
Hayden Noriega, *Vice Pres*
Damien Eastwood, *Admin Sec*
Abhishek Girish, *Sr Software Eng*
EMP: 260
SQ FT: 55,000
SALES (est): 156.4MM **Privately Held**
SIC: 7371 Computer software development

(P-14928)
MARKET SCAN INFO SYSTEMS INC (PA)
815b Camarillo Springs Rd, Camarillo
(93012-9472)
PHONE.....................805 823-4258
Stephen Smythe, *CEO*
Rusty West, *President*
Rustie G West, *CEO*
Carsten Preisz, *Chief Mktg Ofcr*
Vincent Esposito, *Executive*
EMP: 150
SQ FT: 14,000
SALES (est): 20.2MM **Privately Held**
SIC: 7371 8732 Computer software development; market analysis, business & economic research

(P-14929)
MARKETO INC (DH)
901 Mariners Island Blvd # 200, San Mateo
(94404-1573)
PHONE.....................650 376-2300
Steve Lucas, *CEO*
Kate Fitzgerald, *President*
Yasutaka Fukuda, *President*
Brady Holcomb, *President*
Mika Yamamoto, *President*
EMP: 148
SQ FT: 102,670
SALES: 209.8MM
SALES (corp-wide): 9B **Publicly Held**
SIC: 7371 7372 Computer software development; computer software writing services; prepackaged software
HQ: Milestone Holdco, Inc.
901 Mariners Island Blvd
San Mateo CA 94404
650 376-2300

(P-14930)
MARKLOGIC CORPORATION (PA)
999 Skyway Rd Ste 200, San Carlos
(94070-2722)
PHONE.....................650 655-2300
Gary Bloom, *President*
Peter Norman, *CFO*
David Ponzini, *CFO*
Matt Biear, *Vice Pres*
Scott Cameron, *Vice Pres*
EMP: 130 **EST:** 2004
SQ FT: 40,000
SALES (est): 98.2MM **Privately Held**
WEB: www.cerisent.com
SIC: 7371 Computer software development

(P-14931)
MARKMONITOR HOLDINGS INC
425 Market St Ste 500, San Francisco
(94105-2464)
PHONE.....................415 278-8400
Irfan Salim, *President*
Tom Ryden, *Vice Pres*
EMP: 427
SALES (est): 19.8MM **Privately Held**
WEB: www.ftftech.com
SIC: 7371 Computer software development

(P-14932)
MAXPLORE TECHNOLOGIES INC
4450 Rosewood Dr Ste 200, Pleasanton
(94588-3061)
PHONE.....................925 621-1400
Sam Mukherjee, *Principal*

EMP: 100
SALES (est): 1.7MM **Privately Held**
SIC: 7371 Computer software development

(P-14933)
MEGA PROFESSIONAL INTL
Also Called: Mpic
995 Montague Expy Ste 121, Milpitas
(95035-6827)
PHONE.....................408 946-1500
Monali Mehta, *CEO*
Bob Mehta, *President*
EMP: 52 **EST:** 1994
SALES (est): 3.1MM **Privately Held**
WEB: www.mpic.com
SIC: 7371 Computer software systems analysis & design, custom

(P-14934)
MENLO SECURITY INC (PA)
2300 Geng Rd Ste 200, Palo Alto
(94303-3354)
PHONE.....................650 614-1705
Amir Ben-Efraim, *CEO*
Todd Vender, *President*
Young-SAE Song, *Chief Mktg Ofcr*
Schultz Doug, *Vice Pres*
Douglas Schultz, *Vice Pres*
EMP: 56
SALES (est): 12.9MM **Privately Held**
SIC: 7371 7382 Computer software development; security systems services

(P-14935)
METASWITCH NETWORKS
1751 Harbor Bay Pkwy # 125, Alameda
(94502-3034)
PHONE.....................415 513-1500
John Lazar, *CEO*
Thomas L Cronan III, *CFO*
Graeme Macarthur, *Exec VP*
Chris Todd, *Exec VP*
Aaron Tazza, *Vice Pres*
EMP: 50
SALES (est): 9MM
SALES (corp-wide): 355.8K **Privately Held**
SIC: 7371 Computer software development
HQ: Metaswitch Limited
100 Church Street
Enfield MIDDX EN2 6
208 366-1177

(P-14936)
METRON-ATHENE INC (PA)
23046 Avnida De La Crlota Carlota, Laguna
Hills (92653)
PHONE.....................949 588-5757
Paul Malton, *President*
David Kitley, *CFO*
John Howorth, *Senior VP*
Sarah Roper, *Software Engr*
Paul Shimell, *Director*
EMP: 75
SQ FT: 25,000
SALES (est): 4.2MM **Privately Held**
WEB: www.metron-athene.com
SIC: 7371 Computer software development

(P-14937)
MINDSOURCE INC
555 Clyde Ave Ste 100, Mountain View
(94043-2269)
PHONE.....................650 314-6400
David Clark, *President*
Gabriel Meza, *CFO*
Mark Loftus, *Vice Pres*
Puneet Sehgal, *Business Dir*
Dan Miller, *General Mgr*
EMP: 55
SQ FT: 3,200
SALES (est): 7MM **Privately Held**
WEB: www.mindsource.com
SIC: 7371 7372 Computer software development; application computer software

(P-14938)
MINERVA NETWORKS INC (PA)
1600 Technology Dr Fl 8, San Jose
(95110-1382)
PHONE.....................800 806-9594
Mauro Bonomi, *President*
Dr Jean-Georges Fritsch, *COO*

John Doerner, *CFO*
John Campos, *Vice Pres*
Todd Clayton, *Vice Pres*
EMP: 69
SQ FT: 25,600
SALES (est): 19.4MM **Privately Held**
SIC: 7371 Software programming applications

(P-14939)
MIRNAVSEH INC
Also Called: World For US
8436 Florissant Ct, San Diego
(92129-4408)
PHONE.....................858 335-2470
Vitaly Serov, *CEO*
Michael Morozov, *Chief Engr*
EMP: 90
SQ FT: 2,500
SALES (est): 5MM **Privately Held**
SIC: 7371 Computer software development

(P-14940)
MITCHELL INTERNATIONAL INC (HQ)
6220 Greenwich Dr, San Diego
(92122-5913)
P.O. Box 229001 (92192-9001)
PHONE.....................858 368-7000
James Lindner, *Vice Ch Bd*
Jack Farnan, *President*
Alex Sun, *President*
Arthur J Long, *CFO*
Jesse Herrera, *Exec VP*
EMP: 148
SQ FT: 141,000
SALES (est): 1.4B **Publicly Held**
WEB: www.mitchell.com
SIC: 7371 Computer software development

(P-14941)
MIXPANEL INC (PA)
1 Front St Ste 2800, San Francisco
(94111-5385)
PHONE.....................415 688-4001
Suhail M Doshi, *President*
Michelle Denman, *Vice Pres*
Cassie Gamm, *Vice Pres*
Clinton Obrien, *Executive*
Robbie Sparno, *Executive*
EMP: 53
SALES (est): 20.9MM **Privately Held**
SIC: 7371 Computer software systems analysis & design, custom; computer software development & applications

(P-14942)
MOBILITYWARE LLC (PA)
440 Exchange Ste 100, Irvine
(92602-1390)
PHONE.....................949 788-9900
John Libby, *President*
Kathy De Lay, *Vice Pres*
John Heard, *Sr Software Eng*
Ken Mason, *Sr Software Eng*
Douglas Libby, *Software Dev*
EMP: 58
SALES (est): 12.2MM **Privately Held**
SIC: 7371 Computer software development

(P-14943)
MODRINE LIMITED
750 N Diamond Bar Blvd, Diamond Bar
(91765-1023)
PHONE.....................213 269-5466
Fang He, *Sales Mgr*
Lisa Cagnolatti, *Vice Pres*
EMP: 69
SALES (est): 275K **Privately Held**
SIC: 7371 Computer software development & applications

(P-14944)
MOJO NETWORKS INC (PA)
5453 Great America Pkwy, Santa Clara
(95054-3645)
PHONE.....................650 961-1111
Rick Wilmer, *CEO*
Tushar Saxena, *Partner*
Mike Anthofer, *CFO*
Freddy Mangum, *Chief Mktg Ofcr*
Anthony Paladino, *Managing Dir*
EMP: 116

SALES (est): 36.9MM **Privately Held**
WEB: www.airtightnetworks.net
SIC: 7371 Computer software development

(P-14945)
MOOV CORPORATION
Also Called: Moovweb
123 Mission St Ste 1000, San Francisco
(94105-5126)
PHONE.....................877 666-8932
Ajay Kapur, *CEO*
Fady Awada, *Info Tech Mgr*
Tj Eilau, *Marketing Staff*
Paul Dunham, *Director*
EMP: 105
SALES (est): 12.7MM **Privately Held**
SIC: 7371 Computer software development

(P-14946)
MOTIGA INC
100 Rdwood Shres Pkwy 4, Redwood City
(94065)
PHONE.....................425 748-8509
Christopher Chung, *CEO*
Patrick Lambright, *CTO*
EMP: 77 **EST:** 2010
SQ FT: 1,400
SALES (est): 7MM **Privately Held**
SIC: 7371 Computer software development

(P-14947)
MOTION MATH INC
582 Market St Ste 511, San Francisco
(94104-5306)
PHONE.....................415 590-2961
Jacob Klein, *CEO*
Gabriel Adauto, *CTO*
EMP: 120 **EST:** 2010
SALES (est): 3.5MM
SALES (corp-wide): 14MM **Privately Held**
SIC: 7371 Computer software development & applications
PA: Curriculum Associates, Llc
153 Rangeway Rd
North Billerica MA 01862
978 667-8000

(P-14948)
MOVOCASH INC
530 Lytton Ave Fl 2, Palo Alto
(94301-1541)
PHONE.....................650 722-3990
Eric A Solis, *CEO*
EMP: 50
SALES (est): 81.7K **Privately Held**
SIC: 7371 Computer software development

(P-14949)
MOZILLA FOUNDATION (PA)
331 E Evelyn Ave, Mountain View
(94041-1550)
PHONE.....................650 903-0800
Mark Surman, *CEO*
Alan Davidson, *Vice Pres*
Mary Ellen, *Vice Pres*
Shani Higgins, *Vice Pres*
Laura Thomson, *Sr Software Eng*
EMP: 588
SALES (est): 421.2MM **Privately Held**
WEB: www.mozilla.com
SIC: 7371 Computer software development

(P-14950)
MSHIFT INC
39899 Balentine Dr # 235, Newark
(94560-5358)
PHONE.....................408 437-2740
Scott Moeller, *CEO*
Jeff Chen, *Vice Pres*
Alan Finke, *Vice Pres*
Jacqueline Snell, *Vice Pres*
Tien Ha, *Administration*
EMP: 50
SALES (est): 6.8MM **Privately Held**
WEB: www.mobileshift.com
SIC: 7371 Computer software development & applications

(P-14951)
N MODEL INC (PA)
777 Mariners Island Blvd, San Mateo
(94404-5008)
PHONE...................650 610-4600
Jason Blessing, *CEO*
David Barter, *CFO*
Dave Michaud, *Chief Mktg Ofcr*
Mark Anderson, *Senior VP*
Neeraj Gokhale, *Senior VP*
EMP: 142
SQ FT: 35,000
SALES: 154.6MM **Publicly Held**
WEB: www.modeln.com
SIC: 7371 Computer software development; computer software development &
applications

(P-14952)
NANTMOBILE LLC
9920 Jefferson Blvd, Culver City
(90232-3506)
PHONE...................310 883-7888
Patrick Soon-Shiong,
Benjamin Weaver, *Planning*
Matthew Avila, *Manager*
EMP: 200
SALES (est): 3.7MM **Privately Held**
SIC: 7371 Computer software development

(P-14953)
NAVIS HOLDINGS LLC
55 Harrison St Ste 600, Oakland
(94607-3776)
PHONE...................510 267-5000
John Dillon, *CEO*
Anburaja Sangumani, *Sr Software Eng*
Jonathan Shields PHD, *CTO*
Rafay Khawaja, *Engineer*
Almer Mendoza, *Controller*
EMP: 139
SALES (est): 7MM
SALES (corp-wide): 3.7B **Privately Held**
SIC: 7371 Computer software development
HQ: Hiab Usa Inc.
　　12233 Williams Rd
　　Perrysburg OH 43551
　　419 482-6000

(P-14954)
NEONROOTS LLC
8560 W Sunset Blvd # 500, West Hollywood (90069-2311)
PHONE...................310 907-9210
Benjamin C Lee, *CEO*
EMP: 125 EST: 2012
SALES (est): 4.7MM **Privately Held**
SIC: 7371 Computer software development & applications

(P-14955)
NETEASE INFORMATION TECH CORP
2000 Sierra Point Pkwy # 800, Brisbane
(94005-1889)
PHONE...................415 612-7866
Zhuo Huang, *CEO*
EMP: 60 EST: 2014
SALES (est): 4.6MM **Privately Held**
SIC: 7371 Computer software development
& applications

(P-14956)
NETSKOPE INC (PA)
2445 Augustine Dr Fl 3, Santa Clara
(95054-3032)
PHONE...................800 979-6988
Sanjay Beri, *CEO*
Andrew Del Matto, *CFO*
Lebin Cheng, *Vice Pres*
Hicks-Frazer Craig, *Vice Pres*
Bob Gilbert, *Vice Pres*
EMP: 93
SALES (est): 39.2MM **Privately Held**
SIC: 7371 Computer software development

(P-14957)
NETZERO INC (DH)
21301 Burbank Blvd Fl 3, Woodland Hills
(91367-6697)
P.O. Box 5004 (91365-5004)
PHONE...................805 418-2000
Mark R Goldston, *Ch of Bd*

Charles S Hilliard, *CFO*
Gerald Popek, *CTO*
EMP: 250 EST: 1997
SQ FT: 48,000
SALES (est): 29.8MM **Publicly Held**
WEB: www.netzero.net
SIC: 7371 Computer software systems
analysis & design, custom
HQ: United Online, Inc.
　　21255 Burbank Blvd # 400
　　Woodland Hills CA 91367
　　818 287-3000

(P-14958)
NEUINTEL LLC (PA)
Also Called: Price Spider
20 Pacifica Ste 1000, Irvine (92618-7462)
PHONE...................949 625-6117
Parsa Rohani,
Jon Pfortmiller, *President*
Anthony Ferry, *CEO*
Sean Reiter, *VP Mktg*
Tim Marshall,
EMP: 80
SQ FT: 17,000
SALES: 16.5MM **Privately Held**
SIC: 7371 Computer software development

(P-14959)
NEVERSOFT ENTERTAINMENT INC
21255 Burbank Blvd # 600, Woodland Hills
(91367-6610)
PHONE...................818 610-4100
Joel Jewett, *President*
Sandy Jewett, *Data Proc Staff*
EMP: 170
SALES (est): 9.5MM
SALES (corp-wide): 7.5B **Publicly Held**
WEB: www.blizzard.com
SIC: 7371 7372 Computer code authors;
prepackaged software
PA: Activision Blizzard, Inc.
　　3100 Ocean Park Blvd
　　Santa Monica CA 90405
　　310 255-2000

(P-14960)
NEXGENIX INC (PA)
2 Peters Canyon Rd # 200, Irvine
(92606-1798)
PHONE...................714 665-6240
Rick Dutta, *CEO*
Don Ganguly, *Ch of Bd*
Mark Iwanowski, *COO*
Carol Munroe, *Vice Pres*
Ravi Renduchintala, *Vice Pres*
EMP: 258
SQ FT: 14,264
SALES (est): 25.1MM **Privately Held**
SIC: 7371 8748 4813 Computer software
development; systems analysis or design;

(P-14961)
NEXTGEN HEALTHCARE INFO SYSTEM (HQ)
18111 Von Karman Ave, Irvine
(92612-0199)
PHONE...................949 255-2600
John Frantz, *President*
Paul Holt, *CFO*
John Stumpf, *CFO*
John Beck, *Exec VP*
Michael Lovett, *Senior VP*
EMP: 65
SALES: 400MM
SALES (corp-wide): 529.1MM **Publicly Held**
SIC: 7371 5072 Computer software systems analysis & design, custom; hardware
PA: Nextgen Healthcare, Inc.
　　18111 Von Karman Ave # 8
　　Irvine CA 92612
　　949 255-2600

(P-14962)
NISUM TECHNOLOGIES INC
71 Stevenson St Ste 446, San Francisco
(94105-2934)
PHONE...................714 619-7989
EMP: 603

SALES (corp-wide): 6.2MM **Privately Held**
SIC: 7371 Computer software development
PA: Nisum Technologies, Inc.
　　500 S Kraemer Blvd # 301
　　Brea CA
　　714 579-7979

(P-14963)
NISUM TECHNOLOGIES INC
46231 Landing Pkwy, Fremont
(94538-6407)
PHONE...................714 579-7979
EMP: 603
SALES (corp-wide): 6.2MM **Privately Held**
SIC: 7371 Computer software development
PA: Nisum Technologies, Inc.
　　500 S Kraemer Blvd # 301
　　Brea CA
　　714 579-7979

(P-14964)
NITAI PARTNERS INC
1761 Reichert Way, Chula Vista
(91913-4345)
PHONE...................855 879-2847
Aditya Satsangi, *CEO*
Konisha Satsangi, *Principal*
EMP: 80 EST: 2011
SALES (est): 5MM **Privately Held**
SIC: 7371 7373 7372 7374 Computer
software systems analysis & design, custom; systems integration services; business oriented computer software; data
processing & preparation

(P-14965)
NITRO SOFTWARE INC
150 Spear St Ste 1500, San Francisco
(94105-5115)
PHONE...................415 632-4894
Sam Chandler, *President*
Claudia Guerrera, *CEO*
Gina O Reilly, *COO*
Peter Bardwick, *CFO*
Bardwick Peter, *CFO*
▼ EMP: 125
SALES (est): 20.7MM **Privately Held**
WEB: www.nitropdf.com
SIC: 7371 Computer software development
PA: Nitro Software Limited
　　L 4 246 Bourke St
　　Melbourne VIC 3000

(P-14966)
NOODLE ANALYTICS INC
Also Called: Noodle.ai
115 Sansome St Fl 8, San Francisco
(94104-3609)
PHONE...................415 412-2139
Stephen Pratt, *CEO*
Gail Moody-Byrd, *Chief Mktg Ofcr*
Deepinder Dhingra,
Chelsea Hardaway, *Officer*
EMP: 100
SALES: 10MM **Privately Held**
SIC: 7371 Computer software development
& applications

(P-14967)
NORTHROP GRUMMAN SYSTEMS CORP
9326 Spectrum Center Blvd, San Diego
(92123-1443)
PHONE...................858 514-0400
James F Harvey, *General Mgr*
EMP: 260 **Publicly Held**
SIC: 7371 7379 Computer software development; computer related consulting
services
HQ: Northrop Grumman Systems Corporation
　　2980 Fairview Park Dr
　　Falls Church VA 22042
　　703 280-2900

(P-14968)
NORTHSTAR TECHNOLOGY CORP (PA)
32 Mauchly Ste C, Irvine (92618-2336)
PHONE...................949 788-0738

Frances Chiang, *CEO*
Warren Matthews, *COO*
David Wills, *Project Mgr*
Phyllis Chang, *Human Resources*
EMP: 250
SQ FT: 1,500
SALES (est): 21.6MM **Privately Held**
SIC: 7371 Computer software development

(P-14969)
NOVALOGIC INC (PA)
27489 Agoura Rd Ste 300, Agoura Hills
(91301-2419)
PHONE...................818 880-1997
John Garcia, *Ch of Bd*
John Butrovich, *Vice Pres*
Kyle Freeman, *Vice Pres*
David Seeholzer, *Vice Pres*
EMP: 100
SALES (est): 5.5MM **Privately Held**
WEB: www.novalogic.com
SIC: 7371 5734 7372 Computer software
development & applications; software,
business & non-game; prepackaged software

(P-14970)
NPARIO INC
350 Cambridge Ave Ste 330, Palo Alto
(94306-1578)
PHONE...................650 461-9696
Bassel Ojjeh, *CEO*
EMP: 53
SALES (est): 2.5MM **Privately Held**
SIC: 7371 Computer software systems
analysis & design, custom

(P-14971)
NTENT INC
1808 Aston Ave Ste 170, Carlsbad
(92008-7367)
PHONE...................760 930-7600
Patti Stewart, *Manager*
Tony Pecora, *VP Bus Dvlpt*
Jermar Burton, *Manager*
Bill Desmedt, *Consultant*
EMP: 60
SALES (corp-wide): 9.2MM **Privately Held**
WEB: www.concera.com
SIC: 7371 Computer software development
PA: Ntent, Inc.
　　135 W 41st St Frnt 2
　　New York NY
　　212 967-9502

(P-14972)
NTS IT CARE INC
1605 S Main St Ste 125, Milpitas
(95035-6270)
PHONE...................408 480-4083
Jagmeet Singh Virk, *President*
EMP: 180
SALES: 2MM **Privately Held**
SIC: 7371 Computer software development

(P-14973)
NUANCE COMMUNICATIONS INC
1005 Hamilton Ct, Menlo Park
(94025-1422)
PHONE...................650 847-0000
Doug Neilsson, *Principal*
Mark Erwich, *Executive*
EMP: 150 **Publicly Held**
WEB: www.nuance.com
SIC: 7371 Computer software development
PA: Nuance Communications, Inc.
　　1 Wayside Rd
　　Burlington MA 01803

(P-14974)
NUNA INCORPORATED
Also Called: Nuna Health
370 Townsend St, San Francisco
(94107-1607)
PHONE...................415 942-5200
Jini Kim, *CEO*
Neil Austin, *Business Dir*
Amanda Worley, *Office Mgr*
Katja Gussmann, *Executive Asst*

Misu Tasnim, *Technical Staff*
EMP: 100
SQ FT: 25,000
SALES: 5MM **Privately Held**
SIC: 7371 Computer software development

(P-14975)
NUTANIX INC (PA)
1740 Tech Dr Ste 150, San Jose (95110)
PHONE..................................408 216-8360
Dheeraj Pandey, *Ch of Bd*
Duston M Williams, *CFO*
Tyler Wall,
David Sangster, *Exec VP*
Sammy Zoghlami, *Senior VP*
EMP: 623
SQ FT: 326,000
SALES: 1.2B **Publicly Held**
SIC: 7371 Computer software development

(P-14976)
OBJECTIVE SYSTEMS INTEGRATORS (HQ)
Also Called: OSI
2365 Iron Point Rd # 170, Folsom (95630-8713)
PHONE..................................916 467-1500
Mounir Ladki, *Principal*
Bob Franzetta, *CFO*
Cheri Simko, *Vice Pres*
William Burdgick, *Sr Software Eng*
Danny Ho, *Software Engr*
EMP: 50
SQ FT: 14,000
SALES (est): 24.9MM
SALES (corp-wide): 5.3MM **Privately Held**
SIC: 7371 Computer software development
PA: Mycom France
6 A 8
Puteaux 92800
149 037-730

(P-14977)
OBLONG INDUSTRIES INC (HQ)
923 E 3rd St Ste 111, Los Angeles (90013-1867)
PHONE..................................213 683-8863
Peter Holst, *CEO*
Gabriel Abejon, *Vice Pres*
David Kung, *Vice Pres*
Darrin Montague, *Vice Pres*
Justin Shrake, *Vice Pres*
EMP: 109
SALES (est): 9.2MM **Publicly Held**
SIC: 7371 Computer software development & applications

(P-14978)
OMNIUPDATE INC
1320 Flynn Rd Ste 100, Camarillo (93012-8745)
PHONE..................................805 484-9400
Lance Merker, *President*
Dennis Esguerra, *Vice Pres*
Tom Nalevanko, *Vice Pres*
Juston Points, *Vice Pres*
Owen Savage, *Vice Pres*
EMP: 60
SQ FT: 6,600
SALES: 10MM **Privately Held**
WEB: www.omniedit.com
SIC: 7371 7372 Computer software development; prepackaged software

(P-14979)
ONEBILL SOFTWARE INC
3080 Olcott St Ste D230, Santa Clara (95054-3271)
PHONE..................................844 462-7638
Jk Chelladurai, *CEO*
Barathi Balakrishnan, *Vice Pres*
Rajesh Jadhev, *Vice Pres*
Bob Maguire, *Vice Pres*
Kathy Mori, *Vice Pres*
EMP: 70
SALES (est): 2.1MM **Privately Held**
SIC: 7371 5734 Computer software development; computer software & accessories

(P-14980)
ONSOLVE LLC
3398 Carmel Mountain Rd # 100, San Diego (92121-1044)
PHONE..................................858 724-1200
Wain Kellum, *Branch Mgr*
EMP: 90
SALES (corp-wide): 1B **Privately Held**
SIC: 7371 Computer software development & applications
HQ: Onsolve, Llc
780 W Granada Blvd
Ormond Beach FL 32174

(P-14981)
OOYALA INC (HQ)
2099 Gateway Pl Ste 600, San Jose (95110-1048)
PHONE..................................650 961-3400
Jonathan Huberman, *CEO*
David Wilson, *CFO*
Jonas Flodh, *Vice Pres*
Jonathan Wilner, *Vice Pres*
Juan Garza, *Executive*
EMP: 97
SALES (est): 76.1MM **Privately Held**
SIC: 7371 Software programming applications
PA: Ooyala Holdings, Inc.
2099 Gateway Pl Ste 600
San Jose CA 95110
650 961-3400

(P-14982)
OPEN TEXT INC (HQ)
Also Called: Hightail
2950 S Delaware St, San Mateo (94403-2199)
PHONE..................................650 645-3000
Louis Goldner, *Partner*
Mark J Barrenechea, *CEO*
Gordon Davies, *Officer*
Simon T Harrison, *Exec VP*
James McGourlay, *Exec VP*
EMP: 109
SALES (est): 392.4MM
SALES (corp-wide): 2.8B **Privately Held**
SIC: 7371 Computer software development
PA: Open Text Corporation
275 Frank Tompa Dr
Waterloo ON N2L 0
519 888-7111

(P-14983)
OPERATION TECHNOLOGY INC (PA)
Also Called: Etap
17 Goodyear Ste 100, Irvine (92618-1822)
PHONE..................................949 462-0100
Farrokh Shokooh, *President*
Ben Boronow, *Vice Pres*
Nikta Nikzad Shokooh, *Admin Sec*
EMP: 90
SQ FT: 32,000
SALES (est): 18.2MM **Privately Held**
WEB: www.etap.com
SIC: 7371 8732 8249 Computer software development; research services, except laboratory; business training services

(P-14984)
OPSWAT INC (PA)
398 Kansas St, San Francisco (94103-5130)
P.O. Box 77878 (94107-0878)
PHONE..................................415 590-7300
Benjamin Czarny, *President*
Patrick Tan, *CFO*
Frank Cohen, *Vice Pres*
Jeanelle Narine, *Office Mgr*
McKenzie Earley, *Executive Asst*
EMP: 58
SQ FT: 15,000
SALES (est): 10.8MM **Privately Held**
SIC: 7371 Computer software development

(P-14985)
OPTIMIZELY INC (PA)
631 Howard St Ste 100, San Francisco (94105-3934)
PHONE..................................415 376-4598
Jay Larson, *CEO*
Dan Siroker, *Chairman*

Carl Tsukahara, *Chief Mktg Ofcr*
John Leonard, *Program Mgr*
Sarah Lubecki, *Executive Asst*
EMP: 280
SQ FT: 76,000
SALES (est): 81.7MM **Privately Held**
SIC: 7371 Computer software development

(P-14986)
OPUS INSPECTION INC
1410 S Acacia Ave Ste A, Fullerton (92831-5309)
PHONE..................................714 999-6727
Mike Golway, *Branch Mgr*
EMP: 55 **Privately Held**
WEB: www.esp-global.com
SIC: 7371 Computer software development
PA: Opus Inspection, Inc.
7 Kripes Rd
East Granby CT 06026

(P-14987)
ORANGE HEALTH SOLUTIONS INC
28480 Ave Stnford Ste 300, Valencia (91355)
PHONE..................................661 310-9333
Nicole Bradberry, *Branch Mgr*
EMP: 67
SALES (corp-wide): 11.3MM **Privately Held**
SIC: 7371 Custom computer programming services
PA: Orange Health Solutions, Inc.
500 Southborough Dr # 105
South Portland ME 04106
207 253-2131

(P-14988)
ORIGIN SYSTEMS INC
209 Redwood Shores Pkwy, Redwood City (94065-1175)
PHONE..................................650 628-1500
EMP: 270
SQ FT: 175,000
SALES (est): 9.1MM
SALES (corp-wide): 4.5B **Publicly Held**
SIC: 7371
PA: Electronic Arts Inc.
209 Redwood Shores Pkwy
Redwood City CA 94065
650 628-7272

(P-14989)
OSHYN INC
100 W Broadway Ste 330, Long Beach (90802-4431)
PHONE..................................213 483-1770
Diego Rebosio, *CEO*
Taylor Turkeltaub, *Marketing Staff*
Jennifer Posthumus, *Consultant*
EMP: 75
SALES (est): 5.6MM **Privately Held**
WEB: www.oshyn.com
SIC: 7371 Computer software development & applications

(P-14990)
OSISOFT LLC (PA)
Also Called: OSI Software
1600 Alvarado St, San Leandro (94577-2600)
PHONE..................................510 297-5800
Dr J Patrick Kennedy, *Ch of Bd*
Jenny Linton, *President*
Bob Guilbault, *COO*
Susanna Kass, *COO*
Gary Zies S, *Officer*
▲ **EMP:** 418
SQ FT: 55,000
SALES (est): 308.8MM **Privately Held**
WEB: www.osisoft.com
SIC: 7371 7372 7373 Computer software development; application computer software; computer integrated systems design

(P-14991)
P MURPHY & ASSOCIATES INC
359 E Magnolia Blvd Ste G, Burbank (91502-3211)
PHONE..................................818 841-2002
Phyliss Murphy, *President*

EMP: 121
SQ FT: 1,200
SALES (est): 8.8MM
SALES (corp-wide): 67.7MM **Privately Held**
WEB: www.pmurphy.com
SIC: 7371 7361 Computer software development; employment agencies; executive placement
PA: Intelliswift Software, Inc.
39600 Balentine Dr # 200
Newark CA 94560
510 490-9240

(P-14992)
PACKET DESIGN INC
1 Almaden Blvd Ste 1150, San Jose (95113-2249)
PHONE..................................408 490-1000
Judy Estrin, *Chairman*
Jack Bradley, *CEO*
Steve Ackley, *Exec VP*
Jeff Raice, *Exec VP*
Daniel Ley, *Senior VP*
EMP: 56
SALES (est): 5.4MM **Privately Held**
WEB: www.packetdesign.com
SIC: 7371 Computer software development

(P-14993)
PACKETVIDEO CORPORATION (HQ)
10350 Science Center Dr, San Diego (92121-1129)
PHONE..................................858 731-5300
James C Brailean, *CEO*
John Driver, *Chief Mktg Ofcr*
Corbett Kull, *Vice Pres*
Kazunori Takagi, *Vice Pres*
EMP: 100 **EST:** 1998
SQ FT: 22,000
SALES (est): 15.1MM **Privately Held**
WEB: www.packetvideo.com
SIC: 7371 7374 4812 Computer software development; data processing & preparation; radio telephone communication

(P-14994)
PALANTIR TECHNOLOGIES INC (PA)
100 Hamilton Ave Ste 300, Palo Alto (94301-1651)
PHONE..................................650 815-0200
Alex Karp, *President*
Geoff Belknap, *Officer*
Stephen Cohen, *Exec VP*
Nan Burton, *Executive Asst*
Colleen E Crawford, *Executive Asst*
EMP: 148
SQ FT: 65,000
SALES (est): 389.8MM **Privately Held**
WEB: www.palantirtech.com
SIC: 7371 Computer software development

(P-14995)
PALANTIR USG INC (HQ)
635 Waverley St, Palo Alto (94301-2550)
PHONE..................................650 815-0200
Akash Jain, *President*
EMP: 190
SQ FT: 4,000
SALES: 3MM
SALES (corp-wide): 389.8MM **Privately Held**
SIC: 7371 Computer software development
PA: Palantir Technologies Inc.
100 Hamilton Ave Ste 300
Palo Alto CA 94301
650 815-0200

(P-14996)
PANASAS INC (PA)
969 W Maude Ave, Sunnyvale (94085-2802)
PHONE..................................408 215-6800
Faye Pairman, *President*
Tom Shea, *COO*
Stephanie Vinella, *CFO*
Jim Donovan, *Chief Mktg Ofcr*
Barbara Murphy, *Chief Mktg Ofcr*
▲ **EMP:** 100 **EST:** 2000
SQ FT: 20,000

SALES (est): 31.4MM **Privately Held**
WEB: www.panasas.com
SIC: 7371 Computer software development

(P-14997)
PATIENTSAFE SOLUTIONS INC (PA)
9330 Scranton Rd Ste 325, San Diego
(92121-7718)
PHONE..................858 746-3100
Si Luo, *President*
Bill Roof, *President*
Mark Young, *COO*
Balaji Sekar, *CFO*
Kathleen Harmon, *Ch Credit Ofcr*
EMP: 83
SALES (est): 17.3MM **Privately Held**
WEB: www.patientsafesolutions.com
SIC: 7371 Software programming applications

(P-14998)
PATTERSON DENTAL SUPPLY INC
Also Called: Dolphin Imaging MGT Solutions
9200 Oakdale Ave Ste 500, Chatsworth
(91311-6556)
PHONE..................818 435-1368
Sonya Lester, *Branch Mgr*
EMP: 50
SALES (corp-wide): 5.5B **Publicly Held**
SIC: 7371 Computer software development & applications; computer software development
HQ: Patterson Dental Supply, Inc.
1031 Mendota Heights Rd
Saint Paul MN 55120
651 686-1600

(P-14999)
PAYMENT PROCESSING INC
Also Called: Paypros
8200 Central Ave, Newark (94560-3448)
PHONE..................510 795-2290
Charles R Smith, *CEO*
Eddie Myers, *President*
John Malnar, *CFO*
Chuck Riegel, *Exec VP*
Joe Monteil, *CIO*
EMP: 150
SQ FT: 59,000
SALES (est): 8.5MM
SALES (corp-wide): 3.3B **Publicly Held**
WEB: www.paypros2.com
SIC: 7371 Computer software development & applications
PA: Global Payments Inc.
3550 Lenox Rd Ne Ste 3000
Atlanta GA 30326
770 829-8000

(P-15000)
PAYSTACK INC
201 Spear St Ste 1100, San Francisco
(94105-6164)
PHONE..................415 941-8102
Olusola Akinlade, *CEO*
Ezra Olubi, *President*
EMP: 70
SQ FT: 8,698
SALES (est): 1MM **Privately Held**
SIC: 7371 Computer software development

(P-15001)
PDF SOLUTIONS INC (PA)
2858 De La Cruz Blvd, Santa Clara
(95050-2619)
PHONE..................408 280-7900
John K Kibarian, *President*
Christine A Russell, *CFO*
Kimon Michaels, *Exec VP*
EMP: 98
SQ FT: 20,800
SALES: 85.7MM **Publicly Held**
WEB: www.pdf.com
SIC: 7371 Computer software development

(P-15002)
PEOPLEAI INC
475 Brannan St Ste 320, San Francisco
(94107-5420)
PHONE..................888 997-3675
Oleg Rogynskyy, *CEO*

Dana Ray, *Senior VP*
John Gilman, *Risk Mgmt Dir*
Andrey Akselrod, *CTO*
EMP: 92
SQ FT: 14,794
SALES: 5MM **Privately Held**
SIC: 7371 Computer software development & applications

(P-15003)
PERFECT WORLD ENTRMT INC
101 Redwood Shr Pkwy # 400, Redwood
City (94065-1180)
PHONE..................650 590-7700
Alan Chen, *CEO*
Bryan Huang, *Vice Pres*
Yan Ji, *Vice Pres*
Bill Wang, *Vice Pres*
Robert Desmond, *IT/INT Sup*
EMP: 150 EST: 2007
SQ FT: 10,000
SALES (est): 26.7MM
SALES (corp-wide): 260.6K **Privately Held**
SIC: 7371 Computer software development & applications
HQ: Perfect World Co., Ltd.
701-14, Floor 7, Building 5, No.1
Courtyard, Shangdi E. Road, Ha
Beijing 10010
105 780-5623

(P-15004)
PERNIXDATA INC
1740 Tech Dr Ste 150, San Jose (95110)
PHONE..................408 724-8413
Poojan Kumar, *CEO*
Bala Narasimhan, *Vice Pres*
Mike Munoz, *Risk Mgmt Dir*
Armando Muniz, *IT/INT Sup*
Judy Kent, *Director*
EMP: 75
SALES (est): 10.4MM **Publicly Held**
SIC: 7371 Computer software development & applications
PA: Nutanix, Inc.
1740 Tech Dr Ste 150
San Jose CA 95110

(P-15005)
PERSISTENT SYSTEMS INC (HQ)
2055 Laurelwood Rd # 210, Santa Clara
(95054-2727)
PHONE..................408 216-7010
Anand Deshpande, *CEO*
Jitendra Gokhale, *President*
Atul Khadilkar, *President*
Sudhir Kulkarni, *President*
Kiran Naik, *President*
EMP: 65
SQ FT: 25,500
SALES (est): 158MM
SALES (corp-wide): 276.6MM **Privately Held**
WEB: www.persistentsystems.com
SIC: 7371 Computer software development
PA: Persistent Systems Limited
Bhageerath, 402 Senapati Bapat
Road,
Pune MH 41101
206 703-0000

(P-15006)
PERSISTENT TLCOM SOLUTIONS INC
Also Called: Persistant Systems
2055 Laurelwood Rd # 210, Santa Clara
(95054-2729)
PHONE..................408 216-7010
Dr Anand Suresh Deshpande, *CEO*
Jitendra Gokhale, *President*
Hari Haran, *President*
Atul Khadilkar, *President*
Sudhir Kulkarni, *President*
EMP: 50
SQ FT: 25,500
SALES: 4.4MM
SALES (corp-wide): 276.6MM **Privately Held**
SIC: 7371 Computer software development

HQ: Persistent Systems Inc.
2055 Laurelwood Rd # 210
Santa Clara CA 95054
408 216-7010

(P-15007)
PERSONAGRAPH CORPORATION
920 Stewart Dr Ste 100, Sunnyvale
(94085-3923)
PHONE..................408 616-1600
Mandar Shinde, *CEO*
Jason Davis, *Treasurer*
William Rainey, *Admin Sec*
EMP: 55 EST: 2012
SQ FT: 1,500
SALES (est): 183.9K **Privately Held**
SIC: 7371 Computer software systems analysis & design, custom

(P-15008)
PHILIPS HLTHCARE INFRMTICS INC (DH)
4430 Rosewood Dr Ste 200, Pleasanton
(94588-3050)
PHONE..................650 293-2300
Deborah Disanzo, *CEO*
Davidi Gilo, *Ch of Bd*
Oran Muduroglu, *President*
Douglas Sinclair, *CFO*
Dana Cambra, *Vice Pres*
EMP: 148
SQ FT: 31,523
SALES (est): 83.2MM
SALES (corp-wide): 20.8B **Privately Held**
WEB: www.stentor.com
SIC: 7371 Computer software development & applications
HQ: Philips North America Llc
3000 Minuteman Rd Ms1203
Andover MA 01810
978 659-3000

(P-15009)
PHILOTIC INC
524 3rd St, San Francisco (94107-1805)
PHONE..................510 730-1740
Jimmy Kittiyachavalit, *Mng Member*
EMP: 62
SALES (est): 3.6MM **Privately Held**
SIC: 7371 Custom computer programming services

(P-15010)
PICSART INC
1 Market St Fl 32, San Francisco
(94105-1420)
PHONE..................415 757-6800
Hovhannes Avoyan, *CEO*
Artavazd Mehrabyan, *COO*
Tammy H Nam, *COO*
Alan Chinn, *CFO*
Argam Derhartunian, *Vice Pres*
EMP: 100
SALES (est): 264K **Privately Held**
SIC: 7371 Computer software development

(P-15011)
PILLAR DATA SYSTEMS INC
2840 Junction Ave, San Jose (95134-1922)
PHONE..................408 503-4000
Michael L Workman, *CEO*
Nancy Holleran, *President*
Edward Hayes, *CFO*
Warren Webster, *Treasurer*
Adrian Jones, *Senior VP*
EMP: 409
SQ FT: 80,000
SALES (est): 29.7MM
SALES (corp-wide): 39.5B **Publicly Held**
WEB: www.pillardata.com
SIC: 7371 Custom computer programming services
PA: Oracle Corporation
500 Oracle Pkwy
Redwood City CA 94065
650 506-7000

(P-15012)
PIVOT SYSTEMS INC
4320 Stevens Creek Blvd, San Jose
(95129-1202)
PHONE..................408 435-1000
Rajesh Nair, *CEO*
Smita Nair, *Admin Sec*

EMP: 160
SQ FT: 40,000
SALES (est): 10.9MM **Privately Held**
WEB: www.pivotsys.com
SIC: 7371 Computer software development & applications

(P-15013)
PIVOTAL SOFTWARE INC (HQ)
Also Called: DELL TECHNOLOGIES
875 Howard St Fl 5, San Francisco
(94103-3021)
PHONE..................415 777-4868
Robert Mee, *CEO*
Paul Maritz, *Ch of Bd*
William Cook, *President*
Cynthia Gaylor, *CFO*
Andrew Cohen, *Senior VP*
EMP: 148
SQ FT: 66,510
SALES: 657.4MM
SALES (corp-wide): 90.6B **Publicly Held**
SIC: 7371 Computer software development & applications
PA: Dell Technologies Inc.
1 Dell Way
Round Rock TX 78682
800 289-3355

(P-15014)
PIVOTCLOUD INC
1230 Midas Way Ste 210, Sunnyvale
(94085-4068)
P.O. Box 620094, Redwood City (94062-0094)
PHONE..................408 475-6090
Richard Gorman, *CEO*
Lorne Boden, *Vice Pres*
EMP: 50 EST: 2011
SALES (est): 1.8MM **Privately Held**
SIC: 7371 Computer software development & applications

(P-15015)
PIXELMAGS INC
1800 Century Park E # 600, Los Angeles
(90067-1508)
PHONE..................310 598-7303
Mark Stubbs, *CEO*
Ryan Marquis, *COO*
Philip Lunn, *Chairman*
Benjamin Miller, *CTO*
EMP: 70
SQ FT: 5,425
SALES: 48MM **Privately Held**
WEB: www.pixelmags.com
SIC: 7371 Software programming applications

(P-15016)
PLAYPHONE INC
3031 Tisch Way Ste 110pw, San Jose
(95128-2584)
PHONE..................408 261-6200
Takahito Yasuki, *Chairman*
Ron Czerny, *CEO*
Bhaskar Roy,
Rick Liu, *Officer*
Thara Edson, *Vice Pres*
EMP: 61
SALES (est): 11.6MM **Privately Held**
WEB: www.playphone.com
SIC: 7371 Computer software development

(P-15017)
POINT OF VIEW INC
947 N Del Sol Ln, Diamond Bar
(91765-1108)
PHONE..................909 860-0705
Chris Warner, *President*
Mark Nausha, *Vice Pres*
Michael Terlecki, *Vice Pres*
EMP: 54
SQ FT: 10,000
SALES (est): 6.2MM **Privately Held**
WEB: www.pov-inc.com
SIC: 7371 Computer software development

(P-15018)
POLARIS NETWORKS INCORPORATED
14856 Holden Way, San Jose
(95124-4515)
PHONE..................408 625-7273

Buddhadeb Biswas, *CEO*
EMP: 85
SQ FT: 2,000
SALES (est): 2.6MM **Privately Held**
SIC: 7371 7373 Computer software development; computer integrated systems design

(P-15019)
POLARIS WIRELESS INC
301 N Whisman Rd, Mountain View (94043-3969)
PHONE..........................408 492-8900
Manlio Allegra, *President*
Victor C Chun, *CFO*
Victor Chun, *CFO*
Rodrigo Alonso, *Vice Pres*
Sridhar Kolar, *Vice Pres*
EMP: 50
SALES (est): 8.1MM **Privately Held**
WEB: www.polariswireless.com
SIC: 7371 8711 Computer software development; engineering services

(P-15020)
POLEXIS INC
10680 Treena St Fl 6, San Diego (92131-2487)
PHONE..........................858 812-7300
Eric M Demarco, *President*
Deanna H Lund, *CFO*
Laura L Siegal, *Treasurer*
Michael W Fink, *Vice Pres*
Deborah Butera, *Admin Sec*
▲ **EMP:** 55
SQ FT: 20,000
SALES (est): 3MM **Publicly Held**
WEB: www.polexis.com
SIC: 7371 8742 Computer software development; management consulting services
HQ: Kratos Technology & Training Solutions, Inc.
10680 Treena St Fl 6
San Diego CA 92131
858 812-7300

(P-15021)
POLTEX COMPANY INC
Also Called: Interpoltex
14748 Wild Colt Pl, Jamul (91935-2121)
PHONE..........................619 669-1846
Andy Denysiak, *President*
Andy Novak, *Vice Pres*
EMP: 96
SALES (est): 6.8MM **Privately Held**
SIC: 7371 Computer software development

(P-15022)
PONYAI INC
3501 Gateway Blvd, Fremont (94538-6585)
PHONE..........................650 281-4639
Jun Peng, *CEO*
Tiancheng Lou, *Principal*
EMP: 150
SQ FT: 50,000
SALES (est): 218.8K **Privately Held**
SIC: 7371 Computer software development

(P-15023)
PORTWORX INC
4940 El Camino Real # 200, Los Altos (94022-1481)
PHONE..........................650 386-0766
Murli Thirumale, *CEO*
Steve Ackley, *Officer*
Ganesh Sangle, *Software Dev*
Paul Theunis, *Software Engr*
EMP: 90
SALES (est): 89.7K **Privately Held**
SIC: 7371 Software programming applications

(P-15024)
POSTMAN INC
595 Market St Ste 1130, San Francisco (94105-2818)
PHONE..........................415 796-6470
Abhinav Asthana, *President*
Kasey Byrne, *VP Mktg*
Claire Riley, *Manager*
EMP: 60

SALES (est): 294.8K **Privately Held**
SIC: 7371 Computer software development

(P-15025)
POWERREVIEWS OC LLC
180 Montgomery St # 1800, San Francisco (94104-4205)
PHONE..........................415 315-9208
Ken Comee, *President*
Pete Lipovsek, *Vice Pres*
Matt Parsons, *Vice Pres*
David Hummel, *CTO*
Kira Meinzer, *VP Human Res*
EMP: 95
SALES (est): 5.7MM
SALES (corp-wide): 25MM **Privately Held**
WEB: www.powerreviews.com
SIC: 7371 Computer software development
PA: Powerreviews, Inc.
1 N Dearborn St Ste 800
Chicago IL 60602
312 447-6100

(P-15026)
PRACTICE FUSION INC (DH)
Also Called: Ringadoc
731 Market St Ste 400, San Francisco (94103-2009)
PHONE..........................415 346-7700
Tom Langan, *CEO*
Jonathan Malek, *Senior VP*
John Hluboky, *Vice Pres*
Mike Sneeringer, *Vice Pres*
Derrick Tan, *Vice Pres*
▲ **EMP:** 102
SALES (est): 29.5MM
SALES (corp-wide): 1.7B **Publicly Held**
WEB: www.practicefusion.com
SIC: 7371 Computer software development
HQ: Allscripts Healthcare, Llc
305 Church At N Hills St
Raleigh NC 27609
919 847-8102

(P-15027)
PRIME CLINICAL SYSTEMS (PA)
3675 Huntington Dr Ste A, Pasadena (91107-5648)
PHONE..........................626 449-1705
Barry Ardelan, *President*
Madari Mike, *CFO*
Hamid Amjadi, *Vice Pres*
Mike Madri, *Vice Pres*
Jose Moure, *Engineer*
EMP: 60
SQ FT: 5,000
SALES (est): 8MM **Privately Held**
SIC: 7371 Computer software development

(P-15028)
PRIMERO SYSTEMS INCORPORATED
14123 Rasmussen Way, San Diego (92129-3825)
P.O. Box 720490 (92172-0490)
PHONE..........................866 426-0779
Gary Saner, *President*
Melissa Saner, *Admin Sec*
Julie Jepson, *Manager*
EMP: 60
SALES (est): 7.5MM **Privately Held**
WEB: www.primerosystems.com
SIC: 7371 7389 Computer software development;

(P-15029)
PRIYO INC
605 Tumbleweed Cmn, Fremont (94539-6810)
PHONE..........................408 248-2507
Atm Zakaria, *CEO*
Abul Nuruzzaman, *CFO*
EMP: 50
SALES: 60K **Privately Held**
SIC: 7371 Computer software development & applications

(P-15030)
PRN LLC (HQ)
600 Montgomery St # 1800, San Francisco (94111-2720)
PHONE..........................415 805-2525
Kevin Carbone, *CEO*
Jonathan Rosen, *Senior VP*
EMP: 51
SQ FT: 46,000
SALES: 12MM **Privately Held**
SIC: 7371 Computer software development & applications

(P-15031)
PROACTIVE TECHNICAL SVCS INC
2350 Mission College Blvd # 246, Santa Clara (95054-1547)
PHONE..........................408 531-6040
Nitin Seth, *CEO*
Ashish Choudhary, *President*
EMP: 50
SQ FT: 350
SALES (est): 356.1K
SALES (corp-wide): 67.4MM **Privately Held**
WEB: www.ptsius.com
SIC: 7371 Computer software development
PA: Incedo Inc.
170 Wood Ave S
Iselin NJ 08830
408 531-6040

(P-15032)
PROCERA NETWORKS INC (HQ)
2055 Junction Ave Ste 105, San Jose (95131-2115)
PHONE..........................510 230-2777
Lyndon Cantor, *CEO*
Andrew Kowal, *President*
Charles Constanti, *CFO*
Richard Deggs, *CFO*
Andy Lovit, *Senior VP*
▲ **EMP:** 62
SQ FT: 18,000
SALES (est): 37.2MM **Privately Held**
WEB: www.proceranetworks.com
SIC: 7371 7372 Computer software development; prepackaged software
PA: Kdr Holding, Inc.
47448 Fremont Blvd
Fremont CA 94538
510 230-2777

(P-15033)
PROCORE TECHNOLOGIES INC (PA)
6309 Carpinteria Ave, Carpinteria (93013-2924)
PHONE..........................866 477-6267
Craig F Courtemanche Jr, *CEO*
Steve Zahm, *President*
Paul Lyandres, *CFO*
Benjamin Singer,
Ani Abrahamian, *Senior VP*
EMP: 850
SALES: 186.3MM **Privately Held**
SIC: 7371 Computer software development

(P-15034)
PRODEGE LLC (PA)
Also Called: Swagbucks
100 N Pacific Coast Hwy # 800, El Segundo (90245-4300)
PHONE..........................310 294-9599
Chuck Davis, *CEO*
Jay Hoag, *General Ptnr*
Mendy Pinson, *President*
Ron Leshem, *Chief Mktg Ofcr*
Mark Bell, *Vice Pres*
EMP: 88 EST: 2005
SALES (est): 53.9MM **Privately Held**
SIC: 7371 8742 Computer software development & applications; marketing consulting services

(P-15035)
PROGRESSIVE COMPUTING LLC
3615 Krny Vlla Rd Ste 105, San Diego (92123)
PHONE..........................858 707-0707
Edward Miller, *Chairman*

EMP: 90
SALES (est): 7MM **Privately Held**
WEB: www.megamates.com
SIC: 7371 Computer software systems analysis & design, custom

(P-15036)
PROLIFICS TESTING INC
24025 Park Sorrento # 405, Calabasas (91302-4018)
PHONE..........................925 485-9535
Danis Yadegar, *President*
Claude Fenner, *Vice Pres*
Dale Lampson, *Vice Pres*
Rutesh Shah, *Vice Pres*
Armen Tekerian, *Vice Pres*
EMP: 60
SQ FT: 6,500
SALES (est): 7.9MM **Privately Held**
SIC: 7371 7372 Custom computer programming services; prepackaged software
HQ: Prolifics Application Services, Inc.
24025 Park Sorrento # 405
Calabasas CA 91302
646 201-4967

(P-15037)
PROOFPOINT INC (PA)
892 Ross Dr, Sunnyvale (94089-1443)
PHONE..........................408 517-4710
Gary Steele, *CEO*
Klaus Oestermann, *COO*
Paul Auvil, *CFO*
Dana Evan, *Bd of Directors*
Jonathan Feiber, *Bd of Directors*
EMP: 148
SQ FT: 95,557
SALES: 716.9MM **Publicly Held**
WEB: www.proofpoint.com
SIC: 7371 Custom computer programming services; computer software systems analysis & design, custom; computer software development & applications

(P-15038)
PROSPANCE INC (PA)
4221 Bus Ctr Dr Ste 1, Fremont (94538)
PHONE..........................925 415-2394
Manish Bhardwaj, *President*
Kirk Muhlenbruck, *President*
Peter Anand, *CFO*
Manpreet Bajaj, *Vice Pres*
Rajesh Sinha, *Vice Pres*
EMP: 79
SQ FT: 2,400
SALES (est): 11.8MM **Privately Held**
SIC: 7371 Computer software development

(P-15039)
PSI FIRE
820 Eschenburg Dr, Gilroy (95020-5613)
PHONE..........................408 842-9308
Thomas Strickland, *Partner*
EMP: 50
SALES (est): 2.1MM **Privately Held**
WEB: www.psifire.com
SIC: 7371 Computer software development

(P-15040)
PUBNUB INC (PA)
460 Bryant St Fl 2, San Francisco (94107-2595)
PHONE..........................415 223-7552
Todd Greene, *CEO*
Stephen Blum, *COO*
Russ Lemelin, *CFO*
Wendy Schott, *Vice Pres*
Doron Sherman, *VP Bus Dvlpt*
EMP: 60 EST: 2011
SALES (est): 12.4MM **Privately Held**
SIC: 7371 Computer software development

(P-15041)
PULSE SECURE LLC (HQ)
2700 Zanker Rd Ste 200, San Jose (95134-2140)
PHONE..........................408 372-9600
Sudhakar Ramakrishna, *CEO*
Doug Erickson, *Partner*
Nicole Kensicki, *Partner*
Corey Mitchell, *CEO*
Jeffrey C Key, *CFO*

EMP: 85 EST: 2014
SALES (est): 34.4MM
SALES (corp-wide): 603MM **Privately Held**
SIC: **7371** 4899 Computer software development & applications; communication signal enhancement network system
PA: Siris Capital Group, Llc
601 Lexington Ave Fl 59
New York NY 10022
212 231-0095

(P-15042)
QUADRIGA INC
Also Called: Taller Technologies
555 Clfornia Ave Ste 4925, San Francisco (94104)
PHONE...................650 270-6326
Lucas E Fuller, *CEO*
Isabela Felix, *COO*
EMP: 70
SALES (est): 1.5MM **Privately Held**
SIC: **7371** Custom computer programming services

(P-15043)
QUALYS INC (PA)
919 E Hillsdale Blvd Fl 4, Foster City (94404-2112)
PHONE...................650 801-6100
Philippe F Courtot, *Ch of Bd*
Sumedh S Thakar,
Sonu Agarwal, *Vice Pres*
Peter Marcisz, *Vice Pres*
Bruce K Posey, *Vice Pres*
EMP: 148
SQ FT: 76,922
SALES: 278.8MM **Publicly Held**
WEB: www.qualys.com
SIC: **7371** 7372 Custom computer programming services; software programming applications; prepackaged software

(P-15044)
QUANTCAST CORPORATION (PA)
795 Folsom St Fl 5, San Francisco (94107-4226)
PHONE...................800 293-5706
Konrad Feldman, *President*
Michael Kamprath, *President*
Rob Horler, *COO*
Julio Pekarovic, *CFO*
Sam Barnett, *Officer*
EMP: 57
SALES (est): 193.5MM **Privately Held**
SIC: **7371** Computer software development & applications

(P-15045)
QUICKEN INC
Also Called: Quicken Sub, LLC
3760 Haven Ave, Menlo Park (94025-1012)
PHONE...................650 564-3399
Eric Dunn, *CEO*
EMP: 120 EST: 2015
SQ FT: 10,000
SALES: 100MM **Privately Held**
SIC: **7371** Computer software development & applications
PA: Hig Capital Management, Inc.
1450 Brickell Ave Fl 31
Miami FL 33131

(P-15046)
RADIANT LOGIC INC (PA)
75 Rowland Way Ste 300, Novato (94945-5060)
PHONE...................415 209-6800
Michel Prompt, *President*
Claude Samuelson, *Vice Pres*
Joseph Caplan, *Software Dev*
Nicolas Guyot, *Software Dev*
Lipee Hathi, *Software Dev*
EMP: 59 EST: 1995
SQ FT: 10,718
SALES: 26MM **Privately Held**
WEB: www.radiantlogic.com
SIC: **7371** Computer software development

(P-15047)
RAINFOREST QA INC
600 Battery St Fl 2, San Francisco (94111-1820)
PHONE...................650 866-1407
Fred Stevens Smith, *CEO*
Russell Smith, *President*
Heather Doshay, *Vice Pres*
Kristina Tran, *Office Mgr*
Morgan Zan, *Recruiter*
EMP: 120
SALES (est): 2MM **Privately Held**
SIC: **7371** Computer software development; software programming applications

(P-15048)
RAINTREE SYSTEMS INC
27307 Via Industria, Temecula (92590-3699)
PHONE...................951 252-9400
Richard V Welty, *CEO*
Terrence Sims, *COO*
Kimberly Becker, *Chief Mktg Ofcr*
Christopher Benson, *VP Bus Dvlpt*
Grace Rodriguez, *Executive Asst*
EMP: 58
SQ FT: 4,500
SALES (est): 8.2MM **Privately Held**
SIC: **7371** 5045 5734 Computer software development; computer software; computer & software stores

(P-15049)
RAPID SOLUTIONS CONSULTING LLC
1900 S Norfolk St Ste 350, San Mateo (94403-1171)
PHONE...................415 226-1131
Philip Martin, *CEO*
Mark Israelsen, *Vice Pres*
EMP: 50
SQ FT: 6,500
SALES (est): 1.5MM **Privately Held**
SIC: **7371** Computer software development & applications

(P-15050)
REAL ESTATE DIGITAL LLC
27081 Aliso Creek Rd # 200, Aliso Viejo (92656-5365)
PHONE...................800 234-2139
Jay Gaskill, *CEO*
Brent Marchbanks, *Info Tech Mgr*
John Hensley, *Technology*
Shawn Brown, *Manager*
Ancio Robinson, *Manager*
EMP: 108
SALES (est): 11MM
SALES (corp-wide): 3B **Privately Held**
SIC: **7371** Software programming applications
HQ: Constellation Homebuilder Systems Corp
75 Frontenac Dr
Markham ON L3R 6

(P-15051)
REAL-TIME INNOVATIONS INC
Also Called: R T I
232 E Java Dr, Sunnyvale (94089-1318)
PHONE...................408 990-7400
Stanley Schneider, *CEO*
Supreet Oberoi, *President*
Jody Schneider, *CFO*
David Barnett, *Vice Pres*
Mekler Catherine, *Vice Pres*
EMP: 90
SQ FT: 1,000
SALES (est): 13.5MM **Privately Held**
WEB: www.scopetools.com
SIC: **7371** 7379 Computer software development; computer related consulting services

(P-15052)
RECIPROCITY INC
3043 Mission St, San Francisco (94110-4501)
PHONE...................415 851-8667
Kenneth Lynch, *CEO*
Michael Knighten, *Vice Pres*
Korina Lealiiee, *Office Mgr*
Amy Peterson, *Opers Mgr*
Than Tran, *Director*
EMP: 50

SQ FT: 5,300
SALES (est): 1.9MM **Privately Held**
SIC: **7371** Computer software systems analysis & design, custom

(P-15053)
RED CONDOR INC
1300 Valley House Dr # 115, Rohnert Park (94928-4930)
PHONE...................707 569-7419
Ron Longo, *President*
EMP: 60
SALES (est): 4.3MM **Privately Held**
WEB: www.redcondor.com
SIC: **7371** Custom computer programming services

(P-15054)
REDIS LABS INC
700 E El Camino Real # 250, Mountain View (94040-2813)
PHONE...................415 930-9666
Ofer Bengal, *CEO*
Elad Ash, *Vice Pres*
Itai Raz, *Vice Pres*
Oren Yaqobi, *Vice Pres*
Jason Forget, *Risk Mgmt Dir*
EMP: 51
SALES (est): 356.4K **Privately Held**
SIC: **7371** Computer software development
PA: Redis Labs Ltd
94 Alon Igal
Tel Aviv-Jaffa
732 805-177

(P-15055)
REFLEKTION INC (PA)
1510 Fashion Island Blvd # 100, San Mateo (94404-1557)
PHONE...................650 293-0800
Rajeev Madhavan, *CEO*
Ray Villeneuve, *President*
Kurt Heinemann, *Chief Mktg Ofcr*
Vivek Gupta, *Vice Pres*
Jody Stoehr, *Vice Pres*
EMP: 50
SALES (est): 6.5MM **Privately Held**
SIC: **7371** Computer software systems analysis & design, custom

(P-15056)
RELATED TECHNOLOGIES INC
81 Blue Ravine Rd Ste 230, Folsom (95630-4766)
P.O. Box 6975 (95763-6975)
PHONE...................916 357-5900
Cheryl Mal, *President*
Joel Solomon, *Vice Pres*
Cheryl Borgonah, *Marketing Staff*
EMP: 85 EST: 2001
SALES (est): 4.2MM **Privately Held**
WEB: www.relatedtechnologies.com
SIC: **7371** Computer software development

(P-15057)
RENOVATE AMERICA INC
Also Called: Hero
15073 Ave Of Science # 200, San Diego (92128-3453)
PHONE...................858 605-5333
Shawn Stone, *CEO*
Adam Garfinkle, *CFO*
Paige Wisdom, *CFO*
ARI Matusiak, *Exec VP*
Scott McKinlay, *Exec VP*
EMP: 119
SQ FT: 23,500
SALES (est): 25.4MM **Privately Held**
SIC: **7371** 8742 Computer software development & applications; banking & finance consultant

(P-15058)
RESOLVE SYSTEMS LLC (PA)
2302 Martin Ste 225, Irvine (92612-1493)
PHONE...................949 325-0120
Martin B Savitt, *CEO*
Jim Livergood, *President*
Marin Sakhri, *Vice Pres*
Paul Gibson, *Admin Sec*
Thomas Tan, *Marketing Staff*
EMP: 65
SQ FT: 6,000

SALES (est): 19MM **Privately Held**
WEB: www.generationetech.com
SIC: **7371** Computer software development

(P-15059)
RESONATE INC (PA)
90 Great Oaks Blvd # 205, San Jose (95119-1314)
PHONE...................408 545-5500
Peter R Watkins, *Ch of Bd*
Richard Hornstein, *CFO*
David Wheatley, *CFO*
Christopher Marino, *Founder*
Jason Schneider, *Officer*
EMP: 188
SQ FT: 38,000
SALES (est): 13.3MM **Privately Held**
SIC: **7371** 7372 Computer software development & applications; business oriented computer software

(P-15060)
RESPONSYS INC (DH)
Also Called: Responsys.com
1100 Grundy Ln Ste 300, San Bruno (94066-3066)
PHONE...................650 745-1700
Daniel D Springer, *CEO*
Christian A Paul, *CFO*
Scott V Olrich, *Chief Mktg Ofcr*
Julian Ong, *Senior VP*
Michael Della Penna, *Senior VP*
EMP: 97
SQ FT: 72,000
SALES (est): 82.4MM
SALES (corp-wide): 39.5B **Publicly Held**
WEB: www.responsys.com
SIC: **7371** 7372 Computer software development; business oriented computer software
HQ: Oc Acquisition Llc
500 Oracle Pkwy
Redwood City CA 94065
650 506-7000

(P-15061)
RETAIL PRO INTERNATIONAL LLC (PA)
Also Called: Retail Pro Software
400 Plaza Dr Ste 200, Folsom (95630-4746)
PHONE...................916 605-7200
Kerry Lemos, *CEO*
Shaff Kassam, *Vice Pres*
Peter Latona, *Vice Pres*
Kathleen Thompson, *Vice Pres*
Jennifer Lacey, *Administration*
EMP: 70
SQ FT: 7,500
SALES (est): 13.6MM
SALES (corp-wide): 14.4MM **Privately Held**
WEB: www.retailpro.com
SIC: **7371** 7372 Computer software development; prepackaged software

(P-15062)
RETAILNEXT INC (PA)
60 S Market St Ste 1000, San Jose (95113-2336)
PHONE...................408 884-2162
Alexei Agratchev, *CEO*
Michael Manlapas, *President*
Kenton D Chow, *COO*
David Tognotti, *COO*
Marc Dietz, *Chief Mktg Ofcr*
EMP: 77 EST: 2007
SQ FT: 12,000
SALES (est): 56.3MM **Privately Held**
SIC: **7371** Computer software development

(P-15063)
REVINATE INC
1 Letterman Dr, San Francisco (94129-1494)
PHONE...................415 671-4703
Jay Ashton, *Principal*
Wayne Huang, *President*
Kyle Duffy, *Vice Pres*
Kenny Lee, *Vice Pres*
Nick Ferris, *Executive*
EMP: 59

SALES (est): 8.7MM **Privately Held**
SIC: 7371 Computer software development

(P-15064)
RHYTHMONE LLC
800 W El Camino Real, Mountain View (94040-2567)
PHONE..................................650 961-9024
EMP: 70
SALES (corp-wide): 214.9MM **Privately Held**
SIC: 7371
HQ: Rhythmone, Llc
   1 Market St Ste 1810
   San Francisco CA 94111
   415 655-1450

(P-15065)
RIGHTSCALE INC (PA)
402 E Gutierrez St, Santa Barbara (93101-1709)
PHONE..................................805 500-4164
Michael Crandel, *President*
Bailey Caldwell, *President*
Josh Fraser, *President*
Ida Kane, *CFO*
Tim Miller, *Vice Pres*
EMP: 88 EST: 2007
SALES (est): 32.5MM **Privately Held**
SIC: 7371 Computer software development & applications

(P-15066)
RIOSOFT HOLDINGS INC
Also Called: Rio Seo
9255 Towne Centre Dr # 750, San Diego (92121-3017)
PHONE..................................858 529-5005
Dema Zlotin, *CEO*
EMP: 50 EST: 2012
SALES (est): 167.9K **Privately Held**
SIC: 7371 Computer software development & applications

(P-15067)
RIOT GAMES INC (DH)
12333 W Olympic Blvd, Los Angeles (90064-1021)
PHONE..................................310 207-1444
Brandon Beck, *CEO*
Mark Marrill, *President*
A Dyoan Jadeja, *CFO*
Dylan A Jadeja, *CFO*
Ron Williams, *Vice Pres*
▲ EMP: 148 EST: 2006
SALES (est): 516.3MM **Privately Held**
SIC: 7371 7993 Custom computer programming services; video game arcade

(P-15068)
ROSE INTERNATIONAL INC
450 N Brand Blvd Fl 6, Glendale (91203-2349)
PHONE..................................636 812-4000
EMP: 151 **Privately Held**
SIC: 7371 8748 Computer software development; systems engineering consultant, ex. computer or professional
PA: Rose International, Inc.
   16401 Swingley Ridge Rd
   Chesterfield MO 63017

(P-15069)
RUNA HR HOLDINGS INC
3067 E 1st St, Long Beach (90803-2536)
PHONE..................................562 883-3546
Courtney McColgan, *CEO*
EMP: 55
SALES: 120K **Privately Held**
SIC: 7371 Computer software development & applications

(P-15070)
SAAMA TECHNOLOGIES INC (PA)
900 E Hamilton Ave # 200, Campbell (95008-0664)
PHONE..................................408 371-1900
Suresh Katta, *President*
Ken Coleman, *Ch of Bd*
Simon Ho, *CFO*
Scott Kleinberg, *CFO*
Sagar Anisingaraju, *Officer*
EMP: 237

SQ FT: 10,000
SALES (est): 75MM **Privately Held**
SIC: 7371 Computer software development

(P-15071)
SAGAN SYSTEMS INC
201 California St # 1300, San Francisco (94111-5015)
PHONE..................................650 387-8485
Yolanda Ruiz, *VP Finance*
EMP: 60
SALES (est): 72.5K **Privately Held**
SIC: 7371 Computer software development & applications

(P-15072)
SAMBREEL SERVICES LLC
5857 Owens Ave Ste 300, Carlsbad (92008-5507)
PHONE..................................760 266-5090
Kai Hankinson, *CEO*
Shawn E Bridgeman, *President*
EMP: 50
SALES (est): 5.4MM **Privately Held**
WEB: www.finialservices.com
SIC: 7371 Computer software development

(P-15073)
SAMSUNG SDS AMERICA INC
2665 N 1st St Ste 110, San Jose (95134-2033)
PHONE..................................408 638-8800
Jh Kim, *Manager*
Kevin Gould, *Counsel*
EMP: 72 **Privately Held**
SIC: 7371 Computer software development
HQ: Samsung Sds Global Scl America, Inc.
   100 Challenger Rd Ste 601
   Ridgefield Park NJ 07660
   201 229-4456

(P-15074)
SANZARU GAMES INC
1065 E Hillsdale Blvd, Foster City (94404-1613)
PHONE..................................650 312-1000
Glen Egan, *President*
Mat Kraemer, *Creative Dir*
Judah Baron, *Principal*
Martin Gerarro, *Principal*
Dave Grace, *Principal*
EMP: 50 EST: 2006
SALES (est): 4.7MM **Privately Held**
SIC: 7371 Computer software development

(P-15075)
SAP LABS LLC
3475 Deer Creek Rd, Palo Alto (94304-1316)
PHONE..................................650 849-4000
Ben Frommherz, *Manager*
Negar Naderi, *Program Mgr*
Jedd Go, *Administration*
Michael Sawi, *Project Mgr*
Stephanie Lee, *Maintence Staff*
EMP: 53
SALES (corp-wide): 28.2B **Privately Held**
SIC: 7371 Custom computer programming services
HQ: Sap Labs, Llc
   3410 Hillview Ave
   Palo Alto CA 94304

(P-15076)
SAP LABS LLC (DH)
3410 Hillview Ave, Palo Alto (94304-1395)
PHONE..................................650 849-4000
Heinz Roggemkemper,
Almer Podbicanin, *Vice Pres*
Elena Hartlieb, *Business Dir*
Larry Ding, *Engineer*
Karen Herrerias, *Marketing Staff*
◆ EMP: 300
SQ FT: 200,000
SALES (est): 68.1MM
SALES (corp-wide): 28.2B **Privately Held**
WEB: www.saplabs.com
SIC: 7371 Computer software development

HQ: Sap America, Inc.
   3999 West Chester Pike
   Newtown Square PA 19073
   610 661-1000

(P-15077)
SAPHO INC
1150 Bayhill Dr Ste 325, San Bruno (94066-3004)
PHONE..................................650 597-2746
Fouad Elnaggar, *President*
Natalie Lambert, *VP Mktg*
EMP: 52
SALES (est): 4.3MM **Privately Held**
SIC: 7371 Computer software development

(P-15078)
SATMETRIX SYSTEMS INC
1820 Gateway Dr Ste 300, San Mateo (94404-4024)
PHONE..................................650 227-8300
Richard Owen, *President*
Brian Curry, *COO*
Raymond Yue, *CFO*
Sally Henry, *Surgery Dir*
Erik Carlstrom, *Analyst*
EMP: 250
SQ FT: 20,000
SALES (est): 40MM **Privately Held**
SIC: 7371 Software programming applications

(P-15079)
SAVVIUS INC (HQ)
1340 Treat Blvd Ste 500, Walnut Creek (94597-7961)
PHONE..................................925 937-3200
Larry Zulch, *President*
Ron Lloyd, *Vice Pres*
Chuck Gray, *Engineer*
Brad Hall, *Regl Sales Mgr*
Jay Botelho, *Products*
EMP: 55
SQ FT: 30,000
SALES (est): 3.2MM **Privately Held**
WEB: www.wildpackets.com
SIC: 7371 Custom computer programming services

(P-15080)
SCALE AI INC
398 11th St, San Francisco (94103-4314)
PHONE..................................617 803-5667
Alexander Wang, *Admin Sec*
EMP: 100
SALES (est): 251.1K **Privately Held**
SIC: 7371 8748 Custom computer programming services; systems analysis or design

(P-15081)
SCALELAB LLC (DH)
6255 W Sunset Blvd # 850, Los Angeles (90028-7470)
PHONE..................................310 526-7524
David Brenner, *CEO*
Maximilien Desmarais, *President*
George Paskalev, *COO*
Tyler Wells, *Exec VP*
Ruben Ochoa, *Vice Pres*
EMP: 50
SALES (est): 4.6MM
SALES (corp-wide): 72MM **Privately Held**
SIC: 7371 7375 Computer software development & applications; on-line data base information retrieval
HQ: Yeah1 Entertainment Corporation
   39 Le Duan Street,
   Ho Chi Minh
   190 060-71

(P-15082)
SCENE7 INC
6 Hamilton Landing # 150, Novato (94949-8264)
PHONE..................................415 506-6000
EMP: 75
SALES (est): 4.3MM **Privately Held**
WEB: www.scene7.com
SIC: 7371

(P-15083)
SECUREAUTH CORPORATION (PA)
8845 Irvine Center Dr # 200, Irvine (92618-4248)
PHONE..................................949 777-6959
Ahmed Rubaie, *CEO*
Craig J Lund, *CEO*
Justin Dolly, *COO*
Jeffrey Kukowski, *COO*
Tom Moyes, *CFO*
EMP: 96
SQ FT: 27,113
SALES: 12MM **Privately Held**
SIC: 7371 Computer software development

(P-15084)
SELECT DATA INC
4155 E La Palma Ave # 250, Anaheim (92807-1863)
PHONE..................................714 577-1000
Edward A Buckley, *CEO*
Pete Poulis, *CFO*
Stacy Ashworth, *Officer*
Ted Schulte, *Exec VP*
Martha Case, *Vice Pres*
EMP: 121
SQ FT: 18,000
SALES (est): 19.4MM **Privately Held**
WEB: www.selectdata.com
SIC: 7371 7372 Computer code authors; prepackaged software

(P-15085)
SENTIENT TECHNOLOGIES USA LLC
611 Mission St Fl 6, San Francisco (94105-3536)
PHONE..................................415 422-9886
Antoine Blondeau, *CEO*
Julian Tandler, *President*
Fabrice Fischer, *CFO*
Tom Whittaker, *CTO*
EMP: 50
SALES (est): 177.1K **Privately Held**
SIC: 7371 Computer software development; computer software development & applications
PA: Sentient Technologies (Hk) Limited
   Dominion Ctr
   Wan Chai HK

(P-15086)
SENTINEL ACQSTION HOLDINGS INC
2000 Avenue Of The Stars, Los Angeles (90067-4700)
PHONE..................................310 201-4100
Matt Cwiertnia, *President*
EMP: 1463
SALES (est): 42.3MM **Privately Held**
SIC: 7371 7379 Computer software systems analysis & design, custom;

(P-15087)
SEQUOIA RETAIL SYSTEMS INC (DH)
2400 Wyandotte St B103, Mountain View (94043-2373)
PHONE..................................650 237-9000
Jim Zaorski, *CEO*
John Diaz, *COO*
Alan Vu, *Manager*
EMP: 52
SALES (est): 7.8MM
SALES (corp-wide): 2.6MM **Privately Held**
WEB: www.sequoiap.com
SIC: 7371 5942 5961 4813 Computer software development; college book stores;
HQ: Blackboard Inc.
   1111 19th St Nw
   Washington DC 20036
   202 463-4860

(P-15088)
SERVICEMAX INC (PA)
4450 Rosewood Dr Ste 200, Pleasanton (94588-3061)
PHONE..................................925 965-7859
Neil Barua, *CEO*
Cory Ayers, *Partner*

Sean Ryan, *Partner*
Denis Susko, *Partner*
Scott Berg, *COO*
EMP: 70
SQ FT: 7,000
SALES (est): 48.8MM **Privately Held**
WEB: www.maxplore.com
SIC: 7371 Computer software development

(P-15089)
SERVICETITAN INC (PA)
801 N Brand Blvd Ste 700, Glendale
(91203-1237)
PHONE......................855 899-0970
ARA Mahdessian, *CEO*
Rafi Kurkdjian, *Partner*
Guy Longworth, *Chief Mktg Ofcr*
Chris Trombetta,
Vach Hovsepyan, *Vice Pres*
EMP: 63
SALES (est): 3.7MM **Privately Held**
SIC: 7371 Computer software development

(P-15090)
SES LLC
26561 Rancho Pkwy S, Lake Forest
(92630-8301)
PHONE......................949 727-3200
Jim Griffith, *Principal*
Rashesh Mody, *Vice Pres*
Abhijeet Shegokar, *Program Mgr*
Krishnan Iyer, *Director*
Terry Owens, *Director*
EMP: 748
SALES (est): 19.7MM
SALES (corp-wide): 177.9K **Privately Held**
SIC: 7371 Computer software development & applications
HQ: Schneider Electric Systems Usa Inc
10900 Equity Dr
Houston TX 77041
713 329-1600

(P-15091)
SFUSD JROTC BRIGADE
2162 24th Ave, San Francisco
(94116-1723)
PHONE......................415 242-2546
Robert Powell, *Director*
EMP: 55
SALES (est): 2.1MM **Privately Held**
SIC: 7371 Computer software development

(P-15092)
SHIELDX NETWORKS INC
Also Called: Apeiro
4093 Oceanside Blvd Ste A, Oceanside
(92056-5816)
PHONE......................760 724-2700
Ratinder Paul Singh Ahuja, *CEO*
Harjinder Singh, *President*
Manuel Nedbal, *Chief Engr*
Neny Hill, *Director*
EMP: 50
SALES (est): 4MM **Privately Held**
SIC: 7371 Computer software development & applications

(P-15093)
SHOPKICK INC
2317 Broadway St Fl 3, Redwood City
(94063-1659)
PHONE......................650 763-8727
Cyriac Roeding, *CEO*
Alexis Rask, *CFO*
Kristy Stromberg, *Chief Mktg Ofcr*
Jim Clark, *Vice Pres*
James Weinberg, *Vice Pres*
EMP: 70
SALES (est): 13MM
SALES (corp-wide): 31.6MM **Privately Held**
SIC: 7371 Computer software development
PA: Trax Technology Solutions Pte. Ltd.
65 Chulia Street
Singapore 04951
622 491-45

(P-15094)
SIEMENS PRODUCT LIFE MGMT SFTW
Also Called: Siemens PLM Software
10824 Hope St, Cypress (90630-5214)
PHONE......................714 952-6500
Mike Sayen, *Manager*
Richard Bandurian, *Administration*
Sarang Baheti, *Software Dev*
Bill King, *Engineer*
Matt Kelly, *Manager*
EMP: 75
SALES (corp-wide): 95B **Privately Held**
WEB: www.ugs.com
SIC: 7371 3695 Computer software development; magnetic & optical recording media
HQ: Siemens Industry Software Inc.
5800 Granite Pkwy Ste 600
Plano TX 75024
972 987-3000

(P-15095)
SIFT SCIENCE INC
123 Mission St Fl 20, San Francisco
(94105-1592)
PHONE......................415 882-7709
Jason Tan, *CEO*
Marc Olesen, *President*
Warren Harper, *Design Engr*
Jacob Burnim, *Engineer*
Gary Lee, *Engineer*
EMP: 65
SALES (est): 6.4MM **Privately Held**
SIC: 7371 Computer software development

(P-15096)
SIGNALDEMAND INC
101 Montgomery St Ste 400, San Francisco
(94104-4145)
PHONE......................415 356-0800
Mark Tice, *CEO*
Scott C Friend, *Partner*
Douglas Hickey, *Partner*
John G Simon, *Partner*
Bill Rupp, *President*
EMP: 50
SALES (est): 3MM **Publicly Held**
WEB: www.signaldemand.com
SIC: 7371 Computer software development
PA: Pros Holdings, Inc.
3100 Main St Ste 900
Houston TX 77002

(P-15097)
SILICON PRIME TECHNOLOGIES INC
4154 W 172nd St, Torrance (90504-1002)
PHONE......................310 279-0222
Quoc Dinh Tran Dinh, *CEO*
EMP: 50
SALES: 200K **Privately Held**
SIC: 7371 Computer software development & applications

(P-15098)
SILICON VALLEY SFTWR GROUP LLC
74 Tehama St, San Francisco
(94105-3110)
PHONE......................844 946-7874
Matt Swanson,
Eric Leppo, *COO*
Dylan Steinman, *Opers Staff*
EMP: 50 **EST:** 2013
SALES: 3.4MM **Privately Held**
SIC: 7371 Computer software systems analysis & design, custom

(P-15099)
SKIRE INC
500 Oracle Pkwy, Redwood City
(94065-1677)
PHONE......................650 289-2600
Massy Mendipour, *CEO*
Steve Apfelberg, *Chief Mktg Ofcr*
EMP: 70
SALES (est): 6.1MM
SALES (corp-wide): 39.5B **Publicly Held**
WEB: www.skire.com
SIC: 7371 Computer software development

PA: Oracle Corporation
500 Oracle Pkwy
Redwood City CA 94065
650 506-7000

(P-15100)
SKYBOX SECURITY INC (PA)
2077 Gateway Pl Ste 200, San Jose
(95110-1016)
PHONE......................408 441-8060
Gideon Cohen, *CEO*
Lior Barak, *CFO*
Stewart Fox, *Exec VP*
Rob Rosiello, *Exec VP*
Ravid Circus, *Vice Pres*
EMP: 74
SALES: 53MM **Privately Held**
WEB: www.skyboxsecurity.com
SIC: 7371 Computer software development

(P-15101)
SKYLITE NETWORKS
761 Mabury Rd Ste 75, San Jose
(95133-1018)
PHONE......................403 934-9349
Idress M Munir, *CEO*
EMP: 70
SALES (est): 89.9K **Privately Held**
SIC: 7371 Computer software development & applications

(P-15102)
SLEEPY GIANT ENTERTAINMENT INC
4 San Joaquin Plz Ste 200, Newport Beach
(92660-5934)
PHONE......................949 464-7986
EMP: 150 **EST:** 2007
SALES (est): 11.2MM **Privately Held**
SIC: 7371

(P-15103)
SMART ENERGY SYSTEMS LLC (PA)
19900 Macarthur Blvd, Irvine (92612-2445)
PHONE......................909 703-9609
Ray Howlett,
EMP: 150
SALES: 70MM **Privately Held**
SIC: 7371 Computer software development & applications

(P-15104)
SMART ENERGY SYSTEMS LLC
Michelson Dr Ste 3370, Irvine (92612)
PHONE......................909 703-9609
Ray Howlett,
EMP: 150
SALES (corp-wide): 70MM **Privately Held**
SIC: 7371 Computer software development & applications
PA: Smart Energy Systems, Inc.
19900 Macarthur Blvd
Irvine CA 92612
909 703-9609

(P-15105)
SMARTDRIVE SYSTEMS INC (PA)
4790 Estgate Mall Ste 200, San Diego
(92121)
PHONE......................858 225-5550
Steve Mitgang, *CEO*
Michael J Baker, *Vice Pres*
Michael Baker, *Vice Pres*
Nicholas Brookins, *Vice Pres*
Andy Deninger, *Vice Pres*
▲ **EMP:** 96
SQ FT: 18,000
SALES (est): 68.7MM **Privately Held**
WEB: www.smartdrive.net
SIC: 7371 Computer software development & applications

(P-15106)
SNAP INC (PA)
Also Called: Snapchat
2772 Dnald Douglas Loop N, Santa Monica
(90405-2951)
PHONE......................310 399-3339
Evan Spiegel, *CEO*
Derek Andersen, *CFO*
Tim Stone, *CFO*

Jeremi Gorman, *Officer*
Jared Grusd, *Officer*
EMP: 148
SQ FT: 485,000
SALES: 1.1B **Publicly Held**
SIC: 7371 7372 Computer software development & applications; software programming applications; application computer software

(P-15107)
SNAPDOCS INC
100 Montgomery St # 2400, San Francisco
(94104-4356)
PHONE......................415 967-0136
Aaron King, *President*
EMP: 50 **EST:** 2013
SALES (est): 3.1MM **Privately Held**
SIC: 7371 Computer software development & applications

(P-15108)
SNOWFLAKE INC (PA)
450 Concar Dr, San Mateo (94402-2681)
PHONE......................844 766-9355
Frank Slootman, *CEO*
Thomas Tuchscherer, *CFO*
Denise Persson, *Chief Mktg Ofcr*
Margo Smith,
Barbara Walkowski,
EMP: 117
SALES (est): 94.4MM **Privately Held**
SIC: 7371 Computer software development & applications; computer software development; software programming applications

(P-15109)
SOFA HOLDCO DEV LLC
Also Called: Software Dev & Technical Svc
470 S Market St, San Jose (95113-2819)
PHONE......................847 713-0680
Donald Scott, *CEO*
EMP: 55
SALES (est): 832.1K **Privately Held**
SIC: 7371 Computer software development & applications

(P-15110)
SOFTSOL RESOURCES INC (HQ)
42808 Christy St Ste 100, Fremont
(94538-3156)
PHONE......................510 824-2000
Srini Madala, *President*
Rk Ghanta, *Vice Pres*
Kris Yalavarthy, *Vice Pres*
Santhosh Latikar, *Tech Recruiter*
Krishna Magam, *Tech Recruiter*
▲ **EMP:** 100
SALES (est): 15MM **Privately Held**
WEB: www.softsolusa.com
SIC: 7371 Computer software development

(P-15111)
SOFTWARE AG USA INC
1198 E Arques Ave, Sunnyvale
(94085-4602)
P.O. Box 2000, Alviso (95002-2000)
PHONE......................703 860-5050
Phillip Merrick, *CEO*
Michael Gesmann, *Marketing Staff*
EMP: 160
SALES (corp-wide): 991MM **Privately Held**
SIC: 7371 Computer software development
HQ: Software Ag Usa, Inc.
11700 Plaza America Dr # 700
Reston VA 20190
703 860-5050

(P-15112)
SOFTWARE MANAGEMENT CONS INC
Also Called: Smci
959 S Coast Dr Ste 415, Costa Mesa
(92626-7839)
PHONE......................714 662-1841
Cesar Sanchez, *Principal*
EMP: 58
SALES (corp-wide): 54.8MM **Privately Held**
SIC: 7371 Computer software systems analysis & design, custom

PA: Software Management Consultants,
Inc.
500 Nth Brn Blvd Ste 1100
Glendale CA 91203
818 240-3177

(P-15113)
SOLARTIS LLC
1601 N Sepulveda Blvd, Manhattan Beach
(90266-5111)
PHONE....................310 251-4861
Nicholas Richardson, *President*
Siby Nidhiry, *CTO*
EMP: 238
SALES (est): 12.3MM **Privately Held**
SIC: 7371 7374 7372 Computer software
development; data processing & prepara-
tion; business oriented computer software

(P-15114)
SOLIDCORE SYSTEMS INC (DH)
3965 Freedom Cir, Santa Clara
(95054-1206)
PHONE....................408 387-8400
Anne Bonaparte, *President*
David Walker, *Senior VP*
Steve Albertolle, *Vice Pres*
Monico Mallari, *Vice Pres*
Tom Marron, *Vice Pres*
EMP: 100
SQ FT: 2,000
SALES (est): 10MM **Privately Held**
WEB: www.solidcore.com
SIC: 7371 Computer software develop-
ment
HQ: Mcafee, Llc
2821 Mission College Blvd
Santa Clara CA 95054
888 847-8766

(P-15115)
SOLIMAR SYSTEMS INC (PA)
1515 2nd Ave, San Diego (92101-3005)
PHONE....................619 849-2800
Drew Sprague, *President*
Steven Bailey, *Executive*
John Flynn, *Executive*
Deanne Demner, *Admin Asst*
Jason Floquet, *Software Engr*
EMP: 74
SQ FT: 5,414
SALES (est): 11.9MM **Privately Held**
WEB: www.solimarsystems.com
SIC: 7371 Computer software develop-
ment

(P-15116)
SOLIX TECHNOLOGIES INC (PA)
4701 Patrick Henry Dr # 2001, Santa Clara
(95054-1864)
PHONE....................408 654-6446
SAI Gundavelli, *CEO*
Kishore Gadiraju, *Vice Pres*
Jim Lee, *Vice Pres*
Raghunath Pasumarthi, *Software Engr*
Sudhakar Chandu, *Project Mgr*
▼ EMP: 60
SQ FT: 17,000
SALES: 10MM **Privately Held**
WEB: www.solix.com
SIC: 7371 Computer software develop-
ment

(P-15117)
**SONATA SOFTWARE NORTH
AMER INC (HQ)**
2201 Walnut Ave Ste 180, Fremont
(94538-2334)
PHONE....................510 791-7220
P Srikar Reddy, *Principal*
Ravi Aithal, *Partner*
N E Devasahayam, *Assoc VP*
N Sridhara, *Assoc VP*
Shankarnaraya Balasubramanian, *Director*
EMP: 66
SQ FT: 2,500
SALES: 47.2MM
SALES (corp-wide): 116.8MM **Privately
Held**
WEB: www.odsi.com
SIC: 7371 Computer software develop-
ment
PA: Sonata Software Limited
1/4, A.P.S Trust Building
Bengaluru KA 56001
802 662-0358

(P-15118)
**SONY CORPORATION OF
AMERICA**
Sony Interactive Studios Amer
2207 Bridgepointe Pkwy, Foster City
(94404-5060)
PHONE....................650 655-8000
Kelly Flock, *Manager*
Julie Currie, *Vice Pres*
Kristie Parnell, *Program Mgr*
Michael Conklin, *Administration*
Staci Sanders, *Administration*
EMP: 350
SALES (est): 200 **Privately Held**
SIC: 7371 Computer software develop-
ment
HQ: Sony Corporation Of America
25 Madison Ave Fl 27
New York NY 10010
212 833-8000

(P-15119)
SOUNDHOUND INC (PA)
Also Called: Mobile Application
5400 Betsy Ross Dr, Santa Clara
(95054-1101)
PHONE....................408 441-3200
Keyvan Mohajer, *CEO*
Amir Arbabi, *Vice Pres*
Seyed Majid Emami, *Vice Pres*
James Hom, *Vice Pres*
Kathleen McMahon, *Vice Pres*
EMP: 61
SQ FT: 61,000
SALES (est): 27.8MM **Privately Held**
WEB: www.melodis.com
SIC: 7371 Software programming applica-
tions

(P-15120)
SPERASOFT INC
2033 Gateway Pl Ste 500, San Jose
(95110-3712)
PHONE....................408 715-6615
Igor Efremov, *CEO*
Alexei Kudriashov, *CFO*
Anna Limarenko, *Project Mgr*
EMP: 375
SQ FT: 15,000
SALES: 16MM
SALES (corp-wide): 287.1MM **Privately
Held**
SIC: 7371 Software programming applica-
tions
HQ: Keywords International Limited
Whelan House
Dublin D18 T

(P-15121)
SPRUCE TECHNOLOGY INC
3516 Browntail Way, San Ramon
(94582-5245)
PHONE....................925 415-8160
Muttu Nagubandi, *Branch Mgr*
EMP: 72
SALES (corp-wide): 13.7MM **Privately
Held**
SIC: 7371 Computer software develop-
ment & applications
PA: Spruce Technology Inc
1149 Bloomfield Ave Ste G
Clifton NJ 07012
201 693-8843

(P-15122)
STARTEL CORPORATION (PA)
16 Goodyear B-125, Irvine (92618-3758)
PHONE....................949 863-8700
William Lane, *President*
David Abrams, *Purch Mgr*
Rachel Hayes, *Marketing Staff*
Steve Newell, *Manager*
Myrna Nunez, *Manager*
EMP: 60
SQ FT: 27,000
SALES (est): 10.5MM **Privately Held**
WEB: www.startelcorp.com
SIC: 7371 3661 Computer software devel-
opment; communication headgear, tele-
phone

(P-15123)
STARTUP FARMS INTL LLC
Also Called: Sufi
45690 Northport Loop E, Fremont
(94538-6477)
PHONE....................510 440-0110
Jasvir Gill, *President*
Kaval Kaur, *CFO*
Sheena Malhotra, *Manager*
EMP: 350
SALES (est): 287K **Privately Held**
WEB: www.startupfarms.com
SIC: 7371 Computer software develop-
ment

(P-15124)
STONERIVER INC
770 The Cy Dr S Ste 5000, Orange
(92868)
PHONE....................714 705-8227
John Grundman, *Principal*
EMP: 333
SALES (corp-wide): 163.3MM **Privately
Held**
SIC: 7371 Computer software develop-
ment
HQ: Stoneriver, Inc.
20 Horseneck Ln Ste 1
Greenwich CT 06830
303 729-7500

(P-15125)
**STRANDS INC A DELAWARE
CORP**
999 Baker Way Ste 430, San Mateo
(94404-1581)
P.O. Box 331639, Miami FL (33233-1639)
PHONE....................541 753-4426
Edward Chang, *CEO*
David Silverman, *President*
Jordi Teixido, *COO*
Mercedes Blanch, *Project Mgr*
EMP: 50
SQ FT: 3,000
SALES (est): 3.8MM **Privately Held**
WEB: www.strands.com
SIC: 7371 Software programming applica-
tions

(P-15126)
STRANDS LABS INC
Also Called: Strands Finance
999 Baker Way Ste 430, San Mateo
(94404-1581)
PHONE....................415 398-4333
EMP: 50
SALES (est): 3.1MM **Privately Held**
SIC: 7371

(P-15127)
STRATACARE LLC
17838 Gillette Ave Ste D, Irvine
(92614-6502)
P.O. Box 19600 (92623-9600)
PHONE....................949 743-1200
Scott R Green, *CEO*
Steve Ditman, *CFO*
Robert McCaffrey, *Officer*
John Zavoli, *Officer*
Michael Josephs, *Vice Pres*
EMP: 250 EST: 1998
SALES (est): 989K
SALES (corp-wide): 5.3B **Publicly Held**
WEB: www.gensourcecorp.com
SIC: 7371 Computer software develop-
ment & applications
HQ: Conduent Workers Compensation
Holdings, Inc.
17838 Gillette Ave
Irvine CA 92614

(P-15128)
STREAMVECTOR INC
4701 Patrick Henry Dr # 2, Santa Clara
(95054-1819)
PHONE....................415 870-8395
Lokesh Anand, *President*
Piyush Khemka, *Vice Pres*
EMP: 170
SALES (est): 1MM **Privately Held**
SIC: 7371 Computer software develop-
ment & applications

(P-15129)
STRIIM INC
575 Middlefield Rd, Palo Alto (94301-2150)
PHONE....................425 894-1998
Ali Kutay, *President*
Katherine Rincon, *Senior VP*
Michelle Monica, *Executive Asst*
Steve Wilkes, *CTO*
Nicholas Keene, *Software Engr*
EMP: 50
SALES: 1MM **Privately Held**
SIC: 7371 Computer software develop-
ment & applications

(P-15130)
STRIVR LABS INC
90 Middlefield Rd Ste 101, Menlo Park
(94025-3510)
PHONE....................650 656-9987
Derek Belch, *President*
Danny Belch, *Vice Pres*
EMP: 75 EST: 2015
SALES (est): 5MM **Privately Held**
SIC: 7371 Computer software develop-
ment & applications

(P-15131)
SUCCESSFACTORSCOM INC
2000 Alameda De Las Pulga, San Mateo
(94403-1269)
PHONE....................650 645-2000
Mark Pecoraro, *President*
Andy Athanur, *Partner*
Jackie Ato, *Executive*
Piya Paintal, *Executive*
Kerri Brown, *Practice Mgr*
EMP: 83
SALES (est): 4.1MM **Privately Held**
SIC: 7371 Computer software develop-
ment

(P-15132)
SUGARCRM INC (PA)
10050 N Wolfe Rd Sw2130, Cupertino
(95014-2528)
PHONE....................408 454-6900
Craig Charlton, *CEO*
Andrew Chmyz, *CFO*
John Donaldson, *CFO*
Steve Valenzuela, *CFO*
Chris Pennington, *Ch Credit Ofcr*
EMP: 110
SQ FT: 40,000
SALES (est): 68.9MM **Privately Held**
WEB: www.sugarcrm.com
SIC: 7371 Computer software develop-
ment

(P-15133)
SUMO LOGIC INC
305 Main St Fl 3, Redwood City
(94063-1729)
PHONE....................650 810-8700
Vance Marc Loiselle, *CEO*
Ramin Sayar, *President*
Sydney Carey, *CFO*
Aaron Feigin, *Ch Credit Ofcr*
Suku Krishnaraj, *Chief Mktg Ofcr*
EMP: 400
SALES (est): 13.6MM **Privately Held**
SIC: 7371 Computer software develop-
ment

(P-15134)
SVMK INC
3050 S Delaware St, San Mateo
(94403-2392)
PHONE....................503 225-1202
EMP: 793
SALES (corp-wide): 254.3MM **Publicly
Held**
SIC: 7371 Custom computer programming
services; custom computer programming
services; computer software systems
analysis & design, custom; computer software writing services
PA: Svmk Inc.
1 Curiosity Way
San Mateo CA 94403
650 543-8400

(P-15135)
SYMITAR SYSTEMS INC
8985 Balboa Ave, San Diego (92123-1507)
PHONE....................619 542-6700
Kathy Burress, *Principal*

Amy Goodrich, *Admin Sec*
John Clark, *Info Tech Dir*
Colleen Elliott, *Info Tech Dir*
Eben Maat, *Systs Prg Mgr*
EMP: 220
SALES (est): 22.9MM
SALES (corp-wide): 1.5B **Publicly Held**
SIC: 7371 Computer software development
PA: Jack Henry & Associates, Inc.
663 W Highway 60
Monett MO 65708
417 235-6652

(P-15136)
SYSDIG INC (PA)
85 2nd St Ste 800, San Francisco
(94105-3466)
PHONE....................415 872-9473
Suresh Vasudevan, *CEO*
Janet Matsuda, *Chief Mktg Ofcr*
Sandor Klein, *Vice Pres*
Carol Junsay, *Office Mgr*
Brooke Treseder, *Opers Staff*
EMP: 51
SALES (est): 31.3MM **Privately Held**
SIC: 7371 Computer software development

(P-15137)
SYSINTELLI INC
9466 Black Mountain Rd # 200, San Diego
(92126-4550)
PHONE....................858 271-1600
Ravindra Hanumara, *President*
Raja Yalamanchili, *Project Mgr*
Ajay Kumar, *Technology*
Rushikesh Reddy, *Technical Staff*
EMP: 123
SQ FT: 2,400
SALES: 4.5MM **Privately Held**
WEB: www.sysintelli.com
SIC: 7371 7379 Computer related consulting services; custom computer programming services

(P-15138)
SYSTECH SOLUTIONS INC (PA)
500 N Brand Blvd Ste 1900, Glendale
(91203-3308)
PHONE....................818 550-9690
Arun Gollapudi, *President*
Ashish Parikh, *CFO*
Srinivasan Ramaswamy, *Vice Pres*
EMP: 81
SQ FT: 1,500
SALES (est): 25.1MM **Privately Held**
WEB: www.systechusa.com
SIC: 7371 Computer software systems analysis & design, custom

(P-15139)
SYSTEMS AND SOFTWARE ENTPS LLC (HQ)
Also Called: Zodiac Inflight Innovations US
2929 E Imperial Hwy # 170, Brea
(92821-6716)
PHONE....................714 854-8600
Matt Smith, *CEO*
Ed Barrera, *CFO*
Harry Gray, *Vice Pres*
Steve Hawkins, *CTO*
Edison Fabian, *Manager*
EMP: 73
SQ FT: 90,000
SALES (est): 67.8MM
SALES (corp-wide): 833.4MM **Privately Held**
WEB: www.imsinflight.com
SIC: 7371 Computer software systems analysis & design, custom
PA: Safran
2 Bd Du General Martial Valin
Paris 15e Arrondissement 75015
140 608-080

(P-15140)
T AND D COMMUNICATIONS INC (PA)
6761 Sierra Ct Ste F, Dublin (94568-2692)
PHONE....................510 824-0010
Phillip Ernest Croan, *President*
Andrew Vargas, *CFO*
Patrick Croan, *Vice Pres*
James Vollmer, *Vice Pres*
Johnny Reyna, *Branch Mgr*

EMP: 65
SQ FT: 3,000
SALES (est): 17.1MM **Privately Held**
WEB: www.t-and-d.com
SIC: 7371 Software programming applications

(P-15141)
TALENT & ACQUISITION LLC
Also Called: Stand 8
100 W Broadway Ste 650, Long Beach
(90802-4466)
PHONE....................213 742-1972
Quinn Fillmon, *Exec Dir*
Scott Banks, *Tech Recruiter*
Jennifer Gordon, *Director*
EMP: 150
SALES (est): 2.3MM **Privately Held**
SIC: 7371 7379 7363 7361 Custom computer programming services; computer related consulting services; help supply services; employment agencies

(P-15142)
TAMTRON CORPORATION (DH)
6203 San Ignacio Ave # 110, San Jose
(95119-1371)
PHONE....................408 323-3303
Fax: 408 246-5415
EMP: 60
SQ FT: 2,600
SALES (est): 3.8MM
SALES (corp-wide): 1.3B **Privately Held**
SIC: 7371
HQ: Impac Medical Systems, Inc
100 Mathilda Pl Fl 5
Sunnyvale CA 94086
408 830-8000

(P-15143)
TAPESTRY SOLUTIONS INC (HQ)
5643 Copley Dr, San Diego (92111-7903)
PHONE....................858 503-1990
Geoff Evans, *President*
Sam Deford, *President*
Jeremy Lowe, *President*
Mary Ann Wagner, *COO*
Mark Young, *CFO*
EMP: 125
SQ FT: 36,073
SALES (est): 75MM
SALES (corp-wide): 101.1B **Publicly Held**
SIC: 7371 5045 Custom computer programming services; computer software
PA: The Boeing Company
100 N Riverside Plz
Chicago IL 60606
312 544-2000

(P-15144)
TAULIA INC (PA)
250 Montgomery St Ste 400, San Francisco
(94104-3427)
PHONE....................415 376-8280
Cedric Bru, *CEO*
Jonathan Lowenhar, *President*
Courtney Ring, *President*
Rik Thorbecke, *CFO*
Barbara Holzapfel, *Chief Mktg Ofcr*
EMP: 85
SALES (est): 55.7MM **Privately Held**
SIC: 7371 Computer software development

(P-15145)
TAVANT TECHNOLOGIES INC (PA)
3965 Freedom Cir Ste 750, Santa Clara
(95054-1285)
PHONE....................408 519-5400
Sarvesh Mahesh, *CEO*
Venkata Devana, *CFO*
Raj Menon, *Chief Mktg Ofcr*
Krishnan Pp, *Officer*
Hassan Rashid, *Senior VP*
EMP: 107
SALES: 108MM **Privately Held**
WEB: www.tavant.com
SIC: 7371 Computer software development; computer software systems analysis & design, custom

(P-15146)
TAX COMPLIANCE INC
10089 Willow Creek Rd # 300, San Diego
(92131-1699)
PHONE....................858 547-4100
Dave Shea, *CEO*
Jennifer Cortes, *Department Mgr*
Kevin Buckhouse, *VP Info Sys*
Anna Hagel, *Info Tech Dir*
Christine Ponnwitz, *Info Tech Dir*
EMP: 52
SQ FT: 10,000
SALES (est): 8.5MM **Privately Held**
WEB: www.taxcomp.com
SIC: 7371 Computer software development
HQ: Mlm Information Services, Llc
780 3rd Ave
New York NY 10017
212 245-5310

(P-15147)
TCG SOFTWARE SERVICES INC
320 Commerce Ste 200, Irvine
(92602-1363)
PHONE....................714 665-6200
Greg Blevins, *Branch Mgr*
EMP: 50 **Privately Held**
SIC: 7371 Custom computer programming services; computer software development
PA: Tcg Software Services, Inc.
265 Davidson Ave Ste 220
Somerset NJ 08873

(P-15148)
TECH TOWN INC
1157 N Brand Blvd, Glendale (91202-2503)
PHONE....................818 621-2744
Shant Chorbadjian, *CEO*
EMP: 50
SALES (est): 3.3MM **Privately Held**
SIC: 7371 Custom computer programming services

(P-15149)
TECHEXCEL INC (PA)
3675 Mt Diablo Blvd # 200, Lafayette
(94549-3793)
PHONE....................925 871-3900
Tieren Zhou, *President*
James Zhou, *CFO*
Rickard Jonsson, *Vice Pres*
Xiaojie Liu, *Software Engr*
Tingjin Xu, *Software Engr*
EMP: 51
SQ FT: 11,187
SALES (est): 13MM **Privately Held**
WEB: www.techexcel.com
SIC: 7371 Computer software development

(P-15150)
TELESTREAM LLC (PA)
848 Gold Flat Rd, Nevada City
(95959-3208)
PHONE....................530 470-1300
Scott Puopolo, *CEO*
Jim Leighton, *Partner*
Gary Petruzzi, *Partner*
Mark Cuny, *CFO*
Barbara Dehart, *Vice Pres*
▲ **EMP:** 110
SALES (est): 57MM **Privately Held**
WEB: www.telestream.net
SIC: 7371 Computer software development & applications

(P-15151)
TELESYS SOFTWARE
1900 S Norfolk St Ste 221, San Mateo
(94403-1172)
PHONE....................650 522-9922
Bobby Bahl, *President*
Klaus Kiiemank, *Vice Pres*
Ed Lee, *Vice Pres*
EMP: 50
SQ FT: 4,000
SALES (est): 4.8MM **Privately Held**
WEB: www.telesys.com
SIC: 7371 Computer software development

(P-15152)
TEXXIS LIMITED
400 Spectrum Center Dr # 1, Irvine
(92618-4934)
PHONE....................213 631-3547
Wenwu Hu, *Director*
EMP: 72
SALES: 250K **Privately Held**
SIC: 7371 Computer software development & applications

(P-15153)
THISMOMENT INC
690 Market St Unit 1101, San Francisco
(94105-5123)
PHONE....................415 200-4730
Vince Broady, *CEO*
Raffy Kaloustian, *President*
Trey Walker, *President*
John Walliser, *President*
Steve Bach, *CFO*
EMP: 135
SQ FT: 15,000
SALES (est): 17.9MM **Privately Held**
SIC: 7371 Computer software development

(P-15154)
THOMAS GALLAWAY CORPORATION (PA)
Also Called: TECHNOLOGENT
100 Spectrum Center Dr # 700, Irvine
(92618-4970)
PHONE....................949 716-9500
Lezlie L Gallaway, *CEO*
Rod Wright, *Vice Pres*
Judd Borggreve, *Executive*
Dan Fitzgerald, *Executive*
David Lipnick, *Executive*
EMP: 70
SQ FT: 4,500
SALES (est): 100.9MM **Privately Held**
WEB: www.technologent.com
SIC: 7371 Custom computer programming services

(P-15155)
THREATMETRIX INC
160 W Santa Clara St # 1400, San Jose
(95113-1701)
PHONE....................408 200-5700
Reed Taussig, *President*
Frank Teruel, *CFO*
Armen Najarian, *Chief Mktg Ofcr*
Alisdair Faulkner, *Officer*
Phil Steffora, *Officer*
EMP: 165
SQ FT: 10,000
SALES (est): 28.5MM
SALES (corp-wide): 9.6B **Privately Held**
SIC: 7371 7374 7382 Computer software development & applications; computer processing services; security systems services
HQ: Lexisnexis Risk Solutions Inc.
1000 Alderman Dr
Alpharetta GA 30005
678 694-6000

(P-15156)
TIBCO SOFTWARE INC (HQ)
3307 Hillview Ave, Palo Alto (94304-1204)
PHONE....................650 846-1000
Dan Streetman, *CEO*
Sumati Natarajan, *Partner*
Matt Quinn, *COO*
Tom Berquist, *CFO*
Fred Studer, *Chief Mktg Ofcr*
EMP: 148
SQ FT: 292,000
SALES (est): 849.4MM
SALES (corp-wide): 885.6MM **Privately Held**
WEB: www.tibco.com
SIC: 7371 7373 Computer software development; systems integration services
PA: Balboa Intermediate Holdings Llc
3307 Hillview Ave
Palo Alto CA 94304
650 846-1000

(P-15157)
TIKTOK INC (DH)
1920 Olympic Blvd, Santa Monica
(90404-3816)
PHONE....................844 523-3993

Jun Zhu, *CEO*
Luyu Yang, *Treasurer*
Patrick Nommensen, *Admin Sec*
May Guo, *Finance*
EMP: 150 **EST:** 2015
SALES: 16MM
SALES (corp-wide): 176.1K **Privately Held**
SIC: 7371 7389 Software programming applications; music & broadcasting services

(P-15158)
TOOLWIRE INC
7031 Koll Center Pkwy # 220, Pleasanton (94566-3128)
PHONE..................925 227-8500
John Valencia, *President*
John Catanzaro, *Vice Pres*
Cameron Crowe, *Vice Pres*
Nancy Bissonnette, *Office Mgr*
Chris Thompson, *Director*
EMP: 56
SQ FT: 12,500
SALES (est): 9.9MM **Privately Held**
WEB: www.toolwire.com
SIC: 7371 Computer software development

(P-15159)
TOWNS END STUDIOS LLC
699 8th St, San Francisco (94103-4901)
PHONE..................415 802-7936
Mark Pincus,
EMP: 1000
SALES (est): 9.8MM
SALES (corp-wide): 907.2MM **Publicly Held**
SIC: 7371 Computer software development & applications
PA: Zynga Inc.
699 8th St
San Francisco CA 94103
855 449-9642

(P-15160)
TRADE DESK INC (PA)
Also Called: THETRADEDESK
42 N Chestnut St, Ventura (93001-2662)
PHONE..................805 585-3434
Jeff T Green, *Ch of Bd*
Robert D Perdue, *COO*
Paul E Ross, *CFO*
Susan M Vobejda, *Chief Mktg Ofcr*
Vivian W Yang, *CFO*
EMP: 130
SQ FT: 25,000
SALES: 477.2MM **Publicly Held**
SIC: 7371 7372 Software programming applications; prepackaged software; business oriented computer software; publishers' computer software

(P-15161)
TREASURE DATA INC
2565 Leghorn St, Mountain View (94043-1613)
PHONE..................866 899-5386
Hiro Yoshikawa, *CEO*
Dan Weirich, *CFO*
Daniel Weirich, *CFO*
Rob Glickman, *Chief Mktg Ofcr*
Noah Barr, *Vice Pres*
EMP: 100
SALES (est): 12MM **Privately Held**
SIC: 7371 7374 Custom computer programming services; optical scanning data service

(P-15162)
TRENDSHIFT LLC
13274 Fiji Way Ste 250, Marina Del Rey (90292-7298)
P.O. Box 691233, West Hollywood (90069-9233)
PHONE..................866 644-8877
Ryan Weirich, *VP Finance*
EMP: 55
SALES (est): 2MM **Privately Held**
SIC: 7371 Computer software development & applications

(P-15163)
TRINUS CORPORATION
225 S Lake Ave Ste 1080, Pasadena (91101-4892)
PHONE..................818 246-1143
Sanjay Kucheria, *CEO*
Harshada Kucheria, *President*
EMP: 50
SALES: 10MM **Privately Held**
SIC: 7371 Custom computer programming services

(P-15164)
TRUECAR INC (PA)
120 Broadway Ste 200, Santa Monica (90401-2385)
PHONE..................800 200-2000
Michael Darrow, *CEO*
Noel Watson, *CFO*
Neeraj Gunsagar, *Chief Mktg Ofcr*
Jeffrey J Swart, *Exec VP*
EMP: 50
SQ FT: 38,000
SALES: 353.5MM **Publicly Held**
WEB: www.zag.com
SIC: 7371 7299 Custom computer programming services; information services, consumer

(P-15165)
TRYFACTA INC
Also Called: Systems America Public Sector
4637 Chabot Dr Ste 100, Pleasanton (94588-2753)
PHONE..................408 419-9200
Ratika Tyagi, *CEO*
Nikhil Upadhyay, *Recruiter*
EMP: 351
SALES: 34.4MM **Privately Held**
SIC: 7371 7361 7373 8748 Computer software systems analysis & design, custom; labor contractors (employment agency); systems software development services; systems engineering consultant, ex. computer or professional

(P-15166)
TUNARI CORP INC
Also Called: Hara
2755 Campus Dr Ste 300, San Mateo (94403-2538)
PHONE..................650 249-6740
Rodrigo J Prudencio, *CEO*
EMP: 59
SALES (est): 2.7MM
SALES (corp-wide): 6.4B **Publicly Held**
SIC: 7371 Computer software development
HQ: Verisae, Inc.
730 2nd Ave S Ste 600
Minneapolis MN 55402
612 455-2300

(P-15167)
UBICS INC
1050 Bridgeway, Sausalito (94965-2173)
PHONE..................415 289-1400
Vijay Mallya, *Branch Mgr*
EMP: 140 **Privately Held**
SIC: 7371 Custom computer programming services
PA: Ubics, Inc.
400 Sthpinte Blvd Ste 425
Canonsburg PA 15317

(P-15168)
ULTIMO SOFTWARE SOLUTIONS INC
33268 Central Ave 2, Union City (94587-2010)
PHONE..................408 943-1490
Venkatasubhash Pasumarthy, *President*
Smita Pasumarthi, *CFO*
Aikta Verma, *Opers Staff*
Saurabh Srivastava, *Consultant*
EMP: 127
SQ FT: 4,000
SALES (est): 11.1MM **Privately Held**
WEB: www.ultimosoft.com
SIC: 7371 Computer software development & applications

(P-15169)
UNISYS CORPORATION
9701 Jeronimo Rd Ste 100, Irvine (92618-2076)
PHONE..................949 380-5000
Carmen Lynch, *Manager*
Derek Paul, *Engrg Dir*
Chris Liebsack, *Technology*
Jesus Contreras, *Production*
Andy Beale, *Manager*
EMP: 1000
SALES (corp-wide): 2.8B **Publicly Held**
WEB: www.unisys.com
SIC: 7371 Computer software development
PA: Unisys Corporation
801 Lakeview Dr Ste 100
Blue Bell PA 19422
215 986-4011

(P-15170)
UNITY SOFTWARE INC (HQ)
Also Called: Unity Technologies
30 3rd St, San Francisco (94103-3104)
PHONE..................415 848-2533
Oren Tversky, *Vice Pres*
Ryan Hintze, *Partner*
Daniel Kim, *Partner*
Kim Jabal, *CFO*
Anne Evans, *Vice Pres*
EMP: 50 **EST:** 2009
SALES: 18.7MM
SALES (corp-wide): 418.9K **Privately Held**
SIC: 7371 Computer software development & applications

(P-15171)
UNX INC A DELAWARE CORP
Also Called: Universal Network Exchange
175 E Olive Ave Fl 2, Burbank (91502-1821)
PHONE..................818 333-3300
J Scott Harrison, *CEO*
Andre Perold, *Ch of Bd*
David Collett, *CFO*
EMP: 95 **EST:** 1997
SQ FT: 16,000
SALES (est): 6.5MM **Privately Held**
WEB: www.unx.com
SIC: 7371 4813 6211 Computer software development & applications; ; security brokers & dealers

(P-15172)
USER ZOOM INC
10 Almaden Blvd Ste 250, San Jose (95113-2226)
PHONE..................408 533-8619
Alfonso De La Nuez, *CEO*
Xavier Mestres, *COO*
John Crouch, *Vice Pres*
Arthur Moan, *Vice Pres*
Matthew Paulus, *Vice Pres*
EMP: 80 **EST:** 2007
SALES (est): 13.6MM **Privately Held**
SIC: 7371 Computer software development

(P-15173)
UST GLOBAL INC (PA)
5 Polaris Way, Aliso Viejo (92656-5374)
PHONE..................949 716-8757
Paras Chandaria, *Chairman*
Gopikrishnan Jagadeesalu, *Partner*
Sajan Pillai, *CEO*
Arun Narayanan, *COO*
Krishna Sudheendra, *CFO*
EMP: 100
SQ FT: 20,000
SALES (est): 784.8MM **Privately Held**
WEB: www.ust-global.com
SIC: 7371 Computer software development

(P-15174)
UTC FIRE SEC AMERICAS CORP INC
Also Called: Utc, Mas
2955 Red Hill Ave Ste 100, Costa Mesa (92626-1207)
PHONE..................949 737-7800
Shin Voeks, *General Mgr*
Frances Lee, *Sr Software Eng*
Leslie Cushing, *Software Dev*
Alan Harper, *Software Dev*

Mike Kenney, *Software Engr*
EMP: 60
SALES (corp-wide): 66.5B **Publicly Held**
SIC: 7371 5063 Computer software development & applications; computer software systems analysis & design, custom; alarm systems
HQ: Utc Fire & Security Americas Corporation, Inc.
8985 Town Center Pkwy
Lakewood Ranch FL 34202

(P-15175)
UTILITY SYSTEMS SCIENCE (PA)
Also Called: US 3
601 Parkcenter Dr Ste 209, Santa Ana (92705-3542)
PHONE..................714 542-1004
Gabriel A Chavez, *CEO*
Anthony Chavez, *CFO*
Tony Chavez, *CFO*
Mark Serres, *Vice Pres*
Bret Houston, *Software Engr*
EMP: 53
SALES (est): 7.9MM **Privately Held**
SIC: 7371 Computer software development

(P-15176)
VAGARO INC
4120 Dublin Blvd Ste 250, Dublin (94568-7759)
PHONE..................800 919-0157
Fred Helou, *CEO*
Keoni Bail, *Sales Staff*
EMP: 78
SALES (est): 4.8MM **Privately Held**
SIC: 7371 Custom computer programming services

(P-15177)
VCOMPLY TECHNOLOGIES INC
808 N Hampton Dr, Palo Alto (94303)
PHONE..................650 319-8842
Harsh Kariwala, *CEO*
EMP: 100
SALES (est): 1.4MM **Privately Held**
SIC: 7371 Computer software development

(P-15178)
VEGATEK CORPORATION
Also Called: Intellective
470 Wald Ste 100, Irvine (92618-4638)
P.O. Box 436057, Louisville KY (40253-6057)
PHONE..................949 502-0090
Matthew Barnickle, *CEO*
Alexander Kiperman, *Software Dev*
Ray Shafer, *Prgrmr*
Max Zhilin, *IT/INT Sup*
Brijesh Tripathi, *Technical Staff*
EMP: 70
SQ FT: 6,000
SALES (est): 2MM **Privately Held**
WEB: www.vegaecm.com
SIC: 7371 7379 6411 Computer software development; computer software systems analysis & design, custom; computer software development & applications; computer related consulting services; computer related maintenance services; insurance information & consulting services

(P-15179)
VELOCIOUS TECHNOLOGIES INC
6520 N Irwindale Ave A, Irwindale (91702-2801)
PHONE..................650 434-7118
Hanzhong Ye, *CEO*
EMP: 100
SQ FT: 300
SALES: 100K **Privately Held**
SIC: 7371 Computer software development & applications

(P-15180)
VENDINI INC (PA)
55 Francisco St Ste 350, San Francisco (94133-2112)
PHONE..................415 693-9611
Mark Tacchi, *President*
Michael Farrow, *CFO*

Susan Hollingshead,
Keith Goldberg, *Officer*
Ken Foster, *Executive*
EMP: 81
SALES (est): 24.9MM **Privately Held**
SIC: 7371 Computer software development

(P-15181)
VERINT AMERICAS INC
Blue Pumpkin
2250 Walsh Ave Ste 120, Santa Clara
(95050-2514)
PHONE.....................408 830-5400
Doron Aspitz, *Branch Mgr*
Ron Conway, *Bd of Directors*
Andi Fant, *Vice Pres*
Michael Maoz, *Vice Pres*
Elizabeth Ussher, *Vice Pres*
EMP: 100 **Publicly Held**
WEB: www.witness.com
SIC: 7371 8742 7372 Computer software
writers, freelance; management consulting services; prepackaged software
HQ: Verint Americas Inc.
800 North Point Pkwy
Alpharetta GA 30005

(P-15182)
VERITAS TECHNOLOGIES LLC (DH)
2625 Augustine Dr, Santa Clara
(95054-2956)
PHONE.....................866 837-4827
Greg Hughes, *CEO*
Nancy Taylor, *Partner*
Mick Lopez, *CFO*
Todd Forsythe, *Chief Mktg Ofcr*
Ben Gibson, *Chief Mktg Ofcr*
EMP: 200
SALES (est): 146.1MM
SALES (corp-wide): 2.4B **Publicly Held**
SIC: 7371 7372 Computer software development & applications; information retrieval services; data base information retrieval

(P-15183)
VERITAS US INC
500 E Middlefield Rd, Mountain View
(94043-4000)
PHONE.....................650 933-1000
William T Coleman, *CEO*
EMP: 200 **EST:** 2014
SALES: 1.2B **Privately Held**
SIC: 7371 Computer software development & applications

(P-15184)
VERIZON CONNECT NWF INC
9868 Scranton Rd Ste 1000, San Diego
(92121-1791)
PHONE.....................858 450-3245
Keith Schneider, *President*
Brad Lackey, *Administration*
Eric Simon, *Info Tech Dir*
Mark Hunt, *Engineer*
Leonardo Gomez, *Accounting Mgr*
▲ **EMP:** 95
SQ FT: 13,000
SALES (est): 20.4MM
SALES (corp-wide): 130.8B **Publicly Held**
WEB: www.networkcar.com
SIC: 7371 Computer software development & applications
HQ: Verizon Connect Inc.
2002 Summit Blvd Ste 1800
Brookhaven GA 30319
404 573-5800

(P-15185)
VIDA HEALTH INC
100 Montgomery St Ste 750, San Francisco
(94104-4302)
PHONE.....................408 203-7959
Stephanie Tilenius, *CEO*
Cynthia Mark, *Ch Credit Ofcr*
Chris Mosunic, *Vice Pres*
EMP: 60
SALES (est): 655.2K **Privately Held**
SIC: 7371 Computer software development & applications

(P-15186)
VIDHWAN INC
2 N Market St Ste 410, San Jose
(95113-1211)
PHONE.....................408 521-0167
EMP: 112
SALES (corp-wide): 25.5MM **Privately Held**
SIC: 7371 Custom computer programming services
PA: Vidhwan, Inc.
2 N Market St Ste 400
San Jose CA 95113
408 289-8200

(P-15187)
VISION SOLUTIONS INC (PA)
15300 Barranca Pkwy # 100, Irvine
(92618-2256)
PHONE.....................949 253-6500
Nicolaas Vlok, *President*
Maureen Eubeler, *Partner*
Don Scott, *CFO*
Wm Edward Vesely, *Chief Mktg Ofcr*
Alan Arnold, *Exec VP*
EMP: 90
SQ FT: 25,000
SALES: 145MM **Privately Held**
WEB: www.visionsolutions.com
SIC: 7371 7373 Computer software development; systems integration services

(P-15188)
VISUAL CONCEPTS ENTERTAINMENT
10 Hamilton Landing, Novato (94949-8207)
PHONE.....................415 479-3634
Gregory Thomas, *President*
Brian Ramagli, *Software Engr*
Visual Yu, *Project Mgr*
EMP: 200
SALES (est): 14.2MM **Publicly Held**
SIC: 7371 Computer software development
PA: Take-Two Interactive Software, Inc.
110 W 44th St
New York NY 10036

(P-15189)
VM SERVICES INC
1051 S East St, Anaheim (92805-5749)
PHONE.....................714 678-5200
Bernie Chong, *Branch Mgr*
EMP: 50
SALES (corp-wide): 2.5B **Privately Held**
WEB: www.venturemfg-usa.com
SIC: 7371 5734 3999 Computer software development; computer & software stores; barber & beauty shop equipment
HQ: Vm Services, Inc.
6701 Mowry Ave
Newark CA 94560
510 744-3720

(P-15190)
VM SERVICES INC (DH)
6701 Mowry Ave, Newark (94560-4927)
PHONE.....................510 744-3720
Chin Tong Wong, *CEO*
▲ **EMP:** 120
SQ FT: 4,300
SALES (est): 106.6MM
SALES (corp-wide): 2.5B **Privately Held**
WEB: www.venturemfg-usa.com
SIC: 7371 Computer software development
HQ: Cebelian Holdings Pte Ltd
5006 Ang Mo Kio Avenue 5
Singapore
648 217-55

(P-15191)
VMWARE INC
3305 Hillview Ave, Palo Alto (94304-1204)
P.O. Box 52100 (94303-0751)
PHONE.....................650 812-8200
George Symons, *Branch Mgr*
Sachin Prasad, *Administration*
EMP: 180
SALES (corp-wide): 90.6B **Publicly Held**
SIC: 7371 7375 Computer software development; information retrieval services

HQ: Vmware, Inc.
3401 Hillview Ave
Palo Alto CA 94304
650 427-5000

(P-15192)
VOXIFY INC
1151 Marina Village Pkwy, Alameda
(94501-1017)
PHONE.....................510 545-3011
Madhu Ranganathan, *President*
John Gengarella, *President*
John Longinotti, *CFO*
EMP: 65
SALES (est): 6.4MM **Privately Held**
WEB: www.voxify.com
SIC: 7371 Computer software development

(P-15193)
VWISE INC
85 Enterprise Ste 320, Aliso Viejo
(92656-2504)
PHONE.....................949 716-1276
Tony F Mingo, *CEO*
Dave Ferrigno, *CFO*
EMP: 60
SALES (est): 3.2MM **Privately Held**
SIC: 7371 Computer software development

(P-15194)
VYSHNAVI INFORMATION TECHN
2603 Camino Ramon Ste 200, San Ramon
(94583-9137)
PHONE.....................408 454-6218
Ravi H Krishnamurthy, *CEO*
EMP: 150
SALES: 5.7MM **Privately Held**
SIC: 7371 7372 7373 Computer software development & applications; computer software systems analysis & design, custom; application computer software; business oriented computer software; systems software development services

(P-15195)
WALKME INC (PA)
525 Market St Lbby, San Francisco
(94105-2709)
PHONE.....................855 492-5563
Dan Adika, *CEO*
Rephael Sweary, *President*
Eyal Cohen, *Exec VP*
Richard Woolf, *Exec VP*
Amir M Farhi, *Vice Pres*
EMP: 60 **EST:** 2012
SALES: 5.1MM **Privately Held**
SIC: 7371 Computer software development

(P-15196)
WALZ GROUP LLC (HQ)
Also Called: Walz Postal Solutions
27398 Via Industria, Temecula
(92590-3699)
PHONE.....................951 491-6800
Rod Walz, *President*
Kevin Miller, *CFO*
Maria Moskver, *Ch Credit Ofcr*
Brad Knapp, *Exec VP*
Carlo Mitchel, *Vice Pres*
EMP: 117
SQ FT: 40,000
SALES (est): 35.1MM
SALES (corp-wide): 102MM **Privately Held**
SIC: 7371 Computer software development & applications
PA: Lenderlive Network, Llc
710 S Ash St Ste 200
Denver CO 80246
303 226-8000

(P-15197)
WATERLINE DATA SCIENCE INC
615 National Ave Ste 100, Mountain View
(94043-2227)
PHONE.....................650 868-4409
Kailash Ambwani, *CEO*
Kaycee Lai, *President*
Myoung Kang, *CFO*
Todd Goldman, *Chief Mktg Ofcr*
Alex Gorelik, *Officer*
EMP: 75

SALES: 1.4MM **Privately Held**
SIC: 7371 Computer software development & applications

(P-15198)
WAYFORWARD TECHNOLOGIES INC
28738 The Old Rd, Valencia (91355-1084)
PHONE.....................661 286-2769
Voldi Way, *President*
Matt Bozon, *Creative Dir*
Walter Hecht, *Software Engr*
Andrew Aitchison, *Prgrmr*
Edward Fleischman, *Prgrmr*
EMP: 50
SQ FT: 10,000
SALES (est): 7.3MM **Privately Held**
WEB: www.wayforward.com
SIC: 7371 Computer software development

(P-15199)
WEBYOG INC
2900 Gordon Ave 100-7p, Santa Clara
(95051)
PHONE.....................408 512-1434
Rohit Nadhani, *CEO*
EMP: 250
SALES (est): 7.4MM
SALES (corp-wide): 124.3MM **Privately Held**
SIC: 7371 Computer software development
PA: Idera, Inc.
2950 North Loop W Ste 700
Houston TX 77092
713 523-4433

(P-15200)
WETRANSFER CORPORATION
2116 Zeno Pl, Venice (90291-4855)
PHONE.....................626 626-5565
Damian J Bradfield, *CEO*
EMP: 51
SALES (est): 2.7MM **Privately Held**
SIC: 7371 Computer software development & applications

(P-15201)
WIDEORBIT INC (PA)
1160 Battery St Ste 300, San Francisco
(94111-1212)
PHONE.....................415 675-6700
Eric Mathewson, *CEO*
Nathan Gans, *COO*
Mark Moeder, *COO*
Mickey McClay Wilson, *Officer*
Mike Zinsmeister, *Exec VP*
EMP: 88
SQ FT: 9,000
SALES (est): 62.5MM **Privately Held**
WEB: www.wideorbit.com
SIC: 7371 Computer software development

(P-15202)
WINMAX SYSTEMS CORPORATION
1900 Mccarthy Blvd # 301, Milpitas
(95035-7440)
PHONE.....................408 894-9000
Suparna Bhattacharya, *President*
Bhattacharya Pam, *COO*
Vinnie Bandla, *Executive*
Afton Usry-Papesh, *Opers Staff*
Pam Bhattacharya, *Director*
EMP: 120
SQ FT: 1,900
SALES (est): 9.8MM **Privately Held**
WEB: www.winmaxcorp.com
SIC: 7371 8742 Computer software development; management consulting services

(P-15203)
WISE COMMERCE INC
1730 S El Camino Real # 500, San Mateo
(94402-3085)
PHONE.....................855 469-4737
Arie Shpanya, *CEO*
Raaid Hossain, *Vice Pres*
Chris Angell, *VP Mktg*
EMP: 90
SALES (est): 230.4K **Privately Held**
SIC: 7371 Computer software development

(P-15204)
WORKDAY INC (PA)
6110 Stoneridge Mall Rd, Pleasanton
(94588-3211)
PHONE....................925 951-9000
Aneel Bhusri, *CEO*
Chano Fernandez, *President*
Robynne D Sisco, *President*
James J Bozzini, *COO*
Michael A Stankey, *Vice Ch Bd*
EMP: 148
SALES: 2.8B **Publicly Held**
WEB: www.workday.com
SIC: 7371 7374 Custom computer programming services; computer software development; data processing & preparation

(P-15205)
WORKFORCELOGIC
425 California St, San Francisco
(94104-2102)
PHONE....................707 939-4300
Catherine Candland, *CEO*
Steve Furtado, *CFO*
Gary D Nelson, *Chairman*
Stuart Thompto, *Senior VP*
Catherine Wingate, *Senior VP*
EMP: 100
SALES (est): 4.3MM
SALES (corp-wide): 1.8B **Privately Held**
SIC: 7371 7361 Computer software development; executive placement
PA: Workforce Logiq
420 S Orange Ave Ste 600
Orlando FL 32801
877 937-6242

(P-15206)
WYNNE SYSTEMS INC (DH)
2601 Main St Ste 270, Irvine (92614-4203)
PHONE....................949 224-6300
John Bureau, *President*
Mike Stilwagner, *Vice Pres*
Peter Bergstrom, *Software Dev*
Demetrio Robles, *Software Dev*
Craig Stanley, *Prgrmr*
EMP: 62
SALES (est): 8MM
SALES (corp-wide): 3B **Privately Held**
WEB: www.unitedrentals.com
SIC: 7371 7372 Computer software development; prepackaged software
HQ: Volaris Group Inc
5060 Spectrum Way Suite 110
Mississauga ON L4W 5
905 267-5400

(P-15207)
XACTLY CORPORATION (HQ)
505 S Market St, San Jose (95113-2827)
PHONE....................408 977-3132
Christopher W Cabrera, *CEO*
L Evan Ellis Jr, *President*
Joseph C Consul, *CFO*
Elizabeth Salomon, *CFO*
Scott R Broomfield, *Chief Mktg Ofcr*
EMP: 101
SALES (est): 95.4MM
SALES (corp-wide): 19MM **Privately Held**
WEB: www.xactlycorp.com
SIC: 7371 7372 Software programming applications; prepackaged software
PA: Excalibur Parent, Llc
300 Park Ave Ste 1700
San Jose CA 95110
408 977-3132

(P-15208)
XAP CORPORATION (PA)
600 Crprate Pinte Ste 220, Culver City
(90230)
PHONE....................310 743-0450
Eddie Monnier, *CEO*
EMP: 50
SALES: 10MM **Privately Held**
WEB: www.xap.com
SIC: 7371 Computer software development

(P-15209)
XYKA INC
5201 Great America Pkwy # 320, Santa
Clara (95054-1122)
PHONE....................408 340-1923
Rakesh Hegde, *CEO*
Nirav Chhaprapati, *President*
EMP: 50
SQ FT: 1,500
SALES (est): 2.7MM **Privately Held**
WEB: www.xyka.com
SIC: 7371 Computer software development

(P-15210)
YARDI SYSTEMS INC (PA)
430 S Fairview Ave, Santa Barbara
(93117-3637)
PHONE....................805 699-2040
Anant Yardi, *President*
Jonathan Delong, *President*
Gordon Morrell, *COO*
John Pendergast, *Senior VP*
Fritz Schindelbeck, *Senior VP*
EMP: 380
SQ FT: 160,000
SALES (est): 489.6MM **Privately Held**
SIC: 7371 Computer software development

(P-15211)
YOU TECHNOLOGY LLC
2001 Junipero Serra Blvd # 400, Daly City
(94014-3894)
PHONE....................650 624-3800
Cheryl Black, *CEO*
Hemanga Nath, *Senior VP*
Corinne Chiu, *Vice Pres*
Cassie Davis, *Vice Pres*
Sandi Lomeli-Rose, *Vice Pres*
EMP: 65
SALES (est): 6.8MM
SALES (corp-wide): 1.4B **Privately Held**
SIC: 7371 7373 Computer software development & applications; systems software development services
HQ: Inmar, Inc.
635 Vine St
Winston Salem NC 27101
800 765-1277

(P-15212)
ZEND TECHNOLOGIES USA INC
19200 Stevens Creek Blvd # 100, Cupertino (95014-2530)
PHONE....................408 253-8800
Andi Gutmans, *CEO*
Stu Schmidt, *President*
Curt Disibio, *CFO*
Daniel Moskowitz, *Treasurer*
Elaine Lennox, *Chief Mktg Ofcr*
EMP: 130
SALES (est): 15.6MM
SALES (corp-wide): 90.4MM **Privately Held**
SIC: 7371 Computer software development
PA: Rogue Wave Software, Inc.
1315 W Century Dr Ste 150
Louisville CO 80027
303 473-9118

(P-15213)
ZENTEK CORPORATION
3031 Stnfrd Rnch Rd 2, Rocklin (95765)
PHONE....................916 749-3610
Kristi Woehl, *Principal*
Michael Prendergast, *Business Mgr*
EMP: 100
SALES (est): 4.8MM **Privately Held**
SIC: 7371 8741 Computer software development & applications; management services

(P-15214)
ZIGNAL LABS INC
600 California St Fl 18, San Francisco
(94108-2711)
PHONE....................415 683-7871
Bob Deppisch, *Director*
Josh Ginsberg, *CEO*
Chris Krook, *CFO*
Yolis Ruiz, *Vice Pres*
Michael Venet, *Executive*
EMP: 60 EST: 2011
SALES (est): 10.4MM **Privately Held**
SIC: 7371 Computer software development & applications

(P-15215)
ZL TECHNOLOGIES INC (PA)
860 N Mccarthy Blvd # 100, Milpitas
(95035-5110)
PHONE....................408 240-8989
Kon Leong, *President*
Melinda Watts, *Senior VP*
Arvind Srinivasan, *CTO*
Nack Jung, *Software Engr*
Bikramjit Mandal, *Software Engr*
EMP: 51
SQ FT: 1,860
SALES (est): 14.8MM **Privately Held**
WEB: www.zlti.com
SIC: 7371 5045 Computer software systems analysis & design, custom; computer software

(P-15216)
ZONE24X7 INC (PA)
3150 Almaden Expy Ste 234, San Jose
(95118-1250)
PHONE....................408 268-8589
Llavaya Fernando, *President*
Tim Becera, *President*
Saw-Chin Fernando, *CFO*
Neschae Fernando, *Vice Pres*
Schayne Jallow, *Bus Dvlpt Dir*
EMP: 285
SQ FT: 1,000
SALES: 13MM **Privately Held**
WEB: www.zone24x7.com
SIC: 7371 Computer software development

(P-15217)
ZOOM VIDEO COMMUNICATIONS INC (PA)
55 Almaden Blvd Fl 6, San Jose
(95113-1608)
PHONE....................888 799-9666
Eric S Yuan, *Ch of Bd*
Kelly Steckelberg, *CFO*
Janine Pelosi, *Chief Mktg Ofcr*
Wendi Hurley, *Executive*
Janelle Raney, *Executive*
EMP: 148
SQ FT: 66,000
SALES: 330.5MM **Publicly Held**
SIC: 7371 Computer software development

(P-15218)
ZSCALER INC (PA)
110 Rose Orchard Way, San Jose
(95134-1358)
PHONE....................408 533-0288
Jagtar S Chaudhry, *Ch of Bd*
Robert Schlossman,
Amit Sinha, *Exec VP*
Manoj Apte, *Senior VP*
EMP: 146
SQ FT: 56,000
SALES: 302.8MM **Publicly Held**
SIC: 7371 7372 Custom computer programming services; prepackaged software

---
7372 Prepackaged Software

(P-15219)
1ON1 LLC
12015 Waterfront Dr # 261, Playa Vista
(90094-2536)
PHONE....................310 448-5376
Susan Josephson, *Mng Member*
Todd Cherniawsky,
Nicole David,
Lorri Goddard,
Stephane Medam,
EMP: 50
SQ FT: 5,000
SALES: 20MM **Privately Held**
SIC: 7372 Application computer software

(P-15220)
ABB ENTERPRISE SOFTWARE INC
60 Spear St, San Francisco (94105-1506)
PHONE....................415 527-2850
Greg Dukat, *Branch Mgr*
EMP: 175

SALES (corp-wide): 36.4B **Privately Held**
WEB: www.indusinternational.com
SIC: 7372 Business oriented computer software
HQ: Abb Enterprise Software Inc.
305 Gregson Dr
Cary NC 27511
919 856-2360

(P-15221)
ACCELA INC (PA)
2633 Camino Ramon Ste 500, San Ramon
(94583-9149)
PHONE....................925 659-3200
Gary Kovacs, *CEO*
Mark Jung, *Ch of Bd*
Maury Blackman, *CEO*
Ed Daihl, *CFO*
Jeffrey Toung, *COO*
EMP: 150
SALES: 80MM **Privately Held**
WEB: www.accela.com
SIC: 7372 Business oriented computer software

(P-15222)
ACTIVISION BLIZZARD INC
4 Hamilton Landing, Novato (94949-8256)
PHONE....................415 881-9100
EMP: 209
SALES (corp-wide): 7.5B **Publicly Held**
SIC: 7372 Home entertainment computer software
PA: Activision Blizzard, Inc.
3100 Ocean Park Blvd
Santa Monica CA 90405
310 255-2000

(P-15223)
ACTIVISION BLIZZARD INC (PA)
3100 Ocean Park Blvd, Santa Monica
(90405-3032)
PHONE....................310 255-2000
Robert A Kotick, *CEO*
Brian Kelly, *Ch of Bd*
Dennis Durkin, *President*
Collister Johnson, *President*
Rob Kostich, *President*
EMP: 333
SQ FT: 152,431
SALES: 7.5B **Publicly Held**
WEB: www.blizzard.com
SIC: 7372 Home entertainment computer software

(P-15224)
ACTIVISION BLIZZARD INC
Blizzard Entertainment
3 Blizzard, Irvine (92618-3628)
P.O. Box 18979 (92623-8979)
PHONE....................949 955-1380
Frank Pearce, *Principal*
Michael Maggio, *Engineer*
Stephen Raub, *Engineer*
Luke Tomlinson, *Engineer*
Rob Tomson, *Engineer*
EMP: 85
SALES (corp-wide): 7.5B **Publicly Held**
WEB: www.blizzard.com
SIC: 7372 Prepackaged software
PA: Activision Blizzard, Inc.
3100 Ocean Park Blvd
Santa Monica CA 90405
310 255-2000

(P-15225)
ACTIVISION PUBLISHING INC (HQ)
3100 Ocean Park Blvd, Santa Monica
(90405-3032)
PHONE....................310 255-2000
Michael Griffith, *President*
Dave Cowling, *President*
Dan Rosensweig, *President*
Colin Schiller, *President*
Eric Hirshberg, *CEO*
▲ EMP: 1306
SALES (est): 98.4MM
SALES (corp-wide): 7.5B **Publicly Held**
SIC: 7372 Home entertainment computer software
PA: Activision Blizzard, Inc.
3100 Ocean Park Blvd
Santa Monica CA 90405
310 255-2000

(P-15226)
ADAPTIVE INSGHTS LLC A WORKDAY (HQ)
2300 Geng Rd Ste 100, Palo Alto (94303-3352)
PHONE.....................650 528-7500
Thomas F Bogan, *CEO*
Amy Reichanadter, *Officer*
Melanie D Vinson, *Admin Sec*
Bob McDiarmid, *Software Dev*
Ravinder Redd Rallagudam, *Software Dev*
EMP: 200
SALES: 106.5MM
SALES (corp-wide): 2.8B **Publicly Held**
WEB: www.adaptiveplanning.com
SIC: 7372 Business oriented computer software
PA: Workday, Inc.
6110 Stoneridge Mall Rd
Pleasanton CA 94588
925 951-9000

(P-15227)
ADEXA INC (PA)
5777 W Century Blvd # 1100, Los Angeles (90045-5643)
PHONE.....................310 642-2100
Khosrow Cyrus Hadavi, *CEO*
Kameron Hadavi, *Vice Pres*
John Hosford, *Vice Pres*
William Green, *VP Business*
Tim Field, *CTO*
EMP: 50
SQ FT: 31,000
SALES (est): 18MM **Privately Held**
WEB: www.adexa.com
SIC: 7372 Business oriented computer software

(P-15228)
ADOBE INC
601 And 625 Townsend St, San Francisco (94103)
PHONE.....................415 832-2000
Les Schmidt, *Vice Pres*
EMP: 1000
SALES (corp-wide): 9B **Publicly Held**
SIC: 7372 Prepackaged software
PA: Adobe Inc.
345 Park Ave
San Jose CA 95110
408 536-6000

(P-15229)
ADOBE INC (PA)
345 Park Ave, San Jose (95110-2704)
PHONE.....................408 536-6000
Shantanu Narayen, *Ch of Bd*
Ann Lewnes, *Chief Mktg Ofcr*
Scott Belsky,
Bryan Lamkin, *Exec VP*
Donna Morris, *Exec VP*
EMP: 600
SQ FT: 989,000
SALES: 9B **Publicly Held**
WEB: www.adobe.com
SIC: 7372 Application computer software

(P-15230)
ADVENT RESOURCES INC
235 W 7th St, San Pedro (90731-3321)
PHONE.....................310 241-1500
Ysidro Salinas, *Ch of Bd*
Timothy Gill, *CEO*
Vishal Ghelani, *Vice Pres*
Benjamin Gill, *Vice Pres*
Mitch Stahl, *Exec Dir*
EMP: 80
SQ FT: 22,000
SALES (est): 12.2MM **Privately Held**
WEB: www.adventresources.com
SIC: 7372 Prepackaged software

(P-15231)
AGENCYCOM LLC
5353 Grosvenor Blvd, Los Angeles (90066-6913)
PHONE.....................415 817-3800
Chan Suh, *CEO*
Jordan Warren, *President*
Rob Elliott, *CFO*
EMP: 400
SQ FT: 130,000

SALES (est): 20.2MM
SALES (corp-wide): 15.2B **Publicly Held**
WEB: www.agency.com
SIC: 7372 Application computer software
PA: Omnicom Group Inc.
437 Madison Ave
New York NY 10022
212 415-3600

(P-15232)
ALERTENTERPRISE INC
4350 Starboard Dr, Fremont (94538-6434)
PHONE.....................510 440-0840
Jasvir Gill, *CEO*
Kaval Kaur, *COO*
Ehsan Hameed, *Vice Pres*
Srini Kakkera, *Vice Pres*
Willem Ryan, *Vice Pres*
EMP: 140
SQ FT: 24,000
SALES (est): 15.6MM **Privately Held**
SIC: 7372 Prepackaged software

(P-15233)
ALIENVAULT LLC (DH)
1100 Park Pl Ste 300, San Mateo (94403-7108)
PHONE.....................650 713-3333
Barmak Meftah, *President*
J Alberto Yepez, *Ch of Bd*
Chris Murphy, *President*
Brian Robins, *CFO*
Rita Selvaggi, *Chief Mktg Ofcr*
EMP: 56
SALES (est): 37.8MM
SALES (corp-wide): 170.7B **Publicly Held**
SIC: 7372 Business oriented computer software
HQ: Alienvault, Inc.
1100 Park Pl Ste 300
San Mateo CA 94403
650 713-3333

(P-15234)
ALLDATA LLC
9650 W Taron Dr Ste 100, Elk Grove (95757-8197)
PHONE.....................916 684-5200
Stephen Odland,
Bob Olsen,
EMP: 76
SQ FT: 35,000
SALES (est): 43.3MM
SALES (corp-wide): 11.8B **Publicly Held**
WEB: www.alldata.com
SIC: 7372 Business oriented computer software
PA: Autozone, Inc.
123 S Front St
Memphis TN 38103
901 495-6500

(P-15235)
ALTIUM LLC
4275 Executive Sq Ste 825, La Jolla (92037-1478)
PHONE.....................800 544-4186
Aram Mirkazemi,
Martin Ive, *Treasurer*
EMP: 75
SALES (est): 2.2MM **Privately Held**
SIC: 7372 Prepackaged software

(P-15236)
APPDIRECT INC (PA)
650 California St Fl 25, San Francisco (94108-2606)
PHONE.....................415 852-3924
Nicolas Desmarais, *Ch of Bd*
Daniel Saks, *President*
Michael Difilippo, *CFO*
Mark Beebe, *Vice Pres*
Francois Duquette, *Sr Software Eng*
EMP: 59
SQ FT: 10,000
SALES (est): 28.4MM **Privately Held**
SIC: 7372 7371 Application computer software; computer software development & applications

(P-15237)
APPDYNAMICS INC (HQ)
303 2nd St Fl 8, San Francisco (94107-1366)
PHONE.....................415 442-8400

David Wadhwani, *President*
Daniel J Wright, *Senior VP*
Arpit Patel, *Vice Pres*
Keith Scott, *Executive*
Kurt Thompson, *Executive*
EMP: 148
SQ FT: 83,500
SALES: 150.5MM
SALES (corp-wide): 51.9B **Publicly Held**
SIC: 7372 Prepackaged software
PA: Cisco Systems, Inc.
170 W Tasman Dr
San Jose CA 95134
408 526-4000

(P-15238)
APPETIZE TECHNOLOGIES INC
6601 Center Dr W Ste 700, Los Angeles (90045-1545)
PHONE.....................877 559-4225
Max Roper, *CEO*
Jason Pratts, *COO*
Dan Machock, *CFO*
Mark Eastwood, *Officer*
Kevin Anderson, *Senior VP*
EMP: 110 **EST:** 2011
SALES (est): 257.6K **Privately Held**
SIC: 7372 Application computer software

(P-15239)
APPFOLIO INC (PA)
50 Castilian Dr Ste 101, Goleta (93117-5578)
PHONE.....................805 364-6093
Jason Randall, *President*
Andreas Von Blottnitz, *Ch of Bd*
Ida Kane, *CFO*
Janet Kerr, *Bd of Directors*
James Peters, *Bd of Directors*
EMP: 139
SQ FT: 79,200
SALES: 190MM **Publicly Held**
SIC: 7372 Business oriented computer software

(P-15240)
APPFOLIO INC
Also Called: Mycase
9201 Spectrum, San Diego (92123)
PHONE.....................866 648-1536
Troy Alford, *Engineer*
EMP: 573
SALES (corp-wide): 190MM **Publicly Held**
SIC: 7372 Prepackaged software
PA: Appfolio, Inc.
50 Castilian Dr Ste 101
Goleta CA 93117
805 364-6093

(P-15241)
APTELIGENT INC
1100 La Avenida St Ste A, Mountain View (94043-1453)
PHONE.....................415 371-1402
Pat Gelsinger, *CEO*
Scott Bajtos, *COO*
Sanjay Poonen, *COO*
Raghu Raghuram, *COO*
Rajiv Ramaswami, *COO*
EMP: 60
SALES (est): 4.2MM
SALES (corp-wide): 90.6B **Publicly Held**
SIC: 7372 Prepackaged software
HQ: Vmware, Inc.
3401 Hillview Ave
Palo Alto CA 94304
650 427-5000

(P-15242)
APTIV DIGITAL LLC
2160 Gold St, San Jose (95002-3700)
PHONE.....................818 295-6789
Neil Jones, *President*
Christine Otto, *Director*
EMP: 85
SALES (est): 3.5MM
SALES (corp-wide): 695.8MM **Publicly Held**
WEB: www.tvguideinc.com
SIC: 7372 Home entertainment computer software
HQ: Rovi Guides, Inc.
2233 N Ontario St Ste 100
Burbank CA 91504

(P-15243)
ARENA SOLUTIONS INC
Also Called: Omnify Software
989 E Hillsdale Blvd # 250, Foster City (94404-4201)
PHONE.....................978 988-3800
Brad Paul, *Treasurer*
EMP: 50
SALES (corp-wide): 19.6MM **Privately Held**
SIC: 7372 Prepackaged software
PA: Arena Solutions, Inc.
989 E Hillsdale Blvd # 250
Foster City CA 94404
650 513-3500

(P-15244)
ARIBA INC (DH)
3420 Hillview Ave Bldg 3, Palo Alto (94304-1355)
PHONE.....................650 849-4000
Alex Atzberger, *CEO*
Marc Malone, *CFO*
Alicia Tillman, *Chief Mktg Ofcr*
Brad Brubaker, *Admin Sec*
Kimberly Truong, *Administration*
EMP: 105
SQ FT: 86,000
SALES (est): 384.4MM
SALES (corp-wide): 28.2B **Privately Held**
WEB: www.ariba.com
SIC: 7372 Business oriented computer software
HQ: Sap America, Inc.
3999 West Chester Pike
Newtown Square PA 19073
610 661-1000

(P-15245)
ASPECT SOFTWARE INC
101 Academy Ste 130, Irvine (92617-3081)
PHONE.....................408 595-5002
James Foy, *Owner*
EMP: 50
SALES (corp-wide): 303.2MM **Privately Held**
SIC: 7372 Prepackaged software
HQ: Aspect Software, Inc.
2325 E Camelback Rd # 700
Phoenix AZ 85016
978 250-7900

(P-15246)
ATHOC INC (DH)
3001 Bishop Dr Ste 400, San Ramon (94583-5005)
PHONE.....................925 242-5660
Guy Miasnik, *President*
Douglas Doyle, *Officer*
Aviv Siegel, *Exec VP*
Ly Tran, *Exec VP*
Karen Garavatti, *Vice Pres*
EMP: 61
SALES (est): 15.3MM
SALES (corp-wide): 904MM **Privately Held**
WEB: www.athoc.com
SIC: 7372 Prepackaged software
HQ: Blackberry Corporation
3001 Bishop Dr
San Ramon CA 94583
972 650-6126

(P-15247)
ATLASSIAN INC (DH)
350 Bush St Ste 13, San Francisco (94104-2879)
PHONE.....................415 701-1110
Scott Farquhar, *CEO*
Jeff Diana,
Carilu Dietrich, *Vice Pres*
Audra Eng, *Vice Pres*
Daniel Freeman, *Vice Pres*
EMP: 101
SALES (est): 43.3MM
SALES (corp-wide): 873.9MM **Privately Held**
WEB: www.atlassian.com
SIC: 7372 Business oriented computer software

(P-15248)
ATYPON SYSTEMS LLC (PA)
5201 Great America Pkwy # 215, Santa Clara (95054-1177)
PHONE.....................408 988-1240

Georgios Papadopoulos, *CEO*
Colin Caprani, *Partner*
Chao Zhang, *Partner*
Joshua Pyle, *President*
Gordon Tibbitts, *President*
EMP: 60
SQ FT: 6,000
SALES (est): 12.3MM **Privately Held**
WEB: www.atypon.com
SIC: 7372 Application computer software

(P-15249)
AUDATEX NORTH AMERICA INC (DH)
Also Called: Audaexplore
15030 Ave Of, San Diego (92128)
PHONE...................................858 946-1900
Don Tartre, *Vice Pres*
Jack Pearlstein, *CFO*
Ryan Hager, *Vice Pres*
Richard Palmer, *Vice Pres*
Steve Poeschl, *Software Engr*
EMP: 200
SQ FT: 35,000
SALES (est): 130MM
SALES (corp-wide): 849MM **Privately Held**
SIC: 7372 Business oriented computer software

(P-15250)
AUTODESK INC
1 Market St, San Francisco (94105-1420)
PHONE...................................415 356-0700
Chris Bradshaw, *Branch Mgr*
Yvonne Cekel, *Partner*
Wes Hamerstadt, *Partner*
Lisa Campbell, *Chief Mktg Ofcr*
Lee Pisacano, *Vice Pres*
EMP: 61
SALES (corp-wide): 2.5B **Publicly Held**
WEB: www.autodesk.com
SIC: 7372 Application computer software
PA: Autodesk, Inc.
111 Mcinnis Pkwy
San Rafael CA 94903
415 507-5000

(P-15251)
AUTODESK INC (PA)
111 Mcinnis Pkwy, San Rafael (94903-2700)
PHONE...................................415 507-5000
Andrew Anagnost, *President*
Stacy J Smith, *Ch of Bd*
R Scott Herren, *CFO*
Pascal W Di Fronzo,
Carmel Galvin, *Officer*
◆ **EMP:** 400 **EST:** 1982
SQ FT: 189,000
SALES: 2.5B **Publicly Held**
WEB: www.autodesk.com
SIC: 7372 Application computer software

(P-15252)
AUTODESK INC
3950 Civic Center Dr, San Rafael (94903-5901)
PHONE...................................415 507-5000
Kathryn Najafi-Tagol, *Manager*
Thomas Georgens, *Bd of Directors*
EMP: 250
SALES (corp-wide): 2.5B **Publicly Held**
WEB: www.autodesk.com
SIC: 7372 Application computer software
PA: Autodesk, Inc.
111 Mcinnis Pkwy
San Rafael CA 94903
415 507-5000

(P-15253)
AZUL SYSTEMS INC (PA)
385 Moffett Park Dr # 115, Sunnyvale (94089-1217)
PHONE...................................650 230-6500
Scott Sellers, *President*
Anya Chernyak, *Vice Pres*
Michael J Field, *Vice Pres*
George W Gould, *Vice Pres*
George Gould, *Vice Pres*
EMP: 65
SALES (est): 21.7MM **Privately Held**
WEB: www.azulsystems.com
SIC: 7372 Operating systems computer software

(P-15254)
BARRA LLC (HQ)
Also Called: Msci Barra
2100 Milvia St, Berkeley (94704-1861)
PHONE...................................510 548-5442
Kamal Duggirala, *CEO*
Andrew Rudd, *Ch of Bd*
Aamir Sheikh, *President*
Greg Stockett, *CFO*
Susan Gledhill, *General Mgr*
▲ **EMP:** 280
SQ FT: 35,000
SALES (est): 29MM **Publicly Held**
WEB: www.barra.com
SIC: 7372 8741 6282 Business oriented computer software; financial management for business; investment advisory service

(P-15255)
BARRACUDA NETWORKS INC (HQ)
3175 Winchester Blvd, Campbell (95008-6557)
PHONE...................................408 342-5400
William D Jenkins Jr, *President*
Dustin Driggs, *CFO*
Erin Hintz, *Chief Mktg Ofcr*
Zachary Levow, *Exec VP*
Fleming Shi, *Technology*
EMP: 225
SQ FT: 61,400
SALES: 352.6MM
SALES (corp-wide): 44.8MM **Privately Held**
WEB: www.barracudanetworks.com
SIC: 7372 7373 Prepackaged software; computer integrated systems design
PA: Barracuda Holdings, Llc
3175 Winchester Blvd
Campbell CA 95008
408 342-5400

(P-15256)
BEATS MUSIC LLC
235 2nd St, San Francisco (94105-3124)
PHONE...................................415 590-5104
Timothy Cook, *CEO*
EMP: 95
SALES (est): 8.5MM
SALES (corp-wide): 260.1B **Publicly Held**
SIC: 7372 Prepackaged software
PA: Apple Inc.
1 Apple Park Way
Cupertino CA 95014
408 996-1010

(P-15257)
BETTERWORKS SYSTEMS INC
999 Main St, Redwood City (94063-2152)
PHONE...................................650 656-9013
Doug Dennerline, *CEO*
Diane Strohfus, *Officer*
Karen Richter, *Vice Pres*
Mathew Geist, *Software Engr*
Justin Huang, *Software Engr*
EMP: 75
SALES: 8MM **Privately Held**
SIC: 7372 Publishers' computer software

(P-15258)
BIG SWITCH NETWORKS INC (PA)
3111 Coronado Dr Bldg A, Santa Clara (95054-3206)
PHONE...................................650 322-6510
Douglas Murray, *CEO*
Jeffrey Wang, *President*
Seamus Hennessy, *CFO*
Wendell Laidley, *CFO*
Gregg Holzrichter, *Chief Mktg Ofcr*
EMP: 58
SALES (est): 42.8MM **Privately Held**
SIC: 7372 Prepackaged software

(P-15259)
BILLCOM INC
1810 Embarcadero Rd, Palo Alto (94303-3308)
PHONE...................................650 353-3301
Rene Lacerte, *CEO*
Jennifer Mohoney, *Partner*
Becky Riffis, *Partner*
Mark Orttung, *COO*
John Rettig, *CFO*

EMP: 140
SALES (est): 40.9MM **Privately Held**
SIC: 7372 Application computer software

(P-15260)
BIZMATICS INC (PA)
4010 Moorpark Ave Ste 222, San Jose (95117-1843)
PHONE...................................408 873-3030
Vinay Deshpande, *CEO*
Chris Ferguson, *President*
Sneha Baing, *Executive*
Parag Deshpande, *Analyst*
Cheri Yeung, *Accountant*
EMP: 250
SQ FT: 2,000
SALES: 5.9MM **Privately Held**
SIC: 7372 Business oriented computer software

(P-15261)
BLACKBERRY CORPORATION (HQ)
3001 Bishop Dr, San Ramon (94583-5005)
PHONE...................................972 650-6126
John Chen, *CEO*
Rashad Munawar, *Senior Mgr*
Coray Runge, *Manager*
▲ **EMP:** 79
SALES (est): 268.2MM
SALES (corp-wide): 904MM **Privately Held**
WEB: www.osgcorp.com
SIC: 7372 Prepackaged software
PA: Blackberry Limited
2200 University Ave E
Waterloo ON N2K 0
519 888-7465

(P-15262)
BLACKLINE SYSTEMS INC (HQ)
21300 Victory Blvd Fl 12, Woodland Hills (91367-7734)
PHONE...................................877 777-7750
Therese Tucker, *CEO*
Jennifer T Pottle, *Partner*
Dorothy Scofield, *Partner*
Charles Best, *CFO*
Mark Partin, *CFO*
EMP: 108
SQ FT: 66,447
SALES (est): 99.6MM
SALES (corp-wide): 227.7MM **Publicly Held**
WEB: www.blackline.com
SIC: 7372 Business oriented computer software
PA: Blackline, Inc.
21300 Victory Blvd Fl 12
Woodland Hills CA 91367
818 223-9008

(P-15263)
BLIZZARD ENTERTAINMENT INC (HQ)
1 Blizzard, Irvine (92618-3628)
P.O. Box 18979 (92623-8979)
PHONE...................................949 955-1380
Mike Morhaime, *President*
Paul Sams, *President*
Frank Pearce, *Exec VP*
Chris Metzen, *Senior VP*
Robert Bridenbecker, *Vice Pres*
▲ **EMP:** 85
SALES (est): 74.5MM
SALES (corp-wide): 7.5B **Publicly Held**
SIC: 7372 5734 7819 Prepackaged software; software, computer games; reproduction services, motion picture production
PA: Activision Blizzard, Inc.
3100 Ocean Park Blvd
Santa Monica CA 90405
310 255-2000

(P-15264)
BLUE COAT LLC
350 Ellis St, Mountain View (94043-2202)
PHONE...................................408 220-2200
Michael Fey, *President*
Thomas Seifert, *CFO*
Fran Rosch, *Exec VP*
Scott Taylor, *Exec VP*
Balaji Yelamanchili, *Exec VP*
EMP: 1583

SALES (est): 96.8MM
SALES (corp-wide): 4.7B **Publicly Held**
SIC: 7372 Prepackaged software
PA: Nortonlifelock Inc.
60 E Rio Salado Pkwy # 1
Tempe AZ 85281
650 527-8000

(P-15265)
BLUE COAT SYSTEMS LLC (HQ)
350 Ellis St, Mountain View (94043-2202)
PHONE...................................650 527-8000
Michael Fey, *President*
Donald W Alford, *President*
David Yntemai, *President*
Nicholas R Noviello, *CFO*
Thomas Seifert, *CFO*
▲ **EMP:** 81
SQ FT: 234,000
SALES (est): 35.1MM
SALES (corp-wide): 4.7B **Publicly Held**
WEB: www.cacheflow.com
SIC: 7372 Prepackaged software
PA: Nortonlifelock Inc.
60 E Rio Salado Pkwy # 1
Tempe AZ 85281
650 527-8000

(P-15266)
BORLAND SOFTWARE CORPORATION
951 Mariners Isl Blvd # 460, San Mateo (94404-1558)
PHONE...................................650 286-1900
Gina Rosenberger, *Branch Mgr*
Anil Peres-Da-Silva, *Senior Mgr*
EMP: 100 **Privately Held**
WEB: www.borland.com
SIC: 7372 Business oriented computer software
HQ: Borland Software Corporation
8310 N Cpitl Of Texas Hwy
Austin TX 78731
512 340-2200

(P-15267)
BOX INC (PA)
900 Jefferson Ave, Redwood City (94063-1837)
PHONE...................................877 729-4269
Aaron Levie, *Ch of Bd*
Chase Roberts, *Partner*
Stephanie Carullo, *COO*
Dylan Smith, *CFO*
Daniel Levin, *Bd of Directors*
EMP: 148 **EST:** 2005
SQ FT: 340,000
SALES: 608.3MM **Publicly Held**
SIC: 7372 Application computer software

(P-15268)
BQE SOFTWARE INC
3825 Del Amo Blvd Trrance Torrance, Torrance (90503)
PHONE...................................310 602-4020
Shafat Qazi, *CEO*
Sharone Strauss, *Vice Pres*
Kari Weinberger, *Marketing Staff*
Jason Burkley, *Sales Staff*
Humza Khan, *Sales Staff*
EMP: 95
SQ FT: 20,000
SALES (est): 13.1MM **Privately Held**
WEB: www.billquick.com
SIC: 7372 5734 Application computer software; software, business & non-game

(P-15269)
BROADVISION INC (PA)
460 Seaport Ct Ste 102, Redwood City (94063-5548)
PHONE...................................650 331-1000
Pehong Chen, *Ch of Bd*
Sandra Adams, *Vice Pres*
Lisheng Zhang, *Engineer*
May He, *Accounting Mgr*
Combi Serena, *Finance*
EMP: 95
SQ FT: 16,399
SALES: 5MM **Publicly Held**
WEB: www.broadvision.com
SIC: 7372 Prepackaged software

(P-15270)
C3AI INC (PA)
Also Called: C3 Iot
1300 Seaport Blvd Ste 500, Redwood City
(94063-5592)
PHONE..................................650 503-2200
Thomas M Siebel, *CEO*
Ed Abbo, *President*
Jordan Marchetto, *Software Dev*
Dylan Ferris, *Software Engr*
EMP: 122
SQ FT: 35,000
SALES (est): 55.3MM **Privately Held**
SIC: 7372 Business oriented computer
software

(P-15271)
CA INC
3965 Freedom Cir Fl 6, Santa Clara
(95054-1286)
PHONE..................................800 225-5224
EMP: 166
SALES (corp-wide): 20.8B **Publicly Held**
SIC: 7372 Business oriented computer
software
HQ: Ca, Inc.
520 Madison Ave
New York NY 10022
800 225-5224

(P-15272)
**CADENCE DESIGN SYSTEMS
INC (PA)**
2655 Seely Ave Bldg 5, San Jose
(95134-1931)
PHONE..................................408 943-1234
Lip-Bu Tan, *CEO*
John B Shoven, *Ch of Bd*
Anirudh Devgan, *President*
John M Wall, *CFO*
Thomas P Beckley, *Senior VP*
▲ **EMP:** 700
SALES: 2.1B **Publicly Held**
WEB: www.cadence.com
SIC: 7372 Prepackaged software; applica-
tion computer software

(P-15273)
CARPARTS TECHNOLOGIES
32122 Camn Capistrano # 100, San Juan
Capistrano (92675-3734)
PHONE..................................949 488-8860
Charles Ruban, *CEO*
Cynthia Robbins, *President*
EMP: 163 **EST:** 2004
SQ FT: 1,400
SALES (est): 6.3MM **Privately Held**
WEB: www.crcs.com
SIC: 7372 Prepackaged software

(P-15274)
**CATALYST DEVELOPMENT
CORP**
56925 Yucca Trl, Yucca Valley
(92284-7913)
PHONE..................................760 228-9653
Cary Harwin, *President*
Brian Rich, *Managing Prtnr*
Mike Stefanik, *Senior VP*
Kapil Desai, *Analyst*
Samantha Lexton, *Sr Associate*
EMP: 50
SALES (est): 3MM **Privately Held**
WEB: www.catalyst.com
SIC: 7372 Business oriented computer
software

(P-15275)
CELIGO INC (PA)
1820 Gateway Dr Ste 260, San Mateo
(94404-4068)
PHONE..................................650 579-0210
Jan K Arendtsz, *CEO*
Mark Simon, *Vice Pres*
Lisa Lorenz, *Office Mgr*
Laura Sherman, *Administration*
Swapna Vemparala, *Software Engr*
EMP: 50
SALES (est): 14.8MM **Privately Held**
SIC: 7372 Business oriented computer
software

(P-15276)
CFS TAX SOFTWARE
Also Called: CFS Income Tax
1445 E Los Angeles Ave # 214, Simi Valley
(93065-2828)
P.O. Box 941659 (93094-1659)
PHONE..................................805 522-1157
Ted Sullivan, *President*
Duy Tran, *Vice Pres*
Tyler Monroe, *Software Dev*
Juliana Caizzo, *MIS Staff*
Greg Hatfield, *Prgrmr*
EMP: 60
SALES (est): 6MM **Privately Held**
WEB: www.taxtools.com
SIC: 7372 8721 Business oriented com-
puter software; accounting, auditing &
bookkeeping

(P-15277)
**CHECK POINT SOFTWARE TECH
INC (HQ)**
959 Skyway Rd Ste 300, San Carlos
(94070-2723)
PHONE..................................650 628-2000
John Slavitt, *CEO*
Eyal Desheh, *CFO*
Julie Parrish, *Chief Mktg Ofcr*
Asheem Chandna, *Vice Pres*
Dorit Dor, *Vice Pres*
▲ **EMP:** 120
SALES (est): 247.1MM
SALES (corp-wide): 517.3MM **Privately
Held**
WEB: www.checkpoint.com
SIC: 7372 Operating systems computer
software
PA: Check Point Software Technologies
Ltd.
5 Shlomo Kaplan
Tel Aviv-Jaffa 67891
375 345-55

(P-15278)
CHOWNOW INC
12181 Bluff Creek Dr # 200, Playa Vista
(90094-2992)
PHONE..................................888 707-2469
Eric Jaffe, *President*
Christopher Schnack, *Executive*
Mike Wang, *Executive*
Ha Lam, *Software Engr*
Tom Pumilia, *Sales Mgr*
EMP: 100
SQ FT: 25,000
SALES (est): 2.1MM **Privately Held**
SIC: 7372 Business oriented computer
software

(P-15279)
CIPHERCLOUD INC (PA)
2581 Junction Ave Ste 200, San Jose
(95134-1923)
PHONE..................................408 519-6930
Pravin Kothari, *CEO*
Stanley Chan, *Vice Pres*
Paul Culpepper, *Vice Pres*
Harnish Kanani, *Vice Pres*
Ramesh Rathi, *Vice Pres*
EMP: 90
SQ FT: 21,800
SALES (est): 36MM **Privately Held**
SIC: 7372 Business oriented computer
software

(P-15280)
**CISCO IRONPORT SYSTEMS
LLC (HQ)**
170 W Tasman Dr, San Jose (95134-1706)
PHONE..................................650 989-6500
Scott Weiss, *CEO*
Renee Kremer, *Partner*
Tom Peterson, *President*
Craig Collins, *CFO*
Bob Kavner, *Chairman*
EMP: 260
SALES (est): 50.6MM
SALES (corp-wide): 51.9B **Publicly Held**
WEB: www.ironport.com
SIC: 7372 5045 Prepackaged software;
computers, peripherals & software
PA: Cisco Systems, Inc.
170 W Tasman Dr
San Jose CA 95134
408 526-4000

(P-15281)
CITRIX SYSTEMS INC
4988 Great America Pkwy, Santa Clara
(95054-1200)
PHONE..................................408 790-8000
Klaus Oerstermann, *Principal*
Huzaifah Saifee, *Partner*
Rajiv Sinha, *Vice Pres*
Gil Rosario, *Executive*
Daljit Singh, *Principal*
EMP: 95
SALES (corp-wide): 2.9B **Publicly Held**
WEB: www.citrix.com
SIC: 7372 Prepackaged software
PA: Citrix Systems, Inc.
851 W Cypress Creek Rd
Fort Lauderdale FL 33309
954 267-3000

(P-15282)
CLEARSLIDE INC (DH)
45 Fremont St Fl 32, San Francisco
(94105-2258)
PHONE..................................877 360-3366
Dustin Grosse, *CEO*
Jim Benton, *Officer*
Sandra Wright, *Vice Pres*
Bobby Schluter, *Executive*
Lawrence Bruhmuller, *Engineer*
EMP: 84
SALES (est): 27.5MM
SALES (corp-wide): 303.2MM **Privately
Held**
SIC: 7372 Business oriented computer
software
HQ: Corel Corporation
1600 Carling Ave Suite 100
Ottawa ON K1Z 8
613 728-8200

(P-15283)
CLEARWELL SYSTEMS INC
350 Ellis St, Mountain View (94043-2202)
PHONE..................................877 253-2793
Aaref Hilaly, *CEO*
Anup Singh, *CFO*
Venkat Rangan, *CTO*
▼ **EMP:** 110
SQ FT: 17,000
SALES (est): 9.1MM
SALES (corp-wide): 4.7B **Publicly Held**
WEB: www.clearwellsystems.com
SIC: 7372 Business oriented computer
software
PA: Nortonlifelock Inc.
60 E Rio Salado Pkwy # 1
Tempe AZ 85281
650 527-8000

(P-15284)
CLOUDFLARE INC (PA)
101 Townsend St, San Francisco
(94107-1934)
PHONE..................................888 993-5273
Matthew Prince, *Ch of Bd*
EMP: 129
SALES: 192.6MM **Publicly Held**
SIC: 7372 Prepackaged software

(P-15285)
COLORTOKENS INC
2101 Tasman Dr Ste 201, Santa Clara
(95054-1020)
PHONE..................................408 341-6030
Rajesh Parekh, *President*
EMP: 50
SALES (est): 1.3MM **Privately Held**
SIC: 7372 Business oriented computer
software

(P-15286)
COMMERCE VELOCITY LLC
1 Technology Dr Ste J725, Irvine
(92618-2353)
PHONE..................................949 756-8950
Umesh Verma,
Ajay Chopra,
EMP: 50
SQ FT: 5,000
SALES (est): 16MM
SALES (corp-wide): 7.5B **Publicly Held**
WEB: www.cvelocity.com
SIC: 7372 Business oriented computer
software

PA: Fidelity National Financial, Inc.
601 Riverside Ave Fl 4
Jacksonville FL 32204
904 854-8100

(P-15287)
**COMPOSITE SOFTWARE LLC
(HQ)**
755 Sycamore Dr, Milpitas (95035-7411)
PHONE..................................800 553-6387
Jim Green, *CEO*
Jon Bode, *CFO*
Marc Breissinger, *Exec VP*
Robert Eve, *Exec VP*
Che Wijesinghe, *Exec VP*
EMP: 74
SQ FT: 14,000
SALES (est): 17.7MM
SALES (corp-wide): 51.9B **Publicly Held**
WEB: www.compositesw.com
SIC: 7372 Prepackaged software
PA: Cisco Systems, Inc.
170 W Tasman Dr
San Jose CA 95134
408 526-4000

(P-15288)
**COMPULINK BUSINESS
SYSTEMS INC (PA)**
Also Called: Compulink Healthcare Solutions
1100 Business Center Cir, Newbury Park
(91320-1124)
PHONE..................................805 446-2050
Link Wilson, *President*
Mark Young, *COO*
Aundria Hyer, *Vice Pres*
Cole Galbarith, *Info Tech Mgr*
Jose Melendez, *Technology*
EMP: 54
SQ FT: 15,000
SALES (est): 13.5MM **Privately Held**
WEB: www.compulink-software.com
SIC: 7372 Business oriented computer
software

(P-15289)
**COMPULINK MANAGEMENT
CTR INC**
Also Called: Laserfiche Document Imaging
3545 Long Beach Blvd, Long Beach
(90807-3941)
PHONE..................................562 988-1688
Nien-Ling Wacker, *President*
Henk Eisner, *CFO*
Hedy Aref, *Vice Pres*
Karl Chan, *Vice Pres*
Jim Haney, *Vice Pres*
▲ **EMP:** 170
SQ FT: 30,000
SALES (est): 36.9MM **Privately Held**
WEB: www.laserfiche.com
SIC: 7372 Business oriented computer
software

(P-15290)
CONTACTUAL INC
810 W Maude Ave, Sunnyvale
(94085-2910)
PHONE..................................650 292-4408
Mansour Salame, *CEO*
David Sohm, *President*
David Chen, *Vice Pres*
Dani Shomron, *Vice Pres*
Richard W Southwick, *Vice Pres*
EMP: 50
SQ FT: 5,000
SALES (est): 3.3MM
SALES (corp-wide): 352.5MM **Publicly
Held**
WEB: www.contactual.com
SIC: 7372 Prepackaged software
PA: 8x8, Inc.
2125 Onel Dr
San Jose CA 95131
408 727-1885

(P-15291)
**CONVERSIONPOINT HOLDINGS
INC**
840 Newport Center Dr # 450, Newport
Beach (92660-6384)
PHONE..................................888 706-6764
Robert Tallack, *President*
Jonathan Gregg, *President*
Don Walker Barrett III, *COO*

Raghu Kilambi, *CFO*
Tom Furukawa, *CTO*
EMP: 85
SALES (est): 1.2MM **Privately Held**
SIC: 7372 Prepackaged software

(P-15292)
COPPER CRM INC (PA)
301 Howard St Ste 600, San Francisco
(94105-6600)
PHONE...................415 231-6360
Jonathan Lee, *CEO*
Charles Ashworth,
Steve Holm, *Vice Pres*
Jun Hu, *Vice Pres*
Oberbauer Justin, *Vice Pres*
EMP: 104 **EST:** 2011
SQ FT: 15,000
SALES (est): 41.6MM **Privately Held**
SIC: 7372 Application computer software

(P-15293)
CORNERSTONE ONDEMAND INC (PA)
1601 Cloverf Blvd 620s, Santa Monica
(90404-4178)
PHONE...................310 752-0200
Adam L Miller, *CEO*
Jeffrey Lautenbach, *President*
Brian L Swartz, *CFO*
Adrianna Burrows, *Chief Mktg Ofcr*
Adam Weiss, *Officer*
EMP: 148
SQ FT: 94,000
SALES: 537.8MM **Publicly Held**
WEB: www.cornerstoneondemand.com
SIC: 7372 Business oriented computer
software

(P-15294)
COUPA SOFTWARE INCORPORATED (PA)
1855 S Grant St, San Mateo (94402-7016)
PHONE...................650 931-3200
Robert Bernshteyn, *Ch of Bd*
Steven Winter, *Risk Mgmt Dir*
EMP: 148
SQ FT: 69,220
SALES: 260.3MM **Publicly Held**
WEB: www.coupa.com
SIC: 7372 Business oriented computer
software

(P-15295)
CROWDSTRIKE HOLDINGS INC (PA)
150 Mathilda Pl Ste 300, Sunnyvale
(94086-6012)
PHONE...................888 512-8906
George Kurtz, *President*
Gerhard Watzinger, *Ch of Bd*
Michael Carpenter, *President*
Shawn Henry, *President*
Colin Black, *COO*
EMP: 120
SQ FT: 30,331
SALES: 249.8MM **Publicly Held**
SIC: 7372 7379 Prepackaged software;
computer related maintenance services

(P-15296)
CRYSTAL DYNAMICS INC (DH)
1400a Saport Blvd Ste 300, Redwood City
(94063)
PHONE...................650 421-7600
Philip Rogers, *CEO*
John Miller, *President*
Kun Chen, *Info Tech Mgr*
Santiago Velez, *Software Engr*
Grant Ricks, *Project Mgr*
EMP: 90
SQ FT: 26,000
SALES (est): 13.1MM **Privately Held**
WEB: www.crystald.com
SIC: 7372 Business oriented computer
software
HQ: Square Enix Limited
240 Blackfriars Road
London SE1 8
208 636-3000

(P-15297)
CUMULUS NETWORKS INC (PA)
185 E Dana St, Mountain View
(94041-1507)
PHONE...................650 383-6700
Jame Rivers, *CEO*
Nolan Leake, *Co-Owner*
Reza Malekzadeh, *Vice Pres*
Edward Leake, *Principal*
Elizabeth Seamans, *Software Engr*
EMP: 124
SALES (est): 26.7MM **Privately Held**
SIC: 7372 7371 Publishers' computer soft-
ware; computer software development

(P-15298)
CYBREX CONSULTING INC
4470 W Sunset Blvd, Los Angeles
(90027-6302)
PHONE...................513 999-2109
James Whitmore, *Managing Dir*
EMP: 100 **EST:** 2010
SQ FT: 1,000
SALES: 2MM **Privately Held**
SIC: 7372 8742 Prepackaged software;
real estate consultant

(P-15299)
CYLANCE INC (DH)
400 Spectrum Center Dr, Irvine
(92618-4934)
PHONE...................949 375-3380
Stuart McClure, *CEO*
Rick Stojak, *Partner*
Daniel Doimo, *President*
Felix Marquardt, *President*
Brian Robins, *CFO*
EMP: 148
SALES: 200MM
SALES (corp-wide): 904MM **Privately
Held**
SIC: 7372 Application computer software
HQ: Blackberry Corporation
3001 Bishop Dr
San Ramon CA 94583
972 650-6126

(P-15300)
D3PUBLISHER OF AMERICA INC
Also Called: D3 Go
15910 Ventura Blvd # 800, Encino
(91436-2810)
PHONE...................310 268-0820
Yoji Takenaka, *President*
Yuji ITOH, *Ch of Bd*
Hidetaka Tachibana, *CFO*
Arthur Kawamoto, *Manager*
EMP: 63
SQ FT: 6,129
SALES (est): 8.4MM **Privately Held**
SIC: 7372 Home entertainment computer
software
HQ: D3 Publisher Inc.
1-9-5, Dogenzaka
Shibuya-Ku TKY 150-0
-

(P-15301)
DEEM INC (DH)
642 Harrison St Fl 2, San Francisco
(94107-1323)
PHONE...................415 590-8300
John F Rizzo, *President*
David Shiba, *CFO*
Eddie Bridgers, *Senior VP*
Todd Kaiser, *Senior VP*
Neil Markey, *Senior VP*
▲ **EMP:** 65
SQ FT: 133,000
SALES (est): 90.3MM
SALES (corp-wide): 4.5B **Privately Held**
WEB: www.reardencommerce.com
SIC: 7372 Prepackaged software
HQ: Enterprise Holdings, Inc.
600 Corporate Park Dr
Saint Louis MO 63105
314 512-5000

(P-15302)
DELPHIX CORP (PA)
1400 Saport Blvd Ste 200a, Redwood City
(94063)
PHONE...................650 494-1645
Chris Cook, *CEO*
Stewart Grierson, *CFO*

Monika Saha, *Chief Mktg Ofcr*
Jedidiah Yueh, *Officer*
Jason Binder, *Vice Pres*
EMP: 50
SQ FT: 18,000
SALES (est): 28.9MM **Privately Held**
SIC: 7372 Business oriented computer
software

(P-15303)
DEMANDBASE INC
680 Folsom St Ste 400, San Francisco
(94107-2159)
PHONE...................415 683-2660
Chris Golec, *CEO*
Peter Isaacson, *Chief Mktg Ofcr*
Alan Fletcher, *Officer*
Fatima Khan, *Officer*
Mike Hilts, *Vice Pres*
EMP: 251
SALES (est): 50.6MM **Privately Held**
WEB: www.demandbase.com
SIC: 7372 Business oriented computer
software

(P-15304)
DINCLOUD INC
27520 Hawthorne Blvd # 185, Rllng HLS
Est (90274-3576)
PHONE...................310 929-1101
Mark Briggs, *CEO*
Mike L Chase, *Exec VP*
Ali M Dincmo, *Vice Pres*
David Graffia, *Vice Pres*
Alex Orton, *Consultant*
EMP: 53
SQ FT: 1,500
SALES: 4MM
SALES (corp-wide): 43.1MM **Privately
Held**
SIC: 7372 Business oriented computer
software
PA: Premier Bpo, Inc.
128 N 2nd St Ste 210
Clarksville TN 37040
931 551-8888

(P-15305)
DISTILLERY INC
90 Heron Ct, San Quentin (94964)
PHONE...................415 505-5446
Adrian Szwarcburg, *President*
EMP: 55
SALES (est): 1.9MM **Privately Held**
SIC: 7372 Prepackaged software

(P-15306)
DOCTOR ON DEMAND INC
275 Battery St Ste 650, San Francisco
(94111-3332)
PHONE...................415 935-4447
Adam Jackson, *CEO*
Robin Cherry Glass, *President*
Jennifer Nuckles, *Chief Mktg Ofcr*
Barry Becker, *Vice Pres*
David Deane, *Vice Pres*
EMP: 100
SALES (est): 328.6K **Privately Held**
SIC: 7372 Application computer software

(P-15307)
DOCUSIGN INC (PA)
221 Main St Ste 1550, San Francisco
(94105-1947)
PHONE...................415 489-4940
Daniel D Springer, *President*
Michael J Sheridan, *CFO*
Kirsten O Wolberg, *Officer*
Ben Chuba, *Vice Pres*
Pedro Martins, *Vice Pres*
EMP: 300
SQ FT: 146,000
SALES: 700.9MM **Publicly Held**
WEB: www.docusign.com
SIC: 7372 Prepackaged software

(P-15308)
DORADO NETWORK SYSTEMS CORP
Also Called: Corelogic Dorado
555 12th St Ste 1100, Oakland
(94607-4049)
PHONE...................650 227-7300
Dain Ehring, *CEO*
Karen Camp, *CFO*
Adam Springer, *Vice Pres*

Dave Parker, *VP Bus Dvlpt*
Rob Carpenter PHD, *CTO*
EMP: 140
SQ FT: 19,000
SALES (est): 11.7MM
SALES (corp-wide): 1.7B **Publicly Held**
WEB: www.dorado.com
SIC: 7372 Application computer software
PA: Corelogic, Inc.
40 Pacifica Ste 900
Irvine CA 92618
949 214-1000

(P-15309)
DOUBLEDUTCH INC (PA)
350 Rhode Island St # 375, San Francisco
(94103-5181)
PHONE...................800 748-9024
Bryan Parker, *CEO*
Brad Roberts, *CFO*
Lawrence Coburn, *Officer*
Lucian Beebe, *Vice Pres*
Taylor McLoughlin, *Program Mgr*
EMP: 65
SALES: 28MM **Privately Held**
SIC: 7372 Application computer software

(P-15310)
DRIVEAI INC
365 Ravendale Dr, Mountain View
(94043-5217)
P.O. Box 57, Los Altos (94023-0057)
PHONE...................408 693-0765
Sameep Tandon, *CEO*
Swati Dube, *Co-Owner*
Brody Huval, *Co-Owner*
Jeff Kinske, *Co-Owner*
Joel Pazhayampallil, *Co-Owner*
EMP: 150 **EST:** 2015
SALES (est): 368.1K **Privately Held**
SIC: 7372 Prepackaged software

(P-15311)
DROPBOX INC (PA)
1800 Owens St Ste 200, San Francisco
(94158-2381)
PHONE...................415 857-6800
Andrew W Houston, *Ch of Bd*
EMP: 148
SALES: 1.3B **Publicly Held**
SIC: 7372 Prepackaged software

(P-15312)
DRUVA INC (HQ)
800 W California Ave # 100, Sunnyvale
(94086-3608)
PHONE...................650 241-3501
Jaspreet Singh, *CEO*
Mahesh Patel, *CFO*
Thomas Been, *Chief Mktg Ofcr*
Sherry Lowe, *Chief Mktg Ofcr*
Wynn White, *Chief Mktg Ofcr*
EMP: 58
SALES (est): 23.5MM **Privately Held**
SIC: 7372 Business oriented computer
software

(P-15313)
DWA NOVA LLC
1000 Flower St, Glendale (91201-3007)
PHONE...................818 695-5000
Lincoln Wallen, *CEO*
Derek Chan, *COO*
EMP: 75
SQ FT: 10,000
SALES (est): 1.4MM **Privately Held**
SIC: 7372 Business oriented computer
software

(P-15314)
ECRIO INC
19925 Stevens Creek Blvd # 100, Cuper-
tino (95014-2300)
PHONE...................408 973-7290
Randy Granovetter, *CEO*
Tad Bogdan, *COO*
Nagesh Challa, *Officer*
Ted Goldstein, *Officer*
Lina Martin, *Vice Pres*
EMP: 90
SALES (est): 6.5MM **Privately Held**
WEB: www.ecrio.com
SIC: 7372 Prepackaged software

P R O D U C T S & S V C S

(P-15315)
EGAIN CORPORATION (PA)
1252 Borregas Ave, Sunnyvale
(94089-1309)
PHONE.....................408 636-4500
Ashutosh Roy, *Ch of Bd*
Eric Smit, *CFO*
Promod Narang, *Senior VP*
Todd Woodstra, *Senior VP*
Chris Krystalowich, *Vice Pres*
EMP: 111
SQ FT: 42,541
SALES: 67.2MM **Publicly Held**
WEB: www.egain.com
SIC: 7372 7371 Prepackaged software;
application computer software; custom
computer programming services

(P-15316)
EIS GROUP INC
731 Sansome St Fl 4, San Francisco
(94111-1723)
PHONE.....................415 402-2622
Alec Miloslavsky, *CEO*
Sergiy Synyanskyy, *CFO*
Mary A Gillespie, *Exec VP*
Slava Kritov, *Senior VP*
Grosso Anthony, *Vice Pres*
EMP: 128
SQ FT: 16,803
SALES (est): 22.7MM **Privately Held**
SIC: 7372 Business oriented computer
software

(P-15317)
ELECTRONIC ARTS INC (PA)
Also Called: EA
209 Redwood Shores Pkwy, Redwood City
(94065-1175)
PHONE.....................650 628-1500
Andrew Wilson, *CEO*
Lawrence F Probst III, *Ch of Bd*
Blake Jorgensen, *COO*
Christopher Bruzzo, *Chief Mktg Ofcr*
Patrick Sderlund, *Officer*
▲ EMP: 475
SQ FT: 660,000
SALES: 4.9B **Publicly Held**
WEB: www.ea.com
SIC: 7372 Home entertainment computer
software

(P-15318)
ELLIE MAE INC (HQ)
4420 Rosewood Dr Ste 500, Pleasanton
(94588-3059)
PHONE.....................855 224-8572
Jonathan Corr, *President*
Dan Madden, *CFO*
Susan Chenoweth Beermann, *Chief Mktg Ofcr*
Selim Aissi, *Officer*
Brian Brown, *Exec VP*
EMP: 148 EST: 1997
SQ FT: 280,680
SALES: 480.2MM
SALES (corp-wide): 41.6MM **Privately Held**
WEB: www.elliemae.com
SIC: 7372 7371 Prepackaged software;
computer software systems analysis &
design, custom; computer software devel-
opment & applications
PA: Em Eagle Purchaser, Llc
4420 Rosewood Dr Ste 500
Pleasanton CA 94588
855 224-8572

(P-15319)
ENGAGIO INC
181 2nd Ave Ste 200, San Mateo
(94401-3816)
PHONE.....................650 265-2264
Jon Miller, *CEO*
Heidi Bullock, *Chief Mktg Ofcr*
Cheryl Chavez, *Officer*
Inger Rarick, *Vice Pres*
Corey Marcel, *Executive*
EMP: 50 EST: 2015
SALES: 531K **Privately Held**
SIC: 7372 Business oriented computer
software

(P-15320)
ENTCO LLC (DH)
Also Called: Autonomy Interwoven
1140 Enterprise Way, Sunnyvale
(94089-1412)
PHONE.....................312 580-9100
Jeremy K Cox,
John E Calonico Jr, *Senior VP*
Mercedes De Luca, *VP Info Sys*
Rishi Varma,
EMP: 329
SQ FT: 110,000
SALES (est): 44.4MM **Privately Held**
WEB: www.iwov.com
SIC: 7372 Business oriented computer
software
HQ: Micro Focus (Us), Inc.
700 King Farm Blvd # 125
Rockville MD 20850
301 838-5000

(P-15321)
ENTERPRISE SIGNAL INC
Also Called: Kloudgin
440 N Wolfe Rd, Sunnyvale (94085-3869)
PHONE.....................877 256-8303
Vikram Takru, *CEO*
Dharnesh Sethi, *CFO*
Vikas Bansal, *CTO*
Pushkala Venkateswaran, *Director*
Julie Stafford, *Manager*
EMP: 65
SALES (est): 155.9K **Privately Held**
SIC: 7372 Business oriented computer
software

(P-15322)
EPICOR SOFTWARE
CORPORATION
4120 Dublin Blvd Ste 300, Dublin
(94568-7759)
PHONE.....................925 361-9900
Pervez Qureshi, *Branch Mgr*
EMP: 101 **Publicly Held**
SIC: 7372 Prepackaged software
HQ: Epicor Software Corporation
804 Las Cimas Pkwy # 200
Austin TX 78746
-

(P-15323)
ESQ BUSINESS SERVICES INC
(PA)
Also Called: E S Q
20660 Stevens, Cupertino (95014)
PHONE.....................925 734-9800
Iqbal S Sandhu, *Director*
Joe Haggarty, *President*
Neil Butani, *Officer*
Maria Mendoza, *Business Dir*
Shridhar Venkatraman, *CTO*
EMP: 95
SQ FT: 300
SALES (est): 11.4MM **Privately Held**
WEB: www.esq.com
SIC: 7372 7379 Prepackaged software;
computer related consulting services

(P-15324)
EXADEL INC (PA)
1340 Treat Blvd, Walnut Creek
(94597-2101)
PHONE.....................925 363-9510
Fima Katz, *President*
Lev Shur, *President*
Alex Kreymer, *COO*
Dmitry Binunsky, *Vice Pres*
Jonathan Fries, *Vice Pres*
EMP: 62
SALES (est): 22.5MM **Privately Held**
WEB: www.exadel.com
SIC: 7372 Application computer software

(P-15325)
FAIR ISAAC INTERNATIONAL
CORP (HQ)
200 Smith Ranch Rd, San Rafael
(94903-5551)
PHONE.....................415 446-6000
Thomas G Grudnowski, *President*
Cheryl St John, *Cust Svc Dir*
EMP: 600

SALES (est): 51.2MM
SALES (corp-wide): 1B **Publicly Held**
SIC: 7372 Business oriented computer
software
PA: Fair Isaac Corporation
181 Metro Dr Ste 700
San Jose CA 95110
408 535-1500

(P-15326)
FIORANO SOFTWARE INC
230 California Ave # 103, Palo Alto
(94306-1637)
PHONE.....................650 326-1136
Atul Saini, *CEO*
Madhav Vodnala, *President*
Anjali Saini, *CFO*
William La Forge, *Vice Pres*
Tony George, *Manager*
◆ EMP: 85
SALES (est): 8.2MM **Privately Held**
SIC: 7372 7371 Prepackaged software;
custom computer programming services;
computer software development

(P-15327)
FIREEYE INC (PA)
601 Mccarthy Blvd, Milpitas (95035-7932)
PHONE.....................408 321-6300
Kevin R Mandia, *CEO*
William T Robbins, *Exec VP*
EMP: 148
SQ FT: 190,000
SALES: 830.9MM **Publicly Held**
WEB: www.fireeye.com
SIC: 7372 3577 Prepackaged software;
computer peripheral equipment

(P-15328)
FIVE9 INC (PA)
4000 Executive Pkwy # 400, San Ramon
(94583-4206)
PHONE.....................925 201-2000
Rowan Trollope, *CEO*
Michael Burkland, *Ch of Bd*
Daniel Burkland, *President*
Barry Zwarenstein, *CFO*
David Milam, *Chief Mktg Ofcr*
EMP: 148
SQ FT: 79,600
SALES: 257.6MM **Publicly Held**
WEB: www.five9.com
SIC: 7372 7374 Prepackaged software;
data processing & preparation

(P-15329)
FORGEROCK US INC (HQ)
201 Mission St, San Francisco
(94105-1831)
PHONE.....................415 599-1100
John Fernandez, *CFO*
Pola Lobello, *Partner*
Robert Humphrey, *Chief Mktg Ofcr*
Lasse Andresen, *CTO*
EMP: 73
SQ FT: 15,744
SALES (est): 14MM
SALES (corp-wide): 89.9MM **Privately Held**
SIC: 7372 5045 Prepackaged software;
computer software
PA: Forgerock, Inc.
201 Mission St Ste 2900
San Francisco CA 94105
415 599-1100

(P-15330)
FORMATION INC
Also Called: Formation Systems
35 Stillman St, San Francisco
(94107-1361)
PHONE.....................650 257-2277
Christian Hansen, *CEO*
Christian Selchau-Hansen, *CEO*
Ammon Haggerty, *Vice Pres*
EMP: 87
SQ FT: 10,000
SALES (est): 1.3MM **Privately Held**
SIC: 7372 Business oriented computer
software

(P-15331)
FOUNDATION 9
ENTERTAINMENT INC (PA)
30211 A De Las Bandera200, Rancho
Santa Margari (92688)
PHONE.....................949 698-1500
James N Hearn, *CEO*
John Goldman, *Ch of Bd*
David Mann, *President*
EMP: 200
SALES (est): 38.1MM **Privately Held**
SIC: 7372 Home entertainment computer
software

(P-15332)
FOUNDSTONE INC
27201 Puerta Real Ste 400, Mission Viejo
(92691-8517)
PHONE.....................949 297-5600
George Kurtz, *CEO*
Stuart McClure, *President*
Larry McIntosh, *Chief Mktg Ofcr*
William Chan, *Vice Pres*
Chris Prosise, *Vice Pres*
EMP: 80
SQ FT: 15,000
SALES (est): 4.9MM **Privately Held**
WEB: www.foundstone.com
SIC: 7372 Application computer software
HQ: Mcafee, Llc
2821 Mission College Blvd
Santa Clara CA 95054
888 847-8766

(P-15333)
FRONTAPP INC
525 Brannan St Ste 300, San Francisco
(94107-1632)
PHONE.....................415 680-3048
Mathilde Collin, *CEO*
Laurent Perrin, *CTO*
EMP: 71
SQ FT: 11,000
SALES: 5MM **Privately Held**
SIC: 7372 Application computer software

(P-15334)
G7 PRODUCTIVITY SYSTEMS
Also Called: Versacheck
16885 W Bernardo Dr # 290, San Diego
(92127-1618)
P.O. Box 270459 (92198-2459)
PHONE.....................858 675-1095
Thomas Priebus, *President*
Teri Pfarr, *COO*
Jim Danforth, *CFO*
EMP: 60
SQ FT: 18,000
SALES (est): 3.9MM **Privately Held**
WEB: www.g7ps.com
SIC: 7372 Prepackaged software

(P-15335)
GE DIGITAL LLC (HQ)
2623 Camino Ramon, San Ramon
(94583-9130)
PHONE.....................925 242-6200
Vineet Shrivastava, *Surgery Dir*
Luke Tresnicky, *Technical Staff*
Shirley D'Souza, *Opers Staff*
Lili Mokhtari, *Manager*
EMP: 67
SALES (est): 46.3MM
SALES (corp-wide): 121.6B **Publicly Held**
SIC: 7372 Business oriented computer
software
PA: General Electric Company
41 Farnsworth St
Boston MA 02210
617 443-3000

(P-15336)
GENERAL ELECTRIC COMPANY
2623 Camino Ramon, San Ramon
(94583-9130)
PHONE.....................925 242-6200
Holly Gilthorpe, *Ch Credit Ofcr*
Rebecca Lawson, *Vice Pres*
Jennifer Schulze, *Vice Pres*
Ashima Puri, *Program Mgr*
Lavanya Mallikharjuna, *Software Engr*
EMP: 72

SALES (corp-wide): 121.6B **Publicly Held**
SIC: 7372 Business oriented computer software
PA: General Electric Company
41 Farnsworth St
Boston MA 02210
617 443-3000

(P-15337)
GENESYS TELECOM LABS INC (HQ)
Also Called: Genesys Telecom Labs
2001 Junipero Serra Blvd, Daly City
(94014-3891)
PHONE.....................650 466-1100
Tony Bates, *CEO*
Rex Lofland, *Partner*
Tom Eggemeier, *President*
Paul Segre, *Chairman*
David Sudbey, *Ch Credit Ofcr*
EMP: 450
SQ FT: 156,000
SALES (est): 622.6MM
SALES (corp-wide): 34.6MM **Privately Held**
WEB: www.genesyslabs.com
SIC: 7372 Business oriented computer software
PA: Permira Advisers Llp
80 Pall Mall
London SW1Y
207 632-1000

(P-15338)
GIGAMON INC (HQ)
3300 Olcott St, Santa Clara (95054-3005)
PHONE.....................408 831-4000
Paul A Hooper, *CEO*
Michelle Hodges, *Partner*
Shane Buckley, *President*
Dave Arkley, *CFO*
Karl Van Den Bergh, *Chief Mktg Ofcr*
▲ **EMP:** 145
SQ FT: 105,600
SALES: 310.8MM **Privately Held**
WEB: www.gigamon.com
SIC: 7372 3577 Prepackaged software; computer peripheral equipment
PA: Ginsberg Holdco, Inc.
3300 Olcott St
Santa Clara CA 95054
408 831-4000

(P-15339)
GOVERNMENTJOBSCOM INC
Also Called: Neogov
300 Continental Blvd # 565, El Segundo
(90245-5042)
PHONE.....................310 426-6304
Damir Davidovic, *CEO*
Scott Letourneau, *President*
Chris Rosenberger, *Info Tech Mgr*
George Gerbi, *Software Dev*
Ashish Srivastava, *Software Dev*
EMP: 130
SQ FT: 5,000
SALES (est): 20.8MM **Privately Held**
WEB: www.governmentjobs.com
SIC: 7372 Prepackaged software

(P-15340)
GRAYPAY LLC
6345 Balboa Blvd Ste 115, Encino
(91316-1517)
PHONE.....................818 387-6735
Marc Geolina, *Mng Member*
Bryan Rainey,
Jaimie Smith, *Manager*
EMP: 60 EST: 2015
SALES (est): 2.4MM **Privately Held**
SIC: 7372 Business oriented computer software

(P-15341)
GREEN HILLS SOFTWARE LLC (HQ)
30 W Sola St, Santa Barbara (93101-2599)
PHONE.....................805 965-6044
Daniel O Dowd, *CEO*
Dave Kleidermacher, *President*
Michael W Liacko, *President*
Daniel O'Dowd, *CEO*
Matt Fechtman, *CFO*
EMP: 105

SALES (est): 77.1MM
SALES (corp-wide): 23.4MM **Privately Held**
WEB: www.ghs.com
SIC: 7372 Prepackaged software
PA: Ghs Holding Company
30 W Sola St
Santa Barbara CA 93101
805 965-6044

(P-15342)
GRIDGAIN SYSTEMS INC (PA)
1065 E Hillsdale Blvd, Foster City
(94404-1613)
PHONE.....................650 241-2281
Abe Kleinfeld, *President*
Eoin Connor, *CFO*
Andy Sacks, *Exec VP*
Terry Erisman, *Vice Pres*
Jon Webster, *VP Bus Dvlpt*
EMP: 54
SALES (est): 17.8MM **Privately Held**
SIC: 7372 Prepackaged software

(P-15343)
GUAVUS INC (HQ)
2125 Zanker Rd, San Jose (95131-2109)
PHONE.....................650 243-3400
Anukool Lakhina, *CEO*
Michael Crane, *President*
Ty Nam, *COO*
Anupam Rastogi, *CTO*
EMP: 53
SALES (est): 25.6MM
SALES (corp-wide): 262.1MM **Privately Held**
WEB: www.guavus.com
SIC: 7372 7371 Prepackaged software; computer software development & applications
PA: Thales
Tour Carpe Diem Esplanade Nord
Courbevoie 92400
157 778-000

(P-15344)
GUCK ARIBA
807 Eleventh Ave, Sunnyvale
(94089-4731)
PHONE.....................650 390-1445
Chris Cavanaugh, *Vice Pres*
Leigh Interthal, *Vice Pres*
Dave Johnston, *Vice Pres*
Brian Krieger, *Vice Pres*
Darlene French, *Executive*
EMP: 147
SALES (est): 7MM **Privately Held**
SIC: 7372 Business oriented computer software

(P-15345)
GUIDANCE SOFTWARE INC (HQ)
1055 E Colo Blvd Ste 400, Pasadena
(91106)
PHONE.....................626 229-9191
Patrick Dennis, *President*
Barry Plaga, *COO*
Michael Harris, *Chief Mktg Ofcr*
Alfredo Gomez, *Senior VP*
Michael Macguire, *Vice Pres*
EMP: 215 EST: 1997
SQ FT: 90,000
SALES: 110.5MM
SALES (corp-wide): 2.8B **Privately Held**
WEB: www.guidancesoftware.com
SIC: 7372 3572 Business oriented computer software; computer storage devices
PA: Open Text Corporation
275 Frank Tompa Dr
Waterloo ON N2L 0
519 888-7111

(P-15346)
GUIDEWIRE SOFTWARE INC (PA)
2850 S Del St Ste 400, San Mateo (94403)
PHONE.....................650 357-9100
Mike Rosenbaum, *President*
Marcus S Ryu, *Ch of Bd*
Priscilla Hung, *COO*
Curtis Smith, *CFO*
Ali Kheirolomoom, *Officer*
EMP: 148
SQ FT: 97,674

SALES: 719.5MM **Publicly Held**
WEB: www.guidewire.com
SIC: 7372 Business oriented computer software

(P-15347)
H2 WELLNESS INCORPORATED
15414 Milldale Dr, Los Angeles
(90077-1601)
PHONE.....................310 362-1888
Hooman Fakki, *CEO*
Houman Arasteh, *COO*
Russ Nash, *Bd of Directors*
EMP: 55
SALES (est): 3.6MM **Privately Held**
SIC: 7372 Application computer software

(P-15348)
HEALTHSTREAM INC
Also Called: Echo, A Heatlhstream Company
9605 Scranton Rd Ste 200, San Diego
(92121-1768)
PHONE.....................800 733-8737
Robert A Frist Jr, *Ch of Bd*
EMP: 193
SALES (corp-wide): 231.6MM **Publicly Held**
SIC: 7372 7371 Prepackaged software; custom computer programming services
PA: Healthstream, Inc.
500 11th Ave N Ste 1000
Nashville TN 37203
615 301-3100

(P-15349)
HEARSAY SOCIAL INC (PA)
185 Berry St Ste 3800, San Francisco
(94107-1725)
PHONE.....................888 990-3777
Clara Shih, *CEO*
Michael H Lock, *President*
Steve Garrity, *COO*
William Salisbury, *CFO*
Dave Peterson, *Chief Mktg Ofcr*
EMP: 60
SALES (est): 13.5MM **Privately Held**
SIC: 7372 Publishers' computer software

(P-15350)
HEAT SOFTWARE INTERMEDIATE INC
2590 N 1st St Ste 360, San Jose
(95131-1057)
PHONE.....................408 601-2800
Jon Temple, *CEO*
Cary Baker, *CFO*
David Puglia, *Chief Mktg Ofcr*
Roberto Casetta, *Vice Pres*
Fred Johannessen, *Vice Pres*
EMP: 383
SALES (est): 10.2MM **Privately Held**
SIC: 7372 7371 Prepackaged software; computer software systems analysis & design, custom

(P-15351)
HEWLETT PACKARD ENTERPRISE CO (PA)
Also Called: Hpe
6280 America Center Dr, San Jose
(95002-2563)
PHONE.....................650 687-5817
Antonio F Neri, *President*
Patricia F Russo, *Ch of Bd*
Philip Davis, *President*
Keerti Melkote, *President*
Tarek A Robbiati, *CFO*
EMP: 148 EST: 1939
SALES: 30.8B **Publicly Held**
SIC: 7372 7379 3572 Business oriented computer software; computer related maintenance services; computer storage devices

(P-15352)
HORTONWORKS INC (HQ)
5470 Great America Pkwy, Santa Clara
(95054-3644)
PHONE.....................408 916-4121
Scott Aronson, *Risk Mgmt Dir*
Linda Morales, *Partner*
Sean Roberts, *Partner*
Scott Davidson, *CFO*
Jim Frankola, *CFO*
EMP: 725
SQ FT: 92,000

SALES (est): 221.8MM
SALES (corp-wide): 479.9MM **Publicly Held**
SIC: 7372 Application computer software
PA: Cloudera, Inc.
395 Page Mill Rd Ste 300
Palo Alto CA 94306
650 362-0488

(P-15353)
IFWE INC (HQ)
848 Battery St, San Francisco
(94111-1504)
PHONE.....................415 946-1850
Dash Gopinath, *CEO*
Greg Tseng, *CEO*
Nick Hermansader, *Vice Pres*
Misha Nasledov, *Sr Software Eng*
Johann Schleier Smith, *CTO*
EMP: 87
SQ FT: 13,000
SALES (est): 30.7MM
SALES (corp-wide): 178.6MM **Publicly Held**
WEB: www.tagged.com
SIC: 7372 Application computer software
PA: The Meet Group Inc
100 Union Square Dr
New Hope PA 18938
215 862-1162

(P-15354)
ILLUMINATE EDUCATION INC (PA)
6531 Irvine Center Dr # 100, Irvine
(92618-2145)
PHONE.....................949 656-3133
Christine Willig, *CEO*
Dick Davidson, *CFO*
Jane Snyder, *Chief Mktg Ofcr*
Shawn Mahoney, *Officer*
Spencer Kerrigan, *Vice Pres*
EMP: 65 EST: 2009
SALES (est): 15.4MM **Privately Held**
SIC: 7372 Educational computer software

(P-15355)
IMAGEWARE SYSTEMS INC (PA)
13500 Evening Creek Dr N # 550, San Diego (92128-8125)
PHONE.....................858 673-8600
S James Miller Jr, *Ch of Bd*
Wayne Wetherell, *CFO*
David Harding, *Senior VP*
David Somerville, *Senior VP*
EMP: 96
SQ FT: 8,511
SALES: 4.4MM **Publicly Held**
WEB: www.iwsinc.com
SIC: 7372 3699 Business oriented computer software; security control equipment & systems

(P-15356)
INDIUM SOFTWARE INC
1250 Oakmead Pkwy Ste 210, Sunnyvale
(94085-4035)
PHONE.....................408 501-8844
Harsha Nutalapati, *CEO*
Vijay Shankar Balaji, *President*
Shailesh Khanapur, *Assoc VP*
Bala S Selva, *Senior VP*
EMP: 250
SALES (est): 10.4MM **Privately Held**
WEB: www.indiumsoft.com
SIC: 7372 Prepackaged software
HQ: Indium Software (India) Limited
2nd Floor Vds House,
Chennai TN 60008
-

(P-15357)
INFOR (US) INC
Also Called: MAI Systems
26250 Entp Way Ste 220, Lake Forest
(92630)
PHONE.....................678 319-8000
Barbara Nolan, *President*
Marvin Perkins, *Sales Staff*
Christine Greiner, *Manager*
EMP: 190
SALES (corp-wide): 3.1B **Privately Held**
SIC: 7372 Business oriented computer software

HQ: Infor (Us), Inc.
13560 Morris Rd Ste 4100
Alpharetta GA 30004
678 319-8000

(P-15358)
INFOR (US) INC
Also Called: Hansen Information Tech
11000 Olson Dr Ste 201, Rancho Cordova
(95670-5642)
PHONE....................916 921-0883
Charles Hansen, *Manager*
EMP: 225
SALES (corp-wide): 3.1B **Privately Held**
SIC: 7372 Application computer software
HQ: Infor (Us), Inc.
13560 Morris Rd Ste 4100
Alpharetta GA 30004
678 319-8000

(P-15359)
INFOR PUBLIC SECTOR INC (DH)
11092 Sun Center Dr, Rancho Cordova
(95670-6109)
PHONE....................916 921-0883
Charles Hansen, *CEO*
Mark Watts, *President*
Bob Benstead, *Principal*
EMP: 160
SQ FT: 28,000
SALES (est): 22.2MM
SALES (corp-wide): 3.1B **Privately Held**
SIC: 7372 Application computer software
HQ: Infor (Us), Inc.
13560 Morris Rd Ste 4100
Alpharetta GA 30004
678 319-8000

(P-15360)
INFORMATICA LLC (PA)
2100 Seaport Blvd, Redwood City
(94063-5596)
PHONE....................650 385-5000
Anil Chakravarthy, *CEO*
Maryanne Cotrone, *Partner*
Monie Tenbroeck, *Partner*
Nick Voll, *Partner*
Chris Sortzi, *President*
EMP: 148
SQ FT: 290,000
SALES (est): 801.2MM **Privately Held**
WEB: www.metadataexchange.com
SIC: 7372 Prepackaged software

(P-15361)
INSIDEVIEW TECHNOLOGIES INC
444 De Haro St Ste 210, San Francisco
(94107-2398)
PHONE....................415 728-9309
Umberto Milletti, *CEO*
Jim Lightsey, *CFO*
Tracy Eiler, *Chief Mktg Ofcr*
Lisa Bailey, *Vice Pres*
Marc Perramond, *Vice Pres*
EMP: 150
SALES (est): 26.3MM **Privately Held**
SIC: 7372 Business oriented computer software

(P-15362)
INTEGRAL DEVELOPMENT CORP (PA)
Also Called: Integral Engineering
850 Hansen Way, Palo Alto (94304-1017)
PHONE....................650 424-4500
Harpal Sandhu, *President*
Albert Yau, *CFO*
Vikas Srivastava, *Officer*
Patrick Barkhordarian, *Vice Pres*
Ian Doull, *Vice Pres*
EMP: 200
SQ FT: 35,000
SALES (est): 31.5MM **Privately Held**
WEB: www.integral.com
SIC: 7372 Business oriented computer software

(P-15363)
INTOUCH TECHNOLOGIES INC (PA)
Also Called: Intouch Health
7402 Hollister Ave, Goleta (93117-2583)
PHONE....................805 562-8686

Yulun Wang, *CEO*
Susan Wang, *Shareholder*
David Adornetto, *COO*
Stephen L Wilson, *CFO*
Paul Evans, *Exec VP*
EMP: 148
SQ FT: 1,600
SALES (est): 90.1MM **Privately Held**
WEB: www.intouchhealth.com
SIC: 7372 Business oriented computer software

(P-15364)
INTUIT INC (PA)
2700 Coast Ave, Mountain View
(94043-1140)
P.O. Box 7850 (94039-7850)
PHONE....................650 944-6000
Brad D Smith, *Ch of Bd*
Michelle M Clatterbuck, *CFO*
Scott D Cook, *Chairman*
Laura A Fennell, *Exec VP*
Laura Fennell, *Exec VP*
EMP: 70
SQ FT: 712,000
SALES: 6.7B **Publicly Held**
WEB: www.intuit.com
SIC: 7372 Business oriented computer software

(P-15365)
INTUIT INC
2700 Coast Ave Bldg 7, Mountain View
(94043-1140)
PHONE....................650 944-6000
Brad Smith, *Branch Mgr*
EMP: 128
SALES (corp-wide): 6.7B **Publicly Held**
WEB: www.intuit.com
SIC: 7372 Business oriented computer software
PA: Intuit Inc.
2700 Coast Ave
Mountain View CA 94043
650 944-6000

(P-15366)
INTUIT INC
2535 Garcia Ave, Mountain View
(94043-1111)
PHONE....................650 944-6000
Connie Berg, *Branch Mgr*
Jeff Brewer, *Vice Pres*
Brian Curran, *Executive*
Adam Reed, *Creative Dir*
Nita Acosta, *Executive Asst*
EMP: 128
SALES (corp-wide): 6.7B **Publicly Held**
WEB: www.intuit.com
SIC: 7372 Business oriented computer software
PA: Intuit Inc.
2700 Coast Ave
Mountain View CA 94043
650 944-6000

(P-15367)
INTUIT INC
141 Corona Way, Portola Valley
(94028-7437)
PHONE....................650 944-2840
EMP: 136
SALES (corp-wide): 6.7B **Publicly Held**
WEB: www.intuit.com
SIC: 7372 Business oriented computer software
PA: Intuit Inc.
2700 Coast Ave
Mountain View CA 94043
650 944-6000

(P-15368)
INTUIT INC
180 Jefferson Dr, Menlo Park (94025-1115)
PHONE....................650 944-6000
Brad Smith, *Branch Mgr*
Jason Yip, *Business Anlyst*
Betsy Kha, *Marketing Staff*
Lisa Leib, *Manager*
EMP: 128
SALES (corp-wide): 6.7B **Publicly Held**
WEB: www.intuit.com
SIC: 7372 Business oriented computer software

PA: Intuit Inc.
2700 Coast Ave
Mountain View CA 94043
650 944-6000

(P-15369)
INTUIT INC
Also Called: Turbotax
7545 Torrey Santa Fe Rd, San Diego
(92129-5704)
PHONE....................858 215-8000
Jason Jackson, *Branch Mgr*
Manny Ruiz, *Sr Software Eng*
Sheri Dombrow, *Software Dev*
Wolf Paulus, *Software Engr*
Elizabeth Trinh, *Database Admin*
EMP: 300
SALES (corp-wide): 6.7B **Publicly Held**
WEB: www.intuit.com
SIC: 7372 Business oriented computer software
PA: Intuit Inc.
2700 Coast Ave
Mountain View CA 94043
650 944-6000

(P-15370)
IPAYABLES INC (PA)
95 Argonaut Ste 270, Aliso Viejo
(92656-4140)
PHONE....................949 215-9122
Kenneth L Virgin, *CEO*
Robert L Ripley, *COO*
Jon Titel, *CTO*
Ryan Gibson, *Info Tech Dir*
EMP: 63
SALES (est): 1MM **Privately Held**
WEB: www.ipayables.com
SIC: 7372 Business oriented computer software

(P-15371)
IPOLIPO INC
Also Called: Jifflenow
440 N Wolfe Rd, Sunnyvale (94085-3869)
PHONE....................408 916-5290
Hari Shetty, *President*
Arun Kumar, *Administration*
Chopra Anil, *Software Dev*
Nayak Anusha, *Software Dev*
Francis Arun, *Software Dev*
EMP: 75 **EST:** 2006
SALES (est): 3.6MM **Privately Held**
SIC: 7372 Application computer software

(P-15372)
IQMS (HQ)
2231 Wisteria Ln, Paso Robles
(93446-9820)
PHONE....................805 227-1122
Gary Nemmers, *President*
Matt Ouska, *CFO*
Steve Bieszczat, *Chief Mktg Ofcr*
Shannon Holloway, *Officer*
Rocky Morrison, *Exec VP*
EMP: 130
SQ FT: 60,000
SALES: 37MM
SALES (corp-wide): 1.8B **Privately Held**
WEB: www.iqms.com
SIC: 7372 Prepackaged software
PA: Dassault Systemes
10 Rue Marcel Dassault
Velizy-Villacoublay 78140
161 623-000

(P-15373)
ISOLUTECOM INC (PA)
9 Northam Ave, Newbury Park
(91320-3323)
PHONE....................805 498-6259
Byron Nutley, *Ch of Bd*
Don Hyun, *President*
Thomas Mangle, *CFO*
Michael Brown, *CTO*
EMP: 50
SALES (est): 5.1MM **Privately Held**
WEB: www.isolute.com
SIC: 7372 Business oriented computer software

(P-15374)
IXSYSTEMS INC (PA)
2490 Kruse Dr, San Jose (95131-1234)
PHONE....................408 943-4100
Mike Lauth, *CEO*

Andrew Madrid, *COO*
Brett Davis, *Exec VP*
Morgan Littlewood, *Senior VP*
Jeff Kaminsky, *General Mgr*
EMP: 60
SQ FT: 20,000
SALES (est): 21.4MM **Privately Held**
WEB: www.ixsystems.com
SIC: 7372 Operating systems computer software

(P-15375)
KANA SOFTWARE INC (HQ)
Also Called: Verint
2550 Walsh Ave Ste 120, Santa Clara
(95051-1345)
PHONE....................650 614-8300
Mark Duffell, *CEO*
Brett White, *President*
Jeff Wylie, *CFO*
James Norwood, *Chief Mktg Ofcr*
Jim Bureau, *Senior VP*
EMP: 100
SQ FT: 40,000
SALES (est): 79.7MM **Publicly Held**
SIC: 7372 Application computer software

(P-15376)
KHAN ACADEMY INC
1200 Villa St Ste 200, Mountain View
(94041-2922)
P.O. Box 1630 (94042-1630)
PHONE....................650 336-5426
Salman Khan, *Exec Dir*
Shantanu Sinha, *President*
Esther Cho, *Executive Asst*
Nada Abdelhamid, *Software Engr*
Joe Raedle, *Software Engr*
EMP: 85
SALES (est): 27.9MM **Privately Held**
SIC: 7372 Educational computer software

(P-15377)
KHOROS LLC (PA)
1 Pier Ste 1a, San Francisco (94111-2003)
PHONE....................415 757-3100
Jack Blaha, *CEO*
Jim Cox, *CFO*
Sam Monti, *CFO*
Katherine Calvert, *Chief Mktg Ofcr*
Scott Shepherd,
EMP: 50
SALES (est): 76.2MM **Privately Held**
WEB: www.lithium.com
SIC: 7372 Business oriented computer software

(P-15378)
KINGCOM(US) LLC (HQ)
3100 Ocean Park Blvd, Santa Monica
(90405-3032)
PHONE....................424 744-5697
EMP: 200
SALES (est): 17.7MM
SALES (corp-wide): 7.5B **Publicly Held**
SIC: 7372 Home entertainment computer software
PA: Activision Blizzard, Inc.
3100 Ocean Park Blvd
Santa Monica CA 90405
310 255-2000

(P-15379)
KINTERA INC (HQ)
Also Called: Blackbaud Internet Solutions
9605 Scranton Rd Ste 200, San Diego
(92121-1768)
PHONE....................858 795-3000
Marc E Chardon, *CEO*
Alfred R Berkeley III, *Ch of Bd*
Richard Labarbera, *President*
Richard Davidson, *CFO*
Richard R Davidson, *Treasurer*
EMP: 68
SQ FT: 38,000
SALES: 34.2MM
SALES (corp-wide): 848.6MM **Publicly Held**
WEB: www.kintera.org
SIC: 7372 Prepackaged software
PA: Blackbaud, Inc.
2000 Daniel Island Dr
Daniel Island SC 29492
843 216-6200

(P-15380)
KNO INC
2200 Mission College Blvd, Santa Clara
(95054-1537)
PHONE....................408 844-8120
Ronald D Dickel, *CEO*
Babur Habib, *CTO*
EMP: 70
SQ FT: 35,000
SALES (est): 9MM
SALES (corp-wide): 70.8B **Publicly Held**
SIC: 7372 Educational computer software
PA: Intel Corporation
    2200 Mission College Blvd
    Santa Clara CA 95054
    408 765-8080

(P-15381)
KONAMI DIGITAL ENTRMT INC (DH)
2381 Rosecrans Ave # 200, El Segundo
(90245-4922)
PHONE....................310 220-8100
Tomohiro Uesugi, *President*
Takahiro Azuma, *Vice Pres*
Chris Bartee, *Principal*
Kazumi Kitaue, *Principal*
Cesar Pardini, *Info Tech Dir*
▲ EMP: 68
SQ FT: 53,596
SALES (est): 34.5MM **Privately Held**
SIC: 7372 Home entertainment computer
    software

(P-15382)
KPISOFT INC
50 California St Ste 1500, San Francisco
(94111-4612)
PHONE....................415 439-5228
Ravee Ramamoothie, *CEO*
EMP: 80
SQ FT: 4,000
SALES (est): 2.9MM **Privately Held**
SIC: 7372 Prepackaged software

(P-15383)
KRANEM CORPORATION
560 S Winchester Blvd, San Jose
(95128-2560)
PHONE....................650 319-6743
Ajay Batheja, *Ch of Bd*
Edward Miller, *CFO*
Luigi Caramico, *Vice Pres*
Christopher L Rasmussen, *Admin Sec*
EMP: 190
SALES: 8.3MM **Privately Held**
SIC: 7372 Business oriented computer
    software

(P-15384)
KRATOS TECH TRNING SLTIONS INC (HQ)
10680 Treena St Fl 6, San Diego
(92131-2487)
PHONE....................858 812-7300
Eric M Demarco, *President*
Kenneth Reagan, *President*
Deanna H Lund, *CFO*
Laura L Siegal, *Treasurer*
Jane Judd, *Bd of Directors*
EMP: 139
SQ FT: 25,000
SALES (est): 94.3MM **Publicly Held**
WEB: www.sys.com
SIC: 7372 Business oriented computer
    software

(P-15385)
KRONOS INCORPORATED
240 Commerce, Irvine (92602-5004)
PHONE....................800 580-7374
Kaylee Uribe, *Branch Mgr*
Richard Bak, *Software Engr*
Glen Gerber, *Software Engr*
EMP: 56
SALES (corp-wide): 1B **Privately Held**
SIC: 7372 Business oriented computer
    software
HQ: Kronos Incorporated
    900 Chelmsford St # 312
    Lowell MA 01851
    978 250-9800

(P-15386)
KYRIBA CORP (PA)
9620 Towne Cntre Dr 200, San Diego
(92121)
PHONE....................858 210-3560
Jean-Luc Robert, *CEO*
Timothy Ray, *President*
Didier Martineau, *COO*
Fabrice Lvy, *CFO*
Remy Dubois, *Exec VP*
EMP: 50
SALES (est): 75.6MM **Privately Held**
WEB: www.kyriba.com
SIC: 7372 Prepackaged software

(P-15387)
LASTLINE INC
6950 Hollister Ave # 101, Goleta
(93117-2896)
PHONE....................805 456-7075
EMP: 168 **Privately Held**
SIC: 7372 Prepackaged software
PA: Lastline, Inc.
    203 Redwood Shores Pkwy
    Redwood City CA 94065

(P-15388)
LASTLINE INC (PA)
203 Redwood Shores Pkwy, Redwood City
(94065-1198)
PHONE....................805 456-7075
John Dilullo, *CEO*
Ananth Avva, *CFO*
Claire Trimble, *Chief Mktg Ofcr*
Christopher Kruegel, *Officer*
Bert Rankin, *Officer*
EMP: 52
SALES (est): 43.3MM **Privately Held**
SIC: 7372 Prepackaged software

(P-15389)
LAWINFOCOM INC
5901 Priestly Dr Ste 200, Carlsbad
(92008-8825)
PHONE....................800 397-3743
Gunter Enz, *President*
Cara Mae Harrison, *COO*
EMP: 68 EST: 1989
SQ FT: 10,000
SALES: 4.6MM **Privately Held**
WEB: www.lawinfo.com
SIC: 7372 8111 7375 Publishers' com-
    puter software; legal services; information
    retrieval services

(P-15390)
LIVEOFFICE LLC
Also Called: Advisorsquare
900 Corporate Pointe, Culver City
(90230-7609)
PHONE....................877 253-2793
Alexander Rusich,
Matt Hardy,
Jeffrey W Hausman,
Nikhil Menta,
Matt Smith,
EMP: 77
SQ FT: 15,000
SALES (est): 5.5MM
SALES (corp-wide): 4.7B **Publicly Held**
WEB: www.advisorsquare.com
SIC: 7372 Prepackaged software
PA: Nortonlifelock Inc.
    60 E Rio Salado Pkwy # 1
    Tempe AZ 85281
    650 527-8000

(P-15391)
LIVETIME SOFTWARE INC
276 Avocado St Apt C102, Costa Mesa
(92627-7302)
PHONE....................415 905-4009
Darren Williams, *President*
EMP: 50
SALES (est): 2.7MM **Privately Held**
SIC: 7372 Prepackaged software

(P-15392)
LOGINEXT SOLUTIONS INC
5002 Spring Crest Ter, Fremont
(94536-6525)
PHONE....................339 244-0380
Dhruvil Sanghvi, *CEO*
Manisha Raisinghani, *Chief Engr*
EMP: 100

SALES (est): 124.1K **Privately Held**
SIC: 7372 7371 7379 8243 Prepackaged
    software; computer software systems
    analysis & design, custom; computer soft-
    ware development & applications; soft-
    ware programming applications; computer
    related consulting services; software
    training, computer

(P-15393)
LPA INSURANCE AGENCY INC
Also Called: Sat
3800 Watt Ave Ste 147, Sacramento
(95821-2676)
PHONE....................916 286-7850
Michael Winkel, *President*
EMP: 56
SALES (est): 3.4MM
SALES (corp-wide): 8.4B **Publicly Held**
WEB: www.sungard.com
SIC: 7372 Application computer software
HQ: Fis Data Systems Inc.
    200 Campus Dr
    Collegeville PA 19426
    484 582-2000

(P-15394)
LYNX SOFTWARE TECHNOLOGIES INC (PA)
855 Embedded Way, San Jose
(95138-1030)
PHONE....................408 979-3900
Inder Singh, *Chairman*
Gurjot Singh, *President*
Will Keegan, *CTO*
Ingrid Osborne, *Controller*
Lee Cresswell, *Sales Dir*
EMP: 52
SQ FT: 30,000
SALES (est): 15.6MM **Privately Held**
WEB: www.lynuxworks.com
SIC: 7372 Business oriented computer
    software

(P-15395)
MALIKCO LLC
2121 N Calif Blvd Ste 290, Walnut Creek
(94596-7351)
PHONE....................925 974-3555
Stephynie R Malik, *CEO*
Dennis J Dunnigan, *Director*
Ragean Kennedy, *Accounts Exec*
EMP: 50
SQ FT: 1,000
SALES (est): 4.8MM **Privately Held**
WEB: www.malikco.com
SIC: 7372 Operating systems computer
    software

(P-15396)
MAXIMUS HOLDINGS INC
2475 Hanover St, Palo Alto (94304-1114)
PHONE....................650 935-9500
Dominic Gallello, *CEO*
Jim Johnson, *CFO*
Anshul Singh, *Executive*
EMP: 1006
SALES (est): 21.9MM
SALES (corp-wide): 604.2MM **Privately
Held**
SIC: 7372 Prepackaged software
PA: Symphony Technology Group, L.L.C.
    428 University Ave
    Palo Alto CA 94301
    650 935-9500

(P-15397)
MCAFEE INC
6707 Barnhurst Dr, San Diego
(92117-4208)
PHONE....................858 967-2342
EMP: 82 **Privately Held**
SIC: 7372 Prepackaged software
HQ: Mcafee, Llc
    2821 Mission College Blvd
    Santa Clara CA 95054
    888 847-8766

(P-15398)
MCAFEE LLC (HQ)
2821 Mission College Blvd, Santa Clara
(95054-1838)
PHONE....................888 847-8766
Christopher Young, *CEO*
Jean-Claude Broido, *President*
Tom Miglis, *President*

Michael Berry, *CFO*
Thomas Gann, *Officer*
▲ EMP: 148
SQ FT: 208,000
SALES (est): 1.5B **Privately Held**
WEB: www.mcafee.com
SIC: 7372 Application computer software

(P-15399)
MCAFEE FINANCE 2 LLC
2821 Mission College Blvd, Santa Clara
(95054-1838)
PHONE....................888 847-8766
EMP: 1129
SALES (est): 10.3MM
SALES (corp-wide): 277.9MM **Privately
Held**
SIC: 7372 Prepackaged software
HQ: Mcafee Finance 1, Llc
    2821 Mission College Blvd
    Santa Clara CA 95054
    888 847-8766

(P-15400)
MCAFEE SECURITY LLC
2821 Mission College Blvd, Santa Clara
(95054-1838)
PHONE....................866 622-3911
Michael Decesare, *President*
Bob Kelly, *CFO*
Edward Hayden, *Senior VP*
Louis Riley, *Senior VP*
EMP: 5030 EST: 2006
SQ FT: 208,000
SALES (est): 98.4MM **Privately Held**
SIC: 7372 Application computer software
HQ: Mcafee, Llc
    2821 Mission College Blvd
    Santa Clara CA 95054
    888 847-8766

(P-15401)
MEDALLIA INC (PA)
575 Market St Ste 1850, San Francisco
(94105-5803)
PHONE....................650 321-3000
Leslie J Stretch, *President*
Borge Hald, *Ch of Bd*
Roxanne M Oulman, *CFO*
Jimmy C Duan, *Ch Credit Ofcr*
Mikael J Ottosson, *Exec VP*
EMP: 145
SALES (est): 376.3MM **Publicly Held**
WEB: www.medallia.com
SIC: 7372 8732 Business oriented com-
    puter software; market analysis, business
    & economic research

(P-15402)
MEDATA INC (PA)
5 Peters Canyon Rd # 250, Irvine
(92606-1793)
PHONE....................714 918-1310
Cy King, *CEO*
Tom Herndon, *President*
Thomas Herndon, *COO*
Bryan Lowe, *CFO*
T Don Theis, *Senior VP*
EMP: 51 EST: 1975
SQ FT: 17,192
SALES (est): 114.3MM **Privately Held**
WEB: www.medata.com
SIC: 7372 6411 Business oriented com-
    puter software; medical insurance claim
    processing, contract or fee basis

(P-15403)
MEDICAL TRANSCRIPTION BILLING
405 Kenyon St Ste 300, San Diego (92110)
PHONE....................800 869-3700
EMP: 561
SALES (corp-wide): 50.5MM **Publicly
Held**
SIC: 7372 Prepackaged software
PA: Medical Transcription Billing, Corp.
    7 Clyde Rd
    Somerset NJ 08873
    732 873-5133

(P-15404)
MEDITAB SOFTWARE INC
333 Hegenberger Rd # 800, Oakland
(94621-1416)
PHONE....................510 632-2021
Mike Patel, *President*

Kal Patel, *COO*
Marc Beaniza, *Executive*
Sumair Sidhu, *Info Tech Dir*
Jigar Varmora, *Prgrmr*
EMP: 250
SQ FT: 10,000
SALES (est): 27.9MM **Privately Held**
SIC: 7372 Business oriented computer software

(P-15405)
METRICSTREAM INC (PA)
Also Called: Complianceonline
2479 E Byshore Rd Ste 260, Palo Alto (94303)
PHONE..................650 620-2900
Mikael Hagstroem, *CEO*
Gaurave Kapoor, *COO*
Steven R Springsteel, *CFO*
Gunjan Sinha, *Chairman*
Venky Yerrapotu, *Exec VP*
EMP: 150
SALES (est): 214.3MM **Privately Held**
SIC: 7372 Application computer software

(P-15406)
MICROSOFT CORPORATION
1085 La Avenida St, Mountain View (94043-1421)
PHONE..................650 964-7200
Susan Peletta, *Executive*
Jeff Asis, *Partner*
Jim Hogan, *Vice Pres*
John Stevans, *Program Mgr*
Zulfi Alam, *General Mgr*
EMP: 76
SALES (corp-wide): 125.8B **Publicly Held**
SIC: 7372 Prepackaged software
PA: Microsoft Corporation
1 Microsoft Way
Redmond WA 98052
425 882-8080

(P-15407)
MICROSOFT CORPORATION
7007 Friars Rd, San Diego (92108-1148)
PHONE..................619 849-5872
EMP: 100
SALES (corp-wide): 125.8B **Publicly Held**
SIC: 7372 Application computer software
PA: Microsoft Corporation
1 Microsoft Way
Redmond WA 98052
425 882-8080

(P-15408)
MICROSOFT CORPORATION
1020 Entp Way Bldg B, Sunnyvale (94089)
PHONE..................650 693-1009
William H Gates III, *Branch Mgr*
Swathi Shenoy, *Software Engr*
EMP: 103
SALES (corp-wide): 125.8B **Publicly Held**
SIC: 7372 Prepackaged software
PA: Microsoft Corporation
1 Microsoft Way
Redmond WA 98052
425 882-8080

(P-15409)
MICROSOFT CORPORATION
3 Park Plz Ste 1800, Irvine (92614-8541)
PHONE..................949 263-3000
Sandy Thomas, *General Mgr*
Rohit Malhotra, *Software Engr*
Juliet Helms, *Technical Staff*
Amine Brahimi, *Engineer*
Pouya Torabi, *Senior Mgr*
EMP: 125
SALES (corp-wide): 125.8B **Publicly Held**
WEB: www.microsoft.com
SIC: 7372 Application computer software
PA: Microsoft Corporation
1 Microsoft Way
Redmond WA 98052
425 882-8080

(P-15410)
MICROSOFT CORPORATION
13031 W Jefferson Blvd # 200, Playa Vista (90094-7001)
PHONE..................213 806-7300

Evelyn Morgan, *Manager*
Adam Foxman, *Software Dev*
Matthew Fraser, *Software Dev*
Pratap Ladhani, *Software Dev*
Josette Huang, *Software Engr*
EMP: 100
SALES (corp-wide): 125.8B **Publicly Held**
WEB: www.microsoft.com
SIC: 7372 Application computer software
PA: Microsoft Corporation
1 Microsoft Way
Redmond WA 98052
425 882-8080

(P-15411)
MICROSOFT CORPORATION
555 California St Ste 200, San Francisco (94104-1504)
PHONE..................415 972-6400
Teeka Miller, *Branch Mgr*
Vance Frankiewicz, *Technical Staff*
Vandan Kaushik, *Technical Staff*
Rupert Scammell, *Engineer*
Paulo Viralhadas, *Engineer*
EMP: 160
SALES (corp-wide): 125.8B **Publicly Held**
WEB: www.microsoft.com
SIC: 7372 Application computer software
PA: Microsoft Corporation
1 Microsoft Way
Redmond WA 98052
425 882-8080

(P-15412)
MICROSOFT CORPORATION
2045 Lafayette St, Santa Clara (95050-2901)
PHONE..................408 987-9608
Jim Brown, *President*
EMP: 100
SALES (corp-wide): 125.8B **Publicly Held**
WEB: www.microsoft.com
SIC: 7372 Application computer software
PA: Microsoft Corporation
1 Microsoft Way
Redmond WA 98052
425 882-8080

(P-15413)
MOBILEIRON INC (PA)
401 E Middlefield Rd, Mountain View (94043-4005)
PHONE..................650 919-8100
Simon Biddiscombe, *President*
Tae Hea Nahm, *Ch of Bd*
Scott D Hill, *CFO*
Kenneth Klein, *Bd of Directors*
James Tolonen, *Bd of Directors*
EMP: 148
SQ FT: 78,000
SALES: 193.1MM **Publicly Held**
SIC: 7372 Prepackaged software

(P-15414)
MSCSOFTWARE CORPORATION (HQ)
4675 Macarthur Ct Ste 900, Newport Beach (92660-1845)
PHONE..................714 540-8900
Dominic Gallello, *President*
Hugues Jeancolas, *Vice Pres*
Leo Kilfoy, *General Mgr*
Celia Arcos, *Office Admin*
Hiroko Shirai, *Executive Asst*
EMP: 245 **EST:** 1963
SALES (est): 146.4MM
SALES (corp-wide): 4.3B **Privately Held**
WEB: www.mscsoftware.com
SIC: 7372 Business oriented computer software
PA: Hexagon Ab
Lilla Bantorget 15
Stockholm 111 2
860 126-20

(P-15415)
MULESOFT INC
50 Fremont St Ste 300, San Francisco (94105-2231)
PHONE..................415 229-2009
Greg Schott, *CEO*
Matt Langdon, *CFO*
Vidya Peters, *Chief Mktg Ofcr*

Mark Dao, *Officer*
Brent Grimes, *Vice Pres*
EMP: 841
SQ FT: 41,500
SALES: 296.4MM
SALES (corp-wide): 13.2B **Publicly Held**
WEB: www.mulesource.com
SIC: 7372 7371 Prepackaged software; computer software development
PA: Salesforce.Com, Inc.
415 Mission St Fl 3
San Francisco CA 94105
415 901-7000

(P-15416)
MURSION INC (PA)
303 2nd St Ste 460, San Francisco (94107-1366)
PHONE..................415 746-9631
Mark Atkinson, *CEO*
Dovid Gurevich, *CFO*
Arjun Nagendran, *Vice Pres*
Greg Ayers, *Training Spec*
EMP: 54
SALES (est): 8.3MM **Privately Held**
SIC: 7372 Educational computer software; publishers' computer software

(P-15417)
MUSICMATCH INC
16935 W Bernardo Dr # 270, San Diego (92127-1634)
PHONE..................858 485-4300
Dennis Mudd, *CEO*
Peter Csathy, *President*
Gary Acord, *CFO*
Chris Allen, *Senior VP*
Don Leigh, *Senior VP*
EMP: 140
SQ FT: 20,000
SALES (est): 6.9MM **Privately Held**
WEB: www.musicmatch.com
SIC: 7372 5734 Prepackaged software; software, business & non-game
PA: Altaba Inc.
140 E 45th St Ste 15a
New York NY 10017

(P-15418)
NC INTERACTIVE LLC
1900 S Norfolk St Ste 125, San Mateo (94403-1175)
PHONE..................650 393-2200
Songyee Yoon, *CEO*
Eric Garay, *CFO*
Janet Lin, *General Counsel*
EMP: 99 **EST:** 2016
SQ FT: 16,692
SALES (est): 1.4MM **Privately Held**
SIC: 7372 Prepackaged software

(P-15419)
NET OPTICS INC
Also Called: Ixia
5301 Stevens Creek Blvd, Santa Clara (95051-7201)
PHONE..................408 737-7777
Thomas B Miller, *CEO*
Robert Shaw, *President*
Dennis Omanoff, *COO*
Burt Podbere, *CFO*
Nadine Matityahu, *Corp Secy*
EMP: 85
SQ FT: 39,000
SALES (est): 9MM
SALES (corp-wide): 3.8B **Publicly Held**
WEB: www.netoptics.com
SIC: 7372 Operating systems computer software
HQ: Ixia
26601 Agoura Rd
Calabasas CA 91302
818 871-1800

(P-15420)
NETCUBE SYSTEMS INC
1275 Arbor Ave, Los Altos (94024-5330)
PHONE..................650 862-7858
Mallikarjuna Reddy, *President*
EMP: 75
SQ FT: 1,000

SALES: 35MM **Privately Held**
SIC: 7372 7379 7371 7361 Application computer software; computer related consulting services; custom computer programming services; employment agencies

(P-15421)
NETSUITE INC (DH)
Also Called: Oracle
2955 Campus Dr Ste 100, San Mateo (94403-2539)
PHONE..................650 627-1000
Dorian Daley, *President*
Erica Prado, *President*
Evan Goldberg, *Exec VP*
Jim McGeever, *Exec VP*
Gary Wiessinger, *Exec VP*
EMP: 148
SQ FT: 165,000
SALES: 741.1MM
SALES (corp-wide): 39.5B **Publicly Held**
SIC: 7372 Business oriented computer software
HQ: Oc Acquisition Llc
500 Oracle Pkwy
Redwood City CA 94065
650 506-7000

(P-15422)
NETWORK AUTOMATION INC
3530 Wilshire Blvd # 1800, Los Angeles (90010-2335)
PHONE..................213 738-1700
Dustin Snell, *CEO*
Graham Taylor, *CTO*
Carmiel Banasky, *Marketing Staff*
Esther Suh, *Agent*
EMP: 50
SQ FT: 9,000
SALES (est): 3.6MM
SALES (corp-wide): 79.8MM **Privately Held**
WEB: www.networkautomation.com
SIC: 7372 Business oriented computer software
PA: Help/Systems, Llc
6455 City West Pkwy
Eden Prairie MN 55344
952 933-0609

(P-15423)
NEW BI US GAMING LLC
10920 Via Frontera # 420, San Diego (92127-1729)
PHONE..................858 592-2472
Ian Bonner, *CEO*
Kimberly Armstrong, *Vice Pres*
Russell Schechter, *Vice Pres*
EMP: 92 **EST:** 2012
SALES (est): 6MM **Privately Held**
SIC: 7372 Prepackaged software

(P-15424)
NEW CAM COMMERCE SOLUTIONS LLC
5555 Garden Grove Blvd # 100, Westminster (92683-8227)
PHONE..................714 338-0200
Doug Roberson, *Mng Member*
EMP: 77
SQ FT: 26,000
SALES (est): 5.9MM
SALES (corp-wide): 21.3MM **Privately Held**
SIC: 7372 Business oriented computer software
PA: Celerant Technology Corp.
4830 Arthur Kill Rd Ste 3
Staten Island NY 10309
718 351-2000

(P-15425)
NEW RELIC INC (PA)
188 Spear St Ste 1200, San Francisco (94105-1750)
PHONE..................650 777-7600
Lewis Cirne, *CEO*
Ana Valarezo, *Partner*
Peter Fenton, *Ch of Bd*
Mark Sachleben, *CFO*
Matthew Flaming, *Vice Pres*
EMP: 148
SQ FT: 73,391
SALES: 479.2MM **Publicly Held**
SIC: 7372 Application computer software

(P-15426)
NEXTGEN HEALTHCARE INC (PA)
18111 Von Karman Ave # 8, Irvine (92612-0199)
PHONE..................949 255-2600
John R Frantz, *President*
Craig A Barbarosh, *Vice Ch Bd*
Jeffrey D Linton, *Exec VP*
David A Metcalfe, *Exec VP*
Bailey Bachman, *Executive*
EMP: 148
SQ FT: 83,100
SALES: 529.1MM **Publicly Held**
WEB: www.qsii.com
SIC: 7372 7373 Prepackaged software; computer integrated systems design

(P-15427)
NIGHTINGALE VANTAGEMED CORP (HQ)
10670 White Rock Rd, Rancho Cordova (95670-6095)
PHONE..................916 638-4744
Steven Curd, *CEO*
Mark Cameron, *COO*
Liesel Loesch, *CFO*
Richard Altinger, *Vice Pres*
Jennifer Bentley, *VP Mktg*
EMP: 55
SALES (est): 10.6MM **Privately Held**
WEB: www.vantagemed.com
SIC: 7372 Business oriented computer software
PA: Nexia Health Technologies Inc
15 Allstate Prkwy 6th Fl
Markham ON L3R 5
905 415-3063

(P-15428)
NOMINUM INC
3355 Scott Blvd Fl 3, Santa Clara (95054-3127)
PHONE..................650 381-6000
Garry Messiana, *CEO*
Gopala Tumuluri, *COO*
Bob Verheecke, *CFO*
Pete Wisowaty, *Exec VP*
Srini Avirneni, *Senior VP*
EMP: 50
SQ FT: 15,000
SALES (est): 26.9MM
SALES (corp-wide): 2.7B **Publicly Held**
WEB: www.nominum.com
SIC: 7372 Prepackaged software
PA: Akamai Technologies, Inc.
150 Broadway Ste 100
Cambridge MA 02142
617 444-3000

(P-15429)
NTN BUZZTIME INC (PA)
1800 Aston Ave Ste 100, Carlsbad (92008-7399)
PHONE..................760 438-7400
Allen Wolff, *CEO*
Gregg Thomas, *Ch of Bd*
Steve Mitgang, *Bd of Directors*
Sandra Gurrola, *VP Finance*
▲ EMP: 137
SQ FT: 28,000
SALES: 23.3MM **Publicly Held**
WEB: www.ntnwireless.com
SIC: 7372 7922 7929 7359 Application computer software; entertainment promotion; entertainment service; equipment rental & leasing

(P-15430)
NTRUST INFOTECH INC
230 Commerce Ste 180, Irvine (92602-1336)
PHONE..................562 207-1600
Srikanth Ramachandran, *CEO*
Kevin C Harrigan, *Vice Pres*
Manoj Kumar, *Vice Pres*
Ramesh Narayanan, *Vice Pres*
Sameer Sarvate, *Vice Pres*
EMP: 65 EST: 2003
SALES (est): 6.5MM **Privately Held**
SIC: 7372 7371 Business oriented computer software; computer software development & applications

PA: Ntrust Infotech Private Limited
3rd Floor Ganesh Towers
Chennai TN 60000

(P-15431)
NWP SERVICES CORPORATION (HQ)
535 Anton Blvd Ste 1100, Costa Mesa (92626-7699)
P.O. Box 19661, Irvine (92623-9661)
PHONE..................949 253-2500
Ron Reed, *President*
Lana Reeve,
Mike Haviken, *Exec VP*
Monique Black, *Human Resources*
Bob Smolarski, *Opers Staff*
EMP: 141
SQ FT: 21,171
SALES (est): 48.8MM
SALES (corp-wide): 869.4MM **Publicly Held**
WEB: www.nwpco.com
SIC: 7372 8721 Utility computer software; billing & bookkeeping service
PA: Realpage, Inc.
2201 Lakeside Blvd
Richardson TX 75082
972 820-3000

(P-15432)
ODDWORLD INHABITANTS INC
869 Monterey St, San Luis Obispo (93401-3224)
PHONE..................805 503-3000
Sherry McKenna, *CEO*
Lorne Lanning, *President*
Maurice Konkle, *COO*
Raymond Swanland, *Production*
EMP: 60
SQ FT: 15,000
SALES (est): 2.4MM **Privately Held**
WEB: www.oddworld.com
SIC: 7372 Application computer software

(P-15433)
OKTA INC (PA)
100 1st St Ste 600, San Francisco (94105-2634)
PHONE..................888 722-7871
Todd McKinnon, *Ch of Bd*
Natasha Bhargava, *Partner*
Charles Race, *President*
J Frederic Kerrest, *COO*
William E Losch, *CFO*
EMP: 148
SQ FT: 207,066
SALES: 399.2MM **Publicly Held**
SIC: 7372 7371 Prepackaged software; software programming applications

(P-15434)
ON24 INC (PA)
50 Beale St Ste 800, San Francisco (94105-1863)
PHONE..................877 202-9599
Sharat Sharan, *President*
Ian Halifax, *CFO*
Joe Hyland, *Chief Mktg Ofcr*
Mike Badgis, *Vice Pres*
Mahesh Kheny, *Vice Pres*
EMP: 350
SQ FT: 28,353
SALES (est): 81.9MM **Privately Held**
WEB: www.on24.com
SIC: 7372 Business oriented computer software

(P-15435)
OPENTV INC (DH)
Also Called: Nagra
275 Sacramento St Ste Sl1, San Francisco (94111-3831)
PHONE..................415 962-5000
Yves Pitton, *CEO*
Andr Kudelski, *CEO*
Wesley O Hoffman, *COO*
Pamela Creamer, *CFO*
Shum Mukherjee, *CFO*
EMP: 150
SALES (est): 78.6MM
SALES (corp-wide): 919.6MM **Privately Held**
SIC: 7372 Prepackaged software

(P-15436)
OPTIMUM SOLUTIONS GROUP LLC
419 Ponderosa Ct, Lafayette (94549-1812)
PHONE..................415 954-7100
G John Houtary,
Lisa Massman,
EMP: 109
SQ FT: 3,300
SALES (est): 4.6MM
SALES (corp-wide): 3.3B **Privately Held**
WEB: www.optimumsolutions.com
SIC: 7372 7371 8243 7374 Prepackaged software; computer software systems analysis & design, custom; data processing schools; computer graphics service
PA: Kpmg Llp
345 Park Ave Lowr Ll4
New York NY 10154
212 758-9700

(P-15437)
ORACLE AMERICA INC
Also Called: Sun Microsystems
4220 Network Cir, Santa Clara (95054-1780)
PHONE..................408 276-4300
Mark Toliver, *President*
Daniele Knab, *Technical Staff*
Peter Lam, *Technical Staff*
Valerie Peng, *Technical Staff*
Hang Vo, *Technical Staff*
EMP: 187
SALES (corp-wide): 39.5B **Publicly Held**
SIC: 7372 Prepackaged software
HQ: Oracle America, Inc.
500 Oracle Pkwy
Redwood City CA 94065
650 506-7000

(P-15438)
ORACLE AMERICA INC
475 Sansome St Fl 15, San Francisco (94111-3166)
PHONE..................415 908-3609
EMP: 58
SALES (corp-wide): 39.5B **Publicly Held**
SIC: 7372 Prepackaged software
HQ: Oracle America, Inc.
500 Oracle Pkwy
Redwood City CA 94065
650 506-7000

(P-15439)
ORACLE AMERICA INC
4120 Network Cir, Santa Clara (95054-1778)
PHONE..................408 276-3331
Scott G McNealy, *Ch of Bd*
Ashok Krishnamurthi, *CEO*
Karen Willem, *CFO*
Rick Fabiano, *Principal*
Mark Leslie, *Principal*
EMP: 150
SALES (est): 16.3MM **Privately Held**
WEB: www.xsigo.com
SIC: 7372 Prepackaged software

(P-15440)
ORACLE AMERICA INC
Also Called: Sun Microsystems
5815 Owens Dr, Pleasanton (94588-3939)
PHONE..................925 694-3314
Terri Beck, *Manager*
EMP: 75
SALES (corp-wide): 39.5B **Publicly Held**
SIC: 7372 Prepackaged software
HQ: Oracle America, Inc.
500 Oracle Pkwy
Redwood City CA 94065
650 506-7000

(P-15441)
ORACLE AMERICA INC
Also Called: Sun Microsystems
9540 Towne Centre Dr, San Diego (92121-1988)
PHONE..................858 625-5044
Steven Nathan, *Manager*
EMP: 77
SALES (corp-wide): 39.5B **Publicly Held**
SIC: 7372 Prepackaged software
HQ: Oracle America, Inc.
500 Oracle Pkwy
Redwood City CA 94065
650 506-7000

(P-15442)
ORACLE AMERICA INC
Also Called: Sun Microsystems
4230 Leonard Stocking Dr, Santa Clara (95054-1777)
PHONE..................408 276-7534
Denise Shiffman, *VP Mktg*
Larry Williams, *COO*
Joe Fuentes, *Comms Mgr*
Michael Connaughton, *General Mgr*
William H Howard, *CIO*
EMP: 250
SALES (corp-wide): 39.5B **Publicly Held**
SIC: 7372 Prepackaged software
HQ: Oracle America, Inc.
500 Oracle Pkwy
Redwood City CA 94065
650 506-7000

(P-15443)
ORACLE CORPORATION
279 Barnes Rd, Tustin (92782-3748)
PHONE..................713 654-0919
John Czapko, *Branch Mgr*
EMP: 191
SALES (corp-wide): 39.5B **Publicly Held**
SIC: 7372 Business oriented computer software
PA: Oracle Corporation
500 Oracle Pkwy
Redwood City CA 94065
650 506-7000

(P-15444)
ORACLE CORPORATION
214 Clarence Ave, Sunnyvale (94086-5907)
PHONE..................650 607-5402
Jitendra Chinthakindi, *Principal*
EMP: 302
SALES (corp-wide): 39.5B **Publicly Held**
SIC: 7372 Business oriented computer software
PA: Oracle Corporation
500 Oracle Pkwy
Redwood City CA 94065
650 506-7000

(P-15445)
ORACLE CORPORATION
1408 Antigua Ln, Foster City (94404-3970)
PHONE..................650 678-3612
ARA Michaelian, *Principal*
EMP: 302
SALES (corp-wide): 39.5B **Publicly Held**
SIC: 7372 Business oriented computer software
PA: Oracle Corporation
500 Oracle Pkwy
Redwood City CA 94065
650 506-7000

(P-15446)
ORACLE CORPORATION
1490 Newhall St, Santa Clara (95050-6135)
PHONE..................408 421-2890
Stephanie Camarda, *Principal*
EMP: 302
SALES (corp-wide): 39.5B **Publicly Held**
SIC: 7372 Business oriented computer software
PA: Oracle Corporation
500 Oracle Pkwy
Redwood City CA 94065
650 506-7000

(P-15447)
ORACLE CORPORATION
231 Kerry Dr, Santa Clara (95050-6603)
PHONE..................408 276-5552
Annie Van Dalen, *Principal*
Abhijit Kumar, *Technology*
EMP: 302
SALES (corp-wide): 39.5B **Publicly Held**
SIC: 7372 Business oriented computer software
PA: Oracle Corporation
500 Oracle Pkwy
Redwood City CA 94065
650 506-7000

(P-15448)
ORACLE CORPORATION
3084 Thurman Dr, San Jose (95148-3143)
PHONE..................408 276-3822

Alasdair Rendall, *Principal*
Mehdi Syed, *Software Engr*
EMP: 302
SALES (corp-wide): 39.5B **Publicly Held**
SIC: 7372 Business oriented computer
software
PA: Oracle Corporation
500 Oracle Pkwy
Redwood City CA 94065
650 506-7000

(P-15449)
ORACLE CORPORATION
9890 Towne Centre Dr # 150, San Diego
(92121-1999)
PHONE...................858 202-0648
EMP: 191
SALES (corp-wide): 39.5B **Publicly Held**
SIC: 7372 Business oriented computer
software
PA: Oracle Corporation
500 Oracle Pkwy
Redwood City CA 94065
650 506-7000

(P-15450)
ORACLE CORPORATION
3532 Eastin Pl, Santa Clara (95051-2600)
PHONE...................650 506-9864
Maneesh Jain, *Principal*
Gia Nguyen, *Senior Engr*
EMP: 302
SALES (corp-wide): 39.5B **Publicly Held**
SIC: 7372 Business oriented computer
software
PA: Oracle Corporation
500 Oracle Pkwy
Redwood City CA 94065
650 506-7000

(P-15451)
ORACLE CORPORATION
372 Calero Ave, San Jose (95123-4315)
PHONE...................408 390-8623
Aileen F Casanave, *Principal*
EMP: 302
SALES (corp-wide): 39.5B **Publicly Held**
SIC: 7372 Business oriented computer
software
PA: Oracle Corporation
500 Oracle Pkwy
Redwood City CA 94065
650 506-7000

(P-15452)
ORACLE CORPORATION
525 Market St, San Francisco
(94105-2708)
PHONE...................415 402-7200
Victor Coskey, *Principal*
Rafiul Ahad, *Vice Pres*
Trey Parsons, *Vice Pres*
Sivarami Pothula, *Administration*
Eric Tran, *Administration*
EMP: 191
SALES (corp-wide): 39.5B **Publicly Held**
SIC: 7372 Business oriented computer
software
PA: Oracle Corporation
500 Oracle Pkwy
Redwood City CA 94065
650 506-7000

(P-15453)
ORACLE CORPORATION
6224 Hummingbird Ln, Rocklin
(95765-5929)
P.O. Box 3442 (95677-8469)
PHONE...................916 435-8342
Richard Gless, *Principal*
Elishia Duran, *Analyst*
EMP: 302
SALES (corp-wide): 39.5B **Publicly Held**
SIC: 7372 Business oriented computer
software
PA: Oracle Corporation
500 Oracle Pkwy
Redwood City CA 94065
650 506-7000

(P-15454)
ORACLE CORPORATION
5805 Owens Dr, Pleasanton (94588-3939)
PHONE...................877 767-2253
Bor R Fu, *Senior VP*
Clement Sciammas, *Vice Pres*

Kevin Zhou, *Sr Software Eng*
David Laux, *Technical Staff*
Meena Palani, *Technical Staff*
EMP: 315
SALES (corp-wide): 39.5B **Publicly Held**
SIC: 7372 Business oriented computer
software
PA: Oracle Corporation
500 Oracle Pkwy
Redwood City CA 94065
650 506-7000

(P-15455)
ORACLE CORPORATION
3925 Emerald Isle Ln, San Jose
(95135-1708)
PHONE...................925 694-6258
Johnson Aremu, *Principal*
EMP: 306
SALES (corp-wide): 39.5B **Publicly Held**
SIC: 7372 Business oriented computer
software
PA: Oracle Corporation
500 Oracle Pkwy
Redwood City CA 94065
650 506-7000

(P-15456)
ORACLE CORPORATION
5863 Carmel Way, Union City
(94587-5170)
PHONE...................510 471-6971
Renzo Zagni, *Principal*
Terry Bowen, *Software Engr*
Roger Chan, *Software Engr*
Mark Chaney, *Software Engr*
John Holder, *Software Engr*
EMP: 302
SALES (corp-wide): 39.5B **Publicly Held**
SIC: 7372 Business oriented computer
software
PA: Oracle Corporation
500 Oracle Pkwy
Redwood City CA 94065
650 506-7000

(P-15457)
ORACLE CORPORATION
200 Crprate Pinte Ste 200, Culver City
(90230)
PHONE...................310 258-7500
EMP: 302
SALES (corp-wide): 39.5B **Publicly Held**
SIC: 7372 Business oriented computer
software
PA: Oracle Corporation
500 Oracle Pkwy
Redwood City CA 94065
650 506-7000

(P-15458)
ORACLE CORPORATION
200 N Pacific Coast Hwy # 400, El Se-
gundo (90245-5628)
PHONE...................310 343-7405
EMP: 306
SALES (corp-wide): 39.5B **Publicly Held**
SIC: 7372 Business oriented computer
software
PA: Oracle Corporation
500 Oracle Pkwy
Redwood City CA 94065
650 506-7000

(P-15459)
ORACLE CORPORATION
1001 Sunset Blvd, Rocklin (95765-3702)
PHONE...................916 315-3500
Chris Wilson, *Branch Mgr*
Liz Brock, *Administration*
Pavel Buenitsky, *Info Tech Dir*
Steve Fitzgerald, *Info Tech Dir*
Marion Smith, *Info Tech Dir*
EMP: 500
SALES (corp-wide): 39.5B **Publicly Held**
SIC: 7372 7371 Business oriented com-
puter software; custom computer pro-
gramming services
PA: Oracle Corporation
500 Oracle Pkwy
Redwood City CA 94065
650 506-7000

(P-15460)
**ORACLE SYSTEMS
CORPORATION**
200 Crprate Pinte Ste 200, Culver City
(90230)
PHONE...................818 817-2900
Elizabeth Deitz, *General Mgr*
Ram Ramachandran, *Sr Software Eng*
Kamal Fazah, *Technical Staff*
Lisa Schwartz, *Marketing Staff*
EMP: 70
SALES (corp-wide): 39.5B **Publicly Held**
WEB: www.forcecapital.com
SIC: 7372 Prepackaged software
HQ: Oracle Systems Corporation
500 Oracle Pkwy
Redwood City CA 94065
650 506-7000

(P-15461)
**ORACLE SYSTEMS
CORPORATION**
102 Santa Barbara Ave, Daly City
(94014-1045)
PHONE...................650 506-8648
EMP: 92
SALES (corp-wide): 39.5B **Publicly Held**
WEB: www.forcecapital.com
SIC: 7372 Prepackaged software
HQ: Oracle Systems Corporation
500 Oracle Pkwy
Redwood City CA 94065
650 506-7000

(P-15462)
**ORACLE SYSTEMS
CORPORATION**
301 Island Pkwy, Belmont (94002-4109)
PHONE...................650 654-7606
EMP: 304
SALES (corp-wide): 39.5B **Publicly Held**
SIC: 7372 Prepackaged software
HQ: Oracle Systems Corporation
500 Oracle Pkwy
Redwood City CA 94065
650 506-7000

(P-15463)
**ORACLE SYSTEMS
CORPORATION**
500 Oracle Pwky, San Mateo (94403)
PHONE...................650 506-6780
Sayekumar Arumugam, *Principal*
EMP: 108
SALES (corp-wide): 39.5B **Publicly Held**
WEB: www.forcecapital.com
SIC: 7372 Prepackaged software
HQ: Oracle Systems Corporation
500 Oracle Pkwy
Redwood City CA 94065
650 506-7000

(P-15464)
**ORACLE SYSTEMS
CORPORATION**
10 Twin Dolphin Dr, Redwood City
(94065-1035)
PHONE...................650 506-0300
EMP: 252
SALES (corp-wide): 39.5B **Publicly Held**
WEB: www.forcecapital.com
SIC: 7372 Prepackaged software
HQ: Oracle Systems Corporation
500 Oracle Pkwy
Redwood City CA 94065
650 506-7000

(P-15465)
**ORACLE SYSTEMS
CORPORATION**
5840 Owens Dr, Pleasanton (94588-3900)
PHONE...................925 694-3000
Apu Gupta, *Principal*
Peter Chen, *Manager*
Daniel Wright, *Consultant*
EMP: 252
SALES (corp-wide): 39.5B **Publicly Held**
WEB: www.forcecapital.com
SIC: 7372 5734 Prepackaged software;
software, business & non-game
HQ: Oracle Systems Corporation
500 Oracle Pkwy
Redwood City CA 94065
650 506-7000

(P-15466)
**ORACLE SYSTEMS
CORPORATION**
2010 Main St Ste 450, Irvine (92614-7260)
PHONE...................949 224-1000
Dawn Lotez, *Manager*
Jeff Hollenshead, *Network Enginr*
EMP: 100
SALES (corp-wide): 39.5B **Publicly Held**
WEB: www.forcecapital.com
SIC: 7372 Prepackaged software
HQ: Oracle Systems Corporation
500 Oracle Pkwy
Redwood City CA 94065
650 506-7000

(P-15467)
**ORACLE SYSTEMS
CORPORATION**
17901 Von Karman Ave # 800, Irvine
(92614-6297)
PHONE...................949 623-9460
EMP: 275
SALES (corp-wide): 39.5B **Publicly Held**
WEB: www.forcecapital.com
SIC: 7372 5045 Prepackaged software;
computers, peripherals & software
HQ: Oracle Systems Corporation
500 Oracle Pkwy
Redwood City CA 94065
650 506-7000

(P-15468)
ORACLE TALEO LLC
4140 Dublin Blvd Ste 400, Dublin
(94568-7757)
PHONE...................925 452-3000
Dorian Daley, *President*
Eric Ball, *CFO*
Guy Gauvin, *Exec VP*
Neil Hudspith, *Exec VP*
Jason Blessing, *Senior VP*
EMP: 1164
SQ FT: 47,500
SALES (est): 95MM
SALES (corp-wide): 39.5B **Publicly Held**
WEB: www.taleo.com
SIC: 7372 Business oriented computer
software
PA: Oracle Corporation
500 Oracle Pkwy
Redwood City CA 94065
650 506-7000

(P-15469)
PACIOLAN LLC (DH)
Also Called: Ticketswest
5291 California Ave # 100, Irvine
(92617-3220)
PHONE...................866 722-4652
Dave Butler, *CEO*
Jane Kleinberger, *Ch of Bd*
Kimberly Boren, *CFO*
Steve Shaw, *CFO*
Teri Clark, *Admin Sec*
EMP: 85 **EST:** 1980
SALES (est): 28.5MM **Privately Held**
WEB: www.paciolan.com
SIC: 7372 5045 Business oriented com-
puter software; computers
HQ: Learfield Communications, Llc
2400 Dallas Pkwy Ste 510
Plano TX 75093
336 464-0224

(P-15470)
PAGERDUTY INC (PA)
600 Townsend St Ste 200e, San Francisco
(94103-5690)
PHONE...................844 800-3889
Jennifer G Tejada, *Ch of Bd*
Howard Wilson, *CFO*
Steven Chung, *Senior VP*
Stacey A Giamalis, *Senior VP*
Jonathan Rende, *Senior VP*
EMP: 143
SQ FT: 59,000
SALES: 117.8MM **Publicly Held**
WEB: www.pagerduty.com
SIC: 7372 Prepackaged software

(P-15471)
PATIENTPOP INC
214 Wilshire Blvd, Santa Monica
(90401-1202)
PHONE...................844 487-8399
Travis Schneider, *CEO*
Jason Gardner, *CFO*
Luke Kervin, *Co-CEO*
Jeb Burrows, *Vice Pres*
Thomas Le Blan, *Vice Pres*
EMP: 51 **EST:** 2015
SALES (est): 1.1MM **Privately Held**
SIC: 7372 Business oriented computer
software

(P-15472)
PATRON SOLUTIONS LLC
5171 California Ave # 200, Irvine
(92617-3068)
PHONE...................949 823-1700
Steve Shaw, *Owner*
EMP: 245
SALES (est): 17.4MM **Privately Held**
SIC: 7372 Application computer software

(P-15473)
PAXATA INC
1800 Seaport Blvd 1, Redwood City
(94063-5543)
PHONE...................650 542-7897
Prakasa Nanduri, *CEO*
David Brewster, *Co-Owner*
John Botros, *CFO*
Nenshad Bardoliwalla, *Vice Pres*
Manu Chadha, *Vice Pres*
EMP: 90
SALES (est): 10.6MM **Privately Held**
SIC: 7372 Business oriented computer
software

(P-15474)
PAYLOCITY HOLDING CORPORATION
2107 Livingston St, Oakland (94606-5218)
PHONE...................847 956-4850
Lisa Formicola, *Director*
Janine Howard, *Manager*
EMP: 498
SALES (corp-wide): 467.6MM **Publicly Held**
SIC: 7372 Prepackaged software
PA: Paylocity Holding Corporation
1400 American Ln
Schaumburg IL 60173
847 463-3200

(P-15475)
PEOPLE CENTER INC
Also Called: Rippling
2443 Fillmore St 380-7, San Francisco
(94115-1814)
PHONE...................781 864-1232
Parker Conrad, *CEO*
Persona Sankaranarayana, *CTO*
Oscar London, *Sales Staff*
EMP: 50
SQ FT: 4,000
SALES: 1MM **Privately Held**
SIC: 7372 Business oriented computer
software

(P-15476)
PLANGRID INC (HQ)
Also Called: Loupe
2111 Mission St Ste 400, San Francisco
(94110-6349)
PHONE...................800 646-0796
Tracy Young, *CEO*
Douglas Leone, *Managing Prtnr*
Kevin Halter, *President*
Michael Galvin, *CFO*
David Cain, *Chief Mktg Ofcr*
EMP: 76
SQ FT: 16,000
SALES (est): 16.4MM
SALES (corp-wide): 2.5B **Publicly Held**
SIC: 7372 Application computer software
PA: Autodesk, Inc.
111 Mcinnis Pkwy
San Rafael CA 94903
415 507-5000

(P-15477)
PLX TECHNOLOGY INC
1320 Ridder Park Dr, San Jose
(95131-2313)
PHONE...................408 435-7400
Hock Tan, *President*
Anthony Maslowski, *CFO*
Charlie Kawwas, *Senior VP*
Boon Chye Ooi, *Senior VP*
Andy Nallappan, *Vice Pres*
▲ **EMP:** 157
SQ FT: 55,000
SALES (est): 12.4MM
SALES (corp-wide): 20.8B **Publicly Held**
WEB: www.plxtech.com
SIC: 7372 3674 Business oriented com-
puter software; integrated circuits, semi-
conductor networks, etc.
HQ: Avago Technologies Wireless (U.S.A.)
Manufacturing Llc
4380 Ziegler Rd
Fort Collins CO 80525
970 288-2575

(P-15478)
POLARION SOFTWARE INC
1001 Marina Village Pkwy # 403, Alameda
(94501-6401)
PHONE...................877 572-4005
Frank Schrder, *CEO*
George Briner, *CFO*
Stefano Rizzo, *Senior VP*
Nikolay Entin, *Vice Pres*
Jiri Walek, *Vice Pres*
EMP: 90
SALES (est): 7.2MM **Privately Held**
SIC: 7372 Prepackaged software

(P-15479)
PORTELLUS INC
2522 Chambers Rd Ste 100, Tustin
(92780-6962)
PHONE...................949 250-9600
John Le, *President*
EMP: 80
SALES: 3.6MM **Privately Held**
WEB: www.portellus.com
SIC: 7372 Prepackaged software

(P-15480)
POWERSCHOOL GROUP LLC (HQ)
150 Parkshore Dr, Folsom (95630-4710)
PHONE...................916 288-1636
Hardeep Gulati, *CEO*
Mark Oldemeyer, *CFO*
Edward Dedic, *Vice Pres*
SAI Rangarajan, *Vice Pres*
Mike Rhein, *Vice Pres*
EMP: 148
SALES (est): 84.2MM
SALES (corp-wide): 5B **Privately Held**
SIC: 7372 Prepackaged software
PA: Vista Equity Partners Management, Llc
4 Embarcadero Ctr Fl 20
San Francisco CA 94111
415 765-6500

(P-15481)
QAD INC (PA)
100 Innovation Pl, Santa Barbara
(93108-2268)
PHONE...................805 566-6000
Anton Chilton, *CEO*
Pamela M Lopker, *Ch of Bd*
Daniel Lender, *CFO*
John Neale, *Treasurer*
Kara Bellamy, *Senior VP*
EMP: 148
SQ FT: 120,000
SALES: 333MM **Publicly Held**
WEB: www.qad.com
SIC: 7372 7371 Business oriented com-
puter software; custom computer pro-
gramming services

(P-15482)
QUEST SOFTWARE INC
Packettrap Networks
118 2nd St Fl 6, San Francisco
(94105-3620)
PHONE...................415 373-2222
Steven M Goodman, *President*
EMP: 65
SALES (corp-wide): 1.5B **Privately Held**
SIC: 7372 Prepackaged software

HQ: Quest Software, Inc.
4 Polaris Way
Aliso Viejo CA 92656
949 754-8000

(P-15483)
QUEST SOFTWARE INC
Also Called: Cloud Automation Division
4 Polaris Way, Aliso Viejo (92656-5356)
PHONE...................949 754-8000
Angela Morales, *Partner*
Katherine Tate, *Officer*
Doug Wright, *Surgery Dir*
Mark Lomas, *Admin Mgr*
Pierre Nguyen, *Administration*
EMP: 80
SALES (corp-wide): 1.5B **Privately Held**
SIC: 7372 Prepackaged software
HQ: Quest Software, Inc.
4 Polaris Way
Aliso Viejo CA 92656
949 754-8000

(P-15484)
QUMU INC (HQ)
1100 Grundy Ln Ste 110, San Bruno
(94066-3072)
PHONE...................650 396-8530
Jim Stewart, *CFO*
Taimur Mirza, *Sr Software Eng*
David Higuera, *Info Tech Mgr*
Naureen Moon, *Software Engr*
David Bukhan, *VP Engrg*
EMP: 56
SQ FT: 13,000
SALES (est): 8.5MM
SALES (corp-wide): 25MM **Publicly Held**
WEB: www.mediapublisher.com
SIC: 7372 Business oriented computer
software
PA: Qumu Corporation
510 1st Ave N Ste 305
Minneapolis MN 55403
612 638-9100

(P-15485)
REAL SOFTWARE SYSTEMS LLC (PA)
21255 Burbank Blvd # 220, Woodland Hills
(91367-6610)
PHONE...................818 313-8000
Kent Sahin, *Mng Member*
Jenny Gonzales, *Consultant*
EMP: 60
SALES (est): 8MM **Privately Held**
WEB: www.realsoftwaresystems.com
SIC: 7372 Business oriented computer
software

(P-15486)
REDSEAL INC
1600 Technology Dr Fl 4, San Jose
(95110-1382)
PHONE...................408 641-2200
Ray Rothrock, *CEO*
Greg Straughn, *CFO*
Gordon Adams, *Officer*
Jay Miller, *Vice Pres*
Sundar Raj, *Vice Pres*
EMP: 100
SQ FT: 6,500
SALES (est): 22.1MM **Privately Held**
WEB: www.redseal.net
SIC: 7372 Prepackaged software

(P-15487)
REVJET
981 Industrial Rd Ste F, San Carlos
(94070-4150)
PHONE...................650 508-2215
Patrick McNenny, *Vice Pres*
Bradley McKeon, *Vice Pres*
David Mackay, *Risk Mgmt Dir*
Andriy Gusyev, *Engrg Dir*
Derek Gavigan, *Sales Dir*
EMP: 110 **EST:** 2017
SALES (est): 2.3MM **Privately Held**
SIC: 7372 Application computer software

(P-15488)
ROBLOX CORPORATION
970 Park Pl, San Mateo (94403-1907)
PHONE...................888 858-2569
David Baszucki, *CEO*
Michael Poon, *CFO*
Scott Rubin, *Vice Pres*

Andrew Francis, *Sr Software Eng*
Dinghao LI, *Software Engr*
EMP: 500
SALES (est): 4MM **Privately Held**
SIC: 7372 Prepackaged software

(P-15489)
SABA SOFTWARE INC (PA)
4120 Dublin Blvd Ste 200, Dublin
(94568-7759)
PHONE...................877 722-2101
Phil Saunders, *President*
Allison Wudel, *Partner*
Pete Low, *CFO*
Debbie Shotwell,
Paige Newcombe, *Officer*
EMP: 100
SQ FT: 36,000
SALES (est): 177MM **Privately Held**
WEB: www.saba.com
SIC: 7372 7371 Application computer soft-
ware; computer software development &
applications

(P-15490)
SAGE SOFTWARE INC
1380 Tatan Trail Rd, Burlingame (94010)
PHONE...................650 579-3628
Mau Chung Chang, *Branch Mgr*
EMP: 245
SALES (corp-wide): 2.3B **Privately Held**
SIC: 7372 Business oriented computer
software
HQ: Sage Software, Inc.
271 17th St Nw Ste 1100
Atlanta GA 30363
866 996-7243

(P-15491)
SAGE SOFTWARE HOLDINGS INC (HQ)
6561 Irvine Center Dr, Irvine (92618-2118)
PHONE...................866 530-7243
Stev Swenson, *CEO*
Mack Lout, *CFO*
Bill Feder, *Vice Pres*
Doug Meyer, *Vice Pres*
Dion Diroma, *IT/INT Sup*
EMP: 400
SALES (est): 464.7MM
SALES (corp-wide): 2.3B **Privately Held**
SIC: 7372 7371 Business oriented com-
puter software; custom computer pro-
gramming services
PA: The Sage Group Plc.
North Park Avenue
Newcastle-Upon-Tyne NE13
191 294-3000

(P-15492)
SALESFORCECOM INC (PA)
415 Mission St Fl 3, San Francisco
(94105-2533)
PHONE...................415 901-7000
Marc Benioff, *Ch of Bd*
Christina Kirkpatrick, *Partner*
Bob Stutz, *Partner*
Keith Block, *President*
Mark Hawkins, *President*
EMP: 600 **EST:** 1999
SALES: 13.2B **Publicly Held**
WEB: www.salesforce.com
SIC: 7372 7375 Business oriented com-
puter software; information retrieval serv-
ices

(P-15493)
SAS INSTITUTE INC
Salesstock.com
1148 N Lemon St, Orange (92867-4701)
PHONE...................949 250-9999
Shawn Anthony Stiltz, *Vice Pres*
EMP: 56
SALES (corp-wide): 3B **Privately Held**
SIC: 7372 Application computer software;
business oriented computer software; ed-
ucational computer software
PA: Sas Institute Inc.
100 Sas Campus Dr
Cary NC 27513
919 677-8000

(P-15494)
SCHOOL INNOVATIONS ACHIEVEMENT (PA)
5200 Golden Foothill Pkwy, El Dorado Hills (95762-9610)
PHONE...................916 933-2290
Jeffrey C Williams, *CEO*
Gemma Ball, *Partner*
Susan Cook, *COO*
Joe Steele, *CFO*
Jerry Wooden, *Exec VP*
EMP: 95
SQ FT: 25,000
SALES: 14.8MM **Privately Held**
WEB: www.sia-us.com
SIC: 7372 8742 Prepackaged software; management consulting services

(P-15495)
SCOPELY INC (PA)
3530 Hayden Ave Ste A, Culver City (90232-2413)
PHONE...................323 400-6618
Walter Driver III, *President*
JC Bornaghi, *Vice Pres*
Eytan Elbaz, *Vice Pres*
Eric Futoran, *Vice Pres*
Divya Sankaran, *Sr Software Eng*
EMP: 200
SALES (est): 10.3MM **Privately Held**
SIC: 7372 Home entertainment computer software

(P-15496)
SHAREDATA INC
Also Called: Sharedta/E Trade Bus Solutions
2465 Augustine Dr, Santa Clara (95054)
PHONE...................408 490-2500
Laura Fay, *President*
EMP: 53
SALES (est): 1.9MM **Privately Held**
SIC: 7372 Business oriented computer software

(P-15497)
SHOTSPOTTER INC
Also Called: SST
7979 Gateway Blvd Ste 210, Newark (94560-1158)
PHONE...................510 794-3100
Ralph A Clark, *President*
Paul S Ames, *Senior VP*
Nasim Golzadeh, *Senior VP*
Joseph O Hawkins, *Senior VP*
Sonya L Strickler, *VP Finance*
EMP: 76
SQ FT: 12,020
SALES: 34.7MM **Privately Held**
WEB: www.shotspotter.com
SIC: 7372 7382 Prepackaged software; security systems services

(P-15498)
SIGHT MACHINE INC
243 Vallejo St, San Francisco (94111-1511)
PHONE...................888 461-5739
Jon Sobel, *CEO*
John Stone, *President*
Syed Hoda, *Chief Mktg Ofcr*
Kurt Demaagd, *Vice Pres*
Brian Gillespie, *Vice Pres*
EMP: 60
SQ FT: 6,500
SALES (est): 2.4MM **Privately Held**
SIC: 7372 Business oriented computer software

(P-15499)
SLACK TECHNOLOGIES INC (PA)
500 Howard St Ste 100, San Francisco (94105-3031)
PHONE...................415 902-5526
Stewart Butterfield, *Ch of Bd*
Allen Shim, *CFO*
Tamar Yehoshua,
Robert Frati, *Senior VP*
David Schellhase, *Admin Sec*
EMP: 148
SQ FT: 228,998
SALES: 400.5MM **Publicly Held**
SIC: 7372 Business oriented computer software

(P-15500)
SNAPLOGIC INC (PA)
1825 S Grant St Ste 550, San Mateo (94402-2719)
PHONE...................888 494-1570
Gaurav Dhillon, *CEO*
Bob Parker, *CFO*
Robert J Parker, *CFO*
David Downing, *Chief Mktg Ofcr*
Vaikom Krishnan, *Vice Pres*
EMP: 140
SALES (est): 30.4MM **Privately Held**
SIC: 7372 Business oriented computer software

(P-15501)
SOCIALIZE INC
450 Townsend St 102, San Francisco (94107-1510)
PHONE...................415 529-4019
Daniel R Odio, *CEO*
Sean Shadmand, *President*
Isaac Mosquera, *CTO*
EMP: 50
SALES (est): 2.8MM
SALES (corp-wide): 11.9MM **Privately Held**
SIC: 7372 Business oriented computer software
PA: Sharethis, Inc.
3000 El Camino Real 5-150
Palo Alto CA 94306
650 641-0191

(P-15502)
SOFTWARE AG INC
Also Called: Software AG of Virginia
2901 Tasman Dr Ste 219, Santa Clara (95054-1138)
PHONE...................408 490-5300
Karl-Heinz Streibich, *Branch Mgr*
EMP: 119
SALES (corp-wide): 991MM **Privately Held**
SIC: 7372 Application computer software
HQ: Software Ag, Inc.
11700 Plaza America Dr # 700
Reston VA 20190
703 860-5050

(P-15503)
SOLV INC
Also Called: Swinerton Builders
16798 W Bernardo Dr, San Diego (92127-1904)
PHONE...................858 622-4040
EMP: 124
SALES (corp-wide): 32MM **Privately Held**
SIC: 7372 Prepackaged software
PA: Solv, Inc.
260 Townsend St
San Francisco CA 94107
858 622-4040

(P-15504)
SONIC SOLUTIONS HOLDINGS INC
2830 De La Cruz Blvd, Santa Clara (95050-2619)
PHONE...................408 562-8400
EMP: 84
SALES (est): 120.6K
SALES (corp-wide): 695.8MM **Publicly Held**
SIC: 7372 Home entertainment computer software
PA: Tivo Corporation
2160 Gold St
San Jose CA 95002
408 519-9100

(P-15505)
SPLUNK INC (PA)
270 Brannan St, San Francisco (94107-2007)
PHONE...................415 848-8400
Douglas Merritt, *President*
Scott Morgan,
David Conte, *Senior VP*
Jacob Loomis, *Senior VP*
Timothy Tully, *Senior VP*
EMP: 160
SQ FT: 182,000

SALES: 1.8B **Publicly Held**
WEB: www.splunk.com
SIC: 7372 Business oriented computer software

(P-15506)
SQUARE INC (PA)
1455 Market St Ste 600, San Francisco (94103-1332)
PHONE...................415 375-3176
Jack Dorsey, *Ch of Bd*
Ajmere Dale, *Officer*
Dj Ortua, *Trust Officer*
Tyler Doremus, *General Mgr*
Sarah Cook, *Executive Asst*
EMP: 50
SQ FT: 338,910
SALES: 3.3B **Publicly Held**
SIC: 7372 Prepackaged software

(P-15507)
SRA OSS INC
5201 Great America Pkwy # 419, Santa Clara (95054-1143)
PHONE...................408 855-8200
RAO Papolu, *President*
EMP: 160
SQ FT: 5,000
SALES (est): 15.6MM **Privately Held**
WEB: www.sraoss.com
SIC: 7372 Publishers' computer software
HQ: Software Research Associates, Inc.
2-32-8, Minamiikebukuro
Toshima-Ku TKY 171-0

(P-15508)
STACKLA INC
33 New Mont, San Francisco (94105)
PHONE...................415 789-3304
Damien Mahoney, *CEO*
Peter Cassaidy,
Mallory Walsh, *VP Mktg*
EMP: 65
SALES (est): 2.7MM **Privately Held**
SIC: 7372 Application computer software

(P-15509)
STALKER SOFTWARE INC
Also Called: Communigate Systems
125 Park Pl Ste 210, Richmond (94801-3980)
PHONE...................415 569-2280
Vladimir Butenko, *President*
Philip Slater, *Engineer*
Naomi Nelson, *VP Opers*
Simon Obrien, *Marketing Staff*
Azdio Ballesteros, *Director*
EMP: 50
SALES (est): 5.6MM **Privately Held**
WEB: www.communigate.com
SIC: 7372 7371 Prepackaged software; custom computer programming services

(P-15510)
STRATEGIC INSIGHTS INC
Also Called: Brightscope
9191 Towne Centre Dr # 401, San Diego (92122-1225)
PHONE...................858 452-7500
Chris Riggio, *Officer*
Jeremy Ross, *Exec VP*
David Gaunt, *Vice Pres*
Keith Sjgren, *Managing Dir*
Nicole Hoggar, *Executive Asst*
EMP: 65 **Privately Held**
SIC: 7372 Business oriented computer software
PA: Strategic Insights, Inc.
805 3rd Ave
New York NY 10022

(P-15511)
STRATEGY COMPANION CORP
3240 El Camino Real # 120, Irvine (92602-1384)
PHONE...................714 460-8398
Robert Sterling, *President*
Eric Halverson, *Partner*
Grace Lin, *Office Admin*
Bill Tang, *Manager*
EMP: 70
SALES (est): 5.5MM **Privately Held**
SIC: 7372 Prepackaged software

PA: Strategy Companion Corp.
Scotia Centre 4th Floor
George Town GR CAYMAN

(P-15512)
STREVUS INC
455 Market St Ste 1670, San Francisco (94105-2472)
PHONE...................415 704-8182
Ken Hoang, *CEO*
Gregg Loos, *President*
Dmitri Korablev, *Vice Pres*
Ken Price, *Vice Pres*
Jennifer Turcotte, *Vice Pres*
EMP: 60
SALES (est): 5MM **Privately Held**
SIC: 7372 7371 Business oriented computer software; computer software development

(P-15513)
SYAPSE INC
303 2nd St Ste N500, San Francisco (94107-3639)
PHONE...................650 924-1461
Gary J Kurtzman MD, *CEO*
Jonathan Hirsch, *President*
Fletcher Payne, *CFO*
Dennis Shin, *Ch Credit Ofcr*
Thomas D Brown, *Chief Mktg Ofcr*
EMP: 180
SALES (est): 4.3MM **Privately Held**
SIC: 7372 Prepackaged software

(P-15514)
SYNERGEX INTERNATIONAL CORP
2355 Gold Meadow Way # 200, Gold River (95670-6326)
PHONE...................916 635-7300
Michele C Wong, *CEO*
Serena Channel, *Partner*
Vigfus A Asmundson, *Shareholder*
Georgia Petersen, *Shareholder*
Thomas J Powers, *Shareholder*
EMP: 55
SALES (est): 7.9MM **Privately Held**
WEB: www.synergex.com
SIC: 7372 Business oriented computer software

(P-15515)
SYNOPSYS INC (PA)
690 E Middlefield Rd, Mountain View (94043-4033)
PHONE...................650 584-5000
Aart J De Geus, *Ch of Bd*
Trac Pham, *CFO*
Joseph W Logan, *Officer*
John F Runkel Jr, *Admin Sec*
EMP: 500
SQ FT: 341,000
SALES: 3.1B **Publicly Held**
WEB: www.synopsys.com
SIC: 7372 7371 Prepackaged software; computer software development

(P-15516)
SYNOPSYS INC
199 S Los Robles Ave # 400, Pasadena (91101-4634)
PHONE...................626 795-9101
George Bayz, *CEO*
Daren Reid, *Research*
Qingran Zheng, *Research*
Padma Kolli, *Engineer*
EMP: 90
SALES (corp-wide): 3.1B **Publicly Held**
SIC: 7372 8711 Application computer software; engineering services
PA: Synopsys, Inc.
690 E Middlefield Rd
Mountain View CA 94043
650 584-5000

(P-15517)
SYNPLICITY INC (HQ)
690 E Middlefield Rd, Mountain View (94043-4010)
PHONE...................650 584-5000
Gary Meyers, *President*
Alisa Yaffa, *President*
Andrew Dauman, *President*
John J Hanlon, *CFO*
Roy Vallee, *Bd of Directors*

EMP: 160
SQ FT: 66,212
SALES (est): 17.8MM
SALES (corp-wide): 3.1B **Publicly Held**
WEB: www.synplicity.com
SIC: 7372 Prepackaged software
PA: Synopsys, Inc.
　　690 E Middlefield Rd
　　Mountain View CA 94043
　　650 584-5000

(P-15518)
TALIX INC
660 3rd St Ste 302, San Francisco
(94107-1921)
PHONE....................628 220-3885
Derek Gordon, *President*
Bob Hetchler, *Senior VP*
Paul Clip, *Vice Pres*
Shahyan Currimbhoy, *Vice Pres*
Tim England, *Vice Pres*
EMP: 70
SALES (est): 2.2MM **Privately Held**
SIC: 7372 8099 Application computer software; blood related health services

(P-15519)
TANGOE US INC
9920 Pcf Hts Blvd Ste 200, San Diego
(92121)
PHONE....................858 452-6800
Sandy Jimenez, *Branch Mgr*
EMP: 100
SALES (corp-wide): 491.5MM **Privately Held**
SIC: 7372 Application computer software
HQ: Tangoe Us, Inc.
　　1 Waterview Dr Ste 200
　　Shelton CT 06484
　　973 257-0300

(P-15520)
TEKEVER CORPORATION
5201 Great America Pkwy, Santa Clara
(95054-1122)
PHONE....................408 730-2617
Michael L Margolis, *CEO*
Robert Whitehouse, *Business Dir*
EMP: 70
SALES (est): 3.3MM **Privately Held**
WEB: www.tekever.com
SIC: 7372 Prepackaged software

(P-15521)
THOUGHTSPOT INC
910 Hermosa Ct, Sunnyvale (94085-4199)
PHONE....................800 508-7008
Sudheesh Nair, *CEO*
Ajeet Singh, *Ch of Bd*
David Freeman, *Senior VP*
Brian McCarthy, *Senior VP*
Chris Brozek, *Vice Pres*
EMP: 452
SALES (est): 4.3MM **Privately Held**
SIC: 7372 Business oriented computer software

(P-15522)
THOUSANDEYES INC (PA)
201 Mission St Ste 1700, San Francisco
(94105-8102)
PHONE....................415 513-4526
Mohit Lad, *CEO*
Paul Kizakevich, *Vice Pres*
Prabha Krishna, *Vice Pres*
David Stokey, *Vice Pres*
Craig Thomas, *Vice Pres*
EMP: 75
SALES (est): 18.9MM **Privately Held**
SIC: 7372 Business oriented computer software

(P-15523)
TI LIMITED LLC (PA)
20335 Ventura Blvd, Woodland Hills
(91364-2444)
PHONE....................323 877-5991
ARI Daniels,
Alberto Gamez,
EMP: 52 **EST:** 2016
SQ FT: 9,000
SALES: 9MM **Privately Held**
SIC: 7372 8748 Business oriented computer software; business consulting

(P-15524)
TOTAL CMMNICATOR SOLUTIONS INC
Also Called: Spark Compass
11150 Santa Monica Blvd # 600, Los Angeles (90025-3380)
PHONE....................619 277-1488
Brent Erik Bjojegard, *CEO*
EMP: 95
SALES: 5MM **Privately Held**
SIC: 7372 Application computer software

(P-15525)
TRIBEWORX LLC
4 San Joaquin Plz Ste 150, Newport Beach
(92660-5934)
PHONE....................800 949-3432
EMP: 75
SQ FT: 10,000
SALES (est): 4.9MM **Privately Held**
SIC: 7372

(P-15526)
TUBEMOGUL INC
1250 53rd St Ste 1, Emeryville
(94608-2965)
PHONE....................510 653-0126
Brett Wilson, *President*
Robert Gatto, *COO*
Ron Will, *CFO*
Keith Eadie, *Chief Mktg Ofcr*
Paul Joachim, *Officer*
EMP: 68
SQ FT: 49,000
SALES: 180.7MM
SALES (corp-wide): 9B **Publicly Held**
SIC: 7372 Application computer software
PA: Adobe Inc.
　　345 Park Ave
　　San Jose CA 95110
　　408 536-6000

(P-15527)
TZ HOLDINGS LP
567 San Nicolas Dr # 120, Newport Beach
(92660-6513)
PHONE....................949 719-2200
Regina Paolillo, *Principal*
EMP: 2000
SALES (est): 46.9MM **Privately Held**
SIC: 7372 Prepackaged software

(P-15528)
UPSTANDING LLC
Also Called: Mobilityware
440 Exchange Ste 100, Irvine
(92602-1390)
PHONE....................949 788-9900
Dave Yonamine, *CEO*
Claudia Avitabile, *Office Mgr*
Carrie Collins, *Admin Asst*
Lee H McElroy, *Finance*
John Libby,
EMP: 180
SQ FT: 48,000
SALES (est): 2.5MM **Privately Held**
WEB: www.upstanding.com
SIC: 7372 Business oriented computer software

(P-15529)
URBAN TRADING SOFTWARE INC
21227 Foothill Blvd, Hayward
(94541-1517)
PHONE....................877 633-6171
Soufyan Abouahmed, *Principal*
EMP: 50
SALES (est): 1.2MM **Privately Held**
SIC: 7372 Prepackaged software

(P-15530)
VEEVA SYSTEMS INC (PA)
4280 Hacienda Dr, Pleasanton
(94588-2719)
PHONE....................925 452-6500
Peter P Gassner, *CEO*
Gordon Ritter, *Ch of Bd*
Matthew J Wallach, *President*
Timothy S Cabral, *CFO*
E Nitsa Zuppas, *Chief Mktg Ofcr*
EMP: 145

SALES: 862.2MM **Publicly Held**
SIC: 7372 7371 7379 Prepackaged software; software programming applications; computer related consulting services

(P-15531)
VINDICIA INC
2988 Campus Dr Ste 300, San Mateo
(94403-2531)
PHONE....................650 264-4700
Kris Nagel, *CEO*
Mark Elrod, *Exec VP*
Jack Bullock, *Senior VP*
Hurst Arthur, *Vice Pres*
Charles Breed, *Vice Pres*
EMP: 135
SQ FT: 9,000
SALES (est): 15.3MM **Privately Held**
SIC: 7372 Business oriented computer software
HQ: Amdocs, Inc.
　　1390 Tmberlake Manor Pkwy
　　Chesterfield MO 63017
　　314 212-7000

(P-15532)
VISUALON INC
2590 N 1st St Ste 100, San Jose
(95131-1021)
PHONE....................408 645-6618
Andy Lin, *President*
Bill Lin, *Senior VP*
Sean Torsney, *Senior VP*
Shawn O'Farrell, *Vice Pres*
Judy LI, *Finance*
EMP: 120
SALES (est): 25MM **Privately Held**
WEB: www.visualon.com
SIC: 7372 Prepackaged software

(P-15533)
VMWARE INC (DH)
3401 Hillview Ave, Palo Alto (94304-1383)
PHONE....................650 427-5000
Patrick Gelsinger, *CEO*
Jared Byrd, *Partner*
Suzanne Hensley, *Partner*
Michael Dell, *Ch of Bd*
Sanjay Poonen, *COO*
▲ **EMP:** 148
SQ FT: 1,604,769
SALES: 8.9B
SALES (corp-wide): 90.6B **Publicly Held**
SIC: 7372 Prepackaged software
HQ: Emc Corporation
　　176 South St
　　Hopkinton MA 01748
　　508 435-1000

(P-15534)
WEST COAST CONSULTING LLC
9233 Research Dr Ste 200, Irvine
(92618-4294)
PHONE....................949 250-4102
Rajat Khurana,
Puja Budhani, *Tech Recruiter*
Yogesh Tomar, *Tech Recruiter*
Karam Singh, *Technical Staff*
Reena Rawat, *Business Mgr*
EMP: 125
SALES (est): 11.7MM **Privately Held**
WEB: www.westcoastllc.com
SIC: 7372 Prepackaged software

(P-15535)
WIND RIVER SYSTEMS INC (HQ)
500 Wind River Way, Alameda
(94501-1162)
PHONE....................510 748-4100
Jim Douglas, *CEO*
Scot Morrision, *President*
Barry R Mainz, *COO*
Jane Bon, *CFO*
Richard Kraber, *CFO*
EMP: 148
SQ FT: 273,000
SALES (est): 325.9MM **Privately Held**
WEB: www.windriver.com
SIC: 7372 7373 Application computer software; systems software development services

(P-15536)
WIND RIVER SYSTEMS INC
10505 Sorrento Valley Rd, San Diego
(92121-1618)
PHONE....................858 824-3100
Brad Murdoch, *Vice Pres*
Michelle Moselina, *Analyst*
EMP: 100 **Privately Held**
WEB: www.windriver.com
SIC: 7372 Prepackaged software
HQ: Wind River Systems, Inc.
　　500 Wind River Way
　　Alameda CA 94501
　　510 748-4100

(P-15537)
WME BI LLC
17075 Camino, San Diego (92127)
PHONE....................877 592-2472
EMP: 60
SALES (est): 1.4MM **Privately Held**
SIC: 7372 Operating systems computer software

(P-15538)
WORDSMART CORPORATION
10025 Mesa Rim Rd, San Diego
(92121-2913)
P.O. Box 366, La Jolla (92038-0366)
PHONE....................858 565-8068
David Kay, *CEO*
Subhash Katbamna, *Controller*
EMP: 70
SQ FT: 12,375
SALES (est): 9.4MM **Privately Held**
WEB: www.wordsmart.com
SIC: 7372 Educational computer software

(P-15539)
WORKSHARE TECHNOLOGY INC
650 California St Fl 7, San Francisco
(94108-2737)
PHONE....................415 590-7700
Brad Anthony Foy, *CEO*
Thomas C Hoster, *CFO*
Nick Thomson, *Officer*
Barrie Hadfield, *Vice Pres*
Billy Lucas, *Executive*
EMP: 140
SQ FT: 15,000
SALES (est): 21.3MM
SALES (corp-wide): 23.4MM **Privately Held**
WEB: www.workshare.com
SIC: 7372 Prepackaged software
HQ: Workshare Limited
　　10-20 Fashion Street, Whitechapel
　　London E1 6P
　　207 426-0000

(P-15540)
XAVIENT DIGITAL LLC
Also Called: Xavient Info Systems Inc
21700 Oxnard St Ste 1700, Woodland Hills
(91367-7590)
PHONE....................805 955-4111
Rajeev Tandon, *CEO*
Saif Ahmad, *President*
Arshad Majeed, *Exec VP*
Kurt Eltz, *Senior VP*
Matt Dimarsico, *Vice Pres*
EMP: 1800
SALES (corp-wide): 10.6B **Privately Held**
SIC: 7372 Business oriented computer software
HQ: Telus International (U.S) Corp.
　　2251 S Decatur Blvd
　　Las Vegas NV 89102
　　702 238-7900

(P-15541)
XCELMOBILITY INC
2225 E Byshore Rd Ste 200, Palo Alto
(94303)
PHONE....................650 320-1728
Zhixiong WEI, *Ch of Bd*
LI Ouyang, *CFO*
Ying Yang, *Admin Sec*
EMP: 98
SALES: 384.5K **Privately Held**
SIC: 7372 7999 Business oriented computer software; gambling & lottery services

(P-15542)
YOURPEOPLE INC
Also Called: Zenefits
50 Beale St, San Francisco (94105-1813)
PHONE..................................888 249-3263
Parker Conrad, *CEO*
Jessica Hoffman, *Partner*
Avinash Anand, *President*
David Sacks, *CEO*
Laks Srini, *Officer*
EMP: 700 EST: 2004
SALES: 158.4MM **Privately Held**
SIC: 7372 8741 6411 Business oriented
computer software; administrative man-
agement; insurance brokers

(P-15543)
YUJA INC
84 W Santa Clara St # 690, San Jose
(95113-1809)
PHONE..................................888 257-2278
Ajit Singh, *President*
Nannette Don, *Sales Staff*
Boudreau Kline, *Manager*
Smith Isaac, *Accounts Mgr*
Zayn Mashat, *Accounts Mgr*
EMP: 125
SALES (est): 1MM **Privately Held**
SIC: 7372 Prepackaged software

(P-15544)
ZENDESK INC (PA)
1019 Market St, San Francisco
(94103-1612)
PHONE..................................415 418-7506
Mikkel Svane, *Ch of Bd*
Adrian McDermott, *President*
Elena Gomez, *CFO*
Inamarie Johnson,
John Geschke, *Senior VP*
EMP: 148
SQ FT: 18,000
SALES: 598.7MM **Publicly Held**
SIC: 7372 Business oriented computer
software

(P-15545)
ZENPAYROLL INC (PA)
Also Called: Gusto
525 20th St, San Francisco (94107-4345)
PHONE..................................800 936-0383
Joshua D Reeves, *CEO*
Katharine Kinney, *Partner*
Ashley Prince, *Partner*
Tom Roberts, *Partner*
Nate Watson, *Partner*
EMP: 250
SALES (est): 74.9MM **Privately Held**
SIC: 7372 Business oriented computer
software

(P-15546)
ZINIO SYSTEMS INC
114 Sansome St Fl 4, San Francisco
(94104-3803)
PHONE..................................415 494-2700
Rusty Lewis, *CEO*
Michelle Bottomley, *President*
Richard A Maggiotto, *President*
Virendra Vase, *COO*
Tom Nofziger, *CFO*
EMP: 75 EST: 2000
SALES (est): 8MM **Privately Held**
WEB: www.zinio.com
SIC: 7372 Publishers' computer software

(P-15547)
ZYRION INC
440 N Wolfe Rd, Sunnyvale (94085-3869)
PHONE..................................408 524-7424
EMP: 75
SQ FT: 6,000
SALES (est): 4.7MM **Privately Held**
SIC: 7372
PA: Kaseya Global Ireland Limited
Commerzbank House
Dublin

7373 Computer Integrated Systems Design

(P-15548)
10UP INC
2765 Carradale Dr, Roseville (95661-4089)
PHONE..................................888 571-7130
Jacob Goldman, *Owner*
Veronica Bruce, *Finance Dir*
Adam Edgerton, *Director*
Taylor Lovett, *Director*
EMP: 95
SQ FT: 1,300
SALES (est): 6.1MM **Privately Held**
SIC: 7373 Systems software development
services

(P-15549)
3D INFOTECH (PA)
7 Hubble, Irvine (92618-4209)
PHONE..................................949 988-0200
Rohit Khanna, *President*
Paul Oberle, *Engineer*
Luke Santangelo, *Marketing Staff*
EMP: 50
SALES (est): 10.5MM **Privately Held**
SIC: 7373 Computer integrated systems
design

(P-15550)
A10 NETWORKS INC (PA)
3 W Plumeria Dr, San Jose (95134-2111)
PHONE..................................408 325-8668
Lee Chen, *Ch of Bd*
Tom Constantino, *CFO*
Alan Henricks, *Bd of Directors*
Robert Cochran, *Exec VP*
Neil Wu Becker, *Vice Pres*
▲ **EMP:** 148
SQ FT: 79,803
SALES: 232.2MM **Publicly Held**
WEB: www.a10networks.com
SIC: 7373 Systems integration services;
systems software development services;
computer system selling services

(P-15551)
ACOM SOLUTIONS INC (PA)
2850 E 29th St, Long Beach (90806-2313)
PHONE..................................562 424-7899
Patrick S McMahon, *President*
Edward J Kennedy, *Chairman*
Mark Firmin, *Vice Pres*
James Scott, *Vice Pres*
Claude Rosay, *Regional Mgr*
▲ **EMP:** 50
SQ FT: 23,000
SALES (est): 32.9MM **Privately Held**
WEB: www.acom.com
SIC: 7373 Systems software development
services

(P-15552)
ACTIAN CORPORATION (PA)
2300 Geng Rd Ste 150, Palo Alto
(94303-3353)
PHONE..................................650 587-5500
Steve Shine, *CEO*
Lewis Black, *CFO*
Steven Springsteel, *CFO*
Tony Kavanagh, *Chief Mktg Ofcr*
Melissa Ribeiro,
EMP: 70
SQ FT: 20,000
SALES (est): 107MM **Privately Held**
WEB: www.ingres.com
SIC: 7373 7372 Systems software devel-
opment services; business oriented com-
puter software

(P-15553)
ACUMEN LLC
Also Called: Medric
500 Airport Blvd Ste 100, Burlingame
(94010-1980)
PHONE..................................650 558-8882
Thomas Macurdy, *Mng Member*
Kelly Macurdy, *Administration*
Christian Torio, *Administration*
Evan Yip, *Administration*
Zhaoyi Zhou, *Software Engr*
EMP: 166

SALES (est): 29.9MM Privately Held
WEB: www.acumenllc.com
SIC: 7373 7379 8742 Systems software
development services; computer related
consulting services; data processing consultant; management consulting services;
administrative services consultant

(P-15554)
AEROHIVE NETWORKS INC
(HQ)
1011 Mccarthy Blvd, Milpitas (95035-7920)
PHONE..................................408 510-6100
Ed Meyercord, *President*
▲ **EMP:** 131
SALES: 154.9MM **Publicly Held**
WEB: www.aerohive.com
SIC: 7373 Local area network (LAN) sys-
tems integrator

(P-15555)
ALEXANDRIA CLAYTON
Also Called: Net Eternity
2051 Hilltop Dr Ste A16c, Redding
(96002-0264)
PHONE..................................530 262-5961
Alexandria Clayton, *Owner*
EMP: 50
SALES (est): 915K **Privately Held**
SIC: 7373 5961 Systems integration serv-
ices;

(P-15556)
AMSNET INC (PA)
502 Commerce Way, Livermore
(94551-7812)
PHONE..................................925 245-6100
Robert Tocci, *CEO*
Tom Vasconi, *Vice Pres*
Joe Moomau, *Admin Sec*
Paul Payumo, *Technical Staff*
EMP: 50
SQ FT: 15,000
SALES: 69.5MM **Privately Held**
SIC: 7373 1731 7378 Systems integration
services; computer installation; computer
maintenance & repair

(P-15557)
APRISO CORPORATION
301 E Ocean Blvd Ste 1200, Long Beach
(90802-4839)
PHONE..................................562 951-8000
James Henderson, *CEO*
Carey Tokirio, *CFO*
Chris Brecher, *Exec VP*
Tom Comstock, *Exec VP*
Yves Vergnolle, *Senior VP*
EMP: 200
SALES (est): 6.7MM
SALES (corp-wide): 1.8B **Privately Held**
WEB: www.apriso.com
SIC: 7373 Computer integrated systems
design
PA: Dassault Systemes
10 Rue Marcel Dassault
Velizy-Villacoublay 78140
161 623-000

(P-15558)
APTTUS CORPORATION (PA)
1400 Fashion Island Blvd # 100, San Mateo
(94404-2061)
PHONE..................................650 445-7700
Frank Holland, *CEO*
Carlos Enriquez, *Partner*
Charles Mackenna, *Partner*
Alexandra Ortiz, *Partner*
Allison Wudel, *Partner*
EMP: 148
SALES (est): 201MM **Privately Held**
SIC: 7373 Systems software development
services

(P-15559)
ART & LOGIC INC
Also Called: Artlogic
87 N Raymond Ave, Pasadena
(91103-3932)
PHONE..................................818 500-1933
Bob Bajoras, *President*
Paul Hershenson, *Co-Owner*
Tom Bajoras, *Owner*
Andrew Sherbrooke, *Vice Pres*
Jason Bagley, *Sr Software Eng*
EMP: 55

SQ FT: 1,500
SALES (est): 8MM **Privately Held**
WEB: www.artlogic.com
SIC: 7373 7371 7379 Systems software
development services; custom computer
programming services; computer related
consulting services

(P-15560)
ATAC (PA)
2770 De La Cruz Blvd, Santa Clara
(95050-2624)
PHONE..................................408 736-2822
Mark Cochran, *Chairman*
Scott Simcox, *President*
Charles Winkleman, *CFO*
Alan C Sharp, *Vice Pres*
Eric Boyajian, *Program Mgr*
EMP: 65
SQ FT: 31,000
SALES: 21.5MM **Privately Held**
WEB: www.atac.com
SIC: 7373 7376 7379 8711 Computer in-
tegrated systems design; computer facili-
ties management; computer related
maintenance services; engineering serv-
ices; physical research, noncommercial

(P-15561)
AUTOMATION ENGRG SYSTEMS
INC
10815 Rancho Bernardo Rd, San Diego
(92127-2186)
PHONE..................................858 967-8650
Leo Castaneda, *President*
Gary Mitchell, *Engineer*
Doug Strohl, *Engineer*
EMP: 80
SALES (est): 2.9MM **Privately Held**
SIC: 7373 Systems integration services

(P-15562)
AVEVA SOFTWARE LLC (DH)
Also Called: Wonderware
26561 Rancho Pkwy S, Lake Forest
(92630-8301)
PHONE..................................949 727-3200
Ravi Gopinath, *President*
Paul Forney, *Vice Pres*
Rashesh Mody, *Vice Pres*
Mike Pring, *Vice Pres*
Pat Cupo, *Executive*
EMP: 350
SALES (est): 290.7MM **Privately Held**
SIC: 7373 Computer integrated systems
design
HQ: Aveva Inc.
10350 Richmond Ave # 400
Houston TX 77042
713 977-1225

(P-15563)
CACI INC - FEDERAL
1455 Frazee Rd Ste 700, San Diego
(92108-4308)
PHONE..................................619 881-6000
J P London, *Ch of Bd*
EMP: 50
SALES (corp-wide): 4.9B **Publicly Held**
WEB: www.inventure.com
SIC: 7373 Computer integrated systems
design
HQ: Caci, Inc. - Federal
1100 N Glebe Rd Ste 200
Arlington VA 22201
703 841-7800

(P-15564)
CADENT INC
Also Called: Orthocad
2560 Orchard Pkwy, San Jose
(95131-1033)
PHONE..................................408 470-1000
Timothy Mack, *President*
Roger Blanchette, *CFO*
▲ **EMP:** 130
SQ FT: 24,000
SALES (est): 12.4MM
SALES (corp-wide): 1.9B **Publicly Held**
WEB: www.orthocad.com
SIC: 7373 Computer systems analysis &
design
HQ: Cadent Holdings, Inc.
2560 Orchard Pkwy
San Jose CA

(P-15565)
CALCULI CORPORATION
3945 Freedom Cir, Santa Clara
(95054-1223)
PHONE..................408 970-0007
Basheer Janjua, *CEO*
EMP: 50
SALES (est): 1MM **Privately Held**
SIC: 7373 8711 Systems engineering,
computer related; engineering services

(P-15566)
CAPTIVA SOFTWARE CORPORATION (DH)
10145 Pacific Hts Blvd, San Diego
(92121-4234)
PHONE..................858 320-1000
Reynolds C Bish, *President*
Patrick L Edsell, *Ch of Bd*
Rick E Russo, *CFO*
Howard Dratler, *Exec VP*
Jim Nicol, *Exec VP*
EMP: 80
SQ FT: 25,000
SALES (est): 19.7MM
SALES (corp-wide): 90.6B **Publicly Held**
SIC: 7373 7372 Office computer automa-
tion systems integration; prepackaged
software
HQ: Emc Corporation
176 South St
Hopkinton MA 01748
508 435-1000

(P-15567)
CARLISLE RESEARCH CORPORATION
7100 Hayvenhurst Ave Ph F, Van Nuys
(91406-3804)
PHONE..................818 785-8677
Jimmy Carlisle, *President*
EMP: 54
SQ FT: 52,250
SALES (est): 4.1MM **Privately Held**
WEB: www.cri-corp.com
SIC: 7373 7379 7372 7371 Computer in-
tegrated systems design; data processing
consultant; prepackaged software; com-
puter software systems analysis & design,
custom; software, business & non-game

(P-15568)
CELESTIX NETWORKS INC
215 Fourier Ave Ste 140, Fremont
(94539-7837)
PHONE..................510 668-0700
Yong Thye Lin, *CEO*
Gabriele Sartori, *CTO*
Bobby Chen, *Finance Dir*
Payal Thakkar, *Marketing Staff*
Yong Ping Lin, *Director*
EMP: 70
SQ FT: 9,000
SALES (est): 12.3MM **Privately Held**
WEB: www.celestix.com
SIC: 7373 Systems software development
services; systems engineering, computer
related; systems integration services;
local area network (LAN) systems integra-
tor
PA: Celestix Networks Pte Ltd
62 Ubi Road 1
Singapore 40873

(P-15569)
CELLMATICS
2309 Masters Rd, Carlsbad (92008-3843)
PHONE..................760 692-2424
Rose Thomas, *CEO*
EMP: 50
SALES: 250K **Privately Held**
SIC: 7373 Computer integrated systems
design

(P-15570)
CEREBRAS SYSTEMS INC
175 S San Antonio Rd # 1, Los Altos
(94022-3759)
PHONE..................650 933-4980
Andrew Feldman, *CEO*
Michael James, *CFO*
Dhiraj Mallick, *Vice Pres*
Vinay Srinivas, *Vice Pres*
Gary Lauterbach, *Admin Sec*

EMP: 150
SALES (est): 329.4K **Privately Held**
SIC: 7373 7389 Systems software devel-
opment services;

(P-15571)
CGTECH (PA)
Also Called: Cgtech Vericut
9000 Research Dr, Irvine (92618-4214)
PHONE..................949 753-1050
Jon L Prun, *President*
Frankie Cates, *Admin Asst*
Heidi Edmonston, *Admin Asst*
Jia Yan, *Sr Software Eng*
Kelly Anderson, *Info Tech Mgr*
EMP: 50
SQ FT: 27,000
SALES: 26.5MM **Privately Held**
WEB: www.cgtech.com
SIC: 7373 8243 Computer-aided design
(CAD) systems service; software training,
computer

(P-15572)
CLINICOMP INTERNATIONAL INC (PA)
9655 Towne Centre Dr, San Diego
(92121-1964)
PHONE..................858 546-8202
Chris Haudenschild, *Ch of Bd*
Eloisa Haudenschild, *CFO*
Sarah Crouch Chavez, *Vice Pres*
Jiao Fan, *Vice Pres*
Kelley Malott, *Vice Pres*
EMP: 100
SQ FT: 42,000
SALES (est): 22.6MM **Privately Held**
WEB: www.clinicomp.com
SIC: 7373 7371 3571 Systems software
development services; custom computer
programming services; electronic comput-
ers

(P-15573)
CNET NETWORKS INC
235 2nd St, San Francisco (94105-3100)
PHONE..................415 344-2000
Mehdi Maghsoodnia, *Bd of Directors*
Debbie Andrews, *Vice Pres*
Eric Schuldt, *Vice Pres*
Joanne Scott, *Vice Pres*
Jane Goldman, *VP Mngmt*
EMP: 889
SALES (est): 11.8MM
SALES (corp-wide): 25.9B **Publicly Held**
SIC: 7373 7371 Systems software devel-
opment services; computer software de-
velopment & applications
HQ: Cbs Interactive Inc.
235 2nd St
San Francisco CA 94105

(P-15574)
COGNIX AUTOMATION INC
3423 Torlano Pl, Pleasanton (94566-2114)
PHONE..................925 464-8822
Prasad Dasari, *President*
EMP: 50
SALES (est): 915K **Privately Held**
SIC: 7373 Office computer automation sys-
tems integration

(P-15575)
COMGLOBAL SYSTEMS INC (DH)
1315 Dell Ave, Campbell (95008-6609)
PHONE..................619 321-6000
Fax: 408 374-5209
EMP: 68
SQ FT: 600
SALES (est): 14.9MM
SALES (corp-wide): 335.6MM **Privately Held**
WEB: www.comglobal.com
SIC: 7373
HQ: Analex Corporation
11091 Sunset Hills Rd # 200
Reston VA 20171
703 956-8243

(P-15576)
CORDOBA CORPORATION
1401 N Broadway, Los Angeles
(90012-1410)
PHONE..................213 895-0224

George Pla, *President*
Maria Mehranian, *COO*
EMP: 65
SALES (est): 5.4MM **Privately Held**
SIC: 7373 Computer integrated systems
design

(P-15577)
CUBIC CORPORATION
Also Called: Cubic Defense Systems
9233 Balboa Ave, San Diego (92123-1513)
PHONE..................858 277-6780
Brigitte Jen, *Branch Mgr*
John Moran, *Officer*
Rick Kent, *Engineer*
Mark Woodhouse, *QC Mgr*
George Mc Lachlan, *Opers Staff*
EMP: 2000
SALES (corp-wide): 1.2B **Publicly Held**
SIC: 7373 Computer integrated systems
design
PA: Cubic Corporation
9333 Balboa Ave
San Diego CA 92123
858 277-6780

(P-15578)
DATA CONTROL CORPORATION
P.O. Box 2069, Granite Bay (95746-2069)
PHONE..................916 774-4000
J Dale Debber, *President*
EMP: 67
SQ FT: 15,000
SALES (est): 3.5MM **Privately Held**
SIC: 7373 Systems software development
services

(P-15579)
DATA DOMAIN LLC
2421 Mission College Blvd, Santa Clara
(95054-1214)
PHONE..................408 980-4800
Frank Slootman, *President*
Michael P Scarpelli, *CFO*
John Egan, *Bd of Directors*
Nick Bacica, *Senior VP*
Daniel R McGee, *Senior VP*
EMP: 777
SQ FT: 200,000
SALES (est): 88.6MM
SALES (corp-wide): 90.6B **Publicly Held**
WEB: www.datadomain.com
SIC: 7373 Computer integrated systems
design
HQ: Emc Corporation
176 South St
Hopkinton MA 01748
508 435-1000

(P-15580)
DATAPARK INC
1631 Neptune Dr, San Leandro
(94577-3162)
PHONE..................510 483-7275
Steve Haralambiew, *President*
Lorenza Tomaz, *CFO*
EMP: 60
SQ FT: 9,900
SALES (est): 8.7MM **Privately Held**
WEB: www.dataparkgroup.com
SIC: 7373 Computer integrated systems
design

(P-15581)
DELEGATA CORPORATION
2450 Venture Oaks Way # 400, Sacra-
mento (95833-3292)
PHONE..................916 609-5400
Kais Menoufy, *President*
Romy Haddad, *Marketing Mgr*
Jacquelyn Silver, *Manager*
EMP: 100
SQ FT: 5,000
SALES (est): 13.8MM **Privately Held**
WEB: www.delegata.com
SIC: 7373 Computer integrated systems
design

(P-15582)
DIGITAL KEYSTONE INC
21631 Stevns Crk Blvd A, Cupertino
(95014-1169)
PHONE..................650 938-7301
Paolo Siccardo, *CEO*
Jim Hankle, *Vice Pres*
EMP: 50

SQ FT: 27,000
SALES (est): 4.4MM **Privately Held**
WEB: www.dkeystone.com
SIC: 7373 Computer integrated systems
design

(P-15583)
DIGITALIST USA LTD
128 Spear St Lbby, San Francisco
(94105-5160)
PHONE..................949 278-1354
Jo Javier, *Vice Pres*
EMP: 1000
SALES (est): 43.3MM
SALES (corp-wide): 60.3MM **Privately Held**
SIC: 7373 8731 Systems software devel-
opment services; computer (hardware)
development
HQ: Digitalist Group Oyj
Arkadiankatu 2
Helsinki 00100
505 814-075

(P-15584)
DIMENSION DATA NORTH AMER INC
5000 Hopyard Rd, Pleasanton
(94588-3348)
PHONE..................925 226-8378
Scott Chudy, *Branch Mgr*
Sharyl Fleming, *Manager*
EMP: 89 **Privately Held**
SIC: 7373 Computer integrated systems
design
HQ: Dimension Data North America, Inc.
1 Penn Plz
New York NY 10119
212 613-1220

(P-15585)
DYNCORP
Nas Nrth Is Bldg 1479, San Diego (92135)
P.O. Box 189002, Coronado (92178-9002)
PHONE..................619 522-2222
Mike Johnson, *Manager*
EMP: 115
SALES (corp-wide): 16.3B **Privately Held**
WEB: www.dyncorp.com
SIC: 7373 Systems software development
services
PA: Dyncorp Llc
1700 Old Meadow Rd
Mc Lean VA 22102
571 722-0210

(P-15586)
E2 CORP
Also Called: E2 Solutions
8121 Van Nuys Blvd # 308, Panorama City
(91402-5105)
PHONE..................818 904-5660
Sonia Keshap, *President*
Lolita Munsayac, *Accountant*
Avni Keshap, *Opers Staff*
EMP: 75
SQ FT: 1,550
SALES (est): 6.8MM **Privately Held**
WEB: www.e2solutions.com
SIC: 7373 7371 Computer integrated sys-
tems design; computer software systems
analysis & design, custom

(P-15587)
ELECTRONIC DATA CARE INC
Also Called: E D C
23670 Hawthorne Blvd # 208, Torrance
(90505-8207)
PHONE..................310 791-2600
Nabil Salem, *President*
Aref Rashad, *Vice Pres*
Jeff Woods, *Vice Pres*
Amy Riddle, *VP Human Res*
Robert Jalen, *Manager*
EMP: 70
SQ FT: 2,500
SALES: 800K **Privately Held**
WEB: www.edatacare.com
SIC: 7373 8299 Systems integration serv-
ices; educational services

(P-15588)
ELITE INFORMATION GROUP INC (DH)
5100 W Goldleaf Cir # 100, Los Angeles (90056-1284)
PHONE....................323 642-5200
Christopher K Poole, *President*
Daniel Tacone, *COO*
Barry D Emerson, *CFO*
EMP: 400
SQ FT: 40,000
SALES (est): 28.6MM
SALES (corp-wide): 10.6B **Publicly Held**
WEB: www.eliteis.com
SIC: 7373 7372 Computer integrated systems design; systems software development services; systems integration services; business oriented computer software
HQ: Thomson Reuters Corporation
3 Times Sq
New York NY 10036
646 223-4000

(P-15589)
EMR CPR LLC
48511 Warm Springs Blvd # 206, Fremont (94539-7746)
PHONE....................408 471-6804
Edward Ohara, *CEO*
David Ohara, *COO*
Nima Mahanloo, *Technology*
Sukhwinder Mann, *Technology*
John Vasquez, *Technology*
EMP: 412
SALES (est): 1.2MM **Privately Held**
SIC: 7373 7374 Systems engineering, computer related; systems integration services; local area network (LAN) systems integrator; data entry service; data verification service

(P-15590)
ENQUERO INC
1551 Mccarthy Blvd # 207, Milpitas (95035-7442)
PHONE....................408 406-3203
Arvinder Pal Singh, *CEO*
Hemant Asher, *CFO*
Gaurav Dembla, *Sr Consultant*
EMP: 80
SALES (est): 292.5K **Privately Held**
SIC: 7373 7379 Systems software development services;

(P-15591)
ERICSSON INC
100 Headquarters Dr, San Jose (95134-1370)
PHONE....................408 597-3600
Kevin A Denuccio, *Branch Mgr*
EMP: 1100
SALES (corp-wide): 23.4B **Privately Held**
SIC: 7373 Computer integrated systems design
HQ: Ericsson Inc.
6300 Legacy Dr
Plano TX 75024
972 583-0000

(P-15592)
FASTXCHANGE INC
4640 Admiralty Way # 710, Marina Del Rey (90292-6621)
PHONE....................310 827-2445
George Fan, *President*
Paul Postel, *President*
Frank Murnane, *CFO*
Murali Adimoolam, *Info Tech Mgr*
Shepal Patel, *Finance*
EMP: 50
SQ FT: 5,000
SALES (est): 2.2MM **Privately Held**
SIC: 7373 Systems software development services

(P-15593)
FORCE10 NETWORKS INC
Also Called: Dell
350 Holger Way, San Jose (95134-1362)
PHONE....................800 289-3355
Michael Dell, *CEO*
James Hanley, *President*
Luu Nguyen, *President*
Sachi Sambandan, *President*
Robert Tatnall, *President*

▲ EMP: 582 EST: 1999
SQ FT: 97,000
SALES (est): 61.3MM
SALES (corp-wide): 90.6B **Publicly Held**
WEB: www.force10networks.com
SIC: 7373 Computer integrated systems design
HQ: Dell Inc.
1 Dell Way
Round Rock TX 78682
800 289-3355

(P-15594)
FRANCISCO PARTNERS LP (HQ)
Also Called: FP
1 Letterman Dr Bldg C, San Francisco (94129-2402)
PHONE....................415 418-2900
Dipanjan Deb, *Managing Prtnr*
Chris Adams, *Partner*
Ben Ball, *Partner*
Peter Christodoulo, *Partner*
Neil Garfinkel, *Partner*
EMP: 60
SALES (est): 163.6MM
SALES (corp-wide): 1.5B **Privately Held**
SIC: 7373 7372 Systems integration services; prepackaged software
PA: Francisco Partners Management, L.P.
1 Letterman Dr Ste 410
San Francisco CA 94129
415 418-2900

(P-15595)
FRANCONNECT LLC
300 Carlsbad Village Dr 302a, Carlsbad (92008-2990)
PHONE....................760 720-5354
EMP: 101
SALES (corp-wide): 13.8MM **Privately Held**
SIC: 7373 Systems software development services
PA: Franconnect, Llc
11800 Sunrise Valley Dr # 900
Reston VA 20191
703 390-9300

(P-15596)
FRONTECH N FUJITSU AMER INC (DH)
Also Called: Ffna
27121 Towne Centre Dr # 100, Foothill Ranch (92610-2826)
PHONE....................949 855-5500
Yoshihiko Masuda, *President*
Tatsuo Horibe, *CFO*
Pat Cathey, *Senior VP*
Larry Fandel, *Senior VP*
Dick Zarski, *Senior VP*
EMP: 210
SQ FT: 90,000
SALES (est): 211.6MM **Privately Held**
WEB: www.fjicl.com
SIC: 7373 Computer systems analysis & design

(P-15597)
FUJITSU AMERICA INC (DH)
1250 E Arques Ave, Sunnyvale (94085-5401)
P.O. Box 3470 (94088-3470)
PHONE....................408 746-6000
Mike Foster, *CEO*
Robert D Pryor, *President*
Naomi Hadatsuki, *CFO*
ARI Hovsepyan, *CFO*
Tom Duffy, *Officer*
▲ EMP: 400
SALES (est): 1.7B **Privately Held**
SIC: 7373 Computer integrated systems design; systems software development services; systems integration services

(P-15598)
FUJITSU AMERICA INC
3113 Knights Bridge Rd, San Jose (95132-1734)
PHONE....................408 746-8419
Ratan Mohla, *Principal*
EMP: 100 **Privately Held**
SIC: 7373 Computer integrated systems design

HQ: Fujitsu America Inc
1250 E Arques Ave
Sunnyvale CA 94085
408 746-6000

(P-15599)
FUJITSU AMERICA INC
2250 E Imperial Hwy # 200, El Segundo (90245-3543)
PHONE....................310 563-7000
Bob Pryor, *Branch Mgr*
EMP: 140 **Privately Held**
SIC: 7373 Computer integrated systems design
HQ: Fujitsu America Inc
1250 E Arques Ave
Sunnyvale CA 94085
408 746-6000

(P-15600)
GEMALTO COGENT INC (DH)
639 N Rosemead Blvd, Pasadena (91107-2147)
PHONE....................626 325-9600
Olivier Piou, *CEO*
Michael Hollowich, *Exec VP*
Heather Pertel, *Marketing Staff*
EMP: 90
SQ FT: 151,000
SALES (est): 77.4MM
SALES (corp-wide): 262.1MM **Privately Held**
WEB: www.cogentsystem.com
SIC: 7373 Computer-aided system services

(P-15601)
GENEA ENERGY PARTNERS INC
19100 Von Karman Ave # 550, Irvine (92612-6571)
PHONE....................714 694-0536
Jon Haahr, *Chairman*
David Balkin, *President*
Joseph Nugent, *President*
Keith Voysey, *CEO*
Cari Nicholson, *Executive Asst*
EMP: 85
SQ FT: 10,000
SALES (est): 14.5MM **Privately Held**
WEB: geneaenergy.com
SIC: 7373 Systems software development services

(P-15602)
GOBIG INC
338 Main St Unit 5c, San Francisco (94105-2184)
PHONE....................415 513-3029
Joachim Klein, *COO*
EMP: 50
SALES (est): 915K **Privately Held**
SIC: 7373 Systems software development services

(P-15603)
GREEN BITS INC
75 E Santa Clara St # 93, San Jose (95113-1826)
PHONE....................408 596-3341
Benjamin Curren, *CEO*
Matt Beckley, *Business Dir*
Bridgett Thurston, *VP Finance*
EMP: 60
SQ FT: 40,000
SALES (est): 253.3K **Privately Held**
SIC: 7373 Value-added resellers, computer systems

(P-15604)
GROUPWARE TECHNOLOGY INC (PA)
541 Division St, Campbell (95008-6905)
PHONE....................408 540-0090
Mike Thompson, *CEO*
Scott Sutter, *Officer*
Josh Avila, *Vice Pres*
John Barnes, *Vice Pres*
Anthony Miley, *Vice Pres*
EMP: 50
SQ FT: 14,000
SALES (est): 324MM **Privately Held**
WEB: www.groupwaretechnology.com
SIC: 7373 5045 Computer-aided system services; computers, peripherals & software; computer software

(P-15605)
HANDS-ON MOBILE AMERICAS INC (PA)
208 Utah St Ste 300, San Francisco (94103-4890)
PHONE....................415 580-6400
Jonathan Sacks, *CEO*
Dan Kranzler, *Ch of Bd*
Dave Arnold, *President*
Niccolo De Masi, *President*
Kevin Dent, *President*
EMP: 50 EST: 2001
SALES (est): 32.7MM **Privately Held**
WEB: www.mforma.com
SIC: 7373 Computer system selling services

(P-15606)
HARMAN CNNCTED SVCS HOLDG CORP (DH)
636 Ellis St, Mountain View (94043-2207)
PHONE....................650 623-9400
Sanjay Dhawan, *President*
Luigi Sanna, *President*
Pradeep Chaudhry, *CFO*
Subash A K RAO, *Exec VP*
Andrew Till, *CTO*
EMP: 53
SALES (est): 102.4MM **Privately Held**
WEB: www.symphonyservices.com
SIC: 7373 Systems software development services
HQ: Harman International Industries Incorporated
400 Atlantic St Ste 15
Stamford CT 06901
203 328-3500

(P-15607)
HEARTFLOW INC (PA)
1400 Seaport Blvd Bldg B, Redwood City (94063-5594)
PHONE....................650 241-1221
Dana G Mead Jr, *President*
Yoshiki Kawabata, *President*
Baird Radford, *CFO*
John Stevens, *Chairman*
Michael Buck, *Ch Credit Ofcr*
EMP: 62
SQ FT: 3,400
SALES (est): 23.6MM **Privately Held**
SIC: 7373 Systems software development services

(P-15608)
HENRY BROS ELECTRONICS INC
Also Called: National Safe
1511 E Orangethorpe Ave A, Fullerton (92831-5204)
PHONE....................714 525-4350
Eric Demarco, *President*
Deanna Lund, *CEO*
Laura Siegal, *Treasurer*
Michael Fink, *Vice Pres*
Deborah Butera, *Admin Sec*
EMP: 200
SQ FT: 10,000
SALES (est): 17.2MM **Publicly Held**
WEB: www.hbe-ca.com
SIC: 7373 7382 5063 Computer integrated systems design; security systems services; burglar alarm systems
HQ: Henry Bros. Electronics, Inc.
17-01 Pollitt Dr Ste 5
Fair Lawn NJ 07410
201 794-6500

(P-15609)
HID GLOBAL SAFE INC
3590 N 1st St Ste 320, San Jose (95134-1812)
PHONE....................408 453-1008
Stefan Widing, *CEO*
Greg Adkins, *Partner*
Rodney Glass, *COO*
Laura Crumbley, *CFO*
Tina Huston, *Vice Pres*
EMP: 55
SALES (est): 9.7MM
SALES (corp-wide): 9.3B **Privately Held**
WEB: www.quantumsecure.com
SIC: 7373 7371 Systems software development services; computer software development & applications

HQ: Hid Global Corporation
611 Center Ridge Dr.
Austin TX 78753
800 237-7769

(P-15610)
HUBB SYSTEMS LLC
Also Called: Data 911
12305 Crosthwaite Cir, Poway
(92064-6817)
PHONE..................510 865-9100
Abigail Baker, *CEO*
Donald R Hubbard, *President*
Brian McCown, *CFO*
Doug Mosby, *General Mgr*
Charles Hodgkins, *IT/INT Sup*
EMP: 75
SALES (est): 12.3MM
SALES (corp-wide): 30.4MM **Privately Held**
SIC: 7373 7379 Turnkey vendors, computer systems; computer related consulting services
PA: Broadcast Microwave Services, Inc
12305 Crosthwaite Cir
Poway CA 92064
858 391-3050

(P-15611)
I LAN SYSTEMS INC
237 S Raymond Ave, Alhambra
(91801-3131)
PHONE..................626 304-9021
Tom Reynolds, *President*
Virginia Reynolds, *Treasurer*
Mae LI Woo, *Admin Sec*
Trudy Woo, *Purch Agent*
EMP: 55
SQ FT: 1,000
SALES (est): 3.1MM **Privately Held**
SIC: 7373 Systems integration services

(P-15612)
ICYGEN LLC
940 Dwight Way Ste 13b, Berkeley
(94710-2528)
PHONE..................510 540-7122
Milena Badjova,
Krasimir Koeff, *Project Mgr*
Kari Taneva, *Project Mgr*
EMP: 80 EST: 1999
SALES (est): 4.4MM **Privately Held**
WEB: www.icygen.com
SIC: 7373 8742 Computer systems analysis & design; marketing consulting services

(P-15613)
IDONDEMAND INC
Also Called: ID On Demand
1900 Carnegie Ave Ste B, Santa Ana
(92705-5557)
PHONE..................415 200-4546
Jennifer A Grigg, *Vice Pres*
Matthew Herscovitzh, *Principal*
EMP: 290
SALES (est): 53.5MM **Publicly Held**
SIC: 7373 Local area network (LAN) systems integrator
PA: Identiv, Inc.
2201 Walnut Ave Ste 100
Fremont CA 94538

(P-15614)
INDEPENDA INC
11455 El Camino Real # 365, San Diego
(92130-3036)
PHONE..................800 815-7829
Kian Saneii, *CEO*
Gary Gilmore, *CFO*
Pat Kinshofer, *Opers Staff*
Chrysta Henson, *Consultant*
EMP: 50
SALES (est): 5.5MM **Privately Held**
SIC: 7373 Systems software development services

(P-15615)
INSEEGO NORTH AMERICA LLC (HQ)
Also Called: 1-Carasight Surveillance
9605 Scranton Rd Ste 300, San Diego
(92121-1789)
PHONE..................541 685-9045
Michael Newman, *Admin Sec*

Dave Dohna, *Vice Pres*
Mohammad Toossi, *Engineer*
Kaley Macandrew, *Accounting Mgr*
Anna Affleje, *Accountant*
EMP: 65
SQ FT: 36,000
SALES: 25MM
SALES (corp-wide): 202.4MM **Publicly Held**
WEB: www.feeneywireless.com
SIC: 7373 Computer integrated systems design
PA: Inseego Corp.
12600 Drfeld Pkwy Ste 100
Alpharetta GA 30004
858 812-3400

(P-15616)
INTEGRATED DECISION SYSTEMS
11150 W Olympic Blvd # 600, Los Angeles
(90064-1817)
PHONE..................310 954-5530
Jerald Jackrel, *President*
Donald Potter, *CEO*
Philip Alford, *CFO*
Shahram Zaman, *Vice Pres*
Lawrence Kramer, *Principal*
EMP: 75 EST: 1981
SALES (est): 4.4MM **Privately Held**
SIC: 7373 7372 Systems software development services; prepackaged software

(P-15617)
INTELLICUS TECH PVT LTD
720 University Ave # 130, Los Gatos
(95032-7609)
PHONE..................408 213-3314
Praveen Kankiria, *CEO*
Jerry Malec, *President*
Anand Raman, *Vice Pres*
Pankaj Mittal, *CTO*
Rajesh Murthy, *VP Engrg*
EMP: 60
SQ FT: 1,000
SALES: 2MM **Privately Held**
SIC: 7373 Computer integrated systems design

(P-15618)
INTERNATIONAL BUS MCHS CORP
Also Called: IBM
30501 Agoura Rd Ste 100, Agoura Hills
(91301-4399)
PHONE..................914 499-1900
Ricky Kurtz, *Manager*
John Aylesworth, *Executive*
Ralph Capria, *Executive*
Elijah Fonseca, *Principal*
Veronica Lopez, *Principal*
EMP: 61
SALES (corp-wide): 79.5B **Publicly Held**
WEB: www.ibm.com
SIC: 7373 7379 Systems software development services; computer systems analysis & design; computer related consulting services
PA: International Business Machines Corporation
1 New Orchard Rd Ste 1 # 1
Armonk NY 10504
914 499-1900

(P-15619)
INTERNET CORP FOR ASSIGNED NAM (PA)
Also Called: I Cann
12025 Waterfront Dr # 300, Los Angeles
(90094-3220)
PHONE..................310 823-9358
Cherine Chalaby, *Chairman*
Chris Gift, *Vice Pres*
Nigel Hickson, *Vice Pres*
Matt Larson, *Vice Pres*
Becky Nash, *Vice Pres*
EMP: 160
SALES (est): 219.5MM **Privately Held**
WEB: www.icann.org
SIC: 7373 Systems software development services

(P-15620)
INTERSTATE ELECTRONICS CORP
3033 Science Park Rd, San Diego
(92121-1167)
PHONE..................858 552-9500
Andrew Leuthe, *Principal*
EMP: 53
SALES (corp-wide): 6.8B **Publicly Held**
SIC: 7373 7379 5045 Systems engineering, computer related; computer related consulting services; computer software
HQ: Interstate Electronics Corporation
602 E Vermont Ave
Anaheim CA 92805
714 758-0500

(P-15621)
IP INFUSION INC (HQ)
3965 Freedom Cir Ste 200, Santa Clara
(95054-1293)
PHONE..................408 400-1900
Koichi Narasaki, *Chairman*
Amit Chatterjee, *President*
Kiyo Oishi, *CEO*
Atsushi Ogata, *COO*
Shane Rigby, *COO*
EMP: 53
SQ FT: 11,900
SALES (est): 8.1MM **Privately Held**
WEB: www.ipinfusion.com
SIC: 7373 Systems software development services

(P-15622)
IPASS INC
15241 Laguna Canyon Rd # 100, Irvine
(92618-3146)
PHONE..................650 232-4100
John Drosshan, *Manager*
EMP: 90
SALES (corp-wide): 13.5MM **Publicly Held**
SIC: 7373 Computer integrated systems design
HQ: Ipass Inc.
3800 Bridge Pkwy
Redwood City CA 94065

(P-15623)
JACKSON TULL CHRTRED ENGINEERS
550 Continental Blvd # 195, El Segundo
(90245-5049)
PHONE..................310 658-2132
Knox Tull, *President*
EMP: 50
SALES (corp-wide): 20MM **Privately Held**
WEB: www.jacksonandtull.com
SIC: 7373 8711 Systems engineering, computer related; civil engineering
PA: Jackson And Tull Chartered Engineers
2705 Bladensburg Rd Ne
Washington DC 20018
202 333-9100

(P-15624)
JADE GLOBAL INC (PA)
1731 Tech Dr Ste 350, San Jose (95110)
PHONE..................408 899-7200
Karan Yaramada, *CEO*
Rajeev Handa, *President*
Rama Karanam, *CFO*
Sudipta Bhattacharjee, *Vice Pres*
Craig Vidal, *Business Dir*
EMP: 52
SQ FT: 2,200
SALES (est): 20.8MM **Privately Held**
WEB: www.usjadecorp.com
SIC: 7373 Systems software development services

(P-15625)
JUNIPER NETWORKS INC
Also Called: Proof of Concept Poc Lab
1137 Innovation Way B, Sunnyvale
(94089-1228)
PHONE..................408 745-2000
Florin A Oprescu, *Principal*
Melissa Beauparlant, *Partner*
Phil Larson, *Partner*
Domenico Di Mola, *Vice Pres*
Jerry Ibrahim, *Vice Pres*

EMP: 2000 **Publicly Held**
WEB: www.juniper.net
SIC: 7373 7372 Computer integrated systems design; prepackaged software
PA: Juniper Networks, Inc.
1133 Innovation Way
Sunnyvale CA 94089

(P-15626)
JUNIPER NETWORKS INC
Aurrion
6868 Cortona Dr Ste C, Goleta
(93117-1363)
PHONE..................805 880-2000
EMP: 60 **Publicly Held**
SIC: 7373 Computer integrated systems design
PA: Juniper Networks, Inc.
1133 Innovation Way
Sunnyvale CA 94089

(P-15627)
JUNIPER NETWORKS INC
1215 K St Fl 17, Sacramento (95814-3954)
PHONE..................916 503-1593
Gerald Chavez, *Branch Mgr*
Ben Baker, *Marketing Staff*
EMP: 72 **Publicly Held**
WEB: www.juniper.net
SIC: 7373 7372 Computer integrated systems design; prepackaged software
PA: Juniper Networks, Inc.
1133 Innovation Way
Sunnyvale CA 94089

(P-15628)
JUNIPER NETWORKS INC
Also Called: Executive Briefing Center
1133 Innovation Way A, Sunnyvale
(94089-1228)
PHONE..................888 586-4737
Kannan Kothandaraman, *Vice Pres*
Yuriy Voynalovych, *Software Engr*
Tony Wang, *IT/INT Sup*
Amy Cherubino, *Project Mgr*
Mithun Mahale, *Technical Staff*
EMP: 638 **Publicly Held**
WEB: www.juniper.net
SIC: 7373 7372 Computer integrated systems design; prepackaged software
PA: Juniper Networks, Inc.
1133 Innovation Way
Sunnyvale CA 94089

(P-15629)
KG OLDCO INC (HQ)
2270 Martin Ave, Santa Clara
(95050-2704)
PHONE..................408 980-8550
Jeff Kaiser, *CEO*
Jason Gress, *President*
EMP: 50
SQ FT: 13,130
SALES (est): 38.2MM
SALES (corp-wide): 38.8MM **Privately Held**
WEB: www.intervision.com
SIC: 7373 8712 Systems integration services; architectural services
PA: Netelligent Corporation
16401 Swingley Ridge Rd
Chesterfield MO 63017
314 392-6900

(P-15630)
KOAM ENGINEERING SYSTEMS INC
Also Called: K E S
7807 Convoy Ct Ste 200, San Diego
(92111-1213)
PHONE..................858 292-0922
John S Yi, *President*
Richard Comber, *Vice Pres*
Erica Tofson, *Vice Pres*
Doreen Carpenter, *Administration*
Jim Meadows, *Director*
EMP: 105 EST: 1994
SQ FT: 5,700
SALES (est): 26.1MM **Privately Held**
SIC: 7373 Computer integrated systems design

PRODUCTS & SVCS

(P-15631)
KRAFT & KENNEDY INC
1 Post St Ste 2600, San Francisco
(94104-5230)
PHONE....................415 956-4000
Peter Kennedy, *CEO*
EMP: 60
SALES (corp-wide): 15.5MM **Privately
Held**
WEB: www.kklsystems.com
SIC: **7373** 7379 Computer integrated sys-
tems design; computer related consulting
services
PA: Kraft & Kennedy, Inc.
630 3rd Ave Rm 1400
New York NY 10017
212 986-4700

(P-15632)
KRATOS RT LOGIC INC
10680 Treena St Ste 600, San Diego
(92131-2440)
PHONE....................858 812-7300
EMP: 88 **Publicly Held**
SIC: **7373** Computer integrated systems
design
HQ: Kratos Rt Logic, Inc.
12515 Academy Ridge Vw
Colorado Springs CO 80921
719 598-2801

(P-15633)
L3 TECHNOLOGIES INC
117 S Gold Canyon St, Ridgecrest
(93555-4121)
PHONE....................760 375-0390
Jai Gupta, *Manager*
EMP: 100
SALES (corp-wide): 6.8B **Publicly Held**
SIC: **7373** 8731 3761 1731 Systems engineering, computer related; computer
systems analysis & design; systems integration services; commercial physical research; guided missiles & space vehicles;
electrical work
HQ: L3 Technologies, Inc.
600 3rd Ave Fl 34
New York NY 10016
212 697-1111

(P-15634)
LANLOGIC INC (HQ)
248 Rickenbacker Cir, Livermore
(94551-7615)
PHONE....................925 273-2300
Dan Ferguson, *President*
Wilma Smith, *CFO*
Bayani Natividad, *Network Enginr*
Russell Feagley, *IT/INT Sup*
EMP: 50
SQ FT: 6,000
SALES (est): 7.2MM **Privately Held**
WEB: www.lanlogic.com
SIC: **7373** 4813 Computer integrated sys-
tems design;
PA: Addressable Networks, Inc.
3170 Orthello Way
Santa Clara CA 95051
408 241-7446

(P-15635)
LATTICE ENGINES INC (DH)
1820 Gateway Dr Ste 200, San Mateo
(94404-4059)
PHONE....................877 460-0010
Shashi Upadhyay, *CEO*
Timothy Carruthers, *President*
Kent McCormick, *President*
Howie Shohet, *CFO*
Ian J Scott, *Vice Pres*
EMP: 92
SALES (corp-wide): 1.7B **Privately Held**
SIC: **7373** 7372 Computer system selling
services; business oriented computer
software

(P-15636)
LEIDOS INC
3800 Watt Ave Ste 210, Sacramento
(95821-2622)
PHONE....................916 974-8800
Kate Jacobson, *Manager*
EMP: 400

SALES (corp-wide): 10.1B **Publicly Held**
WEB: www.saic.com
SIC: **7373** Systems engineering, computer
related
HQ: Leidos, Inc.
11951 Freedom Dr Ste 500
Reston VA 20190
571 526-6000

(P-15637)
LIFERAY INC (PA)
1400 Montefino Ave # 100, Diamond Bar
(91765-5501)
PHONE....................877 543-3729
Bryan Cheung, *CEO*
Karen Newnam, *Partner*
Scott Tachiki, *CFO*
Paul Hinz, *Chief Mktg Ofcr*
Matt Poladian, *Vice Pres*
EMP: 75
SALES: 3MM **Privately Held**
WEB: www.liferay.com
SIC: **7373** Systems software development
services

(P-15638)
LIGHTCREST LLC
1112 Montana Ave Ste 705, Santa Monica
(90403-1652)
PHONE....................888 320-8495
Zachary Fierstadt,
Denice Legree, *Admin Asst*
Thomas Swigert, *Administration*
Stephen Richter, *Database Admin*
Zeke Dauer, *Engineer*
EMP: 50
SALES (est): 10MM **Privately Held**
SIC: **7373** Computer integrated systems
design

(P-15639)
LILIEN LLC (HQ)
17 E Sir Francis Dr # 110, Larkspur
(94939-1708)
PHONE....................415 389-7500
Geoffrey I Lilien, *Mng Member*
Eric Borsky, *President*
Dhruv Gulati,
Wilson Lochridge,
Brett Osborn,
EMP: 50
SQ FT: 6,200
SALES (est): 11.8MM
SALES (corp-wide): 62.9MM **Privately
Held**
SIC: **7373** Computer integrated systems
design
PA: Sysorex International, Inc
335 E Middlefield Rd
Mountain View CA 94043
650 967-2200

(P-15640)
LIQUIDATE DIRECT LLC
Also Called: Solid Commerce
2929 Washington Blvd Fl 2, Marina Del Rey
(90292-5546)
PHONE....................800 750-7617
Eran Pick, *CEO*
Alon Berkovich, *COO*
Shawna Snukst, *Bus Dvlpt Dir*
EMP: 50 EST: 2003
SALES (est): 5.6MM **Privately Held**
SIC: **7373** 7371 7379 Computer inte-
grated systems design; custom computer
programming services; computer related
maintenance services

(P-15641)
LUCID DESIGN GROUP INC
55 Harrison St 200, Oakland (94607-3790)
PHONE....................510 907-0400
Will Coleman, *CEO*
Vladisoav Shunturov, *President*
Kevin Burns, *Vice Pres*
Shelly Davenport, *Vice Pres*
Sarah Diegnan, *Vice Pres*
EMP: 80
SALES (est): 11.9MM
SALES (corp-wide): 3.6B **Publicly Held**
WEB: www.luciddesigngroup.com
SIC: **7373** Systems software development
services

PA: Acuity Brands, Inc.
1170 Peachtree St Ne # 23
Atlanta GA 30309
404 853-1400

(P-15642)
MACKEVISION CORPORATION
1255 Treat Blvd Ste 250, Walnut Creek
(94597-7997)
PHONE....................248 656-6566
Armin Pohl, *CEO*
Lindy Brodeur, *CFO*
Ross Delconte, *Managing Dir*
Beatrix Frisch, *General Mgr*
Yinai Sun, *Project Mgr*
EMP: 120
SQ FT: 8,000
SALES (est): 20.9MM **Privately Held**
SIC: **7373** Computer-aided design (CAD)
systems service
HQ: Mackevision Medien Design Gmbh
Forststr. 7
Stuttgart 70174
711 933-0480

(P-15643)
**MANTECH INTERNATIONAL
CORP**
8328 Clairemont Mesa Blvd, San Diego
(92111-1328)
PHONE....................858 492-9938
Ronald Renfro, *Exec Dir*
Erik Berg, *Division Mgr*
Jon Trebing, *Administration*
Jennie Black, *Analyst*
Nick Look, *Analyst*
EMP: 200
SALES (corp-wide): 1.9B **Publicly Held**
SIC: **7373** Systems software development
services
PA: Mantech International Corporation
2251 Corporate Park Dr
Herndon VA 20171
703 218-6000

(P-15644)
**MANTECH INTERNATIONAL
CORP**
615 N Nash St Ste 200, El Segundo
(90245-2851)
PHONE....................310 765-9324
EMP: 200
SALES (corp-wide): 1.9B **Publicly Held**
SIC: **7373** Systems software development
services
PA: Mantech International Corporation
2251 Corporate Park Dr
Herndon VA 20171
703 218-6000

(P-15645)
**MILESTONE TECHNOLOGIES
INC (PA)**
3101 Skyway Ct, Fremont (94539-5910)
PHONE....................510 651-2454
Nelson Eng, *President*
Edward Reginelli, *CFO*
Gary Bilovesky, *Vice Pres*
Natalie Heroux, *Vice Pres*
Kristi H Ledwein, *Vice Pres*
EMP: 116
SQ FT: 6,500
SALES (est): 133.1MM **Privately Held**
WEB: www.milestn.com
SIC: **7373** 7374 Computer integrated sys-
tems design; data processing & prepara-
tion

(P-15646)
MIST SYSTEMS INC
1601 S De Anza Blvd # 248, Cupertino
(95014-5347)
PHONE....................408 326-0346
Sujai Hajela, *CEO*
Brett Galloway, *Ch of Bd*
Laura Perrone, *CFO*
Bob Friday, *CTO*
Neal Castagnoli, *Technical Staff*
EMP: 125
SALES (est): 9.2MM **Publicly Held**
SIC: **7373** Local area network (LAN) sys-
tems integrator
PA: Juniper Networks, Inc.
1133 Innovation Way
Sunnyvale CA 94089

(P-15647)
MOBICA US INC
2570 N 1st St Fl 2, San Jose (95131-1035)
PHONE....................650 450-6654
Marcin Kloda, *CEO*
Rafael Janczyk, *COO*
Jenny Vang, *Office Mgr*
Radoslaw Dumanski, *Technical Staff*
EMP: 900 EST: 2012
SALES (est): 482.3K
SALES (corp-wide): 66.3MM **Privately
Held**
SIC: **7373** Systems software development
services
HQ: Mobica Limited
Crown House
Wilmslow SK9 1
-

(P-15648)
MORPHOTRAK LLC (DH)
Also Called: Safran
5515 E La Palma Ave # 100, Anaheim
(92807-2127)
PHONE....................714 238-2000
Celeste Thomasson, *CEO*
Clark Nelson, *Vice Pres*
Hieu Tran, *Vice Pres*
Katie Murphy, *Admin Sec*
Michael Klaassen, *Software Dev*
EMP: 175
SQ FT: 32,000
SALES (est): 94.4MM
SALES (corp-wide): 4.6B **Privately Held**
WEB: www.morpho.com
SIC: **7373** Computer integrated systems
design

(P-15649)
MOZILLA CORPORATION (HQ)
331 E Evelyn Ave, Mountain View
(94041-1550)
PHONE....................650 903-0800
Chris Beard, *CEO*
Denelle Dixon, *COO*
Jascha Kaykaswolff, *Chief Mktg Ofcr*
Michael Deangelo, *Officer*
Gervase Markham, *Officer*
EMP: 588
SQ FT: 58,500
SALES (est): 98.4MM
SALES (corp-wide): 421.2MM **Privately
Held**
WEB: www.mozilla.com
SIC: **7373** Systems software development
services
PA: Mozilla Foundation
331 E Evelyn Ave
Mountain View CA 94041
650 903-0800

(P-15650)
MSCSOFTWARE CORPORATION
Costa Mesa Office
4675 Macarthur Ct Ste 900, Newport Beach
(92660-1845)
PHONE....................714 540-8900
Frank Perna, *President*
EMP: 350
SQ FT: 81,000
SALES (corp-wide): 4.3B **Privately Held**
SIC: **7373** 8711 7372 7371 Computer-
aided engineering (CAE) systems service;
engineering services; prepackaged soft-
ware; custom computer programming
services
HQ: Msc.Software Corporation
4675 Macarthur Ct Ste 900
Newport Beach CA 92660
714 540-8900

(P-15651)
MY ALLY INC
1000 Elwell Ct Ste 105, Palo Alto
(94303-4306)
PHONE....................650 387-9118
Deepti Yenireddy, *CEO*
Carter Perez, *Vice Pres*
EMP: 70
SALES (est): 1.5MM **Privately Held**
SIC: **7373** Systems software development
services

(P-15652)
NAGARRO INC (DH)
Also Called: Projistics
2001 Gateway Pl Ste 100w, San Jose
(95110-1046)
PHONE..................................408 436-6170
Vikram Sehgal, *President*
Anurag Vashisht, *Program Mgr*
Avinash Shukla, *Project Mgr*
Mohit Bhardwaj, *Technical Staff*
Firoz Khan, *Technical Staff*
EMP: 67 **EST:** 1999
SQ FT: 3,000
SALES (est): 99.8MM
SALES (corp-wide): 787.6MM **Privately Held**
WEB: www.nagarro.com
SIC: 7373 Computer-aided system services
HQ: Allgeier Nagarro Holding Gmbh
    Wehrlestr. 12
    Munchen 81679
    899 984-210

(P-15653)
NANTHEALTH INC (HQ)
9920 Jefferson Blvd, Culver City
(90232-3506)
PHONE..................................310 883-1300
Patrick Soon-Shiong, *Ch of Bd*
EMP: 77
SQ FT: 8,000
SALES: 89.4MM
SALES (corp-wide): 154.7MM **Publicly Held**
SIC: 7373 Computer integrated systems design
PA: Nantworks, Llc
    9920 Jefferson Blvd
    Culver City CA 90232
    310 883-1300

(P-15654)
NANTWORKS LLC (PA)
9920 Jefferson Blvd, Culver City
(90232-3506)
PHONE..................................310 883-1300
Charles N Kenworthy, *Mng Member*
Regina Guerrero, *IT/INT Sup*
Jen Hodson, *Pub Rel Dir*
EMP: 91
SALES (est): 154.7MM **Publicly Held**
SIC: 7373 Computer-aided system services

(P-15655)
NET EXPRESS
32 Snyder Way, Fremont (94536-1675)
PHONE..................................510 887-4395
Roland H Baker III, *President*
EMP: 65
SALES (est): 4.5MM **Privately Held**
SIC: 7373 Computer systems analysis & design

(P-15656)
NETAPP INC
300 Spectrum Center Dr # 900, Irvine
(92618-4925)
PHONE..................................949 754-6600
Chris White, *Branch Mgr*
Mujtaba Ghouse, *Engineer*
JP Hernandez, *Engineer*
Steve McCallum, *Business Mgr*
Lucy Chang, *Finance Mgr*
EMP: 209 **Publicly Held**
SIC: 7373 Computer integrated systems design
PA: Netapp, Inc.
    1395 Crossman Ave
    Sunnyvale CA 94089

(P-15657)
NETAPP INC
1299 Orleans Dr, Sunnyvale (94089-1138)
PHONE..................................408 822-3402
Joe McKinney, *Accounts Mgr*
EMP: 215 **Publicly Held**
SIC: 7373 Computer integrated systems design
PA: Netapp, Inc.
    1395 Crossman Ave
    Sunnyvale CA 94089

(P-15658)
NETAPP INC
6320 Canoga Ave Ste 1500, Woodland Hills
(91367-2563)
PHONE..................................818 227-5025
EMP: 209
SALES (corp-wide): 6.3B **Publicly Held**
SIC: 7373
PA: Netapp, Inc.
    495 E Java Dr
    Sunnyvale CA 94089
    408 822-6000

(P-15659)
NETAPP INC
1345 Crossman Ave, Sunnyvale
(94089-1114)
PHONE..................................408 419-5301
Pam Teshera, *Branch Mgr*
Pamela Hutcheson, *Opers Staff*
Tracy Windsor, *Director*
EMP: 209 **Publicly Held**
WEB: www.netapp.com
SIC: 7373 Computer integrated systems design
PA: Netapp, Inc.
    1395 Crossman Ave
    Sunnyvale CA 94089

(P-15660)
NETAPP INC
3334 Meadowlands Ln, San Jose
(95135-1624)
PHONE..................................408 822-3803
EMP: 203
SALES (corp-wide): 6.3B **Publicly Held**
SIC: 7373
PA: Netapp, Inc.
    495 E Java Dr
    Sunnyvale CA 94089
    408 822-6000

(P-15661)
NETWORK INTGRTION PARTNERS INC
Also Called: Nic Partners
11981 Jack Benny Dr # 103, Rancho Cucamonga (91739-9232)
PHONE..................................909 919-2800
Franklin P Spaeth, *President*
EMP: 80
SQ FT: 6,000
SALES (est): 22.1MM **Privately Held**
SIC: 7373 Local area network (LAN) systems integrator

(P-15662)
NEW DIRECTIONS TECH INC (PA)
Also Called: Ndti
137 W Drummond Ave Ste A, Ridgecrest
(93555-3583)
PHONE..................................760 384-2444
Cedric Knight, *President*
Eric Bleau, *Administration*
Russell Tan, *Prgrmr*
Patrick McCombs, *IT/INT Sup*
Diego Rivera, *IT/INT Sup*
EMP: 65
SQ FT: 6,000
SALES (est): 26MM **Privately Held**
WEB: www.ndti.net
SIC: 7373 7374 8711 7371 Systems software development services; data processing & preparation; engineering services; computer software development & applications; computer facilities management

(P-15663)
NORTHROP GRUMMAN SYSTEMS CORP
Also Called: Technical Services
P.O. Box 81, Moffett Field (94035-0081)
PHONE..................................650 604-6056
James R Blount, *Manager*
EMP: 120 **Publicly Held**
SIC: 7373 7374 Computer systems analysis & design; computer processing services

HQ: Northrop Grumman Systems Corporation
    2980 Fairview Park Dr
    Falls Church VA 22042
    703 280-2900

(P-15664)
NORTHROP GRUMMAN SYSTEMS CORP
5161 Verdugo Way, Camarillo
(93012-8603)
PHONE..................................805 987-9739
Jim Lueck, *Branch Mgr*
EMP: 60 **Publicly Held**
WEB: www.logicon.com
SIC: 7373 8731 8711 7371 Computer systems analysis & design; commercial physical research; engineering services; custom computer programming services
HQ: Northrop Grumman Systems Corporation
    2980 Fairview Park Dr
    Falls Church VA 22042
    703 280-2900

(P-15665)
NTT DATA INC
1000 Corporate Center Dr # 140, Monterey Park (91754-7610)
PHONE..................................213 228-2500
Fax: 323 261-3030
EMP: 93
SALES (corp-wide): 93.3B **Privately Held**
SIC: 7373
HQ: Ntt Data, Inc.
    5601 Gran Pkwy Ste 1000
    Plano TX 75024
    800 745-3263

(P-15666)
NURLOGIC DESIGN INC (DH)
5580 Morehouse Dr, San Diego
(92121-1709)
PHONE..................................858 455-7570
Rich Shine, *Manager*
David Matty, *President*
Hugh D Gerfin, *Treasurer*
Mike Brunolli, *CTO*
EMP: 60
SQ FT: 34,000
SALES (est): 2.9MM **Privately Held**
SIC: 7373 Computer integrated systems design

(P-15667)
O2 MICRO INC
3118 Patrick Henry Dr, Santa Clara
(95054-1850)
PHONE..................................408 987-5920
Lynn Lin, *CEO*
Sterling Du, *President*
George Simion, *COO*
Perry Kuo, *CFO*
Johnny Chiang, *Vice Pres*
EMP: 100
SQ FT: 37,000
SALES (est): 15.9MM **Privately Held**
WEB: www.o2micro.com
SIC: 7373 Computer integrated systems design
PA: O2micro International Limited
    The Grand Pavillion
    George Town GR CAYMAN KY1-1

(P-15668)
OASIS TECHNOLOGY INC
601 E Daily Dr Ste 226, Camarillo
(93010-5840)
PHONE..................................805 445-4833
George M Baldonado, *President*
Deborah Johnson, *Vice Pres*
Violeta Baldonado, *Admin Sec*
Michael Meyers, *Technology*
EMP: 65
SQ FT: 2,800
SALES: 3MM **Privately Held**
WEB: www.oasistechnology.com
SIC: 7373 5734 Computer system selling services; personal computers

(P-15669)
OBERMAN TIVOLI & PICKERT INC
Also Called: Media Services
500 S Sepulveda Blvd # 500, Los Angeles
(90049-3551)
PHONE..................................310 440-9600
Robert Oberman, *President*
Sanaa Wadsworth, *CFO*
EMP: 230
SALES (est): 24.8MM **Privately Held**
WEB: www.media-services.com
SIC: 7373 8721 8741 Systems software development services; payroll accounting service; business management

(P-15670)
PACIFIC CROSSING LLC
95 Argonaut Ste 100, Aliso Viejo
(92656-4139)
PHONE..................................949 679-2588
Phyllis Johnson,
Walter Johnson,
EMP: 225
SQ FT: 1,500
SALES (est): 9.5MM **Privately Held**
WEB: www.pacificcrossing.com
SIC: 7373 Computer integrated systems design

(P-15671)
PANZURA INC
695 Campbell Tech Pkwy # 225, Campbell
(95008-5076)
PHONE..................................408 457-8504
Randy Chou, *CEO*
Mark Santora, *Ch of Bd*
Criss Marshall, *Chief Mktg Ofcr*
Rich Weber, *Vice Pres*
Darren Daugherty, *Principal*
EMP: 57 **EST:** 2008
SALES (est): 15MM **Privately Held**
SIC: 7373 5734 Computer integrated systems design; computer software & accessories

(P-15672)
PERSPECTA ENGINEERING INC
1315 Dell Ave, Campbell (95008-6609)
PHONE..................................408 961-3250
Joe Harris, *General Mgr*
Frank Anstett, *Vice Pres*
Jeff Bohling, *Vice Pres*
Brett Dody, *Vice Pres*
Alan Mankofsky, *Vice Pres*
EMP: 100
SALES (corp-wide): 11.5B **Publicly Held**
WEB: www.comglobal.com
SIC: 7373 1731 Systems software development services; electrical work
HQ: Perspecta Engineering Inc.
    15050 Conference Ctr Dr
    Chantilly VA 20151
    571 313-6000

(P-15673)
PINNACLE TELECOM INC (PA)
Also Called: Pti Solutions
8100 Sierra College Blvd, Roseville
(95661-9411)
PHONE..................................916 426-1000
Cecelia Lakatos Sullivan, *CEO*
Barbara Winters, *Chairman*
Eileen Parr, *Risk Mgmt Dir*
Mike Boltz, *Area Mgr*
Michael Sula, *Auditor*
EMP: 50
SQ FT: 20,000
SALES: 12MM **Privately Held**
WEB: www.pinnacle-telecom.com
SIC: 7373 8741 1731 1623 Computer integrated systems design; management services; electronic controls installation; electric power line construction; computer facilities management; computer related maintenance services

(P-15674)
PIXIM INC
1730 N 1st St, San Jose (95112-4642)
PHONE..................................650 934-0550
Chris Adams, *CEO*
Randy Strahan, *President*
John Monti, *Vice Pres*
EMP: 51
SQ FT: 13,560

SALES (est): 6.3MM Privately Held
WEB: www.pixim.com
SIC: 7373 7361 Local area network (LAN) systems integrator; employment agencies

(P-15675)
PLANET GROUP INC
5796 Armada Dr Ste 300, Carlsbad (92008-4694)
PHONE..................402 491-3560
Tom Nichting, *President*
David Gerheauser Jr, *Treasurer*
Sherry Magwire, *CTO*
EMP: 99
SALES: 950K Privately Held
SIC: 7373 Computer integrated systems design

(P-15676)
PLUME DESIGN INC
Also Called: Plume Wifi
290 California Ave # 200, Palo Alto (94306-1618)
PHONE..................408 498-5512
Fahri Diner, *CEO*
Andrew Hartland, *CFO*
EMP: 54
SQ FT: 4,500
SALES (est): 1.1MM Privately Held
SIC: 7373 Systems engineering, computer related

(P-15677)
QCT LLC
1010 Rincon Cir, San Jose (95131-1325)
PHONE..................510 270-6111
Alan Lam, *Mng Member*
Gary TSE, *Software Engr*
Olivia Chen, *Comp Spec*
Michael Quan, *Engineer*
Mike Wagner, *Sales Dir*
▲ EMP: 1000
SALES (est): 6.5MM Privately Held
SIC: 7373 Systems integration services
PA: Quanta Computer Inc.
188, Wenhua 2nd Rd.,
Taoyuan City TAY 33383

(P-15678)
QSOLV INC
440 N Wolfe Rd Ste 26, Sunnyvale (94085-3869)
PHONE..................408 429-0918
Sujaya Viswanathan, *CEO*
Shell Scripting, *Partner*
Shyam Gopal, *President*
Keerthi Vasagan, *Tech Recruiter*
EMP: 112
SALES (est): 3.9MM Privately Held
WEB: www.qsolv.net
SIC: 7373 7379 7371 Computer systems analysis & design; computer related consulting services; software programming applications

(P-15679)
QUEST MEDIA & SUPPLIES INC (PA)
9000 Fthills Blvd Ste 100, Roseville (95747)
P.O. Box 910 (95678-0910)
PHONE..................916 338-7070
Timothy Burke, *CEO*
Cindy P Burke, *President*
Kathy Campbell, *COO*
Francine Walrath, *CFO*
Carlos Romo, *Executive*
EMP: 92
SQ FT: 9,500
SALES: 159.4MM Privately Held
WEB: www.questsys.com
SIC: 7373 Systems integration services

(P-15680)
QUEST SOFTWARE INC (HQ)
4 Polaris Way, Aliso Viejo (92656-5356)
PHONE..................949 754-8000
Jeff Hawn, *CEO*
Gary Broadwater, *President*
Kevin E Brooks, *Vice Pres*
Thomas R Patterson Jr, *Vice Pres*
Philip Walsh, *Vice Pres*
EMP: 600
SQ FT: 170,000

SALES (est): 826.9MM
SALES (corp-wide): 1.5B Privately Held
WEB: www.quest.com
SIC: 7373 7379 7372 Computer integrated systems design; computer related consulting services; business oriented computer software
PA: Francisco Partners Management, L.P.
1 Letterman Dr Ste 410
San Francisco CA 94129
415 418-2900

(P-15681)
R SYSTEMS INC (HQ)
5000 Windplay Dr Ste 5, El Dorado Hills (95762-9319)
PHONE..................916 939-9696
Satinder S Rekhi, *CEO*
Sartaj Singh Rekhi, *Exec Dir*
EMP: 100
SQ FT: 7,000
SALES: 23.5MM
SALES (corp-wide): 44.3MM Privately Held
WEB: www.rsystems.com
SIC: 7373 Computer integrated systems design
PA: R Systems International Limited
C 40, Sector 59
Noida UP 20130
120 258-8191

(P-15682)
RAVENSWOOD SOLUTIONS INC (HQ)
3065 Skyway Ct, Fremont (94539-5909)
PHONE..................650 241-3661
Daniel Donoghue, *CEO*
Christopher Terndrup, *Exec Dir*
Craig Tucker, *Program Mgr*
Marlene Curiel, *Administration*
Stacy Corcoran, *Sr Software Eng*
EMP: 99 EST: 2015
SQ FT: 12,878
SALES (est): 8.3MM
SALES (corp-wide): 461.4MM Privately Held
SIC: 7373 7379 3679 8711 Systems engineering, computer related; computer related maintenance services; antennas, receiving; engineering services
PA: Sri International
333 Ravenswood Ave
Menlo Park CA 94025
650 859-2000

(P-15683)
RAYV INC
6380 Wilshire Blvd # 1006, Los Angeles (90048-5003)
PHONE..................310 600-2959
Ron Zuckerman, *CEO*
Morris Azulay, *CFO*
Ori Birnbaum, *Vice Pres*
Omer Luzzatti, *CTO*
EMP: 50
SQ FT: 4,000
SALES (est): 3.2MM Privately Held
SIC: 7373 Computer integrated systems design

(P-15684)
RESULT GROUP INC
2603 Main St Ste 710, Irvine (92614-4263)
PHONE..................480 777-7130
William Derick Robson, *President*
David Griffiths, *Admin Sec*
EMP: 70
SALES (est): 4.8MM
SALES (corp-wide): 3B Privately Held
SIC: 7373 7372 Systems software development services; business oriented computer software
HQ: Wynne Systems, Inc.
2601 Main St Ste 270
Irvine CA 92614

(P-15685)
SAUCE LABS INC (PA)
116 New Montgomery St # 3, San Francisco (94105-3639)
PHONE..................855 677-0011
Aled Miles, *CEO*
Paul Joachim, *CFO*
Joe Alfaro, *Vice Pres*

Heather McLinden, *Vice Pres*
Manuel Ruiz, *Vice Pres*
EMP: 76
SALES (est): 34.7MM Privately Held
SIC: 7373 Systems software development services

(P-15686)
SCALEFLUX INC
97 E Brokaw Rd Ste 260, San Jose (95112-1032)
PHONE..................408 628-2291
Hao Zhong, *CEO*
Thad Omura, *VP Bus Dvlpt*
EMP: 60 EST: 2014
SALES: 5MM Privately Held
SIC: 7373 Systems engineering, computer related

(P-15687)
SCIENCE APPLICATIONS INTL CORP
Also Called: Saic
4015 Hancock St, San Diego (92110-5121)
PHONE..................858 826-3061
Gordon Saakamodo, *Manager*
Anthony Moraco, *CEO*
Charlie Mathis, *CFO*
Michael Larouche, *Exec VP*
Chris Donaghey, *Vice Pres*
EMP: 600
SALES (corp-wide): 4.6B Publicly Held
WEB: www.saic.com
SIC: 7373 Systems engineering, computer related
PA: Science Applications International Corporation
12010 Sunset Hills Rd
Reston VA 20190
703 676-4300

(P-15688)
SECOM INTERNATIONAL (PA)
15905 S Broadway, Gardena (90248-2405)
PHONE..................310 641-1290
Ted Burton, *President*
Amir Behic, *CFO*
Terry Bixler, *Vice Pres*
Linda Vose, *Admin Sec*
George Horner, *Software Engr*
EMP: 52
SALES (est): 9MM Privately Held
WEB: www.secomintl.com
SIC: 7373 3446 3559 7371 Turnkey vendors, computer systems; architectural metalwork; parking facility equipment & supplies; computer software systems analysis & design, custom

(P-15689)
SECURITY ON-DEMAND INC
12121 Scripps Summit Dr # 320, San Diego (92131-4609)
PHONE..................858 563-5655
Peter Bybee, *CEO*
William Lyman, *CFO*
Glenn Dodds, *Vice Pres*
Traci Esteve, *Vice Pres*
Nathaniel Kelly, *Vice Pres*
EMP: 50 EST: 2001
SQ FT: 12,000
SALES: 3MM Privately Held
SIC: 7373 Computer integrated systems design

(P-15690)
SELLIGENT INC (HQ)
1300 W Island Dr Ste 200, Redwood City (94065-5171)
PHONE..................650 421-4255
John Hernandez, *CEO*
Frank Addante, *President*
Tricia Robinson-Pridemore, *President*
Chris Botting, *COO*
Steve Pantelick, *CFO*
EMP: 90
SALES (est): 36.3MM
SALES (corp-wide): 132.9MM Privately Held
WEB: www.strongmailsystems.com
SIC: 7373 Systems software development services
PA: Hggc, Llc
1950 University Ave # 350
East Palo Alto CA 94303
650 321-4910

(P-15691)
SEMANTIC AI INC (PA)
Also Called: Semantic Research
4922 N Harbor Dr, San Diego (92106-2306)
PHONE..................619 222-4050
Richard Harrison, *CEO*
Thomas Waltz, *CFO*
Molly Ryan, *Human Res Dir*
Erica Davis, *Training Dir*
Dorie Kelly, *Manager*
EMP: 70
SQ FT: 2,600
SALES (est): 12MM Privately Held
WEB: www.semanticresearch.com
SIC: 7373 Systems software development services

(P-15692)
SILVACO INC (PA)
Also Called: Invarian
2811 Mission College Blvd # 6, Santa Clara (95054-1884)
PHONE..................408 567-1000
Babak Taheri, *CEO*
Sungwon Kong, *Engineer*
EMP: 55
SALES (est): 30.9MM Privately Held
SIC: 7373 Office computer automation systems integration

(P-15693)
SOFTWARE DYNAMICS INCORPORATED
8501 Fllbrook Ave Ste 200, Canoga Park (91304)
PHONE..................818 992-3299
Matthew Hale, *President*
Christopher J Stein, *Treasurer*
Richard Dobb, *Admin Sec*
EMP: 164
SQ FT: 40,000
SALES (est): 5.9MM Publicly Held
WEB: www.s1.com
SIC: 7373 7371 Computer systems analysis & design; computer software development
HQ: S1 Corporation
705 Westech Dr
Norcross GA 30092
678 966-9499

(P-15694)
SOLESTAGE INC
Also Called: Store & Online
17651 Railroad St, City of Industry (91748-1194)
PHONE..................909 576-1309
Lane Wang, *CEO*
EMP: 50
SALES: 15MM Privately Held
SIC: 7373 7371 Value-added resellers, computer systems; computer software development & applications

(P-15695)
SONICWALL INC (PA)
1033 Mccarthy Blvd, Milpitas (95035-7920)
PHONE..................888 557-6642
Bill Conner, *President*
Evan Kaplan, *President*
Ravi Chopra, *CFO*
Joe Nguyenle, *Officer*
John Gmuender, *Vice Pres*
▲ EMP: 124
SQ FT: 86,000
SALES (est): 123.7MM Privately Held
WEB: www.sonicwall.com
SIC: 7373 Systems software development services

(P-15696)
SPARXENT INC (PA)
65 Enterprise, Aliso Viejo (92656-2705)
PHONE..................949 222-2287
Steve Dewindt, *CEO*
Andrew Hyde, *CFO*
EMP: 50
SALES (est): 2.6MM Privately Held
SIC: 7373 Systems software development services

(P-15697)
SPIKE TECHNOLOGIES INC
2386 Lacey Dr, Milpitas (95035-6121)
PHONE..................408 410-0624

Nikhil Modi, *President*
Pradeep Vajram, *COO*
Finney Tsai, *Vice Pres*
EMP: 50
SALES (est): 3.2MM **Privately Held**
SIC: 7373 Systems engineering, computer related

(P-15698)
STRIPE INC
Also Called: Stripe Payments Company
510 Townsend St, San Francisco
(94103-4918)
PHONE................................888 963-8955
Patrick Collison, *CEO*
Lachlan Fletcher, *Executive*
Amrit Ayalur, *Software Engr*
Connie Chen, *Software Engr*
Zachary Yellin Flaherty, *Software Engr*
EMP: 1100
SALES (est): 98.4MM **Privately Held**
SIC: 7373 Systems software development services

(P-15699)
SYSOREX USA (HQ)
101 Larkspur Landing Cir # 120, Larkspur
(94939-1749)
PHONE................................415 389-7500
Nadir Ali, *CEO*
EMP: 58
SQ FT: 2,800
SALES (est): 3.8MM
SALES (corp-wide): 3.7MM **Publicly Held**
WEB: www.lilien.com
SIC: 7373 Systems integration services
PA: Inpixon
2479 E Byshore Rd Ste 195
Palo Alto CA 94303
408 702-2167

(P-15700)
SYSTEM INTEGRATORS INC
(HQ)
Also Called: Netlinx Publishing Solutions
1740 N Market Blvd, Sacramento
(95834-1997)
PHONE................................916 830-2400
Paul Donlan, *President*
Allan Katzen, *Vice Pres*
EMP: 140
SQ FT: 70,000
SALES (est): 9.7MM
SALES (corp-wide): 177.9MM **Privately Held**
SIC: 7373 7372 7371 Computer integrated systems design; prepackaged software; custom computer programming services
PA: Net-Linx Ag
Kathe-Kollwitz-Ufer 76-79
Dresden
351 318-750

(P-15701)
TALARI NETWORKS INC (PA)
4230 Leonard Stocking Dr, Santa Clara
(95054-1777)
PHONE................................408 689-0400
Patrick Sweeney, *CEO*
Emerick Woods, *President*
Kevin Gavin, *Chief Mktg Ofcr*
Patrick Reilly, *Vice Pres*
Adrian Tate, *Vice Pres*
EMP: 57
SALES (est): 11.9MM **Privately Held**
SIC: 7373 Computer integrated systems design

(P-15702)
TALEND INC (HQ)
800 Bridge Pkwy Ste 200, Redwood City
(94065-1156)
PHONE................................650 539-3200
Mike Tuchen, *CEO*
Laurent Bride, *COO*
Thomas Tuchscherer, *CFO*
Nanci Caldwell, *Bd of Directors*
Brian Lillie, *Bd of Directors*
EMP: 124
SQ FT: 1,200
SALES (est): 144MM
SALES (corp-wide): 79MM **Privately Held**
SIC: 7373 Computer systems analysis & design

PA: Talend
9 Rue Pages
Suresnes 92150
140 999-704

(P-15703)
TIBCO SOFTWARE INC
Spotfire Division
3307 Hillview Ave, Palo Alto (94304-1204)
P.O. Box 51565 (94303-0710)
PHONE................................650 846-1000
EMP: 52
SALES (corp-wide): 885.6MM **Privately Held**
SIC: 7373 7371 Systems integration services; custom computer programming services
HQ: Tibco Software Inc.
3307 Hillview Ave
Palo Alto CA 94304
-

(P-15704)
TRADESHIFT INC (DH)
Also Called: Trade Shift APS
612 Howard St Ste 100, San Francisco
(94105-3927)
PHONE................................800 381-3585
Christian Lanng, *President*
Jeppe Rindom, *CFO*
Amer Moorhead,
Roy Anderson,
Kevin Wilbur, *Senior VP*
EMP: 53
SALES (est): 8.8MM
SALES (corp-wide): 34.7MM **Privately Held**
SIC: 7373 Local area network (LAN) systems integrator
HQ: Tradeshift Holdings Inc.
221 Main St Ste 250
San Francisco CA 94105
800 381-3585

(P-15705)
TRAMS INC (DH)
5777 W Century Blvd # 1200, Los Angeles
(90045-5674)
PHONE................................310 641-8726
Lee B Rosen, *President*
Ronald Larson, *Vice Pres*
EMP: 65
SQ FT: 14,500
SALES (est): 5.4MM **Publicly Held**
WEB: www.clientbase.com
SIC: 7373 Systems software development services
HQ: Sabre Glbl Inc.
3150 Sabre Dr
Southlake TX 76092
682 605-1000

(P-15706)
TRINITY TECHNOLOGY GROUP
INC
2015 J St Ste 105, Sacramento
(95811-3124)
PHONE................................916 779-0201
Randall E Duart, *CEO*
Timothy Purdy, *CFO*
Jane Duart, *Treasurer*
Stephen Williamson, *Vice Pres*
EMP: 59
SQ FT: 2,800
SALES: 14.8MM **Privately Held**
WEB: www.trinitytg.com
SIC: 7373 Systems software development services

(P-15707)
UNITEK INC
Also Called: Interket Enterprise
41350 Christy St, Fremont (94538-3115)
PHONE................................510 623-8544
Philip Kim, *CEO*
Russ Morrow, *Vice Pres*
EMP: 65
SQ FT: 20,000
SALES (est): 9.3MM **Privately Held**
WEB: www.unitekinc.com
SIC: 7373 3679 3672 Turnkey vendors, computer systems; electronic circuits; printed circuit boards

(P-15708)
V-TEK SYSTEMS CORPORATION
21045 Ridge Park Dr, Yorba Linda
(92886-7808)
PHONE................................909 396-5355
Bernard D Abrams, *President*
Mary Ellen Turino, *Human Resources*
EMP: 65
SQ FT: 19,000
SALES (est): 8.6MM **Privately Held**
WEB: www.v-tek.com
SIC: 7373 Systems integration services

(P-15709)
VERTISYSTEM INC
39300 Civic Center Dr # 160, Fremont
(94538-5397)
PHONE................................510 794-8099
Shaloo Jeswani, *CEO*
Rakesh Sadhwani, *President*
Deebali Syed, *Vice Pres*
Hariom Bisopia, *Manager*
EMP: 110
SQ FT: 2,744
SALES (est): 8.8MM **Privately Held**
SIC: 7373 Systems software development services

(P-15710)
VICOR INC
855 Marina Bay Pkwy # 100, Richmond
(94804-6413)
PHONE................................510 621-2000
Robert Kirk, *CEO*
Garry Mah, *CFO*
EMP: 72
SALES (est): 6.9MM
SALES (corp-wide): 8.4B **Publicly Held**
WEB: www.vicor.com
SIC: 7373 7371 Systems engineering, computer related; computer software development
HQ: Metavante Corporation
4900 W Brown Deer Rd
Milwaukee WI 53223
-

(P-15711)
WAVESTRONG INC
5674 Stoneridge Dr # 225, Pleasanton
(94588-8500)
PHONE................................925 549-2882
Harpreet Walia, *CEO*
Raj Khanna, *COO*
Mandeet Dhoat, *Vice Pres*
Janet Anderson, *Human Res Mgr*
EMP: 94
SQ FT: 5,200
SALES (est): 13.7MM **Privately Held**
SIC: 7373 7379 Computer integrated systems design; computer related consulting services

(P-15712)
WESCON TECHNOLOGY INC
4699 Old Ironsides Dr # 290, Santa Clara
(95054-1859)
PHONE................................408 727-8818
Fred MA, *President*
Anthony Chan, *Vice Pres*
Jason Huang, *Vice Pres*
Julie Wang, *Vice Pres*
EMP: 140
SQ FT: 1,610
SALES (est): 13.4MM **Privately Held**
WEB: www.wescongroup.com
SIC: 7373 7371 Computer integrated systems design; computer software writing services

(P-15713)
WEST PUBLISHING
CORPORATION
Also Called: Elite
800 Crprate Pinte Ste 150, Culver City
(90230)
P.O. Box 51606, Los Angeles (90051-5906)
PHONE................................424 243-2100
Salim Sunderji, *Vice Pres*
EMP: 174
SALES (corp-wide): 10.6B **Publicly Held**
WEB: www.ruttergroup.com
SIC: 7373 7371 Computer integrated systems design; custom computer programming services

HQ: West Publishing Corporation
610 Opperman Dr
Eagan MN 55123
651 687-7000

(P-15714)
XDIMENSIONAL
TECHNOLOGIES INC
145 S State College Blvd # 160, Brea
(92821-5824)
PHONE................................714 672-8960
Michael Walther, *Branch Mgr*
EMP: 60 **Privately Held**
WEB: www.xdimensional.com
SIC: 7373 Systems integration services
PA: Xdimensional Technologies Inc
450a Apollo St Ste A
Brea CA 92821

(P-15715)
XP SYSTEMS CORPORATION
(HQ)
405 Science Dr, Moorpark (93021-2247)
PHONE................................805 532-9100
John Edwards, *President*
Diane Atkins, *Vice Pres*
Drew Foley, *Principal*
Tina Laramie, *Executive Asst*
Teresa Farrow, *Human Res Mgr*
EMP: 200
SQ FT: 109,256
SALES (est): 21.9MM
SALES (corp-wide): 5.8B **Publicly Held**
WEB: www.xpsystems.com
SIC: 7373 Computer integrated systems design
PA: Fiserv, Inc.
255 Fiserv Dr
Brookfield WI 53045
262 879-5000

(P-15716)
ZENITH INFOTECH LIMITED
39675 Cedar Blvd Ste 240b, Newark
(94560-8541)
PHONE................................510 687-1943
EMP: 145
SALES: 7.5MM **Privately Held**
WEB: www.zenithinfotech.com
SIC: 7373
PA: Zenith Infotech Limited
29 & 30 Zenith House
Mumbai MH 40009

(P-15717)
ZMICRO INC (PA)
Also Called: Z Microsystems
9820 Summers Ridge Rd, San Diego
(92121-3083)
PHONE................................858 831-7000
Jack Wade, *CEO*
Jason Wade, *President*
John Howell, *COO*
Rick Schmidt, *CFO*
Rick Elliot, *Vice Pres*
EMP: 57
SQ FT: 36,800
SALES (est): 20.1MM **Privately Held**
WEB: www.zmicro.com
SIC: 7373 3577 3572 Computer integrated systems design; computer peripheral equipment; computer storage devices

7374 Data & Computer Processing & Preparation

(P-15718)
A S E C INTERNATIONAL INC
Also Called: Asec Group
11400 W Olympic Blvd, Los Angeles
(90064-1550)
PHONE................................803 939-4809
Evan Green, *President*
Del Snyder, *Exec VP*
Steve Seiler, *Admin Sec*
EMP: 700
SQ FT: 25,000
SALES (est): 21.8MM **Privately Held**
WEB: www.asecusa.com
SIC: 7374 Data processing service

(P-15719)
ACTIVIDENTITY CORPORATION
6623 Dumbarton Cir, Fremont
(94555-3603)
PHONE....................510 574-0100
Grant Evans, *Ch of Bd*
Jacques Kerrest, *COO*
John Boyer, *Senior VP*
Jerome Becquart, *Vice Pres*
Ben Erwin, *Technical Staff*
▲ **EMP:** 218
SQ FT: 41,000
SALES (est): 14.8MM
SALES (corp-wide): 9.3B **Privately Held**
WEB: www.actividentity.com
SIC: 7374 Data verification service
HQ: Hid Global Corporation
611 Center Ridge Dr
Austin TX 78753
800 237-7769

(P-15720)
ALORICA INC (PA)
Also Called: Priority One Support
5161 California Ave # 100, Irvine
(92617-8002)
PHONE....................949 527-4600
Andy Lee, *President*
Kyle Baker, *President*
Colleen Beers, *President*
Jay King, *President*
Greg Haller, *COO*
▲ **EMP:** 100
SALES (est): 6.6B **Privately Held**
WEB: www.alorica.com
SIC: 7374 7389 7373 Data processing
service; telephone answering service;
telemarketing services; computer inte-
grated systems design

(P-15721)
AUTOMATIC DATA PROCESSING INC
Also Called: ADP
7000 Village Dr Ste 200, Buena Park
(90621-2287)
PHONE....................714 690-7000
Joseph Leung, *Principal*
Liz Coulter, *Vice Pres*
Jay Dutcher, *District Mgr*
Jessica Glass, *District Mgr*
Lauren Komppa, *District Mgr*
EMP: 117
SALES (corp-wide): 14.1B **Publicly Held**
SIC: 7374 8721 Data processing service;
payroll accounting service
PA: Automatic Data Processing, Inc.
1 Adp Blvd Ste 1 # 1
Roseland NJ 07068
973 974-5000

(P-15722)
AUTOMATIC DATA PROCESSING INC
Also Called: ADP
9445 Fairway View Pl # 200, Rancho Cuca-
monga (91730-0931)
PHONE....................800 225-5237
Bill Crawford, *Manager*
Vicki Lehman, *Consultant*
EMP: 200
SALES (corp-wide): 14.1B **Publicly Held**
SIC: 7374 Data processing service
PA: Automatic Data Processing, Inc.
1 Adp Blvd Ste 1 # 1
Roseland NJ 07068
973 974-5000

(P-15723)
AUTOMATIC DATA PROCESSING INC
Also Called: ADP
5153 Camino Ruiz Ste 100, Camarillo
(93012-8656)
PHONE....................805 383-8630
Erich Hillig, *Director*
Ashley Johnson, *District Mgr*
Jon Rust, *Technology*
Vivek Dabholkar, *Director*
Teresa Baker, *Manager*
EMP: 117
SALES (corp-wide): 14.1B **Publicly Held**
SIC: 7374 Data processing service

PA: Automatic Data Processing, Inc.
1 Adp Blvd Ste 1 # 1
Roseland NJ 07068
973 974-5000

(P-15724)
AUTOMATIC DATA PROCESSING INC
Also Called: ADP
600 California St Fl 11, San Francisco
(94108-2727)
PHONE....................800 225-5237
Steve Kapusta, *Manager*
Christine Schindelwolf, *District Mgr*
Gregg Franklin, *Technical Staff*
Lisa Kavanaugh, *Technical Staff*
EMP: 50
SALES (corp-wide): 14.1B **Publicly Held**
SIC: 7374 Data processing service
PA: Automatic Data Processing, Inc.
1 Adp Blvd Ste 1 # 1
Roseland NJ 07068
973 974-5000

(P-15725)
AUTOMATIC DATA PROCESSING INC
Also Called: ADP
620 W Covina Blvd, San Dimas
(91773-2956)
PHONE....................909 592-6411
Melanie Hardin, *Branch Mgr*
Victor Mak, *Vice Pres*
Yan Zhang, *Administration*
Sharon Suh, *Finance*
Rick Weber, *VP Mktg*
EMP: 130
SALES (corp-wide): 14.1B **Publicly Held**
SIC: 7374 Data processing service
PA: Automatic Data Processing, Inc.
1 Adp Blvd Ste 1 # 1
Roseland NJ 07068
973 974-5000

(P-15726)
AUTOMATIC DATA PROCESSING INC
Also Called: ADP
720 Bay Rd, Redwood City (94063-2479)
PHONE....................800 225-5237
EMP: 130
SALES (corp-wide): 14.1B **Publicly Held**
SIC: 7374 Data processing service
PA: Automatic Data Processing, Inc.
1 Adp Blvd Ste 1 # 1
Roseland NJ 07068
973 974-5000

(P-15727)
AUTOMATIC DATA PROCESSING INC
Also Called: ADP
505 San Marin Dr Ste A110, Novato
(94945-1302)
PHONE....................415 899-7300
EMP: 130
SALES (corp-wide): 11.6B **Publicly Held**
SIC: 7374
PA: Automatic Data Processing, Inc.
1 Adp Blvd Ste 1
Roseland NJ 07068
973 974-5000

(P-15728)
AUTOMATIC DATA PROCESSING INC
Also Called: ADP
3972 Barranca Pkwy J610, Irvine
(92606-1204)
PHONE....................949 751-0360
EMP: 165
SALES (corp-wide): 14.1B **Publicly Held**
SIC: 7374 Data processing service
PA: Automatic Data Processing, Inc.
1 Adp Blvd Ste 1 # 1
Roseland NJ 07068
973 974-5000

(P-15729)
AUTOMATIC DATA PROCESSING INC
Also Called: ADP
820 N Mccarthy Blvd # 120, Milpitas
(95035-5115)
PHONE....................408 876-6600

Robert Thomas, *Branch Mgr*
Meghan Giz, *Vice Pres*
Chris Canales, *District Mgr*
Megan Rice, *District Mgr*
EMP: 450
SALES (corp-wide): 14.1B **Publicly Held**
SIC: 7374 8721 Data processing service;
accounting, auditing & bookkeeping
PA: Automatic Data Processing, Inc.
1 Adp Blvd Ste 1 # 1
Roseland NJ 07068
973 974-5000

(P-15730)
AUTOMATIC DATA PROCESSING INC
Also Called: ADP
5355 Orangethorpe Ave, La Palma
(90623-1095)
PHONE....................714 994-2000
Jim Wassik, *Branch Mgr*
John Oravitz, *District Mgr*
Wanda Mamaradlo, *Info Tech Dir*
Megan Shepler, *Sales Executive*
EMP: 78
SALES (corp-wide): 14.1B **Publicly Held**
SIC: 7374 Data processing service
PA: Automatic Data Processing, Inc.
1 Adp Blvd Ste 1 # 1
Roseland NJ 07068
973 974-5000

(P-15731)
AUTOMATIC DATA PROCESSING INC
Also Called: ADP
400 W Covina Blvd, San Dimas
(91773-2954)
PHONE....................800 225-5237
Rodney Hroblak, *Principal*
Robert Barnett, *Vice Pres*
Jorge Gonzalez, *District Mgr*
Mike Tsao, *Programmer Anys*
Susan Gabriel, *Business Anlyst*
EMP: 117
SALES (corp-wide): 14.1B **Publicly Held**
SIC: 7374 8721 Data processing service;
accounting, auditing & bookkeeping
PA: Automatic Data Processing, Inc.
1 Adp Blvd Ste 1 # 1
Roseland NJ 07068
973 974-5000

(P-15732)
AUTOMATIC DATA PROCESSING INC
Also Called: ADP
600 Crprate Pinte Ste 450, Los Angeles
(90230)
PHONE....................800 225-5237
Kevin Gramian, *Manager*
Harsit Patel, *Vice Pres*
Alex Lara Pmp, *Project Mgr*
Ajit Kumar, *Chief*
Luisa Quezada, *Accounts Mgr*
EMP: 70
SALES (corp-wide): 14.1B **Publicly Held**
SIC: 7374 8721 Data processing service;
payroll accounting service
PA: Automatic Data Processing, Inc.
1 Adp Blvd Ste 1 # 1
Roseland NJ 07068
973 974-5000

(P-15733)
AUTOMATIC DATA PROCESSING INC
Also Called: ADP
1450 Frazee Rd Ste 601, San Diego
(92108-4340)
PHONE....................619 293-4800
David Manriquez, *Branch Mgr*
Jason Ducoffe, *District Mgr*
EMP: 100
SALES (corp-wide): 14.1B **Publicly Held**
SIC: 7374 Data processing service
PA: Automatic Data Processing, Inc.
1 Adp Blvd Ste 1 # 1
Roseland NJ 07068
973 974-5000

(P-15734)
BLEACHER REPORT INC
609 Mission St, San Francisco
(94105-3506)
PHONE....................415 777-5505
Mike Jacobsen, *CFO*
Miguel Deavila, *Vice Pres*
Chris Nguyen, *Vice Pres*
Alex Vargas, *Vice Pres*
Joe Yanarella, *Vice Pres*
EMP: 65
SALES: 5.4MM **Privately Held**
SIC: 7374 Computer graphics service

(P-15735)
CALIFORNIA SURVEY RES SVCS
19849 Nordhoff St, Northridge
(91324-3331)
PHONE....................818 780-2777
William Kaplan, *CEO*
Kenneth Gross, *President*
Terrie Kerr, *Research*
EMP: 125
SALES (est): 8.4MM **Privately Held**
WEB: www.calsurvey.com
SIC: 7374 8732 Data processing service;
market analysis or research

(P-15736)
CALIFRNIA HLTH HUMN SRVCS AGCY
Also Called: Hhsa Data Center
3301 S St, Sacramento (95816-7019)
PHONE....................916 739-7640
John Moise, *Director*
EMP: 500 **Privately Held**
SIC: 7374 9431 Data processing & prepa-
ration; administration of public health pro-
grams;
HQ: California Health & Human Services
Agency
1600 9th St Ste 460
Sacramento CA 95814

(P-15737)
CASTLIGHT HEALTH INC (PA)
150 Spear St Ste 400, San Francisco
(94105-1535)
PHONE....................415 829-1400
Maeve O'Meara, *CEO*
Siobhan Nolan Mangini, *President*
Seth Cohen, *Bd of Directors*
Ed Park, *Bd of Directors*
David Singer, *Bd of Directors*
EMP: 109
SQ FT: 44,580
SALES: 156.4MM **Publicly Held**
SIC: 7374 7372 Data processing & prepa-
ration; prepackaged software

(P-15738)
CCH INCORPORATED
Also Called: Cch Computax
20101 Hamilton Ave # 200, Torrance
(90502-1371)
PHONE....................310 800-9800
Jessica Perez, *Human Res Mgr*
Srinivas Lingineni, *Technology*
EMP: 350
SQ FT: 280,000
SALES (corp-wide): 4.8B **Privately Held**
WEB: www.cch.com
SIC: 7374 7372 7371 Data processing &
preparation; prepackaged software; cus-
tom computer programming services
HQ: Cch Incorporated
2700 Lake Cook Rd
Riverwoods IL 60015
847 267-7000

(P-15739)
CHANGE HLTHCARE OPERATIONS LLC
241 Lombard St, Thousand Oaks
(91360-5807)
PHONE....................805 777-7773
Bob Ashworth, *Branch Mgr*
EMP: 75
SALES (corp-wide): 214.3B **Publicly Held**
SIC: 7374 8742 Data processing service;
hospital & health services consultant

HQ: Change Healthcare Operations, Llc
3055 Lebanon Pike # 1000
Nashville TN 37214
-

(P-15740)
COMMUNITY HOSPITALS CENTL CAL
Also Called: Information Services Dept
1140 T St, Fresno (93721-1413)
P.O. Box 9732 (93794-9732)
PHONE.................................559 459-2916
Terri Lutz, *Branch Mgr*
Steven Nichols, *Administration*
Eric Rystad, *Sr Ntwrk Engine*
Joshua Powell, *Programmer Anys*
Michael Childs, *Manager*
EMP: 150
SALES (corp-wide): 1.6B **Privately Held**
SIC: 7374 8741 8062 Data processing & preparation; hospital management; hospital, AMA approved residency
PA: Community Hospitals Of Central California
2823 Fresno St
Fresno CA 93721
559 459-6000

(P-15741)
CORRECTONS RHBLTATION CAL DEPT
Also Called: Data Center
1920 Alabama Ave, Sacramento (95825)
P.O. Box 942883 (94283-0001)
PHONE.................................916 358-2319
Joe Penora, *Director*
EMP: 200 **Privately Held**
SIC: 7374 9223 Data processing service; correctional institutions;
HQ: California Department Of Corrections & Rehabilitation
1515 S St
Sacramento CA 95811
-

(P-15742)
COUNTY OF LOS ANGELES
Also Called: Voter Precinct Voter Reg Off
12400 Imperial Hwy, Norwalk (90650-3134)
PHONE.................................562 462-2094
Connie McCormack, *Branch Mgr*
EMP: 800 **Privately Held**
WEB: www.co.la.ca.us
SIC: 7374 9111 Data entry service; executive offices
PA: County Of Los Angeles
500 W Temple St Ste 437
Los Angeles CA 90012
213 974-1101

(P-15743)
COUNTY OF MARIN
Also Called: Computer Programming Dept
371 Bel Marin Keys Blvd # 100, Novato (94949-5662)
PHONE.................................415 499-7060
Daze Hill, *Director*
EMP: 80 **Privately Held**
SIC: 7374 9111 Data processing service; county supervisors' & executives' offices
PA: County Of Marin
3501 Civic Center Dr # 258
San Rafael CA 94903
415 473-6358

(P-15744)
COUNTY OF SONOMA
Also Called: Sonoma County Data Processing
2615 Paulin Dr, Santa Rosa (95403-2804)
PHONE.................................707 527-2911
Daniel Fruchey, *Info Tech Dir*
EMP: 150
SQ FT: 13,000 **Privately Held**
WEB: www.sonomacompost.com
SIC: 7374 Data processing service
PA: County Of Sonoma
585 Fiscal Dr 100
Santa Rosa CA 95403
707 565-2431

(P-15745)
COUNTY OF SONOMA
Also Called: Information Systems Department
2300 Prof Dr Rear Door B, Santa Rosa (95403)
PHONE.................................707 527-2911
Mark Walsh, *Branch Mgr*
EMP: 75 **Privately Held**
WEB: www.sonomacompost.com
SIC: 7374 Data processing & preparation
PA: County Of Sonoma
585 Fiscal Dr 100
Santa Rosa CA 95403
707 565-2431

(P-15746)
COUNTY OF TUOLUMNE
Also Called: Information Systems & Services
2 S Green St, Sonora (95370-4618)
PHONE.................................209 533-5561
Gregg Jacob, *Manager*
Jacob Gregg, *Manager*
EMP: 500 **Privately Held**
WEB: www.tuolumne.courts.ca.gov
SIC: 7374 9111 7376 Data processing & preparation; county supervisors' & executives' offices; computer facilities management
PA: County Of Tuolumne
2 S Green St
Sonora CA 95370
209 533-5521

(P-15747)
CYBERSOURCE CORPORATION (HQ)
900 Metro Center Blvd, Foster City (94404-2172)
P.O. Box 8999, San Francisco (94128-8999)
PHONE.................................650 432-7350
Alfred F Kelly Jr, *President*
Scott R Cruickshank, *President*
Steven D Pellizzer, *CFO*
Robert J Ford, *Exec VP*
Perry Dembner, *Senior VP*
EMP: 85
SALES (est): 92.9MM **Publicly Held**
WEB: www.cybersource.com
SIC: 7374 Data processing service

(P-15748)
DECISION MINDS
1525 Mccarthy Blvd # 224, Milpitas (95035-7453)
PHONE.................................408 309-8051
Murali Pabbisetty, *Owner*
Balati Ratagocalan, *Co-Owner*
Vidhya Sridaran, *Opers Mgr*
EMP: 135
SALES: 10MM **Privately Held**
SIC: 7374 Data entry service

(P-15749)
DELUXE MEDIA SERVICES
2130 N Hollywood Way, Burbank (91505-1522)
PHONE.................................818 526-3700
Joe Bigley, *General Mgr*
Eric Goetz, *Opers Staff*
EMP: 500
SALES (est): 33.1MM **Privately Held**
SIC: 7374 Computer graphics service

(P-15750)
DOCLER MEDIA LLC (DH)
8000 Beverly Blvd, Los Angeles (90048-4504)
PHONE.................................424 777-3999
Balazs Sipocz, *CEO*
David Duel, *Director*
EMP: 62
SQ FT: 30,000
SALES: 22.3MM
SALES (corp-wide): 94.4K **Privately Held**
SIC: 7374 8741 Computer graphics service; computer processing services; administrative management
HQ: Docler Holding
Av. J.-F. Kennedy 44
Luxembourg 1855
261 118-1

(P-15751)
DOCUMENT PROC SOLUTIONS INC (PA)
Also Called: Southern California Document
590 W Lambert Rd, Brea (92821-3914)
PHONE.................................714 482-2060
Felipe Heras, *President*
Dave Sherman, *Info Tech Dir*
Rodolfo Gutierrez, *Info Tech Mgr*
Guadalupe Garcia, *Project Mgr*
Lisa Ritter, *Accounting Mgr*
EMP: 85
SALES (est): 8.5MM **Privately Held**
WEB: www.dpsx.com
SIC: 7374 Data processing service

(P-15752)
E C WISE INC (PA)
1299 4th St Ste 505, San Rafael (94901-3031)
PHONE.................................415 355-9473
Jack Hakim, *CEO*
Tom Spitzer, *CFO*
Jereff Ye, *Software Dev*
EMP: 100 EST: 1998
SQ FT: 6,600
SALES (est): 8.5MM **Privately Held**
WEB: www.ecwise.com
SIC: 7374 Data processing service

(P-15753)
EDATA SOLUTIONS INC
39180 Liberty St Ste 125, Fremont (94538-2581)
PHONE.................................510 574-5380
Manan Kothari, *CEO*
EMP: 1000
SQ FT: 6,000
SALES: 4.7MM **Privately Held**
SIC: 7374 7371 Data processing service; computer software development & applications

(P-15754)
EMERALD CONNECT LLC (HQ)
15050 Avenue Of Sci 200, San Diego (92128)
PHONE.................................800 233-2834
Adam D Amsterdam, *Mng Member*
Sharon Greener, *Exec VP*
Heather Hinkle, *Exec VP*
Heidi Saucier, *Exec VP*
Travis Mayne, *Vice Pres*
EMP: 100
SQ FT: 35,000
SALES (est): 19.1MM
SALES (corp-wide): 4.3B **Publicly Held**
WEB: emeraldconnect.com
SIC: 7374 7331 Data processing service; mailing service
PA: Broadridge Financial Solutions, Inc.
5 Dakota Dr Ste 300
New Hyde Park NY 11042
516 472-5400

(P-15755)
EMOVE EXPRESS COMPANY
Also Called: Emovexpress.com
688 Matsonia Dr, Foster City (94404-1337)
PHONE.................................650 377-0913
Anthony Chiu, *Ch of Bd*
Steve Argyres, *President*
Teresa Hall, *CFO*
EMP: 56
SQ FT: 2,760
SALES (est): 2MM **Privately Held**
WEB: www.emoveexpress.com
SIC: 7374 Computer graphics service

(P-15756)
ENTERPRISE SERVICES LLC
3215 Prospect Park Dr, Rancho Cordova (95670-6017)
PHONE.................................916 636-1000
Dennis Dormen, *Manager*
EMP: 800
SALES (corp-wide): 11.5B **Publicly Held**
WEB: www.eds.com
SIC: 7374 Data processing service
HQ: Perspecta Enterprise Solutions Llc
13600 Eds Dr A3s
Herndon VA 20171
703 245-9675

(P-15757)
ENTERPRISE SERVICES LLC
3990 Sherman St, San Diego (92110-4324)
PHONE.................................619 817-3851
Javier Berellez, *Manager*
EMP: 350
SALES (corp-wide): 11.5B **Publicly Held**
WEB: www.eds.com
SIC: 7374 Data processing & preparation
HQ: Perspecta Enterprise Solutions Llc
13600 Eds Dr A3s
Herndon VA 20171
703 245-9675

(P-15758)
ENTERPRISE SERVICES LLC
1 Hornet Way, El Segundo (90245-2804)
PHONE.................................310 331-1074
Nelson Lee, *Branch Mgr*
EMP: 138
SALES (corp-wide): 11.5B **Publicly Held**
WEB: www.eds.com
SIC: 7374 Data processing service
HQ: Perspecta Enterprise Solutions Llc
13600 Eds Dr A3s
Herndon VA 20171
703 245-9675

(P-15759)
EPOCHCOM LLC
3110 Main St Ste 220, Santa Monica (90405-5353)
PHONE.................................310 664-5700
Joel Hall, *Mng Member*
Esther Martinez, *COO*
Harmik Gharapetian, *Vice Pres*
Christine Hull, *Vice Pres*
David Bonsukan, *Risk Mgmt Dir*
EMP: 150
SQ FT: 22,000
SALES (est): 14.9MM **Privately Held**
SIC: 7374 Data processing service

(P-15760)
FIERCE WOMBAT GAMES INC
910 E Hamilton Ave Fl 6, Campbell (95008-0655)
PHONE.................................408 745-5400
Jonathan Buckheit, *CEO*
EMP: 50 EST: 2010
SQ FT: 10,000
SALES: 50MM **Privately Held**
SIC: 7374 7371 Computer graphics service; computer software development & applications

(P-15761)
FIGURE EIGHT TECHNOLOGIES INC
940 Howard St, San Francisco (94103-4114)
PHONE.................................415 471-1920
Lukas Biewald, *CEO*
Christopher Van Pelt, *COO*
Ryan Ferrier, *Vice Pres*
Sheel Gupta, *Vice Pres*
Alyssa Simpson Rochwerger, *Vice Pres*
EMP: 60
SQ FT: 8,400
SALES: 7.5MM **Privately Held**
SIC: 7374 Computer graphics service

(P-15762)
FIRST DATABANK INC
701 Gateway Blvd Ste 600, San Francisco (94188)
PHONE.................................650 588-5454
Joe Hirshmann, *Branch Mgr*
Joseph Palermo, *President*
Amanda Johnston, *Office Mgr*
EMP: 100
SQ FT: 3,000
SALES (corp-wide): 8.3B **Privately Held**
WEB: www.firstdatabank.com
SIC: 7374 Data processing service
HQ: First Databank, Inc.
701 Gateway Blvd Ste 600
South San Francisco CA 94080
800 633-3453

(P-15763)
FISERV INC
19935 E Walnut Dr N, City of Industry (91789-2818)
PHONE.................................909 595-9074
Mark Breithaupt, *Manager*

P R O D U C T S & S V C S

EMP: 79
SALES (corp-wide): 5.8B **Publicly Held**
WEB: www.fiserv.com
SIC: 7374 Data processing service
PA: Fiserv, Inc.
    255 Fiserv Dr
    Brookfield WI 53045
    262 879-5000

(P-15764)
FISERV INC
19935 E Walnut Dr N, Walnut
(91789-2818)
PHONE.....................909 598-8700
Bill Costello, *Manager*
EMP: 72
SALES (corp-wide): 5.8B **Publicly Held**
SIC: 7374 Data processing service
PA: Fiserv, Inc.
    255 Fiserv Dr
    Brookfield WI 53045
    262 879-5000

(P-15765)
FISERV INC
525 Almanor Ave, Sunnyvale (94085-3542)
PHONE.....................408 242-3011
EMP: 70
SALES (corp-wide): 5.8B **Publicly Held**
SIC: 7374 Data processing service
PA: Fiserv, Inc.
    255 Fiserv Dr
    Brookfield WI 53045
    262 879-5000

(P-15766)
FISERV INC
405 Science Dr, Moorpark (93021-2247)
PHONE.....................805 532-9100
John Edwards, *Branch Mgr*
EMP: 71
SALES (corp-wide): 5.8B **Publicly Held**
SIC: 7374 7371 Data processing service;
    computer software development & appli-
    cations
PA: Fiserv, Inc.
    255 Fiserv Dr
    Brookfield WI 53045
    262 879-5000

(P-15767)
FISERV INC
8413 Fallbrook Ave, West Hills
(91304-3226)
PHONE.....................818 226-4400
William Braden, *Senior VP*
EMP: 100
SALES (corp-wide): 5.8B **Publicly Held**
SIC: 7374 Data processing service
PA: Fiserv, Inc.
    255 Fiserv Dr
    Brookfield WI 53045
    262 879-5000

(P-15768)
FISERV INC
19935 E Walnut Dr N, Walnut
(91789-2818)
PHONE.....................909 595-9074
Jeff Conte, *Manager*
EMP: 62
SALES (corp-wide): 5.8B **Publicly Held**
WEB: www.fiserv.com
SIC: 7374 Data processing service
PA: Fiserv, Inc.
    255 Fiserv Dr
    Brookfield WI 53045
    262 879-5000

(P-15769)
GENERAL SERVICES CAL DEPT
Office Physical Plg & Dev Csu
4665 Lampson Ave, Los Alamitos
(90720-5187)
PHONE.....................562 342-7212
James K Hightower, *Branch Mgr*
EMP: 100 **Privately Held**
WEB: www.4c.net
SIC: 7374 9199 Data processing service;
    general government administration;
HQ: California Department Of General
    Services
    707 3rd St
    West Sacramento CA 95605

(P-15770)
GLINT INC
1100 Island Dr Ste 101, Redwood City
(94065-5187)
PHONE.....................650 817-7240
Jim Barnett, *CEO*
Dennis Jang, *CFO*
Mary Poppen, *Ch Credit Ofcr*
Jim Bell, *Chief Mktg Ofcr*
Marc Maloy, *Officer*
EMP: 100
SQ FT: 12,500
SALES: 5MM **Privately Held**
SIC: 7374 Data processing & preparation

(P-15771)
GREENSOFT TECHNOLOGY INC
155 S El Molino Ave # 100, Pasadena
(91101-2563)
PHONE.....................323 254-5961
Larry Yen, *President*
Jon Wu, *Vice Pres*
Jill Zhou, *Project Engr*
EMP: 121
SALES (est): 1.7MM **Privately Held**
SIC: 7374 Data processing service

(P-15772)
HACKERONE INC (PA)
22 4th St Fl 5, San Francisco (94103-3173)
P.O. Box 166 (94104-0166)
PHONE.....................415 891-0777
Alex Rice, *CTO*
Marten Mickos, *CEO*
Elizabeth Brittain, *CFO*
Timothy Darosa, *Vice Pres*
Meredith Baker, *Executive Asst*
EMP: 260
SQ FT: 16,374
SALES (est): 8.4MM **Privately Held**
SIC: 7374 Data processing & preparation

(P-15773)
HEALTH DATA VISION INC (PA)
425 W Broadway Ste 100, Glendale
(91204-1269)
PHONE.....................866 969-3222
Jay Ackerman, *President*
Rita Young, *COO*
Ryan Peterson, *Senior VP*
EMP: 67
SQ FT: 2,200
SALES (est): 9.9MM **Privately Held**
WEB: www.healthdatavision.com
SIC: 7374 Data processing & preparation

(P-15774)
HONK TECHNOLOGIES INC
2251 Barry Ave, Los Angeles (90064-1401)
PHONE.....................800 979-3162
Corey Brundage, *CEO*
Dan Rosenthal, *Exec VP*
Rochelle Thielen, *Exec VP*
EMP: 85
SQ FT: 8,000
SALES: 24MM **Privately Held**
SIC: 7374 7372 7371 Data processing &
    preparation; business oriented computer
    software; custom computer programming
    services

(P-15775)
HYVE SOLUTIONS CORPORATION (HQ)
44201 Nobel Dr, Fremont (94538-3178)
PHONE.....................855 869-6873
Kevin Murai, *CEO*
Peter Larocque, *President*
Fili Ledezma, *Vice Pres*
Sarah Lin, *Admin Sec*
Julia Fu, *Software Engr*
▲ EMP: 3645
SALES (est): 4.4MM
SALES (corp-wide): 20B **Publicly Held**
SIC: 7374 Data processing & preparation
PA: Synnex Corporation
    44201 Nobel Dr
    Fremont CA 94538
    510 656-3333

(P-15776)
I HOT LEADS
19671 Beach Blvd Ste 204, Huntington
Beach (92648-5905)
PHONE.....................714 960-8028
EMP: 56

SALES (est): 1.9MM **Privately Held**
WEB: www.ihotleads.com
SIC: 7374

(P-15777)
I MERIT INC
14435c Big Basin Way, Saratoga
(95070-6008)
PHONE.....................504 226-2427
Rahda Basu, *CEO*
EMP: 1965
SALES (corp-wide): 9.5MM **Privately Held**
SIC: 7374 Data processing & preparation
PA: I Merit Inc.
    1515 Poydras St Ste 2400
    New Orleans LA 70112
    650 777-7857

(P-15778)
IKANO COMMUNICATIONS INC (PA)
Also Called: A & S Technologies
9221 Corbin Ave Ste 260, Northridge
(91324-1625)
PHONE.....................801 924-0900
Jim Murphy, *CEO*
Sam Ghahremanpour, *President*
George Mitsopoulos, *COO*
Dean Russ, *Vice Pres*
EMP: 91
SQ FT: 50,000
SALES (est): 32.7MM **Privately Held**
WEB: www.ikano.com
SIC: 7374 Data processing & preparation

(P-15779)
IMAGESCAN INC
390 S Fair Oaks Ave, Pasadena
(91105-2540)
PHONE.....................626 844-2050
Basker S Krishnan, *President*
Hanoz Kateli, *CIO*
Meher Kateli, *Manager*
EMP: 90
SQ FT: 4,000
SALES (est): 5MM **Privately Held**
WEB: www.imagescan-inc.com
SIC: 7374 Data entry service

(P-15780)
INFLECTION RISK SOLUTIONS LLC
Also Called: Goodhire
555 Twin Dolphin Dr # 63, Redwood City
(94065-2129)
PHONE.....................650 618-9910
Matthew Monahan, *Mng Member*
Jeff Newcombe, *Regl Sales Mgr*
David Brown, *Sales Staff*
EMP: 50
SQ FT: 7,000
SALES: 5MM
SALES (corp-wide): 7.5MM **Privately Held**
SIC: 7374 Data processing & preparation
PA: Inflection.Com, Inc.
    555 Twin Dolphin Dr # 630
    Redwood City CA 94065
    650 618-9910

(P-15781)
INKO INDUSTRIAL CORPORATION
695 Vaqueros Ave, Sunnyvale
(94085-3524)
PHONE.....................408 830-1040
George Kuo, *President*
Teresa Kuo, *Executive*
Charlie Chau, *Facilities Mgr*
▲ EMP: 100
SQ FT: 80,000
SALES (est): 9.9MM **Privately Held**
WEB: www.pellicle-inko.com
SIC: 7374 Computer graphics service

(P-15782)
INTERNET BRANDS INC (PA)
909 N Pacific Coast Hwy # 11, El Segundo
(90245-2727)
PHONE.....................310 280-4000
Robert N Brisco, *CEO*
Paul Austin, *Partner*
Gregory T Perrier, *President*
Lisa Morita, *COO*

Scott Friedman, *CFO*
▲ EMP: 148
SQ FT: 54,000
SALES (est): 284.6MM **Privately Held**
WEB: www.carsdirect.com
SIC: 7374 Computer graphics service

(P-15783)
LEIDOS INC
Also Called: Sissc
1550 N Norma St, Ridgecrest
(93555-2556)
PHONE.....................858 826-7670
Doreen Ross, *Branch Mgr*
EMP: 253
SALES (corp-wide): 10.1B **Publicly Held**
WEB: www.saic.com
SIC: 7374 7373 Data processing & prepa-
    ration; systems integration services
HQ: Leidos, Inc.
    11951 Freedom Dr Ste 500
    Reston VA 20190
    571 526-6000

(P-15784)
LENDER PROCESSING SERVICES INC
3100 New York Dr Ste 200, Pasadena
(91107-1524)
PHONE.....................626 808-9000
Brian Mushaney, *Vice Pres*
Aimee Hartmann, *Principal*
EMP: 99
SALES (est): 6MM **Privately Held**
SIC: 7374 Data processing & preparation

(P-15785)
LOS ANGELES UNIFIED SCHOOL DST
Also Called: Information Technology Agency
200 N Main St Ste 1400, Los Angeles
(90012-4127)
PHONE.....................213 847-6911
Jesse Juarros, *Manager*
EMP: 700
SALES (corp-wide): 4B **Privately Held**
WEB: www.lausd.k12.ca.us
SIC: 7374 Data processing service
PA: Los Angeles Unified School District
    333 S Beaudry Ave Ste 209
    Los Angeles CA 90017
    213 241-1000

(P-15786)
MARIN SOFTWARE INCORPORATED (PA)
123 Mission St Fl 27, San Francisco
(94105-1681)
PHONE.....................415 399-2580
Christopher Lien, *Ch of Bd*
Nicklas Wandel, *Administration*
Brian Cary, *Sr Software Eng*
Jonathan Chase, *Sr Software Eng*
Claire Choe, *Sr Software Eng*
EMP: 137
SQ FT: 43,000
SALES: 58.6MM **Publicly Held**
SIC: 7374 Data processing & preparation

(P-15787)
MERCHANT SERVICES INC (PA)
1 S Van Ness Ave Fl 5, San Francisco
(94103-5416)
PHONE.....................817 725-0900
Lorraine Stimmell, *CEO*
Le Tran-Tl, *Senior VP*
Beth Dobyns, *Human Res Mgr*
Andrew Kellerman, *Accounts Exec*
EMP: 400
SQ FT: 58,336
SALES (est): 34MM **Privately Held**
WEB: www.msimerchantservices.com
SIC: 7374 Data processing service

(P-15788)
MERCURY DEFENSE SYSTEMS INC (HQ)
Also Called: Mercury Systems
10855 Bus Ctr Dr Bldg A, Cypress (90630)
PHONE.....................714 898-8200
Mark Aslett, *CEO*
Brian Perry, *President*
Kevin M Bisson, *CFO*
Emma Woodthorpe, *Officer*
Gerald M Haines II, *Senior VP*

EMP: 84
SQ FT: 35,000
SALES (est): 17.6MM
SALES (corp-wide): 654.7MM **Publicly Held**
WEB: www.korelectronics.com
SIC: 7374 Data processing service
PA: Mercury Systems, Inc.
50 Minuteman Rd
Andover MA 01810
978 256-1300

(P-15789)
MICRO HOLDING CORP
1 Maritime Plz Fl 12, San Francisco (94111-3404)
PHONE..............415 788-5111
Warren Hellman, *President*
EMP: 650
SALES (est): 144.2MM **Privately Held**
SIC: 7374 7389 Computer graphics service; advertising, promotional & trade show services
PA: Hellman & Friedman Llc
1 Maritime Plz Ste 1200
San Francisco CA 94111

(P-15790)
MINDBODY INC (PA)
4051 Broad St Ste 220, San Luis Obispo (93401-8723)
PHONE..............877 755-4279
Richard Stollmeyer, *Ch of Bd*
Michael Mansbach, *President*
Josh McCarter, *President*
Michelle Benich, *COO*
Brett White, *COO*
EMP: 109
SQ FT: 160,000
SALES (est): 182.6MM **Privately Held**
SIC: 7374 7372 8741 Data processing & preparation; business oriented computer software; business management

(P-15791)
MOCANA CORPORATION
111 W Evelyn Ave Ste 210, Sunnyvale (94086-6129)
PHONE..............415 617-0055
James Isaacs, *CEO*
Najib Khouri-Haddad, *President*
Jeanne Angelo-Pardo, *CFO*
Hope Frank, *Chief Mktg Ofcr*
Steve Adelman, *Vice Pres*
EMP: 67
SALES (est): 10MM **Privately Held**
WEB: www.mocana.com
SIC: 7374 7379 Computer graphics service;

(P-15792)
MOCEAN LLC
2440 S Sepulveda Blvd # 150, Los Angeles (90064-1786)
PHONE..............310 481-0808
Craig R Murray, *Mng Member*
Stuart Boone, *President*
Michael McIntyre, *President*
Cori Sessions, *Executive Asst*
Tim Baker, *Technical Staff*
EMP: 200 EST: 2000
SALES (est): 27.1MM **Privately Held**
SIC: 7374 7822 Computer graphics service; motion picture distribution

(P-15793)
MOCHANIN LLC
Also Called: Mochahost.com
2880 Zanker Rd Ste 203, San Jose (95134-2122)
PHONE..............408 432-7259
Hristo Angelov, *Mng Member*
Chris Angelov, *Project Mgr*
Jim Truong, *VP Sales*
Radostin Savov, *Mng Member*
EMP: 60
SALES (est): 211.3K **Privately Held**
SIC: 7374 Computer graphics service

(P-15794)
NETBASE SOLUTIONS INC (PA)
3960 Freedom Cir 201, Santa Clara (95054-1449)
PHONE..............650 810-2100
Peter M Caswell, *CEO*

David Pefley, *CFO*
Paige Leidig, *Chief Mktg Ofcr*
EMP: 65
SQ FT: 23,344
SALES (est): 29MM **Privately Held**
WEB: www.accelovation.com
SIC: 7374 Data processing service

(P-15795)
OOMA INC (PA)
525 Almanor Ave Ste 200, Sunnyvale (94085-3542)
PHONE..............650 566-6600
Eric B Stang, *Ch of Bd*
Ravi Narula, *CFO*
Jenny C Yeh, *Vice Pres*
James A Gustke, *VP Mktg*
▲ EMP: 148
SQ FT: 33,400
SALES (est): 129.2MM **Publicly Held**
WEB: www.ooma.com
SIC: 7374 4813 Data processing & preparation;

(P-15796)
PANTHEON SYSTEMS INC (PA)
717 California St, San Francisco (94108-2455)
PHONE..............855 927-9387
Zachary Rosen, *CEO*
David Strauss, *Founder*
Mark Etchin, *Vice Pres*
Steven Juanes, *Info Tech Mgr*
Michelle Krejci, *Software Engr*
EMP: 93
SALES (est): 10MM **Privately Held**
SIC: 7374 Data processing & preparation

(P-15797)
PINE DATA PROCESSING INC
Also Called: Pine Company
10559 Jefferson Blvd, Culver City (90232-3526)
P.O. Box 641836, Los Angeles (90064-6836)
PHONE..............310 815-5700
Ben Pine, *Chairman*
Ken Holsenbeck, *President*
Carol Lewis, *Vice Pres*
EMP: 72
SQ FT: 11,500
SALES (est): 3.9MM **Privately Held**
WEB: www.pinedata.com
SIC: 7374 Data processing service

(P-15798)
PLANET LABS INC (PA)
645 Harrison St Fl 4, San Francisco (94107-3624)
PHONE..............415 829-3313
William Marshall, *CEO*
Leeza Frantz, *Partner*
Shireen Khan, *Partner*
Tom Barton, *COO*
Nate Dickerman, *Officer*
EMP: 92
SQ FT: 25,000
SALES (est): 105.6MM **Privately Held**
SIC: 7374 Data processing service

(P-15799)
PLEX SYSTEMS INC
4305 Hacienda Dr Ste 500, Pleasanton (94588-8586)
PHONE..............248 391-8001
EMP: 139 **Privately Held**
SIC: 7374 Data processing & preparation
PA: Plex Systems, Inc.
900 Tower Dr Ste 1500
Troy MI 48098

(P-15800)
PRICEMETRIX USA INC
3 Bridgeport Rd, Newport Coast (92657-1014)
PHONE..............714 357-6192
Brent Geddes, *CFO*
Doug Trott, *President*
EMP: 50
SALES (est): 1.5MM **Privately Held**
SIC: 7374 Data processing service

(P-15801)
PROSUM INC (PA)
Also Called: Prosum Technology Services
2201 Park Pl Ste 102, El Segundo (90245-5167)
PHONE..............310 426-0600
Ravi Chatwani, *CEO*
Emily Fortenberry, *Partner*
Jimmy Lee, *Partner*
John Petri, *CFO*
Ken Aster, *Vice Pres*
EMP: 57 EST: 1996
SALES (est): 31.1MM **Privately Held**
WEB: www.prosum.com
SIC: 7374 8748 Computer graphics service; systems engineering consultant, ex. computer or professional

(P-15802)
PROTECTIVE BUSINESS & HEALTH
Also Called: Pbs Paymaster Sales & Service
3785 Brickway Blvd # 200, Santa Rosa (95403-9033)
PHONE..............845 354-5372
Jay Levine, *President*
Jenny Liu, *Prgrmr*
Roxanne Zettler, *Marketing Staff*
Kelli Pulido, *Director*
Leah Berlin, *Receptionist*
EMP: 90
SALES (est): 7.5MM **Privately Held**
SIC: 7374 8742 Computer graphics service; marketing consulting services

(P-15803)
PROTOSOURCE CORPORATION
2511 W Shaw Ave Ste 102, Fresno (93711-3325)
PHONE..............559 490-8600
Andy Chu, *Principal*
EMP: 54
SALES (corp-wide): 9.3MM **Publicly Held**
SIC: 7374 Data processing service
PA: Protosource Corporation
1236 Main St Ste 3
Hellertown PA 18055
610 814-0550

(P-15804)
QUALITY INV PRPTS SCRMENTO LLC
Also Called: Quality Tech Svcs Sacramento
1100 N Market Blvd, Sacramento (95834-1931)
PHONE..............916 679-2100
EMP: 78
SALES (est): 1.4MM
SALES (corp-wide): 446.5MM **Privately Held**
SIC: 7374
HQ: Qualitytech, Lp
12851 Foster St
Overland Park KS 66213

(P-15805)
QUESTUS INC (PA)
3350 E Birch St Ste 110, Brea (92821-6290)
PHONE..............415 677-5719
Jordan Berg, *CEO*
Will Chamberlin, *Vice Pres*
Debbie Dumont, *Vice Pres*
Jeff Wagener, *Vice Pres*
Sheila Ang, *Admin Asst*
EMP: 50
SQ FT: 4,000
SALES (est): 11.7MM **Privately Held**
WEB: www.questus.com
SIC: 7374 Computer graphics service

(P-15806)
RESEARCH OF AMERICA
1232 Q St Ste 100, Sacramento (95811-5801)
PHONE..............916 443-4722
Rob Porber, *Owner*
Robert Proctor, *Vice Pres*
EMP: 135
SQ FT: 7,300
SALES (est): 7.4MM **Privately Held**
WEB: www.emhopinions.com
SIC: 7374 Data verification service

(P-15807)
RINGCENTRAL INC (PA)
20 Davis Dr, Belmont (94002-3002)
PHONE..............650 472-4100
Vladimir Shmunis, *Ch of Bd*
David Sipes, *COO*
Mitesh Dhruv, *CFO*
John Marlow, *Officer*
Ritu Mukherjee, *Assoc VP*
▲ EMP: 80
SQ FT: 110,000
SALES: 673.6MM **Publicly Held**
WEB: www.ringcentral.com
SIC: 7374 4899 Data processing & preparation; data communication services

(P-15808)
ROCKSTAR SAN DIEGO
2200 Faraday Ave Ste 200, Carlsbad (92008-7233)
PHONE..............760 929-0700
Allan Wasserman, *President*
Kelly Gibson, *Human Res Dir*
David Counts, *Facilities Mgr*
EMP: 125
SQ FT: 24,000
SALES (est): 7.7MM **Publicly Held**
WEB: www.rockstarsandiego.com
SIC: 7374 7372 Computer graphics service; prepackaged software
PA: Take-Two Interactive Software, Inc.
110 W 44th St
New York NY 10036

(P-15809)
RUBRIK INC (PA)
1001 Page Mill Rd Bldg 2, Palo Alto (94304-1008)
PHONE..............650 300-5862
Bipul Sinha, *CEO*
Arvind Jain, *Founder*
Arvind Nithrakashyap, *Founder*
Wendy Bahr, *Ch Credit Ofcr*
Peter McGoff,
EMP: 83
SQ FT: 54,000
SALES (est): 172.4MM **Privately Held**
SIC: 7374 7371 Data processing & preparation; computer software development & applications

(P-15810)
SANTA CRUZ COUNTY OF
Also Called: Information Services
701 Ocean St Rm 530, Santa Cruz (95060-4015)
PHONE..............831 454-2030
Kevin Bowling, *Director*
EMP: 70 **Privately Held**
WEB: www.scsheriff.com
SIC: 7374 Computer processing services
PA: County Of Santa Cruz
701 Ocean St Rm 520
Santa Cruz CA 95060
831 454-2100

(P-15811)
SECURE ONE DATA SOLUTIONS LLC
11090 Artesia Blvd Ste D, Cerritos (90703-2545)
PHONE..............562 924-7056
David Sandobal, *President*
EMP: 50 **Privately Held**
SIC: 7374 Data punch service; data processing service
PA: Secure One Data Solutions, Llc
2801 N 33rd Ave Ste 1
Phoenix AZ 85009

(P-15812)
SHOPPINGCOM INC
199 Fremont St Fl 4, San Francisco (94105-6634)
PHONE..............650 616-6500
Gautam Thakar, *CEO*
Amir Ashkenazi, *President*
Hendrik Krampe, *CFO*
Robert J Krolik, *CFO*
EMP: 230
SALES (est): 14.2MM **Publicly Held**
SIC: 7374 Data processing & preparation

PA: Ebay Inc.
2025 Hamilton Ave
San Jose CA 95125

(P-15813)
SOCIABLE LABS INC
25 Division St, San Mateo (94402)
PHONE.....................................415 225-8740
Naifan Gabbay, *President*
Sebastien Brault, *Vice Pres*
EMP: 50
SQ FT: 1,500
SALES (est): 3MM **Privately Held**
SIC: 7374 Computer graphics service

(P-15814)
SOCIETY6 LLC
1655 26th St, Santa Monica (90404-4016)
PHONE.....................................310 394-6400
Sean Moriarty,
Andrea Stanford, *Vice Pres*
Dennis Yu, *Business Dir*
Rory Wood, *Marketing Staff*
EMP: 50
SQ FT: 25,000
SALES (est): 2.1MM **Publicly Held**
SIC: 7374 Computer graphics service
PA: Demand One Media Llc
1655 26th St
Santa Monica CA 90404

(P-15815)
SONY PICTURES IMAGEWORKS INC
9050 Washington Blvd, Culver City
(90232-2518)
PHONE.....................................310 840-8000
Bob Osher, *President*
Ken Ralston, *Principal*
Ryan Cushman, *Info Tech Mgr*
Laide Agunbiade, *Technical Staff*
Craig Feifarek, *Technical Staff*
EMP: 1000 EST: 1992
SALES (est): 98.4MM **Privately Held**
WEB: www.sonypictures.com
HQ: Sony Pictures Entertainment, Inc.
10202 Washington Blvd
Culver City CA 90232
310 244-4000

(P-15816)
SOUTHBAY WEBSITE DESIGN LLC
Also Called: Phone App Company, The
1601 Pcf Cast Hwy Ste 290, Hermosa
Beach (90254)
PHONE.....................................310 370-4043
Allen Rubin,
EMP: 60
SQ FT: 250
SALES (est): 500K **Privately Held**
SIC: 7374 7371 Computer graphics serv-
ice; computer software development &
applications

(P-15817)
STARK SERVICES
12444 Victory Blvd # 300, North Hollywood
(91606-3173)
PHONE.....................................818 985-2003
Maricel Zabel, *President*
Steve Pugh, *Vice Pres*
Carl David, *Marketing Staff*
Lori Stark, *Agent*
EMP: 75
SALES (est): 5.6MM **Privately Held**
WEB: www.starkservices.com
SIC: 7374 Data processing service

(P-15818)
STUBHUB INC (HQ)
Also Called: Stubhub.com
199 Fremont St Fl 4, San Francisco
(94105-6634)
PHONE.....................................415 222-8400
Scott Cutler, *CEO*
Noah Goldberg, *COO*
Ajay Gopal, *CFO*
Jennifer Betka, *Chief Mktg Ofcr*
Raji Arasu, *Vice Pres*
EMP: 107
SQ FT: 20,000

SALES (est): 64.5MM **Publicly Held**
SIC: 7374 7922 Data processing & preparation; ticket agency, theatrical

(P-15819)
SUPPORTCOM INC (PA)
1200 Crossman Ave Ste 210, Sunnyvale
(94089-1123)
PHONE.....................................650 556-9440
Richard A Bloom, *President*
Joshua E Schechter, *Ch of Bd*
Eric Singer, *Bd of Directors*
Eric Hagen, *Vice Pres*
Michelle Johnson, *Vice Pres*
EMP: 88
SQ FT: 6,283
SALES (est): 69.5MM **Publicly Held**
WEB: www.supportsoft.com
SIC: 7374 7372 Data processing & prepa-
ration; business oriented computer soft-
ware

(P-15820)
SURVEYMONKEY INC (HQ)
1 Curiosity Way, San Mateo (94403-2396)
PHONE.....................................650 543-8400
Zander Lurie, *CEO*
David Ebersman, *Ch of Bd*
Tom Hale, *President*
Tim Maly, *COO*
Debbie Clifford, *CFO*
EMP: 60
SQ FT: 200,000
SALES (est): 39.9MM
SALES (corp-wide): 254.3MM **Publicly
Held**
SIC: 7374 8732 Data processing service;
survey service; marketing, location, etc.
PA: Svmk Inc.
1 Curiosity Way
San Mateo CA 94403
650 543-8400

(P-15821)
TASKUS INC (PA)
3221 Donald Douglas, Santa Monica
(90405-3213)
PHONE.....................................888 400-8275
Bryce Maddock, *CEO*
Jaspar Weir, *President*
Joe Buggy, *COO*
Balaji Sekar, *CFO*
Jarrod Johnson, *Ch Credit Ofcr*
EMP: 67 EST: 2008
SQ FT: 17,000
SALES (est): 180.1MM **Privately Held**
SIC: 7374 Data processing service

(P-15822)
TEALIUM INC (PA)
11095 Torreyana Rd Fl 2, San Diego
(92121-1104)
PHONE.....................................858 779-1344
Jeffrey W Lunsford, *CEO*
Sean Browning, *Partner*
Ali Behnam, *President*
Doug Lindroth, *CFO*
Jay Calavas, *Officer*
EMP: 99
SQ FT: 40,864
SALES (est): 46.5MM **Privately Held**
SIC: 7374 7371 Computer graphics serv-
ice; computer software development

(P-15823)
TECHNOLOGY SERVICES CAL DEPT
Also Called: Teale Data Center
10860 Gold Center Dr # 100, Rancho Cor-
dova (95670-6024)
PHONE.....................................916 464-3747
Carlos Ramos, *Exec Dir*
EMP: 50 **Privately Held**
WEB: www.osi.ca.gov
SIC: 7374 9199 Data processing & prepa-
ration; general government administra-
tion;
HQ: California Department Of Technology
Services
1325 J St Ste 1600
Sacramento CA 95814

(P-15824)
TECHNOSOCIALWORKCOM LLC
Also Called: Stria
4300 Resnik Ct Unit 103, Bakersfield
(93313-4836)
P.O. Box 21660 (93390-1660)
PHONE.....................................661 617-6601
Jim Damian, *Mng Member*
Garrison Scott, *Vice Pres*
Deanna Kelly, *Controller*
Scott Garrison, *VP Sales*
Rory Banks,
EMP: 75
SQ FT: 10,000
SALES (est): 9.5MM **Privately Held**
WEB: www.goodsamaritanhospital.net
SIC: 7374 Computer graphics service

(P-15825)
TERIS LLC
600 W Broadway Ste 300, San Diego
(92101-3352)
PHONE.....................................619 231-3282
Adam Wells, *Branch Mgr*
EMP: 50
SALES (corp-wide): 5MM **Privately Held**
SIC: 7374 Data processing & preparation
PA: Teris, Llc
2455 Faber Pl Ste 200
Palo Alto CA
650 213-9922

(P-15826)
TIVO CORPORATION
2233 N Ontario St Ste 200, Burbank
(91504-4500)
PHONE.....................................303 273-7800
Cora Locke, *Manager*
EMP: 84
SALES (corp-wide): 695.8MM **Publicly
Held**
SIC: 7374 Data processing & preparation
PA: Tivo Corporation
2160 Gold St
San Jose CA 95002
408 519-9100

(P-15827)
TRULIA INC (HQ)
535 Mission St Fl 7, San Francisco
(94105-3223)
PHONE.....................................415 648-4358
Peter Flint, *CEO*
Lloyd Frink, *President*
Jeff McConathy, *President*
Paul Levine, *COO*
Prashant Aggarwal, *CFO*
EMP: 357
SQ FT: 32,000
SALES: 251.9MM
SALES (corp-wide): 1.3B **Publicly Held**
SIC: 7374 Data processing & preparation
PA: Zillow Group, Inc.
1301 2nd Ave Fl 31
Seattle WA 98101
206 470-7000

(P-15828)
TURBO DATA SYSTEMS INC (PA)
18302 Irvine Blvd Ste 200, Tustin
(92780-3464)
PHONE.....................................714 573-5757
Roberta J Rosen, *President*
Carlos Mendez, *Treasurer*
EMP: 50
SQ FT: 10,000
SALES (est): 6.7MM **Privately Held**
WEB: www.turbodata.com
SIC: 7374 Data processing service

(P-15829)
UCC DIRECT SERVICES INC
330 N Brand Blvd Ste 700, Glendale
(91203-2336)
PHONE.....................................818 662-4100
Walt Powell, *President*
EMP: 80
SALES (est): 2MM **Privately Held**
WEB: www.uccdirectservices.com
SIC: 7374 Data processing service

(P-15830)
UNITAS GLOBAL LLC (PA)
453 S Spring St Ste 201, Los Angeles
(90013-2566)
PHONE.....................................213 785-6200
Patrick Shutt, *CEO*
Ian Gillott, *COO*
Bob Pollan, *CFO*
Grant A Kirkwood, *Founder*
Scott Walker, *Chief Mktg Ofcr*
EMP: 100
SQ FT: 9,000
SALES (est): 80MM **Privately Held**
SIC: 7374 Service bureau, computer

(P-15831)
UNIVERSITY CAL SAN DIEGO
Also Called: San Diego Supercomputer Cen-
ter
10100 Hopkins Dr, La Jolla (92093-0001)
P.O. Box 85608, San Diego (92186-5608)
PHONE.....................................858 534-5000
Michael Norman, *Director*
John Moreland, *Prgrmr*
Susan Rathbun, *Business Mgr*
Nick Feller, *Marketing Staff*
Ilya Zaslavsky, *Director*
EMP: 300 **Privately Held**
WEB: www.generalatomics.com
SIC: 7374 8731 8221 9411 Data pro-
cessing & preparation; commercial physi-
cal research; university; administration of
educational programs;
HQ: University Of California, San Diego
9500 Gilman Dr
La Jolla CA 92093
858 534-2230

(P-15832)
VELOCITY TECH SOLUTIONS INC
111 Pacifica Ste 320, Irvine (92618-7428)
PHONE.....................................949 417-0260
EMP: 70
SALES (corp-wide): 158.9MM **Privately
Held**
SIC: 7374 Data processing & preparation
PA: Velocity Technology Solutions, Inc.
1901 Roxborough Rd # 406
Charlotte NC 28211
704 357-7705

(P-15833)
VERITONE INC (PA)
575 Anton Blvd Ste 900, Costa Mesa
(92626-7665)
PHONE.....................................888 507-1737
Chad Steelberg, *Ch of Bd*
Ryan Steelberg, *President*
Peter F Collins, *CFO*
Jeff Maerov, *Officer*
Pete Collins, *Exec VP*
EMP: 69
SALES: 27MM **Publicly Held**
SIC: 7374 Data processing & preparation

(P-15834)
VERIZON CONNECT TELO INC (DH)
20 Enterprise Ste 100, Aliso Viejo
(92656-7104)
PHONE.....................................949 389-5500
Ralph Mason, *CTO*
Jason Koch, *President*
David Mitchell, *President*
A Newth Morris IV, *President*
Susan Heystee, *Exec VP*
▼ EMP: 150 EST: 2001
SQ FT: 55,700
SALES (est): 89MM
SALES (corp-wide): 130.8B **Publicly
Held**
WEB: www.telogis.com
SIC: 7374 Data processing & preparation
HQ: Verizon Connect Inc.
2002 Summit Blvd Ste 1800
Brookhaven GA 30319
404 573-5800

(P-15835)
VITESSE LLC
1601 Willow Rd, Menlo Park (94025-1452)
PHONE.....................................650 543-4800
Christopher R Gardner, *CEO*
EMP: 3000

SALES (est): 53.9MM
SALES (corp-wide): 55.8B **Publicly Held**
SIC: 7374 Data processing service
PA: Facebook, Inc.
  1 Hacker Way Bldg 10
  Menlo Park CA 94025
  650 543-4800

(P-15836)
VOICE MAIL BROADCASTING CORP
Also Called: Vmbc
5 Columbia, Aliso Viejo (92656-1460)
PHONE....................714 437-0600
Jesse Crowe, *CEO*
Joseph Cox, *Vice Pres*
EMP: 76
SALES (est): 7.3MM **Privately Held**
SIC: 7374 Service bureau, computer

(P-15837)
WYLE INFORMATION SYSTEMS LLC
970 W 190th St Ste 890, Torrance
(90502-1057)
PHONE....................310 563-6800
George Melton, *CEO*
EMP: 500
SALES (est): 178.7K **Publicly Held**
WEB: www.rsis.com
SIC: 7374 7379 Data processing & preparation; computer related consulting services
HQ: Wyle Services Corporation
  1960 E Grand Ave Ste 900
  El Segundo CA 90245
  -

(P-15838)
ZILLOW GROUP INC
Also Called: New Home Feed
4100 Redwood Rd, Oakland (94619-2363)
PHONE....................415 836-6760
EMP: 987
SALES (corp-wide): 1.3B **Publicly Held**
SIC: 7374 7371 Computer graphics service; software programming applications
PA: Zillow Group, Inc.
  1301 2nd Ave Fl 31
  Seattle WA 98101
  206 470-7000

(P-15839)
ZYNGA INC (PA)
699 8th St, San Francisco (94103-4901)
PHONE....................855 449-9642
Frank Gibeau, *CEO*
Dmitriy Makiyevskiy, *Partner*
Mark Pincus, *Ch of Bd*
Bernard Kim, *President*
Matthew S Bromberg, *COO*
EMP: 242
SQ FT: 669,000
SALES: 907.2MM **Publicly Held**
SIC: 7374 7372 Data processing & preparation; application computer software

> ### 7375 Information Retrieval Svcs

(P-15840)
23ANDME INC
349 Oyster Point Blvd # 100, South San Francisco (94080-1980)
PHONE....................510 381-7237
Ted Pederson, *Sr Software Eng*
EMP: 225 **Privately Held**
SIC: 7375 Information retrieval services
PA: 23andme, Inc.
  223 N Mathilda Ave
  Sunnyvale CA 94086

(P-15841)
23ANDME INC (PA)
223 N Mathilda Ave, Sunnyvale
(94086-4830)
PHONE....................650 961-7152
Anne Wojcicki, *CEO*
Richard Scheller, *Officer*
Chris Castro, *Vice Pres*
Ruby Gadelrab, *Vice Pres*
Robert Gentleman, *Vice Pres*
EMP: 143

SALES (est): 118.5MM **Privately Held**
WEB: www.23andme.com
SIC: 7375 Information retrieval services

(P-15842)
ACCESS INFO HOLDINGS LLC
2021 E Locust Ct, Ontario (91761-7618)
PHONE....................909 459-1417
EMP: 1477
SALES (corp-wide): 119.7MM **Privately Held**
SIC: 7375 Information retrieval services
PA: Access Information Holdings, Llc
  500 Unicorn Park Dr # 500
  Woburn MA 01801
  925 583-0100

(P-15843)
ACCURATE BACKGROUND LLC (PA)
Also Called: Selectforce
7515 Irvine Center Dr, Irvine (92618-2930)
PHONE....................800 784-3911
David C Dickerson, *CEO*
David Dickson,
Aaron Charbonnet, *Senior VP*
Damian Villegas, *Security Dir*
Naomi Mc Eachen, *VP Human Res*
EMP: 315
SQ FT: 98,024
SALES: 117.6MM **Privately Held**
WEB: www.accuratebackground.com
SIC: 7375 Information retrieval services

(P-15844)
ACXIOM CORPORATION
8801 Elmer Ln, Garden Grove
(92841-1039)
PHONE....................714 636-3093
Renee Heston, *Manager*
EMP: 50
SALES (corp-wide): 9.7B **Publicly Held**
WEB: www.acxiom.com
SIC: 7375 On-line data base information retrieval
HQ: Acxiom Llc
  301 E Dave Ward Dr
  Conway AR 72032
  501 342-1000

(P-15845)
ACXIOM CORPORATION
100 Redwood Shores Pkwy, Redwood City
(94065-1155)
PHONE....................650 356-3400
Michael Gorman, *Senior VP*
David Mariani, *VP Engrg*
EMP: 72
SALES (corp-wide): 9.7B **Publicly Held**
SIC: 7375 Information retrieval services
HQ: Acxiom Llc
  301 E Dave Ward Dr
  Conway AR 72032
  501 342-1000

(P-15846)
AUTOWEB INC (PA)
18872 Macarthur Blvd, Irvine (92612-1408)
PHONE....................949 225-4500
Jared Rowe, *CEO*
Michael J Fuchs, *Ch of Bd*
William A Ferriolo, *COO*
Dan Ingle, *COO*
Kimberly S Boren, *CFO*
EMP: 148
SQ FT: 26,000
SALES: 125.5MM **Publicly Held**
WEB: www.autobytel.com
SIC: 7375 On-line data base information retrieval

(P-15847)
CHANGEORG INC
383 Rhode Island St # 300, San Francisco
(94103-5178)
PHONE....................415 817-1840
Benj Rattay, *CEO*
Jennifer Dulski, *President*
Benj Rattray, *CEO*
Rahoul Seth, *CFO*
Marcy Mirkin, *Managing Dir*
EMP: 114
SQ FT: 10,000
SALES: 22MM **Privately Held**
SIC: 7375 On-line data base information retrieval

(P-15848)
COMPS INC
4535 Towne Centre Ct, San Diego
(92121-8801)
PHONE....................858 658-0576
Andrew Florance, *President*
Craig Farrington, *COO*
EMP: 175
SALES (est): 5.1MM
SALES (corp-wide): 1.1B **Publicly Held**
SIC: 7375 Information retrieval services
PA: Costar Group, Inc.
  1331 L St Nw Ste 2
  Washington DC 20005
  202 346-6500

(P-15849)
CONFI-CHEK INC (PA)
1915 21st St, Sacramento (95811-6813)
PHONE....................800 718-8997
Rob Miller, *President*
EMP: 70
SQ FT: 6,000
SALES: 32MM **Privately Held**
WEB: www.confi-chek.com
SIC: 7375 Data base information retrieval

(P-15850)
CONVERSANT LLC (HQ)
30699 Russell Ranch Rd # 250, Westlake Village (91362-7319)
PHONE....................818 575-4500
John Giuliani, *President*
Oded Benyo, *President*
John Pitstick, *CFO*
Scott Eagle, *Chief Mktg Ofcr*
Scott P Barlow, *Vice Pres*
EMP: 148
SQ FT: 41,500
SALES (est): 417.8MM **Publicly Held**
WEB: www.valueclick.com
SIC: 7375 4813 On-line data base information retrieval;

(P-15851)
CORVENTIS INC (PA)
2033 Gateway Pl Ste 100, San Jose
(95110-3713)
PHONE....................408 790-9300
John Russell, *President*
Abhi Chavan, *Vice Pres*
Kathy Lundberg, *Vice Pres*
Murali Srivathsa, *Vice Pres*
EMP: 61
SALES (est): 14.9MM **Privately Held**
SIC: 7375 Information retrieval services

(P-15852)
COUNTY OF LOS ANGELES
Also Called: Department of Mental Health
320 W Temple St Fl 9, Los Angeles
(90012-3217)
PHONE....................213 974-0515
Jacqueline Criddell, *Manager*
Kenneth Bjork, *Network Mgr*
Karen Goldberg, *Director*
Tony Kuo, *Director*
Victor Elliott, *Manager*
EMP: 150 **Privately Held**
WEB: www.co.la.ca.us
SIC: 7375 9131 Information retrieval services;
PA: County Of Los Angeles
  500 W Temple St Ste 437
  Los Angeles CA 90012
  213 974-1101

(P-15853)
DIGITAL INSIGHT CORPORATION
5601 Lindero Canyon Rd # 100, Westlake Village (91362-6494)
PHONE....................818 879-1010
Paul Nieman, *Principal*
Woody Woodruff, *Info Tech Mgr*
Brad Ennis, *Project Mgr*
EMP: 150
SALES (corp-wide): 6.4B **Publicly Held**
WEB: www.digitalinsight.com
SIC: 7375 Information retrieval services
HQ: Digital Insight Corporation
  1300 Seaport Blvd Ste 300
  Redwood City CA 94063

(P-15854)
DIGITAL INSIGHT CORPORATION (HQ)
Also Called: Intuit Financial Services
1300 Seaport Blvd Ste 300, Redwood City
(94063-5591)
PHONE....................818 879-1010
Jeffrey E Stiefler, *President*
Joseph M McDoniel, *Exec VP*
Tom Shen, *Exec VP*
Robert R Surridge, *Senior VP*
Chandra Elindram, *Sr Software Eng*
EMP: 200
SQ FT: 46,000
SALES (est): 137.3MM
SALES (corp-wide): 6.4B **Publicly Held**
WEB: www.digitalinsight.com
SIC: 7375 7372 7371 Information retrieval services; prepackaged software; custom computer programming services
PA: Ncr Corporation
  864 Spring St Nw
  Atlanta GA 30308
  937 445-5000

(P-15855)
DISCOVERORG DATA LLC
Dept La 24789, Pasadena (91185-0001)
PHONE....................360 783-6924
Henry Schuck, *Mng Member*
EMP: 98
SALES (corp-wide): 2MM **Privately Held**
SIC: 7375 Information retrieval services
PA: Discoverorg Data, Llc
  805 Broadway St Ste 900
  Vancouver WA 98660
  360 783-6800

(P-15856)
DRIVESAVERS INC
Also Called: Drivesavers Data Recovery
400 Bel Marin Keys Blvd, Novato
(94949-5642)
PHONE....................415 382-2000
Jay Hagan, *CEO*
Victoria O'Hara, *Partner*
Scott Moyer, *President*
Michael Hall, *CIO*
Chris Lyons, *Technology*
EMP: 90
SQ FT: 4,400
SALES: 20MM **Privately Held**
WEB: www.drivesavers.com
SIC: 7375 Information retrieval services

(P-15857)
E-TIMES CORPORATION LTD
601 S Figueroa St # 5000, Los Angeles
(90017-3883)
PHONE....................213 452-6720
Chiharu Nakahara, *President*
EMP: 300
SALES (est): 12.5MM **Privately Held**
WEB: www.etimesltd.com
SIC: 7375 7374 8742 Information retrieval services; computer graphics service; administrative services consultant

(P-15858)
EDMUNDS HOLDING COMPANY (PA)
Also Called: Edmunds.com
2401 Colorado Ave, Santa Monica
(90404-3585)
PHONE....................310 309-6300
AVI Steinlauf, *CEO*
Seth Berkowitz, *President*
Charles Farrell, *CFO*
Stephen Felisan, *CTO*
EMP: 650
SALES (est): 212MM **Privately Held**
SIC: 7375 Information retrieval services

(P-15859)
ELAVON INC
1281 9th Ave Unit 706, San Diego
(92101-4645)
PHONE....................954 776-7990
Kimberly Layton, *Manager*
Jeanna Presnell, *Analyst*
David Dowling, *Production*
Jacqueline Flowers, *Director*
Melanie Miller, *Director*
EMP: 514

SALES (corp-wide): 25.7B **Publicly Held**
SIC: 7375 Information retrieval services
HQ: Elavon, Inc.
2 Concourse Pkwy Ste 800
Atlanta GA 30328
678 731-5000

(P-15860)
ELAVON INC
4234 Hacienda Dr Ste 250, Pleasanton
(94588-2789)
PHONE..................................925 734-8939
EMP: 400
SALES (corp-wide): 25.7B **Publicly Held**
SIC: 7375 Information retrieval services
HQ: Elavon, Inc.
2 Concourse Pkwy Ste 800
Atlanta GA 30328
678 731-5000

(P-15861)
EXABLOX CORPORATION
1156 Sonora Ct, Sunnyvale (94086-5308)
PHONE..................................408 773-8477
Douglas Brockett, *CEO*
Ramesh Iyer Balan, *Vice Pres*
Ramesh Balan, *Vice Pres*
Shridar Subramanian, *Vice Pres*
Meagan Banning, *Office Mgr*
EMP: 51 EST: 2010
SALES (est): 6.6MM **Privately Held**
SIC: 7375 Data base information retrieval
PA: Storagecraft Technology Corporation
380 W Data Dr Ste 300
Draper UT 84020

(P-15862)
FACEBOOK INC (PA)
1 Hacker Way Bldg 10, Menlo Park
(94025-1456)
PHONE..................................650 543-4800
Mark Zuckerberg, *Ch of Bd*
Kevin Carr, *Partner*
Stephane Crozatier, *Partner*
David B Fischer, *Partner*
Nikki Harding, *Partner*
EMP: 800
SQ FT: 6,000,000
SALES: 55.8B **Publicly Held**
SIC: 7375 On-line data base information
retrieval

(P-15863)
**GLOBAL RISK MGT SOLUTIONS
LLC**
660 Nwport Ctr Dr Ste 600, Newport Beach
(92660)
PHONE..................................949 759-8500
Gerard Smith, *President*
EMP: 200
SQ FT: 2,700
SALES (est): 14MM **Privately Held**
SIC: 7375 Information retrieval services

(P-15864)
GO2 SYSTEMS INC
Also Called: Go2systems
18400 Von Karman Ave Fl 9, Irvine
(92612-1514)
PHONE..................................949 553-0800
S Lee Hancock, *President*
Scott Goldman, *COO*
Mark Buckner, *CFO*
Ward Kennedy, *CFO*
Edwin De Ferrante, *VP Mktg*
EMP: 75
SQ FT: 18,955
SALES (est): 3.2MM **Privately Held**
SIC: 7375 Information retrieval services

(P-15865)
**GROUNDWORK OPEN SOURCE
INC**
23332 Mill Creek Dr # 155, Laguna Hills
(92653-7911)
PHONE..................................415 992-4500
Dave Lilly, *CEO*
Thomas Stocking, *Vice Pres*
Laura Hurd, *Executive*
Roger Ruttimann, *Engineer*
Hans Kriel, *Opers Staff*
EMP: 100

SALES (est): 8.9MM
SALES (corp-wide): 79.8MM **Privately
Held**
WEB: www.groundworkopensource.com
SIC: 7375 7371 On-line data base infor-
mation retrieval; custom computer pro-
gramming services
HQ: Fox Technologies, Inc.
6455 City West Pkwy
Eden Prairie MN 55344
800 328-1000

(P-15866)
GUIDANCE SOLUTIONS INC
4134 Del Rey Ave, Marina Del Rey
(90292-5604)
PHONE..................................310 754-4000
Jason Meugniot, *CEO*
Jeff Herrera, *Partner*
John Provisor, *President*
Mike Hill, *Exec VP*
EMP: 50
SQ FT: 10,000
SALES (est): 8.8MM **Privately Held**
WEB: www.guidance.com
SIC: 7375 4813 On-line data base infor-
mation retrieval;

(P-15867)
HIRERIGHT LLC (HQ)
3349 Michelson Dr Ste 150, Irvine
(92612-8881)
PHONE..................................949 428-5800
Jurgen Leijdekker, *CEO*
David Logsdon, *Vice Pres*
Dan Shoemaker, *Vice Pres*
Natasha Hampton, *Executive*
Robin Hart, *Executive*
EMP: 148
SQ FT: 63,440
SALES (est): 136MM **Privately Held**
WEB: www.hireright.com
SIC: 7375 7374 Data base information re-
trieval; data verification service

(P-15868)
IAC SEARCH & MEDIA INC (HQ)
Also Called: Ask.com
555 12th St Ste 500, Oakland
(94607-3699)
PHONE..................................510 985-7400
Doug Leeds, *CEO*
George S Lichter, *President*
Shane McGilloway, *COO*
Dominic Butera, *CFO*
Steven J Sordello, *CFO*
EMP: 200
SQ FT: 76,000
SALES (est): 107.4MM
SALES (corp-wide): 4.2B **Publicly Held**
WEB: www.ask.com
SIC: 7375 On-line data base information
retrieval
PA: Iac/Interactivecorp
555 W 18th St
New York NY 10011
212 314-7300

(P-15869)
**INSURANCE SERVICES OFFICE
INC**
Also Called: INSURANCE SERVICES OF-
FICE INC
388 Market St Ste 750, San Francisco
(94111-5352)
PHONE..................................415 874-4361
Jim Masek, *Branch Mgr*
Glen Brooks, *Vice Pres*
Robert Colvin, *Info Tech Dir*
Eric Good, *Engineer*
Joseph Pasco, *Representative*
EMP: 326 **Publicly Held**
SIC: 7375 Information retrieval services
HQ: Insurance Services Office, Inc.
545 Washington Blvd
Jersey City NJ 07310
201 469-2153

(P-15870)
INTERNET ARCHIVE
300 Funston Ave, San Francisco
(94118-2116)
PHONE..................................415 561-6767
Brewster Kahle, *Director*
Kyrie Whitsett, *Partner*
Caitlin Olson, *Executive Asst*

Bz Phr, *Human Res Dir*
Kathleen Burch, *Director*
EMP: 173
SALES: 17.8MM **Privately Held**
SIC: 7375 On-line data base information
retrieval

(P-15871)
JEPPESEN DATAPLAN INC
225 W Santa Clara St # 1, San Jose
(95113-1748)
PHONE..................................408 961-2825
Mark Van Tine, *President*
Jepson Fuller, *CFO*
Steve Altus, *Senior Mgr*
Jeff Harris, *Manager*
EMP: 118
SQ FT: 20,000
SALES (est): 9.9MM
SALES (corp-wide): 101.1B **Publicly
Held**
WEB: www.jetplan.com
SIC: 7375 Information retrieval services
HQ: Boeing Digital Solutions, Inc
55 Inverness Dr E
Englewood CO 80112
303 799-9090

(P-15872)
LINKEDIN CORPORATION (HQ)
1000 W Maude Ave, Sunnyvale
(94085-2810)
PHONE..................................650 687-3600
Jeff Weiner, *CEO*
Jian Lu, *President*
Maria Robinson, *President*
Steve Sordello, *CFO*
Shannon Stubo, *Chief Mktg Ofcr*
EMP: 148
SQ FT: 373,000
SALES (est): 2.6B
SALES (corp-wide): 125.8B **Publicly
Held**
WEB: www.linkedin.com
SIC: 7375 On-line data base information
retrieval
PA: Microsoft Corporation
1 Microsoft Way
Redmond WA 98052
425 882-8080

(P-15873)
LOGICMONITOR INC (PA)
820 State St Fl 5, Santa Barbara
(93101-3271)
PHONE..................................805 617-3884
Kevin McGibben, *CEO*
Steven Francis,
Tom Kress, *Vice Pres*
Dipan Mann, *Vice Pres*
Lauren Thurman, *Executive*
EMP: 114
SALES (est): 51MM **Privately Held**
SIC: 7375 Information retrieval services

(P-15874)
NEXTDOORCOM INC
875 Stevenson St Ste 100, San Francisco
(94103-0906)
PHONE..................................415 236-0000
Nirav Tolia, *CEO*
Flora Hsu, *Partner*
Prakash Janakiraman, *Vice Pres*
Sarah Leary, *Vice Pres*
Dan Masquelier, *Vice Pres*
EMP: 100 EST: 2011
SALES (est): 20MM **Privately Held**
SIC: 7375 On-line data base information
retrieval

(P-15875)
ONBOARDIQ INC
Also Called: Fountain
275 Sacramento St Ste 300, San Francisco
(94111-3855)
PHONE..................................480 433-1197
Kibaek Ryu, *President*
Nico Roberts, *COO*
EMP: 50
SALES: 5.5MM **Privately Held**
SIC: 7375 7371 Information retrieval serv-
ices; computer software development &
applications

(P-15876)
**PERFORMANT FINANCIAL
CORP (PA)**
333 N Canyons Pkwy # 100, Livermore
(94551-9478)
PHONE..................................925 960-4800
Lisa C Im, *Ch of Bd*
EMP: 94
SQ FT: 50,000
SALES: 155.6MM **Publicly Held**
WEB: www.performantcorp.com
SIC: 7375 Information retrieval services

(P-15877)
PINTEREST INC (PA)
808 Brannan St, San Francisco
(94103-4904)
PHONE..................................415 617-5585
Benjamin Silbermann, *Ch of Bd*
Abby Fromm, *Partner*
Rachel Goodman, *Partner*
Justine Higueras, *Partner*
Jackie Klimes, *Partner*
EMP: 148 EST: 2008
SQ FT: 490,000
SALES: 755.9MM **Publicly Held**
SIC: 7375 On-line data base information
retrieval

(P-15878)
PLAID INC (PA)
1098 Harrison St, San Francisco
(94103-4521)
PHONE..................................415 799-1354
George Zachary Perret, *President*
William Hockey, *CTO*
Brian Jacokes, *Software Engr*
Sandy Wong, *Controller*
EMP: 57
SALES: 2.5MM **Privately Held**
SIC: 7375 Information retrieval services

(P-15879)
PROCTORU INC
3687 Old Sta, Pleasanton (94588)
PHONE..................................205 870-8122
EMP: 382
SALES (corp-wide): 17.4MM **Privately
Held**
SIC: 7375 Information retrieval services
PA: Proctoru, Inc.
2200 Riverchase Ctr # 600
Hoover AL 35244
925 273-7588

(P-15880)
RELATIONEDGE LLC
10120 Pacific Heights Blv, San Diego
(92121-4210)
PHONE..................................858 451-4665
Matthew Stoyka, *CEO*
EMP: 125
SALES: 17.4MM
SALES (corp-wide): 1.4B **Privately Held**
SIC: 7375 On-line data base information
retrieval
HQ: Rackspace Us, Inc.
1 Fanatical Pl
Windcrest TX 78218
210 312-4000

(P-15881)
RELX INC
Also Called: Lexisnexis
555 W 5th St Ste 4500, Los Angeles
(90013-3003)
PHONE..................................213 627-1130
Tim Dawson, *Branch Mgr*
EMP: 70
SALES (corp-wide): 9.6B **Privately Held**
WEB: www.lexis-nexis.com
SIC: 7375 Information retrieval services
HQ: Relx Inc.
230 Park Ave Ste 700
New York NY 10169
212 309-8100

(P-15882)
**RENWOOD REALTYTRAC LLC
(PA)**
Also Called: Attom Data Solutions
1 Venture Ste 300, Irvine (92618-7416)
PHONE..................................949 502-8300
Rob Barber, *CEO*
Richard Lombardi, *COO*

Cabell Cobbs, *CFO*
David Dam, *CFO*
Richard Sawicky, *Officer*
EMP: 88
SALES (est): 20.4MM **Privately Held**
SIC: 7375 Data base information retrieval

(P-15883)
REPRINTS DESK INC
15821 Ventura Blvd # 165, Encino
(91436-5208)
PHONE..................................310 477-0354
Peter Derycz, *President*
Alan Urban, *CFO*
Alan Beckhard, *Executive*
Timothy Burleson, *Technology*
Marie Nyblom, *Technology*
EMP: 92
SQ FT: 2,500
SALES (est): 20.7MM **Publicly Held**
SIC: 7375 Information retrieval services
PA: Research Solutions, Inc.
15821 Ventura Blvd # 165
Encino CA 91436

(P-15884)
RESEARCH LIBRARIES GROUP INC
Also Called: R L G
777 Mariners Island Blvd # 550, San Mateo
(94404-5048)
PHONE..................................650 288-1288
James P Michalko, *President*
Robert J Scott, *Treasurer*
Shaun Flaherty, *Admin Sec*
Ed Chiu, *Administration*
Jake Irland, *Sales Mgr*
EMP: 100
SQ FT: 25,000
SALES (est): 4.4MM **Privately Held**
WEB: www.rlg.com
SIC: 7375 8731 7372 On-line data base
information retrieval; commercial physical
research; prepackaged software

(P-15885)
SAGE SOFTWARE INC
7595 Irvine Center Dr # 200, Irvine
(92618-2957)
PHONE..................................949 753-1222
John Kang, *Branch Mgr*
Linda Brizendine, *Executive Asst*
Ron Fliege, *Software Engr*
Brandon Lowe, *Software Engr*
Diane Bull, *Technical Staff*
EMP: 82
SALES (corp-wide): 2.3B **Privately Held**
SIC: 7375 7374 7372 3089 Information
retrieval services; data processing &
preparation; prepackaged software; plas-
tic processing
HQ: Sage Software, Inc.
271 17th St Nw Ste 1100
Atlanta GA 30363
866 996-7243

(P-15886)
SALON MEDIA GROUP INC (PA)
870 Market St Ste 442, San Francisco
(94102-3018)
PHONE..................................415 870-7566
Richard Macwilliams, *CEO*
John Warnock, *Ch of Bd*
Trevor Calhoun, *CFO*
David Daley, *Chief*
▲ **EMP:** 53
SQ FT: 2,405
SALES (est): 4.5MM **Publicly Held**
SIC: 7375 7383 On-line data base infor-
mation retrieval; news feature syndicate;
news pictures, gathering & distributing

(P-15887)
SCRIBD INC
460 Bryant St Fl 1, San Francisco
(94107-2595)
PHONE..................................415 896-9890
John Adler, *CEO*
Eric Shoup, *COO*
Simon Bond, *Chief Mktg Ofcr*
Sabeen Minns, *Vice Pres*
Andrew Weinstein, *Vice Pres*
EMP: 60
SALES (est): 10.5MM **Privately Held**
SIC: 7375 Information retrieval services

(P-15888)
SPIRE GLOBAL INC (PA)
575 Florida St Ste 150, San Francisco
(94110-7421)
PHONE..................................415 356-3400
Peter Platzer, *CEO*
Carl Harris, *COO*
Christopher Wake, *Vice Pres*
Russell Muzzolini, *Principal*
Russell Muzzolini Cto, *Business Mgr*
EMP: 75
SQ FT: 4,000
SALES (est): 18.3MM **Privately Held**
SIC: 7375 On-line data base information
retrieval

(P-15889)
TEUTONIC HOLDINGS LLC
9221 Corbin Ave Ste 260, Northridge
(91324-1625)
PHONE..................................818 264-4400
James Murphy, *CEO*
Sam Ghahremanpour, *President*
Doreen Paisano, *Human Resources*
EMP: 140
SALES (est): 41.7MM **Privately Held**
SIC: 7375 Data base information retrieval

(P-15890)
TINTRI INC
303 Ravendale Dr, Mountain View
(94043-5228)
PHONE..................................650 810-8200
Kieran Harty, *CTO*
Jagan Raghu, *Vice Pres*
Tim Saunders, *Vice Pres*
Robert J Duffy, *Risk Mgmt Dir*
Brian Houlihan, *Creative Dir*
EMP: 277
SQ FT: 127,000
SALES (est): 125.9MM
SALES (corp-wide): 251.7MM **Privately Held**
SIC: 7375 7374 Data base information re-
trieval; on-line data base information re-
trieval; data processing & preparation
PA: Datadirect Networks, Inc.
9351 Deering Ave
Chatsworth CA 91311
818 700-7600

(P-15891)
TROJAN PROFESSIONAL SVCS INC
4410 Cerritos Ave, Los Alamitos
(90720-2549)
P.O. Box 1270 (90720-1270)
PHONE............(714 816-7169
Mark Dunn, *CEO*
Ingrid M Kidd, *President*
Chris Iseri, *Admin Sec*
Nikki Myers, *Software Dev*
EMP: 99
SQ FT: 12,000
SALES (est): 11.8MM **Privately Held**
WEB: www.trojanonline.com
SIC: 7375 Data base information retrieval

(P-15892)
VESTEK SYSTEMS INC (DH)
425 Market St Fl 6, San Francisco
(94105-2470)
PHONE..................................415 344-6000
Sam Campopiano, *President*
Virginia Chung, *Exec VP*
Lynn Roy PH, *Director*
EMP: 79
SQ FT: 18,000
SALES (est): 4MM
SALES (corp-wide): 117.6MM **Privately Held**
WEB: www.vestek.com
SIC: 7375 On-line data base information
retrieval

(P-15893)
WATER RESOURCES CAL DEPT
1416 9th St Rm 1225, Sacramento
(95814-5511)
PHONE..................................916 324-3812
Karen Bates, *President*
EMP: 50 **Privately Held**
WEB: www.water.ca.gov
SIC: 7375 9511 Data base information re-
trieval; water control & quality agency,
government;

HQ: California Department Of Water Resources
1416 9th St
Sacramento CA 95814
916 653-9394

(P-15894)
WESTERN FELD INVSTIGATIONS INC (PA)
Also Called: Releasepoint
405 W Foothill Blvd # 204, Claremont
(91711-2786)
P.O. Box 246, Glendora (91740-0246)
PHONE..................................800 999-9589
Gerard F Halvey, *President*
Clair Halvey, *Vice Pres*
Derrick Halvey, *Vice Pres*
Sharon Oliver, *Manager*
EMP: 100
SALES (est): 54MM **Privately Held**
WEB: www.wfi-inc.com
SIC: 7375 Information retrieval services

(P-15895)
YELP INC (PA)
140 New Montgomery St # 900, San Fran-
cisco (94105-3822)
PHONE..................................415 908-3801
Jeremy Stoppelman, *CEO*
Charles Baker, *CFO*
Laurence Wilson, *Officer*
Todd Miner, *Vice Pres*
Laura Beller, *Executive*
EMP: 93
SALES: 942.7MM **Publicly Held**
SIC: 7375 On-line data base information
retrieval

(P-15896)
ZYME SOLUTIONS INC (PA)
240 Twin Dolphin Dr Ste D, Redwood City
(94065-1403)
PHONE..................................650 585-2258
Chandran Sankaran, *President*
Jarett Janik, *CFO*
Peter Hantman, *Officer*
Laura L Fese, *Exec VP*
Pawan Joshi, *Exec VP*
EMP: 100
SALES (est): 33.1MM **Privately Held**
SIC: 7375 Information retrieval services

7376 Computer Facilities Management Svcs

(P-15897)
ALLIED DIGITAL SERVICES LLC (HQ)
680 Knox St Ste 200, Torrance
(90502-1358)
PHONE..................................310 431-2375
Paresh Shah, *CEO*
Gaurav Bahirvani, *Chief Mktg Ofcr*
Kapil Mehta, *Officer*
Sair Muhammad, *Exec VP*
Manoj Shah, *CIO*
EMP: 110
SQ FT: 14,516
SALES (est): 28.9MM
SALES (corp-wide): 10.5MM **Privately Held**
WEB: www.allieddigital.net
SIC: 7376 Computer facilities management
PA: Allied Digital Services Limited
Premises No.13a ,13th Floor, Earnest
House
Mumbai MH 40002
226 681-6400

(P-15898)
CONTEMPORARY SERVICES CORP
4365 E Lowell St Ste A, Ontario
(91761-2226)
PHONE..................................909 740-3834
EMP: 65
SALES (corp-wide): 302.9MM **Privately Held**
SIC: 7376 Computer facilities management
PA: Contemporary Services Corporation
17101 Superior St
Northridge CA 91325
818 885-5150

(P-15899)
COUNTY OF SACRAMENTO
Also Called: Communication & Info Tech
799 G St, Sacramento (95814-1212)
PHONE..................................916 874-7752
Rami Zakaria, *Branch Mgr*
EMP: 395 **Privately Held**
WEB: www.sna.com
SIC: 7376 9631 Computer facilities man-
agement; communications commission,
government;
PA: County Of Sacramento
700 H St Ste 7650
Sacramento CA 95814
916 874-5544

(P-15900)
CSRA LLC
4045 Hancock St, San Diego (92110-5126)
PHONE..................................619 225-2600
Art Schrubb, *Manager*
Mike Wingo, *Technology*
EMP: 600
SALES (corp-wide): 36.1B **Publicly Held**
WEB: www.csc.com
SIC: 7376 Computer facilities management
HQ: Csra Llc
3170 Fairview Park Dr
Falls Church VA 22042
703 641-2000

(P-15901)
ECIFM SOLUTIONS INC
3160 Crow Canyon Rd # 240, San Ramon
(94583-1331)
PHONE..................................925 830-1925
Vimaljit Uberoi, *President*
Annette Farrell, *Office Admin*
Ann Welch, *Administration*
Bisrat Tafesse, *Analyst*
EMP: 100
SQ FT: 3,750
SALES: 6.5MM **Privately Held**
WEB: www.ecifm.com
SIC: 7376 7373 8712 Computer facilities
management; computer integrated sys-
tems design; architectural services

(P-15902)
GLOBAL BLUE DVBE INC
5930 Price Ave, McClellan (95652-2402)
PHONE..................................916 632-2583
Dave Hornbeck, *President*
Michael Terpstra, *Vice Pres*
EMP: 75
SQ FT: 4,135
SALES (est): 11.1MM **Privately Held**
SIC: 7376 7379 7371 Computer facilities
management; computer related consult-
ing services; computer related mainte-
nance services; computer software
development & applications

(P-15903)
HCL AMERICA INC (DH)
330 Potrero Ave, Sunnyvale (94085-4194)
PHONE..................................408 733-0480
Shiv Nadar, *Director*
Srinivas Bollepalli, *Partner*
Manish Anand, *CEO*
Sreedhar Chittamuri, *Vice Pres*
Ayut Patel, *Vice Pres*
EMP: 200
SQ FT: 31,000
SALES: 3.7B **Privately Held**
SIC: 7376 7371 8741 Computer facilities
management; computer software devel-
opment; management services

(P-15904)
NTT DATA SERVICES CORPORATION
6701 Center Dr W Ste 1000, Los Angeles
(90045-1566)
PHONE..................................310 342-3200
Sherry Cowan, *Manager*
EMP: 70 **Privately Held**
WEB: www.perotsystems.com
SIC: 7376 7379 Computer facilities management; computer related consulting
services
HQ: Ntt Data Services Holdings Corporation
7950 Legacy Dr
Plano TX 75024
972 577-0000

(P-15905)
RAGINGWIRE DATA CENTERS INC (HQ)
Also Called: Raging Wire
1625 National Dr, Sacramento (95834-2901)
P.O. Box 348060 (95834-8060)
PHONE..................................916 286-3000
Douglas S Adams, *President*
Kevin Dalton, *Senior VP*
Joe Goldsmith, *Senior VP*
Judi A Lee, *Senior VP*
Rice Siouxsie, *Executive Asst*
▲ EMP: 275
SALES (est): 128.7MM **Privately Held**
WEB: www.ragingwire.com
SIC: 7376 Computer facilities management

(P-15906)
VERIZON BUS NETWRK SVCS INC
4340 Solar Way, Fremont (94538-6335)
PHONE..................................510 497-2500
Randy Cade, *Manager*
EMP: 75
SALES (corp-wide): 130.8B **Publicly Held**
WEB: www.gtl.net
SIC: 7376 Computer facilities management
HQ: Verizon Business Network Services Inc.
　1 Verizon Way
　Basking Ridge NJ 07920
　908 559-2000

7377 Computer Rental & Leasing

(P-15907)
2NDGEAR LLC (DH)
611 Anton Blvd Ste 700, Costa Mesa (92626-7050)
PHONE..................................714 702-1023
John W Ford, *CEO*
Norman Brown, *IT/INT Sup*
EMP: 105
SALES (est): 2.3MM **Privately Held**
SIC: 7377 5045 Computer peripheral equipment rental & leasing; computer peripheral equipment
HQ: Insight Investments Llc
　611 Anton Blvd Ste 700
　Costa Mesa CA 92626
　714 939-2300

(P-15908)
INSIGHT INVESTMENTS LLC (HQ)
611 Anton Blvd Ste 700, Costa Mesa (92626-7050)
PHONE..................................714 939-2300
John W Ford, *CEO*
Michael Dundon, *Vice Pres*
Yeung Calvin, *Planning*
Ruth Ford, *Analyst*
Linda Watterson, *Analyst*
EMP: 148
SQ FT: 30,000
SALES (est): 151.4MM **Privately Held**
WEB: www.insightinvestments.com
SIC: 7377 5045 Computer peripheral equipment rental & leasing; computer peripheral equipment

7378 Computer Maintenance & Repair

(P-15909)
ALQUEST TECHNOLOGIES INC
1760 Yeager Ave, La Verne (91750-5850)
PHONE..................................909 592-8708
Henry J Wojcik, *CEO*
Henry Wojcik, *President*
David Miranda, *Admin Asst*
EMP: 70 EST: 2000
SALES (est): 9MM **Privately Held**
WEB: www.alquestonline.com
SIC: 7378 Computer maintenance & repair

(P-15910)
AMKOTRON INC
12620 Hiddencreek Way, Cerritos (90703-2116)
PHONE..................................562 921-3330
Sunja Lee, *Branch Mgr*
EMP: 60
SALES (corp-wide): 8.5MM **Privately Held**
SIC: 7378 5065 Computer peripheral equipment repair & maintenance; electronic parts & equipment
PA: Amkotron, Inc.
　16220 Bloomfield Ave
　Cerritos CA 90703
　562 921-3330

(P-15911)
APEX COMPUTER SYSTEMS INC
13875 Cerritos Corprt Dr A, Cerritos (90703-2470)
P.O. Box 4859 (90703-4859)
PHONE..................................562 926-6820
Philip C Chen, *CEO*
Dennis Rice, *President*
Jessica C Chow, *CFO*
Michael Da Silva, *Vice Pres*
Ira Klein, *General Mgr*
EMP: 60
SQ FT: 18,146
SALES: 23.6MM **Privately Held**
WEB: www.acsi2000.com
SIC: 7378 5734 Computer maintenance & repair; computer & software stores

(P-15912)
BCP SYSTEMS INC
1560 S Sinclair St, Anaheim (92806-5933)
PHONE..................................714 202-3900
Carlos P Torres, *CEO*
William W Price, *President*
Trace Dibble, *Engineer*
David Garcia, *Engineer*
Edward Yap, *Engineer*
EMP: 60
SALES (est): 10.1MM **Privately Held**
WEB: www.bcpsystems.com
SIC: 7378 3571 5063 Computer & data processing equipment repair/maintenance; computer peripheral equipment repair & maintenance; electronic computers; electrical apparatus & equipment

(P-15913)
COKEVA INC
Also Called: Applied Materials
9000 Foothills Blvd, Roseville (95747-4411)
PHONE..................................916 462-6001
Ann D Nguyen, *CEO*
Dominick Derosa, *CFO*
Kevin Nguyen, *Vice Pres*
Lee Nguyen, *Vice Pres*
Qui Nguyen, *Vice Pres*
▲ EMP: 181
SQ FT: 175,000
SALES (est): 30.5MM **Privately Held**
SIC: 7378 Computer maintenance & repair

(P-15914)
DST OUTPUT CALIFORNIA INC
5220 Rbert J Mathews Pkwy, El Dorado Hills (95762-5705)
PHONE..................................916 939-4617
Kenneth Taylor, *Manager*
Adam Miller, *Admin Asst*
Marcus Lapilusa, *Administration*
Matthew Franklin, *Software Dev*
Jeff Weatherly, *Software Engr*
EMP: 95
SALES (est): 21MM
SALES (corp-wide): 4.3B **Publicly Held**
SIC: 7378 Computer maintenance & repair
HQ: Broadridge Customer Communications, Llc
　2600 Southwest Blvd
　Kansas City MO 64108

(P-15915)
ESL TECHNOLOGIES INC
8875 Washington Blvd B, Roseville (95678-6214)
PHONE..................................916 677-4500
Donna Kwidzinski, *CEO*
Tjeu Blommaert, *President*
EMP: 350
SQ FT: 100,000
SALES (est): 23.3MM
SALES (corp-wide): 2.6MM **Privately Held**
WEB: www.eslt.com
SIC: 7378 Computer peripheral equipment repair & maintenance
HQ: Teleplan Holding Usa, Inc.
　8875 Washington Blvd B
　Roseville CA 95678
　916 677-4500

(P-15916)
FAKOURI ELECTRICAL ENGRG INC
Also Called: F E E
30001 Comercio, Rcho STA Marg (92688-2106)
PHONE..................................949 888-2400
Maryam Ewalt, *President*
Charles Ewalt, *COO*
John Oveisi, *CFO*
▲ EMP: 79 EST: 1979
SQ FT: 15,000
SALES (est): 11.8MM **Privately Held**
WEB: www.fee-ups.com
SIC: 7378 8742 Computer maintenance & repair; maintenance management consultant

(P-15917)
FALCONWOOD INC
1011 Camino Del Rio S, San Diego (92108-3531)
PHONE..................................619 297-9080
Bill Severi, *Principal*
EMP: 61
SALES (corp-wide): 21MM **Privately Held**
SIC: 7378 8741 Computer & data processing equipment repair/maintenance; management services
PA: Falconwood
　2231 Crystal Dr Ste 801
　Arlington VA 22202
　703 888-4300

(P-15918)
GENERAL DYNAMICS INFO TECH INC
1700 E Walnut Ave Ste 210, El Segundo (90245-2651)
PHONE..................................310 662-3202
Tom Nutly, *Manager*
EMP: 50
SALES (corp-wide): 36.1B **Publicly Held**
SIC: 7378 Computer maintenance & repair
HQ: General Dynamics Information Technology, Inc.
　3150 Frview Pk Dr Ste 100
　Falls Church VA 22042
　703 995-8700

(P-15919)
GENERAL ELECTRIC COMPANY
1303 Bloomdale St, Duarte (91010-2501)
PHONE..................................626 359-7988
Edward Tabin, *Principal*
Richard Burke, *President*
Ryan Zorko, *Program Mgr*
EMP: 200
SALES (corp-wide): 121.6B **Publicly Held**
SIC: 7378 Computer maintenance & repair
PA: General Electric Company
　41 Farnsworth St
　Boston MA 02210
　617 443-3000

(P-15920)
GUARDIAN COMPUTER SUPPORT
7075 Commerce Cir Ste D, Pleasanton (94588-8015)
P.O. Box 5440, Walnut Creek (94596-1440)
PHONE..................................925 251-8800
David Costa, *Principal*
Randy Swanson, *Principal*
EMP: 125
SQ FT: 24,000
SALES (est): 5.1MM **Privately Held**
WEB: www.guardiancomputer.com
SIC: 7378 Computer & data processing equipment repair/maintenance

(P-15921)
INHOUSEIT INC
400 Exchange Ste 100, Irvine (92602-1340)
PHONE..................................949 660-5655
Glen Ackerman, *CEO*
Steve Bender, *President*
Scott V Essen, *Director*
EMP: 70
SALES (est): 10.9MM **Privately Held**
WEB: www.inhouseit.com
SIC: 7378 Computer & data processing equipment repair/maintenance

(P-15922)
LOS ANGELES UNIFIED SCHOOL DST
Also Called: Information Technology
200 N Main St Ste 1400, Los Angeles (90012-4127)
PHONE..................................213 485-3691
Marry K Kotzman, *Manager*
EMP: 150
SALES (corp-wide): 4B **Privately Held**
WEB: www.lausd.k12.ca.us
SIC: 7378 Computer & data processing equipment repair/maintenance
PA: Los Angeles Unified School District
　333 S Beaudry Ave Ste 209
　Los Angeles CA 90017
　213 241-1000

(P-15923)
ON-SITE LASERMEDIC CORPORATION (PA)
21540 Prairie St Ste D, Chatsworth (91311-5821)
PHONE..................................818 775-9111
Gail Solomon, *CEO*
Jerry Richardson, *Admin Mgr*
Heber Gutierrez, *Technician*
EMP: 51
SQ FT: 6,000
SALES (est): 7.6MM **Privately Held**
WEB: www.onsitelasermedic.com
SIC: 7378 Computer & data processing equipment repair/maintenance

(P-15924)
QUEST INTL MONITOR SVC INC (PA)
60-65 Parker, Irvine (92618)
PHONE..................................949 581-9900
Shahnam Arshadi, *President*
Perry Aminzadeh, *CFO*
Kamyar Katouzian, *Vice Pres*
Ron McCray, *Executive*
Johanna Atman, *IT/INT Sup*
▲ EMP: 60
SALES (est): 27.7MM **Privately Held**
WEB: www.questinc.com
SIC: 7378 7379 7371 7373 Computer maintenance & repair; computer related maintenance services; custom computer programming services; systems integration services; cathode ray tubes, including rebuilt; computer & software stores

(P-15925)
RAKWORX INC
23122 Alcalde Dr Ste C, Laguna Hills (92653-1459)
PHONE..................................949 215-1362
Yue Cong, *Vice Pres*
Zhiyong Ding, *President*
EMP: 150
SALES (est): 4.2MM **Privately Held**
SIC: 7378 3577 Computer & data processing equipment repair/maintenance; data conversion equipment, media-to-media: computer

(P-15926)
TELEPLAN SERVICE SOLUTIONS INC
8875 Washington Blvd B, Roseville (95678-6214)
PHONE..................................916 677-4500
Russell Sproull, *CEO*
Jan Piet Valk, *CFO*

Jack Rockwood, *Vice Pres*
Andrew Chandler, *Business Dir*
Donna Kwidzinski, *Admin Sec*
▲ **EMP:** 75
SALES (est): 13.7MM
SALES (corp-wide): 2.6MM **Privately Held**
SIC: 7378 Computer maintenance & repair
HQ: Teleplan Holding Usa, Inc.
8875 Washington Blvd B
Roseville CA 95678
916 677-4500

(P-15927)
THIRDWAVE TECHNOLOGY SERVICES
4054 Del Rey Ave Ste 207, Marina Del Rey (90292-5680)
PHONE.................310 563-2160
Sharmila Herr, *President*
EMP: 50
SALES (est): 1.4MM **Privately Held**
WEB: www.thirdwavets.com
SIC: 7378 Computer maintenance & repair

(P-15928)
TURNER TECHTRONICS INC
17845 Sky Park Cir, Irvine (92614-6112)
PHONE.................949 724-1339
Randy Hower, *Branch Mgr*
EMP: 118
SALES (corp-wide): 15.2MM **Privately Held**
WEB: www.turnertech.com
SIC: 7378 7372 Computer maintenance & repair; prepackaged software
PA: Turner Techtronics, Inc.
7675 N San Fernando Rd
Burbank CA 91505
818 973-1060

(P-15929)
TURNER TECHTRONICS INC (PA)
7675 N San Fernando Rd, Burbank (91505-1073)
PHONE.................818 973-1060
Brendan Turner, *President*
Charles Turner, *CFO*
Ellen Turner, *Vice Pres*
EMP: 140
SQ FT: 7,500
SALES (est): 15.2MM **Privately Held**
WEB: www.turnertech.com
SIC: 7378 5734 Computer & data processing equipment repair/maintenance; computer & software stores

(P-15930)
TUSA INC (PA)
Also Called: Terix Computer Service
986 Walsh Ave, Santa Clara (95050-2649)
PHONE.................888 848-3749
Bernd Appleby, *CEO*
EMP: 105
SALES: 30MM **Privately Held**
SIC: 7378 Computer maintenance & repair

7379 Computer Related Svcs, NEC

(P-15931)
24 7AI INC (PA)
2001 All Programable # 200, San Jose (95124-4356)
PHONE.................650 385-2247
Pallipuram V Kannan, *Ch of Bd*
Rohan Ganeson, *COO*
Bill Robbins, *COO*
Brent Bowman, *CFO*
Tim Pebworth, *CFO*
EMP: 126
SQ FT: 5,000
SALES (est): 831.3MM **Privately Held**
WEB: www.247customer.com
SIC: 7379

(P-15932)
A P R CONSULTING INC
17852 17th St Ste 206, Tustin (92780-2143)
PHONE.................714 544-3696
Darryl Stone, *Branch Mgr*
EMP: 590

SALES (corp-wide): 74.8MM **Privately Held**
SIC: 7379 7371 Computer related maintenance services; custom computer programming services
PA: A P R Consulting, Inc.
1370 Valley Vista Dr # 280
Diamond Bar CA 91765
909 396-5375

(P-15933)
ABTECH TECHNOLOGIES INC
Also Called: Abtech Support
2042 Corte Del Nogal D, Carlsbad (92011-1438)
PHONE.................760 827-5100
Robert Russell, *President*
Robert Wright, *CEO*
William Green, *Vice Pres*
Paul Storck, *Vice Pres*
Brandon Banks, *Executive*
EMP: 88
SALES (est): 18.4MM **Privately Held**
WEB: www.abtechsupport.com
SIC: 7379 Computer related consulting services

(P-15934)
ACER AMERICA CORPORATION (DH)
333 W San Carlos St, San Jose (95110-2726)
PHONE.................408 533-7700
Emmanuel Fromont, *CEO*
Ming Wang, *CFO*
Nga Ly, *Treasurer*
Harish Kohli, *Officer*
Tim Hesse, *Planning Mgr*
◆ **EMP:** 100
SALES (est): 87.9MM **Privately Held**
WEB: www.acersupport.com
SIC: 7379
HQ: Gateway, Inc.
7565 Irvine Center Dr # 150
Irvine CA 92618
949 471-7000

(P-15935)
ADCOM INTERACTIVE MEDIA INC
Also Called: Admedia
901 W Alameda Ave Ste 102, Burbank (91506-2849)
PHONE.................800 296-7104
Danny E Bibi, *Principal*
AVI N Bibi, *Principal*
Daniel E Bibi, *Principal*
Lacey Stanford, *Principal*
Sumeet Kamat, *Software Dev*
EMP: 52
SALES (est): 6.9MM **Privately Held**
SIC: 7379

(P-15936)
ADD2NET INC (PA)
Also Called: Lunarpages
931 E La Habra Blvd, La Habra (90631-5505)
PHONE.................714 521-8150
George Natzic, *President*
Anoop Boonyarattapan, *Exec VP*
Sanit Khurasi, *Exec VP*
EMP: 50
SQ FT: 7,000
SALES (est): 9.9MM **Privately Held**
SIC: 7379

(P-15937)
ADVANCED RSRVATION SYSTEMS INC
2445 Truxtun Rd Ste 205, San Diego (92106-6154)
PHONE.................619 501-7000
Alan Suchodolski, *President*
Alan Suchdolski, *President*
Wayne Blum, *Vice Pres*
Keith Bockmier, *Vice Pres*
Rob Kazmierski, *Vice Pres*
EMP: 65
SQ FT: 3,000
SALES (est): 7.8MM **Privately Held**
WEB: www.aresdirect.com
SIC: 7379

(P-15938)
ADVANTIS GLOBAL INC (PA)
20 Sunnyside Ave Ste E, Mill Valley (94941-1928)
PHONE.................415 850-1500
Bryan Barber, *CEO*
Jeff Taylor, *COO*
Randi Haaker, *Vice Pres*
Bennett Sabrina, *Accounting Mgr*
Kelly Clawson, *Business Mgr*
EMP: 110 **EST:** 2007
SALES: 40MM **Privately Held**
WEB: www.advantisglobal.com
SIC: 7379 Computer related consulting services;

(P-15939)
AGRIAN INC (PA)
352 W Spruce Ave, Clovis (93611)
PHONE.................559 437-5700
Nishan Majarian, *CEO*
Andriana Majarian, *COO*
Joseph Middione, *COO*
Jeff Dearborn, *Officer*
Luke Deniston, *Vice Pres*
EMP: 99
SQ FT: 3,500
SALES (est): 7.1MM **Privately Held**
SIC: 7379

(P-15940)
AICENT INC
900 E Hamilton Ave # 600, Campbell (95008-0671)
PHONE.................408 324-1316
Lynn Lui, *CEO*
Kallen Chan, *CFO*
EMP: 106 **EST:** 2000
SALES (est): 386.4K **Privately Held**
WEB: www.aicent.net
SIC: 7379 Data processing consultant

(P-15941)
ALLIANZ TECHNOLOGY AMERICA INC
Also Called: Allianz Global Corporate &
1465 N Mcdowell Blvd, Petaluma (94954-6516)
PHONE.................415 899-2713
Axel Shell, *CEO*
Olav Spiegel, *COO*
Michael Schiebel, *CFO*
Ryan Gibson, *Admin Sec*
Dominique Bourdon, *Director*
EMP: 120
SQ FT: 15,000
SALES (est): 32.4MM
SALES (corp-wide): 24.9B **Privately Held**
SIC: 7379
HQ: Allianz Technology International B.V.
Keizersgracht 484
Amsterdam 1017
205 569-715

(P-15942)
ANAPLAN INC (PA)
50 Hawthorne St, San Francisco (94105-3902)
PHONE.................415 742-8199
Frank Calderoni, *President*
Ram Krishnan, *Partner*
Karstin Valadez, *Partner*
David H Morton Jr, *CFO*
Ana Pinczuk, *Senior VP*
EMP: 141 **EST:** 2008
SQ FT: 55,000
SALES: 240.6MM **Publicly Held**
SIC: 7379

(P-15943)
APN SOFTWARE SERVICES INC (PA)
39899 Balentine Dr # 385, Newark (94560-5391)
PHONE.................510 623-5050
Aslam Chandiwalli, *President*
Harish Poojari, *Executive*
Nandkumar Misal, *Administration*
Daya Poojary, *Administration*
Maria Victoria, *Administration*
EMP: 71
SQ FT: 3,500

SALES (est): 26.3MM **Privately Held**
WEB: www.apninc.com
SIC: 7379 Computer related consulting services

(P-15944)
ASANA INC (PA)
1550 Bryant St Ste 200, San Francisco (94103-4853)
PHONE.................415 525-3888
Dustin Moskovitz, *CEO*
Marc Hedlund, *President*
Justin Rosenstein, *President*
Anne Raimondi, *Principal*
Rachel Miller, *Software Engr*
EMP: 93
SALES (est): 17.3MM **Privately Held**
WEB: www.asana.com
SIC: 7379 Computer related consulting services

(P-15945)
ASSIGN CORPORATION
200 N Maryland Ave # 204, Glendale (91206-4274)
PHONE.................818 247-7100
Umesh Lalwani, *CEO*
Tanuj Nigam, *Vice Pres*
Rachel Wagoner, *Admin Asst*
EMP: 120
SQ FT: 1,300
SALES (est): 8MM **Privately Held**
WEB: www.assigncorp.com
SIC: 7379

(P-15946)
AVENTE INC
200 Spectrum Dr Ste 300, Irvine (92618)
PHONE.................844 385-1556
Jason Pammer, *CEO*
EMP: 50
SALES (est): 1.4MM **Privately Held**
SIC: 7379

(P-15947)
BAIDU USA LLC
1195 Bordeaux Dr, Sunnyvale (94089-1210)
PHONE.................669 224-6400
Lydia Liu, *Mng Member*
EMP: 187 **EST:** 2010
SALES (est): 1MM **Privately Held**
SIC: 7379
HQ: Baidu Japan Inc.
6-10-1, Roppongi
Minato-Ku TKY 106-0
-

(P-15948)
BESTITCOM INC (PA)
1464 Madera Rd, Simi Valley (93065-3077)
PHONE.................602 667-5613
Harry Curtin, *CEO*
Susan Silberstein, *COO*
Rich Hybner, *CFO*
Fred Chen, *CTO*
John Yu, *Opers Staff*
EMP: 65
SQ FT: 20,000
SALES (est): 13.1MM **Privately Held**
WEB: www.bestit.com
SIC: 7379 Computer related consulting services; computer related maintenance services

(P-15949)
BIARCA INC (PA)
333 W San Carlos St # 600, San Jose (95110-2731)
PHONE.................408 564-4465
Subhashini Rajana, *CEO*
Kris Rajana, *President*
EMP: 75 **EST:** 2016
SALES (est): 4.8MM **Privately Held**
SIC: 7379 7371 Computer related consulting services; custom computer programming services

(P-15950)
BLYTHECO LLC
23161 Mill Creek Dr # 200, Laguna Hills (92653-1649)
PHONE.................813 854-3388
Bruce Menter,
EMP: 50

SALES (est): 3.1MM **Privately Held**
SIC: 7379 Computer related consulting services

(P-15951)
BMR APPS INC
548 Market St, San Francisco (94104-5401)
PHONE...................954 651-1412
William Schonbrun, *President*
EMP: 68
SALES (est): 4.9MM **Privately Held**
SIC: 7379

(P-15952)
BODHTREE SOLUTIONS INC
74 W Neal St Ste 100, Pleasanton (94566-6661)
PHONE...................844 409-0510
Palaniappan Natarajan, *CEO*
Madhavi Tammineedi, *President*
Trivikram Kolukuluri, *Senior VP*
Rama Krishna, *Senior VP*
Sindhu Mansanpally, *Administration*
EMP: 235
SALES (est): 18MM **Privately Held**
SIC: 7379 Computer related consulting services

(P-15953)
BRICSNET FM AMERICA INC
1820 Harvest Rd, Pleasanton (94566-5417)
PHONE...................202 756-1840
Farid Jinian, *CEO*
Hector Rodriguez, *Ch of Bd*
Stuart Turner, *President*
EMP: 70
SALES (est): 6.2MM **Privately Held**
SIC: 7379 Computer related maintenance services

(P-15954)
CALIFRNIA CRTIVE SOLUTIONS INC (PA)
Also Called: CCS Global Tech
13475 Danielson St # 220, Poway (92064-8855)
PHONE...................858 208-4143
Raminder Singh, *CEO*
Hitesh Jain, *CFO*
David Abdelgawad, *Software Dev*
Deepika Mishra, *Tech Recruiter*
Pooja RAO, *Technical Staff*
EMP: 68
SALES (est): 10.9MM **Privately Held**
WEB: www.ccsglobaltech.com
SIC: 7379 Computer related consulting services

(P-15955)
CAPGEMINI AMERICA INC
427 Brannan St, San Francisco (94107-1715)
PHONE...................415 796-6777
EMP: 100
SALES (corp-wide): 355MM **Privately Held**
SIC: 7379 Computer related consulting services
HQ: Capgemini America, Inc.
79 5th Ave Fl 3
New York NY 10003
212 314-8000

(P-15956)
CELLARSTONE INC (PA)
Also Called: Qcommission
1650 Borel Pl Ste 100, San Mateo (94402-3529)
PHONE...................650 242-0008
Gopi Mattel, *CEO*
Srini Rekapalli, *Vice Pres*
EMP: 60
SQ FT: 800
SALES (est): 7.7MM **Privately Held**
WEB: www.cellarstone.com
SIC: 7379 8742 Computer related consulting services; management consulting services

(P-15957)
CENTRAL BUSINESS SOLUTIONS INC
37600 Central Ct Ste 214, Newark (94560-3456)
PHONE...................510 573-5500
Anjul Katare, *President*
Akash Kumar, *Tech Recruiter*
Digendra Singh, *Tech Recruiter*
Shikha Katare, *Technology*
Bitopi Ghosh, *Human Res Mgr*
EMP: 70
SALES (est): 7MM **Privately Held**
SIC: 7379

(P-15958)
CGI TECHNOLOGIES SOLUTIONS INC
505 14th St Fl 9, Oakland (94612-1406)
PHONE...................510 238-5300
Shelley Bergum, *Branch Mgr*
Jose Guzman, *Info Tech Mgr*
EMP: 56
SALES (corp-wide): 8.8B **Privately Held**
SIC: 7379 Computer related consulting services
HQ: Cgi Technologies And Solutions Inc.
11325 Random Hills Rd
Fairfax VA 22030
703 267-8000

(P-15959)
CIVICACTIONS INC
3470 Shangri La Rd, Lafayette (94549-2134)
PHONE...................510 408-7510
Henry Poole, *President*
Victoria Van Ysseldyk, *Manager*
EMP: 70
SALES: 15MM **Privately Held**
SIC: 7379 Computer related consulting services

(P-15960)
CLOSINGCORP INC
3111 Camino Del Rio N # 200, San Diego (92108-5722)
PHONE...................858 551-1500
Bob Jennings, *CEO*
Pat Carney, *Officer*
EMP: 63
SQ FT: 13,823
SALES (est): 14.2MM **Privately Held**
SIC: 7379 7375 4813 ; information retrieval services;

(P-15961)
CLOUDTECH INCORPORATED
601 S Figueroa St 40501, Los Angeles (90017-5704)
PHONE...................213 230-2616
David Bruce, *Principal*
Joseph Murrary, *Principal*
John Shortz, *Principal*
EMP: 126
SALES (est): 3.3MM **Privately Held**
SIC: 7379 Computer related consulting services

(P-15962)
COMERIT INC
2201 Francisco Dr # 140283, El Dorado Hills (95762-3713)
PHONE...................888 556-5990
Greg Clark, *CEO*
Jesper Christensen, *Senior Partner*
Jeff Johnston, *CFO*
Bjarne Berg, *CIO*
Cathy Simko, *Manager*
EMP: 120 EST: 2008
SQ FT: 3,500
SALES (est): 4.4MM **Privately Held**
SIC: 7379

(P-15963)
COMITY DESIGNS INC
41 Marvin Ave, Los Altos (94022-3709)
PHONE...................415 967-1530
Dushyant Pandya, *CEO*
Piyush Pandya, *CTO*
EMP: 100

SALES: 5MM
SALES (corp-wide): 120MM **Privately Held**
SIC: 7379 Computer related consulting services
PA: Brillio, Llc
399 Thornall St Ste 1
Edison NJ 08837
800 317-0575

(P-15964)
COMMERCIAL PRGRM SYSTEMS INC (PA)
Also Called: CPS
4400 Cldwtr Cyn Ave, Studio City (91604-1480)
P.O. Box 3436, Pls Vrds Pnsl (90274-9436)
PHONE...................818 308-8560
Alan Strong, *CEO*
Phil Sawyer, *President*
Marjorie Kram, *Vice Pres*
Michele Stewart, *Vice Pres*
EMP: 150
SQ FT: 8,000
SALES (est): 13.3MM **Privately Held**
SIC: 7379 Data processing consultant

(P-15965)
COMPUTER SCIENCES CORPORATION
1111 Broadway Fl 13, Oakland (94607-4139)
PHONE...................510 645-3000
William Cunningham, *Manager*
EMP: 100
SALES (corp-wide): 20.7B **Publicly Held**
WEB: www.csc.com
SIC: 7379 7373 Computer related consulting services; systems integration services
HQ: Computer Sciences Corporation
1775 Tysons Blvd Ste 1000
Tysons VA 22102
703 245-9675

(P-15966)
CONCENTRIX CORPORATION
44201 Nobel Dr, Fremont (94538-3178)
PHONE...................510 668-3717
John Vitalie, *Branch Mgr*
Murali Jayaraman, *Vice Pres*
Stephen Patton, *Vice Pres*
Steve Richie, *Vice Pres*
Jasvinder Sagoo, *Executive*
EMP: 70
SALES (corp-wide): 20B **Publicly Held**
SIC: 7379 8742 7331 7311 Computer related maintenance services; management consulting services; direct mail advertising services; advertising agencies
HQ: Concentrix Corporation
3750 Monroe Ave
Pittsford NY 14534
585 218-5300

(P-15967)
CORE BTS INC
5250 Lankershim Blvd, North Hollywood (91601-3186)
PHONE...................818 766-2400
EMP: 106
SALES (corp-wide): 143MM **Privately Held**
SIC: 7379 Computer related consulting services
HQ: Core Bts, Inc.
5875 Castle Creek Parkway
Indianapolis IN 46250
317 566-6200

(P-15968)
COUNTY OF RIVERSIDE
6147 River Crest Dr, Riverside (92507-0768)
PHONE...................951 486-7700
Kevin Crawford, *Branch Mgr*
EMP: 50 **Privately Held**
SIC: 7379 Computer related consulting services
PA: County Of Riverside
4080 Lemon St Fl 11
Riverside CA 92501
951 955-1110

(P-15969)
COYOTE CREEK CONSULTING INC
1551 Mccarthy Blvd # 115, Milpitas (95035-7437)
PHONE...................408 383-9200
Michael R Faster, *CEO*
Anthony Coral, *Data Proc Staff*
Jeff Severance, *Engineer*
Matt Starr, *Senior Engr*
EMP: 65
SQ FT: 3,000
SALES (est): 11.2MM **Privately Held**
WEB: www.coyotecrk.com
SIC: 7379

(P-15970)
CROWDSTRIKE INC (HQ)
150 Mathilda Pl Ste 300, Sunnyvale (94086-6012)
PHONE...................888 512-8906
George Kurtz, *CEO*
Michael Carpenter, *President*
Mike Carpenter, *President*
Colin Black, *COO*
Johanna Flower, *Chief Mktg Ofcr*
EMP: 167
SQ FT: 16,000
SALES (est): 25.9MM
SALES (corp-wide): 249.8MM **Publicly Held**
SIC: 7379 Computer related maintenance services
PA: Crowdstrike Holdings, Inc.
150 Mathilda Pl Ste 300
Sunnyvale CA 94086
888 512-8906

(P-15971)
CSRA SYSTEMS & SOLUTIONS LLC
2727 Hamner Ave, Norco (92860-1927)
PHONE...................951 735-3300
Kenneth Gunn, *Manager*
EMP: 50
SALES (corp-wide): 36.1B **Publicly Held**
SIC: 7379 Computer related consulting services
HQ: Csra Systems & Solutions Llc
3170 Fairview Park Dr
Falls Church VA 22042

(P-15972)
CUSTOMER SRVC DLVRY PLTFRM CRP
Also Called: C S D P
15615 Alton Pkwy Ste 310, Irvine (92618-3308)
PHONE...................717 896-8489
Jerry Edinger, *President*
David Englund, *CFO*
Dave Dorret, *CTO*
Donna Michael, *Marketing Mgr*
EMP: 50
SQ FT: 5,000
SALES (est): 3.8MM **Privately Held**
WEB: www.csdpcorp.com
SIC: 7379 7373 Computer related consulting services; systems software development services

(P-15973)
DCM LIMITED
Also Called: Dcm Data Systems
39159 Paseo Padre Pkwy # 303, Fremont (94538-1698)
PHONE...................510 494-2321
Ashok Choudhury, *President*
EMP: 60
SQ FT: 1,500 **Privately Held**
WEB: www.dcmusa.com
SIC: 7379 Computer related consulting services
PA: D C M Limited
6th Floor, Vikrant Tower
New Delhi DL 11000

(P-15974)
DEALERTRACK COLLTE MANAG SERVI
Also Called: Fdi Collateral Management
9750 Goethe Rd, Sacramento
(95827-3500)
PHONE..................916 368-5300
Mark O'Neil, *CEO*
Daniel L Wollenberg, *President*
Beverly Devine, *Exec VP*
Tony Panganiban, *Vice Pres*
Rob Barron, *IT/INT Sup*
EMP: 220
SQ FT: 84,900
SALES (est): 33.3MM
SALES (corp-wide): 32.3B **Privately Held**
WEB: www.fdielt.com
SIC: 7379 Computer related consulting services
HQ: Trivin, Inc.
115 Poheganut Dr Ste 201
Groton CT 06340
860 448-3177

(P-15975)
DECLARA INC
977 Commercial St, Palo Alto
(94303-4908)
PHONE..................650 800-7695
Ramona Pierson, *CEO*
Theresa Matacia, *CFO*
James Stanbridge, *Vice Pres*
Debra Chrapaty, *Executive*
Nelson Gonzalez, *Security Dir*
EMP: 68
SQ FT: 3,000
SALES (est): 4MM **Privately Held**
SIC: 7379 Data processing consultant

(P-15976)
DEL REY SYSTEMS AND TECH INC (PA)
7844 Convoy Ct, San Diego (92111-1210)
PHONE..................858 874-8992
Nancy S Miller, *President*
Edward Stith, *Financial Analy*
EMP: 100
SQ FT: 5,000
SALES (est): 24.4MM **Privately Held**
WEB: www.drst.net
SIC: 7379 8732 ; merger, acquisition & reorganization research

(P-15977)
DELTA COMPUTER CONSULTING
25550 Hawthorne Blvd # 106, Torrance
(90505-6831)
PHONE..................310 541-9440
Marzieh Daneshvar, *President*
Masih Hakimpour, *Vice Pres*
EMP: 180
SQ FT: 2,000
SALES (est): 13.7MM **Privately Held**
WEB: www.deltacomputerconsulting.com
SIC: 7379 Computer related consulting services

(P-15978)
DELTA MAX
23 Curl Dr, Corona Del Mar (92625-1416)
P.O. Box 7188, Newport Beach (92658-7188)
PHONE..................949 759-8529
Robert Swanson, *Owner*
EMP: 50
SALES (est): 2.2MM **Privately Held**
WEB: www.deltamax.com
SIC: 7379 Computer related consulting services

(P-15979)
DHARNE & COMPANY
19200 Von Karman Ave # 400, Irvine
(92612-8553)
PHONE..................949 293-5675
Nitin Dharne, *President*
Sahil Borate, *Officer*
Gina Wu, *Officer*
EMP: 80
SALES (est): 2.5MM **Privately Held**
SIC: 7379 Computer related services

(P-15980)
DIGITAL FOUNDRY INC
1707 Tiburon Blvd, Belvedere Tiburon
(94920-2513)
PHONE..................415 789-1600
Bradley W Stauffer, *President*
Robert Fraik, *Chairman*
Bonnie Albin Fraik, *Vice Pres*
Andrew Lee, *Software Engr*
Brandon Levinger, *Software Engr*
EMP: 50
SQ FT: 7,500
SALES (est): 5.3MM **Privately Held**
WEB: www.digitalfoundry.com
SIC: 7379 7371 Computer related consulting services; computer software development & applications

(P-15981)
DIGITAL NETWORKS GROUP INC
20382 Hermana Cir, Lake Forest
(92630-8701)
PHONE..................949 428-6333
Jeff Davis, *CEO*
Michael Stammire, *President*
Bart Moran, *Vice Pres*
Chris Ursetta, *Admin Sec*
John Robins, *Info Tech Mgr*
EMP: 100
SALES (est): 27.3MM **Privately Held**
WEB: www.digitalnetworksgroup.com
SIC: 7379 Computer related consulting services
HQ: Telerent Leasing Corporation
4191 Fayetteville Rd
Raleigh NC 27603
919 772-8604

(P-15982)
DIGITAL REALTY TRUST INC (PA)
4 Embarcadero Ctr # 3200, San Francisco
(94111-4188)
PHONE..................415 738-6500
Laurence A Chapman, *Ch of Bd*
A William Stein, *CEO*
Andrew P Power, *CFO*
Andy Power, *CFO*
A Stein, *CFO*
EMP: 150
SALES: 3B **Privately Held**
WEB: www.digitalrealtytrust.com
SIC: 7379 7374 Data processing consultant; data processing service

(P-15983)
DIRECTAPPS INC (PA)
Also Called: Direct Technology
3009 Douglas Blvd Ste 300, Roseville
(95661-3895)
PHONE..................916 787-2200
Rick Nelson, *CEO*
Federico Michanie, *President*
Casey Stenzel, *CFO*
John Sercu, *Treasurer*
Jason Adge, *Vice Pres*
EMP: 125
SQ FT: 19,000
SALES (est): 39.7MM **Privately Held**
WEB: www.directapps.com
SIC: 7379

(P-15984)
DROISYS INC
4657 Hedgewick Ave, Fremont
(94538-3327)
PHONE..................408 329-1761
Sanjiv Goyal, *Branch Mgr*
EMP: 175
SALES (corp-wide): 28.4MM **Privately Held**
SIC: 7379 Computer related consulting services
PA: Droisys Inc.
46540 Fremont Blvd # 516
Fremont CA 94538
408 874-8333

(P-15985)
DTI SERVICES INC (PA)
601 S Figueroa St # 4300, Los Angeles
(90017-5757)
PHONE..................213 670-1100
Satoru Amano, *President*
Chad D Harmon, *CEO*
Ken Yasuda, *CFO*
Michael Frick, *Info Tech Dir*
EMP: 60 EST: 1996
SALES (est): 8.7MM **Privately Held**
WEB: www.dtiserv.com
SIC: 7379 4813 7374 7389 ; ; computer graphics service; business services

(P-15986)
DYNTEK INC (PA)
5241 California Ave # 150, Irvine
(92617-3215)
PHONE..................949 271-6700
Ron Ben-Yishay, *CEO*
Karen S Rosenberger, *CFO*
Michael Gullard, *Chairman*
Leslie Brown, *Executive*
Thomas Fox, *Executive*
EMP: 105
SQ FT: 10,250
SALES (est): 61.5MM **Publicly Held**
WEB: www.dyntek.com
SIC: 7379 ; computer related consulting services

(P-15987)
EA CONSULTING INC
1024 Iron Point Rd, Folsom (95630-8013)
PHONE..................916 357-6767
Chin K Wong, *CEO*
Robitah Mohd-Khatib, *President*
EMP: 50
SQ FT: 12,000
SALES (est): 3.5MM **Privately Held**
WEB: www.ea-inc.com
SIC: 7379 8748 Computer related consulting services; business consulting

(P-15988)
ECLIPSE SOLUTIONS INC
2150 River Plaza Dr # 380, Sacramento
(95833-4138)
PHONE..................916 565-8090
John Willis, *CEO*
Mike Watson, *President*
EMP: 84
SALES (est): 4.7MM
SALES (corp-wide): 459.1MM **Privately Held**
WEB: www.eclipsesolutions.com
SIC: 7379 8748 8742 8322 Computer related consulting services; business consulting; management consulting services; disaster service
PA: Public Consulting Group, Inc.
148 State St Fl 10
Boston MA 02109
617 426-2026

(P-15989)
EDMIN OPEN SYSTEMS INC (PA)
5471 Krny Vlla Rd Ste 310, San Diego
(92123)
PHONE..................858 712-9341
Peter Sibley, *CEO*
Rick Wells, *CFO*
Richard Datz, *Vice Pres*
Clayton Hoyle, *Vice Pres*
Sage Ann Scheer, *Vice Pres*
EMP: 54
SQ FT: 15,000
SALES (est): 10.2MM **Privately Held**
WEB: www.edmin.com
SIC: 7379 7373 7371 Computer related consulting services; value-added resellers, computer systems; software programming applications

(P-15990)
ELITE TEK SERVICES INC
131 Mercer Way, Costa Mesa
(92627-3797)
PHONE..................714 881-5301
Stephanie Duplex, *President*
Scott Duplex, *Vice Pres*
Dora Sequeira, *Nutritionist*
EMP: 54
SALES (est): 4.8MM **Privately Held**
SIC: 7379 7361 Computer related consulting services; employment agencies

(P-15991)
EMERGE DIGITAL INC
Also Called: Emerge Digital Group
543 Howard St Lbby, San Francisco
(94105-3015)
PHONE..................415 839-5055
Chase Norlin, *CEO*
Alexander Rowland, *President*
EMP: 88 EST: 2009
SALES (est): 6.2MM **Privately Held**
SIC: 7379

(P-15992)
ENEXUS GLOBAL INC
39510 Paseo Padre Pkwy # 390, Fremont
(94538-2368)
PHONE..................510 936-4044
Dinesh Puri, *President*
Ridhima Puri, *Principal*
EMP: 74
SALES (est): 154.1K **Privately Held**
SIC: 7379 Computer related services

(P-15993)
ETAIROS CONSULTING
6711 Studio Pl, Riverside (92509-5900)
PHONE..................844 219-7027
EMP: 50
SQ FT: 4,000
SALES (est): 1.9MM **Privately Held**
SIC: 7379

(P-15994)
ETHERWAN SYSTEMS INC
2301 E Winston Rd, Anaheim
(92806-5542)
PHONE..................714 779-3800
Mitch Yang, *President*
John Marchiando, *President*
Cara Rising, *Administration*
Mars Pao, *Engineer*
Jim Toepper, *Products*
▲ EMP: 100 EST: 1996
SQ FT: 5,000
SALES (est): 9.6MM
SALES (corp-wide): 2.5B **Privately Held**
WEB: www.etherwan.com
SIC: 7379 3577 Computer related maintenance services; computer peripheral equipment
HQ: Etherwan Systems, Inc.
8f, No. 2, Alley 6, Lane 235, Baoqiao Rd.
New Taipei City TAP 23145

(P-15995)
ETOUCH SYSTEMS CORP
6627 Dumbarton Cir, Fremont
(94555-3603)
PHONE..................510 795-4800
Aniruddha Gadre, *CEO*
Sachin Bhoinkar, *Executive*
Santharam Chimili, *Sr Software Eng*
Sachin Lokare, *Sr Software Eng*
Rob Nelson, *Sr Software Eng*
EMP: 600
SQ FT: 12,800
SALES: 75MM
SALES (corp-wide): 1.2B **Publicly Held**
WEB: www.etouch.net
SIC: 7379 ; computer related consulting services
PA: Virtusa Corporation
132 Turnpike Rd Ste 300
Southborough MA 01772
508 389-7300

(P-15996)
EVENTBRITE INC (PA)
155 5th St Fl 7, San Francisco
(94103-2919)
PHONE..................415 692-7779
Julia Hartz, *CEO*
Kevin Hartz, *Ch of Bd*
Randy Befumo, *CFO*
Omer Cohen,
Casey Winters,
EMP: 396
SQ FT: 48,812
SALES: 291.6MM **Publicly Held**
SIC: 7379

(P-15997)
EVOTEK INC (PA)
Also Called: Evotek Solutions
6150 Lusk Blvd Ste 204, San Diego
(92121-2738)
PHONE....................................858 362-5083
Didi Gur, *CEO*
Cesar Enciso, *Managing Prtnr*
Jeff Klenner, *President*
Susan Bullwinkle, *Vice Pres*
Mari Rodish, *General Mgr*
EMP: 59
SALES: 100MM **Privately Held**
SIC: 7379 Computer related consulting
　services

(P-15998)
EXPERTS EXCHANGE LLC
Also Called: Experts Exch Exprts-Xchange-
com
2701 Mcmillan Ave Ste 160, San Luis
Obispo (93401-4744)
P.O. Box 1229 (93406-1229)
PHONE....................................805 787-0603
Randy Redberg, *Mng Member*
Kristin Mehiel, *Partner*
Gene Richardson, *Officer*
Andrew Alsup, *Info Tech Dir*
Brian Bermingham, *Info Tech Mgr*
EMP: 55
SQ FT: 13,400
SALES (est): 5.5MM **Privately Held**
SIC: 7379

(P-15999)
FMT CONSULTANTS LLC (PA)
Also Called: F M T
2310 Camino Vida Roble # 101, Carlsbad
(92011-1561)
PHONE....................................844 369-4593
Eric Casazza, *CEO*
EMP: 51
SQ FT: 6,500
SALES: 9MM **Privately Held**
WEB: www.fmtconsultants.com
SIC: 7379

(P-16000)
FNTI FIDELITY NAT TECH
IMAGIN
2123 Ringwood Ave, San Jose
(95131-1725)
PHONE....................................408 942-1780
John Knight, *CEO*
Timothy L Plette, *CFO*
David L Walker, *Vice Pres*
EMP: 50
SQ FT: 8,000
SALES (est): 3MM **Privately Held**
SIC: 7379 Disk & diskette conversion serv-
ice

(P-16001)
FORSYS INC
6036 Stevenson Blvd, Fremont
(94538-5250)
PHONE....................................408 409-2567
Jayaprasad Vejendla, *President*
Vijay Kiran, *Senior Mgr*
EMP: 75 EST: 2015
SQ FT: 3,000
SALES (est): 20MM **Privately Held**
SIC: 7379 Computer related consulting
　services

(P-16002)
FORSYTHE TECHNOLOGY LLC
222 N Pacific Coast Hwy # 1426, El Se-
gundo (90245-5648)
PHONE....................................424 217-6500
EMP: 64
SALES (corp-wide): 3.1B **Privately Held**
SIC: 7379 Computer related maintenance
　services
HQ: Forsythe Technology, Llc
　7770 Frontage Rd
　Skokie IL 60077
　847 213-7000

(P-16003)
FUNNY OR DIE INC
1041 N Formosa Ave, West Hollywood
(90046-6703)
PHONE....................................650 461-3929
Richard Glover, *CEO*
Mitch Galbraith, *COO*

Chris Bruss, *Vice Pres*
Irina Ancevska, *Office Mgr*
Sebastian Rasino, *Information Mgr*
EMP: 50
SALES (est): 7.5MM **Privately Held**
SIC: 7379

(P-16004)
FUSIONZONE AUTOMOTIVE INC
1011 Swarthmore Ave, Pacific Palisades
(90272-2552)
PHONE....................................888 576-1136
Brett Sutherlin, *CEO*
Steve Greenfield, *President*
Karen Sutherlin, *COO*
Kevin Maloy, *CFO*
Emily Sander, *Vice Pres*
EMP: 50
SQ FT: 3,000
SALES (est): 3.6MM **Privately Held**
SIC: 7379 Computer related consulting
　services

(P-16005)
FUTURE DIAL INCORPORATED
392 Potrero Ave, Sunnyvale (94085-4116)
PHONE....................................408 245-8880
George C Huang, *CEO*
Sung L Choi, *President*
Steve Chan, *CEO*
Steve Manning, *Officer*
Dwight Huang, *Vice Pres*
▲ EMP: 80 EST: 1999
SQ FT: 8,000
SALES (est): 11.8MM **Privately Held**
WEB: www.futuredial.com
SIC: 7379 Computer related maintenance
　services

(P-16006)
FUTURE STATE
2101 Webster St Ste 520, Oakland
(94612-3050)
PHONE....................................925 956-4200
Steven Laine, *President*
Shari McAneney, *Office Mgr*
Elizabeth Rutherfurd, *Manager*
Maria Potapov, *Consultant*
EMP: 90
SALES: 19.2MM **Privately Held**
SIC: 7379 8742 Data processing consult-
ant; management consulting services

(P-16007)
GA SERVICES LLC
1681 Kettering, Irvine (92614-5613)
PHONE....................................949 752-6515
Fax: 949 606-1990
EMP: 50
SQ FT: 10,500
SALES (est): 3.6MM **Privately Held**
WEB: www.gasllc.com
SIC: 7379 7378

(P-16008)
GAMEFLY HOLDINGS LLC (PA)
6080 Center Dr Ste 800, Los Angeles
(90045-9205)
PHONE....................................310 568-8224
Dave Hodess, *President*
John Cmar, *Sr Software Eng*
Chris Gee, *Sr Software Eng*
Jack Karapetyan, *Sr Software Eng*
Nick Koier, *Sr Software Eng*
EMP: 115
SALES (est): 36.5MM **Privately Held**
SIC: 7379

(P-16009)
GDR GROUP INC
3 Park Plz Ste 1700, Irvine (92614-8540)
PHONE....................................949 453-8818
Ellen Dorse, *Principal*
Lacie Oots, *COO*
Bruce Greenburg, *Principal*
Robert Redwitz, *Principal*
Christensen Pham, *Technician*
EMP: 76
SALES (est): 18.1MM **Privately Held**
WEB: www.gdrgroup.com
SIC: 7379

(P-16010)
GEBBS SOFTWARE INTL INC
4640 Admiralty Way Fl 9, Marina Del Rey
(90292-6630)
PHONE....................................201 227-0088
Nitin Thakor, *CEO*
EMP: 85
SQ FT: 2,500
SALES: 15.4MM **Privately Held**
WEB: www.gebbs.com
SIC: 7379 Computer related consulting
　services
PA: Gebbs Software International Private
　Limited
　Gebbs House
　Mumbai MH 40009
　-

(P-16011)
GEEK SQUAD INC
2300 N Rose Ave, Oxnard (93036-2628)
PHONE....................................805 278-9555
Jonathan Roach, *Manager*
EMP: 88
SALES (corp-wide): 42.8B **Publicly Held**
SIC: 7379 Computer related consulting
　services
HQ: Geek Squad, Inc.
　1213 Washington Ave N
　Minneapolis MN 55401

(P-16012)
GEEK SQUAD INC
120 Imperial Hwy, Fullerton (92835-1019)
PHONE....................................800 433-5778
EMP: 88
SALES (corp-wide): 42.8B **Publicly Held**
SIC: 7379 Computer related consulting
　services
HQ: Geek Squad, Inc.
　1213 Washington Ave N
　Minneapolis MN 55401

(P-16013)
GEEK SQUAD INC
1490 Fitzgerald Dr, Pinole (94564-2227)
PHONE....................................800 433-5778
Rex Santacera, *Branch Mgr*
Brett Henke, *Analyst*
EMP: 88
SALES (corp-wide): 42.8B **Publicly Held**
SIC: 7379 Computer related consulting
　services
HQ: Geek Squad, Inc.
　1213 Washington Ave N
　Minneapolis MN 55401

(P-16014)
GEEK SQUAD INC
901 S Coast Dr Ste F, Costa Mesa
(92626-1783)
PHONE....................................714 434-0132
EMP: 88
SALES (corp-wide): 42.8B **Publicly Held**
SIC: 7379 Computer related consulting
　services
HQ: Geek Squad, Inc.
　1213 Washington Ave N
　Minneapolis MN 55401

(P-16015)
GEEK SQUAD INC
3741 W Chapman Ave, Orange
(92868-1608)
PHONE....................................714 938-0380
EMP: 88
SALES (corp-wide): 42.8B **Publicly Held**
SIC: 7379 Computer related consulting
　services
HQ: Geek Squad, Inc.
　1213 Washington Ave N
　Minneapolis MN 55401

(P-16016)
GENERAL DYNAMICS INFO
TECH INC
1615 Murray Canyon Rd # 600, San Diego
(92108-4314)
PHONE....................................619 881-8989
Dan Morrissey, *Branch Mgr*
Steve Ikeoka, *Software Engr*

Dennis Cristobal, *Engineer*
EMP: 50
SALES (corp-wide): 36.1B **Publicly Held**
SIC: 7379 Computer related maintenance
　services
HQ: General Dynamics Information Tech-
　nology, Inc.
　3150 Frview Pk Dr Ste 100
　Falls Church VA 22042
　703 995-8700

(P-16017)
GENERAL NETWORKS
CORPORATION
3524 Ocean View Blvd, Glendale
(91208-1212)
PHONE....................................818 249-1962
Robert Todd Withers, *President*
Randall C Wise, *Ch of Bd*
Todd Withers, *President*
Cort Baker, *Vice Pres*
David Horwatt, *Vice Pres*
EMP: 60
SQ FT: 3,600
SALES: 12MM **Privately Held**
WEB: www.gennet.com
SIC: 7379 5045 7372 Computer related
consulting services; terminals, computer;
prepackaged software

(P-16018)
GLOBAL SOFTWARE
RESOURCES INC (PA)
Also Called: G S R
4447 Stoneridge Dr Ste 1, Pleasanton
(94588-8325)
PHONE....................................925 249-2200
Prem J Hinduja, *President*
Diane Walker, *COO*
Satya Pappur, *Sr Software Eng*
Suzanne Griffith, *Human Res Dir*
EMP: 50
SALES (est): 6.7MM **Privately Held**
WEB: www.gsr-inc.com
SIC: 7379 7371 Computer related consult-
ing services; custom computer program-
ming services

(P-16019)
GLOBALWAYS INC (PA)
42808 Christy St Ste 202, Fremont
(94538-3119)
PHONE....................................510 580-1974
Uma Uppalapati, *President*
EMP: 68
SQ FT: 3,500
SALES (est): 5.8MM **Privately Held**
WEB: www.globalways.com
SIC: 7379 Computer related consulting
　services

(P-16020)
GRAYMETA INC
350 Via Las Brisas # 230, Newbury Park
(91320-7045)
PHONE....................................855 202-2270
Tom Szabo, *CEO*
Tim Henderson, *President*
Rory Donnelly, *COO*
Gina Corona, *Surgery Dir*
Josh Wiggins, *Risk Mgmt Dir*
EMP: 50
SQ FT: 2,500
SALES (est): 811.3K **Privately Held**
SIC: 7379 7374 7378 7371 Computer re-
lated maintenance services; data pro-
cessing & preparation; computer & data
processing equipment repair/mainte-
nance; computer software development &
applications

(P-16021)
HEADSTRONG CORPORATION
150 Mathilda Pl Ste 200, Sunnyvale
(94086-6011)
PHONE....................................408 732-8700
Sandip Sahai, *Manager*
EMP: 60 **Privately Held**
WEB: www.headstrong.com
SIC: 7379 8711 1731 Computer related
consulting services; engineering services;
electrical work
HQ: Headstrong Corporation
　11921 Freedom Dr Ste 550
　Reston VA 20190
　703 272-6761

▲ = Import ▼=Export
◆ =Import/Export

(P-16022)
HOMESTAR SYSTEMS INC
Also Called: Izmocars
251 Post St Ste 302, San Francisco
(94108-5020)
PHONE...............................415 694-6000
Tej Soni, *CEO*
Wang Xin, *Vice Pres*
Layton Judd, *Principal*
Soni Tej, *Director*
EMP: 85
SALES (est): 8.4MM **Privately Held**
WEB: www.izmocars.com
SIC: 7379 Computer related consulting
services

(P-16023)
HUMBOLDT DEV LLC
2804 Gateway Oaks Dr # 100, Sacramento
(95833-4345)
PHONE...............................213 295-2890
Eric Walker, *Mng Member*
EMP: 57
SALES (est): 9.3MM **Privately Held**
SIC: 7379 7371 Computer related serv-
ices; computer software development &
applications

(P-16024)
IDRIVE INC
Also Called: Ibackup.com
26115 Mureau Rd Ste A, Calabasas
(91302-3179)
PHONE...............................818 594-5972
Raghu Kulkarni, *Principal*
Ajit Sirohi, *Software Engr*
Jennifer Carver, *Manager*
Maryam Mousavi, *Manager*
Corey Loftus, *Accounts Exec*
EMP: 70
SALES (est): 12.4MM **Privately Held**
WEB: www.pro-softnet.com
SIC: 7379 Computer related maintenance
services; computer related consulting
services

(P-16025)
INCALUS INC
41829 Albrae St Ste 212, Fremont
(94538-3144)
PHONE...............................510 209-4064
Ashok Shetty, *CEO*
EMP: 50
SALES (est): 187.4K **Privately Held**
SIC: 7379 Computer related consulting
services

(P-16026)
INFOGAIN CORPORATION (PA)
485 Alberto Way Ste 100, Los Gatos
(95032-5476)
PHONE...............................408 355-6000
Sunil Bhatia, *CEO*
Ayan Mukerji, *President*
Kapil K Nanda, *President*
Brian Rogan, *President*
Kulesh Bansal, *CFO*
▲ **EMP:** 186
SQ FT: 14,487
SALES: 127.2MM **Privately Held**
WEB: www.infogain.com
SIC: 7379 7373 8742 8748 Computer re-
lated consulting services; computer inte-
grated systems design; management
information systems consultant; systems
engineering consultant, ex. computer or
professional; data processing & prepara-
tion; electrical work

(P-16027)
INFOGEN LABS INC
18223 Charlton Ln, Porter Ranch
(91326-3617)
PHONE...............................818 825-5024
Sanjeev Kuwadeker, *President*
Sid Patti, *VP Sales*
EMP: 70
SALES: 5MM **Privately Held**
SIC: 7379 Computer related consulting
services

(P-16028)
INFORMATION TECH PARTNERS INC
Also Called: I T P
505 N Lake Shore Dr 102, Burbank
(91504)
PHONE...............................800 789-7487
Michael Thompson, *President*
Chuck Newberry, *Software Dev*
EMP: 60
SQ FT: 10,000
SALES (est): 12.1MM **Privately Held**
WEB: www.itpnet.com
SIC: 7379 Computer related consulting
services

(P-16029)
INNOVA SOLUTIONS INC
3211 Scott Blvd Ste 202, Santa Clara
(95054-3009)
PHONE...............................408 889-2020
Rajiv Sardana, *CEO*
EMP: 1100 EST: 2014
SQ FT: 4,656
SALES (est): 47.3MM
SALES (corp-wide): 830.9MM **Privately Held**
SIC: 7379 Computer related consulting
services
PA: American Cybersystems, Inc.
2400 Meadowbrook Pkwy
Duluth GA 30096
770 493-5588

(P-16030)
INQBRANDS INC
Also Called: Ft USA
1801 E Holt Blvd Unit 101, Ontario
(91761-2114)
PHONE...............................909 390-7788
Jinhua Shen, *CEO*
Kim Smith, *Senior Mgr*
▲ **EMP:** 55
SQ FT: 34,000
SALES (est): 10.3MM
SALES (corp-wide): 126MM **Privately Held**
SIC: 7379
PA: Focus Technology Co., Ltd.
12f, Block A, Software Building,
Xinghuo Road, High-Tech Develop
Nanjing 21003
258 699-1866

(P-16031)
INTEGRITS CORPORATION (PA)
5205 Kearny Villa Way # 200, San Diego
(92123-1420)
PHONE...............................858 300-1600
Clarence M Carter Jr, *President*
Ivy Y Carter, *Vice Pres*
Michael Sosamon, *Vice Pres*
James Lyon, *Info Tech Dir*
Stephen Browning, *Engineer*
EMP: 50
SQ FT: 12,600
SALES: 6MM **Privately Held**
WEB: www.integrits.com
SIC: 7379 Computer related consulting
services

(P-16032)
INTELLIPRO GROUP INC
3120 Scott Blvd 301, Santa Clara
(95054-3326)
PHONE...............................408 200-9891
Grace MA, *CEO*
Xiaodong Wang, *Sr Software Eng*
Vivi Chen, *Tech Recruiter*
Shivani Sharma, *Tech Recruiter*
Sherry Wang, *Tech Recruiter*
EMP: 380
SALES (est): 18.3MM **Privately Held**
SIC: 7379 Computer related consulting
services

(P-16033)
INTERMEDIA HOLDINGS INC (PA)
100 Mathilda Pl Ste 600, Sunnyvale
(94086-6081)
PHONE...............................650 641-4000
Michael Gold, *CEO*
Amy Byrd, *Partner*
Christian Daugaard, *Partner*

Matthew Garcia, *Partner*
David Gomez, *Partner*
EMP: 72
SALES (est): 31.9MM **Privately Held**
SIC: 7379

(P-16034)
INTERNATIONAL BUS MCHS CORP
Also Called: IBM
2350 Mission College Blvd, Santa Clara
(95054-1532)
PHONE...............................408 850-8999
EMP: 529
SALES (corp-wide): 79.5B **Publicly Held**
SIC: 7379 Computer related consulting
services
PA: International Business Machines Cor-
poration
1 New Orchard Rd Ste 1 # 1
Armonk NY 10504
914 499-1900

(P-16035)
INTERNATIONAL BUS MCHS CORP
Also Called: IBM
1540 Scenic Ave, Costa Mesa
(92626-1408)
PHONE...............................714 327-3501
William Kreidler, *Branch Mgr*
EMP: 381
SALES (corp-wide): 79.5B **Publicly Held**
SIC: 7379 Computer related consulting
services
PA: International Business Machines Cor-
poration
1 New Orchard Rd Ste 1 # 1
Armonk NY 10504
914 499-1900

(P-16036)
INTERNATIONAL BUS MCHS CORP
Also Called: IBM
1001 E Hillsdale Blvd, Foster City
(94404-1643)
PHONE...............................800 426-4968
Jessica Knuckles, *President*
Monica Delbello, *Vice Pres*
Monique Ouellette, *Vice Pres*
Judy Kearney, *Prgrmr*
Sung Kang, *Research*
EMP: 396
SALES (corp-wide): 79.5B **Publicly Held**
SIC: 7379 7371 3571 3572 Computer related consulting services; computer software development; software
programming applications; minicomputers; mainframe computers; personal computers (microcomputers); computer
storage devices; drum drives, computer;
tape storage units, computer; semiconductors & related devices; microcircuits,
integrated (semiconductor)
PA: International Business Machines Corporation
1 New Orchard Rd Ste 1 # 1
Armonk NY 10504
914 499-1900

(P-16037)
INTERNET-JOURNALS LLC
Also Called: Berkeley Electronic Press
2100 Milvia St Ste 300, Berkeley
(94704-1862)
PHONE...............................510 665-1200
Jean-Gabriel Bankier, *CEO*
EMP: 52 EST: 1999
SALES (est): 6.6MM
SALES (corp-wide): 9.6B **Privately Held**
WEB: www.bepress.com
SIC: 7379
HQ: Elsevier Inc.
230 Park Ave Fl 8
New York NY 10169
212 989-5800

(P-16038)
INTRATEK COMPUTER INC
9950 Irvine Center Dr, Irvine (92618-4357)
PHONE...............................949 334-4200
Parviz Ramezani, *CEO*
Mohsen Fahami, *Shareholder*
Rodney Holdren, *Shareholder*
Bahman Ghobbeh, *CFO*

Allen Fahami, *Chairman*
EMP: 150
SQ FT: 9,800
SALES: 14.5MM **Privately Held**
WEB: www.intrapc.com
SIC: 7379

(P-16039)
IP ACCESS INTERNATIONAL
31831 Cmno Capistrno 300a, San Juan
Capistrano (92675)
PHONE...............................949 655-1000
Bryan Hill, *President*
Mike Gregg, *Director*
John Lewis, *Director*
Michael Weaver, *Director*
EMP: 50
SQ FT: 10,000
SALES (est): 5.6MM **Privately Held**
WEB: www.ipinternational.net
SIC: 7379

(P-16040)
IP INTERNATIONAL INC
Also Called: Info Plus International
1510 Fashion Island Blvd # 104, San Mateo
(94404-1557)
PHONE...............................650 403-7800
Margaret Schaninger, *President*
Agustin Ramirez, *CFO*
EMP: 50
SQ FT: 2,500
SALES (est): 5.6MM **Privately Held**
WEB: www.infoplusintl.com
SIC: 7379 8748 Computer related consult-
ing services; business consulting

(P-16041)
ISPACE INC
2381 Rosecrans Ave # 110, El Segundo
(90245-4920)
PHONE...............................310 563-3800
Suresh Kothapalli, *CEO*
Ram Davaloor, *Vice Pres*
Ebrahim Mohammed, *Administration*
Vinod Kottapalli, *Technical Mgr*
Rajiv Radhakrishnan, *Data Proc Staff*
EMP: 120
SALES (est): 17.1MM **Privately Held**
WEB: www.ispace.com
SIC: 7379

(P-16042)
ISTS WORLDWIDE INC
2201 Walnut Ave Ste 210, Fremont
(94538-2355)
PHONE...............................510 794-1400
Viren Rana, *CEO*
Akash Jain, *President*
Linda S Perry, *Exec VP*
EMP: 106
SALES (est): 8.3MM **Privately Held**
WEB: www.istsinc.com
SIC: 7379 Computer related consulting
services

(P-16043)
ITALENT CORPORATION (PA)
Also Called: Italent Digital
27 Devine St Ste 20, San Jose
(95110-2279)
PHONE...............................408 496-6200
Renee Lalonde, *Partner*
Mark W Ciotek, *Ch of Bd*
Leslie Ottavi, *Exec VP*
Fred Walters, *Exec VP*
Brion Lau, *Vice Pres*
EMP: 150
SQ FT: 200,000
SALES (est): 20.4MM **Privately Held**
SIC: 7379 Computer related consulting
services

(P-16044)
ITCO SOLUTIONS INC
1003 Whitehall Ln, Redwood City
(94061-3687)
P.O. Box 610090 (94061-0090)
PHONE...............................650 367-0514
Ryan Edwards, *Director*
Chris Middleton, *Vice Pres*
Surendra Goud, *Technology*
Harpreet Sandhu, *Technology*
Tom Kramer, *Manager*
EMP: 295

SALES (est): 21.7MM **Privately Held**
WEB: www.itcosolutions.com
SIC: 7379

(P-16045)
ITEK SERVICES INC
25501 Arctic Ocean Dr, Lake Forest
(92630-8827)
PHONE....................................949 770-4835
Donald W Rowley, *CEO*
Jon Thornton, *Project Mgr*
Ken Frank, *Business Mgr*
Mark K Brown, *Human Res Dir*
John Conti, *Opers Staff*
EMP: 100
SQ FT: 12,000
SALES: 24MM **Privately Held**
WEB: www.itekservice.com
SIC: 7379 Computer related maintenance
services

(P-16046)
ITRENEW INC (HQ)
8356 Central Ave, Newark (94560-3432)
PHONE....................................408 744-9600
Aidin Aghamiri, *CEO*
▲ EMP: 50
SQ FT: 72,000
SALES (est): 20.8MM
SALES (corp-wide): 3.6MM **Privately
Held**
SIC: 7379 7378 ; computer maintenance
& repair
PA: Intercept Parent, Inc.
110 E 59th St Fl 24
New York NY 10022
212 223-1383

(P-16047)
JOYENT INC
655 Montgomery St # 1600, San Francisco
(94111-2684)
PHONE....................................415 400-0600
Eric Hahm, *Principal*
EMP: 120
SQ FT: 11,408
SALES (est): 22.1MM **Privately Held**
WEB: www.joyent.com
SIC: 7379 Computer related consulting
services
HQ: Samsung Semiconductor, Inc.
3655 N 1st St
San Jose CA 95134
408 544-4000

(P-16048)
**KML ENTERPRISES CAREER
DEV LLC**
1900 S State College Blvd, Anaheim
(92806-0101)
PHONE....................................714 221-3100
Kevin M Landry,
EMP: 120
SQ FT: 20,000
SALES: 16.5MM **Privately Held**
SIC: 7379 8243 Computer related consult-
ing services; operator training, computer

(P-16049)
KORE1 INC
530 Technology Dr Ste 150, Irvine
(92618-1368)
PHONE....................................949 706-6990
Brian Hunt, *CEO*
EMP: 100
SALES: 8MM **Privately Held**
SIC: 7379

(P-16050)
LITTLETHINGS INC
642 Harrison St Fl 3, San Francisco
(94107-1323)
PHONE....................................917 364-9277
Joseph Speiser, *CEO*
Gretchen Tibbits, *President*
Clare Macgoey, *Officer*
Evan Gotlib, *Senior VP*
Cory Crowther, *Software Engr*
EMP: 95
SALES: 35MM **Privately Held**
SIC: 7379

(P-16051)
**LOCKHEED MARTIN
GOVERNMENT SER**
500 N Via Val Verde, Montebello
(90640-2358)
PHONE....................................323 721-6979
Nate Sadorian, *Branch Mgr*
EMP: 50
SALES (corp-wide): 10.1B **Publicly Held**
SIC: 7379 7372 Computer related consult-
ing services; prepackaged software
HQ: Leidos Government Services, Inc.
700 N Frederick Ave
Gaithersburg MD 20879
856 486-5156

(P-16052)
LOGICTIER INC
7 41st Ave 76, San Mateo (94403-5105)
PHONE....................................650 235-6600
Mary Ann Byrnes, *CEO*
Omar Ahmad, *President*
Bill Zerella, *CFO*
Amanda Reed, *Exec VP*
Patrick Whalen, *Exec VP*
EMP: 200
SALES (est): 8.1MM **Privately Held**
SIC: 7379 1731 ; electrical work

(P-16053)
**LOGIN CONSULTING SERVICES
INC**
300 Continental Blvd # 530, El Segundo
(90245-5042)
PHONE....................................310 607-9091
Elece J Otten, *President*
Lisa Borsa, *Executive*
Normally Ellis, *Administration*
Marvin Johnson, *Prgrmr*
Lesley Saunders, *Business Mgr*
EMP: 75
SQ FT: 3,200
SALES (est): 8.7MM **Privately Held**
WEB: www.loginconsult.com
SIC: 7379

(P-16054)
MARKMONITOR INC (DH)
50 California St Ste 200, San Francisco
(94111-4605)
PHONE....................................415 278-8400
Hemant Gandhi, *Treasurer*
EMP: 86
SQ FT: 25,500
SALES (est): 43.9MM
SALES (corp-wide): 328.1K **Privately
Held**
WEB: www.markmonitor.com
SIC: 7379
HQ: Camelot Uk Bidco Limited
Friars House
London SE1 8
207 433-4041

(P-16055)
MAXONIC INC
2542 S Bascom Ave Ste 190, Campbell
(95008-5542)
PHONE....................................408 739-4900
Ajay Narain, *CEO*
Nitin Khanna, *President*
Tracia Chan, *Regional Mgr*
Nina Schindler, *Technical Staff*
Deepti Vanvari, *Accountant*
EMP: 65
SQ FT: 3,499
SALES: 14.5MM **Privately Held**
WEB: www.maxonic.com
SIC: 7379 7371 Computer related consult-
ing services; computer software develop-
ment & applications

(P-16056)
METABYTE INC
Also Called: Hotdoodle.com
39300 Civic Center Dr # 260, Fremont
(94538-2324)
PHONE....................................510 405-1117
Manu Mehta, *President*
Vijay Parjan, *Finance*
EMP: 100
SQ FT: 3,000
SALES: 12MM **Privately Held**
WEB: www.metabyte.com
SIC: 7379

(P-16057)
MULTIVEN INC
303 Twin Dolphin Dr # 600, Redwood City
(94065-1497)
P.O. Box 394, San Carlos (94070-0394)
PHONE....................................408 828-2715
EMP: 50
SQ FT: 2,000
SALES (est): 2.2MM **Privately Held**
WEB: www.multiven.com
SIC: 7379

(P-16058)
**MURPHY MCKAY & ASSOCIATES
INC**
3468 Mt Diablo Blvd B108, Lafayette
(94549-7103)
PHONE....................................925 283-9555
David D McKay, *Ch of Bd*
Timothy J Murphy, *President*
EMP: 50
SQ FT: 2,000
SALES (est): 7.5MM **Privately Held**
WEB: www.murphymckay.com
SIC: 7379 Computer related consulting
services

(P-16059)
NC INTERACTIVE LLC
Also Called: Ncsoft
1 Polaris Way Ste 110, Aliso Viejo
(92656-5358)
PHONE....................................512 623-8700
Songyee Yoon, *Principal*
EMP: 100 **Privately Held**
SIC: 7379 Computer related consulting
services
HQ: Nc Interactive Llc
3180 139th Ave Se Ste 500
Bellevue WA 98005
206 588-7200

(P-16060)
NCC GROUP INC (HQ)
123 Mission St Ste 1020, San Francisco
(94105-5126)
PHONE....................................415 268-9300
Rob Cotton, *President*
Craig Motta, *President*
Craig Foster, *CFO*
Andy Grant, *Vice Pres*
Tiffany Alston, *Executive*
EMP: 90
SQ FT: 12,000
SALES (est): 40.1MM **Privately Held**
SIC: 7379 Computer data escrow service

(P-16061)
NETENRICH INC (PA)
2590 N 1st St Ste 300, San Jose
(95131-1021)
PHONE....................................408 436-5900
Raju Chekuri, *President*
Courtney Cook, *Partner*
Satish Raju, *Partner*
Bala Muppaneni, *President*
Ray Solari, *CFO*
EMP: 54
SALES (est): 26.8MM **Privately Held**
SIC: 7379 Computer related consulting
services

(P-16062)
NETPACE INC
5000 Executive Pkwy # 530, San Ramon
(94583-4282)
PHONE....................................925 543-7760
Omar Khan, *President*
Rudy Aguirre, *Creative Dir*
Salman Ahmed, *General Mgr*
Yaser Barlas, *Sr Software Eng*
Feroz Gul, *Software Engr*
EMP: 55
SQ FT: 4,000
SALES (est): 5.3MM **Privately Held**
WEB: www.netpace.com
SIC: 7379 Computer related consulting
services

(P-16063)
NEUDESIC LLC (PA)
Also Called: Neuron Esb
200 Spectrum Center Dr # 2000, Irvine
(92618-5013)
PHONE....................................949 754-4500
Parsa Rohani, *CEO*

Manny Singh, *Partner*
Dan Alecia, *Executive*
Alexis Butler, *Tech Recruiter*
Julie Chao, *Technical Staff*
EMP: 125
SQ FT: 15,150
SALES (est): 91.1MM **Privately Held**
SIC: 7379 Computer related consulting
services

(P-16064)
NORLAND GROUP
3350 Scott Blvd Ste 6501, Santa Clara
(95054-3125)
PHONE....................................408 855-8255
Mayling Liang, *President*
Sophie Kuo, *Accounting Mgr*
Reginald Malla, *Recruiter*
Karen Sandoval, *Recruiter*
EMP: 105
SQ FT: 2,200
SALES (est): 10.2MM **Privately Held**
WEB: www.norlandgroup.com
SIC: 7379 7361 Computer related consult-
ing services; employment agencies

(P-16065)
NOWCOM CORPORATION
Also Called: Hankey Group
4751 Wilshire Blvd # 205, Los Angeles
(90010-3860)
PHONE....................................323 938-6449
Don R Hankey, *President*
Capm Siddiqui, *Department Mgr*
Letty Aguiar, *Administration*
Oliver Baes, *Administration*
Rosa Martinez, *Administration*
EMP: 54
SQ FT: 4,800
SALES (est): 14MM **Privately Held**
WEB: www.nowcom.com
SIC: 7379

(P-16066)
ODESUS INC (PA)
11766 Wilshire Blvd # 400, Los Angeles
(90025-6551)
PHONE....................................310 473-4600
Robert P Michaels, *President*
Lisa McCarthy, *Executive*
Teresa Boggs, *Admin Asst*
Jose Galvez, *Tech Recruiter*
Cynthia Yoon, *Technical Staff*
EMP: 100
SQ FT: 3,000
SALES: 9MM **Privately Held**
WEB: www.odesus.com
SIC: 7379

(P-16067)
OLSON & ASSOC
3448 Lupine Cir Ste 102, Costa Mesa
(92626-1723)
PHONE....................................714 878-6649
Steven Olson, *CEO*
EMP: 60
SQ FT: 1,500
SALES (est): 4.7MM **Privately Held**
WEB: www.strategicgrowthsolutions.com
SIC: 7379 7389 Computer related consult-
ing services; personal service agents,
brokers & bureaus

(P-16068)
OMNIKRON SYSTEMS INC
20920 Warner Center Ln A, Woodland Hills
(91367-6526)
PHONE....................................818 591-7890
EMP: 100
SALES (est): 4.9MM **Privately Held**
WEB: www.omnikron.com
SIC: 7379 7375 5045 8243

(P-16069)
ONEHEALTH SOLUTIONS INC
420 Stevens Ave Ste 200, Solana Beach
(92075-2078)
PHONE....................................858 947-6333
Bruce Springer, *President*
John Shade, *COO*
Jeff Goe, *Senior VP*
Chuck Mitchell, *Vice Pres*
EMP: 100

SALES (est): 7.6MM
SALES (corp-wide): 56.4MM **Privately Held**
SIC: 7379
PA: Viverae, Inc.
10670 N Cntl Expy Ste 700
Dallas TX 75231
214 827-4400

(P-16070)
OPAL SOFT INC
Also Called: Opalsoft
1288 Kifer Rd Ste 201, Sunnyvale
(94086-5326)
PHONE...............................408 267-2211
Omprakash Choudhary, *President*
Alkesh Choudhary, *CFO*
EMP: 80
SQ FT: 2,450
SALES: 13.3MM **Privately Held**
WEB: www.opalsoft.com
SIC: 7379 8748 7371 8713 ; business
consulting; custom computer programming services; computer software systems analysis & design, custom;
surveying services; photogrammetric engineering; data processing & preparation;
service bureau, computer; computer facilities management

(P-16071)
ORACLE CORPORATION (PA)
500 Oracle Pkwy, Redwood City
(94065-1677)
PHONE...............................650 506-7000
Safra A Catz, *CEO*
Lawrence J Ellison, *Ch of Bd*
Mark V Hurd, *CEO*
Jeffrey O Henley, *Vice Ch Bd*
Dorian E Daley, *Exec VP*
EMP: 2300
SQ FT: 2,100,000
SALES: 39.5B **Publicly Held**
WEB: www.oracle.com
SIC: 7379 8243 3571 3674 Computer re-
lated consulting services; software train-
ing, computer; minicomputers;
microprocessors; business oriented com-
puter software

(P-16072)
ORACLE SYSTEMS CORPORATION (HQ)
500 Oracle Pkwy, Redwood City
(94065-1677)
PHONE...............................650 506-7000
Safra A Catz, *CEO*
Lawrence J Ellison, *Ch of Bd*
Jeffrey O Henley, *Ch of Bd*
Mark V Hurd, *President*
Mark Hurd, *CEO*
EMP: 2300
SQ FT: 2,200,000
SALES (est): 5.9B
SALES (corp-wide): 39.5B **Publicly Held**
WEB: www.forcecapital.com
SIC: 7379 8243 7372 Data processing
consultant; software training, computer;
business oriented computer software
PA: Oracle Corporation
500 Oracle Pkwy
Redwood City CA 94065
650 506-7000

(P-16073)
ORGANIC INC
390 Amapola Ave Ste 8, Torrance
(90501-1400)
PHONE...............................310 543-4600
EMP: 71
SALES (corp-wide): 15.3B **Publicly Held**
SIC: 7379
HQ: Organic, Inc.
600 California St Fl 8
San Francisco CA 94108
415 581-5300

(P-16074)
ORGANIC INC (HQ)
600 California St Fl 8, San Francisco
(94108-2726)
PHONE...............................415 581-5300
Conor Brady, *Ch Credit Ofcr*
David Bryant, *Officer*
Mark Murata, *Officer*
Tina Leone Webber, *Controller*

Nicole Craine, *Opers Dir*
EMP: 142 EST: 1993
SQ FT: 23,000
SALES (est): 30.1MM
SALES (corp-wide): 15.2B **Publicly Held**
WEB: www.organic.com
SIC: 7379 8742 ; computer related con-
sulting services; marketing consulting
services
PA: Omnicom Group Inc.
437 Madison Ave
New York NY 10022
212 415-3600

(P-16075)
OSI DIGITAL INC
2525 Main St Ste 350, Irvine (92614-6685)
PHONE...............................949 724-8300
Kumar Yamani, *Owner*
Sriram Ranganathan, *Vice Pres*
Candace Bracht, *Sr Consultant*
EMP: 50 **Privately Held**
SIC: 7379 ; computer related consulting
services
PA: Osi Digital Inc.
5950 Canoga Ave Ste 300
Woodland Hills CA 91367

(P-16076)
OUTLOOK AMUSEMENTS INC
2900 W Alameda Ave # 400, Burbank
(91505-4241)
PHONE...............................818 433-3800
Jason Freeland, *CEO*
Cyrus Pejoumand, *President*
Tim Youd, *Co-President*
Tom Wszalek, *Senior VP*
Thomas Wszalek, *Vice Pres*
EMP: 150
SQ FT: 8,000
SALES (est): 26.1MM **Privately Held**
SIC: 7379

(P-16077)
PARTNERS INFORMATION TECH INC (HQ)
Also Called: Calance
7101 Village Dr, Buena Park (90621-2260)
PHONE...............................714 736-4487
Amit Govil, *Chairman*
Bill Darden, *CFO*
Asit Govil, *Treasurer*
Robert Dlugos, *Info Tech Mgr*
EMP: 100
SQ FT: 46,000
SALES (est): 73.8MM **Privately Held**
SIC: 7379 ; computer related consulting
services

(P-16078)
PEGASUS SQUIRE INC
12021 Wilshire Blvd Ste 7, Los Angeles
(90025-1206)
PHONE...............................866 208-6837
Scott Cooper, *CEO*
EMP: 100 EST: 2002
SALES (est): 4.6MM **Privately Held**
SIC: 7379 Computer related consulting
services

(P-16079)
PERFORMANCE TECH PARTNERS LLC
500 Capitol Mall Ste 2350, Sacramento
(95814-4760)
PHONE...............................800 787-4143
John Podlipnik,
Jeff Forderer,
EMP: 106
SALES: 30MM **Privately Held**
WEB: www.performtechnology.com
SIC: 7379

(P-16080)
PEXS INTERNATIONAL INC
1400 Midvale Ave Apt 408, Los Angeles
(90024-7812)
PHONE...............................626 365-6706
Shi Chang Lin, *CEO*
Pien LI, *CFO*
EMP: 124 EST: 2017
SALES (est): 2.2MM **Privately Held**
SIC: 7379 7371 Computer related consult-
ing services; computer software develop-
ment & applications

(P-16081)
PLANNET CONSULTING LLC
2951 Saturn St Ste E, Brea (92821-6206)
PHONE...............................714 982-5800
Steve Miano, *CEO*
Andrew Harrod, *President*
Gary Cox, *Principal*
EMP: 52
SQ FT: 10,800
SALES (est): 4.7MM **Privately Held**
WEB: www.plannetconsulting.com
SIC: 7379 8742 8748 Computer related
consulting services; management consult-
ing services; telecommunications consult-
ant

(P-16082)
POINTSPEED INC
135 Wyndham Dr, Portola Valley
(94028-7240)
PHONE...............................650 638-3720
Norman Goldfarb, *President*
Ron Croce, *COO*
Michael Baltazar, *Vice Pres*
Sabet Chowdbury, *Vice Pres*
Jonathan Lewis, *Vice Pres*
EMP: 71
SALES (est): 2.7MM **Privately Held**
SIC: 7379 Computer related consulting
services

(P-16083)
PRAETORIAN GROUP (PA)
Also Called: Policeone Academy
200 Green St Ste 200 # 200, San Francisco
(94111-1356)
PHONE...............................415 962-8310
Mike Herning, *Ch of Bd*
Bob Bradley, *Vice Pres*
Chip Scarborough, *Executive Asst*
Ryan Houghtelling, *Info Tech Dir*
Shawn Conrad, *Technology*
EMP: 50
SALES (est): 9.1MM **Privately Held**
WEB: www.policeone.com
SIC: 7379

(P-16084)
PRAGITI INC
3312 Woodward Ave, Santa Clara
(95054-2627)
PHONE...............................408 689-7214
Praveen Pahwa, *CEO*
EMP: 55
SALES (est): 3.7MM
SALES (corp-wide): 359.2MM **Privately Held**
SIC: 7379 Computer related consulting
services
PA: Digital Management, Llc
6550 Rock Spring Dr Fl 7
Bethesda MD 20817
240 223-4800

(P-16085)
PRAMIRA INC
1422 Edinger Ave Ste 250, Tustin
(92780-6299)
PHONE...............................800 678-1169
Omar Houari, *CEO*
Edward Krol, *Vice Pres*
EMP: 125 EST: 2014
SQ FT: 6,000
SALES (est): 7.9MM **Privately Held**
SIC: 7379 8711 Computer related consult-
ing services; engineering services

(P-16086)
PRECISEQ INC
11601 Wilshire Blvd Fl 5, Los Angeles
(90025-1995)
PHONE...............................310 709-6094
Mark Dorner, *Partner*
Guy Livneh, *Managing Prtnr*
EMP: 80
SQ FT: 1,200
SALES (est): 560K **Privately Held**
SIC: 7379 Computer related consulting
services

(P-16087)
PRELUDE SYSTEMS INC (PA)
Also Called: PRELUDESYS
5 Corporate Park Ste 140, Irvine
(92606-3163)
PHONE...............................949 208-7126

Kiran B Chandra, *CEO*
Rajamannar Abboy, *President*
Rangesh Rajaram, *Vice Pres*
Manoj K Chandra, *Sr Software Eng*
Selva Pandian, *Project Mgr*
EMP: 121
SQ FT: 4,900
SALES: 16.3MM **Privately Held**
SIC: 7379

(P-16088)
PRIMITIVE LOGIC INC
704 Sansome St, San Francisco
(94111-1704)
PHONE...............................415 391-8080
Jill P Reber, *CEO*
Kevin Moos, *President*
Anisha Weber, *COO*
Mike McDermott, *Senior VP*
Eric Greenfeder, *Vice Pres*
EMP: 63 EST: 1996
SQ FT: 10,000
SALES (est): 12.6MM **Privately Held**
WEB: www.primitivelogic.com
SIC: 7379 Computer related consulting
services

(P-16089)
PRO-TEK CONSULTING (PA)
21300 Victory Blvd # 240, Woodland Hills
(91367-2525)
PHONE...............................805 807-5571
Raj Kessireddy, *CEO*
Divya Reddy Pyreddy, *Chairman*
EMP: 110 EST: 2010
SQ FT: 2,400
SALES (est): 14MM **Privately Held**
SIC: 7379

(P-16090)
PRODUCT QUALITY PARTNERS INC
450 Main St Ste 207, Pleasanton
(94566-7071)
PHONE...............................925 484-6491
Debra Levesque, *President*
Debra Hodtens, *President*
EMP: 54
SQ FT: 20,000
SALES: 600K **Privately Held**
WEB: www.qpqa.com
SIC: 7379 Computer related maintenance
services

(P-16091)
PROLIFICS INC (DH)
24025 Park Sorrento # 405, Calabasas
(91302-4037)
PHONE...............................212 267-7722
Satya Bolli, *CEO*
Biju Nair, *CFO*
Vivek Kalra, *Officer*
David Mogel, *Admin Sec*
EMP: 255
SQ FT: 7,000
SALES (est): 37.5MM **Privately Held**
WEB: www.jyacc.com
SIC: 7379 7371 Computer related consult-
ing services; computer software develop-
ment
HQ: Prolifics Application Services, Inc.
24025 Park Sorrento # 405
Calabasas CA 91302
646 201-4967

(P-16092)
PROPEL SOFTWARE CORPORATION
1010 Rincon Cir, San Jose (95131-1325)
PHONE...............................408 571-6300
Steven T Kirsch, *President*
Steven Manser, *COO*
Steve Strange, *Vice Pres*
EMP: 130
SQ FT: 30,000
SALES (est): 9.6MM **Privately Held**
WEB: www.propel.com
SIC: 7379 Computer related consulting
services

(P-16093)
QUANTUM SOLUTIONS INC
5146 Douglas Fir Rd # 205, Calabasas
(91302-1405)
PHONE...............................818 577-4555
Hamid Akhavan, *CEO*

EMP: 50
SQ FT: 14,641
SALES (est): 4.9MM Privately Held
SIC: 7379 8742 ; business consultant

(P-16094)
QUBERA SOLUTIONS INC
676 Gail Ave Apt 26, Sunnyvale
(94086-8134)
PHONE...................650 294-4460
Prasad Jayaraman, *President*
Jacob Pszonowsky, *Vice Pres*
EMP: 50
SQ FT: 2,900
SALES (est): 8MM Privately Held
SIC: 7379 Computer related consulting
   services

(P-16095)
R S SOFTWARE INDIA LIMITED
1900 Mccarthy Blvd # 103, Milpitas
(95035-7413)
PHONE...................408 382-1200
Rajnit Jain, *President*
Bibek Das, *Vice Pres*
Garry Singer, *Regl Sales Mgr*
Srishti Jain, *Marketing Staff*
EMP: 96
SQ FT: 3,100
SALES (est): 11.1MM
SALES (corp-wide): 8.6MM Privately
   Held
WEB: www.rssoftware.com
SIC: 7379 7371 Computer related consult-
   ing services; computer software develop-
   ment
PA: R S Software (India) Limited
   A - 2, Fmc Fortuna
   Kolkata WB 70002
   983 090-5060

(P-16096)
RIGHTPOINT CONSULTING LLC
1453 3rd Street Promenade, Santa Monica
(90401-2397)
PHONE...................310 451-4619
EMP: 117 Privately Held
SIC: 7379
PA: Rightpoint Consulting, Llc
   29 N Wacker Dr Fl 4
   Chicago IL 60606

(P-16097)
RISKALYZE INC
373 Elm Ave, Auburn (95603-4524)
PHONE...................530 748-1660
Aaron Klein, *CEO*
Kyle Van Pelt, *Partner*
Andrew Palmer, *CFO*
Duncan Powell, *CFO*
Lori Hardwick, *Chairman*
EMP: 112
SALES (est): 7MM Privately Held
SIC: 7379

(P-16098)
SADA SYSTEMS INC
5250 Lankershim Blvd # 620, North Holly-
wood (91601-3188)
PHONE...................818 766-2400
Tony Safoian, *CEO*
Dana Berg, *COO*
Matt Lawrence, *CFO*
Annie Safoian, *CFO*
Patrick Monaghan,
EMP: 106
SQ FT: 10,503
SALES (est): 28MM Privately Held
SIC: 7379 Computer related consulting
   services

(P-16099)
SAGE INTACCT INC (HQ)
300 Park Ave Ste 1400, San Jose
(95110-2774)
PHONE...................408 878-0900
Robert Kleinschmidt, *President*
Scott Lumish, *President*
Marc Linden, *CFO*
Robert K Reid, *Exec VP*
Kathleen Lord, *Vice Pres*
EMP: 50
SQ FT: 6,000

SALES (est): 26.3MM
SALES (corp-wide): 2.3B Privately Held
WEB: www.intacct.com
SIC: 7379 7371 Computer related consult-
   ing services; custom computer program-
   ming services
PA: The Sage Group Plc.
   North Park Avenue
   Newcastle-Upon-Tyne NE13
   191 294-3000

(P-16100)
**SAPPHIRE SOFTECH
SOLUTIONS LLC**
123 E 9th St Ste 323, Upland
(91786-6050)
P.O. Box 6220, Corona (92878-6220)
PHONE...................888 357-5222
Nitin Makkar,
Jasmeer Oberoi,
Rajdeep Singh Oberoi,
EMP: 60
SALES (est): 47.1K Privately Held
SIC: 7379 Computer related maintenance
   services

(P-16101)
SCALEMATRIX HOLDINGS INC
5775 Kearny Villa Rd, San Diego
(92123-1111)
PHONE...................888 349-9994
Chris Orlando, *CEO*
Emily Stebing, *CFO*
Jenny Friederichs, *Executive*
Alex Lee, *Executive*
Linnette Hollman, *Administration*
EMP: 75 EST: 2011
SQ FT: 85,461
SALES (est): 17.1MM Privately Held
SIC: 7379 Computer related consulting
   services

(P-16102)
**SCIENCE APPLICATIONS INTL
CORP**
Also Called: Saic Government Solutions
4065 Hancock St Ste 110, San Diego
(92110-5151)
PHONE...................703 676-4300
Jeff Ferguson, *CEO*
Anthony Morraco, *CEO*
EMP: 99
SALES (corp-wide): 4.6B Publicly Held
SIC: 7379 Computer related consulting
   services
PA: Science Applications International Cor-
   poration
   12010 Sunset Hills Rd
   Reston VA 20190
   703 676-4300

(P-16103)
SCIENCE EXCHANGE INC (PA)
435 Tasso St Ste 100, Palo Alto
(94301-1546)
PHONE...................562 665-8978
Elizabeth Iorns, *CEO*
Daniel Knox, *COO*
Jim Emerich, *CFO*
Clifford Culver, *Vice Pres*
Andrew Gutierrez, *Vice Pres*
EMP: 55
SALES (est): 15.6MM Privately Held
SIC: 7379

(P-16104)
**SEATECH CONSULTING GROUP
INC**
609 Deep Valley Dr # 200, Rllng HLS Est
(90274-3614)
PHONE...................310 356-6828
EMP: 50
SALES: 3.5MM Privately Held
SIC: 7379

(P-16105)
SEAVER INTERNATIONAL
4169 Green Valley Schl Rd, Sebastopol
(95472-8944)
PHONE...................707 291-4929
Jesse Seaver, *Owner*
EMP: 89
SALES (est): 2.6MM Privately Held
SIC: 7379 Computer related consulting
   services

(P-16106)
SENTEK CONSULTING INC
Also Called: Sentek Global
2811 Nimitz Blvd Ste G, San Diego
(92106-4311)
PHONE...................619 543-9550
Eric Basu, *CEO*
Jason Galetti, *COO*
Theresa Thomas, *Executive*
Brigitte Carino, *Admin Asst*
Jill Lesher, *Administration*
EMP: 132 EST: 2001
SALES (est): 22.5MM Privately Held
WEB: www.sentekconsulting.com
SIC: 7379

(P-16107)
SERENE AST LLC (HQ)
3211 Scott Blvd Ste 201, Santa Clara
(95054-3009)
PHONE...................408 986-8544
Shaji Zechariah, *President*
Govind Patwa, *Sr Consultant*
Sachin Ganorkar, *Director*
EMP: 90
SQ FT: 4,816
SALES (est): 20.2MM
SALES (corp-wide): 56.2MM Privately
   Held
WEB: www.serenecorp.com
SIC: 7379 Computer related consulting
   services
PA: Applications Software Technology Llc
   4343 Commerce Ct Ste 701
   Lisle IL 60532
   630 778-0707

(P-16108)
SHOWPAD INC (HQ)
301 Howard St Ste 500, San Francisco
(94105-6603)
PHONE...................415 800-2033
Pieterjan Bouten, *CEO*
Lenz Briana, *President*
Jason Holmes, *President*
Hendrik Isebaert, *CEO*
Alan Gurock, *Senior VP*
EMP: 350
SALES (est): 4.9MM
SALES (corp-wide): 19.2MM Privately
   Held
SIC: 7379 Computer related maintenance
   services
PA: Showpad
   Moutstraat 62
   Gent 9000
   230 939-17

(P-16109)
SITELITE HOLDINGS INC
111 Theory Fl 2, Irvine (92617-3039)
PHONE...................949 265-6200
Reddy Marri, *President*
Kumar Yamani, *Chairman*
EMP: 135 EST: 1999
SQ FT: 30,000
SALES (est): 6.2MM Privately Held
SIC: 7379 8742 Computer related consult-
   ing services; management consulting
   services

(P-16110)
SIZMEK DSP INC (DH)
2000 Seaport Blvd Ste 400, Redwood City
(94063-5584)
PHONE...................650 595-1300
Mark Grether, *CEO*
Stephen Snyder, *CFO*
Eric Duerr, *Chief Mktg Ofcr*
Jennifer Trzepacz, *Exec VP*
Yasmine Decosterd, *Vice Pres*
EMP: 148
SALES: 456.2MM
SALES (corp-wide): 463.4MM Privately
   Held
SIC: 7379 7371 Computer related consult-
   ing services; computer software develop-
   ment & applications

(P-16111)
SKYSLOPE INC
825 K St Fl 2, Sacramento (95814-3547)
PHONE...................916 833-2390
Tyler Smith, *CEO*
Buck Avey, *Vice Pres*
Emilee Johnson, *Vice Pres*

Amanda Nunes, *Executive*
Arielle Percival, *Executive Asst*
EMP: 100
SQ FT: 23,000
SALES: 5.8MM
SALES (corp-wide): 7.5B Publicly Held
SIC: 7379
PA: Fidelity National Financial, Inc.
   601 Riverside Ave Fl 4
   Jacksonville FL 32204
   904 854-8100

(P-16112)
SMASHON INC
1754 Tech Dr Ste 234, San Jose (95110)
PHONE...................855 762-7466
Tasawar Jalali, *CEO*
EMP: 50
SALES (est): 2.5MM Privately Held
SIC: 7379 Computer related maintenance
   services; computer consulting
   services

(P-16113)
SOFT HQ HOLDINGS LLC
Also Called: Softhq
6494 Weathers Pl Ste 200, San Diego
(92121-2938)
PHONE...................858 658-9200
Sindhura Thummalasetty, *Principal*
Kranti Ponnam, *Director*
Shaun Smith, *Manager*
EMP: 50
SALES (est): 9.4MM Privately Held
SIC: 7379

(P-16114)
**SOFTWARE MANAGEMENT
CONS INC (PA)**
Also Called: Smci
500 Nth Brn Blvd Ste 1100, Glendale
(91203)
PHONE...................818 240-3177
Spencer L Karpf, *CEO*
Alden Metz, *President*
Bob Maltzman, *COO*
Susanna Dashknyan, *Vice Pres*
Siddhant Singh, *Tech Recruiter*
EMP: 320
SQ FT: 4,500
SALES (est): 54.8MM Privately Held
WEB: www.smci.com
SIC: 7379 7361 Computer related consult-
   ing services; placement agencies

(P-16115)
SOLUGENIX CORPORATION
225 N Barranca St, West Covina
(91791-1688)
PHONE...................866 749-7658
EMP: 58
SALES (corp-wide): 43.9MM Privately
   Held
SIC: 7379 Computer related maintenance
   services
PA: Solugenix Corporation
   601 Valencia Ave
   Brea CA 92823
   866 749-7658

(P-16116)
SONICOCOM INC
2202 S Figueroa St, Los Angeles
(90007-2049)
PHONE...................213 291-0475
Rodrigo Teijeiro, *President*
Gustavo Victorica, *CFO*
EMP: 90
SQ FT: 400
SALES (est): 3.6MM Privately Held
SIC: 7379

(P-16117)
SPARTA CONSULTING INC
111 Woodmere Rd Ste 200, Folsom
(95630-4750)
PHONE...................916 985-0300
Lokesh Sikaria, *CEO*
Paul Freudenberg, *Ch of Bd*
Vaibhav Nadgauda, *President*
Denise Ferre, *CFO*
Brent Kelton, *Exec VP*
EMP: 300 EST: 2007
SQ FT: 7,200

SALES (est): 38.4MM
SALES (corp-wide): 141.4MM **Privately Held**
SIC: 7379 Computer related consulting services
PA: Birlasoft Limited
Plot No-35 & 36, Rajiv Gandhi Infotech Park,
Pune MH 41105
206 652-5000

(P-16118)
SPRINGML INC
6200 Stoneridge Mall Rd, Pleasanton (94588-3242)
PHONE..................916 316-1566
Charles Landry, *CEO*
Girish Reddy, *Admin Sec*
EMP: 80
SQ FT: 1,200
SALES (est): 3.1MM **Privately Held**
SIC: 7379 7371 Computer related consulting services; computer software development & applications

(P-16119)
SRK GLOBAL CONSULTING
7225 Crescent Park W # 255, Los Angeles (90094-2718)
PHONE..................310 295-2524
Steven Kahn, *Exec Dir*
EMP: 60
SALES (est): 500K **Privately Held**
SIC: 7379 Computer related consulting services

(P-16120)
SRS CONSULTING INC
39465 Paseo Padre P, Fremont (94538)
PHONE..................510 252-0625
Sangeetha Chowhan, *CEO*
Shankar Chowhan, *President*
EMP: 58
SQ FT: 1,250
SALES (est): 7.9MM **Privately Held**
WEB: www.srsconsultinginc.com
SIC: 7379 7371 Computer related consulting services; computer software development

(P-16121)
STELLA TECHNOLOGY INCORPORATED
6203 San Ignacio Ave # 100, San Jose (95119-1358)
PHONE..................402 350-1681
Christopher Henkenius, *CEO*
David Jones, *President*
Krishna Khadloya, *President*
Sandra Sarnoff, *COO*
Salim Kizaraly, *CFO*
EMP: 90 **EST:** 2012
SALES (est): 7MM **Privately Held**
SIC: 7379

(P-16122)
STRATA INFORMATION GROUP INC
3935 Harney St Ste 203, San Diego (92110-2849)
PHONE..................619 296-0170
Henry A Eimstad, *President*
Kari Blinn, *Executive*
Michael Fox, *Executive*
Linda Bettencourt, *Administration*
Edward Ahrens, *Database Admin*
EMP: 93
SQ FT: 2,000
SALES (est): 17.4MM **Privately Held**
WEB: www.sigcorp.com
SIC: 7379

(P-16123)
SYNECTIC SOLUTIONS INC (PA)
Also Called: S S I
1701 Pacific Ave Ste 260, Oxnard (93033-1887)
PHONE..................805 483-4800
Lynn Dines, *President*
Joel Dines, *CFO*
Toby Doane, *Vice Pres*
Pam Pullman, *Director*
EMP: 78 **EST:** 1997
SQ FT: 5,000

SALES (est): 14.9MM **Privately Held**
WEB: www.synecsolu.com
SIC: 7379 8331 ; job training services

(P-16124)
SYNIVERSE TECHNOLOGIES LLC
181 Metro Dr Ste 450, San Jose (95110-1344)
PHONE..................408 324-1830
EMP: 106
SALES (corp-wide): 306.2MM **Privately Held**
SIC: 7379 Data processing consultant
HQ: Syniverse Technologies, Llc
8125 Highwoods Palm Way
Tampa FL 33647

(P-16125)
SYNOPTEK INC (PA)
19520 Jamboree Rd Ste 110, Irvine (92612-2429)
PHONE..................949 241-8600
Tim Britt, *CEO*
Phil Crippen, *Officer*
Brandon Maas, *Officer*
Jeff Pagano, *Officer*
Michael Bank, *Vice Pres*
EMP: 67
SALES (est): 90.1MM **Privately Held**
WEB: www.netsolutionsinc.com
SIC: 7379 Computer related consulting services

(P-16126)
SYSTECH INTEGRATORS INC
2050 Gateway Pl, San Jose (95110-1011)
PHONE..................408 441-2700
Sam Tyagi, *CEO*
Rajeev Tyagi, *COO*
EMP: 240
SALES (est): 14.7MM **Privately Held**
WEB: www.systechi.com
SIC: 7379 Computer related consulting services
HQ: Valores Corporativos Softtek, S.A. De C.V.
Jaime Balmes No. 11 Torre C Piso 6
Ciudad De Mexico CDMX 11510

(P-16127)
T & T SOLUTIONS INC
7018 Owensmouth Ave # 201, Canoga Park (91303-2073)
PHONE..................818 676-1786
Fax: 818 676-1272
EMP: 70
SQ FT: 2,100
SALES (est): 6.2MM **Privately Held**
WEB: www.ttsus.com
SIC: 7379

(P-16128)
TACTICAL ENGRG & ANALIS INC (PA)
6050 Santo Rd Ste 250, San Diego (92124-6104)
P.O. Box 421425 (92142-1425)
PHONE..................858 573-9869
Robert Rosado, *President*
Lawrence Massaro, *CFO*
Julie Rapolla, *Executive*
David Andersen, *Business Dir*
Larry Stevens, *Technical Mgr*
EMP: 104
SQ FT: 14,000
SALES: 25MM **Privately Held**
WEB: www.tac-eng.com
SIC: 7379 8711 Computer related consulting services; engineering services

(P-16129)
TAOS MOUNTAIN LLC (PA)
121 Daggett Dr, San Jose (95134-2110)
PHONE..................408 324-2800
Hamilton Yu, *CEO*
Paul Smith, *Partner*
Ricardo Urrutia, *Ch of Bd*
Jeff Lucchesi, *COO*
Mary Hale, *CFO*
EMP: 335
SQ FT: 45,000

SALES (est): 86.2MM **Privately Held**
SIC: 7379 Computer related consulting services

(P-16130)
TATA AMERICA INTL CORP
Also Called: Tata Consulting Services
5201 Great America Pkwy # 400, Santa Clara (95054-1143)
PHONE..................408 569-5845
S K Bhattacharjee, *Manager*
Dhanam Palanivel, *Technical Mgr*
Archana Kulkarni, *Manager*
EMP: 100
SALES (corp-wide): 1.2B **Privately Held**
SIC: 7379 Computer related consulting services
HQ: Tata America International Corporation
101 Park Ave Rm 2603
New York NY 10178
212 557-8038

(P-16131)
TECH-ED NETWORKS INC
10000 Allantown Dr # 175, Roseville (95678-5996)
PHONE..................916 784-2005
Stephen Fassler, *President*
Ross Ramsey, *Vice Pres*
EMP: 111
SQ FT: 67,800
SALES (est): 6.6MM **Privately Held**
WEB: www.techednetworks.com
SIC: 7379 Computer related consulting services

(P-16132)
TECHNOLOGY SERVICES CAL DEPT
Also Called: Office of Technology
3101 Gold Camp Dr, Rancho Cordova (95670-6099)
PHONE..................916 464-3747
Amy Tom, *Branch Mgr*
Pam Haase, *Data Proc Staff*
EMP: 200 **Privately Held**
SIC: 7379
HQ: California Department Of Technology Services
1325 J St Ste 1600
Sacramento CA 95814

(P-16133)
TECHNOLOGY SERVICES CAL DEPT (DH)
Also Called: Dts
1325 J St Ste 1600, Sacramento (95814-2941)
P.O. Box 1810, Rancho Cordova (95741-1810)
PHONE..................916 319-9223
Marybel Batjer, *Admin Sec*
EMP: 92
SALES (est): 23.3MM **Privately Held**
WEB: www.osi.ca.gov
SIC: 7379

(P-16134)
TECTURA CORPORATION (PA)
951 Old County Rd 2-317, Belmont (94002-2773)
PHONE..................650 273-4249
Duane W Bell, *CEO*
Dave Kempski, *CFO*
EMP: 50
SALES (est): 61.4MM **Privately Held**
SIC: 7379 Computer related consulting services

(P-16135)
TIGERCONNECT INC
2110 Broadway, Santa Monica (90404-2912)
PHONE..................310 401-1820
Jeffrey Evans, *CEO*
Justin Nelson, *Officer*
Sarah Shillington, *Senior VP*
Cary Dobeck, *Vice Pres*
Sheila Saldana, *Vice Pres*
EMP: 50 **EST:** 2010
SALES (est): 1MM **Privately Held**
SIC: 7379 Computer related maintenance services

(P-16136)
TILLSTER INC (PA)
Also Called: Emn8
5959 Cornerstone Ct W # 100, San Diego (92121-3764)
PHONE..................858 784-0800
Perse Faily, *CEO*
Ravi Singh, *President*
John Redding, *CFO*
Trevor Chong, *Senior VP*
Chris Deaton, *Vice Pres*
EMP: 70
SQ FT: 18,642
SALES (est): 15.8MM **Privately Held**
WEB: www.emn8.com
SIC: 7379 7373 Computer related maintenance services; systems integration services; computer system selling services

(P-16137)
TRADEBEAM INC
303 Twin Dolphin Dr # 600, Redwood City (94065-1497)
PHONE..................650 653-4800
Fax: 650 653-4801
EMP: 100
SQ FT: 26,000
SALES (est): 4.8MM
SALES (corp-wide): 481.7MM **Privately Held**
WEB: www.tradebeam.com
SIC: 7379
HQ: Cdc Software, Inc.
4325 Alexander Dr
Alpharetta GA 30022

(P-16138)
TRALIANT LLC
1600 Rosecrans Ave, Manhattan Beach (90266-3708)
PHONE..................323 774-1325
Andrew Rawson, *President*
Michael Pallatta, *CEO*
EMP: 60
SALES: 10MM **Privately Held**
SIC: 7379 Computer related services

(P-16139)
TRIAGE PARTNERS LLC
15717 Texaco Ave, Paramount (90723-3923)
PHONE..................562 634-0058
EMP: 78
SALES (corp-wide): 25.6MM **Privately Held**
SIC: 7379
PA: Triage Partners, L.L.C.
1715 N West Shore Blvd # 250
Tampa FL 33607
813 801-9869

(P-16140)
TRIANZ INC (HQ)
2350 Mission College Blvd, Santa Clara (95054-1532)
PHONE..................408 387-5800
Srikanth Manchala, *President*
Ira Horowitz, *Partner*
Abhineet Jha, *Partner*
Lalit Kumar, *Partner*
Savio Rodrigues, *Partner*
EMP: 120 **EST:** 2000
SQ FT: 18,000
SALES: 65.2MM **Privately Held**
WEB: www.trianz.com
SIC: 7379

(P-16141)
TRIFACTA INC (PA)
575 Market St Ste 1100, San Francisco (94105-5816)
PHONE..................415 429-7570
Adam Wilson, *CEO*
Sachin Chawla, *President*
Michael Dooley, *Vice Pres*
Dan Niemann, *Vice Pres*
WEI Zheng, *Vice Pres*
EMP: 76
SQ FT: 3,000
SALES (est): 17.2MM **Privately Held**
SIC: 7379 7374 Data processing consultant; data processing & preparation

P R O D U C T S & S V C S

(P-16142)
TRIFECTA MULTIMEDIA LLC (PA)
Also Called: Trifecta Clinical
725 S Figueroa St # 4050, Los Angeles
(90017-5482)
PHONE.....................626 355-1303
David Young,
Ericka Atkinson, *Vice Pres*
Ward Rick, *Vice Pres*
Jessica Deroux, *Admin Asst*
Ed Sahakian, *CTO*
EMP: 50
SQ FT: 7,000
SALES (est): 7.6MM **Privately Held**
WEB: www.TRIFECTAMULTIMEDIA.com
SIC: 7379

(P-16143)
TRUSTARC INC
Also Called: Truste
835 Market St Ste 800, San Francisco
(94103-1906)
PHONE.....................415 520-3400
Christopher Babel, *CEO*
Tim Sullivan, *CFO*
Michelle Hines, *Vice Pres*
Matthew Rinkert, *Executive*
Kate Freeman, *Comms Mgr*
EMP: 100 EST: 2008
SQ FT: 7,000
SALES (est): 15.5MM
SALES (corp-wide): 371.7K **Privately Held**
WEB: www.truste.com
SIC: 7379 8742 Computer related consulting services; management consulting services; marketing consulting services
PA: Truste Europe Ltd.
3rd Floor
London

(P-16144)
TRUTHMD LLC
32932 Pacific Coast Hwy, Dana Point
(92629-3466)
PHONE.....................949 637-4296
Gemma Turi,
Charles Rosen MD,
EMP: 54
SALES (est): 133.1K **Privately Held**
SIC: 7379

(P-16145)
UNISH CORPORATION
4300 Stevens Creek Blvd # 126, San Jose
(95129-1263)
PHONE.....................408 708-9300
Basavaraj Ullagaddi, *President*
EMP: 50
SALES (est): 2.4MM **Privately Held**
SIC: 7379

(P-16146)
UNITED STATES TECHNICAL SVCS
Also Called: Usts
16541 Gothard St Ste 214, Huntington Beach (92647-4436)
PHONE.....................714 374-6300
Bob Polk, *President*
John Courtney, *CEO*
Cynthia Dugger, *Treasurer*
Dianne Cooper, *Admin Asst*
EMP: 122
SQ FT: 2,500
SALES (est): 17.7MM **Privately Held**
WEB: www.usts.net
SIC: 7379

(P-16147)
UNITEK INFORMATION SYSTEMS INC (PA)
Also Called: Unitek It Education
4670 Auto Mall Pkwy, Fremont
(94538-3197)
PHONE.....................510 249-1060
Janis Paulson, *CEO*
Shiva Jahan, *CFO*
Navraj Bawa, *Vice Pres*
Ena Hull, *Vice Pres*
Aparna Shikaripur, *Recruiter*
EMP: 55
SQ FT: 27,000

SALES (est): 21.2MM **Privately Held**
WEB: www.abriasoft.com
SIC: 7379 7371 Computer related consulting services; custom computer programming services

(P-16148)
US DATA MANAGEMENT LLC (PA)
Also Called: Usdm Life Science
535 Chapala St, Santa Barbara
(93101-3411)
PHONE.....................888 231-0816
Kevin Brown, *Mng Member*
Bryan Coddington, *Vice Pres*
Erin Northington, *Vice Pres*
Chris Waltrip, *Info Tech Mgr*
Sarah Schultz, *Payroll Mgr*
EMP: 100
SQ FT: 4,000
SALES (est): 20.5MM **Privately Held**
WEB: www.usdatamanagement.com
SIC: 7379 Computer related consulting services

(P-16149)
VALLEY US INC
888 Saratoga Ave Ste 201, San Jose
(95129-2639)
PHONE.....................408 260-7342
Sunita Kumari, *President*
EMP: 70
SALES (est): 2.8MM **Privately Held**
SIC: 7379 Computer related consulting services

(P-16150)
VENTRUM LLC
2033 Gateway Pl Ste 500, San Jose
(95110-3712)
PHONE.....................510 304-0852
Rahul Misra,
Jyoti Joshi, *Project Mgr*
Rohita Misra,
EMP: 75
SALES (est): 8MM **Privately Held**
WEB: www.ventrum.com
SIC: 7379 Computer related consulting services

(P-16151)
VERIZON DIGITAL MEDIA SVCS INC (HQ)
13031 W Jefferson Blvd # 900, Los Angeles (90094-7000)
PHONE.....................310 396-7400
Ralf Jacob, *President*
Christie Van Dyke, *Executive Asst*
Julie Williams, *Executive Asst*
Virgus Hunt, *Administration*
Adam Menchaca, *Administration*
EMP: 117
SQ FT: 50,000
SALES (est): 363.5MM
SALES (corp-wide): 130.8B **Publicly Held**
WEB: www.edgecast.com
SIC: 7379
PA: Verizon Communications Inc.
1095 Ave Of The Americas
New York NY 10036
212 395-1000

(P-16152)
VIRTIUM LLC
30052 Tomas, Rcho STA Marg
(92688-2127)
PHONE.....................949 888-2444
Robert P Healy,
Scott Phillips, *Vice Pres*
Scott Lawrence, *Business Dir*
Anly Nguyen, *Administration*
Chuck Brackman, *Info Tech Dir*
EMP: 100
SALES (est): 51.8K **Privately Held**
SIC: 7379 Computer data escrow service

(P-16153)
VIRTUAL INSTRUMENTS CORP (PA)
2331 Zanker Rd, San Jose (95131-1109)
PHONE.....................408 579-4000
Philippe Vincent, *CEO*
Ray Villeneuve, *President*
Peter Dayton, *CFO*

Kevin O'Donnell, *CFO*
Jeff Jordan, *Vice Pres*
EMP: 80
SALES (est): 34.5MM **Privately Held**
SIC: 7379 7371 Computer related consulting services; computer software development

(P-16154)
VISION SOLUTIONS INC
Also Called: Itera Software
15300 Barranca Pkwy # 100, Irvine
(92618-2200)
PHONE.....................949 253-6500
Daniel Neville, *Branch Mgr*
EMP: 52 **Privately Held**
WEB: www.visionsolutions.com
SIC: 7379 7371 Computer related consulting services; data processing consultant; computer software development & applications
PA: Vision Solutions, Inc.
15300 Barranca Pkwy # 100
Irvine CA 92618

(P-16155)
VORMETRIC INC (HQ)
Also Called: AES Networks
2860 Junction Ave, San Jose (95134-1922)
PHONE.....................408 433-6000
Alan Kessler, *President*
Wayne Lewandowski, *President*
Greg Paulsen, *CFO*
Sol Cates, *Officer*
Gary Clark, *Vice Pres*
▼ EMP: 79 EST: 2001
SQ FT: 56,000
SALES (est): 43.7MM
SALES (corp-wide): 262.1MM **Privately Held**
WEB: www.vormetric.com
SIC: 7379 Computer related maintenance services
PA: Thales
Tour Carpe Diem Esplanade Nord
Courbevoie 92400
157 778-000

(P-16156)
WHITEGOLD SOLUTIONS INC
43 Fernwood Way Ste 210, San Rafael
(94901-2528)
PHONE.....................415 456-4493
Jack Zoken, *President*
EMP: 50
SALES (est): 3MM **Privately Held**
WEB: www.sift.com
SIC: 7379 Data processing consultant

(P-16157)
WHITEHAT SECURITY INC
1741 Tech Dr Ste 300, San Jose (95110)
PHONE.....................408 343-8300
Craig Hinkley, *CEO*
Terry Murphy, *CFO*
Kevin Flynn, *Vice Pres*
David Gerry, *Vice Pres*
Setumadhav Kulkarni, *Vice Pres*
EMP: 55
SALES (est): 14.4MM **Privately Held**
WEB: www.whitehatsec.com
SIC: 7379
HQ: Ntt Security Corporation
4-14-1, Sotokanda
Chiyoda-Ku TKY 101-0
-

(P-16158)
WINCERE INC
2350 Mission College Blvd # 290, Santa Clara (95054-1575)
PHONE.....................408 841-4355
Himanshi Kansara, *President*
EMP: 210
SQ FT: 3,000
SALES (est): 13.6MM **Privately Held**
SIC: 7379 Computer related consulting services
PA: Wincere Solutions Private Limited
Regus Business Centre, Level 2
New Delhi DL 11002

(P-16159)
WORK TRUCK SOLUTIONS INC
2485 Notre Dame Blvd, Chico
(95928-7161)
PHONE.....................855 987-4544
Kathryn Schifferle, *CEO*
Gretchen Krugler, *CFO*
Tony Solano, *Vice Pres*
EMP: 80
SALES (est): 6.5MM **Privately Held**
SIC: 7379 Computer related services

(P-16160)
WYNDGATE TECHNOLOGIES
4925 Robert J Mathews Pkw, El Dorado Hills (95762-5700)
PHONE.....................916 404-8400
Michael Ruxnin, *Ch of Bd*
Tom Marcinek, *COO*
Morgan Polcheni, *Vice Pres*
EMP: 83
SALES (est): 5.3MM
SALES (corp-wide): 967.5MM **Publicly Held**
WEB: www.sttx.net
SIC: 7379 7371 7372 Computer related consulting services; custom computer programming services; prepackaged software
HQ: Global Med Technologies, Inc.
4925 Robert J Mathews Pkw
El Dorado Hills CA 95762
916 404-8400

(P-16161)
XANTRION INCORPORATED
651 Thomas L Berkley Way, Oakland
(94612-1344)
PHONE.....................510 272-4701
Tom Snyder, *COO*
Anne Bisagno, *President*
Sean Cameron, *Administration*
Royden Luis, *Administration*
Kevin Krotzer, *IT/INT Sup*
EMP: 50 EST: 2000
SQ FT: 10,000
SALES: 15.1MM **Privately Held**
SIC: 7379 ; computer related consulting services

(P-16162)
XAVOR CORPORATION
300 Spectrum Center Dr # 400, Irvine
(92618-4925)
PHONE.....................949 529-7372
Humayun Rashid, *President*
Dr Das Gupta, *Vice Pres*
Amara Masood, *Vice Pres*
EMP: 100
SQ FT: 14,000
SALES (est): 7.7MM **Privately Held**
SIC: 7379 1731 Computer related consulting services; electrical work

(P-16163)
XCOMMERCE INC (HQ)
Also Called: Magento
3640 Holdrege Ave, Los Angeles
(90016-4304)
PHONE.....................310 954-8012
Mark Lavelle, *President*
Meagan Dollins, *Partner*
Craig Jackson, *Partner*
Ryan Murden, *Partner*
Amy Schade, *Partner*
▼ EMP: 62
SQ FT: 4,000
SALES (est): 103.6MM
SALES (corp-wide): 9B **Publicly Held**
SIC: 7379 5961 ; catalog sales
PA: Adobe Inc.
345 Park Ave
San Jose CA 95110
408 536-6000

(P-16164)
XORIANT CORPORATION (PA)
1248 Reamwood Ave, Sunnyvale
(94089-2225)
PHONE.....................408 743-4400
Girish Gaitonde, *CEO*
Arun Tendulkar, *COO*
Mahesh Nalavade, *CFO*
Chandra N Singla, *Officer*
Saranath Kandadai, *Assoc VP*
EMP: 120

▲ = Import ▼=Export
◆ =Import/Export

SALES: 200.7MM **Privately Held**
WEB: www.xoriant.com
SIC: 7379 7371 Computer related consulting services; computer software development

(P-16165)
YAMMER INC
410 Townsend St, San Francisco
(94107-1537)
PHONE.................................415 796-7400
Keith R Dolliver, *CEO*
Dee Anna McPherson, *Vice Pres*
EMP: 160
SALES (est): 18.7MM
SALES (corp-wide): 125.8B **Publicly Held**
WEB: www.yammer.com
SIC: 7379 Computer related maintenance services
PA: Microsoft Corporation
1 Microsoft Way
Redmond WA 98052
425 882-8080

(P-16166)
ZIONTECH SOLUTIONS INC
1900 Mccarthy Blvd # 415, Milpitas
(95035-7457)
PHONE.................................408 434-6001
Hymavathi Pentaparthi, *Principal*
Ashok Anumandla, *CEO*
Nagaraju Tirunagaru, *Executive*
Amit Sethi, *Sr Software Eng*
EMP: 60 **EST:** 2008
SALES (est): 477.6K **Privately Held**
SIC: 7379

7381 Detective & Armored Car Svcs

(P-16167)
A1 PROTECTIVE SERVICES INC
5 Thomas Mellon Cir, San Francisco
(94134-2501)
PHONE.................................415 467-7200
Paula Jones, *President*
EMP: 84
SQ FT: 900
SALES: 2MM **Privately Held**
SIC: 7381 Security guard service

(P-16168)
A1 PROTECTIVE SERVICES LLC
7000 Franklin Blvd # 665, Sacramento
(95823-1881)
PHONE.................................916 421-3000
Paula Jones,
Brajah Norris,
EMP: 50
SALES (est): 250.6K **Privately Held**
SIC: 7381 Security guard service

(P-16169)
ABC SECURITY SERVICE INC (PA)
1840 Embarcadero, Oakland (94606-5220)
P.O. Box 1709 (94604-1709)
PHONE.................................510 436-0666
Ana Chretien, *President*
Roger Chretien, *Vice Pres*
EMP: 226
SQ FT: 17,000
SALES (est): 6.4MM **Privately Held**
WEB: www.abcsecurityinc.com
SIC: 7381 Security guard service

(P-16170)
ACTION FORCE SECURITY
1212 W Gardena Blvd Ste C, Gardena
(90247-4896)
PHONE.................................310 715-6053
Pedro Villatoro, *Owner*
EMP: 50
SALES (est): 880K **Privately Held**
SIC: 7381 Security guard service

(P-16171)
ALL ACTION SECURITY INC
20501 Ventura Blvd # 275, Woodland Hills
(91364-6413)
PHONE.................................800 482-7371
John Ayam, *President*
Maryam Ayam, *General Mgr*

Abbas Kosh, *Human Res Mgr*
EMP: 75
SALES (est): 2.1MM **Privately Held**
WEB: www.allactionsecurity.com
SIC: 7381 Security guard service

(P-16172)
ALL NATION SECURITY SVCS INC (PA)
3701 Wilshire Blvd # 530, Los Angeles
(90010-2818)
PHONE.................................213 769-4510
Kathy Thabet, *President*
Torres Sandra, *General Mgr*
Mike Thabet, *General Mgr*
EMP: 250
SQ FT: 4,250
SALES (est): 4.8MM **Privately Held**
SIC: 7381 Security guard service

(P-16173)
ALLIED PROTECTION SERVICES INC
19164 Van Ness Ave, Torrance
(90501-1101)
PHONE.................................310 330-8314
Leon Brooks, *President*
EMP: 78
SALES (est): 3.3MM **Privately Held**
WEB: www.alliedprotection.com
SIC: 7381 Security guard service

(P-16174)
ALLIED RISK MANAGEMENT INC
2010 W Avenue K 395, Lancaster
(93536-5229)
PHONE.................................661 305-0455
Howard Fuchs, *Director*
EMP: 99
SALES (est): 950K **Privately Held**
SIC: 7381 Security guard service

(P-16175)
ALLIEDBARTON SECURITY SVCS LLC
765 The City Dr S Ste 150, Orange
(92868-6920)
PHONE.................................626 213-3100
Janet Melendez, *Manager*
EMP: 127
SALES (corp-wide): 5.2B **Privately Held**
SIC: 7381 Security guard service
HQ: Alliedbarton Security Services Llc
8 Tower Bridge 161 Wshgtn
Conshohocken PA 19428
610 239-1100

(P-16176)
ALLIEDBARTON SECURITY SVCS LLC
637 E Albertoni St # 202, Carson
(90746-1539)
PHONE.................................310 324-1219
Chris Rike, *District Mgr*
EMP: 127
SALES (corp-wide): 5.2B **Privately Held**
SIC: 7381 Security guard service
HQ: Alliedbarton Security Services Llc
8 Tower Bridge 161 Wshgtn
Conshohocken PA 19428
610 239-1100

(P-16177)
ALLIEDBARTON SECURITY SVCS LLC
8950 Cal Center Dr # 150, Sacramento
(95826-3236)
PHONE.................................916 489-8280
Rodney Carter, *Branch Mgr*
EMP: 150
SALES (corp-wide): 5.2B **Privately Held**
WEB: www.alliedsecurity.com
SIC: 7381 Security guard service
HQ: Alliedbarton Security Services Llc
8 Tower Bridge 161 Wshgtn
Conshohocken PA 19428
610 239-1100

(P-16178)
ALLIEDBARTON SECURITY SVCS LLC
300 E Esplanade Dr # 1510, Oxnard
(93036-1238)
PHONE.................................805 983-1204

Jenny Nelson, *Branch Mgr*
Tyna Sorenson, *Data Proc Staff*
EMP: 93
SALES (corp-wide): 5.2B **Privately Held**
SIC: 7381 Security guard service
HQ: Alliedbarton Security Services Llc
8 Tower Bridge 161 Wshgtn
Conshohocken PA 19428
610 239-1100

(P-16179)
ALLIEDBARTON SECURITY SVCS LLC
Also Called: Initial Security
10330 Pioneer Blvd # 235, Santa Fe
Springs (90670-6012)
PHONE.................................562 906-4800
Larry Link, *Vice Pres*
EMP: 500
SALES (corp-wide): 5.2B **Privately Held**
SIC: 7381 Security guard service
HQ: Alliedbarton Security Services Llc
8 Tower Bridge 161 Wshgtn
Conshohocken PA 19428
610 239-1100

(P-16180)
ALLIEDBARTON SECURITY SVCS LLC
1600 Riviera Ave Ste 375, Walnut Creek
(94596-7377)
PHONE.................................510 839-4041
Kiet Phan, *District Mgr*
EMP: 300
SALES (corp-wide): 5.2B **Privately Held**
WEB: www.alliedsecurity.com
SIC: 7381 Security guard service
HQ: Alliedbarton Security Services Llc
8 Tower Bridge 161 Wshgtn
Conshohocken PA 19428
610 239-1100

(P-16181)
ALLIEDBARTON SECURITY SVCS LLC
2540 N 1st St Ste 101, San Jose
(95131-1016)
PHONE.................................408 954-8274
Nanette Jacoby, *Principal*
Paul Gordon, *District Mgr*
Jason Brown, *Business Mgr*
Thyen Lloyd, *Business Mgr*
Lloyd Thyen, *Business Mgr*
EMP: 500
SALES (corp-wide): 5.2B **Privately Held**
WEB: www.alliedsecurity.com
SIC: 7381 Security guard service; protective services, guard; private investigator; detective agency
HQ: Alliedbarton Security Services Llc
8 Tower Bridge 161 Wshgtn
Conshohocken PA 19428
610 239-1100

(P-16182)
ALLIEDBARTON SECURITY SVCS LLC
7670 Opportunity Rd # 210, San Diego
(92111-2274)
PHONE.................................858 874-8200
Melone Widy, *Manager*
EMP: 400
SALES (corp-wide): 5.2B **Privately Held**
WEB: www.alliedsecurity.com
SIC: 7381 Security guard service
HQ: Alliedbarton Security Services Llc
8 Tower Bridge 161 Wshgtn
Conshohocken PA 19428
610 239-1100

(P-16183)
ALLIEDBARTON SECURITY SVCS LLC
3701 Wilshire Blvd # 600, Los Angeles
(90010-2804)
PHONE.................................800 418-6423
Veroin Higbee, *Manager*
EMP: 300
SALES (corp-wide): 5.2B **Privately Held**
WEB: www.alliedsecurity.com
SIC: 7381 Security guard service; protective services, guard; private investigator

HQ: Alliedbarton Security Services Llc
8 Tower Bridge 161 Wshgtn
Conshohocken PA 19428
610 239-1100

(P-16184)
ALLIEDBARTON SECURITY SVCS LLC
765 The City Dr S Ste 105, Orange
(92868-6911)
PHONE.................................714 260-0805
Larry Crowl, *Principal*
William Evans, *Officer*
EMP: 160
SALES (corp-wide): 5.2B **Privately Held**
WEB: www.alliedsecurity.com
SIC: 7381 Security guard service
HQ: Alliedbarton Security Services Llc
8 Tower Bridge 161 Wshgtn
Conshohocken PA 19428
610 239-1100

(P-16185)
AMERICAN CORPORATE SEC INC (PA)
1 World Trade Ctr # 1240, Long Beach
(90831-1240)
PHONE.................................562 216-7440
Larry J Saye, *CEO*
Clifford Muzzi, *Branch Mgr*
Tim Lovette, *Human Res Mgr*
EMP: 67
SALES (est): 35.5MM **Privately Held**
SIC: 7381 8721 Security guard service; payroll accounting service

(P-16186)
AMERICAN CSTM PRIVATE SEC INC
446 E Vine St Ste A, Stockton
(95202-1116)
P.O. Box 8513 (95208-0513)
PHONE.................................209 369-1200
Rajesh Patti, *President*
Carl Murray, *VP Opers*
EMP: 80
SQ FT: 1,100
SALES: 300K **Privately Held**
SIC: 7381 Security guard service

(P-16187)
AMERICAN EAGLE PROTCTVE SVCS
Also Called: American Eagle Protective Svcs
425 W Kelso St, Inglewood (90301-2539)
PHONE.................................310 412-0019
Veronica Bautista, *CEO*
Joelle Epoh, *Principal*
Alma Serrano, *Admin Sec*
EMP: 90 **EST:** 2011
SALES (est): 1.3MM **Privately Held**
SIC: 7381 Guard services

(P-16188)
AMERICAN FORCE PRIVATE SEC INC
1585 S D St Ste 208, San Bernardino
(92408-3236)
PHONE.................................909 384-9820
Shehab Abdelazim, *CEO*
Sam Gal, *Opers Staff*
EMP: 75
SALES (est): 1.7MM **Privately Held**
SIC: 7381 Security guard service

(P-16189)
AMERICAN GUARD SERVICES INC (PA)
1125 W 190th St, Gardena (90248-4303)
PHONE.................................310 645-6200
Sherine Assal, *President*
Sherif Assal, *Vice Pres*
John Fletcher, *Info Tech Mgr*
Arnold Garcia, *Technician*
Francisco Bennett, *Project Mgr*
EMP: 400
SQ FT: 28,000
SALES: 82.7MM **Privately Held**
SIC: 7381 Security guard service

(P-16190)
AMERICAN PATRIOT SECURITY
10293 Rockingham Dr # 104, Sacramento
(95827-2529)
P.O. Box 980071, West Sacramento
(95798-0071)
PHONE..............................916 706-2449
Scott Jacobs, *President*
Kelly Rochester, *Vice Pres*
EMP: 75
SQ FT: 1,200
SALES (est): 2.1MM **Privately Held**
WEB: www.americanpatriotsecurity.com
SIC: 7381 Security guard service

(P-16191)
AMERICAN POWER SEC SVC INC
1451 Rimpau Ave Ste 207, Corona
(92879-7522)
PHONE..............................866 974-9994
Mohamed Faty, *President*
EMP: 85
SALES: 550K **Privately Held**
SIC: 7381 Security guard service

(P-16192)
AMERICAN PROTECTION GROUP INC (PA)
Also Called: Apg
8551 Vesper Ave, Panorama City
(91402-2914)
PHONE..............................818 279-2433
Anthony Brown, *President*
EMP: 107
SQ FT: 3,000
SALES: 5.4MM **Privately Held**
SIC: 7381 5063 7382 Guard services;
burglary protection service; security guard
service; detective agency; alarm systems;
burglar alarm maintenance & monitoring

(P-16193)
AMERICAN SECURITY FORCE INC
5400 E Olympic Blvd # 225, Commerce
(90022-5154)
PHONE..............................323 722-8585
Albert Williams, *President*
EMP: 157
SQ FT: 3,700
SALES (est): 2.5MM **Privately Held**
SIC: 7381 7382 Protective services,
guard; private investigator; guard dog
rental; detective agency; burglar alarm
maintenance & monitoring

(P-16194)
AMERICAN-1 AIRTIGHT SEC CO
2510 N Grand Ave Ste 207, Santa Ana
(92705-8754)
P.O. Box 23130 (92711-3130)
PHONE..............................714 997-0605
Sid Asghari, *President*
EMP: 50
SALES: 1,000K **Privately Held**
WEB: www.spearsecurity.com
SIC: 7381 Security guard service

(P-16195)
ANDREWS INTERNATIONAL INC
455 N Moss St, Burbank (91502-1727)
PHONE..............................818 260-9586
EMP: 177
SALES (corp-wide): 139.5MM **Privately Held**
SIC: 7381
PA: Andrews International, Inc.
455 N Moss St
Burbank CA 91502
818 487-4060

(P-16196)
ANDREWS INTERNATIONAL INC
3396 Willow Ln, Thousand Oaks
(91361-4937)
PHONE..............................805 409-4160
Frank Alverez, *Branch Mgr*
EMP: 177
SALES (corp-wide): 145.5MM **Privately Held**
SIC: 7381 Security guard service

PA: Andrews International, Inc.
455 N Moss St
Burbank CA 91502
818 487-4060

(P-16197)
ANDREWS INTERNATIONAL INC (PA)
455 N Moss St, Burbank (91502-1727)
PHONE..............................818 487-4060
Randy Andrews, *President*
Ty Richmond, *COO*
James Wood, *COO*
Michael Topf, *CFO*
Evert Arriola, *Officer*
EMP: 1700
SQ FT: 5,000
SALES (est): 145.5MM **Privately Held**
WEB: www.andrewinternational.com
SIC: 7381 Protective services, guard; security guard service

(P-16198)
ANDREWS INTERNATIONAL INC
706 E Arrow Hwy, Covina (91722-2123)
PHONE..............................626 407-2290
Mike Wibben, *Vice Pres*
EMP: 200
SALES (corp-wide): 145.5MM **Privately Held**
SIC: 7381 Security guard service
PA: Andrews International, Inc.
455 N Moss St
Burbank CA 91502
818 487-4060

(P-16199)
ASSET PRIVATE SECURITY INC
36 Quail Run Cir Ste O, Salinas
(93907-2351)
PHONE..............................831 809-9779
Jay A Agamao, *CEO*
Allan Tucker, *COO*
Jorge Sareli, *CFO*
EMP: 77
SALES: 2.5MM **Privately Held**
SIC: 7381 Security guard service

(P-16200)
ATLAS SECURITY & PATROL INC
39465 Paseo Padre Pkwy # 2800, Fremont
(94538-1631)
PHONE..............................510 791-7380
Jason Solorzano, *Manager*
EMP: 50
SALES (corp-wide): 4MM **Privately Held**
SIC: 7381 Security guard service; private investigator
PA: Atlas Security & Patrol, Inc.
3851 Charter Park Dr V
San Jose CA
408 972-2099

(P-16201)
BACO REALTY CORPORATION
6310 Stockton Blvd, Sacramento
(95824-4003)
PHONE..............................916 974-9898
EMP: 86
SALES (corp-wide): 37.1MM **Privately Held**
SIC: 7381 Guard services
PA: Baco Realty Corporation
51 Federal St Ste 202
San Francisco CA 94107
415 281-3700

(P-16202)
BAECHLER INVESTIGATIVE SVCS
1935 N Marshall Ave Ste C, El Cajon
(92020-1132)
PHONE..............................619 464-5600
Anthony Baechler, *President*
EMP: 53
SQ FT: 5,200
SALES (est): 1MM **Privately Held**
WEB: www.junes.com
SIC: 7381 Private investigator

(P-16203)
BALD EAGLE SECURITY SVCS INC
3626 Main St, San Diego (92113-3805)
P.O. Box 131350 (92170-1350)
PHONE..............................619 230-0022
Andrea Robinson, *President*
Dean Heilmann, *Manager*
EMP: 75
SALES (est): 234.2K **Privately Held**
SIC: 7381 Security guard service

(P-16204)
BARCOTT FRANK A SEC INVSTGTONS
Also Called: Barcott SEC & Investigations
6446 San Andres Ave, Cypress
(90630-5324)
P.O. Box 2278 (90630-1778)
PHONE..............................714 891-8556
Frank A Barcott, *President*
Carolyn Barcott, *Vice Pres*
EMP: 200
SALES (est): 5.2MM **Privately Held**
SIC: 7381 Security guard service; detective services

(P-16205)
BARRYS SECURITY SERVICES INC (PA)
16739 Van Buren Blvd, Riverside
(92504-5744)
PHONE..............................951 789-7575
Michelle Barry, *CEO*
Martin Morales, *Vice Pres*
EMP: 188
SQ FT: 5,000
SALES: 8.3MM **Privately Held**
WEB: www.weguard.biz
SIC: 7381 Security guard service

(P-16206)
BARRYS SECURITY SERVICES INC
5480 Katella Ave Ste 203, Los Alamitos
(90720-6823)
PHONE..............................562 493-7007
Carlos Nunez, *Branch Mgr*
EMP: 125
SALES (corp-wide): 8.3MM **Privately Held**
WEB: www.weguard.biz
SIC: 7381 Guard services
PA: Barry's Security Services, Inc.
16739 Van Buren Blvd
Riverside CA 92504
951 789-7575

(P-16207)
BEACH CITIES INVEST & PROTCTN
2500 Via Cabrillo Marina, San Pedro
(90731-7224)
PHONE..............................310 322-4724
Kevin R Hackie, *CEO*
Norma Chavarria, *Treasurer*
Nicholas Hackie, *Vice Pres*
Shana Alexander, *Admin Sec*
EMP: 300
SQ FT: 2,000
SALES (est): 4.1MM **Privately Held**
SIC: 7381 Detective services; private investigator

(P-16208)
BELL PRIVATE SECURITY INC
Also Called: R M B SEC Cnslting Invstgtons
18030 Brookhurst St, Fountain Valley
(92708-6756)
PHONE..............................714 964-9381
Robert M Bell, *President*
EMP: 90
SALES (est): 1.4MM **Privately Held**
WEB: www.bellprivatesecurity.com
SIC: 7381 Security guard service; private investigator

(P-16209)
BLACK BEAR SECURITY SERVICES
Also Called: Montana Investigation
2016 Oakdale Ave Ste B, San Francisco
(94124-2041)
PHONE..............................415 559-5159

Moura Borisova, *President*
EMP: 125
SQ FT: 3,000
SALES (est): 3.6MM **Privately Held**
WEB: www.blackbearsecurity.com
SIC: 7381 7382 Security guard service; security systems services

(P-16210)
BORGENS & BORGENS INC
Also Called: Delta Protective Services
141 E Acacia St Ste D, Stockton
(95202-1400)
P.O. Box 8633 (95208-0633)
PHONE..............................209 547-2980
L D Borgens, *President*
K R Borgens, *Vice Pres*
EMP: 85 EST: 1993
SQ FT: 2,475
SALES (est): 1.8MM **Privately Held**
WEB: www.deltaprotectiveservices.com
SIC: 7381 Security guard service

(P-16211)
BORUNDA PRIVATE SEC PATROL INC
1308 Clovis Ave, Clovis (93612-2701)
PHONE..............................559 299-2662
Ben Borunda, *CEO*
EMP: 50
SALES (est): 183.8K **Privately Held**
SIC: 7381 Security guard service

(P-16212)
BOYD & ASSOCIATES
445 E Esplanade Dr # 210, Oxnard
(93036-2126)
PHONE..............................805 988-8298
Kathy Correll, *Manager*
EMP: 100
SALES (corp-wide): 17.2MM **Privately Held**
WEB: www.boydsecurity.com
SIC: 7381 Security guard service
PA: Boyd & Associates
2191 E Thompson Blvd
Ventura CA 93001
818 752-1888

(P-16213)
BOYD & ASSOCIATES (PA)
2191 E Thompson Blvd, Ventura
(93001-3538)
PHONE..............................818 752-1888
Raymond G Boyd Sr, *Ch of Bd*
Daniel Boyd, *President*
Barbara K Boyd, *Vice Pres*
EMP: 160
SQ FT: 8,000
SALES (est): 19.1MM
SALES (corp-wide): 17.2MM **Privately Held**
WEB: www.boydsecurity.com
SIC: 7381 7382 Security guard service; detective services; security systems services

(P-16214)
BOYD & ASSOCIATES
3151 Airway Ave Ste K105, Costa Mesa
(92626-4613)
PHONE..............................714 835-5423
Fax: 714 835-5641
EMP: 150
SQ FT: 3,012
SALES (corp-wide): 19.4MM **Privately Held**
SIC: 7381
PA: Boyd & Associates
2191 E Thompson Blvd
Ventura CA 93001
818 752-1888

(P-16215)
BRINKS INCORPORATED
1120 Venice Blvd, Los Angeles
(90015-3289)
PHONE..............................818 503-8630
Dennis Dwyer, *Executive*
EMP: 136
SALES (corp-wide): 3.4B **Publicly Held**
WEB: www.brinksinc.com
SIC: 7381 Armored car services

HQ: Brink's, Incorporated
1801 Bayberry Ct Ste 400
Richmond VA 23226
804 289-9600

(P-16216)
BRINKS INCORPORATED
8178 Alpine Ave Unit A, Sacramento
(95826-4707)
PHONE.....................................916 452-5279
Steve Morss, *Manager*
Bridgett Bagwill, *Administration*
EMP: 133
SALES (corp-wide): 3.4B **Publicly Held**
WEB: www.brinksinc.com
SIC: 7381 Armored car services
HQ: Brink's, Incorporated
1801 Bayberry Ct Ste 400
Richmond VA 23226
804 289-9600

(P-16217)
BRINKS INCORPORATED
4520 Federal Blvd Ste A, San Diego
(92102-2516)
PHONE.....................................619 263-6615
Eric Holman, *Manager*
EMP: 120
SALES (corp-wide): 3.4B **Publicly Held**
WEB: www.brinksinc.com
SIC: 7381 Armored car services
HQ: Brink's, Incorporated
1801 Bayberry Ct Ste 400
Richmond VA 23226
804 289-9600

(P-16218)
BRINKS INCORPORATED
1630 Old Bayshore Hwy, San Jose
(95112-4304)
PHONE.....................................408 436-7717
George Geovanni, *Manager*
EMP: 80
SALES (corp-wide): 3.4B **Publicly Held**
WEB: www.brinksinc.com
SIC: 7381 Armored car services
HQ: Brink's, Incorporated
1801 Bayberry Ct Ste 400
Richmond VA 23226
804 289-9600

(P-16219)
BRINKS INCORPORATED
1821 S Soto St, Los Angeles (90023-4210)
PHONE.....................................323 262-2646
Eva Salas, *Manager*
EMP: 50
SALES (corp-wide): 3.4B **Publicly Held**
WEB: www.brinksinc.com
SIC: 7381 Armored car services
HQ: Brink's, Incorporated
1801 Bayberry Ct Ste 400
Richmond VA 23226
804 289-9600

(P-16220)
C & C SECURITY PATROL INC (PA)
4615 Enterprise Cmn, Fremont
(94538-6345)
PHONE.....................................510 713-1260
Hermenegildo Couoh, *CEO*
Marcel Lopez, *Vice Pres*
EMP: 120
SALES (est): 5.9MM **Privately Held**
SIC: 7381 Security guard service

(P-16221)
C S I PATROL SERVICES
3605 Long Beach Blvd # 205, Long Beach
(90807-4013)
PHONE.....................................562 981-8988
Dennis Cook, *President*
EMP: 55
SQ FT: 600
SALES (est): 1.6MM **Privately Held**
WEB: www.csipatrol.com
SIC: 7381 Protective services, guard; security guard service

(P-16222)
CALIFORNIA GUARD INC
Also Called: Ad Force Private Security
3108 N Cherryland Ave, Stockton
(95215-2222)
P.O. Box 55331 (95205-8831)
PHONE.....................................209 465-8420
George Garcia, *CEO*
Surinder Singh Sandhu, *President*
EMP: 100
SALES (est): 3.5MM **Privately Held**
SIC: 7381 Security guard service

(P-16223)
CALIFORNIA SAFETY AGENCY
8932 Katella Ave Ste 108, Anaheim
(92804-6299)
PHONE.....................................866 996-6990
EMP: 50
SALES (est): 1MM **Privately Held**
SIC: 7381

(P-16224)
CALIFORNIA SECURITY CONS
3108 N Cherryland Ave, Stockton
(95215-2222)
P.O. Box 55331 (95205-8831)
PHONE.....................................209 465-8420
George Garcia, *President*
EMP: 200
SALES (est): 2.6MM **Privately Held**
SIC: 7381 Security guard service

(P-16225)
CEED SECURITY CORP
Also Called: Security Systems & Services
1525 3rd St Ste K, Riverside (92507-3429)
PHONE.....................................951 222-2233
EMP: 50 EST: 2012
SALES (est): 59.5K **Privately Held**
SIC: 7381 Security guard service

(P-16226)
CENTURION SECURITY INC
Also Called: Centurion Group, The
11454 San Vicente Blvd, Los Angeles
(90049-6208)
PHONE.....................................818 755-0202
Steven Lemmer, *President*
David Rosenberg, *Corp Secy*
Daniel Cambell, *Vice Pres*
EMP: 200
SQ FT: 3,200
SALES (est): 6.4MM **Privately Held**
SIC: 7381 Security guard service

(P-16227)
CENTURION SECURITY SVCS INC (PA)
20102 Sw Cypress St, Newport Beach
(92660-0713)
PHONE.....................................949 474-0444
Robyn Hamilton, *President*
Jeff Hamilton, *Vice Pres*
EMP: 54
SALES: 1.8MM **Privately Held**
SIC: 7381 Security guard service

(P-16228)
CHG SECURITY INC
16431 Grayville Dr, La Mirada
(90638-2719)
PHONE.....................................562 284-6260
Owusu Boateng, *CEO*
EMP: 50
SALES (est): 227.8K **Privately Held**
SIC: 7381 Protective services, guard

(P-16229)
CHIEF PROTECTIVE SERVICES INC
Also Called: Assure Detective Agency
1344 W 6th St Ste 300, Corona
(92882-1641)
P.O. Box 1806 (92878-1806)
PHONE.....................................951 738-0881
Steven Fernandez, *President*
EMP: 100
SQ FT: 3,000
SALES: 2.9MM **Privately Held**
SIC: 7381 Security guard service; private investigator

(P-16230)
CITADEL SECURITY INC
5199 E Pcf Cast Hwy 200, Long Beach
(90804)
PHONE.....................................562 248-2300
Brian Kelley, *CEO*
EMP: 150
SQ FT: 4,500
SALES (est): 2.7MM **Privately Held**
WEB: www.citadelsecurityinc.com
SIC: 7381 Security guard service

(P-16231)
CITY NATIONAL SEC SVCS INC
5901 W Century Blvd # 806, Los Angeles
(90045-5411)
PHONE.....................................310 641-6666
Chiraz Zouaoui, *Manager*
EMP: 80
SALES (est): 950K **Privately Held**
SIC: 7381 Security guard service

(P-16232)
CITY SECURITY CO INC
430 S Grfield Ave Ste 401, Alhambra
(91801)
PHONE.....................................626 458-2325
Bob Rysdon, *President*
EMP: 70
SALES (est): 1.3MM **Privately Held**
SIC: 7381 Security guard service

(P-16233)
CLASSIC PROTECTION INC
3208 Royal St, Los Angeles (90007-3657)
PHONE.....................................213 742-1238
Richard Ullman, *President*
EMP: 50
SQ FT: 1,000
SALES (est): 1.3MM **Privately Held**
SIC: 7381 Guard services; security guard service

(P-16234)
COMMAND INTERNATIONAL SEC SVCS
6819 Sepulveda Blvd, Van Nuys
(91405-4463)
PHONE.....................................818 997-1666
Nafees Memon, *Owner*
EMP: 55
SQ FT: 700
SALES: 1.2MM **Privately Held**
SIC: 7381 Security guard service

(P-16235)
COMMAND SECURITY CORPORATION
8840 Warner Ave Ste 301, Fountain Valley
(92708-3234)
PHONE.....................................714 557-9355
John Dunlevy, *Regl Sales Mgr*
EMP: 168
SALES (corp-wide): 187.9MM **Privately Held**
SIC: 7381 Security guard service
PA: Command Security Corporation
512 Herndon Pkwy Ste A
Herndon VA 20170
703 464-4735

(P-16236)
COMMAND SECURITY CORPORATION
890 Hillview Ct Ste 100, Milpitas
(95035-4573)
PHONE.....................................510 623-2355
Larry Reid, *President*
EMP: 168
SALES (corp-wide): 187.9MM **Privately Held**
SIC: 7381 Security guard service
PA: Command Security Corporation
512 Herndon Pkwy Ste A
Herndon VA 20170
703 464-4735

(P-16237)
COMMAND SECURITY CORPORATION
Also Called: Aviation Safeguards
8929 S Sepulveda Blvd # 300, Los Angeles
(90045-3616)
PHONE.....................................310 981-4530
Sunny Williams, *Vice Pres*

Joe Conlon, *President*
EMP: 800
SALES (corp-wide): 187.9MM **Privately Held**
WEB: www.cscny.com
SIC: 7381 7382 Security guard service; security systems services
PA: Command Security Corporation
512 Herndon Pkwy Ste A
Herndon VA 20170
703 464-4735

(P-16238)
COMMAND SECURITY CORPORATION
Also Called: Aviation Safeguards
1701 Airport Blvd Ste 205, San Jose
(95110-1236)
PHONE.....................................650 574-0911
Earl Hartfield, *Manager*
EMP: 80
SALES (corp-wide): 187.9MM **Privately Held**
WEB: www.cscny.com
SIC: 7381 Security guard service
PA: Command Security Corporation
512 Herndon Pkwy Ste A
Herndon VA 20170
703 464-4735

(P-16239)
COMMERCIAL PROTECTIVE SVCS INC
Also Called: CPS Security
3400 E Airport Way, Long Beach
(90806-2412)
PHONE.....................................310 515-5290
Christopher Coffey, *President*
William R Babcock, *CFO*
EMP: 1800
SQ FT: 10,000
SALES (est): 36MM **Privately Held**
SIC: 7381 Protective services, guard

(P-16240)
COMMONWEALTH INTERNATIONAL
968 Durfee Ave, South El Monte
(91733-4408)
PHONE.....................................626 279-9201
Jose Velasco, *President*
Emil Ayad, *Vice Pres*
EMP: 50
SALES (est): 1.3MM **Privately Held**
SIC: 7381 Armored car services

(P-16241)
COMPREHENSIVE SEC SVCS INC (PA)
10535 E Stockton Blvd G, Elk Grove
(95624-9758)
P.O. Box 246719, Sacramento (95824-6719)
PHONE.....................................916 683-3605
Bashir A Choudry, *President*
Jamal-Eddine Kabbaj, *Exec VP*
Nash Yakoub, *Manager*
EMP: 75
SQ FT: 3,300
SALES: 8.7MM **Privately Held**
WEB: www.comprehensivesecurity.net
SIC: 7381 7382 Security guard service; security systems services

(P-16242)
CONTACT SECURITY INC
3000 E Birch St Ste 111, Brea
(92821-6261)
PHONE.....................................714 572-6760
Michelle Quesada, *President*
EMP: 250
SQ FT: 2,500
SALES (est): 4MM **Privately Held**
WEB: www.contactsecurity.com
SIC: 7381 Security guard service

(P-16243)
CONTEMPORARY SERVICES CORP
Also Called: Crowd Management
2650 E Shaw Ave, Fresno (93710-8284)
PHONE.....................................559 225-9325
Robert Humphrey, *Manager*
EMP: 200

(PA)=Parent Co (HQ)=Headquarters (DH)=Div Headquarters

✿ = New Business established in last 2 years

2019 Directory of California
Wholesalers and Services Companies

689

PRODUCTS & SVCS

SALES (corp-wide): 302.9MM **Privately Held**
WEB: www.csc-usa.com
SIC: 7381 Protective services, guard
PA: Contemporary Services Corporation
17101 Superior St
Northridge CA 91325
818 885-5150

(P-16244)
COURTESY SECURITY INC
Also Called: Securelion Security
37420 Cedar Blvd Ste D, Newark
(94560-4159)
PHONE.............................888 572-5545
Ajmal Boomwal, *Principal*
EMP: 60
SALES (est): 263K **Privately Held**
SIC: 7381 Detective & armored car services

(P-16245)
COVENANT AVIATION SECURITY LLC
1000 Marina Blvd Ste 100, Brisbane
(94005-1839)
PHONE.............................650 219-3473
Brian O Apos, *Manager*
EMP: 1100
SALES (corp-wide): 42.7MM **Privately Held**
SIC: 7381 Security guard service
HQ: Covenant Aviation Security, Llc
400 Quadrangle Dr Ste A
Bolingbrook IL 60440
630 771-0800

(P-16246)
CPS SECURITY SOLUTIONS INC (PA)
3400 E Airport Way, Long Beach
(90806-2412)
PHONE.............................310 818-1030
Chris Coffey, *President*
William Babcock, *CFO*
Scott R Barnes, *Exec VP*
EMP: 67
SQ FT: 14,000
SALES (est): 47.9MM **Privately Held**
SIC: 7381 Security guard service

(P-16247)
CREATIVE SECURITY COMPANY INC
150 S Autumn St Ste B, San Jose
(95110-2515)
PHONE.............................408 295-2600
Charles Wall, *President*
Brian Wall, *Vice Pres*
Mike Mattocks, *Security Dir*
Kristina Davidson, *Accounting Mgr*
Cpp C Fife, *Opers Staff*
EMP: 350
SQ FT: 12,000
SALES (est): 13MM **Privately Held**
WEB: www.creativesecurity.com
SIC: 7381 Security guard service; private investigator

(P-16248)
CRIME IMPACT SECURITY PATROL
Also Called: Crime Impact Security & Patrol
3860 Crenshaw Blvd # 223, Los Angeles
(90008-1816)
PHONE.............................323 296-6406
Darrin Jenkins, *President*
EMP: 55
SALES (est): 993.4K **Privately Held**
SIC: 7381 Security guard service

(P-16249)
CRIMETEK SECURITY
3448 N Golden State Blvd, Turlock
(95382-9709)
P.O. Box 845 (95381-0845)
PHONE.............................209 668-6208
Edward Esmaili, *President*
Ed Esmaili, *Partner*
Rosy Esmaili, *Partner*
Randall Turner, *Officer*
EMP: 420 EST: 1999
SQ FT: 2,200

SALES (est): 12MM **Privately Held**
SIC: 7381 Security guard service; guard services

(P-16250)
CYPRESS SECURITY LLC (PA)
478 Tehama St, San Francisco
(94103-4141)
PHONE.............................866 345-1277
Kes Narbutas,
Veronica Brown, *Controller*
EMP: 83
SQ FT: 3,500
SALES (est): 30.5MM **Privately Held**
WEB: www.cypress-security.com
SIC: 7381 Security guard service

(P-16251)
CYPRESS SECURITY LLC
9926 Pioneer Blvd Ste 106, Santa Fe Springs (90670-6243)
PHONE.............................562 222-4197
Kes Narbutas, *CEO*
EMP: 80
SALES (corp-wide): 30.5MM **Privately Held**
SIC: 7381 Security guard service
PA: Cypress Security, Llc
478 Tehama St
San Francisco CA 94103
866 345-1277

(P-16252)
DAN CONNOLLY INC
Also Called: Armed Courier Service
855 Civic Center Dr Ste 5, Santa Clara
(95050-3962)
PHONE.............................408 241-0910
Dan Connolly, *President*
EMP: 60
SQ FT: 6,000
SALES (est): 1.4MM **Privately Held**
WEB: www.armedcourierservice.com
SIC: 7381 Armored car services

(P-16253)
DANSK ENTERPRISES INC
Also Called: Nordic Security Services
3419 Via Lido 345, Newport Beach
(92663-3908)
PHONE.............................714 751-0347
Peter Jensen, *President*
Eric Reinholtz, *Executive*
Katrina Hernandez, *Office Mgr*
EMP: 100
SALES (est): 2.8MM **Privately Held**
WEB: www.nordicsec.com
SIC: 7381 Security guard service

(P-16254)
DAVID SHIELD SECURITY INC
Also Called: Dss
23945 Calabasas Rd # 102, Calabasas
(91302-1552)
PHONE.............................310 849-4950
Athan Bazaz, *President*
Snir Warshaziak, *CEO*
EMP: 100 EST: 2015
SALES (est): 5MM **Privately Held**
SIC: 7381 Security guard service

(P-16255)
DELTA HAWKEYE SECURITY INC
7400 Shoreline Dr Ste 2, Stockton
(95219-5498)
PHONE.............................209 957-3333
Dallas Faulkner, *Vice Pres*
Frank Passadore, *President*
Brian Millin, *Vice Pres*
EMP: 58
SQ FT: 2,000
SALES (est): 1.5MM
SALES (corp-wide): 86.7MM **Privately Held**
WEB: www.deltahawkeye.com
SIC: 7381 Security guard service
PA: The Grupe Company
3255 W March Ln Ste 400
Stockton CA 95219
209 473-6000

(P-16256)
DELTA ONE SECURITY INC
342 Acacia St, Fairfield (94533-3766)
PHONE.............................707 425-9346
Robert Edwards, *President*

Betty Edwards, *CFO*
Charlotte Gear, *Data Proc Exec*
EMP: 60 EST: 2010
SALES (est): 1.4MM **Privately Held**
SIC: 7381 Security guard service

(P-16257)
DELTA PERSONNEL SERVICES INC
Also Called: Guardian Security Agency
1820 Galindo St Ste 3, Concord
(94520-2447)
PHONE.............................925 356-3034
Judith Travers, *CEO*
EMP: 80
SQ FT: 4,300
SALES (est): 5.1MM **Privately Held**
SIC: 7381 Guard services

(P-16258)
DIEHARD SECURITY SOLUTIONS INC
1151 Harbor Bay Pkwy # 140, Alameda
(94502-6540)
PHONE.............................510 995-8450
Joseph Bando, *President*
Morgan Sorensen, *Office Mgr*
EMP: 107
SALES (est): 141.3K **Privately Held**
SIC: 7381 Guard services

(P-16259)
DLO ENTERPRISES INC
Also Called: Colt Security Services
41865 Boardwalk Ste 216, Palm Desert
(92211-9033)
PHONE.............................760 346-8033
Dennis L Oliver, *President*
EMP: 55
SALES (est): 1.1MM **Privately Held**
WEB: www.coltsecurity.com
SIC: 7381 Protective services, guard; security guard service

(P-16260)
DREW CHAIN SECURITY CORP
55 S Raymond Ave Ste 303, Alhambra
(91801-7100)
PHONE.............................626 457-8626
Kenneth Y Lee, *President*
Art Kasabyan, *COO*
EMP: 71
SQ FT: 800
SALES (est): 1MM **Privately Held**
WEB: www.alhambrahospital.com
SIC: 7381 Security guard service

(P-16261)
DRUM SECURITY SERVICE INC
4509 Callada Pl, Tarzana (91356-5101)
PHONE.............................818 708-7914
Charles R Drum, *President*
EMP: 60
SALES (est): 947.1K **Privately Held**
SIC: 7381 Security guard service

(P-16262)
DUNBAR ARMORED INC
629 Whitney St, San Leandro (94577-1115)
PHONE.............................510 569-7400
Ted Nguyen, *Manager*
John Alltop, *Vice Pres*
Tristan Houghton, *Vice Pres*
Kathy Cash, *Executive*
Cory Harvey, *Branch Mgr*
EMP: 100
SALES (corp-wide): 3.4B **Publicly Held**
WEB: www.dunbararmored.com
SIC: 7381 Armored car services
HQ: Dunbar Armored, Inc.
50 Schilling Rd
Hunt Valley MD 21031
410 584-9800

(P-16263)
EAGLE SECURITY SERVICE INC
12903 S Normandie Ave, Gardena
(90249-2123)
PHONE.............................310 532-1626
Mohsen Kamel, *President*
EMP: 150
SQ FT: 5,000
SALES (est): 4.2MM **Privately Held**
SIC: 7381 Security guard service

(P-16264)
EASTSIDE GROUP CORPORATION
Also Called: Prudential Security Services
1830 W Olympic Blvd # 202, Los Angeles
(90006-3734)
P.O. Box 531, Lynwood (90262-0531)
PHONE.............................213 368-9777
Fernando Gonzales, *President*
Manny Martinez, *Vice Pres*
EMP: 125
SALES: 2.5MM **Privately Held**
SIC: 7381 Security guard service

(P-16265)
ELITE ENFRCMENT SEC SLTONS INC
29970 Technology Dr, Murrieta
(92563-2645)
PHONE.............................866 354-8308
Kevin Roncevich, *Branch Mgr*
EMP: 50
SALES (corp-wide): 5.6MM **Privately Held**
SIC: 7381 Security guard service
PA: Elite Enforcement Security Solutions Inc
1290 N Hancock St Ste 101
Anaheim CA 92807
866 354-8308

(P-16266)
ELITE SECURITY SERVICES INC
18006 Sky Park Cir # 205, Irvine
(92614-6406)
P.O. Box 18073 (92623-8073)
PHONE.............................949 222-2203
Betty Kaminski, *President*
Gene Kaminski, *Exec VP*
EMP: 450
SQ FT: 2,400
SALES (est): 5.2MM **Privately Held**
WEB: www.elitesecurityservices.net
SIC: 7381 7382 Guard services; security systems services

(P-16267)
ELITE SHOW SERVICES INC
2878 Camino Del Rio S # 260, San Diego
(92108-3855)
PHONE.............................619 574-1589
John Kontopuls, *President*
Gus Kontopuls, *Vice Pres*
Donna Forsyth, *Manager*
Stephanie Logan, *Assistant*
Scottie Warren, *Accounts Mgr*
EMP: 3123
SALES (est): 75.2MM **Privately Held**
WEB: www.eliteshowservices.com
SIC: 7381 Security guard service

(P-16268)
EXECUSHELD PRTECTION GROUP LLC
301 Georgia St Ste 307, Vallejo
(94590-5993)
PHONE.............................707 439-6351
Michael Manibusan, *Principal*
Richard Berrios, *Principal*
Daniel Gonzalez, *Principal*
EMP: 75
SALES (est): 515K **Privately Held**
SIC: 7381 9221 Protective services, guard; security guard service; police protection

(P-16269)
EXECUSHIELD INC
4104 24th St Ste 501, San Francisco
(94114-3615)
PHONE.............................415 508-0825
Daniel Gonzalez, *President*
Joshua Carlberg, *Director*
EMP: 55
SALES (est): 1.1MM **Privately Held**
WEB: www.execushield.com
SIC: 7381 Security guard service

(P-16270)
EXECUTIVE PROTECTION AGENCY K-
Also Called: Epak9
1175 N 2nd St Ste 102, El Cajon
(92021-5033)
PHONE.............................619 442-5771

Frank Whiteley, *President*
EMP: 50
SQ FT: 3,600
SALES (est): 993.4K **Privately Held**
SIC: 7381 Security guard service; guard services

(P-16271)
FIDELITY SECURITY SERVICES INC
25133 Avenue Tibbitts H, Valencia (91355-3494)
PHONE..........................661 295-5007
Ahmadshah Ahmadi, *President*
Nazifa Ahmadi, *CFO*
EMP: 105
SQ FT: 1,000
SALES: 675K **Privately Held**
WEB: www.fidelitysecurityservices.com
SIC: 7381 Security guard service; guard services

(P-16272)
FIRST INTERSTATE SECURITY INC
20548 Ventura Blvd # 118, Woodland Hills (91364-6225)
PHONE..........................818 995-6664
Mike Ahmed, *President*
EMP: 210
SQ FT: 5,000
SALES (est): 3.4MM **Privately Held**
WEB: www.firstinterstateinc.com
SIC: 7381 Security guard service

(P-16273)
FIRSTCALL (PA)
Also Called: Steele Corp SEC Advisory Svcs
1 Sansome St Ste 3500, San Francisco (94104-4436)
PHONE..........................415 781-4300
Kenneth Kurtz, *CEO*
EMP: 138
SQ FT: 5,000
SALES (est): 49.8MM **Privately Held**
SIC: 7381 8742 8748 Security guard service; management consulting services; agricultural consultant

(P-16274)
FPK SECURITY INC
Also Called: Fpk Investigaions
28348 Constellation Rd # 880, Valencia (91355-5097)
P.O. Box 55597 (91385-0597)
PHONE..........................661 702-9091
Mark David, *CEO*
Robert Esquivel, *President*
EMP: 365
SQ FT: 1,200
SALES (est): 8.8MM **Privately Held**
SIC: 7381 Private investigator

(P-16275)
FRASCO INC (PA)
Also Called: Frasco Investigative Services
215 W Alameda Ave, Burbank (91502-3060)
PHONE..........................818 848-3888
John C Simmers, *President*
Laura Pfaffman, *CFO*
Todd Savar, *Officer*
Scott Cornelison, *Vice Pres*
Noelle Harling, *Vice Pres*
EMP: 65
SQ FT: 10,000
SALES (est): 18.5MM **Privately Held**
WEB: www.frasco.com
SIC: 7381 Private investigator

(P-16276)
FRESNO COUNTY PRIVATE SECURITY
2150 Tulare St, Fresno (93721-2103)
PHONE..........................559 233-9800
Ronald Sawl, *President*
EMP: 100
SALES (est): 2.2MM **Privately Held**
SIC: 7381 Security guard service

(P-16277)
G4S SECURE SOLUTIONS (USA)
4400 Ashe Rd Ste 206, Bakersfield (93313-2036)
PHONE..........................661 834-3454

Thomas Robinson, *Branch Mgr*
EMP: 125 **Privately Held**
SIC: 7381 Security guard service
HQ: G4s Secure Solutions (Usa) Inc.
1395 University Blvd
Jupiter FL 33458
561 622-5656

(P-16278)
G4S SECURE SOLUTIONS (USA)
4929 Wilshire Blvd # 601, Los Angeles (90010-3808)
PHONE..........................323 938-9100
Yvonne Herod, *Manager*
EMP: 300 **Privately Held**
SIC: 7381 Security guard service
HQ: G4s Secure Solutions (Usa) Inc.
1395 University Blvd
Jupiter FL 33458
561 622-5656

(P-16279)
G4S SECURE SOLUTIONS (USA)
1450 Iowa Ave, Riverside (92507-0522)
PHONE..........................951 341-3000
Richard McDale, *Manager*
Bob Schriener, *Business Mgr*
EMP: 300 **Privately Held**
SIC: 7381 Security guard service
HQ: G4s Secure Solutions (Usa) Inc.
1395 University Blvd
Jupiter FL 33458
561 622-5656

(P-16280)
G4S SECURE SOLUTIONS (USA)
1 Annabel Ln Ste 208, San Ramon (94583-4360)
PHONE..........................925 543-0008
EMP: 119
SALES (corp-wide): 11.8B **Privately Held**
SIC: 7381
HQ: G4s Secure Solutions (Usa) Inc
1395 University Blvd
Jupiter FL 33458
561 622-5656

(P-16281)
G4S SECURE SOLUTIONS USA INC
5030 Camino De La Siesta # 404, San Diego (92108-3120)
PHONE..........................619 295-2394
Steven Fisher, *Systems Staff*
Erin Fujioka, *Business Mgr*
EMP: 250
SQ FT: 1,500 **Privately Held**
SIC: 7381 Security guard service
HQ: G4s Secure Solutions (Usa) Inc.
1395 University Blvd
Jupiter FL 33458
561 622-5656

(P-16282)
G4S SECURE SOLUTIONS USA INC
200 Pine St Fl 7, San Francisco (94104-2707)
PHONE..........................415 591-0780
Stanley Lee, *Branch Mgr*
Kim Whitworth, *Manager*
EMP: 119 **Privately Held**
SIC: 7381 Security guard service
HQ: G4s Secure Solutions (Usa) Inc.
1395 University Blvd
Jupiter FL 33458
561 622-5656

(P-16283)
G4S SECURE SOLUTIONS USA INC
2300 E Katella Ave # 150, Anaheim (92806-6061)
PHONE..........................714 939-4900
John Mc Elhaney, *Manager*
EMP: 119 **Privately Held**
SIC: 7381 Security guard service
HQ: G4s Secure Solutions (Usa) Inc.
1395 University Blvd
Jupiter FL 33458
561 622-5656

(P-16284)
G4S SECURE SOLUTIONS USA INC
5655 Lindero Canyon Rd # 504, Westlake Village (91362-4016)
PHONE..........................818 889-1113
Yvonne Herrod, *Manager*
EMP: 119 **Privately Held**
SIC: 7381 Security guard service
HQ: G4s Secure Solutions (Usa) Inc.
1395 University Blvd
Jupiter FL 33458
561 622-5656

(P-16285)
GARDA CL TECHNICAL SVCS INC
15640 Roxford St, Sylmar (91342-1265)
PHONE..........................818 362-7011
Ken Krogman, *Manager*
EMP: 55
SALES (corp-wide): 1.5MM **Privately Held**
WEB: www.gocashlink.com
SIC: 7381 Armored car services
HQ: Garda Cl Technical Services, Inc.
700 S Federal Hwy Ste 300
Boca Raton FL 33432

(P-16286)
GARDA CL WEST INC
372 S Arrowhead Ave, San Bernardino (92408-1307)
PHONE..........................909 574-2676
Jim Chadwick, *Branch Mgr*
EMP: 50
SALES (corp-wide): 1.5MM **Privately Held**
SIC: 7381 Armored car services
HQ: Garda Cl West, Inc.
1612 W Pico Blvd
Los Angeles CA 90015
213 383-3611

(P-16287)
GARDA CL WEST INC (DH)
Also Called: Gcl W
1612 W Pico Blvd, Los Angeles (90015-2410)
PHONE..........................213 383-3611
Stephan Cretier, *President*
Chris W Jamroz, *President*
Chantal Baril, *Vice Pres*
Jean-Michel Filiatrault, *Vice Pres*
Christian Paradis, *Vice Pres*
EMP: 375
SQ FT: 25,000
SALES (est): 53.8MM
SALES (corp-wide): 1.5MM **Privately Held**
SIC: 7381 Armored car services

(P-16288)
GARDA CL WEST INC
301 N Lake Ave Ste 600, Pasadena (91101-5129)
PHONE..........................800 883-8305
Duncan Longworth, *Branch Mgr*
Debbie Ray, *Vice Pres*
Linda Lanier, *Human Res Dir*
Ken Rose, *Human Res Mgr*
Ruben Blanco, *Manager*
EMP: 70
SALES (corp-wide): 16.5MM **Privately Held**
SIC: 7381 Armored car services; security guard service
PA: Garda Cl West Inc
20325 E Walnut Dr N
Walnut CA 91789
323 668-2712

(P-16289)
GATEWAY SECURITY INC
5757 W Century Blvd, Los Angeles (90045-6401)
PHONE..........................310 410-0790
Stephan Glassman, *Branch Mgr*
EMP: 818
SALES (corp-wide): 100.4MM **Privately Held**
SIC: 7381 Security guard service

PA: Gateway Security Inc.
604 Market St 608
Newark NJ 07105
973 465-8006

(P-16290)
GEIL ENTERPRISES INC
Also Called: CIS Security
1945 N Helm Ave Ste 102, Fresno (93727-1670)
PHONE..........................559 495-3000
Sam Geil, *CEO*
Ryan Geil, *President*
EMP: 107
SQ FT: 10,000
SALES (est): 36.4MM **Privately Held**
WEB: www.geilenterprises.com
SIC: 7381 7349 Protective services, guard; janitorial service, contract basis; building maintenance, except repairs

(P-16291)
GREEN VALLEY SECURITY INC
6049 Douglas Blvd Ste 28, Granite Bay (95746-6275)
PHONE..........................916 797-4058
Anthony Urbancic, *President*
EMP: 60
SQ FT: 300
SALES (est): 1.2MM **Privately Held**
SIC: 7381 Security guard service

(P-16292)
GS1 GROUP INC
70 S Lake Ave Ste 945, Pasadena (91101-4991)
PHONE..........................626 510-6384
Michael Vincent Severo, *CEO*
Ernesto Garcia, *President*
Enrique Garcia, *Director*
EMP: 68 **EST:** 2011
SALES: 1.2MM **Privately Held**
SIC: 7381 Security guard service; private investigator

(P-16293)
GUARD MANAGEMENT INC
Also Called: G M I
8001 Vickers St, San Diego (92111-1917)
PHONE..........................858 279-8282
Larry Abrams, *President*
Bryan Allen, *Administration*
Paloma Jacobo, *Opers Mgr*
Brian Wiley, *Security Mgr*
Ryan Keltner, *Manager*
EMP: 510
SALES (est): 11.1MM **Privately Held**
SIC: 7381 Security guard service

(P-16294)
GUARD-SYSTEMS INC
1910 S Archibald Ave M2, Ontario (91761-8502)
PHONE..........................909 947-5400
Patrick Crawford, *Manager*
EMP: 300
SALES (corp-wide): 25MM **Privately Held**
WEB: www.guardsystemsinc.com
SIC: 7381 Protective services, guard; guard services; security guard service
PA: Guard-Systems, Inc.
1190 Monterey Pass Rd
Monterey Park CA 91754
626 443-0031

(P-16295)
GUARD-SYSTEMS INC
Also Called: Guard Systems District 1
1190 Monterey Pass Rd, Monterey Park (91754-3615)
PHONE..........................323 881-6715
Theodore Haas, *Owner*
EMP: 300
SALES (est): 2MM
SALES (corp-wide): 25MM **Privately Held**
WEB: www.guardsystemsinc.com
SIC: 7381 Security guard service
PA: Guard-Systems, Inc.
1190 Monterey Pass Rd
Monterey Park CA 91754
626 443-0031

(P-16296)
GUARDCO SECURITY SERVICES
1360 W 18th St, Merced (95340-4402)
PHONE.....................209 723-4273
David Williams, *Owner*
EMP: 71
SQ FT: 1,000
SALES: 1.7MM **Privately Held**
WEB: www.guardcosecurity.com
SIC: 7381 Security guard service

(P-16297)
GUARDIAN EAGLE SECURITY INC
11400 W Olympic Blvd Fl 2, Los Angeles (90064-1579)
PHONE.....................888 990-0002
Hassan M Galal, *CEO*
Fadwa Galal, *President*
Hassan Galal, *CEO*
Fathi M Galal, *Vice Pres*
EMP: 500
SQ FT: 3,000
SALES (est): 8.1MM **Privately Held**
WEB: www.ges.net
SIC: 7381 Security guard service

(P-16298)
GUARDIAN NATIONAL INC
Also Called: Guardian National Security
20361 Prairie St Ste 1, Chatsworth (91311-8100)
PHONE.....................800 700-1467
Abraham Ramzan, *CEO*
Jay Helman, *Supervisor*
▲ EMP: 50
SALES (est): 1.4MM **Privately Held**
SIC: 7381 Security guard service

(P-16299)
GUARDNOW INC (PA)
18663 Ventura Blvd # 217, Tarzana (91356-4100)
P.O. Box 67, Manhattan Beach (90267-0067)
PHONE.....................877 482-7366
Mike Kator, *President*
EMP: 50 EST: 2011
SQ FT: 115
SALES: 5MM **Privately Held**
SIC: 7381 Security guard service

(P-16300)
GUARDSMARK LLC
4713 1st St Ste 215, Pleasanton (94566-7363)
PHONE.....................925 484-4412
Charles Parker, *Manager*
EMP: 350
SALES (corp-wide): 686.6MM **Privately Held**
WEB: www.guardsmark.com
SIC: 7381 Security guard service
HQ: Guardsmark, Llc
  1551 N Tustin Ave Ste 650
  Santa Ana CA 92705
  714 619-9700

(P-16301)
GUARDSMARK LLC
1225 W 190th St Ste 280, Gardena (90248-4305)
PHONE.....................310 522-9603
EMP: 60
SALES (corp-wide): 741.7MM **Privately Held**
SIC: 7381
HQ: Guardsmark, Llc
  1551 N Tustin Ave Ste 650
  Santa Ana CA 92705
  714 619-9700

(P-16302)
GUARDSMARK LLC
3000 S Robertson Blvd # 150, Los Angeles (90034-3144)
PHONE.....................310 287-3103
Rebekah Wells, *Principal*
Heather Nowaske, *Info Tech Mgr*
EMP: 111
SALES (corp-wide): 686.6MM **Privately Held**
WEB: www.guardsmark.com
SIC: 7381 Security guard service

HQ: Guardsmark, Llc
  1551 N Tustin Ave Ste 650
  Santa Ana CA 92705
  714 619-9700

(P-16303)
GUARDSMARK LLC (DH)
1551 N Tustin Ave Ste 650, Santa Ana (92705-8664)
PHONE.....................714 619-9700
Steven S Jones, *CEO*
Joshua Lipman, *Vice Chairman*
EMP: 148
SQ FT: 32,107
SALES (est): 258.6MM
SALES (corp-wide): 686.6MM **Privately Held**
WEB: www.guardsmark.com
SIC: 7381 8742 2721 Security guard service; private investigator; industry specialist consultants; periodicals publishing only
HQ: Universal Protection Service, Lp
  1551 N Tustin Ave Ste 650
  Santa Ana CA 92705
  714 619-9700

(P-16304)
GUARDSMARK LLC
350 Sansome St, San Francisco (94104-1304)
PHONE.....................415 956-6070
Coley Buellesfeld, *Vice Pres*
EMP: 300
SALES (corp-wide): 686.6MM **Privately Held**
WEB: www.guardsmark.com
SIC: 7381 Security guard service
HQ: Guardsmark, Llc
  1551 N Tustin Ave Ste 650
  Santa Ana CA 92705
  714 619-9700

(P-16305)
GUARDSMARK LLC
3701 Wilshire Blvd, Los Angeles (90010-2804)
PHONE.....................818 841-0288
Bob Carpenter, *Manager*
EMP: 118
SALES (corp-wide): 686.6MM **Privately Held**
WEB: www.guardsmark.com
SIC: 7381 7382 Security guard service; security systems services
HQ: Guardsmark, Llc
  1551 N Tustin Ave Ste 650
  Santa Ana CA 92705
  714 619-9700

(P-16306)
GUARDSMARK LLC
100 Hegenberger Rd # 130, Oakland (94621-1447)
PHONE.....................510 562-7606
Ben Atkins, *Manager*
EMP: 250
SALES (corp-wide): 686.6MM **Privately Held**
WEB: www.guardsmark.com
SIC: 7381 Security guard service; private investigator
HQ: Guardsmark, Llc
  1551 N Tustin Ave Ste 650
  Santa Ana CA 92705
  714 619-9700

(P-16307)
GUARDSMARK LLC
4970 El Camino Real, Los Altos (94022-1460)
PHONE.....................800 238-5878
Rania Terry, *Manager*
EMP: 118
SALES (corp-wide): 686.6MM **Privately Held**
SIC: 7381 Security guard service
HQ: Universal Protection Service, Lp
  1551 N Tustin Ave Ste 650
  Santa Ana CA 92705
  714 619-9700

(P-16308)
GUARDSMARK LLC
5300 Lennox Ave Ste 102, Bakersfield (93309-1662)
PHONE.....................661 325-5906
EMP: 111
SALES (corp-wide): 928.7MM **Privately Held**
SIC: 7381
HQ: Guardsmark, Llc
  6363 Poplar Ave Ste 300
  Memphis TN 92705
  901 761-2288

(P-16309)
GUARDSMARK LLC
5095 Murphy Canyon Rd # 301, San Diego (92123-4346)
PHONE.....................858 499-0025
Ira Lipman, *Branch Mgr*
EMP: 111
SALES (corp-wide): 686.6MM **Privately Held**
WEB: www.guardsmark.com
SIC: 7381 Security guard service
HQ: Guardsmark, Llc
  1551 N Tustin Ave Ste 650
  Santa Ana CA 92705
  714 619-9700

(P-16310)
GUARDSMARK LLC
600 W Shaw Ave Ste 200, Fresno (93704-2420)
PHONE.....................559 243-1217
Ricardo Franco, *Branch Mgr*
EMP: 111
SALES (corp-wide): 686.6MM **Privately Held**
WEB: www.guardsmark.com
SIC: 7381 Security guard service
HQ: Guardsmark, Llc
  1551 N Tustin Ave Ste 650
  Santa Ana CA 92705
  714 619-9700

(P-16311)
GUARDSMARK LLC
1200 Wilshire Blvd # 620, Los Angeles (90017-1920)
PHONE.....................818 841-0288
Scott Carpenter, *Manager*
EMP: 111
SALES (corp-wide): 686.6MM **Privately Held**
WEB: www.guardsmark.com
SIC: 7381 Security guard service
HQ: Guardsmark, Llc
  1551 N Tustin Ave Ste 650
  Santa Ana CA 92705
  714 619-9700

(P-16312)
GUARDSMARK LLC
30 E San Joaquin St # 204, Salinas (93901-2947)
PHONE.....................831 769-8981
Ira Litman,
EMP: 111
SALES (corp-wide): 686.6MM **Privately Held**
WEB: www.guardsmark.com
SIC: 7381 Security guard service
HQ: Guardsmark, Llc
  1551 N Tustin Ave Ste 650
  Santa Ana CA 92705
  714 619-9700

(P-16313)
GUARDSMARK LLC
533 Airport Blvd Ste 303, Burlingame (94010-2040)
PHONE.....................650 685-2400
David Connor, *Manager*
EMP: 111
SALES (corp-wide): 686.6MM **Privately Held**
WEB: www.guardsmark.com
SIC: 7381 Security guard service
HQ: Guardsmark, Llc
  1551 N Tustin Ave Ste 650
  Santa Ana CA 92705
  714 619-9700

(P-16314)
GUARDSMARK LLC
1601 Bayshore Hwy Ste 350, Burlingame (94010-1522)
PHONE.....................650 652-9130
EMP: 145
SALES (corp-wide): 928.7MM **Privately Held**
SIC: 7381
HQ: Guardsmark, Llc
  6363 Poplar Ave Ste 300
  Memphis TN 92705
  901 761-2288

(P-16315)
GUARDSMARK LLC
101 S 1st St Ste 408, Burbank (91502-1938)
PHONE.....................818 841-0288
Seth Rapaport, *Manager*
EMP: 175
SALES (corp-wide): 686.6MM **Privately Held**
WEB: www.guardsmark.com
SIC: 7381 Security guard service
HQ: Guardsmark, Llc
  1551 N Tustin Ave Ste 650
  Santa Ana CA 92705
  714 619-9700

(P-16316)
GUARDSMARK LLC
2900 Adams St Ste C10a, Riverside (92504-8315)
PHONE.....................909 989-5345
Gary Parks, *Manager*
Roger Langner, *Vice Pres*
EMP: 295
SALES (corp-wide): 686.6MM **Privately Held**
WEB: www.guardsmark.com
SIC: 7381 7382 Security guard service; security systems services
HQ: Guardsmark, Llc
  1551 N Tustin Ave Ste 650
  Santa Ana CA 92705
  714 619-9700

(P-16317)
HAL-MAR-JAC ENTERPRISES
Also Called: McCoy's Patrol Service
1044 Potrero Cir, Suisun City (94585-4139)
PHONE.....................415 467-1470
EMP: 110
SALES (est): 2.3MM **Privately Held**
SIC: 7381

(P-16318)
HARVEST V CITIZENS PATROL
25098 Avenida Valencia, Homeland (92548-9318)
P.O. Box 2255 (92548-2255)
PHONE.....................951 926-9763
Robert Gibbons, *Chairman*
Laura Daniels, *Treasurer*
Winn Barker, *Vice Pres*
John Lauda, *Principal*
Roy Yost, *Principal*
EMP: 127
SALES (est): 1.5MM **Privately Held**
SIC: 7381 Protective services, guard

(P-16319)
HIGHCOM SECURITY SERVICES
1900 Webster St Ste B, Oakland (94612-2946)
PHONE.....................510 893-7600
Sammy Joselewitz, *President*
EMP: 60
SALES (est): 1.9MM **Privately Held**
WEB: www.highcomsecurityservices.com
SIC: 7381 8742 Security guard service; management consulting services

(P-16320)
HMI ASSOCIATES INC
6800 Owensmouth Ave # 330, Canoga Park (91303-3159)
PHONE.....................818 887-6800
EMP: 200
SALES (est): 1.8MM **Privately Held**
SIC: 7381

(P-16321)
HORSEMEN INC
16911 Algonquin St, Huntington Beach
(92649-3812)
PHONE...............................714 847-4243
Patrick Carroll, *President*
Cheryl Gall, *Consultant*
EMP: 100 **EST:** 1995
SALES (est): 3.9MM **Privately Held**
WEB: www.horsemeninc.com
SIC: 7381 Private investigator

(P-16322)
HYLTON SECURITY INC
1015 2nd St Fl 2, Sacramento
(95814-3255)
PHONE...............................916 442-1000
David J Hylton, *President*
Mindy A Hylton, *Senior VP*
EMP: 107
SQ FT: 1,500
SALES: 250K **Privately Held**
WEB: www.hyltonsecurity.com
SIC: 7381 Security guard service

(P-16323)
INTELLIGUARD SECURITY SERVICES
Also Called: Safety Dynamics
4663 Harbord Dr, Oakland (94618-2210)
PHONE...............................510 547-7656
John Weir, *President*
EMP: 130
SALES (est): 3.6MM **Privately Held**
SIC: 7381 Security guard service

(P-16324)
INTER-CON INVESTIGATORS INC
Also Called: Inter Con Systems
210 S De Lacey Ave, Pasadena
(91105-2048)
PHONE...............................626 535-2200
Enrique Hernandez Jr, *President*
Roland Hernandez, *Vice Pres*
EMP: 100
SQ FT: 17,000
SALES (est): 2.5MM **Privately Held**
SIC: 7381 Security guard service

(P-16325)
INTER-CON SECURITY SYSTEMS INC (PA)
210 S De Lacey Ave, Pasadena
(91105-2048)
PHONE...............................626 535-2200
Enrique Hernandez Jr, *Ch of Bd*
Roland A Hernandez, *Treasurer*
Brian Faulkner, *Exec VP*
Arron Money, *Instructor*
Andrea Hernandez, *Assistant*
EMP: 140
SQ FT: 17,000
SALES (est): 487.8MM **Privately Held**
SIC: 7381 Security guard service

(P-16326)
INTERSTATE PROTECTIVE SERVICES
Also Called: Ips
20548 Ventura Blvd # 118, Woodland Hills
(91364-6225)
PHONE...............................818 995-6664
Nabila Helal, *CEO*
Michael Ahmed, *President*
Wil Hanna, *Principal*
Nancy Saenz, *Principal*
EMP: 99
SQ FT: 5,100
SALES: 4.8MM **Privately Held**
SIC: 7381 Security guard service

(P-16327)
IRONCLAD SECURITY SERVICES INC
3561 Homestead Rd Ste 600, Santa Clara
(95051-5161)
PHONE...............................408 773-2800
Bruce McAllister, *President*
Aner Medar, *Opers Staff*
EMP: 75
SQ FT: 4,000

SALES (est): 1MM **Privately Held**
SIC: 7381 7389 Protective services, guard; security guard service; personal investigation service

(P-16328)
IUNLIMITED INCORPORATED
7801 Folsom Blvd Ste 203, Sacramento
(95826-2620)
P.O. Box 276390 (95827-6390)
PHONE...............................916 218-6198
Todd M Tano, *CEO*
Keith Jacobs, *President*
Jeff Walters, *Officer*
Erin Frame, *Department Mgr*
Leonard Watson, *Opers Mgr*
EMP: 115
SALES: 8MM **Privately Held**
SIC: 7381 Private investigator

(P-16329)
J & E PRIVATE SECURITY CORP
3227 Producer Way Ste 110, Pomona
(91768-3919)
PHONE...............................909 594-1111
Megan Hsu, *Admin Sec*
Edwin Inocencio, *CFO*
EMP: 60
SALES (est): 1.7MM **Privately Held**
SIC: 7381 Security guard service

(P-16330)
J WATERS INC
Also Called: Achates Security
75 San Miguel Ave Ste 5, Salinas
(93901-3059)
PHONE...............................866 424-1946
Kristine Waters, *Branch Mgr*
EMP: 65
SALES (corp-wide): 5.2MM **Privately Held**
SIC: 7381 Armored car services
PA: J. Waters, Inc.
10000 Ne 7th Ave
Vancouver WA 98685
831 424-1946

(P-16331)
JONES BOLD SECURITY INC
Also Called: Jbsprotection
7520 Sleepy Creek Ave, Fontana
(92336-2192)
PHONE...............................562 316-6552
Brandon Jones, *Principal*
EMP: 100
SALES (est): 393.1K **Privately Held**
SIC: 7381 Guard services

(P-16332)
K TECH SECURITY & PROTECT SVC
665 Alvin St, San Diego (92114-1817)
PHONE...............................619 858-5832
Kelly J Steppe, *Owner*
EMP: 127
SALES (est): 2.9MM **Privately Held**
WEB: www.k-techsecurity.com
SIC: 7381 Security guard service

(P-16333)
KAISER MED SECURITY SERVICES
2241 Geary Blvd, San Francisco
(94115-3415)
PHONE...............................415 833-3683
Dennis Hyams, *Director*
EMP: 100
SALES (est): 1.1MM **Privately Held**
SIC: 7381 Security guard service

(P-16334)
KING SECURITY SERVICES INC
1159 7th St, Novato (94945-2207)
PHONE...............................415 556-5464
Kimberly King, *President*
Jolanta King, *CFO*
Louis Siracusa, *Vice Pres*
EMP: 528
SQ FT: 2,000
SALES (est): 13.1MM **Privately Held**
WEB: www.kingsecurity.com
SIC: 7381 Security guard service; private investigator

(P-16335)
KYSMET SECURITY & PATROL INC
21 W Laurel Dr Ste 49, Salinas
(93906-3498)
PHONE...............................831 710-2425
Esteban Garcia, *CEO*
EMP: 50 **EST:** 2015
SALES (est): 1.1MM **Privately Held**
SIC: 7381 Guard services

(P-16336)
LAKE TAHOE SECRET WITNESS
1051 Al Tahoe Blvd, South Lake Tahoe
(96150-4502)
P.O. Box 14282 (96151-4282)
PHONE...............................530 541-6800
Pam Sullivan, *Owner*
EMP: 90 **EST:** 1997
SALES (est): 952.3K **Privately Held**
SIC: 7381 Detective services

(P-16337)
LANDMARK EVENT STAFFING
4790 Irvine Blvd Ste 105, Irvine
(92620-1998)
PHONE...............................714 293-4248
Peter Kranske, *President*
EMP: 916 **Privately Held**
SIC: 7381 Security guard service
PA: Landmark Event Staffing Services, Inc.
4131 Harbor Walk Dr
Fort Collins CO 80525

(P-16338)
LANTZ SECURITY SYSTEMS INC
101 N Westlake Blvd # 200, Westlake Village (91362-3753)
PHONE...............................805 496-5775
Terry Oestreich, *Manager*
EMP: 300 **Privately Held**
WEB: www.lantzsecurity.com
SIC: 7381 7382 Security guard service; security systems services
PA: Lantz Security Systems Inc
43440 Sahuayo St
Lancaster CA 93535

(P-16339)
LANTZ SECURITY SYSTEMS INC (PA)
43440 Sahuayo St, Lancaster
(93535-4659)
PHONE...............................661 949-3565
Jack E Lantz, *President*
Jose Reyes, *Vice Pres*
EMP: 60
SQ FT: 2,100
SALES (est): 13.2MM **Privately Held**
WEB: www.lantzsecurity.com
SIC: 7381 Security guard service

(P-16340)
LEGIONS PROTECTIVE SVCS LLC
17201 S Figueroa St, Gardena
(90248-3022)
PHONE...............................310 819-8881
Gregorio Campos, *CEO*
Armando Ojeda Jr, *Vice Pres*
EMP: 50
SQ FT: 1,000
SALES (est): 403.6K **Privately Held**
SIC: 7381 Security guard service

(P-16341)
LEVEL 9 SECURITY SERVICES
9020 Slauson Ave Ste 206, Pico Rivera
(90660-4578)
PHONE...............................562 949-7180
Jose Tellez, *Owner*
EMP: 50
SALES (est): 999.6K **Privately Held**
SIC: 7381 Security guard service

(P-16342)
LOCATOR SERVICES INC
Also Called: Able Patrol & Guard
4616 Mission Gorge Pl, San Diego
(92120-4133)
PHONE...............................619 229-6100
George Grauer,
Diane G Edwards, *Vice Pres*

George Grauer Jr, *Vice Pres*
Deborah L Kopki, *Vice Pres*
Christine Lowe, *Admin Asst*
EMP: 120
SQ FT: 4,500
SALES: 1.9MM **Privately Held**
WEB: www.ablepatrolandguard.com
SIC: 7381 Security guard service

(P-16343)
LOOMIS ARMORED US LLC
3555 Aero Ct, San Diego (92123-1710)
PHONE...............................619 232-5106
Tim Bong, *Manager*
EMP: 70
SALES (corp-wide): 2.1B **Privately Held**
WEB: www.loomisfargo.com
SIC: 7381 Armored car services
HQ: Loomis Armored Us, Llc
2500 Citywest Blvd # 900
Houston TX 77042
713 435-6700

(P-16344)
LOOMIS ARMORED US LLC
315 12th St, Sacramento (95814-0900)
PHONE...............................916 441-1091
Daryl Balko, *General Mgr*
EMP: 70
SALES (corp-wide): 2.1B **Privately Held**
WEB: www.loomisfargo.com
SIC: 7381 Armored car services
HQ: Loomis Armored Us, Llc
2500 Citywest Blvd # 900
Houston TX 77042
713 435-6700

(P-16345)
LYONS SECURITY SERVICE INC
655 University Ave # 240, Sacramento
(95825-6746)
PHONE...............................916 925-9667
Robin Cheatam, *Branch Mgr*
EMP: 55 **Privately Held**
SIC: 7381 Protective services, guard
PA: Lyons Security Service, Inc.
505 S Villa Real Ste 203a
Anaheim CA 92807

(P-16346)
M & S SECURITY SERVICES INC
Also Called: Westside Security Patrol
2900 L St, Bakersfield (93301-2351)
PHONE...............................661 397-9616
Marvin Fuller Jr, *President*
Steve Fuller, *President*
Darlene Fuller, *Corp Secy*
EMP: 100
SQ FT: 3,000
SALES (est): 3.4MM **Privately Held**
WEB: www.mssecurityservices.com
SIC: 7381 7382 1731 Protective services, guard; security systems services; burglar alarm maintenance & monitoring; fire detection & burglar alarm systems specialization

(P-16347)
MADERA PRIVATE SECURITY PATROL
910 W Yosemite Ave, Madera
(93637-4555)
PHONE...............................559 662-1546
Timothy Supple, *Partner*
Michael Gonzalez, *Partner*
Rebecca Supple, *Partner*
EMP: 78
SALES (est): 1.8MM **Privately Held**
WEB: www.maderaprivatesecurity.com
SIC: 7381 Protective services, guard; security guard service

(P-16348)
MAGNUS SECURITY
2667 Camino Del Rio S, San Diego
(92108-3707)
PHONE...............................619 546-7789
Marques Oliver, *Principal*
Marcus Oliver, *Owner*
EMP: 50 **EST:** 2013
SALES (est): 228.7K **Privately Held**
SIC: 7381 Security guard service

(P-16349)
MAZAR CORP
Also Called: Gladiator Security Services
3200 E Guasti Rd Ste 100, Ontario
(91761-8661)
PHONE....................................909 292-8269
Mukhtar Ahmad Peerzay, *President*
Hares Kabir, *CFO*
Lamonte Sanders, *Vice Pres*
EMP: 62
SALES (est): 1.1MM **Privately Held**
SIC: 7381 Armored car services; security
guard service

(P-16350)
MEMON AAMIR
Also Called: American Hritg Protection Svcs
20832 Roscoe Blvd Ste 207, Winnetka
(91306-2058)
PHONE....................................818 339-8810
Aamir Memon, *Owner*
EMP: 50 EST: 2011
SQ FT: 500
SALES (est): 887K **Privately Held**
SIC: 7381 Security guard service

(P-16351)
METROPOLITAN DST PRIVATE SEC
44262 Division St Ste A, Lancaster
(93535-3548)
PHONE....................................661 942-3999
Frederick Porras, *President*
EMP: 93
SQ FT: 1,200
SALES (est): 696.5K **Privately Held**
SIC: 7381 Security guard service

(P-16352)
MICHAEL MCCARTHY
Also Called: Loyal Svc Unt Spec Team
3233 E Broadway, Long Beach
(90803-5817)
PHONE....................................310 800-5367
Michael McCarthy, *Owner*
EMP: 50
SQ FT: 1,500
SALES (est): 292.8K **Privately Held**
SIC: 7381 4119 7361 Security guard serv-
ice; local passenger transportation; em-
ployment agencies

(P-16353)
MISSION SECURITY AND PATROL
27 W Anapamu St Ste 141, Santa Barbara
(93101-3107)
PHONE....................................805 899-3039
Marcu Abandis, *Owner*
Marcus Abundis, *President*
Brian Fairrington, *Director*
EMP: 100 EST: 1997
SALES (est): 2.1MM **Privately Held**
SIC: 7381 6411 Security guard service;
patrol services, insurance

(P-16354)
MONUMENT SECURITY INC
24301 Suthland Dr Ste 312, Hayward
(94545)
PHONE....................................510 430-3540
EMP: 150 **Privately Held**
SIC: 7381
PA: Monument Security, Inc.
4926 43rd St Ste 10
Mcclellan CA 95652

(P-16355)
MONUMENT SECURITY INC (PA)
4926 43rd St Ste 10, McClellan
(95652-2618)
P.O. Box 399, North Highlands (95660-
0399)
PHONE....................................916 564-4234
EMP: 150
SQ FT: 2,500
SALES (est): 36.3MM **Privately Held**
SIC: 7381

(P-16356)
MULHOLLAND SEC & PATROL INC
Also Called: Centurion Group, The
11454 San Vicente Blvd Fi, Los Angeles
(90049-6208)
PHONE....................................818 755-0202
David Rosenberg, *President*
Daniel Campbell, *Vice Pres*
Steven Lemmer, *Vice Pres*
EMP: 350
SQ FT: 2,500
SALES (est): 8.5MM **Privately Held**
WEB: www.mulhollandsecurity.com
SIC: 7381 Protective services, guard; se-
curity guard service

(P-16357)
MURANO GROUP
Also Called: Officer Off Duty
30211 Ave De Las Bndra, Rcho STA Marg
(92688-2147)
PHONE....................................949 409-1079
Tristan Murano, *President*
EMP: 52
SQ FT: 2,000
SALES (est): 1.2MM **Privately Held**
SIC: 7381 7389 Security guard service;
explosives recovery or extraction services

(P-16358)
NATIONAL PUB SFETY SEC SVCS IN
490 N Magnolia Ave, El Cajon
(92020-3607)
PHONE....................................619 579-1660
Natasha Frost, *CEO*
Douglas Frost, *President*
EMP: 56
SALES (est): 1.5MM **Privately Held**
SIC: 7381 Security guard service

(P-16359)
NATIONAL SECURITY INDUSTRIES
Also Called: National Security Santa Cruz
501 Mission St Ste 1a, Santa Cruz
(95060-3661)
PHONE....................................831 425-2052
James Clarke,
EMP: 300
SALES (est): 3.2MM **Privately Held**
SIC: 7381 Security guard service

(P-16360)
NATIONWIDE GUARD SERVICES INC
9327 Fairway View Pl # 200, Rancho Cuca-
monga (91730-0969)
PHONE....................................909 608-1112
John Woolen, *President*
Veronica Kemp, *Administration*
Mari Bennett, *Director*
Johnathan Sullivan, *Supervisor*
EMP: 56
SALES (est): 1.1MM **Privately Held**
WEB: www.nationwideguardservices.com
SIC: 7381 Security guard service

(P-16361)
NORTH AMERICAN SECURITY INC
550 E Carson Plaza Dr # 222, Carson
(90746-3229)
PHONE....................................310 630-4840
Arthur L Lopez, *President*
Kenneth Hillman, *Vice Pres*
Gillian Watanabe, *Accounting Mgr*
Brandon Dangelo, *Controller*
Anthony Vasquez, *Real Est Agnt*
EMP: 420
SQ FT: 1,000
SALES (est): 12.8MM **Privately Held**
SIC: 7381 Security guard service

(P-16362)
NORTH AMRCN SEC INVESTIGATIONS
550 E Carson Plaza Dr, Carson
(90746-3229)
PHONE....................................323 634-1911
Kenny Hillman, *President*
Arthur Lopez, *CEO*
EMP: 100

SQ FT: 6,000
SALES (est): 4.7MM **Privately Held**
SIC: 7381 Security guard service

(P-16363)
NORTH STATE SECURITY INC
1970 Hartnell Ave, Redding (96002-2214)
P.O. Box 991348 (96099-1348)
PHONE....................................530 243-0295
Lance Boek, *President*
EMP: 100
SQ FT: 1,500
SALES (est): 1.4MM **Privately Held**
SIC: 7381 Security guard service

(P-16364)
NORTHEAST PROTECTIVE SVCS INC
Also Called: Neps Worldwide
16040 Peppertree Ln, La Mirada
(90638-3460)
PHONE....................................800 577-0899
Alan Burton, *President*
Frank Widder, *CFO*
Brenda Chavez, *Officer*
Alex Burton, *Director*
EMP: 65
SALES (est): 1.5MM **Privately Held**
WEB:
www.northeastprotectiveservices.com
SIC: 7381 Protective services, guard; se-
curity guard service

(P-16365)
OC SPECIAL EVENTS SEC INC
Also Called: Firearms Academy
1232 Village Way Ste K, Santa Ana
(92705-4746)
PHONE....................................714 541-4111
Richard Allum, *President*
David S Andersen, *Shareholder*
EMP: 102
SALES (est): 1.9MM **Privately Held**
SIC: 7381 Security guard service; guard
services

(P-16366)
ODONA CENTRAL SECURITY INC
71 N San Gabriel Blvd, Pasadena
(91107-3749)
PHONE....................................323 728-8818
Fred Chen, *President*
EMP: 150
SQ FT: 2,000
SALES (est): 3.1MM **Privately Held**
WEB: www.odona.com
SIC: 7381 Security guard service

(P-16367)
OFF DUTY OFFICERS INC
2365 La Mirada Dr, Vista (92081-7863)
PHONE....................................888 408-5900
Aram Minasian, *President*
Terry Degelder, *Managing Prtnr*
Paul Jones, *CEO*
Kevin Hansen, *CFO*
Marc Lapointe, *General Mgr*
EMP: 1300
SQ FT: 4,000
SALES (est): 29.6MM **Privately Held**
WEB: www.offdutyofficers.com
SIC: 7381 8742 Security guard service;
management consulting services

(P-16368)
OMEGA SECURITY SERVICES & CONS
10611 Garden Grove Ave # 2, Northridge
(91326-3211)
PHONE....................................818 831-1100
Motti Ben-Haim, *President*
Motti S Benhaim, *Office Mgr*
EMP: 70
SALES (est): 1.7MM **Privately Held**
WEB: www.omegasec.net
SIC: 7381 Guard services; security guard
service

(P-16369)
ON-SCENE SECURITY SERVICES INC
P.O. Box 800147, Santa Clarita (91380-
0147)
PHONE....................................661 263-2343

Larry Wilson, *President*
Deborah Wilson, *Vice Pres*
EMP: 50
SALES (est): 701.9K **Privately Held**
SIC: 7381 Security guard service

(P-16370)
ONTEL SECURITY SERVICES INC
2125 Wylie Dr Ste 11, Modesto
(95355-3847)
P.O. Box 579730 (95357-9730)
PHONE....................................209 521-0200
David Ackerman, *CEO*
David McCann, *COO*
Michael Ackerman, *CFO*
Roberta Gray, *Treasurer*
John Collins, *Commander*
EMP: 71
SQ FT: 2,500
SALES (est): 2.4MM **Privately Held**
WEB: www.ontelsecurity.com
SIC: 7381 Security guard service

(P-16371)
OPSEC SPECIALIZED PROTECTION
44262 Division St Ste A, Lancaster
(93535-3548)
PHONE....................................661 942-3999
Fred Porras, *Owner*
Jeannie Groff, *Owner*
Sue Imperial, *General Mgr*
EMP: 99
SALES: 950K **Privately Held**
WEB:
www.opsecspecializedprotection.com
SIC: 7381 Security guard service

(P-16372)
OVERTON SECURITY SERVICES INC
39300 Civic Center Dr # 370, Fremont
(94538-2338)
PHONE....................................510 791-7380
Andrew Overton, *President*
Vicki Greiner, *CFO*
Paul Baria, *Officer*
Sandra Overton, *Vice Pres*
Oliver Casillas, *QC Mgr*
EMP: 215
SALES (est): 20.2MM **Privately Held**
SIC: 7381 Security guard service

(P-16373)
PACIFIC PROTECTION SERVICES
22144 Clarendon St # 110, Woodland Hills
(91367-8201)
PHONE....................................818 313-9369
Melvin Staples, *Branch Mgr*
EMP: 97
SALES (corp-wide): 8.1MM **Privately
Held**
SIC: 7381 Security guard service
PA: Pacific Protection Services Inc
22144 Clarendon St # 110
Woodland Hills CA 91367
818 313-9369

(P-16374)
PALADIN PRTCTION SPCALISTS INC
Also Called: Paladin Private Security
320 Commerce Cir, Sacramento
(95815-4213)
PHONE....................................916 331-3175
Louis G Aljens, *CEO*
Joshua Morris, *Officer*
Matthew Carroll, *Vice Pres*
EMP: 135
SALES (est): 9.3MM **Privately Held**
WEB: www.paladinprivatesecurity.com
SIC: 7381 Security guard service

(P-16375)
PATROL MASTERS INC
1651 E 4th St Ste 150, Santa Ana
(92701-5173)
PHONE....................................714 426-2526
Samir Ahmad, *President*
Peter Costello, *Sales Staff*
EMP: 150 EST: 2006
SALES (est): 4.1MM **Privately Held**
SIC: 7381 Security guard service

(P-16376)
PEACE KEEPERS PRIVATE SECURITY
2734b Delta Fair Blvd, Antioch (94509-4100)
PHONE..........................925 978-4140
Stuart M Welch, *President*
Stuart Welch, *President*
EMP: 60 **EST:** 1993
SALES: 800K **Privately Held**
SIC: 7381 Security guard service

(P-16377)
PERSONAL PROTECTIVE SVCS INC (PA)
398 Beach Rd Fl 2, Burlingame (94010-2004)
P.O. Box 14007, Oakland (94614-2007)
PHONE..........................650 344-3302
Stan Teets, *President*
Corbby Johnson, *Opers Staff*
EMP: 100
SQ FT: 1,500
SALES (est): 2.4MM **Privately Held**
WEB: www.personalprotective.com
SIC: 7381 Protective services, guard; private investigator

(P-16378)
PLATINUM PROTECTION GROUP INC
8018 E Santa Ana Cyn Rd, Anaheim (92808-1102)
PHONE..........................800 824-1097
Mark Van Holt,
EMP: 90
SALES: 500K **Privately Held**
WEB: www.platinumprotectiongroup.com
SIC: 7381 Security guard service; protective services, guard

(P-16379)
PLATT SECURITY SYSTEMS INC
Also Called: Platt Security Services
3275 E Grant St Ste D, Long Beach (90755-1293)
PHONE..........................562 986-4484
Robert E Platt, *President*
Tamara Platt, *Treasurer*
Mark Platt, *Vice Pres*
EMP: 150 **EST:** 1977
SQ FT: 2,200
SALES (est): 3.6MM **Privately Held**
WEB: www.plattsecurity.com
SIC: 7381 7382 Security guard service; security systems services

(P-16380)
PRE-EMPLOYCOM
3655 Meadow View Dr, Redding (96002-9715)
P.O. Box 491570 (96049-1570)
PHONE..........................800 300-1821
Robert Mather, *CEO*
EMP: 100
SALES: 10MM **Privately Held**
SIC: 7381 8742 Private investigator; human resource consulting services

(P-16381)
PRESTIGE SECURITY SERVICE INC
5721 W Slauson Ave # 120, Culver City (90230-6581)
PHONE..........................310 670-5999
George Bernaba, *Owner*
Jay Bernaba, *Opers Staff*
EMP: 400
SALES (est): 6.9MM **Privately Held**
SIC: 7381 Security guard service

(P-16382)
PRIME INTERNATIONAL SECURITY
Also Called: Prime Security
1630 Centinela Ave # 209, Inglewood (90302-6948)
P.O. Box 18348, Los Angeles (90018-0348)
PHONE..........................310 670-4565
Akubuo Okorie, *President*
Boniesace Nworgu, *Vice Pres*
EMP: 60
SALES (est): 1.5MM **Privately Held**
SIC: 7381 Security guard service

(P-16383)
PROBE INFORMATION SERVICES INC
6375 Auburn Blvd, Citrus Heights (95621-5270)
P.O. Box 418429, Sacramento (95841-8429)
PHONE..........................916 676-1826
Ross O Stewart, *President*
Renea Abdin, *Vice Pres*
Stephany Leyva, *Admin Asst*
Ryan Parino, *Admin Asst*
Paige Wilson, *Admin Asst*
EMP: 101
SQ FT: 6,000
SALES: 7.3MM **Privately Held**
WEB: www.probeinfo.com
SIC: 7381 Private investigator

(P-16384)
PROFESSIONAL SECURITY CONS (PA)
11454 San Vicente Blvd # 2, Los Angeles (90049-6208)
PHONE..........................310 207-7729
Moshe Alon, *President*
Israr Syed, *Vice Pres*
Grant Erickson, *Exec Dir*
Glen Blaylock, *Security Dir*
Rocco Loccisano, *Security Dir*
EMP: 103
SALES (est): 82MM **Privately Held**
SIC: 7381 7382 Security guard service; security systems services

(P-16385)
PROFESSONAL TECHNICAL SEC SVCS
1970 Broadway Ste 840, Oakland (94612-2299)
PHONE..........................510 645-9200
EMP: 380
SALES (corp-wide): 11.2MM **Privately Held**
SIC: 7381 Guard services
PA: Professional Technical Security Services Inc
625 Market St Fl 9
San Francisco CA 94105
415 243-2100

(P-16386)
PROTECT-US
12397 Lewis St Ste 202, Garden Grove (92840-4696)
PHONE..........................714 721-8127
Nadiya Aziz, *Principal*
EMP: 180
SALES (est): 624.3K **Privately Held**
SIC: 7381 Security guard service

(P-16387)
PROTECTED OUTCOMES CORPORATION
9663 Santa Monica Blvd, Beverly Hills (90210-4303)
PHONE..........................203 545-9565
EMP: 87
SALES: 950K **Privately Held**
SIC: 7381

(P-16388)
PROTECTION SPECIALISTS
Also Called: Chad Garrett Investigations
6841 Whitsett Ave Apt 104, North Hollywood (91605-5456)
PHONE..........................818 503-1306
Chad Garrett, *Principal*
EMP: 500
SALES (est): 3.5MM **Privately Held**
SIC: 7381 Protective services, guard

(P-16389)
PUBLIC SECURITY INC
3860 Crenshaw Blvd # 223, Los Angeles (90008-1816)
PHONE..........................323 293-9884
Darrin Jenkins, *Principal*
EMP: 50
SALES: 950K **Privately Held**
SIC: 7381 Security guard service

(P-16390)
R STANLEY SECURITY SERVICE
403 18th St, Bakersfield (93301-4930)
PHONE..........................661 634-9283
Rachelle Stanley, *President*
Charles Thompson, *Vice Pres*
EMP: 65
SQ FT: 3,000
SALES: 1MM **Privately Held**
SIC: 7381 7389 Security guard service; convention & show services

(P-16391)
RANCHO SANTA FE PROTECTIVE SVC
Also Called: Rsf Protective Services
1991 Village Park Way # 100, Encinitas (92024-1994)
PHONE..........................760 433-8887
Ron Boever, *President*
Denise Mueller, *Shareholder*
EMP: 50
SQ FT: 4,000
SALES: 1.2MM **Privately Held**
SIC: 7381 Security guard service

(P-16392)
REEL SECURITY CALIFORNIA INC
15303 Ventura Blvd # 1080, Sherman Oaks (91403-5800)
PHONE..........................818 928-4737
Mario Inez Ramirez, *CEO*
Bradley Bush, *COO*
EMP: 99
SALES (est): 787.8K **Privately Held**
SIC: 7381 Guard services

(P-16393)
REV ENTERPRISES
Also Called: O & R
417 Arden Ave Ste 103, Glendale (91203-4046)
PHONE..........................818 551-7111
J Antonio Revilla, *Principal*
EMP: 50
SALES: 1.1MM **Privately Held**
SIC: 7381 Detective & armored car services

(P-16394)
RJN INVESTIGATIONS INC
360 E 1st St Ste 696, Tustin (92780-3211)
P.O. Box 55451, Riverside (92517-0451)
PHONE..........................951 686-7638
Robert Nagle, *President*
Michael Gomez, *President*
Fred Martino, *Administration*
Miriam Lawrence, *QC Mgr*
Ty Montoya, *Client Mgr*
EMP: 80
SALES (est): 4.8MM **Privately Held**
SIC: 7381 Detective agency; private investigator

(P-16395)
RMI INTERNATIONAL INC
Also Called: Rodbat Security Services
1919 Torrance Blvd, Torrance (90501-2722)
PHONE..........................310 781-6768
Elena Rabinovich, *Branch Mgr*
EMP: 65
SALES (corp-wide): 28.1MM **Privately Held**
WEB: www.rmiintl.com
SIC: 7381 Security guard service; protective services, guard
PA: Rmi International Inc
8125 Somerset Blvd
Paramount CA 90723
562 806-9098

(P-16396)
RODGERS SECURITY SERVICE INC
Also Called: Rss
8726 S Sepulveda Blvd, Los Angeles (90045-4014)
PHONE..........................310 684-3016
Tyrone Rodgers, *CEO*
EMP: 180
SQ FT: 3,500

SALES: 2.5MM **Privately Held**
SIC: 7381 7382 Private investigator; security guard service; protective services, guard; detective services; burglar alarm maintenance & monitoring

(P-16397)
ROYAL INVESTIGATION PATROL INC
2950 Merced St Ste 108, San Leandro (94577-5636)
PHONE..........................510 352-6800
Edmund Young, *President*
EMP: 58 **EST:** 1974
SQ FT: 2,000
SALES (est): 1.2MM **Privately Held**
SIC: 7381 Protective services, guard; private investigator

(P-16398)
S C SECURITY INC
Also Called: Copper Eagle Patrol & Security
26752 Oak Ave Ste C, Santa Clarita (91351-6620)
PHONE..........................661 251-6999
Isaiah Tally, *President*
William Corbett, *President*
George Streb, *Exec VP*
Deborah Corbett, *Admin Sec*
EMP: 50
SQ FT: 2,000
SALES (est): 1.3MM **Privately Held**
SIC: 7381 Security guard service; guard services

(P-16399)
SAFETY SECURITY PATROL LLC
560 N Arrowhead Ave 3b, San Bernardino (92401-1219)
PHONE..........................909 888-7778
EMP: 63
SALES (est): 86.1K **Privately Held**
SIC: 7381

(P-16400)
SECTRAN SECURITY INCORPORATED (PA)
Also Called: Sectran Armored Truck Service
7633 Industry Ave, Pico Rivera (90660-4301)
P.O. Box 7267, Los Angeles (90022-0967)
PHONE..........................562 948-1446
Fred Kunik, *President*
Irving Barr, *Admin Sec*
Leonard Karsana, *CIO*
Kevin Tang, *Info Tech Dir*
Ramona Lopez, *Human Res Dir*
EMP: 141
SQ FT: 19,736
SALES (est): 13.9MM **Privately Held**
SIC: 7381 Armored car services

(P-16401)
SECURE NET ALLIANCE
Also Called: Security Company
601 S Glenoaks Blvd # 409, Burbank (91502-1474)
PHONE..........................818 848-4900
Levi Quintana, *CEO*
EMP: 50
SALES (est): 957.9K **Privately Held**
SIC: 7381 Security guard service; protective services, guard

(P-16402)
SECURITAS CRITICAL INFRASTRUCT
3914 Murphy Canyon Rd A120, San Diego (92123-4491)
PHONE..........................858 560-0448
John Tucke, *Branch Mgr*
EMP: 868
SALES (corp-wide): 11.2B **Privately Held**
SIC: 7381 Security guard service
HQ: Securitas Critical Infrastructure Services, Inc.
13900 Lincoln Park Dr # 37
Herndon VA 20171

(P-16403)
SECURITAS CRITICAL INFRASTRUCT
1835 W Orangewood Ave # 250, Orange
(92868-2044)
PHONE..................310 817-2177
Elijah Kimble, *Manager*
EMP: 1002
SALES (corp-wide): 11.2B **Privately Held**
SIC: 7381 Security guard service
HQ: Securitas Critical Infrastructure Services, Inc.
13900 Lincoln Park Dr # 37
Herndon VA 20171

(P-16404)
SECURITAS CRITICAL INFRASTRUCT
Rm 117 Bldg 7525, Vandenberg Afb
(93437)
PHONE..................805 685-1100
Paul Jensen, *Branch Mgr*
EMP: 885
SALES (corp-wide): 11.2B **Privately Held**
SIC: 7381 Security guard service
HQ: Securitas Critical Infrastructure Services, Inc.
13900 Lincoln Park Dr # 37
Herndon VA 20171

(P-16405)
SECURITAS CRITICAL INFRASTRUCT
360 N Pacific Coast Hwy, El Segundo
(90245-4460)
PHONE..................310 426-3300
Michael Kemppainen, *Branch Mgr*
EMP: 1750
SALES (corp-wide): 11.2B **Privately Held**
SIC: 7381 Security guard service
HQ: Securitas Critical Infrastructure Services, Inc.
13900 Lincoln Park Dr # 37
Herndon VA 20171

(P-16406)
SECURITAS SEC SVCS USA INC
5700 Ralston St, Ventura (93003-6050)
PHONE..................805 650-6285
Silvia Portillo, *Manager*
EMP: 116
SALES (corp-wide): 11.2B **Privately Held**
SIC: 7381 Security guard service
HQ: Securitas Security Services Usa, Inc.
9 Campus Dr
Parsippany NJ 07054
973 267-5300

(P-16407)
SECURITAS SEC SVCS USA INC
Also Called: Northern California Region
1650 Borel Pl Ste 227, San Mateo
(94402-3508)
PHONE..................650 358-1556
George King, *Branch Mgr*
EMP: 114
SALES (corp-wide): 11.2B **Privately Held**
WEB: www.securitasinc.com
SIC: 7381 Security guard service
HQ: Securitas Security Services Usa, Inc.
9 Campus Dr
Parsippany NJ 07054
973 267-5300

(P-16408)
SECURITAS SEC SVCS USA INC
2045 Hurley Way, Sacramento
(95825-3220)
PHONE..................916 564-2009
Joe Saputo, *President*
Greg K Cpp, *Branch Mgr*
Helen Brumfield, *Administration*
Norma Negron, *Controller*
Chris Carlson, *Manager*
EMP: 181
SALES (corp-wide): 11.2B **Privately Held**
SIC: 7381 Security guard service
HQ: Securitas Security Services Usa, Inc.
9 Campus Dr
Parsippany NJ 07054
973 267-5300

(P-16409)
SECURITAS SEC SVCS USA INC
Also Called: Northern California Region
3115 W March Ln Ste A, Stockton
(95219-2393)
PHONE..................209 943-1401
Kelly Davis, *Manager*
William Barthelemy, *COO*
Helena Andreas, *Vice Pres*
EMP: 120
SALES (corp-wide): 11.2B **Privately Held**
WEB: www.securitasinc.com
SIC: 7381 Protective services, guard
HQ: Securitas Security Services Usa, Inc.
9 Campus Dr
Parsippany NJ 07054
973 267-5300

(P-16410)
SECURITAS SEC SVCS USA INC
Also Called: Northern California Region
10 E River Park Pl E # 220, Fresno
(93720-1535)
PHONE..................559 221-2302
Cotten Kellee, *Human Res Mgr*
Roxana Quillen, *Human Res Mgr*
Daniel Reeves, *Human Res Mgr*
EMP: 116
SALES (corp-wide): 11.2B **Privately Held**
WEB: www.securitasinc.com
SIC: 7381 Security guard service
HQ: Securitas Security Services Usa, Inc.
9 Campus Dr
Parsippany NJ 07054
973 267-5300

(P-16411)
SECURITAS SEC SVCS USA INC
750 Terrado Plz Ste 107, Covina
(91723-3419)
PHONE..................571 321-0913
Michael Persaud, *Branch Mgr*
EMP: 185
SALES (corp-wide): 11.2B **Privately Held**
SIC: 7381 Security guard service
HQ: Securitas Security Services Usa, Inc.
9 Campus Dr
Parsippany NJ 07054
973 267-5300

(P-16412)
SECURITAS SEC SVCS USA INC
505 Montgomery St, San Francisco
(94111-6529)
PHONE..................510 568-6818
Brad Lauer, *Assoc VP*
EMP: 188
SALES (corp-wide): 11.2B **Privately Held**
SIC: 7381 Security guard service
HQ: Securitas Security Services Usa, Inc.
9 Campus Dr
Parsippany NJ 07054
973 267-5300

(P-16413)
SECURITAS SEC SVCS USA INC
Also Called: Automotive Services Division
430 N Vineyard Ave # 335, Ontario
(91764-5494)
PHONE..................909 974-3160
Dave Knutson, *Branch Mgr*
Mark De Ville, *Human Res Mgr*
Albert Jackson, *Supervisor*
EMP: 100
SALES (corp-wide): 11.2B **Privately Held**
WEB: www.securitasinc.com
SIC: 7381 Security guard service
HQ: Securitas Security Services Usa, Inc.
9 Campus Dr
Parsippany NJ 07054
973 267-5300

(P-16414)
SECURITAS SEC SVCS USA INC
Also Called: Southern California / Hawa Reg
2344 S 2nd St Ste C, El Centro
(92243-5606)
PHONE..................760 353-8177
Manuel Andrade, *Branch Mgr*
EMP: 116
SALES (corp-wide): 11.2B **Privately Held**
WEB: www.securitasinc.com
SIC: 7381 Security guard service

(P-16415)
SECURITAS SEC SVCS USA INC
Also Called: Northern California Region
2415 Larkspur Ln Ste B, Redding
(96002-0643)
PHONE..................530 245-0256
Keith Adams, *Branch Mgr*
EMP: 75
SALES (corp-wide): 11.2B **Privately Held**
SIC: 7381 Security guard service; protective services, guard; detective services
HQ: Securitas Security Services Usa, Inc.
9 Campus Dr
Parsippany NJ 07054
973 267-5300

(P-16416)
SECURITAS SEC SVCS USA INC
Southern California / Hawa Reg
1550 Hotel Cir N Ste 440, San Diego
(92108-2933)
PHONE..................619 641-0049
Kelly Senados, *Branch Mgr*
Lauren Winter, *Branch Mgr*
EMP: 178
SQ FT: 2,600
SALES (corp-wide): 11.2B **Privately Held**
WEB: www.securitasinc.com
SIC: 7381 Security guard service
HQ: Securitas Security Services Usa, Inc.
9 Campus Dr
Parsippany NJ 07054
973 267-5300

(P-16417)
SECURITAS SEC SVCS USA INC
Also Called: Western Operations Center
4330 Park Terrace Dr, Westlake Village
(91361-4630)
PHONE..................818 706-6800
Edie Stafford, *Manager*
Paul R Amour, *President*
Tricia Stone, *Vice Pres*
Norman Chavosky, *Branch Mgr*
Nathan Coyle, *Branch Mgr*
EMP: 350
SALES (corp-wide): 11.2B **Privately Held**
WEB: www.securitasinc.com
SIC: 7381 Security guard service
HQ: Securitas Security Services Usa, Inc.
9 Campus Dr
Parsippany NJ 07054
973 267-5300

(P-16418)
SECURITAS SEC SVCS USA INC
Also Called: Northern California Region
1304 Sthpint Blvd Ste 110, Petaluma
(94954)
PHONE..................707 586-1393
Michael Jack, *Branch Mgr*
EMP: 172
SALES (corp-wide): 11.2B **Privately Held**
WEB: www.securitasinc.com
SIC: 7381 Security guard service
HQ: Securitas Security Services Usa, Inc.
9 Campus Dr
Parsippany NJ 07054
973 267-5300

(P-16419)
SECURITAS SEC SVCS USA INC
Also Called: Southern California / Hawa Reg
5276 Hollister Ave # 204, Goleta
(93111-2073)
PHONE..................805 967-8987
Linda Garcia, *Manager*
EMP: 116
SALES (corp-wide): 11.2B **Privately Held**
WEB: www.securitasinc.com
SIC: 7381 Security guard service
HQ: Securitas Security Services Usa, Inc.
9 Campus Dr
Parsippany NJ 07054
973 267-5300

(P-16420)
SECURITAS SEC SVCS USA INC
Also Called: Northern California Region
1606 Koster St Ste A, Eureka
(95501-0179)
PHONE..................707 445-5463
Chris Peters, *Branch Mgr*
EMP: 82
SALES (corp-wide): 11.2B **Privately Held**
WEB: www.securitasinc.com
SIC: 7381 Security guard service
HQ: Securitas Security Services Usa, Inc.
9 Campus Dr
Parsippany NJ 07054
973 267-5300

(P-16421)
SECURITAS SEC SVCS USA INC
Northern California Region
2045 Hurley Way Ste 175, Sacramento
(95825-3220)
PHONE..................916 569-4500
Wallace Lavery, *Principal*
EMP: 200
SALES (corp-wide): 11.2B **Privately Held**
WEB: www.securitasinc.com
SIC: 7381 Security guard service
HQ: Securitas Security Services Usa, Inc.
9 Campus Dr
Parsippany NJ 07054
973 267-5300

(P-16422)
SECURITAS SEC SVCS USA INC
27450 Ynez Rd Ste 315, Temecula
(92591-4681)
PHONE..................951 676-3954
Pat Mac Arthur, *Manager*
EMP: 116
SALES (corp-wide): 11.2B **Privately Held**
SIC: 7381 Security guard service
HQ: Securitas Security Services Usa, Inc.
9 Campus Dr
Parsippany NJ 07054
973 267-5300

(P-16423)
SECURITAS SEC SVCS USA INC
Also Called: Northern California Region
43-00 Cook St Ste 100, Palm Desert
(92211)
PHONE..................559 221-2302
Kiet Phan, *Branch Mgr*
EMP: 200
SALES (corp-wide): 11.2B **Privately Held**
WEB: www.securitasinc.com
SIC: 7381 Security guard service
HQ: Securitas Security Services Usa, Inc.
9 Campus Dr
Parsippany NJ 07054
973 267-5300

(P-16424)
SECURITAS SEC SVCS USA INC
Also Called: Northern California Region
1611 Bunker Hill Way # 100, Salinas
(93906-6004)
PHONE..................831 444-9607
Joseph Santos, *Manager*
EMP: 116
SALES (corp-wide): 11.2B **Privately Held**
WEB: www.securitasinc.com
SIC: 7381 Security guard service
HQ: Securitas Security Services Usa, Inc.
9 Campus Dr
Parsippany NJ 07054
973 267-5300

(P-16425)
SECURITAS SEC SVCS USA INC
Also Called: Southern California / Hawa Reg
1101 W Mckinley Ave, Pomona
(91768-1639)
PHONE..................909 865-4356
Barry Gillies, *Branch Mgr*
EMP: 116
SALES (corp-wide): 11.2B **Privately Held**
WEB: www.securitasinc.com
SIC: 7381 Security guard service
HQ: Securitas Security Services Usa, Inc.
9 Campus Dr
Parsippany NJ 07054
973 267-5300

(P-16426)
SECURITAS SEC SVCS USA INC
Also Called: Southern California / Hawa Reg
6055 E Wash Blvd Ste 155, Commerce
(90040-2418)
PHONE...................................323 832-9074
Mike Kelly, *Branch Mgr*
EMP: 116
SALES (corp-wide): 11.2B **Privately Held**
WEB: www.securitasinc.com
SIC: 7381 Security guard service
HQ: Securitas Security Services Usa, Inc.
    9 Campus Dr
    Parsippany NJ 07054
    973 267-5300

(P-16427)
SECURITAS SEC SVCS USA INC
Also Called: Southern California / Hawa Reg
1055 Wilshire Blvd, Los Angeles
(90017-2431)
PHONE...................................213 580-8825
Jeff Winter, *Principal*
EMP: 116
SALES (corp-wide): 11.2B **Privately Held**
WEB: www.securitasinc.com
SIC: 7381 Security guard service
HQ: Securitas Security Services Usa, Inc.
    9 Campus Dr
    Parsippany NJ 07054
    973 267-5300

(P-16428)
SECURITAS SEC SVCS USA INC
Also Called: Southern California / Hawa Reg
1500 W Carson St Ste 109, Long Beach
(90810-1401)
PHONE...................................562 427-2737
Ivory Phillips, *Assoc VP*
Nathan Coyle, *Branch Mgr*
EMP: 116
SALES (corp-wide): 11.2B **Privately Held**
WEB: www.securitasinc.com
SIC: 7381 Security guard service
HQ: Securitas Security Services Usa, Inc.
    9 Campus Dr
    Parsippany NJ 07054
    973 267-5300

(P-16429)
SECURITAS SEC SVCS USA INC
Also Called: Shared Services
400 Crenshaw Blvd Ste 200, Torrance
(90503-1736)
PHONE...................................310 787-0747
EMP: 181
SALES (corp-wide): 9.4B **Privately Held**
SIC: 7381
HQ: Securitas Security Services Usa, Inc.
    2 Campus Dr
    Parsippany NJ 07054
    973 267-5300

(P-16430)
SECURITAS SEC SVCS USA INC
2870 Skypark Dr Ste 315, Torrance
(90505)
PHONE...................................714 385-9745
Steven Lindsey, *Owner*
EMP: 116
SALES (corp-wide): 11.2B **Privately Held**
WEB: www.securitasinc.com
SIC: 7381 Security guard service
HQ: Securitas Security Services Usa, Inc.
    9 Campus Dr
    Parsippany NJ 07054
    973 267-5300

(P-16431)
SECURITAS SEC SVCS USA INC
Also Called: Southern California / Hawa Reg
15428 Civic Dr Ste 305, Victorville
(92392-9772)
PHONE...................................760 245-1915
Bob Dorian, *Branch Mgr*
EMP: 150
SALES (corp-wide): 11.2B **Privately Held**
WEB: www.securitasinc.com
SIC: 7381 Security guard service
HQ: Securitas Security Services Usa, Inc.
    9 Campus Dr
    Parsippany NJ 07054
    973 267-5300

(P-16432)
SECURITAS SEC SVCS USA INC
Also Called: Automotive Services Division
16909 Parthenia St # 202, Northridge
(91343-4551)
PHONE...................................818 891-0458
Pat Salter, *Branch Mgr*
EMP: 150
SALES (corp-wide): 11.2B **Privately Held**
WEB: www.securitasinc.com
SIC: 7381 8742 8741 Security guard
   service; industry specialist consultants;
   management services
HQ: Securitas Security Services Usa, Inc.
    9 Campus Dr
    Parsippany NJ 07054
    973 267-5300

(P-16433)
SECURITAS SEC SVCS USA INC
4330 Park Terrace Dr, Westlake Village
(91361-4630)
PHONE...................................818 706-6800
EMP: 116
SALES (corp-wide): 10.9B **Privately Held**
SIC: 7381
HQ: Securitas Security Services Usa, Inc.
    9 Campus Dr
    Parsippany NJ 07054
    973 267-5300

(P-16434)
**SECURITECH SECURITY
SERVICES**
2733 N San Fernando Rd, Los Angeles
(90065-1318)
P.O. Box 65097 (90065-0097)
PHONE...................................213 387-5050
Serge Tachdjian, *President*
Marianna Amirkhanyan, *CFO*
Adriana Alvarez, *Admin Sec*
EMP: 110
SALES (est): 9.2MM **Privately Held**
WEB: www.securitechguards.com
SIC: 7381 Security guard service

(P-16435)
**SECURITY INDUST SPCIALISTS
INC**
477 N Oak St, Inglewood (90302-3314)
PHONE...................................323 924-9147
Todd Perkins, *Opers Mgr*
EMP: 250
SALES (corp-wide): 49MM **Privately
Held**
SIC: 7381 Detective services
PA: Security Industry Specialists, Inc.
    6071 Bristol Pkwy
    Culver City CA 90230
    310 215-5100

(P-16436)
**SECURITY INDUST SPCIALISTS
INC (PA)**
6071 Bristol Pkwy, Culver City
(90230-6601)
PHONE...................................310 215-5100
John Spesak, *President*
Tom Seltz, *President*
Gary Davenport, *COO*
Kit Knudsen, *COO*
Chuck Calderhead, *Officer*
EMP: 148
SQ FT: 9,000
SALES (est): 49MM **Privately Held**
WEB: www.securityindustryspecialists.com
SIC: 7381 5065 Security guard service;
   security control equipment & systems

(P-16437)
SECURITY ONE INC
1859 Streiff Ln, Santa Rosa (95403-2326)
PHONE...................................800 778-3017
Tom Kasnick, *President*
Valerie Kasnick, *Vice Pres*
EMP: 65 EST: 1998
SQ FT: 1,000
SALES (est): 1MM **Privately Held**
SIC: 7381 Guard services; security guard
   service; private investigator

(P-16438)
SEGURA ENTERPRISES INC
Also Called: Segura Security Services
1011 W Mccoy Ln, Santa Maria
(93455-1107)
PHONE...................................805 349-0550
Raul Segura, *CEO*
EMP: 100
SQ FT: 1,500
SALES (est): 7.3MM **Privately Held**
SIC: 7381 7382 Security guard service;
   security systems services

(P-16439)
SERVEXO
Also Called: Servexo Protective Service
1515 W 190th St Ste 170, Gardena
(90248-4927)
P.O. Box 9017, San Pedro (90734-9017)
PHONE...................................323 527-9994
John Palmer, *CEO*
EMP: 50
SALES: 3MM **Privately Held**
SIC: 7381 Protective services, guard; se-
   curity guard service

(P-16440)
SHARP GUARD SERVICES INC
3450 Wilshire Blvd # 1000, Los Angeles
(90010-2208)
PHONE...................................213 739-1900
Ilham Chaouir, *President*
Mike Thabet, *Treasurer*
EMP: 521 EST: 1999
SALES (est): 4MM **Privately Held**
WEB: www.sharpgs.com
SIC: 7381 Security guard service

(P-16441)
SHERMAN SECURITY
7218 Hermosa Ave, Rancho Cucamonga
(91701-5929)
PHONE...................................909 941-4167
Daryl Enoch, *Partner*
Clarence Tanner, *Partner*
EMP: 102
SALES (est): 156.3K **Privately Held**
SIC: 7381 7389 Guard services;

(P-16442)
SHIELD SECURITY INC (DH)
1551 N Tustin Ave Ste 650, Santa Ana
(92705-8664)
PHONE...................................714 210-1501
Ed Klosterman Jr, *President*
Kenneth Klosterman, *Vice Pres*
EMP: 300
SQ FT: 5,500
SALES (est): 22.2MM
SALES (corp-wide): 686.6MM **Privately
Held**
SIC: 7381 Security guard service
HQ: Universal Protection Service, Lp
    1551 N Tustin Ave Ste 650
    Santa Ana CA 92705
    714 619-9700

(P-16443)
SHIELD SECURITY INC
21110 Vanowen St, Canoga Park
(91303-2821)
PHONE...................................818 239-5800
Kenneth Klosterman, *Branch Mgr*
EMP: 200
SALES (corp-wide): 686.6MM **Privately
Held**
SIC: 7381 Security guard service
HQ: Shield Security, Inc.
    1551 N Tustin Ave Ste 650
    Santa Ana CA 92705
    714 210-1501

(P-16444)
SHIELD SECURITY INC
150 E Wardlow Rd, Long Beach (90807)
PHONE...................................562 283-1100
Leo Green, *Manager*
EMP: 450
SALES (corp-wide): 686.6MM **Privately
Held**
SIC: 7381 Security guard service
HQ: Shield Security, Inc.
    1551 N Tustin Ave Ste 650
    Santa Ana CA 92705
    714 210-1501

(P-16445)
SHIELD SECURITY INC
265 N Euclid Ave, Upland (91786-6038)
PHONE...................................909 920-1173
Paul Srankowski, *Manager*
EMP: 300
SALES (corp-wide): 686.6MM **Privately
Held**
SIC: 7381 Security guard service
HQ: Shield Security, Inc.
    1551 N Tustin Ave Ste 650
    Santa Ana CA 92705
    714 210-1501

(P-16446)
SIGNAL 88 LLC
821 S Rockefeller Ave, Ontario
(91761-8119)
PHONE...................................714 713-5306
Mark Anderson, *Branch Mgr*
EMP: 942
SALES (corp-wide): 34.2MM **Privately
Held**
SIC: 7381 Guard services
PA: Signal 88, Llc
    3880 S 149th St Ste 102
    Omaha NE 68144
    877 498-8494

(P-16447)
**SILICON VLY SEC & PATROL INC
(PA)**
1131 Luchessi Dr Ste 2, San Jose
(95118-3770)
PHONE...................................408 267-1539
Ray Higdon, *CEO*
Lisa Higdon, *President*
Gary Mills, *Vice Pres*
Julianne Hinson, *Finance Mgr*
EMP: 150
SQ FT: 4,000
SALES (est): 9.7MM **Privately Held**
WEB: www.svsp.com
SIC: 7381 Security guard service

(P-16448)
SILVER SHIELD SECURITY
2107 N 1st St Ste 100, San Jose
(95131-2026)
PHONE...................................408 435-1111
Sabrina Wagner, *President*
Jay Wagner, *Vice Pres*
EMP: 105
SQ FT: 3,500
SALES (est): 1.3MM
SALES (corp-wide): 686.6MM **Privately
Held**
WEB: www.silvershieldsecurity.com
SIC: 7381 Security guard service
HQ: Universal Protection Service, Lp
    1551 N Tustin Ave Ste 650
    Santa Ana CA 92705
    714 619-9700

(P-16449)
**SINTEX SECURITY SERVICES
INC**
501 Bangs Ave Ste D, Modesto
(95356-8978)
PHONE...................................209 543-9044
Jerry Sterner, *President*
EMP: 75
SQ FT: 2,500
SALES (est): 2.6MM **Privately Held**
WEB: www.sintexsecurity.com
SIC: 7381 Security guard service

(P-16450)
SOS SECURITY INCORPORATED
2601 Ocean Park Blvd # 208, Santa Monica
(90405-5229)
PHONE...................................310 392-9600
Doug Hamilton, *Manager*
EMP: 140
SALES (corp-wide): 103.4MM **Privately
Held**
SIC: 7381 Security guard service; detec-
   tive agency
PA: Sos Security Incorporated
    1915 Us Highway 46 Ste 1
    Parsippany NJ 07054
    973 402-6600

(P-16451)
SOS SECURITY INCORPORATED
26250 Industrial Blvd # 48, Hayward
(94545-2922)
PHONE................510 782-4900
Michael Boone, *Vice Pres*
EMP: 140
SALES (corp-wide): 103.4MM **Privately Held**
SIC: 7381 Security guard service; detective agency
PA: Sos Security Incorporated
1915 Us Highway 46 Ste 1
Parsippany NJ 07054
973 402-6600

(P-16452)
SOS SECURITY LLC
331 N Beverly Dr Ste 3, Beverly Hills
(90210-4729)
PHONE................310 859-8248
EMP: 70
SALES (corp-wide): 107MM **Privately Held**
SIC: 7381 Security guard service
PA: Sos Security Llc
1915 Us Highway 46 Ste 2
Parsippany NJ 07054
973 402-6600

(P-16453)
SPECTRUM SECURITY SERVICES INC
1633 E 4th St Ste 238, Santa Ana
(92701-5144)
PHONE................714 542-9600
Sam B Ersan, *President*
EMP: 97
SALES (corp-wide): 7.5MM **Privately Held**
SIC: 7381 Security guard service
PA: Spectrum Security Services, Inc.
13967 Campo Rd Ste 101
Jamul CA 91935
619 669-6660

(P-16454)
STAFF PRO INC
675 Convention Way, San Diego
(92101-7805)
PHONE................619 544-1774
Mike Hernandez, *Manager*
EMP: 198
SALES (est): 2.2MM
SALES (corp-wide): 98.4MM **Privately Held**
WEB: www.staffpro.com
SIC: 7381 Security guard service
PA: Staff Pro Inc.
1400 N Harbor Blvd # 700
Fullerton CA 92835
714 230-7200

(P-16455)
STAR PROTECTION AGENCY LLC
Also Called: Star Protection Agency CA
8201 Edgewater Dr Ste 102, Oakland
(94621-2021)
PHONE................510 635-1732
Edward Lynd, *President*
EMP: 159
SALES (corp-wide): 16.9MM **Privately Held**
SIC: 7381 7389 Security guard service; personal investigation service
PA: Star Protection Agency Llc
846 S Hotel St Ste 200
Honolulu HI 96813
808 792-2086

(P-16456)
STRATEGIC SECURITY SERVICES
Also Called: Strategic Secuirty Services
48521 Warm Springs Blvd # 302, Fremont
(94539-7792)
PHONE................510 623-2355
Larry Reid, *Manager*
EMP: 190
SALES (corp-wide): 187.9MM **Privately Held**
WEB: www.strategicsecurity.net
SIC: 7381 Security guard service

HQ: Strategic Security Services, Inc
3152 University Ave
San Diego CA
619 283-3976

(P-16457)
SUPREME SECURITY SERVICES INC
3517 Cameo Dr Unit 84, Oceanside
(92056-6372)
PHONE................760 415-7399
Lorenzo Middlebrook, *President*
Sharon Middlebrook, *Vice Pres*
EMP: 60
SALES (est): 121.1K **Privately Held**
WEB: www.supremesecurityservices.net
SIC: 7381 7389 Security guard service;

(P-16458)
TRANS WEST INVESTIGATIONS INC
3255 Wilshire Blvd, Los Angeles
(90010-1404)
PHONE................213 381-1500
Edward W Beyer, *President*
James T Walsh, *CEO*
EMP: 57
SQ FT: 2,900
SALES (est): 1.2MM **Privately Held**
SIC: 7381 8111 Private investigator; legal services

(P-16459)
TRANS-WEST SECURITY SVCS INC
8503 Crippen St, Bakersfield (93311-8993)
PHONE................661 381-2900
Brooke L Antonioni, *President*
Duane Williams, *Exec VP*
Katy Williams, *Vice Pres*
Gilbert Cota, *Opers Mgr*
EMP: 300
SQ FT: 8,500
SALES (est): 11.2MM **Privately Held**
WEB: www.twsecurity.com
SIC: 7381 Security guard service

(P-16460)
TRANSCENDENT SECURITY SERVICES
3553 Atl Ave Ste 1197, Long Beach
(90807)
PHONE................562 850-3313
John Harris, *President*
EMP: 50 **EST:** 2018
SALES (est): 227.8K **Privately Held**
SIC: 7381 Security guard service

(P-16461)
TRIUMPH PROTECTION GROUP INC
853 Cotting Ct Ste D, Vacaville
(95688-8701)
P.O. Box 852 (95696-0852)
PHONE................800 224-0286
Jeffrey Fields, *CEO*
Lisa Godden, *Accountant*
Igor Boyko, *Opers Mgr*
Steve Johnson, *Marketing Mgr*
EMP: 150 **EST:** 2013
SQ FT: 2,200
SALES (est): 5.9MM **Privately Held**
SIC: 7381 Security guard service

(P-16462)
TURNER SECURITY SYSTEMS INC
Also Called: Don Turner and Associates
120 W Shields Ave, Fresno (93705-4101)
PHONE................559 486-3466
Donald A Turner, *President*
Michael Garaffa, *Office Mgr*
Dennis Baker, *Accounts Mgr*
Mike Moua, *Accounts Mgr*
EMP: 190
SQ FT: 3,700
SALES (est): 7.2MM **Privately Held**
WEB: www.turnersec.com
SIC: 7381 Security guard service

(P-16463)
TYAN INC
Also Called: Security Specialists
1500 Glenoaks Blvd, San Fernando
(91340-1780)
P.O. Box 3472, Van Nuys (91407-3472)
PHONE................818 785-5831
Nick Tsotsikyan, *President*
EMP: 55
SQ FT: 2,000
SALES (est): 2MM **Privately Held**
WEB: www.capatrol.com
SIC: 7381 Security guard service

(P-16464)
U S PRIVATE PROTECTION SEC INC
5555 Inglewood Blvd # 205, Culver City
(90230-6250)
PHONE................310 301-0010
Dave Solomon, *President*
EMP: 180
SALES (est): 3.8MM **Privately Held**
SIC: 7381 Protective services, guard

(P-16465)
UNITED FACILITY SOLUTIONS INC
Also Called: Command Guard
16835 Algonquin St # 429, Huntington Beach (92649-3810)
PHONE................310 743-3000
Martin Benom, *CEO*
Mark Myers, *President*
EMP: 400
SALES (est): 2.1MM **Privately Held**
SIC: 7381 7349 Security guard service; janitorial service, contract basis

(P-16466)
UNITY SEC & PROTECTIVE SVC
619 E Washington Blvd, Pasadena
(91104-2260)
PHONE................323 695-7234
Jayson Lee, *President*
EMP: 78
SQ FT: 3,000
SALES (est): 1.4MM **Privately Held**
WEB: www.unitedprotection.com
SIC: 7381 Security guard service

(P-16467)
UNIVERSAL PROTECTION SVC LP
Also Called: Prestige Protection
2415 San Ramon Vly Blvd, San Ramon
(94583-5381)
PHONE................805 496-4401
EMP: 61
SALES (corp-wide): 741.7MM **Privately Held**
SIC: 7381
HQ: Universal Protection Service, Lp
1551 N Tustin Ave Ste 650
Santa Ana CA 92705
714 619-9700

(P-16468)
UNIVERSAL PROTECTION SVC LP
340 Golden Shore Ste 100, Long Beach
(90802-4237)
PHONE................562 981-5700
Steve Salyer, *Owner*
Brian Neimeyer, *Vice Pres*
Jessica Smith, *Division Mgr*
EMP: 58
SALES (corp-wide): 686.6MM **Privately Held**
SIC: 7381 Security guard service
HQ: Universal Protection Service, Lp
1551 N Tustin Ave Ste 650
Santa Ana CA 92705
714 619-9700

(P-16469)
UNIVERSAL PROTECTION SVC LP
21300 Victory Blvd # 230, Woodland Hills
(91367-2525)
PHONE................818 227-1240
Jerry McConnell, *Branch Mgr*
EMP: 58

SALES (corp-wide): 686.6MM **Privately Held**
SIC: 7381 Security guard service
HQ: Universal Protection Service, Lp
1551 N Tustin Ave Ste 650
Santa Ana CA 92705
714 619-9700

(P-16470)
UNIVERSAL PROTECTION SVC LP (HQ)
Also Called: Allied Universal Security Svcs
1551 N Tustin Ave Ste 650, Santa Ana
(92705-8664)
PHONE................714 619-9700
Brian Cescolini, *Partner*
Steve Jones, *Partner*
Louis Boulgarides, *President*
Paul Sova, *President*
Ron Allen, *Vice Pres*
EMP: 148
SALES (est): 707.4MM
SALES (corp-wide): 686.6MM **Privately Held**
SIC: 7381 Security guard service
PA: Universal Protection Gp, Llc
1551 N Tustin Ave Ste 650
Santa Ana CA 92705
714 619-9700

(P-16471)
UNIVERSAL PROTECTION SVC LP
1208 Vicente St, San Francisco
(94116-3044)
PHONE................415 759-5056
David Nagle, *CEO*
EMP: 250
SALES (corp-wide): 686.6MM **Privately Held**
SIC: 7381 Security guard service
HQ: Universal Protection Service, Lp
1551 N Tustin Ave Ste 650
Santa Ana CA 92705
714 619-9700

(P-16472)
UNIVERSAL SERVICES AMERICA LP (DH)
Also Called: Allied Universal
1551 N Tustin Ave Fl 6, Santa Ana
(92705-8634)
P.O. Box 101034, Pasadena (91189-0003)
PHONE................714 619-9700
Steven Jones, *CEO*
Toni Ippolito, *CEO*
Chris Johnson, *Officer*
Alexis Williams, *Officer*
Bill Krob, *Vice Pres*
EMP: 100
SALES: 2B
SALES (corp-wide): 5.2B **Privately Held**
SIC: 7381 7349 Security guard service; janitorial service, contract basis
HQ: Allied Universal Holdco Llc
1551 N Tustin Ave Ste 650
Santa Ana CA 92705
866 877-1965

(P-16473)
UNLIMITED SEC SPECIALISTS INC
13636 Ventura Blvd # 206, Sherman Oaks
(91423-3700)
PHONE................877 310-4877
Jose Cardona, *Principal*
Alberto Alvarez, *Accounts Mgr*
EMP: 50
SALES: 2.5MM **Privately Held**
SIC: 7381 Security guard service

(P-16474)
US INVESTIGATIONS SERVICES LLC (HQ)
Also Called: Usis
3349 Michelson Dr Ste 150, Irvine
(92612-8881)
P.O. Box 618, Boyers PA (16018-0618)
PHONE................724 458-1750
Donald I Buzinkai, *Vice Pres*
William Mixon, *President*
Jeremy Wensinger, *President*
Sterling Phillips, *CEO*
Francis Meyer, *Senior VP*
EMP: 1300

SALES (est): 205.2MM **Privately Held**
SIC: 7381 Private investigator

(P-16475)
VERNON SECURITY INC
15317 Parmnt Blvd Ste 201, Paramount
(90723)
PHONE..................................562 790-8993
Jay Ellsworth, *President*
Dan Vincent, *Vice Pres*
EMP: 100
SALES (est): 5.6MM **Privately Held**
SIC: 7381 Guard services

(P-16476)
W S B & ASSOCIATES INC
150 Executive Park Blvd # 4700, San Fran-
cisco (94134-3303)
PHONE..................................510 444-6266
EMP: 100 **Privately Held**
SIC: 7381
PA: W S B & Associates Inc
1390 Market St Ste 314
San Francisco CA 94134

(P-16477)
W S B & ASSOCIATES INC
150 Executive Park Blvd # 4700, San Fran-
cisco (94134-3341)
PHONE..................................415 864-3510
Bobby Sisk, *CEO*
EMP: 177
SALES (est): 4.3MM **Privately Held**
SIC: 7381 Security guard service

(P-16478)
WE TEAM SECURITY FIRM INC
12655 W Jefferson Blvd, Los Angeles
(90066-7008)
PHONE..................................800 745-9051
Charli Beth Brown, *President*
EMP: 65
SALES (est): 139.2K **Privately Held**
SIC: 7381 Guard services

(P-16479)
WINDWALKER SECURITY PATROL INC
23987 Nw Frontage Rd, Acampo (95220)
P.O. Box 488 (95220-0488)
PHONE..................................209 333-3953
Richard V Edwards, *CEO*
Bb Edwards, *Shareholder*
EMP: 75
SALES (est): 1.4MM **Privately Held**
SIC: 7381 Security guard service

(P-16480)
WORLD PRIVATE SECURITY INC
16921 Parthenia St # 201, Northridge
(91343-4568)
PHONE..................................818 894-1800
Fred Youssif, *President*
Jeannette Youssif, *Co-Owner*
EMP: 200
SALES: 4MM **Privately Held**
SIC: 7381 Security guard service

(P-16481)
WORLDWIDE SECURITY ASSOCIATES (HQ)
10311 S La Cienega Blvd, Los Angeles
(90045-6109)
PHONE..................................310 743-3000
Andres Martinez, *President*
EMP: 300
SQ FT: 5,000
SALES (est): 23.1MM
SALES (corp-wide): 31.7MM **Privately Held**
WEB: www.wsainc.net
SIC: 7381 Security guard service
PA: Wsa Group Inc
19208 S Vermont Ave 200
Gardena CA 90248
310 743-3000

(P-16482)
WSA GROUP INC (PA)
19208 S Vermont Ave 200, Gardena
(90248-4414)
PHONE..................................310 743-3000
Andres Martinez, *President*
James E Bush, *Vice Pres*

EMP: 50
SQ FT: 10,000
SALES (est): 31.7MM **Privately Held**
WEB: www.wsagroup.com
SIC: 7381 7349 Security guard service;
janitorial service, contract basis

(P-16483)
XTREME SECURITY SERVICES INC
337 N Vineyard Ave # 210, Ontario
(91764-5669)
PHONE..................................909 390-6818
Lawrence Polzin, *President*
EMP: 50
SALES: 1.2MM **Privately Held**
SIC: 7381 Security guard service

(P-16484)
YOSH ENTERPRISES INC
Also Called: Orion Security
675 E Gish Rd, San Jose (95112-2708)
PHONE..................................408 287-4411
Yosh Gahramani, *President*
EMP: 400
SQ FT: 6,800
SALES (est): 8.8MM **Privately Held**
WEB: www.orionsecurity.com
SIC: 7381 6531 8742 0782 Security
guard service; private investigator; real
estate managers; industrial & labor con-
sulting services; lawn & garden services

7382 Security Systems Svcs

(P-16485)
3VR SECURITY INC
814 Mission St Fl 4, San Francisco
(94103-3034)
PHONE..................................415 513-4577
Robert A Shipp, *CEO*
Charles F Ryan III, *CFO*
James Hudson, *Vice Pres*
Valerie Wehler, *Marketing Staff*
Tony Montes, *Sales Staff*
EMP: 90
SALES (est): 16.6MM **Publicly Held**
WEB: www.3vrsecurity.com
SIC: 7382 Protective devices, security
PA: Identiv, Inc.
2201 Walnut Ave Ste 100
Fremont CA 94538

(P-16486)
ACALVIO TECHNOLOGIES INC
2520 Mission College Blvd # 110, Santa
Clara (95054-1238)
PHONE..................................408 931-6160
Nat Natraj, *President*
Rick Moy, *Chief Mktg Ofcr*
Chad Scrupps, *Vice Pres*
EMP: 52
SQ FT: 4,166
SALES (est): 59.9K **Privately Held**
SIC: 7382 Security systems services

(P-16487)
ACS SECURITY INDUSTRIES INC
Also Called: A C S Security
1964 Westwood Blvd # 235, Los Angeles
(90025-4651)
PHONE..................................310 475-9016
Al Radi, *President*
EMP: 60
SALES (est): 5.2MM **Privately Held**
SIC: 7382 Security systems services

(P-16488)
ADMIRAL SECURITY SERVICES INC
2151 Salvio St Ste 260, Concord
(94520-2406)
PHONE..................................888 471-1128
Mohamed S Ahmed, *CEO*
Youssef Abdallah, *President*
EMP: 400
SQ FT: 1,500
SALES (est): 41.7MM **Privately Held**
SIC: 7382 7381 Security systems serv-
ices; protective services, guard; security
guard service; guard services

(P-16489)
ADT SECURITY CORPORATION
2150 John Glenn Dr # 100, Concord
(94520-5671)
PHONE..................................925 251-9088
Pete Sitch, *Branch Mgr*
EMP: 50
SALES (corp-wide): 4.5B **Publicly Held**
WEB: www.protectionone.com
SIC: 7382 5063 Burglar alarm mainte-
nance & monitoring; alarm systems
HQ: The Adt Security Corporation
1501 W Yamato Rd
Boca Raton FL 33431
561 988-3600

(P-16490)
AERO PORT SERVICES INC (PA)
216 W Florence Ave, Inglewood
(90301-1213)
PHONE..................................310 623-8230
Chris Paik, *President*
Jake Yoon, *CFO*
Julie Hong, *Treasurer*
Walter Vergara, *Chief Mktg Ofcr*
Robert Yim, *Vice Pres*
▲ EMP: 53
SALES (est): 34.8MM **Privately Held**
WEB: www.aeroportservices.com
SIC: 7382 Security systems services

(P-16491)
AM-TEC TOTAL SECURITY INC (PA)
Also Called: Am-TEC Security
4075 Schaefer Ave, Chino (91710-5446)
PHONE..................................909 573-4678
Jeff Torok, *President*
EMP: 55
SQ FT: 7,000
SALES: 280K **Privately Held**
SIC: 7382 Security systems services

(P-16492)
AMERICAN SERVICE INDUSTRIES
2930 W Imperial Hwy # 332, Inglewood
(90303-3143)
PHONE..................................323 779-4000
Tony Caminiti, *President*
Stephen E Kulp, *CEO*
John Congleton, *Senior VP*
EMP: 100
SQ FT: 1,200
SALES (est): 3.9MM **Privately Held**
SIC: 7382 7349 Protective devices, secu-
rity; janitorial service, contract basis

(P-16493)
ANDURIL INDUSTRIES INC (PA)
2722 Michelson Dr Ste 150, Irvine
(92612-8904)
PHONE..................................949 891-1607
Brian Schimpf, *CEO*
Matthew Grimm, *COO*
Phil Hall, *VP Finance*
EMP: 82 EST: 2017
SQ FT: 155,000
SALES (est): 18.2MM **Privately Held**
SIC: 7382 7371 Security systems serv-
ices; computer software development

(P-16494)
ANIXTER INC
7140 Opportunity Rd, San Diego
(92111-2202)
PHONE..................................800 854-2088
Marshall Merrifield, *Branch Mgr*
Larry Clark,
Chuck Connolly, *Manager*
EMP: 76
SALES (corp-wide): 8.4B **Publicly Held**
WEB: www.clarksecurity.com
SIC: 7382 Security systems services
HQ: Anixter Inc.
2301 Patriot Blvd
Glenview IL 60026
800 323-8167

(P-16495)
ASSERTIVE SECURITY SERVICES &
20501 Ventura Blvd # 150, Woodland Hills
(91364-2330)
PHONE..................................818 888-2405

Maryam Ayam, *President*
EMP: 550
SALES (est): 28.1MM **Privately Held**
WEB: www.assertivesecurity.com
SIC: 7382 7381 Security systems serv-
ices; security guard service

(P-16496)
ATLAS SECURITY INC
11862 Balboa Blvd Ste 395, Granada Hills
(91344-2753)
PHONE..................................323 876-1401
Jack Boyd, *President*
EMP: 50
SALES (est): 2.2MM **Privately Held**
SIC: 7382 Security systems services

(P-16497)
AUTHORIZED TAXI CAB
Also Called: A T S
6150 W 96th St, Los Angeles (90045-5218)
PHONE..................................323 776-5324
Behzad Bitaraf, *President*
EMP: 60
SALES: 8.9MM **Privately Held**
SIC: 7382 Security systems services

(P-16498)
BAYER PROTECTIVE SERVICES INC
3436 Amrcn Rver Dr Ste 10, Sacramento
(95864)
PHONE..................................916 486-5800
Bryon A Bayer, *President*
Bryon Bayer, *President*
EMP: 165
SQ FT: 1,600
SALES (est): 10.8MM
SALES (corp-wide): 13.5MM **Privately Held**
WEB: www.bayerprotectiveservices.com
SIC: 7382 Security systems services
PA: First Security Services
850 San Jose Ave Ste 128
Clovis CA 93612
559 297-1444

(P-16499)
BLUEGILL TECHNOLOGIES LLC
Also Called: Bluegill Solar
11884 Welby Pl Ste 101, Moreno Valley
(92557-6444)
PHONE..................................877 765-2770
Aman Chowdhry, *President*
EMP: 60
SQ FT: 1,100
SALES: 12MM **Privately Held**
SIC: 7382 7373 Security systems serv-
ices; systems integration services

(P-16500)
BRIGHTCLOUD INC
4370 La Jolla Village Dr # 820, San Diego
(92122-1277)
PHONE..................................858 652-4803
Quinn Curtis, *President*
Hal Lonas, *President*
EMP: 125
SALES (est): 3.6MM
SALES (corp-wide): 296.4MM **Publicly Held**
SIC: 7382 Security systems services
HQ: Webroot Inc.
385 Interlocken Cres # 800
Broomfield CO 80021
303 442-3813

(P-16501)
CALLAN MANAGEMENT CORPORATION
Also Called: Western Area Security Services
2919 W Burbank Blvd Ste C, Burbank
(91505-2351)
PHONE..................................818 846-2215
Michael Butler, *President*
EMP: 300
SQ FT: 2,000
SALES (est): 14.5MM **Privately Held**
WEB: www.westernarea.com
SIC: 7382 7381 Security systems serv-
ices; detective & armored car services

(P-16502)
CHRONICLE LLC (HQ)
250 Mayfield Ave, Mountain View (94043)
PHONE..................................650 214-5199

Ben Heben, *CFO*
Jan Kang,
EMP: 65
SALES (est): 1MM
SALES (corp-wide): 136.8B **Publicly Held**
SIC: 7382 Security systems services
PA: Alphabet Inc.
1600 Amphitheatre Pkwy
Mountain View CA 94043
650 253-0000

(P-16503)
COAST2COAST PUBLIC SAFETY LLC
575 Birch Ct Ste J, Colton (92324-3248)
PHONE..................................833 262-7877
John Cox,
Sean Riley,
Jason Villa,
EMP: 50
SALES (est): 670.5K **Privately Held**
SIC: 7382 7363 Security systems services; medical help service

(P-16504)
CONTEMPORARY SERVICES CORP
369 Van Ness Way Ste 702, Torrance
(90501-6245)
PHONE..................................310 320-8418
Roy Sukimoto, *Branch Mgr*
Kelly Allison, *Manager*
EMP: 195
SALES (corp-wide): 302.9MM **Privately Held**
SIC: 7382 7381 7299 Security systems services; guard services; party planning service
PA: Contemporary Services Corporation
17101 Superior St
Northridge CA 91325
818 885-5150

(P-16505)
CONVERGINT TECHNOLOGIES LLC
5860 W Las Positas Blvd # 7, Pleasanton
(94588-8557)
PHONE..................................510 300-2800
Doug Lyle, *Branch Mgr*
EMP: 50
SALES (corp-wide): 13.4MM **Privately Held**
SIC: 7382 Security systems services
HQ: Convergint Technologies Llc
1 Commerce Dr
Schaumburg IL 60173
847 620-5000

(P-16506)
CORPORATE ALNCE STRATEGIES INC
3410 La Sierra Ave F244, Riverside
(92503-5270)
PHONE..................................877 777-7487
Leah Pinto, *CEO*
Zeriah McKnight, *Advisor*
EMP: 115
SALES (est): 25K **Privately Held**
SIC: 7382 Security systems services

(P-16507)
DELTA SCIENTIFIC CORPORATION (PA)
40355 Delta Ln, Palmdale (93551-3616)
PHONE..................................661 575-1100
Harry D Dickinson, *CEO*
Richard I Winger, *CFO*
Keith Bobrosky, *Senior VP*
David Dickinson, *Vice Pres*
Greg Hamm, *Vice Pres*
◆ **EMP:** 200 **EST:** 1974
SQ FT: 200,000
SALES (est): 29.3MM **Privately Held**
WEB: www.deltascientific.com
SIC: 7382 Security systems services

(P-16508)
DIAL SECURITY (PA)
Also Called: Dial Communications
760 W Ventura Blvd, Camarillo
(93010-8382)
P.O. Box 34781, Bethesda MD (20827-0781)
PHONE..................................805 389-6700
William H Dundas, *President*
Erica Ayala, *Admin Asst*
EMP: 250
SQ FT: 12,000
SALES (est): 20.2MM **Privately Held**
WEB: www.dialcomm.com
SIC: 7382 7381 Protective devices, security; detective & armored car services

(P-16509)
ECAMSECURE
3400 E Airport Way, Long Beach
(90806-2412)
PHONE..................................888 246-0556
Christopher Coffey, *President*
William R Babcock, *CFO*
EMP: 67
SQ FT: 3,500
SALES (est): 6.3MM **Privately Held**
SIC: 7382 5065 Security systems services; electronic parts & equipment

(P-16510)
EMAGINED SECURITY INC
2816 San Simeon Way, San Carlos
(94070-3611)
PHONE..................................415 944-2977
David Sockol, *President*
Julianna Sockol, *Info Tech Mgr*
Patrick Cleary, *Sr Consultant*
Cory Dixon, *Consultant*
Ishmael Malik, *Consultant*
EMP: 50
SALES (est): 6.3MM **Privately Held**
WEB: www.emagined.com
SIC: 7382 Security systems services

(P-16511)
EMERGENCY TECHNOLOGIES INC
Also Called: American Two-Way
7345 Varna Ave, North Hollywood
(91605-4009)
PHONE..................................818 765-4421
Christopher Baskin, *CEO*
Ty Davis, *Vice Pres*
EMP: 72
SQ FT: 13,000
SALES (est): 8MM **Privately Held**
WEB: www.americantwoway.com
SIC: 7382 Security systems services

(P-16512)
EON INNOVATIVE TECHNOLOGY INC
Also Called: Korea Tchnlgy Cmmnications USA
10645 W Vanowen St, Burbank
(91505-1136)
PHONE..................................213 381-0061
Jason JC Ra, *President*
H S Kwon, *CEO*
Joe Troiano, *Vice Pres*
Daniel Choi, *Sales Executive*
Silvana Kim, *Sales Mgr*
▲ **EMP:** 120 **EST:** 2000
SALES (est): 6.6MM **Privately Held**
WEB: www.ktncusa.com
SIC: 7382 Security systems services
PA: Kt&C Co., Ltd.
7 Yangcheon-Ro 11-Gil, Gangseo-Gu
Seoul 07516

(P-16513)
FED AIR SECURITY CORPORATION
210 S De Lacey Ave, Pasadena
(91105-2048)
PHONE..................................626 535-2200
Enrique Hernandez Jr, *CEO*
Chris R Sherman, *CFO*
EMP: 100
SQ FT: 16,000
SALES (est): 3.7MM **Privately Held**
SIC: 7382 Security systems services

(P-16514)
FIRST ALARM (PA)
1111 Estates Dr, Aptos (95003-3572)
PHONE..................................831 476-1111
Jarl E Saal, *Chairman*
David Hood, *President*
Chris De, *COO*
Thomas Alexander, *Officer*
Douglas Castro, *Officer*
EMP: 120
SQ FT: 14,000
SALES (est): 45.8MM **Privately Held**
WEB: www.firstalarm.com
SIC: 7382 Burglar alarm maintenance & monitoring

(P-16515)
FIRST ALARM SEC & PATROL INC
5250 Claremont Ave, Stockton
(95207-5700)
PHONE..................................209 473-1110
EMP: 587
SALES (corp-wide): 52.6MM **Privately Held**
SIC: 7382 5063 Security systems services; transformers & transmission equipment
PA: First Alarm Security & Patrol, Inc.
1731 Tech Dr Ste 800
San Jose CA 95110
408 866-1111

(P-16516)
FIRST ALARM SEC & PATROL INC
1801 Oakland Blvd Ste 315, Walnut Creek
(94596-7017)
PHONE..................................925 295-1260
EMP: 294
SALES (corp-wide): 52.6MM **Privately Held**
SIC: 7382 Security systems services
PA: First Alarm Security & Patrol, Inc.
1731 Tech Dr Ste 800
San Jose CA 95110
408 866-1111

(P-16517)
FIRST ALARM SEC & PATROL INC
1240 Briggs Ave, Santa Rosa
(95401-4760)
PHONE..................................707 584-1110
EMP: 440
SALES (corp-wide): 52.6MM **Privately Held**
SIC: 7382 Security systems services
PA: First Alarm Security & Patrol, Inc.
1731 Tech Dr Ste 800
San Jose CA 95110
408 866-1111

(P-16518)
FIRST ALARM SEC & PATROL INC (PA)
Also Called: First Security Services
1731 Tech Dr Ste 800, San Jose (95110)
PHONE..................................408 866-1111
Cal Horton, *President*
Jarl E Saal, *Chairman*
Jj Amdjadi, *Branch Mgr*
Mark Pichel, *Branch Mgr*
Mahesh Chand, *Security Mgr*
EMP: 250
SALES (est): 52.6MM **Privately Held**
SIC: 7382 Security systems services

(P-16519)
FIRST FIRE SYSTEMS INC (PA)
5947 Burchard Ave, Los Angeles
(90034-1701)
PHONE..................................310 559-0900
Juda Roshanzamir, *President*
Robbie Kashani, *Executive*
Richard Velasco, *Technician*
Abraham Velasco, *Project Mgr*
Cecil Christian, *Technology*
EMP: 100 **EST:** 1980
SQ FT: 9,400
SALES (est): 14.9MM **Privately Held**
WEB: www.firstfiresystems.com
SIC: 7382 Security systems services

(P-16520)
G4S JUSTICE SERVICES LLC
Also Called: G4s Government Services
1290 N Hancock St Ste 103, Anaheim
(92807-1925)
PHONE..................................800 589-6003
Robert Contestabile, *CEO*
EMP: 220
SALES (est): 11.5MM
SALES (corp-wide): 71.6MM **Privately Held**
SIC: 7382 3669 Fire alarm maintenance & monitoring; emergency alarms
PA: Sentinel Offender Services Llc
1290 N Hancock St Ste 103
Anaheim CA 92807
949 453-1550

(P-16521)
GO GET EM INC
45248 Trevor Ave, Lancaster (93534-1614)
PHONE..................................702 985-5637
Michael Sprague, *President*
EMP: 60 **Privately Held**
SIC: 7382 Security systems services

(P-16522)
GREATER ALARM COMPANY INC (DH)
3750 Schaufele Ave # 200, Long Beach
(90808-1779)
PHONE..................................949 474-0555
George De Marco, *President*
James De Marco, *Vice Pres*
Ken McDowell, *Regl Sales Mgr*
EMP: 71
SQ FT: 11,500
SALES (est): 4MM
SALES (corp-wide): 103.4MM **Privately Held**
SIC: 7382 Security systems services
HQ: Interface Security Systems, Llc
3773 Corporate Centre Dr
Earth City MO 63045
314 595-0100

(P-16523)
GUARD FORCE INC
Also Called: Guard Force International
6135 Tam O Shanter Dr 2, Stockton
(95210-3303)
P.O. Box 284, Austin TX (78767-0284)
PHONE..................................951 233-0206
Gordon Brooks, *President*
EMP: 50
SALES (est): 4MM **Privately Held**
SIC: 7382 7381 Protective devices, security; guard services

(P-16524)
HIKVISION USA INC (HQ)
18639 Railroad St, City of Industry
(91748-1317)
PHONE..................................909 895-0400
Jeffrey He, *CEO*
Nick Tang, *Vice Pres*
Ning Tang, *Admin Sec*
Michael Hendrix, *Technical Staff*
Armen Barseghyan, *Engineer*
▲ **EMP:** 175 **EST:** 2007
SALES: 75MM
SALES (corp-wide): 7.1B **Privately Held**
SIC: 7382 Confinement surveillance systems maintenance & monitoring
PA: Hangzhou Hikvision Digital Technology Co., Ltd.
No.555, Qianmo Road, Binjiang District
Hangzhou 31005
571 880-7599

(P-16525)
HOMELAND SECURITY SERVICES INC
31805 Temecula Pkwy, Temecula
(92592-8203)
P.O. Box 26052, Anaheim (92825-6052)
PHONE..................................714 956-2200
Leonard Bacani, *President*
Florencia Bacani, *Vice Pres*
EMP: 400
SQ FT: 250

SALES: 437.9K Privately Held
WEB: www.homelandsecurityservices.com
SIC: 7382 7381 Protective devices, security; detective & armored car services; detective services

(P-16526)
HONEYWELL INTERNATIONAL INC
1740 Creekside Oaks 150, Sacramento (95833)
PHONE..................916 923-7851
Mike Bishop, *Manager*
EMP: 100
SALES (corp-wide): 41.8B **Publicly Held**
WEB: www.honeywell.com
SIC: 7382 5075 Burglar alarm maintenance & monitoring; warm air heating & air conditioning
PA: Honeywell International Inc.
300 S Tryon St
Charlotte NC 28202
973 455-2000

(P-16527)
ID ANALYTICS LLC
15253 Ave Of Science, San Diego (92128-3437)
PHONE..................858 312-6200
Scott Carter, *CEO*
Peter Boyes, *COO*
George Gelly, *Officer*
Daniel Rawlings, *Officer*
Carrie Bennett, *Vice Pres*
EMP: 140 **EST:** 2002
SQ FT: 32,000
SALES (est): 19.9MM
SALES (corp-wide): 4.7B **Publicly Held**
WEB: www.idanalytics.com
SIC: 7382 Protective devices, security
HQ: Lifelock, Inc.
60 E Rio Salado Pkwy Fl 4
Tempe AZ 85281
480 682-5100

(P-16528)
IRON MOUNTAIN INCORPORATED
30481 Whipple Rd, Union City (94587-1531)
P.O. Box 326 (94587-0326)
PHONE..................510 798-6387
Keven Artis, *Manager*
Patrick Waters, *Finance*
Jennifer Jones, *Opers Spvr*
EMP: 75
SALES (corp-wide): 4.2B **Publicly Held**
SIC: 7382 4226 3572 Security systems services; special warehousing & storage; computer storage devices
PA: Iron Mountain Incorporated
1 Federal St Fl 7
Boston MA 02110
617 535-4766

(P-16529)
JOHNSON CNTRLS SEC SLTIONS LLC
104 E Graham Pl, Burbank (91502-2027)
PHONE..................818 428-6669
Carlo Alarc, *Branch Mgr*
John Sickafoose, *Manager*
EMP: 200 **Privately Held**
WEB: www.adt.com
SIC: 7382 Burglar alarm maintenance & monitoring
HQ: Johnson Controls Security Solutions Llc
6600 Congress Ave
Boca Raton FL 33487
561 264-2071

(P-16530)
JOHNSON CNTRLS SEC SLTIONS LLC
1120 Palmyrita Ave # 280, Riverside (92507-1744)
PHONE..................951 787-0420
Tom Mannon, *Manager*
EMP: 100 **Privately Held**
WEB: www.adt.com
SIC: 7382 Burglar alarm maintenance & monitoring; fire alarm maintenance & monitoring

HQ: Johnson Controls Security Solutions Llc
6600 Congress Ave
Boca Raton FL 33487
561 264-2071

(P-16531)
JOHNSON CNTRLS SEC SLTIONS LLC
3870 Murphy Canyon Rd # 140, San Diego (92123-4446)
PHONE..................561 988-3600
Greg Pavlicek, *Manager*
EMP: 122 **Privately Held**
WEB: www.adt.com
SIC: 7382 Burglar alarm maintenance & monitoring; fire alarm maintenance & monitoring
HQ: Johnson Controls Security Solutions Llc
6600 Congress Ave
Boca Raton FL 33487
561 264-2071

(P-16532)
JOHNSON CNTRLS SEC SLTIONS LLC
150 N Hill Dr Ste 3, Brisbane (94005-1024)
PHONE..................650 634-9000
Dan Zahhos, *Manager*
EMP: 60 **Privately Held**
WEB: www.adt.com
SIC: 7382 Burglar alarm maintenance & monitoring
HQ: Johnson Controls Security Solutions Llc
6600 Congress Ave
Boca Raton FL 33487
561 264-2071

(P-16533)
JOHNSON CNTRLS SEC SLTIONS LLC
3825 Bay Center Pl B, Hayward (94545-3619)
PHONE..................510 246-2862
Leo Brancheau, *General Mgr*
EMP: 70 **Privately Held**
WEB: www.adt.com
SIC: 7382 Burglar alarm maintenance & monitoring; fire alarm maintenance & monitoring
HQ: Johnson Controls Security Solutions Llc
6600 Congress Ave
Boca Raton FL 33487
561 264-2071

(P-16534)
JOHNSON CNTRLS SEC SLTIONS LLC
7565 Irvine Center Dr # 100, Irvine (92618-4918)
PHONE..................714 223-2300
Nels Jenson, *Manager*
EMP: 135 **Privately Held**
WEB: www.adt.com
SIC: 7382 Burglar alarm maintenance & monitoring
HQ: Johnson Controls Security Solutions Llc
6600 Congress Ave
Boca Raton FL 33487
561 264-2071

(P-16535)
JOHNSON CONTROLS
12728 Shoemaker Ave, Santa Fe Springs (90670-6345)
PHONE..................562 405-3817
Andy Bernot, *Manager*
EMP: 150 **Privately Held**
WEB: www.simplexgrinnell.com
SIC: 7382 1731 1711 Security systems services; fire detection & burglar alarm systems specialization; plumbing, heating, air-conditioning contractors
HQ: Johnson Controls Fire Protection Lp
6600 Congress Ave
Boca Raton FL 33487
561 988-7200

(P-16536)
KERN SECURITY CORPORATION
Also Called: Kern Security Systems
2701 Fruitvale Ave, Bakersfield (93308-5905)
PHONE..................661 363-6874
John Affeld, *President*
Ronald C McVicar, *CFO*
EMP: 100
SQ FT: 4,000
SALES (est): 6.8MM
SALES (corp-wide): 55.1MM **Privately Held**
WEB: www.kernsecurity.com
SIC: 7382 5999 1731 Burglar alarm maintenance & monitoring; fire alarm maintenance & monitoring; alarm signal systems; closed circuit television installation
PA: Security Signal Devices, Inc.
1740 N Lemon St
Anaheim CA 92801
800 888-0444

(P-16537)
KIMBERLITE CORPORATION
Sonitrol of Stockton
3728 Imperial Way, Stockton (95215-9686)
PHONE..................209 948-2551
Russ Borse, *Manager*
EMP: 55
SQ FT: 6,500
SALES (corp-wide): 11.7MM **Privately Held**
SIC: 7382 1731 7359 5063 Burglar alarm maintenance & monitoring; fire detection & burglar alarm systems specialization; electronic equipment rental, except computers; burglar alarm systems
PA: Kimberlite Corporation
3621 W Beechwood Ave
Fresno CA 93711
559 264-9730

(P-16538)
KIMBERLITE CORPORATION (PA)
Also Called: Sonitrol Security Systems
3621 W Beechwood Ave, Fresno (93711-0648)
P.O. Box 9189 (93791-9189)
PHONE..................559 264-9730
Joey RAO Russell, *CEO*
Marselle Nikkel, *CFO*
Julie Beach, *Vice Pres*
Kenneth Berry, *Vice Pres*
Brian Petrille, *Vice Pres*
EMP: 58
SQ FT: 3,500
SALES (est): 11.7MM **Privately Held**
SIC: 7382 Burglar alarm maintenance & monitoring; fire alarm maintenance & monitoring; protective devices, security

(P-16539)
LANTZ SECURITY SYSTEMS INC
4111 Las Virgenes Rd # 202, Calabasas (91302-1886)
PHONE..................818 871-0193
EMP: 114
SALES (corp-wide): 9.7MM **Privately Held**
SIC: 7382
PA: Lantz Security Systems Inc
43440 Sahuayo St
Lancaster CA 93535
661 949-3565

(P-16540)
LAW ENFORCEMENT OFFICERS INC
24000 Alicia Pkwy 17-229, Mission Viejo (92691-3929)
PHONE..................855 477-3536
Erick Reyes, *CEO*
EMP: 130
SALES (est): 4.1MM **Privately Held**
SIC: 7382 Protective devices, security

(P-16541)
LIFE ALERT EMERGENCY RESPONSE (PA)
16027 Ventura Blvd # 400, Encino (91436-2747)
PHONE..................800 247-0000

Isaac Shepher, *President*
Miriam Shepher, *Senior VP*
Richard Chen, *Vice Pres*
Russ States, *Info Tech Dir*
Martin Yasin, *Software Engr*
▲ **EMP:** 175
SQ FT: 29,489
SALES (est): 48.9MM **Privately Held**
WEB: www.lifealert.com
SIC: 7382 5731 Confinement surveillance systems maintenance & monitoring; consumer electronic equipment

(P-16542)
LOOKOUT INC (PA)
Also Called: Flexilis
1 Front St Ste 3100, San Francisco (94111-5360)
PHONE..................650 241-2358
James Dolce, *CEO*
Mark Nasiff, *CFO*
Deborah Wolf, *Chief Mktg Ofcr*
Alex Abey, *Vice Pres*
Amit Gupta, *Vice Pres*
EMP: 113
SALES: 100MM **Privately Held**
SIC: 7382 Protective devices, security

(P-16543)
LYONS SECURITY SERVICE INC
P.O. Box 18955 (92817-8955)
PHONE..................714 401-4850
Kathleen Guidice, *Branch Mgr*
EMP: 75 **Privately Held**
SIC: 7382 Security systems services
PA: Lyons Security Service, Inc.
505 S Villa Real Ste 203a
Anaheim CA 92807

(P-16544)
NATIONAL SECURITY INDUSTRIES
1217 Del Paso Blvd Ste A, Sacramento (95815-3660)
PHONE..................916 779-0640
EMP: 277 **Privately Held**
SIC: 7382 Security systems services
PA: National Security Industries
940 Park Ave Frnt Frnt
San Jose CA 95126
-

(P-16545)
NETCONTINUUM INC
1454 Almaden Valley Dr, San Jose (95120-3801)
PHONE..................408 961-5600
Varun Nagaraj, *CEO*
Gene Banman, *President*
EMP: 80
SQ FT: 31,000
SALES: 7.4MM **Privately Held**
SIC: 7382 Security systems services

(P-16546)
NOZOMI NETWORKS INC (HQ)
575 Market St Ste 3650, San Francisco (94105-5823)
PHONE..................800 314-6114
Edgard Capdevielle, *CEO*
Kim Legelis, *Chief Mktg Ofcr*
Andrea Carcano,
Moreno Carullo, *CTO*
EMP: 85 **EST:** 2016
SALES (est): 464.9K
SALES (corp-wide): 654.3K **Privately Held**
SIC: 7382 Security systems services
PA: Nozomi Holding Sagl
Via Penate 4
Mendrisio TI
916 470-406

(P-16547)
OLIVE US BIDCO INC (DH)
25341 Commercentre Dr, Lake Forest (92630-8856)
PHONE..................800 662-1711
Martin Scott, *President*
Lara Dyllon, *Treasurer*
Bela Sworts, *Vice Pres*
EMP: 50
SALES (est): 7.9MM **Privately Held**
SIC: 7382 Burglar alarm maintenance & monitoring

P R O D U C T S & S V C S

(P-16548)
PACIFIC WEST SECURITY INC
Also Called: Sonitrol
1587 Schallenberger Rd, San Jose
(95131-2434)
PHONE..................................801 748-1034
Paul Schumate, *President*
Kari Herzig, *COO*
Sandra Oswalt, *Corp Secy*
EMP: 60
SQ FT: 8,000
SALES (est): 6.7MM **Privately Held**
WEB: www.sonitrolsafetyzone.com
SIC: 7382 1731 Burglar alarm mainte-
nance & monitoring; fire alarm mainte-
nance & monitoring; fire detection &
burglar alarm systems specialization

(P-16549)
PLEXICOR INC (PA)
3598 Cadillac Ave, Costa Mesa
(92626-1416)
PHONE..................................714 918-8700
Robert Klemme, *CEO*
EMP: 50
SALES (est): 4MM **Privately Held**
SIC: 7382 5063 1731 Security systems
services; electric alarms & signaling
equipment; safety & security specializa-
tion

(P-16550)
POST ALARM SYSTEMS (PA)
Also Called: Post Alarm Systems Patrol Svcs
47 E Saint Joseph St, Arcadia
(91006-2861)
PHONE..................................626 446-7159
William Post, *President*
Bill Post, *Owner*
Lois Post, *Treasurer*
Robert Jennison, *Business Dir*
Gina Post-Franco, *General Mgr*
EMP: 98
SQ FT: 10,500
SALES (est): 12.6MM **Privately Held**
WEB: www.postalarm.com
SIC: 7382 1731 5063 Burglar alarm main-
tenance & monitoring; fire alarm mainte-
nance & monitoring; protective devices,
security; fire detection & burglar alarm
systems specialization; electrical appara-
tus & equipment

(P-16551)
**PROTECT-FOR-LESS SECURITY
SVCS**
Also Called: Pfl Security
72877 Dinah Shore Dr, Rancho Mirage
(92270-2763)
PHONE..................................760 343-1192
Norman Southerby, *CEO*
Evelyn Frances Southerby, *President*
EMP: 50
SALES (est): 2.4MM **Privately Held**
SIC: 7382 Security systems services

(P-16552)
REALDEFENSE LLC
Also Called: Mycleanpc
1541 Ocean Ave Ste 200, Santa Monica
(90401-2104)
PHONE..................................310 693-5935
Gary Guseinov, *Mng Member*
EMP: 100
SALES (est): 1.5MM **Privately Held**
SIC: 7382 Security systems services

(P-16553)
**RED HAWK FIRE & SECURITY
LLC**
2705 Media Center Dr, Los Angeles
(90065-1700)
PHONE..................................323 276-3100
James Rider, *Branch Mgr*
Richard Tampier, *Vice Pres*
Jasun Boles, *Project Mgr*
John Reyes, *Project Mgr*
Ryan Castillo, *Opers Staff*
EMP: 51
SALES (corp-wide): 4.5B **Publicly Held**
SIC: 7382 7699 1711 7389 Fire alarm
maintenance & monitoring; fire control
(military) equipment repair; fire sprinkler
system installation; fire protection service
other than forestry or public

HQ: Red Hawk Fire & Security, Llc
5100 Town Center Cir # 350
Boca Raton FL 33486
877 387-0188

(P-16554)
REPUTATIONCOM INC (PA)
1400 A Sport Blvd Ste 401, Redwood City
(94063)
PHONE..................................650 381-3056
Joe Fuca, *CEO*
Mark Phillips, *CFO*
Howard Bragman, *Vice Ch Bd*
Jason Grier, *Ch Credit Ofcr*
Colleen McCreary, *Officer*
EMP: 114
SALES (est): 32.4MM **Privately Held**
SIC: 7382 Security systems services

(P-16555)
SAFE SECURITY INC
2440 Camino Ramon Ste 200, San Ramon
(94583-4326)
P.O. Box 5164 (94583-5164)
PHONE..................................925 830-4777
Paul F Sargenti, *President*
Wayne Jordan, *Director*
Sarah Ratcliffe, *Director*
EMP: 455
SALES (est): 48.3MM **Privately Held**
SIC: 7382 7539 Burglar alarm mainte-
nance & monitoring; automotive sound
system service & installation

(P-16556)
SECTEK INC
Bldg 15, Mountain View (94035)
PHONE..................................650 604-1785
Wilfred D Blood, *Branch Mgr*
EMP: 55 **Privately Held**
WEB: www.sectek.com
SIC: 7382 Security systems services
PA: Sectek, Inc.
1930 Isaac Newton Sq W # 100
Reston VA 20190

(P-16557)
**SECURITAS ELECTRONIC SEC
INC**
7002 Convoy Ct, San Diego (92111-1017)
PHONE..................................858 812-7349
EMP: 99
SALES (corp-wide): 11.2B **Privately Held**
SIC: 7382 Security systems services
HQ: Securitas Electronic Security Inc.
3800 Tabs Dr
Uniontown OH 44685
855 331-0359

(P-16558)
**SECURITY ALARM FING ENTPS
INC**
2440 Camino Ramon Ste 200, San Ramon
(94583-4326)
P.O. Box 5164 (94583-5164)
PHONE..................................925 830-4786
Paul Sargenti, *President*
EMP: 70
SQ FT: 20,000
SALES (est): 10.7MM **Privately Held**
WEB: www.safefinancial.com
SIC: 7382 6141 Security systems serv-
ices; financing; automobiles, furniture,
etc., not a deposit bank

(P-16559)
**SECURITY ON-SITE SERVICES
INC**
2210 Plaza Dr Ste 300, Rocklin
(95765-4406)
PHONE..................................916 988-6500
Martin A Steiner, *CEO*
Michael A McConnell, *COO*
EMP: 75 EST: 2013
SALES (est): 361K **Privately Held**
SIC: 7382 Security systems services

(P-16560)
**SECURITY SIGNAL DEVICES
INC (PA)**
Also Called: Ssd Systems
1740 N Lemon St, Anaheim (92801-1047)
PHONE..................................800 888-0444
John F Affeld, *CEO*

Sheila Rossi, *Admin Sec*
Jim Sanchez, *Purch Mgr*
Christopher Clark, *Opers Mgr*
Greg Denton, *Opers Mgr*
EMP: 50 EST: 1969
SQ FT: 20,000
SALES (est): 55.1MM **Privately Held**
WEB: www.ssdsystems.com
SIC: 7382 1731 Security systems serv-
ices; safety & security specialization; ac-
cess control systems specialization;
closed circuit television installation; fire
detection & burglar alarm systems spe-
cialization

(P-16561)
**SENTINEL MONITORING CORP
(HQ)**
220 Technology Dr Ste 200, Irvine
(92618-2424)
PHONE..................................949 453-1550
Robert Contestabile, *President*
EMP: 200
SALES (est): 5.6MM
SALES (corp-wide): 71.6MM **Privately
Held**
WEB: www.sentrak.com
SIC: 7382 Confinement surveillance sys-
tems maintenance & monitoring
PA: Sentinel Offender Services Llc
1290 N Hancock St Ste 103
Anaheim CA 92807
949 453-1550

(P-16562)
**SENTINEL OFFENDER
SERVICES LLC (PA)**
1290 N Hancock St Ste 103, Anaheim
(92807-1925)
PHONE..................................949 453-1550
Robert Contestabile, *President*
Salman Qureshi, *CTO*
Hans Kintsch, *Manager*
EMP: 85
SALES (est): 71.6MM **Privately Held**
WEB: www.sentrak.com
SIC: 7382 Confinement surveillance sys-
tems maintenance & monitoring

(P-16563)
SKYHIGH NETWORKS INC (DH)
900 E Hamilton Ave # 400, Campbell
(95008-0670)
PHONE..................................408 564-0278
Christopher D Young, *CEO*
Judy Kent, *Partner*
Michael Berry, *CFO*
Allison Cerra, *Chief Mktg Ofcr*
Dawn Smith,
EMP: 99
SALES (est): 2.6MM **Privately Held**
SIC: 7382 Security systems services
HQ: Mcafee, Llc
2821 Mission College Blvd
Santa Clara CA 95054
888 847-8766

(P-16564)
**SPECTRUM SECURITY
SERVICES INC (PA)**
13967 Campo Rd Ste 101, Jamul
(91935-3232)
P.O. Box 744 (91935-0744)
PHONE..................................619 669-6660
Sam Ersan, *President*
Porter Erent, *President*
Porter Trent, *COO*
Lyndie Ersan, *CFO*
Alex Robinson, *Officer*
EMP: 212
SQ FT: 1,200
SALES (est): 7.5MM **Privately Held**
WEB: www.spectrumsecurityservices.com
SIC: 7382 Security systems services

(P-16565)
STAFF PRO INC (PA)
Also Called: Allied Universal Event Svcs
1400 N Harbor Blvd # 700, Fullerton
(92835-4109)
PHONE..................................714 230-7200
Cory Meredith, *CEO*
EMP: 2200

SALES (est): 98.4MM **Privately Held**
WEB: www.staffpro.com
SIC: 7382 8741 Security systems serv-
ices; management services

(P-16566)
TAD GROUP LLC
5000 Birch St Ste 3000, Newport Beach
(92660-2140)
PHONE..................................949 476-3601
Izan Todorov,
EMP: 150
SALES (est): 1.7MM **Privately Held**
SIC: 7382 7373 Security systems serv-
ices; computer integrated systems design

(P-16567)
**TALON EXECUTIVE SERVICES
INC**
151 Kalmus Dr Ste A103, Costa Mesa
(92626-5900)
PHONE..................................714 434-7476
Ronald William, *CEO*
Laurie Virtue, *Office Mgr*
Kain Guercci, *Opers Staff*
EMP: 50
SQ FT: 2,000
SALES (est): 4.7MM **Privately Held**
WEB: www.talonexec.com
SIC: 7382 8742 Security systems serv-
ices; management consulting services

(P-16568)
**WARREN SECURITY SYSTEMS
INC**
1305 Francisco Blvd E, San Rafael
(94901-5501)
P.O. Box 3210 (94912-3210)
PHONE..................................415 456-7034
Warren V Glass III, *President*
Patty Boudreau, *Executive*
EMP: 50
SALES (est): 2.9MM **Privately Held**
SIC: 7382 1731 Burglar alarm mainte-
nance & monitoring; protective devices,
security; electrical work

(P-16569)
**WEST CAST FIRE INTEGRATION
INC**
1474 Miller Dr, Colton (92324-2457)
PHONE..................................909 824-7980
EMP: 71
SALES (corp-wide): 784.5K **Privately
Held**
SIC: 7382 Security systems services
PA: West Coast Fire & Integration, Inc.
3199 Airport Loop Dr D
Costa Mesa CA 92626
714 957-5750

7383 News Syndicates

(P-16570)
ASSOCIATED PRESS
221 S Figueroa St Ste 300, Los Angeles
(90012-2553)
PHONE..................................213 626-1200
Anthony Marquez, *Manager*
Frank Baker, *Chief*
EMP: 60
SALES (corp-wide): 510.1MM **Privately
Held**
WEB: www.apme.com
SIC: 7383 News reporting services for
newspapers & periodicals
PA: The Associated Press
200 Liberty St Fl 19
New York NY 10281
212 621-1500

(P-16571)
BLOOMBERG LP
345 California St Fl 35, San Francisco
(94104-2624)
PHONE..................................415 912-2960
Curtis McCool, *Planning*
Ebru Boysan, *Sales Executive*
Chris Lachmann, *Manager*
Nick Turner, *Editor*
Steve West, *Editor*
EMP: 100

SALES (corp-wide): 1.8B **Privately Held**
WEB: www.bloomberg.com
SIC: 7383 News reporting services for newspapers & periodicals
PA: Bloomberg L.P.
731 Lexington Ave Fl Ll2
New York NY 10022
212 318-2000

(P-16572)
BUENA VISTA TELEVISION (DH)
Also Called: Buena Vista TV Advg Sls
500 S Buena Vista St, Burbank (91521-0001)
PHONE..............................818 560-1878
Janice Marinelli, *CEO*
Jed Cohen, *Exec VP*
Marsha Reed, *Admin Sec*
EMP: 129
SALES (est): 6.4MM
SALES (corp-wide): 90.2B **Publicly Held**
SIC: 7383 News feature syndicate
HQ: Disney Enterprises, Inc.
500 S Buena Vista St
Burbank CA 91521
818 560-1000

(P-16573)
GIGA OMNI MEDIA INC
1613a Lyon St, San Francisco (94115-2414)
PHONE..............................415 974-6355
Paul Walborsky, *CEO*
EMP: 75
SALES (est): 7.8MM **Privately Held**
SIC: 7383 News pictures, gathering & distributing; press service

(P-16574)
MARKETWATCH INC (DH)
Also Called: C B S Marketwatch
201 California St Fl 13, San Francisco (94111-5002)
PHONE..............................415 439-6400
Larry S Kramer, *Ch of Bd*
Kathleen B Yates, *President*
Paul Mattison, *CFO*
William Bishop, *Exec VP*
Doug Appleton, *Admin Sec*
EMP: 51 EST: 1997
SQ FT: 24,000
SALES (est): 10.4MM
SALES (corp-wide): 10B **Publicly Held**
WEB: www.marketwatch.com
SIC: 7383 News ticker service
HQ: Dow Jones & Company, Inc.
1211 Avenue Of The Americ
New York NY 10036
609 627-2999

(P-16575)
MARKETWIRE INC (HQ)
100 N Pacific Coast Hwy, El Segundo (90245-4359)
PHONE..............................310 765-3200
Michael Nowlan, *President*
James H Delaney, *COO*
Stephen Devito, *CFO*
Michael Shuler, *Senior VP*
Suresh Kumar, *Vice Pres*
EMP: 55 EST: 1998
SALES (est): 11.4MM
SALES (corp-wide): 4.2B **Publicly Held**
WEB: www.marketwire.com
SIC: 7383 Press service
PA: Nasdaq, Inc.
1 Liberty Plz Ste 4900
New York NY 10006
212 401-8700

(P-16576)
MELTWATER NEWS US INC (DH)
225 Bush St Ste 1000, San Francisco (94104-4215)
P.O. Box 123408, Dallas TX (75312-3408)
PHONE..............................415 829-5900
Jorn Lyseggen, *CEO*
Adam Dealy, *COO*
Martin Hernandez, *CFO*
Ambera Cruz, *Business Dir*
Shikul Narula, *Business Dir*
EMP: 54
SALES (est): 218.7MM
SALES (corp-wide): 315.5MM **Privately Held**
SIC: 7383 News syndicates

(P-16577)
WRAP NEWS INC
Also Called: Wrap, The
2260 S Centinela Ave # 150, Los Angeles (90064-1007)
PHONE..............................424 248-0612
Sharon Waxman, *President*
EMP: 50
SALES: 7.5MM **Privately Held**
SIC: 7383 News correspondents, independent; news pictures, gathering & distributing

7384 Photofinishing Labs

(P-16578)
ICON EXPOSURE INC
5450 Wilshire Blvd, Los Angeles (90036-4218)
PHONE..............................323 933-1666
Ramesh Venugopal, *President*
EMP: 57 EST: 1998
SQ FT: 11,600
SALES (est): 4.5MM **Privately Held**
SIC: 7384 Photofinishing laboratory

(P-16579)
J H MADDOCKS PHOTOGRAPHY
Also Called: Photocenter Imaging
40 E Verdugo Ave, Burbank (91502-1931)
PHONE..............................818 842-7150
Joe H Maddocks, *President*
Janet Maddocks, *Shareholder*
Vance Maddocks, *CEO*
Scott Maddocks, *Vice Pres*
Boris Winogradow, *Vice Pres*
EMP: 61
SQ FT: 15,000
SALES (est): 4.2MM **Privately Held**
WEB: www.photocenter.net
SIC: 7384 Film processing & finishing laboratory; film developing & printing

(P-16580)
JAKE HEY INCORPORATED
Also Called: A & I Color Laboratory
257 S Lake St, Burbank (91502-2111)
PHONE..............................323 856-5280
David Alexander, *President*
John Gaeta, *CFO*
James Ishihara, *Vice Pres*
EMP: 144
SQ FT: 16,000
SALES (est): 7.2MM **Privately Held**
SIC: 7384 Photofinish laboratories

(P-16581)
PHOTO TLC INC
3925 Cypress Dr, Petaluma (94954-5900)
PHONE..............................415 462-0010
EMP: 125
SQ FT: 30,000
SALES (est): 4.3MM **Privately Held**
SIC: 7384 Photographic services

(P-16582)
PICTURE IT ON CANVAS INC
1800 Seaport Blvd, Redwood City (94063-5543)
PHONE..............................858 679-1200
Robert McKeon, *CEO*
Monica Denosta, *Senior VP*
Merete McCarthy, *Human Res Mgr*
Jason Richey, *Mktg Dir*
EMP: 65
SQ FT: 33,000
SALES (est): 10.7MM **Privately Held**
SIC: 7384 Photograph developing & retouching

(P-16583)
SHUTTERFLY INC (PA)
2800 Bridge Pkwy Ste 100, Redwood City (94065-1193)
PHONE..............................650 610-5200
Ryan O'Hara, *President*
Sarah Allbritten, *Partner*
James Hilt, *President*
Dwayne Black, *COO*
Michael Pope, *CFO*
EMP: 148
SQ FT: 100,000

SALES: 1.9B **Privately Held**
WEB: www.shutterfly.com
SIC: 7384 5946 Photofinishing laboratory; film developing & printing; camera & photographic supply stores; cameras; photographic supplies

(P-16584)
TECHNICOLOR INC
Also Called: Technicolor Lab
2255 N Ontario St Ste 180, Burbank (91524-4509)
PHONE..............................818 260-4577
Joe Berchtold, *President*
EMP: 400
SALES (est): 38.4MM **Privately Held**
SIC: 7384 Photofinish laboratories

7389 Business Svcs, NEC

(P-16585)
1111 6TH AVE LLC
1111 6th Ave Ste 102, San Diego (92101-5214)
PHONE..............................312 283-3683
William Bennett, *Mng Member*
Kayley Dicicco, *Mng Member*
EMP: 75
SALES (est): 943.1K **Privately Held**
SIC: 7389 Office facilities & secretarial service rental

(P-16586)
2DREAM INC
5729 Sonoma Dr Ste Z, Pleasanton (94566-7782)
PHONE..............................650 943-2366
Hongfei Yin, *Principal*
EMP: 70
SALES (est): 1.9MM **Privately Held**
SIC: 7389

(P-16587)
A F EVANS COMPANY INC
Also Called: Byron Park
1700 Tice Valley Blvd Ofc, Walnut Creek (94595-1654)
PHONE..............................925 937-1700
Kirsten Korhsege, *Manager*
EMP: 70
SALES (corp-wide): 60.5MM **Privately Held**
WEB: www.afevans.com
SIC: 7389 Personal service agents, brokers & bureaus
PA: A. F. Evans Company, Inc.
2033 N Main St Ste 340
Walnut Creek CA 94596
510 891-9400

(P-16588)
A J PARENT COMPANY INC (PA)
Also Called: Americas Printer.com
6910 Aragon Cir Ste 6, Buena Park (90620-8103)
PHONE..............................714 521-1100
Arthur Parent, *CEO*
Mel Lewis, *President*
Mike Roccio, *Vice Pres*
Theresa Fatino, *Administration*
Julio Sandoval, *Technician*
EMP: 67
SALES (est): 18.1MM **Privately Held**
WEB: www.americaprinter.com
SIC: 7389 2752 Printers' services: folding, collating; commercial printing, lithographic

(P-16589)
AAA RESTAURANT FIRE CTRL INC
Also Called: AAA Fire Protection Service
30113 Union City Blvd, Union City (94587-1511)
P.O. Box 3626, Hayward (94540-3626)
PHONE..............................510 786-9555
Brent Patterson, *President*
Jeanne Patterson, *Treasurer*
Karen Patterson, *Treasurer*
Brian Patterson, *Vice Pres*
Charisse Filteau, *Office Mgr*
EMP: 90
SQ FT: 10,000

SALES (est): 10MM **Privately Held**
WEB: www.aaafireprotection.com
SIC: 7389 Fire extinguisher servicing

(P-16590)
AARON THOMAS COMPANY INC (PA)
7421 Chapman Ave, Garden Grove (92841-2115)
PHONE..............................714 894-4468
James T Chang, *Ch of Bd*
Thomas Bacon, *President*
Linda Bacon, *Treasurer*
Brian Robinson, *Principal*
Jean Chang, *Admin Sec*
▲ EMP: 125 EST: 1973
SQ FT: 207,000
SALES (est): 48.4MM **Privately Held**
WEB: www.packaging.com
SIC: 7389 Packaging & labeling services

(P-16591)
ABBA BAIL BONDS (PA)
900 Avila Cir Ste 2, Los Angeles (90012-3871)
PHONE..............................213 680-1400
Scott Esparza, *Principal*
Fernando Banuelos, *Mktg Dir*
Linda Olmeda, *Manager*
EMP: 50
SALES (est): 5.8MM **Privately Held**
SIC: 7389 Bail bonding

(P-16592)
ABI DOCUMENT SUPPORT SVCS LLC
11010 White Rock Rd # 160, Rancho Cordova (95670-6083)
PHONE..............................909 793-0613
Maggie Dragna, *Branch Mgr*
EMP: 50 **Privately Held**
SIC: 7389 5044 Microfilm recording & developing service; office equipment
HQ: Abi Document Support Services, Llc
3534 E Sunshine St Ste L
Springfield MO 65809

(P-16593)
ABI DOCUMENT SUPPORT SVCS LLC
10459 Mountain View Ave E, Loma Linda (92354-2033)
PHONE..............................909 793-0613
David Benge, *Branch Mgr*
EMP: 100 **Privately Held**
SIC: 7389 5044 Microfilm recording & developing service; office equipment
HQ: Abi Document Support Services, Llc
3534 E Sunshine St Ste L
Springfield MO 65809

(P-16594)
ABSOLUTDATA TECHNOLOGIES INC
1320 Harbor Bay Pkwy # 170, Alameda (94502-6506)
PHONE..............................510 748-9922
Anil Kaul, *President*
Rangan Bandyopadhyay, *Vice Pres*
Sudeshna Datta, *Vice Pres*
Alice Goodwill, *Vice Pres*
Suhale Kapoor, *Vice Pres*
EMP: 75
SQ FT: 1,600
SALES (est): 7.6MM **Privately Held**
WEB: www.absolutdata.com
SIC: 7389 7374 Personal service agents, brokers & bureaus; data processing service

(P-16595)
ABSOLUTE EXHIBITS INC (PA)
Also Called: Meroform Systems USA
1382 Valencia Ave Ste H, Tustin (92780-6472)
PHONE..............................714 685-2800
Todd Koren, *President*
Jan Koren, *Co-President*
▲ EMP: 65
SQ FT: 15,500

SALES (est): 23.8MM **Privately Held**
WEB: www.absoluteexhibits.com
SIC: 7389 Promoters of shows & exhibitions

(P-16596)
ACCESS BUSINESS GROUP INTL LLC
6500 Beach Blvd, Buena Park (90621)
PHONE..................................800 879-2732
EMP: 120
SALES (corp-wide): 8.7B **Privately Held**
WEB: www.accessbusinessgroupinternational.com
SIC: 7389 Personal service agents, brokers & bureaus
HQ: Access Business Group International Llc
7575 Fulton St E
Ada MI 49355
616 787-6000

(P-16597)
ACCESS FINANCE INC
3415 S Sepulveda Blvd # 400, Los Angeles (90034-6094)
PHONE..................................310 826-4000
EMP: 50
SALES (est): 184.3K **Privately Held**
SIC: 7389 Financial services

(P-16598)
ACCO ENGINEERED SYSTEMS INC
6446 E Washington Blvd, Commerce (90040-1820)
PHONE..................................323 201-0931
Matt Deluca, *Principal*
Ashley Widmar, *Design Engr*
Amanda Shade, *Project Mgr*
Nick Gagliardi, *Engineer*
Nathan Paduraru, *Buyer*
EMP: 50
SALES (corp-wide): 777.3MM **Privately Held**
SIC: 7389 Automobile recovery service
PA: Acco Engineered Systems, Inc.
888 E Walnut St
Pasadena CA 91101
818 244-6571

(P-16599)
ACCT HOLDINGS LLC
5949 Fair Oaks Blvd, Carmichael (95608-5221)
PHONE..................................916 971-1981
Alicia James, *Supervisor*
EMP: 594
SALES (corp-wide): 373.6MM **Privately Held**
SIC: 7389 Telemarketing services
PA: Acct Holdings Llc
1235 Westlakes Dr Ste 160
Berwyn PA 19312
610 695-0500

(P-16600)
ACCU-COUNT INVENTORY SVCS INC
Also Called: MSI Invntory Srvce-Los Angeles
1024 N Citrus Ave, Covina (91722-2739)
P.O. Box 814, Moorpark (93020-0814)
PHONE..................................805 231-6310
Mike M Naderi, *President*
EMP: 59
SQ FT: 800
SALES (est): 945.5K **Privately Held**
SIC: 7389 Inventory computing service

(P-16601)
ACCURATE FIRESTOP INC
1057 Serpentine Ln Ste A, Pleasanton (94566-8465)
PHONE..................................510 886-1169
Gabrielle Lucatero, *Principal*
Javier Lucatero, *Principal*
EMP: 150
SALES (est): 2MM **Privately Held**
SIC: 7389 Fire protection service other than forestry or public

(P-16602)
ACTION SPORTS RETAILER
Also Called: Asr
31910 Del Obispo St # 200, San Juan Capistrano (92675-3182)
PHONE..................................949 226-5744
Greg Farrar, *Principal*
EMP: 60
SALES (est): 1.4MM **Privately Held**
SIC: 7389 Trade show arrangement

(P-16603)
ACTIVEHOURS INC
Also Called: Earnin Hq
260 Sheridan Ave Ste 300, Palo Alto (94306-2010)
PHONE..................................650 272-4083
Ram Palaniappan, *CEO*
Sangeepha Raghunathan, *Ch Credit Ofcr*
Gauraz Bhargaza, *Risk Mgmt Dir*
Ramaneek Khanna, *CTO*
EMP: 150
SALES (est): 15MM **Privately Held**
SIC: 7389 Financial services

(P-16604)
ADMINISTRATIVE SYSTEMS INC
1651 Response Rd Ste 350, Sacramento (95815-5255)
P.O. Box 15437 (95851-0437)
PHONE..................................916 563-1121
Donald J Robinson, *President*
Geraldine M Fong, *Corp Secy*
Keith Crane, *Vice Pres*
James R Powell, *Vice Pres*
EMP: 75
SALES (est): 11.8MM **Privately Held**
WEB: www.asipay.com
SIC: 7389 Personal service agents, brokers & bureaus

(P-16605)
AFFILIATED COMMUNICATIONS INC
Also Called: Alert Communications
3601 Calle Tecate Ste 200, Camarillo (93012-5058)
P.O. Box 5720, Ventura (93005-0720)
PHONE..................................805 650-4949
Richard Starr, *President*
Kim Starr, *Vice Pres*
Monte L Widders, *Vice Pres*
Chris Hall, *Software Dev*
Frances Starr, *Sales Staff*
EMP: 50
SQ FT: 5,000
SALES (est): 7.5MM **Privately Held**
WEB: www.alertcommunications.com
SIC: 7389 5999 Telephone answering service; telephone & communication equipment

(P-16606)
AFFINITY AUTO PROGRAMS INC
Also Called: Costco Auto Program
10251 Vista Cerento Pkwy, San Diego (92121)
PHONE..................................858 643-9324
Jeff Skeen, *President*
Bill Gregory, *President*
Gary Drean, *COO*
Joey Herschel, *Vice Pres*
Rob Hannon, *Technology*
EMP: 80 EST: 1988
SQ FT: 34,000
SALES (est): 7.8MM **Privately Held**
WEB: www.costcoauto.com
SIC: 7389 Advertising, promotional & trade show services

(P-16607)
AFM & SAG-AFTRA INTELLECTUAL
4705 Laurel Canyon Blvd # 400, Valley Village (91607-5904)
PHONE..................................818 255-7980
Dennis Dreith, *Director*
Shari Hoffman, *COO*
Jennifer Leblanc, *CFO*
Eric Cowden, *Associate Dir*
John Felikian, *Associate Dir*
EMP: 70
SQ FT: 21,600

SALES: 68.5MM **Privately Held**
SIC: 7389 Fund raising organizations

(P-16608)
ALBANY INVENTORY SERVICES
11490 Burbank Blvd Ste 1, North Hollywood (91601-2391)
P.O. Box 292, Watervliet NY (12189-0292)
PHONE..................................818 986-5705
Marykay Connors, *President*
EMP: 50
SALES (est): 3MM **Privately Held**
SIC: 7389 Inventory stocking service; inventory computing service

(P-16609)
ALFREDS PICTURES FRAMES INC
Also Called: Heather Ann Creations
1580 Sunflower Ave, Costa Mesa (92626-1511)
PHONE..................................714 434-4838
Pat Cochrane, *President*
Sandra Adams, *Manager*
▲ EMP: 50
SQ FT: 40,000
SALES (est): 5.5MM **Privately Held**
WEB: www.heatherann.com
SIC: 7389 Interior decorating

(P-16610)
ALL-PRO BAIL BONDS INC (PA)
512 Via De La Valle # 302, Solana Beach (92075-2715)
PHONE..................................858 481-1200
Steffan Gibbs, *CEO*
Myrna Chevrie, *Human Resources*
EMP: 63 EST: 2006
SALES (est): 16.5MM **Privately Held**
SIC: 7389 Bail bonding

(P-16611)
ALL-PRO BAIL BONDS INC
530 Hacienda Dr Ste 104d, Vista (92081-6640)
PHONE..................................760 941-4100
Steffan Gibbs, *President*
EMP: 100
SALES (est): 6.9MM **Privately Held**
SIC: 7389 Bail bonding

(P-16612)
ALOM TECHNOLOGIES CORPORATION (PA)
48105 Warm Springs Blvd, Fremont (94538-7498)
PHONE..................................510 360-3600
Hannah Kain, *President*
Jack Sexton, *CFO*
Dana Hicks, *Vice Pres*
Tony Chiu, *Administration*
Sonia Sharma, *Web Dvlpr*
▲ EMP: 144
SQ FT: 300,000
SALES (est): 45.8MM **Privately Held**
WEB: www.alom.com
SIC: 7389 4783 7374 7331 Packaging & labeling services; packing goods for shipping; data processing & preparation; direct mail advertising services

(P-16613)
ALORICA CUSTOMER CARE INC
8885 Rio San Diego Dr, San Diego (92108-1624)
PHONE..................................619 298-7103
EMP: 563
SALES (corp-wide): 6.6B **Privately Held**
SIC: 7389 Telemarketing services
HQ: Alorica Customer Care, Inc.
5085 W Park Blvd Ste 300
Plano TX

(P-16614)
ALPHA SWIMMING POOL & SPA
2600 Athena Pl, Fullerton (92833-2005)
PHONE..................................714 879-4667
Kim Moon, *Owner*
EMP: 51
SALES (est): 1.5MM **Privately Held**
SIC: 7389 Swimming pool & hot tub service & maintenance

(P-16615)
ALTA RESOURCES CORP
Also Called: Tmw Marketing
975 W Imperial Hwy # 200, Brea (92821-3846)
PHONE..................................800 424-9378
Jim Maguire, *Manager*
EMP: 100 **Privately Held**
SIC: 7389 8742 Telemarketing services; training & development consultant; marketing consulting services
PA: Alta Resources Corp.
120 N Commercial St
Neenah WI 54956

(P-16616)
ALTAF ZAHID ENGINEERING SVCS
42051 Orange Blossom Dr, Temecula (92591-5543)
PHONE..................................760 481-9072
Shafiq Rassuli, *Director*
EMP: 50
SALES (est): 1.7MM **Privately Held**
SIC: 7389 Pipeline & power line inspection service

(P-16617)
ALTEC PRODUCTS INC (PA)
23422 Mill Creek Dr # 225, Laguna Hills (92653-7910)
PHONE..................................949 727-1248
Mark Ford, *CEO*
Brandt Morell, *President*
Frank Sansone, *CFO*
Mark Tague, *CFO*
Bill Brown, *Exec VP*
EMP: 80
SQ FT: 12,500
SALES (est): 17.1MM **Privately Held**
SIC: 7389 Telemarketing services; printing broker

(P-16618)
AMERICA SHREDDING
6565 Smith Ave, Newark (94560-4217)
PHONE..................................702 262-3607
John Groenewold, *Vice Pres*
Kevin Duncomed, *President*
EMP: 90
SALES (est): 3.1MM **Privately Held**
WEB: www.americashredding.com
SIC: 7389 Document & office record destruction

(P-16619)
AMERICAN HEALTH CONNECTION
8484 Wilshire Blvd # 501, Beverly Hills (90211-3243)
PHONE..................................424 226-0420
Yuriy Koltyar, *CEO*
Azabeh Williamson, *President*
EMP: 850
SQ FT: 3,500
SALES (est): 12.3MM **Privately Held**
SIC: 7389 Telemarketing services

(P-16620)
AMERICAS LEMONADE STAND INC
Also Called: Institutional Financing Svcs
5100 Park Rd, Benicia (94510-1136)
PHONE..................................707 745-1274
James M Cascino, *CEO*
Jose Ferreira Jr, *Ch of Bd*
Jack Hood, *CFO*
EMP: 250
SQ FT: 140,000
SALES (est): 10.7MM **Privately Held**
SIC: 7389 5094 5199 5145 Fund raising organizations; jewelry & precious stones; gifts & novelties; calendars; candy

(P-16621)
AMOEBA MUSIC INC
1855 Haight St, San Francisco (94117-2790)
PHONE..................................415 831-1200
Joe Goldmark, *Manager*
EMP: 70

SALES (corp-wide): 8.9MM Privately Held
WEB: www.ameebamusic.com
SIC: 7389 5999 5932 5735 Personal service agents, brokers & bureaus; posters; records, secondhand; video discs & tapes, prerecorded
PA: Amoeba Music Inc.
2455 Telegraph Ave
Berkeley CA 94704
510 549-1125

(P-16622)
AMYRIS INC
5850 Hollis St, Emeryville (94608-2016)
PHONE...................................510 597-4839
EMP: 63
SALES (corp-wide): 63.6MM Publicly Held
SIC: 7389 Automobile recovery service
PA: Amyris, Inc.
5885 Hollis St Ste 100
Emeryville CA 94608
510 450-0761

(P-16623)
ANAHEIM/ORANGE CNTY VISITOR BU (PA)
Also Called: Visit Anaheim
2099 S State College Blvd, Anaheim (92806-6142)
P.O. Box 4270 (92803-4270)
PHONE...................................714 765-8888
Jay Burress, CEO
Janine Troy, Partner
Charles Ahlers, President
Mindy Abel, Vice Pres
Christina Dawson, Vice Pres
EMP: 56
SQ FT: 3,000
SALES: 16.5MM Privately Held
SIC: 7389 Convention & show services; tourist information bureau

(P-16624)
ANDREW LAUREN COMPANY INC
15225 Alton Pkwy Unit 300, Irvine (92618-2345)
PHONE...................................949 861-4222
Mark Noonan, Principal
EMP: 189 Privately Held
SIC: 7389 5713 Interior design services; carpets
PA: The Andrew Lauren Company Inc
8909 Kenamar Dr Ste 101
San Diego CA 92121

(P-16625)
ANSIRA PARTNERS INC
Also Called: Co-Optimum
5000 Van Nuys Blvd, Sherman Oaks (91403-1793)
PHONE...................................818 461-6100
EMP: 60
SALES (corp-wide): 73.9MM Privately Held
SIC: 7389 7331
PA: Ansira Partners, Inc.
2300 Locust St
Saint Louis MO 63103
314 783-2300

(P-16626)
ANSWER FINANCIAL INC (HQ)
15910 Ventura Blvd Fl 6, Encino (91436-2803)
PHONE...................................818 644-4000
Robert J Slingerland, CEO
Darren Howard, Chief Mktg Ofcr
Jimmy Lee, Chief Mktg Ofcr
Daniel John Bryce, Senior VP
Peter Foley, Senior VP
EMP: 200
SQ FT: 45,000
SALES: 80MM Publicly Held
WEB: www.answerfinancial.com
SIC: 7389 6411 Brokers, business: buying & selling business enterprises; property & casualty insurance agent

(P-16627)
APPLEBEE LEASING INC
4 Maidstone Dr, Newport Beach (92660-4271)
P.O. Box 9878 (92658-1878)
PHONE...................................818 612-6218
William Applebee, Administration
EMP: 56
SALES (est): 2.7MM Privately Held
SIC: 7389 Personal service agents, brokers & bureaus

(P-16628)
APPLIED LANGUAGE SOLUTIONS LLC
1250 W Sunflower, La Habra (90631-9286)
PHONE...................................800 579-5010
Gavin Wheeldon, Mng Member
EMP: 102
SALES (est): 4.3MM Privately Held
WEB: www.appliedlanguage.com
SIC: 7389 Translation services

(P-16629)
ARAMARK SERVICES INC
17044 Montanero Ave Ste 4, Carson (90746-1338)
PHONE...................................310 635-5000
Chris Leonard, Manager
EMP: 67 Publicly Held
SIC: 7389 Coffee service
HQ: Aramark Services, Inc.
2400 Market St Ste 600
Philadelphia PA 19103
215 238-3000

(P-16630)
ARCANA CORPORATION
118 Nopalitos Way, Santa Barbara (93103-3629)
P.O. Box 4400 (93140-4400)
PHONE...................................805 882-1305
Scot Smigel, President
EMP: 50
SALES (est): 3.6MM Privately Held
SIC: 7389 Hotel & motel reservation service

(P-16631)
ASPIRIANT LLC
50 California St Ste 2600, San Francisco (94111-4704)
PHONE...................................415 371-7800
Raymond Edwards, Branch Mgr
EMP: 50 Privately Held
SIC: 7389 Financial services
PA: Aspiriant, Llc
11100 Santa Monica Blvd
Los Angeles CA 90025

(P-16632)
ASSIST 65 PLUS
111 W 7th St Ste 211, Los Angeles (90014-3933)
PHONE...................................323 557-4426
Kirbi Toure, Partner
EMP: 50 EST: 2011
SALES (est): 1.1MM Privately Held
SIC: 7389

(P-16633)
ASSOCIATED LANDSCAPE
Also Called: Associated Group
2420 S Eastern Ave, Commerce (90040-1415)
PHONE...................................714 558-6100
Laurie Resnick, President
Patrick Skalka, COO
Greg Salmeri, Vice Pres
Stephanie Cervantes, Project Mgr
EMP: 90
SQ FT: 30,000
SALES (est): 13.1MM Privately Held
WEB: www.associatedgroup.biz
SIC: 7389 0781 Plant care service; decoration service for special events; landscape services

(P-16634)
AT&T CORP
5130 Hacienda Dr Fl 1, Dublin (94568-7598)
PHONE...................................925 560-5011
Louis Casali, Principal

Lloyd V Antwerp, Senior Mgr
EMP: 305
SALES (corp-wide): 170.7B Publicly Held
SIC: 7389 Personal service agents, brokers & bureaus
HQ: At&T Corp.
1 At&T Way
Bedminster NJ 07921
800 403-3302

(P-16635)
ATEL CORPORATION
600 Montgomery St Ste 900, San Francisco (94111-2711)
PHONE...................................415 989-8800
Dean L Cash, President
Vasco Morais, Exec VP
Paritosh Choksi, Vice Pres
Jim Ryan, Vice Pres
Janet Nicolas, Controller
EMP: 61
SQ FT: 2,000
SALES (est): 2.8MM Privately Held
SIC: 7389 Office facilities & secretarial service rental
PA: Atel Capital Group
600 Montgomery St Fl 9
San Francisco CA 94111

(P-16636)
AURA FINANCIAL CORPORATION
303 2nd St Ste N550, San Francisco (94107-3614)
PHONE...................................415 391-2431
James Michael Gutierrez, CEO
Jeff Hilton, CFO
Chris Motes, Vice Pres
Devender Gollapally, Sr Software Eng
Akshay Buradkar, Engineer
EMP: 60
SALES: 3.3MM Privately Held
SIC: 7389 Financial services

(P-16637)
AUTHORITY TAX SERVICES LLC
Also Called: Tax Problem Center
777 S Figueroa St # 1900, Los Angeles (90017-5817)
PHONE...................................213 486-5135
EMP: 60
SALES (est): 3.9MM Privately Held
SIC: 7389

(P-16638)
AUTOCRIB INC
2882 Dow Ave, Tustin (92780-7258)
PHONE...................................714 274-0400
Stephen Pixley, CEO
James McMahon, Vice Pres
Jason Racette, Vice Pres
Mark Van Bloem, Vice Pres
Jennie Vaage, Opers Staff
▲ EMP: 150
SQ FT: 58,000
SALES (est): 26.2MM Privately Held
SIC: 7389 3581 Inventory computing service; automatic vending machines

(P-16639)
AVANTI AGENCY CORPORATION
282 S Anita Dr, Orange (92868-3308)
P.O. Box 5406 (92863-5406)
PHONE...................................714 935-0900
Kenneth Thompson, President
Art Olson, Marketing Staff
EMP: 400
SALES (est): 14.6MM Privately Held
SIC: 7389 Personal service agents, brokers & bureaus

(P-16640)
AVAYA INC (HQ)
4655 Great America Pkwy, Santa Clara (95054-1236)
PHONE...................................908 953-6000
Jim Chirico, President
Michael M Runda, President
Patrick O'Malley, CFO
Shefali Shah, Officer
Amy Fliegelman Olli, Senior VP
EMP: 148

SALES (est): 1.7B Publicly Held
WEB: www.avaya.com
SIC: 7389 Telephone answering service; telephone directory distribution, contract or fee basis; telephone services

(P-16641)
AVITAS SYSTEMS INC
2882 Sand Hill Rd Ste 240, Menlo Park (94025-7057)
PHONE...................................650 233-3900
Kenneth Alferez,
EMP: 51 EST: 2017
SQ FT: 6,000
SALES (est): 651.2K Privately Held
SIC: 7389 Industrial & commercial equipment inspection service; petroleum refinery inspection service; pipeline & power line inspection service

(P-16642)
B RILEY FINANCIAL INC (PA)
21255 Burbank Blvd # 400, Woodland Hills (91367-6747)
PHONE...................................818 884-3737
Bryant R Riley, Ch of Bd
Alan N Forman, Exec VP
Howard Weitzman, Senior VP
EMP: 143
SALES: 422.9MM Publicly Held
SIC: 7389 Financial services; merchandise liquidators

(P-16643)
BAD BOYS BAIL BONDS INC (PA)
595 Park Ave Ste 200, San Jose (95110-2641)
PHONE...................................408 298-3333
Clifford J Stanley, President
Craig A Stanley, Vice Pres
George Wallace, General Mgr
▲ EMP: 75
SQ FT: 3,000
SALES (est): 16MM Privately Held
SIC: 7389 Bail bonding

(P-16644)
BANK OF NEW YORK MELLON CORP
Also Called: Bny Mellon Asset Servicing
100 Pine St Ste 3200, San Francisco (94111-5218)
PHONE...................................415 399-4450
John Wetherill, Director
EMP: 60
SALES (corp-wide): 16.3B Publicly Held
SIC: 7389 6733 Financial services; trusts, except educational, religious, charity: management
PA: The Bank Of New York Mellon Corporation
240 E Greenwich St
New York NY 10007
212 495-1784

(P-16645)
BANKCARD SERVICES (PA)
21281 S Western Ave, Torrance (90501-2958)
PHONE...................................213 365-1122
EMP: 200
SALES (est): 17.1MM Privately Held
SIC: 7389 Credit card service

(P-16646)
BATES SAMPLE CASE COMPANY INC
Also Called: Bates Display & Packaging
5995 W Park Dr, Chino Hills (91709-6301)
PHONE...................................951 371-4922
Robert Sherman, President
Emmagene Sherman, Corp Secy
▲ EMP: 60
SQ FT: 36,000
SALES (est): 8MM Privately Held
WEB: www.batesdisplay.com
SIC: 7389 Packaging & labeling services

(P-16647)
BENCHMARK-TECH CORPORATION
Also Called: Chaminade of Santa Cruz
1 Chaminade Ln, Santa Cruz (95065-1524)
PHONE...................................831 475-5600

Tom O'Shea, *Vice Pres*
Rebecca Stimler, *Sales Staff*
Aaron Ackerman, *Clerk*
EMP: 200
SQ FT: 61,000
SALES (est): 12.4MM **Privately Held**
SIC: 7389 Convention & show services

(P-16648)
BENEFICENT TECHNOLOGY INC
Also Called: Benetech
480 California Ave # 201, Palo Alto
(94306-1623)
PHONE...................650 644-3400
James R Fruchterman, *CEO*
Betsy Beaumon, *President*
Jane Poole, *Vice Pres*
Teresa Jenna, *Program Mgr*
Lisa Wadors, *Program Mgr*
EMP: 50 **EST:** 2001
SALES: 12.9MM **Privately Held**
WEB: www.benetech.org
SIC: 7389 Personal service agents, brokers & bureaus

(P-16649)
BERSHTEL ENTERPRISES LLC (PA)
Also Called: We Pack It All
2745 Huntington Dr, Duarte (91010-2302)
PHONE...................626 301-9214
Jack Bershtel, *President*
Sharon Bershtel, *CFO*
Gaby Gaiz, *Treasurer*
George Gellert, *Vice Pres*
Robert Gellert, *Vice Pres*
EMP: 145
SQ FT: 50,000
SALES (est): 31.5MM **Privately Held**
WEB: www.wepackitall.com
SIC: 7389 Packaging & labeling services

(P-16650)
BEVERLY HILLS LINGUAL INST
8383 Wilshire Blvd # 250, Beverly Hills
(90211-2425)
PHONE...................323 651-5000
Nevena Martinovic, *Consultant*
Aleksa Martinovic, *President*
EMP: 50
SALES (est): 1.9MM **Privately Held**
WEB: www.bhlingual.com
SIC: 7389 Translation services

(P-16651)
BEX PORTFOLIO LLC
925 E Meadow Dr, Palo Alto (94303-4233)
PHONE...................650 494-3700
EMP: 92
SALES (est): 74.7K
SALES (corp-wide): 1.4B **Privately Held**
SIC: 7389 Financial services
HQ: Essex Portfolio, L.P.
　　925 E Meadow Dr
　　Palo Alto CA 94303

(P-16652)
BLAINE CONVENTION SERVICES INC
114 S Berry St, Brea (92821-4826)
PHONE...................714 522-8270
Thomas W Blaine Sr, *President*
Dustin Blaine, *Vice Pres*
Lola Alvitre, *Manager*
EMP: 960
SQ FT: 107,000
SALES (est): 10.7MM **Privately Held**
WEB: www.blaineconventionservices.com
SIC: 7389 7359 2542 4731 Exhibit construction by industrial contractors; trade show arrangement; equipment rental & leasing; partitions & fixtures, except wood; domestic freight forwarding

(P-16653)
BLUE CHIP INVENTORY SERVICE
14852 Ventura Blvd # 112, Sherman Oaks
(91403-3499)
PHONE...................818 461-1765
Gerard J Walsh, *President*
Carol F Edgington, *Vice Pres*
Steve Keppler, *Vice Pres*

EMP: 70
SQ FT: 1,800
SALES (est): 3.7MM **Privately Held**
WEB: www.inventoryalliance.com
SIC: 7389 Inventory computing service

(P-16654)
BLUE LAGOON TEXTILE INC
737 Crocker St, Los Angeles (90021-1411)
PHONE...................213 590-4545
Kamran Amirianfar, *CEO*
John Malonie, *Vice Pres*
EMP: 50
SALES (est): 121.5K **Privately Held**
SIC: 7389 Textile & apparel services

(P-16655)
BLX GROUP LLC (PA)
777 S Figueroa St Ste 800, Los Angeles
(90017-5804)
PHONE...................213 612-2200
Jeff Smith, *Director*
Robert Kronman, *Chief Mktg Ofcr*
Rosanne Lehman, *Associate Dir*
Greg Rowan, *Associate Dir*
Nicole Assa, *Managing Dir*
EMP: 60 **EST:** 2000
SALES (est): 5.6MM **Privately Held**
SIC: 7389 Financial services

(P-16656)
BONHAMS BTTRFLDS ACTNEERS CORP (DH)
220 San Bruno Ave, San Francisco
(94103-5018)
PHONE...................415 861-7500
Robert Brooks, *Principal*
Malcom Barber, *CEO*
Pactric Meade, *COO*
Susan Abeles, *Vice Pres*
Rupert Banner, *Vice Pres*
▲ **EMP:** 150 **EST:** 1793
SQ FT: 45,000
SALES (est): 25.8MM
SALES (corp-wide): 555.1K **Privately Held**
SIC: 7389 Auctioneers, fee basis
HQ: Bonhams 1793 Limited
　　101 New Bond Street
　　London W1S 1
　　207 447-7447

(P-16657)
BONHAMS CORPORATION
220 San Bruno Ave, San Francisco
(94103-5018)
PHONE...................415 861-7500
EMP: 140
SALES (est): 8.7MM **Privately Held**
SIC: 7389

(P-16658)
BOSHART AUTOMOTIVE TSTG SVCS
1840 S Carlos Ave 15, Ontario
(91761-8005)
PHONE...................909 466-1602
Ken Boshart, *President*
Lynn Boshart, *Vice Pres*
EMP: 54
SQ FT: 13,567
SALES (est): 3.2MM **Privately Held**
SIC: 7389 7549 Inspection & testing services; emissions testing without repairs, automotive

(P-16659)
BOULEVARD ENTERTAINMENT INC
903 S Lake St Ste 202, Burbank
(91502-2435)
P.O. Box 1188 (91507-1188)
PHONE...................818 840-6969
Scott Jacobson, *President*
David Jacobson, *Vice Pres*
EMP: 108
SALES (est): 4.5MM **Privately Held**
WEB: www.blvdent.com
SIC: 7389 Telephone services

(P-16660)
BOX BROS CORP
825 Wilshire Blvd, Santa Monica
(90401-1809)
PHONE...................310 394-8660
John Simpson,

Mark Frydman, *Branch Mgr*
EMP: 50
SQ FT: 6,930
SALES (corp-wide): 13.4MM **Privately Held**
SIC: 7389 Mailbox rental & related service; packaging & labeling services
PA: Box Bros. Corp.
　　22124 Ventura Blvd
　　Woodland Hills CA 91364
　　818 703-9393

(P-16661)
BRADFORD MESSENGER SERVICE
4955 E Andersen Ave # 118, Fresno
(93727-1543)
PHONE...................559 252-0775
Liner Bluron, *Manager*
EMP: 60
SQ FT: 1,500
SALES (est): 1.6MM **Privately Held**
SIC: 7389 Courier or messenger service

(P-16662)
BRAGG INVESTMENT COMPANY INC (PA)
Also Called: Bragg Crane & Rigging
6251 N Paramount Blvd, Long Beach
(90805-3713)
P.O. Box 727 (90801-0727)
PHONE...................562 984-2400
Marilynn Bragg, *CEO*
Craig Geiger, *Exec VP*
Mike Roy, *Exec VP*
Scott Bragg, *Vice Pres*
Joseph Damico, *Vice Pres*
EMP: 580
SQ FT: 50,000
SALES (est): 381.4MM **Privately Held**
SIC: 7389 7353 1791 Crane & aerial lift service; heavy construction equipment rental; structural steel erection

(P-16663)
BRIGHTCURRENT INC
426 17th St Ste 700, Oakland
(94612-2850)
PHONE...................877 896-3306
John Bourne, *CEO*
EMP: 75
SQ FT: 20,000
SALES (est): 5.1MM
SALES (corp-wide): 16.5MM **Privately Held**
SIC: 7389 Telemarketing services
PA: Lpsh Holdings, Inc.
　　27368 Via Industria
　　Temecula CA 92590
　　855 647-5061

(P-16664)
BUTTER PADDLE
Also Called: Butter Paddle, The
33 N Santa Cruz Ave, Los Gatos
(95030-5916)
PHONE...................408 395-1678
Doris Beccia, *President*
Mumuna Ali, *President*
Mary Ann Jeffri, *Store Mgr*
EMP: 70 **EST:** 1967
SQ FT: 2,000
SALES (est): 5.5MM **Privately Held**
SIC: 7389 Fund raising organizations

(P-16665)
CADFORCE INC
10811 Wash Blvd Ste 302, Culver City
(90232-3660)
PHONE...................310 876-1800
James Katz, *Vice Pres*
Robert W Vanech, *Principal*
EMP: 800
SALES: 35MM **Privately Held**
WEB: www.cadforce.com
SIC: 7389 Drafting service, except temporary help

(P-16666)
CALIFORNIA CREDITS GROUP LLC
87 N Raymond Ave Ste 526, Pasadena
(91103-3904)
PHONE...................626 584-9800
John Simpson,

Marianne Serpa, *Associate Dir*
Richard Mayer, *Info Tech Mgr*
Lan Hai, *Opers Staff*
Mark Dabell, *Director*
EMP: 50
SALES (est): 5.3MM **Privately Held**
WEB: www.ccg.com
SIC: 7389 Personal service agents, brokers & bureaus

(P-16667)
CALIFORNIA HLTH COLLABORATIVE (PA)
1680 W Shaw Ave, Fresno (93711-3504)
PHONE...................559 221-6315
Gary Erickson, *Chairman*
Sharon Johnson, *Exec Dir*
Stephen Ramirez, *Exec Dir*
Stephanie Chandler, *Program Mgr*
Marisol Zamora, *Program Mgr*
EMP: 68
SQ FT: 11,400
SALES: 7.2MM **Privately Held**
WEB: www.california.hometownlocator.com
SIC: 7389 Fund raising organizations

(P-16668)
CALIFORNIA SKATEPARKS
285 N Benson Ave, Upland (91786-5614)
PHONE...................909 949-1601
Joseph M Ciaglia Jr, *President*
Bill Minadeo, *Vice Pres*
Brian Pino, *Project Mgr*
Mario Rodriguez, *Project Mgr*
Ashley Ciaglia, *Marketing Mgr*
EMP: 150
SALES (est): 5.6MM **Privately Held**
SIC: 7389

(P-16669)
CALIFORNIA TRAFFIC CONTROL
Also Called: California Traffic Ctrl Svcs
3333 Cherry Ave, Long Beach
(90807-4901)
PHONE...................562 595-7575
Delores Kepl, *CFO*
EMP: 70
SALES (est): 6.5MM **Privately Held**
SIC: 7389 Flagging service (traffic control)

(P-16670)
CALL CENTER SERVICES INTL LLC
809 Bowsprit Rd Ste 204, Chula Vista
(91914-4527)
PHONE...................858 427-8500
Jose Erick Esparza, *President*
Mariana Alford, *Shareholder*
Jaime Edgar Esparza, *Shareholder*
Veronica Anguiano, *President*
Jorge Oros, *COO*
EMP: 60
SQ FT: 1,200
SALES (est): 6.2MM **Privately Held**
SIC: 7389 Telemarketing services

(P-16671)
CAMARILLO RANCH FOUNDATION
201 Camarillo Ranch Rd, Camarillo
(93012-5081)
PHONE...................805 389-8182
Bruce Fuhrman, *Vice Pres*
EMP: 75
SALES: 842.2K **Privately Held**
SIC: 7389 Fund raising organizations

(P-16672)
CANON SOLUTIONS AMERICA INC
2382 Faraday Ave Ste 250, Carlsbad
(92008-7262)
PHONE...................760 438-6990
EMP: 79
SALES (corp-wide): 43.8B **Privately Held**
SIC: 7389
HQ: Canon Solutions America, Inc.
　　1 Canon Park
　　Melville NY 11747
　　631 330-5000

(P-16673)
CAPITOL RECORDS LLC
Also Called: EMI Music Distribution
1750 Vine St, Los Angeles (90028-5274)
PHONE..........................213 462-6252
Colin Finkelstein, *Mng Member*
EMP: 1500
SQ FT: 200,000
SALES (est): 98.4MM
SALES (corp-wide): 78.1MM **Privately Held**
WEB: www.capitolrecords.com
SIC: 7389 8999 Music & broadcasting services; music arranging & composing
HQ: Universal Music Group, Inc.
2220 Colorado Ave
Santa Monica CA 90404
310 865-4000

(P-16674)
CARBON 38 INC
10000 Wash Blvd Ste 800, Culver City (90232-2784)
PHONE..........................888 723-5838
Katie Warner Johnson, *CEO*
Lisa Kraynak, *Chief Mktg Ofcr*
Jenny Neymark, *Creative Dir*
Caroline Gogolak, *Principal*
Nicole Andrews, *Retailers*
EMP: 90
SALES (est): 1.3MM **Privately Held**
SIC: 7389 Styling of fashions, apparel, furniture, textiles, etc.

(P-16675)
CARDFLEX INC
2900 Bristol St Bldg F, Costa Mesa (92626-5981)
PHONE..........................714 361-1900
Andrew M Phillips, *President*
Todd Gordon, *Manager*
Martin Phillips, *Manager*
EMP: 75
SALES (est): 7.5MM **Privately Held**
SIC: 7389 Credit card service

(P-16676)
CARDSERVICE INTERNATIONAL INC
Also Called: C S I
4565 Industrial St Ste 7k, Simi Valley (93063-3464)
PHONE..........................800 217-4622
Chuck Burtzloft, *Branch Mgr*
EMP: 650
SALES (corp-wide): 5.8B **Publicly Held**
WEB: www.creditcardresults.com
SIC: 7389 7371 6153 Credit card service; custom computer programming services; short-term business credit
HQ: Cardservice International, Inc.
5898 Condor Dr 220
Moorpark CA 93021

(P-16677)
CARDSERVICE INTERNATIONAL INC
Also Called: Csi
1538 W Commonwealth Ave, Fullerton (92833-2754)
PHONE..........................714 773-1778
EMP: 56
SALES (corp-wide): 2B **Privately Held**
SIC: 7389
HQ: Cardservice International, Inc.
5898 Condor Dr 220
Moorpark CA 93021
805 648-1425

(P-16678)
CARECREDIT LLC
555 Anton Blvd Ste 700, Costa Mesa (92626-7659)
PHONE..........................800 300-3046
Kurt Grossheim, *Principal*
Mario Cozzi, *President*
Gregory Pierce, *Vice Pres*
Denise Rogers, *Vice Pres*
Kirk Sweigard, *Vice Pres*
EMP: 120

SALES (est): 9.5MM
SALES (corp-wide): 18.2B **Publicly Held**
WEB: www.carecredit.com
SIC: 7389 8742 Financial services; banking & finance consultant
PA: Synchrony Financial
777 Long Ridge Rd
Stamford CT 06902
203 585-2400

(P-16679)
CASECENTRAL INC (DH)
Also Called: Casecentral.com
1055 E Colo Blvd Ste 400, Pasadena (91106)
PHONE..........................415 989-2300
Christopher S Kruse, *President*
Peter H Kruse, *Vice Pres*
Jay O'Connor, *Vice Pres*
Philip Sakakihara, *Vice Pres*
Ted Sergott, *Vice Pres*
EMP: 60
SALES (est): 7.5MM
SALES (corp-wide): 2.2B **Privately Held**
WEB: www.casecentral.com
SIC: 7389 4813 4226 Legal & tax services; ; document & office records storage
HQ: Guidance Software, Inc.
1055 E Colo Blvd Ste 400
Pasadena CA 91106
626 229-9191

(P-16680)
CASHEDGE INC
525 Almanor Ave Ste 150, Sunnyvale (94085-3545)
PHONE..........................408 541-3900
McKenzie Lyons, *Principal*
EMP: 100
SALES (corp-wide): 5.8B **Publicly Held**
WEB: www.cashedge.com
SIC: 7389 Financial services
HQ: Cashedge Inc.
255 Fiserv Dr
Brookfield WI 53045
262 879-5000

(P-16681)
CATATI ROHNERT PARK INC
1400 Magnolia Ave, Rohnert Park (94928-8129)
PHONE..........................707 792-4531
Jane Wheeler, *Principal*
Alicia Cartwright, *Librarian*
Monica Fong, *Assistant*
EMP: 50
SALES (est): 2MM **Privately Held**
SIC: 7389 Personal service agents, brokers & bureaus

(P-16682)
CATCHPOINT SYSTEMS INC
6080 Center Dr Ste 715, Los Angeles (90045-9227)
PHONE..........................646 727-4557
Mehdi Daoudi, *Branch Mgr*
EMP: 136 **Privately Held**
SIC: 7389 Automobile recovery service
PA: Catchpoint Systems, Inc.
150 W 30th St Fl 3
New York NY 10001

(P-16683)
CENTRAL PAYMENT CO LLC
2350 Kerner Blvd Ste 300, San Rafael (94901-5597)
PHONE..........................415 462-8335
Matthew Hyman, *Managing Prtnr*
Eric Barth, *COO*
John Hinkle, *CFO*
Joseph Astobiza, *Executive*
Bryan Brahms, *Executive*
EMP: 99
SALES (est): 13.1MM **Privately Held**
WEB: www.centralpaymentcorp.com
SIC: 7389 Credit card service

(P-16684)
CENTRAL SVC CTR & EXEC OFFS
1751 Plum Ln, Redlands (92374-4505)
PHONE..........................909 307-6555
Cynthia Harnish Breunig, *CEO*
EMP: 50

SALES (est): 851.3K **Privately Held**
SIC: 7389 Personal service agents, brokers & bureaus

(P-16685)
CENTRELINK INSUR & FINCL SVCS
Also Called: Centrelink Ins & Fincl Svcs
20750 Ventura Blvd # 300, Woodland Hills (91364-2338)
PHONE..........................818 587-2001
Barry Wolfe, *President*
EMP: 90
SALES (est): 3.3MM **Privately Held**
SIC: 7389 8741 Financial services; financial management for business

(P-16686)
CENTURY BANKCARD SERVICES
25129 The Old Rd Ste 222, Stevenson Ranch (91381-2281)
PHONE..........................818 700-3100
Scott Scherr, *President*
EMP: 55
SQ FT: 4,200
SALES (est): 2.7MM
SALES (corp-wide): 323.5MM **Publicly Held**
WEB: www.centurybankcard.com
SIC: 7389 Credit card service
HQ: Pace Payment Systems, Inc.
30 Burton Hills Blvd
Nashville TN

(P-16687)
CERAMIC DECORATING COMPANY INC
4651 Sheila St, Commerce (90040-1003)
PHONE..........................323 268-5135
Chad A Johnson, *CEO*
Allan Johnson, *President*
W Allan Johnson, *CEO*
Burnell D Johnson, *Admin Sec*
Anthony Castillo, *Opers Staff*
EMP: 50 EST: 1934
SQ FT: 30,290
SALES (est): 8.1MM **Privately Held**
WEB: www.ceramicdecoratingco.com
SIC: 7389 2396 Labeling bottles, cans, cartons, etc.; lettering service; automotive & apparel trimmings

(P-16688)
CESARS PRODUCTIONS
91 Miguel St, San Francisco (94131-2605)
PHONE..........................415 821-1156
Cesar Ascarrunz, *Owner*
EMP: 50
SALES (est): 2MM **Privately Held**
WEB: www.cesarsproductions.com
SIC: 7389 Music recording producer

(P-16689)
CETERA FINANCIAL GROUP INC (PA)
200 N Pacific Coast Hwy # 11, El Segundo (90245-5628)
PHONE..........................866 489-3100
Robert Moore, *CEO*
George Barker, *Partner*
Adam Antoniades, *President*
Thomas B Taylor, *President*
Catherine Bonneau, *COO*
EMP: 148
SQ FT: 70,000
SALES (est): 290.6MM **Privately Held**
SIC: 7389 6282 Financial services; investment advisory service

(P-16690)
CHANGE HEALTHCARE TECH LLC
5110 E Clinton Way # 101, Fresno (93727-2040)
PHONE..........................559 455-4000
Glenda Josey, *Principal*
Denise Thompson, *Manager*
EMP: 120
SALES (corp-wide): 214.3B **Publicly Held**
WEB: www.per-se.com
SIC: 7389 Personal service agents, brokers & bureaus

HQ: Change Healthcare Technologies, Llc
5995 Windward Pkwy
Alpharetta GA 30005

(P-16691)
CHARLES SCHWAB CORPORATION
27580 Ynez Rd Ste A, Temecula (92591-4667)
PHONE..........................951 587-2840
Mark Morgan, *Manager*
EMP: 104
SALES (corp-wide): 10.1B **Publicly Held**
SIC: 7389 6282 6211 Financial services; investment advice; stock brokers & dealers
PA: The Charles Schwab Corporation
211 Main St Fl 17
San Francisco CA 94105
415 667-7000

(P-16692)
CHERRY AVENUE AUCTION INC
4640 S Cherry Ave, Fresno (93706-5717)
PHONE..........................559 266-9856
William Mitchell, *President*
Margaret Mitchell, *Treasurer*
EMP: 50
SQ FT: 1,500
SALES (est): 3.6MM **Privately Held**
WEB: www.cherryavenueauction.com
SIC: 7389 Flea market

(P-16693)
CIRTECH INC
250 E Emerson Ave, Orange (92865-3317)
PHONE..........................714 921-0860
Brad Reese, *President*
Frank E Reese, *CEO*
Karen Bever, *Manager*
EMP: 50
SQ FT: 30,000
SALES (est): 1.7MM
SALES (corp-wide): 7MM **Privately Held**
WEB: www.cirtech.com
SIC: 7389 3672 Printed circuitry graphic layout; printed circuit boards; wiring boards
PA: Apct Holdings, Llc
3495 De La Cruz Blvd
Santa Clara CA 95054
408 727-6442

(P-16694)
CISCO SYSTEMS CAPITAL CORP (HQ)
170 W Tasman Dr, San Jose (95134-1706)
PHONE..........................610 386-5870
Kristine A Snow, *President*
David A Rogan, *President*
Prat Bhatt, *Treasurer*
David K Holland, *Treasurer*
John T Chambers, *Principal*
EMP: 132
SALES (est): 38.7MM
SALES (corp-wide): 51.9B **Publicly Held**
SIC: 7389 Financial services
PA: Cisco Systems, Inc.
170 W Tasman Dr
San Jose CA 95134
408 526-4000

(P-16695)
CISCO WEBEX LLC (HQ)
Also Called: Webex.com
170 W Tasman Dr, San Jose (95134-1706)
PHONE..........................408 435-7000
Subrah S Iyar, *President*
Jeffrey Schmidt, *Vice Pres*
Praful Shah, *Vice Pres*
Philip A Long, *Info Tech Dir*
Jennifer Mann, *Info Tech Mgr*
EMP: 1108
SQ FT: 160,000
SALES (est): 199.1MM
SALES (corp-wide): 51.9B **Publicly Held**
WEB: www.webex.com
SIC: 7389 4813 Teleconferencing services; data telephone communications; voice telephone communications
PA: Cisco Systems, Inc.
170 W Tasman Dr
San Jose CA 95134
408 526-4000

PRODUCTS & SVCS

(P-16696)
CITY OF FRESNO
Also Called: Fresno Convention Center
700 M St, Fresno (93721-2715)
PHONE..................................559 445-8200
Michael Swinney, *Director*
Lyn Higginson, *Finance*
EMP: 60 Privately Held
WEB: www.fresnocitizencorps.org
SIC: 7389 9111 Convention & show serv-
ices; mayors' offices
PA: City Of Fresno
2600 Fresno St
Fresno CA 93721
559 621-7001

(P-16697)
CITY OF LONG BEACH
Also Called: Long Bch Convention Entrmt Ctr
300 E Ocean Blvd, Long Beach
(90802-4825)
PHONE..................................562 436-3636
David Gordon, *Manager*
EMP: 300 Privately Held
WEB: www.polb.com
SIC: 7389 8611 6512 Convention & show
services; business associations; nonresi-
dential building operators
PA: City Of Long Beach
411 W Ocean Blvd
Long Beach CA 90802
562 570-6450

(P-16698)
CITY OF PALO ALTO
Also Called: Water Quality Control Plant
2501 Embarcadero Way, Palo Alto
(94303-3326)
PHONE..................................650 329-2598
Richard Wetzel, *Branch Mgr*
EMP: 70 Privately Held
SIC: 7389 9111 8748 Sewer inspection
service; cloth cutting, bolting or winding;
city & town managers' offices; ; business
consulting
PA: City Of Palo Alto
250 Hamilton Ave
Palo Alto CA 94301
650 329-2571

(P-16699)
CITY OF RIVERSIDE
Also Called: Riverside Convention Center
3485 Mission Inn Ave, Riverside
(92501-3304)
PHONE..................................951 346-4700
Scott Megna, *General Mgr*
EMP: 100 Privately Held
SIC: 7389 Convention & show services
PA: City Of Riverside
3900 Main St Fl 7
Riverside CA 92522
951 826-5311

(P-16700)
CITY OF SAN JOSE
Also Called: Conventions Arts & Entrmt
408 Almaden Blvd, San Jose (95110-2709)
PHONE..................................408 277-5277
Nancy Johnson, *Branch Mgr*
Dave Costain, *COO*
Sonia Basa, *Admin Asst*
Tom Gallagher, *Project Mgr*
Atlanta Ngo, *Technology*
EMP: 300 Privately Held
WEB: www.csjfinance.org
SIC: 7389 9512 Convention & show serv-
ices; land, mineral & wildlife conservation;
PA: City Of San Jose
200 E Santa Clara St
San Jose CA 95113
408 535-3500

(P-16701)
CITY OF SUNNYVALE
221 Commercial St, Sunnyvale
(94085-4509)
P.O. Box 3707 (94088-3707)
PHONE..................................408 730-7510
James Craig, *Superintendent*
EMP: 200 Privately Held
SIC: 7389 Field warehousing
PA: City Of Sunnyvale
456 W Olive Ave
Sunnyvale CA 94086
408 730-7415

(P-16702)
CITY OF VISALIA
Also Called: Visalia Convention Center
303 E Acequia Ave, Visalia (93291-6341)
PHONE..................................559 713-4000
Wally Roeben, *General Mgr*
EMP: 60 Privately Held
SIC: 7389 Convention & show services
PA: Visalia, City Of (Inc)
707 W Acequia Ave
Visalia CA 93291
559 713-4565

(P-16703)
CITY RISE INC (PA)
Also Called: City Rise Services
1225 S Sacramento St, Lodi (95240-5703)
PHONE..................................209 333-0807
Nicole Beadles, *CEO*
EMP: 112 EST: 2014
SQ FT: 250,000
SALES: 1.5MM Privately Held
SIC: 7389 Flagging service (traffic control)

(P-16704)
CK ENTERPRISES INC
Also Called: World Tuned Radio
102 Copperwood Way Ste H, Oceanside
(92058-3866)
PHONE..................................760 967-8863
Christopher Parks, *President*
EMP: 87
SALES (est): 2.5MM Privately Held
SIC: 7389

(P-16705)
CLUB SPORT OF FREMONT
46650 Landing Pkwy, Fremont
(94538-6420)
PHONE..................................510 226-8500
Angela Grissar, *Business Mgr*
Guin Cloninger, *Partner*
EMP: 200
SALES (est): 13.8MM Privately Held
SIC: 7389 Artists' agents & brokers

(P-16706)
**CLUM MORFORD DISTRIBUTING
(PA)**
Also Called: Can-West Directory Distrs
20 Ragsdale Dr Ste 100, Monterey
(93940-7812)
PHONE..................................831 333-1100
Woodworth B Clum Jr, *President*
David Forey, *Senior VP*
Judy Carrillo, *Admin Sec*
Kristi Smaby, *Human Res Dir*
EMP: 100
SALES (est): 4.4MM Privately Held
SIC: 7389 Telephone directory distribution,
contract or fee basis

(P-16707)
CMG FINANCIAL SERVICES
3160 Crow Canyon Rd # 400, San Ramon
(94583-1368)
PHONE..................................925 983-3073
Christopher M George, *CEO*
Nora Garcia, *Partner*
Nicole Schorno, *Partner*
Cindy Brown, *Officer*
Sean Martin, *Officer*
EMP: 76
SALES (est): 12.1MM Privately Held
SIC: 7389 Financial services

(P-16708)
COAST ENVIRONMENTAL INC
2221 Las Palmas Dr Ste J, Carlsbad
(92011-1528)
PHONE..................................760 929-9570
Dan Hughes, *President*
Pat Foltz, *Sales Staff*
Adam Ramos, *Manager*
Lisa Smith, *Manager*
▲ EMP: 60
SQ FT: 25,000
SALES (est): 6.7MM Privately Held
WEB: www.coastenvironmental.com
SIC: 7389 Safety inspection service

(P-16709)
COASTAL CLOSEOUTS INC
Also Called: West Coast Rags
100 Oceangate Ste 1200, Long Beach
(90802-4324)
PHONE..................................323 589-7900
EMP: 52
SQ FT: 68,000
SALES (est): 4.1MM Privately Held
SIC: 7389

(P-16710)
**COASTAL INTERNATIONAL INC
(PA)**
Also Called: Coastal Intl Cnstr Svcs
2832 Walnut Ave Ste B, Tustin
(92780-7002)
PHONE..................................415 339-1700
Bruce Green, *CEO*
Rick Broyles, *COO*
Jim Bell, *Vice Pres*
Jesus Lopez, *Vice Pres*
Rich Rebecky, *Vice Pres*
EMP: 65
SQ FT: 12,000
SALES (est): 47MM Privately Held
WEB: www.coastlintl.com
SIC: 7389 1542 1522 Trade show
arrangement; nonresidential construction;
residential construction

(P-16711)
COHESITY INC (PA)
300 Park Ave Ste 1700, San Jose
(95110-2774)
PHONE..................................855 926-4374
Mohit Aron, *CEO*
Robert Salmon, *COO*
Lynn Lucas, *Chief Mktg Ofcr*
William Ho, *Vice Pres*
Nick Oberhuber, *Vice Pres*
EMP: 500
SQ FT: 98,000
SALES (est): 182.6MM Privately Held
SIC: 7389 Document storage service

(P-16712)
COMPLEX STUDIOS
Also Called: Complex The
2323 Corinth Ave, Los Angeles
(90064-1701)
PHONE..................................310 477-1938
Walter Ulloa, *Owner*
EMP: 50
SQ FT: 19,000
SALES (est): 2.6MM Privately Held
SIC: 7389 Recording studio, noncommer-
cial records

(P-16713)
**COMPUMAIL INFORMATION
SVCS INC**
4057 Port Chicago Hwy # 300, Concord
(94520-1160)
P.O. Box 6756 (94524-1756)
PHONE..................................925 689-7100
Monte G Bish, *President*
Frank Fribley, *CFO*
Michelle Lee Chung, *Controller*
▲ EMP: 75
SQ FT: 22,000
SALES (est): 10MM Privately Held
WEB: www.compumailinc.com
SIC: 7389 Printers' services: folding, collat-
ing

(P-16714)
CONFIRE J P A
1743 Miro Way, Rialto (92376-8630)
PHONE..................................909 356-2375
Richard Britt, *Director*
EMP: 60
SALES (est): 7.4MM Privately Held
SIC: 7389 Personal service agents, bro-
kers & bureaus

(P-16715)
**CONSOLDTED FIRE
PROTECTION LLC (HQ)**
153 Technology Dr Ste 200, Irvine
(92618-2461)
PHONE..................................949 727-3277
Rob Salek, *CEO*
Jonathan King, *Administration*
Jeff Murtari, *Info Tech Dir*
Steve Schwartz, *Project Mgr*
Thet Aung, *Accountant*
EMP: 800
SALES (est): 89.4MM Privately Held
SIC: 7389 Fire protection service other
than forestry or public

(P-16716)
CONTI LIFE COMM PLEA LLC
Also Called: Stoneridge Creek Pleasanton
3300 Stoneridge Creek Way, Pleasanton
(94588-2200)
PHONE..................................925 227-6800
Francis X Rodgers, *Exec Dir*
Troy Bourne, *Vice Pres*
David Tsan, *Opers Staff*
EMP: 51
SALES: 8.1MM Privately Held
SIC: 7389 Personal service agents, bro-
kers & bureaus

(P-16717)
**CONTINENTAL EXCH
SOLUTIONS INC**
Also Called: Ria Financial Services
7001 Village Dr Ste 200, Buena Park
(90621-2232)
PHONE..................................562 345-2100
EMP: 70 Publicly Held
SIC: 7389 Financial services
HQ: Continental Exchange Solutions Inc.
6565 Knott Ave
Buena Park CA 90620
714 522-7044

(P-16718)
**CORPORATE RISK HLDINGS III
INC**
Also Called: Hireright
3349 Michelson Dr Ste 150, Irvine
(92612-8881)
PHONE..................................949 428-5839
John Fennelley, *CEO*
Jerey Wahba, *CFO*
Jim Weber, *Officer*
Paty Doverspike, *Executive*
Angela McElyea, *Executive*
EMP: 1700
SALES (est): 15MM Privately Held
SIC: 7389 Personal investigation service

(P-16719)
COUNTRY VILLA SERVICE CORP
39950 Vista Del Sol, Rancho Mirage
(92270-3206)
PHONE..................................760 340-0053
Georgeanne Slapper, *Branch Mgr*
Penny Beltran, *Records Dir*
Richard Welts, *Info Tech Mgr*
Scott Gillis,
EMP: 83
SALES (corp-wide): 125.3MM Privately
Held
SIC: 7389 Personal service agents, bro-
kers & bureaus
PA: Country Villa Service Corp.
2400 E Katella Ave # 800
Anaheim CA 92806
310 574-3733

(P-16720)
COUNTY OF LOS ANGELES
Also Called: Internal Services Dept
1100 N Eastern Ave, Los Angeles
(90063-3200)
PHONE..................................323 267-2771
Linnette Bookman, *Superintendent*
EMP: 200 Privately Held
WEB: www.co.la.ca.us
SIC: 7389 9631 Telephone services; com-
munications commission, government;
PA: County Of Los Angeles
500 W Temple St Ste 437
Los Angeles CA 90012
213 974-1101

(P-16721)
COUNTY OF MODOC
Also Called: Treasurer/Tax Collector
204 S Court St Ste 6, Alturas (96101-4138)
PHONE..................................530 233-6223
Cheryl Knoch, *Treasurer*
EMP: 250 Privately Held
WEB: www.modoccounty.us
SIC: 7389 Tax collection agency

PA: County Of Modoc
202 W 4th St Ste A
Alturas CA 96101
530 233-6400

(P-16722)
COUNTY OF MONTEREY
Also Called: Telecommunications Dept
855 E Laurel Dr Ste D, Salinas
(93905-1300)
PHONE..................................831 755-4944
Chin Lavonne, *Branch Mgr*
EMP: 100 **Privately Held**
WEB: www.montereycountyfarmbureau.org
SIC: 7389 Personal service agents, bro-
kers & bureaus
PA: County Of Monterey
168 W Alisal St Fl 2
Salinas CA 93901
831 755-5040

(P-16723)
COUNTY OF MONTEREY
Also Called: Dept of Building Inspection
240 Church St Ste 116, Salinas
(93901-2683)
P.O. Box 1208 (93902-1208)
PHONE..................................831 755-5027
Scott Hennessy, *Director*
EMP: 100 **Privately Held**
WEB: www.montereycountyfarmbureau.org
SIC: 7389 9111 8111 Building inspection
service; county supervisors' & executives'
offices; legal services
PA: County Of Monterey
168 W Alisal St Fl 2
Salinas CA 93901
831 755-5040

(P-16724)
**CRAFTWORKS REST
BREWERIES INC**
600 Polk St, San Francisco (94102-3328)
PHONE..................................415 292-5800
Alex Smith, *President*
EMP: 102 **Privately Held**
SIC: 7389 Personal service agents, bro-
kers & bureaus
PA: Craftworks Restaurants & Breweries,
Inc.
8001 Arista Pl Fl 5
Broomfield CO 80021

(P-16725)
CREATE MUSIC GROUP INC
1320 N Wilton Pl, Los Angeles
(90028-8527)
PHONE..................................310 623-0696
Jonathan Strauss, *CEO*
Alexandre Williams, *COO*
EMP: 85
SALES: 30MM **Privately Held**
SIC: 7389 7371 Music distribution sys-
tems; computer software development &
applications

(P-16726)
**CREATIVE DESIGN CONS INC
(PA)**
Also Called: C D C
2915 Red Hill Ave G201, Costa Mesa
(92626-5916)
PHONE..................................714 641-4868
Dana Eggerts, *Principal*
Brian Richardson, *Info Tech Mgr*
Rick Betts, *Project Mgr*
Shawna Bong, *Project Mgr*
Cassandra Hanhart, *Project Mgr*
EMP: 100 **EST:** 1994
SQ FT: 9,988
SALES (est): 11.7MM **Privately Held**
WEB: www.cdcdesigns.com
SIC: 7389 Interior designer

(P-16727)
**CREATIVE TECHNOLOGY
GROUP INC (DH)**
14000 Arminta St, Panorama City
(91402-6080)
PHONE..................................818 779-2400
Graham Andrews, *President*
Stephen Gray, *COO*
Bruce Thurston, *Business Dir*
Augie Dellapi, *General Mgr*

Sim Elwood, *General Mgr*
▲ EMP: 80
SALES (est): 43.8MM
SALES (corp-wide): 25.9MM **Privately
Held**
WEB: www.avesco.com
SIC: 7389 Teleconferencing services
HQ: Creative Technology Group Limited
F T V, Unit E2
Crawley W SUSSEX
129 358-3400

(P-16728)
**CREDIT CARD SERVICES INC
(PA)**
Also Called: Bankcard Services
21281 S Western Ave, Torrance
(90501-2958)
PHONE..................................213 365-1122
Patrick S Hong, *CEO*
Joe Kim, *Technical Staff*
Glen Lim, *Technical Staff*
John Lee, *Director*
EMP: 95
SQ FT: 17,000
SALES (est): 19.8MM **Privately Held**
WEB: www.e-bankcard.com
SIC: 7389 Credit card service

(P-16729)
CREDIT KARMA INC (PA)
760 Market St Ste 500, San Francisco
(94102-2410)
PHONE..................................415 510-5059
Kenneth Lin, *CEO*
Yitao Wang, *Engineer*
Matthew Dobos, *Accountant*
Susannah Wright, *General Counsel*
Gael Gates, *Counsel*
EMP: 148
SQ FT: 245,000
SALES (est): 133.2MM **Privately Held**
SIC: 7389 Credit card service

(P-16730)
CROSSCHECK INC (PA)
1440 N Mcdowell Blvd, Petaluma
(94954-6515)
P.O. Box 6008 (94955-6008)
PHONE..................................707 665-2100
J David Siembieda, *President*
Harry Clark, *Partner*
Brandes Elitch, *Partner*
Janet Cipriano, *President*
Christina Erasmy, *President*
EMP: 155
SALES (est): 22.5MM **Privately Held**
WEB: www.checksbynet.com
SIC: 7389 Credit card service

(P-16731)
CRUZ HOFFSTETTER LLC
Also Called: Royal Crest Healthcare
519 W Badillo St, Covina (91722-3763)
PHONE..................................626 915-5621
Lydia Cruz, *President*
EMP: 60
SALES (est): 3.1MM **Privately Held**
SIC: 7389 Personal service agents, bro-
kers & bureaus

(P-16732)
CSUB NURSING CLASS OF 2006
9001 Stockdale Hwy, Bakersfield
(93311-1022)
PHONE..................................408 219-5914
Michelle Concuora, *President*
EMP: 71
SALES: 2.3MM **Privately Held**
SIC: 7389 Fund raising organizations

(P-16733)
CURRENT TV LLC
118 King St, San Francisco (94107-1905)
PHONE..................................415 995-8328
David Bohrman,
Harry Wu, *Vice Pres*
Guy Barbaro,
Mark Golmon,
Paul Hollerbach,
EMP: 200
SQ FT: 27,000
SALES (est): 6.9MM
SALES (corp-wide): 10.3B **Privately Held**
WEB: www.currentmedia.com
SIC: 7389 Field audits, cable television

PA: Al Jazeera Media Network
Qatar Television Building Khalifa
Street
Doha

(P-16734)
CUSTOMFAB INC
Also Called: Fullclip USA
7345 Orangewood Ave, Garden Grove
(92841-1411)
PHONE..................................714 891-9119
Donald Martin Alhanati, *President*
Sharon Benson, *Office Mgr*
Jill Alhanati, *Purch Mgr*
Howard Alhanati, *Sales Mgr*
▲ EMP: 250
SQ FT: 47,000
SALES (est): 28.9MM **Privately Held**
SIC: 7389 Sewing contractor

(P-16735)
CUTLER GROUP LP
101 Montgomery St Ste 700, San Francisco
(94104-4125)
PHONE..................................415 645-6745
Trent Cutler, *Managing Prtnr*
Anand Prakash, *Partner*
Nader Sharabati, *CFO*
Johanna Van, *Accounting Mgr*
Alex Budilovsky, *Manager*
EMP: 50
SALES (est): 5.8MM **Privately Held**
SIC: 7389 Financial services

(P-16736)
CWPFL INC
1682 Langley Ave, Irvine (92614-5620)
PHONE..................................714 564-7900
Matthew K Stewart, *President*
Jeff Gunhus, *CEO*
Spencer Pepe, *CEO*
Jason Reed, *CEO*
Derrick Jackson, *Program Mgr*
EMP: 50
SALES (est): 1.6MM **Privately Held**
WEB: www.kleen-sales.com
SIC: 7389 Personal service agents, bro-
kers & bureaus

(P-16737)
D2J INC
6351 Regent St Ste 100, Huntington Park
(90255-3567)
PHONE..................................323 589-1374
Richard Kim, *President*
▲ EMP: 90
SALES (est): 4MM **Privately Held**
SIC: 7389 Sewing contractor

(P-16738)
DAILYLOOK INC
2445 E 12th St Ste B, Los Angeles
(90021-2937)
PHONE..................................888 888-6645
Brian Ree, *CEO*
Richard Nam, *Finance Mgr*
Frank Estrada, *Client Mgr*
Henry Barahona, *Director*
Michelle Gonzalez, *Supervisor*
EMP: 86 **EST:** 2011
SALES (est): 1MM **Privately Held**
SIC: 7389 Styling of fashions, apparel, fur-
niture, textiles, etc.

(P-16739)
DAVID SANTOS FARMING
720 Jefferson Ave, Los Banos
(93635-4713)
PHONE..................................209 826-1065
David Santos, *Owner*
EMP: 60
SALES (est): 5.6MM **Privately Held**
SIC: 7389 Personal service agents, bro-
kers & bureaus

(P-16740)
DECIMAL INC
Also Called: Ubiquity
1160 Battery St Ste 350, San Francisco
(94111-1238)
PHONE..................................855 980-6612
Chad Parks, *President*
Christopher Jasinski, *Partner*
Mary Torgerson, *COO*
Joe Chan, *Controller*

Jason Gross, *Sales Staff*
EMP: 82
SQ FT: 5,000
SALES (est): 6.7MM **Privately Held**
WEB: www.decimal.com
SIC: 7389 Financial services

(P-16741)
**DEDICATED MANAGEMENT
GROUP LLC**
3876 E Childs Ave, Merced (95341-9520)
PHONE..................................209 385-0694
EMP: 141
SALES (corp-wide): 15.7MM **Privately
Held**
SIC: 7389
PA: Dedicated Management Group Llc
3651 Mars Hill Rd Ste 400
Watkinsville GA 30677
404 564-1201

(P-16742)
DEE SIGN CO
Also Called: American Sign
7950 Woodley Ave, Van Nuys
(91406-1260)
PHONE..................................818 904-3400
Braden Huenefeld, *Principal*
EMP: 55
SQ FT: 28,900
SALES (est): 3.2MM **Privately Held**
SIC: 7389 3993 Sign painting & lettering
shop; signs & advertising specialties

(P-16743)
DEKRA-LITE INDUSTRIES INC
Also Called: DI Imaging
3102 W Alton Ave, Santa Ana
(92704-6817)
PHONE..................................714 436-0705
Jeffrey Lopez, *CEO*
▲ EMP: 80
SQ FT: 30,000
SALES (est): 13.3MM **Privately Held**
WEB: www.dekra-lite.com
SIC: 7389 5999 3999 Decoration service
for special events; art, picture frames &
decorations; Christmas lights & decora-
tions; advertising curtains

(P-16744)
DENIOS ROSEVILLE FARMERS
2013 Opportunity Dr, Roseville
(95678-3023)
PHONE..................................916 782-2704
Jeff Ronten, *CEO*
Ken Denio, *President*
Marilee Denio, *Corp Secy*
EMP: 120
SQ FT: 18,212
SALES (est): 9.4MM **Privately Held**
WEB: www.denios.org
SIC: 7389 Flea market

(P-16745)
DFA OF CALIFORNIA
1050 Diamond St, Stockton (95205-7020)
P.O. Box 1727 (95201-1727)
PHONE..................................209 465-2289
Debra Pennell, *Principal*
EMP: 60
SALES (corp-wide): 9.7MM **Privately
Held**
WEB: www.dfaofca.com
SIC: 7389 Inspection & testing services
PA: Dfa Of California
710 Striker Ave
Sacramento CA 95834
916 561-5900

(P-16746)
**DIABLO VLY COLLEGE
FOUNDATION (PA)**
321 Golf Club Rd, Pleasant Hill
(94523-1544)
PHONE..................................925 685-1230
Mark G Edelstein, *President*
John Freytag, *Ch of Bd*
Katherine Guptill, *CEO*
Tom Barber, *Professor*
Nicole White, *Instructor*
EMP: 112
SQ FT: 1,000

SALES: 1MM **Privately Held**
WEB: www.dvc.edu
SIC: 7389 8221 Fund raising organizations; colleges universities & professional schools

(P-16747)
DMCG INC (PA)
Also Called: Bail Hotline Bail Bonds
3605 10th St, Riverside (92501-3619)
PHONE....................951 683-9685
Daniel McGuire, *CEO*
Ben Srinivas, *CFO*
Cesar McGuire, *Exec VP*
Gilbert McGuire, *Exec VP*
Marco McGuire, *Exec VP*
EMP: 50
SQ FT: 15,000
SALES (est): 11.1MM **Privately Held**
SIC: 7389 Bail bonding

(P-16748)
DOCMAGIC INC
Also Called: Document Systems
1800 W 213th St, Torrance (90501-2832)
PHONE....................800 649-1362
Dominic Iannitti, *President*
Melanie Feliciano, *Officer*
Robert Madsen, *Executive*
Shandi Smith, *Executive*
Jimmy Chen, *Administration*
EMP: 79
SQ FT: 20,000
SALES (est): 18MM **Privately Held**
WEB: www.docmagic.com
SIC: 7389 Legal & tax services

(P-16749)
DOCUMENT TECHNOLOGIES LLC
275 Battery St Ste 250, San Francisco (94111-3318)
PHONE....................415 495-4100
Jonathan Kafka, *Branch Mgr*
EMP: 63
SALES (corp-wide): 589.6MM **Privately Held**
SIC: 7389 Document storage service
PA: Document Technologies, Llc
2 Ravinia Dr Ste 850
Atlanta GA 30346
770 390-2700

(P-16750)
DOCUMENT TECHNOLOGIES LLC
350 S Figueroa St Ste 750, Los Angeles (90071-1313)
PHONE....................213 892-9000
John Davenport Jr, *Branch Mgr*
EMP: 71
SALES (corp-wide): 589.6MM **Privately Held**
SIC: 7389 Document storage service
PA: Document Technologies, Llc
2 Ravinia Dr Ste 850
Atlanta GA 30346
770 390-2700

(P-16751)
DOCUMENT TECHNOLOGIES LLC
3600 W Bayshore Rd, Palo Alto (94303-4239)
PHONE....................650 485-2705
Victor Tan, *Branch Mgr*
EMP: 71
SALES (corp-wide): 589.6MM **Privately Held**
SIC: 7389 Document storage service
PA: Document Technologies, Llc
2 Ravinia Dr Ste 850
Atlanta GA 30346
770 390-2700

(P-16752)
DOUBLELINE CAPITAL LP
333 S Grand Ave Fl 18, Los Angeles (90071-1504)
PHONE....................213 633-8200
Jeffery E Gundlach, *Partner*
Philip A Barach, *Partner*
Henry V Chase, *Partner*
Louis Lucido, *COO*
Cris Ana, *Officer*

EMP: 111
SQ FT: 35,000
SALES (est): 20MM **Privately Held**
SIC: 7389 6719 Financial services; investment holding companies, except banks

(P-16753)
DRIVER SPG
1501 S Harris Ct, Anaheim (92806-5932)
PHONE....................855 300-4774
Dana J Roberts, *CEO*
Karl Kreutziger, *President*
Matt Loorya, *Senior VP*
Aimee Siemianowsk, *Senior VP*
Adam Kingsbury, *Project Engr*
EMP: 50
SQ FT: 7,000
SALES: 74MM **Privately Held**
SIC: 7389 Drive-a-way automobile service

(P-16754)
DUFF & PHELPS LLC
345 California St # 2100, San Francisco (94104-2663)
PHONE....................415 693-5300
Michael Lloyd, *Director*
David Larsen, *Managing Dir*
McGovern Mike, *Analyst*
Joe Lee, *Sr Associate*
EMP: 53
SALES (corp-wide): 312.4MM **Privately Held**
SIC: 7389 Financial services
PA: Duff & Phelps, Llc
55 E 52nd St Fl 31
New York NY 10055
212 871-2000

(P-16755)
DUN & BRADSTREET EMERGING (DH)
22761 Pacific Coast Hwy # 226, Malibu (90265-5064)
PHONE....................310 456-8271
Stephen C Daffron, *President*
Bryan Hipsher, *Treasurer*
Joe Reinhardt, *Officer*
Susan D Beriont, *Vice Pres*
Christopher Iannucci, *Vice Pres*
EMP: 145
SALES (est): 54MM
SALES (corp-wide): 1.7B **Privately Held**
SIC: 7389 Financial services
HQ: Dun & Bradstreet, Inc
103 John F Kennedy Pkwy
Short Hills NJ 07078
973 921-5500

(P-16756)
DURINI LUIS CARLOS ESTRADA
Also Called: Alltoss
100 W Broadway Ste 100 # 100, Glendale (91210-1230)
PHONE....................502 474-3112
Luis Estrada, *Owner*
EMP: 50
SALES (est): 978.2K **Privately Held**
SIC: 7389 Personal service agents, brokers & bureaus

(P-16757)
E & C FASHION INC
Also Called: Pacific Concept Laundry
1420 Esperanza St, Los Angeles (90023-3914)
PHONE....................323 262-0099
William Moo Han Bae, *CEO*
Maria Bae, *President*
Elizabeth Bae, *Vice Pres*
Claudia Kye, *Vice Pres*
▲ **EMP:** 300
SALES (est): 31.3MM **Privately Held**
SIC: 7389 Sewing contractor

(P-16758)
E TRADESHOWGIRLSCOM
1 Ocean Rdg, Laguna Niguel (92677-9231)
PHONE....................949 661-4177
Shelley Tippetts, *Owner*
EMP: 100
SALES (est): 2.7MM **Privately Held**
SIC: 7389 Advertising, promotional & trade show services

(P-16759)
EAST BAY INNOVATIONS
2450 Washington Ave # 240, San Leandro (94577-5996)
PHONE....................510 618-1580
Tom Heinz, *Exec Dir*
Kiera Swan, *Payroll Mgr*
Nicole Manzana, *Human Res Mgr*
Bret Hatcher-Santiag, *Asst Director*
Christine Grabowski, *Director*
EMP: 60
SALES: 8.4MM **Privately Held**
WEB: www.eastbayinnovations.com
SIC: 7389 Personal service agents, brokers & bureaus

(P-16760)
ECONTACTLIVE INC
Also Called: Telecontact Resource Services
6436 Oakdale Rd, Riverbank (95367-9648)
PHONE....................209 548-4300
Julie Hutchings, *CEO*
June Griffith, *Vice Pres*
Alice Martinez, *CTO*
David Schwerd, *Info Tech Mgr*
Katie Griffith, *Human Res Dir*
EMP: 80
SQ FT: 42,000
SALES (est): 4MM **Privately Held**
WEB: www.eContactLive.com
SIC: 7389 Telemarketing services

(P-16761)
ELAINE NULL
1388 Sutter St Fl 11, San Francisco (94109-5427)
PHONE....................415 345-4428
Elaine Null, *Principal*
EMP: 133
SALES (est): 9.1MM **Privately Held**
SIC: 7389 Personal service agents, brokers & bureaus

(P-16762)
ELLIE FASHION GROUP INC
1735 Stewart St Fl 2, Santa Monica (90404-4021)
PHONE....................818 355-3812
Marcus Greinke, *CEO*
EMP: 56
SQ FT: 7,000
SALES: 4MM **Privately Held**
SIC: 7389 Apparel designers, commercial

(P-16763)
EMAGIA CORPORATION
4701 P Henry Dr Bldg 20, Santa Clara (95054)
PHONE....................408 654-6575
Veena Gundavelli, *CEO*
Gss Prabhakar, *Manager*
EMP: 50
SALES (est): 3.4MM **Privately Held**
WEB: www.emagia.com
SIC: 7389 Financial services

(P-16764)
EMERALD EXPOSITIONS LLC (HQ)
31910 Del Obispo St # 200, San Juan Capistrano (92675-3182)
PHONE....................949 226-5700
Kosty Gilis, *CEO*
David Loechner,
▲ **EMP:** 252
SQ FT: 6,500
SALES (est): 125.4MM
SALES (corp-wide): 380.7MM **Publicly Held**
SIC: 7389 Trade show arrangement
PA: Emerald Expositions Events Inc.
31910 Del Obispo St # 20
San Juan Capistrano CA 92675
949 226-5700

(P-16765)
ENCORE EVENTS RENTALS INC
20 Mill St, Healdsburg (95448-4010)
PHONE....................707 431-3500
Bridget Doherty, *CEO*
Tom McCallister, *General Mgr*
Kendall Burger, *Marketing Mgr*
Shelly Gillean, *Manager*
Alyssa Taylor, *Accounts Mgr*
EMP: 100

SALES (est): 437.5K **Privately Held**
SIC: 7389 Decoration service for special events

(P-16766)
ENTREPRENEURIAL HOSPITALITY
Also Called: Riverside Convention Center
3485 Mission Inn Ave, Riverside (92501-3304)
PHONE....................951 346-4700
Duane Roberts, *Ch of Bd*
Richard Shippie, *President*
Ted Weggeland, *President*
Scott Megna, *Vice Pres*
EMP: 200
SQ FT: 75,000
SALES (est): 8.8MM **Privately Held**
SIC: 7389 Convention & show services

(P-16767)
EPHONAMATIONCOM INC
Also Called: Ansafone Contact Centers
145 E Columbine Ave, Santa Ana (92707-4401)
P.O. Box 4678, Ocala FL (34478-4678)
PHONE....................714 560-1000
Randy Harmat, *CEO*
Jennifer Oliveros, *Vice Pres*
Kameron Alexander, *Executive Asst*
Eliseo Lomeli, *Technology*
Steven Rowell, *Technology*
EMP: 175
SQ FT: 18,900
SALES (est): 20.9MM **Privately Held**
SIC: 7389 Telephone answering service

(P-16768)
EQUILAR INC
1100 Marshall St, Redwood City (94063-2595)
PHONE....................877 441-6090
David Chun, *CEO*
Timothy Ranzetta, *President*
Jason Augustine, *Manager*
EMP: 110 **EST:** 2000
SALES (est): 21.3MM **Privately Held**
SIC: 7389 Financial services

(P-16769)
EREPUBLIC INC (PA)
Also Called: Government Technology
100 Blue Ravine Rd, Folsom (95630-4509)
PHONE....................916 932-1300
Dennis McKenna, *CEO*
Margaret Mohr, *Chief Mktg Ofcr*
Cathilea Robinett, *Exec VP*
John Flynn, *Vice Pres*
Dee Pearson, *Vice Pres*
EMP: 120
SQ FT: 36,000
SALES (est): 30.7MM **Privately Held**
WEB: www.erepublic.com
SIC: 7389 2759 2721 Convention & show services; publication printing; magazines: printing; periodicals

(P-16770)
ETC BUILDING & DESIGN INC (PA)
Also Called: Essrig Taylor Constructions
6805 Nancy Ridge Dr, San Diego (92121-2233)
PHONE....................858 554-1150
Michael Essrig, *President*
Tom Ross, *Shareholder*
Chris Taylor, *Shareholder*
John Mentzer, *Vice Pres*
Chloe Sanossian, *Creative Dir*
EMP: 143
SQ FT: 9,000
SALES (est): 21.5MM **Privately Held**
SIC: 7389 1711 1542 Safety inspection service; heating & air conditioning contractors; hospital construction

(P-16771)
EXCELLENCE VENTURES INC
149 S Mednik Ave, Los Angeles (90022-1606)
PHONE....................323 262-6800
Recardo Davila, *CEO*
Manuel Davila, *President*
Ricardo Davila, *CEO*
EMP: 70
SQ FT: 4,000

SALES (est): 2.6MM **Privately Held**
SIC: 7389 Financial services

(P-16772)
EZCARETECH USA INC
21081 S Wstn Ave Ste 130, Torrance
(90501)
PHONE..................................424 558-3191
Justin Chung, *CEO*
Justin Park, *Administration*
Kyungho Min, *Manager*
EMP: 350
SALES (est): 57K **Privately Held**
SIC: 7389 Business services

(P-16773)
FACT FOUNDATION
Also Called: FREDERICKA MANOR CARE
CENTER
303 N Glenoaks Blvd, Burbank
(91502-1116)
PHONE..................................818 729-8105
Donna Shaw, *Principal*
Tim Detmen, *President*
EMP: 75
SALES: 816.1K
SALES (corp-wide): 165.1MM **Privately Held**
SIC: 7389 Fund raising organizations
PA: Front Porch Communities And Services
- Casa De Manana, Llc
800 N Brand Blvd Fl 19
Glendale CA 91203
818 729-8100

(P-16774)
FACTER DIRECT LTD
4751 Wilshire Blvd # 140, Los Angeles
(90010-3827)
PHONE..................................323 634-1999
Larry Keefer, *Controller*
EMP: 170
SALES (est): 4.6MM
SALES (corp-wide): 9.6MM **Privately Held**
WEB: www.giftplanningdirect.com
SIC: 7389 8742 Telemarketing services;
marketing consulting services
PA: Facter Direct Ltd
11500 W Olympic Blvd
Los Angeles CA
310 788-9000

(P-16775)
FALLBROOK FIRE PROTECTION DST
315 E Ivy St, Fallbrook (92028-2138)
PHONE..................................760 723-2010
Kermit Harrison, *President*
Nancy Goss, *Human Resources*
Herbert A Gaetjens, *Director*
Jsteve Johnson, *Director*
Pete Merritt, *Director*
EMP: 69
SALES (est): 3.8MM **Privately Held**
SIC: 7389 Fire protection service other
than forestry or public

(P-16776)
FAMILY PLG ASSOC MED GROUP
2777 Long Beach Blvd # 150, Long Beach
(90806-1571)
PHONE..................................562 595-5653
Edward C Allred, *Branch Mgr*
EMP: 83
SALES (corp-wide): 36.1MM **Privately Held**
SIC: 7389 Personal service agents, bro-
kers & bureaus
PA: Family Planning Associates Medical
Group
3050 E Airport Way
Long Beach CA 90806
213 738-7283

(P-16777)
FARMEX LAND MANAGEMENT INC
11156 E Annadale Ave, Sanger
(93657-9727)
PHONE..................................559 875-7181
James Yakligian, *President*
EMP: 125

SALES (est): 9.9MM **Privately Held**
SIC: 7389 Packaging & labeling services

(P-16778)
FEDERAL EXPRESS CORPORATION
Also Called: Fedex
2495 Faraday Ave, Carlsbad (92010-7225)
PHONE..................................800 463-3339
EMP: 167
SALES (corp-wide): 69.6B **Publicly Held**
WEB: www.federalexpress.com
SIC: 7389 Personal service agents, bro-
kers & bureaus
HQ: Federal Express Corporation
3610 Hacks Cross Rd
Memphis TN 38125
901 369-3600

(P-16779)
FEDERAL EXPRESS CORPORATION
Also Called: Fedex
200 N Pacific Coast Hwy # 800, El Se-
gundo (90245-4340)
PHONE..................................800 463-3339
EMP: 500
SALES (corp-wide): 69.6B **Publicly Held**
WEB: www.federalexpress.com
SIC: 7389 Mailing & messenger services
HQ: Federal Express Corporation
3610 Hacks Cross Rd
Memphis TN 38125
901 369-3600

(P-16780)
FEDERAL EXPRESS CORPORATION
Also Called: Fedex
7275 Johnson Dr, Pleasanton
(94588-3861)
PHONE..................................800 463-3339
EMP: 99
SALES (corp-wide): 69.6B **Publicly Held**
SIC: 7389 Courier or messenger service
HQ: Federal Express Corporation
3610 Hacks Cross Rd
Memphis TN 38125
901 369-3600

(P-16781)
FEDERAL EXPRESS CORPORATION
Also Called: Fedex
7000 Barranca Pkwy, Irvine (92618-3112)
PHONE..................................800 463-3339
EMP: 350
SALES (corp-wide): 47.4B **Publicly Held**
SIC: 7389 4731 4581 4513
HQ: Federal Express Corporation
3610 Hacks Cross Rd
Memphis TN 38125
901 369-3600

(P-16782)
FEDERAL EXPRESS CORPORATION
Also Called: Fedex
3371 E Francis St, Ontario (91761-2914)
PHONE..................................800 463-3339
Vivian Ewing, *Sales Executive*
EMP: 275
SALES (corp-wide): 69.6B **Publicly Held**
WEB: www.federalexpress.com
SIC: 7389 4513 4215 Courier or messen-
ger service; air courier services; courier
services, except by air
HQ: Federal Express Corporation
3610 Hacks Cross Rd
Memphis TN 38125
901 369-3600

(P-16783)
FEDEX CORPORATION
50 Cypress Ln, Brisbane (94005-1217)
PHONE..................................415 657-0403
EMP: 50
SALES (corp-wide): 47.4B **Publicly Held**
SIC: 7389
PA: Fedex Corporation
942 Shady Grove Rd S
Memphis TN 38120
901 818-7500

(P-16784)
FIRST AMERICAN CARD SERVICE
25060 Hancock Ave Ste 103, Murrieta
(92562-5959)
PHONE..................................951 677-8720
Brian Rommele, *President*
EMP: 50
SALES (est): 1.5MM **Privately Held**
WEB: www.1stamericancardservice.com
SIC: 7389 Credit card service

(P-16785)
FLAGSHIP CREDIT ACCEPTANCE LLC
7525 Irvine Center Dr, Irvine (92618-3066)
PHONE..................................949 748-7172
EMP: 125 **Privately Held**
SIC: 7389 Financial services
PA: Flagship Credit Acceptance Llc
3 Christy Dr Ste 203
Chadds Ford PA 19317

(P-16786)
FREEMAN EXPOSITIONS LLC
2170 S Towne Centre Pl, Anaheim
(92806-6127)
PHONE..................................714 254-3400
Pattie Balding, *Manager*
EMP: 200
SALES (corp-wide): 3.5B **Privately Held**
SIC: 7389 Trade show arrangement
HQ: Freeman Expositions, Llc
1600 Viceroy Dr Ste 100
Dallas TX 75235
214 445-1000

(P-16787)
FREEMAN EXPOSITIONS LLC
245 S Spruce Ave, South San Francisco
(94080-4581)
PHONE..................................650 878-6023
Glenn Wyer, *Manager*
EMP: 95
SALES (corp-wide): 3.5B **Privately Held**
SIC: 7389 Trade show arrangement
HQ: Freeman Expositions, Llc
1600 Viceroy Dr Ste 100
Dallas TX 75235
214 445-1000

(P-16788)
FRESNO METRO FLOOD CTRL DST
5469 E Olive Ave, Fresno (93727-2541)
PHONE..................................559 456-3292
Bob Van Wyk, *General Mgr*
Jerry Lakeman, *Principal*
Robert McIntyre, *Info Tech Dir*
Jason Clarke, *Project Mgr*
Michael Maxwell, *Technical Staff*
EMP: 75 EST: 1955
SQ FT: 12,965
SALES (est): 7.4MM **Privately Held**
SIC: 7389 Personal service agents, bro-
kers & bureaus

(P-16789)
FULL THROTTLE ENERGY COMPANY
125 E 56th St, Los Angeles (90011-5125)
PHONE..................................323 474-8417
EMP: 210
SALES (est): 161.6K
SALES (corp-wide): 3.8B **Publicly Held**
SIC: 7389
PA: Monster Beverage Corporation
1 Monster Way
Corona CA 92879
951 739-6200

(P-16790)
FUNGIBLE INC
3201 Scott Blvd, Santa Clara (95054-3008)
PHONE..................................669 292-5522
Pradeep Sindhu, *CEO*
EMP: 80
SALES (est): 7.6MM **Privately Held**
SIC: 7389

(P-16791)
GALICE INC
30140 Tuttle Ct, Tehachapi (93561-7483)
PHONE..................................323 731-8200

Cathrine A Lutz, *President*
EMP: 69 EST: 1991
SALES (est): 3.6MM **Privately Held**
WEB: www.galice.com
SIC: 7389 Interior decorating

(P-16792)
GARY R EDWARDS INC
3930 Utah St Ste C, San Diego
(92104-2939)
PHONE..................................619 299-8700
Gary R Edwards, *President*
EMP: 70
SALES (est): 4.3MM **Privately Held**
WEB: www.greinc.com
SIC: 7389 Subscription fulfillment services:
magazine, newspaper, etc.

(P-16793)
GBS FINANCIAL CORP
Also Called: Wagner Financials
904 Manhattan Ave Ste 3, Manhattan
Beach (90266-5538)
PHONE..................................310 937-0073
EMP: 60
SALES (est): 1.9MM **Privately Held**
SIC: 7389

(P-16794)
GDF PARENT LLC
Also Called: Import Whl Univ Fund Raising
1510 1/2 W 228th St, Torrance
(90501-5105)
PHONE..................................714 743-7209
Yoelie Barag,
EMP: 75
SALES (est): 2.2MM **Privately Held**
SIC: 7389 Fund raising organizations

(P-16795)
GELFAND RENNERT & FELDMAN LLP (PA)
1880 Century Park E # 1600, Los Angeles
(90067-1661)
PHONE..................................310 553-1707
Marshall M Gelfand, *Managing Prtnr*
Tyson Beem, *Partner*
Todd Gelfand, *Partner*
Cary Macmiller, *Managing Dir*
Dan Trockey, *Data Proc Staff*
EMP: 200
SALES: 5K **Privately Held**
WEB: www.grfllp.com
SIC: 7389 8721 8741 Legal & tax serv-
ices; accounting, auditing & bookkeeping;
business management

(P-16796)
GENERAL ENVIRONMENTAL
Also Called: Stericycles Envmtl Solutions
11855 White Rock Rd, Rancho Cordova
(95742-6603)
PHONE..................................916 351-0980
Matt Dickson, *Partner*
EMP: 55
SALES (corp-wide): 3.4B **Publicly Held**
SIC: 7389 Personal service agents, bro-
kers & bureaus
HQ: Psc Environmental Services, Llc
5151 San Felipe St # 1100
Houston TX 77056
713 623-8777

(P-16797)
GENGO INC
307 2nd Ave, San Mateo (94401-3905)
PHONE..................................650 585-4390
Matthew Romaine, *CEO*
Matthew Skyrm, *COO*
Spencer Huddleston, *Executive*
Alexandra Nguyen, *Sales Mgr*
Ken N Yamada, *Marketing Staff*
EMP: 50
SALES (est): 778K **Privately Held**
SIC: 7389 Translation services

(P-16798)
GENTLE GIANT STUDIOS INC
7511 N San Fernando Rd, Burbank
(91505-1044)
PHONE..................................818 504-3555
Karl Z Meyer, *President*
Aaron White, *Manager*
▲ EMP: 56
SQ FT: 20,000

SALES (est): 7.2MM **Publicly Held**
WEB: www.gentlegiantstudios.com
SIC: 7389 Design services
HQ: 3d Systems, Inc.
333 Three D Systems Cir
Rock Hill SC 29730
803 326-3900

(P-16799)
GETFEEDBACK INC
123 Mission St Fl 26, San Francisco
(94105-5140)
PHONE...................888 684-8821
Kraig Swensrud, *CEO*
EMP: 60
SALES (est): 200.6K
SALES (corp-wide): 254.3MM **Publicly Held**
SIC: 7389
HQ: Surveymonkey Inc.
1 Curiosity Way
San Mateo CA 94403
650 543-8400

(P-16800)
GLARE TECHNOLOGY USA INC
38340 Innovation Ct, Murrieta
(92563-2621)
PHONE...................909 437-6999
Laith Salih, *CEO*
EMP: 120
SALES (est): 127.1K **Privately Held**
SIC: 7389

(P-16801)
GLOBAL CHECK SERVICE
1524 Graves Ave Ste C, El Cajon
(92021-2991)
PHONE...................619 449-5150
David James Homoki, *Partner*
Dalila Homoki, *Partner*
Dan White, *Supervisor*
EMP: 200
SQ FT: 2,500
SALES (est): 8.5MM **Privately Held**
WEB: www.globalcheck.com
SIC: 7389 Check validation service; credit card service

(P-16802)
GLOBAL DEBT MANAGEMENT LLC (PA)
18881 Von Karman Ave # 1500, Irvine
(92612-1582)
PHONE...................949 825-7800
Banir Ganatra, *Mng Member*
Ashutosh Bisht, *Research*
Chris Dong, *Research*
EMP: 60
SQ FT: 3,400
SALES (est): 2.2MM **Privately Held**
SIC: 7389 Financial services

(P-16803)
GLOBAL EXPRNCE SPECIALISTS INC
500 N Brand Blvd Ste 1860, Glendale
(91203-3375)
PHONE...................818 638-5959
Eddie Newquist, *Exec VP*
EMP: 65 **Publicly Held**
WEB: www.beckergroup.com
SIC: 7389 Design services
HQ: Global Experience Specialists, Inc.
7000 Lindell Rd
Las Vegas NV 89118
702 515-5500

(P-16804)
GLOBAL EXPRNCE SPECIALISTS INC
Also Called: Ges
491 C St, Chula Vista (91910-1604)
PHONE...................619 498-6300
Tom Robins, *Manager*
EMP: 170 **Publicly Held**
WEB: www.gesexpo.com
SIC: 7389 Convention & show services
HQ: Global Experience Specialists, Inc.
7000 Lindell Rd
Las Vegas NV 89118
702 515-5500

(P-16805)
GLOBAL LANGUAGE SOLUTIONS LLC
19800 Macarthur Blvd, Irvine (92612-2421)
PHONE...................949 798-1400
Olga Smirnova, *CEO*
Inna Kassatkina, *President*
Judit Kulcsar, *Office Mgr*
Volga Aksoy, *Sr Software Eng*
Andrew Welch, *Sr Software Eng*
EMP: 100
SQ FT: 7,500
SALES (est): 5.7MM **Privately Held**
WEB: www.globallanguages.com
SIC: 7389 Translation services
PA: Welocalize, Inc.
241 E 4th St Ste 207
Frederick MD 21701

(P-16806)
GO WEST HOLDINGS LLC
795 Folsom St, San Francisco
(94107-1243)
PHONE...................888 670-0080
Victor Goree,
EMP: 145
SALES (est): 1.8MM **Privately Held**
SIC: 7389 Decoration service for special events

(P-16807)
GOODWILL SRVNG THE PPL OF STHR (PA)
Also Called: Links Sgn Lngg Intrprtng, Shrd
800 W Pacific Coast Hwy, Long Beach
(90806-5243)
PHONE...................562 435-3411
Janet McCarthy, *CEO*
EMP: 100
SQ FT: 80,000
SALES (est): 24.4MM **Privately Held**
WEB: www.goodwill-lbsb.org
SIC: 7389 8331 5932 Translation services; job training & vocational rehabilitation services; vocational training agency; used merchandise stores

(P-16808)
GOOGLE PAYMENT CORP
Also Called: Google Checkout
1600 Amphitheatre Pkwy, Mountain View
(94043-1351)
PHONE...................650 253-0000
EMP: 50
SALES (est): 6.6MM
SALES (corp-wide): 74.9B **Publicly Held**
SIC: 7389
HQ: Google Inc.
1600 Amphitheatre Pkwy
Mountain View CA 94043
650 253-0000

(P-16809)
GORDON & SCHWENKMEYER INC
1860 Howe Ave Ste 300, Sacramento
(95825-1098)
PHONE...................916 569-1740
Brett Carter, *Exec VP*
EMP: 70
SALES (corp-wide): 11.2MM **Privately Held**
WEB: www.gsitel.com
SIC: 7389 Personal service agents, brokers & bureaus
PA: Gordon & Schwenkmeyer Inc
20300 S Vt Ave Ste 210
Torrance CA 90502
310 615-2300

(P-16810)
GRAND PACIFIC RESORTS INC
Also Called: Resortime.com
5900 Pasteur Ct Ste 200, Carlsbad
(92008-7336)
PHONE...................760 431-8500
Sherri Weks, *Manager*
Cathy Fuchs, *Executive Asst*
Loren Mehl, *Technology*
EMP: 200 **Privately Held**
WEB: www.grandpacificresorts.com
SIC: 7389 Personal service agents, brokers & bureaus

PA: Grand Pacific Resorts, Inc.
5900 Pasteur Ct Ste 200
Carlsbad CA 92008

(P-16811)
GRAND PERFORMANCES
350 S Grand Ave Ste A4, Los Angeles
(90071-3461)
PHONE...................213 687-2190
Craig Bloomgardner, *President*
Craig Bloomgarden, *President*
Mari Riddle, *Exec Dir*
Zindy Landeros, *Office Mgr*
Katie Luna, *Administration*
EMP: 55
SALES (est): 1.8MM **Privately Held**
SIC: 7389 Promoters of shows & exhibitions

(P-16812)
GRILL ON THE ALLEY THE INC
6801 Hollywood Blvd, Los Angeles
(90028-6136)
PHONE...................323 856-5530
Katherine Sy, *Branch Mgr*
EMP: 1125
SALES (corp-wide): 24.9MM **Privately Held**
SIC: 7389 Design services
PA: Grill On The Alley, The, Inc
11661 San Vicente Blvd # 404
Los Angeles CA
-

(P-16813)
GRILL RECORDING STUDIO
4770 San Pablo Ave Ste C, Emeryville
(94608-3028)
PHONE...................510 531-4351
Levberlak Mhg, *Owner*
EMP: 51
SALES (est): 2MM **Privately Held**
SIC: 7389 Recording studio, noncommercial records

(P-16814)
GSA DESIGN INC
4551 San Fernando Rd # 102, Glendale
(91204-3227)
PHONE...................818 241-2558
Grigor Grigoryan, *President*
Narine Khachatryan, *CFO*
EMP: 150
SQ FT: 20,000
SALES: 7MM **Privately Held**
SIC: 7389 2386 Sewing contractor; garments, leather

(P-16815)
GUTHY-RENKER LLC
25892 Towne Centre Dr, Foothill Ranch
(92610-3437)
PHONE...................949 454-1400
Olly Efthyvoulos, *Branch Mgr*
EMP: 100
SALES (corp-wide): 270.2MM **Privately Held**
SIC: 7389 7374 Telemarketing services; data processing service
PA: Guthy-Renker Llc
100 N Pacific Coast Hwy
El Segundo CA 90245
760 773-9022

(P-16816)
HARINGA INC (PA)
Also Called: Premier Packaging/Assembly
14422 Best Ave, Santa Fe Springs
(90670-5133)
P.O. Box 4707, Cerritos (90703-4707)
PHONE...................800 499-9991
Victoria Haringa, *CEO*
Vicki Haringa, *President*
Randy Haringa, *General Mgr*
Candice Olson, *Opers Mgr*
Nineth Vera, *Warehouse Mgr*
▲ EMP: 77
SQ FT: 200,000
SALES (est): 13.2MM **Privately Held**
WEB: www.premierpkg.com
SIC: 7389 Packaging & labeling services

(P-16817)
HARRIS DIRECT
21250 Califa St Ste 114, Woodland Hills
(91367-5023)
PHONE...................818 357-2040
James Harris, *President*
EMP: 62
SQ FT: 3,800
SALES: 1.8MM **Privately Held**
SIC: 7389 7331 Telemarketing services; direct mail advertising services

(P-16818)
HARTMANN STUDIOS INC
1150 Brickyard Cove Rd # 202, Point Richmond (94801-4181)
PHONE...................510 232-5030
Thomas J Mahoney, *CEO*
EMP: 150
SALES (est): 1.5MM
SALES (corp-wide): 131.3MM **Privately Held**
SIC: 7389 Convention & show services
PA: Ita Group, Inc
4600 Westown Pkwy Ste 100
West Des Moines IA 50266
515 326-3400

(P-16819)
HCT PACKAGING INC (DH)
2800 28th St Ste 240, Santa Monica
(90405-6214)
PHONE...................310 260-7680
Tim Thorpe, *President*
Tara Corcoran, *Controller*
Christina Blanchard, *Director*
◆ EMP: 125
SQ FT: 1,500
SALES (est): 27.2MM **Privately Held**
WEB: www.hctpackaging.com
SIC: 7389 Packaging & labeling services

(P-16820)
HEARTLAND PAYMENT SYSTEMS LLC
548 Shorebird Cir # 3101, Redwood City
(94065-1038)
PHONE...................650 678-2824
Gary Friedman, *Principal*
EMP: 99
SALES (corp-wide): 3.3B **Publicly Held**
SIC: 7389 Personal service agents, brokers & bureaus
HQ: Heartland Payment Systems, Llc
10 Glenlake Pkwy Ste 324
Atlanta GA 30328
609 683-3831

(P-16821)
HEARTLAND PAYMENT SYSTEMS LLC
35804 Octopus Ln, Wildomar
(92595-8095)
PHONE...................909 609-1836
EMP: 97
SALES (corp-wide): 3.3B **Publicly Held**
SIC: 7389 Credit card service
HQ: Heartland Payment Systems, Llc
10 Glenlake Pkwy Ste 324
Atlanta GA 30328
609 683-3831

(P-16822)
HEARTLAND PAYMENT SYSTEMS LLC
1007 W College Ave Ste B, Santa Rosa
(95401-5046)
PHONE...................707 338-0510
Gregory Arena, *Principal*
EMP: 99
SALES (corp-wide): 3.3B **Publicly Held**
SIC: 7389 Personal service agents, brokers & bureaus
HQ: Heartland Payment Systems, Llc
10 Glenlake Pkwy Ste 324
Atlanta GA 30328
609 683-3831

(P-16823)
HEARTLAND PAYMENT SYSTEMS LLC
207 S Broadway, Redondo Beach
(90277-3674)
PHONE...................424 247-8521
Gilbert Dowling, *Principal*

EMP: 99
SALES (corp-wide): 3.3B **Publicly Held**
SIC: 7389 Personal service agents, brokers & bureaus
HQ: Heartland Payment Systems, Llc
10 Glenlake Pkwy Ste 324
Atlanta GA 30328
609 683-3831

(P-16824)
HEARTLAND PAYMENT SYSTEMS LLC
2225 Buena Vista Ave A, Walnut Creek (94597-3513)
PHONE...................925 360-3258
Paul Bramblet, *Principal*
EMP: 99
SALES (corp-wide): 3.3B **Publicly Held**
SIC: 7389 Personal service agents, brokers & bureaus
HQ: Heartland Payment Systems, Llc
10 Glenlake Pkwy Ste 324
Atlanta GA 30328
609 683-3831

(P-16825)
HEARTLAND PAYMENT SYSTEMS LLC
5325 Elkhorn Blvd, Sacramento (95842-2526)
PHONE...................916 844-9548
James Bramblet, *Principal*
EMP: 99
SALES (corp-wide): 3.3B **Publicly Held**
SIC: 7389 Personal service agents, brokers & bureaus
HQ: Heartland Payment Systems, Llc
10 Glenlake Pkwy Ste 324
Atlanta GA 30328
609 683-3831

(P-16826)
HEARTLAND PAYMENT SYSTEMS INC
510 Cerritos Way, Cathedral City (92234-1617)
PHONE...................760 324-0133
EMP: 97
SALES (corp-wide): 2B **Publicly Held**
SIC: 7389
PA: Heartland Payment Systems, Inc.
90 Nassau St
Princeton NJ 30328
609 683-3831

(P-16827)
HEARTLAND PAYMENT SYSTEMS INC
Also Called: HEARTLAND PAYMENT SYSTEMS, INC.
1460 Golden Gate Ave # 5, San Francisco (94115-4658)
PHONE...................415 518-4810
David Evan, *Principal*
EMP: 99
SALES (corp-wide): 3.3B **Publicly Held**
SIC: 7389 Personal service agents, brokers & bureaus
HQ: Heartland Payment Systems, Llc
10 Glenlake Pkwy Ste 324
Atlanta GA 30328
609 683-3831

(P-16828)
HERBS POOL SERVICE INC
3769 Redwood Hwy, San Rafael (94903-3998)
PHONE...................415 479-4040
Sandra Louise Scott, *CEO*
EMP: 55 EST: 1958
SQ FT: 3,000
SALES (est): 6.6MM **Privately Held**
SIC: 7389 Swimming pool & hot tub service & maintenance

(P-16829)
HIRED INC (PA)
303 2nd St Ste S600, San Francisco (94107-3633)
PHONE...................415 813-4987
Douglas Feirstein, *Principal*
Mehul Patel, *CEO*
Michelle Weaver, *CFO*
Clay Kellogg, *Officer*
Kelly Dragovich, *Senior VP*

EMP: 50
SALES (est): 13.6MM **Privately Held**
SIC: 7389 7361 Auctioneers, fee basis; employment agencies

(P-16830)
HIRSCH/BEDNER INTL INC (PA)
Also Called: Hba International
3216 Nebraska Ave, Santa Monica (90404-4214)
PHONE...................310 829-9087
Rene G Kaerskov, *CEO*
Caren Disney,
Sayeli Ayaydin, *Managing Prtnr*
Michael J Bedner, *Ch of Bd*
Howard Pharr, *President*
EMP: 70
SQ FT: 14,000
SALES (est): 28.7MM
SALES (corp-wide): 31.6MM **Privately Held**
WEB: www.hbadesign.com
SIC: 7389 Interior designer; interior design services

(P-16831)
HOLLISTER PROCESS SERVICE
Also Called: Steven Snyder
341 Tres Pinos Rd Ste 201, Hollister (95023-5582)
PHONE...................831 634-1479
Stephen Snyder, *Owner*
Gawnette Snyder, *Co-Owner*
EMP: 50
SALES (est): 65K **Privately Held**
SIC: 7389 Process serving service

(P-16832)
HOLLYWOOD SPORTS PARK LLC
Also Called: Giant Sportz Paintball Park
9030 Somerset Blvd, Bellflower (90706-3402)
PHONE...................562 867-9600
Dennis Bukowski, *Mng Member*
Giovanni D'Egido,
▲ EMP: 100
SQ FT: 20,000
SALES (est): 8.8MM **Privately Held**
WEB: www.hollywoodsportspark.com
SIC: 7389 Personal service agents, brokers & bureaus

(P-16833)
HOOVER INSTITUTION
434 Galvez Mall, Stanford (94305-6003)
PHONE...................650 723-0603
John Raisian, *Director*
Jenny Mayfield, *President*
Laureen Schieron, *Executive Asst*
Olivia Witting, *Research*
Victor Hanson, *Teacher*
EMP: 200
SALES (est): 11.7MM **Privately Held**
SIC: 7389 Personal service agents, brokers & bureaus

(P-16834)
HOSPITAL BUSINESS SERVICES INC
3300 E Guasti Rd, Ontario (91761-8655)
PHONE...................909 235-4400
Mike Sarian, *President*
Ken Wheeler, *Vice Pres*
EMP: 101
SALES (est): 3.6MM **Privately Held**
SIC: 7389 7349 Financial services; building maintenance services

(P-16835)
HOSPITLITY PRCH GROUP INTL LLC (PA)
Also Called: Hpg International
350 N Wiget Ln Ste 210, Walnut Creek (94598-5903)
PHONE...................925 949-5706
Cary T Schirmer, *CEO*
Benjamin O'Connor, *President*
Sharon Arduini, *Vice Pres*
Wallace McPherson, *Vice Pres*
Raymond Leung, *Managing Dir*
◆ EMP: 150
SALES (est): 29.3MM **Privately Held**
WEB: www.higginspurchasing.com
SIC: 7389 Purchasing service

(P-16836)
HUSTLE DIGITAL INC
12777 W Jefferson Blvd, Los Angeles (90066-7048)
PHONE...................310 882-2680
Josh Mandel, *Vice Pres*
EMP: 50
SALES (est): 1.5MM **Privately Held**
SIC: 7389 Advertising, promotional & trade show services

(P-16837)
HYDROPROCESSING ASSOCIATES LLC
Also Called: Hpa-USA
19122 S Santa Fe Ave, Compton (90221-5910)
PHONE...................310 667-6456
Kees Ooms, *Branch Mgr*
EMP: 50 **Privately Held**
SIC: 7389 Petroleum refinery inspection service
HQ: Hydroprocessing Associates, Llc
6016 Highway 63
Moss Point MS 39563

(P-16838)
ICON DESIGN AND DISPLAY INC
645 4th St Ste 212, Santa Rosa (95404-4435)
PHONE...................707 284-3400
Mark Richard, *Ch of Bd*
Max Blum, *CEO*
▲ EMP: 90
SQ FT: 44,000
SALES (est): 10.2MM **Privately Held**
WEB: www.icondisplay.com
SIC: 7389 Personal service agents, brokers & bureaus

(P-16839)
IDEO LP
28 The Embarcadero Annex, San Francisco (94105-1252)
PHONE...................415 615-5000
Gretchen Addi, *Partner*
EMP: 52
SALES (corp-wide): 40MM **Privately Held**
WEB: www.ideo.com
SIC: 7389 Design, commercial & industrial
PA: Ideo Lp
780 High St
Palo Alto CA 94301
650 289-3400

(P-16840)
IMG (PA)
Also Called: Demo Deluxe
4560 Dorinda Rd, Yorba Linda (92887-1800)
PHONE...................714 974-1700
Jim Smith, *Partner*
Jerry Smith, *Partner*
Nicole Goldberg, *Comms Dir*
Heather Ford, *Administration*
Hossain Uddin, *IT/INT Sup*
EMP: 50
SQ FT: 3,600
SALES (est): 78.1MM **Privately Held**
WEB: www.demodeluxe.com
SIC: 7389 Demonstration service

(P-16841)
INLAND INSPECTIONS CONSULTING
7338 Sycamore Canyon Blvd, Riverside (92508-2334)
PHONE...................951 697-1000
Carol Schumacher, *Manager*
EMP: 50
SALES (est): 1.7MM **Privately Held**
SIC: 7389 Safety inspection service

(P-16842)
INLAND-METRO SERVICES INC
1059 W 14th St, Upland (91786-2678)
PHONE...................909 373-6810
Robert Ayala Sr, *President*
EMP: 55 EST: 2010
SQ FT: 750
SALES (est): 3.7MM **Privately Held**
SIC: 7389 Inspection & testing services

(P-16843)
INNOVATED PACKAGING COMPANY
38505 Cherry St Ste C, Newark (94560-4700)
PHONE...................510 713-3560
Ben F Polando, *President*
Adele Daszko, *Exec VP*
Donna Fernandez, *Senior VP*
Santina Polando, *Exec Sec*
EMP: 148
SQ FT: 110,000
SALES (est): 13.2MM **Privately Held**
WEB: www.innovpak.com
SIC: 7389 3086 Packaging & labeling services; packaging & shipping materials, foamed plastic

(P-16844)
INNOVATIVE MERCH SOLUTIONS LLC
Also Called: IMS
21215 Burbank Blvd, Woodland Hills (91367-7090)
PHONE...................818 936-7800
Joe Kaplan,
Tim Jochner,
EMP: 250 EST: 1999
SQ FT: 50,000
SALES (est): 12.8MM
SALES (corp-wide): 6.7B **Publicly Held**
WEB: www.innovativeclub.com
SIC: 7389 Credit card service
PA: Intuit Inc.
2700 Coast Ave
Mountain View CA 94043
650 944-6000

(P-16845)
INNOVATIVE SILICON INC
4800 Great America Pkwy # 500, Santa Clara (95054-1221)
P.O. Box 391657, Mountain View (94039-1657)
PHONE...................408 572-8700
Mark-Eric Jones, *CEO*
Michael Van Buskirk, *COO*
Jeff Lewis, *Senior VP*
Ken Kundert, *Technical Mgr*
EMP: 80
SQ FT: 11,000
SALES (est): 3.4MM **Privately Held**
WEB: www.innovativesilicon.com
SIC: 7389 Personal service agents, brokers & bureaus

(P-16846)
INSPECTORATE AMERICA CORP
3401 Jack Northrop Ave, Hawthorne (90250-4428)
PHONE...................800 424-0099
EMP: 148
SALES (corp-wide): 280.5MM **Privately Held**
SIC: 7389 Petroleum refinery inspection service
HQ: Inspectorate America Corp
12000 Aerospace Ave # 200
Houston TX 77034
713 944-2000

(P-16847)
INTERIOR OFFICE SOLUTIONS INC (PA)
Also Called: Peoplespace
17800 Mitchell N, Irvine (92614-6004)
PHONE...................949 724-9444
Jesse Bagley, *CEO*
Brian Airth, *Founder*
Caroline Schmidt, *Executive*
Melissa Leonard, *Executive Asst*
Monique Ramirez, *Executive Asst*
EMP: 50
SQ FT: 11,000
SALES: 87.8MM **Privately Held**
WEB: www.iosinc.com
SIC: 7389 5712 Design services; office furniture

(P-16848)
INTERIOR OFFICE SOLUTIONS INC
444 S Flower St Ste 200, Los Angeles (90071-2903)
PHONE...................310 726-9067

Shireen Nadjlessi, *Branch Mgr*
EMP: 50
SALES (corp-wide): 87.8MM **Privately Held**
SIC: 7389 5712 Design services; office furniture
PA: Interior Office Solutions, Inc.
　　17800 Mitchell N
　　Irvine CA 92614
　　949 724-9444

(P-16849)
INTERIORS BY LINDA
49585 Brian Ct, La Quinta (92253-8127)
PHONE..................................760 341-9651
Linda Martin, *Owner*
EMP: 50 EST: 1999
SALES (est): 1.8MM **Privately Held**
SIC: 7389 Interior design services

(P-16850)
INTERPAC TECHNOLOGIES INC
Also Called: Interpac Distribution Center
260 N Pioneer Ave, Woodland (95776-5934)
PHONE..................................530 662-6363
Roderick W Miner, *President*
Corinne Christenson, *Vice Pres*
EMP: 75
SALES (est): 10.1MM **Privately Held**
WEB: www.interpactechnologies.com
SIC: 7389 Packaging & labeling services

(P-16851)
INTERTEK USA INC
Also Called: Intertek Caleb Brett
1941 Freeman Ave Ste A, Signal Hill (90755-1236)
PHONE..................................562 494-4999
Mark Phoreson, *Branch Mgr*
EMP: 50
SQ FT: 1,600
SALES (corp-wide): 3.6B **Privately Held**
WEB: www.itscb.com
SIC: 7389 Pipeline & power line inspection service
HQ: Intertek Usa Inc.
　　200 Westlke Prk Blvd 40
　　Houston TX 77079
　　713 543-3600

(P-16852)
INTRADO CORPORATION
170 N Church Ln, Los Angeles (90049-2044)
PHONE..................................310 481-7878
Rick Patten, *Branch Mgr*
EMP: 198
SALES (corp-wide): 2.2B **Privately Held**
SIC: 7389 Telephone services
HQ: Intrado Corporation
　　11808 Miracle Hills Dr
　　Omaha NE 68154

(P-16853)
INTRADO CORPORATION
3063 W Chapman Ave # 2353, Orange (92868-1738)
PHONE..................................949 294-2801
Gavino D Bautista, *Principal*
EMP: 198
SALES (corp-wide): 2.2B **Privately Held**
SIC: 7389 Telephone services
HQ: Intrado Corporation
　　11808 Miracle Hills Dr
　　Omaha NE 68154

(P-16854)
INVESTLINC GROUP LLC (PA)
Also Called: Investlinc Group, The
1230 Rosecrans Ave # 600, Manhattan Beach (90266-2477)
PHONE..................................310 997-0580
Troy D Wiseman,
Jean-Marc Plantier, *Finance*
Luis Cifuentes, *Accountant*
Leroy H Paris II,
EMP: 85
SALES (est): 2.9MM **Privately Held**
WEB: www.bfd-usa.com
SIC: 7389 Financial services

(P-16855)
IPAYMENT INC (DH)
30721 Russell Ranch Rd # 200, Westlake Village (91362-7383)
PHONE..................................212 802-7200
Mark C Monaco, *CFO*
Philip J Ragona, *Exec VP*
Philip Ragona, *Exec VP*
Robert N Purcell,
Alex Perlovich, *Director*
EMP: 74
SQ FT: 3,800
SALES: 666.8MM
SALES (corp-wide): 85.6K **Privately Held**
WEB: www.ipaymentinc.com
SIC: 7389 Credit card service

(P-16856)
ISI INSPECTION SERVICES INC (PA)
1798 University Ave, Berkeley (94703-1514)
PHONE..................................510 900-2101
Leslie A Sakai, *President*
Ed King, *Exec VP*
Terri Klepp, *Office Mgr*
Kasandra Horcasitas, *Admin Asst*
Mike Everson, *Project Mgr*
EMP: 70
SQ FT: 9,700
SALES (est): 14MM **Privately Held**
WEB: www.inspectionservices.net
SIC: 7389 Inspection & testing services

(P-16857)
J & J PRODUCTIONS INCORPORATED
1775 E Lincoln Ave # 205, Anaheim (92805-4324)
PHONE..................................714 535-0951
Jack D George, *President*
Jessica George, *Vice Pres*
EMP: 50
SQ FT: 1,800
SALES (est): 2.8MM **Privately Held**
SIC: 7389 Fund raising organizations

(P-16858)
JAPANESE ASSISTANCE NETWRK INC
Also Called: Jan
11135 Magnolia Blvd # 140, North Hollywood (91601-3183)
PHONE..................................818 505-6080
Genichi Kadono, *President*
Jj Nishikawa, *Controller*
EMP: 298
SQ FT: 1,700
SALES (est): 12.4MM **Privately Held**
WEB: www.jannetwork.com
SIC: 7389 Translation services
HQ: Relocation International,Inc.
　　4-3-25, Shinjuku
　　Shinjuku-Ku TKY 160-0

(P-16859)
JELEM LLC
1455 Frazee Rd Ste 500, San Diego (92108-4350)
PHONE..................................858 457-2202
Edisena Rodriguez,
EMP: 50
SALES (est): 641.1K **Privately Held**
SIC: 7389 Business services

(P-16860)
JENCO PRODUCTIONS INC (PA)
401 S J St, San Bernardino (92410-2605)
PHONE..................................909 381-9453
Jennifer Imbriani, *President*
Carlos Escobar, *Manager*
Kari Fry, *Manager*
◆ **EMP:** 160 EST: 1995
SQ FT: 50,000
SALES (est): 1.7MM **Privately Held**
WEB: www.jencoprod.com
SIC: 7389 Packaging & labeling services

(P-16861)
JILLIANS SAN FRANCISCO CA
101 4th St Ste 170, San Francisco (94103-3003)
PHONE..................................415 369-6100
Darren Daroches, *General Mgr*

Dan Smith, *President*
Marty Ryan, *General Mgr*
Bryan Galope, *Manager*
EMP: 60
SQ FT: 50,000
SALES (est): 2.9MM **Privately Held**
SIC: 7389 Personal service agents, brokers & bureaus

(P-16862)
JIMMYS FASHIONS
3135 Chadney Dr, Glendale (91206-1004)
PHONE..................................818 790-8932
Young Seok OH, *Owner*
EMP: 50
SALES (est): 2.3MM **Privately Held**
SIC: 7389 Sewing contractor

(P-16863)
JOMAR INDUSTRIES INC
1500 W 139th St, Gardena (90249-2604)
PHONE..................................323 770-0505
John H Stern, *President*
Margaret H Stern, *Corp Secy*
Jeff Stern, *Vice Pres*
EMP: 50
SQ FT: 25,000
SALES (est): 3.3MM **Privately Held**
SIC: 7389 3089 Packaging & labeling services; coloring & finishing of plastic products

(P-16864)
JOPARI SOLUTIONS INC
1855 Gateway Blvd Ste 500, Concord (94520-3277)
PHONE..................................925 459-5200
John Stevens II, *CEO*
John Gilmartin, *COO*
Scott A Hefner, *Senior VP*
EMP: 65
SALES: 8.7MM **Privately Held**
WEB: www.jopari.com
SIC: 7389 Financial services

(P-16865)
JPMORGAN CHASE BANK NAT ASSN
1995 Santa Ana Ave, Costa Mesa (92627-2252)
PHONE..................................949 429-6071
EMP: 103
SALES (corp-wide): 131.4B **Publicly Held**
SIC: 7389 Personal service agents, brokers & bureaus
HQ: Jpmorgan Chase Bank, National Association
　　1111 Polaris Pkwy
　　Columbus OH 43240
　　614 436-3055

(P-16866)
JPMORGAN CHASE BANK NAT ASSN
502 Las Posas Rd, Camarillo (93010-5705)
PHONE..................................805 482-2902
Jane Morel, *Branch Mgr*
EMP: 223
SALES (corp-wide): 131.4B **Publicly Held**
SIC: 7389 6029 Financial services; commercial banks
HQ: Jpmorgan Chase Bank, National Association
　　1111 Polaris Pkwy
　　Columbus OH 43240
　　614 436-3055

(P-16867)
KDS PRINTING AND PACKAGING INC
13397 Marlay Ave Ste A, Fontana (92337-6946)
PHONE..................................909 770-5400
Raymond Fecteau, *President*
Ray Fecteau, *Sales Staff*
EMP: 50
SQ FT: 35,000
SALES (est): 2.5MM **Privately Held**
WEB: www.kdspackaging.com
SIC: 7389 Printing broker

(P-16868)
KENNETH BRDWICK INTR DSGNS INC
Also Called: Beverly Hills Luxury Interiors
1615 Westwood Blvd # 201, Los Angeles (90024-5653)
PHONE..................................310 274-9999
Kenneth Bordewick, *CEO*
Vivian Petreca, *Manager*
EMP: 73
SALES (est): 3.2MM **Privately Held**
WEB: www.kennethbordewickinteriordesigns.com
SIC: 7389 Interior designer

(P-16869)
KILCREW PRODUCTIONS
32811 Wesley St, Wildomar (92595-9759)
PHONE..................................619 564-2080
Robert G Kilbride, *CEO*
Debora Kilbride, *CFO*
EMP: 57
SALES (est): 3.6MM **Privately Held**
SIC: 7389 Convention & show services

(P-16870)
KIM CHONG
Also Called: Union 76
2105 E 25th St, Los Angeles (90058-1125)
PHONE..................................323 581-4700
Chong Kim, *Owner*
EMP: 59
SQ FT: 10,300
SALES (est): 4.7MM **Privately Held**
SIC: 7389 2395 Embroidering of advertising on shirts, etc.; embroidery products, except schiffli machine

(P-16871)
KING-REYNOLDS VENTURES LLC
Also Called: Costanoa
2001 Rossi Rd, Pescadero (94060-9732)
PHONE..................................650 879-2136
John King,
Teri Giordani, *Sales Dir*
Thomas Reynolds,
EMP: 75
SALES (est): 6.7MM **Privately Held**
WEB: www.costanoa.com
SIC: 7389 Financial services

(P-16872)
KIRSCHENMAN ENTERPRISES SLS LP
12826 Edison Hwy, Edison (93220)
P.O. Box 27 (93220-0027)
PHONE..................................661 366-5736
Wayde Kirschenman, *General Ptnr*
EMP: 300
SQ FT: 5,000
SALES: 100MM **Privately Held**
SIC: 7389 Brokers, business: buying & selling business enterprises

(P-16873)
KOBEY CORPORATION INC (PA)
Also Called: Kobey Swap Meet At Spt Arena
3740 Sports Arena Blvd # 2, San Diego (92110-5128)
P.O. Box 81492 (92138-1492)
PHONE..................................619 523-2700
Kimberly Kobey Pretto, *President*
Chuck Pretto, *Vice Pres*
Chris Haesloop, *General Mgr*
Joseph Pretto, *Opers Staff*
EMP: 55
SQ FT: 1,800
SALES (est): 5.7MM **Privately Held**
SIC: 7389 Flea market

(P-16874)
KOOS MANUFACTURING INC
Also Called: Big Star
2741 Seminole Ave, South Gate (90280-5550)
PHONE..................................323 249-1000
U Yul Ku, *President*
Kee H Fong, *Vice Pres*
John Hur, *Vice Pres*
Nan J Ku, *Admin Sec*
David Gumpel, *Business Anlyst*
EMP: 800
SQ FT: 180,000

SALES (est): 98.4MM **Privately Held**
WEB: www.koos.com
SIC: 7389 Sewing contractor

(P-16875)
KOUNTABLE INC
321 Pacific Ave Fl 3, San Francisco
(94111-1701)
PHONE..............................310 613-5481
Chris Hale, *CEO*
Cherry Allen, *Exec VP*
Ian Goudy, *Exec VP*
Maika Hemphill, *Vice Pres*
Joel Onodera, *VP Finance*
EMP: 85
SALES (est): 5.5MM **Privately Held**
SIC: 7389 Financial services

(P-16876)
KOURY ENGRG TSTG & INSPTN
14280 Euclid Ave, Chino (91710-8803)
PHONE..............................310 851-8685
Richard Koury, *President*
EMP: 75
SQ FT: 5,000
SALES: 9MM **Privately Held**
WEB: www.kouryengineering.com
SIC: 7389 Building inspection service

(P-16877)
KPWR RADIO LLC
9550 Firestone Blvd # 105, Downey
(90241-5560)
PHONE..............................562 745-2300
Alex Meruelo, *Mng Member*
EMP: 150
SALES: 27MM **Privately Held**
SIC: 7389 Music & broadcasting services
PA: Meruelo Group Llc
9550 Firestone Blvd # 105
Downey CA 90241
562 745-2300

(P-16878)
L LYON DISTRIBUTING INC
254 W Stuart Ave, Redlands (92374-3136)
P.O. Box 8968 (92375-2168)
PHONE..............................909 798-7129
Michael Lyon, *President*
Lori Lyon, *Vice Pres*
EMP: 50
SQ FT: 5,000
SALES (est): 4.1MM **Privately Held**
SIC: 7389 Merchandise liquidators

(P-16879)
LA INC CONVENTION VISTORS BUR
333 S Hope St Ste 1800, Los Angeles
(90071-1430)
PHONE..............................213 236-2301
Mark Liberman, *Exec Dir*
Tia Sanford, *Sales Staff*
▲ EMP: 75
SALES (est): 19.4MM **Privately Held**
WEB: www.lacvb.com
SIC: 7389 Advertising, promotional & trade
show services

(P-16880)
LA JOLLA GROUP INC (PA)
Also Called: Ljg
14350 Myford Rd, Irvine (92606-1002)
PHONE..............................949 428-2800
Daniel Neukomm, *CEO*
Cristy Abella, *CFO*
Jamie Foote, *Vice Pres*
Michelle Riell, *Admin Sec*
Cedar Carter, *Marketing Staff*
▲ EMP: 59
SALES (est): 24.6MM **Privately Held**
SIC: 7389 6794 2326 Apparel designers,
commercial; copyright buying & licensing;
franchises, selling or licensing; patent
buying, licensing, leasing; men's & boys'
work clothing

(P-16881)
LAKESIDE FIRE PROTECTION DST
12216 Lakeside Ave, Lakeside
(92040-1715)
PHONE..............................619 390-2350
Andy Parr, *Chief*
Tung Nguyen, *Business Anlyst*
Robert Schiwitz, *Comptroller*

EMP: 70
SALES: 16.8MM **Privately Held**
WEB: www.lakesidefire.com
SIC: 7389 Fire protection service other
than forestry or public

(P-16882)
LAKESIDE TAX & FINANCIAL SVCS
9748 Los Coches Rd Ste 3, Lakeside
(92040-4253)
PHONE..............................619 561-2681
Jodie Herzig, *President*
EMP: 68
SALES (est): 293.6K **Privately Held**
SIC: 7389 Financial services

(P-16883)
LAKEWOOD PARK HEALTH CENTER (PA)
12023 Lakewood Blvd, Downey
(90242-2699)
PHONE..............................562 869-0978
Daniel Zilafro, *President*
EMP: 285
SALES (est): 11MM **Privately Held**
SIC: 7389 Personal service agents, bro-
kers & bureaus

(P-16884)
LANGUAGE LINE SERVICES INC (DH)
Also Called: Teleinterpreters
1 Lower Ragsdale Dr # 2, Monterey
(93940-5747)
P.O. Box 202567, Dallas TX (75320-2567)
PHONE..............................800 752-6096
Scott W Klein, *CEO*
Jeffrey Grace, *CFO*
Solange Jerolimov, *CFO*
Michael Schmidt, *CFO*
Dennis G Dracup, *Chairman*
EMP: 53
SALES (est): 10.6MM
SALES (corp-wide): 123.7MM **Privately Held**
SIC: 7389 Translation services
HQ: Language Line Holdings, Inc.
1 Lower Ragsdale Dr # 2
Monterey CA 93940
831 648-5800

(P-16885)
LARK INDUSTRIES INC (HQ)
Also Called: Residential Design Service
4900 E Hunter Ave, Anaheim (92807-2057)
PHONE..............................714 701-4200
Tyron Johnson, *CEO*
Beverly Messemer, *Vice Pres*
Raj Singh, *Vice Pres*
Don Zahnle, *Vice Pres*
Monique Burr, *Admin Mgr*
EMP: 121
SALES (est): 70.4MM
SALES (corp-wide): 489.7MM **Publicly Held**
WEB: www.larkindustries.com
SIC: 7389 3281 Interior design services;
cut stone & stone products
PA: Select Interior Concepts, Inc.
400 Galleria Pkwy Se # 17
Atlanta GA 30339
714 701-4200

(P-16886)
LAX INTERNATIONAL SERVICE CTR
Also Called: Worldway Airmail Center
5800 W Century Blvd, Los Angeles
(90009-5601)
PHONE..............................310 337-8764
Karen Padden, *General Mgr*
EMP: 65
SALES (est): 1.8MM **Privately Held**
SIC: 7389 Post office contract stations

(P-16887)
LEGEND MERCHANT GROUP INC
201 Mission St Ste 230, San Francisco
(94105-1883)
PHONE..............................415 957-9555
Chip Unsworth, *President*
EMP: 50

SALES (est): 3.2MM **Privately Held**
SIC: 7389 Financial services

(P-16888)
LEGION INDUSTRIES
748 Lakemead Way, Emerald Hills
(94062-3923)
PHONE..............................650 743-6358
Zach Micheletti, *Principal*
Ryan Micheletti, *Principal*
EMP: 50
SALES (est): 641.1K **Privately Held**
SIC: 7389

(P-16889)
LENDINGCLUB CORPORATION (PA)
595 Market St Fl 4, San Francisco
(94105-2807)
PHONE..............................415 632-5600
Scott Sanborn, *CEO*
Steven Allocca, *President*
Thomas Casey, *CFO*
Timothy Bogan, *Officer*
Valerie Kay, *Officer*
EMP: 148
SQ FT: 127,000
SALES: 694.8MM **Publicly Held**
SIC: 7389 6153 Financial services; work-
ing capital financing

(P-16890)
LENNAR PARTNERS OF LOS ANGELES (PA)
4350 Von Karman Ave # 200, Newport
Beach (92660-2041)
PHONE..............................949 885-8500
David Team, *Division Pres*
James Camp, *Vice Pres*
EMP: 50
SALES (est): 9.5MM **Privately Held**
WEB: www.lennarpartners.com
SIC: 7389 Personal service agents, bro-
kers & bureaus

(P-16891)
LFP ECOMMERCE LLC
210 N Sunset Ave, West Covina
(91790-2257)
PHONE..............................314 428-5069
EMP: 87
SALES (corp-wide): 379.5K **Privately Held**
SIC: 7389 Personal service agents, bro-
kers & bureaus
PA: Lfp Ecommerce, Llc
8484 Wilshire Blvd # 900
Beverly Hills CA
323 651-5400

(P-16892)
LIFESIGNS NOW INC (PA)
2222 Laverna Ave Fl 1, Los Angeles
(90041-2654)
PHONE..............................323 550-4210
Dr Patricia Hughes, *Director*
EMP: 259 EST: 1986
SALES (est): 3.3MM **Privately Held**
WEB: www.lifesigns.com
SIC: 7389 Translation services

(P-16893)
LINDSAY FRUIT COMPANY LLC
Also Called: Yokohl Valley Packing
247 N Mount Vernon Ave, Lindsay
(93247-2440)
P.O. Box 930 (93247-0930)
PHONE..............................559 562-1327
Tim Bentley,
Larry Larson, *Sales Mgr*
EMP: 75
SALES (est): 5.7MM **Privately Held**
SIC: 7389 Packaging & labeling services

(P-16894)
LITIGTION RSRCES OF AMERICA-CA (PA)
Also Called: Legal Enterprise
4232-1 Las Virgenes Rd, Calabasas
(91302-3589)
PHONE..............................818 878-9227
Tony Maddocks, *President*
Rick Matsumoto, *Manager*
EMP: 75

SALES (est): 5.9MM **Privately Held**
SIC: 7389 8111 Document storage service; general practice attorney, lawyer

(P-16895)
LIVE NATION ENTERTAINMENT INC (PA)
9348 Civic Center Dr Lbby, Beverly Hills
(90210-3642)
PHONE..............................800 653-8000
Michael Rapino, *President*
Arthur Fogel, *President*
Amy Howe, *President*
Bob Roux, *President*
Jared Smith, *President*
▲ EMP: 200
SALES: 10.7B **Publicly Held**
WEB: www.livenation.com
SIC: 7389 7922 7941 Promoters of shows
& exhibitions; entertainment promotion;
theatrical production services; theatrical
companies; legitimate live theater produc-
ers; sports clubs, managers & promoters

(P-16896)
LMS CORPORATION
300 Crprate Pinte Ste 301, Culver City
(90230)
PHONE..............................310 641-4222
EMP: 50
SQ FT: 2,712
SALES (est): 1.6MM **Privately Held**
WEB: www.thelmscorp.com
SIC: 7389 8742

(P-16897)
LONG BEACH UNIFIED SCHOOL DST
Also Called: Newcomb Academy
3351 Val Verde Ave, Long Beach
(90808-4456)
PHONE..............................562 493-3596
EMP: 955
SALES (corp-wide): 865.3MM **Privately Held**
SIC: 7389 Fund raising organizations
PA: Long Beach Unified School District
1515 Hughes Way
Long Beach CA 90810
562 997-8000

(P-16898)
LOS ANGELES UNIFIED SCHOOL DST
Also Called: L A U S D
8525 Rex Rd, Pico Rivera (90660-6702)
PHONE..............................562 654-9007
Marc Monforte, *Branch Mgr*
Mar Tigno, *Principal*
EMP: 59
SALES (corp-wide): 4B **Privately Held**
WEB: www.lausd.k12.ca.us
SIC: 7389 Purchasing service
PA: Los Angeles Unified School District
333 S Beaudry Ave Ste 209
Los Angeles CA 90017
213 241-1000

(P-16899)
LOS ANGLES TRISM CONVENTION BD (PA)
633 W 5th St Ste 1800, Los Angeles
(90071-2087)
PHONE..............................213 624-7300
Ernest Wooden Jr, *CEO*
Alan I Rothenberg, *Ch of Bd*
Stefan J Dietrich, *CFO*
Adam Burke, *Officer*
Jamie Foley, *Vice Pres*
EMP: 77 EST: 1971
SALES (est): 43.7MM **Privately Held**
SIC: 7389 Convention & show services;
tourist information bureau

(P-16900)
LOYAL3 HOLDINGS INC
150 California St Ste 400, San Francisco
(94111-4566)
P.O. Box 26027 (94126-6027)
PHONE..............................415 981-0700
Barry L Schneider, *CEO*
James Iry, *President*
Peter Coleman, *CFO*
Dana Schmidt, *Ch Credit Ofcr*
Jeff Modisett, *Officer*

PRODUCTS & SVCS

EMP: 80
SQ FT: 8,900
SALES (est): 10.8MM **Privately Held**
SIC: **7389** Financial services

(P-16901)
LYELL IMMUNOPHARMA INC
401 E Jamie Ct, South San Francisco
(94080)
PHONE.................................650 383-5381
Richard Klausner, *Principal*
EMP: 150
SALES (est): 157.1K **Privately Held**
SIC: **7389**

(P-16902)
MABIE MARKETING GROUP INC
Also Called: California Marketing
8352 Clairemont Mesa Blvd, San Diego
(92111-1302)
PHONE.................................858 279-5585
John Mabie, *President*
Ramyar Ravansari, *CFO*
Nate Ames, *Info Tech Dir*
Heather Tremble, *Prdtn Dir*
Bo Cline, *Marketing Staff*
EMP: 200
SALES (est): 21MM **Privately Held**
WEB: www.calmarketing.com
SIC: **7389** Telemarketing services

(P-16903)
MACRO-PRO INC (PA)
Also Called: Micro-Pro Microfilming Svcs
2400 Grand Ave, Long Beach
(90815-1762)
P.O. Box 90459 (90809-0459)
PHONE.................................562 595-0900
Patty Waldeck, *President*
Zuly Arguello, *Clerk*
EMP: 140
SQ FT: 24,000
SALES (est): 12.1MM **Privately Held**
WEB: www.macropro.com
SIC: **7389** 7334 Legal & tax services; microfilm recording & developing service; photocopying & duplicating services

(P-16904)
MADDEN CORPORATION
Also Called: Pam's Delivery Svc & Nat Msgnr
733 W Taft Ave, Orange (92865-4229)
PHONE.................................714 922-1670
Donald L Madden, *President*
EMP: 100
SQ FT: 7,000
SALES (est): 10.3MM **Privately Held**
SIC: **7389** Courier or messenger service

(P-16905)
MAGNOLIA VENTURES LTD
Also Called: C/O Longwood Management
4032 Wilshire Blvd Fl 6, Los Angeles
(90010-3425)
PHONE.................................213 389-6900
Jacob Freedman, *President*
EMP: 100
SALES (est): 3.7MM **Privately Held**
SIC: **7389** Personal service agents, brokers & bureaus

(P-16906)
MARINE TECHNICAL SERVICES INC
Also Called: Dockside Machine & Ship Repair
211 N Marine Ave, Wilmington
(90744-5724)
P.O. Box 1301, San Pedro (90733-1301)
PHONE.................................310 549-8030
Dianne Marie Hawke, *President*
Telvis Artis, *General Mgr*
▼ EMP: 75
SQ FT: 20,000
SALES (est): 11MM **Privately Held**
WEB: www.marinetechserv.com
SIC: **7389** 7699 Crane & aerial lift service; nautical repair services

(P-16907)
MARINER SYSTEMS INC (PA)
114 C Ave, Coronado (92118-1435)
PHONE.................................305 266-7255
Carlos M Collazo, *President*
Neil Park, *CEO*
Sawyer Van Horn, *Accounts Mgr*
EMP: 66

SALES (est): 4.1MM **Privately Held**
WEB: www.marinersystems.net
SIC: **7389** 7374 7372 7371 Telephone services; data processing service; prepackaged software; custom computer programming services

(P-16908)
MARMALADE LLC
Also Called: Marmalade Cafes
3894 Cross Creek Rd, Malibu
(90265-4933)
PHONE.................................310 317-4242
Paul McGinley, *Branch Mgr*
EMP: 50
SALES (corp-wide): 22MM **Privately Held**
WEB: www.marmaladecafe.com
SIC: **7389** Personal service agents, brokers & bureaus
PA: Marmalade, Llc
6800 Owensmouth Ave # 350
Canoga Park CA 91303
310 829-0093

(P-16909)
MARQUEZ BROTHERS ADVG AGCY
5801 Rue Ferrari, San Jose (95138-1857)
PHONE.................................408 960-2700
Gustavo Marquez, *President*
EMP: 100
SALES (est): 2.9MM **Privately Held**
SIC: **7389** Advertising, promotional & trade show services

(P-16910)
MARSH CONSULTING GROUP
2626 Summer Ranch Rd, Paso Robles
(93446-8473)
PHONE.................................239 433-5500
Brad Heinrichs, *President*
Robin Schwartz, *Corp Comm Staff*
Geoffrey Marsh, *Consultant*
EMP: 70
SALES (est): 194.1K
SALES (corp-wide): 2.3MM **Privately Held**
WEB: www.mcgteam.com
SIC: **7389** Financial services
PA: Foster & Foster Consulting Actuaries, Inc.
13420 Parker Commons Blvd
Fort Myers FL 33912
239 246-7168

(P-16911)
MARTYS CUTTING INC
Also Called: Marty's Cutting Service
2615 Fruitland Ave, Vernon (90058-2219)
PHONE.................................323 582-5758
Fax: 323 582-5272
EMP: 80
SQ FT: 57,000
SALES (est): 3.8MM **Privately Held**
WEB: www.marty-howard.com
SIC: **7389**

(P-16912)
MASSDROP INC (PA)
710 Sansome St, San Francisco
(94111-1704)
PHONE.................................415 340-2999
Steve El-Hage, *CEO*
Anne Morrissey, *Vice Pres*
Jonathan Liu, *Software Engr*
Albertina Chu, *Project Mgr*
Michael Billeci, *Business Mgr*
EMP: 63
SQ FT: 11,839
SALES (est): 23.2MM **Privately Held**
SIC: **7389** Design services

(P-16913)
MB COATINGS INC
571 N Poplar St Ste G, Orange
(92868-1023)
PHONE.................................714 625-2118
Michael Bartle, *President*
Amanda Bartle, *Vice Pres*
EMP: 80
SQ FT: 2,000
SALES: 5.9MM **Privately Held**
SIC: **7389** Hand painting, textile

(P-16914)
MEDIA ALL STARS INC
8525 Gibbs Dr Ste 206, San Diego
(92123-1765)
PHONE.................................858 300-9600
Buddy Cummings, *President*
Joel Davies, *COO*
Mike McIntosh, *Sales Mgr*
EMP: 53
SALES (est): 6.2MM **Privately Held**
WEB: www.mediaallstars.com
SIC: **7389** Fund raising organizations

(P-16915)
MEDUSIND SOLUTIONS INC (HQ)
31103 Rancho Viejo Rd, San Juan Capistrano (92675-1759)
PHONE.................................949 240-8895
Rajiv Sahney, *Chairman*
Robert Beck, *President*
Vipul Bansal, *CEO*
Dhiren Kapadia, *CFO*
Kranti Munje, *Senior VP*
EMP: 900
SALES (est): 50MM **Privately Held**
WEB: www.medusind.com
SIC: **7389** Personal service agents, brokers & bureaus

(P-16916)
MEGA APPRAISERS INC
14724 Ventura Blvd # 800, Sherman Oaks
(91403-3508)
PHONE.................................818 246-7370
Levon Hairapetian, *President*
EMP: 600
SALES: 1.2MM **Privately Held**
SIC: **7389** Appraisers, except real estate

(P-16917)
MERCURY MESSENGER SERVICE INC
Also Called: Bestway Delivery
16735 Saticoy St Ste 104, Van Nuys
(91406-2700)
PHONE.................................818 989-3115
Lionel Senker, *President*
EMP: 50
SQ FT: 1,500
SALES (est): 6.3MM **Privately Held**
SIC: **7389** 4212 Courier or messenger service; delivery service, vehicular

(P-16918)
MERIBEAR PRODUCTIONS INC
Also Called: Meredith Baer & Associates
4100 Ardmore Ave, South Gate
(90280-3246)
PHONE.................................310 204-5353
Meridith Baer, *President*
Alexandra Parrish, *Creative Dir*
Anna Viola, *Office Mgr*
Anna Tichon, *Purch Mgr*
Brianna Smith, *Sales Associate*
▲ EMP: 90
SQ FT: 55,000
SALES (est): 13.9MM **Privately Held**
SIC: **7389** Interior design services; interior decorating

(P-16919)
MERICAL LLC (PA)
2995 E Miraloma Ave, Anaheim
(92806-1805)
PHONE.................................714 238-7225
Mark Walsh, *CEO*
Jeffrey Stallings, *President*
Richard Gates, *COO*
Michael Smith, *CFO*
Brent Moore, *Exec VP*
EMP: 95
SQ FT: 92,000
SALES (est): 56.8MM **Privately Held**
SIC: **7389** Packaging & labeling services

(P-16920)
MERICAL LLC
447 W Freedom Ave, Orange
(92865-2644)
PHONE.................................714 685-0977
Jeffrey Stallings, *Branch Mgr*
EMP: 58

SALES (corp-wide): 56.8MM **Privately Held**
SIC: **7389** Packaging & labeling services
PA: Merical, Llc
2995 E Miraloma Ave
Anaheim CA 92806
714 238-7225

(P-16921)
MERICAL LLC
Also Called: Merical/Vita-Pak
233 E Bristol Ln, Orange (92865-2715)
PHONE.................................714 283-9551
Tom Bovich, *Exec VP*
Claudia Ruffin, *Vice Pres*
Neil Fournier, *Human Res Mgr*
Kim Butler, *Purchasing*
Brent Moore, *VP Opers*
EMP: 127
SALES (corp-wide): 56.8MM **Privately Held**
SIC: **7389** Packaging & labeling services
PA: Merical, Llc
2995 E Miraloma Ave
Anaheim CA 92806
714 238-7225

(P-16922)
MESSAGE BROADCAST LLC
4685 Macarthur Ct Ste 250, Newport Beach
(92660-1893)
PHONE.................................949 428-3111
William H Potter, *Mng Member*
Bill Joiner, *Officer*
Jim Peterson, *CTO*
Scott Wendrick, *IT/INT Sup*
Tiffany Trinh, *Controller*
EMP: 50
SQ FT: 8,000
SALES: 5.7MM **Privately Held**
SIC: **7389** Telemarketing services

(P-16923)
MESSAGE CENTER COMMUNICATION
6779 Mesa Ridge Rd # 100, San Diego
(92121-2996)
PHONE.................................858 974-7419
Gary Schaumann, *Owner*
EMP: 50
SALES (est): 1.8MM **Privately Held**
SIC: **7389** Telephone answering service

(P-16924)
METRICUS INC
P.O. Box 458 (94302-0458)
PHONE.................................650 328-2500
EMP: 119
SALES (est): 3.1MM **Privately Held**
WEB: www.metricus.com
SIC: **7389**

(P-16925)
MICKWEE GROUP INC
Also Called: Mgi
5600 Mowry School Rd # 230, Newark
(94560-5806)
PHONE.................................510 651-5527
Ronald Mickwee, *President*
EMP: 52
SALES (est): 2.9MM **Privately Held**
WEB: www.mickwee.com
SIC: **7389** 8742 Telemarketing services; management consulting services

(P-16926)
MINIMALISMS INC
49 Missouri St Apt 10, San Francisco
(94107-2484)
PHONE.................................415 309-3108
George Arriola, *President*
EMP: 52 EST: 2014
SALES: 250K **Privately Held**
SIC: **7389** Design services

(P-16927)
MISSION COURIER INC
3204 Orange Grove Ave, North Highlands
(95660-5806)
PHONE.................................916 484-1992
Marc Raty, *President*
Andy French, *Vice Pres*
EMP: 55
SQ FT: 11,000
SALES (est): 5.7MM **Privately Held**
SIC: **7389** Courier or messenger service

(P-16928)
MISSION LANE LLC
101 2nd St Ste 350, San Francisco
(94105-3669)
PHONE...................408 505-3081
Shane Holdaway, *CEO*
Monika Mantri,
EMP: 85
SALES: 50MM **Privately Held**
SIC: 7389 Credit card service

(P-16929)
MODERN DEV CO A LTD PARTNR
Also Called: Paramount Swap Meet
7900 All America City Way, Paramount
(90723-3400)
PHONE...................949 646-6400
Darren Kurkowski, *Branch Mgr*
EMP: 98
SALES (corp-wide): 17.7MM **Privately Held**
SIC: 7389 Flea market
PA: Modern Development Co, A Limited
    Partnership
    3146 Red Hill Ave Ste 220
    Costa Mesa CA 92626
    949 646-6400

(P-16930)
MOLD TESTING AND INSPECTION
Also Called: MT&i
4785 Sequoia Pl, Oceanside (92057-6126)
PHONE...................760 643-1834
K W Huntington, *President*
Keith William Huntington, *President*
EMP: 75
SALES (est): 4.1MM **Privately Held**
SIC: 7389 Inspection & testing services

(P-16931)
MONTRENES FINANCIAL SVCS INC
Also Called: U S Merchant Services
27 Montpellier, Newport Beach
(92660-6844)
PHONE...................562 795-0450
Dan Montrenes, *President*
EMP: 100
SQ FT: 30,000
SALES (est): 5.2MM **Privately Held**
SIC: 7389 Credit card service

(P-16932)
MOTIVATIONAL MARKETING INC (PA)
Also Called: Motivtnal Flfllment Lgstics Sv
15820 Euclid Ave, Chino (91708-9162)
PHONE...................909 517-2200
Hal Altman, *CEO*
Anthony Altman, *Senior VP*
Tony Altman, *Vice Pres*
Cheryl Nataren, *Vice Pres*
Jessie Ortiz, *Vice Pres*
▲ EMP: 88
SQ FT: 300,000
SALES (est): 55.1MM **Privately Held**
WEB: www.mfpsinc.com
SIC: 7389 8748 4225 Telephone services; mailing & messenger services; business consulting; general warehousing & storage

(P-16933)
MULTI-PAK CORPORATION
Also Called: Multipak
20131 Bahama St, Chatsworth
(91311-6202)
PHONE...................818 709-0508
Randall B Unthank, *President*
Victor Sandoval, *Manager*
EMP: 60
SQ FT: 20,000
SALES (est): 5.5MM **Privately Held**
WEB: www.multi-pak.com
SIC: 7389 Packaging & labeling services

(P-16934)
MULTIVISION INC (DH)
Also Called: Bacon's Multivision
66 Franklin St Fl 3, Oakland (94607-3728)
PHONE...................510 740-5600
Babak Farahi, *President*
EMP: 70

SALES (est): 7.9MM
SALES (corp-wide): 730.3MM **Publicly Held**
WEB: www.multivision.com
SIC: 7389 Press clipping service
HQ: Cision Us Inc.
    130 E Randolph St Fl 7
    Chicago IL 60601
    312 922-2400

(P-16935)
MUSCOLINO INVENTORY SVC INC
1620 N Carptr Rd Ste D50, Modesto
(95351)
PHONE...................209 576-8469
Fax: 209 576-8469
EMP: 50
SALES (corp-wide): 67MM **Privately Held**
SIC: 7389
HQ: Muscolino Inventory Service, Inc.
    320 W Chestnut Ave
    Monrovia CA 91016
    626 357-8600

(P-16936)
MVENTIX INC (PA)
21600 Oxnard St Ste 1700, Woodland Hills
(91367-4972)
PHONE...................818 337-3747
Kristian Fatzov, *CEO*
Scott Kleiman, *Exec Dir*
Pavel Monev, *CTO*
Koh Mina, *Accountant*
Shamas Ulhaq, *Marketing Staff*
EMP: 386
SALES (est): 35.4MM **Privately Held**
WEB: www.mventix.com
SIC: 7389 8742 Advertising, promotional & trade show services; marketing consulting services

(P-16937)
MX COURIER SYSTEMS INC
Also Called: Medical Ex Courier Systems
990 N Tustin St, Orange (92867-5908)
PHONE...................714 288-8622
Mohammad A Zadsham, *President*
Akbar Heidarinia, *President*
EMP: 50
SQ FT: 1,200
SALES: 1.5MM **Privately Held**
SIC: 7389 4212 Courier or messenger service; delivery service, vehicular

(P-16938)
MZA EVENTS INC (PA)
3550 Wilshire Blvd # 1012, Los Angeles
(90010-2412)
PHONE...................213 201-1348
Craig R Miller, *CEO*
EMP: 50
SALES (est): 4.1MM **Privately Held**
WEB: www.mzainc.com
SIC: 7389 8742 Fund raising organizations; business planning & organizing services

(P-16939)
NATIONAL BUS INVESTIGATIONS
Also Called: MPS Security
25020 Las Brisas Rd Ste A, Murrieta
(92562-4064)
PHONE...................951 677-3500
Michael D Julian, *President*
Valerie Dovifaaz, *Accounts Mgr*
Sam Grothe, *Accounts Mgr*
EMP: 60 EST: 1967
SQ FT: 2,000
SALES (est): 6.3MM **Privately Held**
SIC: 7389 7381 Personal investigation service; private investigator

(P-16940)
NATIONAL LGAL STUDIES INST INC
Also Called: Nlsi
23962 Alssndro Blvd Ste P, Moreno Valley
(92553-8806)
P.O. Box 7562, Riverside (92513-7562)
PHONE...................951 653-4240
Thersea Thompson, *CEO*
EMP: 50

SQ FT: 2,000
SALES (est): 2.4MM **Privately Held**
SIC: 7389 Paralegal service

(P-16941)
NATIONS DIRECT LENDER & IN
160 S Old Springs Rd # 260, Anaheim
(92808-1229)
PHONE...................800 969-7779
Jeff Store, *President*
Hal Lamm, *CFO*
EMP: 114
SQ FT: 18,000
SALES (est): 8.1MM **Privately Held**
WEB: www.signing-services.com
SIC: 7389 Drafting service, except temporary help

(P-16942)
NEFAB PACKAGING WEST LLC
8477 Central Ave, Newark (94560-3431)
PHONE...................408 678-2516
Fredrik Solspher,
EMP: 60
SALES (est): 10MM
SALES (corp-wide): 496.7MM **Privately Held**
SIC: 7389 Packaging & labeling services
HQ: Nefab Companies, Inc.
    204 Airline Dr Ste 100
    Coppell TX 75019
    866 332-4425

(P-16943)
NESTWISE LLC
9785 Towne Centre Dr, San Diego
(92121-1968)
PHONE...................855 444-6378
Esther Stearns, *CEO*
Beth Stelluto, *Chief Mktg Ofcr*
Burt White, *Ch Invest Ofcr*
Kandis Bates, *Officer*
Rudy Bethea, *Officer*
EMP: 266
SALES (est): 11.7MM **Publicly Held**
SIC: 7389 Financial services
PA: Lpl Financial Holdings Inc.
    75 State St Ste 2401
    Boston MA 02109

(P-16944)
NETBALL AMERICA INC
5101 Audrey Dr, Huntington Beach
(92649-2404)
P.O. Box 11531, Westminster (92685-1531)
PHONE...................888 221-3650
Sonya Ottaway, *President*
EMP: 50
SALES (est): 63.5K **Privately Held**
SIC: 7389 Business services

(P-16945)
NETWORK TELEPHONE SERVICES INC (PA)
Also Called: N T S
21135 Erwin St, Woodland Hills
(91367-3713)
PHONE...................800 742-5687
Joseph Preston, *Ch of Bd*
Gary Passon, *President*
Dan Coleman, *Vice Pres*
Marlene Tanner, *Vice Pres*
Robert Alba, *Info Tech Mgr*
EMP: 500
SQ FT: 70,000
SALES (est): 45.4MM **Privately Held**
WEB: nts.net/index.php
SIC: 7389 4813 7374 Telephone services; ; data processing & preparation

(P-16946)
NEW CREW PRODUCTION CORP
1100 W 135th St, Gardena (90247-1919)
PHONE...................323 234-8880
Kris Park, *President*
Joseph Park, *Admin Sec*
▲ EMP: 110
SALES (est): 10.3MM **Privately Held**
WEB: www.newcrewproductioncorp.com
SIC: 7389 Sewing contractor

(P-16947)
NEWPORT DIVERSIFIED INC
Santa Fe Springs Swap Meet
13963 Alondra Blvd, Santa Fe Springs
(90670-5814)
PHONE...................562 921-4359
Rick Landis, *Sales & Mktg St*
Ron Westphal, *General Mgr*
Chris Woodson, *Opers Mgr*
EMP: 200
SQ FT: 10,846
SALES (corp-wide): 1.1MM **Privately Held**
WEB: www.nd-inc.com
SIC: 7389 5932 Flea market; used merchandise stores
PA: Newport Diversified, Inc.
    4695 Macarthur Ct # 1420
    Newport Beach CA 92660
    949 851-1355

(P-16948)
NEWPORT DIVERSIFIED INC
Also Called: The Boardwalk
1286 Fletcher Pkwy, El Cajon
(92020-1826)
PHONE...................619 449-7800
Ron Westphal, *Manager*
EMP: 100
SALES (corp-wide): 1.1MM **Privately Held**
WEB: www.nd-inc.com
SIC: 7389 7996 Flea market; amusement parks
PA: Newport Diversified, Inc.
    4695 Macarthur Ct # 1420
    Newport Beach CA 92660
    949 851-1355

(P-16949)
NIELSEN MOBILE LLC (DH)
1010 Battery St, San Francisco
(94111-1224)
PHONE...................917 435-9301
Sid Gorham, *President*
Tom Stahl, *COO*
Jim Wandrey, *Treasurer*
Jagdish Patil, *Vice Pres*
Julie Oberhausen-Clar, *Engineer*
EMP: 180 EST: 2000
SQ FT: 38,000
SALES (est): 16.8MM
SALES (corp-wide): 6.5B **Privately Held**
WEB: www.telephia.com
SIC: 7389 Inspection & testing services

(P-16950)
NLC ENTERPRISES INCORPORATED
15710 Leffingwell Rd, Whittier
(90604-3325)
PHONE...................562 693-3590
Norman Carter, *Principal*
EMP: 50
SALES (est): 1.6MM **Privately Held**
SIC: 7389 Business services

(P-16951)
NNA SERVICES LLC
Also Called: Nna Insurance Services
9350 De Soto Ave, Chatsworth
(91311-4926)
PHONE...................818 739-4071
Milton G Valera, *Ch of Bd*
Thomas A Heymann, *CEO*
Robert A Clarke, *CFO*
Deborah M Thaw, *Exec VP*
EMP: 204
SQ FT: 55,000
SALES (est): 3.2MM **Privately Held**
SIC: 7389 6411 Notary publics; insurance agents, brokers & service

(P-16952)
NNNCC RANCH
7602 Monson Ave, Orange Cove
(93646-9307)
PHONE...................559 626-4890
Richard Nicholas, *Partner*
Richard M Nicholas, *Owner*
EMP: 50 EST: 2000
SQ FT: 2,238
SALES (est): 3.5MM **Privately Held**
SIC: 7389 Packaging & labeling services

(P-16953)
NOR-CAL BEVERAGE CO INC
Also Called: Norcal Beverage Co
1226 N Olive St, Anaheim (92801-2543)
PHONE...................714 526-8600
William McFarland, *Manager*
EMP: 200
SALES (corp-wide): 248.5MM **Privately Held**
SIC: 7389 2033 Packaging & labeling services; canned fruits & specialties
PA: Nor-Cal Beverage Co., Inc.
2150 Stone Blvd
West Sacramento CA 95691
916 372-0600

(P-16954)
NOVATO FIRE PROTECTION DIST
95 Rowland Way, Novato (94945-5001)
PHONE...................415 878-2690
Daniel Hom, *Finance*
Marc Revere, *Fire Chief*
EMP: 90
SALES (est): 6.1MM **Privately Held**
SIC: 7389 Fire protection service other than forestry or public

(P-16955)
NTH DEGREE INC
Also Called: N Th Degree
27092 Burbank, Foothill Ranch (92610-2508)
PHONE...................714 734-4155
Scott Bennett, *Branch Mgr*
Jennifer Bannerman, *Manager*
EMP: 50
SALES (corp-wide): 46.3MM **Privately Held**
WEB: www.nthdegree.com
SIC: 7389 Convention & show services
PA: Nth Degree, Inc.
3237 Satellite Blvd # 600
Duluth GA 30096
404 296-5282

(P-16956)
NUCOMPASS MOBILITY SVCS INC (PA)
6800 Koll Center Pkwy, Pleasanton (94566-7045)
PHONE...................925 734-3434
Frank Patitucci, *CEO*
Lesley Dehoney, *Vice Pres*
Douglas Fritz, *Vice Pres*
Ken Klein, *Vice Pres*
Serena Torvik, *Vice Pres*
EMP: 90
SALES (est): 17MM **Privately Held**
SIC: 7389 Relocation service

(P-16957)
OC ACCESSORIES LLC
4533 Macarthur Blvd A-2032, Newport Beach (92660-2059)
PHONE...................949 229-2410
Don Seawell, *Principal*
Yesenia Cruz,
Tracy Zieve,
EMP: 58
SQ FT: 2,485
SALES (est): 871.9K **Privately Held**
SIC: 7389 Personal service agents, brokers & bureaus

(P-16958)
OCEAN BREEZE MANUFACTURING
1961 Hawkins Cir, Los Angeles (90001-2255)
PHONE...................323 586-8760
Jamshid Daneshrad, *President*
Jackline Daneshrad, *Shareholder*
John Daneshrad, *Shareholder*
Shain Daneshrad, *Shareholder*
EMP: 80
SQ FT: 60,000
SALES (est): 1.5MM **Privately Held**
SIC: 7389 Sewing contractor

(P-16959)
OCEANX LLC (HQ)
100 N Pacific Coast Hwy, El Segundo (90245-4359)
PHONE...................310 774-4088

Steve Adams, *Mng Member*
Tony Arteaga, *Vice Pres*
George Morris, *Vice Pres*
Matthew Wall, *Administration*
Charlie Malone, *Engineer*
EMP: 98
SALES: 137MM
SALES (corp-wide): 270.2MM **Privately Held**
SIC: 7389 4731 Subscription fulfillment services: magazine, newspaper, etc.; freight transportation arrangement
PA: Guthy-Renker Llc
100 N Pacific Coast Hwy
El Segundo CA 90245
760 773-9022

(P-16960)
ON-SITE MANAGER INC (HQ)
307 Orchard Cy Dr Ste 110, Campbell (95008)
PHONE...................866 266-7483
Jake Harrington, *CEO*
Monte Jones, *President*
Scott Jones, *CTO*
EMP: 50
SALES (est): 11.2MM
SALES (corp-wide): 869.4MM **Publicly Held**
WEB: www.on-sitemanager.com
SIC: 7389 Tenant screening service
PA: Realpage, Inc.
2201 Lakeside Blvd
Richardson TX 75082
972 820-3000

(P-16961)
ONE HEART WORLD WHICH WILL DO
1818 Pacheco St, San Francisco (94116-1223)
PHONE...................415 379-4762
Arlene Samen, *CEO*
EMP: 80
SALES (est): 928K **Privately Held**
SIC: 7389

(P-16962)
ONE LEGAL INC
350 S Figueroa St Ste 385, Los Angeles (90071-1208)
PHONE...................213 617-1212
Robert Battaglia, *President*
Josh Hanft, *Info Tech Dir*
Visnu Ghosh, *Business Anlyst*
EMP: 60
SALES (est): 4.2MM **Privately Held**
SIC: 7389 Legal & tax services

(P-16963)
ONTARIO CONVENTION CENTER CORP
Also Called: Smg Management Facility
2000 E Convention Ctr Way, Ontario (91764-5633)
PHONE...................909 937-3000
Dick Walsh, *Mayor*
Michael K Krouse, *CEO*
EMP: 130
SQ FT: 225,000
SALES (est): 8.1MM **Privately Held**
WEB: www.ontariocc.com
SIC: 7389 9111 Convention & show services; city & town managers' offices
PA: City Of Ontario
303 E B St
Ontario CA 91764
909 395-2012

(P-16964)
OPENTABLE INC (HQ)
1 Montgomery St Ste 700, San Francisco (94104-4536)
PHONE...................415 344-4200
Christa Quarles, *CEO*
Matthew Roberts, *Ch of Bd*
Jeff McCombs, *CFO*
I Duncan Robertson, *CFO*
Scott Day, *Vice Pres*
EMP: 123 EST: 1998
SQ FT: 50,965
SALES: 190MM
SALES (corp-wide): 14.5B **Publicly Held**
WEB: www.opentable.com
SIC: 7389 Restaurant reservation service

PA: Booking Holdings Inc.
800 Connecticut Ave
Norwalk CT 06854
203 299-8000

(P-16965)
OPORTUN FINANCIAL CORPORATION (PA)
2 Circle Star Way, San Carlos (94070-6200)
PHONE...................650 810-8823
Raul Vazquez, *CEO*
Matthew Jenkins, *COO*
Joan Aristei, *Ch Credit Ofcr*
Patrick Kirscht, *Ch Credit Ofcr*
Jonathan Coblentz, *Officer*
EMP: 513
SQ FT: 100,000
SALES (est): 457.4MM **Publicly Held**
SIC: 7389 Financial services

(P-16966)
OPUS 2 INTERNATIONAL INC
100 Pine St Ste 775, San Francisco (94111-5126)
PHONE...................888 960-3117
Graham Smith-Bernal, *CEO*
Clare Foley, *Vice Pres*
Kenneth Poliran, *Administration*
Chris Finley, *Project Mgr*
Liza Pestillos-Ocat, *Opers Staff*
EMP: 50
SALES (est): 398.5K **Privately Held**
SIC: 7389 Automobile recovery service

(P-16967)
ORA PACIFIC REGIONAL FIELD OFF
Also Called: Pacific Regional Laboratory SW
19701 Fairchild, Irvine (92612-2506)
PHONE...................949 608-2907
William Martin, *Director*
EMP: 85 **Publicly Held**
SIC: 7389 9431 Safety inspection service;
HQ: Ora Pacific Regional Field Office
1301 Clay St Ste 1180n
Oakland CA 94612

(P-16968)
ORANGE CNTY ADULT ACHVMNT CTR
Also Called: MY DAY COUNTS
225 W Carl Karcher Way, Anaheim (92801-2499)
PHONE...................714 744-5301
Michael Galliano, *CEO*
Patrick Faraday, *Vice Pres*
Richard Farmer, *Vice Pres*
Laurie Vinkavich, *Vice Pres*
Martin Campos, *Opers Staff*
▲ EMP: 135
SQ FT: 57,000
SALES (est): 10.5MM **Privately Held**
WEB: www.orangecountyarc.org
SIC: 7389 Packaging & labeling services

(P-16969)
ORANGE COAST TITLE COMPANY (PA)
1551 N Tustin Ave Ste 300, Santa Ana (92705-8638)
P.O. Box 11825 (92711-1825)
PHONE...................714 558-2836
John L Marconi, *CEO*
Rich Mac Aluso, *President*
Fred Nilsen, *President*
Ed Cross, *COO*
Macaluso Rich, *Bd of Directors*
EMP: 100
SQ FT: 24,000
SALES (est): 156.4MM **Privately Held**
SIC: 7389 6361 6541 Personal service agents, brokers & bureaus; title insurance; title & trust companies

(P-16970)
ORANGE COURIER INC
3731 W Warner Ave, Santa Ana (92704-5218)
P.O. Box 5308 (92704-0308)
PHONE...................714 384-3600
Evell T Stanley, *President*
Diane Smith, *Sales Staff*
Michelle Cannon,

▲ EMP: 300
SQ FT: 150,000
SALES (est): 34.6MM **Privately Held**
WEB: www.orangecourier.com
SIC: 7389 4213 4225 Courier or messenger service; trucking, except local; general warehousing & storage

(P-16971)
OST TRUCKS AND CRANES INC
Also Called: Ost Crane Service
2951 N Ventura Ave, Ventura (93001-1210)
P.O. Box 237 (93002-0237)
PHONE...................805 643-9963
L Dennis Zermeno, *President*
Don D Zermeno, *Vice Pres*
Ron J Zermeno, *Vice Pres*
EMP: 73
SQ FT: 3,000
SALES (est): 11.5MM **Privately Held**
WEB: www.ostcranes.com
SIC: 7389 4212 4225 Crane & aerial lift service; local trucking, without storage; general warehousing & storage

(P-16972)
OSTERHOUT GROUP INC
Also Called: Osterhout Design Group
200 Brannan St Apt 326, San Francisco (94107-6025)
PHONE...................415 644-4000
Ralph F Osterhout, *President*
Mike Huynh, *Engineer*
Manuel Sanchez, *Director*
EMP: 50
SALES (est): 10.6MM **Privately Held**
SIC: 7389 Design, commercial & industrial

(P-16973)
OUR LADY OF GRACE P T G
2766 Navajo Rd, El Cajon (92020-2121)
PHONE...................619 466-0055
Susan Husc, *President*
Gloria Green, *Treasurer*
Stephanie Hagenburger, *Treasurer*
Timothy Phariss, *Vice Pres*
Coleen Robinson, *Admin Sec*
EMP: 50
SALES (est): 3.5MM **Privately Held**
WEB: www.ourladyofkazanchurch.org
SIC: 7389 Fund raising organizations

(P-16974)
OVERLAND PACIFIC & CUTLER LLC (PA)
Also Called: Pacific Relocation Consultants
3750 Schaufele Ave # 150, Long Beach (90808-1779)
PHONE...................800 400-7356
Ray Armstrong, *CEO*
Marty Zvirbulis, *Officer*
Mark Labonte Sr, *Vice Pres*
Barry McDaniel, *Vice Pres*
Steve Oliver, *Vice Pres*
▲ EMP: 55
SQ FT: 7,000
SALES (est): 20MM **Privately Held**
WEB: www.opcservices.com
SIC: 7389 Relocation service

(P-16975)
OXNARD PERFRMN ARTS & CONVTN
Also Called: CITY OF OXNARD PERFORMING ARTS
800 Hobson Way, Oxnard (93030-6723)
PHONE...................805 486-2424
Robert Holden, *CEO*
EMP: 50
SALES: 1.6MM **Privately Held**
SIC: 7389 Convention & show services; tourist information bureau

(P-16976)
PACIFIC COAST COMPANIES INC
10600 White Rock Rd # 100, Rancho Cordova (95670-6294)
P.O. Box 419074 (95741-9074)
PHONE...................916 631-6500
David J Lucchetti, *President*
Dale Waldschmitt, *COO*
Joshua Kimerer, *CFO*
Daniel Yanagihara, *Vice Pres*
Ken Kerrick, *CIO*

EMP: 125
SALES (est): 18.9MM
SALES (corp-wide): 1.5B **Privately Held**
SIC: 7389 8742 Legal & tax services;
human resource consulting services
PA: Pacific Coast Building Products, Inc.
10600 White Rock Rd # 100
Rancho Cordova CA 95670
916 631-6500

(P-16977)
PACIFIC COAST PRODUCERS
650 S Guild Ave, Lodi (95240-3114)
PHONE..................................209 365-9982
Jim Farmer, *Branch Mgr*
Dan Newhall, *Manager*
EMP: 500
SALES (corp-wide): 806.2MM **Privately Held**
SIC: 7389 5141 Packaging & labeling
services; groceries, general line
PA: Pacific Coast Producers
631 N Cluff Ave
Lodi CA 95240
209 367-8800

(P-16978)
PACIFIC MEDICAL INC (PA)
1700 N Chrisman Rd, Tracy (95304-9314)
P.O. Box 149 (95378-0149)
PHONE..................................800 726-9180
John M Petlansky, *CEO*
Jeffrey Leonard, *CFO*
James Parsons,
Bob McCune, *Vice Pres*
Kyle Scott, *Practice Mgr*
EMP: 116
SQ FT: 18,000
SALES (est): 67.5MM **Privately Held**
WEB: www.pacmedical.com
SIC: 7389 7352 Brokers, contract serv-
ices; medical equipment rental

(P-16979)
PALADIN TECHNOLOGIES INC
Also Called: Tekworks
13000 Gregg St Ste B, Poway
(92064-7151)
PHONE..................................858 668-1705
EMP: 145
SALES (corp-wide): 13.1MM **Privately Held**
SIC: 7389 1731 Advertising, promotional &
trade show services; electrical work
PA: Paladin Technologies Inc
3001 Wayburne Dr Suite 201
Burnaby BC V5G 4
604 677-8700

(P-16980)
PARADIGM INDUSTRIES INC
2522 E 37th St, Vernon (90058-1725)
PHONE..................................310 965-1900
William Jun, *CEO*
Chu Kim, *President*
▲ EMP: 80
SALES (est): 5.2MM **Privately Held**
WEB: www.paradigmindustries.com
SIC: 7389 Textile & apparel services

(P-16981)
PARALLEL ADVISORS LLC
150 Spear St Ste 950, San Francisco
(94105-5154)
PHONE..................................866 627-6984
Jerry E Rendic, *Mng Member*
CJ Rendic, *CEO*
Diane Gabianelli, *CFO*
Brian O'Keefe, *Ch Invest Ofcr*
Robert Higgins,
EMP: 51
SALES: 11MM **Privately Held**
SIC: 7389 Financial services

(P-16982)
PARTNER HERO INC
1001 Avenida Pico C260, San Clemente
(92673-6957)
PHONE..................................888 968-2767
Shervin Talieh, *Administration*
EMP: 50 EST: 2014
SALES (est): 938.7K **Privately Held**
SIC: 7389 Telephone answering service

(P-16983)
PARTNERS CAPITAL GROUP INC (PA)
201 Sandpointe Ave # 500, Santa Ana
(92707-8716)
PHONE..................................949 916-3900
Mark Davin, *CEO*
Brian Even, *Vice Pres*
Darrell Fleming, *Vice Pres*
David Frank, *Vice Pres*
Mat Hennings, *Vice Pres*
EMP: 80
SQ FT: 25,000
SALES (est): 66.9MM **Privately Held**
SIC: 7389 Financial services

(P-16984)
PARTOS AGENCY LLC
Also Called: Partos Company, The
247 Windward Ave, Venice (90291-3764)
PHONE..................................310 458-7800
Walter Partos,
Laura Roman, *Office Mgr*
Martijn Hostetler, *Agent*
EMP: 70
SALES (est): 4.1MM **Privately Held**
WEB: www.partos.com
SIC: 7389 7922 Authors' agents & bro-
kers; talent agent, theatrical

(P-16985)
PASADENA CENTER OPERATING CO
Also Called: Pasadena Convention Center
300 E Green St, Pasadena (91101-2399)
PHONE..................................626 795-9311
Michael Ross, *CEO*
Mary Collins, *Executive Asst*
Phuong Wong, *Finance*
Gail Anderson, *Opers Staff*
Taylor Fry, *Natl Sales Mgr*
EMP: 116
SQ FT: 32,000
SALES: 23.6MM **Privately Held**
WEB: www.pasadenacal.com
SIC: 7389 Convention & show services

(P-16986)
PASSPRT ACCEPT FCLTY LOS ANGEL
Also Called: Sunset Station
1425 N Cherokee Ave, Los Angeles
(90093-2108)
PHONE..................................323 460-4811
Gerald Padilla, *General Mgr*
EMP: 60 EST: 2014
SALES (est): 1.3MM **Privately Held**
SIC: 7389 Post office contract stations

(P-16987)
PATRICK K WILLIS COMPANY INC
Also Called: American Recovery Service
5118 Rbert J Mathews Pkwy, El Dorado
Hills (95762-5703)
PHONE..................................800 398-6480
David Baker, *Senior VP*
Jennifer Valperga, *President*
John Foster, *Officer*
Christian Beyer, *Vice Pres*
Michael Lusk, *Vice Pres*
EMP: 300
SQ FT: 10,000
SALES (est): 3.2MM **Privately Held**
SIC: 7389 Repossession service

(P-16988)
PAYPAL HOLDINGS INC (PA)
2211 N 1st St, San Jose (95131-2021)
PHONE..................................408 967-1000
Daniel H Schulman, *President*
William J Ready, *COO*
John D Rainey, *CFO*
John Rainey, *CFO*
Jonathan Christodoro, *Bd of Directors*
EMP: 63
SQ FT: 700,000
SALES: 15.4B **Publicly Held**
SIC: 7389 6099 7374 Financial services;
automated clearinghouses; clearinghouse
associations, bank or check; electronic
funds transfer network, including switch-
ing; data processing & preparation; data
processing service

(P-16989)
PB CAR MOVERS
5510 W 120th St, Hawthorne (90250-3406)
PHONE..................................310 283-2741
Jose Desiderio, *Owner*
EMP: 60
SALES (est): 1.9MM **Privately Held**
SIC: 7389 Automobile recovery service

(P-16990)
PERMITS TODAY LLC
140 S Lake Ave Ste 323, Pasadena
(91101-4787)
PHONE..................................626 585-2931
Scott Daves,
Margaret Sargent,
Carla Street,
EMP: 75 EST: 1998
SALES: 2.5MM **Privately Held**
WEB: www.permitstoday.com
SIC: 7389 Personal service agents, bro-
kers & bureaus

(P-16991)
PHOENIX INTL HOLDINGS INC
127 Press Ln, Chula Vista (91910-1011)
PHONE..................................619 207-0871
Kelvin Hall, *Branch Mgr*
EMP: 143 **Privately Held**
SIC: 7389 Marine reporting
PA: Phoenix International Holdings, Inc.
9301 Largo Dr W
Largo MD 20774

(P-16992)
PHOENIX TEXTILE INC
910 S Los Angeles St, Los Angeles
(90015-1726)
PHONE..................................213 239-9640
Fax: 213 228-1109
EMP: 70
SALES (corp-wide): 42.4MM **Privately Held**
SIC: 7389
PA: Phoenix Textile, Inc.
14600 S Broadway
Gardena CA 90248
310 715-7090

(P-16993)
PHONE WARE INC
8902 Activity Rd Ste A, San Diego
(92126-4471)
PHONE..................................858 530-8550
William J Nassir, *President*
Bolden Ellen, *CFO*
Hazel Nassir, *Exec VP*
Jim Rochford, *Vice Pres*
Bill Kyle, *VP Mktg*
EMP: 366
SQ FT: 20,000
SALES (est): 36.6MM **Privately Held**
WEB: www.phoneware.com
SIC: 7389 8742 Telemarketing services;
marketing consulting services

(P-16994)
PIONEER THEATRES INC
Also Called: Roadium Open Air Market
2500 Redondo Beach Blvd, Torrance
(90504-1529)
PHONE..................................310 532-8183
William Fleischman, *President*
William Warnick, *Vice Pres*
EMP: 110
SQ FT: 3,000
SALES (est): 10.3MM **Privately Held**
WEB: www.pioneertheatre.org
SIC: 7389 5431 Flea market; fruit & veg-
etable markets

(P-16995)
PITNEY BOWES PRESORT SVCS INC
18550 S Broadwick St, Compton
(90220-6439)
PHONE..................................310 763-4615
Lori Butcher, *Branch Mgr*
EMP: 115
SALES (corp-wide): 3.5B **Publicly Held**
WEB: www.psigroupinc.com
SIC: 7389 Presorted mail service

HQ: Pitney Bowes Presort Services, Inc.
10110 I St
Omaha NE 68127

(P-16996)
PITNEY BOWES PRESORT SVCS INC
125 Valley Dr, Brisbane (94005-1317)
PHONE..................................415 468-1660
Nick Saribalis, *Vice Pres*
Nichol003 Saribalis, *President*
EMP: 70
SALES (corp-wide): 3.5B **Publicly Held**
WEB: www.psigroupinc.com
SIC: 7389 Presorted mail service
HQ: Pitney Bowes Presort Services, Inc.
10110 I St
Omaha NE 68127

(P-16997)
PIXIOR LLC (PA)
5901 S Eastern Ave, Commerce
(90040-4003)
PHONE..................................323 721-2221
Yassine Amallal, *Mng Member*
James Burley, *Managing Prtnr*
Elena Pickett, *Senior VP*
Kiet Huynh, *Accounting Mgr*
Galina Turetskaya, *Accountant*
▲ EMP: 89
SQ FT: 192,000
SALES (est): 15.9MM **Privately Held**
WEB: www.pixior.com
SIC: 7389 Advertising, promotional & trade
show services

(P-16998)
PLASTIFLEX COMPANY INC (DH)
601 E Palomar St Ste 424, Chula Vista
(91911-6976)
PHONE..................................619 662-8792
Gerald Green, *President*
Robert Sakiyama, *President*
David McIvor, *CEO*
Richard Loh, *Vice Pres*
Mark Monper, *Vice Pres*
▲ EMP: 130
SQ FT: 48,000
SALES (est): 18.7MM
SALES (corp-wide): 242.1K **Privately Held**
WEB: www.plastiflex.com
SIC: 7389 Swimming pool & hot tub serv-
ice & maintenance
HQ: Plastiflex Group
Buntjesstraat 13
Beringen 3583
114 358-00

(P-16999)
PLUM HEALTHCARE GROUP LLC
Also Called: Redlands Health Care Group
1620 W Fern Ave, Redlands (92373-4918)
PHONE..................................909 793-2609
Mark Baliff,
Vicenta Hollingshead, *Records Dir*
Breanna Knight, *Records Dir*
Caprice Gillespie, *Office Mgr*
Eddie Cook, *Technology*
EMP: 80
SALES (est): 3.9MM **Privately Held**
WEB: www.plum.ca
SIC: 7389 Personal service agents, bro-
kers & bureaus

(P-17000)
PRE-EMPLOYCOM INC
3655 Meadow View Dr, Redding
(96002-9715)
P.O. Box 491570 (96049-1570)
PHONE..................................800 300-1821
Robert V Mather, *President*
Michael Hough, *Finance*
Shelby Chase, *Human Resources*
EMP: 100
SQ FT: 10,500
SALES (est): 3.2MM **Privately Held**
WEB: www.pre-employ.com
SIC: 7389 Personal investigation service

(P-17001)
PRECISION IDEO INC
780 High St, Palo Alto (94301-2420)
PHONE..................................650 688-3400
Tim Brown, *President*
Duane Bray, *Partner*
Fred Dust, *Partner*
Tom Eich, *Partner*
Whitney Mortimer, *Partner*
EMP: 400
SALES (est): 19.3MM **Privately Held**
SIC: 7389 Design services

(P-17002)
PREMIER OFFICE CENTERS
LLC (PA)
Also Called: Premier Business Centers
2102 Business Center Dr, Irvine
(92612-1001)
PHONE..................................949 253-4616
Jeffrey Reinstein, *CEO*
Amy Fuller, *Officer*
Nancy Colella, *General Mgr*
Vanessa Decker, *General Mgr*
Jake Khoury, *General Mgr*
▲ **EMP:** 50
SALES (est): 57.4MM
SALES (corp-wide): 59.4MM **Privately**
Held
SIC: 7389 Office facilities & secretarial
service rental

(P-17003)
PREVENT LIFE SAFETY SVCS
INC
1410 Stealth St, Livermore (94551-9358)
PHONE..................................925 667-2088
Carol D Cohan, *President*
Jodi Clem, *Vice Pres*
Jeff Norman, *Executive*
Peter Frenzel, *Sales Engr*
Sam Moreno, *Manager*
EMP: 50
SALES (est): 2.4MM **Privately Held**
SIC: 7389 Fire protection service other
than forestry or public

(P-17004)
PRO-TECH DESIGN & MFG INC
14561 Marquardt Ave, Santa Fe Springs
(90670-5137)
PHONE..................................562 207-1680
Pamela Mc Master, *CEO*
Aaron Swanson, *President*
David Mc Master, *CFO*
Jeff Swanson, *Vice Pres*
▲ **EMP:** 60
SALES (est): 9MM **Privately Held**
WEB: www.protechdesign.net
SIC: 7389 8711 Packaging & labeling
services; industrial engineers

(P-17005)
PRODUCT DEVELOPMENT
CORP (PA)
30 Ragsdale Dr Ste 101, Monterey
(93940-5772)
PHONE..................................831 333-1100
Tim Dinovo, *President*
David Forey, *CFO*
Mario Bertolucci, *Vice Pres*
Vince Gage, *Vice Pres*
Shauna Falk, *Admin Asst*
EMP: 144
SQ FT: 10,700
SALES (est): 118.5MM **Privately Held**
WEB: www.pdceast.com
SIC: 7389 Telephone directory distribution,
contract or fee basis

(P-17006)
PROFESSIONAL EXCHANGE
SVC
4747 N 1st St Ste 140, Fresno
(93726-0517)
P.O. Box 1071 (93714-1071)
PHONE..................................559 229-6249
Cynthia Downing, *CEO*
Peggy Matsoura, *CFO*
Russell Nakaguchio, *Corp Secy*
Paul Bateman, *Principal*
Hien Huynh, *Administration*
EMP: 50 **EST:** 1980
SQ FT: 3,700

SALES (est): 5.5MM **Privately Held**
WEB: www.pesc.com
SIC: 7389 Telephone answering service

(P-17007)
PROFESSNAL CMMNCTONS
NETWRK LP (PA)
6774 Magnolia Ave, Riverside
(92506-2908)
PHONE..................................951 275-9149
Diann K Johnston, *Partner*
Brian White, *Partner*
Jeff White, *Partner*
Diann Johnston, *General Mgr*
Andrew Holybee, *Info Tech Mgr*
EMP: 50
SQ FT: 4,000
SALES (est): 3.9MM **Privately Held**
SIC: 7389 Telephone answering service

(P-17008)
PROJECT SIX
13130 Burbank Blvd, Sherman Oaks
(91401-6037)
PHONE..................................818 781-0360
Barbera Firestone, *President*
EMP: 55
SALES: 3.4MM **Privately Held**
SIC: 7389 Tax title dealers

(P-17009)
PROLOGIC RDMPTION
SLUTIONS INC (PA)
2121 Rosecrans Ave, El Segundo
(90245-4743)
PHONE..................................310 322-7774
William Atkinson, *CEO*
Paul Cooley, *President*
Robb Warwick, *CFO*
Kelly Fuller, *Ch Credit Ofcr*
Ross Ely, *Chief Mktg Ofcr*
EMP: 700
SALES (est): 38.4MM **Privately Held**
SIC: 7389 Coupon redemption service

(P-17010)
PS ENVIRONMENTAL SVCS INC
23775 Madison St, Torrance (90505-6006)
P.O. Box 7000, Redondo Beach (90277-
8710)
PHONE..................................310 373-6259
Joseph Gaglione, *President*
EMP: 62
SALES (est): 5.1MM **Privately Held**
WEB: www.psenvironmental.com
SIC: 7389 Air pollution measuring service

(P-17011)
PUNCTUS TEMPORIS
TRANSLATIONS
5201 Great America Pkwy, Santa Clara
(95054-1122)
PHONE..................................510 309-0888
Jessica Cade, *Owner*
EMP: 50 **EST:** 2016
SALES (est): 641.1K **Privately Held**
SIC: 7389 Translation services

(P-17012)
QUALFAX INC
3605 Long Beach Blvd # 428, Long Beach
(90807-6020)
PHONE..................................562 988-1272
Daniel Wayne, *Vice Pres*
Jim Wolf, *CEO*
EMP: 60
SALES (est): 2.5MM **Privately Held**
WEB: www.qualfax.com
SIC: 7389 8741 Tenant screening service;
management services

(P-17013)
QUINSTREET INC (PA)
950 Tower Ln Ste 600, Foster City
(94404-4253)
PHONE..................................650 578-7700
Douglas Valenti, *Ch of Bd*
Gregory Wong, *CFO*
Martin J Collins, *Ch Credit Ofcr*
Brett Moses, *Senior VP*
Andreja Stevanovic, *Senior VP*
EMP: 50
SQ FT: 63,998

SALES: 455.1MM **Publicly Held**
WEB: www.quinstreet.com
SIC: 7389 7372 Advertising, promotional &
trade show services; prepackaged software; business oriented computer software

(P-17014)
R G CANNING ENTERPRISES
INC
4515 E 59th Pl, Maywood (90270-3201)
PHONE..................................323 560-7469
Richard G Canning, *President*
Charles R Canning, *Vice Pres*
EMP: 215
SQ FT: 50,000
SALES (est): 12.1MM **Privately Held**
WEB: www.rgcshows.com
SIC: 7389 Promoters of shows & exhibi-
tions

(P-17015)
RALPH COLLAZO PACKING INC
72 E Main St Ste A, Heber (92249)
P.O. Box 271 (92249-0271)
PHONE..................................760 353-0856
Ralph Collazo, *President*
EMP: 100
SALES (est): 7.9MM **Privately Held**
SIC: 7389 Packaging & labeling services

(P-17016)
RAYTHEON COMPANY
75 Coromar Dr, Goleta (93117-3088)
PHONE..................................805 562-2941
EMP: 66
SALES (corp-wide): 23.2B **Publicly Held**
SIC: 7389
PA: Raytheon Company
870 Winter St
Waltham MA 02451
781 522-3000

(P-17017)
RECOLOGY SONOMA MARIN
3400 Standish Ave, Santa Rosa
(95407-8112)
PHONE..................................707 586-8261
Fred Stemmler, *General Mgr*
EMP: 450
SALES (est): 16.2MM **Privately Held**
SIC: 7389

(P-17018)
REGISTRATION CTRL SYSTEMS
INC (PA)
Also Called: Rcs World Travel
1833 Portola Rd Unit B, Ventura
(93003-7797)
PHONE..................................805 654-0171
Edgar A Bolton, *President*
Gary Bolton, *Vice Pres*
Chris Cummings, *Vice Pres*
Sam Hamilton, *Vice Pres*
Gary Palmer, *Vice Pres*
EMP: 65 **EST:** 1971
SQ FT: 15,000
SALES (est): 3.3MM **Privately Held**
WEB: www.rcsreg.com
SIC: 7389 Convention & show services

(P-17019)
RESEARCH SOLUTIONS INC
(PA)
15821 Ventura Blvd # 165, Encino
(91436-2915)
PHONE..................................310 477-0354
Peter Victor Derycz, *President*
John Regazzi, *Ch of Bd*
Scott Ahlberg, *COO*
Alan Louis Urban, *CFO*
Yohann Georgel, *Chief Mktg Ofcr*
EMP: 120
SQ FT: 3,200
SALES: 28MM **Publicly Held**
SIC: 7389 7375 Copyright protection serv-
ice; information retrieval services

(P-17020)
RESMEX PARTNERS LLC
438 Geary St, San Francisco (94102-1223)
PHONE..................................415 440-2737
Rallo Edwardo,
EMP: 50

SALES: 3MM **Privately Held**
SIC: 7389 Automobile recovery service

(P-17021)
RETAIL SERVICES WIS CORP
Also Called: W I S
13800 Heacock St D135c, Moreno Valley
(92553-3339)
PHONE..................................951 653-1472
Jeff Ferririak, *Manager*
EMP: 80
SALES (corp-wide): 69.5MM **Privately**
Held
WEB: www.wisusa.com
SIC: 7389 Inventory computing service
HQ: Retail Services Wis Corporation
9265 Sky Park Ct Ste 100
San Diego CA 92123
858 565-8111

(P-17022)
RETAIL SERVICES WIS CORP
3800 Watt Ave Ste 101, Sacramento
(95821-2622)
PHONE..................................916 485-3427
Craig Rust, *President*
EMP: 120
SALES (corp-wide): 69.5MM **Privately**
Held
WEB: www.wisusa.com
SIC: 7389 Inventory stocking service; in-
ventory computing service
HQ: Retail Services Wis Corporation
9265 Sky Park Ct Ste 100
San Diego CA 92123
858 565-8111

(P-17023)
RETAIL SERVICES WIS CORP
1838 N Tustin St Ste A, Orange
(92865-4650)
PHONE..................................714 637-3431
Rubin Vega, *Manager*
EMP: 65
SALES (corp-wide): 69.5MM **Privately**
Held
WEB: www.wisusa.com
SIC: 7389 Inventory computing service
HQ: Retail Services Wis Corporation
9265 Sky Park Ct Ste 100
San Diego CA 92123
858 565-8111

(P-17024)
RETAIL SERVICES WIS CORP
21354 Nordhoff St Ste 108, Chatsworth
(91311-6910)
PHONE..................................818 772-4969
Mary Booher, *Branch Mgr*
EMP: 50
SALES (corp-wide): 69.5MM **Privately**
Held
WEB: www.wisusa.com
SIC: 7389 Inventory computing service
HQ: Retail Services Wis Corporation
9265 Sky Park Ct Ste 100
San Diego CA 92123
858 565-8111

(P-17025)
RETAIL SERVICES WIS CORP
19420 Business Center Dr, Northridge
(91324-3541)
PHONE..................................818 407-2680
Scott Lopez, *Manager*
EMP: 80
SALES (corp-wide): 69.5MM **Privately**
Held
WEB: www.wisusa.com
SIC: 7389 Inventory computing service
HQ: Retail Services Wis Corporation
9265 Sky Park Ct Ste 100
San Diego CA 92123
858 565-8111

(P-17026)
RETAIL SERVICES WIS CORP
1932 Eastman Ave, Ventura (93003-7706)
PHONE..................................805 644-5422
Paul Russ, *Branch Mgr*
EMP: 69
SALES (corp-wide): 69.5MM **Privately**
Held
WEB: www.wisusa.com
SIC: 7389 Inventory computing service

▲ = Import ▼=Export
◆ =Import/Export

HQ: Retail Services Wis Corporation
9265 Sky Park Ct Ste 100
San Diego CA 92123
858 565-8111

(P-17027)
RGIS LLC
5500 Ming Ave Ste 185, Bakersfield
(93309-4623)
PHONE.............................661 827-9195
Laine Martin, *Manager*
EMP: 51
SALES (corp-wide): 6.8B **Publicly Held**
WEB: www.rgisinv.com
SIC: 7389 Inventory computing service
HQ: Rgis, Llc
2000 Taylor Rd
Auburn Hills MI 48326
248 651-2511

(P-17028)
RGIS LLC
1787 Mesa Verde Ave, Ventura
(93003-6531)
PHONE.............................805 644-0454
Darin Coupland, *Manager*
EMP: 75
SALES (corp-wide): 6.8B **Publicly Held**
WEB: www.rgisinv.com
SIC: 7389 Inventory computing service
HQ: Rgis, Llc
2000 Taylor Rd
Auburn Hills MI 48326
248 651-2511

(P-17029)
RGIS LLC
8801 Folsom Blvd Ste 173, Sacramento
(95826-3249)
PHONE.............................916 387-9692
Chris Massoni, *Vice Pres*
Marcus Duran, *Manager*
EMP: 100
SALES (corp-wide): 6.8B **Publicly Held**
WEB: www.rgisinv.com
SIC: 7389 Inventory computing service
HQ: Rgis, Llc
2000 Taylor Rd
Auburn Hills MI 48326
248 651-2511

(P-17030)
RGIS LLC
500 E Olive Ave Ste 240, Burbank
(91501-2171)
PHONE.............................248 651-2511
Bruce Hemingway, *Branch Mgr*
EMP: 140
SALES (corp-wide): 6.8B **Publicly Held**
WEB: www.rgisinv.com
SIC: 7389 Inventory computing service
HQ: Rgis, Llc
2000 Taylor Rd
Auburn Hills MI 48326
248 651-2511

(P-17031)
RGIS LLC
7567 Amador Valley Blvd, Dublin
(94568-2441)
PHONE.............................925 829-2875
Majid Jafarkhani, *Branch Mgr*
EMP: 85
SALES (corp-wide): 6.8B **Publicly Held**
WEB: www.rgisinv.com
SIC: 7389 Inventory computing service
HQ: Rgis, Llc
2000 Taylor Rd
Auburn Hills MI 48326
248 651-2511

(P-17032)
RGIS LLC
4320 Stevens Creek Blvd, San Jose
(95129-1202)
PHONE.............................408 243-9141
EMP: 65
SALES (corp-wide): 5.1B **Publicly Held**
SIC: 7389
HQ: Rgis, Llc
2000 Taylor Rd
Auburn Hills MI 48326
248 651-2511

(P-17033)
RGIS LLC
25115 Avenue Stanford, Valencia
(91355-1290)
PHONE.............................661 702-8987
Becky Conde, *Manager*
EMP: 79
SALES (corp-wide): 6.8B **Publicly Held**
WEB: www.rgisinv.com
SIC: 7389 Inventory stocking service
HQ: Rgis, Llc
2000 Taylor Rd
Auburn Hills MI 48326
248 651-2511

(P-17034)
RGIS LLC
20 Landing Cir Ste 100, Chico
(95973-7889)
PHONE.............................530 898-1015
Jacquelyn Pacconi, *Branch Mgr*
EMP: 65
SALES (corp-wide): 6.8B **Publicly Held**
WEB: www.rgisinv.com
SIC: 7389 Inventory computing service
HQ: Rgis, Llc
2000 Taylor Rd
Auburn Hills MI 48326
248 651-2511

(P-17035)
RHUMBIX INC
1169 Howard St, San Francisco
(94103-3952)
PHONE.............................435 764-3014
Zachary Scheel, *CEO*
Drew Dewalt, *CFO*
Emily Stember, *Executive Asst*
Isaac Dan, *Manager*
EMP: 59
SALES (est): 246.2K **Privately Held**
SIC: 7389 8748 8711 8742 ; business
consulting; building construction consult-
ant; personnel management consultant;
construction project management consult-
ant; commercial physical research

(P-17036)
RIVER CITY AUTO RECOVERY
INC
3401 Fitzgerald Rd, Rancho Cordova
(95742-6815)
PHONE.............................916 851-1100
David Schmidt, *CFO*
EMP: 71
SQ FT: 15,000
SALES (est): 2.2MM
SALES (corp-wide): 577MM **Privately Held**
WEB: www.unitedroad.com
SIC: 7389 Repossession service
PA: United Road Services, Inc.
10701 Middlebelt Rd
Romulus MI 48174
734 946-3232

(P-17037)
ROAD SAFETY INC
4335 Pacific St Ste A, Rocklin
(95677-2104)
PHONE.............................916 543-4600
Melissa L Bamberg, *President*
Jason Bamberg, *CEO*
Andrea West, *Human Res Dir*
EMP: 120
SQ FT: 6,000
SALES (est): 15.7MM **Privately Held**
SIC: 7389 Flagging service (traffic control)

(P-17038)
RONSIN PHOTOCOPY INC (PA)
215 Lemon Creek Dr, Walnut (91789-2643)
PHONE.............................909 594-5995
Dennis Grant, *President*
Robert Alkema, *Ch of Bd*
Cheryl Alkema, *Corp Secy*
Dave Thomas, *Marketing Mgr*
Darren Wong, *Marketing Staff*
EMP: 60
SQ FT: 12,000
SALES (est): 9.4MM **Privately Held**
WEB: www.ronsinphotocopy.com
SIC: 7389 Microfilm recording & develop-
ing service

(P-17039)
ROSE & SHORE INC
5151 Alcoa Ave, Vernon (90058-3715)
P.O. Box 58225 (90058-0225)
PHONE.............................323 826-2144
Irwin Miller, *President*
Irma Espinosa, *Officer*
James Craig, *Vice Pres*
Carol Miller, *Admin Sec*
Carlos Enriquez, *Info Tech Dir*
EMP: 320
SQ FT: 60,000
SALES (est): 54MM **Privately Held**
WEB: www.rose-shore.com
SIC: 7389 5147 Packaging & labeling
services; meats, cured or smoked

(P-17040)
RYAN SHROADS
5110 E Washington Blvd, Commerce
(90040-1239)
P.O. Box 78850, Los Angeles (90016-0850)
PHONE.............................310 936-5966
Marquesha Green, *Principal*
Monique Palmer, *Principal*
EMP: 50
SALES (est): 641.1K **Privately Held**
SIC: 7389

(P-17041)
SALT OF EARTH PRODUCTIONS
INC
Also Called: Salt Catering
1437 S Robertson Blvd, Los Angeles
(90035-3414)
PHONE.............................818 399-1860
Tomas Rivera, *President*
EMP: 108
SALES (est): 1.6MM **Privately Held**
SIC: 7389 Decoration service for special
events

(P-17042)
SAN DIEGO TOURISM
AUTHORITY (PA)
750 B St Ste 1500, San Diego
(92101-8131)
PHONE.............................619 232-3101
Joseph Terzi, *CEO*
Reint Reinders, *President*
Rick Meza, *CFO*
Christine Shimasaki, *Exec VP*
Sal Giametta, *Vice Pres*
EMP: 75
SQ FT: 2,100
SALES: 42.1MM **Privately Held**
SIC: 7389 Convention & show services;
tourist information bureau

(P-17043)
SAN FRANCISCO FOUNDATION
1 Embarcadero Ctr # 1400, San Francisco
(94111-3703)
PHONE.............................415 733-8500
Sandra Hernandez MD, *Director*
EMP: 60 EST: 1948
SQ FT: 22,000
SALES: 174.8MM **Privately Held**
SIC: 7389 Fund raising organizations

(P-17044)
SAN FRANCISCO TRAVEL ASSN
Also Called: Ss Travel
1 Front St Ste 2900, San Francisco
(94111-5333)
PHONE.............................415 974-6900
Joe D'Alessandro, *President*
Tina Wu, *CFO*
Bill Poland, *Treasurer*
Howard Pickett, *Chief Mktg Ofcr*
Paul Frentsos, *Exec VP*
EMP: 70
SQ FT: 15,000
SALES: 32.9MM **Privately Held**
SIC: 7389 Convention & show services;
tourist information bureau

(P-17045)
SANTA BARBARA CITY OF
Also Called: Pub Works/Community Dev
630 Garden St, Santa Barbara
(93101-1656)
PHONE.............................805 564-5485
Paul Casey, *Director*
Brenda Nielsen, *Supervisor*

EMP: 200 **Privately Held**
WEB: www.citytv18.com
SIC: 7389 Safety inspection service
PA: City Of Santa Barbara
735 Anacapa St
Santa Barbara CA 93101
805 564-5334

(P-17046)
SARPA-FELDMAN
ENTERPRISES INC
Also Called: Progressive Solutions
650 N King Rd, San Jose (95133-1715)
PHONE.............................408 982-1790
Mark E Sarpa, *CEO*
Scott R Feldman, *CFO*
Scott Feldman, *CFO*
Trang Nguyen, *Accountant*
▲ EMP: 56
SQ FT: 13,000
SALES (est): 9.3MM **Privately Held**
WEB: www.printhq.com
SIC: 7389 Printing broker

(P-17047)
SCA ENTERPRISES INC (PA)
Also Called: Southern Cal Appraisal Co
3817 W Magnolia Blvd, Burbark
(91505-2820)
P.O. Box 1455 (91507-1455)
PHONE.............................818 845-7621
Timothy S Davis, *CEO*
Severino Dejesus, *Executive*
Dan Karlson, *Info Tech Mgr*
Linda Pineda, *Accountant*
Robert Smidl, *Opers Staff*
EMP: 107
SQ FT: 1,200
SALES (est): 11.6MM **Privately Held**
SIC: 7389 Appraisers, except real estate

(P-17048)
SCHERZER INTERNATIONAL
CORP (PA)
21650 Oxnard St Ste 300, Woodland Hills
(91367-4989)
PHONE.............................818 227-2770
Larry S Scherzer, *President*
Carol Scherzer, *Admin Sec*
Andrew Duong, *Admin Asst*
Angela Galish, *Research Analys*
Holly Legron, *Research Analys*
EMP: 60
SQ FT: 11,400
SALES (est): 10.1MM **Privately Held**
SIC: 7389 Financial services

(P-17049)
SCILEX PHARMACEUTICALS
INC (DH)
4955 Directors Pl Ste 100, San Diego
(92121-3837)
PHONE.............................949 441-2270
Anthony P Mack, *President*
Jaisim Shah, *CEO*
Jiong Shao, *CFO*
EMP: 65
SQ FT: 3,000
SALES (est): 1.4MM
SALES (corp-wide): 21.1MM **Publicly Held**
SIC: 7389 5122 2834 Packaging & label-
ing services; pharmaceuticals; pharma-
ceutical preparations
HQ: Scilex Holding Company
4955 Directors Pl
San Diego CA 92121
858 203-4100

(P-17050)
SCRIP ADVANTAGE INC
4273 W Richert Ave # 110, Fresno
(93722-6333)
P.O. Box 13238 (93794-3238)
PHONE.............................559 320-0052
John Coyle, *President*
Robert Coyle, *CFO*
Bob Coyle, *Vice Pres*
EMP: 54 EST: 1999
SQ FT: 2,000
SALES: 136MM **Privately Held**
WEB: www.scripadvantage.com
SIC: 7389 Fund raising organizations

PRODUCTS & SVCS

(P-17051)
SEASIDE HOTEL LESSEE INC
Also Called: Viceroy Santa Monica
1819 Ocean Ave, Santa Monica
(90401-3215)
PHONE.....................310 260-7500
Janne Clare, *General Mgr*
Todd Yamakoa, *General Mgr*
Jay Thorson, *Finance*
EMP: 178
SALES: 26MM **Privately Held**
SIC: 7389 Hotel & motel reservation service; restaurant reservation service

(P-17052)
SEAVIEW INDUSTRIES
2501 Harbor Blvd, Costa Mesa
(92626-6143)
PHONE.....................714 957-5073
Tom Thomas, *Manager*
EMP: 50
SALES (est): 1.4MM **Privately Held**
WEB: www.seaviewgolf.com
SIC: 7389 Packaging & labeling services

(P-17053)
SERVICE MASTER INDUSTRIES INC
2342 Meyers Ave, Escondido (92029-1008)
PHONE.....................760 480-0208
Mark Bower, *General Mgr*
Philip Fitzpatrick, *President*
Eylse Fitzpatrick, *Vice Pres*
Gerald Farley, *Principal*
EMP: 60
SALES (est): 4.1MM **Privately Held**
SIC: 7389 Personal service agents, brokers & bureaus

(P-17054)
SEVEN ONE INC (PA)
Also Called: Professional Tele Answering Svc
21540 Prairie St Ste E, Chatsworth
(91311-5814)
PHONE.....................818 904-3435
James Thompson, *President*
EMP: 83
SQ FT: 4,000
SALES (est): 5.1MM **Privately Held**
WEB: www.sevenone.com
SIC: 7389 Telephone answering service

(P-17055)
SHINWOO P&C USA INC (PA)
2177 Britannia Blvd # 203, San Diego
(92154-8307)
PHONE.....................619 407-7164
IL Kim, *CEO*
▲ EMP: 600
SQ FT: 300
SALES: 57.6MM **Privately Held**
SIC: 7389 Packaging & labeling services

(P-17056)
SIGUE CORPORATION (PA)
13190 Telfair Ave, Sylmar (91342-3573)
PHONE.....................818 837-5939
Guillermo Dela Vina, *CEO*
Alfredo Dela Vina, *CFO*
Alfredo Vina, *CFO*
Christina Pappas, *Bd of Directors*
Camilo Moncayo, *Officer*
EMP: 100
SQ FT: 3,000
SALES (est): 44.1MM **Privately Held**
SIC: 7389 4822 Financial services; telegraph & other communications

(P-17057)
SINECERA INC
Also Called: Crown Vly Precision Machining
5397 3rd St, Irwindale (91706-2085)
PHONE.....................626 962-1087
Donald Brown, *CEO*
Dale B Mikus, *CFO*
EMP: 80
SQ FT: 10,500
SALES (est): 9.7MM
SALES (corp-wide): 59.4MM **Privately Held**
SIC: 7389 3492 Grinding, precision: commercial or industrial; control valves, aircraft: hydraulic & pneumatic

PA: H-D Advanced Manufacturing Company
2200 Georgetown Dr # 300
Sewickley PA 15143
724 759-2850

(P-17058)
SKYBLUE SEWING MANUFACTURING
960 Mission St Fl 2, San Francisco
(94103-2911)
PHONE.....................415 777-9978
Huang Zhem, *President*
Freda Lau, *Vice Pres*
EMP: 50
SALES (est): 3MM **Privately Held**
SIC: 7389 Sewing contractor

(P-17059)
SMG FOOD AND BEVERAGE LLC (PA)
Also Called: Ontario Convention Center
2000 E Convention Ctr Way, Ontario
(91764-5633)
PHONE.....................909 937-3000
Victoria Van Damme, *Mng Member*
Dick Walsh, *Mayor*
John Burns,
Maureen Ginty,
EMP: 64
SALES (est): 12MM **Privately Held**
SIC: 7389 Convention & show services

(P-17060)
SMG HOLDINGS INC
848 M St Fl 2nd, Fresno (93721-2760)
PHONE.....................559 445-8100
William Overfelt, *General Mgr*
EMP: 336
SALES (corp-wide): 23.7B **Privately Held**
SIC: 7389 Convention & show services
HQ: Smg Holdings, Llc
300 Cnshohckn State Rd # 450
Conshohocken PA 19428

(P-17061)
SMITH-EMERY SAN FRANCISCO INC
1940 Oakdale Ave, San Francisco
(94124-2004)
P.O. Box 880550 (94188-0550)
PHONE.....................415 642-7326
James E Partridge, *President*
Helen Choe, *CFO*
EMP: 113
SQ FT: 10,160
SALES (est): 11.4MM **Privately Held**
SIC: 7389 8711 Inspection & testing services; engineering services

(P-17062)
SOBOBA BAND LUISENO INDIANS
Also Called: Soboba Casino
22777 Soboba Rd, San Jacinto
(92583-2935)
PHONE.....................951 665-1000
Toll Free:.....................888
Richard Kline, *Branch Mgr*
Dominic Abbondanza, *Administration*
Jose Rangel, *Technology*
Maggie Flynn, *Purch Dir*
Shannon Hanna, *Food Svc Dir*
EMP: 900 **Privately Held**
WEB: www.soboba.com
SIC: 7389 7011 Personal service agents, brokers & bureaus; casino hotel
PA: Soboba Band Of Luiseno Indians
23906 Soboba Rd
San Jacinto CA 92583
951 654-2765

(P-17063)
SONY INTERACTIVE ENTRMT LLC (DH)
Also Called: Smss
2207 Bridgepointe Pkwy, Foster City
(94404-5060)
PHONE.....................310 981-1500
Jim Ryan, *President*
John Kodera, *President*
Kazuhiko Takeda, *CFO*
Rob Scheschareg, *Sales Executive*
Jim Kass, *Senior Mgr*

EMP: 148
SALES (est): 109.2MM **Privately Held**
SIC: 7389 Music distribution systems
HQ: Sony Corporation Of America
25 Madison Ave Fl 27
New York NY 10010
212 833-8000

(P-17064)
SOROPTMIST INTL HUNTINGTON BCH
212 Utica Ave, Huntington Beach
(92648-2804)
PHONE.....................714 271-9305
Terry Rose, *Partner*
EMP: 50
SALES (est): 641.1K **Privately Held**
SIC: 7389

(P-17065)
SOUTHWEST DEALER SERVICES INC
1001 G St Ste 113, Sacramento
(95814-0834)
PHONE.....................925 753-0696
EMP: 146 **Privately Held**
SIC: 7389 Brokers, contract services
PA: Southwest Dealer Services, Inc.
8659 Research Dr Ste 100
Irvine CA 92618

(P-17066)
SOUTHWEST INSPECTION AND TSTG
Also Called: Southwest Inspection Testing
441 Commercial Way, La Habra
(90631-6168)
PHONE.....................562 941-2990
Steven L Godbey, *President*
Kathy Godbey, *Treasurer*
Charles L Godbey, *Vice Pres*
EMP: 75
SQ FT: 2,400
SALES (est): 8MM **Privately Held**
SIC: 7389 Building inspection service

(P-17067)
STAGE II INC
Also Called: Stage II Design & Production
21 Channel Dr, Corte Madera
(94925-1845)
PHONE.....................415 285-8400
Chris McGregor, *President*
EMP: 50
SQ FT: 3,800
SALES (est): 3.5MM **Privately Held**
SIC: 7389 Decoration service for special events

(P-17068)
STANFORD LAW SCHL OFF FNCL AID
Crown Quadrangle 559, Stanford (94305)
PHONE.....................650 723-9247
Dewayne Barnes, *Principal*
Bao Tran, *Technical Mgr*
David Johnson, *Professor*
Mark Lemley, *Professor*
Shawn Miller, *Professor*
EMP: 99
SALES: 950K **Privately Held**
SIC: 7389 Financial services

(P-17069)
STERICYCLE COMM SOLUTIONS INC
2255 Watt Ave Ste 50, Sacramento
(95825-0504)
PHONE.....................888 370-6711
Gail Dawson, *Branch Mgr*
EMP: 54
SALES (corp-wide): 3.4B **Publicly Held**
SIC: 7389 Telephone answering service
HQ: Stericycle Communication Solutions, Inc.
4010 Commercial Ave
Northbrook IL 60062
866 783-9820

(P-17070)
STERICYCLE COMM SOLUTIONS INC
612 S Harbor Blvd, Anaheim (92805-4526)
PHONE.....................714 991-9595
Jamie Lloyd, *Branch Mgr*
EMP: 50
SALES (corp-wide): 3.4B **Publicly Held**
SIC: 7389 Telephone answering service
HQ: Stericycle Communication Solutions, Inc.
4010 Commercial Ave
Northbrook IL 60062
866 783-9820

(P-17071)
STERLING HSA INC
475 14th St Ste 120, Oakland
(94612-1900)
P.O. Box 71107 (94612-7207)
PHONE.....................800 617-4729
Cora M Tellez, *President*
Duarte Vatista, *COO*
Robin Katherman, *CFO*
Mark Maltun, *CFO*
Chris Bettner, *Exec VP*
EMP: 50
SALES (est): 7.2MM **Privately Held**
WEB: www.sterlinghsa.com
SIC: 7389 Financial services

(P-17072)
STRATEGIC OPERATIONS INC
4705 Ruffin Rd, San Diego (92123-1611)
PHONE.....................858 244-0559
Stuart Segall, *CEO*
EMP: 250
SQ FT: 12,000
SALES (est): 30.8MM **Privately Held**
WEB: www.strategic-operations.com
SIC: 7389 Personal service agents, brokers & bureaus

(P-17073)
SUGAR FOODS CORPORATION
Also Called: Sygma Network, The
9500 El Dorado Ave, Sun Valley
(91352-1339)
PHONE.....................818 768-7900
Stephen Odell, *Partner*
EMP: 200
SALES (corp-wide): 286.3MM **Privately Held**
WEB: www.sugarfoods.com
SIC: 7389 2099 2062 Packaging & labeling services; food preparations; cane sugar refining
PA: Sugar Foods Corporation
950 3rd Ave Fl 21
New York NY 10022
212 753-6900

(P-17074)
SUGAR FOODS CORPORATION
Also Called: General Brands Packing
9500 El Dorado Ave, Sun Valley
(91352-1339)
PHONE.....................818 768-7900
Steven Odell, *Branch Mgr*
EMP: 100
SQ FT: 60,000
SALES (corp-wide): 294.2MM **Privately Held**
WEB: www.sugarfoods.com
SIC: 7389 Packaging & labeling services
PA: Sugar Foods Corporation
950 3rd Ave Fl 21
New York NY 10022
212 753-6900

(P-17075)
SUN LIGHT & POWER
1035 Folger Ave, Berkeley (94710-2819)
PHONE.....................510 845-2997
Gary Gerber, *President*
Troy Tyler, *COO*
Barb Gerber, *Officer*
Zachary Gill, *Officer*
Harry Payne, *Vice Pres*
EMP: 70
SQ FT: 10,000
SALES: 17MM **Privately Held**
WEB: www.sunlightandpower.com
SIC: 7389 1796 3433 Design services; power generating equipment installation; solar heaters & collectors

(P-17076)
SUPERHERO APP LLC
1517 W Carson St Apt 11, Torrance
(90501-3961)
P.O. Box 1271, Canyon Country (91386-1271)
PHONE....................................562 341-0784
Michael King, *Principal*
EMP: 55
SALES (est): 691.1K **Privately Held**
SIC: 7389 Business services

(P-17077)
TACTICAL TELESOLUTIONS INC
2121 N Calif Blvd Ste 260, Walnut Creek
(94596-3572)
PHONE....................................415 788-8808
Laura Hylton, *President*
Jennifer Kallman, *Vice Pres*
Kurt Stenzel, *Vice Pres*
Kathy O'Toole, *Technology*
Kema Riley, *Technology*
EMP: 130
SQ FT: 15,000
SALES (est): 11.9MM **Privately Held**
WEB: www.tts-sf.com
SIC: 7389 Telemarketing services

(P-17078)
TAKEUCHI FINANCIAL SERVICES
475 Sansome St, San Francisco
(94111-3103)
PHONE....................................706 693-3600
EMP: 53
SALES (est): 3.1MM **Privately Held**
SIC: 7389 Financial services

(P-17079)
TALENTBURST INC
575 Market St Ste 3025, San Francisco
(94105-5840)
PHONE....................................415 813-4011
EMP: 115
SALES (corp-wide): 26.7MM **Privately Held**
SIC: 7389 7375 Check validation service; information retrieval services
PA: Talentburst, Inc.
679 Worcester St Ste 1
Natick MA 01760
508 628-7516

(P-17080)
TATA COMMUNICATIONS AMER INC
Also Called: Bitgravity
700 Airport Blvd Ste 100, Burlingame
(94010-1931)
PHONE....................................650 262-0004
Boris T Lopez, *Technical Staff*
Leigh Walgate, *Engineer*
Gustavo P Barreto, *Opers Staff*
Carl Smith, *Sales Dir*
Michael Jones, *Senior Mgr*
EMP: 62 **Privately Held**
SIC: 7389 Music & broadcasting services
HQ: Tata Communications (America) Inc.
2355 Dulles Corner Blvd # 700
Herndon VA 20171
703 657-8400

(P-17081)
TAX RISE INC
Also Called: Fidelity Tax Relief
19900 Macarthur Blvd, Irvine (92612-2445)
PHONE....................................877 697-4732
Essam Abdullah, *President*
Emily Nguyen, *CFO*
EMP: 80
SQ FT: 15,000
SALES: 5.1MM **Privately Held**
SIC: 7389 Legal & tax services

(P-17082)
TBWA CHIAT/DAY INC
5353 Grosvenor Blvd, Los Angeles
(90066-6913)
PHONE....................................310 305-5000
Lee Clow, *Branch Mgr*
Gary Scheiner, *Exec VP*
Christine Petterson, *Executive*
Renato Fernandez, *Creative Dir*
Kyle Luhr, *Planning*
EMP: 88

SALES (corp-wide): 15.2B **Publicly Held**
SIC: 7389 Interior design services
HQ: Tbwa Chiat/Day Inc.
488 Madison Ave Fl 7
New York NY 10022
212 804-1000

(P-17083)
TEAM SAN JOSE
408 Almaden Blvd, San Jose (95110-2709)
PHONE....................................408 295-9600
Karolyn Kirchgesler, *CEO*
Dave Costain, *COO*
Janette Divol, *CFO*
Janette Sutton, *CFO*
Vijay Sammeta, *Vice Pres*
EMP: 900
SQ FT: 300,000
SALES: 8MM **Privately Held**
SIC: 7389 Convention & show services

(P-17084)
TECH PACKAGING INC
9545 Santa Anita Ave A, Rancho Cucamonga (91730-6110)
PHONE....................................909 243-7047
Steve Andrews, *Manager*
EMP: 80
SALES (corp-wide): 21.8MM **Privately Held**
SIC: 7389 Packaging & labeling services
PA: Tech Packaging, Inc.
13241 Bartram Park Blvd # 101
Jacksonville FL 32258
904 288-6403

(P-17085)
TECHNICON DESIGN CORPORATION
26522 La Alameda Ste 150, Mission Viejo
(92691-6545)
PHONE....................................949 218-1300
David Shall, *President*
Helen Thomas, *Exec VP*
Brenda Ramirez, *Consultant*
EMP: 120
SQ FT: 1,000
SALES (est): 11.6MM
SALES (corp-wide): 20.9MM **Privately Held**
WEB: www.techniconims.com
SIC: 7389 Design services
PA: Technicon Design Limited
Technicon House
Luton BEDS LU1 3
158 250-6600

(P-17086)
TELE-DIRECT COMMUNICATIONS
4741 Madison Ave Ste 200, Sacramento
(95841-2580)
PHONE....................................916 348-2170
A James Puff, *Chairman*
Thomas Coshow, *CEO*
Sandra Coggeshall, *Exec VP*
Jamei Puff, *Sales/Mktg Mgr*
EMP: 75
SQ FT: 6,000
SALES (est): 6.5MM **Privately Held**
WEB: www.tele-direct.com
SIC: 7389 5999 Telemarketing services; telephone & communication equipment

(P-17087)
TELE-INTERPRETERS LLC
1 Lower Ragsdale Dr # 2, Monterey
(93940-5747)
P.O. Box 202572, Dallas TX (75320-2572)
PHONE....................................800 811-7881
Melanie Coto-Trevor,
EMP: 500
SQ FT: 10,000
SALES (est): 11.7MM
SALES (corp-wide): 123.7MM **Privately Held**
WEB: www.teleinterpreters.com
SIC: 7389 Translation services
HQ: Language Line, Llc
1 Lower Ragsdale Dr # 2
Monterey CA 93940
831 648-5800

(P-17088)
TELECNTRIC COMMUNICATIONS INTL
12070 Telg Rd Ste 107, Santa Fe Springs
(90670)
PHONE....................................562 906-2555
CM Lee, *Owner*
EMP: 75
SALES (est): 920.2K **Privately Held**
SIC: 7389 Financial services

(P-17089)
TELECOM EVOLUTIONS LLC
9221 Corbin Ave Ste 260, Northridge
(91324-1625)
PHONE....................................818 264-4400
James Murphy, *Mng Member*
EMP: 50 EST: 2010
SALES: 22MM **Privately Held**
SIC: 7389 Telephone services

(P-17090)
TELECOM INC
2201 Broadway Ste 103, Oakland
(94612-3028)
PHONE....................................510 873-8283
Jon Martin, *President*
Carlos Amaya, *Opers Mgr*
Lani Stackel, *Mktg Dir*
Ashleigh McCullough, *Sr Project Mgr*
EMP: 100
SALES (est): 8.7MM **Privately Held**
WEB: www.telecominc.com
SIC: 7389 4813 8742 Telemarketing services; data telephone communications; marketing consulting services

(P-17091)
TEXAS INSTRUMENTS SUNNYVALE
165 Gibraltar Ct, Sunnyvale (94089-1301)
PHONE....................................408 541-9900
Andrew Hartland, *CFO*
EMP: 50
SQ FT: 12,070
SALES (est): 1.6MM
SALES (corp-wide): 15.7B **Publicly Held**
WEB: www.ti.com
SIC: 7389 Design services
PA: Texas Instruments Incorporated
12500 Ti Blvd
Dallas TX 75243
214 479-3773

(P-17092)
THOMPSON & RICH CRANE SERVICE
2373 E Mariposa Rd, Stockton
(95205-7811)
P.O. Box 30035 (95213-0035)
PHONE....................................209 465-3161
EMP: 50 EST: 1988
SALES (est): 2.5MM **Privately Held**
SIC: 7389

(P-17093)
THOMSON REUTERS (MARKETS) LLC
1 Sansome St, San Francisco
(94104-4448)
PHONE....................................415 677-2500
Ben Silverman, *Manager*
EMP: 60
SALES (corp-wide): 10.6B **Publicly Held**
WEB: www.reuters.com
SIC: 7389 Personal service agents, brokers & bureaus
HQ: Reuters America Llc
3 Times Sq
New York NY 10036
646 223-4000

(P-17094)
THOUSAND OAKS PRTG & SPC INC
Also Called: T/O Printing
5334 Sterling Center Dr, Westlake Village
(91361-4612)
PHONE....................................818 706-8330
Steve Mahr, *President*
Beth Digirolamo, *Human Res Dir*
Timothy Hayes, *Purch Mgr*
Kendall Bradford, *VP Opers*
Lori Abrams, *Manager*

▲ EMP: 140
SQ FT: 60,000
SALES (est): 21.8MM
SALES (corp-wide): 6.8B **Publicly Held**
WEB: www.toprinting.com
SIC: 7389 2752 Printing broker; commercial printing, offset
HQ: Consolidated Graphics, Inc.
5858 Westheimer Rd # 200
Houston TX 77057
713 787-0977

(P-17095)
THYDE INC (PA)
300 El Sobrante Rd, Corona (92879-5757)
PHONE....................................951 817-2300
Tim Hyde, *President*
EMP: 250
SQ FT: 70,000
SALES (est): 52.5MM **Privately Held**
WEB: www.hydeandhyde.com
SIC: 7389 Packaging & labeling services

(P-17096)
TIDAVATER INC
Also Called: Le Courier
2107 W Alameda Ave, Burbank
(91506-2934)
PHONE....................................818 848-4151
Fax: 818 848-5294
EMP: 150
SQ FT: 3,000
SALES (est): 5.2MM **Privately Held**
SIC: 7389 4513 4215

(P-17097)
TOMMY BAHAMA GROUP INC
610 Ventura Blvd Ste 1340, Camarillo
(93010-5869)
PHONE....................................805 482-8868
Janet Infante, *Branch Mgr*
EMP: 112
SALES (corp-wide): 1.1B **Publicly Held**
SIC: 7389 Apparel designers, commercial
HQ: Tommy Bahama Group, Inc.
400 Fairview Ave N # 488
Seattle WA 98109

(P-17098)
TOMMY BAHAMA GROUP INC
1720 Redwood Hwy Spc A019, Corte
Madera (94925-1249)
PHONE....................................415 737-0400
EMP: 112
SALES (corp-wide): 1.1B **Publicly Held**
SIC: 7389 Apparel designers, commercial
HQ: Tommy Bahama Group, Inc.
400 Fairview Ave N # 488
Seattle WA 98109

(P-17099)
TOUCHOFMODERN INC
30063 Ahern Ave, Union City (94587-1234)
PHONE....................................888 868-1232
EMP: 155
SALES (corp-wide): 72.9MM **Privately Held**
SIC: 7389 Interior design services
PA: Touchofmodern, Inc.
1025 Sansome St
San Francisco CA 94111
415 230-0750

(P-17100)
TOWN & COUNTRY EVENT RENTALS
1 N Calle Cesar Chavez # 7, Santa Barbara
(93103-3662)
PHONE....................................305 770-5729
EMP: 398
SALES (corp-wide): 28MM **Privately Held**
SIC: 7389 Personal service agents, brokers & bureaus
PA: Town & Country Event Rentals, Inc
7725 Airport Bus Pkwy
Van Nuys CA 91406
818 908-4211

(P-17101)
TRAFFIC MANAGEMENT INC
Also Called: TMI
690 Quinn Ave, San Jose (95112-2635)
PHONE....................................877 763-5999

PRODUCTS & SVCS

Tina Becker, *Branch Mgr*
EMP: 50 **Privately Held**
SIC: 7389 8741 Flagging service (traffic control); management services
PA: Traffic Management, Inc.
2435 Lemon Ave
Signal Hill CA 90755

(P-17102)
TRAFFIC MANAGEMENT INC (PA)
2435 Lemon Ave, Signal Hill (90755-3462)
PHONE...................562 595-4278
Christopher H Spano, *CEO*
Jonathan Spano, *COO*
William Kearney, *Vice Pres*
Micheel Spreuse, *Vice Pres*
John McKay, *Regional Mgr*
▲ **EMP:** 144
SQ FT: 20,000
SALES (est): 155.2MM **Privately Held**
SIC: 7389 8741 Flagging service (traffic control); business management

(P-17103)
TRANS-PAK INCORPORATED
Also Called: Transpak Los Angeles
2601 S Garnsey St, Santa Ana (92707-3338)
PHONE...................310 618-6937
Charles Frasier, *Principal*
EMP: 108
SALES (corp-wide): 187.9MM **Privately Held**
SIC: 7389 Packaging & labeling services
PA: Transpak, Inc.
520 Marburg Way
San Jose CA 95133
408 254-0500

(P-17104)
TRANSPAK INC (PA)
520 Marburg Way, San Jose (95133-1619)
PHONE...................408 254-0500
Arlene Inch, *Chairman*
Bob Lally, *President*
Bert Inch, *CEO*
Ray Horner, *COO*
Chris Lee, *CFO*
◆ **EMP:** 175
SALES (est): 187.9MM **Privately Held**
WEB: www.transpak.com
SIC: 7389 Packaging & labeling services

(P-17105)
TRAP
Also Called: Task Force For Reg Autostaff
1833 S Mountain Ave, Monrovia (91016-4270)
PHONE...................626 572-5610
EMP: 80
SALES (est): 2.4MM **Privately Held**
SIC: 7389

(P-17106)
TRILLIANT NETWORKS INC (PA)
1100 Island Dr Ste 201, Redwood City (94065-5187)
PHONE...................650 204-5050
Andy White, *Principal*
Mike Mortimer, *Exec VP*
Norma Formanek, *Senior VP*
Ryan Gerbrandt, *Senior VP*
Paul Karr, *Senior VP*
EMP: 65
SALES (est): 43.7MM **Privately Held**
SIC: 7389 Meter readers, remote

(P-17107)
TRILOGY FINANCIAL SERVICES INC (PA)
17011 Beach Blvd Ste 800, Huntington Beach (92647-5995)
PHONE...................714 843-9977
Jeff Motske, *President*
Ed Ghulamali, *Managing Prtnr*
Sean Kennedy, *President*
Doug Stroot, *President*
Kevin Mackintosh, *Exec VP*
EMP: 150
SQ FT: 6,500

SALES (est): 15.6MM
SALES (corp-wide): 21.9MM **Privately Held**
WEB: www.asktrilogy.com
SIC: 7389 Financial services

(P-17108)
TRILOGY FINANCIAL SERVICES INC
12520 High Bluff Dr # 140, San Diego (92130-2061)
PHONE...................858 755-6696
Doug Stroot, *Manager*
Diego De Santos, *Advisor*
Sheryl Stern, *Advisor*
EMP: 50
SALES (corp-wide): 21.9MM **Privately Held**
WEB: www.asktrilogy.com
SIC: 7389 Financial services
PA: Trilogy Financial Services, Inc.
17011 Beach Blvd Ste 800
Huntington Beach CA 92647
714 843-9977

(P-17109)
TRIMARK RAYGAL LLC
Also Called: Trimark Orange County
210 Commerce, Irvine (92602-1318)
PHONE...................949 474-1000
Michael Anthony Costanzo, *President*
Dirk Hallett, *Treasurer*
Eric Smith, *Vice Pres*
Agatha Aguila, *Administration*
Gail Garvin-Golley, *Administration*
EMP: 220
SQ FT: 62,850
SALES: 153MM
SALES (corp-wide): 1B **Privately Held**
WEB: www.raygal.com
SIC: 7389 Design, commercial & industrial
PA: Trimark Usa, Llc
9 Hampshire St
Mansfield MA 02048
508 399-2400

(P-17110)
TRINITY PACKING COMPANY INC (PA)
18700 E South Ave, Reedley (93654-9711)
P.O. Box 28905, Fresno (93729-8905)
PHONE...................559 433-3785
David E White, *CEO*
Brian Hiett, *Vice Pres*
Lance Shebelut, *Vice Pres*
▲ **EMP:** 300
SALES (est): 30MM **Privately Held**
SIC: 7389 Packaging & labeling services

(P-17111)
TRINITY PACKING COMPANY INC
7612 S Reed Ave, Reedley (93654-9712)
PHONE...................559 743-3913
Sam Gomez, *Branch Mgr*
EMP: 300
SALES (corp-wide): 30MM **Privately Held**
SIC: 7389 Packaging & labeling services
PA: Trinity Packing Company, Inc.
18700 E South Ave
Reedley CA 93654
559 433-3785

(P-17112)
TWO JINN INC (PA)
Also Called: Aladdin Bail Bonds
1000 Aviara Dr Ste 300, Carlsbad (92011-4218)
PHONE...................760 431-9911
Robert H Hayes, *Ch of Bd*
Herb Mutter, *CFO*
Dave Edwards, *Info Tech Dir*
Carlos Licerio, *Technology*
Leah Taniguchi, *Controller*
EMP: 75
SALES (est): 53MM **Privately Held**
WEB: www.twojinn.com
SIC: 7389 Bail bonding

(P-17113)
TYLIE JONES & ASSOCIATES INC (PA)
58 E Santa Anita Ave, Burbank (91502-1923)
PHONE...................818 955-7600
Sheri Lawrence, *President*
Tylie Jones, *CEO*
Vincent Grennan, *CFO*
Joanne Eckert, *Vice Pres*
John Dohren, *Manager*
EMP: 50
SQ FT: 45,000
SALES (est): 6.2MM **Privately Held**
SIC: 7389 Music & broadcasting services

(P-17114)
UBS FINANCIAL SERVICES INC
50 W San Fernando St Fl 8, San Jose (95113-2414)
PHONE...................408 282-8402
Kirk Mandlin, *Manager*
Nancy Ubaldi, *Vice Pres*
Jacqueline A Kobinski, *Agent*
EMP: 50
SALES (corp-wide): 29.6B **Privately Held**
SIC: 7389 Financial services
HQ: Ubs Financial Services Inc.
1285 Ave Of The Americas
New York NY 10019
212 713-2000

(P-17115)
UBS FINANCIAL SERVICES INC
3801 University Ave # 300, Riverside (92501-3264)
PHONE...................951 684-6300
James Gallegos, *Manager*
EMP: 50
SALES (corp-wide): 29.6B **Privately Held**
SIC: 7389 Brokers, business: buying & selling business enterprises; authors' agents & brokers; speakers' bureau
HQ: Ubs Financial Services Inc.
1285 Ave Of The Americas
New York NY 10019
212 713-2000

(P-17116)
UBS FINANCIAL SERVICES INC
1200 Prospect St Ste 100, La Jolla (92037-3608)
P.O. Box 2268 (92038-2268)
PHONE...................858 454-9181
Lee Tripodi, *Manager*
Douglas Bradley, *Vice Pres*
Kurt Hoffman, *Vice Pres*
John Seiber, *Manager*
Stephen Seiber, *Vice Pres*
EMP: 60
SALES (corp-wide): 29.6B **Privately Held**
SIC: 7389 Financial services; authors' agents & brokers; speakers' bureau
HQ: Ubs Financial Services Inc.
1285 Ave Of The Americas
New York NY 10019
212 713-2000

(P-17117)
UBS FINANCIAL SERVICES INC
200 S Los Robles Ave # 600, Pasadena (91101-4600)
PHONE...................626 449-1501
Donald Gorsch, *Manager*
EMP: 50
SALES (corp-wide): 29.6B **Privately Held**
SIC: 7389 Financial services
HQ: Ubs Financial Services Inc.
1285 Ave Of The Americas
New York NY 10019
212 713-2000

(P-17118)
UFS INTERNATIONAL LLC
10775 Bus Ctr Dr 100, Cypress (90630)
PHONE...................714 713-6311
Travis Phan, *Owner*
Robert Hrifko, *COO*
EMP: 150
SALES (est): 8.7MM **Privately Held**
SIC: 7389 5044 7371 Financial services; office equipment; custom computer programming services

(P-17119)
UNITED EXCHANGE CORP (PA)
Also Called: Uec
5836 Corp Ave Ste 200, Cypress (90630)
PHONE...................562 977-4500
Eugene W Choi, *CEO*
Carol J Choi, *President*
Sean Akutagawa, *Technology*
Lynn Chang, *Controller*
Elizabeth Lee, *Purchasing*
◆ **EMP:** 62
SQ FT: 100,000
SALES (est): 64.8MM **Privately Held**
WEB: www.ueccorp.com
SIC: 7389 5122 Packaging & labeling services; drugs, proprietaries & sundries

(P-17120)
UNITED EXPRESS MESSENGERS INC
1801 Century Park E # 520, Los Angeles (90067-2307)
PHONE...................310 261-2000
Shahin Abrishamchian, *President*
EMP: 60
SQ FT: 3,000
SALES (est): 4.8MM **Privately Held**
SIC: 7389 4212 Courier or messenger service; delivery service, vehicular

(P-17121)
UNITED PARCEL SERVICE INC
Also Called: UPS
22 Brookline, Aliso Viejo (92656-1461)
PHONE...................949 643-6634
EMP: 316
SALES (corp-wide): 71.8B **Publicly Held**
SIC: 7389 Telephone services
HQ: United Parcel Service, Inc.
55 Glenlake Pkwy
Atlanta GA 30328
404 828-6000

(P-17122)
UNITED PARCEL SERVICE INC
Also Called: UPS
14592 Palmdale Rd, Victorville (92392-2754)
PHONE...................760 241-5540
Hannah Chung, *Principal*
EMP: 1700
SALES (corp-wide): 71.8B **Publicly Held**
SIC: 7389 Mailbox rental & related service
PA: United Parcel Service, Inc.
55 Glenlake Pkwy
Atlanta GA 30328
404 828-6000

(P-17123)
UNITED PARCEL SERVICE INC
Also Called: UPS
201 W Garvey Ave Ste 102, Monterey Park (91754-7425)
PHONE...................626 280-8012
Francis Fong, *Owner*
EMP: 635
SALES (corp-wide): 71.8B **Publicly Held**
WEB: www.upsscs.com
SIC: 7389 Mailbox rental & related service
HQ: United Parcel Service, Inc.
55 Glenlake Pkwy
Atlanta GA 30328
404 828-6000

(P-17124)
UNITED PARCEL SERVICE INC
Also Called: UPS
4607 Lakeview Canyon Rd, Westlake Village (91361-4028)
PHONE...................818 735-0945
Jim Penna, *Manager*
EMP: 635
SALES (corp-wide): 71.8B **Publicly Held**
WEB: www.upsscs.com
SIC: 7389 Mailbox rental & related service
HQ: United Parcel Service, Inc.
55 Glenlake Pkwy
Atlanta GA 30328
404 828-6000

(P-17125)
UNITED PARCEL SERVICE INC OH
Also Called: UPS
3331 Industrial Dr Ste C, Santa Rosa (95403-2062)
PHONE................678 339-3171
Karen Geerdes, *Manager*
EMP: 635
SALES (corp-wide): 71.8B **Publicly Held**
SIC: 7389 Mailbox rental & related service
HQ: United Parcel Service, Inc.
55 Glenlake Pkwy
Atlanta GA 30328
404 828-6000

(P-17126)
UNITED PARCEL SERVICE INC OH
Also Called: UPS
2747 Vail Ave, Commerce (90040-2611)
PHONE................323 837-1220
Steven Hill, *Principal*
EMP: 316
SALES (corp-wide): 71.8B **Publicly Held**
SIC: 7389 Mailing & messenger services
HQ: United Parcel Service, Inc.
55 Glenlake Pkwy
Atlanta GA 30328
404 828-6000

(P-17127)
UNITED PARCEL SERVICE INC OH
Also Called: UPS
6060 Cornerstone Ct W, San Diego (92121-3712)
PHONE................858 455-8800
Minda McAllister, *Officer*
Anne Bowen-Long, *Vice Pres*
Jeff Giboney, *Vice Pres*
Phil Thomison, *Vice Pres*
Glenda Humphrey, *Administration*
EMP: 158
SALES (corp-wide): 71.8B **Publicly Held**
SIC: 7389 Mailing & messenger services
HQ: United Parcel Service, Inc.
55 Glenlake Pkwy
Atlanta GA 30328
404 828-6000

(P-17128)
UNITED PARCEL SERVICE INC OH
Also Called: UPS
3221 E Jurupa, Ontario (91764)
PHONE................909 974-7250
Richard Ricardo, *General Mgr*
EMP: 635
SALES (corp-wide): 71.8B **Publicly Held**
WEB: www.upsscs.com
SIC: 7389 Mailbox rental & related service
HQ: United Parcel Service, Inc.
55 Glenlake Pkwy
Atlanta GA 30328
404 828-6000

(P-17129)
UNITED PARCEL SERVICE INC OH
Also Called: UPS
1746 D St, South Lake Tahoe (96150-6227)
PHONE................800 742-5877
EMP: 316
SALES (corp-wide): 71.8B **Publicly Held**
SIC: 7389 Personal service agents, brokers & bureaus
HQ: United Parcel Service, Inc.
55 Glenlake Pkwy
Atlanta GA 30328
404 828-6000

(P-17130)
UNITED PARCEL SERVICE INC OH
Also Called: UPS
11811 Landon Dr, Eastvale (91752-4002)
PHONE................951 749-3400
Paul Slater, *Principal*
EMP: 316
SALES (corp-wide): 71.8B **Publicly Held**
SIC: 7389 Mailing & messenger services

HQ: United Parcel Service, Inc.
55 Glenlake Pkwy
Atlanta GA 30328
404 828-6000

(P-17131)
UNITED PARCEL SERVICE INC OH
Also Called: UPS
48921 Warm Springs Blvd, Fremont (94539-7767)
PHONE................800 742-5877
EMP: 316
SALES (corp-wide): 71.8B **Publicly Held**
SIC: 7389 Personal service agents, brokers & bureaus
HQ: United Parcel Service, Inc.
55 Glenlake Pkwy
Atlanta GA 30328
404 828-6000

(P-17132)
UNITED PARCEL SERVICE INC OH
Also Called: UPS
91 W Easy St, Simi Valley (93065-1601)
PHONE................866 553-1069
Louis Moody, *Principal*
EMP: 316
SALES (corp-wide): 71.8B **Publicly Held**
SIC: 7389 Mailing & messenger services
HQ: United Parcel Service, Inc.
55 Glenlake Pkwy
Atlanta GA 30328
404 828-6000

(P-17133)
UNITY COURIER SERVICE INC
1132 Beecher St, San Leandro (94577-1252)
PHONE................510 568-8890
Michael Wynant, *Branch Mgr*
Louis Lipson, *Controller*
EMP: 60
SALES (corp-wide): 45.8MM **Privately Held**
WEB: www.unitycourier.com
SIC: 7389 Courier or messenger service
PA: Unity Courier Service, Inc.
3231 Fletcher Dr
Los Angeles CA 90065
323 255-9800

(P-17134)
UNIVERSAL CARD INC
Also Called: Merchant Services
9012 Research Dr Ste 200, Irvine (92618-4254)
PHONE................949 861-4000
Jason W Moore, *President*
Robert Parisi, *Regional Mgr*
Paul Burt, *Recruiter*
Nathan Jurczyk, *VP Opers*
Michael Kimball, *Opers Mgr*
EMP: 400
SQ FT: 40,000
SALES (est): 32.9MM **Privately Held**
WEB: www.merchantsvcs.com
SIC: 7389 Credit card service

(P-17135)
UNIVERSAL MUS INVESTMENTS INC (HQ)
2220 Colorado Ave, Santa Monica (90404-3506)
PHONE................818 577-4700
Lucian C Grainge, *CEO*
Wendy Goldstein, *Vice Pres*
Alasdair J McMullan, *Vice Pres*
Bernie Tan, *Associate Dir*
Marcella Gaither, *Principal*
▲ EMP: 80
SALES (est): 24.9MM
SALES (corp-wide): 78.1MM **Privately Held**
SIC: 7389 7929 Music recording producer; musical entertainers; musicians
PA: Vivendi
42 Avenue De Friedland
Paris 8e Arrondissement 75008
145 639-909

(P-17136)
UNIVERSAL MUSIC GROUP INC (HQ)
2220 Colorado Ave, Santa Monica (90404-3506)
PHONE................310 865-4000
Lucian Grainge, *Co-CEO*
Mauro Deceglie, *Partner*
Jules Ferree, *Partner*
Mike Marshino, *Partner*
Darcus Beese, *President*
▲ EMP: 100
SALES (est): 551.8MM
SALES (corp-wide): 78.1MM **Privately Held**
SIC: 7389 2741 Music recording producer; miscellaneous publishing
PA: Vivendi
42 Avenue De Friedland
Paris 8e Arrondissement 75008
145 639-909

(P-17137)
UNIVERSAL MUSIC GROUP INC
10 Universal City Plz, Universal City (91608)
PHONE................818 286-4000
Kent Earls, *Branch Mgr*
Chris Monaco, *Vice Pres*
Justin Pillay, *Project Mgr*
Jason Northrop, *Finance Mgr*
Sarah Palmer, *Human Res Mgr*
EMP: 50
SALES (corp-wide): 78.1MM **Privately Held**
SIC: 7389 Music recording producer
HQ: Universal Music Group, Inc.
2220 Colorado Ave
Santa Monica CA 90404
310 865-4000

(P-17138)
UNIVERSITY STUDENT UNION INC
5151 State University Dr, Los Angeles (90032-4226)
PHONE................323 343-2450
Joseph Aguirre, *Exec Dir*
Rowena Tran, *Asst Director*
EMP: 110
SALES: 5.9MM **Privately Held**
SIC: 7389 Personal service agents, brokers & bureaus

(P-17139)
UPS STORE INC (HQ)
Also Called: Mail Boxes Etc
6060 Cornerstone Ct W, San Diego (92121-3712)
PHONE................858 455-8800
Walter T Davis, *CEO*
Tim Davis, *President*
Chris Adkins, *Vice Pres*
Jeffrey Alianiello, *Vice Pres*
Steve Dandrea, *Vice Pres*
EMP: 148
SQ FT: 66,000
SALES (est): 82.3MM
SALES (corp-wide): 71.8B **Publicly Held**
WEB: www.ups.com
SIC: 7389 8742 4783 Mailbox rental & related service; printers' services: folding, collating; packaging & labeling services; business consultant; packing goods for shipping
PA: United Parcel Service, Inc.
55 Glenlake Pkwy
Atlanta GA 30328
404 828-6000

(P-17140)
US BANKCARD SERVICES INC
17171 Gale Ave Ste 110, City of Industry (91745-1822)
PHONE................888 888-8872
Christopher J Chang, *President*
Martin Lanyan, *Vice Pres*
Iris Chang, *Products*
Chuck Shin, *Accounts Exec*
▲ EMP: 75 EST: 1996
SQ FT: 3,000
SALES (est): 7.4MM **Privately Held**
WEB: www.topmsp.com
SIC: 7389 Credit card service

(P-17141)
V A ANDERSON ENTERPRISES INC (PA)
Also Called: Kopy Kat Attorney Service
400 Atlas St, Brea (92821-3117)
P.O. Box 1029 (92822-1029)
PHONE................714 990-6100
Pat Flynn, *President*
Bob Flynn, *Vice Pres*
Chuck Cunningham, *Sales Executive*
Perry Miller, *Manager*
EMP: 62
SQ FT: 10,000
SALES (est): 7.4MM **Privately Held**
WEB: www.kopykat.net
SIC: 7389 Microfilm recording & developing service

(P-17142)
V G CARELLI INTERNATIONAL CORP
1 Park Plz Ste 600, Irvine (92614-5987)
PHONE................310 247-8410
Vittorio G Carelli, *President*
Rebecca Mansdorf, *Director*
EMP: 50
SALES (est): 1.6MM **Privately Held**
SIC: 7389 Personal service agents, brokers & bureaus

(P-17143)
VALLEY INVENTORY SERVICE INC
1180 Horizon Dr Ste B, Fairfield (94533-1693)
P.O. Box 503 (94533-0050)
PHONE................707 422-6050
Jeffrey J Link, *President*
Veronica Link, *President*
Jack Link, *General Mgr*
Darian Dixon, *Info Tech Dir*
EMP: 100
SALES (est): 8.2MM **Privately Held**
WEB: www.valleycount.com
SIC: 7389 Inventory computing service

(P-17144)
VALLEY MOON FRE PRTCT DIST
Also Called: Sonoma Vly Fire & Rescue Auth
630 2nd St W, Sonoma (95476-6901)
PHONE................707 996-2102
Stephen Akre, *Principal*
Georgette Darcy, *Analyst*
EMP: 89
SALES (est): 161.2K **Privately Held**
SIC: 7389 Fire protection service other than forestry or public

(P-17145)
VASTEK INC
1230 Columbia St Ste 1180, San Diego (92101-8520)
PHONE................925 948-5701
Vikash Mishra, *CEO*
Vinay Koppula, *Business Anlyst*
EMP: 171
SQ FT: 1,600
SALES: 10.7MM **Privately Held**
SIC: 7389 7371 Air pollution measuring service; custom computer programming services

(P-17146)
VENTURE DESIGN SERVICES INC
451 Aviation Blvd Ste 215, Santa Rosa (95403-1055)
PHONE................707 524-8368
Robert Eves, *Branch Mgr*
EMP: 89
SALES (corp-wide): 12.7MM **Privately Held**
SIC: 7389 Design services
PA: Venture Design Services Inc.
1051 S East St
Anaheim CA 92805
714 765-3740

(P-17147)
VERIZON COMMUNICATIONS INC
2801 Townsgate Rd Ste 300, Westlake Village (91361-3040)
PHONE................805 390-5417

Connie Murphree, *General Mgr*
EMP: 120
SALES (corp-wide): 130.8B **Publicly Held**
WEB: www.verizon.com
SIC: 7389 4812 Telemarketing services; radio telephone communication
PA: Verizon Communications Inc.
1095 Ave Of The Americas
New York NY 10036
212 395-1000

(P-17148)
VIAD CORP
5560 Katella Ave, Cypress (90630-5001)
PHONE..................................562 370-1500
Frank Carbone, *Branch Mgr*
EMP: 85 **Publicly Held**
WEB: www.viad.com
SIC: 7389 Promoters of shows & exhibitions
PA: Viad Corp
1850 N Central Ave # 1900
Phoenix AZ 85004

(P-17149)
VIAN ENTERPRISES INC
1501 Industrial Dr, Auburn (95603-9018)
PHONE..................................530 885-1997
Christopher R Vian, *CEO*
Liz Popsicle, *President*
William Kirby, *CFO*
Carol Ann Vian, *Vice Pres*
Pam Vian, *Vice Pres*
EMP: 50
SALES (est): 8.7MM **Privately Held**
WEB: www.vianenterprises.com
SIC: 7389 Personal service agents, brokers & bureaus

(P-17150)
VISIONFUND INTERNATIONAL
Also Called: VISION FUND INTERNATIONAL
800 W Chestnut Ave, Monrovia (91016-3106)
PHONE..................................626 303-8811
Scott Brown, *CEO*
EMP: 85
SALES: 26.5MM
SALES (corp-wide): 1B **Privately Held**
SIC: 7389 Financial services
HQ: World Vision International
800 W Chestnut Ave
Monrovia CA 91016
626 303-8811

(P-17151)
VISUAL PAK SAN DIEGO LLC
2320 Paseo De Las Ave 2, San Diego (92154)
PHONE..................................847 689-1000
David Waldron, *Mng Member*
Clayton Bolke,
▲ EMP: 250
SALES (est): 20.8MM **Privately Held**
SIC: 7389 Packaging & labeling services

(P-17152)
VITAL FARMLAND HOLDINGS LLC
3 Corte Las Casas, Belvedere Tiburon (94920-2012)
PHONE..................................415 465-2400
Craig Wichner, *Mng Member*
EMP: 54
SALES (est): 1.1MM **Privately Held**
SIC: 7389 Financial services

(P-17153)
VIVID SOLUTION
5959 W Century Blvd, Los Angeles (90045-6517)
PHONE..................................310 498-2559
Steve Huwang, *Principal*
EMP: 99
SALES (est): 1.9MM **Privately Held**
SIC: 7389 Business services

(P-17154)
VIVOPOOLS LLC
Also Called: North Bay Pool and Spa
245 W Foothill Blvd, Monrovia (91016-2152)
PHONE..................................888 702-8486
William Johnson, *Mng Member*

EMP: 63
SQ FT: 4,000
SALES (est): 7.6MM **Privately Held**
SIC: 7389 3589 5734 5091 Swimming pool & hot tub service & maintenance; swimming pool & water conditioning systems; computer software & accessories; swimming pools, equipment & supplies; swimming pool chemicals, equipment & supplies

(P-17155)
VOLCOM LLC (PA)
Also Called: Stone Entertainment
1740 Monrovia Ave, Costa Mesa (92627-4407)
PHONE..................................949 646-2175
Todd Hymel, *CEO*
Josh Douglas, *Admin Sec*
Jeffrey Gonzales, *Admin Sec*
Amy Cole, *Planning*
Paulo Braga, *Technology*
EMP: 200
SQ FT: 104,000
SALES (est): 102.3MM **Privately Held**
WEB: www.volcoment.com
SIC: 7389 2253 7822 5136 Design services; bathing suits & swimwear, knit; motion picture & tape distribution; men's & boys' clothing; women's & children's clothing

(P-17156)
VXI GLOBAL SOLUTIONS LLC (PA)
220 W 1st St Fl 3, Los Angeles (90012-4105)
PHONE..................................213 739-4720
Eva Yi Hui Wang, *President*
Mark Hauge, *President*
Jared Morrison, *COO*
David Zhou, *COO*
Steven Wang, *CFO*
EMP: 1200 EST: 1998
SALES (est): 1B **Privately Held**
WEB: www.vxi.com
SIC: 7389 Telemarketing services

(P-17157)
W SCOTT BLLARD DSIGN ARCH INC
Also Called: Ballard Clothing Design
1800 Century Park E # 600, Los Angeles (90067-1501)
PHONE..................................323 386-4740
W Scott Ballard, *CEO*
EMP: 50
SALES (est): 1.4MM **Privately Held**
SIC: 7389 Design services

(P-17158)
WALLIS FASHIONS INC
1100 8th Ave, Oakland (94606-3613)
PHONE..................................510 763-8018
Fax: 510 832-6882
EMP: 110
SALES (est): 5.2MM **Privately Held**
WEB: www.wallisfashions.com
SIC: 7389

(P-17159)
WARFIGHTER & FAMILY SERVICES
Also Called: Warfighter & Family Services C
2375 Recreation Way, San Diego (92136-5518)
PHONE..................................619 556-7168
A Quezada-Rmirez, *Accounting Mgr*
Anabel Quezada-Ramirez, *Accounting Mgr*
Olivia Austria, *Business Mgr*
EMP: 70
SALES (est): 1.6MM **Privately Held**
SIC: 7389 Personal service agents, brokers & bureaus

(P-17160)
WARNER BROS RECORDS INC (DH)
777 S Santa Fe Ave, Los Angeles (90021-1750)
PHONE..................................818 846-9090
Todd Moscowitz, *President*
Rob Cavallo, *Ch of Bd*
Livia Tortella, *President*
Marty Greenfield, *CFO*

Ben Larsen, *Assoc VP*
EMP: 460
SALES (est): 93.8MM **Privately Held**
WEB: www.warnerbrosrecords.com
SIC: 7389 Music recording producer; recording studio, noncommercial records

(P-17161)
WASHINGTON INVENTORY SERVICE (DH)
Also Called: Wis
9265 Sky Park Ct Ste 100, San Diego (92123-4375)
PHONE..................................858 565-8111
Jim Rose, *CEO*
Howard L Madden, *President*
Trey Graham, *CFO*
Deborah Williams, *Division VP*
Chris Forsberg, *Exec VP*
EMP: 135 EST: 1960
SQ FT: 30,000
SALES (est): 89.3MM **Publicly Held**
WEB: www.wisusa.com
SIC: 7389 Inventory computing service
HQ: Western Inventory Service Ltd
3770 Nashua Dr Suite 5
Mississauga ON L4V 1
905 677-1947

(P-17162)
WASHINGTON INVENTORY SERVICE
Also Called: Wis
7150 El Cajon Blvd, San Diego (92115-1895)
PHONE..................................619 461-8198
Fax: 619 465-0362
EMP: 70
SALES (corp-wide): 671MM **Publicly Held**
SIC: 7389
HQ: Washington Inventory Service Inc
9265 Sky Park Ct Ste 100
San Diego CA 92123
858 565-8111

(P-17163)
WAWONA PACKING CO LLC
12133 Avenue 408, Cutler (93615-2056)
PHONE..................................559 528-4699
EMP: 400
SQ FT: 85,000
SALES (est): 19.3MM **Privately Held**
SIC: 7389 Packaging & labeling services

(P-17164)
WEBLY SYSTEMS INC
2603 Camino Ramon Ste 200, San Ramon (94583-9137)
PHONE..................................888 444-6400
Taj Reneau, *CEO*
Bob McConnell, *CFO*
EMP: 50
SALES (est): 2MM **Privately Held**
SIC: 7389 Telephone services

(P-17165)
WEST COAST LEGAL SERVICE INC
1245 S Winchester Blvd # 208, San Jose (95128-3908)
PHONE..................................408 938-6520
Donald Russi, *President*
Susan Wertz, *Admin Sec*
EMP: 50 EST: 1972
SQ FT: 4,000
SALES (est): 3.6MM **Privately Held**
WEB: www.westcoastlegal.com
SIC: 7389 Legal & tax services; process serving service

(P-17166)
WEST SAFETY SOLUTIONS CORP
3009 Douglas Blvd Ste 300, Roseville (95661-3895)
PHONE..................................514 340-3314
Beth Meek, *President*
Chris Buxler, *Vice Pres*
EMP: 50
SALES (est): 36K
SALES (corp-wide): 2.2B **Privately Held**
SIC: 7389 Telephone services

HQ: Intrado Corporation
11808 Miracle Hills Dr
Omaha NE 68154

(P-17167)
WESTPOINT MARKETING INTL INC
5901 Avalon Blvd, Los Angeles (90003-1309)
P.O. Box 30144 (90030-0144)
PHONE..................................323 233-0233
EMP: 85
SALES (est): 2.9MM **Privately Held**
SIC: 7389

(P-17168)
WET (PA)
10847 Sherman Way, Sun Valley (91352-4829)
PHONE..................................818 769-6200
Mark W Fuller, *CEO*
Shemi Hart, *CFO*
Kenneth Wynn, *Officer*
Tania Avedissian, *Senior VP*
Helen Park, *Senior VP*
▲ EMP: 148
SQ FT: 112,000
SALES (est): 74.7MM **Privately Held**
WEB: www.wetdesign.com
SIC: 7389 8711 3443 Design services; engineering services; metal parts

(P-17169)
WILLITS PERPETUAL LLC
21600 Oxnard St, Woodland Hills (91367-4976)
PHONE..................................818 668-6800
EMP: 75
SALES (est): 3.2MM **Privately Held**
SIC: 7389

(P-17170)
WILMAY INC
893 Oak Ave, Fillmore (93015-9621)
PHONE..................................805 524-2603
EMP: 80
SALES (est): 2.2MM **Privately Held**
SIC: 7389

(P-17171)
WINNING PERFORMANCE PDTS INC
Also Called: Diplomat Packaging
13010 Bradley Ave, Sylmar (91342-3831)
PHONE..................................818 367-1041
Todd J Harding, *President*
Kim Harding, *Officer*
Barbara Rogers, *Officer*
▲ EMP: 50
SQ FT: 60,000
SALES (est): 5.7MM **Privately Held**
WEB: www.diplomatpackaging.com
SIC: 7389 5013 Packaging & labeling services; motorcycle parts

(P-17172)
WORLDLINK LLC (PA)
Also Called: Worldlink East
6100 Wilshire Blvd # 1400, Los Angeles (90048-5111)
PHONE..................................323 866-5900
Toni E Knight, *Mng Member*
Georgette Demarte, *Executive*
Gina Perez, *Executive*
Kevin Moran, *IT/INT Sup*
Michael Crutchfield, *Analyst*
EMP: 72
SQ FT: 20,000
SALES (est): 8.5MM **Privately Held**
WEB: www.worldlinkmedia.com
SIC: 7389 Personal service agents, brokers & bureaus

(P-17173)
YAPSTONE INC (PA)
Also Called: Rentpayment.com
2121 N Calif Blvd Ste 400, Walnut Creek (94596-7305)
PHONE..................................866 289-5977
Tom Villante, *Ch of Bd*
Kelly Kay, *President*
Bryan Murphy, *President*
Mary Hentges, *CFO*
John Malnar, *CFO*
EMP: 125

SALES (est): 33.4MM **Privately Held**
WEB: www.rentpayment.com
SIC: 7389 Credit card service

(P-17174)
YC CABLE USA INC (HQ)
44061 Nobel Dr, Fremont (94538-3162)
PHONE.................................510 824-2788
Gary Hsu, *President*
KAO Y Fang, *Shareholder*
Thuy Diep, *Technician*
Jimmy Kuang, *Engineer*
Wilson Tong, *Engineer*
▲ EMP: 70
SQ FT: 45,000
SALES (est): 21MM **Privately Held**
SIC: 7389 3643 Field audits, cable television; power line cable

(P-17175)
YELLOWPAGESCOM LLC (HQ)
Also Called: Dexyp
611 N Brand Blvd Ste 500, Glendale (91203-1221)
PHONE.................................818 937-5500
David Krantz,
Williams Clenney, *CFO*
Brad Mohs, *CTO*
Laura Thatcher, *Data Proc Staff*
EMP: 260
SALES (est): 51MM
SALES (corp-wide): 1.6B **Privately Held**
WEB: www.yellowpages.com
SIC: 7389 Telephone directory distribution, contract or fee basis
PA: Thryv, Inc.
2200 W Airfield Dr
Dfw Airport TX 75261
972 453-7000

(P-17176)
ZAYO GROUP LLC
3700 Old Redwood Hwy, Santa Rosa (95403-5738)
PHONE.................................707 284-4000
Shawn Shaw, *Branch Mgr*
Robert Guth, *President*
EMP: 72
SALES (corp-wide): 2.5B **Publicly Held**
SIC: 7389 4813 Telephone services; local & long distance telephone communications
HQ: Zayo Group, Llc
1805 29th St Unit 2050
Boulder CO 80301

(P-17177)
ZS ASSOCIATES INC
400 S El Camino Real # 1500, San Mateo (94402-1733)
PHONE.................................650 762-7800
Ty Curry, *Manager*
Graham Webster, *CFO*
Craig Stinebaugh, *Admin Mgr*
Timur Shalizi, *Technical Mgr*
Alexis Steger, *Business Anlyst*
EMP: 80
SALES (corp-wide): 317.9MM **Privately Held**
WEB: www.zsassociates.com
SIC: 7389 8742 Mapmaking services; marketing consulting services
PA: Zs Associates, Inc.
1560 Sherman Ave Ste 800
Evanston IL 60201
847 492-3600

7513 Truck Rental & Leasing, Without Drivers

(P-17178)
PACCAR LEASING CORPORATION
Also Called: PacLease
2892 E Jensen Ave, Fresno (93706-5111)
PHONE.................................559 268-4344
Warren Auwae, *Manager*
EMP: 160
SALES (corp-wide): 23.5B **Publicly Held**
WEB: www.glsayre.com
SIC: 7513 Truck leasing, without drivers

HQ: Paccar Leasing Corporation
777 106th Ave Ne
Bellevue WA 98004
425 468-7400

(P-17179)
PARTS
2445 Evergreen Ave, West Sacramento (95691-3011)
P.O. Box 716 (95691-0716)
PHONE.................................916 371-3115
Tim Hollman, *Principal*
EMP: 82
SALES (est): 1MM **Privately Held**
SIC: 7513 Truck rental & leasing, no drivers

(P-17180)
PENSKE AUTOMOTIVE GROUP INC
4750 Kearny Mesa Rd, San Diego (92111-2405)
PHONE.................................858 430-2320
Dan Collins, *Branch Mgr*
Paul Ramplin, *General Mgr*
Ron Kinsey, *Sales Staff*
Tom Swapp, *Sales Staff*
Tina Celaya, *Manager*
EMP: 200 **Publicly Held**
SIC: 7513 5531 7539 Truck rental & leasing, no drivers; automotive accessories; automotive parts; automotive repair shops
PA: Penske Automotive Group, Inc.
2555 S Telegraph Rd
Bloomfield Hills MI 48302

(P-17181)
PENSKE AUTOMOTIVE GROUP INC
17 Woodland Ave, San Rafael (94901-5301)
PHONE.................................415 492-1922
Jason Golpad, *Principal*
Buskirk Earl, *Sales Associate*
EMP: 50 **Publicly Held**
SIC: 7513 Truck rental & leasing, no drivers
PA: Penske Automotive Group, Inc.
2555 S Telegraph Rd
Bloomfield Hills MI 48302

(P-17182)
PENSKE AUTOMOTIVE GROUP INC
803 S 1st St, San Jose (95110-3123)
PHONE.................................408 293-7688
Ngoc Tran, *Branch Mgr*
EMP: 50 **Publicly Held**
SIC: 7513 Truck rental & leasing, no drivers
PA: Penske Automotive Group, Inc.
2555 S Telegraph Rd
Bloomfield Hills MI 48302

(P-17183)
PENSKE TRUCK LEASING CO LP
2300 E Olympic Blvd, Los Angeles (90021-2537)
PHONE.................................213 628-1255
Alfred McCandless, *Vice Pres*
EMP: 50
SALES (corp-wide): 2.4B **Privately Held**
WEB: www.pensketruckleasing.com
SIC: 7513 Truck rental & leasing, no drivers
PA: Penske Truck Leasing Co., L.P.
2675 Morgantown Rd
Reading PA 19607
610 775-6000

(P-17184)
PENSKE TRUCK LEASING CO LP
19646 Figueroa St, Long Beach (90745-1001)
PHONE.................................310 327-3116
Chris Reynolds, *Manager*
Christina Darlak, *Branch Mgr*
EMP: 60
SQ FT: 9,680

SALES (corp-wide): 2.4B **Privately Held**
WEB: www.pensketruckleasing.com
SIC: 7513 Truck rental & leasing, no drivers
PA: Penske Truck Leasing Co., L.P.
2675 Morgantown Rd
Reading PA 19607
610 775-6000

(P-17185)
PENSKE TRUCK LEASING CO LP
3080 E Malaga Ave, Fresno (93725-9212)
PHONE.................................559 268-7000
Adam Hemmes, *Principal*
EMP: 50
SALES (corp-wide): 2.4B **Privately Held**
WEB: www.pensketruckleasing.com
SIC: 7513 Truck rental & leasing, no drivers
PA: Penske Truck Leasing Co., L.P.
2675 Morgantown Rd
Reading PA 19607
610 775-6000

(P-17186)
RYDER INTEGRATED LOGISTICS INC
19133 Parthenia St, Northridge (91324-3626)
PHONE.................................818 701-9332
Jerry Conrrad, *Branch Mgr*
Pat Hinich, *Cust Mgr*
EMP: 50
SQ FT: 12,100
SALES (corp-wide): 8.4B **Publicly Held**
SIC: 7513 Truck rental, without drivers
HQ: Ryder Integrated Logistics, Inc.
11690 Nw 105th St
Medley FL 33178
305 500-3726

(P-17187)
RYDER TRUCK RENTAL INC
2700 3rd St, San Francisco (94107-3101)
PHONE.................................415 285-0756
Don Kelley, *Manager*
Jonathan Griffith, *Cust Mgr*
EMP: 110
SQ FT: 14,320
SALES (corp-wide): 8.4B **Publicly Held**
SIC: 7513 Truck rental, without drivers
HQ: Ryder Truck Rental, Inc.
11690 Nw 105th St
Medley FL 33178
305 500-3726

(P-17188)
RYDER TRUCK RENTAL INC
13530 Firestone Blvd, Santa Fe Springs (90670-5600)
PHONE.................................562 921-0033
Adrianna Ducante, *Manager*
Joel Lindgren, *Business Dir*
Nicolas Mansour, *Software Dev*
Randy Womack, *Technician*
Brett Robert, *Technology*
EMP: 100
SQ FT: 15,680
SALES (corp-wide): 8.4B **Publicly Held**
SIC: 7513 Truck rental, without drivers
HQ: Ryder Truck Rental, Inc.
11690 Nw 105th St
Medley FL 33178
305 500-3726

(P-17189)
RYDER TRUCK RENTAL INC
9608 Santa Anita Ave, Rancho Cucamonga (91730-6121)
PHONE.................................909 980-3137
Doreen Coddington, *Branch Mgr*
Bowman Richard, *Project Engr*
EMP: 75
SALES (corp-wide): 8.4B **Publicly Held**
SIC: 7513 4212 4213 4225 Truck leasing, without drivers; truck rental, without drivers; local trucking, without storage; trucking, except local; general warehousing; school buses; management services
HQ: Ryder Truck Rental, Inc.
11690 Nw 105th St
Medley FL 33178
305 500-3726

(P-17190)
U-HAUL CO OF CALIFORNIA (DH)
44511 S Grimmer Blvd, Fremont (94538-6309)
PHONE.................................800 528-0463
Dave Adams, *President*
EMP: 150
SALES (est): 39.6MM
SALES (corp-wide): 3.7B **Publicly Held**
SIC: 7513 7519 4226 Truck rental & leasing, no drivers; trailer rental; special warehousing & storage
HQ: U-Haul International, Inc.
2727 N Central Ave
Phoenix AZ 85004
602 263-6011

(P-17191)
UNITED HAULING CORP
Also Called: National Cement
2620 Buena Vista St, Duarte (91010-3338)
PHONE.................................626 358-9417
Alfred Delmonte, *Branch Mgr*
EMP: 70
SALES (est): 1.8MM **Privately Held**
SIC: 7513 Truck rental & leasing, no drivers

(P-17192)
WILLIAM WARREN GROUP INC (PA)
201 Wilshire Blvd Ste 102, Santa Monica (90401-1220)
P.O. Box 2034 (90406-2034)
PHONE.................................310 451-2130
William Warren Hobin, *President*
Kent Christensen, *COO*
Clark W Porter, *CFO*
Clark Porter, *CFO*
Zinke Edward, *Vice Pres*
EMP: 72
SQ FT: 1,500
SALES (est): 31.4MM
SALES (corp-wide): 33.9MM **Privately Held**
SIC: 7513 Truck rental & leasing, no drivers

(P-17193)
WINNRESIDENTIAL LTD PARTNR
2350 W Shaw Ave Ste 148, Fresno (93711-3400)
PHONE.................................559 435-3434
EMP: 443
SALES (corp-wide): 6.9MM **Privately Held**
SIC: 7513 Truck rental & leasing, no drivers
PA: Winnresidential Limited Partnership
6 Faneuil Hall Market Pl
Boston MA 02109
617 742-4500

7514 Passenger Car Rental

(P-17194)
ALAMO RENTAL (US) INC
Also Called: Alamo Rent A Car
9020 Aviation Blvd, Inglewood (90301-2907)
PHONE.................................310 649-2242
Cesar Saurez, *Manager*
EMP: 100
SALES (corp-wide): 4.5B **Privately Held**
WEB: www.area-code-330.info
SIC: 7514 Rent-a-car service
HQ: Alamo Rental (Us) Inc.
600 Corporate Park Dr
Saint Louis MO 63105

(P-17195)
ALAMO RENTAL (US) INC
Also Called: Alamo Rent A Car
4500 Campus Dr Ste 300, Newport Beach (92660-1815)
PHONE.................................949 852-0403
Gordon Schmierer, *Manager*
EMP: 50
SALES (corp-wide): 4.5B **Privately Held**
WEB: www.area-code-330.info
SIC: 7514 Rent-a-car service

HQ: Alamo Rental (Us) Inc.
600 Corporate Park Dr
Saint Louis MO 63105

(P-17196)
AVIS RENT A CAR SYSTEM INC
3450 E Airport Dr Ste 500, Ontario
(91761-7681)
PHONE..............................909 974-2192
Richard Kuehner, *Manager*
EMP: 80
SALES (corp-wide): 9.1B **Publicly Held**
WEB: www.avis.com
SIC: 7514 Rent-a-car service
HQ: Avis Rent A Car System, Inc.
6 Sylvan Way Ste 1
Parsippany NJ 07054
973 496-3500

(P-17197)
AVIS RENT A CAR SYSTEM INC
Also Called: Avis Budget Car Rentals
390 Doolittle Dr, San Leandro
(94577-1015)
PHONE..............................510 562-8828
Marie Peraida, *Manager*
EMP: 200
SALES (corp-wide): 9.1B **Publicly Held**
WEB: www.avis.com
SIC: 7514 Rent-a-car service
HQ: Avis Rent A Car System, Inc.
6 Sylvan Way Ste 1
Parsippany NJ 07054
973 496-3500

(P-17198)
AVIS RENT A CAR SYSTEM INC
1 Airport Dr, Oakland (94621-1430)
PHONE..............................510 577-6360
EMP: 80
SALES (corp-wide): 9.1B **Publicly Held**
WEB: www.cendant.com
SIC: 7514 Rent-a-car service
HQ: Avis Rent A Car System, Inc.
6 Sylvan Way Ste 1
Parsippany NJ 07054
973 496-3500

(P-17199)
AVIS RENT A CAR SYSTEM INC
Also Called: Avis Rent A Car Systems
6520 Mcnair Cir, Sacramento (95837-1120)
PHONE..............................916 922-5601
David McMillan, *Manager*
EMP: 200
SALES (corp-wide): 9.1B **Publicly Held**
SIC: 7514 Rent-a-car service
HQ: Avis Rent A Car System, Inc.
6 Sylvan Way Ste 1
Parsippany NJ 07054
973 496-3500

(P-17200)
AVIS RENT A CAR SYSTEM INC
513 Eccles Ave Ste A, South San Francisco
(94080-1906)
PHONE..............................650 616-0150
Bob Salermo, *Branch Mgr*
Andrew Jaksich, *Technology*
Alexandra Sweeney, *Manager*
EMP: 100
SALES (corp-wide): 9.1B **Publicly Held**
WEB: www.cendant.com
SIC: 7514 Rent-a-car service
HQ: Avis Rent A Car System, Inc.
6 Sylvan Way Ste 1
Parsippany NJ 07054
973 496-3500

(P-17201)
AVIS RENT A CAR SYSTEM INC
4209 W Vanowen Pl, Burbank
(91505-1139)
PHONE..............................818 566-3001
Don Shelton, *Branch Mgr*
EMP: 80
SALES (corp-wide): 9.1B **Publicly Held**
WEB: www.avis.com
SIC: 7514 Rent-a-car service
HQ: Avis Rent A Car System, Inc.
6 Sylvan Way Ste 1
Parsippany NJ 07054
973 496-3500

(P-17202)
BHRAC LLC
Also Called: Beverly
9777 Wilshire Blvd # 517, Beverly Hills
(90212-1910)
PHONE..............................310 862-1933
David Sajasi,
Hugo Vargas, *Controller*
Ani Bsiabanian,
Allan Jerry Siemons,
Blair Stover,
EMP: 65
SALES: 13MM **Privately Held**
SIC: 7514 7515 Passenger car rental;
passenger car leasing

(P-17203)
ENTERPRISE HOLDINGS INC
780 W Pinedale Ave, Fresno (93711-5744)
PHONE..............................559 261-9221
Al Buroquez, *Branch Mgr*
EMP: 53
SALES (corp-wide): 4.5B **Privately Held**
SIC: 7514 Rent-a-car service
HQ: Enterprise Holdings, Inc.
600 Corporate Park Dr
Saint Louis MO 63105
314 512-5000

(P-17204)
ENTERPRISE RENT A CAR
33949 Camino Capistrano, San Juan
Capistrano (92675-4800)
PHONE..............................949 240-7000
Orval Paul, *President*
Steve Paul, *Vice Pres*
EMP: 110
SQ FT: 17,000
SALES (est): 3MM **Privately Held**
WEB: www.capistranoford.com
SIC: 7514 Passenger car rental

(P-17205)
ENTERPRISE RENT-A-CAR
78385 Varner Rd Ste D, Palm Desert
(92211-4118)
PHONE..............................760 772-0281
Jennifer Apruzzese, *Manager*
EMP: 51
SALES (corp-wide): 4.5B **Privately Held**
SIC: 7514 Passenger car rental
HQ: Enterprise Rent-A-Car Company Of
Los Angeles, Llc
333 City Blvd W Ste 1000
Orange CA 92868
657 221-4400

(P-17206)
ENTERPRISE RENT-A-CAR
2942 Kettner Blvd, San Diego
(92101-1111)
PHONE..............................619 297-0311
Doreen Bonner, *Manager*
EMP: 60
SALES (corp-wide): 4.5B **Privately Held**
WEB: www.area-code-330.info
SIC: 7514 Passenger car rental
HQ: Enterprise Rent-A-Car Company Of
Los Angeles, Llc
333 City Blvd W Ste 1000
Orange CA 92868
657 221-4400

(P-17207)
ENTERPRISE RENT-A-CAR (DH)
333 City Blvd W Ste 1000, Orange
(92868-5917)
PHONE..............................657 221-4400
Jack C Taylor, *Ch of Bd*
Pamela Nicholson, *COO*
William W Snyder, *CFO*
Andrew C Taylor, *Chairman*
Rose Langhorst, *Treasurer*
▲ EMP: 90
SQ FT: 30,000
SALES (est): 158MM
SALES (corp-wide): 4.5B **Privately Held**
SIC: 7514 7513 5511 Passenger car
rental; truck rental & leasing, no drivers;
trucks, tractors & trailers: new & used
HQ: Enterprise Holdings, Inc.
600 Corporate Park Dr
Saint Louis MO 63105
314 512-5000

(P-17208)
ENTERPRISE RENT-A-CAR
28112 Camino Capistrano, Laguna Niguel
(92677-1136)
PHONE..............................949 373-9350
Sebrina Rokozit, *Manager*
EMP: 100
SALES (corp-wide): 4.5B **Privately Held**
SIC: 7514 Passenger car rental
HQ: Enterprise Rent-A-Car Company Of
Los Angeles, Llc
333 City Blvd W Ste 1000
Orange CA 92868
657 221-4400

(P-17209)
ENTERPRISE RENT-A-CAR COMPAN
6320 Mcnair Cir, Sacramento (95837-1118)
PHONE..............................916 576-3164
Alfred Husary, *Manager*
EMP: 65
SALES (corp-wide): 4.5B **Privately Held**
WEB: www.area-code-330.info
SIC: 7514 Rent-a-car service
HQ: Enterprise Rent-A-Car Company Of
Sacramento, Llc
150 N Sunrise Ave
Roseville CA 95661

(P-17210)
ENTERPRISE RENT-A-CAR COMPAN (DH)
150 N Sunrise Ave, Roseville (95661-2905)
PHONE..............................916 787-4500
Pamela Nicholson, *President*
Susan Irwin, *Vice Pres*
Theo Curtis, *Controller*
▲ EMP: 50
SALES (est): 59.8MM
SALES (corp-wide): 4.5B **Privately Held**
SIC: 7514 5511 Passenger car rental; au-
tomobiles, new & used
HQ: Enterprise Holdings, Inc.
600 Corporate Park Dr
Saint Louis MO 63105
314 512-5000

(P-17211)
FOX RENT A CAR INC (PA)
5500 W Century Blvd, Los Angeles
(90045-5914)
PHONE..............................310 342-5155
Allen Rezapour, *President*
Mike Jaberi, *Treasurer*
Jerame Jackson, *Vice Pres*
Scott Leibow, *Vice Pres*
Mark Mirtorabi, *Principal*
EMP: 50
SQ FT: 73,500
SALES (est): 114.6MM **Privately Held**
SIC: 7514 Passenger car rental

(P-17212)
GETAROUND INC (PA)
55 Green St, San Francisco (94111-1434)
PHONE..............................866 438-2768
Sam Zaid, *CEO*
Juan Torres, *Exec VP*
Allan Obiocoro, *Administration*
Brian Haberer, *Sr Software Eng*
Dhruv Raturi, *Software Engr*
EMP: 116
SALES (est): 29.2MM **Privately Held**
SIC: 7514 Rent-a-car service

(P-17213)
HERTZ CLAIM MANAGEMENT CORP
2923 Bradley St Ste 190, Pasadena
(91107-1502)
P.O. Box 7857, Burbank (91510)
PHONE..............................626 296-4760
Fax: 626 296-4799
EMP: 84
SALES (corp-wide): 8.8B **Publicly Held**
SIC: 7514
HQ: Hertz Claim Management Corporation
8501 Williams Rd
Estero FL 33928
239 301-7000

(P-17214)
HERTZ CORPORATION
2627 N Hollywood Way # 8, Burbank
(91505-1062)
PHONE..............................818 997-0414
James D Botsch, *Manager*
EMP: 50
SALES (corp-wide): 9.5B **Publicly Held**
WEB: www.hertz.com
SIC: 7514 Rent-a-car service
HQ: The Hertz Corporation
8501 Williams Rd
Estero FL 33928
239 301-7000

(P-17215)
HERTZ CORPORATION
1000 Walsh Ave, Santa Clara
(95050-2615)
PHONE..............................408 450-6025
Orland Savio, *Manager*
Annie Truong, *Human Resources*
EMP: 100
SQ FT: 12,230
SALES (corp-wide): 9.5B **Publicly Held**
WEB: www.hertz.com
SIC: 7514 Rent-a-car service
HQ: The Hertz Corporation
8501 Williams Rd
Estero FL 33928
239 301-7000

(P-17216)
HERTZ CORPORATION
30 S Buchanan Cir, Pacheco (94553-5116)
PHONE..............................925 680-0316
Gerry Plescia, *President*
EMP: 99
SALES (corp-wide): 9.5B **Publicly Held**
SIC: 7514 Rent-a-car service
HQ: The Hertz Corporation
8501 Williams Rd
Estero FL 33928
239 301-7000

(P-17217)
HERTZ CORPORATION
177 S Airport Blvd, South San Francisco
(94080-6003)
PHONE..............................650 624-6391
Chuck Paterson, *Manager*
Dwayne Okabayashi, *General Mgr*
EMP: 82
SALES (corp-wide): 9.5B **Publicly Held**
WEB: www.hertz.com
SIC: 7514 Rent-a-car service
HQ: The Hertz Corporation
8501 Williams Rd
Estero FL 33928
239 301-7000

(P-17218)
HERTZ CORPORATION
3111 N Kenwood St, Burbank
(91505-1041)
PHONE..............................818 569-6900
Rashida Barner, *Manager*
EMP: 99
SALES (corp-wide): 9.5B **Publicly Held**
SIC: 7514 Rent-a-car service
HQ: The Hertz Corporation
8501 Williams Rd
Estero FL 33928
239 301-7000

(P-17219)
MIDWAY MOTORS
6151 W Century Blvd # 100, Los Angeles
(90045-5307)
PHONE..............................310 649-5549
Don Hankey, *Owner*
Gene Brown, *Vice Pres*
Sandra Perrichon, *Sales Mgr*
EMP: 53
SALES (corp-wide): 30.8MM **Privately Held**
WEB: www.midwaycarrental.com
SIC: 7514 Rent-a-car service
PA: Midway Motors
200 N Vermont Ave
Los Angeles CA
213 385-1411

(P-17220)
MIDWAY RENT A CAR INC
Also Called: Midway Clinic Cars
1800 S Sepulveda Blvd, Los Angeles
(90025-4314)
PHONE...................310 445-4355
Steve Rosen, *Manager*
EMP: 55 **Privately Held**
WEB: www.midway-group.com
SIC: 7514 Rent-a-car service
PA: Midway Rent A Car, Inc.
4751 Wilshire Blvd # 120
Los Angeles CA 90010

(P-17221)
NATIONAL RENTAL (US) INC
Also Called: National Rent A Car
7600 Earhart Rd Ste 4, Oakland
(94621-4558)
PHONE...................510 877-4507
Babara Chappelle, *Principal*
EMP: 65
SALES (corp-wide): 4.5B **Privately Held**
WEB: www.specialtyrentals.com
SIC: 7514 Rent-a-car service
HQ: National Rental (Us) Llc
14002 E 21st Ste 1500
Tulsa OK 74134

(P-17222)
NATIONAL RENTAL (US) INC
Also Called: National Rent A Car
2752 De La Cruz Blvd, Santa Clara
(95050-2624)
PHONE...................408 492-0501
Thomas Currier, *Principal*
EMP: 100
SALES (corp-wide): 4.5B **Privately Held**
WEB: www.specialtyrentals.com
SIC: 7514 Rent-a-car service
HQ: National Rental (Us) Llc
14002 E 21st Ste 1500
Tulsa OK 74134

(P-17223)
STAR LAX LLC
Also Called: Budget Rent-A-Car
150 S Doheny Dr, Beverly Hills
(90211-2545)
PHONE...................310 642-4500
Jeffery Mirkin,
Linda King, *Principal*
EMP: 125
SALES (est): 9MM **Privately Held**
SIC: 7514 Rent-a-car service

(P-17224)
T C R LIMITED PARTNERSHIP
Also Called: Thrifty Car Rental
5440 W Century Blvd, Los Angeles
(90045-5912)
PHONE...................310 645-1881
Brett Thomas, *Partner*
EMP: 120
SQ FT: 5,000
SALES (est): 3.2MM **Privately Held**
SIC: 7514 Rent-a-car service

(P-17225)
THRIFTY CAR RENTAL
780 Mcdonnell Rd Ste 1, San Francisco
(94128-3152)
PHONE...................877 283-0898
James S Tennant, *President*
John Tennant, *Treasurer*
Lawrence Lindisch, *Human Res Dir*
EMP: 140
SQ FT: 6,000
SALES (est): 4.9MM **Privately Held**
SIC: 7514 7513 7519 Rent-a-car service;
truck rental, without drivers; recreational
vehicle rental

(P-17226)
THRIFTY RENT-A-CAR SYSTEM INC
Also Called: Thrifty Car Rental
3500 Irvine Ave, Newport Beach
(92660-3106)
PHONE...................949 757-0659
Marion Landazuri, *Manager*
EMP: 50

SALES (corp-wide): 9.5B **Publicly Held**
WEB: www.casinomagic.com
SIC: 7514 Rent-a-car service
HQ: Thrifty Rent-A-Car System, Inc.
8501 Williams Rd
Estero FL 33928
239 301-7000

7515 Passenger Car Leasing

(P-17227)
CITY LEASING & RENTALS
2111 Morena Blvd, San Diego
(92110-3440)
PHONE...................619 276-6171
John Nieman, *President*
Dick Paullin, *Vice Pres*
Kenneth M Nieman, *Director*
EMP: 200
SALES (est): 3.9MM **Privately Held**
SIC: 7515 7514 5521 Passenger car
leasing; passenger car rental; used car
dealers

(P-17228)
EL CAJON MOTORS (PA)
Also Called: El Cajon Ford
1595 E Main St, El Cajon (92021-5902)
P.O. Box 1236 (92022-1236)
PHONE...................619 579-8888
Paul F Leader, *President*
Andrew Breech, *Vice Pres*
John Blake, *Admin Sec*
Klayton Belden, *Sales Mgr*
▲ **EMP:** 100
SQ FT: 311,226
SALES (est): 11.9MM **Privately Held**
WEB: www.elcajonford.com
SIC: 7515 5511 Passenger car leasing;
automobiles, new & used; pickups, new &
used; vans, new & used

(P-17229)
MARTY FRANICH LEASING CO
Also Called: Chrysler Plymouth Dodge Jeep
555 Auto Center Dr, Watsonville
(95076-3745)
PHONE...................831 724-2463
Steven Franich, *President*
Robert H Culbertson, *Vice Pres*
Ken Hubert, *Parts Mgr*
EMP: 50 **EST:** 1960
SQ FT: 15,500
SALES (est): 2.5MM **Privately Held**
SIC: 7515 7513 Passenger car leasing;
truck leasing, without drivers

(P-17230)
MIDWAY RENT A CAR INC
Also Called: Midway Car Rental
4201 Lankershim Blvd, North Hollywood
(91602-2856)
PHONE...................818 985-9770
Jeff Riesenberg, *Branch Mgr*
Caroline Kim, *Department Mgr*
Arbi Ghazarian, *Asst Mgr*
EMP: 160 **Privately Held**
SIC: 7515 7514 Passenger car leasing;
passenger car rental
PA: Midway Rent A Car, Inc.
4751 Wilshire Blvd # 120
Los Angeles CA 90010

(P-17231)
MISSION TRUCK SALES
Also Called: Mission Valley Truck Center
780 E Brokaw Rd, San Jose (95112-1007)
PHONE...................408 436-2920
Ernie Speno, *President*
Jeff Speno, *Vice Pres*
EMP: 75
SALES (est): 2.2MM **Privately Held**
WEB: www.missionvalleyford.com
SIC: 7515 5511 5083 Passenger car leas-
ing; automobiles, new & used; farm & gar-
den machinery

7519 Utility Trailers & Recreational Vehicle Rental

(P-17232)
EL MONTE RENTS INC (HQ)
Also Called: El Monte Rv
12818 Firestone Blvd, Santa Fe Springs
(90670-5404)
PHONE...................562 404-9300
Kenneth Schork, *CEO*
Valerie Luongo, *Project Mgr*
Annemarie De Cort, *Marketing Mgr*
Lynn Van Geene, *Marketing Mgr*
EMP: 110
SALES (est): 43.2MM
SALES (corp-wide): 295.1MM **Privately Held**
WEB: www.elmonterv.com
SIC: 7519 5561 Motor home rental; motor
homes
PA: Tourism Holdings Limited
Level 1
Auckland 1010
933 642-99

(P-17233)
QUIXOTE STUDIOS LLC
11473 Penrose St, Sun Valley
(91352-3922)
PHONE...................818 252-7722
Mikel Elliott, *Mng Member*
EMP: 50
SALES (corp-wide): 23.3MM **Privately Held**
SIC: 7519 5561 Trailer rental; travel trail-
ers: automobile, new & used
PA: Quixote Studios Llc
1011 N Fuller Ave
West Hollywood CA 90046
323 851-5030

7521 Automobile Parking Lots & Garages

(P-17234)
ACE PARKING MANAGEMENT INC
1901 Harrison St Ste 102, Oakland
(94612-3589)
PHONE...................510 589-2313
EMP: 78
SALES (corp-wide): 306.4MM **Privately Held**
SIC: 7521 Automobile parking
PA: Ace Parking Management, Inc.
645 Ash St
San Diego CA 92101
619 233-6624

(P-17235)
ACE PARKING MANAGEMENT INC
4352 La Jolla Village Dr, San Diego
(92122-1233)
PHONE...................858 552-0237
John Morgan, *Branch Mgr*
EMP: 137
SALES (corp-wide): 306.4MM **Privately Held**
SIC: 7521 Parking lots
PA: Ace Parking Management, Inc.
645 Ash St
San Diego CA 92101
619 233-6624

(P-17236)
ACE PARKING MANAGEMENT INC
2101 Webster St, Oakland (94612-3011)
PHONE...................510 272-9788
L Nick Dillard, *Principal*
EMP: 96
SALES (corp-wide): 306.4MM **Privately Held**
SIC: 7521 Parking lots
PA: Ace Parking Management, Inc.
645 Ash St
San Diego CA 92101
619 233-6624

(P-17237)
ACE PARKING MANAGEMENT INC
1330 Broadway Ste 915, Oakland
(94612-2508)
PHONE...................510 251-0509
EMP: 115
SALES (corp-wide): 306.4MM **Privately Held**
SIC: 7521 Parking lots
PA: Ace Parking Management, Inc.
645 Ash St
San Diego CA 92101
619 233-6624

(P-17238)
ACE PARKING MANAGEMENT INC
71 Fortune Dr Ste 916, Irvine (92618-2927)
PHONE...................949 727-1470
John Duanno, *Manager*
EMP: 130
SALES (corp-wide): 306.4MM **Privately Held**
WEB: www.aceparking.com
SIC: 7521 Parking lots
PA: Ace Parking Management, Inc.
645 Ash St
San Diego CA 92101
619 233-6624

(P-17239)
ACE PARKING MANAGEMENT INC (PA)
645 Ash St, San Diego (92101-3299)
PHONE...................619 233-6624
Scott A Jones, *Chairman*
Steve Burton, *President*
John Baumgardner, *CEO*
Charles Blottin, *CFO*
Sasha Bradley, *Vice Pres*
EMP: 50
SQ FT: 10,000
SALES (est): 306.4MM **Privately Held**
WEB: www.aceparking.com
SIC: 7521 Parking lots; parking structure

(P-17240)
ACE PARKING MANAGEMENT INC
2050 Gateway Pl, San Jose (95110-1011)
PHONE...................408 437-2185
Gregory V Wolcott, *Administration*
EMP: 57
SALES (corp-wide): 306.4MM **Privately Held**
SIC: 7521 Parking lots
PA: Ace Parking Management, Inc.
645 Ash St
San Diego CA 92101
619 233-6624

(P-17241)
ACE PARKING MANAGEMENT INC
350 Bush St, San Francisco (94104-2804)
PHONE...................415 421-8800
EMP: 78
SALES (corp-wide): 306.4MM **Privately Held**
SIC: 7521 Parking lots
PA: Ace Parking Management, Inc.
645 Ash St
San Diego CA 92101
619 233-6624

(P-17242)
ACE PARKING MANAGEMENT INC
21500 Pacific Coast Hwy, Huntington
Beach (92648-5300)
PHONE...................714 845-8000
Trevor Waiton, *Branch Mgr*
EMP: 69
SALES (corp-wide): 306.4MM **Privately Held**
SIC: 7521 Parking lots
PA: Ace Parking Management, Inc.
645 Ash St
San Diego CA 92101
619 233-6624

P R O D U C T S & S V C S

(P-17243)
ACE PARKING MANAGEMENT INC
1 Market Pl, San Diego (92101-7714)
PHONE..........................619 232-1234
EMP: 78
SALES (corp-wide): 306.4MM Privately Held
SIC: 7521 Parking lots
PA: Ace Parking Management, Inc.
645 Ash St
San Diego CA 92101
619 233-6624

(P-17244)
AIRPORT PARKING SERVICE INC
Also Called: Skypark
1000 San Mateo Ave, San Bruno
(94066-1526)
PHONE..........................650 875-6655
Kim Kasser, President
Joseph Galligan, Ch of Bd
Essayas Araya, Office Mgr
Helen Galligan, Admin Sec
Shirley Krouse, Admin Sec
EMP: 75
SQ FT: 430,000
SALES (est): 5.5MM Privately Held
WEB: www.skypark.com
SIC: 7521 Automobile parking

(P-17245)
AUTOMATE PARKING INC
8405 Pershing Dr Ste 301, Playa Del Rey
(90293-7861)
PHONE..........................310 674-3396
EMP: 60
SQ FT: 1,000
SALES (est): 1MM Privately Held
SIC: 7521

(P-17246)
CAR PARK INC
6541 Hollywood Blvd, Hollywood
(90028-6256)
PHONE..........................323 462-6060
Joseph Gharib, President
Rick Wilson, Senior VP
Isidro Mocon, Finance
Susan Charif, Human Res Dir
Susan Charis, Human Resources
EMP: 110
SALES (est): 314.1K Privately Held
SIC: 7521 7299 Outdoor parking services;
valet parking

(P-17247)
CENTRAL PARKING CORPORATION
1624 Franklin St Ste 722, Oakland
(94612-2823)
PHONE..........................510 832-7227
EMP: 100
SALES (corp-wide): 1.5B Publicly Held
SIC: 7521
HQ: Central Parking Corporation
507 Mainstream Dr
Nashville TN 37228
615 297-4255

(P-17248)
CENTRAL PARKING SYSTEM INC
3420 Bristol St Ste 225, Costa Mesa
(92626-7136)
PHONE..........................714 751-2855
Peter Cho, Manager
EMP: 70
SALES (corp-wide): 1.4B Publicly Held
SIC: 7521 Parking garage
HQ: Central Parking System, Inc.
507 Mainstream Dr
Nashville TN 37228
615 297-4255

(P-17249)
CENTRAL PARKING SYSTEM INC
716 10th St Ste 101, Sacramento
(95814-1807)
PHONE..........................916 441-1074
EMP: 60

SALES (corp-wide): 1.5B Publicly Held
SIC: 7521
HQ: Central Parking System, Inc.
1225 I St Nw Ste C100
Washington DC 20005
202 496-9650

(P-17250)
CENTURY PLAZA GARAGE
Also Called: American Building Maintenance
2049 Century Park E Ste D, Los Angeles
(90067-3104)
PHONE..........................310 226-7495
Jose Ramos, General Mgr
JP Morgan Investment Mgmnt,
EMP: 135
SQ FT: 2,000
SALES (est): 3MM Privately Held
SIC: 7521 Outdoor parking services

(P-17251)
CITY OF BEVERLY HILLS
342 Foothill Rd, Beverly Hills (90210-3608)
PHONE..........................310 285-2552
Dan Pack, Branch Mgr
EMP: 500 Privately Held
WEB: www.bhcpr.org
SIC: 7521 9111 Automobile parking; may-
ors' offices
PA: City Of Beverly Hills
455 N Rexford Dr
Beverly Hills CA 90210
310 285-1000

(P-17252)
CLASSIC PARKING INC
34 S Autumn St, San Jose (95110-2513)
P.O. Box 720781 (95172-0781)
PHONE..........................408 278-1444
Richard Flores, CFO
EMP: 690
SALES (corp-wide): 39.2MM Privately Held
SIC: 7521 Parking garage
PA: Classic Parking, Inc.
3208 Royal St
Los Angeles CA 90007
213 742-1238

(P-17253)
FIVE STAR PARKING-SAN DIEGO
3585 Corporate Ct, San Diego
(92123-2415)
PHONE..........................619 235-4500
Paul Chacon, General Mgr
EMP: 120
SQ FT: 3,300
SALES (est): 4.8MM Privately Held
SIC: 7521 Parking lots; parking garage

(P-17254)
IMPERIAL PARKING (US) LLC
Also Called: City Park
1740 Cesar Chavez Fl 2, San Francisco
(94124-1134)
PHONE..........................415 495-3909
Tim Leonoudakis, Branch Mgr
EMP: 650
SALES (corp-wide): 443.7MM Privately Held
SIC: 7521 Parking lots; parking garage
PA: Imperial Parking (U.S.), Llc
900 Haddon Ave Unit 333
Collingswood NJ 08108
856 854-7111

(P-17255)
IMPERIAL PARKING (US) LLC
195 N Access Rd, South San Francisco
(94080-6905)
PHONE..........................650 871-5423
David Castagnola, Branch Mgr
EMP: 63
SALES (corp-wide): 443.7MM Privately Held
SIC: 7521 4724 4111 Automobile parking;
travel agencies; airport transportation
PA: Imperial Parking (U.S.), Llc
900 Haddon Ave Unit 333
Collingswood NJ 08108
856 854-7111

(P-17256)
IMPERIAL PARKING (US) LLC
Also Called: Sfo Shuttle Bus Company
360 Oak Rd Ste 1, Stanford (94305-4500)
PHONE..........................650 724-4309
Dave Gottlieb, Branch Mgr
EMP: 50
SALES (corp-wide): 443.7MM Privately Held
SIC: 7521 Parking lots; parking garage
PA: Imperial Parking (U.S.), Llc
900 Haddon Ave Unit 333
Collingswood NJ 08108
856 854-7111

(P-17257)
IMPERIAL PARKING (US) LLC
Also Called: Sfo Shuttle Bus Company
7801 Earhart Rd, Oakland (94621-4529)
PHONE..........................510 382-2140
Dave Gottlieb, Manager
EMP: 50
SALES (corp-wide): 443.7MM Privately Held
SIC: 7521 Parking lots; parking garage
PA: Imperial Parking (U.S.), Llc
900 Haddon Ave Unit 333
Collingswood NJ 08108
856 854-7111

(P-17258)
IMPERIAL PARKING INDUSTRIES (PA)
Also Called: I P I
6404 Wilshire Blvd B, Los Angeles
(90048-5501)
PHONE..........................323 651-5588
Ali Yeganeh, President
Paul Gnasso, Vice Pres
EMP: 100
SALES (est): 6.5MM Privately Held
SIC: 7521 Parking garage

(P-17259)
JIM & DOUG CARTERS AUTOMOTIVE
Also Called: Carters Details Plus
2612 N Hollywood Way, Burbank
(91505-1020)
PHONE..........................818 842-5702
Douglas A Carter, President
Joan Carter, Treasurer
Derek Sweet, Vice Pres
Jason Gunnels, General Mgr
EMP: 50
SQ FT: 10,000
SALES (est): 2.2MM Privately Held
SIC: 7521 Parking lots

(P-17260)
L AND R AUTO PARKS INC
Also Called: Joe's Auto Parks
707 Wilshire Blvd # 4700, Los Angeles
(90017-3601)
PHONE..........................213 784-3018
Charles Bassett, President
Mark Funk, CFO
Gabriel Rubin, Corp Secy
Jeff Matsuno, Vice Pres
EMP: 250
SQ FT: 5,000
SALES (est): 13.3MM Privately Held
WEB: www.joesautoparks.com
SIC: 7521 7542 7371 Parking lots; car-
washes; computer software development
& applications

(P-17261)
L R INVESTMENT COMPANY
515 S Flower St Ste 3200, Los Angeles
(90071-2215)
PHONE..........................213 627-8211
Scott Hutchison, Partner
Kenneth Oldam, Partner
EMP: 99
SALES (est): 6.2MM Privately Held
SIC: 7521 Automobile parking

(P-17262)
LINDBERGH PARKING INC
3705 N Harbor Dr, San Diego
(92101-1021)
PHONE..........................619 291-1508
Maurice Gray, President
Scott Jones, Corp Secy

EMP: 150
SQ FT: 800
SALES (est): 3MM Privately Held
SIC: 7521 Parking lots

(P-17263)
LRW INVESTMENTS LLC
Also Called: Wally Park
9700 Bellanca Ave, Los Angeles
(90045-5510)
PHONE..........................310 337-1944
Gilad Lumer, Branch Mgr
EMP: 60
SALES (corp-wide): 8MM Privately Held
WEB: www.wallypark.com
SIC: 7521 Automobile parking
PA: Lrw Investments Llc
990 W 8th St Ste 600
Los Angeles CA 90017
213 629-3263

(P-17264)
MODERN PARKING INC
14110 Palawan Way, Marina Del Rey
(90292-6231)
PHONE..........................310 821-1081
Arisur Rahnan, Principal
EMP: 80 Privately Held
SIC: 7521 Parking garage
PA: Modern Parking, Inc.
303 S Union Ave Fl 1
Los Angeles CA 90017

(P-17265)
PARK N FLY INC
Also Called: Park One Lax
6351 W Century Blvd, Los Angeles
(90045-5355)
PHONE..........................310 417-3566
Yusef Dini, Branch Mgr
EMP: 51
SALES (corp-wide): 67.5MM Privately Held
WEB: www.parkholding.com
SIC: 7521 Parking lots
HQ: Park 'n Fly, Llc.
2060 Mount Paran Rd Nw # 207
Atlanta GA 30327
404 264-1000

(P-17266)
PARKING COMPANY OF AMERICA
Also Called: Pcamp
523 W 6th St Ste 528, Los Angeles
(90014-1225)
PHONE..........................562 862-2118
Alex Martin Chaves Jr, President
Eric Chaves, President
Lupe Alvarado, Human Resources
Ricardo Delgado, Opers Staff
Edward Lee, Director
EMP: 100 EST: 1990
SQ FT: 4,000
SALES (est): 2.3MM Privately Held
SIC: 7521 Parking lots

(P-17267)
PARKING CONCEPTS INC
1036 Broxton Ave, Los Angeles
(90024-2824)
PHONE..........................310 208-1611
Jorge Lopez, Manager
David Martil, Manager
EMP: 50
SALES (corp-wide): 58.5MM Privately Held
WEB: www.parkingconcepts.net
SIC: 7521 Parking lots
PA: Parking Concepts, Inc.
12 Mauchly Ste I
Irvine CA 92618
949 753-7525

(P-17268)
PARKING CONCEPTS INC
1801 Georgia St, Los Angeles
(90015-3477)
PHONE..........................213 746-5764
Bob Hindle, Manager
Richard Inthavong, Accountant
EMP: 50

SALES (corp-wide): 58.5MM **Privately Held**
WEB: www.parkingconcepts.net
SIC: 7521 8748 Parking lots; traffic consultant
PA: Parking Concepts, Inc.
12 Mauchly Ste I
Irvine CA 92618
949 753-7525

(P-17269)
PARKING CONCEPTS INC
14110 Palawan Way, Venice (90292-6231)
PHONE....................310 821-1081
Frank Vargas, *General Mgr*
EMP: 180
SALES (corp-wide): 58.5MM **Privately Held**
WEB: www.parkingconcepts.net
SIC: 7521 8741 Parking lots; management services
PA: Parking Concepts, Inc.
12 Mauchly Ste I
Irvine CA 92618
949 753-7525

(P-17270)
PARKING CONCEPTS INC
800 Wilshire Blvd, Los Angeles (90017-2604)
PHONE....................213 623-2661
Juan Cortes, *Branch Mgr*
EMP: 50
SALES (corp-wide): 58.5MM **Privately Held**
WEB: www.parkingconcepts.net
SIC: 7521 Parking garage
PA: Parking Concepts, Inc.
12 Mauchly Ste I
Irvine CA 92618
949 753-7525

(P-17271)
PARKING CONCEPTS INC
12001 Vista Del Mar, Playa Del Rey (90293-8518)
PHONE....................310 322-5008
Zahid Hossian, *Branch Mgr*
EMP: 57
SALES (corp-wide): 58.5MM **Privately Held**
WEB: www.parkingconcepts.net
SIC: 7521 Parking lots
PA: Parking Concepts, Inc.
12 Mauchly Ste I
Irvine CA 92618
949 753-7525

(P-17272)
PREFERRED VALET PARKING LLC
2568 Violet St, San Diego (92105-4567)
PHONE....................619 233-7275
Nick Bernal,
Tim Davis, *Manager*
EMP: 50
SALES (est): 976.7K **Privately Held**
SIC: 7521 7299 Parking lots; valet parking

(P-17273)
PRG PARKING CENTURY LLC
Also Called: Parking Spot, The
5701 W Century Blvd, Los Angeles (90045-5629)
PHONE....................310 642-0947
Geoffrey Okamoto, *General Mgr*
Prg Parking Holding LLC,
EMP: 100
SQ FT: 620,000
SALES (est): 3MM **Privately Held**
SIC: 7521 Parking garage

(P-17274)
RESORT PARKING SERVICES INC
39755 Berkey Dr B, Palm Desert (92211-1106)
PHONE....................760 328-4041
Mario Gardner, *President*
EMP: 120
SQ FT: 1,100
SALES (est): 4.3MM **Privately Held**
SIC: 7521 7299 Parking lots; indoor parking services; personal item care & storage services

(P-17275)
SERVICE PARKING CORPORATION
Also Called: Service Cleaning and Maint
3800 Barham Blvd Ste P1, Los Angeles (90068-3097)
PHONE....................323 851-2416
Aziz Azimi, *CEO*
Philip Chirino, *Vice Pres*
EMP: 65
SQ FT: 1,500
SALES (est): 1.8MM **Privately Held**
SIC: 7521 Parking garage

(P-17276)
SP PLUS CORPORATION
3470 Wilshire Blvd # 400, Los Angeles (90010-2207)
PHONE....................213 488-3100
Marjorie Jones, *Branch Mgr*
Samir Elayyan, *Senior Mgr*
EMP: 60
SALES (corp-wide): 1.4B **Publicly Held**
SIC: 7521 Parking garage
PA: Sp Plus Corporation
200 E Randolph St # 7700
Chicago IL 60601
312 274-2000

(P-17277)
TPS PARKING MANAGEMENT LLC
Also Called: Parking Spot, The
9101 S Sepulveda Blvd, Los Angeles (90045-4803)
PHONE....................310 846-4747
Chris Fincutter, *Manager*
EMP: 70
SALES (corp-wide): 68.2MM **Privately Held**
SIC: 7521 Parking garage
PA: Tps Parking Management, Llc
200 W Monroe St Ste 1500
Chicago IL 60606
312 781-9396

(P-17278)
UNIFIED VALET PARKING INC
99 S Chester Ave Fl 2, Pasadena (91106-5805)
PHONE....................818 822-5807
Mike Madjid Sabet, *President*
EMP: 57
SALES (est): 6.5MM **Privately Held**
SIC: 7521 Automobile parking

(P-17279)
VALET PARKING SVC A CAL PARTNR (PA)
6933 Hollywood Blvd, Los Angeles (90028-6146)
PHONE....................323 465-5873
Anthony Policella, *CEO*
EMP: 1268 EST: 1946
SQ FT: 10,000
SALES (est): 24.4MM **Privately Held**
WEB: www.valetparkingservice.com
SIC: 7521 7299 Parking lots; valet parking

7532 Top, Body & Upholstery Repair & Paint Shops

(P-17280)
ANAHEIM HILLS AUTO BODY INC
3500 E La Palma Ave, Anaheim (92806-2116)
PHONE....................714 632-8266
Robert Smith, *President*
Patrick Smith, *Vice Pres*
Janelle Rogers, *Auditor*
EMP: 60
SQ FT: 33,000
SALES (est): 5.8MM **Privately Held**
WEB: www.anaheimhillsautobody.com
SIC: 7532 Body shop, automotive

(P-17281)
AUTO BODY MANAGEMENT INC
Also Called: Precision Auto Body
7654 Tampa Ave, Reseda (91335-1735)
PHONE....................818 888-7654
Audrey Vasquev, *President*
EMP: 50
SALES: 4MM **Privately Held**
SIC: 7532 Body shop, automotive

(P-17282)
CALIBER BODYWORKS TEXAS INC
1100 Colorado Ave, Santa Monica (90401-3010)
PHONE....................310 392-7662
EMP: 100
SALES (corp-wide): 59.1MM **Privately Held**
SIC: 7532 Body shop, automotive
PA: Caliber Bodyworks Of Texas, Inc.
401 E Corp Dr Ste 150
Lewisville TX 75057
469 948-9500

(P-17283)
CALIBER BODYWORKS TEXAS INC
1399 Logan Ave, Costa Mesa (92626-4006)
PHONE....................714 436-5010
EMP: 150
SALES (corp-wide): 59.1MM **Privately Held**
SIC: 7532 Body shop, automotive
PA: Caliber Bodyworks Of Texas, Inc.
401 E Corp Dr Ste 150
Lewisville TX 75057
469 948-9500

(P-17284)
CALIBER BODYWORKS TEXAS INC
Also Called: Caliber Collision Centers
5 Auto Center Dr, Tustin (92782-8402)
PHONE....................714 665-3905
David Adams, *Branch Mgr*
EMP: 100
SALES (corp-wide): 59.1MM **Privately Held**
SIC: 7532 Body shop, automotive
PA: Caliber Bodyworks Of Texas, Inc.
401 E Corp Dr Ste 150
Lewisville TX 75057
469 948-9500

(P-17285)
CALIBER BODYWORKS TEXAS INC
Also Called: Caliber Collision Centers
3517 Hillcap Ave, San Jose (95136-1391)
PHONE....................408 972-0300
Abel Silva, *Branch Mgr*
EMP: 100
SALES (corp-wide): 59.1MM **Privately Held**
SIC: 7532 Body shop, automotive
PA: Caliber Bodyworks Of Texas, Inc.
401 E Corp Dr Ste 150
Lewisville TX 75057
469 948-9500

(P-17286)
CALIBER BODYWORKS TEXAS INC
20601 Valley Blvd, Walnut (91789-2731)
PHONE....................909 598-1113
Brad Wilson, *Manager*
Cindy Sanders, *Human Res Dir*
EMP: 50
SALES (corp-wide): 59.1MM **Privately Held**
SIC: 7532 Body shop, automotive
PA: Caliber Bodyworks Of Texas, Inc.
401 E Corp Dr Ste 150
Lewisville TX 75057
469 948-9500

(P-17287)
CALIBER HOLDINGS CORPORATION
Also Called: Classic Collision Center 2
3020 Riverside Dr, Los Angeles (90039-2014)
P.O. Box 39437 (90039-0437)
PHONE....................323 913-4000
Madjid Berenji, *Branch Mgr*
EMP: 60 **Privately Held**
WEB: www.classicpasadena.com
SIC: 7532 Body shop, automotive
PA: Caliber Holdings Corporation
2941 Lake Vista Dr
Lewisville TX 75067

(P-17288)
EUGENE N TOWNSEND
Also Called: Gene Townsend's Auto Body
609 S Marshall Ave, El Cajon (92020-4214)
PHONE....................619 442-8807
Eugene N Townsend, *Owner*
EMP: 55
SQ FT: 60,000
SALES (est): 3.4MM **Privately Held**
SIC: 7532 Body shop, automotive; paint shop, automotive

(P-17289)
FAITH QUALITY AUTO BODY INC
41130 Nick Ln, Murrieta (92562-7012)
PHONE....................951 698-8215
Lee Amaradio, *President*
EMP: 60
SALES (est): 6MM **Privately Held**
WEB: www.faithqualityautobody.com
SIC: 7532 Body shop, automotive

(P-17290)
FORNACA INC (PA)
Also Called: Frank Toyota & Scion
2400 National City Blvd, National City (91950-6628)
P.O. Box 540 (91951-0540)
PHONE....................866 308-9461
James Fornaca, *CEO*
Gary Fenelli, *Vice Pres*
Ronald Fornaca, *Vice Pres*
Gary Finneli, *General Mgr*
Janice Ulrich, *Administration*
EMP: 140
SQ FT: 150,000
SALES (est): 28.6MM **Privately Held**
WEB: www.frankmotors.com
SIC: 7532 5531 5511 Top & body repair & paint shops; automotive & home supply stores; automobiles, new & used

(P-17291)
FOUNTAIN VALLEY BODY WORKS M2
Also Called: Fvbw
17481 Newhope St, Fountain Valley (92708-4277)
PHONE....................714 751-8812
David March, *President*
Laurie March, *Vice Pres*
EMP: 50 EST: 1975
SQ FT: 50,000
SALES: 6MM **Privately Held**
WEB: www.fountainvalleybodyworks.com
SIC: 7532 Body shop, automotive; paint shop, automotive

(P-17292)
GOLDEN STATE COLLISION CENTERS
841 Galleria Blvd, Roseville (95678-1331)
PHONE....................916 772-1666
Dave Finkelstein, *President*
Michelle Finkelstein, *Vice Pres*
EMP: 75
SQ FT: 14,000
SALES: 11MM **Privately Held**
WEB: www.goldenstatecollision.com
SIC: 7532 Paint shop, automotive; body shop, automotive

(P-17293)
GREENWALDS AUTOBODY FRAMEWORKS (PA)
1814 Roosevelt Ave, National City (91950-5537)
PHONE....................619 477-2600

PRODUCTS & SVCS

Karen Greenwald, *Owner*
Daniel Greenwald, *Owner*
EMP: 70
SQ FT: 13,325
SALES (est): 6MM **Privately Held**
SIC: 7532 Body shop, automotive

(P-17294)
HARRYS AUTO BODY INC
Also Called: Harry's Auto Collision
1013 S La Brea Ave, Los Angeles
(90019-6902)
PHONE.............................323 933-4600
Harry Barseghian, *President*
Anna Sarti, *Exec Dir*
Vic Soghomonian, *Opers Staff*
Sally Courtois, *Marketing Staff*
▲ **EMP:** 65
SQ FT: 5,000
SALES (est): 9.4MM **Privately Held**
SIC: 7532 Body shop, automotive

(P-17295)
HOLMES BODY SHOP INC (PA)
466 Foothill Blvd, La Canada Flintridge
(91011-3518)
PHONE.............................626 795-6447
Thomas V Holmes, *President*
EMP: 64
SQ FT: 300,000
SALES (est): 8.1MM **Privately Held**
WEB: www.holmesbodyshop.com
SIC: 7532 Body shop, automotive; collision
shops, automotive

(P-17296)
KNIESELS AUTO COLLISION CENTER
4680 Pacific St, Rocklin (95677-2406)
PHONE.............................916 315-8888
Tom Kniesel, *Owner*
John Estrada, *General Mgr*
Tom Jeung, *General Mgr*
Justin Yttrup, *General Mgr*
Justin Kniesel, *Opers Staff*
EMP: 50
SALES (est): 5.2MM **Privately Held**
SIC: 7532 Body shop, automotive

(P-17297)
LABAYA BEACHCOMBER LP
3101 Sturgis Rd, Oxnard (93030-7971)
PHONE.............................805 278-6688
Daniel Mohr, *Managing Prtnr*
Edward Mohr, *Partner*
EMP: 50
SQ FT: 25,000
SALES (est): 1.9MM **Privately Held**
SIC: 7532 Collision shops, automotive

(P-17298)
MARCOS AUTO BODY INC (PA)
1390 E Palm St, Altadena (91001-2042)
PHONE.............................626 286-5691
Marco G Maimone, *President*
Mike Gregorian, *President*
Lillian Maimone, *Treasurer*
Carl Canzano, *Vice Pres*
EMP: 100
SQ FT: 14,000
SALES (est): 4.7MM **Privately Held**
WEB: www.marcosautobody.com
SIC: 7532 7539 Body shop, automotive;
frame & front end repair services

(P-17299)
MARINA AUTO BODY SHOP INC
721 Washington Blvd, Marina Del Rey
(90292-5542)
PHONE.............................310 822-6615
Tom Williamson, *President*
Bill Hubbard, *Manager*
EMP: 50
SQ FT: 24,000
SALES (est): 2.2MM **Privately Held**
WEB: www.marinaautobody.com
SIC: 7532 Body shop, automotive; paint
shop, automotive

(P-17300)
MIKE ROSES AUTO BODY INC
Also Called: Meks's Auto Body
2001 Fremont St, Concord (94520-2616)
PHONE.............................925 686-1739
Michelle Banducci, *Manager*
EMP: 50

SALES (corp-wide): 10.4MM **Privately
Held**
SIC: 7532 Upholstery & trim shop, automo-
tive; body shop, trucks
PA: Mike Rose's Auto Body, Inc.
2260 Via De Mercados
Concord CA 94520
925 689-1739

(P-17301)
PK AUTOBODY INC
Also Called: Z J'S Auto Body
361 N Minnewawa Ave, Clovis
(93612-0208)
PHONE.............................559 298-9691
Pam Hartley, *CEO*
Jay Bruno, *President*
Ed Bruno, *CFO*
David Rodriguez, *CFO*
Horace Bruno, *Vice Pres*
EMP: 50
SQ FT: 23,000
SALES (est): 4MM **Privately Held**
SIC: 7532 Body shop, automotive

(P-17302)
PLATINUM EQUITY PARTNERS INC
3131 S Standard Ave, Santa Ana
(92705-5642)
PHONE.............................714 444-3100
Hamid Hojati, *President*
Ingrid Cramer, *Vice Pres*
Elham Hojati, *Vice Pres*
EMP: 145
SQ FT: 45,000
SALES (est): 5.1MM **Privately Held**
SIC: 7532 Body shop, automotive

(P-17303)
PRESTIGE AUTO COLLISION INC
23726 Via Fabricante, Mission Viejo
(92691-3145)
PHONE.............................949 470-6031
Bernie Gates, *President*
Laurie Gates, *Treasurer*
Amy Beckner, *Info Tech Mgr*
EMP: 65
SQ FT: 10,000
SALES (est): 4.7MM **Privately Held**
WEB: www.prestigeautocollision.com
SIC: 7532 Collision shops, automotive

(P-17304)
PRESTIGE TOO AUTO BODY INC
11899 Woodruff Ave, Downey
(90241-5631)
PHONE.............................310 787-8852
Ben L Guerra, *President*
EMP: 50
SALES (est): 4.7MM **Privately Held**
WEB: www.prestigetooautobody.com
SIC: 7532 Body shop, automotive; collision
shops, automotive

(P-17305)
PRIDE COLLISION CENTERS INC (PA)
Also Called: Pride Auto Body
7950 Haskell Ave, Van Nuys (91406-1923)
PHONE.............................818 909-0660
Randy Stabler, *President*
Jay Russell, *Vice Pres*
Robert Turchan, *Vice Pres*
Shawn Sgambellone, *Parts Mgr*
EMP: 65
SQ FT: 44,000
SALES (est): 11.2MM **Privately Held**
SIC: 7532 Body shop, automotive

(P-17306)
REDLANDS FORD INC
1121 W Colton Ave, Redlands
(92374-2935)
PHONE.............................909 793-3211
Steve Rojas, *President*
Tracey Hooper, *Treasurer*
Monica Alvarado, *Sales Staff*
Trever Desherlia, *Manager*
EMP: 85
SALES (est): 9.5MM **Privately Held**
WEB: www.redlandsford.com
SIC: 7532 5511 Body shop, automotive;
automobiles, new & used

(P-17307)
SERVICE KING HOLDINGS LLC
Also Called: Service King Cllision Repr Ctr
7801 Oakport St, Oakland (94621-2024)
PHONE.............................510 562-9650
EMP: 82
SALES (corp-wide): 366.8MM **Privately
Held**
SIC: 7532 Body shop, automotive
PA: Service King Holdings, Llc
2375 N Glenville Dr
Richardson TX 75082
972 960-7595

(P-17308)
SERVICE KING HOLDINGS LLC
Also Called: Service King Cllision Repr Ctr
4660 Alvarado Canyon Rd, San Diego
(92120-4304)
PHONE.............................619 219-3927
EMP: 59
SALES (corp-wide): 366.8MM **Privately
Held**
SIC: 7532 Body shop, automotive
PA: Service King Holdings, Llc
2375 N Glenville Dr
Richardson TX 75082
972 960-7595

(P-17309)
SERVICE KING HOLDINGS LLC
Also Called: Service King Cllision Repr Ctr
18065 Euclid St, Fountain Valley
(92708-6107)
PHONE.............................714 962-2600
Tim Wolf, *General Mgr*
Anna Hernandez, *Finance Dir*
EMP: 71
SALES (corp-wide): 366.8MM **Privately
Held**
SIC: 7532 Body shop, automotive
PA: Service King Holdings, Llc
2375 N Glenville Dr
Richardson TX 75082
972 960-7595

(P-17310)
SERVICE KING PAINT & BODY LLC
6080 Dublin Blvd, Dublin (94568-7581)
PHONE.............................925 301-8481
EMP: 150
SALES (corp-wide): 6.8B **Publicly Held**
SIC: 7532 Body shop, automotive
HQ: Service King Paint & Body, Llc
2375 N Glenville Dr
Richardson TX 75082
972 960-7595

(P-17311)
SONSHINE COLLISION SERVICES
Also Called: Sonshine Auto Body
17200 Jasmine St, Victorville (92395-5836)
PHONE.............................760 243-3185
Gary L Cooper, *CEO*
Darlene T Cooper, *Treasurer*
Terry Thomas, *Vice Pres*
Aaron P Cooper, *Admin Sec*
EMP: 60
SALES (est): 4.7MM **Privately Held**
SIC: 7532 Collision shops, automotive

(P-17312)
STERLING COLLISION CENTER LLC (PA)
Also Called: Sea Breeze Collision
1111 Bell Ave Ste A, Tustin (92780-6463)
PHONE.............................714 259-1111
Ray Shaai, *General Ptnr*
EMP: 65
SALES (est): 6.6MM **Privately Held**
SIC: 7532 Body shop, automotive

(P-17313)
WILLIAMSON ENTERPRISES INC
Also Called: Marina Autobody
721 Washington Blvd, Marina Del Rey
(90292-5542)
PHONE.............................310 822-6615
Thomas C Williamson, *President*
Abbie Woods, *Executive*
Kathlene R Williamson, *Admin Sec*
EMP: 51

SQ FT: 24,000
SALES (est): 5.3MM **Privately Held**
WEB: www.williamsonenterprises.com
SIC: 7532 Body shop, automotive

(P-17314)
Y & S ENTERPRISES INC (PA)
Also Called: Y & S Auto Body Shop
1441 N Gaffey St, San Pedro (90731-1325)
PHONE.............................310 548-1120
Younan Safar, *CEO*
Rose Safar, *Director*
EMP: 50
SQ FT: 71,000
SALES (est): 5.1MM **Privately Held**
WEB: www.yandsautobody.com
SIC: 7532 Body shop, automotive

(P-17315)
ZIKAKIS AUTO HOLDINGS LLC
Also Called: Lompoc Honda Body Shop
1224 N H St, Lompoc (93436-3302)
PHONE.............................805 736-4595
Christopher A Zikakis, *Mng Member*
Ron Hirzel, *Branch Mgr*
EMP: 50
SQ FT: 10,000
SALES (est): 3.6MM **Privately Held**
WEB: www.lompochonda.com
SIC: 7532 Body shop, automotive

7534 Tire Retreading & Repair Shops

(P-17316)
AAA SIGNS INC
Also Called: Total Tire Recycling
2020 Railroad Dr, Sacramento
(95815-3515)
PHONE.............................916 568-3456
Gary Matranga, *President*
Danny L Matranga, *Officer*
Nancy Gray, *Office Mgr*
Steve Horell, *Sales Staff*
EMP: 54
SQ FT: 14,000
SALES (est): 5.6MM **Privately Held**
SIC: 7534 7353 Tire retreading & repair
shops; cranes & aerial lift equipment,
rental or leasing

(P-17317)
NEW PRIDE TIRE INC
1511 E Orangethorpe Ave D, Fullerton
(92831-5204)
PHONE.............................310 631-7000
Edward Eunjong Kim, *President*
EMP: 50 **Privately Held**
SIC: 7534 1799 Rebuilding & retreading
tires; antenna installation
HQ: New Pride Tire, Inc.
333 Hegenberger Rd # 307
Oakland CA 94621
510 567-8800

(P-17318)
RUBBER DUST INC (PA)
Also Called: J & O'S Commercial Tire Center
533 S 13th St, Richmond (94804-3702)
PHONE.............................510 237-6344
Charlie T Talbot, *CEO*
John A Talbot, *President*
Bonnie Talbot, *Corp Secy*
Edward Talbot, *Vice Pres*
▼ **EMP:** 57
SQ FT: 40,000
SALES (est): 7.3MM **Privately Held**
WEB: www.jandotire.com
SIC: 7534 7538 Tire repair shop; general
automotive repair shops

7536 Automotive Glass Replacement Shops

(P-17319)
ALL STAR GLASS INC (PA)
1845 Morena Blvd, San Diego
(92110-3699)
PHONE.............................619 275-3343
Bob Scharaga, *CEO*
Mark V Doren, *COO*
Hermeen Scharaga, *Treasurer*

▲ = Import ▼=Export
◆ =Import/Export

Janet Scharaga, *Vice Pres*
Michele Linhardt, *Controller*
▲ EMP: 50
SQ FT: 15,512
SALES: 24.1MM **Privately Held**
SIC: 7536 Automotive glass replacement shops

(P-17320)
SAFELITE FULFILLMENT INC
Also Called: Safelite Autoglass
261 Richards Blvd, Sacramento (95811-0216)
PHONE....................916 442-4715
Frank Primer, *Manager*
Kay White, *Branch Mgr*
EMP: 80
SALES (corp-wide): 3.7B **Privately Held**
WEB: www.belronus.com
SIC: 7536 4225 Automotive glass replacement shops; general warehousing & storage
HQ: Safelite Fulfillment, Inc.
7400 Safelite Way
Columbus OH 43235
614 210-9000

7537 Automotive Transmission Repair Shops

(P-17321)
PDQ AUTOMATIC TRANSM PARTS INC
8380 Tiogawoods Dr, Sacramento (95828-5048)
PHONE....................916 681-7701
John G Hicks Jr, *President*
John Hicks Sr, *Treasurer*
Tracy Hicks, *Vice Pres*
Amy Hicks, *Admin Sec*
▲ EMP: 62
SQ FT: 33,600
SALES (est): 11.8MM **Privately Held**
WEB: www.pdqparts.com
SIC: 7537 Automotive transmission repair shops

7538 General Automotive Repair Shop

(P-17322)
AUTO TOWN INC
2150 E Hammer Ln, Stockton (95210-4122)
P.O. Box 690368 (95269-0368)
PHONE....................209 473-2513
Paul C Wondries, *President*
EMP: 70 EST: 1947
SQ FT: 40,000
SALES (est): 2.1MM **Privately Held**
SIC: 7538 5511 General automotive repair shops; automobiles, new & used

(P-17323)
BAE SYS SIERRA DETROIT ALLISON (DH)
1755 Adams Ave, San Leandro (94577-1001)
PHONE....................510 635-8991
Cindy Bergstrom, *President*
Wade Sperry, *Vice Pres*
EMP: 95
SQ FT: 45,000
SALES (est): 6.8MM
SALES (corp-wide): 2.9B **Publicly Held**
SIC: 7538 5084 5085 Diesel engine repair: automotive; engines & parts, diesel; industrial supplies
HQ: Bae Systems Resolution Inc.
1000 La St Ste 4950
Houston TX 77002
713 868-7700

(P-17324)
BREWSTERS AUTOMOTIVE INC
17357 Los Angeles St, Yorba Linda (92886-1723)
PHONE....................714 528-4683
John M Brewster, *President*
Karen Brewster, *Treasurer*
EMP: 70 EST: 1973

SALES (est): 2MM **Privately Held**
SIC: 7538 7542 General automotive repair shops; carwashes

(P-17325)
CITY OF LONG BEACH
Also Called: Long Beach City Fleet Services
2600 Temple Ave, Long Beach (90806-2209)
PHONE....................562 570-2828
Dan Burlenbach, *General Mgr*
EMP: 250 **Privately Held**
WEB: www.polb.com
SIC: 7538 9111 General automotive repair shops; mayors' offices
PA: City Of Long Beach
411 W Ocean Blvd
Long Beach CA 90802
562 570-6450

(P-17326)
CRYSTAL CHRYSLER PLYMUTH DODGE
36444 Auto Park Dr, Cathedral City (92234-6500)
PHONE....................760 324-9375
Robert Sherr, *President*
Jorge Aceves, *General Mgr*
EMP: 78
SALES (est): 8.3MM **Privately Held**
WEB: www.crystalchrysler.com
SIC: 7538 5511 General automotive repair shops; automobiles, new & used

(P-17327)
FLT INC
Also Called: Folsom Lake Toyota
12747 Folsom Blvd, Folsom (95630-8097)
PHONE....................916 355-1500
Charles G Peterson, *President*
Pam Peterson, *Admin Sec*
Tim Stockwell, *Cust Mgr*
John Key, *Manager*
EMP: 125
SALES (est): 9.2MM **Publicly Held**
SIC: 7538 5511 7532 5531 General automotive repair shops; automobiles, new & used; pickups, new & used; body shop, automotive; automotive parts; automobiles, used cars only
PA: Group 1 Automotive, Inc.
800 Gessner Rd Ste 500
Houston TX 77024
-

(P-17328)
FORTRESS RESOURCES LLC (HQ)
Also Called: Royal Truck Body
24200 Main St, Carson (90745-6325)
PHONE....................562 633-9951
Daryl Adams, *President*
EMP: 132
SQ FT: 53,000
SALES (est): 59.6MM
SALES (corp-wide): 816.1MM **Publicly Held**
SIC: 7538 General truck repair
PA: Spartan Motors, Inc.
1541 Reynolds Rd
Charlotte MI 48813
517 543-6400

(P-17329)
GARRICK MOTORS INC
559 S Pine St, Escondido (92025-4021)
PHONE....................760 489-2656
Gary Myers, *Branch Mgr*
Chris Bunn, *Sales Staff*
Barry Murray, *Sales Staff*
Andrew Mueller, *Advisor*
EMP: 138
SALES (corp-wide): 107MM **Privately Held**
SIC: 7538 7532 General automotive repair shops; body shop, automotive
PA: Garrick Motors, Inc.
231 E Lincoln Ave
Escondido CA 92026
760 746-0601

(P-17330)
GIBBS INTERNATIONAL INC (PA)
Also Called: Gibbs International Truck Ctrs
2201 Ventura Blvd, Oxnard (93036-7902)
P.O. Box 5206 (93031-5206)
PHONE....................805 485-0551
Edward A Gibbs, *President*
Mark S Rapin, *Sales Mgr*
John Limoli, *Sales Staff*
George Wishart, *Sales Staff*
Patti Gibbs, *Manager*
EMP: 135
SQ FT: 25,000
SALES: 59MM **Privately Held**
WEB: www.gibbstrucks.com
SIC: 7538 5511 4212 Truck engine repair, except industrial; trucks, tractors & trailers: new & used; local trucking, without storage

(P-17331)
GRAND AUTO CARE
Also Called: Grand Auto Repair
744 N Grand Ave, Covina (91724-2402)
PHONE....................626 331-8390
Ellie Fingerfield, *Owner*
EMP: 50
SALES (est): 1MM **Privately Held**
SIC: 7538 7539 7542 General automotive repair shops; brake repair, automotive; washing & polishing, automotive

(P-17332)
GRIMMWAY ENTERPRISES INC
2171 W Bannister Rd, Brawley (92227-9653)
PHONE....................760 344-0204
Cheryl Chaney, *Principal*
EMP: 170
SALES (corp-wide): 1.8B **Privately Held**
SIC: 7538 General automotive repair shops
PA: Grimmway Enterprises, Inc.
14141 Di Giorgio Rd
Arvin CA 93203
800 301-3101

(P-17333)
HAMBLINS BDY PNT FRAME SP INC
Also Called: Hamblin's Auto & Body Shop
7590 Cypress Ave, Riverside (92503-1904)
PHONE....................951 689-8440
Rod Perry, *President*
EMP: 70
SALES (est): 5.9MM **Privately Held**
WEB: www.hamblinsbodyandpaint.com
SIC: 7538 7532 General automotive repair shops; body shop, automotive

(P-17334)
HAWTHORNE MACHINERY CO
Also Called: Caterpillar
16945 Camino San Bernardo, San Diego (92127-2499)
PHONE....................858 674-7000
Bob Price, *Manager*
Elizabeth F Abeyta, *Sales Staff*
Tim Chatfield, *Sales Staff*
Brent Christenson, *Sales Staff*
Brian Fuse, *Sales Staff*
EMP: 100
SALES (corp-wide): 195.6MM **Privately Held**
SIC: 7538 5084 7359 5085 Diesel engine repair: automotive; engines & parts, air-cooled; equipment rental & leasing; industrial supplies; marine crafts & supplies
PA: Hawthorne Machinery Co.
16945 Camino San Bernardo
San Diego CA 92127
858 674-7000

(P-17335)
J&R FLEET SERVICES LLC
210 Saint Katherine Dr, La Canada Flintridge (91011-4109)
PHONE....................909 820-7000
Javier G Rodriguez,
Ricardo Rodriguez,
Roberto Rodriguez,
EMP: 70
SQ FT: 30,000

SALES (est): 7.9MM **Privately Held**
SIC: 7538 General truck repair

(P-17336)
LANCASTER COMM SRVCS FNDTN
Also Called: Development Services
46008 7th St W, Lancaster (93534-7602)
PHONE....................661 723-6230
Randy Williams, *Manager*
EMP: 70 **Privately Held**
WEB: www.poppyfestival.com
SIC: 7538 9111 General automotive repair shops; mayors' offices
PA: The Lancaster Community Services Foundation Inc
44933 Fern Ave
Lancaster CA 93534
661 723-6000

(P-17337)
LITHIA MOTORS INC
Also Called: Nissan of Stockton
3077 E Hammer Ln, Stockton (95212-2801)
PHONE....................209 956-1930
David Maldonado, *Branch Mgr*
EMP: 50
SALES (corp-wide): 11.8B **Publicly Held**
SIC: 7538 General automotive repair shops
PA: Lithia Motors, Inc.
150 N Bartlett St
Medford OR 97501
541 776-6401

(P-17338)
OC IV A CALIFORNIA LP
Also Called: Oil Changers
4511 Willow Rd Ste 1, Pleasanton (94588-2735)
PHONE....................925 734-5800
Lawrence Read, *CEO*
LMC Properties IV, *General Ptnr*
Charles Pass, *CFO*
EMP: 50
SALES (est): 663.3K **Privately Held**
SIC: 7538 General automotive repair shops

(P-17339)
PAPE TRUCKS INC
Also Called: Pape' Kenworth
2892 E Jensen Ave, Fresno (93706-5111)
P.O. Box 407, Eugene OR (97440-0407)
PHONE....................559 268-4344
Charles Davis, *General Mgr*
Dave Laird, *Vice Pres*
Bob Pilon, *General Mgr*
John Kreman, *Info Tech Dir*
Jeff Harris, *Finance Mgr*
EMP: 77
SALES (corp-wide): 640.9MM **Privately Held**
SIC: 7538 5511 5531 General truck repair; trucks, tractors & trailers: new & used; truck equipment & parts
HQ: Pape' Trucks, Inc.
355 Goodpasture Island Rd
Eugene OR 97401
-

(P-17340)
PEP BOYS MANNY MOE JACK OF CAL
11456 Washington Blvd, Whittier (90606)
PHONE....................562 908-4400
Luis Suarez, *Manager*
EMP: 50
SQ FT: 35,341
SALES (corp-wide): 11.7B **Publicly Held**
WEB: www.apdnow.com
SIC: 7538 5531 7549 General automotive repair shops; automotive parts; inspection & diagnostic service, automotive
HQ: The Pep Boys Manny Moe & Jack Of California
3111 W Allegheny Ave
Philadelphia PA 19132
215 430-9095

(P-17341)
PREMIER AUTO W COVINA LLC
777 W Orangethorpe Ave, Placentia (92870-6824)
PHONE....................626 858-7202

Troy Duhon, *Mng Member*
EMP: 60
SQ FT: 10,000
SALES: 5.7MM **Privately Held**
SIC: 7538 General automotive repair shops

(P-17342)
QUALITY AUTO CRAFT INC
3295 Bernal Ave Ste B, Pleasanton (94566-6298)
PHONE..................................925 426-0120
Ivo Soares, *President*
EMP: 1614
SQ FT: 10,000
SALES (est): 30MM **Privately Held**
SIC: 7538 7532 General automotive repair shops; body shop, automotive

(P-17343)
RAYMAK AUTOMOTIVE INC
Also Called: Falcon Auto Repair
15600 S Main St, Gardena (90248-2219)
PHONE..................................310 329-8910
Kamyar Najmi, *President*
EMP: 50
SQ FT: 38,000
SALES: 7.4MM **Privately Held**
SIC: 7538 General automotive repair shops

(P-17344)
ROCKET SMOG INC
11413 W Washington Blvd, Los Angeles (90066-6012)
PHONE..................................310 390-7664
Ann Sadeck, *President*
EMP: 59
SQ FT: 9,000
SALES (est): 287.3K **Privately Held**
SIC: 7538 General automotive repair shops

(P-17345)
SEIDNER-MILLER AUTOMOTIVE INC
1253 S Lone Hill Ave, Glendora (91740-4507)
PHONE..................................909 394-3500
Peter Miller, *Vice Pres*
Robert Kakish, *Sales Mgr*
EMP: 50
SALES (est): 1.8MM **Privately Held**
SIC: 7538 General automotive repair shops

(P-17346)
SIEMENS MOBILITY INC
5301 Price Ave, McClellan (95652-2401)
PHONE..................................916 621-2700
Christopher Maynard, *Vice Pres*
EMP: 100
SALES (corp-wide): 95B **Privately Held**
SIC: 7538 3743 General truck repair; train cars & equipment, freight or passenger
HQ: Siemens Mobility, Inc.
　　1 Penn Plz Ste 1100
　　New York NY 10119
　　212 672-4000

(P-17347)
SOUTHERN CALIFORNIA FLEET SVC
6726 Nicolett St, Riverside (92504-1843)
PHONE..................................951 272-8655
Tom Franchina, *CEO*
Darrell Hull, *Supervisor*
EMP: 50
SALES (est): 2.1MM **Privately Held**
WEB: www.socalfleet.com
SIC: 7538 General truck repair

(P-17348)
SOUTHERN CALIFORNIA MAR ASSN
3333 Fairview Rd, Costa Mesa (92626-1610)
PHONE..................................714 850-4004
Betty Chew, *Director*
Greg Backley, *Vice Pres*
Jim Doran, *Empl Rel Mgr*
Jensen Rei-NA, *Marketing Mgr*
Ewa Goetz, *Manager*
EMP: 58

SALES (est): 9.6MM **Privately Held**
SIC: 7538 General automotive repair shops

(P-17349)
TEAMROSS INC
Also Called: Team Superstores
301 Auto Mall Pkwy, Vallejo (94591-3870)
PHONE..................................707 643-9000
Kenneth B Ross, *President*
Trish Gress, *Treasurer*
Michael Drinker, *Vice Pres*
EMP: 95
SQ FT: 57,000
SALES (est): 7.9MM **Privately Held**
SIC: 7538 5511 General automotive repair shops; automobiles, new & used

(P-17350)
TED FORD JONES INC (PA)
Also Called: Ken Grody Ford
6211 Beach Blvd, Buena Park (90621-2307)
P.O. Box 2154 (90621-0654)
PHONE..................................714 521-3110
Kenneth B Grody, *President*
Ken Grody, *President*
Billy Raymond, *CFO*
Curt Maletych, *Vice Pres*
Kurt Maletych, *Vice Pres*
▼ EMP: 110
SQ FT: 4,500
SALES (est): 32MM **Privately Held**
WEB: www.kengrody.com
SIC: 7538 5511 General automotive repair shops; automobiles, new & used

(P-17351)
TOYOTA-SUNNYVALE INC (PA)
898 W El Camino Real, Sunnyvale (94087-1153)
PHONE..................................408 245-6640
Adam Simms, *President*
Tom Price, *Vice Pres*
Najaf Ali, *Finance Mgr*
Daniel Radcliffe, *Finance Mgr*
Jordan Mehdian, *Sales Mgr*
EMP: 120
SQ FT: 35,000
SALES (est): 19.5MM **Privately Held**
WEB: www.toyotasunnyvale.com
SIC: 7538 5511 5521 5531 General automotive repair shops; automobiles, new & used; used car dealers; automotive & home supply stores

---
7539 Automotive Repair Shops, NEC

(P-17352)
ALASKA DIESEL ELECTRIC
425 S Hacienda Blvd, City of Industry (91745-1123)
PHONE..................................626 934-6211
Peter B Hill Jr, *President*
EMP: 119
SALES (est): 3.1MM
SALES (corp-wide): 181.2MM **Privately Held**
SIC: 7539 Automotive repair shops
PA: Valley Power Systems, Inc.
　　425 S Hacienda Blvd
　　City Of Industry CA 91745
　　626 333-1243

(P-17353)
DISCOUNT TIRE CTR
Also Called: Discount Tire Center
19545 Parthenia St Ste 3, Northridge (91324-3462)
PHONE..................................818 993-4758
Sebouh Donoyan, *CEO*
Steve Donoyan, *Manager*
EMP: 66 EST: 2002
SQ FT: 500
SALES (est): 3.5MM **Privately Held**
SIC: 7539 5531 Automotive repair shops; automotive tires

(P-17354)
EDF RENEWABLES SERVICES INC (HQ)
Also Called: Enxco
15445 Innovation Dr, San Diego (92128-3432)
PHONE..................................858 521-3575
Tristan Grimbert, *President*
John Marchand, *President*
EMP: 65
SQ FT: 70,000
SALES (est): 104MM
SALES (corp-wide): 971.6MM **Privately Held**
SIC: 7539 Alternators & generators, rebuilding & repair
PA: Edf Renewables, Inc.
　　15445 Innovation Dr
　　San Diego CA 92128
　　858 521-3300

(P-17355)
HIGH SUMMIT LLC
Also Called: Special Events
6909 Las Positas Rd Ste D, Livermore (94551-5113)
PHONE..................................925 605-2900
Weston Cook,
Christine Cook, *Manager*
Danielle Landman, *Manager*
EMP: 50
SALES (est): 3.3MM **Privately Held**
SIC: 7539 Automotive repair shops

(P-17356)
SACRAMENTO MUNICPL UTILITY DST
6201 S St, Sacramento (95817-1818)
P.O. Box 15830 (95852-0830)
PHONE..................................916 452-3211
Jan Shoory, *General Mgr*
EMP: 2000
SALES (corp-wide): 1.6B **Privately Held**
SIC: 7539 Electrical services
PA: Sacramento Municipal Utility District
　　6201 S St
　　Sacramento CA 95817
　　916 452-3211

(P-17357)
SAN FRANCISCO CITY & COUNTY
200 Paul Ave B, San Francisco (94124-3100)
PHONE..................................415 550-4600
EMP: 110 **Privately Held**
SIC: 7539 9311 7538
PA: City & County Of San Francisco
　　1 Dr Carlton B Goodlett P
　　San Francisco CA 94102
　　415 554-7500

(P-17358)
VERNON AUTOPARTS INC
1559 W 134th St, Gardena (90249-2215)
PHONE..................................323 249-7545
Mike Klapper, *President*
Mary Ann Klapper, *Corp Secy*
David Klapper, *Vice Pres*
EMP: 54
SQ FT: 100,000
SALES (est): 468.6K
SALES (corp-wide): 7.2MM **Privately Held**
SIC: 7539 3714 3694 3592 Machine shop, automotive; motor vehicle parts & accessories; engine electrical equipment; carburetors, pistons, rings, valves; power transmission equipment; pumps & pumping equipment
PA: Electrical Rebuilders Sales, Inc.
　　1559 W 134th St
　　Gardena CA 90249
　　323 249-7545

7542 Car Washes

(P-17359)
ALL HNDS CRWASH DTAIL CTR LUBE
22952 Pacific Park Dr, Aliso Viejo (92656-3389)
PHONE..................................949 716-3600

Raul Valerio, *President*
Carlos Valerio, *CFO*
EMP: 60
SQ FT: 92,000
SALES (est): 1.3MM **Privately Held**
WEB: www.allhandscarwash.com
SIC: 7542 Washing & polishing, automotive

(P-17360)
AUTO WORLD CAR WASH LLC
15951 Los Gatos Blvd, Los Gatos (95032-3428)
PHONE..................................408 345-6532
EMP: 1597
SALES (est): 2.7MM
SALES (corp-wide): 66.5MM **Privately Held**
SIC: 7542
PA: California Secured Investments, Llc
　　14225 Lora Dr Apt 96
　　Los Gatos CA

(P-17361)
BEACH AND LA MIRADA CAR WASH
5231 Beach Blvd, Buena Park (90621-1229)
PHONE..................................714 994-1099
Efrain Garcia, *Manager*
Harry Acebedo, *Systs Prg Mgr*
EMP: 50
SALES (est): 1.4MM **Privately Held**
SIC: 7542 Carwashes

(P-17362)
BODY BEAUTIFUL CAR WASH INC
13236 Poway Rd, Poway (92064-4614)
PHONE..................................858 748-4400
Dennis McKnight, *Vice Pres*
Alex Alvarado, *Office Mgr*
EMP: 95
SALES (corp-wide): 49.8MM **Privately Held**
SIC: 7542 Washing & polishing, automotive
PA: Body Beautiful Car Wash, Inc.
　　4282 Camino Del Rio N
　　San Diego CA
　　619 563-5566

(P-17363)
BOWIE ENTERPRISES
Also Called: Red Carpet Car Wash
1920 S Mooney Blvd, Visalia (93277-4450)
PHONE..................................559 732-2988
Scott Rotse, *Manager*
EMP: 53
SALES (corp-wide): 13.7MM **Privately Held**
WEB: www.redcarpetcarwash.com
SIC: 7542 Washing & polishing, automotive
PA: Bowie Enterprises
　　4411 N Blackstone Ave
　　Fresno CA 93726
　　559 227-6221

(P-17364)
BOWIE ENTERPRISES (PA)
Also Called: Red Carpet Car Wash
4411 N Blackstone Ave, Fresno (93726-1904)
PHONE..................................559 227-6221
David Bowie, *President*
James M Bowie, *Ch of Bd*
Karen Bowie, *Treasurer*
Kathryn Bowie, *Admin Sec*
EMP: 60
SQ FT: 7,700
SALES (est): 13.7MM **Privately Held**
WEB: www.redcarpetcarwash.com
SIC: 7542 5541 Carwash, automatic; filling stations, gasoline

(P-17365)
BOWIE ENTERPRISES
Also Called: Red Carpet Car Wash
801 W Shaw Ave, Clovis (93612-3218)
PHONE..................................559 292-6565
EMP: 65

SALES (corp-wide): 13.7MM **Privately Held**
WEB: www.redcarpetcarwash.com
SIC: 7542 Washing & polishing, automotive
PA: Bowie Enterprises
4411 N Blackstone Ave
Fresno CA 93726
559 227-6221

(P-17366)
CAR WASH PARTNERS INC
3201 Panama Ln, Bakersfield
(93313-3732)
PHONE..................................661 837-9485
John Lai, *President*
EMP: 150
SALES (corp-wide): 10.6MM **Privately Held**
SIC: 7542 Carwashes
PA: Car Wash Partners, Inc.
222 E 5th St
Tucson AZ 85705
520 615-4000

(P-17367)
CHARLES FENLEY ENTERPRISES
Also Called: Chevron
1109 Oakdale Rd, Modesto (95355-4065)
P.O. Box 577200 (95357-7200)
PHONE..................................209 523-2832
Gene Rooney, *Manager*
EMP: 50
SALES (corp-wide): 9.1MM **Privately Held**
SIC: 7542 5541 5948 7549 Carwash, automatic; filling stations, gasoline; luggage, except footlockers & trunks; leather goods, except luggage & shoes; lubrication service, automotive
PA: Charles Fenley Enterprises
1121 Oakdale Rd Ste 7
Modesto CA 95355
209 576-0381

(P-17368)
CIRCLE MARINA CAR WASH INC
Also Called: Circle Marina Hand Car Wash
4800 E Pacific Coast Hwy, Long Beach
(90804-3243)
PHONE..................................562 494-4698
John C Wang, *President*
EMP: 50
SALES (est): 1.9MM **Privately Held**
SIC: 7542 Washing & polishing, automotive

(P-17369)
CLASSIC CAR WASH INC (PA)
871 E Hamilton Ave Ste C, Campbell
(95008-0602)
P.O. Box 5993, San Jose (95150-5993)
PHONE..................................408 371-2414
Frank Dorsa, *President*
Robert Miller, *CFO*
EMP: 150
SQ FT: 1,500
SALES (est): 4.7MM **Privately Held**
WEB: www.classiccarwash.net
SIC: 7542 Carwash, automatic; washing & polishing, automotive

(P-17370)
COAST CARWASH LP
Also Called: Coast Hand Car Wash
5677 E 7th St, Long Beach (90804-4430)
PHONE..................................562 961-5555
James Yang, *Partner*
Gregory Yang, *Partner*
Jerry Yang, *Partner*
Peter Yang, *Partner*
EMP: 50 **EST:** 1998
SALES (est): 3MM **Privately Held**
WEB: www.coastcarwash.com
SIC: 7542 7538 Carwashes; general automotive repair shops

(P-17371)
DUCKYS OF SAN CARLOS INC
Also Called: Ducky's Car Wash
1301 Old County Rd, San Carlos
(94070-5201)
PHONE..................................650 637-1301
Steve Munkdale, *President*
EMP: 50

SALES (est): 907.9K **Privately Held**
SIC: 7542 Washing & polishing, automotive

(P-17372)
DYNAMIC AUTO IMAGES INC
Also Called: Dynamic Detail
1407 N Batavia St Ste 102, Orange
(92867-3525)
PHONE..................................714 981-4367
Tom Miller, *President*
EMP: 300
SQ FT: 2,500
SALES (est): 13.2MM **Privately Held**
WEB: www.dynamicautoimages.com
SIC: 7542 7532 Washing & polishing, automotive; collision shops, automotive

(P-17373)
ENCINO CENTER CAR WASH INC
16300 Ventura Blvd, Encino (91436-2116)
PHONE..................................818 788-6300
EMP: 60
SALES (est): 1MM **Privately Held**
SIC: 7542 5541 5947

(P-17374)
GEORGE FASCHING
Also Called: Faschings Car Wash
425 N Santa Anita Ave, Arcadia
(91006-2876)
PHONE..................................626 446-0654
George Fasching, *Owner*
Geri Fasching, *Co-Owner*
EMP: 50 **EST:** 1977
SQ FT: 60,000
SALES (est): 1.8MM **Privately Held**
SIC: 7542 5541 Carwash, automatic; washing & polishing, automotive; filling stations, gasoline

(P-17375)
GIEG CHEVRON LLC
Also Called: Splash Fast Lube
905 Abbott St 945, Salinas (93901-4361)
PHONE..................................831 755-8000
Ron Gieg, *Mng Member*
Dale Gieg, *Co-Owner*
EMP: 60 **EST:** 1998
SALES (est): 1.3MM **Privately Held**
SIC: 7542 5541 Carwashes; filling stations, gasoline

(P-17376)
IN & OUT CAR WASH INC
Also Called: Spot Free Car Wash
3615 Monte Real, Escondido (92029-7911)
PHONE..................................619 316-8492
Donald Macek, *President*
Denis McKnight, *Vice Pres*
EMP: 50
SQ FT: 20,000
SALES (est): 2MM **Privately Held**
WEB: www.inoutcarwash.com
SIC: 7542 Washing & polishing, automotive

(P-17377)
JACKS CAR WASH 3
6745 N West Ave, Fresno (93711-4304)
PHONE..................................559 438-8201
EMP: 60
SALES (est): 129.2K **Privately Held**
SIC: 7542 5947 5812 Carwash, self-service; gift shop; coffee shop

(P-17378)
JEMTOWN INC
Also Called: Five Star Auto Repr & Car Wash
6818 Five Star Blvd, Rocklin (95677-2660)
PHONE..................................916 315-0555
James A Sperlazza, *President*
Mary Sperlazza, *Vice Pres*
Kieran Griffin, *Manager*
EMP: 50
SALES (est): 2.1MM **Privately Held**
SIC: 7542 Washing & polishing, automotive

(P-17379)
JKF AUTO SERVICE INC
Also Called: Five Star Auto Repair and Wash
6818 Five Star Blvd, Rocklin (95677-2660)
PHONE..................................916 315-0555
Jeff Finerman, *President*

Karen W Finerman, *Vice Pres*
EMP: 60
SALES (est): 1.3MM **Privately Held**
SIC: 7542 7549 7539 Washing & polishing, automotive; lubrication service, automotive; automotive repair shops

(P-17380)
LAKEWOOD SOUTH CAR WASH LLC
Also Called: Rossmoor Carwash
11031 Alamitos Ave, Los Alamitos (90720)
PHONE..................................562 430-4975
Foster A Hooper, *Principal*
EMP: 50 **EST:** 1965
SALES (est): 1.2MM **Privately Held**
SIC: 7542 Washing & polishing, automotive

(P-17381)
LARK AVENUE CAR WASH
Also Called: Chevron
5005 Almaden Expy, San Jose
(95118-2049)
P.O. Box 5993 (95150-5993)
PHONE..................................408 371-2565
Chuck Mina, *Site Mgr*
EMP: 72
SQ FT: 7,859
SALES (corp-wide): 40.6MM **Privately Held**
SIC: 7542 Carwashes
PA: Lark Avenue Car Wash
871 E Hamilton Ave
Campbell CA 95008
408 371-2414

(P-17382)
LITTLE SISTERS TRUCK WASH INC
72189 Varner Rd, Thousand Palms
(92276-3364)
PHONE..................................760 343-3448
Bob Crogan, *Manager*
EMP: 60 **Privately Held**
SIC: 7542 Washing & polishing, automotive; truck wash
PA: Little Sisters Truck Wash Inc
25 Rolling View Ln
Fallbrook CA 92028

(P-17383)
LITTLE SISTERS TRUCK WASH INC
8899 Three Flags Ave, Oak Hills
(92344-0497)
PHONE..................................760 947-4448
Joe McSann, *Manager*
EMP: 65 **Privately Held**
SIC: 7542 Washing & polishing, automotive; truck wash
PA: Little Sisters Truck Wash Inc
25 Rolling View Ln
Fallbrook CA 92028

(P-17384)
LITTLE SISTERS TRUCK WASH INC
14264 Valley Blvd, Fontana (92335-5293)
PHONE..................................909 549-1862
Tod Kerns, *Manager*
EMP: 65 **Privately Held**
SIC: 7542 Washing & polishing, automotive; truck wash
PA: Little Sisters Truck Wash Inc
25 Rolling View Ln
Fallbrook CA 92028

(P-17385)
LITTLE SISTERS TRUCK WASH INC
2960 Lenwood Rd, Barstow (92311-9571)
PHONE..................................760 253-2277
B J Elmanza, *Manager*
EMP: 70
SQ FT: 2,482 **Privately Held**
SIC: 7542 Washing & polishing, automotive; truck wash
PA: Little Sisters Truck Wash Inc
25 Rolling View Ln
Fallbrook CA 92028

(P-17386)
LITTLE SISTERS TRUCK WASH INC (PA)
Also Called: Little Sister's Truck Wash
25 Rolling View Ln, Fallbrook (92028-9234)
P.O. Box 1530, Bonsall (92003-1530)
PHONE..................................760 731-3170
Renald J Anelle, *President*
Cathy Anelle, *Corp Secy*
William F Wire, *Vice Pres*
EMP: 69
SALES (est): 8.1MM **Privately Held**
SIC: 7542 Washing & polishing, automotive; truck wash

(P-17387)
LOZANO INC
Also Called: Lozano Car Wash
2690 W El Camino Real, Mountain View
(94040-1117)
PHONE..................................650 941-0590
Manuel J Lozano, *President*
Claudia Rozriduez, *Manager*
EMP: 107
SQ FT: 500
SALES (est): 3.5MM **Privately Held**
WEB: www.lozano.net
SIC: 7542 Carwash, automatic

(P-17388)
M K H INC
Also Called: Cruisers Carwash & Diner
8870 Tampa Ave, Northridge (91324-3519)
PHONE..................................818 882-9274
Mike Harn, *President*
EMP: 60
SALES (est): 1.2MM **Privately Held**
SIC: 7542 5812 Washing & polishing, automotive; diner

(P-17389)
MISSION CAR WASH
Also Called: Mission Car Wash & Quik Lube
59 Mission Cir, Santa Rosa (95409-5304)
PHONE..................................707 537-2040
Tim Mitchell, *Owner*
EMP: 50
SQ FT: 6,157
SALES (est): 1.4MM **Privately Held**
SIC: 7542 Washing & polishing, automotive

(P-17390)
NORCO HILLS CAR WASH
Also Called: Norco Auto Wash
18020 Magnolia St, Fountain Valley
(92708-5603)
PHONE..................................951 279-4398
Steve Hart, *Partner*
Robert Keane, *Partner*
EMP: 50
SALES (est): 2.4MM **Privately Held**
SIC: 7542 Washing & polishing, automotive

(P-17391)
PETROLEUM SALES INC (PA)
1475 2nd St, San Rafael (94901-2754)
PHONE..................................415 256-1600
Ben Shimek, *President*
EMP: 120
SALES (est): 15.5MM **Privately Held**
SIC: 7542 5541 Carwashes; gasoline service stations

(P-17392)
PLAZA HAND CARWASH INC
Also Called: Prime Stop
23100 Alssndro Blvd Ste B, Moreno Valley
(92553-9670)
PHONE..................................951 697-4420
Bob Sherrick, *President*
EMP: 50
SQ FT: 15,000
SALES (est): 1.1MM **Privately Held**
SIC: 7542 5087 Carwash, automatic; carwash equipment & supplies

(P-17393)
PRECISION AUTO DETAILING LLC
700 Serramonte Blvd, Colma (94014-3220)
PHONE..................................650 992-9775
Anthony Caprini, *Principal*
James Grasso, *Manager*

PRODUCTS & SVCS

EMP: 80
SALES (est): 2MM **Privately Held**
SIC: 7542 5087 Washing & polishing, automotive; carwash equipment & supplies

(P-17394)
PRESTIGE CAR WASH LAFAYETTE LP
Also Called: Lafayette Car Wash
3319 Mt Diablo Blvd, Lafayette (94549-4011)
PHONE..........................925 283-1190
Jesse Wellen, *Partner*
EMP: 50
SQ FT: 2,000
SALES (est): 1.6MM **Privately Held**
WEB: www.lafayettecarwash.com
SIC: 7542 7532 Washing & polishing, automotive; body shop, automotive

(P-17395)
RUSSELL FISHER PARTNERSHIP
Also Called: Bella Terra Carwash
16061 Beach Blvd, Huntington Beach (92647-3802)
PHONE..........................714 842-4453
Ruben Hernandez, *Site Mgr*
Alphonso Perez, *Manager*
Juan Rojas, *Manager*
EMP: 50
SALES (est): 2.5MM
SALES (corp-wide): 3.6MM **Privately Held**
SIC: 7542 Washing & polishing, automotive
PA: Russell Fisher Partnership
18971 Beach Blvd
Huntington Beach CA 92648
909 930-5420

(P-17396)
RUSSELL FISHER PARTNERSHIP (PA)
Also Called: Huntington Beach Car Wash
18971 Beach Blvd, Huntington Beach (92648-2009)
PHONE..........................909 930-5420
Eddie R Fischer, *Partner*
EMP: 80
SQ FT: 3,000
SALES (est): 3.6MM **Privately Held**
SIC: 7542 Washing & polishing, automotive

(P-17397)
SOAPY JOES INC (PA)
11465 Woodside Ave, Santee (92071-4725)
PHONE..........................619 660-1113
Talal P Sheena, *President*
EMP: 51 EST: 2011
SALES (est): 5.8MM **Privately Held**
SIC: 7542 Washing & polishing, automotive

(P-17398)
SUDS CAR WASH INC
4620 Post St, El Dorado Hills (95762-7102)
PHONE..........................916 673-6300
Jeffery A Lowe, *President*
Ashley Lowe, *Vice Pres*
EMP: 50
SALES (est): 1.7MM **Privately Held**
SIC: 7542 Washing & polishing, automotive

(P-17399)
TEAM DYKSPRA (PA)
2315 California Ave, Corona (92881-6655)
PHONE..........................951 898-6482
Lenny Dykstra, *President*
EMP: 60
SALES (est): 3.1MM **Privately Held**
SIC: 7542 7549 Carwashes; automotive maintenance services

(P-17400)
TRUCK TUB INTERNATIONAL INC
P.O. Box 2111, Pismo Beach (93448-2111)
PHONE..........................805 474-8680
Brian Brady, *President*
Phyllis Molnar, *Manager*
EMP: 53

SALES (est): 577.8K **Privately Held**
SIC: 7542 Truck wash

(P-17401)
VERNON TRUCK WASH INC
3308 Bandini Blvd, Vernon (90058-4113)
PHONE..........................323 267-0706
Armen Keshishyan, *President*
EMP: 105
SQ FT: 800
SALES (est): 2.6MM **Privately Held**
SIC: 7542 Truck wash

(P-17402)
VLADIGOR INVESTMENT INC
Also Called: Tower Car Wash
1601 Mission St, San Francisco (94103-2413)
PHONE..........................415 558-9274
Igor Paskhover,
Lisa Syelsky, *Vice Pres*
Steve Matijevich, *General Mgr*
EMP: 90
SQ FT: 25,000
SALES (est): 3.4MM **Privately Held**
SIC: 7542 Washing & polishing, automotive

(P-17403)
WEST LAKE TOUCHLESS CAR WASH
223 87th St, Daly City (94015-1644)
PHONE..........................650 992-5344
Fred Tautenhan, *Owner*
Dean Tautenhahn, *Persnl Dir*
EMP: 50
SALES (est): 1.1MM **Privately Held**
WEB: www.westlaketouchlesscarwash.com
SIC: 7542 5541 Carwash, automatic; gasoline service stations

7549 Automotive Svcs, Except Repair & Car Washes

(P-17404)
AA AUTMTIVE PERSONNEL SVCS INC
2251 Federal Ave, Los Angeles (90064-1403)
PHONE..........................310 914-3012
Alvaro Marcin, *President*
EMP: 200
SALES (est): 4.1MM **Privately Held**
SIC: 7549 Automotive maintenance services

(P-17405)
ABSOLUTE TOWING-HOLLENBECK DIV
4760 Valley Blvd, Los Angeles (90032-3834)
PHONE..........................323 225-9294
Todd Q Smart, *President*
EMP: 50 EST: 1998
SQ FT: 111,000
SALES (est): 3.9MM **Privately Held**
SIC: 7549 Towing service, automotive

(P-17406)
ALAMITOS ENTERPRISES LLC (PA)
Also Called: Jiffy Lube
3311 Katella Ave, Los Alamitos (90720-2337)
PHONE..........................562 596-1827
Michael Biddle, *Mng Member*
Leslie Lopez, *Controller*
Robert Curry,
EMP: 70 EST: 1998
SQ FT: 2,500
SALES (est): 10.3MM **Privately Held**
SIC: 7549 Lubrication service, automotive

(P-17407)
ALLIED GARDENS TOWING INC (HQ)
9150 Chesapeake Dr # 240, San Diego (92123-1061)
PHONE..........................619 563-4060
Edward S Bischop, *President*

EMP: 60 EST: 1970
SQ FT: 1,500
SALES (est): 2.3MM
SALES (corp-wide): 711.7MM **Publicly Held**
SIC: 7549 Towing service, automotive
PA: Miller Industries, Inc.
8503 Hilltop Dr Ste 100
Ooltewah TN 37363
423 238-4171

(P-17408)
ALLIED LUBE TEXAS LP (PA)
4440 Von Karman Ave # 100, Newport Beach (92660-2011)
PHONE..........................949 486-4008
Anthony Fancicola, *Owner*
Tiffany Preijers-Pompa, *HR Admin*
EMP: 57 EST: 2005
SALES (est): 11.9MM **Privately Held**
SIC: 7549 Lubrication service, automotive

(P-17409)
AMERIT FLEET SOLUTIONS INC (HQ)
1331 N Calif Blvd Ste 150, Walnut Creek (94596-4535)
PHONE..........................877 512-6374
Nick Healing, *CTO*
Dan Williams, *CEO*
Amein Punjani, *COO*
Karen Vinton, *Vice Pres*
Charles Ortiz, *Analyst*
EMP: 100
SALES: 160MM **Privately Held**
SIC: 7549 4785 Inspection & diagnostic service, automotive; transportation inspection services

(P-17410)
ARS WEST LLC
780 W El Norte Pkwy, Escondido (92026-3984)
PHONE..........................760 480-6631
Jennie Anderson, *President*
EMP: 86
SALES (corp-wide): 39.2MM **Privately Held**
SIC: 7549 5499 Automotive maintenance services; dried fruit
PA: Ars West Llc
2204 S El Camino Real # 314
Oceanside CA 92054
760 730-5137

(P-17411)
AUTOMOTIVE TSTG & DEV SVCS INC (PA)
400 Etiwanda Ave, Ontario (91761-8637)
PHONE..........................909 390-1100
Devon Larry Smith, *CEO*
Kay Smith, *Corp Secy*
Devon Smith, *Exec VP*
Steve Arnold, *Vice Pres*
Linwood Farmer, *Vice Pres*
▲ EMP: 200
SQ FT: 24,000
SALES (est): 18.4MM **Privately Held**
WEB: www.automotivetesting.com
SIC: 7549 8734 8711 Emissions testing without repairs, automotive; testing laboratories; engineering services

(P-17412)
BOWIE ENTERPRISES
Also Called: Red Carpet Car Wash
4411 N Blackstone Ave, Fresno (93726-1904)
PHONE..........................559 227-3400
EMP: 72
SALES (corp-wide): 13.7MM **Privately Held**
SIC: 7549 7538 Lubrication service, automotive; general automotive repair shops
PA: Bowie Enterprises
4411 N Blackstone Ave
Fresno CA 93726
559 227-6221

(P-17413)
CA STE ATOM ASSOC INTR-INS BUR
Also Called: AAA
4400 Capitola Rd Ste 100, Capitola (95010-3571)
P.O. Box 250 (95010-0250)
PHONE..........................831 824-9128
Donald Foley, *Branch Mgr*
EMP: 100
SALES (corp-wide): 907.9MM **Privately Held**
WEB: www.viamagazine.com
SIC: 7549 Towing services
HQ: California State Automobile Association Inter-Insurance Bureau
1276 S California Blvd
Walnut Creek CA 94596
925 287-7600

(P-17414)
CAR SPA INC
Also Called: Chevron
996 Mountain Ave, Norco (92860-3160)
PHONE..........................951 279-1422
Jesus Medina, *Manager*
EMP: 50
SALES (corp-wide): 43.8MM **Privately Held**
WEB: www.car-spa.com
SIC: 7549 7542 Lubrication service, automotive; washing & polishing, automotive
PA: Car Spa, Inc.
4835 Lyndo B Johns Fwy St
Dallas TX 75244
469 374-0280

(P-17415)
COMPLETE COACH WORKS (HQ)
Also Called: John Deere Authorized Dealer
1863 Service Ct, Riverside (92507-2341)
PHONE..........................951 682-2557
Dale E Carson, *President*
Aaron Timlick, *General Mgr*
Natalie Esparza, *Admin Asst*
Camelia Cocan, *Administration*
Amber Piccinonno, *Administration*
▲ EMP: 280
SALES (est): 28.4MM
SALES (corp-wide): 58.9MM **Privately Held**
SIC: 7549 5082 Trailer maintenance; construction & mining machinery
PA: D/T Carson Enterprises, Inc.
42882 Ivy St
Murrieta CA 92562
951 684-9585

(P-17416)
COUNTY OF MADERA
Also Called: Madera County Road Department
2037 W Cleveland Ave, Madera (93637-8720)
PHONE..........................559 675-7811
Johannes Hoeversz, *Manager*
EMP: 84 **Privately Held**
WEB: www.madera-county.com
SIC: 7549 Road service, automotive
PA: County Of Madera
209 W Yosemite Ave
Madera CA 93637
559 675-7726

(P-17417)
COVEY AUTO EXPRESS INC (PA)
Also Called: Pacific Towing
1444 El Pinal Dr, Stockton (95205-2642)
PHONE..........................253 826-0461
Michael D Covey, *President*
Kathy Covey, *Vice Pres*
EMP: 150
SQ FT: 19,000
SALES (est): 21.5MM **Privately Held**
SIC: 7549 Towing service, automotive; towing services

(P-17418)
EVGO SERVICES LLC
11835 W Olympic Blvd 900e, Los Angeles (90064-5088)
P.O. Box 642830 (90064-8287)
PHONE..........................310 954-2900

Cathy Zoi, *CEO*
Christoper O'Donnell, *CFO*
Jay Goldman, *Vice Pres*
Jonathan Levy, *Vice Pres*
Olga Shevorenkova, *Vice Pres*
EMP: 75
SQ FT: 10,000
SALES (est): 4.2MM **Publicly Held**
SIC: 7549 Automotive maintenance services
PA: Nrg Energy, Inc.
804 Carnegie Ctr
Princeton NJ 08540
-

(P-17419)
HIGH STREET HAND CAR WASH INC
Also Called: High St Car Wash Lube & Oil
569 High St, Oakland (94601-3905)
PHONE..................................510 536-4333
Chong B Kim, *President*
EMP: 51
SQ FT: 3,123
SALES (est): 2MM **Privately Held**
SIC: 7549 7542 Lubrication service, automotive; carwashes

(P-17420)
J C TOWING INC
2501 Faivre St, Chula Vista (91911-4603)
PHONE..................................619 429-1492
Gardner J Clark IV, *President*
EMP: 52
SQ FT: 2,000
SALES (est): 3.2MM **Privately Held**
SIC: 7549 Towing services

(P-17421)
METROPRO ROAD SERVICES INC (PA)
Also Called: A & P Towing-Metropro Rd Svcs
2550 S Garnsey St, Santa Ana (92707-3337)
PHONE..................................714 556-7600
Bradley T Humphreys, *CEO*
Jody Campbell, *President*
Jean Noutary, *General Mgr*
Brad Humphries, *Information Mgr*
EMP: 100
SQ FT: 85,000
SALES (est): 7.3MM **Privately Held**
SIC: 7549 Towing services

(P-17422)
MOC PRODUCTS COMPANY INC
9840 Kitty Ln, Oakland (94603-1070)
PHONE..................................510 635-1230
George Logan, *Branch Mgr*
Vidyalakshmi Raman, *Office Mgr*
EMP: 68
SALES (corp-wide): 64.6MM **Privately Held**
WEB: www.mocproducts.com
SIC: 7549 Automotive maintenance services
PA: Moc Products Company, Inc.
12306 Montague St
Pacoima CA 91331
818 794-3500

(P-17423)
POISON SPYDER CUSTOMS INC
Also Called: Transamerican Auto Parts
2360 Boswell Rd, Chula Vista (91914-3510)
PHONE..................................951 849-5911
Larry McRae, *President*
Cheri McRae, *CFO*
◆ **EMP:** 712 **EST:** 2009
SALES (est): 26.7MM **Privately Held**
SIC: 7549 Automotive customizing services, non-factory basis
PA: Tap Worldwide, Llc
400 W Artesia Blvd
Compton CA 90220
-

(P-17424)
S AND R TOWING INC (PA)
1060 Airport Rd, Oceanside (92058-1209)
P.O. Box 4366, Carlsbad (92018-4366)
PHONE..................................760 722-6686
Steve Dugan, *President*
Rusty Russell, *COO*
Charles Russell, *CFO*

Ric Johnsen, *Info Tech Mgr*
Vickie Roberts, *Finance Dir*
EMP: 50
SQ FT: 2,400
SALES (est): 8.3MM **Privately Held**
WEB: www.srtow.com
SIC: 7549 Towing service, automotive; towing services

(P-17425)
SEARS ROEBUCK AND CO
1001 Sunvalley Blvd, Concord (94520-5802)
PHONE..................................925 246-1996
Mike Corona, *Manager*
EMP: 83
SALES (corp-wide): 22.2B **Publicly Held**
SIC: 7549 Automotive maintenance services
HQ: Sears, Roebuck And Co.
3333 Beverly Rd
Hoffman Estates IL 60179
847 286-2500

(P-17426)
SEARS ROEBUCK AND CO
40680 Winchester Rd, Temecula (92591-5504)
PHONE..................................951 719-3528
Dan Larue, *Manager*
EMP: 93
SALES (corp-wide): 22.2B **Publicly Held**
SIC: 7549 Automotive maintenance services
HQ: Sears, Roebuck And Co.
3333 Beverly Rd
Hoffman Estates IL 60179
847 286-2500

(P-17427)
SEARS ROEBUCK AND CO
1235 Colusa Ave, Yuba City (95991-3693)
PHONE..................................530 751-4628
Cathy Nicholls, *Branch Mgr*
EMP: 100
SALES (corp-wide): 22.2B **Publicly Held**
SIC: 7549 Automotive maintenance services
HQ: Sears, Roebuck And Co.
3333 Beverly Rd
Hoffman Estates IL 60179
847 286-2500

(P-17428)
STRLNG PATH MEDCL CORP
3030 Old Ranch Pkwy # 430, Seal Beach (90740-2760)
PHONE..................................562 799-8900
Changgao Yang, *President*
EMP: 50
SALES (est): 532.6K **Privately Held**
SIC: 7549 Inspection & diagnostic service, automotive

(P-17429)
SUNBELT TOWING INC (PA)
Also Called: Western Towing
4370 Pacific Hwy, San Diego (92110-3106)
PHONE..................................619 297-8697
Steven Hendrickson, *President*
Carlos Guerrero, *Sales Staff*
Cindy Florian, *Manager*
Linda Beltran, *Representative*
EMP: 70
SALES (est): 8.5MM **Privately Held**
WEB: www.perfectionautobody.net
SIC: 7549 7532 Towing service, automotive; top & body repair & paint shops

(P-17430)
TOYOTA LOGISTICS SERVICES
785 Edison Ave, Long Beach (90813-2657)
PHONE..................................562 437-6767
Audie Freeman, *Manager*
EMP: 289 **Privately Held**
SIC: 7549 Automotive maintenance services
HQ: Toyota Logistics Services, Inc
19001 S Western Ave
Torrance CA 90501
310 618-5009

(P-17431)
UNITED ROAD TOWING INC
1516 S Bon View Ave, Ontario (91761-4407)
PHONE..................................909 923-6100
Gabriel Ramirez, *Manager*
EMP: 56
SALES (est): 881.6K
SALES (corp-wide): 573.9MM **Privately Held**
WEB: www.unitedroad.com
SIC: 7549 Towing service, automotive; towing services
HQ: United Road Towing, Inc.
9550 Bormet Dr Ste 304
Mokena IL 60448
708 390-2200

(P-17432)
UNITED ROAD TOWING INC
945 W Brockton Ave, Redlands (92374-2903)
PHONE..................................909 798-4863
Gabriel Ramirez, *Manager*
EMP: 56
SALES (corp-wide): 573.9MM **Privately Held**
WEB: www.unitedroad.com
SIC: 7549 Towing service, automotive
HQ: United Road Towing, Inc.
9550 Bormet Dr Ste 304
Mokena IL 60448
708 390-2200

(P-17433)
VALVOLINE INTERNATIONAL INC
Also Called: Valvoline Instant Oil Change
9520 John St, Santa Fe Springs (90670-2904)
PHONE..................................562 906-6200
Brian Nichols, *Branch Mgr*
EMP: 50
SALES (corp-wide): 2.2B **Publicly Held**
SIC: 7549 Automotive maintenance services
HQ: Valvoline Llc
100 Valvoline Way
Lexington KY 40509
-

7622 Radio & TV Repair Shops

(P-17434)
BLACK & WHITE TV INC
8756 Dorrington Ave, West Hollywood (90048-1724)
PHONE..................................310 855-1040
Jeffrey Fischgrund, *President*
EMP: 50
SALES (est): 771.8K **Privately Held**
SIC: 7622 Television repair shop

(P-17435)
JVC AMERICAS CORP
Also Called: Jvc Service & Engineering
11925 Pike St, Santa Fe Springs (90670-2955)
PHONE..................................562 463-8110
EMP: 80 **Privately Held**
SIC: 7622

(P-17436)
MINILEC SERVICE INC
Also Called: Minilec Service-Los Angeles BR
9207 Deering Ave Ste A, Chatsworth (91311-6959)
PHONE..................................818 341-1125
EMP: 50
SQ FT: 7,000
SALES (corp-wide): 6.6MM **Privately Held**
SIC: 7622 4812
PA: Minilec Service Inc.
9207 Deering Ave Ste A
Chatsworth CA 91311
818 773-6300

(P-17437)
PRECISION TELEVISION INC
Also Called: Precision TV
2350 Stanwell Dr, Concord (94520-4822)
PHONE..................................925 825-5296

Derrick W Behrens, *CEO*
Robert Behrens, *Vice Pres*
EMP: 54
SQ FT: 5,500
SALES (est): 7.2MM **Privately Held**
SIC: 7622 Television repair shop

(P-17438)
SOHNEN ENTERPRISES INC (PA)
13225 Marquardt Ave, Santa Fe Springs (90670-4831)
P.O. Box 2884 (90670-0884)
PHONE..................................562 903-4957
Barry Sohnen, *President*
Nathan Balsam, *Vice Pres*
Bryan Chase, *Admin Sec*
Carlos Ruiz, *Production*
Peter Demirakian, *Sales Staff*
◆ **EMP:** 50
SQ FT: 132,000
SALES (est): 11.1MM **Privately Held**
WEB: www.sohnen.com
SIC: 7622 5065 7629 Radio repair shop; video repair; communication equipment repair; sound equipment, electronic; video equipment, electronic; telephone equipment; communication equipment; electrical repair shops

(P-17439)
SYNTELESYS INC
Also Called: Ytech
2550 Corp Pl Ste C108, Monterey Park (91754)
PHONE..................................323 859-2160
Carey Chrisman, *President*
▼ **EMP:** 50
SALES (est): 3.2MM **Privately Held**
SIC: 7622 7313 Antenna repair & installation; electronic media advertising representatives

7623 Refrigeration & Air Conditioning Svc & Repair Shop

(P-17440)
ACCO ENGINEERED SYSTEMS INC
3421 S Malt Ave, Commerce (90040-3127)
PHONE..................................323 727-7765
Eric Porras, *Exec Dir*
Minh Phan, *Design Engr*
Michael Gamet, *Manager*
Brian Icban, *Supervisor*
EMP: 70
SQ FT: 77,399
SALES (corp-wide): 777.3MM **Privately Held**
WEB: www.accoair.com
SIC: 7623 1711 Air conditioning repair; plumbing, heating, air-conditioning contractors
PA: Acco Engineered Systems, Inc.
888 E Walnut St
Pasadena CA 91101
818 244-6571

(P-17441)
BROWER MECHANICAL INC
Also Called: Honeywell Authorized Dealer
4060 Alvis Ct, Rocklin (95677-4012)
PHONE..................................530 749-0808
Jeff Brower, *President*
Duane Knickerbocker, *Vice Pres*
Debra Dickmeyer, *Executive*
Bob Rogers, *Project Mgr*
EMP: 75
SQ FT: 5,000
SALES (est): 17.2MM **Privately Held**
WEB: www.browermechanical.com
SIC: 7623 7629 Air conditioning repair; electrical household appliance repair

(P-17442)
CARRIER CORPORATION
Also Called: Carrier Commercial Service
1168 National Dr Ste 60, Sacramento (95834-1979)
PHONE..................................916 928-9500
Craig Sweeney, *Branch Mgr*

EMP: 50
SALES (corp-wide): 66.5B **Publicly Held**
WEB: www.carrier.com
SIC: 7623 Air conditioning repair
HQ: Carrier Corporation
      13995 Pasteur Blvd
      Palm Beach Gardens FL 33418
      800 379-6484

(P-17443)
CITY MECHANICAL INC
724 Alfred Nobel Dr, Hercules
(94547-1805)
PHONE....................510 724-9088
Russell Will Jr, *CEO*
Ronald Tinkey, *Corp Secy*
Helene Banares, *Office Mgr*
EMP: 70
SALES (est): 12.3MM **Privately Held**
WEB: www.citymechanical.com
SIC: 7623 1711 Refrigeration service & re-
    pair; heating systems repair & mainte-
    nance; ventilation & duct work contractor

(P-17444)
CLIMA-TECH INC
1820 Town And Country Dr, Norco
(92860-3616)
PHONE....................909 613-5513
William C Valenzuela, *CEO*
Ada Roberts, *CFO*
Husein Aziz, *Exec VP*
Dolores Garcia, *Administration*
Jessica Hernandez, *Administration*
EMP: 89
SALES (est): 12.3MM **Privately Held**
SIC: 7623 1711 Refrigeration service & re-
    pair; refrigeration contractor; heating & air
    conditioning contractors

(P-17445)
**COMMERCIAL MECHANICAL
SVC INC (PA)**
Also Called: C M Service
981 Bing St, San Carlos (94070-5321)
PHONE....................650 610-8440
Thomas Fewell, *President*
Rick Kirkpatrick, *Opers Staff*
EMP: 50
SALES (est): 5MM **Privately Held**
WEB: www.fm-svcs.com
SIC: 7623 Refrigeration repair service; air
    conditioning repair

(P-17446)
GMH INC
Also Called: West Coast Air Conditioning
561 Kinetic Dr Ste A, Oxnard (93030-7947)
PHONE....................805 485-1410
Michael C Haase, *President*
Jim Clower, *Vice Pres*
Gina Haase, *Vice Pres*
Todd Smith, *General Mgr*
Anna Coronado, *Project Mgr*
EMP: 50 EST: 1976
SQ FT: 5,600
SALES (est): 13.4MM **Privately Held**
WEB: www.westcoast-air.com
SIC: 7623 1711 Refrigeration repair serv-
    ice; air conditioning repair; refrigeration
    contractor; warm air heating & air condi-
    tioning contractor

(P-17447)
RECURVE INC
220 Montgomery St Ste 820, San Francisco
(94104-3439)
PHONE....................510 540-4860
Andy Leventhal, *CEO*
Matthew Golden, *President*
EMP: 52
SQ FT: 8,000
SALES (est): 3.3MM **Privately Held**
SIC: 7623 Air conditioning repair

(P-17448)
SUNBELT CONTROLS INC
Also Called: Honeywell Authorized Dealer
4511 Willow Rd Ste 4, Pleasanton
(94588-2735)
PHONE....................925 660-3900
Josh Reding, *Branch Mgr*
Noah Taber, *Project Engr*
Vincent Darrigo, *Opers Staff*
Thomas Hemby, *Sales Staff*
EMP: 50

SALES (corp-wide): 777.3MM **Privately
Held**
SIC: 7623 1711 Refrigeration service & re-
    pair; septic system construction
HQ: Sunbelt Controls, Inc.
      4511 Willow Rd Ste 4
      Pleasanton CA 94588
      -

(P-17449)
**WESTERN ALLIED SERVICE
COMPANY**
12046 Florence Ave, Santa Fe Springs
(90670-4406)
P.O. Box 3628 (90670-1628)
PHONE....................562 941-3243
Steve Kieve, *CEO*
Laurens Vaneveld, *Chief Engr*
Zachary Russi, *Marketing Staff*
EMP: 300
SQ FT: 15,000
SALES (est): 10.4MM **Privately Held**
SIC: 7623 Air conditioning repair

┌─────────────────────────────┐
│ **7629 Electrical & Elex** │
│ **Repair Shop, NEC**   │
└─────────────────────────────┘

(P-17450)
AAR MANUFACTURING INC
AAR Composites
5307 Luce Ave Bldg 243e, McClellan
(95652-2440)
PHONE....................916 830-7011
Eloy Herrera, *Branch Mgr*
EMP: 73
SALES (corp-wide): 2B **Publicly Held**
SIC: 7629 Electronic equipment repair
HQ: Aar Manufacturing, Inc.
      1100 N Wood Dale Rd
      Wood Dale IL 60191
      630 227-2000

(P-17451)
AAR MANUFACTURING INC
AAR Mobility Systems
5239 Luce Ave Bldg 243d, McClellan
(95652-2427)
PHONE....................800 422-2213
Lee Krantz, *Branch Mgr*
Eloy Herrera, *Business Dir*
EMP: 73
SALES (corp-wide): 2B **Publicly Held**
SIC: 7629 Electronic equipment repair
HQ: Aar Manufacturing, Inc.
      1100 N Wood Dale Rd
      Wood Dale IL 60191
      630 227-2000

(P-17452)
ABLE CABLE INC (PA)
Also Called: A C I Communications
5115 Douglas Fir Rd Ste A, Calabasas
(91302-2588)
PHONE....................818 223-3600
Russell Ramas, *CEO*
David Gardner, *CFO*
Michael Collette, *Vice Pres*
Kim Carpenter, *Asst Controller*
Anthony Buschelman, *Personnel*
EMP: 175
SQ FT: 3,500
SALES (est): 14.8MM **Privately Held**
WEB: www.acicommunications.com
SIC: 7629 1731 4813 Telephone set re-
    pair; telephone & telephone equipment in-
    stallation; fiber optic cable installation;
    telephone communication, except radio

(P-17453)
CPI ECONCO DIVISION (DH)
Also Called: Econco Broadcast Service
1318 Commerce Ave, Woodland
(95776-5908)
PHONE....................530 662-7553
David P Elliot, *President*
Joel Littman, *Corp Secy*
Heidi Lindberg, *Info Tech Mgr*
Paul Cochran, *Engineer*
David Reed, *Safety Mgr*
◆ EMP: 73
SQ FT: 50,000

SALES (est): 9MM
SALES (corp-wide): 399.2MM **Privately
Held**
SIC: 7629 3671 Electrical repair shops;
    vacuum tubes

(P-17454)
DACOR
14525 Clark Ave, City of Industry
(91745-1236)
PHONE....................626 961-2256
Jaime Morales, *Branch Mgr*
EMP: 53 **Privately Held**
SIC: 7629 Electrical household appliance
    repair
HQ: Dacor
      14425 Clark Ave
      City Of Industry CA 91745
      626 799-1000

(P-17455)
**DUTHIE ELECTRIC SERVICE
CORP**
Also Called: Duthie Power Services
2335 E Cherry Indus Cir, Long Beach
(90805-4416)
PHONE....................562 790-1772
Christina Duthie, *President*
Richard Duthie, *Corp Secy*
Erik Duthie, *Vice Pres*
Johnny Bradford, *Technician*
Garrett Talbott, *Sales Engr*
EMP: 50
SQ FT: 17,000
SALES (est): 13.5MM **Privately Held**
WEB: www.duthiepower.com
SIC: 7629 7359 Generator repair; equip-
    ment rental & leasing

(P-17456)
GDSA-LINCOLN INC (PA)
Also Called: Weco Aerospace Systems
1501 Aviation Blvd, Lincoln (95648-9388)
PHONE....................916 645-8961
William Weygandt, *President*
Robert Weygandt, *CFO*
Kathleen Weygandt, *Admin Sec*
▲ EMP: 55 EST: 1971
SQ FT: 7,800
SALES (est): 4.2MM **Privately Held**
SIC: 7629 5088 Aircraft electrical equip-
    ment repair; aircraft equipment & supplies

(P-17457)
JJR ENTERPRISES INC (PA)
Also Called: Caltronics Business Systems
10491 Old Placerville Rd # 150, Sacra-
mento (95827-2531)
PHONE....................916 363-2666
Daniel F Reilly, *CEO*
Anne Long, *CFO*
John J Reilly, *Chairman*
Mark Demee, *Branch Mgr*
Megan Burcham, *Administration*
EMP: 95
SQ FT: 30,000
SALES (est): 53.7MM **Privately Held**
WEB: www.caltronics.net
SIC: 7629 5044 7359 Business machine
    repair, electric; office equipment; equip-
    ment rental & leasing

(P-17458)
NSG TECHNOLOGY INC
Also Called: Hon Hai Precision Industry
1705 Junction Ct Ste 200, San Jose
(95112-1023)
PHONE....................408 547-8770
Ted Dubbs, *CEO*
Aaron Tsai, *Executive*
Cindy LI, *Program Mgr*
Scott Ho, *Administration*
Acacio Filho, *Info Tech Mgr*
▲ EMP: 429 EST: 1995
SALES (est): 52MM **Privately Held**
SIC: 7629 Electronic equipment repair
HQ: Maxwell Holdings Limited
      C/O Vistra (Cayman) Limited
      George Town GR CAYMAN

(P-17459)
RAYTHEON COMPANY
988 Inner Loop Rd, Fort Irwin (92310)
P.O. Box 10079 (92310-0079)
PHONE....................760 386-2572

Denise Lapage, *Branch Mgr*
Lorena Jimenez, *Administration*
Phuong Nguyen, *Electrical Engi*
Richard Stikkers, *Manager*
EMP: 500
SALES (corp-wide): 27B **Publicly Held**
SIC: 7629 1731 Electrical equipment re-
    pair services; electrical work
PA: Raytheon Company
      870 Winter St
      Waltham MA 02451
      781 522-3000

(P-17460)
SCHROFF INC
Also Called: Pentair Equipment Protection
7328 Trade St, San Diego (92121-3435)
PHONE....................858 740-2400
Robert Bradley, *Branch Mgr*
EMP: 120 **Privately Held**
SIC: 7629 3469 Telecommunication equip-
    ment repair (except telephones); elec-
    tronic enclosures, stamped or pressed
    metal
HQ: Schroff, Inc.
      170 Commerce Dr
      Warwick RI 02886
      763 204-7700

(P-17461)
SCOTTEL VOICE & DATA INC
Also Called: Black Box Network Services
6100 Center Dr Ste 720, Los Angeles
(90045-9228)
PHONE....................310 737-7300
George Robertson, *General Mgr*
Alex Kobe, *Administration*
Linda Hunt, *Engineer*
EMP: 130
SQ FT: 5,200
SALES (est): 7.7MM **Privately Held**
WEB: www.scottel.com
SIC: 7629 1731 Telecommunication equip-
    ment repair (except telephones); tele-
    phone & telephone equipment installation
HQ: Black Box Corporation
      1000 Park Dr
      Lawrence PA 15055
      724 746-5500

(P-17462)
SEARS ROEBUCK AND CO
Also Called: Sears Service Center
1406 N Johnson Ave, El Cajon
(92020-1681)
PHONE....................619 590-3812
EMP: 142
SALES (corp-wide): 16.7B **Publicly Held**
SIC: 7629
HQ: Sears, Roebuck And Co.
      3333 Beverly Rd
      Hoffman Estates IL 60179
      847 286-2500

(P-17463)
**SERVICE SOLUTIONS GROUP
LLC**
Also Called: Barkers Food Machinery
5367 2nd St, Irwindale (91706-6608)
PHONE....................626 960-9390
Robert Zachary Barasch, *Branch Mgr*
EMP: 60
SALES (corp-wide): 2.9B **Privately Held**
SIC: 7629 7623 5046 5078 Electrical
    equipment repair services; refrigeration
    repair service; restaurant equipment &
    supplies; commercial refrigeration equip-
    ment; plumbing fittings & supplies; elec-
    tronic parts & equipment
HQ: Service Solutions Group, Llc
      800 Aviation Pkwy
      Smyrna TN 37167
      615 462-4000

(P-17464)
SIMCO ELECTRONICS (PA)
3131 Jay St Ste 100, Santa Clara
(95054-3336)
PHONE....................408 734-9750
Brian Kenna, *CEO*
Todd Lee, *Opers Spvr*
Michael Watts, *Director*
EMP: 75 EST: 1962
SQ FT: 24,222

▲ = Import ▼=Export
◆ =Import/Export

SALES (est): 55.6MM **Privately Held**
WEB: www.simco.com
SIC: 7629 8734 5045 7379 Electrical repair shops; calibration & certification; computer software; computer related consulting services; computer related maintenance services

(P-17465)
TELENET VOIP INC
850 N Park View Dr, El Segundo
(90245-4914)
PHONE....................310 253-9000
Asghar Ghassemy, *President*
Nicol Payab, *Vice Pres*
Jose Pino, *Technician*
Augie Besa, *Project Mgr*
Mike Kohsari, *Project Mgr*
EMP: 65
SQ FT: 11,000
SALES (est): 12.2MM **Privately Held**
WEB: www.telenetusa.net
SIC: 7629 7379 7382 3612 Telephone set repair; computer related consulting services; security systems services; transmission & distribution voltage regulators

(P-17466)
TESTEQUITY LLC (PA)
6100 Condor Dr, Moorpark (93021-2608)
PHONE....................805 498-9933
Neil McKinnon, *CFO*
John Glass, *Chief Mktg Ofcr*
Karla Ksan, *Vice Pres*
Phil Orin, *CIO*
Josh Arellano, *IT/INT Sup*
▲ EMP: 168
SQ FT: 75,000
SALES (est): 129.2MM **Privately Held**
SIC: 7629 3825 Electrical equipment repair services; test equipment for electronic & electrical circuits

(P-17467)
TOSHIBA BUS SOLUTIONS USA INC (DH)
9740 Irvine Blvd, Irvine (92618-1608)
PHONE....................949 462-6000
Mark Mathews, *CEO*
EMP: 118
SALES (est): 128.9MM **Privately Held**
SIC: 7629 5044 5999 Business machine repair, electric; office equipment; business machines & equipment
HQ: Toshiba America Business Solutions, Inc.
25530 Commercentre Dr
Lake Forest CA 92630
949 462-6000

(P-17468)
USACO SERVICE CORP
Also Called: Kenwood Service Center West
16205 Distribution Way, Cerritos (90703-2329)
PHONE....................562 483-8747
Stewart Park, *President*
▲ EMP: 150
SALES (est): 6.4MM **Privately Held**
WEB: www.usacoservice.com
SIC: 7629 Electrical repair shops

7631 Watch, Clock & Jewelry Repair

(P-17469)
ADVANCE SERVICES INC
8021 Kern Ave, Gilroy (95020-4051)
PHONE....................408 767-2797
Vanessa Valencia, *Manager*
EMP: 2166 **Privately Held**
SIC: 7631 Watch, clock & jewelry repair
PA: Advance Services, Inc.
12702 Wsport Pkwy Ste 201
La Vista NE 68138

(P-17470)
M & G JEWELERS INC
10823 Edison Ct, Rancho Cucamonga (91730-3868)
PHONE....................909 989-2929
Juan Guevara, *President*

Michael Insalago, *Vice Pres*
Tom Nevin, *General Mgr*
Adolfo Burbano, *Info Tech Mgr*
Brian Groce, *Accounting Mgr*
EMP: 68
SQ FT: 8,432
SALES (est): 10.7MM **Privately Held**
WEB: www.mandgjewelers.com
SIC: 7631 Watch, clock & jewelry repair

7641 Reupholstery & Furniture Repair

(P-17471)
CHURCH OF JSUS CHRST OF LD STS
Also Called: Los Angeles Deseret Industries
2720 E 11th St, Los Angeles (90023-3404)
PHONE....................323 268-7281
Dessin Meyer, *Director*
EMP: 130
SALES (corp-wide): 3.5B **Privately Held**
WEB: www.lds.org
SIC: 7641 5932 7629 8331 Furniture repair & maintenance; furniture, second-hand; household appliances, used; electrical household appliance repair; job training & vocational rehabilitation services
PA: Corporation Of The President Of The Church Of Jesus Christ Of Latter-Day Saints
50 E North Temple
Salt Lake City UT 84150
801 240-1000

(P-17472)
MOYES CUSTOM FURNITURE INC
3431 E La Palma Ave Ste 3, Anaheim (92806-2022)
PHONE....................714 729-0234
Brian Moyes, *President*
Jane Moyes, *Corp Secy*
David Moyes, *Administration*
EMP: 50
SQ FT: 59,000
SALES (est): 3.7MM **Privately Held**
WEB: www.moyesfurniture.com
SIC: 7641 2512 Reupholstery; upholstered household furniture

7692 Welding Repair

(P-17473)
HAYES WELDING INC (PA)
Also Called: Valew Welding & Fabrication
12522 Violet Rd, Adelanto (92301-2704)
P.O. Box 310 (92301-0310)
PHONE....................760 246-4878
Roger L Hayes, *CEO*
Velma D Hayes, *President*
Vernon L Hayes, *Vice Pres*
Keseloff Manya, *Clerk*
▲ EMP: 86
SQ FT: 45,000
SALES (est): 14.5MM **Privately Held**
WEB: www.valew.com
SIC: 7692 3465 3714 3713 Welding repair; automotive stampings; body parts, automobile: stamped metal; fenders, automobile: stamped or pressed metal; fuel systems & parts, motor vehicle; truck & bus bodies; fabricated plate work (boiler shop)

(P-17474)
JABIL SILVER CREEK INC (HQ)
Also Called: Wolfe Engineering, Inc.
5981 Optical Ct, San Jose (95138-1400)
PHONE....................669 255-2900
John P Wolfe, *CEO*
Rita Wolfe, *Vice Pres*
▲ EMP: 115
SQ FT: 76,000
SALES (est): 25.7MM
SALES (corp-wide): 25.2B **Publicly Held**
WEB: www.wolfe-engr.com
SIC: 7692 8711 3674 3317 Welding repair; engineering services; semiconductors & related devices; steel pipe & tubes; fabricated pipe & fittings

---

PA: Jabil Inc.
10560 Dr Mrtn Lther King
Saint Petersburg FL 33716
727 577-9749

(P-17475)
SOUTHCOAST WELDING & MFG LLC
2591 Faivre St Ste 1, Chula Vista (91911-7146)
PHONE....................619 429-1337
Patrick Shoup, *President*
Leo Mathieu, *CFO*
Jay Parast, *Vice Pres*
David Lerma, *Admin Sec*
Gary Cathcart, *Controller*
EMP: 270
SQ FT: 82,000
SALES (est): 30.7MM **Privately Held**
SIC: 7692 Welding repair

(P-17476)
WELDLOGIC INC
2651 Lavery Ct, Newbury Park (91320-1502)
PHONE....................805 375-1670
Robert Elizarraz, *President*
Jack Froschauer, *Vice Pres*
Rick Heminuk, *Vice Pres*
▲ EMP: 65
SQ FT: 25,000
SALES (est): 11.6MM **Privately Held**
WEB: www.weldlogic.com
SIC: 7692 Welding repair

7694 Armature Rewinding Shops

(P-17477)
SULZER ELECTRO-MECHANICAL SERV
620 S Rancho Ave, Colton (92324-3243)
PHONE....................909 825-7971
Gary Patton, *Branch Mgr*
EMP: 50
SALES (corp-wide): 3.3B **Privately Held**
SIC: 7694 5063 Electric motor repair; motors, electric
HQ: Sulzer Electro-Mechanical Services (Us) Inc.
1910 Jasmine Dr
Pasadena TX 77503
713 473-3231

7699 Repair Shop & Related Svcs, NEC

(P-17478)
24 HOUR ELEVATOR INC
4837 Mercury St, San Diego (92111-2104)
PHONE....................858 279-8900
Kenneth Dixon, *CEO*
William Schassberger, *President*
Frank Rowland, *Vice Pres*
John Armet, *Principal*
Tim Brown, *Principal*
EMP: 53
SQ FT: 2,700
SALES: 8MM **Privately Held**
SIC: 7699 Elevators: inspection, service & repair

(P-17479)
AER TECHNOLOGIES INC
650 Columbia St, Brea (92821-2912)
PHONE....................714 871-7357
Kim Quick, *CEO*
Michael McGroarty, *President*
Ingrid Osborne, *Admin Sec*
Travis Nichols, *Sales Staff*
Cameron Quick, *Sales Staff*
EMP: 320
SQ FT: 50,000
SALES (est): 32.9MM **Privately Held**
SIC: 7699 Precision instrument repair

(P-17480)
AERO-ENGINES INC
2641 Roseview Ave, Los Angeles (90065-1123)
PHONE....................323 663-3961
Otis Perera, *President*

Antonio Ortega, *Vice Pres*
▲ EMP: 60
SQ FT: 41,000
SALES (est): 4.6MM **Privately Held**
SIC: 7699 3724 Aircraft & heavy equipment repair services; aircraft engines & engine parts

(P-17481)
AL-TAR SERVICES INC
823 Kifer Rd, Sunnyvale (94086-5204)
P.O. Box 1929, Evergreen CO (80437-1929)
PHONE....................866 522-3499
Melissa Mia Castro, *President*
Dustin Castro, *COO*
EMP: 54
SQ FT: 15,000
SALES (est): 4.9MM **Privately Held**
WEB: www.al-tar.com
SIC: 7699 Laboratory instrument repair

(P-17482)
ALL AMERICAN SERVICE & SUPS
1776 All American Way, Corona (92879-2070)
P.O. Box 2229 (92878-2229)
PHONE....................951 736-3880
Daniel D Sisemore, *President*
Mark A Luer, *Principal*
Thomas Toscas, *Admin Sec*
EMP: 90
SALES (est): 7.8MM **Privately Held**
SIC: 7699 Construction equipment repair

(P-17483)
AMERICAN RESIDENTIAL SVCS LLC
Also Called: Rescue Rooter Bay Area South
2305 Paragon Dr, San Jose (95131-1309)
P.O. Box 640845 (95164-0845)
PHONE....................408 435-3810
Earnest Bell, *Manager*
EMP: 60
SALES (corp-wide): 2.3B **Privately Held**
WEB: www.ars.com
SIC: 7699 1711 Sewer cleaning & rodding; plumbing contractors
PA: American Residential Services Llc
965 Ridge Lake Blvd # 201
Memphis TN 38120
901 271-9700

(P-17484)
AMERICAN VISION WINDOWS INC
2125 N Madera Rd Ste A, Simi Valley (93065-7709)
PHONE....................805 582-1833
William Herren, *CEO*
Gabriela Herrera, *COO*
Al Alfieri, *Vice Pres*
Monica Estrada, *Vice Pres*
Kathleen Herren, *Vice Pres*
EMP: 215
SALES (est): 31.9MM **Privately Held**
SIC: 7699 1799 5031 Door & window repair; home/office interiors finishing, furnishing & remodeling; metal doors, sash & trim

(P-17485)
ANCON MARINE
2209 Zeus Ct, Bakersfield (93308-6867)
PHONE....................310 952-8160
Bill Boyd, *Principal*
EMP: 72
SALES (corp-wide): 186.6MM **Privately Held**
SIC: 7699 7349 Tank repair & cleaning services; cleaning service, industrial or commercial
PA: Ancon Marine
22707 Wilmington Ave
Carson CA 90745
310 522-5110

(P-17486)
ARNIES SUPPLIES SERVICE LTD
1501 N Ditman Ave, Los Angeles (90063-2501)
P.O. Box 26, Philadelphia PA (19105-0026)
PHONE....................323 263-1696
Arnold Espino, *President*

EMP: 60
SQ FT: 806
SALES (corp-wide): 6.6MM **Privately Held**
SIC: 7699 Pallet repair
PA: Arnie's Supply Service Ltd.
1541 N Ditman Ave
Los Angeles CA 90063
323 263-1696

(P-17487)
AUTOMATED SYSTEMS AMERICA INC
Also Called: Asai
101 N Brand Blvd Ste 1230, Glendale (91203-2677)
PHONE..................877 500-0002
John Thomas Steely, *President*
Jackie Steely, *CFO*
Tomas Sanchez, *Project Mgr*
EMP: 52
SQ FT: 1,200
SALES (est): 42.3MM **Privately Held**
WEB: www.asaiatm.com
SIC: 7699 3578 6099 Automated teller machine (ATM) repair; automatic teller machines (ATM); automated teller machine (ATM) network

(P-17488)
CDSRVS LLC
840 W Grove Ave, Orange (92865-3216)
PHONE..................714 912-8353
Steven Fenzel, *President*
Jim Philipps, *Exec VP*
Danielle Thompson, *Admin Asst*
Mia Ferrante, *Human Res Mgr*
Gordon McTavish,
EMP: 56
SQ FT: 10,000
SALES: 6MM **Privately Held**
SIC: 7699 Metal reshaping & replating services; plastics products repair

(P-17489)
CHROMALLOY SAN DIEGO CORP
7007 Consolidated Way, San Diego (92121-2604)
PHONE..................858 877-2800
Armand F Lauzon Jr, *CEO*
Bob Shambaugh, *COO*
David G Albert, *Vice Pres*
Michael Beffel, *Vice Pres*
Andrea Colombo, *Vice Pres*
EMP: 120
SQ FT: 120,000
SALES (est): 17.5MM
SALES (corp-wide): 2.4B **Publicly Held**
WEB: www.chromalloysatx.com
SIC: 7699 3724 Aircraft & heavy equipment repair services; aircraft engines & engine parts
HQ: Chromalloy American Llc
330 Blaisdell Rd
Orangeburg NY 10962
845 230-7355

(P-17490)
CLEAN ENVIROMENT
4570 Alvarado Canyon Rd C, San Diego (92142-4317)
PHONE..................619 521-0543
Steve G Ottman, *Owner*
Stephen Ottman, *Principal*
Gloria Fernandes, *Admin Sec*
EMP: 60
SALES (est): 1.3MM **Privately Held**
SIC: 7699 Cleaning services

(P-17491)
CLEAN HRBORS ES INDUS SVCS INC
Also Called: Brand Precision
4501 California Ct, Benicia (94510-1021)
PHONE..................707 745-1581
Mark Davis, *Manager*
EMP: 60
SALES (corp-wide): 3.3B **Publicly Held**
WEB: www.onyxindustrial.com
SIC: 7699 8748 Waste cleaning services; sewer cleaning & rodding; environmental consultant

HQ: Clean Harbors Es Industrial Services, Inc.
4760 World Houston Pkwy # 100
Houston TX 77032
713 672-8004

(P-17492)
CLEAN POWER FINANCE INC
50 Osgood Pl Ste 400, San Francisco (94133-4644)
PHONE..................899 525-2123
Gary Kremen, *President*
Rajiv Ghatalia, *Ch of Bd*
Michael Pope, *CFO*
Shawn Tabak, *CFO*
Kristian Hanelt, *Senior VP*
EMP: 137 EST: 2006
SALES (est): 15MM
SALES (corp-wide): 1.1MM **Privately Held**
SIC: 7699 7389 Cleaning services; financial services
HQ: Spruce Finance Inc.
50 Osgood Pl Ste 400
San Francisco CA 94133
866 525-2123

(P-17493)
CLEANING SERVICES
7828 Monterey St, Gilroy (95020-4537)
PHONE..................408 778-9251
Michael Jones, *President*
EMP: 50
SALES (est): 1.7MM **Privately Held**
WEB: www.makeitclean.com
SIC: 7699 Cleaning services

(P-17494)
COLLECTORS UNIVERSE INC (PA)
1610 E Saint Andrew Pl, Santa Ana (92705-4941)
P.O. Box 6280, Newport Beach (92658-6280)
PHONE..................949 567-1234
Joseph J Orlando, *CEO*
Bruce A Stevens, *Ch of Bd*
Joseph J Wallace, *CFO*
Mindy Kinner, *Creative Dir*
Lauren Buckles, *Executive Asst*
EMP: 97
SQ FT: 62,755
SALES: 72.4MM **Publicly Held**
WEB: www.collectors.com
SIC: 7699 Hobby & collectors services

(P-17495)
D S R INC
Also Called: Mr Rooter
3503 Arundell Cir Ste A, Ventura (93003-4916)
PHONE..................805 275-0039
Richard Svestak, *President*
EMP: 70
SQ FT: 6,200
SALES (est): 2MM **Privately Held**
SIC: 7699 Sewer cleaning & rodding

(P-17496)
DESIGN MACHINE AND MFG
2491 Simpson St, Kingsburg (93631-9501)
PHONE..................559 897-7374
Abe Wiabe, *Owner*
Abe Wiebe, *Managing Prtnr*
John Zweigle, *General Mgr*
EMP: 50
SALES (est): 282.9K **Privately Held**
SIC: 7699 Industrial machinery & equipment repair

(P-17497)
DICALITE MINERALS CORP (HQ)
36994 Summit Lake Rd, Burney (96013-9636)
PHONE..................530 335-5451
Raymond Perlman, *President*
Ben Lazar, *Controller*
Derek J Cusack, *VP Opers*
◆ EMP: 59
SQ FT: 3,000
SALES (est): 8.5MM
SALES (corp-wide): 34.9MM **Privately Held**
WEB: www.dicalite-dicaperl.com
SIC: 7699 Filter cleaning

PA: Dicalite Management Group, Inc.
1 Bala Ave Ste 310
Bala Cynwyd PA 19004
610 660-8808

(P-17498)
FOSTER DAIRY FARMS
1472 Hall Rd, Hickman (95323-9615)
PHONE..................209 874-9605
Ronald Hill, *Manager*
EMP: 200
SALES (corp-wide): 397.9MM **Privately Held**
SIC: 7699 Farm machinery repair
PA: Foster Dairy Farms
529 Kansas Ave
Modesto CA 95351
209 576-3400

(P-17499)
GENERAL ELECTRIC COMPANY
2264 E Avion Ave, Ontario (91761-7794)
PHONE..................909 605-7603
Bob Ritch, *Manager*
Christopher Jennings, *Manager*
EMP: 500
SALES (corp-wide): 121.6B **Publicly Held**
SIC: 7699 4581 5088 Aircraft & heavy equipment repair services; airports, flying fields & services; aircraft & parts
PA: General Electric Company
41 Farnsworth St
Boston MA 02210
617 443-3000

(P-17500)
GENESIS TECH PARTNERS LLC
21540 Plummer St Ste A, Chatsworth (91311-4143)
PHONE..................800 950-2647
Sandy D Morford,
Haresh Satiani,
EMP: 175
SQ FT: 3,000
SALES (est): 3.5MM
SALES (corp-wide): 25.3B **Privately Held**
SIC: 7699 Medical equipment repair, non-electric
HQ: Cohr, Inc.
10510 Twin Lakes Pkwy
Charlotte NC 28269
704 948-5700

(P-17501)
GLOBAL DEV STRATEGIES INC
9985 Businesspark Ave A, San Diego (92131-1132)
P.O. Box 26997 (92196-0997)
PHONE..................858 408-1173
Marlene Stephens, *President*
Brandon Campbell, *CFO*
EMP: 60
SALES (est): 14.7MM **Privately Held**
WEB: www.globalstrategy.biz
SIC: 7699 Garage door repair

(P-17502)
GROWITH INC
Also Called: Mr Rooter
1069 Camero Way, Fremont (94539-3785)
PHONE..................805 650-6650
Aung Oo, *CEO*
EMP: 68
SALES (est): 938.2K **Privately Held**
SIC: 7699 Sewer cleaning & rodding

(P-17503)
HAWKER PACIFIC AEROSPACE
11240 Sherman Way, Sun Valley (91352-4942)
PHONE..................818 765-6201
Bernd Riggers, *CEO*
Troy Trower, *CFO*
Blas Maidagan, *Exec VP*
Brian Carr, *Vice Pres*
Valerie Fortner, *Managing Dir*
◆ EMP: 355
SQ FT: 193,000
SALES (est): 51.6MM
SALES (corp-wide): 41B **Privately Held**
WEB: www.hawker.com
SIC: 7699 5088 3728 Hydraulic equipment repair; aircraft & parts; aircraft parts & equipment

HQ: Lufthansa Technik Ag
Weg Beim Jager 193
Hamburg 22335
405 070-3667

(P-17504)
HOFFMAN SOUTHWEST CORP
Also Called: Roto-Rooter
1183 N Kraemer Pl, Anaheim (92806-1923)
PHONE..................714 630-0404
Don Hatcher, *Manager*
EMP: 50
SALES (corp-wide): 34.1MM **Privately Held**
SIC: 7699 1711 Sewer cleaning & rodding; plumbing contractors
PA: Hoffman Southwest Corp.
23311 Madero
Mission Viejo CA 92691
949 380-4161

(P-17505)
HOFFMAN SOUTHWEST CORP (PA)
Also Called: Roto Rooter Plumbing & Svc Co
23311 Madero, Mission Viejo (92691-2730)
PHONE..................949 380-4161
Mark Burel, *CEO*
Bruce Lux, *CFO*
John Andros, *Info Tech Mgr*
Elizabeth Roybal, *Supervisor*
EMP: 60
SQ FT: 14,000
SALES (est): 34.1MM **Privately Held**
SIC: 7699 1711 Sewer cleaning & rodding; plumbing contractors

(P-17506)
HOFFMAN SOUTHWEST CORP
Also Called: Roto-Rooter
8930 Center Ave, Rancho Cucamonga (91730-5328)
PHONE..................909 397-0567
Dan Chavez, *Manager*
EMP: 52
SALES (corp-wide): 34.1MM **Privately Held**
SIC: 7699 Sewer cleaning & rodding
PA: Hoffman Southwest Corp.
23311 Madero
Mission Viejo CA 92691
949 380-4161

(P-17507)
HOFFMAN TEXAS INC
24971 Avenue Stanford, Valencia (91355-1278)
PHONE..................661 257-9200
Gary Thomas, *Manager*
EMP: 50
SQ FT: 6,936
SALES (corp-wide): 34.1MM **Privately Held**
WEB: www.rw-rotorooter.com
SIC: 7699 Sewer cleaning & rodding
HQ: Hoffman Texas, Inc.
23311 Madero
Mission Viejo CA 92691
949 380-4161

(P-17508)
HRD AERO SYSTEMS INC
Also Called: Hrd Oxygens
25555 Avenue Stanford, Valencia (91355-1101)
PHONE..................661 295-0670
Tom Salamone, *President*
EMP: 65
SQ FT: 8,000
SALES (est): 1.2MM **Privately Held**
WEB: www.hrd-aerosystems.com
SIC: 7699 Aircraft & heavy equipment repair services; aircraft flight instrument repair; aviation propeller & blade repair

(P-17509)
HRD AERO SYSTEMS INC (PA)
25555 Avenue Stanford, Valencia (91355-1101)
PHONE..................661 295-0670
Tom Salamone, *President*
Tim McBride, *CFO*
Rich OHM, *Officer*
Paul Zapata, *Regional Mgr*
Louie Lewis, *Department Mgr*
◆ EMP: 110

SQ FT: 70,000
SALES (est): 19.1MM **Privately Held**
SIC: **7699** 8711 Aircraft & heavy equipment repair services; aircraft flight instrument repair; aviation propeller & blade repair; aviation &/or aeronautical engineering

(P-17510)
HYDRATECH LLC (HQ)
1331 S West Ave, Fresno (93706-2530)
PHONE.....................559 233-0876
John J McMahon Jr,
Ginny Zhou, *Executive*
Terrie Lassen, *Purch Mgr*
Matt Rivera, *Purch Mgr*
David Ogen, *VP Sales*
▲ EMP: 56
SQ FT: 40,000
SALES (est): 9.3MM
SALES (corp-wide): 501.5MM **Privately Held**
WEB: www.mvphydratech.com
SIC: **7699** Hydraulic equipment repair; cash register repair
PA: Ligon Industries, Llc
    1927 1st Ave N Ste 500
    Birmingham AL 35203
    205 322-3302

(P-17511)
IMAGE 2000 (PA)
26037 Huntington Ln, Valencia (91355-1145)
PHONE.....................818 781-2200
Joe Blatchford, *CEO*
Richard Campbell, *President*
EMP: 50
SQ FT: 22,557
SALES: 28MM **Privately Held**
SIC: **7699** 5999 Photographic equipment repair; photocopy machines

(P-17512)
INDUS LIGHT & MAGIC (VANCO) LL
1110 Gorgas Ave, San Francisco (94129-1406)
PHONE.....................415 292-4671
Steve Condiotti, *CEO*
Randal Shore, *Executive*
Ben Morris, *Creative Dir*
Mary Hinman, *Administration*
Cary Phillips, *Research*
▲ EMP: 88
SALES (est): 19.4MM
SALES (corp-wide): 90.2B **Publicly Held**
SIC: **7699** Industrial equipment services
HQ: Lucasfilm Ltd. Llc
    1110 Gorgas Ave Bldg C-Hr
    San Francisco CA 94129
    415 623-1000

(P-17513)
INLAND BUSINESS MACHINES INC (DH)
1326 N Market Blvd, Sacramento (95834-1912)
PHONE.....................916 928-0770
Liz Stafford, *President*
EMP: 79
SALES (est): 14.5MM
SALES (corp-wide): 405.1MM **Publicly Held**
WEB: www.ibs-team.com
SIC: **7699** 5044 5999 Printing trades machinery & equipment repair; office equipment; photocopy machines

(P-17514)
INNOVATIVE MEDICAL SOLUTIONS
3002 Dow Ave Ste 110, Tustin (92780-7247)
PHONE.....................714 505-7070
James Stevens, *President*
Stephen Ohare, *Officer*
Elizabeth Stevens, *Vice Pres*
EMP: 58
SALES: 3MM **Privately Held**
SIC: **7699** 5047 Hospital equipment repair services; medical & hospital equipment

(P-17515)
KERN STEEL FABRICATION INC (PA)
627 Williams St, Bakersfield (93305-5445)
PHONE.....................661 327-9588
Tom Champness, *President*
Terri Benyon, *Vice Pres*
Gene Panelli, *Vice Pres*
Josh Perales, *Project Mgr*
Chris Balsillie, *Chief Engr*
◆ EMP: 80
SQ FT: 50,000
SALES (est): 17.6MM **Privately Held**
WEB: www.kernsteel.com
SIC: **7699** Industrial machinery & equipment repair

(P-17516)
LA HYDRO-JET ROOTER SVC INC
Also Called: La Hydrojet
10639 Wixom St, Sun Valley (91352-4603)
PHONE.....................818 768-4225
Daniel Baldwin, *President*
Lori Baldwin, *CFO*
Janet Parker, *Assistant*
EMP: 68 EST: 1991
SALES (est): 9.9MM **Privately Held**
SIC: **7699** Sewer cleaning & rodding

(P-17517)
MATTHEWS INTERNATIONAL CORP
580 S State St Ste 8, San Jacinto (92583-4035)
PHONE.....................951 654-9123
Robert Ochoa, *Manager*
EMP: 50 EST: 1850
SQ FT: 1,200
SALES (est): 392.2K **Privately Held**
SIC: **7699** Industrial equipment services

(P-17518)
N & S TRACTOR CO (PA)
600 S St 59, Merced (95341-6543)
P.O. Box 910 (95341-0910)
PHONE.....................209 383-5888
Arthur R Nutcher, *CEO*
Mary Wallace, *Corp Secy*
Stephanie Nutcher, *Vice Pres*
BJ Cook, *Director*
Anna Perez, *Manager*
▲ EMP: 60
SQ FT: 8,700
SALES (est): 12.5MM **Privately Held**
WEB: www.nstractor.com
SIC: **7699** 5083 Farm machinery repair; agricultural machinery & equipment

(P-17519)
NIACC-AVITECH TECHNOLOGIES INC (PA)
245 W Dakota Ave, Clovis (93612-5608)
PHONE.....................559 291-2500
Jeff Andrews, *CEO*
Thomas S Irwin, *Treasurer*
Todd Rose, *General Mgr*
Elizabeth R Letendre, *Admin Sec*
Bill Fenne, *Administration*
EMP: 80
SALES (est): 13.7MM **Privately Held**
WEB: www.niacctech.com
SIC: **7699** 3471 Aircraft flight instrument repair; plating of metals or formed products

(P-17520)
NORTHFIELD MEDICAL INC
13631 Pawnee Rd, Apple Valley (92308-5880)
PHONE.....................248 268-2500
EMP: 104 **Privately Held**
SIC: **7699** Hospital equipment repair services
PA: Northfield Medical, Inc.
    30275 Hudson Dr
    Novi MI 48377
    -

(P-17521)
OTIS ELEVATOR COMPANY
Also Called: United Technologies
711 E Ball Rd Ste 200, Anaheim (92805-5960)
PHONE.....................714 758-9593

Bob McLeese, *Branch Mgr*
Joe Marquez, *Purchasing*
EMP: 50
SALES (corp-wide): 66.5B **Publicly Held**
WEB: www.otis.com
SIC: **7699** 1796 Elevators: inspection, service & repair; elevator installation & conversion
HQ: Otis Elevator Company
    1 Carrier Pl
    Farmington CT 06032
    860 674-3000

(P-17522)
OTIS ELEVATOR COMPANY
444 Spear St Ste 100, San Francisco (94105-1642)
PHONE.....................415 546-0880
Rob Neill, *Branch Mgr*
George V Klan, *Analyst*
EMP: 150
SALES (corp-wide): 66.5B **Publicly Held**
WEB: www.otis.com
SIC: **7699** 1796 Miscellaneous building item repair services; elevators: inspection, service & repair; elevator installation & conversion
HQ: Otis Elevator Company
    1 Carrier Pl
    Farmington CT 06032
    860 674-3000

(P-17523)
OVERMILLER INC
Also Called: Roto-Rooter
195 Mason Cir, Concord (94520-1213)
PHONE.....................925 798-2122
Billy Joe Bristol, *President*
Mardell A Bristol, *Vice Pres*
EMP: 53
SQ FT: 12,000
SALES (est): 7MM **Privately Held**
SIC: **7699** 1711 Sewer cleaning & rodding; plumbing contractors

(P-17524)
PACIFIC GAS TURBINE CENTER LLC
7007 Consolidated Way, San Diego (92121-2604)
PHONE.....................858 877-2910
Graham Bell,
◆ EMP: 101
SQ FT: 110,000
SALES (est): 4MM **Privately Held**
SIC: **7699** Industrial equipment services; engine repair & replacement, non-automotive

(P-17525)
PACWEST INSTRUMENT LABS INC
Also Called: Pacific Southwest Instruments
1721 Railroad St, Corona (92880-2511)
PHONE.....................951 737-0790
Jim Joubert, *President*
Boon Lee, *CFO*
Ray McDonald, *Vice Pres*
EMP: 51
SQ FT: 37,000
SALES (est): 12.2MM **Privately Held**
WEB: www.psilabs.com
SIC: **7699** 7629 Aircraft flight instrument repair; aircraft electrical equipment repair

(P-17526)
PEGGS COMPANY INC (PA)
4851 Felspar St, Riverside (92509-3024)
PHONE.....................253 584-9548
Chresten Revelle Nelson, *CEO*
John L Peggs, *President*
Frank Loera, *Purchasing*
Nick Corea, *Natl Sales Mgr*
◆ EMP: 100
SQ FT: 80,000
SALES (est): 28.4MM **Privately Held**
WEB: www.thepeggscompany.com
SIC: **7699** 3496 5046 7359 Shopping cart repair; miscellaneous fabricated wire products; commercial equipment; equipment rental & leasing

(P-17527)
PETERSON HYDRAULICS INC (PA)
1653 W El Segundo Blvd, Gardena (90249-2009)
PHONE.....................310 323-3155
Daniel G Peterson II, *CEO*
Dan Peterson, *President*
Pegeen Peterson, *Vice Pres*
EMP: 55
SQ FT: 25,853
SALES (est): 4.5MM **Privately Held**
SIC: **7699** 5172 5084 5013 Hydraulic equipment repair; service station supplies, petroleum; hydraulic systems equipment & supplies; automotive servicing equipment

(P-17528)
PKL SERVICES INC
14265 Danielson St C1, Poway (92064-8818)
PHONE.....................858 679-1755
Samuel Flores Jr, *President*
Paul Callan, *Exec VP*
David K Howell, *Vice Pres*
Mike Naylor, *Vice Pres*
Michael Nisley, *Vice Pres*
EMP: 160
SQ FT: 6,000
SALES (est): 16.8MM **Privately Held**
WEB: www.pklservices.com
SIC: **7699** Aircraft & heavy equipment repair services

(P-17529)
POMONA VALLEY MOTORCYCLES INC
Also Called: Pomona Valley Harley-Davidson
8710 Central Ave, Montclair (91763-5100)
PHONE.....................909 981-9500
Barbara Pennell, *President*
Barbara E Pennell, *President*
David A Pennell, *CFO*
EMP: 53
SQ FT: 26,000
SALES (est): 4.8MM **Privately Held**
WEB: www.pvhd.com
SIC: **7699** 5571 Motorcycle repair service; motorcycle parts & accessories

(P-17530)
PROPAK LOGISTICS INC
1300 S F St, Porterville (93257-5969)
PHONE.....................559 782-8696
EMP: 62 **Privately Held**
SIC: **7699** Pallet repair
PA: Propak Logistics, Inc.
    1100 Garrison Ave
    Fort Smith AR 72901

(P-17531)
PROPULSION CONTROLS ENGRG (PA)
1620 Rigel St, San Diego (92113-3832)
P.O. Box 13606 (92170-3606)
PHONE.....................619 235-0961
David P Clapp, *CEO*
John P Reilly III, *Treasurer*
Ken Barr, *General Mgr*
Maria Naputi, *Administration*
Omar Orona, *Administration*
EMP: 70
SQ FT: 22,000
SALES (est): 23.4MM **Privately Held**
WEB: www.pcehawaii.com
SIC: **7699** Boiler repair shop

(P-17532)
PSC INDUSTRIAL OUTSOURCING LP
Also Called: Hydrochempsc
19340 Van Ness Ave, Torrance (90501-1103)
PHONE.....................310 325-1600
EMP: 137
SALES (corp-wide): 750MM **Privately Held**
SIC: **7699**
PA: Psc Industrial Outsourcing, Lp
    900 Georgia Ave
    Deer Park TX 77536
    713 393-5600

PRODUCTS & SVCS

(P-17533)
RAYMOND HANDLING CONCEPTS CORP (DH)
Also Called: Rhcc
41400 Boyce Rd, Fremont (94538-3113)
PHONE..................510 745-7500
James Wilcox, President
Donald Jones, Vice Pres
Al Seiler, Vice Pres
Samantha Barrows, Administration
Danielle Quinones, Administration
EMP: 60
SQ FT: 32,000
SALES (est): 44.7MM Privately Held
WEB: www.raymondhandling.com
SIC: 7699 5084 7359 7629 Industrial machinery & equipment repair; materials handling machinery; equipment rental & leasing; electrical repair shops
HQ: The Raymond Corporation
22 S Canal St
Greene NY 13778
607 656-2311

(P-17534)
RETRONIX INTERNATIONAL INC
Also Called: Retronix Semiconductors
65 Enterprise, Aliso Viejo (92656-2705)
PHONE..................949 388-6930
Anthony Boswell, President
Mark Diamond, COO
Stuart Proctor, Vice Pres
EMP: 90
SQ FT: 5,000
SALES: 7.8MM Privately Held
SIC: 7699 Industrial machinery & equipment repair

(P-17535)
ROTO ROOTER PLUMBING & DRAIN S
2141 Industrial Ct Ste B, Vista (92081-7905)
PHONE..................951 658-8541
Craig Nunez, General Mgr
EMP: 50
SALES (est): 1.4MM Privately Held
SIC: 7699 Sewer cleaning & rodding

(P-17536)
ROTO-ROOTER SERVICES COMPANY
220 Demeter St, East Palo Alto (94303-1303)
PHONE..................650 322-2366
Cory Feverson, Branch Mgr
EMP: 75
SALES (corp-wide): 1.7B Publicly Held
SIC: 7699 Sewer cleaning & rodding
HQ: Roto-Rooter Services Company
255 E 5th St Ste 2500
Cincinnati OH 45202
513 762-6690

(P-17537)
RS CALIBRATION SERVICES INC
1047 Serpentine Ln # 500, Pleasanton (94566-4786)
PHONE..................925 462-4217
Ralph Sabiel, President
EMP: 50
SQ FT: 5,000
SALES (est): 11.2MM Privately Held
WEB: www.rscalibration.com
SIC: 7699 8734 Professional instrument repair services; calibration & certification

(P-17538)
S A CAMP PUMP COMPANY
Also Called: SA Camp Pump and Drilling Co
17876 Zerker Rd, Bakersfield (93308-9221)
P.O. Box 82575 (93380-2575)
PHONE..................661 399-2976
James S Camp, President
Jim McGowen, Sales Engr
John Reiland, Sales Staff
Warren Richardson, Superintendent
Valerie Bailey, Clerk
EMP: 60 EST: 1952
SQ FT: 10,000

SALES (est): 11.5MM
SALES (corp-wide): 18.1MM Privately Held
WEB: www.sacamp.net
SIC: 7699 Agricultural equipment repair services; pumps & pumping equipment
PA: S A Camp Companies
17876 Zerker Rd
Bakersfield CA 93308
661 399-4451

(P-17539)
SCHINDLER ELEVATOR CORPORATION
2000 Avenue Of The Stars, Los Angeles (90067-4700)
PHONE..................310 785-9775
EMP: 88
SALES (corp-wide): 10.9B Privately Held
SIC: 7699 Elevators: inspection, service & repair
HQ: Schindler Elevator Corporation
20 Whippany Rd
Morristown NJ 07960
973 397-6500

(P-17540)
SCHINDLER ELEVATOR CORPORATION
16450 Fthill Blvd Ste 200, Sylmar (91342)
PHONE..................818 336-3000
Lance Howard, Manager
EMP: 240
SALES (corp-wide): 10.9B Privately Held
WEB: www.us.schindler.com
SIC: 7699 Elevators: inspection, service & repair
HQ: Schindler Elevator Corporation
20 Whippany Rd
Morristown NJ 07960
973 397-6500

(P-17541)
SCIENTIFIC CONCEPTS INC
303 Vintage Park Dr # 220, Foster City (94404-1166)
PHONE..................650 578-1142
Charles Morrison Sr, President
Klahn Gboloh Jorbah, Vice Pres
Carol Morrison, Admin Sec
EMP: 350
SQ FT: 23,000
SALES (est): 20.4MM Privately Held
WEB: www.scientificconceptsinc.com
SIC: 7699 Cleaning services

(P-17542)
SEARS ROEBUCK AND CO
100 Brea Mall, Brea (92821-5796)
PHONE..................714 256-7328
EMP: 200
SALES (corp-wide): 16.7B Publicly Held
SIC: 7699
HQ: Sears, Roebuck And Co.
3333 Beverly Rd
Hoffman Estates IL 60179
847 286-2500

(P-17543)
SEARS ROEBUCK AND CO
Also Called: Direct Delivery Center
5691 E Philadelphia St, Ontario (91761-2805)
PHONE..................909 390-4210
EMP: 125
SALES (corp-wide): 16.7B Publicly Held
SIC: 7699 7629
HQ: Sears, Roebuck And Co.
3333 Beverly Rd
Hoffman Estates IL 60179
847 286-2500

(P-17544)
SECURITY CENTRAL INC
Also Called: Reed Brothers Security
4432 Telegraph Ave, Oakland (94609-2018)
PHONE..................510 652-2477
Ronald Reed, President
Michael Salk, Vice Pres
EMP: 51
SQ FT: 19,000

SALES (est): 10.3MM Privately Held
SIC: 7699 5099 3446 5999 Locksmith shop; locks & lock sets; fences or posts, ornamental iron or steel; electronic parts & equipment

(P-17545)
SOUTH BAY SAND BLASTING AND TA
Also Called: Sbsbtc
326 W 30th St, National City (91950-7206)
P.O. Box 13009, San Diego (92170-3009)
PHONE..................619 238-8338
Canuto Lopez, CEO
EMP: 100
SQ FT: 60,000
SALES (est): 13.5MM Privately Held
SIC: 7699 4212 Ship boiler & tank cleaning & repair, contractors; ship scaling, contractors; hazardous waste transport

(P-17546)
SOUTHBAY SNDBLST & TANK CLG
3589 Dalbergia St, San Diego (92113-3810)
P.O. Box 13009 (92170-3009)
PHONE..................619 238-8338
Adam Juarez, President
EMP: 100 EST: 2015
SALES (est): 703.1K Privately Held
SIC: 7699 4212 Ship boiler & tank cleaning & repair, contractors; ship scaling, contractors; hazardous waste transport

(P-17547)
SPEEDY LOCKSMITH
429 Avnida De La Estrella, San Clemente (92672)
P.O. Box 5075, Oceanside (92052-5075)
PHONE..................760 439-5000
Micky Abdallah, Owner
EMP: 70
SALES: 320K Privately Held
WEB: www.speedylocksmith.com
SIC: 7699 Locksmith shop

(P-17548)
SUNVAIR AEROSPACE GROUP INC (PA)
29145 The Old Rd, Valencia (91355-1015)
PHONE..................661 294-3777
Udo Reider, CEO
Glenn Miller, CFO
Bob Byrd, Opers Staff
EMP: 80 EST: 2014
SQ FT: 77,000
SALES: 30MM Privately Held
SIC: 7699 Aircraft & heavy equipment repair services

(P-17549)
SURVIVAL SYSTEMS INTL INC (PA)
Also Called: Ssi
34140 Valley Center Rd, Valley Center (92082-6017)
P.O. Box 1855 (92082-1855)
PHONE..................760 749-6800
Mark Beatty, Vice Pres
George Beatty, Shareholder
Helen Beatty, Shareholder
Colin Hooper, Vice Pres
Barbara Parker, Accountant
▲ EMP: 95
SQ FT: 100,000
SALES (est): 21.7MM Privately Held
WEB: www.survivalsystemsint.net
SIC: 7699 3531 3086 Industrial equipment services; winches; plastics foam products

(P-17550)
TARSCO HOLDINGS LLC
11905 Regentview Ave, Downey (90241-5515)
PHONE..................562 869-0200
Terry S Warren, Mng Member
Chris Williams, Project Mgr
Malcom Tuggle, Technology
Virjinia Harp, Project Engr
Bill Alumbaugh, Chief Engr
EMP: 121

SALES (est): 4.6MM
SALES (corp-wide): 164.4MM Privately Held
SIC: 7699 Tank repair
PA: T.F. Warren Group Inc
57 Old Onondaga Rd W
Brantford ON N3T 5
519 756-8222

(P-17551)
TECH KNOWLEDGE ASSOCIATES LLC
Also Called: Tka
1 Centerpointe Dr Ste 200, La Palma (90623-2529)
PHONE..................714 735-3810
Joe Randolph, CEO
Ed Wong, CFO
Steve Gilbert, Exec VP
EMP: 80
SALES: 45.2MM
SALES (corp-wide): 15.2B Privately Held
SIC: 7699 Medical equipment repair, non-electric
HQ: St. Joseph Health System
3345 Michelson Dr Ste 100
Irvine CA 92612
949 381-4000

(P-17552)
TED LEVINE DRUM CO (PA)
1817 Chico Ave, South El Monte (91733-2943)
P.O. Box 3246 (91733-0246)
PHONE..................626 579-1084
Ozzie Levine, President
Harvey Kale, COO
Mario Hernandez, Department Mgr
Guillermo Sandoval, Business Mgr
Tom Campbell, Plant Mgr
EMP: 80
SQ FT: 200,000
SALES (est): 14.5MM Privately Held
WEB: www.tldrumco.com
SIC: 7699 4959 3412 Industrial equipment services; sanitary services; metal barrels, drums & pails

(P-17553)
THARP TRUCK RENTAL INC (PA)
Also Called: Depot
15243 Road 192, Porterville (93257-8967)
PHONE..................559 782-5800
Morris A Tharp, CEO
Carol R Tharp, Corp Secy
Casey O Tharp, Vice Pres
◆ EMP: 125
SQ FT: 5,000
SALES (est): 10.1MM Privately Held
WEB: www.emtharp.com
SIC: 7699 5013 5511 5012 Agricultural equipment repair services; motor vehicle supplies & new parts; trucks, tractors & trailers: new & used; automobiles & other motor vehicles

(P-17554)
THYSSENKRUPP ELEVATOR CORP
30984 Santana St, Hayward (94544-7058)
PHONE..................510 476-1900
Homer Guerra, Principal
EMP: 50
SALES (corp-wide): 39.8B Privately Held
SIC: 7699 Elevators: inspection, service & repair
HQ: Thyssenkrupp Elevator Corporation
11605 Haynes Bridge Rd # 650
Alpharetta GA 30009
678 319-3240

(P-17555)
THYSSENKRUPP ELEVATOR CORP
16290 Shoemaker Ave, Cerritos (90703-2241)
PHONE..................323 278-9888
Toll Free:..................877 -
Joe Gonzalles, Manager
Marie Beth Der, Vice Pres
EMP: 50

SALES (corp-wide): 39.8B **Privately Held**
WEB: www.thyssenkruppelevator.com
SIC: 7699 1796 Miscellaneous building item repair services; elevator installation & conversion
HQ: Thyssenkrupp Elevator Corporation
11605 Haynes Bridge Rd # 650
Alpharetta GA 30009
678 319-3240

(P-17556)
TURBINE REPAIR SERVICES LLC (PA)
1838 E Cedar St, Ontario (91761-7763)
PHONE.....................................909 947-2256
Victor M Sanchez, *Mng Member*
Dave Meyer,
Danny Sanchez,
Cesar Siordia,
Michael Dorrel, *Mng Member*
EMP: 56
SQ FT: 12,000
SALES (est): 10.8MM **Privately Held**
WEB: www.steamandgas.com
SIC: 7699 Mechanical instrument repair

(P-17557)
UNITED CALIFORNIA GLASS & DOOR
745 Cesar Chavez, San Francisco
(94124-1211)
PHONE.....................................415 824-8500
Judith Ticktin, *President*
▲ EMP: 70
SQ FT: 31,000
SALES (est): 10.2MM **Privately Held**
WEB: www.ucgd.com
SIC: 7699 1793 Door & window repair; glass & glazing work

(P-17558)
UNITED SERVICE TECH INC
21801 Cactus Ave Ste A, Riverside
(92518-3020)
PHONE.....................................714 224-1406
Robert J Heidkamp, *CEO*
Sandra Smelcer, *Treasurer*
Rodger Smelcer, *Vice Pres*
Greg Haan, *General Mgr*
Terrie Heidkamp, *Admin Sec*
EMP: 56
SQ FT: 2,400
SALES (est): 8.8MM **Privately Held**
SIC: 7699 5963 Industrial equipment services; food services, direct sales

(P-17559)
UNIVERSITY ART CENTER INC (PA)
2550 El Camino Real, Redwood City
(94061-3813)
PHONE.....................................650 328-3500
Lauretta Cappiello, *CEO*
Cornelia Pendleton, *Treasurer*
Charlie Affrunti, *Vice Pres*
Todd Ayers, *General Mgr*
Virginia Biondi, *Admin Sec*
EMP: 75
SQ FT: 24,000
SALES (est): 8.5MM **Privately Held**
SIC: 7699 5947 5999 Picture framing, custom; gift shop; artists' supplies & materials; drafting equipment & supplies

(P-17560)
UPWIND BLADE SOLUTIONS INC
2869 Historic Decatur Rd # 100, San Diego
(92106-6176)
PHONE.....................................866 927-3142
Marty Crotty, *CEO*
Bo Thisted, *President*
Bryan Coggins, *CFO*
EMP: 149 EST: 2011
SALES (est): 3MM
SALES (corp-wide): 11.6B **Privately Held**
SIC: 7699 Pumps & pumping equipment repair
HQ: Upwind Solutions, Inc.
2869 Historic Decatur Rd # 100
San Diego CA 92106

(P-17561)
VSS SALES INC (PA)
Also Called: Vss Compressor Service
16220 Garfield Ave, Paramount
(90723-4804)
PHONE.....................................562 630-0606
Thomas F Vaughan, *President*
David Newton, *Treasurer*
Keven Vaughan, *Vice Pres*
Patricia Vaughan, *Vice Pres*
EMP: 60
SQ FT: 10,000
SALES (est): 4.5MM **Privately Held**
WEB: www.vsssales.com
SIC: 7699 1796 1711 Industrial equipment services; installing building equipment; mechanical contractor

(P-17562)
WARDLOW 2 LP (PA)
333 S Grand Ave Ste 4070, Los Angeles
(90071-1544)
PHONE.....................................562 432-8066
Steven B McLeod, *Partner*
Joe Gregorio, *Partner*
Alvin Adams, *Vice Pres*
Scott Baker, *General Mgr*
Sean Nicolello, *General Mgr*
EMP: 99
SALES (est): 53.3MM **Privately Held**
WEB: www.brockwaymoran.com
SIC: 7699 Construction equipment repair

(P-17563)
WESTERN PUMP INC (PA)
3235 F St, San Diego (92102-3315)
PHONE.....................................619 239-9988
Dennis Rethmeier, *CEO*
Ryan Rethmeier, *President*
Janice C Rethmeier, *Corp Secy*
Vania Defrates, *Accountant*
Janet Rethmeier, *Human Res Dir*
▲ EMP: 55
SQ FT: 10,000
SALES (est): 13.9MM **Privately Held**
WEB: www.westernpump.com
SIC: 7699 5084 1799 3728 Tank repair & cleaning services; petroleum industry machinery; petroleum storage tanks, pumping & draining; aircraft parts & equipment

(P-17564)
WEYGANDT & ASSOCIATES
Also Called: Weco Aerospace Systems
1501 Avi Blvd Ste 100, Lincoln (95648)
PHONE.....................................916 543-0431
William Weygandt, *President*
Harold Weygandt, *President*
EMP: 50
SQ FT: 7,800
SALES (est): 3.3MM **Privately Held**
SIC: 7699 Aircraft & heavy equipment repair services

7812 Motion Picture & Video Tape Production

(P-17565)
A ITS LAUGH PRODUCTIONS INC
Also Called: Would You Rather - Season 1
914 N Victory Blvd, Burbank (91502-1632)
PHONE.....................................818 848-8787
Amanda C Ramey, *CEO*
EMP: 100
SALES (est): 410.7K **Privately Held**
SIC: 7812 Video production

(P-17566)
ABC FAMILY WORLDWIDE INC (DH)
500 S Buena Vista St, Burbank
(91521-0001)
PHONE.....................................818 560-1000
Robert A Iger, *President*
EMP: 500
SALES (est): 45.9MM
SALES (corp-wide): 90.2B **Publicly Held**
SIC: 7812 4841 Cartoon production, television; cable & other pay television services

(P-17567)
ABM DISTRIBUTORS INC
811 W 7th St Ste 1040, Los Angeles
(90017-3408)
PHONE.....................................310 401-0434
Alander Pulliam, *CEO*
EMP: 87
SALES (est): 555K **Privately Held**
SIC: 7812 Television film production

(P-17568)
ACCESS HOLLYWOOD LLC
100 Universal City Plz, Universal City
(91608-1002)
PHONE.....................................818 684-7000
Tom Cast, *Mng Member*
Rahul Singh, *Vice Pres*
Ofri Afek, *Associate Dir*
Christopher Boone, *Associate Dir*
Johnathon Britz, *Associate Dir*
EMP: 91
SALES (est): 2.4MM **Privately Held**
SIC: 7812 7313 Video production; electronic media advertising representatives

(P-17569)
ADVANCED DIGITAL SERVICES INC (PA)
Also Called: A D S
948 N Cahuenga Blvd, Los Angeles
(90038-2615)
PHONE.....................................323 962-8585
Thomas Engdahl, *President*
Andrew McIntyre, *Ch of Bd*
Brad Weyl, *COO*
Valerie Kroll, *Vice Pres*
Han Nguyen, *Technology*
▲ EMP: 87
SQ FT: 33,000
SALES (est): 8.8MM **Privately Held**
WEB: www.adshollywood.com
SIC: 7812 7819 Video tape production; film processing, editing & titling: motion picture

(P-17570)
ALLDAYEVERYDAY PRODUCTIONS LLC
2028 E 7th St, Los Angeles (90021-1302)
PHONE.....................................323 556-6200
Arrow Kruse,
Ross Vinstein, *CFO*
Michael Karbelnikoff, *Finance*
EMP: 50 EST: 2014
SQ FT: 5,000
SALES (est): 1MM **Privately Held**
SIC: 7812 Video production

(P-17571)
ALLIED ENTERTAINMENT GROUP INC (PA)
Also Called: Allied Artists International
273 W Allen Ave, City of Industry (91746)
PHONE.....................................626 330-0600
Greg Hammond, *President*
Robert Fitzpatrick, *Treasurer*
John Mason, *Vice Pres*
Ashley D Posner, *Vice Pres*
Kim Richards, *Admin Sec*
◆ EMP: 900
SQ FT: 60,000
SALES: 30MM **Privately Held**
SIC: 7812 Motion picture & video production

(P-17572)
AMBLIN/RELIANCE HOLDING CO LLC
Also Called: Story Teller
100 Universal City Plz, Universal City
(91608-1002)
PHONE.....................................818 733-6272
Lindson Harding, *Mng Member*
EMP: 99
SALES (est): 2.5MM **Privately Held**
SIC: 7812 7929 Motion picture production; entertainment group

(P-17573)
AND SYNDICATED PRODUCTIONS INC
3500 W Olive Ave Ste 1000, Burbank
(91505-5515)
PHONE.....................................818 308-5200

▲ EMP: 100
SALES (est): 6.2MM **Privately Held**
SIC: 7812

(P-17574)
ANE PRODUCTIONS INC
3500 W Olive Ave Ste 1000, Burbank
(91505-5515)
PHONE.....................................818 972-0777
EMP: 60
SALES (est): 883.9K **Privately Held**
SIC: 7812 Motion picture production & distribution, television

(P-17575)
ANONYMOUS CONTENT LLC (PA)
3532 Hayden Ave, Culver City
(90232-2413)
PHONE.....................................310 558-6000
Steven Golin,
Matthew Velkes, *COO*
Carolyn Govers, *Manager*
Kami Putnam-Heist, *Agent*
▲ EMP: 60 EST: 1999
SALES: 250MM **Privately Held**
WEB: www.anonymouscontent.com
SIC: 7812 Video production

(P-17576)
ARTISAN ENTERTAINMENT INC
2700 Colorado Ave Ste 200, Santa Monica
(90404-5502)
PHONE.....................................310 449-9200
Wayne Levin, *President*
James W Barge, *CFO*
Brian James Gladstone, *Exec VP*
Kristine Klimczak, *Exec VP*
Nicolas Van Dyk, *Exec VP*
EMP: 1000
SALES: 341MM
SALES (corp-wide): 3.6B **Privately Held**
SIC: 7812 Motion picture production; motion picture production & distribution; music video production; video tape production
HQ: Lions Gate Entertainment Inc.
2700 Colorado Ave Ste 200
Santa Monica CA 90404
310 449-9200

(P-17577)
ASSOCIATED ENTRMT RELEASING (PA)
Also Called: Associated Television Intl
4401 Wilshire Blvd, Los Angeles
(90010-3703)
P.O. Box 4180 (90078-4180)
PHONE.....................................323 934-7044
David McKenzie, *President*
Murray Drechsler, *CFO*
Murray Dreschler, *CFO*
Richard Casares, *Exec VP*
Barry Thurston, *Administration*
EMP: 50 EST: 1976
SQ FT: 35,000
SALES (est): 10.5MM **Privately Held**
WEB: www.associatedtelevision.com
SIC: 7812 Motion picture production & distribution

(P-17578)
ATLAS DIGITAL LLC (PA)
170 S Flower St, Burbank (91502-2122)
P.O. Box 4110 (91503-4110)
PHONE.....................................323 762-2626
Shawn Sanbar, *Owner*
Carrie Iino, *Admin Mgr*
Steve Sauber, *Software Dev*
Greg Evanski, *Technician*
Ryan Hammer, *Technician*
EMP: 75
SQ FT: 13,000
SALES (est): 12.8MM **Privately Held**
SIC: 7812 Video production

(P-17579)
ATLAS ENTERTAINMENT INC
9200 W Sunset Blvd Ste 10, West Hollywood (90069-3608)
PHONE.....................................310 786-4900
Charles V Roven, *President*
Dennis Gore, *Executive*
Rebecca Roven, *Executive*
EMP: 50

SALES (est): 3.2MM **Privately Held**
SIC: 7812 Motion picture production & distribution

(P-17580)
AVOCA PRODUCTIONS INC
Also Called: The Newly Wed
10202 Washington Blvd, Culver City
(90232-3119)
PHONE..................310 244-4000
Steve Mosko, *President*
EMP: 60
SALES (est): 1.1MM **Privately Held**
WEB: www.sonypictures.com
SIC: 7812 Television film production
HQ: Sony Pictures Entertainment, Inc.
10202 Washington Blvd
Culver City CA 90232
310 244-4000

(P-17581)
BACHELOR PRODUCTIONS INC
2121 Avenue Of The Stars, Los Angeles
(90067-5010)
PHONE..................310 567-9249
Desiree Varni, *Accountant*
EMP: 99
SALES (est): 850.1K **Privately Held**
SIC: 7812 Motion picture & video production

(P-17582)
BENTO BOX ENTERTAINMENT LLC
5161 Lankershim Blvd, North Hollywood
(91601-4962)
PHONE..................818 333-7700
Scott Greenberg, *CEO*
Joel Kuwahara, *President*
Brett Coker, *COO*
Kyel White, *Production*
EMP: 300
SALES (est): 7.3MM
SALES (corp-wide): 11.3B **Publicly Held**
SIC: 7812 Motion picture production & distribution
HQ: Fox Television Stations, Inc.
1999 S Bundy Dr
Los Angeles CA 90025
310 584-2000

(P-17583)
BLAIR TELEVISION INC
Also Called: Blair TV Communication
11111 Santa Monica Blvd # 1900, Los Angeles (90025-3333)
PHONE..................714 537-5923
Nancy Dodson, *Manager*
EMP: 55 **Privately Held**
SIC: 7812 Motion picture & video production
HQ: Blair Television Inc
200 Park Ave Fl 17
New York NY 10166
212 230-5900

(P-17584)
BRENTWOOD CMMNCATIONS INTL INC
Also Called: BCII
16135 Roscoe Blvd, North Hills
(91343-6226)
PHONE..................818 333-3680
Bud W Brutsman, *President*
EMP: 50
SALES (est): 5.8MM **Privately Held**
SIC: 7812 Television film production

(P-17585)
BRILLSTEIN ENTRMT PARTNERS LLC (PA)
Also Called: Brillstein Grey Entertainment
9150 Wilshire Blvd # 350, Beverly Hills
(90212-3427)
PHONE..................310 205-5100
Brad Grey, *President*
Eliza Walper, *Manager*
EMP: 290
SALES (est): 19.9MM **Privately Held**
SIC: 7812 Television film production

(P-17586)
BUNIM-MURRAY PRODUCTIONS
Also Called: Bmp
1015 Grandview Ave, Glendale
(91201-2205)
PHONE..................818 756-5100
Jonathan Murray, *CEO*
▲ EMP: 150
SQ FT: 20,000
SALES (est): 18.9MM
SALES (corp-wide): 12.6MM **Privately Held**
SIC: 7812 Television film production
HQ: Banijay Entertainment
5 Rue Francois 1er
Paris 75008
143 189-191

(P-17587)
BVS ENTERTAINMENT INC (DH)
500 S Buena Vista St, Burbank
(91521-0001)
PHONE..................818 460-6917
Griffith Foxley, *President*
David K Thompson, *Admin Sec*
EMP: 50
SQ FT: 111,000
SALES (est): 5.8MM
SALES (corp-wide): 90.2B **Publicly Held**
SIC: 7812 7822 Cartoon production, television; motion picture distribution; television & video tape distribution
HQ: Abc Family Worldwide, Inc.
500 S Buena Vista St
Burbank CA 91521
818 560-1000

(P-17588)
CAFFEINE PRODUCTIONS
1040 N Las Palmas Ave, Los Angeles
(90038-2409)
PHONE..................323 860-8111
Jen Gore, *Director*
Greg Choa, *Owner*
EMP: 80
SQ FT: 10,000
SALES (est): 890.6K
SALES (corp-wide): 13.2B **Publicly Held**
WEB: www.caffeineproductions.com
SIC: 7812 Television film production
HQ: Comedy Partners
345 Hudson St Fl 9
New York NY 10014

(P-17589)
CARA COMMUNICATIONS CORP
Also Called: Vin Dibona Productions
12233 W Olympic Blvd # 170, Los Angeles
(90064-1034)
PHONE..................310 442-5600
Vincent Dibona, *President*
Lisa Black, *Exec VP*
Sharon Arnett, *Vice Pres*
Bayard Jones, *Vice Pres*
Philip Shafran, *Director*
EMP: 50
SALES (est): 4.4MM **Privately Held**
SIC: 7812 7819 7922 Television film production; directors, independent; motion picture; television program, including commercial producers

(P-17590)
CINOVATION INC
6527 San Fernando Rd, Glendale
(91201-2108)
P.O. Box 909, Pacific Palisades (90272-0909)
PHONE..................818 246-3160
Rick Baker, *President*
EMP: 100
SQ FT: 24,000
SALES (est): 1.9MM **Privately Held**
SIC: 7812 Motion picture production

(P-17591)
CNX MEDIA INC
1 Beach St Ste 300, San Francisco
(94133-1228)
PHONE..................415 229-8300
James Hornthal, *Ch of Bd*
Allan Horlick, *President*
Angela Pumo Cohen, *Exec VP*
EMP: 90
SQ FT: 15,000

SALES (est): 5.1MM **Privately Held**
SIC: 7812 Video tape production

(P-17592)
COLUMBIA PICTURES INDS INC (DH)
10202 Washington Blvd, Culver City
(90232-3119)
PHONE..................310 244-4000
Michael Lynton, *CEO*
Doug Belgrad, *President*
Andrew Gumpert, *President*
Hannah Minghella, *President*
Matt Tolmach, *President*
EMP: 200
SALES (est): 70.1MM **Privately Held**
WEB: www.columbiapictures.com
SIC: 7812 Motion picture production & distribution
HQ: Sony Pictures Entertainment, Inc.
10202 Washington Blvd
Culver City CA 90232
310 244-4000

(P-17593)
CORPORATE PRODUCTION DESIGNS
1427 Goodman Ave, Redondo Beach
(90278-4004)
PHONE..................310 937-9663
Bill Ganz, *President*
EMP: 50 EST: 1997
SALES (est): 1.7MM **Privately Held**
SIC: 7812 Video production

(P-17594)
CYBERNET ENTERTAINMENT LLC (PA)
1800 Mission St, San Francisco
(94103-3502)
PHONE..................415 865-0230
Peter Ackworth, *Mng Member*
Matthew Devney, *Administration*
Adam Boyd, *HR Admin*
Matt Slusarenko, *Director*
EMP: 93
SALES (est): 11.6MM **Privately Held**
SIC: 7812 Video production

(P-17595)
DALAKLIS MCKEOWN ENTERTAINMENT
2517 Crest Dr, Manhattan Beach
(90266-2135)
PHONE..................310 545-0120
Charles Dalaklis, *President*
Theresa McKeown, *COO*
EMP: 75
SQ FT: 12,000
SALES (est): 13.5MM **Privately Held**
WEB: www.dmetv.net
SIC: 7812 Television film production

(P-17596)
DCP RIGHTS LLC
2900 Olympic Blvd, Santa Monica
(90404-4127)
PHONE..................310 255-4600
Allen Shapiro, *President*
Kyla Druckman, *Sales Mgr*
EMP: 50
SQ FT: 45,637
SALES (est): 403.6K **Privately Held**
SIC: 7812 Motion picture & video production

(P-17597)
DELUXE MEDIA SERVICES LLC
1377 N Serrano Ave, Los Angeles
(90027-5623)
PHONE..................323 462-6171
John Suh, *Principal*
EMP: 900 EST: 2012
SALES (est): 44.2MM **Privately Held**
SIC: 7812 Video production

(P-17598)
DIGITAL DOMAIN 30 INC (PA)
12641 Beatrice St, Los Angeles
(90066-7003)
PHONE..................310 314-2800
Daniel Seah, *CEO*
Frank Ming WEI, *Vice Chairman*
Od Welch, *President*
Amit Chopra, *COO*

Samantha McConnell, *Technical Staff*
EMP: 300
SALES: 75MM **Privately Held**
SIC: 7812 Video production

(P-17599)
DIGITAL KITCHEN LLC
3585 Hayden Ave, Culver City
(90232-2412)
PHONE..................310 499-9255
Cythia Bimon, *Manager*
EMP: 50 **Privately Held**
SIC: 7812 7819 Video production; services allied to motion pictures
HQ: Digital Kitchen, Llc
600 W Fulton St Ste 400
Chicago IL 60661

(P-17600)
DISNEY ENTERPRISES INC
3235 S Buena Vista St, Burbank
(91521-0001)
PHONE..................818 560-3692
EMP: 300
SALES (corp-wide): 90.2B **Publicly Held**
SIC: 7812 Television film production
HQ: Disney Enterprises, Inc.
500 S Buena Vista St
Burbank CA 91521
818 560-1000

(P-17601)
DISNEY INCORPORATED (DH)
500 S Buena Vista St, Burbank
(91521-0001)
PHONE..................818 560-1000
Matthew L McGinnis, *CEO*
▲ EMP: 150
SALES (est): 30.3MM
SALES (corp-wide): 90.2B **Publicly Held**
WEB: www.wdwnews.com
SIC: 7812 Motion picture production & distribution
HQ: Disney Enterprises, Inc.
500 S Buena Vista St
Burbank CA 91521
818 560-1000

(P-17602)
DUCKPUNK PRODUCTIONS INC
10728 Westminster Ave, Los Angeles
(90034-5516)
PHONE..................310 836-3818
Mellissa Tong, *President*
EMP: 100
SALES: 202.3K **Privately Held**
SIC: 7812 7311 7335 7819 Commercials, television: tape or film; advertising agencies; commercial photography; services allied to motion pictures; directors, independent: motion picture

(P-17603)
DW STUDIOS PRODUCTIONS LLC (PA)
Also Called: Blades of Glory
100 Universal City Plz, Universal City
(91608-1002)
PHONE..................818 733-9631
Mark Sayles, *Mng Member*
EMP: 50
SALES (est): 831.7K **Privately Held**
WEB: www.bladesofglory.com
SIC: 7812 Motion picture production

(P-17604)
DWA HOLDINGS LLC (HQ)
1000 Flower St, Glendale (91201-3007)
PHONE..................818 695-5000
Mellody Hobson, *Ch of Bd*
Ann Daly, *President*
Jeffrey Katzenberg, *CEO*
Fazal Merchant, *CFO*
Steven A Adams,
EMP: 61
SQ FT: 500,000
SALES (est): 824.2MM
SALES (corp-wide): 94.5B **Publicly Held**
WEB: www.dreamworksanimation.com
SIC: 7812 Cartoon motion picture production
PA: Comcast Corporation
1701 Jfk Blvd
Philadelphia PA 19103
215 286-1700

(P-17605)
EARTHBOUND PRODUCTIONS LLC
849 N Occidental Blvd, Los Angeles (90026-2925)
PHONE....................504 734-3337
Mandy M Gagliardi,
EMP: 100
SALES (est): 984.1K Privately Held
SIC: 7812 Television film production

(P-17606)
EFILM LLC
Also Called: E Film Digital Labratories
1144 N Las Palmas Ave, Los Angeles (90038-1209)
PHONE....................323 463-7041
Aria Mehrabi,
Terry Morrison, Senior Engr
Mitch P Infuses, Opers Staff
Brian Shinkle, Facilities Mgr
Dominik J Schmidt,
EMP: 150
SALES (est): 14.2MM Privately Held
WEB: www.efilm.com
SIC: 7812 Video production
HQ: Deluxe Laboratories, Inc.
2400 W Empire Ave
Burbank CA 91504
323 462-6171

(P-17607)
FILM ROMAN LLC
6320 Canoga Ave Ste 450, Woodland Hills (91367-2561)
PHONE....................818 748-4000
Dana Booton, Manager
EMP: 200
SQ FT: 87,000
SALES (corp-wide): 3.6B Privately Held
SIC: 7812 Cartoon motion picture production; cartoon production, television
HQ: Film Roman, Llc.
8900 Liberty Cir
Englewood CO 80112
720 852-6327

(P-17608)
FILM ROMAN LLC
6320 Canoga Ave Ste 450, Woodland Hills (91367-2561)
PHONE....................818 748-4000
EMP: 200
SQ FT: 81,000
SALES (est): 7.5MM Privately Held
SIC: 7812 Television film production

(P-17609)
FILMQUEST PICTURES CORPORATION
15331 Stonewood Ter, Sherman Oaks (91403-4917)
PHONE....................818 905-1006
Eric Steven Stahl, President
EMP: 175
SALES (est): 3.6MM Privately Held
SIC: 7812 Motion picture production & distribution

(P-17610)
FOX ANIMATION STUDIOS INC
5700 Wilshire Blvd # 325, Los Angeles (90036-3659)
PHONE....................323 857-8800
John McKenna, President
▲ EMP: 310
SALES (est): 7.4MM
SALES (corp-wide): 90.2B Publicly Held
WEB: www.foxmovies.com
SIC: 7812 Motion picture production & distribution; video tape production; motion picture production & distribution, television; cartoon motion picture production
HQ: Twentieth Century Fox Film Corporation
10201 W Pico Blvd
Los Angeles CA 90064
310 369-1000

(P-17611)
FRIENDS OF MAX ROSE LLC
1639 11th St Ste 260, Santa Monica (90404-3759)
PHONE....................424 901-1260
Paul Currie,

EMP: 58 EST: 2011
SALES (est): 1MM Privately Held
SIC: 7812 Motion picture production

(P-17612)
GLOBAL ASYLUM INCORPORATED
Also Called: Asylum, The
440 W Los Feliz Rd, Glendale (91204-2776)
PHONE....................323 850-1214
Paul Bales, CFO
EMP: 50 EST: 1997
SALES: 3.9MM Privately Held
SIC: 7812 Motion picture production & distribution

(P-17613)
GLOBAL EAGLE ENTERTAINMENT INC
2941 Alton Pkwy, Irvine (92606-5142)
PHONE....................949 608-8700
Rick Warren,
EMP: 140 Publicly Held
SIC: 7812 Video production
PA: Global Eagle Entertainment Inc.
6080 Center Dr Ste 1200
Los Angeles CA 90045

(P-17614)
HARPO PRODUCTIONS INC
Also Called: Harpo Entertainment Group
1041 N Formosa Ave, West Hollywood (90046-6703)
PHONE....................312 633-1000
Oprah Winfrey, Ch of Bd
Tim Bennett, President
Doug Pattison, CFO
Bill Becker, Vice Pres
EMP: 200
SQ FT: 100,000
SALES (est): 15.5MM Privately Held
SIC: 7812 Television film production; video tape production

(P-17615)
HELINET AVIATION SERVICES LLC (PA)
16303 Waterman Dr, Van Nuys (91406-1222)
PHONE....................818 902-0229
Jim McGowan, President
Kathryn Purwin, Ch of Bd
EMP: 53
SQ FT: 10,000
SALES (est): 9MM Privately Held
SIC: 7812 7359 4522 Motion picture & video production; aircraft & industrial truck rental services; helicopter carriers, nonscheduled

(P-17616)
HIGHPOINT PRODUCTIONS INC
13400 Rverside Dr Ste 300, Sherman Oaks (91423)
PHONE....................818 728-7600
Gary Benz, President
Michael Branton, Vice Pres
EMP: 100
SALES (est): 9.4MM Privately Held
WEB: www.grbtv.com
SIC: 7812 Television film production

(P-17617)
HISTORIC TW INC
Also Called: Time Warner
106 Disney Productions, Burbank (91521-0001)
PHONE....................818 954-3096
Alan Horn, CEO
EMP: 50
SALES (corp-wide): 170.7B Publicly Held
SIC: 7812 3652 Motion picture & video production; master records or tapes, preparation of
HQ: Historic Tw Inc.
75 Rockefeller Plz
New York NY 10019
-

(P-17618)
IGNITION CREATIVE LLC
12959 Coral Tree Pl, Los Angeles (90066-7020)
PHONE....................310 315-6300
Ron Moler,
Jenna Doneen, Vice Pres
Paul Spencer, Creative Dir
Madeleine Schnell, Production
Jason Wright, Facilities Mgr
EMP: 65
SALES (est): 12MM Privately Held
WEB: www.ignitionla.com
SIC: 7812 Video production

(P-17619)
JEOPARDY PRODUCTIONS INC
10202 Washington Blvd, Culver City (90232-3119)
PHONE....................310 244-8855
Rocky Schmitt, CEO
EMP: 125 EST: 1984
SALES (est): 2MM Privately Held
WEB: www.jeopardy.com
SIC: 7812 Television film production
HQ: Sony Pictures Entertainment, Inc.
10202 Washington Blvd
Culver City CA 90232
310 244-4000

(P-17620)
JIM HENSON COMPANY INC (PA)
Also Called: Henson Recording Studio
1416 N La Brea Ave, Los Angeles (90028-7506)
PHONE....................323 856-6680
Lisa Henson, CEO
Cheryl Henson, President
Peter Schube, President
Halle Stanford, President
Brian Henson, CEO
EMP: 55
SQ FT: 7,000
SALES (est): 8.5MM Privately Held
WEB: www.farscape.com
SIC: 7812 Motion picture production & distribution; television film production

(P-17621)
KINGDOM ENTERPRISE FILMS LLC
10812 Bothwell Rd, Chatsworth (91311-1915)
PHONE....................818 963-2513
Gregory Nalbandian,
Armando Talian,
EMP: 50
SALES (est): 250.6K Privately Held
SIC: 7812 Motion picture & video production

(P-17622)
LEGEND3D INC
1500 N El Centro Ave # 100, Los Angeles (90028-9229)
PHONE....................858 793-4420
Ian Jessel, President
Tom Sinnott, COO
Steven Wolkenstein, CFO
Barry Sandrew, Ch Credit Ofcr
Matt Akey, Chief Mktg Ofcr
EMP: 86 EST: 2002
SQ FT: 50,000
SALES (est): 15MM Privately Held
SIC: 7812 Motion picture & video production

(P-17623)
LEMONLIGHT MEDIA INC
226 S Glasgow Ave, Inglewood (90301-2106)
PHONE....................310 402-0275
Hope Horner, CEO
EMP: 67
SALES (est): 445.9K Privately Held
SIC: 7812 Video tape production

(P-17624)
LINNE ENTERTAINMENT LLC
1250 N June St Apt 305, Los Angeles (90038-1387)
PHONE....................213 425-1146
Eric Hall,
EMP: 50

SALES (est): 15.2K Privately Held
SIC: 7812 7389 Motion picture & video production;

(P-17625)
LIONS GATE ENTERTAINMENT INC (HQ)
2700 Colorado Ave Ste 200, Santa Monica (90404-5502)
PHONE....................310 449-9200
Jon Feltheimer, Ch of Bd
Steven Beeks, President
Joseph Drake, President
Erik Feig, President
Jared Goetz, President
EMP: 55
SALES (est): 2.1B
SALES (corp-wide): 3.6B Privately Held
SIC: 7812 Motion picture production & distribution
PA: Lions Gate Entertainment Corp
250 Howe St Fl 20
Vancouver BC V6C 3
877 848-3866

(P-17626)
LIONS GATE FILMS INC
2700 Colorado Ave Ste 200, Santa Monica (90404-5502)
PHONE....................310 449-9200
Jon Feltheimer, President
Steve Beeks, COO
James Keegan, CFO
Eli Cotham, Vice Pres
David Diamond, Vice Pres
EMP: 147
SQ FT: 30,000
SALES (est): 10MM
SALES (corp-wide): 3.6B Privately Held
WEB: www.lionsgatefilms.com
SIC: 7812 Motion picture production
HQ: Lions Gate Entertainment Inc.
2700 Colorado Ave Ste 200
Santa Monica CA 90404
310 449-9200

(P-17627)
LMNO PRODUCTIONS INC
Also Called: Lmno Cable Group
15821 Ventura Blvd # 320, Encino (91436-2928)
PHONE....................818 995-5555
Eric Schotz, President
Reggie Carter, Partner
Ned Davis, Vice Pres
Ed Horowitz, Vice Pres
David Reed, Info Tech Mgr
EMP: 200
SALES (est): 14.6MM Privately Held
SIC: 7812 Television film production

(P-17628)
LOOKOUT PRODUCTIONS LLC
3748 W 9th St Apt 403, Los Angeles (90019-2117)
PHONE....................310 408-5687
Gustavo Morales, Mng Member
Douglas Wirth,
EMP: 50
SQ FT: 1,500
SALES (est): 559.9K Privately Held
SIC: 7812 Motion picture & video production

(P-17629)
LUCASFILM LTD LLC (DH)
Also Called: Lucasfilm Coml Productions
1110 Gorgas Ave Bldg C-Hr, San Francisco (94129-1406)
P.O. Box 29901 (94129-0901)
PHONE....................415 623-1000
Kathleen Kennedy, President
Doug Chiang, Vice Pres
Rayne Roberts, Executive
Hank Foo, Executive Asst
Kathleen Rodriguez, Executive Asst
▲ EMP: 250
SALES (est): 59.6MM
SALES (corp-wide): 90.2B Publicly Held
WEB: www.lucasfilm.com
SIC: 7812 6794 Motion picture production & distribution; television film production; patent owners & lessors

P
R
O
D
U
C
T
S

&

S
V
C
S

(P-17630)
MARK HERZOG & COMPANY INC
4640 Lankershim Blvd, North Hollywood (91602-1841)
PHONE..................818 762-4640
Mark Herzog, *President*
Raleigh Stewart, *Creative Dir*
EMP: 64
SQ FT: 12,500
SALES (est): 6.3MM **Privately Held**
WEB: www.herzogproductions.com
SIC: 7812 Television film production

(P-17631)
MEDIA VNTURES ENTRMT GROUP LLC
1547 14th St, Santa Monica (90404-3302)
PHONE..................310 260-3171
Hans Zimmer, *President*
Blane Snyder, *Accounts Exec*
EMP: 50
SALES (est): 1.3MM **Privately Held**
SIC: 7812 Video tape production

(P-17632)
MEDIAPLATFORM INC
Also Called: Vcall
8383 Wilshire Blvd # 460, Beverly Hills (90211-2446)
PHONE..................310 909-8410
Jim McGovern, *CEO*
Mike Newman, *President*
Dena Kendros, *Vice Pres*
Craig Myers, *Vice Pres*
Eugene Kovnatsky, *CTO*
EMP: 60
SALES (est): 3.2MM **Publicly Held**
WEB: www.vodium.com
SIC: 7812 7819 7822 8743 Motion picture & video production; services allied to motion pictures; motion picture & tape distribution; public relations services
HQ: Precisionir Group Inc.
601 Moorefield Park Dr
North Chesterfield VA

(P-17633)
MERLOT FILM PRODUCTIONS INC
Also Called: CBS Network News
7800 Beverly Blvd, Los Angeles (90036-2112)
PHONE..................323 575-2906
Bruce C Taub, *CEO*
Lesile Moondes, *President*
David Strauss, *CFO*
Claudia E Morf, *Treasurer*
Leo Gorius, *Vice Pres*
EMP: 200
SALES (est): 6MM
SALES (corp-wide): 25.9B **Publicly Held**
SIC: 7812 4833 Motion picture & video production; television broadcasting stations
HQ: Cbs Broadcasting Inc.
524 W 57th St
New York NY 10019
212 975-4321

(P-17634)
METHOD STUDIOS LLC
3401 Exposition Blvd, Santa Monica (90404-5050)
PHONE..................310 434-6500
Ed Ulbrich, *President*
Deborah Giarratana, *Vice Pres*
Aidan Thomas, *Creative Dir*
Andrew Bell, *Managing Dir*
David Toepfer, *Technology*
EMP: 68 EST: 2007
SALES (est): 5.2MM **Privately Held**
SIC: 7812 Video production
HQ: Deluxe Entertainment Services Group Inc.
2400 W Empire Ave
Burbank CA 91504

(P-17635)
METRO-GOLDWYN-MAYER INC (DH)
Also Called: MGM
245 N Beverly Dr, Beverly Hills (90210-5319)
PHONE..................310 449-3000
Gary Barber, *CEO*
Ken Schapiro, *COO*
Kenneth Kay, *CFO*
Katie Martin Kelley, *Officer*
John Bryan, *Exec VP*
EMP: 300
SQ FT: 131,400
SALES (est): 116.9MM
SALES (corp-wide): 1.1B **Privately Held**
WEB: www.mgm.com
SIC: 7812 Motion picture production & distribution; motion picture production & distribution, television; television film production; video production
HQ: Mgm Holdings Ii, Inc.
245 N Beverly Dr
Beverly Hills CA 90210
310 449-3000

(P-17636)
MIRAMAX FILM NY LLC (HQ)
1901 Avenue Of The Stars # 2000, Los Angeles (90067-6021)
PHONE..................310 409-4321
Steven Schoch, *CEO*
EMP: 80
SALES (est): 8MM
SALES (corp-wide): 9.3MM **Privately Held**
SIC: 7812 Video production
PA: Bein Media Group Wll
Behind Ahli Hospital, Al Asmakh
Tower No. 864, Zone 63
Doha
445 770-11

(P-17637)
NEP GROUP INC
Screenworks Nep
1580 Magnolia Ave, Corona (92879-2073)
PHONE..................951 279-8877
Tom McCracken, *Branch Mgr*
EMP: 50
SALES (corp-wide): 119.2MM **Privately Held**
SIC: 7812 Television film production
PA: Nep Group, Inc.
2 Beta Dr
Pittsburgh PA 15238
412 826-1414

(P-17638)
NEP GROUP INC
7635 Airport Bus Pkwy, Van Nuys (91406)
PHONE..................412 423-1354
EMP: 100
SALES (corp-wide): 119.2MM **Privately Held**
SIC: 7812 Television film production
PA: Nep Group, Inc.
2 Beta Dr
Pittsburgh PA 15238
412 826-1414

(P-17639)
NETFLIX PRODUCTIONS LLC
Also Called: Black Excellence
5555 Melrose Ave, Los Angeles (90038-3989)
PHONE..................323 960-3457
Donald Wygal, *CEO*
EMP: 200
SALES (est): 556.3K **Privately Held**
SIC: 7812 Television film production

(P-17640)
NEW PARADIGM PRODUCTIONS INC (PA)
Also Called: Edelman Productions
39 Mesa St Ste 212, San Francisco (94129-1019)
PHONE..................415 924-8000
Steve Edelman, *President*
EMP: 100
SQ FT: 8,500
SALES (est): 19.7MM **Privately Held**
WEB: www.edelmanproductions.com
SIC: 7812 Video production

(P-17641)
NEW REGENCY PRODUCTIONS INC (PA)
Also Called: Regency Enterprises
10201 W Pico Blvd Bldg 12, Los Angeles (90064-2606)
PHONE..................310 369-8300
Arnon Milchan, *Principal*
Yariv Milchan, *President*
Brad Weston, *CEO*
Jonathan Fischer, *COO*
Mimi Mtseng, *CFO*
▼ EMP: 60
SQ FT: 13,000
SALES (est): 8.4MM **Privately Held**
WEB: www.newregency.com
SIC: 7812 Video production

(P-17642)
NOVASTAR POST INC
23466 Hatteras St, Woodland Hills (91367-3020)
P.O. Box 25724, Miami FL (33102-5724)
PHONE..................323 467-5020
Greg Geddes, *President*
Bob Sky, *Vice Pres*
EMP: 50
SQ FT: 7,900
SALES (est): 1.5MM **Privately Held**
WEB: www.novastarpost.com
SIC: 7812 Audio-visual program production

(P-17643)
NW ENTERTAINMENT INC (PA)
Also Called: New Wave Entertainment
2660 W Olive Ave, Burbank (91505-4525)
PHONE..................818 295-5000
Paul Apel, *CEO*
Brian Volk-Weiss, *President*
Kieran Dotti, *COO*
Greg Woertz, *CFO*
Gary Lister, *Senior VP*
▲ EMP: 101
SQ FT: 40,000
SALES (est): 16.6MM **Privately Held**
WEB: www.newwaveent.com
SIC: 7812 Motion picture production

(P-17644)
ORION PICTURES CORPORATION
245 N Beverly Dr, Beverly Hills (90210-5319)
PHONE..................310 449-3000
Alex Yemenidjian, *Ch of Bd*
Daniel J Taylor, *Treasurer*
EMP: 1000
SALES (est): 89.2K
SALES (corp-wide): 1.1B **Privately Held**
SIC: 7812 Motion picture production & distribution
HQ: Metro-Goldwyn-Mayer, Inc.
245 N Beverly Dr
Beverly Hills CA 90210

(P-17645)
PARAMOUNT PICTURES CORPORATION (HQ)
Also Called: Paramount Studios
5555 Melrose Ave, Los Angeles (90038-3197)
PHONE..................323 956-5000
Jim Gianopulos, *Ch of Bd*
Fred T Gallo, *President*
Adam Goodman, *President*
Dennis Maguire, *President*
David Stainton, *President*
◆ EMP: 1700 EST: 1912
SALES (est): 260.6MM
SALES (corp-wide): 12.9B **Publicly Held**
WEB: www.paramount.com
SIC: 7812 5099 4833 7829 Motion picture production & distribution, television; motion picture production & distribution; video cassettes, accessories & supplies; television broadcasting stations; motion picture distribution services
PA: Viacom Inc.
1515 Broadway
New York NY 10036
212 258-6000

(P-17646)
PARAMOUNT TELEVISION SERVICE
Also Called: Paramount Pictures
5555 Melrose Ave Rm 204, Los Angeles (90038-3996)
PHONE..................323 956-5000
Brad Grey, *CEO*
Brian Agboh, *Senior VP*
Liz Miller, *Senior VP*
Rob Ortiz, *Senior VP*
Brian Segna, *Senior VP*
EMP: 1800
SALES (est): 9.9MM
SALES (corp-wide): 12.9B **Publicly Held**
WEB: www.paramount.com
SIC: 7812 Motion picture production & distribution, television; motion picture production & distribution
HQ: Paramount Pictures Corporation
5555 Melrose Ave
Los Angeles CA 90038
323 956-5000

(P-17647)
PARTICIPANT MEDIA LLC (PA)
331 Foothill Rd Fl 3, Beverly Hills (90210-3669)
PHONE..................310 550-5100
Jeff Skoll, *CEO*
Joshua Couch, *President*
Jeffrey Ivers, *COO*
Andy Kim, *CFO*
Diane Weyermann, *Ch Credit Ofcr*
EMP: 65
SALES (est): 11.8MM **Privately Held**
WEB: www.participantproductions.com
SIC: 7812 Video production

(P-17648)
PICKLEBACK NOLA LLC
1102 7th Pl, Hermosa Beach (90254-4911)
PHONE..................504 605-0911
EMP: 50
SALES (est): 275.6K **Privately Held**
SIC: 7812 Television film production

(P-17649)
PIE TOWN PRODUCTIONS INC
5433 Laurel Canyon Blvd, North Hollywood (91607-2114)
PHONE..................818 255-9300
Tara Sandler, *President*
Dana Besnoy, *Vice Pres*
Drew Hallmann, *Executive*
Laura Stover, *Executive*
Samantha Leonard, *Exec Dir*
EMP: 160
SALES (est): 8.3MM **Privately Held**
WEB: www.pietownproductions.com
SIC: 7812 Television film production

(P-17650)
PIXAR (DH)
Also Called: Pixar Animation Studios
1200 Park Ave, Emeryville (94608-3677)
PHONE..................510 922-3000
James W Morris, *CEO*
Tyler Fazakerley, *Technology*
Leila Chesloff, *Technical Staff*
Farhez Rayani, *Technical Staff*
Mark Vandewettering, *Technical Staff*
▲ EMP: 850
SQ FT: 247,000
SALES (est): 120.7MM
SALES (corp-wide): 90.2B **Publicly Held**
WEB: www.martinreddy.net
SIC: 7812 7372 7371 Cartoon motion picture production; commercials; television: tape or film; prepackaged software; computer software development

(P-17651)
PLAYBOY ENTERPRISES INC (PA)
Also Called: Playboy Magazine
9346 Civic Center Dr # 200, Beverly Hills (90210-3604)
PHONE..................310 424-1800
Ben Kohn, *CEO*
David Israel, *President*
Bob Meyers, *President*
Randy A Nicolau, *President*
Alex L Vaickus, *President*
▲ EMP: 96 EST: 1953

SALES (est): 45.6MM **Privately Held**
WEB: www.playboy.com
SIC: 7812 4841 2721 Motion picture production; video production; cable & other pay television services; periodicals

(P-17652)
PLAYBOY ENTRMT GROUP INC (HQ)
2300 W Empire Ave, Burbank (91504-3341)
PHONE.....................323 276-4000
Brinda Viloa, *Director*
James Griffiths, *President*
Rebecca Pizzello, *Executive Asst*
EMP: 139
SALES (est): 7.9MM
SALES (corp-wide): 45.6MM **Privately Held**
SIC: 7812 Video tape production
PA: Playboy Enterprises, Inc.
   9346 Civic Center Dr # 200
   Beverly Hills CA 90210
   310 424-1800

(P-17653)
POST MODERN EDIT LLC
4551 Glencoe Ave Ste 210, Marina Del Rey (90292-7930)
PHONE.....................310 396-7375
EMP: 70
SALES (est): 853.1K **Privately Held**
SIC: 7812 Video production
PA: Post Modern Edit, Llc
   2941 Alton Pkwy
   Irvine CA 92606

(P-17654)
POST MODERN EDIT LLC (PA)
2941 Alton Pkwy, Irvine (92606-5142)
PHONE.....................949 608-8700
Rick Warren,
Hamid Samnani,
◆ EMP: 51
SQ FT: 22,000
SALES (est): 7.2MM **Privately Held**
WEB: www.postmoderngroup.com
SIC: 7812 Video production

(P-17655)
PRG (CALIFORNIA) INC
Also Called: Fourth Phase Los Angeles
1245 Aviation Pl, San Fernando (91340-1459)
PHONE.....................818 252-2600
Jeremiah Harris, *President*
John Wolf, *Exec VP*
James Riendeau, *Vice Pres*
Nicole Scano, *Vice Pres*
Tim Wiley, *Vice Pres*
▲ EMP: 50
SALES (est): 6.7MM **Privately Held**
SIC: 7812 Video production

(P-17656)
QUADRA PRODUCTIONS INC
Also Called: Wheel of Forturne
10202 Washington Blvd, Culver City (90232-3119)
PHONE.....................310 244-1234
Harry Friedman, *President*
EMP: 130
SALES (est): 5.3MM **Privately Held**
WEB: www.sonypictures.com
SIC: 7812 Television film production
HQ: Sony Pictures Entertainment, Inc.
   10202 Washington Blvd
   Culver City CA 90232
   310 244-4000

(P-17657)
RADLEYS
3780 Wilshire Blvd, Los Angeles (90010-2805)
PHONE.....................310 765-2223
Christian Thompson, *COO*
Brandon Hill, *Partner*
Elizabeth Lisk, *Controller*
Brandon Pleus, *Production*
Sara Cimino, *Producer*
EMP: 50
SALES (est): 1.9MM **Privately Held**
SIC: 7812 Television film production

(P-17658)
RANCH HAND ENTERTAINMENT INC
11333 Moorpark St Pmb 441, Studio City (91602-2618)
PHONE.....................612 396-2632
Peter Williams, *President*
Jonathan Ward, *Vice Pres*
EMP: 68
SALES (est): 784K **Privately Held**
SIC: 7812 7389 Television film production;

(P-17659)
REGENT WORLDWIDE SALES LLC
10990 Wilshire Blvd, Los Angeles (90024-3913)
PHONE.....................310 806-4288
Stephen P Jarchow,
Ann Derwin, *Project Mgr*
Staci Porter, *Project Mgr*
Michelle Hefflin, *Technical Staff*
Paul Colichman,
EMP: 50
SALES (est): 12MM **Privately Held**
SIC: 7812 Motion picture production & distribution

(P-17660)
REILLY WORLDWIDE INC
3000 Olympic Blvd, Santa Monica (90404-5073)
PHONE.....................310 449-4065
James M Burnett, *President*
EMP: 50
SALES (est): 1MM **Privately Held**
SIC: 7812 Television film production

(P-17661)
REMOTE CONTROL PRODUCTIONS INC (PA)
1547 14th St, Santa Monica (90404-3302)
PHONE.....................310 260-0171
Hans Zimmer, *President*
Lee Rossignol, *Technology*
EMP: 50
SALES (est): 6MM **Privately Held**
SIC: 7812 Video tape production

(P-17662)
RESPOND 2 LLC
Also Called: R2c Group
727 Ansome St, San Francisco (94111)
PHONE.....................415 398-4200
Mark Yesayian, *Branch Mgr*
EMP: 62
SALES (corp-wide): 22.5MM **Privately Held**
SIC: 7812 Video production
PA: Respond 2 Llc
   207 Nw Park Ave
   Portland OR 97209
   503 222-0025

(P-17663)
ROCK PAPER SCISSORS LLC
2308 Broadway, Santa Monica (90404-2916)
PHONE.....................310 586-0600
Angus Wall,
Rob Larose, *Engineer*
Kevin Bass, *Chief Engr*
Julianne Cort, *Production*
Shayna Rubin, *Production*
EMP: 50
SQ FT: 9,000
SALES (est): 6.9MM **Privately Held**
WEB: www.a52.com
SIC: 7812 8999 Commercials, television: tape or film; editorial service

(P-17664)
ROUNDABOUT ENTERTAINMENT INC
Also Called: Secuto Music
217 S Lake St, Burbank (91502-2111)
PHONE.....................818 842-9300
Craig S Clark, *CEO*
Paul Rodriguez, *Vice Pres*
Isabel Olmos, *Admin Asst*
James Jan, *Info Tech Dir*
Ross Millard, *Info Tech Mgr*
EMP: 84
SQ FT: 6,000

SALES (est): 9.9MM **Privately Held**
WEB: www.roundabout.com
SIC: 7812 Video production

(P-17665)
RSA FILMS INC (PA)
634 N La Peer Dr, West Hollywood (90069-5602)
PHONE.....................310 659-1577
Jules Daly, *President*
Raymond Chu, *CIO*
Marlene Muller, *Project Mgr*
Autumn Hymes, *Production*
Elicia Laport, *Production*
EMP: 57
SALES (est): 8.3MM **Privately Held**
WEB: www.rsafilms.com
SIC: 7812 Commercials, television: tape or film; music video production

(P-17666)
SCRIPT TO SCREEN INC
200 N Tustin Ave Ste 200 # 200, Santa Ana (92705-3817)
PHONE.....................714 558-3287
Barbara L Kerry, *Ch of Bd*
W E Mitchell, *President*
Alex Dinsmoor, *Exec VP*
Kenneth P Kerry, *Vice Pres*
Catherine Gudvangen, *Producer*
EMP: 75
SQ FT: 6,000
SALES (est): 7MM **Privately Held**
WEB: www.scripttoscreen.com
SIC: 7812 Video production; motion picture production

(P-17667)
SDI MEDIA USA INC (DH)
Also Called: Sdi Media USA
6060 Center Dr Ste 100, Los Angeles (90045-8835)
PHONE.....................323 602-5455
Walter Schonfeld, *CEO*
Rick Sanchez, *CFO*
Mary Ann Fialkowski, *Exec VP*
Scott Rose, *Exec VP*
Olivier Christmann, *Vice Pres*
EMP: 87
SQ FT: 13,000
SALES (est): 30.6MM **Privately Held**
WEB: www.sdimediagroup.com
SIC: 7812 Motion picture & video production
HQ: Sdi Media Group Limited
   1000 Great West Road
   Brentford MIDDX
   208 232-4930

(P-17668)
SHADOW ANIMATION LLC
940 N Mansfield Ave, Los Angeles (90038-2312)
PHONE.....................323 466-7771
Alex Bulkley, *Owner*
Corey Campodonico,
Chris Lee, *Sr Project Mgr*
Don Schwarz, *Director*
EMP: 50
SALES (est): 3.2MM **Privately Held**
WEB: www.shadowmachine.com
SIC: 7812 Audio-visual program production

(P-17669)
SMUK INC
3800 Barham Blvd Ste 410, Los Angeles (90068-1042)
PHONE.....................323 904-4680
Nick Emmerson, *President*
EMP: 200
SALES (est): 2MM **Privately Held**
SIC: 7812 Television film production

(P-17670)
SONY ELECTRONICS INC
Also Called: Urban Sony Service Center
14450 Myford Rd, Irvine (92606-1001)
PHONE.....................714 508-7634
Jim Whitehouse, *Principal*
EMP: 101 **Privately Held**
SIC: 7812 7622 5731 Motion picture & video production; video repair; high fidelity stereo equipment

HQ: Sony Electronics Inc.
   16535 Via Esprillo Bldg 1
   San Diego CA 92127
   858 942-2400

(P-17671)
SONY ELECTRONICS INC
835 Howard St, San Francisco (94103-3009)
PHONE.....................415 833-4796
Yvonne Miranda, *Principal*
EMP: 300 **Privately Held**
SIC: 7812 7832 Motion picture production & distribution; motion picture production & distribution, television; motion picture theaters, except drive-in
HQ: Sony Electronics Inc.
   16535 Via Esprillo Bldg 1
   San Diego CA 92127
   858 942-2400

(P-17672)
SONY PICTURES ENTRMT INC
9050 Washington Blvd, Culver City (90232-2518)
PHONE.....................310 840-8000
Kym Wulfe, *President*
Kevin Noel, *Exec Dir*
EMP: 500 **Privately Held**
WEB: www.sonypictures.com
SIC: 7812 Video production
HQ: Sony Pictures Entertainment, Inc.
   10202 Washington Blvd
   Culver City CA 90232
   310 244-4000

(P-17673)
SONY PICTURES ENTRMT INC (DH)
Also Called: Sony Pictures Studios
10202 Washington Blvd, Culver City (90232-3119)
PHONE.....................310 244-4000
Tony Vinciquerra, *CEO*
Kristine Belson, *President*
David Bishop, *President*
Rory Bruer, *President*
Dwight Caines, *President*
▲ EMP: 3000
SALES (est): 432.6MM **Privately Held**
WEB: www.sonypictures.com
SIC: 7812 7822 7832 Motion picture production & distribution; motion picture production & distribution, television; distribution, exclusive of production: motion picture; distribution for television: motion picture; motion picture theaters, except drive-in
HQ: Sony Corporation Of America
   25 Madison Ave Fl 27
   New York NY 10010
   212 833-8000

(P-17674)
SONY PICTURES STUDIOS INC
1250 S Beverly Glen Blvd # 112, Los Angeles (90024-5204)
PHONE.....................310 244-4000
Jack Kindberg, *President*
Jared Jussim, *Admin Sec*
EMP: 380
SALES (est): 7.3MM **Privately Held**
WEB: www.sonypictures.com
SIC: 7812 Motion picture production
HQ: Sony Pictures Entertainment, Inc.
   10202 Washington Blvd
   Culver City CA 90232
   310 244-4000

(P-17675)
SONY PICTURES TELEVISION INC (DH)
10202 Washington Blvd, Culver City (90232-3119)
PHONE.....................310 244-7625
Steve Mosko, *CEO*
Drew Shearer, *CFO*
Jennifer Gerstenblatt, *Senior VP*
Linda Bershad, *Vice Pres*
Lori Drum, *Vice Pres*
▲ EMP: 300
SALES: 6MM **Privately Held**
WEB: www.sonypicturestelevision.com
SIC: 7812 Motion picture production & distribution, television

P R O D U C T S & S V C S

HQ: Sony Pictures Entertainment, Inc.
10202 Washington Blvd
Culver City CA 90232
310 244-4000

(P-17676)
SPORTVISION INC
6657 Kaiser Dr, Fremont (94555-3608)
PHONE..................510 736-2925
Rhonda Brewer, *Opers Staff*
EMP: 50
SALES (corp-wide): 38.6MM **Privately Held**
SIC: 7812 7371 Commercials, television: tape or film; custom computer programming services
HQ: Sportvision, Inc.
4619 N Ravenswood Ave # 304
Chicago IL 60640
773 293-4300

(P-17677)
STARGATE FILMS INC
Also Called: Stargate Digital
1001 El Centro St, South Pasadena (91030-5206)
PHONE..................626 403-8403
Sam Nicholson, *President*
Jason Lucas, *CFO*
Jim Riley, *Exec VP*
Darren Frankel, *Vice Pres*
Pete Ware, *Principal*
EMP: 65
SQ FT: 50,000
SALES (est): 7.4MM **Privately Held**
SIC: 7812 Motion picture production; television film production

(P-17678)
STU SEGALL PRODUCTIONS INC
4705 Ruffin Rd, San Diego (92123-1611)
PHONE..................858 974-8988
Stu Segall, *President*
Kevin Waskow, *Vice Pres*
EMP: 200
SQ FT: 1,000
SALES (est): 14MM **Privately Held**
WEB: www.stusegall.com
SIC: 7812 Video production

(P-17679)
STUDY TAPES
Also Called: PINE KNOLL PUBLICATIONS
1341 Pine Knoll Cres, Redlands (92373-6545)
PHONE..................909 792-0111
Dr Gerald A Kirk, *Partner*
Cheryl J Kirk, *Partner*
▲ EMP: 52
SALES (est): 231.7K **Privately Held**
WEB: www.pineknoll.org
SIC: 7812 5735 Video tape production; audio tapes, prerecorded

(P-17680)
TALL PONY PRODUCTIONS INC
300 Loma Metisse Rd, Malibu (90265-3059)
P.O. Box 1026 (90265-1026)
PHONE..................310 456-7495
Anthony Eaton, *President*
EMP: 150
SQ FT: 2,000
SALES (est): 3.4MM **Privately Held**
WEB: www.tallponyproductions.com
SIC: 7812 Television film production

(P-17681)
TECHNICOLOR NEW MEDIA INC
250 E Olive Ave Ste 300, Burbank (91502-1211)
PHONE..................818 480-5100
Dave Weaphers, *President*
Robin Boyarsky, *Manager*
EMP: 50
SALES (est): 3.4MM **Privately Held**
SIC: 7812 Audio-visual program production

(P-17682)
TOPANGA PRODUCTIONS INC
10202 Wash Blvd Ste 1132, Culver City (90232-3119)
PHONE..................310 244-4000
Steve Mosko, *CEO*
EMP: 50

SALES (est): 66.5K **Privately Held**
WEB: www.sonypictures.com
SIC: 7812 Motion picture & video production
HQ: Sony Pictures Entertainment, Inc.
10202 Washington Blvd
Culver City CA 90232
310 244-4000

(P-17683)
TOUCHSTONE TELEVISION PROD LLC (PA)
500 S Buena Vista St, Burbank (91521-0001)
PHONE..................323 671-5116
Mark Pedowitz, *President*
EMP: 50
SALES (est): 11.9MM **Privately Held**
SIC: 7812 Non-theatrical motion picture production, television

(P-17684)
TRIAGE ENTERTAINMENT LLC
6701 Center Dr W Ste 300, Los Angeles (90045-2482)
PHONE..................310 417-4800
Stuart M Schreiberg, *President*
Stephen Kroopnick, *Exec VP*
John Bravakis, *Vice Pres*
EMP: 60
SQ FT: 15,000
SALES (est): 7.6MM **Privately Held**
WEB: www.triageinc.com
SIC: 7812 Motion picture & video production

(P-17685)
TRICOR ENTERTAINMENT INC
Also Called: Chinaamerica Film Distributors
1613 Chelsea Rd, San Marino (91108-2419)
PHONE..................626 282-5184
Craig Darian, *Chairman*
Howard Kazanjian, *Co-COB*
Sally Austin, *Exec VP*
William E Wegner, *General Counsel*
EMP: 240
SQ FT: 350,000
SALES (est): 3.6MM **Privately Held**
SIC: 7812 Motion picture production; television film production

(P-17686)
TTT WEST COAST INC
3000 W Alameda Ave # 125, Burbank (91505-4437)
PHONE..................818 972-0500
Mike Darnell, *President*
EMP: 200
SALES (est): 5.5MM
SALES (corp-wide): 3.1B **Publicly Held**
SIC: 7812 Motion picture production; television film production
HQ: Ti Gotham Inc.
225 Liberty St
New York NY 10281
212 522-1212

(P-17687)
TURNER BROADCASTING SYSTEM INC
Also Called: TNT Originals
3500 W Olive Ave Ste 1500, Burbank (91505-4630)
PHONE..................818 977-5452
Sandra Dewey, *Vice Pres*
EMP: 50
SALES (corp-wide): 170.7B **Publicly Held**
WEB: www.turner.com
SIC: 7812 Television film production
HQ: Turner Broadcasting System, Inc.
1 Cnn Ctr Nw 14sw
Atlanta GA 30303
404 575-7250

(P-17688)
TWDC ENTERPRISES 18 CORP
601 Circle Seven Dr, Glendale (91201-2332)
PHONE..................818 553-4222
Jan Smith, *Branch Mgr*
EMP: 120

SALES (corp-wide): 90.2B **Publicly Held**
SIC: 7812 Motion picture production & distribution; motion picture production & distribution, television; video tape production; television film production
HQ: Twdc Enterprises 18 Corp.
500 S Buena Vista St
Burbank CA 91521

(P-17689)
TWENTIETH CENTURY FOX HOME E (DH)
10201 W Pico Blvd, Los Angeles (90064-2651)
PHONE..................310 369-1000
K Rupert Murdoch,
Eileen Ige, *Vice Pres*
EMP: 1000
SQ FT: 25,000
SALES (est): 68.7MM
SALES (corp-wide): 90.2B **Publicly Held**
SIC: 7812 Television film production
HQ: Twentieth Century Fox Film Corporation
10201 W Pico Blvd
Los Angeles CA 90064
310 369-1000

(P-17690)
TWENTIETH CNTURY FOX FILM CORP (DH)
Also Called: Fox Films Entertainment
10201 W Pico Blvd, Los Angeles (90064-2606)
P.O. Box 900, Beverly Hills (90213-0900)
PHONE..................310 369-1000
K Rupert Murdoch, *Ch of Bd*
Florence Grace, *Vice Pres*
◆ EMP: 75 EST: 1915
SQ FT: 25,000
SALES (est): 252.2MM
SALES (corp-wide): 90.2B **Publicly Held**
WEB: www.foxmovies.com
SIC: 7812 Motion picture production & distribution; video tape production; motion picture production & distribution, television; television film production
HQ: Fox Entertainment Group, Llc
1211 Ave Of The Americas
New York NY 10036
212 852-7000

(P-17691)
UNIVERSAL CITY STUDIOS LLC (DH)
Also Called: Universal Creative
100 Universal City Plz, Universal City (91608-1085)
PHONE..................800 864-8377
Kimberley D Harris,
Nicki Richards, *President*
Eliot Sekuler, *President*
Donna Langley, *Bd of Directors*
Scott Nemes, *Exec VP*
EMP: 58
SALES (est): 19.4MM
SALES (corp-wide): 94.5B **Publicly Held**
SIC: 7812 Motion picture production & distribution
HQ: Nbcuniversal Media, Llc
30 Rockefeller Plz Fl 2
New York NY 10112
212 664-4444

(P-17692)
UNIVERSAL STUDIOS INC
1295 Los Angeles St Ste 1, Glendale (91204-2403)
PHONE..................818 262-4301
Kate Sullivan, *Branch Mgr*
EMP: 155
SALES (corp-wide): 94.5B **Publicly Held**
WEB: www.universalstudios.com
SIC: 7812 Motion picture & video production
HQ: Universal Studios Company Llc
100 Universal City Plz
North Hollywood CA 91608
818 777-1000

(P-17693)
UNIVERSAL STUDIOS INC
MCA Music
4123 Lankershim Blvd, North Hollywood (91602-2828)
PHONE..................818 753-0000
George Smith, *Manager*
EMP: 100
SALES (corp-wide): 94.5B **Publicly Held**
WEB: www.universalstudios.com
SIC: 7812 Motion picture & video production
HQ: Universal Studios Company Llc
100 Universal City Plz
North Hollywood CA 91608
818 777-1000

(P-17694)
UNIVERSAL STUDIOS INC
3900 Lankershim Blvd, Studio City (91604)
PHONE..................818 777-2351
Edgar Bromfrom Jr, *Manager*
EMP: 155
SALES (corp-wide): 94.5B **Publicly Held**
WEB: www.universalstudios.com
SIC: 7812 Motion picture & video production
HQ: Universal Studios Company Llc
100 Universal City Plz
North Hollywood CA 91608
818 777-1000

(P-17695)
UNIVERSAL STUDIOS COMPANY LLC
Also Called: MCA Music
1000 Univ Studio Blvd 2, Universal City (91608-1008)
PHONE..................818 622-4455
James Warren, *Manager*
Kathy Mandato, *Senior VP*
EMP: 400
SALES (corp-wide): 94.5B **Publicly Held**
WEB: www.universalstudios.com
SIC: 7812 Motion picture & video production
HQ: Universal Studios Company Llc
100 Universal City Plz
North Hollywood CA 91608
818 777-1000

(P-17696)
UNIVERSAL STUDIOS COMPANY LLC (DH)
100 Universal City Plz, North Hollywood (91608-1002)
PHONE..................818 777-1000
Adam Fogelson, *Chairman*
Ron Meyer, *Vice Chairman*
Sean Gamble, *CFO*
Donna Langley, *Chairman*
Michael Daruty, *Vice Pres*
▲ EMP: 168 EST: 1924
SQ FT: 100,000
SALES (est): 1.1B
SALES (corp-wide): 94.5B **Publicly Held**
WEB: www.universalstudios.com
SIC: 7812 3652 2741 5947 Motion picture production & distribution; television film production; phonograph records, prerecorded; magnetic tape (audio): prerecorded; compact laser discs, prerecorded; music, sheet: publishing & printing; gift shop; novelties; jewelry stores; gift items, mail order; novelty merchandise, mail order; jewelry, mail order
HQ: Nbcuniversal Media, Llc
30 Rockefeller Plz Fl 2
New York NY 10112
212 664-4444

(P-17697)
UNIVERSAL STUDIOS COMPANY LLC
MCA Music
100 Universal City Plz # 3, Universal City (91608-1002)
PHONE..................818 777-1000
Larry Miller, *Manager*
EMP: 155
SALES (corp-wide): 94.5B **Publicly Held**
WEB: www.universalstudios.com
SIC: 7812 Motion picture & video production

HQ: Universal Studios Company Llc
100 Universal City Plz
North Hollywood CA 91608
818 777-1000

(P-17698)
UNIVERSAL STUDIOS COMPANY LLC
2440 S Sepulveda Blvd # 100, Los Angeles
(90064-1784)
PHONE..................310 235-4749
David Renzer, *Principal*
Caryn Tomlinson, *Vice Pres*
Amy Kersey, *Credit Staff*
Dave Porter, *Director*
Samantha Iufer, *Manager*
EMP: 125
SALES (corp-wide): 94.5B **Publicly Held**
WEB: www.universalstudios.com
SIC: 7812 Motion picture & video production
HQ: Universal Studios Company Llc
100 Universal City Plz
North Hollywood CA 91608
818 777-1000

(P-17699)
UNIVERSAL STUDIOS COMPANY LLC
Also Called: Universal City
2220 Colorado Ave, Santa Monica
(90404-3506)
PHONE..................310 865-5000
Darcey Graver, *Principal*
EMP: 100
SALES (corp-wide): 94.5B **Publicly Held**
SIC: 7812 Motion picture production & distribution
HQ: Universal Studios Company Llc
100 Universal City Plz
North Hollywood CA 91608
818 777-1000

(P-17700)
UP STAGE INC
Also Called: Stage Right Production Svcs
30757 Canwood St, Agoura (91301-2022)
PHONE..................818 879-8781
Thomas Peachee, *President*
Lisa Peachee, *Admin Sec*
EMP: 50
SALES (est): 895.5K **Privately Held**
SIC: 7812 Commercials, television: tape or film

(P-17701)
VIACOM NETWORKS
Also Called: Mtv Networks
1575 N Gower St Ste 100, Los Angeles
(90028-6488)
PHONE..................310 752-8000
Anthony Disanto, *President*
Jeremy Gonzalez, *President*
Babak Siar, *COO*
David Waggoner, *Director*
EMP: 3645
SALES (est): 106.8MM **Privately Held**
SIC: 7812 7822 Television film production; motion picture & tape distribution

(P-17702)
VILLAGE RDSHOW ENTRMT GROUP US
9268 W 3rd St, Beverly Hills (90210-3713)
PHONE..................310 867-8000
James P Moore, *CEO*
EMP: 50
SALES (est): 250.6K
SALES (corp-wide): 3.6MM **Privately Held**
SIC: 7812 Motion picture & video production
PA: Village Roadshow Entertainment Group Usa Inc.
10100 Santa Monica Blvd
Los Angeles CA 90067
310 385-4300

(P-17703)
WAD PRODUCTIONS INC
Also Called: Ellen Degeneres Show, The
3500 W Olive Ave Ste 1000, Burbank
(91505-5515)
PHONE..................818 260-5673
Greg Gorden, *President*

Jonathan Norman, *Producer*
Corey Palent, *Producer*
Melissa McKeon, *Marketing Staff*
Liz Patrick, *Director*
EMP: 99
SALES (est): 5.4MM **Privately Held**
SIC: 7812 Motion picture & video production

(P-17704)
WALT DISNEY RECORDS DIRECT (DH)
500 S Buena Vista St, Burbank
(91521-0007)
PHONE..................818 560-1000
Alan H Bergman, *Senior VP*
Rob Moore, *CFO*
Nick Franklin, *Senior VP*
Marsha Reed, *Admin Sec*
◆ EMP: 2990
SQ FT: 600,000
SALES (est): 112.3MM
SALES (corp-wide): 90.2B **Publicly Held**
WEB: www.radiodisney.com
SIC: 7812 Motion picture production & distribution; motion picture production & distribution, television; non-theatrical motion picture production; non-theatrical motion picture production, television
HQ: Disney Enterprises, Inc.
500 S Buena Vista St
Burbank CA 91521
818 560-1000

(P-17705)
WARNER BROS ENTERTAINMENT INC
Also Called: Warner Bros. Paint Department
4000 Warner Blvd, Burbank (91522-0002)
PHONE..................818 954-1817
Ron Stansberry, *Manager*
EMP: 120
SALES (corp-wide): 170.7B **Publicly Held**
SIC: 7812 7384 Television film production; home movies, developing & processing
HQ: Warner Bros. Entertainment Inc.
4000 Warner Blvd
Burbank CA 91522
818 954-6000

(P-17706)
WARNER BROS ENTERTAINMENT INC
Also Called: Warner Bros. Legal Department
4000 W Alameda Ave, Burbank
(91505-4305)
PHONE..................818 954-7232
Peter Roch, *President*
Isabelle Renaud, *VP Prdtn*
Alexis Smith, *Director*
EMP: 447
SALES (corp-wide): 170.7B **Publicly Held**
SIC: 7812 8111 Television film production; specialized legal services
HQ: Warner Bros. Entertainment Inc.
4000 Warner Blvd
Burbank CA 91522
818 954-6000

(P-17707)
WARNER BROS ENTERTAINMENT INC
Also Called: Warner Bros Studio Facilities
4000 Warner Blvd, Burbank (91522-0002)
PHONE..................818 954-3000
David Camp, *Manager*
EMP: 168
SALES (corp-wide): 170.7B **Publicly Held**
SIC: 7812 Motion picture production; television film production
HQ: Warner Bros. Entertainment Inc.
4000 Warner Blvd
Burbank CA 91522
818 954-6000

(P-17708)
WARNER BROS ENTERTAINMENT INC
Also Called: Warner Bros Domestic TV Dist
4000 Warner Blvd Bldg 118, Burbank
(91522-0002)
PHONE..................818 954-5301

Mike Troxler, *Branch Mgr*
EMP: 168
SALES (corp-wide): 170.7B **Publicly Held**
SIC: 7812 Motion picture production & distribution, television
HQ: Warner Bros. Entertainment Inc.
4000 Warner Blvd
Burbank CA 91522
818 954-6000

(P-17709)
WARNER BROS ENTERTAINMENT INC
DC Entertainment
4000 Warner Blvd, Burbank (91522-0002)
PHONE..................818 954-6000
Diane Nelson, *President*
EMP: 125
SALES (corp-wide): 170.7B **Publicly Held**
SIC: 7812 Motion picture & video production
HQ: Warner Bros. Entertainment Inc.
4000 Warner Blvd
Burbank CA 91522
818 954-6000

(P-17710)
WARNER BROS ENTERTAINMENT INC (DH)
Also Called: Victory Studio
4000 Warner Blvd, Burbank (91522-0002)
PHONE..................818 954-6000
Ann Sarnoff, *CEO*
Alan Horn, *President*
Jeff Brown, *Exec VP*
Tom Cerio, *Exec VP*
Jeff Goldstein, *Exec VP*
◆ EMP: 835
SALES (est): 706.6MM
SALES (corp-wide): 170.7B **Publicly Held**
SIC: 7812 Television film production

(P-17711)
WARNER BROS ENTERTAINMENT INC
Warner Bros. Animation
15301 Ventura Blvd, Sherman Oaks
(91403-3102)
PHONE..................818 954-3000
Nina Naranja, *Branch Mgr*
Britton Payne, *Director*
Eddie Scannell, *Manager*
EMP: 168
SALES (corp-wide): 170.7B **Publicly Held**
SIC: 7812 Cartoon motion picture production
HQ: Warner Bros. Entertainment Inc.
4000 Warner Blvd
Burbank CA 91522
818 954-6000

(P-17712)
WARNER BROS ENTERTAINMENT INC
4000 Warner Blvd Bldg 30, Burbank
(91522-0002)
PHONE..................818 954-2181
EMP: 168
SALES (corp-wide): 170.7B **Publicly Held**
SIC: 7812 Motion picture production & distribution, television
HQ: Warner Bros. Entertainment Inc.
4000 Warner Blvd
Burbank CA 91522
818 954-6000

(P-17713)
WARNER BROS HOME ENTRMT INC (DH)
4000 Warner Blvd Bldg 160, Burbank
(91522-0002)
P.O. Box 9153, Canton MA (02021-9153)
PHONE..................818 954-6000
James Cardwell, *President*
David Haddad, *Senior VP*
Jeff Baker, *Vice Pres*
Alisa Bergman, *Vice Pres*
Shari Black, *Vice Pres*
▲ EMP: 80
SQ FT: 12,000

SALES (est): 58.1MM
SALES (corp-wide): 170.7B **Publicly Held**
SIC: 7812 Motion picture & video production
HQ: Warner Bros. Entertainment Inc.
4000 Warner Blvd
Burbank CA 91522
818 954-6000

(P-17714)
WARNER BROS INTL TV DIST INC
4000 Warner Blvd, Burbank (91522-0002)
PHONE..................818 954-6000
Robert Blair, *President*
Monique Esclavissat, *Exec VP*
Sarah Godfrey, *Senior Mgr*
Margee Schubert, *Director*
EMP: 99
SALES (est): 2MM
SALES (corp-wide): 170.7B **Publicly Held**
SIC: 7812 Motion picture & video production
HQ: Warner Bros. Entertainment Inc.
4000 Warner Blvd
Burbank CA 91522
818 954-6000

(P-17715)
WATCHIT MEDIA INC
655 Montgomery St # 1000, San Francisco
(94111-2635)
PHONE..................702 740-1700
James R Lavelle, *Ch of Bd*
John Dong, *CFO*
No L McDaniel, *Marketing Mgr*
EMP: 140
SALES (est): 2.7MM **Privately Held**
WEB: www.cotl.com
SIC: 7812 7822 Motion picture production & distribution, television; film exchange for television: motion picture

(P-17716)
WEINSTEIN COMPANY LLC
9100 Wilshire Blvd 700w, Beverly Hills
(90212-3466)
PHONE..................424 204-4800
Harvey Weinstein, *Manager*
EMP: 60
SALES (corp-wide): 37.6MM **Privately Held**
SIC: 7812 Audio-visual program production
PA: The Weinstein Company Llc
99 Hudson St Fl 4
New York NY 10013
212 845-8600

(P-17717)
WESTWIND MEDIA INC
100 W Alameda Ave, Burbank
(91502-2208)
PHONE..................818 972-9000
John A Bidasio, *President*
EMP: 55
SQ FT: 20,000
SALES (est): 3.4MM **Privately Held**
SIC: 7812 Non-theatrical motion picture production, television

(P-17718)
WESTWIND STUDIOS LLC
Also Called: Westwind Media
100 W Alameda Ave, Burbank
(91502-2208)
PHONE..................818 972-9000
John A Bidasio, *Mng Member*
Stephen Cannell,
Leland Postil,
EMP: 50
SQ FT: 20,000
SALES: 9MM **Privately Held**
SIC: 7812 Motion picture production; television film production

(P-17719)
YES VIDEOCOM INC (PA)
2805 Bowers Ave Ste 230, Santa Clara
(95051-0971)
PHONE..................408 907-7600
Michael Chang, *CEO*
▲ EMP: 350
SQ FT: 36,000

SALES (est): 33.1MM **Privately Held**
WEB: www.yesvideo.com
SIC: 7812 Motion picture production

(P-17720)
ZEFR INC
Also Called: Movieclips.com
4101 Redwood Ave, Los Angeles
(90066-5603)
PHONE..........................310 392-3555
Rich Raddon, *President*
Alan Joos, *Partner*
Toby Byrne, *President*
Robert Cukierman, *Vice Pres*
Adam Goldstein, *Vice Pres*
EMP: 200 EST: 2010
SALES (est): 16.6MM **Privately Held**
SIC: 7812 Motion picture production

(P-17721)
ZOIC INC
Also Called: Zoic Studios
3582 Eastham Dr, Culver City
(90232-2409)
PHONE..........................310 838-0770
Loni Peristere, *CEO*
Chris Jones, *President*
Tim McBride, *Treasurer*
Patrick Mooney, *General Mgr*
Cynthia Fary, *Office Mgr*
EMP: 125
SQ FT: 15,000
SALES (est): 14MM **Privately Held**
WEB: www.zoicstudios.com
SIC: 7812 Video production

7819 Services Allied To Motion Picture Prdtn

(P-17722)
A FILML INC
Also Called: Filml.a
6255 W Sunset Blvd Fl 12, Los Angeles
(90028-7428)
PHONE..........................213 977-8600
Paul Audley, *President*
Denise Gutches, *CFO*
Donna Washington, *Vice Pres*
Philip Sokoloski, *Comms Dir*
Daniel Poissant, *Office Admin*
EMP: 70
SALES: 12.7MM **Privately Held**
WEB: www.filmla.com
SIC: 7819 Services allied to motion pictures

(P-17723)
ACADEMY FOUNDATION (HQ)
8949 Wilshire Blvd, Beverly Hills
(90211-1907)
PHONE..........................310 247-3000
Bruce Davis, *Exec Dir*
Dawn Mori, *Director*
EMP: 60
SQ FT: 35,000
SALES: 111.2MM
SALES (corp-wide): 123.6MM **Privately Held**
WEB: www.academyfoundation.com
SIC: 7819 Services allied to motion pictures
PA: Academy Of Motion Picture Arts & Sciences
8949 Wilshire Blvd
Beverly Hills CA 90211
310 247-3000

(P-17724)
ALLIANCE FUNDING GROUP
Also Called: Alliance Capital Markets
17542 17th St Ste 200, Tustin
(92780-1960)
PHONE..........................800 978-8817
Brijesh Ashok Patel, *President*
Shawn M Donohue, *Vice Pres*
Vishal V Masani, *Vice Pres*
EMP: 80 EST: 1998

SALES (est): 18.9MM **Privately Held**
WEB: www.alliancefunds.com
SIC: 7819 7377 6159 7353 Equipment & prop rental, motion picture production; computer rental & leasing; equipment & vehicle finance leasing companies; machinery & equipment finance leasing; earth moving equipment, rental or leasing; equipment rental & leasing

(P-17725)
AVONGARD PRODUCTS USA LTD
Also Called: Hydraulx
12855 Runway Rd Apt 1208, Playa Vista
(90094-2666)
PHONE..........................310 319-2300
David Strause, *President*
Gregor D Strause, *CEO*
Colin Strause, *Vice Pres*
Linda Strause, *Admin Sec*
Dawn Begun, *Finance Mgr*
EMP: 50
SALES (est): 7.8MM **Privately Held**
WEB: www.avongard.com
SIC: 7819 Visual effects production

(P-17726)
BAY AREA VIDEO COALITION INC
Also Called: BAVC
2727 Mariposa St Fl 2, San Francisco
(94110-1401)
PHONE..........................415 861-3282
Ken Ikeda, *Director*
Innesa Goldman, *Accountant*
Vicki Nunez, *Controller*
Jennifer Tanguay, *Human Res Mgr*
Christine Sugrue, *Opers Staff*
EMP: 55 EST: 1977
SQ FT: 25,000
SALES: 5.3MM **Privately Held**
WEB: www.bavc.org
SIC: 7819 8249 Video tape or disk reproduction; vocational schools

(P-17727)
BEAR NASH PRODUCTIONS
521 E Sycamore Ave, El Segundo
(90245-2406)
PHONE..........................310 428-5167
Albert CHI, *Principal*
EMP: 65
SALES (est): 422K **Privately Held**
SIC: 7819 Developing & laboratory services, motion picture

(P-17728)
CHAPMAN/LEONARD STUDIO EQP INC (PA)
12950 Raymer St, North Hollywood
(91605-4211)
PHONE..........................323 877-5309
Leonard Chapman, *President*
Michael Chapman, *Corp Secy*
Christine Chapman-Hueneng, *Vice Pres*
Elsa Echeverria, *Personnel Assit*
▲ EMP: 145
SQ FT: 300,000
SALES (est): 24.3MM **Privately Held**
WEB: www.chapman-leonard.com
SIC: 7819 Studio property rental, motion picture; equipment rental, motion picture

(P-17729)
CINELEASE INC (HQ)
5375 W San Fernando Rd, Los Angeles
(90039-1013)
PHONE..........................855 441-5500
Steven Ortiz, *President*
Brian Macdonald, *President*
Scott Massengill, *Treasurer*
Joseph Ball, *Vice Pres*
J Jeffrey Zimmerman, *Admin Sec*
▲ EMP: 50
SALES (est): 10.6MM
SALES (corp-wide): 1.9B **Publicly Held**
SIC: 7819 Equipment rental, motion picture
PA: Herc Holdings Inc.
27500 Riverview Center Bl
Bonita Springs FL 34134
239 301-1000

(P-17730)
CMS LLNL
7000 East Ave Msl090, Livermore
(94550-9698)
PHONE..........................925 422-5584
Stan Stone,
EMP: 50
SALES (est): 7.9MM **Privately Held**
SIC: 7819 Laboratory service, motion picture

(P-17731)
COMPANY 3 INC
1661 Lincoln Blvd Ste 400, Santa Monica
(90404-3741)
PHONE..........................310 255-6600
Stefan Sonnenfeld, *President*
Tom Gehring, *Opers Staff*
Brian Anderson, *Producer*
Alexis Guajardo, *Producer*
Kayla Kossi, *Client Mgr*
EMP: 59
SALES (est): 6.5MM
SALES (corp-wide): 2B **Publicly Held**
SIC: 7819 Services allied to motion pictures
PA: Deluxe Corporation
3680 Victoria St N
Shoreview MN 55126
651 483-7111

(P-17732)
CONDOR PRODUCTIONS LLC
245 N Beverly Dr, Beverly Hills
(90210-5319)
PHONE..........................310 449-3000
Kathryn Rose-Remlinger, *Accountant*
EMP: 99
SQ FT: 5,000
SALES (est): 401.6K **Privately Held**
SIC: 7819 TV tape services: editing, transfers, etc.

(P-17733)
DELUXE DIGITAL DIST INC
Also Called: D3, Deluxe Ondemand
2400 W Empire Ave Ste 200, Los Angeles
(90027)
PHONE..........................818 260-6202
Cyril Drabinsky, *CEO*
Warren Stein, *Exec VP*
Jeff Cuneo, *Engineer*
EMP: 50
SALES (est): 4.5MM **Privately Held**
SIC: 7819 Services allied to motion pictures

(P-17734)
DELUXE LABORATORIES INC (DH)
Also Called: Color By Deluxe
2400 W Empire Ave, Burbank
(91504-3331)
PHONE..........................323 462-6171
Cyril Drabinsky, *CEO*
Mike Gunter, *CFO*
Scott Ehrlich, *Exec VP*
Dashiell Morrison, *Exec VP*
Warren Stein, *Exec VP*
▲ EMP: 626 EST: 1990
SQ FT: 150,000
SALES (est): 37.8MM **Privately Held**
SIC: 7819 Film processing, editing & titling: motion picture

(P-17735)
DIRECTORS GUILD AMERICA INC (PA)
Also Called: D G A
7920 W Sunset Blvd # 600, Los Angeles
(90046-3334)
PHONE..........................310 289-2000
Jay D Roth, *Exec Dir*
Michael Apted, *President*
Brian O'Rourke, *CFO*
Scott Berger, *Treasurer*
Gilbert Cates, *Corp Secy*
EMP: 110
SQ FT: 100,000
SALES: 26.2MM **Privately Held**
WEB: www.directors-guild.com
SIC: 7819 8631 Directors, independent: motion picture; labor unions & similar labor organizations

(P-17736)
DTS INC (HQ)
5220 Las Virgenes Rd, Calabasas
(91302-1064)
PHONE..........................818 436-1000
Jon E Kirchner, *CEO*
Michael Quiroz, *Partner*
Brian D Towne, *President*
Melvin L Flanigan, *CFO*
Sue Molina, *Bd of Directors*
▲ EMP: 150
SQ FT: 89,000
SALES: 138.2MM
SALES (corp-wide): 406.1MM **Publicly Held**
WEB: www.dtsonline.com
SIC: 7819 3651 Services allied to motion pictures; household audio & video equipment
PA: Xperi Corporation
3025 Orchard Pkwy
San Jose CA 95134
408 321-6000

(P-17737)
DX HOLDINGS LLC
1377 N Serrano Ave, Los Angeles
(90027-5623)
PHONE..........................323 462-6171
Cyril Drabinsky, *CEO*
EMP: 809
SALES (est): 60.9K **Privately Held**
SIC: 7819 Film processing, editing & titling: motion picture
PA: Macandrews & Forbes Incorporated
35 E 62nd St
New York NY 10065

(P-17738)
EDGEBROOK PRODUCTIONS INC
10806 Ventura Blvd, Studio City
(91604-3300)
PHONE..........................818 766-6789
Alan O Grady, *President*
EMP: 52
SALES (est): 415.9K **Privately Held**
SIC: 7819 Developing & laboratory services, motion picture

(P-17739)
ESC ENTERTAINMENT INC
4000 Warner Blvd, Burbank (91522-0001)
PHONE..........................818 954-1018
Tom Davila, *President*
Ed Jones, *CEO*
Tom Settle, *CFO*
EMP: 250
SQ FT: 61,000
SALES (est): 16.1MM **Privately Held**
SIC: 7819 Visual effects production

(P-17740)
FOTO-KEM INDUSTRIES INC (PA)
Also Called: Foto Kem Film & Video
2801 W Alameda Ave, Burbank
(91505-4405)
P.O. Box 7755 (91510-7755)
PHONE..........................818 846-3102
William F Brodersen, *CEO*
Kam Schumacher, *Bd of Directors*
Rosanna Marino, *Senior VP*
Gerald D Brodersen Jr, *Vice Pres*
Ellen Ostoich, *Vice Pres*
▲ EMP: 486
SQ FT: 43,000
SALES (est): 74.1MM **Privately Held**
WEB: www.fotokem.com
SIC: 7819 Laboratory service, motion picture; developing & printing of commercial motion picture film

(P-17741)
FOTO-KEM INDUSTRIES INC
Also Called: Fotokem
2801 W Olive Ave, Burbank (91505-4578)
PHONE..........................818 846-3102
William Brodersen, *President*
Ronnie Bordey, *Technical Mgr*
Shawn Leonard, *Engineer*
EMP: 500

▲ = Import ▼=Export
◆ =Import/Export

SALES (corp-wide): 74.1MM **Privately Held**
WEB: www.fotokem.com
SIC: 7819 Laboratory service, motion picture; developing & printing of commercial motion picture film
PA: Foto-Kem Industries, Inc.
2801 W Alameda Ave
Burbank CA 91505
818 846-3102

(P-17742)
FUSEFX LLC
14823 Califa St, Van Nuys (91411-3108)
PHONE..................................818 237-5052
David Altenau, *CEO*
Tim Jacobsen, *Officer*
Jason Fotter, *Principal*
EMP: 300
SQ FT: 12,500
SALES (est): 1.9MM **Privately Held**
SIC: 7819 Visual effects production

(P-17743)
HIGH TECHNOLOGY VIDEO INC
Also Called: H T V
10900 Ventura Blvd, Studio City (91604-3340)
PHONE..................................323 969-8822
Jim Hardy, *CEO*
Steve Weiner, *Chairman*
Steve Galloway, *Senior VP*
Richard Gelles, *Vice Pres*
Sandy Crawford, *General Mgr*
EMP: 73
SQ FT: 30,000
SALES (est): 11.5MM **Privately Held**
WEB: www.htvinc.net
SIC: 7819 Video tape or disk reproduction

(P-17744)
HOLLYWOOD RNTALS PROD SVCS LLC (PA)
5300 Melrose Ave, Los Angeles (90038-5111)
PHONE..................................818 407-7800
Mark A Rosenthal, *Mng Member*
▲ **EMP:** 100
SQ FT: 100,000
SALES (est): 13.7MM **Privately Held**
WEB: www.hollywoodrentals.com
SIC: 7819 Equipment rental, motion picture

(P-17745)
INDUSTRIAL MEDIA INC
6007 Sepulveda Blvd, Van Nuys (91411-2502)
PHONE..................................310 777-1940
Peter Hurwitz, *CEO*
Scott Frosch, *CFO*
EMP: 250
SALES: 150MM **Privately Held**
SIC: 7819 Reproduction services, motion picture production

(P-17746)
JACKSON SHRUB SUPPLY INC
11505 Vanowen St, North Hollywood (91605-6232)
PHONE..................................818 982-0100
Gary Jackson, *President*
EMP: 60
SQ FT: 16,000
SALES (est): 4.1MM **Privately Held**
WEB: www.jacksonshrub.com
SIC: 7819 Services allied to motion pictures

(P-17747)
LEGEND FILMS
2200 Faraday Ave Ste 100, Carlsbad (92008-7233)
PHONE..................................858 793-4420
Barry Sandrew, *Founder*
EMP: 350
SALES (est): 224.1K **Privately Held**
SIC: 7819 Services allied to motion pictures

(P-17748)
LUMA PICTURES INC
1424 2nd St, Santa Monica (90401-2345)
PHONE..................................310 888-8738
Payam Shohadai, *President*
John Betdul, *Principal*
Myles Wright, *Administration*

Kevin McCartney, *Info Tech Mgr*
EMP: 171
SQ FT: 5,500
SALES (est): 2.7MM **Privately Held**
WEB: www.lumapictures.com
SIC: 7819 Visual effects production

(P-17749)
MBS EQUIPMENT COMPANY (PA)
Also Called: Tm Motion Picture Eqp Rentals
12800 Foothill Blvd, Sylmar (91342-5315)
PHONE..................................310 558-3100
Tom May, *President*
EMP: 81
SALES (est): 22.8MM **Privately Held**
SIC: 7819 Equipment rental, motion picture

(P-17750)
MODERN VIDEOFILM INC
Also Called: Mod Vid Film
1733 Flower St, Glendale (91201-2022)
PHONE..................................818 637-6800
Mark Smirnoff, *Manager*
EMP: 125
SALES (corp-wide): 30.7MM **Privately Held**
WEB: www.mvfinc.com
SIC: 7819 Video tape or disk reproduction; film processing, editing & titling: motion picture; TV tape services: editing, transfers, etc.
PA: Modern Videofilm, Inc.
2300 W Empire Ave
Burbank CA 91504
818 840-1700

(P-17751)
MODERN VIDEOFILM INC (PA)
Also Called: Mvf World Wide Services
2300 W Empire Ave, Burbank (91504-3341)
PHONE..................................818 840-1700
Scott Avila, *CEO*
Cooper Crouse, *President*
Roxanna Sassanian, *CFO*
Brett Pooley, *Admin Sec*
Lisa Dewey, *Director*
EMP: 230
SQ FT: 100,000
SALES (est): 30.7MM **Privately Held**
WEB: www.mvfinc.com
SIC: 7819 Video tape or disk reproduction; film processing, editing & titling: motion picture; TV tape services: editing, transfers, etc.

(P-17752)
MUSIC COLLECTIVE LLC
12711 Ventura Blvd # 110, Studio City (91604-2431)
PHONE..................................818 508-3303
Alan Ett, *Owner*
Irl Sanders, *Editor*
EMP: 50
SALES (est): 1.9MM **Privately Held**
WEB: www.aemg.com
SIC: 7819 Sound (effects & music production), motion picture

(P-17753)
NATIONAL FILM LABORATORIES
Also Called: Crest Digital
900 Glenneyre St, Laguna Beach (92651-2707)
PHONE..................................323 466-0281
Stephen R Stein, *CEO*
Ronald Stein, *President*
Lorraine Ross, *Corp Secy*
EMP: 157
SQ FT: 50,000
SALES (est): 7.4MM **Privately Held**
WEB: www.concorddisc.com
SIC: 7819 7812 Film processing, editing & titling: motion picture; reproduction services, motion picture production; motion picture & video production

(P-17754)
NEW DEAL STUDIOS INC
1812 W Burbank Blvd, Burbank (91506-1315)
PHONE..................................310 578-9929
Shannon Gans, *CEO*
Matthew Gratzner, *Vice Pres*

Ian Hunter, *Admin Sec*
David Sanger, *Production*
Celeste Masters, *Manager*
EMP: 52
SQ FT: 20,000
SALES (est): 3.8MM **Privately Held**
SIC: 7819 Visual effects production

(P-17755)
OMEGA/CINEMA PROPS INC
5857 Santa Monica Blvd, Los Angeles (90038-2001)
PHONE..................................323 466-8201
E Jay Krause, *President*
Cheryl Jordan, *Corp Secy*
Allan Songer, *Opers Mgr*
Ryan Pritchard, *Asst Mgr*
▲ **EMP:** 90
SQ FT: 300,000
SALES (est): 11.6MM **Privately Held**
WEB: www.omegacinemaprops.com
SIC: 7819 Equipment rental, motion picture

(P-17756)
PIXELOGIC MEDIA PARTNERS LLC
4000 W Alameda Ave # 110, Burbank (91505-4305)
PHONE..................................818 861-2001
John Suh,
Robert Seidel,
EMP: 250
SQ FT: 20,000
SALES (est): 4.8MM **Privately Held**
SIC: 7819 Reproduction services, motion picture production

(P-17757)
POINT360
1133 N Hollywood Way, Burbank (91505-2528)
PHONE..................................818 556-5700
Brian Ehrlich, *Manager*
EMP: 100
SALES (corp-wide): 37.5MM **Publicly Held**
WEB: www.vdimultimedia.com
SIC: 7819 Editing services, motion picture production; equipment & prop rental, motion picture production
PA: Point.360
2701 Media Center Dr
Los Angeles CA 90065
818 565-1400

(P-17758)
POINT360 (PA)
Also Called: Digital Film Labs
2701 Media Center Dr, Los Angeles (90065-1700)
PHONE..................................818 565-1400
Haig S Bagerdjian, *Ch of Bd*
Alan R Steel, *CFO*
Sally Fenton, *Managing Dir*
David Tuszynski, *General Mgr*
Debbie Collins, *Technician*
EMP: 111
SQ FT: 64,600
SALES: 37.5MM **Publicly Held**
WEB: www.vdimultimedia.com
SIC: 7819 7822 7829 Video tape or disk reproduction; motion picture & tape distribution; television & video tape distribution; motion picture distribution services

(P-17759)
POST GROUP INC (PA)
1415 N Cahuenga Blvd, Los Angeles (90028-8198)
PHONE..................................323 462-2300
Frederic Rheinstein, *Chairman*
Lloyd Guillen, *President*
Vincent Lyons, *President*
Winston Whitmarsh, *Office Mgr*
Duke Gallagher, *Admin Sec*
EMP: 110 **EST:** 1974
SQ FT: 40,000
SALES (est): 12.7MM **Privately Held**
WEB: www.postgroup.com
SIC: 7819 7812 Editing services, motion picture production; film processing, editing & titling: motion picture; TV tape services: editing, transfers, etc.; motion picture & video production

(P-17760)
PRIME FOCUS NORTH AMERICA INC (PA)
Also Called: Prime Focus World
5750 Hannum Ave Ste 100, Culver City (90230-6666)
PHONE..................................323 461-7887
Namit Malhotra, *CEO*
Robert Hummel, *CEO*
Oliver Welch, *COO*
Sue Murphree, *CFO*
Atul Saxena, *Vice Pres*
EMP: 85
SQ FT: 50,000
SALES (est): 9.5MM **Privately Held**
WEB: www.postlogic.com
SIC: 7819 Sound (effects & music production), motion picture

(P-17761)
QUIXOTE MM LLC
Also Called: Movie Movers
1011 N Fuller Ave Ste B, West Hollywood (90046-6658)
PHONE..................................323 851-5030
Mikel Elliott, *Mng Member*
Michael Elliott, *Mng Member*
EMP: 50
SALES (est): 3.6MM **Privately Held**
SIC: 7819 Equipment rental, motion picture

(P-17762)
RALEIGH ENTERPRISES INC
Also Called: Raleigh Studios
5300 Melrose Ave Fl 3, Los Angeles (90038-5113)
PHONE..................................323 466-3111
Michael Moore, *Branch Mgr*
EMP: 130
SQ FT: 68,388
SALES (corp-wide): 43.7MM **Privately Held**
WEB: www.raleighenterprises.com
SIC: 7819 7359 6512 Services allied to motion pictures; equipment rental & leasing; nonresidential building operators
PA: Raleigh Enterprises, Inc.
5300 Melrose Ave Fl 4
Los Angeles CA 90038
310 899-8900

(P-17763)
SIX POINT HARNESS
1759 Glendale Blvd, Los Angeles (90026-1761)
PHONE..................................323 462-3344
Brendan Burch, *Principal*
EMP: 50
SALES (est): 2.5MM **Privately Held**
SIC: 7819 Services allied to motion pictures

(P-17764)
SKYLAR FILM STUDIOS LLC
13589 Mindanao Way # 11, Marina Del Rey (90292-6950)
PHONE..................................424 653-8902
Jamie Skylar, *CEO*
Dylan Johnson, *Managing Dir*
EMP: 200 **EST:** 2010
SQ FT: 200,000
SALES (est): 2.7MM **Privately Held**
SIC: 7819 Services allied to motion pictures

(P-17765)
STAN WINSTON INC
Also Called: Stan Winston Studio
340 Parkside Dr, San Fernando (91340-3035)
PHONE..................................818 782-0870
Stan Winston, *President*
Brian Gilbert, *Vice Pres*
EMP: 80
SQ FT: 10,538
SALES (est): 2.1MM **Privately Held**
WEB: www.stanwinston.com
SIC: 7819 Visual effects production

(P-17766)
STEREO D LLC
Also Called: Stereod
3355 W Empire Ave Fl 1, Burbank (91504-3160)
P.O. Box 892164, Temecula (92589-2164)
PHONE..................................818 861-3100

William Sherak, *President*
Aaron Parry, *Exec VP*
Milton Adamou, *Vice Pres*
Prafull Gade, *Vice Pres*
Alex Macdonald, *Administration*
EMP: 275
SQ FT: 55,000
SALES (est): 16.3MM **Privately Held**
SIC: 7819 Editing services, motion picture production
HQ: Deluxe Entertainment Services Group Inc.
2400 W Empire Ave
Burbank CA 91504

(P-17767)
TECHNCLOR CRATIVE SVCS USA INC (DH)
6040 W Sunset Blvd, Los Angeles (90028-6402)
PHONE..................818 260-3800
Timothy Sarnoff, *CEO*
Richard Andrews, *President*
Claude Gagnon, *CEO*
John Hancock, *Admin Sec*
EMP: 300
SQ FT: 25,000
SALES (est): 27.8MM
SALES (corp-wide): 62.9MM **Privately Held**
WEB: www.vidfilm.com
SIC: 7819 Video tape or disk reproduction
HQ: Technicolor Thomson Group, Inc
2233 N Ontario St Ste 300
Burbank CA 91504
818 260-3600

(P-17768)
TECHNCLOR CRATIVE SVCS USA INC
Technicolor Complete Post
6040 W Sunset Blvd, Los Angeles (90028-6402)
PHONE..................323 467-1244
Mike Doggett, *Manager*
Heather Sanchez, *Personnel Exec*
EMP: 150
SALES (corp-wide): 62.9MM **Privately Held**
WEB: www.vidfilm.com
SIC: 7819 TV tape services: editing, transfers, etc.; sound (effects & music production), motion picture
HQ: Technicolor Creative Services Usa, Inc.
6040 W Sunset Blvd
Los Angeles CA 90028
818 260-3800

(P-17769)
TECHNCLOR VDOCASSETTE MICH INC (DH)
Also Called: Technicolor Video Service
3233 Mission Oaks Blvd, Camarillo (93012-5138)
PHONE..................805 445-1122
Lanni Ormonvo, *President*
John H Oliphant, *Admin Sec*
▲ **EMP:** 500
SQ FT: 300,000
SALES (est): 42.2MM
SALES (corp-wide): 62.9MM **Privately Held**
SIC: 7819 Video tape or disk reproduction
HQ: Technicolor Thomson Group, Inc
2233 N Ontario St Ste 300
Burbank CA 91504
818 260-3600

(P-17770)
TECHNICOLOR INC (DH)
3233 Mission Oaks Blvd, Camarillo (93012-5097)
PHONE..................805 445-1122
Quinton Lily, *President*
▲ **EMP:** 55
SALES (est): 11.8MM
SALES (corp-wide): 62.9MM **Privately Held**
WEB: www.technicolor.com
SIC: 7819 Video tape or disk reproduction
HQ: Technicolor Thomson Group, Inc
2233 N Ontario St Ste 300
Burbank CA 91504
818 260-3600

(P-17771)
TECHNICOLOR HM ENTRMT SVCS INC
Also Called: Technicolor - Funimation Ent
1778 Zinetta Rd Ste F, Calexico (92231-9510)
PHONE..................760 357-3372
EMP: 268
SALES (corp-wide): 62.9MM **Privately Held**
SIC: 7819 Video tape or disk reproduction
HQ: Technicolor Home Entertainment Services, Inc.
3233 Mission Oaks Blvd
Camarillo CA 93012

(P-17772)
TECHNICOLOR HM ENTRMT SVCS INC
Also Called: Accounts Payable Department
5491 E Philadelphia St, Ontario (91761-2807)
P.O. Box 2459, Rancho Cucamonga (91729-2459)
PHONE..................909 974-2016
EMP: 301
SALES (corp-wide): 62.9MM **Privately Held**
SIC: 7819 Video tape or disk reproduction
HQ: Technicolor Home Entertainment Services, Inc.
3233 Mission Oaks Blvd
Camarillo CA 93012

(P-17773)
TECHNICOLOR HM ENTRMT SVCS INC (HQ)
Also Called: Technicolor Video Services
3233 Mission Oaks Blvd, Camarillo (93012-5097)
PHONE..................805 445-1122
Lanny Raimondo, *CEO*
Orlando F Raimondo, *President*
Patricia Dave, *CFO*
▲ **EMP:** 500
SQ FT: 5,000
SALES (est): 352.6MM
SALES (corp-wide): 62.9MM **Privately Held**
SIC: 7819 Video tape or disk reproduction

(P-17774)
TECHNICOLOR THOMSON GROUP
Also Called: Technicolor Hollywood
6040 W Sunset Blvd, Los Angeles (90028-6402)
PHONE..................323 817-6600
Michael Doggett, *Manager*
Tom Cotton, *President*
Jennifer Boyack, *Vice Pres*
Michael Stiles, *Vice Pres*
Pat Taylor, *Executive Asst*
EMP: 573
SALES (corp-wide): 62.9MM **Privately Held**
SIC: 7819 Video tape or disk reproduction; developing & printing of commercial motion picture film
HQ: Technicolor Thomson Group, Inc
2233 N Ontario St Ste 300
Burbank CA 91504
818 260-3600

(P-17775)
TECHNICOLOR THOMSON GROUP
2255 N Ontario St Ste 100, Burbank (91504-3194)
PHONE..................818 260-3600
Juliana Bacchus, *Branch Mgr*
EMP: 301
SQ FT: 200,000
SALES (corp-wide): 62.9MM **Privately Held**
WEB: www.technicolor.com
SIC: 7819 2759 Film processing, editing & titling: motion picture; TV tape services: editing, transfers, etc.; commercial printing

HQ: Technicolor Thomson Group, Inc
2233 N Ontario St Ste 300
Burbank CA 91504
818 260-3600

(P-17776)
TECHNICOLOR THOMSON GROUP
Technicolor Entertainment Svcs
5491 E Philadelphia St, Ontario (91761-2807)
PHONE..................909 974-2222
Mary Nakagawa, *Manager*
EMP: 300
SALES (corp-wide): 62.9MM **Privately Held**
WEB: www.technicolor.com
SIC: 7819 Video tape or disk reproduction; developing & printing of commercial motion picture film
HQ: Technicolor Thomson Group, Inc
2233 N Ontario St Ste 300
Burbank CA 91504
818 260-3600

(P-17777)
TECHNICOLOR THOMSON GROUP
3301 Mission Oaks Blvd, Camarillo (93012-5048)
PHONE..................805 445-1122
Orlando Raimondo, *CEO*
EMP: 2000
SALES (corp-wide): 62.9MM **Privately Held**
WEB: www.technicolor.com
SIC: 7819 Video tape or disk reproduction; developing & printing of commercial motion picture film
HQ: Technicolor Thomson Group, Inc
2233 N Ontario St Ste 300
Burbank CA 91504
818 260-3600

(P-17778)
TEN PUBLISHING MEDIA LLC (PA)
831 S Douglas St Ste 100, El Segundo (90245-4956)
PHONE..................310 531-9900
Scott P Dickey, *CEO*
Peter H Englehart, *Ch of Bd*
Chris Argentieri, *President*
Bill Sutman, *CFO*
Jonathan Anastas, *Chief Mktg Ofcr*
EMP: 230
SALES (est): 66.9MM **Privately Held**
WEB: www.sourceinterlink.com
SIC: 7819 Visual effects production

(P-17779)
THINKWELL DESIGN & PROD INC
Also Called: Thinkwell Design & Productions
2710 Media Center Dr, Los Angeles (90065-1746)
PHONE..................818 333-3444
Cliff Warner, *CEO*
Craig Hanna, *CTO*
Kris Springer, *Info Tech Mgr*
Yoli Romeo, *Opers Mgr*
EMP: 115 **EST:** 2001
SALES (est): 158.3K **Privately Held**
SIC: 7819 Services allied to motion pictures; visual effects production

(P-17780)
WALT DISNEY IMAGINEERING (DH)
1401 Flower St, Glendale (91201-2421)
P.O. Box 25020 (91221-5020)
PHONE..................818 544-6500
Thomas O Staggs, *CEO*
Martin A Sklar, *Vice Ch Bd*
Craig Russell, *Exec VP*
Markus Gross, *Vice Pres*
Jessica Hodgins, *Vice Pres*
▲ **EMP:** 1011
SQ FT: 100,000
SALES (est): 106.3MM
SALES (corp-wide): 90.2B **Publicly Held**
SIC: 7819 8712 1542 8741 Visual effects production; architectural services; custom builders, non-residential; management services; engineering services

HQ: Disney Enterprises, Inc.
500 S Buena Vista St
Burbank CA 91521
818 560-1000

(P-17781)
WALT DISNEY PICTURES
811 Sonora Ave, Glendale (91201-2433)
PHONE..................818 409-2200
Meredith Roberts, *Senior VP*
EMP: 300 **EST:** 1983
SQ FT: 461,000
SALES (est): 8.8MM
SALES (corp-wide): 90.2B **Publicly Held**
SIC: 7819 TV tape services: editing, transfers, etc.
PA: The Walt Disney Company
500 S Buena Vista St
Burbank CA 91521
818 560-1000

7822 Motion Picture & Video Tape Distribution

(P-17782)
ABC CABLE NETWORKS GROUP
Also Called: Buena Vista Pictures Dist
698 S Buena Vista St, Burbank (91521-0001)
PHONE..................818 560-4365
Cindy Cohen-Hiller, *Vice Pres*
Chuch Viane, *President*
EMP: 190
SALES (corp-wide): 90.2B **Publicly Held**
WEB: www.breakbar.com
SIC: 7822 Distribution, exclusive of production: motion picture
HQ: Abc Cable Networks Group
500 S Buena Vista St
Burbank CA 91521
818 460-7477

(P-17783)
BLEACHER REPORT INC
153 Kearny St Fl 2, San Francisco (94108-4808)
PHONE..................415 777-5505
Dave Finocchio, *CEO*
Sam Toles, *Officer*
Josh Abrams, *Vice Pres*
Bill McCandless, *Vice Pres*
Rich Calacci, *Principal*
EMP: 104
SALES (est): 10MM
SALES (corp-wide): 170.7B **Publicly Held**
SIC: 7822 4833 4841 7812 Motion picture distribution; television broadcasting stations; cable television services; motion picture production
HQ: Turner Broadcasting System, Inc.
1 Cnn Ctr Nw 14sw
Atlanta GA 30303
404 575-7250

(P-17784)
BUENA VISTA INTERNATIONAL INC (DH)
500 S Buena Vista St, Burbank (91521-0001)
PHONE..................818 560-1000
David M Hollis, *CEO*
Mark D Zoradi, *President*
David Hughes, *Treasurer*
▲ **EMP:** 50
SALES (est): 8.3MM
SALES (corp-wide): 90.2B **Publicly Held**
WEB: www.filmes.net
SIC: 7822 Distribution, exclusive of production: motion picture; distribution for television: motion picture

(P-17785)
DISNEY INTERFINANCE CORP
500 S Buena Vista St, Burbank (91521-0001)
PHONE..................818 560-1000
David K Thompson, *President*
EMP: 360
SALES (est): 1.5MM
SALES (corp-wide): 90.2B **Publicly Held**
SIC: 7822 Distribution, exclusive of production: motion picture

HQ: Disney Enterprises, Inc.
500 S Buena Vista St
Burbank CA 91521
818 560-1000

(P-17786)
ERO-TECH CORP
2301 S El Camino Real, San Mateo
(94403-2213)
PHONE..................................415 468-5600
David Sturman, *President*
▲ EMP: 100
SALES (est): 2.6MM **Privately Held**
SIC: 7822 5192 Video tapes, recorded:
wholesale; magazines

(P-17787)
IMAGE ENTERTAINMENT INC
(DH)
6320 Canoga Ave Ste 790, Woodland Hills
(91367-2561)
PHONE..................................818 407-9100
Miguel Penella, *COO*
Drew Wilson, *CFO*
▲ EMP: 57
SQ FT: 30,000
SALES (est): 9.8MM
SALES (corp-wide): 2.9B **Publicly Held**
WEB: www.image-entertainment.com
SIC: 7822 Motion picture & tape distribu-
tion
HQ: Rlj Entertainment, Inc.
8515 Georgia Ave Ste 650
Silver Spring MD 20910
301 608-2115

(P-17788)
METROLUX THEATRES
Also Called: Metrolux 14 Theatres
8727 W 3rd St, Los Angeles (90048-3843)
PHONE..................................310 858-2800
EMP: 70
SALES (est): 2.5MM **Privately Held**
SIC: 7822 Motion picture & tape distribu-
tion

(P-17789)
MORGAN CREEK
PRODUCTIONS (PA)
10351 Santa Monica Blvd # 200, Los Ange-
les (90025-6937)
PHONE..................................310 432-4848
James Robinson, *Ch of Bd*
Barbara Wall, *Vice Pres*
EMP: 60
SQ FT: 3,497
SALES (est): 3.2MM **Privately Held**
SIC: 7822 Motion picture & tape distribu-
tion

(P-17790)
REVOLUTION STUDIOS DIST CO
LP (PA)
225 Santa Monica Blvd # 900, Santa Mon-
ica (90401-2209)
PHONE..................................310 255-7000
Joe Roth, *Mng Member*
▲ EMP: 60
SALES (est): 2.4MM **Privately Held**
SIC: 7822 Motion picture & tape distribu-
tion

(P-17791)
SONY DADC NEW MDIA
SLTIONS INC
4499 Glencoe Ave, Marina Del Rey
(90292-6357)
PHONE..................................310 760-8500
Scott Hamilton, *President*
EMP: 200 **EST:** 2015
SQ FT: 20,000
SALES (est): 401.6K **Privately Held**
SIC: 7822 7374 Motion picture & tape dis-
tribution; data processing & preparation

(P-17792)
TWENTIETH CNTURY FOX INTL
CORP (DH)
Also Called: Fox Corporation
10201 W Pico Blvd Bldg 1, Los Angeles
(90064-2606)
Rural Route 900, Beverly Hills (90213)
PHONE..................................310 969-5300
Pat Wyatt, *Ch of Bd*
Bob Delellis, *President*

Craig Sloan, *President*
Dean Hallett, *CFO*
David Miller, *Treasurer*
◆ EMP: 324
SQ FT: 115,000
SALES (est): 59.7MM
SALES (corp-wide): 90.2B **Publicly Held**
SIC: 7822 7922 Motion picture distribu-
tion; television program, including com-
mercial producers
HQ: Twentieth Century Fox Film Corpora-
tion
10201 W Pico Blvd
Los Angeles CA 90064
310 369-1000

(P-17793)
UNITED ARTISTS
PRODUCTIONS INC
10250 Constellation Blvd # 19, Los Angeles
(90067-6200)
PHONE..................................310 449-3000
Christopher McGurk, *President*
EMP: 200
SALES (est): 1MM
SALES (corp-wide): 1.1B **Privately Held**
WEB: www.unitedartists.com
SIC: 7822 Distribution, exclusive of pro-
duction: motion picture; distribution for tel-
evision: motion picture
HQ: United Artists Pictures Inc.
10250 Constellation Blvd
Los Angeles CA 90067

(P-17794)
UNITED ARTISTS TELEVISION
CORP
10250 Constellation Blvd # 27, Los Angeles
(90067-6200)
PHONE..................................310 449-3000
EMP: 150
SALES (est): 448.9K
SALES (corp-wide): 1.1B **Privately Held**
SIC: 7822 Distribution, exclusive of pro-
duction: motion picture; distribution for tel-
evision: motion picture
HQ: United Artists Pictures Inc.
10250 Constellation Blvd
Los Angeles CA 90067

(P-17795)
VUBIQUITY INC
15301 Ventura Blvd Bldg E, Sherman Oaks
(91403-5885)
PHONE..................................818 526-5000
Darcy Antonellis, *Branch Mgr*
EMP: 200 **Privately Held**
SIC: 7822 Motion picture & tape distribu-
tion
HQ: Vubiquity, Inc.
3900 W Alameda Ave Ste 17
Burbank CA 91505

(P-17796)
WARNER BROS
TRANSATLANTIC INC (DH)
4000 Warner Blvd, Burbank (91522-0002)
PHONE..................................818 977-0018
Barry M Meyer, *CEO*
Jeremy Williams, *President*
Ralph Peterson, *Treasurer*
Dean Hale, *Officer*
Scott Phelan, *Officer*
▲ EMP: 729
SALES (est): 344.1MM
SALES (corp-wide): 170.7B **Publicly
Held**
WEB: www.juwannamann.com
SIC: 7822 Distribution, exclusive of pro-
duction: motion picture

(P-17797)
WARNER BROS
TRANSATLANTIC INC
3300 W Olive Ave Ste 200, Burbank
(91505-4658)
PHONE..................................818 977-6384
Scott Levy, *Branch Mgr*
Lawrence Smith, *Info Tech Dir*
EMP: 515

SALES (corp-wide): 170.7B **Publicly
Held**
SIC: 7822 Distribution, exclusive of pro-
duction: motion picture
HQ: Warner Bros. (Transatlantic), Inc.
4000 Warner Blvd
Burbank CA 91522
818 977-0018

(P-17798)
WARNER BROS
TRANSATLANTIC INC
Also Called: Telepictures
3500 W Olive Ave Ste 1000, Burbank
(91505-5515)
PHONE..................................818 972-0777
Khuyem Phan, *Branch Mgr*
Joshua Barber, *Counsel*
EMP: 515
SALES (corp-wide): 170.7B **Publicly
Held**
SIC: 7822 Distribution, exclusive of pro-
duction: motion picture
HQ: Warner Bros. (Transatlantic), Inc.
4000 Warner Blvd
Burbank CA 91522
818 977-0018

**7829 Services Allied To
Motion Picture Distribution**

(P-17799)
PACIFIC THEATERS
Also Called: Northridge Fashion Center 10
9400 Shirley Ave, Northridge (91324-2413)
PHONE..................................818 501-5121
Joshua Watts, *Manager*
EMP: 60
SALES (est): 1.1MM **Privately Held**
SIC: 7829 Motion picture distribution serv-
ices

(P-17800)
WALT DISNEY PICTURES AND
TV
500 S Buena Vista St, Burbank
(91521-0007)
PHONE..................................818 560-1000
Bob Iger, *CEO*
Robert Matschullat, *Vice Chairman*
Ravi Ahuja, *President*
Alan Bergman, *President*
Richard W Cook, *Chairman*
▲ EMP: 56
SALES (est): 5.4MM
SALES (corp-wide): 90.2B **Publicly Held**
SIC: 7829 Motion picture distribution serv-
ices
HQ: Disney Enterprises, Inc.
500 S Buena Vista St
Burbank CA 91521
818 560-1000

**7832 Motion Picture
Theaters, Except Drive-In**

(P-17801)
AMC ENTERTAINMENT INC
4549 Mills Cir, Ontario (91764-5220)
PHONE..................................909 476-1288
Adam Aron, *Owner*
EMP: 50
SALES (corp-wide): 7.3MM **Publicly Held**
SIC: 7832 Exhibitors, itinerant: motion pic-
ture
HQ: Amc Entertainment Inc.
11500 Ash St
Leawood KS 66211
913 213-2000

(P-17802)
AMERICAN MULTI-CINEMA INC
Also Called: AMC
125 E Palm Ave, Burbank (91502-1834)
PHONE..................................818 953-4020
EMP: 70

SALES (corp-wide): 7.3MM **Publicly Held**
WEB: www.arrowheadtowncenter.com
SIC: 7832 Motion picture theaters, except
drive-in
HQ: American Multi-Cinema, Inc.
1 Amc Way
Leawood KS 66211
913 213-2000

(P-17803)
AMERICAN MULTI-CINEMA INC
Also Called: AMC
7037 Friars Rd, San Diego (92108-1129)
PHONE..................................619 296-0370
Brian Fuller, *Manager*
Donald Griffith, *Facilities Mgr*
EMP: 50
SALES (corp-wide): 7.3MM **Publicly Held**
WEB: www.arrowheadtowncenter.com
SIC: 7832 Exhibitors, itinerant: motion pic-
ture
HQ: American Multi-Cinema, Inc.
1 Amc Way
Leawood KS 66211
913 213-2000

(P-17804)
AMERICAN MULTI-CINEMA INC
Also Called: AMC
450 N Atlantic Blvd, Monterey Park
(91754-1057)
PHONE..................................626 407-0240
EMP: 61
SALES (corp-wide): 7.3MM **Publicly Held**
SIC: 7832 Exhibitors, itinerant: motion pic-
ture
HQ: American Multi-Cinema, Inc.
1 Amc Way
Leawood KS 66211
913 213-2000

(P-17805)
AMERICAN MULTI-CINEMA INC
Also Called: AMC
1414 N Azusa Ave, Covina (91722-1251)
PHONE..................................626 974-8624
John Eisner, *Manager*
EMP: 60
SALES (corp-wide): 7.3MM **Publicly Held**
WEB: www.arrowheadtowncenter.com
SIC: 7832 Exhibitors, itinerant: motion pic-
ture
HQ: American Multi-Cinema, Inc.
1 Amc Way
Leawood KS 66211
913 213-2000

(P-17806)
AMERICAN MULTI-CINEMA INC
Also Called: AMC
2591 Airport Dr, Torrance (90505-6137)
PHONE..................................310 326-5011
Craig Adams, *Sales/Mktg Mgr*
EMP: 120
SALES (corp-wide): 7.3MM **Publicly Held**
WEB: www.arrowheadtowncenter.com
SIC: 7832 Exhibitors, itinerant: motion pic-
ture
HQ: American Multi-Cinema, Inc.
1 Amc Way
Leawood KS 66211
913 213-2000

(P-17807)
AMERICAN MULTI-CINEMA INC
Also Called: AMC
1565 S Disneyland Dr Frnt, Anaheim
(92802-2324)
PHONE..................................714 630-2410
EMP: 50
SALES (corp-wide): 7.3MM **Publicly Held**
WEB: www.arrowheadtowncenter.com
SIC: 7832 Motion picture theaters, except
drive-in
HQ: American Multi-Cinema, Inc.
1 Amc Way
Leawood KS 66211
913 213-2000

(P-17808)
AMERICAN MULTI-CINEMA INC
Also Called: AMC
20 City Blvd W Ste E1, Orange
(92868-3130)
PHONE..................................714 769-4288
Scott Shellenbergar, *Manager*

Jeremy Acosta, *Cashier*
EMP: 90
SALES (corp-wide): 7.3MM **Publicly Held**
WEB: www.arrowheadtownecenter.com
SIC: 7832 Motion picture theaters, except drive-in
HQ: American Multi-Cinema, Inc.
1 Amc Way
Leawood KS 66211
913 213-2000

(P-17809)
AMERICAN MULTI-CINEMA INC
Also Called: AMC
1001 S Lemon St Ste A, Fullerton (92832-3007)
PHONE..................................714 992-6961
Brian Lind, *Manager*
Casey Cawelti, *General Mgr*
EMP: 50
SALES (corp-wide): 7.3MM **Publicly Held**
WEB: www.arrowheadtownecenter.com
SIC: 7832 Exhibitors, itinerant: motion picture
HQ: American Multi-Cinema, Inc.
1 Amc Way
Leawood KS 66211
913 213-2000

(P-17810)
AMERICAN MULTI-CINEMA INC
Also Called: AMC
42 Miller Aly, Pasadena (91103-3643)
PHONE..................................626 585-8900
EMP: 50 **Publicly Held**
SIC: 7832
HQ: American Multi-Cinema, Inc.
1 Amc Way
Leawood KS 66211
913 213-2000

(P-17811)
AMERICAN MULTI-CINEMA INC
Also Called: AMC
12300 Civic Center Dr, Norwalk (90650-3171)
PHONE..................................562 864-6206
Gary Orland, *Executive*
EMP: 50
SALES (corp-wide): 7.3MM **Publicly Held**
WEB: www.arrowheadtownecenter.com
SIC: 7832 Exhibitors, itinerant: motion picture
HQ: American Multi-Cinema, Inc.
1 Amc Way
Leawood KS 66211
913 213-2000

(P-17812)
AMERICAN MULTI-CINEMA INC
Also Called: AMC
10250 Snta Mnca Bld, Los Angeles (90067)
PHONE..................................310 228-5500
Rick Walsh, *Branch Mgr*
EMP: 50
SALES (corp-wide): 7.3MM **Publicly Held**
SIC: 7832 Motion picture theaters, except drive-in
HQ: American Multi-Cinema, Inc.
1 Amc Way
Leawood KS 66211
913 213-2000

(P-17813)
AMERICAN MULTI-CINEMA INC
Also Called: AMC
1640 Cmino Del Rio N 20, San Diego (92108)
PHONE..................................619 296-2737
Kathy Dominguez, *Manager*
EMP: 75
SALES (corp-wide): 7.3MM **Publicly Held**
WEB: www.arrowheadtownecenter.com
SIC: 7832 Exhibitors, itinerant: motion picture
HQ: American Multi-Cinema, Inc.
1 Amc Way
Leawood KS 66211
913 213-2000

(P-17814)
AMERICAN MULTI-CINEMA INC
Also Called: AMC
1560 S Azusa Ave, City of Industry (91748-1603)
PHONE..................................626 810-7949
Favio Adane, *General Mgr*
EMP: 59
SALES (corp-wide): 7.3MM **Publicly Held**
SIC: 7832 Exhibitors, itinerant: motion picture
HQ: American Multi-Cinema, Inc.
1 Amc Way
Leawood KS 66211
913 213-2000

(P-17815)
AMERICAN MULTI-CINEMA INC
Also Called: AMC
1475 N Montebello Blvd, Montebello (90640-2584)
PHONE..................................323 722-4583
Rachell Hatton, *General Mgr*
EMP: 50
SALES (corp-wide): 7.3MM **Publicly Held**
WEB: www.arrowheadtownecenter.com
SIC: 7832 Exhibitors, itinerant: motion picture
HQ: American Multi-Cinema, Inc.
1 Amc Way
Leawood KS 66211
913 213-2000

(P-17816)
ARCLIGHT CINEMA COMPANY
15301 Ventura Blvd Bldg A, Sherman Oaks (91403-3102)
PHONE..................................818 501-0753
Christopher S Forman, *Branch Mgr*
EMP: 92
SALES (corp-wide): 12.5MM **Privately Held**
SIC: 7832 Motion picture theaters, except drive-in
PA: Arclight Cinema Company
6360 W Sunset Blvd
Los Angeles CA 90028
323 464-4226

(P-17817)
ARCLIGHT CINEMA COMPANY
120 N Robertson Blvd Fl 3, Los Angeles (90048-3115)
PHONE..................................323 464-1465
Christopher S Forman, *Branch Mgr*
EMP: 170
SALES (corp-wide): 12.5MM **Privately Held**
SIC: 7832 Motion picture theaters, except drive-in
PA: Arclight Cinema Company
6360 W Sunset Blvd
Los Angeles CA 90028
323 464-4226

(P-17818)
BAYOU CINEMAS LP
500 Citadel Dr Ste 300, Commerce (90040-1575)
PHONE..................................213 235-2244
EMP: 246
SALES (est): 63.7K
SALES (corp-wide): 309.3MM **Publicly Held**
SIC: 7832 Motion picture theaters, except drive-in
PA: Reading International, Inc.
5995 Sepulveda Blvd Fl 3
Culver City CA 90230
213 235-2240

(P-17819)
BRENDEN THEATRE CORPORATION
531 Davis St, Vacaville (95688-4632)
PHONE..................................707 469-0180
Tim Kruse, *Branch Mgr*
EMP: 70
SALES (corp-wide): 16.9MM **Privately Held**
WEB: www.brendantheaters.com
SIC: 7832 Exhibitors, itinerant: motion picture

PA: Brenden Theatre Corporation
1985 Willow Pass Rd Ste C
Concord CA 94520
925 677-0462

(P-17820)
BRENDEN THEATRE CORPORATION
1021 10th St Frnt, Modesto (95354-0888)
PHONE..................................209 491-7770
Saul Trujllo, *General Mgr*
EMP: 100
SALES (corp-wide): 16.9MM **Privately Held**
WEB: www.brendantheaters.com
SIC: 7832 Exhibitors, itinerant: motion picture
PA: Brenden Theatre Corporation
1985 Willow Pass Rd Ste C
Concord CA 94520
925 677-0462

(P-17821)
BRENDEN THEATRE CORPORATION (PA)
1985 Willow Pass Rd Ste C, Concord (94520-2533)
PHONE..................................925 677-0462
John Brenden, *President*
EMP: 189
SQ FT: 70,000
SALES (est): 16.9MM **Privately Held**
WEB: www.brendantheaters.com
SIC: 7832 Motion picture theaters, except drive-in

(P-17822)
CAL GRAN THEATRES LLC
Also Called: Valley Drive-In Theatre
3170 Santa Maria Way, Santa Maria (93455-2102)
PHONE..................................805 934-1582
Bob Gran, *President*
Diane Gran, *General Mgr*
EMP: 50
SQ FT: 1,200
SALES (est): 1MM **Privately Held**
SIC: 7832 7833 Motion picture theaters, except drive-in; drive-in motion picture theaters

(P-17823)
CINEMA CITY THEATERS
5635 E La Palma Ave, Anaheim (92807-2109)
PHONE..................................714 970-0865
Meghan Walsh, *Manager*
EMP: 50
SALES (est): 1.1MM **Privately Held**
WEB: www.cinemacitytheatres.com
SIC: 7832 Motion picture theaters, except drive-in

(P-17824)
CINEMARK USA INC
15555 E 14th St Ste 600, San Leandro (94578-1970)
PHONE..................................510 276-9684
Anthony Tan, *Branch Mgr*
EMP: 60 **Publicly Held**
SIC: 7832 Motion picture theaters, except drive-in
HQ: Cinemark Usa, Inc.
3900 Dallas Pkwy Ste 500
Plano TX 75093
972 665-1000

(P-17825)
CINEMARK USA INC
Also Called: Century Stadium 21
1590 Ethan Way, Sacramento (95825-2298)
PHONE..................................916 922-4241
Donna Sheila, *Branch Mgr*
EMP: 73 **Publicly Held**
SIC: 7832 Motion picture theaters, except drive-in
HQ: Cinemark Usa, Inc.
3900 Dallas Pkwy Ste 500
Plano TX 75093
972 665-1000

(P-17826)
CINEMARK USA INC
Also Called: Century Huntington Beach & Xd
7777 Edinger Ave Ste 170, Huntington Beach (92647-8690)
PHONE..................................714 373-4573
Kevin Cron, *Branch Mgr*
EMP: 90 **Publicly Held**
SIC: 7832 Motion picture theaters, except drive-in
HQ: Cinemark Usa, Inc.
3900 Dallas Pkwy Ste 500
Plano TX 75093
972 665-1000

(P-17827)
CINEMASTAR LUXURY THEATERS
1949 Avenida Del Oro # 100, Oceanside (92056-5829)
PHONE..................................760 945-2500
Jack R Crosby, *President*
EMP: 350
SALES (est): 4.1MM **Privately Held**
WEB: www.cinemastar.com
SIC: 7832 Motion picture theaters, except drive-in

(P-17828)
CINEPOLIS LUXURY CINEMAS
6420 Wilshire Blvd # 900, Los Angeles (90048-5502)
PHONE..................................323 556-6340
Jay Bhatt, *Project Mgr*
Luis Orozco, *Controller*
David Alvarado, *Opers Staff*
Carlos Barrera, *Marketing Mgr*
Annelise Holyoak, *Marketing Staff*
EMP: 87
SALES (est): 396.1K **Privately Held**
SIC: 7832 Motion picture theaters, except drive-in

(P-17829)
COMMERCE CENTER THEATRES
Also Called: Pacific Thtres Cmmerce Theatre
950 Goodrich Blvd, Commerce (90022-4110)
PHONE..................................323 722-5577
Roberta Sanchez, *Manager*
EMP: 60
SALES (est): 562.8K **Privately Held**
SIC: 7832 Motion picture theaters, except drive-in

(P-17830)
DE ANZA LAND & LEISURE CORP
Also Called: South Bay Drive In Theatre
2170 Coronado Ave, San Diego (92154-2022)
PHONE..................................619 423-2727
Veronica Sarabia, *Branch Mgr*
EMP: 50
SALES (corp-wide): 12.6MM **Privately Held**
SIC: 7832 Motion picture theaters, except drive-in
PA: De Anza Land & Leisure Corp.
4407 State St
Montclair CA 91763
909 628-0019

(P-17831)
DECURION CORPORATION (PA)
120 N Robertson Blvd Fl 3, Los Angeles (90048-3115)
PHONE..................................310 659-9432
Michael R Forman, *President*
Jeffrey Koblentz, *COO*
James Cotter, *Vice Pres*
Jerome Forman, *Vice Pres*
Jerry Forman, *Vice Pres*
EMP: 100
SQ FT: 31,000
SALES (est): 180.2MM **Privately Held**
SIC: 7832 7833 Motion picture theaters, except drive-in; drive-in motion picture theaters

(P-17832)
EDWARDS THEATRES CIRCUIT INC
Also Called: Jurupa Stadium Cinema 14
8032 Limonite Ave, Riverside (92509-6107)
PHONE..........................951 361-1917
EMP: 62 **Privately Held**
SIC: **7832** Motion picture theaters, except drive-in
HQ: Edwards Theatres Circuit, Inc.
 300 Newport Center Dr
 Newport Beach CA 92660
 949 640-4600

(P-17833)
EDWARDS THEATRES CIRCUIT INC
Also Called: Mesa Pointe Stadium 12
901 S Coast Dr, Costa Mesa (92626-1747)
PHONE..........................714 428-0962
Minh Duong, *Branch Mgr*
EMP: 62 **Privately Held**
SIC: **7832** Motion picture theaters, except drive-in
HQ: Edwards Theatres Circuit, Inc.
 300 Newport Center Dr
 Newport Beach CA 92660
 949 640-4600

(P-17834)
EDWARDS THEATRES CIRCUIT INC
Also Called: Rancho San Diego Cinema 16
2951 Jamacha Rd, El Cajon (92019-4342)
PHONE..........................619 660-3460
EMP: 62 **Privately Held**
SIC: **7832** Motion picture theaters, except drive-in
HQ: Edwards Theatres Circuit, Inc.
 300 Newport Center Dr
 Newport Beach CA 92660
 949 640-4600

(P-17835)
EDWARDS THEATRES CIRCUIT INC
Also Called: Kaleidioscope Stadium Cinema
27741 Crown Valley Pkwy # 323, Mission Viejo (92691-6532)
PHONE..........................949 582-4078
EMP: 62 **Privately Held**
SIC: **7832** Motion picture theaters, except drive-in
HQ: Edwards Theatres Circuit, Inc.
 300 Newport Center Dr
 Newport Beach CA 92660
 949 640-4600

(P-17836)
EDWARDS THEATRES CIRCUIT INC
Also Called: Mira Mesa Stadium 18
10733 Westview Pkwy, San Diego (92126-2963)
PHONE..........................858 635-7716
Peter Brandon, *Branch Mgr*
EMP: 62 **Privately Held**
SIC: **7832** Motion picture theaters, except drive-in
HQ: Edwards Theatres Circuit, Inc.
 300 Newport Center Dr
 Newport Beach CA 92660
 949 640-4600

(P-17837)
EDWARDS THEATRES CIRCUIT INC
Also Called: South Coast Village
1561 W Sunflower Ave, Santa Ana (92704-7436)
PHONE..........................714 557-5701
EMP: 62 **Privately Held**
SIC: **7832** Motion picture theaters, except drive-in
HQ: Edwards Theatres Circuit, Inc.
 300 Newport Center Dr
 Newport Beach CA 92660
 949 640-4600

(P-17838)
EDWARDS THEATRES CIRCUIT INC (DH)
300 Newport Center Dr, Newport Beach (92660-7529)
PHONE..........................949 640-4600
W James Edwards III, *Ch of Bd*
Steve Coffey, *President*
Joan Randolph, *Vice Pres*
Marcella Sheldon, *Admin Sec*
EMP: 118
SQ FT: 30,000
SALES (est): 78.3MM **Privately Held**
SIC: **7832** Motion picture theaters, except drive-in
HQ: Regal Cinemas, Inc.
 101 E Blount Ave Ste 100
 Knoxville TN 37920
 865 922-1123

(P-17839)
EDWARDS THEATRES CIRCUIT INC
Also Called: San Marcos Stadium Cinema 18
1180 W San Marcos Blvd, San Marcos (92078-4009)
PHONE..........................760 471-3734
Jerry Jorgensen, *Manager*
EMP: 100 **Privately Held**
SIC: **7832** Motion picture theaters, except drive-in
HQ: Edwards Theatres Circuit, Inc.
 300 Newport Center Dr
 Newport Beach CA 92660
 949 640-4600

(P-17840)
EDWARDS THEATRES CIRCUIT INC
Also Called: Cerritos Cinemas 10
12761 Towne Center Dr, Artesia (90703-8545)
PHONE..........................562 403-1133
James Edwards III, *Branch Mgr*
EMP: 60 **Privately Held**
SIC: **7832** Motion picture theaters, except drive-in
HQ: Edwards Theatres Circuit, Inc.
 300 Newport Center Dr
 Newport Beach CA 92660
 949 640-4600

(P-17841)
EDWARDS THEATRES CIRCUIT INC
Also Called: Temecula Stadium Cinemas 15
40750 Winchester Rd, Temecula (92591-5524)
PHONE..........................951 296-0144
EMP: 62 **Privately Held**
SIC: **7832** Motion picture theaters, except drive-in
HQ: Edwards Theatres Circuit, Inc.
 300 Newport Center Dr
 Newport Beach CA 92660
 949 640-4600

(P-17842)
EDWARDS THEATRES CIRCUIT INC
Also Called: Edwards Cinemas University
4245 Campus Dr, Irvine (92612-2752)
PHONE..........................949 854-8811
Mike Peterson, *Branch Mgr*
EMP: 62 **Privately Held**
SIC: **7832** Motion picture theaters, except drive-in
HQ: Edwards Theatres Circuit, Inc.
 300 Newport Center Dr
 Newport Beach CA 92660
 949 640-4600

(P-17843)
EDWARDS THEATRES CIRCUIT INC
Also Called: Simi Valley Plaza 10
1457 E Los Angeles Ave, Simi Valley (93065-2807)
PHONE..........................805 526-4329
Dominiqua Lint, *Branch Mgr*
EMP: 62 **Privately Held**
SIC: **7832** Motion picture theaters, except drive-in

HQ: Edwards Theatres Circuit, Inc.
 300 Newport Center Dr
 Newport Beach CA 92660
 949 640-4600

(P-17844)
EDWARDS THEATRES CIRCUIT INC
Also Called: Santa Maria Cinema 10
1521 S Bradley Rd, Santa Maria (93454-8014)
PHONE..........................805 347-1164
Santa Edwards, *Manager*
EMP: 62 **Privately Held**
SIC: **7832** Motion picture theaters, except drive-in
HQ: Edwards Theatres Circuit, Inc.
 300 Newport Center Dr
 Newport Beach CA 92660
 949 640-4600

(P-17845)
HARKINS THEATRES INC
3100 Chino Ave, Chino Hills (91709)
PHONE..........................909 627-8010
Sarah Yeats, *Principal*
EMP: 56 **Privately Held**
SIC: **7832** Motion picture theaters, except drive-in
PA: Harkins Theatres, Inc.
 7511 E Mcdonald Dr
 Scottsdale AZ 85250

(P-17846)
IMAX CORPORATION (HQ)
Also Called: Imax Theatre Marketing
12582 Millennium, Los Angeles (90094-2823)
PHONE..........................310 255-5559
Richard Gelfond, *CEO*
Greg Foster, *President*
◆ EMP: 97
SALES (est): 16.3MM
SALES (corp-wide): 374.4MM **Privately Held**
WEB: www.imaxcorporation.com
SIC: **7832** Motion picture theaters, except drive-in
PA: Imax Corporation
 2525 Speakman Dr
 Mississauga ON L5K 1
 905 403-6500

(P-17847)
KRIKORIAN PREMIERE THEATRE LLC
8290 La Palma Ave, Buena Park (90620)
PHONE..........................626 305-7469
Ted Goldbeck, *Branch Mgr*
Todd Cummings, *VP Opers*
EMP: 108
SALES (corp-wide): 63.1MM **Privately Held**
WEB: www.krikorianmetroplex.com
SIC: **7832** Motion picture theaters, except drive-in
PA: Krikorian Premiere Theatre Llc
 2275 W 190th St
 Torrance CA 90504
 310 856-1270

(P-17848)
KRIKORIAN PREMIERE THEATRE LLC
25 Main St, Vista (92083-5800)
PHONE..........................760 945-7469
EMP: 108
SALES (corp-wide): 63.1MM **Privately Held**
SIC: **7832** Motion picture theaters, except drive-in
PA: Krikorian Premiere Theatre Llc
 2275 W 190th St
 Torrance CA 90504
 310 856-1270

(P-17849)
KRIKORIAN PREMIERE THEATRE LLC
8540 Whittier Blvd, Pico Rivera (90660-2520)
PHONE..........................562 205-3456
Todd Cummings, *Branch Mgr*
EMP: 65

HQ: Edwards Theatres Circuit, Inc.
 300 Newport Center Dr
 Newport Beach CA 92660
 949 640-4600

(P-17844)
EDWARDS THEATRES CIRCUIT INC

SALES (corp-wide): 63.1MM **Privately Held**
SIC: **7832** Motion picture theaters, except drive-in
PA: Krikorian Premiere Theatre Llc
 2275 W 190th St
 Torrance CA 90504
 310 856-1270

(P-17850)
METROPLEX THEATRES LLC
2275 W 190th St Ste 201, Torrance (90504-6007)
PHONE..........................310 856-1270
George Krikorian,
EMP: 600
SALES (est): 8.9MM **Privately Held**
SIC: **7832** Motion picture theaters, except drive-in

(P-17851)
NORTH AMERICAN CINEMAS INC
Also Called: Airport Cinemas 12
409 Aviation Blvd, Santa Rosa (95403-1069)
PHONE..........................707 571-1412
Nicholas Mann, *General Mgr*
EMP: 365 **Privately Held**
WEB: www.northamericacinemas.com
SIC: **7832** Motion picture theaters, except drive-in
PA: North American Cinemas, Inc.
 816 4th St
 Santa Rosa CA 95404

(P-17852)
PACIFIC THEATERS INC (PA)
120 N Robertson Blvd Fl 3, Los Angeles (90048-3113)
PHONE..........................310 657-8420
Michael Forman, *Ch of Bd*
Christopher Forman, *CEO*
Gary Marcotte, *CFO*
Kevin Elms, *Treasurer*
EMP: 120 EST: 1950
SQ FT: 25,000
SALES (est): 8.3MM **Privately Held**
SIC: **7832** Exhibitors, itinerant: motion picture; motion picture production & distribution, television

(P-17853)
PACIFIC THEATERS INC
Also Called: Beach Cities 16 Cinemas
831 S Nash St, El Segundo (90245-4708)
PHONE..........................310 607-0007
Gaye Clemson, *Manager*
EMP: 55
SALES (corp-wide): 7.2MM **Privately Held**
SIC: **7832** Motion picture theaters, except drive-in
PA: Pacific Theaters, Inc
 120 N Robertson Blvd Fl 3
 Los Angeles CA 90048
 310 657-8420

(P-17854)
PACIFIC THEATERS INC
4821 Del Amo Blvd, Lakewood (90712-2504)
PHONE..........................562 634-1183
Bill Bayam, *Manager*
Todd Neuman, *Risk Mgmt Dir*
Penny McNamee, *Manager*
EMP: 80
SALES (corp-wide): 7.2MM **Privately Held**
SIC: **7832** Exhibitors, itinerant: motion picture
PA: Pacific Theaters, Inc
 120 N Robertson Blvd Fl 3
 Los Angeles CA 90048
 310 657-8420

(P-17855)
PACIFIC THEATRES ENTRMT CORP (HQ)
120 N Robertson Blvd Fl 3, Los Angeles (90048-3113)
PHONE..........................310 659-9432
Christopher Forman, *Ch of Bd*
Joe Robinson, *Administration*
EMP: 100 EST: 1962

PRODUCTS & SVCS

SQ FT: 3,000
SALES (est): 7.8MM
SALES (corp-wide): 180.2MM **Privately Held**
WEB: www.pacifictheatres.com
SIC: **7832** Motion picture theaters, except drive-in
PA: The Decurion Corporation
120 N Robertson Blvd Fl 3
Los Angeles CA 90048
310 659-9432

(P-17856)
PARAMOUNT THEATRE OF ARTS INC
2025 Broadway, Oakland (94612-2303)
PHONE..................510 893-2300
Leslee Stewart, *Director*
Chris Bahara, *Manager*
Sherre Giles, *Manager*
EMP: 60
SQ FT: 37,000
SALES: 4.4MM **Privately Held**
SIC: **7832** Motion picture theaters, except drive-in

(P-17857)
READING ENTERTAINMENT INC (HQ)
500 Citadel Dr Ste 300, Commerce (90040-1575)
PHONE..................213 235-2226
Robert F Smerling, *President*
John Hunter, *COO*
Andrzej Matyczynski, *CFO*
Craig Tompkins, *Exec VP*
Terri Alvarez, *Vice Pres*
▲ EMP: 78
SQ FT: 3,300
SALES (est): 3.2MM
SALES (corp-wide): 309.3MM **Publicly Held**
SIC: **7832** Motion picture theaters, except drive-in
PA: Reading International, Inc.
5995 Sepulveda Blvd Fl 3
Culver City CA 90230
213 235-2240

(P-17858)
READING INTERNATIONAL INC
41090 California Oaks Rd, Murrieta (92562-5749)
PHONE..................951 696-7045
Dolly Woodland, *General Mgr*
EMP: 50
SALES (corp-wide): 309.3MM **Publicly Held**
SIC: **7832** Motion picture theaters, except drive-in
PA: Reading International, Inc.
5995 Sepulveda Blvd Fl 3
Culver City CA 90230
213 235-2240

(P-17859)
READING INTERNATIONAL INC
Also Called: Angelika Film Center and Cafe
11620 Carmel Mountain Rd, San Diego (92128-4621)
PHONE..................858 207-2606
Chris Herbert, *General Mgr*
EMP: 60
SALES (corp-wide): 309.3MM **Publicly Held**
SIC: **7832** 5812 5182 Motion picture theaters, except drive-in; cafe; wine & distilled beverages
PA: Reading International, Inc.
5995 Sepulveda Blvd Fl 3
Culver City CA 90230
213 235-2240

(P-17860)
READING INTERNATIONAL INC
2508 Land Park Dr, Sacramento (95818-2224)
PHONE..................916 442-0985
EMP: 205
SALES (corp-wide): 309.3MM **Publicly Held**
SIC: **7832** Motion picture theaters, except drive-in

PA: Reading International, Inc.
5995 Sepulveda Blvd Fl 3
Culver City CA 90230
213 235-2240

(P-17861)
READING INTERNATIONAL INC (PA)
5995 Sepulveda Blvd Fl 3, Culver City (90230-6400)
PHONE..................213 235-2240
Ellen M Cotter, *Ch of Bd*
Robert F Smerling, *President*
Gilbert Avanes, *CFO*
Margaret Cotter, *Vice Ch Bd*
Michael Wrotniak, *Bd of Directors*
EMP: 85
SQ FT: 11,700
SALES: 309.3MM **Publicly Held**
SIC: **7832** 7922 6512 6531 Motion picture theaters, except drive-in; theatrical producers & services; nonresidential building operators; real estate agents & managers

(P-17862)
REGAL CINEMAS INC
Also Called: Natomas Marketplace 16
3561 Truxel Rd, Sacramento (95834-3641)
PHONE..................916 419-0205
Ricks Hescock, *Manager*
EMP: 60 **Privately Held**
WEB: www.regalcinemas.com
SIC: **7832** Motion picture theaters, except drive-in
HQ: Regal Cinemas, Inc.
101 E Blount Ave Ste 100
Knoxville TN 37920
865 922-1123

(P-17863)
REGAL CINEMAS INC
550 Deep Valley Dr # 339, Rllng HLS Est (90274-7603)
PHONE..................310 544-3042
Christy Alexander, *Manager*
EMP: 80 **Privately Held**
WEB: www.regalcinemas.com
SIC: **7832** Motion picture theaters, except drive-in
HQ: Regal Cinemas, Inc.
101 E Blount Ave Ste 100
Knoxville TN 37920
865 922-1123

(P-17864)
REGENCY THEATRES INC
26901 Agoura Rd Ste 150, Agoura Hills (91301-5114)
PHONE..................818 224-3825
Lyndon H Golin, *President*
Monica Golin, *CFO*
Angie Haziza, *Marketing Staff*
Crystal Whittaker, *Marketing Staff*
EMP: 50
SQ FT: 1,000
SALES: 4MM **Privately Held**
WEB: www.regencymovies.com
SIC: **7832** Motion picture theaters, except drive-in

(P-17865)
SANBORN THEATRES INC
41090 Calif Oaks Rd, Murrieta (92562-5749)
PHONE..................909 296-9728
Arthur Sanborn, *Branch Mgr*
EMP: 70
SALES (corp-wide): 10.9MM **Privately Held**
SIC: **7832** Motion picture theaters, except drive-in
PA: Sanborn Theatres Inc
13 Corporate Plaza Dr # 110
Newport Beach CA 92660
949 640-2370

(P-17866)
SILVER CINEMAS ACQUISITION CO (HQ)
Also Called: Landmark Theatres
2222 S Barrington Ave, Los Angeles (90064-1206)
PHONE..................310 473-6701
George T Mundorff, *CEO*
Paul Serwitz, *President*

Sky Hansen, *CFO*
Dale Friddell, *Vice Pres*
David Barlow, *General Mgr*
EMP: 52
SALES (est): 76.1MM **Privately Held**
SIC: **7832** Motion picture theaters, except drive-in
PA: Cohen Media Group Llc
750 Lexington Ave Ste 500
New York NY 10022
646 380-7929

(P-17867)
UA GALAXY LOS CERRITOS
Also Called: Ua Galaxy Los Cerritos 33
4900 E 4th St, Ontario (91764-5229)
PHONE..................562 865-6499
Mike Friextad, *Manager*
EMP: 70
SALES (est): 939.4K **Privately Held**
SIC: **7832** Motion picture theaters, except drive-in

(P-17868)
WESTSTAR CINEMAS INC
Also Called: Mann's Theatres
6801 Hollywood Blvd # 335, Los Angeles (90028-6136)
PHONE..................323 461-3331
Laval How, *Manager*
EMP: 95
SALES (corp-wide): 26.5MM **Privately Held**
WEB: www.manntheatres.com
SIC: **7832** Motion picture theaters, except drive-in
PA: Weststar Cinemas, Inc
16530 Ventura Blvd # 500
Encino CA 91436
818 784-6266

(P-17869)
WF CINEMA HOLDINGS LP
Also Called: Village 8
180 Promenade Way Ste R, Westlake Village (91362-3826)
PHONE..................805 379-8966
Joseph Leptore, *Manager*
EMP: 50
SALES (corp-wide): 29.1MM **Privately Held**
WEB: www.manntheatres.com
SIC: **7832** Motion picture theaters, except drive-in
PA: Weststar Cinemas, Inc
16530 Ventura Blvd # 500
Encino CA 91436
818 784-6266

(P-17870)
WF CINEMA HOLDINGS LP
Also Called: Mann Theaters
3500 W Olive Ave Ste 890, Burbank (91505-4667)
PHONE..................818 784-6266
Peter Dobson, *CEO*
EMP: 2000 EST: 2000
SALES (est): 9.1MM
SALES (corp-wide): 170.7B **Publicly Held**
SIC: **7832** Motion picture theaters, except drive-in
HQ: Historic Tw Inc.
75 Rockefeller Plz
New York NY 10019

7833 Drive-In Motion Picture Theaters

(P-17871)
CENTURY THEATRES INC
Also Called: Century 14
1555 Eureka Rd, Roseville (95661-3040)
PHONE..................916 797-3466
Ray Syufy, *President*
EMP: 70 **Publicly Held**
WEB: www.centurytheaters.com
SIC: **7833** 7832 Drive-in motion picture theaters; motion picture theaters, except drive-in

HQ: Century Theatres, Inc
3900 Dallas Pkwy Ste 500
Plano TX 75093
972 665-1000

(P-17872)
CENTURY THEATRES INC
3200 Klose Way, Richmond (94806-5792)
PHONE..................510 758-9626
Makisha Jones, *Manager*
EMP: 90 **Publicly Held**
WEB: www.centurytheaters.com
SIC: **7833** 7832 Drive-in motion picture theaters; motion picture theaters, except drive-in
HQ: Century Theatres, Inc
3900 Dallas Pkwy Ste 500
Plano TX 75093
972 665-1000

(P-17873)
CENTURY THEATRES INC
Also Called: Century 8
12827 Victory Blvd, North Hollywood (91606-3012)
PHONE..................818 508-1943
Terrell Hammack, *Branch Mgr*
EMP: 60 **Publicly Held**
WEB: www.centurytheaters.com
SIC: **7833** 7832 Drive-in motion picture theaters; motion picture theaters, except drive-in
HQ: Century Theatres, Inc
3900 Dallas Pkwy Ste 500
Plano TX 75093
972 665-1000

(P-17874)
MISSION DRIVE-IN THEATRE CO
Also Called: Los Angeles Dr-In Theatre Co
4407 State St, Montclair (91763-6034)
PHONE..................909 465-9219
William Oldknow, *Managing Prtnr*
Charles P Skouras III, *Partner*
Charles P Skouras Jr, *Partner*
Diane M Skouras, *Partner*
Christianna Skouras-Marin, *Partner*
EMP: 60
SQ FT: 500
SALES (est): 3.2MM **Privately Held**
WEB: www.missiontiki.com
SIC: **7833** 6515 5932 Drive-in motion picture theaters; mobile home site operators; used merchandise stores

(P-17875)
NATIONWIDE THEATRES CORP (HQ)
120 N Robertson Blvd Fl 3, Los Angeles (90048-3115)
PHONE..................310 657-8420
Christopher Forman, *President*
Nora Dashwood, *COO*
EMP: 75
SQ FT: 25,000
SALES (est): 38.5MM
SALES (corp-wide): 180.2MM **Privately Held**
SIC: **7833** 7832 Drive-in motion picture theaters; motion picture theaters, except drive-in
PA: The Decurion Corporation
120 N Robertson Blvd Fl 3
Los Angeles CA 90048
310 659-9432

7841 Video Tape Rental

(P-17876)
NETFLIX INC
121 Albright Way, Los Gatos (95032-1801)
PHONE..................408 540-3700
EMP: 2000 **Publicly Held**
SIC: **7841** Video disk/tape rental to the general public
PA: Netflix, Inc.
100 Winchester Cir
Los Gatos CA 95032

(P-17877)
SABAN FILMS LLC
10100 Santa Monica Blvd # 2525, Los Angeles (90067-4160)
PHONE...................310 203-5850
Bill Bromiley, *President*
Shanan Becker, *CFO*
Jonathan Saba, *Senior VP*
Azniv Tashchyan, *Senior VP*
Ness Saban, *Vice Pres*
EMP: 63
SALES (est): 206.6K
SALES (corp-wide): 17.4MM **Privately Held**
SIC: 7841 Film or tape rental, motion picture
PA: Saban Capital Group, Inc.
10100 Santa Monica Blvd
Los Angeles CA 90067
310 557-5100

7911 Dance Studios, Schools & Halls

(P-17878)
CLOVIS UNIFIED SCHOOL DISTRICT
885 Gettysburg Ave, Clovis (93612-3906)
PHONE...................559 327-3900
EMP: 635
SALES (corp-wide): 316MM **Privately Held**
SIC: 7911 Dance instructor & school services
PA: Clovis Unified School District
1450 Herndon Ave
Clovis CA 93611
559 327-9000

(P-17879)
FOUNDATION FOR DANCE EDUCATION
Also Called: INLAND PACIFIC BALLET
9061 Central Ave, Montclair (91763-1622)
PHONE...................909 482-1590
Victoria Koenig, *Exec Dir*
▲ EMP: 51
SALES: 679.9K **Privately Held**
SIC: 7911 Dance instructor & school services

(P-17880)
GABRIELLA FOUNDATION
639 S Commwl Ave Ste B, Los Angeles (90005)
PHONE...................213 365-2491
Liza Bercovici, *Exec Dir*
Jen Mathews, *Opers Staff*
EMP: 82
SALES: 1.7MM **Privately Held**
WEB: www.gabriellaaxelradfoundation.org
SIC: 7911 8211 Children's dancing school; elementary & secondary schools

(P-17881)
ODC (PA)
351 Shotwell St, San Francisco (94110-1324)
PHONE...................415 863-6606
Bartley Deamer, *CEO*
Constance Geisler, *Development*
EMP: 98
SQ FT: 33,000
SALES: 3.9MM **Privately Held**
SIC: 7911 7922 6512 Dance studios, schools & halls; legitimate live theater producers; nonresidential building operators

---

7922 Theatrical Producers & Misc Theatrical Svcs

(P-17882)
42ND STREET MOON
601 Van Ness Ave, San Francisco (94102-3200)
PHONE...................415 255-8207
J Patterson McBaine, *President*
Greg Mackellan, *Director*

EMP: 50
SALES: 700.4K **Privately Held**
SIC: 7922 Theatrical producers & services

(P-17883)
ADVENTIST MEDIA CENTER INC (PA)
Also Called: It Is Written
11291 Pierce St, Riverside (92505-2705)
P.O. Box 101, Simi Valley (93062-0101)
PHONE...................805 955-7777
Daniel R Jackson, *CEO*
Daniel Jackson, *Ch of Bd*
Marshall Chase, *President*
Charles Reel, *Treasurer*
Warren Judd, *Vice Pres*
▲ EMP: 72 EST: 1972
SQ FT: 76,000
SALES (est): 14.5MM **Privately Held**
WEB: www.sdamedia.org
SIC: 7922 Television program, including commercial producers

(P-17884)
AEG PRESENTS LLC (DH)
425 W 11th St, Los Angeles (90015-3459)
PHONE...................323 930-5700
Randy Phillips,
Brooke Kain, *Officer*
Scott Campbell, *Vice Pres*
Ron Chiu, *Vice Pres*
Colin Conway, *Vice Pres*
▲ EMP: 140
SQ FT: 16,400
SALES (est): 32.1MM **Privately Held**
SIC: 7922 Entertainment promotion
HQ: Anschutz Entertainment Group, Inc.
800 W Olympic Blvd # 305
Los Angeles CA 90015
213 337-5052

(P-17885)
AGENCY FOR PERFORMING ARTS INC (PA)
405 S Beverly Dr Ste 500, Beverly Hills (90212-4425)
PHONE...................310 557-9049
James Gosnell, *President*
Stuart Nichols, *CFO*
Jeff Witjas, *Senior VP*
Jay Gilbert, *Vice Pres*
Marc Kamler, *Vice Pres*
EMP: 100 EST: 1962
SALES (est): 17.9MM **Privately Held**
WEB: www.apa-agency.com
SIC: 7922 Theatrical producers & services; talent agent, theatrical

(P-17886)
AMERICAN CONSERVATORY
415 Geary St, San Francisco (94102-1222)
PHONE...................415 749-2228
Roger Wahther, *Manager*
EMP: 70
SALES (corp-wide): 27.4MM **Privately Held**
WEB: www.acts-at.com
SIC: 7922 Repertory, road or stock companies: theatrical
PA: American Conservatory Theatre Foundation
30 Grant Ave Fl 7
San Francisco CA 94108
415 834-3200

(P-17887)
AMERICAN CONSERVATORY
Also Called: A C T Box Office
405 Geary St, San Francisco (94102-1222)
PHONE...................415 749-2228
Cheryl Sorokin, *Branch Mgr*
EMP: 70
SALES (corp-wide): 27.4MM **Privately Held**
WEB: www.acts-at.com
SIC: 7922 Repertory, road or stock companies: theatrical
PA: American Conservatory Theatre Foundation
30 Grant Ave Fl 7
San Francisco CA 94108
415 834-3200

(P-17888)
BEN BOLLINGER PRODUCTIONS INC
Also Called: Bollingers Candelight Pavilion
455 W Foothill Blvd, Claremont (91711-2701)
PHONE...................909 626-3296
Ben Bollinger, *President*
EMP: 70
SALES (est): 3.3MM **Privately Held**
SIC: 7922 8999 Legitimate live theater producers; music arranging & composing

(P-17889)
BREAK FLOOR PRODUCTIONS LLC (PA)
Also Called: Jump Dance Convention
5446 Satsuma Ave, North Hollywood (91601-2837)
PHONE...................818 432-1234
Jacquelyn Stroming, *Mng Member*
George Gregory, *Prdtn Dir*
EMP: 50
SALES: 5MM **Privately Held**
WEB: www.breakthefloor.com
SIC: 7922 Theatrical producers

(P-17890)
BROADWAY BY BAY
853 Industrial Rd Ste H, San Carlos (94070-3324)
P.O. Box 728 (94070-0728)
PHONE...................650 579-5565
Waren Doan, *President*
Alicia Jeffrey, *Director*
Alexis Lazear, *Director*
EMP: 140
SQ FT: 1,600
SALES (est): 1.2MM **Privately Held**
WEB: www.bbbay.org
SIC: 7922 Ticket agency, theatrical

(P-17891)
BROADWAY SACRAMENTO (PA)
Also Called: Music Circus
1510 J St Ste 200, Sacramento (95814-2099)
PHONE...................916 446-5880
Richard Lewis, *President*
Matt Hessburg, *Marketing Staff*
Laura Hunter, *Manager*
Michael Hunter, *Manager*
John Lewitzke, *Manager*
▲ EMP: 150
SQ FT: 7,000
SALES: 18.4MM **Privately Held**
WEB: www.calmt.com
SIC: 7922 Theatrical companies

(P-17892)
BULLY PICTURES INC (PA)
1220 Cabrillo Ave, Venice (90291-3704)
PHONE...................310 395-6500
Jason Forest, *Principal*
Collin Tokarsky, *Producer*
EMP: 103
SALES (est): 2MM **Privately Held**
SIC: 7922 Television program, including commercial producers

(P-17893)
CALIFORNIA REPERTORY COMPANY
Also Called: California University Long Bch
1250 N Bellflower Blvd # 124, Long Beach (90840-0124)
PHONE...................562 985-7891
Joanne Gordon, *Director*
Pamela Poppin, *General Mgr*
Arlene Reyes, *Finance Mgr*
Howard Burman, *Director*
Alan Shockley, *Director*
EMP: 50
SALES: 2.2MM **Privately Held**
SIC: 7922 6512 Theatrical producers & services; theater building, ownership & operation

(P-17894)
CALIFORNIA SHAKESPEARE THEATER
Also Called: CAL SHAKES
701 Heinz Ave, Berkeley (94710-2732)
PHONE...................510 548-3422
Jonathan Moscone, *Director*

Susie Falk, *Managing Dir*
Sam Agarwal, *Finance*
Lisa Evans, *Director*
Eric Ting, *Director*
EMP: 225 EST: 1974
SALES: 4.9MM **Privately Held**
WEB: www.calshakes.org
SIC: 7922 Plays, road & stock companies

(P-17895)
CALIFORNIA TICKETSCOM INC
1855 Gateway Blvd Ste 630, Concord (94520-3200)
PHONE...................925 671-4000
Terry Wojtulewicz, *Branch Mgr*
Ed Gow, *Vice Pres*
John Burns, *Info Tech Mgr*
EMP: 200
SALES (corp-wide): 191.3MM **Privately Held**
WEB: www.tickets.com
SIC: 7922 7999 Ticket agency, theatrical; ticket sales office for sporting events, contract
HQ: California Tickets.Com Inc.
555 Anton Blvd Fl 11
Costa Mesa CA 92626
714 327-5400

(P-17896)
CALIFORNIA TICKETSCOM INC (DH)
555 Anton Blvd Fl 11, Costa Mesa (92626-7811)
PHONE...................714 327-5400
Joe Choti, *President*
Derek Goodnature, *President*
Chris Hurley, *CFO*
Cristine Hurley, *CFO*
Derek Palmer, *Exec VP*
▲ EMP: 89
SALES (est): 18.5MM
SALES (corp-wide): 191.3MM **Privately Held**
WEB: www.tickets.com
SIC: 7922 7999 5961 5045 Ticket agency, theatrical; ticket sales office for sporting events, contract; catalog & mail-order houses; computers, peripherals & software
HQ: Mlb Advanced Media, L.P.
75 9th Ave Fl 5
New York NY 10011
212 485-3444

(P-17897)
CENTER THTRE GROUP LOS ANGELES (PA)
601 W Temple St, Los Angeles (90012-2621)
PHONE...................213 972-7344
Michael Ritchie, *CEO*
Dawn Holiski, *Owner*
William Ahmanson, *Ch of Bd*
Kiki Ramos Gindler, *President*
Jason Martin, *President*
▲ EMP: 130
SQ FT: 20,000
SALES: 48.8MM **Privately Held**
WEB: www.ctgla.org
SIC: 7922 Theatrical companies

(P-17898)
CITY & COUNTY OF SAN FRANCISCO
Also Called: Zellerbach Rehearsal Hall
401 Van Ness Ave Ste 110, San Francisco (94102-4521)
PHONE...................415 621-6600
Elizabeth Maury, *Manager*
Jenna Lee, *Human Res Mgr*
Elizabeth Murray, *Manager*
Khan Wong, *Manager*
Claudia Leung, *Associate*
EMP: 100 **Privately Held**
SIC: 7922 9199 Performing arts center production; general government administration; ;
PA: City & County Of San Francisco
1 Dr Carlton B Goodlett P
San Francisco CA 94102
415 554-7500

(P-17899)
CITY & COUNTY OF SAN FRANCISCO
Also Called: War Memorial Prfrmg Art Ctr
401 Van Ness Ave Ste 110, San Francisco
(94102-4521)
PHONE...............................415 621-6600
Elizabeth Murray, *Manager*
Wae Seruge, *Officer*
Tony Winnicker, *Comms Dir*
Amdur Kelley, *Exec Dir*
Anmarie Rodgers, *Planning*
EMP: 100 **Privately Held**
SIC: 7922 9199 6512 Performing arts
center production; general government
administration; ; ; nonresidential building
operators
PA: City & County Of San Francisco
1 Dr Carlton B Goodlett P
San Francisco CA 94102
415 554-7500

(P-17900)
CITY OF CONCORD
Also Called: Concord Pavillion
2000 Kirker Pass Rd, Concord
(94521-1642)
PHONE...............................925 692-2400
Doug Warrick, *General Mgr*
EMP: 400 **Privately Held**
WEB: www.cpd.ci.concord.ca.us
SIC: 7922 6512 Theatrical companies;
theater building, ownership & operation
PA: City Of Concord
1950 Parkside Dr
Concord CA 94519
925 671-3000

(P-17901)
CITY OF DOWNEY
Also Called: Downey Civic Theatre
8435 Firestone Blvd, Downey
(90241-3843)
P.O. Box 607 (90241-0607)
PHONE...............................562 861-8211
Gerald Caton, *Manager*
EMP: 97 **Privately Held**
WEB: www.dpoa.org
SIC: 7922 Legitimate live theater produc-
ers
PA: City Of Downey
11111 Brookshire Ave
Downey CA 90241
562 869-7331

(P-17902)
COVENANT PLAYERS (PA)
1741 Fiske Pl, Oxnard (93033-1864)
P.O. Box 2900 (93034-2900)
PHONE...............................805 486-7155
Robin Johnson-Tanner, *Owner*
Peter Iverson, *Vice Pres*
Gary Barcus, *Finance*
Gail Crabtree, *Director*
Bobbi Johnson-Tanner, *Director*
EMP: 220
SQ FT: 19,424
SALES: 405.2K **Privately Held**
WEB: www.covenantplayers.org
SIC: 7922 8661 Performing arts center
production; religious organizations

(P-17903)
CREATING ARTS COMPANY
Also Called: Cac Studios
4380 Hillview Dr, Malibu (90265-2832)
PHONE...............................310 804-0223
Shannon Sukovaty, *CEO*
Todd Skinner, *President*
EMP: 50
SALES: 250K **Privately Held**
SIC: 7922 Theatrical companies

(P-17904)
CREATIVE ARTISTS AGENCY LLC (PA)
Also Called: C A A
2000 Avenue Of The Stars # 100, Los An-
geles (90067-4705)
PHONE...............................424 288-2000
Steve Hasker, *CEO*
Kevin Gelbard, *Partner*
Steve Lafferty, *Managing Prtnr*
Rick Nicita, *Chairman*
Mark Cheatham, *Vice Pres*

EMP: 800
SALES (est): 112.7MM **Privately Held**
WEB: www.caa.com
SIC: 7922 Agent or manager for entertain-
ers

(P-17905)
CROSSROADS LIVE INC
3900 W Alameda Ave Fl 12, Burbank
(91505-4316)
PHONE...............................818 247-0400
Dan Miller, *President*
EMP: 51
SALES (est): 169.3K **Privately Held**
SIC: 7922 7929 Legitimate live theater
producers; musical entertainers

(P-17906)
DAVIE BROWN ENTERTAINMENT INC
12777 W Jefferson Blvd # 120, Los Angeles
(90066-7048)
PHONE...............................310 979-1980
James Davie, *CEO*
Stephanie Cohen, *President*
Tom Meyer, *President*
Russell Meisels, *CFO*
Adam Smith, *Exec VP*
EMP: 60
SQ FT: 16,100
SALES: 18.5MM
SALES (corp-wide): 15.2B **Publicly Held**
WEB: www.davie-brown.com
SIC: 7922 Entertainment promotion
HQ: The Marketing Arm Inc
1999 Bryan St Fl 18
Dallas TX 75201

(P-17907)
DELICATE PRODUCTIONS INC (PA)
874 Verdulera St, Camarillo (93010-8371)
PHONE...............................415 484-1174
James Steve Dabbs, *CEO*
Christopher Smyth, *CFO*
Angus Thomson, *Vice Pres*
Steven I Gilbard, *Principal*
Preston Soper, *Engineer*
EMP: 79
SQ FT: 19,937
SALES (est): 7MM **Privately Held**
WEB: www.delicate.com
SIC: 7922 7359 Equipment rental, theatri-
cal; sound & lighting equipment rental

(P-17908)
ENDEMOL
9255 W Sunset Blvd # 1100, West Holly-
wood (90069-3309)
PHONE...............................310 860-9914
David Goldberg, *Chairman*
EMP: 70 **EST:** 2012
SALES: 170MM **Privately Held**
SIC: 7922 Television program, including
commercial producers

(P-17909)
EPICENTER LIVE INC
4040 Mahaila Ave Unit A, San Diego
(92122-5807)
PHONE...............................424 235-4835
Devon Joseph, *President*
Keith A Joseph, *Exec Dir*
EMP: 150
SALES (est): 2.6MM **Privately Held**
SIC: 7922 Concert management service

(P-17910)
FRIENDS OF CULTURAL CENTER INC
Also Called: McCallum Theatre
73000 Fred Waring Dr, Palm Desert
(92260-2800)
PHONE...............................760 346-6505
Ted Giatas, *President*
William Towers, *Chairman*
Ron Gregroire, *Treasurer*
EMP: 100
SQ FT: 66,000
SALES: 15.3MM **Privately Held**
WEB: www.mccallum-theatre.org
SIC: 7922 Legitimate live theater produc-
ers

(P-17911)
GERSH AGENCY INC (PA)
9465 Wilshire Blvd Fl 6, Beverly Hills
(90212-2605)
PHONE...............................310 274-6611
Robert Gersh, *President*
Beatrice Gersh, *Vice Pres*
David Gersh, *Vice Pres*
Sandra Lucchesi, *Manager*
Bobby Myerow, *Assistant*
EMP: 100 **EST:** 1949
SQ FT: 15,000
SALES (est): 11.1MM **Privately Held**
WEB: www.gershagency.com
SIC: 7922 Talent agent, theatrical

(P-17912)
GREAT AMERICAN MUSIC HALL
859 Ofarrell St, San Francisco
(94109-7005)
PHONE...............................415 885-0750
Dawn Holiday, *CEO*
Kit Carter, *Manager*
Amie Kraft, *Relations*
EMP: 50
SQ FT: 6,000
SALES (est): 1.3MM **Privately Held**
WEB: www.musichallsf.com
SIC: 7922 5813 Entertainment promotion;
cocktail lounge

(P-17913)
GREENWAY ARTS ALLIANCE INC
544 N Fairfax Ave, Los Angeles
(90036-1771)
PHONE...............................323 655-7679
Molly Miles, *Chairman*
D Pierson Blaetz, *Manager*
Whitney Weston, *Manager*
EMP: 79
SALES: 1.7MM **Privately Held**
SIC: 7922 8299 Theatrical companies; art
school, except commercial

(P-17914)
HARPO INC
Also Called: Harpo Studios
1041 N Formosa Ave, West Hollywood
(90046-6703)
PHONE...............................312 633-1000
Oprah Winfrey, *President*
Erik Logan, *President*
Sheri Salata, *President*
Douglas J Pattison, *CFO*
Jon Sinclair, *Vice Pres*
EMP: 70
SQ FT: 88,000
SALES (est): 8.2MM **Privately Held**
SIC: 7922 Television program, including
commercial producers

(P-17915)
INNOVATIVE ARTISTS TALENT AGNY (PA)
1505 10th St, Santa Monica (90401-2805)
PHONE...............................310 656-0400
Scott Harris, *President*
Cecilia Banck, *Agent*
Craig Mizrahi, *Agent*
EMP: 75
SALES (est): 6MM **Privately Held**
WEB: www.iany.com
SIC: 7922 7819 Talent agent, theatrical;
casting bureau, motion picture

(P-17916)
INTERNATIONAL CREATIVE MGT INC (HQ)
Also Called: I C M
10250 Constellation Blvd, Los Angeles
(90067-6200)
PHONE...............................310 550-4000
Jeff Berg, *Ch of Bd*
Esther Newberg, *Partner*
Robert Murphy, *CFO*
Nancy Josephson, *Co-President*
Ed Limato, *Co-President*
▲ **EMP:** 220
SQ FT: 72,000
SALES (est): 33.7MM **Privately Held**
WEB: www.icmtalent.com
SIC: 7922 8699 Talent agent, theatrical; lit-
erary, film or cultural club

PA: Icm Holdings Inc
40 W 57th St Fl 16
New York NY 10019
212 556-5600

(P-17917)
INTERNATIONAL CREATIVE MGT INC
Also Called: I C M
10250 Constellation Blvd # 1, Los Angeles
(90067-6200)
PHONE...............................310 550-4000
Jeff Derg, *Manager*
EMP: 200
SALES (corp-wide): 33.7MM **Privately Held**
SIC: 7922 Booking agency, theatrical
HQ: International Creative Management,
Inc.
10250 Constellation Blvd
Los Angeles CA 90067
310 550-4000

(P-17918)
J C ENTERTAINMENT LTG SVCS INC
Also Called: E L S
5435 W San Fernando Rd, Los Angeles
(90039-1014)
PHONE...............................818 252-7481
John Allen Chuck, *CEO*
Todd Richards, *CFO*
Kevin Dowling, *Vice Pres*
Derek Smith, *Vice Pres*
EMP: 80
SQ FT: 69,000
SALES (est): 9.6MM **Privately Held**
WEB: www.elslights.com
SIC: 7922 5719 Equipment rental, theatri-
cal; lighting, lamps & accessories

(P-17919)
JOHN GORE ORGANIZATION INC
255 S B St, San Mateo (94401-4017)
PHONE...............................650 340-0469
EMP: 78
SALES (corp-wide): 555.1MM **Privately Held**
SIC: 7922 Entertainment promotion
PA: The John Gore Organization Inc
1619 Broadway Fl 9
New York NY 10019
917 421-5400

(P-17920)
KID STOCK INC
1539 Funston Ave, San Francisco
(94122-3530)
PHONE...............................415 753-3737
Jane Sullivan, *Deputy Dir*
Noel Donahue, *Deputy Dir*
EMP: 80
SALES: 432.5K **Privately Held**
WEB: www.kidstockinc.org
SIC: 7922 Community theater production

(P-17921)
LA LIVE PROPERTIES LLC
800 W Olympic Blvd # 305, Los Angeles
(90015-1360)
PHONE...............................213 763-7700
Donna Johnson, *VP Finance*
Ruebn Lechuga, *Security Dir*
EMP: 50
SALES (est): 6.4MM **Privately Held**
WEB: www.lalive.com
SIC: 7922 6512 Theatrical producers &
services; property operation, auditoriums
& theaters
HQ: Anschutz Entertainment Group, Inc.
800 W Olympic Blvd # 305
Los Angeles CA 90015
213 337-5052

(P-17922)
LAGUNA PLAYHOUSE (PA)
606 Laguna Canyon Rd, Laguna Beach
(92651-1837)
P.O. Box 1747 (92652-1747)
PHONE...............................949 497-2787
Karen Wood, *CEO*
Bob Crowson, *CFO*
Richard Stein, *Exec Dir*
Louisa Balch, *General Mgr*

Irene Samadoff, *Controller*
EMP: 250
SQ FT: 19,000
SALES: 8MM **Privately Held**
WEB: www.lagunaplayhouse.com
SIC: 7922 Community theater production

(P-17923)
LIVE NATION WORLDWIDE INC
6500 Wilshire Blvd # 200, Los Angeles
(90048-4920)
PHONE..............................323 966-5066
Terry Dreher, *Principal*
EMP: 130
SALES (corp-wide): 10.7B **Publicly Held**
WEB: www.sfx.com
SIC: 7922 Theatrical producers & services
HQ: Live Nation Worldwide, Inc.
430 W 15th St
New York NY 10011
917 421-5100

(P-17924)
LIVE NATION WORLDWIDE INC
9348 Civic Center Dr Lbby, Beverly Hills
(90210-3642)
PHONE..............................310 867-7000
Kathy Willard, *CEO*
Jimmy Iovine, *Bd of Directors*
John Hopmans, *Exec VP*
EMP: 8800
SALES (est): 291K
SALES (corp-wide): 10.7B **Publicly Held**
SIC: 7922 Theatrical producers & services
PA: Live Nation Entertainment, Inc.
9348 Civic Center Dr Lbby
Beverly Hills CA 90210
800 653-8000

(P-17925)
LUTHER BURBANK MEM FOUNDATION
50 Mark West Springs Rd, Santa Rosa
(95403-1457)
PHONE..............................707 546-3600
Richard Nowlin, *Exec Dir*
J David Siembieda, *Director*
Audrey Rosado, *Manager*
Melanie Weir, *Manager*
EMP: 74
SQ FT: 120,000
SALES: 15.3MM **Privately Held**
WEB: www.lbc.net
SIC: 7922 8299 6519 Performing arts center production; music & drama schools; real property lessors

(P-17926)
MAGIC MOUNTAIN LLC
Also Called: Six Flags Magic Mountain
26101 Magic Mountain Pkwy, Valencia
(91355-1052)
P.O. Box 5500 (91380-5500)
PHONE..............................661 255-4100
Bonnie Rabjohn,
Tim Tim Burkhart, *Vice Pres*
Scott McClellan, *Finance*
Ronald DOE, *Supervisor*
▲ **EMP:** 300
SALES (est): 11.1MM
SALES (corp-wide): 1.4B **Publicly Held**
SIC: 7922 7996 Entertainment promotion; theme park, amusement
PA: Six Flags Entertainment Corp
924 E Avenue J
Grand Prairie TX 75050
972 595-5000

(P-17927)
MCGUIRE TALENT INC
8608 Utica Ave Ste 220, Rancho Cuca-
monga (91730-4879)
PHONE..............................909 527-7006
EMP: 80
SQ FT: 2,200
SALES: 2MM **Privately Held**
SIC: 7922

(P-17928)
MOUNTAIN PLAY ASSOCIATION
1556 4th St B, San Rafael (94901-2713)
PHONE..............................415 383-1100
Sara Pearson, *Director*
EMP: 50
SQ FT: 650

SALES: 985.3K **Privately Held**
SIC: 7922 Theatrical producers & services

(P-17929)
NEWPORT TELEVISION LLC
4880 N 1st St, Fresno (93726-0514)
PHONE..............................559 761-0243
EMP: 123
SALES (corp-wide): 51.2MM **Privately Held**
SIC: 7922 Television program, including commercial producers
PA: Newport Television Llc
460 Nichols Rd Ste 250
Kansas City MO 64112
816 751-0200

(P-17930)
NFL PROPERTIES LLC
Also Called: Nfl Network
10950 Wash Blvd Ste 100, Culver City
(90232-4032)
PHONE..............................310 840-4635
Steve Bernstein, *Principal*
Shona Holagh, *Planning*
Amy Lee, *Software Engr*
Wade Marshall, *Prdtn Mgr*
Tara Deeker, *Production*
EMP: 300
SALES (corp-wide): 55.7MM **Privately Held**
SIC: 7922 Television program, including commercial producers
PA: Nfl Properties Llc
345 Park Ave Bsmt Lc1
New York NY 10154
212 450-2000

(P-17931)
ODC THEATER
351 Shotwell St, San Francisco
(94110-1324)
PHONE..............................415 863-6606
Carma Zisman, *Exec Dir*
Malia Connor, *Admin Asst*
Jason Dinneen, *Technical Staff*
Leigh Lehman, *Director*
EMP: 55
SQ FT: 10,000
SALES: 907K
SALES (corp-wide): 3.9MM **Privately Held**
SIC: 7922 7911 Theatrical companies; dance studio & school
PA: Odc
351 Shotwell St
San Francisco CA 94110
415 863-6606

(P-17932)
OLD GLOBE THEATRE
1363 Old Globe Way, San Diego
(92101-1696)
P.O. Box 122171 (92112-2171)
PHONE..............................619 234-5623
Michael G Murphy, *CEO*
Louis Spisto, *CEO*
Mark Somers, *CFO*
Kristina Keeler, *Associate Dir*
Manny Bejarano, *Hum Res Coord*
▲ **EMP:** 500
SALES (est): 21.6MM **Privately Held**
WEB: www.theoldglobe.org
SIC: 7922 Performing arts center production

(P-17933)
OPERA SAN JOSE INC
2149 Paragon Dr, San Jose (95131-1312)
PHONE..............................408 437-4450
Irene Dalis, *Exec Dir*
George Crow, *President*
Bryan Ferraro, *Comms Mgr*
Larry Hancock, *General Mgr*
Donna Lara, *Admin Asst*
EMP: 100
SQ FT: 25,000
SALES: 6.2MM **Privately Held**
SIC: 7922 7929 Opera company; enter-
tainers & entertainment groups

(P-17934)
PARADIGM MUSIC LLC (PA)
360 N Crescent Dr, Beverly Hills
(90210-4874)
PHONE..............................310 288-8000

Sam Gores, *Ch of Bd*
Lucy Stille, *Partner*
Colby Casoria, *Chairman*
Brad Turell, *Exec VP*
Michael Dates, *Vice Pres*
EMP: 70
SALES (est): 8.2MM **Privately Held**
WEB: www.michaelokeefe.com
SIC: 7922 Talent agent, theatrical

(P-17935)
PERFORMING ARTS CENTER OF LA C
Also Called: MUSIC CENTER UNIFIED FUND
135 N Grand Ave, Los Angeles
(90012-3013)
PHONE..............................213 972-7211
John Emerson, *Ch of Bd*
Lisa Specht, *Ch of Bd*
Stephen Rountree, *President*
Howard Sherman, *COO*
William Meyerchak, *CFO*
▲ **EMP:** 250
SQ FT: 24,000
SALES: 74.5MM **Privately Held**
WEB: www.musiccenter.org
SIC: 7922 Theatrical producers & services;
equipment rental, theatrical; concert man-
agement service; ticket agency, theatrical
PA: The Music Center Of Los Angeles
County Inc
135 N Grand Ave Ste 201
Los Angeles CA 90012
213 972-8007

(P-17936)
PLAYWRIGHTS FOUNDATION INC
1616 16th St Ste 350, San Francisco
(94103-5164)
PHONE..............................415 626-2176
Amy Mueller, *Director*
Linda Brewer, *President*
Marcy Straw, *General Mgr*
Sara Sparks, *Office Mgr*
Tessa King, *Opers Mgr*
EMP: 73
SQ FT: 1,200
SALES: 354.9K **Privately Held**
SIC: 7922 Legitimate live theater produc-
ers

(P-17937)
PRDCTIONS N FREMANTLE AMER INC (DH)
Also Called: Fremantle Media
2900 W Alameda Ave # 800, Burbank
(91505-4220)
PHONE..............................818 748-1100
Thom Beers, *CEO*
Donna Redier Linsk, *COO*
Dan Goldberg, *Exec VP*
Mark Deetjen, *Senior VP*
Ellen Goldstein, *Vice Pres*
EMP: 100
SALES (est): 18.1MM
SALES (corp-wide): 75.3MM **Privately Held**
SIC: 7922 Television program, including
commercial producers
HQ: Fremantlemedia Group Limited
1 Stephen Street
London W1T 1
207 691-6000

(P-17938)
PREMIERE RADIO NETWORK INC (DH)
Also Called: Prn Radio Networks
15260 Ventura Blvd # 400, Sherman Oaks
(91403-5307)
PHONE..............................818 377-5300
Stephen C Lehman, *CEO*
Kraig T Kitchin, *President*
Timothy M Kelly, *Exec VP*
David Kolin, *Exec VP*
Bill Cahill, *Vice Pres*
EMP: 200
SQ FT: 15,000
SALES (est): 20.5MM **Publicly Held**
WEB: www.premrad.com
SIC: 7922 7389 4832 Radio producers;
advertising, promotional & trade show
services; radio broadcasting stations

HQ: Jacor Communications Company
200 E Basse Rd
San Antonio TX 78209
210 822-2828

(P-17939)
PRODUCTION SPECIAL EVENTS SVCS
17326 Devonshire St, Northridge
(91325-1543)
PHONE..............................818 831-5326
Wendy Moodie, *President*
Terry Merkle, *Vice Pres*
EMP: 50 **EST:** 1997
SALES (est): 2.1MM **Privately Held**
SIC: 7922 Entertainment promotion

(P-17940)
RADFORD STUDIO CENTER INC
Also Called: CBS Studio Center
4024 Radford Ave, Studio City
(91604-2101)
PHONE..............................818 655-5000
Michael Klausman, *President*
Nina Tassler, *Ch of Bd*
John Lu, *Info Tech Mgr*
Robert Sheldon, *Chief Engr*
Barbara Mannina, *VP Finance*
EMP: 300
SALES (est): 31.3MM
SALES (corp-wide): 25.9B **Publicly Held**
WEB: www.cbssc.com
SIC: 7922 6512 7999 Television program,
including commercial producers; nonresi-
dential building operators; martial arts
school
HQ: Cbs Broadcasting Inc.
524 W 57th St
New York NY 10019
212 975-4321

(P-17941)
ROSE BRAND WIPERS INC
11440 Sheldon St, Sun Valley
(91352-1121)
PHONE..............................818 505-6290
Tina Carlin, *Principal*
EMP: 82
SALES (corp-wide): 106.4MM **Privately Held**
SIC: 7922 Costume & scenery design
services
PA: Rose Brand Wipers, Inc.
4 Emerson Ln
Secaucus NJ 07094
201 809-1730

(P-17942)
SACRAMENTO THEATRICAL LTG LTD
Also Called: S T L
950 Richards Blvd, Sacramento
(95811-0333)
PHONE..............................916 447-3258
John W Cox, *CEO*
Kaye Newton, *Vice Pres*
Dianne Jared, *Finance*
Bobbie Odehnal, *Manager*
EMP: 65
SQ FT: 60,000
SALES (est): 6.5MM **Privately Held**
WEB: www.stl-ltd.com
SIC: 7922 5063 Equipment rental, theatri-
cal; lighting fixtures

(P-17943)
SAN DIEGO OPERA ASSOCIATION (PA)
233 A St Ste 500, San Diego (92101-4095)
PHONE..............................619 232-7636
Michael Lowry, *Finance*
Michael Lowery, *Officer*
Eric French, *Administration*
Cliff Thrasher, *Director*
Toni Read, *Manager*
EMP: 50 **EST:** 1945
SQ FT: 11,000
SALES: 9.3MM **Privately Held**
SIC: 7922 Opera company

(P-17944)
SAN FRANCISCO BALLET ASSN
455 Franklin St, San Francisco
(94102-4471)
PHONE..............................415 865-2000

Glenn McCoy, *CEO*
Kim Carim, *CFO*
Donald B Paterson, *CFO*
J Stuart Francis, *Treasurer*
Kera Jewett, *Sr Corp Ofcr*
▲ **EMP:** 250
SQ FT: 70,000
SALES: 25.3MM **Privately Held**
SIC: 7922 7911 Ballet production; dance
studio & school

(P-17945)
SAN FRANCISCO OPERA ASSN
301 Van Ness Ave, San Francisco
(94102-4509)
PHONE....................415 861-4008
John A Gunn, *Chairman*
Karl O Mills, *Vice Chairman*
Keith B Geeslin, *President*
David Gockley, *CEO*
Michael Simpson, *CFO*
▲ **EMP:** 1050 **EST:** 1932
SALES: 33.1MM **Privately Held**
SIC: 7922 Opera company

(P-17946)
SHOW CALL PRODUCTIONS INC
5212 Lenore Dr, San Diego (92115-1638)
P.O. Box 13333, La Jolla (92039-3333)
PHONE....................619 602-0656
Gary Zugel, *CEO*
EMP: 400 **EST:** 2006
SALES (est): 2.6MM **Privately Held**
SIC: 7922 Concert management service

(P-17947)
SOUTH COAST REPERTORY INC
Also Called: SCR
655 Town Center Dr, Costa Mesa
(92626-1918)
P.O. Box 2197 (92628-2197)
PHONE....................714 708-5500
Martin Benson, *Art Dir*
Lauren Hovey, *Social Dir*
Kim Fleming, *Executive Asst*
David Wynn, *Info Tech Dir*
Dean Lissner, *Info Tech Mgr*
EMP: 60
SQ FT: 40,000
SALES: 11.5MM **Privately Held**
SIC: 7922 Repertory, road or stock compa-
nies: theatrical

(P-17948)
STEVE SILVER PRODUCTIONS INC
678 Green St Ste 2, San Francisco
(94133-3846)
PHONE....................415 421-4284
EMP: 94
SALES (corp-wide): 3.7MM **Privately
Held**
SIC: 7922
PA: Silver Steve Productions Inc
470 Columbus Ave Ste 204
San Francisco CA 94133
415 421-4284

(P-17949)
TENNIS CHANNEL INC (HQ)
2850 Ocean Park Blvd # 150, Santa Monica
(90405-6217)
PHONE....................310 392-1920
Ken Solomon, *CEO*
William Simon, *COO*
EMP: 70
SALES (est): 8.8MM
SALES (corp-wide): 3B **Publicly Held**
WEB: www.thetennischannel.com
SIC: 7922 Television program, including
commercial producers
PA: Sinclair Broadcast Group, Inc.
10706 Beaver Dam Rd
Hunt Valley MD 21030
410 568-1500

(P-17950)
THINKWELL GROUP INC
2710 Media Center Dr, Los Angeles
(90065-1746)
PHONE....................818 333-3444
Joseph Zenas, *CEO*
James Clark, *Vice Pres*
Aamna Jalal, *Vice Pres*
Diane Michioka, *Vice Pres*

Ron Morissette, *Vice Pres*
▲ **EMP:** 75
SQ FT: 23,000
SALES (est): 9MM **Privately Held**
SIC: 7922 7389 Theatrical producers &
services; interior design services

(P-17951)
TICKETSCOM LLC (DH)
Also Called: Tickets.com, Inc.
535 Anton Blvd Ste 250, Costa Mesa
(92626-7694)
PHONE....................714 327-5400
Joe Choti, *President*
Larry D Witherspoon, *President*
Cristine Hurley, *CFO*
John Walker, *Principal*
Curt Clausen, *Admin Sec*
EMP: 50
SALES: 75MM
SALES (corp-wide): 191.3MM **Privately
Held**
SIC: 7922 7372 Ticket agency, theatrical;
application computer software
HQ: Mlb Advanced Media, L.P.
75 9th Ave Fl 5
New York NY 10011
212 485-3444

(P-17952)
TRISTAR TELEVISION MUSIC INC
10202 Washington Blvd, Culver City
(90232-3119)
PHONE....................310 244-4000
Eric Tannenbaum, *President*
EMP: 50
SALES (est): 696.3K **Privately Held**
WEB: www.paulleydenonline.com
SIC: 7922 Television program, including
commercial producers
HQ: Sony Pictures Releasing International
Corporation
10202 Washington Blvd
Culver City CA
310 244-4000

(P-17953)
TURNING POINT FOR GOD
Also Called: Turning Point Ministries
10007 Riverford Rd, Lakeside
(92040-2772)
PHONE....................619 258-3600
David P Jeremiah, *CEO*
Michael Guzik, *CFO*
Jenny Neighbour, *Officer*
EMP: 55
SALES: 51.8MM **Privately Held**
SIC: 7922 Radio producers

(P-17954)
WILLIAM MORRIS ENDEAVOR
Also Called: William Morris Agency
2624 Military Ave, Los Angeles
(90064-3132)
PHONE....................310 285-9000
Mark Edkins, *Manager*
Erik Seastrand, *Vice Pres*
Max Wagner, *Executive Asst*
Theresa Kang, *Director*
Alexis Garcia, *Agent*
EMP: 500
SALES (corp-wide): 98.6MM **Privately
Held**
WEB: www.rupaul.com
SIC: 7922 Talent agent, theatrical
PA: William Morris Endeavor Entertain-
ment, Llc
11 Madison Ave Fl 18
New York NY 10010
212 586-5100

(P-17955)
WILLIAM MORRIS ENDEAVOR
Also Called: William Morris Consulting
9601 Wilshire Blvd Fl 3, Beverly Hills
(90210-5219)
PHONE....................310 285-9000
Chris Newman, *Vice Pres*
Erik Seastrand, *Vice Pres*
Lisa Reiter, *Assistant*
Abby Baas, *Agent*
EMP: 393

SALES (corp-wide): 98.6MM **Privately
Held**
WEB: www.rupaul.com
SIC: 7922 Talent agent, theatrical
PA: William Morris Endeavor Entertain-
ment, Llc
11 Madison Ave Fl 18
New York NY 10010
212 586-5100

(P-17956)
WILLIAM MRRIS ENDVOR ENTRMT FN (HQ)
9601 Wilshire Blvd Fl 3, Beverly Hills
(90210-5219)
PHONE....................310 285-9000
Tom Strickler, *Mng Member*
Peter Klein, *CFO*
Corey Fitelson, *Vice Pres*
Joel Karansky, *Vice Pres*
June Horton, *Executive*
EMP: 180
SALES (est): 15.8MM
SALES (corp-wide): 98.6MM **Privately
Held**
WEB: www.endeavorla.com
SIC: 7922 Talent agent, theatrical
PA: William Morris Endeavor Entertain-
ment, Llc
11 Madison Ave Fl 18
New York NY 10010
212 586-5100

**7929 Bands, Orchestras,
Actors & Entertainers**

(P-17957)
19 ENTERTAINMENT WORLDWIDE LLC
Also Called: 19 Management
401 Wilshire Blvd Lbby, Santa Monica
(90401-1453)
PHONE....................310 777-1940
Iain Pirie, *President*
Maria Diaz, *Finance Dir*
Ginger Ramsey, *Manager*
EMP: 60
SALES (est): 2.7MM **Privately Held**
WEB: www.19.co.uk
SIC: 7929 Entertainment service

(P-17958)
51 MINDS ENTERTAINMENT LLC
Also Called: Mindless Entertainment
5200 Lankershim Blvd # 200, North Holly-
wood (91601-3180)
PHONE....................323 466-9200
Mark Cronin,
Courtland Cox, *Vice Pres*
Isabella Jorbajian, *Executive Asst*
Ruba Zarour, *Executive Asst*
Spencer Wierwille, *Graphic Designe*
◆ **EMP:** 60
SALES (est): 2.5MM
SALES (corp-wide): 2.1B **Privately Held**
WEB: www.51minds.com
SIC: 7929 7812 Entertainers; television
film production
HQ: Endemol Usa Holding, Inc.
5161 Lankershim Blvd # 400
North Hollywood CA 91601
310 860-9914

(P-17959)
ANSCHUTZ ENTRMT GROUP INC (HQ)
Also Called: AEG Worldwide
800 W Olympic Blvd # 305, Los Angeles
(90015-1366)
PHONE....................213 337-5052
Tim Leiweke, *President*
Sean Ryan, *President*
Dan Beckerman, *CFO*
Dennis Dennehy, *Ch Credit Ofcr*
Kevin McDowell, *Officer*
EMP: 148
SALES (est): 50.4MM **Privately Held**
SIC: 7929 Entertainment service

(P-17960)
ARAMARK SPT & ENTRMT GROUP LLC
525 W Santa Clara St, San Jose
(95113-1520)
PHONE....................408 999-5735
John Heberden, *Principal*
EMP: 106 **Publicly Held**
WEB: www.aramarksports.com
SIC: 7929 Entertainers & entertainment
groups
HQ: Aramark Sports And Entertainment
Group, Llc
2400 Market St
Philadelphia PA 19103
215 238-3000

(P-17961)
ARAMARK SPT & ENTRMT GROUP LLC
3400 S Figueroa St, Los Angeles
(90007-4348)
PHONE....................213 740-1224
EMP: 120 **Publicly Held**
SIC: 7929 Entertainment service
HQ: Aramark Sports And Entertainment
Group, Llc
2400 Market St
Philadelphia PA 19103
215 238-3000

(P-17962)
ARAMARK SPT & ENTRMT GROUP LLC
886 Cannery Row, Monterey (93940-1023)
PHONE....................831 648-9809
EMP: 106 **Publicly Held**
SIC: 7929 Entertainers & entertainment
groups
HQ: Aramark Sports And Entertainment
Group, Llc
2400 Market St
Philadelphia PA 19103
215 238-3000

(P-17963)
ARAMARK SPT & ENTRMT GROUP LLC
5001 Great America Pkwy, Santa Clara
(95054-1119)
PHONE....................408 748-7030
Jerry McCarthy, *Manager*
EMP: 100 **Publicly Held**
WEB: www.aramarksports.com
SIC: 7929 Entertainment service
HQ: Aramark Sports And Entertainment
Group, Llc
2400 Market St
Philadelphia PA 19103
215 238-3000

(P-17964)
ARTISTIC ENTRMT SVCS LLC
120 N Aspan Ave, Azusa (91702-4224)
PHONE....................626 334-9388
Craig Bugajski, *Mng Member*
Jonathan Broom, *Project Mgr*
Jason Degrande, *Project Mgr*
Aram Dergevorkian, *Engineer*
Albert Lopez, *Production*
EMP: 60
SALES (est): 10MM **Privately Held**
SIC: 7929 Entertainers & entertainment
groups

(P-17965)
BAKERSFIELD SYMPHONY ORCH
1328 34th St Ste A, Bakersfield
(93301-2154)
PHONE....................661 323-7928
Kari Heilman, *Exec Dir*
Nile Kinney, *CFO*
Jerome Kleinsasser, *Bd of Directors*
Elaine Lecain, *Vice Pres*
Jean Dodson, *VP Mktg*
EMP: 75
SALES: 938.1K **Privately Held**
WEB: www.bakersfieldsymphony.org
SIC: 7929 Symphony orchestras

(P-17966)
BERKELEY SYMPHONY ORCHESTRA
1942 University Ave # 207, Berkeley (94704-1246)
PHONE..................510 841-2800
Gary Ginstling, *Exec Dir*
Ian Harwood, *Associate Dir*
Theresa Gabel, *Exec Dir*
James Kleinmann, *Exec Dir*
Cindy Michael, *Finance*
EMP: 50
SALES: 1.8MM **Privately Held**
SIC: 7929 Symphony orchestras

(P-17967)
BONANZA PRODUCTIONS INC
4000 Warner Blvd, Burbank (91522-0001)
P.O. Box 1667 (91507-1667)
PHONE..................818 954-4212
John A Rogovin, *CEO*
Jonathan Rosenfeld, *Director*
EMP: 1000 EST: 1991
SALES (est): 13.6MM **Privately Held**
SIC: 7929 Entertainment group

(P-17968)
CZND INC
8444 Wilshire Blvd Fl 5, Beverly Hills (90211-3200)
PHONE..................323 378-6505
Luigi Picarazzi, *President*
EMP: 68
SALES (est): 140.1K **Privately Held**
SIC: 7929 Entertainment service

(P-17969)
DANNY MAHAGNA SHAPPRIE
73280 Highway 111, Palm Desert (92260-3915)
PHONE..................760 341-5070
Danny M Shapprie, *Principal*
EMP: 50
SALES (est): 265.2K **Privately Held**
SIC: 7929 Entertainment service

(P-17970)
DELUXE ENTRMT SVCS GROUP INC (PA)
2400 W Empire Ave Ste 200, Burbank (91504-3355)
PHONE..................818 565-3600
EMP: 98 EST: 1932
SALES (est): 38.3MM **Privately Held**
SIC: 7929

(P-17971)
DOUBLE G PRODUCTIONS LTD
11301 W Olympic Blvd # 115, Los Angeles (90064-1653)
PHONE..................310 479-0978
Louie Irizarry, *Branch Mgr*
EMP: 75
SALES (corp-wide): 2.3MM **Privately Held**
WEB: www.doubleg.com
SIC: 7929 Disc jockey service
PA: Double G Productions Ltd
1055 Stewart Ave Fl 2
Bethpage NY 11714
516 932-8342

(P-17972)
ENTERTINMENT STUDIOS MEDIA INC (PA)
1925 Century Park E # 1025, Los Angeles (90067-2701)
PHONE..................310 277-3500
Byron Allen Folks, *CEO*
Nora Zimmett, *Ch Credit Ofcr*
Eric Gould Evp, *CIO*
EMP: 65
SQ FT: 5,000
SALES: 10MM **Privately Held**
SIC: 7929 Entertainers & entertainment groups

(P-17973)
ENTITLEMENT LLC
1236 Euclid St, Santa Monica (90404-1041)
PHONE..................224 336-2669
Ted Lauck,
EMP: 50

SALES (est): 117.4K **Privately Held**
SIC: 7929 Entertainment service

(P-17974)
FORUM ENTERPRISES INC
333 W Florence Ave, Inglewood (90301-1103)
PHONE..................310 330-7300
Gerard McCallum, *Exec VP*
EMP: 50
SALES (est): 545.7K **Privately Held**
WEB: www.thelaforum.com
SIC: 7929 4832 Entertainment service; sports

(P-17975)
FRAMESTORE INC (PA)
Also Called: Creative Gallery
8616 National Blvd, Culver City (90232-2473)
PHONE..................310 975-7300
William Sargent, *CEO*
Jon Collins, *President*
Mel Sullivan, *COO*
Mike McGee, *Officer*
Steve Macpherson, *Principal*
EMP: 50
SALES (est): 2.9MM **Privately Held**
SIC: 7929 Entertainment service

(P-17976)
GENTRY GROUP LLC
555 N Rockingham Ave, Los Angeles (90049-2639)
PHONE..................310 968-5399
Brandon Kahen,
EMP: 50
SALES (est): 117.4K **Privately Held**
SIC: 7929 Entertainment service

(P-17977)
HOB ENTERTAINMENT LLC
1350 Disneyland Dr, Anaheim (92802)
PHONE..................714 778-2583
Kristen Kowlminsky, *Branch Mgr*
EMP: 240
SALES (corp-wide): 10.7B **Publicly Held**
WEB: www.hob.ca
SIC: 7929 Entertainment service
HQ: Hob Entertainment, Llc
7060 Hollywood Blvd
Los Angeles CA 90028

(P-17978)
HOB ENTERTAINMENT LLC
8430 W Sunset Blvd, West Hollywood (90069-1910)
PHONE..................323 848-5100
Arich Berghammer, *Principal*
EMP: 230
SALES (corp-wide): 10.7B **Publicly Held**
WEB: www.hob.ca
SIC: 7929 Entertainment service
HQ: Hob Entertainment, Llc
7060 Hollywood Blvd
Los Angeles CA 90028

(P-17979)
HOB ENTERTAINMENT LLC
1055 5th Ave, San Diego (92101-5101)
PHONE..................619 299-2583
Jim Biasore, *Manager*
EMP: 220
SALES (corp-wide): 10.7B **Publicly Held**
WEB: www.hob.ca
SIC: 7929 Entertainment service
HQ: Hob Entertainment, Llc
7060 Hollywood Blvd
Los Angeles CA 90028

(P-17980)
HOB ENTERTAINMENT LLC (DH)
Also Called: House of Blues
7060 Hollywood Blvd, Los Angeles (90028-6014)
PHONE..................323 769-4600
Michael Rapino, *CEO*
Joseph C Kaczorowski, *President*
Peter Cyffka, *Senior VP*
EMP: 172
SQ FT: 53,000

SALES (est): 102MM
SALES (corp-wide): 10.7B **Publicly Held**
WEB: www.hob.ca
SIC: 7929 Entertainment service
HQ: Live Nation Worldwide, Inc.
430 W 15th St
New York NY 10011
917 421-5100

(P-17981)
IMPERIAL PROJECT INC
Also Called: Bare Elegance
1947 S Myrtle Ave, Monrovia (91016-4854)
PHONE..................310 671-3263
Michael Woods, *Treasurer*
David Amos, *President*
EMP: 60
SQ FT: 1,500
SALES (est): 809.1K **Privately Held**
WEB: www.bareelegance.com
SIC: 7929 5813 Entertainment service; night clubs

(P-17982)
INSOMNIAC INC
9441 W Olympic Blvd, Beverly Hills (90212-4541)
PHONE..................323 874-7020
Pasquale Rotella, *CEO*
Simon Rust Lamb, *CFO*
John Boyle, *Officer*
Matt Muir, *Vice Pres*
Bunny Eachon, *Creative Dir*
▲ EMP: 86
SALES (est): 6MM **Privately Held**
SIC: 7929 Entertainment service

(P-17983)
INSOMNIAC HOLDINGS LLC
9441 W Olympic Blvd, Beverly Hills (90212-4541)
PHONE..................310 867-7041
Michael Rapino,
George Chan, *Accounting Mgr*
Pasquale Rotella,
EMP: 125
SQ FT: 5,000
SALES: 120MM
SALES (corp-wide): 10.7B **Publicly Held**
SIC: 7929 Entertainers & entertainment groups
PA: Live Nation Entertainment, Inc.
9348 Civic Center Dr Lbby
Beverly Hills CA 90210
800 653-8000

(P-17984)
ISRAEL POPS ORCHESTRA
4841 Alonzo Ave, Encino (91316-3607)
PHONE..................818 343-6450
Michael Isaacson, *President*
EMP: 50
SALES (est): 439.4K **Privately Held**
SIC: 7929 Orchestras or bands

(P-17985)
KADEN CASH LLC
15845 Jackson Dr, Fontana (92336-1763)
PHONE..................818 714-4665
Kevin Buckley,
EMP: 50 EST: 2017
SALES (est): 127.4K **Privately Held**
SIC: 7929 Entertainment service

(P-17986)
LIVE MEDIA LLC
1580 Magnolia Ave, Corona (92879-2073)
PHONE..................951 279-8877
Tom McCracken,
EMP: 50
SALES: 14.5MM
SALES (corp-wide): 119.2MM **Privately Held**
SIC: 7929 Entertainment service
PA: Nep Group, Inc.
2 Beta Dr
Pittsburgh PA 15238
412 826-1414

(P-17987)
LIVE NATION ENTERTAINMENT INC
7060 Hollywood Blvd Ste 2, Los Angeles (90028-6030)
PHONE..................213 639-6178
Michael Rapino, *Branch Mgr*

Dan Kemer, *Vice Pres*
Cory Shakarian, *Vice Pres*
Matthew Stein, *Vice Pres*
Jon O'Hara, *Director*
EMP: 89
SALES (corp-wide): 10.7B **Publicly Held**
SIC: 7929 Entertainers & entertainment groups
PA: Live Nation Entertainment, Inc.
9348 Civic Center Dr Lbby
Beverly Hills CA 90210
800 653-8000

(P-17988)
LIVE NATION ENTERTAINMENT INC
151 El Camino Dr Fl 3, Beverly Hills (90212-2704)
PHONE..................323 462-4785
Brooke Stanley, *Branch Mgr*
EMP: 70
SALES (corp-wide): 10.7B **Publicly Held**
SIC: 7929 Entertainers & entertainment groups
PA: Live Nation Entertainment, Inc.
9348 Civic Center Dr Lbby
Beverly Hills CA 90210
800 653-8000

(P-17989)
LOS ANGELES CHMBER ORCHSTRA
350 S Figueroa St Ste 183, Los Angeles (90071-1117)
PHONE..................213 622-7001
Andrea Laguni, *Exec Dir*
Thomas Mallen, *CFO*
EMP: 60
SALES: 4.5MM **Privately Held**
WEB: www.laco.org
SIC: 7929 Orchestras or bands

(P-17990)
LOS ANGELES PHILHARMONIC ASSN (PA)
Also Called: L A Philharmonic
151 S Grand Ave, Los Angeles (90012-3034)
P.O. Box 1951 (90078-1951)
PHONE..................213 972-7300
Chad Smith, *CEO*
Thomas L Beckmen, *Ch of Bd*
Robert Albini, *Associate Dir*
Gail Samuel, *General Mgr*
Alan Wayte, *Admin Sec*
EMP: 2000 EST: 1934
SQ FT: 13,467
SALES (est): 137.3MM **Privately Held**
WEB: www.laphil.com
SIC: 7929 Symphony orchestras

(P-17991)
MAKER STUDIOS INC (DH)
3515 Eastham Dr, Culver City (90232-2440)
PHONE..................310 606-2182
Courtney Holt, *CEO*
Lisa Donovan, *CFO*
EMP: 250
SQ FT: 20,000
SALES (est): 21MM
SALES (corp-wide): 90.2B **Publicly Held**
SIC: 7929 Entertainment service

(P-17992)
MARINE BAND SAN DIEGO
1400 Russell Ave, San Diego (92140-5594)
PHONE..................619 524-1754
Edward Hayes, *Chief*
EMP: 50
SALES (est): 339.7K **Privately Held**
WEB: www.marines.mil
SIC: 7929 Entertainers

(P-17993)
MPC PRODUCTIONS LLC
12035 Killion St, Sherman Oaks (91401)
PHONE..................310 418-8115
Rick Nicolet,
EMP: 75
SALES (est): 176.9K **Privately Held**
SIC: 7929 Entertainment service

(P-17994)
ORCHARD HORROR FILM LLC
15715 Woodvale Rd, Encino (91436-3416)
PHONE...........................212 203-6147
Brandon Menchen, *Mng Member*
EMP: 50 **EST:** 2017
SALES (est): 117.4K **Privately Held**
SIC: 7929 Entertainment service

(P-17995)
PACIFIC SYMPHONY
17620 Fitch Ste 100, Irvine (92614-6081)
PHONE...........................714 755-5788
Jjohn Forsyte, *President*
John E Forsyte, *CEO*
Rhonda Halverson, *Vice Pres*
Kelli Frager, *Manager*
Jennise Hwang, *Assistant*
EMP: 60
SQ FT: 5,750
SALES: 24.3MM **Privately Held**
WEB: www.psyo.org
SIC: 7929 Symphony orchestras

(P-17996)
PALA BAND OF MISSION INDIANS
3478 Sunset Dr, Fallbrook (92028-9579)
PHONE...........................760 207-2603
Ryan McQueen Rusnell, *Branch Mgr*
EMP: 173 **Privately Held**
SIC: 7929 Entertainers & entertainment groups
PA: Pala Band Of Mission Indians
12196 Pala Mission Rd
Pala CA 92059
760 891-3500

(P-17997)
POP MEDIA NETWORKS LLC (DH)
Also Called: Tvguide.com
5510 Lincoln Blvd Ste 400, Playa Vista (90094-1900)
PHONE...........................323 856-4000
Allen Shapiro, *Chairman*
Ryan O'Hara, *President*
Brad Schwartz, *President*
Debra Wichser, *CFO*
David Mandell, *Exec VP*
EMP: 51
SALES (est): 8.1MM
SALES (corp-wide): 25.9B **Publicly Held**
SIC: 7929 7313 7379 Entertainment service; electronic media advertising representatives;
HQ: Cbs Corporation
51 W 52nd St Bsmt 1
New York NY 10019
212 975-4321

(P-17998)
PRIMX ENTERTAINMENT LLC
9664 Andora Ave, Chatsworth (91311-2611)
PHONE...........................818 324-5229
Ryan Christopher Johnson,
EMP: 50
SALES: 153K **Privately Held**
SIC: 7929 7371 7389 Entertainment service; computer software development & applications;

(P-17999)
SAN BERNARDINO SYMPHONY
198 N Arrowhead Ave 2b, San Bernardino (92408-1011)
P.O. Box 109 (92402-0109)
PHONE...........................909 381-5388
Mary Schnepp, *President*
Charles Bradley, *Exec Dir*
EMP: 80
SALES: 514.6K **Privately Held**
WEB: www.sanbernardinosymphony.org
SIC: 7929 Symphony orchestras

(P-18000)
SAN DIEGO SYMPHONY ORCHESTRA
1245 7th Ave, San Diego (92101-4398)
PHONE...........................619 235-0800
Edward B Gill, *Exec Dir*
EMP: 110

SALES: 27MM **Privately Held**
SIC: 7929 Symphony orchestras; orchestras or bands

(P-18001)
SAN FRANCISCO SYMPHONY INC (PA)
201 Van Ness Ave, San Francisco (94102-4585)
PHONE...........................415 552-8000
Brent Assink, *CEO*
James Kirk, *CFO*
Mark Koenig, *CFO*
Christina Coughlin, *Treasurer*
Ruth Goldfine, *Vice Pres*
▲ **EMP:** 400 **EST:** 1911
SALES: 91.1MM **Privately Held**
SIC: 7929 Symphony orchestras

(P-18002)
SANTA CRUZ COUNTY SYMPHONY
307 Church St, Santa Cruz (95060-3811)
PHONE...........................831 462-0553
Mary James, *President*
Virginia Wright, *Exec Dir*
Jan Derecho, *Director*
EMP: 50
SALES: 1.2MM **Privately Held**
WEB: www.santacruzsymphony.com
SIC: 7929 Symphony orchestras

(P-18003)
SANTA ROSA RNCHRIA GAMING COMM
17225 Jersey Ave, Lemoore (93245-9760)
P.O. Box 668 (93245-0668)
PHONE...........................559 924-6948
Abby Ramirez, *Principal*
EMP: 55
SALES (est): 1.2MM **Privately Held**
SIC: 7929 Entertainment service

(P-18004)
SAS ENTERTAINMENT PARTNERS INC
6224 Greenleaf Ave, Whittier (90601-3528)
PHONE...........................213 400-1901
Miles Williams, *President*
EMP: 50
SALES (est): 117.4K **Privately Held**
SIC: 7929 Entertainment service

(P-18005)
SKY ZONE LLC (HQ)
1201 W 5th St Ste T340, Los Angeles (90017-1489)
PHONE...........................310 734-0300
Jeffrey Platt, *CEO*
Pam Tuohey, *Partner*
Julie Petritsch, *CFO*
Matt Lambeth, *Vice Pres*
Stefan Hedgren, *General Mgr*
▲ **EMP:** 65
SALES (est): 12MM
SALES (corp-wide): 38MM **Privately Held**
SIC: 7929 Entertainment service

(P-18006)
SLEEPY GIANT ENTERTAINMENT INC
3501 Jamboree Rd Ste 5000, Newport Beach (92660-2959)
PHONE...........................714 460-4113
Matthew Hannus, *CEO*
David S Lee, *Admin Sec*
◆ **EMP:** 58
SALES: 1.5MM **Privately Held**
SIC: 7929 Entertainment service

(P-18007)
SOCAL SPORTSNET LLC
100 Park Blvd, San Diego (92101-7405)
PHONE...........................619 795-5000
Caroline Perry, *General Counsel*
EMP: 600 **EST:** 2012
SALES (est): 1.3MM
SALES (corp-wide): 18.6MM **Privately Held**
SIC: 7929 Entertainment service
PA: Padre Time, Llc
100 Park Blvd
San Diego CA 92101
619 795-5000

(P-18008)
SONY PICTURES ENTRMT INC
9336 Washington Blvd, Culver City (90232-2628)
PHONE...........................310 202-1234
Margi Bertram, *Manager*
EMP: 500 **Privately Held**
WEB: www.sonypictures.com
SIC: 7929 Entertainers
HQ: Sony Pictures Entertainment, Inc.
10202 Washington Blvd
Culver City CA 90232
310 244-4000

(P-18009)
SONY PICTURES ENTRMT INC
6527 W 82nd St, Los Angeles (90045-2841)
PHONE...........................310 244-3558
Kriege Janz, *Branch Mgr*
EMP: 500 **Privately Held**
SIC: 7929 Entertainers
HQ: Sony Pictures Entertainment, Inc.
10202 Washington Blvd
Culver City CA 90232
310 244-4000

(P-18010)
SPSV ENTERTAINMENT LLC
Also Called: Skypark At Santa's Village
28950 State Highway 18, Skyforest (92385-0460)
P.O. Box 369 (92385-0369)
PHONE...........................909 744-9373
William Johnson, *Mng Member*
EMP: 99
SALES (est): 25.3K **Privately Held**
SIC: 7929 Entertainers & entertainment groups

(P-18011)
STREAMRAY INC
Also Called: Hotbox
910 E Hamilton Ave Fl 6, Campbell (95008-0655)
PHONE...........................408 745-5449
Mallorie Burak, *CEO*
EMP: 315
SALES (est): 697.3K **Privately Held**
SIC: 7929 Entertainment group

(P-18012)
STRIKING DISTANCE STUDIOS INC
2430 Cmino Rmon Ste 122s, San Ramon (94583)
PHONE...........................925 355-5131
Glen Schofield, *CEO*
EMP: 50
SALES (est): 117.4K **Privately Held**
SIC: 7929 Entertainment group

(P-18013)
TURTLE ENTERTAINMENT AMERICA
Also Called: Esl
1212 Chestnut St, Burbank (91506-1627)
PHONE...........................818 861-7315
Han Park, *President*
Yvette Marinez-Ray, *COO*
Craig Levine, *Exec VP*
Paul Brewer, *Vice Pres*
Kevin Rosenblatt, *Vice Pres*
EMP: 50
SALES (est): 2MM
SALES (corp-wide): 2.1B **Privately Held**
SIC: 7929 Entertainment service
HQ: Esl Gaming Gmbh
Schanzenstr. 23
Koln 51063
221 880-4490

(P-18014)
TWDC ENTERPRISES 18 CORP
3900 W Alameda Ave Rm 845, Burbank (91505-4316)
PHONE...........................818 567-5590
Ramona Barnes, *Principal*
EMP: 2002
SALES (corp-wide): 90.2B **Publicly Held**
SIC: 7929 Entertainment service
HQ: Twdc Enterprises 18 Corp.
500 S Buena Vista St
Burbank CA 91521

(P-18015)
TWENTY MILE PRODUCTIONS LLC
11833 Miss Ave Ste 101, Los Angeles (90025-6135)
PHONE...........................412 251-0767
Karen Wacker,
Margaret Ellison,
EMP: 150
SALES (est): 716K **Privately Held**
SIC: 7929 Entertainment group

(P-18016)
UBI SOFT ENTERTAINMENT
625 3rd St Fl 3, San Francisco (94107-1918)
PHONE...........................415 547-4000
Yves Guillemot, *President*
Yannis Mallat, *Chief Mktg Ofcr*
Alex Methot, *Admin Sec*
Vincent Paquet, *Project Mgr*
Adam Novickas, *Mktg Dir*
EMP: 51 **EST:** 2011
SALES (est): 4.5MM
SALES (corp-wide): 1.2B **Privately Held**
SIC: 7929 Entertainers & entertainment groups
PA: Ubisoft Entertainment
107 Avenue Henri Freville
Rennes 35200
299 932-068

(P-18017)
UNIVERSAL MUSIC GROUP INC
Also Called: Verve Music Group
2220 Colorado Ave, Santa Monica (90404-3506)
PHONE...........................310 865-4000
Charles Ciongoli, *Exec VP*
Rob Cromar, *President*
Jay Thompson, *Analyst*
EMP: 100
SALES (corp-wide): 78.1MM **Privately Held**
SIC: 7929 Entertainment service
HQ: Universal Music Group, Inc.
2220 Colorado Ave
Santa Monica CA 90404
310 865-4000

(P-18018)
US AIRFORCE BAND OF GOLDEN W
551 Waldron St Bldg 240, Travis Afb (94535)
PHONE...........................707 424-2263
Michael Manch, *Principal*
EMP: 50
SALES (est): 488.9K **Privately Held**
SIC: 7929 Orchestras or bands

(P-18019)
WERM INVESTMENTS LLC
Also Called: Exchange La
14242 Ventura Blvd # 212, Sherman Oaks (91423-2771)
PHONE...........................213 627-8070
ADI McBain, *Mng Member*
Camil Sayadeh,
EMP: 50
SALES (est): 297.4K **Privately Held**
SIC: 7929 Entertainment service

7933 Bowling Centers

(P-18020)
3900 WEST LANE BOWL INC
3900 West Ln, Stockton (95204-2436)
PHONE...........................209 466-6100
Richard Ghio, *President*
Rudy Antonini, *Corp Secy*
EMP: 50
SQ FT: 20,000
SALES (est): 2.1MM **Privately Held**
WEB: www.westlanebowl.net
SIC: 7933 5812 5813 Ten pin center; American restaurant; beer garden (drinking places)

(P-18021)
AMF BOWLING CENTERS INC
1201 W Beverly Blvd, Montebello (90640-4142)
PHONE...........................323 728-9161

Norris Runnels, *Manager*
EMP: 50
SALES (corp-wide): 343.5MM **Privately Held**
WEB: www.kidsports.org
SIC: 7933 7999 Ten pin center; tourist attractions, amusement park concessions & rides
HQ: Amf Bowling Centers, Inc.
7313 Bell Creek Rd
Mechanicsville VA 23111

(P-18022)
AMF BOWLING CENTERS INC
1819 30th St, Bakersfield (93301-1928)
PHONE.................................661 324-4966
Rick Mossman, *Branch Mgr*
EMP: 50
SALES (corp-wide): 343.5MM **Privately Held**
WEB: www.kidsports.org
SIC: 7933 7999 Ten pin center; tourist attractions, amusement park concessions & rides
HQ: Amf Bowling Centers, Inc.
7313 Bell Creek Rd
Mechanicsville VA 23111

(P-18023)
AMF BOWLING CENTERS INC
22771 Centre Dr, Lake Forest (92630-1747)
PHONE.................................949 770-0055
Darryl Messiah, *Branch Mgr*
EMP: 50
SALES (corp-wide): 343.5MM **Privately Held**
WEB: www.kidsports.org
SIC: 7933 5813 Ten pin center; bar (drinking places)
HQ: Amf Bowling Centers, Inc.
7313 Bell Creek Rd
Mechanicsville VA 23111

(P-18024)
BDP BOWL INC
Also Called: Classic Bowling Center
900 King Plz, Daly City (94015-4450)
PHONE.................................650 878-0300
Robert Devincenzi, *President*
Richard J Bocci, *Treasurer*
Rob Petroni, *General Mgr*
Steven Devinchenzi, *Admin Sec*
Steve Devinchenzi, *Sales Executive*
EMP: 50
SQ FT: 50,000
SALES (est): 1.9MM **Privately Held**
WEB: www.classicbowling.com
SIC: 7933 Ten pin center

(P-18025)
BOWLERO CORP
Also Called: Brunswick Covino Lanes
1060 W San Bernardino Rd, Covina (91722-4160)
PHONE.................................626 339-1286
Javier Guzman, *Manager*
EMP: 53
SALES (corp-wide): 343.5MM **Privately Held**
SIC: 7933 Bowling centers
PA: Bowlero Corp.
222 W 44th St
New York NY 10036
212 777-2214

(P-18026)
BOWLERO CORP
Also Called: West Covina Lanes
675 S Glendora Ave, West Covina (91790-3705)
PHONE.................................626 960-3636
Joe Carridoza, *Manager*
EMP: 55
SQ FT: 57,259
SALES (corp-wide): 343.5MM **Privately Held**
SIC: 7933 Ten pin center
PA: Bowlero Corp.
222 W 44th St
New York NY 10036
212 777-2214

(P-18027)
BOWLERO CORP
Also Called: Brunswick Deer Creks Lnes 213
7930 Haven Ave Ste 101, Rancho Cucamonga (91730-3056)
PHONE.................................909 945-9392
Venesa Boudreau, *Assistant VP*
EMP: 50
SALES (corp-wide): 343.5MM **Privately Held**
SIC: 7933 Ten pin center
PA: Bowlero Corp.
222 W 44th St
New York NY 10036
212 777-2214

(P-18028)
BOWLERO CORP
Also Called: Brunswick Cal Oaks Bowl
40440 California Oaks Rd, Murrieta (92562-5828)
PHONE.................................951 698-2202
John Tang, *Branch Mgr*
EMP: 50
SALES (corp-wide): 343.5MM **Privately Held**
SIC: 7933 Ten pin center
PA: Bowlero Corp.
222 W 44th St
New York NY 10036
212 777-2214

(P-18029)
CAL BOWL ENTERPRISES LLC
2500 Carson St, Lakewood (90712-4198)
PHONE.................................562 421-8448
Charles Knistler,
EMP: 50
SALES (est): 836.6K **Privately Held**
SIC: 7933 Bowling centers

(P-18030)
COVINA BOWL INC
675 S Glendora Ave, West Covina (91790-3705)
PHONE.................................626 339-1286
Leonard A Brutocao, *President*
Angelo Brutocao, *Treasurer*
James Parker, *Bd of Directors*
EMP: 80
SQ FT: 60,000
SALES (est): 1.3MM **Privately Held**
SIC: 7933 5812 5813 7999 Ten pin center; American restaurant; drinking places; billiard parlor

(P-18031)
CRENSHAW BOWLING
Also Called: Palos Verdes Bowl
24600 Crenshaw Blvd, Torrance (90505-5307)
PHONE.................................310 326-5120
George Brant, *Vice Pres*
EMP: 50
SQ FT: 40,000
SALES (est): 1.6MM **Privately Held**
SIC: 7933 5812 5813 Ten pin center; snack bar; bar (drinking places)

(P-18032)
FOLSOM RECREATION CORP
Also Called: Lake Bowl
511 E Bidwell St, Folsom (95630-3118)
PHONE.................................916 983-4411
Wally Dreher, *President*
Sue Dreher, *Vice Pres*
Dan Dreher, *General Mgr*
Jeremy Dreher, *General Mgr*
Carly Dreher, *Bookkeeper*
EMP: 70
SQ FT: 18,000
SALES (est): 4.1MM **Privately Held**
SIC: 7933 Ten pin center

(P-18033)
FOURTH STREET BOWL
1441 N 4th St, San Jose (95112-4716)
PHONE.................................408 453-5555
Ken Nakatsu, *President*
Cathie Judy, *General Mgr*
EMP: 50
SQ FT: 31,450
SALES (est): 3.1MM **Privately Held**
WEB: www.4thstreetbowl.com
SIC: 7933 5813 5812 Bowling centers; bar (drinking places); coffee shop

(P-18034)
FREMONT SPORTS INC
Also Called: Cloverleaf Bowl
40645 Fremont Blvd Ste 3, Fremont (94538-4368)
PHONE.................................510 656-4411
James Chambers, *CEO*
Donald F Hillman, *President*
Mike Hillman, *Manager*
EMP: 50
SQ FT: 40,000
SALES (est): 2.4MM **Privately Held**
WEB: www.cloverleafbowl.com
SIC: 7933 5812 5813 Ten pin center; food bars; bar (drinking places)

(P-18035)
GABLE HOUSE INC
Also Called: Gable House Bowl
22501 Hawthorne Blvd, Torrance (90505-2509)
PHONE.................................310 378-2265
Michael Cogan, *President*
EMP: 100
SQ FT: 80,000
SALES (est): 4.7MM **Privately Held**
WEB: www.gablehousebowl.com
SIC: 7933 5813 5812 Ten pin center; bar (drinking places); snack bar

(P-18036)
LUCKY STRIKE ENTERTAINMENT LLC
Also Called: LUCKY STRIKE ENTERTAINMENT, L.L.C.
6801 Hollywood Blvd # 143, Los Angeles (90028-6138)
PHONE.................................818 933-3752
David Bradley, *General Mgr*
EMP: 87
SALES (corp-wide): 61.2MM **Privately Held**
SIC: 7933 Bowling centers
PA: Lucky Strike Entertainment, Llc
15260 Ventura Blvd # 1110
Sherman Oaks CA 91403
323 467-7776

(P-18037)
LUCKY STRIKE ENTERTAINMENT LLC
Also Called: LUCKY STRIKE ENTERTAINMENT, L.L.C.
15260 Ventura Blvd # 1110, Sherman Oaks (91403-5346)
PHONE.................................818 933-0872
Mark P'Pool, *Branch Mgr*
EMP: 131
SALES (corp-wide): 61.2MM **Privately Held**
SIC: 7933 Bowling centers
PA: Lucky Strike Entertainment, Llc
15260 Ventura Blvd # 1110
Sherman Oaks CA 91403
323 467-7776

(P-18038)
LUCKY STRIKE ENTERTAINMENT LLC
Also Called: LUCKY STRIKE ENTERTAINMENT, L.L.C.
20 City Blvd W Ste G2, Orange (92868-3131)
PHONE.................................248 374-3420
Ismail Saleem, *Branch Mgr*
EMP: 88
SALES (corp-wide): 61.2MM **Privately Held**
SIC: 7933 Ten pin center
PA: Lucky Strike Entertainment, Llc
15260 Ventura Blvd # 1110
Sherman Oaks CA 91403
323 467-7776

(P-18039)
MCHENRY BOWL INC
3700 Mchenry Ave, Modesto (95356-1597)
PHONE.................................209 571-2695
Garrard Marsh, *President*
Dallas Kadry, *Treasurer*
W Jerry Marsh, *Vice Pres*
Maxine Marsh, *Admin Sec*
EMP: 50
SQ FT: 52,000

SALES (est): 1.6MM **Privately Held**
WEB: www.mchenrybowl.com
SIC: 7933 5813 5941 Ten pin center; bar (drinking places); bowling equipment & supplies

(P-18040)
NATIONWIDE THEATRES CORP
Also Called: Cal Coffee Shop
2500 Carson St, Lakewood (90712-4107)
PHONE.................................562 421-8448
Tom Moeller, *Manager*
EMP: 60
SALES (corp-wide): 180.2MM **Privately Held**
SIC: 7933 5813 5812 Ten pin center; cocktail lounge; coffee shop
HQ: Nationwide Theatres Corp.
120 N Robertson Blvd Fl 3
Los Angeles CA 90048
310 657-8420

(P-18041)
PINSETTERS INC
Also Called: Country Club Lanes
2600 Watt Ave, Sacramento (95821-6296)
PHONE.................................916 488-7545
Greg Kassis, *Ch of Bd*
Dave Haness, *President*
Jim Kassis, *Corp Secy*
Dave Kassis, *Vice Pres*
Kerry Kassis, *Vice Pres*
EMP: 70
SQ FT: 70,000
SALES (est): 2.7MM **Privately Held**
SIC: 7933 5812 5813 Ten pin center; snack bar; bar (drinking places)

(P-18042)
SPARE-TIME INC
429 W Lockeford St, Lodi (95240-2058)
PHONE.................................209 371-0241
Dennis Kaufman, *Principal*
EMP: 226
SALES (corp-wide): 38.3MM **Privately Held**
SIC: 7933 Ten pin center
PA: Spare-Time, Inc.
11344 Coloma Rd Ste 350
Gold River CA 95670
916 859-5910

(P-18043)
STARS RECREATION CENTER LP
155 Browns Valley Pkwy, Vacaville (95688-3011)
PHONE.................................707 455-7827
Ernest E Sousa, *Partner*
Kenneth Sousa, *Partner*
EMP: 50
SQ FT: 65,000
SALES (est): 2.2MM **Privately Held**
SIC: 7933 Ten pin center

(P-18044)
STRIKES UNLIMITED INC
5681 Lonetree Blvd, Rocklin (95765-3735)
PHONE.................................916 626-3600
Kari Pegram, *CEO*
Kathi Miller, *General Mgr*
Armando Pacheco, *General Mgr*
Prakash Chandra, *Controller*
Annette Turek, *Human Res Dir*
EMP: 90 **EST:** 2011
SQ FT: 54,000
SALES (est): 3.5MM **Privately Held**
SIC: 7933 5812 Ten pin center; eating places

7941 Professional Sports Clubs & Promoters

(P-18045)
ACE HIGH ENTERTAINNMENT LLC
125 Sconce Way, Sacramento (95838-4744)
PHONE.................................916 243-5515
Rodney Shead, *CEO*
EMP: 50

PRODUCTS & SVCS

SALES (est): 403.3K **Privately Held**
SIC: 7941 5812 7922 Sports field or stadium operator, promoting sports events; Sushi bar; ethnic food restaurants; Chinese restaurant; theatrical talent & booking agencies

(P-18046)
ANAHEIM ARENA MANAGEMENT LLC
Also Called: AAM
2695 E Katella Ave, Anaheim (92806-5904)
PHONE.................................714 704-2400
Tim Ryan, *President*
Ryan Cordes, *Partner*
Michael Schulman, *Ch of Bd*
Nestor Blanco, *Officer*
Chris Johnston, *Vice Pres*
EMP: 600
SQ FT: 106,000
SALES (est): 37.9MM **Privately Held**
WEB: www.hondacenter.com
SIC: 7941 Sports field or stadium operator, promoting sports events

(P-18047)
ANAHEIM DUCKS HOCKEY CLUB LLC
2101 E Coast Hwy Fl 3, Corona Del Mar (92625-1900)
PHONE.................................714 940-2900
Michel Schulman, *Mng Member*
EMP: 68 **Privately Held**
SIC: 7941 Sports clubs, managers & promoters
PA: Anaheim Ducks Hockey Club, Llc
2695 E Katella Ave
Anaheim CA 92806

(P-18048)
ANAHEIM DUCKS HOCKEY CLUB LLC (PA)
2695 E Katella Ave, Anaheim (92806-5904)
PHONE.................................714 940-2900
Michel Schulman, *Mng Member*
John Viola, *Vice Pres*
Jamie Hernandez, *Executive*
Doug Shearer, *Executive*
Doug Heller, *Financial Exec*
EMP: 82
SALES (est): 12.7MM **Privately Held**
SIC: 7941 Sports clubs, managers & promoters

(P-18049)
ANGELS BASEBALL LP (PA)
Also Called: Los Angeles Angels of Anaheim
2000 E Gene Autry Way, Anaheim (92806-6143)
PHONE.................................714 940-2000
Dennis Kuhl, *General Ptnr*
Bill Beverage, *Partner*
Molly Jolly, *Partner*
Richard McClemmy, *Partner*
Tim Mead, *Partner*
EMP: 1000 EST: 1996
SALES (est): 61.7MM **Privately Held**
SIC: 7941 Baseball club, professional & semi-professional

(P-18050)
ANSCHUTZ SO CALIF SPORTS COMPL
Also Called: Stop Hop Center
18400 Avalon Blvd Ste 100, Carson (90746-2180)
PHONE.................................310 630-2000
Kedie Pendolfo,
Diego Martinez, *Admin Sec*
Anschutz Grp,
EMP: 160
SALES (est): 5.3MM **Privately Held**
SIC: 7941 Soccer club
HQ: Anschutz Entertainment Group, Inc.
800 W Olympic Blvd # 305
Los Angeles CA 90015
213 337-5052

(P-18051)
ATHLETICS INVESTMENT GROUP LLC (PA)
Also Called: Oakland Athletics
7000 Coliseum Way Ste 3, Oakland (94621-1917)
P.O. Box 2220 (94621-0120)
PHONE.................................510 638-4900
Lewis N Wolff, *Mng Member*
Ken Pries, *Vice Pres*
David Rinetti, *Vice Pres*
Mike Selleck, *Vice Pres*
Paul Wong, *Vice Pres*
EMP: 162 EST: 1901
SALES (est): 23.8MM **Privately Held**
SIC: 7941 Baseball club, professional & semi-professional

(P-18052)
BIG LEAGUE DREAMS JURUPA LLC
10550 Cntu Gllano Rnch Rd, Jurupa Valley (91752-3261)
PHONE.................................951 685-6900
Scott Parks Letellier, *CEO*
Jeffrey Odekirk,
Richard Odekirk,
EMP: 57
SALES (est): 2.9MM **Privately Held**
SIC: 7941 7999 Sports field or stadium operator, promoting sports events; recreation center

(P-18053)
BIG LGUE DRAMS CHINO HILLS LLC
16333 Fairfield Ranch Rd, Chino Hills (91709-8816)
PHONE.................................909 287-6900
Rick Odekirk,
Jeff Odekirk,
EMP: 93
SALES (est): 2.2MM **Privately Held**
WEB: www.baseballfirst.com
SIC: 7941 Sports field or stadium operator, promoting sports events

(P-18054)
BIG LGUE DREAMS CONSULTING LLC
2155 Trumble Rd, Perris (92571-9211)
PHONE.................................619 846-8855
EMP: 118
SALES (corp-wide): 45.7MM **Privately Held**
SIC: 7941 Sports field or stadium operator, promoting sports events
PA: Big League Dreams Consulting, Llc
16333 Fairfield Ranch Rd
Chino Hills CA 91709
909 287-1700

(P-18055)
BIG LGUE DREAMS CONSULTING LLC
2100 S Azusa Ave, West Covina (91792-1507)
PHONE.................................626 839-1100
Jeffrey Odekirk, *Principal*
EMP: 118
SALES (corp-wide): 45.7MM **Privately Held**
SIC: 7941 Sports field or stadium operator, promoting sports events
PA: Big League Dreams Consulting, Llc
16333 Fairfield Ranch Rd
Chino Hills CA 91709
909 287-1700

(P-18056)
BIG3 BASKETBALL LLC
644 S Figueroa St, Los Angeles (90017-3411)
PHONE.................................213 417-2013
Jeff Kwatinetz, *CEO*
O'Shea Jackson Sr, *Principal*
EMP: 67
SALES: 5.7MM **Privately Held**
SIC: 7941 Basketball club

(P-18057)
CAA SPORTS LLC (HQ)
2000 Avenue Of The Stars # 100, Los Angeles (90067-4705)
PHONE.................................424 288-2000
Michael A Rubel,
EMP: 67
SALES (est): 13.2MM
SALES (corp-wide): 112.7MM **Privately Held**
SIC: 7941 Sports promotion
PA: Creative Artists Agency, Llc
2000 Avenue Of The Stars # 100
Los Angeles CA 90067
424 288-2000

(P-18058)
CHARGERS FOOTBALL COMPANY LLC (PA)
Also Called: Los Angeles Chargers
3333 Susan St, Costa Mesa (92626-1632)
PHONE.................................619 280-2121
Dean A Spanos, *Mng Member*
Jeanne Bonk, *CFO*
Alex Spanos, *Chairman*
Alexander G Spanos, *Bd of Directors*
Jeanne M Bonk, *Exec VP*
EMP: 70
SALES (est): 15.5MM **Privately Held**
SIC: 7941 Football club

(P-18059)
CITY OF GLENDALE
541 W Chevy Chase Dr, Glendale (91204-1813)
PHONE.................................818 548-3950
Daniel Hardgrove, *Manager*
EMP: 80 **Privately Held**
WEB: www.glendaleca.com
SIC: 7941 9111 Sports clubs, managers & promoters; mayors' offices
PA: City Of Glendale
141 N Glendale Ave Fl 2
Glendale CA 91206
818 548-2085

(P-18060)
COTO DE CAZA GOLF CLUB INC
25291 Vista Del Verde, Trabuco Canyon (92679-4900)
PHONE.................................949 766-7886
Jack Deal, *Director*
Marc Chasman, *Director*
EMP: 135
SALES (est): 2.3MM
SALES (corp-wide): 12.3MM **Privately Held**
WEB: www.coto-de-caza.com
SIC: 7941 5813 7992 7991 Professional & semi-professional sports clubs; drinking places; public golf courses; physical fitness facilities; eating places
PA: Coto De Caza Limited
24800 Chrisanta Dr
Mission Viejo CA

(P-18061)
FORTY NINERS FOOTBALL CO LLC
Also Called: San Francisco 49ers
4949 Mrie P Debartolo Way, Santa Clara (95054-1156)
PHONE.................................408 562-4949
Denise Debartolo York, *Principal*
Patty Inglis, *Exec VP*
Robert Alberino, *Vice Pres*
Keena Turner, *Vice Pres*
Bob Lange, *Comms Dir*
EMP: 99
SALES (est): 13.6MM **Privately Held**
SIC: 7941 Football club

(P-18062)
FOX BSB HOLDCO INC
Also Called: GUGGENHEIM INVESTMENTS
1000 Vin Scully Ave, Los Angeles (90090-1112)
PHONE.................................323 224-1500
Steve Soboroff, *Vice Chairman*
Ron Wheeler, *CEO*
Dannis Mannion, *COO*
Peter Wilhelm, *CFO*
Lon Rosen, *Chief Mktg Ofcr*
EMP: 5173

SQ FT: 20,000
SALES: 5.1MM
SALES (corp-wide): 727.6MM **Privately Held**
WEB: www.ladodgers.com
SIC: 7941 Baseball club, professional & semi-professional
PA: Guggenheim Partners, Llc
330 Madison Ave Rm 201
New York NY 10017
212 739-0700

(P-18063)
GOLDEN STATE WARRIORS LLC
1011 Broadway, Oakland (94607-4027)
PHONE.................................510 986-2200
Christopher Cohan, *Mng Member*
Mike Kitts, *Partner*
Gail Hunter, *Vice Pres*
Phillip Hastings, *Surgery Dir*
Jose Gordon, *Exec Dir*
EMP: 100 EST: 1962
SALES (est): 16.4MM **Privately Held**
WEB: www.gs-warriors.com
SIC: 7941 Basketball club

(P-18064)
HOTROLLERGIRL PRODUCTIONS
11890 Silver Spur St, Ojai (93023-4181)
PHONE.................................530 521-2745
Kristin Longstreet, *Owner*
EMP: 100 EST: 2015
SALES (est): 377.6K **Privately Held**
SIC: 7941 7231 7221 Stadium event operator services; beauty shops; photographer, still or video

(P-18065)
INLAND EMPRE 66ERS BSEBLL CLB
280 S E St, San Bernardino (92401-2009)
PHONE.................................909 888-9922
David Elmore, *CEO*
Donna Tuttle, *President*
Jhon Fonsaker, *CFO*
Dave Oldham, *VP Bus Dvlpt*
John Fonseca, *Controller*
EMP: 110
SQ FT: 600
SALES (est): 5.4MM
SALES (corp-wide): 53.7MM **Privately Held**
WEB: www.ie66ers.com
SIC: 7941 Baseball club, professional & semi-professional
PA: The Elmore Group Ltd
19 N Grant St Ste 2
Hinsdale IL
630 325-6228

(P-18066)
KINGS ARENA LTD PARTNERSHIP
Also Called: Maloof Sport Entertainment
1 Sports Pkwy, Sacramento (95834-2300)
PHONE.................................916 928-0000
Gavin Maloof, *Managing Prtnr*
John Rinehart, *Partner*
John Thomas, *Partner*
EMP: 60 EST: 1992
SALES (est): 7.1MM **Privately Held**
SIC: 7941 Boxing & wrestling arena

(P-18067)
LA SPORTS PROPERTIES INC
Also Called: Los Angeles Clippers
1212 S Flower St Fl 5, Los Angeles (90015-2123)
PHONE.................................213 742-7500
Dick Parsons, *CEO*
EMP: 195 EST: 1946
SQ FT: 5,000
SALES (est): 15.1MM **Privately Held**
WEB: www.clippers.com
SIC: 7941 Basketball club

(P-18068)
LOS ANGELES DODGERS LLC
1000 Vin Scully Ave, Los Angeles (90090-1112)
PHONE.................................323 224-1507
Stan Kasten, *President*
EMP: 1360

SALES (est): 4.2MM Privately Held
SIC: 7941 Stadium event operator services

(P-18069)
LOS ANGELES LAKERS INC
Also Called: La Lakers
2275 E Mariposa Ave, El Segundo
(90245-5029)
PHONE..................................310 426-6000
Jeanie Buss, *President*
Aj Harris, *Asst Controller*
Susan Matson, *Controller*
Carlos Maples, *Manager*
Joe Bucz, *Accounts Exec*
EMP: 150
SQ FT: 12,000
SALES (est): 1.3MM Privately Held
WEB: www.lakers.com
SIC: 7941 Basketball club

(P-18070)
LOS ANGELES RAMS LLC (PA)
Also Called: St Louis Rams
29899 Agoura Rd, Agoura Hills
(91301-2493)
PHONE..................................314 982-7267
E Stanley Kroenke, *General Ptnr*
Lucia Rodriguez, *Owner*
Chip Rosenbloom, *Owner*
Kevin Demoff, *COO*
Bill Consoli, *Vice Pres*
EMP: 100
SALES (est): 28.1MM Privately Held
WEB: www.stlouisrams.com
SIC: 7941 Football club

(P-18071)
LOS ANGELES KINGS HOCKEY CLB LP
555 N Nash St, El Segundo (90245-2818)
P.O. Box 912 (90245-0912)
PHONE..................................310 535-4502
Dean Lombardi, *General Mgr*
Solomon Jeff, *Exec VP*
Nick Grodotzke, *Executive*
Kehly Sloane, *Executive Asst*
Scott Sangrey, *Controller*
EMP: 119 Privately Held
WEB: www.lakings.com
SIC: 7941 Ice hockey club
PA: The Los Angeles Kings Hockey Club L
P
800 W Olympic Blvd
Los Angeles CA 90015
-

(P-18072)
LOS ANGLES KINGS HOCKEY CLB LP (PA)
Also Called: L A Kings
800 W Olympic Blvd, Los Angeles
(90015-1360)
PHONE..................................888 546-4752
Toll Free:...............................888 -
Timothy Leiweke, *Partner*
Joe Leibfried, *Vice Pres*
Johnathan Lowe, *Vice Pres*
Martha Saucedo, *Vice Pres*
Derek Mayfield, *Executive*
EMP: 120
SALES (est): 3.3MM Privately Held
WEB: www.lakings.com
SIC: 7941 Ice hockey club

(P-18073)
MANDALAY SPORTS ENTRMT LLC (PA)
Also Called: Mandalay Baseball Properties
4751 Wilshire Blvd Fl 3, Los Angeles
(90010-3844)
PHONE..................................323 549-4300
Hank Stickney, *CEO*
Anthony Lott, *Ch of Bd*
Peter Guber, *CEO*
Leroy Kim, *Vice Pres*
Shelly Riney, *Vice Pres*
EMP: 65
SALES (est): 6.7MM Privately Held
SIC: 7941 Sports clubs, managers & pro-
moters

(P-18074)
PADRES LP
Also Called: San Diego Padres
100 Park Blvd Petco Park, San Diego
(92101)
P.O. Box 122000 (92112-2000)
PHONE..................................619 795-5000
Mike Dee,
Ronda Sedillo,
Ryan Thorvaldsen, *Manager*
Jeff Gould, *Accounts Exec*
EMP: 1100
SQ FT: 3,000
SALES (est): 398.6K Privately Held
SIC: 7941 Baseball club, professional &
semi-professional

(P-18075)
PSE HOLDING LLC (HQ)
Also Called: Palace Sports & Entrmt LLC
360 N Crescent Dr, Beverly Hills
(90210-4874)
PHONE..................................248 377-0165
Tom Gores,
EMP: 300
SALES (est): 166.9MM
SALES (corp-wide): 17.2MM Privately
Held
WEB: www.palacenet.com
SIC: 7941 7922 Stadium event operator
services; summer theater
PA: Pistons Palace Holdings, Llc
360 N Crescent Dr
Beverly Hills CA 90210
310 228-9521

(P-18076)
RIVER CY BASBAL INV GROUP LLC (PA)
400 Ball Park Dr, West Sacramento
(95691-2824)
PHONE..................................916 376-4700
Art Savage,
Alan Ledford,
Dan Vistica,
EMP: 60
SALES (est): 2.8MM Privately Held
SIC: 7941 7999 6512 Baseball club, pro-
fessional & semi-professional; concession
operator; nonresidential building opera-
tors

(P-18077)
SACRAMENTO RIVER CATS BASEBALL
400 Ball Park Dr, West Sacramento
(95691-2824)
PHONE..................................916 376-4700
Art Savage,
Chip Maxson, *General Mgr*
Brittney Broberg, *Info Tech Mgr*
Madeline Strika, *Controller*
Daniel Emmons, *Opers Staff*
EMP: 50
SALES (est): 6.2MM
SALES (corp-wide): 2.8MM Privately
Held
WEB: www.rivercats.net
SIC: 7941 Baseball club, professional &
semi-professional
PA: River City Baseball Investment Group
Llc
400 Ball Park Dr
West Sacramento CA 95691
916 376-4700

(P-18078)
SAN FRANCISCO FORTY NINERS (PA)
4949 Mrie P Debartolo Way, Santa Clara
(95054-1156)
PHONE..................................408 562-4949
Denise Debartolo York, *Ch of Bd*
Peter Harris, *President*
Andy Dolich, *COO*
Larry Macneil, *CFO*
Patty Inglis, *Exec VP*
EMP: 120
SQ FT: 50,000
SALES (est): 164.5MM Privately Held
WEB: www.sf49ers.com
SIC: 7941 Football club

(P-18079)
SAN JOSE SHARKS LLC
Also Called: HP Pavillion At San Jose
525 W Santa Clara St, San Jose
(95113-1500)
PHONE..................................408 999-6810
Greg Jamison, *President*
Flavil Hampsten, *Exec VP*
Neda Tabatabaie, *Vice Pres*
Jeenette Miller, *Administration*
Patrick Doherty, *Opers Staff*
EMP: 170
SALES (est): 15.1MM Privately Held
WEB: www.hppsj.com
SIC: 7941 Ice hockey club

(P-18080)
SHARKS SPORTS & ENTRMT LLC
Also Called: SSE Merchandise
525 W Santa Clara St, San Jose
(95113-1520)
PHONE..................................408 287-7070
Hasso Plattner, *Mng Member*
Kevin Hilton, *Partner*
Gary Parrish, *Officer*
Charles Faas, *Exec VP*
Jim Goddard, *Exec VP*
EMP: 800
SALES (est): 31.9MM Privately Held
SIC: 7941 Sports field or stadium operator,
promoting sports events

(P-18081)
UNITED STTES OLYMPIC COMMITTEE
Also Called: Arco Olympic Training Center
2800 Olympic Pkwy, Chula Vista
(91915-6002)
PHONE..................................619 656-1500
Tracie Lamb, *Director*
Guy Dragisic, *Manager*
EMP: 50
SALES (corp-wide): 193.9MM Privately
Held
WEB: www.usoc.org
SIC: 7941 Manager of individual profes-
sional athletes
PA: United States Olympic Committee Inc
1 Olympic Plz
Colorado Springs CO 80903
719 632-5551

7948 Racing & Track Operations

(P-18082)
CALIFORNIA SPEEDWAY CORP
Also Called: Auto Club Speedway
9300 Cherry Ave, Fontana (92335-2562)
PHONE..................................909 429-5000
William Miller, *President*
Brian Geye, *Executive*
Erin Macdonald, *Executive*
David Talley, *Comms Mgr*
Nicole McCance, *Executive Asst*
EMP: 50 EST: 1994
SALES (est): 4.8MM
SALES (corp-wide): 675MM Privately
Held
SIC: 7948 Automotive race track operation
HQ: 88 Corporation
1801 W Intl Speedway Blvd
Daytona Beach FL 32114
386 254-2700

(P-18083)
CHURCHILL DOWNS INCORPORATED
800 W El Camino Real # 400, Mountain
View (94040-2589)
PHONE..................................502 638-3879
Ted Gay, *President*
EMP: 900
SALES (corp-wide): 1B Publicly Held
SIC: 7948 7993 Race track operation;
thoroughbred horse racing; gambling ma-
chines, coin-operated
PA: Churchill Downs Incorporated
600 N Hurstbourne Pkwy # 400
Louisville KY 40222
502 636-4400

(P-18084)
DEL MAR THOROUGHBRED CLUB
Also Called: SURFSIDE RACE PLACE AT
DEL MAR
2260 Jimmy Durante Blvd, Del Mar
(92014-2216)
P.O. Box 700 (92014-0700)
PHONE..................................858 755-1141
Joe Harper, *President*
Karl Bupp, *CFO*
Mike Ernst, *CFO*
Craig Dado, *Vice Pres*
Craig Fravel, *Vice Pres*
▲ EMP: 400 EST: 1970
SALES (est): 37.9MM Privately Held
WEB: www.dmtc.com
SIC: 7948 Thoroughbred horse racing

(P-18085)
LOS ANGELES TURF CLUB INC (DH)
Also Called: Santa Anita Park
285 W Huntington Dr, Arcadia
(91007-3439)
P.O. Box 60014 (91066-6014)
PHONE..................................626 574-6330
Gregory C Avioli, *CEO*
Frank Stronach, *Ch of Bd*
George Haines II, *President*
Sherwood Chillingworth, *Exec VP*
Alfredo Arias, *Vice Pres*
▲ EMP: 168 EST: 1964
SALES (est): 33.4MM
SALES (corp-wide): 40.8B Privately Held
WEB: www.santaanita.com
SIC: 7948 Horse race track operation
HQ: Magna Car Top Systems Of America,
Inc.
2725 Commerce Pkwy
Auburn Hills MI 48326
248 836-4500

(P-18086)
NATIONAL HOT ROD ASSOCIATION (PA)
Also Called: Nhra
2035 E Financial Way, Glendora
(91741-4602)
PHONE..................................626 914-4761
Wally Parks, *Director*
Tom Compton, *President*
Leila Fenberg, *Executive Asst*
Richard Wells, *Admin Sec*
Jodee Kennedy, *Admin Asst*
EMP: 200 EST: 1951
SQ FT: 30,000
SALES: 99.2MM Privately Held
WEB: www.nhra.com
SIC: 7948 2711 2741 Automotive race
track operation; newspapers: publishing
only, not printed on site; miscellaneous
publishing

(P-18087)
PACIFIC RACING ASSOCIATION
Also Called: Golden Gate Fields
1100 Eastshore Hwy, Albany (94710-1002)
P.O. Box 6027 (94706-0027)
PHONE..................................510 559-7300
Frank Stronach, *President*
Mary Hile, *Admin Asst*
Juan Leon, *Info Tech Mgr*
Bob Hemmer, *Analyst*
Terry Roberson, *Manager*
EMP: 140
SALES: 63MM Privately Held
WEB: www.goldengatefields.com
SIC: 7948 Horses, racing

(P-18088)
PHILIP DAMATO RACING LLC
28202 Palmada, Mission Viejo
(92692-1422)
PHONE..................................949 830-7027
Philip D'Amato,
EMP: 55 EST: 2014
SALES (est): 227.3K Privately Held
SIC: 7948 Horses, racing

(P-18089)
SMISC HOLDINGS LLC
Hwy 121, Sonoma (95476)
PHONE..................................707 938-8448
Steve Page, *Manager*

EMP: 50
SALES (corp-wide): 461.9MM **Privately Held**
SIC: 7948 Motor vehicle racing & drivers
HQ: Smisc Holdings, Llc
5239 Zmax Blvd
Harrisburg NC 28075
704 455-9453

(P-18090)
SPEEDWAY SONOMA LLC
Also Called: Infineon Raceway
Hwy 37 N, Sonoma (95476)
PHONE.................................707 938-8448
Bruton Smith,
Sarah Grasal,
▲ EMP: 60 EST: 2000
SALES (est): 4.1MM
SALES (corp-wide): 461.9MM **Privately Held**
WEB: www.infineonraceway.com
SIC: 7948 Automotive race track operation
HQ: Speedway Motorsports, Llc
5555 Concord Pkwy S
Concord NC 28027

7991 Physical Fitness Facilities

(P-18091)
24 HOUR FITNESS USA INC
Also Called: Folsom Sport Club
1006 Riley St, Folsom (95630-3266)
PHONE.................................916 984-1924
Doug Coelho, Manager
EMP: 50
SALES (corp-wide): 480.7MM **Privately Held**
SIC: 7991 Health club
HQ: 24 Hour Fitness Usa, Inc.
12647 Alcosta Blvd # 500
San Ramon CA 94583
925 543-3100

(P-18092)
24 HOUR FITNESS USA INC
39300 Paseo Padre Pkwy, Fremont (94538-1629)
PHONE.................................510 795-6666
Tammy Egan, Manager
EMP: 50
SALES (corp-wide): 480.7MM **Privately Held**
SIC: 7991 Health club
HQ: 24 Hour Fitness Usa, Inc.
12647 Alcosta Blvd # 500
San Ramon CA 94583
925 543-3100

(P-18093)
24 HOUR FITNESS USA INC
5964 La Place Ct, Carlsbad (92008-8829)
P.O. Box 2409 (92018-2409)
PHONE.................................760 918-4790
Geoff Singer, Branch Mgr
Jerry Mc Cauley, Manager
EMP: 59
SALES (corp-wide): 480.7MM **Privately Held**
WEB: www.extremephysiques.net
SIC: 7991 Health club
HQ: 24 Hour Fitness Usa, Inc.
12647 Alcosta Blvd # 500
San Ramon CA 94583
925 543-3100

(P-18094)
24 HOUR FITNESS USA INC
Also Called: Boulder Active Club
1265 Laurel Tree Ln # 100, Carlsbad (92011-4221)
PHONE.................................760 602-5001
S Woodard, Principal
EMP: 80
SALES (corp-wide): 480.7MM **Privately Held**
SIC: 7991 Health club
HQ: 24 Hour Fitness Usa, Inc.
12647 Alcosta Blvd # 500
San Ramon CA 94583
925 543-3100

(P-18095)
24 HOUR FITNESS USA INC
Also Called: Beverly Hills Active Club
9911 W Pico Blvd Ste A, Los Angeles (90035-2708)
PHONE.................................310 553-7600
Julian Jekines, Manager
EMP: 60
SALES (corp-wide): 480.7MM **Privately Held**
SIC: 7991 Health club
HQ: 24 Hour Fitness Usa, Inc.
12647 Alcosta Blvd # 500
San Ramon CA 94583
925 543-3100

(P-18096)
24 HOUR FITNESS USA INC
Also Called: Pasadena Sport Club
525 E Colorado Blvd Bsmt, Pasadena (91101-5229)
PHONE.................................626 795-7121
Mike Priebe, General Mgr
EMP: 55
SALES (corp-wide): 480.7MM **Privately Held**
SIC: 7991 Health club
HQ: 24 Hour Fitness Usa, Inc.
12647 Alcosta Blvd # 500
San Ramon CA 94583
925 543-3100

(P-18097)
24 HOUR FITNESS USA INC
Also Called: Rancho Cucamonga Sport Club
11787 Foothill Blvd, Rancho Cucamonga (91730-3907)
PHONE.................................909 944-1000
Bobby Serrano, Branch Mgr
EMP: 100
SALES (corp-wide): 480.7MM **Privately Held**
SIC: 7991 Health club
HQ: 24 Hour Fitness Usa, Inc.
12647 Alcosta Blvd # 500
San Ramon CA 94583
925 543-3100

(P-18098)
24 HOUR FITNESS USA INC
Also Called: West Hollywood Sport Club
8612 Santa Monica Blvd, West Hollywood (90069-4110)
PHONE.................................310 652-7440
Robin Morris, Manager
EMP: 50
SALES (corp-wide): 480.7MM **Privately Held**
SIC: 7991 Health club
HQ: 24 Hour Fitness Usa, Inc.
12647 Alcosta Blvd # 500
San Ramon CA 94583
925 543-3100

(P-18099)
24 HOUR FITNESS USA INC
Also Called: Costa Mesa Sport Club
555 W 19th St, Costa Mesa (92627-2753)
PHONE.................................949 650-3600
Andy Breton, Manager
EMP: 85
SALES (corp-wide): 480.7MM **Privately Held**
SIC: 7991 Health club
HQ: 24 Hour Fitness Usa, Inc.
12647 Alcosta Blvd # 500
San Ramon CA 94583
925 543-3100

(P-18100)
24 HOUR FITNESS USA INC
(HQ)
12647 Alcosta Blvd # 500, San Ramon (94583-4436)
P.O. Box 2689, Carlsbad (92018-2689)
PHONE.................................925 543-3100
Tony Ueber, CEO
▲ EMP: 183
SALES (est): 480.7MM
SALES (corp-wide): 480.7MM **Privately Held**
WEB: www.extremephysiques.net
SIC: 7991 Health club

PA: 24 Hour Fitness Worldwide, Inc.
12647 Alcosta Blvd # 500
San Ramon CA 94583
925 543-3100

(P-18101)
24 HOUR FITNESS USA INC
Also Called: Anaheim Gateway Sport Club
1430 N Lemon St, Anaheim (92801-1200)
PHONE.................................714 525-9924
Dalia Shoham, Manager
EMP: 60
SALES (corp-wide): 480.7MM **Privately Held**
SIC: 7991 Health club
HQ: 24 Hour Fitness Usa, Inc.
12647 Alcosta Blvd # 500
San Ramon CA 94583
925 543-3100

(P-18102)
24 HOUR FITNESS USA INC
Also Called: Chula Vista Active Club
1660 Broadway Ste 19, Chula Vista (91911-4857)
PHONE.................................619 425-6600
Louis Carranza, Manager
EMP: 65
SALES (corp-wide): 480.7MM **Privately Held**
SIC: 7991 Health club
HQ: 24 Hour Fitness Usa, Inc.
12647 Alcosta Blvd # 500
San Ramon CA 94583
925 543-3100

(P-18103)
24 HOUR FITNESS USA INC
Also Called: Glendale Super-Sport Club
450 N Brand Blvd Ste 100, Glendale (91203-2345)
PHONE.................................818 247-4334
David Crisalli, Branch Mgr
EMP: 100
SALES (corp-wide): 480.7MM **Privately Held**
SIC: 7991 Health club
HQ: 24 Hour Fitness Usa, Inc.
12647 Alcosta Blvd # 500
San Ramon CA 94583
925 543-3100

(P-18104)
24 HOUR FITNESS USA INC
Also Called: Citrus Heights Sport Club
12647 Alcosta Blvd # 500, San Ramon (94583-4436)
PHONE.................................916 722-7588
Tom Hatfield, Director
EMP: 70
SALES (corp-wide): 480.7MM **Privately Held**
SIC: 7991 Health club
HQ: 24 Hour Fitness Usa, Inc.
12647 Alcosta Blvd # 500
San Ramon CA 94583
925 543-3100

(P-18105)
24 HOUR FITNESS USA INC
Also Called: Santa Monica Sport Club
2929 31st St, Santa Monica (90405-3036)
PHONE.................................310 450-4464
Tina Rodriguez, Manager
EMP: 98
SALES (corp-wide): 480.7MM **Privately Held**
SIC: 7991 Health club
HQ: 24 Hour Fitness Usa, Inc.
12647 Alcosta Blvd # 500
San Ramon CA 94583
925 543-3100

(P-18106)
24 HOUR FITNESS USA INC
Also Called: Foothill Ranch Sport Club
26781 Rancho Pkwy, Lake Forest (92630-8706)
PHONE.................................949 830-4213
Rick Roe, Manager
EMP: 60
SALES (corp-wide): 480.7MM **Privately Held**
SIC: 7991 Health club

HQ: 24 Hour Fitness Usa, Inc.
12647 Alcosta Blvd # 500
San Ramon CA 94583
925 543-3100

(P-18107)
24 HOUR FITNESS USA INC
Also Called: San Mateo Sport Club
500 El Camino Real, Burlingame (94010-5159)
PHONE.................................650 343-7922
Paul Draubot, Branch Mgr
EMP: 50
SALES (corp-wide): 480.7MM **Privately Held**
SIC: 7991 Health club
HQ: 24 Hour Fitness Usa, Inc.
12647 Alcosta Blvd # 500
San Ramon CA 94583
925 543-3100

(P-18108)
24 HOUR FITNESS USA INC
1640 Camino Del Rio N # 315, San Diego (92108-1506)
PHONE.................................619 294-2424
Denver Warth, Manager
EMP: 50
SALES (corp-wide): 480.7MM **Privately Held**
SIC: 7991 Health club
HQ: 24 Hour Fitness Usa, Inc.
12647 Alcosta Blvd # 500
San Ramon CA 94583
925 543-3100

(P-18109)
24 HOUR FITNESS USA INC
Also Called: Canoga Park/West Hills Club
6653 Fallbrook Ave, Canoga Park (91307-3520)
PHONE.................................818 887-2582
Nichole Lorenz, Branch Mgr
EMP: 68
SALES (corp-wide): 480.7MM **Privately Held**
SIC: 7991 Health club
HQ: 24 Hour Fitness Usa, Inc.
12647 Alcosta Blvd # 500
San Ramon CA 94583
925 543-3100

(P-18110)
24 HOUR FITNESS USA INC
Also Called: Whittier Active Club
10125 Whittwood Dr, Whittier (90603-2314)
PHONE.................................562 943-3771
Bryan Mirchof, Manager
EMP: 60
SALES (corp-wide): 480.7MM **Privately Held**
SIC: 7991 Health club
HQ: 24 Hour Fitness Usa, Inc.
12647 Alcosta Blvd # 500
San Ramon CA 94583
925 543-3100

(P-18111)
24 HOUR FITNESS USA INC
Also Called: Walnut Creek Active Club
2033 N Main St Ste 110, Walnut Creek (94596-3737)
PHONE.................................925 930-7900
Scott Pendel, General Mgr
EMP: 60
SALES (corp-wide): 480.7MM **Privately Held**
WEB: www.extremephysiques.net
SIC: 7991 Health club
HQ: 24 Hour Fitness Usa, Inc.
12647 Alcosta Blvd # 500
San Ramon CA 94583
925 543-3100

(P-18112)
24 HOUR FITNESS USA INC
Also Called: Mountain View Sport Club
550 Showers Dr Ste 1, Mountain View (94040-1438)
PHONE.................................650 941-2268
Oshkar Gobani, General Mgr
EMP: 50
SALES (corp-wide): 480.7MM **Privately Held**
SIC: 7991 Health club

HQ: 24 Hour Fitness Usa, Inc.
12647 Alcosta Blvd # 500
San Ramon CA 94583
925 543-3100

(P-18113)
24 HOUR FITNESS USA INC
Also Called: Rancho Penasquitos Sport Club
10025 Carmel Mountain Rd, San Diego
(92129-3229)
PHONE.....................................858 538-4400
Connie Lauda, *Manager*
EMP: 50
SALES (corp-wide): 480.7MM **Privately Held**
SIC: 7991 Health club
HQ: 24 Hour Fitness Usa, Inc.
12647 Alcosta Blvd # 500
San Ramon CA 94583
925 543-3100

(P-18114)
24 HOUR FITNESS USA INC
Also Called: Hayward Active Club
24727 Amador St, Hayward (94544-1801)
PHONE.....................................510 264-3275
Stephanie Johnson, *Manager*
EMP: 75
SALES (corp-wide): 480.7MM **Privately Held**
SIC: 7991 Health club
HQ: 24 Hour Fitness Usa, Inc.
12647 Alcosta Blvd # 500
San Ramon CA 94583
925 543-3100

(P-18115)
24 HOUR FITNESS WORLDWIDE INC (PA)
12647 Alcosta Blvd # 500, San Ramon
(94583-4436)
PHONE.....................................925 543-3100
Brenden Egen, *Principal*
David Galvan, *Vice Pres*
EMP: 100 EST: 2001
SALES (est): 480.7MM **Privately Held**
WEB: www.24hourfitness.com
SIC: 7991 Health club

(P-18116)
24 HOUR FITNESS WORLDWIDE INC
1601 Pcf Cast Hwy Ste 100, Hermosa
Beach (90254)
PHONE.....................................310 374-4524
Tommy Cassidy, *Manager*
EMP: 50
SALES (corp-wide): 480.7MM **Privately Held**
WEB: www.24hourfitness.com
SIC: 7991 Health club
PA: 24 Hour Fitness Worldwide, Inc.
12647 Alcosta Blvd # 500
San Ramon CA 94583
925 543-3100

(P-18117)
ADDISON-PENZAK JEWISH COMMUNIT
14855 Oka Rd Ste 201, Los Gatos
(95032-1956)
PHONE.....................................408 358-3636
Nate Stein, *CEO*
Rebecca Geshuri, *Vice Chairman*
Stuart Phillips, *CFO*
Josh Boedecker, *Administration*
Sierra Burt, *Administration*
EMP: 236
SALES: 8.3MM **Privately Held**
WEB: www.svjcc.org
SIC: 7991 8299 Physical fitness facilities;
educational services

(P-18118)
ADVENTUREPLEX
1701 Marine Ave, Manhattan Beach
(90266-4100)
PHONE.....................................310 546-7708
Kate Hurley, *Manager*
EMP: 50
SALES (est): 1.7MM **Privately Held**
WEB: www.adventureplex.com
SIC: 7991 Physical fitness facilities

(P-18119)
B A M I INC
Also Called: 24 Hour In Motion Fitness
1293 E 1st Ave, Chico (95926-1548)
PHONE.....................................530 343-5678
Carleton J Sommer, *President*
Lance Baxman, *Accountant*
Lori Pine, *Director*
EMP: 50
SQ FT: 19,400
SALES (est): 2.3MM **Privately Held**
WEB: www.inmotionfitness.net
SIC: 7991 Health club

(P-18120)
BACK STREET FITNESS INC
Also Called: Health Quest
3175 California Blvd, NAPA (94558-3307)
PHONE.....................................707 254-7200
Anthony Giovannoni, *President*
Lisa Ghisletta, *Sales Staff*
EMP: 50
SALES (est): 1.4MM **Privately Held**
WEB: www.napahealthquest.com
SIC: 7991 Exercise facilities

(P-18121)
BAY CLUBS INC
Also Called: Decathlon Club
3250 Central Expy, Santa Clara
(95051-0828)
PHONE.....................................408 738-2582
Erin Rucker, *Manager*
EMP: 90
SALES (corp-wide): 202.6MM **Privately Held**
WEB: www.pacclub.com
SIC: 7991 7997 5813 5812 Athletic club
& gymnasiums, membership; member-
ship sports & recreation clubs; drinking
places; eating places
HQ: The Bay Clubs Company Llc
1 Lombard St
San Francisco CA 94111
415 781-1874

(P-18122)
BAY CLUBS INC
Also Called: Sanctuary, The
200 Redwood Shr Pkwy, Redwood City
(94065-1100)
PHONE.....................................650 593-1112
Erin Cker, *Manager*
EMP: 79
SALES (corp-wide): 202.6MM **Privately Held**
WEB: www.pacclub.com
SIC: 7991 7997 5812 5699 Health club;
swimming club, membership; tennis club,
membership; racquetball club, member-
ship; eating places; sports apparel; sport-
ing goods & bicycle shops
HQ: The Bay Clubs Company Llc
1 Lombard St
San Francisco CA 94111
415 781-1874

(P-18123)
BEING FIT INC (PA)
Also Called: Being Fit Fitness Centers
8292 Mira Mesa Blvd, San Diego
(92126-2604)
PHONE.....................................858 549-3456
Lenny Hecht, *President*
EMP: 60
SALES (est): 700K **Privately Held**
WEB: www.beingfit.net
SIC: 7991 Exercise facilities

(P-18124)
BEING FIT INC
4971 Clairemont Dr Ste A, San Diego
(92117-2785)
PHONE.....................................858 483-9294
Lennie Heck, *President*
EMP: 56
SALES (corp-wide): 700K **Privately Held**
WEB: www.beingfit.net
SIC: 7991 Aerobic dance & exercise
classes; health club
PA: Being Fit, Inc
8292 Mira Mesa Blvd
San Diego CA 92126
858 549-3456

(P-18125)
BLADIUM INC (PA)
Also Called: Bladium Sports Clubs
800 W Tower Ave Bldg 40, Alameda
(94501-5048)
PHONE.....................................510 814-4999
Brad C Shook, *President*
David Walsh, *CFO*
Diogo Gomes, *Director*
EMP: 120
SQ FT: 115,000
SALES (est): 3.5MM **Privately Held**
WEB: www.bladium.com
SIC: 7991 Athletic club & gymnasiums,
membership

(P-18126)
BURN 60 LLC
159 S Barrington Pl, Los Angeles
(90049-3305)
PHONE.....................................310 476-5656
Drew Gerstein, *Owner*
EMP: 50
SALES (est): 351.2K **Privately Held**
SIC: 7991 5993 Aerobic dance & exercise
classes; tobacco stores & stands

(P-18127)
CALIFORNIA FAMILY HEALTH LLC
Also Called: California Family Fitness
8569 Bond Rd Ste 130, Elk Grove
(95624-9522)
PHONE.....................................916 685-3355
Eric Sorenson, *Manager*
Dave Stauffer, *President*
EMP: 50 **Privately Held**
SIC: 7991 Health club
PA: California Family Health Llc
8680 Greenback Ln Ste 108
Orangevale CA 95662

(P-18128)
CALISTOGA SPA INC
Also Called: Calistoga Spa Hot Springs
1006 Washington St, Calistoga
(94515-1499)
PHONE.....................................707 942-6269
Bradley L Barrett, *President*
Michael Lennon, *General Mgr*
Diane Barrett, *Admin Sec*
EMP: 65
SQ FT: 50,000
SALES (est): 2.5MM **Privately Held**
WEB: www.calistogaspa.com
SIC: 7991 Spas

(P-18129)
CANOGA PARK FITNESS LLC
22235 Sherman Way, Canoga Park
(91303-1058)
PHONE.....................................818 884-5034
Curtis Harman,
EMP: 50
SALES (est): 193.6K **Privately Held**
SIC: 7991 Physical fitness facilities

(P-18130)
CAPITAL ATHLETIC CLUB INC
1515 8th St, Sacramento (95814-5503)
PHONE.....................................916 442-3927
Ken Hoffman, *President*
Jane Coolidge, *Admin Mgr*
Veronica Gomez, *Admin Asst*
Bruce Coolidge, *Director*
Jonna Edwinson, *Director*
EMP: 64
SQ FT: 52,000
SALES (est): 2MM **Privately Held**
WEB: www.capitalac.com
SIC: 7991 Health club

(P-18131)
CLUB AT LOS GATOS INC
14428 Big Basin Way Ste A, Saratoga
(95070-6010)
PHONE.....................................408 867-5110
David S Wilson, *CEO*
EMP: 60
SALES (est): 160.6K **Privately Held**
SIC: 7991 Physical fitness clubs with train-
ing equipment; health club

(P-18132)
CLUBSPORT SAN RAMON LLC
Also Called: Oakwood Athletic Club
4000 Mt Diablo Blvd, Lafayette
(94549-3498)
PHONE.....................................925 283-4000
Michael Reardon, *Manager*
Ashley Saputo, *Manager*
EMP: 170
SQ FT: 63,749
SALES (corp-wide): 9.7MM **Privately Held**
WEB: www.clubsportsr.com
SIC: 7991 7997 Athletic club & gymnasi-
ums, membership; membership sports &
recreation clubs
PA: Clubsport San Ramon, Llc
350 Bollinger Canyon Ln
San Ramon CA 94582
925 735-1182

(P-18133)
CLUBSPORT SAN RAMON LLC (PA)
Also Called: Spa At Club Sport
350 Bollinger Canyon Ln, San Ramon
(94582-4592)
PHONE.....................................925 735-1182
Dennis Garrison,
John Moore, *Partner*
Al Schaffer, *Partner*
Mike Reardon, *General Mgr*
Kathy Denton, *Manager*
EMP: 350
SQ FT: 70,000
SALES (est): 9.7MM **Privately Held**
WEB: www.clubsportsr.com
SIC: 7991 Health club

(P-18134)
COURT HOUSE ATHLETIC CLUB (PA)
2514 Bell Rd, Auburn (95603-2502)
PHONE.....................................530 885-1964
Art Chappell Jr, *Owner*
Danielle Covert, *Manager*
EMP: 78
SQ FT: 22,000
SALES (est): 932.5K **Privately Held**
WEB: www.cacfit.com
SIC: 7991 Athletic club & gymnasiums,
membership

(P-18135)
CRUNCH LLC
Also Called: Crunch Fitness
8000 W Sunset Blvd # 220, West Holly-
wood (90046-2439)
PHONE.....................................323 654-4550
Amita Balla, *Branch Mgr*
EMP: 75 **Privately Held**
SIC: 7991 Physical fitness facilities
PA: Crunch, Llc
220 W 19th St
New York NY 10011

(P-18136)
CRUNCH LLC
1190 Saratoga Ave, San Jose
(95129-3438)
PHONE.....................................650 257-8000
Saeid Ghafouri, *CEO*
EMP: 99 **Privately Held**
SIC: 7991 Physical fitness facilities
PA: Crunch, Llc
220 W 19th St
New York NY 10011
-

(P-18137)
CRUNCH LLC
Also Called: Embarcadero, The
345 Spear St Ste 104, San Francisco
(94105-1659)
PHONE.....................................415 495-1939
Mahogany Lenard, *Branch Mgr*
EMP: 124 **Privately Held**
SIC: 7991 Health club
PA: Crunch, Llc
220 W 19th St
New York NY 10011
-

PRODUCTS & SVCS

(P-18138)
CRUNCH FITNESS
19867 Prairie St Ste 200, Chatsworth
(91311-6533)
PHONE..............................805 522-5454
Teresa Frost, *General Mgr*
EMP: 65
SALES (est): 1.5MM **Privately Held**
WEB: www.oakridgefitness.com
SIC: 7991 Athletic club & gymnasiums,
membership

(P-18139)
DECATHLON CLUB INC
3250 Central Expy, Santa Clara
(95051-0873)
PHONE..............................408 738-2582
Kayte Bandcraft, *Manager*
EMP: 200
SQ FT: 100,000
SALES (est): 5MM **Privately Held**
SIC: 7991 5812 Physical fitness clubs with
training equipment; eating places

(P-18140)
DEEPAK CHOPRA LLC
7668 El Camino Real # 101, Carlsbad
(92009-7932)
PHONE..............................760 494-1600
Deepak Chopra,
EMP: 50
SALES (est): 1.6MM **Privately Held**
WEB: www.chopra.com
SIC: 7991 Health club

(P-18141)
EQUINOX HOLDINGS INC
Also Called: Equinox Fitness Club
747 Market St, San Francisco
(94103-2001)
PHONE..............................415 243-0492
Amie Skidmore, *General Mgr*
EMP: 500
SALES (corp-wide): 10.6B **Privately Held**
SIC: 7991 Health club
HQ: Equinox Holdings, Inc.
895 Broadway
New York NY 10003
212 677-0180

(P-18142)
EQUINOX-76TH STREET INC
301 Pine St, San Francisco (94104-3301)
PHONE..............................415 398-0747
Patrick Ahern, *Manager*
EMP: 75
SALES (corp-wide): 10.6B **Privately Held**
SIC: 7991 Health club
HQ: Equinox-76th Street, Inc.
895 Broadway Fl 3
New York NY 10003

(P-18143)
EQUINOX-76TH STREET INC
Also Called: Equinox Fitness Club
19540 Jamboree Rd, Irvine (92612-8448)
PHONE..............................949 296-1700
Herb Umphreyville, *General Mgr*
EMP: 90
SALES (corp-wide): 10.6B **Privately Held**
SIC: 7991 Health club
HQ: Equinox-76th Street, Inc.
895 Broadway Fl 3
New York NY 10003

(P-18144)
EXECUTIVES OUTLET INC
Also Called: Decathalon Club
1 Lombard St Lbby, San Francisco
(94111-1127)
PHONE..............................415 433-6044
James Gerber, *President*
Sandra Hoeffer, *Vice Pres*
Mindy Steiner, *Vice Pres*
David Smith, *Admin Sec*
EMP: 150 **EST:** 1977
SQ FT: 100,000
SALES: 7.8MM
SALES (corp-wide): 46.8MM **Privately
Held**
SIC: 7991 7997 Athletic club & gymnasi-
ums, membership; racquetball club, mem-
bership

PA: Bay Club Holdings Iii, Llc
1 Lombard St Lbby
San Francisco CA 94111
415 781-1874

(P-18145)
FITNESS 2000 INC
35145 Newark Blvd, Newark (94560-1219)
PHONE..............................510 791-2481
Mike Patel, *President*
Sonia Patel, *Principal*
Jay Patel, *Manager*
EMP: 50
SALES (est): 658.3K **Privately Held**
SIC: 7991 Health club

(P-18146)
FITNESS INTERNATIONAL LLC
Also Called: La Fitness
24491 Alicia Pkwy, Mission Viejo
(92691-4506)
PHONE..............................949 421-6082
Lisa Guidno, *Branch Mgr*
EMP: 50
SALES (corp-wide): 175.8MM **Privately
Held**
SIC: 7991 Physical fitness clubs with train-
ing equipment
PA: Fitness International, Llc
3161 Michelson Dr Ste 600
Irvine CA 92612
949 255-7200

(P-18147)
FITNESS INTERNATIONAL LLC
Also Called: L A Fitness Sports Clubs
10535 Heater Ct, San Diego (92121-4111)
PHONE..............................858 550-5912
Joe Torrice, *Manager*
EMP: 50
SALES (corp-wide): 175.8MM **Privately
Held**
WEB: www.proresultsfit.com
SIC: 7991 Physical fitness clubs with train-
ing equipment
PA: Fitness International, Llc
3161 Michelson Dr Ste 600
Irvine CA 92612
949 255-7200

(P-18148)
**GEORGE BROWNS SPORTS
CLUB (PA)**
Also Called: Gb3
1155 N Fowler Ave Ste 500, Clovis
(93611-8192)
PHONE..............................559 297-8656
George Brown, *President*
EMP: 70
SALES (est): 1.2MM **Privately Held**
SIC: 7991 Health club

(P-18149)
**GOLDS GYM INTERNATIONAL
INC**
39 S Altadena Dr, Pasadena (91107-4256)
PHONE..............................626 304-1133
Frank Jordan, *Manager*
EMP: 55
SALES (corp-wide): 1.2B **Privately Held**
SIC: 7991 Physical fitness facilities
HQ: Gold's Gym International, Inc.
125 E J Carpentr Fwy 13
Irving TX 75062
972 444-8527

(P-18150)
HARBOR BAY CLUB INC
200 Packet Landing Rd, Alameda
(94502-6599)
P.O. Box 1450 (94501-0158)
PHONE..............................510 521-5414
C Timothy Hoppen, *President*
Timothy Hoppen, *President*
Louise Howard, *Mktg Dir*
Vince Piro, *Facilities Mgr*
Lonsdale Kiley, *Director*
EMP: 83
SQ FT: 30,000
SALES (est): 2.9MM **Privately Held**
WEB: www.harborbayclub.com
SIC: 7991 5813 5941 5812 Athletic club
& gymnasiums, membership; aerobic
dance & exercise classes; bar (drinking
places); golf goods & equipment; eating
places

PA: Harbor Bay Club Associates, A California Limited Partnership
1141 Harbor Bay Pkwy # 221
Alameda CA 94502

(P-18151)
**HEALTHSPORT LTD A LTD
PARTNR (PA)**
Also Called: Healthsport-Arcata
300 Dr Martin Luther, Arcata (95521)
PHONE..............................707 822-3488
Susan Johnson, *Partner*
EMP: 115
SQ FT: 24,560
SALES (est): 3.4MM **Privately Held**
WEB: www.healthsport.com
SIC: 7991 Health club

(P-18152)
HERCULES FITNESS
600 Alfred Nobel Dr, Hercules
(94547-1834)
PHONE..............................510 724-2900
Steve Buchanan, *Owner*
EMP: 50 **EST:** 2008
SALES (est): 766.1K **Privately Held**
SIC: 7991 Athletic club & gymnasiums,
membership

(P-18153)
HOLLYWOOD SPA INC
Also Called: Hollywood Spa, The
5636 Vineland Ave, North Hollywood
(91601-2028)
PHONE..............................323 464-0445
Rosa Klein, *CEO*
Peter D Sykes, *President*
EMP: 50
SQ FT: 20,000
SALES (est): 1.8MM **Privately Held**
WEB: www.hollywoodspa.com
SIC: 7991 Health club

(P-18154)
**IN SHAPE MANAGEMENT
COMPANY**
Also Called: In Shape Health Clubs
6 S El Dorado St, Stockton (95202-2804)
PHONE..............................209 472-2231
Morton Rothbard, *President*
Paul Rothbard, *CEO*
Rob Farrens, *CFO*
EMP: 300
SQ FT: 60,000
SALES: 9MM **Privately Held**
SIC: 7991 Health club

(P-18155)
IN-SHAPE HEALTH CLUBS LLC
Also Called: In Shape
14601 Valley Center Dr, Victorville
(92395-4216)
PHONE..............................760 381-1200
Derrick Johnson, *Branch Mgr*
EMP: 50
SALES (corp-wide): 17.5MM **Privately
Held**
SIC: 7991 Health club
PA: In-Shape Health Clubs, Llc
6 S El Dorado St Ste 700
Stockton CA 95202
209 472-2231

(P-18156)
**IN-SHAPE HEALTH CLUBS LLC
(PA)**
Also Called: In-Shape City
6 S El Dorado St Ste 700, Stockton
(95202-2804)
PHONE..............................209 472-2231
Francesca Schuler, *CEO*
Rob Farrens, *Vice Pres*
Rachelle Gardette, *Regional Mgr*
Damian Weber, *District Mgr*
Crystal Rosado, *Administration*
EMP: 50
SQ FT: 60,000
SALES (est): 17.5MM **Privately Held**
WEB: www.inshapeclubs.com
SIC: 7991 Health club

(P-18157)
IN-SHAPE HEALTH CLUBS LLC
101 S Tracy Blvd, Tracy (95376-4620)
PHONE..............................209 836-2504
Robin Phillip, *Manager*
EMP: 113
SALES (corp-wide): 17.5MM **Privately
Held**
WEB: www.inshapeclubs.com
SIC: 7991 Health club
PA: In-Shape Health Clubs, Llc
6 S El Dorado St Ste 700
Stockton CA 95202
209 472-2231

(P-18158)
**INSTITUTE FOR ONE WORLD
HEALTH**
600 California St Fl 11, San Francisco
(94108-2727)
PHONE..............................650 392-2510
Victoria G Hale, *Ch of Bd*
EMP: 50 **EST:** 2000
SALES: 30.6MM **Privately Held**
SIC: 7991 Health club

(P-18159)
JAZZERCISE INC (PA)
2460 Impala Dr, Carlsbad (92010-7226)
PHONE..............................760 476-1750
Judi Sheppard Missett, *CEO*
Andrew Blocksidge, *President*
Sally Baldridge, *CFO*
Megan Wakefield, *Officer*
Shanna Missett Nelson, *Exec VP*
EMP: 100
SQ FT: 24,228
SALES (est): 12.2MM **Privately Held**
WEB: www.jazzercise.com
SIC: 7991 6794 5961 Aerobic dance &
exercise classes; franchises, selling or li-
censing; fitness & sporting goods, mail
order

(P-18160)
JEFF STOVER INC
Also Called: Chico Sports Club
260 Cohasset Rd Ste 190, Chico
(95926-2282)
PHONE..............................530 345-9427
Jeff Stover, *President*
EMP: 85
SQ FT: 11,000
SALES (est): 3.2MM **Privately Held**
WEB: www.chicosportsclub.com
SIC: 7991 7997 Health club; membership
sports & recreation clubs

(P-18161)
**JURLIQUE HLISTIC SKIN CARE
INC (PA)**
234 E Colo Blvd Ste 450, Pasadena
(91101)
PHONE..............................914 998-8800
Sam McKay, *CEO*
EMP: 50
SALES (est): 10.2MM **Privately Held**
SIC: 7991 Spas

(P-18162)
KEISERS HOLDINGS LLC
411 S West Ave, Fresno (93706-1320)
PHONE..............................559 265-4700
Dennis Keiser,
EMP: 80
SALES (est): 646.9K **Privately Held**
SIC: 7991 Physical fitness facilities

(P-18163)
KENNEDY ATHLETIC CLUB (PA)
3534 El Camino Real, Atascadero
(93422-2532)
PHONE..............................805 466-6775
Kevin P Kennedy, *General Ptnr*
Barbara Kennedy, *General Ptnr*
EMP: 85
SQ FT: 30,000
SALES (est): 2.7MM **Privately Held**
WEB: www.kennedyclubs.com
SIC: 7991 Health club

(P-18164)
KENNEDY CLUB FITNESS
188 Tank Farm Rd, San Luis Obispo
(93401-7528)
PHONE.............................805 781-3488
Brett Weaver,
Barbara Kennedy,
Kevin Kennedy,
EMP: 70
SQ FT: 50,000
SALES (est): 536K **Privately Held**
SIC: 7991 Health club

(P-18165)
L A FITNESS INTL LLC
Also Called: L A Fitness Sports Clubs
1760 S Victoria Ave, Ventura (93003-6592)
PHONE.............................805 289-9907
Eric Bjerkens, *Manager*
EMP: 60
SALES (corp-wide): 175.8MM **Privately Held**
WEB: www.proresultsfit.com
SIC: 7991 Physical fitness facilities
PA: Fitness International, Llc
3161 Michelson Dr Ste 600
Irvine CA 92612
949 255-7200

(P-18166)
LA BONNE VIE INC
2723 Shell Beach Rd, Shell Beach
(93449-1629)
PHONE.............................805 773-5003
Maureen Raynaud-Loughead, *Principal*
EMP: 100
SALES (est): 128.7K **Privately Held**
SIC: 7991 Spas

(P-18167)
LA BOXING FRANCHISE CORP
1241 E Dyer Rd Ste 100, Santa Ana
(92705-5611)
PHONE.............................714 668-0911
Anthony Geisler, *President*
▲ **EMP:** 163
SALES (est): 5.1MM
SALES (corp-wide): 30.3MM **Privately Held**
SIC: 7991 Physical fitness facilities
PA: U Gym, Llc
1501 Quail St Ste 100
Newport Beach CA 92660
714 668-0911

(P-18168)
LA PETITE BALEEN INC
Also Called: La Petite Baleen Swim School
434 San Mateo Ave, San Bruno
(94066-4417)
PHONE.............................650 588-7665
John Kolbisen, *Owner*
EMP: 80
SALES (corp-wide): 8.1MM **Privately Held**
WEB: www.swimlpb.com
SIC: 7991 7999 Physical fitness facilities; swimming instruction
PA: La Petite Baleen, Inc
775 Main St
Half Moon Bay CA 94019
650 726-7166

(P-18169)
LEISURE SPORTS INC
Also Called: Clubsport of Fremont
46650 Landing Pkwy, Fremont
(94538-6420)
PHONE.............................510 226-8500
Dan Detrick, *General Mgr*
EMP: 200
SALES (corp-wide): 68.8MM **Privately Held**
WEB: www.leisuresportsinc.com
SIC: 7991 Athletic club & gymnasiums, membership
PA: Leisure Sports, Inc.
4670 Willow Rd Ste 100
Pleasanton CA 94588
925 600-1966

(P-18170)
LIVERMORE VALLEY TENNIS CLUB
2000 Arroyo Rd, Livermore (94550-6027)
PHONE.............................925 443-7700

Kim Fuller, *General Ptnr*
Roy Rasmussen, *General Ptnr*
Desiree McMillen, *Opers Staff*
Emily Byrom, *Director*
EMP: 100 **EST:** 1972
SQ FT: 51,758
SALES: 3.1MM **Privately Held**
WEB: www.lvtc.com
SIC: 7991 5941 Athletic club & gymnasiums, membership; sporting goods & bicycle shops; tennis goods & equipment

(P-18171)
LOS ANGELES ATHLETIC CLUB INC
431 W 7th St, Los Angeles (90014-1691)
PHONE.............................213 625-2211
Karen Hathaway, *President*
Bryan Cusworth, *CFO*
EMP: 175
SALES (est): 1.5MM
SALES (corp-wide): 22.6MM **Privately Held**
SIC: 7991 Athletic club & gymnasiums, membership
PA: Laaco, Ltd.
431 W 7th St
Los Angeles CA 90014
213 622-1254

(P-18172)
LOVE LIFTED US YOUTH SERVICES
6356 Van Nuys Blvd # 229, Van Nuys
(91401-2627)
P.O. Box 2131, North Hills (91393-2131)
PHONE.............................818 471-0594
Ashley D Oshilaja, *CEO*
EMP: 50
SALES (est): 52.3K **Privately Held**
SIC: 7991 Physical fitness facilities

(P-18173)
LSI - SILVERCREEK LLC
800 Embedded Way Ste 80, San Jose
(95138-1074)
PHONE.............................408 226-8080
Oscar Bazan,
EMP: 120
SALES: 8MM **Privately Held**
SIC: 7991 7999 Physical fitness facilities; amusement & recreation

(P-18174)
MARINER SQUARE ATHLETIC INC
2227 Mariner Square Loop, Alameda
(94501-1021)
PHONE.............................510 523-8011
Kathy Wagner, *President*
Diana Thomas, *General Mgr*
Kevin Truglio, *General Mgr*
Mike Daniels, *Maintence Staff*
Camille Hammond, *Manager*
EMP: 100 **EST:** 1975
SQ FT: 60,000
SALES (est): 3.6MM **Privately Held**
WEB: www.marinersq.com
SIC: 7991 7997 Athletic club & gymnasiums, membership; membership sports & recreation clubs

(P-18175)
MAXIMUM FITNESS LLC
Also Called: Gold's Gym
135 Dobbins St, Vacaville (95688-3929)
PHONE.............................707 447-0606
Richard A Martindale,
Teresa Conner, *General Mgr*
David Conner,
EMP: 50 **EST:** 1997
SQ FT: 27,000
SALES (est): 2.1MM **Privately Held**
SIC: 7991 Physical fitness facilities

(P-18176)
MILLENIUM ATHLETIC CLUB LLC
Also Called: Goleta Valley Athletic Club
170 Los Carneros Way, Goleta
(93117-3012)
PHONE.............................805 562-3845
Jarrod Schwartz,
Gordon Schwartz,
David Arico, *Manager*

▲ **EMP:** 65
SQ FT: 30,000
SALES (est): 2.4MM **Privately Held**
WEB: www.gvac.com
SIC: 7991 Health club

(P-18177)
MONIQUE SURACI
Also Called: Murrieta Day Spa
41885 Ivy St, Murrieta (92562-8607)
PHONE.............................951 677-8111
Monique Suraci, *Owner*
Adrienne Crane, *Director*
EMP: 60
SALES: 1.7MM **Privately Held**
SIC: 7991 Spas

(P-18178)
MUSCLE IMPROVEMENT INC
Also Called: Gold's Gym
200 N Harbor Dr, Redondo Beach
(90277-2507)
PHONE.............................310 374-5522
Fax: 310 372-4741
EMP: 70
SQ FT: 21,000
SALES (est): 3.2MM **Privately Held**
SIC: 7991

(P-18179)
MUSCLEBOUND INC (PA)
Also Called: Golds Gym
19835 Nordhoff St, Northridge
(91324-3331)
PHONE.............................818 349-0123
Angel J Banos, *President*
William Banos, *Vice Pres*
Jason Taylor, *Facilities Dir*
Ricardo Gomez, *Facilities Mgr*
EMP: 350
SQ FT: 8,625
SALES (est): 12.6MM **Privately Held**
SIC: 7991 Physical fitness facilities

(P-18180)
MV HOSPITALITY INC
Also Called: Mount View Hotel
1457 Lincoln Ave, Calistoga (94515-1417)
PHONE.............................707 942-6877
Steve Carver, *Manager*
Mike Woods, *President*
Rick Howard, *Vice Pres*
EMP: 50
SALES (est): 2.5MM **Privately Held**
WEB: www.mountviewhotel.com
SIC: 7991 7011 Spas; hotels

(P-18181)
NC FIT INC
647 N Santa Cruz Ave C, Los Gatos
(95030-4351)
PHONE.............................408 910-6748
Jason Khalipa, *Branch Mgr*
EMP: 88
SALES (corp-wide): 3.6MM **Privately Held**
SIC: 7991 Physical fitness clubs with training equipment
PA: Nc Fit, Inc.
2280 S Bascom Ave Ste A
Campbell CA 95008
408 822-9597

(P-18182)
OLYMPIX FITNESS LLC
4101 E Olympic Plz, Long Beach
(90803-2807)
PHONE.............................562 366-4600
Eden Paul,
EMP: 91
SALES (est): 89K **Privately Held**
SIC: 7991 Physical fitness facilities

(P-18183)
PERFECT WORKOUT INC (PA)
150 N El Camino Real, Encinitas
(92024-2849)
PHONE.............................949 943-7281
Matt Hedman, *CEO*
EMP: 70
SALES (est): 6.2MM **Privately Held**
SIC: 7991 Athletic club & gymnasiums, membership

(P-18184)
PF WEST LLC
Also Called: Planet Fitness
101 Lucas Valley Rd # 150, San Rafael
(94903-1700)
PHONE.............................415 479-9600
Roger Bates, *Mng Member*
EMP: 105
SQ FT: 1,500
SALES (est): 2.8MM **Privately Held**
SIC: 7991 Physical fitness facilities

(P-18185)
PISMO BEACH ATHLETIC CLUB
1751 Price St, Pismo Beach (93449-2230)
PHONE.............................805 773-3011
Henry F Myers, *President*
Ryan Tomich, *Executive*
EMP: 50
SALES (est): 1.7MM **Privately Held**
WEB: www.pbac.com
SIC: 7991 Health club

(P-18186)
PRESTON WYNNE SPA INC
14567 Big Basin Way A2, Saratoga
(95070-6039)
PHONE.............................408 741-1750
Peggy Wynne-Borgman, *President*
Cat Blohm, *Mktg Coord*
Shelby Bauer, *Manager*
EMP: 56
SQ FT: 4,700
SALES (est): 1.5MM **Privately Held**
WEB: www.prestonwynne.com
SIC: 7991 Spas

(P-18187)
PRIME TIME ATHLETIC CLUB INC
1730 Rollins Rd, Burlingame (94010-2297)
PHONE.............................650 204-3662
John Michael, *President*
EMP: 80 **EST:** 1979
SQ FT: 35,000
SALES (est): 3.3MM **Privately Held**
WEB: www.primetimeathleticclub.com
SIC: 7991 Athletic club & gymnasiums, membership

(P-18188)
REDWOOD HEALTH CLUB (PA)
3101 S State St, Ukiah (95482-6938)
PHONE.............................707 468-0441
Rob Marthe Deomont, *Partner*
EMP: 85
SQ FT: 20,000
SALES (est): 1.2MM **Privately Held**
WEB: www.redwoodhealthclub.com
SIC: 7991 7997 5812 5813 Health club; racquetball club, membership; tennis club, membership; snack bar; drinking places

(P-18189)
SALUTARY SPORTS CLUBS INC
Also Called: Sports Club of El Dorado
4242 Sports Club Dr, Shingle Springs
(95682-9546)
P.O. Box 659 (95682-0659)
PHONE.............................530 677-5705
Don Lynd, *Manager*
EMP: 50
SALES (corp-wide): 7.8MM **Privately Held**
SIC: 7991 Physical fitness facilities
PA: Salutary Sports Clubs, Inc.
3442 Browns Valley Rd # 100
Vacaville CA 95688
707 446-2350

(P-18190)
SALVATION ARMY RAY & JOAN
6845 University Ave, San Diego
(92115-5829)
PHONE.............................619 287-5762
James Knaggs, *President*
David Hudson, *Vice Pres*
EMP: 300
SALES (est): 9.2MM
SALES (corp-wide): 2.3B **Privately Held**
SIC: 7991 8661 7032 7922 Physical fitness clubs with training equipment; miscellaneous denomination church; sporting & recreational camps; community theater production

PA: The Salvation Army National Corporation
615 Slaters Ln
Alexandria VA 22314
703 684-5500

(P-18191)
SAN FRANCISCO TENNIS CLUB
645 5th St, San Francisco (94107-1516)
PHONE..............................415 777-9000
Jim Hinckley, *President*
Thomas Kanar, *Corp Secy*
Jeff Janke, *Vice Pres*
EMP: 100
SQ FT: 300,000
SALES: 209.4K
SALES (corp-wide): 841.1MM **Privately Held**
WEB: www.sftennis.com
SIC: 7991 7997 5813 Physical fitness facilities; membership sports & recreation clubs; drinking places
HQ: Clubcorp Usa, Inc.
3030 Lyndon B Johnson Fwy
Dallas TX 75234
972 243-6191

(P-18192)
SANTA CLARITA ATHLETIC CLUB
23942 Lyons Ave Ste 106, Newhall (91321-2475)
PHONE..............................661 255-3365
Charles Hamilton, *President*
Michelle Marbach, *Vice Pres*
Ann Hamilton, *Admin Sec*
EMP: 78
SQ FT: 64,000
SALES: 5MM **Privately Held**
WEB: www.santaclaritaathleticclub.com
SIC: 7991 5812 8699 Health club; athletic club & gymnasiums, membership; cafe; athletic organizations

(P-18193)
SANTEE SYSTEMS SERVICES II LL
229 E Gage Ave, Los Angeles (90003-1533)
PHONE..............................323 445-0044
EMP: 50 **EST:** 2012
SQ FT: 10,000
SALES (est): 1.4MM **Privately Held**
SIC: 7991

(P-18194)
SIM INVESTMENT CORPORATION
Also Called: Right Stuff Health Club, The
1329 Blossom Hill Rd, San Jose (95118-3801)
PHONE..............................408 445-3310
Enrico Dileonardo, *General Mgr*
EMP: 60
SALES (corp-wide): 8MM **Privately Held**
SIC: 7991 Health club
PA: S.I.M. Investment Corporation
1600 W Campbell Ave
Campbell CA 95008
408 874-0610

(P-18195)
SK SANCTUARY DAY SPA SALON LLC
6919 La Jolla Blvd, La Jolla (92037-5427)
PHONE..............................858 459-2400
Steven Krant, *Mng Member*
Lyn Krant,
EMP: 50
SALES (est): 2.4MM **Privately Held**
WEB: www.sk-sanctuary.com
SIC: 7991 Spas

(P-18196)
SOUND MIND AND BODY INC
117 Via Yella, Newport Beach (92663-5536)
PHONE..............................206 547-2706
Richard Harrington, *President*
Victoria Aldrich, *Vice Pres*
Dennis Rose, *Vice Pres*
EMP: 60
SALES (est): 1.3MM **Privately Held**
WEB: www.smbgym.com
SIC: 7991 Health club

(P-18197)
SPA CAS PALMAS
Also Called: Spa Las Palmas of Marriot Intl
41000 Bob Hope Dr, Rancho Mirage (92270-4416)
PHONE..............................760 836-3106
Dawn Ferraro, *Exec Dir*
EMP: 50
SALES (est): 763.8K **Privately Held**
SIC: 7991 Spas

(P-18198)
SPA DREAMS
6419 Hesperia Ave, Reseda (91335-6225)
PHONE..............................818 298-1120
Yvette Vink, *Owner*
EMP: 100
SALES: 350K **Privately Held**
SIC: 7991 Spas

(P-18199)
SPA HAVENS LP
Also Called: Cal-A-Vie
29402 Spa Haven Way, Vista (92084-2234)
PHONE..............................760 945-2055
John Havens, *Owner*
Gary McGiboney, *Vice Pres*
Gary McGivoney, *Vice Pres*
Cayley Macgregor, *Executive Asst*
James Marin, *Info Tech Dir*
▲ **EMP:** 105
SALES (est): 8.6MM **Privately Held**
WEB: www.calavie.com
SIC: 7991 Spas

(P-18200)
SPA PARTNERS INC
Also Called: Mount View Spa
1457 Lincoln Ave, Calistoga (94515-1417)
PHONE..............................707 942-5789
Thomas M Gottlieb, *President*
EMP: 50
SALES: 4.2MM **Privately Held**
SIC: 7991 Spas

(P-18201)
SPARE-TIME INC
Also Called: Natomas Racquet Club
2450 Natomas Park Dr, Sacramento (95833-2938)
PHONE..............................916 649-0909
Joe Rose, *Manager*
EMP: 70
SALES (corp-wide): 38.3MM **Privately Held**
WEB: www.sparetimeinc.com
SIC: 7991 Health club
PA: Spare-Time, Inc.
11344 Coloma Rd Ste 350
Gold River CA 95670
916 859-5910

(P-18202)
SPORT CENTER FITNESS INC
Also Called: King Harbor Sports Center
819 N Harbor Dr, Redondo Beach (90277-2006)
PHONE..............................310 376-9443
Michael Marinelli, *President*
EMP: 73
SQ FT: 25,000
SALES (est): 514.9K **Privately Held**
WEB: www.sportcenterfitness.com
SIC: 7991 7999 Health club; tennis courts, outdoor/indoor: non-membership

(P-18203)
SWEETWATER GARDENS INC
955 Ukiah, Mendocino (95460)
P.O. Box 337 (95460-0337)
PHONE..............................707 937-4140
Henry McCusker, *President*
Agatha Anne Yount, *Admin Sec*
EMP: 50
SQ FT: 1,250
SALES (est): 1.3MM **Privately Held**
SIC: 7991 5499 7011 7299 Spas; juices, fruit or vegetable; motels; massage parlor

(P-18204)
THINK TOGETHER
12016 Telegraph Rd, Santa Fe Springs (90670-3784)
PHONE..............................562 236-3835
EMP: 704

SALES (corp-wide): 47.1MM **Privately Held**
SIC: 7991 Physical fitness facilities
PA: Think Together
2101 E 4th St Ste 200b
Santa Ana CA 92705
714 543-3807

(P-18205)
TOTAL WOMAN
860 N Rose Dr, Placentia (92870-7522)
PHONE..............................714 993-6003
Lori Colagrossi, *Manager*
EMP: 65
SALES (est): 989.7K **Privately Held**
SIC: 7991 Physical fitness facilities

(P-18206)
TW HOLDINGS INC
10805 Rncho Brnrdo Rd Ste, San Diego (92127)
PHONE..............................858 217-8750
Gene Lamott, *CEO*
Karen Wischmann, *President*
Rob Zielinski, *Principal*
EMP: 600 **EST:** 2007
SALES (est): 8.4MM **Privately Held**
SIC: 7991 Physical fitness clubs with training equipment; spas

(P-18207)
U GYM LLC
470 N Mckinley St, Corona (92879-1291)
PHONE..............................951 808-3850
Adam Sedalck, *Vice Pres*
EMP: 91
SALES (corp-wide): 30.3MM **Privately Held**
SIC: 7991 Health club
PA: U Gym, Llc
1501 Quail St Ste 100
Newport Beach CA 92660
714 668-0911

(P-18208)
U GYM LLC (PA)
Also Called: Ufc Gym
1501 Quail St Ste 100, Newport Beach (92660-2797)
PHONE..............................714 668-0911
Brent Leffel,
Kim Hayoung, *Partner*
Mike Pilatos, *CFO*
Adam Fedlack, *Senior VP*
Shawna Winters, *Vice Pres*
EMP: 70 **EST:** 2008
SALES (est): 30.3MM **Privately Held**
SIC: 7991 5699 6794 Physical fitness facilities; shirts, custom made; franchises, selling or licensing

(P-18209)
US DEPT OF AIR FORCE
Also Called: Edwards Fitness
5 Seller Ave Bldg 3000, Edwards (93524-0001)
PHONE..............................661 277-3432
Robert Evans, *Branch Mgr*
EMP: 99 **Publicly Held**
WEB: www.af.mil
SIC: 7991 Physical fitness facilities
HQ: United States Department Of The Air Force
1000 Air Force Pentagon
Washington DC 20330

(P-18210)
WALSH GROUP INC
Also Called: Sun Oaks Tennis & Fitness
3135 Agassi Ln, Redding (96002-9548)
PHONE..............................530 221-4405
Jo Campbell, *Principal*
Jeremiah Walsh, *Principal*
EMP: 95
SQ FT: 217,800
SALES (est): 416.3K **Privately Held**
SIC: 7991 Physical fitness facilities

(P-18211)
WESTLAKE NAIL SPA
233 Lake Merced Blvd, Daly City (94015-3113)
PHONE..............................650 994-7777
Loi Duong, *Owner*
EMP: 68

SALES (est): 762.9K **Privately Held**
SIC: 7991 Spas

(P-18212)
WI SPA LLC
2700 Wilshire Blvd, Los Angeles (90057-3202)
PHONE..............................213 487-2700
Stuart Whang,
EMP: 50
SALES (est): 1.7MM **Privately Held**
SIC: 7991 Spas

(P-18213)
XI ENTERPRISE INC
2140 E Palmdale Blvd, Palmdale (93550-1202)
PHONE..............................661 266-3200
Shah Roshan, *CEO*
EMP: 75
SALES (est): 1.2MM **Privately Held**
SIC: 7991 Physical fitness facilities

(P-18214)
YOGA WORKS INC (HQ)
Also Called: Yogaworks
5780 Uplander Way, Culver City (90230-6606)
PHONE..............................310 664-6470
Phillip Swain, *CEO*
Aubrey Elizaga, *Partner*
Jay Decoons, *President*
Kurt Donnell, *Exec VP*
Edie Oung, *Vice Pres*
EMP: 50
SQ FT: 6,000
SALES (est): 8.9MM
SALES (corp-wide): 59.5MM **Privately Held**
SIC: 7991 5961 5651 Exercise salon; mail order house; unisex clothing stores
PA: Yogaworks, Inc.
5780 Uplander Way
Culver City CA 90230
310 664-6470

7992 Public Golf Courses

(P-18215)
ALONDRA GOLF COURSE INC
Also Called: Three Rivers Golf Course
16400 Prairie Ave, Lawndale (90260-3037)
PHONE..............................310 217-9915
Steve OH, *President*
Edna Villarina, *Comptroller*
EMP: 52 **EST:** 1984
SQ FT: 12,000
SALES (est): 2.9MM **Privately Held**
SIC: 7992 5941 5812 Public golf courses; golf goods & equipment; restaurant, family: independent

(P-18216)
AMERICAN GOLF CORPORATION
Also Called: Lakewood Country Club
3101 Carson St, Lakewood (90712-4005)
PHONE..............................562 421-0550
Gary Kossick, *General Mgr*
EMP: 50 **Publicly Held**
WEB: www.americangolf.com
SIC: 7992 7997 Public golf courses; golf club, membership
HQ: American Golf Corporation
909 N Pacific Coast Hwy
El Segundo CA 90245
310 664-4000

(P-18217)
AMERICAN GOLF CORPORATION
Also Called: Recreation Park Golf Course 18
5001 Deukmejian Dr, Long Beach (90804-4311)
PHONE..............................562 494-4424
Tim Dunlop, *Branch Mgr*
EMP: 50
SQ FT: 2,000 **Publicly Held**
WEB: www.americangolf.com
SIC: 7992 Public golf courses
HQ: American Golf Corporation
909 N Pacific Coast Hwy
El Segundo CA 90245
310 664-4000

▲ = Import ▼=Export
◆ =Import/Export

(P-18218)
AMERICAN GOLF CORPORATION
Also Called: Wood Ranch Golf Club
301 Wood Ranch Pkwy, Simi Valley (93065-6600)
PHONE..............................805 527-9663
Mark Kelly, *Manager*
EMP: 70 **Publicly Held**
WEB: www.americangolf.com
SIC: 7992 7997 7299 Public golf courses; golf club, membership; banquet hall facilities
HQ: American Golf Corporation
909 N Pacific Coast Hwy
El Segundo CA 90245
310 664-4000

(P-18219)
AMERICAN GOLF CORPORATION
Also Called: Coyote Hills Golf Course
1440 E Bastanchury Rd, Fullerton (92835-2822)
PHONE..............................714 672-6800
Brent Boznanski, *Manager*
EMP: 100 **Publicly Held**
WEB: www.americangolf.com
SIC: 7992 7997 7299 5812 Public golf courses; membership sports & recreation clubs; banquet hall facilities; eating places
HQ: American Golf Corporation
909 N Pacific Coast Hwy
El Segundo CA 90245
310 664-4000

(P-18220)
ANTIOCH PUBLIC GOLF CORP
Also Called: LONE TREE GOLF COURSE
4800 Golf Course Rd, Antioch (94531-8012)
P.O. Box 2115 (94531-2115)
PHONE..............................925 706-4220
Ollie Anderson, *President*
Crystal Biggs, *Relations*
EMP: 58
SALES: 2.8MM **Privately Held**
SIC: 7992 5941 5812 Public golf courses; golf goods & equipment; golf driving range; restaurant, family: independent

(P-18221)
BARONA CREEK GOLF CLUB
1932 Wildcat Canyon Rd, Lakeside (92040-1553)
PHONE..............................619 387-7018
Clifford Lachappa, *Chairman*
Dean Allen, *CFO*
Michael Patterson, *Vice Pres*
Thomas Dullien, *Exec Dir*
Sik Shum, *Administration*
EMP: 60
SALES (est): 3.1MM **Privately Held**
SIC: 7992 Public golf courses

(P-18222)
BIG SKY COUNTRY CLUB LLC
Also Called: Lost Canyons Golf Course
3301 Lost Canyons Dr, Simi Valley (93063-7168)
PHONE..............................805 522-4653
Jay Collaite,
New Delos Ptnr,
EMP: 100 EST: 1997
SQ FT: 30,000
SALES (est): 2.7MM **Privately Held**
WEB: www.lostcanyons.com
SIC: 7992 5941 5812 Public golf courses; golf, tennis & ski shops; eating places

(P-18223)
BLACK GOLD GOLF CLUB
1 Black Gold Dr, Yorba Linda (92886-2383)
PHONE..............................714 961-0060
Eric Lohman, *General Mgr*
Jim Goss, *General Mgr*
Dave Bosak, *Technology*
Homik Gina, *Sales Staff*
Joshua Hunhoff, *Sales Staff*
EMP: 90
SALES (est): 3.1MM **Privately Held**
SIC: 7992 Public golf courses

(P-18224)
BRIAR GOLF LP
Also Called: Cathedral Cyn Golf Tennis CLB
68311 Paseo Real, Cathedral City (92234-6767)
PHONE..............................760 328-6571
Tom Moran, *General Ptnr*
David Flickwir, *General Ptnr*
EMP: 70
SALES (est): 1.4MM **Privately Held**
SIC: 7992 Public golf courses

(P-18225)
BSL GOLF CORP
Also Called: Bayonet/Blackhorse Golf Course
1 Mcclure Way, Seaside (93955-7100)
PHONE..............................831 899-7271
Joe Priddy, *Manager*
Jennifer Cushman, *Administration*
EMP: 150
SALES (corp-wide): 9.1MM **Privately Held**
WEB: www.bayonetblackhorse.com
SIC: 7992 Public golf courses
PA: Bsl Golf Corp.
402 Heights Blvd
Houston TX 77007
713 522-4547

(P-18226)
CALIFORNIA FUJI INTERNATIONAL
Also Called: Malibu Country Club
901 Encinal Canyon Rd, Malibu (90265-2405)
P.O. Box 3126, Westlake Village (91359-0126)
PHONE..............................818 889-6680
Norihisa Koda, *General Mgr*
Takashi Nozu, *President*
Motohiro Nozu, *Vice Pres*
EMP: 50
SQ FT: 11,000
SALES: 4MM **Privately Held**
WEB: www.malibucountryclub.net
SIC: 7992 5812 Public golf courses; eating places
PA: Tokyo Leisure Development Co.,Ltd.
3-12, Kioicho
Chiyoda-Ku TKY 102-0

(P-18227)
CALIFORNIA OAK VALLEY GOLF
Also Called: Oak Valley Golf Club
1888 Golf Club Dr, Beaumont (92223-9700)
PHONE..............................951 769-9771
Mike Pearson, *Manager*
Evlyon Then, *Manager*
EMP: 50
SQ FT: 1,000
SALES (est): 2.4MM **Privately Held**
SIC: 7992 Public golf courses

(P-18228)
CHAMPIONSHIP GOLF SERVICES INC
2340 Silver Oak Cir, Corona (92882-6025)
P.O. Box 79156 (92877-0171)
PHONE..............................951 272-4340
Steven Plummer, *President*
EMP: 145
SALES: 5.9MM **Privately Held**
SIC: 7992 Public golf courses

(P-18229)
CITY OF CONCORD
4050 Port Chicago Hwy, Concord (94520-1121)
PHONE..............................925 686-6262
Joe Fernandez, *Manager*
EMP: 60
SQ FT: 3,200 **Privately Held**
WEB: www.cpd.ci.concord.ca.us
SIC: 7992 9111 Public golf courses; mayors' offices
PA: City Of Concord
1950 Parkside Dr
Concord CA 94519
925 671-3000

(P-18230)
CITY OF DELANO
Also Called: City Corporation Yard
725 S Lexington St, Delano (93215-3617)
PHONE..............................661 721-3350
Phil Newhouse, *Branch Mgr*
Craig Wilson, *Vice Pres*
EMP: 50 **Privately Held**
SIC: 7992 Public golf courses
PA: City Of Delano
1015 11th Ave
Delano CA 93215
661 721-3300

(P-18231)
CITY OF OXNARD
Also Called: River Ridge Gulf Course
2401 W Vineyard Ave, Oxnard (93036-2218)
PHONE..............................805 983-4653
Otto Kenny, *General Mgr*
EMP: 100 **Privately Held**
WEB: www.oxnardtourism.com
SIC: 7992 Public golf courses
PA: City Of Oxnard
300 W 3rd St Uppr Fl4
Oxnard CA 93030
805 385-7803

(P-18232)
CITY OF PASADENA
Also Called: Brookside Golf Course
1133 Rosemont Ave, Pasadena (91103-2401)
PHONE..............................626 543-4708
EMP: 60 **Privately Held**
SIC: 7992 9111
PA: City Of Pasadena
100 N Garfield Ave
Pasadena CA 91101
626 744-4386

(P-18233)
CLUBCORP USA INC
Also Called: Turkey Creek Golf Club
1525 Highway 193, Lincoln (95648-9639)
PHONE..............................916 434-9100
Brent Cohen, *Manager*
EMP: 50
SALES (corp-wide): 841.1MM **Privately Held**
WEB: www.remington-gc.com
SIC: 7992 5941 5813 5812 Public golf courses; sporting goods & bicycle shops; drinking places; eating places
HQ: Clubcorp Usa, Inc.
3030 Lyndon B Johnson Fwy
Dallas TX 75234
972 243-6191

(P-18234)
CONCERT GOLF PARTNERS LLC
1 Coastal Oak, Newport Coast (92657-1655)
PHONE..............................949 715-0602
Peter J Nanula, *Mng Member*
Susan Dunnavant, *COO*
Aaron Straub, *Vice Pres*
Gabby McCalister, *Director*
Yvonne Turnbull, *Director*
EMP: 2000
SALES (est): 1MM **Privately Held**
SIC: 7992 Public golf courses

(P-18235)
COURSECO INC (PA)
1039b N Mcdowell Blvd, Petaluma (94954-1173)
PHONE..............................707 763-0335
Michael Sharp, *CEO*
John C Telischak, *Shareholder*
Tom Bugbee, *President*
Thomas B Isaak, *President*
Tom Isaak, *Info Tech Dir*
EMP: 1025
SALES (est): 35.2MM **Privately Held**
WEB: www.courseco.com
SIC: 7992 Public golf courses

(P-18236)
COYOTE CREEK GOLF CLUB
1 Coyote Creek Golf Dr, Morgan Hill (95037-9052)
P.O. Box 2527 (95038-2527)
PHONE..............................408 463-1400

Stephan Vigiano, *General Mgr*
Christopher Chai, *Mktg Dir*
Don Leone, *Director*
Gabby Mariscal, *Manager*
Donna Steele, *Manager*
EMP: 75
SQ FT: 12,000
SALES (est): 5.2MM **Privately Held**
WEB: www.coyotecreekgolf.com
SIC: 7992 5812 5941 Public golf courses; eating places; sporting goods & bicycle shops

(P-18237)
CROCKETT & COINC
Also Called: Bonita Golf Club
5540 Sweetwater Rd, Bonita (91902-2137)
PHONE..............................619 267-1103
Clayton Crockett, *Principal*
EMP: 58
SALES (corp-wide): 4.9MM **Privately Held**
WEB: www.bonitagolfclub.com
SIC: 7992 5812 Public golf courses; eating places
PA: Crockett & Co.Inc.
5120 Robinwood Rd Ste A22
Bonita CA 91902
619 267-6410

(P-18238)
CRSTB PARTNERS LLC
Also Called: Twelve Bridges Golf Club
3075 Twelve Bridges Dr, Lincoln (95648)
PHONE..............................916 645-7200
Chris S Member, *Principal*
EMP: 110
SALES (est): 1.4MM **Privately Held**
SIC: 7992 Public golf courses

(P-18239)
CYPRESS RIDGE GOLF COURSE
780 Cypress Ridge Pkwy, Arroyo Grande (93420-6524)
PHONE..............................805 474-7979
Dennis Sullivan, *Owner*
EMP: 50
SALES (est): 1.8MM **Privately Held**
SIC: 7992 6531 Public golf courses; real estate agents & managers

(P-18240)
D C GOLF A CA PARTNERSHIP
Also Called: Eaton Canyon Golf Course
1456 E Mendocino St, Altadena (91001-2600)
PHONE..............................626 797-3821
Doug Colliflower, *Managing Prtnr*
EMP: 50
SQ FT: 6,000
SALES (est): 1.7MM **Privately Held**
WEB: www.dcgolf.info
SIC: 7992 5812 Public golf courses; American restaurant

(P-18241)
DESERT WILLOW GOLF RESORT INC
Also Called: Desert Willow Golf Course
38995 Desert Willow Dr, Palm Desert (92260-1674)
PHONE..............................760 346-0015
Richard Mogensen, *General Mgr*
EMP: 150
SQ FT: 33,000
SALES (est): 8.3MM **Privately Held**
WEB: www.desertwillow.com
SIC: 7992 Public golf courses

(P-18242)
DONOVAN BROS GOLF LLC
Also Called: Tierra Rejada Golf Course
15187 Tierra Rejada Rd, Moorpark (93021-9756)
PHONE..............................805 531-9300
Michael Donovan,
Jerry Crumpler,
Ted Kruger,
Walter Rosenthal, *Consultant*
EMP: 60
SALES (est): 3MM **Privately Held**
WEB: www.donovanbrosgolf.com
SIC: 7992 Public golf courses

(P-18243)
DONOVAN GOLF COURSES MGT
Also Called: Western Hills Golf & Cntry CLB
1800 Carbon Canyon Rd, Chino (91708)
PHONE.................................714 528-6400
Michael Donovan, *General Mgr*
EMP: 50
SALES (corp-wide): 6.3MM **Privately Held**
WEB: www.willowickgolf.com
SIC: 7992 Public golf courses
PA: Donovan Golf Courses Management, Inc
3017 W 5th St
Santa Ana CA

(P-18244)
EAGLE GLEN COUNTRY CLUB LLC
Also Called: Eagle Glen Golf Club
1800 Eagle Glen Pkwy, Corona
(92883-0620)
PHONE.................................951 272-4653
Jim Previty, *Chairman*
EMP: 60
SQ FT: 26,000
SALES (est): 4MM **Privately Held**
WEB: www.eagleglengc.com
SIC: 7992 Public golf courses

(P-18245)
EL PRADO GOLF COURSE LP
6555 Pine Ave, Chino (91708-9192)
PHONE.................................909 597-1751
Bruce Jenke, *General Ptnr*
Anthony Foo, *Partner*
G Barton Heuler, *Partner*
Walter Heuler, *Partner*
Kevin Knutson, *Director*
EMP: 80 EST: 1975
SQ FT: 5,000
SALES (est): 4.4MM **Privately Held**
SIC: 7992 Public golf courses

(P-18246)
FARMS GOLF CLUB INC
Also Called: Red Tail Golf Assoc
8500 San Andreas Rd, Rancho Santa Fe
(92067)
P.O. Box 2769 (92067-2769)
PHONE.................................858 756-5585
Scott Heyn, *Manager*
Bruce Bennetts, *Manager*
EMP: 63
SALES (est): 1.9MM **Privately Held**
SIC: 7992 Public golf courses

(P-18247)
FOUNTAIN GROVE GOLF & ATHC CLB
1525 Fountaingrove Pkwy, Santa Rosa
(95403-1778)
PHONE.................................707 701-3050
Greg Sabens, *Manager*
EMP: 75
SQ FT: 33,000
SALES (est): 12.2MM **Privately Held**
WEB: www.fountaingrovegolf.com
SIC: 7992 7299 5941 7997 Public golf
courses; banquet hall facilities; golf goods
& equipment; golf club, membership

(P-18248)
FOUR SEASONS RESORT AVIARA
Also Called: Aviar Golf Club
7447 Batiquitos Dr, Carlsbad (92011-4732)
PHONE.................................760 603-6900
James Bellington, *Manager*
EMP: 74
SALES (corp-wide): 1.9MM **Privately Held**
SIC: 7992 7011 Public golf courses; hotels
HQ: Four Seasons Hotels Limited
1165 Leslie St
North York ON M3C 2
416 449-1750

(P-18249)
GLEN ANNIE GOLF CLUB
405 Glen Annie Rd, Goleta (93117-1427)
PHONE.................................805 968-6400
Richard Nahas, *General Mgr*
EMP: 80

SALES (est): 2.7MM **Privately Held**
SIC: 7992 Public golf courses

(P-18250)
GREEN RIVER GOLF CORPORATION
Also Called: Green River Golf Course
5215 Green River Rd, Corona
(92880-9404)
PHONE.................................714 970-8411
Judy Saguchi, *President*
Glen Chow, *General Mgr*
Frost Tom, *General Mgr*
Stephnie McNulty, *Sales Staff*
Michael Dooley, *Superintendent*
EMP: 100
SQ FT: 30,000
SALES (est): 6.8MM **Privately Held**
WEB: www.playgreenriver.com
SIC: 7992 5941 5813 5812 Public golf
courses; sporting goods & bicycle shops;
drinking places; eating places
PA: Courseco, Inc.
1039b N Mcdowell Blvd
Petaluma CA 94954
-

(P-18251)
HAYWARD AREA RECREATION PKDIST
Also Called: Sky West Golf Course
1401 Golf Course Rd, Hayward
(94541-4619)
PHONE.................................510 317-2300
Dan Eiamana, *Branch Mgr*
EMP: 50
SQ FT: 2,400
SALES (corp-wide): 46.9MM **Privately Held**
SIC: 7992 Public golf courses
PA: Hayward Area Recreation & Pk.Dist
1099 E St
Hayward CA 94541
510 670-1665

(P-18252)
HERITAGE GOLF GROUP INC
Also Called: Valencia Country Club
27330 Tourney Rd, Valencia (91355-1806)
PHONE.................................661 254-4401
Jim Fitzsimmons, *Manager*
EMP: 100
SALES (corp-wide): 472.8MM **Privately Held**
WEB: www.talegagolfclub.com
SIC: 7992 Public golf courses
HQ: Heritage Golf Group, Llc
12750 High Bluff Dr # 400
San Diego CA 92130
858 720-0694

(P-18253)
HERITAGE GOLF GROUP LLC
Also Called: Talega Golf Club
990 Avenida Talega, San Clemente
(92673-6849)
PHONE.................................949 369-6226
David Foster, *Branch Mgr*
EMP: 70
SALES (corp-wide): 472.8MM **Privately Held**
WEB: www.talegagolfclub.com
SIC: 7992 Public golf courses
HQ: Heritage Golf Group, Llc
12750 High Bluff Dr # 400
San Diego CA 92130
858 720-0694

(P-18254)
HIGH TIDE AND GREEN GRASS INC
Also Called: River Ridge Golf Club
2401 W Vineyard Ave, Oxnard
(93036-2218)
PHONE.................................805 981-8722
Carl Kanny, *President*
John Kanny, *Vice Pres*
Otto Kanny, *Vice Pres*
EMP: 84
SQ FT: 27,000
SALES (est): 3.5MM **Privately Held**
SIC: 7992 5812 Public golf courses; snack bar

(P-18255)
INDIAN VALLEY GOLF CLUB INC
3035 Novato Blvd, Novato (94947-1002)
P.O. Box 351 (94948-0351)
PHONE.................................415 897-1118
Jeff Mc Andrew, *President*
Fermin Vergara, *Vice Pres*
EMP: 50
SQ FT: 4,000
SALES: 2.6MM **Privately Held**
WEB: www.ivgc.com
SIC: 7992 Public golf courses; golf
goods & equipment

(P-18256)
INSTITUTE LLC
14830 Foothill Ave, Morgan Hill
(95037-9595)
PHONE.................................408 782-7101
Steven Sorenson, *Owner*
EMP: 50
SQ FT: 200
SALES (est): 2.2MM **Privately Held**
SIC: 7992 Public golf courses

(P-18257)
J G GOLFING ENTERPRISES INC
Also Called: San Bernardino Golf Club
1494 S Waterman Ave, San Bernardino
(92408-2805)
P.O. Box 3632, Running Springs (92382-3632)
PHONE.................................909 885-2414
Tom Shelf, *President*
EMP: 50
SQ FT: 4,000
SALES (est): 2.1MM **Privately Held**
WEB: www.sanbernardinogolfclub.com
SIC: 7992 Public golf courses

(P-18258)
KOLLWOOD GOLF OPERATING LP
Also Called: Kollstar Golf Company
4343 Von Karman Ave, Newport Beach
(92660-2099)
PHONE.................................949 833-3025
Joseph Woodard, *Partner*
Donald M Koll, *Partner*
EMP: 400
SALES (est): 3.8MM **Privately Held**
SIC: 7992 Public golf courses

(P-18259)
LAGUNA BCH GOLF BNGLOW VLG LLC
Also Called: Aliso Creek Inn and Golf Crse
31106 Coast Hwy, Laguna Beach
(92651-8130)
PHONE.................................949 499-2271
Mark Christy, *Mng Member*
Johnny Sanabria, *Accounting Mgr*
Lisa Rosecrans, *Human Resources*
EMP: 65
SQ FT: 10,000
SALES (est): 5.7MM **Privately Held**
WEB: www.alisocreekinn.com
SIC: 7992 7011 Public golf courses; hotels

(P-18260)
LAKESIDE GOLF CLUB
4500 W Lakeside Dr, Burbank
(91505-4088)
P.O. Box 2386, Toluca Lake (91610-0386)
PHONE.................................818 984-0601
Jerry Fard, *Manager*
Michael E Henry, *CEO*
Isabel Cruz, *Controller*
Kristin Okpaise, *Merchandise Mgr*
Lance Sabella, *Manager*
EMP: 98
SQ FT: 25,000
SALES (est): 12.4MM **Privately Held**
WEB: www.lakesidegolfclub.com
SIC: 7992 Public golf courses

(P-18261)
LB HILLS GOLF CLUB LLC
Also Called: Golf Club At Terra Lago, The
84000 Terra Lago Pkwy, Indio
(92203-9706)
PHONE.................................760 775-2000
Jeff Walser, *Partner*
EMP: 100

SALES (est): 4.1MM **Privately Held**
WEB: www.golfclub-terralago.com
SIC: 7992 7991 7299 Public golf courses;
physical fitness facilities; banquet hall facilities

(P-18262)
LINCOLN HILLS GOLF CLUB
1005 Sun City Ln, Lincoln (95648-8443)
PHONE.................................916 543-9200
Marker Brian, *President*
John Reuer, *Manager*
Jason Wolf, *Superintendent*
EMP: 50
SALES (est): 2.2MM **Privately Held**
WEB: www.lincolnhillsclub.com
SIC: 7992 7997 Public golf courses; golf
club, membership

(P-18263)
LOS SERRANOS GOLF CLUB
Also Called: Los Serranos Golf & Cntry CLB
15656 Yorba Ave, Chino Hills (91709-3129)
PHONE.................................909 597-1769
John A Kramer Jr, *CEO*
Gloria Kramer, *Shareholder*
John A Kramer Sr, *President*
David Kramer, *Treasurer*
Ronald Kramer, *Vice Pres*
EMP: 135
SQ FT: 41,896
SALES (est): 9.1MM **Privately Held**
WEB: www.losserranoscountryclub.com
SIC: 7992 5812 5813 Public golf courses;
American restaurant; snack shop; cocktail
lounge

(P-18264)
LOS VERDES MNS GOLF CNTRY CLB
Also Called: Los Verdes Golf Curse
7000 Los Verdes Dr Ste 1, Rancho Palos
Verdes (90275-5600)
PHONE.................................310 377-7370
Bob Lockhart, *General Mgr*
Fred Weibell, *Principal*
EMP: 50
SALES: 87.1K **Privately Held**
SIC: 7992 Public golf courses

(P-18265)
MADERAS GOLF CLUB
17750 Old Coach Rd, Poway (92064-6621)
PHONE.................................858 451-8100
Bill O'Brien, *General Mgr*
EMP: 80
SALES (est): 3MM **Privately Held**
SIC: 7992 Public golf courses

(P-18266)
MADISON CLUB OWNERS ASSN
Also Called: Madison Club, The
53035 Meriwether Way, La Quinta
(92253-5535)
P.O. Box 1558 (92247-1558)
PHONE.................................760 777-9320
Douglas Siebold, *CEO*
Brian Ellis, *Principal*
EMP: 125
SQ FT: 70,000
SALES (est): 10.6MM
SALES (corp-wide): 3.1B **Privately Held**
SIC: 7992 Public golf courses
PA: Discovery Land Company, Llc
14605 N 73rd St
Scottsdale AZ 85260
480 624-5200

(P-18267)
MCMILLIN COMMUNITIES INC
Also Called: Temeku Hills
41687 Temeku Dr, Temecula (92591-3909)
PHONE.................................951 506-3303
Sonia Howard, *Branch Mgr*
EMP: 947
SALES (corp-wide): 129.6MM **Privately Held**
SIC: 7992 Public golf courses
PA: Mcmillin Communities, Inc.
2750 Womble Rd Ste 102
San Diego CA 92106

(P-18268)
MESA VERDE PARTNERS
Also Called: Costa Mesa Country Club
1701 Golf Course Dr, Costa Mesa
(92626-5049)
PHONE..................714 540-7500
Scott Henderson, *Partner*
EMP: 100
SQ FT: 12,000
SALES (est): 3.6MM
SALES (corp-wide): 5.3MM **Privately Held**
SIC: 7992 7997 5813 5812 Public golf courses; membership sports & recreation clubs; drinking places; eating places
PA: Santa Anita Associates
405 S Santa Anita Ave
Arcadia CA 91006
626 447-2764

(P-18269)
MF DAILY OXNARD RANCH PARTNR
Also Called: Soule Park Golf Course
1033 E Ojai Ave, Ojai (93023-3018)
P.O. Box 758 (93024-0758)
PHONE..................805 646-5633
Don Miller, *General Mgr*
Tim Wolfe, *Officer*
EMP: 50
SQ FT: 13,000
SALES (est): 1.3MM **Privately Held**
SIC: 7992 5941 5812 Public golf courses; golf goods & equipment; eating places

(P-18270)
MILE SQUARE GOLF COURSE
10401 Warner Ave, Fountain Valley
(92708-1604)
PHONE..................714 962-5541
David A Rainville, *Partner*
Gail Hirata, *Director*
EMP: 109
SQ FT: 12,000
SALES (est): 5.9MM **Privately Held**
WEB: www.milesquaregolfcourse.com
SIC: 7992 7999 5812 Public golf courses; golf driving range; American restaurant

(P-18271)
MONARCH BAY GOLF RESORT
13800 Monarch Bay Dr, San Leandro
(94577-6401)
PHONE..................510 895-2162
Roland Smith, *CEO*
David Price, *President*
EMP: 100 EST: 1987
SALES (est): 1.7MM **Privately Held**
SIC: 7992 Public golf courses

(P-18272)
MONARCH BEACH GOLF LINKS (HQ)
50 Monarch Beach Resort N, Dana Point
(92629-4084)
PHONE..................949 240-8247
Hale Kelly, *Director*
Brandon Delgado, *Director*
Carrie Matlin, *Director*
EMP: 80
SALES (est): 4.6MM **Privately Held**
WEB: www.monarchbeachgolf.com
SIC: 7992 Public golf courses

(P-18273)
MORTON GOLF LLC
Also Called: Haggin Oaks Golf Shop
3645 Fulton Ave, Sacramento
(95821-1808)
PHONE..................916 481-4653
Terry Daubert, *Principal*
Daya Kraemer, *Executive*
Andrew Wilson, *General Mgr*
Kathleen Morton, *CPA*
Marlene Kawaguchi, *Buyer*
EMP: 100
SQ FT: 13,800
SALES (est): 12.3MM **Privately Held**
WEB: www.mortongolfsales.com
SIC: 7992 5941 5813 5812 Public golf courses; golf goods & equipment; drinking places; eating places

(P-18274)
MOTHERLODE INVESTORS LLC
Also Called: Greenlaw Grupe Jr Operating Co
711 Mccauley Ranch Rd, Angels Camp
(95222-9562)
PHONE..................209 736-8112
EMP: 85
SALES (est): 2.4MM **Privately Held**
SIC: 7992

(P-18275)
NATIONAL GOLF PROPERTIES LLC
Also Called: San Geronimo Golf Course
5800 Sir Francis Drake, San Geronimo
(94963)
P.O. Box 130 (94963-0130)
PHONE..................415 488-4030
Heather Loivos, *Manager*
EMP: 98 **Privately Held**
WEB: www.nationalgolfproperties.com
SIC: 7992 Public golf courses
PA: National Golf Properties Llc
2951 28th St Ste 3000
Santa Monica CA 90405

(P-18276)
NEW DISCOVERY INC
Also Called: Discovery Bay Golf & Cntry CLB
2600 Cherry Hills Dr, Byron (94505-1430)
P.O. Box 907, Concord (94522-0907)
PHONE..................925 634-0505
Keneth H Hofmann, *President*
EMP: 75
SALES (est): 18MM **Privately Held**
SIC: 7992 Public golf courses

(P-18277)
OAKMONT GOLF CLUB INC
7025 Oakmont Dr, Santa Rosa
(95409-6301)
PHONE..................707 538-2454
Michelle Sand, *Sales Staff*
Dann Newton, *Assistant*
EMP: 80
SQ FT: 4,000
SALES: 3.8MM **Privately Held**
WEB: www.oakmontgc.com
SIC: 7992 7997 5941 Public golf courses; golf club, membership; golf goods & equipment

(P-18278)
OCEAN LINKS CORPORATION
Also Called: Half Moon Bay Golf Links
2 Miramontes Point Rd, Half Moon Bay
(94019-2377)
PHONE..................650 726-1800
Mark Kendall, *President*
Clay Mallory, *Director*
Darren Wall, *Manager*
▼ EMP: 100
SQ FT: 6,000
SALES (est): 3.3MM **Privately Held**
SIC: 7992 Public golf courses

(P-18279)
PALM DSERT RCRTL FCLITIES CORP
Also Called: Pdrfc
38995 Desert Willow Dr, Palm Desert
(92260-1674)
P.O. Box 14290 (92255-4290)
PHONE..................760 346-0015
Richard Mogensen, *General Mgr*
Lisa Lozano, *Accountant*
Kathy Anderson, *Controller*
Jodi Shaver, *Marketing Staff*
EMP: 100
SQ FT: 10,000
SALES: 2.5MM **Privately Held**
WEB: www.cityofpalmdesert.com
SIC: 7992 Public golf courses
PA: City Of Palm Desert
73510 Fred Waring Dr
Palm Desert CA 92260
760 346-0611

(P-18280)
POPPY HILLS INC
3200 Lopez Rd, Pebble Beach
(93953-2900)
PHONE..................831 625-1513
Lyn Nelson, *President*

Manny Sousa, *Superintendent*
EMP: 60
SQ FT: 8,000
SALES (est): 1.6MM **Privately Held**
SIC: 7992 5941 5812 Public golf courses; golf goods & equipment; eating places
PA: Poppy Holding Inc
3200 Lopez Rd
Pebble Beach CA 93953

(P-18281)
POPPY RIDGE INC
Also Called: Poppy Ridge Golf Course
4280 Greenville Rd, Livermore
(94550-9720)
PHONE..................925 456-8229
Paul Porter, *President*
Melissa Johnson, *Accountant*
Jennifer Barbara, *Marketing Mgr*
Abby Crandall, *Sales Staff*
EMP: 75
SALES (est): 4.3MM **Privately Held**
SIC: 7992 Public golf courses
PA: Poppy Holding Inc
3200 Lopez Rd
Pebble Beach CA 93953

(P-18282)
PRESERVE GOLF CLUB INC
1 Rancho San Carlos Rd, Carmel
(93923-7999)
PHONE..................831 620-6871
Thomas Gray, *President*
EMP: 50
SQ FT: 20,000
SALES: 4MM **Privately Held**
SIC: 7992 Public golf courses

(P-18283)
PRIMM VALLEY GOLF CLUB
1 Yates Wells Rd, Nipton (92364)
PHONE..................702 679-5509
Keith Flatt, *Director*
▲ EMP: 70
SALES (est): 2.5MM **Privately Held**
SIC: 7992 Public golf courses

(P-18284)
PYJ V A CALIFORNIA LTD PARTNR
Also Called: Westlake Village Golf Course
4812 Lakeview Canyon Rd, Westlake Village (91361-4030)
PHONE..................805 495-8437
Clinton Airey, *General Mgr*
EMP: 60
SQ FT: 7,131
SALES: 3MM **Privately Held**
SIC: 7992 7999 6531 5091 Public golf courses; golf services & professionals; real estate managers; golf equipment

(P-18285)
QUARRY AT LA QUINTA INC (PA)
41865 Boardwalk Ste 214, Palm Desert
(92211-9033)
PHONE..................760 777-1100
William Morrow, *President*
EMP: 60
SALES (est): 5.5MM **Privately Held**
SIC: 7992 Public golf courses

(P-18286)
RANCH GOLF CLUB
4601 Hill Top View Ln, San Jose
(95138-2707)
PHONE..................408 270-0557
Mike Higuera, *Superintendent*
Kristy Park, *General Mgr*
Thomas Mejia,
EMP: 75
SQ FT: 2,880
SALES (est): 5.3MM **Privately Held**
SIC: 7992 Public golf courses

(P-18287)
RAWITSER GOLF SHOP MIKE
Also Called: San Jose Municipal Golf Course
1560 Oakland Rd, San Jose (95131-2430)
PHONE..................408 441-4653
Mike Rawitser, *President*
Berne Finch, *Director*
EMP: 50 EST: 1967
SQ FT: 2,500

SALES (est): 1.9MM **Privately Held**
WEB: www.sjmuni.com
SIC: 7992 Public golf courses

(P-18288)
ROBINSON RANCH GOLF LLC
27734 Sand Canyon Rd, Santa Clarita
(91387-3639)
PHONE..................818 885-0599
Bill McNair,
EMP: 120 EST: 1999
SALES (est): 8.4MM **Privately Held**
WEB: www.robinsonranchgolf.com
SIC: 7992 7997 Public golf courses; membership sports & recreation clubs

(P-18289)
ROOSTER RUN GOLF CLUB INC
2301 E Washington St, Petaluma
(94954-3897)
PHONE..................707 778-1211
Rob Watson, *President*
John Nice, *Vice Pres*
EMP: 50
SALES (est): 2.8MM **Privately Held**
WEB: www.roosterrun.com
SIC: 7992 5812 Public golf courses; eating places

(P-18290)
RUBY HILL GOLF CLUB LLC
3400 W Ruby Hill Dr, Pleasanton
(94566-3604)
PHONE..................925 417-5840
Jim Ghielmetti,
Chef Harold, *Executive*
Eric Jacobsen, *General Mgr*
Michael Rood, *General Mgr*
Janan Ali, *Sales Staff*
EMP: 100 EST: 1994
SALES (est): 8.1MM **Privately Held**
WEB: www.rubyhill.com
SIC: 7992 Public golf courses

(P-18291)
SAN JUAN GOLF INC
Also Called: San Juan Hill Country Club
32120 San Juan Creek Rd, San Juan
Capistrano (92675-3840)
PHONE..................949 493-1167
Tony Kato, *President*
Allan Freeman, *Partner*
Mike Abee, *General Mgr*
Ashley Demein, *Food Svc Dir*
Stacey Strausbaugh, *Director*
EMP: 50
SALES (est): 3.3MM **Privately Held**
SIC: 7992 5812 5941 Public golf courses; eating places; golf goods & equipment

(P-18292)
SAN JUAN OAKS LLC
Also Called: San Juan Oaks Golf Club
3825 Union Rd, Hollister (95023-9135)
PHONE..................831 636-6113
Kenneth Gimelli,
Sandy Vera, *Human Resources*
Amanda Pacheco, *Director*
EMP: 80
SQ FT: 1,800
SALES (est): 6.9MM **Privately Held**
WEB: www.sanjuanoaks.com
SIC: 7992 5941 5812 5813 Public golf courses; golf goods & equipment; eating places; bar (drinking places); banquet hall facilities

(P-18293)
SAND CANYON LLC
Also Called: Strawberry Farms Golf Club
11 Strawberry Farm Rd, Irvine
(92612-2300)
PHONE..................949 551-2560
Doug Decinces, *Partner*
EMP: 80
SALES (est): 4.2MM **Privately Held**
WEB: www.sandcanyon.com
SIC: 7992 Public golf courses

(P-18294)
SANTA ANITA ASSOCIATES (PA)
Also Called: Santa Anita Golf Course
405 S Santa Anita Ave, Arcadia
(91006-3509)
PHONE..................626 447-2764
Scott L Henderson, *Managing Prtnr*

PRODUCTS & SVCS

Mike Donavan, *Partner*
Scott Henderson, *Manager*
Tim Wren, *Superintendent*
EMP: 60
SQ FT: 16,000
SALES (est): 5.3MM **Privately Held**
SIC: 7992 5812 7999 7299 Public golf
courses; American restaurant; golf cart,
power, rental; golf driving range; banquet
hall facilities

(P-18295)
SANTA TERESA GOLF CLUB
Also Called: Santa Teresa Golf Center
260 Bernal Rd, San Jose (95119-1809)
PHONE..................................408 225-2650
Mike Rawitser, *Partner*
Lawrence Lobue, *General Ptnr*
Victor Lobue, *General Ptnr*
John Mc Enery III, *General Ptnr*
Rudy Steadler, *General Ptnr*
EMP: 70
SQ FT: 5,300
SALES (est): 4.3MM **Privately Held**
WEB: www.all-seasons-golf.com
SIC: 7992 Public golf courses

(P-18296)
SCGA GOLF COURSE MGT INC
39500 Robrt Trnt Jnes Pkw, Murrieta
(92563-5849)
PHONE..................................951 677-7446
Jon Bilger, *President*
EMP: 72
SQ FT: 4,000
SALES: 2.5MM
SALES (corp-wide): 7.7MM **Privately
Held**
WEB: www.scgamembersclub.com
SIC: 7992 5812 5941 7999 Public golf
courses; eating places; golf goods &
equipment; golf driving range
PA: Southern California Golf Association
3740 Cahuenga Blvd
North Hollywood CA 91604
818 980-3630

(P-18297)
SIERRA LAKES GOLF CLUB
16600 Clubhouse Dr, Fontana
(92336-5138)
PHONE..................................909 350-2500
Dave Lewis, *President*
Rick Danruther, *Manager*
EMP: 60
SALES (est): 3.4MM **Privately Held**
WEB: www.sierralakes.com
SIC: 7992 Public golf courses

(P-18298)
**SILVER ROCK RESORT GOLF
CLUB**
79179 Ahmanson Ln, La Quinta
(92253-5715)
PHONE..................................760 777-8884
EMP: 100
SALES (est): 4MM **Privately Held**
SIC: 7992 Public golf courses
PA: City Of La Quinta
78495 Calle Tampico
La Quinta CA 92253
760 777-7000

(P-18299)
**SISKIYOU LAKE GOLF RESORT
INC**
Also Called: Mount Shasta Resort
1000 Siskiyou Lake Blvd, Mount Shasta
(96067-9482)
PHONE..................................530 926-3030
John Cullison, *President*
John Fryer, *Director*
EMP: 80
SALES (est): 5.5MM **Privately Held**
WEB: www.mtshastaresort.com
SIC: 7992 5941 7011 5812 Public golf
courses; golf goods & equipment; tourist
camps, cabins, cottages & courts; Ameri-
can restaurant

(P-18300)
SPE GO HOLDINGS INC
Also Called: Mount Woodson Country Club
16422 N Woodson Dr, Ramona
(92065-6800)
PHONE..................................858 638-0672

Steve Dawe, *Exec VP*
Amanda Rangel, *General Mgr*
Scott Hardy, *Superintendent*
EMP: 50
SALES (corp-wide): 13.9B **Publicly Held**
SIC: 7992 Public golf courses
HQ: Spe Go Holdings, Inc.
11575 Great Oaks Way # 210
Alpharetta GA 30022
401 621-4200

(P-18301)
**STEELE CANYON GOLF CLUB
CORP (PA)**
3199 Stonefield Dr, Jamul (91935-1527)
PHONE..................................619 441-6900
Lawrence M Taylor, *CEO*
Jennifer Davis, *Accounting Mgr*
Barry Rice, *Food Svc Dir*
EMP: 53 **EST:** 1991
SALES (est): 6.2MM **Privately Held**
SIC: 7992 Public golf courses

(P-18302)
STONETREE GOLF LLC
Also Called: Stonetree Management
9 Stonetree Ln, Novato (94945-3541)
PHONE..................................415 209-6744
Warren Spieker, *Partner*
Bill Bunce, *Partner*
Dennis Singleton, *Partner*
EMP: 50
SALES (est): 5.1MM **Privately Held**
WEB: www.blackpt.com
SIC: 7992 5941 5812 Public golf courses;
golf, tennis & ski shops; family restau-
rants

(P-18303)
**STRAWBERRY FARMS GOLF
CLUB LLC**
11 Strawberry Farm Rd, Irvine
(92612-2300)
PHONE..................................949 551-2560
Doug Decinese,
EMP: 75
SALES (est): 3.6MM **Privately Held**
WEB: www.strawberryfarmsgolf.com
SIC: 7992 Public golf courses

(P-18304)
**SUN CITY RSVLLE CMNTY ASSN
INC (PA)**
Also Called: TIMBER CREEK GOLF
COURSE
7050 Del Webb Blvd, Roseville
(95747-8040)
PHONE..................................916 774-3880
Dewolfe Emory, *CEO*
Derek Zachman, *Marketing Staff*
Jason Smith, *Director*
Chris Hall, *Manager*
EMP: 200 **EST:** 1994
SALES: 12.4MM **Privately Held**
WEB: www.scr-cc.com
SIC: 7992 5812 Public golf courses; eat-
ing places; caterers

(P-18305)
**SUNOL VLY GOLF &
RECREATION CO**
Also Called: Sunol Valley Golf Course
5117 Mount Tam Cir, Pleasanton
(94588-3676)
PHONE..................................925 862-2404
Ron Ivaldi, *General Ptnr*
Lisa Grannzella, *Partner*
Brian Richardson, *General Mgr*
Carol Richardson, *Office Mgr*
Perry Lee, *Technology*
EMP: 100
SALES (est): 4MM **Privately Held**
WEB: www.sunolvalley.com
SIC: 7992 5812 5813 7997 Public golf
courses; coffee shop; snack shop; cock-
tail lounge; membership sports & recre-
ation clubs; sporting goods & bicycle
shops

(P-18306)
**TAHOE DONNER GOLF COURSE
INC**
11509 Northwoods Blvd, Truckee
(96161-6000)
PHONE..................................530 587-9455

Mike Peters, *Executive Asst*
EMP: 75
SALES: 5MM **Privately Held**
SIC: 7992 5813 5812 Public golf courses;
bar (drinking places); American restaurant

(P-18307)
**TRADITION GOLF CLUB
ASSOCIATES**
78505 Avenue 52, La Quinta (92253-2802)
PHONE..................................760 564-3355
David Champman, *General Mgr*
EMP: 60
SALES (est): 2MM **Privately Held**
SIC: 7992 Public golf courses

(P-18308)
TRADITIONS GOLF LLC
Also Called: Cinnabar Hills Golf Club
23600 Mckean Rd, San Jose (95141-1001)
PHONE..................................408 323-5200
Bill Baron,
D Scott Hoyt, *General Mgr*
Scott Giangreco, *Food Svc Dir*
Lee Brandenburg,
Paul Pugh,
EMP: 100
SQ FT: 25,000
SALES (est): 7.5MM **Privately Held**
WEB: www.cinnabarhills.com
SIC: 7992 Public golf courses

(P-18309)
TRILOGY GOLF AT LA QUINTA
60151 Trilogy Pkwy, La Quinta
(92253-7640)
PHONE..................................760 771-0707
Tom Williams, *Manager*
Ralph Bernhisel, *General Mgr*
Marge Deschaak, *Office Admin*
EMP: 64
SALES (est): 2.4MM
SALES (corp-wide): 2.2B **Privately Held**
WEB: www.jfshea.com
SIC: 7992 Public golf courses
HQ: J.F. Shea Construction, Inc.
655 Brea Canyon Rd
Walnut CA 91789
909 595-4397

(P-18310)
VB GOLF LLC
Also Called: Mariner's Point Golf Course
2401 E 3rd Ave, Foster City (94404-1067)
PHONE..................................650 573-7888
Chris Aliaga, *Manager*
Sergio Garcia, *Partner*
William Verbrugge, *Partner*
Christopher Aliaga, *Executive*
Mick Soli, *Exec Dir*
EMP: 55
SALES (est): 2.7MM **Privately Held**
SIC: 7992 Public golf courses

(P-18311)
VH PROPERTY CORP
1 Ocean Trl, Rancho Palos Verdes (90275)
PHONE..................................310 303-3210
Donald Trump Jr, *Director*
EMP: 300
SQ FT: 39,883
SALES (est): 6.6MM **Privately Held**
SIC: 7992 Public golf courses

(P-18312)
VINTNERS GOLF CLUB
Also Called: Lakeside Grill, The
7901 Solano Ave, Yountville (94599-1453)
PHONE..................................707 944-1992
Mike Stead, *Owner*
Jason Boldt, *Director*
Justin Tews, *Associate*
EMP: 50
SALES (est): 2.2MM **Privately Held**
WEB: www.vintnersgolfclub.com
SIC: 7992 Public golf courses

(P-18313)
WESTRIDGE GOLF INC
1400 S La Habra Hills Dr, La Habra
(90631-6998)
PHONE..................................562 690-4200
J C Song, *General Mgr*
EMP: 75
SQ FT: 15,000

SALES (est): 4.4MM **Privately Held**
WEB: www.westridgegolf.com
SIC: 7992 Public golf courses

(P-18314)
WINDSOR GOLF CLUB INC
1340 19th Hole Dr, Windsor (95492-6829)
PHONE..................................707 838-7888
Charlie Gibson, *General Mgr*
Larry Wasm, *Treasurer*
Brove O'Brien, *Vice Pres*
Alex Wright, *Principal*
Tami Sullberg, *General Mgr*
EMP: 60
SALES (est): 2.8MM **Privately Held**
WEB: www.windsorgolf.com
SIC: 7992 5941 Public golf courses; golf
goods & equipment

(P-18315)
**WOODLEY LAKES GOLF
COURSE**
6331 Woodley Ave, Van Nuys
(91406-6473)
PHONE..................................818 780-6886
Phil Rigs, *Manager*
EMP: 70
SALES (est): 2.6MM **Privately Held**
SIC: 7992 Public golf courses

**7993 Coin-Operated
Amusement Devices &**

(P-18316)
**CAMPO BAND MISSIONS
INDIANS**
Also Called: Golden Acorn Casino & Trvl Ctr
1800 Golden Acorn Way, Campo
(91906-2301)
P.O. Box 310 (91906-0310)
PHONE..................................619 938-6000
Don Trimble, *Manager*
Larry Drouse, *General Mgr*
Katie Wahl, *Accountant*
Patrick Swope, *Manager*
Christopher Thornton, *Manager*
EMP: 330 **Privately Held**
SIC: 7993 5812 Gambling establishments
operating coin-operated machines; Ameri-
can restaurant
PA: Campo Band Of Missions Indians
36190 Church Rd
Campo CA 91906
619 478-9046

(P-18317)
EMOTIV SYSTEMS INC
1770 Post St Ste 350, San Francisco
(94115-3606)
PHONE..................................415 503-3601
Tan Le, *President*
EMP: 50
SALES (est): 1.8MM **Privately Held**
SIC: 7993 Game machines

(P-18318)
INDUSTRY EVENTS
25501 Narbonne Ave, Lomita (90717-2511)
PHONE..................................310 834-3422
John Bayouth, *Principal*
EMP: 50
SALES (est): 1.4MM **Privately Held**
SIC: 7993 Amusement arcade

(P-18319)
LOOFS LITE A LINE
2500 Long Beach Blvd, Long Beach
(90806-3112)
PHONE..................................562 436-2978
Michael Sincola, *Owner*
Ettamay Errock, *Partner*
EMP: 50
SQ FT: 10,005
SALES (est): 1.2MM **Privately Held**
SIC: 7993 Arcades

(P-18320)
MOORETOWN RANCHERIA
Also Called: Feather Falls Casino
3 Alverda Dr, Oroville (95966-9379)
PHONE..................................530 533-3885
Tom Yarbrough, *General Mgr*
Nicole Taylor, *CIO*
Dori Moura, *Human Res Dir*

EMP: 340 **Privately Held**
WEB: www.drumvision.com
SIC: 7993 7999 Gambling establishments operating coin-operated machines; gambling establishment
PA: Mooretown Rancheria
1 Alverda Dr
Oroville CA 95966

(P-18321)
PACHINKO WORLD INC
5912 Bolsa Ave Ste 108, Huntington Beach (92649-1105)
PHONE.....................714 895-7772
Shinichi Hirabayashi, *CEO*
Yoneji Hirabayashi, *Ch of Bd*
Akinori Hirabayashi, *COO*
Haruo Miyano, *Admin Sec*
EMP: 195
SQ FT: 500
SALES (est): 9MM **Privately Held**
SIC: 7993 7999 5812 5194 Game machines; pinball machines; amusement arcade; game parlor; Japanese restaurant; cigarettes

7996 Amusement Parks

(P-18322)
APEX PARKS GROUP LLC (PA)
18575 Jamboree Rd Ste 600, Irvine (92612-2554)
PHONE.....................949 349-8461
John Fitzgerald, *CEO*
Greg Borman, *Vice Pres*
Rebecca Tortorelli, *Vice Pres*
Craig Stieglitz, *General Mgr*
Meleena Loseke, *Marketing Mgr*
EMP: 114
SALES (est): 43.9MM **Privately Held**
SIC: 7996 Amusement parks

(P-18323)
CASINO MORONGO
49500 Seminole Dr, Cabazon (92230-2202)
P.O. Box 366 (92230-0366)
PHONE.....................951 849-3080
Gene Stachowksi, *Principal*
Koehler Daniel, *Training Super*
EMP: 57
SALES: 5MM **Privately Held**
SIC: 7996 Amusement parks

(P-18324)
CEDAR FAIR LP
Great America Theme Park
4701 Great America Pkwy, Santa Clara (95054-1287)
P.O. Box 1776 (95052-1776)
PHONE.....................408 988-1776
David Mannix, *Systems Mgr*
Kanchan Wadhwa, *Technical Mgr*
Luwanna Le, *Finance*
Huynh Lien, *Foreman/Supr*
Danielle Alvarez, *Assistant*
EMP: 120
SALES (corp-wide): 1.3B **Publicly Held**
WEB: www.cedarfair.com
SIC: 7996 Theme park, amusement
PA: Cedar Fair, L.P.
1 Cedar Point Dr
Sandusky OH 44870
419 626-0830

(P-18325)
CITY OF OXNARD
Also Called: Streets Street Tree Inquiries
1060 Pacific Ave, Oxnard (93030-7337)
PHONE.....................805 385-7950
Michael Henderson, *Director*
EMP: 100 **Privately Held**
WEB: www.oxnardtourism.com
SIC: 7996 Amusement parks
PA: City Of Oxnard
300 W 3rd St Uppr Fl4
Oxnard CA 93030
805 385-7803

(P-18326)
CITY OF VALLEJO
Also Called: Marine World/Africa USA
1001 Fairgrounds Dr, Vallejo (94589-4001)
PHONE.....................707 644-4000

Joe Meck, *Vice Pres*
EMP: 350 **Privately Held**
WEB: www.ci.vallejo.ca.us
SIC: 7996 Theme park, amusement
PA: City Of Vallejo
555 Santa Clara St
Vallejo CA 94590
707 648-4575

(P-18327)
COUNTY OF SACRAMENTO
Also Called: Department of Regional Parks
10361 Rockingham Dr # 100, Sacramento (95827-2519)
PHONE.....................916 363-8383
Ron Suter, *Manager*
Janet Baker, *Principal*
Jill Ritzman, *Manager*
EMP: 82 **Privately Held**
WEB: www.sna.com
SIC: 7996 Amusement parks
PA: County Of Sacramento
700 H St Ste 7650
Sacramento CA 95814
916 874-5544

(P-18328)
DISCOVERY SCNCE CTR ORNGE CNTY
2500 N Main St, Santa Ana (92705-6600)
PHONE.....................866 552-2823
Daniel Bolar, *Ch of Bd*
Joseph Adams, *President*
Kellee Preston, *Vice Pres*
Brie Griset Smith, *Vice Pres*
Kafi Blumenfield, *Exec Dir*
▲ **EMP:** 135
SALES (est): 12MM **Privately Held**
WEB: www.discoverycube.org
SIC: 7996 Amusement parks

(P-18329)
DISNEYLAND INTERNATIONAL (DH)
1313 S Harbor Blvd, Anaheim (92802-2309)
PHONE.....................714 781-4565
James Thomas, *President*
David A Hughes, *Asst Treas*
Richard Nunis, *Purch Dir*
Phillip N Smith, *Asst Sec*
EMP: 200
SALES (est): 177.8MM
SALES (corp-wide): 90.2B **Publicly Held**
SIC: 7996 Theme park, amusement
HQ: Disney Enterprises, Inc.
500 S Buena Vista St
Burbank CA 91521
818 560-1000

(P-18330)
FESTIVAL FUN PARKS LLC
3500 Polk St, Riverside (92505-1824)
PHONE.....................951 785-3000
EMP: 68 **Privately Held**
SIC: 7996 Amusement parks
HQ: Festival Fun Parks, Llc
4590 Macarthur Blvd # 400
Newport Beach CA 92660
949 261-0404

(P-18331)
FESTIVAL FUN PARKS LLC
Also Called: Malibu Grand Prix 51
340 Blomquist St, Redwood City (94063-2702)
PHONE.....................949 261-0404
Margi Marshall, *Information Mgr*
Amanda Blazey, *Mktg Coord*
EMP: 50 **Privately Held**
SIC: 7996 Kiddie park
HQ: Festival Fun Parks, Llc
4590 Macarthur Blvd # 400
Newport Beach CA 92660
949 261-0404

(P-18332)
GILROY GARDENS FAMILY THEME PK
3050 Hecker Pass Rd, Gilroy (95020-9411)
PHONE.....................408 840-7100
Michael Bonfante, *Director*
Barb Granter, *President*
Patti Stephens, *Controller*
Liliana Becerra, *Human Resources*

Brenda Romero, *Human Resources*
EMP: 204
SALES: 15.8MM **Privately Held**
SIC: 7996 Amusement parks

(P-18333)
HARDCORE SKATEPARKS INC
285 N Benson Ave, Upland (91786-5614)
PHONE.....................909 949-1601
Joseph M Ciaglia Jr, *CEO*
EMP: 150
SALES (est): 560.8K **Privately Held**
SIC: 7996 Amusement parks

(P-18334)
LEGOLAND CALIFORNIA LLC
1 Legoland Dr, Carlsbad (92008-4610)
PHONE.....................760 918-5346
John Jakobson,
Mary Dougherty, *Executive*
Lauren Paffenback, *Executive*
Mercedes Casey, *Social Dir*
Shawn Greiner, *Social Dir*
▲ **EMP:** 400
SALES (est): 38.2MM
SALES (corp-wide): 2.1B **Privately Held**
WEB: www.legoland.com
SIC: 7996 Theme park, amusement
HQ: Merlin Entertainments Group Limited
Link House
Poole BH15
-

(P-18335)
MALIBU CASTLE
27061 Aliso Creek Rd # 100, Aliso Viejo (92656-5322)
PHONE.....................210 341-6663
EMP: 50
SQ FT: 6,980
SALES: 3.1MM **Privately Held**
SIC: 7996
HQ: Festival Fun Parks, Llc
4590 Macarthur Blvd # 400
Newport Beach CA 92660
949 261-0404

(P-18336)
MOUNTASIA FAMILY FUN CENTER
21516 Golden Triangle Rd, Santa Clarita (91350-2612)
PHONE.....................661 253-4386
David Fleming, *Owner*
Mike Fleming, *Partner*
Mike Henn, *General Mgr*
EMP: 60
SQ FT: 22,000
SALES: 2.4MM **Privately Held**
WEB: www.mountasiafuncenter.com
SIC: 7996 Theme park, amusement

(P-18337)
MULLIGAN LIMITED (PA)
Also Called: Mulligan Family Fun Center
4281 Katella Ave Ste 228, Los Alamitos (90720-6505)
PHONE.....................714 484-6799
Rob Thomas, *Principal*
Georgia Claessens, *Partner*
EMP: 58
SALES (est): 4MM **Privately Held**
WEB: www.mulliganfun.com
SIC: 7996 Amusement parks

(P-18338)
MULLIGAN LTD A CAL LTD PARTNR
Also Called: Mulligan Family Fun Center
24950 Madison Ave, Murrieta (92562-9714)
PHONE.....................951 696-9696
Micheal Brooks, *Manager*
EMP: 95 **Privately Held**
WEB: www.mulliganfun.com
SIC: 7996 7999 Theme park, amusement; tourist attractions, amusement park concessions & rides
PA: Mulligan Limited
4281 Katella Ave Ste 228
Los Alamitos CA 90720
-

(P-18339)
SANTA CRUZ SEASIDE COMPANY (PA)
400 Beach St, Santa Cruz (95060-5416)
PHONE.....................831 423-5590
Charles L Canfield, *President*
Jo Anne Dlott, *Vice Pres*
Bryan Wall, *Exec Dir*
Juana Villar, *Admin Sec*
Patricia Isaak, *Admin Asst*
▲ **EMP:** 299
SQ FT: 8,000
SALES: 55.2MM **Privately Held**
WEB: www.scseaside.com
SIC: 7996 7011 7933 6531 Pier, amusement; motels; bowling centers; real estate agents & managers

(P-18340)
SANTA MONICA AMUSEMENTS LLC
Also Called: Pacific Park
380 Santa Monica Pier, Santa Monica (90401-3128)
PHONE.....................310 451-9641
Mary Ann Powell, *CEO*
David Gillam, *CFO*
Jeff Klocke, *Vice Pres*
Perez Flor, *Executive Asst*
Dorene Goldman, *Controller*
EMP: 325
SQ FT: 70,000
SALES (est): 22.9MM **Privately Held**
WEB: www.pacpark.com
SIC: 7996 Theme park, amusement

(P-18341)
SIX FLAGS ENTERTAINMENT CORP
Also Called: Waterworld USA
1600 Exposition Blvd, Sacramento (95815-5104)
PHONE.....................916 924-3747
Keith Regardons, *Director*
EMP: 300
SALES (corp-wide): 1.4B **Publicly Held**
WEB: www.sixflags.com
SIC: 7996 Theme park, amusement
PA: Six Flags Entertainment Corp
924 E Avenue J
Grand Prairie TX 75050
972 595-5000

(P-18342)
TWDC ENTERPRISES 18 CORP
650 S Buenavista St, Burbank (91501)
PHONE.....................818 553-7333
Sylvian Goessens, *Branch Mgr*
EMP: 250
SALES (corp-wide): 90.2B **Publicly Held**
SIC: 7996 Kiddie park
HQ: Twdc Enterprises 18 Corp.
500 S Buena Vista St
Burbank CA 91521
-

(P-18343)
YANACO INC
Also Called: Waterworks Park
151 N Boulder Dr, Redding (96003-4607)
PHONE.....................530 246-9550
Joe Murphy, *President*
EMP: 176
SQ FT: 1,000
SALES (est): 591K **Privately Held**
SIC: 7996 Amusement parks

7997 Membership Sports & Recreation Clubs

(P-18344)
1334 PARTNERS LP
Also Called: Manhattan Country Club
1330 Park View Ave, Manhattan Beach (90266-3704)
PHONE.....................310 546-5656
Keith Brackpool, *Partner*
EMP: 100
SQ FT: 80,000

PRODUCTS & SVCS

SALES: 54.7K **Privately Held**
WEB: www.manhattancc.com
SIC: 7997 6512 7991 5813 Country club, membership; commercial & industrial building operation; physical fitness facilities; drinking places; eating places

(P-18345)
16700 ROSCOE ASSOCIATES LLC
Also Called: Maguire Aviation
16700 Roscoe Blvd, Van Nuys (91406-1100)
PHONE..................................818 989-2300
Robert F Maguire III, *Mng Member*
Alec Maguire, *President*
Cary Stalding, *CFO*
EMP: 70
SALES: 15MM **Privately Held**
SIC: 7997 Aviation club, membership

(P-18346)
A A A FIVE STAR ADVENTURES
611 S Palm Canyon Dr, Palm Springs (92264-7213)
PHONE..................................760 320-1500
A D Kesson, *Principal*
EMP: 50
SALES (est): 619.2K **Privately Held**
SIC: 7997 Membership sports & recreation clubs

(P-18347)
ACADEMY SWIM CLUB
Also Called: Santa Clarita Swim Club
28079 Smyth Dr, Valencia (91355-4023)
PHONE..................................661 702-8585
Nikki Miller, *President*
Jim Miller, *Vice Pres*
Dakota Miller, *Program Dir*
EMP: 55
SALES (est): 187.7K **Privately Held**
SIC: 7997 7999 Swimming club, membership; swimming instruction

(P-18348)
ADVENTURES IN HOSPITALITY INC
Also Called: Barbara Worth Resort
633 W Canal St, Calexico (92231-3503)
PHONE..................................760 356-2806
Suzanna Esparza, *President*
EMP: 65
SQ FT: 15,000
SALES (est): 3.5MM **Privately Held**
WEB: www.bwresort.com
SIC: 7997 Country club, membership; golf club, membership

(P-18349)
AGI HOLDING CORP (PA)
Also Called: Affinity Group
2575 Vista Del Mar Dr, Ventura (93001-3900)
P.O. Box 6888, Englewood CO (80155-6888)
PHONE..................................805 667-4100
Mr Stephen Adams, *CEO*
Joe McAdams, *President*
Maria Recinos, *COO*
Michael Schneider, *COO*
Mark Boggess, *CFO*
▲ **EMP:** 59
SQ FT: 74,000
SALES (est): 488.7MM **Privately Held**
SIC: 7997 2741 Membership sports & recreation clubs; directories: publishing & printing; newsletter publishing

(P-18350)
AIRPORT CLUB
Also Called: Airport Health Club
432 Aviation Blvd, Santa Rosa (95403-1069)
PHONE..................................707 528-2582
Bob Page, *President*
Vickie Morse, *Corp Secy*
Russell Tow, *Vice Pres*
EMP: 120
SQ FT: 44,000
SALES (est): 6MM **Privately Held**
SIC: 7997 7991 Membership sports & recreation clubs; physical fitness facilities

(P-18351)
ALISO VIEJO GOLF CLUB INC
Also Called: Aliso Viejo Country Club
33 Santa Barbara Dr, Aliso Viejo (92656-1622)
PHONE..................................949 598-9200
Lorraine Grassman, *General Mgr*
Lorraine Gerassman, *General Mgr*
EMP: 110
SQ FT: 8,000
SALES (est): 5.2MM
SALES (corp-wide): 841.1MM **Privately Held**
WEB: www.alisogolf.com
SIC: 7997 Golf club, membership
HQ: Clubcorp Usa, Inc.
3030 Lyndon B Johnson Fwy
Dallas TX 75234
972 243-6191

(P-18352)
ALMADEN GOLF & COUNTRY CLUB
6663 Hampton Dr, San Jose (95120-5536)
PHONE..................................408 323-4812
Robert Osshalem, *General Mgr*
Adrienne Simpson, *Director*
EMP: 60
SQ FT: 26,000
SALES: 6MM **Privately Held**
WEB: www.almadengcc.com
SIC: 7997 Country club, membership; golf club, membership

(P-18353)
ALMADEN VALLEY ATHLETIC CLUB
Also Called: Avac
5400 Camden Ave, San Jose (95124-5897)
PHONE..................................408 445-4900
Joseph Shank, *General Ptnr*
Court Aquatic Sports, *General Ptnr*
EMP: 70
SQ FT: 20,000
SALES (est): 4MM **Privately Held**
SIC: 7997 Tennis club, membership

(P-18354)
ALTA SIERRA COUNTRY CLUB INC
11897 Tammy Way, Grass Valley (95949-6626)
PHONE..................................530 273-2041
Del Clement, *President*
Jim Hansen, *Treasurer*
Doug Bulman, *Vice Pres*
Carl Guastaferro, *Admin Sec*
EMP: 50
SQ FT: 21,500
SALES (est): 3.6MM **Privately Held**
WEB: www.altasierracc.com
SIC: 7997 Golf club, membership

(P-18355)
ALTA VISTA COUNTRY CLUB LLC
777 Alta Vista St, Placentia (92870-5101)
PHONE..................................714 524-1591
Karl Reul, *General Mgr*
Ashley Knorr, *Marketing Staff*
EMP: 60
SQ FT: 6,751,800
SALES (est): 238.8K **Privately Held**
SIC: 7997 Country club, membership

(P-18356)
ALTADENA TOWN AND COUNTRY CLUB
2290 Country Club Dr, Altadena (91001-3202)
PHONE..................................626 345-9088
David Edens, *President*
Stephanie Duran, *Manager*
Margot Flynn, *Manager*
EMP: 80
SQ FT: 50,000
SALES: 4MM **Privately Held**
SIC: 7997 Country club, membership

(P-18357)
AMERICAN GOLF CORPORATION
Also Called: Lomas Santa Fe Country Club
1505 Lomas Santa Fe Dr, Solana Beach (92075-2103)
PHONE..................................858 755-6768
Lynn Ferrer, *Sales/Mktg Mgr*
EMP: 150 **Publicly Held**
WEB: www.americangolf.com
SIC: 7997 Country club, membership; golf club, membership
HQ: American Golf Corporation
909 N Pacific Coast Hwy
El Segundo CA 90245
310 664-4000

(P-18358)
AMERICAN GOLF CORPORATION
Also Called: Sunset Hills Country Club
4155 Erbes Rd, Thousand Oaks (91360-6842)
PHONE..................................805 495-5407
Scott Richmond, *Manager*
Nicole Fredrichs, *Sales Staff*
Janet Smith, *Director*
EMP: 75 **Publicly Held**
WEB: www.americangolf.com
SIC: 7997 Country club, membership; golf club, membership
HQ: American Golf Corporation
909 N Pacific Coast Hwy
El Segundo CA 90245
310 664-4000

(P-18359)
AMERICAN GOLF CORPORATION
Also Called: Rancho San Joaquin Golf Course
1 Ethel Coplen Way, Irvine (92612-1716)
PHONE..................................949 786-1224
Steve Jeffrey, *Manager*
EMP: 125 **Publicly Held**
WEB: www.americangolf.com
SIC: 7997 7992 Golf club, membership; public golf courses
HQ: American Golf Corporation
909 N Pacific Coast Hwy
El Segundo CA 90245
310 664-4000

(P-18360)
AMERICAN GOLF CORPORATION (HQ)
909 N Pacific Coast Hwy, El Segundo (90245-2724)
PHONE..................................310 664-4000
Jim Hinckley, *CEO*
Paul Major, *President*
Keith Brown, *COO*
Mike Moecker, *CFO*
Rick Rosen, *CFO*
EMP: 150 **EST:** 1973
SALES (est): 376.6MM **Publicly Held**
WEB: www.americangolf.com
SIC: 7997 7999 5812 5941 Golf club, membership; tennis club, membership; golf services & professionals; eating places; golf goods & equipment; public golf courses

(P-18361)
AMERICAN GOLF CORPORATION
Also Called: Reserve At Spanos Park, The
6301 W Eight Mile Rd, Stockton (95219-8702)
P.O. Box 7126 (95267-0126)
PHONE..................................209 477-4653
Barry Ruhl, *Manager*
EMP: 50 **Publicly Held**
WEB: www.americangolf.com
SIC: 7997 7992 Golf club, membership; public golf courses
HQ: American Golf Corporation
909 N Pacific Coast Hwy
El Segundo CA 90245
310 664-4000

(P-18362)
AMERICAN GOLF CORPORATION
Also Called: Yorba Linda Country Club
19400 Mountain View Ave, Yorba Linda (92886-5530)
PHONE..................................714 779-2461
Scott Lester, *District Mgr*
Shuji Inada, *Buyer*
EMP: 55
SQ FT: 19,800 **Publicly Held**
WEB: www.americangolf.com
SIC: 7997 Golf club, membership
HQ: American Golf Corporation
909 N Pacific Coast Hwy
El Segundo CA 90245
310 664-4000

(P-18363)
AMERICAN GOLF CORPORATION
Also Called: Desert Rose Golf Course
68311 Paseo Real, Cathedral City (92234-6767)
PHONE..................................702 431-2191
EMP: 78
SALES (corp-wide): 560.6MM **Privately Held**
SIC: 7997 7999 7992
PA: American Golf Corporation
6080 Center Dr Ste 500
Los Angeles CA 90245
310 664-4000

(P-18364)
AMERICAN GOLF CORPORATION
Also Called: Escondido Country Club
17166 Stonerdg Cntry Clb, Poway (92064-1333)
PHONE..................................760 737-9762
Angela Emory, *Manager*
Rose Vossenkemper, *Food Svc Dir*
EMP: 50 **Publicly Held**
WEB: www.americangolf.com
SIC: 7997 Golf club, membership
HQ: American Golf Corporation
909 N Pacific Coast Hwy
El Segundo CA 90245
310 664-4000

(P-18365)
AMERICAN GOLF CORPORATION
Also Called: Black Lake Golf Course
1490 Golf Course Ln, Nipomo (93444-9307)
PHONE..................................805 343-1214
Bill Burney, *Manager*
EMP: 70
SQ FT: 3,000 **Publicly Held**
WEB: www.americangolf.com
SIC: 7997 Country club, membership; golf club, membership
HQ: American Golf Corporation
909 N Pacific Coast Hwy
El Segundo CA 90245
310 664-4000

(P-18366)
AMERICAN GOLF CORPORATION
Also Called: Seacliff Country Club
6501 Palm Ave, Huntington Beach (92648-2611)
PHONE..................................714 536-8866
Mike Cress, *General Mgr*
EMP: 100
SQ FT: 20,000 **Publicly Held**
WEB: www.americangolf.com
SIC: 7997 Golf club, membership
HQ: American Golf Corporation
909 N Pacific Coast Hwy
El Segundo CA 90245
310 664-4000

(P-18367)
AMERICAN GOLF CORPORATION
Also Called: Diamond Bar Golf Course
22751 Golden Springs Dr, Diamond Bar (91765-2218)
PHONE..................................909 861-5757
Andy Melnyk, *Manager*

EMP: 70 **Publicly Held**
WEB: www.americangolf.com
SIC: 7997 7992 Golf club, membership;
  public golf courses
HQ: American Golf Corporation
  909 N Pacific Coast Hwy
  El Segundo CA 90245
  310 664-4000

(P-18368)
AMERICAN GOLF CORPORATION
Also Called: Oakhurst Country Club
1001 Peacock Creek Dr, Clayton
(94517-2201)
PHONE............................925 672-9737
Craig Wong, *General Mgr*
EMP: 100 **Publicly Held**
WEB: www.americangolf.com
SIC: 7997 Golf club, membership
HQ: American Golf Corporation
  909 N Pacific Coast Hwy
  El Segundo CA 90245
  310 664-4000

(P-18369)
AMERICAN GOLF CORPORATION
Also Called: Summitpointe Golf Club
1500 Country Club Dr, Milpitas
(95035-3456)
PHONE............................408 262-8813
Lance Fong, *General Mgr*
EMP: 50 **Publicly Held**
WEB: www.americangolf.com
SIC: 7997 Golf club, membership
HQ: American Golf Corporation
  909 N Pacific Coast Hwy
  El Segundo CA 90245
  310 664-4000

(P-18370)
AMERICAN GOLF CORPORATION
Also Called: El Camino Country Club
3202 Vista Way, Oceanside (92056-3607)
PHONE............................760 757-2100
Ted Axe, *Manager*
EMP: 75 **Publicly Held**
WEB: www.americangolf.com
SIC: 7997 Golf club, membership
HQ: American Golf Corporation
  909 N Pacific Coast Hwy
  El Segundo CA 90245
  310 664-4000

(P-18371)
AMERICAN GOLF CORPORATION
Also Called: Los Verdes Golf Course
7000 Los Verdes Dr Ste 1, Rancho Palos
Verdes (90275-5600)
PHONE............................310 377-7370
Mike Shank, *Branch Mgr*
EMP: 55 **Publicly Held**
WEB: www.americangolf.com
SIC: 7997 Golf club, membership
HQ: American Golf Corporation
  909 N Pacific Coast Hwy
  El Segundo CA 90245
  310 664-4000

(P-18372)
AMERICAN GOLF CORPORATION
16782 Graham St, Huntington Beach
(92649-3754)
PHONE............................714 846-1364
Brent Boznanski, *Manager*
EMP: 55 **Publicly Held**
WEB: www.americangolf.com
SIC: 7997 Golf club, membership
HQ: American Golf Corporation
  909 N Pacific Coast Hwy
  El Segundo CA 90245
  310 664-4000

(P-18373)
AMERICAN GOLF CORPORATION
Also Called: Seascape Golf Club
610 Clubhouse Dr Rear, Aptos
(95003-4868)
PHONE............................831 688-3213
Steve Argo, *Manager*

EMP: 60 **Publicly Held**
WEB: www.americangolf.com
SIC: 7997 5941 5812 Golf club, membership; golf goods & equipment; eating
  places
HQ: American Golf Corporation
  909 N Pacific Coast Hwy
  El Segundo CA 90245
  310 664-4000

(P-18374)
AMERICAN GOLF CORPORATION
Also Called: Monterey Country Club
41500 Monterey Ave, Palm Desert
(92260-2173)
PHONE............................760 568-9311
Rod Winger, *Manager*
John Kulow, *General Mgr*
EMP: 50 **Publicly Held**
WEB: www.americangolf.com
SIC: 7997 Golf club, membership
HQ: American Golf Corporation
  909 N Pacific Coast Hwy
  El Segundo CA 90245
  310 664-4000

(P-18375)
AMERICAN GOLF CORPORATION
Also Called: La Mirada Country Club
15501 Alicante Rd, La Mirada
(90638-3112)
PHONE............................562 943-7123
Dill Crawford, *Manager*
EMP: 65 **Publicly Held**
WEB: www.americangolf.com
SIC: 7997 Golf club, membership
HQ: American Golf Corporation
  909 N Pacific Coast Hwy
  El Segundo CA 90245
  310 664-4000

(P-18376)
AMERICAN GOLF CORPORATION
Also Called: Simi Hills Golf Course
5031 Alamo St, Simi Valley (93063-1949)
PHONE............................805 522-0803
Brian Reed, *Branch Mgr*
Jackie Cochran, *Director*
EMP: 50 **Publicly Held**
WEB: www.americangolf.com
SIC: 7997 5941 7992 Golf club, member-
  ship; golf goods & equipment; public golf
  courses
HQ: American Golf Corporation
  909 N Pacific Coast Hwy
  El Segundo CA 90245
  310 664-4000

(P-18377)
ANNANDALE GOLF CLUB
1 N San Rafael Ave, Pasadena
(91105-1299)
PHONE............................626 796-6125
Christoff Granger, *General Mgr*
Toni Crockett, *Admin Sec*
Tom Lease, *Controller*
Charie Laugham, *Director*
Rene Morales, *Manager*
EMP: 125
SQ FT: 10,000
SALES: 11.8MM **Privately Held**
WEB: www.annandalegolf.com
SIC: 7997 Golf club, membership

(P-18378)
ANTELOPE VALLEY COUNTRY CLUB
39800 Country Club Dr, Palmdale
(93551-2970)
PHONE............................661 947-3142
Mark Range, *General Mgr*
EMP: 150
SQ FT: 22,000
SALES (est): 3.1MM **Privately Held**
WEB: www.palmdalegolf.com
SIC: 7997 Country club, membership

(P-18379)
ANTIOCH ROTARY CLUB
324 G St, Antioch (94509-1255)
P.O. Box 692 (94509-0069)
PHONE............................925 757-1800

EMP: 50 EST: 2010
SALES (est): 1.7MM **Privately Held**
SIC: 7997

(P-18380)
APPLE VALLEY GOLF CLUB
Also Called: Apple Valley Golf Course
15200 Rancherias Rd, Apple Valley
(92307-5201)
PHONE............................760 242-3653
Ned R Curtis, *CEO*
Todd Edwards, *Principal*
Gregg Campbell, *Office Mgr*
EMP: 170
SQ FT: 21,471
SALES (est): 4.7MM **Privately Held**
WEB: www.applevalleycountryclub.net
SIC: 7997 Country club, membership

(P-18381)
ARDEN HILLS COUNTRY CLUB INC
1220 Arden Hills Ln, Sacramento
(95864-5378)
PHONE............................916 482-6111
Jeralyn Favero, *President*
Brett Favero, *Admin Sec*
Minnetta McAdams, *Controller*
Paige Ricci,
Alex Anders, *Director*
EMP: 70
SALES (est): 5.9MM **Privately Held**
WEB: www.ardenhills.net
SIC: 7997 Country club, membership

(P-18382)
ASSOCIATED KOI CLUBS AMERICA
P.O. Box 10879, Costa Mesa (92627-0272)
PHONE............................949 650-5225
Robert Finnegan, *Chairman*
EMP: 75
SALES (est): 34.1K **Privately Held**
SIC: 7997 Membership sports & recreation
  clubs

(P-18383)
ATSUGI KOKUSAI KANKO USA INC
28095 John F Kennedy Dr, Moreno Valley
(92555-6301)
PHONE............................951 924-4444
Hideo Komuro, *President*
EMP: 55
SQ FT: 21,000
SALES (est): 807.3K **Privately Held**
WEB: www.hawaiikaigolf.com
SIC: 7997 5812 Membership sports &
  recreation clubs; eating places
HQ: Atsugi Kokusai Kanko Co., Ltd.
  1920, Shimoogino
  Atsugi KNG 243-0

(P-18384)
BAKERSFIELD COUNTRY CLUB
4200 Country Club Dr, Bakersfield
(93306-3700)
P.O. Box 6007 (93386-6007)
PHONE............................661 871-4000
Jon Van Boening, *President*
Jack N Zimmerman, *General Mgr*
Christy Solari, *Controller*
Eric Kuhn, *Manager*
EMP: 75
SQ FT: 30,000
SALES: 5.5MM **Privately Held**
WEB: www.bakersfieldcountryclub.com
SIC: 7997 5812 5813 Country club, mem-
  bership; eating places; bar (drinking
  places)

(P-18385)
BALBOA BAY CLUB INC (HQ)
1221 W Coast Hwy Ste 145, Newport
Beach (92663-5092)
PHONE............................949 645-5000
David Wooten, *President*
W D Ray, *CEO*
EMP: 275
SALES (est): 17MM
SALES (corp-wide): 30.2MM **Privately Held**
SIC: 7997 7011 Country club, member-
  ship; resort hotel

PA: International Bay Clubs, Llc
  1221 W Coast Hwy Ste 145
  Newport Beach CA 92663
  949 645-5000

(P-18386)
BALBOA YACHT CLUB
1801 Bayside Dr, Corona Del Mar
(92625-1898)
PHONE............................949 673-3515
Howard Ness, *President*
Erick Flores, *Manager*
EMP: 50 EST: 1924
SQ FT: 23,000
SALES: 6.7MM **Privately Held**
WEB: www.balboayachtclub.com
SIC: 7997 Yacht club, membership

(P-18387)
BAY CLUB GOLDEN GATEWAY LLC
Also Called: Bay Club Golden Gateway Inc
370 Drumm St, San Francisco
(94111-2010)
PHONE............................415 616-8800
Broc Stevens, *General Mgr*
Rachel Ruperto, *President*
David Smith, *Admin Sec*
EMP: 50
SQ FT: 8,000
SALES (est): 1.8MM
SALES (corp-wide): 46.3MM **Privately Held**
WEB: www.ggtsc.com
SIC: 7997 7999 7991 Tennis club, mem-
  bership; swimming club, membership;
  swimming instruction; health club
PA: Bay Club Holdings Iii, Llc
  1 Lombard St Lbby
  San Francisco CA 94111
  415 781-1874

(P-18388)
BAY CLUBS INC
Also Called: Bay Club Marin
220 Corte Madera Town Ctr, Corte Madera
(94925-1208)
PHONE............................415 945-3000
Maegan Devlin, *Manager*
EMP: 68
SALES (corp-wide): 202.6MM **Privately Held**
WEB: www.pacclub.com
SIC: 7997 Membership sports & recreation
  clubs
HQ: The Bay Clubs Company Llc
  1 Lombard St
  San Francisco CA 94111
  415 781-1874

(P-18389)
BAY CLUBS INC
Also Called: Racquetball World
22235 Sherman Way, Canoga Park
(91303-1058)
PHONE............................818 884-5034
Harold Wright, *Branch Mgr*
EMP: 80
SQ FT: 85,294
SALES (corp-wide): 202.6MM **Privately Held**
SIC: 7997 7299 7991 Racquetball club,
  membership; personal appearance serv-
  ices; physical fitness facilities
HQ: The Bay Clubs Company Llc
  1 Lombard St
  San Francisco CA 94111
  415 781-1874

(P-18390)
BEACH CLUB
201 Palisades Beach Rd, Santa Monica
(90402-1401)
PHONE............................310 395-3254
Gregg Patterson, *Exec Dir*
Tania Trombetta, *Director*
EMP: 60 EST: 1923
SQ FT: 35,000
SALES: 7.6MM **Privately Held**
WEB: www.beachclub.org
SIC: 7997 5812 5813 Beach club, mem-
  bership; eating places; bar (drinking
  places)

P R O D U C T S & S V C S

(P-18391)
BEAR CREEK GOLF CLUB INC
Also Called: Bear Creek Golf & Country Club
22640 Bear Creek Dr N, Murrieta
(92562-3015)
PHONE......................951 677-8621
Peter Hanson, *General Mgr*
Rich Gillete, *President*
EMP: 85
SQ FT: 28,000
SALES: 2.9MM **Privately Held**
WEB: www.bearcreekgc.com
SIC: 7997 7992 Golf club, membership;
public golf courses

(P-18392)
BEAR CREEK PARTNERS LLC
22640 Bear Creek Dr N, Murrieta
(92562-3015)
PHONE......................951 677-8621
Richard H Gillette, *Mng Member*
Gary Mineo, *Controller*
EMP: 65
SALES (est): 2.5MM **Privately Held**
SIC: 7997 Golf club, membership

(P-18393)
BEL-AIR BAY CLUB LTD
16801 Pacific Coast Hwy, Pacific Palisades
(90272-3399)
PHONE......................310 230-4700
William Howard, *CEO*
Shannon Griffin, *Executive*
Teresa Kuo, *Accountant*
Charlotte Farrens, *Controller*
Christopher Glaneman, *Purch Mgr*
EMP: 200
SQ FT: 7,500
SALES (est): 10.9MM **Privately Held**
WEB: www.belairbayclub.com
SIC: 7997 Membership sports & recreation
clubs

(P-18394)
BEL-AIR COUNTRY CLUB
10768 Bellagio Rd, Los Angeles
(90077-3799)
PHONE......................310 472-9563
Joseph Wagner, *General Mgr*
Peter Best, *CEO*
Daryn Wood, *Controller*
Karen Decker, *Human Res Mgr*
Martha Gamez, *Purch Dir*
EMP: 140
SQ FT: 10,000
SALES: 13.9MM **Privately Held**
WEB: www.bel-aircc.com
SIC: 7997 5941 Country club, member-
ship; golf goods & equipment

(P-18395)
BELMONT ATHLETIC CLUB
4918 E 2nd St, Long Beach (90803-5318)
PHONE......................562 438-3816
John Doyle, *Partner*
Bill Fraser, *Ltd Ptnr*
Patrick Gormley, *Ltd Ptnr*
Barry Miller, *Ltd Ptnr*
Joyce Pokstaff, *Ltd Ptnr*
EMP: 65 EST: 1980
SQ FT: 25,000
SALES (est): 2.9MM **Privately Held**
WEB: www.belmontathleticclub.com
SIC: 7997 7991 Racquetball club, mem-
bership; athletic club & gymnasiums,
membership

(P-18396)
BERKELEY COUNTRY CLUB
7901 Cutting Blvd, El Cerrito (94530-1877)
P.O. Box 2636 (94530-5636)
PHONE......................510 233-7550
Richard Pettler, *President*
Ken Kipp, *Treasurer*
Charles Ibbotson, *Vice Pres*
Bob Langbein, *Admin Sec*
EMP: 60
SQ FT: 12,000
SALES (est): 4MM **Privately Held**
SIC: 7997 Country club, membership

(P-18397)
BERMUDA DUNES COUNTRY CLUB
42765 Adams St, Bermuda Dunes
(92203-7937)
PHONE......................760 360-2481
Ed Cooney, *CEO*
Steve Hubbard, *President*
Perry Dickey, *COO*
George Neidhardt, *Treasurer*
Leon Webrand, *Vice Pres*
EMP: 50
SQ FT: 40,000
SALES: 4.3MM **Privately Held**
WEB: www.bermudadunescc.com
SIC: 7997 Country club, membership

(P-18398)
BIG CANYON COUNTRY CLUB
1 Big Canyon Dr, Newport Beach
(92660-5299)
PHONE......................949 644-5404
Donald Tippett, *CEO*
William Stamply, *President*
Lisa Curlee, *Comms Mgr*
Lisa Daley, *Comms Mgr*
Gloria Bridges, *Human Res Dir*
EMP: 180
SQ FT: 50,000
SALES: 20.4MM **Privately Held**
WEB: www.bigcanyoncc.org
SIC: 7997 Country club, membership

(P-18399)
BIG LGUE DREAMS CONSULTING LLC
20155 Viking Way, Redding (96003-8293)
PHONE......................530 223-1177
Brandi Merkel, *Principal*
EMP: 109
SALES (corp-wide): 45.7MM **Privately Held**
SIC: 7997 Outdoor field clubs
PA: Big League Dreams Consulting, Llc
16333 Fairfield Ranch Rd
Chino Hills CA 91709
909 287-1700

(P-18400)
BIGHORN GOLF CLUB
255 Palowet Dr, Palm Desert (92260-7311)
PHONE......................760 773-2468
Carl T Cardinalli, *President*
Joe Curtis, *Treasurer*
Greg Proper, *Executive*
Mike Groat, *Project Mgr*
Urrutia Gabriella, *Graphic Designe*
EMP: 190
SALES (est): 16.9MM **Privately Held**
SIC: 7997 7992 Country club, member-
ship; public golf courses

(P-18401)
BIRNAM WOOD GOLF CLUB (PA)
1941 E Valley Rd, Santa Barbara
(93108-1427)
PHONE......................805 969-2223
Robert Thornburgh, *President*
Michael-Mc Gardner, *COO*
Robert Trent Jones, *Principal*
Marcus McMillian, *Human Resources*
Marty Moore, *Superintendent*
EMP: 89
SQ FT: 45,000
SALES (est): 8.9MM **Privately Held**
WEB: www.birnamwoodgolfclub.com
SIC: 7997 7992 5812 Golf club, member-
ship; public golf courses; eating places

(P-18402)
BLACKHAWK COUNTRY CLUB
599 Blackhawk Club Dr, Danville
(94506-4522)
PHONE......................925 736-6500
Michael G Burton, *CEO*
Larry Marx, *President*
Kevin Dunne, *COO*
Erin McDermott, *Director*
Linda Cecchini, *Supervisor*
EMP: 230
SQ FT: 35,743

SALES: 17.2MM **Privately Held**
WEB: www.blackhawkcc.org
SIC: 7997 7992 5812 Golf club, membership; tennis club, membership; public golf
courses; eating places

(P-18403)
BOYS & GIRLS CLB OF PENINSULA
401 Pierce Rd, Menlo Park (94025-1240)
PHONE......................650 322-6255
Peter Fortenbaugh, *Director*
Erin Brannan, *Vice Pres*
Jay Deshetler, *Info Tech Mgr*
Cindy McIntyre, *Finance Dir*
Lauren Labrecque-Jesse, *Recruiter*
EMP: 60 EST: 1975
SQ FT: 2,000
SALES: 14.1MM **Privately Held**
SIC: 7997 Membership sports & recreation
clubs

(P-18404)
BOYS AND GIRLS CLUB
22450 Mulholland Hwy, Calabasas
(91302-5180)
PHONE......................818 225-8406
Natalie Gonzales, *Director*
EMP: 50
SALES (est): 86K **Privately Held**
SIC: 7997 Membership sports & recreation
clubs

(P-18405)
BRAEMAR COUNTRY CLUB INC
4001 Reseda Blvd, Tarzana (91356-5330)
P.O. Box 570217 (91357-0217)
PHONE......................323 873-6880
Steven Held, *Manager*
EMP: 199
SQ FT: 20,000
SALES (est): 8.7MM
SALES (corp-wide): 841.1MM **Privately Held**
WEB: www.braemarclub.com
SIC: 7997 Country club, membership
HQ: Clubcorp Usa, Inc.
3030 Lyndon B Johnson Fwy
Dallas TX 75234
972 243-6191

(P-18406)
BRENTWOOD COUNTRY CLUB
590 S Burlingame Ave, Los Angeles
(90049-4896)
PHONE......................310 451-8011
Linda Briskman, *President*
Allison Kalma, *Executive Asst*
Rosemary Bryan, *Director*
Robert Nagelberg, *Director*
David Smith, *Director*
EMP: 120
SALES: 17.1MM **Privately Held**
SIC: 7997 7999 Country club, member-
ship; golf services & professionals

(P-18407)
BRIDGES AT GALE RANCH LLC
Also Called: Bridges Golf Club, The
9000 S Gale Ridge Rd, San Ramon
(94582-9174)
PHONE......................925 735-4253
Joey Pickavance, *Manager*
Sandy Tijero, *Director*
EMP: 90
SALES (est): 4.9MM **Privately Held**
WEB: www.thebridgesgolf.com
SIC: 7997 Golf club, membership

(P-18408)
BROOKSIDE COUNTRY CLUB
3603 Saint Andrews Dr, Stockton
(95219-1868)
PHONE......................209 956-6200
Barney Kramer, *CEO*
New England Life, *Partner*
EMP: 70
SQ FT: 5,000
SALES: 3.2MM **Privately Held**
WEB: www.brooksidegolf.net
SIC: 7997 7999 5941 5812 Country club,
membership; swimming club, member-
ship; tennis club, membership; golf driving
range; golf goods & equipment; eating
places

(P-18409)
BURLINGAME COUNTRY CLUB
80 New Place Rd, Hillsborough
(94010-6499)
PHONE......................650 696-8100
Ralston P Roberts, *CEO*
EMP: 70 EST: 1893
SALES: 8.2MM **Privately Held**
WEB: www.burlingamecc.org
SIC: 7997 Country club, membership

(P-18410)
BUSINESS AND SUPPORT SERVICES
P.O. Box 6001 (92278-6001)
PHONE......................760 830-6873
EMP: 70 **Publicly Held**
SIC: 7997 Membership sports & recreation
clubs
HQ: Business And Support Services
3044 Catlin Ave
Quantico VA 22134
703 432-0109

(P-18411)
CALABASAS COUNTRY CLUB
4515 Park Entrada, Calabasas
(91302-1469)
PHONE......................818 222-8111
Robert W Linn, *Principal*
EMP: 74
SALES (est): 469.8K
SALES (corp-wide): 8.1MM **Privately Held**
SIC: 7997 Country club, membership
PA: Knight-Calabasas Llc
4515 Park Entrada
Calabasas CA 91302
818 222-3200

(P-18412)
CALIFORNIA COUNTRY CLUB
Also Called: S R Mutual Funds
1509 Workman Mill Rd, City of Industry
(90601-1499)
PHONE......................626 333-4571
Will Bayer, *General Mgr*
Duk He Choduplicate, *CFO*
ARA Cho, *Executive*
Helen Bates, *Administration*
Ted Parker, *Director*
EMP: 60 EST: 1956
SALES (est): 4.9MM **Privately Held**
WEB: www.golfccc.com
SIC: 7997 Country club, membership

(P-18413)
CALIFORNIA MOTORCYCLE CLUB
742 45th Ave, Oakland (94601-4429)
PHONE......................510 534-6222
Mark Norris, *Exec Dir*
Larry Steward, *Principal*
EMP: 75
SQ FT: 2,232
SALES: 88.2K **Privately Held**
WEB: www.oaklandmc.org
SIC: 7997 Membership sports & recreation
clubs

(P-18414)
CALIFRNIA GOLF CLB SAN FRNCSCO
844 W Orange Ave, South San Francisco
(94080-3125)
PHONE......................650 588-9021
Jon McGovern, *CEO*
Junaid Sheikh, *Treasurer*
Henry Bullock, *Vice Pres*
Gregory Spencer, *Exec Dir*
Steven Ruwe, *Admin Sec*
EMP: 74
SQ FT: 30,000
SALES: 7.9MM **Privately Held**
SIC: 7997 Country club, membership

(P-18415)
CAMERON PARK COUNTRY CLUB INC
3201 Royal Dr, Cameron Park
(95682-8559)
PHONE......................530 672-9840
J Poindexter, *Manager*
Jack Mehl, *President*
Mark Carson, *CEO*

Don Seese, *CFO*
Joe William, *Vice Pres*
EMP: 60
SQ FT: 50,000
SALES: 3.8MM **Privately Held**
WEB: www.cameronparkcc.com
SIC: 7997 Country club, membership

(P-18416)
CANYON CREST COUNTRY CLUB INC
Also Called: Golf Pro Shop
975 Country Club Dr, Riverside
(92506-3699)
PHONE................................951 274-7900
Robert H Dedman, *Ch of Bd*
James Maser, *Officer*
Frank Gore, *Exec VP*
Richard S Poole, *Exec VP*
Sidney Simmons, *Exec VP*
EMP: 85
SQ FT: 4,000
SALES (est): 3.8MM
SALES (corp-wide): 841.1MM **Privately Held**
WEB: www.canyoncrestcc.com
SIC: 7997 5812 5813 Golf club, membership; American restaurant; bar (drinking places)
HQ: Clubcorp Usa, Inc.
   3030 Lyndon B Johnson Fwy
   Dallas TX 75234
   972 243-6191

(P-18417)
CASTLEWOOD COUNTRY CLUB
707 Country Club Cir, Pleasanton
(94566-9743)
PHONE................................925 846-2871
Jerry Olson, *CEO*
Rick Hankins, *President*
Jerry Olson, *CEO*
Tom Rutherford, *General Mgr*
Amber Lindsey, *IT/INT Sup*
EMP: 167 **EST:** 1954
SQ FT: 55,000
SALES: 12.2MM **Privately Held**
WEB: www.castlewoodcc.org
SIC: 7997 Country club, membership

(P-18418)
CATTA VERDERA COUNTRY CLUB
1111 Catta Verdera, Lincoln (95648-9649)
PHONE................................916 645-7200
Deke Kastner, *Manager*
EMP: 90
SQ FT: 196,020
SALES (est): 3.5MM **Privately Held**
SIC: 7997 Golf club, membership; country club, membership

(P-18419)
CHAPMAN GOLF DEVELOPMENT LLC
Also Called: TRADITION GOLF CLUB
78505 Avenue 52, La Quinta (92253-2802)
PHONE................................760 564-8723
David Chapman, *General Mgr*
Risk Heidi, *COO*
Victoria Khaligov, *CFO*
Julie Harris,
Donna Long,
EMP: 100
SALES: 10.6MM **Privately Held**
SIC: 7997 Country club, membership

(P-18420)
CHARDONNAY/ CLUB SHAKESPEARE
Also Called: Chardonnay Golf Club
2555 Jamieson Canyon Rd, NAPA (94558)
PHONE................................707 257-1900
Jack Barry, *President*
EMP: 100
SQ FT: 24,000
SALES (est): 3.3MM **Privately Held**
WEB: www.chardonnaygolfclub.com
SIC: 7997 Golf club, membership

(P-18421)
CITIZENS DEVELOPMENT CORP (PA)
Also Called: Lake San Marcos Resort
1105 La Bonita Dr, San Marcos
(92078-5296)
PHONE................................760 744-0120
Ronald N Frazar, *President*
EMP: 59
SALES (est): 3.4MM **Privately Held**
SIC: 7997 Country club, membership

(P-18422)
CITY CLUB LLC
Also Called: City Club of San Francisco
155 Sansome St Fl 9, San Francisco
(94104-3687)
PHONE................................415 362-2480
Martin Brown, *Owner*
Brian Reed, *President*
EMP: 65
SQ FT: 25,000
SALES (est): 3.6MM **Privately Held**
WEB: www.cityclubsf.com
SIC: 7997 8641 5812 Membership sports & recreation clubs; civic social & fraternal associations; caterers

(P-18423)
CLAREMONT COUNTRY CLUB
5295 Broadway Ter, Oakland (94618-1498)
PHONE................................510 653-6789
Harold Peter Smith, *CEO*
Warren Chip Brown, *President*
Richard W Kraber, *Treasurer*
Thomas C Crosby, *Vice Pres*
Alec Churchward, *General Mgr*
EMP: 85 **EST:** 1903
SQ FT: 479,160
SALES: 11.4MM **Privately Held**
WEB: www.claremontcountryclub.org
SIC: 7997 Country club, membership

(P-18424)
CLAREMONT TENNIS CLUB
Also Called: Claremont Club, The
1777 Monte Vista Ave, Claremont
(91711-2916)
PHONE................................909 625-9515
Michael G Alpert, *President*
Philip Pandy, *CFO*
Geoffrey Clark, *Vice Pres*
Antoinette Mara, *Instructor*
Cathleen Garner, *Director*
EMP: 200
SQ FT: 40,000
SALES (est): 11.2MM **Privately Held**
SIC: 7997 7991 5812 Membership sports & recreation clubs; health club; eating places

(P-18425)
CLUB AT SHNNDOAH SPRNG VLG INC
32700 Desert Moon Dr, Thousand Palms
(92276-3713)
PHONE................................760 343-3497
Ronald Safren, *President*
Gary Safren, *Treasurer*
Ronald Edwards, *Vice Pres*
Gary Copp, *Controller*
Lizela Rivera, *Assistant*
EMP: 50 **EST:** 2006
SALES: 3MM **Privately Held**
SIC: 7997 Country club, membership

(P-18426)
CLUB OF SUNRISE COUNTRY
71601 Country Club Dr, Rancho Mirage
(92270-3546)
PHONE................................760 328-6549
Bill Athan, *General Mgr*
EMP: 64
SQ FT: 15,000
SALES: 3.3MM **Privately Held**
SIC: 7997 5812 Country club, membership; American restaurant; golf, tennis & ski shops

(P-18427)
CLUB ONE AT PETALUMA
1201 Redwood Way, Petaluma
(94954-6533)
PHONE................................707 766-8080
Yalda Teranchi, *General Mgr*

EMP: 90
SALES (est): 775.7K **Privately Held**
SIC: 7997 Membership sports & recreation clubs

(P-18428)
CLUBCORP USA INC
5690 Cancha De Golf, Rancho Santa Fe
(92091-4408)
PHONE................................858 756-2471
Jim Macdonough, *General Mgr*
EMP: 180
SALES (corp-wide): 841.1MM **Privately Held**
WEB: www.remington-gc.com
SIC: 7997 Country club, membership
HQ: Clubcorp Usa, Inc.
   3030 Lyndon B Johnson Fwy
   Dallas TX 75234
   972 243-6191

(P-18429)
CONTRA COSTA COUNTRY CLUB
801 Golf Club Rd, Pleasant Hill
(94523-1101)
PHONE................................925 798-7135
Bill Wampler, *Manager*
EMP: 69
SQ FT: 20,000
SALES: 7.5MM **Privately Held**
SIC: 7997 5812 5813 Golf club, membership; American restaurant; drinking places

(P-18430)
COPPER RIVER COUNTRY CLUB LP (PA)
2140 E Clubhouse Dr, Fresno
(93730-7020)
P.O. Box 25850 (93729-5850)
PHONE................................559 434-5200
William R Tatham Sr, *Partner*
Michael F Tatham, *Partner*
William T Tatham Jr, *Partner*
Chris Huerta, *Administration*
Sherry Azevedo,
EMP: 62
SALES (est): 4.2MM **Privately Held**
SIC: 7997 Golf club, membership

(P-18431)
CORDEVALLE GOLF CLUB LLC
1 Cordevalle Club Dr, San Martin
(95046-9472)
PHONE................................408 695-4500
Earl Wilson,
EMP: 250 **EST:** 1999
SALES (est): 8.4MM
SALES (corp-wide): 3.1B **Privately Held**
WEB: www.cordevalle.com
SIC: 7997 Golf club, membership
PA: Discovery Land Company, Llc
   14605 N 73rd St
   Scottsdale AZ 85260
   480 624-5200

(P-18432)
CORRAL DE TIERRA COUNTRY CLUB
81 Corral De Tierra Rd, Salinas
(93908-9477)
PHONE................................831 484-1325
Mike Oprish, *President*
William Bennett, *Executive*
Dominic Guzzo, *General Mgr*
David Webb, *General Mgr*
Gayle Smith, *Controller*
EMP: 100 **EST:** 1959
SQ FT: 15,000
SALES: 7.7MM **Privately Held**
WEB: www.corraldetierracc.com
SIC: 7997 Country club, membership

(P-18433)
CORRAL DEL TIERRA
81 Corral De Tierra Rd, Salinas
(93908-9474)
PHONE................................831 372-6244
Dominic Guzzo, *Manager*
EMP: 70
SALES: 40.3K **Privately Held**
SIC: 7997 Golf club, membership

(P-18434)
COTO DE CAZA GOLF RACQUET CLB
Also Called: Coto De Caza Golf Racquet CLB
25291 Vista Del Verde, Trabuco Canyon
(92679-4900)
PHONE................................949 858-4100
John Rosenbluth, *General Mgr*
EMP: 160
SQ FT: 44,000
SALES (est): 7.6MM
SALES (corp-wide): 841.1MM **Privately Held**
WEB: www.remington-gc.com
SIC: 7997 7992 7991 5813 Racquetball club, membership; public golf courses; physical fitness facilities; drinking places; eating places
HQ: Clubcorp Usa, Inc.
   3030 Lyndon B Johnson Fwy
   Dallas TX 75234
   972 243-6191

(P-18435)
COURTSIDE TENNIS CLUB
Also Called: Courtside Club
14675 Winchester Blvd, Los Gatos
(95032-1890)
PHONE................................408 395-7111
James Hinckley, *President*
Jim Gerber, *President*
EMP: 90
SQ FT: 100,000
SALES (est): 3.4MM
SALES (corp-wide): 841.1MM **Privately Held**
WEB: www.courtsideclub.com
SIC: 7997 7991 5812 Tennis club, membership; physical fitness facilities; eating places
HQ: Clubcorp Usa, Inc.
   3030 Lyndon B Johnson Fwy
   Dallas TX 75234
   972 243-6191

(P-18436)
CROSBY NATIONAL GOLF CLUB LLC
17102 Bing Crosby Blvd, Rancho Santa Fe
(92067)
PHONE................................858 756-6310
Rhonda Hill, *Director*
Ron Cropley, *Principal*
EMP: 70
SALES (est): 4.8MM **Privately Held**
SIC: 7997 Golf club, membership

(P-18437)
CRYSTAL AIRE COUNTRY CLUB GOLF
Also Called: Crystalaire Country Club
15701 Boca Raton Ave, Llano
(93544-1211)
PHONE................................661 944-2112
Mike Carpenter, *President*
Jane Reason, *Treasurer*
Dick McDonald, *Vice Pres*
EMP: 50
SALES (est): 1.9MM **Privately Held**
WEB: www.crystalairecc.com
SIC: 7997 5812 Golf club, membership; American restaurant

(P-18438)
CRYSTAL SPRINGS GOLF PARTNERS
Also Called: Crystal Springs Golf Course
6650 Golf Course Dr, Burlingame
(94010-6543)
PHONE................................650 342-4188
Tom Issak, *President*
John Teleshek, *CFO*
Natalia Aldana, *Director*
EMP: 50
SALES (est): 3.9MM **Privately Held**
WEB: www.playcrystalsprings.com
SIC: 7997 Country club, membership

(P-18439)
CS-PLEASANTON LLC
Also Called: Clubsport of Pleasanton
7090 Johnson Dr, Pleasanton
(94588-3328)
PHONE................................925 463-2822
Steve Gilmour, *President*

EMP: 258
SALES (est): 494.6K
SALES (corp-wide): 68.8MM **Privately Held**
SIC: 7997 Membership sports & recreation clubs
PA: Leisure Sports, Inc.
 4670 Willow Rd Ste 100
 Pleasanton CA 94588
 925 600-1966

(P-18440)
DEL MAR COUNTRY CLUB INC
6001 Clubhouse Dr, Rancho Santa Fe (92067)
P.O. Box 9866 (92067-4866)
PHONE..................858 759-5500
Madeleine Pickens, *President*
EMP: 90
SQ FT: 18,000
SALES (est): 7.5MM **Privately Held**
WEB: www.delmarcountryclub.com
SIC: 7997 Golf club, membership; country club, membership

(P-18441)
DEL PASO COUNTRY CLUB
3333 Marconi Ave, Sacramento (95821-6293)
PHONE..................916 489-3681
Chris Shanks, *Controller*
Eric Hatzenbiler, *CEO*
EMP: 105
SALES: 7.6MM **Privately Held**
WEB: www.delpasocountryclub.com
SIC: 7997 5941 5812 Country club, membership; sporting goods & bicycle shops; eating places

(P-18442)
DEL RIO GOLF & COUNTRY CLUB
Also Called: BRIGHTON
801 Stewart Rd, Modesto (95356-9639)
PHONE..................209 341-2414
John Bellizzi, *Principal*
Duncan Reno, *Officer*
Jay Ward, *Admin Sec*
Emmy Paulos, *Controller*
Lisa Tessaro, *Sales Staff*
EMP: 112
SQ FT: 48,000
SALES: 7.7MM **Privately Held**
WEB: www.delriocountryclub.com
SIC: 7997 5941 Country club, membership; golf club, membership; tennis club, membership; sporting goods & bicycle shops

(P-18443)
DESERT FALLS COUNTRY CLUB INC
1111 Desert Falls Pkwy, Palm Desert (92211-1709)
PHONE..................760 340-5646
Tim Scogan, *President*
EMP: 90
SALES (est): 4.5MM
SALES (corp-wide): 841.1MM **Privately Held**
WEB: www.desert-falls.com
SIC: 7997 5812 7992 7299 Golf club, membership; eating places; public golf courses; banquet hall facilities
HQ: Clubcorp Usa, Inc.
 3030 Lyndon B Johnson Fwy
 Dallas TX 75234
 972 243-6191

(P-18444)
DESERT PRINCESS HOME
28555 Landau Blvd, Cathedral City (92234-3508)
PHONE..................760 322-1655
Lynn Gilliam, *President*
EMP: 50
SALES (est): 2.8MM **Privately Held**
WEB: www.desertprincess.com
SIC: 7997 Country club, membership

(P-18445)
DHCCNP
Also Called: DESERT HORIZONS COUNTRY CLUB
44900 Desert Horizons Dr, Indian Wells (92210-7401)
PHONE..................760 340-4646
Jurgen Gross, *Manager*
Damien Gallardo, *General Mgr*
Armida Trujillo, *Buyer*
Katie Meyer, *Assistant*
EMP: 86 EST: 1979
SQ FT: 30,000
SALES: 5MM **Privately Held**
WEB: www.deserthorizonscc.com
SIC: 7997 7992 5812 Country club, membership; public golf courses; eating places

(P-18446)
DIABLO COUNTRY CLUB
1700 Club House Rd, Diablo (94528)
P.O. Box 777 (94528-0777)
PHONE..................925 837-4221
EMP: 80
SQ FT: 52,000
SALES: 11MM **Privately Held**
WEB: www.diablocc.com
SIC: 7997 5812 5813 5941 Country club, membership; eating places; drinking places; sporting goods & bicycle shops

(P-18447)
DIABLO COUNTRY CLUB
Also Called: Golf Pro. Shop
1700 Clubhouse Rd, Diablo (94528)
PHONE..................925 837-4221
Larry Marx, *General Mgr*
Bob Bodman, *Director*
Jim Collins, *Director*
EMP: 50
SQ FT: 38,199
SALES (est): 1.2MM **Privately Held**
SIC: 7997 Country club, membership

(P-18448)
EAGLE RIDGE GOLF CNTRY CLB LLC
Also Called: Eagle Ridge Golf Club
2951 Club Dr, Gilroy (95020-3043)
PHONE..................408 846-4531
Mark Gurnow, *Mng Member*
EMP: 125
SALES (est): 3.9MM **Privately Held**
WEB: www.eagleridgegc.com
SIC: 7997 7992 5812 Country club, membership; public golf courses; eating places

(P-18449)
EAGLE VNES VNYRDS GOLF CLB LLC
580 S Kelly Rd, American Canyon (94503-5600)
P.O. Box 2398, NAPA (94558-0239)
PHONE..................707 257-4470
Tokutaro Umezawa,
Nobu Mizuhara, *Vice Pres*
David Koo, *Sales Staff*
Michael Stirling, *Director*
John Walsh, *Director*
EMP: 70
SALES (est): 3.7MM **Privately Held**
SIC: 7997 Golf club, membership

(P-18450)
EL CABALLERO COUNTRY CLUB
18300 Tarzana Dr, Tarzana (91356-4216)
PHONE..................818 654-3000
Bary West, *President*
Kristin Charness, *CFO*
Peter Jimenez, *CFO*
Gary Diamond, *Treasurer*
Lauren Manoff, *Sales Staff*
EMP: 125
SQ FT: 20,000
SALES: 11MM **Privately Held**
SIC: 7997 7992 5812 Country club, membership; public golf courses; eating places

(P-18451)
EL DORADO COUNTRY CLUB
46000 Fairway Dr, Indian Wells (92210-8631)
PHONE..................760 346-8081
Geoff Hasley, *President*

Mark Miller, *General Mgr*
Maria Cintron, *Human Resources*
Terry Beardsley, *Director*
Tawny Musashi, *Director*
EMP: 200
SQ FT: 50,000
SALES (est): 13MM **Privately Held**
WEB: www.eldoradocountryclub.com
SIC: 7997 5812 Golf club, membership; eating places

(P-18452)
EL MACERO COUNTRY CLUB INC
44571 Clubhouse Dr, El Macero (95618-1073)
PHONE..................530 753-3363
Steven Backman, *General Mgr*
Rusty Seymour, *General Mgr*
Heidi Arnold, *Director*
Keith Culley, *Director*
Kasey Robinson, *Director*
EMP: 60
SQ FT: 21,000
SALES: 3.8MM **Privately Held**
SIC: 7997 5941 5812 5813 Golf club, membership; golf goods & equipment; American restaurant; bar (drinking places)

(P-18453)
FAIRBANKS RANCH CNTRY CLB INC
15150 San Dieguito Rd, Rancho Santa Fe (92067)
P.O. Box 8586 (92067-8586)
PHONE..................858 259-8811
Mike Kendall, *CEO*
Brad Forrester, *President*
Robert Macier, *CEO*
Stan Kinsey, *Vice Pres*
EMP: 180
SQ FT: 35,000
SALES (est): 12.7MM **Privately Held**
WEB: www.fairbanksranch.com
SIC: 7997 Country club, membership

(P-18454)
FAMILY MRALE WLFARE RECREATION
Also Called: Fmwr
1317 Normandy Dr, Fort Irwin (92310)
P.O. Box 105094 (92310-5094)
PHONE..................760 380-3493
Marion Taylor, *CFO*
Tricia Berg, *Officer*
Sonia Bonet-Betancourt, *Director*
EMP: 99
SALES (est): 385.4K **Privately Held**
SIC: 7997 5812 8361 8351 Membership sports & recreation clubs; family restaurants; residential care for children; child day care services

(P-18455)
FOREST PARK CABANA CLUB
2911 Pruneridge Ave, Santa Clara (95051-5652)
P.O. Box 2151 (95055-2151)
PHONE..................408 244-1884
Jo Ann Frink, *President*
EMP: 50
SALES: 307.3K **Privately Held**
WEB: www.forestparkcabanaclub.com
SIC: 7997 Swimming club, membership

(P-18456)
FORT WASH GOLF & CNTRY CLB
Also Called: FORT, THE
10272 N Millbrook Ave, Fresno (93730-3400)
PHONE..................559 434-1702
Dean Pryor, *President*
Bruce Waltz, *President*
EMP: 95
SALES: 4.4MM **Privately Held**
SIC: 7997 5813 5812 Golf club, membership; cocktail lounge; American restaurant

(P-18457)
FRIENDLY HILLS COUNTRY CLUB
8500 Villaverde Dr, Whittier (90605-1398)
PHONE..................562 698-0331
Dave Goodrich, *COO*

Russ Onizuka, *COO*
Peter Phan, *Executive*
Raj Manni, *Finance*
Gail Heins, *Controller*
EMP: 110 EST: 1969
SQ FT: 42,000
SALES (est): 3.9MM **Privately Held**
WEB: www.friendlyhillscc.com
SIC: 7997 Country club, membership

(P-18458)
FRIENDLY VALLEY RECRTL ASSN
Also Called: FRIENDLY VILLAGE COMMUNITY ASS
19345 Avenue Of The Oaks, Santa Clarita (91321-1406)
PHONE..................661 252-3223
Debbie Makaryk, *Manager*
Ruth Gauthier, *President*
EMP: 50
SQ FT: 1,500
SALES: 2.1MM **Privately Held**
SIC: 7997 Membership sports & recreation clubs

(P-18459)
GLENDORA COUNTRY CLUB
2400 Country Club Dr, Glendora (91741)
PHONE..................626 335-4051
Jack Stoughton, *CEO*
Mike Kerstetter, *President*
Jim Leahy, *CEO*
Bill McKinley, *Treasurer*
Arthur Barajas, *General Mgr*
EMP: 90
SQ FT: 10,000
SALES: 5.2MM **Privately Held**
SIC: 7997 5812 5813 Country club, membership; eating places; drinking places

(P-18460)
GLENROCK GROUP
Also Called: Golf Club At Boulder Ridge
1000 Old Quarry Rd, San Jose (95123-2454)
PHONE..................408 323-9900
Glenda Garcia, *Vice Pres*
Rocke Garcia, *President*
EMP: 75
SALES (est): 988.3K **Privately Held**
SIC: 7997 Membership sports & recreation clubs

(P-18461)
GOLF INVESTMENT LLC (PA)
200 Avenida La Pata, San Clemente (92673-6301)
PHONE..................949 498-6604
Shahin Vosough,
EMP: 100
SQ FT: 42,250
SALES (est): 2.7MM **Privately Held**
WEB: www.golfinvestment.com
SIC: 7997 7992 Golf club, membership; public golf courses

(P-18462)
GRANITE BAY GOLF CLUB
9600 Golf Club Dr, Granite Bay (95746-6721)
PHONE..................916 791-5379
Bob Kunz, *General Mgr*
EMP: 120
SQ FT: 1,440
SALES (est): 5.4MM
SALES (corp-wide): 841.1MM **Privately Held**
WEB: www.granitebayclub.com
SIC: 7997 5812 7299 Golf club, membership; eating places; wedding chapel, privately operated
HQ: Clubcorp Usa, Inc.
 3030 Lyndon B Johnson Fwy
 Dallas TX 75234
 972 243-6191

(P-18463)
GREEN VALLEY COUNTRY CLUB
35 Country Club Dr, Fairfield (94534-1305)
PHONE..................707 864-1101
Tom Snell, *President*
EMP: 75

SALES: 5.9MM **Privately Held**
WEB: www.greenvalleycc.com
SIC: 7997 Country club, membership

(P-18464)
HACIENDA GOLF CLUB
718 East Rd, La Habra Heights
(90631-8155)
PHONE.................................562 694-1081
Frank Cordeiro, *General Mgr*
Daniel Arsenault, *Director*
Casey Wheeler, *Manager*
EMP: 95
SQ FT: 30,000
SALES: 5.8MM **Privately Held**
WEB: www.haciendagolfclub.com
SIC: 7997 5812 5813 Golf club, membership; American restaurant; bar (drinking places)

(P-18465)
HCC INVESTORS LLC
Also Called: Lennar
18550 Seven Bridges Rd, Rancho Santa Fe
(92091-0216)
P.O. Box 1322 (92067-1322)
PHONE.................................858 759-7200
Jon Jaffe,
Patty Aguirre, *Controller*
EMP: 120
SQ FT: 35,000
SALES (est) 3.5MM **Privately Held**
SIC: 7997 Golf club, membership

(P-18466)
HIDEAWAY CLUB
80440 Hideaway Club Ct, La Quinta
(92253-7867)
P.O. Box 1540 (92247-1540)
PHONE.................................760 777-7400
Brian J Ellis, *CEO*
EMP: 1795
SALES (est): 2.3MM
SALES (corp-wide): 3.1B **Privately Held**
SIC: 7997 6531 Membership sports & recreation clubs; real estate agents & managers
PA: Discovery Land Company, Llc
14605 N 73rd St
Scottsdale AZ 85260
480 624-5200

(P-18467)
HILLCREST COUNTRY CLUB
10000 W Pico Blvd, Los Angeles
(90064-3400)
PHONE.................................310 553-8911
John Jameson, *President*
John Goldsmith, *CEO*
Tom Driefus, *CFO*
Chester Firestien, *Principal*
Leonard Fisher, *Principal*
EMP: 180
SQ FT: 69,081
SALES: 22.1MM **Privately Held**
WEB: www.hcc-la.com
SIC: 7997 Country club, membership

(P-18468)
INDIAN WELLS COUNTRY CLUB INC
Also Called: Iw Golf Club, Inc
46000 Club Dr, Indian Wells (92210-8870)
PHONE.................................760 345-2561
Gabe Codding, *General Mgr*
James Hinckley, *President*
Jack Lupton, *Treasurer*
Douglas Howe, *Exec VP*
Erin Dougherty, *General Mgr*
EMP: 60
SQ FT: 65,000
SALES (est): 4.5MM
SALES (corp-wide): 841.1MM **Privately Held**
WEB: www.remington-gc.com
SIC: 7997 Country club, membership
HQ: Clubcorp Usa, Inc.
3030 Lyndon B Johnson Fwy
Dallas TX 75234
972 243-6191

(P-18469)
INTERNATIONAL BAY CLUBS LLC (PA)
Also Called: Balboa Bay Club and Resort
1221 W Coast Hwy Ste 145, Newport Beach (92663-5037)
PHONE.................................949 645-5000
Todd M Pickup, *CEO*
David Wooten, *President*
Elizabeth Stefan, *Marketing Staff*
EMP: 500
SQ FT: 330,000
SALES (est): 30.2MM **Privately Held**
WEB: www.balboabayclub.com
SIC: 7997 4493 6552 7011 Country club, membership; swimming club, membership; beach club, membership; marinas; land subdividers & developers; residential; hotels & motels

(P-18470)
INTERVEC PHOENIX TRAVEL CLUB
1456 Seacoast Dr Unit 4a, Imperial Beach
(91932-3198)
PHONE.................................828 728-5287
Donna Weston, *President*
EMP: 130
SALES (est): 5.5MM **Privately Held**
SIC: 7997 Membership sports & recreation clubs

(P-18471)
JACK KRAMER CLUB
11 Montecillo Dr, Rllng HLS Est
(90274-4297)
PHONE.................................310 326-4404
Craig Purcell, *General Mgr*
Connie Spencer, *President*
Bruce Ostermann, *General Mgr*
EMP: 60
SQ FT: 4,000
SALES (est): 1.2MM **Privately Held**
WEB: www.jackkramerclub.com
SIC: 7997 5941 5812 7999 Tennis club, membership; swimming club, membership; tennis goods & equipment; snack bar; swimming instruction; aerobic dance & exercise classes

(P-18472)
JONATHAN CLUB
Also Called: Jonathan Beach Club
850 Palisades Beach Rd, Santa Monica
(90403-1008)
PHONE.................................310 393-9245
Ernie Dunn, *Manager*
Jeremy Samson, *Finance Mgr*
EMP: 150
SQ FT: 12,784
SALES (corp-wide): 39.4MM **Privately Held**
WEB: www.jc.org
SIC: 7997 5812 8641 Beach club, membership; grills (eating places); civic social & fraternal associations
PA: Jonathan Club
545 S Figueroa St
Los Angeles CA 90071
213 624-0881

(P-18473)
KNIGHT-CALABASAS LLC (PA)
Also Called: Calabasas Country Club
4515 Park Entrada, Calabasas
(91302-1453)
PHONE.................................818 222-3200
Mike Calabassas,
Robert W Linn, *General Mgr*
Pam Lydon, *Accounting Mgr*
Karen Seidman, *Controller*
EMP: 75
SQ FT: 2,000
SALES (est): 8.1MM **Privately Held**
SIC: 7997 Country club, membership

(P-18474)
KNIGHT-CALABASAS LLC
Also Called: Peacock Gap Golf & Country Clb
333 Biscayne Dr, San Rafael (94901-1577)
PHONE.................................415 453-4940
Bobby Yokito, *Partner*
Patrick Devin, *Opers Staff*
EMP: 60

SALES (est): 1.8MM
SALES (corp-wide): 8.1MM **Privately Held**
SIC: 7997 Golf club, membership
PA: Knight-Calabasas Llc
4515 Park Entrada
Calabasas CA 91302
818 222-3200

(P-18475)
LA CANADA FLINTRIDGE CNTRY CLB
5500 Godbey Dr, La Canada (91011-1836)
PHONE.................................818 790-0611
Gilbert Dreyfus, *President*
Shi Wang, *CFO*
Evelyn Dreyfus, *Admin Sec*
Victor Ortega, *Controller*
EMP: 80 EST: 1977
SQ FT: 24,000
SALES (est): 7MM **Privately Held**
SIC: 7997 Country club, membership

(P-18476)
LA CUMBRE COUNTRY CLUB
4015 Via Laguna, Santa Barbara
(93110-2298)
PHONE.................................805 687-2421
Brian Bahman, *General Mgr*
Chuck Pressley, *Facilities Mgr*
Karen Webb, *Director*
Wayne Mills, *Manager*
EMP: 100
SQ FT: 8,000
SALES: 7.9MM **Privately Held**
SIC: 7997 Golf club, membership; country club, membership

(P-18477)
LA JOLLA BCH & TENNIS CLB INC (PA)
Also Called: Marine Room Restaurant
2000 Spindrift Dr, La Jolla (92037-3237)
PHONE.................................858 454-7126
William J Kellogg, *CEO*
John Campbell, *COO*
Jeannie Porter, *CFO*
Rob Walsh, *Vice Pres*
Caitlin Boehrig, *Executive Asst*
▲ EMP: 165
SQ FT: 3,500
SALES (est): 28.2MM **Privately Held**
WEB: www.ljbtc.com
SIC: 7997 8742 Membership sports & recreation clubs; food & beverage consultant

(P-18478)
LA JOLLA COUNTRY CLUB INC
7301 High Ave, La Jolla (92037-5210)
PHONE.................................858 454-9601
Andrew Gorton, *General Mgr*
Mike Mooney, *General Mgr*
Jorge Dominguez, *Facilities Dir*
EMP: 122 EST: 1928
SQ FT: 39,000
SALES: 10.6MM **Privately Held**
WEB: www.lajollacc.com
SIC: 7997 5812 5941 5813 Golf club, membership; eating places; golf goods & equipment; bar (drinking places); public golf courses

(P-18479)
LA QUINTA COUNTRY CLUB
77750 Avenue 50, La Quinta (92253-2204)
PHONE.................................760 564-4151
Ernest Moore, *CFO*
Bruce Zahn, *COO*
Bradd Bennick, *Executive*
Teresa Windsor, *Controller*
Ricardo Prado, *Opers Staff*
EMP: 55
SQ FT: 36,000
SALES: 7MM **Privately Held**
SIC: 7997 Country club, membership

(P-18480)
LA RINCONADA COUNTRY CLUB INC (PA)
Also Called: LA RINCONADA GOLF AND COUNTRY
14595 Clearview Dr, Los Gatos
(95032-1799)
PHONE.................................408 395-4181

Steve Vindasius, *CEO*
Mac Niven, *General Mgr*
Tom Schunn, *General Mgr*
Janett Antle, *Admin Asst*
Rich Baloga, *Controller*
EMP: 78
SQ FT: 100,000
SALES: 10.9MM **Privately Held**
WEB: www.larinconadacc.com
SIC: 7997 5813 5812 Country club, membership; bar (drinking places); eating places

(P-18481)
LAACO LTD
Also Called: California Yacht Club
4469 Admiralty Way, Marina Del Rey
(90292-5415)
PHONE.................................310 823-4567
Steve Hathaway, *President*
Steve Bell, *Director*
Sallie Wolcott, *Director*
EMP: 100
SALES (corp-wide): 22.6MM **Privately Held**
SIC: 7997 4493 Yacht club, membership; marinas
PA: Laaco, Ltd.
431 W 7th St
Los Angeles CA 90014
213 622-1254

(P-18482)
LAGUNA WOODS GOLF CLUB
Also Called: Laguna Woods Village Golf Club
24122 Moulton Pkwy, Laguna Hills
(92637-2781)
PHONE.................................949 597-4336
Joel Walker, *Director*
Roger Teel, *Director*
▲ EMP: 50
SALES (est): 736.9K **Privately Held**
SIC: 7997 Golf club, membership

(P-18483)
LAHONTAN GOLF CLUB
12700 Lodgetrail Dr, Truckee (96161-5125)
PHONE.................................530 550-2400
Jon Madonna, *President*
Kelly Gold, *Branch Mgr*
Steve Harris, *Admin Sec*
Aimee Carlon, *Technical Staff*
Holly Porter, *Director*
EMP: 150 EST: 1996
SQ FT: 500,000
SALES (est): 10.3MM **Privately Held**
SIC: 7997 Golf club, membership

(P-18484)
LAKE MERCED GOLF & COUNTRY CLB
2300 Junipero Serra Blvd, Daly City
(94015-1630)
PHONE.................................650 755-2233
Dale Holub, *CEO*
Nick Bailey, *General Mgr*
EMP: 75
SQ FT: 38,000
SALES: 7MM **Privately Held**
WEB: www.lmgc.org
SIC: 7997 5813 Country club, membership; golf club, membership; tennis club, membership; bars & lounges

(P-18485)
LAKES COUNTRY CLUB ASSN INC (PA)
Also Called: Lakes Country Club, The
161 Old Ranch Rd, Palm Desert
(92211-3211)
PHONE.................................760 568-4321
Gerald Lee Hagood, *President*
Sandy Seddon, *COO*
Ron Phipps, *CFO*
Frank Melon, *Principal*
EMP: 300
SQ FT: 3,600
SALES (est): 14MM **Privately Held**
WEB: www.thelakescc.com
SIC: 7997 5941 5812 Country club, membership; sporting goods & bicycle shops; eating places

P R O D U C T S & S V C S

(PA)=Parent Co (HQ)=Headquarters (DH)=Div Headquarters
✪ = New Business established in last 2 years
2019 Directory of California Wholesalers and Services Companies
781

(P-18486)
LANCASTER JETHAWKS
45116 Valley Central Way, Lancaster
(93536-1508)
PHONE..................661 726-5400
Peter A Carfagna, *CEO*
Pete Carfagna, *President*
Brad Seymour, *President*
Derek Sharp, *General Mgr*
Mike Carfagna, *Controller*
EMP: 80
SALES (est): 2.7MM **Privately Held**
SIC: 7997 Baseball club, except professional & semi-professional

(P-18487)
LAS POSAS CLUB INC
230 Ramona Pl, Camarillo (93010-8406)
P.O. Box 3089 (93011-3089)
PHONE..................805 482-1811
Barbara Stevens, *President*
EMP: 75
SALES: 45.1K **Privately Held**
SIC: 7997 Country club, membership

(P-18488)
LAS POSAS COUNTRY CLUB
Also Called: Lpcc
955 Fairway Dr, Camarillo (93010-8499)
PHONE..................805 482-4518
Sandy McNolty, *Controller*
Charles Burns, *CEO*
Thomas Walling, *CEO*
Dan Meherin, *COO*
Alfonso Arechiga, *Executive*
EMP: 100
SALES: 5.1MM **Privately Held**
SIC: 7997 7992 5812 0781 Country club, membership; tennis club, membership; public golf courses; eating places; landscape counseling & planning

(P-18489)
LOCKEFORD SPRING GOLF COURSE (PA)
16360 N Highway 88, Lodi (95240-9706)
P.O. Box 1315, Lockeford (95237-1315)
PHONE..................209 333-6275
John De Nault, *President*
Gary Reiff, *General Mgr*
Letty Rocha, *Office Mgr*
Wade Isbell, *Manager*
EMP: 125
SQ FT: 2,778
SALES (est): 2.1MM **Privately Held**
WEB: www.lockefordsprings.com
SIC: 7997 7992 Golf club, membership; public golf courses

(P-18490)
LONE CYPRESS COMPANY LLC
Also Called: Beach & Tennis Club
1567 Cypress Dr, Pebble Beach (93953)
P.O. Box 1128 (93953-1128)
PHONE..................831 625-8507
Steve Hurst, *Branch Mgr*
EMP: 100
SALES (corp-wide): 378.4MM **Privately Held**
WEB: www.pebblebeach.com
SIC: 7997 7999 5812 7991 Beach club, membership; swimming club, membership; tennis services & professionals; caterers; physical fitness facilities
PA: Pebble Beach Resort Co Dba Lone Cypress Shop
2700 17 Mile Dr
Pebble Beach CA 93953
831 647-7500

(P-18491)
LONG BEACH YACHT CLUB
6201 E Appian Way, Long Beach
(90803-4199)
PHONE..................562 598-9401
Louis Izurieta, *General Mgr*
Matthew Williston, *Executive*
Louis Izurieta, *General Mgr*
Kim Eastwood, *Personnel Assit*
Andrea Hart,
EMP: 63
SQ FT: 25,000
SALES: 6.2MM **Privately Held**
WEB: www.lbyc.org
SIC: 7997 Yacht club, membership

(P-18492)
LOS ALTOS GOLF AND COUNTRY CLB
1560 Country Club Dr, Los Altos
(94024-5907)
PHONE..................650 947-3100
Bill Schneider, *President*
Yolanda Suess, *Human Resources*
Tracy Goodwin, *Director*
Jenna Su, *Director*
Monica Barclay, *Manager*
EMP: 70
SALES: 17.8MM **Privately Held**
WEB: www.lagcc.com
SIC: 7997 Country club, membership

(P-18493)
LOS AMIGOS COUNTRY CLUB INC
Also Called: Los Amigos Golf Course
7295 Quill Dr, Downey (90242-2001)
PHONE..................562 923-9696
Donald Duffin Sr, *President*
Tina Nunez, *Vice Pres*
Anne Hunter, *Admin Sec*
Yolanda Valencia, *Sales Associate*
Brenda Ueman, *Sales Staff*
EMP: 65
SALES (est): 3.9MM **Privately Held**
WEB: www.losamigoscountryclub.com
SIC: 7997 Golf club, membership

(P-18494)
LOS ANGELES COUNTRY CLUB
10101 Wilshire Blvd, Los Angeles
(90024-4703)
PHONE..................310 276-6104
Kirk O Reese, *Principal*
Alan Green, *Security Dir*
Michael Beam, *General Mgr*
James H Brewer, *General Mgr*
Patrick Volders, *Office Mgr*
EMP: 250 **EST:** 1898
SQ FT: 75,000
SALES: 17.6MM **Privately Held**
WEB: www.thelacc.org
SIC: 7997 Country club, membership; golf club, membership; tennis club, membership

(P-18495)
LOS ANGELES ORGANIZING
10900 Wilshire Blvd # 710, Los Angeles
(90024-6515)
PHONE..................310 407-0539
Casey Wasserman, *Chairman*
EMP: 50 **EST:** 2014
SALES: 17.7MM **Privately Held**
SIC: 7997 Membership sports & recreation clubs

(P-18496)
MARBELLA COUNTRY CLUB
30800 Golf Club Dr, San Juan Capistrano
(92675-5415)
PHONE..................949 248-3700
Dan Riker, *Manager*
Ted Clark, *Treasurer*
Jeffrey Krifle, *General Mgr*
Phil Kempler, *Admin Sec*
EMP: 140
SQ FT: 43,000
SALES (est): 6.8K **Privately Held**
WEB: www.marbellacc.net
SIC: 7997 Country club, membership
PA: National Golf Properties Llc
2951 28th St Ste 3000
Santa Monica CA 90405

(P-18497)
MARBELLA GOLF & COUNTRY CLUB
30800 Golf Club Dr, San Juan Capistrano
(92675-5415)
PHONE..................949 248-3700
Rod Hayden, *President*
Gary Lisenbee, *Treasurer*
David Neish, *Vice Pres*
Larry De Pope, *General Mgr*
Larry D Pope, *General Mgr*
EMP: 114
SQ FT: 43,000
SALES (est): 4MM **Privately Held**
SIC: 7997 Country club, membership

(P-18498)
MARIN COUNTRY CLUB INC
500 Country Club Dr, Novato (94949-5896)
PHONE..................415 382-6700
Ryan Wilson, *CEO*
Tiffany Hutchinson, *Admin Asst*
Linda Mortarotti, *Buyer*
Lou Ayers, *Food Svc Dir*
Kimberly Becker, *Director*
EMP: 75
SQ FT: 5,000
SALES: 8.6MM **Privately Held**
WEB: www.marincountryclub.com
SIC: 7997 5812 Country club, membership; golf club, membership; tennis club, membership; swimming club, membership; eating places

(P-18499)
MAYACAMA GOLF CLUB LLC
1240 Mayacama Club Dr, Santa Rosa
(95403-8251)
PHONE..................707 569-2900
Johnathan Wilhelm, *Managing Prtnr*
Jonathan Wilhelm, *Managing Prtnr*
Greg Brown, *General Mgr*
Jan Bowers, *Human Res Dir*
Tim Hoffmann, *Sales Executive*
EMP: 65
SQ FT: 5,000
SALES (est): 11.4MM **Privately Held**
SIC: 7997 Golf club, membership

(P-18500)
MEADOW CLUB
1001 Bolinas Rd, Fairfax (94930-2200)
P.O. Box 129 (94978-0129)
PHONE..................415 453-3274
John Grehan, *General Mgr*
Jack Grehan, *Executive*
Linda Coiner, *Human Resources*
Anita Law, *Manager*
Kevin Hauschel, *Superintendent*
EMP: 81
SQ FT: 3,000
SALES: 9.4MM **Privately Held**
WEB: www.meadowclub.com
SIC: 7997 Golf club, membership

(P-18501)
MENIFEE MANAGEMENT CORP
Also Called: Menifee Lakes Country Club
3200 E Guasti Rd Ste 100, Ontario
(91761-8661)
PHONE..................951 672-4824
Chiao-Tung Geroge Chang, *CEO*
EMP: 100
SALES (est): 4.7MM **Privately Held**
SIC: 7997 Country club, membership

(P-18502)
MENLO CIRCUS CLUB
190 Park Ln, Atherton (94027-4194)
PHONE..................650 322-4616
Steve De Laet, *CEO*
Nora B Stent, *President*
Matt Quinlan, *CFO*
Susie Frimel, *Admin Sec*
Stephen Gonzales, *Director*
EMP: 70 **EST:** 1923
SQ FT: 14,000
SALES: 9.7MM **Privately Held**
SIC: 7997 Country club, membership

(P-18503)
MENLO COUNTRY CLUB
2300 Woodside Rd, Woodside
(94062-1132)
P.O. Box 729, Redwood City (94064-0729)
PHONE..................650 369-2342
Chris Robinson, *General Mgr*
EMP: 50
SALES (est): 10.6MM **Privately Held**
SIC: 7997 Country club, membership

(P-18504)
MESA VERDE COUNTRY CLUB
3000 Club House Rd, Costa Mesa
(92626-3599)
PHONE..................714 549-0377
John Hayhoe, *CEO*
Robert Heflin, *President*
Patricia Smith, *Controller*
Kate Ball,
Diane Burnes, *Director*
EMP: 125

SQ FT: 34,000
SALES: 8.9MM **Privately Held**
WEB: www.mesaverdecc.com
SIC: 7997 Country club, membership

(P-18505)
METROPOLITAN CLUB
640 Sutter St, San Francisco (94102-1097)
PHONE..................415 673-0600
Clint Prescott, *General Mgr*
Kayne Maynard, *President*
Margaret Handelman, *Treasurer*
Gibbs Freeman, *General Mgr*
EMP: 65
SQ FT: 101,662
SALES: 5.6MM **Privately Held**
WEB: www.metropolitanclubsf.org
SIC: 7997 Membership sports & recreation clubs

(P-18506)
MID VLLEY RACQUETBALL ATHC CLB
Also Called: Mid-Valley Athletic Club
18420 Hart St, Reseda (91335-4317)
PHONE..................818 705-6500
Ray Haizlip, *President*
Harold Wright, *President*
Jeannie Henning, *Vice Pres*
Christina Hughes, *Admin Sec*
EMP: 120 **EST:** 1979
SQ FT: 75,000
SALES (est): 2.2MM **Privately Held**
SIC: 7997 7991 Racquetball club, membership; physical fitness facilities

(P-18507)
MISSION HILLS COUNTRY CLUB INC
34600 Mission Hills Dr, Rancho Mirage
(92270-1300)
PHONE..................760 324-9400
Josh Tanner, *General Mgr*
Doug Howe, *Exec VP*
EMP: 130
SQ FT: 75,000
SALES (est): 9.5MM
SALES (corp-wide): 841.1MM **Privately Held**
WEB: www.remington-gc.com
SIC: 7997 7992 5812 Country club, membership; public golf courses; eating places
HQ: Clubcorp Usa, Inc.
3030 Lyndon B Johnson Fwy
Dallas TX 75234
972 243-6191

(P-18508)
MISSION VIEJO COUNTRY CLUB
26200 Country Club Dr, Mission Viejo
(92691-5905)
PHONE..................949 582-1550
Michael Lance Kennedy, *Mng Member*
Veronica Alva Roman, *Accountant*
Scot Dey, *Superintendent*
EMP: 103
SALES: 6.2MM **Privately Held**
WEB: www.missionviejocc.com
SIC: 7997 7991 5812 7299 Country club, membership; physical fitness facilities; eating places; banquet hall facilities

(P-18509)
MODESTO COURT ROOM INC
2012 Mchenry Ave, Modesto (95350-3212)
PHONE..................209 577-1060
Lloyd Overholtzer, *President*
Sheri Walker, *Vice Pres*
EMP: 90
SQ FT: 43,000
SALES (est): 1.6MM **Privately Held**
WEB: www.modestocourtroom.net
SIC: 7997 5941 Swimming club, membership; racquetball club, membership; handball club, membership; sporting goods & bicycle shops

(P-18510)
MONTEREY PENINSULA COUNTRY CLB
Also Called: Mpcc
3000 Club Rd, Pebble Beach (93953-2542)
PHONE..................831 373-1556
Robert Perry Smith, *CEO*
Lisa Rasmussen, *Executive Asst*

Joan Lucido, *Accounting Mgr*
Brad Spencer, *Asst Controller*
Rick Busman, *Finance*
EMP: 130
SQ FT: 70,000
SALES: 23.6MM **Privately Held**
WEB: www.mpccpb.org
SIC: 7997 Country club, membership

(P-18511)
MORAGA CNTRY CLB HMOWNERS ASSN
1600 Saint Andrews Dr, Moraga (94556-1194)
PHONE....................925 376-2200
Frank Meln, *General Mgr*
Meghan Cullen, *Director*
EMP: 100 **EST:** 1973
SQ FT: 10,000
SALES (est): 6MM **Privately Held**
WEB: www.moragacc.com
SIC: 7997 Country club, membership

(P-18512)
NAPA GOLF ASSOCIATES LLC
Also Called: Chardonnay
2555 Jameson Canyon Rd, NAPA (94558)
P.O. Box 3779 (94558-0377)
PHONE....................707 257-1900
Kenneth E Laird,
Gus Gianulias,
Jim Gianulias,
EMP: 84
SQ FT: 24,000
SALES (est): 2.4MM
SALES (corp-wide): 841.1MM **Privately Held**
WEB: www.remington-gc.com
SIC: 7997 Golf club, membership
HQ: Clubcorp Usa, Inc.
3030 Lyndon B Johnson Fwy
Dallas TX 75234
972 243-6191

(P-18513)
NAPA VALLEY COUNTRY CLUB
3385 Hagen Rd, NAPA (94558-3849)
PHONE....................707 252-1111
Todd Jeffrey Meginness, *CEO*
Todd Meginness, *COO*
Jeorge Hise, *Treasurer*
Mike Wilson, *Vice Pres*
Patrick Smorra, *Admin Sec*
▲ **EMP:** 80 **EST:** 1923
SQ FT: 8,000
SALES: 6.4MM **Privately Held**
WEB: www.napavalleycc.com
SIC: 7997 5813 5812 Country club, membership; bar (drinking places); eating places

(P-18514)
NEW DISCOVERY INC
Also Called: Discovery Bay Ctry Club
1475 Clubhouse Dr, Byron (94505-9241)
PHONE....................925 783-6613
Mark Tissot, *Manager*
Jenelle Tissot, *Manager*
EMP: 60
SALES (corp-wide): 9.3MM **Privately Held**
SIC: 7997 Golf club, membership
PA: New Discovery Inc
1380 Galaxy Way
Concord CA

(P-18515)
NEWPORT BEACH COUNTRY CLUB INC
1 Clubhouse Dr, Newport Beach (92660-7107)
PHONE....................949 644-9550
David Wooten, *President*
Jerry Anderson, *Vice Pres*
EMP: 90
SALES (est): 5.5MM
SALES (corp-wide): 30.2MM **Privately Held**
WEB: www.newportbeachcc.com
SIC: 7997 7991 5941 5813 Country club, membership; physical fitness facilities; sporting goods & bicycle shops; drinking places; eating places

PA: International Bay Clubs, Llc
1221 W Coast Hwy Ste 145
Newport Beach CA 92663
949 645-5000

(P-18516)
NOR-WALL INC (PA)
Also Called: Cal Courts
518 W Clark St, Eureka (95501-0103)
PHONE....................707 445-5445
Agetha Nord, *President*
Glen Wallace, *President*
EMP: 50
SQ FT: 9,000
SALES (est): 1.8MM **Privately Held**
WEB: www.calcourtsfitness.com
SIC: 7997 Tennis club, membership; racquetball club, membership

(P-18517)
NORTH RANCH COUNTRY CLUB
4761 Valley Spring Dr, Westlake Village (91362-4399)
PHONE....................818 889-3531
Mark Bagaaso, *CEO*
Scott London, *Treasurer*
Ashley McCoy, *Comms Mgr*
Jenny Duce, *General Mgr*
Westbrook Jonathan, *Controller*
EMP: 160
SQ FT: 53,000
SALES: 12MM **Privately Held**
SIC: 7997 5812 5941 Country club, membership; eating places; sporting goods & bicycle shops

(P-18518)
NORTH RIDGE COUNTRY CLUB
7600 Madison Ave, Fair Oaks (95628-3400)
PHONE....................916 967-5717
Dennis Tootelian, *CEO*
Rink Sanford, *General Mgr*
Jennifer Colasuonno, *Manager*
Dave Zulaica, *Manager*
EMP: 75
SQ FT: 5,000
SALES: 5.7MM **Privately Held**
WEB: www.northridgegolf.com
SIC: 7997 Country club, membership; golf club, membership

(P-18519)
OAKDALE GOLF AND COUNTRY CLUB
243 N Stearns Rd, Oakdale (95361-9247)
PHONE....................209 847-2984
Tom Brennan, *President*
Rick Schultz, *General Mgr*
Alicia Hawkins, *Admin Asst*
Chris Carroll, *Manager*
Lacey Vieira, *Receptionist*
EMP: 55
SQ FT: 12,000
SALES: 3.9MM **Privately Held**
WEB: www.oakdalegcc.org
SIC: 7997 Country club, membership

(P-18520)
OAKMONT COUNTRY CLUB
3100 Country Club Dr, Glendale (91208-1799)
PHONE....................818 542-4260
Pat Dahlson, *CEO*
John Schiller, *President*
Michael Hyler, *COO*
Kurt Desiderio, *Superintendent*
EMP: 125
SQ FT: 37,000
SALES: 10.3MM **Privately Held**
SIC: 7997 Country club, membership; golf club, membership; swimming club, membership

(P-18521)
OASIS PALM DSERT HMOWNERS ASSN
Also Called: Oasis Country Club
42330 Casbah Way, Palm Desert (92211-7660)
PHONE....................760 345-5661
Robert Masata, *President*
Roy McGowen, *President*
EMP: 52
SALES (est): 2.4MM **Privately Held**
SIC: 7997 Country club, membership

(P-18522)
OLYMPIC CLUB
665 Sutter St, San Francisco (94102-1017)
PHONE....................415 676-1412
Sharon Zimmerman, *Human Res Mgr*
EMP: 78
SALES (corp-wide): 48.3MM **Privately Held**
SIC: 7997 Golf club, membership
PA: The Olympic Club
524 Post St
San Francisco CA 94102
415 345-5100

(P-18523)
OLYMPIC INVESTORS LTD
Also Called: Walnut Creek Spt & Fitnes CLB
1908 Olympic Blvd, Walnut Creek (94596-5023)
PHONE....................925 322-8996
Linda Hansen, *Partner*
Sam Beler, *General Ptnr*
George Valerio, *General Ptnr*
Robert F Wattles, *General Ptnr*
John Jackson, *Manager*
EMP: 90
SQ FT: 25,000
SALES (est): 4.9MM **Privately Held**
WEB: www.wcsf.net
SIC: 7997 7991 5812 7999 Membership sports & recreation clubs; physical fitness facilities; eating places; physical fitness instruction

(P-18524)
ORINDA COUNTRY CLUB
315 Camino Sobrante, Orinda (94563-1899)
PHONE....................925 254-4313
Jeff Bause, *President*
George Parker, *General Mgr*
Dawn Kelly, *Human Res Mgr*
Brian Fields, *Opers Staff*
EMP: 90
SALES: 13MM **Privately Held**
WEB: www.orindacc.org
SIC: 7997 Country club, membership

(P-18525)
PACIFIC CLUB (PA)
4110 Macarthur Blvd, Newport Beach (92660-2012)
PHONE....................949 955-1123
Douglas M Ammerman, *President*
Richard M Ortwein, *Treasurer*
Joe Gatto, *General Mgr*
Thomas R Acklum, *Admin Sec*
Karen Ringer,
EMP: 77
SQ FT: 28,000
SALES: 6.8MM **Privately Held**
WEB: www.pacificclub.org
SIC: 7997 5812 5813 Country club, membership; eating places; bar (drinking places)

(P-18526)
PACIFIC GOLF & COUNTRY CLUB
200 Avenida La Pata, San Clemente (92673-6301)
PHONE....................949 498-6604
Tom Frost, *Manager*
EMP: 90
SQ FT: 27,000
SALES (est): 1.8MM
SALES (corp-wide): 2.7MM **Privately Held**
WEB: www.pacificgc.com
SIC: 7997 7992 Golf club, membership; public golf courses
PA: Golf Investment Llc
200 Avenida La Pata
San Clemente CA 92673
949 498-6604

(P-18527)
PALOMAR GEM & MINERAL CLUB
2120 Mission Rd Ste 260, Escondido (92029-1014)
P.O. Box 1583 (92033-1583)
PHONE....................760 743-0809
Mike Nelson, *Principal*
Don Parsley, *Manager*

EMP: 70
SALES (est): 692.5K **Privately Held**
SIC: 7997 Membership sports & recreation clubs

(P-18528)
PALOS VERDES BEACH & ATHC CLB
389 Paseo Del Mar, Palos Verdes Estates (90274-1267)
P.O. Box 158 (90274-0158)
PHONE....................310 375-8777
Jane Williamson, *Manager*
EMP: 88
SQ FT: 5,000
SALES: 1.7MM **Privately Held**
SIC: 7997 Swimming club, membership

(P-18529)
PASADENA MODEL RAILROAD CLUB
5458 Alhambra Ave, Los Angeles (90032-3102)
PHONE....................323 222-1718
Steve Phillips, *President*
William James, *Principal*
EMP: 55
SQ FT: 6,596
SALES: 52.4K **Privately Held**
SIC: 7997 Membership sports & recreation clubs

(P-18530)
PAUMA VALLEY COUNTRY CLUB
15835 Pauma Valley Dr, Pauma Valley (92061-1612)
PHONE....................760 742-1230
Butt Suze, *President*
Paul Devine, *General Mgr*
EMP: 76 **EST:** 1961
SQ FT: 3,000
SALES (est): 7MM **Privately Held**
SIC: 7997 Country club, membership

(P-18531)
PLANTATION GOLF CLUB INC
50994 Monroe St, Indio (92201-9709)
P.O. Box 1657, La Quinta (92247-1657)
PHONE....................760 775-3688
Art Schillings, *General Mgr*
EMP: 54
SQ FT: 16,000
SALES: 4MM **Privately Held**
SIC: 7997 Golf club, membership

(P-18532)
PORTER VALLEY COUNTRY CLUB
Also Called: Porter Valley Catering
19216 Singing Hills Dr, Northridge (91326-1799)
PHONE....................818 360-1071
Robert H Dedman, *Ch of Bd*
John Beckett, *President*
Doug Howe, *Exec VP*
EMP: 110
SQ FT: 18,000
SALES (est): 5.2MM
SALES (corp-wide): 841.1MM **Privately Held**
WEB: www.remington-gc.com
SIC: 7997 5812 5941 Golf club, membership; steak restaurant; sporting goods & bicycle shops
HQ: Clubcorp Usa, Inc.
3030 Lyndon B Johnson Fwy
Dallas TX 75234
972 243-6191

(P-18533)
RACQUET CLUB OF IRVINE
Also Called: Rci
5 Ethel Coplen Way Ste 5 # 5, Irvine (92612-1797)
PHONE....................949 786-3000
Spearman Industry, *President*
EMP: 54
SQ FT: 15,000
SALES (est): 1.4MM **Privately Held**
SIC: 7997 Tennis club, membership

(P-18534)
RAMS HILL COUNTRY CLUB
1881 Rams Hill Rd, Borrego Springs
(92004-5400)
PHONE....................760 767-4259
Wesley Porter, *President*
Don Davis, *Exec VP*
Debbie Woollet, *Admin Asst*
EMP: 60
SQ FT: 40,000
SALES (est): 2.8MM **Privately Held**
SIC: 7997 Country club, membership

(P-18535)
RANCHO MURIETA COUNTRY CLUB
7000 Alameda Dr, Rancho Murieta
(95683-9148)
PHONE....................916 354-2400
Robert Wright, *CEO*
Vince Lepera, *President*
Buzz Breedlove, *Treasurer*
Dick Stenstrom, *Vice Pres*
Johnny Frink, *Executive*
EMP: 90
SQ FT: 40,000
SALES (est): 6.8MM **Privately Held**
WEB: www.ranchomurietacc.com
SIC: 7997 Country club, membership

(P-18536)
RANCHO SANTA FE ASSOCIATION A
Also Called: Rancho Sante Fe Golf Club
5827 Viadelacumere, Rancho Santa Fe
(92067)
P.O. Box A (92067-0359)
PHONE....................858 756-1182
Stephen Nordstrom, *Manager*
EMP: 100
SALES (corp-wide): 16.3MM **Privately Held**
SIC: 7997 Golf club, membership
PA: Rancho Santa Fe Association
17022 Avenida De Acacias
Rancho Santa Fe CA 92067
858 756-1174

(P-18537)
RB ANGLERS CLUB
12578 Cresta Pl, San Diego (92128-2312)
PHONE....................858 487-6484
Richard Studinka, *President*
EMP: 75
SALES (est): 662.1K **Privately Held**
SIC: 7997 Country club, membership

(P-18538)
RED HILL COUNTRY CLUB
8358 Red Hl Cntry Clb Dr, Rancho Cuca-
monga (91730-1899)
PHONE....................909 982-1358
Rob Mocskley, *President*
Gina Smith, *Corp Comm Staff*
EMP: 92
SQ FT: 20,000
SALES: 4.8MM **Privately Held**
WEB: www.redhillcc.com
SIC: 7997 5812 Country club, member-
ship; eating places

(P-18539)
REDLANDS COUNTRY CLUB
1749 Garden St, Redlands (92373-7248)
PHONE....................909 793-2661
Scott Reding, *President*
Pamela Dvorak, *Comms Dir*
Kurt Burmeister, *General Mgr*
Jason Murphy, *General Mgr*
Jeff Rojanaroj, *Manager*
EMP: 80
SQ FT: 22,000
SALES: 5.6MM **Privately Held**
SIC: 7997 5812 5813 Country club, mem-
bership; tennis club, membership; golf
club, membership; snack shop; diner; bar
(drinking places)

(P-18540)
REDWOOD BRIDGE CLUB
3111 6th Ave, San Diego (92103-5836)
PHONE....................619 296-4274
Warren Edelson, *President*
Evelyn Flowers, *Vice Pres*
EMP: 80

SALES: 28.3K **Privately Held**
WEB: www.redwoodbridgeclub.com
SIC: 7997 Membership sports & recreation
clubs

(P-18541)
RESERVE CLUB
49400 Desert Butte Trl, Indian Wells
(92210-7075)
PHONE....................760 674-2222
Kenneth Novack, *President*
C Ted McCarter, *Treasurer*
EMP: 80
SQ FT: 10,000
SALES: 8.5MM **Privately Held**
SIC: 7997 Country club, membership

(P-18542)
RICHMOND COUNTRY CLUB
1 Markovich Ln, Richmond (94806-1825)
PHONE....................510 231-2241
Mac Niven, *General Mgr*
Amanda Howard, *Manager*
EMP: 57
SQ FT: 30,000
SALES (est): 4MM **Privately Held**
SIC: 7997 Country club, membership

(P-18543)
RIVER ISLAND COUNTRY CLUB INC
31989 River Island Dr, Porterville
(93257-9611)
PHONE....................559 781-2917
Terry Treece, *Director*
Corey Carlson, *Executive*
Irene Zuniga, *Office Mgr*
Jimmy Pettis, *Director*
Patty Brown, *Manager*
EMP: 52
SQ FT: 13,500
SALES (est): 2.8MM **Privately Held**
SIC: 7997 Golf club, membership; country
club, membership

(P-18544)
RIVER RIDGE GOLF CLUB
2401 W Vineyard Ave, Oxnard
(93036-2218)
PHONE....................805 981-8724
Otto Kanny, *General Mgr*
EMP: 92
SALES (est): 1.7MM **Privately Held**
SIC: 7997 Golf club, membership

(P-18545)
RIVERVIEW GOLF AND COUNTRY CLB
4200 Bechelli Ln, Redding (96002-3533)
PHONE....................530 224-2254
Ralph Stroch, *President*
Ralph Storch, *President*
Ashli Helstrom, *Director*
Lynette Trotter, *Manager*
EMP: 72
SQ FT: 30,000
SALES: 3.2MM **Privately Held**
WEB: www.riverviewgolf.net
SIC: 7997 5812 5813 Country club, mem-
bership; eating places; bar (drinking
places)

(P-18546)
RODDY RANCH PBC LLC
Also Called: Golf Club At Roddy Ranch
1 Tour Way, Antioch (94531-9053)
PHONE....................925 978-4653
Jack Roddy,
EMP: 55
SQ FT: 1,400
SALES (est): 5.3MM **Privately Held**
WEB: www.roddyranch.com
SIC: 7997 Golf club, membership

(P-18547)
ROSE BOWL AQUATICS CENTER
360 N Arroyo Blvd, Pasadena
(91103-3201)
PHONE....................626 564-0330
Judy Biggs, *Exec Dir*
Kurt Knop, *Principal*
Alethea Crespo, *Managing Dir*
Sandra Hilts, *Finance*
Tim Unger, *Opers Staff*

EMP: 80
SALES: 7.6MM **Privately Held**
WEB: www.rosebowl.com
SIC: 7997 Swimming club, membership

(P-18548)
ROTARY CLB PCF GROVE CHAR FUND
706 Forest Ave, Pacific Grove
(93950-4283)
PHONE....................831 372-3877
Kenneth Petersen, *Principal*
EMP: 77
SALES: 98.5K **Privately Held**
SIC: 7997 Membership sports & recreation
clubs

(P-18549)
ROUND HILL COUNTRY CLUB
3169 Roundhill Rd, Alamo (94507-1735)
PHONE....................925 934-8211
Bruce Rarter, *President*
Greg Gonsalves, *COO*
Brian Plopner, *CFO*
Michael McDonald, *Vice Pres*
Christine Lindgren, *Human Res Dir*
EMP: 180 **EST:** 1959
SQ FT: 20,000
SALES: 17.9MM **Privately Held**
WEB: www.rhcountryclub.com
SIC: 7997 5813 5812 7371 Country club,
membership; bar (drinking places); Ameri-
can restaurant; computer software devel-
opment & applications

(P-18550)
ROUND HILL COUNTRY CLUB
Also Called: Rh
3169 Roundhill Rd, Alamo (94507-1735)
PHONE....................925 934-8211
Debby Grauman, *CEO*
Greg Tachiera, *CEO*
Marcel Steigerwald, *Merchandising*
John Hattab, *Director*
Janelle Lembeck, *Director*
EMP: 50 **EST:** 1965
SALES (est): 5.6MM **Privately Held**
SIC: 7997 Country club, membership

(P-18551)
SADDLEBACK VLY
25631 Peter A Hartman Way, Mission Viejo
(92691-3142)
PHONE....................949 586-1234
Don Cuzick, *Principal*
EMP: 56
SALES (est): 4MM **Privately Held**
SIC: 7997 Membership sports & recreation
clubs

(P-18552)
SAN DIEGO COUNTRY CLUB INC
88 L St, Chula Vista (91911-1499)
PHONE....................619 422-8895
David Morris, *General Mgr*
EMP: 80
SQ FT: 36,140
SALES (est): 5.1MM **Privately Held**
WEB: www.sdcc.cc
SIC: 7997 Country club, membership; golf
club, membership

(P-18553)
SAN DIMAS GOLF INC
Also Called: Via Verde Country Club
1400 Avenida Entrada, San Dimas
(91773-4004)
PHONE....................909 599-8486
Kwan O Lee, *President*
Dal Eun Lee, *Shareholder*
Dal H Lee, *Vice Pres*
Dal K Lee, *Admin Sec*
EMP: 70 **EST:** 1975
SQ FT: 21,887
SALES (est): 4.5MM **Privately Held**
WEB: www.viaverdecountryclub.com
SIC: 7997 Country club, membership

(P-18554)
SAN GABRIEL COUNTRY CLUB
350 E Hermosa Dr, San Gabriel
(91775-2346)
PHONE....................626 287-9671
Tom Dukes, *President*
EMP: 80

SQ FT: 48,000
SALES: 9.2MM **Privately Held**
WEB: www.sangabrielcc.com
SIC: 7997 Country club, membership

(P-18555)
SAN JOAQUIN COUNTRY CLUB
3484 W Bluff Ave, Fresno (93711-0199)
PHONE....................559 439-3483
Jeffrey Newman, *President*
Melissa Allen, *Manager*
EMP: 63
SQ FT: 39,615
SALES: 3.6MM **Privately Held**
SIC: 7997 5812 5813 Country club, mem-
bership; American restaurant; bar (drink-
ing places)

(P-18556)
SAN JOSE COUNTRY CLUB
15571 Alum Rock Ave, San Jose
(95127-2799)
PHONE....................408 258-4901
Chris Simpson, *General Mgr*
Jason Green, *General Mgr*
UT Lu, *Controller*
Kathleen Knudsen, *Sales Dir*
Kevin Sullivan, *Superintendent*
EMP: 70
SQ FT: 24,000
SALES: 5.6MM **Privately Held**
SIC: 7997 7299 Ice sports; color consult-
ant

(P-18557)
SAN LUIS OBISPO GOLF
Also Called: Slogcc
255 Country Club Dr, San Luis Obispo
(93401-8921)
PHONE....................805 543-3400
David Cole, *President*
Carol Kerwin, *Admin Sec*
Hugh Payne, *Director*
Christopher Simpson, *Manager*
EMP: 110
SQ FT: 10,000
SALES (est): 6MM **Privately Held**
SIC: 7997 Country club, membership

(P-18558)
SANTA ANA COUNTRY CLUB
20382 Newport Blvd, Santa Ana
(92707-5396)
PHONE....................714 556-3000
Joseph J Wagner, *CEO*
Pamela Paulson, *Director*
EMP: 100
SALES: 10.1MM **Privately Held**
SIC: 7997 Country club, membership

(P-18559)
SANTA CLARA WOMENS CLUB
Also Called: Santa Clara Woman's Club
Adobe
3260 The Alameda, Santa Clara
(95050-4329)
P.O. Box 367 (95052-0367)
PHONE....................408 246-8000
Marlene O'Donnell, *President*
EMP: 92
SALES (est): 1.1MM **Privately Held**
SIC: 7997 Membership sports & recreation
clubs

(P-18560)
SANTA LUCIA PRESERVE COMPANY
1 Rancho San Carlos Rd, Carmel
(93923-7999)
PHONE....................831 620-6760
Tom Gray, *Principal*
Andy Simer, *CFO*
Jennifer O'Hara, *General Mgr*
Richard Tanner, *Purch Mgr*
EMP: 99
SALES (est): 8.3MM **Privately Held**
SIC: 7997 Country club, membership

(P-18561)
SANTA ROSA GOLF & COUNTRY CLUB
333 Country Club Dr, Santa Rosa
(95401-5599)
PHONE....................707 546-3485
Eric L Affeldt, *CEO*
EMP: 100

SQ FT: 40,000
SALES (est): 7MM
SALES (corp-wide): 841.1MM **Privately Held**
WEB: www.santarosagolf.com
SIC: 7997 Country club, membership
HQ: Clubcorp Holdings, Inc.
3030 Lbj Fwy Ste 600
Dallas TX 75234
972 243-6191

(P-18562)
SANTALUZ CLUB INC
8170 Caminito Santaluz E, San Diego
(92127-2577)
PHONE................858 759-3120
Steve Cowell, *CEO*
Timothy A Kaehr, *CFO*
Michael Forsum, *Vice Pres*
James Hoselton, *Vice Pres*
Jim Macdonough, *General Mgr*
EMP: 120
SQ FT: 19,000
SALES (est): 11.7MM **Privately Held**
WEB: www.santaluz.com
SIC: 7997 Country club, membership

(P-18563)
SANYO FOODS CORP AMERICA
Also Called: Tustin Ranch Golf Club
12442 Tustin Ranch Rd, Tustin
(92782-1000)
PHONE................714 730-1611
Steve Plummer, *Branch Mgr*
EMP: 105 **Privately Held**
SIC: 7997 Golf club, membership
HQ: Sanyo Foods Corporation Of America
11955 Monarch St
Garden Grove CA 92841
714 891-3671

(P-18564)
SATICOY COUNTRY CLUB
4450 Clubhouse Dr, Somis (93066-9798)
PHONE................805 647-1153
Douglas Taxton, *President*
James R Van Wyck, *CEO*
Kathy Sube, *Financial Exec*
Amy Hogue, *Accountant*
Tom Szwedzinski, *Director*
EMP: 80
SALES (est): 4.2MM **Privately Held**
WEB: www.saticoycountryclub.com
SIC: 7997 Country club, membership; golf club, membership

(P-18565)
SCRIPPS RANCH RECREATION CLUB (PA)
9875 Aviary Dr, San Diego (92131-1701)
PHONE................858 271-6222
Ben Domurat, *President*
Rob Walker, *Vice Pres*
Monica Oates, *Director*
EMP: 100
SQ FT: 19,000
SALES (est): 4.6MM **Privately Held**
WEB: www.srsrc.com
SIC: 7997 Tennis club, membership

(P-18566)
SEQUOIA WOOD COUNTRY CLUB
1000 Cypress Point Dr, Arnold (95223)
P.O. Box 930 (95223-0930)
PHONE................209 795-1000
Norm Kestner, *President*
EMP: 64
SQ FT: 13,000
SALES (est): 2.3MM **Privately Held**
WEB: www.sequoiawoods.com
SIC: 7997 5812 5813 Golf club, membership; eating places; bar (drinking places)

(P-18567)
SERRANO ASSOCIATES LLC
Also Called: Serrano Country Club
5005 Serrano Pkwy, El Dorado Hills
(95762-7511)
PHONE................916 939-3333
Kevitt Sale, *Manager*
EMP: 100

SALES (corp-wide): 10.1MM **Privately Held**
WEB: www.serranoassociates.com
SIC: 7997 5941 5813 5812 Golf club, membership; sporting goods & bicycle shops; drinking places; eating places
PA: Serrano Associates, Llc
4525 Serrano Pkwy
El Dorado Hills CA 95762
916 939-3333

(P-18568)
SERRANO COUNTRY CLUB INC
5005 Serrano Pkwy P, El Dorado Hills
(95762-7511)
PHONE................916 933-5005
Dean Cummings, *President*
Bob Stangroom, *General Mgr*
Lauri Davis, *Accounting Mgr*
Laura Lewis, *Accounting Mgr*
Tazim Venkataya, *Controller*
EMP: 105
SALES (est): 7.8MM **Privately Held**
WEB: www.serranocountryclub.com
SIC: 7997 Golf club, membership

(P-18569)
SEVEN LAKES HM ASSN CNTRY CLB
1 Desert Lakes Dr, Palm Springs
(92264-5520)
PHONE................760 328-2695
Silas Dreher, *General Mgr*
Diane Hale, *Administration*
Linda Starck, *Personnel*
EMP: 50
SQ FT: 6,000
SALES (est): 884.7K **Privately Held**
SIC: 7997 8641 Country club, membership; homeowners' association

(P-18570)
SEVEN OAKS COUNTRY CLUB
2000 Grand Lakes Ave, Bakersfield
(93311-2931)
P.O. Box 11165 (93389-1165)
PHONE................661 664-6404
David H Murdock, *CEO*
Bruce Freeman, *President*
Don Ciota, *General Mgr*
EMP: 125
SQ FT: 39,000
SALES (est): 7.9MM **Privately Held**
WEB: www.sevenoakscountryclub.com
SIC: 7997 Country club, membership

(P-18571)
SHADY CANYON GOLF CLUB INC
100 Shady Canyon Dr, Irvine (92603-0301)
PHONE................949 856-7000
James T Wood, *CEO*
Thomas Heggi, *President*
Robert Leenhouts, *Principal*
Bernard Lee, *Accountant*
Lynne Clarke, *Purch Mgr*
EMP: 114
SALES (est): 186.4K **Privately Held**
WEB: www.shadycanyongolfclub.com
SIC: 7997 Country club, membership

(P-18572)
SHERWOOD COUNTRY CLUB
320 W Stafford Rd, Thousand Oaks
(91361-5087)
PHONE................805 496-3036
Lance Fisher, *General Mgr*
Lenny Fisher, *General Mgr*
Melanie Kohagen, *Executive Asst*
Andrea Sidman, *Admin Asst*
Jean Gojkovich, *Human Res Dir*
EMP: 113 **EST:** 1989
SALES: 14.5MM **Privately Held**
SIC: 7997 Country club, membership

(P-18573)
SIERRA VIEW COUNTRY CLUB
105 Alta Vista Ave, Roseville (95678-1647)
P.O. Box 676 (95678-0676)
PHONE................916 782-3741
Barry Macdonald, *CEO*
Steve Rainwater, *President*
John Welch, *General Mgr*
Steve Dunmore, *Director*
Mark Harris, *Director*
EMP: 75

SQ FT: 5,000
SALES: 1.8MM **Privately Held**
WEB: www.sierraviewcc.com
SIC: 7997 5812 5813 Golf club, membership; American restaurant; bar (drinking places)

(P-18574)
SILVER CREEK VLY CNTRY CLB INC
5460 Country Club Pkwy, San Jose
(95138-2215)
PHONE................408 239-5775
Rene Devos, *General Mgr*
Andy Moshier, *Vice Pres*
Steven Backman, *General Mgr*
Alan Deck, *General Mgr*
Robert E Lee, *General Mgr*
EMP: 180
SALES (est): 9MM **Privately Held**
WEB: www.scvcc.com
SIC: 7997 5941 Country club, membership; sporting goods & bicycle shops

(P-18575)
SILVERADO RESORT AND SPA
1600 Atlas Peak Rd, NAPA (94558-1425)
PHONE................707 257-0200
Setsuo Okawa, *CEO*
Isao Okawa, *Ch of Bd*
EMP: 600
SQ FT: 2,000
SALES (est): 75.8K **Privately Held**
WEB: www.silveradoresort.com
SIC: 7997 Country club, membership
HQ: Silverado Napa Corp
1600 Atlas Peak Rd
Napa CA 94558
707 226-1325

(P-18576)
SNOWBOUNDERS SKI CLUB
5402 Tattershall Ave, Westminster
(92683-3447)
PHONE................714 892-4897
EMP: 80
SALES: 47.9K **Privately Held**
SIC: 7997

(P-18577)
SOUTH HILLS COUNTRY CLUB
2655 S Citrus St, West Covina
(91791-3405)
PHONE................626 339-1231
James Wendoll, *CEO*
Chris Banner, *General Mgr*
Alex Godinez, *Manager*
Terry Wysocki, *Consultant*
EMP: 78
SQ FT: 34,000
SALES: 5.9MM **Privately Held**
WEB: www.southhillscountryclub.org
SIC: 7997 5813 5812 Country club, membership; golf club, membership; bar (drinking places); American restaurant

(P-18578)
SOUTHWESTERN YACHT CLUB INC
2702 Qualtrough St, San Diego
(92106-3415)
PHONE................619 222-0438
Jeff Wheeler, *General Mgr*
EMP: 50 **EST:** 1947
SQ FT: 10,000
SALES: 4.1MM **Privately Held**
WEB: www.southwesternyc.org
SIC: 7997 4493 5812 5813 Yacht club, membership; yacht basins; eating places; bar (drinking places)

(P-18579)
SPANISH HILLS COUNTRY CLUB (PA)
999 Crestview Ave, Camarillo
(93010-8493)
PHONE................805 389-1644
Joe Topper, *President*
Grant Webster, *Controller*
Estella Arguelles, *Human Resources*
Whitney West, *Sales Staff*
Mark Coulter, *Director*
EMP: 150
SQ FT: 42,000

SALES (est): 10.1MM **Privately Held**
WEB: www.spanishhillscc.com
SIC: 7997 Country club, membership

(P-18580)
SPARE-TIME INC
Also Called: Broadstone Racquet Club
820 Halidon Way, Folsom (95630-8406)
PHONE................916 983-9180
Gavin Russo, *General Mgr*
EMP: 80
SALES (corp-wide): 38.3MM **Privately Held**
WEB: www.sparetimeinc.com
SIC: 7997 7991 Racquetball club, membership; health club
PA: Spare-Time, Inc.
11344 Coloma Rd Ste 350
Gold River CA 95670
916 859-5910

(P-18581)
SPARE-TIME INC
Also Called: Johnson Ranch Racquet Club
2501 Eureka Rd, Roseville (95661-6400)
PHONE................916 782-2600
Tim Munson, *General Mgr*
EMP: 60
SQ FT: 21,584
SALES (corp-wide): 38.3MM **Privately Held**
WEB: www.sparetimeinc.com
SIC: 7997 Racquetball club, membership
PA: Spare-Time, Inc.
11344 Coloma Rd Ste 350
Gold River CA 95670
916 859-5910

(P-18582)
SPARE-TIME INC
Also Called: Gold River Racquet Club
2201 Gold Rush Dr, Gold River
(95670-4466)
PHONE................916 638-7001
Mike Burchett, *General Mgr*
EMP: 50
SALES (corp-wide): 38.3MM **Privately Held**
WEB: www.sparetimeinc.com
SIC: 7997 Racquetball club, membership
PA: Spare-Time, Inc.
11344 Coloma Rd Ste 350
Gold River CA 95670
916 859-5910

(P-18583)
SPARE-TIME INC
Also Called: Laguna Creek Racquet Club
9570 Racquet Ct, Elk Grove (95758-4349)
PHONE................916 859-5910
Kimberley Miller, *Manager*
EMP: 59
SALES (corp-wide): 38.3MM **Privately Held**
WEB: www.sparetimeinc.com
SIC: 7997 7999 7991 Racquetball club, membership; racquetball club, non-membership; health club
PA: Spare-Time, Inc.
11344 Coloma Rd Ste 350
Gold River CA 95670
916 859-5910

(P-18584)
SPRING VALLEY LAKE COUNTRY CLB
13229 Spring Valley Pkwy, Victorville
(92395)
PHONE................760 245-5356
Erick Affeldt, *CEO*
Osmar Castro, *General Mgr*
Leo Riley, *General Mgr*
EMP: 90
SALES (est): 4MM
SALES (corp-wide): 841.1MM **Privately Held**
WEB: www.remington-gc.com
SIC: 7997 Country club, membership
HQ: Clubcorp Usa, Inc.
3030 Lyndon B Johnson Fwy
Dallas TX 75234
972 243-6191

(P-18585)
SPRINGS CLUB INC
Also Called: Springs Country Club, The
1 Duke Dr, Rancho Mirage (92270-3647)
PHONE..................................760 328-0254
Robert Middlemas, *CEO*
Rick Cabasal, *COO*
Daniel Cooper, *COO*
Ronda Allen, *Principal*
Douglas R Hart, *Principal*
EMP: 65
SQ FT: 36,000
SALES (est): 5.5MM **Privately Held**
SIC: 7997 5812 5813 Golf club, member-
ship; tennis club, membership; American
restaurant; cocktail lounge

(P-18586)
ST FRANCIS YACHT CLUB
700 Marina Blvd, San Francisco
(94123-1044)
PHONE..................................415 563-6363
Jim Diepenbrock, *CEO*
Gregory Rossmann, *Bd of Directors*
David Sneary, *Bd of Directors*
Anna Hoit, *Comms Mgr*
Kara B Martinez, *Administration*
◆ EMP: 110
SQ FT: 20,000
SALES: 17.2MM **Privately Held**
WEB: www.stfyc.com
SIC: 7997 4493 Yacht club, membership;
marinas

(P-18587)
STOCKDALE COUNTRY CLUB
7001 Stockdale Hwy, Bakersfield
(93309-1313)
P.O. Box 9727 (93389-9727)
PHONE..................................661 832-0310
Sam Monroe, *President*
Michael Davis, *CEO*
Linda Voiland, *Vice Pres*
Susan Greer, *General Mgr*
Linda Turner, *Controller*
EMP: 100 EST: 1925
SQ FT: 12,000
SALES: 6.7MM **Privately Held**
WEB: www.stockdalecountryclub.com
SIC: 7997 Country club, membership

(P-18588)
STONEBRAE LP
Also Called: TPC Stonebrea
222 Country Club Dr, Hayward
(94542-7927)
PHONE..................................510 728-7878
Lisa Hinman, *General Mgr*
Erin Crawford, *Project Mgr*
EMP: 67
SALES (est): 5MM **Privately Held**
SIC: 7997 Country club, membership

(P-18589)
SUNNYSIDE COUNTRY CLUB
Also Called: University Sequoia
5704 E Butler Ave, Fresno (93727-5499)
PHONE..................................559 255-6871
Steve Menchinella, *Manager*
EMP: 85
SQ FT: 24,250
SALES: 2.4MM **Privately Held**
WEB: www.sunnyside-cc.com
SIC: 7997 Country club, membership

(P-18590)
SWELL ATHLETIC CLUB GP
Also Called: Cathedral Oaks Athletic Club
5800 Cathedral Oaks Rd, Goleta
(93117-1829)
PHONE..................................805 964-7762
James Knell, *Partner*
Janice Lesin, *Partner*
Eric Geeb, *General Mgr*
Tom Horne, *General Mgr*
EMP: 75
SQ FT: 11,200
SALES: 3.6MM **Privately Held**
SIC: 7997 7991 Swimming club, member-
ship; athletic club & gymnasiums, mem-
bership

(P-18591)
SYCAMORE CC INC
Also Called: The Golf Club of California
3742 Flowerwood Ln, Fallbrook
(92028-8013)
PHONE..................................760 451-3700
William Lyon, *President*
EMP: 60
SQ FT: 4,320
SALES (est): 2.5MM **Publicly Held**
WEB: www.lyonhomes.com
SIC: 7997 Golf club, membership
PA: William Lyon Homes
4695 Macarthur Ct Ste 800
Newport Beach CA 92660

(P-18592)
TEHAMA GOLF CLUB LLC
4 Tehama, Carmel (93923-9622)
PHONE..................................831 622-2200
Roy D Kaufman,
Howard M Bernstein,
EMP: 95
SALES (est): 5.8MM **Privately Held**
WEB: www.tehamagolfclub.com
SIC: 7997 Golf club, membership

(P-18593)
**TENNIS EVERYONE
INCORPORATED**
Also Called: Rolling Hills Club
351 San Andreas Dr, Novato (94945-1206)
PHONE..................................415 897-2185
Chuk Trieve, *President*
Andrea Pozzi, *Officer*
Marybeth Bradley, *General Mgr*
Bobbie Bukszar, *Director*
Debbie Gleeson, *Director*
EMP: 85 EST: 1973
SQ FT: 19,000
SALES (est): 3MM **Privately Held**
WEB: www.rollinghillsclub.com
SIC: 7997 Swimming club, membership

(P-18594)
**THE VALLEY CLUB OF
MONTECITO**
1901 E Valley Rd, Santa Barbara
(93108-1427)
PHONE..................................805 969-2215
John S Degroot, *CEO*
Palmer Jackson, *President*
EMP: 50 EST: 1931
SQ FT: 3,000
SALES: 8.6MM **Privately Held**
SIC: 7997 Golf club, membership

(P-18595)
**THE WOODBRIDGE GOLF
CNTRY CLB**
800 E Woodbridge Rd, Woodbridge
(95258-9628)
P.O. Box 806 (95258-0806)
PHONE..................................209 369-2371
Jerry Leonard, *CEO*
Ernie Micelli, *General Mgr*
Mindy Adolf, *Admin Asst*
Catherine Kading, *Director*
Kristine Roberson, *Director*
EMP: 79
SQ FT: 20,000
SALES: 3.9MM **Privately Held**
SIC: 7997 Golf club, membership

(P-18596)
THUNDERBIRD COUNTRY CLUB
70737 Country Club Dr, Rancho Mirage
(92270-3500)
P.O. Box 5005 (92270-1065)
PHONE..................................760 328-2161
Brian Rice, *CEO*
David Shepler, *COO*
Potts Donna, *Vice Pres*
Chris Olson, *Executive*
Michaell Crandall, *General Mgr*
EMP: 60
SQ FT: 30,000
SALES: 8.7MM **Privately Held**
WEB: www.thunderbirdcc.org
SIC: 7997 5812 7011 Country club, mem-
bership; eating places; hotels & motels

(P-18597)
TIBURON PENINSULA CLUB INC
1600 Mar West St, Belvedere Tiburon
(94920-1830)
PHONE..................................415 789-7900
Gerry Pang, *Manager*
Julie Coulston, *General Mgr*
Catherine Sanders, *Marketing Staff*
Juliana Moreno, *Rector*
Brent Rodenbeck, *Director*
EMP: 50
SQ FT: 6,674
SALES: 6.1MM **Privately Held**
WEB: www.tiburonpc.org
SIC: 7997 Swimming club, membership;
tennis club, membership

(P-18598)
TIERRA OAKS GOLF CLUB INC
19700 La Crescenta Dr, Redding
(96003-7474)
PHONE..................................530 275-0795
Shawn Sich, *General Mgr*
EMP: 90
SALES (est): 3.5MM **Privately Held**
WEB: www.lockefordsprings.com
SIC: 7997 6531 Golf club, membership;
real estate agents & managers
PA: Spring Lockeford Golf Course Inc
16360 N Highway 88
Lodi CA 95240

(P-18599)
TOSCANA COUNTRY CLUB INC
76009 Via Club Villa, Indian Wells
(92210-7851)
PHONE..................................760 404-1444
Paul K Levy, *CEO*
Lori Benavides, *Office Mgr*
Crista Collins, *Director*
Bill Harmon, *Director*
Dennis Sperat, *Manager*
EMP: 150
SALES (est): 8MM **Privately Held**
SIC: 7997 Country club, membership

(P-18600)
TY INVESTMENT INC
1015 21st St Unit A, Santa Monica
(90403-4567)
PHONE..................................619 448-4242
Toru Mise, *President*
EMP: 75
SALES (est): 3.9MM **Privately Held**
WEB: www.carltonoaksgolf.com
SIC: 7997 Country club, membership; golf
club, membership

(P-18601)
UNITED STATES PONY CLUBS
7010 Hidden Valley Pl, Granite Bay
(95746-9456)
PHONE..................................916 791-1223
Linda Gurnee, *Director*
EMP: 82
SALES: 58.2K **Privately Held**
SIC: 7997 Membership sports & recreation
clubs

(P-18602)
VALLEY-HI COUNTRY CLUB
9595 Franklin Blvd, Elk Grove
(95758-9532)
PHONE..................................916 684-2120
Edgar Gill, *CEO*
Nick West, *Principal*
Judi Santiago, *Office Mgr*
EMP: 50
SQ FT: 20,000
SALES: 3.4MM **Privately Held**
WEB: www.valleyhicc.com
SIC: 7997 Country club, membership

(P-18603)
VILLAGE WEST YACHT CLUB
6633 Embarcadero Dr, Stockton
(95219-3329)
PHONE..................................209 478-8992
Fred Von Helf, *President*
Margaret Armstrong, *CFO*
EMP: 100
SALES (est): 1.8MM **Privately Held**
SIC: 7997 7941 Yacht club, membership;
sports clubs, managers & promoters

(P-18604)
**VILLAGES GOLF AND COUNTRY
CLUB**
Also Called: Villages, The
5000 Cribari Ln, San Jose (95135-1397)
PHONE..................................408 274-4400
Virginia Fanelli, *CEO*
David Gonzales, *Area Spvr*
Luann Busse, *Admin Asst*
Elissa Caruso, *Administration*
Jim White, *Finance Dir*
EMP: 170
SALES (est): 15.5MM **Privately Held**
WEB: www.the-villages.com
SIC: 7997 Country club, membership

(P-18605)
VINTAGE CLUB
75001 Vintage Dr W, Indian Wells
(92210-7304)
PHONE..................................760 340-0500
John Buttemiller Broker, *Sales Executive*
Marc D Ray, *COO*
Carol Daniels, *Comms Dir*
Steve Cenicola, *General Mgr*
Jennifer Latteri, *Office Mgr*
EMP: 90
SQ FT: 86,000
SALES (est): 7.8MM **Privately Held**
WEB: www.thevintageclub.com
SIC: 7997 5813 5812 5941 Country club,
membership; bar (drinking places); Ameri-
can restaurant; golf goods & equipment;
tennis services & professionals; real es-
tate agents & managers

(P-18606)
VIRGINIA COUNTRY CLUB
4602 N Virginia Rd, Long Beach
(90807-1999)
PHONE..................................562 427-0924
Jamie Mulligan, *CEO*
Steve Bendt, *Director*
Dena Turner, *Receptionist*
EMP: 110
SQ FT: 15,000
SALES: 6.8MM **Privately Held**
SIC: 7997 Country club, membership; golf
club, membership

(P-18607)
VISALIA COUNTRY CLUB
625 N Ranch St, Visalia (93291-4317)
P.O. Box 3410 (93278-3410)
PHONE..................................559 734-3733
Steve Beargeon, *Principal*
EMP: 80
SQ FT: 60,000
SALES: 4.5MM **Privately Held**
SIC: 7997 Country club, membership

(P-18608)
VISTA VALLEY COUNTRY CLUB
Also Called: V Vcc Havens
29354 Vista Valley Dr, Vista (92084-2209)
PHONE..................................760 758-2800
John Havens, *President*
Marissa Gerlach, *Executive*
Philip Rodriguez, *General Mgr*
Alexis Jenkins, *Executive Asst*
Constance Ryan, *Sales Staff*
EMP: 70
SQ FT: 15,000
SALES (est): 5.5MM **Privately Held**
WEB: www.vistavalley.com
SIC: 7997 5812 7999 Country club, mem-
bership; eating places; golf cart, power,
rental

(P-18609)
WEST HILLS GOLF ASSOCIATES
Also Called: Western Hills Country Club
1800 Carbon Canyon Rd, Chino Hills
(91709-2300)
PHONE..................................714 528-6400
Michael Donovan, *Partner*
William Donovan, *Ltd Ptnr*
Ron Lane, *Ltd Ptnr*
EMP: 50
SQ FT: 12,000
SALES (est): 2.1MM **Privately Held**
SIC: 7997 7299 Golf club, membership;
banquet hall facilities

(P-18610)
WESTGROUP KONA KAI LLC
Also Called: Kona Kai Resort Hotel
1551 Shelter Island Dr, San Diego
(92106-3102)
PHONE..................................619 221-8000
Kathy Little,
EMP: 99
SALES (est): 5.3MM Privately Held
SIC: 7997 7011 Membership sports & recreation clubs; resort hotel

(P-18611)
WILSHIRE COUNTRY CLUB
301 N Rossmore Ave, Los Angeles
(90004-2499)
PHONE..................................323 934-6050
Jeffrey Ornstein, CEO
Norman Branchflower, President
Todd Keefer, COO
Mirion Bowers MD, Vice Pres
Peter Jimenez, Controller
EMP: 94
SQ FT: 50,000
SALES: 10.6MM Privately Held
WEB: www.wilshirecc.com
SIC: 7997 5941 5812 Country club, membership; sporting goods & bicycle shops; eating places

(P-18612)
YUBA CITY RACQUET CLUB INC
825 Jones Rd, Yuba City (95991-6124)
PHONE..................................530 673-6900
Judie Jacoby, President
▲ EMP: 73 EST: 1975
SQ FT: 40,000
SALES (est): 3.1MM Privately Held
WEB: www.ycrc.com
SIC: 7997 7991 Tennis club, membership; health club

7999 Amusement & Recreation Svcs, NEC

(P-18613)
29 PALMS ENTERPRISES CORP
Also Called: Spotlight 29 Casino
46200 Harrison Pl, Coachella
(92236-2031)
PHONE..................................760 775-5566
Darrel Mike, President
Stephenie Streiff-Process, Analyst
Michael Passarello, Buyer
Richard Montigny, Opers Staff
Matthew Bruce, Marketing Mgr
EMP: 600
SQ FT: 70,000
SALES (est): 33.4MM Privately Held
WEB: www.spotlight29.net
SIC: 7999 5812 Gambling establishment; eating places

(P-18614)
ADRIENNE MATTOS SWIM SCHL INC (PA)
2203 Mariner Square Loop, Alameda
(94501-1021)
PHONE..................................866 633-4147
Adrienne L Mattos, CEO
Heidi Moore, COO
Matthew Mitchell, Manager
EMP: 50
SALES (est): 2MM Privately Held
SIC: 7999 Swimming instruction

(P-18615)
ADVENTURE CITY INC
1238 S Beach Blvd, Anaheim
(92804-4828)
PHONE..................................714 821-3311
Allan Ansdell Jr, President
Yvonne Ansdell, Treasurer
Trina Ansdell, Human Res Mgr
EMP: 100
SALES (est): 3MM Privately Held
WEB: www.adventurecity.com
SIC: 7999 7996 Tourist attractions, amusement park concessions & rides; amusement parks

(P-18616)
ADVENTURE CONNECTION INC
986 Lotus Rd, Lotus (95651)
P.O. Box 475, Coloma (95613-0475)
PHONE..................................530 626-7385
Nathan J Rangel, President
EMP: 60
SQ FT: 2,400
SALES (est): 750K Privately Held
WEB: www.raftcalifornia.com
SIC: 7999 4725 Rafting tours; tour operators

(P-18617)
ALAMEDA COUNTY AG FAIR ASSN
Also Called: ALAMEDA COUNTY FAIR
4501 Pleasanton Ave, Pleasanton
(94566-7001)
PHONE..................................925 426-7600
Rick Pickering, CEO
Randy Maggie, CFO
Richard Sims, Manager
EMP: 75
SQ FT: 125,000
SALES: 23.6MM Privately Held
WEB: www.alamedacountyfair.com
SIC: 7999 Agricultural fair

(P-18618)
ALPINE CAMP CONFERENCE CTR INC
415 Clubhouse Dr, Blue Jay (92317)
P.O. Box 155 (92317-0155)
PHONE..................................909 337-6287
Kim Polson, Administration
Anthony Xepolis, President
Joel Rude, Principal
Mark Gilliland, Accountant
John Gehrig, Director
EMP: 68
SALES (est): 1.7MM Privately Held
SIC: 7999 7032 Instruction schools, camps & services; youth camps

(P-18619)
AMBASSADOR GAMING INC
Also Called: Key Largo Casino
660 Newport Center Dr # 1050, Newport Beach (92660-6401)
PHONE..................................714 969-8730
Stephen K Bone, President
Robert L Mayer Jr, Treasurer
EMP: 112
SALES (est): 4.8MM Privately Held
WEB: www.keylargocasino.com
SIC: 7999 7993 Gambling machines, operation; gambling establishments operating coin-operated machines; slot machines

(P-18620)
AMBROSE RECREATION & PARK DST
3105 Willow Pass Rd, Bay Point
(94565-3149)
PHONE..................................925 458-1601
Travis Stombaugh, General Mgr
Gloria Magleby, Ch of Bd
Veronica Washington, Planning
Judy Dawson,
Greg Enholm, Director
EMP: 100
SALES (est): 2.4MM Privately Held
SIC: 7999 Recreation services

(P-18621)
ANAHEIM ICE
Also Called: Rinks Anaheim Ice, The
300 W Lincoln Ave, Anaheim (92805-2947)
PHONE..................................714 535-7465
Eddie Hawkins, General Mgr
Cindy Frazier, CFO
Art Trottier, Vice Pres
Jill Herzogge, General Mgr
Stacy Witt, Opers Staff
EMP: 70
SALES (est): 1.6MM Privately Held
SIC: 7999 Ice skating rink operation

(P-18622)
ANGELES LOS EQUESTRIAN CENTER
480 W Riverside Dr, Burbank (91506-3209)
PHONE..................................818 840-9063
J Albert Garcia, President
Mina Behboudi, Sales Staff
EMP: 120
SALES (est): 3.4MM Privately Held
SIC: 7999 Riding stable

(P-18623)
APEX PARKS GROUP LLC
Also Called: Malibu Castle
27061 Aliso Creek Rd # 100, Aliso Viejo (92656-5322)
PHONE..................................210 341-6663
EMP: 100
SALES (corp-wide): 39.9MM Privately Held
SIC: 7999 5599
PA: Apex Parks Group, Llc
27061 Aliso Creek Rd # 100
Aliso Viejo CA 92612
949 349-8461

(P-18624)
ARISE LLC
1033 Van Ness Ave, Fresno (93721-2006)
PHONE..................................559 485-0881
Darrell Miers, CEO
EMP: 60
SALES (est): 1.9MM Privately Held
SIC: 7999 Gambling establishment

(P-18625)
ARIZONA CHANNEL ISLA
300 W 9th St, Oxnard (93030-7060)
PHONE..................................480 788-0755
Roger Burt, CEO
Abou Dieng, CFO
EMP: 75
SQ FT: 60,000
SALES (est): 282.9K Privately Held
SIC: 7999 Amusement & recreation

(P-18626)
AROMA SPA & SPORTS LLC
Also Called: Aroma Wilshire Center
3680 Wilshire Blvd # 301, Los Angeles
(90010-2708)
PHONE..................................213 387-2111
Byoung G Choi,
Chris Mader, Officer
Jae Whang, Controller
Keejune Huh,
EMP: 60
SALES (est): 1.9MM Privately Held
SIC: 7999 7991 Recreation center; health club

(P-18627)
ARTICHOKE JOES INC
Also Called: Artichoke Joe's Casino
659 Huntington Ave, San Bruno
(94066-3608)
PHONE..................................650 589-8812
Dennis J Sammut, CEO
Helen Sammut, Corp Secy
Vincent Defrlese, Manager
EMP: 330
SALES (est): 15.2MM Privately Held
WEB: www.artichokejoes.com
SIC: 7999 5812 5813 Game parlor; eating places; tavern (drinking places)

(P-18628)
ARTISTS STUDIO GALLERY
5504 Crestridge Rd, Rancho Palos Verdes
(90275-4905)
PHONE..................................424 206-9902
EMP: 55 Privately Held
SIC: 7999 Art gallery, commercial
PA: Artists Studio Gallery Of The Palos Verdes
550 Deep Valley Dr # 327
Rllng Hls Est CA 90274
-

(P-18629)
AUBURN OLD TOWN GALLERY
Also Called: Old Town Gallery of Fine Art
218 Washington St Ste A, Auburn
(95603-5048)
PHONE..................................530 887-9150
Sonja Hamilton, President
Mike Miller,
Marilyn Russell,
EMP: 60

SALES (est): 2.2MM Privately Held
WEB: www.auburnoldtowngallery.com
SIC: 7999 5999 Art gallery, commercial; art dealers

(P-18630)
BAY AREA SEATING SERVICE INC
Also Called: Bass Tickets
1855 Gateway Blvd Ste 630, Concord
(94520-3200)
PHONE..................................925 671-4000
W Thomas Gimple, President
Doug Levenson, Exec VP
EMP: 300 EST: 1974
SQ FT: 18,000
SALES (est): 1.5MM
SALES (corp-wide): 191.3MM Privately Held
WEB: www.tickets.com
SIC: 7999 Ticket sales office for sporting events, contract
HQ: California Tickets.Com Inc.
555 Anton Blvd Fl 11
Costa Mesa CA 92626
714 327-5400

(P-18631)
BAY CLUB HOLDINGS III LLC
Also Called: Golden Gtwy Tennis & Swim CLB
370 Drumm St, San Francisco
(94111-2010)
PHONE..................................415 433-2936
EMP: 80
SALES (corp-wide): 46.3MM Privately Held
SIC: 7999 Tennis services & professionals
PA: Bay Club Holdings Iii, Llc
1 Lombard St Lbby
San Francisco CA 94111
415 781-1874

(P-18632)
BEAR VALLEY SKI CO
Also Called: Bear Valley Mountain Resort
2280 State Rte 207, Bear Valley (95223)
P.O. Box 5038 (95223-5038)
PHONE..................................209 753-2301
Tim Bottomley, CEO
EMP: 325
SQ FT: 70,000
SALES (est): 14.9MM
SALES (corp-wide): 176MM Privately Held
WEB: www.bearvalley.com
SIC: 7999 5941 Recreation services; ski rental concession; ski instruction; skiing equipment
PA: Skyline Investments Inc
36 King St E Suite 700
Toronto ON M5C 2
416 368-2565

(P-18633)
BELL GARDENS BICYCLE CLUB INC
Also Called: Bicycle Club Casino
888 Bicycle Casino Dr, Bell Gardens
(90201-7617)
PHONE..................................562 806-4646
George Hardie, President
George G Hardie, President
EMP: 1300
SQ FT: 110,000
SALES (est): 35.1MM Privately Held
WEB: www.thebicyclecasino.com
SIC: 7999 5812 Card rooms; coffee shop

(P-18634)
BIG 5 SPORTING GOODS CORP
11310 Crenshaw Blvd, Inglewood
(90303-2807)
PHONE..................................323 755-2663
EMP: 409 Publicly Held
SIC: 7999 5941 5699 5661 Sporting goods rental; sporting goods & bicycle shops; sports apparel; shoe stores
PA: Big 5 Sporting Goods Corp
2525 E El Segundo Blvd
El Segundo CA 90245

(P-18635)
BLACK OAK CASINO
19400 Tuolumne Rd N, Tuolumne
(95379-9696)
PHONE................................209 928-9300
Ron Patel, *General Mgr*
Ernie Ball, *Vice Pres*
Nelson BJ, *Exec Dir*
James Hodge, *General Mgr*
Ronaldo Pascual, *General Mgr*
EMP: 99
SQ FT: 168,000
SALES (est): 8.9MM **Privately Held**
WEB: www.blackoakcasino.com
SIC: 7999 Gambling establishment
PA: Tuolumne Me-Wuk Tribal Council
19595 Mi Wu St
Tuolumne CA 95379
209 928-5300

(P-18636)
BLUE BUS TOURS LLC
Also Called: Grayline of San Francisco
50 Quint St, San Francisco (94124-1424)
PHONE................................415 353-5310
Raman Fargoni, *President*
EMP: 120 EST: 2011
SQ FT: 4,200
SALES: 350K **Privately Held**
SIC: 7999 Tourist attraction, commercial

(P-18637)
BUSINESS AND SUPPORT SERVICES
Also Called: Marine Corps Community Svcs
Mccs Bldg 2273 Elrod Ave, San Diego
(92145-0001)
P.O. Box 452008 (92145-2008)
PHONE................................858 577-1061
Mary Bradford, *Director*
EMP: 800 **Publicly Held**
WEB: www.mccssc.com
SIC: 7999 9711 Recreation center; Marine
Corps;
HQ: Business And Support Services
3044 Catlin Ave
Quantico VA 22134
703 432-0109

(P-18638)
BVK GAMING INC
3466 Broadway St, American Canyon
(94503-1263)
P.O. Box 10078 (94503-0078)
PHONE................................707 644-8853
Brian Altizer, *Admin Sec*
Von Altizer, *President*
EMP: 90 EST: 2005
SALES (est): 785.4K **Privately Held**
SIC: 7999 Card rooms

(P-18639)
CAESARS ENTRTNMENT OPRTING INC
Also Called: Harrah's
777 Harrahs Rincon Way, Valley Center
(92082-5343)
PHONE................................760 751-3100
Janet Deronio, *Branch Mgr*
Albert Lee, *Vice Pres*
Janet Beroino, *General Mgr*
Pom Maldonado, *Info Tech Mgr*
Paul Kenyon, *IT/INT Sup*
EMP: 1400
SALES (corp-wide): 8.3B **Publicly Held**
WEB: www.flamingolv.com
SIC: 7999 7011 Gambling establishment;
casino hotel
HQ: Caesars Entertainment Operating
Company, Inc.
1 Caesars Palace Dr
Las Vegas NV 89109
702 407-6000

(P-18640)
CAHUILLA CREEK REST & CASINO
Also Called: Cahuilla Creek Casino
52702 Us Highway 371, Anza
(92539-8707)
PHONE................................951 763-1200
Leonardo Pasquarelli, *General Mgr*
Robert Liera, *Bd of Directors*
Phillip Madrigal, *Bd of Directors*
Jon Gregory, *General Mgr*

Susan Bellamy, *Mktg Dir*
EMP: 103
SQ FT: 14,000
SALES (est): 8MM **Privately Held**
WEB: www.cahuillacreekcasino.com
SIC: 7999 5812 5813 Gambling establishment; American restaurant; bar (drinking
places); tavern (drinking places)

(P-18641)
CALIFORNIA LAND MGT SVCS CORP (PA)
Also Called: Clm Services
675 Gilman St, Palo Alto (94301-2528)
PHONE................................650 322-1181
Janice Nakaya, *Ch of Bd*
Eric R Mart, *President*
Larry Farquhar, *Software Dev*
Mel Brown, *Site Mgr*
Jace Reed, *Opers Mgr*
EMP: 50
SQ FT: 1,800
SALES: 12.7MM **Privately Held**
WEB: www.clm-services.com
SIC: 7999 5091 Recreation services;
camping equipment & supplies

(P-18642)
CAPITOL CASINO
411 N 16th St, Sacramento (95811-0516)
PHONE................................916 446-0700
Clarke Rosa, *President*
EMP: 150
SQ FT: 7,500
SALES (est): 3.8MM **Privately Held**
WEB: www.capitol-casino.com
SIC: 7999 5813 Card rooms; cocktail
lounge

(P-18643)
CARMICHAEL RECREATION & PK DST
5750 Grant Ave, Carmichael (95608-3779)
PHONE................................916 485-5322
Ronald D Cuppy, *Administration*
EMP: 170
SALES (est): 5.8MM **Privately Held**
WEB: www.carmichaelpark.com
SIC: 7999 Recreation center

(P-18644)
CATALINA BUSINESS ENTPS INC
635 Crescent Ave, Avalon (90704)
P.O. Box 1919 (90704-1919)
PHONE................................310 510-1600
Buddy Wilson, *President*
EMP: 50
SALES (corp-wide): 1.9MM **Privately
Held**
SIC: 7999 Golf cart, power, rental
PA: Catalina Business Enterprises, Inc.
800 Cresent Ave
Avalon CA 90704
310 510-2550

(P-18645)
CHER-AE HEIGHTS INDIAN CMNTY
Also Called: Cher Ae Heights Casino
27 Scenic Dr, Trinidad (95570-9767)
P.O. Box 610 (95570-0610)
PHONE................................707 677-3611
Ron Dadouin, *Manager*
EMP: 196 **Privately Held**
WEB: www.trinidadrancheria.com
SIC: 7999 7011 Card rooms; casino hotel
PA: Cher-Ae Heights Indian Community
1 Cher Ae Ln
Trinidad CA 95570
707 677-0211

(P-18646)
CHICKEN RANCH BINGO & CASINO
16929 Chicken Ranch Rd, Jamestown
(95327-9779)
P.O. Box 1699 (95327-1699)
PHONE................................209 984-3000
Lloyd Matheson, *Owner*
Tim Hawk, *CFO*
Trish Magdaleno, *Human Res Mgr*
EMP: 150
SQ FT: 35,000

SALES: 5.7K **Privately Held**
SIC: 7999 Bingo hall

(P-18647)
CHICO AREA RECREATION & PK DST (PA)
Also Called: Dorothy Johnson Center
545 Vallombrosa Ave, Chico (95926-4037)
PHONE................................530 895-4711
Mary Cahill, *General Mgr*
Heidi Radcliffe, *Finance Asst*
Ryan Arnold, *Mktg Coord*
Marty Bergstedt, *Manager*
Scott Dowel, *Manager*
EMP: 135
SQ FT: 27,000
SALES (est): 4.7MM **Privately Held**
WEB: www.chicorec.com
SIC: 7999 8322 Recreation services; individual & family services

(P-18648)
CHOPRA CNTRE FOR WLL-BEING LLC
Also Called: Chopra Center For Wellbeing
2013 Costa Del Mar Rd, Carlsbad
(92009-6801)
PHONE................................760 494-1600
Deepak Chopra MD, *Principal*
David Simon MD, *Principal*
Treloar Hocking, *Opers Staff*
Gail Vogt, *Marketing Staff*
Christine Day, *Director*
▲ EMP: 51 EST: 1996
SALES (est): 4.6MM **Privately Held**
SIC: 7999 8299 7991 Yoga instruction;
meditation therapy; spas

(P-18649)
CHRISTIANSEN AMUSEMENTS CORP
1725 S Escondido Blvd E, Escondido
(92025-6546)
P.O. Box 997 (92033-0997)
PHONE................................760 735-8542
Stacey Brown, *President*
William Jacob, *Vice Pres*
Mindy Seltmann, *Vice Pres*
EMP: 70
SALES (est): 2.1MM **Privately Held**
WEB: www.carnivalgame.com
SIC: 7999 Carnival operation; amusement
ride

(P-18650)
CHUMASH CASINO RESORT (HQ)
3400 E Highway 246, Santa Ynez
(93460-9405)
PHONE................................805 686-0855
Carol Clearwater, *CFO*
Daniel Breining, *Officer*
David Brents, *Officer*
John Featherstone, *Executive*
Mike Hackett, *Exec Dir*
EMP: 168
SQ FT: 29,000
SALES (est): 28.9MM **Privately Held**
WEB: www.chumashcasino.com
SIC: 7999 7011 Gambling establishment;
resort hotel

(P-18651)
CITY OF COMMERCE
Also Called: Parks & Recreation
2535 Commerce Way, Commerce
(90040-1410)
PHONE................................323 722-4805
Jim Jimenez, *Director*
EMP: 400 **Privately Held**
SIC: 7999 7991 Recreation center; physical fitness facilities
PA: City Of Commerce
2535 Commerce Way
Commerce CA 90040
323 722-4805

(P-18652)
CITY OF COMPTON
Also Called: William Love Swimming Pool
1108 N Oleander Ave, Compton
(90222-4041)
PHONE................................310 635-3484
Vanessa Little, *Principal*
Marvin Hunt, *Director*

EMP: 60 **Privately Held**
SIC: 7999 9111 Swimming pool, nonmembership; mayors' offices
PA: City Of Compton
205 S Willowbrook Ave
Compton CA 90220
310 605-5500

(P-18653)
CITY OF CORONADO
Also Called: Recreation Dept
1845 Strand Way, Coronado (92118-3005)
PHONE................................619 522-7342
Linda Rahn, *Director*
EMP: 100 **Privately Held**
WEB: www.coronadoplayhouse.com
SIC: 7999 7997 Swimming pool, nonmembership; membership sports & recreation clubs
PA: City Of Coronado
1825 Strand Way
Coronado CA 92118
619 522-7300

(P-18654)
CITY OF FOLSOM
Also Called: Park and Recreation
48 Natoma St, Folsom (95630-2614)
PHONE................................916 355-7285
Robert Goss, *Director*
EMP: 75 **Privately Held**
WEB: www.folsompd.com
SIC: 7999 Recreation services
PA: City Of Folsom
50 Natoma St
Folsom CA 95630
916 355-7200

(P-18655)
CITY OF FOSTER CITY
Parks & Recreation
650 Shell Blvd, Foster City (94404-2501)
P.O. Box 4752 (94404-0752)
PHONE................................650 286-3380
Kevin Miller, *Director*
Estelle Gobrera, *Assistant*
EMP: 50 **Privately Held**
WEB: www.fostercitymothersclub.org
SIC: 7999 9111 Recreation services; mayors' offices
PA: City Of Foster City
610 Foster City Blvd
Foster City CA 94404
650 286-3260

(P-18656)
CITY OF GALT
Also Called: Galt Park Recreation
660 Chabolla Ave, Galt (95632)
PHONE................................209 366-7180
Boyce Jeffries, *Director*
EMP: 65 **Privately Held**
WEB: www.ci.galt.ca.us
SIC: 7999 Recreation center
PA: City Of Galt
380 Civic Dr
Galt CA 95632
209 366-7000

(P-18657)
CITY OF INGLEWOOD
Also Called: Edward Vincent Park
700 Warren Ln, Inglewood (90302-3208)
PHONE................................310 412-5370
James Henry, *Manager*
EMP: 65 **Privately Held**
SIC: 7999 9111 Recreation services; mayors' offices
PA: City Of Inglewood
1 W Manchester Blvd
Inglewood CA 90301
310 412-5301

(P-18658)
CITY OF IRVINE
Also Called: Parks-Rcreation-Community
Svcs
6443 Oak Cyn, Irvine (92618-5202)
PHONE................................949 724-7740
EMP: 56 **Privately Held**
SIC: 7999 Recreation services
PA: City Of Irvine
1 Civic Center Plz
Irvine CA 92606
949 724-6000

(P-18659)
CITY OF MILL VALLEY
Also Called: Mill Valley Parks & Recreation
180 Camino Alto, Mill Valley (94941-4603)
PHONE..............................415 383-1370
Christine Som, *Director*
EMP: 50 **Privately Held**
WEB: www.donnadacuti.com
SIC: 7999 9111 Recreation services; mayors' offices
PA: City Of Mill Valley
26 Corte Madera Ave
Mill Valley CA 94941
415 388-4033

(P-18660)
CITY OF MONTEREY PARK
Also Called: City Mnterey Pk Recreation Ctr
320 W Newmark Ave Fl 1, Monterey Park
(91754-2896)
PHONE..............................626 307-1388
Harry Panagiotes, *Director*
EMP: 100 **Privately Held**
SIC: 7999 9111 Recreation center; mayors' offices
PA: City Of Monterey Park
320 W Newmark Ave
Monterey Park CA 91754
626 307-1255

(P-18661)
CITY OF OAKLAND
Also Called: Sports Office
250 Frank H Ogawa Plz # 6300, Oakland
(94612-2052)
PHONE..............................510 238-3494
Michael Hammock, *Principal*
EMP: 50 **Privately Held**
WEB: www.cityofbuellton.com
SIC: 7999 Sports instruction, schools & camps
PA: City Of Oakland
150 Frank H Ogawa Plz # 3332
Oakland CA 94612
510 238-3280

(P-18662)
CITY OF OAKLAND
Also Called: Oakland Ice Center
519 18th St, Oakland (94612-1511)
PHONE..............................510 268-9000
Dave Fies, *General Mgr*
Peggy Young, *Accountant*
EMP: 50 **Privately Held**
WEB: www.cityofbuellton.com
SIC: 7999 Ice skating rink operation
PA: City Of Oakland
150 Frank H Ogawa Plz # 3332
Oakland CA 94612
510 238-3280

(P-18663)
CITY OF ORANGE
Also Called: Parks Recreation Libraries
230 E Chapman Ave, Orange
(92866-1506)
PHONE..............................714 744-7272
Gary Wann, *Director*
EMP: 50 **Privately Held**
WEB: www.cityoforange.org
SIC: 7999 Recreation services
PA: City Of Orange
300 E Chapman Ave
Orange CA 92866
714 744-5500

(P-18664)
CITY OF RICHMOND
Also Called: Convention Center Booking Off
3230 Macdonald Ave Fl 2, Richmond
(94804-3012)
P.O. Box 4046 (94804-0046)
PHONE..............................510 620-6788
Jesse Washington, *Director*
Sue Hartman, *Vice Pres*
EMP: 100 **Privately Held**
WEB: www.kcrt.com
SIC: 7999 Recreation center
PA: City Of Richmond
450 Civic Center Plaza
Richmond CA 94804
510 620-6727

(P-18665)
CITY OF SOUTH LAKE TAHOE
Also Called: Recreation Complex
1180 Rufus Allen Blvd, South Lake Tahoe
(96150-8211)
PHONE..............................530 542-6056
Gary Moore, *Superintendent*
EMP: 78 **Privately Held**
WEB: www.cityofslt.com
SIC: 7999 Swimming pool, non-membership
PA: City Of South Lake Tahoe
1901 Airport Rd Ste 210
South Lake Tahoe CA 96150

(P-18666)
CITY OF TORRANCE
Also Called: Park Maintenance
20500 Madrona Ave, Torrance
(90503-3692)
PHONE..............................310 781-6901
Robert Carson, *General Mgr*
EMP: 55 **Privately Held**
SIC: 7999 Recreation center
PA: City Of Torrance
3031 Torrance Blvd
Torrance CA 90503
310 328-5310

(P-18667)
CITY OF VISTA
Wave Water Park
101 Wave Dr, Vista (92083-5824)
PHONE..............................760 940-9283
Natalie Livingston, *Branch Mgr*
EMP: 150 **Privately Held**
WEB: www.cityofvista.com
SIC: 7999 Tourist attractions, amusement park concessions & rides
PA: City Of Vista
200 Civic Center Dr
Vista CA 92084
760 726-1340

(P-18668)
CITY OF WOODLAND
Also Called: Charles Brooks Cmnty Swim Ctr
2001 East St, Woodland (95776-5183)
PHONE..............................530 661-5878
Dan Gentry, *Director*
EMP: 200 **Privately Held**
WEB: www.ci.woodland.ca.us
SIC: 7999 9111 Swimming pool, non-membership; mayors' offices
PA: City Of Woodland
300 1st St
Woodland CA 95695
530 661-5830

(P-18669)
CONCESSION MANAGEMENT SVCS INC
Also Called: C M S Hospitality
6033 W Century Blvd # 890, Los Angeles
(90045-6414)
P.O. Box 180250 (90018-0717)
PHONE..............................310 846-5830
Clarence A Daniels Jr, *CEO*
EMP: 150
SQ FT: 800
SALES (est) 9.7MM **Privately Held**
SIC: 7999 Concession operator

(P-18670)
CONCESSIONAIRES URBAN PARK (PA)
Also Called: Angel Island Co
2150 Main St Ste 5, Red Bluff
(96080-2372)
PHONE..............................530 529-1512
John W Koeberer, *CEO*
Kris Koeberer, *Vice Pres*
Pamela Koeberrer Pitts, *Vice Pres*
Michele Silva Lane, *Controller*
Dina Del Dotto, *Director*
EMP: 300 EST: 1981
SQ FT: 2,800
SALES (est): 16.2MM **Privately Held**
WEB: www.angelisland.com
SIC: 7999 5941 5812 Beach & water sports equipment rental & services; fishing equipment; snack bar

(P-18671)
CONCESSIONAIRES URBAN PARK
Also Called: Camanche Recreation-North
2000 Camanche Rd Ofc Ofc, Ione
(95640-9420)
PHONE..............................209 763-5121
Chris Cantwell, *Branch Mgr*
EMP: 50
SALES (corp-wide): 16.2MM **Privately Held**
WEB: www.angelisland.com
SIC: 7999 7032 Beach & water sports equipment rental & services; recreational camps
PA: Urban Park Concessionaires
2150 Main St Ste 5
Red Bluff CA 96080
530 529-1512

(P-18672)
CONCESSIONAIRES URBAN PARK
Also Called: Camanche Northshore Store
2000 Camanche Rd Ofc Ofc, Ione
(95640-9420)
PHONE..............................209 763-5166
Chris Cantwell, *Branch Mgr*
EMP: 75
SALES (corp-wide): 16.2MM **Privately Held**
WEB: www.angelisland.com
SIC: 7999 5941 5812 Beach & water sports equipment rental & services; fishing equipment; snack bar
PA: Urban Park Concessionaires
2150 Main St Ste 5
Red Bluff CA 96080
530 529-1512

(P-18673)
CONCESSIONAIRES URBAN PARK
34600 Ardenwood Blvd, Fremont
(94555-3645)
PHONE..............................530 529-1596
Michele Silva Lane, *Branch Mgr*
EMP: 100
SALES (corp-wide): 16.2MM **Privately Held**
WEB: www.angelisland.com
SIC: 7999 5941 5812 Beach & water sports equipment rental & services; fishing equipment; snack bar
PA: Urban Park Concessionaires
2150 Main St Ste 5
Red Bluff CA 96080
530 529-1512

(P-18674)
CONCESSIONAIRES URBAN PARK
Also Called: Ranch At Little Hills, The
18013 Bollinger Canyon Rd, San Ramon
(94583-1501)
PHONE..............................530 529-1513
Michele Silva Lane, *Manager*
EMP: 100
SALES (corp-wide): 16.2MM **Privately Held**
WEB: www.angelisland.com
SIC: 7999 5941 5812 Beach & water sports equipment rental & services; fishing equipment; snack bar
PA: Urban Park Concessionaires
2150 Main St Ste 5
Red Bluff CA 96080
530 529-1512

(P-18675)
COSUMNES COMMUNITY SVCS DST
9355 E Stockton Blvd, Elk Grove
(95624-9476)
PHONE..............................916 405-7150
Rod Brewer, *President*
Rich Lozano, *Vice Pres*
EMP: 387 EST: 1985
SQ FT: 10,000
SALES: 60MM **Privately Held**
SIC: 7999 Recreation services

(P-18676)
COUNTY OF KERN
Parks & Recreation
500 Cascade Pl, Taft (93268-2641)
P.O. Box 1406 (93268-1406)
PHONE..............................661 763-4246
Les Clark, *Superintendent*
EMP: 50 **Privately Held**
WEB: www.kccfc.org
SIC: 7999 Recreation services
PA: County Of Kern
1115 Truxtun Ave Rm 505
Bakersfield CA 93301
661 868-3690

(P-18677)
COUNTY OF RIVERSIDE
Economic Development
82503 Us Highway 111, Indio (92201-5633)
PHONE..............................760 863-8247
Darrell Shippy, *Manager*
EMP: 60 **Privately Held**
SIC: 7999 9611 9512 Fair; economic development agency, government; ; land, mineral & wildlife conservation;
PA: County Of Riverside
4080 Lemon St Fl 11
Riverside CA 92501
951 955-1110

(P-18678)
CRESSE MARK SCHOOL OF BASEBALL
58 Fulmar Ln, Aliso Viejo (92656-1764)
PHONE..............................714 892-6145
Mark E Cresse, *President*
Jeff Courvoisier, *Exec Dir*
EMP: 80
SALES: 1.4MM **Privately Held**
SIC: 7999 Baseball instruction school

(P-18679)
CTOUR HOLIDAY LLC
222 E Huntington Dr # 105, Monrovia
(91016-8006)
PHONE..............................323 261-8811
Charlie Lu, *Mng Member*
EMP: 300 EST: 2016
SALES (est): 1.6MM **Privately Held**
SIC: 7999 Tour & guide services

(P-18680)
DESERT RECREATION DISTRICT (PA)
45305 Oasis St, Indio (92201-4337)
PHONE..............................760 347-3484
Rudy Acosta, *President*
Noelle Furon, *Officer*
Laura McGalliard, *Vice Pres*
Steven Lorick, *Exec Dir*
Manuel Rios, *Technician*
EMP: 55
SQ FT: 40,000
SALES (est): 6MM **Privately Held**
WEB: www.cvrpd.org
SIC: 7999 Recreation center

(P-18681)
DESTINY ARTS CENTER
970 Grace Ave, Oakland (94608-2784)
PHONE..............................510 597-1619
Cristy Johnson, *Exec Dir*
Sarah Crowell, *Exec Dir*
Cristy Johnston-Limon, *Exec Dir*
Eden Feil, *Office Mgr*
Razavi Nasim, *Business Mgr*
EMP: 50
SALES: 1.9MM **Privately Held**
WEB: www.destinyarts.org
SIC: 7999 7911 Martial arts school; golf professionals; dance studio & school

(P-18682)
DISNEY REGIONAL ENTRMT INC (DH)
500 S Buena Vista St, Burbank
(91521-0001)
PHONE..............................818 560-1000
Arthur Levitt, *President*
Gary Marcotte, *CFO*
EMP: 200

SALES (est): 33.7MM
SALES (corp-wide): 90.2B **Publicly Held**
SIC: 7999 5812 5813 Recreation center; eating places; American restaurant; drinking places; bar (drinking places)

(P-18683)
DOWNTOWN SD VENTURES LLC
Also Called: Bassmnt
20162 Sw Birch St Ste 350, Newport Beach (92660-0790)
PHONE....................................619 231-9200
Mike Kinsella, *Mng Member*
EMP: 60
SQ FT: 1,500
SALES (est): 1.1MM **Privately Held**
SIC: 7999 Night club, not serving alcoholic beverages

(P-18684)
DROPZONE WATERPARK
2165 Trumble Rd, Perris (92571-9211)
PHONE....................................951 210-1600
Erica Bice, *Director*
EMP: 150
SALES (est): 164.7K **Privately Held**
SIC: 7999 Recreation services

(P-18685)
EAGLE RAFTING
13226 Sierra Way, Kernville (93238)
P.O. Box 2013 (93238-2013)
PHONE....................................760 376-3648
Loxie Chesney, *Owner*
EMP: 250
SALES (est): 3.5MM **Privately Held**
WEB: www.eaglerafting.com
SIC: 7999 Tour & guide services

(P-18686)
EAST BAY REGIONAL PARK DST
Also Called: East Bay Regional Park Public
17930 Lake Chabot Rd, Castro Valley (94546-1950)
PHONE....................................510 881-1833
Timothy Anderson, *Chief*
EMP: 75
SALES (corp-wide): 201.9MM **Privately Held**
SIC: 7999 Recreation services
PA: East Bay Regional Park District
2950 Peralta Oaks Ct
Oakland CA 94605
888 327-2757

(P-18687)
EAST VALLEY TOURIST DEV AUTH
Also Called: Fantasy Springs Resort Casino
84245 Indio Springs Dr, Indio (92203-3405)
PHONE....................................760 342-5000
John James, *Ch of Bd*
Angela Roosevelt, *Corp Secy*
Mark Benitez, *Vice Ch Bd*
Brenda Soulliere, *Vice Ch Bd*
Don Casper, *Vice Pres*
EMP: 1200
SQ FT: 94,000
SALES (est): 55.2MM **Privately Held**
WEB: www.fantasyspringsresort.com
SIC: 7999 Gambling establishment; off-track betting

(P-18688)
ENCORE INC
Also Called: Encore Gymnstics Dnce Climbing
999 Bancroft Rd, Concord (94518-3911)
P.O. Box 30113, Walnut Creek (94598-9113)
PHONE....................................925 932-1033
Tamara Gerlach, *President*
EMP: 50
SQ FT: 17,000
SALES: 1MM **Privately Held**
SIC: 7999 Gymnastic instruction, non-membership

(P-18689)
FAIRPLEX ENTERPRISES INC
1101 W Mckinley Ave, Pomona (91768-1650)
PHONE....................................909 623-3111
James Henwood, *President*
Michelle Demott, *Vice Pres*
John Gilbert, *Vice Pres*

Lucas Rivera, *Vice Pres*
Dwight Richards, *Executive*
▲ **EMP:** 52
SALES (est): 4.8MM
SALES (corp-wide): 66.3MM **Privately Held**
SIC: 7999 Fair
PA: Los Angeles County Fair Association
1101 W Mckinley Ave
Pomona CA 91768
909 623-3111

(P-18690)
FAZE CLAN INC
1800 Vine St Ste 301, Los Angeles (90028-5234)
PHONE....................................818 538-5204
Lee Trink, *CEO*
Tyler Rayne, *Info Tech Mgr*
EMP: 56
SALES (est): 700K **Privately Held**
SIC: 7999 5961 Games, instruction;

(P-18691)
FEATHER RVER RECREATION PK DST
1875 Feather River Blvd, Oroville (95965-5701)
PHONE....................................530 533-2011
Vicky Smith, *Chairman*
Victoria Coots, *Director*
Gary Emberland, *Director*
EMP: 76
SQ FT: 3,000
SALES (est): 1.7MM **Privately Held**
WEB: www.frrpd.com
SIC: 7999 Recreation center

(P-18692)
FESTIVAL FUN PARKS LLC
Also Called: Boomers
4590 Macarthur Blvd # 400, Newport Beach (92660-2027)
PHONE....................................954 921-1411
EMP: 150 **Privately Held**
SIC: 7999
HQ: Festival Fun Parks, Llc
4590 Macarthur Blvd # 400
Newport Beach CA 92660
949 261-0404

(P-18693)
FESTIVAL FUN PARKS LLC
Also Called: Camelot Park Santa Maria
2250 Preisker Ln, Santa Maria (93458-9060)
PHONE....................................805 922-1574
Jesse Ghormley, *Manager*
EMP: 160 **Privately Held**
SIC: 7999 7993 7991 Miniature golf course operation; arcades; physical fitness facilities
HQ: Festival Fun Parks, Llc
4590 Macarthur Blvd # 400
Newport Beach CA 92660
949 261-0404

(P-18694)
FESTIVAL FUN PARKS LLC
Also Called: Boomers
1525 W Vista Way, Vista (92083-4001)
PHONE....................................760 945-9474
Mark Williams, *Manager*
EMP: 85 **Privately Held**
SIC: 7999 Recreation services
HQ: Festival Fun Parks, Llc
4590 Macarthur Blvd # 400
Newport Beach CA 92660
949 261-0404

(P-18695)
FESTIVAL FUN PARKS LLC
Also Called: Palace Park
3405 Michelson Dr, Irvine (92612-1605)
PHONE....................................949 559-8336
Craig Stieglitz, *General Mgr*
EMP: 100 **Privately Held**
SIC: 7999 7996 Tourist attractions, amusement park concessions & rides; amusement parks
HQ: Festival Fun Parks, Llc
4590 Macarthur Blvd # 400
Newport Beach CA 92660
949 261-0404

(P-18696)
FESTIVAL OF ARTS LAGUNA BEACH
650 Laguna Canyon Rd, Laguna Beach (92651-1899)
PHONE....................................949 494-1145
Fredric Sattler, *CEO*
Gary Fowler, *COO*
David Perry, *Vice Pres*
Monica Daebritz, *Office Mgr*
Pat Kollenda, *Admin Sec*
EMP: 51
SQ FT: 6,500
SALES: 9.6MM **Privately Held**
SIC: 7999 Festival operation

(P-18697)
FINLEY SWIM CENTER
Also Called: Ridgway
2060 W College Ave, Santa Rosa (95401-4458)
PHONE....................................707 543-3760
Don Hicks, *Principal*
EMP: 50
SALES (est): 681.5K **Privately Held**
WEB: www.ridgway.com
SIC: 7999 Swimming pool, non-membership

(P-18698)
FLOATIES SWIM SCHOOL LLC
13180 Poway Rd, Poway (92064-4612)
PHONE....................................877 277-7946
Kira La Forgia, *Director*
EMP: 75
SALES (est): 188.6K **Privately Held**
SIC: 7999 Swimming instruction

(P-18699)
FOOD & AGRICULTURE CAL DEPT
Also Called: 32nd District-Orange Cnty Fair
88 Fair Dr, Costa Mesa (92626-6521)
PHONE....................................714 751-3247
Becky Bailey-Findley, *Branch Mgr*
EMP: 70 **Privately Held**
WEB: www.cmab.net
SIC: 7999 9641 6512 Agricultural fair; regulation of agricultural marketing; ; non-residential building operators
HQ: Food & Agriculture, California Dept
1220 N St Ste 400
Sacramento CA 95814

(P-18700)
FUNTOPIA INC
3700 Brookstone Dr, Turlock (95382-9290)
PHONE....................................510 246-3098
Sukhdeep Garcha, *Administration*
EMP: 60
SALES (est): 165.9K **Privately Held**
SIC: 7999 Tourist attractions, amusement park concessions & rides

(P-18701)
GARDEN CITY INC
Also Called: Garden City Casino & Rest
1887 Matrix Blvd, San Jose (95110-2309)
PHONE....................................408 244-3333
Pete V Lunardi III, *CEO*
Eli Reinhard, *President*
Llene Brandon, *CFO*
Kathy Reiner, *CFO*
Simeon Shigg, *CFO*
EMP: 569 EST: 1974
SQ FT: 22,000
SALES (est): 10.5MM **Privately Held**
SIC: 7999 Card rooms

(P-18702)
GLAD ENTERTAINMENT INC (PA)
Also Called: Blackbeard's Family Fun Center
4055 N Chestnut Ave, Fresno (93726-4701)
PHONE....................................559 292-9000
Greg Florer, *President*
Don Jackley, *Corp Secy*
EMP: 70 EST: 1977
SQ FT: 12,000
SALES (est): 3.4MM **Privately Held**
WEB: www.blackbeardsfresno.com
SIC: 7999 Miniature golf course operation; baseball batting cage; waterslide operation; amusement concession

(P-18703)
GREATER VALLEJO RECREATION DST
395 Amador St, Vallejo (94590-6320)
PHONE....................................707 648-4600
William Pendergast III, *Ch of Bd*
Phillip McCoy, *General Mgr*
Anthony Kenaston, *Admin Sec*
Jazsmine Alzate, *Technician*
Casey Halcro, *Human Res Mgr*
EMP: 150 EST: 1944
SQ FT: 5,000
SALES (est): 7.1MM **Privately Held**
WEB: www.gvrd.org
SIC: 7999 Recreation services

(P-18704)
HIGH DESERT PHOENIX
42980 Staffordshire Dr, Lancaster (93534-6263)
PHONE....................................661 547-5630
Norma Cook, *Principal*
EMP: 50
SALES (est): 316K **Privately Held**
SIC: 7999 Amusement & recreation

(P-18705)
HOPLAND BAND POMO INDIANS INC
Also Called: Casino
13101 Nokomis Rd, Hopland (95449-9793)
PHONE....................................707 744-1395
John O'Neil, *Manager*
EMP: 200
SALES (corp-wide): 17.8MM **Privately Held**
WEB: www.hoplandtribe.com
SIC: 7999 7011 5813 5812 Gambling establishment; casino hotel; drinking places; eating places
PA: Hopland Band Of Pomo Indians Inc.
3000 Shanel Rd
Hopland CA 95449
707 472-2100

(P-18706)
HOUSE OF AIR LLC
926 Mason St, San Francisco (94129-1602)
PHONE....................................415 345-9675
Paul McGeehan,
Shoshanna Moody, *General Mgr*
David Schaeffer,
EMP: 61 EST: 2009
SALES (est): 1.7MM **Privately Held**
SIC: 7999 Recreation center; trampoline operation

(P-18707)
HOWE COMMUNITY CENTER
2201 Cottage Way, Sacramento (95825-1022)
PHONE....................................916 927-3802
Jeff Dubchnasky, *General Mgr*
Jeff Dubchansky, *General Mgr*
EMP: 50
SALES (est): 303.8K **Privately Held**
SIC: 7999 Recreation center

(P-18708)
ICE CENTER ENTERPRISES LLC
Also Called: Ice Center, The
10123 N Wolfe Rd Ste 1020, Cupertino (95014-2585)
P.O. Box 1433, Alameda (94501-0155)
PHONE....................................510 604-8878
Michael Benesh,
Christopher Hathaway, *COO*
Mike Benesh, *Executive*
Chris Hathaway,
EMP: 75
SQ FT: 28,000
SALES (est): 1.7MM **Privately Held**
WEB: www.icecenter.net
SIC: 7999 Ice skating rink operation

(P-18709)
ICE SPECIALTY ENTRMT INC (PA)
Also Called: Iceoplex
409 Santa Monica Blvd E, Santa Monica (90401-2378)
PHONE....................................310 899-3889
Bradford Becken, *President*
EMP: 140

SQ FT: 1,300
SALES: 5MM **Privately Held**
SIC: 7999 Skating rink operation services

(P-18710)
ICE STATION VALENCIA L L C
27745 Smyth Dr, Valencia (91355-4019)
PHONE..............................661 775-8686
Roger Perez, *Principal*
EMP: 60
SALES: 277.6K **Privately Held**
SIC: 7999 7299 Ice skating rink operation;
party planning service

(P-18711)
KAIMANU OUTRIGGER CANOE CLUB
13424 Doolittle Dr, San Leandro
(94577-4141)
PHONE..............................510 895-0435
Debbie Green, *President*
EMP: 60 **EST:** 1977
SALES (est): 2.2MM **Privately Held**
SIC: 7999 Rowboat & canoe rental

(P-18712)
KATHERINE BOUSSON
1015 Palisade St, Hayward (94542-1025)
PHONE..............................510 582-1166
Katherine Bousson, *Owner*
EMP: 85
SQ FT: 1,000
SALES (est): 2.2MM **Privately Held**
WEB: www.palacecardclub.com
SIC: 7999 Card rooms

(P-18713)
KEB KEB MAGIC CLOWN
637 Germaine Dr, Galt (95632-2161)
P.O. Box 163584, Sacramento (95816-9584)
PHONE..............................916 369-6054
Kevin Keller, *Owner*
EMP: 72
SALES: 10MM **Privately Held**
SIC: 7999 Tennis services & professionals

(P-18714)
KERN RIVER TOURS INC
2712 Mayfair Rd, Lake Isabella
(93240-9643)
P.O. Box 3444 (93240-3444)
PHONE..............................760 379-4616
Kenneth Busheing, *President*
Joseph M Kent, *Corp Secy*
EMP: 70
SQ FT: 2,250
SALES: 500K **Privately Held**
WEB: www.kernrivertours.com
SIC: 7999 Tourist guide

(P-18715)
KINGS CASINO MANAGEMENT CORP
6510 Antelope Rd, Citrus Heights
(95621-1077)
PHONE..............................916 560-4405
Ryan Stone, *CEO*
EMP: 350 **EST:** 2013
SALES (est): 8.4MM **Privately Held**
SIC: 7999 Card & game services

(P-18716)
KONOCTI VISTA CASINO (PA)
2755 Mission Rancheria Rd, Lakeport
(95453-9612)
P.O. Box 57, Finley (95435-0057)
PHONE..............................707 262-1900
Sam Dornham, *General Mgr*
Larry Green, *CFO*
EMP: 225
SALES (est): 11.6MM **Privately Held**
SIC: 7999 Gambling establishment

(P-18717)
LEISURE PLANET
Also Called: Jungle Fun & Adventure
1975 Diamond Blvd, Concord
(94520-5792)
PHONE..............................925 687-4386
Olivier Sermet, *President*
EMP: 130
SQ FT: 15,000

SALES (est): 2.6MM **Privately Held**
WEB: www.junglefunadventure.com
SIC: 7999 5947 Tourist attractions,
amusement park concessions & rides;
gifts & novelties

(P-18718)
LIVERMORE AREA RCRATION PK DST
71 Trevarno Rd, Livermore (94551-4931)
PHONE..............................925 373-5700
Doug Bell, *Branch Mgr*
Don Humphrey, *Finance Mgr*
Denise Deprato, *Human Res Mgr*
EMP: 131
SALES (est): 1MM
SALES (corp-wide): 9.5MM **Privately Held**
SIC: 7999 8211 Recreation services; pub-
lic elementary & secondary schools
PA: Livermore Area Recreation & Park Dis-
trict
4444 East Ave
Livermore CA 94550
925 373-5700

(P-18719)
LIVERMORE AREA RCRATION PK DST (PA)
4444 East Ave, Livermore (94550-5053)
PHONE..............................925 373-5700
Tim Barry, *General Mgr*
Jeffrey Schneider, *Admin Mgr*
Sandra Kaya, *Admin Asst*
Maryalice Faltings, *Director*
David Furst, *Director*
EMP: 260 **EST:** 1947
SQ FT: 71,000
SALES (est): 9.5MM **Privately Held**
WEB: www.larpd.dst.ca.us
SIC: 7999 Recreation services

(P-18720)
LOS ANGELES COUNTY FAIR ASSN (PA)
Also Called: Fairplex Rv Park
1101 W Mckinley Ave, Pomona
(91768-1639)
PHONE..............................909 623-3111
Ronald Bolding, *Director*
Micheal Seder, *Vice Pres*
EMP: 100
SALES (est): 66.3MM **Privately Held**
SIC: 7999 8412 Fair; museums & art gal-
leries

(P-18721)
LYTTON RANCHERIA
Also Called: Casino San Pablo
13255 San Pablo Ave, San Pablo
(94806-3907)
PHONE..............................510 215-7888
Michael Gorczynski, *General Mgr*
Cathi Hamel, *Principal*
Michael Gorczynski, *General Mgr*
Jeff Dossey, *Info Tech Mgr*
Marissa Sepagan, *Marketing Staff*
EMP: 547
SALES (est): 20.7MM **Privately Held**
WEB: www.casinosanpablo.com
SIC: 7999 Gambling & lottery services

(P-18722)
MINDFULL BODY
2876 California St, San Francisco
(94115-2545)
PHONE..............................415 931-2639
Roy N Bergmann, *Owner*
Charisse Sharpe, *Human Res Mgr*
EMP: 80
SALES (est): 1.6MM **Privately Held**
SIC: 7999 7299 Yoga instruction; mas-
sage parlor

(P-18723)
MISSION OAKS RECREATION PK DST
3344 Mission Ave, Carmichael
(95608-3111)
PHONE..............................916 488-2810
Daniel Barton, *Administration*
Cindy Paredes, *Director*
Lisa Paredes, *Assistant*
Nicole Plumley, *Assistant*
Rodney Dahlberg, *Supervisor*

EMP: 89
SQ FT: 1,500
SALES (est): 542.4K **Privately Held**
SIC: 7999 Recreation center

(P-18724)
MOORETOWN RANCHERIA (PA)
Also Called: Feather Falls Casino
1 Alverda Dr, Oroville (95966-9379)
PHONE..............................530 533-3625
Gary Archuleta, *Ch of Bd*
Kayla Lobo, *Treasurer*
Melvin Jackson, *Vice Pres*
Julie McIntosh, *Principal*
Penny Palmer, *Admin Sec*
EMP: 50
SALES (est): 23.5MM **Privately Held**
WEB: www.drumvision.com
SIC: 7999 5993 Gambling establishment;
cigar store

(P-18725)
MOUNT SAN JACINTO WIN PK AUTH
Also Called: PALM SPRINGS AERIAL
TRAMWAY
1 Tramway Rd, Palm Springs
(92262-1827)
PHONE..............................760 325-1449
Rob Parkins, *President*
Marjorie Dela Cruz, *Vice Pres*
Nancy Nichols, *Vice Pres*
Marjorie De La Cruz, *HR Admin*
Scott Barrick, *Opers Spvr*
▲ **EMP:** 64 **EST:** 1945
SQ FT: 50,000
SALES: 19.4MM **Privately Held**
WEB: www.pstramway.com
SIC: 7999 Aerial tramway or ski lift, amuse-
ment or scenic

(P-18726)
MUSEUM OF CHILDRENS ART
Also Called: Mocha
1221 Broadway, Oakland (94612-1837)
PHONE..............................510 465-8770
Karen Ransom, *Director*
Roxanne Padgett, *Exec Dir*
Simon Muturi, *Administration*
Haldun Morgan, *Marketing Staff*
Katie Sammon, *Program Dir*
EMP: 50
SQ FT: 4,800
SALES (est): 844.6K **Privately Held**
WEB: www.mocha.org
SIC: 7999 8412 Art gallery, commercial;
instruction schools, camps & services;
museum

(P-18727)
NAPA VALLEY WINE TRAIN LLC (HQ)
Also Called: NAPA Valley Railroad Co
1275 Mckinstry St, NAPA (94559-1925)
PHONE..............................707 253-2160
Anthony J Giaccio,
Vincent M De Deminico Jr, *Vice Pres*
Diana Evensen, *Purchasing*
Yuri Soshizaki, *Marketing Staff*
Denise Perkins, *Sales Staff*
▲ **EMP:** 125
SQ FT: 20,000
SALES (est): 10.1MM **Privately Held**
WEB: www.winetrain.com
SIC: 7999 5812 4011 4119 Scenic rail-
roads for amusement; eating places; rail-
roads, line-haul operating; local
passenger transportation

(P-18728)
NEW COLUSA INDIAN BINGO
Also Called: Colusa Casino Resort
3770 State Highway 45, Colusa
(95932-4021)
PHONE..............................530 458-8844
Steve Gonzales, *Principal*
Bonnie Pullen, *CFO*
Fred Pina, *Vice Pres*
Tammy Harris, *Human Res Mgr*
Jamie Perry, *Opers Staff*
EMP: 450
SALES (est): 1.7MM **Privately Held**
SIC: 7999 Card & game services

(P-18729)
NORMANDIE CLUB LP
Also Called: Normandie Casino & Showroom
57 Via Malona, Rancho Palos Verdes
(90275-4882)
PHONE..............................310 352-3486
Lawrence F Miller, *Managing Prtnr*
Russel Miller Jr, *General Ptnr*
Greg Miller, *Partner*
Steve Miller, *Partner*
Sandi Miller, *Accounting Mgr*
▲ **EMP:** 600
SQ FT: 44,000
SALES (est): 21.6MM **Privately Held**
WEB: www.normandiecasino.com
SIC: 7999 5812 Card & game services;
eating places

(P-18730)
O A OUTFITTING INC
Also Called: Kern River Outfitters
6602 Wofford Heights Blvd, Bayside
(95524)
P.O. Box 91 (95524-0091)
PHONE..............................707 498-2917
James Ritter, *President*
Robert Volpert, *CEO*
EMP: 55
SALES: 1MM **Privately Held**
SIC: 7999 Recreation services

(P-18731)
O C SAILING CLUB INC
Also Called: Olympic Circle Sailing Club
1 Spinnaker Way, Berkeley (94710-1612)
PHONE..............................510 843-4200
Anthony P Sandberg, *President*
Svet Voskoboinik, *Bookkeeper*
EMP: 65
SQ FT: 5,000
SALES (est): 3.4MM **Privately Held**
WEB: www.ocscsailing.com
SIC: 7999 5651 Sailing instruction; pleas-
ure boat rental; family clothing stores

(P-18732)
OCEANSIDE LIFEGUARDS
300 N Coast Hwy, Oceanside
(92054-2824)
PHONE..............................760 435-4500
Ray Duncan, *Manager*
Tracey Bohlen, *Manager*
EMP: 73
SALES (est): 774.8K **Privately Held**
WEB: www.ci.oceanside.ca.us
SIC: 7999 Lifeguard service

(P-18733)
PALACE ENTERTAINMENT INC (DH)
4590 Macarthur Blvd # 400, Newport Beach
(92660-2027)
PHONE..............................949 261-0404
Alexander Weber Jr, *CEO*
- John Cora, *President*
Albert Cabuco, *Vice Pres*
James Judy, *Vice Pres*
Anthony Woods, *Vice Pres*
EMP: 50
SQ FT: 8,000
SALES (est): 88.1MM **Privately Held**
SIC: 7999 7993 Miniature golf course op-
eration; arcades
HQ: Parque De Atracciones Madrid Sa
Lugar Parque Atracciones (Casa De
Campo), S/N
Madrid 28011
902 345-001

(P-18734)
PARC MANAGEMENT LLC
Also Called: Waterworld USA
1950 Waterworld Pkwy, Concord
(94520-2602)
PHONE..............................925 609-1364
Steve Mayer, *Manager*
EMP: 1988
SALES (corp-wide): 77.1MM **Privately Held**
WEB: www.parcmanagement.com
SIC: 7999 Picnic ground operation
PA: Parc Management, Llc
8649 Baypine Rd Ste 101
Jacksonville FL 32256
904 732-7272

P R O D U C T S & S V C S

(P-18735)
PARKS AND RECREATION CAL DEPT
Also Called: Camanche Lake
2000 Camanche Rd Ofc, Ione
(95640-9420)
PHONE..................................209 763-5121
Mary Mendence, *Manager*
EMP: 50 Privately Held
WEB: www.aprpd.org
SIC: 7999 Recreation center; ping pong parlor
HQ: California Department Of Parks And Recreation
1416 9th St Ste 1041
Sacramento CA 95814
800 777-0369

(P-18736)
PAUL MAURER COMPANY
Also Called: Paul Maurer Shows
16081 Warren Ln, Huntington Beach
(92649-2433)
PHONE..................................714 231-8241
Paul Maurer, *Owner*
EMP: 60
SALES (est): 1MM Privately Held
SIC: 7999 Amusement ride

(P-18737)
PERRIS VLY SKYDIVING SCHL INC
2091 Goetz Rd, Perris (92570-9315)
PHONE..................................951 657-1664
Melanie Conatser, *President*
Patrick Conatser, *Vice Pres*
Laura Work, *Accountant*
James Perez, *Instructor*
EMP: 50
SALES (est): 961.9K Privately Held
WEB: www.skydiveperris.com
SIC: 7999 4581 Tennis services & professionals; airport

(P-18738)
PIT RIVER TRIBAL COUNCIL
Also Called: Pit River Casino
20265 Tamarack Ave, Burney
(96013-4064)
PHONE..................................530 335-2334
Nathan Schoofield, *Manager*
Mike Avelar, *Manager*
David Hawkins, *Editor*
EMP: 54
SALES (corp-wide): 4.5MM Privately Held
WEB: www.pitrivercasino.com
SIC: 7999 Card & game services; bingo hall
PA: Pit River Tribal Council
37960 Park Ave
Burney CA 96013
530 335-5487

(P-18739)
PLAYWORKS EDUCATION ENERGIZED (PA)
638 3rd St, Oakland (94607-3551)
PHONE..................................510 893-4180
Jill Vialet, *President*
Elizabeth Cushing, *President*
David Carroll, *CFO*
Phillis Carte, *CFO*
Amanda Casey, *CFO*
EMP: 50
SALES (est): 18.9MM Privately Held
WEB: www.sports4kids.org
SIC: 7999 Recreation services

(P-18740)
PYRAMID ENTERPRISES INC (PA)
Also Called: Lake Piru Marina
28368 Constellation Rd # 380, Valencia
(91355-5005)
PHONE..................................661 702-1420
Chester Roberts, *President*
Traci Roberts, *Admin Sec*
EMP: 60
SQ FT: 1,300
SALES (est): 7MM Privately Held
WEB: www.lake-piru.com
SIC: 7999 4493 Beach & water sports equipment rental & services; marinas

(P-18741)
QUECHAN INDIAN TRIBE
Also Called: Quechan Gaming Commission
450 Quechan Rd, Winterhaven
(92283-9676)
P.O. Box 2737, Yuma AZ (85366-2573)
PHONE..................................760 572-2413
Mike Jackson, *President*
Juan Gabriel Leyva, *Comp Spec*
EMP: 300 Privately Held
SIC: 7999 5812 Gambling establishment; eating places
PA: Quechan Indian Tribe
350 Picacho Rd
Winterhaven CA 92283
760 572-0213

(P-18742)
RAINBOW CAMP INC
26619 Marigold Ct, Calabasas
(91302-2945)
PHONE..................................310 456-3066
EMP: 50
SALES: 165K Privately Held
WEB: www.rainbowcamp.com
SIC: 7999

(P-18743)
RANCHO BERNARDO GOLF CLUB
Also Called: COUNTRY CLUB OF RANCHO BERNARD
17550 Bernardo Oaks Dr, San Diego
(92128-2112)
PHONE..................................858 487-1134
Jeff Grace, *President*
Mike Curry, *President*
Sandy Douglass, *President*
David Mrachek, *Principal*
Richard Park, *Principal*
EMP: 62
SQ FT: 23,000
SALES: 3.6MM Privately Held
WEB: www.ccofrb.com
SIC: 7999 7371 Golf services & professionals; computer software development & applications

(P-18744)
RANCHO JURUPA PARK
4800 Crestmore Rd, Riverside
(92509-6839)
PHONE..................................951 684-7032
Paul Franzen, *President*
EMP: 50
SALES (est): 578.3K Privately Held
SIC: 7999 Recreation center

(P-18745)
RANCHO SIMI RECREATION PK DST (PA)
4201 Guardian St, Simi Valley
(93063-3372)
PHONE..................................805 584-4400
Doug Gale, *Administration*
EMP: 70 EST: 1961
SQ FT: 1,589
SALES (est): 5.3MM Privately Held
WEB: www.rsrpd.org
SIC: 7999 Recreation services

(P-18746)
REDWOOD EMPIRE ICE OPRTONS LLC (PA)
Also Called: Snoopy's Galary and Gift Shop
1667 W Steele Ln, Santa Rosa
(95403-2625)
PHONE..................................707 546-7147
Jean F Schulz, *President*
EMP: 80 EST: 1968
SQ FT: 40,000
SALES (est): 2.7MM Privately Held
SIC: 7999 5947 5812 Ice skating rink operation; gift shop; coffee shop

(P-18747)
ROLLING HLLS ESTTES TENNIS CLB
Also Called: Rolling Hills Estates City of
25851 Hawthorne Blvd, Rllng HLS Est
(90275)
PHONE..................................310 541-4585
Andy Clark, *Director*
EMP: 50

SALES (est): 417.7K Privately Held
WEB: www.ci.rolling-hills-estates.ca.us
SIC: 7999 Tennis courts, outdoor/indoor: non-membership

(P-18748)
ROSEVILLE SPORTWORLD INC
Also Called: Skatetown
1009 Orlando Ave, Roseville (95661-5230)
PHONE..................................916 783-8550
Scott Slavensky, *President*
Althea Slavensky, *Shareholder*
Frank Slavensky, *Shareholder*
Kerry Slavensky, *Corp Secy*
EMP: 83
SQ FT: 61,679
SALES (est): 3.1MM Privately Held
SIC: 7999 5941 Ice skating rink operation; skating equipment

(P-18749)
SAC RIVER OUTFITTERS
1403 Edgewood Dr, Redding (96003-9227)
PHONE..................................530 275-3500
Chris King, *Owner*
EMP: 70
SALES (est): 440.3K Privately Held
WEB: www.sacriveroutfitters.com
SIC: 7999 Outfitters, recreation

(P-18750)
SAN DIEGO GULLS HOCKEY CLB LLC
7676 Hazard Center Dr, San Diego
(92108-4503)
PHONE..................................619 359-4700
Michael Schulman, *Director*
Brian Hartzell, *Executive*
Steven Brown, *Comms Mgr*
Micah Porter, *Controller*
Dave Desrochers, *Opers Staff*
EMP: 65
SQ FT: 2,000
SALES: 8.5MM Privately Held
SIC: 7999 Sports professionals

(P-18751)
SAN FRANCISCO ZOOLOGICAL SOC
1 Zoo Rd, San Francisco (94132-1098)
PHONE..................................415 753-7080
Tanya Peterson, *CEO*
Robert Pedrero, *Chairman*
EMP: 222
SQ FT: 2,000
SALES (est): 24.2MM Privately Held
WEB: www.sfzoo.org
SIC: 7999 7389 Concession operator; amusement ride; fund raising organizations

(P-18752)
SAN MANUEL INDIAN BINGO CASINO (PA)
777 San Manuel Blvd, Highland
(92346-6713)
PHONE..................................909 864-5050
James Ramos, *Chairman*
Peter Watts, *Chief Mktg Ofcr*
Jesse Gardner, *Officer*
Susana Lopez, *Officer*
Brigitte L Saria, *Officer*
▲ **EMP: 3000**
SALES (est): 89.5MM Privately Held
SIC: 7999 Bingo hall; card & game services

(P-18753)
SAN MATEO CNTY EXPO FAIR ASSN
Also Called: SAN MATEO COUNTY EXPO CENTER
2495 S Delaware St, San Mateo
(94403-1902)
PHONE..................................650 574-3247
Chris Carpenter, *General Mgr*
Charlene King, *Officer*
▲ **EMP: 50**
SQ FT: 225,000
SALES: 8.9MM Privately Held
WEB: www.smexpo.com
SIC: 7999 6512 Exhibition operation; exposition operation; fair; nonresidential building operators

(P-18754)
SANTA CLARA COUNTY OF
Parks & Recreation Dept
298 Garden Hill Dr, Los Gatos
(95032-7669)
PHONE..................................408 355-2200
Lisa Killough, *Branch Mgr*
EMP: 140 Privately Held
WEB: www.countyairports.org
SIC: 7999 9512 Recreation services; land, mineral & wildlife conservation;
PA: County Of Santa Clara
3180 Newberry Dr Ste 150
San Jose CA 95118
408 299-5105

(P-18755)
SANTA CLARITA CITY OF
Also Called: Cowboy Poetry
23920 Valencia Blvd # 300, Santa Clarita
(91355-2175)
PHONE..................................661 284-1423
Ken Pulskamp, *Manager*
Carl Newton,
EMP: 350 Privately Held
WEB: www.golfsantaclarita.com
SIC: 7999 Festival operation
PA: Santa Clarita, City Of
23920 Valencia Blvd # 300
Santa Clarita CA 91355
661 259-2489

(P-18756)
SCANDIA SPORTS INC
Also Called: Scandia Family Fun Center
5070 Hillsdale Blvd, Sacramento
(95842-3520)
PHONE..................................916 331-5757
Paul Wood, *Manager*
EMP: 50
SALES (corp-wide): 2.4MM Privately Held
SIC: 7999 Miniature golf course operation; recreation center; trampoline operation
PA: Scandia Sports, Inc
4607 Wardman Bullock Rd
Rancho Cucamonga CA

(P-18757)
SHASTA LAKE RESORTS LP
Also Called: Jones Valley Resorts
22300 Jones Vly Marina Dr, Redding
(96003-7829)
PHONE..................................209 785-3300
David M Smith, *Partner*
Steve Woodward, *Partner*
Water Resorts, *Managing Prtnr*
Tim Newcomer, *Controller*
EMP: 55
SQ FT: 3,500
SALES (est): 3.1MM Privately Held
SIC: 7999 4493 5411 Pleasure boat rental; marinas; grocery stores, independent

(P-18758)
SHINGLE SPRNG TRBAL GMING AUTH
Also Called: Red Hawk Casino
1 Red Hawk Pkwy, Placerville
(95667-8639)
PHONE..................................530 677-7000
Nicholas Fonseca, *Ch of Bd*
Tyrone Huff, *CFO*
Pat Farrington, *Vice Pres*
Marcos Martinez, *Vice Pres*
Evan Smith, *Vice Pres*
EMP: 1200
SQ FT: 278,000
SALES (est): 57.6MM Privately Held
WEB: www.shinglespringsrancheria.com
SIC: 7999 Gambling establishment
PA: Shingle Springs Rancheria
5168 Honpie Rd
Placerville CA 95667

(P-18759)
SKATE ENTERPRISES INC
12356 Central Ave, Chino (91710-2601)
PHONE..................................562 924-0911
Jerry Curran, *President*
Robert E Osborne, *Corp Secy*
David O Clark, *Vice Pres*
Robert E Maurer, *Vice Pres*

EMP: 54
SQ FT: 1,200
SALES (est): 2MM Privately Held
WEB: www.skateenterprises.com
SIC: 7999 Roller skating rink operation

(P-18760)
SKYHIGH WOODLAND HILLS LLC
Also Called: Sky High Sports
6051 De Soto Ave, Woodland Hills
(91367-3707)
PHONE.................................805 484-6300
Ron Rafia, Branch Mgr
EMP: 60
SALES (corp-wide): 400K Privately Held
SIC: 7999 6512 Trampoline operation; nonresidential building operators
PA: Skyhigh Woodland Hills, Llc
6033 De Soto Ave
Woodland Hills CA 91367
818 346-6300

(P-18761)
SNOW SUMMIT SKI CORPORATION
Also Called: Snow Summit Mountain Resort
43101 Goldmine Dr, Big Bear City (92314)
P.O. Box 77, Big Bear Lake (92315-0077)
PHONE.................................909 585-2517
Richard C Kun, Branch Mgr
EMP: 452
SALES (corp-wide): 70.3MM Privately Held
WEB: www.bearmtn.com
SIC: 7999 7011 5941 7992 Aerial tramway or ski lift, amusement or scenic; ski rental concession; ski lodge; skiing equipment; public golf courses
PA: Snow Summit Ski Corporation
880 Summit Blvd
Big Bear Lake CA 92315
909 866-5766

(P-18762)
SPEARMAN CLUBS INC (PA)
Also Called: Laguna Niguel Racquet Club
23500 Clubhouse Dr, Laguna Niguel
(92677-2902)
PHONE.................................949 496-2070
Cecil E Spearman Jr, Ch of Bd
Mark Spearman, President
Steven Spearman, CFO
Jean Spearman, Vice Ch Bd
Scott Spearman, Vice Pres
EMP: 50 EST: 1979
SQ FT: 20,000
SALES (est): 4.9MM Privately Held
WEB: www.spearmanclubs.com
SIC: 7999 7991 Tennis club, non-membership; physical fitness clubs with training equipment

(P-18763)
SPLASH SWIM SCHOOL INC
2411 Old Crow Canyon Rd, San Ramon
(94583-1240)
PHONE.................................925 838-7946
Elisabeth Claytor, President
D Christian Claytor, Admin Sec
EMP: 50
SQ FT: 7,310
SALES (est): 2.3MM Privately Held
SIC: 7999 Swimming instruction

(P-18764)
SYCUAN CASINO
Also Called: Sycuan Resort and Casino
5459 Casino Way, El Cajon (92019)
PHONE.................................619 445-6002
John Denius, General Mgr
Javier Murillo, Senior VP
Andrew Kerzmann, Vice Pres
Jumar Alcantara, Executive
Marilynn Cormier, Admin Asst
EMP: 2000
SQ FT: 236,000
SALES (est): 74.5MM Privately Held
SIC: 7999 7997 Gambling establishment; membership sports & recreation clubs

(P-18765)
TICKETMASTER ENTERTAINMENT LLC
8800 W Sunset Blvd, West Hollywood
(90069-2105)
PHONE.................................800 653-8000
Ron Bension, Mng Member
EMP: 4390
SALES (est): 43.1MM
SALES (corp-wide): 10.7B Publicly Held
SIC: 7999 Ticket sales office for sporting events, contract; tennis club, non-membership
PA: Live Nation Entertainment, Inc.
9348 Civic Center Dr Lbby
Beverly Hills CA 90210
800 653-8000

(P-18766)
TICKETWEB LLC
685 Market St Ste 200, San Francisco
(94105-4203)
PHONE.................................415 901-0210
EMP: 50
SALES (est): 1.2MM
SALES (corp-wide): 10.3B Publicly Held
WEB: www.ticketweb.com
SIC: 7999
HQ: Ticketmaster L.L.C.
7060 Hollywood Blvd Fl 4
Los Angeles CA 90028
323 441-7336

(P-18767)
TIERRA DEL SOL FOUNDATION
Also Called: Tierra Del Soul
250 W 1st St Ste 120, Claremont
(91711-4741)
PHONE.................................909 626-8301
Rebecca Hamm, Branch Mgr
EMP: 85
SALES (corp-wide): 16.6MM Privately Held
SIC: 7999 5999 Art gallery, commercial; art dealers
PA: Tierra Del Sol Foundation
9919 Sunland Blvd
Sunland CA 91040
818 352-1419

(P-18768)
TONAL SYSTEMS INC
325 Vermont St, San Francisco
(94103-5022)
PHONE.................................855 698-6625
Aly Orady, CEO
EMP: 65
SALES (est): 5MM Privately Held
SIC: 7999 Physical fitness instruction

(P-18769)
TOP SEED TENNIS ACADEMY INC
23400 Park Sorrento, Calabasas
(91302-1743)
PHONE.................................818 222-2782
Steve McAvoy, President
EMP: 65 EST: 1996
SALES (est): 1MM Privately Held
WEB: www.topseed.us
SIC: 7999 Tennis services & professionals

(P-18770)
TOPGOLF MEDIA LLC (HQ)
100 California St Ste 650, San Francisco
(94111-4531)
PHONE.................................214 377-0615
Ken May,
EMP: 79
SALES (est): 237.8K
SALES (corp-wide): 221.9MM Privately Held
SIC: 7999 Golf driving range
PA: Topgolf International, Inc.
8750 N Cntl Expy Ste 1200
Dallas TX 75231
214 377-0663

(P-18771)
TOWN OF DANVILLE
420 Front St, Danville (94526-3404)
PHONE.................................925 314-3400
Craig Bowen, Branch Mgr
EMP: 224 Privately Held
SIC: 7999 Recreation center

PA: Town Of Danville
510 La Gonda Way
Danville CA 94526
925 314-3311

(P-18772)
TRICKS GYMNASTIC INC (PA)
4070 Cavitt Stallman Rd, Granite Bay
(95746-9460)
PHONE.................................916 791-4496
Vern Taylor, President
Kenny Aldana, Manager
EMP: 75
SQ FT: 10,000
SALES (est): 2.6MM Privately Held
WEB: www.tricks-gymnastics.com
SIC: 7999 7911 Gymnastic instruction, non-membership; dance instructor & school services

(P-18773)
TRUCKEE DNNER RCREATION PK DST
10981 Truckee Way, Truckee (96161-2904)
PHONE.................................530 582-7720
Steve Randall, General Mgr
Peter Werbel, Chairman
Kevin Murphy, Admin Sec
Elaina Deyo, Admin Asst
Ali Freeman, Office Spvr
EMP: 100 EST: 1962
SQ FT: 10,000
SALES (est): 10.8MM Privately Held
WEB: www.tdrpd.com
SIC: 7999 Recreation services

(P-18774)
TUMBLEWEED EDUCATIONAL ENTPS
Also Called: Tumbleweed Day Camp
1024 Hanley Ave, Los Angeles
(90049-1306)
P.O. Box 49291 (90049-0291)
PHONE.................................310 444-3232
Erin Benfield, President
Liz Kimmelman, Director
Brooks McCall, Director
EMP: 160
SQ FT: 6,500
SALES (est): 9.3MM Privately Held
SIC: 7999 4151 Day camp; school buses

(P-18775)
UCLA MARINA CENTER
111 Deneve Dr, Los Angeles (90095-0001)
PHONE.................................310 825-3671
Steve Tevenajera, Branch Mgr
EMP: 80
SALES (corp-wide): 2.2MM Privately Held
SIC: 7999 Recreation services
PA: Marina Ucla Center
14001 Fiji Way
Marina Del Rey CA 90292
310 823-0048

(P-18776)
UNIVERSITY OF PACIFIC
Also Called: Athletic Department
1040 E Stadium Dr, Stockton (95204)
PHONE.................................209 946-2030
Donald Derosa, President
EMP: 600
SALES (corp-wide): 341.6MM Privately Held
WEB: www.uop.edu
SIC: 7999 8221 Ticket sales office for sporting events, contract; university
PA: University Of The Pacific
3601 Pacific Ave
Stockton CA 95211
209 946-2401

(P-18777)
URBAN PLATES LLC
Also Called: Urban Plates - Playa Vista
12746 W Jefferson Blvd # 3140, Playa Vista
(90094-2778)
PHONE.................................424 256-7274
EMP: 51
SALES (corp-wide): 50MM Privately Held
SIC: 7999 Recreation services

PA: Urban Plates Llc
2053 San Elijo Ave
Cardiff By The Sea CA 92007
760 230-1700

(P-18778)
VALLEY WIDE RECREATION PK DST (PA)
901 W Esplanade Ave, San Jacinto
(92582-4501)
P.O. Box 907 (92581-0907)
PHONE.................................951 654-1505
Nick Schouton, President
Kenneth Hyatt, President
Sam Goepp, General Mgr
EMP: 80
SQ FT: 30,000
SALES: 161.4K Privately Held
WEB: www.vwrpd.org/index.cfm
SIC: 7999 7996 Recreation services; amusement parks

(P-18779)
VILLAGE CLUB
429 Broadway, Chula Vista (91910-4320)
PHONE.................................619 425-3333
Harvey Souza, Owner
Jay Morales, Opers Staff
EMP: 50
SQ FT: 1,200
SALES (est): 1.7MM Privately Held
SIC: 7999 Card rooms

(P-18780)
VOLUME SERVICES INC
Also Called: Centerplate
24 Willie Mays Plz, San Francisco
(94107-2134)
PHONE.................................415 972-1500
Angie Perrilliat, General Mgr
EMP: 97
SALES (corp-wide): 133.3MM Privately Held
WEB: www.volumeservicesamerica.com
SIC: 7999 Concession operator
HQ: Volume Services, Inc.
2187 Atlantic St Ste 6
Stamford CT 06902
-

(P-18781)
VOLUME SERVICES INC
5333 Zoo Dr, Los Angeles (90027-1451)
PHONE.................................323 644-6038
Greg Edgar, Manager
EMP: 97
SALES (corp-wide): 133.3MM Privately Held
WEB: www.volumeservicesamerica.com
SIC: 7999 Concession operator
HQ: Volume Services, Inc.
2187 Atlantic St Ste 6
Stamford CT 06902
-

(P-18782)
VOLUME SERVICES INC
111 W Harbor Dr, San Diego (92101-7822)
PHONE.................................619 525-5800
EMP: 97
SALES (corp-wide): 133.3MM Privately Held
WEB: www.volumeservicesamerica.com
SIC: 7999 Concession operator
HQ: Volume Services, Inc.
2187 Atlantic St Ste 6
Stamford CT 06902
-

(P-18783)
WEST VALLEY JEWISH CMNTY CTR
22622 Vanowen St, Canoga Park
(91307-2646)
PHONE.................................818 348-0048
Anthony Flores, Director
EMP: 60 EST: 2000
SALES (est): 879.9K Privately Held
SIC: 7999 Recreation center

PRODUCTS & SVCS

(P-18784)
WINCHESTER MYSTERY HOUSE LLC
525 S Winchester Blvd, San Jose
(95128-2588)
PHONE.....................408 247-2101
Ray K Farris II,
Walter Magnuson, *General Mgr*
Charles Miranda, *Marketing Staff*
Vakerue Bovone,
Michael Taffe, *Manager*
EMP: 90
SQ FT: 44,000
SALES (est): 5.3MM **Privately Held**
WEB: www.winchestermysteryhouse.com
SIC: 7999 Tourist attraction, commercial

(P-18785)
YOGAWORKS INC (PA)
Also Called: MYYOGAWORKS
5780 Uplander Way, Culver City
(90230-6606)
PHONE.....................310 664-6470
Rosanna C McCollough, *President*
Peter L Garran, *Ch of Bd*
Vance Y Chang, *CFO*
Kurt C Donnell, *Exec VP*
Olivia Greth, *Cust Mgr*
EMP: 60 **EST:** 1987
SALES: 59.5MM **Privately Held**
SIC: 7999 5961 5651 7991 Yoga instruction; mail order house; unisex clothing stores; exercise salon

(P-18786)
YOUNG MENS CHRISTIAN ASSO
Also Called: Simi Valley Family YMCA
3200 Cochran St, Simi Valley (93065-2769)
PHONE.....................805 583-5338
Dan Jaeger, *Director*
EMP: 100
SALES (corp-wide): 10.2MM **Privately Held**
SIC: 7999 8351 8641 7997 Recreation center; child day care services; civic social & fraternal associations; membership sports & recreation clubs
PA: Young Men's Christian Association Of Southeast Ventura County
31105 E Thusand Oaks Blvd
Thousand Oaks CA 91362
805 497-3081

(P-18787)
ZEPHYR RIVER EXPEDITIONS INC
Also Called: Zephyr White Water Expeditions
22517 Parrotts Ferry Rd, Columbia
(95310-9757)
P.O. Box 510 (95310-0510)
PHONE.....................800 431-3636
Bob Ferguson, *President*
EMP: 60
SQ FT: 2,000
SALES (est): 1.2MM **Privately Held**
WEB: www.zrafting.com
SIC: 7999 Rafting tours

8011 Offices & Clinics Of Doctors Of Medicine

(P-18788)
A & C HEALTH CARE SERVICES INC
Also Called: A & C Convatescent Hospital
33 Mateo Ave, Millbrae (94030-2037)
PHONE.....................650 689-5784
Carlos P Ragudo, *President*
Amparo B Ragudo, *CFO*
EMP: 135
SALES (est): 4.6MM **Privately Held**
SIC: 8011 Clinic, operated by physicians

(P-18789)
ADVENTIST HEALTH SYSTEM
Also Called: Adventist Health Cmnty. Care
250 W El Monte Way, Dinuba
(93618-1554)
PHONE.....................559 595-9890
Wayne Ferch, *Branch Mgr*
EMP: 5004 **Privately Held**
SIC: 8011 Offices & clinics of medical doctors

PA: Adventist Health System Sunbelt Healthcare Corporation
900 Hope Way
Altamonte Springs FL 32714

(P-18790)
ADVENTIST HEALTH SYSTEM/WEST
14880 Olympic Dr, Clearlake (95422-9521)
P.O. Box 6710 (95422-6710)
PHONE.....................707 995-4888
Patricia Van Horn, *Manager*
Ron Ryskalczyk, *Sales Staff*
Allyne Brown, *Director*
EMP: 115
SALES (corp-wide): 4.4B **Privately Held**
SIC: 8011 Clinic, operated by physicians
PA: Adventist Health System/West
1 Adventist Health Way
Roseville CA 95661
844 574-5686

(P-18791)
ADVENTIST HEALTH SYSTEM/WEST
Also Called: St Helena Hospital Clearlake
18th Ave Hwy 53, Clearlake (95422)
PHONE.....................707 994-6486
Kendall Fults, *CEO*
Colleen Assavapisitkul, *Officer*
Duane Barnes, *Finance*
EMP: 330
SALES (corp-wide): 4.4B **Privately Held**
WEB: www.sthelenahospital.com
SIC: 8011 Surgeon
PA: Adventist Health System/West
1 Adventist Health Way
Roseville CA 95661
844 574-5686

(P-18792)
ALL CARE MEDICAL GROUP INC
Also Called: Professional Svcs Med Group
31 Crescent St, Huntington Park (90255)
PHONE.....................408 278-3550
Samuel Rotenberg MD, *Director*
EMP: 85 **EST:** 1946
SQ FT: 33,000
SALES (est): 8MM **Privately Held**
WEB: www.allcaremg.com
SIC: 8011 Physicians' office, including specialists

(P-18793)
ALLEN MEDICAL GROUP INC
14416 Victory Blvd # 211, Van Nuys
(91401-1441)
PHONE.....................818 698-8444
Avionne Petal Allen-Singh, *President*
EMP: 50 **EST:** 2008
SALES: 11MM **Privately Held**
SIC: 8011 Offices & clinics of medical doctors

(P-18794)
ALLIANCE MEDICAL CENTER INC
1381 University St, Healdsburg
(95448-3314)
PHONE.....................707 431-8234
Beatrice Bostick, *CEO*
Jack Neureuter, *CEO*
EMP: 99
SALES: 15.8MM **Privately Held**
WEB: www.alliancemedicalcenter.com
SIC: 8011 Clinic, operated by physicians

(P-18795)
ALLIED ANESTHESIA MED GROUP
400 N Tustin Ave, Santa Ana (92705-3813)
P.O. Box 1628, Orange (92856-0628)
PHONE.....................951 830-9816
George Kanaly, *CEO*
Kaveh Matin, *President*
EMP: 99
SALES (est): 3.3MM **Privately Held**
SIC: 8011 Anesthesiologist

(P-18796)
ALTA VISTA HEALTHCARE AND WELL
9020 Garfield St, Riverside (92503-3903)
PHONE.....................951 688-8200
EMP: 105
SALES (est): 5.5MM **Privately Held**
SIC: 8011

(P-18797)
ALTAMED HEALTH SERVICES CORP
5427 Whittier Blvd, Los Angeles
(90022-4101)
PHONE.....................323 980-4466
Irene Avilar, *Principal*
EMP: 80
SALES (corp-wide): 677.8MM **Privately Held**
WEB: www.altamed.org
SIC: 8011 Clinic, operated by physicians
PA: Altamed Health Services Corporation
2040 Camfield Ave
Commerce CA 90040
323 725-8751

(P-18798)
ALTAMED HEALTH SERVICES CORP
1820 W Lincoln Ave, Anaheim
(92801-6730)
PHONE.....................714 635-0593
EMP: 161
SALES (corp-wide): 677.8MM **Privately Held**
SIC: 8011 Gynecologist
PA: Altamed Health Services Corporation
2040 Camfield Ave
Commerce CA 90040
323 725-8751

(P-18799)
ALTAMED HEALTH SERVICES CORP
268 Bloom St, Los Angeles (90012-1973)
PHONE.....................323 276-0267
EMP: 225
SALES (corp-wide): 677.8MM **Privately Held**
SIC: 8011 Clinic, operated by physicians
PA: Altamed Health Services Corporation
2040 Camfield Ave
Commerce CA 90040
323 725-8751

(P-18800)
ALTAMED HEALTH SERVICES CORP (PA)
2040 Camfield Ave, Commerce
(90040-1574)
PHONE.....................323 725-8751
Castulo De La Rocha, *CEO*
Jose U Esparza, *CFO*
Marie S Torres, *Senior VP*
Zoila D Escobar, *Vice Pres*
EMP: 135
SQ FT: 27,345
SALES: 677.8MM **Privately Held**
WEB: www.altamed.org
SIC: 8011 8099 Gynecologist; pediatrician; radiologist; medical services organization

(P-18801)
ALTAMED HEALTH SERVICES CORP
Also Called: Indiana Adhc
5425 Pomona Blvd, Los Angeles
(90022-1716)
PHONE.....................323 980-4000
Irma Wisenberg, *Branch Mgr*
EMP: 50
SALES (corp-wide): 677.8MM **Privately Held**
WEB: www.altamed.org
SIC: 8011 8322 Gynecologist; adult day care center
PA: Altamed Health Services Corporation
2040 Camfield Ave
Commerce CA 90040
323 725-8751

(P-18802)
ALTAMED HEALTH SERVICES CORP
1814 W Lincoln Ave, Anaheim
(92801-6730)
PHONE.....................714 780-5690
EMP: 282
SALES (corp-wide): 677.8MM **Privately Held**
SIC: 8011 Gynecologist
PA: Altamed Health Services Corporation
2040 Camfield Ave
Commerce CA 90040
323 725-8751

(P-18803)
ALTURA CENTERS FOR HEALTH
1201 N Cherry St, Tulare (93274-2233)
PHONE.....................559 686-9097
Graciela Soto-Perez, *President*
Dennis Jungwirth, *Executive*
Evelyn Benson, *Exec Dir*
Yolanda Berlin, *Executive Asst*
Amy Azevedo, *Admin Asst*
EMP: 83
SQ FT: 18,000
SALES: 25.6MM **Privately Held**
WEB: www.tchci.org
SIC: 8011 8021 Clinic, operated by physicians; offices & clinics of dentists

(P-18804)
AMEN CLINICS INC A MED CORP (PA)
3150 Bristol St Ste 400, Costa Mesa
(92626-3054)
PHONE.....................888 564-2700
Daniel Amen, *President*
Kim Schneider, *Executive Asst*
Catherine J Hanlon, *Administration*
▲ **EMP:** 200
SALES (est): 36.9MM **Privately Held**
WEB: www.amenclinics.com
SIC: 8011 Psychiatric clinic; neurologist

(P-18805)
AMEN CLINICS INC A MED CORP
350 N Wiget Ln Ste 105, Walnut Creek
(94598-5960)
PHONE.....................650 416-7830
Daniel G Amen MD, *Owner*
EMP: 50
SALES (est): 1.9MM **Privately Held**
WEB: www.amenclinic.com
SIC: 8011 Psychiatrist

(P-18806)
AMERICAN HEALTH SERVICES LLC
Also Called: Palmdale Med Mental Hlth Svcs
26460 Summit Cir, Santa Clarita
(91350-2991)
P.O. Box 801809 (91380-1809)
PHONE.....................661 254-6630
Stan Sharma, *CEO*
Leni Legaspi, *CFO*
Hamir Sinha, *Treasurer*
Sean Sharma, *Vice Pres*
Arlyn Barner, *Admin Sec*
EMP: 110
SALES: 4.9MM **Privately Held**
SIC: 8011 8361 Offices & clinics of medical doctors; rehabilitation center; residential: health care incidental

(P-18807)
AMIR AHMAD MD
628 California Blvd Ste D, San Luis Obispo
(93401-2558)
PHONE.....................805 545-8100
Amir Ahmad, *Owner*
EMP: 80 **EST:** 2010
SALES (est): 825.7K **Privately Held**
SIC: 8011 General & family practice, physician/surgeon

(P-18808)
AMN HEALTHCARE INC (HQ)
12400 High Bluff Dr, San Diego
(92130-3077)
PHONE.....................858 792-0711
Susan R Nowakowski, *CEO*
Ann Harris, *Bd of Directors*
Martha Marsh, *Bd of Directors*
Andrew Stern, *Bd of Directors*

▲ = Import ▼=Export
◆ =Import/Export

Tien Le, *Officer*
EMP: 168
SALES (est): 196.3MM
SALES (corp-wide): 2.1B **Publicly Held**
WEB: www.amnhealthcare.com
SIC: 8011 Primary care medical clinic
PA: Amn Healthcare Services, Inc.
12400 High Bluff Dr
San Diego CA 92130
866 871-8519

(P-18809)
AMPLA HEALTH
Also Called: Chico Family Health Center
680 Cohasset Rd, Chico (95926-2213)
PHONE..................................530 342-4395
Amalia Bejerano, *Branch Mgr*
EMP: 57
SALES (corp-wide): 50.2MM **Privately Held**
SIC: 8011 Clinic, operated by physicians
PA: Ampla Health
935 Market St
Yuba City CA 95991
530 674-4261

(P-18810)
AMPLA HEALTH
Also Called: Lindhurst Family Health Center
4941 Olivehurst Ave, Olivehurst (95961-4225)
PHONE..................................530 743-4614
Sally Moore, *Branch Mgr*
EMP: 51
SALES (corp-wide): 50.2MM **Privately Held**
SIC: 8011 Health maintenance organization
PA: Ampla Health
935 Market St
Yuba City CA 95991
530 674-4261

(P-18811)
ANAHEIM HARBOR MEDICAL GROUP (PA)
Also Called: Family Urgent Care Center
710 N Euclid St, Anaheim (92801-4122)
PHONE..................................714 533-4511
David L Tsoong MD, *President*
Joseph M Mule MD, *Admin Sec*
EMP: 185
SQ FT: 10,000
SALES (est): 8.1MM **Privately Held**
SIC: 8011 Pediatrician; internal medicine, physician/surgeon; orthopedic physician; obstetrician

(P-18812)
ANAHEIM MEDICAL CENTER
1111 W La Palma Ave, Anaheim (92801-2804)
PHONE..................................714 774-1450
Patrick Petre, *Principal*
Cindy Gross, *COO*
Darrel Brownell, *CFO*
Janet Beutner, *Admin Sec*
Carol Christensen, *Admin Sec*
EMP: 62
SALES (est): 6.9MM **Privately Held**
SIC: 8011 Medical centers

(P-18813)
ANAHEIM REGIONAL MEDICAL CTR
Also Called: Ahmc
1211 W La Palma Ave, Anaheim (92801-2815)
PHONE..................................714 999-3847
Patrick Petre, *Branch Mgr*
Yvonne Lau, *Education*
Lily Hong, *Director*
EMP: 440
SALES (corp-wide): 169.9MM **Privately Held**
SIC: 8011 Medical centers
PA: Anaheim Regional Medical Center
1211 W La Palma Ave
Anaheim CA 92801
714 774-1450

(P-18814)
ANDREW M GOLDEN MD
4647 Zion Ave, San Diego (92120-2507)
PHONE..................................619 528-5342
Andrew Golden, *Principal*

EMP: 51 **EST:** 2013
SALES (est): 4MM **Privately Held**
SIC: 8011 Physicians' office, including specialists

(P-18815)
ANESTHESIA BUSINESS CONS INC
Also Called: Anesthesia Consultants of Cont
1600 Riviera Ave Ste 420, Walnut Creek (94596-7115)
PHONE..................................925 951-1366
Kristina Coster, *Branch Mgr*
EMP: 80
SALES (corp-wide): 5.1MM **Privately Held**
SIC: 8011 8741 Anesthesiologist; management services
PA: Anesthesia Business Consultants, Inc.
8905 Sw Nimbus Ave # 300
Beaverton OR 97008
503 372-2740

(P-18816)
ANESTHESIA SERVICE MED GROUP
Also Called: Asmg
3626 Ruffin Rd, San Diego (92123-1810)
P.O. Box 82807 (92138-2807)
PHONE..................................858 277-4767
Peter Raudaskoski, *President*
Thomas R Farrell MD, *President*
EMP: 50
SQ FT: 11,200
SALES (est): 15.7MM **Privately Held**
WEB: www.asmgmd.com
SIC: 8011 Anesthesiologist

(P-18817)
ANNE M KENT MD
500 Superior Ave Ste 310, Newport Beach (92663-3609)
PHONE..................................949 650-7100
Anne Kent, *Principal*
EMP: 60
SALES (est): 307.4K **Privately Held**
SIC: 8011 General & family practice, physician/surgeon

(P-18818)
ANTELOPE VALLEY HOSPITAL INC
1601 W Avenue J Ste 201, Lancaster (93534-2824)
PHONE..................................661 949-1550
Pradeep Damle, *Branch Mgr*
EMP: 56
SALES (corp-wide): 411.1MM **Privately Held**
SIC: 8011 General & family practice, physician/surgeon
PA: Antelope Valley Hospital, Inc.
1600 W Avenue J
Lancaster CA 93534
661 949-5000

(P-18819)
ANTELOPE VALLEY HOSPITAL INC
Ob Clinic
1600 W Avenue J, Lancaster (93534-2894)
PHONE..................................661 726-6180
Vikki Haley, *Principal*
EMP: 167
SALES (corp-wide): 411.1MM **Privately Held**
SIC: 8011 Offices & clinics of medical doctors
PA: Antelope Valley Hospital, Inc.
1600 W Avenue J
Lancaster CA 93534
661 949-5000

(P-18820)
ANTELOPE VALLEY MEDICAL GROUP
44469 10th St W, Lancaster (93534-3324)
PHONE..................................661 945-2783
Karunyan Arul, *Partner*
Donna Acosta, *Manager*
EMP: 50
SALES (est): 1.4MM **Privately Held**
SIC: 8011 Clinic, operated by physicians

(P-18821)
APLA HEALTH & WELLNESS
Also Called: AIDS PROJECT LA
611 S Kingsley Dr, Los Angeles (90005-2319)
PHONE..................................213 201-1546
Craig Thompson, *CEO*
Robyn Goldman, *CFO*
EMP: 56 **EST:** 2010
SALES: 13.3MM
SALES (corp-wide): 10.3MM **Privately Held**
SIC: 8011 Primary care medical clinic
PA: Aids Project Los Angeles
611 S Kingsley Dr
Los Angeles CA 90005
213 201-1600

(P-18822)
ARBOR MEDICAL GROUP INC (PA)
1502 Marilyn Way, Santa Maria (93454-5945)
PHONE..................................805 614-7591
Gerald Ebner MD, *President*
Margaret Elfering MD, *Vice Pres*
Dennis Shepard MD, *Admin Sec*
EMP: 60
SQ FT: 10,000
SALES (est): 2.2MM **Privately Held**
SIC: 8011 Physicians' office, including specialists

(P-18823)
ARLENE KELLER MD
Also Called: Pacific Interior Medicine
2100 Webster St Ste 423, San Francisco (94115-2380)
PHONE..................................415 923-3598
Arlene Keller, *Principal*
EMP: 50
SALES (est): 1.9MM **Privately Held**
SIC: 8011 General & family practice, physician/surgeon

(P-18824)
ARROYO SECO MEDICAL GROUP (PA)
301 S Fair Oaks Ave # 300, Pasadena (91105-2561)
PHONE..................................626 795-7556
Henry Sideropoulos MD, *President*
Andrew Muller MD, *Vice Pres*
EMP: 65
SQ FT: 9,145
SALES (est): 6.5MM **Privately Held**
WEB: www.arroyoseco.net
SIC: 8011 Internal medicine, physician/surgeon; general & family practice, physician/surgeon

(P-18825)
ASIAN HEALTH SERVICES
270 13th St, Oakland (94612-4801)
PHONE..................................510 986-0601
Sherry Hirota, *Branch Mgr*
EMP: 58
SALES (corp-wide): 42MM **Privately Held**
SIC: 8011 Offices & clinics of medical doctors
PA: Asian Health Services
101 8th St
Oakland CA 94607
510 986-6800

(P-18826)
ASIAN HEALTH SERVICES (PA)
101 8th St, Oakland (94607-4707)
PHONE..................................510 986-6800
Sherry Hirota, *CEO*
Grace Fung, *Executive*
Dong Suh, *Associate Dir*
Dennis Ing, *Internal Med*
Daniel Park, *Internal Med*
EMP: 147
SQ FT: 30,000
SALES: 42MM **Privately Held**
SIC: 8011 Clinic, operated by physicians

(P-18827)
ASSOCIATED STUDENTS UCLA
Also Called: Ucla Mdcn SC Phrmclgy
650 Chrls Yng S Rm 23 120, Los Angeles (90095-0001)
PHONE..................................310 825-9451
Michael Phelps, *Principal*
EMP: 800
SALES (corp-wide): 42.7MM **Privately Held**
SIC: 8011 General & family practice, physician/surgeon
PA: Associated Students U.C.L.A.
308 Westwood Plz
Los Angeles CA 90095
310 825-4321

(P-18828)
ASSOCTED GSTRNTRLOGY MED GROUP (PA)
1211 W La Palma Ave, Anaheim (92801-2815)
PHONE..................................714 778-1300
Michael De Micco MD, *Partner*
Dennis Riff MD, *Partner*
EMP: 52
SQ FT: 2,698
SALES (est): 5.4MM **Privately Held**
SIC: 8011 Gastronomist

(P-18829)
AUDREY ADAMS MD
718 University Ave # 211, Los Gatos (95032-7608)
PHONE..................................408 354-2114
Franklin Chow, *Principal*
Anthony Lin, *Anesthesiology*
EMP: 50
SALES (est): 1.3MM **Privately Held**
SIC: 8011 General & family practice, physician/surgeon

(P-18830)
AXMINSTER MEDICAL GROUP INC (PA)
8540 S Sepulveda Blvd # 818, Los Angeles (90045-3808)
PHONE..................................310 670-3255
Raymond Jing MD, *CEO*
Huey-Jer Su MD, *Treasurer*
Spencer H Wenger MD, *Vice Pres*
Stanley E Golden MD, *Admin Sec*
Ira Smalberg, *Professor*
EMP: 56
SQ FT: 20,000
SALES (est): 12.1MM
SALES (corp-wide): 13.3MM **Privately Held**
WEB: www.axminstermedicalgroup.com
SIC: 8011 Internal medicine, physician/surgeon; pediatrician; gynecologist

(P-18831)
BAY AREA PDATRIC MED GROUP INC (PA)
901 Campus Dr Ste 111, Daly City (94015-4930)
PHONE..................................650 992-4200
James Ferrara MD, *President*
Diane Swabe MD, *Treasurer*
Robert C Zaglin MD, *Vice Pres*
EMP: 70
SQ FT: 1,579
SALES (est): 3MM **Privately Held**
WEB: www.bapmg.com
SIC: 8011 Pediatrician

(P-18832)
BAY AREA SURGICAL MGT LLC
2110 Forest Ave Fl 2, San Jose (95128-1469)
PHONE..................................408 297-3432
Stephanie Halls,
Katherine Altonaga, *Administration*
EMP: 50
SALES (est): 1.5MM **Privately Held**
SIC: 8011 Surgeon

(P-18833)
BAY IMAGING CONS MED GROUP INC (PA)
175 Lennon Ln Ste 100, Walnut Creek (94598-2466)
PHONE..................................925 296-7150
Anton C Pogany, *Director*

Keith Tao, *Partner*
Lisa Woelfel, *Executive*
Reed Smoller, *Info Tech Dir*
Wendy Patton, *Pediatrics*
EMP: 80
SQ FT: 4,500
SALES (est): 7.4MM **Privately Held**
SIC: 8011 Radiologist

(P-18834)
BAY MEDICAL MANAGEMENT LLC
2125 Oak Grove Rd Ste 200, Walnut Creek (94598-2520)
PHONE....................925 296-7150
Mary Gerard, *Mng Member*
Graciela Paguirigan, *Administration*
Christine Puckett, *Administration*
Kurtis Kamm, *Technology*
Merrie Campbell, *Controller*
EMP: 160
SALES (est): 20.9MM **Privately Held**
WEB: www.bmmi.net
SIC: 8011 Radiologist

(P-18835)
BAY VALLEY MEDICAL GROUP INC (PA)
319 Diablo Rd Ste 105, Danville (94526-3428)
PHONE....................510 785-5000
Shelley A Horwitz, *CEO*
Roland J Wong, *Ch of Bd*
Eric S Kohleriter, *President*
Misha Roitshteyn, *Director*
Sheri Task, *Director*
EMP: 93
SALES (est): 16.9MM **Privately Held**
WEB: www.bvmed.com
SIC: 8011 Clinic, operated by physicians

(P-18836)
BAYSPRING MEDICAL GROUP A PRO
1199 Bush St Ste 500, San Francisco (94109-5976)
PHONE....................415 674-2600
Laurel Dawson, *President*
Marilyn Milkman, *Treasurer*
Susan Rosen, *Vice Pres*
Tara Reilly, *Nurse Practr*
Ayesha Denis, *Supervisor*
EMP: 50
SALES (est): 3.8MM **Privately Held**
SIC: 8011 General & family practice, physician/surgeon; internal medicine practitioners; obstetrician; gynecologist

(P-18837)
BEAVER MEDICAL CLINIC INC (PA)
1615 Orange Tree Ln, Redlands (92374-4501)
P.O. Box 10069, San Bernardino (92423-0069)
PHONE....................909 793-3311
Robert Klein, *President*
Douglas Brockmann, *Med Doctor*
EMP: 190 **EST:** 1945
SQ FT: 79,212
SALES: 158.4K **Privately Held**
WEB: www.epiclp.com
SIC: 8011 Clinic, operated by physicians

(P-18838)
BELVILLE ENTERPRISES INC
Also Called: Ron's Pharmacy Services
6225 Nancy Ridge Dr, San Diego (92121-2245)
PHONE....................858 652-6960
Ronald W Belville, *CEO*
EMP: 100 **EST:** 1996
SQ FT: 27,000
SALES (est): 12.5MM **Privately Held**
SIC: 8011 5912 Offices & clinics of medical doctors; drug stores & proprietary stores

(P-18839)
BEVERLY RADIOLOGY MED GROUP (PA)
Also Called: Tower- Imaging Roxanne
465 N Roxbury Dr Ste 101, Beverly Hills (90210-4230)
PHONE....................310 975-1500

Howard G Berger MD, *President*
Michael J Krane MD, *Vice Pres*
EMP: 250
SALES (est): 6.4MM **Privately Held**
SIC: 8011 Radiologist

(P-18840)
BORREGO CMNTY HLTH FOUNDATION
1121 E Washington Ave, Escondido (92025-2214)
PHONE....................760 466-1080
EMP: 139
SALES (corp-wide): 64.3MM **Privately Held**
SIC: 8011 Offices & clinics of medical doctors
PA: Borrego Community Health Foundation
4343 Yaqui Pass Rd
Borrego Springs CA 92004
760 767-5051

(P-18841)
BORREGO CMNTY HLTH FOUNDATION
2721 Washington St, Julian (92036-9233)
P.O. Box 969 (92036-0969)
PHONE....................760 765-1223
Gina Glenn, *Branch Mgr*
EMP: 194
SALES (corp-wide): 64.3MM **Privately Held**
SIC: 8011 Offices & clinics of medical doctors
PA: Borrego Community Health Foundation
4343 Yaqui Pass Rd
Borrego Springs CA 92004
760 767-5051

(P-18842)
BORREGO CMNTY HLTH FOUNDATION (PA)
Also Called: Borrego Medical Center
4343 Yaqui Pass Rd, Borrego Springs (92004)
P.O. Box 2369 (92004-2369)
PHONE....................760 767-5051
Bruce E Smith, *CEO*
Dianna Troncoso, *CFO*
Mikia Wallis, *Officer*
Gary Rotto, *Vice Pres*
Ron Andersen, *Info Tech Dir*
EMP: 140
SQ FT: 8,054
SALES: 64.3MM **Privately Held**
SIC: 8011 Offices & clinics of medical doctors

(P-18843)
BREAST DIAGNOSTIC CENTER
3275 Skypark Dr Ste A, Torrance (90505-5027)
PHONE....................310 517-4709
George Gram, *President*
EMP: 50
SALES (est): 1MM **Privately Held**
SIC: 8011 General & family practice, physician/surgeon

(P-18844)
BRIGHT HEALTH PHYSICIANS (PA)
15725 Whittier Blvd # 500, Whittier (90603-2350)
PHONE....................562 947-8478
William H Stimmler MD, *Ch of Bd*
Keith Miyamoto MD, *President*
Don T Eli, *Principal*
Berent Gray MD, *Admin Sec*
EMP: 140
SQ FT: 50,000
SALES (est): 120.5MM **Privately Held**
WEB: www.brightmedical.com
SIC: 8011 Physicians' office, including specialists

(P-18845)
BROWN & TOLAND MEDICAL GROUP
3905 Sacramento St # 301, San Francisco (94118-1636)
PHONE....................415 752-8038
Jeanne David, *Office Mgr*
Stephen K Lee, *Internal Med*
William Todd, *Podiatrist*

Faviola Munoz, *Assistant*
Maria Pavon, *Assistant*
EMP: 148
SALES (corp-wide): 59.5MM **Privately Held**
SIC: 8011 Physicians' office, including specialists
PA: Brown & Toland Physician Services Organization, Inc.
1221 Broadway Ste 700
Oakland CA 94612
415 972-4162

(P-18846)
BROWN TLAND PHYSCN SVCS ORGNZT (PA)
1221 Broadway Ste 700, Oakland (94612-1898)
P.O. Box 72710 (94612-8910)
PHONE....................415 972-4162
Joel Klompus, *President*
Deborah Keef, *COO*
Michael Gam, *CFO*
Lynn S Grennan, *CFO*
Jackie Bright, *Senior VP*
EMP: 480
SQ FT: 8,000
SALES (est): 59.5MM **Privately Held**
WEB: www.brownandtoland.com
SIC: 8011 Medical centers

(P-18847)
BUENA PARK MEDICAL GROUP INC (PA)
6301 Beach Blvd Ste 101, Buena Park (90621-4030)
P.O. Box 277 (90621-0277)
PHONE....................714 994-5290
Martin Ahn, *CEO*
EMP: 100
SQ FT: 20,000
SALES (est): 5.5MM **Privately Held**
SIC: 8011 General & family practice, physician/surgeon

(P-18848)
BUENAVENTURA MEDICAL GROUP (PA)
888 S Hill Rd, Ventura (93003-8400)
PHONE....................805 477-6000
James Malone, *CEO*
David Grahm, *COO*
Kevin Moore, *CFO*
EMP: 350
SQ FT: 27,000
SALES (est): 5.5MM **Privately Held**
SIC: 8011 Clinic, operated by physicians

(P-18849)
BUENAVENTURA MEDICAL GROUP
2601 E Main St Ste 104, Ventura (93003-2801)
PHONE....................805 477-6220
James Malone, *CEO*
G Dennis Horvath, *Surgeon*
EMP: 100
SALES (corp-wide): 5.5MM **Privately Held**
SIC: 8011 Clinic, operated by physicians
PA: Buenaventura Medical Group Inc
888 S Hill Rd
Ventura CA 93003
805 477-6000

(P-18850)
BUTTE PRIMARY CARE MED GROUP
6585 Clark Rd Ste 200, Paradise (95969-3500)
PHONE....................530 877-0762
D L Miller MD, *President*
Joseph Lee, *CFO*
Thomas Roth MD, *CFO*
Kenneth Logan MD, *Vice Pres*
Donald Smith MD, *Vice Pres*
EMP: 60
SQ FT: 1,150
SALES (est): 3.1MM **Privately Held**
SIC: 8011 General & family practice, physician/surgeon

(P-18851)
BUTTERWICK DR KIMBERLY JANE MD
9339 Genesee Ave Ste 300, San Diego (92121-2122)
PHONE....................858 657-1002
Mitchell Goldman, *Owner*
Lillian Wills, *CFO*
EMP: 95
SALES (est): 2.1MM **Privately Held**
SIC: 8011 Dermatologist

(P-18852)
C E P
400 N Pepper Ave Ste 107, Colton (92324-1801)
PHONE....................909 580-1456
Rodney Burger,
Eugene L Kwong, *Med Doctor*
EMP: 60
SALES (est): 1.7MM **Privately Held**
SIC: 8011 Offices & clinics of medical doctors

(P-18853)
C/O UC SAN FRANCISCO
1245 16th St Ste 225, Santa Monica (90404-1240)
PHONE....................310 794-1841
Greer Gustavson, *Program Mgr*
Sandra Ogbonnaya-Whitt, *Internal Med*
Michelle Aguilar, *Pediatrics*
Sharon M Sikand, *Physician Asst*
EMP: 92
SALES (corp-wide): 49.8MM **Privately Held**
SIC: 8011 8221 Specialized medical practitioners, except internal; university
PA: C/O Uc San Francisco
1111 Franklin St Fl 12
Oakland CA 94607
858 534-7323

(P-18854)
CALIFORNIA ANESTHESIA ASSO MED
400 N Tustin Ave Ste 400 # 400, Santa Ana (92705-3850)
P.O. Box 3493, Laguna Hills (92654-3493)
PHONE....................800 888-2186
Kevin Jones, *President*
Alan Ross, *CEO*
EMP: 60
SALES (est): 1.8MM **Privately Held**
SIC: 8011 Anesthesiologist

(P-18855)
CALIFORNIA CANCER ASSCTES
Also Called: Ccare West
7130 N Millbrook Ave, Fresno (93720-3347)
PHONE....................559 447-4949
Thomas Hackett, *Branch Mgr*
EMP: 80
SALES (corp-wide): 22.8MM **Privately Held**
SIC: 8011 Oncologist; hematologist
PA: California Cancer Associates For Research And Excellence, Inc.
7130 N Millbrook Ave
Fresno CA 93720
800 456-5860

(P-18856)
CALIFORNIA EYE INSTITUTE
Low Vision Dept St Agnes, Fresno (93720)
PHONE....................559 449-5000
Kathy Ploszaj, *Administration*
Gary R Fogg MD, *Shareholder*
Saint Agnes Hospital, *Shareholder*
Larry R Lawrence MD, *Shareholder*
Andrew Maxwell MD, *Shareholder*
EMP: 180
SQ FT: 59,000
SALES (est): 9.6MM **Privately Held**
SIC: 8011 Ophthalmologist

(P-18857)
CALIFORNIA KIDNEY MED GROUP
375 Rolling Oaks Dr # 100, Thousand Oaks (91361-1023)
PHONE....................805 497-7775
Kant Tucker, *President*
Margie Manwell, *Manager*

EMP: 130
SALES (est): 4.4MM **Privately Held**
SIC: 8011 Offices & clinics of medical doctors

(P-18858)
CALIFORNIA PACIFIC CA
2100 Webster St Ste 516, San Francisco (94115-2381)
PHONE..................415 345-0940
Bruce Brent MD, *President*
Richard Francoz MD, *Vice Pres*
Adam Rosenblatt, *Med Doctor*
EMP: 50
SQ FT: 3,500
SALES (est): 3.5MM **Privately Held**
WEB: www.cpcmg.com
SIC: 8011 Offices & clinics of medical doctors

(P-18859)
CALIFORNIA SCHOOLS VEBA
1843 Hotel Cir S, San Diego (92108-3320)
PHONE..................888 276-0250
George McGregor, *Mng Member*
EMP: 60
SALES: 500K **Privately Held**
SIC: 8011 Health maintenance organization

(P-18860)
CALIFRNIA FRNSIC MED GROUP INC
1410 Natividad Rd, Salinas (93906-3102)
PHONE..................831 755-3886
EMP: 175
SALES (corp-wide): 33.7MM **Privately Held**
SIC: 8011 Primary care medical clinic
PA: California Forensic Medical Group, Incorporated
1283 Murfreesboro Pike # 500
Nashville TN 37217
831 649-8994

(P-18861)
CALIFRNIA FRNSIC MED GROUP INC
200 E Hackett Rd, Modesto (95358-9415)
PHONE..................209 525-5670
L Cottrel, *Principal*
EMP: 131
SALES (corp-wide): 33.7MM **Privately Held**
SIC: 8011 Primary care medical clinic
PA: California Forensic Medical Group, Incorporated
1283 Murfreesboro Pike # 500
Nashville TN 37217
831 649-8994

(P-18862)
CALIFRNIA PSYCHTRIC TRNSITIONS
9234n Hinton Ave, Delhi (95315-8200)
P.O. Box 339 (95315-0339)
PHONE..................209 667-9304
John T Hackett MD, *President*
EMP: 70
SQ FT: 25,000
SALES (est): 4.2MM **Privately Held**
SIC: 8011 Psychiatric clinic

(P-18863)
CAMARENA HEALTH
505 E Almond Ave, Madera (93637-5742)
PHONE..................559 664-4000
Paulo A Soares, *CEO*
EMP: 92
SALES (corp-wide): 41.5MM **Privately Held**
SIC: 8011 Health maintenance organization
PA: Camarena Health
344 E 6th St
Madera CA 93638
559 664-4000

(P-18864)
CAMARENA HEALTH
49169 Road 426, Oakhurst (93644-8702)
PHONE..................559 642-6724
Johnny McCrory, *President*
EMP: 74

SALES (corp-wide): 41.5MM **Privately Held**
SIC: 8011 Clinic, operated by physicians
PA: Camarena Health
344 E 6th St
Madera CA 93638
559 664-4000

(P-18865)
CAPITAL EYE MEDICAL GROUP
6620 Coyle Ave Ste 408, Carmichael (95608-6338)
P.O. Box 279, Roseville (95661-0279)
PHONE..................916 241-9378
Mitra Ayazifar, *President*
EMP: 55
SALES (est): 1MM
SALES (corp-wide): 4MM **Privately Held**
SIC: 8011 Surgeon
PA: Nvision Laser Eye Centers Inc.
75 Enterprise Ste 200
Aliso Viejo CA 92656
877 455-9942

(P-18866)
CARDIC ARITHMIAS
Also Called: Cardic Arithmias
770 Welch Rd Ste 100, Palo Alto (94304-1505)
PHONE..................650 617-8100
Michael Ruder MD, *Partner*
Gregory Engel, *Med Doctor*
Hardwi Mead, *Med Doctor*
EMP: 50
SALES (est): 2.2MM **Privately Held**
SIC: 8011 Cardiologist & cardio-vascular specialist

(P-18867)
CARDIOVASCULAR CONSULTANTS HEA
1207 E Herndon Ave, Fresno (93720-3235)
PHONE..................559 432-4303
Kevin L Boran, *President*
William E Hanks MD, *Treasurer*
Donald Gregory MD, *Admin Sec*
EMP: 67
SQ FT: 17,000
SALES (est): 11.5MM **Privately Held**
SIC: 8011 Cardiologist & cardio-vascular specialist

(P-18868)
CARDIVSCLR MDCL GRP OF STHRN
Also Called: Harold L Karpman MD
414 N Camden Dr Ste 1100, Beverly Hills (90210-4517)
PHONE..................310 278-3400
Harold L Karpman, *President*
Selvyn B Bleifer MD, *President*
EMP: 50
SALES (est): 952.9K **Privately Held**
SIC: 8011 Cardiologist & cardio-vascular specialist

(P-18869)
CAREMARK RX INC
Also Called: US Family Care
1851 N Riverside Ave, Rialto (92376-8069)
PHONE..................909 822-1164
Steve Heide, *Administration*
EMP: 70
SALES (corp-wide): 194.5B **Publicly Held**
WEB: www.medpartners.com
SIC: 8011 General & family practice, physician/surgeon; internal medicine, physician/surgeon; obstetrician; gynecologist
HQ: Caremark Rx, Inc.
445 Great Circle Rd
Nashville TN 37228

(P-18870)
CAREMARK RX LLC
Also Called: US Family Care
15576 Main St, Hesperia (92345-3482)
PHONE..................760 948-6606
Rochelle Steen, *Principal*
EMP: 50
SALES (corp-wide): 194.5B **Publicly Held**
WEB: www.medpartners.com
SIC: 8011 General & family practice, physician/surgeon

HQ: Caremark Rx, Inc.
445 Great Circle Rd
Nashville TN 37228

(P-18871)
CAREMARK RX LLC
Also Called: Mullikin Medical Center
800 Douglas Rd, Stockton (95207-3607)
PHONE..................209 957-7050
EMP: 50
SALES (corp-wide): 184.7B **Publicly Held**
SIC: 8011
HQ: Caremark Rx, Inc.
445 Great Circle Rd
Nashville TN 37228
-

(P-18872)
CAREMORE HEALTH PLAN (HQ)
Also Called: Caremore Insurance Services
12900 Park Plaza Dr # 150, Cerritos (90703-9329)
PHONE..................562 622-2950
Toll Free:..................888 -
Leeba R Lessin, *President*
Jason Barker, *President*
John KAO, *President*
Allan Hoops, *CEO*
Vish Sankaran, *COO*
EMP: 89
SALES (est): 39MM
SALES (corp-wide): 92.1B **Publicly Held**
WEB: www.caremore.com
SIC: 8011 6411 Offices & clinics of medical doctors; insurance agents, brokers & service
PA: Anthem, Inc.
220 Virginia Ave
Indianapolis IN 46204
317 488-6000

(P-18873)
CAREONSITE INC
1805 Arnold Dr, Martinez (94553-4182)
PHONE..................562 437-0381
EMP: 70
SALES (corp-wide): 12MM **Privately Held**
SIC: 8011 Occupational & industrial specialist, physician/surgeon
PA: Careonsite, Inc.
1250 Pacific Ave
Long Beach CA 90813
562 437-0831

(P-18874)
CAREONSITE INC (PA)
1250 Pacific Ave, Long Beach (90813-3026)
P.O. Box 11389, Carson (90749-1389)
PHONE..................562 437-0831
Helen Tang, *President*
Brian Tang, *Vice Pres*
EMP: 50
SALES: 12MM **Privately Held**
SIC: 8011 Occupational & industrial specialist, physician/surgeon

(P-18875)
CARES COMMUNITY HEALTH
Also Called: Pharmacy At Cares, The
1500 21st St, Sacramento (95811-5216)
PHONE..................916 443-3299
Christy Ward, *CEO*
Richard Soohoo, *Ch of Bd*
Kathleen Marshall, *COO*
Bob Styron, *CFO*
Mark Thomas, *Admin Sec*
EMP: 105
SALES: 22.6MM **Privately Held**
SIC: 8011 8299 Offices & clinics of medical doctors; educational services

(P-18876)
CASSIDY MEDICAL GROUP INC (PA)
145 Thunder Dr, Vista (92083-6010)
PHONE..................760 630-5487
John Bennett, *President*
EMP: 50
SQ FT: 14,495
SALES (est): 5.3MM **Privately Held**
SIC: 8011 General & family practice, physician/surgeon

(P-18877)
CEDARS-SINAI MEDICAL CENTER
Also Called: Nephrology
8635 W 3rd St Ste 1195, Los Angeles (90048-6146)
P.O. Box 48956 (90048-0956)
PHONE..................310 824-3664
Larry Froch, *Principal*
Theodore Collier, *Office Mgr*
Silvia Guzman, *Executive Asst*
James Hawes, *Administration*
Patricia Lin, *Administration*
EMP: 161
SALES (corp-wide): 3.6B **Privately Held**
SIC: 8011 Nephrologist
PA: Cedars-Sinai Medical Center
8700 Beverly Blvd
West Hollywood CA 90048
310 423-3277

(P-18878)
CEDARS-SINAI MEDICAL CENTER
Also Called: Cardiac Noninvasive Laboratory
127 S San Vicente Blvd # 3417, Los Angeles (90048-3311)
PHONE..................310 423-3849
Timothy Henry, *Director*
Maricela Clemens, *Manager*
EMP: 201
SALES (corp-wide): 3.6B **Privately Held**
SIC: 8011 Cardiologist & cardio-vascular specialist
PA: Cedars-Sinai Medical Center
8700 Beverly Blvd
West Hollywood CA 90048
310 423-3277

(P-18879)
CEDARS-SINAI MEDICAL CENTER
8631 W 3rd St Ste 730, Los Angeles (90048-5911)
P.O. Box 48955 (90048-0955)
PHONE..................323 866-8483
Graham Woolf, *Principal*
EMP: 3824
SALES (corp-wide): 3.6B **Privately Held**
SIC: 8011 Medical centers
PA: Cedars-Sinai Medical Center
8700 Beverly Blvd
West Hollywood CA 90048
310 423-3277

(P-18880)
CENTER MEDICAL COMPANY
12100 Valley Blvd 109a, El Monte (91732-3100)
P.O. Box 6208 (91734-6208)
PHONE..................626 575-7500
Mohammad Rasekhi, *President*
EMP: 50
SALES (est): 663.2K **Privately Held**
SIC: 8011 Medical centers

(P-18881)
CENTRAL ANESTHESIA SERVICE
Also Called: Case Medical Group
3315 Watt Ave, Sacramento (95821-3600)
P.O. Box 660910 (95866-0910)
PHONE..................916 481-6800
David Downs, *President*
Vince Isso, *CFO*
Shaunda Barry, *Executive*
Claudia Halkyer, *Hum Res Coord*
Conrad Arnold, *Anesthesiology*
EMP: 80
SALES (est): 12.4MM **Privately Held**
WEB: www.casemedgroup.com
SIC: 8011 Group health association

(P-18882)
CENTRAL CALIFORNIA EAR NOSE
Also Called: Ent Facial Surgery Center
1351 E Spruce Ave, Fresno (93720-3342)
PHONE..................559 432-3724
Marvin Beil MD, *Partner*
Allan Evans MD, *Partner*
Brent Lanier MD, *Partner*
Jerry Moore MD, *Partner*
Oscar Tamez MD, *Partner*
EMP: 50

PRODUCTS & SVCS

SQ FT: 24,000
SALES (est): 10.6MM **Privately Held**
SIC: 8011 8049 5999 Eyes, ears, nose & throat specialist: physician/surgeon; audiologist; hearing aids

(P-18883)
CENTRAL CALIFORNIA FACULTY MED (PA)
2625 E Divisadero St, Fresno (93721-1431)
PHONE.................................559 453-5200
Karl Van Gundy, *CEO*
Rachel Carder, *CFO*
Randall Stern, *Treasurer*
Joyce Fields-Keene, *Exec Dir*
Jenny Eastman, *Office Mgr*
EMP: 100
SQ FT: 19,053
SALES (est): 53.8MM **Privately Held**
WEB: www.ccfmg.org
SIC: 8011 Medical centers

(P-18884)
CENTRAL CARDIOLOGY MED CLINIC
2901 Sillect Ave Ste 100, Bakersfield (93308-6372)
P.O. Box 1139 (93302-1139)
PHONE.................................661 395-0000
Brijesh Bahmbi, *Partner*
Peter Nalos MD, *Partner*
William Nyitray MD, *Partner*
EMP: 120
SALES (est): 23.2MM **Privately Held**
WEB: www.heart24.com
SIC: 8011 Cardiologist & cardio-vascular specialist; medical centers

(P-18885)
CENTRAL VALLEY INDIAN HLTH INC (PA)
2740 Herndon Ave, Clovis (93611-6813)
PHONE.................................559 299-2578
Chuck Fowler, *CEO*
Julie Ramsey, *Executive*
Arthur Hugues, *Software Dev*
Pao Yang, *Technology*
Paul Bains, *Financial Exec*
EMP: 82 EST: 1974
SQ FT: 14,000
SALES: 20.7MM **Privately Held**
WEB: www.cvih.org
SIC: 8011 8021 8042 8093 Clinic, operated by physicians; dental clinic; offices & clinics of optometrists; substance abuse clinics (outpatient)

(P-18886)
CENTRE CARE MANAGEMENT CO LLC
Also Called: Centre For Health Care
15611 Pomerado Rd Ste 400, Poway (92064-2437)
PHONE.................................858 613-6255
Jerome P Brodkin, *Med Doctor*
Hamed Bayat, *Cardiology*
Stephen Shewmake, *Dermatology*
Stuart Graham, *Med Doctor*
Kamen Zakov, *Med Doctor*
EMP: 200 EST: 1997
SALES (est): 8.4MM
SALES (corp-wide): 502.8MM **Privately Held**
SIC: 8011 General & family practice, physician/surgeon
HQ: Arch Health Partners, Inc.
15611 Pomerado Rd Ste 575
Poway CA 92064
858 675-3100

(P-18887)
CENTURY CITY PRIMARY CARE
2080 Century Park E # 1605, Los Angeles (90067-2019)
PHONE.................................310 553-3189
Jay S Rudin MD, *Principal*
EMP: 50
SALES (est): 4.8MM **Privately Held**
SIC: 8011 Allergist

(P-18888)
CEP AMERICA LLC
Also Called: Vituity
2100 Powell St Ste 400, Emeryville (94608-1826)
PHONE.................................510 350-2691
Theo Koury,
Jaime Rivas, *Partner*
Chris Kuhns, *Vice Pres*
Scott Zeller, *Vice Pres*
Siobhan Gray, *Surgery Dir*
EMP: 90
SALES: 4.1MM **Privately Held**
SIC: 8011 Offices & clinics of medical doctors

(P-18889)
CHADWICK CENTER FOR CHILDREN &
3020 Childrens Way, San Diego (92123-4223)
PHONE.................................858 966-5814
Charles Wlison, *Principal*
EMP: 50
SALES (est): 2.7MM **Privately Held**
SIC: 8011 Primary care medical clinic

(P-18890)
CHAPA-DE INDIAN HEALTH (PA)
11670 Atwood Rd, Auburn (95603-9522)
PHONE.................................530 887-2800
Lisa Davies, *President*
Debbie Arvay, *Practice Mgr*
Aimee Sagan, *Executive Asst*
Gene Whitehouse, *Admin Sec*
Anthony Reyes, *Human Res Dir*
EMP: 85
SQ FT: 65,000
SALES: 21.2MM **Privately Held**
SIC: 8011 8322 8021 8042 Clinic, operated by physicians; outreach program; multi-service center; dentists' office; orthodontist; offices & clinics of optometrists; dietician

(P-18891)
CHARLIE W SHAEFFER JR MD
Also Called: Eisenhower Desert Crdiolgy Ctr
39000 Bob Hope Dr, Rancho Mirage (92270-3221)
PHONE.................................760 346-0642
Charlie Schaeffer MD, *Principal*
Lin Fang, *Cardiology*
Leon A Feldman, *Med Doctor*
Philip J Shaver, *Med Doctor*
Patricia Garcia,
EMP: 61
SALES (est): 2.5MM **Privately Held**
SIC: 8011 General & family practice, physician/surgeon

(P-18892)
CHICO IMMDATE CARE MED CTR INC (PA)
376 Vallombrosa Ave, Chico (95926-3900)
PHONE.................................530 891-1676
Bradley M Smith, *CEO*
David Ricci, *Accountant*
Bradley Smith, *Med Doctor*
EMP: 50
SQ FT: 4,000
SALES (est): 7.1MM **Privately Held**
SIC: 8011 Clinic, operated by physicians

(P-18893)
CHILDRENS CLINIC SERVING CHL
701 E 28th St Ste 200, Long Beach (90806-2784)
PHONE.................................562 264-4638
Elisa A Nicholas, *CEO*
Jina Lee Lawler, *COO*
Maria Y Chandler, *CFO*
Albert P Ocampo, *CFO*
Knut P Thune, *CFO*
EMP: 320
SQ FT: 24,000
SALES: 30.4MM **Privately Held**
SIC: 8011 Clinic, operated by physicians

(P-18894)
CHILDRENS HEALTHCARE CAL
Also Called: Pediatric Cancer Research
455 S Main St, Orange (92868-3835)
P.O. Box 5700 (92863-5700)
PHONE.................................714 997-3000
Kimberly Crite, *CEO*
EMP: 1600 **Privately Held**
SIC: 8011 Pediatrician
PA: Children's Healthcare Of California
1201 W La Veta Ave
Orange CA 92868

(P-18895)
CHILDRENS HOSPITAL LOS ANGELES
Also Called: Division of Rheumatology
4650 W Sunset Blvd, Los Angeles (90027-6062)
PHONE.................................323 361-2119
Andreas O Reiff, *Principal*
EMP: 339
SALES (corp-wide): 1.3B **Privately Held**
SIC: 8011 Pediatrician
PA: The Childrens Hospital Los Angeles
4650 W Sunset Blvd
Los Angeles CA 90027
323 660-2450

(P-18896)
CHILDRENS SPECIALIST OF SAN D (PA)
Also Called: Childrens Associated Med Group
3020 Childrens Way, San Diego (92123-4223)
PHONE.................................858 576-1700
Michael Segall MD, *President*
Betty Hill, *Office Mgr*
Phil Stearns, *Nurse Practr*
Wilma A Robb, *Manager*
EMP: 350
SALES: 283.3K **Privately Held**
SIC: 8011 Physicians' office, including specialists

(P-18897)
CHINO MEDICAL GROUP INC
5475 Walnut Ave, Chino (91710-2699)
PHONE.................................909 591-6446
J A Lira MD, *President*
Fidel F Pinzon MD, *Vice Pres*
Steven Pulverman, *Vice Pres*
Jeffrey R Unger MD, *Vice Pres*
EMP: 100
SQ FT: 36,000
SALES (est): 14.3MM **Privately Held**
WEB: www.chinomedicalgroup.com
SIC: 8011 8031 Clinic, operated by physicians; offices & clinics of osteopathic physicians

(P-18898)
CIRRUS HEALTH II LP
Also Called: Laguna Hills Surgery Center
24331 El Toro Rd Ste 150, Laguna Hills (92637-8818)
PHONE.................................949 855-0562
Kim Wood, *Principal*
EMP: 113
SALES (corp-wide): 12.1MM **Privately Held**
WEB: www.cirrushealth.com
SIC: 8011 Offices & clinics of medical doctors
PA: Cirrus Health Ii, L.P.
2800 E Highway 114 # 300
Trophy Club TX 76262
214 217-0100

(P-18899)
CLINIC INC
Also Called: TO HELP EVERYONE HEALTH AND WE
3834 S Western Ave, Los Angeles (90062-1104)
PHONE.................................323 730-1920
Jamesina E Henderson, *Exec Dir*
Jamesina Henderson, *Exec Dir*
Rise K Phillips, *Technology*
Lilian Alvarez, *Human Res Dir*
Wendy Green, *Pediatrics*
EMP: 85
SQ FT: 26,000
SALES: 14.9MM **Privately Held**
WEB: www.theclinicinc.org
SIC: 8011 Clinic, operated by physicians

(P-18900)
CLINICA MEDICA FAMILIAR
517 N Main St Ste 100, Santa Ana (92701-4684)
PHONE.................................714 541-0870
Ricardo Limon MD, *President*
EMP: 100
SALES (est): 8.9MM **Privately Held**
SIC: 8011 Primary care medical clinic

(P-18901)
CLINICA MSR OSCAR A ROMERO (PA)
123 S Alvarado St, Los Angeles (90057-2201)
PHONE.................................213 989-7700
Carlos Antonio H Vaquerano, *President*
Pablo F Lopez, *Treasurer*
Marcello Villagomez, *Vice Pres*
Jonathan Miranda Canas C, *Admin Sec*
Eduardo Gonzalez, *Director*
EMP: 52
SALES: 13.6MM **Privately Held**
WEB: www.clinicaromero.com
SIC: 8011 Clinic, operated by physicians

(P-18902)
CLINICA POPULAR MEDICAL GROUP
101 S Rossmore Ave, Los Angeles (90004-3736)
PHONE.................................213 381-7175
Daniel Berdakin MD, *President*
EMP: 50 EST: 1977
SQ FT: 7,000
SALES (est): 1.6MM **Privately Held**
SIC: 8011 General & family practice, physician/surgeon

(P-18903)
CLINICA SAGRADO CORAZON
831 S Harbor Blvd, Anaheim (92805-5157)
PHONE.................................714 491-7777
Ivone Alfaro, *Principal*
EMP: 50 EST: 2011
SALES (est): 641 7K **Privately Held**
SIC: 8011 Clinic, operated by physicians

(P-18904)
CLINICA SIERRA VISTA (PA)
Also Called: Lamont Community Health Center
1430 Truxtun Ave Ste 400, Bakersfield (93301-5220)
P.O. Box 1559 (93302-1559)
PHONE.................................661 635-3050
Matthew Clark, *Ch of Bd*
Ana Medina, *COO*
Emily Garcia, *CFO*
Robbie Gerds, *Bd of Directors*
Patricia Miller, *Bd of Directors*
EMP: 90 EST: 1971
SQ FT: 14,599
SALES: 136.6MM **Privately Held**
WEB: www.clinicasierravista.org
SIC: 8011 Clinic, operated by physicians

(P-18905)
CLINICA SIERRA VISTA
1945 N Fine Ave Ste 100, Fresno (93727-1528)
PHONE.................................559 457-5292
Stephen W Schilling, *Branch Mgr*
EMP: 63
SALES (corp-wide): 136.6MM **Privately Held**
SIC: 8011 Clinic, operated by physicians
PA: Clinica Sierra Vista
1430 Truxtun Ave Ste 400
Bakersfield CA 93301
661 635-3050

(P-18906)
CLINICAS DE SLUD DEL PEBLO INC (PA)
1166 K St, Brawley (92227-2737)
P.O. Box 1279 (92227-1279)
PHONE.................................760 344-9951
Yvonne Bell, *CEO*
Dolores Martinez, *COO*
Gloria Santillan, *CFO*

Josie Godinez, *Administration*
Lwbba Chait Llamas, *Pediatrics*
EMP: 62 **EST:** 1970
SQ FT: 15,251
SALES: 34.5MM **Privately Held**
WEB: www.clinicasdesalud.com
SIC: 8011 8049 Clinic, operated by physicians; gynecologist; nutrition specialist; dental hygienist

(P-18907)
CLINICAS DE SLUD DEL PEBLO INC
Also Called: Betty Jimenez
900 Main St, Brawley (92227-2630)
PHONE......................760 344-6471
Betty Jimenez, *Branch Mgr*
EMP: 55
SALES (corp-wide): 39.6MM **Privately Held**
WEB: www.clinicasdesalud.com
SIC: 8011 8049 Clinic, operated by physicians; gynecologist; nutrition specialist; dental hygienist
PA: Clinicas De Salud Del Pueblo, Inc.
1166 K St
Brawley CA 92227
760 344-9951

(P-18908)
CO D L PHAM MD
Also Called: Bolsa Medical Group
10362 Bolsa Ave Ste 110, Westminster
(92683-6763)
PHONE......................714 531-2091
Co L Pham MD, *President*
Tuan V Pham, *Family Practiti*
EMP: 50
SALES (est): 7.2MM **Privately Held**
SIC: 8011 Gynecologist

(P-18909)
COASTAL RADIATION ONCOLOGY MED
1240 S Westlake Blvd, Westlake Village
(91361-1929)
PHONE......................805 494-4483
Kimberly Commins, *Director*
Lauren Lovett, *Director*
EMP: 99
SALES (est): 458.8K **Privately Held**
SIC: 8011 Offices & clinics of medical doctors

(P-18910)
COLORADO RIVER MEDICAL CENTER
1401 Bailey Ave, Needles (92363-3198)
PHONE......................760 326-4531
Steve Lopez, *CEO*
Knaya Tabora, *COO*
Bing Lum, *Exec VP*
Celia Ulibarri, *Radiology Dir*
Ron Chieffo, *CIO*
EMP: 100
SQ FT: 46,000
SALES: 9.7MM **Privately Held**
SIC: 8011 8062 Clinic, operated by physicians; general medical & surgical hospitals

(P-18911)
COMMUNICARE HEALTH CENTERS
2051 John Jones Rd, Davis (95616-9701)
P.O. Box 1260 (95617-1260)
PHONE......................530 758-2060
Melissa Marshall, *CEO*
Carolina Apicella, *CFO*
Dennis Su, *Fmly & Gen Dent*
EMP: 200
SALES: 29.1MM **Privately Held**
SIC: 8011 Clinic, operated by physicians

(P-18912)
COMMUNITY HEALTH CENTERS (PA)
150 Tejas Pl, Nipomo (93444-9123)
P.O. Box 430 (93444-0430)
PHONE......................805 929-3211
Ronald E Castle, *CEO*
Denise Stewart, *COO*
Bob Lotwala, *CFO*
Erica Guijarro, *Office Mgr*
Deanna Schreier, *Controller*

EMP: 55
SQ FT: 10,000
SALES (est): 21.7MM **Privately Held**
SIC: 8011 Clinic, operated by physicians

(P-18913)
COMMUNITY HEALTH GROUP
2420 Fenton St Ste 100, Chula Vista
(91914-3516)
PHONE......................800 224-7766
Norma A Diaz, *CEO*
Mauricio Osorio, *Information Mgr*
Michael Williams, *Software Engr*
Laura Infante, *Business Anlyst*
Jake Disanto, *Financial Analy*
EMP: 140
SQ FT: 26,000
SALES: 52.1MM **Privately Held**
WEB: www.communityhealthgroup.com
SIC: 8011 Health maintenance organization

(P-18914)
COMMUNITY HEALTH SYSTEMS INC
Also Called: Moreno Valley Family Hlth Ctr
22675 Alessandro Blvd # 1, Moreno Valley
(92553-8551)
PHONE......................951 571-2300
Lori Holeman, *CEO*
Yolanda Gomez, *Director*
Rosa Gonzales, *Clerk*
EMP: 130
SALES: 20.8MM **Privately Held**
SIC: 8011 Primary care medical clinic

(P-18915)
COMMUNITY MEDICAL CENTERS INC
Also Called: Channel Medical Center
701 E Channel St, Stockton (95202-2628)
P.O. Box 779 (95201-0779)
PHONE......................209 944-4700
Alice Souligen, *Manager*
Aziz Khambati, *Med Doctor*
EMP: 100
SALES (corp-wide): 44.6MM **Privately Held**
SIC: 8011 Clinic, operated by physicians
PA: Community Medical Centers Inc
7210 Murray Dr
Stockton CA 95210
209 373-2800

(P-18916)
COMMUNITY ORTHOPEDIC MEDICAL
26401 Crown Valley Pkwy # 101, Mission
Viejo (92691-6302)
PHONE......................949 348-4000
Kent Adamson, *President*
EMP: 63
SALES (est): 10.1MM **Privately Held**
WEB: www.comg.com
SIC: 8011 Orthopedic physician

(P-18917)
COMPREHENSIVE CMNTY HLTH CTR
5059 York Blvd, Los Angeles (90042-1713)
PHONE......................323 344-4144
EMP: 50
SALES (est): 78K **Privately Held**
SIC: 8011

(P-18918)
CONGRESS MED SURGERY CTR LLC
800 S Raymond Ave, Pasadena
(91105-3229)
PHONE......................626 396-8100
James A Shankwiler,
Gregory J Adamson,
EMP: 100
SALES (est): 1.4MM **Privately Held**
SIC: 8011 Ambulatory surgical center

(P-18919)
CONRAD A COX
Also Called: Caremore Medical Group
9040 Telegraph Rd, Downey (90240-2393)
PHONE......................562 927-0033
Conrad A Cox, *Owner*
Warren Magalong, *Nurse Practr*
EMP: 50

SALES (est): 3MM **Privately Held**
SIC: 8011 Gastronomist

(P-18920)
COPTIC CLINICS
3803 W Mission Blvd, Pomona
(91766-6823)
PHONE......................562 900-2692
Henry Kirolos, *Director*
Bishop Serapion, *Exec Dir*
EMP: 99
SALES (est): 1.7MM **Privately Held**
SIC: 8011 8021 Offices & clinics of medical doctors; specialized dental practitioners

(P-18921)
CORIZON HEALTH INC
5325 Broder Blvd, Dublin (94568-3309)
PHONE......................925 551-6500
Nomali Toman, *Principal*
Kevin Carreiro,
EMP: 105
SALES (corp-wide): 1.2B **Privately Held**
SIC: 8011 Dispensary, operated by physicians
HQ: Corizon Health, Inc.
103 Powell Ct
Brentwood TN 37027
800 729-0069

(P-18922)
COUNTY OF ALAMEDA
Also Called: Alameda, County Medical Center
2060 Fairmont Dr, San Leandro
(94578-1001)
PHONE......................510 481-4141
Robert Jones, *Director*
Katya Osipova, *Director*
EMP: 220 **Privately Held**
WEB: www.co.alameda.ca.us
SIC: 8011 9431 8361 8093 Psychiatric clinic; mental health agency administration, government; ; residential care; specialty outpatient clinics; psychiatric hospitals
PA: County Of Alameda
1221 Oak St Ste 555
Oakland CA 94612
510 272-6691

(P-18923)
COUNTY OF KERN
Also Called: Admin
1721 Westwind Dr, Bakersfield
(93301-3026)
PHONE......................661 868-8360
Carol Bowman, *Principal*
EMP: 50 **Privately Held**
WEB: www.kccfc.org
SIC: 8011 9111 Medical centers; county supervisors' & executives' offices
PA: County Of Kern
1115 Truxtun Ave Rm 505
Bakersfield CA 93301
661 868-3690

(P-18924)
COUNTY OF LOS ANGELES
1212 Pico St, San Fernando (91340-3503)
PHONE......................818 837-6969
Gretchen McGinley, *Principal*
Hadi Rahnamoon, *Obstetrician*
EMP: 123 **Privately Held**
WEB: www.co.la.ca.us
SIC: 8011 9111 Clinic, operated by physicians; executive offices
PA: County Of Los Angeles
500 W Temple St Ste 437
Los Angeles CA 90012
213 974-1101

(P-18925)
COUNTY OF LOS ANGELES
Also Called: L A County Hospital
1000 W Carson St, Torrance (90502-2004)
PHONE......................310 222-4220
EMP: 119 **Privately Held**
SIC: 8011 Medical centers
PA: County Of Los Angeles
500 W Temple St Ste 437
Los Angeles CA 90012
213 974-1101

(P-18926)
COUNTY OF LOS ANGELES
Also Called: Health Services, Dept of
3834 S Western Ave, Los Angeles
(90062-1104)
PHONE......................323 730-3507
Bernard Wilite, *Administration*
EMP: 100 **Privately Held**
WEB: www.co.la.ca.us
SIC: 8011 9431 8011 Medical centers; administration of public health programs; ; offices & clinics of osteopathic physicians
PA: County Of Los Angeles
500 W Temple St Ste 437
Los Angeles CA 90012
213 974-1101

(P-18927)
COUNTY OF LOS ANGELES
Also Called: Health Services, Dept of
1325 Broad Ave, Wilmington (90744-2604)
PHONE......................310 518-8800
Dr Jesus Gutierrez, *Director*
EMP: 52 **Privately Held**
WEB: www.co.la.ca.us
SIC: 8011 9431 Offices & clinics of medical doctors; administration of public health programs
PA: County Of Los Angeles
500 W Temple St Ste 437
Los Angeles CA 90012
213 974-1101

(P-18928)
COUNTY OF LOS ANGELES
Also Called: Los Angeles County
13300 Van Nuys Blvd, Pacoima
(91331-3004)
PHONE......................818 896-1903
Miriam Sanchez, *Administration*
EMP: 123
SQ FT: 47,532 **Privately Held**
SIC: 8011 Clinic, operated by physicians
PA: County Of Los Angeles
500 W Temple St Ste 437
Los Angeles CA 90012
213 974-1101

(P-18929)
COUNTY OF LOS ANGELES
Also Called: Mental Health Dept of
2600 Redondo Ave 3, Long Beach
(90806-2325)
PHONE......................562 599-9200
Margie Pappas, *Chief*
EMP: 123 **Privately Held**
WEB: www.co.la.ca.us
SIC: 8011 9431 Offices & clinics of medical doctors; administration of public health programs
PA: County Of Los Angeles
500 W Temple St Ste 437
Los Angeles CA 90012
213 974-1101

(P-18930)
COUNTY OF MONTEREY
Also Called: Alisal Health Center
559 E Alisal St Ste 201, Salinas
(93905-2516)
PHONE......................831 769-8800
Len Foster, *Director*
EMP: 50 **Privately Held**
WEB: www.montereycountyfarmbureau.org
SIC: 8011 Offices & clinics of medical doctors
PA: County Of Monterey
168 W Alisal St Fl 2
Salinas CA 93901
831 755-5040

(P-18931)
COUNTY OF RIVERSIDE
Also Called: Rubidoux Family Care Center
5256 Mission Blvd, Riverside (92509-4624)
PHONE......................951 955-0840
Koen Brown, *Exec Dir*
EMP: 84 **Privately Held**
SIC: 8011 Offices & clinics of medical doctors
PA: County Of Riverside
4080 Lemon St Fl 11
Riverside CA 92501
951 955-1110

(P-18932)
COUNTY OF RIVERSIDE
Also Called: Public Social Services
26520 Cactus Ave, Moreno Valley
(92555-3927)
PHONE..................951 486-4000
Donna Matney, *Administration*
Virginia Garcia, *Admin Sec*
Adam Grieder, *Technology*
Bryan Oshiro, *Obstetrician*
David Ninan, *Anesthesiology*
EMP: 84 **Privately Held**
SIC: 8011 9431 Medical centers; mental
health agency administration, govern-
ment;
PA: County Of Riverside
4080 Lemon St Fl 11
Riverside CA 92501
951 955-1110

(P-18933)
COUNTY OF RIVERSIDE
Also Called: Community Health Agency
7140 Indiana Ave, Riverside (92504-4544)
PHONE..................951 358-6000
Ibrahim Sumarli, *Med Doctor*
Peter Lee, *Associate Dir*
Biplav Yadav, *Family Practiti*
Donna Bonelli-Filter, *Counsel*
EMP: 84
SQ FT: 1,276 **Privately Held**
SIC: 8011 9431 Clinic, operated by physi-
cians; administration of public health pro-
grams;
PA: County Of Riverside
4080 Lemon St Fl 11
Riverside CA 92501
951 955-1110

(P-18934)
COUNTY OF RIVERSIDE
Also Called: Community Health Agency
26520 Cactus Ave, Moreno Valley
(92555-3927)
PHONE..................951 486-4000
Jim Watkins, *Principal*
Raul Hermano, *Pharmacist*
EMP: 300 **Privately Held**
SIC: 8011 9431 Medical centers; public
health agency administration, government
PA: County Of Riverside
4080 Lemon St Fl 11
Riverside CA 92501
951 955-1110

(P-18935)
COUNTY OF RIVERSIDE
Also Called: Indio Family Care Center
47923 Oasis St Ste A, Indio (92201-9788)
PHONE..................760 863-8283
Koen Brown, *Exec Dir*
EMP: 84 **Privately Held**
SIC: 8011 Clinic, operated by physicians
PA: County Of Riverside
4080 Lemon St Fl 11
Riverside CA 92501
951 955-1110

(P-18936)
CRIPTS HEALTH CARE
10666 N Torrey Pines Rd, La Jolla
(92037-1027)
PHONE..................858 554-8646
Hubert Greenway MD, *Director*
EMP: 50
SALES (est): 823.2K **Privately Held**
SIC: 8011 Physicians' office, including spe-
cialists

(P-18937)
**CYPRESS CTR FOR FMLY
MEDICINE**
10601 Walker St Ste 250, Cypress
(90630-4733)
PHONE..................562 799-4801
Franklin Lowe, *President*
Scott Brunner, *Vice Pres*
Bethany Gray, *Med Doctor*
EMP: 90
SQ FT: 4,200
SALES (est): 5.6MM **Privately Held**
SIC: 8011 Primary care medical clinic; gen-
eral & family practice, physician/surgeon

(P-18938)
**CYPRESS HALTHCARE
PARTNERS LLC (PA)**
100 Wilson Rd Ste 100 # 100, Monterey
(93940-7885)
PHONE..................831 649-1000
Michael K McMillan,
Judy Cabanban, *Marketing Staff*
William Hines,
EMP: 50
SQ FT: 8,500
SALES (est): 24.7MM **Privately Held**
WEB: www.doctorsonduty.com
SIC: 8011 Clinic, operated by physicians

(P-18939)
DANIEL O MONGIANO MD A PR
Also Called: AV Occupational Medicine
42220 10th St W Ste 109, Lancaster
(93534-7075)
PHONE..................661 951-9195
Daniel Mongiano, *President*
Lionel Mongiano, *Office Mgr*
Kimberly D Lear, *Radiology*
Imelda Rodriguez, *Assistant*
EMP: 50
SALES (est): 3.8MM **Privately Held**
WEB: www.avoccmed.com
SIC: 8011 Physicians' office, including spe-
cialists

(P-18940)
DAO MEDICAL GROUP INC
9191 Westminster Ave # 204, Garden
Grove (92844-2751)
PHONE..................714 899-2000
Michael Dao, *President*
Linh Bui, *Executive*
Peter H Vu, *Pediatrics*
Tao Duong, *Cardiovascular*
EMP: 65
SALES (est): 1.6MM **Privately Held**
SIC: 8011 Cardiologist & cardio-vascular
specialist

(P-18941)
DAVID CIVALIER MD INC
Also Called: Redding Medical Group
2510 Airpark Dr Ste 104, Redding
(96001-2461)
PHONE..................530 244-4034
David Civalier MD, *President*
EMP: 50
SALES (est): 4.1MM **Privately Held**
SIC: 8011 General & family practice, physi-
cian/surgeon

(P-18942)
DAVIS COMMUNITY CLINIC (PA)
Also Called: Davis Cmnty Clnic Dntl Program
2040 Sutter Pl, Davis (95616-6201)
P.O. Box 1260 (95617-1260)
PHONE..................530 758-2060
Sherry Cauchois, *Exec Dir*
EMP: 100
SQ FT: 5,000
SALES (est): 4.7MM **Privately Held**
SIC: 8011 Clinic, operated by physicians

(P-18943)
**DAVITA MAGAN MANAGEMENT
INC (DH)**
Also Called: M M C
420 W Rowland St, Covina (91723-2943)
PHONE..................626 331-6411
Bradley J Rosenberg, *Principal*
Connie Solorza, *Division VP*
Howard Ort MD, *Exec VP*
Miguel Garcia, *Vice Pres*
Richard Fernandez, *Sr Ntwrk Engine*
EMP: 250
SQ FT: 66,000
SALES (est): 27.2MM **Publicly Held**
WEB: www.maganclinic.com
SIC: 8011 Clinic, operated by physicians;
urologist; internal medicine, physician/sur-
geon; ophthalmologist

(P-18944)
**DAVITA MAGAN MANAGEMENT
INC**
330 W Covina Blvd, San Dimas (91773)
PHONE..................909 592-9712
Beth Nunn, *Human Resources*
EMP: 91 **Publicly Held**

WEB: www.maganclinic.com
SIC: 8011 8071 Clinic, operated by physicians; medical laboratories
HQ: Davita Magan Management, Inc.
420 W Rowland St
Covina CA 91723
626 331-6411

(P-18945)
**DAVITA MEDICAL
MANAGEMENT LLC**
Also Called: Healthcare Partners Med Group
2601 Via Campo, Montebello (90640-1807)
PHONE..................323 720-1144
Sonia Flores, *Branch Mgr*
Olga Alarid, *Med Doctor*
Mohindrjit Neelam, *Med Doctor*
Allison Taylor, *Manager*
EMP: 100 **Publicly Held**
WEB: www.davidv.com
SIC: 8011 Clinic, operated by physicians
HQ: Davita Medical Management, Llc
2175 Park Pl
El Segundo CA 90245

(P-18946)
**DAVITA MEDICAL
MANAGEMENT LLC**
Also Called: Healthcare Partners Med Group
3144 Santa Anita Ave # 201, El Monte
(91733-1316)
PHONE..................626 444-0333
Joseph Soto, *Branch Mgr*
EMP: 60 **Publicly Held**
WEB: www.davidv.com
SIC: 8011 Clinic, operated by physicians
HQ: Davita Medical Management, Llc
2175 Park Pl
El Segundo CA 90245

(P-18947)
**DAVITA MEDICAL
MANAGEMENT LLC (HQ)**
Also Called: Healthcare Partners Med Group
2175 Park Pl, El Segundo (90245-4705)
PHONE..................310 354-4200
Robert J Margolis, *CEO*
Matthew Mazdyasni, *Exec VP*
Paula De Almeida, *Vice Pres*
Suzanne Hansen, *Vice Pres*
Zan F Calhoun, *CIO*
EMP: 600
SQ FT: 38,000
SALES (est): 356.1MM **Publicly Held**
WEB: www.davidv.com
SIC: 8011 Group health association

(P-18948)
**DEL PUERTO HEALTH CARE
DST**
Also Called: Del Puerto Health Center
875 E St, Patterson (95363-2670)
P.O. Box 187 (95363-0187)
PHONE..................209 892-9100
Margo Arnold, *Administration*
Paul Willette, *Director*
EMP: 55
SQ FT: 25,000
SALES (est): 9.3MM **Privately Held**
SIC: 8011 Medical centers

(P-18949)
**DESERT CARDIOLOGY
CONSULTANTS**
Also Called: Desert Cardiology Cons Med G
39000 Bob Hope Dr, Rancho Mirage
(92270-3221)
PHONE..................760 346-0642
Keenan F Barber MD, *Vice Pres*
Barry Hackshaw, *President*
Merle R Bolton, *Treasurer*
John Nelson, *Officer*
Andrew Frutkin, *Managing Dir*
EMP: 70
SALES (est): 6MM **Privately Held**
WEB: www.desertcard.com
SIC: 8011 Cardiologist & cardio-vascular
specialist

(P-18950)
**DESERT MEDICAL GROUP INC
(PA)**
Also Called: Desert Oasis Healthcare
275 N El Cielo Rd D-402, Palm Springs
(92262-6972)
PHONE..................760 320-8814
Richard E Merkin MD, *President*
EMP: 240
SQ FT: 13,000
SALES (est): 43.2MM **Privately Held**
WEB: www.oasisipa.com
SIC: 8011 General & family practice, physi-
cian/surgeon; freestanding emergency
medical center

(P-18951)
DESERT MEDICAL GROUP INC
Also Called: Oasis IPA
275 N El Cielo Rd Ste C, Palm Springs
(92262-6972)
PHONE..................760 323-8657
Tammy Torres, *Manager*
EMP: 250
SALES (corp-wide): 43.2MM **Privately
Held**
WEB: www.oasisipa.com
SIC: 8011 General & family practice, physi-
cian/surgeon
PA: Desert Medical Group, Inc.
275 N El Cielo Rd D-402
Palm Springs CA 92262
760 320-8814

(P-18952)
**DESERT ORTHOPDC CENTER A
MDCL (PA)**
39000 Bob Hope Dr W301, Rancho Mirage
(92270-3221)
PHONE..................760 568-2684
Ronald Lamb MD, *President*
Robert Murphy MD, *Ch of Bd*
Stephen O Connell MD, *CFO*
James Bell MD, *Vice Pres*
David Friscia, *Vice Pres*
EMP: 98
SQ FT: 23,000
SALES (est): 9.9MM **Privately Held**
SIC: 8011 Orthopedic physician

(P-18953)
**DESERT VALLEY MED GROUP
INC (PA)**
16850 Bear Valley Rd, Victorville
(92395-5794)
PHONE..................760 241-8000
Prem Reddy MD, *CEO*
Lex Reddy, *President*
M Mansukhani, *CFO*
Diane Van Velkinburg, *Project Mgr*
EMP: 300
SQ FT: 15,000
SALES (est): 46.4MM **Privately Held**
WEB: www.dvmc.com
SIC: 8011 Phys cians' office, including spe-
cialists

(P-18954)
DIAGNOSTIC AND INTERVENTIO
13160 Mindanao Way # 150, Marina Del
Rey (90292-6358)
PHONE..................310 574-0400
Robert S Bray Jr, *President*
Keren Reiter, *COO*
Robert Bray, *Med Doctor*
Susan Koh,
EMP: 100
SALES: 35MM **Privately Held**
SIC: 8011 Surgeon

(P-18955)
DIGNITY HEALTH
8120 Timberlake Way # 201, Sacramento
(95823-5412)
PHONE..................916 667-0000
Daniel Yuen, *Principal*
Brent Keane, *Director*
EMP: 193 **Privately Held**
WEB: www.chw.edu
SIC: 8011 Clinic, operated by physicians
HQ: Dignity Health
185 Berry St Ste 300
San Francisco CA 94107
415 438-5500

(P-18956)
DIGNITY HEALTH
Also Called: James A Kiley MD
1600 Creekside Dr # 3700, Folsom
(95630-3444)
PHONE....................916 983-7988
James Kiley, *Partner*
EMP: 60 **Privately Held**
WEB: www.mercycare.net
SIC: 8011 Offices & clinics of medical doctors
HQ: Dignity Health
185 Berry St Ste 300
San Francisco CA 94107
415 438-5500

(P-18957)
DIGNITY HEALTH
Also Called: Emergency Physicians Med Group
8350 Auburn Blvd Ste 200, Citrus Heights
(95610-0396)
PHONE....................916 536-2420
Art B Wong MD, *Branch Mgr*
Christine Braid, *Family Practiti*
EMP: 90 **Privately Held**
WEB: www.chw.edu
SIC: 8011 Offices & clinics of medical doctors
HQ: Dignity Health
185 Berry St Ste 300
San Francisco CA 94107
415 438-5500

(P-18958)
DINUBA MEDICAL CLINIC (PA)
Also Called: Dinuba Medical Center
271 N L St, Dinuba (93618-2107)
PHONE....................559 591-1820
John Moore, *Manager*
EMP: 61
SALES (est): 5.1MM **Privately Held**
SIC: 8011 Physicians' office, including specialists; general & family practice, physician/surgeon; pediatrician; internal medicine, physician/surgeon

(P-18959)
DISCOVERY PRACTICE MANAGEMENT
Also Called: Center For Discovery
4136 Ann Arbor Rd, Lakewood
(90712-3817)
PHONE....................562 425-6404
Craig M Brown, *President*
Julia Cassidy, *Dietician*
EMP: 50
SQ FT: 2,500
SALES (est): 2.3MM **Privately Held**
SIC: 8011 General & family practice, physician/surgeon

(P-18960)
DOS PALOS MEMORIAL HOSP INC
Also Called: Dos Palos Mem Rur Hlth Clinic
2118 Marguerite St, Dos Palos
(93620-2339)
PHONE....................209 392-6121
Fax: 209 392-8872
EMP: 60
SQ FT: 16,000
SALES (est): 2.7MM **Privately Held**
SIC: 8011 8051

(P-18961)
DOUGLAS W JACKSON MD
2760 Atlantic Ave, Long Beach
(90806-2755)
PHONE....................562 424-6666
Douglas W Jackson MD, *Owner*
EMP: 60
SALES (est): 736.1K **Privately Held**
SIC: 8011 General & family practice, physician/surgeon

(P-18962)
DRUMMOND MEDICAL GROUP INC
Also Called: Indian Wells Vly Surgery Ctr
900 N Heritage Dr Ste A, Ridgecrest
(93555-3196)
PHONE....................760 446-4571
Douglas E Roberts Jr, *President*
EMP: 120 **EST:** 1958

SQ FT: 30,000
SALES (est): 6.2MM **Privately Held**
WEB: www.drummondmedical.com
SIC: 8011 General & family practice, physician/surgeon

(P-18963)
EAST BAY NEPHROLOGY
2089 Vale Rd Ste 32, San Pablo
(94806-3850)
PHONE....................510 235-1057
Ellen Morrissey, *Principal*
EMP: 50 **EST:** 2011
SALES (est): 97.7K **Privately Held**
SIC: 8011 Nephrologist

(P-18964)
EBSC LP
Also Called: Surgery Center of Health South
3875 Telegraph Ave, Oakland
(94609-2428)
PHONE....................510 547-2244
Judy Rich, *Administration*
EMP: 65
SQ FT: 12,500
SALES (est): 7.8MM **Privately Held**
SIC: 8011 Ambulatory surgical center

(P-18965)
EDEN LABS MED GROUP INC
20103 Lake Chabot Rd, Castro Valley
(94546-5305)
PHONE....................510 537-1234
John Carney, *President*
Katherine Thomas, *Admin Sec*
Yolanda Tam, *Anesthesiology*
Kathy Lawrence, *Nursing Dir*
Fe Dizon, *Manager*
EMP: 50
SQ FT: 9,000
SALES (est): 3.3MM **Privately Held**
SIC: 8011 Pathologist

(P-18966)
EDINGER MEDICAL GROUP INC (PA)
9900 Talbert Ave 302, Fountain Valley
(92708-5153)
PHONE....................714 965-2500
Burton F Willis MD, *President*
Bertram N Dias MD, *CFO*
Denise Court, *Officer*
Gary Ahn MD, *Vice Pres*
Stanley W Arnold MD, *Vice Pres*
▲ **EMP:** 101
SALES (est): 15.4MM **Privately Held**
WEB: www.edingermedicalgroup.com
SIC: 8011 General & family practice, physician/surgeon

(P-18967)
EDWARDS LIFESCIENCES LLC (HQ)
1 Edwards Way, Irvine (92614-5688)
PHONE....................949 250-2500
Michael A Mussallem, *CEO*
Huimin Wang MD, *President*
Patricia Garvey, *Vice Pres*
John H Kehl Jr, *Vice Pres*
Sadiq Khanani, *Administration*
▲ **EMP:** 1700
SALES (est): 423.4MM
SALES (corp-wide): 3.7B **Publicly Held**
SIC: 8011 Cardiologist & cardio-vascular specialist
PA: Edwards Lifesciences Corp
1 Edwards Way
Irvine CA 92614
949 250-2500

(P-18968)
EL DORADO COUNTY HEALTH DEPT
Also Called: County of El Dorado
931 Spring St, Placerville (95667-4543)
PHONE....................530 621-6100
Lori Walker, *CFO*
Lynnan Svensson, *Nursing Dir*
EMP: 94
SALES (est): 1.3MM **Privately Held**
SIC: 8011 Primary care medical clinic

(P-18969)
ELDORADO COMMUNITY SERVICE CTR
335 E Manchester Blvd, Inglewood
(90301-1814)
PHONE....................424 227-7971
Stan Sharma, *Principal*
Ararat Alex Yarijanian, *Marketing Staff*
EMP: 99
SALES (est): 996.8K **Privately Held**
SIC: 8011 8049 Physicians' office, including specialists; clinical psychologist

(P-18970)
ELICA HEALTH CENTERS
3701 J St Ste 201, Sacramento
(95816-5542)
PHONE....................916 454-2345
Tamara Miroshniehenko, *Branch Mgr*
David Hughes, *COO*
Laton Fuller, *Info Tech Mgr*
Martha Tapia, *Pediatrics*
Yuriy Shevtsov, *Director*
EMP: 80
SALES (corp-wide): 13.6MM **Privately Held**
SIC: 8011 Clinic, operated by physicians
PA: Elica Health Centers
1860 Howe Ave Ste 455
Sacramento CA 95825
916 569-8484

(P-18971)
EMERGENCY MED GROUP OF FOLSOM
1650 Creekside Dr, Folsom (95630-3400)
PHONE....................916 983-7470
Dwight B Stalker, *Principal*
EMP: 80 **EST:** 2011
SALES (est): 138.6K **Privately Held**
SIC: 8011 Freestanding emergency medical center

(P-18972)
EMERGENT MEDICAL ASSOCIATES (PA)
111 N Sepulveda Blvd # 210, Manhattan Beach (90266-6849)
PHONE....................310 379-2134
Mark Bell, *Principal*
Jeff Ly, *Executive Asst*
David Limoges, *CTO*
Juan King, *Recruiter*
Courtney Boucher, *Physician Asst*
▲ **EMP:** 58
SALES (est): 9.6MM **Privately Held**
WEB: www.emergentmed.com
SIC: 8011 Medical centers

(P-18973)
ENLOE MEDICAL CENTER
Also Called: Payroll Dept.
175 W 5th Ave, Chico (95926)
PHONE....................530 332-7522
Linda Irvine, *Branch Mgr*
EMP: 357
SALES (corp-wide): 480.2MM **Privately Held**
SIC: 8011 Medical centers
PA: Enloe Medical Center
1531 Esplanade
Chico CA 95926
530 332-7300

(P-18974)
ENLOE MEDICAL CENTER
Also Called: Children's Health Center
1515 Sprngfeld Dr Ste 175, Chico (95928)
PHONE....................530 332-6000
Dorothy Chinnock, *Branch Mgr*
EMP: 357
SALES (corp-wide): 480.2MM **Privately Held**
SIC: 8011 Clinic, operated by physicians
PA: Enloe Medical Center
1531 Esplanade
Chico CA 95926
530 332-7300

(P-18975)
ERIC D FELDMAN MD INC
Also Called: Rehab Associates
2760 Atlantic Ave, Long Beach
(90806-2755)
PHONE....................562 424-6666

Eric D Feldman MD, *President*
EMP: 50
SALES (est): 1.5MM **Privately Held**
SIC: 8011 General & family practice, physician/surgeon

(P-18976)
EYE MEDICAL CLINIC FRESNO INC
Also Called: Eye Medical Center of Fresno
1360 E Herndon Ave # 301, Fresno
(93720-3326)
PHONE....................559 486-5000
Richard H Whitten Jr, *CEO*
George Bertolucci M, *President*
Carolyn Sakauye, *Bd of Directors*
Esmeralda Garcia, *Executive*
Juanita Esparza, *Office Mgr*
EMP: 55
SQ FT: 12,000
SALES (est): 6.8MM **Privately Held**
SIC: 8011 8042 Ophthalmologist; offices & clinics of optometrists

(P-18977)
EYE Q VISION CARE (PA)
7075 N Sharon Ave, Fresno (93720-3329)
PHONE....................559 486-2000
Scott Bridgeman, *CEO*
Sarah Jaimenez, *Administration*
Leeann Erl, *Manager*
EMP: 175
SALES (est): 23.1MM **Privately Held**
SIC: 8011 8042 8031 Ophthalmologist; offices & clinics of optometrists; offices & clinics of osteopathic physicians

(P-18978)
FACEY MEDICAL FOUNDATION (PA)
15451 San Fernando Msn, Mission Hills
(91345-1368)
PHONE....................818 365-9531
Bill Gill, *CEO*
Vivek Srinivasan, *COO*
Jim Corwin, *CFO*
Pati Cheesman, *Info Tech Dir*
Paul McCarty, *Technical Staff*
EMP: 170
SQ FT: 306,000
SALES (est): 197.1MM **Privately Held**
WEB: www.facey.com
SIC: 8011 Offices & clinics of medical doctors

(P-18979)
FACEY MEDICAL FOUNDATION
11165 Sepulveda Blvd, Mission Hills
(91345-1125)
PHONE....................818 365-9531
Judy Breen, *Branch Mgr*
Melissa Beaman, *Info Tech Mgr*
Jennifer Decker, *Med Doctor*
Cornelia D Licona, *Med Doctor*
Lily Yip, *Manager*
EMP: 220
SALES (corp-wide): 197.1MM **Privately Held**
SIC: 8011 Physicians' office, including specialists
PA: Facey Medical Foundation
15451 San Fernando Msn
Mission Hills CA 91345
818 365-9531

(P-18980)
FACIAL RECONSTRUCTIVE SURGERY
Also Called: Facial Reconstructive Surg &
1900 University Ave 101e, East Palo Alto
(94303-2212)
PHONE....................650 328-0511
Steven Schendel, *Partner*
Mary Lynn Fouche, *Assistant*
EMP: 50
SALES (est): 3MM **Privately Held**
WEB: www.sleepsurgery.com
SIC: 8011 Plastic surgeon

(P-18981)
FACULTY PHYSCANS SRGEONS LLUSM
11370 Anderson St, Loma Linda
(92354-3450)
P.O. Box 945 (92354-0945)
PHONE..................909 558-4000
Ricardo Peverini, *President*
EMP: 99
SALES (est): 3.9MM **Privately Held**
SIC: 8011 Physicians' office, including specialists

(P-18982)
FAMILY HEALTHCARE NETWORK
Also Called: Porterville Annex
1137 W Poplar Ave, Porterville
(93257-5839)
PHONE..................559 781-7242
EMP: 217
SALES (corp-wide): 114.6MM **Privately Held**
SIC: 8011 Primary care medical clinic
PA: Family Healthcare Network
       305 E Center Ave
       Visalia CA 93291
       559 737-4700

(P-18983)
FAMILY HEALTHCARE NETWORK
250 W 5th St, Hanford (93230-5029)
PHONE..................559 582-2013
EMP: 217
SALES (corp-wide): 114.6MM **Privately Held**
SIC: 8011 Primary care medical clinic
PA: Family Healthcare Network
       305 E Center Ave
       Visalia CA 93291
       559 737-4700

(P-18984)
FAMILY HEALTHCARE NETWORK
33025 159th Rd, Ivanhoe (93235)
PHONE..................559 798-1877
Yterry Abbott, *Manager*
EMP: 103
SALES (corp-wide): 114.6MM **Privately Held**
SIC: 8011 8021 Physicians' office, including specialists; offices & clinics of dentists
PA: Family Healthcare Network
       305 E Center Ave
       Visalia CA 93291
       559 737-4700

(P-18985)
FAMILY PLG ASSOC MED GROUP (PA)
3050 E Airport Way, Long Beach
(90806-2404)
PHONE..................213 738-7283
Edward C Allred MD, *Principal*
EMP: 52
SQ FT: 14,000
SALES (est): 36.1MM **Privately Held**
WEB: www.fpamg.net
SIC: 8011 Clinic, operated by physicians

(P-18986)
FANG INC
12235 Beach Blvd Ste 20h, Stanton
(90680-3965)
PHONE..................714 898-7785
Kaung-King Fang, *President*
Benjamin Fang, *Software Dev*
EMP: 55
SALES (est): 5MM **Privately Held**
WEB: www.fanginc.com
SIC: 8011 Offices & clinics of medical doctors

(P-18987)
FERTILITY & REPRODUCTIVE
Also Called: F R H I
2581 Samaritan Dr Ste 302, San Jose
(95124-4112)
PHONE..................408 358-2500
G D Adamson MD, *Director*
EMP: 60

SALES (est): 3.5MM
SALES (corp-wide): 12.7B **Privately Held**
SIC: 8011 Fertility specialist, physician
HQ: Palo Alto Medical Foundation For
       Health Care, Research And Education
       (Inc)
       795 El Camino Real
       Palo Alto CA 94301
       650 321-4121

(P-18988)
FOOTHILL HEALTH CENTER INC
Also Called: SAN JOSE FOOTHILL FAMILY
2670 S White Rd Ste 200, San Jose
(95148-2073)
PHONE..................408 729-4290
Salvador Chavarin, *CEO*
Marcella Gonzales, *Human Res Mgr*
Jiguett Sanchez, *Human Resources*
EMP: 170
SQ FT: 2,200
SALES: 16.8MM **Privately Held**
WEB: www.sjffcc.org
SIC: 8011 Primary care medical clinic

(P-18989)
FRANK D YELIAN MD PC
Also Called: Life Ivf Center
3500 Barranca Pkwy # 300, Irvine
(92606-8232)
PHONE..................949 788-1133
Frank D Yelian, *CEO*
EMP: 50 **EST:** 2010
SALES: 8MM **Privately Held**
SIC: 8011 Fertility specialist, physician

(P-18990)
FREMONT AMBLTORY SRGERY CTR LP
Also Called: Fremont Surgery Center
39350 Civic Center Dr, Fremont
(94538-2343)
PHONE..................510 456-4600
John Mazoros, *General Ptnr*
EMP: 80
SQ FT: 19,000
SALES (est): 15.1MM **Privately Held**
WEB: www.fremontsurgerycenter.com
SIC: 8011 Ambulatory surgical center; surgeon

(P-18991)
FRIEDMAN PROFESSIONAL MGT CO
Also Called: Post Surgical Recovery Center
17752 Beach Blvd Side, Huntington Beach
(92647-6838)
PHONE..................714 842-1426
EMP: 70 **EST:** 1975
SQ FT: 35,500
SALES (est): 4.1MM **Privately Held**
SIC: 8011

(P-18992)
GARDNER FAMILY HLTH NETWRK INC (PA)
Also Called: Gardner Health Services
160 E Virginia St Ste 100, San Jose
(95112-5865)
PHONE..................408 457-7100
Reymundo C Espinoza, *CEO*
EMP: 50 **EST:** 1968
SALES (est): 18.9MM **Privately Held**
SIC: 8011 Clinic, operated by physicians

(P-18993)
GARY LASK
Also Called: U C L A Dermatology
200 Ucla Medical Plz 4, Los Angeles
(90095-8344)
PHONE..................310 825-0631
EMP: 60
SALES (est): 3.4MM **Privately Held**
SIC: 8011 Offices & clinics of medical doctors

(P-18994)
GASTROENTEROLOGY DIVISION
Also Called: San Francisco General Hospital
1001 Potrero Ave Ste 1e21, San Francisco
(94110-3518)
PHONE..................415 206-8823
Amy Akbarian, *Administration*

EMP: 50
SALES (est): 30.3MM **Privately Held**
SIC: 8011 Gastronomist

(P-18995)
GEORGE M RAJACICH MD PC
Also Called: Valley Eye Center Group
14914 Sherman Way, Van Nuys
(91405-2113)
PHONE..................818 787-2020
George M Rajacich MD, *President*
Dorcas Fikejs, *Office Mgr*
Karen Smith, *Executive Asst*
EMP: 50
SQ FT: 12,000
SALES (est): 6.4MM **Privately Held**
SIC: 8011 Ophthalmologist

(P-18996)
GLENDALE EYE MEDICAL GROUP
500 N Cntl Ave Ste 400, Glendale (91203)
PHONE..................818 956-1010
James M Mc Caffery MD, *President*
EMP: 80
SQ FT: 11,000
SALES (est): 1.9MM **Privately Held**
SIC: 8011 Ophthalmologist

(P-18997)
GLENDALE EYE MEDICAL GROUP (PA)
Also Called: Amsurg
607 N Central Ave Ste 203, Glendale
(91203-1845)
PHONE..................818 956-1010
Richard Weise, *Partner*
Stephen Chang, *Partner*
Candy Sorgani, *Executive*
Heather McKinney,
EMP: 70
SALES (est): 7.6MM **Privately Held**
SIC: 8011 Physicians' office, including specialists; ophthalmologist

(P-18998)
GOLD COAST SURGERY CENTER LLC
Also Called: Center For Specialized Surgery
2927 De La Vina St, Santa Barbara
(93105-3362)
PHONE..................805 324-4555
S David Lippert, *Mng Member*
Nate Snyder, *Mng Member*
EMP: 102
SALES (est): 2.8MM
SALES (corp-wide): 1.7B **Publicly Held**
SIC: 8011 Ambulatory surgical center
HQ: Surgery Partners, Inc.
       310 Sven Sprng Way Ste 50
       Brentwood TN 37027
       615 234-5900

(P-18999)
GOLDEN RAIN FOUNDATION
1661 Golden Rain Rd, Seal Beach
(90740-4999)
P.O. Box 2685 (90740-1685)
PHONE..................562 493-9581
EMP: 83
SALES (corp-wide): 15MM **Privately Held**
SIC: 8011 Geriatric specialist, physician/surgeon
PA: Rain Golden Foundation
       13531 Saint Andrews Dr
       Seal Beach CA 90740
       562 431-6586

(P-19000)
GOOD SAMARITAN HOSPITAL AUX
1225 Wilshire Blvd, Los Angeles
(90017-1901)
PHONE..................213 977-2121
Andrew Leeka, *CEO*
Claus Von Zychlin, *COO*
Barry Hampton, *Project Leader*
David Gil Noel, *Accountant*
Robert Peroutka, *Med Doctor*
EMP: 1500
SALES: 118.6K **Privately Held**
SIC: 8011 Medical centers

(P-19001)
GRAYBILL MEDICAL GROUP INC (PA)
332 S Juniper St Ste 100, Escondido
(92025-4249)
PHONE..................866 228-2236
Floyd Farley, *CEO*
Marvin V Beddoe, *President*
David Borecky, *CEO*
George A Pleitez, *Vice Pres*
Jackie Craw, *Executive*
EMP: 180
SALES (est): 32.8MM **Privately Held**
SIC: 8011 General & family practice, physician/surgeon

(P-19002)
GROSSMONT HOSPITAL CORPORATION (HQ)
5555 Grossmont Center Dr, La Mesa
(91942-3077)
PHONE..................619 740-6000
Dan Gross, *CEO*
Tere Trout, *Ch Radiology*
Jonathan Myer, *Surgeon*
Ahmad Kabakibi, *Internal Med*
Magdalena Ruiz, *Internal Med*
EMP: 1740
SQ FT: 494,000
SALES (est): 105.5MM
SALES (corp-wide): 3.4B **Privately Held**
WEB: www.grossmonthealthcare.com
SIC: 8011 Radiologist
PA: Sharp Healthcare
       8695 Spectrum Center Blvd
       San Diego CA 92123
       858 499-4000

(P-19003)
HAIDER SPINE CTR MED GROUP INC
6276 River Crest Dr Ste A, Riverside
(92507-0754)
PHONE..................951 413-0200
Thomas Haider, *President*
David Siambanes, *Principal*
EMP: 50
SALES (est): 3.6MM **Privately Held**
SIC: 8011 Surgeon

(P-19004)
HEALTHCARE PARTNERS LLC
Also Called: Healthcare Partners Med Group
3932 Long Beach Blvd, Long Beach
(90807-2615)
PHONE..................562 304-2100
Kenny Heine, *Branch Mgr*
EMP: 67 **Publicly Held**
SIC: 8011 Group health association
HQ: Davita Medical Management, Llc
       2175 Park Pl
       El Segundo CA 90245

(P-19005)
HEALTHCARE PARTNERS LLC
Harriman Jones Medical
2600 Redondo Ave Ste 405, Long Beach
(90806-2330)
PHONE..................562 988-7000
Jill R Cortese, *Principal*
Karol Attaway, *Vice Pres*
Alexandre Portet, *Vice Pres*
Sam Wald, *Vice Pres*
Trang Nguyen, *Executive Asst*
EMP: 405 **Publicly Held**
WEB: www.davidv.com
SIC: 8011 Clinic, operated by physicians
HQ: Davita Medical Management, Llc
       2175 Park Pl
       El Segundo CA 90245

(P-19006)
HEALTHPOINTE MEDICAL GROUP INC (PA)
Also Called: Southern Cal Orthopedics
16702 Valley View Ave, La Mirada
(90638-5824)
PHONE..................714 956-2663
Ismael Silva, *President*
Victoria Callaway, *Office Admin*
Floyd Bender, *Info Tech Mgr*
Rebecca Gray, *Director*
Mickie White, *Director*

EMP: 52
SQ FT: 10,000
SALES (est): 13.3MM **Privately Held**
SIC: 8011 Orthopedic physician; sports medicine specialist, physician; surgeon

(P-19007)
HEALTHY BEGINNINGS FRENCH CAMP
Also Called: Women' S Health
500 W Hospital Rd, French Camp
(95231-9693)
P.O. Box 1020, Stockton (95201-3120)
PHONE..................................209 468-6147
Michael Smith, *Principal*
EMP: 80
SALES (est): 2.1MM **Privately Held**
SIC: 8011 Offices & clinics of medical doctors

(P-19008)
HEILWELL GAD MD
625 S Fair Oaks Ave # 280, Pasadena
(91105-2613)
PHONE..................................626 817-4747
Gad Heilwell, *Manager*
EMP: 78
SALES (est): 59.5K
SALES (corp-wide): 32.4MM **Privately Held**
SIC: 8011 Offices & clinics of medical doctors
PA: Doheny Eye Institute
1355 San Pablo St
Los Angeles CA 90033
323 342-7120

(P-19009)
HEMET VALLEY IMAGING MED GROUP (PA)
Also Called: Professional Medical MGT
3292 E Florida Ave Ste F, Hemet
(92544-4941)
P.O. Box 459 (92546-0459)
PHONE..................................951 925-6537
Frederick E White, *President*
EMP: 65
SQ FT: 12,196
SALES (est): 4.1MM **Privately Held**
SIC: 8011 Radiologist

(P-19010)
HENRY MAYO NEWHALL MEM HOSP
23845 Mcbean Pkwy, Valencia
(91355-2001)
PHONE..................................661 253-8112
EMP: 94 EST: 2013
SALES: 245.5MM **Privately Held**
SIC: 8011

(P-19011)
HENRY MAYO NEWHALL MEM HOSP
Also Called: Henry Mayo Diagnostic Imaging
23845 Mcbean Pkwy, Valencia
(91355-2001)
PHONE..................................661 253-8400
Emily Phirman, *Principal*
EMP: 373
SALES (corp-wide): 320MM **Privately Held**
SIC: 8011 Radiologist
PA: Henry Mayo Newhall Memorial Hospital
23845 Mcbean Pkwy
Valencia CA 91355
661 253-8000

(P-19012)
HERALD CHRISTIAN HEALTH CENTER (PA)
8841 Garvey Ave, Rosemead
(91770-3358)
PHONE..................................626 286-8700
David Lee, *CEO*
Carolin Eng, *COO*
Emily Szeto, *CFO*
Alice Wang, *Admin Asst*
Thomas Harang, *Human Res Dir*
EMP: 80
SQ FT: 11,000
SALES: 6.3MM **Privately Held**
SIC: 8011 8021 Primary care medical clinic; dental clinics & offices

(P-19013)
HIGH DESERT MED CORP A MED GRP (PA)
Also Called: Heritage Health Care
43839 15th St W, Lancaster (93534-4756)
P.O. Box 7007 (93539-7007)
PHONE..................................661 945-5984
Richard N Merkin, *CEO*
Rafael Gonzalez, *Administration*
Kimberly Powell, *Administration*
Tawnya Smead, *Database Admin*
Christine Jackson, *Opers Mgr*
EMP: 120
SQ FT: 25,000
SALES (est): 22.6MM **Privately Held**
WEB: www.regalmed.com
SIC: 8011 Clinic, operated by physicians

(P-19014)
HIGH DSERT PTENT CARE SVCS LLC
17095 Main St, Hesperia (92345-6004)
PHONE..................................760 956-4150
Medhi Izadi,
Ziad R El-Hajjaoui,
Zoheir El-Hajjaoui,
EMP: 53
SQ FT: 9,000
SALES: 5MM **Privately Held**
SIC: 8011 Offices & clinics of medical doctors

(P-19015)
HILARY A BRODIE MD PHD
2521 Stockton Blvd 7200, Sacramento
(95817-2207)
PHONE..................................916 734-3744
Hilary Brodie, *Chairman*
EMP: 60
SALES (est): 2.4MM **Privately Held**
SIC: 8011 Ears, nose & throat specialist; physician/surgeon

(P-19016)
HILL PHYSICIANS MED GROUP INC (PA)
2409 Camino Ramon, San Ramon
(94583-4285)
P.O. Box 5080 (94583-0980)
PHONE..................................800 445-5747
David Joyner, *CEO*
Dawn Bell, *Executive*
Leslie Plotner, *Executive Asst*
Denise Monday, *Admin Sec*
Stephan Hookano, *CIO*
EMP: 412
SQ FT: 36,000
SALES: 504.8MM **Privately Held**
SIC: 8011 8031 General & family practice, physician/surgeon; offices & clinics of osteopathic physicians

(P-19017)
HUNTINGTON AMBLTRY SURG CTR
625 S Fair Oaks Ave, Pasadena
(91105-2613)
P.O. Box 840189, Los Angeles (90084-0189)
PHONE..................................626 229-8999
Harry Bowles, *Mng Member*
James Noble,
Stephen Ralph,
Robin Waldvogel, *Director*
EMP: 50
SALES (est): 4.6MM **Privately Held**
SIC: 8011 Surgeon

(P-19018)
HUNTINGTON OTPTENT SURGERY CTR
625 S Fair Oaks Ave # 380, Pasadena
(91105-2613)
PHONE..................................626 535-2434
Sandy Bidlack, *Director*
EMP: 55
SQ FT: 12,030
SALES (est): 3.5MM **Privately Held**
SIC: 8011 Ambulatory surgical center; surgeon

(P-19019)
HUNTINGTON REPRODCTVE CTR INC (PA)
Also Called: Hrc Fertility
135 S Rosemead Blvd, Pasadena
(91107-3955)
PHONE..................................626 204-9699
Timothy J McGinley, *CEO*
John Wilcox, *Treasurer*
Jeffrey R Nelson, *Vice Pres*
Robert Boostanfar, *Managing Dir*
Lydia Chang, *Info Tech Dir*
EMP: 50
SQ FT: 22,394
SALES (est): 20.1MM **Privately Held**
WEB: www.havingbabies.com
SIC: 8011 Fertility specialist, physician

(P-19020)
IGO MEDICAL GROUP A MED CORP (PA)
Also Called: Infertlity Gynclogy Obstetrics
9339 Genesee Ave Ste 220, San Diego
(92121-2196)
PHONE..................................858 455-7520
Benito Villanueva, *President*
Wendy M Buchi, *CEO*
Dr Philip E Young, *CFO*
Dr Stephen Herbert, *Vice Pres*
Dr M E Ted Quigley, *Vice Pres*
EMP: 70
SQ FT: 11,500
SALES (est): 8.5MM **Privately Held**
WEB: www.igomed.com
SIC: 8011 Gynecologist; obstetrician; fertility specialist, physician

(P-19021)
IMAGING HLTHCARE SPCALISTS LLC (PA)
150 W Washington St, San Diego
(92103-2005)
PHONE..................................619 295-9729
Thomas D Cleary, *President*
Thomas Cleary, *COO*
Renee Glass, *Med Doctor*
Donielle Sullivan,
EMP: 65
SALES (est): 16.2MM **Privately Held**
SIC: 8011 Radiologist

(P-19022)
INDIAN HLTH CTR SNTA CLARA VLY
1333 Meridian Ave, San Jose
(95125-5212)
PHONE..................................408 445-3400
Sonya M Tetnowski, *CEO*
EMP: 200
SQ FT: 10,000
SALES: 24.3MM **Privately Held**
WEB: www.ihcscv.org
SIC: 8011 8322 Clinic, operated by physicians; individual & family services

(P-19023)
INLAND EYE INST MED GROUP INC (PA)
1900 E Washington St, Colton
(92324-4698)
P.O. Box 1427 (92324-0836)
PHONE..................................909 825-3425
Loren Denler MD, *President*
Harold P Wallar, *Treasurer*
Wayne B Isaeff, *Vice Pres*
Melissa Goins, *Nursing Dir*
EMP: 70
SQ FT: 12,500
SALES (est): 10MM **Privately Held**
SIC: 8011 Ophthalmologist

(P-19024)
INLAND HLTH ORG OF SO CAL (DH)
1980 Orange Tree Ln # 200, Redlands
(92374-4534)
P.O. Box 10457, San Bernardino (92423-0457)
PHONE..................................909 335-7171
Jeff Winter, *President*
Paula Lamar, *Vice Pres*
EMP: 50
SQ FT: 12,000

SALES (est): 7.8MM **Privately Held**
WEB: www.pulliamgroup.com
SIC: 8011 Clinic, operated by physicians
HQ: Dignity Health
185 Berry St Ste 300
San Francisco CA 94107
415 438-5500

(P-19025)
INSITE DIGESTIVE HEALTH CARE
7320 Woodlake Ave Ste 310, West Hills
(91307-1471)
PHONE..................................818 346-9911
Margarita Joaquin, *Branch Mgr*
EMP: 85
SALES (corp-wide): 10.1MM **Privately Held**
SIC: 8011 Gastronomist
PA: Insite Digestive Health Care
5525 Etiwanda Ave Ste 110
Tarzana CA 91356
818 437-8105

(P-19026)
INSITE DIGESTIVE HEALTH CARE
225 W Broadway Ste 350, Glendale
(91204-1303)
PHONE..................................626 817-2900
Alaa Abousaif, *Branch Mgr*
EMP: 85
SALES (corp-wide): 10.1MM **Privately Held**
SIC: 8011 2834 General & family practice, physician/surgeon; chlorination tablets & kits (water purification)
PA: Insite Digestive Health Care
5525 Etiwanda Ave Ste 110
Tarzana CA 91356
818 437-8105

(P-19027)
INSITE DIGESTIVE HEALTH CARE
200 Jose Figueres Ave, San Jose
(95116-1500)
PHONE..................................408 471-2222
Margarita Joaquin, *Branch Mgr*
EMP: 153
SALES (corp-wide): 10.1MM **Privately Held**
SIC: 8011 Gastronomist
PA: Insite Digestive Health Care
5525 Etiwanda Ave Ste 110
Tarzana CA 91356
818 437-8105

(P-19028)
IPC HEALTHCARE INC (DH)
Also Called: Intrepid Healthcare Svcs Inc
4605 Lankershim Blvd, North Hollywood
(91602-1818)
PHONE..................................888 447-2362
Adam D Singer, *CEO*
R Jeffrey Taylor, *President*
Richard H Kline III, *CFO*
Kerry E Weiner, *Chief Mktg Ofcr*
Richard G Russell, *Exec VP*
EMP: 105
SALES (est): 505.9MM
SALES (corp-wide): 287.4MM **Privately Held**
WEB: www.ipcm.com
SIC: 8011 Physicians' office, including specialists
HQ: Team Health Holdings, Inc.
265 Brookview Centre Way
Knoxville TN 37919
865 693-1000

(P-19029)
JAMES D TATE MD
Also Called: Tate Neurological Surgery
2888 Eureka Way Ste 200, Redding
(96001-0210)
PHONE..................................530 225-8710
James D Tate MD, *Owner*
Tracey Lattimore, *Office Mgr*
EMP: 62
SALES (est): 2.2MM **Privately Held**
SIC: 8011 Surgeon

PRODUCTS & SVCS

(P-19030)
JANET K HARTZLER MD
72057 Dinah Shore Dr D, Rancho Mirage
(92270-1791)
PHONE..............................760 340-3937
Janet Hartzler, *Principal*
Bart Ketover, *Med Doctor*
EMP: 60
SALES (est): 1MM **Privately Held**
SIC: 8011 Ophthalmologist

(P-19031)
JAYASINGHE MEDICAL GROUP INC (PA)
Also Called: Ameri-West Medical Associates
200 S Beach Blvd Ste A2, La Habra
(90631-5181)
PHONE..............................562 267-7000
Walter Jayasinghe MD, *President*
Earla Quisido, *Director*
EMP: 60
SQ FT: 4,000
SALES (est): 2.3MM **Privately Held**
SIC: 8011 Obstetrician; gynecologist

(P-19032)
JERRY S POWELL MD
4501 X St, Sacramento (95817-2229)
PHONE..............................916 734-5959
Jerry S Powell, *Owner*
Jerry Powell, *Med Doctor*
EMP: 70
SALES (est): 1.9MM **Privately Held**
SIC: 8011 Oncologist

(P-19033)
JOHN M ADAMS JR MD
1301 20th St Ste 150, Santa Monica
(90404-2050)
PHONE..............................310 829-2663
Kevin Airheart MD, *Owner*
Natasha Trentacosta, *Surgeon*
EMP: 60
SALES (est): 938.5K **Privately Held**
SIC: 8011 General & family practice, physician/surgeon

(P-19034)
JOHN MUIR PHYSICIAN NETWORK
Also Called: Alamo Medical Group
1505 Saint Alphonsus Way, Alamo
(94507-1570)
PHONE..............................925 838-4633
Judy Hicklin, *Manager*
Nhu Pham,
EMP: 50
SALES (corp-wide): 322.9MM **Privately Held**
SIC: 8011 Pediatrician; internal medicine, physician/surgeon
PA: John Muir Physician Network
1450 Treat Blvd
Walnut Creek CA 94597
925 296-9700

(P-19035)
JUDY MADRIGAL & ASSOCIATES INC
Also Called: J M A
2000 Alameda De Las Pulga, San Mateo
(94403-1289)
PHONE..............................650 873-3444
Judy Madrigal, *President*
Tammy Attard, *Vice Pres*
EMP: 550
SALES (est): 21.8MM **Privately Held**
WEB: www.judymadrigal.com
SIC: 8011 8742 Offices & clinics of medical doctors; management consulting services

(P-19036)
KAISER FOUNDATION HOSPITALS
Also Called: Lakeview Medical Offices
411 N Lakeview Ave, Anaheim
(92807-3028)
PHONE..............................714 279-4675
Suzie Characky, *Manager*
Martha Dispoto, *Executive*
Jose Baeza, *Internal Med*
Emil Dionysian, *Med Doctor*
Henry Hwu, *Med Doctor*
EMP: 105

SALES (corp-wide): 76.5B **Privately Held**
SIC: 8011 Offices & clinics of medical doctors
HQ: Kaiser Foundation Hospitals Inc
1 Kaiser Plz
Oakland CA 94612
510 271-6611

(P-19037)
KAISER FOUNDATION HOSPITALS
Also Called: Aliso Viejo Medical Offices
24502 Pacific Park Dr, Aliso Viejo
(92656-3033)
PHONE..............................949 425-3150
Bruce Sogioka, *Branch Mgr*
EMP: 105
SALES (corp-wide): 76.5B **Privately Held**
SIC: 8011 Offices & clinics of medical doctors
HQ: Kaiser Foundation Hospitals Inc
1 Kaiser Plz
Oakland CA 94612
510 271-6611

(P-19038)
KAISER FOUNDATION HOSPITALS
8889 Rio San Diego Dr, San Diego
(92108-1670)
PHONE..............................619 542-7210
Kate Kessler, *Branch Mgr*
EMP: 55
SALES (corp-wide): 76.5B **Privately Held**
SIC: 8011 Health maintenance organization
HQ: Kaiser Foundation Hospitals Inc
1 Kaiser Plz
Oakland CA 94612
510 271-6611

(P-19039)
KAISER FOUNDATION HOSPITALS
Also Called: Kaiser Permanente Santa
401 Bicentennial Way, Santa Rosa
(95403-2149)
PHONE..............................707 393-4000
Susan Janvirin, *Branch Mgr*
Cyndy Larsen, *Vice Pres*
Mark Brna, *Exec Dir*
Tori Suarez, *Program Mgr*
Judy Coffey, *Area Mgr*
EMP: 2000
SALES (corp-wide): 76.5B **Privately Held**
WEB: www.kaiserpermanente.org
SIC: 8011 Medical centers
HQ: Kaiser Foundation Hospitals Inc
1 Kaiser Plz
Oakland CA 94612
510 271-6611

(P-19040)
KAISER FOUNDATION HOSPITALS
Also Called: Kaiser Prmnnte Antioch Med Ctr
4501 Sand Creek Rd, Antioch
(94531-8687)
PHONE..............................925 813-6500
Albert L Carver, *Branch Mgr*
EMP: 105
SALES (corp-wide): 76.5B **Privately Held**
SIC: 8011 Internal medicine practitioners
HQ: Kaiser Foundation Hospitals Inc
1 Kaiser Plz
Oakland CA 94612
510 271-6611

(P-19041)
KAISER FOUNDATION HOSPITALS
Also Called: Kaiser Permanente
12100 Euclid St, Garden Grove
(92840-3304)
PHONE..............................714 741-3448
Betty Bohner, *Administration*
Melanie Linke, *Family Practiti*
Paul Vollucci, *Family Practiti*
Ashley Brown, *Dermatology*
Leo Maffey, *Internal Med*
EMP: 100
SALES (corp-wide): 76.5B **Privately Held**
WEB: www.kaiserpermanente.org
SIC: 8011 Offices & clinics of medical doctors

HQ: Kaiser Foundation Hospitals Inc
1 Kaiser Plz
Oakland CA 94612
510 271-6611

(P-19042)
KAISER FOUNDATION HOSPITALS
Also Called: Oakland Medical Center
3600 Broadway, Oakland (94611-5730)
P.O. Box 12929 (94604-3010)
PHONE..............................510 752-1000
David J Artenburn, *Manager*
Allan Chu, *Accountant*
Andrew V Slucky, *Surgeon*
Tatiana Chou, *Obstetrician*
Maniza Dhillon, *Anesthesiology*
EMP: 2200
SALES (corp-wide): 76.5B **Privately Held**
WEB: www.kaiserpermanente.org
SIC: 8011 8062 Medical centers; general medical & surgical hospitals
HQ: Kaiser Foundation Hospitals Inc
1 Kaiser Plz
Oakland CA 94612
510 271-6611

(P-19043)
KAISER FOUNDATION HOSPITALS
Also Called: Kaiser Permanente San
2425 Geary Blvd, San Francisco
(94115-3358)
PHONE..............................415 833-2000
Harry Chima, *Branch Mgr*
Cristine Robisch, *Vice Pres*
Tinbet Gizaw, *Analyst*
Mitchell Adachi, *Pathologist*
Junming Fang, *Pathologist*
EMP: 750
SALES (corp-wide): 76.5B **Privately Held**
WEB: www.kaiserpermanente.org
SIC: 8011 8062 Medical centers; general medical & surgical hospitals
HQ: Kaiser Foundation Hospitals Inc
1 Kaiser Plz
Oakland CA 94612
510 271-6611

(P-19044)
KAISER FOUNDATION HOSPITALS
Also Called: Kaiser Permanente
1301 California St, Redlands (92374-2910)
PHONE..............................888 750-0036
Cindy Wong, *Director*
Yohan Shin, *Pediatrics*
EMP: 52
SALES (corp-wide): 76.5B **Privately Held**
WEB: www.kaiserpermanente.org
SIC: 8011 Offices & clinics of medical doctors
HQ: Kaiser Foundation Hospitals Inc
1 Kaiser Plz
Oakland CA 94612
510 271-6611

(P-19045)
KAISER FOUNDATION HOSPITALS
Also Called: Kaiser Permanente
1900 E Lambert Rd, Brea (92821-4371)
PHONE..............................714 672-5100
David Jeng, *Principal*
Alia Khalil, *Family Practiti*
Tiffany Park, *Family Practiti*
Danielle Weiler, *Family Practiti*
Alex Wu, *Family Practiti*
EMP: 52
SQ FT: 9,240
SALES (corp-wide): 76.5B **Privately Held**
WEB: www.kaiserpermanente.org
SIC: 8011 Medical centers
HQ: Kaiser Foundation Hospitals Inc
1 Kaiser Plz
Oakland CA 94612
510 271-6611

(P-19046)
KAISER FOUNDATION HOSPITALS
Also Called: Kaiser Permanente
99 Montecillo Rd, San Rafael
(94903-3308)
PHONE..............................415 444-2000

Patricia Kendall, *Administration*
Kevin F Hile, *Regional Mgr*
Paula Russo, *Nursing Mgr*
Gretchen Klein, *Admin Sec*
Tonya A Loving, *Administration*
EMP: 1500
SALES (corp-wide): 76.5B **Privately Held**
WEB: www.kaiserpermanente.org
SIC: 8011 8062 Medical centers; general medical & surgical hospitals
HQ: Kaiser Foundation Hospitals Inc
1 Kaiser Plz
Oakland CA 94612
510 271-6611

(P-19047)
KAISER FOUNDATION HOSPITALS
Also Called: Kaiser Permanente
901 Nevin Ave, Richmond (94801-3143)
PHONE..............................510 307-1500
Debbie Vachau, *Manager*
Ryona Durham, *Administration*
Monica Brown, *Project Mgr*
Michael Esquibel, *Technology*
Allan Sendaydiego, *Opers Staff*
EMP: 400
SALES (corp-wide): 76.5B **Privately Held**
WEB: www.kaiserpermanente.org
SIC: 8011 8062 Medical centers; general medical & surgical hospitals
HQ: Kaiser Foundation Hospitals Inc
1 Kaiser Plz
Oakland CA 94612
510 271-661

(P-19048)
KAISER FOUNDATION HOSPITALS
Also Called: Kaiser Permanente West
6041 Cadillac Ave, Los Angeles
(90034-1700)
PHONE..............................323 857-2000
Howard Fullman, *Admin Director*
Mannuel Villagomez, *Finance*
Brian E Platz, *Pathologist*
Sally Turla, *Pathologist*
Benjamin B Kim, *Surgeon*
EMP: 2000
SALES (corp-wide): 76.5B **Privately Held**
WEB: www.kaiserpermanente.org
SIC: 8011 Medical centers
HQ: Kaiser Foundation Hospitals Inc
1 Kaiser Plz
Oakland CA 94612
510 271-6611

(P-19049)
KAISER FOUNDATION HOSPITALS
17284 Slover Ave, Fontana (92337-7584)
PHONE..............................909 609-3800
Gregory Christian, *Branch Mgr*
EMP: 106
SALES (corp-wide): 76.5B **Privately Held**
SIC: 8011 General & family practice, physician/surgeon
HQ: Kaiser Foundation Hospitals Inc
1 Kaiser Plz
Oakland CA 94612
510 271-6611

(P-19050)
KAISER FOUNDATION HOSPITALS
Also Called: Vacaville Medical Center
1 Quality Dr, Vacaville (95688-9494)
PHONE..............................707 624-4000
EMP: 593
SALES (corp-wide): 76.5B **Privately Held**
SIC: 8011 Medical centers
HQ: Kaiser Foundation Hospitals Inc
1 Kaiser Plz
Oakland CA 94612
510 271-6611

(P-19051)
KAISER FOUNDATION HOSPITALS
Also Called: Tracy Medical Offices
2185 W Grant Line Rd, Tracy
(95377-7309)
PHONE..............................209 839-3200
Anale Cunningham, *Branch Mgr*
EMP: 593

SALES (corp-wide): 76.5B **Privately Held**
SIC: **8011** Medical centers
HQ: Kaiser Foundation Hospitals Inc
1 Kaiser Plz
Oakland CA 94612
510 271-6611

(P-19052)
KAISER FOUNDATION HOSPITALS
Also Called: Union City Medical Offices
3555 Whipple Rd, Union City (94587-1507)
PHONE.................................510 675-4010
Andrea Wilcox, *President*
EMP: 593
SALES (corp-wide): 76.5B **Privately Held**
SIC: **8011** Medical centers
HQ: Kaiser Foundation Hospitals Inc
1 Kaiser Plz
Oakland CA 94612
510 271-6611

(P-19053)
KAISER FOUNDATION HOSPITALS
Also Called: Rancho Cucamonga Medical Offs
10850 Arrow Rte, Rancho Cucamonga (91730-4833)
PHONE.................................888 750-0036
EMP: 593
SALES (corp-wide): 76.5B **Privately Held**
SIC: **8011** Medical centers
HQ: Kaiser Foundation Hospitals Inc
1 Kaiser Plz
Oakland CA 94612
510 271-6611

(P-19054)
KAISER FOUNDATION HOSPITALS
Also Called: Anaheim Hills Medical Offices
5475 E La Palma Ave, Anaheim (92807-2075)
PHONE.................................888 988-2800
EMP: 593
SALES (corp-wide): 76.5B **Privately Held**
SIC: **8011** Offices & clinics of medical doctors
HQ: Kaiser Foundation Hospitals Inc
1 Kaiser Plz
Oakland CA 94612
510 271-6611

(P-19055)
KAISER FOUNDATION HOSPITALS
Also Called: Central Medical Offices
3733 San Dimas St, Bakersfield (93301-1407)
PHONE.................................877 524-7373
EMP: 593
SALES (corp-wide): 76.5B **Privately Held**
SIC: **8011** Medical centers
HQ: Kaiser Foundation Hospitals Inc
1 Kaiser Plz
Oakland CA 94612
510 271-6611

(P-19056)
KAISER FOUNDATION HOSPITALS
Also Called: Anaheim Kraemer Medical Offs
3460 E La Palma Ave, Anaheim (92806-2020)
PHONE.................................888 988-2800
EMP: 593
SALES (corp-wide): 76.5B **Privately Held**
SIC: **8011** Medical centers
HQ: Kaiser Foundation Hospitals Inc
1 Kaiser Plz
Oakland CA 94612
510 271-6611

(P-19057)
KAISER FOUNDATION HOSPITALS
Also Called: Chester Avenue Medical Offices
2531 Chester Ave, Bakersfield (93301-2012)
PHONE.................................877 524-7373
EMP: 593
SALES (corp-wide): 76.5B **Privately Held**
SIC: **8011** Medical centers

HQ: Kaiser Foundation Hospitals Inc
1 Kaiser Plz
Oakland CA 94612
510 271-6611

(P-19058)
KAISER FOUNDATION HOSPITALS
Also Called: Chester Avenue Medical Offs II
2620 Chester Ave, Bakersfield (93301-2015)
PHONE.................................661 337-7160
EMP: 593
SALES (corp-wide): 76.5B **Privately Held**
SIC: **8011** Offices & clinics of medical doctors
HQ: Kaiser Foundation Hospitals Inc
1 Kaiser Plz
Oakland CA 94612
510 271-6611

(P-19059)
KAISER FOUNDATION HOSPITALS
Also Called: Discovery Plz Med & Admin Offs
1200 Discovery Dr, Bakersfield (93309-7032)
PHONE.................................877 524-7373
EMP: 593
SALES (corp-wide): 76.5B **Privately Held**
SIC: **8011** Medical centers
HQ: Kaiser Foundation Hospitals Inc
1 Kaiser Plz
Oakland CA 94612
510 271-6611

(P-19060)
KAISER FOUNDATION HOSPITALS
Also Called: Cerritos Medical Office Bldg
10820 183rd St, Cerritos (90703-8010)
PHONE.................................800 823-4040
William Sim, *Internal Med*
Kalyn Skiles, *Internal Med*
EMP: 593
SALES (corp-wide): 76.5B **Privately Held**
SIC: **8011** Medical centers
HQ: Kaiser Foundation Hospitals Inc
1 Kaiser Plz
Oakland CA 94612
510 271-6611

(P-19061)
KAISER FOUNDATION HOSPITALS
Also Called: Las Posas Road Medical Offices
2620 Las Posas Rd, Camarillo (93010-3400)
PHONE.................................888 515-3500
EMP: 593
SALES (corp-wide): 76.5B **Privately Held**
SIC: **8011** Medical centers
HQ: Kaiser Foundation Hospitals Inc
1 Kaiser Plz
Oakland CA 94612
510 271-6611

(P-19062)
KAISER FOUNDATION HOSPITALS
Also Called: Ming Medical Offices
8800 Ming Ave, Bakersfield (93311-1308)
PHONE.................................877 524-7373
EMP: 593
SALES (corp-wide): 76.5B **Privately Held**
SIC: **8011** Medical centers
HQ: Kaiser Foundation Hospitals Inc
1 Kaiser Plz
Oakland CA 94612
510 271-6611

(P-19063)
KAISER FOUNDATION HOSPITALS
Also Called: Crossroads Medical Offices
12801 Crossroads Pkwy S, City of Industry (91746-3502)
PHONE.................................562 463-4377
EMP: 593
SALES (corp-wide): 76.5B **Privately Held**
SIC: **8011** Medical centers
HQ: Kaiser Foundation Hospitals Inc
1 Kaiser Plz
Oakland CA 94612
510 271-6611

(P-19064)
KAISER FOUNDATION HOSPITALS
Also Called: Orchard Medical Offices
9449 Imperial Hwy, Downey (90242-2814)
PHONE.................................800 823-4040
Leon Randolph, *President*
EMP: 593
SALES (corp-wide): 76.5B **Privately Held**
SIC: **8011** Medical centers
HQ: Kaiser Foundation Hospitals Inc
1 Kaiser Plz
Oakland CA 94612
510 271-6611

(P-19065)
KAISER FOUNDATION HOSPITALS
Also Called: Diamond Bar Medical Offices
1336 Bridgegate Dr, Diamond Bar (91765-3955)
PHONE.................................800 780-1277
EMP: 593
SALES (corp-wide): 76.5B **Privately Held**
SIC: **8011** Medical centers
HQ: Kaiser Foundation Hospitals Inc
1 Kaiser Plz
Oakland CA 94612
510 271-6611

(P-19066)
KAISER FOUNDATION HOSPITALS
Also Called: Palomar Health Downtown Campus
555 E Valley Pkwy, Escondido (92025-3048)
PHONE.................................760 739-3000
EMP: 593
SALES (corp-wide): 76.5B **Privately Held**
SIC: **8011** Medical centers
HQ: Kaiser Foundation Hospitals Inc
1 Kaiser Plz
Oakland CA 94612
510 271-6611

(P-19067)
KAISER FOUNDATION HOSPITALS
Also Called: Garden Medical Offices
9353 Imperial Hwy, Downey (90242-2812)
PHONE.................................800 823-4040
EMP: 593
SALES (corp-wide): 76.5B **Privately Held**
SIC: **8011** Medical centers
HQ: Kaiser Foundation Hospitals Inc
1 Kaiser Plz
Oakland CA 94612
510 271-6611

(P-19068)
KAISER FOUNDATION HOSPITALS
Also Called: Fairfield Medical Offices
1550 Gateway Blvd, Fairfield (94533-6901)
PHONE.................................707 427-4000
Gregory A Adams, *CEO*
EMP: 593
SALES (corp-wide): 76.5B **Privately Held**
SIC: **8011** Medical centers
HQ: Kaiser Foundation Hospitals Inc
1 Kaiser Plz
Oakland CA 94612
510 271-6611

(P-19069)
KAISER FOUNDATION HOSPITALS
Also Called: Foothill Ranch Medical Offices
26882 Towne Centre Dr # 1, Foothill Ranch (92610-2862)
PHONE.................................800 922-2000
EMP: 593
SALES (corp-wide): 76.5B **Privately Held**
SIC: **8011** Medical centers
HQ: Kaiser Foundation Hospitals Inc
1 Kaiser Plz
Oakland CA 94612
510 271-6611

(P-19070)
KAISER FOUNDATION HOSPITALS
Also Called: Fontana Mental Health Offices
9310 Sierra Ave, Fontana (92335-5711)
PHONE.................................866 205-3595
EMP: 593
SALES (corp-wide): 76.5B **Privately Held**
SIC: **8011** Psychiatrists & psychoanalysts
HQ: Kaiser Foundation Hospitals Inc
1 Kaiser Plz
Oakland CA 94612
510 271-6611

(P-19071)
KAISER FOUNDATION HOSPITALS
Also Called: Folsom Ambulatory Surgery Ctr
285 Palladio Pkwy, Folsom (95630-8741)
PHONE.................................916 986-4178
EMP: 593
SALES (corp-wide): 76.5B **Privately Held**
SIC: **8011** Ambulatory surgical center
HQ: Kaiser Foundation Hospitals Inc
1 Kaiser Plz
Oakland CA 94612
510 271-6611

(P-19072)
KAISER FOUNDATION HOSPITALS
Also Called: Carson Medical Offices
18600 S Figueroa St, Gardena (90248-4505)
PHONE.................................800 780-1230
EMP: 593
SALES (corp-wide): 76.5B **Privately Held**
SIC: **8011** Medical centers
HQ: Kaiser Foundation Hospitals Inc
1 Kaiser Plz
Oakland CA 94612
510 271-6611

(P-19073)
KAISER FOUNDATION HOSPITALS
Also Called: Balboa Plaza Admin Offices
10605 Balboa Blvd Ste 330, Granada Hills (91344-6358)
PHONE.................................818 832-7200
Dennis C Benton, *Exec Dir*
EMP: 593
SALES (corp-wide): 76.5B **Privately Held**
SIC: **8011** Health maintenance organization
HQ: Kaiser Foundation Hospitals Inc
1 Kaiser Plz
Oakland CA 94612
510 271-6611

(P-19074)
KAISER FOUNDATION HOSPITALS
Also Called: Glendale Orange St Med Offs
501 N Orange St, Glendale (91203-1970)
PHONE.................................800 954-8000
EMP: 593
SALES (corp-wide): 76.5B **Privately Held**
SIC: **8011** Offices & clinics of medical doctors
HQ: Kaiser Foundation Hospitals Inc
1 Kaiser Plz
Oakland CA 94612
510 271-6611

(P-19075)
KAISER FOUNDATION HOSPITALS
Also Called: Indio Medical Offices
46900 Monroe St, Indio (92201-4827)
PHONE.................................866 984-7483
EMP: 593
SALES (corp-wide): 76.5B **Privately Held**
SIC: **8011** Medical centers
HQ: Kaiser Foundation Hospitals Inc
1 Kaiser Plz
Oakland CA 94612
510 271-6611

P R O D U C T S & S V C S

(P-19076)
KAISER FOUNDATION HOSPITALS
Also Called: Rancho San Diego Medical Offs
3875 Avocado Blvd, La Mesa (91941-7303)
PHONE...................619 528-5000
EMP: 593
SALES (corp-wide): 76.5B **Privately Held**
SIC: **8011** Medical centers
HQ: Kaiser Foundation Hospitals Inc
1 Kaiser Plz
Oakland CA 94612
510 271-6611

(P-19077)
KAISER FOUNDATION HOSPITALS
Also Called: Lincoln Medical Offices
1900 Dresden Dr, Lincoln (95648-8803)
PHONE...................916 543-5153
EMP: 593
SALES (corp-wide): 76.5B **Privately Held**
SIC: **8011** Medical centers
HQ: Kaiser Foundation Hospitals Inc
1 Kaiser Plz
Oakland CA 94612
510 271-6611

(P-19078)
KAISER FOUNDATION HOSPITALS
Also Called: Behavioral Health
44444 20th St W, Lancaster (93534-2714)
PHONE...................661 951-0070
EMP: 593
SALES (corp-wide): 76.5B **Privately Held**
SIC: **8011** Psychiatrists & psychoanalysts
HQ: Kaiser Foundation Hospitals Inc
1 Kaiser Plz
Oakland CA 94612
510 271-6611

(P-19079)
KAISER FOUNDATION HOSPITALS
Also Called: Lomita Medical Offices
2081 Palos Verdes Dr N, Lomita
(90717-3701)
PHONE...................310 325-6542
EMP: 593
SALES (corp-wide): 76.5B **Privately Held**
SIC: **8011** Medical centers
HQ: Kaiser Foundation Hospitals Inc
1 Kaiser Plz
Oakland CA 94612
510 271-6611

(P-19080)
KAISER FOUNDATION HOSPITALS
Also Called: Lynwood Medical Offices
3830 Martin Luther King, Lynwood
(90262-3625)
PHONE...................310 604-5700
Sepehr Katiraie MD, *CEO*
EMP: 593
SALES (corp-wide): 76.5B **Privately Held**
SIC: **8011** Medical centers
HQ: Kaiser Foundation Hospitals Inc
1 Kaiser Plz
Oakland CA 94612
510 271-6611

(P-19081)
KAISER FOUNDATION HOSPITALS
Also Called: Modesto Medical Offices
4601 Dale Rd, Modesto (95356-9718)
PHONE...................209 735-5000
EMP: 593
SALES (corp-wide): 76.5B **Privately Held**
SIC: **8011** Medical centers
HQ: Kaiser Foundation Hospitals Inc
1 Kaiser Plz
Oakland CA 94612
510 271-6611

(P-19082)
KAISER FOUNDATION HOSPITALS
Also Called: North Hollywood Medical Offs
5250 Lankershim Blvd, North Hollywood
(91601-3186)
PHONE...................888 778-5000

EMP: 593
SALES (corp-wide): 76.5B **Privately Held**
SIC: **8011** Medical centers
HQ: Kaiser Foundation Hospitals Inc
1 Kaiser Plz
Oakland CA 94612
510 271-6611

(P-19083)
KAISER FOUNDATION HOSPITALS
Also Called: Bangs Avenue Medical Offices
4125 Bangs Ave, Modesto (95356-8713)
PHONE...................209 735-5000
EMP: 593
SALES (corp-wide): 76.5B **Privately Held**
SIC: **8011** Offices & clinics of medical doctors
HQ: Kaiser Foundation Hospitals Inc
1 Kaiser Plz
Oakland CA 94612
510 271-6611

(P-19084)
KAISER FOUNDATION HOSPITALS
Also Called: Norwalk Medical Offices
12501 Imperial Hwy, Norwalk (90650-3179)
PHONE...................562 807-6100
EMP: 593
SALES (corp-wide): 76.5B **Privately Held**
SIC: **8011** Offices & clinics of medical doctors
HQ: Kaiser Foundation Hospitals Inc
1 Kaiser Plz
Oakland CA 94612
510 271-6611

(P-19085)
KAISER FOUNDATION HOSPITALS
Also Called: Ontario Vineyard Medical Offs
2295 S Vineyard Ave, Ontario
(91761-7925)
PHONE...................909 724-5000
EMP: 593
SALES (corp-wide): 76.5B **Privately Held**
SIC: **8011** Medical centers
HQ: Kaiser Foundation Hospitals Inc
1 Kaiser Plz
Oakland CA 94612
510 271-6611

(P-19086)
KAISER FOUNDATION HOSPITALS
Also Called: Oxnard 2200 East Gonzales
2200 E Gonzales Rd, Oxnard
(93036-0619)
PHONE...................888 515-3500
EMP: 593
SALES (corp-wide): 76.5B **Privately Held**
SIC: **8011** Medical centers
HQ: Kaiser Foundation Hospitals Inc
1 Kaiser Plz
Oakland CA 94612
510 271-6611

(P-19087)
KAISER FOUNDATION HOSPITALS
Also Called: Kaiser Permanente Member Svcs
73733 Fred Waring Dr, Palm Desert
(92260-2589)
PHONE...................800 777-1256
Virginia McLain, *Branch Mgr*
EMP: 593
SALES (corp-wide): 76.5B **Privately Held**
SIC: **8011** Health maintenance organization
HQ: Kaiser Foundation Hospitals Inc
1 Kaiser Plz
Oakland CA 94612
510 271-6611

(P-19088)
KAISER FOUNDATION HOSPITALS
Also Called: Oxnard 2103 East Gonzales Road
2103 E Gonzales Rd, Oxnard
(93036-3757)
PHONE...................805 988-6300
EMP: 593

SALES (corp-wide): 76.5B **Privately Held**
SIC: **8011** Medical centers
HQ: Kaiser Foundation Hospitals Inc
1 Kaiser Plz
Oakland CA 94612
510 271-6611

(P-19089)
KAISER FOUNDATION HOSPITALS
Also Called: Pinole Medical Offices
1301 Pinole Valley Rd, Pinole
(94564-1384)
PHONE...................510 243-4000
EMP: 593
SALES (corp-wide): 76.5B **Privately Held**
SIC: **8011** Offices & clinics of medical doctors
HQ: Kaiser Foundation Hospitals Inc
1 Kaiser Plz
Oakland CA 94612
510 271-6611

(P-19090)
KAISER FOUNDATION HOSPITALS
Also Called: Palm Desert Medical Offices
University Park Ctr, Palm Desert (92211)
PHONE...................866 984-7483
EMP: 593
SALES (corp-wide): 19.1B **Privately Held**
SIC: **8011**
PA: Kaiser Foundation Hospitals Inc
1 Kaiser Plz Ste 2600
Oakland CA 94612
510 271-5800

(P-19091)
KAISER FOUNDATION HOSPITALS
Also Called: Canyon Crest Mental Hlth Offs
5225 Canyon Crest Dr, Riverside
(92507-6301)
PHONE...................951 248-4000
EMP: 593
SALES (corp-wide): 76.5B **Privately Held**
SIC: **8011** Psychiatrists & psychoanalysts
HQ: Kaiser Foundation Hospitals Inc
1 Kaiser Plz
Oakland CA 94612
510 271-6611

(P-19092)
KAISER FOUNDATION HOSPITALS
Also Called: Meridian Medical Offices
14305 Meridian Pkwy, Riverside
(92518-3034)
PHONE...................866 984-7483
EMP: 593
SALES (corp-wide): 76.5B **Privately Held**
SIC: **8011** Medical centers
HQ: Kaiser Foundation Hospitals Inc
1 Kaiser Plz
Oakland CA 94612
510 271-6611

(P-19093)
KAISER FOUNDATION HOSPITALS
Also Called: Carmel Valley Medical Offices
3851 Shaw Ridge Rd, San Diego
(92130-2807)
PHONE...................858 847-3500
EMP: 593
SALES (corp-wide): 76.5B **Privately Held**
SIC: **8011** Offices & clinics of medical doctors
HQ: Kaiser Foundation Hospitals Inc
1 Kaiser Plz
Oakland CA 94612
510 271-6611

(P-19094)
KAISER FOUNDATION HOSPITALS
Also Called: Kaiser Permanente Kearny
4510 Viewridge Ave, San Diego
(92123-1637)
PHONE...................858 502-1350
EMP: 593
SALES (corp-wide): 76.5B **Privately Held**
SIC: **8011** Specialized medical practitioners, except internal

SALES (corp-wide): 76.5B **Privately Held**
SIC: **8011** Medical centers
HQ: Kaiser Foundation Hospitals Inc
1 Kaiser Plz
Oakland CA 94612
510 271-6611

(P-19095)
KAISER FOUNDATION HOSPITALS
Also Called: Kaiser Permanente San
1000 Franklin Pkwy, San Mateo
(94403-1922)
PHONE...................650 358-7000
David Kvancz, *Vice Pres*
EMP: 593
SALES (corp-wide): 76.5B **Privately Held**
SIC: **8011** Medical centers
HQ: Kaiser Foundation Hospitals Inc
1 Kaiser Plz
Oakland CA 94612
510 271-6611

(P-19096)
KAISER FOUNDATION HOSPITALS
Also Called: Kaiser Permanente San
2500 Merced St, San Leandro
(94577-4201)
PHONE...................510 454-1000
Thomas S Hanenburg, *Senior VP*
EMP: 593
SALES (corp-wide): 76.5B **Privately Held**
SIC: **8011** 8062 Medical centers; general medical & surgical hospitals
HQ: Kaiser Foundation Hospitals Inc
1 Kaiser Plz
Oakland CA 94612
510 271-6611

(P-19097)
KAISER FOUNDATION HOSPITALS
Also Called: San Ramon Medical Offices
2300 Camino Ramon, San Ramon
(94583-1354)
PHONE...................925 244-7600
EMP: 593
SALES (corp-wide): 76.5B **Privately Held**
SIC: **8011** Medical centers
HQ: Kaiser Foundation Hospitals Inc
1 Kaiser Plz
Oakland CA 94612
510 271-6611

(P-19098)
KAISER FOUNDATION HOSPITALS
Also Called: Harbor Corporate Park
3601 S Harbor Blvd, Santa Ana
(92704-7909)
PHONE...................714 223-2606
EMP: 593
SALES (corp-wide): 76.5B **Privately Held**
SIC: **8011** Psychiatric clinic
HQ: Kaiser Foundation Hospitals Inc
1 Kaiser Plz
Oakland CA 94612
510 271-6611

(P-19099)
KAISER FOUNDATION HOSPITALS
Also Called: Canyon Country Medical Offices
26415 Carl Boyer Dr, Santa Clarita
(91350-5824)
PHONE...................888 778-5000
EMP: 593
SALES (corp-wide): 76.5B **Privately Held**
SIC: **8011** Medical centers
HQ: Kaiser Foundation Hospitals Inc
1 Kaiser Plz
Oakland CA 94612
510 271-6611

(P-19100)
KAISER FOUNDATION HOSPITALS
Also Called: Thosand Oaks 145 Hodencamp
145 Hodenkamp Rd, Thousand Oaks
(91360-5810)
PHONE...................888 515-3500
EMP: 593
SALES (corp-wide): 76.5B **Privately Held**
SIC: **8011** Medical centers

HQ: Kaiser Foundation Hospitals Inc
1 Kaiser Plz
Oakland CA 94612
510 271-6611

(P-19101)
KAISER FOUNDATION
HOSPITALS
Also Called: Santa Clara Arques Med Offs
1263 E Arques Ave, Sunnyvale
(94085-4701)
PHONE..............................408 851-1000
EMP: 593
SALES (corp-wide): 76.5B Privately Held
SIC: 8011 Medical centers
HQ: Kaiser Foundation Hospitals Inc
1 Kaiser Plz
Oakland CA 94612
510 271-6611

(P-19102)
KAISER FOUNDATION
HOSPITALS
Also Called: Thousand Oaks 322 E Thousand
322 E Thousand Oaks Blvd, Thousand
Oaks (91360-5804)
PHONE..............................888 515-3500
EMP: 593
SALES (corp-wide): 76.5B Privately Held
SIC: 8011 Medical centers
HQ: Kaiser Foundation Hospitals Inc
1 Kaiser Plz
Oakland CA 94612
510 271-6611

(P-19103)
KAISER FOUNDATION
HOSPITALS
Also Called: Tustin Ranch Medical Offices
2521 Michelle Dr, Tustin (92780-7014)
PHONE..............................888 988-2800
EMP: 593
SALES (corp-wide): 76.5B Privately Held
SIC: 8011 Offices & clinics of medical doc-
tors
HQ: Kaiser Foundation Hospitals Inc
1 Kaiser Plz
Oakland CA 94612
510 271-6611

(P-19104)
KAISER FOUNDATION
HOSPITALS
Also Called: Kaiser Permanente
250 Hospital Pkwy, San Jose (95119-1103)
PHONE..............................408 972-7000
Joann Zimmerman, Branch Mgr
Frederick S Wright, Surgeon
Mark Korkowski, Obstetrician
Thomas T Lin, Obstetrician
Suchada Nopachai, Obstetrician
EMP: 650
SALES (corp-wide): 76.5B Privately Held
WEB: www.kaiserpermanente.org
SIC: 8011 Medical centers
HQ: Kaiser Foundation Hospitals Inc
1 Kaiser Plz
Oakland CA 94612
510 271-6611

(P-19105)
KAISER FOUNDATION
HOSPITALS
Also Called: Kaiser Permanente
1100 Veterans Blvd, Redwood City
(94063-2037)
PHONE..............................650 299-2000
Eric Rasmussen, Manager
Flavio Garcia, Purch Dir
Reza Adineh, Security Mgr
Malika N Kheraj, Infectious Dis
Vinod Chopra, Anesthesiology
EMP: 1500
SALES (corp-wide): 76.5B Privately Held
WEB: www.kaiserpermanente.org
SIC: 8011 8062 Medical centers; general
medical & surgical hospitals
HQ: Kaiser Foundation Hospitals Inc
1 Kaiser Plz
Oakland CA 94612
510 271-6611

(P-19106)
KAISER FOUNDATION
HOSPITALS
Also Called: Kaiser Permanente
1425 S Main St, Walnut Creek
(94596-5318)
PHONE..............................925 295-4000
Michael Tully-Cintron, Branch Mgr
Jessica Arroyo-Bansraj, Technology
Deneen Wohlford, Mktg Dir
Joseph Grondahl, Family Practiti
Birgitta Snyder, Psychologist
EMP: 2000
SQ FT: 11,840
SALES (corp-wide): 76.5B Privately Held
WEB: www.kaiserpermanente.org
SIC: 8011 Medical centers
HQ: Kaiser Foundation Hospitals Inc
1 Kaiser Plz
Oakland CA 94612
510 271-6611

(P-19107)
KAISER FOUNDATION
HOSPITALS
Also Called: Kaiser Permanente
25825 Vermont Ave, Harbor City
(90710-3518)
PHONE..............................310 325-5111
Mary Ann Barnes, Branch Mgr
Michael Kusunoki, Officer
Cristeta L Lozon, Top Exec
Christine Sandaval, Project Mgr
Abir Makarem, Technology
EMP: 1700
SALES (corp-wide): 76.5B Privately Held
WEB: www.kaiserpermanente.org
SIC: 8011 Medical centers
HQ: Kaiser Foundation Hospitals Inc
1 Kaiser Plz
Oakland CA 94612
510 271-6611

(P-19108)
KAISER FOUNDATION
HOSPITALS
Also Called: Kaiser Permanente San Fran
601 Van Ness Ave Ste 2008, San Francisco
(94102-6310)
PHONE..............................415 833-9688
EMP: 105
SALES (corp-wide): 76.5B Privately Held
SIC: 8011 Occupational & industrial spe-
cialist, physician/surgeon
HQ: Kaiser Foundation Hospitals Inc
1 Kaiser Plz
Oakland CA 94612
510 271-6611

(P-19109)
KAISER FOUNDATION
HOSPITALS
Also Called: Kaiser Permanente
9961 Sierra Ave, Fontana (92335-6720)
PHONE..............................909 427-5000
William Meyer, Principal
Preston Lee Wisner, Analyst
Adetunji Adegboyega, Family Practiti
Sourav Das, Family Practiti
Deborah Gililland, Family Practiti
EMP: 1700
SALES (corp-wide): 76.5B Privately Held
WEB: www.kaiserpermanente.org
SIC: 8011 Medical centers
HQ: Kaiser Foundation Hospitals Inc
1 Kaiser Plz
Oakland CA 94612
510 271-6611

(P-19110)
KAISER FOUNDATION
HOSPITALS
Also Called: Milpitas Medical Offices
770 E Calaveras Blvd, Milpitas
(95035-5491)
PHONE..............................408 945-2900
Ellen Sinclair, Manager
Bill Jue, Internal Med
Curtis L Mark, Internal Med
Ravita Saluja, Internal Med
Quang D Dao, Pediatrics
EMP: 50

SALES (corp-wide): 76.5B Privately Held
WEB: www.kaiserpermanente.org
SIC: 8011 8062 Medical centers; general
medical & surgical hospitals
HQ: Kaiser Foundation Hospitals Inc
1 Kaiser Plz
Oakland CA 94612
510 271-6611

(P-19111)
KAISER FOUNDATION
HOSPITALS
Kaiser Permanente
1950 Franklin St, Oakland (94612-5190)
PHONE..............................510 987-1000
Maryanne Williams, Manager
Carol Cardinale,
Mark Tortorich, Vice Pres
Kathy Weiner, Managing Dir
Melissa Gray, Executive Asst
EMP: 793
SALES (corp-wide): 76.5B Privately Held
WEB: www.kaiserpermanente.org
SIC: 8011 Health maintenance organiza-
tion
HQ: Kaiser Foundation Hospitals Inc
1 Kaiser Plz
Oakland CA 94612
510 271-6611

(P-19112)
KAISER FOUNDATION
HOSPITALS
Also Called: La Palma Medical Offices
5 Centerpointe Dr, La Palma (90623-1050)
PHONE..............................714 562-3420
Josefina Guzman-Inouye, Manager
Diane V Pham, Family Practiti
EMP: 50
SALES (corp-wide): 76.5B Privately Held
WEB: www.kaiserpermanente.org
SIC: 8011 Offices & clinics of medical doc-
tors
HQ: Kaiser Foundation Hospitals Inc
1 Kaiser Plz
Oakland CA 94612
510 271-6611

(P-19113)
KAISER FOUNDATION
HOSPITALS
Also Called: Glendale Medical Offices
444 W Glenoaks Blvd, Glendale
(91202-2917)
PHONE..............................818 552-3000
Avetis Tashyan, Branch Mgr
Richard Walburg, Podiatrist
EMP: 50
SALES (corp-wide): 76.5B Privately Held
WEB: www.kaiserpermanente.org
SIC: 8011 Medical centers
HQ: Kaiser Foundation Hospitals Inc
1 Kaiser Plz
Oakland CA 94612
510 271-6611

(P-19114)
KAISER FOUNDATION
HOSPITALS
Also Called: Kaiser Prmnnte Psadena Med
Off
3280 E Foothill Blvd, Pasadena
(91107-3103)
P.O. Box 7005 (91109-7005)
PHONE..............................626 440-5639
Sung Hyon, Psychiatry
EMP: 50
SALES (corp-wide): 76.5B Privately Held
WEB: www.kaiserpermanente.org
SIC: 8011 Medical centers
HQ: Kaiser Foundation Hospitals Inc
1 Kaiser Plz
Oakland CA 94612
510 271-6611

(P-19115)
KAISER FOUNDATION
HOSPITALS
Also Called: Yorba Linda Medical Offices
22550 Savi Ranch Pkwy, Yorba Linda
(92887-4670)
PHONE..............................714 685-3520
Marie Kohl, Administration
Lester Cheng, Family Practiti
Deepti Gandhi, Family Practiti

EMP: 50
SALES (corp-wide): 76.5B Privately Held
WEB: www.kaiserpermanente.org
SIC: 8011 Offices & clinics of medical doc-
tors
HQ: Kaiser Foundation Hospitals Inc
1 Kaiser Plz
Oakland CA 94612
510 271-6611

(P-19116)
KAISER FOUNDATION
HOSPITALS
Also Called: Escondido Medical Offices
732 N Broadway, Escondido (92025-1897)
PHONE..............................619 528-5000
Han Kim, Manager
EMP: 50
SALES (corp-wide): 76.5B Privately Held
WEB: www.kaiserpermanente.org
SIC: 8011 Offices & clinics of medical doc-
tors
HQ: Kaiser Foundation Hospitals Inc
1 Kaiser Plz
Oakland CA 94612
510 271-6611

(P-19117)
KAISER FOUNDATION
HOSPITALS
Also Called: Davis Medical Offices
1955 Cowell Blvd, Davis (95618-6325)
PHONE..............................530 757-7100
Robert Talkington, Manager
EMP: 50
SALES (corp-wide): 76.5B Privately Held
WEB: www.kaiserpermanente.org
SIC: 8011 Medical centers
HQ: Kaiser Foundation Hospitals Inc
1 Kaiser Plz
Oakland CA 94612
510 271-6611

(P-19118)
KAISER FOUNDATION
HOSPITALS
Also Called: Kaiser Prmnnte Hayward Med
Ctr
27400 Hesperian Blvd, Hayward
(94545-4235)
PHONE..............................510 678-4000
Cynthia Seay, Manager
Arcadio Mariano, Administration
Luis Mejia, Opers Staff
Rabiatu Abdullah, Emerg Med Spec
Trupti Mehta MD, Med Doctor
EMP: 1200
SALES (corp-wide): 76.5B Privately Held
WEB: www.kaiserpermanente.org
SIC: 8011 Medical centers
HQ: Kaiser Foundation Hospitals Inc
1 Kaiser Plz
Oakland CA 94612
510 271-6611

(P-19119)
KAISER FOUNDATION
HOSPITALS
Also Called: Permanentee Medical Group
1001 Riverside Ave, Roseville
(95678-5134)
PHONE..............................916 784-4000
Deb Royer, Manager
Diane Dailey, Med Doctor
EMP: 200
SALES (corp-wide): 76.5B Privately Held
WEB: www.kaiserpermanente.org
SIC: 8011 Offices & clinics of medical doc-
tors
HQ: Kaiser Foundation Hospitals Inc
1 Kaiser Plz
Oakland CA 94612
510 271-6611

(P-19120)
KAISER FOUNDATION
HOSPITALS
Also Called: Kaiser Perminente
2155 Iron Point Rd, Folsom (95630-8707)
PHONE..............................916 817-5200
Larry Marini, Manager
Hamid R Kazerouni Zadeh, Internal Med
Darryl Hunter, Oncology
EMP: 200

PRODUCTS & SVCS

SALES (corp-wide): 76.5B **Privately Held**
WEB: www.kaiserpermanente.org
SIC: **8011** Health maintenance organization
HQ: Kaiser Foundation Hospitals Inc
1 Kaiser Plz
Oakland CA 94612
510 271-6611

(P-19121)
KAISER FOUNDATION HOSPITALS
Also Called: Kaiser Permanente
1200 El Camino Real, South San Francisco
(94080-3208)
PHONE..................................650 742-2000
Evelyn Chan, *Branch Mgr*
Brenda Leonard, *Associate Dir*
Terrill Tang, *Business Dir*
Richard Diaz, *Security Dir*
Vangie Cade, *Facilities Mgr*
EMP: 1500
SALES (corp-wide): 76.5B **Privately Held**
WEB: www.kaiserpermanente.org
SIC: **8011 8062** Medical centers; general medical & surgical hospitals
HQ: Kaiser Foundation Hospitals Inc
1 Kaiser Plz
Oakland CA 94612
510 271-6611

(P-19122)
KAISER FOUNDATION HOSPITALS
Also Called: Kaiser Permanente South
6600 Bruceville Rd, Sacramento
(95823-4671)
PHONE..................................916 688-2000
Sarah Krevans, *Branch Mgr*
Sudha Yenumula, *Family Practiti*
Makoto Ono, *Psychologist*
Michael I Chow, *Surgeon*
Christine Jang, *Obstetrician*
EMP: 3600
SALES (corp-wide): 76.5B **Privately Held**
WEB: www.kaiserpermanente.org
SIC: **8011** Medical centers
HQ: Kaiser Foundation Hospitals Inc
1 Kaiser Plz
Oakland CA 94612
510 271-6611

(P-19123)
KAISER FOUNDATION HOSPITALS
Also Called: Kaiser Permanente
39400 Paseo Padre Pkwy, Fremont
(94538-2310)
PHONE..................................510 248-3000
Calvin Wheeler, *Manager*
Peter H D, *IT/INT Sup*
Phil Wald, *Controller*
Linda Twilling, *Psychologist*
Hanlon B Jen, *Surgeon*
EMP: 400
SQ FT: 86,710
SALES (corp-wide): 76.5B **Privately Held**
WEB: www.kaiserpermanente.org
SIC: **8011 8062** Medical centers; general medical & surgical hospitals
HQ: Kaiser Foundation Hospitals Inc
1 Kaiser Plz
Oakland CA 94612
510 271-6611

(P-19124)
KAISER FOUNDATION HOSPITALS
Also Called: Kaiser Permanente
27107 Tourney Rd, Santa Clarita
(91355-1860)
PHONE..................................661 222-2323
Pat Kenney, *Principal*
Magdalena Stevens, *Family Practiti*
Mariam Assaad, *Internal Med*
Mano Thanam, *Med Doctor*
EMP: 52
SQ FT: 70,835
SALES (corp-wide): 76.5B **Privately Held**
WEB: www.kaiserpermanente.org
SIC: **8011** Medical centers
HQ: Kaiser Foundation Hospitals Inc
1 Kaiser Plz
Oakland CA 94612
510 271-6611

(P-19125)
KAISER FOUNDATION HOSPITALS
Also Called: Riverside Medical Center
10800 Magnolia Ave, Riverside
(92505-3000)
PHONE..................................951 353-2000
Vita Willett, *Director*
Caitlin Chau, *Family Practiti*
Mitchell F Howo, *Family Practiti*
Mohammad Qazi, *Family Practiti*
Tracey Thompson, *Family Practiti*
EMP: 1000
SALES (corp-wide): 76.5B **Privately Held**
WEB: www.kaiserpermanente.org
SIC: **8011 8062** Medical centers; general medical & surgical hospitals
HQ: Kaiser Foundation Hospitals Inc
1 Kaiser Plz
Oakland CA 94612
510 271-6611

(P-19126)
KAISER FOUNDATION HOSPITALS
Also Called: Kaiser Permanente San Jose
250 Hospital Pkwy Bldg D, San Jose
(95119-1103)
PHONE..................................408 972-3000
Thomas Hau, *Branch Mgr*
Venny V Lee, *Pediatrics*
Anil Rama, *Psychiatry*
Joseph M Fuentes, *Emerg Med Spec*
Dottie Trusty, *Consultant*
EMP: 105
SQ FT: 5,976
SALES (corp-wide): 76.5B **Privately Held**
WEB: www.kaiserpermanente.org
SIC: **8011** General & family practice, physician/surgeon; general medical & surgical hospitals
HQ: Kaiser Foundation Hospitals Inc
1 Kaiser Plz
Oakland CA 94612
510 271-6611

(P-19127)
KAISER FOUNDATION HOSPITALS
Also Called: Kaiser Permanente
2425 Geary Blvd, San Francisco
(94115-3358)
PHONE..................................415 833-2000
Mike Alexander, *Senior VP*
Mohammad Islam, *Engineer*
Richard Norman, *Chief Engr*
Jason Buenviaje, *Senior Engr*
Karen Kenny, *Psychologist*
EMP: 720
SALES (corp-wide): 76.5B **Privately Held**
WEB: www.kaiserpermanente.org
SIC: **8011** Medical centers
HQ: Kaiser Foundation Hospitals Inc
1 Kaiser Plz
Oakland CA 94612
510 271-6611

(P-19128)
KAISER FOUNDATION HOSPITALS
Also Called: Kaiser Permanente Moreno
27300 Iris Ave, Moreno Valley
(92555-4802)
PHONE..................................951 243-0811
Tom Mc Ciltock, *Manager*
EMP: 400
SALES (corp-wide): 76.5B **Privately Held**
WEB: www.kaiserpermanente.org
SIC: **8011** Medical centers
HQ: Kaiser Foundation Hospitals Inc
1 Kaiser Plz
Oakland CA 94612
510 271-6611

(P-19129)
KAISER FOUNDATION HOSPITALS
Also Called: Kaiser Permanente
110 N La Brea Ave, Inglewood
(90301-1708)
PHONE..................................310 419-3303
Victor Ahaiwe, *President*
Keith Damsker, *Internal Med*
EMP: 450

SALES (corp-wide): 76.5B **Privately Held**
WEB: www.kaiserpermanente.org
SIC: **8011** Offices & clinics of medical doctors
HQ: Kaiser Foundation Hospitals Inc
1 Kaiser Plz
Oakland CA 94612
510 271-6611

(P-19130)
KAISER FOUNDATION HOSPITALS
Also Called: Kaiser Permanente
7300 N Fresno St, Fresno (93720-2941)
PHONE..................................559 448-4500
Susan Ryan, *Senior VP*
Kathy Mulvey,
EMP: 2000
SALES (corp-wide): 76.5B **Privately Held**
WEB: www.kaiserpermanente.org
SIC: **8011** Medical centers
HQ: Kaiser Foundation Hospitals Inc
1 Kaiser Plz
Oakland CA 94612
510 271-6611

(P-19131)
KAISER FOUNDATION HOSPITALS
Also Called: Carlsbad Medical Offices
6860 Avenida Encinas, Carlsbad
(92011-3201)
PHONE..................................760 931-4228
Phong Nguyen, *Manager*
EMP: 105
SALES (corp-wide): 76.5B **Privately Held**
SIC: **8011** Health maintenance organization
HQ: Kaiser Foundation Hospitals Inc
1 Kaiser Plz
Oakland CA 94612
510 271-6611

(P-19132)
KAISER MED CLINIC
555 Castro St, Mountain View
(94041-2009)
PHONE..................................650 903-2103
Patricia Carpenter MGA, *Manager*
EMP: 110
SALES (est): 2.9MM **Privately Held**
SIC: **8011** Clinic, operated by physicians

(P-19133)
KAWEAH DELTA HEALTH CARE DST
1014 San Juan Ave, Exeter (93221-1312)
PHONE..................................559 592-7128
Chris Robertson, *Nurse*
EMP: 118
SALES (corp-wide): 710.9MM **Privately Held**
SIC: **8011** Medical centers
PA: Kaweah Delta Health Care District
400 W Mineral King Ave
Visalia CA 93291
559 624-2000

(P-19134)
KAWEAH DLTA HLTH CARE DST GILD
1110 S Ben Maddox Way, Visalia
(93292-3643)
PHONE..................................559 624-4800
EMP: 177
SALES (corp-wide): 537.4MM **Privately Held**
SIC: **8011** Medical centers
PA: Kaweah Delta Health Care District
400 W Mineral King Ave
Visalia CA 93291
559 624-2000

(P-19135)
KERLAN-JOBE ORTHOPEDIC CLINIC (PA)
6801 Park Ter Ste 500, Los Angeles
(90045-9212)
PHONE..................................310 665-7200
Ralph A Gambardella, *CEO*
EMP: 78
SQ FT: 37,000

SALES (est): 13.7MM
SALES (corp-wide): 15.2MM **Privately Held**
WEB: www.kerlanjobe.com
SIC: **8011** Orthopedic physician

(P-19136)
KERN HEALTH SYSTEMS INC
Also Called: Kern Family Healthcare
9700 Stockdale Hwy, Bakersfield
(93311-3617)
P.O. Box 85000 (93380-5000)
PHONE..................................661 664-5000
Paul Hensler, *Ch of Bd*
Robert Landis, *CFO*
Lamberson Philip, *Administration*
Richard Pruitt, *CIO*
Anita Martin, *Human Res Dir*
EMP: 98
SQ FT: 16,000
SALES (est): 19.5MM **Privately Held**
WEB: www.kernfamilyhealthcare.com
SIC: **8011** Clinic, operated by physicians

(P-19137)
KERN RDLGY IMAGING SYSTEMS INC (PA)
2301 Bahamas Dr, Bakersfield
(93309-0663)
PHONE..................................661 326-9600
David P Schale, *CEO*
Jeff Child MD, *Treasurer*
John Gundzik MD, *Vice Pres*
EMP: 180
SQ FT: 20,000
SALES (est): 17.6MM **Privately Held**
SIC: **8011** Radiologist

(P-19138)
LA CLINICA DE LA RAZA INC
1515 Fruitvale Ave, Oakland (94601-2355)
PHONE..................................510 535-6300
Jim Eitel, *Partner*
Nancy Lewis, *Web Dvlpr*
Vicky Cuevas, *MIS Staff*
Dan Gilliam, *Technology*
Wendy Jeter, *Site Mgr*
EMP: 248
SALES (corp-wide): 112.4MM **Privately Held**
SIC: **8011 8699** Clinic, operated by physicians; charitable organization
PA: La Clinica De La Raza, Inc.
1450 Fruitvale Ave Fl 3
Oakland CA 94601
510 535-4000

(P-19139)
LA CLINICA DE LA RAZA INC
243 Georgia St, Vallejo (94590-5905)
PHONE..................................707 556-8100
Jane Garcia, *Branch Mgr*
EMP: 372
SALES (corp-wide): 112.4MM **Privately Held**
SIC: **8011** Clinic, operated by physicians
PA: La Clinica De La Raza, Inc.
1450 Fruitvale Ave Fl 3
Oakland CA 94601
510 535-4000

(P-19140)
LA CLINICA DE LA RAZA INC
Also Called: Mental Health Department
1601 Fruitvale Ave, Oakland (94601-2418)
PHONE..................................510 535-6200
Jane Garcia, *CEO*
Susanna Moore, *Psychiatry*
Lisa Montang, *Assistant*
EMP: 310
SALES (corp-wide): 112.4MM **Privately Held**
SIC: **8011** Clinic, operated by physicians
PA: La Clinica De La Raza, Inc.
1450 Fruitvale Ave Fl 3
Oakland CA 94601
510 535-4000

(P-19141)
LA COUNTY HIGH DESERT HLTH SYS
44900 60th St W, Lancaster (93536-7618)
PHONE..................................661 945-8461
Beryl Brooks, *Exec Dir*
EMP: 400

SALES (est): 11.9MM **Privately Held**
SIC: **8011** 8062 8093 Ambulatory surgical center; hospital, AMA approved residency; specialty outpatient clinics

(P-19142)
LA JOLLA ORTHOPAEDIC
4120 La Jolla Village Dr, La Jolla (92037-1406)
PHONE...................................858 657-0055
Scott Leggett, *Mng Member*
EMP: 69
SALES (est): 11.3MM **Privately Held**
WEB: www.osclajolla.com
SIC: **8011** Orthopedic physician; surgeon

(P-19143)
LA LASER CENTER PC CPMC
10884 Santa Monica Blvd # 300, Los Angeles (90025-7638)
P.O. Box 16297, Beverly Hills (90209-2297)
PHONE...................................310 446-4400
Mehry Tahery, *Admin Sec*
Keith Guddy, *Accountant*
EMP: 95
SALES (est): 1.4MM **Privately Held**
SIC: **8011** Dermatologist

(P-19144)
LA MAESTRA FAMILY CLINIC INC
Also Called: La Maestra Community Clinic
4060 Fairmount Ave, San Diego (92105-1608)
PHONE...................................619 280-4213
Alejanderina Areizaza, *Manager*
EMP: 100 **Privately Held**
SIC: **8011** Clinic, operated by physicians
PA: La Maestra Family Clinic, Inc.
    4060 Fairmount Ave
    San Diego CA 92105

(P-19145)
LA MAESTRA FAMILY CLINIC INC
4305 University Ave # 120, San Diego (92105-1645)
PHONE...................................619 501-1235
Liv David, *Branch Mgr*
EMP: 100 **Privately Held**
SIC: **8011** Clinic, operated by physicians
PA: La Maestra Family Clinic, Inc.
    4060 Fairmount Ave
    San Diego CA 92105

(P-19146)
LA MAESTRA FAMILY CLINIC INC (PA)
Also Called: La Maestra Community Hlth Ctrs
4060 Fairmount Ave, San Diego (92105-1608)
PHONE...................................619 584-1612
Zara Marselian, *CEO*
Carlos Hanessian, *Ch of Bd*
Alejandrina Areizaga, *COO*
Jeffrey Neumann, *CFO*
Alex Pantoja, *CFO*
EMP: 161
SQ FT: 5,000
SALES: 29.8MM **Privately Held**
SIC: **8011** Clinic, operated by physicians

(P-19147)
LA MESA INTRNL MDC MDCL GR
Also Called: La Mesa Internal Medical Group
5111 Garfield St, La Mesa (91941-5147)
PHONE...................................619 460-4050
Donald Patterson, *President*
John Dapolito, *Shareholder*
Dr Kenneth Hanson, *Shareholder*
James Malinak, *Shareholder*
Dr Roger English, *President*
EMP: 50
SQ FT: 10,000
SALES (est): 2.9MM **Privately Held**
SIC: **8011** Internal medicine, physician/surgeon

(P-19148)
LA PEER SURGERY CENTER LLC
Also Called: La Peer Health Systems
8920 Wilshire Blvd # 101, Beverly Hills (90211-2007)
PHONE...................................310 360-9119
Dr Siamak Tabib, *Mng Member*
Heidi Partida, *Office Mgr*
Juselle Cortes, *Administration*
EMP: 78 **EST:** 2000
SQ FT: 2,300
SALES: 28.3MM **Privately Held**
SIC: **8011** Surgeon

(P-19149)
LA VIDA MLTISPECIALTY MED CTRS
Also Called: Northeast Community Clinics
1400 S Grand Ave, Los Angeles (90015-3048)
PHONE...................................213 765-7500
Amber Crujillo, *Office Mgr*
Chuca Chidi, *President*
EMP: 60 **EST:** 2000
SQ FT: 52,000
SALES: 23MM **Privately Held**
SIC: **8011** Clinic, operated by physicians

(P-19150)
LANCASTER CRDLGY MED GROUP INC (PA)
Also Called: Physicians Referral Service
43847 Heaton Ave Ste B, Lancaster (93534-4936)
PHONE...................................661 726-3058
Shun K Sunder MD, *President*
E Ekong MD, *Vice Pres*
Kanagarath Sivalingam MD, *Admin Sec*
EMP: 90
SQ FT: 30,000
SALES (est): 4MM **Privately Held**
SIC: **8011** Cardiologist & cardio-vascular specialist

(P-19151)
LARCHMONT RADIOLOGY MED GROUP
Also Called: Westcoast Medial Imaging
2010 Wilshire Blvd # 409, Los Angeles (90057-3598)
PHONE...................................213 483-5953
Stewart A Lapin, *President*
EMP: 55
SQ FT: 4,500
SALES (est): 2.2MM **Privately Held**
SIC: **8011** Radiologist

(P-19152)
LAREN D TAN MD
11234 Anderson St, Loma Linda (92354-2804)
PHONE...................................909 558-4444
Laren Tan, *Principal*
EMP: 89
SALES (est): 2.6MM **Privately Held**
SIC: **8011** Physicians' office, including specialists

(P-19153)
LASSEN MEDICAL GROUP INC (PA)
Also Called: Mercy Medical
2450 Sster Mary Clumba Dr, Red Bluff (96080-4356)
PHONE...................................530 527-0414
Kimberli R Frantz, *President*
Dan Mc Daniel MD, *Treasurer*
Richard Wickenheiser, *Principal*
Eugene Plett MD, *Admin Sec*
Danielle Massie, *Admin Asst*
EMP: 57
SALES (est): 10.9MM **Privately Held**
SIC: **8011** 8099 Physicians' office, including specialists; blood related health services

(P-19154)
LELAND STANFORD JUNIOR UNIV
1201 Welch Rd, Stanford (94305-5102)
PHONE...................................650 723-7863
William C Mobley, *Principal*
Bruce Phillips, *IT/INT Sup*

Joachim Hallmayer, *Associate*
EMP: 54
SALES (corp-wide): 11.3B **Privately Held**
SIC: **8011** Radiologist
PA: Leland Stanford Junior University
    450 Jane Stanford Way
    Stanford CA 94305
    650 723-2300

(P-19155)
LELAND STANFORD JUNIOR UNIV
Health Promotion Resource Ctr
211 Quarry Rd N229, Palo Alto (94304-1416)
PHONE...................................650 725-4416
Wes Alles, *Principal*
Katharine Hagerman, *Research*
Sylvia Kreibig, *Research*
O'Neal Patrick, *Accountant*
Deitria Chapman, *Human Res Mgr*
EMP: 54
SALES (corp-wide): 11.3B **Privately Held**
SIC: **8011** 8221 Health maintenance organization; university
PA: Leland Stanford Junior University
    450 Jane Stanford Way
    Stanford CA 94305
    650 723-2300

(P-19156)
LELAND STANFORD JUNIOR UNIV
Also Called: Cowell Student Health Service
870 Campus Dr, Stanford (94305-8508)
PHONE...................................650 723-0821
Dr Ira Friedman, *Director*
EMP: 100
SALES (corp-wide): 11.3B **Privately Held**
SIC: **8011** 8031 8221 Medical centers; offices & clinics of osteopathic physicians; university
PA: Leland Stanford Junior University
    450 Jane Stanford Way
    Stanford CA 94305
    650 723-2300

(P-19157)
LES KELLEY FAMILY HEALTH CTR
1920 Colorado Ave, Santa Monica (90404-3414)
PHONE...................................310 319-4700
Michele Bholat, *Director*
Eric Chamers, *Administration*
EMP: 60
SALES (est): 2.4MM **Privately Held**
SIC: **8011** Clinic, operated by physicians

(P-19158)
LIFELONG MEDICAL CARE (PA)
Also Called: Over 60 Health Center
2344 6th St, Berkeley (94710-2412)
P.O. Box 11247 (94712-2247)
PHONE...................................510 704-6010
Marty A Lynch, *CEO*
Brenda Shipp, *COO*
Rick Clark, *CFO*
EMP: 50
SQ FT: 4,200
SALES (est): 59.1MM **Privately Held**
SIC: **8011** General & family practice, physician/surgeon

(P-19159)
LINDA LOMA UNIV HLTH CARE
Also Called: Loma Linda Faculty Med Group
11370 Anderson St # 2100, Loma Linda (92354-3450)
P.O. Box 626 (92354-0626)
PHONE...................................909 558-2851
Ilene Spencer, *Manager*
Leo Chan-June Jeng, *Pediatrics*
Mary Ann Magoun, *Pediatrics*
John W Mace, *Med Doctor*
EMP: 250 **Privately Held**
SIC: **8011** Offices & clinics of medical doctors
PA: Loma Linda University Health Care
    11175 Campus St
    Loma Linda CA 92350

(P-19160)
LINDA LOMA UNIV HLTH CARE (PA)
11175 Campus St, Loma Linda (92350-1700)
PHONE...................................909 558-4729
Roger Hadley MD, *President*
David B Hinshaw Jr, *Vice Chairman*
Brian Bull MD, *Admin Sec*
EMP: 850
SQ FT: 70,000
SALES: 166.4MM **Privately Held**
SIC: **8011** Clinic, operated by physicians

(P-19161)
LINDA LOMA UNIV HLTH CARE
Also Called: Llu Center For Fertility
11370 Anderson St # 3950, Loma Linda (92354-3450)
P.O. Box 1009 (92354-1009)
PHONE...................................909 558-2840
Linda Moore, *Administration*
EMP: 153 **Privately Held**
SIC: **8011** Fertility specialist, physician
PA: Loma Linda University Health Care
    11175 Campus St
    Loma Linda CA 92350

(P-19162)
LINDEN CREST SURGERY CENTER
9735 Wilshire Blvd # 100, Beverly Hills (90212-2114)
PHONE...................................310 601-3900
Christina Niegos, *Principal*
Manuel Unzueta, *Manager*
EMP: 60
SALES (est): 2.9MM **Privately Held**
WEB: www.lindencrestsurgery.com
SIC: **8011** Surgeon

(P-19163)
LIVINGSTON COMMUNITY HEALTH
Also Called: Livingston Health Center
600 B St Bldg A, Livingston (95334-9593)
PHONE...................................209 394-7913
Leslie McGowan, *CEO*
Selina Montoya, *CFO*
EMP: 101
SALES: 18.1MM **Privately Held**
SIC: **8011** Primary care medical clinic

(P-19164)
LLU ADVNTIST HLTH SCIENCES CTR
Also Called: Risk Management
101 E Redlands Blvd, San Bernardino (92408-3710)
P.O. Box 1770, Loma Linda (92354-0570)
PHONE...................................909 558-4386
Mark Hubbard, *Director*
EMP: 52
SALES (est): 3.4MM **Privately Held**
SIC: **8011** Medical centers

(P-19165)
LODI MEMORIAL HOSP ASSN INC
Also Called: Rehabilitation Center
800 S Lower Sacramento Rd, Lodi (95242-3635)
PHONE...................................209 333-3100
Linda Escobar, *Director*
EMP: 120
SALES (corp-wide): 4.4B **Privately Held**
SIC: **8011** 8069 Specialized medical practitioners, except internal; specialty hospitals, except psychiatric
HQ: Lodi Memorial Hospital Association, Inc.
    975 S Fairmont Ave
    Lodi CA 95240
    209 334-3411

(P-19166)
LOMA LINDA UNIVERSITY
1911 W Park Ave, Redlands (92373-8045)
P.O. Box 1740, Loma Linda (92354-0240)
PHONE...................................909 558-6422
Brian Bull, *President*
EMP: 65

P
R
O
D
U
C
T
S

&

S
V
C
S

SALES: 11.4MM **Privately Held**
SIC: **8011** Pathologist

(P-19167)
LOS ANGELES CARDIOLOGY ASSOC (PA)
1245 Wilshire Blvd # 703, Los Angeles (90017-4810)
PHONE..............................213 977-0419
David S Cannom MD, *Partner*
Anil K Bhandari MD, *Partner*
Steven Burstein MD, *Partner*
Robert D Lerman MD, *Partner*
Charles Pollick MD, *Partner*
EMP: 65
SQ FT: 12,000
SALES (est): 10.4MM **Privately Held**
SIC: **8011** Cardiologist & cardio-vascular specialist

(P-19168)
LOS ANGELES FREE CLINIC (PA)
Also Called: Saban Community Clinic
8405 Beverly Blvd, Los Angeles (90048-3401)
PHONE..............................323 653-8622
Jeffrey Bujer, *CEO*
Elisabeth Normand, *Pharmacy Dir*
Lauren Hill, *Program Mgr*
Brenda Moses, *Nursing Mgr*
Mario Rivas, *Info Tech Mgr*
EMP: 300
SQ FT: 26,615
SALES: 17.4MM **Privately Held**
SIC: **8011** Clinic, operated by physicians

(P-19169)
LOS ANGELES FREE CLINIC
8405 Beverly Blvd, Los Angeles (90048-3401)
PHONE..............................323 653-8622
Abbe Land, *CEO*
EMP: 99
SALES: 32.6K **Privately Held**
SIC: **8011** General & family practice, physician/surgeon

(P-19170)
LUCILE SALTER PACKARD CHIL
Also Called: Bayside Medical Group
5601 Norris Canyon Rd # 230, San Ramon (94583-5407)
PHONE..............................925 277-7550
K C Campion, *CEO*
Douglas Severance, *Family Practiti*
EMP: 187
SALES (corp-wide): 1.6B **Privately Held**
SIC: **8011** Physicians' office, including specialists
PA: Lucile Salter Packard Children's Hospital At Stanford
725 Welch Rd
Palo Alto CA 94304
650 497-8000

(P-19171)
MADISON RADIOLOGY MED GROUP
65 N Madison Ave Ste M250, Pasadena (91101-2000)
PHONE..............................626 793-8189
Terry S Becker, *President*
Eric Becker, *Info Tech Dir*
Jeanette Velasco, *Manager*
EMP: 55
SALES (est): 3.1MM **Privately Held**
SIC: **8011** Radiologist

(P-19172)
MANGROVE MEDICAL GROUP
Also Called: Mangrove Lab & X-Ray
1040 Mangrove Ave, Chico (95926-3509)
PHONE..............................530 345-0064
Dewayne E Caviness MD, *Principal*
Randall E Caviness MD, *Principal*
Kurt E Johnson MD, *Principal*
Dean P Smith MD, *Principal*
Randall S Williams MD, *Principal*
EMP: 50
SQ FT: 12,000
SALES (est): 8.1MM **Privately Held**
SIC: **8011** General & family practice, physician/surgeon

(P-19173)
MARIN COMMUNITY CLINIC
Also Called: Marin Community Clinics
9 Commercial Blvd Ste 100, Novato (94949-6137)
PHONE..............................415 448-1500
Linda Tavaszi, *CEO*
David Klinetobe, *CFO*
John Shen, *Exec Dir*
Daniel Escobar, *Technology*
Len Pukanic, *Accounting Mgr*
EMP: 99
SQ FT: 9,000
SALES: 35.1MM **Privately Held**
SIC: **8011** Clinic, operated by physicians

(P-19174)
MARINOW HARRY MD FACS INC
Also Called: Feiwell, Lawrence MD
3742 Katella Ave Ste 401, Los Alamitos (90720-3172)
PHONE..............................562 430-3561
Korinne Walker, *President*
EMP: 50
SALES (est): 2.6MM **Privately Held**
SIC: **8011** General & family practice, physician/surgeon

(P-19175)
MARK E JACOBSON M D
1260 N Dutton Ave Ste 230, Santa Rosa (95401-7161)
PHONE..............................707 571-4022
Mark Jacobson MD, *President*
EMP: 60
SALES (est): 658.3K **Privately Held**
SIC: **8011** Offices & clinics of medical doctors

(P-19176)
MARK H LEIBENHAUT MD
Also Called: Ras
2800 L St Ste 110, Sacramento (95816-5616)
PHONE..............................916 454-6600
Mark H Leibenhaut, *Partner*
Mark Leibenhaut, *Med Doctor*
EMP: 50
SALES (est): 1.1MM **Privately Held**
SIC: **8011** Offices & clinics of medical doctors

(P-19177)
MARTECH MEDICAL PRODUCTS INC
565 Clara Nofal Rd, Calexico (92231-9533)
PHONE..............................215 256-8833
EMP: 98
SALES (corp-wide): 38.8MM **Privately Held**
SIC: **8011** Offices & clinics of medical doctors
PA: Martech Medical Products, Inc.
1500 Delp Dr
Harleysville PA 19438
215 256-8833

(P-19178)
MARTIN LTHER KING/DREW MED CTR
1670 E 120th St, Los Angeles (90059-3026)
PHONE..............................310 773-4926
Hank Wells, *CEO*
Linda McAuley, *COO*
Anthony Gray, *CFO*
Kate Edmunson, *Human Resources*
Roger Peeks, *Director*
EMP: 74
SALES (est): 19MM **Privately Held**
SIC: **8011** Clinic, operated by physicians

(P-19179)
MCHENRY MEDICAL GROUP INC
1541 Florida Ave Ste 200, Modesto (95350-4438)
PHONE..............................209 577-3388
John Porteous, *President*
Harris M Goodman, *Treasurer*
EMP: 100
SQ FT: 22,000

SALES (est): 9.8MM **Privately Held**
WEB: www.mchenrymedical.com
SIC: **8011** Internal medicine, physician/surgeon; gastronomist; dermatologist; surgeon

(P-19180)
MD IMAGING INC A PROF MED CORP
Also Called: Women's Imaging Center
2020 Court St, Redding (96001-1822)
PHONE..............................530 243-1249
Michael G Davis, *CEO*
Richard J Slepicka, *CFO*
Charlene Cundy, *Human Res Mgr*
Melody Christenson, *Marketing Mgr*
Patricia Hansen, *Med Doctor*
EMP: 100
SALES (est): 20MM **Privately Held**
WEB: www.mdimaging.net
SIC: **8011** Radiologist

(P-19181)
MEDICAL GROUP BVERLY HILLS INC (PA)
Also Called: CEDARS SINAI MEDICAL GROUP
200 N Robertson Blvd, Beverly Hills (90211-1769)
PHONE..............................310 385-3200
Thomas D Gordon, *CEO*
Mary Claire Lingel, *Exec Dir*
Diana Orrantia, *Executive Asst*
Cheryl Charles, *Admin Sec*
Hilary Bettinelli-Olpi, *Project Mgr*
EMP: 50
SQ FT: 14,500
SALES: 441.7MM **Privately Held**
SIC: **8011** Clinic, operated by physicians

(P-19182)
MEDICAL GROUP BVERLY HILLS INC
Also Called: Cedar Sinai Medical Group
250 N Robertson Blvd # 603, Beverly Hills (90211-1788)
PHONE..............................310 247-4646
Tom Gordon, *Branch Mgr*
Nicholas Szumski, *Neurology*
John Andrews, *Med Doctor*
James L Caplan, *Med Doctor*
EMP: 50
SALES (corp-wide): 441.7MM **Privately Held**
SIC: **8011** General & family practice, physician/surgeon
PA: Medical Group Of Beverly Hills, Inc.
200 N Robertson Blvd
Beverly Hills CA 90211
310 385-3200

(P-19183)
MEDICL IMGNG CTR OF SOUTHRN CA
2811 Wilshire Blvd # 100, Santa Monica (90403-4803)
PHONE..............................310 829-9788
Bradley Jabour MD, *President*
Nicole Pelissier, *COO*
EMP: 65
SQ FT: 22,000
SALES (est): 7.4MM **Privately Held**
WEB: www.corbyandcorby.com
SIC: **8011** Radiologist

(P-19184)
MEDNAX INC
225 N Jackson Ave, San Jose (95116-1603)
PHONE..............................408 254-8257
EMP: 188 **Publicly Held**
SIC: **8011** Hematologist
PA: Mednax, Inc.
1301 Concord Ter
Sunrise FL 33323

(P-19185)
MEDNAX INC
300 W Huntington Dr, Arcadia (91007-3402)
PHONE..............................626 574-3050
Ronald Jenkins, *Branch Mgr*
John R Kole, *Principal*
EMP: 191 **Publicly Held**

SIC: **8011** Internal medicine, physician/surgeon
PA: Mednax, Inc.
1301 Concord Ter
Sunrise FL 33323

(P-19186)
MEDNAX INC
24411 Health Center Dr, Laguna Hills (92653-3651)
PHONE..............................949 587-9037
Kathy Roquemore, *Branch Mgr*
EMP: 188 **Publicly Held**
SIC: **8011** Pediatrician
PA: Mednax, Inc.
1301 Concord Ter
Sunrise FL 33323

(P-19187)
MEDNAX INC
23441 Madison St Ste 215, Torrance (90505-4756)
PHONE..............................310 375-7172
Nanette Sanders, *Director*
EMP: 191 **Publicly Held**
SIC: **8011** General & family practice, physician/surgeon
PA: Mednax, Inc.
1301 Concord Ter
Sunrise FL 33323

(P-19188)
MEDNAX INC
2204 Grant Rd, Mountain View (94040-3855)
PHONE..............................650 625-0127
Howard Rosenberg, *Branch Mgr*
EMP: 188 **Publicly Held**
SIC: **8011** Internal medicine, physician/surgeon
PA: Mednax, Inc.
1301 Concord Ter
Sunrise FL 33323

(P-19189)
MEDPOINT MANAGEMENT
6400 Canoga Ave Ste 163, Woodland Hills (91367-2435)
PHONE..............................818 702-0100
Sheldon Lewenfuff Preident, *Principal*
Sheldon Lewenfuf, *President*
Albert Avila, *Officer*
Anne Rohr, *Officer*
Tom Diaz, *Vice Pres*
EMP: 50
SALES (est): 6.9MM **Privately Held**
WEB: www.medpointmanagement.com
SIC: **8011** Health maintenance organization

(P-19190)
MEMOR ORTHO SURGIC GROUP A M
Also Called: Southern California Cen
2760 Atlantic Ave, Long Beach (90806-2755)
PHONE..............................562 424-6666
Peter R Kurzweil, *CEO*
Douglas W Jackson MD, *President*
Curtis W Spencer III, *Vice Pres*
Leang Prum, *Office Mgr*
Lianne Prum, *Office Mgr*
▲ EMP: 70
SQ FT: 12,000
SALES (est): 8.8MM **Privately Held**
SIC: **8011** Orthopedic physician; sports medicine specialist, physician; surgeon; physical medicine, physician/surgeon

(P-19191)
MEMORIAL COUNSELING ASSOC INC
4525 E Atherton St, Long Beach (90815-3700)
PHONE..............................562 961-0155
A Sarkis, *President*
EMP: 80
SALES (est): 3.4MM **Privately Held**
WEB: www.mcapsych.com
SIC: **8011** 8322 Offices & clinics of medical doctors; general counseling services

(P-19192)
MEMORIAL PSYCHIATRIC HLTH SVCS
4525 E Atherton St, Long Beach (90815-3700)
PHONE....................562 494-9243
Lee Yoseloff, *President*
Sarkis Gavin MD, *Principal*
EMP: 50
SALES (est): 3.2MM **Privately Held**
SIC: 8011 Psychiatrist

(P-19193)
MENDOCINO CMNTY HLTH CLNIC INC (PA)
Also Called: McHc
333 Laws Ave, Ukiah (95482-6540)
PHONE....................707 468-1010
John Pavoni, *CEO*
Kathy Macdougall, *CEO*
Diane Behne, *Technician*
Richard McClintock Jr, *Dermatology*
Sarah Alvord, *Internal Med*
EMP: 235
SQ FT: 24,000
SALES: 30.9MM **Privately Held**
WEB: www.mchcinc.org
SIC: 8011 Primary care medical clinic

(P-19194)
MERCY HM SVCS A CAL LTD PARTNR
Also Called: Mercy Hospital of Folsom
1650 Creekside Dr, Folsom (95630-3400)
PHONE....................916 983-7400
Margaret Beck, *Branch Mgr*
EMP: 1080
SALES (est): 35.9K **Privately Held**
WEB: www.mercyhealth.org
SIC: 8011 Offices & clinics of medical doctors
HQ: Mercy Home Services A California Limited Partnership
2175 Rosaline Ave Ste A
Redding CA 96001
530 225-6000

(P-19195)
MICHAEL S DUFFY SR DO INC
1501 5th Ave Ste 100, San Diego (92101-3251)
PHONE....................619 461-3717
Brian Gonzales, *CEO*
David Duffy, *CFO*
Michael Duffy, *Principal*
EMP: 95 EST: 2011
SALES (est): 439.8K **Privately Held**
SIC: 8011 Offices & clinics of medical doctors

(P-19196)
MICHAEL SD NAGATINI
5400 W Hillsdale Ave, Visalia (93291-8222)
PHONE....................559 738-7502
Bill Brower, *CEO*
EMP: 60 EST: 2001
SALES (est): 709.1K **Privately Held**
SIC: 8011 Offices & clinics of medical doctors

(P-19197)
MISSION INTERNAL MED GROUP INC
Also Called: Arthur Loussararian MD
26800 Crown Valley Pkwy # 103, Mission Viejo (92691-6389)
PHONE....................949 364-3570
Arthur Loussararian, *Principal*
EMP: 102
SALES (corp-wide): 21.3MM **Privately Held**
WEB: www.mimg.com
SIC: 8011 Primary care medical clinic
PA: Mission Internal Medical Group, Inc.
26732 Crown Valley Pkwy # 411
Mission Viejo CA 92691
949 282-1600

(P-19198)
MISSION INTERNAL MED GROUP INC
Also Called: West Coast Physical Therapy
27882 Forbes Rd Ste 110, Laguna Niguel (92677-1267)
PHONE....................949 364-3605
Joan Shrum-Brown, *Principal*
EMP: 102
SALES (corp-wide): 21.3MM **Privately Held**
WEB: www.mimg.com
SIC: 8011 8049 Cardiologist & cardio-vascular specialist; physical therapist
PA: Mission Internal Medical Group, Inc.
26732 Crown Valley Pkwy # 411
Mission Viejo CA 92691
949 282-1600

(P-19199)
MISSION NEIGHBORHOOD HLTH CTR (PA)
240 Shotwell St, San Francisco (94110-1323)
PHONE....................415 552-3870
Brenda Storey, *CEO*
Amelia Martinez, *President*
Patty Caplan, *COO*
Charles Moser, *Trustee*
Luisa Eztouerro, *Vice Pres*
EMP: 110
SQ FT: 21,000
SALES: 22.2MM **Privately Held**
WEB: www.mnhc.org
SIC: 8011 Primary care medical clinic

(P-19200)
MISSION PEAK ORTHOPEDICS
5924 Stoneridge Dr # 200, Pleasanton (94588-2887)
PHONE....................510 797-3933
Co V Banh, *Principal*
EMP: 65
SALES (est): 113.3K **Privately Held**
SIC: 8011 Orthopedic physician

(P-19201)
MISSION VALLEY HTS SURGERY CTR
Also Called: Amsurg
7485 Mission Valley Rd # 106, San Diego (92108-4422)
PHONE....................619 291-3737
William S Adsit MD, *Partner*
Drew A Peterson MD, *Partner*
Kevin Smith MD, *Principal*
Jocelyn Day, *Business Mgr*
EMP: 59
SQ FT: 14,000
SALES (est): 6.7MM **Privately Held**
WEB: www.mvhsc.com
SIC: 8011 Surgeon

(P-19202)
MOLINA HEALTHCARE INC
790 E Foothill Blvd, Rialto (92376-5269)
PHONE....................909 546-7116
EMP: 133
SALES (corp-wide): 18.8B **Publicly Held**
SIC: 8011 Health maintenance organization
PA: Molina Healthcare, Inc.
200 Oceangate Ste 100
Long Beach CA 90802
562 435-3666

(P-19203)
MOLINA HEALTHCARE INC
604 Pine Ave, Long Beach (90802-1329)
PHONE....................888 562-5442
EMP: 272
SALES (corp-wide): 18.8B **Publicly Held**
SIC: 8011 Health maintenance organization
PA: Molina Healthcare, Inc.
200 Oceangate Ste 100
Long Beach CA 90802
562 435-3666

(P-19204)
MOLINA HEALTHCARE INC (PA)
200 Oceangate Ste 100, Long Beach (90802-4317)
P.O. Box 22813 (90801-5813)
PHONE....................562 435-3666

Joseph M Zubretsky, *President*
Dale B Wolf, *Ch of Bd*
John Kotal, *President*
Joseph W White, *CFO*
Ronna E Romney, *Vice Ch Bd*
EMP: 2800
SALES: 18.8B **Publicly Held**
WEB: www.molinahealthcare.com
SIC: 8011 6324 Health maintenance organization; hospital & medical service plans; health maintenance organization (HMO), insurance only

(P-19205)
MOLINA HEALTHCARE CALIFORNIA
200 Oceangate Ste 100, Long Beach (90802-4317)
PHONE....................800 526-8196
EMP: 213
SALES (est): 113.8K
SALES (corp-wide): 18.8B **Publicly Held**
SIC: 8011 Offices & clinics of medical doctors
PA: Molina Healthcare, Inc.
200 Oceangate Ste 100
Long Beach CA 90802
562 435-3666

(P-19206)
MONARCH HEALTHCARE A MEDICAL (HQ)
11 Technology Dr, Irvine (92618-2302)
PHONE....................949 923-3200
Bartley Asner, *CEO*
Marcie Greene, *CEO*
Marvin Gordon MD, *CFO*
Jay J Cohen MD, *Vice Pres*
Steven Rudy MD, *Vice Pres*
EMP: 80
SQ FT: 75,000
SALES (est): 43.8MM
SALES (corp-wide): 226.2B **Publicly Held**
WEB: www.mhealth.com
SIC: 8011 Group health association
PA: Unitedhealth Group Incorporated
9900 Bren Rd E Ste 300w
Minnetonka MN 55343
952 936-1300

(P-19207)
MONROVIA HEALTH CENTER
330 W Maple Ave, Monrovia (91016-3387)
PHONE....................626 256-1600
Maxine Liggins, *Director*
EMP: 60
SQ FT: 2,400
SALES (est): 3.6MM **Privately Held**
SIC: 8011 Medical centers

(P-19208)
MONTAGE HEALTH
P.O. Box Hh (93942-6032)
PHONE....................831 625-4821
Judi Sanderlin, *CEO*
EMP: 2500
SALES (est): 6MM **Privately Held**
SIC: 8011 Health maintenance organization

(P-19209)
MUIR ORTHOPEDIC SPECIALISTS
2405 Shadelands Dr # 210, Walnut Creek (94598-5905)
PHONE....................925 939-8585
K C Campion, *CEO*
Ramiro Miranda MD, *President*
Abid A Qureshi, *Med Doctor*
EMP: 177
SALES: 20MM **Privately Held**
SIC: 8011 Orthopedic physician

(P-19210)
NATIVE AMERICAN HEALTH CTR INC (PA)
2950 International Blvd, Oakland (94601-2228)
PHONE....................510 535-4400
Martin Waukazoo, *CEO*
Ana M Oconnor, *COO*
Alan Wong, *CFO*
Dr Joseph Marquis, *Chief Mktg Ofcr*
Karen Harrison, *Office Mgr*

EMP: 80 EST: 1971
SQ FT: 16,000
SALES: 22.3MM **Privately Held**
WEB: www.nativehealth.org
SIC: 8011 8021 8093 Clinic, operated by physicians; dentists' office; mental health clinic, outpatient

(P-19211)
NEIGHBORHOOD HEALTHCARE (PA)
425 N Date St Ste 203, Escondido (92025-3413)
PHONE....................760 520-8372
Tracy Ream, *CEO*
Johnny Watson, *President*
Amparo Mahler, *COO*
Lisa Daigle, *CFO*
Dr James Schultz, *Chief Mktg Ofcr*
EMP: 50
SQ FT: 17,000
SALES: 67.7MM **Privately Held**
SIC: 8011 Clinic, operated by physicians

(P-19212)
NEIGHBORHOOD HEALTHCARE
855 E Madison Ave, El Cajon (92020-3819)
PHONE....................619 440-2751
Alex Nunez, *Director*
Nishwan Jibri, *Family Practiti*
EMP: 100
SQ FT: 9,198
SALES (corp-wide): 57.9MM **Privately Held**
SIC: 8011 General & family practice, physician/surgeon
PA: Neighborhood Healthcare
425 N Date St Ste 203
Escondido CA 92025
760 520-8372

(P-19213)
NEIGHBORHOOD HEALTHCARE
460 N Elm St, Escondido (92025-3002)
PHONE....................760 737-2000
Gail Thomsky, *Manager*
EMP: 88
SQ FT: 9,288
SALES (corp-wide): 57.9MM **Privately Held**
SIC: 8011 Clinic, operated by physicians
PA: Neighborhood Healthcare
425 N Date St Ste 203
Escondido CA 92025
760 520-8372

(P-19214)
NEONATAL MEDICAL ASSOC INC
1022 E Tehachapi Dr, Long Beach (90807-2452)
PHONE....................562 933-8100
Jose M Perez MD, *President*
EMP: 267
SALES (est): 2.7MM **Publicly Held**
SIC: 8011 Medical centers
PA: Mednax, Inc.
1301 Concord Ter
Sunrise FL 33323

(P-19215)
NEW PORT ORTHOPEDIC INSTITUTE
19582 Beach Blvd Ste 118, Huntington Beach (92648-2996)
PHONE....................949 722-5071
Alan Beyer MD, *Principal*
EMP: 60
SALES (est): 4.1MM **Privately Held**
SIC: 8011 Orthopedic physician

(P-19216)
NEWPORT BEACH ORTHOPEDIC INST
22 Corporate Plaza Dr, Newport Beach (92660-7985)
P.O. Box 2597 (92659-1597)
PHONE....................949 722-7038
Alan Beyer MD, *Owner*
EMP: 79
SALES (est): 4.6MM **Privately Held**
SIC: 8011 Orthopedic physician

P
R
O
D
U
C
T
S
&
S
V
C
S

(P-19217)
NEWPORT BEACH SURGERY CTR LLC
361 Hospital Rd Ste 124, Newport Beach (92663-3521)
PHONE..........................949 631-0988
John McNutt, *Managing Dir*
Madonna Molinari, *Exec VP*
Bruce Albert,
Robert Anderson,
Perter Broekelschen, *Mng Member*
EMP: 120
SQ FT: 10,000
SALES (est): 14.5MM **Privately Held**
WEB: www.nbbrewco.com
SIC: 8011 Surgeon

(P-19218)
NEWPORT FMLY MDCNE/A MED GROUP
Also Called: Campion, Catherine A MD
520 Superior Ave, Newport Beach (92663-3637)
PHONE..........................949 644-1025
Maclyn Somers MD, *Partner*
Catherine A Campion MD, *Partner*
Sheryl L Long MD, *Partner*
William R Somers MD, *Partner*
Benjamin B Wright MD, *Partner*
EMP: 65
SQ FT: 9,000
SALES (est): 5.8MM **Privately Held**
WEB: www.newportfamilymedicine.com
SIC: 8011 General & family practice, physician/surgeon

(P-19219)
NEWPORT HARBOR RADIOLOGY ASSOC
Also Called: Newport Imaging Center
360 San Miguel Dr # 105106, Newport Beach (92660-7853)
PHONE..........................949 721-8191
Hurwitz Robert, *Owner*
EMP: 61
SALES (est): 2.2MM **Privately Held**
SIC: 8011 Radiologist

(P-19220)
NORTH BAY EYE ASSOC A MED CORP
Also Called: North Bay Eye Assoc Med Group
50 Professional Center Dr # 210, Rohnert Park (94928-2173)
PHONE..........................707 206-0849
Christian Kim, *Principal*
Michele Clites, *Human Res Mgr*
EMP: 65
SALES (est): 4.5MM **Privately Held**
SIC: 8011 Ophthalmologist

(P-19221)
NORTH COAST SURGERY CENTER
3903 Waring Rd, Oceanside (92056-4405)
PHONE..........................760 940-0997
Dr Bruce Hochman, *Managing Prtnr*
EMP: 79
SQ FT: 11,000
SALES (est): 5.5MM **Privately Held**
SIC: 8011 Surgeon

(P-19222)
NORTH COUNTY HEALTH PRJ INC (PA)
Also Called: NORTH COUNTY SERVICES
150 Valpreda Rd Frnt, San Marcos (92069-2944)
PHONE..........................760 736-6755
Irma Cota, *CEO*
Sheila Brown, *Vice Chairman*
Kathy Martinez, *CFO*
Tracy Elmer, *Officer*
Deizel Sarte, *Officer*
EMP: 221 **EST:** 1973
SQ FT: 69,880
SALES: 77.2MM **Privately Held**
SIC: 8011 Clinic, operated by physicians

(P-19223)
NORTH COUNTY OB-GYN MED GROUP
9850 Genesee Ave Ste 600, La Jolla (92037-1207)
PHONE..........................858 453-0753
Allan Silver, *CEO*
EMP: 50
SQ FT: 2,000
SALES (est): 2.1MM **Privately Held**
WEB: www.ncogmedical.com
SIC: 8011 Gynecologist; obstetrician; specialized medical practitioners, except internal

(P-19224)
NORTH STATE RADIOLOGY
Also Called: North State Imaging
1702 Esplanade, Chico (95926-3315)
PHONE..........................530 898-0504
Scot Woolley, *CEO*
Don Hubbard, *CFO*
Chris Jones, *Info Tech Mgr*
Sara Warner, *Human Res Mgr*
EMP: 50
SALES (est): 13.6MM **Privately Held**
SIC: 8011 Radiologist

(P-19225)
NORTHCOUNTRY CLINIC
Also Called: Dickinson, Diane MD
785 18th St, Arcata (95521-5683)
PHONE..........................707 822-2481
Herrmann Spetzler, *Administration*
Rick Davis, *Info Tech Mgr*
Sheyenne Spetzler, *Director*
Tammy Flint, *Manager*
EMP: 55
SQ FT: 10,000
SALES (est): 3.3MM **Privately Held**
WEB: www.northcoastclinics.org
SIC: 8011 Clinic, operated by physicians

(P-19226)
NORTHEAST COMMUNITY CLINIC
1414 S Grand Ave Ste 380, Los Angeles (90015-3072)
PHONE..........................323 373-9400
Emilio Garza, *Principal*
EMP: 76
SALES (corp-wide): 28MM **Privately Held**
WEB: www.lausd.k12.ca.us
SIC: 8011 Offices & clinics of medical doctors
PA: Northeast Community Clinic
2550 W Main St Ste 301
Alhambra CA 91801
626 457-6900

(P-19227)
NORTHEAST VALLEY HEALTH CORP
Also Called: San Fernando Health Center
1600 San Fernando Rd, San Fernando (91340-3115)
PHONE..........................818 365-8086
Beverly Jenkins, *Manager*
Joy Ahrens, *Director*
EMP: 85
SALES (corp-wide): 89.4MM **Privately Held**
SIC: 8011 Clinic, operated by physicians
PA: Northeast Valley Health Corp
1172 N Maclay Ave
San Fernando CA 91340
818 898-1388

(P-19228)
NORTHEAST VALLEY HEALTH CORP
12756 Van Nuys Blvd, Pacoima (91331-1696)
PHONE..........................818 896-0531
Kathreen Dayanim, *Manager*
David McIntosh, *Family Practiti*
EMP: 100
SQ FT: 11,645
SALES (corp-wide): 89.4MM **Privately Held**
SIC: 8011 8071 Clinic, operated by physicians; medical laboratories

PA: Northeast Valley Health Corp
1172 N Maclay Ave
San Fernando CA 91340
818 898-1388

(P-19229)
NORTHEASTERN RUR HLTH CLINICS (PA)
Also Called: Nrhc
1850 Spring Ridge Dr, Susanville (96130-6100)
PHONE..........................530 251-5000
Phil Nowak, *CEO*
Daniel Kazakos, *CFO*
Richard Hrezo, *Treasurer*
Pamela Robbins, *Admin Sec*
Steven E Braatz, *Med Doctor*
EMP: 65 **EST:** 1977
SQ FT: 27,000
SALES: 12.2MM **Privately Held**
WEB: www.northeasternhealth.org
SIC: 8011 Clinic, operated by physicians

(P-19230)
NORTHWEST MEDICAL GROUP INC
Also Called: Good Neighbor Pharmacy
7355 N Palm Ave Ste 100, Fresno (93711-5770)
PHONE..........................559 271-6302
Cecil Bullard MD, *President*
Diane Hubbard, *Shareholder*
Vivian Hernandez MD, *Admin Sec*
Lisa Jelinek, *Administration*
EMP: 75
SQ FT: 5,000
SALES (est): 7.1MM **Privately Held**
SIC: 8011 5912 Pediatrician; drug stores

(P-19231)
NORTHWEST PHYSICIANS MED GROUP
Also Called: Northwest Medical Pharmacy
7355 N Palm Ave Ste 100, Fresno (93711-5770)
PHONE..........................559 271-6370
David A Wilcox, *Branch Mgr*
EMP: 83
SALES (corp-wide): 4.3MM **Privately Held**
SIC: 8011 Physicians' office, including specialists
PA: Northwest Physicians Medical Group Inc
7355 N Palm Ave Ste 100
Fresno CA 93711
559 271-6300

(P-19232)
NVISION LASER EYE CENTERS INC (PA)
3155d Sedona Ct 100, Ontario (91764)
PHONE..........................909 605-1975
Todd Cooper, *CEO*
Christy Keffeler, *Exec Dir*
EMP: 53 **EST:** 2010
SALES (est): 11.1MM **Privately Held**
SIC: 8011 Ophthalmologist

(P-19233)
NVISION LASER EYE CENTERS INC
711 Van Ness Ave Ste 320, San Francisco (94102-3285)
PHONE..........................415 421-8667
EMP: 65
SALES (corp-wide): 4MM **Privately Held**
SIC: 8011 Ophthalmologist
PA: Nvision Laser Eye Centers Inc.
75 Enterprise Ste 200
Aliso Viejo CA 92656
877 455-9942

(P-19234)
OAK GROVE INST FOUNDATION INC (PA)
Also Called: Oak Grove Center
24275 Jefferson Ave, Murrieta (92562-7285)
PHONE..........................951 677-5599
Tamara L Wilson, *CEO*
Barry Soper, *Ch of Bd*
Fe Santiago, *CFO*
EMP: 388
SQ FT: 39,000
SALES: 19MM **Privately Held**
WEB: www.oak-grove.org
SIC: 8011 8211 8361 Psychiatric clinic; specialty education; residential care

(P-19235)
OAKS DIAGNOSTICS INC (PA)
Also Called: California Imaging Nework
6310 San Vicente Blvd, Los Angeles (90048-5426)
P.O. Box 5355, Beverly Hills (90209-5355)
PHONE..........................310 855-0035
Ronald Grusd MD, *CEO*
EMP: 60
SQ FT: 9,000
SALES (est): 6.8MM **Privately Held**
WEB: www.milleniumimaging.com
SIC: 8011 Radiologist

(P-19236)
OCEAN PARK HEALTH CENTER
Also Called: Community Health Netwrk of San
1351 24th Ave, San Francisco (94122-1616)
PHONE..........................415 753-8100
Lisa Golden, *Director*
EMP: 50
SALES (est): 3MM **Privately Held**
SIC: 8011 Offices & clinics of medical doctors

(P-19237)
OCONNOR IMAGING MED GROUP INC
Also Called: Oconnor Hospital
2105 Forest Ave, San Jose (95128-1425)
PHONE..........................408 947-2992
Charles Griffin MD, *President*
Dr Richard Turner, *Vice Pres*
Jeffrey Anderson, *Surgeon*
Mark Penner, *Med Doctor*
EMP: 60
SQ FT: 2,000
SALES (est): 2.8MM **Privately Held**
SIC: 8011 Radiologist

(P-19238)
OLE HEALTH
1100 Trancas St Ste 300, NAPA (94558-2921)
PHONE..........................707 254-1770
Tanir AMI, *CEO*
Molly Nelson, *CFO*
EMP: 50
SALES (est): 23.5MM **Privately Held**
WEB: www.clinicole.org
SIC: 8011 General & family practice, physician/surgeon

(P-19239)
OLIVE VIEW-UCLA MEDICAL CENTER (PA)
Also Called: Valley Care Olive View Med Ctr
14445 Olive View Dr, Sylmar (91342-1438)
PHONE..........................818 364-1555
Carolyn Rhee, *CEO*
Chisa Aoyama, *Pathologist*
Janice Chew,
EMP: 87
SALES: 357.8MM **Privately Held**
WEB: www.uclasfvp.org
SIC: 8011 Medical centers

(P-19240)
OMNI FAMILY HEALTH (PA)
Also Called: Community Health Center
4900 California Ave 400b, Bakersfield (93309-7081)
P.O. Box 1060, Shafter (93263-1060)
PHONE..........................661 459-1900
Francisco L Castillon, *CEO*
Susan Watkins, *Vice Chairman*
Novira Irawan, *CFO*
David Brust, *Treasurer*
Aurora Cooper, *Officer*
EMP: 80
SQ FT: 14,000
SALES: 66.4MM **Privately Held**
SIC: 8011 Clinic, operated by physicians

(P-19241)
OMNI WOMENS HLTH MED GROUP INC
2550 Merced St, Fresno (93721-1812)
PHONE..................................559 441-4271
Robert Frediani, *Branch Mgr*
EMP: 69
SALES (corp-wide): 12.5MM **Privately Held**
SIC: 8011 Gynecologist
PA: Omni Women's Health Medical Group, Inc.
3812 N 1st St
Fresno CA 93726
559 495-3120

(P-19242)
ON LOK INC
1333 Bush St, San Francisco (94109-5691)
PHONE..................................415 292-8888
Grace Li, *CEO*
EMP: 99
SALES: 7.7MM **Privately Held**
SIC: 8011 Offices & clinics of medical doctors

(P-19243)
ONE MEDICAL GROUP INC (PA)
1 Embarcadero Ctr Ste 500, San Francisco (94111-3610)
PHONE..................................415 578-3100
Thomas H Lee, *CEO*
Michael Sarmiento, *Vice Pres*
Briana Marshall, *District Mgr*
Laura McCaffrey, *District Mgr*
Allan Moss, *Office Mgr*
EMP: 94
SALES (est): 90.6MM **Privately Held**
SIC: 8011 Physical medicine, physician/surgeon

(P-19244)
ONE MEDICAL GROUP INC
3885 24th St, San Francisco (94114-3840)
PHONE..................................415 529-4522
Elizabeth Maier, *Administration*
Russell Alpert, *Family Practiti*
Sayanta Akkad, *Internal Med*
Joanne Dames, *Med Doctor*
EMP: 59
SALES (corp-wide): 90.6MM **Privately Held**
SIC: 8011 Offices & clinics of medical doctors
PA: One Medical Group, Inc.
1 Embarcadero Ctr Ste 500
San Francisco CA 94111
415 578-3100

(P-19245)
ONE MEDICAL GROUP INC
1 Embarcadero Ctr Ste 500, San Francisco (94111-3610)
PHONE..................................212 530-2288
Thomas Lee, *Branch Mgr*
Maribel Cano, *Admin Asst*
Chris Massoud, *Technology*
Morehead Christine, *Human Res Dir*
Karis N Cho, *Family Practiti*
EMP: 68
SALES (corp-wide): 90.6MM **Privately Held**
SIC: 8011 Primary care medical clinic
PA: One Medical Group, Inc.
1 Embarcadero Ctr Ste 500
San Francisco CA 94111
415 578-3100

(P-19246)
ONRAD INC
Also Called: Onrad Medical Group
1770 Iowa Ave Ste 280, Riverside (92507-7401)
PHONE..................................800 848-5876
David Engert, *President*
Samuel Salen, *Ch of Bd*
Joseph Artino, *CFO*
Scott Castle, *CFO*
Lisa Maulit, *Executive*
EMP: 79
SQ FT: 1,500
SALES: 9MM **Privately Held**
SIC: 8011 Radiologist

(P-19247)
OPERATION SAMAHAN INC
Also Called: Camino Ruiz Suite 235
10737 Camino Ruiz Ste 235, San Diego (92126-2375)
PHONE..................................619 477-4451
Dirk Virbel, *CEO*
EMP: 128
SALES (corp-wide): 13.9MM **Privately Held**
SIC: 8011 8021 Clinic, operated by physicians; offices & clinics of dentists
PA: Operation Samahan, Inc.
1428 Highland Ave
National City CA 91950
619 477-4451

(P-19248)
ORANGE COAST WNS MED GROUP INC (PA)
Also Called: Women Obsttrcts Gynocology Ctr
24411 Health Center Dr # 200, Laguna Hills (92653-3651)
PHONE..................................949 829-5500
Susan Mendelsohn, *CEO*
Noreen Norris-Walsh MD, *Shareholder*
Barrie S May MD, *President*
Mark Vincher, *CFO*
Catherine Han, *Vice Pres*
EMP: 100
SQ FT: 16,000
SALES (est): 17.5MM **Privately Held**
WEB: www.ocwmg.com
SIC: 8011 Pediatrician; gynecologist

(P-19249)
OROHEALTH CORPORATION
Also Called: Oroville Hospital
900 Oro Dam Blvd E, Oroville (95965-5832)
PHONE..................................530 534-9183
Mark Heinrich, *Director*
EMP: 1127
SALES (corp-wide): 3.3MM **Privately Held**
WEB: www.orovillehospital.com
SIC: 8011 8062 Internal medicine, physician/surgeon; general medical & surgical hospitals
PA: Orohealth Corporation
2767 Olive Hwy
Oroville CA 95966
530 533-8500

(P-19250)
OROVILLE INTERNAL MEDS GROUP
Also Called: Roy C Shannon MD
2721 Olive Hwy Ste 12, Oroville (95966-6115)
PHONE..................................530 538-3171
Roy Shannon, *President*
EMP: 50
SQ FT: 3,600
SALES (est): 2.9MM **Privately Held**
SIC: 8011 Internal medicine, physician/surgeon; physicians' office, including specialists

(P-19251)
ORTHOPEDIC CONSULTANTS (PA)
16311 Ventura Blvd # 800, Encino (91436-2140)
PHONE..................................818 788-7343
Lester Cohn, *President*
EMP: 50
SQ FT: 8,300
SALES (est): 3.9MM **Privately Held**
WEB: www.ocmgortho.com
SIC: 8011 Orthopedic physician

(P-19252)
OUTPATNT EYE SRGRY CTR OF DSRT
Also Called: Milauskas Eye Institute
72057 Dinah Shore Dr D1, Rancho Mirage (92270-1791)
PHONE..................................760 340-3937
Albert T Milauskas, *President*
EMP: 50
SALES (est): 1.1MM **Privately Held**
SIC: 8011 Ambulatory surgical center; ophthalmologist

(P-19253)
PACIFIC EYE ASSOCIATED INC
2100 Webster St Ste 214, San Francisco (94115-2375)
PHONE..................................415 923-3007
Wayne E Fung MD, *President*
Arthur W Allen Jr, *Vice Pres*
Bee Veeraseati, *General Mgr*
Roger E Atkins, *Ophthalmology*
Laura Inger,
EMP: 60
SQ FT: 8,000
SALES (est): 8.2MM **Privately Held**
SIC: 8011 Ophthalmologist

(P-19254)
PACIFIC INPTIENT MED GROUP INC
9 Jeffrey Ct, Novato (94945-1739)
P.O. Box 573 (94948-0573)
PHONE..................................415 485-8824
Fabiola Cobarrubias, *President*
Christopher M Valentino, *COO*
EMP: 69
SALES (est): 4.5MM **Privately Held**
SIC: 8011 Offices & clinics of medical doctors

(P-19255)
PACIFIC SHORES MED GROUP INC (PA)
1043 Elm Ave Ste 104, Long Beach (90813-3244)
PHONE..................................562 590-0345
Simon Tchekmedyian, *CEO*
Jonathan Rigutto, *District Mgr*
Sarmen Sarkissian, *Internal Med*
Marcy Lebeau, *Med Doctor*
Mark Ngo, *Med Doctor*
EMP: 60
SQ FT: 3,300
SALES (est): 18.4MM **Privately Held**
WEB: www.pacshoresoncology.com
SIC: 8011 Medical centers; oncologist

(P-19256)
PACKARD CHILDRENS HLTH ALIANCE
Also Called: Pcha
725 Welch Rd, Palo Alto (94304-1601)
PHONE..................................650 497-8000
Kim Robert, *CEO*
Lisa Holbrook, *COO*
Rick Vance, *COO*
Whitney Daniels, *Psychiatry*
Anh-Thu Lewis, *Nurse Practr*
EMP: 100
SALES: 81.8MM
SALES (corp-wide): 1.6B **Privately Held**
SIC: 8011 Pediatrician; obstetrician; cardiologist & cardio-vascular specialist; gynecologist
PA: Lucile Salter Packard Children's Hospital At Stanford
725 Welch Rd
Palo Alto CA 94304
650 497-8000

(P-19257)
PACKARD MEDICAL GROUP INC
770 Welch Rd, Palo Alto (94304-1511)
PHONE..................................650 724-3637
Tika Martin, *Human Resources*
EMP: 85
SALES (est): 3.1MM **Privately Held**
SIC: 8011 Obstetrician; pediatrician

(P-19258)
PAIN MANAGEMENT SPECIALISTS PC
1551 Bishop St Ste 230, San Luis Obispo (93401-4661)
PHONE..................................805 544-7246
Borris Pilch MD, *President*
EMP: 50
SALES (est): 950.9K **Privately Held**
SIC: 8011 Specialized medical practitioners, except internal

(P-19259)
PALMDALE CENTER FOR PAIN MGT
819 Auto Center Dr, Palmdale (93551-4599)
PHONE..................................661 267-6876
Shahin Sadik, *Owner*
EMP: 50
SALES (est): 1.4MM **Privately Held**
SIC: 8011 Anesthesiologist

(P-19260)
PALO ALTO MEDICAL CLINIC
795 El Camino Real, Palo Alto (94301-2302)
PHONE..................................650 321-4121
John Cooper, *Principal*
David Yu, *Technology*
Warren King, *Surgeon*
David S Leibowitz, *Hematology*
Cara Barone, *Pediatrics*
EMP: 50
SALES (est): 5.5MM **Privately Held**
SIC: 8011 Primary care medical clinic

(P-19261)
PALO ALTO MEDICAL FOUNDATION (HQ)
Also Called: Palo Alto Clinic
795 El Camino Real, Palo Alto (94301-2302)
P.O. Box 254738, Sacramento (95865-4738)
PHONE..................................650 321-4121
Jeff Gerard, *CEO*
Mara Hook, *Vice Pres*
Linda Harris, *Principal*
Marina Tostado, *Exec Dir*
Alan Worley, *Technician*
EMP: 700
SQ FT: 200,000
SALES (est): 156.5MM
SALES (corp-wide): 12.7B **Privately Held**
SIC: 8011 Clinic, operated by physicians
PA: Sutter Health
2200 River Plaza Dr
Sacramento CA 95833
916 733-8800

(P-19262)
PALO ALTO MEDICAL FOUNDATION
Also Called: Los Altos Center
370 Distel Cir, Los Altos (94022-1404)
PHONE..................................650 254-5200
Sandy Greenberg, *Manager*
A Sastri H Sukhdeo, *Obstetrician*
Julia Martino, *Pediatrics*
Meagan Jennings, *Med Doctor*
Julia Marx, *Med Doctor*
EMP: 60
SQ FT: 32,059
SALES (corp-wide): 12.7B **Privately Held**
SIC: 8011 Pediatrician
HQ: Palo Alto Medical Foundation For Health Care, Research And Education (Inc)
795 El Camino Real
Palo Alto CA 94301
650 321-4121

(P-19263)
PALO ALTO MEDICAL FOUNDATION
Also Called: Steven Rubinstein MD
201 Old San Francisco Rd, Sunnyvale (94086-6385)
P.O. Box 3496 (94088-3496)
PHONE..................................408 730-4390
Kam Yung, *Branch Mgr*
Inderjeet Uppal, *Family Practiti*
Grace Guo, *Internal Med*
Christina Vu, *Pediatrics*
EMP: 62
SALES (corp-wide): 12.7B **Privately Held**
SIC: 8011 Allergist
HQ: Palo Alto Medical Foundation For Health Care, Research And Education (Inc)
795 El Camino Real
Palo Alto CA 94301
650 321-4121

(P-19264)
PALO ALTO MEDICAL FOUNDATION
1085 W El Camino Real, Sunnyvale (94087-1030)
PHONE....................408 524-5900
Tom Frick, *President*
EMP: 62
SALES (corp-wide): 12.7B **Privately Held**
SIC: 8011 Offices & clinics of medical doctors
HQ: Palo Alto Medical Foundation For Health Care, Research And Education (Inc)
795 El Camino Real
Palo Alto CA 94301
650 321-4121

(P-19265)
PAVILION SURGERY CENTER LLC
1140 W La Veta Ave, Orange (92868-4225)
PHONE....................714 744-8850
David Yomtoob, *Ch of Bd*
EMP: 70
SQ FT: 49,000
SALES (est): 72K **Privately Held**
SIC: 8011 Surgeon

(P-19266)
PEACH TREE HEALTHCARE
5730 Packard Ave Ste 500, Marysville (95901-7119)
PHONE....................530 749-3242
Thomas Walther, *President*
EMP: 97
SALES: 11.8MM **Privately Held**
SIC: 8011 Clinic, operated by physicians

(P-19267)
PEACHWOOD MEDICAL GROUP CLOVIS
275 W Herndon Ave, Clovis (93612-0204)
PHONE....................559 324-6200
Lee Copeland MD, *President*
Jeffrey Hubbard, *Vice Pres*
Sue Marino, *Administration*
Jena Torres, *Recruiter*
EMP: 70
SQ FT: 33,595
SALES (est): 13.7MM **Privately Held**
SIC: 8011 Primary care medical clinic

(P-19268)
PENINSULA WOMENS HEALTH (PA)
1828 El Camino Real Ste 8, Burlingame (94010-3103)
PHONE....................650 692-3818
Andrew Jurow MD, *President*
EMP: 50 **EST:** 1952
SQ FT: 2,800
SALES (est): 4.4MM **Privately Held**
WEB: www.peninsulawomenshealth.com
SIC: 8011 Gynecologist; obstetrician

(P-19269)
PEOPLE CREATING SUCCESS INC
380 Arneill Rd, Camarillo (93010-6406)
PHONE....................805 644-9480
Marie McManus, *Branch Mgr*
EMP: 113
SALES (corp-wide): 14.8MM **Privately Held**
SIC: 8011 Offices & clinics of medical doctors
PA: People Creating Success, Inc.
2585 Teller Rd
Newbury Park CA 91320
805 375-9222

(P-19270)
PERMANENTE MEDICAL GROUP INC
7300 N Fresno St, Fresno (93720-2941)
PHONE....................559 448-4500
Irene A Heetebry, *Principal*
EMP: 63
SALES (corp-wide): 76.5B **Privately Held**
SIC: 8011 Offices & clinics of medical doctors

HQ: The Permanente Medical Group Inc
1950 Franklin St Fl 18th
Oakland CA 94612
866 858-2226

(P-19271)
PERMANENTE MEDICAL GROUP INC
6600 Bruceville Rd, Sacramento (95823-4671)
PHONE....................916 688-2055
Kevin L Smith, *Branch Mgr*
EMP: 58
SALES (corp-wide): 76.5B **Privately Held**
WEB: www.permanente.net
SIC: 8011 Gynecologist
HQ: The Permanente Medical Group Inc
1950 Franklin St Fl 18th
Oakland CA 94612
866 858-2226

(P-19272)
PERMANENTE MEDICAL GROUP INC
901 El Camino Real, San Bruno (94066-3009)
PHONE....................650 742-2100
Cheryl Halcovich, *Manager*
EMP: 58
SALES (corp-wide): 76.5B **Privately Held**
SIC: 8011 Offices & clinics of medical doctors
HQ: The Permanente Medical Group Inc
1950 Franklin St Fl 18th
Oakland CA 94612
866 858-2226

(P-19273)
PERMANENTE MEDICAL GROUP INC
3558 Round Barn Blvd, Santa Rosa (95403-1780)
PHONE....................707 393-4000
Pat Henson, *Principal*
Robert Martinez, *Family Practiti*
Jean Lim, *Dermatology*
Christine Kaiser, *Internal Med*
Christopher C Gaut, *Emerg Med Spec*
EMP: 58
SALES (corp-wide): 76.5B **Privately Held**
SIC: 8011 Medical centers
HQ: The Permanente Medical Group Inc
1950 Franklin St Fl 18th
Oakland CA 94612
866 858-2226

(P-19274)
PERMANENTE MEDICAL GROUP INC
275 Hospital Pkwy Ste 470, San Jose (95119-1138)
PHONE....................408 972-6883
Maurice Alfaro, *Director*
EMP: 78
SALES (corp-wide): 76.5B **Privately Held**
SIC: 8011 Offices & clinics of medical doctors
HQ: The Permanente Medical Group Inc
1950 Franklin St Fl 18th
Oakland CA 94612
866 858-2226

(P-19275)
PERMANENTE MEDICAL GROUP INC
200 Muir Rd, Martinez (94553-4614)
PHONE....................925 372-1000
EMP: 69
SALES (corp-wide): 76.5B **Privately Held**
SIC: 8011 Offices & clinics of medical doctors
HQ: The Permanente Medical Group Inc
1950 Franklin St Fl 18th
Oakland CA 94612
866 858-2226

(P-19276)
PERMANENTE MEDICAL GROUP INC
3779 Piedmont Ave, Oakland (94611-5347)
PHONE....................510 752-1000
Ellen P Brennan, *Branch Mgr*
Ravinder S Bains, *Med Doctor*
EMP: 58

SALES (corp-wide): 76.5B **Privately Held**
SIC: 8011 Medical centers
HQ: The Permanente Medical Group Inc
1950 Franklin St Fl 18th
Oakland CA 94612
866 858-2226

(P-19277)
PERMANENTE MEDICAL GROUP INC
39400 Paseo Padre Pkwy, Fremont (94538-2310)
PHONE....................510 248-3000
EMP: 78
SALES (corp-wide): 76.5B **Privately Held**
SIC: 8011 Offices & clinics of medical doctors
HQ: The Permanente Medical Group Inc
1950 Franklin St Fl 18th
Oakland CA 94612
866 858-2226

(P-19278)
PERMANENTE MEDICAL GROUP INC
770 E Calaveras Blvd, Milpitas (95035-5491)
PHONE....................408 945-2900
Bindu Israni, *Branch Mgr*
EMP: 78
SALES (corp-wide): 76.5B **Privately Held**
SIC: 8011 Medical centers
HQ: The Permanente Medical Group Inc
1950 Franklin St Fl 18th
Oakland CA 94612
866 858-2226

(P-19279)
PERMANENTE MEDICAL GROUP INC
4501 Sand Creek Rd, Antioch (94531-8687)
PHONE....................925 813-6149
Kim Daily, *Branch Mgr*
EMP: 78
SALES (corp-wide): 76.5B **Privately Held**
SIC: 8011 Medical centers
HQ: The Permanente Medical Group Inc
1950 Franklin St Fl 18th
Oakland CA 94612
866 858-2226

(P-19280)
PERMANENTE MEDICAL GROUP INC
1150 Veterans Blvd, Redwood City (94063-2037)
PHONE....................650 299-2000
Arlene McCarthy, *Principal*
Janis Turner, *Project Mgr*
Malika N Kheraj, *Infectious Dis*
Alvin Mok, *Orthopedist*
Joanne Marie Nino, *Obstetrician*
EMP: 78
SALES (corp-wide): 76.5B **Privately Held**
SIC: 8011 Medical centers
HQ: The Permanente Medical Group Inc
1950 Franklin St Fl 18th
Oakland CA 94612
866 858-2226

(P-19281)
PERMANENTE MEDICAL GROUP INC
910 Marshall St, Redwood City (94063-2033)
PHONE....................650 299-2015
Christina Apostolakos, *Director*
Kristine Hendrickson, *Med Doctor*
EMP: 59
SALES (corp-wide): 76.5B **Privately Held**
SIC: 8011 Medical centers
HQ: The Permanente Medical Group Inc
1950 Franklin St Fl 18th
Oakland CA 94612
866 858-2226

(P-19282)
PERMANENTE MEDICAL GROUP INC
914 Marina Way S, Richmond (94804-3739)
PHONE....................510 231-5406
C J Bhalla, *Vice Pres*
EMP: 70

SALES (corp-wide): 76.5B **Privately Held**
SIC: 8011 Medical centers
HQ: The Permanente Medical Group Inc
1950 Franklin St Fl 18th
Oakland CA 94612
866 858-2226

(P-19283)
PERMANENTE MEDICAL GROUP INC
2500 Merced St, San Leandro (94577-4201)
PHONE....................510 454-1000
Bryan Waiss, *Obstetrician*
Rik B Smith, *Internal Med*
Peter S Kim, *Nephrology*
Harry J Duh, *Pediatrics*
Aruna Koduri, *Pediatrics*
EMP: 63
SALES (corp-wide): 76.5B **Privately Held**
SIC: 8011 Offices & clinics of medical doctors
HQ: The Permanente Medical Group Inc
1950 Franklin St Fl 18th
Oakland CA 94612
866 858-2226

(P-19284)
PERMANENTE MEDICAL GROUP INC
99 Montecillo Rd, San Rafael (94903-3308)
PHONE....................415 444-2000
EMP: 63
SALES (corp-wide): 76.5B **Privately Held**
SIC: 8011 Medical centers
HQ: The Permanente Medical Group Inc
1950 Franklin St Fl 18th
Oakland CA 94612
866 858-2226

(P-19285)
PERMANENTE MEDICAL GROUP INC
320 Lennon Ln, Walnut Creek (94598-2419)
PHONE....................925 906-2000
Lynn Arsenault, *Med Doctor*
Thomas Connolly, *Med Doctor*
EMP: 63
SALES (corp-wide): 76.5B **Privately Held**
SIC: 8011 Medical centers
HQ: The Permanente Medical Group Inc
1950 Franklin St Fl 18th
Oakland CA 94612
866 858-2226

(P-19286)
PERMANENTE MEDICAL GROUP INC
100 Rowland Way Ste 125, Novato (94945-5012)
PHONE....................415 209-2444
EMP: 69
SALES (corp-wide): 76.5B **Privately Held**
SIC: 8011 Medical centers
HQ: The Permanente Medical Group Inc
1950 Franklin St Fl 18th
Oakland CA 94612
866 858-2226

(P-19287)
PERMANENTE MEDICAL GROUP INC
97 San Marin Dr, Novato (94945-1100)
PHONE....................415 899-7400
Willa Jefferson-Stokes, *Manager*
EMP: 100
SALES (corp-wide): 76.5B **Privately Held**
WEB: www.permanente.net
SIC: 8011 Internal medicine practitioners
HQ: The Permanente Medical Group Inc
1950 Franklin St Fl 18th
Oakland CA 94612
866 858-2226

(P-19288)
PERMANENTE MEDICAL GROUP INC
1600 Eureka Rd, Roseville (95661-3027)
PHONE....................916 784-4000
Craig Green MD, *Director*
EMP: 63

SALES (corp-wide): 76.5B **Privately Held**
SIC: **8011** Offices & clinics of medical doctors
HQ: The Permanente Medical Group Inc
1950 Franklin St Fl 18th
Oakland CA 94612
866 858-2226

(P-19289)
PERMANENTE MEDICAL GROUP INC
1750 2nd St, Berkeley (94710-1705)
PHONE..................................510 559-5338
Dianne Easterwood, *General Mgr*
EMP: 100
SALES (corp-wide): 76.5B **Privately Held**
WEB: www.permanente.net
SIC: **8011** Offices & clinics of medical doctors
HQ: The Permanente Medical Group Inc
1950 Franklin St Fl 18th
Oakland CA 94612
866 858-2226

(P-19290)
PERMANENTE MEDICAL GROUP INC
3900 Lakeville Hwy, Petaluma (94954-5698)
PHONE..................................707 765-3900
Willa Jefferson-Stokes, *Manager*
EMP: 75
SALES (corp-wide): 76.5B **Privately Held**
WEB: www.permanente.net
SIC: **8011** Clinic, operated by physicians
HQ: The Permanente Medical Group Inc
1950 Franklin St Fl 18th
Oakland CA 94612
866 858-2226

(P-19291)
PERMANENTE MEDICAL GROUP INC
1305 Tommydon St, Stockton (95210-3364)
PHONE..................................209 476-2000
Jack Gillimand, *Branch Mgr*
EMP: 50
SALES (corp-wide): 76.5B **Privately Held**
SIC: **8011** Medical centers
HQ: The Permanente Medical Group Inc
1950 Franklin St Fl 18th
Oakland CA 94612
866 858-2226

(P-19292)
PERMANENTE MEDICAL GROUP INC
3000 Las Positas Rd, Livermore (94551-9627)
PHONE..................................925 243-2600
Stan Combs, *Manager*
EMP: 55
SALES (corp-wide): 76.5B **Privately Held**
WEB: www.permanente.net
SIC: **8011** Offices & clinics of medical doctors
HQ: The Permanente Medical Group Inc
1950 Franklin St Fl 18th
Oakland CA 94612
866 858-2226

(P-19293)
PERMANENTE MEDICAL GROUP INC
10725 International Dr, Rancho Cordova (95670-7967)
PHONE..................................916 631-3000
Donald Forrester, *Branch Mgr*
EMP: 130
SALES (corp-wide): 76.5B **Privately Held**
WEB: www.permanente.net
SIC: **8011** Clinic, operated by physicians
HQ: The Permanente Medical Group Inc
1950 Franklin St Fl 18th
Oakland CA 94612
866 858-2226

(P-19294)
PERMANENTE MEDICAL GROUP INC
1000 Franklin Pkwy, San Mateo (94403-1922)
PHONE..................................650 358-7000

Diane Oliver, *Med Doctor*
EMP: 69
SALES (corp-wide): 76.5B **Privately Held**
SIC: **8011** Offices & clinics of medical doctors
HQ: The Permanente Medical Group Inc
1950 Franklin St Fl 18th
Oakland CA 94612
866 858-2226

(P-19295)
PERMANENTE MEDICAL GROUP INC
1617 Broadway St, Vallejo (94590-2406)
PHONE..................................707 765-3930
Robin E Bjorger, *Branch Mgr*
Christian Lopez Reyes, *Internal Med*
EMP: 58
SALES (corp-wide): 76.5B **Privately Held**
SIC: **8011** Medical centers
HQ: The Permanente Medical Group Inc
1950 Franklin St Fl 18th
Oakland CA 94612
866 858-2226

(P-19296)
PERMANENTE MEDICAL GROUP INC
1800 Harrison St Fl 7th, Oakland (94612-3467)
PHONE..................................510 625-6262
Connie Wilson, *Branch Mgr*
Johanna Reneke, *Med Doctor*
EMP: 78
SALES (corp-wide): 76.5B **Privately Held**
SIC: **8011** Offices & clinics of medical doctors
HQ: The Permanente Medical Group Inc
1950 Franklin St Fl 18th
Oakland CA 94612
866 858-2226

(P-19297)
PERMANENTE MEDICAL GROUP INC
235 W Macarthur Blvd, Oakland (94611-5641)
PHONE..................................510 752-1190
Marta Perl, *Branch Mgr*
EMP: 58
SALES (corp-wide): 76.5B **Privately Held**
SIC: **8011** Medical centers
HQ: The Permanente Medical Group Inc
1950 Franklin St Fl 18th
Oakland CA 94612
866 858-2226

(P-19298)
PERMANENTE MEDICAL GROUP INC
7373 West Ln, Stockton (95210-3377)
PHONE..................................209 476-3737
Michael Coleman, *Principal*
EMP: 58
SALES (corp-wide): 76.5B **Privately Held**
SIC: **8011** Medical centers
HQ: The Permanente Medical Group Inc
1950 Franklin St Fl 18th
Oakland CA 94612
866 858-2226

(P-19299)
PERMANENTE MEDICAL GROUP INC
395 Hickey Blvd Fl 1, Daly City (94015-2770)
PHONE..................................650 301-5860
Jennifer Normoyle, *Branch Mgr*
Betty Lee, *Obstetrician*
Yvonne Ong, *Pediatrics*
Laura Prager, *Pediatrics*
Bertha Saucedo, *Pediatrics*
EMP: 78
SALES (corp-wide): 76.5B **Privately Held**
SIC: **8011** Offices & clinics of medical doctors
HQ: The Permanente Medical Group Inc
1950 Franklin St Fl 18th
Oakland CA 94612
866 858-2226

(P-19300)
PETALUMA HEALTH CENTER INC
1179 N Mcdowell Blvd A, Petaluma (94954-1171)
PHONE..................................707 559-7500
Kathryn Powell, *CEO*
Daymon Doss, *COO*
Jane Read, *COO*
Brian Burns, *CFO*
Carlin Chi, *Associate Dir*
EMP: 325
SALES: 42.9MM **Privately Held**
WEB: www.phealthcenter.org
SIC: **8011** Clinic, operated by physicians

(P-19301)
PETER J WOLK MD
2721 Olive Hwy, Oroville (95966-6115)
PHONE..................................530 534-6517
Peter Wolk, *Principal*
EMP: 50 EST: 2001
SALES (est): 719.3K **Privately Held**
SIC: **8011** Offices & clinics of medical doctors

(P-19302)
PIONEER MEDICAL GROUP INC
11411 Brookshire Ave # 108, Downey (90241-5008)
PHONE..................................562 862-2775
Gergie Salsky, *Manager*
EMP: 52
SALES (corp-wide): 40.1MM **Privately Held**
SIC: **8011** 5047 Medical centers; medical equipment & supplies
PA: Pioneer Medical Group, Inc.
17777 Center Court Dr N # 400
Cerritos CA 90703
562 597-4181

(P-19303)
PIONEER MEDICAL GROUP INC
16510 Bloomfield Ave, Cerritos (90703-2115)
PHONE..................................562 229-0902
Tanya Lee-Jordan, *Manager*
Marilyn Kamerer, *Human Res Mgr*
EMP: 78
SALES (corp-wide): 40.1MM **Privately Held**
SIC: **8011** Offices & clinics of medical doctors
PA: Pioneer Medical Group, Inc.
17777 Center Court Dr N # 400
Cerritos CA 90703
562 597-4181

(P-19304)
PIT RIVER TRIBAL COUNCIL
Also Called: Pit River Health Services
36977 Park Ave, Burney (96013-4067)
PHONE..................................530 335-3651
Keith Ratcliff, *Manager*
EMP: 52
SALES (corp-wide): 4.5MM **Privately Held**
WEB: www.pitrivercasino.com
SIC: **8011** 8021 Offices & clinics of medical doctors; offices & clinics of dentists
PA: Pit River Tribal Council
37960 Park Ave
Burney CA 96013
530 335-5487

(P-19305)
PLUMAS DISTRICT HOSPITAL
Also Called: Quincy Family Medicine
1045 Bucks Lake Rd, Quincy (95971-9507)
PHONE..................................530 283-0650
Dan Brandes, *Director*
Lawrence A Price, *Med Doctor*
EMP: 120
SALES (corp-wide): 20.4MM **Privately Held**
SIC: **8011** 8062 Clinic, operated by physicians; general medical & surgical hospitals
PA: Plumas District Hospital
1065 Bucks Lake Rd
Quincy CA 95971
530 283-2121

(P-19306)
PRECISION MEDICAL PRODUCTS INC
2217 Plaza Dr, Rocklin (95765-4421)
PHONE..................................573 474-9302
EMP: 99
SALES (est): 835K **Privately Held**
SIC: **8011**

(P-19307)
PREDICINE INC
3555 Arden Rd, Hayward (94545-3922)
PHONE..................................650 300-2188
Shidong Jia, *CEO*
EMP: 50 EST: 2015
SALES (est): 1.2MM **Privately Held**
SIC: **8011** Health maintenance organization

(P-19308)
PRIMARY CRITICAL CARE MEDICAL
620 N Brand Blvd Ste 500, Glendale (91203-4218)
P.O. Box 998, North Hollywood (91603-0998)
PHONE..................................818 847-9950
EMP: 164 EST: 1995
SALES (est): 1.8MM
SALES (corp-wide): 287.4MM **Privately Held**
SIC: **8011**
HQ: Team Health Holdings, Inc.
265 Brookview Centre Way
Knoxville TN 37919
865 693-1000

(P-19309)
PROFESSIONAL HEALTH TECH
Also Called: Cardio Pulmonary Services
8131 Calle Del Cielo, La Jolla (92037-3148)
PHONE..................................858 449-1599
Stanley Pappelbaum MD, *President*
Searle Turner MD, *Corp Secy*
EMP: 77 EST: 1976
SALES (est): 7MM **Privately Held**
SIC: **8011** 8399 Cardiologist & cardio-vascular specialist; health systems agency

(P-19310)
PROMED HLTH CARE ADMNISTRATORS
9302 Pttsbrgh Ave Ste 220, Rancho Cucamonga (91730)
PHONE..................................909 932-1045
Jeereedi Prasad, *President*
Brian Wederman, *COO*
EMP: 75
SALES (est): 3.3MM
SALES (corp-wide): 1.2B **Privately Held**
SIC: **8011** Offices & clinics of medical doctors
PA: Prospect Medical Holdings, Inc.
3415 S Sepulveda Blvd # 9
Los Angeles CA 90034
310 943-4500

(P-19311)
PROSPECT MEDICAL HOLDINGS INC (PA)
3415 S Sepulveda Blvd # 9, Los Angeles (90034-6060)
PHONE..................................310 943-4500
Samuel S Lee, *Ch of Bd*
Mike Heather, *CFO*
Linda Hodges, *Exec VP*
Donna Vigil, *VP Finance*
Robert Elders, *Counsel*
EMP: 96
SQ FT: 7,154
SALES (est): 1.2B **Privately Held**
WEB: www.prospectmedicalholdings.com
SIC: **8011** Health maintenance organization

(P-19312)
PROVIDENCE HEALTH SYSTEM
15031 Rinaldi St, Mission Hills (91345-1207)
PHONE..................................818 898-4530
Terry Carmondy, *Administration*
EMP: 1200

SALES (corp-wide): 15.2B **Privately Held**
SIC: **8011** Offices & clinics of medical doctors
HQ: Providence Health System-Southern California
1801 Lind Ave Sw
Renton WA 98057
425 525-3355

(P-19313)
PSYCHIATRIC CTRS AT SAN DIEGO (PA)
4542 Ruffner St Ste 200, San Diego (92111-2239)
P.O. Box 609001 (92160-9001)
PHONE............................619 528-4600
Sabah Chammas PHD, *President*
Kristi Romero, *COO*
Dr Sharon McClure, *Treasurer*
Dr Katherine Dixon, *Vice Pres*
Colleen Su, *Administration*
▲ EMP: 68
SQ FT: 2,000
SALES (est): 9.8MM **Privately Held**
WEB: www.psychiatriccenters.com
SIC: **8011** Psychiatrist

(P-19314)
PSYCHIATRIC SOLUTIONS INC
Also Called: Sierra Vista Hospital
8001 Bruceville Rd, Sacramento (95823-2329)
PHONE............................916 288-0300
Mike Zauner, *CEO*
EMP: 125
SALES (corp-wide): 10.7B **Publicly Held**
WEB: www.intermountainhospital.com
SIC: **8011** 8063 Psychiatric clinic; psychiatric hospitals
HQ: Psychiatric Solutions, Inc.
6640 Carothers Pkwy # 500
Franklin TN 37067
615 312-5700

(P-19315)
PSYCHIATRIC SOLUTIONS INC
Fremont Hospital
39001 Sundale Dr, Fremont (94538-2005)
PHONE............................510 796-1100
Toll Free:....................................888
Joan Bettencourt Newman, *Principal*
Crysta Krames, *Mktg Dir*
Perlita Dejesus, *Director*
Frances Fentzke, *Manager*
EMP: 150
SALES (corp-wide): 10.7B **Publicly Held**
WEB: www.intermountainhospital.com
SIC: **8011** 8093 8361 8069 Psychiatric clinic; specialty outpatient clinics; residential care; specialty hospitals, except psychiatric; psychiatric hospitals
HQ: Psychiatric Solutions, Inc.
6640 Carothers Pkwy # 500
Franklin TN 37067
615 312-5700

(P-19316)
PSYCHIATRIC SOLUTIONS INC
17241 Van Buren Blvd, Riverside (92504-5942)
PHONE............................951 789-4405
Joseph McCoy, *Branch Mgr*
EMP: 137
SALES (corp-wide): 10.7B **Publicly Held**
WEB: www.intermountainhospital.com
SIC: **8011** Psychiatric clinic
HQ: Psychiatric Solutions, Inc.
6640 Carothers Pkwy # 500
Franklin TN 37067
615 312-5700

(P-19317)
PUBLIC HEALTH CALIFORNIA DEPT
320 W 4th St Ste 830, Los Angeles (90013-2348)
PHONE............................213 620-6160
Donna Mc Callum, *Principal*
Ivan Zogovic, *Analyst*
EMP: 140 **Privately Held**
SIC: **8011** Clinic, operated by physicians
HQ: California Department Of Public Health
1615 Capitol Ave
Sacramento CA 95814

(P-19318)
PUBLIC HEALTH CALIFORNIA DEPT
Also Called: Wic
2400 Wible Rd Ste 14, Bakersfield (93304-4734)
PHONE............................661 835-4668
EMP: 140 **Privately Held**
SIC: **8011** Clinic, operated by physicians
HQ: California Department Of Public Health
1615 Capitol Ave
Sacramento CA 95814
-

(P-19319)
PUBLIC HEALTH CALIFORNIA DEPT
Also Called: Genetic Dsase Screening Program
850 Marina Bay Pkwy F175, Richmond (94804-6403)
PHONE............................510 412-1502
Melissa Huang, *Manager*
Kathryn Williams, *Associate*
EMP: 140 **Privately Held**
SIC: **8011** 9431 Offices & clinics of medical doctors; administration of public health programs;
HQ: California Department Of Public Health
1615 Capitol Ave
Sacramento CA 95814

(P-19320)
PULMONARY MEDICINE ASSOC
2801 K St Ste 500, Sacramento (95816-5119)
PHONE............................916 733-5040
Geneva Lee, *Manager*
EMP: 54
SALES (corp-wide): 5.5MM **Privately Held**
SIC: **8011** Clinic, operated by physicians
PA: Pulmonary Medicine Associated Medical Group
1300 Ethan Way Ste 600
Sacramento CA 95825
916 482-7623

(P-19321)
QUANTBIOME INC
1475 Veterans Blvd, Redwood City (94063-2611)
PHONE............................408 421-0315
Richard Lin, *CEO*
EMP: 50
SALES (est): 276.4K **Privately Held**
SIC: **8011** Sports medicine specialist, physician

(P-19322)
QUEENSCARE HEALTH CENTERS
Also Called: Queenscare Fmly Clinics-Eastsd
4816 E 3rd St, Los Angeles (90022-1602)
PHONE............................323 780-4510
Evelyn Moody, *Manager*
EMP: 77
SALES (corp-wide): 32.7MM **Privately Held**
SIC: **8011** Clinic, operated by physicians
PA: Queenscare Health Centers
950 S Grand Ave
Los Angeles CA 90015
323 669-4301

(P-19323)
QUEENSCARE HEALTH CENTERS
4618 Fountain Ave, Los Angeles (90029-1977)
PHONE............................323 644-6180
Guillermo Diaz, *Branch Mgr*
Cynthia Borders, *Director*
EMP: 88
SALES (corp-wide): 32.7MM **Privately Held**
SIC: **8011** Clinic, operated by physicians
PA: Queenscare Health Centers
950 S Grand Ave
Los Angeles CA 90015
323 669-4301

(P-19324)
RADIATION MEDICAL GROUP INC (PA)
9333 Genesee Ave Ste 300, San Diego (92121-2114)
P.O. Box 33865 (92163-3865)
PHONE............................619 220-4100
Sara Rosenthal MD, *President*
Donald Fuller MD, *Vice Pres*
Ronald Davis MD, *Admin Sec*
EMP: 50
SQ FT: 2,156
SALES (est): 2.4MM **Privately Held**
WEB: www.rmgmed.com
SIC: **8011** Radiologist

(P-19325)
RADIOLOGY DEPARTMENT CAL HOSP
1338 S Hope St Fl 4, Los Angeles (90015-2902)
PHONE............................213 742-5840
Phil Faircharles, *Manager*
EMP: 50 EST: 2001
SQ FT: 88,284
SALES (est): 1MM **Privately Held**
SIC: **8011** Radiologist

(P-19326)
RADIOLOGY PRTNERS HOLDINGS LLC (PA)
2330 Utah Ave Ste 200, El Segundo (90245-4817)
PHONE............................424 290-8004
Rich Whitney, *CEO*
Jay Bronner, *President*
Anthony Gabriel, *COO*
Steve Tumbarello, *CFO*
Craig Cunningham, *Vice Pres*
EMP: 55
SALES (est): 12.2MM **Privately Held**
SIC: **8011** Radiologist

(P-19327)
RADNET MANAGEMENT INC
8750 Wilshire Blvd # 100, Beverly Hills (90211-2708)
PHONE............................323 549-3000
Taryn D Dartz, *Branch Mgr*
EMP: 100 **Publicly Held**
WEB: www.radnetmgt.com
SIC: **8011** Radiologist
HQ: Radnet Management, Inc.
1510 Cotner Ave
Los Angeles CA 90025
310 445-2800

(P-19328)
REDDING FAMILY MEDICINE ASSOC
2510 Airpark Dr Ste 201, Redding (96001-2461)
PHONE............................530 244-4907
David Civalier MD, *President*
Vance Harris, *Partner*
Jack Kimple, *Partner*
Richard Maples, *Partner*
David Short, *Partner*
EMP: 50
SALES (est): 3.5MM **Privately Held**
WEB: www.reddingaquaticcenter.com
SIC: **8011** General & family practice, physician/surgeon

(P-19329)
REDWOOD COAST MEDICAL SERVICES (PA)
46900 Ocean Dr, Gualala (95445)
P.O. Box 1100 (95445-1100)
PHONE............................707 884-1721
Dianne Agee, *Director*
Don Kemp, *Vice Chairman*
Thomas A Bertolli, *Exec Dir*
EMP: 50 EST: 1977
SQ FT: 5,000
SALES: 6.8MM **Privately Held**
WEB: www.rcms-healthcare.org
SIC: **8011** Clinic, operated by physicians; primary care medical clinic

(P-19330)
REDWOOD REGIONAL MEDICAL GROUP
1165 S Dora St Bldg H, Ukiah (95482-8325)
PHONE............................707 463-3636
Jay Joseph, *Branch Mgr*
EMP: 59
SALES (corp-wide): 11.1MM **Privately Held**
SIC: **8011** General & family practice, physician/surgeon
PA: Redwood Regional Medical Group Drug Company, Llc
990 Sonoma Ave Ste 15
Santa Rosa CA 95404
707 525-4080

(P-19331)
REPRODUCTIVE SCIENCE CENTER
Also Called: Reproductive Science Ctr Bay
100 Park Pl Ste 200, San Ramon (94583-4416)
PHONE............................925 867-1800
Susan Willman, *CEO*
Donald I Galen, *Vice Pres*
Louis Weckstein, *Vice Pres*
Sheldon Josephs, *Exec Dir*
Karen Volpe, *Opers Staff*
EMP: 75
SALES (est): 5MM **Privately Held**
SIC: **8011** Physicians' office, including specialists

(P-19332)
RESPONSIBLE MED SOLUTIONS CORP
Also Called: Temecula 24 Hour Care
41715 Winchester Rd # 101, Temecula (92590-4808)
PHONE............................951 308-0024
Steven J Schutz, *President*
Paul Schutz, *Admin Sec*
Gabrielle Davis, *Manager*
EMP: 50 EST: 2007
SQ FT: 5,000
SALES: 6.5MM **Privately Held**
SIC: **8011** Freestanding emergency medical center

(P-19333)
RETINAL CONSULTANTS INC
Also Called: Vitreo Retinal Medical Group
19 Ilahee Ln, Chico (95973-7205)
PHONE............................530 899-2251
David Telander, *Branch Mgr*
Tony Tsai, *Associate*
EMP: 72
SALES (corp-wide): 11.1MM **Privately Held**
WEB: www.retinalmd.com
SIC: **8011** Ophthalmologist
PA: Retinal Consultants Inc
3939 J St Ste 106
Sacramento CA 95819
916 454-4861

(P-19334)
RETINAL CONSULTANTS INC (PA)
3939 J St Ste 106, Sacramento (95819-3631)
PHONE............................916 454-4861
Neil E Kelly MD, *President*
Arun C Patel, *Shareholder*
Robert T Wendel, *Shareholder*
James W Wells Jr, *Vice Pres*
Thomas C Salzano MD, *Admin Sec*
EMP: 50
SALES (est): 11.1MM **Privately Held**
WEB: www.retinamed.com
SIC: **8011** Ophthalmologist

(P-19335)
RIAD ADOUMIE MD
23560 Madison St Ste 110, Torrance (90505-4709)
PHONE............................310 373-6864
Riad Adoumie MD, *Owner*
EMP: 60
SALES (est): 1MM **Privately Held**
SIC: **8011** Surgeon

(P-19336)
RICHARD BURNS MD
41637 Margarita Rd # 100, Temecula
(92591-2990)
PHONE...................................951 296-9300
Richard Burns, *Principal*
EMP: 70
SALES (est) 1.6MM **Privately Held**
SIC: 8011 Physicians' office, including specialists

(P-19337)
RICHARD J METZ MD INC
2080 Century Park E # 1609, Los Angeles
(90067-2001)
PHONE...................................310 553-3189
Richard J Metz MD, *President*
EMP: 50
SALES (est) 2.3MM **Privately Held**
SIC: 8011 Internal medicine, physician/surgeon

(P-19338)
RICHARD SHAMES MD
25 Mitchell Blvd Ste 8, San Rafael
(94903-2013)
PHONE...................................415 388-0456
Elson Haas, *Director*
EMP: 63
SALES (est) 1.2MM **Privately Held**
SIC: 8011 Physicians' office, including specialists

(P-19339)
RIDGECREST REGIONAL HOSPITAL
Also Called: Specialty Center
1011 N China Lake Blvd, Ridgecrest
(93555-3130)
PHONE...................................760 499-7260
EMP: 404
SALES (corp-wide): 106.3MM **Privately Held**
SIC: 8011 Gastronomist
PA: Ridgecrest Regional Hospital
1081 N China Lake Blvd
Ridgecrest CA 93555
760 446-3551

(P-19340)
RIVERSIDE MEDICAL CLINIC INC
7117 Brockton Ave, Riverside
(92506-2658)
PHONE...................................951 683-6370
Judy Carpenter, *Manager*
EMP: 300
SALES (corp-wide): 110.9MM **Privately Held**
SIC: 8011 Clinic, operated by physicians
PA: Riverside Medical Clinic, Inc.
3660 Arlington Ave
Riverside CA 92506
951 683-6370

(P-19341)
RIVERSIDE MEDICAL CLINIC INC (PA)
Also Called: Riverside Med Clnic Ptient Ctr
3660 Arlington Ave, Riverside
(92506-3987)
PHONE...................................951 683-6370
Steven E Larson, *President*
Judy Carpenter, *President*
Susan Marinaro, *Officer*
Sondra Smith, *Vice Pres*
Ruben Muradyan, *Executive*
EMP: 300
SQ FT: 65,000
SALES (est) 110.9MM **Privately Held**
SIC: 8011 Clinic, operated by physicians

(P-19342)
RIVERSIDE-SAN BERNARDINO (PA)
11980 Mount Vernon Ave, Grand Terrace
(92313-5172)
PHONE...................................909 864-1097
Jackie Wisespirit, *President*
Bill Thomsen, *COO*
Mark Jensen, *CFO*
Brandie Miranda, *Treasurer*
Charles Castello, *Vice Pres*
EMP: 109
SQ FT: 38,000

SALES (est): 35.9MM **Privately Held**
SIC: 8011 8093 Clinic, operated by physicians; specialty outpatient clinics

(P-19343)
RIVERSIDE-SAN BERNARDINO
Also Called: Soboba Indian Health Clinic
607 Donna Way, San Jacinto (92583-5517)
PHONE...................................951 654-0803
Maria Adams, *Manager*
EMP: 60
SALES (corp-wide): 35.9MM **Privately Held**
SIC: 8011 Clinic, operated by physicians
PA: Riverside-San Bernardino County Indian Health, Inc.
11980 Mount Vernon Ave
Grand Terrace CA 92313
909 864-1097

(P-19344)
ROGER L CRUMLEY MD INC
Also Called: University Head Neck Surgeons
101 City Dr S Bldg 56 5, Orange (92868)
PHONE...................................714 456-5750
Roger L Crumley MD, *President*
EMP: 50
SALES (est) 3.2MM **Privately Held**
SIC: 8011 Surgeon; plastic surgeon

(P-19345)
ROUND VALLEY INDIAN HEALTH CTR
Hwy 162 Biggar Ln, Covelo (95428)
P.O. Box 247 (95428-0247)
PHONE...................................707 983-6182
James Russ, *Director*
Barbara Figueroa, *Technician*
EMP: 60 **EST:** 1968
SALES: 4.7MM **Privately Held**
SIC: 8011 8021 Clinic, operated by physicians; dental clinic

(P-19346)
RUSSIAN RIVER HEALTH CENTER
16319 3rd St, Guerneville (95446)
PHONE...................................707 869-2849
Mary Szecsey, *Director*
EMP: 50
SALES (est) 11.4MM **Privately Held**
SIC: 8011 8093 8322 Offices & clinics of medical doctors; mental health clinic, outpatient; individual & family services

(P-19347)
SACRAMENTO EAR NOSE & THROAT (PA)
1111 Expo Blvd Bldg 700, Sacramento
(95815-4314)
PHONE...................................916 736-3399
Ernest E Johnson MD, *President*
Kevin Mc Kennan MD, *Treasurer*
Richard G Areen MD, *Admin Sec*
Michelle Mitzel, *Assistant*
EMP: 55
SQ FT: 12,000
SALES (est) 10.5MM **Privately Held**
SIC: 8011 Ears, nose & throat specialist: physician/surgeon

(P-19348)
SACRAMENTO HEART AND CARDIOVAS (PA)
500 University Ave # 100, Sacramento
(95825-6527)
PHONE...................................916 830-2000
Phillip Bach, *Partner*
Drraye L Bellinger, *Partner*
Raye Bellinger, *Med Doctor*
EMP: 51
SQ FT: 45,000
SALES (est) 10.4MM **Privately Held**
WEB: www.sacheart.com
SIC: 8011 Cardiologist & cardio-vascular specialist

(P-19349)
SACRAMNTO NTIV AMERCN HLTH CTR
2020 J St, Sacramento (95811-3120)
PHONE...................................916 341-0575
Britta Guerrero, *Exec Dir*
Lisa McKay, *Admin Dir*
Britta Guerrero, *Exec Dir*

EMP: 119
SQ FT: 39,573
SALES: 14.3MM **Privately Held**
WEB: www.snahc.org
SIC: 8011 Clinic, operated by physicians

(P-19350)
SAINT JHNS HLTH CTR FOUNDATION
Wayne, John Cancer Institute
2200 Santa Monica Blvd, Santa Monica
(90404-2312)
PHONE...................................310 315-6111
Donald Mortan, *Director*
Lynne Cabus, *Technician*
Fred Sweers, *Opers Spvr*
EMP: 125
SQ FT: 7,100
SALES (corp-wide): 2.7B **Privately Held**
SIC: 8011 8731 Primary care medical clinic; commercial physical research
HQ: Saint John's Health Center Foundation.
2121 Santa Monica Blvd
Santa Monica CA 90404
310 829-5511

(P-19351)
SALINAS MED MNGT SRVCS ORG INC
Also Called: Salinas Valley Prime Care Med
355 Abbott St Ste 100, Salinas
(93901-4484)
PHONE...................................831 751-7070
Gerald W Oehler, *President*
Glen Yoneda, *Treasurer*
Robert Patton, *Vice Pres*
EMP: 70 **EST:** 1997
SQ FT: 6,612
SALES (est) 2.9MM **Privately Held**
SIC: 8011 General & family practice, physician/surgeon

(P-19352)
SALINAS VALLEY MEDICAL CLINIC
236 San Jose St, Salinas (93901-3901)
PHONE...................................831 424-7389
EMP: 414
SALES: 50.5MM
SALES (corp-wide): 494.4MM **Privately Held**
SIC: 8011 Cardiologist & cardio-vascular specialist
PA: Salinas Valley Memorial Healthcare Systems
450 E Romie Ln
Salinas CA 93901
831 757-4333

(P-19353)
SALUD PARA LA GENTE
Also Called: Salud Para La Gnte Hlth Clinic
195 Aviation Way Ste 200, Watsonville
(95076-2059)
PHONE...................................831 728-0222
Dori Rose Inda, *CEO*
Tony Balistreri, *CFO*
Obdulia Landaverry, *Finance Asst*
Guillermina Porraz, *Human Res Dir*
Amy Ross, *Opers Staff*
EMP: 125
SALES: 38MM **Privately Held**
SIC: 8011 Clinic, operated by physicians

(P-19354)
SAN BERNARDINO MED GROUP INC (PA)
1700 N Waterman Ave, San Bernardino
(92404-5115)
PHONE...................................909 883-8611
James Malin, *CEO*
Thomas Hellwig, *President*
James W Malin, *CEO*
Louis Francisco MD, *Treasurer*
Paul G Godfrey MD, *Vice Pres*
EMP: 150
SQ FT: 55,000
SALES (est) 22.6MM **Privately Held**
SIC: 8011 General & family practice, physician/surgeon

(P-19355)
SAN DIEGO FAMILY CARE (PA)
Also Called: Linda Vista Health Care Center
6973 Linda Vista Rd, San Diego
(92111-6342)
PHONE...................................858 279-0925
Roberta L Feinberg, *CEO*
Manuel Quintanar, *CFO*
Kevin Gomez, *Administration*
Margarita Caudillo, *Data Proc Staff*
Jonathan Baker, *Grnl Med Prac*
EMP: 93 **EST:** 1972
SALES: 21.3MM **Privately Held**
WEB: www.lvhcc.com
SIC: 8011 Clinic, operated by physicians

(P-19356)
SAN DIEGO IMAGING - CHULA VIST (PA)
8745 Aero Dr Ste 200, San Diego
(92123-1774)
PHONE...................................858 565-0950
Keth Prince, *Principal*
▲ **EMP:** 53
SALES (est) 4.9MM **Privately Held**
WEB: www.sandiegoimaging.com
SIC: 8011 Radiologist

(P-19357)
SAN DIEGO ORTHOPAEDIC ASSOCIAT
Also Called: S D O A
4060 4th Ave Ste 700, San Diego
(92103-2121)
PHONE...................................619 299-8500
Larry Dodge, *President*
William E Bowman MD, *Principal*
Maneesh Bawa, *Med Doctor*
William H Davidson, *Med Doctor*
EMP: 52 **EST:** 1973
SQ FT: 11,000
SALES (est) 8.2MM **Privately Held**
SIC: 8011 Orthopedic physician; surgeon

(P-19358)
SAN DIEGO PATHOLOGISTS MEDICAL
7592 Metro Dr Ste 406, San Diego (92108)
PHONE...................................619 297-4012
Carla Stayboldt MD, *President*
Slavek Niewiadomski MD, *Treasurer*
David Francis MD, *Exec VP*
Bruce Robbins MD, *Exec VP*
Nancy L Harrison MD, *Vice Pres*
EMP: 120
SQ FT: 3,500
SALES (est) 9MM **Privately Held**
WEB: www.sdpath.com
SIC: 8011 Pathologist

(P-19359)
SAN DIMAS MEDICAL GROUP INC
100 Old River Rd, Bakersfield
(93311-8823)
PHONE...................................661 663-4800
Frank Ynostroza MD, *Ch of Bd*
Cameron Johnson, *Executive*
Wendy Crenshaw MD, *Principal*
Philip H Davis MD, *Principal*
Marietta M Tan MD, *Principal*
EMP: 60
SQ FT: 20,000
SALES (est) 9.8MM **Privately Held**
WEB: www.sandimasmedical.com
SIC: 8011 Obstetrician; gynecologist

(P-19360)
SAN FRANCISCO FERTILITY CTRS
55 Francisco St Ste 300, San Francisco
(94133-2113)
PHONE...................................415 834-3000
Carl Herbert, *Med Doctor*
Maryellen Moore, *CEO*
EMP: 74
SALES (est) 5.6MM **Privately Held**
SIC: 8011 Fertility specialist, physician

(P-19361)
SAN GABRIEL AMBULATORY SUGERY
207 S Santa Anita St G16, San Gabriel (91776-1147)
PHONE...................626 300-5300
Brenda Durgin, *Manager*
EMP: 556
SALES (est): 34.5MM
SALES (corp-wide): 18.3B **Publicly Held**
SIC: 8011 Surgeon
HQ: United Surgical Partners International, Inc.
15305 Dallas Pkwy # 1600
Addison TX 75001
972 713-3500

(P-19362)
SAN JOSE STATE UNIVERSITY
Also Called: Student Health Services
1 Washington Sq, San Jose (95112-3613)
PHONE...................408 924-1000
Robert J Latta MD, *Director*
Susan Arias, *Program Mgr*
Jessie Cai, *Branch Mgr*
Teng Moh, *Branch Mgr*
Cher Jones, *Admin Asst*
EMP: 50 **Privately Held**
WEB: www.sjsu.edu
SIC: 8011 8221 9411 Dispensary, operated by physicians; university;
HQ: San Jose State University
1 Washington Sq
San Jose CA 95192
408 924-1000

(P-19363)
SAN LEANDRO SURGERY CENTER LT
15035 E 14th St, San Leandro (94578-1901)
PHONE...................510 276-2800
Sheila Cook, *Partner*
EMP: 60
SQ FT: 33,000
SALES (est): 6.6MM **Privately Held**
WEB: www.slsurgery.com
SIC: 8011 Surgeon

(P-19364)
SANSUM CLINIC (PA)
470 S Patterson Ave, Santa Barbara (93111-2404)
P.O. Box 1200 (93102-1200)
PHONE...................805 681-7700
Kurt Ransohoff MD, *President*
Chad Hine, *CFO*
Thomas Colbert, *Vice Pres*
Susan Kennedy, *Vice Pres*
Matthew Kunkel, *Vice Pres*
EMP: 60
SQ FT: 10,944
SALES: 303.9MM **Privately Held**
WEB: www.sansum.com
SIC: 8011 Clinic, operated by physicians

(P-19365)
SANTA ANA RADIOLOGY CENTER
Also Called: West Coast Radiology Center
1100 N Tustin Ave Ste A, Santa Ana (92705-3509)
PHONE...................714 835-6055
Tim Chavez, *CEO*
Susan Dalessandro, *Marketing Staff*
EMP: 60
SQ FT: 15,000
SALES (est): 4.8MM **Privately Held**
SIC: 8011 8071 Radiologist; X-ray laboratory, including dental

(P-19366)
SANTA CLARA VALLEY MEDICAL CTR
2400 Moorpark Ave, San Jose (95128-2631)
PHONE...................408 885-6300
Ben Wong, *Internal Med*
Jeffrey Arnold, *Director*
EMP: 449 **Privately Held**
SIC: 8011 Medical centers
PA: Santa Clara Valley Medical Center
751 S Bascom Ave
San Jose CA 95128

(P-19367)
SANTA CLARITA MEDICAL GROUP
25775 Mcbean Pkwy Ste 209, Valencia (91355-3703)
PHONE...................661 255-6802
Kurt Olson, *Branch Mgr*
EMP: 50
SALES (est): 1MM
SALES (corp-wide): 3.3MM **Privately Held**
SIC: 8011 Physicians' office, including specialists
PA: Santa Clarita Medical Group, Inc
1680 S Garfield Ave
Alhambra CA
661 250-0100

(P-19368)
SANTA CRUZ COUNTY OF
Also Called: Watsonville Health Clinic
1430 Freedom Blvd Ste D, Watsonville (95076-2752)
PHONE...................831 763-8400
Michelle Violich, *Director*
EMP: 50 **Privately Held**
WEB: www.scsheriff.com
SIC: 8011 9111 Clinic, operated by physicians; county supervisors' & executives' offices
PA: County Of Santa Cruz
701 Ocean St Rm 520
Santa Cruz CA 95060
831 454-2100

(P-19369)
SANTA CRUZ MEDICAL FOUNDATION (HQ)
2025 Soquel Ave, Santa Cruz (95062-1323)
PHONE...................831 458-5537
Larry De Ghetaldi, *Director*
Shawna Riddle, *Family Practiti*
Scott S Merlo, *Physician Asst*
David A Sofen, *Med Doctor*
Andrew Wu, *Med Doctor*
EMP: 53
SQ FT: 60,000
SALES (est): 31.6MM
SALES (corp-wide): 12.7B **Privately Held**
WEB: www.sutterhealth.org
SIC: 8011 General & family practice, physician/surgeon
PA: Sutter Health
2200 River Plaza Dr
Sacramento CA 95833
916 733-8800

(P-19370)
SANTA MONICA BAY PHYSICANS
881 Alma Real Dr Ste 214, Pacific Palisades (90272-3750)
PHONE...................310 459-2363
Mark R Needham, *President*
EMP: 180
SALES (est): 6.8MM **Privately Held**
SIC: 8011 Physical medicine, physician/surgeon

(P-19371)
SANTA MONICA BAY PHYSICANS HE (PA)
Also Called: Bay Area Community Med Group
5767 W Century Blvd, Los Angeles (90045-5631)
PHONE...................310 417-5900
Eileen McGrath, *President*
Dr Richard Zachrich, *Treasurer*
Dr Steven Seizer, *Vice Pres*
Dr David Cutler, *Admin Sec*
EMP: 85
SALES (est): 15.4MM **Privately Held**
WEB: www.smbp.com
SIC: 8011 Clinic, operated by physicians

(P-19372)
SANTA MONICA ORTHOPEDIC (PA)
2020 Santa Monica Blvd # 230, Santa Monica (90404-2124)
PHONE...................310 315-2018
Ramin M Modabber MD, *President*
Kevin M Erhardt MD, *Vice Pres*
Kenton S Horacek MD, *Admin Sec*

Daniel Cho, *Gastroenterlgy*
Kenton Horacek, *Med Doctor*
EMP: 54
SQ FT: 28,242
SALES (est): 248.9K **Privately Held**
WEB: www.aclprevent.com
SIC: 8011 Orthopedic physician

(P-19373)
SCRIPPS CLINIC CARMEL VALLEY
Also Called: Division Infectious Diseases
10666 N Torrey Pines Rd, La Jolla (92037-1092)
PHONE...................858 554-8096
EMP: 271
SALES (corp-wide): 21.9MM **Privately Held**
SIC: 8011
PA: Scripps Clinic Carmel Valley
3811 Valley Centre Dr
San Diego CA 92130
858 764-3000

(P-19374)
SCRIPPS CLINIC MEDICAL GROUP
10666 N Torrey Pines Rd, La Jolla (92037-1092)
PHONE...................858 554-9606
Thomas Waltz, *CEO*
James Collins, *CFO*
Gilanthony D Ungab, *Principal*
Sunil Rayan, *Managing Dir*
Rhona Fink, *Family Practiti*
EMP: 300
SALES (est): 15MM **Privately Held**
SIC: 8011 Physicians' office, including specialists

(P-19375)
SCRIPPS DIALASYS INC (PA)
Also Called: Scripps Dialysis Center
9870 Genesee Ave, La Jolla (92037-1205)
PHONE...................619 453-9070
John Aalbers, *Principal*
EMP: 50
SQ FT: 10,000
SALES (est): 2.2MM **Privately Held**
SIC: 8011 8092 Clinic, operated by physicians; kidney dialysis centers

(P-19376)
SCRIPPS HEALTH
477 N El Camino Real A208, Encinitas (92024-1328)
PHONE...................760 479-3900
Jennifer Duong, *Family Practiti*
Stacey Lin, *Family Practiti*
Diane Vu, *Family Practiti*
David Ko, *Internal Med*
EMP: 188
SALES (corp-wide): 2.1B **Privately Held**
SIC: 8011 Physicians' office, including specialists
PA: Scripps Health
10140 Campus Point Dr Ax415
San Diego CA 92121
800 727-4777

(P-19377)
SCRIPPS HEALTH
Also Called: Rancho Clinic Rancho San Diego
10862 Calle Verde, La Mesa (91941-7340)
PHONE...................619 670-5400
Yvonne Markovitz, *Manager*
Michael Magpile, *Orthopedist*
Michaela Miller, *Internal Med*
Ziad Allos, *Med Doctor*
Erik Gilbertson, *Manager*
EMP: 70
SALES (corp-wide): 2.1B **Privately Held**
WEB: www.scripps.org
SIC: 8011 Clinic, operated by physicians
PA: Scripps Health
10140 Campus Point Dr Ax415
San Diego CA 92121
800 727-4777

(P-19378)
SCRIPPS HEALTH
Also Called: Scripps Clinic Ob-Gyn
9850 Genesee Ave Ste 600, San Diego (92121)
PHONE...................858 882-8350

EMP: 188
SALES (corp-wide): 2.1B **Privately Held**
SIC: 8011 Gynecologist
PA: Scripps Health
10140 Campus Point Dr Ax415
San Diego CA 92121
800 727-4777

(P-19379)
SCRIPPS HEALTH
Also Called: Scripps Clinic - Encinatas
310 Santa Fe Dr Ste 200, Encinitas (92024-5124)
PHONE...................760 633-6915
Cheryl Suqua, *Administration*
EMP: 60
SQ FT: 38,331
SALES (corp-wide): 2.1B **Privately Held**
WEB: www.scripps.org
SIC: 8011 General & family practice, physician/surgeon
PA: Scripps Health
10140 Campus Point Dr Ax415
San Diego CA 92121
800 727-4777

(P-19380)
SCRIPPS HEALTH
488 E Valley Pkwy Ste 411, Escondido (92025-3380)
PHONE...................760 806-5700
EMP: 220
SALES (corp-wide): 2.1B **Privately Held**
SIC: 8011 Clinic, operated by physicians
PA: Scripps Health
10140 Campus Point Dr Ax415
San Diego CA 92121
800 727-4777

(P-19381)
SCRIPPS HEALTH
9834 Genesee Ave Ste 311, La Jolla (92037-1221)
PHONE...................858 458-5100
Eric Hong, *Internal Med*
Douglas Bolitho, *Plastic Surgeon*
EMP: 251
SALES (corp-wice): 2.1B **Privately Held**
SIC: 8011 Plastic surgeon
PA: Scripps Health
10140 Campus Point Dr Ax415
San Diego CA 92121
800 727-4777

(P-19382)
SCRIPPS HEALTH
9850 Genesee Ave Ste 620, La Jolla (92037-1217)
PHONE...................858 626-5200
EMP: 126
SALES (corp-wide): 2.1B **Privately Held**
SIC: 8011 8059 Offices & clinics of medical doctors; convalescent home
PA: Scripps Health
10140 Campus Point Dr Ax415
San Diego CA 92121
800 727-4777

(P-19383)
SCRIPPS HEALTH
10666 N Torrey Pines Rd, La Jolla (92037-1027)
PHONE...................858 554-8892
Larry Harrison, *President*
Quang Nguyen, *Med Doctor*
Lisa Otte, *Director*
EMP: 60
SQ FT: 99,999
SALES (corp-wide): 2.1B **Privately Held**
SIC: 8011 Physicians' office, including specialists
PA: Scripps Health
10140 Campus Point Dr Ax415
San Diego CA 92121
800 727-4777

(P-19384)
SCRIPPS HEALTH
10666 N Torrey Pines Rd, La Jolla (92037-1027)
PHONE...................858 554-9489
Allan Saven MD, *Principal*
EMP: 60

SALES (corp-wide): 2.1B **Privately Held**
WEB: www.scripps.org
SIC: 8011 Physicians' office, including specialists
PA: Scripps Health
   10140 Campus Point Dr Ax415
   San Diego CA 92121
   800 727-4777

(P-19385)
SCRIPPS HEALTH
3998 Vista Way Ste E, Oceanside
(92056-4514)
PHONE.................................760 901-5200
Karl Steinberg, *Sales Mgr*
John Kroener, *Surgeon*
EMP: 220
SALES (corp-wide): 2.1B **Privately Held**
SIC: 8011 General & family practice, physician/surgeon
PA: Scripps Health
   10140 Campus Point Dr Ax415
   San Diego CA 92121
   800 727-4777

(P-19386)
SCRIPPS HEALTH
Also Called: Clinic Business
10790 Rancho Bernardo Rd, San Diego
(92127-5705)
PHONE.................................858 784-5888
Breaux Castleman, *President*
Susan Erickson, *Director*
Regeorgia Lange, *Manager*
Shirley McCurtis, *Supervisor*
EMP: 100
SALES (corp-wide): 2.1B **Privately Held**
WEB: www.scripps.org
SIC: 8011 Internal medicine practitioners; specialized medical practitioners, except internal
PA: Scripps Health
   10140 Campus Point Dr Ax415
   San Diego CA 92121
   800 727-4777

(P-19387)
SD SPORTS MDCNE&FMLY HLTH CNTR
6699 Alvarado Rd Ste 2100, San Diego
(92120-5238)
PHONE.................................619 229-3910
Jo Baxter, *Manager*
Michelle Look, *Sports Medicine*
Stephen J Rohrer, *Sports Medicine*
Shannon Cheffet, *Pediatrics*
Bill Taylor,
EMP: 52
SALES (est): 3.7MM **Privately Held**
WEB: www.sandiegosportsmed.com
SIC: 8011 Clinic, operated by physicians

(P-19388)
SENECA HEALTHCARE DISTRICT
Also Called: Seneca Hospital Almanor Clinic
199 Reynolds Rd, Chester (96020)
PHONE.................................530 258-1977
Camille Hovellerdale, *Manager*
EMP: 78
SALES (corp-wide): 26.3MM **Privately Held**
SIC: 8011 Clinic, operated by physicians
PA: Seneca Healthcare District
   130 Brentwood Dr
   Chester CA 96020
   530 258-2151

(P-19389)
SEQUOIA SURGICAL CENTER LP
Also Called: Sequoia Surgical Pavilion
2405 Shadelands Dr # 200, Walnut Creek
(94598-5916)
PHONE.................................925 935-6700
Debbie Mack, *General Ptnr*
EMP: 50
SQ FT: 14,750
SALES (est): 5MM
SALES (corp-wide): 1.7B **Publicly Held**
SIC: 8011 Ambulatory surgical center
HQ: National Surgical Hospitals, Inc.
   250 S Wacker Dr Ste 500
   Chicago IL 60606
   312 627-8400

(P-19390)
SERRA COMMUNITY MED CLINIC INC
9375 San Fernando Rd, Sun Valley
(91352-1418)
PHONE.................................818 768-3000
Sadayappa K Durairaj, *CEO*
Kumar Soundar, *CFO*
Dr Arnold Jacobs, *Treasurer*
Renne Applebaum, *Radiology Dir*
Dr Carlos Jimenez, *Admin Sec*
EMP: 163 **EST:** 1975
SQ FT: 60,000
SALES (est): 18.5MM **Privately Held**
SIC: 8011 Clinic, operated by physicians

(P-19391)
SERRA MEDICAL CLINIC INC
9375 San Fernando Rd, Sun Valley
(91352-1418)
PHONE.................................818 768-3000
S K Durairaj MD, *President*
Tamiselvi R Krishnakumar, *Pediatrics*
Liana Volpe, *Med Doctor*
EMP: 100 **EST:** 1974
SQ FT: 62,000
SALES (est): 3.8MM **Privately Held**
SIC: 8011 Internal medicine, physician/surgeon

(P-19392)
SHARP HEALTHCARE
7910 Frost St Ste 280, San Diego
(92123-2752)
PHONE.................................619 398-2988
Geoffrey Weinstein, *Oncology*
Aleksandr Filen, *Physician Asst*
Kevin S Smith, *Med Doctor*
EMP: 128
SALES (corp-wide): 3.4B **Privately Held**
SIC: 8011 Neurologist
PA: Sharp Healthcare
   8695 Spectrum Center Blvd
   San Diego CA 92123
   858 499-4000

(P-19393)
SHARP HEALTHCARE
3575 Euclid Ave, San Diego (92105-2925)
PHONE.................................619 284-1400
Linhkieu Nguyen, *Principal*
Stefanie Winder, *Physician Asst*
Joseph Garvin, *Nurse Practr*
EMP: 53
SALES (corp-wide): 3.4B **Privately Held**
SIC: 8011 Physicians' office, including specialists
PA: Sharp Healthcare
   8695 Spectrum Center Blvd
   San Diego CA 92123
   858 499-4000

(P-19394)
SHARP HEALTHCARE
550 Washington St Ste 701, San Diego
(92103-2229)
PHONE.................................619 297-0008
EMP: 53
SALES (corp-wide): 3.4B **Privately Held**
SIC: 8011 Physicians' office, including specialists
PA: Sharp Healthcare
   8695 Spectrum Center Blvd
   San Diego CA 92123
   858 499-4000

(P-19395)
SHARP HEALTHCARE
Also Called: Eye Physican Medical Group
225 W Madison Ave Ste 1, El Cajon
(92020-3454)
PHONE.................................619 442-0844
Christopher H Hsu, *Med Doctor*
EMP: 53
SALES (corp-wide): 3.4B **Privately Held**
SIC: 8011 General & family practice, physician/surgeon
PA: Sharp Healthcare
   8695 Spectrum Center Blvd
   San Diego CA 92123
   858 499-4000

(P-19396)
SHARP HEALTHCARE
Also Called: Sharp Rees-Stealy Div
300 Fir St, San Diego (92101-2327)
PHONE.................................619 446-1575
Donna Mills, *Administration*
Eric Giroux, *Partner*
Teresa Harris, *Partner*
Stacey Richard, *Partner*
Alicia Bingham, *Admin Sec*
EMP: 150
SQ FT: 61,608
SALES (corp-wide): 3.4B **Privately Held**
SIC: 8011 Medical centers
PA: Sharp Healthcare
   8695 Spectrum Center Blvd
   San Diego CA 92123
   858 499-4000

(P-19397)
SHARP HEALTHCARE
8901 Activity Rd, San Diego (92126-4427)
PHONE.................................858 653-6100
Joy Stewart, *Director*
EMP: 100
SALES (corp-wide): 3.4B **Privately Held**
SIC: 8011 Offices & clinics of medical doctors
PA: Sharp Healthcare
   8695 Spectrum Center Blvd
   San Diego CA 92123
   858 499-4000

(P-19398)
SHARP HEALTHCARE
2020 Genesee Ave Fl 2, San Diego
(92123-4219)
PHONE.................................858 616-8411
Leticia Rawls, *Principal*
Regina Maple-Carley, *Case Mgr*
EMP: 100
SQ FT: 33,244
SALES (corp-wide): 3.4B **Privately Held**
SIC: 8011 Clinic, operated by physicians
PA: Sharp Healthcare
   8695 Spectrum Center Blvd
   San Diego CA 92123
   858 499-4000

(P-19399)
SHARP HEALTHCARE
Also Called: Sharp Reece Stealy Med Group
4510 Viewridge Ave, San Diego
(92123-1637)
PHONE.................................800 827-4277
Don Balfour, *Manager*
EMP: 70
SALES (corp-wide): 3.4B **Privately Held**
SIC: 8011 Clinic, operated by physicians
PA: Sharp Healthcare
   8695 Spectrum Center Blvd
   San Diego CA 92123
   858 499-4000

(P-19400)
SHARP HEALTHCARE
8860 Center Dr Ste 450, La Mesa
(91942-7001)
PHONE.................................619 460-6200
Scott Musicant, *Branch Mgr*
EMP: 83
SALES (corp-wide): 3.4B **Privately Held**
SIC: 8011 General & family practice, physician/surgeon
PA: Sharp Healthcare
   8695 Spectrum Center Blvd
   San Diego CA 92123
   858 499-4000

(P-19401)
SHARP HEALTHCARE
2020 Genesee Ave, San Diego
(92123-4219)
PHONE.................................858 616-8200
Dawn M Long, *Family Practiti*
Joel Mata, *Manager*
EMP: 60
SALES (corp-wide): 3.4B **Privately Held**
SIC: 8011 Medical centers
PA: Sharp Healthcare
   8695 Spectrum Center Blvd
   San Diego CA 92123
   858 499-4000

(P-19402)
SHEPARD EYE CENTER
1418 E Main St Ste 110, Santa Maria
(93454-4836)
PHONE.................................805 925-2637
Dennis D Shepard MD, *President*
James T Franta, *Principal*
EMP: 50
SQ FT: 10,000
SALES (est): 4.8MM **Privately Held**
SIC: 8011 Ophthalmologist

(P-19403)
SIERRA PACIFIC ORTHO
1630 E Herndon Ave, Fresno (93720-3391)
PHONE.................................559 256-5200
Joe Clark, *CEO*
Eric C Hanson, *President*
Paramjeet Gill, *Officer*
Annette Hopkins, *Office Mgr*
Hong Nakphouminh, *Financial Analy*
EMP: 200 **EST:** 2000
SALES (est): 5.1MM **Privately Held**
WEB: www.spoc-ortho.com
SIC: 8011 Orthopedic physician

(P-19404)
SIERRA VIEW DST HOSP LEAG INC (PA)
465 W Putnam Ave, Porterville
(93257-3320)
PHONE.................................559 784-1110
Donna Hefner, *President*
Douglas Dickson, *CFO*
Ruth Gonzalez, *CFO*
Jeff Hudson, *Vice Pres*
Katrina Creekmore, *Executive*
◆ **EMP:** 168 **EST:** 1948
SQ FT: 135,000
SALES: 147.9MM **Privately Held**
WEB: www.sierra-view.com
SIC: 8011 8062 Offices & clinics of medical doctors; general medical & surgical hospitals

(P-19405)
SOBOL PHILIP A MD P C INC
8618 S Sepulveda Blvd # 130, Los Angeles
(90045-4005)
PHONE.................................310 649-5894
Philip A Sobol, *President*
EMP: 50
SALES (est): 2.3MM **Privately Held**
SIC: 8011 Offices & clinics of medical doctors

(P-19406)
SONOMA COUNTY INDIAN HEALTH PR (PA)
Also Called: Scihp
144 Stony Point Rd, Santa Rosa
(95401-4122)
PHONE.................................707 521-4545
Betty Arterverry, *CEO*
Molin T Malicay, *CEO*
Lori Houston, *Planning*
Dr Don Carlos Stele, *Medical Dir*
EMP: 170
SQ FT: 70,000
SALES: 21.8MM **Privately Held**
SIC: 8011 Clinic, operated by physicians

(P-19407)
SOUTH BAY FAMILY MEDICAL GROUP
Also Called: Mellor, Anna B MD
3105 Lomita Blvd, Torrance (90505-5108)
PHONE.................................310 378-2234
Glenn M Wishon MD, *Partner*
Nancy Griffith MD, *Partner*
George A Joseph MD, *Partner*
Lee G Kissel MD, *Partner*
Joseph Mansen, *Partner*
EMP: 70
SQ FT: 6,400
SALES (est): 3.4MM **Privately Held**
WEB: www.sbfmg.com
SIC: 8011 General & family practice, physician/surgeon

(P-19408)
SOUTH CENTRAL FAMILY HLTH CTR
4425 S Central Ave, Los Angeles (90011-3629)
PHONE..................323 908-4200
Richard Veloz, *President*
Paul Ramos, *CFO*
Ruby Raya Morones, *Chief Mktg Ofcr*
Sandra Tatum Green, *Human Res Dir*
EMP: 92
SQ FT: 13,000
SALES: 13.7MM **Privately Held**
WEB: www.scfhc.org
SIC: 8011 Clinic, operated by physicians

(P-19409)
SOUTH COUNTY ORTHOPEDIC SPECIA
Also Called: Moskow, Lonnie J MD
24331 El Toro Rd Ste 200, Laguna Hills (92637-3116)
PHONE..................949 586-3200
James Mullen, *President*
Kyle W Coker, *Principal*
Larry M Gursten, *Principal*
Lance R Montgomery, *Principal*
Lonnie J Moskow, *Principal*
EMP: 75
SALES (est): 9.8MM **Privately Held**
WEB: www.scosortho.com
SIC: 8011 Orthopedic physician

(P-19410)
SOUTHERN CA HLTH & RHBLTN PRG
2610 Industry Way Ste A, Lynwood (90262-4028)
PHONE..................310 631-8004
Dr Jack M Barbour, *CEO*
Rita Floyd, *President*
EMP: 165
SQ FT: 6,000
SALES (est): 10.4MM **Privately Held**
SIC: 8011 Psychiatric clinic

(P-19411)
SOUTHERN CAL ORTHPD INST LP
375 Rolling Oaks Dr, Thousand Oaks (91361-1023)
PHONE..................805 497-7015
David M Auerbach, *Branch Mgr*
EMP: 61 **Privately Held**
SIC: 8011 Orthopedic physician
PA: Southern California Orthopedic Institute, L.P.
6815 Noble Ave Ste 400
Van Nuys CA 91405
-

(P-19412)
SOUTHERN CAL ORTHPD INST LP
Also Called: Satellite Office
6815 Noble Ave Frnt Frnt, Van Nuys (91405-6515)
PHONE..................818 901-6600
Patricia McKeever, *Partner*
EMP: 150 **Privately Held**
WEB: www.scoiclasroom.com
SIC: 8011 Orthopedic physician
PA: Southern California Orthopedic Institute, L.P.
6815 Noble Ave
Van Nuys CA 91405
-

(P-19413)
SOUTHERN CAL ORTHPD INST LP
6815 Noble Ave Ste 112, Westlake Village (91361)
PHONE..................818 901-6600
Dr Mark Friedman, *Partner*
EMP: 66 **Privately Held**
WEB: www.scoiclasroom.com
SIC: 8011 Orthopedic physician
PA: Southern California Orthopedic Institute, L.P.
6815 Noble Ave
Van Nuys CA 91405
-

(P-19414)
SOUTHERN CAL PRMNNTE MED GROUP
6 Willard, Irvine (92604-4694)
PHONE..................949 262-5780
Debra Dannemeyer, *Administration*
EMP: 100
SALES (corp-wide): 3.5B **Privately Held**
WEB: www.permanente.net
SIC: 8011 Clinic, operated by physicians
PA: Southern California Permanente Medical Group
393 Walnut Dr
Pasadena CA 91107
626 405-5704

(P-19415)
SOUTHERN CAL PRMNNTE MED GROUP
3501 Stockdale Hwy, Bakersfield (93309-2150)
PHONE..................661 398-5085
EMP: 54
SALES (corp-wide): 3.5B **Privately Held**
SIC: 8011 Offices & clinics of medical doctors
PA: Southern California Permanente Medical Group
393 Walnut Dr
Pasadena CA 91107
626 405-5704

(P-19416)
SOUTHERN CAL PRMNNTE MED GROUP
Also Called: Kaiser Permanente
4647 Zion Ave, San Diego (92120-2507)
PHONE..................619 528-5000
Terry Belmont, *Principal*
Cheryl Hendershott, *CFO*
Peter Martin, *Top Exec*
Pamela Shatwell, *Executive*
Pamela Reger, *Case Mgmt Dir*
EMP: 53
SALES (corp-wide): 3.5B **Privately Held**
SIC: 8011 Medical centers
PA: Southern California Permanente Medical Group
393 Walnut Dr
Pasadena CA 91107
626 405-5704

(P-19417)
SOUTHERN CAL PRMNNTE MED GROUP
3830 Martin L King Jr Blv, Lynwood (90262-3625)
PHONE..................310 604-5700
Janet Cartmill, *Analyst*
EMP: 53
SALES (corp-wide): 3.5B **Privately Held**
SIC: 8011 Medical centers
PA: Southern California Permanente Medical Group
393 Walnut Dr
Pasadena CA 91107
626 405-5704

(P-19418)
SOUTHERN CAL PRMNNTE MED GROUP
6041 Cadillac Ave, Los Angeles (90034-1702)
PHONE..................323 857-2000
Larry Poston, *Director*
Mitchell Friedman, *Med Doctor*
Stephanie Leong, *Med Doctor*
Karina Maher, *Med Doctor*
Yosef Zibari, *Med Doctor*
EMP: 58
SALES (corp-wide): 3.5B **Privately Held**
SIC: 8011 Radiologist
PA: Southern California Permanente Medical Group
393 Walnut Dr
Pasadena CA 91107
626 405-5704

(P-19419)
SOUTHERN CAL PRMNNTE MED GROUP
25825 Vermont Ave, Harbor City (90710-3518)
PHONE..................800 780-1230
EMP: 58
SALES (corp-wide): 3.5B **Privately Held**
WEB: www.permanente.net
SIC: 8011 Offices & clinics of medical doctors
PA: Southern California Permanente Medical Group
393 Walnut Dr
Pasadena CA 91107
626 405-5704

(P-19420)
SOUTHERN CAL PRMNNTE MED GROUP
4841 Hollywood Blvd, Los Angeles (90027-5301)
PHONE..................323 783-5455
Maria Montes, *Project Mgr*
EMP: 70
SALES (corp-wide): 3.5B **Privately Held**
SIC: 8011 Medical centers
PA: Southern California Permanente Medical Group
393 Walnut Dr
Pasadena CA 91107
626 405-5704

(P-19421)
SOUTHERN CAL PRMNNTE MED GROUP
Also Called: Orthopedics Department
4760 W Sunset Blvd, Los Angeles (90027-6063)
PHONE..................323 783-4893
Dolores Cobbarrubias, *Office Mgr*
EMP: 443
SALES (corp-wide): 3.5B **Privately Held**
SIC: 8011 Orthopedic physician
PA: Southern California Permanente Medical Group
393 Walnut Dr
Pasadena CA 91107
626 405-5704

(P-19422)
SOUTHERN CAL PRMNNTE MED GROUP
Also Called: S C P M G
789 E Cooley Dr, Colton (92324-4007)
PHONE..................909 370-2501
EMP: 50
SALES (corp-wide): 3.5B **Privately Held**
SIC: 8011 Offices & clinics of medical doctors
PA: Southern California Permanente Medical Group
393 Walnut Dr
Pasadena CA 91107
626 405-5704

(P-19423)
SOUTHERN CAL PRMNNTE MED GROUP
18081 Beach Blvd, Huntington Beach (92648-1304)
PHONE..................714 841-7293
Nancy Lee-Hata, *Family Practiti*
EMP: 50
SALES (corp-wide): 3.5B **Privately Held**
WEB: www.permanente.net
SIC: 8011 Offices & clinics of medical doctors
PA: Southern California Permanente Medical Group
393 Walnut Dr
Pasadena CA 91107
626 405-5704

(P-19424)
SOUTHERN CAL PRMNNTE MED GROUP
Also Called: S C P M G
1630 E Main St, El Cajon (92021-5204)
PHONE..................619 528-5000
Brenda Scott-Mead, *Manager*
EMP: 50
SALES (corp-wide): 3.5B **Privately Held**
WEB: www.permanente.net
SIC: 8011 Medical centers
PA: Southern California Permanente Medical Group
393 Walnut Dr
Pasadena CA 91107
626 405-5704

(P-19425)
SOUTHERN CAL PRMNNTE MED GROUP
Also Called: S C P M G
411 N Lakeview Ave, Anaheim (92807-3028)
PHONE..................714 279-4675
Ryan Williams, *Manager*
Janet Hartmann Jones, *Hematology*
EMP: 50
SALES (corp-wide): 3.5B **Privately Held**
WEB: www.permanente.net
SIC: 8011 Offices & clinics of medical doctors
PA: Southern California Permanente Medical Group
393 Walnut Dr
Pasadena CA 91107
626 405-5704

(P-19426)
SOUTHERN CAL PRMNNTE MED GROUP
Also Called: S C P M G
30400 Camino Capistrano, San Juan Capistrano (92675-1300)
PHONE..................949 234-2139
David L Haller, *Family Practiti*
Paula M Richter, *Obstetrician*
EMP: 50
SALES (corp-wide): 3.5B **Privately Held**
WEB: www.permanente.net
SIC: 8011 Offices & clinics of medical doctors
PA: Southern California Permanente Medical Group
393 Walnut Dr
Pasadena CA 91107
626 405-5704

(P-19427)
SOUTHERN CAL PRMNNTE MED GROUP
Also Called: S C P M G
22550 Savi Ranch Pkwy, Yorba Linda (92887-4670)
PHONE..................714 685-3520
Kamil Antonios MD, *Manager*
EMP: 50
SALES (corp-wide): 3.5B **Privately Held**
WEB: www.permanente.net
SIC: 8011 Offices & clinics of medical doctors
PA: Southern California Permanente Medical Group
393 Walnut Dr
Pasadena CA 91107
626 405-5704

(P-19428)
SOUTHERN CAL PRMNNTE MED GROUP
Also Called: S C P M G
1900 E 4th St, Santa Ana (92705-3962)
PHONE..................714 967-4760
Julie White-Dahlgren, *Branch Mgr*
EMP: 60
SALES (corp-wide): 3.5B **Privately Held**
WEB: www.permanente.net
SIC: 8011 8049 Obstetrician; psychiatric social worker
PA: Southern California Permanente Medical Group
393 Walnut Dr
Pasadena CA 91107
626 405-5704

(P-19429)
SOUTHERN CAL PRMNNTE MED GROUP
Also Called: S C P M G
4405 Vandever Ave, San Diego (92120-3315)
PHONE..................619 516-6000
Thomas Volle, *Manager*
EMP: 50
SALES (corp-wide): 3.5B **Privately Held**
WEB: www.permanente.net
SIC: 8011 Medical centers
PA: Southern California Permanente Medical Group
393 Walnut Dr
Pasadena CA 91107
626 405-5704

▲ = Import ▼=Export
◆ =Import/Export

(P-19430)
SOUTHERN CAL PRMNNTE MED GROUP
Also Called: S C P M G
732 N Broadway, Escondido (92025-1870)
PHONE.................................760 839-7200
Alex Anderson, *Manager*
William McKown, *Med Doctor*
EMP: 50
SALES (corp-wide): 3.5B **Privately Held**
WEB: www.permanente.net
SIC: 8011 Medical centers
PA: Southern California Permanente Medical Group
    393 Walnut Dr
    Pasadena CA 91107
    626 405-5704

(P-19431)
SOUTHERN CAL PRMNNTE MED GROUP
Also Called: S C P M G
7825 Atlantic Ave, Cudahy (90201-5022)
PHONE.................................323 562-6459
Maria Gonzalez, *Principal*
EMP: 50
SALES (corp-wide): 3.5B **Privately Held**
WEB: www.permanente.net
SIC: 8011 Offices & clinics of medical doctors
PA: Southern California Permanente Medical Group
    393 Walnut Dr
    Pasadena CA 91107
    626 405-5704

(P-19432)
SOUTHERN CAL PRMNNTE MED GROUP
Also Called: S C P M G
21263 Erwin St, Woodland Hills (91367-3715)
PHONE.................................818 592-3038
Cary Glass, *Branch Mgr*
EMP: 50
SALES (corp-wide): 3.5B **Privately Held**
WEB: www.permanente.net
SIC: 8011 Offices & clinics of medical doctors
PA: Southern California Permanente Medical Group
    393 Walnut Dr
    Pasadena CA 91107
    626 405-5704

(P-19433)
SOUTHERN CAL PRMNNTE MED GROUP
Also Called: S C P M G
27107 Tourney Rd, Santa Clarita (91355-1860)
PHONE.................................661 222-2150
EMP: 50
SALES (corp-wide): 3.5B **Privately Held**
WEB: www.permanente.net
SIC: 8011 Offices & clinics of medical doctors
PA: Southern California Permanente Medical Group
    393 Walnut Dr
    Pasadena CA 91107
    626 405-5704

(P-19434)
SOUTHERN CAL PRMNNTE MED GROUP
5055 California Ave, Bakersfield (93309-0701)
PHONE.................................661 334-2020
Geckeley, *Principal*
EMP: 100
SALES (corp-wide): 3.5B **Privately Held**
WEB: www.permanente.net
SIC: 8011 Offices & clinics of medical doctors
PA: Southern California Permanente Medical Group
    393 Walnut Dr
    Pasadena CA 91107
    626 405-5704

(P-19435)
SOUTHERN CAL STONE CTR LLC
Also Called: So Calif Stone Center
5400 Balboa Blvd Ste 111, Encino (91316-5206)
PHONE.................................818 784-8975
Jerry Garrett MD, *Principal*
James Orecklin MD,
EMP: 56
SALES (est): 4MM **Privately Held**
SIC: 8011 Medical centers

(P-19436)
SOUTHERN INDIAN HEALTH COUNCIL (PA)
4058 Willows Rd, Alpine (91901-1668)
P.O. Box 2128 (91903-2128)
PHONE.................................619 445-1188
Carolina Monsano, *Exec Dir*
Laura Caswell, *COO*
Jimmy Romero, *Vice Pres*
Donna James, *Exec Dir*
Christy Cadena, *Office Mgr*
EMP: 100
SQ FT: 11,000
SALES: 14.6MM **Privately Held**
SIC: 8011 8021 Clinic, operated by physicians; dental clinic

(P-19437)
SOUTHLAND ARTHRITIS OSTEO
949 Calhoun Pl Ste F, Hemet (92543-4403)
PHONE.................................951 672-1866
Chantra V Mehta, *Owner*
Dharmarajan Ramaswamy, *Director*
EMP: 50 **EST:** 2011
SALES (est): 860.5K **Privately Held**
SIC: 8011 Rheumatology specialist, physician/surgeon

(P-19438)
SOUTHWESTERN ORTHPD MED CORP
Also Called: Downey Orthopedic Med Group
15901 Hawthorne Blvd, Lawndale (90260-2655)
P.O. Box 4489, Montebello (90640-9309)
PHONE.................................562 803-0600
Lucy Guttierez, *Branch Mgr*
EMP: 50
SALES (corp-wide): 3.3MM **Privately Held**
SIC: 8011 Orthopedic physician
PA: Southwestern Orthopedic Medical Corporation
    905 S A St
    Oxnard CA 93030
    805 486-4501

(P-19439)
SPALDING SRGCL CTR OF BVRLY HL
Also Called: S&B Surgery Center II
27520 Hawthorne Blvd # 176, Rllng HLS Est (90274-3576)
PHONE.................................949 863-0022
Theordore Goldstrein, *President*
Randy Rosen, *CFO*
EMP: 120
SQ FT: 8,000
SALES (est): 12MM **Privately Held**
WEB: www.snbsurgery.com
SIC: 8011 Surgeon

(P-19440)
SPECIALTY SURGICAL CENTERS
15825 Laguna Canyon Rd # 200, Irvine (92618-2127)
PHONE.................................949 341-3499
Andrew Brooks MD, *President*
Linda Mansfield, *Director*
Terry Weisman, *Director*
EMP: 50
SALES (est): 7.8MM **Privately Held**
SIC: 8011 Physicians' office, including specialists

(P-19441)
SPECILTY SRGICAL CTR ENCINO LP
16501 Ventura Blvd # 103, Encino (91436-2007)
PHONE.................................310 659-6333
Andrew Brooks,
EMP: 100
SALES (est): 480K
SALES (corp-wide): 1.7B **Publicly Held**
SIC: 8011 Surgeon
HQ: Surgery Partners, Inc.
    310 Sven Sprng Way Ste 50
    Brentwood TN 37027
    615 234-5900

(P-19442)
SPH-IRVINE LLC
Also Called: Starpoint Surgery Center
18952 Macarthur Blvd # 103, Irvine (92612-1401)
PHONE.................................949 833-1432
Eric Friedlander, *Mng Member*
EMP: 50 **EST:** 2010
SALES (est): 358.5K **Privately Held**
SIC: 8011 Ambulatory surgical center

(P-19443)
SPINECARE MEDICAL GROUP INC
455 Hickey Blvd Ste 310, Daly City (94015-2630)
PHONE.................................650 985-7500
Arthur H White MD, *Ch of Bd*
James B Reynolds MD, *President*
Noel D Goldthwaite MD, *Treasurer*
Richard Derby MD, *Vice Pres*
Garrett Kine MD, *Vice Pres*
EMP: 57
SQ FT: 82,000
SALES (est): 7.7MM **Privately Held**
WEB: www.spinecare.com
SIC: 8011 Clinic, operated by physicians; surgeon

(P-19444)
ST FRANCIS MEDICAL CENTER (HQ)
Also Called: Sfmc
3630 E Imperial Hwy, Lynwood (90262-2609)
P.O. Box 1168, San Carlos (94070-1168)
PHONE.................................310 900-8900
Richard Adcock, *CEO*
Gerald Kozai, *CEO*
Shan Jordan, *Executive Asst*
Eileen Williams, *CTO*
Richard Hirbe, *Pastor Care Dir*
EMP: 168
SALES (est): 406MM
SALES (corp-wide): 995MM **Privately Held**
SIC: 8011 Medical centers
PA: Verity Health System Of California, Inc.
    2040 E Mariposa Ave
    El Segundo CA 90245
    650 551-6650

(P-19445)
ST JOSEPH HEALTH SYSTEM
Humboldt Medical Speicialists
2280 Harrison Ave Ste B, Eureka (95501-3200)
PHONE.................................707 443-9371
William Stiles, *Manager*
EMP: 50
SALES (corp-wide): 15.2B **Privately Held**
SIC: 8011 Internal medicine practitioners; internal medicine, physician/surgeon
HQ: St. Joseph Health System
    3345 Michelson Dr Ste 100
    Irvine CA 92612
    949 381-4000

(P-19446)
ST JOSEPH SURGERY CENTER LP
1800 N California St # 1, Stockton (95204-6019)
PHONE.................................209 467-6316
Don Wiley, *President*
Lisa Beeman, *Purch Dir*
EMP: 75
SALES (est): 7MM **Privately Held**
SIC: 8011 Surgeon

(P-19447)
ST JUDE HERITAGE MEDICAL GROUP
4300 Rose Dr, Yorba Linda (92886-2026)
PHONE.................................714 528-4211
Lytton Smith MD, *President*
Richard Kenfield MD, *Treasurer*
R S Hall MD, *Vice Pres*
Kenneth Tan MD, *Admin Sec*
Marcia Wilken, *Opers Staff*
EMP: 148
SALES (est): 8.1MM **Privately Held**
SIC: 8011 Clinic, operated by physicians; general & family practice, physician/surgeon

(P-19448)
ST JUDE HOSPITAL YORBA LINDA
Also Called: Bristol Park Medical Group
11420 Warner Ave, Fountain Valley (92708-2529)
PHONE.................................714 665-1797
Helena Rivas, *Manager*
EMP: 200
SALES (corp-wide): 15.2B **Privately Held**
SIC: 8011 8071 Offices & clinics of medical doctors; medical laboratories
HQ: St. Joseph Heritage Healthcare
    200 W Ctr St Promenade
    Anaheim CA 92805
    714 712-3308

(P-19449)
STANFORD HEALTH CARE PRIMARY
Also Called: Stanford Health Services
211 Quarry Rd Fl 3, Palo Alto (94304-1416)
PHONE.................................650 723-6963
Nancy Morioka, *Principal*
Adam Alkhato, *IT/INT Sup*
Norman H Silverman, *Med Doctor*
EMP: 75
SALES (est): 3.1MM **Privately Held**
SIC: 8011 General & family practice, physician/surgeon

(P-19450)
STANLEY M KIRKPATRICK MD
Also Called: Childerns Spec of San Deigo
3020 Childrens Way, San Diego (92123-4223)
PHONE.................................858 966-5855
Stanley M Kirkpatrick MD, *Partner*
Robert Newbury, *Director*
▲ **EMP:** 50
SALES (est): 2.1MM **Privately Held**
SIC: 8011 Pediatrician

(P-19451)
STANLEY R KLEIN MD FACS INC
23451 Madison St Ste 300, Torrance (90505-4737)
PHONE.................................310 373-6864
Stanley Klein, *President*
EMP: 50
SALES (est): 3MM **Privately Held**
SIC: 8011 Surgeon

(P-19452)
STEPHEN B MEISEL MD PC
Also Called: Medfocus Radiology Network
2811 Wilshire Blvd # 900, Santa Monica (90403-4805)
PHONE.................................310 828-8843
Stephen B Meisel, *President*
Frnak Carti, *Business Dir*
EMP: 50
SQ FT: 20,000
SALES (est): 3MM **Privately Held**
WEB: www.medfocuslogin.net
SIC: 8011 Radiologist

(P-19453)
STEPHEN B MEISEL MD A MED CORP (HQ)
Also Called: Med Focus/California Radiology
2811 Wilshire Blvd # 900, Santa Monica (90403-4805)
PHONE.................................310 828-8843
Joseph P Delaney, *President*
Raymond Wong, *Accountant*
EMP: 52
SQ FT: 14,000

SALES (est): 5.1MM **Privately Held**
WEB: www.medfocus.net
SIC: **8011** Radiologist

(P-19454)
STEVEN G FOGG MD
1360 E Herndon Ave # 401, Fresno
(93720-3326)
PHONE...................559 449-5010
Steven G Fogg, *Principal*
EMP: 80
SALES (est): 1.2MM **Privately Held**
SIC: **8011** Ophthalmologist

(P-19455)
STEVEN P ABELOW MD
2311 Lake Tahoe Blvd, South Lake Tahoe
(96150-7129)
PHONE...................530 544-8033
Steven Abelow MD, *Owner*
EMP: 100
SALES (est): 236.7K **Privately Held**
SIC: **8011** Orthopedic physician; general &
family practice, physician/surgeon

(P-19456)
STOCKTON CARDIOLOGY
MEDICAL GR
1148 Norman Dr Ste 3, Manteca
(95336-5961)
PHONE...................209 824-1555
Gina Callegari, *Manager*
Sanjeev Vaishampayan, *Med Doctor*
EMP: 60
SALES (corp-wide): 12.6MM **Privately
Held**
SIC: **8011** Cardiologist & cardio-vascular
specialist
PA: Stockton Cardiology Medical Group
Complete Heart Care, Inc
415 E Harding Way Ste D
Stockton CA 95204
209 994-5750

(P-19457)
STOCKTON CARDIOLOGY
MEDICAL GR (PA)
415 E Harding Way Ste D, Stockton
(95204-6118)
PHONE...................209 994-5750
Rajiv Punjya, *President*
Tuan A Pham, *Treasurer*
John A Bouteller, *Vice Pres*
EMP: 50
SQ FT: 6,500
SALES: 12.6MM **Privately Held**
SIC: **8011** Cardiologist & cardio-vascular
specialist

(P-19458)
STOCKTON ORTHPD MED
GROUP INC
Also Called: Crooks, Jerry C MD
2545 W Hammer Ln, Stockton
(95209-2839)
PHONE...................209 948-1641
Kevin Mikaelian, *Principal*
Scott Bethune, *Treasurer*
Miklein Kevin MD, *Vice Pres*
David Bethune, *Surgeon*
Kevin K Mikaelian, *Med Doctor*
EMP: 50
SALES (est): 4.3MM **Privately Held**
WEB: www.stocktonortho.com
SIC: **8011** Orthopedic physician; surgeon

(P-19459)
STUART LOVETT
350 30th St Ste 208, Oakland
(94609-3425)
PHONE...................510 444-0790
Stuart Lovett, *Owner*
EMP: 51
SALES (est): 444.8K **Privately Held**
SIC: **8011** Obstetrician

(P-19460)
SUN HEALTHCARE GROUP INC
(DH)
27442 Portola Pkwy # 200, Foothill Ranch
(92610-2822)
PHONE...................949 255-7100
George V Hager Jr, *CEO*
Melissa Craig, *President*
Richard Edwards, *Vice Pres*

▲ EMP: 300
SALES (est): 733.9MM **Publicly Held**
WEB: www.sunh.com
SIC: **8011** 8322 Medical insurance plan;
referral service for personal & social prob-
lems
HQ: Genesis Healthcare Corporation
101 E State St
Kennett Square PA 19348
610 444-6350

(P-19461)
SURGERY CENTER OF ALTA
BATES
Also Called: Herrick Hospital
2001 Dwight Way, Berkeley (94704-2608)
PHONE...................510 204-4411
Albert Greene, *Branch Mgr*
Andrea Clark, *Manager*
EMP: 50
SQ FT: 6,750
SALES (corp-wide): 12.7B **Privately Held**
WEB: www.altabates.com
SIC: **8011** 8051 Medical centers; skilled
nursing care facilities
HQ: The Surgery Center Of Alta Bates
Summit Medical Center Llc
2450 Ashby Ave
Berkeley CA 94705
510 204-4444

(P-19462)
SURGERY CENTER OF ALTA
BATES
Also Called: Alta Btes Cmprhnsive Cncer Ctr
2001 Dwight Way, Berkeley (94704-2608)
PHONE...................510 204-1591
Peter H Jessup, *CEO*
Sunil Krishnan, *QA Dir*
Josh Iufer, *Food Svc Dir*
Michael J Cassidy, *Oncology*
Mary Cafareella-Ake, *Director*
EMP: 82
SALES (corp-wide): 12.7B **Privately Held**
SIC: **8011** Offices & clinics of medical doc-
tors
HQ: The Surgery Center Of Alta Bates
Summit Medical Center Llc
2450 Ashby Ave
Berkeley CA 94705
510 204-4444

(P-19463)
SUTTER GOULD MED
FOUNDATION (PA)
600 Coffee Rd, Modesto (95355-4201)
PHONE...................209 948-5940
David Bradley, *CEO*
Maria Dizon, *Executive Asst*
E Lewis Cobb, *Obstetrician*
David Betz, *Anesthesiology*
You-Tan Yeh, *Internal Med*
EMP: 50
SALES (est): 15.6MM **Privately Held**
SIC: **8011** Obstetrician

(P-19464)
SUTTER HEALTH
2068 John Jones Rd # 100, Davis
(95616-9711)
PHONE...................530 747-0389
Craig Blomberg,
EMP: 147
SALES (corp-wide): 12.7B **Privately Held**
SIC: **8011** Internal medicine, physician/sur-
geon
PA: Sutter Health
2200 River Plaza Dr
Sacramento CA 95833
916 733-8800

(P-19465)
SUTTER HEALTH
795 El Camino Real, Palo Alto
(94301-2302)
PHONE...................650 853-2975
Mathew Hernandez, *Shareholder*
Kelvin Chang, *Regional Mgr*
Patrick Furtado, *Analyst*
Rahul Verma, *Gastroenterlgy*
James Ahn, *Ophthalmology*
EMP: 265
SALES (corp-wide): 12.7B **Privately Held**
SIC: **8011** Offices & clinics of medical doc-
tors

PA: Sutter Health
2200 River Plaza Dr
Sacramento CA 95833
916 733-8800

(P-19466)
SUTTER HEALTH
100 Mission Blvd, Jackson (95642-2536)
PHONE...................209 223-5445
Melody Eurbe, *Officer*
Denise Lack, *Nurse Practr*
EMP: 147
SALES (corp-wide): 12.7B **Privately Held**
SIC: **8011** Cardiologist & cardio-vascular
specialist
PA: Sutter Health
2200 River Plaza Dr
Sacramento CA 95833
916 733-8800

(P-19467)
SUTTER HEALTH
3 Medical Plaza Dr # 100, Roseville
(95661-3088)
PHONE...................916 797-4715
Parul Singh, *Family Practiti*
Carla Ellis,
EMP: 236
SALES (corp-wide): 12.7B **Privately Held**
SIC: **8011** Offices & clinics of medical doc-
tors
PA: Sutter Health
2200 River Plaza Dr
Sacramento CA 95833
916 733-8800

(P-19468)
SUTTER HEALTH
8170 Laguna Blvd Ste 210, Elk Grove
(95758-7902)
PHONE...................916 691-5900
Solomon Yeung, *President*
Francisco Prieto, *Family Practiti*
EMP: 177
SALES (corp-wide): 12.7B **Privately Held**
SIC: **8011** General & family practice, physi-
cian/surgeon
PA: Sutter Health
2200 River Plaza Dr
Sacramento CA 95833
916 733-8800

(P-19469)
SUTTER HEALTH
5196 Hill Rd E Ste 300, Lakeport
(95453-6374)
PHONE...................707 263-6885
Harneet Bath, *Branch Mgr*
EMP: 200
SALES (corp-wide): 12.7B **Privately Held**
SIC: **8011** Offices & clinics of medical doc-
tors
PA: Sutter Health
2200 River Plaza Dr
Sacramento CA 95833
916 733-8800

(P-19470)
SUTTER HEALTH
2725 Capitol Ave, Sacramento
(95816-6004)
PHONE...................916 262-9400
Damon Namvar, *Podiatrist*
EMP: 206
SALES (corp-wide): 12.7B **Privately Held**
SIC: **8011** Specialized medical practition-
ers, except internal
PA: Sutter Health
2200 River Plaza Dr
Sacramento CA 95833
916 733-8800

(P-19471)
SUTTER HEALTH
2725 Capitol Ave Dept 304, Sacramento
(95816-6006)
PHONE...................916 262-9414
EMP: 261
SALES (corp-wide): 12.7B **Privately Held**
SIC: **8011** Offices & clinics of medical doc-
tors
PA: Sutter Health
2200 River Plaza Dr
Sacramento CA 95833
916 733-8800

(P-19472)
SUTTER HEALTH
1500 Expo Pkwy, Sacramento
(95815-4227)
PHONE...................916 646-8300
EMP: 1000
SALES (corp-wide): 11B **Privately Held**
SIC: **8011** 8071
PA: Sutter Health
2200 River Plaza Dr
Sacramento CA 95833
916 286-6670

(P-19473)
SUTTER HEALTH
3875 Telegraph Ave, Oakland
(94609-2428)
PHONE...................510 547-2244
Aaron Adams, *Branch Mgr*
Kim Dambrosia, *Administration*
Russell Bran, *Med Doctor*
EMP: 324
SALES (corp-wide): 12.7B **Privately Held**
SIC: **8011** Medical centers
PA: Sutter Health
2200 River Plaza Dr
Sacramento CA 95833
916 733-8800

(P-19474)
SUTTER HEALTH
475 Pioneer Ave Ste 100, Woodland
(95776-4905)
PHONE...................530 406-5600
Judi Monday, *Director*
EMP: 200
SALES (corp-wide): 12.7B **Privately Held**
SIC: **8011** Offices & clinics of medical doc-
tors
PA: Sutter Health
2200 River Plaza Dr
Sacramento CA 95833
916 733-8800

(P-19475)
SUTTER HEALTH
3612 Dale Rd, Modesto (95356-0500)
PHONE...................209 522-0146
EMP: 206
SALES (corp-wide): 12.7B **Privately Held**
SIC: **8011** Offices & clinics of medical doc-
tors
PA: Sutter Health
2200 River Plaza Dr
Sacramento CA 95833
916 733-8800

(P-19476)
SUTTER HEALTH
50 S San Mateo Dr Ste 470, San Mateo
(94401-3833)
PHONE...................650 262-4262
Roger Larsen, *President*
Jenny Breen, *Administration*
Michael Weatherford, *VP Finance*
Cheryl Cummings, *Physician Asst*
Harvey Matlof, *Med Doctor*
EMP: 206
SALES (corp-wide): 12.7B **Privately Held**
SIC: **8011** Orthopedic physician
PA: Sutter Health
2200 River Plaza Dr
Sacramento CA 95833
916 733-8800

(P-19477)
SUTTER HEALTH
999 S Fairmont Ave # 200, Lodi
(95240-5100)
PHONE...................209 334-3333
Carol Nakashima, *Med Doctor*
EMP: 136
SALES (corp-wide): 12.7B **Privately Held**
SIC: **8011** General & family practice, physi-
cian/surgeon
PA: Sutter Health
2200 River Plaza Dr
Sacramento CA 95833
916 733-8800

(P-19478)
SUTTER HEALTH
Also Called: Nguyen, Myhanh MD
325 N Mathilda Ave, Sunnyvale
(94085-4207)
PHONE...................408 733-4380

Connie Conover, *Branch Mgr*
Connie Caraang, *Buyer*
Myhanh Nguyen, *Med Doctor*
April Espaniola, *Supervisor*
EMP: 147
SALES (corp-wide): 12.7B **Privately Held**
SIC: 8011 Occupational & industrial specialist, physician/surgeon
PA: Sutter Health
2200 River Plaza Dr
Sacramento CA 95833
916 733-8800

(P-19479)
SUTTER HEALTH
Also Called: Sutter Pacific Med Foundation
5196 Hill Rd E Ste 300, Lakeport
(95453-6374)
PHONE..................................707 263-6885
EMP: 121
SALES (corp-wide): 11B **Privately Held**
SIC: 8011
PA: Sutter Health
2200 River Plaza Dr
Sacramento CA 95833
916 733-8800

(P-19480)
SUTTER HEALTH
Also Called: Palo Alpo Medical Foudation
795 El Camino Real, Palo Alto
(94301-2302)
PHONE..................................650 853-2904
Nan A Link, *Branch Mgr*
EMP: 106
SALES (corp-wide): 12.7B **Privately Held**
SIC: 8011 Offices & clinics of medical doctors
PA: Sutter Health
2200 River Plaza Dr
Sacramento CA 95833
916 733-8800

(P-19481)
SUTTER HEALTH
Also Called: Breast Imaging Center
3161 L St, Sacramento (95816-5234)
PHONE..................................916 451-3344
Jerry Fosselman, *Branch Mgr*
EMP: 100
SALES (corp-wide): 12.7B **Privately Held**
WEB: www.radiological.com
SIC: 8011 8071 Offices & clinics of medical doctors; medical laboratories
PA: Sutter Health
2200 River Plaza Dr
Sacramento CA 95833
916 733-8800

(P-19482)
SUTTER HEALTH
Also Called: Cpmc Mission Bernal Campus
3555 Cesar Chavez, San Francisco
(94110-4403)
PHONE..................................415 600-6000
Warren Browner MD, *CEO*
Adrian Gutierrez, *Opers Mgr*
EMP: 109
SALES (corp-wide): 12.7B **Privately Held**
WEB: www.sutterhealth.org
SIC: 8011 Offices & clinics of medical doctors
PA: Sutter Health
2200 River Plaza Dr
Sacramento CA 95833
916 733-8800

(P-19483)
SUTTER HEALTH
969 Plumas St Ste 103116, Yuba City
(95991-4011)
PHONE..................................530 749-3585
Aparna Kareti, *Branch Mgr*
EMP: 200
SALES (corp-wide): 12.7B **Privately Held**
WEB: www.sutterhealth.org
SIC: 8011 Medical centers
PA: Sutter Health
2200 River Plaza Dr
Sacramento CA 95833
916 733-8800

(P-19484)
SUTTER HEALTH
Also Called: Sutter Occupational Hlth Svcs
3 Medical Plaza Dr # 100, Roseville
(95661-3088)
PHONE..................................916 797-4700
Dave Gladden, *Branch Mgr*
EMP: 60
SALES (corp-wide): 12.7B **Privately Held**
SIC: 8011 Offices & clinics of medical doctors
PA: Sutter Health
2200 River Plaza Dr
Sacramento CA 95833
916 733-8800

(P-19485)
SUTTER HEALTH
2725 Capitol Ave Dept 404, Sacramento
(95816-6032)
PHONE..................................916 262-9456
EMP: 152
SALES (corp-wide): 12.7B **Privately Held**
SIC: 8011 Medical centers
PA: Sutter Health
2200 River Plaza Dr
Sacramento CA 95833
916 733-8800

(P-19486)
SUTTER HEALTH AT WORK
Also Called: Sutter Hlth At Work - Natomas
1014 N Market Blvd Ste 20, Sacramento
(95834-1986)
PHONE..................................916 565-8607
Judi Monday, *President*
Jona Calitis, *Med Doctor*
Sally Greene, *Director*
EMP: 75
SALES (est): 2.4MM **Privately Held**
SIC: 8011 General & family practice, physician/surgeon

(P-19487)
**SUTTER HLTH SCRMNTO
SIERRA REG**
Also Called: Sutter West Foundation
2030 Sutter Pl Ste 2000, Davis
(95616-6216)
PHONE..................................530 747-5010
Jo Lisa Miller, *Radiology*
EMP: 641
SALES (corp-wide): 12.7B **Privately Held**
SIC: 8011 General & family practice, physician/surgeon
HQ: Sutter Health Sacramento Sierra Region
2200 River Plaza Dr
Sacramento CA 95833
916 733-8800

(P-19488)
**SUTTER HLTH SCRMNTO
SIERRA REG**
Also Called: Sutter Amador Hospital Lab
100 Mission Blvd, Jackson (95642-2536)
PHONE..................................209 223-7540
Margie Souza, *Branch Mgr*
Doug Archer, *Asst Admin*
Jason Rice, *Buyer*
Nancy Leland, *Director*
EMP: 1268
SALES (corp-wide): 12.7B **Privately Held**
SIC: 8011 Radiologist
HQ: Sutter Health Sacramento Sierra Region
2200 River Plaza Dr
Sacramento CA 95833
916 733-8800

(P-19489)
**SUTTER HLTH SCRMNTO
SIERRA REG**
Also Called: Sutter Medical Center
475 Pioneer Ave Ste 100, Woodland
(95776-4905)
PHONE..................................530 406-5616
Leefeldt Randall, *Branch Mgr*
EMP: 641
SALES (corp-wide): 12.7B **Privately Held**
SIC: 8011 Physicians' office, including specialists

HQ: Sutter Health Sacramento Sierra Region
2200 River Plaza Dr
Sacramento CA 95833
916 733-8800

(P-19490)
**SUTTER N MED GROUP A PROF
CORP (PA)**
969 Plumas St Ste 205, Yuba City
(95991-4011)
PHONE..................................530 749-3661
Robert H Wright Jr, *President*
EMP: 84
SQ FT: 30,096
SALES (est): 3.3MM **Privately Held**
SIC: 8011 Offices & clinics of medical doctors

(P-19491)
**SUTTER NORTH MED
FOUNDATION (PA)**
Also Called: Multi Specialty Group Practice
969 Plumas St, Yuba City (95991-4011)
PHONE..................................530 741-1300
Bruce Tigner, *CEO*
Tom Walther, *COO*
Kelly Danna, *CFO*
Barinder Thiara, *Radiology Dir*
Emilio Bethencourt, *Business Dir*
EMP: 160
SALES (est): 27.2MM **Privately Held**
WEB: www.snmf.com
SIC: 8011 General & family practice, physician/surgeon; clinic, operated by physicians

(P-19492)
**SUTTER NORTH MED
FOUNDATION**
480 Plumas Blvd, Yuba City (95991-5005)
PHONE..................................530 749-3635
William G Hoffman MD, *Principal*
Leonard Marks, *Med Doctor*
David Silva, *Med Doctor*
EMP: 100
SALES (corp-wide): 27.2MM **Privately Held**
WEB: www.snmf.com
SIC: 8011 Surgeon
PA: North Sutter Medical Foundation
969 Plumas St
Yuba City CA 95991
530 741-1300

(P-19493)
**SUTTER NORTH MED
FOUNDATION**
Also Called: Home Health Brownsville
16911 Willow Glen Rd, Brownsville (95919)
P.O. Box 609 (95919-0609)
PHONE..................................530 675-1245
Cindy White, *Branch Mgr*
EMP: 55
SALES (corp-wide): 27.2MM **Privately Held**
WEB: www.snmf.com
SIC: 8011 General & family practice, physician/surgeon
PA: North Sutter Medical Foundation
969 Plumas St
Yuba City CA 95991
530 741-1300

(P-19494)
**SUTTER NORTH MED
FOUNDATION**
Also Called: Suttter North Home Health
400 Plumas Blvd Ste 115, Yuba City
(95991-5081)
PHONE..................................530 749-3450
Shelley Sanbury, *Branch Mgr*
EMP: 55
SALES (corp-wide): 27.2MM **Privately Held**
WEB: www.snmf.com
SIC: 8011 Offices & clinics of medical doctors
PA: North Sutter Medical Foundation
969 Plumas St
Yuba City CA 95991
530 741-1300

(P-19495)
**SUTTER REGIONAL MED
FOUNDATION**
770 Mason St, Vacaville (95688-4646)
PHONE..................................707 454-5800
Hon Chan, *Med Doctor*
Sukhjinder Kaur, *Med Doctor*
Paula Grover, *Supervisor*
EMP: 53
SALES (corp-wide): 28.5MM **Privately Held**
WEB: www.sutterdavis.org
SIC: 8011 Offices & clinics of medical doctors
PA: Sutter Regional Medical Foundation Inc
2702 Low Ct
Fairfield CA 94534
707 427-4900

(P-19496)
SWAMINATHA MAHADEVAN MD
701 Welch Rd Bldg C, Palo Alto
(94304-1706)
PHONE..................................650 723-6576
Swaminatha Mahadevan, *Chairman*
EMP: 90
SALES (est): 246.6K **Privately Held**
SIC: 8011 Freestanding emergency medical center

(P-19497)
SYNERMED
Also Called: Ehs Medical Group
1200 Corp Ctr Dr Ste 200, Monterey Park
(91754)
PHONE..................................216 406-2845
Cindy Ehnes, *CEO*
Cindy Ehne, *CEO*
Gina Zwick, *Vice Pres*
Melissa Alexander, *Manager*
Bradley Bonilla, *Supervisor*
EMP: 180
SALES (est): 11MM **Privately Held**
SIC: 8011 Offices & clinics of medical doctors

(P-19498)
**TAHOE FOREST HOSPITAL
DISTRICT**
10710 Donner Pass Rd, Truckee
(96161-4812)
PHONE..................................530 582-7488
Nina Winans, *Branch Mgr*
EMP: 57
SALES (corp-wide): 158.7MM **Privately Held**
SIC: 8011 General & family practice, physician/surgeon
PA: Tahoe Forest Hospital District
10121 Pine Ave
Truckee CA 96161
530 587-6011

(P-19499)
TAMMI R JAMES MD
7273 14th Ave Ste 120b, Sacramento
(95820-3500)
PHONE..................................916 383-6783
Tammi James, *Principal*
EMP: 50
SALES (est): 543.9K **Privately Held**
SIC: 8011 8093 Pediatrician; mental health clinic, outpatient

(P-19500)
**TENET HEALTHSYSTEM
MEDICAL**
414 Cliffside Dr, Danville (94526-4810)
PHONE..................................925 275-8303
Phillip Gustafson, *Director*
EMP: 500
SALES (corp-wide): 18.3B **Publicly Held**
WEB: www.tenenthealth.com
SIC: 8011 Offices & clinics of medical doctors
HQ: Tenet Healthsystem Medical, Inc.
1445 Ross Ave Ste 1400
Dallas TX 75202
469 893-2000

P
R
O
D
U
C
T
S
& SVCS

(P-19501)
TENET HEALTHSYSTEM MEDICAL
Also Called: Lakewood Regional Medical Ctr
3700 South St, Lakewood (90712-1419)
PHONE..........................562 531-2550
Carol Mammolite, *Branch Mgr*
Alfred Yamamoto, *Pathologist*
Irwin Cohen, *Pharmacist*
Mary L Okuhara, *Director*
Joshua Daniels, *Manager*
EMP: 700
SALES (corp-wide): 18.3B **Publicly Held**
WEB: www.tenethealth.com
SIC: 8011 8062 Medical centers; general medical & surgical hospitals
HQ: Tenet Healthsystem Medical, Inc.
   1445 Ross Ave Ste 1400
   Dallas TX 75202
   469 893-2000

(P-19502)
TENET HEALTHSYSTEM MEDICAL
Los Alamitos Med Ctr
3751 Katella Ave, Los Alamitos (90720-3113)
PHONE..........................805 546-7698
Michelle Finney, *Principal*
Kimberly Bartley, *Records Dir*
Maria Murguia, *Technician*
EMP: 625
SALES (corp-wide): 18.3B **Publicly Held**
WEB: www.tenethealth.com
SIC: 8011 8062 Offices & clinics of medical doctors; general medical & surgical hospitals
HQ: Tenet Healthsystem Medical, Inc.
   1445 Ross Ave Ste 1400
   Dallas TX 75202
   469 893-2000

(P-19503)
TENET HEALTHSYSTEM MEDICAL
Also Called: Leisure World Pharmacy
1661 Golden Rain Rd, Seal Beach (90740-4907)
P.O. Box 2685 (90740-1685)
PHONE..........................562 493-9581
Diana Doyle, *Manager*
EMP: 60
SALES (corp-wide): 18.3B **Publicly Held**
WEB: www.tenethealth.com
SIC: 8011 5912 Offices & clinics of medical doctors; drug stores
HQ: Tenet Healthsystem Medical, Inc.
   1445 Ross Ave Ste 1400
   Dallas TX 75202
   469 893-2000

(P-19504)
THE ORTHOPEDIC INSTITUTE OF
616 Witmer St, Los Angeles (90017-2308)
PHONE..........................213 977-2010
Andrew B Leeka, *CEO*
EMP: 681
SALES: 120.9K
SALES (corp-wide): 319.2MM **Privately Held**
SIC: 8011 Orthopedic physician
PA: Good Samaritan Hospital
   1225 Wilshire Blvd
   Los Angeles CA 90017

(P-19505)
TIBURCIO VASQUEZ HLTH CTR INC (PA)
33255 9th St, Union City (94587-2137)
PHONE..........................510 471-5880
David B Vliet, *CEO*
Luis Arenas, *Partner*
Yolanda Triana, *President*
Brent Copen, *CFO*
Malou Martinez, *CFO*
EMP: 50
SQ FT: 15,000
SALES: 23.7MM **Privately Held**
SIC: 8011 Primary care medical clinic

(P-19506)
TIBURCIO VASQUEZ HLTH CTR INC
22331 Mission Blvd, Hayward (94541-3911)
PHONE..........................510 471-5907
Malou Martinez, *Branch Mgr*
EMP: 86
SALES (corp-wide): 23.7MM **Privately Held**
SIC: 8011 Primary care medical clinic
PA: Tiburcio Vasquez Health Center Incorporated
   33255 9th St
   Union City CA 94587
   510 471-5880

(P-19507)
TORRANCE SURGERY CENTER LP
Also Called: Amsurg
23560 Crenshaw Blvd # 104, Torrance (90505-5233)
PHONE..........................310 986-2005
Nick Silvino MD, *Partner*
Ripu Arora MD, *Partner*
Marc Colman MD, *Partner*
Steve Dinsmore MD, *Partner*
Nelman Low MD, *Partner*
EMP: 2202 EST: 2001
SQ FT: 6,300
SALES: 42.9MM
SALES (corp-wide): 643.1MM **Privately Held**
WEB: www.natsurgcare.com
SIC: 8011 Surgeon
HQ: Envision Healthcare Corporation
   1a Burton Hills Blvd
   Nashville TN 37215
   615 665-1283

(P-19508)
TOWER HEMATOLOGY ONCOLOGY MEDI
9090 Wilshire Blvd # 200, Beverly Hills (90211-1848)
P.O. Box 5624 (90209-5605)
PHONE..........................310 888-8680
Robert W Decker MD, *Partner*
Heydi Ellis, *Admin Asst*
Alicia Lopez, *IT/INT Sup*
Robert Decker, *Oncology*
David Hoffman, *Oncology*
EMP: 75
SQ FT: 13,000
SALES (est): 10MM **Privately Held**
WEB: www.toweroncology.com
SIC: 8011 Hematologist; oncologist

(P-19509)
TRACY TRUJILLO MD
200 Porter Dr Ste 300, San Ramon (94583-1524)
PHONE..........................925 838-6511
Tracy Trujillo, *Principal*
EMP: 50
SALES (est): 670.9K **Privately Held**
SIC: 8011 Pediatrician

(P-19510)
TRI CITY ORTHOPEDIC SGY & MDCL
Also Called: Neville Alleyne MD
3905 Waring Rd, Oceanside (92056-4405)
PHONE..........................760 724-9000
James Esch, *President*
Dr Neville Alleyne, *Bd of Directors*
Dr James Helgager, *Bd of Directors*
Dr Norman Kane, *Bd of Directors*
Dr Richard Muir, *Bd of Directors*
▲ EMP: 50
SQ FT: 10,000
SALES (est): 7.3MM **Privately Held**
WEB: www.tricityortho.com
SIC: 8011 Orthopedic physician; surgeon

(P-19511)
TRI-CITY HEALTH CENTER (PA)
39500 Liberty St, Fremont (94538-2211)
PHONE..........................510 770-8040
Kathleen Lievre, *CEO*
EMP: 148 EST: 1972

SALES: 30.3MM **Privately Held**
WEB: www.tri-cityhealth.org
SIC: 8011 Offices & clinics of medical doctors

(P-19512)
TUOLUMNE ME-WUK INDIAN
Also Called: Tuolumne Mewuk Indian Health
18880 Cherry Valley Blvd, Tuolumne (95379-9506)
PHONE..........................209 928-5400
Christopher Gorsky, *Principal*
Darla Merlin, *Ch of Bd*
Tammy Barker, *Finance Dir*
EMP: 90
SQ FT: 11,000
SALES: 7.8MM **Privately Held**
SIC: 8011 Clinic, operated by physicians

(P-19513)
TWIN CITIES COMMUNITY HOSP INC
1100 Las Tablas Rd, Templeton (93465-9704)
PHONE..........................805 434-3500
Mark P Lisa, *CEO*
Paul Posmosga, *CFO*
William Gamba, *Ch Nursing Ofcr*
Myint Singh, *Anesthesiology*
Kelly Branck, *Supervisor*
EMP: 450
SQ FT: 120,000
SALES: 17.7K
SALES (corp-wide): 18.3B **Publicly Held**
WEB: www.tenethealth.com
SIC: 8011 8062 Medical centers; general medical & surgical hospitals
PA: Tenet Healthcare Corporation
   1445 Ross Ave Ste 1400
   Dallas TX 75202
   469 893-2200

(P-19514)
UC REGENTS
Also Called: Ucla Nrpsychtric Bhvioral Hlth
300 Medical Plaza, Los Angeles (90095-0001)
PHONE..........................310 301-8777
Jody Gaspar, *Principal*
Lavonte Hickman, *Principal*
EMP: 99
SALES (est): 4.2MM **Privately Held**
SIC: 8011 8049 Medical centers; clinical psychologist; speech pathologist; psychiatric social worker; psychotherapist, except M.D.

(P-19515)
UNITED FAMILY CARE INC
8110 Mango Ave Ste 104, Fontana (92335-3603)
PHONE..........................909 874-1679
Keith Schauermann, *President*
EMP: 120
SALES (est): 5.8MM **Privately Held**
WEB: www.unitedfamilycare.com
SIC: 8011 Primary care medical clinic

(P-19516)
UNITED INDIAN HEALTH SVCS INC (PA)
Also Called: Potawot Health Clinic
1600 Weeot Way, Arcata (95521-4734)
PHONE..........................707 825-5000
David Rosen, *CFO*
EMP: 150
SQ FT: 46,304
SALES: 26.7MM **Privately Held**
WEB: www.uihs.org
SIC: 8011 8021 8031 5912 Clinic, operated by physicians; primary care medical clinic; dental clinics & offices; offices & clinics of osteopathic physicians; drug stores; mental health clinic, outpatient; community center

(P-19517)
UNITED MEDICAL IMAGING INC
Also Called: Umi of Huntington Beach
16161 Gothard St Ste C, Huntington Beach (92647-3603)
PHONE..........................714 843-6255
Vivian Thai, *Administration*
David Haynes, *Director*
EMP: 78 **Privately Held**
SIC: 8011 Medical centers

PA: United Medical Imaging, Inc.
   1762 Westwood Blvd # 230
   Los Angeles CA 90024

(P-19518)
UNITED STATES DEPT OF NAVY
8808 Balboa Ave, San Diego (92123-1592)
PHONE..........................619 532-6397
Mike Clark, *Branch Mgr*
EMP: 924 **Publicly Held**
SIC: 8011 Medical centers
HQ: United States Department Of The Navy
   1200 Navy Pentagon
   Washington DC 20350

(P-19519)
UNITED STATES DEPT OF NAVY
34800 Bob Wilson Dr # 409, San Diego (92134-1409)
PHONE..........................619 532-8953
Elizabeth Ferrara, *Principal*
EMP: 924 **Publicly Held**
SIC: 8011 Anesthesiologist
HQ: United States Department Of The Navy
   1200 Navy Pentagon
   Washington DC 20350

(P-19520)
UNITED STATES DEPT OF NAVY
Also Called: Naval Dental Center
2310 Craven St, San Diego (92136-5596)
PHONE..........................619 556-8210
Pete Seder, *Branch Mgr*
EMP: 300 **Publicly Held**
SIC: 8011 9711 Health maintenance organization; Navy;
HQ: United States Department Of The Navy
   1200 Navy Pentagon
   Washington DC 20350

(P-19521)
UNITED STATES DEPT OF NAVY
Also Called: US Naval Medical Clinical Lab
162 1st St, Port Hueneme (93043-4316)
PHONE..........................805 982-6392
Sharon West, *Principal*
EMP: 924 **Publicly Held**
SIC: 8011 9711 Primary care medical clinic; Navy;
HQ: United States Department Of The Navy
   1200 Navy Pentagon
   Washington DC 20350

(P-19522)
UNITED STATES DEPT OF NAVY
Naval Med Ctr Crdiolgy Clinic
34730 Bob Wilson Dr, San Diego (92134-3098)
PHONE..........................619 532-7400
Ed Doorn, *Manager*
Anna P Helgeson, *Med Doctor*
EMP: 924 **Publicly Held**
SIC: 8011 9711 Cardiologist & cardio-vascular specialist; Navy;
HQ: United States Department Of The Navy
   1200 Navy Pentagon
   Washington DC 20350

(P-19523)
UNITED STATES DEPT OF NAVY
Also Called: Naval Medical Clinic
162 1st St Bldg 1402, Port Hueneme (93043-4316)
PHONE..........................805 982-6370
J F Murray, *Branch Mgr*
EMP: 924 **Publicly Held**
SIC: 8011 9711 Primary care medical clinic; Navy;
HQ: United States Department Of The Navy
   1200 Navy Pentagon
   Washington DC 20350

(P-19524)
UNITED STATES DEPT OF NAVY
Also Called: Navmedwest
4170 Norman Scott Rd, San Diego (92136-5501)
PHONE..........................619 767-6592
Cdr M Campbell, *Branch Mgr*

Patty Miller, *Director*
EMP: 924 Publicly Held
SIC: 8011 Offices & clinics of medical doctors
HQ: United States Department Of The Navy
1200 Navy Pentagon
Washington DC 20350
-

(P-19525)
UNIVERSITY CAL LOS ANGELES
Also Called: Ucla Primary Care Westlake
1250 Avanta Dr Ste 207, Westlake Village (91361)
PHONE..................805 494-6920
Dina Sarabia, *Branch Mgr*
Sonya Heitmann, *Internal Med*
Anitha Srinivasa, *Internal Med*
EMP: 50 Privately Held
SIC: 8011 8221 9411 Primary care medical clinic; university; administration of educational programs;
HQ: University Of California, Los Angeles
405 Hilgard Av
Los Angeles CA 90095
-

(P-19526)
UNIVERSITY CAL SAN FRANCISCO
Also Called: Ucsf Medical Center
3330 Geary Blvd, San Francisco (94118-3347)
PHONE..................415 353-3155
Monica Seay, *Branch Mgr*
Gemma Bernabe, *Opers Staff*
Jeanette Capitulo, *Opers Staff*
EMP: 60 Privately Held
SIC: 8011 8221 9411 Medical centers; university; administration of educational programs;
HQ: University Cal San Francisco
513 Parnassus Ave 115f
San Francisco CA 94143

(P-19527)
UNIVERSITY CALIFORNIA DAVIS
2315 Stockton Blvd # 6309, Sacramento (95817-2201)
PHONE..................916 734-2846
Valerie Adame, *Branch Mgr*
Joanna Baginski, *Med Doctor*
William C Peve, *Med Doctor*
Kurt Steen,
Emalie Chandras, *Assistant*
EMP: 50 Privately Held
SIC: 8011 8221 9411 Surgeon; university; administration of educational programs;
HQ: University Of California, Davis
1 Shields Ave
Davis CA 95616
-

(P-19528)
UNIVERSITY CALIFORNIA DAVIS
Also Called: Cowell Student Health Center
Student House Ctr, Davis (95616)
PHONE..................530 752-2300
Dr Michelle Famula, *Director*
EMP: 150 Privately Held
WEB: www.ucdavis.edu
SIC: 8011 8221 9411 Medical centers; university; administration of educational programs;
HQ: University Of California, Davis
1 Shields Ave
Davis CA 95616
-

(P-19529)
UNIVERSITY CALIFORNIA IRVINE
Also Called: Uc Irvine Hlth Rgonal Burn Ctr
101 The City Dr S Bldg 1a, Orange (92868-3201)
PHONE..................714 456-6170
Howard Federoff, *Vice Chancellor*
Aaron Nisley, *Practice Mgr*
Elisa Apiz, *Admin Asst*
Linda Ketchersid, *Administration*
Aida Ang, *Programmer Anys*
EMP: 1757 Privately Held

WEB: www.com.uci.edu
SIC: 8011 8221 9411 Medical centers; university; administration of educational programs;
HQ: University Of California, Irvine
510 Aldrich Hall
Irvine CA 92697
949 824-8343

(P-19530)
UNIVERSITY CALIFORNIA IRVINE
Also Called: UCI Family Health Center
800 N Main St, Santa Ana (92701-3576)
PHONE..................714 480-2443
Nancy D Hurtado, *Manager*
Aaron Barth, *Professor*
Marco Angulo, *Family Practiti*
Huy Tran, *Family Practiti*
Ivan Coziahr, *Director*
EMP: 65
SQ FT: 49,361 Privately Held
WEB: www.com.uci.edu
SIC: 8011 8221 9411 Medical centers; university; administration of educational programs;
HQ: University Of California, Irvine
510 Aldrich Hall
Irvine CA 92697
949 824-8343

(P-19531)
UNIVERSITY CALIFORNIA IRVINE
1640 Newport Blvd Ste 340, Costa Mesa (92627-7730)
PHONE..................949 646-2267
Olivia Reil, *Branch Mgr*
EMP: 50 Privately Held
SIC: 8011 8221 9411 Gynecologist; university; administration of educational programs;
HQ: University Of California, Irvine
510 Aldrich Hall
Irvine CA 92697
949 824-8343

(P-19532)
UNIVERSITY CALIFORNIA BERKELEY
Also Called: University Health Services
2222 Bancroft Way, Berkeley (94720-4301)
PHONE..................510 642-2000
Diane Liu MD, *Principal*
Dominic Labanowski, *Vice Pres*
Kniffin Michelle, *Associate Dir*
Teresa Liu, *Division Mgr*
David Zusman, *Professor*
EMP: 370 Privately Held
WEB: www.law.berkeley.edu
SIC: 8011 8221 9411 Dispensary, operated by physicians; university; administration of educational programs;
HQ: The University California Berkeley
200 Clfrnia Hall Spc 1500
Berkeley CA 94720
510 642-6000

(P-19533)
UNIVERSITY SOUTHERN CALIFORNIA
Also Called: Usc Student Health Center
849 W 34th St Ste 208, Los Angeles (90089-0079)
PHONE..................213 743-5339
Dr Steven Gardner, *Principal*
EMP: 60
SALES (corp-wide): 4.9B Privately Held
WEB: www.usc.edu
SIC: 8011 8221 Medical centers; university
PA: University Of Southern California
3720 S Flower St Fl 3
Los Angeles CA 90089
213 740-7762

(P-19534)
UROLOGY ASSOC OF CEN CAL
7014 N Whitney Ave Ste A, Fresno (93720-0155)
PHONE..................559 321-2800
Gilbert Dale MD, *President*
Artin Jibilian MD, *Treasurer*
Irwin S Barg MD, *Vice Pres*
Yuk-Yuen Leung, *Managing Dir*

William Schiff MD, *Admin Sec*
EMP: 90
SQ FT: 28,074
SALES (est): 6.7MM Privately Held
WEB: www.fresnosecurity.us
SIC: 8011 Urologist

(P-19535)
US DEPT OF THE AIR FORCE
Also Called: Sgokc
15301 Warren Shingle Rd, Beale Afb (95903-1907)
PHONE..................530 634-4738
Melvin Antonio, *Branch Mgr*
EMP: 90 Publicly Held
WEB: www.af.mil
SIC: 8011 9711 Pediatrician; Air Force;
HQ: United States Department Of The Air Force
1000 Air Force Pentagon
Washington DC 20330

(P-19536)
US HEALTHWORKS INC (DH)
Also Called: U.S. Healthworks Medical Group
28035 Avenue Stanford, Valencia (91355-1104)
PHONE..................661 678-2300
Keith Newton, *President*
Su Zan Nelson, *CFO*
John Anderson, *Chief Mktg Ofcr*
John Delorimier, *Exec VP*
Jim Talalai, *Senior VP*
EMP: 60
SALES (est): 215.2MM
SALES (corp-wide): 5B Publicly Held
SIC: 8011 Clinic, operated by physicians
HQ: Concentra Inc.
5080 Spectrum Dr Ste 400w
Addison TX 75001
972 364-8000

(P-19537)
USC EMERGENCY MEDICINE ASSOC
1200 N State St Ste 1011, Los Angeles (90033-1029)
PHONE..................323 226-6667
Fax: 323 226-6806
EMP: 80
SALES (est): 3.9MM Privately Held
SIC: 8011

(P-19538)
USC INSTITUTE FOR NEUROIMAGING
Also Called: Usc MARk& Mary Steven Neuro
2001 N Soto St Ste 102, Los Angeles (90032-3675)
PHONE..................323 442-7246
Arthur Toga, *Director*
EMP: 125
SALES (est): 222.8K Privately Held
SIC: 8011 Offices & clinics of medical doctors

(P-19539)
USC SURGEONS INCORPORATED
Also Called: Usc Srgcal Edcatn RES Fndation
1510 San Pablo St Ste 514, Los Angeles (90033-5324)
PHONE..................323 442-5910
Tom Demeester MD, *President*
Eric Alcorn, *Exec VP*
Albert Yellin MD, *Admin Sec*
EMP: 250
SQ FT: 15,000
SALES (est): 11.1MM Privately Held
SIC: 8011 Specialized medical practitioners, except internal

(P-19540)
VALLEY CHILDRENS HEALTHCARE
9300 Valley Childrens Pl, Madera (93636-8761)
PHONE..................559 353-3000
Todd Suntrapak, *CEO*
William Chaltraw, *Vice Pres*
Tami Evers, *Analyst*
Joseph Hernandez, *Analyst*
Dennis Yee, *Recruiter*
EMP: 2800

SALES: 698.2MM Privately Held
SIC: 8011 8069 Physical medicine, physician/surgeon; physicians' office, including specialists; children's hospital

(P-19541)
VALLEY COMMUNITY HEALTHCARE
6801 Coldwater Canyon Ave 1b, North Hollywood (91605-5164)
PHONE..................818 763-8836
Paula Wilson, *CEO*
Lee Huey, *CFO*
Judi Rose, *Vice Pres*
Allaine Herrera, *Controller*
Irina Pogosyan, *Human Res Dir*
EMP: 300
SQ FT: 15,000
SALES: 22.3MM Privately Held
WEB: www.valleycommunityclinic.org
SIC: 8011 Clinic, operated by physicians

(P-19542)
VALLEY MEDICAL GROUP OF LOMPOC
Also Called: Bailey, Rollin C MD
136 N 3rd St, Lompoc (93436-7099)
PHONE..................805 736-1253
William H Gausman Jr, *President*
B J Coughlin MD, *Corp Secy*
Eldon Elam MD, *Vice Pres*
Rollin C Bailey, *Managing Dir*
Thomas E Fritch, *Managing Dir*
EMP: 60 EST: 1965
SQ FT: 10,700
SALES (est): 8.3MM Privately Held
WEB: www.vmglompoc.com
SIC: 8011 Internal medicine, physician/surgeon; general & family practice, physician/surgeon

(P-19543)
VALLEY OB GYN MEDICAL GROUP
400 N Pepper Ave Fl 6, Colton (92324-1801)
PHONE..................909 580-6333
Guillermo Valenzuela, *President*
EMP: 50
SALES (est): 4.3MM Privately Held
SIC: 8011 Gynecologist

(P-19544)
VALLEYCARE HOSPITAL CORP (DH)
Also Called: Valleycare Health
1111 E Stanley Blvd, Livermore (94550-4115)
PHONE..................925 447-7000
Marcelina L Feit, *President*
Tracy McClain, *CFO*
Doreen Montemayor, *Officer*
Chris Faber, *Exec Dir*
Shake Sulikyan, *Exec Dir*
EMP: 67
SALES (est): 68.3MM
SALES (corp-wide): 11.3B Privately Held
SIC: 8011 Primary care medical clinic
HQ: The Hospital Committee For The Livermore-Pleasanton Areas
5555 W Las Positas Blvd
Pleasanton CA 94588
925 847-3000

(P-19545)
VAN GROW JACK S MD
1140 W La Veta Ave # 640, Orange (92868-4225)
PHONE..................714 564-3300
Jack Van Grow, *Partner*
Jack Vangrow, *Partner*
EMP: 50
SALES (est): 723.5K Privately Held
WEB: www.ocheart.com
SIC: 8011 Cardiologist & cardio-vascular specialist

(P-19546)
VANTAGE ONCOLOGY LLC (HQ)
1500 Rosecrans Ave # 400, Manhattan Beach (90266-3754)
P.O. Box 10033 (90267-7533)
PHONE..................310 335-4000
Michael Fiore, *CEO*
Dee Delapp, *President*

P R O D U C T S & S V C S

Marshal Salomon, *COO*
Brian Rizkallah, *CFO*
Leslie E Botnick, *Chief Mktg Ofcr*
EMP: 300
SQ FT: 150,000
SALES (est): 53.3MM
SALES (corp-wide): 214.3B **Publicly Held**
SIC: 8011 Oncologist
PA: Mckesson Corporation
6555 State Highway 161
Irving TX 75039
972 446-4800

(P-19547)
VANTAGE ONCOLOGY INC
1500 Rosecrans Ave # 400, Manhattan Beach (90266-3754)
PHONE................310 335-4000
Michael T Fiore, *CEO*
Eliot Levitt, *Vice Pres*
Sean Reis, *Info Tech Dir*
Christy Harper, *Analyst*
Marjan Kruisheer, *Human Res Dir*
EMP: 60
SALES (est): 1.8MM
SALES (corp-wide): 214.3B **Publicly Held**
SIC: 8011 Oncologist
HQ: Vantage Oncology, Llc
1500 Rosecrans Ave # 400
Manhattan Beach CA 90266
-

(P-19548)
VENICE FAMILY CLINIC (PA)
604 Rose Ave, Venice (90291-2767)
PHONE................310 664-7703
Elizabeth Forer, *CEO*
Andrea Blackbird, *CFO*
Gordon Lee, *Treasurer*
Stewart Seradsky, *Treasurer*
Jeffrey E Sinaiko, *Treasurer*
EMP: 61
SALES: 41.8MM **Privately Held**
SIC: 8011 Primary care medical clinic

(P-19549)
VENTURA COUNTY HEMATOLOGY (PA)
1700 N Rose Ave Ste 320, Oxnard (93030-7648)
PHONE................805 485-8709
Kooros Parsa MD, *Partner*
Kevin Cheng, *Partner*
Ann S Kelley MD, *Partner*
Lynn Kong, *Partner*
Rosemary McIntyre, *Partner*
EMP: 50
SALES (est): 3.9MM **Privately Held**
WEB: www.venturaoncology.com
SIC: 8011 Oncologist

(P-19550)
VENTURA COUNTY MEDICAL CENTER
Also Called: Santa Paula Hospital
845 N 10th St Ste 3, Santa Paula (93060-1348)
PHONE................805 933-8600
EMP: 69
SALES (corp-wide): 371.8MM **Privately Held**
SIC: 8011 Medical centers
PA: Ventura County Medical Center
3291 Loma Vista Rd
Ventura CA 93003
805 652-6000

(P-19551)
VENTURA COUNTY MEDICAL CENTER (PA)
3291 Loma Vista Rd, Ventura (93003-3099)
PHONE................805 652-6000
Ronald O'Halloran, *Principal*
George Paul,
Robert McMahan, *Ch Radiology*
Carla Cross, *Train & Dev Mgr*
Megan Krispinsky, *Family Practiti*
EMP: 138
SALES: 371.8MM **Privately Held**
SIC: 8011 Medical centers

(P-19552)
VENTURA COUNTY MEDICAL CENTER
Also Called: Ana Nacapa Surgical Associates
3291 Loma Vista Rd # 343, Ventura (93003-3099)
PHONE................805 652-6201
Scott Arnold, *Principal*
EMP: 85
SALES (corp-wide): 371.8MM **Privately Held**
SIC: 8011 Medical centers
PA: Ventura County Medical Center
3291 Loma Vista Rd
Ventura CA 93003
805 652-6000

(P-19553)
VERDUGO HILLS URGENT CARE MG
Also Called: Verdugo Hills Medical Assoc
544 N Glendale Ave, Glendale (91206-3311)
PHONE................818 241-4331
Richard A Foullon, *President*
Cynthia Foullon, *Vice Pres*
EMP: 62
SQ FT: 11,000
SALES (est): 4.8MM **Privately Held**
WEB: www.vhma.com
SIC: 8011 Medical centers

(P-19554)
VERITY MEDICAL FOUNDATION (HQ)
Also Called: San Jose Medical Group / MGT
400 Race St, San Jose (95126-3518)
PHONE................408 278-3000
Richard Adcock, *CEO*
Ernest Wallerstein, *CEO*
Christine Hoskinson, *CFO*
Shahida Malik, *Managing Dir*
Arthur Feldman, *Med Doctor*
EMP: 80
SALES (est): 48.6MM
SALES (corp-wide): 995MM **Privately Held**
SIC: 8011 8741 Medical centers; management services
PA: Verity Health System Of California, Inc.
2040 E Mariposa Ave
El Segundo CA 90245
650 551-6650

(P-19555)
VETERANS HEALTH ADMINISTRATION
Also Called: Mare Island Outpatient Clinic
Walnut Ave Bldg 201, Vallejo (94589)
PHONE................707 562-8200
Debra Nathanson, *Manager*
EMP: 264 **Publicly Held**
WEB: www.veterans-ru.org
SIC: 8011 9451 Clinic, operated by physicians; psychiatric clinic;
HQ: Veterans Health Administration
810 Vermont Ave Nw
Washington DC 20420

(P-19556)
VETERANS HEALTH ADMINISTRATION
Also Called: West Los Angeles V A Med Ctr
11301 Wilshire Blvd, Los Angeles (90073-1003)
PHONE................310 478-3711
Donna Beiter, *Director*
Tung Phan, *Network Mgr*
Deniz Ahmadinia, *Psychologist*
Mark Sawicki, *Surgeon*
Natalya Bussel, *Psychiatry*
EMP: 4374 **Publicly Held**
WEB: www.veterans-ru.org
SIC: 8011 9451 Clinic, operated by physicians; psychiatric clinic;
HQ: Veterans Health Administration
810 Vermont Ave Nw
Washington DC 20420
-

(P-19557)
VETERANS HEALTH ADMINISTRATION
Also Called: San Luis Obispo VA Cboc
1288 Morro St Ste 200, San Luis Obispo (93401-6302)
PHONE................805 543-1233
Mark Donaldson, *Branch Mgr*
EMP: 264 **Publicly Held**
SIC: 8011 9451 Clinic, operated by physicians;
HQ: Veterans Health Administration
810 Vermont Ave Nw
Washington DC 20420

(P-19558)
VETERANS HEALTH ADMINISTRATION
Also Called: Sacramento Mental Hlth Clinic
10535 Hospital Way, Mather (95655-4200)
PHONE................916 366-5427
Charles Barnett, *Manager*
EMP: 264 **Publicly Held**
WEB: www.veterans-ru.org
SIC: 8011 9451 Clinic, operated by physicians; psychiatric clinic;
HQ: Veterans Health Administration
810 Vermont Ave Nw
Washington DC 20420

(P-19559)
VETERANS HEALTH ADMINISTRATION
Also Called: Central Cal Healthcare Sys
2615 E Clinton Ave, Fresno (93703-2223)
PHONE................559 225-6100
Al Perry, *Branch Mgr*
EMP: 800 **Publicly Held**
WEB: www.veterans-ru.org
SIC: 8011 9451 Medical centers; administration of veterans' affairs;
HQ: Veterans Health Administration
810 Vermont Ave Nw
Washington DC 20420

(P-19560)
VETERANS HEALTH ADMINISTRATION
Also Called: Redding V A Outpatient Clinic
351 Hartnell Ave, Redding (96002-1845)
PHONE................530 226-7555
Anthony Pineda, *Branch Mgr*
Corsini Templado, *Internal Med*
EMP: 264 **Publicly Held**
WEB: www.veterans-ru.org
SIC: 8011 9451 Clinic, operated by physicians; psychiatric clinic;
HQ: Veterans Health Administration
810 Vermont Ave Nw
Washington DC 20420

(P-19561)
VETERANS HEALTH ADMINISTRATION
Also Called: Palo Alto VA Medical Center
3801 Miranda Ave Bldg 101, Palo Alto (94304-1207)
PHONE................650 493-5000
Elizabeth Freeman, *Director*
Jude Lopez, *Officer*
Katherine Portugal, *Med Doctor*
EMP: 3500 **Publicly Held**
WEB: www.veterans-ru.org
SIC: 8011 9451 Medical centers;
HQ: Veterans Health Administration
810 Vermont Ave Nw
Washington DC 20420

(P-19562)
VETERANS HEALTH ADMINISTRATION
Also Called: Oakland V A Outpatient Clinic
2221 Martin Luther King J, Oakland (94612-1318)
PHONE................510 267-7820
Dr Elmer Anderson, *Principal*
EMP: 264 **Publicly Held**
WEB: www.veterans-ru.org

(P-19563)
VETERANS HEALTH ADMINISTRATION
Also Called: San Francisco Vamc
4150 Clement St 6205, San Francisco (94121-1563)
PHONE................415 750-2009
Brian J Kelly, *Manager*
Ellen Peterson, *Nursing Mgr*
Art Wallace, *Anesthesiology*
Rizwan Aslam, *Radiology*
Harry Lampiris, *Director*
EMP: 85 **Publicly Held**
WEB: www.veterans-ru.org
SIC: 8011 9451 Medical centers; psychiatric clinic;
HQ: Veterans Health Administration
810 Vermont Ave Nw
Washington DC 20420

(P-19564)
VETERANS HEALTH ADMINISTRATION
Also Called: Chico V A Outpatient Clinic
280 Cohasset Rd, Chico (95926-2210)
PHONE................530 879-5000
Sonny Morgan, *Manager*
EMP: 264 **Publicly Held**
WEB: www.veterans-ru.org
SIC: 8011 9451 Clinic, operated by physicians; psychiatric clinic;
HQ: Veterans Health Administration
810 Vermont Ave Nw
Washington DC 20420

(P-19565)
VETERANS HEALTH ADMINISTRATION
Also Called: Santa Rosa Clinic
3315 Chanate Rd, Santa Rosa (95404-1736)
PHONE................707 570-3800
Donald B Dean, *Manager*
EMP: 264 **Publicly Held**
WEB: www.veterans-ru.org
SIC: 8011 9451 Clinic, operated by physicians; psychiatric clinic;
HQ: Veterans Health Administration
810 Vermont Ave Nw
Washington DC 20420

(P-19566)
VETERANS HEALTH ADMINISTRATION
Also Called: Chula Vista Veterans Center
835 Third Ave, Chula Vista (91911-1352)
PHONE................619 409-1600
Harvey Souza, *Manager*
EMP: 264 **Publicly Held**
WEB: www.veterans-ru.org
SIC: 8011 9451 Medical centers; psychiatric clinic;
HQ: Veterans Health Administration
810 Vermont Ave Nw
Washington DC 20420

(P-19567)
VETERANS HEALTH ADMINISTRATION
Also Called: Escondido Veterans Center
815 E Pennsylvania Ave, Escondido (92025-3424)
PHONE................760 745-2000
Jamie Switzer, *Principal*
EMP: 264 **Publicly Held**
WEB: www.veterans-ru.org
SIC: 8011 9451 Medical centers; psychiatric clinic;
HQ: Veterans Health Administration
810 Vermont Ave Nw
Washington DC 20420

(P-19568)
VETERANS HEALTH ADMINISTRATION
Also Called: Oxnard Veterans Center
250 Citrus Grove Ln # 250, Oxnard
(93036-9030)
PHONE..................................805 983-6384
EMP: 263 **Publicly Held**
SIC: 8011 9451
HQ: Veterans Health Administration
810 Vermont Ave Nw
Washington DC 20420
-

(P-19569)
VETERANS HEALTH ADMINISTRATION
Also Called: Mission Valley V A
8810 Rio San Diego Dr, San Diego
(92108-1698)
PHONE..................................619 400-5000
EMP: 264 **Publicly Held**
WEB: www.veterans-ru.org
SIC: 8011 9451 Clinic, operated by physicians; psychiatric clinic;
HQ: Veterans Health Administration
810 Vermont Ave Nw
Washington DC 20420
-

(P-19570)
VETERANS HEALTH ADMINISTRATION
Also Called: Sepulveda Ambulatory Care
16111 Plummer St, North Hills
(91343-2036)
PHONE..................................818 891-7711
Dolly G Whitehead, *Manager*
EMP: 900 **Publicly Held**
WEB: www.veterans-ru.org
SIC: 8011 9451 Medical centers; psychiatric clinic;
HQ: Veterans Health Administration
810 Vermont Ave Nw
Washington DC 20420
-

(P-19571)
VETERANS HEALTH ADMINISTRATION
Also Called: Sacramento V A Medical Center
10535 Hospital Way, Mather (95655-4200)
PHONE..................................916 843-7000
Lawrence Sandlers, *Director*
EMP: 500 **Publicly Held**
WEB: www.veterans-ru.org
SIC: 8011 9451 Medical centers; administration of veterans' affairs;
HQ: Veterans Health Administration
810 Vermont Ave Nw
Washington DC 20420
-

(P-19572)
VETERANS HEALTH ADMINISTRATION
Also Called: Livermore VA Medical Center
4951 Arroyo Rd, Livermore (94550-9650)
PHONE..................................925 447-2560
C H Nixon, *Director*
Val Sia, *Radiology Dir*
EMP: 450 **Publicly Held**
WEB: www.veterans-ru.org
SIC: 8011 9451 Medical centers;
HQ: Veterans Health Administration
810 Vermont Ave Nw
Washington DC 20420
-

(P-19573)
VETERANS HEALTH ADMINISTRATION
Also Called: Loma Linda Healthcare Sys 605
11201 Benton St, Loma Linda
(92357-1000)
PHONE..................................909 825-7084
Debbie Romero, *Branch Mgr*
Michael Miller, *Officer*
EMP: 2000 **Publicly Held**
WEB: www.veterans-ru.org
SIC: 8011 9451 Medical centers; psychiatric clinic;

HQ: Veterans Health Administration
810 Vermont Ave Nw
Washington DC 20420

(P-19574)
VETERANS HEALTH ADMINISTRATION
Also Called: Menlo Park VA Medical Center
795 Willow Rd, Menlo Park (94025-2539)
PHONE..................................650 614-9997
Lisa Freeman, *Director*
EMP: 3000 **Publicly Held**
WEB: www.veterans-ru.org
SIC: 8011 9451 Medical centers; psychiatric clinic;
HQ: Veterans Health Administration
810 Vermont Ave Nw
Washington DC 20420
-

(P-19575)
VETERANS HEALTH ADMINISTRATION
Also Called: VA HSR&d Center of Excellence
16111 Plummer St, North Hills
(91343-2036)
PHONE..................................818 895-9449
Lisa Rubenstein, *Branch Mgr*
EMP: 99 **Publicly Held**
WEB: www.veterans-ru.org
SIC: 8011 9451 Medical centers; administration of veterans' affairs;
HQ: Veterans Health Administration
810 Vermont Ave Nw
Washington DC 20420
-

(P-19576)
VETERANS HEALTH ADMINISTRATION
Also Called: Anaheim V A Clinic
1801 W Romneya Dr Ste 303, Anaheim
(92801-1825)
PHONE..................................714 780-5400
Teresa Carpenter, *Branch Mgr*
EMP: 183 **Publicly Held**
WEB: www.veterans-ru.org
SIC: 8011 9451 Clinic, operated by physicians; administration of veterans' affairs;
HQ: Veterans Health Administration
810 Vermont Ave Nw
Washington DC 20420
-

(P-19577)
VETERANS HEALTH ADMINISTRATION
Also Called: Bakersfield Community Based
1801 Westwind Dr, Bakersfield
(93301-3028)
PHONE..................................661 632-1871
Joan Van Horn, *Manager*
EMP: 50 **Publicly Held**
WEB: www.veterans-ru.org
SIC: 8011 9451 Clinic, operated by physicians; psychiatric clinic;
HQ: Veterans Health Administration
810 Vermont Ave Nw
Washington DC 20420
-

(P-19578)
VETERANS HEALTH ADMINISTRATION
Also Called: Los Angles Ambulatory Care Ctr
351 E Temple St, Los Angeles
(90012-3328)
PHONE..................................213 253-2677
Lane Turzan, *General Mgr*
EMP: 190 **Publicly Held**
WEB: www.veterans-ru.org
SIC: 8011 9451 Medical centers; psychiatric clinic;
HQ: Veterans Health Administration
810 Vermont Ave Nw
Washington DC 20420
-

(P-19579)
VETERANS HEALTH ADMINISTRATION
Also Called: Bakersfield Vet Center
1110 Golden Valley Fwy, Bakersfield
(93301)
PHONE..................................661 323-8387
Jenney Frank, *Office Mgr*
EMP: 264 **Publicly Held**
SIC: 8011 9451 Medical centers; psychiatric clinic;
HQ: Veterans Health Administration
810 Vermont Ave Nw
Washington DC 20420
-

(P-19580)
VETERINARY SURGICAL ASSOCIATES
251 N Amphlett Blvd, San Mateo
(94401-1805)
PHONE..................................650 696-8196
Sharon Ullman, *Manager*
EMP: 60
SALES (est): 736.1K
SALES (corp-wide): 6.1MM **Privately Held**
SIC: 8011 0742 Freestanding emergency medical center; surgeon; veterinarian, animal specialties
PA: Veterinary Surgical Associates
1410 Monu Blvd Ste 100
Concord CA 94520
925 827-1777

(P-19581)
VIA CARE CMNTY HLTH CTR INC
Also Called: Bienvenidos Community Hlth Ctr
507 S Atlantic Blvd, Los Angeles
(90022-2621)
PHONE..................................323 268-9191
Deborah Villar, *CEO*
Joe Gotsill, *CFO*
EMP: 60
SALES (est): 2MM **Privately Held**
SIC: 8011 Primary care medical clinic

(P-19582)
VINOD KUMAR MD
5020 Commerce Dr, Bakersfield
(93309-0631)
P.O. Box 1351 (93302-1351)
PHONE..................................661 324-4100
Vinod Kumar, *Owner*
EMP: 75
SALES (est): 623K **Privately Held**
SIC: 8011 Cardiologist & cardio-vascular specialist

(P-19583)
VISALIA MEDICAL CLINIC INC (PA)
Also Called: Multi Specialty Medical Svc
5400 W Hillsdale Ave, Visalia (93291-5140)
PHONE..................................559 733-5222
Richard E Strid, *CEO*
Susan Rasmussen, *Executive*
Gilbert Sunio, *Managing Dir*
Rebecca Enos, *Office Mgr*
Raul Perez, *Gnrl Med Prac*
EMP: 299
SQ FT: 70,000
SALES (est): 41.1MM **Privately Held**
SIC: 8011 8071 Clinic, operated by physicians; medical laboratories

(P-19584)
VISCENT ORTHPD SOLUTIONS LLC (DH)
2885 Loker Ave E, Carlsbad (92010-6626)
PHONE..................................214 501-0180
Brad Lee, *Mng Member*
EMP: 50
SALES (est): 10.4MM
SALES (corp-wide): 330.2MM **Privately Held**
SIC: 8011 Orthopedic physician
HQ: Breg, Inc.
2885 Loker Ave E
Carlsbad CA 92010
760 599-3000

(P-19585)
VISION CARE CENTER (PA)
Also Called: Vision Care Center Central Cal
7075 N Sharon Ave, Fresno (93720-3329)
PHONE..................................559 486-2000
Julie Cleeland, *CEO*
Ralph Hadley Od, *President*
EMP: 82 EST: 1963
SQ FT: 18,000
SALES (est): 9.9MM **Privately Held**
WEB: www.eyeqvc.com
SIC: 8011 8042 Ophthalmologist; offices & clinics of optometrists

(P-19586)
VISTA COMMUNITY CLINIC
30195 Fraser Dr, Lake Elsinore
(92530-7006)
PHONE..................................951 245-2735
EMP: 52
SALES (corp-wide): 49.2MM **Privately Held**
SIC: 8011 Clinic, operated by physicians
PA: Vista Community Clinic
1000 Vale Terrace Dr
Vista CA 92084
760 631-5000

(P-19587)
WATTS HEALTHCARE CORPORATION
700 W Imperial Hwy, Los Angeles
(90044-4127)
PHONE..................................323 241-1780
EMP: 162
SALES (corp-wide): 34.1MM **Privately Held**
SIC: 8011
PA: Watts Healthcare Corporation
10300 Compton Ave
Los Angeles CA 90002
323 568-3059

(P-19588)
WATTS HEALTHCARE CORPORATION (PA)
10300 Compton Ave, Los Angeles
(90002-3628)
PHONE..................................323 564-4331
Roderick Seamster, *President*
Carroll J McNeely, *CFO*
Earnestene Wilson, *Bd of Directors*
Dolores Gay, *Admin Asst*
Sonny Tran, *Info Tech Mgr*
EMP: 180
SALES: 37.3MM **Privately Held**
WEB: www.wattshealth.com
SIC: 8011 Clinic, operated by physicians

(P-19589)
WAVE PLASTIC SURGERY CTR INC
18433 Colima Rd, La Puente (91748-5815)
PHONE..................................626 964-7788
Peter Lee, *President*
EMP: 160
SALES (corp-wide): 19.4MM **Privately Held**
SIC: 8011 Plastic surgeon
PA: Wave Plastic Surgery Center Inc.
3680 Wilshire Blvd Fl 2
Los Angeles CA 90010
213 383-4800

(P-19590)
WAYNE R KIDDER
915 Via Los Padres, Santa Barbara
(93111-1325)
PHONE..................................805 967-6993
Wayne R Kidder, *Owner*
EMP: 80
SALES (est): 3.6MM **Privately Held**
SIC: 8011 Offices & clinics of medical doctors

(P-19591)
WEST COAST CHILDRENS CENTER
545 Ashbury Ave, El Cerrito (94530-3220)
PHONE..................................510 269-9030
Dr Stacey Kath, *Exec Dir*
Dr Kenneth Parker, *Exec Dir*
EMP: 50

PRODUCTS & SVCS

SALES: 11.4MM **Privately Held**
SIC: 8011 8322 8049 Clinic, operated by physicians; social worker; clinical psychologist

(P-19592)
WEST COVINA MEDICAL CLINIC INC (PA)
1500 W West Covina Pkwy, West Covina (91790-2708)
PHONE.................................626 960-8614
Dr Ziad Dabuni, *President*
Dr Suntheetha Ali, *Treasurer*
Dr Shivani Shah, *Exec VP*
Dr Jose Bautista, *Asst Treas*
Beata A Wicherski, *Pediatrics*
EMP: 225
SQ FT: 50,000
SALES (est): 15.8MM **Privately Held**
SIC: 8011 Clinic, operated by physicians

(P-19593)
WEST DERMATOLOGY MED MGT INC
400 Newport Center Dr # 702, Newport Beach (92660-7601)
PHONE.................................909 793-3000
J Robert West, *President*
EMP: 140
SALES (est): 10.7MM **Privately Held**
SIC: 8011 Dermatologist

(P-19594)
WEST VENTURA FAMILY CARE CTR
Also Called: Rocha, Jill B MD
133 W Santa Clara St, Ventura (93001-2543)
PHONE.................................805 641-5620
Joan E Baumer MD, *Owner*
EMP: 54
SALES (est): 2.9MM **Privately Held**
SIC: 8011 Medical centers

(P-19595)
WESTERN MED ASSOC MED GROUP (PA)
1595 Soquel Dr Ste 330, Santa Cruz (95065-1722)
PHONE.................................831 475-1111
Robert D Keet MD, *Principal*
Statish Chandra MD, *Principal*
Vernon Loverde MD, *Principal*
Nicole Rojas, *Administration*
Thomas Yen, *Surgeon*
EMP: 60
SALES: 7.5MM **Privately Held**
SIC: 8011 Internal medicine, physician/surgeon

(P-19596)
WHITE MEMORIAL MED GROUP INC (PA)
1701 E Cesar E Chavez Ave # 510, Los Angeles (90033-2464)
P.O. Box 51741 (90051-6041)
PHONE.................................323 987-1300
Alan Lau, *President*
EMP: 75
SQ FT: 20,000
SALES (est): 8MM **Privately Held**
SIC: 8011 8742 Medical centers; hospital & health services consultant

(P-19597)
WILLIAM H WARDEN III MD
2760 Atlantic Ave, Long Beach (90806-2755)
PHONE.................................562 424-6666
William Warden, *Principal*
EMP: 75
SALES (est): 978K **Privately Held**
SIC: 8011 Orthopedic physician

(P-19598)
WILLIAM MCGANN MD
1 Shrader St Ste 650, San Francisco (94117-1036)
PHONE.................................415 221-0665
A Noble MD, *President*
Alan Noble MD, *President*
Ray Schmidt, *Office Mgr*
EMP: 54
SQ FT: 7,000

SALES (est): 1.6MM **Privately Held**
SIC: 8011 Internal medicine, physician/surgeon; pediatrician

(P-19599)
ZEITER EYE MEDICAL GROUP INC (PA)
255 E Weber Ave, Stockton (95202-2706)
PHONE.................................209 366-0446
John H Zeiter MD, *President*
Joseph Zeiter MD, *CFO*
Henry J Zeiter MD, *Vice Pres*
Erin K McCarthy, *Office Mgr*
Theresa Slatton, *Administration*
EMP: 95
SQ FT: 11,500
SALES (est): 11.7MM **Privately Held**
WEB: www.zeitereye.com
SIC: 8011 Ophthalmologist

8021 Offices & Clinics Of Dentists

(P-19600)
ACCESS DENTAL PLAN (PA)
Also Called: Access Dental Centers
530 S Main St, Orange (92868-4525)
PHONE.................................916 922-5000
Reza M Abbaszadeh, *President*
Teri Abbaszadeh, *President*
Laura Shively, *Vice Pres*
Armando Chavez, *Office Mgr*
Charlotte Quider, *Admin Asst*
▲ **EMP:** 70
SALES (est): 11.2MM **Privately Held**
SIC: 8021 Dental clinic

(P-19601)
ADVANCED HM HLTH & HOSPICE INC
Also Called: Advanced Home House
4354 Auburn Blvd, Sacramento (95841-4107)
PHONE.................................916 978-0744
Angela Sehr, *CEO*
▲ **EMP:** 100
SALES (est): 2.2MM **Privately Held**
SIC: 8021 Group & corporate practice dentists

(P-19602)
AMERICAN DNTL PARTNERS OF CAL
Also Called: Rouche O Edgar DDS
7251 Magnolia Ave, Riverside (92504-3811)
PHONE.................................951 689-5031
Greg Serrao, *CEO*
EMP: 165
SQ FT: 9,700
SALES (est): 2.8MM **Privately Held**
SIC: 8021 Dentists' office

(P-19603)
AMPLA HEALTH (PA)
935 Market St, Yuba City (95991-4217)
PHONE.................................530 674-4261
Benjamin Flores, *CEO*
Hilton Perez, *COO*
Dale Johnson, *CFO*
Carlos Peralta, *Officer*
Daniel Siri, *Officer*
EMP: 245
SQ FT: 10,200
SALES: 50.2MM **Privately Held**
SIC: 8021 8011 Dental clinic; health maintenance organization; primary care medical clinic; pediatrician

(P-19604)
ANTHONY P GAROFALO A DENTAL
Also Called: Horizon Dental Grp
742 Broadway, El Cajon (92021-4630)
PHONE.................................619 440-0071
Anthony P Garofalo, *Owner*
EMP: 60
SALES (est): 2.6MM **Privately Held**
WEB: www.horizondentalgroup.com
SIC: 8021 Dentists' office

(P-19605)
BUSINESS AND SUPPORT SERVICES
Camp Pendleton Mc Base, Oceanside (92055)
P.O. Box 555221, Camp Pendleton (92055-5221)
PHONE.................................760 725-5187
EMP: 320 **Publicly Held**
WEB: www.mccssc.com
SIC: 8021 9711 Offices & clinics of dentists; Marine Corps;
HQ: Business And Support Services
3044 Catlin Ave
Quantico VA 22134
703 432-0109

(P-19606)
CASTLE DENTAL
Also Called: South Gate Dental Group
4433 Tweedy Blvd, South Gate (90280-6303)
PHONE.................................323 567-1227
Elliott Schlang DDS, *Manager*
EMP: 50
SALES (est): 1.2MM **Privately Held**
SIC: 8021 Specialized dental practitioners

(P-19607)
CHILDRENS HOSPITAL LOS ANGELES
7891 Talbert Ave Ste 103, Huntington Beach (92648-8613)
PHONE.................................714 841-4990
Richard P Mungo DDS, *President*
Richard Mungo, *Fmly & Gen Dent*
EMP: 339
SQ FT: 100
SALES (corp-wide): 1.3B **Privately Held**
SIC: 8021 Dentists' office
PA: The Childrens Hospital Los Angeles
4650 W Sunset Blvd
Los Angeles CA 90027
323 660-2450

(P-19608)
DEDICATED DENTAL SYSTEMS INC
9800 S La Cienega Blvd # 800, Inglewood (90301-4440)
PHONE.................................661 397-5513
Arthur Kaiser, *President*
Heather Martinez, *Manager*
EMP: 65
SQ FT: 5,000
SALES (est): 351K
SALES (corp-wide): 115.2MM **Privately Held**
WEB: www.dedicated-dental.com
SIC: 8021 6324 Offices & clinics of dentists; hospital & medical service plans
HQ: Interdent Service Corporation
9800 S La Cienega Blvd # 800
Inglewood CA 90301

(P-19609)
DHS MEMBER SERVICES
3833 Atlantic Ave, Long Beach (90807-3505)
PHONE.................................562 595-5151
Godfrey Pernell, *Principal*
EMP: 50
SALES (est): 675.4K **Privately Held**
SIC: 8021 Dental insurance plan

(P-19610)
ELIAS ELLIOTT LAMPASI FEHN (PA)
7251 Magnolia Ave, Riverside (92504-3811)
PHONE.................................951 689-5031
Douglass R Gerald, *CEO*
Jay Elliot, *Vice Pres*
Dee Elias, *Admin Sec*
EMP: 59
SALES (est): 4MM **Privately Held**
WEB: www.riversidedentalgroup.com
SIC: 8021 Dentists' office

(P-19611)
INTERDENT INC (HQ)
Also Called: Smile Keepers
9800 S La Cienega Blvd # 800, Inglewood (90301-4442)
PHONE.................................310 765-2400
Ivar S Chhina, *President*
Robert W Hill, *CFO*
Matthew Wickesberg, *CFO*
Mark Backstrom, *Vice Pres*
Judy Dunbar, *Vice Pres*
EMP: 55
SQ FT: 10,000
SALES (est): 115.2MM **Privately Held**
SIC: 8021 Dentists' office
PA: H.I.G. Middle Market Llc
1 Sansome St Fl 37
San Francisco CA 94104
415 439-5500

(P-19612)
INTERDENT SERVICE CORPORATION (DH)
9800 S La Cienega Blvd # 800, Inglewood (90301-4442)
PHONE.................................310 765-2400
Marshal Salomon, *CFO*
Matthew Wickesberg, *CFO*
Irma Duron, *Manager*
EMP: 50
SQ FT: 10,000
SALES (est): 55.8MM
SALES (corp-wide): 115.2MM **Privately Held**
SIC: 8021 Dental clinic
HQ: Interdent, Inc.
9800 S La Cienega Blvd # 800
Inglewood CA 90301
310 765-2400

(P-19613)
JOSEPH A FOROOSH DENTAL CORP (PA)
Also Called: Desert Dental Group
12640 Hesperia Rd Ste A, Victorville (92395-7753)
PHONE.................................760 241-3336
Joseph Foroosh, *Owner*
Elly Foroosh, *Administration*
EMP: 60
SALES (est): 5.9MM **Privately Held**
WEB: www.desertdentalgroup.com
SIC: 8021 Dentists' office

(P-19614)
LA CLINICA DE LA RAZA INC
3050 E 16th St, Oakland (94601-2319)
PHONE.................................510 535-4700
Magnolia Rios, *Office Mgr*
EMP: 310
SQ FT: 5,208
SALES (corp-wide): 112.4MM **Privately Held**
SIC: 8021 Dental clinic
PA: La Clinica De La Raza, Inc.
1450 Fruitvale Ave Fl 3
Oakland CA 94601
510 535-4000

(P-19615)
LA CLINICA DE LA RAZA INC
Also Called: Laclinica
337 E Leland Rd, Pittsburg (94565-4911)
PHONE.................................925 431-1250
Viola Lujan, *Branch Mgr*
Karen Nguyen, *Assistant*
EMP: 310
SALES (corp-wide): 112.4MM **Privately Held**
SIC: 8021 Dental clinic
PA: La Clinica De La Raza, Inc.
1450 Fruitvale Ave Fl 3
Oakland CA 94601
510 535-4000

(P-19616)
LAKE CNTY TRBAL HLTH CNSORTIUM
925 Bevins Ct, Lakeport (95453-9754)
P.O. Box 1950 (95453-1950)
PHONE.................................707 263-8382
Mike Icay, *President*
Crista Ray, *Ch of Bd*
Tanya Michel, *CFO*
Tina Ramos, *Chairman*

Bret Woods, *Executive*
EMP: 80
SQ FT: 10,832
SALES: 28.4MM **Privately Held**
WEB: www.lcthc.org
SIC: 8021 Dental clinic

(P-19617)
LAKEWOOD CERRITOS DENTAL CTR
5819 Adenmoor Ave, Lakewood (90713-1067)
PHONE....................562 860-0388
Kosmas Pappas DDS, *Owner*
EMP: 100
SQ FT: 5,600
SALES (est): 4.1MM **Privately Held**
WEB: www.doctorlopez.com
SIC: 8021 Dentists' office

(P-19618)
LEONID M GLOSMAN DDS A D
Also Called: Dentalville
5021 Florence Ave, Bell (90201-3802)
PHONE....................323 560-4514
EMP: 130
SALES (corp-wide): 3.2MM **Privately Held**
SIC: 8021 Dental clinics & offices
PA: Leonid M. Glosman, D.D.S., A Dental Corporation
7864 Van Nuys Blvd
Panorama City CA
323 266-1000

(P-19619)
LINDHURST DENTAL CLINIC
4941 Olivehurst Ave, Olivehurst (95961-4225)
PHONE....................530 743-4614
Sally Moore, *Manager*
EMP: 50
SQ FT: 13,712
SALES (est): 1.5MM **Privately Held**
SIC: 8021 Dental clinic

(P-19620)
MICHAEL P BYKO DDS A PROF CORP (PA)
164 W Hospitality Ln # 14, San Bernardino (92408-3316)
PHONE....................909 888-7817
Michael Boyko, *President*
◆ **EMP:** 60
SQ FT: 3,000
SALES (est): 4.3MM **Privately Held**
SIC: 8021 Dentists' office; orthodontist

(P-19621)
MONTEREY DENTAL GROUP
333 El Dorado St, Monterey (93940-4606)
PHONE....................831 373-3068
Rick Baldwin, *Principal*
Mark Bayless, *Partner*
Arthur Benoit, *Partner*
S Bhaskar, *Partner*
P Breuleux, *Partner*
EMP: 55
SQ FT: 13,330
SALES (est): 2.2MM **Privately Held**
WEB: www.quantified.com
SIC: 8021 Dentists' office

(P-19622)
MONTEREY PENINSULA DNTL GROUP
333 El Dorado St, Monterey (93940-4645)
PHONE....................831 373-3068
Ronald Faia, *Partner*
J Mark Baliff, *Partner*
S N Bashcor, *Partner*
John Faia III, *Partner*
Mick Falkel, *Partner*
EMP: 60
SQ FT: 13,000
SALES (est): 3.7MM **Privately Held**
WEB: www.mpdg.com
SIC: 8021 Group & corporate practice dentists; dentists' office

(P-19623)
MY KIDS DENTIST
24635 Madison Ave Ste E, Murrieta (92562-7556)
PHONE....................951 600-1062

Theresa Gomez, *Branch Mgr*
EMP: 400
SALES (corp-wide): 5.4MM **Privately Held**
SIC: 8021 Dentists' office
PA: My Kid's Dentist
17000 Red Hill Ave
Irvine CA 92614
909 854-1437

(P-19624)
NADER MEHR DDS INC
555 Anton Blvd Ca, Costa Mesa (92626-7811)
PHONE....................562 634-2477
Nader Mehr, *President*
EMP: 51 EST: 2011
SALES: 8MM **Privately Held**
SIC: 8021 Dentists' office

(P-19625)
NORTHERN VLY INDIAN HLTH INC
845 W East Ave, Chico (95926-2002)
PHONE....................530 896-9400
Maureen Self, *Manager*
Brian Dudar, *Manager*
Jolynn Delgado, *Receptionist*
EMP: 90
SALES (corp-wide): 35.3MM **Privately Held**
WEB: www.nvih.org
SIC: 8021 8011 Dental clinic; primary care medical clinic
PA: Northern Valley Indian Health, Inc.
207 N Butte St
Willows CA
530 934-9293

(P-19626)
PACIFIC DENTAL SERVICES LLC (PA)
Also Called: Pds
17000 Red Hill Ave, Irvine (92614-5626)
P.O. Box 19723 (92623-9723)
PHONE....................714 845-8500
Stephen E Thorne IV, *President*
Dan Burke, *Senior VP*
Joe Feldsien, *Senior VP*
Joanna Rodgers, *Senior VP*
Jon Thorne, *Senior VP*
▲ **EMP:** 300
SQ FT: 40,000
SALES (est): 376.7MM **Privately Held**
WEB: www.pacificdentalservices.com
SIC: 8021 6794 Dental clinic; franchises, selling or licensing

(P-19627)
RANCHO NIGUEL DENTAL GROUP
30140 Town Center Dr, Laguna Niguel (92677-2037)
PHONE....................949 249-4180
Steve Krieger,
Rodney Boyd,
Gary Mar,
Hugh Murray,
Mary Stay,
EMP: 50
SALES (est): 1.8MM **Privately Held**
SIC: 8021 Dental clinic

(P-19628)
SAC HEALTH SYSTEM (PA)
1455 3rd Ave, San Bernardino (92408-0218)
PHONE....................909 382-7100
Richard H Hart MD, *President*
George Cencel, *CFO*
Barry Randolph, *Opers Staff*
EMP: 64
SALES: 17.2MM **Privately Held**
SIC: 8021 8011 8093 Offices & clinics of dentists; offices & clinics of medical doctors; mental health clinic, outpatient

(P-19629)
SANTA ROSA DENTAL GROUP
1820 Sonoma Ave Ste 80, Santa Rosa (95405-6617)
PHONE....................707 545-0944
Allen Barbieri, *Partner*
Perry Bingham, *Partner*
Richard L Blechel, *Partner*

James J Bridges, *Partner*
Ted Degolia, *Partner*
EMP: 64
SQ FT: 8,000
SALES (est): 3MM **Privately Held**
SIC: 8021 Dentists' office

(P-19630)
SCHNIEROW DENTAL CARE
Also Called: Piehl, Joel J DDS
13450 Hawthorne Blvd, Hawthorne (90250-5806)
PHONE....................310 377-6453
Burton Schnierow, *President*
EMP: 50
SQ FT: 3,200
SALES (est): 4.9MM **Privately Held**
SIC: 8021 Dentists' office

(P-19631)
SCOTT JACKS DDS INC
Also Called: Adult & Childrens Dental Group
4444 Tweedy Blvd, South Gate (90280-6392)
PHONE....................323 564-2444
Scott Jacks, *CEO*
Marsha Jacks, *Admin Sec*
EMP: 111
SQ FT: 9,375
SALES (est): 6.7MM **Privately Held**
SIC: 8021 Dentists' office

(P-19632)
ST JOHNS WELL CHILD (PA)
Also Called: SAINT JOHN'S WELL CHILD CENTER
808 W 58th St, Los Angeles (90037-3632)
PHONE....................323 541-1600
James J Mangia, *CEO*
Liz Meisler, *CFO*
EMP: 89
SALES: 63.5MM **Privately Held**
WEB: www.wellchild.org
SIC: 8021 8011 Dental clinic; offices & clinics of medical doctors

(P-19633)
THURSTON MARTIN H DDS MS
11616 Iberia Pl, San Diego (92128-2404)
PHONE....................858 676-5010
Martin Thurston, *Principal*
EMP: 50
SALES (est): 1.1MM **Privately Held**
SIC: 8021 Orthodontist

(P-19634)
TOIYABE INDIAN HEALTH PRJ INC (PA)
250 N See Vee Ln, Bishop (93514-8130)
PHONE....................760 873-8461
David Lent, *CEO*
Mary Daniel, *CFO*
Monty Bengochia, *Chairman*
Rick Frey, *Officer*
Christie Martindale, *Associate Dir*
EMP: 113
SQ FT: 66,300
SALES (est): 16.4MM **Privately Held**
WEB: www.toiyabe.us
SIC: 8021 8011 Dental clinic; clinic, operated by physicians; psychiatric clinic

(P-19635)
UNIVERSITY CAL SAN FRANCISCO
Also Called: Ucsf Dental Center-Buchanan
100 Buchanan St, San Francisco (94102-6147)
PHONE....................415 476-5608
Mark Kirkland DDS, *Administration*
EMP: 50 **Privately Held**
SIC: 8021 Dental clinics & offices; maxillo-facial specialist
HQ: University Cal San Francisco
513 Parnassus Ave 115f
San Francisco CA 94143

(P-19636)
VALLEY OAK DENTAL GROUP
1507 W Yosemite Ave, Manteca (95337-5182)
PHONE....................209 823-9341
Marvin Bledsoe, *President*
Bonnie Morehead DDS, *Corp Secy*
Mark Hochhalter DDS, *Vice Pres*

Ron Joseph, *Fmly & Gen Dent*
EMP: 70
SALES (est): 4.5MM **Privately Held**
SIC: 8021 Dental clinic; specialized dental practitioners; periodontist; dentists' office

(P-19637)
VETERANS HEALTH ADMINISTRATION
Also Called: Dental
3350 La Jolla Village Dr, San Diego (92161-0002)
PHONE....................858 552-7525
EMP: 264 **Publicly Held**
WEB: www.veterans-ru.org
SIC: 8021 9451 Dental clinic;
HQ: Veterans Health Administration
810 Vermont Ave Nw
Washington DC 20420
-

(P-19638)
WESTERN DENTAL SERVICES INC (HQ)
530 S Main St Ste 600, Orange (92868-4544)
P.O. Box 14227 (92863-1227)
PHONE....................714 480-3000
Thomas W Erickson, *CEO*
Samuel H Gruenbaum, *President*
Stuart Gray, *COO*
David Joe, *CFO*
Alex Park, *Ch Credit Ofcr*
EMP: 350
SALES (est): 236.2MM
SALES (corp-wide): 271.2MM **Privately Held**
WEB: www.westerndental.com
SIC: 8021 Dentists' office
PA: Premier Dental Holdings, Inc.
530 S Main St Ste 600
Orange CA 92868
714 480-3000

(P-19639)
WILSHIRE CENTER DENTAL GROUP
3932 Wilshire Blvd # 102, Los Angeles (90010-3334)
PHONE....................213 386-3336
Gregory Kaplan, *Owner*
EMP: 50
SQ FT: 7,000
SALES (est): 1.8MM **Privately Held**
SIC: 8021 Dental clinic; dental surgeon; orthodontist; pedodontist

---

8031 Offices & Clinics Of Doctors Of Osteopathy

(P-19640)
FACEY MEDICAL FOUNDATION
2655 1st St, Simi Valley (93065-1547)
PHONE....................805 206-2000
EMP: 157
SALES (corp-wide): 197.1MM **Privately Held**
SIC: 8031 8011 Offices & clinics of osteopathic physicians; offices & clinics of medical doctors
PA: Facey Medical Foundation
15451 San Fernando Msn
Mission Hills CA 91345
818 365-9531

(P-19641)
FACEY MEDICAL FOUNDATION
191 S Buena Vista St, Burbank (91505-4554)
PHONE....................818 861-7831
Jennifer Sung MD, *Branch Mgr*
Tri Dao, *Family Practiti*
EMP: 126
SALES (corp-wide): 197.1MM **Privately Held**
SIC: 8031 8011 Offices & clinics of osteopathic physicians; offices & clinics of medical doctors
PA: Facey Medical Foundation
15451 San Fernando Msn
Mission Hills CA 91345
818 365-9531

(P-19642)
FCS MEDICAL CORPORATION
1701 E Cesar E Chavez Ave # 230, Los Angeles (90033-2464)
PHONE...................................323 317-9200
Mimi House, *Manager*
EMP: 93
SALES (corp-wide): 14MM **Privately Held**
SIC: 8031 8011 Offices & clinics of osteopathic physicians; offices & clinics of medical doctors
PA: Fcs Medical Corporation
5823 York Blvd Ste 1
Los Angeles CA 90042
323 255-1575

(P-19643)
SUTTER HEALTH
5150 Hill Rd Ste E, Lakeport (95453-5100)
PHONE...................................707 263-3520
EMP: 236
SALES (corp-wide): 12.7B **Privately Held**
SIC: 8031 8011 Offices & clinics of osteopathic physicians; offices & clinics of medical doctors
PA: Sutter Health
2200 River Plaza Dr
Sacramento CA 95833
916 733-8800

(P-19644)
VISTA COMMUNITY CLINIC (PA)
1000 Vale Terrace Dr, Vista (92084-5218)
PHONE...................................760 631-5000
Fernando Sanudo, *CEO*
Michele Lambert, *CFO*
Thomas Van Bui, *Analyst*
Susana Castrellon, *Manager*
Sergio Newsome MBA, *Manager*
EMP: 280
SQ FT: 60,000
SALES: 49.2MM **Privately Held**
WEB: www.vistacommunityclinic.org
SIC: 8031 8011 Offices & clinics of osteopathic physicians; medical centers

(P-19645)
VISTA COMMUNITY CLINIC
134 Grapevine Rd, Vista (92083-4004)
PHONE...................................760 631-5030
Sonia Jimenez, *Branch Mgr*
EMP: 50
SALES (corp-wide): 49.2MM **Privately Held**
SIC: 8031 8011 Offices & clinics of osteopathic physicians; medical centers
PA: Vista Community Clinic
1000 Vale Terrace Dr
Vista CA 92084
760 631-5000

8041 Offices & Clinics Of Chiropractors

(P-19646)
CORNERSTONE MEDICAL GROUP
1881 Commercenter E # 112, San Bernardino (92408-3442)
PHONE...................................909 890-4353
Steve Mansker, *CEO*
Michelle Van Dyke, *Treasurer*
Mark C Hamilton DC, *Vice Pres*
EMP: 50
SQ FT: 6,000
SALES (est): 1.7MM **Privately Held**
WEB: www.cornerstonemedical.com
SIC: 8041 Offices & clinics of chiropractors

(P-19647)
LANDMARK HEALTHCARE SVCS INC (DH)
1610 Arden Way Ste 280, Sacramento (95815-4050)
PHONE...................................800 638-4557
Adam Boehler, *CEO*
Christopher Goldsmith, *President*
Carol Devol, *CFO*
EMP: 120
SQ FT: 330,215

SALES (est): 5.9MM
SALES (corp-wide): 141.6B **Publicly Held**
WEB: www.lmhealthcare.com
SIC: 8041 8049 Offices & clinics of chiropractors; acupuncturist
HQ: Carecore National, Llc
400 Buckwalter Place Blvd
Bluffton SC 29910
800 918-8924

8042 Offices & Clinics Of Optometrists

(P-19648)
FIRSTSIGHT VISION SERVICES INC (DH)
1202 Monte Vista Ave # 17, Upland (91786-8208)
PHONE...................................909 920-5008
Robert K Patton, *President*
Joseph T Heidelman, *CFO*
EMP: 53
SALES (est): 12MM
SALES (corp-wide): 1.5B **Publicly Held**
SIC: 8042 Specialized optometrists
HQ: National Vision, Inc.
2435 Commerce Ave # 2200
Duluth GA 30096
770 822-3600

(P-19649)
LINDEN OPTOMETRY A PROF CORP
Also Called: Pasadena Vision
477 E Colorado Blvd, Pasadena (91101-2024)
PHONE...................................323 681-5678
Allan Linfat, *President*
William J Linden, *Shareholder*
Steve Linden, *Executive*
Elianna Samaniego, *Human Res Mgr*
EMP: 100
SALES (est): 7.1MM **Privately Held**
SIC: 8042 Specialized optometrists

(P-19650)
PACIFIC VISION SERVICES INC
1900 E Washington St, Colton (92324-4614)
PHONE...................................909 824-6090
Christopher Blanton, *President*
EMP: 90
SQ FT: 5,000
SALES (est): 7.4MM **Privately Held**
WEB: www.visioncarebylaser.com
SIC: 8042 Offices & clinics of optometrists

(P-19651)
TOTAL VISION LLC
27271 Las Ramblas 200a, Mission Viejo (92691-8041)
PHONE...................................949 652-7242
Scott Strachan, *President*
Doug Lattime, *Senior VP*
Broke Jakovich, *VP Opers*
EMP: 194
SQ FT: 3,000
SALES: 19MM **Privately Held**
SIC: 8042 Group & corporate practice optometrists
PA: Total Vision Holdings, Llc
277 Park Ave Fl 27
New York NY 10172
212 704-5364

8049 Offices & Clinics Of Health Practitioners, NEC

(P-19652)
A IS FOR APPLE INC
1485 Saratoga Ave Ste 200, San Jose (95129-4965)
PHONE...................................877 991-0009
Marilyn Freeman, *President*
John Freeman, *Vice Pres*
EMP: 113
SALES: 6MM **Privately Held**
SIC: 8049 Speech pathologist

(P-19653)
ADDUS HEALTHCARE INC
2851 Park Marina Dr # 150, Redding (96001-2813)
PHONE...................................530 247-0858
Michele Dugar, *Branch Mgr*
EMP: 80 **Publicly Held**
WEB: www.addus.com
SIC: 8049 8011 Nurses & other medical assistants; clinic, operated by physicians
HQ: Addus Healthcare, Inc.
2300 Warrenville Rd # 100
Downers Grove IL 60515
630 296-3400

(P-19654)
AMN HEALTHCARE SERVICES INC
Also Called: American Mobile Healthcare
12400 High Bluff Dr # 100, San Diego (92130-3077)
PHONE...................................858 792-0711
Ralph Henderson, *President*
Miranda Behrens, *Recruiter*
Lorena Brunson, *Recruiter*
Ashlie Burke, *Recruiter*
Caitlin Casey, *Recruiter*
EMP: 750
SALES (corp-wide): 2.1B **Publicly Held**
WEB: www.amnhealthcare.com
SIC: 8049 Physical therapist; nurses & other medical assistants
PA: Amn Healthcare Services, Inc.
12400 High Bluff Dr
San Diego CA 92130
866 871-8519

(P-19655)
APEX HEALTHCARE MED CTR INC (PA)
Also Called: Apex Medical Group Lab
2390 E Florida Ave # 201, Hemet (92544-4707)
PHONE...................................951 765-0700
Kali P Chaudhuri MD, *President*
Surya Reddy MD, *Treasurer*
Herman Mathia MD, *Admin Sec*
EMP: 60
SALES (est): 2.5MM **Privately Held**
SIC: 8049 Physical therapist

(P-19656)
BACCI GLINN PHYSCL THERAPY INC
5533 W Hillsdale Ave A, Visalia (93291-5366)
P.O. Box 7779 (93290-7779)
PHONE...................................559 733-2478
Robert Bacci, *President*
James Glinn, *Vice Pres*
EMP: 50
SALES (est): 3.2MM **Privately Held**
SIC: 8049 Physiotherapist; physical therapist

(P-19657)
BURGER PHYSCL THERAPY SVCS INC (HQ)
Also Called: Burger Physcl Thrapy Rhbltttion
1301 E Bidwell St Ste 201, Folsom (95630-3565)
PHONE...................................916 983-5900
Carol Burger, *President*
Elizabeth Johnson, *Human Res Dir*
Lauren Bahr,
Aaron Abrams, *Manager*
Felicia Krieger, *Manager*
EMP: 140
SALES (est): 4.6MM **Privately Held**
SIC: 8049 Physical therapist

(P-19658)
BURGER PHYSICAL THERAPY
1301 E Bidwell St Ste 101, Folsom (95630-3565)
PHONE...................................916 983-5900
Carol K Burger, *President*
EMP: 50
SQ FT: 5,800
SALES (est): 1MM **Privately Held**
SIC: 8049 8093 Physical therapist; rehabilitation center, outpatient treatment; speech defect clinic

PA: Burger Rehabilitation Systems, Inc.
1301 E Bidwell St Ste 201
Folsom CA 95630

(P-19659)
BURGER RHBLITATION SYSTEMS INC
2101 Stone Blvd Ste 175, West Sacramento (95691-4055)
PHONE...................................916 617-2400
EMP: 71 **Privately Held**
SIC: 8049 Physical therapist
PA: Burger Rehabilitation Systems, Inc.
1301 E Bidwell St Ste 201
Folsom CA 95630

(P-19660)
BURGER RHBLITATION SYSTEMS INC
6614 Mercy Ct Ste C, Fair Oaks (95628-3167)
PHONE...................................916 863-5785
Carol Burger, *Branch Mgr*
EMP: 71 **Privately Held**
SIC: 8049 Physical therapist
PA: Burger Rehabilitation Systems, Inc.
1301 E Bidwell St Ste 201
Folsom CA 95630

(P-19661)
BURGER RHBLITATION SYSTEMS INC (PA)
1301 E Bidwell St Ste 201, Folsom (95630-3565)
PHONE...................................800 900-8491
Carol K Burger, *President*
Deena Smith, *Recruiter*
Joanne Walder,
Kiara Kim, *Director*
Kathy Pugh, *Consultant*
EMP: 200
SQ FT: 5,000
SALES (est): 11.6MM **Privately Held**
SIC: 8049 Occupational therapist; speech specialist; physical therapist

(P-19662)
CENTER FOR AUTISM & (PA)
21600 Oxnard St Ste 1800, Woodland Hills (91367-7807)
PHONE...................................818 345-2345
Doreen Granpeesheh, *Founder*
Tracy Macgugan, *Technician*
Jennifer Avalos, *Project Mgr*
Trevor Smith, *VP Finance*
Serenita Kumar, *Business Mgr*
EMP: 143
SALES (est): 48.7MM **Privately Held**
WEB: www.centerforautism.com
SIC: 8049 Clinical psychologist

(P-19663)
COMMUNITY THERAPIES
Also Called: Community Therapies Baby Steps
19040 Soledad Canyon Rd, Santa Clarita (91351-3363)
P.O. Box 432, Lancaster (93584-0432)
PHONE...................................661 945-7878
Roy Jensen, *Owner*
EMP: 50 EST: 1996
SALES (est): 474.7K **Privately Held**
WEB: www.babysteps.com
SIC: 8049 Speech therapist

(P-19664)
COMPREHENSIVE AUTISM CTR INC
7839 University Ave # 105, La Mesa (91942-0476)
PHONE...................................951 813-4035
EMP: 60
SALES (corp-wide): 2.2MM **Privately Held**
SIC: 8049 Physical therapist
PA: Comprehensive Autism Center, Inc.
40485 Mrreta Hot Sprng Rd
Murrieta CA 92563
951 813-4034

(P-19665)
ENLOE MEDICAL CENTER
Also Called: Enloe Rehabilitation Center
340 W East Ave, Chico (95926-7238)
PHONE..............................530 332-6138
Diane Jones, *Administration*
Les Doll, *Opers Mgr*
EMP: 100
SQ FT: 61,571
SALES (corp-wide): 480.2MM **Privately Held**
SIC: 8049 Physical therapist
PA: Enloe Medical Center
    1531 Esplanade
    Chico CA 95926
    530 332-7300

(P-19666)
EQUINOX-76TH STREET INC
Also Called: Health Fitness America
1980 Main St Fl 4, Irvine (92614-7200)
PHONE..............................949 975-8400
Ian McFodden, *Manager*
EMP: 300
SALES (corp-wide): 10.6B **Privately Held**
SIC: 8049 7991 Physical therapist; health club
HQ: Equinox-76th Street, Inc.
    895 Broadway Fl 3
    New York NY 10003

(P-19667)
FAMILY HEALTHCARE NETWORK
501 N Bridge St, Visalia (93291-5014)
PHONE..............................559 734-1939
Travis Chapin, *Principal*
Robert M Ayers, *Obstetrician*
Hoang U Le, *Obstetrician*
Elizabeth Enderton, *Director*
Jeanine Bailey, *Manager*
EMP: 145
SALES (corp-wide): 114.6MM **Privately Held**
SIC: 8049 Acupuncturist
PA: Family Healthcare Network
    305 E Center Ave
    Visalia CA 93291
    559 737-4700

(P-19668)
FORTA (PA)
Also Called: Fortanasce & Associates
671 W Naomi Ave, Arcadia (91007-7502)
P.O. Box 661150 (91066-1150)
PHONE..............................626 446-7027
Michael Fortanasce, *President*
EMP: 60
SQ FT: 10,250
SALES (est): 4.8MM **Privately Held**
WEB: www.fortanasce.com
SIC: 8049 Physiotherapist; physical therapist

(P-19669)
HOLMAN FAMILY COUNSELING INC (PA)
Also Called: Holman Group, The
8511 Fllbrook Ave Ste 400, West Hills (91304)
PHONE..............................818 704-1444
Ron Holman PHD, *President*
Elizabeth Holman, *President*
Jane Galvin, *Vice Pres*
Dawn Gray, *Sales Executive*
EMP: 66
SALES (est): 8.1MM **Privately Held**
SIC: 8049 Clinical psychologist

(P-19670)
INLAND EMPIRE THERAPY PROVIDER (PA)
Also Called: Life Enchancing Therapies
1150 N Mountain Ave # 214, Upland (91786-3668)
PHONE..............................909 985-7905
James W Milton, *President*
EMP: 65
SALES (est): 2MM **Privately Held**
SIC: 8049 Physical therapist; speech therapist; occupational therapist

(P-19671)
INLAND VALLEY PARTNERS LLC
Also Called: Inland Valley Care & Rehab Ctr
250 W Artesia St, Pomona (91768-1807)
PHONE..............................909 623-7100
Robert Nelson,
Elizabeth Casey,
Phil Chase,
Susan Chase,
EMP: 250
SALES: 25.9MM **Privately Held**
SIC: 8049 Nurses & other medical assistants

(P-19672)
INSTITUTE FOR APPLIED BEHAVIOR (PA)
Also Called: Iaba
5777 W Century Blvd # 675, Los Angeles (90045-5600)
PHONE..............................310 649-0499
Gary W Lavigna PHD, *President*
Shannon Carleton, *Admin Sec*
Ellen Slaton, *Consultant*
▲ **EMP:** 140
SQ FT: 3,000
SALES (est): 13.1MM **Privately Held**
WEB: www.iaba.com
SIC: 8049 8741 8093 Clinical psychologist; management services; specialty outpatient clinics

(P-19673)
INSTITUTE FOR APPLIED BEHAVIOR
Also Called: Iaba
2310 E Ponderosa Dr Ste 1, Camarillo (93010-4747)
PHONE..............................805 987-5886
Gary Lavigna, *Director*
EMP: 170
SALES (corp-wide): 13.1MM **Privately Held**
WEB: www.iaba.com
SIC: 8049 8399 Clinical psychologist; community development groups
PA: Institute For Applied Behavior Analysis, A Psychological Corporation
    5777 W Century Blvd # 675
    Los Angeles CA 90045
    310 649-0499

(P-19674)
INSTITUTE FOR APPLIED BEHAVIOR
Also Called: Institute Applied Bhvior Anlis
19510 Ventura Blvd # 204, Tarzana (91356-2969)
PHONE..............................818 881-1933
Fax: 818 881-1835
EMP: 61
SALES (corp-wide): 17.3MM **Privately Held**
SIC: 8049 8322 8093
PA: Institute For Applied Behavior Analysis, A Psychological Corporation
    5777 W Century Blvd # 675
    Los Angeles CA 90045
    310 649-0499

(P-19675)
INTERCARE THERAPY INC
4221 Wilshire Blvd 300a, Los Angeles (90010-3537)
PHONE..............................323 866-1880
Naomi Heller, *President*
Eri Heller, *Vice Pres*
Gan Luong, *Supervisor*
EMP: 130
SALES (est): 7.1MM **Privately Held**
SIC: 8049 Psychologist, psychotherapist & hypnotist; occupational therapist; speech specialist

(P-19676)
INTERFACE REHAB INC
774 S Placentia Ave # 200, Placentia (92870-6826)
PHONE..............................714 646-8300
Anant B Desai, *CEO*
Falguni Desai, *Admin Sec*
EMP: 657
SQ FT: 10,000
SALES (est): 31.6MM **Privately Held**
WEB: www.interfacerehab.com
SIC: 8049 Physical therapist; speech specialist

(P-19677)
INTERGRO REHAB SERVICE
1922 N Broadway, Santa Ana (92706-2610)
PHONE..............................714 901-4200
Sherrilyn Tong, *President*
Pooja Jani, *Area Mgr*
Alma Rolle, *Administration*
Katie Jeffery, *Opers Staff*
EMP: 80
SQ FT: 2,000
SALES (est): 6.7MM **Privately Held**
WEB: www.intergrorehab.com
SIC: 8049 Physical therapist; speech specialist; occupational therapist

(P-19678)
LEAD STAFFING CORPORATION
216 S Citrus St Ste 397, West Covina (91791-2144)
PHONE..............................800 928-5561
Lilian Nyamoita, *CEO*
EMP: 225
SALES (est): 3.5MM **Privately Held**
SIC: 8049 7363 Nurses & other medical assistants; medical help service

(P-19679)
LOCUMS UNLIMITED LLC
4141 Jutland Dr Ste 305, San Diego (92117-3658)
PHONE..............................619 550-3763
Sigrid Boring,
Kelly Johnson,
EMP: 347
SALES (est): 43.2K **Privately Held**
SIC: 8049 Nurses & other medical assistants
PA: Aya Healthcare, Inc.
    5930 Cornerstone Ct W # 300
    San Diego CA 92121

(P-19680)
MOUNTAIN VIEW PHYSICAL THERAPY
Also Called: Inland Hand Therapy & Rehab
299 W Fthill Blvd Ste 200, Upland (91786)
PHONE..............................909 949-6235
Catherine Konn, *President*
EMP: 54
SALES (est): 816.5K **Privately Held**
SIC: 8049 Physical therapist

(P-19681)
NVISION LASER EYE CENTERS INC
24022 Calle De La Plata, Laguna Hills (92653-3626)
PHONE..............................949 951-1457
Norman Peterson, *Branch Mgr*
EMP: 65
SALES (corp-wide): 4MM **Privately Held**
SIC: 8049 Nutrition specialist
PA: Nvision Laser Eye Centers Inc.
    75 Enterprise Ste 200
    Aliso Viejo CA 92656
    877 455-9942

(P-19682)
OROVILLE HOSPITAL
Also Called: Golden Vly Occpational Therapy
2353 Myers St Ste B, Oroville (95965-5334)
PHONE..............................530 538-8700
Trish Hopps, *Branch Mgr*
EMP: 100
SALES (corp-wide): 319MM **Privately Held**
SIC: 8049 Physical therapist
PA: Oroville Hospital
    2767 Olive Hwy
    Oroville CA 95966
    530 533-8500

(P-19683)
PHYSICAL REHABILITATION NETWRK
2833 Junction Ave Ste 206, San Jose (95134-1920)
P.O. Box 612260 (95161-2260)
PHONE..............................408 570-0510
Fax: 408 570-0516
EMP: 50 **Privately Held**
SIC: 8049 8742
PA: Physical Rehabilitation Network
    5962 La Place Ct Ste 170
    Carlsbad CA 92011

(P-19684)
PHYSICAL RHBLTATION NETWRK LLC (PA)
3025 Crte Del Ngal Ste 20, Carlsbad (92011)
PHONE..............................760 931-8310
Bruce McDaniel, *CEO*
Galen Danielson, *President*
Craig Rettke, *President*
James Ripp, *President*
Tim Varley, *Vice Pres*
EMP: 75
SALES (est): 50.6MM **Privately Held**
SIC: 8049 8011 8093 Physiotherapist; sports medicine specialist, physician; rehabilitation center, outpatient treatment

(P-19685)
PHYSICAL THERAPY HAND CTRS INC
Also Called: Valley Physical Theraphy
1815 E Valley Pkwy Ste 5, Escondido (92027-2550)
PHONE..............................760 233-9655
Mike Morasel, *Manager*
EMP: 50
SALES (corp-wide): 3.8MM **Privately Held**
WEB: www.pthc-pt.com
SIC: 8049 Physical therapist
PA: Physical Therapy & Hand Centers, Inc.
    540 S Andreasen Dr Ste C
    Escondido CA

(P-19686)
POMONA VALLEY HOSPITAL MED CTR
Also Called: Pamona Valley Physical Therapy
1775 Monte Vista Ave, Claremont (91711-2916)
PHONE..............................909 621-7956
Joseph Bomgardner, *Director*
EMP: 70
SALES (corp-wide): 654.6MM **Privately Held**
WEB: www.pvhmc.org
SIC: 8049 Physical therapist
PA: Pomona Valley Hospital Medical Center
    1798 N Garey Ave
    Pomona CA 91767
    909 865-9500

(P-19687)
QUANTUM BHVIORAL SOLUTIONS INC (PA)
445 S Figueroa St # 3100, Los Angeles (90071-1602)
PHONE..............................626 531-6999
Gevork Gevojanyan, *Principal*
EMP: 71 **EST:** 2012
SALES (est): 7.3MM **Privately Held**
SIC: 8049 Clinical psychologist

(P-19688)
QUANTUM BHVIORAL SOLUTIONS INC
2400 E Katella Ave # 800, Anaheim (92806-5945)
PHONE..............................626 531-6999
EMP: 70
SALES (corp-wide): 7.3MM **Privately Held**
SIC: 8049 Clinical psychologist
PA: Quantum Behavioral Solutions, Inc.
    445 S Figueroa St # 3100
    Los Angeles CA 90071
    626 531-6999

PRODUCTS & SVCS

(P-19689)
R & R PROFESSION
Also Called: R and R Professional Medical
2216 S El Camino Real # 211, Oceanside
(92054-6369)
PHONE..................................760 754-9020
George Hebeler, *President*
Renee Hebeler, *CFO*
Rachel Sterling, *Vice Pres*
EMP: 150
SQ FT: 900
SALES (est): 3.6MM **Privately Held**
SIC: 8049 7363 7361 Nurses, registered
& practical; help supply services; employ-
ment agencies

(P-19690)
R DS FOR HEALTHCARE
Also Called: Body Transformations
1420 W Kettleman Ln N5, Lodi
(95242-4557)
PHONE..................................209 333-2115
Terri Novadinavich, *Owner*
Kim Ishii, *Director*
EMP: 50
SALES (est): 1.2MM **Privately Held**
SIC: 8049 Nutrition specialist

(P-19691)
**RANCHO PHYSICAL THERAPY
INC**
277 Rancheros Dr, San Marcos
(92069-2976)
PHONE..................................760 752-1011
James Lin, *Branch Mgr*
EMP: 177
SALES (corp-wide): 15MM **Privately
Held**
SIC: 8049 8011 Physical therapist; offices
& clinics of medical doctors
PA: Rancho Physical Therapy, Inc.
24630 Washington Ave # 200
Murrieta CA 92562
951 696-9353

(P-19692)
**RANCHO PHYSICAL THERAPY
INC (PA)**
24630 Washington Ave # 200, Murrieta
(92562-6177)
PHONE..................................951 696-9353
John Waite, *CEO*
Greg Smith, *Principal*
Bill Atkins,
Binoy Patel, *Director*
Weston Smith, *Director*
EMP: 52
SALES: 15MM **Privately Held**
SIC: 8049 8093 Physical therapist; respi-
ratory therapy clinic

(P-19693)
**RIVER OAK CENTER FOR
CHILDREN**
9412 Big Horn Blvd Ste 6, Elk Grove
(95758-1101)
PHONE..................................916 226-2800
Laurie Clothier, *Branch Mgr*
EMP: 200
SALES (corp-wide): 17.3MM **Privately
Held**
SIC: 8049 Clinical psychologist
PA: River Oak Center For Children
5445 Laurel Hills Dr
Sacramento CA 95841
916 609-5100

(P-19694)
SCRIPPS HEALTH
237 Church Ave, Chula Vista (91910-2702)
PHONE..................................619 862-6600
EMP: 126
SALES (corp-wide): 2.1B **Privately Held**
SIC: 8049 Acupuncturist
PA: Scripps Health
10140 Campus Point Dr Ax415
San Diego CA 92121
800 727-4777

(P-19695)
**SIMI VLY HOSP & HLTH CARE
SVCS (HQ)**
Also Called: Therapy & Rehabilitation Ctrs
2975 Sycamore Dr, Simi Valley
(93065-1201)
PHONE..................................805 955-6000
Margaret Peterson, *President*
Mitchell Solomon,
Caroline Esparza, *President*
Clif Patten, *CFO*
Ann Svolos, *Risk Mgmt Dir*
EMP: 117
SALES: 163MM
SALES (corp-wide): 4.4B **Privately Held**
SIC: 8049 Physical therapist
PA: Adventist Health System/West
1 Adventist Health Way
Roseville CA 95661
844 574-5686

(P-19696)
SUTTER MEDICAL FOUNDATION
1014 N Market Blvd Ste 20, Sacramento
(95834-1986)
PHONE..................................916 924-7764
Judi Monday, *Branch Mgr*
EMP: 519 **Privately Held**
SIC: 8049 8011 Physical therapist; offices
& clinics of medical doctors
PA: Sutter Valley Medical Foundation
2700 Gateway Oaks Dr
Sacramento CA 95833
-

(P-19697)
**THERAPEUTIC ASSOCIATES
INC**
Also Called: Physical Therapy Unit
Saint Joseph Hospital, Burbank (91505)
PHONE..................................818 843-5111
Julianne Courtney, *Manager*
EMP: 65
SALES (corp-wide): 73.6MM **Privately
Held**
SIC: 8049 Physical therapist
PA: Therapeutic Associates, Inc.
20829 72nd Ave S Ste 710
Kent WA 98032
253 872-6028

(P-19698)
THERAPEUTIC PATHWAYS INC
Also Called: Candle Center The
2775 Cottage Way Ste 8, Sacramento
(95825-1220)
PHONE..................................916 489-1376
Coleen R Sparkman, *Director*
EMP: 70
SALES (corp-wide): 11.9MM **Privately
Held**
SIC: 8049 Clinical psychologist
PA: Therapeutic Pathways, Inc.
1115 14th St
Modesto CA 95354
209 572-2589

(P-19699)
THERAPY FOR KIDS INC
Also Called: Gallagher Pediatric Therapy
233 Orangefair Mall, Fullerton
(92832-3038)
PHONE..................................714 870-6116
Mary K Gallagher, *President*
Jessica Alter,
Stacy Cobbs,
Jennifer Leghart, *Manager*
EMP: 50
SALES (est): 2.7MM **Privately Held**
WEB: www.gptkids.com
SIC: 8049 Occupational therapist

(P-19700)
**TRI COUNTY REGIONAL
CENTER**
2220 E Gonzales Rd 210a, Oxnard
(93036-8294)
PHONE..................................805 485-3177
Gary Feldman, *President*
Sha Azedi, *Director*
EMP: 55
SALES (est): 1.7MM **Privately Held**
WEB: www.garyfeldman.com
SIC: 8049 Psychiatric social worker

(P-19701)
VALLEY NURSES
1450 W 9th St, Pomona (91766-2607)
PHONE..................................714 549-2512
Bob Gill, *Owner*
EMP: 65
SALES (est): 2.5MM **Privately Held**
SIC: 8049 7361 Nurses & other medical
assistants; nurses' registry

(P-19702)
WRIGHT INSTITUTE
2728 Durant Ave, Berkeley (94704-1796)
PHONE..................................510 841-9230
Peter Dybwad, *President*
Hanna Mae Levenson, *Principal*
Luli Emmons, *Exec Dir*
Tricia Oreilly, *General Mgr*
Ann Howard, *Admin Sec*
EMP: 50
SQ FT: 20,000
SALES: 15.2MM **Privately Held**
WEB: www.wrightinst.edu
SIC: 8049 Clinical psychologist

8051 Skilled Nursing Facilities

(P-19703)
**1000 EXECUTIVE PARKWAY
LLC**
Also Called: Oroville Hosp Post Acute Ctr
1000 Executive Pkwy, Oroville
(95966-5100)
PHONE..................................530 533-7335
Tina Nickolas, *Administration*
EMP: 161
SALES: 14.2MM **Privately Held**
SIC: 8051 Mental retardation hospital

(P-19704)
1130 W LA PALMA AVE INC
Also Called: La Palma Nursing Center
4115 E Broadway, Long Beach
(90803-1532)
PHONE..................................562 930-0777
Brenda Mandelbaum, *CEO*
Janet Mandelbaum, *Vice Pres*
Joseph Berkowitz, *Administration*
EMP: 90
SALES (est): 1MM **Privately Held**
SIC: 8051 Skilled nursing care facilities

(P-19705)
1135 N LEISURE CT INC
Also Called: Leisure Court Nursing Center
1135 N Leisure Ct, Anaheim (92801-2939)
PHONE..................................714 772-1353
Patricia Smith, *Director*
Aura Galindo, *Administration*
EMP: 130 EST: 1965
SQ FT: 15,000
SALES: 11.4MM **Privately Held**
SIC: 8051 Skilled nursing care facilities

(P-19706)
3067 ORANGE AVENUE LLC
Also Called: Anaheim Crest Nursing Center
3067 W Orange Ave, Anaheim
(92804-3156)
PHONE..................................714 827-2440
Alireza Talebi,
Joanna Rabanes, *Human Res Dir*
EMP: 120
SALES (est): 3.2MM **Privately Held**
SIC: 8051 Skilled nursing care facilities

(P-19707)
A B C D ASSOCIATES
Also Called: Casa Coloma Health Care Cen-
ter
10410 Coloma Rd, Rancho Cordova
(95670-2108)
PHONE..................................916 363-4843
Deborah Portela, *Administration*
Arden Millermon, *Partner*
Betty Millermon, *Partner*
EMP: 106 EST: 1975
SQ FT: 37,000
SALES: 9.4MM **Privately Held**
SIC: 8051 8052 Convalescent home with
continuous nursing care; intermediate
care facilities

(P-19708)
A F V W HEALTH CENTER
17050 Arnold Dr Ofc, Riverside
(92518-2879)
PHONE..................................951 697-2025
James Melin, *President*
Charlie Lamb, *President*
Bruce Cameron, *COO*
Ervin Reed, *CFO*
EMP: 270
SALES (est): 2.3MM **Privately Held**
SIC: 8051 Convalescent home with contin-
uous nursing care

(P-19709)
**ACCREDITED NURSING
SERVICES**
Also Called: Accredited Nursing Care
80 S Lake Ave Ste 630, Pasadena
(91101-4971)
PHONE..................................626 573-1234
Teresa Salvino, *Manager*
EMP: 80
SALES (corp-wide): 16.8MM **Privately
Held**
WEB: www.accreditednursing.com
SIC: 8051 Skilled nursing care facilities
PA: Accredited Nursing Services
17141 Ventura Blvd # 201
Encino CA
818 986-6017

(P-19710)
AGEMARK CORPORATION (PA)
25 Avenida De Orinda, Orinda
(94563-2305)
PHONE..................................925 257-4671
Richard J Westin, *Ch of Bd*
Jesse A Pittore, *CEO*
James P Tolley, *CFO*
Linda Larkin, *Vice Pres*
Forrest Westin, *Vice Pres*
EMP: 69
SQ FT: 2,100
SALES (est): 12MM **Privately Held**
SIC: 8051 Convalescent home with contin-
uous nursing care

(P-19711)
**AHMC GARFIELD MEDICAL CTR
LP**
525 N Garfield Ave, Monterey Park
(91754-1202)
PHONE..................................626 573-2222
Patrick Petre, *CEO*
Steve Maekewa, *Partner*
Erik Jiang, *Officer*
Jane Petre, *Case Mgmt Dir*
Helen Razon, *Executive Asst*
EMP: 150
SALES (est): 195.3MM
SALES (corp-wide): 570.2MM **Privately
Held**
WEB: www.garfieldmedicalcenter.com
SIC: 8051 8062 Skilled nursing care facili-
ties; general medical & surgical hospitals
PA: Ahmc Healthcare Inc.
1000 S Fremont Ave Unit 6
Alhambra CA 91803
-

(P-19712)
AIR FORCE VILLAGE WEST INC
Also Called: Village West Health Center
17050 Arnold Dr, Riverside (92518-2806)
PHONE..................................951 697-2000
Mary Carruthers, *CEO*
Ervin Reed, *CFO*
Charles Dalton, *Vice Pres*
EMP: 350
SQ FT: 494,000
SALES: 5.7MM **Privately Held**
WEB: www.afvw.com
SIC: 8051 8052 Convalescent home with
continuous nursing care; intermediate
care facilities

(P-19713)
**ALAMEDA HLTHCARE &
WELLNSS CTR**
Also Called: Alameda Halthcare Wellness Ctr
430 Willow St, Alameda (94501-6130)
PHONE..................................510 523-8857
Sharrod Brooks,
Mary Boutelle, *Social Dir*

Brenna McDaniel,
Sol Healthcare LLC,
Sol Majer,
EMP: 99
SALES (est): 4.2MM **Privately Held**
SIC: 8051 Convalescent home with continuous nursing care

(P-19714)
ALAMITOS-BELMONT REHAB INC
Also Called: Alamitos Blmont Rhblttion Hosp
3901 E 4th St, Long Beach (90814-1632)
PHONE..................................562 434-8421
Darian Dahl, *Administration*
Raquel Quijano, *Records Dir*
Arlene Donato, *Human Res Dir*
Rose Posadas, *Nursing Dir*
Traci Torres, *Director*
EMP: 150 EST: 1969
SQ FT: 30,000
SALES: 10.5MM **Privately Held**
WEB: www.alamitosbelmont.com
SIC: 8051 Skilled nursing care facilities

(P-19715)
ALHAMBRA CONVALESCENT HOSP LLC
331 Ilene St, Martinez (94553-2631)
PHONE..................................925 228-2020
Nina Gilbert, *Administration*
Walter Peters, *Director*
EMP: 60
SALES: 3.2MM **Privately Held**
SIC: 8051 8322 Convalescent home with continuous nursing care; rehabilitation services

(P-19716)
ALHAMBRA HEALTHCARE & WELLNESS
415 S Garfield Ave, Alhambra (91801-3838)
PHONE..................................626 282-3151
Sharrod Brooks, *Partner*
EMP: 99 EST: 2012
SALES: 10.4MM **Privately Held**
SIC: 8051 Mental retardation hospital

(P-19717)
ALL SAINTSIDENCE OPCO LLC
Also Called: All Snts Sbcute Trnstonal Care
1652 Mono Ave, San Leandro (94578-2020)
PHONE..................................510 481-3200
Jason Murray, *President*
EMP: 99 EST: 2015
SALES (est): 431.6K **Privately Held**
SIC: 8051 Skilled nursing care facilities

(P-19718)
ALMAVIA OF SAN FRANCISCO
1 Thomas More Way, San Francisco (94132-2914)
PHONE..................................415 337-1339
Janeane Randolph, *Owner*
EMP: 60
SALES (est): 2MM **Privately Held**
SIC: 8051 Skilled nursing care facilities

(P-19719)
AMADA ENTERPRISES INC
Also Called: View Heights Convalescent Hosp
12619 Avalon Blvd, Los Angeles (90061-2727)
PHONE..................................323 757-1881
Shedrick D Jones, *CEO*
John Jones, *Administration*
Charlena Grato, *Social Worker*
EMP: 135 EST: 1968
SQ FT: 36,600
SALES (est): 7.6MM **Privately Held**
WEB: www.viewheights.com
SIC: 8051 Convalescent home with continuous nursing care

(P-19720)
AMERICAN RETIREMENT CORP
2107 Ocean Ave, Santa Monica (90405-2299)
PHONE..................................310 399-3227
EMP: 112
SALES (corp-wide): 4.5B **Publicly Held**
SIC: 8051 Skilled nursing care facilities

HQ: American Retirement Corporation
111 Westwood Pl Ste 200
Brentwood TN 37027
615 221-2250

(P-19721)
APPLE VLY CNVALESCENT HOSP INC
Also Called: Apple Valley Care & Rehab
1035 Gravenstein Hwy N, Sebastopol (95472)
PHONE..................................707 823-7675
Jeff Barbieri, *Administration*
Garrin Obrien, *Records Dir*
Rudy Meza, *Maintenance Dir*
Robert Reyes, *Director*
EMP: 120
SQ FT: 20,000
SALES (est): 8.1MM **Privately Held**
WEB: www.applevalleyrehab.com
SIC: 8051 8322 Convalescent home with continuous nursing care; rehabilitation services

(P-19722)
APPLEWOOD CARE CENTER
1090 Rio Ln, Sacramento (95822-1706)
PHONE..................................916 446-2506
Bill Drennen, *Administration*
EMP: 50
SALES (est): 2.7MM
SALES (corp-wide): 8.4MM **Privately Held**
SIC: 8051 Skilled nursing care facilities
PA: Riverside Health Care Corporation
1469 Humboldt Rd Ste 175
Chico CA 95928
530 897-5100

(P-19723)
AQUINAS CORPORATION
Also Called: San Tomas Convalescent Hosp
3580 Payne Ave, San Jose (95117-2925)
PHONE..................................408 248-7100
Ken Dunton, *Ch of Bd*
Julita Javier, *President*
EMP: 135 EST: 1974
SQ FT: 15,000
SALES (est): 9.9MM **Privately Held**
WEB: www.aquinascorp.com
SIC: 8051 8059 Convalescent home with continuous nursing care; convalescent home

(P-19724)
ARROWHEAD CONVALESCENT HOME
Also Called: Arrowhead Home
4343 N Sierra Way, San Bernardino (92407-3822)
PHONE..................................909 886-4731
Joe Bolton, *President*
Don Popovich, *President*
EMP: 56
SQ FT: 6,000
SALES (est): 3MM **Privately Held**
SIC: 8051 Convalescent home with continuous nursing care

(P-19725)
ARTESIA HEALTHCARE INC
Also Called: Alameda Care Center
925 W Alameda Ave, Burbank (91506-2801)
PHONE..................................818 843-1771
Lori De Kruif, *Administration*
EMP: 99
SALES (est): 3MM **Privately Held**
SIC: 8051 Mental retardation hospital

(P-19726)
ASH HOLDINGS LLC
Also Called: REDLANDS HEALTHCARE CENTER
1620 W Fern Ave, Redlands (92373-4918)
PHONE..................................909 793-2609
Novie Sitanggang, *Administration*
Scott Clawson, *President*
EMP: 85
SALES: 8.9MM **Privately Held**
SIC: 8051 Skilled nursing care facilities

(P-19727)
ASHLEY LTC INC
Also Called: Santa Rosa Convalescent Hosp
446 Arrowood Dr, Santa Rosa (95407-7503)
PHONE..................................707 528-2100
Robert O Benson, *President*
EMP: 60
SQ FT: 18,000
SALES (est): 3.4MM **Privately Held**
WEB: www.santarosaconvalescent.com
SIC: 8051 Convalescent home with continuous nursing care

(P-19728)
ASTORIA CONVALESCENT HOSPITAL
Also Called: Astoria Nursing & Rehab Center
14040 Astoria St, Sylmar (91342-2998)
PHONE..................................818 367-5881
Grace Mercado, *Exec Dir*
EMP: 202
SQ FT: 50,000
SALES (est): 4.9MM **Privately Held**
SIC: 8051 8059 8322 Convalescent home with continuous nursing care; convalescent home; rehabilitation services

(P-19729)
ATHERTON BAPTIST HOMES
214 S Atlantic Blvd, Alhambra (91801-3298)
PHONE..................................626 863-1710
Craig Statton, *President*
Dennis E McFadden, *President*
Jackie Pascual, *CFO*
Dale Torry, *Vice Pres*
Deborah Sanchez, *Executive*
EMP: 200
SQ FT: 42,000
SALES: 20.7MM **Privately Held**
WEB: www.abh.org
SIC: 8051 Convalescent home with continuous nursing care; extended care facility

(P-19730)
ATLANTIC MEM HEALTHCARE ASSOC (PA)
Also Called: ATLANTIC MEMORIAL HEALTHCARE C
2750 Atlantic Ave, Long Beach (90806-2713)
PHONE..................................562 424-8101
Jake Rothey, *Administration*
EMP: 180
SALES: 11MM **Privately Held**
WEB: www.atlanticmemorial.com
SIC: 8051 Convalescent home with continuous nursing care

(P-19731)
AUBURN OAKS CARE CENTER
3400 Bell Rd, Auburn (95603-9241)
PHONE..................................650 949-7777
Ellen Kuykendall, *President*
Kevin Hadfield, *Administration*
EMP: 99
SALES: 12.8MM **Privately Held**
SIC: 8051 Convalescent home with continuous nursing care

(P-19732)
AVALON CARE CEN
Also Called: Hy-Lond Hlth Care Cnter-Merced
3170 M St, Merced (95348-2403)
PHONE..................................209 723-1056
Charles R Kirton,
EMP: 74
SALES (est): 2.2MM
SALES (corp-wide): 713.3MM **Privately Held**
SIC: 8051 Skilled nursing care facilities
PA: Avalon Health Care, Inc.
206 N 2100 W Ste 300
Salt Lake City UT 84116
801 596-8844

(P-19733)
AVALON CARE CENTER
Also Called: Mark Twain Conv. Hospital
900 Mountain Ranch Rd, San Andreas (95249-9713)
PHONE..................................209 754-3823
Larry Washington, *Administration*
EMP: 102

SALES (est): 2.5MM
SALES (corp-wide): 713.3MM **Privately Held**
SIC: 8051 Skilled nursing care facilities
PA: Avalon Health Care, Inc.
206 N 2100 W Ste 300
Salt Lake City UT 84116
801 596-8844

(P-19734)
AVALON CARE CENTER - MERCED
Also Called: Franciscan Conv. Hospital
3169 M St, Merced (95348-2404)
PHONE..................................209 722-6231
Larry Imperial, *Administration*
EMP: 74
SALES (est): 2.5MM
SALES (corp-wide): 713.3MM **Privately Held**
SIC: 8051 Skilled nursing care facilities
PA: Avalon Health Care, Inc.
206 N 2100 W Ste 300
Salt Lake City UT 84116
801 596-8844

(P-19735)
AVALON CARE CENTER - MODESTO
Also Called: Hy-Lond Hlth Care Cntr-Modesto
1900 Coffee Rd, Modesto (95355-2703)
PHONE..................................209 526-1775
Randy Kirton, *CEO*
Gabriel Okere, *Administration*
Leonard Battle, *Maint Spvr*
David Giles, *Director*
Buck Perano, *Manager*
EMP: 93 EST: 2003
SALES (est): 2.1MM
SALES (corp-wide): 713.3MM **Privately Held**
SIC: 8051 Convalescent home with continuous nursing care
PA: Avalon Health Care, Inc.
206 N 2100 W Ste 300
Salt Lake City UT 84116
801 596-8844

(P-19736)
AVALON CARE CTR - CHWCHLLA LLC
Also Called: Chowchilla Conv. Center
1010 Ventura Ave, Chowchilla (93610-2368)
PHONE..................................559 665-4826
EMP: 74
SALES: 4.2MM
SALES (corp-wide): 713.3MM **Privately Held**
SIC: 8051 Skilled nursing care facilities
PA: Avalon Health Care, Inc.
206 N 2100 W Ste 300
Salt Lake City UT 84116
801 596-8844

(P-19737)
AVALON CARE CTR - MADERA LLC
Also Called: Avalon Health Care - Madera
1700 Howard Rd, Madera (93637-5131)
PHONE..................................559 673-9278
Jim Lundy, *Exec Dir*
Yolanda Falcon, *Records Dir*
Mary Lee, *Social Dir*
EMP: 67
SALES (est): 2.4MM **Privately Held**
SIC: 8051 Convalescent home with continuous nursing care

(P-19738)
AVALON CARE CTR - MODESTO LLC
515 E Orangeburg Ave, Modesto (95350-5510)
PHONE..................................209 529-0516
Darla Lorenzen, *Exec Dir*
EMP: 65
SALES (est): 3.3MM
SALES (corp-wide): 713.3MM **Privately Held**
SIC: 8051 Skilled nursing care facilities
PA: Avalon Health Care, Inc.
206 N 2100 W Ste 300
Salt Lake City UT 84116
801 596-8844

(P-19739)
AVALON CARE CTR - NEWMAN LLC
Also Called: San Luis Care Center
709 N St, Newman (95360-1162)
PHONE..................209 862-2862
David Robinson,
Robin Scesa, *Records Dir*
EMP: 65
SALES (est): 1.2MM
SALES (corp-wide): 713.3MM **Privately Held**
SIC: 8051 Convalescent home with continuous nursing care
PA: Avalon Health Care, Inc.
206 N 2100 W Ste 300
Salt Lake City UT 84116
801 596-8844

(P-19740)
AVALON CARE CTR - SONORA LLC
Also Called: AVALON HEALTH CARE GROUP
19929 Greenley Rd, Sonora (95370-5996)
PHONE..................209 533-2500
Faye Lincoln, *Vice Pres*
EMP: 107
SALES: 19.5MM
SALES (corp-wide): 713.3MM **Privately Held**
SIC: 8051 Convalescent home with continuous nursing care
PA: Avalon Health Care, Inc.
206 N 2100 W Ste 300
Salt Lake City UT 84116
801 596-8844

(P-19741)
AVE MARIA CONVALESCENT HOSP
Also Called: Ave Maria Senior Living
1249 Josselyn Canyon Rd, Monterey (93940-5265)
PHONE..................831 373-1216
Barbara Reid, *Exec Dir*
Josefina Pimentel, *Director*
EMP: 62
SALES (est): 2.3MM **Privately Held**
SIC: 8051 8361 Convalescent home with continuous nursing care; residential care

(P-19742)
B-SPRING VALLEY LLC
Also Called: BRIGHTON PLACE SPRING VALLEY
9009 Campo Rd, Spring Valley (91977-1112)
PHONE..................619 797-3991
Sharrod Brooks,
EMP: 91
SALES: 8.6MM **Privately Held**
SIC: 8051 Convalescent home with continuous nursing care

(P-19743)
BAKERSFIELD HEALTHCARE
Also Called: Rehablttion Cntre of Bkrsfield
2211 Mount Vernon Ave, Bakersfield (93306-3309)
PHONE..................661 872-2121
Sharrod Brooks,
EMP: 99
SALES (est): 2.6MM **Privately Held**
SIC: 8051 Mental retardation hospital

(P-19744)
BALBOA ENTERPRISES INC
Also Called: Mountain View Healthcare Ctr
2530 Solace Pl, Mountain View (94040-4309)
PHONE..................650 961-6161
Karl Vitt, *President*
Judith Surbuts, *Principal*
Sue Andersen, *Food Svc Dir*
A Bowline, *Director*
Shakira Dalal, *Director*
EMP: 130
SQ FT: 30,000
SALES (est): 8.8MM **Privately Held**
WEB: www.mvhealthcare.com
SIC: 8051 Convalescent home with continuous nursing care

(P-19745)
BAY VIEW RHBILITATION HOSP LLC
516 Willow St, Alameda (94501-6132)
PHONE..................510 521-5600
Thomas Chambers, *Mng Member*
Ziba Aflak, *CFO*
Adrian Manesh, *CFO*
Brooke Saunders, *Officer*
Earl Nicholson, *Vice Pres*
EMP: 99
SALES: 19.2MM **Privately Held**
SIC: 8051 8062 8361 Skilled nursing care facilities; general medical & surgical hospitals; rehabilitation center, residential: health care incidental

(P-19746)
BAYSHORE HEALTHCARE INC
Also Called: Bella Vsta Trnstional Care Ctr
3033 Augusta St, San Luis Obispo (93401-5820)
PHONE..................805 544-5100
Benjamin Flinders, *CEO*
Paul McLean, *CFO*
Johannah Tamba, *Administration*
EMP: 160
SQ FT: 43,000
SALES: 9.4MM **Privately Held**
SIC: 8051 Convalescent home with continuous nursing care

(P-19747)
BEAVER DAM HEALTH CARE CENTER
Also Called: Beverly Healthcare
850 S Sunkist Ave, West Covina (91790-2534)
PHONE..................626 962-3368
Mary Julienne, *Manager*
EMP: 80
SQ FT: 25,000
SALES (corp-wide): 409.2MM **Privately Held**
WEB: www.nwbeccorp.com
SIC: 8051 8093 Convalescent home with continuous nursing care; rehabilitation center, outpatient treatment
PA: Beaver Dam Health Care Center
5220 Tennyson Pkwy # 400
Plano TX 75024
972 372-6300

(P-19748)
BEAVER DAM HEALTH CARE CENTER
Also Called: Golden Livingcenter - Reedley
1090 E Dinuba Ave, Reedley (93654-3577)
PHONE..................559 638-3577
Julie Whiteside, *Manager*
EMP: 93
SALES (corp-wide): 409.2MM **Privately Held**
SIC: 8051 8082 Skilled nursing care facilities; home health care services
PA: Beaver Dam Health Care Center
5220 Tennyson Pkwy # 400
Plano TX 75024
972 372-6300

(P-19749)
BEGROUP
Also Called: Royal Oaks Manor
1763 Royal Oaks Dr Ofc, Duarte (91010-1989)
PHONE..................626 359-9371
EMP: 79
SALES (corp-wide): 20.3MM **Privately Held**
SIC: 8051 Skilled nursing care facilities
PA: Be.Group
516 Burchett St
Glendale CA 91203
818 638-4563

(P-19750)
BELLA VISTA HEALTHCARE CENTER
Also Called: Kf Bella Vista Health Care
933 E Deodar St, Ontario (91764-1309)
PHONE..................909 985-2731
Doug Ason, *CEO*
Marcella Allard, *Administration*
EMP: 100
SQ FT: 10,000

SALES (est): 4.6MM **Privately Held**
SIC: 8051 Skilled nursing care facilities

(P-19751)
BENT TREE NURSING CENTER INC
Also Called: Garden Terrace Health Care Ctr
247 E Bobier Dr, Vista (92084-3026)
PHONE..................760 945-3033
Arch B Gilbert, *President*
Candy Rowland, *Administration*
EMP: 200
SQ FT: 57,000
SALES (est): 2.3MM **Privately Held**
SIC: 8051 Skilled nursing care facilities

(P-19752)
BERKLEY VLY CNVLSCENT HOSP INC
6600 Sepulveda Blvd, Van Nuys (91411-1203)
PHONE..................818 786-0020
Sol Galper, *President*
EMP: 150
SALES: 7.3MM **Privately Held**
SIC: 8051 Convalescent home with continuous nursing care

(P-19753)
BEVERLY WEST HEALTH CARE INC
1020 S Fairfax Ave, Los Angeles (90019-4401)
PHONE..................323 938-2451
Louise Koss, *President*
Lydia Cruz, *President*
EMP: 85
SQ FT: 23,848
SALES: 8.7MM **Privately Held**
SIC: 8051 Convalescent home with continuous nursing care

(P-19754)
BRASWELLS YUCAIPA VALLEY C
35253 Avenue H, Yucaipa (92399-5415)
PHONE..................909 795-2476
James Braswell, *CEO*
EMP: 59
SALES (est): 879K **Privately Held**
SIC: 8051 Convalescent home with continuous nursing care

(P-19755)
BRIARCREST NURSING CENTER INC
5648 Gotham St, Bell (90201-5413)
PHONE..................562 927-2641
Jack Silverman, *President*
Wilson Park, *CFO*
EMP: 110
SALES: 11.7MM **Privately Held**
SIC: 8051 Skilled nursing care facilities

(P-19756)
BRIGHTON GARDENS INC
13101 Hartfield Ave, San Diego (92130-1511)
PHONE..................858 259-2222
Scott Polzin, *Manager*
EMP: 100
SALES (est): 2.2MM **Privately Held**
SIC: 8051 8052 Skilled nursing care facilities; intermediate care facilities

(P-19757)
BRIGHTON HEALTH ALLIANCE (PA)
Also Called: Brighton Place of San Diego
8322 Clairemont Mesa Blvd, San Diego (92111-1317)
PHONE..................619 461-0376
Berry T Crow, *President*
EMP: 83
SQ FT: 20,000
SALES (est): 3.2MM **Privately Held**
SIC: 8051 Convalescent home with continuous nursing care

(P-19758)
BRIGHTON PLACE EAST INC
8625 Lamar St, Spring Valley (91977-2518)
PHONE..................619 461-3222
Guy Reggev, *Administration*

EMP: 62
SQ FT: 11,500
SALES: 5.1MM **Privately Held**
SIC: 8051 Skilled nursing care facilities

(P-19759)
BRIGHTON PLACE SAN DIEGO
1350 Euclid Ave, San Diego (92105-5424)
PHONE..................619 263-2166
Cristin Whittaker, *Exec Dir*
Eden Zapanta, *Nurse*
EMP: 150
SQ FT: 12,000
SALES: 10.9MM **Privately Held**
SIC: 8051 Convalescent home with continuous nursing care

(P-19760)
BROADVIEW INC
Also Called: HIGH HAVEN
4570 Griffin Ave, Los Angeles (90031-1422)
PHONE..................323 221-9174
Micheal Fisher, *Administration*
EMP: 50
SQ FT: 24,000
SALES: 4.2MM **Privately Held**
SIC: 8051 Skilled nursing care facilities

(P-19761)
BROOKDALE LVING CMMUNITIES INC
Also Called: Brookdale Redwood City
485 Woodside Rd Ofc, Redwood City (94061-3890)
PHONE..................650 366-3900
Diane Morton, *Director*
Michelle Merritt, *Marketing Staff*
EMP: 64
SALES (corp-wide): 4.5B **Publicly Held**
WEB: www.parkplace-spokane.com
SIC: 8051 Skilled nursing care facilities
HQ: Brookdale Living Communities, Inc.
515 N State St Ste 1750
Chicago IL 60654

(P-19762)
BROOKDALE SENIOR LIVING INC
Also Called: Brookdale Elk Grove
6727 Laguna Park Dr, Elk Grove (95758-5069)
PHONE..................916 683-1881
Ricky David, *Exec Dir*
Brenda Chappell, *Director*
EMP: 51
SALES (corp-wide): 4.5B **Publicly Held**
SIC: 8051 Skilled nursing care facilities
PA: Brookdale Senior Living
111 Westwood Pl Ste 400
Brentwood TN 37027
615 221-2250

(P-19763)
BROOKDALE SENIOR LIVING INC
Also Called: Brookdale Folsom
780 Harrington Way, Folsom (95630-3458)
PHONE..................916 983-9300
Rhonda Carter, *Manager*
EMP: 65
SALES (corp-wide): 4.5B **Publicly Held**
SIC: 8051 Skilled nursing care facilities
PA: Brookdale Senior Living
111 Westwood Pl Ste 400
Brentwood TN 37027
615 221-2250

(P-19764)
BUENA VENTURA CARE CENTER INC (PA)
1016 S Record Ave, Los Angeles (90023-2533)
PHONE..................323 268-0106
Vernon Aguirre, *Administration*
Steve Keh, *Vice Pres*
EMP: 75
SQ FT: 15,000
SALES: 6.6MM **Privately Held**
SIC: 8051 Convalescent home with continuous nursing care

(P-19765)
BUENA VISTA CARE CENTER INC
1440 S Euclid St, Anaheim (92802-2156)
PHONE....................714 535-7264
EMP: 90
SQ FT: 27,613
SALES (est): 3.8MM **Privately Held**
WEB: www.buenavistacarecenter.com
SIC: 8051 Skilled nursing care facilities

(P-19766)
BURLINGTON CONVALESCENT HOSP (PA)
Also Called: VIEW PARK CONVALESCENT CENTER
845 S Burlington Ave, Los Angeles (90057-4296)
PHONE.....................213 381-5585
Jacob Friedman, President
Ervin Friedman, Vice Pres
Kathleen Becker, Administration
EMP: 100 EST: 1967
SQ FT: 5,000
SALES: 10.9MM **Privately Held**
SIC: 8051 8059 8052 Skilled nursing care facilities; convalescent home; intermediate care facilities

(P-19767)
BURLINGTON CONVALESCENT HOSP
Also Called: View Park Convalescent Center
3737 Don Felipe Dr, Los Angeles (90008-4210)
PHONE.....................323 295-7737
Joe Voltes, Manager
Shanae Curl, Human Res Dir
EMP: 79
SQ FT: 40,000
SALES (corp-wide): 10.9MM **Privately Held**
SIC: 8051 Skilled nursing care facilities
PA: Burlington Convalescent Hospital
845 S Burlington Ave
Los Angeles CA 90057
213 381-5585

(P-19768)
C J HEALTH SERVICES INC
Also Called: Marina Convalescent Center
38650 Mission Blvd, Fremont (94536-4391)
PHONE.....................510 793-3000
Catherine Joseph, President
EMP: 100
SQ FT: 5,000
SALES (est): 3.3MM **Privately Held**
SIC: 8051 Skilled nursing care facilities

(P-19769)
CAL SOUTHERN PRESBT HOMES
Also Called: Buena Vista Manor
802 Buena Vista St, Duarte (91010-1702)
PHONE.....................626 359-8141
Judy Phornkein, Manager
EMP: 65
SALES (corp-wide): 101.5MM **Privately Held**
WEB: www.scths.com
SIC: 8051 Convalescent home with continuous nursing care
PA: Southern California Presbyterian Homes
516 Burchett St
Glendale CA 91203
818 247-0420

(P-19770)
CAL-COAST HEALTHCARE INC
Also Called: Hillside Care Center
81 Professional Ctr Pkwy, San Rafael (94903-2702)
PHONE.....................415 479-5149
Stephen Rodrigues, Administration
EMP: 100
SQ FT: 28,000
SALES (est): 4.6MM **Privately Held**
SIC: 8051 Skilled nursing care facilities

(P-19771)
CALDWELL VENTURES LLC
Also Called: Prestige Asstd Lvng in Chico
1351 E Lassen Ave Ofc, Chico (95973-7700)
PHONE.....................530 899-0814
Gordon Wiens, Manager
EMP: 50
SALES (corp-wide): 4.5MM **Privately Held**
SIC: 8051 Skilled nursing care facilities
PA: Caldwell Ventures, L.L.C.
7700 Ne Parkway Dr # 300
Vancouver WA 98662
360 735-7155

(P-19772)
CALIFORNIA CONVALESCENT HOSPTL
Also Called: Californian-Pasadena
120 Bellefontaine St, Pasadena (91105-3102)
PHONE.....................626 793-5114
Luis Pages, President
Eva M Casner, Treasurer
Clyde L Casner, Vice Pres
Nancy Bower, Administration
EMP: 100
SQ FT: 30,000
SALES (est): 490.8K **Privately Held**
SIC: 8051 Convalescent home with continuous nursing care

(P-19773)
CALIFORNIA NURSING AND REHAB
Also Called: Califrnia Nrsing Rhblttion Ctr
2299 N Indian Ave, Palm Springs (92262-3098)
PHONE.....................760 325-2937
Kennon Shea, Administration
Victoria Shea, Treasurer
Linda Jackson, Administration
Shlomo Rechnitz,
EMP: 150 EST: 1965
SQ FT: 22,000
SALES: 9.9MM **Privately Held**
SIC: 8051 Convalescent home with continuous nursing care

(P-19774)
CALIMESA OPERATIONS LLC
Also Called: Calimesa Post Acute
13542 2nd St, Yucaipa (92399-5396)
PHONE.....................909 795-2421
Jordan Thompson,
Covey Christensen,
EMP: 105 EST: 2015
SALES (est): 740K **Privately Held**
SIC: 8051 Skilled nursing care facilities

(P-19775)
CAMELLIA GARDENS CARE CTR
Also Called: Camellia Gardens Care Center
1920 N Fair Oaks Ave, Pasadena (91103-1623)
PHONE.....................626 798-6777
Pompeyo Rosales, President
Arlene Rosales, Vice Pres
EMP: 80
SALES: 8.3MM **Privately Held**
WEB: www.arpom.org
SIC: 8051 Convalescent home with continuous nursing care

(P-19776)
CANYON PROPERTIES III LLC
Also Called: Country Manor Health Care
11723 Fenton Ave, Sylmar (91342-6431)
PHONE.....................818 890-0430
Donna Santos, Administration
EMP: 99
SALES (est): 5.1MM **Privately Held**
WEB: www.countrymanorhealthcare.com
SIC: 8051 Skilled nursing care facilities

(P-19777)
CAPISTRANO BEACH EXTENDED
35410 Del Rey, Capistrano Beach (92624-1814)
PHONE.....................949 496-5786
Nora Deleon, Administration
EMP: 60

SALES (est): 1.8MM **Privately Held**
SIC: 8051 Skilled nursing care facilities

(P-19778)
CARE TECH INC
Also Called: Hill Cress Home
4280 Cypress Dr, San Bernardino (92407-2960)
PHONE.....................909 882-2965
Carol Dichman, Administration
Gilbert Beltran, Maintence Staff
EMP: 70
SALES (corp-wide): 3.8MM **Privately Held**
SIC: 8051 Skilled nursing care facilities
PA: Care Tech Inc
401 N Central Ave Ste B
Upland CA 91786
909 373-3766

(P-19779)
CAREAGE INC
Also Called: Mission De La Casa
2501 Alvin Ave, San Jose (95121-1660)
PHONE.....................408 238-9751
Kim Nguyen, Branch Mgr
Huynh Vo, Admin Asst
Josh Hedger, Administration
EMP: 50
SALES (corp-wide): 17.3MM **Privately Held**
SIC: 8051 Convalescent home with continuous nursing care
PA: Careage Construction, Inc.
4411 Point Fosdick Dr Nw
Gig Harbor WA 98335
253 853-4457

(P-19780)
CARMICHAEL CARE INC
Also Called: Rosewood Rehabilitation
6041 Fair Oaks Blvd, Carmichael (95608-4816)
PHONE.....................916 483-8103
John L Sorensen, President
Donald Laws, Shareholder
David Sorensen, Shareholder
EMP: 140
SALES (est): 9.2MM **Privately Held**
SIC: 8051 Extended care facility

(P-19781)
CASAVINA FOUNDATION CORP
2501 Alvin Ave, San Jose (95121-1660)
PHONE.....................408 238-9751
Ngai Nguyen, President
CHI Nguyen, Admin Sec
EMP: 187
SALES (est): 5MM **Privately Held**
SIC: 8051 Convalescent home with continuous nursing care

(P-19782)
CASTLE MANOR INC
Also Called: Castle Manor Convalescent Ctr
541 S V Ave, National City (91950-2828)
PHONE.....................619 791-7900
Ruth Cheneweth, President
J Edwin Cheneweth, Treasurer
EMP: 98
SALES: 10.6MM **Privately Held**
SIC: 8051 Skilled nursing care facilities

(P-19783)
CATHEDRAL PIONEER CHURCH HOMES (PA)
Also Called: Pioneer House
415 P St Ofc, Sacramento (95814-5300)
PHONE.....................916 442-4906
Calvin Hara, Administration
EMP: 96
SQ FT: 52,000
SALES: 3.9K **Privately Held**
SIC: 8051 8699 Skilled nursing care facilities; charitable organization

(P-19784)
CEDAR HOLDINGS LLC
Also Called: HIGHLAND PALMS HEALTHCARE CENT
7534 Palm Ave, Highland (92346-3736)
PHONE.....................909 862-0611
Ryan McCook, Mng Member
Alma Ochoa, Executive
Carroll Collins, Office Mgr
Julie Smith, Info Tech Mgr

Myrna De Guzman,
EMP: 99
SALES: 10.2MM **Privately Held**
SIC: 8051 Skilled nursing care facilities

(P-19785)
CEDAR OPERATIONS LLC
Also Called: Cedar Mountain Post Acute
11970 4th St, Yucaipa (92399-2720)
PHONE.....................909 790-2273
Covey Christensen,
EMP: 140 EST: 2001
SALES (est): 131.6K
SALES (corp-wide): 1.5MM **Privately Held**
SIC: 8051 Skilled nursing care facilities
PA: Madison Creek Partners, Llc
26522 La Alameda Ste 300
Mission Viejo CA 92691
949 449-2500

(P-19786)
CENTER OF REHABILITATION
9021 Knott Ave, Buena Park (90620-4138)
PHONE.....................714 826-2330
Peter Madigan, President
Robert Nelson, President
EMP: 125
SALES: 15.3MM **Privately Held**
SIC: 8051 8059 Convalescent home with continuous nursing care; rest home, with health care

(P-19787)
CENTINELA SKILLED NURSING AND
950 S Flower St, Inglewood (90301-4186)
PHONE.....................310 674-3216
Nichole Tons, Vice Pres
EMP: 99
SQ FT: 6,000
SALES (est): 711.8K **Privately Held**
SIC: 8051 Skilled nursing care facilities

(P-19788)
CENTINELA SKLLD NRSNG & WLLNSS
Also Called: Osage Hlthcare Wellness Centre
1001 S Osage Ave, Inglewood (90301-4116)
PHONE.....................310 674-3216
Chaim Kolodny, Principal
EMP: 99
SALES (est): 4.1MM **Privately Held**
SIC: 8051 Convalescent home with continuous nursing care

(P-19789)
CENTRAL GARDENS INC
Also Called: CENTRAL GARDENS CONVALESCENT H
1355 Ellis St, San Francisco (94115-4215)
PHONE.....................415 567-2967
Irene Lieberman, President
David P Lieberman, Treasurer
Michael Lieberman, Vice Pres
Cleitus Jones, Social Dir
Paula Lieberman, Admin Sec
EMP: 136 EST: 1964
SALES: 8MM **Privately Held**
WEB: www.centralgardenssf.com
SIC: 8051 Convalescent home with continuous nursing care

(P-19790)
CENTURY SKILL CARE
Also Called: Century Skilled Nursing Care
301 Centinela Ave, Inglewood (90302-3231)
PHONE.....................310 672-1012
Oscar Parel, Exec Dir
Christopher Arias, Administration
EMP: 100
SALES (est): 5.5MM **Privately Held**
SIC: 8051 Skilled nursing care facilities

(P-19791)
CF MERCED LA SIERRA LLC
Also Called: La Sierra Care Center
2424 M St, Merced (95340-2808)
PHONE.....................209 723-4224
Carson Day, President
Bryan Tanner, COO
EMP: 82
SQ FT: 15,000

PRODUCTS & SVCS

SALES (est): 29.2MM
SALES (corp-wide): 125.3MM **Privately Held**
WEB: www.countryvillahealth.com
SIC: 8051 Skilled nursing care facilities
PA: Country Villa Service Corp.
2400 E Katella Ave # 800
Anaheim CA 92806
310 574-3733

(P-19792)
CF SAN RAFAEL LLC
81 Professional Ctr Pkwy, San Rafael
(94903-2702)
PHONE...............................415 479-5161
Joel Saltzburg, CFO
EMP: 99
SALES (est): 4.6MM **Privately Held**
SIC: 8051 Convalescent home with contin-
uous nursing care

(P-19793)
CF WATSONVILLE LLC
Also Called: Watsonville Post Acute Center
525 Auto Center Dr, Watsonville
(95076-3745)
PHONE...............................831 724-7505
Doug Easton, Manager
Imelda Gil, Records Dir
Krista Garcia, Social Dir
Angelina Martinez, Office Mgr
Leticia Mayotte, Office Mgr
EMP: 96
SQ FT: 24,000
SALES (est): 1.9MM **Privately Held**
SIC: 8051 Skilled nursing care facilities

(P-19794)
CF WATSONVILLE EAST LLC
Also Called: Watsonville Nursing Center
535 Auto Center Dr, Watsonville
(95076-3745)
PHONE...............................310 574-3733
Joel Saltzburg,
Gordon Buechs, CFO
EMP: 99
SALES: 5.1MM **Privately Held**
SIC: 8051 Convalescent home with contin-
uous nursing care

(P-19795)
CF WATSONVILLE WEST LLC
Also Called: Watsonville Post Acute Center
525 Auto Center Dr, Watsonville
(95076-3745)
PHONE...............................831 724-7505
Doug Easton, CEO
Jacob Wintner, Manager
EMP: 96
SQ FT: 24,000
SALES (est): 1.1MM **Privately Held**
SIC: 8051 Skilled nursing care facilities

(P-19796)
**CHANDLER CONVALESCENT
HOSPITAL**
525 S Central Ave, Glendale (91204-2099)
PHONE...............................818 240-1610
Richard Statler, President
Charles Levine, President
Harry Levine, Vice Pres
EMP: 70
SALES: 5.4MM **Privately Held**
SIC: 8051 Convalescent home with contin-
uous nursing care

(P-19797)
CHAPARRAL FOUNDATION
Also Called: CHAPARRAL HOUSE
1309 Allston Way, Berkeley (94702-1920)
PHONE...............................510 848-8774
K J Paige, Administration
EMP: 90
SQ FT: 21,000
SALES: 6.1MM **Privately Held**
WEB: www.chaparralhouse.org
SIC: 8051 Convalescent home with contin-
uous nursing care

(P-19798)
**CHAPMAN HBR SKLLED
NRSING CARE**
Also Called: Chapmn-Hrbor Sklled Nrsing Ctr
12232 Chapman Ave, Garden Grove
(92840-3717)
PHONE...............................714 971-5517

Lydia Goodell, President
Aaron Victor, President
EMP: 95
SQ FT: 15,000
SALES (est): 3.3MM **Privately Held**
SIC: 8051 Convalescent home with contin-
uous nursing care

(P-19799)
**CHINO VALLEY HEALTHCARE
CENTER**
2351 S Towne Ave, Pomona (91766-6227)
PHONE...............................909 628-1245
Wanita Orkia, Administration
EMP: 85 EST: 1995
SQ FT: 17,684
SALES: 11.6MM **Privately Held**
SIC: 8051 Convalescent home with contin-
uous nursing care

(P-19800)
**CHOWCHILLA MEM HLTH CARE
DST (PA)**
1104 Ventura Ave, Chowchilla
(93610-2244)
PHONE...............................559 665-3781
Cathy Flores, Administration
Leland Decker, Principal
EMP: 55
SQ FT: 23,000
SALES: 1.9MM **Privately Held**
SIC: 8051 Skilled nursing care facilities

(P-19801)
CITRUS VALLEY HOSPICE
Also Called: CITRUS VALLEY HOME
HEALTH
820 N Phillips Ave, West Covina
(91791-1121)
PHONE...............................626 859-2263
Robert Curry, CEO
Felipe Dela Riva, Records Dir
EMP: 100
SQ FT: 16,000
SALES: 9.5MM **Privately Held**
SIC: 8051 8082 Convalescent home with
continuous nursing care; home health
care services

(P-19802)
CLAIREMONT HEALTHCARE
8060 Frost St, San Diego (92123-2703)
PHONE...............................858 278-4750
Sharrod Brooks,
EMP: 99 EST: 2012
SALES: 8.6MM **Privately Held**
SIC: 8051 Mental retardation hospital

(P-19803)
**CLARA BALDWIN STOCKER
HOME**
527 S Valinda Ave, West Covina
(91790-3008)
PHONE...............................626 962-7151
Laura Qualls, Administration
Barabara Giesa, Trustee
Alfred Giese, Trustee
Ann Koecritz, Trustee
Ann E Koeckritz, Administration
EMP: 50
SQ FT: 12,218
SALES: 3.8MM **Privately Held**
SIC: 8051 Skilled nursing care facilities

(P-19804)
CLOISTERS OF LA JOLLA INC
7160 Fay Ave, La Jolla (92037-5511)
PHONE...............................858 459-4361
Kennon S Shea, President
EMP: 75 EST: 1983
SQ FT: 5,000
SALES (est): 4.5MM **Privately Held**
SIC: 8051 Convalescent home with contin-
uous nursing care

(P-19805)
CNRC LLC
Also Called: Califrnia Nrsing Rhbltton Ctr
2299 N Indian Ave, Palm Springs (92262)
PHONE...............................760 325-2937
John Black, Administration
EMP: 99 EST: 2000
SALES (est): 2.5MM **Privately Held**
SIC: 8051 Skilled nursing care facilities

(P-19806)
**COALINGA DSTNGISHED
CMNTY CARE**
834 Maple Rd, Coalinga (93210-1348)
PHONE...............................559 935-5939
EMP: 67
SQ FT: 52,000
SALES (est): 1.1MM **Privately Held**
SIC: 8051

(P-19807)
COASTAL HEALTH CARE INC
Also Called: Brentwood Health Care Center
1321 Franklin St, Santa Monica
(90404-2603)
PHONE...............................310 828-5596
John Sorensen, President
Tim Paulsen, Exec VP
Tanner Mitchell, General Mgr
Jessica Kari, Rector
EMP: 75
SALES (est): 10.9MM **Privately Held**
WEB: www.brentwoodnursing.com
SIC: 8051 Convalescent home with contin-
uous nursing care

(P-19808)
**COLDWATER CARE CENTER
LLC**
Also Called: Sherman Village Hlth Care Ctr
12750 Riverside Dr, North Hollywood
(91607-3319)
PHONE...............................818 766-6105
Brenan Lowery, Manager
EMP: 99
SALES: 12.9MM **Privately Held**
SIC: 8051 Convalescent home with contin-
uous nursing care

(P-19809)
**COMMUNITY CARE & REHAB
CTR LLC**
Also Called: Community Care Rhbltation Ctr
4070 Jurupa Ave, Riverside (92506-2234)
PHONE...............................951 680-6500
Frank Johnson, CEO
Irving Bauman, COO
Kelly Iasparro, Vice Pres
Micah Rhead, Administration
EMP: 190
SALES (est): 16.6MM **Privately Held**
SIC: 8051 Skilled nursing care facilities

(P-19810)
**COMMUNITY CONVALESCENT
CENTER**
9620 Fremont Ave, Montclair (91763-2320)
PHONE...............................909 621-4751
Sim Mndlbum,
EMP: 99
SQ FT: 10,000
SALES (est): 348.7K **Privately Held**
SIC: 8051 Skilled nursing care facilities

(P-19811)
**COMMUNITY CONVALESCENT
HOSPITA**
638 E Colorado Ave, Glendora
(91740-4422)
PHONE...............................626 963-6091
Ledmile Gierowitz, President
EMP: 50
SQ FT: 10,000
SALES (est): 1.1MM **Privately Held**
SIC: 8051 Convalescent home with contin-
uous nursing care

(P-19812)
COMPASS HEALTH INC
Also Called: Danish Care Center
10805 El Camino Real, Atascadero
(93422-8868)
PHONE...............................805 466-9254
Mark Woolpert, President
Sheila Brown, Records Dir
Sharon Ray, Office Mgr
Linda Lindsay, Administration
Vanessa Mansker, Education
EMP: 70
SALES (est): 1.9MM **Privately Held**
SIC: 8051 Skilled nursing care facilities

PA: Compass Health, Inc.
200 S 13th St Ste 208
Grover Beach CA 93433

(P-19813)
**CONGRGTNAL CH RETIREMENT
CMNTY**
Also Called: AUBURN RAVINE TERRACE
750 Auburn Ravine Rd, Auburn
(95603-3820)
PHONE...............................530 823-6131
Deborah Stouff, Admin Sec
Stacie Doebler, Records Dir
Lucia Llamas, Director
EMP: 85
SALES: 7.3MM **Privately Held**
SIC: 8051 Skilled nursing care facilities

(P-19814)
COPPER RIDGE CARE CENTER
Also Called: APPLEWOOD OPERATING
201 Hartnell Ave, Redding (96002-1843)
PHONE...............................530 222-2273
Darrell Thompson, President
Carol Carroll, Administration
Dan Gallegos, Telecom Exec
EMP: 200
SALES: 17.4MM **Privately Held**
SIC: 8051 Convalescent home with contin-
uous nursing care

(P-19815)
**CORECARE V A CAL LTD
PARTNR**
Also Called: PARK VISTA AT MORNINGSIDE
2525 Brea Blvd, Fullerton (92835-2787)
PHONE...............................714 256-1000
Gary R Stork, Principal
Melody Olmstead, Controller
Jennifer Martinez, Education
Karrie Castles, Food Svc Dir
EMP: 200
SALES: 12.9MM **Privately Held**
SIC: 8051 Convalescent home with contin-
uous nursing care

(P-19816)
**COUNTRY HILLS HEALTH CARE
INC**
1580 Broadway, El Cajon (92021-5124)
PHONE...............................619 441-8745
Glen Larson, President
Robert Peacock, Administration
Jane Fontecha, Nursing Dir
EMP: 247
SALES: 27.1MM **Privately Held**
WEB: www.countryhills.com
SIC: 8051 Convalescent home with contin-
uous nursing care

(P-19817)
**COUNTRY OAKS CARE CENTER
INC**
830 E Chapel St, Santa Maria
(93454-4699)
PHONE...............................805 922-6657
John Henning, President
Sharon Henning, Principal
EMP: 70
SQ FT: 14,000
SALES: 4.4MM **Privately Held**
SIC: 8051 Convalescent home with contin-
uous nursing care

(P-19818)
**COUNTRY OAKS PARTNERS
LLC**
Also Called: Country Oaks Care Center
215 W Pearl St, Pomona (91768-3114)
PHONE...............................909 622-1067
Tanner Person, Administration
Kelly Iasparro, Vice Pres
William Presnell, Admin Sec
EMP: 99 EST: 2008
SQ FT: 10,601
SALES (est): 324.2K **Privately Held**
SIC: 8051 8049 Skilled nursing care facili-
ties; physical therapist

(P-19819)
COUNTRY VILLA SERVICE CORP
1208 S Central Ave, Glendale
(91204-2504)
PHONE...............................818 246-5516

Adam Mitchel, *Administration*
Anna Trejo, *Data Proc Staff*
EMP: 70
SALES (corp-wide): 125.3MM **Privately Held**
SIC: 8051 Skilled nursing care facilities
PA: Country Villa Service Corp.
2400 E Katella Ave # 800
Anaheim CA 92806
310 574-3733

(P-19820)
COUNTRY VILLA SERVICE CORP
400 W Huntington Dr, Arcadia
(91007-3470)
PHONE.................626 445-2421
Shelly Andresen, *Principal*
EMP: 70
SALES (corp-wide): 125.3MM **Privately Held**
SIC: 8051 Skilled nursing care facilities
PA: Country Villa Service Corp.
2400 E Katella Ave # 800
Anaheim CA 92806
310 574-3733

(P-19821)
COUNTRY VILLA SERVICE CORP
3611 E Imperial Hwy, Lynwood
(90262-2608)
PHONE.................310 537-2500
Jacob Wintner, *Branch Mgr*
EMP: 70
SALES (corp-wide): 125.3MM **Privately Held**
SIC: 8051 Skilled nursing care facilities
PA: Country Villa Service Corp.
2400 E Katella Ave # 800
Anaheim CA 92806
310 574-3733

(P-19822)
COUNTY OF MODOC
Also Called: Care Wst-Wrner Mtn Nursing Ctr
228 W Mcdowell Ave, Alturas (96101-3934)
PHONE.................530 233-3416
Bonney Markgrass, *Director*
Dick Steyer, *Exec Dir*
EMP: 161 **Privately Held**
WEB: www.modoccounty.us
SIC: 8051 Skilled nursing care facilities
PA: County Of Modoc
202 W 4th St Ste A
Alturas CA 96101
530 233-6400

(P-19823)
COUNTY OF SACRAMENTO
Also Called: Public Health Nursing Service
9616 Micron Ave Ste 750, Sacramento
(95827-2604)
PHONE.................916 875-0900
Jan Peters, *Director*
EMP: 55 **Privately Held**
WEB: www.sna.com
SIC: 8051 9431 Skilled nursing care facilities; administration of public health programs;
PA: County Of Sacramento
700 H St Ste 7650
Sacramento CA 95814
916 874-5544

(P-19824)
COUNTY OF SAN DIEGO
Also Called: Health & Human Services- Aging
655 Park Center Dr, Santee (92071-6957)
PHONE.................619 956-2800
Gwen Marie Hilleary, *Manager*
EMP: 400 **Privately Held**
WEB: www.sdicc.org
SIC: 8051 9431 Skilled nursing care facilities;
PA: County Of San Diego
1600 Pacific Hwy Ste 209
San Diego CA 92101
619 531-5880

(P-19825)
COURTYARD PLAZA
6951 Lennox Ave, Van Nuys (91405-4034)
PHONE.................818 780-5005
Donahue G Vanderhider, *Principal*
EMP: 50
SALES (est): 1.4MM **Privately Held**
SIC: 8051 Skilled nursing care facilities

(P-19826)
COVENANT CARE LLC
Also Called: Pacific Coast Manor
1935 Wharf Rd, Capitola (95010-2606)
PHONE.................831 476-0770
Christine Sims, *Manager*
EMP: 90
SALES (est): 1.9MM **Privately Held**
WEB: www.willowtreenursingcenter.com
SIC: 8051 Convalescent home with continuous nursing care
HQ: Covenant Care California, Llc
27071 Aliso Creek Rd # 100
Aliso Viejo CA 92656

(P-19827)
COVENANT CARE CALIFORNIA LLC
Also Called: Wagner Heights Nursing & Rehab
9289 Branstetter Pl, Stockton
(95209-1700)
PHONE.................209 477-5252
Janey Hargreaves, *Branch Mgr*
Ruby Maes, *Human Res Dir*
Norma Hurick, *Education*
Frank Cervantes, *Director*
EMP: 160 **Privately Held**
WEB: www.willowtreenursingcenter.com
SIC: 8051 Skilled nursing care facilities
HQ: Covenant Care California, Llc
27071 Aliso Creek Rd # 100
Aliso Viejo CA 92656

(P-19828)
COVENANT CARE CALIFORNIA LLC
Also Called: Palo Alto Nursing Center
911 Bryant St, Palo Alto (94301-2711)
PHONE.................415 327-0511
Roland Gandy, *Branch Mgr*
Marina Safro, *Hlthcr Dir*
EMP: 55 **Privately Held**
WEB: www.willowtreenursingcenter.com
SIC: 8051 8059 Skilled nursing care facilities; personal care home, with health care
HQ: Covenant Care California, Llc
27071 Aliso Creek Rd # 100
Aliso Viejo CA 92656

(P-19829)
COVENANT CARE CALIFORNIA LLC
Also Called: Mission Skilled Nursing Home
410 N Winchester Blvd, Santa Clara
(95050-6325)
PHONE.................408 248-3736
Kathleen Glass, *Manager*
Herland Martinez, *Records Dir*
Dae-Wook Kang, *Director*
EMP: 75 **Privately Held**
WEB: www.willowtreenursingcenter.com
SIC: 8051 Skilled nursing care facilities
HQ: Covenant Care California, Llc
27071 Aliso Creek Rd # 100
Aliso Viejo CA 92656

(P-19830)
COVENANT CARE CALIFORNIA LLC
Also Called: Willow Tree Nursing Center
2124 57th Ave, Oakland (94621-4322)
PHONE.................510 261-2628
Tony Moya, *Manager*
EMP: 90 **Privately Held**
WEB: www.willowtreenursingcenter.com
SIC: 8051 Skilled nursing care facilities
HQ: Covenant Care California, Llc
27071 Aliso Creek Rd # 100
Aliso Viejo CA 92656

(P-19831)
COVENANT CARE CALIFORNIA LLC
Also Called: Royal Care Skilled Nursing Ctr
2725 Pacific Ave, Long Beach
(90806-2612)
PHONE.................562 427-7493
Nasreen Pervaiz, *Branch Mgr*
Djuan Jester, *Director*

EMP: 90 **Privately Held**
WEB: www.willowtreenursingcenter.com
SIC: 8051 Convalescent home with continuous nursing care
HQ: Covenant Care California, Llc
27071 Aliso Creek Rd # 100
Aliso Viejo CA 92656

(P-19832)
COVENANT CARE CALIFORNIA LLC
Also Called: Shoreline Care Center
5225 S J St, Oxnard (93033-8320)
PHONE.................805 488-3696
Cindy Poulsen, *Exec Dir*
Melissa Zabala, *Food Svc Dir*
Christian Capili, *Nurse*
Donna Rodriguez, *Nursing Dir*
Elizabeth Salazar, *Director*
EMP: 200 **Privately Held**
WEB: www.willowtreenursingcenter.com
SIC: 8051 Skilled nursing care facilities
HQ: Covenant Care California, Llc
27071 Aliso Creek Rd # 100
Aliso Viejo CA 92656

(P-19833)
COVENANT CARE CALIFORNIA LLC
Also Called: Huntington Park Nursing Center
6425 Miles Ave, Huntington Park
(90255-4348)
PHONE.................323 589-5941
Toni Mazzeo, *Branch Mgr*
Paula Holman, *Purch Agent*
EMP: 140 **Privately Held**
WEB: www.willowtreenursingcenter.com
SIC: 8051 Skilled nursing care facilities
HQ: Covenant Care California, Llc
27071 Aliso Creek Rd # 100
Aliso Viejo CA 92656

(P-19834)
COVENANT CARE CALIFORNIA LLC
Also Called: Pacific Gardens Hlth Care Ctr
577 S Peach Ave, Fresno (93727-3952)
PHONE.................559 251-8463
Bart Vanderwal, *Branch Mgr*
EMP: 150
SQ FT: 40,000 **Privately Held**
WEB: www.willowtreenursingcenter.com
SIC: 8051 Skilled nursing care facilities
HQ: Covenant Care California, Llc
27071 Aliso Creek Rd # 100
Aliso Viejo CA 92656

(P-19835)
COVENANT CARE CALIFORNIA LLC
Also Called: Capital Transitional Care
6821 24th St, Sacramento (95822-4037)
PHONE.................916 391-6011
Richard Thorp, *Branch Mgr*
Lee Nguyen, *Education*
Kaly Vo, *Nursing Dir*
Jasraj Kaur,
EMP: 100 **Privately Held**
WEB: www.willowtreenursingcenter.com
SIC: 8051 Skilled nursing care facilities
HQ: Covenant Care California, Llc
27071 Aliso Creek Rd # 100
Aliso Viejo CA 92656

(P-19836)
COVENANT CARE CALIFORNIA LLC
Also Called: Buena Vista Care Center
160 S Patterson Ave, Santa Barbara
(93111-2006)
PHONE.................805 964-4871
David Hibarger, *Branch Mgr*
Jaime Mejia, *Office Mgr*
Michael Malloy, *Business Anlyst*
Tara Curtis, *Opers Staff*
Lance Hassell, *Opers Staff*
EMP: 150 **Privately Held**
WEB: www.willowtreenursingcenter.com
SIC: 8051 Skilled nursing care facilities

HQ: Covenant Care California, Llc
27071 Aliso Creek Rd # 100
Aliso Viejo CA 92656

(P-19837)
COVENANT CARE CALIFORNIA LLC
Also Called: Turlock Nrsing Rhabilation Ctr
1111 E Tuolumne Rd, Turlock
(95382-1541)
PHONE.................209 632-3821
Loris Gielczyk, *Principal*
Monica Ruiz, *Office Mgr*
Stephanie Morris, *Director*
EMP: 135 **Privately Held**
WEB: www.willowtreenursingcenter.com
SIC: 8051 Convalescent home with continuous nursing care
HQ: Covenant Care California, Llc
27071 Aliso Creek Rd # 100
Aliso Viejo CA 92656

(P-19838)
COVENANT CARE CALIFORNIA LLC
Also Called: Gilroy Health Care
8170 Murray Ave, Gilroy (95020-4605)
PHONE.................408 842-9311
Doreen McGary, *Director*
EMP: 150 **Privately Held**
WEB: www.willowtreenursingcenter.com
SIC: 8051 Skilled nursing care facilities
HQ: Covenant Care California, Llc
27071 Aliso Creek Rd # 100
Aliso Viejo CA 92656

(P-19839)
COVENANT CARE CALIFORNIA LLC (HQ)
27071 Aliso Creek Rd # 100, Aliso Viejo
(92656-5325)
PHONE.................949 349-1200
Robert Levin, *President*
Christine Sims, *CFO*
Therese Domingo, *Officer*
Judy Elmore, *Vice Pres*
Debbie Nix, *Vice Pres*
EMP: 50
SQ FT: 10,000
SALES (est): 169.8MM **Privately Held**
WEB: www.willowtreenursingcenter.com
SIC: 8051 Skilled nursing care facilities

(P-19840)
COVENANT CARE CALIFORNIA LLC
Also Called: Valle Vista Convalescent Hosp
1025 W 2nd Ave, Escondido (92025-3839)
PHONE.................760 745-1288
Kristina Kuizon, *Branch Mgr*
EMP: 50
SQ FT: 15,494 **Privately Held**
WEB: www.willowtreenursingcenter.com
SIC: 8051 Convalescent home with continuous nursing care
HQ: Covenant Care California, Llc
27071 Aliso Creek Rd # 100
Aliso Viejo CA 92656

(P-19841)
COVENANT CARE CALIFORNIA LLC
Also Called: St. Edna Sb-Cute Rhblttion Ctr
1929 N Fairview St, Santa Ana
(92706-2205)
PHONE.................714 554-9700
Joshua Torres, *Manager*
Jon Hooyenga, *Sales Staff*
EMP: 125 **Privately Held**
WEB: www.willowtreenursingcenter.com
SIC: 8051 Convalescent home with continuous nursing care
HQ: Covenant Care California, Llc
27071 Aliso Creek Rd # 100
Aliso Viejo CA 92656

(P-19842)
COVENANT CARE CALIFORNIA LLC
Also Called: Los Alts Sub-Acute Rhbltn
809 Fremont Ave, Los Altos (94024-5617)
PHONE.................................650 941-5255
Annie Buerhaus, *Branch Mgr*
Alfred Tenoso, *Maintence Staff*
Teresa Lopez, *Education*
Donald Thorpe, *Food Svc Dir*
Eunice Pino, *Nursing Dir*
EMP: 200 **Privately Held**
WEB: www.willowtreenursingcenter.com
SIC: 8051 8093 Skilled nursing care facili-
ties; rehabilitation center, outpatient treat-
ment
HQ: Covenant Care California, Llc
27071 Aliso Creek Rd # 100
Aliso Viejo CA 92656

(P-19843)
COVENANT CARE COURTYARD LLC
Also Called: Courtyard Healthcare
1850 E 8th St, Davis (95616-2502)
PHONE.................................530 756-1800
Robert Levin, *CEO*
EMP: 56
SALES (est): 5.2MM **Privately Held**
SIC: 8051 Convalescent home with contin-
uous nursing care
HQ: Covenant Care California, Llc
27071 Aliso Creek Rd # 100
Aliso Viejo CA 92656

(P-19844)
COVENANT CARE INDIANA INC (DH)
27071 Aliso Creek Rd # 100, Aliso Viejo
(92656-5325)
PHONE.................................949 349-1200
Robert Levin, *President*
Christine Sims, *CFO*
Linda Leming, *Director*
EMP: 57
SALES (est): 13.4MM **Privately Held**
WEB:
www.covingtonmanornursingcenter.com
SIC: 8051 Skilled nursing care facilities

(P-19845)
COVENANT CARE LA JOLLA LLC
Also Called: La Jolla Nrsing Rhbltation Ctr
2552 Torrey Pines Rd # 1, La Jolla
(92037-3432)
PHONE.................................858 453-5810
Lisa Parker, *Administration*
Nadia Decastro, *Records Dir*
Rodney Washington, *Social Dir*
Carol Tiaadwai, *Administration*
Laura Klyza, *Education*
EMP: 150
SALES (est): 4.3MM **Privately Held**
WEB: www.willowtreenursingcenter.com
SIC: 8051 Skilled nursing care facilities
HQ: Covenant Care California, Llc
27071 Aliso Creek Rd # 100
Aliso Viejo CA 92656

(P-19846)
COVENANT RTIREMENT COMMUNITIES
325 Kempton St, Spring Valley
(91977-5810)
PHONE.................................619 479-4790
Thad Rothrock, *Branch Mgr*
Richard Miller, *Exec Dir*
EMP: 193
SALES (corp-wide): 4.3MM **Privately
Held**
SIC: 8051 Skilled nursing care facilities
HQ: Covenant Retirement Communities
5700 Old Orchard Rd # 100
Skokie IL 60077

(P-19847)
COVENTRY COURT HEALTH CENTER
2040 S Euclid St, Anaheim (92802-3111)
PHONE.................................714 636-2800
Saun Dohl, *CEO*
Shaun Dahl, *Administration*
Erin Hawley, *Sales Staff*
EMP: 200
SALES: 13MM **Privately Held**
SIC: 8051 Skilled nursing care facilities

(P-19848)
COVINA REHABILITATION CENTER
Also Called: REGENCY HEALTH SERVICES
261 W Badillo St, Covina (91723-1907)
PHONE.................................626 967-3874
Teresa Dearmond, *Director*
Agnes Maron, *Director*
EMP: 110
SQ FT: 27,800
SALES: 11.6MM **Privately Held**
SIC: 8051 Skilled nursing care facilities

(P-19849)
CREEKSIDE CNVALESCENT HOSP INC
850 Sonoma Ave, Santa Rosa
(95404-4715)
PHONE.................................707 544-7750
Robert Bates, *Administration*
Lawrence R De Beni, *President*
EMP: 160
SQ FT: 44,000
SALES (est): 4.9MM **Privately Held**
SIC: 8051 Convalescent home with contin-
uous nursing care

(P-19850)
CREEKSIDE HEALTHCARE CTR
1900 Church Ln, San Pablo (94806-3708)
PHONE.................................510 235-5514
Dianna Haines, *Administration*
EMP: 50
SALES (est): 437.6K **Privately Held**
SIC: 8051 Extended care facility

(P-19851)
CREEKSIDE REHAB AND BEHAVIORAL
850 Sonoma Ave, Santa Rosa
(95404-4715)
PHONE.................................707 524-7030
Paul Duranczsk, *Administration*
Prema Thekkek, *President*
EMP: 208 **EST:** 2000
SALES (est): 7.2MM **Privately Held**
SIC: 8051 Convalescent home with contin-
uous nursing care

(P-19852)
CRESTVIEW CNVALESCENT HOSP INC
1471 S Riverside Ave, Rialto (92376-7703)
PHONE.................................909 877-1361
Roy Berglund MD, *President*
EMP: 220
SQ FT: 44,000
SALES (est): 5.7MM **Privately Held**
WEB: www.crestviewcarecenter.com
SIC: 8051 Convalescent home with contin-
uous nursing care

(P-19853)
CROCUS HOLDINGS LLC
Also Called: Roseville Care Center
1161 Cirby Way, Roseville (95661-4421)
PHONE.................................916 782-1238
James Huish,
Myrna De Guzman, *Controller*
Jessica Abney, *Food Svc Dir*
Amy Griffis, *Nursing Dir*
EMP: 99
SALES: 20.8MM **Privately Held**
SIC: 8051 Convalescent home with contin-
uous nursing care

(P-19854)
CUPERTINO HEALTHCARE
Also Called: Cupertino Hlthcare Wllness Ctr
22590 Voss Ave, Cupertino (95014-2627)
PHONE.................................408 253-9034
Aaron Robin, *Mng Member*

EMP: 99
SALES: 15MM **Privately Held**
SIC: 8051 Convalescent home with contin-
uous nursing care

(P-19855)
DANVILLE LONG-TERM CARE INC
Also Called: Danville Post Acute Rehab
336 Diablo Rd, Danville (94526-3417)
PHONE.................................925 837-4566
John L Sorensen, *President*
Tim Paulsen, *Vice Pres*
Taylor Ellis, *Administration*
Shannon Olmstead, *Human Res Dir*
EMP: 80
SALES (est): 2.6MM **Privately Held**
SIC: 8051 Convalescent home with contin-
uous nursing care

(P-19856)
DANVILLE VILLAGE SKILLED NURSN
Also Called: Danville Rehsbilitation
336 Diablo Rd, Danville (94526-3417)
PHONE.................................925 837-4566
Spencer Brinton, *Administration*
Rosemary Segelke, *Director*
EMP: 65
SQ FT: 13,760
SALES: 9.4MM **Privately Held**
SIC: 8051 Skilled nursing care facilities

(P-19857)
DAVID ROSS INC
Also Called: ROSE GARDEN CONVALES-
CENT CENTE
1899 N Raymond Ave, Pasadena
(91103-1733)
PHONE.................................323 684-7673
Arlene Rosales, *Ch of Bd*
▲ **EMP:** 100
SQ FT: 27,000
SALES: 8.8MM **Privately Held**
SIC: 8051 Skilled nursing care facilities

(P-19858)
DEL AMO GRDNS CNVLSCNT HOSP &
22419 Kent Ave, Torrance (90505-2303)
PHONE.................................310 378-4233
Morris Weiss, *President*
Barry Weiss, *Vice Pres*
Harumi Takeda, *Risk Mgmt Dir*
Daniella Gonzalez, *Office Mgr*
Harry Jacobs, *Admin Sec*
EMP: 92 **EST:** 1960
SQ FT: 21,298
SALES: 8.9MM **Privately Held**
WEB: www.delamogardens.com
SIC: 8051 Convalescent home with contin-
uous nursing care

(P-19859)
DEL RIO HEALTH CARE INC
Also Called: Del Rio Convalescent Center
16016 Rio Florida Dr, Whittier
(90603-1045)
PHONE.................................562 947-5221
Steven Highland, *President*
Mahmood M Moledina, *Treasurer*
EMP: 150
SQ FT: 42,000
SALES (est): 2.6MM **Privately Held**
SIC: 8051 Skilled nursing care facilities

(P-19860)
DEL RIO SANITARIUM INC
Also Called: Del Rio Convalescent
7002 Gage Ave, Bell Gardens
(90201-2014)
PHONE.................................562 927-6586
Joy Thune, *President*
EMP: 150
SALES (est): 8.2MM **Privately Held**
SIC: 8051 Skilled nursing care facilities

(P-19861)
DEL ROSA VILLA INC
2018 Del Rosa Ave, San Bernardino
(92404-5642)
PHONE.................................909 885-3261
Carol Wagner, *Administration*
Thomas S Plott, *President*
Elizabeth Plott, *Corp Secy*

EMP: 85
SQ FT: 20,000
SALES (est): 3.3MM **Privately Held**
SIC: 8051 Convalescent home with contin-
uous nursing care

(P-19862)
DELANO DST SKLLED NRSING FCLTY
1509 Tokay St, Delano (93215-3603)
PHONE.................................661 720-2100
Dennis Karnowski, *Administration*
Janice Calzo, *Business Dir*
EMP: 115
SQ FT: 30,000
SALES (est): 9.7MM **Privately Held**
SIC: 8051 Skilled nursing care facilities

(P-19863)
DELTA NRSING RHBILITATION HOSP
Also Called: Delta Nrsing Rhabilitation Ctr
514 N Bridge St, Visalia (93291-5015)
PHONE.................................559 625-4003
Mark Fisher, *President*
EMP: 60
SALES (est): 1.7MM **Privately Held**
WEB: www.missioncaregroup.com
SIC: 8051 Convalescent home with contin-
uous nursing care

(P-19864)
DEVELOPMENTAL SVCS CAL DEPT
Also Called: Porterville Developmental Ctr
26501 Avenue 140, Porterville
(93257-9109)
P.O. Box 2000 (93258-2000)
PHONE.................................559 782-2222
Theresa Villeci, *Principal*
EMP: 1800 **Privately Held**
WEB: www.ldc.dds.ca.gov
SIC: 8051 9431 Mental retardation hospi-
tal; administration of public health pro-
grams;
HQ: California Department Of Developmen-
tal Services
1600 9th St
Sacramento CA 95814
916 654-1690

(P-19865)
DIGNITY HEALTH
Also Called: Marian Extended Care Cntr
1530 Cypress Way, Santa Maria
(93454-5900)
PHONE.................................805 739-3650
Debbie M Young, *Manager*
Susan Ziemba, *Director*
EMP: 132 **Privately Held**
WEB: www.chw.edu
SIC: 8051 8082 Skilled nursing care facili-
ties; home health care services
HQ: Dignity Health
185 Berry St Ste 300
San Francisco CA 94107
415 438-5500

(P-19866)
DOUGLAS FIR HOLDINGS LLC
Also Called: Huntington Vly Healthcare Ctr
8382 Newman Ave, Huntington Beach
(92647-7038)
PHONE.................................714 842-5551
Brad Truhar, *Administration*
Cara McVey, *Food Svc Dir*
David Price, *Director*
EMP: 145
SALES: 16.8MM **Privately Held**
SIC: 8051 Extended care facility

(P-19867)
DOWNEY COMMUNITY HEALTH CENTER
8425 Iowa St, Downey (90241-4929)
P.O. Box 340 (90241-0340)
PHONE.................................562 862-6506
Rich Coberly, *Administration*
Stanley Diller, *Partner*
EMP: 175
SQ FT: 60,000
SALES: 17.3MM **Privately Held**
SIC: 8051 Convalescent home with contin-
uous nursing care

(P-19868)
E W C H INC
1805 West St, Hayward (94545-1932)
PHONE....................................510 783-4811
Ada Lukban, *Administration*
Mark Costa, *Sales Executive*
EMP: 100
SQ FT: 26,000
SALES (est): 1MM **Privately Held**
SIC: 8051 8069 Convalescent home with
continuous nursing care; specialty hospi-
tals, except psychiatric

(P-19869)
EARLWOOD LLC
Also Called: Earlwood Convalescent Hospital
20820 Earl St, Torrance (90503-4307)
PHONE....................................310 371-1228
Kevin Thomas, *Administration*
EMP: 75 EST: 2003
SALES (est): 1.6MM **Publicly Held**
WEB: www.parkviewnursing.net
SIC: 8051 Skilled nursing care facilities
HQ: Skilled Healthcare, Llc
27442 Portola Pkwy # 200
Foothill Ranch CA 92610
949 282-5800

(P-19870)
EASTERN PLUMAS HEALTH
CARE
700 3rd St, Loyalton (96118)
PHONE....................................530 993-1225
G Koortbojian, *Administration*
EMP: 85 EST: 1951
SQ FT: 20,000
SALES (est): 5.5MM **Privately Held**
SIC: 8051 Skilled nursing care facilities

(P-19871)
EDEN WEST REHABILITATION
1805 West St, Hayward (94545-1932)
PHONE....................................510 783-4811
Ruth Gildea, *Administration*
EMP: 99
SALES (est): 1MM **Privately Held**
SIC: 8051 Convalescent home with contin-
uous nursing care

(P-19872)
EDGEWATER CONVALESCENT
HOSP
Also Called: Edgewater Skilled Nursing Ctr
2625 E 4th St, Long Beach (90814-1299)
PHONE....................................562 434-0974
Debbie Grani, *President*
Norma Cowles, *Vice Pres*
Sylvia Gandara, *Social Worker*
Ace Mendoza, *Director*
Ignacio Torres, *Director*
EMP: 75 EST: 1954
SQ FT: 18,000
SALES: 9.5MM **Privately Held**
SIC: 8051 Convalescent home with contin-
uous nursing care

(P-19873)
EL ENCANTO HEALTHCARE &
REHAB
Also Called: EL ENCANTO HOME HEALTH
CARE
555 El Encanto Rd, City of Industry
(91745-1017)
PHONE....................................626 336-1274
Steve Blackwell, *Administration*
EMP: 212
SQ FT: 70,000
SALES: 12MM **Privately Held**
WEB: www.elencantohealthcare.com
SIC: 8051 Convalescent home with contin-
uous nursing care; mental retardation
hospital

(P-19874)
ELDER CARE ALLIANCE SAN
RAFAEL
1301 Marina Village Pkwy # 210, Alameda
(94501-1082)
PHONE....................................510 769-2700
Jesse Janteen, *President*
EMP: 75
SALES: 10MM **Privately Held**
SIC: 8051 Convalescent home with contin-
uous nursing care

(P-19875)
ELDORADO CARE CENTER LP
Also Called: Avocado Post Acute
510 E Washington Ave, El Cajon
(92020-5324)
PHONE....................................619 440-1211
Jacob Graff, *Owner*
EMP: 298
SALES (est): 17.2MM **Privately Held**
WEB: www.eldoradocarecenterllc.com
SIC: 8051 8322 Convalescent home with
continuous nursing care; adult day care
center

(P-19876)
ELIM ALZHEIMERS & REHAB
668 E Bullard Ave, Fresno (93710-5401)
PHONE....................................559 320-2200
Ronald E Howe, *President*
M K Howe, *Admin Sec*
EMP: 95
SQ FT: 28,000
SALES (est): 1.3MM **Privately Held**
SIC: 8051 Skilled nursing care facilities

(P-19877)
ELMS SANITARIUM INC
Also Called: Elms Convalescent Hospital
3247 Windmist Ave, Thousand Oaks
(91362-1151)
PHONE....................................818 240-6720
Aleck Knell, *President*
Lena Knell, *Treasurer*
William Knell, *Vice Pres*
EMP: 60
SQ FT: 11,000
SALES: 3.8MM **Privately Held**
SIC: 8051 Skilled nursing care facilities

(P-19878)
EMERITUS CORPORATION
Also Called: Brookdale Clairemont
5219 Clairemont Mesa Blvd, San Diego
(92117-2206)
PHONE....................................858 292-8044
S Wheeler, *Exec Dir*
Francis Cabral, *Director*
EMP: 50
SALES (corp-wide): 4.5B **Publicly Held**
SIC: 8051 Skilled nursing care facilities
HQ: Emeritus Corporation
3131 Elliott Ave Ste 500
Milwaukee WI 53214

(P-19879)
EMPRES FINANCIAL SERVICES
LLC
Also Called: Living Centers
1527 Springs Rd, Vallejo (94591-5448)
PHONE....................................707 643-2793
David Hicks, *Manager*
EMP: 61
SALES (corp-wide): 5MM **Privately Held**
SIC: 8051 Skilled nursing care facilities
HQ: Empres Financial Services, Llc
4601 Ne 77th Ave Ste 300
Vancouver WA 98662
360 892-6628

(P-19880)
ENSIGN CLOVERDALE LLC
Also Called: Cloverdale Healthcare Center
300 Cherry Creek Rd, Cloverdale
(95425-3811)
PHONE....................................707 894-5201
Soon Burnam, *Administration*
Misty Robinson, *Social Dir*
Adam Willits, *Administration*
Trang Davis, *Human Res Dir*
Christopher Christensen,
EMP: 66
SALES: 6.6MM
SALES (corp-wide): 2B **Publicly Held**
SIC: 8051 Convalescent home with contin-
uous nursing care
HQ: Northern Pioneer Healthcare, Inc.
27101 Puerta Real
Mission Viejo CA 92691
949 487-9500

(P-19881)
ENSIGN GROUP INC
340 Victoria St, Costa Mesa (92627-1914)
PHONE....................................949 642-0387
Cindy Ramirez, *Director*

EMP: 84
SALES (corp-wide): 2B **Publicly Held**
SIC: 8051 Skilled nursing care facilities
PA: The Ensign Group Inc
27101 Puerta Real Ste 450
Mission Viejo CA 92691
949 487-9500

(P-19882)
ENSIGN GROUP INC
Also Called: Downey Care Center
13007 Paramount Blvd, Downey
(90242-4329)
PHONE....................................562 923-9301
Marc Brian, *Principal*
EMP: 75
SALES (corp-wide): 2B **Publicly Held**
WEB: www.willowtreenursingcenter.com
SIC: 8051 Skilled nursing care facilities
PA: The Ensign Group Inc
27101 Puerta Real Ste 450
Mission Viejo CA 92691
949 487-9500

(P-19883)
ENSIGN GROUP INC
Also Called: Panaroma Gardens
9541 Van Nuys Blvd, Panorama City
(91402-1315)
PHONE....................................818 893-6385
Alicia Gamero, *Executive*
Belen Herrera, *Hlthcr Dir*
Esperanza Hernandez, *Director*
EMP: 115
SALES (corp-wide): 2B **Publicly Held**
WEB: www.theensigngroup.com
SIC: 8051 Convalescent home with contin-
uous nursing care
PA: The Ensign Group Inc
27101 Puerta Real Ste 450
Mission Viejo CA 92691
949 487-9500

(P-19884)
ENSIGN GROUP INC
Also Called: Whittier Hills Health Care Ctr
10426 Bogardus Ave, Whittier
(90603-2642)
PHONE....................................562 947-7817
Lisa Matarazzo, *Administration*
EMP: 150
SQ FT: 36,316
SALES (corp-wide): 2B **Publicly Held**
WEB: www.theensigngroup.com
SIC: 8051 8059 Convalescent home with
continuous nursing care; rest home, with
health care
PA: The Ensign Group Inc
27101 Puerta Real Ste 450
Mission Viejo CA 92691
949 487-9500

(P-19885)
ENSIGN GROUP INC
Also Called: Park View Gardens
3751 Montgomery Dr, Santa Rosa
(95405-5214)
PHONE....................................707 525-1250
Eric Moessing, *Director*
EMP: 110
SALES (corp-wide): 2B **Publicly Held**
WEB: www.theensigngroup.com
SIC: 8051 Convalescent home with contin-
uous nursing care
PA: The Ensign Group Inc
27101 Puerta Real Ste 450
Mission Viejo CA 92691
949 487-9500

(P-19886)
ENSIGN GROUP INC
Also Called: Palomar Vista Healthcare Ctr
201 N Fig St, Escondido (92025-3416)
PHONE....................................760 746-0303
William Adams, *Manager*
Pam Campbell, *Executive*
EMP: 100
SALES (corp-wide): 2B **Publicly Held**
WEB: www.theensigngroup.com
SIC: 8051 Convalescent home with contin-
uous nursing care
PA: The Ensign Group Inc
27101 Puerta Real Ste 450
Mission Viejo CA 92691
949 487-9500

(P-19887)
ENSIGN GROUP INC
Also Called: Mission Care Center
4800 Delta Ave, Rosemead (91770-1127)
PHONE....................................626 607-2400
Tin Nelson, *Director*
Sheila Manapat, *Human Res Dir*
EMP: 60
SALES (corp-wide): 2B **Publicly Held**
WEB: www.missioncareandrehab.com
SIC: 8051 Skilled nursing care facilities
PA: The Ensign Group Inc
27101 Puerta Real Ste 450
Mission Viejo CA 92691
949 487-9500

(P-19888)
ENSIGN PALM I LLC
Also Called: Premier Care Ctr For Palm Sprn
2990 E Ramon Rd, Palm Springs
(92264-7931)
PHONE....................................760 323-2638
Soon Burnam, *Treasurer*
Leeron Hever, *Administration*
Misty Edgemon, *Train & Dev Mgr*
EMP: 90
SALES (est): 3.2MM
SALES (corp-wide): 2B **Publicly Held**
SIC: 8051 Convalescent home with contin-
uous nursing care
PA: The Ensign Group Inc
27101 Puerta Real Ste 450
Mission Viejo CA 92691
949 487-9500

(P-19889)
ENSIGN SERVICES INC
27101 Puerta Real Ste 450, Mission Viejo
(92691-8566)
PHONE....................................949 487-9500
Christopher Christensen, *CEO*
Snapper Suzanne, *CFO*
Beverly B Wittekind, *Treasurer*
Debbie Miller, *Officer*
Chad Keetch, *Admin Sec*
EMP: 90
SALES (est): 10.7MM **Privately Held**
SIC: 8051 Convalescent home with contin-
uous nursing care

(P-19890)
ENSIGN SOUTHLAND LLC
Also Called: Southland Care
29222 Rancho Viejo Rd # 127, San Juan
Capistrano (92675-1049)
PHONE....................................949 487-9500
Allan Norman,
EMP: 150
SALES (est): 1.2MM
SALES (corp-wide): 2B **Publicly Held**
WEB: www.ensigngroup.com
SIC: 8051 Extended care facility
PA: The Ensign Group Inc
27101 Puerta Real Ste 450
Mission Viejo CA 92691
949 487-9500

(P-19891)
EPISCOPAL COMMUNITIES &
SERVIC
Also Called: Canterbury, The
5801 Crestridge Rd, Pls Vrds Pnsl
(90275-4961)
PHONE....................................310 544-2204
Consuelo Haire, *Branch Mgr*
Dave Hone, *Exec Dir*
Jane Salmon, *Education*
EMP: 100
SALES (corp-wide): 62.1MM **Privately
Held**
WEB: www.episcopalhome.org
SIC: 8051 8361 8059 Extended care facil-
ity; home for the aged; personal care
home, with health care
PA: Episcopal Communities & Services For
Seniors
605 E Huntington Dr # 207
Monrovia CA 91016
626 403-5880

(P-19892)
EQUICARE MEDICAL SUPPLY INC
Also Called: Emerald Ter Convalescent Hosp
1154 S Alvarado St, Los Angeles
(90006-4110)
PHONE..................................213 385-1715
Elena Mendoza-Legaspi, *President*
Elena M Mendoza-Legaspi, *President*
Christina Mendoza, *Administration*
EMP: 55
SALES: 3MM **Privately Held**
SIC: 8051 Convalescent home with continuous nursing care

(P-19893)
ESKATON PROPERTIES INC
Also Called: Eskaton Village Care Center
3847 Walnut Ave, Carmichael
(95608-2148)
PHONE..................................916 974-2060
Larry Bahr, *Manager*
Phyllis Johnson, *Accountant*
EMP: 1000
SALES (corp-wide): 102.2MM **Privately Held**
SIC: 8051 Skilled nursing care facilities
PA: Eskaton Properties Incorporated
5105 Manzanita Ave Ste A
Carmichael CA 95608
916 334-0810

(P-19894)
ESKATON PROPERTIES INC
Also Called: Homestead of Fair Oaks
11300 Fair Oaks Blvd, Fair Oaks
(95628-5141)
PHONE..................................916 965-4663
Tom Coffey, *Manager*
EMP: 160
SALES (corp-wide): 102.2MM **Privately Held**
SIC: 8051 Convalescent home with continuous nursing care
PA: Eskaton Properties Incorporated
5105 Manzanita Ave Ste A
Carmichael CA 95608
916 334-0810

(P-19895)
ESKATON PROPERTIES INC
Also Called: Eskaton Center of Greenhaven
455 Florin Rd, Sacramento (95831-2024)
PHONE..................................916 393-2550
Heather Craig, *Manager*
EMP: 180
SALES (corp-wide): 102.2MM **Privately Held**
SIC: 8051 Convalescent home with continuous nursing care
PA: Eskaton Properties Incorporated
5105 Manzanita Ave Ste A
Carmichael CA 95608
916 334-0810

(P-19896)
ESKATON PROPERTIES INC (PA)
Also Called: 0EPI
5105 Manzanita Ave Ste A, Carmichael
(95608-0523)
PHONE..................................916 334-0810
Todd Murch, *President*
Betsy Donovan, *Senior VP*
Bill Pace, *Senior VP*
Sheri Peifer, *Senior VP*
Charles Garcia, *Vice Pres*
▲ EMP: 60
SQ FT: 27,000
SALES: 102.2MM **Privately Held**
SIC: 8051 Skilled nursing care facilities

(P-19897)
ESTRELLA INC
Also Called: Woodruff Convalescent Center
1340 Highland Ave 12, Duarte
(91010-2520)
PHONE..................................562 925-6418
Liberation De Leon MD, *President*
EMP: 110
SALES (est): 6.9MM **Privately Held**
SIC: 8051 Convalescent home with continuous nursing care

(P-19898)
EUREKA REHAB & WELLNESS CENTER
2353 23rd St, Eureka (95501-3201)
PHONE..................................707 445-3261
Sharrod Brooks, *Partner*
Shlomo Rechnitz, *Partner*
EMP: 98 EST: 2011
SALES: 8.1MM **Privately Held**
SIC: 8051 Skilled nursing care facilities

(P-19899)
EVERGREEN AT CHICO LLC
Also Called: Twin Oaks Nrsing Rhbltion Ctr
1200 Springfield Dr, Chico (95928-6340)
PHONE..................................530 342-4885
Barbara Addington, *Manager*
Carla McClintock, *Executive*
Charles Garretson, *Director*
EMP: 150
SALES (corp-wide): 5MM **Privately Held**
SIC: 8051 8069 Convalescent home with continuous nursing care; specialty hospitals, except psychiatric
HQ: Evergreen At Chico, L.L.C.
4601 Ne 77th Ave Ste 300
Vancouver WA 98662

(P-19900)
EVERGREEN AT LAKEPORT LLC (PA)
Also Called: Evergreen Lkport Hlthcare Ctr
1291 Craig Ave, Lakeport (95453-5704)
PHONE..................................707 263-6382
Steve Hendrickson, *Administration*
Rhonda Daughtery, *Executive*
EMP: 100
SQ FT: 36,240
SALES: 8.1B **Privately Held**
SIC: 8051 Convalescent home with continuous nursing care

(P-19901)
EVERGREEN AT LAKEPORT LLC
Also Called: Evergreen Healthcare Center
6212 Tudor Way, Bakersfield (93306-7067)
PHONE..................................661 871-3133
Gloria Melliti, *Manager*
EMP: 125
SALES (corp-wide): 8.1B **Privately Held**
SIC: 8051 Convalescent home with continuous nursing care
PA: Evergreen At Lakeport Llc
1291 Craig Ave
Lakeport CA 95453
707 263-6382

(P-19902)
EVERGREEN AT OROVILLE LLC
Also Called: Olive Ridge Post Acute Care
1000 Executive Pkwy, Oroville
(95966-5100)
PHONE..................................530 533-7335
Dale Patterson,
EMP: 99
SALES (est): 1.8MM **Privately Held**
SIC: 8051 Mental retardation hospital

(P-19903)
EVERGREEN AT PETALUMA LLC
Also Called: EMPRES POST ACUTE REHABILITATION
300 Douglas St, Petaluma (94952-2503)
PHONE..................................707 763-6887
Connie Smith, *Exec Dir*
Ahmed El-Ghoneimy, *Director*
Noel Serrano, *Director*
EMP: 121
SQ FT: 21,965
SALES: 10.9MM
SALES (corp-wide): 553.1K **Privately Held**
SIC: 8051 Skilled nursing care facilities
PA: Empres California Healthcare, Llc
4601 Ne 77th Ave Ste 300
Vancouver WA 98662
360 892-6628

(P-19904)
EVERGREEN HEALTH CARE LLC
323 Campus Dr, Arvin (93203-1047)
PHONE..................................661 854-4475

Cody Rasmussen, *Exec Dir*
Rush Melliti, *Manager*
EMP: 92
SALES: 6.1MM
SALES (corp-wide): 5MM **Privately Held**
SIC: 8051 Skilled nursing care facilities
HQ: Evergreen At Chico, L.L.C.
4601 Ne 77th Ave Ste 300
Vancouver WA 98662

(P-19905)
EXTENDED CARE HOSP WESTMINSTER
206 Hospital Cir, Westminster
(92683-3910)
PHONE..................................714 891-2769
George Rhodes, *Administration*
Connie Black, *Partner*
Fred Landry, *Partner*
Mark Landry, *Partner*
Debbie Odonnell, *Education*
EMP: 115
SALES (est): 6.7MM **Privately Held**
SIC: 8051 8069 Convalescent home with continuous nursing care; specialty hospitals, except psychiatric

(P-19906)
FAIRFIELD NURSING & REHAB CTR
Also Called: Fairfield Healthcare Center
1255 Travis Blvd, Fairfield (94533-4801)
PHONE..................................707 425-0623
Steve Hendrickson, *Administration*
Joanne Van Dyke, *Administration*
Joan Wandyke, *Administration*
Patti Turner, *Info Tech Mgr*
Selmar Himbing, *Director*
EMP: 90
SALES (est): 4.9MM **Privately Held**
SIC: 8051 Convalescent home with continuous nursing care

(P-19907)
FAITH ENTERPRISES INC
545 W Beverly Pl, Tracy (95376-3012)
PHONE..................................209 835-6034
R David Delisle, *President*
EMP: 50
SQ FT: 18,159
SALES (est): 1.4MM **Privately Held**
SIC: 8051 Convalescent home with continuous nursing care

(P-19908)
FALLBROOK SKLLED NRSING FCILTY
325 Potter St, Fallbrook (92028-3068)
PHONE..................................760 728-2330
Larry Payton, *CEO*
EMP: 95
SALES (est): 5MM **Privately Held**
SIC: 8051 Skilled nursing care facilities

(P-19909)
FAR WEST INC
Also Called: Linwood Grdns Convalescent Ctr
4444 W Meadow Ave, Visalia (93277-1652)
PHONE..................................559 627-1241
Robert Barker, *Manager*
Aaron Burrup, *Administration*
Kathy Alfaro, *Human Res Dir*
Jackie Dees, *Education*
Cecilia Ramirez, *Nursing Dir*
EMP: 70
SALES (corp-wide): 103.9MM **Privately Held**
SIC: 8051 8059 Convalescent home with continuous nursing care; convalescent home
HQ: Far West, Inc
4020 Sierra College Blvd
Rocklin CA 95677

(P-19910)
FAR WEST INC
Also Called: South Gate Care Centers
8455 State St, South Gate (90280-2339)
PHONE..................................323 564-7761
James Hagar, *Administration*
EMP: 78

SALES (corp-wide): 103.9MM **Privately Held**
SIC: 8051 8059 Convalescent home with continuous nursing care; convalescent home
HQ: Far West, Inc
4020 Sierra College Blvd
Rocklin CA 95677

(P-19911)
FAR WEST INC
Also Called: Medical Center
467 E Gilbert St, San Bernardino
(92404-5318)
PHONE..................................909 884-4781
Frank De Leosa, *Manager*
EMP: 80
SALES (corp-wide): 103.9MM **Privately Held**
SIC: 8051 8059 Convalescent home with continuous nursing care; rest home, with health care
HQ: Far West, Inc
4020 Sierra College Blvd
Rocklin CA 95677

(P-19912)
FERNVIEW CONVALESCENT HOSPITAL
Also Called: Pinegrove Hlthcare Wllness Ctr
126 N San Gabriel Blvd, San Gabriel
(91775-2499)
PHONE..................................626 285-3131
Benjamin Garret, *President*
EMP: 72 EST: 1964
SQ FT: 38,000
SALES (est): 2.2MM **Privately Held**
SIC: 8051 8322 8399 Convalescent home with continuous nursing care; rehabilitation services; advocacy group

(P-19913)
FIG HOLDINGS LLC
Also Called: GARDEN CITY HEALTHCARE CENTER
1310 W Granger Ave, Modesto
(95350-3911)
PHONE..................................209 524-4817
Gary Collins,
Diana Reyes, *Office Mgr*
Colleen Pittman, *Education*
Kristina Lackey, *Food Svc Dir*
Christyn Young, *Hlthcr Dir*
EMP: 100
SQ FT: 23,000
SALES: 14.8MM
SALES (corp-wide): 40.3MM **Privately Held**
SIC: 8051 Convalescent home with continuous nursing care
PA: Plum Healthcare Group, Llc
100 E San Marcos Blvd # 200
San Marcos CA 92069
760 471-0388

(P-19914)
FIVE STAR QUALITY CARE INC
Also Called: Flagship Health Care Center
466 Flagship Rd, Newport Beach
(92663-3635)
PHONE..................................949 642-8044
Bonny Christino, *Manager*
EMP: 200 **Publicly Held**
WEB: www.fivestarqualitycare.com
SIC: 8051 Skilled nursing care facilities
PA: Five Star Senior Living Inc.
400 Centre St
Newton MA 02458

(P-19915)
FIVE STAR QUALITY CARE INC
Also Called: Remington Club I & II
16925 Hierba Dr, San Diego (92128-2688)
PHONE..................................858 673-6300
Kristen Crinigan, *Exec Dir*
Jennifer Bradford, *Director*
EMP: 300 **Publicly Held**
WEB: www.fivestarqualitycare.com
SIC: 8051 Skilled nursing care facilities
PA: Five Star Senior Living Inc.
400 Centre St
Newton MA 02458

(P-19916)
FIVE STAR QUALITY CARE INC
Also Called: Somerford Place Fresno
6075 N Marks Ave, Fresno (93711-1600)
PHONE.............................559 446-6226
Kathy Gorman, *Exec Dir*
EMP: 84 **Publicly Held**
WEB: www.fivestarqualitycare.com
SIC: 8051 Skilled nursing care facilities
PA: Five Star Senior Living Inc.
400 Centre St
Newton MA 02458

(P-19917)
FIVE STAR QULTY CARE-CA II LLC
Also Called: Lasaltte Hlth Rhbilitation Ctr
537 E Fulton St, Stockton (95204-2227)
PHONE.............................209 466-2066
Gus Ropalidis, *Administration*
Chris Fenicle, *Financial Exec*
EMP: 105 **Publicly Held**
WEB: www.fivestarqualitycare.com
SIC: 8051 Skilled nursing care facilities
PA: Five Star Senior Living Inc.
400 Centre St
Newton MA 02458

(P-19918)
FIVE STAR QULTY CARE-CA II LLC
Also Called: Van Nuys Health Care Center
6835 Hazeltine Ave, Van Nuys (91405-3218)
PHONE.............................818 997-1841
George Martinez Admin, *Branch Mgr*
EMP: 65 **Publicly Held**
WEB: www.fivestarqualitycare.com
SIC: 8051 Skilled nursing care facilities
HQ: Five Star Quality Care-Ca Ii, Llc
93 W Avnida De Los Arbles
Thousand Oaks CA
-

(P-19919)
FIVE STAR SENIOR LIVING INC
Also Called: Somerford Place Encinitas
1350 S El Camino Real, Encinitas (92024-4904)
PHONE.............................760 479-1818
Terry Records, *Manager*
EMP: 50 **Publicly Held**
WEB: www.fivestarqualitycare.com
SIC: 8051 Skilled nursing care facilities
PA: Five Star Senior Living Inc.
400 Centre St
Newton MA 02458

(P-19920)
FIVE STAR SENIOR LIVING INC
Also Called: Somerford Place Stockton
3530 Deer Park Dr, Stockton (95219-2350)
PHONE.............................209 951-6500
Leslie Anderson, *Manager*
EMP: 50 **Publicly Held**
WEB: www.fivestarqualitycare.com
SIC: 8051 Skilled nursing care facilities
PA: Five Star Senior Living Inc.
400 Centre St
Newton MA 02458

(P-19921)
FOOTHILL OAKS CARE CENTER INC
3400 Bell Rd, Auburn (95603-9241)
PHONE.............................530 888-6257
Art Whitney, *CEO*
Ellen Kuykendall, *President*
EMP: 90
SALES (est): 1.9MM
SALES (corp-wide): 103.9MM **Privately Held**
WEB: www.villadelrey.com
SIC: 8051 8093 8062 Convalescent home with continuous nursing care; rehabilitation center, outpatient treatment; general medical & surgical hospitals
HQ: Horizon West Healthcare, Inc.
4020 Sierra College Blvd # 190
Rocklin CA 95677
916 624-6230

(P-19922)
FORUM HEALTHCARE CENTER
23600 Via Esplendor, Cupertino (95014-6571)
PHONE.............................650 944-0200
Lynda Kaser, *Administration*
EMP: 245 EST: 1998
SALES (est): 6.1MM **Privately Held**
SIC: 8051 8052 Convalescent home with continuous nursing care; intermediate care facilities

(P-19923)
FOUR SEASONS HEALTHCARE
5335 Laurel Canyon Blvd, North Hollywood (91607-2711)
PHONE.............................818 985-1814
Sharrod Brooks, *Partner*
Sharon Hernandez, *Human Res Dir*
EMP: 99
SALES (est): 3MM **Privately Held**
SIC: 8051 Mental retardation hospital

(P-19924)
FREEDOM VILLAGE HEALTHCARE CTR
Also Called: Rehabworks At Freedom Village
23442 El Toro Rd Bldg 2, Lake Forest (92630-6992)
PHONE.............................949 472-4733
Joel Niblett, *Administration*
Mary Beth Melby, *Records Dir*
Chery Roscamp, *CFO*
Teresa Leleux, *Administration*
Christine Hall, *Controller*
EMP: 100
SALES (est): 5.1MM **Privately Held**
SIC: 8051 8052 Convalescent home with continuous nursing care; intermediate care facilities

(P-19925)
FRENCH PARK CARE CENTER
Also Called: TENET
600 E Washington Ave, Santa Ana (92701-3843)
P.O. Box 139036, Dallas TX (75313-9036)
PHONE.............................714 973-1656
Talmadge Cline, *Administration*
Candise Nomellini, *Marketing Staff*
EMP: 150
SQ FT: 171,000
SALES: 21.9MM
SALES (corp-wide): 18.3B **Publicly Held**
WEB: www.tenethealth.com
SIC: 8051 Convalescent home with continuous nursing care
PA: Tenet Healthcare Corporation
1445 Ross Ave Ste 1400
Dallas TX 75202
469 893-2200

(P-19926)
FRESNO HERITAGE PARTNERS
Also Called: Somerford Place
6075 N Marks Ave, Fresno (93711-1600)
PHONE.............................559 446-6226
Sharol Hutchison, *Exec Dir*
Fresno Surgery Center, *General Ptnr*
EMP: 50
SQ FT: 26,166
SALES (est): 1.4MM **Privately Held**
SIC: 8051 Skilled nursing care facilities

(P-19927)
FRESNO SKILLED NURSING
Also Called: Healthcare Centre of Fresno
1665 M St, Fresno (93721-1121)
PHONE.............................559 268-5361
Sharrod Brooks,
EMP: 99
SALES (est): 6.5MM **Privately Held**
SIC: 8051 Mental retardation hospital

(P-19928)
FRONT PORCH COMMUNITIES
Also Called: Kingsley Manor
1055 N Kingsley Dr, Los Angeles (90029-1207)
PHONE.............................323 661-1128
Cindy Gonzales, *Principal*
Emily Ruyes, *Office Mgr*
Jeannie Weber, *Sales Staff*
Ritsime Janikyan, *Hlthcr Dir*
EMP: 130
SQ FT: 106,521

SALES (corp-wide): 165.1MM **Privately Held**
SIC: 8051 Convalescent home with continuous nursing care
PA: Front Porch Communities And Services - Casa De Manana, Llc
800 N Brand Blvd Fl 19
Glendale CA 91203
818 729-8100

(P-19929)
FRONT PORCH COMMUNITIES & SVCS
Also Called: Apple Valley Care Center
11959 Apple Valley Rd, Apple Valley (92308-7507)
PHONE.............................760 240-5051
Terry Blumer, *Manager*
EMP: 80
SQ FT: 36,151
SALES (corp-wide): 165.1MM **Privately Held**
SIC: 8051 Convalescent home with continuous nursing care
PA: Front Porch Communities And Services - Casa De Manana, Llc
800 N Brand Blvd Fl 19
Glendale CA 91203
818 729-8100

(P-19930)
FRUITVALE LONG TERM CARE LLC
3020 E 15th St, Oakland (94601-2305)
PHONE.............................510 261-5613
Kam McGavock,
EMP: 75
SALES (est): 838.7K **Privately Held**
SIC: 8051 Mental retardation hospital

(P-19931)
GARDEN CREST CONVALESCE
Also Called: Garden Crest Rtrment Residence
909 Lucile Ave, Los Angeles (90026-1598)
PHONE.............................323 663-8281
Paul Barron, *CEO*
Vera Barron, *Vice Pres*
EMP: 90
SQ FT: 30,000
SALES (est): 7.3MM **Privately Held**
WEB: www.gardencrestweb.com
SIC: 8051 8059 8322 Convalescent home with continuous nursing care; convalescent home; old age assistance

(P-19932)
GARDEN VIEW CARE CENTER INC
14475 Garden View Ln, Baldwin Park (91706-6000)
PHONE.............................626 962-7095
John Sorensen, *President*
EMP: 80 EST: 1990
SALES (est): 12MM **Privately Held**
WEB: www.gardenviewcarecenter.com
SIC: 8051 Convalescent home with continuous nursing care

(P-19933)
GARDENA FLORES INC
Also Called: Las Flores Convalescent Hosp
14165 Purche Ave, Gardena (90249-2824)
PHONE.............................310 323-4570
Keith Fortune, *Director*
Diana Fortune, *Treasurer*
EMP: 90
SQ FT: 10,000
SALES (est): 5MM **Privately Held**
SIC: 8051 Skilled nursing care facilities

(P-19934)
GARFIELD NURSING HOME INC
Also Called: Morton Bakar Center
1100 Marina Village Pkwy # 100, Alameda (94501-6461)
PHONE.............................510 582-7676
Ann Bakar, *CEO*
Robert H Guttman, *President*
Marshall D Langfeld, *CFO*
Ross C Peterson, *Vice Pres*
EMP: 125

SALES (est): 2.1MM
SALES (corp-wide): 205.4MM **Privately Held**
WEB: www.telecare.com
SIC: 8051 Convalescent home with continuous nursing care
PA: Telecare Corporation
1080 Marina Village Pkwy # 100
Alameda CA 94501
510 337-7950

(P-19935)
GEM TRANSITIONAL CARE CENTER
Also Called: Gem Trans Care
716 S Fair Oaks Ave, Pasadena (91105-2618)
PHONE.............................626 737-0560
Rupert Ouano, *Director*
Manuel Dellana, *Administration*
EMP: 80
SALES (est): 3.7MM **Privately Held**
SIC: 8051 Convalescent home with continuous nursing care

(P-19936)
GENESIS HEALTHCARE CORPORATION
Also Called: Meadowbrook Bhavioral Hlth Ctr
3951 East Blvd, Los Angeles (90066-4605)
PHONE.............................310 391-8266
Michael Mayer, *Branch Mgr*
EMP: 85 **Publicly Held**
SIC: 8051 Skilled nursing care facilities
HQ: Genesis Healthcare Corporation
101 E State St
Kennett Square PA 19348
610 444-6350

(P-19937)
GENESIS HEALTHCARE CORPORATION
Also Called: Laurel Park
1425 Laurel Ave, Pomona (91768-2837)
PHONE.............................909 622-1069
Gerald Bogard, *Branch Mgr*
EMP: 50 **Publicly Held**
SIC: 8051 Skilled nursing care facilities
HQ: Genesis Healthcare Corporation
101 E State St
Kennett Square PA 19348
610 444-6350

(P-19938)
GENESIS HEALTHCARE CORPORATION
Also Called: Olive Vista, Center
2335 S Towne Ave, Pomona (91766-6227)
PHONE.............................909 628-6024
Richard Escontrias, *Branch Mgr*
EMP: 120 **Publicly Held**
SIC: 8051 8361 Convalescent home with continuous nursing care; residential care
HQ: Genesis Healthcare Corporation
101 E State St
Kennett Square PA 19348
610 444-6350

(P-19939)
GEORGIA ATKISON SNF LLC
Also Called: Alliance Nrsing Rhbltation Ctr
3825 Durfee Ave, El Monte (91732-2505)
PHONE.............................626 444-2535
Eli Quinones, *Mng Member*
EMP: 125
SQ FT: 30,000
SALES (est): 9MM **Privately Held**
WEB: www.alliancenursingrehab.com
SIC: 8051 Skilled nursing care facilities

(P-19940)
GERI CARE INC
Also Called: HARBOR CARE CENTER
21521 S Vermont Ave, Torrance (90502-1939)
PHONE.............................310 320-0961
Emmanuel David, *President*
EMP: 100 EST: 1975
SQ FT: 30,000
SALES: 10MM **Privately Held**
SIC: 8051 Convalescent home with continuous nursing care

(P-19941)
GLADIOLUS HOLDINGS LLC
Also Called: Pines At Plcrvlle Hlthcare Ctr
1040 Marshall Way, Placerville
(95667-5706)
PHONE....................530 622-3400
Nick Anderson, *President*
Victoria Rapoza, *Records Dir*
Jared Edmunds, *General Mgr*
EMP: 99
SALES: 950K **Privately Held**
SIC: 8051 Convalescent home with continuous nursing care

(P-19942)
GLENDALE HEALTHCARE CENTER
Also Called: COUNTRY VILLA GLENDALE HEALTHC
1208 S Central Ave, Glendale
(91204-2504)
PHONE....................818 246-5516
Adam Mitchel, *Administration*
Bernie Lozano, *Chf Purch Ofc*
EMP: 70
SALES: 5.5MM **Privately Held**
SIC: 8051 Convalescent home with continuous nursing care

(P-19943)
GLENWOOD CORPORATION
Also Called: Glenwood Care Center
1300 N C St, Oxnard (93030-4006)
PHONE....................805 983-0305
Jerry E Wells, *President*
Frank Chung MD, *Treasurer*
Wallace Tamoyose MD, *Vice Pres*
Harvey Wilson, *Admin Sec*
EMP: 70
SQ FT: 30,000
SALES: 12.1MM **Privately Held**
SIC: 8051 Skilled nursing care facilities

(P-19944)
GLENWOOD GARDENS
Also Called: A E W/Careage Ops
350 Calloway Dr Unit A1, Bakersfield
(93312-2966)
PHONE....................661 587-0221
Cindy Boudreaux, *Business Mgr*
EMP: 260
SALES (est): 9.6MM **Privately Held**
SIC: 8051 Skilled nursing care facilities

(P-19945)
GOLD COUNTRY HEALTH CENTER INC (PA)
4301 Golden Center Dr, Placerville
(95667-6260)
PHONE....................530 621-1100
Suzanne Valoppi, *Administration*
Sandra Haskins, *Exec Dir*
Lorraine Wells, *Food Svc Dir*
Carol Schroeder, *Nursing Dir*
Bonnie Berndt, *Director*
EMP: 130
SQ FT: 57,000
SALES: 13.5MM **Privately Held**
SIC: 8051 Skilled nursing care facilities

(P-19946)
GOLDEN CROSS CARE II INC
Also Called: Golden Cross Hlth Care Fresno
1233 A St, Fresno (93706-3299)
PHONE....................559 268-3023
Marlene Z Robertson, *President*
Melanie Balubar, *Food Svc Dir*
EMP: 70
SALES (est): 2.9MM **Privately Held**
SIC: 8051 Skilled nursing care facilities

(P-19947)
GOLDEN CROSS CARE INC
Also Called: GOLDEN CROSS HEALTH CARE
1450 N Fair Oaks Ave, Pasadena
(91103-1801)
PHONE....................626 791-1948
Marlene Robertson, *President*
Joe Arevalo, *Administration*
EMP: 160
SQ FT: 30,000
SALES: 7.1MM **Privately Held**
SIC: 8051 Skilled nursing care facilities

(P-19948)
GOLDEN LIVING LLC
Also Called: Beverly
1715 S Cedar Ave, Fresno (93702-4331)
PHONE....................559 237-8377
Ed Johnson, *Exec Dir*
EMP: 93
SALES (corp-wide): 409.2MM **Privately Held**
SIC: 8051 8361 8063 8082 Skilled nursing care facilities; residential care; psychiatric hospitals; home health care services
PA: Beaver Dam Health Care Center
  5220 Tennyson Pkwy # 400
  Plano TX 75024
  972 372-6300

(P-19949)
GOLDEN LIVING LLC
Also Called: Beverly
1306 E Sumner Ave, Fowler (93625-2627)
PHONE....................559 834-2542
Christine Clark, *Branch Mgr*
EMP: 60
SALES (corp-wide): 409.2MM **Privately Held**
SIC: 8051 8082 Skilled nursing care facilities; home health care services
PA: Beaver Dam Health Care Center
  5220 Tennyson Pkwy # 400
  Plano TX 75024
  972 372-6300

(P-19950)
GOLDEN LIVING LLC
Also Called: Beverly Healthcare
340 Victoria St, Costa Mesa (92627-1914)
P.O. Box 1933, San Marcos (92079-1933)
PHONE....................949 642-0387
David Sedgwick, *Exec Dir*
EMP: 100
SALES (corp-wide): 409.2MM **Privately Held**
WEB: www.nwbeccorp.com
SIC: 8051 Convalescent home with continuous nursing care
PA: Beaver Dam Health Care Center
  5220 Tennyson Pkwy # 400
  Plano TX 75024
  972 372-6300

(P-19951)
GOLDEN LIVING LLC
Also Called: Golden Living Center - Chateau
1221 Rosemarie Ln, Stockton
(95207-6703)
PHONE....................707 546-0471
Susan Morgan, *Manager*
EMP: 100
SALES (corp-wide): 409.2MM **Privately Held**
SIC: 8051 Convalescent home with continuous nursing care
PA: Beaver Dam Health Care Center
  5220 Tennyson Pkwy # 400
  Plano TX 75024
  972 372-6300

(P-19952)
GOLDEN LIVING LLC
Also Called: Golden Livingctr-Country View
925 N Cornelia Ave, Fresno (93706-1031)
PHONE....................559 275-4785
Deann Walters, *Manager*
EMP: 93
SALES (corp-wide): 409.2MM **Privately Held**
SIC: 8051 8059 Skilled nursing care facilities; convalescent home
PA: Beaver Dam Health Care Center
  5220 Tennyson Pkwy # 400
  Plano TX 75024
  972 372-6300

(P-19953)
GOLDEN LIVING LLC
Also Called: Beverly Healthcare
1477 Grove St, San Francisco
(94117-1421)
PHONE....................415 563-0565
Simon Chen, *Manager*
Sean De Ocampo, *Social Dir*
EMP: 100

SALES (corp-wide): 409.2MM **Privately Held**
WEB: www.nwbeccorp.com
SIC: 8051 Skilled nursing care facilities
PA: Beaver Dam Health Care Center
  5220 Tennyson Pkwy # 400
  Plano TX 75024
  972 372-6300

(P-19954)
GOLDEN LIVING LLC
Also Called: Beverly Healthcare
14966 Terreno De Flores, Los Gatos
(95032-2023)
PHONE....................408 356-8136
Richard Gotmaster, *Branch Mgr*
EMP: 70
SALES (corp-wide): 409.2MM **Privately Held**
WEB: www.nwbeccorp.com
SIC: 8051 Skilled nursing care facilities
PA: Beaver Dam Health Care Center
  5220 Tennyson Pkwy # 400
  Plano TX 75024
  972 372-6300

(P-19955)
GOLDEN LIVING LLC
Also Called: Golden Lvngcnter - Bakersfield
3601 San Dimas St, Bakersfield
(93301-1405)
PHONE....................661 323-2894
Will Maloney, *Director*
EMP: 70
SALES (corp-wide): 409.2MM **Privately Held**
SIC: 8051 Skilled nursing care facilities
PA: Beaver Dam Health Care Center
  5220 Tennyson Pkwy # 400
  Plano TX 75024
  972 372-6300

(P-19956)
GOLDEN LIVING LLC
Also Called: Beverly Healthcare
1300 N C St, Oxnard (93030-4006)
PHONE....................805 983-0305
David Banks, *Ch of Bd*
EMP: 100
SALES (corp-wide): 409.2MM **Privately Held**
WEB: www.nwbeccorp.com
SIC: 8051 Skilled nursing care facilities
PA: Beaver Dam Health Care Center
  5220 Tennyson Pkwy # 400
  Plano TX 75024
  972 372-6300

(P-19957)
GOLDEN LIVING LLC
Also Called: Beverly Healthcare
5445 Everglades St, Ventura (93003-6523)
PHONE....................805 642-1736
Jay Brady, *Branch Mgr*
EMP: 100
SALES (corp-wide): 409.2MM **Privately Held**
WEB: www.nwbeccorp.com
SIC: 8051 Skilled nursing care facilities
PA: Beaver Dam Health Care Center
  5220 Tennyson Pkwy # 400
  Plano TX 75024
  972 372-6300

(P-19958)
GOLDEN LIVING LLC
Also Called: Beverly Healthcare
950 S Fairmont Ave, Lodi (95240-5131)
PHONE....................209 368-0693
Beverly Mannon, *Principal*
EMP: 70
SALES (corp-wide): 409.2MM **Privately Held**
WEB: www.nwbeccorp.com
SIC: 8051 Convalescent home with continuous nursing care
PA: Beaver Dam Health Care Center
  5220 Tennyson Pkwy # 400
  Plano TX 75024
  972 372-6300

(P-19959)
GOLDEN LIVING LLC
Also Called: Golden Lvngcenter - Santa Rosa
4650 Hoen Ave, Santa Rosa (95405-9407)
PHONE....................707 546-0471

Georgia Otterson, *Exec Dir*
Constance Smith, *Director*
EMP: 100
SALES (corp-wide): 409.2MM **Privately Held**
SIC: 8051 8069 Skilled nursing care facilities; specialty hospitals, except psychiatric
PA: Beaver Dam Health Care Center
  5220 Tennyson Pkwy # 400
  Plano TX 75024
  972 372-6300

(P-19960)
GOLDEN LIVING LLC
Also Called: Golden Livingcenter - Petaluma
217 Lakeville St Apt 3, Petaluma
(94952-3166)
PHONE....................707 763-4109
Monica Choperena, *General Mgr*
EMP: 72
SALES (corp-wide): 409.2MM **Privately Held**
SIC: 8051 Skilled nursing care facilities
PA: Beaver Dam Health Care Center
  5220 Tennyson Pkwy # 400
  Plano TX 75024
  972 372-6300

(P-19961)
GOLDEN LIVING LLC
Also Called: Golden Livingcenter - San Jose
401 Ridge Vista Ave, San Jose
(95127-1501)
PHONE....................408 923-7232
Almaroos Apapira, *Exec Dir*
EMP: 105
SALES (corp-wide): 409.2MM **Privately Held**
SIC: 8051 Skilled nursing care facilities
PA: Beaver Dam Health Care Center
  5220 Tennyson Pkwy # 400
  Plano TX 75024
  972 372-6300

(P-19962)
GOLDEN LIVING LLC
Also Called: Beverly Healthcare
35410 Del Rey, Capistrano Beach
(92624-1814)
PHONE....................949 496-5786
Nora Saulietis, *Administration*
EMP: 60
SALES (corp-wide): 409.2MM **Privately Held**
WEB: www.nwbeccorp.com
SIC: 8051 Extended care facility
PA: Beaver Dam Health Care Center
  5220 Tennyson Pkwy # 400
  Plano TX 75024
  972 372-6300

(P-19963)
GOLDEN LIVING LLC
3510 E Shields Ave, Fresno (93726-6909)
PHONE....................559 222-4807
Kara Pappanduros, *Manager*
EMP: 100
SALES (corp-wide): 409.2MM **Privately Held**
WEB: www.nwbeccorp.com
SIC: 8051 Skilled nursing care facilities
PA: Beaver Dam Health Care Center
  5220 Tennyson Pkwy # 400
  Plano TX 75024
  972 372-6300

(P-19964)
GOLDEN LIVING LLC
Also Called: Golden Livingcenter - Clovis
111 Barstow Ave, Clovis (93612-2225)
PHONE....................559 299-2591
Michelle Tathem, *Manager*
EMP: 93
SALES (corp-wide): 409.2MM **Privately Held**
SIC: 8051 Convalescent home with continuous nursing care
PA: Beaver Dam Health Care Center
  5220 Tennyson Pkwy # 400
  Plano TX 75024
  972 372-6300

(P-19965)
GOLDEN LIVING LLC
Also Called: Beverly Healthcare
3672 N 1st St, Fresno (93726-6810)
PHONE.....................................559 227-5383
Kristine Clark, *Manager*
EMP: 65
SALES (corp-wide): 409.2MM **Privately Held**
WEB: www.nwbeccorp.com
SIC: 8051 Skilled nursing care facilities
PA: Beaver Dam Health Care Center
5220 Tennyson Pkwy # 400
Plano TX 75024
972 372-6300

(P-19966)
GOLDEN LIVING LLC
Also Called: Beverly Healthcare
1900 Coffee Rd, Modesto (95355-2703)
PHONE.....................................209 548-0318
Belinda Guzman, *CEO*
Kim Damale, *Vice Pres*
EMP: 108
SALES (corp-wide): 409.2MM **Privately Held**
WEB: www.nwbeccorp.com
SIC: 8051 Skilled nursing care facilities
PA: Beaver Dam Health Care Center
5220 Tennyson Pkwy # 400
Plano TX 75024
972 372-6300

(P-19967)
GOLDEN LIVING LLC
Also Called: Beverly Healthcare
350 De Soto Dr, Los Gatos (95032-2402)
PHONE.....................................408 356-9151
Julie Okada, *Exec Dir*
EMP: 60
SALES (corp-wide): 409.2MM **Privately Held**
WEB: www.nwbeccorp.com
SIC: 8051 Convalescent home with contin-
uous nursing care
PA: Beaver Dam Health Care Center
5220 Tennyson Pkwy # 400
Plano TX 75024
972 372-6300

(P-19968)
GOLDEN LIVING LLC
Also Called: Golden Livingcenter - Portside
2740 N California St, Stockton
(95204-5529)
PHONE.....................................209 466-3522
Judy Thornhill, *Director*
EMP: 100
SALES (corp-wide): 409.2MM **Privately Held**
SIC: 8051 Convalescent home with contin-
uous nursing care
PA: Beaver Dam Health Care Center
5220 Tennyson Pkwy # 400
Plano TX 75024
972 372-6300

(P-19969)
GOLDEN LIVING LLC
Also Called: Golden Livingcenter
678 2nd St W, Sonoma (95476-6901)
PHONE.....................................707 938-1096
Keith Gold, *Administration*
EMP: 72
SALES (corp-wide): 409.2MM **Privately Held**
SIC: 8051 Skilled nursing care facilities
PA: Beaver Dam Health Care Center
5220 Tennyson Pkwy # 400
Plano TX 75024
972 372-6300

(P-19970)
GOLDEN LIVING LLC
Also Called: Beverly Healthcare
188 Cohasset Ln, Chico (95926-2206)
PHONE.....................................530 343-6084
John Crowley, *Administration*
Barbara Juede Santos, *Director*
EMP: 80
SALES (corp-wide): 409.2MM **Privately Held**
WEB: www.nwbeccorp.com
SIC: 8051 Extended care facility

PA: Beaver Dam Health Care Center
5220 Tennyson Pkwy # 400
Plano TX 75024
972 372-6300

(P-19971)
GOLDEN LIVING LLC
Also Called: Beverly Healthcare
709 N St, Newman (95360-1162)
PHONE.....................................209 862-2862
Darla Larinda, *Exec Dir*
EMP: 69
SALES (corp-wide): 409.2MM **Privately Held**
WEB: www.nwbeccorp.com
SIC: 8051 Convalescent home with contin-
uous nursing care
PA: Beaver Dam Health Care Center
5220 Tennyson Pkwy # 400
Plano TX 75024
972 372-6300

(P-19972)
GOLDEN STATE HABILITATION CONV (PA)
Also Called: Golden State Care Center
1758 Big Dalton Ave, Baldwin Park
(91706-5910)
PHONE.....................................626 962-3274
Eden Salceda, *President*
Claudio Hernandez, *Vice Pres*
Emmanual David, *Admin Sec*
EMP: 400
SALES (est): 8.6MM **Privately Held**
SIC: 8051 8361 8052 Convalescent home
with continuous nursing care; residential
care; intermediate care facilities

(P-19973)
GOLDEN STATE HEALTH CTRS INC (PA)
13347 Ventura Blvd, Sherman Oaks
(91423-3979)
PHONE.....................................818 385-3200
Martin J Weiss, *CEO*
Ronald Mayer, *CFO*
David B Weiss, *Chairman*
Bernard Friedman, *Exec Dir*
Howard Weiss, *Admin Sec*
EMP: 121
SQ FT: 2,000
SALES: 62.1MM **Privately Held**
WEB: www.goldenstatehealth.com
SIC: 8051 Skilled nursing care facilities

(P-19974)
GOLDEN STATE WEST VALLEY
7057 Shoup Ave, Canoga Park
(91307-2335)
PHONE.....................................818 348-8422
Susan Henry, *President*
Rose Kasirer, *Admin Sec*
EMP: 110 EST: 1968
SQ FT: 26,937
SALES (est): 3.7MM
SALES (corp-wide): 62.1MM **Privately Held**
WEB: www.goldenstatehealth.com
SIC: 8051 Skilled nursing care facilities
PA: Golden State Health Centers, Inc.
13347 Ventura Blvd
Sherman Oaks CA 91423
818 385-3200

(P-19975)
GOOD SHEPHERD HEALTH CARE CE
1131 Arizona Ave, Santa Monica
(90401-2009)
PHONE.....................................310 451-4809
Jeong Lee, *CEO*
EMP: 55
SQ FT: 8,136
SALES (est): 2.2MM **Privately Held**
SIC: 8051 Convalescent home with contin-
uous nursing care

(P-19976)
GOODMAN GROUP INC
Also Called: Alamitos Convalescent Hospital
3902 Katella Ave, Los Alamitos
(90720-3304)
PHONE.....................................562 596-5561
Pradeep Muley, *Exec Dir*
EMP: 65

SALES (corp-wide): 31.8MM **Privately Held**
WEB: www.thepalmsoflargo.com
SIC: 8051 Skilled nursing care facilities
PA: The Goodman Group Inc
1107 Hazeltine Blvd # 200
Chaska MN 55318
952 361-8000

(P-19977)
GR8 CARE INC
14518 Los Angeles St, Baldwin Park
(91706-2636)
PHONE.....................................626 337-7229
Edwin Raquel, *CEO*
Napoleon Garcia, *Principal*
EMP: 73
SQ FT: 9,710
SALES (est): 1.6MM **Privately Held**
SIC: 8051 Skilled nursing care facilities

(P-19978)
GRANADA HEALTHCRE & REHAB CNTR
2885 Harris St, Eureka (95503-4808)
PHONE.....................................707 443-1627
Maria Coda,
Ted Chigaros,
EMP: 99
SALES: 950K **Privately Held**
SIC: 8051 Skilled nursing care facilities

(P-19979)
GRANADA HLLS CONVALESCENT HOSP
Also Called: Granada Hills Care Center
16123 Chatsworth St, Granada Hills
(91344-7045)
PHONE.....................................818 891-1745
Seid Sadat, *President*
Abraham Birnbaum, *President*
Kim Marconet, *Vice Pres*
EMP: 64 EST: 1963
SQ FT: 96,680
SALES (est): 2MM **Privately Held**
SIC: 8051 Convalescent home with contin-
uous nursing care

(P-19980)
GRANCARE LLC
Also Called: Vale Healthcare Center
13484 San Pablo Ave, San Pablo
(94806-3904)
PHONE.....................................510 232-5945
Tim Neal, *Principal*
Remy Rhodes, *President*
Kenneth Tabler, *President*
EMP: 277
SALES (corp-wide): 1B **Privately Held**
SIC: 8051 Skilled nursing care facilities
HQ: Grancare Llc
1 Ravinia Dr Ste 1400
Atlanta GA 30346
770 393-0199

(P-19981)
GRAND PARK CONVALESCENT HOSP
2312 W 8th St, Los Angeles (90057-3955)
PHONE.....................................213 382-7315
Barry Kohn, *President*
Toby Kohn, *Vice Pres*
EMP: 135 EST: 1976
SQ FT: 60,000
SALES (est): 6.3MM **Privately Held**
SIC: 8051 8361 Convalescent home with
continuous nursing care; rehabilitation
center, residential; health care incidental

(P-19982)
GRAND TERRACE CARE CENTER
Also Called: Sunbridge Care Ctr - Grnd Ter
12000 Mount Vernon Ave, Grand Terrace
(92313-5174)
PHONE.....................................909 825-5221
Darlene Simonias, *Branch Mgr*
EMP: 53
SALES (corp-wide): 9.2MM **Privately Held**
SIC: 8051 Convalescent home with contin-
uous nursing care

PA: Grand Terrace Care Center
12000 Mount Vernon Ave
Grand Terrace CA 92313
909 825-5221

(P-19983)
GRAND VALLEY HEALTH CARE CTR
13524 Sherman Way, Van Nuys
(91405-2830)
PHONE.....................................818 786-3470
Janet Mandelbaum, *Mng Member*
Elizabeth Solis, *Social Dir*
Joanna Walker, *Office Mgr*
Liza Mariano, *Food Svc Dir*
Brenda Mandelbaum, *Mng Member*
EMP: 108
SALES (est): 3.9MM **Privately Held**
SIC: 8051 Skilled nursing care facilities

(P-19984)
GRANITE HILLS HEALTHCARE
1340 E Madison Ave, El Cajon
(92021-8501)
PHONE.....................................619 447-1020
Sharrod Brooks,
EMP: 99 EST: 2012
SALES: 9.7MM **Privately Held**
SIC: 8051 Skilled nursing care facilities

(P-19985)
GRIFFITH PK RHBLTATION CTR LLC
Also Called: Griffith Park Healthcare Ctr
201 Allen Ave, Glendale (91201-2803)
PHONE.....................................818 845-8507
Crystal Solorzano,
EMP: 75 EST: 2015
SALES: 11.3MM **Privately Held**
SIC: 8051 Skilled nursing care facilities

(P-19986)
GROSS CONVALESCENT HOSPITAL
321 W Turner Rd, Lodi (95240-0517)
PHONE.....................................209 334-3760
Paul Gross, *Vice Pres*
Elsie Gross, *Corp Secy*
Oscar Gross, *Principal*
EMP: 73
SQ FT: 10,000
SALES (est): 2.8MM **Privately Held**
SIC: 8051 Convalescent home with contin-
uous nursing care

(P-19987)
GUARDIANS OF THE LOS ANGELES
10780 Santa Monica Blvd # 225, Los Ange-
les (90025-4749)
PHONE.....................................310 479-2468
Shannon Slater, *Manager*
EMP: 67
SALES: 595.8K **Privately Held**
SIC: 8051 Skilled nursing care facilities

(P-19988)
GVA ENTERPRISES INC
Also Called: Angels Nursing Center
415 S Union Ave, Los Angeles
(90017-1007)
PHONE.....................................213 484-0784
Marco Cortes, *Manager*
EMP: 57
SALES (corp-wide): 5.3MM **Privately Held**
SIC: 8051 Skilled nursing care facilities
PA: Gva Enterprises Inc
316 S Westlake Ave
Los Angeles CA 90057
213 484-0510

(P-19989)
H C C S INC
Also Called: Sherwood Healthcare Center
4700 Elvas Ave, Sacramento (95819-2250)
PHONE.....................................916 454-5752
David Hilburn, *Director*
John Lund, *Director*
EMP: 70
SALES (est): 2.7MM **Privately Held**
WEB: www.sherwoods.com
SIC: 8051 Convalescent home with contin-
uous nursing care

(P-19990)
HACIENDA REHABILITATION & HEAL (PA)
1440 S State College Blvd 2a, Anaheim (92806-5724)
PHONE.................................714 778-0221
Rex Moore, *President*
Robert L Stotts, *Ch of Bd*
Donna Stotts, *Treasurer*
Michael H Camp, *Principal*
Kenny Teranishi, *Site Mgr*
EMP: 126
SALES (est): 5MM **Privately Held**
SIC: 8051 Skilled nursing care facilities

(P-19991)
HACIENDA REHABILITATION & HEAL
Also Called: Hacienda Health Care
361 E Grangeville Blvd, Hanford (93230-3054)
PHONE.................................559 582-9221
Rex Moore, *Branch Mgr*
EMP: 120
SALES (est): 3.6MM
SALES (corp-wide): 5MM **Privately Held**
SIC: 8051 8069 Convalescent home with continuous nursing care; specialty hospitals, except psychiatric
PA: Hacienda Rehabilitation & Health Care Center, Inc
1440 S State College Blvd 2a
Anaheim CA 92806
714 778-0221

(P-19992)
HANCOCK PK RHBLITATION CTR LLC
505 N La Brea Ave, Los Angeles (90036-2015)
PHONE.................................323 937-4860
EMP: 135
SALES (est): 3.9MM **Privately Held**
SIC: 8051 Skilled nursing care facilities

(P-19993)
HARBOR GLEN CARE CENTER
1033 E Arrow Hwy, Glendora (91740-6110)
PHONE.................................626 963-7531
Kevin Thomas, *Owner*
EMP: 100 EST: 2000
SALES (est): 2.9MM
SALES (corp-wide): 2B **Publicly Held**
WEB: www.theensigngroup.com
SIC: 8051 Convalescent home with continuous nursing care
PA: The Ensign Group Inc
27101 Puerta Real Ste 450
Mission Viejo CA 92691
949 487-9500

(P-19994)
HAWTHORNE HEALTHCARE
11630 Grevillea Ave, Hawthorne (90250-2231)
PHONE.................................310 679-9732
Sharrod Brooks, *Managing Prtnr*
EMP: 99 EST: 2011
SALES (est): 365K **Privately Held**
SIC: 8051 Skilled nursing care facilities

(P-19995)
HB HEALTHCARE ASSOCIATES LLC
Also Called: Sea Cliff Healthcare Center
18811 Florida St, Huntington Beach (92648-1920)
PHONE.................................714 887-0144
Mike Williams,
Kirk Lindahl, *Administration*
Jose Lemus, *QC Dir*
EMP: 90
SALES: 16.2MM **Privately Held**
SIC: 8051 Convalescent home with continuous nursing care

(P-19996)
HCR MANORCARE INC
Also Called: In Home Health
1575 Bayshore Hwy Ste 200, Burlingame (94010-1616)
PHONE.................................419 252-5743
Thomas R Kile, *Treasurer*
EMP: 55

SALES (corp-wide): 8.2B **Privately Held**
SIC: 8051 Skilled nursing care facilities
HQ: Hcr Manorcare, Inc.
333 N Summit St
Toledo OH 43604
419 252-5743

(P-19997)
HCR MANORCARE MED SVCS FLA LLC
Also Called: Manorcare Health Services
1975 Tice Valley Blvd, Walnut Creek (94595-2201)
PHONE.................................925 274-1325
Roger Hogan, *Branch Mgr*
Gilbert Castro, *Records Dir*
Jonathan Frank, *Director*
EMP: 125
SQ FT: 53,335
SALES (corp-wide): 8.2B **Privately Held**
WEB: www.manorcare.com
SIC: 8051 Convalescent home with continuous nursing care
HQ: Hcr Manorcare Medical Services Of Florida, Llc
333 N Summit St Ste 100
Toledo OH 43604
419 252-5500

(P-19998)
HCR MANORCARE MED SVCS FLA LLC
Also Called: Manor Care
11680 Warner Ave, Fountain Valley (92708-2513)
PHONE.................................714 241-9800
Mark Shaffer, *Administration*
EMP: 195
SALES (corp-wide): 8.2B **Privately Held**
WEB: www.manorcare.com
SIC: 8051 Convalescent home with continuous nursing care
HQ: Hcr Manorcare Medical Services Of Florida, Llc
333 N Summit St Ste 100
Toledo OH 43604
419 252-5500

(P-19999)
HCR MANORCARE MED SVCS FLA LLC
Also Called: Manor Care
7807 Uplands Way, Citrus Heights (95610-7500)
PHONE.................................916 967-2929
Terri Ballesteros, *Principal*
EMP: 180
SALES (corp-wide): 8.2B **Privately Held**
WEB: www.manorcare.com
SIC: 8051 Convalescent home with continuous nursing care
HQ: Hcr Manorcare Medical Services Of Florida, Llc
333 N Summit St Ste 100
Toledo OH 43604
419 252-5500

(P-20000)
HCR MANORCARE MED SVCS FLA LLC
Also Called: Manorcare Health Svcs Hemet
1717 W Stetson Ave, Hemet (92545-6882)
PHONE.................................951 925-9171
Ron Ellenich, *Branch Mgr*
EMP: 180
SALES (corp-wide): 8.2B **Privately Held**
WEB: www.manorcare.com
SIC: 8051 Convalescent home with continuous nursing care
HQ: Hcr Manorcare Medical Services Of Florida, Llc
333 N Summit St Ste 100
Toledo OH 43604
419 252-5500

(P-20001)
HCR MANORCARE MED SVCS FLA LLC
Also Called: Manor Care
1150 Tilton Dr, Sunnyvale (94087-2440)
PHONE.................................408 735-7200
Arthur Spencer, *Branch Mgr*
EMP: 100

SALES (corp-wide): 8.2B **Privately Held**
WEB: www.manorcare.com
SIC: 8051 Convalescent home with continuous nursing care
HQ: Hcr Manorcare Medical Services Of Florida, Llc
333 N Summit St Ste 100
Toledo OH 43604
419 252-5500

(P-20002)
HCR MANORCARE MED SVCS FLA LLC
Also Called: Manorcare Health Svcs Rossmoor
1226 Rossmoor Pkwy, Walnut Creek (94595-2538)
PHONE.................................925 975-5000
John Gallick, *Manager*
Richard Kolecki, *Vice Pres*
EMP: 105
SQ FT: 69,382
SALES (corp-wide): 8.2B **Privately Held**
WEB: www.manorcare.com
SIC: 8051 Convalescent home with continuous nursing care
HQ: Hcr Manorcare Medical Services Of Florida, Llc
333 N Summit St Ste 100
Toledo OH 43604
419 252-5500

(P-20003)
HCR MANORCARE MED SVCS FLA LLC
Also Called: Manorcare Hlth Svcs Encinitas
944 Regal Rd, Encinitas (92024-4634)
PHONE.................................760 944-0331
James Elton, *Manager*
EMP: 100
SQ FT: 38,890
SALES (corp-wide): 8.2B **Privately Held**
SIC: 8051 Convalescent home with continuous nursing care
HQ: Hcr Manorcare Medical Services Of Florida, Llc
333 N Summit St Ste 100
Toledo OH 43604
419 252-5500

(P-20004)
HEALTH & REHABILITATION CENTER
Also Called: Mariner
2065 Los Gatos Almaden Rd, San Jose (95124-5417)
PHONE.................................408 377-9275
James Brende, *Administration*
EMP: 50
SALES (est): 528.3K **Privately Held**
SIC: 8051 Skilled nursing care facilities

(P-20005)
HEALTH CARE INVESTMENTS INC
Also Called: Rosecrans Care Center
1140 W Rosecrans Ave, Gardena (90247-2664)
PHONE.................................310 323-3194
Pompeyo Rosales, *President*
Gonzalo Delrosario, *Admin Sec*
EMP: 106
SALES: 11.1MM **Privately Held**
SIC: 8051 Skilled nursing care facilities

(P-20006)
HEALTHCARE CTR OF DOWNEY LLC
Also Called: Lakewood Healthcare Center
12023 Lakewood Blvd, Downey (90242-2635)
PHONE.................................562 869-0978
Vince Hambright, *CEO*
Ken Lehmann,
EMP: 250
SQ FT: 1,076,391
SALES: 21.6MM **Privately Held**
SIC: 8051 Mental retardation hospital

(P-20007)
HEALTHCARE FULLERTON & WELL
Also Called: EVERGREEN FULLERTON HEALTHCARE
2222 N Harbor Blvd, Fullerton (92835-2605)
PHONE.................................714 992-5701
Shlomo Rechnitz,
Sharrod Brooks, *Senior VP*
Wesley Jones, *Administration*
EMP: 125
SALES: 22.7MM **Privately Held**
SIC: 8051 Skilled nursing care facilities

(P-20008)
HEALTHCARE MGT SYSTEMS INC
Also Called: Bradley Grdns Convalescent Ctr
980 W 7th St, San Jacinto (92582-3814)
PHONE.................................951 654-9347
Dyan Lewis, *Manager*
EMP: 55
SALES (corp-wide): 3.5MM **Privately Held**
SIC: 8051 Convalescent home with continuous nursing care
PA: Healthcare Management Systems, Inc.
900 Lane Ave Ste 190
Chula Vista CA 91914

(P-20009)
HEBREW HOME FOR AGED DISABLED
Also Called: JEWISH HOME FOR THE AGED
302 Silver Ave, San Francisco (94112-1510)
PHONE.................................415 334-2500
Daniel Ruth, *President*
Kevin T Potter, *CFO*
Ashley Teal, *Administration*
Helen Colombo, *Research*
Ken Diep, *Engineer*
EMP: 600 EST: 1889
SALES: 81MM **Privately Held**
WEB: www.jhsf.org
SIC: 8051 Skilled nursing care facilities

(P-20010)
HELIOS HEALTHCARE LLC
Also Called: El Camino Care Center
2540 Carmichael Way, Carmichael (95608-5314)
PHONE.................................916 482-0465
Evelyn McGraff, *Administration*
Roxanne L Henry, *Social Dir*
David Gram, *Administration*
Suzanne Brazier, *Nursing Dir*
Danette Perkins, *Director*
EMP: 140
SALES (corp-wide): 24.1MM **Privately Held**
SIC: 8051 Skilled nursing care facilities
PA: Helios Healthcare, Llc
520 Capitol Mall Ste 800
Sacramento CA 95814
916 471-2241

(P-20011)
HELIOS HEALTHCARE LLC
Also Called: Sunridge Care & Rehabilitation
350 Iris Dr, Salinas (93906-3514)
PHONE.................................831 449-1515
Rachael Bruton, *Administration*
EMP: 150
SALES (corp-wide): 24.1MM **Privately Held**
SIC: 8051 Skilled nursing care facilities
PA: Helios Healthcare, Llc
520 Capitol Mall Ste 800
Sacramento CA 95814
916 471-2241

(P-20012)
HELIOS HEALTHCARE LLC
Also Called: Chico Creek Care Rhabilitation
587 Rio Lindo Ave, Chico (95926-1816)
PHONE.................................530 345-1306
Carl Lewis, *Manager*
EMP: 170
SQ FT: 51,457
SALES (corp-wide): 24.1MM **Privately Held**
SIC: 8051 Skilled nursing care facilities

PA: Helios Healthcare, Llc
520 Capitol Mall Ste 800
Sacramento CA 95814
916 471-2241

(P-20013)
HELPING HANDS SANCTUARY OF IDA
Also Called: Helping Hands of Westminster
240 Hospital Cir, Westminster
(92683-3953)
PHONE...................714 892-6686
Jon Peralez, *Administration*
Cristina Saril, *Director*
EMP: 100
SQ FT: 24,214
SALES (est): 2.6MM **Privately Held**
SIC: 8051 Skilled nursing care facilities

(P-20014)
HERITAGE HEALTH CARE INC
Also Called: Heritage Gardens Hlth Care Ctr
25271 Barton Rd, Loma Linda
(92354-3013)
PHONE...................909 796-0216
Stephen Flood, *CEO*
Gregory S Goings, *CEO*
Jim Kilian, *CFO*
Cathy Aceres, *Director*
EMP: 150
SALES: 11.6MM **Privately Held**
SIC: 8051 8059 Skilled nursing care facilities; rest home, with health care

(P-20015)
HERITAGE MANOR INC
610 N Garfield Ave, Monterey Park
(91754-1103)
PHONE...................626 573-3141
Janie Campos, *Administration*
Cathriene Mc Dowell, *Financial Exec*
EMP: 80
SALES: 9.3MM **Privately Held**
SIC: 8051 Skilled nursing care facilities

(P-20016)
HERMAN SANITARIUM
Also Called: Herman Health Care Center
2295 Plummer Ave, San Jose
(95125-4767)
PHONE...................408 269-0701
Mandy S Sollis, *President*
Steve Marcus, *Administration*
Mandy Sollis, *Mktg Dir*
Mike Bottarini, *Food Svc Dir*
EMP: 104
SQ FT: 4,500
SALES (est): 3.3MM **Privately Held**
SIC: 8051 Convalescent home with continuous nursing care

(P-20017)
HIGHLAND PARK SKILLED NURSING
5125 Monte Vista St, Los Angeles
(90042-3931)
PHONE...................323 254-6125
Shlomo Rechnitz,
EMP: 72 EST: 2008
SALES: 7MM **Privately Held**
SIC: 8051 Convalescent home with continuous nursing care

(P-20018)
HILLVIEW CONVALESCENT HOSPITAL
530 W Dunne Ave, Morgan Hill
(95037-4823)
PHONE...................408 779-3633
James Ross, *Owner*
Richard Ross, *Co-Owner*
Steve Ross, *Administration*
EMP: 50
SQ FT: 10,000
SALES: 3.9MM **Privately Held**
SIC: 8051 Convalescent home with continuous nursing care

(P-20019)
HONEY FLOWER HOLDINGS LLC
Also Called: ARLINGTON GARDENS CARE CENTER
3688 Nye Ave, Riverside (92505-1818)
PHONE...................951 351-2800

Mark Ballif, *Mng Member*
Paul Hubbard, *Mng Member*
Gary Angeles, *Director*
Brett Hill, *Director*
Jose Rodriguez, *Director*
EMP: 170
SALES: 15.5MM **Privately Held**
SIC: 8051 Convalescent home with continuous nursing care

(P-20020)
HORIZON WEST INC
Also Called: Walnut Whtney Convalecent Hosp
3529 Walnut Ave, Carmichael
(95608-3049)
PHONE...................916 488-8601
Kathy Spake, *Branch Mgr*
EMP: 130
SALES (corp-wide): 103.9MM **Privately Held**
SIC: 8051 Convalescent home with continuous nursing care
PA: Horizon West, Inc.
4020 Sierra College Blvd
Rocklin CA 95677
916 624-6230

(P-20021)
HORIZON WEST INC
Also Called: Heritage Conalescent Hospital
5255 Hemlock St, Sacramento
(95841-3017)
PHONE...................916 331-4590
Randy Balecha, *Manager*
EMP: 100
SALES (corp-wide): 103.9MM **Privately Held**
SIC: 8051 8361 8059 Skilled nursing care facilities; residential care; convalescent home
PA: Horizon West, Inc.
4020 Sierra College Blvd
Rocklin CA 95677
916 624-6230

(P-20022)
HORIZON WEST HEALTHCARE INC (HQ)
4020 Sierra College Blvd # 190, Rocklin
(95677-3906)
PHONE...................916 624-6230
Martine D Harmon, *CEO*
Dennis Roccaforte, *Corp Secy*
Bernice Schrabeck, *Vice Pres*
EMP: 59
SQ FT: 6,000
SALES (est): 52.6MM
SALES (corp-wide): 103.9MM **Privately Held**
WEB: www.villadelrey.com
SIC: 8051 Convalescent home with continuous nursing care
PA: Horizon West, Inc.
4020 Sierra College Blvd
Rocklin CA 95677
916 624-6230

(P-20023)
HORIZON WEST HEALTHCARE INC
Also Called: Valley View Skilled Nursing
1162 S Dora St, Ukiah (95482-6340)
PHONE...................707 462-1436
Paul Medlin, *Administration*
EMP: 60
SALES (corp-wide): 103.9MM **Privately Held**
WEB: www.villadelrey.com
SIC: 8051 Convalescent home with continuous nursing care
HQ: Horizon West Healthcare, Inc.
4020 Sierra College Blvd # 190
Rocklin CA 95677
916 624-6230

(P-20024)
HOSPICE OF SAN JOAQUIN
3888 Pacific Ave, Stockton (95204-1953)
PHONE...................209 957-3888
Stephen L Guasco, *CEO*
Kerrie Biddle, *CFO*
Stephen Guasco, *Exec Dir*
Becky Burnett, *Nursing Dir*
Steve Parsons, *Director*
EMP: 90

SQ FT: 5,000
SALES: 15.1MM **Privately Held**
WEB: www.hospicesj.org
SIC: 8051 8641 Skilled nursing care facilities; social associations

(P-20025)
HOVLID SKILLED NURSING
240 Spruce St, Gridley (95948-2216)
PHONE...................530 846-9065
John Turner, *Director*
EMP: 50
SALES (est): 440.4K **Privately Held**
SIC: 8051 Convalescent home with continuous nursing care

(P-20026)
HUNTINGTON BCH CNVLESCENT HOSP
Also Called: Sea Cliff Health Care
18811 Florida St, Huntington Beach
(92648-1920)
PHONE...................714 847-3515
Michael Williams, *Administration*
Evelyn Aranton, *Nursing Dir*
EMP: 300
SALES (est): 8.3MM **Privately Held**
SIC: 8051 Convalescent home with continuous nursing care

(P-20027)
HYDE PARK CONVALESCENT HOSP
6520 West Blvd, Los Angeles
(90043-4393)
PHONE...................323 753-1354
Jeff Mendell, *President*
Elaine Wiesel, *Admin Sec*
EMP: 50
SQ FT: 15,258
SALES: 7.2MM **Privately Held**
SIC: 8051 Skilled nursing care facilities

(P-20028)
IMAGINATIVE HORIZONS INC
Also Called: Hillcrest Manor Sanitarium
1889 National City Blvd, National City
(91950-5517)
PHONE...................619 477-1176
Gary Byrnes, *President*
Rosella Byrnes, *Treasurer*
Dan Byrnes, *Info Tech Dir*
EMP: 84
SQ FT: 30,000
SALES (est): 6.1MM **Privately Held**
WEB: www.specialized-care.com
SIC: 8051 Skilled nursing care facilities

(P-20029)
INDIO HLTHCARE WLLNESS CTR LLC
Also Called: DESERT SPRINGS HEALTHCARE & WE
82262 Valencia Ave, Indio (92201-3120)
PHONE...................760 347-6000
Sharrod Brooks,
EMP: 99
SALES: 6.2MM **Privately Held**
SIC: 8051 Skilled nursing care facilities

(P-20030)
INFINITY CARE OF EAST LA
101 S Fickett St, Los Angeles
(90033-4017)
PHONE...................323 261-8108
Dr Bina Kambar, *President*
Douglas Cooper, *CFO*
Boyd B Fowler, *Vice Pres*
Rani Magboo, *Executive*
Bruce Willy, *Program Mgr*
EMP: 98
SALES: 8.4MM **Privately Held**
SIC: 8051 Skilled nursing care facilities

(P-20031)
INLAND CHRISTIAN HOME INC
1950 S Mountain Ave Ofc, Ontario
(91762-6709)
PHONE...................909 395-9322
David Stienstra, *President*
Mary Wolff, *Administration*
Joe Whitford, *Opers Staff*
Jennifer Dreiling, *Marketing Staff*
Lisa Armstrong, *Director*
EMP: 114 EST: 1973

SQ FT: 100,000
SALES: 11MM **Privately Held**
WEB: www.ichome.org
SIC: 8051 8052 6513 8361 Skilled nursing care facilities; intermediate care facilities; retirement hotel operation; residential care

(P-20032)
INTEGRTED CARE COMMUNITIES INC
Also Called: Inegrated Care Communities
11751 Davis St, Moreno Valley
(92557-6316)
PHONE...................951 243-3837
Carl Rowe, *President*
Sarah Saucedo, *Finance Mgr*
EMP: 50
SALES (est): 2.7MM **Privately Held**
WEB: www.icare.bz
SIC: 8051 Skilled nursing care facilities

(P-20033)
INTERCOMMUNITY CARE CENTERS
2626 Grand Ave, Long Beach
(90815-1707)
PHONE...................562 427-8915
Russel Boydston, *Branch Mgr*
Rosemary Valentin, *Office Mgr*
Monique Robinette, *Human Res Dir*
Armida Faessler, *Director*
Tina Ray, *Director*
EMP: 120
SQ FT: 32,159
SALES (corp-wide): 9.5MM **Privately Held**
WEB: www.iccare.org
SIC: 8051 Mental retardation hospital
PA: Intercommunity Care Centers Inc
2660 Grand Ave
Long Beach CA
562 426-1368

(P-20034)
J P H CONSULTING INC (PA)
1101 Crenshaw Blvd, Los Angeles
(90019-3112)
PHONE...................323 934-5660
Jeoung H Lee, *President*
Greda Bernabe, *CFO*
Kyle Watanabe, *Director*
EMP: 50
SALES (est): 22.8MM **Privately Held**
SIC: 8051 Skilled nursing care facilities

(P-20035)
J P H CONSULTING INC
4515 Huntington Dr S, Los Angeles
(90032-1940)
PHONE...................323 934-5660
EMP: 206
SALES (corp-wide): 22.8MM **Privately Held**
SIC: 8051 Skilled nursing care facilities
PA: J P H Consulting, Inc.
1101 Crenshaw Blvd
Los Angeles CA 90019
323 934-5660

(P-20036)
JEFFREY PINE HOLDINGS LLC
Also Called: VILLA LAS PALMAS HEALTH-CARE CE
622 S Anza St, El Cajon (92020-6602)
PHONE...................619 442-0544
Myrna De Guzman,
Melinda Astudillo, *Records Dir*
Adriana Bernal, *Social Dir*
Arlene Diche, *Office Mgr*
Lizbeth Hernandez, *Hlthcr Dir*
EMP: 99
SALES: 16.3MM **Privately Held**
SIC: 8051 Convalescent home with continuous nursing care

(P-20037)
JEWISH HOME FOR THE AGING OF O
Also Called: Heritage Pointe
27356 Bellogente, Mission Viejo
(92691-6341)
PHONE...................949 364-0010
David Zarnow, *Vice Pres*
Brad Plose, *President*

Rena Loveless, *Administration*
Patti Gardner, *Director*
EMP: 120
SQ FT: 88,928
SALES: 10.8MM **Privately Held**
SIC: 8051 Skilled nursing care facilities

(P-20038)
JOHNRE CARE LLC
461 E Johnston Ave, Hemet (92543-7113)
PHONE..................951 658-6374
Johnny Sicat, *Mng Member*
EMP: 60
SALES (est): 1.9MM **Privately Held**
SIC: 8051 Skilled nursing care facilities

(P-20039)
KARMA INC
Also Called: Manteca Care Rhabilitation Ctr
410 Eastwood Ave, Manteca (95336-3167)
PHONE..................209 239-1222
Antony Thekkek, *President*
Prema Thekkek, *Vice Pres*
EMP: 165
SQ FT: 29,700
SALES (est): 5.9MM
SALES (corp-wide): 12.1MM **Privately Held**
WEB: www.paksn.com
SIC: 8051 Convalescent home with continuous nursing care
PA: Paksn, Inc.
540 W Monte Vista Ave
Vacaville CA 95688
707 449-3400

(P-20040)
KATELLA PROPERTIES
Also Called: Alamitos W Convalescent Hosp
3902 Katella Ave, Los Alamitos (90720-3304)
PHONE..................562 596-5561
Marilyn Gelgincolin, *Director*
Luis Pages, *Exec Dir*
Dora Hernandez, *Technology*
Arnold Venlensza, *Chf Purch Ofc*
Christina Marquez, *Marketing Staff*
EMP: 170
SALES (est): 4.7MM
SALES (corp-wide): 4MM **Privately Held**
WEB: www.katellamanor.com
SIC: 8051 Convalescent home with continuous nursing care
PA: Katella Properties
3952 Katella Ave
Los Alamitos CA 90720
562 596-2773

(P-20041)
KIMBERLY CARE CENTER INC
Also Called: SANTA MARIA CARE CENTER
820 W Cook St, Santa Maria (93458-5414)
PHONE..................805 925-8877
Walter Matjasic, *President*
EMP: 75
SQ FT: 20,000
SALES: 3.7MM **Privately Held**
SIC: 8051 Skilled nursing care facilities

(P-20042)
KINDRED HEALTHCARE OPER INC
Also Called: Kindred Nrsing Hlthcre- Bybrry
1800 Adobe St, Concord (94520-2313)
PHONE..................925 692-5886
J Seawell, *Exec Dir*
EMP: 106
SQ FT: 25,780
SALES (corp-wide): 6B **Privately Held**
WEB: www.salemhaven.com
SIC: 8051 Skilled nursing care facilities
HQ: Kindred Healthcare Operating, Llc
680 S 4th St
Louisville KY 40202
502 596-7300

(P-20043)
KINDRED HEALTHCARE OPER INC
4700 Elvas Ave, Sacramento (95819-2250)
PHONE..................916 454-5752
David Hilburn, *Director*
EMP: 75
SALES (corp-wide): 6B **Privately Held**
WEB: www.salemhaven.com
SIC: 8051 Skilled nursing care facilities

HQ: Kindred Healthcare Operating, Llc
680 S 4th St
Louisville KY 40202
502 596-7300

(P-20044)
KINDRED HEALTHCARE OPER INC
Also Called: Kindred Hospital - Brea
875 N Brea Blvd, Brea (92821-2606)
PHONE..................714 529-6842
Donna Hoover, *Administration*
Danielle Carter, *Radiology Dir*
Steve Aird, *Director*
EMP: 79
SALES (corp-wide): 6B **Privately Held**
WEB: www.salemhaven.com
SIC: 8051 Extended care facility
HQ: Kindred Healthcare Operating, Llc
680 S 4th St
Louisville KY 40202
502 596-7300

(P-20045)
KINDRED HEALTHCARE OPER INC
7534 Palm Ave, Highland (92346-3736)
PHONE..................909 862-0611
Lance Squire, *Administration*
EMP: 161
SALES (corp-wide): 6B **Privately Held**
WEB: www.salemhaven.com
SIC: 8051 8069 Skilled nursing care facilities; specialty hospitals, except psychiatric
HQ: Kindred Healthcare Operating, Llc
680 S 4th St
Louisville KY 40202
502 596-7300

(P-20046)
KINDRED HEALTHCARE OPER INC
Also Called: Kindred Nursng & Healthcare
76 Fenton St, Livermore (94550-4144)
PHONE..................925 443-1800
Canbice Hale, *Branch Mgr*
EMP: 90
SALES (corp-wide): 6B **Privately Held**
WEB: www.salemhaven.com
SIC: 8051 Skilled nursing care facilities
HQ: Kindred Healthcare Operating, Llc
680 S 4th St
Louisville KY 40202
502 596-7300

(P-20047)
KINDRED HEALTHCARE OPER LLC
Also Called: Saylor Lane Healthcare Center
3500 Folsom Blvd, Sacramento (95816-6615)
PHONE..................916 457-6521
David Hilburn, *Manager*
EMP: 127
SALES (corp-wide): 6B **Privately Held**
WEB: www.salemhaven.com
SIC: 8051 Skilled nursing care facilities
HQ: Kindred Healthcare Operating, Llc
680 S 4th St
Louisville KY 40202
502 596-7300

(P-20048)
KINDRED HEALTHCARE OPER LLC
1586 W San Marcos Blvd, San Marcos (92078-4019)
PHONE..................760 471-2986
Daicel Gasperian, *Manager*
EMP: 130
SALES (corp-wide): 6B **Privately Held**
WEB: www.salemhaven.com
SIC: 8051 Convalescent home with continuous nursing care
HQ: Kindred Healthcare Operating, Llc
680 S 4th St
Louisville KY 40202
502 596-7300

(P-20049)
KINDRED HEALTHCARE OPER LLC
Also Called: Pacific Coast Care Center
720 E Romie Ln, Salinas (93901-4208)
PHONE..................831 424-8072
EMP: 165
SALES (corp-wide): 6B **Privately Held**
WEB: www.salemhaven.com
SIC: 8051 Convalescent home with continuous nursing care
HQ: Kindred Healthcare Operating, Llc
680 S 4th St
Louisville KY 40202
502 596-7300

(P-20050)
KINDRED HEALTHCARE OPER LLC
Also Called: Kindred Nursing
2121 Pine St, San Francisco (94115-2829)
PHONE..................415 922-5085
Melissa Jones, *Director*
EMP: 100
SALES (corp-wide): 6B **Privately Held**
WEB: www.salemhaven.com
SIC: 8051 Convalescent home with continuous nursing care
HQ: Kindred Healthcare Operating, Llc
680 S 4th St
Louisville KY 40202
502 596-7300

(P-20051)
KINDRED HEALTHCARE OPER LLC
1575 7th Ave, San Francisco (94122-3704)
PHONE..................415 566-1200
Melissa Jones, *Administration*
Jennifer Knight, *Director*
EMP: 218
SALES (corp-wide): 6B **Privately Held**
SIC: 8051 Skilled nursing care facilities
HQ: Kindred Healthcare Operating, Llc
680 S 4th St
Louisville KY 40202
502 596-7300

(P-20052)
KINDRED HEALTHCARE OPERATING
2211 Mount Vernon Ave, Bakersfield (93306-3309)
PHONE..................661 872-2121
Lori Hay, *Manager*
EMP: 200
SALES (corp-wide): 6B **Privately Held**
WEB: www.salemhaven.com
SIC: 8051 Skilled nursing care facilities
HQ: Kindred Healthcare Operating, Llc
680 S 4th St
Louisville KY 40202
502 596-7300

(P-20053)
KINDRED HEALTHCARE OPERATING
223 Fargo Way, Folsom (95630-2961)
PHONE..................916 351-9151
Meridith Taylor, *Administration*
EMP: 150
SALES (corp-wide): 6B **Privately Held**
WEB: www.salemhaven.com
SIC: 8051 Skilled nursing care facilities
HQ: Kindred Healthcare Operating, Llc
680 S 4th St
Louisville KY 40202
502 596-7300

(P-20054)
KINDRED NURSING CENTERS W LLC
Also Called: Kindred Transitional Care
516 Willow St, Alameda (94501-6132)
PHONE..................510 521-5600
Richard Espinosa, *Administration*
Christine Christopher, *Executive*
Tom Wood, *Finance Mgr*
Norbu Sangpo, *Chf Purch Ofc*
Frank Rynig, *Director*
EMP: 89
SALES (corp-wide): 6B **Privately Held**
WEB: www.salemhaven.com
SIC: 8051 Skilled nursing care facilities

HQ: Kindred Nursing Centers West Llc
3128 Boxelder Dr
Cheyenne WY 82001
307 634-7901

(P-20055)
KINDRED NURSING CENTERS W LLC
Also Called: Kindred Transitional Care
2120 Benton Dr, Redding (96003-2151)
PHONE..................530 243-6317
Michael Sowerby, *Manager*
Gary W Crawford, *Med Doctor*
EMP: 127
SALES (corp-wide): 6B **Privately Held**
WEB: www.salemhaven.com
SIC: 8051 Skilled nursing care facilities
HQ: Kindred Nursing Centers West Llc
3128 Boxelder Dr
Cheyenne WY 82001
307 634-7901

(P-20056)
KINDRED NURSING CENTERS W LLC
Also Called: Kindred Transitional
1517 Knickerbocker Dr, Stockton (95210-3119)
PHONE..................209 957-4539
Keith Braley, *Administration*
EMP: 101
SALES (corp-wide): 6B **Privately Held**
WEB: www.salemhaven.com
SIC: 8051 Skilled nursing care facilities
HQ: Kindred Nursing Centers West Llc
3128 Boxelder Dr
Cheyenne WY 82001
307 634-7901

(P-20057)
KISSITO HEALTH CASE INC
Also Called: Arbor Vly Nrsing Rhbltion Ctr
1310 W Granger Ave, Modesto (95350-3911)
PHONE..................209 524-4817
Al Johnson, *Branch Mgr*
EMP: 127
SALES (corp-wide): 2.3MM **Privately Held**
SIC: 8051 8361 Convalescent home with continuous nursing care; rehabilitation center, residential: health care incidental
PA: Kissito Healthcare, Inc.
5228 Valleypointe Pkwy
Roanoke VA 24019
540 265-0322

(P-20058)
KNOLLS CONVALESCENT HOSPITAL (PA)
Also Called: Desert Knlls Convalescent Hosp
16890 Green Tree Blvd, Victorville (92395-5618)
PHONE..................760 245-5361
Gary L Bechtold, *President*
Fred Bechtold, *Vice Pres*
Larry Bechtold, *Vice Pres*
EMP: 130
SQ FT: 5,421
SALES (est): 6.5MM **Privately Held**
SIC: 8051 8052 Convalescent home with continuous nursing care; intermediate care facilities

(P-20059)
KNOLLS CONVALESCENT HOSPITAL
Also Called: Desert Knolls Convalescent
14973 Hesperia Rd, Victorville (92395-3923)
PHONE..................760 245-6477
Gary Bechtold, *General Mgr*
EMP: 80
SALES (corp-wide): 6.5MM **Privately Held**
SIC: 8051 6513 Convalescent home with continuous nursing care; apartment building operators
PA: Knolls Convalescent Hospital Inc
16890 Green Tree Blvd
Victorville CA 92395
760 245-5361

(P-20060)
KSM HEALTHCARE INC
Also Called: Dreier's Nursing Care Center
1400 W Glenoaks Blvd, Glendale
(91201-1911)
PHONE.................................818 242-1183
John Haedrich, *President*
EMP: 76
SQ FT: 40,000
SALES: 4.7MM **Privately Held**
WEB: www.nursing-care.com
SIC: 8051 Skilled nursing care facilities

(P-20061)
KU KYOUNG
Also Called: Eden Villa
Unknown, Redding (96003)
P.O. Box 590428
PHONE.................................510 582-2765
Kyoung Ku, *Owner*
EMP: 170
SQ FT: 37,157
SALES (est): 4MM **Privately Held**
SIC: 8051 1522 Convalescent home with
continuous nursing care; residential con-
struction

(P-20062)
**LA JOLLA VILLAGE TOWERS
500**
8515 Costa Verde Blvd Ofc, San Diego
(92122-1152)
PHONE.................................858 646-7700
Steve Brudnick, *Administration*
Vicki Simpson, *Administration*
EMP: 65
SQ FT: 900,000
SALES (est): 1.4MM **Privately Held**
SIC: 8051 Skilled nursing care facilities

(P-20063)
LA PALMA CARE CENTER
Also Called: La Palma Nursing Center
1130 W La Palma Ave, Anaheim
(92801-2803)
PHONE.................................714 772-7480
Sim Mandelbaum, *President*
Joseph Berkowitc, *Administration*
EMP: 75
SQ FT: 20,000
SALES (est): 3.5MM **Privately Held**
SIC: 8051 Convalescent home with contin-
uous nursing care

(P-20064)
**LAFALTTE RHBILITATION CARE
CTR**
537 E Fulton St, Stockton (95204-2227)
PHONE.................................209 466-2066
Gus Ropalidas, *Administration*
EMP: 100
SALES (est): 1.1MM **Privately Held**
SIC: 8051 Convalescent home with contin-
uous nursing care

(P-20065)
LAKEWOOD MANOR NORTH INC
831 S Lake St, Los Angeles (90057-4013)
PHONE.................................213 380-9175
Kim C Elliott, *Administration*
EMP: 74 EST: 1971
SQ FT: 23,000
SALES (est): 3.4MM **Privately Held**
SIC: 8051 Skilled nursing care facilities

(P-20066)
**LANTERN OF CRESCENT CITY
LLC**
1280 Marshall St, Crescent City
(95531-2217)
PHONE.................................949 445-1000
Spencer Samuelian, *Mng Member*
EMP: 99
SQ FT: 45,000
SALES: 1.7MM **Privately Held**
SIC: 8051 Skilled nursing care facilities

(P-20067)
LAS VILLAS DEL NORTE
Also Called: Healthcare Group
1325 Las Villas Way, Escondido
(92026-1946)
PHONE.................................760 741-1047
John Helpsley, *Director*
EMP: 100

SALES (corp-wide): 3MM **Privately Held**
SIC: 8051 8052 Skilled nursing care facilities; intermediate care facilities
PA: Las Villas Del Norte
416 W Spruce St
Junction City KS 66441
760 741-1046

(P-20068)
**LAWNDALE HLTHCARE
WLLNESS CTR**
1700 Santa Fe Ave Ste 100, Long Beach
(90813-1201)
PHONE.................................310 679-3344
Sharrod Brooks,
EMP: 99 EST: 2011
SALES: 6.8MM **Privately Held**
SIC: 8051 Mental retardation hospital

(P-20069)
LEGACY AND NURSING REHAB
1790 Muir Rd, Martinez (94553-4718)
PHONE.................................925 228-8383
Dipa Gupta, *Owner*
Thomas Joseph, *Principal*
Burnadett Joseph, *Admin Asst*
Sherry Jansen, *Director*
EMP: 90
SALES (est): 2MM **Privately Held**
SIC: 8051 Skilled nursing care facilities

(P-20070)
**LIBERTY HEALTHCARE OF
OKLAHOMA**
Also Called: Regency
4463 San Felipe Rd Ofc, San Jose
(95135-1515)
PHONE.................................408 532-7677
Aliyan Montose, *Manager*
EMP: 80 **Privately Held**
SIC: 8051 Skilled nursing care facilities
PA: Liberty Healthcare Of Oklahoma Inc
3073 Horseshoe Dr S # 100
Naples FL 34104

(P-20071)
**LIFE CARE CENTERS AMERICA
INC**
Also Called: Life Care Center of La Habra
1233 W La Habra Blvd, La Habra
(90631-5226)
PHONE.................................562 690-0852
Daniel Husband, *Administration*
Marilyn Mallari, *Records Dir*
Lupe Rosas, *Hlthcr Dir*
Juan Jimenez, *Director*
EMP: 90
SALES (corp-wide): 144MM **Privately
Held**
SIC: 8051 Convalescent home with contin-
uous nursing care
PA: Life Care Centers Of America, Inc.
3570 Keith St Nw
Cleveland TN 37312
423 472-9585

(P-20072)
**LIFE CARE CENTERS AMERICA
INC**
Also Called: Mirada Hills Rehb & Conva
12200 La Mirada Blvd, La Mirada
(90638-1306)
PHONE.................................562 947-8691
EMP: 150
SALES (corp-wide): 144MM **Privately
Held**
SIC: 8051 Skilled nursing care facilities
PA: Life Care Centers Of America, Inc.
3570 Keith St Nw
Cleveland TN 37312
423 472-9585

(P-20073)
**LIFE CARE CENTERS AMERICA
INC**
Also Called: Life Care Center San Gabriel
909 W Santa Anita Ave, San Gabriel
(91776-1018)
PHONE.................................626 289-5365
Eunice Fletcher, *Manager*
EMP: 90

SALES (corp-wide): 144MM **Privately
Held**
SIC: 8051 Convalescent home with contin-
uous nursing care
PA: Life Care Centers Of America, Inc.
3570 Keith St Nw
Cleveland TN 37312
423 472-9585

(P-20074)
**LIFE CARE CENTERS AMERICA
INC**
Also Called: Life Care Centers of Escondido
1980 Felicita Rd, Escondido (92025-5922)
PHONE.................................760 741-6109
Trent Weaver, *Administration*
Debbie Woitas, *Marketing Staff*
Hafiza Resstom, *Food Svc Dir*
EMP: 200
SALES (corp-wide): 144MM **Privately
Held**
SIC: 8051 Convalescent home with contin-
uous nursing care
PA: Life Care Centers Of America, Inc.
3570 Keith St Nw
Cleveland TN 37312
423 472-9585

(P-20075)
**LIFE CARE CENTERS AMERICA
INC**
Also Called: Lake Forest Nursing Center
25652 Old Trabuco Rd, Lake Forest
(92630-2776)
PHONE.................................949 380-9380
Kim Le, *Branch Mgr*
Kaye Browe, *Human Res Dir*
EMP: 200
SALES (corp-wide): 144MM **Privately
Held**
SIC: 8051 Convalescent home with contin-
uous nursing care
PA: Life Care Centers Of America, Inc.
3570 Keith St Nw
Cleveland TN 37312
423 472-9585

(P-20076)
**LIFE CARE CENTERS AMERICA
INC**
Also Called: Imperial Convalescent
11926 La Mirada Blvd, La Mirada
(90638-1303)
PHONE.................................562 943-7156
Ted Stultz, *Manager*
EMP: 150
SALES (corp-wide): 144MM **Privately
Held**
SIC: 8051 8741 Convalescent home with
continuous nursing care; management
services
PA: Life Care Centers Of America, Inc.
3570 Keith St Nw
Cleveland TN 37312
423 472-9585

(P-20077)
**LIFE CARE CENTERS AMERICA
INC**
Also Called: Life Care Center of Bellflower
16910 Woodruff Ave, Bellflower
(90706-6036)
PHONE.................................562 867-1761
Tooren Bel, *Manager*
Mary Helen Gomez, *Director*
EMP: 100
SALES (corp-wide): 144MM **Privately
Held**
SIC: 8051 Convalescent home with contin-
uous nursing care
PA: Life Care Centers Of America, Inc.
3570 Keith St Nw
Cleveland TN 37312
423 472-9585

(P-20078)
**LIFE CARE CENTERS AMERICA
INC**
Also Called: Life Care Center of Norwalk
12350 Rosecrans Ave, Norwalk
(90650-5064)
PHONE.................................562 921-6624
Steve Ramsdel, *Vice Pres*
EMP: 60

SALES (corp-wide): 144MM **Privately
Held**
SIC: 8051 Convalescent home with contin-
uous nursing care
PA: Life Care Centers Of America, Inc.
3570 Keith St Nw
Cleveland TN 37312
423 472-9585

(P-20079)
**LIFE CARE CENTERS AMERICA
INC**
27555 Rimrock Rd, Barstow (92311-4230)
PHONE.................................760 252-2515
Denise Kuhn, *Director*
EMP: 366
SALES (corp-wide): 144MM **Privately
Held**
SIC: 8051 Convalescent home with contin-
uous nursing care
PA: Life Care Centers Of America, Inc.
3570 Keith St Nw
Cleveland TN 37312
423 472-9585

(P-20080)
**LIFE GNERATIONS
HEALTHCARE LLC**
Also Called: Stanford Court Nursing Center
7800 Parkway Dr, La Mesa (91942-2001)
PHONE.................................619 460-2330
Lisa Lowe, *Records Dir*
EMP: 110
SALES (est): 2.7MM
SALES (corp-wide): 63.1MM **Privately
Held**
SIC: 8051 Convalescent home with contin-
uous nursing care
PA: Life Generations Healthcare Llc
6 Hutton Cntre Dr Ste 400
Santa Ana CA 92707
714 241-5600

(P-20081)
LIFECARE SYSTEMS INC
Also Called: Medical Inst of Little Co Mary
4101 Torrance Blvd, Torrance
(90503-4607)
PHONE.................................310 540-7676
Karl Carrier, *President*
Henry G Walker, *President*
EMP: 150
SALES: 17.6MM **Privately Held**
SIC: 8051 Skilled nursing care facilities

(P-20082)
**LIGHTHOUSE HEALTHCARE
CTR LLC**
2222 Santa Ana S, Los Angeles
(90059-1350)
PHONE.................................323 564-4461
Sharrod Brooks,
EMP: 99
SALES (est): 3MM **Privately Held**
SIC: 8051 Skilled nursing care facilities

(P-20083)
LILY HOLDINGS LLC
Also Called: Oakwood Gardens Care Center
3510 E Shields Ave, Fresno (93726-6909)
PHONE.................................559 222-4807
Ashley Specht,
Lisa Perez, *Office Mgr*
Benjamin Carter, *Administration*
EMP: 99
SALES (est): 2MM **Privately Held**
SIC: 8051 Convalescent home with contin-
uous nursing care

(P-20084)
LINDA VISTA MANOR INC
Also Called: Kearny Mesa Convalescent
Hosp
7675 Family Cir, San Diego (92111-5304)
PHONE.................................858 278-8121
Richard Hebbel, *President*
Jeanette Hebbel, *Vice Pres*
EMP: 109
SQ FT: 30,000
SALES (est): 7.5MM **Privately Held**
WEB: www.kearnymesaconvalescent.com
SIC: 8051 6411 Skilled nursing care facili-
ties; insurance agents, brokers & service

**P
R
O
D
U
C
T
S
&
S
V
C
S**

(P-20085)
LITTLE SISTERS THE POOR OF LA
Also Called: JEANNE JUGAN, A RESIDENCE
2100 S Western Ave, San Pedro (90732-4389)
PHONE..................310 548-0625
Margaret McArthy, *President*
Clotilde Jardim, *Treasurer*
Michael Mugan, *Vice Pres*
Victor Salcido, *Human Res Dir*
EMP: 100
SQ FT: 145,530
SALES: 5.5MM **Privately Held**
SIC: 8051 8361 8052 Extended care facility; residential care; intermediate care facilities

(P-20086)
LONE TREE CONVALESCENT HOSP
4001 Lone Tree Way, Antioch (94509-6232)
PHONE..................925 754-0470
Lowell Callaway, *President*
Mark Callaway, *Corp Secy*
Velda C Pierce, *Vice Pres*
EMP: 135 EST: 1968
SQ FT: 10,000
SALES (est): 8.6MM **Privately Held**
SIC: 8051 Convalescent home with continuous nursing care

(P-20087)
LONG BEACH CARE CENTER INC
2615 Grand Ave, Long Beach (90815-1708)
PHONE..................562 426-6141
William A Nelson, *President*
EMP: 108
SQ FT: 43,962
SALES: 14.6MM **Privately Held**
WEB: www.longbeachcarecenter.com
SIC: 8051 Convalescent home with continuous nursing care

(P-20088)
LONGWOOD MANAGEMENT CORP
Also Called: Imperial Crest Healthcare Ctr
11834 Inglewood Ave, Hawthorne (90250-0107)
PHONE..................310 679-1461
Robert Villalub, *Administration*
Priscilla Quizon, *Office Mgr*
Margie Linder, *Nursing Dir*
Rahul Dhakwadar, *Director*
EMP: 150
SALES (corp-wide): 170MM **Privately Held**
SIC: 8051 Convalescent home with continuous nursing care
PA: Longwood Management Corp.
4032 Wilshire Blvd Fl 6
Los Angeles CA 90010
213 389-6900

(P-20089)
LONGWOOD MANAGEMENT CORP
Also Called: Magnolia Grdns Convalescent HM
17922 San Frnando Msn, Granada Hills (91344-4043)
PHONE..................818 360-1864
Ojijoji Gervacio, *Principal*
Annalynn Barrion, *Executive*
EMP: 100
SALES (corp-wide): 170MM **Privately Held**
SIC: 8051 Convalescent home with continuous nursing care
PA: Longwood Management Corp.
4032 Wilshire Blvd Fl 6
Los Angeles CA 90010
213 389-6900

(P-20090)
LONGWOOD MANAGEMENT CORP
Also Called: Green Acres Lodge
8101 Hill Dr, Rosemead (91770-4169)
PHONE..................626 280-2293
Karen Fugate, *Administration*
EMP: 60
SALES (corp-wide): 170MM **Privately Held**
SIC: 8051 Convalescent home with continuous nursing care
PA: Longwood Management Corp.
4032 Wilshire Blvd Fl 6
Los Angeles CA 90010
213 389-6900

(P-20091)
LONGWOOD MANAGEMENT CORP
Also Called: San Gabriel Convalescent Ctr
8035 Hill Dr, Rosemead (91770-4116)
PHONE..................626 280-4820
Gigi Garcia, *Branch Mgr*
EMP: 150
SALES (corp-wide): 170MM **Privately Held**
SIC: 8051 Convalescent home with continuous nursing care
PA: Longwood Management Corp.
4032 Wilshire Blvd Fl 6
Los Angeles CA 90010
213 389-6900

(P-20092)
LONGWOOD MANAGEMENT CORP
Also Called: Crenshaw Nursing
1900 S Longwood Ave, Los Angeles (90016-1408)
PHONE..................323 933-1560
Gilbert Fimbres, *Manager*
EMP: 50
SALES (corp-wide): 170MM **Privately Held**
SIC: 8051 8052 Convalescent home with continuous nursing care; intermediate care facilities
PA: Longwood Management Corp.
4032 Wilshire Blvd Fl 6
Los Angeles CA 90010
213 389-6900

(P-20093)
LONGWOOD MANOR
Also Called: Longwood Manor Convalescent HM
4853 W Washington Blvd, Los Angeles (90016-1501)
PHONE..................323 935-1157
Jacob Friedman, *President*
Lea Friedman, *Corp Secy*
Irving Friedman, *Vice Pres*
EMP: 200
SQ FT: 30,000
SALES: 16.3MM **Privately Held**
SIC: 8051 Convalescent home with continuous nursing care

(P-20094)
LOS ANGLES JEWISH HM FOR AGING (PA)
Also Called: Grancell Village
7150 Tampa Ave, Reseda (91335-3700)
PHONE..................818 774-3000
Andrew Berman, *Ch of Bd*
Joyce Brandman, *Vice Chairman*
Les Granow, *Vice Chairman*
Danny Rosett, *Vice Chairman*
Molly Forrest, *CEO*
EMP: 760
SQ FT: 35,000
SALES (est): 172.6MM **Privately Held**
WEB: www.jha.org
SIC: 8051 8361 Skilled nursing care facilities; residential care

(P-20095)
LOS ANGLES JEWISH HM FOR AGING
Also Called: Eisenberg Village
18855 Victory Blvd, Reseda (91335-6445)
PHONE..................818 774-3000
Annette Brinnon, *Manager*
Hadi Pourbeheshtian, *Engineer*

Anna Haro, *Human Res Dir*
EMP: 350
SALES (est): 8.5MM
SALES (corp-wide): 172.6MM **Privately Held**
WEB: www.jha.org
SIC: 8051 Convalescent home with continuous nursing care
PA: Los Angeles Jewish Home For The Aging
7150 Tampa Ave
Reseda CA 91335
818 774-3000

(P-20096)
MADERA CONVALESCENT HOSPITAL (PA)
517 S A St, Madera (93638-3896)
PHONE..................559 673-9228
Arden Bennett, *CEO*
Dennis Albers, *Ch of Bd*
Mathilde Albers, *Corp Secy*
Emile Damia, *Vice Pres*
Paula Asaro, *Social Dir*
EMP: 160 EST: 1965
SQ FT: 1,500
SALES (est): 5.6MM **Privately Held**
SIC: 8051 Convalescent home with continuous nursing care

(P-20097)
MADERA CONVALESCENT HOSPITAL
Also Called: Auburn Gardens Care Center
260 Racetrack St, Auburn (95603-5422)
PHONE..................530 885-7051
Clayton Green, *Administration*
EMP: 78
SALES (est): 413.1K
SALES (corp-wide): 5.6MM **Privately Held**
SIC: 8051 Skilled nursing care facilities
PA: Madera Convalescent Hospital, Inc
517 S A St
Madera CA 93638
559 673-9228

(P-20098)
MADISON CARE CENTER LLC
1391 E Madison Ave, El Cajon (92021-8568)
PHONE..................619 444-1107
Emmanuel David, *President*
Liz Contreras, *Human Res Dir*
Sarah Donley, *Human Res Dir*
Jeanette Laplant, *Director*
EMP: 100
SALES (est): 1.9MM **Privately Held**
SIC: 8051 Skilled nursing care facilities

(P-20099)
MANCHSTER MNOR CNVLESCENT HOSP
837 W Manchester Ave, Los Angeles (90044-4913)
PHONE..................323 753-1789
Phadra Johnson-Fenton, *Administration*
Wilisha Jackson, *Office Mgr*
Phadra Fenton, *Administration*
Mary Morales, *Human Res Dir*
EMP: 65 EST: 1963
SQ FT: 10,000
SALES (est): 3MM **Privately Held**
WEB: www.manchestermanorch.com
SIC: 8051 Skilled nursing care facilities

(P-20100)
MANNING GARDENS INC
Also Called: Manning Grdns Cnvalescent Hosp
2113 E Manning Ave, Fresno (93725-9681)
PHONE..................559 834-2586
Cary Hanson, *Administration*
Jacob Kizirian, *President*
Norman Kizirian, *Vice Pres*
Ron Kinnersley, *Director*
EMP: 50
SQ FT: 15,000
SALES (est): 2.2MM **Privately Held**
SIC: 8051 Skilled nursing care facilities

(P-20101)
MANNING GARDENS CARE CTR INC
2113 E Manning Ave, Fresno (93725-9681)
PHONE..................559 834-2586
Ronald Kinnersley, *President*
EMP: 82 EST: 2011
SALES (est): 1.7MM **Privately Held**
SIC: 8051 Skilled nursing care facilities

(P-20102)
MANOR CARE SUNNYVALE CA LLC
Also Called: Manorcare Hlth Svcs Sunnyvale
1150 Tilton Dr, Sunnyvale (94087-2440)
PHONE..................408 735-7200
EMP: 89 EST: 2016
SALES (est): 60.8K
SALES (corp-wide): 8.2B **Privately Held**
SIC: 8051 Convalescent home with continuous nursing care
HQ: Hcr Manorcare, Inc.
333 N Summit St
Toledo OH 43604
419 252-5743

(P-20103)
MARIN CNVLSCENT RHBLTTION HOSP
30 Hacienda Dr, Belvedere Tiburon (94920-1127)
PHONE..................415 435-4554
Mary Wollam, *President*
Debbie Litchfield,
EMP: 60
SQ FT: 5,000
SALES (est): 3.3MM **Privately Held**
WEB: www.marinconvalescent.com
SIC: 8051 Convalescent home with continuous nursing care

(P-20104)
MARINER HEALTH CARE INC
Also Called: Driftwood Health Care Ctr
4109 Emerald St, Torrance (90503-3105)
PHONE..................310 371-4628
Jennifer Torgrude, *Manager*
EMP: 100
SALES (corp-wide): 1B **Privately Held**
WEB: www.marinerhealth.com
SIC: 8051 Extended care facility
HQ: Mariner Health Care, Inc.
1 Ravinia Dr Ste 1500
Atlanta GA 30346
678 443-7000

(P-20105)
MARINER HEALTH CARE INC
Also Called: Freemont Health Care Center
39022 Presidio Way, Fremont (94538-1221)
PHONE..................510 792-3743
Carinagayle Gorospe, *Administration*
Mary Grace Abuan, *Chf Purch Ofc*
EMP: 170
SALES (corp-wide): 1B **Privately Held**
WEB: www.marinerhealth.com
SIC: 8051 Extended care facility
HQ: Mariner Health Care, Inc.
1 Ravinia Dr Ste 1500
Atlanta GA 30346
678 443-7000

(P-20106)
MARINER HEALTH CARE INC
Also Called: Gilroy Health & Rehab Ctr
8170 Murray Ave, Gilroy (95020-4605)
PHONE..................408 842-9311
Gerald Hunter, *Administration*
Hector Yanez, *Facilities Dir*
EMP: 145
SALES (corp-wide): 1B **Privately Held**
WEB: www.marinerhealth.com
SIC: 8051 Extended care facility
HQ: Mariner Health Care, Inc.
1 Ravinia Dr Ste 1500
Atlanta GA 30346
678 443-7000

(P-20107)
MARINER HEALTH CARE INC
Also Called: Skyline Health Care Center
2065 Forest Ave, San Jose (95128-4807)
PHONE..................408 298-3950
Richard Park, *Administration*

EMP: 250
SALES (corp-wide): 1B **Privately Held**
SIC: 8051 Extended care facility
HQ: Mariner Health Care, Inc.
   1 Ravinia Dr Ste 1500
   Atlanta GA 30346
   678 443-7000

(P-20108)
MARINER HEALTH CARE INC
7400 24th St, Sacramento (95822-5350)
PHONE....................................916 422-4825
Robert Lorenzo, *Manager*
EMP: 120
SALES (corp-wide): 1B **Privately Held**
WEB: www.marinerhealth.com
SIC: 8051 Extended care facility
HQ: Mariner Health Care, Inc.
   1 Ravinia Dr Ste 1500
   Atlanta GA 30346
   678 443-7000

(P-20109)
MARINER HEALTH CARE INC
Also Called: Vale Healthcare Center
13484 San Pablo Ave, San Pablo
(94806-3904)
PHONE....................................510 232-5945
Remy Dise, *Director*
Kathleen Lovato, *Vice Pres*
David Groch-Tochman, *Director*
EMP: 210
SALES (corp-wide): 1B **Privately Held**
WEB: www.marinerhealth.com
SIC: 8051 Extended care facility
HQ: Mariner Health Care, Inc.
   1 Ravinia Dr Ste 1500
   Atlanta GA 30346
   678 443-7000

(P-20110)
MARINER HEALTH CARE INC
Also Called: Inglewood Health Care Center
100 S Hillcrest Blvd, Inglewood
(90301-1313)
PHONE....................................310 677-9114
Amanda Arevalo, *Administration*
Tessie Fagarang, *Records Dir*
Hieldeen Bonsall, *Nursing Dir*
EMP: 128
SALES (corp-wide): 1B **Privately Held**
WEB: www.marinerhealth.com
SIC: 8051 Extended care facility
HQ: Mariner Health Care, Inc.
   1 Ravinia Dr Ste 1500
   Atlanta GA 30346
   678 443-7000

(P-20111)
MARINER HEALTH CARE INC
Also Called: Skyline Health Care Ctr
3032 Rowena Ave, Los Angeles
(90039-2005)
PHONE....................................323 665-1185
Kathleen Glass, *Administration*
Marilyn Washington, *Nurse*
EMP: 100
SALES (corp-wide): 1B **Privately Held**
WEB: www.marinerhealth.com
SIC: 8051 Extended care facility
HQ: Mariner Health Care, Inc.
   1 Ravinia Dr Ste 1500
   Atlanta GA 30346
   678 443-7000

(P-20112)
MARINER HEALTH CARE INC
Also Called: Driftwood Convalescent Hosp
1850 E 8th St, Davis (95616-2502)
PHONE....................................530 756-1800
David Ormiston, *Principal*
EMP: 150
SALES (corp-wide): 1B **Privately Held**
WEB: www.marinerhealth.com
SIC: 8051 Extended care facility
HQ: Mariner Health Care, Inc.
   1 Ravinia Dr Ste 1500
   Atlanta GA 30346
   678 443-7000

(P-20113)
MARINER HEALTH CARE INC
Also Called: Autumn Hills Convalescent
Home
430 N Glendale Ave, Glendale
(91206-3309)
PHONE....................................818 246-5677
Jenik Akopian, *Principal*
EMP: 120
SALES (corp-wide): 1B **Privately Held**
WEB: www.marinerhealth.com
SIC: 8051 Extended care facility
HQ: Mariner Health Care, Inc.
   1 Ravinia Dr Ste 1500
   Atlanta GA 30346
   678 443-7000

(P-20114)
MARINER HEALTH CARE INC
675 24th Ave, Santa Cruz (95062-4205)
PHONE....................................831 475-6323
EMP: 85
SALES (corp-wide): 1B **Privately Held**
WEB: www.marinerhealth.com
SIC: 8051 Extended care facility
HQ: Mariner Health Care, Inc.
   1 Ravinia Dr Ste 1500
   Atlanta GA 30346
   678 443-7000

(P-20115)
MARINER HEALTH CARE INC
Also Called: Hayward Hills Health Care Ctr
1768 B St, Hayward (94541-3102)
PHONE....................................510 538-4424
Annamarie Magna, *Branch Mgr*
EMP: 99
SALES (corp-wide): 1B **Privately Held**
WEB: www.marinerhealth.com
SIC: 8051 Extended care facility
HQ: Mariner Health Care, Inc.
   1 Ravinia Dr Ste 1500
   Atlanta GA 30346
   678 443-7000

(P-20116)
MARINER HEALTH CARE INC
Also Called: Driftwood Healthcare Center
19700 Hesperian Blvd, Hayward
(94541-4704)
PHONE....................................510 785-2880
Ellen Renner, *Administration*
EMP: 135
SALES (corp-wide): 1B **Privately Held**
WEB: www.marinerhealth.com
SIC: 8051 Extended care facility
HQ: Mariner Health Care, Inc.
   1 Ravinia Dr Ste 1500
   Atlanta GA 30346
   678 443-7000

(P-20117)
MARINER HEALTH CARE INC
Also Called: El Rancho Vista Hlth Care Ctr
8925 Mines Ave, Pico Rivera (90660-3006)
PHONE....................................562 942-7019
Richard Widerynski, *Sales/Mktg Mgr*
EMP: 100
SALES (corp-wide): 1B **Privately Held**
WEB: www.marinerhealth.com
SIC: 8051 Extended care facility
HQ: Mariner Health Care, Inc.
   1 Ravinia Dr Ste 1500
   Atlanta GA 30346
   678 443-7000

(P-20118)
MARINER HEALTH CARE INC
Also Called: Pinedridge Care Ctr
45 Professional Ctr Pkwy, San Rafael
(94903-2702)
PHONE....................................415 479-3610
Louise Kalchek, *Director*
Conrad Bustamante, *Facilities Dir*
Marivic Yumul, *Nursing Dir*
EMP: 70
SALES (corp-wide): 1B **Privately Held**
WEB: www.marinerhealth.com
SIC: 8051 Extended care facility
HQ: Mariner Health Care, Inc.
   1 Ravinia Dr Ste 1500
   Atlanta GA 30346
   678 443-7000

(P-20119)
MARINER HEALTH CARE INC
Also Called: Almaden Health & Rehab Ctr
2065 Los Gatos Almaden Rd, San Jose
(95124-5417)
PHONE....................................408 377-9275
Yvette Bonnet, *Branch Mgr*
EMP: 100
SALES (corp-wide): 1B **Privately Held**
WEB: www.marinerhealth.com
SIC: 8051 Extended care facility
HQ: Mariner Health Care, Inc.
   1 Ravinia Dr Ste 1500
   Atlanta GA 30346
   678 443-7000

(P-20120)
MARINER HEALTH CARE INC
Also Called: Excell Care Ctr
3025 High St, Oakland (94619-1807)
PHONE....................................510 261-5200
Elma Conway, *Administration*
EMP: 100
SALES (corp-wide): 1B **Privately Held**
WEB: www.marinerhealth.com
SIC: 8051 Extended care facility
HQ: Mariner Health Care, Inc.
   1 Ravinia Dr Ste 1500
   Atlanta GA 30346
   678 443-7000

(P-20121)
MARINER HEALTH CARE INC
Also Called: La Salette Rehab Convlesc Hos
537 E Fulton St, Stockton (95204-2227)
PHONE....................................209 466-2066
Karol Ford, *Manager*
EMP: 125
SALES (corp-wide): 1B **Privately Held**
WEB: www.marinerhealth.com
SIC: 8051 Extended care facility
HQ: Mariner Health Care, Inc.
   1 Ravinia Dr Ste 1500
   Atlanta GA 30346
   678 443-7000

(P-20122)
MARINER HEALTH CARE INC
Also Called: Windsor Gardens Hea
13000 Victory Blvd, North Hollywood
(91606-2926)
PHONE....................................818 985-5990
Dolly Piper, *Manager*
EMP: 100
SALES (corp-wide): 1B **Privately Held**
WEB: www.marinerhealth.com
SIC: 8051 Extended care facility
HQ: Mariner Health Care, Inc.
   1 Ravinia Dr Ste 1500
   Atlanta GA 30346
   678 443-7000

(P-20123)
MARINER HEALTH CARE INC
Also Called: Verdugo Vista Healthcare Ctr
3050 Montrose Ave, La Crescenta
(91214-3619)
PHONE....................................818 957-0850
Jeri-Enn Shelton, *Administration*
EMP: 90
SALES (corp-wide): 1B **Privately Held**
WEB: www.marinerhealth.com
SIC: 8051 Extended care facility
HQ: Mariner Health Care, Inc.
   1 Ravinia Dr Ste 1500
   Atlanta GA 30346
   678 443-7000

(P-20124)
MARINER HEALTH CARE INC
Also Called: Arden Health & Rehab Ctr
3400 Alta Arden Expy, Sacramento
(95825-2103)
PHONE....................................916 481-5500
John Pritchard, *Manager*
EMP: 150
SALES (corp-wide): 1B **Privately Held**
WEB: www.marinerhealth.com
SIC: 8051 8069 Extended care facility;
  specialty hospitals, except psychiatric
HQ: Mariner Health Care, Inc.
   1 Ravinia Dr Ste 1500
   Atlanta GA 30346
   678 443-7000

(P-20125)
MARK & FRED ENTERPRISES
Also Called: West Anaheim Care Center
645 S Beach Blvd, Anaheim (92804-3102)
PHONE....................................714 821-1993
Mark Landry, *Managing Prtnr*
Connie Black, *Partner*
George Rodes, *CFO*
Donna Meyer, *Officer*
Mary Loether, *Social Dir*
EMP: 125
SQ FT: 39,000
SALES (est): 9.7MM **Privately Held**
SIC: 8051 Convalescent home with contin-
  uous nursing care

(P-20126)
MARLORA INVESTMENTS LLC
Also Called: MARLORA POST ACCUTE RE-
HABLITAT
3801 E Anaheim St, Long Beach
(90804-4004)
PHONE....................................562 494-3311
Marilyn A Hauser,
Cathy Hernandez, *Marketing Staff*
EMP: 100
SQ FT: 22,118
SALES: 8.6MM **Privately Held**
SIC: 8051 Convalescent home with contin-
  uous nursing care

(P-20127)
**MARY HLTH SCK CNVLSCNT
&NRSNG**
2929 Theresa Dr, Newbury Park
(91320-3136)
PHONE....................................805 498-3644
Jody Rupp, *Administration*
Sister Purificaion Fererro, *CEO*
Diane Zimanski, *Office Mgr*
EMP: 92
SQ FT: 5,000
SALES: 7.2MM **Privately Held**
SIC: 8051 Convalescent home with contin-
  uous nursing care

(P-20128)
**MARYSVLLE NRSING REHAB
CTR LLC**
Also Called: MARYSVILLE CARE CENTER
1617 Ramirez St, Marysville (95901-4334)
PHONE....................................530 742-7311
Jim Bursey, *Administration*
Joseph Palli,
EMP: 90
SALES: 8.3MM **Privately Held**
SIC: 8051 Skilled nursing care facilities

(P-20129)
**MAYWOOD HALTHCARE
WELLNESS CTR**
Also Called: Pine Crest
6025 Pine Ave, Maywood (90270-3108)
PHONE....................................323 560-0720
Emmanuel Bernabe, *President*
EMP: 50 **EST:** 1995
SALES (est): 4.3MM **Privately Held**
SIC: 8051 Convalescent home with contin-
  uous nursing care

(P-20130)
MEADOW VIEW MANOR INC
396 Dorsey Dr, Grass Valley (95945-5368)
PHONE....................................530 272-2273
Jim Bursey, *Administration*
EMP: 100
SQ FT: 22,000
SALES (est): 726K
SALES (corp-wide): 103.9MM **Privately
Held**
WEB: www.villadelrey.com
SIC: 8051 Skilled nursing care facilities
HQ: Horizon West Healthcare, Inc.
   4020 Sierra College Blvd # 190
   Rocklin CA 95677
   916 624-6230

(P-20131)
**MEADOWOOD HLTH
REHABILITATION**
Also Called: Meadowood Care Center
3110 Wagner Heights Rd, Stockton
(95209-4848)
PHONE....................................209 956-3444
Keith Berry, *President*

Chard Hardcastle, *President*
Alex Kim, *General Mgr*
Jose Aguilera, *Director*
EMP: 370
SQ FT: 43,800
SALES (est): 5.8MM **Privately Held**
SIC: 8051 Skilled nursing care facilities

(P-20132)
MEDICAL CARE PROFESSIONALS
363 El Cmino Real Ste 215, South San Francisco (94080)
PHONE.....................650 583-9898
Sharon Youngberg, *President*
EMP: 100
SQ FT: 550
SALES (est): 3.2MM **Privately Held**
WEB: www.medicalcareprofessionals.com
SIC: 8051 8082 Skilled nursing care facilities; home health care services

(P-20133)
MEDICREST OF CALIFORNIA 1
Also Called: Montclair Mnor Cnvlescent Hosp
5119 Bandera St, Montclair (91763-4410)
PHONE.....................909 626-1294
Melinda Mabini, *Administration*
EMP: 60
SALES (corp-wide): 103.9MM **Privately Held**
SIC: 8051 Convalescent home with continuous nursing care
HQ: Medicrest Of California 1, Inc
4020 Sierra College Blvd
Rocklin CA 95677
916 624-6238

(P-20134)
MEK NORWOOD PINES LLC
500 Jessie Ave, Sacramento (95838-2609)
PHONE.....................916 922-7177
Bobby Federico, *Manager*
EMP: 99
SALES (est): 3.8MM **Privately Held**
SIC: 8051 Convalescent home with continuous nursing care

(P-20135)
MELON HOLDINGS LLC
Also Called: Marysville Post-Acute
1617 Ramirez St, Marysville (95901-4334)
PHONE.....................530 742-7311
Joseph Cunliffe, *Administration*
Nicklas Anderson, *President*
Matt Jackson, *President*
Melody Welch, *Chf Purch Ofc*
EMP: 99 **EST:** 2016
SALES (est): 985.7K **Privately Held**
SIC: 8051 Convalescent home with continuous nursing care

(P-20136)
MENTAL HLTH CNVLSCENT SVCS INC
Also Called: Lakewood Park Health Center
12023 Lakewood Blvd, Downey (90242-2635)
PHONE.....................562 869-0978
Daniel C Zilafro, *President*
Daniel Zilafro, *Administration*
EMP: 300
SQ FT: 60,000
SALES: 11.4MM **Privately Held**
SIC: 8051 Skilled nursing care facilities

(P-20137)
MESA VERDE CONVALESCENT HOSP
Also Called: Mesa Verde Prosecute Care
661 Center St, Costa Mesa (92627-2708)
PHONE.....................949 548-5584
Rita Simms, *Administration*
Joseph Munoz, *Administration*
Joye Tsuchiyama, *Administration*
Christina Flores, *Hlthcr Dir*
Greg Katz, *Director*
EMP: 200
SALES (est): 8.5MM **Privately Held**
WEB: www.mesaverdehealthcare.com
SIC: 8051 Convalescent home with continuous nursing care

(P-20138)
MID WILSHIRE HEALTH CARE CTR
676 S Bonnie Brae St, Los Angeles (90057-3710)
PHONE.....................213 483-9921
Jeoung Hie Lee, *President*
EMP: 60
SQ FT: 17,469
SALES: 4.6MM **Privately Held**
SIC: 8051 Skilled nursing care facilities

(P-20139)
MIRAMONTE ENTERPRISES LLC
Also Called: San Jacinto Healthcare
275 N San Jacinto St, Hemet (92543-4453)
PHONE.....................951 658-9441
Emmanuel B David, *President*
EMP: 134
SQ FT: 22,968
SALES: 8.2MM **Privately Held**
SIC: 8051 Skilled nursing care facilities

(P-20140)
MISSION HILLS HEALTHCARE INC
Also Called: Mission Hills Healthcare Ctr
726 Torrance St, San Diego (92103-3813)
PHONE.....................619 297-4086
Patrick Higgins, *CEO*
Leah Higgins, *President*
EMP: 92
SALES: 7.6MM **Privately Held**
SIC: 8051 Convalescent home with continuous nursing care

(P-20141)
MISSION MEDICAL ENTPS INC
Also Called: Hanford Nursing Rehabilitation
1007 W Lacey Blvd, Hanford (93230-4331)
PHONE.....................559 582-2871
Mark Fisher, *General Mgr*
EMP: 120
SALES (corp-wide): 9MM **Privately Held**
WEB: www.missioncaregroup.com
SIC: 8051 Convalescent home with continuous nursing care
PA: Mission Medical Enterprises, Inc.
1007 W Lacey Blvd
Hanford CA 93230
559 582-2871

(P-20142)
MISSION MEDICAL ENTPS INC
Also Called: Kings Nrsing Rhabilitation Ctr
851 Leslie Ln, Hanford (93230-5643)
PHONE.....................559 582-4414
Mark Fisher, *Branch Mgr*
EMP: 82
SALES (corp-wide): 9MM **Privately Held**
SIC: 8051 Skilled nursing care facilities
PA: Mission Medical Enterprises, Inc.
1007 W Lacey Blvd
Hanford CA 93230
559 582-2871

(P-20143)
MJB PARTNERS LLC
Also Called: Pomona Vista Care Center
651 N Main St, Pomona (91768-3110)
PHONE.....................909 623-2481
Frank Johnson,
Kelly Iasparro, *Vice Pres*
EMP: 62
SQ FT: 8,844
SALES (est): 207.3K **Privately Held**
SIC: 8051 Skilled nursing care facilities

(P-20144)
MONROVIA CONVALESCENT HOSPITAL
1220 Huntington Dr, Duarte (91010-2477)
PHONE.....................626 359-6618
Lydia Cruz, *President*
EMP: 63 **EST:** 1967
SQ FT: 15,000
SALES (est): 1.5MM **Privately Held**
SIC: 8051 Skilled nursing care facilities

(P-20145)
MONTECITO RETIREMENT ASSN
Also Called: Casa Dorinda
300 Hot Springs Rd, Santa Barbara (93108-2037)
PHONE.....................805 969-8011
Robin Drew, *CFO*
Claudia Bott, *Admin Sec*
Rose Flores, *Admin Asst*
Travis Dunn, *Graphic Designe*
Alan Blaver, *Broker*
EMP: 265
SQ FT: 350,000
SALES: 27.7MM **Privately Held**
WEB: www.casadorinda.com
SIC: 8051 8052 8361 Skilled nursing care facilities; personal care facility; rest home, with health care incidental

(P-20146)
MONTEREY HEALTHCARE & WELLNESS
1267 San Gabriel Blvd, Rosemead (91770-4237)
PHONE.....................626 280-3220
Shlomo Rechnitz, *CEO*
Sharrod Brooks, *Senior VP*
EMP: 90 **EST:** 2013
SALES: 12.9MM **Privately Held**
SIC: 8051 Mental retardation hospital

(P-20147)
MONTEREY PINES SKLLD NURSG FAC
Also Called: Horizon West
1501 Skyline Dr, Monterey (93940-4110)
PHONE.....................831 373-3716
Gene Sajcich, *Administration*
Kevin Hadfield, *Administration*
Michelle Ramirez, *Human Res Mgr*
EMP: 94
SQ FT: 32,000
SALES (est): 1.9MM
SALES (corp-wide): 103.9MM **Privately Held**
WEB: www.villadelrey.com
SIC: 8051 Convalescent home with continuous nursing care
HQ: Horizon West Healthcare, Inc.
4020 Sierra College Blvd # 190
Rocklin CA 95677
916 624-6230

(P-20148)
MORNINGSIDE CORECARE ASSOC LP
2180 Sand Hill Rd Ste 200, Menlo Park (94025-6949)
PHONE.....................650 854-5600
Justin Wilson, *Partner*
Carl Wilson, *Director*
EMP: 200
SALES (est): 2MM **Privately Held**
SIC: 8051 Skilled nursing care facilities

(P-20149)
MOUNT RBDOUX CONVALESCENT HOSP
Also Called: Plott Family Care Center
6401 33rd St, Riverside (92509-1404)
PHONE.....................951 681-2200
Thomas Plott, *President*
EMP: 150 **EST:** 1971
SALES: 6.2MM **Privately Held**
SIC: 8051 8059 Convalescent home with continuous nursing care; convalescent home

(P-20150)
MOUNTAIN VIEW CNVALESCENT HOSP
13333 Fenton Ave, Sylmar (91342-3113)
PHONE.....................818 367-1033
Ray Talebi, *Owner*
EMP: 50
SALES (est): 2.2MM **Privately Held**
SIC: 8051 Convalescent home with continuous nursing care

(P-20151)
MOYLES CENTRAL VLY HLTH CARE (PA)
999 N M St, Tulare (93274-2019)
PHONE.....................559 688-0288

Ken Moyel III, *President*
EMP: 340
SALES (est): 6.6MM **Privately Held**
WEB: www.portervillecon.com
SIC: 8051 Skilled nursing care facilities

(P-20152)
MOYLES CENTRAL VLY HLTH CARE
Also Called: Porterville Convalescent Hosp
1100 W Morton Ave, Porterville (93257-1947)
PHONE.....................559 782-1509
James Higbee, *CFO*
EMP: 120
SALES (corp-wide): 6.6MM **Privately Held**
WEB: www.portervillecon.com
SIC: 8051 Convalescent home with continuous nursing care
PA: Moyles Central Valley Health Care Inc
999 N M St
Tulare CA 93274
559 688-0288

(P-20153)
NAPA NURSING CENTER INC
3275 Villa Ln, NAPA (94558-3094)
PHONE.....................707 257-0931
Martine D Harmon, *CEO*
Tim Motooka, *President*
Georgia Otterros, *Administration*
Krizelle Cabaltera, *Hlthcr Dir*
EMP: 130
SQ FT: 48,000
SALES (est): 5.1MM
SALES (corp-wide): 103.9MM **Privately Held**
WEB: www.napayellowpages.com
SIC: 8051 Convalescent home with continuous nursing care
HQ: Horizon West Healthcare, Inc.
4020 Sierra College Blvd # 190
Rocklin CA 95677
916 624-6230

(P-20154)
NEW BTHNY RSDNTL CRE&SKLLD
1441 Berkeley Dr, Los Banos (93635-9599)
PHONE.....................209 827-8933
Lucinda Fonseca, *Exec Dir*
EMP: 80
SALES (est): 2.4MM **Privately Held**
SIC: 8051 Skilled nursing care facilities

(P-20155)
NEW COVENANT CARE OF DINUBA
Also Called: NEW COVENANT CARE CENTER OF DI
1730 S College Ave, Dinuba (93618-2812)
PHONE.....................559 591-3300
Gary V Guarisco, *President*
EMP: 100
SQ FT: 26,692
SALES: 6.2MM **Privately Held**
SIC: 8051 Skilled nursing care facilities

(P-20156)
NICE AVENUE LLC
Also Called: Mill Creek Manor
2278 Nice Ave, Mentone (92359-9655)
PHONE.....................909 794-1189
Jason Bell, *Administration*
EMP: 65
SALES (est): 343.1K **Privately Held**
SIC: 8051 Skilled nursing care facilities

(P-20157)
NORTH PT HLTH WELLNESS CTR LLC
Also Called: Northpointe Healthcare Centre
668 E Bullard Ave, Fresno (93710-5401)
PHONE.....................559 320-2200
Stephen Reissman,
Janet Bamper,
Cheryl Petterson,
EMP: 99
SALES (est): 3.7MM **Privately Held**
SIC: 8051 Skilled nursing care facilities

(P-20158)
NORTH SHORE INVESTMENT INC
Also Called: Crescent Cy Convalescent Hosp
1280 Marshall St, Crescent City
(95531-2217)
PHONE...................707 464-6151
Jeffery Davis, *President*
Armando Rafailan, *Office Mgr*
EMP: 100
SQ FT: 35,000
SALES: 5.4MM **Privately Held**
SIC: 8051 Convalescent home with continuous nursing care

(P-20159)
NORTHERN CALIFORNIA PRESBYTERI
Also Called: Sequos-San Frncsco Residential
1400 Geary Blvd, San Francisco
(94109-6561)
PHONE...................415 922-9700
Michael Daugherty, *Branch Mgr*
Steve Martinez, *Human Res Dir*
Donna Ficarrotta, *Marketing Staff*
EMP: 277
SALES (corp-wide): 73.3MM **Privately Held**
SIC: 8051 Convalescent home with continuous nursing care
PA: Sequoia Living
1525 Post St
San Francisco CA 94109
415 922-0200

(P-20160)
NORWALK MEADOWS NURSING CTR LP
10625 Leffingwell Rd, Norwalk
(90650-3434)
PHONE...................562 864-2541
Pnina Graff, *Partner*
Jacob Graff, *Partner*
Lisa Thomashow, *Administration*
EMP: 152
SQ FT: 23,632
SALES (est): 9.2MM **Privately Held**
SIC: 8051 Convalescent home with continuous nursing care

(P-20161)
NOVATO HEALTHCARE CENTER LLC
1565 Hill Rd, Novato (94947-4063)
PHONE...................415 897-6161
Michael J Torgan,
Joseph Lavitoria, *Opers Staff*
Sharrod Brooks,
EMP: 200 **EST:** 2007
SALES: 19.9MM **Privately Held**
SIC: 8051 Convalescent home with continuous nursing care

(P-20162)
NUEVACARE LLC
2100 Geng Rd Ste 210, Palo Alto
(94303-3307)
PHONE...................650 396-3596
EMP: 82
SALES (corp-wide): 3.6MM **Privately Held**
SIC: 8051 Skilled nursing care facilities
PA: Nuevacare Llc
1900 S Norfolk St Ste 350
San Mateo CA 94403
650 539-2000

(P-20163)
OAK KNOLL CONVALESCENT CENTER
Also Called: Oaks, The
450 Hayes Ln, Petaluma (94952-4010)
PHONE...................707 778-8686
Ann Abbott, *President*
Tony Meyers, *CEO*
EMP: 72
SQ FT: 36,000
SALES: 4.9MM **Privately Held**
SIC: 8051 Convalescent home with continuous nursing care

(P-20164)
OAK RIVER REHABILITATION
3300 Franklin St, Anderson (96007-3279)
PHONE...................530 365-0025
Andy Tanner, *Manager*
Krista Brown, *Executive*
Dan Funk, *Administration*
David Terry, *Administration*
EMP: 150
SQ FT: 3,000
SALES: 19.6MM **Privately Held**
SIC: 8051 Convalescent home with continuous nursing care

(P-20165)
OAKDALE HEIGHTS SENIOR LIVING
3209 Brookside Dr, Bakersfield
(93311-3459)
PHONE...................661 663-9671
Mike Laudon, *President*
EMP: 50
SALES (est): 1.4MM **Privately Held**
SIC: 8051 Skilled nursing care facilities

(P-20166)
OAKHURST SKILLED NURSING WELLN
Also Called: OAKHURST HEALTHCARE & WELLNESS
40131 Highway 49, Oakhurst (93644-9560)
PHONE...................559 683-2244
Stepan Sarmazian, *Administration*
EMP: 99
SALES: 5.6MM **Privately Held**
SIC: 8051 Mental retardation hospital

(P-20167)
OAKLAND HEALTHCARE & WELLNESS
Also Called: Akland Healthcare Wellness Ctr
3030 Webster St, Oakland (94609-3411)
PHONE...................323 330-6572
Sol Majer, *Mng Member*
EMP: 131
SQ FT: 20,000
SALES: 427.9K **Privately Held**
SIC: 8051 Convalescent home with continuous nursing care

(P-20168)
OCADIAN CARE CENTERS LLC
Also Called: Northern Cal Rehabilitation
2801 Eureka Way, Redding (96001-0222)
PHONE...................530 246-9000
Chris Jones, *Exec Dir*
Jody Carter, *Radiology Dir*
Kevin Rainsford, *Director*
Debbie Wiechman, *Director*
EMP: 250
SALES (corp-wide): 4.8MM **Privately Held**
WEB: www.ocadian.com
SIC: 8051 5912 8069 Skilled nursing care facilities; drug stores & proprietary stores; specialty hospitals, except psychiatric
PA: Ocadian Care Centers, Llc
104 Main St
Belvedere Tiburon CA 94920
415 789-5427

(P-20169)
OCADIAN CARE CENTERS LLC
Also Called: Medical Hill Rehabilitation
475 29th St, Oakland (94609-3510)
PHONE...................510 832-3222
Robert G Peirce, *President*
EMP: 100
SALES (corp-wide): 4.8MM **Privately Held**
WEB: www.ocadian.com
SIC: 8051 Convalescent home with continuous nursing care
PA: Ocadian Care Centers, Llc
104 Main St
Belvedere Tiburon CA 94920
415 789-5427

(P-20170)
OCADIAN CARE CENTERS LLC
Also Called: Greenbrea Care Center
1220 S Eliseo Dr, Greenbrae (94904-2006)
PHONE...................415 461-9700
Susan Weaver, *Manager*
EMP: 75

SALES (corp-wide): 4.8MM **Privately Held**
WEB: www.ocadian.com
SIC: 8051 8069 8052 Skilled nursing care facilities; specialty hospitals, except psychiatric; intermediate care facilities
PA: Ocadian Care Centers, Llc
104 Main St
Belvedere Tiburon CA 94920
415 789-5427

(P-20171)
OCADIAN CARE CENTERS LLC
1550 Silveira Pkwy, San Rafael
(94903-4879)
PHONE...................415 499-1000
Linda Creekmoore, *Manager*
EMP: 90
SALES (corp-wide): 4.8MM **Privately Held**
WEB: www.ocadian.com
SIC: 8051 8361 Skilled nursing care facilities; residential care
PA: Ocadian Care Centers, Llc
104 Main St
Belvedere Tiburon CA 94920
415 789-5427

(P-20172)
OCADIAN CARE CENTERS LLC
Also Called: Homewood Care Center
75 N 13th St, San Jose (95112-3439)
PHONE...................408 295-2665
David Martinez, *Administration*
EMP: 50
SALES (corp-wide): 4.8MM **Privately Held**
WEB: www.ocadian.com
SIC: 8051 Skilled nursing care facilities
PA: Ocadian Care Centers, Llc
104 Main St
Belvedere Tiburon CA 94920
415 789-5427

(P-20173)
ODYSSEY HEALTHCARE INC
525 Cabrillo Park Dr # 150, Santa Ana
(92701-5017)
PHONE...................714 245-7420
EMP: 52
SALES (corp-wide): 6B **Privately Held**
SIC: 8051
HQ: Odyssey Healthcare, Inc.
7801 Mesquite Bend Dr # 105
Irving TX 75063

(P-20174)
ODYSSEY HEALTHCARE INC
1500 E Hamilton Ave # 212, Campbell
(95008-0809)
PHONE...................408 626-4868
Elaine Fritz, *Principal*
EMP: 52
SALES (corp-wide): 1.5B **Privately Held**
SIC: 8051 Extended care facility
HQ: Odyssey Healthcare, Inc.
7801 Mesquite Bend Dr # 105
Irving TX 75063

(P-20175)
OLEANDER HOLDINGS LLC
Also Called: Sacramento Post-Acute
5255 Hemlock St, Sacramento
(95841-3017)
PHONE...................916 331-4590
James Huish,
Rita Brown, *Records Dir*
David Terry, *Administration*
Myrna De Guzman, *Controller*
Nick Anderson,
EMP: 99
SALES (est): 1.5MM **Privately Held**
SIC: 8051 Convalescent home with continuous nursing care

(P-20176)
ORANGE HEALTHCARE & WELLNESS
920 W La Veta Ave, Orange (92868-4302)
PHONE...................714 633-3568
Jonathan Weiss,
Slusser Kathy, *Human Resources*
Sharrod Brooks,
Linda Mendoza, *Social Worker*

Maricris Guray, *Director*
EMP: 110
SALES (est): 6.5MM **Privately Held**
SIC: 8051 Skilled nursing care facilities

(P-20177)
ORCHARD - POST ACUTE CARE CTR
12385 Washington Blvd, Whittier
(90606-2502)
PHONE...................562 693-7701
Rich Jorgensen, *Principal*
EMP: 1674
SALES: 15.6MM
SALES (corp-wide): 2B **Publicly Held**
SIC: 8051 Convalescent home with continuous nursing care
PA: The Ensign Group Inc
27101 Puerta Real Ste 450
Mission Viejo CA 92691
949 487-9500

(P-20178)
OUR LADY OF FATIMA VILLA INC
20400 Srtoga Los Gatos Rd, Saratoga
(95070-5997)
PHONE...................408 741-2950
Bella Mahoney, *Administration*
EMP: 90
SQ FT: 45,123
SALES: 12.5MM **Privately Held**
WEB: www.fatimavilla.org
SIC: 8051 Skilled nursing care facilities

(P-20179)
OXNARD MANOR HEALTHCARE CTR LP
1400 W Gonzales Rd, Oxnard
(93036-3392)
PHONE...................805 983-0324
Steven Rieder, *Ltd Ptnr*
Carlo Oleta, *Records Dir*
Sharrod Brooks, *Partner*
Bertie Krieger, *Partner*
Cassy Clayton, *Social Dir*
EMP: 99
SALES: 10.1MM **Privately Held**
SIC: 8051 Skilled nursing care facilities

(P-20180)
P R N CONVALESCENT HOSPITAL
Also Called: HIGH VALLEY LODGE
7912 Topley Ln, Sunland (91040-3336)
PHONE...................818 352-3158
Pauline Albert, *President*
Luis Albert Jr, *Vice Pres*
EMP: 54
SQ FT: 11,712
SALES: 3.7MM **Privately Held**
SIC: 8051 Skilled nursing care facilities

(P-20181)
PACIFIC REHABILITATION & WEL
2211 Harrison Ave, Eureka (95501-3214)
PHONE...................707 443-9767
Sharrod Brooks, *Senior VP*
EMP: 65 **EST:** 2011
SQ FT: 20,000
SALES: 6.1MM **Privately Held**
SIC: 8051 8322 Mental retardation hospital; rehabilitation services

(P-20182)
PACIFICA CARE CENTER
Also Called: Pacifica Nursing & Rehab Ctr
385 Esplanade Ave, Pacifica (94044-1882)
PHONE...................650 355-5622
Jacob Beaman, *Administration*
Elizabeth De Guzman, *Records Dir*
Filipina Atienza, *Director*
EMP: 150
SALES: 17MM **Privately Held**
WEB: www.pacifica-rehab.com
SIC: 8051 Convalescent home with continuous nursing care

(P-20183)
PACIFICA LINDA MAR INC
Also Called: Linda Mar Care Center
751 San Pedro Terrace Rd, Pacifica
(94044-4101)
PHONE...................650 359-4800

David Mahrt, *Administration*
Carmen Paz, *Director*
EMP: 85
SQ FT: 10,000
SALES: 5.8MM **Privately Held**
WEB: www.lawgate.byu.edu
SIC: 8051 Convalescent home with contin-
uous nursing care

(P-20184)
PALMCREST GRAND CARE CTR INC
3501 Cedar Ave, Long Beach
(90807-3809)
PHONE..................562 595-4551
William Nelson, *President*
EMP: 99
SALES (est): 5.7MM **Privately Held**
SIC: 8051 Skilled nursing care facilities

(P-20185)
PANORAMA MADOWS NURSING CTR LP
Also Called: Sun-Air Convalescent Hospital
14857 Roscoe Blvd, Panorama City
(91402-4617)
PHONE..................818 894-5707
Glen Bennett, *Administration*
Brenda Mandelbaum, *Treasurer*
Uri Mandelbaum, *Vice Pres*
EMP: 80 **EST:** 1969
SQ FT: 25,000
SALES (est): 5.4MM **Privately Held**
SIC: 8051 Skilled nursing care facilities

(P-20186)
PARA & PALLI INC
Also Called: LOS BANOS NURSING AND REHAB
931 Idaho Ave, Los Banos (93635-3405)
PHONE..................209 826-0790
Joseph Palli, *President*
▲ **EMP:** 65
SQ FT: 1,000
SALES: 3.7MM **Privately Held**
SIC: 8051 Skilled nursing care facilities

(P-20187)
PARADISE VLY HLTH CARE CTR INC
2575 E 8th St, National City (91950-2913)
PHONE..................619 470-6700
Kenneth Michael Funk, *President*
Jason Murray, *CEO*
Mark Hancock, *CFO*
Aaron Burrup, *Director*
EMP: 59
SALES (est): 5.7MM **Privately Held**
SIC: 8051 Skilled nursing care facilities

(P-20188)
PARK CNTL CARE RHBLITATION CTR
2100 Parkside Dr, Fremont (94536-5326)
PHONE..................510 797-5300
Anthony P Thekkek, *President*
Prema Thekkek, *Vice Pres*
EMP: 100
SALES (est): 4.2MM **Privately Held**
SIC: 8051 Skilled nursing care facilities

(P-20189)
PARKSIDE SPECIAL CARE CENTER
444 W Lexington Ave, El Cajon
(92020-4416)
PHONE..................619 442-7744
Edd Long, *Administration*
EMP: 75
SALES (est): 4.7MM **Privately Held**
SIC: 8051 Convalescent home with contin-
uous nursing care

(P-20190)
PARKVIEW JLIAN CNVLESCENT HOSP
1801 Julian Ave, Bakersfield (93304-6419)
PHONE..................661 831-9150
Ligia Denham, *Vice Pres*
Douglas Rice, *Administration*
EMP: 130
SQ FT: 8,000

SALES: 12.3MM **Privately Held**
WEB: www.parkviewjulian.com
SIC: 8051 Convalescent home with contin-
uous nursing care

(P-20191)
PASADENA HOSPITAL ASSN LTD
Also Called: Huntington Extended Care Ctr
716 S Fair Oaks Ave, Pasadena
(91105-2618)
PHONE..................626 397-3322
Ken Hoff, *Manager*
EMP: 75
SALES (corp-wide): 654.4MM **Privately Held**
WEB: www.huntingtonhospital.com
SIC: 8051 Skilled nursing care facilities
PA: Pasadena Hospital Association, Ltd.
100 W California Blvd
Pasadena CA 91105
626 397-5000

(P-20192)
PASADENA MADOWS NURSING CTR LP
150 Bellefontaine St, Pasadena
(91105-3102)
PHONE..................626 796-1103
Pnina Graff, *Partner*
EMP: 99
SALES (est): 5.6MM **Privately Held**
SIC: 8051 Skilled nursing care facilities

(P-20193)
PATER DIGINTAS INC
Also Called: Carmel Hills Care Center
23795 Holman Hwy, Monterey
(93940-5903)
PHONE..................831 624-1875
Robert Bowersox, *President*
Kim Bowersox, *CFO*
EMP: 90
SQ FT: 30,000
SALES: 11.5MM **Privately Held**
WEB: www.carmelhillscarecenter.com
SIC: 8051 Convalescent home with contin-
uous nursing care

(P-20194)
PINE GROVE HEALTHCARE
126 N San Gabriel Blvd, San Gabriel
(91775-2427)
PHONE..................626 285-3131
Sharrod Brooks, *Partner*
EMP: 99 **EST:** 2012
SALES (est): 3.9MM **Privately Held**
SIC: 8051 Mental retardation hospital

(P-20195)
PINERS NURSING HOME INC
Also Called: Piner's Medical Supply
1800 Pueblo Ave, NAPA (94558-4751)
PHONE..................707 224-7925
Gary Piner, *President*
Starr Piner, *Treasurer*
Malinda Meeker, *Controller*
Jeremy Piner, *Opers Mgr*
EMP: 65 **EST:** 1944
SQ FT: 20,000
SALES (est): 5.2MM **Privately Held**
SIC: 8051 4119 5999 Convalescent home
with continuous nursing care; ambulance
service; medical apparatus & supplies

(P-20196)
PITTSBURG CARE CENTER LTD
535 School St, Pittsburg (94565-3937)
PHONE..................925 432-3831
Abby Tiller, *Owner*
EMP: 50
SQ FT: 20,000
SALES (est): 2.2MM **Privately Held**
SIC: 8051 Extended care facility

(P-20197)
PITTSBURG SKILLED NURSING
535 School St, Pittsburg (94565-3937)
PHONE..................925 808-6540
Allen Leung, *Admin Sec*
EMP: 67
SQ FT: 12,140
SALES (est): 1.3MM **Privately Held**
SIC: 8051 Skilled nursing care facilities

(P-20198)
PLEASANT CARE OF VISTA
247 E Bobier Dr, Vista (92084-3026)
PHONE..................760 945-3033
Thomas Delucia, *Administration*
Diane Thibodeau, *Administration*
EMP: 180
SALES (est): 5.1MM **Privately Held**
SIC: 8051 Skilled nursing care facilities

(P-20199)
PLOTT MANAGEMENT CO
Also Called: Plott Family Home Care
264 E 18th St, San Bernardino
(92404-4708)
PHONE..................909 883-0288
EMP: 88
SALES (est): 3.6MM **Privately Held**
SIC: 8051

(P-20200)
PLUM HEALTHCARE GROUP LLC (PA)
100 E San Marcos Blvd # 200, San Marcos
(92069-2987)
PHONE..................760 471-0388
Toby Tilford, *Principal*
Rick Burke, *Creative Dir*
Ross Shutt, *Finance Mgr*
Myrna De Guzman, *Controller*
Renee Pugh, *Controller*
EMP: 100
SALES (est): 40.3MM **Privately Held**
SIC: 8051 Skilled nursing care facilities

(P-20201)
PLUM HEALTHCARE GROUP LLC
Also Called: White Blossom Care Center
1990 Fruitdale Ave, San Jose
(95128-2709)
PHONE..................408 998-8447
Mark Lamb, *Manager*
Virend Prasad, *Food Svc Dir*
Jose Iniguez, *Director*
EMP: 100
SALES (corp-wide): 40.3MM **Privately Held**
SIC: 8051 Skilled nursing care facilities
PA: Plum Healthcare Group, Llc
100 E San Marcos Blvd # 200
San Marcos CA 92069
760 471-0388

(P-20202)
PLUM HEALTHCARE GROUP LLC
Also Called: Cottonwood Cyn Healthcare Ctr
1391 E Madison Ave, El Cajon
(92021-8568)
PHONE..................619 873-2500
Leticia Guerrero, *Business Mgr*
Linell Serquina, *Records Dir*
Liz Contreras, *Human Res Dir*
EMP: 120
SALES (corp-wide): 40.3MM **Privately Held**
SIC: 8051 8059 Skilled nursing care facili-
ties; nursing home, except skilled & inter-
mediate care facility
PA: Plum Healthcare Group, Llc
100 E San Marcos Blvd # 200
San Marcos CA 92069
760 471-0388

(P-20203)
POINT LOMA CONVALESCENT HOSP
3202 Duke St, San Diego (92110-5401)
PHONE..................619 224-4141
Samuel Horowitz, *Partner*
Joseph Fisch, *General Ptnr*
Reena Horowitz, *General Ptnr*
J Axelrod, *Ltd Ptnr*
B Crow, *Ltd Ptnr*
EMP: 160
SQ FT: 25,402
SALES: 12.4MM **Privately Held**
WEB: www.pointlomarehab.com
SIC: 8051 Convalescent home with contin-
uous nursing care

(P-20204)
POINT LOMA RHBLITATION CTR LLC
Also Called: Point Loma Post Acute Care Ctr
3202 Duke St, San Diego (92110-5401)
PHONE..................619 224-4141
Guy Reggev,
Luchie Diwa, *Manager*
EMP: 130
SQ FT: 30,895
SALES (est): 5.2MM **Privately Held**
SIC: 8051 Skilled nursing care facilities

(P-20205)
POMERADO OPERATIONS LLC
Also Called: Boulder Creek Post Acute
12696 Monte Vista Rd, Poway
(92064-2500)
PHONE..................858 487-6242
Covey Christensen, *CEO*
James Gamett, *President*
Leland Bruce, *COO*
Travis Greenwood, *CFO*
EMP: 99
SALES (est): 1.1MM **Privately Held**
SIC: 8051 Convalescent home with contin-
uous nursing care

(P-20206)
QUALITY LONG TERM CARE NEV INC
Also Called: Eineridge Care Center
14122 Hubbard St, Sylmar (91342-4712)
PHONE..................818 361-0191
Scott Dale, *Branch Mgr*
EMP: 65 **Privately Held**
SIC: 8051 Skilled nursing care facilities
PA: Quality Long Term Care Of Nevada,
Inc.
2800 W Sahara Ave
Las Vegas NV 89102

(P-20207)
R FELLEN INC
Also Called: Sunnyside Convalescent Hosp
2939 S Peach Ave, Fresno (93725-9302)
PHONE..................559 233-6248
Michael Fellen, *President*
Steven Fellen, *Vice Pres*
EMP: 95
SQ FT: 10,000
SALES (est): 7MM **Privately Held**
SIC: 8051 Convalescent home with contin-
uous nursing care

(P-20208)
RAMONA CARE CENTER INC
Also Called: Ramona Nrsing Rhbilitation Ctr
11900 Ramona Blvd, El Monte
(91732-2314)
PHONE..................626 442-5721
John Sorensen, *Vice Pres*
Jan Stine, *Administration*
Sheila Severo, *Phys Thrpy Dir*
EMP: 140
SQ FT: 35,000
SALES: 16.5MM **Privately Held**
SIC: 8051 Convalescent home with contin-
uous nursing care

(P-20209)
RAZAVI CORPORATION
Also Called: Hilldale Habilitation Center
7979 La Mesa Blvd, La Mesa
(91942-5565)
PHONE..................619 465-8010
Darius Razavi, *President*
Maria Razavi, *Vice Pres*
▲ **EMP:** 60
SQ FT: 20,080
SALES: 2MM **Privately Held**
SIC: 8051 Convalescent home with contin-
uous nursing care

(P-20210)
REBECCA TERLEY
Also Called: Sunbrdge Care Ctr - Bellflower
9028 Rose St, Bellflower (90706-6418)
PHONE..................562 925-4252
Andrew Ashton, *Exec Dir*
EMP: 53
SALES (est): 966.2K **Privately Held**
SIC: 8051 Skilled nursing care facilities

(P-20211)
RECHE CYN RHBLITATION HLTH CTR
Also Called: Reche Cyn Regional Rehab Ctr
1350 Reche Canyon Rd, Colton
(92324-9528)
PHONE...............................909 370-4411
Fred Frank, *Administration*
Benjamin Atkins, *CEO*
EMP: 350
SALES: 25.9MM **Privately Held**
SIC: 8051 Convalescent home with continuous nursing care

(P-20212)
REGENCY CENTERS LP
40 Main St, Vista (92083-5831)
PHONE...............................760 724-9795
Darrell Musick, *Principal*
EMP: 507
SALES (est): 63.4K **Publicly Held**
WEB: www.regencycenters.com
SIC: 8051 Skilled nursing care facilities
HQ: Regency Centers Texas Llc
1 Independent Dr Ste 102
Jacksonville FL 32202
904 598-7000

(P-20213)
REGENCY OAKS CARE CENTER
3850 E Esther St, Long Beach
(90804-2009)
PHONE...............................562 498-3368
Vince Hambright, *President*
Lori Johnson, *Manager*
EMP: 110
SALES (est): 5.3MM **Privately Held**
SIC: 8051 Convalescent home with continuous nursing care

(P-20214)
REHABLTION CNTRE OF BVRLY HLLS
580 S San Vicente Blvd, Los Angeles
(90048-4621)
PHONE...............................323 782-1500
Eldon Teper, *President*
EMP: 200
SALES (est): 14.1MM **Privately Held**
SIC: 8051 Convalescent home with continuous nursing care

(P-20215)
RIVER BEND HOLDINGS LLC
Also Called: River Bend Nursing Center
2215 Oakmont Way, West Sacramento
(95691-3022)
PHONE...............................916 371-1890
Nell Stamm,
Bryan Boeher,
Richard Martin,
EMP: 153
SQ FT: 34,000
SALES (est): 3.9MM **Privately Held**
WEB: www.somersetnursingcenter.com
SIC: 8051 Convalescent home with continuous nursing care

(P-20216)
RIVERA SANITARIUM INC
Also Called: Colonial Gardens Nursing Home
7246 Rosemead Blvd, Pico Rivera
(90660-4010)
P.O. Box 2098 (90662-2098)
PHONE...............................562 949-2591
Elizabeth Stephens, *President*
Kent Stephens, *Administration*
EMP: 86
SQ FT: 30,000
SALES (est): 4.8MM **Privately Held**
SIC: 8051 Convalescent home with continuous nursing care

(P-20217)
RIVERSIDE CARE INC
Also Called: VALENCIA GARDENS HEALTH CARE CENTER
4301 Caroline Ct, Riverside (92506-2902)
PHONE...............................951 683-7111
Ted Holt, *President*
Spencer E Olsen, *Treasurer*
Jenny Ortiz, *Office Mgr*
EMP: 130

SALES: 6.9MM
SALES (corp-wide): 62.4MM **Privately Held**
SIC: 8051 Convalescent home with continuous nursing care
PA: North American Client Services, Inc.
5150 E A Palma Ave 206
Anaheim CA 92807
949 240-2423

(P-20218)
RIVERSIDE EQUITIES LLC
Also Called: MISSION CARE CENTER
8487 Magnolia Ave, Riverside
(92504-3222)
PHONE...............................951 688-2222
Frank Johnson, *CEO*
Irving Bauman, *COO*
Carey Van Boxtel, *Administration*
EMP: 93
SALES: 7.7MM **Privately Held**
SIC: 8051 Mental retardation hospital

(P-20219)
RIVERSIDE HEALTH CARE CORP
1090 Rio Ln, Sacramento (95822-1706)
PHONE...............................916 446-2506
Larry Meyer, *Administration*
EMP: 65
SALES (corp-wide): 8.4MM **Privately Held**
SIC: 8051 Skilled nursing care facilities
PA: Riverside Health Care Corporation
1469 Humboldt Rd Ste 175
Chico CA 95928
530 897-5100

(P-20220)
RIVERSIDE SANITARIUM LLC
Also Called: Riverside Bhvral Heathcare Ctr
4580 Palm Ave, Riverside (92501-3950)
PHONE...............................951 684-7701
Ira Smedra,
Jacob Wintner,
EMP: 99
SALES (est): 2.5MM **Privately Held**
SIC: 8051 Skilled nursing care facilities

(P-20221)
RIVIERA NURSING & CONVA
Also Called: Riviera Health Care Center
8203 Telegraph Rd, Pico Rivera
(90660-4905)
PHONE...............................562 806-2576
Morris Weiss, *President*
Bessie Weiss, *Vice Pres*
Dov Jacobs, *Administration*
Gerhard Najera, *Manager*
EMP: 118
SQ FT: 60,000
SALES (est): 6.3MM **Privately Held**
WEB: www.rivierahealthcare.com
SIC: 8051 8059 Convalescent home with continuous nursing care; convalescent home

(P-20222)
ROWLAND CONVALESCENT HOSP INC
Also Called: ROWLAND, THE
330 W Rowland St, Covina (91723-2941)
PHONE...............................626 967-2741
Anthony Kalomas, *President*
EMP: 100
SQ FT: 30,000
SALES: 8.3MM **Privately Held**
SIC: 8051 Convalescent home with continuous nursing care

(P-20223)
ROYAL CONVALESCENT HOSPITAL
320 Cattle Call Dr, Brawley (92227-3198)
P.O. Box 1380 (92227-1380)
PHONE...............................760 344-5431
Tobias Friedman, *President*
Ida Friedman, *Admin Sec*
Fred Friedman, *Administration*
Tobias Friedman, *Agent*
EMP: 80
SQ FT: 25,000
SALES (est): 1.6MM **Privately Held**
SIC: 8051 Skilled nursing care facilities

(P-20224)
ROYAL TERRACE HEALTHCARE
1340 Highland Ave, Duarte (91010-2520)
PHONE...............................626 256-4654
Eloisa Heiser, *Director*
Alma Hechanova, *Director*
Anabell Reyes, *Director*
EMP: 60 **EST:** 2003
SALES (est): 1.7MM **Privately Held**
SIC: 8051 Skilled nursing care facilities

(P-20225)
RRT ENTERPRISES LP
855 N Fairfax Ave, Los Angeles
(90046-7207)
PHONE...............................323 653-1521
Stephen Reissman, *Branch Mgr*
EMP: 344
SALES (corp-wide): 18.2MM **Privately Held**
SIC: 8051 Skilled nursing care facilities
PA: Rrt Enterprises Lp
3966 Marcasel Ave
Los Angeles CA 90066
310 397-2372

(P-20226)
S L H C C INC
Also Called: Saylor Lane Healthcare Center
3500 Folsom Blvd, Sacramento
(95816-6615)
PHONE...............................916 457-6521
Dave Hilburn, *President*
EMP: 50
SALES (est): 2.6MM **Privately Held**
SIC: 8051 Convalescent home with continuous nursing care

(P-20227)
S&F MANAGEMENT COMPANY INC
2030 Evergreen Ave, Modesto
(95350-3785)
PHONE...............................209 846-9744
EMP: 904 **Privately Held**
SIC: 8051 Convalescent home with continuous nursing care
PA: S&F Management Company, Llc
9200 W Sunset Blvd # 700
West Hollywood CA 90069

(P-20228)
S&F MANAGEMENT COMPANY LLC
442 E Hampton St, Stockton (95204-5519)
PHONE...............................209 466-0456
EMP: 2598 **Privately Held**
SIC: 8051 Skilled nursing care facilities
PA: S&F Management Company, Llc
9200 W Sunset Blvd # 700
West Hollywood CA 90069

(P-20229)
S&F MANAGEMENT COMPANY LLC (PA)
9200 W Sunset Blvd # 700, West Hollywood (90069-3502)
PHONE...............................310 385-1090
Lee C Samson,
EMP: 118
SALES (est): 25.8MM **Privately Held**
WEB: www.snfmgt.com
SIC: 8051 Convalescent home with continuous nursing care

(P-20230)
SACRAMENTO OPERATING CO LP
Also Called: Double Tree Past Acute
7400 24th St, Sacramento (95822-5350)
PHONE...............................916 422-4825
Kenneth Tabler, *Partner*
Cynthia Mitchell,
EMP: 120
SALES (est): 2.7MM **Privately Held**
SIC: 8051 Extended care facility

(P-20231)
SAINT CLAIRES NURSING CTR LLC
6248 66th Ave, Sacramento (95823-2733)
PHONE...............................916 392-4440

Kathryn J Hill, *President*
Michael Maderas, *Administration*
EMP: 124
SALES: 6.5MM **Privately Held**
SIC: 8051 Skilled nursing care facilities

(P-20232)
SAN DIEGO HEBREW HOMES (PA)
Also Called: Leichtag Assisted Living
211 Saxony Rd, Encinitas (92024-2791)
PHONE...............................760 942-2695
Yehudi Gaffen, *Chairman*
Pam Ferris, *President*
Robin Weiner, *CFO*
Brad Blose, *Vice Pres*
Kimberly Fuson, *Vice Pres*
EMP: 180
SQ FT: 219,000
SALES: 20.6MM **Privately Held**
WEB: www.seacrestvillage.com
SIC: 8051 8059 6513 Skilled nursing care facilities; rest home, with health care; retirement hotel operation

(P-20233)
SAN JOSES HEALTHCARE & WELL
Also Called: San Jose Hlthcare Wellness Ctr
75 N 13th St, San Jose (95112-3439)
PHONE...............................408 295-2665
Sole Majer, *Mng Member*
Aaron Robins,
EMP: 90
SALES (est): 6MM **Privately Held**
SIC: 8051 Convalescent home with continuous nursing care

(P-20234)
SAN LEANDRO HEALTHCARE CENTER
368 Juana Ave, San Leandro (94577-4811)
PHONE...............................510 357-4015
Pat Poddatoori, *President*
Laslo Hites, *Director*
EMP: 70
SALES (est): 2.8MM **Privately Held**
SIC: 8051 Convalescent home with continuous nursing care

(P-20235)
SAN MARCOS OPERATING CO LP
Also Called: Village Square Healthcare Ctr
1586 W Square Marcos Blvd, San Marcos
(92078)
PHONE...............................760 471-2986
Kristina Kuizon,
EMP: 85
SALES (est): 300.8K **Privately Held**
SIC: 8051 Skilled nursing care facilities

(P-20236)
SAN MATEO HEALTHCARE & WELLNES
Also Called: Burlingame Long Term Care
1100 Trousdale Dr, Burlingame
(94010-3207)
PHONE...............................650 692-3758
Sharrod Brooks,
Bryan Guillermo, *Administration*
EMP: 99
SALES (est): 6.4MM **Privately Held**
SIC: 8051 Mental retardation hospital

(P-20237)
SAN PABLO HEALTHCARE
13328 San Pablo Ave, San Pablo
(94806-3902)
PHONE...............................510 235-3720
Suzette Cheatham, *Mng Member*
EMP: 130
SALES: 11.7MM **Privately Held**
SIC: 8051 Skilled nursing care facilities

(P-20238)
SAN PEDRO CONVALESCENT HM INC
Also Called: Los Palos Convalescent Hosp
1430 W 6th St, San Pedro (90732-3503)
PHONE...............................310 832-6431
Celia Valdomar, *President*
Ruth Angeles, *Office Mgr*
Christine Yim, *Hlthcr Dir*

PRODUCTS & SVCS

Nestor Alegre, *Director*
EMP: 90
SQ FT: 10,000
SALES (est): 5.6MM **Privately Held**
SIC: 8051 Convalescent home with continuous nursing care

(P-20239)
SANDHURST CONVALES GRP LTD A
Also Called: Windsor Garden Conv Ctr Hwthrn
13922 Cerise Ave, Hawthorne (90250-8688)
PHONE..................................310 675-3304
Anne Josafat, *Principal*
EMP: 50
SALES (est): 990K **Privately Held**
SIC: 8051 Convalescent home with continuous nursing care

(P-20240)
SANHYD INC
Also Called: Kyakamena Sklled Nrsing Fcilty
2131 Carleton St, Berkeley (94704-3213)
PHONE..................................510 843-2131
Pat Poddatoori, *President*
EMP: 52 **EST:** 1965
SQ FT: 15,000
SALES (est): 2.3MM **Privately Held**
SIC: 8051 Convalescent home with continuous nursing care

(P-20241)
SANTA ANITA CONVALESCENT HOSPI
5522 Gracewood Ave, Temple City (91780)
PHONE..................................626 579-0310
Miriam Weiss, *President*
Jacob Kasirer, *Vice Pres*
EMP: 150
SQ FT: 88,615
SALES (est): 4.8MM
SALES (corp-wide): 62.1MM **Privately Held**
WEB: www.goldenstatehealth.com
SIC: 8051 Skilled nursing care facilities
PA: Golden State Health Centers, Inc.
13347 Ventura Blvd
Sherman Oaks CA 91423
818 385-3200

(P-20242)
SANTA ROSAIDENCE OPCO LLC
Also Called: Santa Rosa Post Acute
4650 Hoen Ave, Santa Rosa (95405-9407)
PHONE..................................707 546-0471
Jason Murray, *Principal*
Mark Hancock, *Principal*
EMP: 135
SALES (est): 3.2MM **Privately Held**
SIC: 8051 Skilled nursing care facilities

(P-20243)
SCRIPPS HEALTH
122 Civic Center Dr # 101, Vista (92084-6040)
PHONE..................................760 806-9263
EMP: 251
SALES (corp-wide): 2.1B **Privately Held**
SIC: 8051 Skilled nursing care facilities
PA: Scripps Health
10140 Campus Point Dr Ax415
San Diego CA 92121
800 727-4777

(P-20244)
SCRIPPS HEALTH
Also Called: Scripps Shared Services
10790 Rancho Bernardo Rd, San Diego (92127-5705)
P.O. Box 85105 (92186-5105)
PHONE..................................858 657-4218
Vickie Tickel, *Director*
Spencer Alexander, *Analyst*
Diane Ogorman, *Nurse*
Daniel Kehl, *Director*
Gregory Bantigue, *Manager*
EMP: 150
SALES (corp-wide): 2.1B **Privately Held**
WEB: www.scripps.org
SIC: 8051 8082 Skilled nursing care facilities; home health care services

PA: Scripps Health
10140 Campus Point Dr Ax415
San Diego CA 92121
800 727-4777

(P-20245)
SEA BREEZE HEALTH CARE INC
Also Called: Beachside Nursing Center
7781 Garfield Ave, Huntington Beach (92648-2026)
PHONE..................................714 847-9671
Tim Paulson, *President*
Nathan Nguyen, *Case Mgmt Dir*
Nate Beck, *Administration*
Seth Braithwaite, *Administration*
ARI Corona, *Payroll Mgr*
EMP: 132
SQ FT: 14,895
SALES (est): 9.9MM
SALES (corp-wide): 62.4MM **Privately Held**
SIC: 8051 Convalescent home with continuous nursing care
PA: North American Client Services, Inc.
5150 E A Palma Ave 206
Anaheim CA 92807
949 240-2423

(P-20246)
SEACREST CONVALESCENT HOSP INC
1416 W 6th St, San Pedro (90732-3550)
PHONE..................................310 833-3526
Cecelia Valdomar, *President*
Cecelia D Valdomar, *President*
Joy Nacionales, *Admin Sec*
Pearl Wells, *QC Dir*
Chris Tui, *Director*
EMP: 70
SALES (est): 3.2MM **Privately Held**
SIC: 8051 Convalescent home with continuous nursing care

(P-20247)
SELA HEALTHCARE INC (PA)
Also Called: Holiday Manor Care Center
867 E 11th St, Upland (91786-4867)
PHONE..................................909 985-1981
Philip Weinberger, *CEO*
Marylynn Mahan, *CFO*
EMP: 140
SQ FT: 60,000
SALES (est): 8.5MM **Privately Held**
SIC: 8051 Skilled nursing care facilities

(P-20248)
SERRANO COVALESCENT HOSPITAL
5401 Fountain Ave, Los Angeles (90029-1006)
PHONE..................................323 465-2106
Lydia Cruz, *Manager*
EMP: 80
SALES (est): 1.5MM **Privately Held**
SIC: 8051 Skilled nursing care facilities

(P-20249)
SHADOW HLLS CNVLSCENT HOSP INC
10158 Sunland Blvd, Sunland (91040-1651)
PHONE..................................818 352-4438
Orlando Clarizio Jr, *President*
Dino Clarizio, *Treasurer*
Michale Clarizio, *Admin Sec*
EMP: 67
SQ FT: 13,000
SALES: 3.8MM **Privately Held**
SIC: 8051 Convalescent home with continuous nursing care

(P-20250)
SHADOWBROOK HEALTH CARE INC
1 Gilmore Ln, Oroville (95966-5147)
PHONE..................................530 534-1353
Sharon Jennings, *President*
EMP: 50
SQ FT: 10,100
SALES: 3.4MM
SALES (corp-wide): 8.4MM **Privately Held**
SIC: 8051 Skilled nursing care facilities

(P-20251)
SHARON CARE CENTER LLC
8167 W 3rd St, Los Angeles (90048-4314)
PHONE..................................323 655-2023
Isaac Shabat, *Exec Dir*
EMP: 108
SALES (est): 1.6MM **Publicly Held**
WEB: www.parkviewnursing.net
SIC: 8051 8059 Skilled nursing care facilities; convalescent home
HQ: Genesis Healthcare Corporation
101 E State St
Kennett Square PA 19348
610 444-6350

(P-20252)
SHARP HEALTHCARE
Also Called: Birch Ptrick Convalescent Cntr
751 Medical Center Ct, Chula Vista (91911-6617)
PHONE..................................858 499-2000
Lily Reyes, *Director*
Terry Chan, *Pharmacist*
Erlynda Borja, *Director*
Laurie Godfrey, *Manager*
Katherine Muth, *Manager*
EMP: 140
SALES (corp-wide): 3.4B **Privately Held**
SIC: 8051 Skilled nursing care facilities
PA: Sharp Healthcare
8695 Spectrum Center Blvd
San Diego CA 92123
858 499-4000

(P-20253)
SHATTUCK HEALTH CARE INC
Also Called: Elmwood Care Center
2829 Shattuck Ave, Berkeley (94705-1037)
PHONE..................................510 665-2800
Pat Podatorri, *President*
Terry McGregor, *Vice Pres*
EMP: 97
SQ FT: 34,404
SALES (est): 2.9MM **Privately Held**
SIC: 8051 Convalescent home with continuous nursing care

(P-20254)
SHERWOOD OAKS ENTERPRISES
Also Called: Sherwood Oaks Health Center
130 Dana St, Fort Bragg (95437-4506)
PHONE..................................707 964-6333
Melanie Reding, *President*
Joe Reding, *Corp Secy*
EMP: 90 **EST:** 1975
SQ FT: 19,000
SALES (est): 5.1MM **Privately Held**
SIC: 8051 Convalescent home with continuous nursing care

(P-20255)
SHIELDS NURSING CENTERS INC (PA)
606 Alfred Nobel Dr, Hercules (94547-1834)
PHONE..................................510 724-9911
William Shields Jr, *CEO*
EMP: 150
SQ FT: 6,100
SALES (est): 11.1MM **Privately Held**
WEB: www.shieldsnursingcenters.com
SIC: 8051 Convalescent home with continuous nursing care

(P-20256)
SHIELDS NURSING CENTERS INC
3230 Carlson Blvd, El Cerrito (94530-3907)
PHONE..................................510 525-3212
William Shields, *Administration*
EMP: 58
SALES (corp-wide): 11.1MM **Privately Held**
WEB: www.shieldsnursingcenters.com
SIC: 8051 Convalescent home with continuous nursing care

(P-20257)
SIERRA CARE REHABILITATION CTR
310 Oak Ridge Dr, Roseville (95661-3420)
PHONE..................................916 782-3188
Alice Mills, *Principal*
Rachelle McCoure, *Admin Asst*
EMP: 90
SALES (est): 1MM **Privately Held**
SIC: 8051 Skilled nursing care facilities

(P-20258)
SIERRA VIEW CARE HOLDINGS LLC
Also Called: Sierra View Care Center
14318 Ohio St, Baldwin Park (91706-2553)
PHONE..................................626 960-1971
Jordan Fishman, *Mng Member*
Irving Bauman, *President*
Matheson Chambers, *Principal*
David Johnson, *Principal*
Eli Marmur, *Principal*
EMP: 99
SALES (est): 8MM **Privately Held**
SIC: 8051 Skilled nursing care facilities

(P-20259)
SIERRA VIEW HOMES
Also Called: SIERRA VIEW HOMES RESIDENTIAL
1155 E Springfield Ave, Reedley (93654-3225)
PHONE..................................559 637-2256
Vito Genna, *Exec Dir*
Janice Gray, *Office Mgr*
Kecia Friesen, *Admin Asst*
Crystal Rogalsky, *Marketing Staff*
Estella Pena, *Nursing Dir*
EMP: 140 **EST:** 1960
SQ FT: 63,600
SALES: 9.1MM **Privately Held**
WEB: www.sierraview.org
SIC: 8051 8059 6513 Skilled nursing care facilities; personal care home, with health care; apartment hotel operation

(P-20260)
SILVERADO SENIOR LIVING INC
Also Called: Beach Cities Memory Care Cmnty
514 N Prospect Ave # 120, Redondo Beach (90277-3036)
PHONE..................................424 257-6418
Dorothy Washington, *Comms Dir*
Sammy Hassan, *Administration*
EMP: 87
SALES (corp-wide): 180.3MM **Privately Held**
SIC: 8051 Skilled nursing care facilities
PA: Senior Silverado Living Inc
6400 Oak Cyn Ste 200
Irvine CA 92618
949 240-7200

(P-20261)
SILVERSCREEN HEALTHCARE INC
Also Called: Golden State Colonial Convales
10830 Oxnard St, North Hollywood (91606-5021)
PHONE..................................818 763-8247
Philip Weinberger, *President*
Marylynn Mahan, *CFO*
Klara Elekes, *Admin Sec*
EMP: 58 **EST:** 1964
SQ FT: 16,477
SALES (est): 2.2MM **Privately Held**
SIC: 8051 8059 Convalescent home with continuous nursing care; convalescent home

(P-20262)
SKILLED HEALTHCARE LLC (DH)
27442 Portola Pkwy # 200, Foothill Ranch (92610-2822)
PHONE..................................949 282-5800
George V Hager Jr,
Richard Edwards, *Vice Pres*
EMP: 58

PA: Riverside Health Care Corporation
1469 Humboldt Rd Ste 175
Chico CA 95928
530 897-5100

PA: Shields Nursing Centers, Inc.
606 Alfred Nobel Dr
Hercules CA 94547
510 724-9911

SQ FT: 22,000
SALES (est): 116MM **Publicly Held**
WEB: www.skilledhealthcare.com
SIC: **8051** 6513 5122 Skilled nursing care facilities; retirement hotel operation; drugs, proprietaries & sundries

(P-20263)

SKILLED HEALTHCARE LLC

Also Called: Brier Oak On Sunset Rehab
5154 W Sunset Blvd, Los Angeles
(90027-5708)
PHONE....................323 663-3951
Douglas Lehnhoff, *Exec Dir*
EMP: 100 **Publicly Held**
WEB: www.skilledhealthcare.com
SIC: **8051** 8049 8059 Skilled nursing care facilities; physical therapist; personal care home, with health care
HQ: Skilled Healthcare, Llc
27442 Portola Pkwy # 200
Foothill Ranch CA 92610
949 282-5800

(P-20264)

SKYLINE HEALTHCARE & WELLNESS

Also Called: Skyline Healthcare Center
3032 Rowena Ave, Los Angeles
(90039-2005)
PHONE....................323 665-1185
Bernon Aguilar, *Administration*
Sharrod Brooks,
EMP: 99
SALES (est): 4.8MM **Privately Held**
SIC: **8051** Mental retardation hospital

(P-20265)

SLCH INC (PA)

Also Called: Sophia Lyn Convalescent Hosp
1920 N Fair Oaks Ave, Pasadena
(91103-1623)
PHONE....................626 798-0558
Phillip Rosales, *President*
Lolita Asero, *Administration*
EMP: 50
SQ FT: 16,757
SALES: 3.2MM **Privately Held**
WEB: www.slch.com
SIC: **8051** Extended care facility

(P-20266)

SOLEDAD CMNTY HLTH CARE DST

Also Called: Soledad Medical Group
612 Main St, Soledad (93960-2533)
PHONE....................831 678-2462
Steven Pritt, *CEO*
Ralph Sarmento, *President*
Rosemary Guidotti, *Admin Sec*
Jack Franscioni, *Director*
EMP: 80
SALES: 30.2K **Privately Held**
WEB: www.schcd.com
SIC: **8051** Skilled nursing care facilities

(P-20267)

SOUTH COAST HEALTH WELLNESS

Also Called: Community Care On Palm
4768 Palm Ave, Riverside (92501-4012)
PHONE....................951 686-9001
Cheryl B Jumonville, *President*
Tony Hunter, *Administration*
Peter Anes, *Maint Spvr*
EMP: 50
SALES (est): 388K **Privately Held**
SIC: **8051** Skilled nursing care facilities

(P-20268)

SPRING VALLEY POST ACUTE LLC

14973 Hesperia Rd, Victorville
(92395-3923)
PHONE....................760 245-6477
David Johnson, *Mng Member*
Matheson Chambers, *Mng Member*
Thomas Chambers, *Mng Member*
EMP: 200
SALES: 11.5MM **Privately Held**
SIC: **8051** Convalescent home with continuous nursing care

(P-20269)

SSC CARMICHAEL OPERATING CO LP

Also Called: SAVA SENIOR CARE
3630 Mission Ave, Carmichael
(95608-2933)
PHONE....................916 485-4793
Anne Gilles, *Administration*
Wayne M Sanner, *Partner*
EMP: 99
SALES: 12.2MM
SALES (corp-wide): 588.8MM **Privately Held**
SIC: **8051** Skilled nursing care facilities
PA: Savaseniorcare, Llc
1 Ravinia Dr Ste 1500
Atlanta GA 30346
770 829-5100

(P-20270)

SSC NEWPORT BEACH OPER CO LP

Also Called: Flagship Healthcare Center
466 Flagship Rd, Newport Beach
(92663-3635)
PHONE....................949 642-8044
Scott Harris, *Partner*
Wayne Sanner, *Partner*
Wynn Sims, *Partner*
Julio Saldago, *Director*
Annika Sanders, *Director*
EMP: 133
SQ FT: 21,903
SALES (est): 3.5MM **Privately Held**
SIC: **8051** Convalescent home with continuous nursing care

(P-20271)

SSC OAKLAND EXCELL OPER CO LP

Also Called: Excell Health Care Center
3025 High St, Oakland (94619-1807)
PHONE....................510 261-5200
Elma Conway, *Manager*
Wayne M Sanner,
EMP: 99
SALES (est): 1.2MM **Privately Held**
SIC: **8051** Skilled nursing care facilities

(P-20272)

SSC SAN JOSE OPERATING CO LP

Also Called: Courtyard Care Center
340 Northlake Dr, San Jose (95117-1251)
PHONE....................408 249-0344
Luz Bester, *Personnel Exec*
Wayne M Sanner,
Remedios B Tibayan, *Director*
EMP: 94
SALES (est): 6.3MM
SALES (corp-wide): 588.8MM **Privately Held**
SIC: **8051** Skilled nursing care facilities
PA: Savaseniorcare, Llc
1 Ravinia Dr Ste 1500
Atlanta GA 30346
770 829-5100

(P-20273)

ST LUKE HLTHCR & REHAB CTR LL

2321 Newburg Rd, Fortuna (95540-2815)
PHONE....................707 725-4467
Ted Chigaros,
EMP: 100
SALES: 1,000K **Privately Held**
SIC: **8051** Convalescent home with continuous nursing care

(P-20274)

ST MICHAEL CONVALESCENT HOSP

Also Called: Vintage Estates of Hayward
25919 Gading Rd, Hayward (94544-2798)
PHONE....................510 782-8424
Sally Rapp, *CEO*
Roland Rapp, *Treasurer*
Cheryl A Rapp, *Principal*
EMP: 99
SQ FT: 6,000
SALES (est): 2.4MM **Privately Held**
WEB: www.vintage-estates.com
SIC: **8051** Skilled nursing care facilities

(P-20275)

STANDARDBEARER INSUR CO LTD

27101 Puerta Real Ste 450, Mission Viejo
(92691-8566)
PHONE....................949 487-9500
EMP: 478
SALES (est): 682.9K
SALES (corp-wide): 2B **Publicly Held**
SIC: **8051** Skilled nursing care facilities
PA: The Ensign Group Inc
27101 Puerta Real Ste 450
Mission Viejo CA 92691
949 487-9500

(P-20276)

STJOHN GOD RTIREMENT CARE CTR

2468 S St Andrews Pl, Los Angeles
(90018-2042)
PHONE....................323 731-0641
Michael Bessimer, *Administration*
Jonathon Harris, *Human Res Dir*
Marinor Ifurung, *Human Res Dir*
Edemidia Vasquez, *Supervisor*
EMP: 200
SQ FT: 99,392
SALES (est): 16MM **Privately Held**
SIC: **8051** 8052 Skilled nursing care facilities; intermediate care facilities

(P-20277)

STONEBROOK CONVALESCENT CENTER

Also Called: Stonebrook Health Care Center
4367 Concord Blvd, Concord (94521-1100)
PHONE....................925 689-7457
James D Hightower, *President*
Glenna Buford, *Director*
EMP: 206
SQ FT: 44,000
SALES (est): 14.1MM **Privately Held**
WEB: www.healthmarkservices.com
SIC: **8051** Convalescent home with continuous nursing care
PA: Healthmark Services Inc
217 Lakewood Rd
Van Buren AR 72956
479 471-9797

(P-20278)

SUN HAVEN CARE INC

Also Called: Terrace View Care Center
201 E Bastanchury Rd, Fullerton
(92835-2604)
PHONE....................714 870-0060
John Sworenson, *CEO*
Brendon Bahl, *Vice Pres*
EMP: 60
SALES (est): 3MM **Privately Held**
SIC: **8051** Convalescent home with continuous nursing care

(P-20279)

SUN MAR MANAGEMENT SERVICES

8171 Magnolia Ave, Riverside
(92504-3409)
PHONE....................951 687-3842
Robert Ginn, *Administration*
EMP: 100
SALES (corp-wide): 50.5MM **Privately Held**
WEB: www.extendedcarehospital.com
SIC: **8051** Skilled nursing care facilities
PA: Sun Mar Management Services
3050 Saturn St Ste 201
Brea CA 92821
714 577-3880

(P-20280)

SUN VILLA INC

350 N Villa St, Porterville (93257-3211)
PHONE....................559 784-6644
David Green, *Administration*
Mark Mann, *Manager*
EMP: 120 EST: 1971
SQ FT: 50,000
SALES (est): 4.7MM **Privately Held**
SIC: **8051** Convalescent home with continuous nursing care

(P-20281)

SUNBRIDGE BRITTANY REHAB CENTR

Also Called: American River Care
3900 Garfield Ave, Carmichael
(95608-6647)
PHONE....................916 484-1393
Andrew Turner, *President*
Carly Migdal, *Social Dir*
Anne Butler, *Administration*
Sultan Yusufzai, *Director*
EMP: 120
SALES (est): 3.5MM **Publicly Held**
SIC: **8051** 8069 Skilled nursing care facilities; specialty hospitals, except psychiatric
HQ: Regency Health Services, Inc.
5100 Sun Ave Ne
Albuquerque NM 87109
505 821-3355

(P-20282)

SUNBRIDGE CARE ENTPS W INC

Also Called: Kingsburg Center
1101 Stroud Ave, Kingsburg (93631-1016)
PHONE....................559 897-5881
Ron Kennersly, *Manager*
J Richard Edwards, *Treasurer*
EMP: 100 **Publicly Held**
SIC: **8051** Skilled nursing care facilities
HQ: Sunbridge Care Enterprises West, Inc.
101 Sun Ave Ne
Albuquerque NM

(P-20283)

SUNBRIDGE CARE ENTPS W LLC

Also Called: KINGSBURG CENTER
1101 Stroud Ave, Kingsburg (93631-1016)
PHONE....................559 897-5881
Ron Kinnersly, *Administration*
EMP: 2002
SALES: 7.6MM **Publicly Held**
SIC: **8051** Skilled nursing care facilities
HQ: Genesis Healthcare Llc
101 E State St
Kennett Square PA 19348

(P-20284)

SUNBRIDGE HARBOR VIEW

Also Called: Harbor View Rehabilitation Ctr
490 W 14th St, Long Beach (90813-2943)
PHONE....................562 989-9907
Rick Matros, *President*
Wendy McLearie, *Administration*
EMP: 200
SALES (est): 4.6MM **Publicly Held**
SIC: **8051** 8361 Skilled nursing care facilities; residential care
HQ: Regency Health Services, Inc.
5100 Sun Ave Ne
Albuquerque NM 87109
505 821-3355

(P-20285)

SUNBRIDGE HEALTHCARE LLC

Also Called: Sunbridge Elmhaven Care Center
6940 Pacific Ave, Stockton (95207-2602)
PHONE....................209 477-4817
Mike Blaufus, *Administration*
Beth Clark, *Office Mgr*
Karen Smith, *Administration*
Richard Gonzales, *Facilities Dir*
Suzie Vargas, *Director*
EMP: 99 **Publicly Held**
SIC: **8051** Convalescent home with continuous nursing care
HQ: Sunbridge Healthcare, Llc
101 Sun Ave Ne
Albuquerque NM 87109
505 821-3355

(P-20286)

SUNNYSIDE RHBLTTION NRSING CTR

22617 S Vermont Ave, Torrance
(90502-2550)
PHONE....................310 320-4130
Judy Narloda, *President*
Jaime Deutsch, *Vice Pres*
Shane Dahl, *Administration*

EMP: 220
SQ FT: 35,000
SALES (est): 9.3MM **Privately Held**
SIC: 8051 8361 8069 8052 Convalescent home with continuous nursing care; residential care; specialty hospitals, except psychiatric; intermediate care facilities

(P-20287)
SUNNYVALE HEALTHCARE CENTER
Also Called: Sunnyvale Health Care
1291 S Bernardo Ave, Sunnyvale
(94087-2060)
PHONE..................................408 245-8070
Hermina Chavez, *CEO*
Maricel De Guzman, *Records Dir*
Vanessa Chavez, *Treasurer*
Mario Chavez, *Vice Pres*
John Chavez, *Admin Sec*
EMP: 75
SQ FT: 26,679
SALES (est): 4.2MM **Privately Held**
WEB: www.svhcc.com
SIC: 8051 Convalescent home with continuous nursing care

(P-20288)
SUNRISE OF PETALUMA
815 Wood Sorrel Dr, Petaluma
(94954-6857)
PHONE..................................707 776-2885
Erin Carlson, *Director*
EMP: 70
SALES (est): 1.5MM **Privately Held**
SIC: 8051 Skilled nursing care facilities

(P-20289)
SUNRISE SENIOR LIVING INC
Also Called: Sunrise At Alta Loma
9519 Baseline Rd, Rancho Cucamonga
(91730-1313)
PHONE..................................909 941-3001
Carol Lininger, *Exec Dir*
Luis Rodriquez, *Exec Dir*
Gloria Tafesh, *Marketing Staff*
Billy Davis, *Food Svc Dir*
Jenna Altshule, *Nursing Dir*
EMP: 60
SALES (corp-wide): 4.7B **Publicly Held**
WEB: www.sunrise.com
SIC: 8051 8322 Skilled nursing care facilities; senior citizens' center or association
HQ: Sunrise Senior Living, Llc
7902 Westpark Dr
Mc Lean VA 22102

(P-20290)
SUNRISE SENIOR LIVING INC
Also Called: Brighton Gardens of Sunrise
72201 Country Club Dr, Palm Desert
(92210)
PHONE..................................760 340-5999
Ernie Schaffer, *Director*
EMP: 58
SALES (corp-wide): 4.7B **Publicly Held**
WEB: www.sunrise.com
SIC: 8051 8361 Skilled nursing care facilities; residential care
HQ: Sunrise Senior Living, Llc
7902 Westpark Dr
Mc Lean VA 22102

(P-20291)
SUNRISE SENIOR LIVING INC
Also Called: Sunrise of Petaluma
815 Wood Sorrel Dr, Petaluma
(94954-6857)
PHONE..................................707 776-2885
Carla Sanchez, *Exec Dir*
EMP: 62
SALES (corp-wide): 4.7B **Publicly Held**
WEB: www.sunrise.com
SIC: 8051 8361 Skilled nursing care facilities; residential care
HQ: Sunrise Senior Living, Llc
7902 Westpark Dr
Mc Lean VA 22102

(P-20292)
SUNRISE SENIOR LIVING INC
Also Called: Sunrise Asssted Lving San Mteo
955 S El Camino Real, San Mateo
(94402-2346)
PHONE..................................650 558-8555
Andrew Smith, *Manager*
Vicki Boe, *Director*
EMP: 65
SALES (corp-wide): 4.7B **Publicly Held**
WEB: www.sunrise.com
SIC: 8051 8361 Skilled nursing care facilities; home for the aged
HQ: Sunrise Senior Living, Llc
7902 Westpark Dr
Mc Lean VA 22102

(P-20293)
SUNRISE SENIOR LIVING INC
3840 Lampson Ave, Seal Beach
(90740-2797)
PHONE..................................562 594-5788
Bonnie Christie, *Branch Mgr*
EMP: 58
SALES (corp-wide): 4.7B **Publicly Held**
WEB: www.sunrise.com
SIC: 8051 8361 Skilled nursing care facilities; residential care
HQ: Sunrise Senior Living, Llc
7902 Westpark Dr
Mc Lean VA 22102

(P-20294)
SUNRISE SENIOR LIVING INC
Also Called: Sunrise of Woodland Hills
5501 Newcastle Ave # 130, Encino
(91316-2147)
PHONE..................................818 346-9046
Tom Colomaria, *Manager*
EMP: 50
SALES (corp-wide): 4.7B **Publicly Held**
WEB: www.sunrise.com
SIC: 8051 8361 Skilled nursing care facilities; residential care
HQ: Sunrise Senior Living, Llc
7902 Westpark Dr
Mc Lean VA 22102

(P-20295)
SUNRISE SENIOR LIVING INC
Also Called: Sunrise of Palo Alto
201 N Crescent Dr Apt 503, Beverly Hills
(90210-6184)
PHONE..................................650 326-1108
Ken Claire, *Branch Mgr*
EMP: 65
SALES (corp-wide): 4.7B **Publicly Held**
WEB: www.sunrise.com
SIC: 8051 8361 Skilled nursing care facilities; residential care
HQ: Sunrise Senior Living, Llc
7902 Westpark Dr
Mc Lean VA 22102

(P-20296)
SUNRISE SENIOR LIVING INC
Also Called: Sunrise At Sterling Canyon
25815 Mcbean Pkwy Ofc, Valencia
(91355-2071)
PHONE..................................661 253-3551
Pamela Sellers, *Director*
EMP: 65
SALES (corp-wide): 4.7B **Publicly Held**
WEB: www.sunrise.com
SIC: 8051 8361 Skilled nursing care facilities; home for the aged
HQ: Sunrise Senior Living, Llc
7902 Westpark Dr
Mc Lean VA 22102

(P-20297)
SUNRISE SENIOR LIVING INC
Also Called: Fountains At Sea Bluffs
25421 Sea Bluffs Dr, Dana Point
(92629-2196)
PHONE..................................949 234-3000
David Omalley, *Branch Mgr*
EMP: 58

(P-20298)
SUNRISE SENIOR LIVING INC
Also Called: Sunrise of Beverly Hills
201 N Crescent Dr, Beverly Hills
(90210-4898)
PHONE..................................310 274-4479
Brandy Velencia, *Manager*
EMP: 58
SALES (corp-wide): 4.7B **Publicly Held**
WEB: www.sunrise.com
SIC: 8051 Skilled nursing care facilities
HQ: Sunrise Senior Living, Llc
7902 Westpark Dr
Mc Lean VA 22102

(P-20299)
SUNRISE SENIOR LIVING INC
Also Called: Sunrise of Playa Vista
5555 Playa Vista Dr, Los Angeles
(90094-2234)
PHONE..................................310 437-7178
Wendy McIlnay, *Manager*
EMP: 59
SALES (corp-wide): 4.7B **Publicly Held**
WEB: www.sunrise.com
SIC: 8051 8361 Skilled nursing care facilities; home for the aged
HQ: Sunrise Senior Living, Llc
7902 Westpark Dr
Mc Lean VA 22102

(P-20300)
SUNRISE SENIOR LIVING INC
1601 19th Ave, San Francisco
(94122-3468)
PHONE..................................415 664-6264
Jeannie Hung, *Branch Mgr*
EMP: 58
SALES (corp-wide): 4.7B **Publicly Held**
WEB: www.sunrise.com
SIC: 8051 8361 Skilled nursing care facilities; home for the aged
HQ: Sunrise Senior Living, Llc
7902 Westpark Dr
Mc Lean VA 22102

(P-20301)
SUNRISE SENIOR LIVING INC
Also Called: Vintage Silver Creek
4855 San Felipe Rd, San Jose
(95135-1287)
PHONE..................................408 223-1312
Rick Qwaza, *Branch Mgr*
Caroline Deguzman, *Office Mgr*
EMP: 58
SALES (corp-wide): 4.7B **Publicly Held**
WEB: www.sunrise.com
SIC: 8051 8361 Skilled nursing care facilities; home for the aged
HQ: Sunrise Senior Living, Llc
7902 Westpark Dr
Mc Lean VA 22102

(P-20302)
SUNRISE SENIOR LIVING INC
Also Called: Villa Valencia Health Care Ctr
24552 Paseo De Valencia, Laguna Hills
(92653-4236)
PHONE..................................949 581-6111
Terry Records, *Chief*
EMP: 58
SALES (corp-wide): 4.7B **Publicly Held**
WEB: www.sunrise.com
SIC: 8051 8361 Skilled nursing care facilities; home for the aged
HQ: Sunrise Senior Living, Llc
7902 Westpark Dr
Mc Lean VA 22102

(P-20303)
SUNRISE SENIOR LIVING INC
Also Called: Sunrise of Carmichael
5451 Fair Oaks Blvd, Carmichael
(95608-5748)
PHONE..................................916 485-4500
EMP: 58
SALES (corp-wide): 4.7B **Publicly Held**
WEB: www.sunrise.com
SIC: 8051 8361 Skilled nursing care facilities; home for the aged
HQ: Sunrise Senior Living, Llc
7902 Westpark Dr
Mc Lean VA 22102

(P-20304)
SUNRISE SENIOR LIVING INC
Also Called: Sunrise of Monterey
1110 Carmelo St, Monterey (93940-4508)
PHONE..................................831 643-2400
Susan Sundell, *Branch Mgr*
EMP: 58
SALES (corp-wide): 4.7B **Publicly Held**
WEB: www.sunrise.com
SIC: 8051 8361 Skilled nursing care facilities; home for the aged
HQ: Sunrise Senior Living, Llc
7902 Westpark Dr
Mc Lean VA 22102

(P-20305)
SUNRISE SENIOR LIVING INC
Also Called: Sunrise of Santa Rosa
3250 Chanate Rd Ofc, Santa Rosa
(95404-1771)
PHONE..................................707 575-7503
Rob Komorowski, *Manager*
EMP: 50
SALES (corp-wide): 4.7B **Publicly Held**
WEB: www.sunrise.com
SIC: 8051 8361 Skilled nursing care facilities; home for the aged
HQ: Sunrise Senior Living, Llc
7902 Westpark Dr
Mc Lean VA 22102

(P-20306)
SUNRISE SENIOR LIVING LLC
Also Called: Sunrise of Danville
1027 Diablo Rd, Danville (94526-1923)
PHONE..................................925 309-4178
Sol Spencer, *Director*
Harmony Venturelli, *Office Mgr*
Jessica Flores, *Director*
EMP: 80
SALES (corp-wide): 4.7B **Publicly Held**
WEB: www.sunrise.com
SIC: 8051 Skilled nursing care facilities
HQ: Sunrise Senior Living, Llc
7902 Westpark Dr
Mc Lean VA 22102

(P-20307)
SUNRISE SENIOR LIVING LLC
Also Called: Sunrise Assistd Lving of Wlnt
2175 Ygnacio Valley Rd, Walnut Creek
(94598-3385)
PHONE..................................925 932-3500
Kathlyn McParron, *Manager*
Ron Havens, *Director*
EMP: 50
SALES (corp-wide): 4.7B **Publicly Held**
WEB: www.sunrise.com
SIC: 8051 Skilled nursing care facilities
HQ: Sunrise Senior Living, Llc
7902 Westpark Dr
Mc Lean VA 22102

(P-20308)
SUNRISE SENIOR LIVING LLC
17650 Devonshire St, Northridge
(91325-1445)
PHONE..................................818 886-1616
Susan Nasraty, *General Mgr*
EMP: 58
SALES (corp-wide): 4.7B **Publicly Held**
WEB: www.sunrise.com
SIC: 8051 8361 Skilled nursing care facilities; residential care

HQ: Sunrise Senior Living, Llc
  7902 Westpark Dr
  Mc Lean VA 22102
  -

(P-20309)
SUNRISE SENIOR LIVING LLC
Also Called: Sunrise of Oakland Hills
  11889 Skyline Blvd, Oakland (94619-2418)
  PHONE...................................510 531-7190
  Bill Keck, *Branch Mgr*
  EMP: 65
  SQ FT: 64,421
  SALES (corp-wide): 4.7B **Publicly Held**
  WEB: www.sunrise.com
  SIC: 8051 8361 Skilled nursing care facilities; residential care
  HQ: Sunrise Senior Living, Llc
    7902 Westpark Dr
    Mc Lean VA 22102
    -

(P-20310)
SUNRISE SENIOR LIVING LLC
Also Called: Sunrise of Mission Viejo
  26151 Country Club Dr, Mission Viejo
  (92691-5907)
  PHONE...................................949 582-2010
  Lynn Piglao, *Director*
  EMP: 60
  SALES (corp-wide): 4.7B **Publicly Held**
  WEB: www.sunrise.com
  SIC: 8051 Skilled nursing care facilities
  HQ: Sunrise Senior Living, Llc
    7902 Westpark Dr
    Mc Lean VA 22102
    -

(P-20311)
SUNRISE SENIOR LIVING LLC
Also Called: Sunrise of Hermosa Beach
  1837 Pacific Coast Hwy, Hermosa Beach
  (90254-3160)
  PHONE...................................310 937-0959
  Josie Hecht, *Manager*
  EMP: 50
  SALES (corp-wide): 4.7B **Publicly Held**
  WEB: www.sunrise.com
  SIC: 8051 8361 Skilled nursing care facilities; home for the aged
  HQ: Sunrise Senior Living, Llc
    7902 Westpark Dr
    Mc Lean VA 22102
    -

(P-20312)
SUNRISE SENIOR LIVING LLC
Also Called: Sunrise At La Costa
  7020 Manzanita St, Carlsbad (92011-5123)
  PHONE...................................760 930-0060
  Euginia Whelch, *Director*
  EMP: 100
  SALES (corp-wide): 4.7B **Publicly Held**
  WEB: www.sunrise.com
  SIC: 8051 8361 Skilled nursing care facilities; home for the aged
  HQ: Sunrise Senior Living, Llc
    7902 Westpark Dr
    Mc Lean VA 22102
    -

(P-20313)
SUNRISE SENIOR LIVING LLC
Also Called: Sunrise At Bonita
  3302 Bonita Rd, Chula Vista (91910-3207)
  PHONE...................................619 470-2220
  Gwen Krushensky, *Manager*
  EMP: 55
  SALES (corp-wide): 4.7B **Publicly Held**
  WEB: www.sunrise.com
  SIC: 8051 8361 Skilled nursing care facilities; residential care
  HQ: Sunrise Senior Living, Llc
    7902 Westpark Dr
    Mc Lean VA 22102
    -

(P-20314)
SUNRISE SENIOR LIVING LLC
Also Called: Sunrise of Sacramento
  345 Munroe St, Sacramento (95825-6459)
  PHONE...................................916 486-0200
  Lyndee Whaley, *Manager*
  EMP: 50

SALES (corp-wide): 4.7B **Publicly Held**
  WEB: www.sunrise.com
  SIC: 8051 8361 Skilled nursing care facilities; residential care
  HQ: Sunrise Senior Living, Llc
    7902 Westpark Dr
    Mc Lean VA 22102

(P-20315)
SUNRISE SENIOR LIVING LLC
  530 Water St Fl 5, Oakland (94607-3532)
  PHONE...................................303 410-0500
  Shanelle Armas, *Manager*
  EMP: 58
  SALES (corp-wide): 4.7B **Publicly Held**
  WEB: www.sunrise.com
  SIC: 8051 Skilled nursing care facilities
  HQ: Sunrise Senior Living, Llc
    7902 Westpark Dr
    Mc Lean VA 22102

(P-20316)
SUNRISE SENIOR LIVING LLC
Also Called: Sunrise of Sunnyvale
  633 S Knickerbocker Dr # 263, Sunnyvale
  (94087-1034)
  PHONE...................................408 749-8600
  Tina Bagheri, *Manager*
  EMP: 65
  SALES (corp-wide): 4.7B **Publicly Held**
  WEB: www.sunrise.com
  SIC: 8051 8361 Skilled nursing care facilities; home for the aged
  HQ: Sunrise Senior Living, Llc
    7902 Westpark Dr
    Mc Lean VA 22102

(P-20317)
SUNRISE SENIOR LIVING LLC
Also Called: Sunrise of Westlake Village
  3101 Townsgate Rd, Westlake Village
  (91361-5835)
  PHONE...................................805 557-1100
  Angela Ling, *Branch Mgr*
  EMP: 58
  SALES (corp-wide): 4.7B **Publicly Held**
  WEB: www.sunrise.com
  SIC: 8051 8361 Skilled nursing care facilities; residential care
  HQ: Sunrise Senior Living, Llc
    7902 Westpark Dr
    Mc Lean VA 22102

(P-20318)
SUNRISE SENIOR LIVING LLC
Also Called: Sunrise of Studio City
  4610 Coldwater Canyon Ave, Studio City
  (91604-1031)
  PHONE...................................818 505-8484
  Jason Malone, *Manager*
  EMP: 58
  SALES (corp-wide): 4.7B **Publicly Held**
  WEB: www.sunrise.com
  SIC: 8051 8361 Skilled nursing care facilities; residential care
  HQ: Sunrise Senior Living, Llc
    7902 Westpark Dr
    Mc Lean VA 22102

(P-20319)
SUNRISE SENIOR LIVING LLC
Also Called: Sunrise of Fresno
  7444 N Cedar Ave, Fresno (93720-3636)
  PHONE...................................559 325-8170
  Jessica Lopez, *Director*
  EMP: 70
  SALES (corp-wide): 4.7B **Publicly Held**
  WEB: www.sunrise.com
  SIC: 8051 8361 Skilled nursing care facilities; residential care
  HQ: Sunrise Senior Living, Llc
    7902 Westpark Dr
    Mc Lean VA 22102

(P-20320)
SUNRISE SENIOR LIVING LLC
Also Called: Sunrise of La Palma
  5321 La Palma Ave Fl 2, La Palma
  (90623-1703)
  PHONE...................................714 739-8111

Jennifer Munoz, *Mayor*
  EMP: 60
  SALES (corp-wide): 4.7B **Publicly Held**
  WEB: www.sunrise.com
  SIC: 8051 Skilled nursing care facilities
  HQ: Sunrise Senior Living, Llc
    7902 Westpark Dr
    Mc Lean VA 22102

(P-20321)
SUNRISE SENIOR LIVING LLC
  31741 Rancho Viejo Rd, San Juan Capistrano (92675-6722)
  PHONE...................................949 248-8855
  Tiffany Calahan, *Manager*
  EMP: 58
  SALES (corp-wide): 4.7B **Publicly Held**
  WEB: www.sunrise.com
  SIC: 8051 8361 Convalescent home with continuous nursing care; residential care
  HQ: Sunrise Senior Living, Llc
    7902 Westpark Dr
    Mc Lean VA 22102

(P-20322)
SUNRISE SENIOR LIVING LLC
Also Called: Sunrise of Palm Springs
  1780 E Baristo Rd, Palm Springs
  (92262-7114)
  PHONE...................................760 322-3444
  Lisa Kennedy, *Exec Dir*
  EMP: 80
  SALES (corp-wide): 4.7B **Publicly Held**
  WEB: www.sunrise.com
  SIC: 8051 8361 Skilled nursing care facilities; residential care
  HQ: Sunrise Senior Living, Llc
    7902 Westpark Dr
    Mc Lean VA 22102

(P-20323)
SUNRISE SENIOR LIVING LLC
  1301 Ralston Ave Ste A, Belmont
  (94002-1961)
  PHONE...................................650 654-9700
  Bradford Liebman, *Branch Mgr*
  EMP: 58
  SALES (corp-wide): 4.7B **Publicly Held**
  WEB: www.sunrise.com
  SIC: 8051 8361 Skilled nursing care facilities; home for the aged
  HQ: Sunrise Senior Living, Llc
    7902 Westpark Dr
    Mc Lean VA 22102

(P-20324)
SUNRISE SENIOR LIVING LLC
Also Called: Brighton Gardens of Camarillo
  6000 Santa Rosa Rd Ofc, Camarillo
  (93012-7121)
  PHONE...................................805 388-8086
  Stan Main, *Branch Mgr*
  EMP: 58
  SALES (corp-wide): 4.7B **Publicly Held**
  WEB: www.sunrise.com
  SIC: 8051 8361 Convalescent home with continuous nursing care; home for the aged
  HQ: Sunrise Senior Living, Llc
    7902 Westpark Dr
    Mc Lean VA 22102

(P-20325)
SUNRISE SENIOR LIVING LLC
Also Called: Sunrise of Hemet
  1177 S Palm Ave, Hemet (92543-7817)
  PHONE...................................951 929-5988
  Kent K Goforth, *Branch Mgr*
  EMP: 58
  SALES (corp-wide): 4.7B **Publicly Held**
  WEB: www.sunrise.com
  SIC: 8051 Skilled nursing care facilities
  HQ: Sunrise Senior Living, Llc
    7902 Westpark Dr
    Mc Lean VA 22102

(P-20326)
SUNRISE SENIOR LIVING LLC
Also Called: Sunrise of Rocklin
  6100 Sierra College Blvd, Rocklin
  (95677-3505)
  PHONE...................................916 632-3003
  Josh Lancaster, *Branch Mgr*
  EMP: 59
  SALES (corp-wide): 4.7B **Publicly Held**
  WEB: www.sunrise.com
  SIC: 8051 Skilled nursing care facilities
  HQ: Sunrise Senior Living, Llc
    7902 Westpark Dr
    Mc Lean VA 22102

(P-20327)
SUNRISE SENIOR LIVING LLC
Also Called: Fountains At The Carlotta
  41505 Carlotta Dr, Palm Desert
  (92211-3279)
  PHONE...................................760 346-5420
  EMP: 58
  SALES (corp-wide): 4.7B **Publicly Held**
  WEB: www.sunrise.com
  SIC: 8051 8361 Skilled nursing care facilities; home for the aged
  HQ: Sunrise Senior Living, Llc
    7902 Westpark Dr
    Mc Lean VA 22102

(P-20328)
SUNRISE SENIOR LIVING LLC
Also Called: Sunrise At Raincross Village
  5232 Central Ave, Riverside (92504-1825)
  PHONE...................................951 785-1200
  Christi Steichen, *Branch Mgr*
  EMP: 58
  SALES (corp-wide): 4.7B **Publicly Held**
  WEB: www.sunrise.com
  SIC: 8051 8361 Skilled nursing care facilities; home for the aged
  HQ: Sunrise Senior Living, Llc
    7902 Westpark Dr
    Mc Lean VA 22102
    -

(P-20329)
SUTTER HEALTH
  3707 Schriever Ave, Mather (95655-4202)
  PHONE...................................916 454-8200
  Sheila Black, *Branch Mgr*
  Teddy Halidy, *Analyst*
  Theron Seitz, *Analyst*
  Doug Angove, *Manager*
  Sheryll Parsons, *Manager*
  EMP: 60
  SALES (corp-wide): 12.7B **Privately Held**
  WEB: www.sutterhealth.org
  SIC: 8051 8062 Skilled nursing care facilities; general medical & surgical hospitals
  PA: Sutter Health
    2200 River Plaza Dr
    Sacramento CA 95833
    916 733-8800

(P-20330)
SUTTER VSTING NRSE ASSN HSPICE
  1651 Alvarado St, San Leandro
  (94577-2636)
  PHONE...................................510 618-5277
  Rosemarie Avery, *Manager*
  EMP: 100
  SALES (corp-wide): 12.7B **Privately Held**
  WEB: www.suttervnaandhospice.com
  SIC: 8051 8082 Skilled nursing care facilities; home health care services
  HQ: Sutter Visiting Nurse Association & Hospice
    1900 Powell St Ste 300
    Emeryville CA 94608
    866 652-9178

(P-20331)
T C H P INC
Also Called: Palm Terrace Care Center
  11162 Palm Terrace Ln, Riverside
  (92505-2338)
  PHONE...................................951 687-7330
  Jeremy Jergensen, *Administration*
  David Gunnell, *Administration*
  Kolee Knoefler, *Director*
  Madisyn Norman, *Director*
  Christian Torres, *Director*

EMP: 75
SALES: 10.9MM
SALES (corp-wide): 62.4MM **Privately Held**
WEB: www.palmterracecare.com
SIC: 8051 Skilled nursing care facilities
PA: North American Client Services, Inc.
5150 E A Palma Ave 206
Anaheim CA 92807
949 240-2423

(P-20332)
TLC OF BAY AREA INC
Also Called: Valley House Care Center
991 Clyde Ave, Santa Clara (95054-1905)
P.O. Box 607, Indiana PA (15701-0607)
PHONE...........................408 988-7667
Marcy Colkitt, *President*
Merlin Davey, *Exec Dir*
EMP: 51
SALES (est): 5.7MM **Privately Held**
SIC: 8051 Skilled nursing care facilities

(P-20333)
TORRANCE CARE CENTER WEST INC
4333 Torrance Blvd, Torrance
(90503-4401)
PHONE...........................310 370-4561
Vicki P Rollins, *President*
EMP: 180
SALES: 17.8MM **Privately Held**
SIC: 8051 Skilled nursing care facilities

(P-20334)
TOWN & COUNTRY MANOR OF THE CH
555 E Memory Ln Ofc Ofc, Santa Ana
(92706-1708)
PHONE...........................714 547-7581
Dirk De Wolfe, *Administration*
Gina Kolb, *CFO*
Shauna Stratton, *Admin Sec*
Taylor Wilson, *Marketing Staff*
Christine Nguyen, *Education*
EMP: 210 **EST:** 1975
SQ FT: 208,000
SALES: 18.9MM **Privately Held**
SIC: 8051 8059 8052 Skilled nursing care facilities; nursing home, except skilled & intermediate care facility; intermediate care facilities

(P-20335)
TRINITY HEALTH SYSTEMS
Also Called: Villa Maria Care Center
723 E 9th St, Long Beach (90813-4611)
PHONE...........................562 437-2797
Jordan Fishman, *Administration*
EMP: 57
SALES (corp-wide): 9.1MM **Privately Held**
SIC: 8051 8059 Convalescent home with continuous nursing care; nursing home, except skilled & intermediate care facility
PA: Trinity Health Systems
14318 Ohio St
Baldwin Park CA 91706
626 960-1971

(P-20336)
TRINITY HEALTH SYSTEMS (PA)
Also Called: Villa Maria Care Center
14318 Ohio St, Baldwin Park (91706-2553)
PHONE...........................626 960-1971
Randal Kleis, *President*
Ron Kroll, *CFO*
Susan Biddlecombe, *Principal*
Donna Brooking, *Principal*
Shelley Jackson, *Principal*
EMP: 80
SQ FT: 35,000
SALES (est): 9.1MM **Privately Held**
SIC: 8051 Skilled nursing care facilities

(P-20337)
TULARE NRSING RHBLITATION HOSP
Also Called: Tulare Nrsing Rhbilitation Ctr
680 E Merritt Ave, Tulare (93274-2135)
PHONE...........................559 686-8581
Mark Fisher, *President*
Norm Christianson, *CFO*
Sharon A Fisher, *Admin Sec*
EMP: 125

SALES (est): 3.9MM **Privately Held**
WEB: www.missioncaregroup.com
SIC: 8051 Skilled nursing care facilities

(P-20338)
TUTERA GROUP INC
Also Called: Kit Carson Nursing & Rehab
811 Court St, Jackson (95642-2131)
PHONE...........................209 223-2231
Shawn Moody, *Manager*
EMP: 100
SALES (corp-wide): 12.7MM **Privately Held**
WEB: www.tutera.com
SIC: 8051 Skilled nursing care facilities
PA: Tutera Group Inc.
7611 State Line Rd # 301
Kansas City MO 64114
816 444-0900

(P-20339)
TWILIGHT HAVEN
1717 S Winery Ave, Fresno (93727-5011)
PHONE...........................559 251-8417
David Viancourt, *Administration*
Kenneth Karle, *President*
Kamaljit Kaur, *Officer*
Robert Herman, *Vice Pres*
Vicente Magallon, *Social Dir*
EMP: 95 **EST:** 1957
SQ FT: 70,000
SALES: 5.5MM **Privately Held**
WEB: www.twilighthaven.com
SIC: 8051 8052 8361 Convalescent home with continuous nursing care; personal care facility; rest home, with health care incidental

(P-20340)
UNITED COM SERVE
Also Called: FOUNTAINS, THE
1260 Williams Way, Yuba City
(95991-2400)
PHONE...........................530 790-3000
Ryan Dickerson, *President*
Chris Parker, *Administration*
EMP: 100
SQ FT: 40,000
SALES: 17.5MM
SALES (corp-wide): 26.9MM **Privately Held**
SIC: 8051 Skilled nursing care facilities
PA: Freemont Rideout Health Group
989 Plumas St
Yuba City CA 95991
530 751-4010

(P-20341)
UNITED HEALTH SYSTEMS INC
Also Called: ALDERSON CONVALESCENT HOSPITAL
124 Walnut St, Woodland (95695-3137)
PHONE...........................530 662-9161
Santiago M S Miguel, *CEO*
Thomas E Mullen, *President*
Lynn Mullen, *Admin Sec*
Ann M Joule, *Director*
EMP: 154
SQ FT: 40,000
SALES: 10.9MM **Privately Held**
WEB: www.unitedhealthsystems.com
SIC: 8051 Convalescent home with continuous nursing care

(P-20342)
US SKILLSERVE INC
Also Called: Communty Convlscnt Hosp Mntclr
9620 Fremont Ave, Montclair (91763-2320)
PHONE...........................909 621-4751
Johannes Simanjuntak, *Manager*
EMP: 140
SALES (corp-wide): 74.8MM **Privately Held**
SIC: 8051 Convalescent home with continuous nursing care
PA: U.S. Skillserve Inc
4115 E Broadway Ste A
Long Beach CA 90803
562 930-0777

(P-20343)
V S N F INC
Also Called: Valley Skilled Nursing Care
2120 Stockton Blvd, Sacramento
(95817-1337)
PHONE...........................916 452-6631
John Sorensen, *President*
EMP: 55
SALES (est): 2MM **Privately Held**
SIC: 8051 Extended care facility

(P-20344)
VALLEY CAREIDENCE OPCO LLC
Also Called: Gateway Post Acute
661 W Poplar Ave, Porterville
(93257-5926)
PHONE...........................559 784-8371
Jason Murray, *CEO*
Mark Hancock, *CFO*
EMP: 75
SALES (est): 231.3K
SALES (corp-wide): 951.8K **Privately Held**
SIC: 8051 Skilled nursing care facilities
PA: Providence Group Of California, Llc
140 N Union Ave Ste 320
Farmington UT 84025
619 756-6800

(P-20345)
VALLEY HEALTHCARE CENTER LLC
4840 E Tulare Ave, Fresno (93727-3062)
PHONE...........................559 251-7161
George V Hagaer Jr, *CEO*
EMP: 100 **EST:** 2003
SALES (est): 574.4K **Publicly Held**
SIC: 8051 Skilled nursing care facilities
HQ: Genesis Healthcare Llc
101 E State St
Kennett Square PA 19348

(P-20346)
VALLEY HEALTHCARE CENTER LLC
4840 E Tulare Ave, Fresno (93727-3062)
PHONE...........................559 251-7161
Leila Malicoat, *Administration*
EMP: 105
SALES: 7.6MM **Publicly Held**
SIC: 8051 Skilled nursing care facilities
HQ: Skilled Healthcare, Llc
27442 Portola Pkwy # 200
Foothill Ranch CA 92610
949 282-5800

(P-20347)
VALLEY VIEW SKLLED NURSING CTR
1162 S Dora St, Ukiah (95482-6340)
PHONE...........................707 462-1436
Rosemary Brown, *Administration*
EMP: 58
SALES (est): 1.1MM
SALES (corp-wide): 103.9MM **Privately Held**
WEB: www.villadelrey.com
SIC: 8051 Convalescent home with continuous nursing care
HQ: Horizon West Healthcare, Inc.
4020 Sierra College Blvd # 190
Rocklin CA 95677
916 624-6230

(P-20348)
VALLEY VISTA NURSING AND TRANS
6120 Vineland Ave, North Hollywood
(91606-4914)
PHONE...........................818 763-6275
Crystal Solorzano,
EMP: 170
SALES (est): 2.1MM **Privately Held**
SIC: 8051 Skilled nursing care facilities

(P-20349)
VALLEY WEST HEALTH CARE INC
Also Called: Valley View Care Center
2649 Topeka St, Riverbank (95367-2248)
PHONE...........................209 869-2569
Terry Bane, *Principal*

EMP: 80
SALES (corp-wide): 4.2MM **Privately Held**
SIC: 8051 8062 Convalescent home with continuous nursing care; general medical & surgical hospitals
PA: Valley West Health Care Inc
1224 E St
Williams CA 95987
530 473-5321

(P-20350)
VAN INN II INC (PA)
25 Avenida De Orinda, Orinda
(94563-2305)
PHONE...........................510 548-6600
Richard J Westin, *Principal*
Jesse Pittore, *Principal*
EMP: 55
SQ FT: 2,000
SALES (est): 696.4K **Privately Held**
SIC: 8051 6513 Skilled nursing care facilities; retirement hotel operation

(P-20351)
VETERANS AFFAIRS CAL DEPT
Also Called: Redding Veterans Home, The
3400 Knighton Rd, Redding (96002-9657)
PHONE...........................530 224-3300
Tim Bouseman, *Administration*
EMP: 200 **Privately Held**
SIC: 8051 Skilled nursing care facilities
HQ: California Department Of Veterans Affairs
1227 O St Ste 105
Sacramento CA 95814
800 952-5626

(P-20352)
VETERANS HOME CAL - FRESNO
2811 W California Ave, Fresno
(93706-2306)
PHONE...........................559 493-4400
Stanley Jones, *Director*
Shayna Richards, *Analyst*
Donna Corkill, *Manager*
EMP: 99 **EST:** 2012
SALES (est): 3.7MM **Privately Held**
SIC: 8051 Skilled nursing care facilities

(P-20353)
VICTORIA CARE CENTER
5445 Everglades St, Ventura (93003-6523)
PHONE...........................805 642-1736
Scott Porter, *Exec Dir*
Jay Brady, *President*
EMP: 100
SQ FT: 85,000
SALES: 16.9MM **Privately Held**
WEB: www.victoriacarecenter.com
SIC: 8051 Convalescent home with continuous nursing care
PA: Beverly Health Care Corporation
5445 Everglades St
Ventura CA 93003

(P-20354)
VIENNA CONVALESCENT HOSPITAL
800 S Ham Ln, Lodi (95242-3543)
PHONE...........................209 368-7141
Kenneth Heffel, *President*
Diana Heffel, *Admin Sec*
Alfred Loza, *Supervisor*
EMP: 131
SQ FT: 25,000
SALES: 827MM **Privately Held**
SIC: 8051 Skilled nursing care facilities

(P-20355)
VILLA CONVALESCENT HOSP INC
8965 Magnolia Ave, Riverside
(92503-4432)
PHONE...........................951 689-5788
Jacob Paulson, *Administration*
Spencer E Olsen, *CFO*
Stephanie Rivera, *Social Dir*
Holly Christensen, *Marketing Staff*
Cindy Aleman, *Hlthcr Dir*
EMP: 90 **EST:** 1971
SQ FT: 25,000

SALES (est): 9.2MM **Privately Held**
WEB: www.villahealthcare.com
SIC: 8051 Convalescent home with continuous nursing care

(P-20356)
VILLA RANCHO BRNO HLTH CR LLC
Also Called: VILLA RANCHO BERNARDO CARE CEN
15720 Bernardo Center Dr, San Diego (92127-5861)
PHONE...................................858 672-3900
Irving Bauman,
Brank Johnson,
EMP: 200
SALES: 27.3MM **Privately Held**
SIC: 8051 Skilled nursing care facilities

(P-20357)
VILLA SERENA HEALTHCARE CENTER
723 E 9th St, Long Beach (90813-4611)
PHONE...................................562 437-2797
Matt Carp, *President*
EMP: 70
SALES (est): 42K **Privately Held**
SIC: 8051 Skilled nursing care facilities

(P-20358)
VILLAGE PACIFIC MGT GROUP
Also Called: Village At Sydney Creek
1234 Laurel Ln, San Luis Obispo (93401-5860)
PHONE...................................805 543-2350
Leona Baker, *Manager*
EMP: 55 **Privately Held**
SIC: 8051 Skilled nursing care facilities
PA: Village Pacific Management Group Inc
55 Broad St
San Luis Obispo CA 93405

(P-20359)
VILLAGE PACIFIC MGT GROUP (PA)
Also Called: Village At Sydney Creek
55 Broad St, San Luis Obispo (93405-1745)
PHONE...................................805 543-2300
Patrick Smith, *Principal*
EMP: 55
SALES (est): 9MM **Privately Held**
SIC: 8051 Skilled nursing care facilities

(P-20360)
VILLAGE SQUARE NURSING CENTER
1586 W San Marcos Blvd, San Marcos (92078-4019)
PHONE...................................760 471-2986
G Wiswell, *Exec Dir*
Gavin Wiswell, *Exec Dir*
Pam Turner, *Administration*
EMP: 140
SALES (est): 9MM **Privately Held**
SIC: 8051 8093 Convalescent home with continuous nursing care; rehabilitation center, outpatient treatment

(P-20361)
VINDRA INC
Also Called: Meadowood Nursing Center
3805 Dexter Ln, Clearlake (95422-8850)
PHONE...................................707 994-7738
Calvin Baker Jr, *President*
Gloria Ghiringhelli, *Office Mgr*
EMP: 100
SQ FT: 30,250
SALES (est): 6.1MM **Privately Held**
SIC: 8051 8069 Convalescent home with continuous nursing care; specialty hospitals, except psychiatric

(P-20362)
VIRGIL SNTRIUM CNVLESCENT HOSP
Also Called: Virgil Convalescent Hospital
975 N Virgil Ave, Los Angeles (90029-2944)
PHONE...................................323 665-5793
Miriam Weiss, *President*
EMP: 150

SALES (est): 5.3MM
SALES (corp-wide): 62.1MM **Privately Held**
WEB: www.goldenstatehealth.com
SIC: 8051 Convalescent home with continuous nursing care
PA: Golden State Health Centers, Inc.
13347 Ventura Blvd
Sherman Oaks CA 91423
818 385-3200

(P-20363)
VISTA COVE CARE CENTER AT LONG
3401 Cedar Ave, Long Beach (90807-4422)
PHONE...................................562 426-4461
Bonaparte Liu, *Principal*
Sean Brophy, *Principal*
Floyd Rhoades, *Principal*
Marcela Rodriguez, *Principal*
EMP: 99
SALES (est): 4.9MM **Privately Held**
SIC: 8051 Mental retardation hospital

(P-20364)
VISTA COVE CARE CTR - RIALTO
1471 S Riverside Ave, Rialto (92376-7703)
PHONE...................................909 877-1361
Sean William Brophy, *Admin Sec*
EMP: 99
SALES (est): 13.1MM **Privately Held**
SIC: 8051 Skilled nursing care facilities

(P-20365)
VISTA KNOLL INC
2000 Westwood Rd, Vista (92083-5123)
PHONE...................................760 630-2273
Gary R Byrnes, *President*
Gary Byrnes, *President*
Carol Byrnes, *Officer*
Leo Halpins, *Vice Pres*
Kylie Day, *Hlthcr Dir*
EMP: 70
SQ FT: 45,000
SALES (est): 2.3MM **Privately Held**
WEB: www.vistaknoll.com
SIC: 8051 Skilled nursing care facilities

(P-20366)
VISTA PACIFICA ENTERPRISES INC (PA)
Also Called: VISTA PACIFICA CONVALESCENT CE
3662 Pacific Ave, Riverside (92509-1923)
PHONE...................................951 682-4833
Cheryl Jumonville, *CEO*
James Braswell, *Shareholder*
Ruth Braswell, *Shareholder*
A L Braswell Jr, *President*
Josefa Briseno, *COO*
EMP: 180
SALES: 3.7MM **Privately Held**
SIC: 8051 8059 Skilled nursing care facilities; domiciliary care

(P-20367)
VISTA WOODS HEALTH ASSOC LLC
Also Called: Vista Knoll Spclzed Care Fclty
2000 Westwood Rd, Vista (92083-5123)
PHONE...................................760 630-2273
Ron Cook, *Mng Member*
Clay Gardner,
EMP: 130
SALES: 15.2MM
SALES (corp-wide): 2B **Publicly Held**
WEB: www.theensigngroup.com
SIC: 8051 Convalescent home with continuous nursing care
PA: The Ensign Group Inc
27101 Puerta Real Ste 450
Mission Viejo CA 92691
949 487-9500

(P-20368)
W H C INC
Also Called: Woodside Healthcare Center
2240 Northrop Ave, Sacramento (95825-7408)
PHONE...................................916 927-9300
John Lund, *CEO*
Judy Cantrell, *Principal*
Jay Anderson, *Administration*

EMP: 75
SALES (est): 2MM **Privately Held**
SIC: 8051 Convalescent home with continuous nursing care

(P-20369)
WALNUT WHTNEY CNVALESCENT HOSP
3529 Walnut Ave, Carmichael (95608-3049)
PHONE...................................916 488-8601
Jesse Barrios, *Administration*
Sharon Laidley, *Administration*
EMP: 110
SALES (est): 2.2MM
SALES (corp-wide): 103.9MM **Privately Held**
WEB: www.villadelrey.com
SIC: 8051 Convalescent home with continuous nursing care
HQ: Horizon West Healthcare, Inc.
4020 Sierra College Blvd # 190
Rocklin CA 95677
916 624-6230

(P-20370)
WASHINGTON ENTERPRISES 3 LLC
Also Called: St Andrews Health Care
2300 W Washington Blvd, Los Angeles (90018-1445)
PHONE...................................323 731-0861
Emmanuel David,
Gloria Fonicer, *Treasurer*
Dolores N Chivi, *Admin Sec*
EMP: 68
SQ FT: 5,000
SALES: 5.3MM **Privately Held**
SIC: 8051 Skilled nursing care facilities

(P-20371)
WATERMAN CONVALESCENT HOSPITAL (PA)
Also Called: Mt Rubidoux Convalescent Hosp
1850 N Waterman Ave, San Bernardino (92404-4895)
PHONE...................................909 882-1215
Thomas Plott, *President*
Elizabeth Plott, *Corp Secy*
Mr Terry Steege, *Account Dir*
EMP: 109
SQ FT: 13,000
SALES (est): 11.1MM **Privately Held**
SIC: 8051 Convalescent home with continuous nursing care

(P-20372)
WATERMARK RTRMENT CMMNTIES INC
Also Called: Fountains At The Carlotta, The
41505 Carlotta Dr, Palm Desert (92211-3279)
PHONE...................................760 346-5420
Misty Hansen, *CFO*
Lisa Hollinger, *Exec Dir*
Richard M Howell, *Managing Dir*
Cathy Lubanski, *Managing Dir*
Bill Zachau, *Sales Staff*
EMP: 70 **Privately Held**
SIC: 8051 8052 Skilled nursing care facilities; intermediate care facilities
HQ: Watermark Retirement Communities, Inc.
2020 W Rudasill Rd
Tucson AZ 85704
520 797-4000

(P-20373)
WATERS EDGE INC
Also Called: Waters Edge Nursing Home
2401 Blanding Ave, Alameda (94501-1503)
PHONE...................................510 748-4300
Christian Zimmerman, *Vice Pres*
John C Zimmerman, *President*
Virginia Zimmerman, *Corp Secy*
EMP: 110
SQ FT: 24,000
SALES (est): 6.9MM **Privately Held**
SIC: 8051 Skilled nursing care facilities

(P-20374)
WELLS HSE HSPICE FUNDATION INC
245 Cherry Ave, Long Beach (90802-3901)
PHONE...................................714 952-3795

Ronald Morgan, *President*
EMP: 60 EST: 1997
SALES (est): 1.9MM **Privately Held**
WEB: www.wellshousehospice.com
SIC: 8051 Convalescent home with continuous nursing care

(P-20375)
WESCORDON INCORPORATED (PA)
Also Called: Valley Care Center
661 W Poplar Ave, Porterville (93257-5926)
P.O. Box 3566 (93258-3566)
PHONE...................................559 784-8371
Donald C Smith, *President*
EMP: 150 EST: 1948
SQ FT: 14,000
SALES (est): 4.6MM **Privately Held**
SIC: 8051 Convalescent home with continuous nursing care

(P-20376)
WEST CNTINELA VLY CARE CTR INC
Also Called: Centinela Skld Nrng Wlns Cntr
950 S Flower St, Inglewood (90301-4186)
PHONE...................................310 674-3216
Koom S Son, *CEO*
Karen Tanedo, *Records Dir*
Nancy Aguillar, *Social Dir*
Dave Ares, *Human Res Dir*
Faye Sorianosos, *Nursing Dir*
EMP: 99
SALES (est): 5.7MM **Privately Held**
SIC: 8051 Skilled nursing care facilities

(P-20377)
WEST ESCONDIDO HEALTHCARE LLC
Also Called: Palomar Vista Healthcare Ctr
201 N Fig St, Escondido (92025-3416)
PHONE...................................760 746-0303
Mike Conrad,
Soon Burnam,
David Mayo,
Richard Mallo, *Director*
EMP: 95
SALES: 6.8MM **Privately Held**
SIC: 8051 Convalescent home with continuous nursing care

(P-20378)
WESTERN HEALTHCARE MANAGEMENT
Also Called: Western Healthcare Center
1700 E Washington St, Colton (92324-4619)
PHONE...................................909 824-1530
Everett Goings, *Owner*
EMP: 102
SALES (est): 3.9MM **Privately Held**
SIC: 8051 Skilled nursing care facilities

(P-20379)
WESTERN SLOPE HEALTH CENTER
Also Called: Western Slope Health Care
3280 Washington St, Placerville (95667-5838)
PHONE...................................530 622-6842
Jeff Maggard, *Owner*
Wendy Witek, *Office Mgr*
EMP: 90
SALES: 12.6MM **Privately Held**
WEB: www.eldoradocounty.org
SIC: 8051 Convalescent home with continuous nursing care

(P-20380)
WESTGATE GARDENS CARE CENTER
4525 W Tulare Ave, Visalia (93277-1560)
PHONE...................................559 733-0901
Eric Tolman, *Administration*
Tiffini Garcia, *Food Svc Dir*
Cathy Meis, *Director*
EMP: 127
SALES (corp-wide): 103.9MM **Privately Held**
WEB: www.horizonwest.com
SIC: 8051 Skilled nursing care facilities

HQ: Westgate Gardens Care Center, Inc
4020 Sierra College Blvd # 190
Rocklin CA 95677
916 624-6230

(P-20381)
WESTLAKE HEALTH CARE CENTER
1101 Crenshaw Blvd, Los Angeles
(90019-3112)
PHONE..............................805 494-1233
Jeoung Lee, *President*
EMP: 250
SALES (est): 9.9MM
SALES (corp-wide): 22.8MM **Privately Held**
SIC: 8051 Skilled nursing care facilities
PA: J P H Consulting, Inc.
1101 Crenshaw Blvd
Los Angeles CA 90019
323 934-5660

(P-20382)
WESTVIEW HEALH CARE CENTER
Also Called: Kerria
12225 Shale Ridge Ln, Auburn
(95602-8870)
PHONE..............................530 885-7511
Edmund Erapt, *Administration*
Deanna Jones, *Executive*
Lynda Rogers, *Education*
Venessa Suetos, *Hlthcr Dir*
EMP: 222
SALES (est): 6.2MM
SALES (corp-wide): 40.3MM **Privately Held**
SIC: 8051 Convalescent home with continuous nursing care
PA: Plum Healthcare Group, Llc
100 E San Marcos Blvd # 200
San Marcos CA 92069
760 471-0388

(P-20383)
WESTVIEW SERVICES INC
Also Called: Westview Cmnty Arts Program
1701 S Euclid St Ste E, Anaheim
(92802-2408)
PHONE..............................714 956-4199
Britain Semain, *Manager*
EMP: 205
SALES (corp-wide): 16.6MM **Privately Held**
SIC: 8051 8322 Mental retardation hospital; adult day care center
PA: Westview Services, Inc
10522 Katella Ave
Anaheim CA 92804
714 517-6606

(P-20384)
WESTWOOD HEALTHCARE CENTER LP
Also Called: COUNTRY VILLA WESTWOOD NURSING
12121 Santa Monica Blvd, Los Angeles
(90025-2515)
PHONE..............................310 826-0821
Stephen Reissman, *General Ptnr*
Hillard Torgan, *Partner*
Ann Truitt, *Treasurer*
Jerry Allgood, *Administration*
Louis Florin, *Administration*
EMP: 75 EST: 1970
SQ FT: 18,000
SALES: 10.2MM **Privately Held**
SIC: 8051 Skilled nursing care facilities

(P-20385)
WILD KARMA INC
Also Called: Divine Home Care
2365 Hagen Oaks Dr, Alamo (94507-2208)
PHONE..............................510 639-9088
Robbin R Beebe, *CEO*
Robin Beebe, *CEO*
Dmitri Ostromuhov, *Manager*
EMP: 270 EST: 2007
SALES (est): 8.2MM **Privately Held**
SIC: 8059 Convalescent home with continuous nursing care; personal care home, with health care

(P-20386)
WILLOW CREEK HALTHCARE CTR LLC
650 W Alluvial Ave, Clovis (93611-6716)
PHONE..............................559 323-6200
George V Hager Jr, *CEO*
EMP: 2335
SALES (est): 5.8MM **Publicly Held**
SIC: 8051 Skilled nursing care facilities
HQ: Genesis Healthcare Llc
101 E State St
Kennett Square PA 19348
-

(P-20387)
WILLOW CREEK HALTHCARE CTR LLC
Also Called: Willow Creek Care Center
650 W Alluvial Ave, Clovis (93611-6716)
PHONE..............................559 323-6200
Lillian Werntz, *President*
EMP: 99
SALES (est): 1.3MM **Publicly Held**
WEB: www.parkviewnursing.net
SIC: 8051 Convalescent home with continuous nursing care
HQ: Skilled Healthcare, Llc
27442 Portola Pkwy # 200
Foothill Ranch CA 92610
949 282-5800

(P-20388)
WILMON CORPORATION
Also Called: Millers Progressive Care
8951 Granite Hill Dr, Riverside
(92509-1104)
PHONE..............................951 685-7474
Wilmer W Miller, *President*
EMP: 65
SQ FT: 16,000
SALES (est): 4.2MM **Privately Held**
SIC: 8051 Skilled nursing care facilities

(P-20389)
WINDFLOWER HOLDINGS LLC
Also Called: Rocky Point Care Center
625 16th St, Lakeport (95453-3501)
PHONE..............................707 263-6101
Mark Ballif, *Mng Member*
Paul Hubbard,
EMP: 80 EST: 1965
SQ FT: 5,000
SALES (est): 3.1MM
SALES (corp-wide): 40.3MM **Privately Held**
WEB: www.villadelrey.com
SIC: 8051 Convalescent home with continuous nursing care
PA: Plum Healthcare Group, Llc
100 E San Marcos Blvd # 200
San Marcos CA 92069
760 471-0388

(P-20390)
WINDSOR ANAHEIM HEALTHCARE (PA)
Also Called: Windsor Grdns Cnvlescent Ctr A
3415 W Ball Rd, Anaheim (92804-3708)
PHONE..............................714 826-8950
Lee Samson, *President*
EMP: 264
SQ FT: 37,245
SALES (est): 6.2MM **Privately Held**
SIC: 8051 Skilled nursing care facilities

(P-20391)
WINDSOR CONVALESCENT
Also Called: WINDSOR MANOR REHABILITATION CENTER OF CO
3806 Clayton Rd, Concord (94521-2516)
PHONE..............................925 689-2266
Lee Samson, *Mng Member*
EMP: 133
SALES (est): 22.4MM **Privately Held**
SIC: 8051 Convalescent home with continuous nursing care
PA: Lexington Group International, Inc
9200 W Sunset Blvd # 700
West Hollywood CA 90069

(P-20392)
WINDSOR CONVALESCENT
Also Called: Windsor Park Care Ctr Fremont
2400 Parkside Dr, Fremont (94536-5332)
PHONE..............................510 793-7222
Lee Samson, *Mng Member*
EMP: 133
SALES (est): 3.7MM **Privately Held**
SIC: 8051 Convalescent home with continuous nursing care
PA: Lexington Group International, Inc
9200 W Sunset Blvd # 700
West Hollywood CA 90069

(P-20393)
WINDSOR CONVALESCENT
Also Called: Windsor Gardens
637 E Romie Ln, Salinas (93901-4205)
PHONE..............................831 424-0687
Lee Samson, *Mng Member*
EMP: 133
SALES (est): 13.5MM **Privately Held**
SIC: 8051 Convalescent home with continuous nursing care
PA: Lexington Group International, Inc
9200 W Sunset Blvd # 700
West Hollywood CA 90069

(P-20394)
WINDSOR GARDENS
Also Called: Windsor Gardens of Long Beach
4333 Torrance Blvd, Torrance
(90503-4401)
PHONE..............................562 422-9219
Calcin Warren, *Administration*
EMP: 100 **Privately Held**
SIC: 8051 Skilled nursing care facilities
PA: Windsor Anaheim Healthcare, Ltd
3415 W Ball Rd
Anaheim CA 92804

(P-20395)
WINDSOR GARDENS
Also Called: Southwest Convalesant
13922 Cerise Ave, Hawthorne
(90250-8688)
PHONE..............................310 675-3304
Michael Gamet, *Administration*
EMP: 100 **Privately Held**
SIC: 8051 Skilled nursing care facilities
PA: Windsor Anaheim Healthcare, Ltd
3415 W Ball Rd
Anaheim CA 92804

(P-20396)
WINDSOR GARDENS CONVALESCNT
915 Crenshaw Blvd, Los Angeles
(90019-1938)
PHONE..............................323 937-5466
Nathan Alyeshmerni, *Administration*
Lee Samson, *President*
EMP: 99
SALES: 12.9MM **Privately Held**
SIC: 8051 8742 Convalescent home with continuous nursing care; hospital & health services consultant

(P-20397)
WINDSOR GARDNS HEALTHCARE CNTR
Also Called: WINDSOR GARDENS OF FULLERTON
245 E Wilshire Ave, Fullerton (92832-1935)
PHONE..............................714 871-6020
Lee Samson,
EMP: 133
SALES: 10.7MM **Privately Held**
SIC: 8051 Convalescent home with continuous nursing care
PA: Lexington Group International, Inc
9200 W Sunset Blvd # 700
West Hollywood CA 90069

(P-20398)
WINDSOR HEALTHCARE MANAGEMENT
Also Called: Windsor Gardens Convalescnt
220 E 24th St, National City (91950-6705)
PHONE..............................619 474-6741

Lee Samson, *President*
EMP: 115
SALES: 8.6MM **Privately Held**
SIC: 8051 Convalescent home with continuous nursing care

(P-20399)
WINDSOR MONTEREY CARE CTR LLC
1575 Skyline Dr, Monterey (93940-4110)
PHONE..............................831 373-2731
Lawrence Feigen,
EMP: 95
SALES (est): 4.4MM **Privately Held**
SIC: 8051 Skilled nursing care facilities

(P-20400)
WINDSOR RDGE RHBLTTION CTR LLC
350 Iris Dr, Salinas (93906-3514)
PHONE..............................831 449-1515
Lee C Samson,
Lawrence E Feigen,
EMP: 99
SALES: 13.4MM **Privately Held**
SIC: 8051 Skilled nursing care facilities

(P-20401)
WINDSOR SKYLINE CARE CTR LLC
348 Iris Dr, Salinas (93906-3514)
PHONE..............................831 449-5496
Patricia Roels, *Vice Pres*
Nikki Thomas, *Office Mgr*
EMP: 91
SALES: 8.9MM **Privately Held**
SIC: 8051 Skilled nursing care facilities
PA: S&F Management Company, Llc
9200 W Sunset Blvd # 700
West Hollywood CA 90069

(P-20402)
WINDSOR TWIN PALMS HLTHCARE
Also Called: Windsor Palms Care Ctr Artesia
11900 Artesia Blvd, Artesia (90701-4039)
PHONE..............................562 865-0271
John Ryan, *Administration*
Lee Samson, *Partner*
Carrie Marigny, *Social Worker*
EMP: 133
SALES (est): 6.8MM **Privately Held**
WEB: www.windsor.com
SIC: 8051 Convalescent home with continuous nursing care
PA: Lexington Group International, Inc
9200 W Sunset Blvd # 700
West Hollywood CA 90069

(P-20403)
WINSOR HOUSE COMPALESSANT
Also Called: Winsor House Convalescent Hosp
101 S Orchard Ave, Vacaville (95688-3635)
PHONE..............................707 448-6458
Prema Thekkek, *President*
Joe Niccoli, *Administration*
Pam Lopez, *Director*
EMP: 77 EST: 1972
SALES (est): 2.1MM **Privately Held**
SIC: 8051 Convalescent home with continuous nursing care

(P-20404)
WINTER CARE CENTER SACRAMENTO
501 Jessie Ave, Sacramento (95838-2608)
PHONE..............................916 922-8855
Ariane Swick, *Administration*
EMP: 120
SQ FT: 25,000
SALES (est): 2.8MM **Privately Held**
SIC: 8051 8322 Skilled nursing care facilities; rehabilitation services

(P-20405)
WISH I AH CARE CENTER INC
1665 M St, Fresno (93721-1121)
PHONE..............................559 855-2211
Janice Harshman, *President*
John E Harshman II, *Vice Pres*

EMP: 118
SQ FT: 60,000
SALES (est): 4.9MM Privately Held
WEB: www.fmaaa.org
SIC: 8051 Extended care facility

(P-20406)
WISH-I-AH HLTHCRE & WELLNESS
1665 M St, Fresno (93721-1121)
PHONE..................................559 855-2211
Maceo Garcia, *Principal*
EMP: 99
SALES (est): 2.3MM Privately Held
SIC: 8051 Skilled nursing care facilities

(P-20407)
WISH-I-AH SKILLED NURSING
Also Called: Wish-Ah Skilled
1665 M St, Fresno (93721-1121)
PHONE..................................949 285-8859
Aaron Robin, *COO*
EMP: 145 EST: 2008
SALES (est): 2.4MM Privately Held
SIC: 8051 Skilled nursing care facilities

(P-20408)
YUBA CITY NURSING & REHAB LLC
1220 Plumas St, Yuba City (95991-3411)
PHONE..................................530 671-0550
Joseph Pallivathucal,
Babu Parayil,
James Paul,
EMP: 75
SALES (est): 4.5MM Privately Held
SIC: 8051 Skilled nursing care facilities

8052 Intermediate Care Facilities

(P-20409)
834 W ARROW HIGHWAY LP
4032 Wilshire Blvd # 600, Los Angeles (90010-3405)
PHONE..................................213 355-1024
David Friedman, *Vice Pres*
Scott Hayashi, *Finance*
EMP: 99
SALES (est): 839.6K Privately Held
SIC: 8052 Intermediate care facilities

(P-20410)
ALLIANCE FOR HOUSING & HEALING (PA)
Also Called: AID FOR AIDS
825 Colorado Blvd Ste 100, Los Angeles (90041-1741)
PHONE..................................323 344-4885
Terry Goddard, *Exec Dir*
Warren R Wimmer, *President*
Edgar Guevara, *Case Mgr*
Chris Murillo, *Case Mgr*
Maricor Lopez, *Assistant*
EMP: 63
SQ FT: 1,620
SALES (est): 10.2MM Privately Held
SIC: 8052 Personal care facility

(P-20411)
ARCADIA GARDENS MGT CORP
Also Called: Indepndnt Asstd Lvng & Memory
720 W Camino Real Ave, Arcadia (91007-7839)
PHONE..................................626 574-8571
Julie Chirikian, *President*
David Chirikian, *Vice Pres*
EMP: 100
SQ FT: 120,320
SALES (est): 5.4MM Privately Held
SIC: 8052 Intermediate care facilities

(P-20412)
BAYBERRY INC (PA)
Also Called: SUPPORTED LIVING SERVICES
1700 2nd St Ste 350, NAPA (94559-2409)
PHONE..................................707 252-5587
Linda Washington, *Exec Dir*
Iris Cloudt, *President*
Isabel Harris, *Corp Secy*
William Miller, *Chief*
EMP: 95

SQ FT: 400
SALES: 6.5MM Privately Held
SIC: 8052 8322 Intermediate care facilities; individual & family services

(P-20413)
BEST CONSULTING INC
8795 Folsom Blvd Ste 103, Sacramento (95826-3720)
PHONE..................................916 448-2050
Sergio E Pinto, *President*
Danielle Nuzum, *COO*
Jaclyn Shandy-Pinto, *Vice Pres*
Sergio Pinto, *Principal*
EMP: 50
SALES (est): 2.2MM Privately Held
SIC: 8052 Home for the mentally retarded, with health care

(P-20414)
BIG HEALTH INC
Also Called: Sleepio
461 Bush St Ste 200, San Francisco (94108-3716)
PHONE..................................415 867-3473
Peter Andrew, *CEO*
EMP: 51
SALES (est): 106.6K Privately Held
SIC: 8052 Home for the mentally retarded, with health care

(P-20415)
CARE INC
15315 Magnolia Blvd # 306, Sherman Oaks (91403-1173)
PHONE..................................818 232-7940
Yue LI, *Principal*
EMP: 50
SALES (est): 1.6MM Privately Held
SIC: 8052 Home for the mentally retarded, with health care

(P-20416)
CC-PALO ALTO INC
Also Called: VI At Palo Alto
620 Sand Hill Rd, Palo Alto (94304-2002)
PHONE..................................650 853-5000
Penny Pritzker, *President*
EMP: 225
SALES (est): 11.4MM Privately Held
SIC: 8052 8322 8361 Personal care facility; adult day care center; rehabilitation center, residential: health care incidental

(P-20417)
CHARTER HOSPICE COLTON LLC
1007 E Cooley Dr Ste 100, Colton (92324-3901)
PHONE..................................909 825-2969
Fred Frank, *President*
Meagan Huynh, *Human Res Dir*
Sabina Del Rosario, *Sales Staff*
EMP: 120
SALES (est): 11.9MM Privately Held
SIC: 8052 Personal care facility

(P-20418)
COMMUNITY HOME PARTNERS LLC
Also Called: Pacific Gardens
2384 Pacific Dr, Santa Clara (95051-1458)
PHONE..................................408 985-5252
Maxine Brookner,
EMP: 85
SQ FT: 56,300
SALES: 4MM Privately Held
SIC: 8052 Intermediate care facilities

(P-20419)
COMMUNITY HOSPICE INC (PA)
Also Called: C H I
4368 Spyres Way, Modesto (95356-9259)
PHONE..................................209 578-6300
Harold A Peterson III, *CEO*
Rick Dahlseid, *CFO*
Gary Ervin, *Treasurer*
Monica Ojcius, *Exec Dir*
Karen Aiello, *Admin Asst*
EMP: 125
SQ FT: 24,000
SALES: 22.8MM Privately Held
SIC: 8052 8069 Personal care facility; specialty hospitals, except psychiatric

---

(P-20420)
COMMUNITY HOSPICE INC
2201 Euclid Ave, Hughson (95326-9183)
PHONE..................................209 578-6380
Laura Miller, *Administration*
EMP: 50
SALES (corp-wide): 22.8MM Privately Held
SIC: 8052 Personal care facility
PA: Community Hospice, Inc.
4368 Spyres Way
Modesto CA 95356
209 578-6300

(P-20421)
COUNTY OF ORANGE
405 W 5th St Ofc, Santa Ana (92701-4519)
PHONE..................................714 834-6021
David L Riley, *Director*
EMP: 2500 Privately Held
SIC: 8052 Intermediate care facilities
PA: County Of Orange
333 W Santa Ana Blvd 3f
Santa Ana CA 92701
714 834-6200

(P-20422)
COUNTY OF SOLANO
Also Called: Adult Mddlhlth Otptient Clinic
2101 Courage Dr, Fairfield (94533-6717)
PHONE..................................707 784-2080
Rod Kennedy, *Manager*
EMP: 100 Privately Held
SIC: 8052 5719 Intermediate care facilities; linens
PA: County Of Solano
675 Texas St Ste 2600
Fairfield CA 94533
707 784-6706

(P-20423)
CYPRESS GARDEN AT CITRUS HTS
7375 Stock Ranch Rd, Citrus Heights (95621-5616)
PHONE..................................916 729-2722
Pepper Bell, *Exec Dir*
Sondra Campbell, *Deputy Dir*
EMP: 50
SALES (est): 1.6MM Privately Held
SIC: 8052 Personal care facility

(P-20424)
ELIZABETH HOSPICE INC (PA)
500 La Terraza Blvd # 130, Escondido (92025-3876)
PHONE..................................760 737-2050
Jan Jones, *President*
Laura Miller, *President*
Andrea Goodwin, *COO*
Kiprian Skavinski, *CFO*
Holly Swiger, *Officer*
EMP: 200
SQ FT: 14,000
SALES: 40.3MM Privately Held
WEB: www.elizabethhospice.org
SIC: 8052 Personal care facility

(P-20425)
EMERITUS CORPORATION
2261 Tuolumne St, Vallejo (94589-2560)
PHONE..................................707 552-3336
EMP: 50
SALES (corp-wide): 4.5B Publicly Held
SIC: 8052 Personal care facility
HQ: Emeritus Corporation
3131 Elliott Ave Ste 500
Milwaukee WI 53214

(P-20426)
EMERITUS CORPORATION
800 Oregon St, Sonoma (95476-6445)
PHONE..................................707 996-7101
Melon Rivera, *Hlthcr Dir*
EMP: 50
SALES (corp-wide): 4.5B Publicly Held
SIC: 8052 8361 Personal care facility; geriatric residential care
HQ: Emeritus Corporation
3131 Elliott Ave Ste 500
Milwaukee WI 53214

(P-20427)
EMERITUS CORPORATION
Also Called: Emeritus At Villa Colima
19850 Colima Rd, Walnut (91789-3411)
PHONE..................................909 595-5030
Wanda Reynolds, *Branch Mgr*
EMP: 50
SALES (corp-wide): 4.5B Publicly Held
SIC: 8052 Intermediate care facilities
HQ: Emeritus Corporation
3131 Elliott Ave Ste 500
Milwaukee WI 53214

(P-20428)
ESKATON
11390 Coloma Rd Ofc, Gold River (95670-6324)
PHONE..................................916 852-7900
Tonae Hasik, *Manager*
David Van Reusen, *Administration*
EMP: 60
SALES (est): 1.6MM
SALES (corp-wide): 142MM Privately Held
SIC: 8052 Intermediate care facilities
PA: Eskaton
5105 Manzanita Ave Ste D
Carmichael CA 95608
916 334-0296

(P-20429)
GENTIVA HOSPICE
5001 E Commercecenter Dr # 140, Bakersfield (93309-1687)
PHONE..................................661 324-1232
EMP: 155
SALES (est): 507.9K
SALES (corp-wide): 6B Privately Held
SIC: 8052 Personal care facility
HQ: Kindred Healthcare, Llc
680 S 4th St
Louisville KY 40202
502 596-7300

(P-20430)
HILLSIDE HOUSE INC
1235 Veronica Springs Rd, Santa Barbara (93105-4522)
PHONE..................................805 687-4818
Pam Flynt, *Administration*
Chuck Klein, *Principal*
Peter Troesch, *Principal*
Bernard Mines, *Accounting Mgr*
Craig Olson, *Controller*
EMP: 88 EST: 1945
SQ FT: 24,000
SALES: 4.8MM Privately Held
WEB: www.hillsidehousesb.org
SIC: 8052 Home for the mentally retarded, with health care

(P-20431)
HOFFMAN HOSPICE OF THE VALLEY
8501 Brimhall Rd Bldg 100, Bakersfield (93312-2327)
PHONE..................................661 410-1010
Beth Hosman, *President*
Sheila Fryer, *Admin Sec*
Don Leonard, *Controller*
EMP: 67
SQ FT: 8,500
SALES: 14.7MM Privately Held
SIC: 8052 Personal care facility

(P-20432)
HOSPICE AND PALLIATIVE CARE
Also Called: Hospice of The East Bay
2849 Miranda Ave, Alamo (94507-1443)
PHONE..................................925 945-8924
Laura Pakar, *Branch Mgr*
EMP: 75
SALES (corp-wide): 1.5MM Privately Held
SIC: 8052 Personal care facility
PA: Hospice And Palliative Care
3470 Buskirk Ave
Concord CA 94523
925 887-5678

(P-20433)
HOSPICE OF VALLEYS SC (PA)
Also Called: HOSPICE OF VALLEYS
25240 Hancock Ave Ste 120, Murrieta
(92562-5991)
PHONE..........................951 200-7800
Terry Azkoul, *Exec Dir*
Lynette Cvar, *General Mgr*
Leslee Cochrane, *Director*
Gina Isaac, *Director*
Gina Obryant, *Director*
EMP: 70
SALES: 5.8MM **Privately Held**
SIC: 8052 Personal care facility

(P-20434)
**JONBEC CARE INCORPORATED
(PA)**
1711 Plum Ln, Redlands (92374-2874)
P.O. Box 10788, San Bernardino (92423-0788)
PHONE..........................909 798-4003
Jonathan Joseph, *President*
Cindy Collins, *Treasurer*
Becky Joseph, *Vice Pres*
Oynnie Joseph, *Admin Sec*
EMP: 52
SQ FT: 13,000
SALES: 12.2MM **Privately Held**
SIC: 8052 Home for the mentally retarded, with health care

(P-20435)
**KERN CNTY MNTAL HLTH CHILD
SYS**
1111 Columbus St Ste 3000, Bakersfield
(93305-1939)
P.O. Box 1000 (93302-1000)
PHONE..........................661 868-8300
James Waterman, *Director*
EMP: 62
SALES (est): 1MM **Privately Held**
SIC: 8052 Home for the mentally retarded, with health care

(P-20436)
LEISURE CARE LLC
Also Called: Fairwinds-West Hills
8138 Woodlake Ave, West Hills
(91304-3500)
PHONE..........................818 713-0900
Pat Luc, *General Mgr*
EMP: 60
SALES (corp-wide): 112.4K **Privately Held**
WEB: www.leisurecare.com
SIC: 8052 Intermediate care facilities
HQ: Leisure Care, Llc
999 3rd Ave Ste 4550
Seattle WA 98104
206 436-7827

(P-20437)
**LOS ANGELES CTY RNCH LOS
AMGOS**
7601 Imperial Hwy, Downey (90242-3456)
PHONE..........................562 385-7111
Jorge Orozco, *CEO*
EMP: 1400
SALES (est): 112.3K **Privately Held**
SIC: 8052 Personal care facility

(P-20438)
**MAGNOLIA SPECIAL CARE
CENTER**
Also Called: Magnolia Post Acute Care
635 S Magnolia Ave, El Cajon
(92020-6012)
PHONE..........................619 442-8826
Kennon S Shea, *President*
EMP: 99
SQ FT: 24,088
SALES (est): 4.7MM **Privately Held**
SIC: 8052 8059 8051 Personal care facility; convalescent home; nursing home, except skilled & intermediate care facility; skilled nursing care facilities

(P-20439)
MARYMOUNT VILLA LLC
345 Davis St Ofc, San Leandro
(94577-2795)
PHONE..........................510 895-5007
Jasbir Walia, *Mng Member*
Arjun Bhagat, *Mng Member*

EMP: 65
SALES (est): 2.4MM **Privately Held**
SIC: 8052 8059 Personal care facility; convalescent home

(P-20440)
**MILESTONES OF
DEVELOPMENT INC**
1 Florida St, Vallejo (94590-5000)
PHONE..........................707 644-0496
Cynthia Mack, *Director*
Joan Yates, *Ch of Bd*
Faith Ohara, *Admin Sec*
EMP: 55
SQ FT: 7,564
SALES: 5.1MM **Privately Held**
SIC: 8052 Home for the mentally retarded, with health care

(P-20441)
**MOUNTAIN SHADOWS
SUPPORT GROUP (PA)**
Also Called: MOUNTAIN SHADOWS COM-MUNITY HOM
2067 W El Norte Pkwy, Escondido
(92026-1899)
PHONE..........................760 743-3714
Richard W Marrs, *President*
David Erickson, *Bd of Directors*
Wade Wilde, *Exec Dir*
Toni Albright, *Human Res Dir*
Fabiola Fuller, *Human Res Mgr*
EMP: 81
SQ FT: 3,000
SALES: 18MM **Privately Held**
WEB: www.mtnshadows.org
SIC: 8052 8059 Personal care facility; rest home, with health care

(P-20442)
**MOUNTAIN VALLEY CHILD AND
FAMI**
24077 State Highway 49, Nevada City
(95959-8519)
PHONE..........................530 265-9057
Daniel Petrie, *CEO*
Richard Milhous, *CFO*
Janet Milhous, *Business Mgr*
Teresa Petrie, *Food Svc Dir*
Kathleen Benson, *Director*
EMP: 220
SQ FT: 22,000
SALES: 11.2MM **Privately Held**
SIC: 8052 8361 Intermediate care facilities; residential care

(P-20443)
**MURRIETA GARDENS SENIOR
LIVING**
18878 E Armstead St, Azusa (91702-4805)
PHONE..........................951 600-7676
Michelle Tehlam, *Director*
EMP: 60
SALES (est): 3MM **Privately Held**
SIC: 8052 Intermediate care facilities

(P-20444)
**NEW VISTA BEHAVIORAL HLTH
LLC**
3 Park Plz Ste 550, Irvine (92614-2537)
PHONE..........................949 284-0095
Jennifer Hale, *Branch Mgr*
EMP: 99
SALES (corp-wide): 3MM **Privately Held**
SIC: 8052 Home for the mentally retarded, with health care
PA: New Vista Behavioral Health, Llc
1901 Newport Blvd Ste 204
Costa Mesa CA
888 316-3665

(P-20445)
PRAIRIE CITY COMMONS LLC
Also Called: Prairie City Landing
645 Willard Dr, Folsom (95630-4048)
PHONE..........................916 458-0303
Eric Hostetter, *Mng Member*
EMP: 85 EST: 2016
SALES (est): 807K **Privately Held**
SIC: 8052 Intermediate care facilities

(P-20446)
**QUAIL PARK RETIREMENT
VILLAGE**
4520 W Cypress Ave, Visalia (93277-1577)
PHONE..........................559 624-3500
Denis Bryant, *Manager*
Valerie White, *Exec Dir*
EMP: 65
SALES (est): 4.1MM **Privately Held**
WEB: www.quail-park.com
SIC: 8052 6513 Intermediate care facilities; apartment building operators

(P-20447)
**RANCHO VISTA HEALTH
CENTER**
200 Grapevine Rd Apt 15, Vista
(92083-4042)
PHONE..........................760 941-1480
Alan Shigley, *Exec Dir*
EMP: 205
SALES (est): 8.8MM **Privately Held**
SALES (corp-wide): 35.4MM **Privately
Held**
WEB: www.healthcaregrp.com
SIC: 8052 8051 8361 Intermediate care facilities; skilled nursing care facilities; residential care
PA: Activcare Living, Inc.
10603 Rancho Bernardo Rd
San Diego CA 92127
858 565-4424

(P-20448)
RES-CARE INC
611 S Central Ave, Glendale (91204-2008)
PHONE..........................818 637-7727
Michael Sowerby, *Manager*
EMP: 130
SALES (corp-wide): 2B **Privately Held**
WEB: www.rescare.com
SIC: 8052 Home for the mentally retarded, with health care
HQ: Res-Care, Inc.
805 N Whittington Pkwy
Louisville KY 40222
502 394-2100

(P-20449)
RES-CARE CALIFORNIA INC
Also Called: Edgewood Center
200 W Paramount St, Azusa (91702-4422)
PHONE..........................626 334-7862
Danny Soto, *Branch Mgr*
EMP: 50
SQ FT: 78,991
SALES (corp-wide): 2B **Privately Held**
SIC: 8052 Home for the mentally retarded, with health care
HQ: Res-Care California, Inc.
6170 Purple Hills Dr
San Jose CA 95119

(P-20450)
ROSS VALLEY HOMES INC
Also Called: TAMALPAIS
501 Via Casitas, Greenbrae (94904-1901)
PHONE..........................415 461-2300
David Berg, *CEO*
Don Meninga, *CFO*
Valerie Peterson, *Social Dir*
Belinda Ong, *Controller*
EMP: 100
SALES: 24.5MM **Privately Held**
WEB: www.rossvalleyhomes.com
SIC: 8052 Personal care facility

(P-20451)
**SCOTT STREET SENIOR
HOUSING CO**
Also Called: RHODA GOLDMAN PLAZA
2180 Post St, San Francisco (94115-6013)
PHONE..........................415 345-5083
Marrianne Nannesthad, *Director*
Eric Luu, *CFO*
Ira Kurtz, *Exec Dir*
Candiece Milford, *Managing Dir*
Simeon Meyer, *Director*
EMP: 105
SQ FT: 195,000
SALES: 14MM **Privately Held**
WEB: www.rgplaza.org
SIC: 8052 Personal care facility

(P-20452)
**SENIOR LIVING SOLUTIONS
LLC**
1725 S Bascom Ave Apt 105, Campbell
(95008-0676)
PHONE..........................408 385-1835
Daniel P Schneider,
EMP: 120
SALES (est): 1.9MM **Privately Held**
SIC: 8052 Personal care facility

(P-20453)
**SHORELINE S INTERMEDIATE
CARE**
Also Called: Alameda Care Center
430 Willow St, Alameda (94501-6130)
PHONE..........................510 523-8857
Jack E Easterday, *President*
EMP: 200
SQ FT: 38,000
SALES (est): 5.2MM **Privately Held**
SIC: 8052 8051 Intermediate care facilities; skilled nursing care facilities

(P-20454)
**SIERRA HILLS CARE CENTER
INC**
1139 Cirby Way, Roseville (95661-4421)
PHONE..........................916 782-7007
Ellen L Kuykendall, *President*
Brad Wilcox, *Treasurer*
EMP: 53
SQ FT: 30,000
SALES (est): 1.9MM
SALES (corp-wide): 103.9MM **Privately
Held**
WEB: www.villadelrey.com
SIC: 8052 Personal care facility
HQ: Horizon West Healthcare, Inc.
4020 Sierra College Blvd # 190
Rocklin CA 95677
916 624-6230

(P-20455)
SILVERADO SENIOR LIVING INC
Also Called: Newport Mesa Memory Care
Cmnty
350 W Bay St, Costa Mesa (92627-2020)
PHONE..........................949 945-0189
Michelle Egrer, *Principal*
Lee Riggs, *COO*
Jamie Langston, *Hlthcr Dir*
EMP: 70
SQ FT: 20,331
SALES (corp-wide): 180.3MM **Privately
Held**
WEB: www.silveradosenior.com
SIC: 8052 Personal care facility
PA: Senior Silverado Living Inc
6400 Oak Cyn Ste 200
Irvine CA 92618
949 240-7200

(P-20456)
**SNOWLINE HSPC ELDORADO
CNTY**
6520 Pleasant Valley Rd, Diamond Springs
(95619-9512)
PHONE..........................916 817-2338
Tom Heflin, *President*
William Fisher, *Treasurer*
Mary Newton, *Exec Dir*
Michael Schmidt, *Exec Dir*
Leah Hall, *Admin Sec*
EMP: 140
SQ FT: 8,900
SALES: 8.7MM **Privately Held**
SIC: 8052 Personal care facility

(P-20457)
**SNOWLINE HSPICE EL DORADO
CNTY**
6520 Pleasant Valley Rd, Diamond Springs
(95619-9512)
PHONE..........................530 621-7820
Michael Sehmidt, *Exec Dir*
Richard B Esposito, *President*
William Fisher, *Treasurer*
Jon Lehrman, *Vice Pres*
Leah Hall, *Admin Sec*
EMP: 140
SQ FT: 8,900
SALES: 11.7MM **Privately Held**
SIC: 8052 Personal care facility

(P-20458)
SOMERSET SPECIAL CARE CENTER
Also Called: Shea Family Care Somerset
151 Claydelle Ave, El Cajon (92020-4505)
PHONE....................619 442-0245
Kennon S Shea, *President*
EMP: 56
SALES (est): 3.6MM **Privately Held**
SIC: 8052 Personal care facility

(P-20459)
SPECIAL HOME NEEDS
1440 Jackson St, Santa Clara
(95050-4210)
PHONE....................408 985-8666
Vivian Ascusion, *President*
EMP: 51
SALES (est): 500K **Privately Held**
SIC: 8052 Home for the mentally retarded, with health care

(P-20460)
STRATGIES TO EMPWER PEOPLE INC (PA)
Also Called: Step
2330 Glendale Ln, Sacramento
(95825-2455)
PHONE....................916 679-1527
Jacquine Difoss, *President*
Claudia Loveless, *Controller*
Lydia Edinborough, *Human Res Mgr*
Lynn Heitner, *Director*
Sisson Stacy, *Director*
EMP: 53
SALES (est): 14.9MM **Privately Held**
SIC: 8052 Personal care facility

(P-20461)
SUNBRIDGE HEALTHCARE LLC
Also Called: Willows Care Rhabilitation Ctr
320 N Crawford St, Willows (95988-2326)
PHONE....................530 934-2834
Tina Brey, *Manager*
EMP: 99 **Publicly Held**
WEB: www.innoventurehealthcare.com
SIC: 8052 8051 Intermediate care facilities; skilled nursing care facilities
HQ: Sunbridge Healthcare, Llc
101 Sun Ave Ne
Albuquerque NM 87109
505 821-3355

(P-20462)
SUNBRIDGE HEALTHCARE LLC
Also Called: Harbor View Community Svcs Ctr
850 E Wardlow Rd, Long Beach
(90807-4628)
PHONE....................562 981-9392
Dan Thorne, *Branch Mgr*
EMP: 200 **Publicly Held**
WEB: www.innoventurehealthcare.com
SIC: 8052 8051 Intermediate care facilities; skilled nursing care facilities
HQ: Sunbridge Healthcare, Llc
101 Sun Ave Ne
Albuquerque NM 87109
505 821-3355

(P-20463)
SUNBRIDGE HEALTHCARE LLC
Also Called: Sunbridge Care Ctr For Downey
9300 Telegraph Rd, Downey (90240-2425)
PHONE....................562 869-2567
Wendy Johnson, *Principal*
EMP: 119 **Publicly Held**
SIC: 8052 8051 Intermediate care facilities; skilled nursing care facilities
HQ: Sunbridge Healthcare, Llc
101 Sun Ave Ne
Albuquerque NM 87109
505 821-3355

(P-20464)
SUNBRIDGE HEALTHCARE LLC
Also Called: San Lndro Care Rhblitation Ctr
14766 Washington Ave, San Leandro
(94578-4220)
PHONE....................510 352-2211
Joe Gengilcore, *Administration*
Danielle Houston, *Human Res Dir*
EMP: 100
SQ FT: 28,635 **Publicly Held**
WEB: www.innoventurehealthcare.com

SIC: 8052 8093 8051 Intermediate care facilities; rehabilitation center, outpatient treatment; skilled nursing care facilities
HQ: Sunbridge Healthcare, Llc
101 Sun Ave Ne
Albuquerque NM 87109
505 821-3355

(P-20465)
SUTTER HEALTH
1651 Alvarado St, San Leandro
(94577-2636)
PHONE....................510 618-5200
EMP: 118
SALES (corp-wide): 12.7B **Privately Held**
SIC: 8052 Personal care facility
PA: Sutter Health
2200 River Plaza Dr
Sacramento CA 95833
916 733-8800

(P-20466)
TUSTIN CARE CENTER CORP
1051 Bryan Ave, Tustin (92780-4419)
PHONE....................714 832-6780
Jeoung H Lee, *President*
EMP: 60
SALES (est): 3.2MM **Privately Held**
SIC: 8052 Intermediate care facilities

(P-20467)
VITAS HEALTHCARE CORP CAL
355 Lennon Ln Ste 150, Walnut Creek
(94598-2475)
PHONE....................925 930-9373
Shirley Blethen, *Branch Mgr*
EMP: 95
SALES (corp-wide): 1.7B **Publicly Held**
WEB: www.vitasinnovativehospicecare.com
SIC: 8052 Personal care facility
HQ: Vitas Healthcare Corporation Of California
7888 Mission Grove Pkwy S
Riverside CA 92508
305 374-4143

(P-20468)
VITAS HEALTHCARE CORP CAL
1343 N Grand Ave Ste 100, Covina
(91724-4043)
PHONE....................626 918-2273
Thomas E Combs, *Owner*
Bruce Schlecter, *Director*
EMP: 80
SALES (corp-wide): 1.7B **Publicly Held**
WEB: www.vitasinnovativehospicecare.com
SIC: 8052 Personal care facility
HQ: Vitas Healthcare Corporation Of California
7888 Mission Grove Pkwy S
Riverside CA 92508
305 374-4143

(P-20469)
VITAS HEALTHCARE CORPORATION
333 N Lantana St Ste 124, Camarillo
(93010-9007)
PHONE....................805 437-2100
Rita Peddycoart, *Manager*
EMP: 95
SALES (corp-wide): 1.7B **Publicly Held**
WEB: www.vitasinnovativehospicecare.com
SIC: 8052 Personal care facility
HQ: Vitas Healthcare Corporation
201 S Biscayne Blvd # 400
Miami FL 33131
305 374-4143

(P-20470)
WATTS HEALTH FOUNDATION INC (HQ)
Also Called: Uhp Healthcare
3405 W Imperial Hwy # 304, Inglewood
(90303-2219)
PHONE....................310 424-2220
Dr Clyde W Oden, *President*
Jennifer Stapalding, *CEO*
Dr Darryl Leong, *MIS Dir*
EMP: 400 **EST:** 1967

SALES (est): 17.4MM
SALES (corp-wide): 31.9MM **Privately Held**
WEB: www.sonnytran.com
SIC: 8052 8011 8741 Intermediate care facilities; health maintenance organization; management services
PA: Watts Health Systems, Inc
3405 W Imperial Hwy
Inglewood CA
310 424-2220

(P-20471)
XCITE STEPS CORP
3978 Sorrento Valley Blvd # 100, San Diego
(92121-1436)
PHONE....................858 722-1948
Matthew Winkley, *Principal*
Marianne Bernaldo, *Director*
Darryn Robinson, *Case Mgr*
EMP: 140 **EST:** 2012
SALES (est): 3MM **Privately Held**
SIC: 8052 Home for the mentally retarded, with health care

8059 Nursing & Personal Care Facilities, NEC

(P-20472)
14766 WASH AVE OPERATIONS LLC
14766 Washington Ave, San Leandro
(94578-4220)
PHONE....................510 352-2211
Jeanine Allspaw, *Administration*
EMP: 552
SALES (est): 293.5K **Publicly Held**
SIC: 8059 Nursing home, except skilled & intermediate care facility
HQ: Sun Healthcare Group, Inc.
27442 Portola Pkwy # 200
Foothill Ranch CA 92610

(P-20473)
8520 WESTERN AVE INC
Also Called: Buena Park Nursing Center
10811 Kiowa Rd Apt 2a, Apple Valley
(92308-7989)
PHONE....................714 828-8222
Sim Mandelbaum, *President*
Brenda Mandelbaum, *Principal*
EMP: 135
SQ FT: 31,474
SALES (est): 7.4MM **Privately Held**
SIC: 8059 8051 Convalescent home; skilled nursing care facilities

(P-20474)
A CORI PARTNERSHIP
Also Called: Casitas Care Center
10826 Balboa Blvd, Granada Hills
(91344-6329)
PHONE....................818 368-2802
Claire Badama, *Partner*
EMP: 90 **EST:** 1982
SALES (est): 2.8MM **Privately Held**
SIC: 8059 8051 Convalescent home; nursing home, except skilled & intermediate care facility; skilled nursing care facilities

(P-20475)
A T ASSOCIATES INC
Also Called: Berkeley Pines Care Center
2223 Ashby Ave, Berkeley (94705-1907)
PHONE....................510 649-6670
Natalie Montijo, *Director*
EMP: 50
SALES (est): 1.1MM **Privately Held**
SIC: 8059 Personal care home, with health care
PA: A T Associates, Inc
535 School St
Pittsburg CA 94565

(P-20476)
A T ASSOCIATES INC
Also Called: Oakridge Care Center
2919 Fruitvale Ave, Oakland (94602-2108)
PHONE....................510 261-8564
Abby Tiller, *Manager*
EMP: 100 **Privately Held**

SIC: 8059 8051 Convalescent home; skilled nursing care facilities
PA: A T Associates, Inc
535 School St
Pittsburg CA 94565

(P-20477)
A T ASSOCIATES INC (PA)
535 School St, Pittsburg (94565-3937)
PHONE....................925 808-6540
Alba F Tiller, *President*
EMP: 75
SALES (est): 2.5MM **Privately Held**
SIC: 8059 8011 Convalescent home; free-standing emergency medical center

(P-20478)
AG FACILITIES OPERATIONS LLC
6380 Wilshire Blvd # 800, Los Angeles
(90048-5003)
PHONE....................323 651-1808
Jacob Winter, *President*
Leo Krieger, *CFO*
Scott Krieger, *Director*
EMP: 1000
SALES (est): 7.4MM **Privately Held**
SIC: 8059 Nursing home, except skilled & intermediate care facility

(P-20479)
AG REDLANDS LLC
Also Called: Highland Care Center Redlands
700 E Highland Ave, Redlands
(92374-6233)
PHONE....................909 793-2678
Tyrus Lefler, *Director*
Doug Easton, *CEO*
EMP: 110
SALES (est): 4.9MM **Privately Held**
SIC: 8059 Nursing home, except skilled & intermediate care facility

(P-20480)
ALAIDANDREW CORPORATION
1205 8th St, Bakersfield (93304-2123)
PHONE....................661 334-2200
Julita A Javier, *President*
EMP: 79
SALES (est): 2MM
SALES (corp-wide): 3.4MM **Privately Held**
SIC: 8059 Convalescent home
PA: Bettec Corporation
3210 W Pico Blvd
Los Angeles CA
323 734-2171

(P-20481)
ALDERWOOD INC
115 Bridge St, San Gabriel (91775-2719)
PHONE....................626 289-4439
Ben Garrett, *President*
Eva Mae Casner, *Treasurer*
Christin Garret, *Admin Sec*
Louis Pages, *Administration*
EMP: 90 **EST:** 1974
SALES (est): 5.4MM **Privately Held**
SIC: 8059 Convalescent home

(P-20482)
ALEXANDRIA CARE CENTER LLC
1515 N Alexandria Ave, Los Angeles
(90027-5203)
PHONE....................323 660-1800
Robert Snukal, *President*
Edwin Evangelista, *Director*
Julio Guzman, *Director*
EMP: 140
SQ FT: 30,000
SALES (est): 9MM **Publicly Held**
WEB: www.parkviewnursing.net
SIC: 8059 8051 Convalescent home; skilled nursing care facilities
PA: Genesis Healthcare, Inc.
101 E State St
Kennett Square PA 19348

(P-20483)
ALTA CARE CENTER LLC
13075 Blackbird St, Garden Grove
(92843-2902)
PHONE....................714 530-6322

EMP: 118
SALES (est): 788.6K **Publicly Held**
WEB: www.parkviewnursing.net
SIC: **8059** 8051 Convalescent home;
skilled nursing care facilities
HQ: Skilled Healthcare, Llc
27442 Portola Pkwy # 200
Foothill Ranch CA 92610
949 282-5800

(P-20484)
AMDAL IN-HOME CARE INC (PA)
147 N K St, Tulare (93274-4003)
P.O. Box 1318 (93275-1318)
PHONE...............................559 686-6611
Deanne Martin Soares, *CEO*
Julian Mack, *Shareholder*
Charles Mack, *Admin Sec*
EMP: 50
SALES (est): 3.7MM **Privately Held**
WEB: www.amdalinhome.com
SIC: **8059** Personal care home, with health
care

(P-20485)
AMDAL IN-HOME CARE INC
3410 Mccall Ave Ste 107, Selma
(93662-2500)
PHONE...............................559 227-1701
Deanne Martin-Soares, *Manager*
EMP: 55
SALES (corp-wide): 3.7MM **Privately
Held**
WEB: www.amdalinhome.com
SIC: **8059** Personal care home, with health
care
PA: Amdal In-Home Care, Inc.
147 N K St
Tulare CA 93274
559 686-6611

(P-20486)
**AMERICAN BAPTIST HOMES OF
WEST**
Also Called: Rosewood Retirement Commu-
nity
1401 New Stine Rd, Bakersfield
(93309-3530)
PHONE...............................661 834-0620
Ellen Renner, *Branch Mgr*
Rebecca Humes, *Records Dir*
Diane Kimbrough, *Social Dir*
Brenda Ocheao, *Office Mgr*
Rowena Lopez, *Nursing Dir*
EMP: 150
SALES (corp-wide): 21.8MM **Privately
Held**
WEB: www.abhow.com
SIC: **8059** 8052 8051 Rest home, with
health care; intermediate care facilities;
skilled nursing care facilities
HQ: American Baptist Homes Of The West
6120 Stoneridge Mall Rd # 300
Pleasanton CA 94588
925 924-7100

(P-20487)
**AMERICAN BAPTIST HOMES OF
WEST**
Also Called: Plymouth Village
900 Salem Dr, Redlands (92373-6147)
PHONE...............................909 793-1233
Keith Kasin, *Branch Mgr*
EMP: 250
SQ FT: 8,000
SALES (corp-wide): 21.8MM **Privately
Held**
WEB: www.abhow.com
SIC: **8059** 8051 Rest home, with health
care; skilled nursing care facilities
HQ: American Baptist Homes Of The West
6120 Stoneridge Mall Rd # 300
Pleasanton CA 94588
925 924-7100

(P-20488)
**AMERICAN BAPTIST HOMES OF
WEST**
Also Called: Pilgrim Haven Retirement Home
373 Pine Ln, Los Altos (94022-1694)
PHONE...............................650 948-8291
Rae Holt, *Manager*
EMP: 120
SQ FT: 95,130

SALES (corp-wide): 21.8MM **Privately
Held**
WEB: www.abhow.com
SIC: **8059** 8052 8051 Convalescent
home; intermediate care facilities; skilled
nursing care facilities
HQ: American Baptist Homes Of The West
6120 Stoneridge Mall Rd # 300
Pleasanton CA 94588
925 924-7100

(P-20489)
**AMERICAN BAPTIST HOMES OF
WEST**
Also Called: Terraces of Los Gatos Agei
800 Blossom Hill Rd Ofc, Los Gatos
(95032-3563)
PHONE...............................408 357-1100
A Candalla, *Exec Dir*
Patty Lopez, *Food Svc Dir*
EMP: 115
SALES (corp-wide): 21.8MM **Privately
Held**
WEB: www.abhow.com
SIC: **8059** 8052 8051 6513 Rest home,
with health care; intermediate care facili-
ties; skilled nursing care facilities; apart-
ment building operators
HQ: American Baptist Homes Of The West
6120 Stoneridge Mall Rd # 300
Pleasanton CA 94588
925 924-7100

(P-20490)
**ANTELOPE VLY RETIREMENT
HM INC**
Also Called: Antelope Vly Convalecent Hosp
44445 15th St W, Lancaster (93534-2801)
PHONE...............................661 948-7501
Marsha Weldon, *Director*
EMP: 400
SALES (corp-wide): 11.4MM **Privately
Held**
SIC: **8059** 8051 Convalescent home;
skilled nursing care facilities
PA: Antelope Valley Retirement Home, Inc.
44523 15th St W
Lancaster CA 93534
661 949-5584

(P-20491)
**ANTELOPE VLY RETIREMENT
HM INC**
Also Called: A V Nursing Care Center
44567 15th St W, Lancaster (93534-2803)
PHONE...............................661 949-5524
Alfred Jones, *Manager*
EMP: 200
SALES (corp-wide): 11.4MM **Privately
Held**
SIC: **8059** 8051 Convalescent home;
skilled nursing care facilities
PA: Antelope Valley Retirement Home, Inc.
44523 15th St W
Lancaster CA 93534
661 949-5584

(P-20492)
**ARARAT HOME OF LOS
ANGELES**
Also Called: Ararat Nursing Facility
15099 Mission Hills Rd, Mission Hills
(91345-1102)
PHONE...............................818 837-1800
M Kebhichien, *Administration*
EMP: 250
SALES (corp-wide): 32MM **Privately
Held**
SIC: **8059** 8051 Nursing home, except
skilled & intermediate care facility; skilled
nursing care facilities
PA: Ararat Home Of Los Angeles Inc
15105 Mission Hills Rd
Mission Hills CA 91345
818 365-3000

(P-20493)
**ARCADIA CONVALESCENT
HOSP INC (PA)**
Also Called: Arcadia Health Care Center
1601 S Baldwin Ave, Arcadia (91007-7910)
PHONE...............................323 681-1504
Orlando Clarizio Jr, *CEO*
EMP: 191
SQ FT: 21,342

SALES (est): 10.3MM **Privately Held**
SIC: **8059** 8051 Convalescent home;
skilled nursing care facilities

(P-20494)
ARIZONA AND 21ST CORP
Also Called: Berkley East Convalescent Hosp
2021 Arizona Ave, Santa Monica
(90404-1335)
PHONE...............................310 829-5377
Sol Galper, *President*
Steven Galper, *Corp Secy*
EMP: 60
SALES: 17.1MM **Privately Held**
SIC: **8059** Convalescent home

(P-20495)
ARTESIA CHRISTIAN HOME INC
11614 183rd St, Artesia (90701-5506)
PHONE...............................562 865-5218
Elroy Van Derley, *Exec Dir*
Sharon Kim, *Exec Dir*
Carol Smidt, *Technology*
Deborah Rouwenhorst, *Accountant*
Joy Bunyi, *Human Res Dir*
EMP: 140
SQ FT: 43,223
SALES: 10.8MM **Privately Held**
SIC: **8059** 8052 8051 Convalescent
home; intermediate care facilities; skilled
nursing care facilities

(P-20496)
**ASBURY PK NRSING
RHBLTTION CTR**
2257 Fair Oaks Blvd, Sacramento
(95825-5501)
PHONE...............................916 649-2000
John Lund, *President*
Austin Brickner, *Manager*
EMP: 130 EST: 1997
SQ FT: 30,000
SALES: 10.9MM **Privately Held**
SIC: **8059** Nursing home, except skilled &
intermediate care facility

(P-20497)
**B & E CONVALESCENT CENTER
INC (PA)**
Also Called: Gardena Convalescent Center
11627 Telg Rd Ste 200, Santa Fe Springs
(90670)
PHONE...............................562 923-9449
Barry J Weiss, *President*
Esther Weiss, *Treasurer*
EMP: 60
SALES (est): 4.8MM **Privately Held**
WEB:
www.gardenaconvalescentcenter.com
SIC: **8059** Convalescent home

(P-20498)
**BASSARD CONVALESCENT &
MED HM (PA)**
Also Called: Bassard Convalscent Home
3269 D St, Hayward (94541-4599)
PHONE...............................510 537-6700
Prema Thekkek, *President*
Bobby Singh, *Administration*
Heather Vance, *Accountant*
EMP: 65
SQ FT: 25,000
SALES (est): 1.6MM **Privately Held**
SIC: **8059** Convalescent home

(P-20499)
**BEAVER DAM HEALTH CARE
CENTER**
Also Called: Golden Livingcenter - NAPA
705 Trancas St, NAPA (94558-3014)
PHONE...............................707 255-6060
Jerry Wells, *Manager*
EMP: 55
SALES (corp-wide): 409.2MM **Privately
Held**
SIC: **8059** 8051 Convalescent home;
skilled nursing care facilities
PA: Beaver Dam Health Care Center
5220 Tennyson Pkwy # 400
Plano TX 75024
972 372-6300

(P-20500)
**BEAVER DAM HEALTH CARE
CENTER**
Also Called: Beverly Healthcare
515 E Orangeburg Ave, Modesto
(95350-5510)
PHONE...............................209 529-0516
Belinda Guzman, *Exec Dir*
EMP: 76
SALES (corp-wide): 409.2MM **Privately
Held**
WEB: www.nwbeccorp.com
SIC: **8059** Convalescent home
PA: Beaver Dam Health Care Center
5220 Tennyson Pkwy # 400
Plano TX 75024
972 372-6300

(P-20501)
BEGROUP (PA)
516 Burchett St, Glendale (91203-1014)
PHONE...............................818 638-4563
John H Cochrane III, *President*
David L Pierce, *CFO*
Daniel S Ogus, *Exec VP*
EMP: 59
SALES (est): 20.3MM **Privately Held**
SIC: **8059** Nursing home, except skilled &
intermediate care facility

(P-20502)
BELMONT VILLAGE LP
Also Called: Belmont Village At Sabre Sprng
13075 Evening Creek Dr S, San Diego
(92128-8101)
PHONE...............................858 486-5020
Inan Linton, *Manager*
EMP: 85
SALES (corp-wide): 41.3MM **Privately
Held**
SIC: **8059** Nursing home, except skilled &
intermediate care facility
PA: Belmont Village, L.P.
7660 Woodway Dr Ste 400
Houston TX 77063
713 463-1700

(P-20503)
BEN BENNETT INC (PA)
Also Called: Community Care Rhblitation Ctr
3419 Via Lido 646, Newport Beach
(92663-3908)
PHONE...............................949 209-9712
Bruce Bennett, *President*
▲ EMP: 200
SQ FT: 50,000
SALES (est): 9MM **Privately Held**
WEB: www.commcare.org
SIC: **8059** 8069 8051 Convalescent
home; specialty hospitals, except psychi-
atric; skilled nursing care facilities

(P-20504)
**BERNARDO HTS HEALTHCARE
INC**
Also Called: Carmel Mtn Rhab Healthcare Ctr
11895 Avenue Of Industry, San Diego
(92128-3423)
PHONE...............................858 673-0101
Christopher R Christensen, *CEO*
Covey C Christensen, *President*
Laura Sargent, *Chf Purch Ofc*
EMP: 99
SALES (est): 3.9MM
SALES (corp-wide): 2B **Publicly Held**
SIC: **8059** 8051 8011 Nursing home, ex-
cept skilled & intermediate care facility;
skilled nursing care facilities; clinic, oper-
ated by physicians
PA: The Ensign Group Inc
27101 Puerta Real Ste 450
Mission Viejo CA 92691
949 487-9500

(P-20505)
BERRYMAN HEALTH INC
Also Called: Ukiah Convalescent Hospital
1349 S Dora St, Ukiah (95482-6512)
PHONE...............................707 462-8864
Barbara Jimenez, *Principal*
EMP: 63
SALES (corp-wide): 2.4MM **Privately
Held**
WEB: www.ukiahconvalescent.com
SIC: **8059** Convalescent home

PA: Berryman Health Inc
615 E Chapman Ave Ste 3
Orange CA
-

(P-20506)
BETHEL LUTHERAN HOME INC
2280 Dockery Ave, Selma (93662-3898)
PHONE...................................559 896-4900
C Kaylene Steele, *Administration*
EMP: 100 **EST:** 1928
SQ FT: 33,000
SALES (est): 4MM **Privately Held**
SIC: 8059 8051 Domiciliary care; extended care facility

(P-20507)
BETHEL RETIREMENT COMMUNITY
2345 Scenic Dr, Modesto (95355-4574)
PHONE...................................209 577-1901
Tony Musolino, *General Ptnr*
Kenneth Lemmings DDS, *Partner*
Robert Pirtle, *Partner*
Stephen P Thomas, *Partner*
EMP: 100
SQ FT: 120,000
SALES (est): 4.2MM **Privately Held**
WEB: www.bethelretirement.com
SIC: 8059 8361 Nursing home, except skilled & intermediate care facility; home for the aged

(P-20508)
BLYTHE NURSING CARE CENTER
Also Called: Corprate Office
285 W Chanslor Way, Blythe (92225-1246)
PHONE...................................760 922-8176
Sandra Blessing, *Owner*
David Shellmann, *Administration*
EMP: 64
SQ FT: 12,000
SALES: 3.8MM **Privately Held**
WEB: www.blythenursing.com
SIC: 8059 Nursing home, except skilled & intermediate care facility

(P-20509)
BMB 1 LLC
Also Called: Ride At Home Care
495 E Rincon St Ste 211, Corona (92879-1379)
PHONE...................................951 272-6200
Michael Barboza, *Mng Member*
EMP: 65
SALES (est): 781.6K **Privately Held**
SIC: 8059 8051 Nursing & personal care; convalescent home with continuous nursing care

(P-20510)
BONNIE BRAE CNVLSCENT HOSP INC (PA)
Also Called: California Convalescent Center
420 S Bonnie Brae St, Los Angeles (90057-3010)
PHONE...................................213 483-8144
Elma Cayton, *CEO*
Albert Ballo, *Treasurer*
Divina Matabalan-Billing, *Clerk*
EMP: 60 **EST:** 1960
SALES (est): 6.7MM **Privately Held**
SIC: 8059 8051 Convalescent home; skilled nursing care facilities

(P-20511)
BRASWELL COL CARE REDLANDS CA
1618 Laurel Ave, Redlands (92373-4838)
PHONE...................................909 792-6050
James Braswell, *Partner*
EMP: 245
SALES (est): 10.6MM **Privately Held**
SIC: 8059 8051 Rest home, with health care; skilled nursing care facilities

(P-20512)
BRASWELLS VILLA MONTE VISTA
12696 Monte Vista Rd, Poway (92064-2500)
PHONE...................................858 487-6242
James Braswell, *Partner*
EMP: 160

SALES: 7.3MM **Privately Held**
SIC: 8059 8051 Convalescent home; skilled nursing care facilities

(P-20513)
BRENTWOOD SKILL NURSNG & REHAB
Also Called: Brentwood Sklled Nursng Rhbltn
1795 Walnut St, Red Bluff (96080-3645)
PHONE...................................530 527-2046
Phil Sullivan, *Administration*
Daniel McNeal, *Maint Spvr*
Terri Sullivan, *Nursing Dir*
Stephen Datu, *Director*
Becky Taroli, *Receptionist*
EMP: 66
SQ FT: 1,600
SALES (est): 1.8MM **Privately Held**
SIC: 8059 Convalescent home

(P-20514)
BRIARWOOD HEALTH CARE INC
5901 Lemon Hill Ave, Sacramento (95824-3231)
PHONE...................................916 383-2741
Sharron Jennings, *President*
EMP: 50
SALES: 3.4MM **Privately Held**
SIC: 8059 Convalescent home

(P-20515)
BRIER OAK ON SUNSET LLC
Also Called: BRIER OAK ON SUNSET REHAB CENTER
5154 W Sunset Blvd, Los Angeles (90027-5708)
PHONE...................................323 663-3951
Hazel Delacruz, *Marketing Staff*
Claudia Velasquez, *Director*
EMP: 120
SALES: 3.2MM **Publicly Held**
SIC: 8059 8051 8361 Convalescent home; skilled nursing care facilities; rehabilitation center, residential: health care incidental
HQ: Skilled Healthcare, Llc
27442 Portola Pkwy # 200
Foothill Ranch CA 92610
949 282-5800

(P-20516)
BRIGHTON CONVALESCENT CENTER
1836 N Fair Oaks Ave, Pasadena (91103-1619)
PHONE...................................626 798-9124
Alex Makabuhay, *Administration*
Pat Capello, *Administration*
Rose Wilson, *Systems Mgr*
EMP: 100
SALES: 9.4MM **Privately Held**
SIC: 8059 8051 Convalescent home; skilled nursing care facilities

(P-20517)
BROOKDALE SENIOR LIVING INC
72750 Country Club Dr, Rancho Mirage (92270-4083)
PHONE...................................760 346-7772
EMP: 87
SALES (corp-wide): 4.5B **Publicly Held**
SIC: 8059 6513 Nursing home, except skilled & intermediate care facility; retirement hotel operation
PA: Brookdale Senior Living
111 Westwood Pl Ste 400
Brentwood TN 37027
615 221-2250

(P-20518)
BROOKDALE SENIOR LIVING INC
Also Called: Brookdale Sunwest
1001 N Lyon Ave, Hemet (92545-1753)
PHONE...................................951 744-9861
T Byington, *Exec Dir*
EMP: 65
SALES (corp-wide): 4.5B **Publicly Held**
SIC: 8059 Nursing home, except skilled & intermediate care facility
PA: Brookdale Senior Living
111 Westwood Pl Ste 400
Brentwood TN 37027
615 221-2250

(P-20519)
BUENA VENTURA CARE CENTER INC
Also Called: Leisure Glen Convalescent Ctr
1505 Colby Dr, Glendale (91205-3307)
PHONE...................................818 247-4476
Yolanda Wise, *Administration*
EMP: 80
SALES (corp-wide): 6.6MM **Privately Held**
SIC: 8059 8051 Convalescent home; skilled nursing care facilities
PA: Buena Ventura Care Center Inc
1016 S Record Ave
Los Angeles CA 90023
323 268-0106

(P-20520)
BV GENERAL INC
Also Called: Kennedy Care Center
619 N Fairfax Ave, Los Angeles (90036-1714)
PHONE...................................323 651-0043
James Kargol, *Branch Mgr*
EMP: 70
SALES (corp-wide): 14.4MM **Privately Held**
WEB: www.hmscal.com
SIC: 8059 Rest home, with health care
PA: B.V. General, Inc.
1332 S Glendale Ave
Glendale CA 91205
760 747-0430

(P-20521)
CALIFORNIA CONVALESCENT HOSP
Also Called: Santa Barbara Convalescent Ctr
2225 De La Vina St, Santa Barbara (93105-3815)
PHONE...................................805 682-1355
Dorothy Shea, *President*
Laurie Shea, *President*
Roger Shea, *Treasurer*
S Laurie Anderson, *Admin Sec*
Kathleen Shea, *Admin Sec*
EMP: 70
SQ FT: 25,000
SALES (est): 6.2MM **Privately Held**
SIC: 8059 Convalescent home

(P-20522)
CALIFORNIA HM FOR THE AGED INC
Also Called: CALIFORNIA ARMENIAN HOME
6720 E Kings Canyon Rd, Fresno (93727-3603)
PHONE...................................559 251-8414
Ray Wark, *Administration*
EMP: 165 **EST:** 1950
SQ FT: 39,000
SALES: 13MM **Privately Held**
SIC: 8059 Convalescent home; nursing home, except skilled & intermediate care facility

(P-20523)
CALIFORNIA VOCATIONS INC
Also Called: Arthur Schawlow Center
564 Rio Lindo Ave Ste 204, Chico (95926-1852)
P.O. Box 538, Paradise (95967-0538)
PHONE...................................530 877-0937
Bob Irvine, *Exec Dir*
Richard Welsh, *President*
George Dailey, *Treasurer*
Lisa Nixon, *Officer*
Paul Johnson, *Admin Sec*
EMP: 195
SQ FT: 5,700
SALES: 7.5MM **Privately Held**
WEB: www.calvoc.org
SIC: 8059 Home for the mentally retarded, exc. skilled or intermediate

(P-20524)
CALIFRNIA-NEVADA METHDST HOMES
Also Called: Lake Park Retirment Residence
1850 Alice St Ofc, Oakland (94612-4169)
PHONE...................................510 835-5511
Steve Jacobson, *Manager*
Barbara Conlon, *Executive*
EMP: 100

SALES (est): 3.2MM
SALES (corp-wide): 19.4MM **Privately Held**
WEB: www.foresthillmanor.com
SIC: 8059 Rest home, with health care
PA: California-Nevada Methodist Homes
201 19th St Ste 100
Oakland CA 94612
510 893-8989

(P-20525)
CARE CHOICE HEALTH SYSTEMS INC
Also Called: Care Choice Home Care
338 Via Vera Cruz Ste 120, San Marcos (92078-2647)
PHONE...................................760 798-4508
Tara Pardo, *CEO*
EMP: 60
SALES (est): 982K **Privately Held**
SIC: 8059 8082 Personal care home, with health care; home health care services

(P-20526)
CHANCELLOR HLTH CARE CAL I INC (PA)
Also Called: Linda Valley Care Center
25383 Cole St, Loma Linda (92354-3103)
PHONE...................................909 796-0235
Corbin Swafford, *Exec Dir*
Edmond Peters, *Vice Ch Bd*
Ferney Zuluaga, *Exec Dir*
Hoselito Acuna, *Office Mgr*
Dave Green, *Administration*
EMP: 70
SQ FT: 32,000
SALES (est): 6.2MM **Privately Held**
SIC: 8059 6513 8051 Convalescent home; nursing home, except skilled & intermediate care facility; apartment building operators; skilled nursing care facilities

(P-20527)
CHANNING HOUSE
850 Webster St Ofc, Palo Alto (94301-2859)
PHONE...................................650 327-0950
Melvin Matsumoto, *CEO*
Honey Faustino, *Records Dir*
Dr Thomas Fiene, *Trustee*
Trinh Quach, *Executive*
Carl Braginsky, *Exec Dir*
EMP: 100
SQ FT: 300,000
SALES: 21.1MM **Privately Held**
WEB: www.channinghouse.com
SIC: 8059 Rest home, with health care

(P-20528)
CHASE CARE CENTER INC
1101 Crenshaw Blvd, Los Angeles (90019-3112)
PHONE...................................323 935-8490
Jeoung H Lee, *President*
John Yoo, *Administration*
EMP: 121
SQ FT: 83,000
SALES (est): 5.6MM **Privately Held**
SIC: 8059 8051 Convalescent home; skilled nursing care facilities

(P-20529)
COASTAL VIEW HALTHCARE CTR LLC
4904 Telegraph Rd, Ventura (93003-4109)
PHONE...................................805 642-4101
Sim Mandelbaum,
Beverly Bragado, *Administration*
Debbie Smith, *Marketing Staff*
Frances Foy, *Director*
EMP: 96
SALES (est): 4MM **Privately Held**
SIC: 8059 Convalescent home

(P-20530)
COMPASS HEALTH INC
Also Called: Mission View Health Center
1425 Woodside Dr, San Luis Obispo (93401-5936)
PHONE...................................805 543-0210
Linda Lindsey, *Manager*
Marcy Woolpert, *Administration*
EMP: 99 **Privately Held**

SIC: 8059 Nursing home, except skilled & intermediate care facility
PA: Compass Health, Inc.
200 S 13th St Ste 208
Grover Beach CA 93433
-

(P-20531)
COMPASS HEALTH INC
Also Called: Bayside Care Center
1405 Teresa Dr, Morro Bay (93442-2458)
PHONE.........................805 772-7372
Harold Carder, *Manager*
Mindi Martin, *Executive*
Cindi Murray, *Social Dir*
Rebecca Nolan, *Office Mgr*
Erica Gomez, *Human Res Dir*
EMP: 131 **Privately Held**
SIC: 8059 Nursing home, except skilled & intermediate care facility
PA: Compass Health, Inc.
200 S 13th St Ste 208
Grover Beach CA 93433

(P-20532)
COMPASS HEALTH INC
Also Called: Arroyo Grande Care Center
1212 Farroll Ave, Arroyo Grande (93420-3718)
PHONE.........................805 489-8137
Harold Carder, *Administration*
Tammy Risner, *Food Svc Dir*
Melissa Myers, *Director*
Sonja Rogers, *Director*
EMP: 131 **Privately Held**
SIC: 8059 Nursing home, except skilled & intermediate care facility
PA: Compass Health, Inc.
200 S 13th St Ste 208
Grover Beach CA 93433

(P-20533)
COUNTRY VILLA BLMNT HGHT HLTH
Also Called: BELMONT CONVALESCENT HOSPITAL
1730 Grand Ave, Long Beach (90804-2011)
PHONE.........................562 597-8817
Sherry Gradon, *Administration*
Janice Connelly, *Psychologist*
EMP: 70
SALES: 14.5MM **Privately Held**
SIC: 8059 Convalescent home

(P-20534)
COUNTRY VILLA EAST LP
Also Called: Country Vlla Nrsing Rhbltation
5916 W Pico Blvd, Los Angeles (90035-2615)
PHONE.........................323 939-3184
Stephen Reissman, *Partner*
Steve Reissmann, *Partner*
Cherrie Villanueva, *VP Human Res*
Tristan Viola, *Human Res Dir*
Bevye Bressant, *Education*
EMP: 200
SALES (est): 8.3MM **Privately Held**
SIC: 8059 8051 Convalescent home; skilled nursing care facilities

(P-20535)
COUNTRY VILLA SERVICE CORP
112 E Broadway, San Gabriel (91776-1805)
PHONE.........................626 285-2165
J Caballero, *Administration*
EMP: 188
SALES (corp-wide): 125.3MM **Privately Held**
SIC: 8059 Nursing home, except skilled & intermediate care facility
PA: Country Villa Service Corp.
2400 E Katella Ave # 800
Anaheim CA 92806
310 574-3733

(P-20536)
COUNTRY VILLA TERRACE (PA)
Also Called: Country Vlla Convalescent Hosp
6050 W Pico Blvd, Los Angeles (90035-2647)
PHONE.........................323 653-3980
Steven Reissman, *President*

Diana Reissman, *Vice Pres*
Jessica Arenivas, *Director*
Myung Moreno, *Director*
David Ramin, *Director*
EMP: 75
SQ FT: 6,000
SALES (est): 5.4MM **Privately Held**
SIC: 8059 8361 Convalescent home; residential care

(P-20537)
COUNTRY VILLA TERRACE
Also Called: Flora Ter Convalescent Hosp
5916 W Pico Blvd, Los Angeles (90035-2615)
PHONE.........................323 939-3184
Lydia Reyes, *Manager*
EMP: 50
SQ FT: 15,240
SALES (corp-wide): 5.4MM **Privately Held**
SIC: 8059 Convalescent home
PA: Country Villa Terrace
6050 W Pico Blvd
Los Angeles CA 90035
323 653-3980

(P-20538)
COVENANT CARE CALIFORNIA LLC
Also Called: Vintage Faire Nrsng Rhbltn
3620 Dale Rd Ste B, Modesto (95356-0598) .
PHONE.........................209 521-2094
Julie Abram, *Administration*
Jaime Ochoa, *Director*
Carol Sparks, *Director*
EMP: 105 **Privately Held**
WEB: www.willowtreenursingcenter.com
SIC: 8059 8051 Convalescent home; skilled nursing care facilities
HQ: Covenant Care California, Llc
27071 Aliso Creek Rd # 100
Aliso Viejo CA 92656

(P-20539)
CPCC INC
Also Called: Chatsworth Park Hlth Care Ctr
10610 Owensmouth Ave, Chatsworth (91311-2151)
PHONE.........................818 882-3200
John Sorensen, *President*
Greg Ethington, *Administration*
Leticia Wong, *Food Svc Dir*
EMP: 99
SALES (est): 4.2MM **Privately Held**
SIC: 8059 8051 Convalescent home; skilled nursing care facilities

(P-20540)
CRESCENT COURT NURSING HOME
1334 S Ham Ln, Lodi (95242-3903)
PHONE.........................209 367-7400
Kerry Bains, *President*
Terry Jen, *President*
Sharon Jennings, *President*
Bea Halsell, *Principal*
Mary Chow, *Director*
EMP: 50
SQ FT: 5,000
SALES (est): 1.9MM
SALES (corp-wide): 8.4MM **Privately Held**
SIC: 8059 8052 Convalescent home; intermediate care facilities
PA: Riverside Health Care Corporation
1469 Humboldt Rd Ste 175
Chico CA 95928
530 897-5100

(P-20541)
CULVER WEST HEALTH CENTER LLC
4035 Grand View Blvd, Los Angeles (90066-5211)
PHONE.........................310 390-9506
Harry Jacobs,
EMP: 90
SQ FT: 25,000
SALES (est): 8.1MM **Privately Held**
SIC: 8059 Convalescent home

(P-20542)
CYPRESS GARDENS CONVALESCENT H
9025 Colorado Ave, Riverside (92503-2167)
PHONE.........................951 688-3643
Stanley Angermeir, *President*
Edward Erzen, *Vice Pres*
EMP: 115
SALES: 10.9MM **Privately Held**
SIC: 8059 8051 Convalescent home; skilled nursing care facilities

(P-20543)
D & C CARE CENTER INC
Also Called: Sunrise Convalescent Hospital
1640 N Fair Oaks Ave, Pasadena (91103-1615)
PHONE.........................626 798-1175
Felipe T Chu, *CEO*
June Cayabyab, *Administration*
June Ceayabyab, *Administration*
EMP: 75
SALES (est): 5.9MM **Privately Held**
SIC: 8059 Convalescent home

(P-20544)
D K FORTUNE & ASSOCIATES INC
Also Called: Marina Care Center
5240 Sepulveda Blvd, Culver City (90230-5214)
PHONE.........................310 391-7266
Fax: 310 397-4998
EMP: 130
SALES: 9.2MM **Privately Held**
SIC: 8059 8051

(P-20545)
DAVID KING CONVALESCENT HOSP
1340 15th St, Santa Monica (90404-1802)
PHONE.........................310 451-9706
Miriam Weiss, *President*
EMP: 99
SQ FT: 62,075
SALES (est): 1MM
SALES (corp-wide): 62.1MM **Privately Held**
WEB: www.goldenstatehealth.com
SIC: 8059 Nursing & personal care
PA: Golden State Health Centers, Inc.
13347 Ventura Blvd
Sherman Oaks CA 91423
818 385-3200

(P-20546)
DEVONSHIRE CARE CENTER LLC
1350 E Devonshire Ave, Hemet (92544-8629)
P.O. Box 1405, Riverside (92502-1405)
PHONE.........................951 925-2571
Jose Lynch, *Mng Member*
Andrea Abbes, *Mng Member*
EMP: 90
SALES: 8MM **Privately Held**
SIC: 8059 Convalescent home

(P-20547)
DIVERSIFIED HEALTH SVCS DEL (PA)
136 Washington Ave, Richmond (94801-3947)
PHONE.........................510 231-6200
Garrett Loube, *President*
EMP: 200 EST: 1968
SALES (est): 5.3MM **Privately Held**
SIC: 8059 Convalescent home

(P-20548)
EL MONTE CONVALESCENT HOSPITAL
4096 Easy St, El Monte (91731-1054)
PHONE.........................626 442-1500
Jesse Telles, *CEO*
Nhu Devera, *Nursing Dir*
David Gu, *Director*
Linda Torres, *Receptionist*
EMP: 75 EST: 1964
SQ FT: 21,208
SALES: 5.9MM **Privately Held**
WEB: www.elmonteconvalescent.com
SIC: 8059 Convalescent home

(P-20549)
ELENA VILLA HEALTHCARE CENTER
13226 Studebaker Rd, Norwalk (90650-2532)
PHONE.........................562 868-0591
Floyd Loupot, *President*
Everett E Goings, *Vice Pres*
EMP: 90
SQ FT: 24,000
SALES (est): 4.1MM **Privately Held**
SIC: 8059 8051 Convalescent home; skilled nursing care facilities

(P-20550)
EMPRESS CARE CENTER
1299 S Bascom Ave, San Jose (95128-3514)
PHONE.........................408 287-0616
Ben Laub, *Director*
Kin Mohamed, *Director*
EMP: 65
SALES (est): 3.4MM **Privately Held**
SIC: 8059 Convalescent home

(P-20551)
ENGLISH OAKS CONVALESCENT
Also Called: English Oaks Convalescent & RE
2633 W Rumble Rd, Modesto (95350-0154)
PHONE.........................209 577-1001
Terry L Mundy, *President*
Pamela Mundy, *Admin Sec*
EMP: 225
SQ FT: 57,000
SALES: 22.2MM **Privately Held**
SIC: 8059 Convalescent home

(P-20552)
FAR WEST INC
Also Called: Westgage Grdn Convalescent Ctr
4525 W Tulare Ave, Visalia (93277-1560)
PHONE.........................559 733-0901
Ellen Rioux, *Principal*
EMP: 113
SALES (corp-wide): 103.9MM **Privately Held**
SIC: 8059 8051 Convalescent home; skilled nursing care facilities
HQ: Far West, Inc.
4020 Sierra College Blvd
Rocklin CA 95677
-

(P-20553)
FILLMORE CONVALESCENT CTR LLC
118 B St, Fillmore (93015-1763)
PHONE.........................805 524-0083
Fax: 805 524-7260
EMP: 80
SQ FT: 13,800
SALES (est): 4.5MM **Privately Held**
WEB: www.fillmoreconvalescentcenter.com
SIC: 8059 8051

(P-20554)
FOWLER CONVALESCENT HOSPITAL
1306 E Sumner Ave, Fowler (93625-2697)
PHONE.........................559 834-2542
Roy Delacerda, *Administration*
EMP: 50
SALES (est): 917.2K **Privately Held**
SIC: 8059 8051 Convalescent home; skilled nursing care facilities

(P-20555)
FRAN-JOM INC
Also Called: Temple City Convalescent Hosp
5101 Tyler Ave, Temple City (91780-3682)
PHONE.........................626 443-3028
Gary Elliott, *President*
Bryan Elliott, *Vice Pres*
Frank Elliott, *Vice Pres*
EMP: 60
SQ FT: 15,000
SALES (est): 2.5MM **Privately Held**
SIC: 8059 Convalescent home

(P-20556)

FRONT PORCH COMMUNITIES
Also Called: Walnut Manor Care Center
1401 W Ball Rd, Anaheim (92802-1711)
PHONE..................................714 776-7150
Sondra Coughlin, *Manager*
Maria Reynoso, *Facilities Dir*
EMP: 159
SALES (corp-wide): 165.1MM **Privately Held**
SIC: 8059 8051 Rest home, with health care; skilled nursing care facilities
PA: Front Porch Communities And Services - Casa De Manana, Llc
800 N Brand Blvd Fl 19
Glendale CA 91203
818 729-8100

(P-20557)

FRONT PORCH COMMUNITIES (PA)
Also Called: Fredericka Manor Care Center
800 N Brand Blvd Fl 19, Glendale (91203-1231)
PHONE..................................818 729-8100
Gary Wheeler, *CEO*
Roberta Jacobsen, *President*
Bill Jennings, *CFO*
Mary Miller, *CFO*
Ed Salvador, *CFO*
EMP: 100
SQ FT: 20,000
SALES: 165.1MM **Privately Held**
SIC: 8059 8051 Rest home, with health care; skilled nursing care facilities

(P-20558)

FRONT PORCH COMMUNITIES
Also Called: Claremont Manor
650 Harrison Ave, Claremont (91711-4538)
PHONE..................................909 626-1227
Joseph Peduzzi, *Branch Mgr*
Kari Miner, *President*
EMP: 150
SQ FT: 167,053
SALES (corp-wide): 165.1MM **Privately Held**
SIC: 8059 8052 6513 Convalescent home; intermediate care facilities; apartment building operators
PA: Front Porch Communities And Services - Casa De Manana, Llc
800 N Brand Blvd Fl 19
Glendale CA 91203
818 729-8100

(P-20559)

FRONT PORCH COMMUNITIES
Also Called: Fredericka Manor Care Center
111 Third Ave, Chula Vista (91910-1822)
PHONE..................................619 427-2777
Loraine Wiencek, *Administration*
Tess Liangco, *Records Dir*
Jolene Hall, *Human Res Dir*
Cindy Ross, *Marketing Staff*
Lita Luansing, *Nursing Dir*
EMP: 178
SALES (corp-wide): 165.1MM **Privately Held**
SIC: 8059 8051 Convalescent home; skilled nursing care facilities
PA: Front Porch Communities And Services - Casa De Manana, Llc
800 N Brand Blvd Fl 19
Glendale CA 91203
818 729-8100

(P-20560)

FRONT PORCH COMMUNITIES & SVCS
Also Called: Lutheran Health Facility
303 N Glenoaks Blvd # 1000, Burbank (91502-1116)
PHONE..................................818 729-8100
Bob Moses, *Director*
EMP: 60
SALES (corp-wide): 165.1MM **Privately Held**
SIC: 8059 8011 Rest home, with health care; clinic, operated by physicians
PA: Front Porch Communities And Services - Casa De Manana, Llc
800 N Brand Blvd Fl 19
Glendale CA 91203
818 729-8100

(P-20561)

FRONT PORCH COMMUNITIES & SVCS
Also Called: Southland Lutheran Home
11701 Studebaker Rd, Norwalk (90650-7544)
PHONE..................................562 868-9761
Covy Christiansen, *Manager*
EMP: 200
SALES (corp-wide): 165.1MM **Privately Held**
SIC: 8059 8011 8052 8051 Rest home, with health care; geriatric specialist, physician/surgeon; intermediate care facilities; skilled nursing care facilities
PA: Front Porch Communities And Services - Casa De Manana, Llc
800 N Brand Blvd Fl 19
Glendale CA 91203
818 729-8100

(P-20562)

FRONT PRCH CMMUNITIES/SERVICES
3775 Modoc Rd, Santa Barbara (93105-4474)
PHONE..................................805 687-0793
Roberta Jacobsen, *Branch Mgr*
Laurie Yttri, *Exec Dir*
EMP: 250
SQ FT: 68,000
SALES (corp-wide): 165.1MM **Privately Held**
SIC: 8059 8051 Rest home, with health care; skilled nursing care facilities
PA: Front Porch Communities And Services - Casa De Manana, Llc
800 N Brand Blvd Fl 19
Glendale CA 91203
818 729-8100

(P-20563)

FRONT ST INC
Also Called: FRONT ST RESIDENTIAL CARE
2115 7th Ave, Santa Cruz (95062-1663)
PHONE..................................831 420-0120
Anne Butler, *President*
EMP: 115
SALES: 1.3MM **Privately Held**
WEB: www.frontst.com
SIC: 8059 Personal care home, with health care

(P-20564)

GAITHERS FAMILY HOME
1408 S Newcomb St, Porterville (93257-9354)
PHONE..................................559 781-0301
Henrietta Gaithers, *President*
EMP: 50
SALES (est): 1.5MM **Privately Held**
SIC: 8059 Home for the mentally retarded, exc. skilled or intermediate

(P-20565)

GARDEN GROVE CONVALES
12882 Shackelford Ln, Garden Grove (92841-5109)
PHONE..................................714 638-9470
Aurea Sarigan, *Administration*
Percy Miranda, *Records Dir*
Uri Mandelbaum, *President*
Carol Bercich, *Social Dir*
Letty Vasquez, *Social Dir*
EMP: 125
SQ FT: 6,000
SALES (est): 5MM **Privately Held**
SIC: 8059 8051 Convalescent home; skilled nursing care facilities

(P-20566)

GENERATION CLOVIS LLC
Also Called: Carmel Village At Clovis
1650 Shaw Ave, Clovis (93611-4201)
PHONE..................................559 297-4900
Erik Schuck, *Administration*
EMP: 150
SALES (est): 778.5K **Privately Held**
SIC: 8059 Nursing & personal care

(P-20567)

GENESIS HEALTHCARE LLC
Also Called: Fountain View Cnvalescent Hosp
5310 Fountain Ave, Los Angeles (90029-1005)
PHONE..................................323 461-9961
Jennifer Gans, *Records Dir*
Claire Padama, *Vice Pres*
Jamila Gaines, *Social Dir*
Rogaciaonno Morales, *Envir Svcs Dir*
Pia Banaag, *Office Mgr*
EMP: 150 **Publicly Held**
SIC: 8059 8051 8069 Convalescent home; skilled nursing care facilities; specialty hospitals, except psychiatric
HQ: Genesis Healthcare Llc
101 E State St
Kennett Square PA 19348

(P-20568)

GERI-CARE II INC
Also Called: Vermont Care Center
22035 S Vermont Ave, Torrance (90502-2120)
P.O. Box 6069 (90504-0069)
PHONE..................................310 328-0812
Emmanuel David, *President*
Engelica Vivillanueva, *Vice Pres*
EMP: 250
SQ FT: 40,000
SALES: 10.7MM **Privately Held**
SIC: 8059 8051 Convalescent home; skilled nursing care facilities

(P-20569)

GHC OF SUNNYVALE LLC
Also Called: CEDAR CREST NURSING & REHABILITATION CENTER
797 E Fremont Ave, Sunnyvale (94087-2805)
PHONE..................................408 738-4880
Thomas Olds Jr,
Scott Morley, *Food Svc Dir*
Jose Contreras, *Director*
Nelia Montojo, *Director*
EMP: 140 EST: 2000
SALES: 12.7MM
SALES (corp-wide): 63.1MM **Privately Held**
SIC: 8059 8051 Nursing home, except skilled & intermediate care facility; skilled nursing care facilities
PA: Life Generations Healthcare Llc
6 Hutton Cntre Dr Ste 400
Santa Ana CA 92707
714 241-5600

(P-20570)

GIBRALTER CONVALESCENT HOSP
Also Called: Sunset Manor Convalescent Hosp
2720 Nevada Ave, El Monte (91733-2318)
PHONE..................................626 443-9425
Marcel Morales, *Manager*
EMP: 100
SALES (corp-wide): 828.1MM **Privately Held**
SIC: 8059 8051 Convalescent home; skilled nursing care facilities
PA: Gibralter Convalescent Hospital
600 E Washington Ave
Santa Ana CA
-

(P-20571)

GOLDEN LIVING LLC
Also Called: Beverly Healthcare
9541 Van Nuys Blvd, Panorama City (91402-1315)
PHONE..................................818 893-6385
Christopher Christenson, *Sales/Mktg Mgr*
EMP: 100
SALES (corp-wide): 409.2MM **Privately Held**
WEB: www.nwbeccorp.com
SIC: 8059 8051 Convalescent home; skilled nursing care facilities
PA: Beaver Dam Health Care Center
5220 Tennyson Pkwy # 400
Plano TX 75024
972 372-6300

(P-20572)

GOLDEN LIVING LLC
Also Called: Beverly Healthcare
2123 Verdugo Blvd, Montrose (91020-1628)
PHONE..................................818 249-3925
Shahid Chaudhry, *Manager*
EMP: 51
SALES (corp-wide): 409.2MM **Privately Held**
WEB: www.nwbeccorp.com
SIC: 8059 Convalescent home
PA: Beaver Dam Health Care Center
5220 Tennyson Pkwy # 400
Plano TX 75024
972 372-6300

(P-20573)

GOLDEN LIVING LLC
Also Called: Beverly Healthcare
19929 Greenley Rd, Sonora (95370-5996)
PHONE..................................209 533-2500
Michael Ramstead, *Manager*
EMP: 105
SALES (corp-wide): 409.2MM **Privately Held**
WEB: www.nwbeccorp.com
SIC: 8059 8051 Convalescent home; skilled nursing care facilities
PA: Beaver Dam Health Care Center
5220 Tennyson Pkwy # 400
Plano TX 75024
972 372-6300

(P-20574)

GOLDEN LIVING LLC
Also Called: Beverly Healthcare
3000 N Gate Rd, Seal Beach (90740-2535)
PHONE..................................562 598-2477
Lory Heredia, *Director*
Alfredo Cervantes, *Maint Spvr*
EMP: 80
SALES (corp-wide): 409.2MM **Privately Held**
WEB: www.nwbeccorp.com
SIC: 8059 8051 8721 Convalescent home; skilled nursing care facilities; billing & bookkeeping service
PA: Beaver Dam Health Care Center
5220 Tennyson Pkwy # 400
Plano TX 75024
972 372-6300

(P-20575)

GOLDEN LIVING LLC
Also Called: Beverly Healthcare
1700 Howard Rd, Madera (93637-5131)
PHONE..................................559 673-9278
Ken Evans, *Principal*
EMP: 65
SALES (corp-wide): 409.2MM **Privately Held**
WEB: www.nwbeccorp.com
SIC: 8059 Convalescent home
PA: Beaver Dam Health Care Center
5220 Tennyson Pkwy # 400
Plano TX 75024
972 372-6300

(P-20576)

GOLDEN LIVING LLC
Also Called: Golden Livingcenter - Redding
1836 Gold St, Redding (96001-1817)
PHONE..................................530 241-6756
Pam Eiszele, *Manager*
EMP: 55
SALES (corp-wide): 409.2MM **Privately Held**
SIC: 8059 8051 Convalescent home; skilled nursing care facilities
PA: Beaver Dam Health Care Center
5220 Tennyson Pkwy # 400
Plano TX 75024
972 372-6300

(P-20577)

GOLDEN LIVING LLC
Also Called: Golden Livingcenter - Fresno
2715 Fresno St, Fresno (93721-1304)
PHONE..................................559 486-4433
Debbie Witt, *Manager*
EMP: 55
SALES (corp-wide): 409.2MM **Privately Held**
SIC: 8059 8051 Convalescent home; skilled nursing care facilities

PA: Beaver Dam Health Care Center
5220 Tennyson Pkwy # 400
Plano TX 75024
972 372-6300

(P-20578)
GOLDEN LIVING LLC
Also Called: Golden Livingcenter - Hyland
3408 E Shields Ave, Fresno (93726-6907)
PHONE..............................559 227-4063
Michelle Tatham, *Administration*
EMP: 55
SALES (corp-wide): 409.2MM **Privately Held**
SIC: 8059 Convalescent home
PA: Beaver Dam Health Care Center
5220 Tennyson Pkwy # 400
Plano TX 75024
972 372-6300

(P-20579)
GOLDEN LIVING LLC
Also Called: Beverly Healthcare
3169 M St, Merced (95348-2404)
PHONE..............................209 722-6231
Mary Imperial, *Manager*
EMP: 70
SALES (corp-wide): 409.2MM **Privately Held**
WEB: www.nwbeccorp.com
SIC: 8059 Convalescent home
PA: Beaver Dam Health Care Center
5220 Tennyson Pkwy # 400
Plano TX 75024
972 372-6300

(P-20580)
GOLDEN LIVING LLC
Also Called: Golden Livingcenter - Sanger
2550 9th St, Sanger (93657-2716)
PHONE..............................559 875-6501
Leslie Cotham, *Branch Mgr*
EMP: 100
SALES (corp-wide): 409.2MM **Privately Held**
SIC: 8059 8051 Convalescent home; skilled nursing care facilities
PA: Beaver Dam Health Care Center
5220 Tennyson Pkwy # 400
Plano TX 75024
972 372-6300

(P-20581)
GOLDEN STATE HEALTH CTRS INC
5522 Gracewood Ave, Temple City (91780)
PHONE..............................626 579-0310
David Schachter, *VP Opers*
EMP: 153
SALES (corp-wide): 62.1MM **Privately Held**
WEB: www.goldenstatehealth.com
SIC: 8059 8051 Convalescent home; skilled nursing care facilities
PA: Golden State Health Centers, Inc.
13347 Ventura Blvd
Sherman Oaks CA 91423
818 385-3200

(P-20582)
GOLDEN STATE HEALTH CTRS INC
Also Called: Chatsworth Health & Rehab
21820 Craggy View St, Chatsworth (91311-2909)
P.O. Box 3909 (91313-3909)
PHONE..............................818 882-8233
Emmanuel Ruiz, *Manager*
EMP: 105
SALES (corp-wide): 62.1MM **Privately Held**
WEB: www.goldenstatehealth.com
SIC: 8059 8051 Convalescent home; skilled nursing care facilities
PA: Golden State Health Centers, Inc.
13347 Ventura Blvd
Sherman Oaks CA 91423
818 385-3200

(P-20583)
GOLDSTAR HLTHCR CNTR OF CHTSWR
145 S Fairfax Ave Ste 200, Los Angeles (90036-2186)
P.O. Box 3909, Chatsworth (91313-3909)
PHONE..............................818 882-8233
Miriam Weiss, *President*
David Weiss, *Ch of Bd*
Rose Kasirer, *Vice Pres*
EMP: 147
SQ FT: 26,650
SALES: 7.5MM
SALES (corp-wide): 62.1MM **Privately Held**
WEB: www.goldenstatehealth.com
SIC: 8059 Convalescent home
PA: Golden State Health Centers, Inc.
13347 Ventura Blvd
Sherman Oaks CA 91423
818 385-3200

(P-20584)
GREAT WSTN CNVLESCENT HOSP INC
Also Called: Verdugo Vly Convalescent Hosp
2635 Honolulu Ave, Montrose (91020-1706)
PHONE..............................818 248-6856
Ishkhan Khatchadurian, *President*
Barbara Khatchadurian, *Vice Pres*
EMP: 130
SQ FT: 22,000
SALES (est): 3.7MM **Privately Held**
SIC: 8059 8361 8051 Convalescent home; residential care; skilled nursing care facilities

(P-20585)
GUARDIAN REHABILITATION HOSP
533 S Fairfax Ave, Los Angeles (90036-3129)
PHONE..............................323 930-4815
Uri Mandelbaum, *President*
EMP: 90
SQ FT: 10,000
SALES (est): 5.7MM **Privately Held**
SIC: 8059 8069 8051 Convalescent home; specialty hospitals, except psychiatric; skilled nursing care facilities

(P-20586)
GVA ENTERPRISES INC (PA)
Also Called: Angels Nursing Center
316 S Westlake Ave, Los Angeles (90057-4500)
PHONE..............................213 484-0510
George Rabinowitz, *President*
Aileen Delmo, *Nursing Dir*
EMP: 53
SQ FT: 22,578
SALES (est): 5.3MM **Privately Held**
SIC: 8059 Convalescent home

(P-20587)
HANK FISHER PROPERTIES INC
Also Called: Chateau At River's Edge
641 Feature Dr Apt 233, Sacramento (95825-8331)
PHONE..............................916 921-1970
Jeff Hertzig, *Director*
EMP: 92
SALES (est): 3.7MM
SALES (corp-wide): 17.5MM **Privately Held**
SIC: 8059 8052 Convalescent home; intermediate care facilities
PA: Hank Fisher Properties, Inc.
641 Fulton Ave Ste 200
Sacramento CA 95825
916 485-1441

(P-20588)
HARBOR VILLA CARE CENTER
861 S Harbor Blvd, Anaheim (92805-5157)
PHONE..............................714 635-8131
Ramon Martinez, *Administration*
EMP: 90
SQ FT: 25,000
SALES (est): 2.9MM **Privately Held**
SIC: 8059 Convalescent home

(P-20589)
HEALTH INFORMATION PARTNERS
4041 Macarthur Blvd # 360, Newport Beach (92660-2512)
P.O. Box 10129 (92658-0129)
PHONE..............................949 261-5000
Joseph A Farris, *CEO*
EMP: 125
SALES: 7MM **Privately Held**
WEB: www.hip-inc.com
SIC: 8059 Rest home, with health care

(P-20590)
HELIOS HEALTHCARE LLC
Also Called: Windsor Vallejo Care Center
2200 Tuolumne St, Vallejo (94589-2523)
PHONE..............................707 644-7401
Laura Curly, *Manager*
EMP: 180
SALES (corp-wide): 24.1MM **Privately Held**
SIC: 8059 8051 Convalescent home; skilled nursing care facilities
PA: Helios Healthcare, Llc
520 Capitol Mall Ste 800
Sacramento CA 95814
916 471-2241

(P-20591)
HERMITAGE HLTHCR MNKN MNR
400 Circle Dr, Angwin (94508-9806)
PHONE..............................410 651-0011
Bonnie Stone,
EMP: 165
SQ FT: 52,000
SALES (est): 1.6MM **Privately Held**
SIC: 8059 8051 Convalescent home; skilled nursing care facilities

(P-20592)
HILLCREST CARE INC
4280 Cypress Dr, San Bernardino (92407-2960)
PHONE..............................909 882-2965
C David Benfield, *President*
EMP: 100 **EST:** 1977
SALES (est): 4.9MM **Privately Held**
SIC: 8059 Nursing home, except skilled & intermediate care facility

(P-20593)
HILLCREST CNVALESCENT HOSP INC
3401 Cedar Ave, Long Beach (90807-4422)
PHONE..............................323 636-3462
Rosalyn Zisman, *CEO*
Gaby Chacanas, *Treasurer*
Brad D Hann, *Administration*
EMP: 130
SQ FT: 37,500
SALES (est): 3.3MM **Privately Held**
SIC: 8059 Convalescent home

(P-20594)
HILLSDALE GROUP LP
Also Called: Sherman Village Hlth Care Ctr
12750 Riverside Dr, North Hollywood (91607-3319)
PHONE..............................818 623-2170
Rich Terrell, *Principal*
EMP: 100
SALES (corp-wide): 14.5MM **Privately Held**
WEB: www.greenhillsretirement.com
SIC: 8059 8051 8093 8011 Convalescent home; skilled nursing care facilities; rehabilitation center, outpatient treatment; clinic, operated by physicians
PA: The Hillsdale Group L P
1199 Howard Ave Ste 200
Burlingame CA

(P-20595)
HILLSDALE GROUP LP
Also Called: Green Hills Retirement Center
1201 Broadway Ofc, Millbrae (94030-1976)
PHONE..............................650 742-9150
Pooja Sadarangani, *Manager*
EMP: 50

SALES (corp-wide): 14.5MM **Privately Held**
WEB: www.greenhillsretirement.com
SIC: 8059 8051 Nursing home, except skilled & intermediate care facility; skilled nursing care facilities
PA: The Hillsdale Group L P
1199 Howard Ave Ste 200
Burlingame CA
-

(P-20596)
HILLSDALE GROUP LP
Also Called: Hayward Convalescent Hospital
1832 B St, Hayward (94541-3140)
PHONE..............................510 538-3866
Mark Bornta, *Manager*
EMP: 80
SALES (corp-wide): 14.5MM **Privately Held**
WEB: www.greenhillsretirement.com
SIC: 8059 8051 Nursing home, except skilled & intermediate care facility; convalescent home with continuous nursing care
PA: The Hillsdale Group L P
1199 Howard Ave Ste 200
Burlingame CA
-

(P-20597)
HORIZON WEST HEALTHCARE INC
Also Called: Hilltop Manor
12225 Shale Ridge Ln, Auburn (95602-8870)
PHONE..............................530 885-7511
Sheilia Waddell, *Director*
EMP: 180
SALES (corp-wide): 103.9MM **Privately Held**
WEB: www.villadelrey.com
SIC: 8059 8051 Convalescent home; skilled nursing care facilities
HQ: Horizon West Healthcare, Inc.
4020 Sierra College Blvd # 190
Rocklin CA 95677
916 624-6230

(P-20598)
HUMANGOOD (PA)
Also Called: TERRACES AT SQUAW PEAK
6120 Stoneridge Mall Rd, Pleasanton (94588-3296)
PHONE..............................602 906-4024
John Cochran, *CEO*
EMP: 57 **EST:** 1959
SQ FT: 161,000
SALES: 21.8MM **Privately Held**
WEB: www.abhow.com
SIC: 8059 8051 8322 Rest home, with health care; skilled nursing care facilities; old age assistance

(P-20599)
INDEPENDENT QUALITY CARE INC
Also Called: Northgate Convalescent Hosp
40 Professional Ctr Pkwy, San Rafael (94903-2703)
PHONE..............................415 479-1230
Theresa D Guzman, *Principal*
Zeke Griffin, *Administration*
Dawn Bright, *Director*
Debra Koonce, *Director*
Linda Pearson, *Director*
EMP: 75
SALES (corp-wide): 11.6MM **Privately Held**
WEB: www.iqcare.com
SIC: 8059 Convalescent home
PA: Independent Quality Care, Inc
3 Crow Canyon Ct
San Ramon CA 94583
925 855-0881

(P-20600)
INDEPENDENT QUALITY CARE INC (PA)
Also Called: Woodland Lfytte Cnvlscent Hosp
3 Crow Canyon Ct, San Ramon (94583-1619)
PHONE..............................925 855-0881
Daniel W Alger, *President*
Jeremy Grimes, *Vice Pres*
▲ **EMP:** 75

SALES (est): 11.6MM **Privately Held**
WEB: www.iqcare.com
SIC: 8059 Convalescent home

(P-20601)
INDEPENDENT QUALITY CARE INC
Also Called: McClure Convalescent Hospital
2910 Mcclure St, Oakland (94609-3505)
PHONE..........................510 836-3677
Hung-Chee Chan, *Manager*
EMP: 55
SQ FT: 5,000
SALES (corp-wide): 11.6MM **Privately Held**
WEB: www.iqcare.com
SIC: 8059 Convalescent home
PA: Independent Quality Care, Inc
3 Crow Canyon Ct
San Ramon CA 94583
925 855-0881

(P-20602)
INDEPENDENT QUALITY CARE INC
Also Called: Woodland Lfyett Sklled Nursing
3721 Mt Diablo Blvd, Lafayette (94549-3538)
PHONE..........................925 284-5544
Christine Nacion, *Branch Mgr*
EMP: 75
SALES (corp-wide): 11.6MM **Privately Held**
WEB: www.iqcare.com
SIC: 8059 Convalescent home
PA: Independent Quality Care, Inc
3 Crow Canyon Ct
San Ramon CA 94583
925 855-0881

(P-20603)
INSTITUTE ON AGING
881 Fremont Ave Ste A2, Los Altos (94024-5637)
PHONE..........................510 536-3377
Tara Bradley, *Director*
EMP: 139 **Privately Held**
SIC: 8059 Convalescent home
PA: Institute On Aging
3575 Geary Blvd
San Francisco CA 94118

(P-20604)
KENNEDY CARE CENTER
Also Called: Kennedy Care Ctr Kosher Certif
619 N Fairfax Ave, Los Angeles (90036-1714)
PHONE..........................323 651-0043
Alisa Berdnik, *Administration*
EMP: 98 **EST:** 1968
SQ FT: 25,000
SALES (est): 4.8MM **Privately Held**
SIC: 8059 Convalescent home

(P-20605)
KF COMMUNITY CARE LLC
Also Called: Community Care Center
2335 Mountain Ave, Duarte (91010-3559)
PHONE..........................626 357-3207
Barbara O'Connor, *Administration*
Gordon Buechs, *CFO*
Barbara Oconnor, *General Mgr*
EMP: 170
SQ FT: 11,000
SALES (est): 6.7MM **Privately Held**
SIC: 8059 Convalescent home

(P-20606)
KF ONTARIO HEALTHCARE LLC
Also Called: Ontario Healthcare Center
1661 S Euclid Ave, Ontario (91762-5826)
PHONE..........................909 984-6713
Jacob Wintner, *CEO*
Edward S Shea, *President*
Gordon Buechs, *CFO*
EMP: 50
SALES (est): 2MM **Privately Held**
SIC: 8059 8051 Convalescent home; nursing home, except skilled & intermediate care facility; skilled nursing care facilities

(P-20607)
KF SUNRAY LLC
Also Called: Sunray Healthcare Center
3210 W Pico Blvd, Los Angeles (90019-3643)
PHONE..........................323 734-2171
Douglas Easton, *Owner*
Daniel Wintner, *General Mgr*
Vandana Desai, *Administration*
EMP: 99
SALES (est): 4.3MM **Privately Held**
SIC: 8059 Convalescent home

(P-20608)
KINDRED HEALTHCARE OPER INC
Also Called: Maywood Acres Health Care Ctr
2641 S C St, Oxnard (93033-4502)
PHONE..........................805 487-7840
Bonnie Velal, *Manager*
EMP: 100
SALES (corp-wide): 6B **Privately Held**
WEB: www.salemhaven.com
SIC: 8059 8051 Convalescent home; skilled nursing care facilities
HQ: Kindred Healthcare Operating, Llc
680 S 4th St
Louisville KY 40202
502 596-7300

(P-20609)
KINDRED HEALTHCARE OPERATING
Also Called: Alta Vista Healthcare Center
9020 Garfield St, Riverside (92503-3903)
PHONE..........................951 688-8200
Jeff Henson, *Director*
EMP: 100
SALES (corp-wide): 6B **Privately Held**
WEB: www.salemhaven.com
SIC: 8059 8051 Nursing home, except skilled & intermediate care facility; skilled nursing care facilities
HQ: Kindred Healthcare Operating, Llc
680 S 4th St
Louisville KY 40202
502 596-7300

(P-20610)
KNOLLS WEST POST ACUTE LLC
16890 Green Tree Blvd, Victorville (92395-5618)
PHONE..........................760 245-5361
David Johnson, *Mng Member*
Thomas Chambers,
Ryan O'Hara,
EMP: 99
SALES (est): 1.9MM **Privately Held**
SIC: 8059 Nursing home, except skilled & intermediate care facility

(P-20611)
L C C H ASSOCIATES INC
Also Called: Health Care Group
4311 3rd Ave B, San Diego (92103-1407)
PHONE..........................858 565-4424
William M Chance, *President*
Renee Barnard, *COO*
Ronald McElloit, *Exec VP*
Rn Case, *Manager*
EMP: 50
SQ FT: 10,000
SALES (est): 2.3MM **Privately Held**
SIC: 8059 Convalescent home

(P-20612)
LEE JOHNSON
Also Called: Casa Palmera Care Center
14750 El Camino Real, Del Mar (92014-4204)
PHONE..........................858 481-4411
Lee Johnson, *Owner*
▲ **EMP:** 132
SQ FT: 36,000
SALES (est): 10.7MM **Privately Held**
SIC: 8059 8051 Convalescent home; skilled nursing care facilities

(P-20613)
LIFE CARE CENTERS AMERICA INC
Also Called: Vista Del Mar Health Centers
304 N Melrose Dr, Vista (92083-4814)
PHONE..........................760 724-8222
Michael Ramstead, *Branch Mgr*
Nada Elaile, *Food Svc Dir*
Sunni Bullock, *Director*
EMP: 170
SALES (corp-wide): 144MM **Privately Held**
SIC: 8059 8051 Convalescent home; skilled nursing care facilities
PA: Life Care Centers Of America, Inc.
3570 Keith St Nw
Cleveland TN 37312
423 472-9585

(P-20614)
LIFE GNERATIONS HEALTHCARE LLC
Also Called: Stanford Crt Nrsing Cntr-Sntee
8778 Cuyamaca St, Santee (92071-4255)
PHONE..........................619 449-5555
Andy Ashton, *Administration*
Najat Ailey, *Records Dir*
Patricia Clark, *Social Dir*
Manuel Lopez, *Director*
EMP: 100
SALES (corp-wide): 63.1MM **Privately Held**
SIC: 8059 8051 8049 Convalescent home; skilled nursing care facilities; physical therapist
PA: Life Generations Healthcare Llc
6 Hutton Cntre Dr Ste 400
Santa Ana CA 92707
714 241-5600

(P-20615)
LINCOLN GLEN MANOR
Also Called: LINCOLN GLEN SKILLED NURSING
2671 Plummer Ave Ste A, San Jose (95125-4877)
PHONE..........................408 267-1492
Loren Kroeker, *Exec Dir*
Barbara Filler, *Administration*
Anne Phoenix, *Info Tech Mgr*
Rick Hendrickson, *Plant Mgr*
Raul Lorenzo, *Food Svc Dir*
EMP: 110
SQ FT: 68,000
SALES: 7.4MM **Privately Held**
WEB: www.lgmanor.org
SIC: 8059 Convalescent home

(P-20616)
LOMITA VERDE INC
Also Called: Lomita Care Center
1955 Lomita Blvd, Lomita (90717-1807)
PHONE..........................310 325-1970
Donald G Laws, *President*
David E Sorenson, *Treasurer*
Roy Ruiz, *Food Svc Dir*
Nabil El Sayad, *Director*
EMP: 60
SALES: 9.9MM **Privately Held**
WEB: www.lomitacare.com
SIC: 8059 8322 Convalescent home; individual & family services

(P-20617)
LONGWOOD MANAGEMENT CORP
Also Called: Sunny View Care Center
2000 W Washington Blvd, Los Angeles (90018-1637)
PHONE..........................323 735-5146
Amber Gooden, *Administration*
EMP: 80
SALES (corp-wide): 170MM **Privately Held**
SIC: 8059 Convalescent home
PA: Longwood Management Corp.
4032 Wilshire Blvd Fl 6
Los Angeles CA 90010
213 389-6900

(P-20618)
LONGWOOD MANAGEMENT CORP
Also Called: Broadway Manor Care Center
605 W Broadway, Glendale (91204-1007)
PHONE..........................818 246-7174
Dolly Piper, *Manager*
EMP: 70
SQ FT: 7,000

SALES (corp-wide): 170MM **Privately Held**
SIC: 8059 8051 Convalescent home; skilled nursing care facilities
PA: Longwood Management Corp.
4032 Wilshire Blvd Fl 6
Los Angeles CA 90010
213 389-6900

(P-20619)
LONGWOOD MANAGEMENT CORP
Also Called: Western Convelescence
2190 W Adams Blvd, Los Angeles (90018-2039)
PHONE..........................323 737-7778
Emma Camanag, *Administration*
EMP: 80
SALES (corp-wide): 170MM **Privately Held**
SIC: 8059 6512 Convalescent home; commercial & industrial building operation
PA: Longwood Management Corp.
4032 Wilshire Blvd Fl 6
Los Angeles CA 90010
213 389-6900

(P-20620)
LONGWOOD MANAGEMENT CORP
Also Called: Aldon Ter Convalsent Hosptial
1240 S Hoover St, Los Angeles (90006-3606)
PHONE..........................213 382-8461
John Sicat, *Principal*
EMP: 170
SALES (corp-wide): 170MM **Privately Held**
SIC: 8059 8051 Convalescent home; skilled nursing care facilities
PA: Longwood Management Corp.
4032 Wilshire Blvd Fl 6
Los Angeles CA 90010
213 389-6900

(P-20621)
LONGWOOD MANAGEMENT CORP
Also Called: Imperial Care Center
11429 Ventura Blvd, Studio City (91604-3143)
PHONE..........................818 980-8200
Emma Dellanuoni, *Manager*
EMP: 200
SQ FT: 29,525
SALES (corp-wide): 170MM **Privately Held**
SIC: 8059 8051 Convalescent home; skilled nursing care facilities
PA: Longwood Management Corp.
4032 Wilshire Blvd Fl 6
Los Angeles CA 90010
213 389-6900

(P-20622)
LONGWOOD MANAGEMENT CORP
Also Called: Live Oak Rehab
537 W Live Oak St, San Gabriel (91776-1149)
PHONE..........................626 289-3763
Ranita Phan, *Manager*
EMP: 100
SALES (corp-wide): 170MM **Privately Held**
SIC: 8059 8051 Convalescent home; skilled nursing care facilities
PA: Longwood Management Corp.
4032 Wilshire Blvd Fl 6
Los Angeles CA 90010
213 389-6900

(P-20623)
LONGWOOD MANAGEMENT CORP
Also Called: Colonial Care Center
1913 E 5th St, Long Beach (90802-2024)
PHONE..........................562 432-5751
Laura McCuphen, *Manager*
EMP: 150
SALES (corp-wide): 170MM **Privately Held**
SIC: 8059 8051 Convalescent home; skilled nursing care facilities

PRODUCTS & SVCS

PA: Longwood Management Corp.
4032 Wilshire Blvd Fl 6
Los Angeles CA 90010
213 389-6900

(P-20624)
LOS GATOS SENIOR LIVING LLC
Also Called: Los Gtos Oaks Cnvalescent Hosp
16605 Lark Ave, Los Gatos (95032-7642)
PHONE..........................408 356-9146
Brad Heap, *Mng Member*
EMP: 50
SQ FT: 5,600
SALES (est): 1.6MM Privately Held
SIC: 8059 8051 Convalescent home; convalescent home with continuous nursing care

(P-20625)
MADERA CONVALESCENT HOSPITAL
Also Called: Merced Convalescent Hospital
510 W 26th St, Merced (95340-2804)
PHONE..........................209 723-2911
Dave Yarborough, *Manager*
EMP: 130
SALES (corp-wide): 5.6MM **Privately Held**
SIC: 8059 8051 Convalescent home; skilled nursing care facilities
PA: Madera Convalescent Hospital, Inc
517 S A St
Madera CA 93638
559 673-9228

(P-20626)
MAGNOLIA RHBLTTION NURSING CTR
Also Called: Magnolia Convalescent Hospital
8133 Magnolia Ave, Riverside (92504-3409)
PHONE..........................951 688-4321
Larry Mays, *President*
Grant Edgeson, *Treasurer*
Bennie J Mays, *Vice Pres*
Vanessa Romo, *Executive*
Bobbie N Mays, *Admin Sec*
EMP: 140
SQ FT: 25,000
SALES: 9.4MM **Privately Held**
SIC: 8059 8051 Convalescent home; skilled nursing care facilities

(P-20627)
MARK ONE CORPORATION
Also Called: Ha-Le Aloha Convalescent Hosp
1711 Richland Ave, Ceres (95307-4509)
PHONE..........................209 537-4581
Fax: 209 537-0035
EMP: 50
SALES (corp-wide): 12.7MM **Privately Held**
SIC: 8059
PA: Mark One Corporation
812 W Main St
Turlock CA
209 667-2484

(P-20628)
MARLINDA MANAGEMENT INC (PA)
Also Called: Sherwood Guest Home
3351 E Imperial Hwy, Lynwood (90262-3305)
PHONE..........................310 631-6122
Martha Lang, *President*
Linda Gassoumis, *CFO*
EMP: 120
SALES (est): 2.8MM **Privately Held**
SIC: 8059 Convalescent home

(P-20629)
MARNA HEALTH SERVICES INC
Also Called: SILLCREST NURSING HOME
4280 Cypress Dr, San Bernardino (92407-2960)
PHONE..........................909 882-2965
Maria Barrios, *President*
Napoleon Garcia, *Vice Pres*
EMP: 70
SQ FT: 120

SALES: 4.6MM **Privately Held**
SIC: 8059 7389 8049 Personal care home, with health care; ; physical therapist

(P-20630)
MARYCREST MANOR
10664 Saint James Dr, Culver City (90230-5498)
PHONE..........................310 838-2778
SIS V Del Carmen, *Administration*
SIS Veronica Del Carmen, *Administration*
EMP: 86
SQ FT: 43,449
SALES: 6.3MM **Privately Held**
SIC: 8059 8051 Convalescent home; skilled nursing care facilities

(P-20631)
MBK SENIOR LIVING LLC
Also Called: Sterling Senior Communities
41780 Btterfield Stage Rd, Temecula (92592-9206)
PHONE..........................951 506-5555
Nancy Halleck, *Director*
EMP: 60
SALES (corp-wide): 1.9MM **Privately Held**
SIC: 8059 Rest home, with health care
PA: Senior Mbk Living Llc
895 Dove St Ste 450
Newport Beach CA

(P-20632)
MEDICAL INVESTMENT CO
Also Called: Rinaldi Convalescent Hospital
16553 Rinaldi St, Granada Hills (91344-3762)
PHONE..........................818 360-1003
Glen Padama, *Principal*
EMP: 175
SQ FT: 25,000
SALES (est): 5.9MM **Privately Held**
SIC: 8059 8051 Convalescent home; skilled nursing care facilities

(P-20633)
MILLBRAE SERRA SANITARIUM
Also Called: Millbrae Srra Cnvalescent Hosp
150 Serra Ave, Millbrae (94030-2629)
P.O. Box 789 (94030-0789)
PHONE..........................650 697-8386
Fax: 650 697-3058
EMP: 125
SQ FT: 10,000
SALES: 4.6MM **Privately Held**
SIC: 8059 8051

(P-20634)
MONTEREY PK CONVALESCENT HOSP
Also Called: Sun Mar Management Service
416 N Garfield Ave, Monterey Park (91754-1203)
PHONE..........................626 280-0280
Irving Bauman, *President*
William Presnell, *Treasurer*
Frank Johnson, *Principal*
Eli Marmur, *Principal*
EMP: 85
SQ FT: 22,000
SALES (est): 3.3MM **Privately Held**
SIC: 8059 8051 Convalescent home; skilled nursing care facilities

(P-20635)
MOYLES HEALTH CARE INC
604 E Merritt Ave, Tulare (93274-2135)
PHONE..........................559 686-1601
Kensett J Moyle III, *President*
Kensett J Moyle IV, *Vice Pres*
Mark Harris, *Admin Sec*
EMP: 550
SALES: 3MM **Privately Held**
SIC: 8059 Convalescent home

(P-20636)
MT MIQUEL COVENANT VILLAGE
325 Kempton St, Spring Valley (91977-5810)
PHONE..........................619 479-4790
Rich Miller, *Director*
EMP: 241
SQ FT: 316,465

SALES: 18.4MM
SALES (corp-wide): 4.3MM **Privately Held**
SIC: 8059 Rest home, with health care
PA: Covenant Retirement Communities, Inc.
5700 Old Orchard Rd
Skokie IL 60077
773 878-2294

(P-20637)
NEW VISA HEALTH SERVICES INC
3414 Preakness Ct, Fallbrook (92028-9096)
PHONE..........................760 723-0053
Robert Craig, *President*
EMP: 500
SALES (est): 3.8MM **Privately Held**
SIC: 8059 Nursing home, except skilled & intermediate care facility

(P-20638)
NEW VISTA HEALTH SERVICES
Also Called: New Vista Pst Act Care Cntr
1516 Sawtelle Blvd, Los Angeles (90025-3207)
PHONE..........................310 477-5501
Eugene Tipo, *Administration*
Joel Waldman, *CFO*
Crystal Quinonez, *Vice Pres*
Gracie Johnson, *Social Dir*
Eugene Tito, *Administration*
EMP: 150
SALES (corp-wide): 8.1MM **Privately Held**
WEB: www.newvista.us
SIC: 8059 8051 Nursing home, except skilled & intermediate care facility; skilled nursing care facilities
PA: New Vista Health Services, Inc
1987 Vartikian Ave
Clovis CA 93611
559 298-3236

(P-20639)
NEW VISTA HEALTH SERVICES
Also Called: New Vsta Nrsng Rhbltation Cntr
8647 Fenwick St, Sunland (91040-1957)
PHONE..........................818 352-1421
Robert Craig, *President*
Alexis Remington-Perez, *Vice Pres*
Michael Yago, *Administration*
EMP: 130
SALES (est): 2.5MM
SALES (corp-wide): 8.1MM **Privately Held**
WEB: www.newvista.us
SIC: 8059 8361 Nursing home, except skilled & intermediate care facility; rehabilitation center, residential: health care incidental
PA: New Vista Health Services, Inc
1987 Vartikian Ave
Clovis CA 93611
559 298-3236

(P-20640)
NEW VISTA HEALTH SERVICES (PA)
1987 Vartikian Ave, Clovis (93611-0634)
PHONE..........................559 298-3236
Robert Craig, *President*
Steve Saunders, *CFO*
Arnold Delantar, *Vice Pres*
Honey Gayares, *Vice Pres*
Ronald Palma, *Maintence Staff*
EMP: 450
SALES (est): 8.1MM **Privately Held**
WEB: www.newvista.us
SIC: 8059 8361 8351 Nursing home, except skilled & intermediate care facility; rehabilitation center, residential: health care incidental; child day care services

(P-20641)
NORCAL CARE CENTERS INC
Also Called: Antioch Convalescent Hospital
1210 A St, Antioch (94509-2327)
PHONE..........................925 757-8787
Thaylene Sunga, *Manager*
EMP: 80
SALES (corp-wide): 2.2MM **Privately Held**
SIC: 8059 Convalescent home

PA: Norcal Care Centers Inc
3788 Fairway Dr
Cameron Park CA
530 677-9477

(P-20642)
NORTHERN CA CNGRGTNL RTMT
Also Called: CARMEL VALLEY MANOR
8545 Carmel Valley Rd, Carmel (93923-9556)
PHONE..........................831 624-1281
Roger D Bolgard, *Ch of Bd*
Jane Ipsen, *CEO*
Richard Boluga, *CFO*
Maria Williams, *Executive*
Mary Gates, *Office Mgr*
EMP: 162 **EST:** 1960
SQ FT: 196,800
SALES: 17.9MM **Privately Held**
WEB: www.cvmanor.com
SIC: 8059 Convalescent home

(P-20643)
NORTHERN CALIFORNIA PRESBYTERI
Also Called: Tamal Pais
501 Via Casitas Ofc, Greenbrae (94904-1958)
PHONE..........................415 464-1767
Nan Boyd, *CFO*
David Latina, *Officer*
Michael Cataldo, *Exec Dir*
Glen Goddard, *Exec Dir*
EMP: 100
SALES (corp-wide): 73.3MM **Privately Held**
WEB: www.contracostasbdc.com
SIC: 8059 8062 8051 8052 Rest home, with health care; general medical & surgical hospitals; skilled nursing care facilities; intermediate care facilities
PA: Sequoia Living
1525 Post St
San Francisco CA 94109
415 922-0200

(P-20644)
NORTHGATE CARE CENTER
40 Professional Ctr Pkwy, San Rafael (94903-2703)
PHONE..........................415 479-1230
Jeremy Zrimes, *President*
EMP: 52 **EST:** 1970
SQ FT: 11,000
SALES (est): 3.3MM
SALES (corp-wide): 11.6MM **Privately Held**
WEB: www.iqcare.com
SIC: 8059 Convalescent home
PA: Independent Quality Care, Inc
3 Crow Canyon Ct
San Ramon CA 94583
925 855-0881

(P-20645)
NOTELLAGE CORPORATION
Also Called: College Vsta Convalescent Hosp
4681 Eagle Rock Blvd, Los Angeles (90041-3036)
PHONE..........................323 257-8151
Michael Stifere, *Administration*
EMP: 50
SQ FT: 10,000
SALES (est): 2.3MM **Privately Held**
SIC: 8059 Convalescent home

(P-20646)
OAKVIEW CONVALESCENT HOSPITAL
9166 Tujunga Canyon Blvd, Tujunga (91042-3498)
PHONE..........................818 352-4426
Ben Garrett, *President*
Christen Garrett, *Treasurer*
Clyde Casner, *Vice Pres*
Eva Casner, *Admin Sec*
EMP: 50
SALES (est): 1.7MM **Privately Held**
SIC: 8059 Convalescent home

(P-20647)
ODYSSEY HEALTHCARE INC
74350 Country Club Dr, Palm Desert
(92260-1608)
PHONE..............................760 674-0066
Candice Heldenbrand, *Manager*
EMP: 50
SALES (corp-wide): 1.5B **Privately Held**
SIC: 8059 Convalescent home
HQ: Odyssey Healthcare, Inc.
 7801 Mesquite Bend Dr # 105
 Irving TX 75063

(P-20648)
OLYMPIA CONVALESCENT HOSPITAL
1100 S Alvarado St, Los Angeles
(90006-4110)
PHONE..............................213 487-3000
Otto Schwartz, *Administration*
Sam Lidell, *Ltd Ptnr*
Andre Pollak, *Ltd Ptnr*
Marco Cantoreggi, *Director*
EMP: 115
SQ FT: 25,000
SALES (est): 3.9MM **Privately Held**
SIC: 8059 8051 Convalescent home;
 skilled nursing care facilities

(P-20649)
ON MY OWN INDEPEDENT LIVING
920 1st St W, Sonoma (95476-7417)
PHONE..............................707 938-9156
EMP: 60
SALES (est): 427.9K **Privately Held**
SIC: 8059 Nursing & personal care

(P-20650)
ORANGE COUNTY ROYALE CONVLSCNT (PA)
1030 W Warner Ave, Santa Ana
(92707-3147)
PHONE..............................714 546-6450
Mitchell Kantor, *President*
Donald Connelly, *Administration*
Luis Pinedo, *Maintence Staff*
Midge Smith, *Education*
Debra Sanchez, *Food Svc Dir*
EMP: 330
SQ FT: 87,000
SALES (est): 17MM **Privately Held**
WEB: www.royalehealth.com
SIC: 8059 8051 Convalescent home;
 skilled nursing care facilities

(P-20651)
ORINDA CONVALESCENT HOSPITAL
11 Altarinda Rd, Orinda (94563-2602)
PHONE..............................925 254-6500
David Cronin, *President*
Charles Speers, *Administration*
EMP: 52
SQ FT: 5,000
SALES (est): 3.5MM **Privately Held**
SIC: 8059 Convalescent home

(P-20652)
OUR HUSE RSDNTIAL CARE CTR INC
109 E Central Ave, Madera (93638-3109)
PHONE..............................559 674-8670
Carolyn Pipes, *President*
EMP: 70
SALES (est): 2.6MM **Privately Held**
SIC: 8059 Rest home, with health care

(P-20653)
PACIFIC GROVE CNVALESCENT HOSP
200 Lighthouse Ave, Pacific Grove
(93950-3022)
PHONE..............................831 375-2695
John Lund, *Owner*
John P Jones, *Manager*
EMP: 60
SALES (est): 1.2MM **Privately Held**
SIC: 8059 Convalescent home

(P-20654)
PACIFIC HAVEN CONVALESCENT HM
Also Called: Pacific Haven Convalescent HM
12072 Trask Ave, Garden Grove
(92843-3881)
PHONE..............................714 534-1942
Mike Uranga, *Administration*
Allan Chou, *Director*
EMP: 100
SALES (est): 8.7MM **Privately Held**
SIC: 8059 8051 Convalescent home;
 skilled nursing care facilities

(P-20655)
PACIFIC HOMES FOUNDATION
303 N Lennox Glenoaks1000 # 1000, Burbank (91502)
PHONE..............................818 729-8106
Gary Wheeler, *CEO*
Mort Swales, *CEO*
EMP: 70 EST: 2001
SALES: 1.8MM **Privately Held**
SIC: 8059 Nursing home, except skilled &
 intermediate care facility

(P-20656)
PALADIN HOME CARE
555 Pierce St Ste Cml 4, Albany
(94706-1078)
PHONE..............................510 526-2273
Shaun M Charles, *Principal*
EMP: 50
SALES (est): 431.6K **Privately Held**
SIC: 8059 Personal care home, with health
 care

(P-20657)
PALM HARBOR RESIDENCY LP
Also Called: Palmcrest North Convalescent
3501 Cedar Ave, Long Beach
(90807-3809)
PHONE..............................562 595-4551
Leonard Muskin, *General Ptnr*
EMP: 200 EST: 1971
SQ FT: 120,000
SALES: 2.5MM **Privately Held**
SIC: 8059 8052 Convalescent home; intermediate care facilities

(P-20658)
PARAMUNT CNVALESCENT GROUP INC
Also Called: Paramount Convalescent Hosp
8558 Rosecrans Ave, Paramount
(90723-3644)
PHONE..............................562 634-6895
Irving Bauman, *President*
Zeny Evaldez, *Manager*
EMP: 65
SQ FT: 12,000
SALES (est): 2.1MM **Privately Held**
SIC: 8059 Nursing home, except skilled &
 intermediate care facility

(P-20659)
PARK MARINO CONVALESCENT CTR
2585 E Washington Blvd, Pasadena
(91107-1446)
PHONE..............................626 463-4105
William Kite, *Administration*
EMP: 50 EST: 1966
SALES (est): 828K
SALES (corp-wide): 5.3MM **Privately Held**
SIC: 8059 8051 Convalescent home;
 skilled nursing care facilities
PA: Diversified Health Services (Del)
 136 Washington Ave
 Richmond CA 94801
 510 231-6200

(P-20660)
PILGRIM PLACE IN CLAREMONT (PA)
625 Mayflower Rd, Claremont
(91711-4240)
PHONE..............................909 399-5500
William R Cunitz, *President*
Sue Fairley, *Vice Pres*
Rich Rodas, *Vice Pres*
Bernard Valek, *Vice Pres*
Joyce Yarborough, *Vice Pres*
EMP: 205

SQ FT: 2,000
SALES: 19.5MM **Privately Held**
WEB: www.pilgrimplace.org
SIC: 8059 8051 8052 Rest home, with
 health care; skilled nursing care facilities;
 intermediate care facilities

(P-20661)
PLACERVLLE PNES CNVLSCENT HOSP
1040 Marshall Way, Placerville
(95667-5706)
PHONE..............................530 622-3400
Jared Edmunds, *Administration*
EMP: 130 EST: 1963
SQ FT: 40,000
SALES (est): 2.8MM
SALES (corp-wide): 103.9MM **Privately Held**
WEB: www.villadelrey.com
SIC: 8059 8051 Convalescent home;
 skilled nursing care facilities
HQ: Horizon West Healthcare, Inc.
 4020 Sierra College Blvd # 190
 Rocklin CA 95677
 916 624-6230

(P-20662)
PLEASANT VIEW CONVALESCENT HOS
22590 Voss Ave, Cupertino (95014-2627)
PHONE..............................408 253-9034
Jack Easterday, *President*
Jet Rupisan, *Administration*
EMP: 140
SQ FT: 55,000
SALES (est): 4.5MM **Privately Held**
SIC: 8059 8069 8051 Convalescent
 home; specialty hospitals, except psychiatric; skilled nursing care facilities

(P-20663)
PORCHLIGHT INC
Also Called: Scan
3800 Kilroy Airport Way, Long Beach
(90806-2494)
P.O. Box 22616 (90801-5616)
PHONE..............................562 989-5100
EMP: 100
SALES (est): 9.4MM
SALES (corp-wide): 329.7MM **Privately Held**
WEB: www.scanhealthplan.com
SIC: 8059 Personal care home, with health
 care
PA: Senior Care Action Network Foundation
 3800 Kilroy Airport Way
 Long Beach CA 90806
 562 989-5100

(P-20664)
PRUITTHEALTH INC
Also Called: United Care Homes
1982 Camwood Ave, City of Industry
(91748-4044)
PHONE..............................626 810-5567
Susana Tubianosa, *Branch Mgr*
EMP: 50
SALES (corp-wide): 268.8MM **Privately Held**
WEB: www.peachtreechristianhospice.com
SIC: 8059 Convalescent home
PA: Pruitthealth, Inc.
 1626 Jeurgens Ct
 Norcross GA 30093
 770 279-6200

(P-20665)
RAFAEL CONVALESCENT HOSPITAL
234 N San Pedro Rd, San Rafael
(94903-2858)
PHONE..............................415 479-3450
Timothy J Egan, *President*
Michael Egan, *Admin Sec*
EMP: 180
SQ FT: 9,000
SALES (est): 10.6MM **Privately Held**
SIC: 8059 8051 Convalescent home;
 skilled nursing care facilities

(P-20666)
RCC FACILITY INCORPORATED
Also Called: Rounseville Rehabilitation Ctr
210 40th Street Way, Oakland
(94611-5612)
PHONE..............................510 658-2041
Jack Easterday, *President*
EMP: 70
SQ FT: 10,000
SALES: 6.7MM **Privately Held**
SIC: 8059 Convalescent home

(P-20667)
REDLANDS CMNTY HOSP FOUNDATION
Also Called: Asistencia Villa
1875 Barton Rd, Redlands (92373-5308)
PHONE..............................909 793-1382
Ron Dahlgren, *Manager*
EMP: 101
SALES (corp-wide): 1.1MM **Privately Held**
WEB: www.redlandshospital.com
SIC: 8059 8051 8093 Convalescent
 home; skilled nursing care facilities; rehabilitation center, outpatient treatment
PA: Redlands Community Hospital Foundation
 350 Terracina Blvd
 Redlands CA 92373
 909 335-5540

(P-20668)
REDWOOD CONVALESCENT HOSPITAL
22103 Redwood Rd, Castro Valley
(94546-7173)
PHONE..............................510 537-8848
Frank V Kreske MD, *President*
Elizabeth Kreske, *Vice Pres*
EMP: 56
SQ FT: 10,000
SALES (est): 4MM **Privately Held**
SIC: 8059 Convalescent home

(P-20669)
REYNOLDS HEALTH INDUSTRIES
Also Called: SKYLIGHT CONVALESCENT CENTER
1201 Walnut Ave, Long Beach
(90813-3822)
PHONE..............................562 591-7621
Caul Murayama, *President*
Vicki Reynolds, *Vice Pres*
EMP: 70
SQ FT: 21,000
SALES: 9.4MM **Privately Held**
SIC: 8059 Convalescent home

(P-20670)
RIVER OAK CENTER FOR CHILDREN
5445 Laurel Hills Dr, Sacramento
(95841-3105)
PHONE..............................916 550-5600
EMP: 94
SALES (corp-wide): 13.5MM **Privately Held**
SIC: 8059 8063
PA: River Oak Center For Children
 5445 Laurel Hills Dr
 Sacramento CA 95841
 916 609-5100

(P-20671)
RIVERSIDE CNVALESCENT HOSP INC
375 Cohasset Rd, Chico (95926-2211)
PHONE..............................530 343-5595
Gladys Jennings, *President*
EMP: 72 EST: 1963
SQ FT: 50,000
SALES (est): 2.5MM **Privately Held**
SIC: 8059 Convalescent home

(P-20672)
RIVERSIDE HEALTH CARE CORP
Also Called: Scenic Circle Care Center
1611 Scenic Dr, Modesto (95355-4907)
PHONE..............................209 523-5667
Jim Dickinson, *Branch Mgr*
EMP: 80

SALES (corp-wide): 8.4MM **Privately Held**
SIC: 8059 Nursing home, except skilled & intermediate care facility
PA: Riverside Health Care Corporation
1469 Humboldt Rd Ste 175
Chico CA 95928
530 897-5100

(P-20673)
RIVERSIDE HEALTH CARE CORP (PA)
1469 Humboldt Rd Ste 175, Chico (95928-9204)
PHONE..................530 897-5100
Sharon Jennings Kearns, *CEO*
EMP: 60
SQ FT: 9,000
SALES (est): 8.4MM **Privately Held**
SIC: 8059 Convalescent home

(P-20674)
SABU ENTERPRISES INC
Also Called: IDLE ACRES CONVALESCENT HOSPIT
5044 Buffington Rd, El Monte (91732-1466)
PHONE..................626 443-1351
Solomon Silverberg, *President*
Uri Mendelbaum, *Vice Pres*
Barry Silverberg, *Director*
EMP: 50
SQ FT: 17,000
SALES: 4.8MM **Privately Held**
SIC: 8059 Convalescent home

(P-20675)
SAN BERNARDINO CARE COMPANY
467 E Gilbert St, San Bernardino (92404-5318)
PHONE..................909 884-4781
Jenq Chen, *President*
EMP: 110
SALES (est): 196.3K **Privately Held**
SIC: 8059 Convalescent home

(P-20676)
SAN DIEGO CENTER FOR CHILDREN (PA)
3002 Armstrong St, San Diego (92111-5702)
PHONE..................858 277-9550
Moises Baron, *CEO*
Davery Jones, *Partner*
Pamela Ross, *Human Res Dir*
Amy Sorensen, *Personnel Assit*
Harman Sarky, *Opers Staff*
EMP: 90
SQ FT: 38,000
SALES: 21.5MM **Privately Held**
WEB: www.centerforchildren.org
SIC: 8059 8361 Personal care home, with health care; residential care

(P-20677)
SAN MARINO MANOR
6812 Oak Ave, San Gabriel (91775-2099)
PHONE..................626 446-5263
Michael Elbert, *Administration*
Mike Elbert, *Administration*
EMP: 50
SALES: 3.3MM **Privately Held**
SIC: 8059 Convalescent home

(P-20678)
SECROM INC
Also Called: Carson Senior Assisted Living
345 E Carson St, Carson (90745-2709)
PHONE..................310 830-4010
Shlomo Rechnitz, *CEO*
EMP: 55
SALES (est): 950.8K **Privately Held**
SIC: 8059 Rest home, with health care

(P-20679)
SHASTA CONVALESCENT CENTER
Also Called: Shasta Convalescent Hospital
3550 Churn Creek Rd, Redding (96002-2718)
PHONE..................530 222-3630
Donald Ostrom, *President*
Marlene Ostrom, *Vice Pres*
EMP: 180

SQ FT: 38,000
SALES (est): 4.2MM **Privately Held**
SIC: 8059 8051 Convalescent home; nursing home, except skilled & intermediate care facility; skilled nursing care facilities

(P-20680)
SIERRA VALLEY REHAB CENTER
301 W Putnam Ave, Porterville (93257-3429)
PHONE..................559 784-7375
Steve Brown, *Administration*
Emmanuel B David, *President*
Ramona Villaluz, *Treasurer*
EMP: 170
SQ FT: 26,000
SALES (est): 5.7MM **Privately Held**
SIC: 8059 8051 Convalescent home; skilled nursing care facilities

(P-20681)
SILVERADO SENIOR LIVING INC
Also Called: Bay Area At Home
1301 Ralston Ave Ste A, Belmont (94002-1961)
PHONE..................650 226-8017
Kevin Gunter, *Vice Pres*
Robert De, *Analyst*
EMP: 54
SALES (corp-wide): 180.3MM **Privately Held**
SIC: 8059 Personal care home, with health care
PA: Senior Silverado Living Inc
6400 Oak Cyn Ste 200
Irvine CA 92618
949 240-7200

(P-20682)
SILVERADO SENIOR LIVING INC (PA)
6400 Oak Cyn Ste 200, Irvine (92618-5233)
PHONE..................949 240-7200
George L Chapman, *CEO*
Daizel Gasperian, *President*
Kathy Greene, *President*
Shannon Gutierrez, *President*
Loren B Shook, *President*
EMP: 65 **EST:** 1996
SQ FT: 65,000
SALES (est): 180.3MM **Privately Held**
WEB: www.silveradosenior.com
SIC: 8059 Personal care home, with health care

(P-20683)
SILVERADO SENIOR LIVING INC
Also Called: Sierra Vista Memory Care Cmnty
125 W Sierra Madre Ave, Azusa (91702-2023)
P.O. Box 636 (91702-0636)
PHONE..................626 650-9891
Bida Gwinn, *Manager*
EMP: 54
SALES (corp-wide): 180.3MM **Privately Held**
WEB: www.silveradosenior.com
SIC: 8059 8051 Personal care home, with health care; skilled nursing care facilities
PA: Senior Silverado Living Inc
6400 Oak Cyn Ste 200
Irvine CA 92618
949 240-7200

(P-20684)
SILVERADO SENIOR LIVING INC
Also Called: Huntington Memory Care Cmnty
1118 N Stoneman Ave, Alhambra (91801-1007)
PHONE..................626 872-3941
Vida Gwin, *Administration*
Tamra Mitchell, *Human Res Dir*
Maria Quizon, *Director*
EMP: 50
SALES (corp-wide): 180.3MM **Privately Held**
WEB: www.silveradosenior.com
SIC: 8059 Personal care home, with health care
PA: Senior Silverado Living Inc
6400 Oak Cyn Ste 200
Irvine CA 92618
949 240-7200

(P-20685)
SILVERADO SENIOR LIVING INC
Also Called: Escondido Memory Care Cmnty
1500 Borden Rd, Escondido (92026-2373)
PHONE..................760 456-5137
Jean Busher, *Administration*
Thomas V Croal, *Technology*
EMP: 91
SQ FT: 33,000
SALES (corp-wide): 180.3MM **Privately Held**
WEB: www.silveradosenior.com
SIC: 8059 Personal care home, with health care
PA: Senior Silverado Living Inc
6400 Oak Cyn Ste 200
Irvine CA 92618
949 240-7200

(P-20686)
SILVERADO SENIOR LIVING INC
Also Called: Encinitas Memory Care Cmnty
335 Saxony Rd, Encinitas (92024-2723)
PHONE..................760 270-9917
Dina Trester, *Director*
Thomas V Croal, *CFO*
Jolene Farish, *Asst Director*
EMP: 70
SALES (corp-wide): 180.3MM **Privately Held**
WEB: www.silveradosenior.com
SIC: 8059 Personal care home, with health care
PA: Senior Silverado Living Inc
6400 Oak Cyn Ste 200
Irvine CA 92618
949 240-7200

(P-20687)
SILVERADO SENIOR LIVING INC
Also Called: Beverly Pl Memory Care Cmnty
330 N Hayworth Ave, Los Angeles (90048-2702)
PHONE..................323 984-7313
Beth Medina, *Principal*
EMP: 70
SALES (corp-wide): 180.3MM **Privately Held**
SIC: 8059 Personal care home, with health care
PA: Senior Silverado Living Inc
6400 Oak Cyn Ste 200
Irvine CA 92618
949 240-7200

(P-20688)
SILVERSCREEN HEALTHCARE INC
Also Called: Asistencia Villa Rehab & Care
1875 Barton Rd, Redlands (92373-5308)
PHONE..................909 793-1382
Philip Weinberger, *CEO*
Marylynn Mahan, *CFO*
EMP: 135
SALES (est): 4.4MM **Privately Held**
SIC: 8059 8322 Convalescent home; rehabilitation services

(P-20689)
SISTERS OF NAZARETH
Also Called: Nazareth House
245 Nova Albion Way, San Rafael (94903-3539)
PHONE..................415 479-8282
Sister Rose Hoye, *Principal*
Sister John Berchmans, *Administration*
EMP: 91
SALES (est): 3.9MM **Privately Held**
SIC: 8059 8051 Rest home, with health care; skilled nursing care facilities

(P-20690)
SPRINGHILL MANOR REHABILITATIO
Also Called: Spring Hl Mnor Cnvlescent Hosp
355 Joerschke Dr, Grass Valley (95945-5288)
PHONE..................530 273-7247
Brian Collier, *Principal*
Patricia Vixie, *Treasurer*
Gregory Vixie, *Vice Pres*
EMP: 50 **EST:** 1966
SQ FT: 14,000
SALES: 8.5MM **Privately Held**
SIC: 8059 Convalescent home

(P-20691)
SSC PITTSBURG OPERATING CO LP
Also Called: Diamond Ridge Healthcare Ctr
2351 Loveridge Rd, Pittsburg (94565-5117)
PHONE..................925 427-4444
Wayne M Sanner,
Mandy Garcia, *Director*
EMP: 2728
SALES (est): 14MM
SALES (corp-wide): 588.8MM **Privately Held**
SIC: 8059 Nursing home, except skilled & intermediate care facility
PA: Savaseniorcare, Llc
1 Ravinia Dr Ste 1500
Atlanta GA 30346
770 829-5100

(P-20692)
ST FRANCIS EXTENDED CARE INC
718 Bartlett Ave, Hayward (94541-3698)
PHONE..................510 785-3630
Sally Rapp, *President*
Roland Rapp, *Vice Pres*
EMP: 67
SQ FT: 13,120
SALES: 5.9MM **Privately Held**
SIC: 8059 Convalescent home

(P-20693)
ST FRANCIS HTS CONVALESCENT
35 Escuela Dr, Daly City (94015-4003)
PHONE..................650 755-9515
Kordel Erickson, *Administration*
Evelyn Goddard, *Principal*
Kathleen Lovato, *Administration*
Glen Gotter, *Director*
EMP: 100 **EST:** 1967
SQ FT: 12,000
SALES (est): 2.7MM **Privately Held**
WEB: www.sfhouseprices.net
SIC: 8059 8051 Convalescent home; skilled nursing care facilities

(P-20694)
ST JOHNS RETIREMENT VILLAGE
Also Called: STOLLWOOD CONVALESCENT HOSPITA
135 Woodland Ave, Woodland (95695-2701)
PHONE..................530 662-9674
John Prichard, *Administration*
Barbara Fleck, *Manager*
EMP: 142 **EST:** 1964
SALES: 10.3MM **Privately Held**
SIC: 8059 8361 Convalescent home; convalescent home with continuous nursing care; geriatric residential care; home for the aged; rest home, with health care incidental

(P-20695)
STOCKTON EDSON HEALTHCARE CORP
Also Called: GOOD SAMARITAN REHAB AND CARE
1630 N Edison St, Stockton (95204-5633)
PHONE..................209 948-8762
Emanuel Bernabe, *President*
Gilda Dizon, *Treasurer*
Sedy Demesa, *Exec VP*
EMP: 100
SQ FT: 4,000
SALES: 9MM **Privately Held**
SIC: 8059 8051 Nursing home, except skilled & intermediate care facility; skilled nursing care facilities

(P-20696)
SUN MAR NURSING CENTER INC
Also Called: SUN MAR MANAGEMENT SERVICES
1720 W Orange Ave, Anaheim (92804-2699)
PHONE..................714 776-1720
Chris William, *Administration*
Blaine Hendrickson, *President*
Bill Presnell, *Corp Secy*
EMP: 75

SQ FT: 10,000
SALES: 8.2MM **Privately Held**
SIC: 8059 Nursing home, except skilled & intermediate care facility

(P-20697)
SUNNY RETIREMENT HOME
22445 Cupertino Rd, Cupertino (95014-1052)
PHONE.....................408 454-5600
Sally Plank, *Exec Dir*
Tess Balaan, *Nursing Dir*
EMP: 140 EST: 1964
SQ FT: 112,000
SALES: 2.9MM **Privately Held**
WEB: www.sunny4care.com
SIC: 8059 Rest home, with health care

(P-20698)
SYCAMORE PARK CARE CENTER LLC
Also Called: SYCAMORE PARK CONVALESCENT HOSPITAL
4585 N Figueroa St, Los Angeles (90065-3026)
PHONE.....................323 223-3441
Robert Snukal, *President*
Consolacion Padama, *Corp Secy*
Manuel Padama, *Vice Pres*
Sheila Snukal, *Vice Pres*
▲ EMP: 80
SQ FT: 20,000
SALES (est): 5.1MM **Publicly Held**
WEB: www.skilledhealthcare.com
SIC: 8059 8051 Convalescent home; skilled nursing care facilities
PA: Genesis Healthcare, Inc.
101 E State St
Kennett Square PA 19348
-

(P-20699)
TEMPLE PARK CONVALESCENT HOSP
2411 W Temple St, Los Angeles (90026-4899)
PHONE.....................213 380-2035
Barry Kohn, *President*
Toby Kohn, *Vice Pres*
EMP: 77
SALES (est): 4.2MM **Privately Held**
SIC: 8059 Convalescent home

(P-20700)
TJD LLC
Also Called: Anberry Rehabilitation Hosp
1685 Shaffer Rd, Atwater (95301-4456)
PHONE.....................209 357-3420
Donald W Gormly Jr,
Suzanne Carvalho, *Records Dir*
Joshua Ooka, *Office Mgr*
Nancy Romero, *Education*
Jerry Holloway,
EMP: 140
SQ FT: 40,000
SALES: 11.9MM **Privately Held**
WEB: www.anberryhospital.com
SIC: 8059 8051 8093 Nursing home, except skilled & intermediate care facility; convalescent home with continuous nursing care; rehabilitation center, outpatient treatment

(P-20701)
TRANQUILITY INCORPORATED
Also Called: SAN MIGUEL VILLA
1050 San Miguel Rd, Concord (94518-2094)
PHONE.....................925 825-4280
Velda Pierce, *CEO*
EMP: 180
SQ FT: 20,000
SALES: 17.3MM **Privately Held**
SIC: 8059 8051 Convalescent home; skilled nursing care facilities

(P-20702)
TRINITY HEALTH SYSTEMS
Also Called: Valley Palms Convalescent Hosp
13400 Sherman Way, North Hollywood (91605-4415)
PHONE.....................818 983-0103
Roland Santos, *Manager*
EMP: 100

SALES (corp-wide): 9.1MM **Privately Held**
SIC: 8059 8051 Convalescent home; skilled nursing care facilities
PA: Trinity Health Systems
14318 Ohio St
Baldwin Park CA 91706
626 960-1971

(P-20703)
TWO PALMS NURSING CENTER INC (PA)
2637 E Washington Blvd, Pasadena (91107-1412)
PHONE.....................626 798-8991
Marthann Demchuk, *CEO*
EMP: 50
SALES (est): 7.7MM **Privately Held**
SIC: 8059 Convalescent home

(P-20704)
TWO PALMS NURSING CENTER INC
Also Called: Marlinda Imperial Hospital
150 Bellefontaine St, Pasadena (91105-3102)
PHONE.....................626 796-1103
EMP: 85
SQ FT: 28,955
SALES (corp-wide): 7.7MM **Privately Held**
SIC: 8059 8051 Convalescent home; skilled nursing care facilities
PA: Two Palms Nursing Center, Inc.
2637 E Washington Blvd
Pasadena CA 91107
626 798-8991

(P-20705)
TZIPPY CARE INC
Also Called: Western Convalescent Hospital
2190 W Adams Blvd, Los Angeles (90018-2039)
PHONE.....................323 737-7778
David Friedman, *President*
Ken Lehman, *Corp Secy*
Aaron Friedman, *Vice Pres*
EMP: 95
SALES: 12.8MM **Privately Held**
SIC: 8059 Convalescent home

(P-20706)
UNITED CONVALESCENT FACILITIES
Also Called: University Park Healthcare Ctr
230 E Adams Blvd, Los Angeles (90011-1426)
PHONE.....................626 629-6950
Doug Easton, *Owner*
Patricia Patterson, *Social Dir*
Victor Espinoza, *Director*
EMP: 80
SQ FT: 1,300
SALES: 4MM **Privately Held**
SIC: 8059 Nursing home, except skilled & intermediate care facility

(P-20707)
UNITED CP/S CHLDRNS FNDN LA
Also Called: Ucp Dronfield North
13272 Dronfield Ave, Sylmar (91342-2961)
PHONE.....................818 364-5911
Liz McLaughlin, *Administration*
EMP: 70
SALES (corp-wide): 24.2MM **Privately Held**
SIC: 8059 Home for the mentally retarded, exc. skilled or intermediate
PA: United Cerebral Palsy/Spastic Children's Foundation Of Los Angeles And Ventura Counties
6430 Independence Ave
Woodland Hills CA 91367
818 782-2211

(P-20708)
UNITED MEDICAL MANAGEMENT INC
Also Called: Valley Healthcare
1680 N Waterman Ave, San Bernardino (92404-5113)
PHONE.....................909 886-5291
Alan Hull, *Administration*
Aurelia Romero, *Food Svc Dir*

EMP: 125
SQ FT: 30,000
SALES (est): 5.3MM **Privately Held**
WEB: www.healthcare-centers.com
SIC: 8059 8051 8322 Convalescent home; skilled nursing care facilities; rehabilitation services

(P-20709)
UPLAND COMMUNITY CARE INC
Also Called: Upland Rehabilitation Care Ctr
1221 E Arrow Hwy, Upland (91786-4911)
PHONE.....................909 985-1903
Owen Hammond, *CEO*
Nora Moscozo, *Human Res Dir*
EMP: 99
SALES (est): 3.3MM
SALES (corp-wide): 2B **Publicly Held**
SIC: 8059 Convalescent home
PA: The Ensign Group Inc
27101 Puerta Real Ste 450
Mission Viejo CA 92691
949 487-9500

(P-20710)
VACAVLLE CNVALESCENT REHAB CTR
585 Nut Tree Ct, Vacaville (95687-3353)
PHONE.....................707 449-8000
Joe Nicolli, *President*
EMP: 120
SQ FT: 38,000
SALES (est): 6MM **Privately Held**
SIC: 8059 Convalescent home

(P-20711)
VALENCIA HEALTH CARE INC
Also Called: Santa Clarita Convalescent HM
23801 Newhall Ave, Newhall (91321-3126)
PHONE.....................661 254-2425
Ishkhan Khatchadurian, *President*
Armand Masongsong, *Director*
EMP: 75 EST: 1969
SQ FT: 24,000
SALES (est): 3.9MM **Privately Held**
SIC: 8059 Convalescent home

(P-20712)
VALLE VSTA CNVLESCENT HOSP INC
1025 W 2nd Ave, Escondido (92025-3839)
PHONE.....................760 745-1288
Kristina Kuivon, *CEO*
Tammy Wimbish, *Nursing Dir*
Katrina Lopez, *Hlthcr Dir*
Nittly Chahal, *Director*
Rick Tedesco, *Director*
EMP: 85 EST: 1961
SQ FT: 19,000
SALES (est): 2.7MM **Privately Held**
SIC: 8059 Convalescent home; nursing home, except skilled & intermediate care facility
PA: Covenant Care, Llc
27071 Aliso Creek Rd # 100
Aliso Viejo CA 92656

(P-20713)
VALLEY WEST HEALTH CARE INC (PA)
Also Called: Valley West Care Center
1224 E St, Williams (95987)
P.O. Box 1059 (95987-1059)
PHONE.....................530 473-5321
Sharon Jennings, *President*
Gladys Jennings, *CFO*
EMP: 95
SQ FT: 32,000
SALES (est): 4.2MM **Privately Held**
SIC: 8059 Convalescent home

(P-20714)
VAN NUYS CARE CENTER INC
Also Called: Lake Balboa Care Center
16955 Vanowen St, Van Nuys (91406-4542)
PHONE.....................818 343-0700
Chad Thornton, *President*
John Thornton, *President*
Wayne A Evans, *Vice Pres*
Ana Rosa Aguilar, *Director*
Paolo Andres, *Director*
EMP: 88

SQ FT: 12,500
SALES (est): 3.9MM **Privately Held**
SIC: 8059 8051 Convalescent home; skilled nursing care facilities

(P-20715)
VICTORIA POST ACUTE CARE
654 S Anza St, El Cajon (92020-6602)
PHONE.....................619 440-5005
Ed Dove, *Administration*
EMP: 150
SALES (est): 6.6MM **Privately Held**
SIC: 8059 8361 Convalescent home; rehabilitation center, residential: health care incidental

(P-20716)
VILLA SIENA
1855 Miramonte Ave 117, Mountain View (94040-4029)
PHONE.....................650 961-6484
Corrine Bernard, *CEO*
Corine Bernard, *Exec Dir*
Mary Ellen Barber, *Nursing Dir*
EMP: 68
SQ FT: 40,000
SALES: 228.7K **Privately Held**
WEB: www.villasiena.com
SIC: 8059 Nursing home, except skilled & intermediate care facility

(P-20717)
VINCENT HAYLEY ENTERPRISES
Also Called: ST VINCENT HEALTH CARE
1810 N Fair Oaks Ave, Pasadena (91103-1619)
PHONE.....................626 398-8182
Rob Barrett, *President*
Cipriano Baustista, *Administration*
Tina M Erhardt, *Research*
EMP: 75
SALES: 8.1MM **Privately Held**
SIC: 8059 Nursing home, except skilled & intermediate care facility

(P-20718)
VISTA PACIFICA ENTERPRISES INC
Also Called: Vista Pcifica Convalescent Ctr
3662 Pacific Ave, Riverside (92509-1923)
PHONE.....................951 682-4867
Cheryl Jumonville, *Director*
EMP: 200 **Privately Held**
SIC: 8059 Convalescent home
PA: Vista Pacifica Enterprises, Inc.
3662 Pacific Ave
Riverside CA 92509
-

(P-20719)
VOCH INC
Also Called: Villa Oaks Convalescent Homes
1920 N Fair Oaks Ave, Pasadena (91103-1623)
PHONE.....................626 798-1111
Pompeyo Rosales, *Owner*
EMP: 60
SQ FT: 16,000
SALES (est): 2.3MM
SALES (corp-wide): 3.2MM **Privately Held**
WEB: www.slch.com
SIC: 8059 Convalescent home
PA: Slch, Inc
1920 N Fair Oaks Ave
Pasadena CA 91103
626 798-0558

(P-20720)
WEST COAST HOSPITALS INC
Also Called: Valley Convalescent Hospital
919 Freedom Blvd, Watsonville (95076-3804)
P.O. Box 1242 (95077-1242)
PHONE.....................831 722-3581
Richard Murphy, *Treasurer*
EMP: 65
SQ FT: 20,000
SALES: 6.5MM **Privately Held**
SIC: 8059 Convalescent home

(P-20721)
WESTMINSTER GARDENS
1420 Santo Domingo Ave, Duarte
(91010-2698)
PHONE..................626 359-2571
Judy Thorndyke, *Exec Dir*
EMP: 54
SQ FT: 1,306,800
SALES: 6.3MM **Privately Held**
WEB: www.westgardens.org
SIC: 8059 Rest home, with health care

(P-20722)
WICORO INC (HQ)
Also Called: COLONIAL MANOR CONVA-
LESCENT HOSPITAL
919 N Sunset Ave, West Covina
(91790-1244)
PHONE..................626 962-4489
C David Benfield, *President*
Amber Felix, *Manager*
EMP: 50
SQ FT: 15,000
SALES: 3.3MM
SALES (corp-wide): 3.8MM **Privately
Held**
SIC: 8059 Convalescent home
PA: Care Tech Inc
401 N Central Ave Ste B
Upland CA 91786
909 373-3766

(P-20723)
**WILLOW TREE NURSING
CENTER**
Also Called: WILLOW TREE CONVALES-
CENT HOSPI
2124 57th Ave, Oakland (94621-4322)
PHONE..................510 261-2628
Preston SOO, *Administration*
Breta Conroy, *Director*
EMP: 90 **EST:** 1976
SQ FT: 18,000
SALES: 8.6MM **Privately Held**
SIC: 8059 8052 Convalescent home; in-
termediate care facilities

(P-20724)
**WILSHIRE HEALTH AND CMNTY
SVCS**
Also Called: Wilshire Nursing & Rehab
290 Heather Ct, Templeton (93465-9738)
PHONE..................805 434-3035
Jack Doria, *Manager*
EMP: 100
SALES (corp-wide): 13MM **Privately
Held**
SIC: 8059 8051 Convalescent home;
skilled nursing care facilities
PA: Wilshire Health And Community Serv-
ices, Inc.
285 South St Ste J
San Luis Obispo CA 93401
805 547-7025

(P-20725)
**WILSHIRE HLTH & CMNTY SVCS
INC**
Also Called: Hawthorne Convalescent Center
11630 Grevillea Ave, Hawthorne
(90250-2231)
PHONE..................310 679-9732
Theresa Reyes, *Director*
EMP: 100
SALES (corp-wide): 13MM **Privately
Held**
SIC: 8059 8051 Convalescent home;
skilled nursing care facilities
PA: Wilshire Health And Community Serv-
ices, Inc.
285 South St Ste J
San Luis Obispo CA 93401
805 547-7025

(P-20726)
**WILSHIRE HLTH & CMNTY SVCS
INC**
Also Called: Kings Nrsing Rhabilitaion Hosp
851 Leslie Ln, Hanford (93230-5643)
PHONE..................559 582-4414
Mark Fisher, *Owner*
EMP: 74
SALES (corp-wide): 13MM **Privately
Held**
SIC: 8059 Convalescent home

PA: Wilshire Health And Community Services, Inc.
285 South St Ste J
San Luis Obispo CA 93401
805 547-7025

(P-20727)
**WOODLAND CARE CENTER
LLC**
7120 Corbin Ave, Reseda (91335-3618)
PHONE..................818 881-4540
Ailean Yosmco, *Principal*
Yuri Guardado, *Office Mgr*
Gwendy Hernandez, *Director*
EMP: 100
SALES: 12.2MM **Publicly Held**
WEB: www.parkviewnursing.net
SIC: 8059 8051 Convalescent home;
skilled nursing care facilities
HQ: Skilled Healthcare, Llc
27442 Portola Pkwy # 200
Foothill Ranch CA 92610
949 282-5800

**8062 General Medical &
Surgical Hospitals**

(P-20728)
**1125 SIR FRANCIS DRAKE
BOULEVA**
Also Called: Kentfield Rehabilation Hosp
1125 Sir Francis Drake Bl, Kentfield
(94904-1418)
PHONE..................415 456-9680
Brad Hollinger,
Denise Mace, *Radiology Dir*
Deborah Doherty, *Exec Dir*
Chris Yarnovich, *Office Mgr*
Lutchman Perumal, *Human Res Dir*
EMP: 250
SALES (est): 35.8MM **Privately Held**
WEB: www.kentfieldrehab.com
SIC: 8062 General medical & surgical hos-
pitals

(P-20729)
**ADVENTIST HEALTH
CLEARLAKE (HQ)**
Also Called: Saint Helena Hosp Clearlake
15630 18th Ave, Clearlake (95422-9336)
PHONE..................707 994-6486
David Santos, *CEO*
Carlton Jacobson, *CFO*
Meredith Jobe, *Admin Sec*
Vlad Toca, *Opers Mgr*
Kimberly Fordham, *Obstetrician*
EMP: 287
SQ FT: 41,750
SALES: 111MM
SALES (corp-wide): 4.4B **Privately Held**
SIC: 8062 8011 Hospital, affiliated with
AMA residency; medical centers
PA: Adventist Health System/West
1 Adventist Health Way
Roseville CA 95661
844 574-5686

(P-20730)
ADVENTIST HEALTH SELMA
Also Called: Urgent Care-Selma Dst Hosp
1141 Rose Ave, Selma (93662-3241)
PHONE..................559 891-1000
Wayne Ferch, *President*
Christine Pickering, *Pub Rel Dir*
James C Forsythe, *Radiology*
Bethlyn Buchanan, *Manager*
EMP: 339 **EST:** 1962
SQ FT: 67,000
SALES (est): 30.6MM **Privately Held**
SIC: 8062 8051 General medical & surgi-
cal hospitals; skilled nursing care facilities

(P-20731)
**ADVENTIST HEALTH SONORA
(HQ)**
1000 Greenley Rd, Sonora (95370-5200)
PHONE..................209 532-5000
Michelle Fuentes, *President*
David Larsen, *CFO*
Greg McCulloch, *CFO*
Julie Kline, *Vice Pres*
Jeffrey Nash, *Info Tech Dir*
EMP: 712

SQ FT: 60,000
SALES: 267MM
SALES (corp-wide): 4.4B **Privately Held**
SIC: 8062 8051 General medical & surgi-
cal hospitals; skilled nursing care facilities
PA: Adventist Health System/West
1 Adventist Health Way
Roseville CA 95661
844 574-5686

(P-20732)
**ADVENTIST HEALTH
SYSTEM/WEST**
Also Called: Adventist Hlth Med Foundation
381 Merrill Ave, Glendale (91206-4178)
PHONE..................818 409-8540
Iris Weil, *CEO*
Sara Kim, *Med Doctor*
EMP: 50
SALES (corp-wide): 4.4B **Privately Held**
SIC: 8062 General medical & surgical hos-
pitals
PA: Adventist Health System/West
1 Adventist Health Way
Roseville CA 95661
844 574-5686

(P-20733)
**ADVENTIST HEALTH
SYSTEM/WEST**
Also Called: Feather River Home Health
6626 Clark Rd Ste P, Paradise
(95969-3523)
PHONE..................530 872-3378
Gregg Quattlevaum, *Manager*
Albert Deininger, *Facilities Mgr*
Bena Baybayan, *Manager*
EMP: 60
SALES (corp-wide): 4.4B **Privately Held**
SIC: 8062 8082 General medical & surgi-
cal hospitals; home health care services
PA: Adventist Health System/West
1 Adventist Health Way
Roseville CA 95661
844 574-5686

(P-20734)
**ADVENTIST HEALTH
SYSTEM/WEST**
Also Called: Clearlake Family Health Center
15230 Lakeshore Dr, Clearlake
(95422-8107)
PHONE..................707 995-4500
Ilona Horton, *Director*
Raymond Jennings, *Med Doctor*
EMP: 50
SALES (corp-wide): 4.4B **Privately Held**
SIC: 8062 General medical & surgical hos-
pitals
PA: Adventist Health System/West
1 Adventist Health Way
Roseville CA 95661
844 574-5686

(P-20735)
**ADVINTIST HLTH CLEARLAKE
HOSP**
Also Called: St Helana Hospital Clearlake
18th Ave & Hwy 53, Clearlake (95422)
PHONE..................707 994-6486
Terry Newmeyer, *CEO*
Jeniffer Swenson, *Vice Pres*
Shelly Mascari, *Director*
EMP: 340
SQ FT: 62,000
SALES: 65.9MM **Privately Held**
WEB: www.rchea.org
SIC: 8062 General medical & surgical hos-
pitals

(P-20736)
AHM GEMCH INC
Also Called: GREATER EL MONTE COMMU-
NITY HOSPITAL
1701 Santa Anita Ave, El Monte
(91733-3411)
PHONE..................626 579-7777
Jeffrey Flocken, *CEO*
Patrick Steinhauser, *COO*
Gary Louis, *CFO*
Victor Lange, *QA Dir*
Pasha Dourseau, *Opers Staff*
EMP: 180
SQ FT: 71,500

SALES: 50.5MM
SALES (corp-wide): 570.2MM **Privately
Held**
WEB: www.greaterelmonte.com
SIC: 8062 General medical & surgical hos-
pitals
PA: Ahmc Healthcare Inc.
1000 S Fremont Ave Unit 6
Alhambra CA 91803

(P-20737)
AHMC HEALTHCARE INC
1701 Santa Anita Ave, South El Monte
(91733-3411)
PHONE..................626 579-7777
Linda Du, *Controller*
EMP: 601
SALES (corp-wide): 570.2MM **Privately
Held**
SIC: 8062 General medical & surgical hos-
pitals
PA: Ahmc Healthcare Inc.
1000 S Fremont Ave Unit 6
Alhambra CA 91803

(P-20738)
**AHMC WHITTIER HOSP MED
CTR LP**
9080 Colima Rd, Whittier (90605-1600)
PHONE..................562 945-3561
Richard Castro, *CEO*
Mary A Monje, *COO*
Lee Panton, *Lab Dir*
Abegail Camus, *Controller*
Linda Castellanet, *Director*
EMP: 850
SQ FT: 16,782
SALES (est): 41.9MM
SALES (corp-wide): 570.2MM **Privately
Held**
WEB: www.ahmchealth.com
SIC: 8062 General medical & surgical hos-
pitals
PA: Ahmc Healthcare Inc.
1000 S Fremont Ave Unit 6
Alhambra CA 91803

(P-20739)
ALAKOR HEALTHCARE LLC
Also Called: Monrovia Memorial Hospital
323 S Heliotrope Ave, Monrovia
(91016-2914)
PHONE..................626 408-9800
Kevin Smith,
Frank Adomitis, *CFO*
Katty Johnson, *Human Res Mgr*
Jon Woods, *General Counsel*
EMP: 126
SQ FT: 10,000
SALES: 47.2MM **Privately Held**
SIC: 8062 General medical & surgical hos-
pitals

(P-20740)
**ALAMEDA HEALTH SYSTEM
(PA)**
Also Called: Highland Hosp Hghland Well-
ness
1411 E 31st St, Oakland (94602-1018)
PHONE..................510 437-4800
Daniel Boggan Jr, *CEO*
Lynda Wilson, *Ch of Bd*
Mark S Fratzke, *COO*
Peter Hohl, *COO*
David Cox, *CFO*
EMP: 99
SALES (est): 52.7MM **Privately Held**
SIC: 8062 General medical & surgical hos-
pitals

(P-20741)
**ALHAMBRA HOSPITAL MED CTR
LP**
100 S Raymond Ave, Alhambra
(91801-3166)
PHONE..................626 570-1606
Iris Lai, *Marketing Staff*
Suh Wang, *Business Dir*
Elizabeth Sabandit, *Exec Dir*
Juan Rodriquez, *Purchasing*
Diane Wong, *Marketing Staff*
EMP: 160 **EST:** 1920
SQ FT: 200,000

SALES: 81.7MM
SALES (corp-wide): 570.2MM **Privately Held**
SIC: 8062 General medical & surgical hospitals
PA: Ahmc Healthcare Inc.
1000 S Fremont Ave Unit 6
Alhambra CA 91803
-

(P-20742)
ALTA HOSPITALS SYSTEM LLC
Also Called: Los Angeles Community Hospital
4081 E Olympic Blvd, Los Angeles (90023-3330)
PHONE..................................323 267-0477
Remy Hart, *Branch Mgr*
Farrel Johnson, *Engineer*
Carlos Mota, *Purch Mgr*
David Guerrero, *Hlthcr Dir*
Robert Vasquez, *Director*
EMP: 250
SQ FT: 64,024
SALES (corp-wide): 1.2B **Privately Held**
SIC: 8062 General medical & surgical hospitals
HQ: Alta Hospitals System, Llc
3415 S Sepulveda Blvd # 900
Los Angeles CA 90034
-

(P-20743)
ALTA HOSPITALS SYSTEM LLC
Also Called: Foothill Regional Medical Ctr
14662 Newport Ave, Tustin (92780-6064)
PHONE..................................714 619-7700
EMP: 575
SALES (corp-wide): 1.2B **Privately Held**
SIC: 8062 General medical & surgical hospitals
HQ: Alta Hospitals System, Llc
3415 S Sepulveda Blvd # 900
Los Angeles CA 90034
-

(P-20744)
ALTA HOSPITALS SYSTEM LLC (HQ)
3415 S Sepulveda Blvd # 900, Los Angeles (90034-6981)
PHONE..................................310 943-4500
Samuel S Lee, *Mng Member*
Ralph Uribe, *President*
Fred Capozello, *Vice Pres*
Bruce Grimshaw, *Vice Pres*
Berril Kenoly, *Admin Asst*
EMP: 143
SALES (est): 95.4MM
SALES (corp-wide): 1.2B **Privately Held**
SIC: 8062 General medical & surgical hospitals
PA: Prospect Medical Holdings, Inc.
3415 S Sepulveda Blvd # 9
Los Angeles CA 90034
310 943-4500

(P-20745)
ALVARADO HOSPITAL LLC (DH)
6655 Alvarado Rd, San Diego (92120-5208)
PHONE..................................619 287-3270
Tracey Tally, *CFO*
Darlene Wetton, *COO*
Natalie Mercille, *Lab Dir*
Tony Sangermano, *Technician*
Marilyn Anderson, *Controller*
EMP: 62
SALES: 154.2K
SALES (corp-wide): 3.4B **Privately Held**
SIC: 8062 General medical & surgical hospitals

(P-20746)
AMERICAN HOSPITAL MGT CORP (PA)
Also Called: MAD RIVER COMMUNITY HOSPITAL
3800 Janes Rd, Arcata (95521-4742)
P.O. Box 1115 (95518-1115)
PHONE..................................707 822-3621
Allen E Shaw, *President*
Michael Young, *CFO*
Doug A Shaw, *Vice Pres*
Charles F Forbes, *Admin Sec*
Pamela Floyd, *QA Dir*
EMP: 500

SQ FT: 60,000
SALES: 66.8MM **Privately Held**
WEB: www.madriverhospital.com
SIC: 8062 General medical & surgical hospitals

(P-20747)
AMI-HTI TARZANA ENCINO JOINT V
Also Called: A M I Encn-Trzana Rgnal Med Ce
18321 Clark St, Tarzana (91356-3501)
PHONE..................................818 881-0800
Dale Surowitz, *Managing Prtnr*
Nick Lymberopoulos, *CFO*
Bryan Tzy Young Lin, *Pathologist*
Jo Ann Lewis, *Director*
EMP: 1800
SQ FT: 180,000
SALES: 14.6MM **Privately Held**
SIC: 8062 General medical & surgical hospitals

(P-20748)
AMISUB (IRVINE REGIONAL HOSPI)
1400 S Douglass Rd # 250, Anaheim (92806-6904)
PHONE..................................949 916-7556
EMP: 590
SQ FT: 244,000
SALES (est): 17.9MM **Privately Held**
SIC: 8062 5912 General medical & surgical hospitals; drug stores

(P-20749)
AMISUB OF CALIFORNIA INC (DH)
18321 Clark St, Tarzana (91356-3501)
PHONE..................................818 881-0800
Dale Surowitz, *CEO*
Don Kreitz, *COO*
Nick Lymberopolous, *CFO*
EMP: 900 **EST:** 1979
SQ FT: 180,000
SALES (est): 480K
SALES (corp-wide): 18.3B **Publicly Held**
SIC: 8062 General medical & surgical hospitals
HQ: Tenet Healthsystem Medical, Inc.
1445 Ross Ave Ste 1400
Dallas TX 75202
469 893-2000

(P-20750)
ANAHEIM GLOBAL MEDICAL CENTER
1025 S Anaheim Blvd, Anaheim (92805-5806)
PHONE..................................714 533-6220
Marven E Howard, *CEO*
Jason Liu, *Principal*
EMP: 500
SALES (est): 14MM
SALES (corp-wide): 407.3MM **Privately Held**
SIC: 8062 General medical & surgical hospitals
PA: Kpc Healthcare, Inc.
1301 N Tustin Ave
Santa Ana CA 92705
714 953-3652

(P-20751)
ANAHEIM REGIONAL MEDICAL CTR
Also Called: Cardiac Unit
1111 W La Palma Ave, Anaheim (92801-2804)
PHONE..................................714 774-1450
EMP: 705
SALES (corp-wide): 169.9MM **Privately Held**
WEB: www.cardiacunit.com
SIC: 8062 General medical & surgical hospitals
PA: Anaheim Regional Medical Center
1111 W La Palma Ave
Anaheim CA 92801
714 774-1450

(P-20752)
ANTELOPE VALLEY HOSPITAL INC (PA)
Also Called: Antelope Valley Healthcare Dst
1600 W Avenue J, Lancaster (93534-2894)
P.O. Box 7001 (93539-7001)
PHONE..................................661 949-5000
Edward Mirzabegian, *CEO*
Patalappa Chandrashekar, *Jennifer Hill, Ch Radiology*
Jack Burke, *COO*
Dennis Empey, *CFO*
EMP: 1660 **EST:** 1953
SQ FT: 300,000
SALES (est): 411.1MM **Privately Held**
WEB: www.avhospital.com
SIC: 8062 General medical & surgical hospitals

(P-20753)
ARCH HEALTH PARTNERS INC (HQ)
15611 Pomerado Rd Ste 575, Poway (92064-2438)
PHONE..................................858 675-3100
Deanna Kyrimis, *CEO*
Matt Niedzwiecki, *COO*
Hugh King, *CFO*
Vicky Lister, *Exec Dir*
Kristen Napierskie, *Executive Asst*
EMP: 92 **EST:** 2009
SALES: 49.5MM
SALES (corp-wide): 502.8MM **Privately Held**
SIC: 8062 General medical & surgical hospitals
PA: Palomar Health
456 E Grand Ave
Escondido CA 92025
442 281-5000

(P-20754)
ARROWHEAD REGIONAL MEDICAL CTR
Also Called: Armc
400 N Pepper Ave, Colton (92324-1819)
PHONE..................................909 580-1000
Patrick Petre, *Director*
William Gilbert, *Officer*
Theodore Friedman, *Lab Dir*
Cliff Hiroshige, *Pharmacy Dir*
Mari Craig, *Executive Asst*
EMP: 2500
SQ FT: 950,000
SALES: 468.9MM **Privately Held**
SIC: 8062 General medical & surgical hospitals
PA: County Of San Bernardino
385 N Arrowhead Ave
San Bernardino CA 92415
909 387-3841

(P-20755)
AURORA HEALTHCARE INC
Also Called: Aurora Behavioral Hlth Care
11878 Avenue Of Industry, San Diego (92128-3423)
PHONE..................................858 487-3200
James S Plummer, *CEO*
Cordova Sheila, *COO*
Vicki Thomsen, *Human Res Dir*
Marret Funk, *Human Res Mgr*
Vincent Reid, *Opers Mgr*
EMP: 50
SALES (est): 3.8MM **Privately Held**
SIC: 8062 General medical & surgical hospitals

(P-20756)
AUXILIARY OF MISSION
27700 Medical Center Rd, Mission Viejo (92691-6426)
PHONE..................................949 364-1400
Eduardo Jordan, *Ch of Bd*
Kenn McFarland, *President*
Vicki J Veal, *CEO*
Shawn Bullock, *Anesthesiology*
Christopher Romig, *Anesthesiology*
EMP: 54
SALES: 516.9K
SALES (corp-wide): 547.3MM **Privately Held**
SIC: 8062 General medical & surgical hospitals

PA: Mission Hospital Regional Medical Center Inc
27700 Medical Center Rd
Mission Viejo CA 92691
949 364-1400

(P-20757)
AZALEA HOLDINGS LLC
Also Called: MCKINLEY PARK CARE CENTER
3700 H St, Sacramento (95816-4611)
PHONE..................................916 452-3592
Radio Shey, *Administration*
Jared Bake, *Principal*
Gary Weemers, *Administration*
EMP: 85
SALES: 12.5MM **Privately Held**
SIC: 8062 General medical & surgical hospitals

(P-20758)
BAKERSFIELD MEMORIAL HOSPITAL
Also Called: Memorial Center
420 34th St, Bakersfield (93301-2237)
P.O. Box 1888 (93303-1888)
PHONE..................................661 327-1792
Jon Van Boening, *CEO*
Gordon K Foster, *Ch of Bd*
R Mark R Root, *Vice Pres*
Renee Brooks, *Purch Dir*
Rachel Larsen, *Dietician*
EMP: 1100
SQ FT: 364,000
SALES: 401.3MM **Privately Held**
SIC: 8062 Hospital, affiliated with AMA residency
HQ: Dignity Health
185 Berry St Ste 300
San Francisco CA 94107
415 438-5500

(P-20759)
BANNER HEALTH
1800 Spring Ridge Dr, Susanville (96130-6100)
PHONE..................................530 251-3147
Dan Bandy, *Radiology*
Fred Nielson, *Pharmacist*
Kelsey Rinaudo,
Paul Holmes, *Director*
Pam Novosad, *Director*
EMP: 165
SALES (corp-wide): 8.5B **Privately Held**
WEB: www.bannerhealth.com
SIC: 8062 General medical & surgical hospitals
PA: Banner Health
2901 N Central Ave # 160
Phoenix AZ 85012
602 747-4000

(P-20760)
BANNER LASSEN MEDICAL CENTER
1800 Spring Ridge Dr, Susanville (96130-6100)
PHONE..................................530 252-2000
Bob Edwards, *CEO*
Shelby Diede, *CFO*
Kimberly Hamelton, *Radiology Dir*
Deborah Ingle, *Financial Analy*
EMP: 200
SALES: 41.5MM **Privately Held**
SIC: 8062 8051 General medical & surgical hospitals; skilled nursing care facilities

(P-20761)
BARTON HOSPITAL
2170 South Ave, South Lake Tahoe (96150-7026)
P.O. Box 9578 (96158-9578)
PHONE..................................530 543-5685
Clint Purvance, *CEO*
Darcy Wallace, *Vice Pres*
EMP: 1200 **EST:** 2014
SALES (est): 107.1K **Privately Held**
SIC: 8062 General medical & surgical hospitals

P R O D U C T S & S V C S

(P-20762)
BEAR VLY CMNTY HEALTHCARE DST (PA)
41870 Garstin Dr, Big Bear Lake (92315-2088)
PHONE..................909 866-6501
Raymond Hino, *CEO*
Barbara Espinoza, *Vice Pres*
Donna Nicely, *Vice Pres*
Shelly Egerer, *General Mgr*
Christopher Fagan, *Admin Sec*
EMP: 150
SQ FT: 25,000
SALES: 26.2K **Privately Held**
SIC: 8062 General medical & surgical hospitals

(P-20763)
BEVERLY COMMUNITY HOSP ASSN
101 E Beverly Blvd # 104, Montebello (90640-4300)
PHONE..................323 889-2452
Norma Valdez, *Principal*
EMP: 322
SALES (corp-wide): 205.6MM **Privately Held**
SIC: 8062 8011 General medical & surgical hospitals; clinic, operated by physicians
PA: Beverly Community Hospital Association
309 W Beverly Blvd
Montebello CA 90640
323 726-1222

(P-20764)
BEVERLY COMMUNITY HOSP ASSN (PA)
Also Called: BEVERLY HOSPITAL
309 W Beverly Blvd, Montebello (90640-4308)
PHONE..................323 726-1222
Gary Kiff, *CEO*
Luis Sanchez, *President*
Larry Pugh, *CFO*
Renee D Martinez, *Treasurer*
Wendy Beesley, *Vice Pres*
EMP: 136 **EST:** 1949
SQ FT: 274,000
SALES: 205.6MM **Privately Held**
WEB: www.beverly.org
SIC: 8062 General medical & surgical hospitals

(P-20765)
BEVERLY COMMUNITY HOSP ASSN
Also Called: Kelpien Health Care
1920 W Whittier Blvd, Montebello (90640-4009)
PHONE..................323 725-1519
Wendy Torres, *Manager*
EMP: 537
SALES (corp-wide): 205.6MM **Privately Held**
WEB: www.beverly.org
SIC: 8062 General medical & surgical hospitals
PA: Beverly Community Hospital Association
309 W Beverly Blvd
Montebello CA 90640
323 726-1222

(P-20766)
CALIFORNIA PACIFIC MEDICAL CTR
2100 Webster St Ste 115, San Francisco (94115-2374)
PHONE..................415 600-1378
Matthew Poland, *Principal*
Michelle Haynes, *Osteopathy*
Sarah T Love, *Director*
EMP: 99
SALES (est): 5.5MM **Privately Held**
SIC: 8062 General medical & surgical hospitals

(P-20767)
CALIFRNIA HOSP MED CTR FNDTION
1401 S Grand Ave, Los Angeles (90015-3010)
PHONE..................213 748-2411
Phillip C Hill, *Ch of Bd*
Nathan R Nusbaum, *President*
Margaret R Peterson, *President*
Harold Newton, *COO*
Clark Underwood, *CFO*
▲ **EMP:** 1500
SQ FT: 800,000
SALES: 396.8MM **Privately Held**
WEB: www.chw.edu
SIC: 8062 Hospital, medical school affiliated with nursing & residency
HQ: Dignity Health
185 Berry St Ste 300
San Francisco CA 94107
415 438-5500

(P-20768)
CASA COLINA HOSPITAL AND CENTE (HQ)
Also Called: Casa Clina Ctrs For Rhbltation
255 E Bonita Ave, Pomona (91767-1933)
P.O. Box 6001 (91769-6001)
PHONE..................909 596-7733
Felice Loverso, *CEO*
Bill Loverso, *COO*
Steve Norin, *Chairman*
Randy Blackman, *Treasurer*
Stephen Graeber, *Treasurer*
▲ **EMP:** 500
SQ FT: 90,000
SALES: 53.4MM
SALES (corp-wide): 111.2MM **Privately Held**
WEB: www.casacolina.org
SIC: 8062 General medical & surgical hospitals
PA: Casa Colina, Inc.
255 E Bonita Ave
Pomona CA 91767
909 596-7733

(P-20769)
CEDARS-SINAI MEDICAL CENTER
Also Called: Health System Medical Network
250 N Robertson Blvd # 101, Beverly Hills (90211-1788)
PHONE..................310 385-3400
Tom Gordon, *CEO*
Ruchi Mathur, *Med Doctor*
Clement Yang, *Med Doctor*
EMP: 200
SALES (corp-wide): 3.6B **Privately Held**
SIC: 8062 8011 General medical & surgical hospitals; offices & clinics of medical doctors
PA: Cedars-Sinai Medical Center
8700 Beverly Blvd
West Hollywood CA 90048
310 423-3277

(P-20770)
CENTRAL VLY SPECIALTY HOSP INC
730 17th St, Modesto (95354-1209)
PHONE..................209 248-7700
Gia Smith, *CEO*
Chioma Nwokike, *Director*
Chris Lowey, *Case Mgr*
EMP: 99 **EST:** 2012
SALES: 40.7MM **Privately Held**
SIC: 8062 General medical & surgical hospitals

(P-20771)
CFHS HOLDINGS INC
Also Called: Centinela Frman Rgonal Med Ctr
4650 Lincoln Blvd, Marina Del Rey (90292-6306)
PHONE..................310 823-8911
EMP: 650
SQ FT: 150,000
SALES (corp-wide): 3.6B **Privately Held**
SIC: 8062 General medical & surgical hospitals
HQ: Cfhs Holdings, Inc.
4650 Lincoln Blvd
Marina Del Rey CA 90292
310 823-8911

(P-20772)
CFHS HOLDINGS INC
Also Called: Centinela Frman Rgonal Med Ctr
4640 Admiralty Way # 650, Marina Del Rey (90292-6667)
PHONE..................310 448-7800
Bob Bokern, *Principal*
EMP: 1940
SALES (corp-wide): 3.6B **Privately Held**
SIC: 8062 General medical & surgical hospitals
HQ: Cfhs Holdings, Inc.
4650 Lincoln Blvd
Marina Del Rey CA 90292
310 823-8911

(P-20773)
CFHS HOLDINGS INC
Also Called: Centinela Frman Rgonal Med Ctr
555 E Hardy St, Inglewood (90301-4011)
PHONE..................310 673-4660
Michael Rembis, *Branch Mgr*
EMP: 1200
SALES (corp-wide): 3.6B **Privately Held**
SIC: 8062 General medical & surgical hospitals
HQ: Cfhs Holdings, Inc.
4650 Lincoln Blvd
Marina Del Rey CA 90292
310 823-8911

(P-20774)
CHA HOLLYWOOD MEDICAL CTR LP (PA)
Also Called: Hollywood Presbyterian Med Ctr
1300 N Vermont Ave, Los Angeles (90027-6098)
PHONE..................213 413-3000
Jeff A Nelson, *CEO*
Romeo Velasco,
Galen Gorman, *CFO*
Angela Salinas, *Supervisor*
▲ **EMP:** 1500
SQ FT: 900,000
SALES: 288.9MM **Privately Held**
WEB: www.hollywoodpresbyterian.com
SIC: 8062 8351 Hospital, affiliated with AMA residency; child day care services

(P-20775)
CHAPMAN GLOBAL MEDICAL CENTER
Also Called: Chapman Family Health
2601 E Chapman Ave, Orange (92869-3206)
PHONE..................714 633-0011
Don Kreitz, *CEO*
Kelvin Nguyen,
Lori Firman, *President*
Kenneth K Westbrook, *CEO*
Robert Heinemeier, *CFO*
EMP: 425
SQ FT: 96,000
SALES: 46.3MM
SALES (corp-wide): 407.3MM **Privately Held**
WEB: www.chapmanmedicalcenter.com
SIC: 8062 General medical & surgical hospitals
PA: Kpc Healthcare, Inc.
1301 N Tustin Ave
Santa Ana CA 92705
714 953-3652

(P-20776)
CHHP MANAGEMENT LLC
Also Called: Community Hosp Huntington Pk
2623 E Slauson Ave, Huntington Park (90255-2926)
PHONE..................323 583-1931
Joel Freedman, *Principal*
Mark Bell, *Principal*
Jamie Macpherson, *Principal*
EMP: 99 **EST:** 2010
SALES: 49.7MM
SALES (corp-wide): 264.6MM **Privately Held**
SIC: 8062 General medical & surgical hospitals
HQ: Chhp Holdings Ii, Llc
2623 E Slauson Ave
Huntington Park CA 90255
323 583-1931

(P-20777)
CHILDRENS HOSPITAL LOS ANGELES
Also Called: Childrens Laboratory
5359 Balboa Blvd, Encino (91316-2819)
PHONE..................818 728-4930
Paul Pattengale, *Director*
EMP: 185
SALES (corp-wide): 1.3B **Privately Held**
SIC: 8062 General medical & surgical hospitals
PA: The Childrens Hospital Los Angeles
4650 W Sunset Blvd
Los Angeles CA 90027
323 660-2450

(P-20778)
CHILDRENS HOSPITAL LOS ANGELES
5000 W Sunset Blvd # 400, Los Angeles (90027-5865)
PHONE..................323 361-2153
EMP: 247
SALES (corp-wide): 1.3B **Privately Held**
SIC: 8062 General medical & surgical hospitals
PA: The Childrens Hospital Los Angeles
4650 W Sunset Blvd
Los Angeles CA 90027
323 660-2450

(P-20779)
CHILDRENS HOSPITAL LOS ANGELES
468 E Santa Clara St, Arcadia (91006-7228)
PHONE..................626 795-7177
Bianca Edison, *Sports Medicine*
EMP: 247
SALES (corp-wide): 1.3B **Privately Held**
SIC: 8062 General medical & surgical hospitals
PA: The Childrens Hospital Los Angeles
4650 W Sunset Blvd
Los Angeles CA 90027
323 660-2450

(P-20780)
CHILDRENS HOSPITAL LOS ANGELES
Also Called: Santa Monica Outpatient Center
1301 20th St Ste 460, Santa Monica (90404-2090)
PHONE..................310 820-8608
Ronald J Gowey, *President*
EMP: 185
SALES (corp-wide): 1.3B **Privately Held**
SIC: 8062 General medical & surgical hospitals
PA: The Childrens Hospital Los Angeles
4650 W Sunset Blvd
Los Angeles CA 90027
323 660-2450

(P-20781)
CHILDRENS HOSPITAL LOS ANGELES
Foundation Division
4650 W Sunset Blvd, Los Angeles (90027-6062)
PHONE..................323 660-2450
Claudia Looney, *Vice Pres*
EMP: 80
SALES (corp-wide): 1.3B **Privately Held**
SIC: 8062 8641 General medical & surgical hospitals; civic social & fraternal associations
PA: The Childrens Hospital Los Angeles
4650 W Sunset Blvd
Los Angeles CA 90027
323 660-2450

(P-20782)
CHILDRENS HOSPITAL ORANGE CNTY
Also Called: Choc Mission
455 S Main St, Orange (92868-3835)
PHONE..................949 365-2416
Kerri Ruppert Schiller, *Principal*
Susan Burrows, *Vice Pres*
James Fabella, *Vice Pres*
Waldo Romero, *Vice Pres*
Barbara Sanchez, *Vice Pres*
EMP: 1168

SALES (corp-wide): 523.1MM **Privately Held**
SIC: **8062** General medical & surgical hospitals
PA: Children's Hospital Of Orange County
1201 W La Veta Ave
Orange CA 92868
714 997-3000

(P-20783)
CHILDRENS HOSPITAL ORANGE CNTY
980 Roosevelt, Irvine (92620-3672)
PHONE.................................949 387-2586
EMP: 1036
SALES (corp-wide): 523.1MM **Privately Held**
SIC: **8062** 8099 8082 6321 General medical & surgical hospitals; childbirth preparation clinic; home health care services; accident & health insurance
PA: Children's Hospital Of Orange County
1201 W La Veta Ave
Orange CA 92868
714 997-3000

(P-20784)
CHILDRENS HOSPOTAL & RESEARCH (PA)
Also Called: Ucsf Benioff Chld Hosp Oakland
747 52nd St, Oakland (94609-1809)
PHONE.................................510 428-3000
Bertram Lubin, *President*
Harold Davis, *Ch of Bd*
Kathleen Cain, *CFO*
Rina Smith, *CFO*
Betsy Biern, *Senior VP*
EMP: 1900
SQ FT: 160,000
SALES: 178.6MM **Privately Held**
SIC: **8062** Hospital, AMA approved residency

(P-20785)
CHINESE HOSPITAL ASSOCIATION (PA)
845 Jackson St, San Francisco (94133-4899)
PHONE.................................415 982-2400
Brenda Yee, *CEO*
Thomas Bolger, *CFO*
Helen Lee, *Systs Prg Mgr*
Lisa Glaser, *Technician*
Christina Lee, *Technology*
EMP: 279
SQ FT: 54,000
SALES: 216.8MM **Privately Held**
WEB: www.cchphmo.com
SIC: **8062** General medical & surgical hospitals

(P-20786)
CITRUS VALLEY MEDICAL CTR INC (PA)
1115 S Sunset Ave, West Covina (91790-3940)
P.O. Box 6108, Covina (91722-5108)
PHONE.................................626 962-4011
Robert Curry, *President*
Elvia Foulke, *COO*
Roger Sharma, *CFO*
Ryan Burke, *Officer*
Annette Macias, *Mktg Dir*
EMP: 1229
SQ FT: 285,000
SALES: 502.7MM **Privately Held**
WEB: www.cvpg.org
SIC: **8062** General medical & surgical hospitals

(P-20787)
CITRUS VALLEY MEDICAL CTR INC
Also Called: Human Resources Department
140 W College St, Covina (91723-2007)
PHONE.................................626 858-8515
Robert H Curry, *Administration*
EMP: 746
SALES (corp-wide): 502.7MM **Privately Held**
SIC: **8062** General medical & surgical hospitals

PA: Citrus Valley Medical Center, Inc.
1115 S Sunset Ave
West Covina CA 91790
626 962-4011

(P-20788)
CITRUS VALLEY MEDICAL CTR INC
Also Called: Queen of The Valley Hospital
1115 S Sunset Ave, West Covina (91790-3940)
PHONE.................................626 963-8411
Robert Curry, *President*
EMP: 2000
SALES (corp-wide): 502.7MM **Privately Held**
WEB: www.cvpg.org
SIC: **8062** General medical & surgical hospitals
PA: Citrus Valley Medical Center, Inc.
1115 S Sunset Ave
West Covina CA 91790
626 962-4011

(P-20789)
CITRUS VALLEY MEDICAL CTR INC
Also Called: Inter Community Hospital
210 W San Bernardino Rd, Covina (91723-1515)
PHONE.................................626 331-7331
Toll Free:.................................877 -
Jim Yoshioka, *President*
EMP: 1000
SALES (corp-wide): 502.7MM **Privately Held**
WEB: www.cvpg.org
SIC: **8062** General medical & surgical hospitals
PA: Citrus Valley Medical Center, Inc.
1115 S Sunset Ave
West Covina CA 91790
626 962-4011

(P-20790)
CITRUS VLY HLTH PARTNERS INC
Also Called: Queen of The Valley Campus
1115 S Sunset Ave, West Covina (91790-3940)
PHONE.................................626 962-4011
Debbie Segaram, *Branch Mgr*
EMP: 501 **Privately Held**
SIC: **8062** General medical & surgical hospitals
PA: Emanate Health Inter-Community Hospital
210 W San Bernardino Rd
Covina CA 91723

(P-20791)
CITY & COUNTY OF SAN FRANCISCO
Also Called: San Francisco General Hospital
1001 Potrero Ave, San Francisco (94110-3518)
PHONE.................................415 206-8000
Susan Currin, *Principal*
Sarah Haynes, *Principal*
Jean O'Connel, *Principal*
Lisa Steven, *Business Anlyst*
Porsche Bunton, *Recruiter*
EMP: 5000 **Privately Held**
SIC: **8062** General medical & surgical hospitals
PA: City & County Of San Francisco
1 Dr Carlton B Goodlett P
San Francisco CA 94102
415 554-7500

(P-20792)
CITY ALAMEDA HEALTH CARE CORP
Also Called: Alameda Hospital
2070 Clinton Ave, Alameda (94501-4399)
PHONE.................................510 522-3700
Deborah E Stebbins, *CEO*
Rosemarie Delahaye, *Director*
Katy Silverman, *Director*
EMP: 520
SQ FT: 150,000

SALES (est): 94.5MM **Privately Held**
WEB: www.alamedahospital.com
SIC: **8062** 8051 General medical & surgical hospitals; skilled nursing care facilities

(P-20793)
CITY HOPE NATIONAL MEDICAL CTR
1500 Duarte Rd, Duarte (91010-3012)
PHONE.................................626 256-4673
Michael A Friedman, *CEO*
Mick Protopapas, *Database Admin*
Matthew Parsons, *Project Mgr*
Sarmad Bahrani, *Research*
Alyssa Gonzalez, *Research*
EMP: 1900
SALES (est): 774.5MM
SALES (corp-wide): 1.3B **Privately Held**
SIC: **8062** General medical & surgical hospitals
PA: City Of Hope
1500 Duarte Rd
Duarte CA 91010
626 256-4673

(P-20794)
COALINGA REGIONAL MEDICAL CENT
Also Called: Crmc
1191 Phelps Ave, Coalinga (93210-9609)
PHONE.................................559 935-6400
EMP: 230 EST: 1947
SALES: 20.1MM **Privately Held**
WEB: www.coalingamedicalcenter.com
SIC: **8062** 8051 Hospital, affiliated with AMA residency; skilled nursing care facilities

(P-20795)
COAST PLAZA DOCTORS HOSPITAL (PA)
13100 Studebaker Rd, Norwalk (90650-2531)
PHONE.................................562 868-3751
John Ferrelli, *CEO*
Craig B Garner, *CEO*
Mihi Lee, *CFO*
Joel Freedman, *Principal*
EMP: 59
SQ FT: 58,000
SALES (est): 18.7MM **Privately Held**
WEB: www.coastplazahospital.com
SIC: **8062** Hospital, medical school affiliation

(P-20796)
COMMUNITY HLTH ALANCE PASADENA (PA)
Also Called: Chap
1855 N Fair Oaks Ave # 200, Pasadena (91103-1620)
P.O. Box 94873 (91109-4873)
PHONE.................................626 398-6300
Margaret Martinez, *CEO*
Deborah Villar, *Vice Chairman*
Sergio Bautista, *COO*
Michael P Hernandez, *Treasurer*
Sumayya Aasi, *Bd of Directors*
EMP: 56
SALES: 9.9MM **Privately Held**
SIC: **8062** General medical & surgical hospitals

(P-20797)
COMMUNITY HOSP SAN BERNARDINO (DH)
1805 Medical Center Dr, San Bernardino (92411-1217)
PHONE.................................909 887-6333
June Collisone, *President*
Gonzalo Cazas,
Ed Sorenson, *CFO*
Faviola Garcia, *Admin Sec*
Daniel Osias, *Administration*
EMP: 350
SALES: 244.8MM **Privately Held**
SIC: **8062** Hospital, affiliated with AMA residency
HQ: Dignity Health
185 Berry St Ste 300
San Francisco CA 94107
415 438-5500

(P-20798)
COMMUNITY HOSPITALS CENTL CAL (PA)
Also Called: COMMUNITY HEALTH SYSTEM
2823 Fresno St (93721-1324)
P.O. Box 1232 (93715-1232)
PHONE.................................559 459-6000
Tim A Joslin, *CEO*
Robin Gonzales,
Gordon Webster Jr, *Vice Chairman*
Phyllis Baltz, *COO*
Craig S Castro, *COO*
EMP: 3400
SQ FT: 200,000
SALES: 1.6B **Privately Held**
SIC: **8062** 8011 8051 General medical & surgical hospitals; ambulatory surgical center; clinic, operated by physicians; extended care facility

(P-20799)
COMMUNITY HOSPITALS CENTL CAL
Also Called: Community Regional Medical Ctr
2823 Fresno St, Fresno (93721-1324)
PHONE.................................559 459-6000
Tim Joslin, *President*
Hap Morrissey, *Lab Dir*
Matthew Joslin, *Administration*
Jagmeet Singh, *Database Admin*
Melissa Davis, *Human Res Dir*
EMP: 1000
SALES: 1.5B **Privately Held**
SIC: **8062** General medical & surgical hospitals

(P-20800)
COMMUNITY MEDICAL CENTER
Also Called: Clovis Community Living
3003 N Mariposa St, Fresno (93703-1127)
PHONE.................................559 222-7416
EMP: 150
SALES (corp-wide): 1.6B **Privately Held**
SIC: **8062** 8051
PA: Community Hospitals Of Central California
2823 Fresno St
Fresno CA 93721
559 459-6000

(P-20801)
COMMUNITY MEDICAL CENTERS
Also Called: Alzheimer's Living Center
668 E Bullard Ave, Fresno (93710-5401)
PHONE.................................559 320-2200
Patrick Uribe, *Manager*
EMP: 110
SQ FT: 28,845
SALES (corp-wide): 1.6B **Privately Held**
SIC: **8062** 8051 General medical & surgical hospitals; skilled nursing care facilities
PA: Community Hospitals Of Central California
2823 Fresno St
Fresno CA 93721
559 459-6000

(P-20802)
COMMUNITY MEDICAL CENTERS
Also Called: Advanced Medical Imaging
6297 N Fresno St, Fresno (93710-5209)
PHONE.................................559 447-4000
Donna Moora, *Director*
Hans Hildebrandt, *Med Doctor*
EMP: 70
SALES (corp-wide): 1.6B **Privately Held**
SIC: **8062** 8011 8093 General medical & surgical hospitals; radiologist; specialty outpatient clinics
PA: Community Hospitals Of Central California
2823 Fresno St
Fresno CA 93721
559 459-6000

(P-20803)
COMMUNITY MEM HSP/SN BENUA
Also Called: Purchasing Department
147 N Brent St, Ventura (93003-2809)
PHONE.................................805 652-5072
Chuck Gray, *Manager*
▲ EMP: 99

SALES: 285MM **Privately Held**
WEB: www.cmhhospital.org
SIC: **8062** General medical & surgical hospitals

(P-20804)
COMMUNITY MEMORIAL HEALTH SYS
Also Called: Ojai Valley Community Hospital
1306 Maricopa Hwy, Ojai (93023-3131)
PHONE...................................805 646-1401
Gary Wilde, *President*
EMP: 120
SALES (corp-wide): 432.7MM **Privately Held**
SIC: **8062** General medical & surgical hospitals
PA: Community Memorial Health System
147 N Brent St
Ventura CA 93003
805 652-5011

(P-20805)
CORCORAN DISTRICT HOSPITAL
1310 Hanna Ave, Corcoran (93212-2314)
P.O. Box 758 (93212-0758)
PHONE...................................559 992-3300
Mike Graville, *CEO*
Jonathan Brain, *CEO*
Alan Macphee, *CFO*
Jess Martinez, *Admin Sec*
EMP: 100 EST: 1951
SQ FT: 35,000
SALES (est): 7MM **Privately Held**
SIC: **8062** General medical & surgical hospitals

(P-20806)
CORRECTONS RHBLTATION CAL DEPT
Also Called: Cdcr Cal Instn For Men Hosp
14901 Central Ave, Chino (91710-9500)
P.O. Box 128 (91708-0128)
PHONE...................................909 597-1821
ME Poulls, *Warden*
Wasil Aqil, *Family Practiti*
Boles Bishay, *Family Practiti*
Mohan Garikaparthi, *Family Practiti*
Victor Gomez, *Family Practiti*
EMP: 179 **Privately Held**
SIC: **8062** 9223 General medical & surgical hospitals; house of correction, government;
HQ: California Department Of Corrections & Rehabilitation
1515 S St
Sacramento CA 95811

(P-20807)
COTTAGE CARE CENTER
Also Called: Santa Barbara Cottage Care Ctr
2415 De La Vina St, Santa Barbara (93105-3819)
P.O. Box 689 (93102-0689)
PHONE...................................805 682-7111
Dr Peter Macdougall, *Ch of Bd*
James L Ash, *President*
Reece Duca, *CFO*
EMP: 160
SQ FT: 45,000
SALES: 7.8MM **Privately Held**
SIC: **8062** General medical & surgical hospitals

(P-20808)
COTTAGE HEALTH (PA)
400 W Pueblo St, Santa Barbara (93105-4353)
P.O. Box 689 (93102-0689)
PHONE...................................805 682-7111
Ronald C Werft, *President*
James Benzian, *Ch Radiology*
Thomas J Cusack, *Vice Chairman*
Gregory F Faulkner, *Vice Chairman*
Edmund Wroblewski, *Chief Mktg Ofcr*
EMP: 2422
SQ FT: 202,500
SALES (est): 549.4MM **Privately Held**
SIC: **8062** 8741 General medical & surgical hospitals; hospital management

(P-20809)
COTTAGE HEALTH
2050 Viborg Rd, Solvang (93463-2220)
PHONE...................................805 688-6432
John Blaustein, *Ch Pathology*
Wende Cappetta, *Vice Pres*
Judy Blokdyk, *Purchasing*
EMP: 171
SALES (est): 3.9MM
SALES (corp-wide): 549.4MM **Privately Held**
SIC: **8062** General medical & surgical hospitals
PA: Cottage Health
400 W Pueblo St
Santa Barbara CA 93105
805 682-7111

(P-20810)
COTTAGE HEALTH SYSTEM
351 S Patterson Ave, Goleta (93111-2403)
PHONE...................................805 967-3411
EMP: 1389
SALES (corp-wide): 549.4MM **Privately Held**
SIC: **8062** General medical & surgical hospitals
PA: Cottage Health
400 W Pueblo St
Santa Barbara CA 93105
805 682-7111

(P-20811)
COUNTY OF CONTRA COSTA
Also Called: Department of Health Services
2500 Alhambra Ave, Martinez (94553-3156)
PHONE...................................925 370-5000
Jeff Smith, *CEO*
Anna Roth, *Officer*
Fernando Mendoza, *Lab Dir*
Xiaohui Xiong, *Lab Dir*
Hye Kim, *Pathologist*
EMP: 200 **Privately Held**
WEB: www.cccounty.us
SIC: **8062** 9431 General medical & surgical hospitals; administration of public health programs
PA: County Of Contra Costa
625 Court St Ste 100
Martinez CA 94553
925 957-5280

(P-20812)
COUNTY OF KERN
Public Health Dept
1700 Mount Vernon Ave, Bakersfield (93306-4018)
PHONE...................................661 326-2054
Peter Bryan, *CEO*
Manish Amin, *Emerg Med Spec*
EMP: 800 **Privately Held**
WEB: www.kccfc.org
SIC: **8062** 9431 General medical & surgical hospitals; administration of public health programs
PA: County Of Kern
1115 Truxtun Ave Rm 505
Bakersfield CA 93301
661 868-3690

(P-20813)
COUNTY OF LOS ANGELES
Health Services, Dept of
14445 Olive View Dr 2b, Sylmar (91342-1437)
PHONE...................................818 364-1555
Melinda Anderson, *CEO*
Jack Williams, *Supervisor*
EMP: 200 **Privately Held**
WEB: www.co.la.ca.us
SIC: **8062** 9431 General medical & surgical hospitals;
PA: County Of Los Angeles
500 W Temple St Ste 437
Los Angeles CA 90012
213 974-1101

(P-20814)
COUNTY OF LOS ANGELES
Also Called: Health Services Dept
1000 W Carson St Fl 8 Flr 8, Palos Verdes Peninsu (90274)
PHONE...................................310 222-2401
Miguel Ortiz Marroquin, *CEO*
EMP: 300 **Privately Held**

WEB: www.co.la.ca.us
SIC: **8062** 9431 General medical & surgical hospitals; administration of public health programs
PA: County Of Los Angeles
500 W Temple St Ste 437
Los Angeles CA 90012
213 974-1101

(P-20815)
COUNTY OF LOS ANGELES
Also Called: Health Services, Dept of
12025 Wilmington Ave, Los Angeles (90059)
PHONE...................................310 668-4545
Willie T May, *Exec Dir*
EMP: 197 **Privately Held**
WEB: www.co.la.ca.us
SIC: **8062** 9431 General medical & surgical hospitals; administration of public health programs
PA: County Of Los Angeles
500 W Temple St Ste 437
Los Angeles CA 90012
213 974-1101

(P-20816)
COUNTY OF LOS ANGELES
Also Called: Health Services Dept
1100 N Mission Rd Rm 236, Los Angeles (90033-1017)
PHONE...................................323 226-6021
Scott Drewgan, *Director*
EMP: 200 **Privately Held**
WEB: www.co.la.ca.us
SIC: **8062** 9431 General medical & surgical hospitals; administration of public health programs
PA: County Of Los Angeles
500 W Temple St Ste 437
Los Angeles CA 90012
213 974-1101

(P-20817)
COUNTY OF LOS ANGELES
Also Called: Los Angles Cnty Cntl Jail Hosp
450 Bauchet St, Los Angeles (90012-2907)
PHONE...................................213 473-6100
Don Knable, *Ch of Bd*
La S Tillman, *Opers-Prdtn-Mfg*
Karen Siscoe, *Psychologist*
Victor Tung, *Internal Med*
EMP: 278 **Privately Held**
WEB: www.co.la.ca.us
SIC: **8062** 9431 General medical & surgical hospitals;
PA: County Of Los Angeles
500 W Temple St Ste 437
Los Angeles CA 90012
213 974-1101

(P-20818)
COUNTY OF MONTEREY
Also Called: Residncy Prgram Natividad Hosp
1441 Constitution Blvd # 100, Salinas (93906-3136)
P.O. Box 81611 (93912-1611)
PHONE...................................831 755-4201
Dr Gary Gray, *Director*
EMP: 600 **Privately Held**
WEB: www.montereycountyfarmbureau.org
SIC: **8062** General medical & surgical hospitals
PA: County Of Monterey
168 W Alisal St Fl 2
Salinas CA 93901
831 755-5040

(P-20819)
COUNTY OF SAN DIEGO
Also Called: Medical Examiner
9320 Farnham St, San Diego (92123)
PHONE...................................858 694-2895
Brian Blackburn, *Branch Mgr*
EMP: 50 **Privately Held**
WEB: www.sdlcc.org
SIC: **8062** 9431 General medical & surgical hospitals;
PA: County Of San Diego
1600 Pacific Hwy Ste 209
San Diego CA 92101
619 531-5880

(P-20820)
COUNTY OF SONOMA
Also Called: Palm Drive Healthcare District
501 Petaluma Ave, Sebastopol (95472-4215)
PHONE...................................707 823-8511
Shawndra Nimtz, *CEO*
EMP: 200
SQ FT: 3,684 **Privately Held**
WEB: www.sonomacompost.com
SIC: **8062** 8051 General medical & surgical hospitals; skilled nursing care facilities
PA: County Of Sonoma
585 Fiscal Dr 100
Santa Rosa CA 95403
707 565-2431

(P-20821)
COUNTY OF STANISLAUS
Also Called: Stanislaus Medical Center
830 Scenic Dr, Modesto (95350-6131)
P.O. Box 3271 (95353-3271)
PHONE...................................209 525-7000
Beverly M Finley, *Manager*
EMP: 600
SQ FT: 1,866 **Privately Held**
WEB: www.co.stanislaus.ca.us
SIC: **8062** General medical & surgical hospitals
PA: County Of Stanislaus
1010 10th St Ste 5100
Modesto CA 95354
209 525-6398

(P-20822)
COVENANT CARE CALIFORNIA LLC
Also Called: Grant-Cuesta Nursing Center
1949 Grant Rd, Mountain View (94040-3217)
PHONE...................................650 964-0543
Cheryl Cartney, *Branch Mgr*
Rachel Johnson, *Purchasing*
EMP: 100 **Privately Held**
WEB: www.willowtreenursingcenter.com
SIC: **8062** 8051 8069 General medical & surgical hospitals; skilled nursing care facilities; specialty hospitals, except psychiatric
HQ: Covenant Care California, Llc
27071 Aliso Creek Rd # 100
Aliso Viejo CA 92656

(P-20823)
CPH HOSPITAL MANAGEMENT LLC
Also Called: Coast Plaza Hospital
13100 Studebaker Rd, Norwalk (90650-2531)
PHONE...................................562 838-3751
James Paul Macpherson,
EMP: 781
SALES (est): 6.8MM
SALES (corp-wide): 264.6MM **Privately Held**
SIC: **8062** General medical & surgical hospitals
PA: Avanti Hospitals, Llc
898 N Pacific Coast Hwy # 700
El Segundo CA 90245
310 356-0550

(P-20824)
DAMERON HOSPITAL ASSOCIATION (PA)
525 W Acacia St, Stockton (95203-2484)
PHONE...................................209 944-5550
Lorraine Auerbach, *CEO*
Albert Siu, *Ch Pathology*
David Kerrins, *CFO*
Elizabeth Propp, *CFO*
Debbie Hill, *Bd of Directors*
EMP: 1003
SQ FT: 136,061
SALES (est): 190.4MM **Privately Held**
WEB: www.dameronhospital.org
SIC: **8062** General medical & surgical hospitals

(P-20825)
DEANCO HEALTHCARE LLC
Also Called: Mission Community Hospital
14850 Roscoe Blvd, Panorama City
(91402-4618)
PHONE..................................818 787-2222
James Theiring,
Dianne Wagner, *COO*
Nate Hart, *Vice Pres*
Joe Magpantay, *Lab Dir*
Liza Lee, *Business Dir*
EMP: 700 **EST:** 2010
SALES (est): 86MM **Privately Held**
SIC: 8062 General medical & surgical hospitals

(P-20826)
DEL MAR CONVALESCENT HOSPITAL
3136 Del Mar Ave, Rosemead
(91770-2326)
PHONE..................................626 288-8353
Walter Chameides, *Principal*
EMP: 60
SALES: 7.9MM **Privately Held**
SIC: 8062 8051 8322 General medical & surgical hospitals; skilled nursing care facilities; rehabilitation services

(P-20827)
DESERT REGIONAL MED CTR INC (HQ)
Also Called: Tenet
1150 N Indian Canyon Dr, Palm Springs
(92262-4872)
P.O. Box 2739 (92263-2739)
PHONE..................................760 323-6511
Toll Free:................................888   -
Carolyn Caldwell, *CEO*
Robert Rosser, *Ch Pathology*
Frank Ercoli, *Chairman*
Raymond Foster, *Radiology Dir*
Ralph M Steiger, *Principal*
EMP: 1200
SQ FT: 400,000
SALES (est): 518.1MM
SALES (corp-wide): 18.3B **Publicly Held**
SIC: 8062 General medical & surgical hospitals
PA: Tenet Healthcare Corporation
1445 Ross Ave Ste 1400
Dallas TX 75202
469 893-2200

(P-20828)
DESERT VALLEY HOSPITAL INC (DH)
16850 Bear Valley Rd, Victorville
(92395-5794)
PHONE..................................760 241-8000
Margaret R Peterson, *CEO*
Kristina Woodworth, *Hum Res Coord*
▲ **EMP:** 95
SQ FT: 63,000
SALES (est): 126.5MM
SALES (corp-wide): 3.4B **Privately Held**
SIC: 8062 General medical & surgical hospitals

(P-20829)
DIGNITY HEALTH
2131 W 3rd St, Los Angeles (90057-1901)
PHONE..................................213 484-7111
William Parente, *President*
EMP: 500 **Privately Held**
WEB: www.chw.edu
SIC: 8062 General medical & surgical hospitals
HQ: Dignity Health
185 Berry St Ste 300
San Francisco CA 94107
415 438-5500

(P-20830)
DIGNITY HEALTH
1650 Creekside Dr, Folsom (95630-3400)
PHONE..................................916 983-7400
Karl L Silberstein, *Manager*
Joshua Freilich, *Ch Nursing Ofcr*
Richard Mattern, *Engineer*
James Majewski, *Security Mgr*
Goldie Smith, *Director*
EMP: 193 **Privately Held**
WEB: www.chw.edu

SIC: 8062 General medical & surgical hospitals
HQ: Dignity Health
185 Berry St Ste 300
San Francisco CA 94107
415 438-5500

(P-20831)
DIGNITY HEALTH
Also Called: Marian Regional Medical Center
1400 E Church St, Santa Maria
(93454-5906)
PHONE..................................805 739-3000
Charles Cova, *President*
Vickie Berry, *Radiology Dir*
Rachel Alvarez, *Admin Asst*
Tayari Anderson, *Technology*
Brian Crisp, *Obstetrician*
EMP: 400 **Privately Held**
WEB: www.chw.edu
SIC: 8062 8011 General medical & surgical hospitals; offices & clinics of medical doctors
HQ: Dignity Health
185 Berry St Ste 300
San Francisco CA 94107
415 438-5500

(P-20832)
DIGNITY HEALTH
7601 Hospital Dr Ste 103, Sacramento
(95823-5408)
PHONE..................................916 681-1600
Amir Sweha MD, *Branch Mgr*
EMP: 50 **Privately Held**
SIC: 8062 General medical & surgical hospitals
HQ: Dignity Health
185 Berry St Ste 300
San Francisco CA 94107
415 438-5500

(P-20833)
DIGNITY HEALTH
Also Called: Mercy San Juan Med Trauma Ctr
6501 Coyle Ave Fl 6, Carmichael
(95608-0306)
PHONE..................................916 537-5151
Donna Utley, *Director*
Julie Meylor, *Manager*
EMP: 1700 **Privately Held**
WEB: www.mercycare.net
SIC: 8062 General medical & surgical hospitals
HQ: Dignity Health
185 Berry St Ste 300
San Francisco CA 94107
415 438-5500

(P-20834)
DIGNITY HEALTH
5051 Verdugo Way Ste 100, Camarillo
(93012-8681)
PHONE..................................805 384-8071
Tom Lowry, *Branch Mgr*
Naser Jamal, *Internal Med*
Mark Stokols, *Internal Med*
Cynthia Fiacco, *Nurse*
EMP: 452 **Privately Held**
SIC: 8062 General medical & surgical hospitals
HQ: Dignity Health
185 Berry St Ste 300
San Francisco CA 94107
415 438-5500

(P-20835)
DIGNITY HEALTH
3400 Data Dr, Rancho Cordova
(95670-7956)
PHONE..................................916 851-2153
Rick Canning, *Principal*
David Schnitzer, *Technology*
Tammie Jones, *Manager*
EMP: 193 **Privately Held**
WEB: www.chw.edu
SIC: 8062 General medical & surgical hospitals
HQ: Dignity Health
185 Berry St Ste 300
San Francisco CA 94107
415 438-5500

(P-20836)
DIGNITY HEALTH
Also Called: Arroyo Grande Community Hosp
345 S Halcyon Rd, Arroyo Grande
(93420-3817)
PHONE..................................805 473-7626
Sue Anderson, *CFO*
Ken Dalebout, *Officer*
Christina Squires, *Vice Pres*
Brad Groh, *QA Dir*
Amber Rogers, *Opers Staff*
EMP: 400 **Privately Held**
SIC: 8062 General medical & surgical hospitals
HQ: Dignity Health
185 Berry St Ste 300
San Francisco CA 94107
415 438-5500

(P-20837)
DIGNITY HEALTH
1700 Montgomery St # 300, San Francisco
(94111-1021)
PHONE..................................415 438-5500
Parmod Garg, *Finance*
Tracy Sklar, *Vice Pres*
Cyndi Melden, *Technical Staff*
John Cerato, *Finance Mgr*
EMP: 474 **Privately Held**
WEB: www.chw.edu
SIC: 8062 General medical & surgical hospitals
HQ: Dignity Health
185 Berry St Ste 300
San Francisco CA 94107
415 438-5500

(P-20838)
DIGNITY HEALTH
Also Called: Saint Mary Medical Center
1050 Linden Ave, Long Beach
(90813-3321)
PHONE..................................562 491-9000
Chris Diccio, *Principal*
Ann Marie Levan, *Ch Radiology*
Alfred V Budris, *Anesthesiology*
Ken Henderson, *Pharmacist*
Ni WEI Chu, *Director*
EMP: 1450 **Privately Held**
WEB: www.chw.edu
SIC: 8062 General medical & surgical hospitals
HQ: Dignity Health
185 Berry St Ste 300
San Francisco CA 94107
415 438-5500

(P-20839)
DIGNITY HEALTH (HQ)
185 Berry St Ste 300, San Francisco
(94107-1773)
PHONE..................................415 438-5500
Lloyd Dean, *President*
Michael Blaszyk, *CFO*
Lisa Zuckerman, *Treasurer*
Kevin E Lofton, *Co-CEO*
Linda Hunt, *Officer*
▲ **EMP:** 120
SALES (est): 5.6B **Privately Held**
WEB: www.chw.edu
SIC: 8062 General medical & surgical hospitals

(P-20840)
DIGNITY HEALTH
Also Called: California Hospital Med Ctr
1401 S Grand Ave, Los Angeles
(90015-3010)
PHONE..................................213 748-2411
Julie Sprengel, *President*
Nicole Kerns, *Administration*
Kelley Ford, *Opers Mgr*
Aung Zin, *Internal Med*
Scott Beasley, *Pediatrics*
EMP: 1500 **Privately Held**
WEB: www.chw.edu
SIC: 8062 8741 General medical & surgical hospitals; management services
HQ: Dignity Health
185 Berry St Ste 300
San Francisco CA 94107
415 438-5500

(P-20841)
DIGNITY HEALTH
Also Called: Mercy San Juan Medical Center
6501 Coyle Ave, Carmichael (95608-0306)
PHONE..................................916 537-5000
Rian Ivie, *Director*
Jay Conner, *Facilities Mgr*
Nabil Majid, *Internal Med*
Jacob A Bair, *Emerg Med Spec*
Tiffany Heu, *Emerg Med Spec*
EMP: 1500 **Privately Held**
WEB: www.mercycare.net
SIC: 8062 8011 General medical & surgical hospitals; offices & clinics of medical doctors
HQ: Dignity Health
185 Berry St Ste 300
San Francisco CA 94107
415 438-5500

(P-20842)
DIGNITY HEALTH
Mercy Hospital of Folsom
1650 Creekside Dr, Folsom (95630-3400)
PHONE..................................916 983-7400
Donald Hudson, *President*
Aaron T Breit, *Emerg Med Spec*
Robert Jackson, *Director*
Ahmad Polad, *Supervisor*
EMP: 400 **Privately Held**
WEB: www.mercycare.net
SIC: 8062 4119 General medical & surgical hospitals; ambulance service
HQ: Dignity Health
185 Berry St Ste 300
San Francisco CA 94107
415 438-5500

(P-20843)
DIGNITY HEALTH
Also Called: Mercy Medical Center Redding
2175 Rosaline Ave Ste A, Redding
(96001-2549)
PHONE..................................530 225-6345
Scott Foster, *Branch Mgr*
Robert Folden, *Lab Dir*
Deborah Wilson-Ferguson, *Lab Dir*
Henry Niessink, *Info Tech Dir*
Lisa Leblanc, *Facilities Mgr*
EMP: 193 **Privately Held**
SIC: 8062 General medical & surgical hospitals
HQ: Dignity Health
185 Berry St Ste 300
San Francisco CA 94107
415 438-5500

(P-20844)
DIGNITY HEALTH
20 N Cottonwood St, Woodland
(95695-2585)
PHONE..................................530 666-8828
Dawn M Purkey, *Branch Mgr*
Salil Kharat, *Technology*
David Ditler, *Engineer*
Alborz Alali, *Med Doctor*
Dawnese Kindelt, *Director*
EMP: 187 **Privately Held**
SIC: 8062 General medical & surgical hospitals
HQ: Dignity Health
185 Berry St Ste 300
San Francisco CA 94107
415 438-5500

(P-20845)
DIGNITY HEALTH
1555 Soquel Dr, Santa Cruz (95065-1705)
PHONE..................................831 462-7700
Nanette Mickiewicz, *Principal*
Lauren Smith, *Chief Engr*
Kevin Keith, *Plant Mgr*
EMP: 1500 **Privately Held**
WEB: www.chw.edu
SIC: 8062 General medical & surgical hospitals
HQ: Dignity Health
185 Berry St Ste 300
San Francisco CA 94107
415 438-5500

(P-20846)
DIGNITY HEALTH
Also Called: Mark Twain St Josephs Hospital
768 Mountain Ranch Rd, San Andreas
(95249-9707)
PHONE...................................209 754-3521
Katherine McCoy, *Vice Pres*
EMP: 193 Privately Held
WEB: www.chw.edu
SIC: 8062 General medical & surgical hospitals
HQ: Dignity Health
185 Berry St Ste 300
San Francisco CA 94107
415 438-5500

(P-20847)
DIGNITY HEALTH
Also Called: Methodist Hospital Sacramento
7500 Hospital Dr, Sacramento
(95823-5403)
PHONE...................................916 423-5940
William J Hunt, *Principal*
Anita Kennedy, *Vice Pres*
Denise Bragg, *Business Dir*
Michael Stern, *QA Dir*
Leonard Gold, *Info Tech Dir*
EMP: 193 Privately Held
WEB: www.chw.edu
SIC: 8062 General medical & surgical hospitals
HQ: Dignity Health
185 Berry St Ste 300
San Francisco CA 94107
415 438-5500

(P-20848)
DIGNITY HEALTH
Also Called: Mercy General Hospital Bus Off
4001 J St, Sacramento (95819-3626)
P.O. Box 3008, Rancho Cordova (95741-3008)
PHONE...................................916 453-4545
Thomas Peterson, *Director*
Page West, *Vice Pres*
EMP: 1600 Privately Held
WEB: www.mercycare.net
SIC: 8062 General medical & surgical hospitals
HQ: Dignity Health
185 Berry St Ste 300
San Francisco CA 94107
415 438-5500

(P-20849)
DIGNITY HEALTH
551 Shanley Ct, Bakersfield (93311-1306)
PHONE...................................661 663-6767
Mike Depetro, *Manager*
EMP: 50 Privately Held
WEB: www.chw.edu
SIC: 8062 General medical & surgical hospitals
HQ: Dignity Health
185 Berry St Ste 300
San Francisco CA 94107
415 438-5500

(P-20850)
DIGNITY HEALTH
Also Called: St. Johns Pleasant Valley Hosp
2309 Antonio Ave, Camarillo (93010-1414)
PHONE...................................805 389-5800
Daniel Herlinger, *Branch Mgr*
Dean Black, *Ch Radiology*
M Eugene Fussell, *Vice Pres*
EMP: 250 Privately Held
WEB: www.chw.edu
SIC: 8062 General medical & surgical hospitals
HQ: Dignity Health
185 Berry St Ste 300
San Francisco CA 94107
415 438-5500

(P-20851)
DIGNITY HEALTH
Also Called: Marian West
505 Plaza Dr, Santa Maria (93454-6907)
PHONE...................................805 739-3100
Kathleen Sullivan, *Manager*
EMP: 1400 Privately Held
WEB: www.chw.edu
SIC: 8062 General medical & surgical hospitals

HQ: Dignity Health
185 Berry St Ste 300
San Francisco CA 94107
415 438-5500

(P-20852)
DIGNITY HEALTH
Also Called: St Johns Regional Medical Ctr
1600 N Rose Ave, Oxnard (93030-3722)
PHONE...................................805 988-2500
George West, *Vice Pres*
Vance Kalcic,
Teeya Davis, *Volunteer Dir*
Henry Montes, *Bd of Directors*
Chris Champlin, *Vice Pres*
EMP: 1900 Privately Held
SIC: 8062 General medical & surgical hospitals
HQ: Dignity Health
185 Berry St Ste 300
San Francisco CA 94107
415 438-5500

(P-20853)
DIGNITY HEALTH
Also Called: St. Mary's Medical Center
450 Stanyan St, San Francisco
(94117-1019)
PHONE...................................415 668-1000
John Allen, *President*
Scott Robin Mangari, *Vice Pres*
Amy Carrillo, *Executive Asst*
Sarah Williams, *Executive Asst*
Jeffrey Stoner, *Admin Asst*
EMP: 1100 Privately Held
SIC: 8062 8322 General medical & surgical hospitals; adult day care center
HQ: Dignity Health
185 Berry St Ste 300
San Francisco CA 94107
415 438-5500

(P-20854)
DIGNITY HEALTH
Also Called: Pedi Center
400 Old River Rd, Bakersfield
(93311-9781)
P.O. Box 119 (93302-0119)
PHONE...................................661 632-5279
Kirk Douglas, *Branch Mgr*
Rodrigo Vazquez, *Analyst*
Sandy Doucette, *Marketing Staff*
EMP: 120 Privately Held
WEB: www.chw.edu
SIC: 8062 8099 8011 General medical & surgical hospitals; childbirth preparation clinic; offices & clinics of medical doctors
HQ: Dignity Health
185 Berry St Ste 300
San Francisco CA 94107
415 438-5500

(P-20855)
DIGNITY HEALTH
Also Called: Mercy Hospital
2215 Truxtun Ave, Bakersfield
(93301-3602)
PHONE...................................661 632-5000
Rodney B Winegarner, *Branch Mgr*
Colleen Goodman, *Lab Dir*
Stacy Close, *Nursing Mgr*
Michael Gong, *Pharmacist*
EMP: 474 Privately Held
SIC: 8062 General medical & surgical hospitals
HQ: Dignity Health
185 Berry St Ste 300
San Francisco CA 94107
415 438-5500

(P-20856)
DIGNITY HEALTH MED FOUNDATION (DH)
Also Called: Dignity Hlth Med Grp-Dominican
3400 Data Dr, Rancho Cordova
(95670-7956)
PHONE...................................916 379-2840
Laurie Schwarctz, *President*
Theresa Hylen, *CFO*
Sherry Penlesky, *Admin Asst*
Sonja Greene, *Financial Analy*
Yvette Thompson, *Recruiter*
EMP: 200
SQ FT: 45,000

SALES: 570.1MM Privately Held
WEB: www.chwmedicalfoundation.com
SIC: 8062 General medical & surgical hospitals
HQ: Dignity Health
185 Berry St Ste 300
San Francisco CA 94107
415 438-5500

(P-20857)
DOCTORS HOSPITAL RIVERSIDE LLC (PA)
3865 Jackson St, Riverside (92503-3919)
PHONE...................................951 354-7404
Jonathan Wu, *CEO*
EMP: 50
SALES (est): 162.7MM Privately Held
SIC: 8062 General medical & surgical hospitals

(P-20858)
DOCTORS HOSPITAL W COVINA INC
Also Called: WEST COVINA PHYSICAL THERAPY
725 S Orange Ave, West Covina
(91790-2614)
PHONE...................................626 338-8481
Pareed Mohamed, *CEO*
Carmen Silva, *COO*
Cami Horvat, *CFO*
Jong Kim MD, *Treasurer*
Akbar Omar MD, *Vice Pres*
EMP: 155
SQ FT: 50,000
SALES: 16MM Privately Held
SIC: 8062 8049 General medical & surgical hospitals; physical therapist

(P-20859)
DOCTORS MED CTR MODESTO INC (HQ)
Also Called: TENET
1441 Florida Ave, Modesto (95350-4404)
P.O. Box 139036, Dallas TX (75313-9036)
PHONE...................................209 578-1211
Warren J Kirk, *CEO*
Greg Berry, *CFO*
Veronica Ortiz, *Internal Med*
Edward W Verde, *Med Doctor*
Linda Hawkins, *Nurse*
EMP: 67
SALES: 587.9MM
SALES (corp-wide): 18.3B Publicly Held
SIC: 8062 General medical & surgical hospitals
PA: Tenet Healthcare Corporation
1445 Ross Ave Ste 1400
Dallas TX 75202
469 893-2200

(P-20860)
DOMINICAN HOSPITAL FOUNDATION (DH)
1555 Soquel Dr, Santa Cruz (95065-1794)
PHONE...................................831 462-7700
Beverly Grova, *CEO*
Chuck Maffia, *President*
Jon Sisk, *President*
Sam Leask, *CEO*
Ted Burke, *Vice Pres*
EMP: 114
SQ FT: 110,000
SALES: 2.9MM Privately Held
SIC: 8062 8051 General medical & surgical hospitals; skilled nursing care facilities
HQ: Dignity Health
185 Berry St Ste 300
San Francisco CA 94107
415 438-5500

(P-20861)
EAST VALLEY GLENDORA HOSP LLC
Also Called: East Valley Hospital Med Ctr
150 W Route 66, Glendora (91740-6207)
PHONE...................................626 852-5000
C Joseph Chang, *Ch of Bd*
Jinny Kim, *Business Dir*
Robert Gordon,
EMP: 300
SQ FT: 60,592

SALES: 29.3MM Privately Held
WEB: www.evhmc.org
SIC: 8062 General medical & surgical hospitals

(P-20862)
EISENHOWER MEDICAL CENTER (PA)
Also Called: Eisenhower Health
39000 Bob Hope Dr, Rancho Mirage
(92270-3221)
PHONE...................................760 340-3911
G Aubrey Serfling, *CEO*
Barbara Comess, *Ch Pathology*
Caryn C Hawthorne, *CFO*
Kimberly Osborne, *CFO*
Joel Fischer, *Trustee*
▲ **EMP: 2000**
SQ FT: 240,000
SALES (est): 640.2MM Privately Held
SIC: 8062 8082 General medical & surgical hospitals; home health care services

(P-20863)
EL CAMINO SURGERY CENTER LLC
15046 Karl Ave, Monte Sereno
(95030-2211)
PHONE...................................650 961-1200
Lisa Cooper, *Exec Dir*
Marla Marlow, *Mng Member*
EMP: 70
SALES: 15K Privately Held
WEB: www.ecsc.com
SIC: 8062 General medical & surgical hospitals

(P-20864)
EL CENTRO REGIONAL MEDICAL CTR (PA)
Also Called: E C R M C
1415 Ross Ave, El Centro (92243-4306)
PHONE...................................760 339-7100
Robert R Frantz, *President*
Kathy Farmer, *CFO*
Mark Nellis, *CFO*
Cathy Kennerson, *Officer*
David Jones, *Exec VP*
EMP: 673
SQ FT: 187,044
SALES (est): 127.8MM Privately Held
WEB: www.ecrmc.org
SIC: 8062 General medical & surgical hospitals

(P-20865)
ELADH LP
Also Called: East Los Angeles Doctors Hosp
4060 Whittier Blvd, Los Angeles
(90023-2526)
PHONE...................................323 268-5514
Gerald Clute, *CEO*
Hector Hernandez, *Managing Prtnr*
EMP: 99
SALES: 72.1MM
SALES (corp-wide): 264.6MM Privately Held
SIC: 8062 General medical & surgical hospitals
PA: Avanti Hospitals, Llc
898 N Pacific Coast Hwy # 700
El Segundo CA 90245
310 356-0550

(P-20866)
EMANATE HLTH INTR-CMMNITY HOSP (PA)
Also Called: Inter Community Hospital
210 W San Bernardino Rd, Covina
(91723-1515)
P.O. Box 6108 (91722-5108)
PHONE...................................626 331-7331
Robert Curry, *CEO*
James Yoshioka, *President*
Alvia Polk, *COO*
Lois Conyers, *CFO*
Paveljit Bindra, *Chief Mktg Ofcr*
EMP: 1200
SQ FT: 237,000
SALES: 606.3MM Privately Held
WEB: www.cvhp.com
SIC: 8062 General medical & surgical hospitals

(P-20867)
EMANUEL MEDICAL CENTER INC
Also Called: Brandel Manor
1801 N Olive Ave, Turlock (95382-2568)
PHONE..................................209 667-5600
Dawn Sughruel, *Director*
EMP: 160
SQ FT: 58,282
SALES (corp-wide): 18.3B **Publicly Held**
WEB: www.emanuelmedicalcenter.com
SIC: **8062** 8051 General medical & surgical hospitals; convalescent home with continuous nursing care
HQ: Emanuel Medical Center, Inc.
825 Delbon Ave
Turlock CA 95382
209 667-4200

(P-20868)
EMANUEL MEDICAL CENTER INC (DH)
825 Delbon Ave, Turlock (95382-2016)
PHONE..................................209 667-4200
Susan Micheletti, *CEO*
Huy Dao,
Ronald Arakelian MD,
Joseph L Higgins, *Ch Radiology*
Julie Riddick, *President*
EMP: 850
SQ FT: 200,000
SALES: 209.5MM
SALES (corp-wide): 18.3B **Publicly Held**
WEB: www.emanuelmedicalcenter.com
SIC: **8062** General medical & surgical hospitals
HQ: Doctors Medical Center Of Modesto, Inc.
1441 Florida Ave
Modesto CA 95350
209 578-1211

(P-20869)
EMANUEL MEDICAL CENTER INC
Also Called: Turlock Diagnostic Center
2121 Colorado Ave Ste A, Turlock (95382-2012)
PHONE..................................209 664-2520
Michael Iltis, *Manager*
EMP: 103
SALES (corp-wide): 18.3B **Publicly Held**
WEB: www.emanuelmedicalcenter.com
SIC: **8062** 8011 General medical & surgical hospitals; medical centers
HQ: Emanuel Medical Center, Inc.
825 Delbon Ave
Turlock CA 95382
209 667-4200

(P-20870)
EMERGENCY MEDICINE SPECIALIST
Also Called: Emsoc
1010 W La Veta Ave # 755, Orange (92868-4306)
PHONE..................................714 543-8911
James Pierog, *Chairman*
EMP: 90
SALES (est): 5.8MM **Privately Held**
SIC: **8062** General medical & surgical hospitals

(P-20871)
ENCINO HOSPITAL MEDICAL CENTER
16237 Ventura Blvd, Encino (91436-2272)
PHONE..................................818 995-5000
Bockhi Park, *CEO*
Prem Reddy, *President*
David Asplund, *Administration*
EMP: 400
SALES: 52.4MM
SALES (corp-wide): 3.4B **Privately Held**
SIC: **8062** General medical & surgical hospitals
HQ: Prime Healthcare Services Inc
3300 E Guasti Rd Ste 300
Ontario CA 91761

(P-20872)
ENCINO TRZANA REGIONAL MED CTR
16237 Ventura Blvd, Encino (91436-2201)
PHONE..................................818 995-5000
EMP: 450
SALES: 41.7MM **Privately Held**
SIC: **8062**

(P-20873)
ENLOE HOSPT-PHYS THRPY
1444 Magnolia Ave, Chico (95926-3227)
PHONE..................................530 891-7300
Brenda Logan, *Director*
EMP: 173
SALES (corp-wide): 4.3MM **Privately Held**
SIC: **8062** General medical & surgical hospitals
PA: Enloe Hospital - Physical Therapy Dept
1600 Esplanade
Chico CA 95926
530 891-7300

(P-20874)
ENLOE MEDICAL CENTER
Also Called: E E G and E P
560 Cohasset Rd, Chico (95926-2281)
PHONE..................................530 332-4111
Joan Lilly, *Principal*
Sandra Bernstein, *Nursing Mgr*
Andrea Rodriguez, *Accountant*
Gary Lautt, *Pharmacist*
Gail Cunha,
EMP: 53
SALES (corp-wide): 480.2MM **Privately Held**
SIC: **8062** General medical & surgical hospitals
PA: Enloe Medical Center
1531 Esplanade
Chico CA 95926
530 332-7300

(P-20875)
ENLOE MEDICAL CENTER
Also Called: Enloe Outpatient Center
888 Lakeside Vlg Cmns, Chico (95928-3979)
PHONE..................................530 332-6400
Joleen Nixon, *Director*
Kathy Buck, *Director*
EMP: 130
SQ FT: 44,171
SALES (corp-wide): 480.2MM **Privately Held**
SIC: **8062** 8093 General medical & surgical hospitals; specialty outpatient clinics
PA: Enloe Medical Center
1531 Esplanade
Chico CA 95926
530 332-7300

(P-20876)
FAMILY MDCINE RSIDENCY PROGRAM
155 N Fresno St Ste 326, Fresno (93701-2302)
PHONE..................................559 499-6450
Ivan Gomez, *Director*
EMP: 60
SALES (est): 871.4K **Privately Held**
SIC: **8062** Hospital, AMA approved residency

(P-20877)
FOOTHILL HSPTL-MRRIS L JHNSTON (PA)
Also Called: Foothill Presbyterian Hospital
250 S Grand Ave, Glendora (91741-4218)
PHONE..................................626 857-3145
Robert Curry, *President*
Roger Sharma, *CFO*
Melissa Howard, *Ch Nursing Ofcr*
Diana Zenner, *Administration*
Ed Tronez,
EMP: 97
SQ FT: 104,371
SALES: 110.1MM **Privately Held**
SIC: **8062** Hospital, affiliated with AMA residency

(P-20878)
FOUNTAIN VALLEY REGL HOSPL
17100 Euclid St, Fountain Valley (92708-4043)
P.O. Box 8010 (92728-8010)
PHONE..................................714 966-7200
Kenneth McFarlin, *CEO*
Edward F Littlejohn, *COO*
Ken Jordan, *CFO*
Kenneth McFarland, *Officer*
Glenda Rivera, *Admin Asst*
EMP: 1200
SALES (est): 478.1K
SALES (corp-wide): 18.3B **Publicly Held**
WEB: www.tenenthealth.com
SIC: **8062** Hospital, affiliated with AMA residency
HQ: Tenet Healthsystem Medical, Inc.
1445 Ross Ave Ste 1400
Dallas TX 75202
469 893-2000

(P-20879)
FREMONT HOSPITAL
Also Called: Fremont Medical Center
620 J St, Marysville (95901-5413)
PHONE..................................530 751-4000
Thomas P Hayes, *CEO*
Jeanne Martin, *Admin Sec*
EMP: 598
SQ FT: 121,000
SALES (est): 17.8MM
SALES (corp-wide): 26.9MM **Privately Held**
SIC: **8062** General medical & surgical hospitals
PA: Freemont Rideout Health Group
989 Plumas St
Yuba City CA 95991
530 751-4010

(P-20880)
FRENCH HOSP MED CTR FOUNDATION (DH)
1911 Johnson Ave, San Luis Obispo (93401-4131)
PHONE..................................805 543-5353
Jim Copeland, *Chairman*
Allan Iftiniuk, *President*
Sue Anderson, *CFO*
Julia Fogelson, *Ch Nursing Ofcr*
Patricia Herrera, *Benefits Mgr*
EMP: 480
SQ FT: 80,000
SALES: 126.7MM **Privately Held**
SIC: **8062** Hospital, affiliated with AMA residency
HQ: Dignity Health
185 Berry St Ste 300
San Francisco CA 94107
415 438-5500

(P-20881)
FRESNO CMNTY HOSP & MED CTR
Also Called: Clovis Community Medical Ctr
2755 Herndon Ave, Clovis (93611-6800)
PHONE..................................559 324-4000
Phyllis Baltz, *Manager*
Joseph Boado, *Lab Dir*
Paul Luchi, *Food Svc Dir*
Patricia Young, *Director*
EMP: 95
SQ FT: 36,000
SALES (corp-wide): 1.6B **Privately Held**
SIC: **8062** General medical & surgical hospitals
HQ: Fresno Community Hospital And Medical Center
2823 Fresno St
Fresno CA 93721
559 459-3948

(P-20882)
FRESNO CMNTY HOSP & MED CTR (HQ)
2823 Fresno St, Fresno (93721-1324)
P.O. Box 1232 (93715-1232)
PHONE..................................559 459-3948
Phillip Hinton, *President*
William Grigg, *CFO*
Roger Fretwell, *Treasurer*
Mike Kingbury, *Senior VP*
Stephen Walter, *Senior VP*
EMP: 3000
SQ FT: 2,469
SALES (est): 1.2B
SALES (corp-wide): 1.6B **Privately Held**
SIC: **8062** General medical & surgical hospitals
PA: Community Hospitals Of Central California
2823 Fresno St
Fresno CA 93721
559 459-6000

(P-20883)
FRESNO HEART HOSPITAL LLC
15 E Audubon Dr, Fresno (93720-1542)
PHONE..................................559 433-8000
Wanda Holderman, *Mng Member*
Tim A Joslin, *CEO*
Patrick Rafferty, *Exec VP*
Peg Breen, *Senior VP*
Mitzi Whigan, *Infect Cntl Dir*
EMP: 330
SQ FT: 140,000
SALES (est): 42.2MM
SALES (corp-wide): 1.6B **Privately Held**
WEB: www.fresnoheart.com
SIC: **8062** General medical & surgical hospitals
PA: Community Hospitals Of Central California
2823 Fresno St
Fresno CA 93721
559 459-6000

(P-20884)
FRESNO SURGERY CENTER LP (PA)
Also Called: Fresno Surgical Hospital
6125 N Fresno St, Fresno (93710-5207)
PHONE..................................559 431-8000
Kristine Kassahn, *CEO*
Bruce Cecil, *CFO*
Paramjeet Gill, *Chairman*
Alejandra Contreras, *Officer*
Sandra Kneefel, *Pharmacy Dir*
EMP: 213
SQ FT: 32,000
SALES: 74MM **Privately Held**
WEB: www.fresnosurgerycenter.com
SIC: **8062** 8011 General medical & surgical hospitals; orthopedic physician; gynecologist; surgeon

(P-20885)
GARDENA HOSPITAL LP
Also Called: MEMORIAL HOSPITAL OF GARDENA
1145 W Redondo Beach Blvd, Gardena (90247-3511)
PHONE..................................310 532-4200
Kathy Wojno, *CEO*
John N Loizeaux-Witte, *Partner*
David Lee, *CFO*
Michael Ditommaso, *Facilities Mgr*
Rachel Gonzalez, *Director*
EMP: 760
SALES: 143.5MM
SALES (corp-wide): 264.6MM **Privately Held**
SIC: **8062** General medical & surgical hospitals
PA: Avanti Hospitals, Llc
898 N Pacific Coast Hwy # 700
El Segundo CA 90245
310 356-0550

(P-20886)
GATEWAYS HOSP MENTAL HLTH CTR
340 N Madison Ave, Los Angeles (90004-3504)
PHONE..................................323 644-2026
Mara Pelsman, *Branch Mgr*
Priscilla Ortega, *Systems Dir*
EMP: 92
SALES (corp-wide): 29.1MM **Privately Held**
SIC: **8062** General medical & surgical hospitals
PA: Gateway's Hospital And Mental Health Center Inc
1891 Effie St
Los Angeles CA 90026
323 644-2000

PRODUCTS & SVCS

(P-20887)
**GLENDALE ADVENTIST
MEDICAL CTR (HQ)**
1509 Wilson Ter, Glendale (91206-4007)
PHONE.................818 409-8000
Kevin A Roberts, *President*
Irene Bourdon, *President*
Warren Tetz, *COO*
Judy Blair, *Senior VP*
Kelly Turner, *Senior VP*
EMP: 2550
SQ FT: 700,000
SALES: 502MM
SALES (corp-wide): 4.4B **Privately Held**
WEB: www.glendaleadventist.com
SIC: 8062 8093 8011 General medical &
surgical hospitals; mental health clinic,
outpatient; freestanding emergency med-
ical center
PA: Adventist Health System/West
1 Adventist Health Way
Roseville CA 95661
844 574-5686

(P-20888)
GLENN MEDICAL CENTER INC
1133 W Sycamore St, Willows
(95988-2601)
PHONE.................530 934-4681
William Casey, *CEO*
Gary Pea, *CFO*
Andrea Miller,
Nancy Ehorn, *Director*
EMP: 99
SQ FT: 62,000
SALES: 13.7MM **Privately Held**
SIC: 8062 General medical & surgical hos-
pitals

(P-20889)
**GLENOAKS CONVALESCENT
HOSP LP**
409 W Glenoaks Blvd, Glendale
(91202-2916)
PHONE.................818 240-4300
Elaine Levine, *Partner*
EMP: 85 **EST:** 1984
SQ FT: 22,306
SALES: 5.3MM **Privately Held**
SIC: 8062 General medical & surgical hos-
pitals

(P-20890)
**GOLDEN EMPIRE
CONVALESCENT HOS**
121 Dorsey Dr, Grass Valley (95945-5201)
PHONE.................530 273-1316
Vicki Young, *Partner*
Chan Sinsaeng, *Social Dir*
Shari Antonucci, *Nursing Dir*
EMP: 180
SALES (est): 12.9MM **Privately Held**
WEB: www.goldenempiresnf.com
SIC: 8062 General medical & surgical hos-
pitals

(P-20891)
**GOLETA VALLEY COTTAGE
HOSPITAL**
Also Called: COTTAGE HEALTH SYSTEM
351 S Patterson Ave, Santa Barbara
(93111-2403)
P.O. Box 689 (93102-0689)
PHONE.................805 681-6468
Ronald C Werft, *President*
Robert Knight, *Ch of Bd*
Joan Bricher, *CFO*
Ron Biscaro, *Vice Pres*
Diane Wisby, *Vice Pres*
EMP: 275
SQ FT: 92,273
SALES: 79MM **Privately Held**
SIC: 8062 General medical & surgical hos-
pitals

(P-20892)
GOOD SAMARITAN HOSPITAL
901 Olive Dr, Bakersfield (93308-4144)
P.O. Box 85002 (93380-5002)
PHONE.................661 399-4461
Andrew B Leeka, *CEO*
David Huff, *Partner*
Sakrepatna Manohara, *President*
Anand Manohara, *CEO*
Canesh Acharya, *CFO*
EMP: 400 **EST:** 1965
SQ FT: 49,001
SALES (est): 43.7MM **Privately Held**
SIC: 8062 8063 8069 General medical &
surgical hospitals; psychiatric hospitals;
specialty hospitals, except psychiatric

(P-20893)
**GOOD SAMARITAN HOSPITAL
LP (DH)**
Also Called: HOSPITAL COPORATION OF
AMERICA
2425 Samaritan Dr, San Jose
(95124-3985)
P.O. Box 550, Nashville TN (37202-0550)
PHONE.................408 559-2011
Paul Beaupre, *CEO*
Jordan Herget, *COO*
Lana Arad, *CFO*
Darrel Neuenschwander, *CFO*
Paul Deaupre, *Officer*
EMP: 1200
SALES: 618.4MM **Publicly Held**
WEB: www.goodsamsj.org
SIC: 8062 General medical & surgical hos-
pitals
HQ: Hca Inc.
1 Park Plz
Nashville TN 37203
615 344-9551

(P-20894)
**GOOD SAMARITAN HOSPITAL
LP**
Also Called: Mission Oaks Hospital
15891 Los Gtos Almaden Rd, Los Gatos
(95032-3742)
PHONE.................408 356-4111
Brian Knecht, *COO*
Ron Terras, *Director*
EMP: 200 **Publicly Held**
WEB: www.goodsamsj.org
SIC: 8062 General medical & surgical hos-
pitals
HQ: Good Samaritan Hospital, L.P.
2425 Samaritan Dr
San Jose CA 95124
408 559-2011

(P-20895)
**GORDON LANE
CONVALESCENT HOSP**
1821 E Chapman Ave, Fullerton
(92831-4102)
PHONE.................714 879-7301
Lee Shannon, *President*
Toni Spencer, *Business Dir*
EMP: 65 **EST:** 1971
SQ FT: 24,180
SALES (est): 5.5MM **Privately Held**
SIC: 8062 8051 General medical & surgi-
cal hospitals; skilled nursing care facilities

(P-20896)
**GROSSMONT HOSPITAL
CORPORATION**
Also Called: Grossmont Home Hlth & Hospice
8881 Fletcher Pkwy # 105, La Mesa
(91942-3134)
PHONE.................619 667-1900
Jean Cruise, *Manager*
EMP: 150
SALES (corp-wide): 3.4B **Privately Held**
WEB: www.grossmonthealthcare.com
SIC: 8062 8082 General medical & surgi-
cal hospitals; home health care services
HQ: Grossmont Hospital Corporation
5555 Grossmont Center Dr
La Mesa CA 91942
619 740-6000

(P-20897)
HALSEN HEALTHCARE LLC
Also Called: Watsonville Community Hospital
75 Neilson St, Watsonville (95076-2468)
PHONE.................831 724-4741
Sean Fowler, *CEO*
EMP: 820
SALES (corp-wide): 8.8MM **Privately
Held**
SIC: 8062 General medical & surgical hos-
pitals

PA: Halsen Healthcare, Llc
1872 Sharon Ln
Santa Ana CA 92705
714 726-6189

(P-20898)
**HANFORD COMMUNITY
HOSPITAL (HQ)**
Also Called: ADVENTIST HEALTH
115 Mall Dr, Hanford (93230-5786)
P.O. Box 619002, Roseville (95661-9002)
PHONE.................559 582-9000
Scott Reiner, *Chairman*
Dawn Silva, *Buyer*
Lori Ruffner, *Opers Staff*
Stephen M Avalos, *Pathologist*
Michael Crawford, *Pathologist*
EMP: 640
SQ FT: 52,060
SALES: 321MM
SALES (corp-wide): 4.4B **Privately Held**
WEB: www.hanford.ah.org
SIC: 8062 General medical & surgical hos-
pitals
PA: Adventist Health System/West
1 Adventist Health Way
Roseville CA 95661
844 574-5686

(P-20899)
**HARBOR-CLA MED CTR DEPT
SRGERY**
1000 W Carson St 25, Torrance
(90502-2004)
PHONE.................310 222-2701
Christian De Virgillo, *Chairman*
Kyle Mock, *Principal*
Alexander Schwed, *Principal*
EMP: 99
SALES (est): 947.5K **Privately Held**
SIC: 8062 General medical & surgical hos-
pitals

(P-20900)
**HAYWARD SISTERS HOSPITAL
(HQ)**
Also Called: St Rose Hospital
27200 Calaroga Ave, Hayward
(94545-4339)
PHONE.................510 264-4000
Michael Mahoney, *President*
Leeann Schierburg, *Records Dir*
Ken Henkelman, *COO*
Clifford Tschetter, *Lab Dir*
Laura Stephens, *Business Dir*
EMP: 842
SQ FT: 173,000
SALES: 136.8MM
SALES (corp-wide): 1.3B **Privately Held**
WEB: www.aboutinfectioncontrol.com
SIC: 8062 Hospital, affiliated with AMA res-
idency
PA: Alecto Healthcare Services Llc
16310 Bake Pkwy Ste 200
Irvine CA 92618
323 938-3161

(P-20901)
HCA INC
Also Called: Main Hospital
225 N Jackson Ave, San Jose
(95116-1603)
PHONE.................408 729-2801
Trey Abshier, *COO*
Elaine Nelson, *Vice Chairman*
David Hutto, *Op Rm Dir*
Jesse Nath, *Information Mgr*
Nancy Clark, *Human Res Dir*
EMP: 115 **Publicly Held**
SIC: 8062 General medical & surgical hos-
pitals
HQ: Hca Inc.
1 Park Plz
Nashville TN 37203
615 344-9551

(P-20902)
HCA INC
Also Called: Columbia San Clemente Hospital
654 Camino De Los Mares, San Clemente
(92673-2827)
PHONE.................949 496-1122
Patricia Wolfram, *CEO*
EMP: 250 **Publicly Held**
SIC: 8062 General medical & surgical hos-
pitals

HQ: Hca Inc.
1 Park Plz
Nashville TN 37203
615 344-9551

(P-20903)
HEALTH RESOURCES CORP
Also Called: Coastal Community Hospital
2701 S Bristol St, Santa Ana (92704-6201)
PHONE.................714 754-5454
Trevor Fetter, *President*
EMP: 400
SALES (corp-wide): 407.3MM **Privately
Held**
WEB: www.ihhioc.com
SIC: 8062 General medical & surgical hos-
pitals
PA: Kpc Healthcare, Inc.
1301 N Tustin Ave
Santa Ana CA 92705
714 953-3652

(P-20904)
**HEALTHCARE BARTON SYSTEM
(PA)**
2170 South Ave, South Lake Tahoe
(96150-7026)
P.O. Box 9578 (96158-9578)
PHONE.................530 541-3420
John Williams, *CEO*
Dick Derby, *CFO*
Richard Derby, *CFO*
Sharon Bishop, *Branch Mgr*
Barton Audiology, *Cardiology*
EMP: 554 **EST:** 1960
SQ FT: 112,190
SALES: 179.5MM **Privately Held**
SIC: 8062 General medical & surgical hos-
pitals

(P-20905)
HEALTHCARE BARTON SYSTEM
2270 South, South Lake Tahoe (96150)
PHONE.................530 543-5685
Sharon Bishop, *Branch Mgr*
EMP: 50
SALES (corp-wide): 179.5MM **Privately
Held**
SIC: 8062 General medical & surgical hos-
pitals
PA: Barton Healthcare System
2170 South Ave
South Lake Tahoe CA 96150
530 541-3420

(P-20906)
**HEALTHSMART PACIFIC INC
(PA)**
Also Called: Long Beach Pain Center
5150 E Pacific Cst Hwy # 200, Long Beach
(90804-3312)
PHONE.................562 595-1911
Michael Ddrobot, *CEO*
Michael D Drobot, *CEO*
EMP: 610
SALES (est): 80.5MM **Privately Held**
SIC: 8062 General medical & surgical hos-
pitals

(P-20907)
HEART HOSPITAL OF BK LLC
Also Called: Bakersfield Heart Hospital
3001 Sillect Ave, Bakersfield (93308-6337)
PHONE.................661 316-6000
Michelle Oxford, *President*
Judy Littrell, *Vice Pres*
Paul Sauvola, *Senior Engr*
Cherie Cadena, *Analyst*
Keshav Khadka,
EMP: 336 **EST:** 1996
SALES: 443MM **Privately Held**
SIC: 8062 General medical & surgical hos-
pitals

(P-20908)
**HENRY MAYO NEWHALL MEM
HLTH**
Also Called: Henrymayo Newhall Mem Hosp
23845 Mcbean Pkwy, Valencia
(91355-2001)
P.O. Box 55279 (91385-0279)
PHONE.................661 253-8000
Roger Seaver, *President*
Deal Christin, *Admin Asst*

Rodriguez Anabel, *Network Analyst*
EMP: 1500
SALES: 251.8MM **Privately Held**
SIC: 8062 General medical & surgical hospitals

(P-20909)
HI-DESERT MEM HLTH CARE DST (PA)
Also Called: Hi-Desert Medical Center
6530 Lcontenpa Rd Ste 100, Yucca Valley (92284)
PHONE...................................760 820-9229
Jacqueline Combs, *CEO*
EMP: 70 **EST:** 1964
SALES: 62.8MM **Privately Held**
WEB: www.carolyager.com
SIC: 8062 General medical & surgical hospitals

(P-20910)
HOAG MEMORIAL HOSPITAL PRESBT (PA)
1 Hoag Dr, Newport Beach (92663-4162)
P.O. Box 6100 (92658-6100)
PHONE...................................949 764-4624
Robert Braithwaite, *President*
Leslie Scarborough, *Records Dir*
Robert Evans, *Vice Chairman*
Kris Iyer, *Bd of Directors*
Richard Taketa, *Bd of Directors*
EMP: 3600
SALES: 894MM **Privately Held**
SIC: 8062 General medical & surgical hospitals

(P-20911)
HOLLYWOOD COMMUNITY HOSPITAL M
Also Called: Hollywood Cmnty Hosp Hollywood
6245 De Longpre Ave, Los Angeles (90028-8253)
PHONE...................................323 462-2271
Robert Starling, *CEO*
Kenneth Auguster, *Records Dir*
Ron Messenger, *President*
Manfred Krukemeyer, *Vice Ch Bd*
Catherine Shitara, *Officer*
EMP: 220
SQ FT: 100,000
SALES (est): 54.8MM **Privately Held**
WEB: www.clarenthospital.com
SIC: 8062 Hospital, affiliated with AMA residency

(P-20912)
HOLLYWOOD MEDICAL CENTER LP
Also Called: Hollywood Presbyterian Med Ctr
1300 N Vermont Ave, Los Angeles (90027-6098)
PHONE...................................213 413-3000
Jeff Nelson, *Partner*
EMP: 1250
SALES: 281.2MM **Privately Held**
WEB: www.qahpmc.com
SIC: 8062 General medical & surgical hospitals
PA: Cha Health Systems, Inc
3731 Wilshire Blvd # 850
Los Angeles CA 90010
213 487-3211

(P-20913)
HOSPITAL OF BARSTOW INC
Also Called: Barstow Community Hospital
820 E Mountain View St, Barstow (92311-3004)
PHONE...................................760 256-1761
Kane Dawson, *CEO*
EMP: 215
SQ FT: 54,000
SALES (est): 16.9MM
SALES (corp-wide): 1.8B **Publicly Held**
WEB: www.barstowhospital.com
SIC: 8062 Hospital, affiliated with AMA residency
PA: Quorum Health Corporation
1573 Mallory Ln Ste 100
Brentwood TN 37027
615 221-1400

(P-20914)
INDIAN VALLEY HEALTH CARE DIST
Also Called: Indian Valley Hospital
184 Hot Springs Rd, Greenville (95947-9747)
PHONE...................................530 284-7191
Sue Neer, *CEO*
Wick Viswell, *Administration*
EMP: 80
SQ FT: 20,000
SALES (est): 3.2MM **Privately Held**
WEB: www.ivhcd.com
SIC: 8062 General medical & surgical hospitals

(P-20915)
INLAND VLY RGIONAL MED CTR INC
36485 Inland Valley Dr, Wildomar (92595-9681)
PHONE...................................951 677-1111
Alan B Miller, *CEO*
Barry Thorfinnson, *CFO*
Ginny Ince, *Nursing Dir*
Peggy Kiolbasa, *Manager*
EMP: 74
SQ FT: 77,000
SALES (est): 56.3MM
SALES (corp-wide): 10.7B **Publicly Held**
SIC: 8062 8011 General medical & surgical hospitals; clinic, operated by physicians
PA: Universal Health Services, Inc.
367 S Gulph Rd
King Of Prussia PA 19406
610 768-3300

(P-20916)
INSTITUTE FOR HEALTH & HEALING
2300 California St # 101, San Francisco (94115-2754)
P.O. Box 7999 (94120-7999)
PHONE...................................415 600-3503
William B Stewart, *Owner*
EMP: 50
SALES (est): 1.3MM **Privately Held**
SIC: 8062 General medical & surgical hospitals

(P-20917)
INTERHEALTH CORP (PA)
Also Called: Pih Health
12401 Washington Blvd, Whittier (90602-1006)
PHONE...................................562 698-0811
Jane Dicus, *Ch of Bd*
Richard Atwood, *Vice Chairman*
Kenton Woods, *Treasurer*
Ronald Yoshihara, *Vice Pres*
Efrain Aceves, *Admin Sec*
EMP: 1100
SQ FT: 500,000
SALES: 27.7MM **Privately Held**
SIC: 8062 8011 General medical & surgical hospitals; offices & clinics of medical doctors

(P-20918)
JOHN C FREMONT HEALTHCARE DST
Also Called: FREMONT HOSPITAL
5189 Hospital Rd, Mariposa (95338-9524)
P.O. Box 216 (95338-0216)
PHONE...................................209 966-3631
Matthew Matthiessen, *CEO*
Dana Oster, *Bd of Directors*
Bonnie Newman, *Radiology Dir*
Kathy Blalock, *Pharmacy Dir*
Craig Burchfiel, *Network Analyst*
EMP: 250
SQ FT: 59,112
SALES: 26.2MM **Privately Held**
SIC: 8062 General medical & surgical hospitals

(P-20919)
JOHN F KENNEDY MEMORIAL HOSP
Also Called: John F Knnedy Mem Hosp Emrgncy
47111 Monroe St, Indio (92201-6799)
PHONE...................................760 347-6191
Gary Honts, *CEO*

Jorge Cebreros, *Buyer*
Toni Rutherford, *Director*
Jose Vasquez, *Director*
Carolyn Stratton, *Case Mgr*
EMP: 650
SALES: 125.8MM
SALES (corp-wide): 471MM **Privately Held**
WEB: www.jfkfoundation.org
SIC: 8062 Hospital, affiliated with AMA residency
HQ: St. Luke's Des Peres Episcopal-Presbyterian Hospital
2345 Dougherty Ferry Rd
Saint Louis MO 63122
314 966-9100

(P-20920)
JOHN MUIR HEALTH
5003 Commercial Cir, Concord (94520-1268)
PHONE...................................925 692-5600
Cynthia Liedstrand, *Branch Mgr*
EMP: 775
SALES (corp-wide): 322.9MM **Privately Held**
SIC: 8062 General medical & surgical hospitals
HQ: John Muir Health
1601 Ygnacio Valley Rd
Walnut Creek CA 94598
925 947-4449

(P-20921)
JOHN MUIR HEALTH
380 Civic Dr Ste 100, Pleasant Hill (94523-1946)
PHONE...................................925 952-2887
EMP: 940
SALES (corp-wide): 322.9MM **Privately Held**
SIC: 8062 General medical & surgical hospitals
HQ: John Muir Health
1601 Ygnacio Valley Rd
Walnut Creek CA 94598
925 947-4449

(P-20922)
JOHN MUIR HEALTH (HQ)
1601 Ygnacio Valley Rd, Walnut Creek (94598-3122)
P.O. Box 9023 (94596-9023)
PHONE...................................925 947-4449
Calvin Knight, *CEO*
Michael S Thomas, *President*
Jane A Willemsen, *President*
Malcolm McAuley, *Treasurer*
Michael Kern, *Chief Mktg Ofcr*
EMP: 1600
SQ FT: 5,500
SALES: 1.8B
SALES (corp-wide): 322.9MM **Privately Held**
WEB: www.johnmuirmtdiablo.com
SIC: 8062 General medical & surgical hospitals
PA: John Muir Physician Network
1450 Treat Blvd
Walnut Creek CA 94597
925 296-9700

(P-20923)
JOHN MUIR HEALTH
Also Called: Outpatient Rehabilitation Svcs
1981 N Broadway Ste 180, Walnut Creek (94596-3817)
PHONE...................................925 947-5300
Sid Hsu, *Manager*
EMP: 50
SALES (corp-wide): 322.9MM **Privately Held**
WEB: www.johnmuirmtdiablo.com
SIC: 8062 8049 8093 General medical & surgical hospitals; clinical psychologist; rehabilitation center, outpatient treatment
HQ: John Muir Health
1601 Ygnacio Valley Rd
Walnut Creek CA 94598
925 947-4449

(P-20924)
JOHN MUIR HEALTH
Also Called: John Muir Medical Center
1601 Ygnacio Valley Rd, Walnut Creek (94598-3122)
PHONE...................................925 939-3000
Vicki C Lee, *Administration*
Craig Devinney, *Officer*
Lee Huskin, *Vice Pres*
Lee Huskins, *Vice Pres*
Linda Jaffe, *Vice Pres*
EMP: 775
SALES (corp-wide): 322.9MM **Privately Held**
SIC: 8062 General medical & surgical hospitals
HQ: John Muir Health
1601 Ygnacio Valley Rd
Walnut Creek CA 94598
925 947-4449

(P-20925)
JOHN MUIR HEALTH
Also Called: John Muir Med Ctr Cncord Cmpus
2540 East St, Concord (94520-1906)
PHONE...................................925 682-8200
EMP: 1500
SALES (corp-wide): 322.9MM **Privately Held**
SIC: 8062 General medical & surgical hospitals
HQ: John Muir Health
1601 Ygnacio Valley Rd
Walnut Creek CA 94598
925 947-4449

(P-20926)
JOHN MUIR PHYSICIAN NETWORK
112 La Casa Via Ste 300, Walnut Creek (94598-3059)
PHONE...................................925 952-2701
EMP: 634
SALES (corp-wide): 322.9MM **Privately Held**
SIC: 8062 General medical & surgical hospitals
PA: John Muir Physician Network
1450 Treat Blvd
Walnut Creek CA 94597
925 296-9700

(P-20927)
JOHN MUIR PHYSICIAN NETWORK
91 Gregory Ln Ste 15, Pleasant Hill (94523-4927)
PHONE...................................925 685-0843
Aileen Mirabel, *Branch Mgr*
Philip Rush, *Med Doctor*
EMP: 634
SALES (corp-wide): 322.9MM **Privately Held**
SIC: 8062 General medical & surgical hospitals
PA: John Muir Physician Network
1450 Treat Blvd
Walnut Creek CA 94597
925 296-9700

(P-20928)
JOHN MUIR PHYSICIAN NETWORK
Also Called: Mount Diablo Medical Center
2540 East St, Concord (94520-1906)
PHONE...................................925 682-8200
Deborah Kolhede, *Vice Pres*
Sue Ellen Thompson, *Cardiology*
EMP: 1500
SALES (corp-wide): 322.9MM **Privately Held**
SIC: 8062 8011 General medical & surgical hospitals; offices & clinics of medical doctors
PA: John Muir Physician Network
1450 Treat Blvd
Walnut Creek CA 94597
925 296-9700

(P-20929)
JOHN MUIR PHYSICIAN NETWORK (PA)
Also Called: John Muir Medical Center
1450 Treat Blvd, Walnut Creek
(94597-2168)
PHONE...............................925 296-9700
Cal Knight, *Principal*
Laura Kazaglis, *Admin Asst*
Jatinder S Dhillon, *Surgeon*
Andreas Kamlot, *Surgeon*
Tanveer A Khan, *Surgeon*
EMP: 1601
SQ FT: 83,579
SALES: 322.9MM **Privately Held**
SIC: 8062 8069 8093 7363 General medical & surgical hospitals; substance abuse hospitals; substance abuse clinics (outpatient); medical help service

(P-20930)
JOHN MUIR PHYSICIAN NETWORK
Also Called: Mt Diablo Medical Center
1601 Ygnacio Valley Rd, Walnut Creek
(94598-3122)
PHONE...............................925 939-3000
J Kendall Anderson, *President*
Dave Hook, *Exec Dir*
Tran Pham, *Pharmacist*
Lisa McCrary, *Manager*
Lindsay Sandberg, *Manager*
EMP: 399
SALES (corp-wide): 322.9MM **Privately Held**
SIC: 8062 General medical & surgical hospitals
PA: John Muir Physician Network
1450 Treat Blvd
Walnut Creek CA 94597
925 296-9700

(P-20931)
JOHN MUIR PHYSICIAN NETWORK
Also Called: Mt Diablo Heart Health Center
2720 Grant St, Concord (94520-2294)
PHONE...............................925 674-2200
Elizabeth Stalling, *Branch Mgr*
George Melendez, *Technology*
Ayman A Hosny, *Cardiovascular*
EMP: 634
SALES (corp-wide): 322.9MM **Privately Held**
SIC: 8062 General medical & surgical hospitals
PA: John Muir Physician Network
1450 Treat Blvd
Walnut Creek CA 94597
925 296-9700

(P-20932)
KAISER FOUNDATION HOSPITALS
Also Called: Barranca Medical Offices
6 Willard, Irvine (92604-4694)
PHONE...............................949 262-5780
George Disalvo, *Owner*
EMP: 105
SQ FT: 51,080
SALES (corp-wide): 76.5B **Privately Held**
SIC: 8062 General medical & surgical hospitals
HQ: Kaiser Foundation Hospitals Inc
1 Kaiser Plz
Oakland CA 94612
510 271-6611

(P-20933)
KAISER FOUNDATION HOSPITALS
Also Called: Kaiser Permanente Eye
1680 E Roseville Pkwy, Roseville
(95661-3988)
PHONE...............................916 746-3937
Daniel Rule, *Branch Mgr*
Don R Robinson, *Psychiatry*
EMP: 105
SALES (corp-wide): 76.5B **Privately Held**
SIC: 8062 General medical & surgical hospitals
HQ: Kaiser Foundation Hospitals Inc
1 Kaiser Plz
Oakland CA 94612
510 271-6611

(P-20934)
KAISER FOUNDATION HOSPITALS
Also Called: Kaiser Permanente
5601 De Soto Ave, Woodland Hills
(91367-6701)
PHONE...............................818 719-2000
Cathy Casas, *Senior VP*
Antonia Kovachev, *Project Mgr*
Nabil Odeh, *Technology*
Andrew Perez, *Technology*
Shan-Fu Huang, *Family Practiti*
EMP: 1200
SALES (corp-wide): 76.5B **Privately Held**
WEB: www.kaiserpermanente.org
SIC: 8062 General medical & surgical hospitals
HQ: Kaiser Foundation Hospitals Inc
1 Kaiser Plz
Oakland CA 94612
510 271-6611

(P-20935)
KAISER FOUNDATION HOSPITALS
Also Called: Kaiser Permanente
12620 Prescott Ave, Tustin (92782-1066)
PHONE...............................951 353-4000
Danh V Le, *Director*
EMP: 789
SALES (corp-wide): 76.5B **Privately Held**
WEB: www.kaiserpermanente.org
SIC: 8062 General medical & surgical hospitals
HQ: Kaiser Foundation Hospitals Inc
1 Kaiser Plz
Oakland CA 94612
510 271-6611

(P-20936)
KAISER FOUNDATION HOSPITALS
Also Called: Kaiser Permanente
43112 15th St W, Lancaster (93534-6219)
PHONE...............................661 726-2500
Barbara Fordice, *General Mgr*
Cynthia Mackey, *Emerg Med Spec*
Mohamed Gudal, *Med Doctor*
Nareshkumar Arulampalam,
Adoracion Thompson, *Manager*
EMP: 175
SALES (corp-wide): 76.5B **Privately Held**
WEB: www.kaiserpermanente.org
SIC: 8062 Hospital, affiliated with AMA residency
HQ: Kaiser Foundation Hospitals Inc
1 Kaiser Plz
Oakland CA 94612
510 271-6611

(P-20937)
KAISER FOUNDATION HOSPITALS
Also Called: Kaiser Permanente
4867 W Sunset Blvd, Los Angeles
(90027-5969)
PHONE...............................323 783-4011
Vicken Aharonian, *Director*
Brian Herzberger, *Administration*
Leonard Champion, *Project Mgr*
Kelly Malone, *Project Mgr*
Tomic Hacopian, *Pathologist*
EMP: 60
SALES (corp-wide): 76.5B **Privately Held**
WEB: www.kaiserpermanente.org
SIC: 8062 8099 6321 6324 General medical & surgical hospitals; physical examination service, insurance; health insurance carriers; hospital & medical service plans
HQ: Kaiser Foundation Hospitals Inc
1 Kaiser Plz
Oakland CA 94612
510 271-6611

(P-20938)
KAISER FOUNDATION HOSPITALS
Also Called: Park Shadelands Medical Offs
320 Lennon Ln, Walnut Creek
(94598-2419)
PHONE...............................925 906-2380
David Nievr, *President*
EMP: 52

(P-20939)
KAISER FOUNDATION HOSPITALS
Also Called: Kaiser Permanente
1011 Baldwin Park Blvd, Baldwin Park
(91706-5806)
PHONE...............................626 851-1011
Linda Margarita Gutierrez, *Principal*
Shirley Lac, *Project Mgr*
Lee Diers, *Materials Mgr*
Richard Hill, *Family Practiti*
Cristiane Guberman De and, *Obstetrician*
EMP: 793
SALES (corp-wide): 76.5B **Privately Held**
WEB: www.kaiserpermanente.org
SIC: 8062 General medical & surgical hospitals
HQ: Kaiser Foundation Hospitals Inc
1 Kaiser Plz
Oakland CA 94612
510 271-6611

(P-20940)
KAISER FOUNDATION HOSPITALS
Also Called: Kaiser Prmnente Downey Med Ctr
9333 Imperial Hwy, Downey (90242-2812)
PHONE...............................562 657-9000
Gemma Abad, *Branch Mgr*
Roger Preciado, *Technician*
Connie Pinkerton, *Project Mgr*
Joan Duffy, *Family Practiti*
Luis E Fletes, *Family Practiti*
EMP: 410
SALES (corp-wide): 76.5B **Privately Held**
SIC: 8062 General medical & surgical hospitals
HQ: Kaiser Foundation Hospitals Inc
1 Kaiser Plz
Oakland CA 94612
510 271-6611

(P-20941)
KAISER FOUNDATION HOSPITALS (HQ)
Also Called: Kaiser Permanente
1 Kaiser Plz, Oakland (94612-3610)
P.O. Box 12929 (94604-3010)
PHONE...............................510 271-6611
Bernard J Tyson, *President*
Kathryn Beiser, *President*
Janet Liang, *President*
Kathy Lancaster, *CFO*
Patrick Courneya, *Exec VP*
▲ **EMP:** 250 **EST:** 1948
SQ FT: 90,000
SALES (corp-wide): 76.5B **Privately Held**
WEB: www.kaiserpermanente.org
SIC: 8062 8011 General medical & surgical hospitals; medical centers
PA: Kaiser Foundation Health Plan, Inc.
1 Kaiser Plz
Oakland CA 94612
510 271-5800

(P-20942)
KAISER FOUNDATION HOSPITALS
Also Called: Kaiser Permanente
280 W Macarthur Blvd, Oakland
(94611-5642)
PHONE...............................510 752-1000
Bettie Coles, *Manager*
Monica Sugg, *Human Res Dir*
Miriam E Dunham, *Family Practiti*
Brad A Becker, *Dermatology*
Anna Maguire, *Internal Med*
EMP: 708
SALES (corp-wide): 76.5B **Privately Held**
SIC: 8062 General medical & surgical hospitals

SALES (corp-wide): 76.5B **Privately Held**
WEB: www.kaiserpermanente.org
SIC: 8062 8011 General medical & surgical hospitals; general & family practice, physician/surgeon
HQ: Kaiser Foundation Hospitals Inc
1 Kaiser Plz
Oakland CA 94612
510 271-6611

(P-20943)
KAISER FOUNDATION HOSPITALS
Also Called: Kaiser Permanente
1255 W Arrow Hwy, San Dimas
(91773-2340)
PHONE...............................909 394-2530
Will Tatum, *Manager*
Jennie Chang, *Obstetrician*
EMP: 52
SQ FT: 23,801
SALES (corp-wide): 76.5B **Privately Held**
WEB: www.kaiserpermanente.org
SIC: 8062 8011 General medical & surgical hospitals; general & family practice, physician/surgeon
HQ: Kaiser Foundation Hospitals Inc
1 Kaiser Plz
Oakland CA 94612
510 271-6611

(P-20944)
KAISER FOUNDATION HOSPITALS
Also Called: Kaiser Permanente
4405 Vandever Ave Fl 5, San Diego
(92120-3315)
PHONE...............................619 528-2583
David Mandler, *Manager*
Catherine G Pattengill, *Obstetrician*
Aaron Harper, *Pediatrics*
Mark E Nunes, *Pediatrics*
Joanne Wong, *Pediatrics*
EMP: 52
SALES (corp-wide): 76.5B **Privately Held**
WEB: www.kaiserpermanente.org
SIC: 8062 General medical & surgical hospitals
HQ: Kaiser Foundation Hospitals Inc
1 Kaiser Plz
Oakland CA 94612
510 271-6611

(P-20945)
KAISER FOUNDATION HOSPITALS
Also Called: Kaiser Permanente
13651 Willard St, Panorama City (91402)
PHONE...............................818 375-2000
Dev Mahadevan, *Principal*
Suzy Ghadarossin, *Lab Dir*
Michael Flores, *Radiology Dir*
Jane Ryang, *Business Dir*
Eugene Kenigsberg, *Research*
EMP: 3000
SALES (corp-wide): 76.5B **Privately Held**
WEB: www.kaiserpermanente.org
SIC: 8062 General medical & surgical hospitals
HQ: Kaiser Foundation Hospitals Inc
1 Kaiser Plz
Oakland CA 94612
510 271-6611

(P-20946)
KAISER FOUNDATION HOSPITALS
280 Hospital Pkwy, San Jose (95119-1103)
PHONE...............................408 972-6010
Rajan Bhandari, *Branch Mgr*
EMP: 267
SALES (corp-wide): 76.5B **Privately Held**
SIC: 8062 General medical & surgical hospitals
HQ: Kaiser Foundation Hospitals Inc
1 Kaiser Plz
Oakland CA 94612
510 271-6611

(P-20947)
KAISER FOUNDATION HOSPITALS
Also Called: San Joaquin Community Hospital
2615 Chester Ave, Bakersfield
(93301-2014)
PHONE...............................661 395-3000
EMP: 267

SALES (corp-wide): 76.5B **Privately Held**
SIC: **8062** General medical & surgical hospitals
HQ: Kaiser Foundation Hospitals Inc
1 Kaiser Plz
Oakland CA 94612
510 271-6611

(P-20948)
KAISER FOUNDATION HOSPITALS
Also Called: Palomar Medical Center
2185 Citracado Pkwy, Escondido
(92029-4159)
PHONE.................................442 281-5000
EMP: 593
SALES (corp-wide): 76.5B **Privately Held**
SIC: **8062** General medical & surgical hospitals
HQ: Kaiser Foundation Hospitals Inc
1 Kaiser Plz
Oakland CA 94612
510 271-6611

(P-20949)
KAISER FOUNDATION HOSPITALS
Also Called: Antelope Valley Hospital
1600 W Avenue J, Lancaster (93534-2814)
PHONE.................................661 949-5000
Harriet R Lee, *Administration*
EMP: 267
SALES (corp-wide): 76.5B **Privately Held**
SIC: **8062** General medical & surgical hospitals
HQ: Kaiser Foundation Hospitals Inc
1 Kaiser Plz
Oakland CA 94612
510 271-6611

(P-20950)
KAISER FOUNDATION HOSPITALS
Also Called: Kaiser Prmante Internet Svcs
5820 Owens Dr Bldg E-2, Pleasanton
(94588-3900)
PHONE.................................925 598-2799
EMP: 267
SALES (corp-wide): 76.5B **Privately Held**
SIC: **8062** General medical & surgical hospitals
HQ: Kaiser Foundation Hospitals Inc
1 Kaiser Plz
Oakland CA 94612
510 271-6611

(P-20951)
KAISER FOUNDATION HOSPITALS
Also Called: Kaiser Permanente
1650 Response Rd, Sacramento
(95815-4807)
PHONE.................................916 973-5000
Sandra Lee Panora, *Branch Mgr*
Vong M Lee, *Internal Med*
Jeffrey S Skilling, *Oncology*
Colleen Hendershott, *Med Doctor*
Cindy Green, *Representative*
EMP: 52
SALES (corp-wide): 76.5B **Privately Held**
WEB: www.kaiserpermanente.org
SIC: **8062** General medical & surgical hospitals
HQ: Kaiser Foundation Hospitals Inc
1 Kaiser Plz
Oakland CA 94612
510 271-6611

(P-20952)
KAISER FOUNDATION HOSPITALS
10990 San Dego Mission Rd, San Diego
(92108-2417)
PHONE.................................619 641-4663
Caroline Bonner, *Director*
Claudia F De Carvalho, *Pharmacist*
Inga X Garmanyan, *Pharmacist*
Christina T Nguyen, *Pharmacist*
Chris J Sando, *Pharmacist*
EMP: 410
SALES (corp-wide): 76.5B **Privately Held**
WEB: www.kaiserpermanente.org
SIC: **8062** General medical & surgical hospitals

(P-20953)
KAISER FOUNDATION HOSPITALS
Also Called: La Mesa Medical Offices
8080 Parkway Dr, La Mesa (91942-2104)
PHONE.................................619 528-5000
Caroline Wu, *Principal*
Ronny Kalasho, *Family Practiti*
Angela Kutsunis, *Family Practiti*
Shreya Chandra, *Internal Med*
EMP: 50
SALES (corp-wide): 76.5B **Privately Held**
WEB: www.kaiserpermanente.org
SIC: **8062** General medical & surgical hospitals
HQ: Kaiser Foundation Hospitals Inc
1 Kaiser Plz
Oakland CA 94612
510 271-6611

(P-20954)
KAISER FOUNDATION HOSPITALS
Also Called: Stockdale Medical Offices
3501 Stockdale Hwy, Bakersfield
(93309-2150)
PHONE.................................661 398-5011
KY P Ho, *Principal*
Jinsun Kim, *Family Practiti*
EMP: 50
SALES (corp-wide): 76.5B **Privately Held**
WEB: www.kaiserpermanente.org
SIC: **8062** General medical & surgical hospitals
HQ: Kaiser Foundation Hospitals Inc
1 Kaiser Plz
Oakland CA 94612
510 271-6611

(P-20955)
KAISER FOUNDATION HOSPITALS
Also Called: Wildomar Medical Offices
36450 Inland Valley Dr # 204, Wildomar
(92595-9583)
PHONE.................................951 353-2000
Geoffrey Gomez, *Principal*
Keith Hamilton, *Family Practiti*
EMP: 50
SALES (corp-wide): 76.5B **Privately Held**
WEB: www.kaiserpermanente.org
SIC: **8062** General medical & surgical hospitals
HQ: Kaiser Foundation Hospitals Inc
1 Kaiser Plz
Oakland CA 94612
510 271-6611

(P-20956)
KAISER FOUNDATION HOSPITALS
Also Called: Bostonia Medical Offices
1630 E Main St, El Cajon (92021-5204)
PHONE.................................619 528-5000
Jennifer Park, *Med Doctor*
EMP: 50
SALES (corp-wide): 76.5B **Privately Held**
WEB: www.kaiserpermanente.org
SIC: **8062** General medical & surgical hospitals
HQ: Kaiser Foundation Hospitals Inc
1 Kaiser Plz
Oakland CA 94612
510 271-6611

(P-20957)
KAISER FOUNDATION HOSPITALS
Also Called: Cudahy Medical Offices
7825 Atlantic Ave, Cudahy (90201-5022)
PHONE.................................323 562-6400
Karen Warren, *Manager*
Robert L Escalera, *Family Practiti*
Vicki L Cordts, *Obstetrician*
Juan C Ruiz, *Pediatrics*
EMP: 100
SALES (corp-wide): 76.5B **Privately Held**
WEB: www.kaiserpermanente.org
SIC: **8062** General medical & surgical hospitals

(P-20958)
KAISER FOUNDATION HOSPITALS
Also Called: El Cajon Medical Offices
250 Travelodge Dr, El Cajon (92020-4126)
PHONE.................................619 528-5000
Carolyn Bonner, *Administration*
EMP: 50
SQ FT: 47,486
SALES (corp-wide): 76.5B **Privately Held**
WEB: www.kaiserpermanente.org
SIC: **8062** General medical & surgical hospitals
HQ: Kaiser Foundation Hospitals Inc
1 Kaiser Plz
Oakland CA 94612
510 271-6611

(P-20959)
KAISER FOUNDATION HOSPITALS
Also Called: Kaiser Permanente
1249 S Sunset Ave, West Covina
(91790-3960)
PHONE.................................866 319-4269
Jane Lau, *Manager*
Chan Kiet Wong, *Pharmacist*
EMP: 50
SALES (corp-wide): 76.5B **Privately Held**
WEB: www.kaiserpermanente.org
SIC: **8062** General medical & surgical hospitals
HQ: Kaiser Foundation Hospitals Inc
1 Kaiser Plz
Oakland CA 94612
510 271-6611

(P-20960)
KAISER FOUNDATION HOSPITALS
Also Called: Gardena Medical Offices
15446 S Western Ave, Gardena
(90249-4319)
PHONE.................................310 517-2956
Mary Mauch, *Manager*
Agnes E Chen, *Family Practiti*
Keila Cox, *Pediatrics*
Thuy Lu, *Med Doctor*
EMP: 50
SQ FT: 114,575
SALES (corp-wide): 76.5B **Privately Held**
WEB: www.kaiserpermanente.org
SIC: **8062** General medical & surgical hospitals
HQ: Kaiser Foundation Hospitals Inc
1 Kaiser Plz
Oakland CA 94612
510 271-6611

(P-20961)
KAISER FOUNDATION HOSPITALS
Also Called: Erwin Street Medical Offices
21263 Erwin St, Woodland Hills
(91367-3715)
PHONE.................................818 592-3100
Karen Kim, *Executive*
Sylva Murdaian, *Family Practiti*
Donald Eknoyan, *Psychiatry*
Alisha Kohm, *Psychiatry*
EMP: 50
SQ FT: 28,398
SALES (corp-wide): 76.5B **Privately Held**
WEB: www.kaiserpermanente.org
SIC: **8062** General medical & surgical hospitals
HQ: Kaiser Foundation Hospitals Inc
1 Kaiser Plz
Oakland CA 94612
510 271-6611

(P-20962)
KAISER FOUNDATION HOSPITALS
Also Called: Rancho Cordova Medical Offices
10725 International Dr, Rancho Cordova
(95670-7967)
PHONE.................................916 631-3088
David Haddad, *Principal*
Ethan Cutts, *Pediatrics*

Alex Kriegshauser, *Manager*
EMP: 50
SALES (corp-wide): 76.5B **Privately Held**
WEB: www.kaiserpermanente.org
SIC: **8062** General medical & surgical hospitals
HQ: Kaiser Foundation Hospitals Inc
1 Kaiser Plz
Oakland CA 94612
510 271-6611

(P-20963)
KAISER FOUNDATION HOSPITALS
Also Called: Petaluma Medical Offices
3900 Lakeville Hwy, Petaluma
(94954-5698)
PHONE.................................707 765-3900
Claudia R Viazzoli, *Principal*
Dorothea Lorimer, *Pharmacy Dir*
Susan Gross, *Family Practiti*
Amos Yew, *Psychologist*
Karen Bloom, *Internal Med*
EMP: 50
SQ FT: 39,000
SALES (corp-wide): 76.5B **Privately Held**
WEB: www.kaiserpermanente.org
SIC: **8062** General medical & surgical hospitals
HQ: Kaiser Foundation Hospitals Inc
1 Kaiser Plz
Oakland CA 94612
510 271-6611

(P-20964)
KAISER FOUNDATION HOSPITALS
Also Called: Novato Medical Offices
97 San Marin Dr, Novato (94945-1100)
PHONE.................................415 899-7400
Margaret R Hill, *Principal*
Willa Jefferson-Stoke, *Manager*
EMP: 50
SALES (corp-wide): 76.5B **Privately Held**
WEB: www.kaiserpermanente.org
SIC: **8062** General medical & surgical hospitals
HQ: Kaiser Foundation Hospitals Inc
1 Kaiser Plz
Oakland CA 94612
510 271-6611

(P-20965)
KAISER FOUNDATION HOSPITALS
Also Called: Permanente Medical Group
555 Castro St Fl 3, Mountain View
(94041-2009)
PHONE.................................650 903-3000
Patricia Carpenter, *Director*
Sindey Chung, *Med Doctor*
Andrea Forgy, *Med Doctor*
EMP: 200
SALES (corp-wide): 76.5B **Privately Held**
WEB: www.kaiserpermanente.org
SIC: **8062** Hospital, affiliated with AMA residency
HQ: Kaiser Foundation Hospitals Inc
1 Kaiser Plz
Oakland CA 94612
510 271-6611

(P-20966)
KAISER FOUNDATION HOSPITALS
Also Called: Kaiser Permanente
501 Lennon Ln, Walnut Creek
(94598-2414)
PHONE.................................925 906-2000
Christina Robinson, *Principal*
Charu Gupta, *Family Practiti*
James Ferry, *Obstetrician*
Michael Jordan, *Obstetrician*
Gita M Moarefi, *Internal Med*
EMP: 1000
SALES (corp-wide): 76.5B **Privately Held**
WEB: www.kaiserpermanente.org
SIC: **8062** General medical & surgical hospitals
HQ: Kaiser Foundation Hospitals Inc
1 Kaiser Plz
Oakland CA 94612
510 271-6611

PRODUCTS & SVCS

(P-20967)
KAISER FOUNDATION HOSPITALS
Also Called: Kaiser Permanente
7601 Stoneridge Dr, Pleasanton (94588-4501)
PHONE....................925 847-5000
Linsey Dicks, *Admin Director*
Todd W Dillard, *Obstetrician*
Jerome Deck Jr, *Internal Med*
Muniza Muzaffar, *Internal Med*
Amy L Gruber, *Pediatrics*
EMP: 350
SALES (corp-wide): 76.5B **Privately Held**
WEB: www.kaiserpermanente.org
SIC: 8062 General medical & surgical hospitals
HQ: Kaiser Foundation Hospitals Inc
1 Kaiser Plz
Oakland CA 94612
510 271-6611

(P-20968)
KAISER FOUNDATION HOSPITALS
Also Called: Kaiser Permanente Division RES
2000 Brdwy, Oakland (94612)
PHONE....................510 891-3400
Joe Shelby MD, *Director*
Victoria Peckham, *Business Anlyst*
Alyce Adams, *Research*
Assiamira Ferrara, *Research*
Nicole Rutkowski, *Sales Staff*
EMP: 400
SQ FT: 86,875
SALES (corp-wide): 76.5B **Privately Held**
WEB: www.kaiserpermanente.org
SIC: 8062 General medical & surgical hospitals
HQ: Kaiser Foundation Hospitals Inc
1 Kaiser Plz
Oakland CA 94612
510 271-6611

(P-20969)
KAISER FOUNDATION HOSPITALS
Also Called: Kaiser Permanente
5055 California Ave # 110, Bakersfield (93309-0701)
P.O. Box 12099 (93389-2099)
PHONE....................661 334-2020
EMP: 105
SALES (corp-wide): 76.5B **Privately Held**
SIC: 8062 General medical & surgical hospitals
HQ: Kaiser Foundation Hospitals Inc
1 Kaiser Plz
Oakland CA 94612
510 271-6611

(P-20970)
KAISER FOUNDATION HOSPITALS
Also Called: Kaiser Prmnnte Vallejo Med Ctr
975 Sereno Dr, Vallejo (94589-2441)
PHONE....................707 651-1000
Katie Rickleff, *Principal*
McSweeney Brian, *Engineer*
Gabriel Flaxman, *Family Practiti*
Nizar Kajani, *Pathologist*
Ronald V Stradiotto, *Surgeon*
EMP: 2700
SALES (corp-wide): 76.5B **Privately Held**
WEB: www.kaiserpermanente.org
SIC: 8062 General medical & surgical hospitals
HQ: Kaiser Foundation Hospitals Inc
1 Kaiser Plz
Oakland CA 94612
510 271-6611

(P-20971)
KAISER FOUNDATION HOSPITALS
Also Called: Kaiser Permanente
12470 Whittier Blvd, Whittier (90602-1017)
PHONE....................866 340-5974
Beth Lopez, *Principal*
EMP: 50
SALES (corp-wide): 76.5B **Privately Held**
WEB: www.kaiserpermanente.org
SIC: 8062 General medical & surgical hospitals

(P-20972)
KAISER FOUNDATION HOSPITALS
Also Called: Bonita Medical Offices
3955 Bonita Rd, Bonita (91902-1230)
PHONE....................619 409-6405
James Lentz, *Principal*
EMP: 72
SQ FT: 67,760
SALES (corp-wide): 76.5B **Privately Held**
WEB: www.kaiser.com
SIC: 8062 General medical & surgical hospitals
HQ: Kaiser Foundation Hospitals Inc
1 Kaiser Plz
Oakland CA 94612
510 271-6611

(P-20973)
KAISER FOUNDATION HOSPITALS
Also Called: Kaiser Prmnnte Manteca Med Ctr
1777 W Yosemite Ave, Manteca (95337-5187)
PHONE....................209 825-3700
Anita Kennedy, *COO*
EMP: 593
SALES (corp-wide): 76.5B **Privately Held**
SIC: 8062 General medical & surgical hospitals
HQ: Kaiser Foundation Hospitals Inc
1 Kaiser Plz
Oakland CA 94612
510 271-6611

(P-20974)
KAISER FOUNDATION HOSPITALS
Also Called: Kaiser Permanente San
275 Hospital Pkwy 765a, San Jose (95119-1106)
PHONE....................408 972-6700
Diana Ochoa, *Branch Mgr*
Fauzia Basit, *Family Practiti*
EMP: 105
SALES (corp-wide): 76.5B **Privately Held**
WEB: www.kaiserpermanente.org
SIC: 8062 8021 General medical & surgical hospitals; offices & clinics of dentists
HQ: Kaiser Foundation Hospitals Inc
1 Kaiser Plz
Oakland CA 94612
510 271-6611

(P-20975)
KAISER FOUNDATION HOSPITALS
Also Called: Kaiser Permanente
1055 E Colo Blvd Ste 100, Pasadena (91106)
PHONE....................626 440-5659
Jeanine Boudakian, *Branch Mgr*
George Di Salvo, *CFO*
Laurel Junk, *Senior VP*
Jodie Lesh, *Vice Pres*
Sami Chan, *Administration*
EMP: 500
SALES (corp-wide): 76.5B **Privately Held**
WEB: www.kaiserpermanente.org
SIC: 8062 General medical & surgical hospitals
HQ: Kaiser Foundation Hospitals Inc
1 Kaiser Plz
Oakland CA 94612
510 271-6611

(P-20976)
KAISER FOUNDATION HOSPITALS
Also Called: Kaiser Permanente
1600 Eureka Rd, Roseville (95661-3027)
PHONE....................916 784-4000
Douglas Freeman, *Branch Mgr*
Karen Martins, *Human Res Dir*
Cheryl Kenner, *Education*
Irina Badalyan, *Family Practiti*
Rakhshi Khan, *Family Practiti*
EMP: 2300

(P-20977)
KAISER FOUNDATION HOSPITALS
Also Called: Kaiser Foundation Health Plan
7300 N Fresno St, Fresno (93720-2941)
PHONE....................559 448-4500
Jeffrey Collins, *Manager*
Arshad Ahad, *Hematology*
Karl Quinn, *Internal Med*
Don M Yoshimura, *Neurology*
Huiwen Hao, *Psychiatry*
EMP: 2300
SALES (corp-wide): 76.5B **Privately Held**
WEB: www.kaiser.com
SIC: 8062 General medical & surgical hospitals
HQ: Kaiser Foundation Hospitals Inc
1 Kaiser Plz
Oakland CA 94612
510 271-6611

(P-20978)
KAISER FOUNDATION HOSPITALS
Also Called: Kaiser Permanente
250 W San Jose Ave, Claremont (91711-5295)
PHONE....................888 750-0036
Bell Pacific, *Manager*
EMP: 267
SQ FT: 17,908
SALES (corp-wide): 76.5B **Privately Held**
WEB: www.kaiserpermanente.org
SIC: 8062 General medical & surgical hospitals
HQ: Kaiser Foundation Hospitals Inc
1 Kaiser Plz
Oakland CA 94612
510 271-6611

(P-20979)
KAISER FOUNDATION HOSPITALS
Also Called: Kaiser Permanente Advice
7300 Wyndham Dr, Sacramento (95823-4913)
PHONE....................916 525-6300
Tony Le, *Manager*
Amal Hagen, *Office Mgr*
Humberto Temporini, *Psychiatry*
EMP: 105
SALES (corp-wide): 76.5B **Privately Held**
SIC: 8062 General medical & surgical hospitals
HQ: Kaiser Foundation Hospitals Inc
1 Kaiser Plz
Oakland CA 94612
510 271-6611

(P-20980)
KAISER FOUNDATION HOSPITALS
Also Called: Kaiser Permanente
7373 West Ln, Stockton (95210-3377)
PHONE....................209 476-3101
Gene Long, *Branch Mgr*
Lulu Esau, *Project Mgr*
EMP: 175
SALES (corp-wide): 76.5B **Privately Held**
WEB: www.kaiserpermanente.org
SIC: 8062 General medical & surgical hospitals
HQ: Kaiser Foundation Hospitals Inc
1 Kaiser Plz
Oakland CA 94612
510 271-6611

(P-20981)
KAISER FOUNDATION HOSPITALS
Also Called: Kaiser Permanente Santa
710 Lawrence Expy, Santa Clara (95051-5173)
PHONE....................408 851-1000
Ana Herdocia, *Executive Asst*
Ninad R Dabadghav, *Surgeon*

Jemmy C Hwang, *Surgeon*
Judith Keddington, *Surgeon*
Lucy J Kim, *Surgeon*
EMP: 593
SALES (corp-wide): 76.5B **Privately Held**
SIC: 8062 General medical & surgical hospitals
HQ: Kaiser Foundation Hospitals Inc
1 Kaiser Plz
Oakland CA 94612
510 271-6611

(P-20982)
KAISER FOUNDATION HOSPITALS
Also Called: Kaiser Permanente
1900 E 4th St, Santa Ana (92705-3962)
PHONE....................714 967-4700
Martha Bieser, *Principal*
Stephanie Du, *Family Practiti*
Melissa Toffel, *Family Practiti*
Eric Nguyen, *Psychiatry*
Paul C Rosandich, *Psychiatry*
EMP: 50
SALES (corp-wide): 76.5B **Privately Held**
WEB: www.kaiserpermanente.org
SIC: 8062 General medical & surgical hospitals
HQ: Kaiser Foundation Hospitals Inc
1 Kaiser Plz
Oakland CA 94612
510 271-6611

(P-20983)
KAISER PERMANENTE
3505 Broadway, Oakland (94611-5798)
PHONE....................510 450-2109
T Raine Bennett, *Med Doctor*
Andrew Geranio, *Officer*
Rich E Smith, *Vice Pres*
Gregory A Hughes, *Executive*
Haley Donaldson, *Administration*
EMP: 72
SALES (est): 3.1MM **Privately Held**
SIC: 8062 General medical & surgical hospitals

(P-20984)
KAWEAH DELTA HEALTH CARE DST
355 Monte Vista Dr, Dinuba (93618-9228)
PHONE....................559 591-5513
Gary K Herbst, *CFO*
EMP: 236
SALES (corp-wide): 710.9MM **Privately Held**
SIC: 8062 Hospital, AMA approved residency
PA: Kaweah Delta Health Care District
400 W Mineral King Ave
Visalia CA 93291
559 624-2000

(P-20985)
KAWEAH DELTA HEALTH CARE DST (PA)
Also Called: KAWEAH DELTA DISTRICT HOSPITAL
400 W Mineral King Ave, Visalia (93291-6237)
PHONE....................559 624-2000
Donna Archer, *CEO*
Lindsay K Mann, *CEO*
Thomas Rayner, *COO*
Gary Herbst, *CFO*
Mark Garfield, *Chief Mktg Ofcr*
EMP: 1800 EST: 1961
SQ FT: 250,255
SALES: 710.9MM **Privately Held**
SIC: 8062 Hospital, AMA approved residency

(P-20986)
KECK HOSPITAL OF USC
1500 San Pablo St, Los Angeles (90033-5313)
PHONE....................800 872-2273
Thomas E Jackiewicz, *CEO*
Holly Muir,
Mike Fong, *Records Dir*
Angela Niparko, *Records Dir*
Rodney B Hanners, *COO*
▲ EMP: 77
SALES (est): 761.1MM **Privately Held**
SIC: 8062 General medical & surgical hospitals

(P-20987)
KEIRO NURSING HOME
2221 Lincoln Park Ave, Los Angeles (90031-2998)
PHONE...............................323 276-5700
Janie Teshima, *Administration*
EMP: 150
SALES (corp-wide): 16.5MM **Privately Held**
SIC: 8062 8052 8051 General medical & surgical hospitals; intermediate care facilities; skilled nursing care facilities
PA: Keiro Nursing Home
325 S Boyle Ave
Los Angeles CA 90033
323 263-9655

(P-20988)
KENNETH CORP
Also Called: GARDEN GROVE HOSPITAL
12601 Garden Grove Blvd, Garden Grove (92843-1908)
PHONE...............................714 537-5160
Edward Mirzabegian, *CEO*
Hassan Alkhouli, *Ch of Bd*
EMP: 615
SQ FT: 133,083
SALES: 108.4MM **Privately Held**
SIC: 8062 General medical & surgical hospitals

(P-20989)
KERN COUNTY HOSPITAL AUTHORITY
1700 Mount Vernon Ave, Bakersfield (93306-4018)
PHONE...............................661 326-2102
Russell Judd, *CEO*
Andrew Cantu, *CFO*
Tyler Whitezell, *VP Admin*
EMP: 1000 **EST:** 1865
SQ FT: 29,800
SALES (est) 711.8K **Privately Held**
SIC: 8062 General medical & surgical hospitals

(P-20990)
KINDRED HEALTHCARE OPER INC
Also Called: Kindred Hospital
2800 Benedict Dr, San Leandro (94577-6840)
PHONE...............................510 357-8300
Wendy Mamoon, *CEO*
Virgil Williams, *Ch Radiology*
Patty Levin, *Phys Thrpy Dir*
Tito Aquino, *Director*
Aamir Faruqui, *Director*
EMP: 450
SALES (corp-wide): 6B **Privately Held**
WEB: www.salemhaven.com
SIC: 8062 General medical & surgical hospitals
HQ: Kindred Healthcare Operating, Llc
680 S 4th St
Louisville KY 40202
502 596-7300

(P-20991)
KINDRED HEALTHCARE OPER INC
Also Called: Ontario Community Hospital
550 N Monterey Ave, Ontario (91764-3318)
PHONE...............................909 391-0333
Peter Adamo, *CEO*
Carol Kirk, *Planning*
Debi Walker, *Purchasing*
Michael Williams, *Buyer*
Hector Cisneros, *Food Svc Dir*
EMP: 275
SALES (corp-wide): 6B **Privately Held**
WEB: www.salemhaven.com
SIC: 8062 General medical & surgical hospitals
HQ: Kindred Healthcare Operating, Llc
680 S 4th St
Louisville KY 40202
502 596-7300

(P-20992)
KINDRED HEALTHCARE OPER LLC
Also Called: Kindred Hospital San Diego
1940 El Cajon Blvd, San Diego (92104-1005)
PHONE...............................502 596-7300
EMP: 222
SALES (corp-wide): 6B **Privately Held**
WEB: www.salemhaven.com
SIC: 8062 General medical & surgical hospitals
HQ: Kindred Healthcare Operating, Llc
680 S 4th St
Louisville KY 40202
502 596-7300

(P-20993)
KINDRED HEALTHCARE OPERATING
5525 W Slauson Ave, Los Angeles (90056-1047)
PHONE...............................310 642-0325
Adam Darvish, *Manager*
Elizabeth Robinson, *Records Dir*
Noris Aleman, *Ch Credit Ofcr*
Evelyn McLauglin, *Officer*
Alex Nava, *Purchasing*
EMP: 280
SALES (corp-wide): 6B **Privately Held**
WEB: www.salemhaven.com
SIC: 8062 General medical & surgical hospitals
HQ: Kindred Healthcare Operating, Llc
680 S 4th St
Louisville KY 40202
502 596-7300

(P-20994)
KINDRED NURSING CENTERS W LLC
Also Called: Kindred Nursing and Reha
1601 5th Ave, San Rafael (94901-1808)
PHONE...............................415 456-7170
Richard Espinoza, *Manager*
EMP: 65
SALES (corp-wide): 6B **Privately Held**
WEB: www.salemhaven.com
SIC: 8062 General medical & surgical hospitals
HQ: Kindred Nursing Centers West Llc
3128 Boxelder Dr
Cheyenne WY 82001
307 634-7901

(P-20995)
KND DEVELOPMENT 55 LLC
Also Called: Kindred Hospital - Rancho
10841 White Oak Ave, Rancho Cucamonga (91730-3817)
PHONE...............................909 581-6400
Miller Debroah, *Director*
Tessie Mancilla, *Human Res Mgr*
Joseph Flores, *Purch Dir*
Cesar Tirado, *Director*
Leonard Wolfe, *Director*
EMP: 61
SALES (est) 45.1MM **Privately Held**
SIC: 8062 General medical & surgical hospitals

(P-20996)
LA PALMA HOSPITAL MEDICAL CTR
Also Called: LA PALMA INTERCOMMUNITY HOSPITAL
7901 Walker St, La Palma (90623-1764)
PHONE...............................714 670-7400
Virg Narbutas, *CEO*
Sami Shoukair, *Chairman*
Marlene Pritchard, *Vice Pres*
Hilda Manzo-Luna, *Ch Nursing Ofcr*
Mark Fatemi, *Med Doctor*
EMP: 400 **EST:** 1970
SQ FT: 94,000
SALES: 56.9MM
SALES (corp-wide): 3.4B **Privately Held**
SIC: 8062 General medical & surgical hospitals
HQ: Prime Healthcare Services Inc
3300 E Guasti Rd Ste 300
Ontario CA 91761

(P-20997)
LAST FRONTIER HEALTHCARE DST
Also Called: MODOC MEDICAL CENTER
228 W Mcdowell Ave, Alturas (96101-3934)
PHONE...............................530 233-5131
Kevin Kramer, *CEO*
Jo Knoch, *CFO*
Patrick Fields, *Finance Dir*
Diane Hagelthorne, *Human Resources*
EMP: 190
SQ FT: 56,094
SALES: 18.5MM **Privately Held**
WEB: www.modoccounty.us
SIC: 8062 General medical & surgical hospitals

(P-20998)
LEGACY LIFEPOINT HEALTH INC
Also Called: Colorado River Medical Center
1401 Bailey Ave, Needles (92363-3103)
PHONE...............................760 326-7100
James Arp, *Manager*
EMP: 215
SALES (corp-wide): 713.4MM **Privately Held**
WEB: www.ennisregional.com
SIC: 8062 General medical & surgical hospitals
HQ: Legacy Lifepoint Health, Inc.
330 Seven Springs Way
Brentwood TN 37027
615 920-7000

(P-20999)
LELAND STANFORD JUNIOR UNIV
Also Called: Cantor Art Ctr Stanford Univ
328 Lomita Dr, Palo Alto (94305-5006)
PHONE...............................650 723-2997
Jesse Cool, *Manager*
EMP: 50
SALES (corp-wide): 11.3B **Privately Held**
SIC: 8062 8069 8221 General medical & surgical hospitals; children's hospital; university
PA: Leland Stanford Junior University
450 Jane Stanford Way
Stanford CA 94305
650 723-2300

(P-21000)
LELAND STANFORD JUNIOR UNIV
Also Called: Stanford Hospitals and Clinics
820 Quarry Rd, Palo Alto (94304-2202)
PHONE...............................650 725-2377
Roy King, *Branch Mgr*
Benjamin Elkins, *Director*
EMP: 2285
SALES (corp-wide): 11.3B **Privately Held**
SIC: 8062 8221 General medical & surgical hospitals; university
PA: Leland Stanford Junior University
450 Jane Stanford Way
Stanford CA 94305
650 723-2300

(P-21001)
LELAND STANFORD JUNIOR UNIV
Also Called: Stanford Medical Center
2680 Hanover St, Palo Alto (94304-1117)
PHONE...............................650 723-4000
Elizabeth Eilers, *Director*
Joyce Kaufman, *Nurse Practr*
EMP: 2285
SALES (corp-wide): 11.3B **Privately Held**
SIC: 8062 8221 General medical & surgical hospitals; university
PA: Leland Stanford Junior University
450 Jane Stanford Way
Stanford CA 94305
650 723-2300

(P-21002)
LELAND STANFORD JUNIOR UNIV
Also Called: Stanford University Med Ctr
1000 Welch Rd, Palo Alto (94304-1811)
PHONE...............................650 725-4617
Kate Lorig, *Principal*
Tatiana Pannetta, *Executive Asst*

Joseph Baylan, *Surgeon*
Neyssa Marina, *Hematology*
Nathan Luna, *Pediatrics*
EMP: 2285
SALES (corp-wide): 11.3B **Privately Held**
SIC: 8062 8221 Hospital, medical school affiliation; university
PA: Leland Stanford Junior University
450 Jane Stanford Way
Stanford CA 94305
650 723-2300

(P-21003)
LELAND STANFORD JUNIOR UNIV
Also Called: Stanford University
473 Via Ortega, Stanford (94305-4121)
PHONE...............................650 725-2386
Richard Luthy, *Branch Mgr*
EMP: 2285
SALES (corp-wide): 11.3B **Privately Held**
SIC: 8062 8069 8221 General medical & surgical hospitals; children's hospital; university
PA: Leland Stanford Junior University
450 Jane Stanford Way
Stanford CA 94305
650 723-2300

(P-21004)
LELAND STANFORD JUNIOR UNIV
Also Called: Stanford University
243 Panama St, Stanford (94305-4102)
PHONE...............................650 725-6127
Phil Reese, *Branch Mgr*
Michelle Collette, *Technical Mgr*
Lisa McPherson, *Research*
Anthony D Wagner, *Professor*
Jonjon Blanco, *Director*
EMP: 2285
SALES (corp-wide): 11.3B **Privately Held**
SIC: 8062 8069 8221 General medical & surgical hospitals; children's hospital; university
PA: Leland Stanford Junior University
450 Jane Stanford Way
Stanford CA 94305
650 723-2300

(P-21005)
LELAND STANFORD JUNIOR UNIV
Also Called: Stanford University Medical
300 Pasteur Dr, Stanford (94305-2200)
PHONE...............................650 723-4000
Martha Marsh, *Administration*
Gabiola Julieta, *Managing Dir*
Irena Koziol, *Technician*
Lawrence Hofmann, *Professor*
Paul Khavari, *Professor*
EMP: 6120
SQ FT: 33,503
SALES (corp-wide): 11.3B **Privately Held**
SIC: 8062 8011 8221 General medical & surgical hospitals; offices & clinics of medical doctors; university
PA: Leland Stanford Junior University
450 Jane Stanford Way
Stanford CA 94305
650 723-2300

(P-21006)
LINDA LOMA UNIV HLTH CARE (HQ)
11370 Anderson St # 3900, Loma Linda (92350-1715)
P.O. Box 2000 (92354-0200)
PHONE...............................909 558-2806
Richard Hart, *President*
Rosita Fike, *CEO*
Subhas Gupta, *Executive*
Padmini Davamony, *Exec Dir*
Ivan Buchheim, *Analyst*
EMP: 64 **EST:** 1967
SALES (est) 184.5MM
SALES (corp-wide): 269.1MM **Privately Held**
SIC: 8062 8011 8051 5999 Hospital, medical school affiliated with residency; medical centers; extended care facility; convalescent equipment & supplies

PA: Loma Linda University
11060 Anderson St
Loma Linda CA 92350
909 558-4540

(P-21007)
LITTLE COMPANY MARY HOSPITAL
Also Called: Leader Drug Store
4101 Torrance Blvd, Torrance
(90503-4664)
PHONE..................310 540-7676
Joseph Zanetta, *CEO*
Elizabeth Zuanich, *CFO*
Traci Smith, *Info Tech Mgr*
Nick Orr, *Project Mgr*
Kasey Lai, *Internal Med*
▲ **EMP:** 1200 **EST:** 1957
SQ FT: 300,000
SALES (est): 10.3MM
SALES (corp-wide): 15.2B **Privately Held**
WEB: www.lcmhs.org
SIC: 8062 8051 General medical & surgical hospitals; skilled nursing care facilities
HQ: Providence Health System-Southern California
1801 Lind Ave Sw
Renton WA 98057
425 525-3355

(P-21008)
LODI MEMORIAL HOSP ASSN INC (HQ)
Also Called: Adventist Health Lodi Memorial
975 S Fairmont Ave, Lodi (95240-5118)
P.O. Box 3004 (95241-1908)
PHONE..................209 334-3411
Daniel Wolcott, *CEO*
Roland Simeon,
Nagui N Sorour,
Sarah Beasley, *Volunteer Dir*
Joseph P Harrington, *President*
EMP: 700
SQ FT: 97,057
SALES: 256MM
SALES (corp-wide): 4.4B **Privately Held**
SIC: 8062 Hospital, affiliated with AMA residency
PA: Adventist Health System/West
1 Adventist Health Way
Roseville CA 95661
844 574-5686

(P-21009)
LODI MEMORIAL HOSP ASSN INC
Also Called: Conrad Lab, The
1200 W Vine St, Lodi (95240-5136)
PHONE..................209 339-7583
Dave Mack, *Director*
Sue Anderson, *Admin Sec*
Jackie Vollmer, *Supervisor*
EMP: 50
SALES (corp-wide): 4.4B **Privately Held**
SIC: 8062 General medical & surgical hospitals
HQ: Lodi Memorial Hospital Association, Inc.
975 S Fairmont Ave
Lodi CA 95240
209 334-3411

(P-21010)
LOMA LINDA UNIVERSITY MED CTR
Also Called: Craniofacial Department
11370 Anderson St 2100, Loma Linda
(92350-1715)
P.O. Box 982 (92354-0982)
PHONE..................909 558-2100
Leonard Bailey MD, *Principal*
Ravi Raghavan, *Professor*
EMP: 105
SALES (corp-wide): 269.1MM **Privately Held**
WEB: www.llumc.com
SIC: 8062 8221 Hospital, medical school affiliation; university
HQ: Loma Linda University Medical Center
11234 Anderson St
Loma Linda CA 92354
909 558-4000

(P-21011)
LOMA LINDA UNIVERSITY MED CTR (DH)
Also Called: LLUMC
11234 Anderson St, Loma Linda
(92354-2871)
P.O. Box 2000 (92354-0200)
PHONE..................909 558-4000
Richard H Hart, *Vice Chairman*
David Hinshaw Jr, *Ch Radiology*
James Jesse, *President*
Steven Mohr, *CFO*
Noni Patchett, *Treasurer*
EMP: 4600
SQ FT: 630,000
SALES: 35.6MM
SALES (corp-wide): 269.1MM **Privately Held**
WEB: www.llumc.com
SIC: 8062 8011 8051 5999 Hospital, medical school affiliated with residency; medical centers; extended care facility; medical apparatus & supplies
HQ: Loma Linda University Health Care
11370 Anderson St # 3900
Loma Linda CA 92350
909 558-2806

(P-21012)
LOMA LINDA UNIVERSITY MED CTR
Also Called: Loma Linda Catering Center
11175 Campus St, Loma Linda
(92350-1700)
PHONE..................909 558-8244
Najwa Medina, *Manager*
Janelle Pyke, *Records Dir*
Barbara Sharp, *Exec Dir*
Jim White, *Info Tech Dir*
Fred Williams, *Prgrmr*
EMP: 100
SALES (corp-wide): 269.1MM **Privately Held**
WEB: www.llumc.com
SIC: 8062 Hospital, medical school affiliation
HQ: Loma Linda University Medical Center
11234 Anderson St
Loma Linda CA 92354
909 558-4000

(P-21013)
LOMA LINDA UNIVERSITY MED CTR
Also Called: Behavioral Medicine Center
1710 Barton Rd, Redlands (92373-5304)
PHONE..................909 558-9275
Ruthita Fike, *Manager*
Edward L Field, *Exec Dir*
Carol Barnes-Reid, *Food Svc Dir*
Ricardo Whyte, *Psychiatry*
Bryan Wick, *Psychiatry*
EMP: 310
SQ FT: 62,476
SALES (corp-wide): 269.1MM **Privately Held**
WEB: www.llumc.com
SIC: 8062 8221 Hospital, medical school affiliation; university
HQ: Loma Linda University Medical Center
11234 Anderson St
Loma Linda CA 92354
909 558-4000

(P-21014)
LOMA LINDA UNIVERSITY MED CTR
Also Called: Loma Linda Pharmacy
11223 Campus St, Loma Linda
(92354-3203)
PHONE..................909 558-4216
Bill Robinson, *Manager*
EMP: 200
SALES (corp-wide): 269.1MM **Privately Held**
WEB: www.llumc.com
SIC: 8062 General medical & surgical hospitals
HQ: Loma Linda University Medical Center
11234 Anderson St
Loma Linda CA 92354
909 558-4000

(P-21015)
LOMA LINDA UNIVERSITY MED CTR
Also Called: Loma Linda Community Hospital
25333 Barton Rd, Loma Linda
(92350-0210)
PHONE..................909 796-0167
Todd Nelson, *Manager*
Mark Hubbard, *Vice Pres*
Jody Hughes, *Office Mgr*
EMP: 172
SQ FT: 79,580
SALES (corp-wide): 269.1MM **Privately Held**
WEB: www.llumc.com
SIC: 8062 General medical & surgical hospitals
HQ: Loma Linda University Medical Center
11234 Anderson St
Loma Linda CA 92354
909 558-4000

(P-21016)
LOMPOC VALLEY MEDICAL CENTER
Also Called: Mammography Center
1111 E Ocean Ave Ste 2, Lompoc
(93436-2500)
PHONE..................805 735-9229
Jim Raggio, *Branch Mgr*
Christopher Lumsdaine, *Med Doctor*
EMP: 197
SALES (corp-wide): 93.2MM **Privately Held**
SIC: 8062 General medical & surgical hospitals
PA: Lompoc Valley Medical Center
1515 E Ocean Ave
Lompoc CA 93436
805 737-3300

(P-21017)
LOMPOC VALLEY MEDICAL CENTER (PA)
Also Called: Lompoc Skilled Care Center
1515 E Ocean Ave, Lompoc (93436-7092)
P.O. Box 1058 (93438-1058)
PHONE..................805 737-3300
Jim Raggio, *CEO*
Naishadh Buch, *COO*
Jim White, *Exec VP*
Jayne Scalise, *Principal*
Eric Lykens, *Systs Prg Mgr*
EMP: 325
SQ FT: 150,000
SALES: 93.2MM **Privately Held**
SIC: 8062 8051 Hospital, affiliated with AMA residency; skilled nursing care facilities

(P-21018)
LOMPOC VALLEY MEDICAL CENTER
Also Called: Lompoc Convlsnt Care Ctr
216 N 3rd St, Lompoc (93436-6104)
PHONE..................805 736-3466
Judy Smith, *Principal*
EMP: 150
SALES (corp-wide): 93.2MM **Privately Held**
SIC: 8062 General medical & surgical hospitals
PA: Lompoc Valley Medical Center
1515 E Ocean Ave
Lompoc CA 93436
805 737-3300

(P-21019)
LONG BEACH MEMORIAL MED CTR (HQ)
Also Called: Miller Children's Hospital
2801 Atlantic Ave Fl 2, Long Beach
(90806-1701)
PHONE..................562 933-2000
John Bishop, *CEO*
Barry Arbuckle PHD, *President*
Tamra Kaplan, *COO*
Suize Reinsvold, *COO*
Wendy Dorchester,
EMP: 2000
SQ FT: 1,100,000

SALES: 633.6MM
SALES (corp-wide): 2.4B **Privately Held**
WEB: www.longbeachstate.com
SIC: 8062 General medical & surgical hospitals
PA: Memorial Health Services
17360 Brookhurst St # 160
Fountain Valley CA 92708
714 377-6748

(P-21020)
LONGWOOD MANAGEMENT CORP
Also Called: Shea Convalescent Hospital
7716 Pickering Ave, Whittier (90602-2001)
PHONE..................562 693-5240
Richard Esconrias, *Manager*
EMP: 100
SALES (corp-wide): 170MM **Privately Held**
SIC: 8062 8051 8011 General medical & surgical hospitals; skilled nursing care facilities; offices & clinics of medical doctors
PA: Longwood Management Corp.
4032 Wilshire Blvd Fl 6
Los Angeles CA 90010
213 389-6900

(P-21021)
LONGWOOD MANAGEMENT CORP
Also Called: Northridge Nursing Center
7836 Reseda Blvd, Reseda (91335-1902)
PHONE..................818 881-7414
Deffie Biczi, *General Mgr*
EMP: 80
SALES (corp-wide): 170MM **Privately Held**
SIC: 8062 General medical & surgical hospitals
PA: Longwood Management Corp.
4032 Wilshire Blvd Fl 6
Los Angeles CA 90010
213 389-6900

(P-21022)
LOS ALAMITOS MEDICAL CTR INC (HQ)
3751 Katella Ave, Los Alamitos
(90720-3113)
P.O. Box 533 (90720-0533)
PHONE..................714 826-6400
Kent Clayton, *CEO*
Alice Livingood, *President*
Margaret Watkins, *President*
Rosa Espinoza, *Human Res Dir*
Joan Blake, *Manager*
EMP: 1100 **EST:** 1970
SQ FT: 900
SALES: 210.5MM
SALES (corp-wide): 18.3B **Publicly Held**
SIC: 8062 General medical & surgical hospitals
PA: Tenet Healthcare Corporation
1445 Ross Ave Ste 1400
Dallas TX 75202
469 893-2200

(P-21023)
LOS ROBLES HOSPITAL & MED CTR (DH)
Also Called: HOSPITAL COPORATION OF AMERICA
215 W Janss Rd, Thousand Oaks
(91360-1899)
P.O. Box 550, Nashville TN (37202-0550)
PHONE..................805 497-2727
Greg Angle, *CEO*
Maureen Nicols, *CEO*
Tony Antonelli, *Business Dir*
Don Adler, *Administration*
Alex Bryar, *MIS Dir*
◆ **EMP:** 94
SQ FT: 475
SALES: 474.6MM **Publicly Held**
SIC: 8062 General medical & surgical hospitals
HQ: Hca Inc.
1 Park Plz
Nashville TN 37203
615 344-9551

(P-21024)
LUCILE PACKARD CHILDRENS HOSP
730 Welch Rd Ste B, Palo Alto
(94304-1504)
PHONE.................................650 321-2545
Christophe Dawes, *CEO*
EMP: 51
SALES (est): 7.6MM **Privately Held**
SIC: 8062 General medical & surgical hospitals

(P-21025)
MADERA COMMUNITY HOSPITAL
Also Called: Family Health Services Clinic
1210 E Almond Ave Ste A, Madera
(93637-5606)
PHONE.................................559 675-5530
Robert Kelly, *CEO*
EMP: 228
SALES (corp-wide): 81.3MM **Privately Held**
SIC: 8062 General medical & surgical hospitals
PA: Madera Community Hospital
1250 E Almond Ave
Madera CA 93637
559 675-5555

(P-21026)
MADERA COMMUNITY HOSPITAL
Also Called: Chowchilla Medical Center
285 Hospital Dr, Chowchilla (93610-2041)
PHONE.................................559 665-3768
Mark J Foote, *CEO*
EMP: 209
SALES (corp-wide): 81.3MM **Privately Held**
SIC: 8062 General medical & surgical hospitals
PA: Madera Community Hospital
1250 E Almond Ave
Madera CA 93637
559 675-5555

(P-21027)
MADERA COMMUNITY HOSPITAL (PA)
Also Called: Mch
1250 E Almond Ave, Madera (93637-5696)
P.O. Box 1328 (93639-1328)
PHONE.................................559 675-5555
Evan J Rayner, *CEO*
Connie Wise, *Officer*
Mary Aguirre, *Vice Pres*
Rhonda Valdivia, *Nurse*
Francette Roberts, *Supervisor*
EMP: 345
SQ FT: 66,300
SALES: 81.3MM **Privately Held**
SIC: 8062 General medical & surgical hospitals

(P-21028)
MAIN STREET SPECIALTY SURGERY
280 S Mn St Ste 100, Orange (92868)
PHONE.................................714 704-1900
Betty Hoogenban, *Director*
Tammy Tanner, *Manager*
EMP: 92
SALES (est): 13.1MM **Privately Held**
WEB: www.msssc.com
SIC: 8062 General medical & surgical hospitals

(P-21029)
MARIN GENERAL HOSPITAL
250 Bon Air Rd, Kentfield (94904-1784)
PHONE.................................415 925-7000
Lee Domanico, *CEO*
David Bradley, *CEO*
Theresa Daughton, *CFO*
Linda Lang, *Officer*
Rich Hayden, *Lab Dir*
EMP: 1100 **EST:** 1947
SQ FT: 125,000

SALES: 470.1MM
SALES (corp-wide): 23MM **Privately Held**
WEB: www.sutterhealth.org
SIC: 8062 8011 General medical & surgical hospitals; offices & clinics of medical doctors
PA: Marin Healthcare District
100b Drakes Landing Rd
Greenbrae CA 94904
415 464-2090

(P-21030)
MARK TWAIN MEDICAL CENTER (DH)
Also Called: Mark Twain St Josephs Hospital
768 Mountain Ranch Rd, San Andreas
(95249-9707)
PHONE.................................209 754-3521
Craig J Marks, *CEO*
Greg Jordan, *President*
Jacob Lews, *CFO*
Linda Lewis, *Treasurer*
Dean Kelaita, *Bd of Directors*
EMP: 225
SQ FT: 40,000
SALES: 62.8MM **Privately Held**
SIC: 8062 General medical & surgical hospitals
HQ: Dignity Health
185 Berry St Ste 300
San Francisco CA 94107
415 438-5500

(P-21031)
MARK TWAIN MEDICAL CENTER
Also Called: Silver Service
768 Mountain Ranch Rd, San Andreas
(95249-9707)
PHONE.................................209 754-1487
Mike Lawson, *President*
EMP: 300 **Privately Held**
SIC: 8062 8322 General medical & surgical hospitals; geriatric social service
HQ: Mark Twain Medical Center
768 Mountain Ranch Rd
San Andreas CA 95249

(P-21032)
MARSHALL MEDICAL CENTER
1100 Marshall Way, El Dorado Hills
(95762)
PHONE.................................916 933-2273
EMP: 221
SALES (corp-wide): 238.8MM **Privately Held**
SIC: 8062 General medical & surgical hospitals
PA: Marshall Medical Center
1100 Marshall Way
Placerville CA 95667
530 622-1441

(P-21033)
MARSHALL MEDICAL CENTER (PA)
Also Called: Marshall Hospital
1100 Marshall Way, Placerville
(95667-6533)
P.O. Box 872 (95667-0872)
PHONE.................................530 622-1441
James Whipple, *CEO*
Shannon Truesdell, *COO*
Laurie Eldridge, *CFO*
Maia Schneider, *Exec Dir*
Marlene Markowich, *General Mgr*
EMP: 1000
SQ FT: 124,000
SALES: 238.8MM **Privately Held**
SIC: 8062 8071 8082 General medical & surgical hospitals; medical laboratories; X-ray laboratory, including dental; home health care services

(P-21034)
MATER MISERICORDIAE HOSPITAL (PA)
Also Called: MERCY MEDICAL CENTER MERCED
333 Mercy Ave, Merced (95340-8319)
PHONE.................................209 564-5000
David Dunham, *CEO*
Mika Grisham, *Risk Mgmt Dir*
Michael Aldrich, *Engrg Dir*
Paul Feltz, *Marketing Staff*

Jacqueline Craig, *Family Practiti*
EMP: 668
SQ FT: 60,000
SALES: 298.8MM **Privately Held**
SIC: 8062 General medical & surgical hospitals

(P-21035)
MEMORIALCARE SURGICAL CENTER A
Also Called: Orange Coast Ctr For Surgl Cr
18111 Brookhurst St # 3200, Fountain Valley (92708-6728)
PHONE.................................714 369-1100
Dana Pratt, *CEO*
EMP: 60
SALES (est): 7.9MM **Privately Held**
SIC: 8062 General medical & surgical hospitals

(P-21036)
MENDOCINO COAST DISTRICT HOSP (PA)
700 River Dr, Fort Bragg (95437-5403)
PHONE.................................707 961-1234
Jonathan Baker, *CEO*
Mark Smith, *CFO*
Patricia Jauregui Darland, *Chairman*
Tom Birdsell, *Treasurer*
Camille Ranker, *Treasurer*
▲ **EMP:** 320
SQ FT: 71,500
SALES: 54.4MM **Privately Held**
SIC: 8062 General medical & surgical hospitals

(P-21037)
MENDOCINO COAST DISTRICT HOSP
Also Called: Mendicino Cast Otpient Surgery
700 River Dr, Fort Bragg (95437-5403)
PHONE.................................707 961-4736
Jonathan Baker, *Branch Mgr*
EMP: 167
SALES (corp-wide): 54.4MM **Privately Held**
SIC: 8062 8011 General medical & surgical hospitals; surgeon
PA: Mendocino Coast District Hospital
700 River Dr
Fort Bragg CA 95437
707 961-1234

(P-21038)
MERCY HM SVCS A CAL LTD PARTNR
2215 Truxtun Ave, Bakersfield
(93301-3602)
PHONE.................................661 632-5234
Russel Judd, *President*
EMP: 200 **Privately Held**
WEB: www.mercyhealth.org
SIC: 8062 General medical & surgical hospitals
HQ: Mercy Home Services A California Limited Partnership
2175 Rosaline Ave Ste A
Redding CA 96001
530 225-6000

(P-21039)
MERCY HM SVCS A CAL LTD PARTNR (DH)
Also Called: Mercy Medical Center - Redding
2175 Rosaline Ave Ste A, Redding
(96001-2549)
P.O. Box 496009 (96049-6009)
PHONE.................................530 225-6000
George A Govier, *CEO*
Brian Moon,
Peggy Podliska, *Buyer*
Brenden Hanks, *Anesthesiology*
Jonathan Kombrinck, *Anesthesiology*
EMP: 700
SQ FT: 250,000
SALES: 446.3MM **Privately Held**
WEB: www.mercyhealth.org
SIC: 8062 Hospital, affiliated with AMA residency
HQ: Dignity Health
185 Berry St Ste 300
San Francisco CA 94107
415 438-5500

(P-21040)
MERCY HM SVCS A CAL LTD PARTNR
Also Called: Administrative Office
2175 Rosaline Ave Ste A, Redding
(96001-2549)
PHONE.................................530 225-6000
Ronald Cloud, *Branch Mgr*
Steven Bleiweiss, *Ch Pathology*
Peter Halt, *Radiology Dir*
Jamie Santis, *Pharmacy Dir*
Sean Anderson, *Director*
EMP: 340 **Privately Held**
SIC: 8062 General medical & surgical hospitals
HQ: Mercy Home Services A California Limited Partnership
2175 Rosaline Ave Ste A
Redding CA 96001
530 225-6000

(P-21041)
MERCY HM SVCS A CAL LTD PARTNR
914 Pine St, Mount Shasta (96067-2143)
PHONE.................................530 926-6111
Kenneth Platou, *CEO*
EMP: 340 **Privately Held**
WEB: www.mercyhealth.org
SIC: 8062 General medical & surgical hospitals
HQ: Mercy Home Services A California Limited Partnership
2175 Rosaline Ave Ste A
Redding CA 96001
530 225-6000

(P-21042)
MERCY HM SVCS A CAL LTD PARTNR
Also Called: Mercy General Hospital
4001 J St, Sacramento (95819-3626)
PHONE.................................916 453-4545
Edmundo Castaneda, *President*
Conrad Megia, *Vice Pres*
Cynthia Kirch, *VP Human Res*
Jane Crable, *Maintence Staff*
EMP: 1000 **Privately Held**
WEB: www.mercyhealth.org
SIC: 8062 Hospital, affiliated with AMA residency
HQ: Mercy Home Services A California Limited Partnership
2175 Rosaline Ave Ste A
Redding CA 96001
530 225-6000

(P-21043)
MERCY HM SVCS A CAL LTD PARTNR
Also Called: Mercy Medical Center
2740 M St, Merced (95340-2813)
PHONE.................................209 564-4200
Lisa Wegley, *Manager*
Kingshuk Sharma, *Med Doctor*
EMP: 340 **Privately Held**
WEB: www.mercyhealth.org
SIC: 8062 General medical & surgical hospitals
HQ: Mercy Home Services A California Limited Partnership
2175 Rosaline Ave Ste A
Redding CA 96001
530 225-6000

(P-21044)
METHODIST HOSP SOUTHERN CAL (PA)
300 W Huntington Dr, Arcadia
(91007-3402)
PHONE.................................626 898-8000
Dan F Ausman, *CEO*
Bridgett Didier, *Records Dir*
Clifford R Daniels, *Senior VP*
William E Grigg, *Senior VP*
Steven A Sisto, *Senior VP*
EMP: 2200
SQ FT: 100,000
SALES: 300MM **Privately Held**
SIC: 8062 General medical & surgical hospitals

(P-21045)
METHODIST HOSPITAL OF S CA
300 W Huntington Dr, Arcadia
(91007-3402)
P.O. Box 60016 (91066-6016)
PHONE................................626 574-3755
Dennis Lee, *Principal*
Jason Aranda, *Manager*
EMP: 61
SALES (est): 7.2MM **Privately Held**
SIC: 8062 General medical & surgical hospitals

(P-21046)
MISSION HOSP REGIONAL MED CTR (PA)
27700 Medical Center Rd, Mission Viejo
(92691-6426)
PHONE................................949 364-1400
Seth Peigen, *CEO*
Robert Deshaies, *Treasurer*
Katherine Davis, *Officer*
Terry Wooten, *Officer*
Mark Jablonski, *Vice Pres*
EMP: 1349
SQ FT: 750,000
SALES (est): 547.3MM **Privately Held**
WEB: www.drvonmaur.com
SIC: 8062 General medical & surgical hospitals

(P-21047)
MOFFITT H C HOSPITAL
505 Parnassus Ave, San Francisco
(94143-2204)
PHONE................................415 476-1000
EMP: 148 EST: 2008
SALES (est): 283.3K
SALES (corp-wide): 9.5B **Privately Held**
SIC: 8062
HQ: University Of California, San Francisco
505 Parnassus Ave
San Francisco CA 94143
415 476-9000

(P-21048)
MONTEREY PARK HOSPITAL
Also Called: Monterey Park Hospital
900 S Atlantic Blvd, Monterey Park
(91754-4780)
PHONE................................626 570-9000
Philip A Cohen, *CEO*
Robert M Dubbs, *President*
Robert W Fleming Jr, *Senior VP*
Minerva Mandujano, *Administration*
Gretchen Lindeman, *Human Res Dir*
EMP: 150
SQ FT: 90,575
SALES: 74.7MM
SALES (corp-wide): 570.2MM **Privately Held**
WEB: www.montereyparkhosp.com
SIC: 8062 General medical & surgical hospitals
PA: Ahmc Healthcare Inc.
1000 S Fremont Ave Unit 6
Alhambra CA 91803

(P-21049)
MONTEREY PENINSULA HOSPITAL
Also Called: Community Hosp Recovery Ctr
576 Hartnell St Ste 260, Monterey
(93940-2887)
PHONE................................831 373-0924
Oscar Reyes, *Director*
Wayne Lavengood, *Manager*
EMP: 50
SALES (est): 1.7MM
SALES (corp-wide): 145.4MM **Privately Held**
SIC: 8062 General medical & surgical hospitals
PA: Montage Health
23625 Holman Hwy
Monterey CA 93940
831 625-4830

(P-21050)
MOTION PICTURE AND TV FUND (PA)
Also Called: Bob Hope Health Center
23388 Mulholland Dr # 200, Woodland Hills
(91364-2733)
P.O. Box 51151, Los Angeles (90051-5451)
PHONE................................818 876-1777
Robert Beitcher, *CEO*
Bob Pisano, *Ch of Bd*
Jay Roth, *Treasurer*
Scott Kaiser, *Officer*
Mike Kuehl, *Vice Pres*
EMP: 688 EST: 1924
SQ FT: 50,000
SALES: 23MM **Privately Held**
WEB: www.mptvfund.org
SIC: 8062 8051 8011 8351 General medical & surgical hospitals; convalescent home with continuous nursing care; medical centers; child day care services; individual & family services; retirement hotel operation

(P-21051)
MOUNTAIN COMM HLTH CRE DIST
Also Called: Trinity Hospital
410 N Taylor St, Weaverville (96093)
P.O. Box 1229 (96093-1229)
PHONE................................530 623-5541
David Yarbrough, *Director*
EMP: 130
SALES (corp-wide): 15.2MM **Privately Held**
SIC: 8062 General medical & surgical hospitals
PA: Mountain Communities Health Care District
60 Easter Ave
Weaverville CA 96093
530 623-5541

(P-21052)
MOUNTAIN COMM HLTH CRE DIST (PA)
Also Called: Trinity Hospital
60 Easter Ave, Weaverville (96093)
P.O. Box 1229 (96093-1229)
PHONE................................530 623-5541
Aaron Rogers, *CEO*
Julia Mooney, *Med Doctor*
EMP: 108
SALES: 15.2MM **Privately Held**
WEB: www.mcmedical.org
SIC: 8062 General medical & surgical hospitals

(P-21053)
MOUNTAIN VIEW CHILD CARE INC (PA)
Also Called: Totally Kids Rhbilitation Hosp
1720 Mountain View Ave, Loma Linda
(92354-1799)
PHONE................................909 796-6915
Doug Pagett, *CEO*
Irwin Hansen, *COO*
Cynthia Capetillo, *CFO*
Donald Nydam, *Vice Pres*
Loma Linda, *Principal*
EMP: 490
SALES (est): 46.3MM **Privately Held**
SIC: 8062 8052 8051 General medical & surgical hospitals; intermediate care facilities; skilled nursing care facilities

(P-21054)
MOUNTAINS COMMUNITY HOSP FNDTN
29101 Hospital Rd, Lake Arrowhead
(92352-9706)
P.O. Box 70 (92352-0070)
PHONE................................909 336-3651
Don Willerth, *CEO*
Kim McGuire, *Director*
EMP: 180
SQ FT: 18,500
SALES: 520.9K **Privately Held**
WEB: www.mchcares.com
SIC: 8062 8051 General medical & surgical hospitals; skilled nursing care facilities

(P-21055)
MUIR LABS
Also Called: Muirlab
1601 Ygnacio Valley Rd, Walnut Creek
(94598-3122)
PHONE................................925 947-3335
Pat Morgan, *Director*
Deborah Droker, *Director*
EMP: 400
SALES (est): 5.4MM **Privately Held**
SIC: 8062 General medical & surgical hospitals

(P-21056)
NATIVIDAD MEDICAL CENTER
Also Called: Occupational Medicine
1441 Constitution Blvd, Salinas
(93906-3100)
PHONE................................831 755-4111
Gary Gray, *CEO*
EMP: 659
SALES: 211.3MM **Privately Held**
WEB: www.natividad.com
SIC: 8062 8011 8093 General medical & surgical hospitals; offices & clinics of medical doctors; specialty outpatient clinics

(P-21057)
NORTH SONOMA COUNTY HOSP DST
Also Called: Healdsburg District Hospital
1375 University St, Healdsburg
(95448-3382)
PHONE................................707 431-6500
Evan J Rayner, *CEO*
Chung LI, *Records Dir*
Regina Novello, *COO*
Dan Hull, *CFO*
Lynda Guthrie, *Exec Dir*
EMP: 171
SALES (est): 41.3MM **Privately Held**
SIC: 8062 General medical & surgical hospitals

(P-21058)
NORTHBAY HEALTHCARE CORP (PA)
Also Called: Northbay Healthcare System
1200 B Gale Wilson Blvd, Fairfield
(94533-3552)
PHONE................................707 646-5000
Gary J Passama, *President*
Nicole Brocato, *Vice Pres*
Wayne Gietz, *Vice Pres*
Jerry Simmers, *Lab Dir*
Kathy Richerson, *Ch Nursing Ofcr*
EMP: 114
SQ FT: 24,000
SALES (est): 69.9MM **Privately Held**
SIC: 8062 8011 General medical & surgical hospitals; offices & clinics of medical doctors

(P-21059)
NORTHBAY HEALTHCARE GROUP (PA)
Also Called: Northbay Medical Center
1200 B Gale Wilson Blvd, Fairfield
(94533-3552)
PHONE................................707 646-5000
Toll Free:................................888 -
Deborah Sugiyama, *CEO*
Christopher Timbers, *Vice Pres*
Traci Duncan, *Ch Nursing Ofcr*
Kathy Halkett, *Technician*
Darrin Salswedel, *Purch Mgr*
EMP: 900
SQ FT: 125,000
SALES: 530.8MM **Privately Held**
SIC: 8062 General medical & surgical hospitals

(P-21060)
NORTHBAY HEALTHCARE GROUP
Also Called: Vaca Valley Hospital
1000 Nut Tree Rd, Vacaville (95687-4100)
PHONE................................707 446-4000
Debra Sugiyama, *President*
Lynn McCormick, *Records Dir*
Elnora Cameron, *Vice Pres*
Dave Mathews, *Engineer*
Lorie Jarvis, *Personnel Assit*
EMP: 1200

SQ FT: 59,000
SALES (corp-wide): 530.8MM **Privately Held**
SIC: 8062 General medical & surgical hospitals
PA: Northbay Healthcare Group
1200 B Gale Wilson Blvd
Fairfield CA 94533
707 646-5000

(P-21061)
NORTHERN CALIFORNIA REHAB
2801 Eureka Way, Redding (96001-0222)
PHONE................................530 246-9000
Brad Hollinger, *Mng Member*
Penny Booth, *Info Tech Dir*
Lisa Stevens, *Opers Staff*
Stephen Marcus,
Mark Cardenas, *Manager*
EMP: 250
SALES: 39.2MM
SALES (corp-wide): 330.4MM **Privately Held**
SIC: 8062 General medical & surgical hospitals
PA: Vibra Healthcare, Llc
4600 Lena Dr Ste 100
Mechanicsburg PA 17055
717 591-5700

(P-21062)
NORTHERN INYO HEALTHCARE DST
Also Called: NORTHERN INYO HOSPITAL
150 Pioneer Ln, Bishop (93514-2556)
PHONE................................760 873-5811
Victoria Alexander-Lane, *CEO*
M C Hubbard, *President*
Peter Watercott, *Treasurer*
Evelyn Camposdiaz, *Officer*
Kathryn Erickson, *Officer*
EMP: 402
SQ FT: 55,000
SALES: 88MM **Privately Held**
WEB: www.nih.org
SIC: 8062 General medical & surgical hospitals

(P-21063)
NORWALK COMMUNITY HOSPITAL
13222 Bloomfield Ave, Norwalk
(90650-3200)
PHONE................................562 863-4763
David Topper, *President*
David Herrera, *Vice Pres*
EMP: 100
SQ FT: 18,935
SALES (est): 11.2MM
SALES (corp-wide): 1.2B **Privately Held**
SIC: 8062 General medical & surgical hospitals
HQ: Alta Healthcare System Llc
4081 E Olympic Blvd
Los Angeles CA 90023
323 267-0477

(P-21064)
OAK VALLEY HOSPITAL DISTRICT (DH)
350 S Oak Ave, Oakdale (95361-3519)
PHONE................................209 847-3011
John McCormick, *CEO*
Bob Wikoff, *Ch of Bd*
Gail Sward, *Vice Ch Bd*
Sherry Arndt, *Legal Exec*
EMP: 325
SQ FT: 55,000
SALES: 66.4MM **Privately Held**
WEB: www.ovhd.com
SIC: 8062 8051 General medical & surgical hospitals; skilled nursing care facilities
HQ: Dignity Health
185 Berry St Ste 300
San Francisco CA 94107
415 438-5500

(P-21065)
OCONNOR HOSPITAL
Also Called: O'Connor Hospital Pedia Center
2039 Forest Ave, San Jose (95128-4817)
P.O. Box 1347, San Carlos (94070-7347)
PHONE................................408 947-2929
James F Dover, *President*

▲ = Import ▼=Export
◆ =Import/Export

EMP: 58 **Privately Held**
SIC: 8062 General medical & surgical hospitals
HQ: O'connor Hospital
2105 Forest Ave
San Jose CA 95128
408 947-2500

(P-21066)
OCONNOR HOSPITAL (HQ)
Also Called: O'Connor Wound Care Clinic
2105 Forest Ave, San Jose (95128-1471)
PHONE.................................408 947-2500
Richard Adcock, *CEO*
James F Dover, *CEO*
David W Carroll, *Senior VP*
Craig Rucker, *Vice Pres*
Dennnis Kim, *Pharmacist*
EMP: 1000
SQ FT: 750,000
SALES (est): 216MM **Privately Held**
SIC: 8062 General medical & surgical hospitals
PA: County Of Santa Clara
3180 Newberry Dr Ste 150
San Jose CA 95118
408 299-5105

(P-21067)
OLYMPIA HEALTH CARE LLC
Also Called: Olympia Medical Center
5900 W Olympic Blvd, Los Angeles
(90036-4671)
PHONE.................................323 938-3161
John A Calderone, *CEO*
Babur Ozkan, *CFO*
Sheryl Howland, *Ch Nursing Ofcr*
Maria Shah, *CTO*
Jason Williams, *Info Tech Mgr*
EMP: 875 EST: 2004
SQ FT: 500,000
SALES (est): 37.7MM
SALES (corp-wide): 1.3B **Privately Held**
SIC: 8062 Hospital, affiliated with AMA residency
PA: Alecto Healthcare Services Llc
16310 Bake Pkwy Ste 200
Irvine CA 92618
323 938-3161

(P-21068)
ORANGE COAST MEMORIAL MED CTR (HQ)
9920 Talbert Ave, Fountain Valley
(92708-5153)
PHONE.................................714 378-7000
Toll Free:.................................888 -
Marcia Manker, *President*
David Steward, *Records Dir*
Aaron Coley, *CFO*
Steve McNamara, *CFO*
Francis Sirotnak, *Lab Dir*
EMP: 79
SQ FT: 40,361
SALES: 245.8MM
SALES (corp-wide): 2.4B **Privately Held**
SIC: 8062 General medical & surgical hospitals
PA: Memorial Health Services
17360 Brookhurst St # 160
Fountain Valley CA 92708
714 377-6748

(P-21069)
ORANGE COUNTY ROYALE CONVLSCNT
Also Called: Royale Hlth Care Mission Viejo
23228 Madero, Mission Viejo (92691-2706)
PHONE.................................949 458-6346
William Arellanes, *Exec Dir*
Jenny Forkey, *Manager*
EMP: 100
SQ FT: 54,500
SALES (corp-wide): 17MM **Privately Held**
WEB: www.royalehealth.com
SIC: 8062 General medical & surgical hospitals
PA: Orange County Royale Convalescent Hospital, Inc.
1030 W Warner Ave
Santa Ana CA 92707
714 546-6450

(P-21070)
ORCHARD HOSPITAL
240 Spruce St, Gridley (95948-2216)
P.O. Box 97 (95948-0097)
PHONE.................................530 846-9000
Steve Stark, *CEO*
Kristina Sanke, *CFO*
Kirsten Stome, *Social Dir*
Matt Washburn, *Safety Mgr*
Catherine Smith,
EMP: 235
SQ FT: 12,000
SALES: 24.4MM **Privately Held**
SIC: 8062 General medical & surgical hospitals

(P-21071)
ORTHOPAEDIC HOSPITAL (PA)
Also Called: Orthopaedic Inst For Children
403 W Adams Blvd, Los Angeles
(90007-2664)
P.O. Box 60132 (90060-0132)
PHONE.................................213 742-1000
Anthony A Scaduto, *President*
Diane Moon, *CFO*
Nicholas V McClure, *Bd of Directors*
EMP: 180
SQ FT: 105,000
SALES: 48.7MM **Privately Held**
SIC: 8062 8011 General medical & surgical hospitals; primary care medical clinic

(P-21072)
PACIFIC HEALTH CORPORATION
Also Called: Anaheim General Hospital
3699 Wilshire Blvd # 540, Los Angeles
(90010-2723)
PHONE.................................714 619-7797
Fax: 714 761-1295
EMP: 500
SALES (corp-wide): 93MM **Privately Held**
SIC: 8062
HQ: Pacific Health Corporation
14642 Newport Ave
Tustin CA 92780
714 838-9600

(P-21073)
PACIFIC OCCPTNAL MEDICINE SVCS
2776 Pacific Ave, Long Beach
(90806-2613)
PHONE.................................562 997-2290
Michael PH, *Principal*
Kathy Gerard, *Principal*
EMP: 50
SALES (est): 753.3K **Privately Held**
SIC: 8062 General medical & surgical hospitals

(P-21074)
PACIFICA OF VALLEY CORPORATION
Also Called: Pacifica Hospital of Valley
9449 San Fernando Rd, Sun Valley
(91352-1421)
PHONE.................................818 767-3310
Paul Tuft, *Ch of Bd*
Ayman Mousa, *CEO*
Pat Golden, *Nursing Dir*
Jay Santos, *Supervisor*
EMP: 607
SQ FT: 148,020
SALES (est): 109.8MM **Privately Held**
WEB: www.pacificahospital.com
SIC: 8062 Hospital, affiliated with AMA residency

(P-21075)
PALO ALTO MED FNDTION STA CRUZ
2025 Soquel Ave, Santa Cruz
(95062-1323)
PHONE.................................831 458-5670
Larry Beghttaldi, *President*
Howard Salvay MD, *Admin Sec*
Gail Hoover, *Relations*
Pia Zoliniak, *Supervisor*
EMP: 2000
SALES (est): 69.1MM **Privately Held**
SIC: 8062 General medical & surgical hospitals

(P-21076)
PALO VERDE HEALTH CARE DST
Also Called: Palo Verde Hospital
250 N 1st St, Blythe (92225-1702)
PHONE.................................760 922-4115
Sandra J Anaya, *CEO*
Dennis Rutherford, *CFO*
EMP: 180 EST: 1938
SALES: 23.8MM **Privately Held**
WEB: www.paloverdehospital.com
SIC: 8062 8069 General medical & surgical hospitals; specialty hospitals, except psychiatric

(P-21077)
PALO VERDE HOSPITAL ASSN
250 N 1st St, Blythe (92225-1702)
PHONE.................................760 922-4115
Sandra J Anaya, *CEO*
Jim Carney, *President*
Larry Blitz, *CEO*
Samuel Burton, *Treasurer*
Beatrice Pinon, *Vice Pres*
EMP: 135
SQ FT: 44,000
SALES (est): 23.4MM **Privately Held**
SIC: 8062 General medical & surgical hospitals

(P-21078)
PALOMAR HEALTH
Also Called: Patient Business Services
555 E Valley Pkwy 6, Escondido
(92025-3048)
PHONE.................................858 675-5360
Laurie Rose, *Manager*
Timothy Barlow, *Lab Dir*
Dennis Dechant, *Administration*
Lauren Van Winkle, *Analyst*
Joseph Parker, *Nurse*
EMP: 300
SALES (corp-wide): 502.8MM **Privately Held**
WEB: www.sunbridge.com
SIC: 8062 General medical & surgical hospitals
PA: Palomar Health
456 E Grand Ave
Escondido CA 92025
442 281-5000

(P-21079)
PALOMAR HEALTH (PA)
Also Called: Palomar Medical Center
456 E Grand Ave, Escondido (92025-3319)
PHONE.................................442 281-5000
Doug Moir, *Principal*
Jerry Kolins, *Ch Pathology*
Robert McCaulley, *Officer*
Prudence August, *Vice Pres*
Bill Tench, *Associate Dir*
EMP: 180
SQ FT: 66,000
SALES (est): 502.8MM **Privately Held**
WEB: www.sunbridge.com
SIC: 8062 8059 General medical & surgical hospitals; convalescent home

(P-21080)
PALOMAR HEALTH
Also Called: Palomar Medical Center
2185 Citracado Pkwy, Escondido
(92029-4159)
PHONE.................................760 739-3000
Michael Covert, *CEO*
Lachlan Macleay, *Associate Dir*
Tye Stewart, *Office Mgr*
Suzanne Martin, *Nursing Mgr*
Deborah Hollick, *Executive Asst*
EMP: 1200
SALES (corp-wide): 502.8MM **Privately Held**
WEB: www.sunbridge.com
SIC: 8062 General medical & surgical hospitals
PA: Palomar Health
456 E Grand Ave
Escondido CA 92025
442 281-5000

(P-21081)
PALOMAR HEALTH
Also Called: Pomerado Hospital
15615 Pomerado Rd, Poway (92064-2405)
PHONE.................................858 613-4000

Jim Flinn, *Administration*
Larry Labossiere, *Ch Nursing Ofcr*
Gil Carson, *Administration*
Elainne Payumo,
Nina Kim, *Manager*
EMP: 300
SALES (corp-wide): 502.8MM **Privately Held**
WEB: www.sunbridge.com
SIC: 8062 General medical & surgical hospitals
PA: Palomar Health
456 E Grand Ave
Escondido CA 92025
442 281-5000

(P-21082)
PAMC LTD (PA)
Also Called: Pamc Health Foundation
531 W College St, Los Angeles
(90012-2315)
PHONE.................................213 624-8411
John Edwards, *CEO*
EMP: 530
SQ FT: 75,600
SALES (est): 56.7MM **Privately Held**
SIC: 8062 General medical & surgical hospitals

(P-21083)
PARACELSUS LOS ANGELES COMM
4081 E Olympic Blvd, Los Angeles
(90023-3330)
PHONE.................................323 267-0477
Lou Rubino, *Acting CEO*
Omar Ramirez, *COO*
Keith Levy, *Analyst*
Janine Yoshida, *Human Res Dir*
Hector Enriquez, *Purch Dir*
EMP: 250
SALES: 141.6MM **Privately Held**
SIC: 8062 General medical & surgical hospitals

(P-21084)
PARADISE VALLEY HOSPITAL
Also Called: West Health Care
180 Otay Lakes Rd Ste 100, Bonita
(91902-2464)
PHONE.................................619 472-7474
Connie Mayo, *Director*
Fredd Delost, *Manager*
EMP: 80
SALES (corp-wide): 144.4MM **Privately Held**
WEB: www.paradisevalleyhospital.org
SIC: 8062 General medical & surgical hospitals
PA: Paradise Valley Hospital
2400 E 4th St
National City CA 91950
619 470-4100

(P-21085)
PARKVIEW CMNTY HOSP MED CTR
3865 Jackson St, Riverside (92503-3919)
PHONE.................................951 354-7404
Norm Martin, *President*
Doug Drumwright, *CEO*
Catherine O Dell, *Admin Sec*
EMP: 1149
SQ FT: 132,651
SALES: 162.7MM **Privately Held**
SIC: 8062 8011 General medical & surgical hospitals; offices & clinics of medical doctors
PA: Doctors Hospital Of Riverside Llc
3865 Jackson St
Riverside CA 92503
951 354-7404

(P-21086)
PASADENA CYTO PATHOLOGY LAB
Also Called: Huntington Med Pathology Group
100 W Calif Blvd Fl 3, Pasadena
(91105-3010)
PHONE.................................626 397-8616
Susan Murakami MD, *President*
Henry Slosser MD, *Vice Pres*
Steve Ralph, *Director*
EMP: 300

PRODUCTS & SVCS

SALES (est): 7.3MM **Privately Held**
SIC: **8062** General medical & surgical hospitals

(P-21087)
PATIENTS HOSPITAL
2900 Eureka Way, Redding (96001-0220)
PHONE..................................530 225-8700
James D Tate MD, *President*
Shari Lejsek, *Administration*
Ezra Hemping, *Engineer*
EMP: 80
SALES: 5.9MM **Privately Held**
WEB: www.patientshospital.com
SIC: **8062** General medical & surgical hospitals

(P-21088)
PERMANENTE MEDICAL GROUP INC
Also Called: Labratory
2425 Geary Blvd, San Francisco (94115-3358)
PHONE..................................415 833-2000
Harry Chima, *Manager*
EMP: 100
SALES (corp-wide): 76.5B **Privately Held**
WEB: www.permanente.net
SIC: **8062** General medical & surgical hospitals
HQ: The Permanente Medical Group Inc
1950 Franklin St Fl 18th
Oakland CA 94612
866 858-2226

(P-21089)
PERMANENTE MEDICAL GROUP INC
1550 Gateway Blvd, Fairfield (94533-6901)
PHONE..................................707 427-4000
Laura Coffman, *Branch Mgr*
Seema Rizvi, *Internal Med*
Pat Van Nordstrom, *Manager*
EMP: 50
SALES (corp-wide): 76.5B **Privately Held**
WEB: www.permanente.net
SIC: **8062** General medical & surgical hospitals
HQ: The Permanente Medical Group Inc
1950 Franklin St Fl 18th
Oakland CA 94612
866 858-2226

(P-21090)
PERRIS VALLEY CMNTY HOSP LLC (PA)
Also Called: Vista Specialty Hosp Riverside
2224 Medical Center Dr, Perris (92571-2638)
PHONE..................................951 436-5000
James Linhares, *Mng Member*
Tawanda Whitaker, *Records Dir*
Marc C Ferrell, *Mng Member*
Marc A Furstman, *Mng Member*
ARA Tavitian, *Mng Member*
EMP: 260
SALES (est): 6.1MM **Privately Held**
SIC: **8062** General medical & surgical hospitals

(P-21091)
PERRIS VALLEY CMNTY HOSP LLC
Also Called: Vista Hospital Riverside
10841 White Oak Ave, Rancho Cucamonga (91730-3817)
PHONE..................................909 581-6400
Edward L Kuntz, *CEO*
EMP: 234 **Privately Held**
SIC: **8062** General medical & surgical hospitals
PA: Perris Valley Community Hospital, Llc
2224 Medical Center Dr
Perris CA 92571

(P-21092)
PHYSICIANS FOR HEALTHY HOSPITA (HQ)
Also Called: PHH
1117 E Devonshire Ave, Hemet (92543-3083)
PHONE..................................951 652-2811
Kali Chaudhuri, *CEO*
Sreenivasa Nakka, *President*

Ashok Agarwal, *Vice Pres*
Kali Priyo Chaudhuri, *Vice Pres*
Neelam Gupta, *Vice Pres*
EMP: 57 EST: 2009
SALES: 150.8MM
SALES (corp-wide): 407.3MM **Privately Held**
SIC: **8062** General medical & surgical hospitals
PA: Kpc Healthcare, Inc.
1301 N Tustin Ave
Santa Ana CA 92705
714 953-3652

(P-21093)
PHYSICIANS FOR HEALTHY HOSPITA
Also Called: Menifee Valley Hospital Center
28400 Mccall Blvd, Sun City (92585-9658)
PHONE..................................951 679-8888
Jeffrey Lang, *CEO*
EMP: 300
SALES (corp-wide): 407.3MM **Privately Held**
SIC: **8062** General medical & surgical hospitals
HQ: Physicians For Healthy Hospitals, Inc.
1117 E Devonshire Ave
Hemet CA 92543
951 652-2811

(P-21094)
PHYSICIANS FOR HEALTHY HOSPITA
Also Called: Leland Health Care Services
371 N Weston Pl, Hemet (92543-3006)
PHONE..................................951 652-2811
Carol Wood, *Director*
EMP: 110
SALES (corp-wide): 407.3MM **Privately Held**
SIC: **8062** 8051 8059 General medical & surgical hospitals; skilled nursing care facilities; nursing home, except skilled & intermediate care facility
HQ: Physicians For Healthy Hospitals, Inc.
1117 E Devonshire Ave
Hemet CA 92543
951 652-2811

(P-21095)
PHYSICIANS FOR HEALTHY HOSPITA
1280 S Buena Vista St, San Jacinto (92583-4604)
PHONE..................................951 652-2811
Tim Murray, *Manager*
EMP: 180
SALES (corp-wide): 407.3MM **Privately Held**
SIC: **8062** General medical & surgical hospitals
HQ: Physicians For Healthy Hospitals, Inc.
1117 E Devonshire Ave
Hemet CA 92543
951 652-2811

(P-21096)
PIH HEALTH HOSPITAL - DOWNEY
Also Called: General Acute Care Hospital
11500 Brookshire Ave, Downey (90241-4917)
PHONE..................................562 698-0811
James R West, *President*
Bryan Smolskis, *COO*
Greg Williams, *CFO*
Kenton Woods, *Treasurer*
Rosalio Lopez MD, *Senior VP*
EMP: 1150
SQ FT: 225,000
SALES: 126.8MM
SALES (corp-wide): 457.5MM **Privately Held**
SIC: **8062** General medical & surgical hospitals
PA: Pih Health Hospital - Whittier
12401 Washington Blvd
Whittier CA 90602
562 698-0811

(P-21097)
PIH HEALTH HOSPITAL - WHITTI
122 N Primrose Ave Apt A, Monrovia (91016-2162)
PHONE..................................626 357-6876
EMP: 399
SALES (corp-wide): 457.5MM **Privately Held**
SIC: **8062** 8011 General medical & surgical hospitals; clinic, operated by physicians
PA: Pih Health Hospital - Whittier
12401 Washington Blvd
Whittier CA 90602
562 698-0811

(P-21098)
PIH HEALTH HOSPITAL - WHITTI
Also Called: Downey Regional Medical Center
11500 Brookshire Ave, Downey (90241-4917)
PHONE..................................562 904-5482
James R West, *CEO*
EMP: 1150
SALES (corp-wide): 457.5MM **Privately Held**
SIC: **8062** 8071 General medical & surgical hospitals; medical laboratories
PA: Pih Health Hospital - Whittier
12401 Washington Blvd
Whittier CA 90602
562 698-0811

(P-21099)
PIH HEALTH HOSPITAL - WHITTIER (PA)
Also Called: General Acute Care Hospital
12401 Washington Blvd, Whittier (90602-1006)
PHONE..................................562 698-0811
James R West, *CEO*
Mitchell Thomas, *CFO*
Greg Williams, *CFO*
Peggy Chulack, *Officer*
Ramona Pratt, *Officer*
EMP: 1900
SQ FT: 500,000
SALES (est): 457.5MM **Privately Held**
SIC: **8062** General medical & surgical hospitals

(P-21100)
PIONEERS MEM HEALTHCARE DST (PA)
Also Called: PIONEERS MEMORIAL HOSPITAL
207 W Legion Rd, Brawley (92227-7780)
PHONE..................................760 351-3333
Richard L Mendoza, *CEO*
Roger Armstrong, *CFO*
Daniel Heckathorne, *CFO*
Justina Aguirre, *Vice Pres*
Bill Railsback, *Lab Dir*
EMP: 571
SQ FT: 171,445
SALES: 126.5MM **Privately Held**
WEB: www.pioneersmemorialhospital.com
SIC: **8062** Hospital, affiliated with AMA residency

(P-21101)
PLUMAS DISTRICT HOSPITAL (PA)
1065 Bucks Lake Rd, Quincy (95971-9599)
PHONE..................................530 283-2121
Doug Lafferty, *President*
Tiffany Leonhardt, *Marketing Mgr*
Susan Brown, *Nurse*
▲ EMP: 180 EST: 1959
SQ FT: 30,000
SALES: 20.4MM **Privately Held**
SIC: **8062** Hospital, affiliated with AMA residency

(P-21102)
POMONA VALLEY HOSPITAL MED CTR (PA)
Also Called: PVHMC
1798 N Garey Ave, Pomona (91767-2918)
PHONE..................................909 865-9500
Richard E Yochum, *CEO*
Jasvir Sandhu,
James Dale, *Vice Chairman*
Rosie Rieger, *President*

Kurt Weinmeister, *COO*
EMP: 2121
SQ FT: 362,000
SALES: 654.6MM **Privately Held**
WEB: www.pvhmc.org
SIC: **8062** Hospital, medical school affiliated with residency

(P-21103)
POMONA VALLEY HOSPITAL MED CTR
Also Called: Claremont Outpatient Clinic
1601 Monte Vista Ave, Claremont (91711-2962)
PHONE..................................909 865-9104
Joan Harper, *Manager*
EMP: 728
SALES (corp-wide): 654.6MM **Privately Held**
SIC: **8062** Hospital, medical school affiliated with residency
PA: Pomona Valley Hospital Medical Center
1798 N Garey Ave
Pomona CA 91767
909 865-9500

(P-21104)
POMONA VALLEY HOSPITAL MED CTR
Also Called: Montclair Physical Therapy
1601 Monte Vista Ave # 270, Claremont (91711-2962)
PHONE..................................909 865-9977
Antoinette Fernandez, *Director*
EMP: 728
SALES (corp-wide): 654.6MM **Privately Held**
WEB: www.montclairphysicaltherapy.com
SIC: **8062** Hospital, medical school affiliated with residency
PA: Pomona Valley Hospital Medical Center
1798 N Garey Ave
Pomona CA 91767
909 865-9500

(P-21105)
PRESBYTERIAN HEALTH PHYSICIANS
6557 Greenleaf Ave, Whittier (90601-4108)
PHONE..................................562 464-4717
Marvin Rice, *President*
Walter Price, *Director*
EMP: 173
SQ FT: 72,000
SALES: 82.7MM
SALES (corp-wide): 27.7MM **Privately Held**
SIC: **8062** General medical & surgical hospitals
PA: Interhealth Corp.
12401 Washington Blvd
Whittier CA 90602
562 698-0811

(P-21106)
PRIME HEALTH CARE SVCS GRDN GR
Also Called: Garden Grove Hospital Med Ctr
12601 Garden Grove Blvd, Garden Grove (92843-1908)
PHONE..................................714 537-5160
Mike Sarian, *President*
Kevan Metcalfe, *CEO*
Alan Smith, *CFO*
Sofia Abrina, *Administration*
EMP: 500
SALES: 101.8MM **Privately Held**
SIC: **8062** General medical & surgical hospitals

(P-21107)
PRIME HEALTHCARE ANAHEIM LLC
Also Called: WEST ANAHEIM MEDICAL CENTER
3033 W Orange Ave, Anaheim (92804-3156)
PHONE..................................714 827-3000
Virg Narbutas, *CEO*
Mylinh Bui, *CFO*
Kora Guoyavatin, *CFO*
David Lang, *Executive*
Reena Mahadevan, *Engineer*
EMP: 800 EST: 1963
SQ FT: 180,000

SALES: 123.9MM
SALES (corp-wide): 3.4B **Privately Held**
SIC: 8062 Hospital, affiliated with AMA residency
HQ: Prime Healthcare Services Inc
3300 E Guasti Rd Ste 300
Ontario CA 91761
-

(P-21108)
PRIME HEALTHCARE CENTINELA LLC
Also Called: Centinela Hospital Medical Ctr
555 E Hardy St, Inglewood (90301-4011)
PHONE.....................310 673-4660
Linda Bradley, *CEO*
Jeffrey Benson, *Administration*
Matt Ewert, *Technician*
Kavya Kandula, *Technology*
Tommy Lasorda, *Surgeon*
EMP: 1500
SALES: 259.6MM
SALES (corp-wide): 3.4B **Privately Held**
SIC: 8062 General medical & surgical hospitals
HQ: Prime Healthcare Services Inc
3300 E Guasti Rd Ste 300
Ontario CA 91761
-

(P-21109)
PRIME HEALTHCARE SERVICES
Also Called: Shasta Regional Med Ctr Srmc
1100 Butte St, Redding (96001-0852)
P.O. Box 491810 (96049-1810)
PHONE.....................530 244-5400
Cyndy Gordon, *CEO*
Paul Beck,
Paul Mazur,
Linda Leaell, *COO*
Glen Hayward, *Bd of Directors*
EMP: 850
SALES: 152.3MM
SALES (corp-wide): 3.4B **Privately Held**
SIC: 8062 8011 General medical & surgical hospitals; offices & clinics of medical doctors
HQ: Prime Healthcare Services Inc
3300 E Guasti Rd Ste 300
Ontario CA 91761
-

(P-21110)
PRIME HEALTHCARE SERVS SH
1450 Liberty St, Redding (96001-0838)
P.O. Box 491810 (96049-1810)
PHONE.....................530 244-5458
Cindy Gordon, *CEO*
EMP: 902
SALES: 50MM **Privately Held**
SIC: 8062 General medical & surgical hospitals

(P-21111)
PRIME HEALTHCARE SVCS II LLC
Also Called: Sherman Oaks Hospital
4929 Van Nuys Blvd, Sherman Oaks
(91403-1702)
PHONE.....................818 981-7111
Prem Reddy, *CEO*
John Deady, *CFO*
Edgar Nunes, *Research*
EMP: 500
SQ FT: 36,000
SALES: 62.4MM
SALES (corp-wide): 3.4B **Privately Held**
SIC: 8062 General medical & surgical hospitals
HQ: Prime Healthcare Services Inc
3300 E Guasti Rd Ste 300
Ontario CA 91761
-

(P-21112)
PRIME HEALTHCARE SVCS III LLC (DH)
Also Called: MONTCLAIR HOSPITAL MEDICAL CENTER
5000 San Bernardino St, Montclair
(91763-2326)
PHONE.....................909 625-5411
Jennifer Ramirez, *Exec Sec*
Prem Reddy, *Chairman*
David Chu, *Manager*
EMP: 102

SALES: 55.5MM
SALES (corp-wide): 3.4B **Privately Held**
WEB: www.dhmcm.com
SIC: 8062 General medical & surgical hospitals

(P-21113)
PRIME HEALTHCARE-SAN DIMAS LLC
Also Called: SAN DIMAS COMMUNITY HOSPITAL
1350 W Covina Blvd, San Dimas
(91773-3245)
PHONE.....................909 599-6811
Gregory Brentano, *CEO*
Dan Galles, *CFO*
Maria Cordon,
EMP: 350
SQ FT: 90,000
SALES: 60MM
SALES (corp-wide): 3.4B **Privately Held**
SIC: 8062 General medical & surgical hospitals
HQ: Prime Healthcare Services Inc
3300 E Guasti Rd Ste 300
Ontario CA 91761
-

(P-21114)
PRIME HLTHCARE HNTNGTON BCH
Also Called: Huntington Beach Hospital
17772 Beach Blvd, Huntington Beach
(92647-6819)
PHONE.....................714 843-5000
Prem Reddy, *CEO*
Eileen Fisler, *CEO*
Ravi Alla, *Vice Pres*
Mark Bell, *Med Doctor*
David Bloom, *Med Doctor*
EMP: 480 EST: 1957
SQ FT: 100,000
SALES (est): 52.5MM
SALES (corp-wide): 3.4B **Privately Held**
WEB: www.hbhospital.com
SIC: 8062 General medical & surgical hospitals
HQ: Prime Healthcare Services Inc
3300 E Guasti Rd Ste 300
Ontario CA 91761
-

(P-21115)
PROVIDENCE HEALTH & SERVICES F
Also Called: Providnce Holy Cross Fundation
501 S Buena Vista St, Burbank
(91505-4809)
PHONE.....................818 843-5111
Patricia Modrzejewski, *CEO*
James Reiner, *CFO*
Lee Kanon Alpert, *Chairman*
Alexander Koretz, *Principal*
Rich Snader, *Controller*
EMP: 2000
SALES: 19.1MM **Privately Held**
SIC: 8062 General medical & surgical hospitals

(P-21116)
PROVIDENCE HEALTH & SERVICES S
Also Called: Providence Little Company of M
1300 W 7th St, San Pedro (90732-3505)
PHONE.....................310 832-3311
EMP: 99
SALES (est): 4.7MM **Privately Held**
SIC: 8062

(P-21117)
PROVIDENCE HEALTH & SVCS - ORE
540 23rd St, Oakland (94612-1724)
PHONE.....................510 444-0839
Tim Zaricznyj, *Director*
EMP: 360
SALES (corp-wide): 15.2B **Privately Held**
WEB: www.providence.org
SIC: 8062 General medical & surgical hospitals
HQ: Providence Health & Services - Oregon
1801 Lind Ave Sw
Renton WA 98057
425 525-3355

(P-21118)
PROVIDENCE HEALTH & SVCS - ORE
Also Called: Providence Holy Cross Med Ctr
15031 Rinaldi St, Mission Hills
(91345-1207)
PHONE.....................818 365-8051
David Mast, *Branch Mgr*
Rowena Chin, *Education*
Henry Yoo, *Pharmacist*
Georgia Colkitt, *Director*
Andrew Mircovich, *Manager*
EMP: 360
SALES (corp-wide): 15.2B **Privately Held**
SIC: 8062 General medical & surgical hospitals
HQ: Providence Health & Services - Oregon
1801 Lind Ave Sw
Renton WA 98057
425 525-3355

(P-21119)
PROVIDENCE HEALTH SYSTEM
Also Called: Providence Holy Cross Med Ctr
15031 Rinaldi St, Mission Hills
(91345-1207)
PHONE.....................818 898-4561
Kerry Carmody, *Administration*
EMP: 1000
SALES (corp-wide): 15.2B **Privately Held**
SIC: 8062 8661 General medical & surgical hospitals; Catholic Church
HQ: Providence Health System-Southern California
1801 Lind Ave Sw
Renton WA 98057
425 525-3355

(P-21120)
PROVIDENCE HEALTH SYSTEM
Also Called: San Pedro Peninsula Hospital
1300 W 7th St, San Pedro (90732-3505)
PHONE.....................310 832-3311
Hero Nishi, *Principal*
Andrea Viggers, *Human Res Dir*
Kathryn Sprague, *Mktg Dir*
Mary J Jones, *Nursing Dir*
EMI Ariura, *Pharmacist*
EMP: 880
SALES (corp-wide): 15.2B **Privately Held**
SIC: 8062 8051 5912 General medical & surgical hospitals; skilled nursing care facilities; drug stores
HQ: Providence Health System-Southern California
1801 Lind Ave Sw
Renton WA 98057
425 525-3355

(P-21121)
PROVIDENCE HEALTH SYSTEM
Providence St Joseph Med Ctr
501 S Buena Vista St, Burbank
(91505-4809)
PHONE.....................818 843-5111
Georgianne Johnson, *COO*
Arnie Schaffer, *CEO*
Patty Williams, *Exec Dir*
Andrew Werts, *Marketing Staff*
EMP: 2000
SALES (corp-wide): 15.2B **Privately Held**
SIC: 8062 General medical & surgical hospitals
HQ: Providence Health System-Southern California
1801 Lind Ave Sw
Renton WA 98057
425 525-3355

(P-21122)
PROVIDENCE HEALTH SYSTEM
Also Called: San Pedro Hospital Pavilion
1322 W 6th St, San Pedro (90732-3501)
PHONE.....................310 514-5270
Julie Theiring, *Principal*
EMP: 100
SALES (corp-wide): 15.2B **Privately Held**
SIC: 8062 8051 General medical & surgical hospitals; convalescent home with continuous nursing care
HQ: Providence Health System-Southern California
1801 Lind Ave Sw
Renton WA 98057
425 525-3355

(P-21123)
PROVIDENCE HOLY CROSS (PA)
15031 Rinaldi St, Mission Hills
(91345-1207)
PHONE.....................818 365-8051
Lee Kanon Alpert, *Chairman*
June E Drake, *CEO*
Michael White, *COO*
Bob Sampson, *Vice Pres*
Cynthia Simmons, *Executive Asst*
▲ EMP: 70 EST: 1960
SALES (est): 255.5MM **Privately Held**
SIC: 8062 General medical & surgical hospitals

(P-21124)
PROVIDENCE ST JOHNS HLTH CTR
2121 Santa Monica Blvd, Santa Monica
(90404-2303)
PHONE.....................310 829-6562
Marcel Loh, *CEO*
Donald Larsen Jr, *Officer*
Virginia Borncamp, *Vice Pres*
Leanne Park, *Risk Mgmt Dir*
Liga Mezaraups, *Ch Nursing Ofcr*
EMP: 350
SQ FT: 60,000
SALES (est): 366.7K **Privately Held**
SIC: 8062 General medical & surgical hospitals

(P-21125)
PROVIDENCE TARZANA MEDICAL CTR
18321 Clark St, Tarzana (91356-3501)
PHONE.....................818 881-0800
Dale Surowitz, *CEO*
Kathy Evans, *CEO*
Nick Lymberopoulos, *COO*
EMP: 1300
SALES: 199.1MM **Privately Held**
SIC: 8062 General medical & surgical hospitals

(P-21126)
QUEEN OF ANGELS HOLLYWOOD PRES
1300 N Vermont Ave, Los Angeles
(90027-6300)
PHONE.....................213 413-3000
John Fenton, *President*
EMP: 1200
SALES: 23.7MM **Privately Held**
SIC: 8062 Hospital, affiliated with AMA residency

(P-21127)
QUEEN OF VALLEY HOSPITAL
1115 S Sunset Ave, West Covina
(91790-3940)
PHONE.....................626 962-4011
Louis Conyers, *CEO*
Robert Curry, *CEO*
Elvia Foulke, *COO*
EMP: 900
SALES (est): 37.5MM **Privately Held**
SIC: 8062 General medical & surgical hospitals

(P-21128)
QUEEN OF VALLEY MEDICAL CENTER (DH)
1000 Trancas St, NAPA (94558-2906)
PHONE.....................707 252-4411
Lawrence Michael Coomes, *President*
Vincent Morgese, *COO*
Bob Diehl, *CFO*
Don Miller, *CFO*
Mich Riccioni, *CFO*
EMP: 653 EST: 1953
SQ FT: 278,500
SALES: 268.1MM
SALES (corp-wide): 15.2B **Privately Held**
SIC: 8062 General medical & surgical hospitals
HQ: St. Joseph Health System
3345 Michelson Dr Ste 100
Irvine CA 92612
949 381-4000

PRODUCTS & SVCS

(P-21129)
R M MATOVU MEMORIAL
327 Consuelo Dr, Santa Barbara
(93110-1419)
PHONE......................412 337-5975
Annette Ndagano, *President*
EMP: 50 EST: 2016
SALES (est): 286.2K **Privately Held**
SIC: 8062 General medical & surgical hospitals

(P-21130)
RADY CHLD HOSPITAL-SAN DIEGO (HQ)
3020 Childrens Way, San Diego
(92123-4223)
PHONE......................858 576-1700
Donald Kearns, *CEO*
David Frankville,
Debbie Smith, *Admin Asst*
Anna Delgado, *Administration*
Christine Farnsworth, *Research*
EMP: 2000 EST: 1952
SQ FT: 276,000
SALES: 1.3B **Privately Held**
SIC: 8062 General medical & surgical hospitals

(P-21131)
RAMONA REHABILITATION AND POST
485 W Johnston Ave, Hemet (92543-7012)
PHONE......................951 652-0011
Stan Leland, *President*
Heidi Vickers, *Admin Sec*
EMP: 120
SQ FT: 30,000
SALES (est): 7.2MM **Privately Held**
SIC: 8062 8051 General medical & surgical hospitals; convalescent home with continuous nursing care

(P-21132)
RANCHO CCAMONGA CMNTY HOSP LLC
Also Called: Rancho Speciality Hospital
10841 White Oak Ave, Rancho Cucamonga (91730-3817)
PHONE......................909 581-6400
Marc C Ferrell,
Debroah Miller, *Business Dir*
Mark Ferrell,
Vartan Hovsetian,
ARA Tavitian,
EMP: 110
SQ FT: 100,000
SALES (est): 8.5MM **Privately Held**
SIC: 8062 Hospital, affiliated with AMA residency

(P-21133)
REDLANDS COMMUNITY HOSPITAL (PA)
350 Terracina Blvd, Redlands
(92373-4897)
PHONE......................909 335-5500
James R Holmes, *CEO*
Michelle Mok, *Vice Pres*
Josephine Dudeck, *Personnel Assit*
Alvin Umeda, *Otolaryngology*
Steve Mera, *Med Doctor*
EMP: 99
SALES: 174.1MM **Privately Held**
SIC: 8062 General medical & surgical hospitals

(P-21134)
REDWOOD MEMORIAL HOSP FORTUNA (PA)
3300 Renner Dr, Fortuna (95540-3120)
PHONE......................707 725-7327
Thomas McConnell, *CEO*
Bob Branigan, *COO*
Kevin Clouder, *CFO*
Stanley Hino, *Pathologist*
Philip Vogelsang, *Pathologist*
EMP: 150
SQ FT: 65,000
SALES: 55.5MM **Privately Held**
SIC: 8062 Hospital, affiliated with AMA residency

(P-21135)
RIDEOUT MEMORIAL HOSPITAL (HQ)
726 4th St, Marysville (95901-5656)
P.O. Box 2128 (95901-0075)
PHONE......................530 749-4416
Ronald M Sweeney, *Chairman*
Theresa Hamilton, *CEO*
John Cary, *Treasurer*
Lisa Del Pero, *Admin Sec*
EMP: 700
SQ FT: 100,000
SALES: 335MM
SALES (corp-wide): 26.9MM **Privately Held**
SIC: 8062 8082 General medical & surgical hospitals; home health care services
PA: Freemont Rideout Health Group
989 Plumas St
Yuba City CA 95991
530 751-4010

(P-21136)
RIDGECREST REGIONAL HOSPITAL (PA)
Also Called: Southern Sierra Medical Clinic
1081 N China Lake Blvd, Ridgecrest
(93555-3130)
PHONE......................760 446-3551
James A Suver, *CEO*
Donna Kiser, *CFO*
Lisa Sparland, *Radiology Dir*
Tammy Lilly, *Office Mgr*
Christy Lofing, *Admin Asst*
EMP: 77
SQ FT: 80,000
SALES: 106.3MM **Privately Held**
WEB: www.rrh.org
SIC: 8062 General medical & surgical hospitals

(P-21137)
RIVERSIDE CMNTY HLTH SYSTEMS (DH)
Also Called: Riverside Community Hospital
4445 Magnolia Ave Fl 6, Riverside
(92501-4135)
PHONE......................951 788-3000
Partrick Brilliant, *President*
Doug Long, *COO*
Tracey Fernandez, *CFO*
Kathy Torres, *Vice Pres*
Paul Woerz, *VP Human Res*
EMP: 91
SQ FT: 386,100
SALES: 435.8MM **Publicly Held**
WEB: www.rchc.org
SIC: 8062 8011 General medical & surgical hospitals; offices & clinics of medical doctors
HQ: Hca Inc.
1 Park Plz
Nashville TN 37203
615 344-9551

(P-21138)
RIVERSIDE HEALTHCARE SYSTEM LP
Also Called: Riverside Community Hospital
4445 Magnolia Ave, Riverside
(92501-4135)
PHONE......................951 788-3000
Patrick Brilliant, *Managing Prtnr*
EMP: 1600
SALES (est): 28.7MM **Publicly Held**
SIC: 8062 General medical & surgical hospitals
HQ: Hca Inc.
1 Park Plz
Nashville TN 37203
615 344-9551

(P-21139)
RIVERSIDE UNIVERSITY HEALTH (PA)
Also Called: Riverside Cnty Rgional Med Ctr
4065 County Circle Dr, Riverside
(92503-3410)
PHONE......................951 358-5000
Douglas D Bagley, *CEO*
Ellie Bennett, *COO*
David Runke, *CFO*
Gregory Prouty, *Business Dir*
Donna Bennett, *Exec Dir*
EMP: 77

SALES (est): 1.5MM **Privately Held**
SIC: 8062 General medical & surgical hospitals

(P-21140)
RIVERSIDE UNIVERSITY HEALTH
Also Called: Ruhs-Emergency Department
26520 Cactus Ave, Moreno Valley
(92555-3927)
PHONE......................951 486-4000
Bret Powers Do, *Principal*
EMP: 723 **Privately Held**
SIC: 8062 General medical & surgical hospitals
PA: Riverside University Health System Foundation
4065 County Circle Dr
Riverside CA 92503

(P-21141)
SADDLEBACK MEMORIAL MED CTR (HQ)
24451 Health Center Dr # 1, Laguna Hills
(92653-3689)
PHONE......................949 837-4500
Steve Geidt, *CEO*
Kathleen Sullivan,
Barry Arbuckle, *President*
Catherine Shitara, *COO*
Adolfo Chanez, *CFO*
EMP: 1020 EST: 1969
SQ FT: 195,000
SALES (est): 349.1MM
SALES (corp-wide): 2.4B **Privately Held**
SIC: 8062 8011 8093 8099 General medical & surgical hospitals; medical centers; diabetes specialist, physician/surgeon; cardiologist & cardio-vascular specialist; pediatrician; rehabilitation center, outpatient treatment; blood related health services; medical laboratories; cancer hospital; maternity hospital; orthopedic hospital
PA: Memorial Health Services
17360 Brookhurst St # 160
Fountain Valley CA 92708
714 377-6748

(P-21142)
SAFEOP SURGICAL INC
5818 El Camino Real, Carlsbad
(92008-8816)
PHONE......................760 494-6752
EMP: 82
SALES (est): 17.2MM
SALES (corp-wide): 91.6MM **Publicly Held**
SIC: 8062 General medical & surgical hospitals
PA: Alphatec Holdings, Inc.
5818 El Camino Real
Carlsbad CA 92008
760 431-9286

(P-21143)
SAINT AGNES MEDICAL CENTER (HQ)
1303 E Herndon Ave, Fresno (93720-3309)
PHONE......................559 450-3000
Nancy R Hollingsworth, *CEO*
Tai-PO Tschang, *Ch Pathology*
Tom Anderson,
Jason Fellows,
Joan Marie Steadman, *Trustee*
EMP: 1688
SQ FT: 200,000
SALES: 513.9MM
SALES (corp-wide): 18.3B **Privately Held**
SIC: 8062 General medical & surgical hospitals
PA: Trinity Health Corporation
20555 Victor Pkwy
Livonia MI 48152
734 343-1000

(P-21144)
SAINT JHNS HLTH CTR FOUNDATION
Also Called: St John's Health Centre
2020 Santa Monica Blvd 3rdfl3, Santa Monica (90404-2023)
PHONE......................310 829-8970
Lou Laztin, *CEO*

EMP: 297
SALES (corp-wide): 2.7B **Privately Held**
SIC: 8062 General medical & surgical hospitals
HQ: Saint John's Health Center Foundation.
2121 Santa Monica Blvd
Santa Monica CA 90404
310 829-5511

(P-21145)
SAINT LOUISE HOSPITAL
9400 N Name Uno, Gilroy (95020-3528)
PHONE......................408 848-2000
Jim Dober, *CEO*
Terry Curley, *Vice Pres*
Joanne Allan, *Principal*
EMP: 500
SALES: 90.6MM **Privately Held**
SIC: 8062 General medical & surgical hospitals

(P-21146)
SALINAS VALLEY MEMORIAL HLTHCA
440 E Romie Ln, Salinas (93901-4033)
PHONE......................831 759-3236
EMP: 251
SALES (corp-wide): 494.4MM **Privately Held**
SIC: 8062 General medical & surgical hospitals
PA: Salinas Valley Memorial Healthcare Systems
450 E Romie Ln
Salinas CA 93901
831 757-4333

(P-21147)
SALINAS VALLEY MEMORIAL HLTHCA
5 Lower Ragsdle Dr 102, Monterey
(93940)
PHONE......................831 884-5048
EMP: 351
SALES (corp-wide): 494.4MM **Privately Held**
SIC: 8062 General medical & surgical hospitals
PA: Salinas Valley Memorial Healthcare Systems
450 E Romie Ln
Salinas CA 93901
831 757-4333

(P-21148)
SALINAS VALLEY MEMORIAL HLTHCA (PA)
Also Called: Salinas Valley Memorial Hosp
450 E Romie Ln, Salinas (93901-4029)
P.O. Box 4760 (93912-4760)
PHONE......................831 757-4333
Pete Delgado, *President*
Maria Fuenzalida, *Social Dir*
Mary Stepien, *Nursing Mgr*
Kathie Haines, *Admin Asst*
Carol Kidder, *Admin Asst*
▲ EMP: 77
SQ FT: 187,942
SALES: 494.4MM **Privately Held**
SIC: 8062 Hospital, affiliated with AMA residency

(P-21149)
SALINAS VALLEY MEMORIAL HLTHCA
Also Called: Salinas Urgent Care
558 Abbott St, Salinas (93901-4326)
PHONE......................831 755-7880
Angela Mendez, *Office Mgr*
Karina A Rusk, *Corp Comm Staff*
Joseph D Zakar, *Pharmacist*
EMP: 301
SALES (corp-wide): 494.4MM **Privately Held**
WEB: www.salinasurgentcare.com
SIC: 8062 General medical & surgical hospitals
PA: Salinas Valley Memorial Healthcare Systems
450 E Romie Ln
Salinas CA 93901
831 757-4333

(P-21150)
SAN ANTONIO COMMUNITY HOSPITAL
Also Called: Rancho San Antonio Medical Ctr
7777 Milliken Ave Ste A, Rancho Cuca-
monga (91730-7489)
PHONE......................909 948-8000
Jullian Doxon, *Director*
Amanda Jones, *Assistant*
EMP: 50
SALES (corp-wide): 364.9MM **Privately
Held**
WEB: www.sach.com
SIC: 8062 General medical & surgical hos-
pitals
PA: San Antonio Regional Hospital
999 San Bernardino Rd
Upland CA 91786
909 985-2811

(P-21151)
SAN ANTONIO REGIONAL HOSPITAL (PA)
999 San Bernardino Rd, Upland
(91786-4920)
PHONE......................909 985-2811
John Chapman, *CEO*
Cindy McClain, *Records Dir*
Roger Parsons, *CFO*
Jim Milhiser, *Chairman*
Martin Jarzombek, *Officer*
▲ **EMP:** 1900 **EST:** 1906
SQ FT: 349,000
SALES: 364.9MM **Privately Held**
WEB: www.sach.com
SIC: 8062 5912 General medical & surgi-
cal hospitals; drug stores & proprietary
stores

(P-21152)
SAN BENITO HEALTH CARE DST (PA)
Also Called: HAZEL HAWKINS MEMORIAL
HOSPITA
911 Sunset Dr Ste A, Hollister
(95023-5608)
PHONE......................831 637-5711
Ken Underwood, *CEO*
Alice Oliveira, *Volunteer Dir*
Beth Ivy, *President*
Mark Robinson, *CFO*
Lynn Gomez, *Vice Pres*
▲ **EMP:** 270
SQ FT: 42,000
SALES: 115.7MM **Privately Held**
WEB: www.hazelhawkins.com
SIC: 8062 8051 8059 General medical &
surgical hospitals; skilled nursing care fa-
cilities; convalescent home

(P-21153)
SAN CLEMENTE MEDICAL CTR LLC
Also Called: Saddleback Memorial Hospital
654 Camino De Los Mares, San Clemente
(92673-2827)
PHONE......................949 496-1122
Ronald McGee,
William Van Derreis,
Adolfo Chanez, *CFO*
Mary Olson, *Analyst*
Gus Gialamas MD,
EMP: 300
SQ FT: 65,000
SALES (est): 20.2MM **Privately Held**
SIC: 8062 8011 General medical & surgi-
cal hospitals; offices & clinics of medical
doctors

(P-21154)
SAN GBRIEL VLY MED CTR FNDTION
438 W Las Tunas Dr, San Gabriel
(91776-1216)
PHONE......................626 289-5454
Thomas Mone, *CEO*
Harold Way, *CFO*
Richard Polver, *Treasurer*
Edward Shuey, *Admin Sec*
EMP: 850
SQ FT: 42,000
SALES: 2.5K **Privately Held**
WEB: www.sgvmc.com
SIC: 8062 General medical & surgical hos-
pitals

HQ: Dignity Health
185 Berry St Ste 300
San Francisco CA 94107
415 438-5500

(P-21155)
SAN GORGONIO MEMORIAL HOSPITAL (PA)
600 N Highland Sprng Ave, Banning
(92220-3046)
PHONE......................951 845-1121
Steven Barron, *CEO*
Devin Borna,
Ha Le, *Ch Radiology*
Dave Recupero, *CFO*
Dorothy Ellis, *Chairman*
EMP: 250
SQ FT: 76,000
SALES: 56.1MM **Privately Held**
WEB: www.sgmh.org
SIC: 8062 Hospital, affiliated with AMA res-
idency

(P-21156)
SAN JOAQUIN COMMUNITY HOSPITAL (PA)
2615 Chester Ave, Bakersfield
(93301-2014)
PHONE......................661 395-3000
Sharlet Briggs, *President*
Brent Soper, *CFO*
Georgia McCormick, *Admin Sec*
Nancy Garcia, *CTO*
Jack Houston, *Human Res Dir*
EMP: 850 **EST:** 1910
SQ FT: 137,000
SALES: 368.6MM **Privately Held**
SIC: 8062 8011 General medical & surgi-
cal hospitals; offices & clinics of medical
doctors

(P-21157)
SAN JOAQUIN GENERAL HOSPITAL
Also Called: Healthcare Services
500 W Hospital Rd, French Camp
(95231-9693)
PHONE......................209 468-6000
David Colberson, *CEO*
Ronald Kruetner, *CFO*
Usman Ali, *Director*
EMP: 1300 **EST:** 2001
SALES: 313MM **Privately Held**
SIC: 8062 General medical & surgical hos-
pitals

(P-21158)
SAN JOSE MEDICAL SYSTEMS LP
Also Called: Regional Medical Ctr San Jose
225 N Jackson Ave, San Jose
(95116-1603)
PHONE......................408 259-5000
Mike Johnson, *Partner*
Darrel Odell, *MIS Dir*
Amir Matityahu, *Surgeon*
Cheung Leung, *Cardiology*
Kenneth Smith, *Nutritionist*
EMP: 1200
SQ FT: 203,685
SALES: 446.9MM **Publicly Held**
SIC: 8062 General medical & surgical hos-
pitals
HQ: Hca Inc.
1 Park Plz
Nashville TN 37203
615 344-9551

(P-21159)
SAN LEANDRO HOSPITAL LP
13855 E 14th St, San Leandro
(94578-2600)
PHONE......................510 357-6500
Ronnie Bayduza, *CEO*
Gloria Coats, *Social Dir*
EMP: 475
SALES (est): 13.7K **Privately Held**
WEB: www.triadhospitals.com
SIC: 8062 8361 General medical & surgi-
cal hospitals; residential care
PA: Alameda Health System
1411 E 31st St
Oakland CA 94602

(P-21160)
SAN RAMON REGIONAL MED CTR LLC
6001 Norris Canyon Rd, San Ramon
(94583-5400)
PHONE......................925 275-9200
Shawn Dewers,
Pam Yoo, *Officer*
Jennifer Brasiel, *Pharmacist*
Ruth Burk,
Lee Huskins,
EMP: 600 **EST:** 1983
SALES: 195.5K
SALES (corp-wide): 18.3B **Publicly Held**
WEB: www.tenethealth.com
SIC: 8062 8093 General medical & surgi-
cal hospitals; rehabilitation center, outpa-
tient treatment
PA: Tenet Healthcare Corporation
1445 Ross Ave Ste 1400
Dallas TX 75202
469 893-2200

(P-21161)
SANTA BARBARA COTTAGE HOSPITAL
Pathology Department
400 W Pueblo St, Santa Barbara
(93105-4353)
P.O. Box 689 (93102-0689)
PHONE......................805 569-7367
Ron Werdt, *President*
Rick Donovan, *Director*
Mary Puryear, *Director*
EMP: 578
SALES (corp-wide): 646.4MM **Privately
Held**
WEB:
www.santabarbaracottagehospital.com
SIC: 8062 General medical & surgical hos-
pitals
PA: Santa Barbara Cottage Hospital
400 W Pueblo St
Santa Barbara CA 93105
805 682-7111

(P-21162)
SANTA BARBARA COTTAGE HOSPITAL (PA)
Also Called: Cottage Hospital Childrens Ctr
400 W Pueblo St, Santa Barbara
(93105-4353)
P.O. Box 689 (93102-0689)
PHONE......................805 682-7111
Gretchen Milligan, *Chairman*
Patricia Dooley, *Volunteer Dir*
Ronald C Werft, *President*
Steven Fellow, *Exec VP*
Steven Fellows, *Exec VP*
EMP: 60
SQ FT: 485,874
SALES: 646.4MM **Privately Held**
SIC: 8062 Hospital, AMA approved resi-
dency

(P-21163)
SANTA BARBARA COTTAGE HOSPITAL
Also Called: Santa Barbara Cnty Social Svcs
2125 Centerpointe Pkwy, Santa Maria
(93455-1337)
PHONE......................805 346-7135
Charlene Chase, *Director*
EMP: 210
SALES (corp-wide): 646.4MM **Privately
Held**
SIC: 8062 General medical & surgical hos-
pitals
PA: Santa Barbara Cottage Hospital
400 W Pueblo St
Santa Barbara CA 93105
805 682-7111

(P-21164)
SANTA CLARA COUNTY OF
Also Called: Santa Clara Valley Health & Ho
2325 Enborg Ln Ste 380, San Jose
(95128-2649)
PHONE......................408 885-6818
Kim Roberts, *Finance*
EMP: 50 **Privately Held**
WEB: www.countyairports.org

SIC: 8062 9431 9311 Hospital, medical
school affiliated with nursing & residency;
administration of public health programs; ;
finance, taxation & monetary policy;
PA: County Of Santa Clara
3180 Newberry Dr Ste 150
San Jose CA 95118
408 299-5105

(P-21165)
SANTA ROSA MEMORIAL HOSPITAL (DH)
Also Called: Sjhs Sonoma County
1165 Montgomery Dr, Santa Rosa
(95405-4897)
P.O. Box 522 (95402-0522)
PHONE......................707 546-3210
Todd Salnas, *CEO*
Mich Riccioni, *CFO*
Gary Greensweig, *Vice Pres*
Kathrine Hardin, *Ch Nursing Ofcr*
Spencer S Snyder, *Regional Mgr*
EMP: 1500 **EST:** 1948
SQ FT: 163,692
SALES: 518MM
SALES (corp-wide): 15.2B **Privately Held**
WEB: www.stjosephhealth.org
SIC: 8062 General medical & surgical hos-
pitals
HQ: St. Joseph Health System
3345 Michelson Dr Ste 100
Irvine CA 92612
949 381-4000

(P-21166)
SANTA ROSA SURGERY CENTER LP
Also Called: Sutter Health
1111 Sonoma Ave Ste 214, Santa Rosa
(95405-4833)
PHONE......................707 575-5831
Dan Peterson, *Administration*
Jiries Mogannam, *Principal*
EMP: 75
SQ FT: 8,000
SALES (est): 5.3MM **Privately Held**
WEB: www.srsurgerycenter.com
SIC: 8062 General medical & surgical hos-
pitals

(P-21167)
SANTA TERESA CONV HOSPITAL
9140 Verner St, Pico Rivera (90660-2741)
PHONE......................562 948-1961
Nick Cardenas, *Director*
EMP: 85
SALES (est): 1.3MM **Privately Held**
SIC: 8062 5912 General medical & surgi-
cal hospitals; drug stores & proprietary
stores

(P-21168)
SANTA TERESITA INC (PA)
Also Called: Manor At Santa Teresita Hosp
819 Buena Vista St, Duarte (91010-1703)
PHONE......................626 359-3243
Sister Mary Clare Mancini, *CEO*
EMP: 278
SQ FT: 232,165
SALES: 13.2MM **Privately Held**
WEB: www.santa-teresita.org
SIC: 8062 8051 General medical & surgi-
cal hospitals; skilled nursing care facilities

(P-21169)
SANTA YNEZ VALLEY COTTAGE HOSP
2050 Viborg Rd, Solvang (93463-2220)
P.O. Box 689, Santa Barbara (93102-0689)
PHONE......................805 688-6431
Ron Werft, *President*
Gary Blum, *Ch Radiology*
Wende Cappetta, *Vice Pres*
Mary Meola, *Admin Dir*
Carla Long, *Director*
EMP: 75 **EST:** 1962
SQ FT: 30,000
SALES: 19.4MM **Privately Held**
WEB: www.cottagehealthsystem.org
SIC: 8062 General medical & surgical hos-
pitals

PRODUCTS & SVCS

(PA)=Parent Co (HQ)=Headquarters (DH)=Div Headquarters   2019 Directory of California
✪ = New Business established in last 2 years   Wholesalers and Services Companies

895

(P-21170)
SCHMIDT PHYLLIS MD CORPORATION
711 W College St, Los Angeles (90012-1163)
PHONE..................213 613-1163
Phyllis Schmidt MD, *President*
EMP: 600
SALES (est): 4.5MM **Privately Held**
SIC: 8062 General medical & surgical hospitals

(P-21171)
SCRIPPS CLINIC
12395 El Camino Real, San Diego (92130-3082)
P.O. Box 2469, La Jolla (92038-2469)
PHONE..................858 794-1250
Chris Van Gorder, *CEO*
James Collins, *President*
Dr Hubert Greenway, *CEO*
Ken Fujioka, *Med Doctor*
EMP: 116 EST: 1999
SALES (est): 20.3MM **Privately Held**
SIC: 8062 General medical & surgical hospitals

(P-21172)
SCRIPPS HEALTH
Also Called: Scripps Ambulatory Surgery Ctr
320 Santa Fe Dr Ste 310, Encinitas (92024-5140)
PHONE..................760 753-8413
Donna Danley, *Principal*
Sunil Rayan, *Surgeon*
Lawrence Eisenhauer, *Obstetrician*
Roy Kaplan, *Rheumtlgy Spec*
Roy Avalos, *Med Doctor*
EMP: 60
SALES (corp-wide): 2.1B **Privately Held**
SIC: 8062 General medical & surgical hospitals
PA: Scripps Health
10140 Campus Point Dr Ax415
San Diego CA 92121
800 727-4777

(P-21173)
SCRIPPS HEALTH
Also Called: Scripps Whttier Dbetes Program
10140 Campus Point Dr, San Diego (92121-1520)
PHONE..................858 622-9076
Athena Philis-Tsimikas, *Branch Mgr*
Bruce Rainey, *Vice Pres*
Kathyrn Libby,
EMP: 60
SALES (corp-wide): 2.1B **Privately Held**
SIC: 8062 General medical & surgical hospitals
PA: Scripps Health
10140 Campus Point Dr Ax415
San Diego CA 92121
800 727-4777

(P-21174)
SCRIPPS HEALTH
Also Called: Scripps Mercy Hospital
4077 5th Ave, San Diego (92103-2105)
PHONE..................619 294-8111
Jacqueline Saucier, *Director*
Melissa Studds, *Vice Pres*
Lisa Thakur, *Vice Pres*
Chris Nicholson, *Lab Dir*
Gayosso Aliscia, *Technology*
EMP: 99
SALES (corp-wide): 2.1B **Privately Held**
WEB: www.scripps.org
SIC: 8062 General medical & surgical hospitals
PA: Scripps Health
10140 Campus Point Dr Ax415
San Diego CA 92121
800 727-4777

(P-21175)
SCRIPPS HEALTH
Also Called: Scripps Rancho Bernardo
15004 Innovation Dr, San Diego (92128-3491)
PHONE..................858 271-9770
Melody Stewart, *Administration*
Michael D Lee, *Family Practiti*
Lon Manson, *Family Practiti*
Charles Edwards, *Obstetrician*
Katrina Kelly, *Obstetrician*

EMP: 259
SALES (corp-wide): 2.1B **Privately Held**
WEB: www.scripps.org
SIC: 8062 General medical & surgical hospitals
PA: Scripps Health
10140 Campus Point Dr Ax415
San Diego CA 92121
800 727-4777

(P-21176)
SCRIPPS HEALTH
7565 Mission Valley Rd # 200, San Diego (92108-4431)
PHONE..................619 245-2350
Sevil Brahme, *Branch Mgr*
Aleksandr M Itkin, *Dermatology*
Mahlet Alula, *Internal Med*
EMP: 377
SALES (corp-wide): 2.1B **Privately Held**
SIC: 8062 General medical & surgical hospitals
PA: Scripps Health
10140 Campus Point Dr Ax415
San Diego CA 92121
800 727-4777

(P-21177)
SCRIPPS HEALTH
Also Called: Scripps Mem Hosp - Encinatas
354 Santa Fe Dr, Encinitas (92024-5142)
P.O. Box 230817 (92023-0817)
PHONE..................760 753-6501
Rebecca Ropchan, *Branch Mgr*
Grace Conlon,
Kris Vanlom, *Ch Radiology*
Sally Margulis, *Partner*
Barbara Walker, *CFO*
EMP: 250
SALES (corp-wide): 2.1B **Privately Held**
WEB: www.scripps.org
SIC: 8062 5912 General medical & surgical hospitals; drug stores
PA: Scripps Health
10140 Campus Point Dr Ax415
San Diego CA 92121
800 727-4777

(P-21178)
SCRIPPS HEALTH
Also Called: Scripps Mercy Hospitals
435 H St, Chula Vista (91910-4307)
PHONE..................619 691-7000
Pott Hoff, *COO*
Juan Tovar MD, *Vice Chairman*
Carole Groyer, *Technology*
Denise Schultz, *Technology*
Ron Mc Clean, *Purchasing*
EMP: 1000
SALES (corp-wide): 2.1B **Privately Held**
WEB: www.scripps.org
SIC: 8062 General medical & surgical hospitals
PA: Scripps Health
10140 Campus Point Dr Ax415
San Diego CA 92121
800 727-4777

(P-21179)
SCRIPPS HEALTH (PA)
10140 Campus Point Dr Ax415, San Diego (92121-1520)
PHONE..................800 727-4777
Chris D Van Gorder, *President*
Richard K Rothberger, *CFO*
Mary J Anderson, *Trustee*
A B Eastman MD, *Officer*
Kelly Hardiman, *Officer*
EMP: 2514
SQ FT: 95,000
SALES (est): 2.1B **Privately Held**
WEB: www.scripps.org
SIC: 8062 8049 8042 8043 General medical & surgical hospitals; physical therapist; psychologist, psychotherapist & hypnotist; offices & clinics of optometrists; offices & clinics of podiatrists

(P-21180)
SCRIPPS HEALTH
Also Called: Scripps Green Hospital
10666 N Torrey Pines Rd, La Jolla (92037-1027)
PHONE..................858 455-9100
Robin Brown, *Branch Mgr*
Athena Philis-Tsimikas, *Vice Pres*

Nicole Reynolds, *Social Dir*
Michael Fache, *Admin Asst*
Linda Powell, *Comp Spec*
EMP: 326
SALES (corp-wide): 2.1B **Privately Held**
WEB: www.scripps.org
SIC: 8062 General medical & surgical hospitals
PA: Scripps Health
10140 Campus Point Dr Ax415
San Diego CA 92121
800 727-4777

(P-21181)
SCRIPPS HEALTH
Also Called: Scripps Mercy Hospital
4077 Fifth Ave, San Diego (92103-2105)
PHONE..................619 294-8111
Medical Records, *Manager*
Janmar Ramirez, *Technology*
Joseph Blatt, *Cardiology*
Lloyd Chang, *Cardiology*
Barry Handler, *Plastic Surgeon*
EMP: 300
SQ FT: 3,062
SALES (corp-wide): 2.1B **Privately Held**
WEB: www.scripps.org
SIC: 8062 General medical & surgical hospitals
PA: Scripps Health
10140 Campus Point Dr Ax415
San Diego CA 92121
800 727-4777

(P-21182)
SCRIPPS HEALTH
Also Called: Scripps Torrey Pines
10666 N Torrey Pines Rd, La Jolla (92037-1027)
PHONE..................800 727-4777
Larry Harrison, *Manager*
Pat Kirkeby, *Engineer*
Phataraporn Thorson, *Pathologist*
EMP: 200
SALES (corp-wide): 2.1B **Privately Held**
WEB: www.scripps.org
SIC: 8062 General medical & surgical hospitals
PA: Scripps Health
10140 Campus Point Dr Ax415
San Diego CA 92121
800 727-4777

(P-21183)
SCRIPPS HEALTH
Also Called: Scripps Mem Hospital-La Jolla
9888 Genesee Ave, La Jolla (92037-1205)
PHONE..................858 626-6150
James Bruffey, *Branch Mgr*
Margaret Moreno, *Technology*
Sandy Hughes, *Human Res Dir*
Carol Kashefi, *Surgeon*
Walter Coyle, *Gastroenterlgy*
EMP: 326
SALES (corp-wide): 2.1B **Privately Held**
SIC: 8062 General medical & surgical hospitals
PA: Scripps Health
10140 Campus Point Dr Ax415
San Diego CA 92121
800 727-4777

(P-21184)
SCRIPPS HEALTH
Also Called: Scripps Mem Hosp - La Jolla
9888 Genesee Ave, La Jolla (92037-1205)
PHONE..................858 626-4123
Gary Fybel, *CEO*
Kim Whitlock, *Records Dir*
Larry Juarez, *Admin Sec*
Carol Steele-Johnson, *Technology*
Elizabeth Eisenberg, *Train & Dev Mgr*
EMP: 200
SALES (corp-wide): 2.1B **Privately Held**
WEB: www.scripps.org
SIC: 8062 General medical & surgical hospitals
PA: Scripps Health
10140 Campus Point Dr Ax415
San Diego CA 92121
800 727-4777

(P-21185)
SCRIPPS MERCY HOSPITAL
4077 5th Ave Mer35, San Diego (92103-2105)
PHONE..................619 294-8111
Andrew C Ping, *Principal*
Jerry Cunningham, *General Mgr*
Paula Rintye, *Administration*
Veronica Esparza, *Human Res Dir*
Anthony Roman, *Security Mgr*
EMP: 77
SALES: 750.4MM **Privately Held**
SIC: 8062 General medical & surgical hospitals

(P-21186)
SENECA HEALTHCARE DISTRICT (PA)
Also Called: SHD
130 Brentwood Dr, Chester (96020)
P.O. Box 737 (96020-0737)
PHONE..................530 258-2151
Linda Wagner, *CEO*
David Slusher Jr, *President*
Cheryl Darnell, *CFO*
William Howe, *Treasurer*
David Walls, *Treasurer*
EMP: 105 EST: 1952
SQ FT: 12,417
SALES: 26.3MM **Privately Held**
SIC: 8062 General medical & surgical hospitals

(P-21187)
SEQUOIA HEALTH SERVICES (DH)
Also Called: SEQUOIA HOSPITAL
170 Alameda De Las Pulgas, Redwood City (94062-2751)
PHONE..................650 369-5811
Glenna Vaskellas, *Administration*
Michael Hollett, *Ch Radiology*
Helen Monk, *Radiology Dir*
Marian Marcella, *Ch Nursing Ofcr*
Scott Sherr, *Internal Med*
EMP: 88 EST: 1947
SQ FT: 350,000
SALES: 258.7MM **Privately Held**
WEB: www.sequoiahealthcaredistrict.com
SIC: 8062 General medical & surgical hospitals
HQ: Dignity Health
185 Berry St Ste 300
San Francisco CA 94107
415 438-5500

(P-21188)
SETON MEDICAL CENTER (HQ)
1900 Sullivan Ave, Daly City (94015-2229)
PHONE..................650 992-4000
Mark S Fratzke, *President*
Liz Ingwersen, *Surgery Dir*
Alicia Antonio, *Director*
Suzy Beeler, *Director*
Ilze Pleisa-Musaev, *Director*
EMP: 1099
SQ FT: 400,000
SALES (est): 213.3MM
SALES (corp-wide): 995MM **Privately Held**
WEB: www.sportsmedshop.com
SIC: 8062 8051 General medical & surgical hospitals; skilled nursing care facilities
PA: Verity Health System Of California, Inc.
2040 E Mariposa Ave
El Segundo CA 90245
650 551-6650

(P-21189)
SETON MEDICAL CENTER
Also Called: Seton Medical Center Coastside
600 Marine Blvd, Moss Beach (94038-9641)
PHONE..................650 563-7100
Judy Cook, *Director*
Sue Desoto, *Radiology Dir*
Robert Telfer MD, *Med Doctor*
Davida Corpuz, *Director*
EMP: 160
SALES (corp-wide): 995MM **Privately Held**
WEB: www.sportsmedshop.com
SIC: 8062 5812 8051 General medical & surgical hospitals; eating places; skilled nursing care facilities

HQ: Seton Medical Center
1900 Sullivan Ave
Daly City CA 94015
650 992-4000

(P-21190)
SETON MEDICAL CENTER
West Bay HM Hlth & Cmnty Svcs
1784 Sullivan Ave Ste 200, Daly City
(94015-2067)
PHONE..................................650 992-4000
Fax: 650 991-4146
EMP: 60
SALES (corp-wide): 225.4MM **Privately Held**
SIC: **8062** 7361 8082
HQ: Seton Medical Center
1900 Sullivan Ave
Daly City CA 94015
650 992-4000

(P-21191)
SHARP CHULA VISTA MEDICAL CTR
Also Called: Sharp Chula Vista Medical Ctr
751 Medical Center Ct, Chula Vista
(91911-6617)
PHONE..................................619 502-5800
Chris Boyd, *CEO*
Kara Yu, *Records Dir*
Michael Murphy, *President*
Rick King, *CFO*
Vennie Henderson, *General Mgr*
EMP: 1600
SQ FT: 270,205
SALES: 367.2MM
SALES (corp-wide): 3.4B **Privately Held**
SIC: **8062** General medical & surgical hospitals
PA: Sharp Healthcare
8695 Spectrum Center Blvd
San Diego CA 92123
858 499-4000

(P-21192)
SHARP CHULA VISTA MEDICAL CTR
8695 Spectrum Center Blvd, San Diego
(92123-1489)
PHONE..................................858 499-5150
Chris Boyd, *CEO*
Dolly Delarosa, *Admin Asst*
Lori Moody, *Recruiter*
Kimberly Castillo, *Director*
EMP: 99
SALES: 407.7MM **Privately Held**
SIC: **8062** General medical & surgical hospitals

(P-21193)
SHARP HEALTHCARE
Also Called: Sharp Rees-Stealy
8008 Frost St Ste 106, San Diego
(92123-4229)
PHONE..................................858 939-5434
Lori Allshouse, *Training Spec*
Alfred Saleh, *Oncology*
Carola Romero, *Physician Asst*
Bill Raymond, *Supervisor*
EMP: 53
SALES (corp-wide): 3.4B **Privately Held**
SIC: **8062** General medical & surgical hospitals
PA: Sharp Healthcare
8695 Spectrum Center Blvd
San Diego CA 92123
858 499-4000

(P-21194)
SHARP HEALTHCARE
Also Called: Sharp Health Care
3554 Ruffin Rd Ste Soca, San Diego
(92123-2596)
PHONE..................................858 627-5152
Alison Fleury, *Finance Other*
EMP: 150
SALES (corp-wide): 3.4B **Privately Held**
SIC: **8062** General medical & surgical hospitals
PA: Sharp Healthcare
8695 Spectrum Center Blvd
San Diego CA 92123
858 499-4000

(P-21195)
SHARP HEALTHCARE
Also Called: Sharp Mission Park Medical Ctr
130 Cedar Rd, Vista (92083-5102)
PHONE..................................760 806-5600
Meredith Acosta, *Branch Mgr*
EMP: 59
SALES (corp-wide): 3.4B **Privately Held**
SIC: **8062** General medical & surgical hospitals
PA: Sharp Healthcare
8695 Spectrum Center Blvd
San Diego CA 92123
858 499-4000

(P-21196)
SHARP MARY BIRCH H
3003 Health Center Dr, San Diego
(92123-2700)
PHONE..................................858 939-3400
Trisha Khaleghi, *CEO*
Samantha Heddy, *Admin Sec*
Lolie Fromm, *Emerg Med Spec*
Caryn Arnold,
Roxane Braun, *Manager*
EMP: 73
SALES (est): 13.8MM **Privately Held**
SIC: **8062** General medical & surgical hospitals

(P-21197)
SHARP MEMORIAL HOSPITAL (HQ)
Also Called: SHARP REES-STEALY PHARMACY
7901 Frost St, San Diego (92123-2701)
PHONE..................................858 939-3636
Tim Smith, *CEO*
Geoffrey Thompson,
Alison J Fleury, *Vice Pres*
Ken Lawonn, *Vice Pres*
Bill Littlejohn, *Vice Pres*
▲ EMP: 3000 EST: 1957
SALES: 1.3B
SALES (corp-wide): 3.4B **Privately Held**
SIC: **8062** General medical & surgical hospitals
PA: Sharp Healthcare
8695 Spectrum Center Blvd
San Diego CA 92123
858 499-4000

(P-21198)
SHERMAN OAKS HEALTH SYSTEM
4929 Van Nuys Blvd, Sherman Oaks
(91403-1702)
PHONE..................................818 981-7111
David Levinsohn, *CEO*
EMP: 51
SALES: 341.2K **Privately Held**
SIC: **8062** General medical & surgical hospitals

(P-21199)
SHRINERS HSPITALS FOR CHILDREN
2425 Stockton Blvd, Sacramento
(95817-2215)
PHONE..................................916 453-2050
Margaret Bryan, *Administration*
Debra Popejoy, *Pediatrics*
Karen Howes, *Nurse*
Tracey Padilla, *Pharmacist*
Robert Tolbert, *Manager*
EMP: 500 **Privately Held**
SIC: **8062** General medical & surgical hospitals
HQ: Shriners Hospitals For Children
12502 Usf Pine Dr
Tampa FL 33612
813 972-2250

(P-21200)
SIERRA VIEW LOCAL HOSPITAL DST
Also Called: Sierra View District Hospital
283 Pearson Dr, Porterville (93257-3353)
PHONE..................................559 781-7877
Dennis Coleman, *Branch Mgr*
Marcy Wallace, *Director*
EMP: 432

SALES (corp-wide): 147.9MM **Privately Held**
SIC: **8062** General medical & surgical hospitals
PA: Sierra View District Hospital League, Inc.
465 W Putnam Ave
Porterville CA 93257
559 784-1110

(P-21201)
SIERRA VISTA HOSPITAL INC (HQ)
Also Called: Sierra Vista Regional Med Ctr
1010 Murray Ave, San Luis Obispo
(93405-8801)
P.O. Box 1367 (93406-1367)
PHONE..................................805 546-7600
Joseph Deschryver, *CEO*
Candace Markwith, *President*
Ikenna Mmeje, *COO*
Richard Phillips, *CFO*
Rollie Pirkl, *CFO*
EMP: 575
SQ FT: 138,690
SALES: 150MM
SALES (corp-wide): 18.3B **Publicly Held**
WEB: www.raslowe.com
SIC: **8062** General medical & surgical hospitals
PA: Tenet Healthcare Corporation
1445 Ross Ave Ste 1400
Dallas TX 75202
469 893-2200

(P-21202)
SISKIYOU HOSPITAL INC
Also Called: Fairchild Medical Center
444 Bruce St, Yreka (96097-3450)
PHONE..................................530 842-4121
Dwayne Jones, *CEO*
Steven Nelson,
Marcus Issoglio, *President*
Jonathon C Andrus, *CEO*
Arvid Magnuson, *Lab Dir*
EMP: 450
SALES: 81.7MM **Privately Held**
WEB: www.fairchildmed.org
SIC: **8062** General medical & surgical hospitals

(P-21203)
SOMA SURGICENTER
1580 Valencia St, San Francisco
(94110-4423)
PHONE..................................415 641-6889
Mary Sherman, *Manager*
EMP: 50
SALES (est): 543.5K **Privately Held**
SIC: **8062** General medical & surgical hospitals

(P-21204)
SONOMA VALLEY HEALTH CARE DST (PA)
Also Called: SONOMA VALLEY HOSPITAL
347 Andrieux St, Sonoma (95476-6811)
PHONE..................................707 935-5000
Carl Gerlach, *CEO*
Timothy Noakes, *CFO*
Pauline Headley, *Bd of Directors*
Courtney McMahon, *Infect Cntl Dir*
Dave Pier, *Exec Dir*
EMP: 445
SQ FT: 115,000
SALES: 55.8MM **Privately Held**
WEB: www.svh.com
SIC: **8062** General medical & surgical hospitals

(P-21205)
SOUTHERN CAL PRMNNTE MED GROUP
26415 Carl Boyer Dr, Santa Clarita
(91350-5824)
PHONE..................................661 290-3100
EMP: 78
SALES (corp-wide): 3.5B **Privately Held**
SIC: **8062** General medical & surgical hospitals
PA: Southern California Permanente Medical Group
393 Walnut Dr
Pasadena CA 91107
626 405-5704

(P-21206)
SOUTHERN CAL PRMNNTE MED GROUP
Also Called: S C P M G
9961 Sierra Ave, Fontana (92335-6720)
PHONE..................................909 427-5000
Gerald McCall, *Branch Mgr*
Aaron L Rubin, *Med Doctor*
Arlene Sarocca, *Med Doctor*
EMP: 50
SALES (corp-wide): 3.5B **Privately Held**
WEB: www.permanente.net
SIC: **8062** General medical & surgical hospitals
PA: Southern California Permanente Medical Group
393 Walnut Dr
Pasadena CA 91107
626 405-5704

(P-21207)
SOUTHERN CAL SPCIALTY CARE INC
Also Called: Kindred Hospital La Mirada
845 N Lark Ellen Ave, West Covina
(91791-1069)
PHONE..................................626 339-5451
Nenda Estudillo, *Director*
Elvira Gonzalez, *Food Svc Dir*
EMP: 100
SQ FT: 34,082
SALES (corp-wide): 6B **Privately Held**
SIC: **8062** General medical & surgical hospitals
HQ: Southern California Specialty Care, Inc.
14900 Imperial Hwy
La Mirada CA 90638
-

(P-21208)
SOUTHERN CAL SPCIALTY CARE INC
1901 College Ave, Santa Ana
(92706-2334)
PHONE..................................714 564-7800
Morgan Topper, *CEO*
Elaine Pardee, *Director*
EMP: 146
SALES (corp-wide): 6B **Privately Held**
SIC: **8062** General medical & surgical hospitals
HQ: Southern California Specialty Care, Inc.
14900 Imperial Hwy
La Mirada CA 90638
-

(P-21209)
SOUTHERN CAL SPCIALTY CARE INC (DH)
Also Called: Kindred Hospital La Mirada
14900 Imperial Hwy, La Mirada
(90638-2172)
PHONE..................................562 944-1900
Ty Richardson, *President*
George Burkley, *COO*
Robin Rapp, *COO*
Judie Sheldon, *Ch Credit Ofcr*
Susan Hung, *Admin Asst*
EMP: 100
SQ FT: 74,074
SALES: 109.3MM
SALES (corp-wide): 6B **Privately Held**
SIC: **8062** General medical & surgical hospitals
HQ: Specialty Healthcare Services, Inc
680 S 4th St
Louisville KY 40202
502 596-7300

(P-21210)
SOUTHERN HMBLDT CMNTY DST HOSP
Also Called: Southern Humboldt Cmnty Clinic
733 Cedar St, Garberville (95542-3201)
PHONE..................................707 923-3921
Deborah Scaife, *President*
EMP: 95
SQ FT: 17,000
SALES (est): 5.9MM **Privately Held**
SIC: **8062** General medical & surgical hospitals

PRODUCTS & SVCS

(P-21211)
SOUTHERN HUMBOLDT COMM HLTH CR
733 Cedar St, Garberville (95542-3201)
PHONE....................................707 923-3925
Matt Rees, *CEO*
Kent Sown, *COO*
Paul Eves, *CFO*
Judy Gallagher, *Ch Nursing Ofcr*
Margo Acuna, *Manager*
EMP: 85 **EST:** 2001
SALES (est): 323.2K **Privately Held**
SIC: 8062 General medical & surgical hospitals

(P-21212)
SOUTHERN INYO HEALTHCARE DST
501 E Locust St, Lone Pine (93545-8044)
PHONE....................................760 876-5501
Lee Barron, *CEO*
EMP: 106
SQ FT: 29,000
SALES (est): 16.8MM **Privately Held**
WEB: www.sihd.org
SIC: 8062 General medical & surgical hospitals

(P-21213)
SOUTHERN MNTEREY CNTY MEM HOSP (PA)
Also Called: George L Mee Memorial Hospital
300 Canal St, King City (93930-3431)
PHONE....................................831 385-6000
Lex T Smith, *CEO*
James Ewart, *Vice Chairman*
Roger Borzini, *Treasurer*
Susan Childers, *Officer*
Karen Wong, *Officer*
EMP: 495
SQ FT: 5,000
SALES (est): 71.8MM **Privately Held**
WEB: www.meememorial.com
SIC: 8062 Hospital, affiliated with AMA residency

(P-21214)
SOUTHERN MNTEREY CNTY MEM HOSP
467 El Camino Real, Greenfield (93927-4915)
PHONE....................................831 674-0112
Camille Sanz, *Director*
EMP: 146
SALES (corp-wide): 71.8MM **Privately Held**
SIC: 8062 Hospital, affiliated with AMA residency
PA: Southern Monterey County Memorial Hospital Inc
300 Canal St
King City CA 93930
831 385-6000

(P-21215)
SOUTHERN MONO HEALTHCARE DST
Also Called: MAMMOTH HOSPITAL
85 Sierra Park Rd, Mammoth Lakes (93546-2073)
P.O. Box 660 (93546-0660)
PHONE....................................760 934-3311
Helen Shepherd, *Chairman*
Gary Myers, *CEO*
Stephen Swisher M D, *Treasurer*
Christy Mc Millan, *Director*
EMP: 350
SQ FT: 20,000
SALES: 73MM **Privately Held**
SIC: 8062 General medical & surgical hospitals

(P-21216)
SOUTHWEST HEALTHCARE SYS AUX
Also Called: Business Department
38977 Sky Canyon Dr # 200, Murrieta (92563-2681)
PHONE....................................800 404-6627
Paula Dalbeck, *Controller*
EMP: 50
SALES (corp-wide): 10.7B **Publicly Held**
SIC: 8062 General medical & surgical hospitals

HQ: Southwest Healthcare System Auxiliary
25500 Medical Center Dr
Murrieta CA 92562

(P-21217)
SOUTHWEST HEALTHCARE SYS AUX (HQ)
Also Called: Rancho Springs Medical Center
25500 Medical Center Dr, Murrieta (92562-5965)
PHONE....................................951 696-6000
Brad Neet, *CEO*
Vimi Kapur,
Diane Moon, *CFO*
Barry Thorfenson, *CFO*
Anne Marie Watkins, *Ch Nursing Ofcr*
▲ **EMP:** 450
SALES: 51.1K
SALES (corp-wide): 10.7B **Publicly Held**
SIC: 8062 8051 8059 4119 General medical & surgical hospitals; skilled nursing care facilities; convalescent home; ambulance service
PA: Universal Health Services, Inc.
367 S Gulph Rd
King Of Prussia PA 19406
610 768-3300

(P-21218)
SRM ALLIANCE HOSPITAL SERVICES (PA)
Also Called: Petaluma Valley Hospital
400 N Mcdowell Blvd, Petaluma (94954-2339)
PHONE....................................707 778-1111
Deborah A Proctor, *President*
Jane Reed, *Vice Pres*
Katy Hillenmeyer, *Executive*
Gary Toavs, *Chief Engr*
Jane Read, *Mktg Dir*
EMP: 400
SQ FT: 98,000
SALES: 89.2MM **Privately Held**
SIC: 8062 General medical & surgical hospitals

(P-21219)
ST ELIZABETH COMMUNITY HOSP (DH)
2550 Sister Mary Clumba Dr, Red Bluff (96080-4327)
PHONE....................................530 529-7760
Todd Smith, *CEO*
John Halfhide, *President*
Tammy Fuller, *Mktg Dir*
Brooke Halford, *Director*
Kristine Kuebli, *Director*
EMP: 94 **EST:** 1901
SQ FT: 98,000
SALES: 95.6MM **Privately Held**
SIC: 8062 6513 General medical & surgical hospitals; retirement hotel operation
HQ: Dignity Health
185 Berry St Ste 300
San Francisco CA 94107
415 438-5500

(P-21220)
ST HELENA HOSPITAL (HQ)
Also Called: Deer Park Pharmacy
10 Woodland Rd, Saint Helena (94574-9554)
PHONE....................................707 963-3611
Steven Herber, *CEO*
Whie OH,
Timothy J Kares, *CFO*
Wendell Bobst, *Info Tech Dir*
Paul Selivanoff, *Finance*
EMP: 750
SQ FT: 200,000
SALES: 255MM
SALES (corp-wide): 4.4B **Privately Held**
WEB: www.sthelenahospital.com
SIC: 8062 8063 General medical & surgical hospitals; psychiatric hospitals
PA: Adventist Health System/West
1 Adventist Health Way
Roseville CA 95661
844 574-5686

(P-21221)
ST JOSEPH HEALTH SYSTEM
101 E Valencia Mesa Dr, Fullerton (92835-3809)
PHONE....................................714 992-3000
Deborah Proctor, *Principal*
Teresa Frey, *Vice Pres*
Jeff Harpster, *Exec Dir*
Sandy Quillin, *Executive Asst*
Rogelio Murillo, *Technician*
EMP: 65
SALES (est): 3.9MM **Privately Held**
SIC: 8062 General medical & surgical hospitals

(P-21222)
ST JOSEPH HEALTH SYSTEM
Also Called: Petaluma Valley Hospital
400 N Mcdowell Blvd Fl 1, Petaluma (94954-2339)
PHONE....................................707 778-2505
Hollis Belwaey, *Manager*
Miranda Prescott, *Nurse*
EMP: 50
SALES (corp-wide): 15.2B **Privately Held**
SIC: 8062 General medical & surgical hospitals
HQ: St. Joseph Health System
3345 Michelson Dr Ste 100
Irvine CA 92612
949 381-4000

(P-21223)
ST JOSEPH HERITAGE HEALTHCARE
27800 Medical Center Rd, Mission Viejo (92691-6410)
PHONE....................................949 365-2492
Nicki Levitt, *Manager*
EMP: 50
SALES (corp-wide): 15.2B **Privately Held**
SIC: 8062 General medical & surgical hospitals
HQ: St. Joseph Heritage Healthcare
200 W Ctr St Promenade
Anaheim CA 92805
714 712-3308

(P-21224)
ST JOSEPH HERITAGE MED GROUP (PA)
Also Called: Yorba Park Medical Group
2212 E 4th St Ste 201, Santa Ana (92705-3872)
PHONE....................................714 633-1011
Charles Foster, *President*
C R Burke, *CFO*
Dennis Long MD, *Treasurer*
Marc Bennette MD, *Vice Pres*
Joseph Brown MD, *Vice Pres*
▲ **EMP:** 134
SQ FT: 58,000
SALES (est): 16.2MM **Privately Held**
WEB: www.sjhmg.org
SIC: 8062 General medical & surgical hospitals

(P-21225)
ST JOSEPH HOSPITAL (PA)
2700 Dolbeer St, Eureka (95501-4799)
PHONE....................................707 445-8121
Toll Free:.............................888　-
Joseph Mark, *CEO*
David O'Brien, *President*
David Southerland, *COO*
Andrew Rybolt, *CFO*
Donald Baird, *Bd of Directors*
▲ **EMP:** 79 **EST:** 1920
SQ FT: 125,000
SALES: 248.2MM **Privately Held**
WEB: www.meyerinsure.com
SIC: 8062 General medical & surgical hospitals

(P-21226)
ST JOSEPH HOSPITAL
Also Called: Neurosurgery
2752 Harrison Ave Ste A, Eureka (95501-4738)
PHONE....................................707 268-0190
Maureen Lawlor, *Manager*
Edward Emmons, *Surgeon*
Daniel Farnum, *Surgeon*
Asa Stockton, *Surgeon*
John Biteman, *Otolaryngology*

EMP: 674
SALES (corp-wide): 248.2MM **Privately Held**
SIC: 8062 General medical & surgical hospitals
PA: St. Joseph Hospital
2700 Dolbeer St
Eureka CA 95501
707 445-8121

(P-21227)
ST JOSEPH HOSPITAL OF EUREKA
2700 Dolbeer St, Eureka (95501-4736)
P.O. Box 5600, Orange (92863-5600)
PHONE....................................707 445-8121
Sherie Henderson-Bialo, *Engineer*
Megan Zagone, *Pathologist*
Dennis Knoernschild, *Anesthesiology*
Bruce Boswick, *Oncology*
Dusten Macdonald, *Oncology*
EMP: 970
SALES: 292.2MM
SALES (corp-wide): 15.2B **Privately Held**
SIC: 8062 General medical & surgical hospitals
HQ: St. Joseph Hospital Of Orange
1100 W Stewart Dr
Orange CA 92868
714 633-9111

(P-21228)
ST JOSEPH HOSPITAL OF ORANGE (DH)
1100 W Stewart Dr, Orange (92868-3891)
P.O. Box 5600 (92863-5600)
PHONE....................................714 633-9111
Larry K Ainsworth, *President*
Tina Nycroft, *CFO*
Jim Cora, *Chairman*
Warren D Johnson, *Vice Ch Bd*
Terry Alvarez, *Vice Pres*
EMP: 2100 **EST:** 1929
SQ FT: 448,000
SALES: 627.2MM
SALES (corp-wide): 15.2B **Privately Held**
SIC: 8062 General medical & surgical hospitals
HQ: St. Joseph Health System
3345 Michelson Dr Ste 100
Irvine CA 92612
949 381-4000

(P-21229)
ST JOSEPH HOSPITAL OF ORANGE
Also Called: Renal Center
1100 W Stewart Dr, Orange (92868-3891)
P.O. Box 5600 (92863-5600)
PHONE....................................714 771-8037
Mary McKenzie, *Director*
EMP: 100
SALES (corp-wide): 15.2B **Privately Held**
SIC: 8062 General medical & surgical hospitals
HQ: St. Joseph Hospital Of Orange
1100 W Stewart Dr
Orange CA 92868
714 633-9111

(P-21230)
ST JOSEPHS MED CTR STOCKTON
1800 N California St, Stockton (95204-6019)
P.O. Box 213008 (95213-9008)
PHONE....................................209 943-2000
Donald J Wiley, *President*
EMP: 2366
SALES (est): 4.2MM **Privately Held**
WEB: www.chw.edu
SIC: 8062 General medical & surgical hospitals
HQ: Dignity Health
185 Berry St Ste 300
San Francisco CA 94107
415 438-5500

(P-21231)
ST JOSEPHS MEDICAL CENTER
1800 N California St, Stockton (95204-6019)
P.O. Box 213008 (95213-9008)
PHONE....................................209 943-2000
Donald J Wiley, *President*

Dr Susan McDonald, *Vice Pres*
Terry Spring, *Vice Pres*
Kathy Tohrnan, *Vice Pres*
Rae Charos, *Executive*
EMP: 150
SQ FT: 18,000
SALES: 478MM **Privately Held**
WEB: www.chw.edu
SIC: 8062 General medical & surgical hospitals
HQ: Dignity Health
185 Berry St Ste 300
San Francisco CA 94107
415 438-5500

(P-21232)
ST JUDE HOSPITAL (DH)
Also Called: ST JUDE MEDICAL CENTER
101 E Valencia Mesa Dr, Fullerton
(92835-3875)
PHONE.................................714 871-3280
Robert Fraschetti, *President*
Pamela Frey, *Records Dir*
Doreen Dann, *CEO*
Lee Penrose, *CEO*
Leslee Mc Gregor, *Admin Asst*
▲ **EMP:** 2582
SQ FT: 190,000
SALES: 557.5MM
SALES (corp-wide): 15.2B **Privately Held**
WEB: www.stjudemedicalcenter.com
SIC: 8062 General medical & surgical hospitals
HQ: St. Joseph Health System
3345 Michelson Dr Ste 100
Irvine CA 92612
949 381-4000

(P-21233)
ST JUDE HOSPITAL
Also Called: Administration
279 Imperial Hwy Ste 770, Fullerton
(92835-1059)
PHONE.................................714 578-8544
Claudette Desforges, *Principal*
Monica Hacker, *Finance*
EMP: 120
SALES (corp-wide): 15.2B **Privately Held**
WEB: www.stjudemedical.com
SIC: 8062 General medical & surgical hospitals
HQ: St. Jude Hospital
101 E Valencia Mesa Dr
Fullerton CA 92835
714 871-3280

(P-21234)
ST JUDE HOSPITAL
Also Called: St Jude Medical Ctr Purch Dept
101 E Valencia Mesa Dr, Fullerton
(92835-3875)
PHONE.................................714 992-3057
David Saffert, *Director*
EMP: 2500
SALES (corp-wide): 15.2B **Privately Held**
WEB: www.stjudemedical.com
SIC: 8062 General medical & surgical hospitals
HQ: St. Jude Hospital
101 E Valencia Mesa Dr
Fullerton CA 92835
714 871-3280

(P-21235)
ST MARY MEDICAL CENTER (DH)
Also Called: ST MARY'S SCHOOL OF NURSING
1050 Linden Ave, Long Beach
(90813-3321)
P.O. Box 887 (90801-0887)
PHONE.................................562 491-9000
Trammie McMann, *CEO*
Alan Garrett, *CEO*
Tammie McMann, *CEO*
Carolyn Caldwell, *Officer*
Stephen Dunn, *Lab Dir*
EMP: 1929
SQ FT: 700,000
SALES: 254.7MM **Privately Held**
SIC: 8062 Hospital, medical school affiliated with nursing & residency
HQ: Dignity Health
185 Berry St Ste 300
San Francisco CA 94107
415 438-5500

(P-21236)
ST MARY MEDICAL CENTER (PA)
18300 Us Highway 18, Apple Valley
(92307-2206)
PHONE.................................760 242-2311
David Klein, *President*
Kelly Linden, *COO*
Tracey Fernandez, *CFO*
Mark Lauron, *Treasurer*
Diana Carloni - O'Malley, *Trustee*
EMP: 1350
SQ FT: 92,000
SALES: 333.5MM **Privately Held**
WEB: www.stmaryapplevalley.com
SIC: 8062 General medical & surgical hospitals

(P-21237)
ST MARYS MED CTR FOUNDATION
450 Stanyan St, San Francisco
(94117-1019)
PHONE.................................415 668-1000
Ken Steele, *President*
James Wentz, *CFO*
Dee Mostofi, *Marketing Staff*
EMP: 1067 **EST:** 1983
SALES: 5.2MM **Privately Held**
WEB: www.chw.edu
SIC: 8062 Hospital, professional nursing school
HQ: Dignity Health
185 Berry St Ste 300
San Francisco CA 94107
415 438-5500

(P-21238)
STANFORD HEALTH CARE
Also Called: Quality Management
300 Pasteur Dr, Stanford (94305-2200)
PHONE.................................650 723-4000
Bert Hurlbut, *Vice Pres*
Helen Wilmot, *Vice Pres*
Jorge Wilson, *Vice Pres*
Thomas Bruynell, *Lab Dir*
Judy Kaufman, *Associate Dir*
EMP: 2523
SALES (corp-wide): 11.3B **Privately Held**
SIC: 8062 8099 Hospital, medical school affiliated with residency; childbirth preparation clinic
HQ: Stanford Health Care
300 Pasteur Dr
Stanford CA 94305
650 723-4000

(P-21239)
STANFORD HEALTH CARE
Also Called: Stanford Cancer Center S Bay
2589 Samaritan Dr, San Jose
(95124-4102)
PHONE.................................408 426-4900
Patrick Swift, *Med Doctor*
Duane Fernandez, *IT/INT Sup*
Eduard Tesnado, *Supervisor*
EMP: 2523
SALES (corp-wide): 11.3B **Privately Held**
SIC: 8062 Hospital, medical school affiliated with residency
HQ: Stanford Health Care
300 Pasteur Dr
Stanford CA 94305
650 723-4000

(P-21240)
STANFORD HEALTH CARE (HQ)
Also Called: Stanford Medical Center
300 Pasteur Dr, Stanford (94305-2200)
PHONE.................................650 723-4000
David Entwistle, *CEO*
Barbara Clemons, *President*
Quinn L McKenna, *COO*
Tracey Lewis Taylor, *COO*
David Connor, *CFO*
▲ **EMP:** 2392
SALES: 4.9B
SALES (corp-wide): 11.3B **Privately Held**
WEB: www.stanfordmedicalcenter.com
SIC: 8062 Hospital, medical school affiliated with residency
PA: Leland Stanford Junior University
450 Jane Stanford Way
Stanford CA 94305
650 723-2300

(P-21241)
STANFORD HEALTH CARE
Also Called: Shc Reference Laboratory
3375 Hillview Ave, Palo Alto (94304-1204)
PHONE.................................650 736-7844
Wendy Eilers, *Admin Asst*
Carin Milligan, *Senior Mgr*
Martha Aragon, *Director*
Susan Larry, *Manager*
EMP: 2523
SALES (corp-wide): 11.3B **Privately Held**
SIC: 8062 General medical & surgical hospitals
HQ: Stanford Health Care
300 Pasteur Dr
Stanford CA 94305
650 723-4000

(P-21242)
STANFORD HOSPITAL AND CLINICS
1510 Page Mill Rd Ste 2, Palo Alto
(94304-1133)
PHONE.................................650 213-8360
Martha Marsh, *President*
Katie Lipovsky, *Corp Comm Staff*
Lisa Levin, *Nurse*
Yvonne Rodrigues, *Vice Pres*
Hoi Yeung, *Manager*
EMP: 2523
SALES (corp-wide): 11.3B **Privately Held**
SIC: 8062 Hospital, medical school affiliated with residency
HQ: Stanford Health Care
300 Pasteur Dr
Stanford CA 94305
650 723-4000

(P-21243)
STANISLAUS SURGICAL HOSP LLC (PA)
Also Called: STANISLAUS SURGICAL CENTER
1421 Oakdale Rd, Modesto (95355-3356)
PHONE.................................209 572-2700
Douglas V Johnson, *CEO*
Leslie Konkin,
Timothy J Noakes, *Mng Member*
EMP: 230
SQ FT: 50,000
SALES: 36MM **Privately Held**
WEB: www.stanislaussurgical.com
SIC: 8062 General medical & surgical hospitals

(P-21244)
SURGERY CENTER OF ALTA BATES (HQ)
Also Called: Alta Bates Summit Medical Ctr
2450 Ashby Ave, Berkeley (94705-2067)
PHONE.................................510 204-4444
Warren Kirk, *President*
Annette Shaieb, *Pathologist*
Horacio Cruz, *Surgeon*
David H Irwin, *Hematology*
Ilan Remler, *Internal Med*
EMP: 653
SQ FT: 749,000
SALES (est): 410.8MM
SALES (corp-wide): 12.7B **Privately Held**
WEB: www.altabates.com
SIC: 8062 General medical & surgical hospitals
PA: Sutter Health
2200 River Plaza Dr
Sacramento CA 95833
916 733-8800

(P-21245)
SURPRISE VALLEY HLTH CARE DST
741 N Main St, Cedarville (96104)
P.O. Box 246 (96104-0246)
PHONE.................................530 279-6111
Wanda Grove, *CEO*
Jason Diven, *President*
Megan Grove, *CFO*
Cindy Linker, *Treasurer*
Carl Quigley, *Vice Pres*
EMP: 72
SQ FT: 13,330
SALES (est): 3.9MM **Privately Held**
SIC: 8062 General medical & surgical hospitals

(P-21246)
SUTTER BAY HOSPITALS (HQ)
Also Called: California Pacific Medical Ctr
633 Folsom St Fl 5, San Francisco
(94107-3623)
P.O. Box 7999 (94120-7999)
PHONE.................................415 600-6000
Jeff Gerard, *CEO*
Martin Brotman, *President*
Jamey Schmidt, *Administration*
Mike Souza, *Info Tech Dir*
Jeffrey Ziarno, *Analyst*
EMP: 2578
SALES: 1.5B
SALES (corp-wide): 12.7B **Privately Held**
WEB: www.cpmc.org
SIC: 8062 General medical & surgical hospitals
PA: Sutter Health
2200 River Plaza Dr
Sacramento CA 95833
916 733-8800

(P-21247)
SUTTER CENTRAL VLY HOSPITALS (HQ)
Also Called: Memorial Medical Center
1700 Coffee Rd, Modesto (95355-2803)
P.O. Box 942 (95353-0942)
PHONE.................................209 526-4500
James Conforti, *CEO*
Todd Smith, *Ch of Bd*
David P Benn, *CEO*
Sutter Pat Fry, *CEO*
Steve Mitchell, *COO*
EMP: 112 **EST:** 1947
SQ FT: 180,000
SALES: 772MM
SALES (corp-wide): 12.7B **Privately Held**
WEB: www.memorialmedicalcenter.org
SIC: 8062 General medical & surgical hospitals
PA: Sutter Health
2200 River Plaza Dr
Sacramento CA 95833
916 733-8800

(P-21248)
SUTTER COAST HOSPITAL (HQ)
Also Called: SUTTER C H S
800 E Washington Blvd, Crescent City
(95531-8359)
PHONE.................................707 464-8511
Eugene Suksi, *President*
Jim Strong, *CFO*
Candi Owens, *Planning*
Debra Faulk, *Systems Mgr*
Hamzeh Nasri, *Pediatrics*
▲ **EMP:** 250
SQ FT: 70,000
SALES: 89MM
SALES (corp-wide): 12.7B **Privately Held**
WEB: www.suttercoast.com
SIC: 8062 General medical & surgical hospitals
PA: Sutter Health
2200 River Plaza Dr
Sacramento CA 95833
916 733-8800

(P-21249)
SUTTER DELTA MEDICAL CTR AUX
3901 Lone Tree Way, Antioch
(94509-6200)
P.O. Box 3225 (94531-3225)
PHONE.................................925 779-7200
Linda Lee Rovai, *President*
Linda Horn, *Administration*
Janice Falzano, *Finance*
Phil Gardiner, *Human Resources*
Tim Bouslog, *Purch Mgr*
EMP: 53
SQ FT: 150,000
SALES (est): 9.9MM **Privately Held**
WEB: www.sutterdelta.com
SIC: 8062 8082 8093 8069 General medical & surgical hospitals; home health care services; specialty outpatient clinics; orthopedic hospital

(P-21250)
SUTTER HEALTH
1625 Stockton Blvd # 207, Sacramento
(95816-7092)
PHONE.................................916 733-1025

PRODUCTS & SVCS

Brian Betschart, *Partner*
Katie Scott, *Human Resources*
EMP: 265
SALES (corp-wide): 12.7B **Privately Held**
SIC: 8062 General medical & surgical hospitals
PA: Sutter Health
2200 River Plaza Dr
Sacramento CA 95833
916 733-8800

(P-21251)
SUTTER HEALTH
Also Called: Mamone James M
2 Medical Plaza Dr, Roseville
(95661-3043)
PHONE.....................916 797-4725
Kooyer Sharyl, *Administration*
Martin Neft, *Med Doctor*
Karen Nishimura, *Med Doctor*
EMP: 265
SALES (corp-wide): 12.7B **Privately Held**
SIC: 8062 General medical & surgical hospitals
PA: Sutter Health
2200 River Plaza Dr
Sacramento CA 95833
916 733-8800

(P-21252)
SUTTER HEALTH
Also Called: Cpmc
P.O. Box 7999 (94120-7999)
PHONE.....................415 600-7034
Suzann Samet, *Supervisor*
EMP: 324
SALES (corp-wide): 12.7B **Privately Held**
SIC: 8062 8051 8011 6513 General medical & surgical hospitals; skilled nursing care facilities; offices & clinics of medical doctors; retirement hotel operation
PA: Sutter Health
2200 River Plaza Dr
Sacramento CA 95833
916 733-8800

(P-21253)
SUTTER HEALTH
1020 29th St Ste 600, Sacramento
(95816-5126)
PHONE.....................916 733-9588
Connie Tam, *Office Mgr*
Ronda Willis, *Admin Asst*
Adriana Edeza, *Accountant*
Sara Dionne, *Counsel*
EMP: 177
SALES (corp-wide): 12.7B **Privately Held**
SIC: 8062 General medical & surgical hospitals
PA: Sutter Health
2200 River Plaza Dr
Sacramento CA 95833
916 733-8800

(P-21254)
SUTTER HEALTH
2734 El Camino Real, Santa Clara
(95051-3007)
PHONE.....................408 524-5952
Deborah Yim, *Analyst*
Medina Irene,
EMP: 324
SALES (corp-wide): 12.7B **Privately Held**
SIC: 8062 General medical & surgical hospitals
PA: Sutter Health
2200 River Plaza Dr
Sacramento CA 95833
916 733-8800

(P-21255)
SUTTER HEALTH
2000 Sutter Pl, Davis (95616-6201)
PHONE.....................530 757-5111
EMP: 348
SALES (corp-wide): 12.7B **Privately Held**
SIC: 8062 General medical & surgical hospitals
PA: Sutter Health
2200 River Plaza Dr
Sacramento CA 95833
916 733-8800

(P-21256)
SUTTER HEALTH
3901 Lone Tree Way, Antioch
(94509-6200)
PHONE.....................925 779-7273
Susan Bumatay, *Asst Admin*
Dan Baer, *Human Res Dir*
Alfort Santos, *Family Practiti*
Kyla Yee, *Obstetrician*
Michael Mann, *Anesthesiology*
EMP: 765
SALES (corp-wide): 12.7B **Privately Held**
SIC: 8062 General medical & surgical hospitals
PA: Sutter Health
2200 River Plaza Dr
Sacramento CA 95833
916 733-8800

(P-21257)
SUTTER HEALTH
3468 California St, San Francisco
(94118-1837)
PHONE.....................415 345-0100
Santos Dalere, *Officer*
Rene Biba, *Analyst*
Sabrina Butler, *Dermatology*
Dong Hwang, *Med Doctor*
Carmel Keane,
EMP: 294
SALES (corp-wide): 12.7B **Privately Held**
SIC: 8062 General medical & surgical hospitals
PA: Sutter Health
2200 River Plaza Dr
Sacramento CA 95833
916 733-8800

(P-21258)
SUTTER HEALTH
1335 S Fairmont Ave, Lodi (95240-5520)
PHONE.....................209 366-2007
David Duncan, *Principal*
EMP: 147
SALES (corp-wide): 12.7B **Privately Held**
SIC: 8062 General medical & surgical hospitals
PA: Sutter Health
2200 River Plaza Dr
Sacramento CA 95833
916 733-8800

(P-21259)
SUTTER HEALTH
595 Buckingham Way # 515, San Francisco
(94132-1909)
P.O. Box 320427 (94132-0427)
PHONE.....................415 731-6300
Diane Watkins, *Comp Tech*
Sherreah Daniels, *Manager*
EMP: 147
SALES (corp-wide): 12.7B **Privately Held**
SIC: 8062 General medical & surgical hospitals
PA: Sutter Health
2200 River Plaza Dr
Sacramento CA 95833
916 733-8800

(P-21260)
SUTTER HEALTH
Also Called: Sutter Pacific Med Foundation
1375 Sutter St Ste 406, San Francisco
(94109-5467)
PHONE.....................415 600-0110
Karen Earle, *Endocrinology*
EMP: 232
SALES (corp-wide): 12.7B **Privately Held**
SIC: 8062 General medical & surgical hospitals
PA: Sutter Health
2200 River Plaza Dr
Sacramento CA 95833
916 733-8800

(P-21261)
SUTTER HEALTH
2030 Sutter Pl Ste 1000, Davis
(95616-6215)
PHONE.....................530 750-5904
Lydia Lindsay, *Branch Mgr*
EMP: 177
SALES (corp-wide): 12.7B **Privately Held**
SIC: 8062 General medical & surgical hospitals

PA: Sutter Health
2200 River Plaza Dr
Sacramento CA 95833
916 733-8800

(P-21262)
SUTTER HEALTH
110 Stony Point Rd # 200, Santa Rosa
(95401-4189)
PHONE.....................707 535-5600
Pam Carroll, *Manager*
EMP: 177
SALES (corp-wide): 12.7B **Privately Held**
SIC: 8062 General medical & surgical hospitals
PA: Sutter Health
2200 River Plaza Dr
Sacramento CA 95833
916 733-8800

(P-21263)
SUTTER HEALTH
Also Called: Sutter Alhambra Surgery Center
8170 Laguna Blvd Ste 103, Elk Grove
(95758-7902)
PHONE.....................916 455-8137
Katie Askew, *Family Practiti*
Trevor Hacker, *Family Practiti*
Kimberly Buss, *Fmly & Gen Dent*
Dawn Blanton, *Supervisor*
EMP: 324
SALES (corp-wide): 12.7B **Privately Held**
SIC: 8062 General medical & surgical hospitals
PA: Sutter Health
2200 River Plaza Dr
Sacramento CA 95833
916 733-8800

(P-21264)
SUTTER HEALTH
2340 Clay St Rm 121, San Francisco
(94115-1932)
P.O. Box 7999 (94120-7999)
PHONE.....................415 600-1020
Warren Browner, *Vice Pres*
Anjula Singh, *Admin Sec*
Chris Riley, *Sr Ntwrk Engine*
Nelson Yee, *Finance*
Stanley Leong, *Oncology*
EMP: 648
SALES (corp-wide): 12.7B **Privately Held**
SIC: 8062 General medical & surgical hospitals
PA: Sutter Health
2200 River Plaza Dr
Sacramento CA 95833
916 733-8800

(P-21265)
SUTTER HEALTH
2880 Gateway Oaks Dr # 220, Sacramento
(95833-4332)
PHONE.....................916 566-4819
Vicki Flemming, *Branch Mgr*
Tajinder Kaur, *Program Mgr*
Jennifer Sproull, *Director*
Robert Stephens, *Manager*
EMP: 265
SALES (corp-wide): 12.7B **Privately Held**
SIC: 8062 General medical & surgical hospitals
PA: Sutter Health
2200 River Plaza Dr
Sacramento CA 95833
916 733-8800

(P-21266)
SUTTER HEALTH
Also Called: Sutter Elk Grove Surgery Ctr
8200 Laguna Blvd, Elk Grove
(95758-7956)
PHONE.....................916 544-5423
EMP: 589
SALES (corp-wide): 12.7B **Privately Held**
SIC: 8062 General medical & surgical hospitals
PA: Sutter Health
2200 River Plaza Dr
Sacramento CA 95833
916 733-8800

(P-21267)
SUTTER HEALTH
1375 Sutter St Ste 208, San Francisco
(94109-5465)
PHONE.....................415 600-0140
Tanya Watts, *Administration*
Susan Koo,
Sophia Katuta, *Manager*
EMP: 177
SALES (corp-wide): 12.7B **Privately Held**
SIC: 8062 General medical & surgical hospitals
PA: Sutter Health
2200 River Plaza Dr
Sacramento CA 95833
916 733-8800

(P-21268)
SUTTER HEALTH
2015 Steiner St Fl 1, San Francisco
(94115-2627)
PHONE.....................415 600-4280
Dorothy Coleman-Riese MD, *President*
Elizabeth Peralta, *Surgeon*
William Black, *Internal Med*
Vanessa Dumont, *Nurse Practr*
EMP: 1089
SALES (corp-wide): 12.7B **Privately Held**
SIC: 8062 General medical & surgical hospitals
PA: Sutter Health
2200 River Plaza Dr
Sacramento CA 95833
916 733-8800

(P-21269)
SUTTER HEALTH
100 Rowland Way Ste 210, Novato
(94945-5041)
PHONE.....................415 897-8495
Vicki Del, *Branch Mgr*
Peter Sullivan, *Officer*
EMP: 147
SALES (corp-wide): 12.7B **Privately Held**
SIC: 8062 General medical & surgical hospitals
PA: Sutter Health
2200 River Plaza Dr
Sacramento CA 95833
916 733-8800

(P-21270)
SUTTER HEALTH
Also Called: Sutter Medical Center
2825 Capitol Ave, Sacramento
(95816-6039)
PHONE.....................916 887-0000
EMP: 412
SALES (corp-wide): 12.7B **Privately Held**
SIC: 8062 General medical & surgical hospitals
PA: Sutter Health
2200 River Plaza Dr
Sacramento CA 95833
916 733-8800

(P-21271)
SUTTER HEALTH
3000 Telegraph Ave, Oakland
(94609-3218)
PHONE.....................510 869-8777
Stefan Arnold, *Branch Mgr*
Rick Beach, *Manager*
Jessica Romo, *Assistant*
EMP: 177
SALES (corp-wide): 12.7B **Privately Held**
SIC: 8062 General medical & surgical hospitals
PA: Sutter Health
2200 River Plaza Dr
Sacramento CA 95833
916 733-8800

(P-21272)
SUTTER HEALTH (PA)
Also Called: SUTTER C H S
2200 River Plaza Dr, Sacramento
(95833-4134)
PHONE.....................916 733-8800
Patrick Fry, *President*
Jim Gray, *Ch of Bd*
Robert D Reed, *CFO*
Gordon Hunt MD, *Officer*
Gary F Loveridge, *Senior VP*
EMP: 900

▲ = Import ▼=Export
◆ =Import/Export

SALES: 12.7B **Privately Held**
WEB: www.sutterhealth.org
SIC: 8062 8051 8011 6513 General medical & surgical hospitals; skilled nursing care facilities; offices & clinics of medical doctors; retirement hotel operation

(P-21273)
SUTTER HEALTH
475 Pioneer Ave Ste 400, Woodland (95776-4905)
PHONE...............................530 406-5600
Manuel Diaz, *President*
EMP: 265
SALES (corp-wide): 12.7B **Privately Held**
SIC: 8062 General medical & surgical hospitals
PA: Sutter Health
    2200 River Plaza Dr
    Sacramento CA 95833
    916 733-8800

(P-21274)
SUTTER HEALTH
600 Coffee Rd, Modesto (95355-4201)
PHONE...............................209 524-1211
Laurie Scott, *Principal*
Macedo Shannon, *Partner*
Paul Norton, *Technician*
Johanna Dailey, *Buyer*
Audrey Gilbert, *Buyer*
EMP: 200
SALES (corp-wide): 12.7B **Privately Held**
WEB: www.sutterhealth.org
SIC: 8062 General medical & surgical hospitals
PA: Sutter Health
    2200 River Plaza Dr
    Sacramento CA 95833
    916 733-8800

(P-21275)
SUTTER HEALTH
2516 E Whitmore Ave, Ceres (95307-2645)
PHONE...............................209 538-1733
EMP: 147
SALES (corp-wide): 12.7B **Privately Held**
SIC: 8062 General medical & surgical hospitals
PA: Sutter Health
    2200 River Plaza Dr
    Sacramento CA 95833
    916 733-8800

(P-21276)
SUTTER HEALTH
8170 Laguna Blvd Ste 220, Elk Grove (95758-7902)
PHONE...............................916 691-5900
EMP: 265
SALES (corp-wide): 12.7B **Privately Held**
SIC: 8062 General medical & surgical hospitals
PA: Sutter Health
    2200 River Plaza Dr
    Sacramento CA 95833
    916 733-8800

(P-21277)
SUTTER HEALTH
25 W Micheltorena St, Santa Barbara (93101-2509)
PHONE...............................805 966-1600
EMP: 265
SALES (corp-wide): 12.7B **Privately Held**
SIC: 8062 General medical & surgical hospitals
PA: Sutter Health
    2200 River Plaza Dr
    Sacramento CA 95833
    916 733-8800

(P-21278)
SUTTER HEALTH
2880 Soquel Ave Ste 10, Santa Cruz (95062-1423)
PHONE...............................831 477-3600
Kathleen McNupp, *Manager*
EMP: 50
SALES (corp-wide): 12.7B **Privately Held**
WEB: www.sutterhealth.org
SIC: 8062 General medical & surgical hospitals

PA: Sutter Health
    2200 River Plaza Dr
    Sacramento CA 95833
    916 733-8800

(P-21279)
SUTTER HEALTH
Also Called: Sutter Pacific Med Foundation
4702 Hoen Ave, Santa Rosa (95405-7824)
PHONE...............................707 545-2255
EMP: 324
SALES (corp-wide): 12.7B **Privately Held**
SIC: 8062 General medical & surgical hospitals
PA: Sutter Health
    2200 River Plaza Dr
    Sacramento CA 95833
    916 733-8800

(P-21280)
SUTTER HEALTH
1020 29th St Ste 570b, Sacramento (95816-5173)
PHONE...............................916 453-5955
EMP: 118
SALES (corp-wide): 12.7B **Privately Held**
SIC: 8062 General medical & surgical hospitals
PA: Sutter Health
    2200 River Plaza Dr
    Sacramento CA 95833
    916 733-8800

(P-21281)
SUTTER HEALTH
Also Called: Eden Medical Center
P.O. Box 160100 (95816-0100)
PHONE...............................916 731-5672
EMP: 147
SALES (corp-wide): 12.7B **Privately Held**
WEB: www.sutterhealth.org
SIC: 8062 General medical & surgical hospitals
PA: Sutter Health
    2200 River Plaza Dr
    Sacramento CA 95833
    916 733-8800

(P-21282)
SUTTER HEALTH
2449 Summerfield Rd, Santa Rosa (95405-7815)
PHONE...............................707 523-7253
Lisa Cooper, *Internal Med*
Benjamin Fritz, *Nephrology*
EMP: 236
SALES (corp-wide): 12.7B **Privately Held**
SIC: 8062 General medical & surgical hospitals
PA: Sutter Health
    2200 River Plaza Dr
    Sacramento CA 95833
    916 733-8800

(P-21283)
SUTTER HEALTH
Also Called: Shuler, Kurt MD
2030 Sutter Pl Ste 1300, Davis (95616-6215)
PHONE...............................530 750-5888
EMP: 135
SALES (corp-wide): 12.7B **Privately Held**
SIC: 8062 General medical & surgical hospitals
PA: Sutter Health
    2200 River Plaza Dr
    Sacramento CA 95833
    916 733-8800

(P-21284)
SUTTER HEALTH
100 Rowland Way, Novato (94945-5011)
PHONE...............................415 602-5380
Bill Davis, *CEO*
EMP: 145
SALES (corp-wide): 12.7B **Privately Held**
SIC: 8062 General medical & surgical hospitals
PA: Sutter Health
    2200 River Plaza Dr
    Sacramento CA 95833
    916 733-8800

(P-21285)
SUTTER HLTH SCRMNTO SIERRA REG (HQ)
Also Called: Sutter Memorial Hospital
2200 River Plaza Dr, Sacramento (95833-4134)
P.O. Box 160727 (95816-0727)
PHONE...............................916 733-8800
Patrick E Fry, *CEO*
Darling Lones, *President*
Tracy Murphy, *Vice Pres*
Philip Orisek, *Surgeon*
▲ **EMP:** 300 **EST:** 1935
SQ FT: 20,000
SALES: 1.8B
SALES (corp-wide): 12.7B **Privately Held**
SIC: 8062 8063 8052 General medical & surgical hospitals; psychiatric hospitals; intermediate care facilities
PA: Sutter Health
    2200 River Plaza Dr
    Sacramento CA 95833
    916 733-8800

(P-21286)
SUTTER HLTH SCRMNTO SIERRA REG
Also Called: Sutter Davis Hospital
2000 Sutter Pl, Davis (95616-6201)
P.O. Box 1617 (95617-1617)
PHONE...............................530 756-6440
Janet Wagner, *Branch Mgr*
Rose Lizola, *Safety Dir*
Jill Antonides, *Pub Rel Dir*
Jody Boetzer, *Marketing Staff*
Harkamal Sandhu, *Internal Med*
EMP: 350
SALES (corp-wide): 12.7B **Privately Held**
SIC: 8062 8011 General medical & surgical hospitals; offices & clinics of medical doctors
HQ: Sutter Health Sacramento Sierra Region
    2200 River Plaza Dr
    Sacramento CA 95833
    916 733-8800

(P-21287)
SUTTER HLTH SCRMNTO SIERRA REG
Also Called: Sutter Memorial Hospital
5151 F St, Sacramento (95819-3223)
P.O. Box 160727 (95816-0727)
PHONE...............................916 454-2222
Richard Foohoo, *Administration*
John Culver, *QA Dir*
Jim Kubota, *Finance Mgr*
Myra Malkiewicz, *Financial Analy*
Joshua Hoffman, *Director*
EMP: 310
SALES (corp-wide): 12.7B **Privately Held**
SIC: 8062 8011 General medical & surgical hospitals; offices & clinics of medical doctors
HQ: Sutter Health Sacramento Sierra Region
    2200 River Plaza Dr
    Sacramento CA 95833
    916 733-8800

(P-21288)
SUTTER HLTH SCRMNTO SIERRA REG
Also Called: Sutter Senior Care
1234 U St, Sacramento (95818-1433)
PHONE...............................916 446-3100
Janet Tedesco, *Branch Mgr*
EMP: 57
SALES (corp-wide): 12.7B **Privately Held**
SIC: 8062 General medical & surgical hospitals
HQ: Sutter Health Sacramento Sierra Region
    2200 River Plaza Dr
    Sacramento CA 95833
    916 733-8800

(P-21289)
SUTTER HLTH SCRMNTO SIERRA REG
Also Called: Sutter Roseville Medical Ctr
1 Medical Plaza Dr, Roseville (95661-3037)
PHONE...............................916 781-1000
EMP: 1180

SALES (corp-wide): 12.7B **Privately Held**
SIC: 8062 General medical & surgical hospitals
HQ: Sutter Health Sacramento Sierra Region
    2200 River Plaza Dr
    Sacramento CA 95833
    916 733-8800

(P-21290)
SUTTER HLTH SCRMNTO SIERRA REG
Also Called: Sutter Medical Center
2800 L St, Sacramento (95816-5616)
P.O. Box 160727 (95816-0727)
PHONE...............................916 733-3095
Sarah Krevans, *Branch Mgr*
EMP: 2500
SALES (corp-wide): 12.7B **Privately Held**
SIC: 8062 General medical & surgical hospitals
HQ: Sutter Health Sacramento Sierra Region
    2200 River Plaza Dr
    Sacramento CA 95833
    916 733-8800

(P-21291)
SUTTER LAKESIDE HOSPITAL (HQ)
Also Called: SUTTER C H S
5176 Hill Rd E, Lakeport (95453-6357)
PHONE...............................707 262-5000
Siri Nelson,
Bob Anderson, *CFO*
Kelly Mather, *Administration*
Blaze King, *CIO*
William D Duge, *Radiology*
EMP: 340 **EST:** 1945
SQ FT: 26,000
SALES: 80MM
SALES (corp-wide): 12.7B **Privately Held**
SIC: 8062 General medical & surgical hospitals
PA: Sutter Health
    2200 River Plaza Dr
    Sacramento CA 95833
    916 733-8800

(P-21292)
SUTTER MATERNITY & SURGERY CTR
2900 Chanticleer Ave, Santa Cruz (95065-1816)
PHONE...............................831 477-2200
Larry De Ghetaldi, *CEO*
Richard Nichols, *Administration*
Mark Riley, *Mktg Dir*
EMP: 225
SALES: 74.4MM **Privately Held**
SIC: 8062 General medical & surgical hospitals

(P-21293)
SUTTER ROSEVILLE MEDICAL CTR
1 Medical Plaza Dr, Roseville (95661-3037)
PHONE...............................916 781-1000
Patrick Brady, *CEO*
Rebecca Thompson, *Sr Corp Ofcr*
Susan Willson, *Sr Corp Ofcr*
Leslie Shane, *Executive Asst*
Julie Fralick, *Human Res Mgr*
EMP: 1700
SALES: 669.3MM **Privately Held**
SIC: 8062 General medical & surgical hospitals

(P-21294)
SUTTER RSVLLE MED CTR FNDATION
1 Medical Plaza Dr, Roseville (95661-3037)
PHONE...............................916 781-1000
Patricia Marquez, *President*
Pooja Sharma, *Internal Med*
Lance Rossi, *Physician Asst*
Mitch Davenport, *Manager*
EMP: 2000
SALES: 2.6MM **Privately Held**
SIC: 8062 General medical & surgical hospitals

PRODUCTS & SVCS

(P-21295)
SUTTER SURGICAL HOSPITAL N VLY
455 Plumas Blvd, Yuba City (95991-5074)
PHONE..........................530 749-5700
Toni Morris, *Principal*
EMP: 118 **EST:** 2010
SALES (est): 14.8MM
SALES (corp-wide): 1.7B **Publicly Held**
SIC: 8062 General medical & surgical hospitals
HQ: National Surgical Hospitals, Inc.
  250 S Wacker Dr Ste 500
  Chicago IL 60606
  312 627-8400

(P-21296)
SUTTER VALLEY HOSPITALS (HQ)
Also Called: Sutter Amador Hospital
200 Mission Blvd, Jackson (95642-2564)
PHONE..........................209 223-7500
Anne Platt, *CEO*
Jillian Chin, *Administration*
Joanne Hasson, *Education*
Nicki Allen, *Nursing Dir*
Sipho Munyaradzi, *Director*
EMP: 385
SALES (corp-wide): 12.7B **Privately Held**
WEB: www.sutteramador.com
SIC: 8062 General medical & surgical hospitals
PA: Sutter Health
  2200 River Plaza Dr
  Sacramento CA 95833
  916 733-8800

(P-21297)
SUTTER VALLEY MED FOUNDATION (PA)
Also Called: SUTTER HEALTH
2700 Gateway Oaks Dr, Sacramento (95833-4337)
PHONE..........................916 887-7122
Tom Blinn, *CEO*
Tambria Agnew, *Department Mgr*
Steven Coker, *Administration*
Tanya Hughes, *Project Mgr*
Daniel Yucht, *Project Mgr*
EMP: 700
SALES: 1.5B **Privately Held**
SIC: 8062 Hospital, AMA approved residency

(P-21298)
SUTTER WEST BAY HOSPITALS (HQ)
Also Called: SUTTER C H S
180 Rowland Way, Novato (94945-5009)
P.O. Box 1108 (94948-1108)
PHONE..........................415 209-1300
Brian Alexander, *CEO*
David Bradley, *President*
Sherie Hickman, *Administration*
Jonathan Hsiao, *Anesthesiology*
Wendy Davis, *Gastroenterlgy*
▲ **EMP:** 329 **EST:** 1952
SQ FT: 50,000
SALES: 68MM
SALES (corp-wide): 12.7B **Privately Held**
WEB: www.sutterhealth.org
SIC: 8062 General medical & surgical hospitals
PA: Sutter Health
  2200 River Plaza Dr
  Sacramento CA 95833
  916 733-8800

(P-21299)
TAHOE FOREST HOSPITAL DISTRICT
Also Called: Tahoe Workx
10956 Donner Paca Rd, Truckee (96161)
PHONE..........................530 582-3277
Ricardo Fergazo, *Director*
Celia Sutton-Pado, *Family Practiti*
John Swanson, *Med Doctor*
Jackie Griffin,
EMP: 111
SALES (corp-wide): 158.7MM **Privately Held**
SIC: 8062 8071 General medical & surgical hospitals; X-ray laboratory, including dental

---

PA: Tahoe Forest Hospital District
  10121 Pine Ave
  Truckee CA 96161
  530 587-6011

(P-21300)
TAHOE FOREST HOSPITAL DISTRICT (PA)
10121 Pine Ave, Truckee (96161-4856)
PHONE..........................530 587-6011
Robert Schapper, *CEO*
Jeff Dodd,
David Kitts,
Tad Laird, *Ch Radiology*
Tami Prior, *Ch of Bd*
EMP: 302
SQ FT: 120,000
SALES: 158.7MM **Privately Held**
WEB: www.tfhd.com
SIC: 8062 General medical & surgical hospitals

(P-21301)
TEHACHAPI VLY HEALTHCARE DST (PA)
305 S Robinson St, Tehachapi (93561-1726)
P.O. Box 669 (93581-0669)
PHONE..........................661 750-4848
Eugene Suksi, *CEO*
Chet Beedle, *CFO*
Allen Burgess, *Principal*
Bridget Thomason, *Controller*
Elizabeth McGehee,
EMP: 132
SQ FT: 18,000
SALES (est): 329.1K **Privately Held**
SIC: 8062 General medical & surgical hospitals

(P-21302)
TENET HEALTH SYSTEMS NORRIS
Also Called: Kenneth Norris Cancer Hospital
1441 Eastlake Ave, Los Angeles (90089-1019)
PHONE..........................323 865-3000
Scott Evans, *CEO*
Brian Harper, *President*
Strawn Steele, *CFO*
Carol Geffner, *Executive*
Brian Wilson, *Exec Dir*
EMP: 352
SQ FT: 175,000
SALES: 179.2MM **Privately Held**
SIC: 8062 General medical & surgical hospitals

(P-21303)
TENET HEALTHSYSTEM MEDICAL
13032 Earlham St, Santa Ana (92705-2113)
PHONE..........................714 966-8191
Tim Smith, *CEO*
EMP: 1500
SALES (corp-wide): 18.3B **Publicly Held**
WEB: www.tenenthealth.com
SIC: 8062 General medical & surgical hospitals
HQ: Tenet Healthsystem Medical, Inc.
  1445 Ross Ave Ste 1400
  Dallas TX 75202
  469 893-2000

(P-21304)
TENET HEALTHSYSTEM MEDICAL
16331 Arthur St, Cerritos (90703-2128)
PHONE..........................562 531-2550
John R Nickens, *Principal*
EMP: 509
SALES (corp-wide): 18.3B **Publicly Held**
WEB: www.tenenthealth.com
SIC: 8062 8011 General medical & surgical hospitals; offices & clinics of medical doctors
HQ: Tenet Healthsystem Medical, Inc.
  1445 Ross Ave Ste 1400
  Dallas TX 75202
  469 893-2000

(P-21305)
TENET HEALTHSYSTEM MEDICAL
Also Called: Tenet Health System Hospital
1205 E North St, Manteca (95336-4932)
PHONE..........................209 823-3111
Brenden Panzarello, *Branch Mgr*
Debra Garcia, *Records Dir*
Shawn Collins, *Recruiter*
Jody Gary,
EMP: 474
SALES (corp-wide): 18.3B **Publicly Held**
SIC: 8062 General medical & surgical hospitals
HQ: Tenet Healthsystem Medical, Inc.
  1445 Ross Ave Ste 1400
  Dallas TX 75202
  469 893-2000

(P-21306)
TENET HEALTHSYSTEM MEDICAL
Also Called: Irvine Regional Hospital
1400 S Duglaca Rd Ste 250, Anaheim (92806)
PHONE..........................714 428-6800
Donald Lorack, *CEO*
EMP: 509
SALES (corp-wide): 18.3B **Publicly Held**
WEB: www.tenethealth.com
SIC: 8062 General medical & surgical hospitals
HQ: Tenet Healthsystem Medical, Inc.
  1445 Ross Ave Ste 1400
  Dallas TX 75202
  469 893-2000

(P-21307)
TENET HEALTHSYSTEM MEDICAL
Cnty HSP/Rhb Ctr/Ls GTS-Srtg
815 Pollard Rd, Los Gatos (95032-1438)
PHONE..........................408 378-6131
Toll Free:..........................888
Gary Honts, *CEO*
EMP: 750
SALES (corp-wide): 18.3B **Publicly Held**
WEB: www.tenenthealth.com
SIC: 8062 8011 General medical & surgical hospitals; offices & clinics of medical doctors
HQ: Tenet Healthsystem Medical, Inc.
  1445 Ross Ave Ste 1400
  Dallas TX 75202
  469 893-2000

(P-21308)
THC - ORANGE COUNTY INC
5525 W Slauson Ave, Los Angeles (90056-1047)
PHONE..........................310 642-0325
Arthur L Rothgerber, *Principal*
EMP: 116
SALES (est): 318.5K
SALES (corp-wide): 6B **Privately Held**
SIC: 8062 General medical & surgical hospitals
HQ: Kindred Healthcare, Llc
  680 S 4th St
  Louisville KY 40202
  502 596-7300

(P-21309)
THOUSAND OAKS SURGICAL HOSP LP
401 Rolling Oaks Dr, Thousand Oaks (91361-1050)
PHONE..........................805 777-7750
Micheal Bass, *Partner*
Marissa Mc Arthur, *Exec Sec*
EMP: 100
SQ FT: 50,000
SALES (est): 13.9MM **Privately Held**
WEB: www.toshospital.com
SIC: 8062 General medical & surgical hospitals

(P-21310)
TORRANCE HEALTH ASSN INC (PA)
Also Called: PHYSICIAN OFFICE SUPPORT SERVI
3330 Lomita Blvd, Torrance (90505-5002)
P.O. Box 13717 (90503-0717)
PHONE..........................310 325-9110

Craig Leach, *CEO*
Sally Eberhard, *Senior VP*
John McNamara, *Senior VP*
Robin Camrin, *Vice Pres*
James Mollenkamp, *Vice Pres*
EMP: 3000
SQ FT: 180,000
SALES: 186.2MM **Privately Held**
SIC: 8062 General medical & surgical hospitals

(P-21311)
TORRANCE MEMORIAL MEDICAL CTR (HQ)
Also Called: PHYSICIAN OFFICE SUPPORT SERVI
3330 Lomita Blvd, Torrance (90505-5002)
P.O. Box 13717 (90503-0717)
PHONE..........................310 325-9110
Craig Leach, *President*
Eric Milefchik, *Infectious Dis*
Behzad Noorian, *Infectious Dis*
Mark V Ancheta, *Anesthesiology*
Steven Giles, *Anesthesiology*
EMP: 1500
SALES: 681.1MM
SALES (corp-wide): 186.2MM **Privately Held**
WEB: www.torrancememorial.org
SIC: 8062 Hospital, affiliated with AMA residency
PA: Torrance Health Association, Inc.
  3330 Lomita Blvd
  Torrance CA 90505
  310 325-9110

(P-21312)
TRACY SUTTER COMMUNITY HOSP
1420 N Tracy Blvd, Tracy (95376-3451)
PHONE..........................209 835-1500
David Thompson, *President*
Eric Dalton, *Administration*
J Lee, *Gnrl Med Prac*
Stephen Wesely, *Med Doctor*
Dave Bowlsby, *Director*
▲ **EMP:** 400
SQ FT: 80,000
SALES (est): 54.9MM
SALES (corp-wide): 12.7B **Privately Held**
WEB: www.suttertracy.org
SIC: 8062 8051 8011 General medical & surgical hospitals; skilled nursing care facilities; offices & clinics of medical doctors
PA: Sutter Health
  2200 River Plaza Dr
  Sacramento CA 95833
  916 733-8800

(P-21313)
TRI-CITY HOME CARE SERVICES
2095 W Vista Way Ste 220, Vista (92083-6029)
PHONE..........................760 940-5800
Vernon Petelle, *Director*
EMP: 140
SALES (est): 3.9MM **Privately Held**
SIC: 8062 General medical & surgical hospitals

(P-21314)
TRI-CITY HOSPITAL DISTRICT (PA)
Also Called: Tri-City Medical Center
4002 Vista Way, Oceanside (92056-4506)
PHONE..........................760 724-8411
Larry Schallock, *Chairman*
Casey Fatch, *CEO*
Robert Wardwell, *CFO*
Rosemarie V Reno, *Treasurer*
David Bennett, *Chief Mktg Ofcr*
EMP: 2100
SQ FT: 50,000
SALES: 319.2MM **Privately Held**
WEB: www.tcmccareers.com
SIC: 8062 General medical & surgical hospitals

(P-21315)
TULARE LOCAL HEALTH CARE DST
Also Called: TULARE DISTRICT HOSPITAL
869 N Cherry St, Tulare (93274-2207)
PHONE..........................559 685-3462

Shawn Bolouki, *CEO*
Sherrie Bell, *President*
Fred Capozello, *CFO*
Lee Gardner, *Pharmacy Dir*
Prem Camboj, *Admin Sec*
EMP: 700
SQ FT: 140,000
SALES: 14.2MM **Privately Held**
SIC: 8062 General medical & surgical hospitals

(P-21316)
TULARE REGIONAL MEDICAL CENTER
Also Called: Adventist Health Tulare
869 N Cherry St, Tulare (93274-2207)
PHONE....................559 688-0821
Andy Dodd, *CEO*
EMP: 100
SALES (est): 61.8K **Privately Held**
SIC: 8062 General medical & surgical hospitals

(P-21317)
U C MED HUMN RSRCES APLCAT SVC
Also Called: U C Health Systems
2730 Stockton Blvd # 21002500, Sacramento (95817-2217)
PHONE....................916 734-5916
Gloria Alvardo, *Director*
John Gubbels, *Manager*
EMP: 75
SALES (est): 1.8MM **Privately Held**
SIC: 8062 General medical & surgical hospitals

(P-21318)
UC DAVIS HEALTH SYSTEM (PA)
4610 X St, Sacramento (95817-2200)
PHONE....................916 734-1000
Katherine Wesnousky, *Principal*
Claire Pomeroy, *Principal*
Malathy Kapali, *Pathologist*
Mohammad Rasool, *Manager*
EMP: 59
SALES (est): 14MM **Privately Held**
SIC: 8062 General medical & surgical hospitals

(P-21319)
UCLA HEALTH SYSTEM
Also Called: Ronald Reagan Building
757 Westwood Plz, Los Angeles (90095-8358)
PHONE....................310 825-9111
Dr David T Feinberg, *CEO*
Suzie Morrel, *Officer*
Carl Nordstrom, *Associate Dir*
Jocelyn Apodaca, *Corp Comm Staff*
Lauren Beck, *Professor*
EMP: 99
SALES (est): 18.1MM **Privately Held**
SIC: 8062 General medical & surgical hospitals

(P-21320)
UCLA HEALTHCARE
1821 Wilshire Blvd Fl 6, Santa Monica (90403-5618)
PHONE....................310 319-4560
Tami Dennis, *Exec Dir*
EMP: 77
SALES (est): 150.4K **Privately Held**
SIC: 8062 9411 General medical & surgical hospitals; administration of educational programs
HQ: University Of California, Los Angeles
405 Hilgard Ave
Los Angeles CA 90095
-

(P-21321)
UHS-CORONA INC (HQ)
Also Called: Corona Regional Med Ctr Hosp
800 S Main St, Corona (92882-3420)
PHONE....................951 737-4343
Marvin Pember, *CEO*
Alan B Miller, *President*
Ken Rivers, *CEO*
Kevan Metcalf, *Principal*
Diane Holcomb, *Admin Sec*
▲ **EMP:** 900

SALES: 169.5MM
SALES (corp-wide): 10.7B **Publicly Held**
SIC: 8062 General medical & surgical hospitals
PA: Universal Health Services, Inc.
367 S Gulph Rd
King Of Prussia PA 19406
610 768-3300

(P-21322)
UKIAH ADVENTIST HOSPITAL (HQ)
Also Called: Ukiah Valley Medical Center
275 Hospital Dr, Ukiah (95482-4531)
PHONE....................707 462-3111
Terry Burns, *President*
Jeremy Mann, *Bd of Directors*
Janette Wilson, *Admin Sec*
Debra McEntee, *Network Enginr*
Kathy Smith, *Materials Dir*
EMP: 500 **EST:** 1967
SQ FT: 50,000
SALES: 200MM
SALES (corp-wide): 4.4B **Privately Held**
SIC: 8062 General medical & surgical hospitals
PA: Adventist Health System/West
1 Adventist Health Way
Roseville CA 95661
844 574-5686

(P-21323)
UKIAH ADVENTIST HOSPITAL
1120 S Dora St, Ukiah (95482-6340)
PHONE....................707 462-3111
Val Gene Devitt, *Branch Mgr*
EMP: 150
SQ FT: 43,500
SALES (corp-wide): 4.4B **Privately Held**
SIC: 8062 General medical & surgical hospitals
HQ: Ukiah Adventist Hospital
275 Hospital Dr
Ukiah CA 95482
707 462-3111

(P-21324)
UNITED STATES DEPT OF NAVY
Also Called: Navy Hospital
937 Vista Pl, Lemoore (93245)
PHONE....................559 998-4201
Clinton Butler, *Exec Dir*
D V Nostrand, *Director*
EMP: 711 **Publicly Held**
SIC: 8062 9711 General medical & surgical hospitals; Navy;
HQ: United States Department Of The Navy
1200 Navy Pentagon
Washington DC 20350
-

(P-21325)
UNITED STATES DEPT OF NAVY
Also Called: Naval Hospital Lemoore
Bldg 937 Franklin Ave, Lemoore (93246-0001)
PHONE....................559 998-4481
Stephen Mandia, *Director*
Holden Terry, *Info Tech Mgr*
William R Volk, *Orthopedist*
EMP: 600 **Publicly Held**
SIC: 8062 9711 General medical & surgical hospitals; Navy;
HQ: United States Department Of The Navy
1200 Navy Pentagon
Washington DC 20350

(P-21326)
UNITED STATES DEPT OF NAVY
Also Called: Naval Medical Center
34800 Bob Wilson Dr, San Diego (92134-1098)
PHONE....................619 532-6400
Esther Lynn, *Branch Mgr*
Christopher Williams, *Vice Chairman*
J Williams Sparks, *Anesthesiology*
Paula Witherspoon, *Pediatrics*
Jonathan Richardson, *Psychiatry*
EMP: 4250 **Publicly Held**
SIC: 8062 9711 General medical & surgical hospitals; Navy;
HQ: United States Department Of The Navy
1200 Navy Pentagon
Washington DC 20350

(P-21327)
UNITED STATES DEPT OF NAVY
Us Naval Hosp Bldg 1145, Twentynine Palms (92278)
PHONE....................760 830-2190
Mark Bowman,
EMP: 500 **Publicly Held**
SIC: 8062 9711 General medical & surgical hospitals; Navy;
HQ: United States Department Of The Navy
1200 Navy Pentagon
Washington DC 20350

(P-21328)
UNITED STATES DEPT OF NAVY
Also Called: Daps Naval Hosp
937 Franklin Blvd, Lemoore (93246-4700)
PHONE....................559 998-2894
Maryalice Morro, *Principal*
EMP: 400 **Publicly Held**
SIC: 8062 General medical & surgical hospitals
HQ: United States Department Of The Navy
1200 Navy Pentagon
Washington DC 20350
-

(P-21329)
UNIVERS OF CALIF SAN DIEGO HS
200 W Arbor Dr 8201, San Diego (92103-1911)
PHONE....................619 543-3713
Tom McAsee, *Principal*
Margarita Baggett, *CEO*
Duncan Campbell, *COO*
Angela Sciao, *Chief Mktg Ofcr*
EMP: 3281
SALES (est): 121.4MM **Privately Held**
SIC: 8062 General medical & surgical hospitals

(P-21330)
UNIVERSITY CAL LOS ANGELES
Also Called: Ucla Medical Center
200 Ucla Medical Plz, Los Angeles (90095-8344)
PHONE....................310 825-0640
Evelyn Cederbaum, *Branch Mgr*
Rhonda Sena, *Psychologist*
Kirsten Tillisch, *Gastroenterlgy*
Julie Yabu, *Nephrology*
Francy Shu, *Neurology*
EMP: 2056 **Privately Held**
WEB: www.ucla.edu
SIC: 8062 8221 9411 General medical & surgical hospitals; university; administration of educational programs;
HQ: University Of California, Los Angeles
405 Hilgard Ave
Los Angeles CA 90095

(P-21331)
UNIVERSITY CAL LOS ANGELES
Also Called: Ucla Medical Center
14445 Olive View Dr, Sylmar (91342-1437)
PHONE....................818 364-1555
Dr Dennis Cope, *Branch Mgr*
Rashmi RAO, *Obstetrician*
EMP: 3000 **Privately Held**
WEB: www.ucla.edu
SIC: 8062 8221 9411 General medical & surgical hospitals; university; administration of educational programs;
HQ: University Of California, Los Angeles
405 Hilgard Ave
Los Angeles CA 90095

(P-21332)
UNIVERSITY CAL LOS ANGELES
Also Called: Santa Monica Ucla Medical Ctr
1225 15th St, Santa Monica (90404-1101)
PHONE....................310 319-4000
Susan Colley, *Principal*
EMP: 1111
SQ FT: 7,350 **Privately Held**
WEB: www.ucla.edu
SIC: 8062 8221 9411 General medical & surgical hospitals; university; administration of educational programs;

HQ: University Of California, Los Angeles
405 Hilgard Ave
Los Angeles CA 90095

(P-21333)
UNIVERSITY CAL LOS ANGELES
Also Called: Ronald Reagan Ucla Medical Ctr
757 Westwood Plz, Los Angeles (90095-8358)
PHONE....................310 825-9111
Tatiana Orloff, *Branch Mgr*
Richard Frieder, *Obstetrician*
Gary Satou, *Cardiology*
Kyle Kern, *Neurology*
John Chute, *Oncology*
EMP: 2056 **Privately Held**
SIC: 8062 8221 9411 General medical & surgical hospitals; university; administration of educational programs
HQ: University Of California, Los Angeles
405 Hilgard Ave
Los Angeles CA 90095

(P-21334)
UNIVERSITY CAL SAN DIEGO
Also Called: Medical Center
200 W Arbor Dr Frnt, San Diego (92103-9000)
PHONE....................619 543-6654
Richard Likeweg, *Manager*
Barbara Hanks, *Executive Asst*
Sophia Davidson, *Admin Asst*
Yvonne Grobe, *Admin Asst*
Julia Roderick, *Admin Asst*
EMP: 4000 **Privately Held**
WEB: www.medicine.ucsd.edu
SIC: 8062 8221 9411 General medical & surgical hospitals; university; administration of educational programs;
HQ: University Of California, San Diego
9500 Gilman Dr
La Jolla CA 92093
858 534-2230

(P-21335)
UNIVERSITY CAL SAN DIEGO
Also Called: Ucsd Thornton Hospital
9300 Campus Point Dr, La Jolla (92037-1300)
PHONE....................858 657-7000
Paul Hensler, *Director*
John Einck, *Med Doctor*
EMP: 500 **Privately Held**
WEB: www.medicine.ucsd.edu
SIC: 8062 8221 9411 General medical & surgical hospitals; university; administration of educational programs;
HQ: University Of California, San Diego
9500 Gilman Dr
La Jolla CA 92093
858 534-2230

(P-21336)
UNIVERSITY CAL SAN FRANCISCO
Ucsf Langley Porter
401 Parnassus Ave, San Francisco (94143-2211)
PHONE....................415 476-7000
Craig Van Dyke, *Manager*
Tim Greer, *Info Tech Mgr*
Sarah Pennisten, *Project Mgr*
David Bickford, *Research*
Yan Leykin, *Psychologist*
EMP: 1000 **Privately Held**
WEB: www.uchastings.edu
SIC: 8062 8221 9411 General medical & surgical hospitals; university; administration of educational programs;
HQ: University Cal San Francisco
513 Parnassus Ave 115f
San Francisco CA 94143

(P-21337)
UNIVERSITY CAL SAN FRANCISCO
Also Called: Department of Urology
400 Parnassus Ave A633, San Francisco (94143-2202)
P.O. Box 738 (94104-0738)
PHONE....................415 476-1611
Christine McDevitt, *Manager*
EMP: 50 **Privately Held**

WEB: www.uchastings.edu
SIC: **8062** 8221 9411 General medical &
surgical hospitals; university; administration of educational programs;
HQ: University Cal San Francisco
513 Parnassus Ave 115f
San Francisco CA 94143

(P-21338)
UNIVERSITY CAL SAN FRANCISCO
Also Called: Ucsf Medical Center At Mt Zion
1600 Divisadero St, San Francisco
(94143-3010)
PHONE.....................................415 567-6600
Mark Laret, *Manager*
Mervyn Maze,
Edmon Obiniana, *Office Mgr*
Ed Torrento, *Purch Mgr*
Calvin Tang, *Opers Spvr*
EMP: 360 **Privately Held**
WEB: www.uchastings.edu
SIC: 8062 8221 9411 General medical &
surgical hospitals; university;
HQ: University Cal San Francisco
513 Parnassus Ave 115f
San Francisco CA 94143

(P-21339)
UNIVERSITY CALIFORNIA DAVIS
Also Called: Medical Centre
4400 V St, Sacramento (95817-1445)
PHONE.....................................916 734-3141
Dr William Ellis, *Principal*
EMP: 3575 **Privately Held**
WEB: www.ucdavis.edu
SIC: 8062 8221 9411 General medical &
surgical hospitals; university; administration of educational programs;
HQ: University Of California, Davis
1 Shields Ave
Davis CA 95616

(P-21340)
UNIVERSITY CALIFORNIA DAVIS
Also Called: Uc Davis Medical Center
2450 48th St Ste 2401, Sacramento
(95817-1538)
PHONE.....................................916 734-2011
Mauda Butte, *Principal*
Praveen Kumar, *Prgrmr*
Madeleine Silva, *Project Mgr*
Roger K Low, *Urology*
Nina Amenta, *Director*
EMP: 3575 **Privately Held**
SIC: 8062 8221 9411 General medical &
surgical hospitals; university; administration of educational programs;
HQ: University Of California, Davis
1 Shields Ave
Davis CA 95616

(P-21341)
UNIVERSITY CALIFORNIA DAVIS
Also Called: Department of Ane
4150 V St Ste 1200, Sacramento
(95817-1460)
PHONE.....................................916 734-5113
Karen Anderson, *Manager*
Pia Anette Hof, *Anesthesiology*
EMP: 3575 **Privately Held**
SIC: 8062 8221 9411 General medical &
surgical hospitals; university; administration of educational programs;
HQ: University Of California, Davis
1 Shields Ave
Davis CA 95616

(P-21342)
UNIVERSITY CALIFORNIA IRVINE
Also Called: Uc Irvine Medical Center
101 The City Dr S, Orange (92868-3201)
PHONE.....................................714 456-6011
Mary Piccione, *Exec Dir*
Janet Shigei, *Admin Dir*
Katie Teetor, *Office Mgr*

Thomas Wen, *Administration*
Kim Ritorto, *Network Enginr*
EMP: 3000 **Privately Held**
WEB: www.com.uci.edu
SIC: 8062 8221 9411 General medical &
surgical hospitals; university;
HQ: University Of California, Irvine
510 Aldrich Hall
Irvine CA 92697
949 824-8343

(P-21343)
UNIVERSITY CALIFORNIA IRVINE
Also Called: Irvine Medical Center
200 S Manchester Ave # 400, Orange
(92868-3220)
PHONE.....................................714 456-5558
Joy Grosse, *Director*
Matt Deines, *Associate*
EMP: 4000 **Privately Held**
WEB: www.com.uci.edu
SIC: 8062 8221 9411 General medical &
surgical hospitals; university; administration of educational programs;
HQ: University Of California, Irvine
510 Aldrich Hall
Irvine CA 92697
949 824-8343

(P-21344)
UNIVERSITY SOUTHERN CALIFORNIA
Also Called: Intergraded Media Systems Ctr
3737 Watt Way Fl 3, Los Angeles
(90089-0096)
PHONE.....................................213 740-4694
Adam Powell, *Branch Mgr*
EMP: 200
SALES (corp-wide): 4.9B **Privately Held**
WEB: www.usc.edu
SIC: 8062 8221 Hospital, medical school
affiliation; university
PA: University Of Southern California
3720 S Flower St Fl 3
Los Angeles CA 90089
213 740-7762

(P-21345)
UNIVERSITY SOUTHERN CALIFORNIA
Also Called: Usc University Hospital
1500 San Pablo St, Los Angeles
(90033-5313)
PHONE.....................................323 442-8500
Paul Vivano, *Director*
Alan Levine, *Managing Prtnr*
Patrick Niemann, *Managing Prtnr*
Jeff Fleeher, *CFO*
Sue Klug, *Chief Mktg Ofcr*
EMP: 875
SALES (corp-wide): 4.9B **Privately Held**
WEB: www.tenenthealth.com
SIC: 8062 8011 General medical & surgical hospitals; offices & clinics of medical
doctors
PA: University Of Southern California
3720 S Flower St Fl 3
Los Angeles CA 90089
213 740-7762

(P-21346)
US DEPT OF THE AIR FORCE
Also Called: 9th Medical Group
15301 Warren Shingle Rd, Marysville
(95903-1907)
PHONE.....................................530 634-4839
Melvin Antonio, *Branch Mgr*
EMP: 400 **Publicly Held**
WEB: www.af.mil
SIC: 8062 9711 General medical & surgical hospitals; Air Force;
HQ: United States Department Of The Air
Force
1000 Air Force Pentagon
Washington DC 20330

(P-21347)
USC CARE MEDICAL GROUP INC
Also Called: CARDIOLOGY DEPARTMENT
1510 San Pablo St Ste 649, Los Angeles
(90033-5404)
PHONE.....................................323 442-5100

Smitha Ravipudi, *CEO*
David Peng, *President*
Eileen Kohan, *Exec Dir*
Angel Padilla, *Office Mgr*
Glenn T Ault, *Med Doctor*
EMP: 80 **EST:** 1995
SALES: 333.5MM **Privately Held**
SIC: 8062 Hospital, medical school affiliated with nursing & residency

(P-21348)
USC VERDUGO HILLS HOSPITAL LLC
1812 Verdugo Blvd, Glendale
(91208-1407)
PHONE.....................................818 790-7100
Paul Craig, *CEO*
Hack Lash, *CFO*
Tracy Valenzuela, *Program Mgr*
Paul Celuch, *VP Human Res*
Andrew Brown, *Buyer*
EMP: 750
SQ FT: 45,000
SALES (est): 58.2MM
SALES (corp-wide): 4.9B **Privately Held**
SIC: 8062 Hospital, affiliated with AMA residency
PA: University Of Southern California
3720 S Flower St Fl 3
Los Angeles CA 90089
213 740-7762

(P-21349)
USC VRDUGO HLLS HOSP FUNDATION (PA)
1812 Verdugo Blvd, Glendale
(91208-1407)
PHONE.....................................800 872-2273
Armand Dorian, *Principal*
Debbie L Walsh, *President*
Paul Craig, *CEO*
Donna Tasker, *Admin Sec*
Marian Mc Cann, *Opers Staff*
EMP: 446
SQ FT: 225,000
SALES (est): 67.6MM **Privately Held**
SIC: 8062 General medical & surgical hospitals

(P-21350)
VALLEY CHILDRENS HOSPITAL
Also Called: Charlie Mitchell Chld Clinic
9300 Valley Childrens Pl, Madera
(93636-8762)
PHONE.....................................559 353-6425
Annette Humphrys, *Manager*
Merideth Robinson, *Psychologist*
Alfredo Garcia, *Pediatrics*
James Ozeran, *Med Doctor*
Robert Saunder, *Nurse*
EMP: 226
SALES (corp-wide): 518.1MM **Privately Held**
SIC: 8062 General medical & surgical hospitals
PA: Valley Children's Hospital
9300 Valley Childrens Pl
Madera CA 93636
559 353-3000

(P-21351)
VALLEY CHILDRENS HOSPITAL (PA)
9300 Valley Childrens Pl, Madera
(93636-8762)
PHONE.....................................559 353-3000
Todd Sunterapak, *President*
Timothy Hansen,
Jessie Hudgins, *COO*
Michele Waldrin, *CFO*
David Krause, *Bd of Directors*
EMP: 1500 **EST:** 1949
SQ FT: 300,000
SALES (est): 518.1MM **Privately Held**
SIC: 8062 General medical & surgical hospitals

(P-21352)
VALLEY HOSPITAL MEDICAL CENTER (DH)
Also Called: Calex
18300 Roscoe Blvd, Northridge
(91325-4105)
PHONE.....................................818 885-8500
Patrick Hawthorne, *President*

Stephen Farnum,
Betsy Hart, *COO*
Pam Alfenito, *Admin Sec*
Megan Lundgren, *Asst Admin*
EMP: 400
SQ FT: 300,000
SALES: 403.2MM **Privately Held**
WEB: www.northridgemg.com
SIC: 8062 General medical & surgical hospitals
HQ: Dignity Health
185 Berry St Ste 300
San Francisco CA 94107
415 438-5500

(P-21353)
VALLEY MEDICAL ONCOLOGY (PA)
5725 W Las Psts Blvd # 100, Pleasanton
(94588-4007)
PHONE.....................................925 734-8130
Rishi Sawney MD, *President*
Rick Da Roza, *CEO*
Shawana Davis, *Human Res Dir*
EMP: 100
SQ FT: 5,000
SALES (est): 11.8MM **Privately Held**
SIC: 8062 General medical & surgical hospitals

(P-21354)
VALLEY PRESBYTERIAN HOSPITAL
Also Called: V P H
15107 Vanowen St, Van Nuys
(91405-4597)
PHONE.....................................818 782-6600
Gustavo Valdespino, *CEO*
Janice Klostermeier, *CFO*
Jose Claudio, *Officer*
Michelle Quigley, *Officer*
Clyde Wesp, *Officer*
EMP: 1600
SQ FT: 400,000
SALES: 319.5MM **Privately Held**
SIC: 8062 General medical & surgical hospitals

(P-21355)
VERITAS HEALTH SERVICES INC
Also Called: CHINO VALLEY MEDICAL CENTER
5451 Walnut Ave, Chino (91710-2609)
PHONE.....................................909 464-8600
Prem Reddy, *CEO*
Irv E Edwards, *President*
Jacob Jensen, *Podiatrist*
Anna Zvansky, *Med Doctor*
EMP: 600 **EST:** 2000
SALES: 92MM
SALES (corp-wide): 3.4B **Privately Held**
WEB: www.cvmc.com
SIC: 8062 General medical & surgical hospitals
HQ: Prime Healthcare Services Inc
3300 E Guasti Rd Ste 300
Ontario CA 91761

(P-21356)
VERITY HEALTH SYSTEM CAL INC
Also Called: St Francis Medical Center
203 Redwood Shores Pkwy, Redwood City
(94065-1198)
PHONE.....................................310 900-8900
Fax: 626 744-3686
EMP: 300
SALES (corp-wide): 225.4MM **Privately Held**
SIC: 8062
PA: Verity Health System Of California, Inc.
2040 E Mariposa Ave
El Segundo CA 90245
650 551-6650

(P-21357)
VERITY HEALTH SYSTEM CAL INC
Also Called: O'Connor Hospital
2105 Forest Ave, San Jose (95128-1425)
PHONE.....................................408 947-2500
Robert Curry, *CEO*
Tara Archibald,

EMP: 200
SALES (corp-wide): 995MM Privately Held
SIC: 8062 General medical & surgical hospitals
PA: Verity Health System of California, Inc.
2040 E Mariposa Ave
El Segundo CA 90245
650 551-6650

(P-21358)
VERITY HEALTH SYSTEM CAL INC
Also Called: Paryroll Department
203 Redwood Shores Pkwy # 700, Redwood City (94065-1198)
PHONE..................650 551-6507
EMP: 200
SALES (corp-wide): 225.4MM Privately Held
SIC: 8062 8721
PA: Verity Health System Of California, Inc.
2040 E Mariposa Ave
El Segundo CA 90245
650 551-6650

(P-21359)
VERITY HEALTH SYSTEM CAL INC
Also Called: St. Louise Regional Hospital
9400 N Name Uno, Gilroy (95020-3528)
PHONE..................408 848-2000
Steven C Sharrer, Officer
Dub Drees, Vice Pres
Lisa Turallo, Executive Asst
Laura Reyes, Admin Asst
Patrick Ycaro, Analyst
EMP: 143
SALES (corp-wide): 995MM Privately Held
SIC: 8062 General medical & surgical hospitals
PA: Verity Health System Of California, Inc.
2040 E Mariposa Ave
El Segundo CA 90245
650 551-6650

(P-21360)
VERITY HEALTH SYSTEM CAL INC
3680 E Imperial Hwy # 306, Lynwood (90262-2659)
PHONE..................310 900-2000
EMP: 100
SALES (corp-wide): 225.4MM Privately Held
SIC: 8062
PA: Verity Health System Of California, Inc.
2040 E Mariposa Ave
El Segundo CA 90245
650 551-6650

(P-21361)
VERITY HEALTH SYSTEM CAL INC
Also Called: St. Francis Medical Center
3630 E Imperial Hwy, Lynwood (90262-2609)
PHONE..................310 900-8900
Gerald Kozai, Manager
EMP: 760
SALES (corp-wide): 995MM Privately Held
SIC: 8062 8011 General medical & surgical hospitals; medical centers
PA: Verity Health System Of California, Inc.
2040 E Mariposa Ave
El Segundo CA 90245
650 551-6650

(P-21362)
VETERANS HEALTH ADMINISTRATION
Also Called: VA Hospital
2615 E Clinton Ave, Fresno (93703-2223)
PHONE..................559 225-6100
Rhonda Aday, CFO
Michael Gatley,
Tanec Thompson, Officer
Josephine Davis, Technology
Sunitha Nalavenkata, Med Doctor
EMP: 961 Publicly Held
SIC: 8062 9451 General medical & surgical hospitals;

HQ: Veterans Health Administration
810 Vermont Ave Nw
Washington DC 20420

(P-21363)
VIBRA HEALTHCARE LLC
1315 Shaw Ave Ste 102, Clovis (93612-3963)
PHONE..................559 325-5601
Scott Mooneyham, Branch Mgr
EMP: 71
SALES (corp-wide): 330.4MM Privately Held
SIC: 8062 General medical & surgical hospitals
PA: Vibra Healthcare, Llc
4600 Lena Dr Ste 100
Mechanicsburg PA 17055
717 591-5700

(P-21364)
VIBRA HEALTHCARE LLC
Also Called: Vibra Hospital Northern Cal
2801 Eureka Way, Redding (96001-0222)
PHONE..................530 246-9000
Ross Domke, Business Dir
Christine A Jones, Administration
Rich Schubert, Food Svc Dir
Jennifer Douglas, Director
Sheba Saelee, Director
EMP: 104
SALES (corp-wide): 330.4MM Privately Held
SIC: 8062 General medical & surgical hospitals
PA: Vibra Healthcare, Llc
4600 Lena Dr Ste 100
Mechanicsburg PA 17055
717 591-5700

(P-21365)
VIBRA HEALTHCARE LLC
7173 N Sharon Ave, Fresno (93720-3329)
PHONE..................559 436-3600
Mary Jacobson, Principal
EMP: 71
SALES (corp-wide): 330.4MM Privately Held
SIC: 8062 General medical & surgical hospitals
PA: Vibra Healthcare, Llc
4600 Lena Dr Ste 100
Mechanicsburg PA 17055
717 591-5700

(P-21366)
VIBRA HEALTHCARE LLC
Also Called: Vibra Hospital of San Diego
555 Washington St, San Diego (92103-2289)
PHONE..................619 260-8300
Meeta Jones, CEO
Stacey Hedrick, Sales Staff
EMP: 141
SALES (corp-wide): 330.4MM Privately Held
WEB: www.vibrahealthcare.com
SIC: 8062 8069 8322 General medical & surgical hospitals; specialty hospitals, except psychiatric; rehabilitation services
PA: Vibra Healthcare, Llc
4600 Lena Dr Ste 100
Mechanicsburg PA 17055
717 591-5700

(P-21367)
VIBRA HOSPITAL SAN DIEGO LLC
555 Washington St, San Diego (92103-2289)
PHONE..................619 260-8300
Martha Heubach, CEO
Joe Leppert, Officer
Stephanie Moenich, Purchasing
Daniel Lample, Materials Mgr
Michael Kaber, Marketing Staff
EMP: 62
SALES (est): 8.7MM
SALES (corp-wide): 5B Publicly Held
SIC: 8062 General medical & surgical hospitals
PA: Select Medical Holdings Corporation
4714 Gettysburg Rd
Mechanicsburg PA 17055
717 972-1100

(P-21368)
VISTA SPECIALTY HOSP CAL LP
Also Called: Vista Hospital San Gabriel Vly
14148 Francisquito Ave, Baldwin Park (91706-6120)
PHONE..................626 388-2700
Marc C Ferrell, Partner
Christine Saltonstall, CFO
EMP: 200
SQ FT: 44,400
SALES (est): 8.6MM Privately Held
WEB: www.vistahealthcare.net
SIC: 8062 General medical & surgical hospitals

(P-21369)
WASHINGTON OUTPATIENT
Also Called: Washington Otpnt Surgery Ctr
2299 Mowry Ave Fl 1, Fremont (94538-1621)
PHONE..................510 791-5374
Gary Charland, Partner
Kimberly Hartz,
Neil Marks,
EMP: 97
SQ FT: 18,000
SALES (est): 12.5MM Privately Held
WEB: www.washosc.com
SIC: 8062 General medical & surgical hospitals
PA: Washington Township Hospital Development Corporation
2000 Mowry Ave
Fremont CA 94538
510 797-1111

(P-21370)
WAVE PLASTIC SURGERY CTR INC
Also Called: Wave Plstic Srgery Ctr Arcadia
400 N Santa Anita Ave, Arcadia (91006-2874)
PHONE..................626 898-9711
EMP: 256
SALES (corp-wide): 19.4MM Privately Held
SIC: 8062 8011 General medical & surgical hospitals; plastic surgeon
PA: Wave Plastic Surgery Center Inc.
3680 Wilshire Blvd Fl 2
Los Angeles CA 90010
213 383-4800

(P-21371)
WEST SIDE DISTRICT HOSPITAL
Also Called: Skilled Nursing Facility
110 E North St, Taft (93268-3606)
PHONE..................805 763-4211
Morgan Clayton, Ch of Bd
John Ruffner, Administration
EMP: 155
SQ FT: 30,000
SALES (est): 6.4MM Privately Held
WEB: www.chw.com
SIC: 8062 8051 8011 General medical & surgical hospitals; skilled nursing care facilities; offices & clinics of medical doctors

(P-21372)
WESTERN MEDICAL CENTER AUX (HQ)
Also Called: Western Med Center-Santa Ana
1301 N Tustin Ave, Santa Ana (92705-8619)
PHONE..................714 835-3555
Dan Brothman, CEO
Patricia Stites, CFO
EMP: 200
SALES (est): 117.6MM
SALES (corp-wide): 407.3MM Privately Held
WEB: www.westernmedanaheim.com
SIC: 8062 General medical & surgical hospitals
PA: Kpc Healthcare, Inc.
1301 N Tustin Ave
Santa Ana CA 92705
714 953-3652

(P-21373)
WHITE MEMORIAL MEDICAL CENTER (HQ)
Also Called: CECILLA GONZALEZ DE AL HOYA CA
1720 E Cesar E Chavez Ave, Los Angeles (90033-2414)
PHONE..................323 268-5000
Beth D Zachary, CEO
Mark J Newmyer, President
John G Raffoul, CEO
Terri Day, CFO
Mara C Bryant, Vice Pres
EMP: 1200 EST: 1913
SQ FT: 454,000
SALES: 504MM
SALES (corp-wide): 4.4B Privately Held
WEB: www.whitememorial.com
SIC: 8062 General medical & surgical hospitals
PA: Adventist Health System/West
1 Adventist Health Way
Roseville CA 95661
844 574-5686

(P-21374)
WHITTIER HOSPITAL MED CTR INC
9080 Colima Rd, Whittier (90605-1600)
PHONE..................562 945-3561
Richard Castro, CEO
Sarkis Vartanian, Ch Nursing Ofcr
Sheilah Creus, QA Dir
EMP: 180
SQ FT: 144,000
SALES (est): 33.5MM
SALES (corp-wide): 570.2MM Privately Held
SIC: 8062 General medical & surgical hospitals
PA: Ahmc Healthcare Inc.
1000 S Fremont Ave Unit 6
Alhambra CA 91803

(P-21375)
WILLITS HOSPITAL INC
Also Called: Howard Frank R Memorial Hosp
1 Marcela Dr, Willits (95490-5769)
PHONE..................707 459-6801
Rich Bockmann, CEO
Diane Moratti, Records Dir
Carlton Jacobsen, CFO
Jason Wells, Officer
Karen Scott Vpres, Vice Pres
EMP: 283
SQ FT: 27,000
SALES: 66MM
SALES (corp-wide): 4.4B Privately Held
WEB: www.howardhospital.com
SIC: 8062 General medical & surgical hospitals
PA: Adventist Health System/West
1 Adventist Health Way
Roseville CA 95661
844 574-5686

(P-21376)
WOODLAND HEALTHCARE
2660 W Covell Blvd, Davis (95616-5645)
PHONE..................530 756-2364
Kevin Mould, Branch Mgr
Philip M Laughlin MD, Med Doctor
Kevin S Mould MD, Med Doctor
EMP: 63 Privately Held
SIC: 8062 8011 General medical & surgical hospitals; offices & clinics of medical doctors
HQ: Woodland Healthcare
1325 Cottonwood St
Woodland CA 95695
530 662-3961

(P-21377)
WOODLAND HEALTHCARE
1207 Fairchild Ct, Woodland (95695-4321)
PHONE..................530 668-2600
Bill Hunt, Principal
Eduardo O Zapata, Med Doctor
EMP: 150 Privately Held
WEB: www.woodlandhealthcare.com
SIC: 8062 8011 General medical & surgical hospitals; offices & clinics of medical doctors

PRODUCTS & SVCS

HQ: Woodland Healthcare
1325 Cottonwood St
Woodland CA 95695
530 662-3961

8063 Psychiatric Hospitals

(P-21378)
7TH AVENUE CENTER LLC
1171 7th Ave, Santa Cruz (95062-2714)
PHONE.................................831 476-1700
Ann Butler,
Tami Toop, *Office Mgr*
Diana Cornell, *Bookkeeper*
EMP: 92
SALES (est): 4.7MM **Privately Held**
WEB: www.insuranceneighborhood.com
SIC: 8063 8361 8011 Psychiatric hospitals; residential care; offices & clinics of medical doctors

(P-21379)
ALTA HOLLYWOOD COMMUNITY HSPTL
14433 Emelita St, Van Nuys (91401-4213)
PHONE.................................818 787-1511
Irving Loube, *President*
Claude Lowen, *Corp Secy*
EMP: 115
SQ FT: 34,192
SALES (est): 4.8MM **Privately Held**
SIC: 8063 Psychiatric hospitals

(P-21380)
AURORA BEHAVIORAL HEALTH
1287 Fulton Rd, Santa Rosa (95401-4923)
PHONE.................................707 800-7700
Susan Rose, *CEO*
EMP: 75 EST: 2000
SQ FT: 50,000
SALES (est): 6.2MM
SALES (corp-wide): 7.3B **Publicly Held**
SIC: 8063 Psychiatric hospitals
HQ: Aurora Behavioral Healthcare Llc
4238 Green River Rd
Corona CA 92880
951 549-8032

(P-21381)
AURORA BEHAVIORAL HEALTH CARE
Also Called: MAGELLAN HEALTH
11878 Avenue Of Industry, San Diego (92128-3423)
PHONE.................................858 487-3200
Jim Plummer, *CEO*
Elizabeth Roods, *Social Dir*
Carol Yuan, *Pharmacy Dir*
Roma Sysyn, *Executive Asst*
Ruben Salazar, *Info Tech Mgr*
EMP: 150
SQ FT: 50,000
SALES: 30.6MM
SALES (corp-wide): 7.3B **Publicly Held**
WEB: www.aurorabehavioral.com
SIC: 8063 8069 Psychiatric hospitals; drug addiction rehabilitation hospital
PA: Magellan Health, Inc.
4800 N Scottsdale Rd Fl 4
Scottsdale AZ 85251
602 572-6050

(P-21382)
AURORA LAS ENCINAS LLC
Also Called: Aurora Las Encinas Hospital
2900 E Del Mar Blvd, Pasadena (91107-4375)
PHONE.................................626 795-9901
James Wilcox,
Brenda Nocon Rn,
EMP: 236
SQ FT: 132,000
SALES (est): 23.5MM **Publicly Held**
WEB: www.lasencinashospital.com
SIC: 8063 8069 Hospital for the mentally ill; alcoholism rehabilitation hospital
HQ: Hca Inc.
1 Park Plz
Nashville TN 37203
615 344-9551

(P-21383)
BAYVIEW HOSPITAL AND MENTAL
330 Moss St, Chula Vista (91911-2005)
PHONE.................................619 426-6311
Robert Bourseau, *Principal*
EMP: 250
SALES (est): 16.3MM **Privately Held**
SIC: 8063 Psychiatric hospitals

(P-21384)
BEACON HEALTHCARE SERVICES
Also Called: Newport Bay Hospital
1501 E 16th St, Newport Beach (92663-5924)
PHONE.................................949 650-9750
James E Parkhurst, *President*
EMP: 60
SALES (est): 10.3MM **Privately Held**
WEB: www.newportbayhospital.com
SIC: 8063 Psychiatric hospitals

(P-21385)
BEHAVIORAL H BAKERSFIELD
5201 White Ln, Bakersfield (93309-6200)
PHONE.................................661 398-1800
Ganesh Acharya, *CEO*
Amber Smithson, *Mktg Dir*
Sergio Herrera, *Food Svc Dir*
Brian Nelson, *Hlthcr Dir*
EMP: 235
SALES (est): 799.4K **Privately Held**
SIC: 8063 8011 Psychiatric hospitals; medical centers

(P-21386)
BEHAVIORAL HEALTH RESOURCES
Also Called: KNOLLWOOD PSYCHIATRIC CENTER
5900 Brockton Ave, Riverside (92506-1862)
PHONE.................................951 275-8400
Robert B Summerour, *President*
Karen Jerotz, *CFO*
EMP: 175
SALES: 7MM **Privately Held**
SIC: 8063 Psychiatric hospitals

(P-21387)
CALIFRNIA DEPT STATE HOSPITALS
Also Called: Coalinga State Hospital
24511 W Jayne Ave, Coalinga (93210-9503)
P.O. Box 5000 (93210-5000)
PHONE.................................559 935-4300
Tom Voss, *Director*
EMP: 300 **Privately Held**
SIC: 8063 9431 Psychiatric hospitals; mental health agency administration, government;
HQ: California Department Of State Hospitals
1600 9th St Ste 350
Sacramento CA 95814

(P-21388)
CALIFRNIA DEPT STATE HOSPITALS
Also Called: Fairview Developmental Center
2501 Harbor Blvd, Costa Mesa (92626-6143)
PHONE.................................714 957-5000
Michael Hatton, *Principal*
EMP: 1500 **Privately Held**
SIC: 8063 9431 Hospital for the mentally ill; mental health agency administration, government;
HQ: California Department Of State Hospitals
1600 9th St Ste 350
Sacramento CA 95814

(P-21389)
CALIFRNIA DEPT STATE HOSPITALS
Also Called: NAPA State Hospital
2100 Napa Vallejo Hwy, NAPA (94558-6234)
PHONE.................................707 253-5000

Sidney Herndon, *Branch Mgr*
Carol A Kuchmak, *Med Doctor*
Beverly De Chavez,
Margie Van Dam,
EMP: 2500 **Privately Held**
SIC: 8063 9431 8361 Hospital for the mentally ill; mental health agency administration, government; ; residential care
HQ: California Department Of State Hospitals
1600 9th St Ste 350
Sacramento CA 95814

(P-21390)
CALIFRNIA DEPT STATE HOSPITALS
Also Called: Patton State Hospital
3102 E Highland Ave, Patton (92369-7813)
PHONE.................................909 425-7000
Bruce Parks, *Director*
Aili W Arias, *Med Doctor*
Chinh Pham, *Med Doctor*
Nguyen Thong, *Med Doctor*
EMP: 2000 **Privately Held**
SIC: 8063 9431 Hospital for the mentally ill; mental health agency administration, government;
HQ: California Department Of State Hospitals
1600 9th St Ste 350
Sacramento CA 95814

(P-21391)
CALIFRNIA DEPT STATE HOSPITALS
Also Called: Atascadero State Hospital
10333 El Camino Real, Atascadero (93422-5808)
P.O. Box 7001 (93423-7001)
PHONE.................................805 468-2000
John De Morales, *Branch Mgr*
EMP: 1600 **Privately Held**
SIC: 8063 9431 8062 Hospital for the mentally ill; mental health agency administration, government; ; general medical & surgical hospitals
HQ: California Department Of State Hospitals
1600 9th St Ste 350
Sacramento CA 95814

(P-21392)
CALIFRONIA DEPARTMENT OF STATE
10333 El Camino Real, Atascadero (93422-5808)
PHONE.................................805 468-2501
Peter Sotello,
Christopher Stuiber, *Partner*
Faith Jewell,
EMP: 1953 EST: 1954
SALES (est): 42.4MM **Privately Held**
SIC: 8063 Psychiatric hospitals

(P-21393)
CANYON RIDGE HOSPITAL INC
Also Called: UHS
5353 G St, Chino (91710-5250)
PHONE.................................909 590-3700
Peggy Minnick, *CEO*
George Wilcox, *Executive*
Maria Patterson, *Safety Mgr*
EMP: 150
SALES (est): 19.1MM
SALES (corp-wide): 10.7B **Publicly Held**
WEB: www.intermountainhospital.com
SIC: 8063 8093 Hospital for the mentally ill; mental health clinic, outpatient
HQ: Psychiatric Solutions, Inc.
6640 Carothers Pkwy # 500
Franklin TN 37067
615 312-5700

(P-21394)
CATASYS INC (PA)
11601 Wilshire Blvd # 1100, Los Angeles (90025-1747)
PHONE.................................310 444-4300
Terren S Peizer, *Ch of Bd*
Richard A Anderson, *President*
Richard Anderson, *COO*
Christopher Shirley, *CFO*
Carol Murdock, *Officer*

EMP: 118
SQ FT: 9,120
SALES: 15.1MM **Publicly Held**
WEB: www.hythiam.com
SIC: 8063 Psychiatric hospitals

(P-21395)
CHARTER BEHAVIORAL HEALTH SYST
Also Called: Charter Oak Hospital
1161 E Covina Blvd, Covina (91724-1523)
PHONE.................................626 966-1632
Todd Smith, *CEO*
Vickie Esquibel, *Records Dir*
Janet Ray Perkins, *Officer*
Christine De La Paz, *Executive*
Mimi Mangune, *Nursing Dir*
EMP: 100
SALES (est): 7.8MM **Privately Held**
SIC: 8063 Psychiatric hospitals

(P-21396)
CHLB LLC
Also Called: College Medical Center
2776 Pacific Ave, Long Beach (90806-2613)
PHONE.................................562 997-2000
Joe Avelino, *CEO*
Rod Bell, *CFO*
Roderick Bell, *CFO*
Gregory Dixon, *Info Tech Dir*
Ray Avila, *IT/INT Sup*
EMP: 132
SALES (est): 15.5MM **Privately Held**
SIC: 8063 Psychiatric hospitals
PA: College Health Enterprises
11627 Telg Rd Ste 200
Santa Fe Springs CA 90670

(P-21397)
COLLEGE HOSPITAL INC (PA)
Also Called: College Hospital Cerritos
10802 College Pl, Cerritos (90703-1579)
PHONE.................................562 924-9581
Stephen A Witt, *President*
Bessie Weiss, *Corp Secy*
EMP: 300
SQ FT: 60,000
SALES: 70.3MM **Privately Held**
WEB: www.collegehospitals.com
SIC: 8063 Hospital for the mentally ill

(P-21398)
COUNTY OF EL DORADO
Also Called: Psychiatric Health Facility
935b Spring St, Placerville (95667-4523)
PHONE.................................530 621-6210
Kathlen Burne, *Branch Mgr*
EMP: 76 **Privately Held**
WEB: www.filmtahoe.com
SIC: 8063 9111 Psychiatric hospitals; executive offices
PA: County Of El Dorado
330 Fair Ln
Placerville CA 95667
530 621-5830

(P-21399)
COUNTY OF SAN DIEGO
Also Called: Health & Human Services
3853 Rosecrans St, San Diego (92110-3115)
PHONE.................................619 692-8200
Karen Hogan, *CEO*
Gonzalo Mendez, *Opers Staff*
Debbie Pasamonte, *Nurse*
Randall Krogman, *Manager*
David Nickel, *Manager*
EMP: 350 **Privately Held**
WEB: www.sdlcc.com
SIC: 8063 9431 Psychiatric hospitals; administration of public health programs;
PA: County Of San Diego
1600 Pacific Hwy Ste 209
San Diego CA 92101
619 531-5880

(P-21400)
COUNTY OF SONOMA
Department Mental Health Svcs
2227 Capricorn Way # 207, Santa Rosa (95407-5478)
PHONE.................................707 565-4850
Marcus Crosdowny, *Director*
Naomi Granvold, *Psychiatry*

Katrina Straight, *Med Doctor*
EMP: 63 **Privately Held**
WEB: www.sonomacompost.com
SIC: 8063 Hospital for the mentally ill
PA: County Of Sonoma
   585 Fiscal Dr 100
   Santa Rosa CA 95403
   707 565-2431

(P-21401)
CRESTWOOD BEHAVIORAL HLTH INC
Also Called: 112 Modesto Snf
1400 Celeste Dr, Modesto (95355-5041)
PHONE..................................209 526-8050
Lauri Blaufus, *Branch Mgr*
EMP: 200
SQ FT: 56,538
SALES (corp-wide): 188.6MM **Privately Held**
WEB: www.dreamcatch.us
SIC: 8063 Psychiatric hospitals
PA: Crestwood Behavioral Health, Inc.
   520 Capitol Mall Ste 800
   Sacramento CA 95814
   510 651-1244

(P-21402)
CRESTWOOD BEHAVIORAL HLTH INC
Also Called: 106 Sacramento Mhrc
2600 Stockton Blvd, Sacramento (95817-2210)
PHONE..................................916 452-1431
Cindy Mataraso, *Administration*
EMP: 120
SALES (corp-wide): 188.6MM **Privately Held**
WEB: www.dreamcatch.us
SIC: 8063 8361 Hospital for the mentally ill; residential care
PA: Crestwood Behavioral Health, Inc.
   520 Capitol Mall Ste 800
   Sacramento CA 95814
   510 651-1244

(P-21403)
CRESTWOOD BEHAVIORAL HLTH INC
Also Called: Fallbrook Healing Center
624 E Elder St, Fallbrook (92028-3004)
PHONE..................................760 451-4165
James M Dobbins Jr, *Branch Mgr*
EMP: 80
SALES (corp-wide): 188.6MM **Privately Held**
SIC: 8063 Psychiatric hospitals
PA: Crestwood Behavioral Health, Inc.
   520 Capitol Mall Ste 800
   Sacramento CA 95814
   510 651-1244

(P-21404)
CRESTWOOD BEHAVIORAL HLTH INC
Also Called: 145 Fresno Bridge
153 N U St, Fresno (93701-2438)
PHONE..................................559 445-9094
Giang T Nguyen, *Principal*
EMP: 89
SALES (corp-wide): 188.6MM **Privately Held**
SIC: 8063 Psychiatric hospitals
PA: Crestwood Behavioral Health, Inc.
   520 Capitol Mall Ste 800
   Sacramento CA 95814
   510 651-1244

(P-21405)
CRESTWOOD BEHAVIORAL HLTH INC
Also Called: Our House
2201 Tuolumne St, Vallejo (94589-2524)
PHONE..................................707 558-1777
Gail McDonald, *Branch Mgr*
EMP: 55
SALES (corp-wide): 188.6MM **Privately Held**
SIC: 8063 8011 Psychiatric hospitals; offices & clinics of medical doctors
PA: Crestwood Behavioral Health, Inc.
   520 Capitol Mall Ste 800
   Sacramento CA 95814
   510 651-1244

(P-21406)
CRESTWOOD BEHAVIORAL HLTH INC
Also Called: 111 Vallejo IMD
115 Oddstad Dr, Vallejo (94589-2520)
PHONE..................................707 552-0215
Minda Bunggay, *Administration*
EMP: 89
SALES (corp-wide): 188.6MM **Privately Held**
SIC: 8063 Psychiatric hospitals
PA: Crestwood Behavioral Health, Inc.
   520 Capitol Mall Ste 800
   Sacramento CA 95814
   510 651-1244

(P-21407)
CRESTWOOD BEHAVIORAL HLTH INC
Also Called: 153 American River PHF
4741 Engle Rd, Carmichael (95608-2223)
PHONE..................................916 977-0949
EMP: 89
SALES (corp-wide): 188.6MM **Privately Held**
SIC: 8063 Psychiatric hospitals
PA: Crestwood Behavioral Health, Inc.
   520 Capitol Mall Ste 800
   Sacramento CA 95814
   510 651-1244

(P-21408)
CRESTWOOD BEHAVIORAL HLTH INC
Also Called: 144 Pleasant Hill The Pathway
550 Patterson Blvd, Pleasant Hill (94523-4155)
PHONE..................................925 938-8050
Cynthia Mathraso, *Branch Mgr*
EMP: 89
SALES (corp-wide): 188.6MM **Privately Held**
SIC: 8063 Psychiatric hospitals
PA: Crestwood Behavioral Health, Inc.
   520 Capitol Mall Ste 800
   Sacramento CA 95814
   510 651-1244

(P-21409)
DEL AMO HOSPITAL INC
Also Called: UHS
23700 Camino Del Sol, Torrance (90505-5000)
P.O. Box 61558, King of Prussia PA (19406-0958)
PHONE..................................310 530-1151
Lisa Moncen, *CEO*
Alan B Miller, *Ch of Bd*
Kirk E Gorman, *Treasurer*
Sidney Miller, *Exec VP*
Jane Tinio, *Administration*
EMP: 300
SQ FT: 88,000
SALES: 42.9MM
SALES (corp-wide): 10.7B **Publicly Held**
WEB: www.uhsinc.com
SIC: 8063 Psychiatric hospitals
PA: Universal Health Services, Inc.
   367 S Gulph Rd
   King Of Prussia PA 19406
   610 768-3300

(P-21410)
GATEWAYS HOSP MENTAL HLTH CTR (PA)
1891 Effie St, Los Angeles (90026-1711)
PHONE..................................323 644-2000
Mara Pelsman, *CEO*
Jeff Emery, *CFO*
George King, *CFO*
Lisa Leist, *Executive Asst*
Phil Wong, *QA Dir*
EMP: 150 **EST:** 1953
SQ FT: 40,000
SALES: 29.1MM **Privately Held**
WEB: www.gatewayshospital.org
SIC: 8063 8093 Hospital for the mentally ill; mental health clinic, outpatient

(P-21411)
GOLDEN STATE HEALTH CTRS INC
Also Called: Sylmar Hlth Rehabilitation Ctr
12220 Foothill Blvd, Sylmar (91342-6001)
PHONE..................................818 834-5082

Cherlyn Hawkins, *Manager*
Michael Freeman, *Manager*
EMP: 250
SALES (corp-wide): 62.1MM **Privately Held**
WEB: www.goldenstatehealth.com
SIC: 8063 8069 Psychiatric hospitals; specialty hospitals, except psychiatric
PA: Golden State Health Centers, Inc.
   13347 Ventura Blvd
   Sherman Oaks CA 91423
   818 385-3200

(P-21412)
HELIX HEALTHCARE INC
Also Called: Alvarado Parkway Institute
7050 Parkway Dr, La Mesa (91942-1535)
PHONE..................................619 465-4411
Roy Rodriguez, *CEO*
Megan Monrgomery -West, *COO*
Mohammed Bari, *Vice Pres*
Patric Ziemer, *General Mgr*
Patty Dela Rosa, *Administration*
EMP: 310
SQ FT: 37,354
SALES (est): 40MM **Privately Held**
WEB: www.alvaradoparkwayinstitute.com
SIC: 8063 Hospital for the mentally ill

(P-21413)
JOHN MUIR BEHAVIORAL HLTH CTR
2740 Grant St, Concord (94520-2265)
PHONE..................................925 674-4100
Elizabeth Stallings, *COO*
Kevin Lane, *Business Dir*
Laura Dungo, *Office Mgr*
Amanda Tucker, *Persnl Dir*
Cindy Bolter, *Opers Staff*
EMP: 165
SQ FT: 40,000
SALES (est): 15.8MM **Privately Held**
SIC: 8063 8051 Psychiatric hospitals; skilled nursing care facilities

(P-21414)
KAISER FOUNDATION HOSPITALS
Also Called: Kaiser Mental Health Center
765 W College St, Los Angeles (90012-1181)
PHONE..................................213 580-7200
Kurt Hastings, *Manager*
Siv Hour, *Psychiatry*
EMP: 200
SQ FT: 66,697
SALES (corp-wide): 76.5B **Privately Held**
WEB: www.kaiserpermanente.org
SIC: 8063 Psychiatric hospitals
HQ: Kaiser Foundation Hospitals Inc
   1 Kaiser Plz
   Oakland CA 94612
   510 271-6611

(P-21415)
KEDREN COMMUNITY HLTH CTR INC (PA)
Also Called: Kedren Acute Psychia Hospit An
4211 Avalon Blvd, Los Angeles (90011-5622)
PHONE..................................323 233-0425
John Griffith, *President*
Robert Lawson, *Treasurer*
Lupe Ross, *Admin Sec*
Debra Thomas, *Admin Asst*
Araceli Lomeli, *Personnel Assit*
EMP: 400
SQ FT: 144,000
SALES: 35.8MM **Privately Held**
WEB: www.kedren.com
SIC: 8063 8093 Hospital for the mentally ill; specialty outpatient clinics

(P-21416)
KNOLLWOOD PSYCHIATRIC AND CHEM
Also Called: Knollwood Center
5900 Brockton Ave, Riverside (92506-1862)
PHONE..................................951 275-8400
Robert B Summerour, *President*
Byron Defour, *Shareholder*
EMP: 100
SQ FT: 50,000

SALES (est): 6.3MM **Privately Held**
SIC: 8063 Psychiatric hospitals

(P-21417)
LANDMARK MEDICAL SERVICES INC
Also Called: Landmark Medical Center
2030 N Garey Ave, Pomona (91767-2722)
PHONE..................................909 593-2585
Rose Horsman, *President*
EMP: 100
SQ FT: 27,500
SALES (est): 7.6MM **Privately Held**
SIC: 8063 Hospital for the mentally ill

(P-21418)
MADERA CONVALESCENT HOSPITAL
1255 B St, Merced (95341-6345)
PHONE..................................209 723-8814
Jerry Allgood, *Principal*
EMP: 80
SALES (corp-wide): 5.6MM **Privately Held**
SIC: 8063 Psychiatric hospitals
PA: Madera Convalescent Hospital, Inc
   517 S A St
   Madera CA 93638
   559 673-9228

(P-21419)
MARIN COUNTY SART PROGRAM
Also Called: Canyon Manor Residential Treat
655 Canyon Rd, Novato (94947-4331)
P.O. Box 865 (94948-0865)
PHONE..................................415 892-1628
Donald Harris, *President*
Ben Lan, *Corp Secy*
EMP: 100
SQ FT: 15,000
SALES (est): 2.4MM **Privately Held**
SIC: 8063 8361 8069 Hospital for the mentally ill; residential care; specialty hospitals, except psychiatric

(P-21420)
MENTAL HEALTH CALIFORNIA DEPT
Also Called: Vacaville Psychiatric Program
1600 California Dr, Vacaville (95696)
P.O. Box 2297 (95696-8297)
PHONE..................................707 449-6504
Victor Brewer, *Director*
EMP: 283 **Privately Held**
SIC: 8063 9431 Hospital for the mentally ill; mental health agency administration, government;
HQ: California Department Of State Hospitals
   1600 9th St Ste 350
   Sacramento CA 95814

(P-21421)
NORTHERN VLY INDIAN HLTH INC
175 W Court St, Woodland (95695-2913)
PHONE..................................530 661-4400
EMP: 52
SALES (est): 82.2K
SALES (corp-wide): 35.3MM **Privately Held**
SIC: 8063 Psychiatric hospitals
PA: Northern Valley Indian Health, Inc.
   207 N Butte St
   Willows CA
   530 934-9293

(P-21422)
OASIS MENTAL HEALTH TRTMNT CTR
47915 Oasis St, Indio (92201-6950)
PHONE..................................760 863-8609
Mary Jane Gross, *President*
EMP: 103 **EST:** 1995
SALES (est): 2.5MM **Privately Held**
SIC: 8063 Hospital for the mentally ill

(P-21423)
PSYCHIATRIC SOLUTIONS INC
Heritage Oaks Hospital
4250 Auburn Blvd, Sacramento
(95841-4100)
PHONE.................916 489-3336
Shawn Silva, *CEO*
EMP: 135
SALES (corp-wide): 10.7B **Publicly Held**
WEB: www.intermountainhospital.com
SIC: 8063 Psychiatric hospitals
HQ: Psychiatric Solutions, Inc.
6640 Carothers Pkwy # 500
Franklin TN 37067
615 312-5700

(P-21424)
SAGE BEHAVIOR SERVICES INC
505 E Commonwealth Ave, Fullerton
(92832-4009)
PHONE.................714 773-0077
Tammy Heo, *Director*
Kimi Ibello, *Analyst*
Cindy Hebert, *Director*
Kareem A Khouri, *Director*
EMP: 60
SQ FT: 6,000
SALES (est): 3.2MM **Privately Held**
SIC: 8063 Psychiatric hospitals

(P-21425)
SAN GBRIEL VLY CNVLESCENT HOSP
Also Called: Pennmar
3938 Cogswell Rd, El Monte (91732-2404)
PHONE.................626 401-1557
Dori Dimla, *Administration*
Carmen Fletcher, *Records Dir*
Mitchel Kantor, *President*
EMP: 65
SALES: 5MM **Privately Held**
WEB: www.pennmar.com
SIC: 8063 Psychiatric hospitals

(P-21426)
SHARP MEMORIAL HOSPITAL
Also Called: Sharp Mesa Vista Hospital
7850 Vista Hill Ave, San Diego
(92123-2717)
PHONE.................858 278-4110
Carolyn Mason, *Director*
Linda Carson, *Volunteer Dir*
Melody White, *Admin Sec*
Raymond Fidaleo, *Psychiatry*
Joseph Minick, *Med Doctor*
EMP: 190
SALES (corp-wide): 3.4B **Privately Held**
SIC: 8063 8069 8093 Psychiatric hospitals; substance abuse hospitals; specialty outpatient clinics
HQ: Sharp Memorial Hospital
7901 Frost St
San Diego CA 92123
858 939-3636

(P-21427)
STAR VIEW ADOLESCENT CENTER
4025 W 226th St, Torrance (90505-2340)
PHONE.................310 373-4556
Mary Jane Gross, *President*
Ryan Chadderton, *Psychologist*
Jennifer Jarbath, *Director*
Deiadra Kearns, *Director*
Rob McKinstry, *Director*
EMP: 80 **EST:** 1996
SALES (est): 5.4MM **Privately Held**
SIC: 8063 Psychiatric hospitals

(P-21428)
SYLMAR HLTH REHABILITATION CTR
Also Called: Sylmar Hlth Rehabilitation Ctr
12220 Foothill Blvd, Sylmar (91342-6001)
PHONE.................818 834-5082
Marty Weiss, *President*
Cherlyn Brintnell, *Administration*
EMP: 200 **EST:** 1969
SALES (est): 8.4MM
SALES (corp-wide): 62.1MM **Privately Held**
WEB: www.goldenstatehealth.com
SIC: 8063 Psychiatric hospitals

PA: Golden State Health Centers, Inc.
13347 Ventura Blvd
Sherman Oaks CA 91423
818 385-3200

(P-21429)
TELECARE CORPORATION
275 Baker St, Costa Mesa (92626-4566)
PHONE.................714 361-6760
Anne Bakar, *Branch Mgr*
EMP: 61
SALES (corp-wide): 205.4MM **Privately Held**
SIC: 8063 Psychiatric hospitals
PA: Telecare Corporation
1080 Marina Village Pkwy # 100
Alameda CA 94501
510 337-7950

(P-21430)
TELECARE CORPORATION
Also Called: Willow Rock Center
2050 Fairmont Dr, San Leandro
(94578-1001)
PHONE.................510 895-5502
Peter Zucker, *Branch Mgr*
EMP: 60
SALES (corp-wide): 205.4MM **Privately Held**
SIC: 8063 Psychiatric hospitals
PA: Telecare Corporation
1080 Marina Village Pkwy # 100
Alameda CA 94501
510 337-7950

(P-21431)
TELECARE CORPORATION
16460 Victor St, Victorville (92395-3918)
PHONE.................760 245-8837
Clarissa Dodd, *Branch Mgr*
EMP: 60
SALES (corp-wide): 205.4MM **Privately Held**
SIC: 8063 8093 Psychiatric hospitals; mental health clinic, outpatient
PA: Telecare Corporation
1080 Marina Village Pkwy # 100
Alameda CA 94501
510 337-7950

(P-21432)
TELECARE CORPORATION
1675 Morena Blvd Ste 100, San Diego
(92110-3703)
PHONE.................619 275-8000
Tara Booth, *Administration*
EMP: 60
SALES (corp-wide): 205.4MM **Privately Held**
SIC: 8063 Psychiatric hospitals
PA: Telecare Corporation
1080 Marina Village Pkwy # 100
Alameda CA 94501
510 337-7950

(P-21433)
TELECARE CORPORATION
Also Called: La Casa Mhrc
6060 N Paramount Blvd, Long Beach
(90805-3711)
PHONE.................562 630-8672
Anne Bakar, *CEO*
EMP: 99
SALES (est): 5.7MM
SALES (corp-wide): 205.4MM **Privately Held**
SIC: 8063 Psychiatric hospitals
PA: Telecare Corporation
1080 Marina Village Pkwy # 100
Alameda CA 94501
510 337-7950

(P-21434)
TELECARE CORPORATION
Also Called: La Casa Mental Health Center
6060 N Paramount Blvd, Long Beach
(90805-3711)
PHONE.................562 634-9534
David Effron, *Branch Mgr*
EMP: 230
SALES (corp-wide): 205.4MM **Privately Held**
WEB: www.telecarecorp.com
SIC: 8063 8011 Psychiatric hospitals; health maintenance organization

PA: Telecare Corporation
1080 Marina Village Pkwy # 100
Alameda CA 94501
510 337-7950

(P-21435)
TELECARE CORPORATION
Also Called: Garfield Nuerobehavioral Ctr
1451 28th Ave, Oakland (94601-1632)
PHONE.................510 261-9191
Alonzo Clemens, *Director*
EMP: 110
SQ FT: 2,117
SALES (corp-wide): 205.4MM **Privately Held**
WEB: www.telecarecorp.com
SIC: 8063 8011 Psychiatric hospitals; health maintenance organization
PA: Telecare Corporation
1080 Marina Village Pkwy # 100
Alameda CA 94501
510 337-7950

(P-21436)
TELECARE CORPORATION
Also Called: Morton Bakar Center
494 Blossom Way, Hayward (94541-1948)
PHONE.................510 582-7676
Mary Thrower, *Branch Mgr*
Kishor Kumar, *Director*
EMP: 125
SALES (corp-wide): 205.4MM **Privately Held**
WEB: www.telecarecorp.com
SIC: 8063 8011 Psychiatric hospitals; health maintenance organization
PA: Telecare Corporation
1080 Marina Village Pkwy # 100
Alameda CA 94501
510 337-7950

(P-21437)
TELECARE CORPORATION
Also Called: Villa Fairmont Mental Hlth Ctr
15200 Foothill Blvd, San Leandro
(94578-1013)
PHONE.................510 352-9690
Regina Scott, *Manager*
EMP: 132
SALES (corp-wide): 205.4MM **Privately Held**
WEB: www.telecarecorp.com
SIC: 8063 8011 Psychiatric hospitals; health maintenance organization
PA: Telecare Corporation
1080 Marina Village Pkwy # 100
Alameda CA 94501
510 337-7950

(P-21438)
TELECARE CORPORATION
Also Called: San Diego Choices
3851 Rosecrans St, San Diego
(92110-3115)
PHONE.................619 692-8225
Scherry Messic, *Branch Mgr*
EMP: 58
SALES (corp-wide): 205.4MM **Privately Held**
WEB: www.telecarecorp.com
SIC: 8063 8011 Psychiatric hospitals; health maintenance organization
PA: Telecare Corporation
1080 Marina Village Pkwy # 100
Alameda CA 94501
510 337-7950

(P-21439)
TELECARE CORPORATION
Also Called: Los Posadas Service Center
1756 S Lewis Rd, Camarillo (93012-8520)
PHONE.................805 383-3669
Tim Kuehnel, *Manager*
EMP: 55
SALES (corp-wide): 205.4MM **Privately Held**
WEB: www.telecarecorp.com
SIC: 8063 8011 Psychiatric hospitals; health maintenance organization
PA: Telecare Corporation
1080 Marina Village Pkwy # 100
Alameda CA 94501
510 337-7950

PA: Telecare Corporation
1080 Marina Village Pkwy # 100
Alameda CA 94501
510 337-7950

(P-21440)
TELECARE CORPORATION
Also Called: Cordilleras Mental Health Ctr
200 Edmonds Rd, Redwood City
(94062-3813)
PHONE.................650 367-1890
Bill Kruse, *Branch Mgr*
EMP: 123
SALES (corp-wide): 205.4MM **Privately Held**
WEB: www.telecarecorp.com
SIC: 8063 8011 Psychiatric hospitals; health maintenance organization
PA: Telecare Corporation
1080 Marina Village Pkwy # 100
Alameda CA 94501
510 337-7950

(P-21441)
TELECARE CORPORATION
Also Called: Cresta Loma
1080 Marina Village Pkwy # 100, Alameda
(94501-1078)
PHONE.................510 337-7950
Becky Clark, *Branch Mgr*
EMP: 101
SQ FT: 44,000
SALES (corp-wide): 205.4MM **Privately Held**
WEB: www.telecarecorp.com
SIC: 8063 8011 Psychiatric hospitals; health maintenance organization
PA: Telecare Corporation
1080 Marina Village Pkwy # 100
Alameda CA 94501
510 337-7950

(P-21442)
TELECARE CORPORATION
Also Called: La Paz Geropsychiatric Center
8835 Vans St, Paramount (90723-4656)
PHONE.................562 633-5111
Rich Widerynski, *Administration*
Faye Bernardo, *Director*
Cynthia Lopez, *Director*
EMP: 150
SALES (corp-wide): 205.4MM **Privately Held**
WEB: www.telecarecorp.com
SIC: 8063 8011 Psychiatric hospitals; health maintenance organization
PA: Telecare Corporation
1080 Marina Village Pkwy # 100
Alameda CA 94501
510 337-7950

(P-21443)
TELECARE CORPORATION
Also Called: Telecare Fsp
300 Harbor Blvd E, Belmont (94002-4018)
P.O. Box 1329, San Carlos (94070-7329)
PHONE.................650 817-9070
Kevin Jones, *Administration*
EMP: 60
SALES (corp-wide): 205.4MM **Privately Held**
SIC: 8063 8621 Psychiatric hospitals; health association
PA: Telecare Corporation
1080 Marina Village Pkwy # 100
Alameda CA 94501
510 337-7950

(P-21444)
TELECARE CORPORATION
Also Called: Heritage Psychiatric Health
2633 E 27th St, Oakland (94601-1912)
PHONE.................510 535-5115
Patty Espeseth, *Branch Mgr*
EMP: 120
SALES (corp-wide): 205.4MM **Privately Held**
WEB: www.telecarecorp.com
SIC: 8063 8011 Psychiatric hospitals; health maintenance organization
PA: Telecare Corporation
1080 Marina Village Pkwy # 100
Alameda CA 94501
510 337-7950

(P-21445)
TENET HEALTHSYSTEM MEDICAL
330 Moss St, Chula Vista (91911-2005)
PHONE.................619 426-6310
EMP: 150

SALES (corp-wide): 11.1B **Publicly Held**
SIC: **8063**
HQ: Tenet Healthsystem Medical, Inc
1445 Ross Ave Ste 1400
Dallas TX 75202
469 893-2000

(P-21446)
VISTA BEHAVIORAL HEALTH INC
Also Called: Pacific Grove Hospital
5900 Brockton Ave, Riverside
(92506-1862)
PHONE..................................800 992-0901
Nelson Smith, *CEO*
EMP: 67 EST: 2015
SALES (est): 2.6MM **Publicly Held**
SIC: **8063** Psychiatric hospitals
PA: Acadia Healthcare Company, Inc.
6100 Tower Cir Ste 1000
Franklin TN 37067

┌─────────────────────────────┐
│ **8069 Specialty Hospitals,** │
│ **Except Psychiatric** │
└─────────────────────────────┘

(P-21447)
ANAHEIM REGIONAL MEDICAL CTR (PA)
1111 W La Palma Ave, Anaheim
(92801-2804)
PHONE..................................714 774-1450
Patrick Petre, *CEO*
Deborah Webber, *COO*
Linda Marsh, *Vice Pres*
Katherine Doi, *Human Res Dir*
Kim Wright, *Human Res Dir*
EMP: 55
SALES (est): 169.9MM **Privately Held**
SIC: **8069** 8062 Children's hospital; general medical & surgical hospitals

(P-21448)
ASIAN AMERCN RECOVERY SVCS INC
Also Called: Place Asian Amrcn Rcovery Svcs
1340 Tully Rd Ste 304, San Jose
(95122-3055)
PHONE..................................408 271-3900
Jeff Mori, *Exec Dir*
EMP: 125
SALES (corp-wide): 6MM **Privately Held**
WEB: www.aars-inc.org
SIC: **8069** Drug addiction rehabilitation hospital
PA: Asian American Recovery Services, Inc.
1115 Mission Rd 2
South San Francisco CA 94080
650 243-4888

(P-21449)
BARLOW GROUP (PA)
Also Called: BARLOW RESPITORY HOSPITAL
2000 Stadium Way, Los Angeles
(90026-2606)
PHONE..................................213 250-4200
Margaret W Crane, *CEO*
Julia Shimizu, *Pub Rel Dir*
EMP: 250
SALES: 3.2MM **Privately Held**
SIC: **8069** 7389 8733 Specialty hospitals, except psychiatric; fund raising organizations; medical research

(P-21450)
BARLOW RESPIRATORY HOSPITAL (PA)
2000 Stadium Way, Los Angeles
(90026-2606)
PHONE..................................213 250-4200
Margaret W Crane, *CEO*
Edward Engesser, *CFO*
Rick Culp, *Engineer*
Donna Kraus, *Purchasing*
Anna Urling, *Manager*
EMP: 250 EST: 1902
SQ FT: 80,000
SALES: 55.2MM **Privately Held**
SIC: **8069** Specialty hospitals, except psychiatric

(P-21451)
BETTY FORD CENTER (HQ)
39000 Bob Hope Dr, Rancho Mirage
(92270-3297)
P.O. Box 1560 (92270-1056)
PHONE..................................760 773-4100
Mark Mishek, *President*
Jim Steinhagen, *Vice Pres*
Jan Hart, *Executive Asst*
Laurie Skochil, *Executive Asst*
Jason Roberson, *Technology*
EMP: 250
SALES: 38.3MM
SALES (corp-wide): 191.3MM **Privately Held**
SIC: **8069** Drug addiction rehabilitation hospital
PA: Hazelden Betty Ford Foundation
15251 Pleasant Valley Rd
Center City MN 55012
651 213-4000

(P-21452)
CALIFORNIA HISPANIC COM
9033 Washington Blvd, Pico Rivera
(90660-3839)
PHONE..................................562 942-9625
Samuel Campbell, *Director*
EMP: 123
SALES (corp-wide): 12.3MM **Privately Held**
SIC: **8069** Alcoholism rehabilitation hospital
PA: California Hispanic Commission On Alcohol And Drug Abuse Inc
9942 13th St
Garden Grove CA 92844
916 443-5473

(P-21453)
CAMP RECOVERY CENTERS LP
Also Called: Azure Acres
2264 Green Hill Rd, Sebastopol
(95472-9034)
PHONE..................................707 823-3385
Shannon Clay, *Manager*
Lynette Grelet, *Human Res Dir*
Jody Livingston, *Nursing Dir*
Ryan Manzano, *Hlthcr Dir*
Timothy Fitzgerald, *Director*
EMP: 4413 **Privately Held**
WEB: www.azureacres.com
SIC: **8069** 8361 Alcoholism rehabilitation hospital; rehabilitation center, residential: health care incidental
PA: The Camp Recovery Centers L P
6100 Tower Cir Ste 1000
Franklin TN 37067

(P-21454)
CBEST INC
11620 Wilshire Blvd # 450, Los Angeles
(90025-1779)
PHONE..................................310 445-2378
Bahador, *President*
EMP: 80 EST: 2011
SALES (est): 710.5K **Privately Held**
SIC: **8069** Children's hospital

(P-21455)
CENTER FOR DSCOVERY ADOLOSCENT
4136 Ann Arbor Rd, Lakewood
(90712-3817)
PHONE..................................562 425-6404
Craig Brown, *Director*
EMP: 50
SALES (est): 640.4K **Privately Held**
SIC: **8069** Drug addiction rehabilitation hospital

(P-21456)
CHILDRENS HEALTHCARE CAL (PA)
1201 W La Veta Ave, Orange (92868-4203)
PHONE..................................714 997-3000
Kimberly C Cripe, *President*
Kerri Ruppert, *CFO*
Ali Edgcomb, *Officer*
Maria Minon MD, *Vice Pres*
Bree Morse, *Associate Dir*
EMP: 1800
SALES: 548.7MM **Privately Held**
SIC: **8069** Children's hospital

(P-21457)
CHILDRENS HOSPITAL LOS ANGELES (PA)
4650 W Sunset Blvd, Los Angeles
(90027-6062)
PHONE..................................323 660-2450
Richard Cordova, *President*
Lannie Tonnu, *CFO*
Owen Lei, *Officer*
Alexandra Carter, *Senior VP*
Steven R Garske, *Vice Pres*
▲ EMP: 79 EST: 1901
SQ FT: 750,000
SALES (est): 1.3B **Privately Held**
SIC: **8069** 8062 Children's hospital; general medical & surgical hospitals

(P-21458)
CHILDRENS HOSPITAL LOS ANGELES
800 N Brand Blvd, Glendale (91203-1245)
PHONE..................................323 361-2215
EMP: 216
SALES (corp-wide): 1.3B **Privately Held**
SIC: **8069** 8093 Children's hospital; specialty outpatient clinics
PA: The Childrens Hospital Los Angeles
4650 W Sunset Blvd
Los Angeles CA 90027
323 660-2450

(P-21459)
CHILDRENS HOSPITAL LOS ANGELES
Also Called: Chidren's Hospital Center
4661 W Sunset Blvd, Los Angeles
(90027-6042)
PHONE..................................323 361-5702
Nikita Tripuraneni, *Principal*
EMP: 160
SALES (corp-wide): 1.3B **Privately Held**
SIC: **8069** Children's hospital
PA: The Childrens Hospital Los Angeles
4650 W Sunset Blvd
Los Angeles CA 90027
323 660-2450

(P-21460)
CHILDRENS HOSPITAL ORANGE CNTY (PA)
Also Called: Choc
1201 W La Veta Ave, Orange (92868-4203)
PHONE..................................714 997-3000
Kimberly Cripe, *President*
Eric Ontiveros,
L Kenneth Heuler DDS, *Ch of Bd*
Sally Gallagher, *President*
Thomas Brotherton, *COO*
EMP: 77 EST: 1950
SQ FT: 328,200
SALES (est): 523.1MM **Privately Held**
SIC: **8069** Children's hospital

(P-21461)
CITY OF SAN DIEGO
Also Called: Park and Recreation
202 C St Ms37c, San Diego (92101-3860)
PHONE..................................619 533-6518
Albert Cuevas, *Administration*
EMP: 99
SALES (est): 486.2K **Privately Held**
SIC: **8069** Specialty hospitals, except psychiatric

(P-21462)
CLARE MATRIX
1849 Sawtelle Blvd # 670, Los Angeles
(90025-7006)
PHONE..................................310 478-6006
EMP: 60
SALES (corp-wide): 7.4MM **Privately Held**
SIC: **8069** Drug addiction rehabilitation hospital
PA: Clare Matrix
2644 30th St Ste 100
Santa Monica CA 90405
310 314-6200

(P-21463)
COUNTY OF LOS ANGELES
Also Called: Health Services, Dept of
30500 Arrastre Canyon Rd, Acton
(93510-2160)
P.O. Box 25 (93510-0025)
PHONE..................................661 223-8700
Suzanna Kassinger, *Administration*
EMP: 100 **Privately Held**
WEB: www.co.la.ca.us
SIC: **8069** 9431 8361 Alcoholism rehabilitation hospital; administration of public health programs; ; residential care
PA: County Of Los Angeles
500 W Temple St Ste 437
Los Angeles CA 90012
213 974-1101

(P-21464)
COUNTY OF LOS ANGELES
515 E 6th St, Los Angeles (90021-1009)
PHONE..................................213 974-7284
Maria Lopez, *Manager*
EMP: 1000 **Privately Held**
WEB: www.co.la.ca.us
SIC: **8069** 9111 Tuberculosis hospital; executive offices
PA: County Of Los Angeles
500 W Temple St Ste 437
Los Angeles CA 90012
213 974-1101

(P-21465)
COUNTY OF LOS ANGELES
Also Called: Department of Health Services
1240 N Mission Rd, Los Angeles
(90033-1019)
PHONE..................................323 226-3468
Barbara Oliver, *Exec Dir*
Robert Moore, *Chief*
Victoria Walsh, *Art Dir*
EMP: 1000 **Privately Held**
WEB: www.co.la.ca.us
SIC: **8069** 9431 8062 Specialty hospitals, except psychiatric; administration of public health programs; ; general medical & surgical hospitals
PA: County Of Los Angeles
500 W Temple St Ste 437
Los Angeles CA 90012
213 974-1101

(P-21466)
CRC HEALTH LLC (DH)
Also Called: CRC Health Corporation
20400 Stevens Creek Blvd # 600, Cupertino (95014-2296)
PHONE..................................877 272-8668
R Andrew Eckert, *Ch of Bd*
Jerome E Rhodes, *CEO*
Leanne M Stewart, *CFO*
Philip L Herschman, *Officer*
Pamela B Burke, *Senior VP*
EMP: 80
SALES (est): 407MM **Publicly Held**
WEB: www.crchealth.com
SIC: **8069** 8099 8322 8093 Drug addiction rehabilitation hospital; medical services organization; general counseling services; substance abuse clinics (outpatient)
HQ: Crc Health Group, Inc.
20400 Stev Creek Blvd 6 Flr 6
Cupertino CA 95014
877 272-8668

(P-21467)
CRESTWOOD BEHAVIORAL HLTH INC
Also Called: 137 Bakersfield Bridge
6744 Eucalyptus Dr, Bakersfield
(93306-6053)
PHONE..................................661 363-6711
Lori Blackburn, *Branch Mgr*
EMP: 200
SALES (corp-wide): 188.6MM **Privately Held**
SIC: **8069** Specialty hospitals, except psychiatric
PA: Crestwood Behavioral Health, Inc.
520 Capitol Mall Ste 800
Sacramento CA 95814
510 651-1244

PRODUCTS & SVCS

(P-21468)
DESERT REGIONAL MED CTR INC
Also Called: Tenet
1695 N Sunrise Way, Palm Springs (92262-3701)
PHONE..................................760 323-6640
Truman Gates, *Manager*
EMP: 190
SALES (corp-wide): 18.3B **Publicly Held**
SIC: 8069 8082 Specialty hospitals, except psychiatric; home health care services
HQ: Desert Regional Medical Center, Inc.
1150 N Indian Canyon Dr
Palm Springs CA 92262
760 323-6511

(P-21469)
DOCTORS HOSPITAL MANTECA INC
1205 E North St, Manteca (95336-4900)
PHONE..................................209 823-3111
Nicholas Tejeda, *CEO*
Mark Lisa, *President*
Katherine Medeiros, *President*
Tracy Roman, *CFO*
Beverly Fick, *Ch Nursing Ofcr*
EMP: 400 EST: 2001
SALES: 90.8MM
SALES (corp-wide): 18.3B **Publicly Held**
SIC: 8069 Specialty hospitals, except psychiatric
PA: Tenet Healthcare Corporation
1445 Ross Ave Ste 1400
Dallas TX 75202
469 893-2200

(P-21470)
EDGEMOOR HOSPITAL
655 Park Center Dr, Santee (92071-3094)
PHONE..................................619 596-5500
Janet Seawell, *CEO*
Gwenmarie Hilleary, *Administration*
Jean Shepphard, *Director*
EMP: 350
SALES (est): 26MM **Privately Held**
SIC: 8069 Specialty hospitals, except psychiatric

(P-21471)
EL CAMINO HOSPITAL
Also Called: Occupational Health Services
1737 N 1st St Ste 220, San Jose (95112-4522)
PHONE..................................650 988-4825
Todd Blancept, *Manager*
EMP: 215
SALES (corp-wide): 973.3MM **Privately Held**
PA: El Camino Hospital
2500 Grant Rd
Mountain View CA 94040
650 940-7000

(P-21472)
ENCOMPASS HEALTH CORPORATION
Also Called: HealthSouth
3875 Telegraph Ave, Oakland (94609-2428)
PHONE..................................510 547-2244
Ann Banchero, *Branch Mgr*
EMP: 55
SALES (corp-wide): 4.2B **Publicly Held**
WEB: www.healthsouth.com
SIC: 8069 Orthopedic hospital
PA: Encompass Health Corporation
9001 Liberty Pkwy
Birmingham AL 35242
205 967-7116

(P-21473)
ENLIGHTICARE INC
Also Called: Elevate Addiction Services
138 Victoria Ln, Aptos (95003-3027)
P.O. Box 1690 (95001-1690)
PHONE..................................831 750-3546
Daniel Manson, *President*
EMP: 90
SALES (est): 1.8MM **Privately Held**
SIC: 8069 Substance abuse hospitals

(P-21474)
EXODUS RECOVERY CTR AT BROTMAN (PA)
3828 Delmas Ter, Culver City (90232-2713)
PHONE..................................310 253-9494
Luana Murphy, *Principal*
EMP: 59
SALES (est): 3MM **Privately Held**
SIC: 8069 Drug addiction rehabilitation hospital

(P-21475)
GUAVA HOLDINGS LLC
Also Called: Yuba City Post-Acute
1220 Plumas St, Yuba City (95991-3411)
PHONE..................................530 671-0550
Toby Tilford, *President*
Dustin Murray, *Administration*
Nicklas Anderson, *Manager*
Naveed Hakim, *Manager*
EMP: 50 EST: 2017
SALES (est): 747.1K **Privately Held**
SIC: 8069 Geriatric hospital

(P-21476)
HEALTHCARE CENTRE OF FRESNO
1665 M St, Fresno (93721-1121)
PHONE..................................559 268-5361
Lucille Epperson, *Administration*
Charles J Enoch, *Partner*
Joyce S Lopez, *Partner*
Laverne E Masten, *Partner*
Barbara H Rose, *Partner*
EMP: 163
SQ FT: 87,000
SALES (est): 4.6MM **Privately Held**
SIC: 8069 8051 Specialty hospitals, except psychiatric; convalescent home with continuous nursing care

(P-21477)
HORIZON WEST HEALTHCARE INC
Also Called: Roseville Convalescent Hosp
1161 Cirby Way, Roseville (95661-4421)
PHONE..................................916 782-1238
James Paul, *Manager*
EMP: 150
SALES (corp-wide): 103.9MM **Privately Held**
WEB: www.villadelrey.com
SIC: 8069 8051 Specialty hospitals, except psychiatric; skilled nursing care facilities
HQ: Horizon West Healthcare, Inc.
4020 Sierra College Blvd # 190
Rocklin CA 95677
916 624-6230

(P-21478)
HOSPITAL OF COMMUNITY (HQ)
23625 Holman Hwy, Monterey (93940-5902)
P.O. Box Hh (93942-6032)
PHONE..................................831 624-5311
Steven J Packer, *President*
Laura Zehm, *CFO*
Steven X Cabrales, *Vice Pres*
Terrill Lowe, *Vice Pres*
Tim Nylen, *Vice Pres*
EMP: 1500
SQ FT: 550,000
SALES: 526.9MM
SALES (corp-wide): 145.4MM **Privately Held**
SIC: 8069 8011 Geriatric hospital; hematologist
PA: Montage Health
23625 Holman Hwy
Monterey CA 93940
831 625-4830

(P-21479)
KINDRED HEALTHCARE OPERATING
Also Called: Hillhaven Convalescent Hosp
1609 Trousdale Dr, Burlingame (94010-4520)
PHONE..................................650 697-1865
Jan Clemons, *Administration*
Parvin Salem, *Director*
EMP: 500

SALES (corp-wide): 6B **Privately Held**
WEB: www.salemhaven.com
SIC: 8069 Specialty hospitals, except psychiatric
HQ: Kindred Healthcare Operating, Llc
680 S 4th St
Louisville KY 40202
502 596-7300

(P-21480)
LIGHTBRIDGE HOSPICE LLC (PA)
Also Called: Lightbrdge Hspice Plltive Care
6155 Cornerstone Ct E, San Diego (92121-4736)
PHONE..................................858 458-2992
Jill Mendlen, *CEO*
Cindy Hutchinson, *Vice Pres*
Nan Johnson, *Vice Pres*
Abigail Dagostino, *Associate Dir*
Maria Danilychev, *Associate Dir*
EMP: 57
SALES (est): 130.2K **Privately Held**
WEB: www.lightbridgehospice.com
SIC: 8069 Specialty hospitals, except psychiatric

(P-21481)
LIVONGO HEALTH INC (PA)
150 W Evelyn Ave Ste 150 # 150, Mountain View (94041-1556)
PHONE..................................866 435-5643
Zane Burke, *CEO*
Glen E Tullman, *Ch of Bd*
Jennifer Schneider, *President*
Lee Shapiro, *CFO*
James Pursley, *Ch Credit Ofcr*
▲ EMP: 50
SQ FT: 30,019
SALES: 68.4MM **Publicly Held**
SIC: 8069 Chronic disease hospital

(P-21482)
LUCILE SALTER PACKARD CHIL
4100 Bohannon Dr, Menlo Park (94025-1013)
PHONE..................................650 736-2142
Fred Y Nishioka, *Director*
Sandy Leow, *Admin Asst*
EMP: 218
SALES (corp-wide): 1.6B **Privately Held**
SIC: 8069 Children's hospital
PA: Lucile Salter Packard Children's Hospital At Stanford
725 Welch Rd
Palo Alto CA 94304
650 497-8000

(P-21483)
LUCILE SALTER PACKARD CHIL (PA)
725 Welch Rd, Palo Alto (94304-1601)
PHONE..................................650 497-8000
Christopher Dawes, *President*
Timothy W Carmack, *CFO*
Susan Costello, *Vice Pres*
Jerry Harris, *Vice Pres*
Michael Lane, *Vice Pres*
▲ EMP: 97
SALES: 1.6B **Privately Held**
SIC: 8069 8082 5912 Children's hospital; home health care services; drug stores & proprietary stores

(P-21484)
LUCILE SALTER PACKARD CHIL
300 Pasteur Dr, Stanford (94305-2200)
PHONE..................................650 723-5791
Jeff Driver, *Principal*
EMP: 249
SALES (corp-wide): 1.6B **Privately Held**
SIC: 8069 Children's hospital
PA: Lucile Salter Packard Children's Hospital At Stanford
725 Welch Rd
Palo Alto CA 94304
650 497-8000

(P-21485)
MARINE CORPS UNITED STATES
Also Called: Camp Pendleton Hospital
Camp Pendleton, Oceanside (92055)
P.O. Box 555191, Camp Pendleton (92055-5191)
PHONE..................................760 725-1304
Richard R Jeffries, *Manager*
EMP: 1000 **Publicly Held**
WEB: www.usmc.mil
SIC: 8069 9711 Specialty hospitals, except psychiatric; Marine Corps;
HQ: United States Marine Corps
Pentagon Rm 4b544
Washington DC 20380

(P-21486)
NEW BRIDGE FOUNDATION INC
1820 Scenic Ave, Berkeley (94709-1395)
PHONE..................................510 548-7270
Kosta Markakis, *Exec Dir*
EMP: 73
SQ FT: 3,000
SALES (est): 6.2MM **Privately Held**
SIC: 8069 Drug addiction rehabilitation hospital

(P-21487)
POMONA VALLEY HOSPITAL MED CTR
Also Called: Pomona Vallley Hospital
1798 N Garey Ave, Pomona (91767-2918)
PHONE..................................909 865-9700
Dee Ann Gibs, *Director*
EMP: 200
SALES (corp-wide): 654.6MM **Privately Held**
WEB: www.pvhmc.org
SIC: 8069 Maternity hospital
PA: Pomona Valley Hospital Medical Center
1798 N Garey Ave
Pomona CA 91767
909 865-9500

(P-21488)
PROGRESSIVE SUB-ACUTE CARE
Also Called: Sub-Acute Saratoga Hospital
13425 Sousa Ln, Saratoga (95070-4637)
PHONE..................................408 378-8875
Michael Zarcone, *President*
Elio Amio, *Food Svc Dir*
Olga Chukhlebova,
Selah Mercado, *Director*
EMP: 130
SQ FT: 10,000
SALES (est): 14.5MM **Privately Held**
WEB: www.subacutesaratoga.com
SIC: 8069 Children's hospital

(P-21489)
RADY CHILDRENS HOSP & HLTH CTR (PA)
3020 Childrens Way, San Diego (92123-4223)
PHONE..................................858 576-1700
Donald B Kearns, *President*
Dorothy O'Hagan, *Records Dir*
Carlos Delgado, *Partner*
Nicholas Holmes, *COO*
Roger G Roux, *CFO*
EMP: 1700
SALES: 1.3B **Privately Held**
SIC: 8069 Children's hospital

(P-21490)
RECOVERY PLACE INC
5000 E Spring St Ste 650, Long Beach (90815-5205)
PHONE..................................954 200-8308
John Cates, *President*
EMP: 100
SALES (est): 7.9MM **Privately Held**
SIC: 8069 Drug addiction rehabilitation hospital

(P-21491)
SALINAS VALLEY MEMORIAL HLTHCA
Also Called: Svmc Precision Orthopedics
611 Abbott St Ste 101, Salinas
(93901-4391)
PHONE..................................831 757-3041
EMP: 401
SALES (corp-wide): 494.4MM **Privately Held**
SIC: 8069 Orthopedic hospital
PA: Salinas Valley Memorial Healthcare
Systems
450 E Romie Ln
Salinas CA 93901
831 757-4333

(P-21492)
SHARP MCDONALD CENTER
7989 Linda Vista Rd, San Diego
(92111-5106)
PHONE..................................858 637-6920
Daniel L Gross, Exec VP
EMP: 800
SALES (est): 31.2MM
SALES (corp-wide): 3.4B **Privately Held**
SIC: 8069 Drug addiction rehabilitation hospital
PA: Sharp Healthcare
8695 Spectrum Center Blvd
San Diego CA 92123
858 499-4000

(P-21493)
SHIELDS FOR FAMILIES (PA)
11601 S Western Ave, Los Angeles
(90047-5006)
P.O. Box 59129 (90059-0129)
PHONE..................................323 242-5000
Kathryn S Icenhower, CEO
Xylina Bean, President
Norma Mtume, CFO
Gerald Phillips, Chairman
Susan Haynes, Treasurer
EMP: 82
SALES: 20.3MM **Privately Held**
SIC: 8069 Drug addiction rehabilitation hospital

(P-21494)
SHRINERS HSPITALS FOR CHILDREN
Also Called: Shriner's Hospital
909 S Fair Oaks Ave, Pasadena
(91105-2625)
PHONE..................................213 388-3151
Terence Cunningham, Principal
G Frank Labonte, Administration
Luz Ramos, Engineer
Robert Cho, Director
Dawn Musser, Director
EMP: 300 **Privately Held**
SIC: 8069 8062 Children's hospital; general medical & surgical hospitals
HQ: Shriners Hospitals For Children
12502 Usf Pine Dr
Tampa FL 33612
813 972-2250

(P-21495)
SOCIAL SCIENCE SERVICE CENTER
Also Called: Cedar House Rehabilitation Ctr
18612 Santa Ana Ave, Bloomington
(92316-2636)
PHONE..................................909 421-7120
Daniel Gakgolla, CEO
EMP: 63
SQ FT: 29,000
SALES (est): 3.8MM **Privately Held**
WEB: www.cedarhouse.org
SIC: 8069 8322 Alcoholism rehabilitation hospital; individual & family services

(P-21496)
SPECIAL NEEDS NETWORK
4401 Crenshaw Blvd # 215, Los Angeles
(90043-1200)
PHONE..................................323 291-7100
Julia Djeke, President
Edguin Castellanos, Officer
Daniel Fausto, Comms Dir
Marcos Aguilar, Administration
Juan Garcia, Opers Staff
EMP: 50 EST: 2013

SALES: 2.8MM **Privately Held**
SIC: 8069 Children's hospital

(P-21497)
SUBACUTE CHLD HOSP CAL INC
Also Called: Childrens Rcvery Ctr Nthrn Cal
3777 S Bascom Ave, Campbell
(95008-7320)
PHONE..................................408 558-3644
Micahel Zarcone, CEO
Christy Bracco, Records Dir
Nasim Zadeh, Chief Mktg Ofcr
Priya Yadav, Human Res Dir
Grace Shih, Food Svc Dir
EMP: 80
SQ FT: 17,000
SALES (est): 8.4MM **Privately Held**
SIC: 8069 Children's hospital

(P-21498)
SURE HAVEN INC
Also Called: Sure Haven Addiction Treatment
1730 Pomona Ave Ste 3, Costa Mesa
(92627-3628)
PHONE..................................949 467-9213
Steve Fennelly, CEO
Elizabeth Perry, Vice Pres
Mark Shandrow, Vice Pres
EMP: 550 EST: 2010
SQ FT: 7,500
SALES (est): 47.7MM **Privately Held**
SIC: 8069 Alcoholism rehabilitation hospital

(P-21499)
TENET HEALTHSYSTEM MEDICAL
Also Called: Placentia Linda Hospital
1301 N Rose Dr, Placentia (92870-3802)
PHONE..................................714 993-2000
Kent Clayton, CEO
Ann Marie Watkins, Ch Nursing Ofcr
Mary Ann Railey, Planning
Freddie Sanchez, MIS Dir
John Kirby, Research
EMP: 400
SALES (corp-wide): 18.3B **Publicly Held**
WEB: www.tenenthealth.com
SIC: 8069 8011 8062 Specialty hospitals, except psychiatric; offices & clinics of medical doctors; general medical & surgical hospitals
HQ: Tenet Healthsystem Medical, Inc.
1445 Ross Ave Ste 1400
Dallas TX 75202
469 893-2000

(P-21500)
THERAPEUTIC ASSOCIATES INC
Also Called: Providence St Joseph Med Ctr
181 S Buena Vista St, Burbank
(91505-4504)
PHONE..................................818 748-4900
EMP: 51
SALES (corp-wide): 73.6MM **Privately Held**
SIC: 8069 Cancer hospital
PA: Therapeutic Associates, Inc.
20829 72nd Ave S Ste 710
Kent WA 98032
253 872-6028

(P-21501)
UNITED CEREBRAL PALSY ASSOC
333 W Benjamin Holt Dr # 1, Stockton
(95207-3906)
PHONE..................................209 956-0290
Ray Call, CEO
Leslie Heier, COO
Lillian Callangan, Finance
EMP: 137
SALES (est): 3.1MM **Privately Held**
SIC: 8069 8322 Chronic disease hospital; individual & family services

(P-21502)
VIBRA HOSPITAL SACRAMENTO LLC
330 Montrose Dr, Folsom (95630-2720)
PHONE..................................916 351-9151
Janet Biedrone, CEO
Mark Blum, Radiology Dir

Tom Root, Business Dir
Deann Stoner, Hum Res Coord
Sarah Olson, Food Svc Dir
EMP: 246
SQ FT: 22,000
SALES (est): 18.3MM
SALES (corp-wide): 330.4MM **Privately Held**
SIC: 8069 Specialty hospitals, except psychiatric
PA: Vibra Healthcare, Llc
4600 Lena Dr Ste 100
Mechanicsburg PA 17055
717 591-5700

(P-21503)
WATERMAN CONVALESCENT HOSPITAL
Mt Rubidoux Convalescent Hosp
6401 33rd St, Riverside (92509-1404)
PHONE..................................951 681-2200
Magda Williams, Director
EMP: 130
SALES (corp-wide): 11.1MM **Privately Held**
SIC: 8069 8051 Specialty hospitals, except psychiatric; skilled nursing care facilities
PA: Waterman Convalescent Hospital, Inc
1850 N Waterman Ave
San Bernardino CA 92404
909 882-1215

8071 Medical Laboratories

(P-21504)
ALLIANCE HEALTHCARE SVCS INC (DH)
18201 Von Karman Ave, Irvine
(92612-1000)
P.O. Box 19532 (92623-9532)
PHONE..................................949 242-5300
Rhonda Longmore-Grund, CEO
Howard Aihara, CFO
Richard W Johns,
Laurie R Miller, Exec VP
Minal Amin, Vice Pres
EMP: 250
SALES: 505.5MM
SALES (corp-wide): 1.4MM **Privately Held**
WEB: www.mvhs.org
SIC: 8071 Ultrasound laboratory
HQ: Thaihot Investment Company Us Limited
18201 Von Karman Ave
Irvine CA 92612
949 242-5300

(P-21505)
AMBRY GENETICS CORPORATION (DH)
Also Called: Konica Minolta Hlthcare
15 Argonaut, Aliso Viejo (92656-1423)
PHONE..................................949 900-5500
Charles Lm Dunlop, President
Ardy Arianpour, President
Julie Holmes, CEO
Linh H Le, COO
Charles Caporale, CFO
EMP: 85 EST: 1999
SQ FT: 20,000
SALES (est): 19.1MM **Privately Held**
WEB: www.ambrygen.com
SIC: 8071 Medical laboratories
HQ: Konica Minolta Healthcare Americas, Inc.
411 Newark Pompton Tpke
Wayne NJ 07470
973 633-1500

(P-21506)
ASCEND CLINICAL LLC (PA)
1400 Industrial Way, Redwood City
(94063-1101)
PHONE..................................800 800-5655
Paul F Beyer, CEO
Jeffrey Vizethann, President
Patricia Hunsader, COO
Olivier Gindraux, CFO
Jeff Vizethann, Exec VP
▲ EMP: 72

SALES (est): 15.6MM **Privately Held**
WEB: www.satellitelabs.com
SIC: 8071 Blood analysis laboratory

(P-21507)
BIO-REFERENCE LABORATORIES INC
2605 Winchester Blvd, Campbell
(95008-5379)
PHONE..................................408 341-8600
Sally Howlett, Vice Pres
Miriam Lieberman, Sales Staff
EMP: 150 **Publicly Held**
SIC: 8071 Testing laboratories
HQ: Bio-Reference Laboratories, Inc.
481 Edward H Ross Dr
Elmwood Park NJ 07407
201 791-2600

(P-21508)
BIOTHERANOSTICS INC (PA)
9640 Towne Centre Dr # 200, San Diego
(92121-1986)
P.O. Box 749249, Los Angeles (90074-9249)
PHONE..................................877 886-6739
Gail Sloan, CFO
Don Hardison, CEO
Macey Johnson, Vice Pres
Nancy Smith, Executive Asst
Karla Kelly, Admin Sec
EMP: 55
SALES (est): 8.6MM **Privately Held**
WEB: www.aviaradx.com
SIC: 8071 2835 Medical laboratories; in vitro diagnostics

(P-21509)
CALIFORNIA LAB SCIENCES LLC
Also Called: West Pacific Medical Lab
10200 Pioneer Blvd # 500, Santa Fe Springs (90670-6000)
PHONE..................................562 758-6900
William McDonald,
EMP: 300
SALES (est): 7.5MM **Privately Held**
SIC: 8071 Medical laboratories

(P-21510)
CAP DIAGNOSTICS LLC
Also Called: Pathnostics
17661 Cowan, Irvine (92614-6031)
PHONE..................................714 966-1221
David A Baunoch,
Matt Tate, Vice Pres
EMP: 73
SALES (est): 8MM **Privately Held**
SIC: 8071 Medical laboratories

(P-21511)
CARDIODX INC
3945 Freedom Cir Ste 560, Santa Clara
(95054-1269)
PHONE..................................650 475-2788
Khush F Mehta, President
Timothy Henn, CFO
David Levison, Officer
Mark Monane, Officer
Cynthia Lee, Software Dev
EMP: 146
SALES: 7.9MM **Privately Held**
WEB: www.cardiodx.com
SIC: 8071 2834 Medical laboratories; drugs acting on the cardiovascular system, except diagnostic

(P-21512)
CAREDX INC (PA)
3260 Bayshore Blvd, Brisbane
(94005-1021)
PHONE..................................415 287-2300
Peter Maag, CEO
Michael D Goldberg, Ch of Bd
Reginald Seeto, President
Michael Bell, CFO
Sasha King, Ch Credit Ofcr
EMP: 145
SQ FT: 46,000
SALES: 76.5MM **Publicly Held**
SIC: 8071 8733 Medical laboratories; non-commercial research organizations

PRODUCTS & SVCS

(P-21513)
CLARIENT DIAGNOSTIC SVCS INC
31 Columbia, Aliso Viejo (92656-1460)
PHONE......................888 443-3310
Cindy Collins, *CEO*
Renika Seghal, *CFO*
Michael Brown, *Vice Pres*
Mark Machulcz, *Vice Pres*
EMP: 313
SALES (est): 1.7MM
SALES (corp-wide): 276.7MM **Publicly Held**
SIC: 8071 Testing laboratories
HQ: Clarient, Inc.
      31 Columbia
      Aliso Viejo CA 92656
      949 445-7300

(P-21514)
COMMUNITY MBL DIAGNOSTICS LLC
Also Called: Tridentcare Imaging
10936 Bigge St, San Leandro (94577-1121)
PHONE......................925 516-6851
William McDonald, *Mng Member*
Joseph Cleberg,
David Smith III,
EMP: 72
SALES (est): 2.6MM **Privately Held**
SIC: 8071 X-ray laboratory, including dental
HQ: Community Mobile Ultrasound, Llc
      10936 Bigge St
      San Leandro CA

(P-21515)
CONSOLDTED MED BO-ANALYSIS INC (PA)
Also Called: Cmb Laboratory
10700 Walker St, Cypress (90630-4703)
P.O. Box 2369 (90630-1869)
PHONE......................714 657-7369
Chin Kuo Fan, *President*
Gloria Fan, *Shareholder*
CAM Chinh Fan, *Senior VP*
Michelle Fan, *Vice Pres*
Maria Polintan, *Human Res Mgr*
EMP: 100
SQ FT: 11,000
SALES: 12MM **Privately Held**
SIC: 8071 Testing laboratories

(P-21516)
CONSOLDTED MED BO-ANALYSIS INC
7631 Wyoming St Ste 105a, Westminster (92683-3904)
PHONE......................714 657-7389
Chin Kuo Fan, *President*
Vincent Stack, *Pathologist*
EMP: 51
SALES (corp-wide): 12MM **Privately Held**
SIC: 8071 Testing laboratories
PA: Consolidated Medical Bio-Analysis, Inc.
      10700 Walker St
      Cypress CA 90630
      714 657-7369

(P-21517)
CONSOLDTED MED BO-ANALYSIS INC
12665 Garden Grove Blvd, Garden Grove (92843-1901)
PHONE......................714 467-0240
Chin Kuo Fan, *Owner*
EMP: 51
SALES (corp-wide): 12MM **Privately Held**
SIC: 8071 Medical laboratories
PA: Consolidated Medical Bio-Analysis, Inc.
      10700 Walker St
      Cypress CA 90630
      714 657-7369

(P-21518)
COUNTY OF ORANGE
Also Called: Health Care Agency
1729 W 17th St, Santa Ana (92706-2316)
PHONE......................714 834-8385
Richard Alexander, *Director*
EMP: 50 **Privately Held**

SIC: 8071 9431 Medical laboratories; administration of public health programs;
PA: County Of Orange
      333 W Santa Ana Blvd 3f
      Santa Ana CA 92701
      714 834-6200

(P-21519)
COUNTY OF SAN BERNARDINO
Arrowhead Regional Medical Ctr
400 N Pepper Ave, Colton (92324-1801)
PHONE......................909 580-1000
Toll Free:......................877 -
June Griffith, *CEO*
Patrick Petre, *CEO*
Joseph Davis, *Osteopathy*
Laura Ellers, *Director*
EMP: 210 **Privately Held**
SIC: 8071 9431 Medical laboratories; administration of public health programs;
PA: County Of San Bernardino
      385 N Arrowhead Ave
      San Bernardino CA 92415
      909 387-3841

(P-21520)
DECIPHER CORP
Also Called: Genomedx Biosciences Corp.
10355 Science Center Dr, San Diego (92121-1157)
PHONE......................888 975-4540
Tina Nova, *CEO*
Elai Davicioni, *President*
William Kachioff, *CFO*
Doug Dolginow, *Principal*
EMP: 85 **EST:** 2012
SQ FT: 15,000
SALES: 7.3MM
SALES (corp-wide): 5.4MM **Privately Held**
SIC: 8071 Biological laboratory
PA: Genomedx Biosciences Inc
      430-1152 Mainland St
      Vancouver BC V6B 4
      888 975-4540

(P-21521)
DEPARTMENT HEALTH CARE SVCS
Also Called: Microbial Diseases Laboratory
850 Marina Bay Pkwy, Richmond (94804-6403)
PHONE......................510 412-3700
Michael Janda, *Branch Mgr*
EMP: 70 **Privately Held**
WEB: www.calsurv.org
SIC: 8071 9431 Medical laboratories; administration of public health programs;
HQ: Department Of Health Care Services
      1501 Capitol Ave
      Sacramento CA 95814

(P-21522)
DIAZYME LABORATORIES INC
12889 Gregg Ct, Poway (92064-6833)
P.O. Box 85608, San Diego (92186-5608)
PHONE......................858 455-4768
Chong Yuan PHD, *Managing Dir*
Jeff Jackson, *Cust Mgr*
EMP: 90
SALES (est): 2.9MM **Privately Held**
SIC: 8071 Medical laboratories

(P-21523)
DIGNITY HEALTH
Health Care Lab
1800 N California St, Stockton (95204-6019)
PHONE......................209 467-6430
Terry Bryan, *Director*
Denise Facaros, *Manager*
EMP: 115 **Privately Held**
WEB: www.chw.edu
SIC: 8071 Testing laboratories
HQ: Dignity Health
      185 Berry St Ste 300
      San Francisco CA 94107
      415 438-5500

(P-21524)
DIGNITY HEALTH
Also Called: Mercy General Hospital
4001 J St, Sacramento (95819-3626)
PHONE......................916 453-4453
Tom Peterson, *President*

EMP: 2000 **Privately Held**
WEB: www.mercycare.net
SIC: 8071 X-ray laboratory, including dental
HQ: Dignity Health
      185 Berry St Ste 300
      San Francisco CA 94107
      415 438-5500

(P-21525)
DUAL DIAGNOSIS TRTMNT CTR INC
Also Called: Sovereign Health of California
12832 Short Ave, Los Angeles (90066-6421)
PHONE......................424 289-9031
EMP: 107
SALES (corp-wide): 68.5MM **Privately Held**
SIC: 8071 Medical laboratories
PA: Dual Diagnosis Treatment Center, Inc.
      1211 Puerta Del Sol # 200
      San Clemente CA 92673
      949 276-5553

(P-21526)
EL CAMINO HOSPITAL
Evergreen Dialisist
2240 Tully Rd, San Jose (95122-1347)
PHONE......................650 940-7000
Chu Nuyen, *Manager*
EMP: 172
SALES (corp-wide): 973.3MM **Privately Held**
SIC: 8071 Medical laboratories
PA: El Camino Hospital
      2500 Grant Rd
      Mountain View CA 94040
      650 940-7000

(P-21527)
ENDOCRINE SCIENCES INC
Also Called: Esoterix Ctr For Clncal Trails
4301 Lost Hills Rd, Calabasas (91301-5358)
PHONE......................818 880-8040
Darrel Mayes, *CEO*
Dennis Griffin, *President*
EMP: 125 **EST:** 1972
SQ FT: 35,000
SALES (est): 6.6MM **Publicly Held**
WEB: www.esoterix.com
SIC: 8071 2869 Medical laboratories; industrial organic chemicals
HQ: Esoterix Inc
      4509 Freidrich Ln Ste 100
      Austin TX 78744
      512 225-1100

(P-21528)
EPIC SCIENCES INC
9381 Judicial Dr Ste 200, San Diego (92121-3832)
PHONE......................858 356-6610
Lloyd Sanders, *President*
Michael Rodriguez, *CFO*
Cevdet Samikoglu, *CFO*
Katherine Atkinson, *Ch Credit Ofcr*
Chris Bernard, *Officer*
EMP: 80
SALES (est): 16.6MM **Privately Held**
SIC: 8071 Blood analysis laboratory

(P-21529)
EXAGEN DIAGNOSTICS INC
1221 Liberty Way Ste A, Vista (92081-8368)
PHONE......................505 272-7966
Robert Mignatti, *President*
EMP: 95
SALES (corp-wide): 32.4MM **Publicly Held**
SIC: 8071 Medical laboratories
PA: Exagen Inc.
      1261 Liberty Way Ste C
      Vista CA 92081
      760 560-1501

(P-21530)
FOCUS DIAGNOSTICS INC
11331 Valley View St # 150, Cypress (90630-5300)
PHONE......................714 220-1900
John Hurrell PHD, *President*
Edward Rusowicz, *General Mgr*
Kathy Roundtree, *Admin Asst*

Anh Ha, *Research*
Huong MAI, *Research*
EMP: 400
SQ FT: 36,000
SALES (est): 3.3MM
SALES (corp-wide): 7.5B **Publicly Held**
WEB: www.focusdx.com
SIC: 8071 Testing laboratories
PA: Quest Diagnostics Incorporated
      500 Plaza Dr Ste G
      Secaucus NJ 07094
      973 520-2700

(P-21531)
FOCUS TECHNOLOGIES HOLDING CO
10703 Progress Way, Cypress (90630-4714)
PHONE......................800 838-4548
Charles C Harwood, *President*
Edward Caffrey, *Vice Pres*
Don Mooney, *Vice Pres*
Laurence R McCarthy, *CTO*
EMP: 454
SQ FT: 28,000
SALES (est): 6.7MM **Privately Held**
WEB: www.focustechnologies.com
SIC: 8071 3826 Testing laboratories; analytical instruments

(P-21532)
FREEMONT RIDEOUT HEALTH GROUP
481 Plumas Blvd Ste 105, Yuba City (95991-5075)
PHONE......................530 671-2883
Karanbir Grewal, *Branch Mgr*
EMP: 59
SALES (corp-wide): 26.9MM **Privately Held**
SIC: 8071 X-ray laboratory, including dental
PA: Freemont Rideout Health Group
      989 Plumas St
      Yuba City CA 95991
      530 751-4010

(P-21533)
GARDEN GROVE ADVANCED IMAGING
1510 Cotner Ave, Los Angeles (90025-3303)
PHONE......................310 445-2800
Steiner Brittany, *Manager*
EMP: 299
SALES (est): 1.1MM **Publicly Held**
SIC: 8071 Medical laboratories
HQ: Radnet Management, Inc.
      1510 Cotner Ave
      Los Angeles CA 90025
      310 445-2800

(P-21534)
GENOMIC HEALTH INC (PA)
301 Penobscot Dr, Redwood City (94063-4700)
PHONE......................650 556-9300
Kimberly J Popovits, *Ch of Bd*
Frederic Pla, *COO*
G Bradley Cole, *CFO*
Phillip Febbo, *Chief Mktg Ofcr*
Jason W Radford,
EMP: 104
SQ FT: 180,700
SALES: 394.1MM **Privately Held**
WEB: www.genomichealth.com
SIC: 8071 8731 Medical laboratories; biotechnical research, commercial

(P-21535)
GENOMIC HEALTH INC
101 University Ave, Palo Alto (94301-1638)
PHONE......................650 269-0545
EMP: 397
SALES (corp-wide): 394.1MM **Privately Held**
SIC: 8071 Medical laboratories
PA: Genomic Health, Inc.
      301 Penobscot Dr
      Redwood City CA 94063
      650 556-9300

(P-21536)
GENOMIC HEALTH INC
101 Galveston Dr, Redwood City
(94063-4734)
PHONE..................................650 556-9300
Kimberly Popovits, *CEO*
Jeremiah Johnson, *Sales Staff*
Keith Gran, *Director*
Megan Gee, *Manager*
Ennio Villaflor, *Assistant*
EMP: 354
SALES (corp-wide): 394.1MM **Privately Held**
SIC: 8071 8731 Medical laboratories; commercial physical research
PA: Genomic Health, Inc.
  301 Penobscot Dr
  Redwood City CA 94063
  650 556-9300

(P-21537)
GENOPTIX INC (PA)
Also Called: Genoptix Medical Laboratory
2131 Faraday Ave, Carlsbad (92008-7252)
PHONE..................................760 268-6200
Joseph M Limber, *CEO*
Mark Spring, *CFO*
Joe Durshaw, *Executive*
Paul Stephensen, *Associate Dir*
Arianne Cruz, *Administration*
EMP: 130
SQ FT: 116,000
SALES (est): 47.6MM **Privately Held**
WEB: www.genoptix.com
SIC: 8071 Medical laboratories

(P-21538)
GENOPTIX INC
Also Called: Genoptix Mdcial Lab A Novartis
2110 Rutherford Rd, Carlsbad
(92008-7328)
PHONE..................................760 268-6200
Christian Itin, *Manager*
Kristen Tuba, *Info Tech Mgr*
Sherry Rocquemore, *Engineer*
Tina Maddox, *Purch Mgr*
Burt De Mill, *VP Sales*
EMP: 272
SALES (corp-wide): 47.6MM **Privately Held**
SIC: 8071 Testing laboratories
PA: Genoptix, Inc.
  2131 Faraday Ave
  Carlsbad CA 92008
  760 268-6200

(P-21539)
GRIFOLS DIAGNSTC SOLUTIONS INC (HQ)
2410 Lillyvale Ave, Los Angeles
(90032-3514)
PHONE..................................323 225-2221
David Bell, *Exec VP*
Christine Wong, *Engineer*
Dennis Cody, *Senior Engr*
Carmalyn Lubawy, *Senior Engr*
Jack Young, *Accounting Mgr*
EMP: 167
SALES (est): 136.8MM
SALES (corp-wide): 741MM **Privately Held**
SIC: 8071 Testing laboratories; biological laboratory; blood analysis laboratory; pathological laboratory
PA: Grifols Sa
  Calle Jesus I Maria 6
  Barcelona 08022
  935 710-196

(P-21540)
GUARDANT HEALTH INC (PA)
505 Penobscot Dr, Redwood City
(94063-4737)
PHONE..................................855 698-8887
Helmy Eltoukhy, *CEO*
Amirali Talasaz, *Ch of Bd*
Derek Bertocci, *CFO*
Richard Lanman, *Chief Mktg Ofcr*
Michael Wiley,
EMP: 275
SQ FT: 114,000
SALES: 90.6MM **Publicly Held**
SIC: 8071 Medical laboratories

(P-21541)
HEALTHQUEST LABORATORIES INC (PA)
18023 Sky Park Cir, Irvine (92614-6521)
PHONE..................................714 418-5867
Thomas Giancursio, *CEO*
Edward Hickey, *CFO*
EMP: 55
SQ FT: 2,043
SALES (est): 1MM **Privately Held**
SIC: 8071 Medical laboratories

(P-21542)
IGENEX INC
Also Called: Igenex Reference Laboratory
556 Gibralter Dr, Milpitas (95035-6315)
PHONE..................................650 424-1191
Jyotsna Shah, *CEO*
EMP: 50
SALES (est): 4.9MM **Privately Held**
WEB: www.igenex.com
SIC: 8071 Testing laboratories

(P-21543)
KAISER MANTECA MEDICAL OFFICE
1721 W Yosemite Ave, Manteca
(95337-5130)
PHONE..................................209 825-3700
Melanie Hatchel, *Owner*
EMP: 115 EST: 1998
SALES (est): 4.2MM **Privately Held**
SIC: 8071 Medical laboratories

(P-21544)
KAISER RADIOLOGY
7300 N Fresno St, Fresno (93720-2941)
PHONE..................................559 448-5541
Quemars Ahmadi, *Manager*
Mary Cooper, *Manager*
EMP: 80 EST: 1986
SALES (est): 4.6MM **Privately Held**
SIC: 8071 X-ray laboratory, including dental

(P-21545)
KAN-DI-KI LLC (HQ)
Also Called: Diagnostic Labs & Rdlgy
2820 N Ontario St, Burbank (91504-2015)
PHONE..................................818 549-1880
David F Smith III, *Mng Member*
Jose Martinez, *Analyst*
Joyce Amande,
Kelly McCullum,
Mark Parrish,
EMP: 164
SQ FT: 7,000
SALES (est): 80.8MM **Privately Held**
SIC: 8071 Testing laboratories; X-ray laboratory, including dental

(P-21546)
LABORATORY CORPORATION AMERICA
14901 Rinaldi St Ste 203, Mission Hills
(91345-1251)
PHONE..................................818 361-7089
Paul Rodriguez, *Manager*
EMP: 84 **Publicly Held**
SIC: 8071 Medical laboratories
HQ: Laboratory Corporation Of America
  358 S Main St Ste 458
  Burlington NC 27215
  336 229-1127

(P-21547)
LABORATORY CORPORATION AMERICA
10930 Bigge St, San Leandro
(94577-1121)
PHONE..................................510 635-4555
Kimberly Williams, *Branch Mgr*
Pu Fung, *Manager*
EMP: 84 **Publicly Held**
SIC: 8071 Testing laboratories
HQ: Laboratory Corporation Of America
  358 S Main St Ste 458
  Burlington NC 27215
  336 229-1127

(P-21548)
LATARA ENTERPRISE INC (PA)
Also Called: Foundation Laboratory
1716 W Holt Ave, Pomona (91768-3333)
PHONE..................................909 623-9301
Stepan Vartanian, *CEO*
Michelle Lewis, *CFO*
ARA Vartanian, *Treasurer*
Lala Vartanian, *Exec VP*
Sam Azatyan, *Executive*
EMP: 120
SQ FT: 19,000
SALES (est): 13.5MM **Privately Held**
WEB: www.foundationlaboratory.com
SIC: 8071 Pathological laboratory

(P-21549)
LATARA ENTERPRISE INC
9610 Stockdale Hwy, Bakersfield
(93311-3625)
PHONE..................................661 665-9780
Rosie Chavez, *Manager*
EMP: 62
SALES (corp-wide): 13.5MM **Privately Held**
SIC: 8071 Testing laboratories
PA: Latara Enterprise, Inc.
  1716 W Holt Ave
  Pomona CA 91768
  909 623-9301

(P-21550)
LATARA ENTERPRISE INC
705 E Virginia Way Ste D, Barstow
(92311-3955)
PHONE..................................760 256-3450
Susan Reese, *Manager*
EMP: 62
SALES (corp-wide): 13.5MM **Privately Held**
SIC: 8071 Testing laboratories
PA: Latara Enterprise, Inc.
  1716 W Holt Ave
  Pomona CA 91768
  909 623-9301

(P-21551)
MAGNETIC IMAGING AFFILATES
5730 Telegraph Ave, Oakland
(94609-1710)
PHONE..................................510 204-1820
Stefan Arnold, *Director*
EMP: 55
SQ FT: 3,500
SALES (est): 2.4MM **Privately Held**
SIC: 8071 Medical laboratories

(P-21552)
MAX MRI IMAGING INC (PA)
17530 Ventura Blvd # 105, Encino
(91316-3883)
PHONE..................................818 382-2220
Rafi Hedvat, *Principal*
Javad Ahmadian, *President*
Cecilia Saldana, *Manager*
EMP: 50
SQ FT: 10,000
SALES (est): 5MM **Privately Held**
WEB: www.maxmriimaging.com
SIC: 8071 X-ray laboratory, including dental

(P-21553)
MAX/MR IMAGING INC
17530 Ventura Blvd # 105, Encino
(91316-3883)
PHONE..................................818 382-2220
Javad Ahmadian, *President*
Rafi Hedvat, *CFO*
Majid Ahmadian, *Vice Pres*
Laura Melendez, *Administration*
Anna Rodriguez, *Administration*
EMP: 100
SALES (est): 2.8MM **Privately Held**
SIC: 8071 X-ray laboratory, including dental

(P-21554)
MID RCKLAND IMGING PRTNRS INC (HQ)
1510 Cotner Ave, Los Angeles
(90025-3303)
PHONE..................................310 445-2800
Howard G Berger, *CEO*
▲ EMP: 50
SQ FT: 1,000
SALES (est): 8.3MM **Publicly Held**
SIC: 8071 Ultrasound laboratory; X-ray laboratory, including dental; neurological laboratory

(P-21555)
MOSS LANDING MARINE LABS
8272 Moss Landing Rd, Moss Landing
(95039-9647)
PHONE..................................831 771-4400
James Harvey, *Director*
David Ebert, *Program Mgr*
Sandy Yarbrough, *Admin Asst*
George Radojevic, *Database Admin*
John Negrey, *Technician*
EMP: 150
SALES (est): 13.6MM **Privately Held**
WEB: www.mlml.calstate.edu
SIC: 8071 Biological laboratory

(P-21556)
MYRIAD WOMENS HEALTH INC
Also Called: Counsyl, Inc.
180 Kimball Way, South San Francisco
(94080-6218)
PHONE..................................888 268-6795
Ramji Srinivasan, *CEO*
Matthew J Meyer, *Senior VP*
Brent Blake, *Vice Pres*
Brenton Blake, *Vice Pres*
John Tan, *Vice Pres*
EMP: 281
SALES: 96.3MM **Publicly Held**
WEB: www.counsyl.com
SIC: 8071 Medical laboratories
PA: Myriad Genetics, Inc.
  320 S Wakara Way
  Salt Lake City UT 84108

(P-21557)
NATERA INC (PA)
201 Industrial Rd Ste 410, San Carlos
(94070-2396)
PHONE..................................650 249-9090
Steve Chapman, *CEO*
Matthew Rabinowitz, *Ch of Bd*
Michael Brophy, *CFO*
Ramesh Hariharan, *Vice Pres*
David Swan, *Vice Pres*
EMP: 215
SQ FT: 113,000
SALES: 257.6MM **Publicly Held**
SIC: 8071 2835 Testing laboratories; in vitro diagnostics

(P-21558)
NEWPORT DIAGNOSTIC CENTER INC (PA)
Also Called: Newport Radio Surgery Center
1605 Avocado Ave, Newport Beach
(92660-7725)
PHONE..................................949 760-3025
Hazem H Chehabi, *President*
Nader Morcos, *Vice Pres*
Gregg Stempson, *Info Tech Dir*
Brigit Lieb, *Technology*
Janet Crider, *Finance*
EMP: 60
SQ FT: 26,000
SALES (est): 9.5MM **Privately Held**
SIC: 8071 Testing laboratories

(P-21559)
NICHOLS INST REFERENCE LABS (DH)
33608 Ortega Hwy, San Juan Capistrano
(92675-2042)
PHONE..................................949 728-4000
Douglas Harrington, *President*
Charles Olson, *CFO*
Jolene Kahn, *Treasurer*
Michael O'Gorman, *Vice Pres*
Murugan R Pandian, *Vice Pres*
EMP: 525
SQ FT: 240,000
SALES (est): 10.8MM
SALES (corp-wide): 7.5B **Publicly Held**
SIC: 8071 Testing laboratories
HQ: Quest Diagnostics Nichols Institute
  33608 Ortega Hwy
  San Juan Capistrano CA 92675
  949 728-4000

(P-21560)
OPTICS LABORATORY INC
9480 Telstar Ave Ste 3, El Monte
(91731-2988)
PHONE..................................626 350-1926
Patricia Chiu, *CEO*

PRODUCTS & SVCS

Shawn Ko, *Chairman*
George Lin, *Business Mgr*
▲ **EMP:** 60
SQ FT: 7,500
SALES (est): 3.3MM **Privately Held**
WEB: www.opticslab.com
SIC: 8071 Testing laboratories

(P-21561)
PENNISULA PTHLOGISTS MED GROUP
Also Called: Peninsula Pathology Associates
393 E Grand Ave Ste I, South San Francisco (94080-6233)
PHONE..................650 616-2940
Leonard A Valentino MD, *President*
Judy Alonzo, *President*
Carolyn Katzen MD, *Treasurer*
Jay A Guichard MD, *Vice Pres*
Martha S Hales, *Admin Sec*
EMP: 60
SALES (est): 3.7MM **Privately Held**
SIC: 8071 Pathological laboratory

(P-21562)
PENTRON CLINICAL TECH LLC
1717 W Collins Ave, Orange (92867-5422)
PHONE..................203 265-7397
EMP: 85
SALES (est): 2.3MM
SALES (corp-wide): 16.8MM **Privately Held**
SIC: 8071
PA: Pentron Corporation
53 N Plains Industrial Rd
Wallingford CT
203 265-7397

(P-21563)
PERSONALIS INC
1330 Obrien Dr, Menlo Park (94025-1436)
PHONE..................650 752-1300
John West, *President*
Jonathan Macquitty, *Ch of Bd*
Aaron Tachibana, *CFO*
Mike Fitzpatrick, *Vice Pres*
Richard Chen, *Security Dir*
EMP: 135
SQ FT: 31,280
SALES (est): 37.7MM **Privately Held**
SIC: 8071 Biological laboratory

(P-21564)
PHIFACTOR TECHNOLOGIES LLC
6415 Surfside Way, Malibu (90265-3627)
PHONE..................424 234-9494
Heiko Schmidt, *CEO*
EMP: 60
SQ FT: 2,700
SALES (est): 6.5MM **Privately Held**
SIC: 8071 3841 8731 Medical laboratories; diagnostic apparatus, medical; biotechnical research, commercial

(P-21565)
PHYSICIANS AUTOMATED LAB INC (DH)
Also Called: Central Coast Pathology Lab
820 34th St Ste 102, Bakersfield (93301-1933)
P.O. Box 1536 (93302-1536)
PHONE..................661 325-0744
Ken Botta, *CEO*
William R Schmalhorst MD, *President*
Bruce Smith, *CEO*
Joyce Hulen, *Admin Sec*
Mimi Breslin, *Finance Dir*
EMP: 69
SQ FT: 63,000
SALES (est): 27.1MM **Privately Held**
SIC: 8071 Medical laboratories

(P-21566)
POLYPEPTIDE LABORATORIES INC (DH)
365 Maple Ave, Torrance (90503-2602)
PHONE..................310 782-3569
Jane Salik, *CEO*
Tim Culbreth, *Vice Pres*
Nagana Goud, *Vice Pres*
Michael Verlander, *Vice Pres*
Brant Zell, *Vice Pres*
▲ **EMP:** 90
SQ FT: 19,200

SALES (est): 14MM **Privately Held**
WEB: www.polypeptide.com
SIC: 8071 8731 Medical laboratories; biotechnical research, commercial
HQ: Polypeptide Laboratories Holding (Ppl) Ab
Soldattorpsv 5
Limhamn 216 1
403 662-00

(P-21567)
PRECISION TOXICOLOGY LLC
4215 Sorrento Valley Blvd, San Diego (92121-1408)
PHONE..................800 635-6901
Jason Hansen, *CEO*
Miguel Gallego, *COO*
Kenton Whitfield, *CFO*
Chrismarie Sanchez, *Technician*
EMP: 60
SALES (est): 7.5MM
SALES (corp-wide): 79.5MM **Privately Held**
SIC: 8071 Testing laboratories
PA: Belhealth Investment Partners, Llc
126 E 56th St Fl 23
New York NY 10022
347 308-7011

(P-21568)
PRIMEX CLINICAL LABS INC (PA)
16742 Stagg St Ste 120, Van Nuys (91406-1641)
PHONE..................818 779-0496
Oshin Hartoonian, *President*
Denisha McQueen, *Officer*
Erik Avaniss-Aghajano, *Vice Pres*
ARA Hartoonian, *Vice Pres*
Andre Aslanian, *Info Tech Dir*
EMP: 80
SQ FT: 3,000
SALES (est): 13MM **Privately Held**
WEB: www.primexlab.com
SIC: 8071 Blood analysis laboratory

(P-21569)
PROGENITY INC (PA)
Also Called: Amdx Laboratory Sciences
4330 La Jolla Village Dr # 200, San Diego (92122-6201)
P.O. Box 674425, Detroit MI (48267-4425)
PHONE..................760 494-1555
Harry Stylli, *CEO*
Sumit Aggarwal, *CFO*
Eric Desparbes, *CFO*
Howard Slutsky, *Senior VP*
Eric Fox, *Vice Pres*
EMP: 168 **EST:** 2002
SALES (est): 40.8MM **Privately Held**
WEB: www.amdxlabs.com
SIC: 8071 8731 Blood analysis laboratory; biotechnical research, commercial

(P-21570)
PROOVE MEDICAL LABS INC
15326 Elton Pkwy, Irvine (92618)
PHONE..................949 427-5303
Brian Meshkin, *CEO*
Sean Roddi, *COO*
Russell Skibsted, *CFO*
EMP: 175
SQ FT: 71,000
SALES: 201MM **Privately Held**
SIC: 8071 Biological laboratory

(P-21571)
QUEST DGNSTICS CLNCAL LABS INC
2369 Bering Dr, San Jose (95131-1125)
PHONE..................408 975-1015
Dennis Hogle, *Manager*
EMP: 320
SALES (corp-wide): 7.5B **Publicly Held**
WEB: www.questcentralab.com
SIC: 8071 Testing laboratories
HQ: Quest Diagnostics Clinical Laboratories, Inc.
1201 S Collegeville Rd
Collegeville PA 19426
610 454-6000

(P-21572)
QUEST DGNSTICS CLNCAL LABS INC
26081 Avenue Hall 150, Valencia (91355-1241)
PHONE..................661 964-6582
Dennis Hogle, *Branch Mgr*
EMP: 350
SQ FT: 40,000
SALES (corp-wide): 7.5B **Publicly Held**
WEB: www.questcentralab.com
SIC: 8071 Medical laboratories
HQ: Quest Diagnostics Clinical Laboratories, Inc.
1201 S Collegeville Rd
Collegeville PA 19426
610 454-6000

(P-21573)
QUEST DIAGNOSTICS INCORPORATED
401 Gregory Ln Ste 146, Pleasant Hill (94523-2836)
PHONE..................925 687-2514
Claire McCrossen, *Manager*
EMP: 450
SALES (corp-wide): 7.5B **Publicly Held**
WEB: www.questdiagnostics.com
SIC: 8071 Testing laboratories
PA: Quest Diagnostics Incorporated
500 Plaza Dr Ste G
Secaucus NJ 07094
973 520-2700

(P-21574)
QUEST DIAGNOSTICS INCORPORATED
33608 Ortega Hwy, Mission Viejo (92675-2042)
PHONE..................949 728-4235
Jon Nakamoto, *Manager*
EMP: 500
SALES (corp-wide): 7.5B **Publicly Held**
WEB: www.questdiagnostics.com
SIC: 8071 Testing laboratories
PA: Quest Diagnostics Incorporated
500 Plaza Dr Ste G
Secaucus NJ 07094
973 520-2700

(P-21575)
QUEST DIAGNOSTICS INCORPORATED
1275 E Spruce Ave Ste 102, Fresno (93720-3372)
PHONE..................559 438-2893
Jeff Owens, *Manager*
EMP: 60
SALES (corp-wide): 7.5B **Publicly Held**
WEB: www.questdiagnostics.com
SIC: 8071 Medical laboratories
PA: Quest Diagnostics Incorporated
500 Plaza Dr Ste G
Secaucus NJ 07094
973 520-2700

(P-21576)
RADNET INC (PA)
1510 Cotner Ave, Los Angeles (90025-3303)
PHONE..................310 445-2800
Howard G Berger, *Ch of Bd*
Mark D Stolper, *CFO*
Joan Brandehoff, *Chairman*
Jeffrey L Linden, *Exec VP*
Michael M Murdock, *Exec VP*
EMP: 150
SQ FT: 21,500
SALES: 975.1MM **Publicly Held**
WEB: www.radnetonline.com
SIC: 8071 Ultrasound laboratory

(P-21577)
REDDING PATHOLOGISTS LAB
2036 Railroad Ave, Redding (96001-1801)
PHONE..................530 225-8050
EMP: 55
SALES (corp-wide): 11.6MM **Privately Held**
SIC: 8071
PA: Redding Pathologists Laboratory
1725 Gold St
Redding CA
530 225-8050

(P-21578)
REDWOOD REGIONAL MEDICAL GROUP (PA)
Also Called: Redwood Regional Oncology Ctr
990 Sonoma Ave Ste 15, Santa Rosa (95404-4813)
PHONE..................707 525-4080
Mike Smith, *CFO*
Allan P Fishbein,
David A Keefer,
EMP: 70
SQ FT: 20,000
SALES (est): 12.3MM **Privately Held**
WEB: www.rrmginc.com
SIC: 8071 8011 X-ray laboratory, including dental; radiologist

(P-21579)
REDWOOD TOXICOLOGY LAB INC
3650 Westwind Blvd, Santa Rosa (95403-1066)
P.O. Box 5680 (95402-5680)
PHONE..................707 577-7958
Albert Berger, *CEO*
Wayne Ross, *Shareholder*
Alber Berger, *CEO*
Barry Chapman, *CFO*
Hollie Glaze, *Sales Mgr*
▲ **EMP:** 120
SQ FT: 23,000
SALES (est): 19.8MM
SALES (corp-wide): 30.5B **Publicly Held**
WEB: www.redwoodtoxicology.com
SIC: 8071 8734 Testing laboratories; testing laboratories
HQ: Alere Inc.
51 Sawyer Rd Ste 200
Waltham MA 02453
781 647-3900

(P-21580)
RHEUMATOLOGY DIAGNOSTICS LAB
Also Called: Rdl Reference Laboratory
10755 Venice Blvd, Los Angeles (90034-6214)
P.O. Box 34020 (90034-0020)
PHONE..................310 253-5455
Morris Robert I, *President*
Laura Lehrhoff, *COO*
Rick Kazdan, *CFO*
Allan Metzger MD, *Vice Pres*
Zina Karayev, *Executive*
EMP: 60
SQ FT: 33,000
SALES (est): 7.7MM **Privately Held**
WEB: www.rdlinc.com
SIC: 8071 Pathological laboratory

(P-21581)
SADDLEBACK MEMORIAL MED CTR
Also Called: Saddleback Mem Med Lab Svcs
24411 Health Center Dr, Laguna Hills (92653-3651)
PHONE..................949 452-3405
Cheryl Dilbeck, *Manager*
EMP: 150
SALES (corp-wide): 2.4B **Privately Held**
SIC: 8071 Medical laboratories
HQ: Saddleback Memorial Medical Center
24451 Health Center Dr # 1
Laguna Hills CA 92653
949 837-4500

(P-21582)
SAMARITAN IMAGING CENTER
1245 Wilshire Blvd # 205, Los Angeles (90017-4812)
PHONE..................213 977-2140
Andrew B Leeka, *CEO*
EMP: 658
SALES: 3.8MM
SALES (corp-wide): 319.2MM **Privately Held**
SIC: 8071 Medical laboratories
PA: Good Samaritan Hospital
1225 Wilshire Blvd
Los Angeles CA 90017

(P-21583)
SANTA BARBRA CTTGE HSPTL
Respiratory Care
400 W Pueblo St, Santa Barbara
(93105-4353)
PHONE.....................805 569-7224
Dr Phillip Michael, *Director*
EMP: 289
SALES (corp-wide): 646.4MM **Privately Held**
SIC: 8071 Medical laboratories
PA: Santa Barbara Cottage Hospital
400 W Pueblo St
Santa Barbara CA 93105
805 682-7111

(P-21584)
SANTA MNICA WLSHIRE IMGING LLC
Also Called: Tower St John Imaging
5455 Wilshire Blvd, Los Angeles
(90036-4201)
PHONE.....................323 549-3055
Gerald Roth MD,
EMP: 50
SALES (est): 5MM **Privately Held**
SIC: 8071 X-ray laboratory, including dental

(P-21585)
SANTA ROSA RADIOLOGY MED GROUP (PA)
121 Sotoyome St, Santa Rosa
(95405-4871)
PHONE.....................707 546-4062
Kim Miranda, *CFO*
Emily Conway, *Cardiovascular*
EMP: 50
SQ FT: 20,000
SALES (est): 4.4MM **Privately Held**
WEB: www.wyominglobbyist.com
SIC: 8071 8011 X-ray laboratory, including dental; radiologist

(P-21586)
SCANTIBODIES CLINICAL LAB INC
9236 Abraham Way, Santee (92071-5611)
PHONE.....................866 249-1212
Thomas L Cantor, *President*
EMP: 50
SALES (est): 2.4MM
SALES (corp-wide): 101.9MM **Privately Held**
SIC: 8071 Testing laboratories
PA: Scantibodies Laboratory, Inc.
9336 Abraham Way
Santee CA 92071
619 258-9300

(P-21587)
SCHRYVER MED SLS & MKTG LLC
526 Mccormick St, San Leandro
(94577-1108)
PHONE.....................303 371-0073
Todd Hubbard, *Manager*
EMP: 120
SALES (corp-wide): 149.4MM **Privately Held**
SIC: 8071 Medical laboratories
HQ: Schryver Medical Sales And Marketing, Llc
12075 E 45th Ave Ste 600
Denver CO 80239

(P-21588)
SCHRYVER MED SLS & MKTG LLC
8545 Arjons Dr, San Diego (92126-4361)
PHONE.....................303 459-8160
Jose Silva, *Branch Mgr*
EMP: 91
SALES (corp-wide): 149.4MM **Privately Held**
SIC: 8071 Ultrasound laboratory; X-ray laboratory, including dental
HQ: Schryver Medical Sales And Marketing, Llc
12075 E 45th Ave Ste 600
Denver CO 80239

(P-21589)
SCHRYVER MED SLS & MKTG LLC
1845 N Case St, Orange (92865-4234)
PHONE.....................303 459-8160
Jose Silva, *Branch Mgr*
EMP: 91
SALES (corp-wide): 149.4MM **Privately Held**
SIC: 8071 Ultrasound laboratory; X-ray laboratory, including dental
HQ: Schryver Medical Sales And Marketing, Llc
12075 E 45th Ave Ste 600
Denver CO 80239

(P-21590)
SCHRYVER MED SLS & MKTG LLC
310 N Cluff Ave Ste 212, Lodi
(95240-0764)
PHONE.....................303 459-8150
Marc Martin, *Branch Mgr*
EMP: 91
SALES (corp-wide): 149.4MM **Privately Held**
SIC: 8071 Ultrasound laboratory; X-ray laboratory, including dental
HQ: Schryver Medical Sales And Marketing, Llc
12075 E 45th Ave Ste 600
Denver CO 80239

(P-21591)
SEQUENOM CENTER FOR MOLECULAR
Also Called: Sequenom Laboratories
3595 John Hopkins Ct, San Diego
(92121-1121)
PHONE.....................858 202-9051
Jeffrey D Linton, *Admin Sec*
Carolyn D Beaver, *Treasurer*
Daniel Grosu, *Vice Pres*
Alexis Parton, *Manager*
◆ **EMP:** 400
SALES: 89.7MM **Publicly Held**
WEB: www.sequenom.com
SIC: 8071 Medical laboratories
HQ: Sequenom, Inc.
3595 John Hopkins Ct
San Diego CA 92121

(P-21592)
SOC PATHOLOGY MED GROUP INC
2374 E Pacifica Pl, Rancho Dominguez
(90220-6214)
PHONE.....................310 225-3244
Meredith Peake, *CEO*
Stanette Kennebrew, *Administration*
EMP: 85
SALES: 1MM **Privately Held**
SIC: 8071 Medical laboratories

(P-21593)
SPECIALTY LABORATORIES INC (DH)
Also Called: Quest Diagn Nichols Inst Valen
27027 Tourney Rd, Valencia (91355-5386)
PHONE.....................661 799-6543
R Keith Laughman, *President*
Vicki Difrancesco, *Vice Pres*
Nicole Larkins, *Administration*
Michael Bond, *Info Tech Mgr*
Sam Hart, *Info Tech Mgr*
▲ **EMP:** 633 **EST:** 1975
SALES (est): 23MM
SALES (corp-wide): 7.5B **Publicly Held**
WEB: www.specialtylabs.com
SIC: 8071 Testing laboratories
HQ: Ameripath, Inc.
7111 Fairway Dr Ste 101
Palm Beach Gardens FL 33418
561 712-6200

(P-21594)
SUTTER HEALTH
Also Called: Roseville Imaging
1640 E Roseville Pkwy, Roseville
(95661-3902)
PHONE.....................916 784-2277
Jerry Fosselman, *Manager*

EMP: 85
SALES (corp-wide): 12.7B **Privately Held**
WEB: www.radiological.com
SIC: 8071 Medical laboratories; specialized medical practitioners, except internal
PA: Sutter Health
2200 River Plaza Dr
Sacramento CA 95833
916 733-8800

(P-21595)
UNCHAINED LABS (PA)
Also Called: Optim
6870 Koll Center Pkwy # 20, Pleasanton
(94566-3176)
PHONE.....................925 587-9800
Tim Harness, *CEO*
Jason Novi, *COO*
Terry Salyer, *Ch Credit Ofcr*
Will Lachnit, *Vice Pres*
Scott Lockard, *Vice Pres*
EMP: 140
SALES (est): 46.5MM **Privately Held**
SIC: 8071 Medical laboratories

(P-21596)
UNILAB CORPORATION (HQ)
Also Called: Quest Diagnostics
8401 Fallbrook Ave, West Hills
(91304-3226)
PHONE.....................818 737-6000
Surya Mohapatra, *CEO*
Robert Moverley, *Managing Dir*
Tony Gouveia, *VP Finance*
Alexis Pacheco, *Training Spec*
Melissa Mahoney, *Director*
EMP: 400
SALES (est): 553.2MM
SALES (corp-wide): 7.5B **Publicly Held**
WEB: www.unilab.com
SIC: 8071 Testing laboratories
PA: Quest Diagnostics Incorporated
500 Plaza Dr Ste G
Secaucus NJ 07094
973 520-2700

(P-21597)
UNILAB CORPORATION
6475 Camden Ave Ste 104, San Jose
(95120-2847)
PHONE.....................408 927-8331
Ian Brotchie, *President*
EMP: 300
SALES (corp-wide): 7.5B **Publicly Held**
WEB: www.unilab.com
SIC: 8071 Testing laboratories
HQ: Unilab Corporation
8401 Fallbrook Ave
West Hills CA 91304
818 737-6000

(P-21598)
VALLEY RADIOLOGY CONSULTANTS (PA)
6185 Paseo Del Norte # 110, Carlsbad
(92011-1152)
PHONE.....................619 797-8248
Allen Nalbandian, *President*
Raymond Sung, *Treasurer*
Marcus Van Demetrie, *Admin Sec*
EMP: 52
SALES (est): 9.6MM
SALES (corp-wide): 8.8MM **Privately Held**
WEB: www.valleyrad.com
SIC: 8071 8011 X-ray laboratory, including dental; radiologist

(P-21599)
VALLEY TOXICOLOGY SERVICE INC
Also Called: Valtox Laboratories
2401 Port St, West Sacramento
(95691-3501)
P.O. Box 427 (95691-0427)
PHONE.....................916 371-5440
Jon Knapp, *President*
Carol Knapp, *Admin Sec*
EMP: 70
SQ FT: 7,000
SALES (est): 2.6MM **Privately Held**
WEB: www.valtox.com
SIC: 8071 Bacteriological laboratory

(P-21600)
VERACYTE INC
6000 Shoreline Ct Ste 300, South San
Francisco (94080-7606)
PHONE.....................650 243-6300
Bonnie H Anderson, *Ch of Bd*
Keith Kennedy, *COO*
Robert Epstein, *Bd of Directors*
Julie Brooks, *Exec VP*
Scott Bland, *Vice Pres*
EMP: 246
SQ FT: 59,000
SALES: 92MM **Privately Held**
SIC: 8071 8733 2835 Medical laboratories; medical research; cytology & histology diagnostic agents

(P-21601)
WEST PACIFIC MEDICAL LAB LLC (PA)
10200 Pioneer Blvd # 500, Santa Fe
Springs (90670-6008)
PHONE.....................818 773-9771
Martin Borish, *President*
Manny Jaime, *Vice Pres*
Brian Patchett, *Officer*
Tony Marquez, *IT/INT Sup*
EMP: 80 **EST:** 2009
SALES (est): 23.6MM **Privately Held**
SIC: 8071 Medical laboratories

(P-21602)
WHITEFIELD MEDICAL LAB INC (PA)
Also Called: Whitefield Medical Lab & Rdlgy
764 Indigo Ct Ste A, Pomona (91767-2269)
PHONE.....................909 625-2114
Jatin Laxpati, *President*
Shaila Laxpati, *Treasurer*
EMP: 50
SQ FT: 7,000
SALES (est): 6.2MM **Privately Held**
SIC: 8071 Testing laboratories

8072 Dental Laboratories

(P-21603)
BURBANK DENTAL LABORATORY INC
2101 Floyd St, Burbank (91504-3411)
PHONE.....................818 841-2256
Anatony Sedler, *CEO*
Tony Sedler, *President*
David French, *Vice Pres*
Robert Vartanian, *Vice Pres*
Tom Perachio, *Info Tech Mgr*
▲ **EMP:** 175
SALES (est): 17.1MM **Privately Held**
SIC: 8072 Dental laboratories

(P-21604)
CALIFORNIA DENTAL ARTS LLC
20421 Pacifica Dr, Cupertino (95014-3013)
PHONE.....................408 255-1020
Leon Frangadakis, *Med Doctor*
Matt Froess, *Vice Pres*
Steve Pavlidakis, *Planning*
Jan Martz, *Controller*
Lonnie Fountain, *Marketing Mgr*
EMP: 58
SQ FT: 4,000
SALES (est): 5.7MM **Privately Held**
WEB: www.caldentalarts.com
SIC: 8072 Crown & bridge production

(P-21605)
CANEW INC
22135 Roscoe Blvd, West Hills
(91304-3885)
PHONE.....................818 703-5100
Dan Materdomini, *President*
EMP: 120
SQ FT: 22,000
SALES (est): 12.5MM **Privately Held**
WEB: www.davincilab.com
SIC: 8072 5047 Crown & bridge production; dental equipment & supplies

(P-21606)
CONTINENTAL DNTL CERAMICS INC
1873 Western Way, Torrance (90501-1124)
PHONE.....................310 618-8821

Jerry Doviack, *President*
Krystina Doviack, *Corp Secy*
Tina Doviack, *Vice Pres*
Karen Chamberlain, *Mktg Dir*
EMP: 50
SQ FT: 12,000
SALES (est): 4.9MM **Privately Held**
SIC: 8072 Crown & bridge production

(P-21607)
DLH DAVINCI LLC
22135 Roscoe Blvd Ste 101, West Hills
(91304-3857)
PHONE..................................818 703-5100
EMP: 65
SALES (est): 294.8K **Privately Held**
SIC: 8072

(P-21608)
DURA METRICS INC (PA)
816 Piner Rd, Santa Rosa (95403-2019)
P.O. Box 873 (95402-0873)
PHONE..................................707 546-5138
Michael Kulwiec, *President*
EMP: 68 **EST:** 1968
SQ FT: 7,500
SALES (est): 4.7MM **Privately Held**
SIC: 8072 Dental laboratories

(P-21609)
EURODENT INC
9310 Topanga Canyon Blvd # 200,
Chatsworth (91311-5713)
PHONE..................................818 832-1325
Adam Adamonis, *President*
V J Lyons, *Vice Pres*
EMP: 60
SQ FT: 1,800
SALES (est): 4.1MM **Privately Held**
WEB: www.eurodentlab.com
SIC: 8072 Crown & bridge production

(P-21610)
GKY DENTAL ARTS INC (PA)
4212 Artesia Blvd, Torrance (90504-3106)
PHONE..................................310 214-8007
Glen Yamamoto, *President*
Kiichi Yamamoto, *Vice Pres*
Emiko Onda, *Accountant*
▲ **EMP:** 79
SQ FT: 4,500
SALES (est): 10MM **Privately Held**
WEB: www.gandhdental.com
SIC: 8072 Crown & bridge production

(P-21611)
JAMES R GLIDEWELL DENTAL
Also Called: Bdl Prosthetics
2181 Dupont Dr, Irvine (92612-1301)
PHONE..................................800 411-9723
Robert Rosen, *Branch Mgr*
Jessica Murga, *Project Mgr*
EMP: 1000
SALES (corp-wide): 327.6MM **Privately Held**
SIC: 8072 Crown & bridge production
PA: James R. Glidewell, Dental Ceramics, Inc.
4141 Macarthur Blvd
Newport Beach CA 92660
949 440-2600

(P-21612)
JAMES R GLIDEWELL DENTAL (PA)
Also Called: Glidewell Laboratories
4141 Macarthur Blvd, Newport Beach
(92660-2015)
PHONE..................................949 440-2600
James R Glidewell, *CEO*
Greg Minzenmayer, *COO*
Rob Grice, *CFO*
Glenn Sasaki, *CFO*
Anna Ameduri, *Vice Pres*
▲ **EMP:** 1100 **EST:** 1969
SQ FT: 72,000
SALES (est): 327.6MM **Privately Held**
WEB: www.glidewelldental.com
SIC: 8072 Crown & bridge production

(P-21613)
KEATING DENTAL ARTS INC
16881 Hale Ave Ste A, Irvine (92606-5068)
PHONE..................................949 955-2100
Shaun Keating, *President*
Dean Tassey, *Manager*

EMP: 105
SQ FT: 26,000
SALES: 13MM **Privately Held**
WEB: www.keatingdentalarts.com
SIC: 8072 Crown & bridge production

(P-21614)
POSCA BROTHERS DENTAL LAB
641 W Willow St, Long Beach
(90806-2832)
PHONE..................................562 427-1811
Alex Posca, *President*
Yanette Posca, *Corp Secy*
Angel Jorge Posca, *Vice Pres*
Greg Muro, *General Mgr*
▲ **EMP:** 55 **EST:** 1965
SQ FT: 5,000
SALES (est): 7.2MM **Privately Held**
WEB: www.poscabrothers.com
SIC: 8072 3843 Dental laboratories; teeth, artificial (not made in dental laboratories)

(P-21615)
TRIDENT LABS LLC
Also Called: Trident Dental Laboratories
12000 Aviation Blvd, Hawthorne
(90250-3438)
PHONE..................................310 915-9121
Laurence K Fishman, *President*
Richard B Mc Donald, *CFO*
Richard B McDonald, *CFO*
▲ **EMP:** 125
SQ FT: 16,000
SALES (est): 16.6MM
SALES (corp-wide): 165.1MM **Privately Held**
WEB: www.tridentlab.com
SIC: 8072 Crown & bridge production
PA: Gdc Holdings, Inc.
11601 Kew Gardens Ave # 200
Palm Beach Gardens FL 33410
763 398-0654

8082 Home Health Care

(P-21616)
24-7 CAREGIVERS REGISTRY INC
6800 Owensmouth Ave # 420, Canoga Park
(91303-4238)
PHONE..................................800 687-8066
Piroska Zalkadi, *CEO*
Richard Weatherman, *CFO*
EMP: 110
SALES: 4.2MM **Privately Held**
SIC: 8082 Home health care services

(P-21617)
24HR HOMECARE LLC (PA)
300 N Pacific Coast Hwy # 1065, El Segundo (90245-4490)
PHONE..................................310 906-3683
Sonia Aouriri, *Principal*
Joey Jacobellis, *Accounts Mgr*
EMP: 65
SALES (est): 12.2MM **Privately Held**
SIC: 8082 Home health care services

(P-21618)
A & A HOME CARE SERVICES
7756 Cntry Clb Dr Bldg A, Palm Springs
(92263)
PHONE..................................760 416-6769
Suzanne O Armstrong, *Owner*
EMP: 60
SALES (est): 588.7K **Privately Held**
SIC: 8082 7299 Home health care services; personal financial services; personal shopping service

(P-21619)
A BETTER LIFE TOGETHER INC
3322 Sweetwater Springs B, Spring Valley
(91977-3142)
PHONE..................................619 741-1548
Kim Wilson, *Principal*
Kimberly Mills, *Owner*
EMP: 90
SALES (est): 2.6MM **Privately Held**
SIC: 8082 Visiting nurse service

(P-21620)
A CAOS MEDICAL CORPORATION
2655 Camino Del R, San Diego (92108)
PHONE..................................800 362-2731
Angel Iscovich, *President*
EMP: 99
SALES (est): 371.5K **Privately Held**
SIC: 8082 Home health care services

(P-21621)
A CAREGIVER LLC
31520 Rr Cyn Rd Ste A, Canyon Lake
(92587-9499)
PHONE..................................951 676-4190
EMP: 50
SALES (est): 841.8K **Privately Held**
SIC: 8082

(P-21622)
A-1 HOSPICE CARE INC
217 E Alameda Ave Ste 306, Burbank
(91502-2621)
PHONE..................................818 237-2700
Femi Samuel, *CFO*
EMP: 65
SQ FT: 2,800
SALES: 1.6MM **Privately Held**
SIC: 8082 Home health care services

(P-21623)
ABC HOME HEALTH CARE LLC
5090 Shoreham Pl Ste 209, San Diego
(92122-5935)
PHONE..................................858 455-5000
Joseph Monteforte, *Exec Dir*
Hamid Alebrahim, *Mng Member*
Hamideh F Panabi, *Mng Member*
EMP: 125
SALES: 1.1MM **Privately Held**
WEB: www.abchomehealthcare.com
SIC: 8082 7371 Home health care services; computer software development & applications

(P-21624)
ABCSP LLC
Also Called: Always Best Care Senior Svcs
1406 Blue Oaks Blvd, Roseville
(95747-5199)
PHONE..................................855 470-2273
Michael Newman, *Ch of Bd*
Jake Brown, *President*
Sheila Davis, *Senior VP*
David J Caesar, *Vice Pres*
Jason Wiedder, *Vice Pres*
EMP: 121
SQ FT: 3,000
SALES (est): 7.7MM **Privately Held**
WEB: www.alwaysbestcare.com
SIC: 8082 Home health care services

(P-21625)
ABLE HANDS INC
18780 Amar Rd Ste 207, Walnut
(91789-4559)
PHONE..................................626 965-2233
Salvador L Abiera, *President*
Cynthia Magtoto, *CFO*
EMP: 100
SALES (est): 1.7MM **Privately Held**
SIC: 8082 Home health care services

(P-21626)
ABOVE HLTH HM CARE SLTIONS LLC
960 S Peregrine Pl, Anaheim (92806-4727)
PHONE..................................714 585-2185
Jesselle Macis,
EMP: 53 **EST:** 2011
SALES (est): 467.9K **Privately Held**
SIC: 8082 Home health care services

(P-21627)
ACCENTCARE INC
5050 Mrphy Knyan Rd St200, San Diego
(92123)
PHONE..................................858 576-7410
EMP: 1587
SALES (corp-wide): 682.7MM **Privately Held**
SIC: 8082 7389 Home health care services; business services

PA: Accentcare, Inc.
17855 Dallas Pkwy
Dallas TX 75287
800 834-3059

(P-21628)
ACCENTCARE HM HLTH SCRMNTO INC
2880 Sunrise Blvd Ste 218, Rancho Cordova (95742-6101)
PHONE..................................916 852-5888
Karin Stark, *President*
Rochelle Ward, *Vice Pres*
EMP: 55
SQ FT: 10,000
SALES (est): 1.5MM
SALES (corp-wide): 682.7MM **Privately Held**
SIC: 8082 Visiting nurse service
HQ: Accentcare Home Health, Inc.
135 Technology Dr Ste 150
Irvine CA 92618

(P-21629)
ACCENTCARE HOME HEALTH
2344 S 2nd St Ste A, El Centro
(92243-5606)
PHONE..................................760 352-4022
Melanie Ihler, *CEO*
EMP: 50
SALES (est): 925.5K
SALES (corp-wide): 682.7MM **Privately Held**
WEB: www.accentcare.com
SIC: 8082 Home health care services
HQ: Accentcare Home Health, Inc.
135 Technology Dr Ste 150
Irvine CA 92618

(P-21630)
ACCENTCARE HOME HEALTH CAL INC
Also Called: Sunplus HM Care - Pleasant Hl
2300 Contra Costa Blvd # 125, Pleasant Hill (94523-3918)
PHONE..................................925 356-6066
Francine Cummings, *Administration*
EMP: 84
SALES (corp-wide): 682.7MM **Privately Held**
WEB: www.dhsi.com
SIC: 8082 Visiting nurse service
HQ: Accentcare Home Health Of California, Inc.
17855 Dallas Pkwy
Dallas TX 75287

(P-21631)
ACCENTCARE HOME HEALTH CAL INC
15455 San Fernando Ste, Mission Hills
(91345)
PHONE..................................818 528-8855
Patricia Haynes, *Administration*
Annette Van As, *Administration*
EMP: 50
SALES (corp-wide): 682.7MM **Privately Held**
WEB: www.dhsi.com
SIC: 8082 8051 Home health care services; skilled nursing care facilities
HQ: Accentcare Home Health Of California, Inc.
17855 Dallas Pkwy
Dallas TX 75287

(P-21632)
ACCENTCARE HOME HEALTH CAL INC
Also Called: Sunplus Home Care - Ontario
1455 Auto Center Dr # 200, Ontario
(91761-2239)
PHONE..................................909 605-7000
EMP: 58
SALES (corp-wide): 682.7MM **Privately Held**
WEB: www.dhsi.com
SIC: 8082 8051 Home health care services; skilled nursing care facilities

HQ: Accentcare Home Health Of California, Inc.
17855 Dallas Pkwy
Dallas TX 75287

(P-21633)
ACCENTCARE HOME HEALTH CAL INC
Also Called: Sunplus Home Care - San Diego
5050 Murphy Canyon Rd # 200, San Diego (92123-4441)
PHONE................................858 576-7410
Joan Laforteza, *Manager*
EMP: 184
SQ FT: 4,000
SALES (corp-wide): 682.7MM **Privately Held**
WEB: www.dhsi.com
SIC: 8082 Visiting nurse service
HQ: Accentcare Home Health Of California, Inc.
17855 Dallas Pkwy
Dallas TX 75287

(P-21634)
ACCENTCARE HOME HEALTH CAL INC
Also Called: Sunplus HM Hlth - Newport Bch
3636 Birch St Ste 195, Newport Beach (92660-2644)
PHONE................................949 250-0133
Mary Lynn, *Manager*
EMP: 56
SALES (corp-wide): 682.7MM **Privately Held**
WEB: www.dhsi.com
SIC: 8082 8051 Home health care services; skilled nursing care facilities
HQ: Accentcare Home Health Of California, Inc.
17855 Dallas Pkwy
Dallas TX 75287

(P-21635)
ACCREDITED NURSING SERVICES
Also Called: Accredited Nursing Care
950 S Coast Dr Ste 215, Costa Mesa (92626-7850)
PHONE................................714 973-1234
Meryll Jones, *Manager*
EMP: 65
SALES (corp-wide): 16.8MM **Privately Held**
WEB: www.accreditednursing.com
SIC: 8082 Home health care services
PA: Accredited Nursing Services
17141 Ventura Blvd # 201
Encino CA
818 986-6017

(P-21636)
ACCUMEN INC (PA)
5414 Oberlin Dr Ste 200, San Diego (92121-4745)
PHONE................................858 777-8160
Jeff Osborne, *President*
Jim Bredy, *COO*
John Adams, *CFO*
Kimberly Macdowell, *Vice Pres*
Cindy Murphy, *Vice Pres*
EMP: 61
SALES (est): 27.4MM **Privately Held**
SIC: 8082 Home health care services

(P-21637)
ACT HOME HEALTH INC
12431 Lewis St Ste 101, Garden Grove (92840-4653)
PHONE................................714 560-0800
Catherine Johnston, *President*
EMP: 60
SQ FT: 2,500
SALES (est): 2.8MM **Privately Held**
WEB: www.acthh.com
SIC: 8082 Visiting nurse service

(P-21638)
ACTION HOME NURSING SERVICES
561 Torero Way, El Dorado Hills (95762-3541)
PHONE................................530 756-2600
J Karen Hahn, *President*
Steven Weishaar, *Vice Pres*
EMP: 70
SALES (est): 2.5MM **Privately Held**
WEB: www.actionhomenursing.com
SIC: 8082 Visiting nurse service

(P-21639)
ADDUS HEALTHCARE INC
817 Coffee Rd Ste B1, Modesto (95355-4241)
PHONE................................209 526-8451
Linda Stinson, *Branch Mgr*
EMP: 100 **Publicly Held**
WEB: www.addus.com
SIC: 8082 Home health care services
HQ: Addus Healthcare, Inc.
2300 Warrenville Rd # 100
Downers Grove IL 60515
630 296-3400

(P-21640)
ADDUS HEALTHCARE INC
196 Cohasset Rd Ste 200, Chico (95926-2287)
PHONE................................530 566-0405
Mary Gorman, *Manager*
EMP: 50 **Publicly Held**
WEB: www.addus.com
SIC: 8082 Home health care services
HQ: Addus Healthcare, Inc.
2300 Warrenville Rd # 100
Downers Grove IL 60515
630 296-3400

(P-21641)
ADDUS HEALTHCARE INC
1730 S Amphlett Blvd, San Mateo (94402-2707)
PHONE................................650 638-7943
Nancy Kline, *Manager*
EMP: 495 **Publicly Held**
WEB: www.addus.com
SIC: 8082 Home health care services
HQ: Addus Healthcare, Inc.
2300 Warrenville Rd # 100
Downers Grove IL 60515
630 296-3400

(P-21642)
ADMIRAL HOME HEALTH INC
4010 Watson Plaza Dr # 140, Lakewood (90712-4047)
PHONE................................562 421-0777
Josie Jones, *President*
Danilo Bautista, *Vice Pres*
Keila Hernandez, *Director*
EMP: 70
SQ FT: 5,900
SALES: 1.4MM **Privately Held**
WEB: www.admiralhomehealth.com
SIC: 8082 Visiting nurse service

(P-21643)
ADVANCE HEALTH SOLUTIONS LLC
7825 Fay Ave Ste 200, La Jolla (92037-4270)
PHONE................................858 876-0136
F Chubak,
Maryam Navaie,
EMP: 60 EST: 2008
SALES (est): 708.7K **Privately Held**
SIC: 8082 Home health care services

(P-21644)
ADVANCED HOME HEALTH INC
4354 Auburn Blvd, Sacramento (95841-4107)
PHONE................................916 978-0744
Angela Sehr, *President*
Angie Macadangdang, *Principal*
Cindy Patrick, *Admin Asst*
Kathleen Boesch, *Info Tech Dir*
Sherah Hernandez,
EMP: 75
SQ FT: 4,000

SALES: 15.7MM **Privately Held**
SIC: 8082 8621 Visiting nurse service; nursing association

(P-21645)
AEGIS SENIOR COMMUNITIES LLC
Also Called: Aegis Gardens
36281 Fremont Blvd, Fremont (94536-3509)
PHONE................................510 739-0909
Emily Poon, *Manager*
EMP: 50
SALES (corp-wide): 102MM **Privately Held**
WEB: www.aegisal.com
SIC: 8082 8051 Home health care services; skilled nursing care facilities
PA: Senior Aegis Communities Llc
415 118th Ave Se
Bellevue WA 98005

(P-21646)
AEGIS SENIOR COMMUNITIES LLC
Also Called: Aegis Living
1660 Oak Park Blvd, Pleasant Hill (94523-4422)
PHONE................................925 588-7030
Fax: 925 939-2785
EMP: 70
SALES (corp-wide): 138.5MM **Privately Held**
SIC: 8082 8051
PA: Senior Aegis Communities Llc
415 118th Ave Se
Bellevue WA 98005
866 688-5829

(P-21647)
AEGIS SENIOR COMMUNITIES LLC
Also Called: Aegis Assisted Living
125 Heather Ter, Aptos (95003-3825)
PHONE................................831 684-2700
Janice Ibaio, *Manager*
Jose Godinez, *Maintence Staff*
EMP: 50
SALES (corp-wide): 102MM **Privately Held**
WEB: www.aegisal.com
SIC: 8082 8051 Home health care services; skilled nursing care facilities
PA: Senior Aegis Communities Llc
415 118th Ave Se
Bellevue WA 98005

(P-21648)
AEGIS SENIOR COMMUNITIES LLC
Also Called: Aegis of Granada Hills
10801 Lindley Ave, Granada Hills (91344-4441)
PHONE................................818 363-3373
Bill Phelps, *Branch Mgr*
Scott Eckstein, *Manager*
EMP: 80
SALES (corp-wide): 102MM **Privately Held**
WEB: www.aegisal.com
SIC: 8082 8052 8051 8361 Home health care services; intermediate care facilities; skilled nursing care facilities; residential care
PA: Senior Aegis Communities Llc
415 118th Ave Se
Bellevue WA 98005

(P-21649)
AGAPE IN HOME CARE INC
4800 District Blvd Ste A, Bakersfield (93313-2325)
PHONE................................661 835-0364
Sandra Oxford, *President*
EMP: 50
SALES (est): 1.2MM **Privately Held**
SIC: 8082 Home health care services

(P-21650)
AGE ADVANTAGE HM CARE SVCS
5480 Baltimore Dr Ste 214, La Mesa (91942-2066)
PHONE................................619 449-5900
Daphne Archer, *President*
Joyce Porterfield, *Exec VP*
Ellen Hanson, *Office Mgr*
EMP: 75 EST: 1998
SQ FT: 1,200
SALES (est): 2.1MM **Privately Held**
SIC: 8082 Home health care services

(P-21651)
ALEGRECARE INC
1375 Sutter St Ste 110, San Francisco (94109-5465)
PHONE................................415 974-3530
Charles Symes II, *President*
Corie Moyers, *Client Mgr*
EMP: 400 EST: 2014
SALES (est): 6MM **Privately Held**
SIC: 8082 Home health care services

(P-21652)
ALL SEASONS HOMECARE
2160 The Alameda Ste C, San Jose (95126-1122)
PHONE................................408 378-0900
Lou Anne Mowry, *Owner*
EMP: 80
SALES (corp-wide): 1.4MM **Privately Held**
SIC: 8082 Home health care services
PA: All Seasons Homecare
5653 Stoneridge Dr # 110
Pleasanton CA 94588
650 368-4040

(P-21653)
ALL VALLEY HOME HLTH CARE INC
Also Called: All Valley Home Care
3665 Ruffin Rd Ste 103, San Diego (92123-1871)
PHONE................................619 276-8001
Glen Amador, *President*
Michael Drake, *Regional Mgr*
EMP: 100
SQ FT: 2,500
SALES (est): 1.6MM **Privately Held**
SIC: 8082 Home health care services

(P-21654)
ALLIANCE HOSPITAL SERVICES
Also Called: Mills-Peninsula Health HM Care
100 S San Mateo Dr, San Mateo (94401-3805)
PHONE................................650 697-6900
Sheila Schubert, *Branch Mgr*
EMP: 50
SALES (corp-wide): 5.6MM **Privately Held**
WEB: www.hospitalconsort.org
SIC: 8082 Home health care services
PA: Alliance Hospital Services, Inc
309 Lennon Ln Ste 200
Walnut Creek CA 94598
925 304-1107

(P-21655)
ALLIANCE HOSPITAL SERVICES (PA)
Also Called: Alliance Home Care Management
309 Lennon Ln Ste 200, Walnut Creek (94598-2445)
PHONE................................925 304-1107
Gregory Capson, *Ch of Bd*
George Cucozza, *Exec VP*
EMP: 350
SQ FT: 7,000
SALES (est): 5.6MM **Privately Held**
WEB: www.hospitalconsort.org
SIC: 8082 Home health care services

(P-21656)
ALLIED PROF NURSING CARE
2345 W Fthlls Blvd Ste 14, Upland (91786)
PHONE................................909 949-1066
Michael Gutierrez, *President*
Karen Gutierrez, *Administration*
EMP: 80 EST: 1996

SALES: 1MM **Privately Held**
SIC: 8082 Visiting nurse service

(P-21657)
ALWAYS HOME NURSING SVC INC
7777 Greenback Ln Ste 208, Citrus Heights (95610-5800)
PHONE..................................916 989-6420
Nancy Giachino, *President*
EMP: 200
SALES (est): 7.8MM **Privately Held**
SIC: 8082 Visiting nurse service

(P-21658)
ALWAYS THERE LIVE IN CARE LLC
7121 Magnolia Ave, Riverside (92504-3805)
PHONE..................................888 606-8880
Anntwonette Howard, *President*
Anntwonette Bonner, *President*
EMP: 72
SALES: 190K **Privately Held**
SIC: 8082 7389 Home health care services;

(P-21659)
ALZHEIMERS CARE SINCE 1983
Also Called: Garden, The
3730 S Greenville St, Santa Ana (92704-7092)
PHONE..................................714 641-0959
Violet Lazarescu, *Administration*
EMP: 50
SALES (est): 477.3K **Privately Held**
SIC: 8082 Home health care services

(P-21660)
AMBIENTE ENTERPRISES INC
Also Called: Home Instead Senior Care
73726 Alessandro Dr # 203, Palm Desert (92260-3640)
PHONE..................................760 674-1905
Rob Costello, *President*
EMP: 120
SQ FT: 2,600
SALES: 1.5MM **Privately Held**
SIC: 8082 Home health care services

(P-21661)
AMERICAN CAREQUEST INC (PA)
819 Cowan Rd Ste C, Burlingame (94010-1220)
PHONE..................................415 885-3324
Margarita Riskin, *President*
Eric Levsky, *Admin Sec*
EMP: 80
SQ FT: 1,100
SALES: 5.4MM **Privately Held**
WEB: www.americancarequest.com
SIC: 8082 5047 Home health care services; medical & hospital equipment

(P-21662)
AMERICAN PRIVATE DUTY INC
Also Called: American Untd HM Care Crp-Priv
13111 Ventura Blvd # 100, Studio City (91604-2218)
PHONE..................................818 386-6358
Ann Koshy, *President*
EMP: 80
SALES (est): 3.7MM **Privately Held**
WEB: www.americanprivateduty.com
SIC: 8082 Visiting nurse service

(P-21663)
AMERICAN SPCLTY HLTH GROUP INC
10221 Wateridge Cir # 201, San Diego (92121-2702)
PHONE..................................858 754-2000
George T Devries, *CEO*
Robert White, *COO*
William M Comer Jr, *CFO*
Kevin E Kujawa, *Exec VP*
R Douglas Metz, *Exec VP*
▲ EMP: 378
SQ FT: 148,000
SALES (est): 14.2MM **Privately Held**
WEB: www.ashbenefits.com
SIC: 8082 Home health care services

PA: American Specialty Health Incorporated
10221 Wateridge Cir # 201
San Diego CA 92121

(P-21664)
ANGEL CARE HOME HEALTH INC
2600 Foothill Blvd # 103, La Crescenta (91214-4578)
PHONE..................................818 248-8811
Vivian A Kono, *President*
EMP: 50
SALES: 1.2MM **Privately Held**
SIC: 8082 Home health care services

(P-21665)
ANGELES HOME HEALTH CARE INC
3701 Wilshire Blvd # 900, Los Angeles (90010-2871)
PHONE..................................213 487-5131
Rita L Doll, *CEO*
EMP: 125
SALES (est): 3.1MM
SALES (corp-wide): 2B **Publicly Held**
SIC: 8082 Visiting nurse service
HQ: Cornerstone Healthcare, Inc.
1675 E Riverside Dr # 200
Eagle ID 83616

(P-21666)
ANGELS IN MOTION LLC
Also Called: Visiting Angels
4091 Riverside Dr Ste 111, Chino (91710-3195)
PHONE..................................909 590-9102
Dominique Alvarez, *Mng Member*
EMP: 70 EST: 2010
SALES (est): 1.6MM **Privately Held**
SIC: 8082 Home health care services

(P-21667)
APEXCARE INC (PA)
1418 Howe Ave Ste B, Sacramento (95825-3230)
PHONE..................................916 924-9111
Kenneth Wang, *President*
EMP: 2000
SALES (est): 17.4MM **Privately Held**
SIC: 8082 Home health care services

(P-21668)
APRIA HEALTHCARE GROUP INC (PA)
26220 Enterprise Ct, Lake Forest (92630-8405)
PHONE..................................949 639-2000
Daniel J Starck, *CEO*
Debra L Morris, *CFO*
Connie Lai, *Officer*
Nichola Denney, *Exec VP*
Debra Morris, *Exec VP*
◆ EMP: 350
SQ FT: 100,000
SALES: 1.1B **Privately Held**
WEB: www.respimed.com
SIC: 8082 Home health care services

(P-21669)
APRIA HEALTHCARE LLC
815 Marlborough Ave # 200, Riverside (92507-2175)
PHONE..................................951 320-1100
Diana Castro, *Manager*
EMP: 83 **Privately Held**
WEB: www.apria.com
SIC: 8082 Home health care services
HQ: Apria Healthcare Llc
26220 Enterprise Ct
Lake Forest CA 92630
949 639-2000

(P-21670)
APRIA HEALTHCARE LLC
2476 Verna Ct, San Leandro (94577-4223)
PHONE..................................510 346-4000
Carl Caldwell, *Branch Mgr*
Jodi Roberts, *Sales Executive*
EMP: 66 **Privately Held**
WEB: www.apria.com
SIC: 8082 Home health care services

HQ: Apria Healthcare Llc
26220 Enterprise Ct
Lake Forest CA 92630
949 639-2000

(P-21671)
ASHLEY HOME CARE SERVICES LLC
200 Spectrum Center Dr # 300, Irvine (92618-5004)
P.O. Box 25321, Overland Park KS (66225-5321)
PHONE..................................323 286-2831
Lance Ashley, *Mng Member*
EMP: 50
SQ FT: 65,672
SALES (est): 2.5MM **Privately Held**
SIC: 8082 Home health care services

(P-21672)
ASIST INC
1974 N Gateway Blvd # 102, Fresno (93727-1632)
PHONE..................................559 251-7701
Amy Anne Sequeira, *Director*
Amy Sequeira, *Director*
EMP: 75 EST: 1999
SALES (est): 1.4MM **Privately Held**
SIC: 8082 Home health care services

(P-21673)
ASPEN HEALTHCARE CORPORATION (PA)
Also Called: SALUS HOME HEALTH
17100 Pioneer Blvd # 310, Artesia (90701-2776)
PHONE..................................562 888-6371
Mark Mortensen, *CEO*
Boad Swanson, *President*
Tyson Manning, *CFO*
Jay Brady, *Director*
Jeffrey Bradshaw, *Manager*
EMP: 60
SALES (est): 4.9MM **Privately Held**
SIC: 8082 Home health care services

(P-21674)
ASSISTA HLTHCARE PRFSSNALS LLC
Also Called: Assita In-Home Care
2006 Pioneer Ct, San Mateo (94403-1720)
P.O. Box 6205 (94403-6205)
PHONE..................................650 393-4293
Bernadette Galvan-Torrejon, *CEO*
Ernie Torrejon, *Officer*
EMP: 115
SQ FT: 1,065
SALES (est): 1.2MM **Privately Held**
SIC: 8082 Home health care services

(P-21675)
ASSISTED HOME RECOVERY INC
1900 W Garvey Ave S # 210, West Covina (91790-2656)
PHONE..................................626 915-5595
EMP: 62
SALES (corp-wide): 10.3MM **Privately Held**
SIC: 8082 Home health care services
PA: Assisted Home Recovery Inc
8550 Balboa Blvd Lbby
Northridge CA 91325
818 894-8117

(P-21676)
ATTENDANT CARE REFERRALS INC
2801 Ocean Park Blvd # 192, Santa Monica (90405-2905)
PHONE..................................310 399-2904
Gail Shaffer, *President*
EMP: 85
SALES (est): 1MM **Privately Held**
WEB: www.tlcacr.com
SIC: 8082 Visiting nurse service

(P-21677)
AVIDA CAREGIVERS INC
11500 W Olympic Blvd # 400, Los Angeles (90064-1524)
PHONE..................................323 498-1500
Chanel N Devlin, *CEO*
Samuel Bradley, *President*
EMP: 855 EST: 2014

HQ: Apria Healthcare Llc
26220 Enterprise Ct
Lake Forest CA 92630
949 639-2000

SALES (est): 428.7K **Privately Held**
SIC: 8082 Home health care services

(P-21678)
AXELACARE HOLDINGS INC
12604 Hiddencreek Way C, Cerritos (90703-2137)
PHONE..................................714 522-8802
EMP: 778 **Privately Held**
SIC: 8082 Home health care services
PA: Axelacare Holdings, Inc.
15529 College Blvd
Lenexa KS 66219

(P-21679)
B H PREMIER INC (PA)
Also Called: Premier Management Company
1141 S Beverly Dr Fl 3, Los Angeles (90035-1119)
PHONE..................................310 286-3074
Jacob Graff, *President*
Pnina Graff, *Admin Sec*
EMP: 58
SQ FT: 1,000
SALES (est): 2.8MM **Privately Held**
SIC: 8082 Home health care services

(P-21680)
BAYWOOD COURT (PA)
Also Called: Baywood Court Retirement Ctr
21966 Dolores St, Castro Valley (94546-6900)
PHONE..................................510 733-2102
Kelly Wiest, *Exec Dir*
EMP: 150
SALES: 19.3MM **Privately Held**
WEB: www.baywoodcourt.org
SIC: 8082 8051 6513 Home health care services; skilled nursing care facilities; retirement hotel operation

(P-21681)
BEAR FLAG MARKETING CORP
Also Called: At Home Caregivers
7599 Redwood Blvd Ste 200, Novato (94945-7706)
PHONE..................................415 899-8466
Peter L Rubens, *CEO*
EMP: 117
SQ FT: 1,200
SALES (est): 3.4MM **Privately Held**
WEB: www.bearflagmarketing.com
SIC: 8082 Home health care services

(P-21682)
BLIZE HEALTHCARE CAL INC
750 Alfred Nobel Dr # 202, Hercules (94547-1837)
PHONE..................................800 343-2549
Ukeje Elendu, *President*
Blessing Elendu, *COO*
EMP: 100
SQ FT: 3,700
SALES: 8.4MM **Privately Held**
SIC: 8082 Home health care services

(P-21683)
BLUEBRIDGE PROFESSIONAL SVCS
Also Called: Comfort Keepers
420 W Baseline Rd Ste D, Claremont (91711-1621)
PHONE..................................909 625-6151
Michael Craig II, *CEO*
EMP: 68
SALES (est): 352.3K **Privately Held**
SIC: 8082 Home health care services

(P-21684)
BRADEN PARTNERS LP A CALIF (HQ)
Also Called: Pacific Pulmonary Services Co
1304 Sthpint Blvd Ste 130, Petaluma (94954)
PHONE..................................415 893-1518
Jane Thomas, *CEO*
Tsutomu Igawa, *Ch of Bd*
Nancy V Natta, *VP Mktg*
▲ EMP: 65
SALES (est): 91.7MM **Privately Held**
SIC: 8082 Home health care services

(P-21685)
BRANLYN PROMINENCE INC
Also Called: Home Instead Senior Care
13334 Amargosa Rd, Victorville
(92392-8504)
PHONE..................................760 843-5655
Chris Parmelee, *General Mgr*
EMP: 130
SQ FT: 1,800 **Privately Held**
SIC: 8082 Home health care services
PA: Branlyn Prominence, Inc.
9213 Archibald Ave
Rancho Cucamonga CA 91730

(P-21686)
BRANLYN PROMINENCE INC (PA)
Also Called: Home Instead Senior Care
9213 Archibald Ave, Rancho Cucamonga
(91730-5207)
PHONE..................................909 476-9030
Brandi Johnson, *CEO*
Lynda Patriquin, *Vice Pres*
EMP: 100
SALES (est): 9.1MM **Privately Held**
SIC: 8082 Home health care services

(P-21687)
BRIGHT EXPECTATIONS INC
8175 Limonite Ave Ste C, Riverside
(92509-6121)
PHONE..................................951 360-2070
Charley Cox, *President*
EMP: 50
SQ FT: 1,000
SALES (est): 2.1MM **Privately Held**
SIC: 8082 Home health care services

(P-21688)
BRITTNEY HOUSE
5401 E Centralia St, Long Beach
(90808-1494)
PHONE..................................562 421-4717
Major Chief, *Owner*
EMP: 72
SALES (est): 295K **Privately Held**
SIC: 8082 8051 Home health care services; skilled nursing care facilities

(P-21689)
BURDETTE DE COCK INC
Also Called: Home Instead Senior Care
3625 Del Amo Blvd Ste 105, Torrance
(90503-1698)
PHONE..................................310 542-0563
Denise De Cock, *President*
EMP: 110
SALES (est): 4.4MM **Privately Held**
SIC: 8082 Home health care services

(P-21690)
BUTTE HOME HEALTH INC
Also Called: BUTTE HOME HEALTH & HOSPICE
10 Constitution Dr, Chico (95973-4903)
P.O. Box 5171 (95927-5171)
PHONE..................................530 895-0462
Brooke Quilici, *President*
Mike Quilici, *Vice Pres*
EMP: 105
SQ FT: 7,100
SALES: 6.6MM **Privately Held**
WEB: www.buttehomehealth.com
SIC: 8082 Visiting nurse service

(P-21691)
CAMBRIAN HOMECARE INC
15401 Anacapa Rd Ste 2, Victorville
(92392-2466)
PHONE..................................760 955-2250
EMP: 60 **Privately Held**
SIC: 8082 Home health care services
PA: Cambrian Homecare Inc
5199 E Pacific Coast Hwy
Long Beach CA 90804

(P-21692)
CARE OPTIONS MANAGEMENT PLANS
7000 Village Pkwy Ste A, Dublin
(94568-2413)
PHONE..................................925 551-3227
Joanne McCarley, *Branch Mgr*

EMP: 77 **Privately Held**
SIC: 8082 Home health care services
PA: Care Options Management Plans And
Supportive Services, Llc
1020 Market St
Redding CA 96001

(P-21693)
CARE OPTIONS MANAGEMENT PLANS (PA)
Also Called: C.O.M.P.A.S.S.
1020 Market St, Redding (96001-0512)
P.O. Box 993753 (96099-3753)
PHONE..................................530 242-8580
Sadie Hess, *Mng Member*
Sadie Huffmaster, *CTO*
Eric Hess,
Joanne McCarley, *Mng Member*
▲ EMP: 63
SALES (est): 8.5MM **Privately Held**
WEB: www.compasscares.com
SIC: 8082 Home health care services

(P-21694)
CARE PLUS HOME CARE INC
22931 Triton Way Ste 133, Laguna Hills
(92653-1237)
PHONE..................................949 716-2273
Carl Buffa, *President*
Maria Buffa, *Admin Sec*
EMP: 250
SALES (est): 4.5MM **Privately Held**
SIC: 8082 Home health care services

(P-21695)
CARE PLUS NURSING SERVICES INC
Also Called: CARE PLUS HOME HEALTH
22931 Triton Way Ste 236, Laguna Hills
(92653-1237)
PHONE..................................949 600-7194
Carl Buffa, *President*
Sharon Henry, *Administration*
Kyle Moffett, *Administration*
Noreen Ozawa, *Comptroller*
EMP: 160
SALES (est): 4.1MM **Privately Held**
SIC: 8082 8051 Visiting nurse service; skilled nursing care facilities

(P-21696)
CARE SOLUTION ASSOCIATES LLC
179 Contractors Ave, Livermore
(94551-8856)
PHONE..................................925 443-1000
Keith Beck, *Exec Dir*
EMP: 100
SALES (est): 275K **Privately Held**
SIC: 8082 Home health care services

(P-21697)
CARE UNLIMITED HEALTH SYSTEMS
1025 W Arrow Hwy Ste 105, Glendora
(91740-5407)
PHONE..................................626 332-3767
Carol Weatherburns, *Owner*
EMP: 75 EST: 1999
SALES (est): 1.9MM **Privately Held**
SIC: 8082 Home health care services

(P-21698)
CAREABILITY HEALTH SVCS CORP
Also Called: All For You Home Care
1329 Howe Ave Ste 100, Sacramento
(95825-3363)
PHONE..................................916 479-8554
Daniel Gourley, *Director*
EMP: 65
SALES: 950K **Privately Held**
SIC: 8082 Home health care services

(P-21699)
CARING COMPANIONS HOME
Also Called: Caring Cmpanions Referral Agcy
116 Las Lunas St, Hemet (92543-4028)
PHONE..................................951 765-1441
Deanna Hosick, *President*
EMP: 80
SQ FT: 700
SALES (est): 3.7MM **Privately Held**
SIC: 8082 Home health care services

(P-21700)
CARLTON SENIOR LIVING
Also Called: Senior Assisted Living Comm Ch
175 Cleaveland Rd, Pleasant Hill
(94523-3875)
PHONE..................................925 935-1001
Jeffrey Dillon, *Manager*
EMP: 65
SALES (corp-wide): 29.6MM **Privately Held**
SIC: 8082 Home health care services
PA: Senior Carlton Living Inc
4005 Port Chicago Hwy # 120
Concord CA 94520
925 338-2434

(P-21701)
CASTRO VALLEY HEALTH INC
Also Called: CVH HOME HEALTH SERVICES
39 Beta Ct, San Ramon (94583-1201)
PHONE..................................510 690-1930
Mark R Parinas, *CEO*
Isobel Parinas, *CFO*
Marc Pineda, *CIO*
Chan Zeb, *Accountant*
EMP: 200
SALES: 17.7MM **Privately Held**
WEB: www.parinashouse.com
SIC: 8082 Visiting nurse service

(P-21702)
CASWELL BAY INC
Also Called: Hillendale Home Care
1777 N Calif Blvd Ste 210, Walnut Creek
(94596-4150)
PHONE..................................925 933-8181
Bridget Waller, *President*
Weldon Waller, *Corp Secy*
EMP: 60
SQ FT: 1,100
SALES (est): 2.3MM **Privately Held**
WEB: www.hillendale.net
SIC: 8082 Home health care services

(P-21703)
CENTRAL COAST CMNTY HLTH CARE
5 Lower Ragsdale Dr # 102, Monterey
(93940-5817)
P.O. Box 2480 (93942-2480)
PHONE..................................831 372-6668
Carol Snow, *President*
EMP: 250
SQ FT: 18,014
SALES (est): 8MM **Privately Held**
SIC: 8082 Home health care services

(P-21704)
CENTRAL COAST CMNTY HLTH CARE
Also Called: Central Cast Vsting Nurse Assn
40 Ragsdale Dr Ste 150, Monterey
(93940-5790)
P.O. Box 2480 (93942-2480)
PHONE..................................831 648-4200
Norma J Harlacher, *President*
EMP: 350
SALES (est): 7.7MM **Privately Held**
SIC: 8082 Home health care services

(P-21705)
CENTRAL COAST VNA & HOSPICE (PA)
5 Lower Ragsdale Dr 102, Monterey
(93940)
P.O. Box 2480 (93942-2480)
PHONE..................................831 372-6668
Carol Snow, *CEO*
Gayle McConnell, *President*
Steven A Johnson, *CEO*
EMP: 175
SALES: 15.4MM **Privately Held**
SIC: 8082 Visiting nurse service

(P-21706)
CENTRAL COAST VNA & HOSPICE
45 Plaza Cir, Salinas (93901-2902)
PHONE..................................831 758-8243
Raul Perez, *Manager*
EMP: 75
SALES (corp-wide): 15.4MM **Privately Held**
SIC: 8082 Visiting nurse service

PA: Central Coast Vna & Hospice, Inc
5 Lower Ragsdale Dr 102
Monterey CA 93940
831 372-6668

(P-21707)
CHAROLAIS CARE V INC
Also Called: San Francisco Bay
1426 Fillmore St Ste 207, San Francisco
(94115-4164)
PHONE..................................415 921-5038
Jim Everton, *CEO*
EMP: 100 EST: 2008
SALES (est): 1.1MM
SALES (corp-wide): 27MM **Privately Held**
SIC: 8082 Home health care services
PA: B.R.P. Health Management Systems, Inc.
275 S 5th Ave Lowr Level
Pocatello ID 83201
208 233-4673

(P-21708)
CK FRANCHISING INC (DH)
Also Called: Comfort Keepers
1 Park Plz Ste 300, Irvine (92614-2510)
PHONE..................................800 498-8144
Sarosh Mistry, *CEO*
Tim Purcey, *Vice Pres*
Carol Carbutti, *General Mgr*
Tony Scapellato, *General Mgr*
Tammara Lacasse, *Human Res Dir*
EMP: 81
SQ FT: 11,160
SALES (est): 13.4MM
SALES (corp-wide): 133.3MM **Privately Held**
SIC: 8082 Home health care services
HQ: Sodexo, Inc.
9801 Washingtonian Blvd # 416
Gaithersburg MD 20878
301 987-4000

(P-21709)
CLINICS ON DEMAND INC
11000 Wilshire Blvd, Los Angeles
(90024-3601)
PHONE..................................310 709-7355
Shahrouz Ghodsian, *CEO*
EMP: 81
SALES (est): 8.5MM **Privately Held**
SIC: 8082 Home health care services

(P-21710)
COASTAL CMNTY SENIOR CARE LLC
Also Called: Home Instead Senior Care
5500 E Atherton St # 216, Long Beach
(90815-4016)
PHONE..................................562 596-4884
Donald Pierce, *Mng Member*
EMP: 140
SQ FT: 2,300
SALES (est): 959.8K **Privately Held**
SIC: 8082 Home health care services

(P-21711)
COLLABRIA CARE
414 S Jefferson St, NAPA (94559-4515)
PHONE..................................707 258-9080
Linda Gibson, *President*
Cathy Poliak, *Human Res Dir*
Caroline Wynne, *Human Res Dir*
Kyle Coburn, *Purchasing*
Celine Regalia, *Director*
EMP: 90
SALES: 15.1MM **Privately Held**
WEB: www.hospiceofnapa.org
SIC: 8082 Home health care services

(P-21712)
COLONIAL HOME CARE SVCS INC
326 W Katella Ave Ste F, Orange
(92867-4756)
PHONE..................................714 289-7220
Catherina Bertaina, *President*
Trevor O'Neil, *Administration*
EMP: 180
SQ FT: 1,200
SALES: 2.5MM **Privately Held**
WEB: www.colonialhomecareservices.com
SIC: 8082 Home health care services

PRODUCTS & SVCS

(P-21713)
COMMUNITY CARE INC
80 Garden Ct Ste 105, Monterey
(93940-5367)
PHONE...........................831 645-1434
Norris Blockhus, *Branch Mgr*
EMP: 72
SALES (corp-wide): 1.1MM **Privately Held**
SIC: **8082** Home health care services
PA: Community Care Inc
80 Garden Ct Ste 106
Monterey CA
-

(P-21714)
COMMUNITY HEALTH NETWORK LLC
25102 Jefferson Ave Ste B, Murrieta
(92562-1708)
PHONE...........................951 265-8281
Greg Maasberg, *Mng Member*
EMP: 55
SALES (est): 355K **Privately Held**
SIC: **8082** Home health care services

(P-21715)
COMPANION HOME HLTH & HOSPICE
Also Called: Companion Hospice
2041 W Orangewood Ave B, Orange
(92868-1902)
PHONE...........................714 560-8177
Michael Uranga, *President*
Eleenor Phillips, *Manager*
EMP: 95
SALES (est): 12.3MM **Privately Held**
WEB: www.companionhospice.com
SIC: **8082** Visiting nurse service

(P-21716)
COMPANION HOSPICE AND
6133 Bristol Parkday 11 # 110, Culver City
(90230)
PHONE...........................310 338-1257
Elo Sahagian,
Eleenor Phillips, *Manager*
EMP: 99
SQ FT: 2,000
SALES (est): 229.3K **Privately Held**
SIC: **8082** Home health care services

(P-21717)
COMPANION HOSPICE CARE LLC
8130 Florence Ave Ste 200, Downey
(90240-3977)
PHONE...........................562 944-2711
Michael A Uranga, *CEO*
Chris Vallandigham, *COO*
EMP: 125
SQ FT: 5,000
SALES (est): 5MM **Privately Held**
SIC: **8082** Home health care services

(P-21718)
COMPANION HOSPICE LLC
8130 Florence Ave Ste 200, Downey
(90240-3977)
PHONE...........................562 944-2711
EMP: 99
SALES (est): 229.3K **Privately Held**
SIC: **8082** Home health care services

(P-21719)
COMPETENT CARE INC
Also Called: Competent Care HM Hlth Nursing
2900 Bristol St Ste D107, Costa Mesa
(92626-5940)
PHONE...........................714 545-4818
Lynett Laroche, *President*
EMP: 70
SALES: 1.2MM **Privately Held**
WEB: www.competentcare.com
SIC: **8082** 7299 Visiting nurse service; information services, consumer

(P-21720)
COMPPARTNERS INC
333 City Blvd W Ste 1500, Orange
(92868-5913)
PHONE...........................949 253-3111
Bruce Carlin, *CEO*
Bernard J Mansheim, *Chief Mktg Ofcr*

Long Doan, *Vice Pres*
Eleanor Marciniak, *CTO*
Mary Mata,
EMP: 70
SQ FT: 15,000
SALES (est): 2.5MM **Privately Held**
WEB: www.comppartners.com
SIC: **8082** Home health care services

(P-21721)
COMPREHENSIVE COMMUNITY HEALTH (PA)
801 S Chevy Chase Dr, Glendale
(91205-4431)
PHONE...........................818 265-2264
Grace Javellana, *CFO*
Kenneth Thompson, *Physician Asst*
Michael Eshaghian, *Med Doctor*
Muhammad Iqbal, *Med Doctor*
Arthur Manoukian, *Med Doctor*
EMP: 50
SALES: 25.5MM **Privately Held**
SIC: **8082** Home health care services

(P-21722)
CONFIDO LLC
Also Called: 123 Home Care
3407 W 6th St Ste 709, Los Angeles
(90020-2554)
PHONE...........................310 361-8558
Graeme Freeman, *CEO*
Ryan Baxter, *Director*
Mark Schellinger, *Director*
EMP: 1900
SALES (est): 1.6MM **Privately Held**
SIC: **8082** Home health care services

(P-21723)
CORNERSTONE FAMILY SVCS LLC
Also Called: Comfort Keepers - 509
1748 W Katella Ave # 207, Orange
(92867-3437)
PHONE...........................714 744-3800
Christopher Gamble, *Managing Prtnr*
EMP: 55
SALES (est): 163.5K **Privately Held**
SIC: **8082** Home health care services

(P-21724)
CORNERSTONE HEALTHCARE INC
143 Triunfo Canyon Rd # 103, Westlake Village (91361-2514)
PHONE...........................805 777-1133
Andre, *Med Doctor*
EMP: 120
SALES (corp-wide): 2B **Publicly Held**
SIC: **8082** Home health care services
HQ: Cornerstone Healthcare, Inc.
1675 E Riverside Dr # 200
Eagle ID 83616

(P-21725)
CORNERSTONE HOSPICE CAL LLC
1461 E Cooley Dr Ste 220, Colton
(92324-3921)
PHONE...........................909 872-8100
Blaine Whitson, *President*
Erick Kerner, *Vice Pres*
Blaine L Whitson, *Administration*
EMP: 60
SALES (est): 3.8MM **Publicly Held**
WEB: www.cornerstonehospice.net
SIC: **8082** Visiting nurse service
PA: Genesis Healthcare, Inc.
101 E State St
Kennett Square PA 19348

(P-21726)
COSMOPRO WEST INC
15773 Gateway Cir, Tustin (92780-6470)
PHONE...........................714 258-8301
Antoine Macoule, *President*
◆ EMP: 50
SALES (est): 1.4MM **Privately Held**
SIC: **8082** Home health care services

(P-21727)
CRESCENT HEALTHCARE INC (DH)
11980 Telg Rd Ste 100, Santa Fe Springs
(90670)
PHONE...........................714 520-6300
Paul Mastrapa, *CEO*
David Zelaskowski, *President*
William P Forster, *CFO*
Pamela Bowen, *CIO*
EMP: 150
SQ FT: 26,000
SALES (est): 21.1MM
SALES (corp-wide): 136.8B **Publicly Held**
WEB: www.crescenthealthcare.com
SIC: **8082** Home health care services
HQ: Walgreen Co.
4010 Commercial Ave
Northbrook IL 60062
800 925-4733

(P-21728)
CUSTOMCARE HOME HLTH SVCS INC
9826 Bond Rd Ste A, Elk Grove
(95624-9419)
P.O. Box 2792 (95759-2792)
PHONE...........................916 714-1155
Audrey Acosta, *CEO*
EMP: 70
SALES (est): 1.4MM **Privately Held**
SIC: **8082** 7361 Home health care services; nurses' registry

(P-21729)
DIGNITY HEALTH
Also Called: Marian Hospital Homecare
1054 E Grand Ave Ste A, Arroyo Grande
(93420-2527)
PHONE...........................805 489-4261
Mike Cornaire, *Manager*
Elva Nava, *Director*
EMP: 73 **Privately Held**
WEB: www.chw.edu
SIC: **8082** Home health care services
HQ: Dignity Health
185 Berry St Ste 300
San Francisco CA 94107
415 438-5500

(P-21730)
DIGNITY HEALTH
Also Called: Marian Home Care and Hospice
124 S College Dr, Santa Maria
(93454-5325)
PHONE...........................805 739-3830
Toll Free:...........................877   -
Cathy Sullivan, *Administration*
EMP: 120 **Privately Held**
WEB: www.chw.edu
SIC: **8082** Home health care services
HQ: Dignity Health
185 Berry St Ste 300
San Francisco CA 94107
415 438-5500

(P-21731)
DIGNITY HEALTH
Home Health Dept of St Joseph
2333 W March Ln Ste B, Stockton
(95207-5272)
PHONE...........................209 943-4663
EMP: 50
SALES (corp-wide): 10.4B **Privately Held**
SIC: **8082**
PA: Dignity Health
185 Berry St Ste 300
San Francisco CA 94107
415 438-5500

(P-21732)
DUNN & BERGER INC
Also Called: Accredited Nursing Care
5955 De Soto Ave Ste 160, Woodland Hills
(91367-5101)
PHONE...........................818 986-1234
Barry Berger, *President*
EMP: 500
SALES (est): 11.7MM **Privately Held**
SIC: **8082** Home health care services

(P-21733)
DYNAMIC HOME CARE SERVICE INC (PA)
14260 Ventura Blvd # 301, Sherman Oaks
(91423-2734)
PHONE...........................818 981-4446
Nissan Pardo, *CEO*
Carol Silver, *President*
Jeff Friedman, *Sales Staff*
Marilyn Flick, *Manager*
EMP: 200
SALES (est): 6MM **Privately Held**
WEB: www.dynamicnursing.com
SIC: **8082** Visiting nurse service

(P-21734)
E R G HOME HEALTH PROVIDER
11700 South St Ste 200, Artesia
(90701-6619)
PHONE...........................562 403-1070
Fax: 562 403-1068
EMP: 60
SALES (est): 2.2MM **Privately Held**
SIC: **8082**

(P-21735)
EL CAMINO HOSPITAL AUXILIARY
2500 Grant Rd, Mountain View
(94040-4378)
P.O. Box 7025 (94039-7025)
PHONE...........................650 940-7214
Linda Heider, *President*
EMP: 600
SQ FT: 2,000
SALES: 104.3K
SALES (corp-wide): 973.3MM **Privately Held**
SIC: **8082** Home health care services
PA: El Camino Hospital
2500 Grant Rd
Mountain View CA 94040
650 940-7000

(P-21736)
EMINENCE HOME HEALTH CARE INC
16921 Parthenia St # 301, Northridge
(91343-4553)
PHONE...........................818 830-7113
Oscar Parel, *CEO*
EMP: 50
SALES (est): 2.6MM **Privately Held**
SIC: **8082** Home health care services

(P-21737)
ENLOE MEDICAL CENTER
Also Called: Enloe Homecare Services
1390 E Lassen Ave, Chico (95973-7823)
PHONE...........................530 332-6050
Leslie Gunghl, *Director*
Kathaleen Chaney, *Supervisor*
EMP: 300
SALES (corp-wide): 480.2MM **Privately Held**
SIC: **8082** Home health care services
PA: Enloe Medical Center
1531 Esplanade
Chico CA 95926
530 332-7300

(P-21738)
EXCEL HOME HEALTH INC
5575 Lake Park Way # 220, La Mesa
(91942-1664)
PHONE...........................619 460-6622
SRI Gopal, *President*
Anidta Krishnan, *Vice Pres*
Sonia Silva, *Executive*
Crystal Kays,
EMP: 50
SALES: 3.2MM **Privately Held**
WEB: www.excelhomehealth.com
SIC: **8082** Visiting nurse service

(P-21739)
EXPERIENCED HOME CARE REGISTRY
110 Civic Center Dr # 206, Vista
(92084-6037)
PHONE...........................760 724-0880
Deborah W Dahlin, *Owner*
EMP: 60
SALES (est): 1.3MM **Privately Held**
SIC: **8082** Home health care services

(P-21740)
FAITH JONES & ASSOCIATES INC (PA)
Also Called: Aall Care In Home Services
7801 Mission Center Ct # 106, San Diego
(92108-1314)
PHONE.....................619 297-9601
Faith Jones, *President*
Norman Jones, *CFO*
EMP: 90
SQ FT: 1,200
SALES (est): 5.2MM **Privately Held**
WEB: www.aallcare.com
SIC: 8082 Home health care services

(P-21741)
FAR EAST HOME CARE INC
3407 W 6th St Ste 710, Los Angeles
(90020-2554)
PHONE.....................949 673-3100
Rosendo Labadlabad, *President*
EMP: 110
SALES (est): 2.5MM **Privately Held**
WEB: www.fareasthomecare.com
SIC: 8082 8322 Home health care serv-
ices; individual & family services

(P-21742)
FIRSTAT NURSING SERVICES INC
411 Camino Del Rio S # 100, San Diego
(92108-3508)
PHONE.....................619 220-7600
Linnea Goodrich, *Owner*
Kathleen Tickle, *President*
EMP: 105
SQ FT: 1,800
SALES (est): 2.8MM **Privately Held**
SIC: 8082 Visiting nurse service

(P-21743)
FORTUNE SENIOR ENTERPRISES
Also Called: Comfort Keepers of Folsom
3941 Park Dr Ste 20265, El Dorado Hills
(95762-4549)
PHONE.....................916 560-9100
Vince Maffeo, *CEO*
Eleanor Maffeo, *President*
Vincent Maffeo, *Info Tech Mgr*
EMP: 72
SALES: 1.5MM **Privately Held**
SIC: 8082 Home health care services

(P-21744)
FOUNDERS HEALTHCARE LLC
Also Called: Lifecare Solutions
170 N Daisy Ave, Pasadena (91107-3465)
PHONE.....................626 683-5401
Rene Moreno, *Principal*
EMP: 57
SALES (corp-wide): 347MM **Privately
Held**
SIC: 8082 Home health care services
HQ: Founders Healthcare, L.L.C.
4601 E Hilton Ave Ste 100
Phoenix AZ 85034
800 636-2123

(P-21745)
GENTIVA HEALTH SERVICES INC
9444 Balboa Ave Ste 290, San Diego
(92123-4901)
PHONE.....................858 565-2499
EMP: 334
SALES (corp-wide): 1.5B **Privately Held**
SIC: 8082 Home health care services
PA: Gentiva Health Services, Inc.
3350 Riverwood Pkwy Se # 1
Atlanta GA 30339
770 951-6450

(P-21746)
GENTIVA HEALTH SERVICES INC
Also Called: Gentiva Home Health Care
3220 S Higuera St Ste 101, San Luis
Obispo (93401-6983)
PHONE.....................805 549-0801
Elaine Clark, *Manager*
EMP: 187

SALES (corp-wide): 1.5B **Privately Held**
WEB: www.gentiva.com
SIC: 8082 Home health care services
PA: Gentiva Health Services, Inc.
3350 Riverwood Pkwy Se # 1
Atlanta GA 30339
770 951-6450

(P-21747)
GLENDALE ADVENTIST MEDICAL CTR
Also Called: Adventist Health Homecare Svcs
281 Harvey Dr Unit B, Glendale
(91206-4112)
PHONE.....................818 409-8379
Bruce Nelson, *Med Doctor*
Edmund Lew, *Director*
EMP: 50
SALES (corp-wide): 4.4B **Privately Held**
SIC: 8082 Home health care services
HQ: Glendale Adventist Medical Center Inc
1509 Wilson Ter
Glendale CA 91206
818 409-8000

(P-21748)
GLOBAL MED SERVICES INC
Also Called: East West
11818 South St Ste 201a, Cerritos
(90703-6831)
PHONE.....................562 207-6970
Kwang Chang, *President*
▲ EMP: 600
SQ FT: 22,250
SALES (est): 10MM **Privately Held**
SIC: 8082 Home health care services

(P-21749)
GOLDEN LIVING LLC
Also Called: Golden Livingcenter - Galt
144 F St, Galt (95632-1833)
PHONE.....................209 745-1537
Brigitte Coleman, *Administration*
EMP: 90
SALES (corp-wide): 409.2MM **Privately
Held**
SIC: 8082 8051 Home health care serv-
ices; skilled nursing care facilities
PA: Beaver Dam Health Care Center
5220 Tennyson Pkwy # 400
Plano TX 75024
972 372-6300

(P-21750)
GOLDEN LIVING LLC
Also Called: California Healthcare
6700 Sepulveda Blvd, Van Nuys
(91411-1248)
PHONE.....................805 494-4949
Jerry Catama, *Exec Dir*
EMP: 100
SALES (corp-wide): 409.2MM **Privately
Held**
WEB: www.nwbeccorp.com
SIC: 8082 Home health care services
PA: Beaver Dam Health Care Center
5220 Tennyson Pkwy # 400
Plano TX 75024
972 372-6300

(P-21751)
GOLDEN LIVING LLC
Also Called: Beverly
1131 N China Lake Blvd, Ridgecrest
(93555-3131)
PHONE.....................760 446-3591
Steven Rodriguez, *Exec Dir*
EMP: 100
SALES (corp-wide): 409.2MM **Privately
Held**
WEB: www.nwbeccorp.com
SIC: 8082 8051 Home health care serv-
ices; skilled nursing care facilities
PA: Beaver Dam Health Care Center
5220 Tennyson Pkwy # 400
Plano TX 75024
972 372-6300

(P-21752)
GOOD WORKS LLC
Also Called: Right At Home
1250 E Walnut St Ste 220, Pasadena
(91106-5118)
PHONE.....................626 584-8130
Renee Concialdi, *Mng Member*
Joseph A Concialdi,

EMP: 65
SQ FT: 1,300
SALES: 2.5MM **Privately Held**
SIC: 8082 Home health care services

(P-21753)
GRANDCARE HEALTH SERVICES LLC (PA)
3452 E Foothill Blvd # 700, Pasadena
(91107-3167)
PHONE.....................866 554-2447
EMP: 150
SALES (est): 4.7MM **Privately Held**
SIC: 8082 Home health care services

(P-21754)
GREATER SOUTH BAY AREA HM HLTH
Also Called: Greater South Bay Home Health
18726 S Wstn Ave Ste 409, Gardena
(90248)
PHONE.....................310 329-4835
Lilia Ramos, *President*
EMP: 50
SALES (est): 2.2MM **Privately Held**
WEB: www.gsbhh.com
SIC: 8082 Visiting nurse service

(P-21755)
H & K ABOUAF CORPORATION
9100 S Sepulveda Blvd # 1, Los Angeles
(90045-4814)
PHONE.....................310 393-1282
Hadas Abouaf, *CEO*
Jeffrey Taylor, *CFO*
EMP: 65
SALES: 950K **Privately Held**
SIC: 8082 Home health care services

(P-21756)
HARMONY HOME HEALTH LLC
Also Called: Harmony Homecare
2500 Ranch Rd Ste 104, Placerville
(95667-9181)
PHONE.....................916 933-9777
Jennifer Jarrett, *Mng Member*
Patrick Philbrick, *Executive*
EMP: 70
SALES: 500K **Privately Held**
SIC: 8082 Home health care services

(P-21757)
HCS HOLDCO LLC (DH)
27071 Aliso Creek Rd # 100, Aliso Viejo
(92656-5327)
PHONE.....................949 349-1200
Robert Levin, *President*
EMP: 219
SALES (est): 5.1MM **Privately Held**
SIC: 8082 Home health care services

(P-21758)
HEALTH BY DESIGN
3029 La Via Way, Sacramento
(95825-1818)
PHONE.....................916 974-3322
Peg Cannon, *President*
▲ EMP: 50
SQ FT: 1,200
SALES (est): 1.6MM **Privately Held**
WEB: www.healthbydesign.net
SIC: 8082 Visiting nurse service

(P-21759)
HEALTH ENTPS LF LONG PLAN
Also Called: Health Entps Life-Long Plans
5805 Sepulveda Blvd, Van Nuys
(91411-2546)
PHONE.....................818 654-0330
Johnathan Istrin, *President*
EMP: 500
SQ FT: 4,000
SALES (est): 6MM **Privately Held**
SIC: 8082 Home health care services

(P-21760)
HEALTHCARE CALIFORNIA
6327 N Fresno St Ste 104, Fresno
(93710-5236)
PHONE.....................559 243-9990
Harry G Harris, *President*
Bevan S Nugent, *COO*
EMP: 70
SALES (est): 3.3MM **Privately Held**
SIC: 8082 Home health care services

(P-21761)
HELP UNLMTED PERSONNEL SVC INC
1765 Goodyear Ave Ste 203, Ventura
(93003-8026)
PHONE.....................805 962-4646
Leanna McNealy, *Manager*
EMP: 150 **Privately Held**
SIC: 8082 7363 Visiting nurse service;
medical help service
PA: Help Unlimited Personnel Service, Inc.
1957 Eastman Ave
Ventura CA 93003

(P-21762)
HERITAGE SENIOR CARE INC
15428 Civic Dr Ste 345, Victorville
(92392-2383)
PHONE.....................800 562-2734
EMP: 67 **Privately Held**
SIC: 8082 8322 Home health care serv-
ices; individual & family services
PA: Heritage Senior Care, Inc.
2755 Jefferson St Ste 101
Carlsbad CA 92008

(P-21763)
HINDS HOSPICE (PA)
2490 W Shaw Ave Ste 100a, Fresno
(93711-3305)
PHONE.....................559 674-0407
Nancy Hinds, *Exec Dir*
Michael Kosareff, *CFO*
Lynne Pietz, *Exec Dir*
Rosa Butler, *Admin Asst*
Rosa Charles-Butler, *Admin Asst*
EMP: 170
SALES: 17.9MM **Privately Held**
SIC: 8082 Home health care services

(P-21764)
HIRED HANDS INC
2901 Cleveland Ave # 203, Santa Rosa
(95403-2785)
PHONE.....................707 575-4700
Lynn Winter, *Branch Mgr*
EMP: 79 **Privately Held**
SIC: 8082 Visiting nurse service
PA: Hired Hands Inc
1744 Novato Blvd Ste 200
Novato CA 94947

(P-21765)
HIS PASSION INC
Also Called: Senior Helpers South Coast
17195 Newhope St Ste 201, Fountain Val-
ley (92708-4211)
PHONE.....................800 760-6389
George Miller, *President*
Dawn Miller, *Vice Pres*
EMP: 50
SALES (est): 896.4K **Privately Held**
SIC: 8082 Home health care services

(P-21766)
HOLLYWOOD HEALTH SYSTEM INC
Also Called: HOLLYWOOD HOME HEALTH
SERVICES
4640 Lankershim Blvd # 100, North Holly-
wood (91602-1841)
PHONE.....................323 662-3731
Siranush Manukyan, *CEO*
EMP: 99
SALES: 10MM **Privately Held**
SIC: 8082 Home health care services

(P-21767)
HOME CARE OF AMERICA INC
Also Called: Home Care America-San Marino
101 W Bennett Ave A, Glendora
(91741-2533)
PHONE.....................626 309-7696
Nymia Cucueco, *President*
EMP: 75
SALES (est): 3MM **Privately Held**
WEB: www.americani.org
SIC: 8082 Visiting nurse service

(P-21768)
HOME HEALTH CARE MANAGEMENT
1398 Ridgewood Dr, Chico (95973-7801)
PHONE.....................530 343-0727
Barbara Hanna, *President*
Carl Watkins, *CFO*
Terry Gordon, *Vice Pres*
Julie Lehmann, *General Mgr*
Amicie Zimmerman, *VP Human Res*
EMP: 100
SQ FT: 27,007
SALES: 3.5MM **Privately Held**
SIC: 8082 8322 Visiting nurse service; general counseling services

(P-21769)
HOME HELPERS SAN MATEO COUNTY
655 Miramontes St, Half Moon Bay (94019-1945)
PHONE.....................650 532-3122
Peggy Milne, *Owner*
EMP: 60
SALES (est): 311.7K **Privately Held**
SIC: 8082 Home health care services

(P-21770)
HOME INSTEAD SENIOR CARE
9665 Gran Rdge Dr Ste 250, San Diego (92123)
PHONE.....................858 277-3722
Robert Perez, *President*
Jessica Perez, *Vice Pres*
Molly Horton, *Manager*
EMP: 60 **EST:** 1997
SQ FT: 900
SALES (est): 3.1MM **Privately Held**
SIC: 8082 Home health care services

(P-21771)
HOME INSTEAD SENIOR CARE
11160 Sun Center Dr, Rancho Cordova (95670-6121)
PHONE.....................916 920-2273
Scott Shaw, *Owner*
EMP: 60
SALES (est): 1.5MM **Privately Held**
WEB: www.scottshaw.com
SIC: 8082 Home health care services

(P-21772)
HOME INSTEAD SENIOR CARE
5360 Jackson Dr Ste 120, La Mesa (91942-6003)
PHONE.....................619 460-6222
Leslie Bojorquez, *President*
Steve Bojorquez, *CFO*
EMP: 50
SQ FT: 1,500
SALES (est): 1.2MM **Privately Held**
SIC: 8082 Home health care services

(P-21773)
HOME INSTEAD SENIOR CARE
405 Court St, Woodland (95695-3421)
PHONE.....................707 678-2005
Thomas Suharik, *President*
EMP: 50
SALES (est): 988.3K **Privately Held**
SIC: 8082 Home health care services

(P-21774)
HOME INSTEAD SENIOR CARE
26 Carmello Rd, Walnut Creek (94597-3402)
P.O. Box 5459 (94596-1459)
PHONE.....................510 686-9940
Ron Macarthur, *President*
Renee Macarthur, *CFO*
EMP: 100
SALES (est): 2.1MM **Privately Held**
SIC: 8082 Home health care services

(P-21775)
HOME INSTEAD SENIOR CARE
28570 Marguerite Pkwy # 221, Mission Viejo (92692-3733)
PHONE.....................949 347-6767
Jim Efzlinger, *Managing Prtnr*
Fred Wollman, *Managing Prtnr*
Joe Sanders, *Principal*
EMP: 50

SALES (est): 1.9MM **Privately Held**
SIC: 8082 8322 Home health care services; senior citizens' center or association

(P-21776)
HOSPICE & HOME HEALTH OF E BAY
Also Called: Pathways
333 Hegenberger Rd # 700, Oakland (94621-1420)
PHONE.....................510 632-4390
Barbara Burgess, *President*
Donna Lopez, *Vice Pres*
EMP: 200
SQ FT: 10,000
SALES (est): 3.3MM **Privately Held**
WEB: www.pathwayshealth.org
SIC: 8082 Home health care services

(P-21777)
HOSPICE BY BAY (PA)
Also Called: Hospice of Marin
17 E Sir Francis Drake Bl, Larkspur (94939-1708)
PHONE.....................415 927-2273
Kitty Whitaker, *CEO*
Mary Taverna, *President*
Mary Whitaker, *COO*
Denis Viscek, *CFO*
Dennis A Gilardi, *Chairman*
EMP: 220
SQ FT: 8,000
SALES: 57.6MM **Privately Held**
SIC: 8082 Home health care services

(P-21778)
HOSPICE CHEERS
625 Fair Oaks Ave Ste 229, South Pasadena (91030-2697)
PHONE.....................626 799-2727
David Friedman, *President*
Vivian Allen, *Opers Staff*
EMP: 95
SALES (est): 1.2MM **Privately Held**
SIC: 8082 Home health care services

(P-21779)
HOSPICE OF FOOTHILLS (PA)
11270 Rough And Ready Hwy, Grass Valley (95945-8530)
PHONE.....................530 272-5739
Vanessa Bengston, *Director*
Sue Hodge, *Exec Dir*
Rene Kronland, *Director*
EMP: 95
SQ FT: 5,000
SALES: 8.9MM **Privately Held**
WEB: www.hospiceofthefoothills.org
SIC: 8082 Visiting nurse service

(P-21780)
HOSPICE OF SANTA CRUZ COUNTY (PA)
Also Called: Hospice Caring Project
940 Disc Dr, Scotts Valley (95066-4544)
PHONE.....................831 430-3000
Michael Milward, *CEO*
Lisa Flores, *Director*
EMP: 110
SQ FT: 2,300
SALES: 21MM **Privately Held**
WEB: www.hospicesantacruz.org
SIC: 8082 Home health care services

(P-21781)
HOSPICE OF SANTA CRUZ COUNTY
Also Called: Hospice Caring Project
65 Neilson St Ste 121, Watsonville (95076-2491)
PHONE.....................831 430-3000
Michael Milward, *CEO*
EMP: 60
SALES (corp-wide): 21MM **Privately Held**
SIC: 8082 Home health care services
PA: Hospice Of Santa Cruz County
　940 Disc Dr
　Scotts Valley CA 95066
　831 430-3000

(P-21782)
HOSPICE OF VALLEY (PA)
4850 Union Ave, San Jose (95124-5156)
PHONE.....................408 947-1233

Sally Adelus, *Director*
Neal E Slatkin, *Chief Mktg Ofcr*
Gary Montrezzo, *Principal*
EMP: 50
SALES: 2.4MM **Privately Held**
WEB: www.hospicevalley.org
SIC: 8082 8322 Home health care services; individual & family services

(P-21783)
HUMAN TOUCH HOME HEALTH
3629 N Sepulveda Blvd, Manhattan Beach (90266-3632)
PHONE.....................424 247-8165
Kameria Ahmed Ibrahim, *Principal*
EMP: 120
SALES: 950K **Privately Held**
SIC: 8082 Home health care services

(P-21784)
HUNTINGTON CARE LLC
Also Called: Huntington Home Care
3452 E Foothill Blvd # 760, Pasadena (91107-6043)
PHONE.....................877 405-6990
Carlo Stepanians, *CEO*
Sergio Varela, *President*
EMP: 350
SALES (est): 4.2MM
SALES (corp-wide): 4.7MM **Privately Held**
SIC: 8082 Home health care services
PA: Grandcare Health Services Llc
　3452 E Foothill Blvd # 700
　Pasadena CA 91107
　866 554-2447

(P-21785)
IN HOME COMFORT AND CARE INC
Also Called: Right At Home
17155 Newhope St Ste O, Fountain Valley (92708-4233)
PHONE.....................714 485-4120
Greg James, *CEO*
EMP: 55
SALES (est): 133.6K **Privately Held**
SIC: 8082 Home health care services

(P-21786)
IN HOME HEALTH INC
Also Called: Home Health Plus
2005 De La Cruz Blvd # 271, Santa Clara (95050-3013)
PHONE.....................408 986-8160
Cheryl Bartin, *Manager*
EMP: 132
SALES (corp-wide): 29MM **Privately Held**
SIC: 8082 Visiting nurse service
PA: In Home Health, Inc.
　333 N Summit St
　Toledo OH
　419 252-5500

(P-21787)
IN HOME HEALTH INC
Also Called: Home Health Plus
1000 Lakes Dr Ste 200, West Covina (91790-2927)
PHONE.....................419 254-7841
Wendy Myers, *Director*
EMP: 60
SALES (corp-wide): 29MM **Privately Held**
SIC: 8082 Home health care services
PA: In Home Health, Inc.
　333 N Summit St
　Toledo OH
　419 252-5500

(P-21788)
INFINITE HOME HEALTH INC
22151 Ventura Blvd # 102, Woodland Hills (91364-1666)
PHONE.....................818 888-7772
Taimoor Bidari, *President*
EMP: 60
SQ FT: 4,000
SALES: 2.5MM **Privately Held**
SIC: 8082 Home health care services

(P-21789)
INTEGRITY HEALTHCARE SERVICES
425 W 5th Ave Ste 101, Escondido (92025-4843)
PHONE.....................760 432-9811
Wendy Olayvar, *President*
Char Talmadge, *Director*
EMP: 75 **Privately Held**
SIC: 8082 Home health care services
PA: Integrity Healthcare Services Inc
　5625 Ruffin Rd Ste 225
　San Diego CA 92123

(P-21790)
INTERHEALTH SERVICES INC (HQ)
Also Called: Presbyterian Inter Cmnty Hosp
12401 Washington Blvd, Whittier (90602-1006)
PHONE.....................562 698-0811
Daniel F Adams, *President*
Jim West, *President*
Gary Koger, *CFO*
Peggy Chulack, *Admin Sec*
Keith Miyamoto, *Pediatrics*
EMP: 53
SQ FT: 1,000
SALES (est): 8.4MM
SALES (corp-wide): 27.7MM **Privately Held**
SIC: 8082 8062 Home health care services; general medical & surgical hospitals
PA: Interhealth Corp.
　12401 Washington Blvd
　Whittier CA 90602
　562 698-0811

(P-21791)
INTERIM ASSISTED CARE OF NORT
Also Called: Interim Services
373 Smile Pl, Redding (96001-3637)
PHONE.....................530 722-1530
Robert Seawright, *President*
EMP: 99
SALES (est): 1.4MM **Privately Held**
SIC: 8082 Home health care services

(P-21792)
JOY SENIOR INC
Also Called: Home Instead Senior Care
6593 Collins Dr Ste D10, Moorpark (93021-1495)
PHONE.....................805 577-0926
Laurie Reid, *CEO*
Austin Reid, *General Mgr*
EMP: 175 **EST:** 1997
SALES (est): 2.1MM **Privately Held**
SIC: 8082 Home health care services

(P-21793)
KAISER FOUNDATION HOSPITAL
4501 Broadway, Oakland (94611-4615)
PHONE.....................510 752-6295
Kirs Holm, *Director*
EMP: 50
SALES (est): 211.9K **Privately Held**
SIC: 8082 Home health care services

(P-21794)
KAISER FOUNDATION HOSPITALS
Also Called: Kaiser Permanente
50 Great Oaks Blvd, San Jose (95119-1381)
PHONE.....................408 361-2100
EMP: 793
SALES (corp-wide): 76.5B **Privately Held**
SIC: 8082 8011 Home health care services; health maintenance organization
HQ: Kaiser Foundation Hospitals Inc
　1 Kaiser Plz
　Oakland CA 94612
　510 271-6611

(P-21795)
KEARN ALTERNATIVE CARE INC (PA)
2029 21st St, Bakersfield (93301-4219)
PHONE.....................661 631-2036
Jean Schamblin, *President*

J R Doty, *Admin Sec*
Jeanne Schamblin, *Telecom Exec*
EMP: 300
SALES (est): 5.6MM **Privately Held**
SIC: 8082 Visiting nurse service

(P-21796)
KERN ALTERNATIVE CARE INC
2029 21st St, Bakersfield (93301-4219)
PHONE..............................661 631-2036
Jeanne Schamblin, *President*
Leo Schamblin, *Vice Pres*
EMP: 160
SQ FT: 1,800
SALES (est): 6.3MM **Privately Held**
SIC: 8082 Visiting nurse service

(P-21797)
KIDS OVERCOMING LLC
40029 St Ste 204, Oakland (94609)
PHONE..............................415 748-8052
Anne Swinney, *Mng Member*
Matt McAlear,
EMP: 75
SALES (est): 1.3MM **Privately Held**
SIC: 8082 Home health care services

(P-21798)
KIND HOMECARE INC
3705 Haven Ave Ste 104, Menlo Park
(94025-1011)
P.O. Box 1914, Mountain View (94042-
1914)
PHONE..............................888 885-5463
Aida Bruun, *CEO*
EMP: 99
SALES (est): 305.3K **Privately Held**
SIC: 8082 7389 Home health care serv-
ices;

(P-21799)
KISSITO HEALTH CARE INC
Also Called: Bay Point Healthcare Center
442 Sunset Blvd, Hayward (94541-3832)
PHONE..............................510 582-8311
Bob Ewing, *Manager*
Robert Ewing, *Administration*
EMP: 100
SALES (corp-wide): 2.3MM **Privately
Held**
SIC: 8082 8051 8052 Home health care
services; skilled nursing care facilities; in-
termediate care facilities
PA: Kissito Healthcare, Inc.
5228 Valleypointe Pkwy
Roanoke VA 24019
540 265-0322

(P-21800)
KISSITO HEALTH CASE INC
Also Called: Willow Pass Healthcare Center
3318 Willow Pass Rd, Concord
(94519-2316)
PHONE..............................925 689-9222
Fax: 925 689-3412
EMP: 100
SALES (corp-wide): 62.4MM **Privately
Held**
SIC: 8082 8051
PA: Kissito Health Care, Inc.
5228 Valleypointe Pkwy
Roanoke VA 24019
540 265-0322

(P-21801)
KISSITO HEALTH CASE INC
Also Called: San Leandro Healthcare Center
368 Juana Ave, San Leandro (94577-4811)
PHONE..............................510 357-4015
Vinny Poddapoori, *Administration*
EMP: 80
SALES (corp-wide): 2.3MM **Privately
Held**
SIC: 8082 8051 Home health care serv-
ices; skilled nursing care facilities
PA: Kissito Healthcare, Inc.
5228 Valleypointe Pkwy
Roanoke VA 24019
540 265-0322

(P-21802)
LANDMARK HEALTH LLC (PA)
7755 Center Ave Ste 630, Huntington
Beach (92647-9152)
PHONE..............................253 394-2566
Adam Boehler,

Christopher Goldsmith, *President*
Brandon Kerns, *CFO*
EMP: 58 EST: 2013
SALES (est): 26.8MM **Privately Held**
SIC: 8082 Home health care services

(P-21803)
LIVHOME INC (PA)
5670 Wilshire Blvd # 500, Los Angeles
(90036-5682)
PHONE..............................800 807-5854
Toll Free:..............................877 -
Mike Nicholson, *Ch of Bd*
Cody D Legler, *Officer*
Gail Zimmerman, *Vice Pres*
Leslie Saller, *Office Mgr*
Aleksandra Rozenfeld, *Accounting Mgr*
EMP: 1299
SQ FT: 7,454
SALES (est): 50.6MM **Privately Held**
SIC: 8082 Home health care services

(P-21804)
LOMA LINDA UNIVERSITY MED
CTR
Loma Linda Home Health Care
11265 Mountain View Ave E, Loma Linda
(92354-3863)
P.O. Box 2000 (92354-0200)
PHONE..............................909 558-3096
Jan Huckins, *Director*
EMP: 120
SALES (corp-wide): 269.1MM **Privately
Held**
WEB: www.llumc.com
SIC: 8082 7361 Home health care serv-
ices; nurses' registry
HQ: Loma Linda University Medical Center
11234 Anderson St
Loma Linda CA 92354
909 558-4000

(P-21805)
LOVELY LIVING HOMECARE
112 Harvard Ave, Claremont (91711-4716)
PHONE..............................909 625-7999
Lee Rodriguez, *President*
EMP: 65
SALES (est): 632.2K **Privately Held**
SIC: 8082 Home health care services

(P-21806)
LUMINA HEALTHCARE LLC (PA)
Also Called: Lumina At Home
5220 Pacific Concourse Dr, Los Angeles
(90045-6277)
PHONE..............................888 958-6462
Mary Ellen Hardin, *President*
Robert C Mathuny, *Vice Pres*
EMP: 55
SALES (est): 8MM **Privately Held**
SIC: 8082 Home health care services

(P-21807)
MANAGED HOMECARE INC
17682 Mitchell N Ste 100, Irvine
(92614-6037)
PHONE..............................951 341-0782
David Ross, *Administration*
EMP: 50
SALES (est): 1.4MM **Privately Held**
SIC: 8082 Home health care services

(P-21808)
MATCHED CAREGIVERS INC
Also Called: Matched Care Gvrs Cntns Care
95 Wilburn Ave, Atherton (94027-3839)
PHONE..............................408 560-2382
Kathryn Janz, *President*
Christina Martinez, *Associate Dir*
Christina Mendez, *Associate Dir*
EMP: 130
SALES (est): 2.4MM **Privately Held**
SIC: 8082 Home health care services

(P-21809)
MAXIM HEALTHCARE SERVICES
INC
500 E Esplanade Dr, Oxnard (93036-2110)
PHONE..............................805 278-4593
EMP: 657
SALES (corp-wide): 1.5B **Privately Held**
SIC: 8082 Home health care services

PA: Maxim Healthcare Services, Inc.
7227 Lee Deforest Dr
Columbia MD 21046
410 910-1500

(P-21810)
MAXIM HEALTHCARE SERVICES
INC
Also Called: Los Angles Homecare Pediatrics
4221 Wilshire Blvd # 130, Los Angeles
(90010-3538)
PHONE..............................323 937-9410
Jeff Poitras, *Manager*
EMP: 250
SALES (corp-wide): 1.5B **Privately Held**
WEB: www.maximstaffing.com
SIC: 8082 Home health care services
PA: Maxim Healthcare Services, Inc.
7227 Lee Deforest Dr
Columbia MD 21046
410 910-1500

(P-21811)
MAXIMUS INC
11050 Olson Dr Ste 100, Rancho Cordova
(95670-5600)
PHONE..............................916 364-6610
Bob Britton, *Principal*
Stephanie Brooks, *Officer*
Albert Wong, *Software Dev*
Greg Hanzelka, *Technology*
Laurie Yamada-Mori, *Graphic Designe*
EMP: 80
SALES (corp-wide): 2.3B **Publicly Held**
SIC: 8082 Home health care services
PA: Maximus, Inc.
1891 Metro Center Dr
Reston VA 20190
703 251-8500

(P-21812)
MERCY HM SVCS A CAL LTD
PARTNR
1544 Market St, Redding (96001-1023)
P.O. Box 496009 (96049-6009)
PHONE..............................530 245-4070
Ginger White, *Exec Dir*
EMP: 80 **Privately Held**
WEB: www.mercyhealth.org
SIC: 8082 Visiting nurse service
HQ: Mercy Home Services A California Lim-
ited Partnership
2175 Rosaline Ave Ste A
Redding CA 96001
530 225-6000

(P-21813)
MILESTONE HOSPICE
1025 W 190th St Ste 450, Gardena
(90248-4339)
PHONE..............................310 782-1177
Harry Mc Namra, *CEO*
Ivette Carrillo, *Executive*
Minda Mc Namra, *Administration*
EMP: 120
SALES: 14MM **Privately Held**
SIC: 8082 Home health care services

(P-21814)
MIRACLE HOME HEALTH
AGENCY
13146 Mungo Ct, Rancho Cucamonga
(91739-9157)
PHONE..............................562 653-0668
Bernice Osunwa, *President*
EMP: 50
SALES (est): 889.2K **Privately Held**
SIC: 8082 Home health care services

(P-21815)
MOMS ORANGE COUNTY
1128 W Santa Ana Blvd, Santa Ana
(92703-3833)
PHONE..............................714 972-2610
Pamela Pimentel Rn, *Exec Dir*
Barbara Overholser, *Executive Asst*
Luisa Santa, *Director*
EMP: 50
SALES: 7.1MM **Privately Held**
WEB: www.oc-moms.org
SIC: 8082 Home health care services

(P-21816)
MSJ HEALTHCARE LLC
Also Called: Grandcare Home Health Serv-
ices
3452 E Fthill Blvd Ste 70, Pasadena
(91107)
PHONE..............................818 244-8446
David Bell, *President*
Bill Chu, *Bd of Directors*
Jay Pamintuan, *Vice Pres*
Douglas Saylor, *Marketing Staff*
Nurmina Banaag, *Director*
EMP: 50
SALES (est): 1.7MM **Privately Held**
SIC: 8082 Home health care services

(P-21817)
MY CHOICE INHOME CARE LLC
31610 Rr Cyn Rd Ste 4, Canyon Lake
(92587-9454)
PHONE..............................951 244-8770
Julie Zimmerer,
EMP: 87
SALES: 480K **Privately Held**
SIC: 8082 Home health care services

(P-21818)
NO ORDINARY MOMENTS INC
16742 Gothard St Ste 115, Huntington
Beach (92647-4564)
PHONE..............................714 848-3800
Luis Pena, *President*
Jason Martinez, *Director*
EMP: 250
SALES (est): 4.7MM **Privately Held**
SIC: 8082 8322 Home health care serv-
ices; emergency social services

(P-21819)
NORTH COAST HOME CARE
INC
Also Called: Homewatch Caregivers
5731 Palmer Way Ste F, Carlsbad
(92010-7247)
PHONE..............................760 260-8700
Tanya Finnerty, *President*
Michael Finnerty, *Admin Sec*
EMP: 70
SQ FT: 1,000
SALES: 1MM **Privately Held**
SIC: 8082 Home health care services

(P-21820)
NORTHERN CALIFORNIA HLTH
CARE
Also Called: Arcadia Healthcare
16201 Plateau Cir, Redding (96001-9720)
PHONE..............................530 223-2332
Tim Araiza, *President*
Ronald Wickershiem, *Info Tech Mgr*
Dan Gazzigli, *Sales Staff*
EMP: 60
SALES (est): 1.1MM **Privately Held**
WEB: www.norcalarcadia.com
SIC: 8082 Home health care services

(P-21821)
NURSES TUCH HM HLTH
PRVDER INC
135 S Jackson St Ste 100, Glendale
(91205-4917)
PHONE..............................818 500-4877
Evangeline Ursua, *President*
EMP: 50
SALES: 1.4MM **Privately Held**
SIC: 8082 Home health care services

(P-21822)
NURSING & REHAB AT HOME
1660 S Amphlett Blvd # 112, San Mateo
(94402-2507)
PHONE..............................650 286-4272
Lorna Beukema, *President*
Lorna Smith, *Executive*
EMP: 54
SQ FT: 3,000
SALES: 3.5MM **Privately Held**
WEB: www.rehabathome.org
SIC: 8082 Home health care services

PRODUCTS & SVCS

(P-21823)
OAK HILL CAPITAL PARTNERS LP
2775 Sand Hill Rd Ste 220, Menlo Park (94025-7085)
PHONE..................650 234-0500
Steven B Gruber, *President*
Karen Capparelli, *Executive Asst*
EMP: 858
SALES (corp-wide): 2.9B **Privately Held**
SIC: 8082 Home health care services
PA: Oak Hill Capital Partners, L.P.
   65 E 55th St Fl 32
   New York NY 10022
   212 527-8400

(P-21824)
ODYSSEY HEALTHCARE INC
9444 Balboa Ave Ste 290, San Diego (92123-4901)
PHONE..................858 565-2499
Diana Thompson, *Manager*
EMP: 70
SALES (corp-wide): 1.5B **Privately Held**
SIC: 8082 Home health care services
HQ: Odyssey Healthcare, Inc.
   7801 Mesquite Bend Dr # 105
   Irving TX 75063

(P-21825)
ODYSSEY HEALTHCARE INC
17290 Jasmine St Ste 104, Victorville (92395-8300)
PHONE..................760 241-7044
Jodi Schmidt, *Branch Mgr*
EMP: 53
SALES (corp-wide): 1.5B **Privately Held**
SIC: 8082 Home health care services
HQ: Odyssey Healthcare, Inc.
   7801 Mesquite Bend Dr # 105
   Irving TX 75063

(P-21826)
ONEBODY INC
Also Called: Consensus Health
2000 Powell St Ste 555, Emeryville (94608-1838)
P.O. Box 6219, Moraga (94570-6219)
PHONE..................510 285-2000
Kendall Lockhart, *Ch of Bd*
Susan M Rowe, *CFO*
EMP: 60 EST: 1996
SALES (est): 2.2MM **Privately Held**
SIC: 8082 Home health care services

(P-21827)
ONMYCARE LLC
Also Called: Onmycare Home Health
39159 Paseo Padre Pkwy # 304, Fremont (94538-1608)
PHONE..................510 858-2273
Hansjeet Gill, *Mng Member*
EMP: 56
SALES (est): 506.3K **Privately Held**
SIC: 8082 Visiting nurse service

(P-21828)
ONTARIO HEALTH EDUCATN CO INC
3130 Sedona Ct, Ontario (91764-6554)
PHONE..................951 817-8553
David Pyle, *President*
EMP: 50 EST: 2008
SALES (est): 510.6K **Privately Held**
SIC: 8082 Home health care services

(P-21829)
OPTIMAL HEALTH SERVICES INC
1227 Chester Ave, Bakersfield (93301-5445)
PHONE..................661 393-4483
Doug Clary, *President*
Sarah Shelbourne, *CFO*
Joe Vega, *Office Mgr*
Shelly Hutsell,
Kevin Fabrizio, *Director*
EMP: 73
SALES (est): 7.4MM **Privately Held**
SIC: 8082 Visiting nurse service

(P-21830)
OPTIMAL HOSPICE FOUNDATION
Also Called: Optimal Hospice Care
1675 Chester Ave Ste 401, Bakersfield (93301-5225)
PHONE..................661 716-4000
Doug Clary, *CEO*
EMP: 129
SALES (corp-wide): 281.2K **Privately Held**
SIC: 8082 Visiting nurse service
PA: Optimal Hospice Foundation
   1227 Chester Ave Ste A
   Bakersfield CA 93301
   661 410-3000

(P-21831)
OPTION CARE HOME CARE INC
9401 Chivers Ave, Sun Valley (91352-2655)
PHONE..................818 351-3000
Jon Pyshny, *Branch Mgr*
EMP: 55
SALES (corp-wide): 136.8B **Publicly Held**
SIC: 8082 Home health care services
HQ: Option Care Home Care, Inc.
   1417 Lake Cook Rd Ste 100
   Deerfield IL 60015

(P-21832)
OUR WATCH
Also Called: Assistance In Home Care
12832 Valley View St # 211, Garden Grove (92845-2524)
PHONE..................714 622-5852
Ramona Streit, *Principal*
EMP: 52
SALES (est): 1.9MM **Privately Held**
SIC: 8082 Home health care services

(P-21833)
PACIFIC CARE INC
Also Called: Pro Care 2000 Home Health Care
1903 Redondo Ave, Long Beach (90755-1226)
PHONE..................562 494-6500
Michael Siller, *President*
Steve Liss, *Vice Pres*
Mike Bladuka MD, *Medical Dir*
EMP: 60
SALES: 1.2MM **Privately Held**
SIC: 8082 Visiting nurse service

(P-21834)
PACIFIC COAST SERVICES INC
Also Called: Pacific Homecare Services
3202 W March Ln Ste D, Stockton (95219-2351)
PHONE..................209 956-2532
Leticia Robles, *President*
Damian Gutierrez, *Vice Pres*
Jorge Robles, *Vice Pres*
EMP: 3043
SQ FT: 2,000
SALES (est): 3.5MM **Privately Held**
SIC: 8082 Visiting nurse service

(P-21835)
PACIFIC PALMS HEALTHCARE LLC
Empress Rehabilitation Center
1020 Termino Ave, Long Beach (90804-4123)
PHONE..................562 433-6791
Emmanuel B David, *Branch Mgr*
EMP: 51
SALES (corp-wide): 8.3MM **Privately Held**
SIC: 8082 Home health care services
PA: Pacific Palms Healthcare, Llc
   1020 Termino Ave
   Long Beach CA 90804
   562 433-6791

(P-21836)
PATHFINDER HEALTH INC
10051 Lampson Ave, Garden Grove (92840-4716)
PHONE..................714 636-5649
Avelina Cumbis, *President*
EMP: 150

SALES (est): 3.4MM **Privately Held**
SIC: 8082 Visiting nurse service

(P-21837)
PEACEFUL HEARTS HOME CARE INC
387 Magnolia Ave Ste 103, Corona (92879-3308)
PHONE..................951 541-9343
Brian McKee, *President*
EMP: 55
SALES (est): 1.1MM **Privately Held**
SIC: 8082 Home health care services

(P-21838)
PEGASUS HOME HEALTH CARE A CA
Also Called: Pegasus Home Health Services
132 N Artsakh St, Glendale (91206-4094)
PHONE..................818 551-1932
Pamela Spiszman, *President*
▼ EMP: 80
SQ FT: 2,800
SALES (est): 3.8MM **Privately Held**
SIC: 8082 Visiting nurse service

(P-21839)
PEOPLES CARE INC
13901 Amargosa Rd Ste 101, Victorville (92392-2409)
PHONE..................760 962-1900
Stacey Minwalla, *Owner*
EMP: 188
SALES (corp-wide): 39.2MM **Privately Held**
SIC: 8082 Home health care services
PA: People's Care Inc.
   13920 City Center Dr # 230
   Chino Hills CA 91709
   855 773-6753

(P-21840)
PERSONLZED HMCARE HMMAKER AGCY
4700 Northgate Blvd, Sacramento (95834-1128)
PHONE..................916 979-4975
Celso Avaricio, *CEO*
Pat Mitchell, *Program Dir*
EMP: 100
SQ FT: 900
SALES (est): 403K **Privately Held**
SIC: 8082 Home health care services

(P-21841)
PHARMACO INC
Also Called: Premier Infusion Care
19500 Normandie Ave, Torrance (90502-1108)
PHONE..................310 328-3897
Saman Rehfahzadeh, *CEO*
EMP: 99
SALES (est): 3.6MM **Privately Held**
SIC: 8082 Home health care services

(P-21842)
PHYSICIANS CHOICE HM HLTH INC
3220 Sepulveda Blvd # 100, Torrance (90505-8160)
PHONE..................310 793-1616
Shari Sunada, *President*
EMP: 50
SQ FT: 2,500
SALES: 3.5MM **Privately Held**
SIC: 8082 Home health care services

(P-21843)
POLARIS HOME CARE LLC
830 Stewart Dr Ste 211, Sunnyvale (94085-4513)
PHONE..................408 400-7020
Gregory Kemper, *Principal*
EMP: 55
SALES (est): 387K **Privately Held**
SIC: 8082 Home health care services

(P-21844)
PREMIER MANAGEMENT COMPANY
Also Called: Jacob Health Care Center
4075 54th St, San Diego (92105-2301)
PHONE..................619 582-5168
Guy Reggeb, *Manager*
EMP: 50 **Privately Held**

SIC: 8082 8051 Home health care services; skilled nursing care facilities
PA: B H Premier Inc
   1141 S Beverly Dr Fl 3
   Los Angeles CA 90035

(P-21845)
PROVIDENCE HEALTH SYSTEM
Also Called: Trinity Home Care
4101 Torrance Blvd, Torrance (90503-4607)
PHONE..................310 370-5895
EMP: 200
SALES (corp-wide): 17.6B **Privately Held**
SIC: 8082 8051
HQ: Providence Health System-Southern California
   1801 Lind Ave Sw
   Renton WA 98057
   425 525-3355

(P-21846)
PW JADE LLC
Also Called: Right At Home
1825 4th St, Santa Rosa (95404-3202)
PHONE..................707 843-5192
Robert Brohmer, *Principal*
EMP: 60
SALES (est): 664K **Privately Held**
SIC: 8082 Home health care services

(P-21847)
QUALITY IN-HMECARE SPECIALISTS
1166 Broadway Ste T, Placerville (95667-5745)
PHONE..................530 303-3477
Pete Messimore, *CEO*
Arlene Secondo, *Treasurer*
Gloria Tingley, *Principal*
Gail Huston, *Opers Staff*
EMP: 99
SQ FT: 597
SALES (est): 2.3MM **Privately Held**
WEB: www.qualityinhomecare.com
SIC: 8082 Visiting nurse service

(P-21848)
RAINBOW HOME CARE SERVICES
1560 Brookhollow Dr # 100, Santa Ana (92705-5411)
PHONE..................714 544-8070
Barbara Hedges, *CEO*
Victoria Lord, *Mktg Dir*
EMP: 55
SALES (est): 2.8MM **Privately Held**
WEB: www.rainbowhomecareservices.com
SIC: 8082 Home health care services

(P-21849)
RAMONA COMMUNITY SERVICES CORP (HQ)
Also Called: RAMONA VNA & HOSPICE
890 W Stetson Ave Ste A, Hemet (92543-7311)
PHONE..................951 658-9288
Patricia McBe, *Branch Mgr*
Patrick Searl, *Ch of Bd*
Carol Wood, *CEO*
Lauien Mahieu, *COO*
John Brudin, *Treasurer*
EMP: 150
SQ FT: 14,000
SALES: 3.9MM
SALES (corp-wide): 22.1MM **Privately Held**
WEB: www.ramonavna.org
SIC: 8082 Visiting nurse service
PA: Kpc Group Llc
   6800 Indiana Ave Ste 130
   Riverside CA 92506
   951 782-8812

(P-21850)
RELIABLE CAREGIVERS INC
1700 California St # 400, San Francisco (94109-0429)
PHONE..................415 436-0100
Linda Leary, *President*
Bobbie Joe Keating, *Finance Dir*
EMP: 120

SALES: 3MM **Privately Held**
WEB: www.reliablecaregivers.net
SIC: 8082 Home health care services

(P-21851)
RES-CARE INC
Also Called: Socal Home Care-Givers Svcs
17291 Irvine Blvd Ste 150, Tustin
(92780-2900)
PHONE........................800 707-8781
Babli Dusttrama, *Branch Mgr*
EMP: 100
SALES (corp-wide): 2B **Privately Held**
SIC: 8082 Home health care services
HQ: Res-Care, Inc.
805 N Whittington Pkwy
Louisville KY 40222
502 394-2100

(P-21852)
RIGHT AT HOME
Also Called: Sierra West Home Care
3435 Ocean Park Blvd # 110, Santa Monica
(90405-3318)
PHONE........................310 313-0600
Timothy Petlin, *Principal*
EMP: 75 EST: 2011
SALES: 1.2MM **Privately Held**
SIC: 8082 Home health care services

(P-21853)
RIGHT CHOICE IN-HOME CARE INC
7104 Owensmouth Ave, Canoga Park
(91303-2007)
PHONE........................818 836-6001
Don Lucas, *Director*
Linda Weinberg, *President*
EMP: 680
SQ FT: 1,800
SALES (est): 10.9MM **Privately Held**
SIC: 8082 Home health care services

(P-21854)
ROBERTS & ASSOCIATES INC
Also Called: Visiting Angels Riverside Cnty
8175 Limonite Ave Ste A1, Riverside
(92509-6121)
PHONE........................951 727-4357
Joan Roberts, *President*
Robert Roberts, *Treasurer*
Benita Roberts, *Vice Pres*
EMP: 55
SQ FT: 400
SALES (est): 1.9MM **Privately Held**
SIC: 8082 Home health care services

(P-21855)
ROCK CANYON HEALTHCARE INC
Also Called: Riverwalk PST-Cute Rhblitation
27101 Puerta Real Ste 450, Mission Viejo
(92691-8566)
PHONE........................719 404-1000
Dave Jorgensen, *President*
Soon Burnam, *Treasurer*
Ron Cook, *Exec Dir*
Beverly Wittekind, *Admin Sec*
EMP: 250 EST: 2014
SALES (est): 2.1MM
SALES (corp-wide): 2B **Publicly Held**
SIC: 8082 Home health care services
PA: The Ensign Group Inc
27101 Puerta Real Ste 450
Mission Viejo CA 92691
949 487-9500

(P-21856)
S B C SENIOR CARE INC
Also Called: Home Instead Senior Care
101 W Anapamu St Ste C, Santa Barbara
(93101-3140)
PHONE........................805 560-6995
Susan Johnson, *Owner*
EMP: 75
SALES (est): 1.4MM **Privately Held**
SIC: 8082 Home health care services

(P-21857)
SAFELY HOME
Also Called: Home Instead Senior Care
461 Tennessee St Ste O, Redlands
(92373-8161)
PHONE........................909 370-0343
Neva Labate, *President*
EMP: 54

SQ FT: 1,000
SALES (est): 178K **Privately Held**
SIC: 8082 Home health care services

(P-21858)
SAN DIEGO HOSPICE
Also Called: San Diego Hospice & Institute
2400 Historic Decatur Rd # 107, San Diego
(92106-6158)
PHONE........................619 688-1600
Fax: 619 688-1599
EMP: 600
SALES (corp-wide): 9.8MM **Privately Held**
SIC: 8082
PA: San Diego Hospice & Palliative Care Corporation
4311 3rd Ave
San Diego CA 92103
619 688-1600

(P-21859)
SANSUM CLINIC
Also Called: Community Home Health Agency
509 E Montecito St # 200, Santa Barbara
(93103-3259)
PHONE........................805 682-6507
Melanie Thompson, *Director*
EMP: 50
SALES (corp-wide): 303.9MM **Privately Held**
WEB: www.sansum.com
SIC: 8082 Home health care services
PA: Sansum Clinic
470 S Patterson Ave
Santa Barbara CA 93111
805 681-7700

(P-21860)
SCRIPPS HEALTH
3811 Valley Centre Dr, San Diego
(92130-3318)
PHONE........................858 764-3000
Robert B Sarnoff MD, *President*
Joanna Benavidez, *Psychologist*
Lorenzo Pacelli, *Surgeon*
Amy Brown, *Obstetrician*
Dimitri Sherev, *Cardiology*
EMP: 314
SALES (corp-wide): 2.1B **Privately Held**
SIC: 8082 Home health care services
PA: Scripps Health
10140 Campus Point Dr Ax415
San Diego CA 92121
800 727-4777

(P-21861)
SELECT HOME CARE
2393 Townsgate Rd Ste 100, Westlake Village (91361-2513)
PHONE........................805 777-3855
Dylan Hull, *CEO*
EMP: 100
SALES (est): 2.8MM **Privately Held**
SIC: 8082 Home health care services

(P-21862)
SENIOR COMPANIONS AT HOME
650 El Camino Real Ste E, Redwood City
(94063-1345)
P.O. Box 5715 (94063-0715)
PHONE........................650 364-1265
Jovie Magbanua, *Director*
EMP: 50
SALES (est): 1.3MM **Privately Held**
SIC: 8082 Home health care services

(P-21863)
SERACADA
Also Called: Home Instead Senior Care
709 E Lavender Way, Azusa (91702-6294)
PHONE........................626 486-0800
Ada Wong, *President*
EMP: 50
SALES: 350K **Privately Held**
SIC: 8082 Home health care services

(P-21864)
SHARP HEALTHCARE
Also Called: Sharp Home Care
8080 Dagget St Ste 200, San Diego
(92111-2333)
PHONE........................858 541-4850
Dan Gross, *Manager*
Marlene Gerendash, *Human Res Mgr*
EMP: 66

SALES (corp-wide): 3.4B **Privately Held**
SIC: 8082 Home health care services
PA: Sharp Healthcare
8695 Spectrum Center Blvd
San Diego CA 92123
858 499-4000

(P-21865)
SHERPAUL CORPORATION
Also Called: Home Instead Senior Care
901 Hacienda Dr Ste B, Vista
(92081-6498)
PHONE........................760 639-6472
Sherry Dziuban, *President*
Paul Dziuban, *Vice Pres*
EMP: 54
SQ FT: 951
SALES (est): 2.1MM **Privately Held**
SIC: 8082 Home health care services

(P-21866)
SIERRA NEVADA MEMORIAL HM CARE
Also Called: Sierra Nevada Home Care
1020 Mccourtney Rd Ste A, Grass Valley
(95949-7453)
P.O. Box 1029 (95945-1029)
PHONE........................530 274-6350
Sharon Turner, *Director*
EMP: 90
SQ FT: 6,200
SALES: 3.7MM **Privately Held**
WEB: www.snhc.org
SIC: 8082 7361 Home health care services; nurses' registry
HQ: Dignity Health
185 Berry St Ste 300
San Francisco CA 94107
415 438-5500

(P-21867)
SMITH RESIDENTIAL CARE FCILTY (PA)
318 E 4th St, Hanford (93230-5125)
P.O. Box 1093 (93232-1093)
PHONE........................559 584-8451
Catherine Smith, *Owner*
EMP: 70
SALES (est): 2MM **Privately Held**
SIC: 8082 Home health care services

(P-21868)
SOUTH BAY SENIOR SERVICES INC
Also Called: Homewatch Caregivers
8929 S Sepulveda Blvd # 314, Los Angeles
(90045-3616)
PHONE........................310 338-8558
Richard Williams, *President*
Patricia Greaney, *Admin Sec*
EMP: 77
SQ FT: 700
SALES (est): 1.8MM **Privately Held**
WEB: www.homewatchcaregivers.com/los-angeles
SIC: 8082 Home health care services

(P-21869)
SOUTH BAY SENIOR SOLUTIONS INC
Also Called: Home Instead Senior Care
1660 Hamilton Ave Ste 204, San Jose
(95125-5434)
PHONE........................408 370-6360
Brian Jackson, *President*
EMP: 65 EST: 1996
SQ FT: 1,500
SALES (est): 2.4MM **Privately Held**
SIC: 8082 Home health care services

(P-21870)
ST JOSEPH COMMUNITY HOME CARE
7400 Shoreline Dr Ste 4, Stockton
(95219-5498)
PHONE........................209 478-9547
Carol Harpman, *Director*
EMP: 75
SALES (est): 2.5MM **Privately Held**
SIC: 8082 Home health care services

(P-21871)
ST JOSEPH HEALTH PER CARE SVCS
1315 Corona Pointe Ct, Corona
(92879-1785)
PHONE........................800 365-1110
Greg Henderson, *Principal*
EMP: 99
SALES (corp-wide): 2.7MM **Privately Held**
SIC: 8082 Home health care services
PA: St Joseph Health Personal Care Services
200 W Center St Promenade
Anaheim CA 92805
714 712-7100

(P-21872)
ST JOSEPH HEALTH SYSTEM HOME
200 W Center St Promenade, Anaheim
(92805-3960)
PHONE........................714 712-9500
Jeffrey Hammond, *Mng Member*
Susan Harvey, *CFO*
Lydia Thangaiyan, *Finance*
EMP: 800
SALES: 71.9MM
SALES (corp-wide): 15.2B **Privately Held**
SIC: 8082 Home health care services
HQ: St. Joseph Health System
3345 Michelson Dr Ste 100
Irvine CA 92612
949 381-4000

(P-21873)
ST JOSEPH HOME HEALTH NETWORK (DH)
441 College Ave, Santa Rosa
(95401-5141)
PHONE........................714 712-9500
Linda Glomp, *Director*
Vincent Castaldo, *CFO*
Michael Robinson, *Exec Dir*
Mary Titus, *Director*
Liz Wessel, *Director*
EMP: 77
SQ FT: 25,000
SALES (est): 27.7MM
SALES (corp-wide): 15.2B **Privately Held**
SIC: 8082 Home health care services
HQ: St. Joseph Health System
3345 Michelson Dr Ste 100
Irvine CA 92612
949 381-4000

(P-21874)
ST JOSEPH HOME HEALTH NETWORK
Also Called: Saint Joseph Hlth Sys HM Hlth
200 W Center St Promenade, Anaheim
(92805-3960)
PHONE........................714 712-9559
Kris Kowlaski, *Director*
Elizabeth Ariosto, *Technology*
Beverly Curtis, *Technical Staff*
Sheree Simpson, *Analyst*
Lisa Muller, *Nurse*
EMP: 50
SALES (corp-wide): 15.2B **Privately Held**
SIC: 8082 Visiting nurse service
HQ: St Joseph Home Health Network
441 College Ave
Santa Rosa CA 95401
714 712-9500

(P-21875)
STAFFING SPECIALISTS INTL
Also Called: Staffing Home Care
2598 Olympic Dr, San Bruno (94066-1251)
PHONE........................650 737-0777
Tina Desuasido, *Owner*
EMP: 50
SALES (est): 842.8K **Privately Held**
SIC: 8082 Home health care services

(P-21876)
STEP UP ON SECOND STREET INC (PA)
1328 2nd St Ofc, Santa Monica
(90401-1123)
PHONE........................310 394-6889
Todd Lipka, *CEO*
Barbara Bloom, *COO*
Kim Carson, *CFO*

Cathia Barrow,
EMP: 60
SQ FT: 7,500
SALES: 9.6MM **Privately Held**
SIC: 8082 8052 8059 Home health care services; home for the mentally retarded, with health care; personal care home, with health care

(P-21877)
SUTTER VSTING NRSE ASSN HSPICE
1625 Van Ness Ave, San Francisco (94109-3370)
PHONE......................415 600-6200
Cindy Brown, *Manager*
EMP: 80
SALES (corp-wide): 12.7B **Privately Held**
SIC: 8082 8049 7361 Visiting nurse service; nurses & other medical assistants; nurses' registry
HQ: Sutter Visiting Nurse Association & Hospice
1900 Powell St Ste 300
Emeryville CA 94608
866 652-9178

(P-21878)
SUTTER VSTING NRSE ASSN HSPICE (HQ)
Also Called: Vnahnc
1900 Powell St Ste 300, Emeryville (94608-1815)
P.O. Box 22250, Salt Lake City UT (84122-0250)
PHONE......................866 652-9178
Marcia Reissig, *CEO*
Maryellen Rota, *COO*
Gregg Davis, *CFO*
Annette Pabilona, *Administration*
Bambi Gallagher, *Manager*
EMP: 50
SQ FT: 24,000
SALES: 171MM
SALES (corp-wide): 12.7B **Privately Held**
WEB: www.suttervnaandhospice.com
SIC: 8082 Visiting nurse service
PA: Sutter Health
2200 River Plaza Dr
Sacramento CA 95833
916 733-8800

(P-21879)
SUTTER VSTING NRSE ASSN HSPICE
Also Called: Sutter Vsiting Nurse Assn Hosp
5099 Commercial Cir # 20594520, Concord (94520-1291)
PHONE......................925 677-4250
Windi Heaton, *Manager*
EMP: 100
SALES (corp-wide): 12.7B **Privately Held**
SIC: 8082 Visiting nurse service
HQ: Sutter Visiting Nurse Association & Hospice
1900 Powell St Ste 300
Emeryville CA 94608
866 652-9178

(P-21880)
TA-KAI HOME CARE INC
22349 La Palma Ave # 105, Yorba Linda (92887-3809)
PHONE......................714 393-4586
Brian Nakamura, *Principal*
EMP: 69
SALES (est): 437.4K **Privately Held**
SIC: 8082 Home health care services

(P-21881)
TENDER HOME HEALTHCARE INC
Also Called: Home Instead Senior Care
3550 Wilshire Blvd # 700, Los Angeles (90010-2401)
PHONE......................323 466-2345
Ben Jarakunnel, *President*
EMP: 80
SALES (est): 2.1MM **Privately Held**
SIC: 8082 Home health care services

(P-21882)
TENET HEALTHSYSTEM MEDICAL
Also Called: Redding Medical Home Care
475 Knollcrest Dr, Redding (96002-0101)
P.O. Box 494130 (96049-4130)
PHONE......................530 222-1992
Judith Moroney, *Manager*
EMP: 60
SALES (corp-wide): 18.3B **Publicly Held**
WEB: www.tenenthealth.com
SIC: 8082 Home health care services
HQ: Tenet Healthsystem Medical, Inc.
1445 Ross Ave Ste 1400
Dallas TX 75202
469 893-2000

(P-21883)
TEXAS HOME HEALTH AMERICA LP (PA)
1455 Auto Center Dr # 200, Ontario (91761-2239)
PHONE......................972 201-3800
Steve Abshire, *Partner*
Judy Bishop, *Partner*
Mark Lamp, *Partner*
Duff Whitaker, *Partner*
Julie Porras, *Nurse*
EMP: 100 **EST:** 1969
SQ FT: 18,000
SALES (est): 118.1MM **Privately Held**
WEB: www.txhha.com
SIC: 8082 Home health care services

(P-21884)
THERAPY IN YOUR HOME O TP TS
147 Vista Del Monte, Los Gatos (95030-6335)
PHONE......................408 358-0201
Julie Groves, *Owner*
EMP: 51
SALES (est): 1.4MM **Privately Held**
WEB: www.therapyinyourhome.net
SIC: 8082 Home health care services

(P-21885)
THOM SHARON & G ENTERPRISES
Also Called: Home Helpers
2620 Larkspur Ln Ste N, Redding (96002-1043)
PHONE......................530 226-8350
Sharon Clark, *President*
EMP: 50
SQ FT: 750
SALES (est): 1.4MM **Privately Held**
SIC: 8082 Home health care services

(P-21886)
THRIVE SUPPORT SERVICES INC
900 Court St, Martinez (94553-1731)
PHONE......................925 682-2273
Eric Partridge, *President*
EMP: 50 **EST:** 2009
SALES (est): 2MM **Privately Held**
SIC: 8082 Home health care services

(P-21887)
TRINITY HOME HEALTH SVCS INC
Also Called: Saint Agnes HM Hlth & Hospice
6729 N Willow Ave Ste 103, Fresno (93710-5952)
PHONE......................559 450-5112
B Smart, *Exec Dir*
Erin Denholm, *President*
Barbara Sears, *Principal*
EMP: 90
SALES (corp-wide): 18.3B **Privately Held**
SIC: 8082 8093 Visiting nurse service; rehabilitation center, outpatient treatment
HQ: Trinity Home Health Services
17410 College Pkwy # 150
Livonia MI 48152
734 542-8200

(P-21888)
TRINITYCARE LLC (PA)
Also Called: Trinity Care & Nutria
13030 Alondra Blvd, Cerritos (90703-2246)
PHONE......................818 709-4221
Peggy Chris,

EMP: 60
SALES (est): 1.9MM **Privately Held**
SIC: 8082 Home health care services

(P-21889)
UCLA HEALTH SYSTEM AUXILIARY
10920 Wilshire Blvd, Los Angeles (90024-6502)
PHONE......................310 267-4327
David T Feinberg, *President*
Patricia Kapur, *Exec VP*
Patty Cuen, *Exec Dir*
Rietta Goodglick, *Instructor*
EMP: 11154 **EST:** 1981
SALES (est): 185.6MM **Privately Held**
SIC: 8082 Home health care services

(P-21890)
UNIVERSAL HOME CARE INC
151 N San Vicente Blvd, Beverly Hills (90211-2323)
PHONE......................323 653-9222
Marina Greenberg, *CEO*
Stephen Shapiro MD, *Vice Pres*
Svetlana Razhavsky, *Office Mgr*
Bonnie Siegal, *Director*
EMP: 200
SALES: 3.5MM **Privately Held**
SIC: 8082 Home health care services

(P-21891)
US CARENET SERVICES LLC
815 Pollard Rd, Los Gatos (95032-1438)
PHONE......................408 378-6131
Carol Parker, *Branch Mgr*
EMP: 50 **Privately Held**
SIC: 8082 Home health care services
HQ: Us Carenet Services, Llc
1 10th St Ste 500
Augusta GA 30901

(P-21892)
VINA HOLDINGS INC
13800 Arizona St, Westminster (92683-3951)
PHONE......................714 622-5334
Cuong Nguyen, *President*
EMP: 80 **EST:** 2015
SALES: 3.7MM **Privately Held**
SIC: 8082 Home health care services

(P-21893)
VISITING CARE & COMPANIONS INC
Also Called: PERSONAL CARE SERVICES
509 E Montecito St # 200, Santa Barbara (93103-3293)
PHONE......................805 690-6202
Lynda Panner, *CEO*
EMP: 84
SALES: 2.8MM **Privately Held**
SIC: 8082 Visiting nurse service

(P-21894)
VISITING NRSE ASSN ORANGE CNTY (PA)
Also Called: Vna Home Health Systems
2520 Redhill Ave, Santa Ana (92705-5542)
PHONE......................949 263-4700
Jeneane A Brian, *President*
Joan Randall, *COO*
Andrea Arambula, *Marketing Mgr*
Diana Greenberg, *Nursing Dir*
▼ **EMP:** 55
SQ FT: 30,000
SALES: 2MM **Privately Held**
WEB: www.vnahhs.com
SIC: 8082 Home health care services

(P-21895)
VISITING NURSE ASSOCI
Also Called: Vna Private Duty Care
150 W 1st St Ste 176, Claremont (91711-4739)
P.O. Box 1208 (91711-1208)
PHONE......................909 621-3961
Marsha Fox, *Director*
Gayle McConnell, *CFO*
Brian Davis, *CTO*
Cindy Cameron, *Agent*
EMP: 100 **EST:** 1984
SALES: 2.8MM **Privately Held**
SIC: 8082 Visiting nurse service

(P-21896)
VISITING NURSE ASSOCIATION
Also Called: Center Coast Home Help Care
5 Lower Ragsdle Dr 102, Monterey (93940)
P.O. Box 2480 (93942-2480)
PHONE......................831 385-1014
Carol Snow, *President*
Gayle McConnell, *CFO*
Gena Gett, *Director*
EMP: 80
SALES (est): 823.2K **Privately Held**
SIC: 8082 Visiting nurse service

(P-21897)
VISITING NURSE ASSOCIATION OF (DH)
2880 Soquel Ave Ste 10, Santa Cruz (95062-1423)
PHONE......................831 477-2600
Bella Hughes, *Exec Dir*
EMP: 100
SQ FT: 19,000
SALES (est): 5.4MM
SALES (corp-wide): 12.7B **Privately Held**
SIC: 8082 Home health care services
HQ: Palo Alto Medical Foundation For Health Care, Research And Education (Inc)
795 El Camino Real
Palo Alto CA 94301
650 321-4121

(P-21898)
VISITNG NURSE ASSN INLND CNT (PA)
Also Called: Vnaic
6235 River Crest Dr Ste L, Riverside (92507-0758)
P.O. Box 1649 (92502-1649)
PHONE......................951 413-1200
Mike A Rusnak, *President*
Norman Lynde, *CFO*
Tanya Del Gado, *Executive Asst*
Gerrard Gier, *Info Tech Dir*
Jennifer Rock, *Graphic Designe*
EMP: 720 **EST:** 1931
SQ FT: 12,000
SALES: 56.8MM **Privately Held**
SIC: 8082 Visiting nurse service

(P-21899)
VISITNG NURSE ASSN INLND CNT
42600 Cook St Ste 202, Palm Desert (92211-5143)
PHONE......................760 346-3982
Anne Tyer, *Director*
EMP: 130
SALES (corp-wide): 56.8MM **Privately Held**
SIC: 8082 8621 Visiting nurse service; nursing association
PA: Visiting Nurse Association Of The Inland Counties
6235 River Crest Dr Ste L
Riverside CA 92507
951 413-1200

(P-21900)
VISTA HOME HEALTH SERVICE INC
343 E Palmdale Blvd Ste 4, Palmdale (93550-7138)
PHONE......................818 701-1877
Alma A Jastia, *President*
EMP: 57
SALES (est): 2.2MM **Privately Held**
WEB: www.vistahomehealth.com
SIC: 8082 Visiting nurse service

(P-21901)
VITAS HEALTHCARE CORP CAL
Also Called: Vitas Innovative Hospice Care
670 N Mccarthy Blcvd 220, Milpitas (95035)
PHONE......................408 964-6800
Roslyn Stenson, *Branch Mgr*
EMP: 80
SALES (corp-wide): 1.7B **Publicly Held**
WEB: www.vitasinnovativehospicecare.com
SIC: 8082 Home health care services

HQ: Vitas Healthcare Corporation Of California
7888 Mission Grove Pkwy S
Riverside CA 92508
305 374-4143

(P-21902)
VITAS HEALTHCARE CORP CAL
2710 Gateway Oaks Dr # 100, Sacramento
(95833-3505)
PHONE.................................916 925-7010
Sharon Rostoker, *Principal*
EMP: 95
SALES (corp-wide): 1.7B Publicly Held
WEB: www.vitasinnovativehospicecare.com
SIC: 8082 Home health care services
HQ: Vitas Healthcare Corporation Of Cali-
fornia
7888 Mission Grove Pkwy S
Riverside CA 92508
305 374-4143

(P-21903)
VITAS HEALTHCARE CORP CAL
Also Called: Vitas Innovative Hospice Care
7888 Mission Grove Pkwy S, Riverside
(92508-5089)
PHONE.................................909 386-6000
Karen Bennett, *Manager*
EMP: 170
SALES (corp-wide): 1.7B Publicly Held
WEB: www.vitasinnovativehospicecare.com
SIC: 8082 8011 Home health care serv-
ices; physical medicine, physician/sur-
geon
HQ: Vitas Healthcare Corporation Of Cali-
fornia
7888 Mission Grove Pkwy S
Riverside CA 92508
305 374-4143

(P-21904)
VITAS HEALTHCARE CORP CAL
990 W 190th St Ste 550, Torrance
(90502-1046)
PHONE.................................310 324-2273
Marie Hagerty, *Principal*
EMP: 70
SALES (corp-wide): 1.7B Publicly Held
WEB: www.vitasinnovativehospicecare.com
SIC: 8082 Home health care services
HQ: Vitas Healthcare Corporation Of Cali-
fornia
7888 Mission Grove Pkwy S
Riverside CA 92508
305 374-4143

(P-21905)
VITAS HEALTHCARE CORP CAL
Also Called: Vitas Innovative Hospice Care
16830 Ventura Blvd # 315, Encino
(91436-1723)
PHONE.................................818 760-2273
Susie Fishenfeld, *Branch Mgr*
Albert Hoston, *Technology*
EMP: 60
SALES (corp-wide): 1.7B Publicly Held
WEB: www.vitasinnovativehospicecare.com
SIC: 8082 Home health care services
HQ: Vitas Healthcare Corporation Of Cali-
fornia
7888 Mission Grove Pkwy S
Riverside CA 92508
305 374-4143

(P-21906)
VN HOME HEALTH CARE LP
2528 Qume Dr Ste 7, San Jose
(95131-1836)
PHONE.................................408 998-0550
Ngai Nguyen, *Principal*
EMP: 62
SALES: 4.9MM Privately Held
SIC: 8082 Home health care services

(P-21907)
VNA HOSPICE & PLLATVE CRE
S CA
Also Called: V N A & Hospice Southern Calif
412 E Vanderbilt Way, San Bernardino
(92408-3552)
PHONE.................................909 384-0737
Toll Free:.................................888 -
Marsha Fox, *President*
Timothy Dauwalder, *Director*
EMP: 150

SQ FT: 3,230
SALES (corp-wide): 40.1MM Privately
Held
WEB: www.vnasocal.org
SIC: 8082 Visiting nurse service
PA: Vna Hospice And Palliative Care Of
Southern California
412 E Vanderbilt Way
San Bernardino CA 92408
909 624-3574

(P-21908)
VNA HOSPICE & PLLATVE CRE
S CA (PA)
Also Called: Vna Private Duty Care
412 E Vanderbilt Way, San Bernardino
(92408-3552)
P.O. Box 908, Claremont (91711-0908)
PHONE.................................909 624-3574
Marsha Fox, *President*
Linda Adams, *Marketing Staff*
Karen Turner,
Kristin Candy, *Director*
Margaret Townsend, *Manager*
EMP: 300
SALES: 40.1MM Privately Held
SIC: 8082 Visiting nurse service

(P-21909)
WAY COOL HOMECARE INC
Also Called: Comfort Keepers
900 N Cuyamaca St Ste 201, El Cajon
(92020-1865)
PHONE.................................619 444-3200
Moura A Everhart, *President*
Benjamin Everhart, *Treasurer*
EMP: 50
SQ FT: 1,650
SALES (est): 1.4MM Privately Held
SIC: 8082 Home health care services

(P-21910)
WELL BEING GROUP INC
7075 N Howard St Ste 102, Fresno
(93720-2922)
PHONE.................................559 432-3737
Mark Dyson, *President*
EMP: 80
SALES (est): 1.3MM Privately Held
SIC: 8082 Home health care services

(P-21911)
WILLOW PASS HLTH CARE CTR
INC
3318 Willow Pass Rd, Concord
(94519-2316)
PHONE.................................925 689-9222
Pratap Poddatoori, *CEO*
Liz Lewis, *Office Mgr*
Mark Pagaduan, *Director*
EMP: 100
SALES (est): 168.3K Privately Held
SIC: 8082 8051 Home health care serv-
ices; skilled nursing care facilities
PA: Hycare, Inc.
524 Callan Ave
San Leandro CA 94577

(P-21912)
YOLO HOSPICE INC (PA)
1909 Galileo Ct Ste A, Davis (95618-4890)
P.O. Box 1014 (95617-1014)
PHONE.................................530 758-5566
Doug Jena, *Exec Dir*
EMP: 60
SALES: 7.3MM Privately Held
WEB: www.yolohospice.org
SIC: 8082 8322 Home health care serv-
ices; individual & family services

8092 Kidney Dialysis Centers

(P-21913)
BIO-MDCAL APPLICATIONS CAL
INC
Also Called: FMC Dialysis Svcs Bellflower
10116 Rosecrans Ave, Bellflower
(90706-2564)
PHONE.................................562 920-2070
Nelly McPhail, *Administration*
EMP: 52

SALES (corp-wide): 18.9B Privately Held
WEB: www.fresenius.org
SIC: 8092 Kidney dialysis centers
HQ: Bio-Medical Applications Of California,
Inc.
920 Winter St
Waltham MA 02451
-

(P-21914)
BIO-MDCAL APPLICATIONS CAL
INC
Also Called: BMA San Gabriel
1801 W Valley Blvd # 102, Alhambra
(91803-2300)
PHONE.................................626 457-9002
Monique Hartell, *Manager*
EMP: 50
SALES (corp-wide): 18.9B Privately Held
SIC: 8092 Kidney dialysis centers
HQ: Bio-Medical Applications Of California,
Inc.
920 Winter St
Waltham MA 02451
-

(P-21915)
BIO-MDCAL APPLICATIONS CAL
INC
Also Called: FMC Dialysis Svcs Riverside
3470 La Sierra Ave Ste E, Riverside
(92503-5223)
PHONE.................................951 343-7700
Gina Harper, *Manager*
EMP: 52
SALES (corp-wide): 18.9B Privately Held
SIC: 8092 Kidney dialysis centers
HQ: Bio-Medical Applications Of California,
Inc.
920 Winter St
Waltham MA 02451
-

(P-21916)
BIO-MDCAL APPLICATIONS RI
INC
Also Called: Fresenius Medical Care
3636 N 1st St Ste 144, Fresno
(93726-6818)
PHONE.................................559 221-6311
Monique Hartell, *Manager*
EMP: 53
SALES (corp-wide): 18.9B Privately Held
SIC: 8092 Kidney dialysis centers
HQ: Bio-Medical Applications Of Rhode Is-
land, Inc.
920 Winter St Ste A
Waltham MA 02451
781 699-9000

(P-21917)
DAVITA INC
15271 Laguna Canyon Rd, Irvine
(92618-3146)
PHONE.................................949 930-4400
Viki Anderson, *Branch Mgr*
David Kolojay, *Regional Mgr*
Patricia Ruiz, *Admin Asst*
Irene Watts, *Administration*
Clark Herrman, *IT/INT Sup*
EMP: 270 Publicly Held
WEB: www.davita.com
SIC: 8092 Kidney dialysis centers
PA: Davita Inc.
2000 16th St
Denver CO 80202

(P-21918)
DAVITA INC
601 Hawaii St, El Segundo (90245-4814)
PHONE.................................310 536-2400
Larry Buckelew, *Principal*
Tim Burke, *Officer*
Edward Stahel, *Vice Pres*
David Van Wyck, *Vice Pres*
Kimberly Vullo, *Vice Pres*
EMP: 85 Publicly Held
SIC: 8092 Kidney dialysis centers
PA: Davita Inc.
2000 16th St
Denver CO 80202

(P-21919)
DIALYSIS CENTERS VENTURA
CNTY
4567 Telephone Rd Ste 101, Ventura
(93003-5665)
PHONE.................................805 658-9211
Laura Norkinson, *Manager*
EMP: 67
SQ FT: 6,000
SALES (est): 1.4MM Privately Held
SIC: 8092 Kidney dialysis centers

(P-21920)
DIALYSIS CLINIC INC
1771 Stockton Blvd # 200, Sacramento
(95816-7040)
PHONE.................................916 453-0803
Cecelia Cronk, *Manager*
EMP: 50
SALES (corp-wide): 760.1MM Privately
Held
WEB: www.dciinc.org
SIC: 8092 Kidney dialysis centers
PA: Dialysis Clinic, Inc.
1633 Church St Ste 500
Nashville TN 37203
615 327-3061

(P-21921)
DVA RENAL HEALTHCARE INC
Also Called: Saddleback Dialysis
23141 Plaza Pointe Dr, Laguna Hills
(92653-1425)
PHONE.................................949 588-9211
Remy Obrt, *Branch Mgr*
EMP: 75 Publicly Held
WEB: www.us.gambro.com
SIC: 8092 Kidney dialysis centers
HQ: Dva Renal Healthcare, Inc.
2000 16th St
Denver CO 80202
253 258-9501

(P-21922)
EL CAMINO HOSPITAL
Also Called: Camino Dialysis Svcs Oak 110
2505 Hospital Dr Ste 1, Mountain View
(94040-4127)
PHONE.................................650 940-7310
George Ting MD, *Director*
Douglas Pulley, *Ophthalmology*
EMP: 75
SALES (corp-wide): 973.3MM Privately
Held
SIC: 8092 Kidney dialysis centers
PA: El Camino Hospital
2500 Grant Rd
Mountain View CA 94040
650 940-7000

(P-21923)
FRESENIUS MED CARE LONG
BEACH
Also Called: BMA Long Beach
440 W Ocean Blvd, Long Beach
(90802-4518)
PHONE.................................562 432-4444
Monique Hartell, *Manager*
EMP: 50
SALES (corp-wide): 18.9B Privately Held
WEB: www.fresenius.org
SIC: 8092 Kidney dialysis centers
HQ: Fresenius Medical Care Long Beach,
Llc
920 Winter St
Waltham MA 02451
781 699-9000

(P-21924)
HEMODIALYSIS INC (PA)
Also Called: Glentrans
710 W Wilson Ave, Glendale (91203-2409)
PHONE.................................818 500-8736
John R Depalma, *President*
EMP: 200
SQ FT: 1,500
SALES (est): 10.4MM Privately Held
SIC: 8092 Kidney dialysis centers

(P-21925)
HEMODIALYSIS INC
14901 Rinaldi St Ste 100, Mission Hills
(91345-1253)
PHONE.................................818 365-6961
John R Depalma, *Branch Mgr*

EMP: 50
SALES (est): 553.4K
SALES (corp-wide): 10.4MM **Privately Held**
SIC: 8092 Kidney dialysis centers
PA: Hemodialysis, Inc.
710 W Wilson Ave
Glendale CA 91203
818 500-8736

(P-21926)
INTERCOMMUNITY DIALYSIS SVCS
Also Called: Intercommunity Dialysis Center
12455 Washington Blvd, Whittier (90602-1006)
P.O. Box 11065 (90603-0065)
PHONE..................562 696-1841
Riad Darwish, *Administration*
Evelyn Sandoval, *Principal*
Dr John Shaib, *Principal*
EMP: 50
SQ FT: 7,400
SALES (est): 3.8MM **Privately Held**
SIC: 8092 8011 Kidney dialysis centers; clinic, operated by physicians

(P-21927)
JAMBOOR MEDICAL CORPORATION
Also Called: Desert Cities Dialysis
12675 Hesperia Rd, Victorville (92395-5878)
PHONE..................760 241-8063
Jay Shankar, *President*
Saguna Jayashankar, *Admin Sec*
EMP: 65
SQ FT: 7,000
SALES (est): 5.8MM **Privately Held**
SIC: 8092 Kidney dialysis centers

(P-21928)
KIDNEY CENTER INC
Also Called: Kidney Dialysis Center Verdugo
50 Moreland Rd, Simi Valley (93065-1659)
P.O. Box 940838 (93094-0838)
PHONE..................805 433-7777
Kant Tucker MD, *CEO*
Ushakant Thakkar, *President*
Raj Thakkar, *Vice Pres*
EMP: 200
SQ FT: 10,000
SALES (est): 14.6MM **Privately Held**
SIC: 8092 Kidney dialysis centers

(P-21929)
LOS ALMTOS HMODIALYSIS CTR INC
Also Called: Los Alamitos Hemo Dialysis Ctr
3810 Katella Ave, Los Alamitos (90720-3302)
PHONE..................562 426-8881
Maher A Azer, *President*
EMP: 60
SQ FT: 15,000
SALES (est): 4.2MM **Privately Held**
WEB: www.dialysisflorence.com
SIC: 8092 Kidney dialysis centers

(P-21930)
MOHAN DIALYSIS CENTER INDUSTRY
15757 E Valley Blvd, City of Industry (91744-3900)
PHONE..................626 333-3801
Krishna Mohan, *Director*
Ana Mohan, *Admin Sec*
EMP: 70
SALES (est): 5MM **Privately Held**
SIC: 8092 Kidney dialysis centers

(P-21931)
MOHAN DIALYSIS CTR OF COVINA
Also Called: Mdcc
158 W College St, Covina (91723-2064)
PHONE..................626 859-2522
Sheri A Pham, *Med Doctor*
▲ EMP: 70
SQ FT: 5,500
SALES (est): 5MM **Privately Held**
WEB: www.mdcc.com
SIC: 8092 Kidney dialysis centers

(P-21932)
RENAL TREATMENT CTRS - CAL INC
Also Called: Brea Dialysis Center
595 Tamarack Ave Ste A, Brea (92821-3125)
PHONE..................714 990-0110
Agnes Henry, *Branch Mgr*
EMP: 70 **Publicly Held**
WEB: www.davita.com
SIC: 8092 Kidney dialysis centers
HQ: Renal Treatment Centers - California, Inc.
2000 16th St
Denver CO 80202
303 405-2100

(P-21933)
RENAL TREATMENT CTRS - CAL INC
Also Called: Davita Dialysis
15271 Laguna Canyon Rd, Irvine (92618-3146)
PHONE..................949 930-6882
Kent Thiry, *CEO*
Christian Orem, *Info Tech Mgr*
Lori Harris, *Manager*
Edna McCoy, *Manager*
EMP: 99
SALES (est): 3.1MM **Privately Held**
SIC: 8092 Kidney dialysis centers

(P-21934)
RIVERSIDE DIALYSIS CENTER
4361 Latham St Ste 100, Riverside (92501-1767)
PHONE..................951 682-2700
Linda Sherman, *Principal*
▲ EMP: 50
SALES (est): 1.1MM **Privately Held**
SIC: 8092 Kidney dialysis centers

(P-21935)
SATELLITE HEALTHCARE INC
Also Called: Satellite Dialysis
3500 Coffee Rd Ste 21, Modesto (95355-1315)
PHONE..................209 578-0691
Susie Phillips, *Branch Mgr*
Janet Luker, *Admin Sec*
EMP: 60
SALES (corp-wide): 188.9MM **Privately Held**
WEB: www.satellitehealth.com
SIC: 8092 8011 Kidney dialysis centers; offices & clinics of medical doctors
PA: Satellite Healthcare, Inc.
300 Santana Row Ste 300 # 300
San Jose CA 95128
650 404-3600

(P-21936)
SATELLITE HEALTHCARE INC (PA)
Also Called: Satellite Dialysis Centers
300 Santana Row Ste 300 # 300, San Jose (95128-2424)
PHONE..................650 404-3600
Rick J Barnett, *President*
Norman S Coplon, *Ch of Bd*
Dave Carter, *COO*
Susan Del Bene, *CFO*
Estrella Parker, *Officer*
EMP: 75
SQ FT: 12,000
SALES (est): 188.9MM **Privately Held**
WEB: www.satellitehealth.com
SIC: 8092 Kidney dialysis centers

(P-21937)
SATELLITE HEALTHCARE INC
2121 Alexian Dr Ste 118, San Jose (95116-1905)
PHONE..................408 258-8720
Mark Carlston, *Manager*
EMP: 80
SALES (corp-wide): 188.9MM **Privately Held**
WEB: www.satellitehealth.com
SIC: 8092 8011 Kidney dialysis centers; clinic, operated by physicians
PA: Satellite Healthcare, Inc.
300 Santana Row Ste 300 # 300
San Jose CA 95128
650 404-3600

(P-21938)
TOTAL RENAL CARE INC
Also Called: TRC Pleasanton Dialysis Cntr
5720 Stoneridge Mall Rd # 160, Pleasanton (94588-2828)
PHONE..................925 737-0120
Connie Edwards, *Administration*
Kari Everson, *Administration*
EMP: 50 **Publicly Held**
WEB: www.davita.com
SIC: 8092 Kidney dialysis centers
HQ: Total Renal Care, Inc.
2000 16th St
Denver CO 80202
303 405-2100

(P-21939)
TOTAL RENAL CARE INC
15271 Laguna Canyon Rd, Irvine (92618-3146)
PHONE..................949 930-6882
Kent Thiry, *President*
Jennifer Werner, *Info Tech Mgr*
EMP: 99
SALES (est): 1.4MM **Publicly Held**
SIC: 8092 Kidney dialysis centers
PA: Davita Inc.
2000 16th St
Denver CO 80202

(P-21940)
TOTAL RENAL CARE INC
Also Called: Carquinez Dialysis
125 Corporate Pl Ste C, Vallejo (94590-6968)
PHONE..................707 556-3637
Agnes Brabek, *CEO*
EMP: 600 **Publicly Held**
WEB: www.davita.com
SIC: 8092 Kidney dialysis centers
HQ: Total Renal Care, Inc.
2000 16th St
Denver CO 80202
303 405-2100

(P-21941)
TOTAL RENAL CARE INC
Also Called: Davita Hesperia Dialysis Ctr
14135 Main St Ste 501, Hesperia (92345-8097)
PHONE..................760 947-7405
EMP: 60
SALES (corp-wide): 12.8B **Publicly Held**
SIC: 8092
HQ: Total Renal Care, Inc.
601 Hawaii St
El Segundo CA 80202
310 536-2400

8093 Specialty Outpatient Facilities, NEC

(P-21942)
21ST CENTURY HEALTH CLUB (PA)
680a E Cotati Ave, Cotati (94931-4092)
PHONE..................707 795-0400
John Ford, *President*
Dr Robert Gardner, *Treasurer*
Frank Ford, *Vice Pres*
Elizabeth Gardner, *Admin Sec*
▲ EMP: 70
SQ FT: 20,000
SALES (est): 3.1MM **Privately Held**
SIC: 8093 7991 Rehabilitation center, outpatient treatment; health club

(P-21943)
ADDICTION RES & TRTMNT INC
433 Turk St, San Francisco (94102-3329)
PHONE..................415 928-7800
Teresa Fleming, *Branch Mgr*
EMP: 56 **Privately Held**
SIC: 8093 Drug clinic, outpatient
PA: Addiction Research And Treatment, Inc.
1145 Market St Fl 10
San Francisco CA 94103

(P-21944)
AEGIS TREATMENT CENTERS LLC (PA)
7246 Remmet Ave, Canoga Park (91303-1531)
PHONE..................818 206-0360
Alex Dodd, *CEO*
James Ferguson, *Accounting Mgr*
David Devine, *Controller*
Jovan Blake, *Recruiter*
Thai Vo, *Counsel*
EMP: 55
SALES (est): 11.1MM **Privately Held**
SIC: 8093 Rehabilitation center, outpatient treatment

(P-21945)
AGENDIA INC
22 Morgan, Irvine (92618-2022)
PHONE..................949 540-6300
Mark R Straley, *CEO*
Glen Fredenberg, *CFO*
Kurt Schmidt, *CFO*
Peter C Wulff, *CFO*
M William Audeh, *Chief Mktg Ofcr*
EMP: 107 EST: 2008
SALES: 18.7MM
SALES (corp-wide): 38.5MM **Privately Held**
SIC: 8093 Drug clinic, outpatient
PA: Agendia N.V.
Science Park 406
Amsterdam
204 621-500

(P-21946)
ALCOHOL DRG PROGRAM YOLO CNTY
137 N Cottonwood St Ste 1, Woodland (95695-6646)
PHONE..................530 666-8650
Karen Gerbasi, *Exec Dir*
EMP: 50 EST: 2001
SALES (est): 1.5MM **Privately Held**
SIC: 8093 Specialty outpatient clinics

(P-21947)
ALGOS INC A MEDICAL CORP (PA)
Also Called: Pasadena Rehabilitation Inst
224 N Fair Oaks Ave, Pasadena (91103-3618)
PHONE..................626 696-1400
Clayton Varga, *President*
Robert Castaneda, *CFO*
Gerri Summe, *CFO*
EMP: 60
SQ FT: 8,000
SALES (est): 8MM **Privately Held**
WEB: www.thebigmd.com
SIC: 8093 8049 8011 Rehabilitation center, outpatient treatment; physical therapist; specialized medical practitioners, except internal

(P-21948)
ALLIANT EDUCATIONAL FOUNDATION
5130 E Clinton Way, Fresno (93727-2014)
PHONE..................559 456-2777
Jennifer Wilson, *Branch Mgr*
EMP: 200
SALES (corp-wide): 71.7MM **Privately Held**
SIC: 8093 8221 Mental health clinic, outpatient; university
PA: Alliant International University, Inc.
10455 Pomerado Rd
San Diego CA 92131
415 955-2000

(P-21949)
ALPINE CONVALESCENT CENTER INC
Also Called: Alpine Special Treatment Ctr
2120 Alpine Blvd, Alpine (91901-2113)
PHONE..................619 659-3120
Michael E Doyle, *CEO*
Kristine Tiernan, *Psychologist*
EMP: 100 EST: 1972
SQ FT: 15,000
SALES (est): 7.1MM **Privately Held**
WEB: www.astci.com
SIC: 8093 Rehabilitation center, outpatient treatment; mental health clinic, outpatient

(P-21950)
AMANECER CMNTY COUNSELING SVC
1200 Wilshire Blvd # 200, Los Angeles (90017-1908)
PHONE...................213 481-7464
Tim Ryder, *Exec Dir*
Frank Chargualaf, *CFO*
Linda Sanner, *CFO*
Laura Gonzalez, *Executive Asst*
Kanisha McReynolds, *QA Dir*
EMP: 100 **EST:** 1975
SALES: 9.1MM **Privately Held**
WEB: www.ccsla.org
SIC: 8093 Mental health clinic, outpatient

(P-21951)
ANKA BEHAVIORAL HEALTH INC (PA)
3840 Buskirk Ave Ste 300, Pleasant Hill (94523)
PHONE...................925 825-4700
EMP: 143
SALES: 40.4MM **Privately Held**
SIC: 8093 Mental health clinic, outpatient

(P-21952)
ANKA BEHAVIORAL HEALTH INC
942 Barbara Ln, Pomona (91767-4118)
PHONE...................909 622-8217
EMP: 130
SALES (corp-wide): 40.4MM **Privately Held**
SIC: 8093 Mental health clinic, outpatient
PA: Anka Behavioral Health, Incorporated
3840 Buskirk Ave Ste 300
Pleasant Hill CA 94523
925 825-4700

(P-21953)
ARC - IMPERIAL VALLEY
340 E 1st St, Calexico (92231-2732)
PHONE...................760 768-1944
Alex King, *Principal*
Ramon Aguirre, *Transportation*
EMP: 58
SALES (corp-wide): 10.8MM **Privately Held**
SIC: 8093 4783 2051 5812 Rehabilitation center, outpatient treatment; packing goods for shipping; bakery: wholesale or wholesale/retail combined; delicatessen (eating places); caterers
PA: Arc - Imperial Valley
298 E Ross Ave
El Centro CA 92243
760 352-0180

(P-21954)
ARC OF VENTURA COUNTY INC
Also Called: ARC Community Enrichment
210 Canada St, Ojai (93023-2523)
PHONE...................805 650-8611
Lisa Emery, *Manager*
EMP: 60
SALES (corp-wide): 13.2MM **Privately Held**
SIC: 8093 8322 Rehabilitation center, outpatient treatment; social services for the handicapped
PA: The Arc Of Ventura County Inc
5103 Walker St
Ventura CA 93003
805 650-8611

(P-21955)
ARC OF VENTURA COUNTY INC
4277 Transport St Ste F, Ventura (93003-5657)
PHONE...................805 644-0880
Alisa Mahrer, *Manager*
EMP: 192
SALES (corp-wide): 13.2MM **Privately Held**
SIC: 8093 8361 8322 8331 Rehabilitation center, outpatient treatment; residential care; individual & family services; sheltered workshop
PA: The Arc Of Ventura County Inc
5103 Walker St
Ventura CA 93003
805 650-8611

(P-21956)
ASIAN COMMUNITY MENTAL HLTH BD
Also Called: Asian Cmnty Mental Hlth Svcs
310 8th St Ste 303, Oakland (94607-4253)
PHONE...................510 869-6000
Lawrence Fong, *President*
John Fong, *Treasurer*
Betty Hong, *Vice Pres*
Sharon Sue, *Admin Sec*
Moira Bowman, *Deputy Dir*
EMP: 95
SALES: 963K **Privately Held**
WEB: www.acmhs.org
SIC: 8093 Mental health clinic, outpatient

(P-21957)
AXIS COMMUNITY HEALTH INC
4361 Railroad Ave, Pleasanton (94566-6611)
PHONE...................925 462-1755
Sue Compton, *CEO*
Christina McFadden, *COO*
Joe Flarity, *CFO*
Kanwar Singh, *CFO*
Sylvia Madrid, *QA Dir*
EMP: 99 **EST:** 1972
SALES: 12.2MM **Privately Held**
WEB: www.axishealth.org
SIC: 8093 Mental health clinic, outpatient

(P-21958)
BAART BEHAVIORAL HLTH SVCS INC
433 Turk St, San Francisco (94102-3329)
PHONE...................415 928-7800
Teresa Fleming, *Branch Mgr*
EMP: 56
SALES (corp-wide): 12.6MM **Privately Held**
SIC: 8093 Substance abuse clinics (outpatient)
HQ: Baart Behavioral Health Services, Inc.
1145 Market St Fl 10
San Francisco CA 94103
415 552-7914

(P-21959)
BAART COMMUNITY HEALTHCARE
433 Turk St, San Francisco (94102-3329)
PHONE...................415 928-7800
Teresa Fleming, *Branch Mgr*
EMP: 56
SALES (corp-wide): 4.4MM **Privately Held**
SIC: 8093 Drug clinic, outpatient
PA: Baart Community Healthcare
1145 Market St Fl 10
San Francisco CA 94103
415 863-3883

(P-21960)
BAKER PLACES INC
101 Gough St, San Francisco (94102-5903)
PHONE...................415 503-3137
EMP: 134
SALES (corp-wide): 15MM **Privately Held**
SIC: 8093 Substance abuse clinics (outpatient)
PA: Baker Places, Inc.
170 9th St
San Francisco CA 94103
415 864-4655

(P-21961)
BASQUEZ TIBURCIO HEALTH CENTER
33255 9th St, Union City (94587-2137)
PHONE...................510 471-5907
Jose J Garcia, *CEO*
EMP: 160
SALES (est): 1.4MM **Privately Held**
SIC: 8093 Specialty outpatient clinics

(P-21962)
BRIDGES AT SN PDRO PNNSLA HSPT
1300 W 7th St Fl 4, San Pedro (90732-3505)
PHONE...................310 514-5359
Vivian Harvey, *Director*

EMP: 55
SALES (est): 804.6K **Privately Held**
SIC: 8093 Mental health clinic, outpatient

(P-21963)
CAMINAR
Also Called: Jobs Plus
376 Rio Lindo Ave, Chico (95926-1914)
PHONE...................530 343-4421
Tracy Watkins, *Branch Mgr*
Charles Huggins, *CEO*
EMP: 65
SALES (corp-wide): 18.6MM **Privately Held**
SIC: 8093 Mental health clinic, outpatient
PA: Caminar
2600 S El Camino Real # 200
San Mateo CA 94403
650 372-4080

(P-21964)
CAMP RECOVERY CENTERS LLP
3192 Glen Canyon Rd, Santa Cruz (95066-4916)
P.O. Box 66569, Scotts Valley (95067-6569)
PHONE...................831 438-1868
Page Bottom, *Exec Dir*
Steve Hanusa, *Director*
EMP: 100
SALES (est): 2.2MM **Privately Held**
WEB: www.camprecovery.com
SIC: 8093 Rehabilitation center, outpatient treatment

(P-21965)
CARLSBAD SURGERY CENTER LLC
6121 Paseo Del Norte # 100, Carlsbad (92011-1161)
PHONE...................760 448-2488
David W Douglas, *Mng Member*
EMP: 50
SALES: 5.4MM **Privately Held**
SIC: 8093 Specialty outpatient clinics

(P-21966)
CARNAHAN OCCUPATIONAL THERAPY
116 E College Ave Ste G, Lompoc (93436-5331)
PHONE...................805 737-1604
Juanita Carnahan, *Owner*
EMP: 50
SALES (est): 800.8K **Privately Held**
WEB: www.carnahantherapy.com
SIC: 8093 Rehabilitation center, outpatient treatment

(P-21967)
CASA COLIN COMPREHENSIVE
255 E Bonita Ave, Pomona (91767-1923)
PHONE...................909 596-7733
Felice Loverso, *CEO*
Ross Lessons, *MIS Dir*
EMP: 150
SQ FT: 35,000
SALES: 2.8MM **Privately Held**
SIC: 8093 Rehabilitation center, outpatient treatment

(P-21968)
CASTLE FAMILY HEALTH CTRS INC (PA)
3605 Hospital Rd Ste H, Atwater (95301-5173)
PHONE...................209 381-2000
Edward H Lujano, *CEO*
Bill Able, *CFO*
Fily Cale, *Executive Asst*
Charles Mook, *Opers Mgr*
Isaac Medina, *Marketing Staff*
EMP: 99
SALES: 19.9MM **Privately Held**
SIC: 8093 Specialty outpatient clinics

(P-21969)
CASTLEWOOD TREATMENT CTR LLC (PA)
Also Called: Alsana
2545 W Hillcrest Dr 205, Thousand Oaks (91320-2296)
PHONE...................805 273-5217
Jennifer Steiner, *CEO*

Clodagh Rafferty, *COO*
Bart Thielen, *CFO*
Nicole Siegfried, *Officer*
Brian Cook, *Vice Pres*
EMP: 91
SQ FT: 5,000
SALES: 1.7MM **Privately Held**
WEB: www.castlewoodtc.com
SIC: 8093 Mental health clinic, outpatient

(P-21970)
CENTER FOR AUTISM &
106 Discovery, Irvine (92618-3131)
PHONE...................949 203-8872
EMP: 50 **Privately Held**
SIC: 8093 Mental health clinic, outpatient
PA: Center For Autism And Related Disorders, Inc.
21600 Oxnard St Ste 1800
Woodland Hills CA 91367

(P-21971)
CENTER FOR AUTSM RSRCH EVLTN
Also Called: Cares
10174 Old Grove Rd, San Diego (92131-1652)
PHONE...................858 444-8823
Olanderia Brown, *Manager*
EMP: 140 **EST:** 2007
SALES (est): 4.4MM
SALES (corp-wide): 29.6MM **Privately Held**
SIC: 8093 Specialty outpatient clinics
PA: Fred Finch Youth Center
3800 Coolidge Ave
Oakland CA 94602
510 773-6669

(P-21972)
CENTRAL VALLEY CLINIC INC
Also Called: Sants Clair Alcohol Meth Prog
2425 Enborg Ln, San Jose (95128-2648)
PHONE...................408 885-5400
Robert Garner, *Director*
EMP: 50 **EST:** 1985
SALES (est): 991.4K **Privately Held**
SIC: 8093 Drug clinic, outpatient

(P-21973)
CENTRAL VLY REGIONAL CTR INC
5441 W Cypress Ave, Visalia (93277-8341)
PHONE...................559 738-2200
Lorraine Bortes, *General Mgr*
Ed Araim, *Technology*
EMP: 120
SALES (est): 1.1MM
SALES (corp-wide): 277.3MM **Privately Held**
SIC: 8093 8399 Mental health clinic, outpatient; social service information exchange
PA: Central Valley Regional Center, Inc.
4615 N Marty Ave
Fresno CA
559 276-4300

(P-21974)
CENTRE FOR NEURO SKILLS (PA)
5215 Ashe Rd, Bakersfield (93313-2069)
PHONE...................661 872-3408
Mark J Ashley, *CEO*
Susan Ashley, *Vice Pres*
Ron Boutte, *Purchasing*
Diana Berry, *Marketing Staff*
Elaine Roberts, *Marketing Staff*
EMP: 168
SQ FT: 14,000
SALES: 320.2K **Privately Held**
SIC: 8093 Rehabilitation center, outpatient treatment

(P-21975)
CENTRO DE SALUD DE LA COMUNI (PA)
Also Called: San Ysidro Health
1601 Precision Park Ln, San Diego (92173-1345)
PHONE...................619 428-4463
Kevin Mattson, *CEO*
M Gutierrez, *President*
Maria Carriedo-Cenice, *Vice Pres*

PRODUCTS & SVCS

Ana Melgoza, *Vice Pres*
Tomas Urtasun, *Vice Pres*
EMP: 80
SQ FT: 2,000
SALES: 87.1MM **Privately Held**
SIC: 8093 8011 Specialty outpatient clinics; offices & clinics of medical doctors

(P-21976)
CENTRO DE SALUD DE LA COMUNI
Also Called: National City Family Clinic
1136 D Ave, National City (91950-3412)
PHONE..........................619 336-2300
Joe Robledo, *Manager*
EMP: 90
SQ FT: 4,712
SALES (corp-wide): 87.1MM **Privately Held**
SIC: 8093 Specialty outpatient clinics
PA: Centro De Salud De La Comunidad De
San Ysidro, Inc.
1601 Precision Park Ln
San Diego CA 92173
619 428-4463

(P-21977)
CHILD AND FAMILY GUIDANCE CTR
Also Called: Valley Child Guidance Clinic
310 E Plmdle Blvd G, Palmdale (93550)
PHONE..........................661 265-8627
Joelle Hunnewell, *Director*
Alpa Patel, *Med Doctor*
Rocio Cabrales, *Director*
EMP: 72
SALES (corp-wide): 29.1MM **Privately Held**
WEB: www.childguidance.org
SIC: 8093 Mental health clinic, outpatient
PA: Child And Family Guidance Center
9650 Zelzah Ave
Northridge CA 91325
818 739-5140

(P-21978)
CHILD AND FAMILY GUIDANCE CTR (PA)
Also Called: Northpoint Day Treatment Sch
9650 Zelzah Ave, Northridge (91325-2003)
PHONE..........................818 739-5140
Roy Marshall, *Exec Dir*
Russell Jones, *Ch of Bd*
Robert Garcia, *President*
Ronald Call, *Treasurer*
Stephen J Howard PHD, *Vice Pres*
EMP: 200
SQ FT: 35,000
SALES: 29.1MM **Privately Held**
WEB: www.childguidance.org
SIC: 8093 Mental health clinic, outpatient

(P-21979)
CHILD AND FAMILY GUIDANCE CTR
Also Called: Family Stress Center
8550 Balboa Blvd Ste 150, Northridge (91325-3579)
PHONE..........................818 830-0200
Jessica Card, *Director*
EMP: 50
SALES (corp-wide): 29.1MM **Privately Held**
WEB: www.childguidance.org
SIC: 8093 8322 Mental health clinic, outpatient; general counseling services
PA: Child And Family Guidance Center
9650 Zelzah Ave
Northridge CA 91325
818 739-5140

(P-21980)
CHOICE IN AGING (PA)
Also Called: MT DIABLO CENTER ADULT
DAY HEA
490 Golf Club Rd, Pleasant Hill (94523-1553)
PHONE..........................925 682-6330
Debbie Toth, *CEO*
Jeaneen McPherson, *Finance*
Joanne McClellan, *Accountant*
Bonnie Price, *Human Resources*
Danielle Lopez, *Nurse*
EMP: 85
SQ FT: 24,335

SALES: 4.9MM **Privately Held**
WEB: www.rsnc-centers.org
SIC: 8093 8331 Rehabilitation center, outpatient treatment; vocational rehabilitation agency

(P-21981)
CHOICE MEDICAL GROUP INC
2322 Butano Dr Ste 205, Sacramento (95825-0657)
PHONE..........................916 483-2885
Lisa Vaughn, *General Mgr*
Laurie Luiza, *Treasurer*
EMP: 70
SALES (est): 1.4MM **Privately Held**
SIC: 8093 Abortion clinic

(P-21982)
CLINICAS DEL CAMINO REAL INC
Also Called: Dental Office
650 Meta St, Oxnard (93030-7182)
PHONE..........................805 487-5351
Patricia Andrade, *General Mgr*
Bob Johnson, *Purchasing*
Jeff Raikes, *Director*
Janet Rasmussen, *Director*
EMP: 73
SALES (corp-wide): 97.9MM **Privately Held**
SIC: 8093 8011 Specialty outpatient clinics; ambulatory surgical center
PA: Clinicas Del Camino Real, Inc.
200 S Wells Rd Ste 200 # 200
Ventura CA 93004
805 647-6322

(P-21983)
CLINICAS DEL CAMINO REAL INC (PA)
200 S Wells Rd Ste 200 # 200, Ventura (93004-1377)
P.O. Box 1270, Camarillo (93011-1270)
PHONE..........................805 647-6322
Roberto S Juarez, *CEO*
Hideto Saito, *Family Practiti*
Veena Verghese,
EMP: 230
SQ FT: 4,000
SALES: 100.6MM **Privately Held**
SIC: 8093 Specialty outpatient clinics

(P-21984)
COMMUNITY ACTION MARIN
Also Called: Community Action Marine
1108 Tamalpais Ave, San Rafael (94901-3247)
PHONE..........................415 459-6330
Michael Payne, *President*
EMP: 212
SALES (corp-wide): 16.3MM **Privately Held**
SIC: 8093 Mental health clinic, outpatient
PA: Community Action Marin
555 Northgate Dr Ste 201
San Rafael CA 94903
415 485-1489

(P-21985)
COMMUNITY FAMILY GUIDANCE CTR (PA)
10929 South St Ste 208b, Cerritos (90703-5391)
PHONE..........................562 865-6444
Richard Murase, *President*
Lesley Watkins, *CFO*
Patricia Taylor PH, *Training Dir*
Lindsay Rosser, *Med Doctor*
EMP: 65
SALES: 6.5MM **Privately Held**
WEB: www.cfgconline.com
SIC: 8093 Mental health clinic, outpatient

(P-21986)
COMMUNITY MEDICAL CENTERS INC (PA)
7210 Murray Dr, Stockton (95210-3339)
PHONE..........................209 373-2800
Kathleen Marshall, *CEO*
Art Feagles, *CFO*
Benjamin Morrison, *Associate Dir*
Michael Kirkpatrick, *General Mgr*
Debra Johnson, *Office Mgr*
EMP: 90 **EST:** 1978
SQ FT: 14,000

SALES: 44.6MM **Privately Held**
SIC: 8093 8011 Specialty outpatient clinics; offices & clinics of medical doctors

(P-21987)
CONSOLIDATED TRIBAL HEALTH PRJ
6991 N State St, Redwood Valley (95470-9629)
P.O. Box 387, Calpella (95418-0387)
PHONE..........................707 485-5115
Michael Knight, *Chairman*
George Provencher, *Treasurer*
Debra Ramirez, *Principal*
Donna Schuler, *Admin Sec*
EMP: 65
SALES: 9.5MM **Privately Held**
WEB: www.cthp.org
SIC: 8093 Mental health clinic, outpatient

(P-21988)
COPPERTOWER FAMILY MEDICAL CTR
Also Called: Alexander Valley Healthcare
100 W 3rd St, Cloverdale (95425-3204)
PHONE..........................707 894-4229
Debbie Howell, *CEO*
Jenine Rose, *CFO*
EMP: 50
SQ FT: 2,700
SALES: 5.9MM **Privately Held**
WEB: www.coppertower.com
SIC: 8093 Specialty outpatient clinics

(P-21989)
CORRECTONS RHBLTATION CAL DEPT
Also Called: Cdcr - California Men's Colony
Hwy 1 N, San Luis Obispo (93409-0001)
P.O. Box 8101 (93403-8101)
PHONE..........................805 547-7900
John Marshall, *Warden*
Tyler Campbell, *Family Practiti*
Scott Lee, *Family Practiti*
Sarah Chisholm, *Psychologist*
Barry Mactarnaghan, *Psychologist*
EMP: 2000 **Privately Held**
SIC: 8093 9223 Specialty outpatient clinics;
HQ: California Department Of Corrections
& Rehabilitation
1515 S St
Sacramento CA 95811

(P-21990)
COUNTY OF BUTTE
Also Called: Butte County Mental Hlth Svcs
107 Parmac Rd Ste 4, Chico (95926-2298)
PHONE..........................530 891-2850
Bradford Luz PHD, *Director*
EMP: 400 **Privately Held**
WEB: www.bcihsspa.org
SIC: 8093 9111 Substance abuse clinics (outpatient); county supervisors' & executives' offices
PA: County Of Butte
25 County Center Dr # 125
Oroville CA 95965
530 538-7701

(P-21991)
COUNTY OF CONTRA COSTA
Also Called: Department of Health Services
1420 Willow Pass Rd # 140, Concord (94520-5823)
PHONE..........................925 646-5480
John Allen, *Director*
EMP: 50 **Privately Held**
WEB: www.cccounty.us
SIC: 8093 9431 Mental health clinic, outpatient; administration of public health programs;
PA: County Of Contra Costa
625 Court St Ste 100
Martinez CA 94553
925 957-5280

(P-21992)
COUNTY OF FRESNO
Also Called: Department Behavioral Health
4417 E Inyo St Bldg 333, Fresno (93702-2977)
PHONE..........................559 600-4600
Sean Patterson, *Business Mgr*

Jennifer Quintana, *Social Worker*
EMP: 99 **EST:** 1872
SQ FT: 4,000
SALES (est): 562.3K **Privately Held**
SIC: 8093 Mental health clinic, outpatient

(P-21993)
COUNTY OF GLENN
Also Called: Department of Mental Health
242 N Villa Ave, Willows (95988-2641)
PHONE..........................530 934-6582
Scott Gruentl, *Director*
EMP: 75 **Privately Held**
WEB: www.countyofglen.net
SIC: 8093 9111 Mental health clinic, outpatient; county supervisors' & executives' offices
PA: County Of Glenn
516 W Sycamore St Fl 2
Willows CA 95988
530 934-6410

(P-21994)
COUNTY OF HUMBOLDT
Also Called: Humboldt County Mental Health
720 Wood St, Eureka (95501-4413)
PHONE..........................707 476-4054
Cindy Moore, *Manager*
EMP: 120 **Privately Held**
SIC: 8093 9111 8063 Mental health clinic, outpatient; county supervisors' & executives' offices; psychiatric hospitals
PA: County Of Humboldt
825 5th St
Eureka CA 95501
707 268-2543

(P-21995)
COUNTY OF IMPERIAL
Also Called: Imperial County Mental Health
202 N 8th St, El Centro (92243-2302)
PHONE..........................760 482-4120
Rudy Lopez, *Director*
Anna Welzein, *Human Res Dir*
Morteza Rahmani, *Neurology*
EMP: 100 **Privately Held**
WEB: www.imperialcounty.net
SIC: 8093 9111 Mental health clinic, outpatient; county supervisors' & executives' offices
PA: County Of Imperial
940 W Main St Ste 208
El Centro CA 92243
760 482-4556

(P-21996)
COUNTY OF LOS ANGELES
Also Called: Health Services, Dept of
7601 Imperial Hwy, Downey (90242-3456)
PHONE..........................562 401-7088
Valeria Orange, *Director*
Aries Limbaga, *Ch Nursing Ofcr*
Ron Chai, *Internal Med*
EMP: 1400 **Privately Held**
WEB: www.co.la.ca.us
SIC: 8093 9431 Rehabilitation center, outpatient treatment;
PA: County Of Los Angeles
500 W Temple St Ste 437
Los Angeles CA 90012
213 974-1101

(P-21997)
COUNTY OF LOS ANGELES
Also Called: Health Dept
5850 S Main St, Los Angeles (90003-1215)
PHONE..........................323 897-6187
Floretta Taylor, *Admin Director*
EMP: 120 **Privately Held**
WEB: www.co.la.ca.us
SIC: 8093 9431 8011 Specialty outpatient clinics; administration of public health programs; ; offices & clinics of medical doctors
PA: County Of Los Angeles
500 W Temple St Ste 437
Los Angeles CA 90012
213 974-1101

(P-21998)
COUNTY OF LOS ANGELES
Also Called: Health Services, Dept of
5205 Melrose Ave, Los Angeles (90038-3144)
PHONE..........................323 769-7800
Rosa Pinon, *Branch Mgr*

EMP: 100 Privately Held
WEB: www.co.la.ca.us
SIC: 8093 9431 Family planning & birth control clinics; administration of public health programs;
PA: County Of Los Angeles
500 W Temple St Ste 437
Los Angeles CA 90012
213 974-1101

(P-21999)
COUNTY OF LOS ANGELES
Also Called: Mental Health Dept of
17707 Studebaker Rd, Artesia (90703-2640)
PHONE..................................562 402-0688
Latisha Guvman, *Manager*
EMP: 50 Privately Held
WEB: www.co.la.ca.us
SIC: 8093 9431 Specialty outpatient clinics; administration of public health programs;
PA: County Of Los Angeles
500 W Temple St Ste 437
Los Angeles CA 90012
213 974-1101

(P-22000)
COUNTY OF LOS ANGELES
Also Called: Antelope Valley Health Center
335 E Avenue K6 Ste B, Lancaster (93535-4645)
PHONE..................................661 524-2005
Mary Nolan, *Manager*
EMP: 59 Privately Held
SIC: 8093 Family planning clinic
PA: County Of Los Angeles
500 W Temple St Ste 437
Los Angeles CA 90012
213 974-1101

(P-22001)
COUNTY OF MARIN
Also Called: Community Mental Health Clinic
250 Bon Air Rd, Greenbrae (94904-1702)
P.O. Box 2728, San Rafael (94912-2728)
PHONE..................................415 448-1500
Bruce Gurganus, *Director*
EMP: 100 Privately Held
SIC: 8093 9111 Mental health clinic, outpatient; county supervisors' & executives' offices
PA: County Of Marin
3501 Civic Center Dr # 258
San Rafael CA 94903
415 473-6358

(P-22002)
COUNTY OF MENDOCINO
860a N Bush St, Ukiah (95482-3919)
PHONE..................................707 463-4396
EMP: 200 Privately Held
SIC: 8093 9111
PA: County Of Mendocino
501 Low Gap Rd Rm 1010
Ukiah CA 95482
707 463-4441

(P-22003)
COUNTY OF NAPA
Also Called: Health Department
2261 Elm St, NAPA (94559-3721)
PHONE..................................707 253-4461
Bruce Heid, *Manager*
EMP: 260 Privately Held
WEB: www.billkeller.com
SIC: 8093 9111 Specialty outpatient clinics; county supervisors' & executives' offices
PA: County Of Napa
1195 Third St Ste 310
Napa CA 94559
707 253-4421

(P-22004)
COUNTY OF PLACER
Also Called: Health & Human Services
3091 County Center Dr # 100, Auburn (95603-2610)
PHONE..................................530 889-7215
Robert Long, *Systems Mgr*
Mark Rideout, *Architect*
EMP: 75 Privately Held
WEB: www.ssvems.com

SIC: 8093 9431 Specialty outpatient clinics; administration of public health programs;
PA: County Of Placer
2986 Richardson Dr
Auburn CA 95603
530 889-4200

(P-22005)
COUNTY OF SAN JOAQUIN
Also Called: Mental Health Services
1212 N California St, Stockton (95202-1552)
PHONE..................................209 468-8750
Bruce Hopperstead, *Principal*
Tony Vartan, *Director*
EMP: 300 Privately Held
WEB: www.sjclawlib.org
SIC: 8093 9111 8361 Mental health clinic, outpatient; county supervisors' & executives' offices; residential care
PA: County Of San Joaquin
44 N San Joaquin St # 640
Stockton CA 95202
209 468-3203

(P-22006)
COUNTY OF SAN LUIS OBISPO
Also Called: Community Mental Health Svcs
2178 Johnson Ave, San Luis Obispo (93401-4535)
PHONE..................................805 781-4700
Tom Omalley, *Principal*
Wilaim Boorman, *Psychologist*
Azarm Ghareman, *Psychologist*
Carolyn Murphy, *Psychologist*
Josefina Ouano, *Psychiatry*
EMP: 250 Privately Held
SIC: 8093 Mental health clinic, outpatient
PA: County Of San Luis Obispo
Government Center Rm. 300
San Luis Obispo CA 93408
805 781-5040

(P-22007)
COUNTY OF SAN MATEO
Also Called: Health System
150 W 20th Ave, San Mateo (94403-1341)
PHONE..................................650 372-8540
Sonia Celmira Lucana, *Principal*
EMP: 100 Privately Held
WEB: www.ci.sanmateo.ca.us
SIC: 8093 9431 Mental health clinic, outpatient;
PA: County Of San Mateo
400 County Ctr
Redwood City CA 94063
650 363-4123

(P-22008)
COUNTY OF SANTA BARBARA ALCOHO
Also Called: Admhs
300 N San Antonio Rd, Santa Barbara (93110-1316)
PHONE..................................805 681-4093
Al Rodriguez, *Principal*
EMP: 90
SALES (est): 2.2MM Privately Held
SIC: 8093 Alcohol clinic, outpatient

(P-22009)
COUNTY OF SISKIYOU
Also Called: Behavioral Health Services
1107 Ream Ave, Mount Shasta (96067-9768)
PHONE..................................530 918-7200
Hap Stemm, *Manager*
Leslie Zane, *QC Mgr*
EMP: 60 Privately Held
WEB: www.siskiyoucounty.org
SIC: 8093 9111 Mental health clinic, outpatient; county supervisors' & executives' offices
PA: County Of Siskiyou
311 4th St Rm 108
Yreka CA 96097
530 841-4100

(P-22010)
COUNTY OF STANISLAUS
Also Called: Stanisluas County Mental Hlth
800 Scenic Dr Bldg B, Modesto (95350-6131)
PHONE..................................209 525-7423
Dennise Han, *Director*

EMP: 200 Privately Held
WEB: www.co.stanislaus.ca.us
SIC: 8093 Specialty outpatient clinics
PA: County Of Stanislaus
1010 10th St Ste 5100
Modesto CA 95354
209 525-6398

(P-22011)
COUNTY OF SUTTER
Also Called: Sutter Yuba Mental Health Svcs
1965 Live Oak Blvd Ste B, Yuba City (95991-8850)
P.O. Box 1520 (95992-1520)
PHONE..................................530 822-7250
Joann Hoss, *Director*
Karin Phagura, *Manager*
EMP: 200 Privately Held
WEB: www.co.yuba.ca.us
SIC: 8093 9431 Mental health clinic, outpatient; mental health agency administration, government;
PA: County Of Sutter
1160 Civic Center Blvd A
Yuba City CA 95993
530 822-7100

(P-22012)
COUNTY OF YOLO
Also Called: Dept of Mental Health
137 N Cottonwood St # 2400, Woodland (95695-6682)
PHONE..................................530 666-8630
Kim Suderman, *Director*
EMP: 80 Privately Held
WEB: www.yctd.org
SIC: 8093 9111 Mental health clinic, outpatient; county supervisors' & executives' offices
PA: County Of Yolo
625 Court St Ste 102
Woodland CA 95695
530 666-8114

(P-22013)
CRASH INC SHORT TERM I
4161 Marlborough Ave, San Diego (92105-1412)
PHONE..................................619 282-7274
Sue Dolby, *Exec Dir*
EMP: 50
SALES (est): 869.7K Privately Held
SIC: 8093 Substance abuse clinics (outpatient)

(P-22014)
CRC HEALTH CORPORATE
Also Called: Recovery Solutions Santa Ana
2101 E 1st St, Santa Ana (92705-4007)
PHONE..................................714 542-3581
Tfu Bach Tran, *Manager*
EMP: 60 Publicly Held
SIC: 8093 Drug clinic, outpatient
HQ: Crc Health Corporate
20400 Stevens
Cupertino CA 95014
408 367-0044

(P-22015)
CRC HEALTH CORPORATE (DH)
Also Called: Willamette Valley Trtmnt Ctr
20400 Stevens, Cupertino (95014)
PHONE..................................408 367-0044
R Andrew Eckert, *CEO*
Kevin Hogge, *CFO*
Gary Fisher, *Chief Mktg Ofcr*
Pamela B Burke, *Vice Pres*
James Hudak, *Vice Pres*
EMP: 60
SALES (est): 55.7MM Publicly Held
SIC: 8093 Substance abuse clinics (outpatient)
HQ: Crc Health Llc
20400 Stevens Creek Blvd # 600
Cupertino CA 95014
877 272-8668

(P-22016)
DEL AMO DIAGNOSTIC CENTER
Also Called: Little Mary Amblatory Care Ctr
5215 Torrance Blvd, Torrance (90503-4009)
PHONE..................................310 316-2424
Steve Magennis, *Director*
EMP: 50

SALES (est): 3MM Privately Held
SIC: 8093 8011 Specialty outpatient clinics; clinic, operated by physicians

(P-22017)
DEVEREUX FOUNDATION
Also Called: Devereux California Center
7055 Seaway Dr, Goleta (93117-4358)
P.O. Box 6784, Santa Barbara (93160-6784)
PHONE..................................805 968-2525
Amy Evans, *Principal*
Veronica Arenas, *Human Res Mgr*
EMP: 400
SALES (corp-wide): 460.5MM Privately Held
SIC: 8093 Mental health clinic, outpatient
PA: Devereux Foundation
444 Devereux Dr
Villanova PA 19085
610 520-3000

(P-22018)
DRUG & ALCOHOL SERVICES OF
2180 Johnson Ave Ste A, San Luis Obispo (93401-4558)
PHONE..................................805 781-4275
Paul Hyman, *Director*
Jeff Hamm, *Director*
EMP: 80
SALES (est): 1.6MM Privately Held
SIC: 8093 Rehabilitation center, outpatient treatment

(P-22019)
DRUG ABUSE ALTERNATIVES CENTER
Also Called: Redwood Empire Addctons Prgram
2403 Prof Dr Ste 103, Santa Rosa (95403)
PHONE..................................707 571-2233
Sushana Taylor, *President*
EMP: 50
SALES (corp-wide): 5.9MM Privately Held
WEB: www.daacinfo.org
SIC: 8093 Drug clinic, outpatient
PA: Drug Abuse Alternatives Center
2403 Prof Dr Ste 102
Santa Rosa CA 95403
707 544-3295

(P-22020)
DUAL DIAGNOSIS TRTMNT CTR INC (PA)
Also Called: Sovereign Health of California
1211 Puerta Del Sol # 200, San Clemente (92673-6342)
PHONE..................................949 276-5553
Tonmoy Sharma, *CEO*
Rishi Barkataki, *President*
Nidhi Grover, *Executive*
Lise Stevens, *Comms Mgr*
Harkirat Singh, *Finance*
EMP: 139
SALES (est): 68.5MM Privately Held
SIC: 8093 Mental health clinic, outpatient

(P-22021)
DUAL DIAGNOSIS TRTMNT CTR INC
6167 Bristol Pkwy, Culver City (90230-6610)
PHONE..................................424 207-2220
Marissa Maldonado, *Branch Mgr*
EMP: 160
SALES (corp-wide): 68.5MM Privately Held
SIC: 8093 Mental health clinic, outpatient
PA: Dual Diagnosis Treatment Center, Inc.
1211 Puerta Del Sol # 200
San Clemente CA 92673
949 276-5553

(P-22022)
EAST LOS ANGELES MENTAL HLTH
1436 Goodrich Blvd, Commerce (90022-5111)
PHONE..................................323 725-1337
Alfredo Lavios, *President*
Rod Shaner, *Director*
EMP: 60

SALES (est): 895.8K **Privately Held**
SIC: 8093 Mental health clinic, outpatient

(P-22023)
EAST VALLEY CMNTY HLTH CTR INC (PA)
420 S Glendora Ave, West Covina (91790-3001)
PHONE..................................626 919-3402
Alicia Mardini, *CEO*
Sophia Shavira, *Ch of Bd*
Alicia Thomas, *CEO*
Vanessa Cuevas, *Purchasing*
EMP: 65
SQ FT: 24,000
SALES: 22.3MM **Privately Held**
SIC: 8093 Family planning clinic

(P-22024)
ELEMENTS BEHAVIORAL HEALTH INC (PA)
5000 Arprt Plz Dr Ste 100, Long Beach (90815)
PHONE..................................562 741-6470
David Sack, *CEO*
Rob Mahan, *CFO*
Keith Arnold, *Exec VP*
Kathleen Burkett, *Vice Pres*
Stuart Chew, *Vice Pres*
EMP: 116
SALES (est): 66.4MM **Privately Held**
SIC: 8093 8049 Substance abuse clinics (outpatient); nutrition specialist

(P-22025)
ENCOMPASS HEALTH CORPORATION
Also Called: HealthSouth
14851 Yorba St, Tustin (92780-2925)
PHONE..................................714 832-9200
Cathline Smith, *Branch Mgr*
Ladonna Butler, *Ch Nursing Ofcr*
EMP: 200
SALES (corp-wide): 4.2B **Publicly Held**
WEB: www.healthsouth.com
SIC: 8093 Rehabilitation center, outpatient treatment
PA: Encompass Health Corporation
9001 Liberty Pkwy
Birmingham AL 35242
205 967-7116

(P-22026)
EXODUS RECOVERY INC (PA)
9808 Venice Blvd Ste 700, Culver City (90232-6824)
PHONE..................................310 945-3350
Luana Murphy, *President*
Leeann Skorohod, *President*
Lezlie Murch, *Senior VP*
Grace Lee, *Vice Pres*
Kathy Shoemaker, *Vice Pres*
EMP: 84
SALES: 4MM **Privately Held**
SIC: 8093 Mental health clinic, outpatient

(P-22027)
FAMILY HLTH CTRS SAN DIEGO INC (PA)
823 Gateway Center Way, San Diego (92102-4541)
PHONE..................................619 515-2303
Fran Butler-Cohen, *President*
Donna Baker, *Vice Pres*
Ruth Cowan, *Office Mgr*
SAI Vulchi, *Business Anlyst*
Omar Somo, *Technology*
EMP: 65 EST: 1972
SQ FT: 32,000
SALES: 147.1MM **Privately Held**
SIC: 8093 Mental health clinic, outpatient

(P-22028)
FAMILY PATHS INC (PA)
Also Called: CHILD ABUSE PREVENTION
1727 M L King Jr Way, Oakland (94612-1327)
PHONE..................................510 893-9230
Lyda Mata, *CFO*
Debbi Sack, *Human Resources*
Denise Jones-Kazan, *Mktg Dir*
Joanne Ruby, *Marketing Staff*
Araceli Varela, *Internal Med*
EMP: 70
SQ FT: 2,300

SALES: 5.6MM **Privately Held**
WEB: www.psshelps.org
SIC: 8093 Mental health clinic, outpatient

(P-22029)
GENESIS HEALTHCARE PARTNERS PC
Also Called: Integrated Medical Specialists
2466 1st Ave Ste B, San Diego (92101-1480)
P.O. Box 33865 (92163-3865)
PHONE..................................619 230-0400
Edward S Cohen, *CEO*
EMP: 113
SALES (corp-wide): 13.3MM **Privately Held**
SIC: 8093 Specialty outpatient clinics
PA: Genesis Healthcare Partners, P.C.
3444 Kearny Villa Rd
San Diego CA 92123
858 810-7200

(P-22030)
GENESIS HEALTHCARE PARTNERS PC (PA)
3444 Kearny Villa Rd, San Diego (92123-1959)
P.O. Box 33865 (92163-3865)
PHONE..................................858 810-7200
Edward Cohen, *CEO*
Kellie Golshan, *CFO*
Monica Vanderwerf, *Administration*
David Cho, *Technology*
Don Counts, *Accounting Mgr*
EMP: 175
SQ FT: 15,000
SALES (est): 13.3MM **Privately Held**
SIC: 8093 Rehabilitation center, outpatient treatment

(P-22031)
GHC OF LOMPOC LLC
Also Called: Lompoc Skilled Nursing & Rehab
1428 W North Ave, Lompoc (93436-3961)
PHONE..................................805 735-4010
Thomas Olds,
Lois Mastrocola,
EMP: 250
SALES (est): 8.1MM
SALES (corp-wide): 63.1MM **Privately Held**
SIC: 8093 Rehabilitation center, outpatient treatment
PA: Life Generations Healthcare Llc
6 Hutton Cntre Dr Ste 400
Santa Ana CA 92707
714 241-5600

(P-22032)
GOLDEN VALLEY HEALTH CENTERS (PA)
737 W Childs Ave, Merced (95341-6805)
PHONE..................................209 383-1848
Tony Weber, *CEO*
Rebecca Cabrera-Reyes, *President*
Lue Thao, *CFO*
Michael Buda, *Officer*
M Henson, *Officer*
EMP: 850
SQ FT: 23,000
SALES: 107.4MM **Privately Held**
SIC: 8093 Specialty outpatient clinics

(P-22033)
GOLDEN VALLEY HEALTH CENTERS
Also Called: Women's Health Center
797 W Childs Ave, Merced (95341-6805)
PHONE..................................209 383-5871
Pierre Scales, *Branch Mgr*
George Alkhouri, *Med Doctor*
EMP: 100
SALES (corp-wide): 107.4MM **Privately Held**
SIC: 8093 8011 Specialty outpatient clinics; clinic, operated by physicians
PA: Golden Valley Health Centers
737 W Childs Ave
Merced CA 95341
209 383-1848

(P-22034)
GREATER SACRAMENTO SUR
Also Called: Greater Sacramento Surgery Ctr
2288 Auburn Blvd Ste 201, Sacramento (95821-1620)
PHONE..................................916 929-7229
Marvin Kamras, *Partner*
EMP: 60
SQ FT: 15,000
SALES (est): 7.6MM **Privately Held**
SIC: 8093 8011 Specialty outpatient clinics; ambulatory surgical center

(P-22035)
GREATER VALLEY MEDICAL GROUP (PA)
11600 Indian Hills Rd # 300, Mission Hills (91345-1225)
PHONE..................................818 838-4500
Don Rebhun MD, *President*
Howard Sawyer MD, *Corp Secy*
Mohyi Soleiman MD, *Vice Pres*
Donald Rebhun, *Med Doctor*
EMP: 255
SALES (est): 6.2MM **Privately Held**
SIC: 8093 Specialty outpatient clinics

(P-22036)
GUARDIAN HEALTH CARE SERVICES
Also Called: D'Amore Healthcare
16541 Gothard St Ste 102, Huntington Beach (92647-4472)
PHONE..................................714 375-1110
Britten Devereux, *CEO*
EMP: 75
SALES (est): 270.5K **Privately Held**
SIC: 8093 Detoxification center, outpatient

(P-22037)
GUIDANCE CENTER (PA)
1301 Pine Ave, Long Beach (90813-3124)
PHONE..................................562 595-1159
David Stotler, *President*
Geneses Davis, *Comms Mgr*
Kristen Martin, *Program Mgr*
Flaviola Gonzalez, *Executive Asst*
Rev Paul Lance, *Admin Sec*
EMP: 125
SQ FT: 11,000
SALES: 16.9MM **Privately Held**
WEB: www.tcgclb.org
SIC: 8093 8322 Mental health clinic, outpatient; child related social services

(P-22038)
HEALTHFIRST MEDICAL GROUP INC (PA)
13440 Imperial Hwy, Santa Fe Springs (90670-4820)
PHONE..................................562 949-9328
Ronald Crowell, *President*
Les Phillips, *Personnel*
Gregory O D, *Med Doctor*
Robin Collier, *Assistant*
EMP: 50
SALES (est): 4.5MM **Privately Held**
SIC: 8093 Rehabilitation center, outpatient treatment

(P-22039)
HELP GROUP WEST (PA)
13130 Burbank Blvd, Sherman Oaks (91401-6000)
PHONE..................................818 781-0360
Barbara Firestone, *President*
Michael Love, *CFO*
Susan Berman PH, *Exec VP*
EMP: 200
SQ FT: 100,000
SALES: 19.3MM **Privately Held**
SIC: 8093 Speech defect clinic

(P-22040)
HENRIETTA WEILL MEMORIAL CHILD (PA)
3628 Stockdale Hwy, Bakersfield (93309-2153)
PHONE..................................661 322-1021
Blake Smith, *President*
Lindsey West, *Treasurer*
Candy Coats, *Executive*
David Camara, *Exec Dir*
Marcie Lesser, *Program Mgr*
EMP: 70

SQ FT: 16,000
SALES: 7.3MM **Privately Held**
SIC: 8093 Mental health clinic, outpatient

(P-22041)
HILLVIEW MENTAL HEALTH CENTER
12450 Van Nuys Blvd # 200, Pacoima (91331-1391)
PHONE..................................818 896-1161
Eva S McCraven, *President*
Carl C Mc Craven, *Treasurer*
Julie E Jones, *Vice Pres*
Beth K Meltzer, *Vice Pres*
Myron Cohen, *Admin Sec*
EMP: 80
SQ FT: 17,600
SALES: 10.8MM **Privately Held**
SIC: 8093 Mental health clinic, outpatient

(P-22042)
HOLLYWOOD MENTAL HEALTH CENTER
1224 Vine St, Los Angeles (90038-1612)
PHONE..................................323 769-6100
Barbara Engleman, *President*
EMP: 65
SALES (est): 1.8MM **Privately Held**
SIC: 8093 Mental health clinic, outpatient

(P-22043)
HOPE OF VALLEY MISSION
19379 Soledad Canyon Rd, Santa Clarita (91351-2630)
PHONE..................................661 673-5951
EMP: 50
SALES (est): 351.7K **Privately Held**
SIC: 8093 Rehabilitation center, outpatient treatment

(P-22044)
I P S SERVICES INC
627 E Foothill Blvd, San Dimas (91773-1208)
PHONE..................................909 305-0250
Robert Hernandez, *CEO*
David Nickel, *Shareholder*
EMP: 60
SALES (est): 4.3MM **Privately Held**
SIC: 8093 Mental health clinic, outpatient

(P-22045)
IMPERIAL COUNTY BEHAVIORAL HLT
2695 S 4th St, El Centro (92243-6012)
PHONE..................................760 482-2149
Michael Horn, *Director*
Mary Esquer, *Program Mgr*
Franciso Ortiz, *Senior Mgr*
EMP: 50
SALES (est): 738.6K **Privately Held**
SIC: 8093 Substance abuse clinics (outpatient); mental health clinic, outpatient

(P-22046)
INTERSTATE RHBLTATION SVCS LLC
333 E Glenoaks Blvd # 204, Glendale (91207-2074)
PHONE..................................818 244-5656
James Pietsch, *Owner*
Beth Cera-Celo,
Sandy Pietsch,
EMP: 120
SALES (est): 4.2MM **Privately Held**
WEB: www.interstaterehab.com
SIC: 8093 Rehabilitation center, outpatient treatment

(P-22047)
KAISER FOUNDATION HOSPITALS
Also Called: Kaiser Permanente
710 S Broadway, Walnut Creek (94596-5294)
PHONE..................................925 295-4145
Vikki Antonelli, *Manager*
Katrina Domingo, *Psychologist*
Ryan E Kolakoski, *Psychologist*
Rebecca Partridge, *Psychologist*
EMP: 793
SALES (corp-wide): 76.5B **Privately Held**
WEB: www.kaiserpermanente.org
SIC: 8093 Mental health clinic, outpatient

HQ: Kaiser Foundation Hospitals Inc
1 Kaiser Plz
Oakland CA 94612
510 271-6611

(P-22048)
KAISER FOUNDATION HOSPITALS
Also Called: Oak Street Physical Therapy
2040 Pacific Coast Hwy, Lomita
(90717-2660)
PHONE....................................424 251-7000
EMP: 192
SALES (corp-wide): 76.5B **Privately Held**
SIC: 8093 Rehabilitation center, outpatient treatment
HQ: Kaiser Foundation Hospitals Inc
1 Kaiser Plz
Oakland CA 94612
510 271-6611

(P-22049)
KAISER FOUNDATION HOSPITALS
Also Called: Positive Choice Wellness Ctr
7035 Convoy Ct, San Diego (92111-1016)
PHONE....................................858 573-0090
Joe Anderson, *Manager*
EMP: 192
SALES (corp-wide): 76.5B **Privately Held**
SIC: 8093 Weight loss clinic, with medical staff
HQ: Kaiser Foundation Hospitals Inc
1 Kaiser Plz
Oakland CA 94612
510 271-6611

(P-22050)
KAISER FOUNDATION HOSPITALS
Also Called: Health Educatn Psychiatry Offs
5105 W Goldleaf Cir, Los Angeles
(90056-1269)
PHONE....................................323 298-3300
Natasha Elliott, *Branch Mgr*
EMP: 200
SALES (corp-wide): 76.5B **Privately Held**
SIC: 8093 Specialty outpatient clinics
HQ: Kaiser Foundation Hospitals Inc
1 Kaiser Plz
Oakland CA 94612
510 271-6611

(P-22051)
KAISER FOUNDATION HOSPITALS
Also Called: Kaiser Permanente
3400 Delta Fair Blvd, Antioch (94509-4004)
PHONE....................................925 779-5000
Dan Sonnier, *Manager*
Ram Thamburaj, *Project Mgr*
Gulshan S Panjwani, *Internal Med*
Carl Ng, *Podiatrist*
Vickrum Chodri, *Med Doctor*
EMP: 200
SQ FT: 47,307
SALES (corp-wide): 76.5B **Privately Held**
WEB: www.kaiserpermanente.org
SIC: 8093 8011 8062 Specialty outpatient clinics; general & family practice, physician/surgeon; general medical & surgical hospitals
HQ: Kaiser Foundation Hospitals Inc
1 Kaiser Plz
Oakland CA 94612
510 271-6611

(P-22052)
KAISER FOUNDATION HOSPITALS
Also Called: Kaiser Permanente
23621 Main St, Carson (90745-5743)
PHONE....................................310 513-6707
Lora Griffin, *Branch Mgr*
Ann La Fever, *Executive*
EMP: 60
SALES (corp-wide): 76.5B **Privately Held**
WEB: www.kaiserpermanente.org
SIC: 8093 8062 Specialty outpatient clinics; general medical & surgical hospitals
HQ: Kaiser Foundation Hospitals Inc
1 Kaiser Plz
Oakland CA 94612
510 271-6611

(P-22053)
KEITH T KUSUNIS MD
Also Called: Family Health Center
91767 N Orange Grv Ave, Pomona (91767)
PHONE....................................909 469-9494
Keith T Kusunas, *Principal*
Keith T Kusunis, *President*
EMP: 65
SALES (est): 627.6K **Privately Held**
SIC: 8093 Family planning clinic

(P-22054)
KIMA W MEDICAL CENTER
535 Airport Rd, Hoopa (95546-9615)
P.O. Box 1288 (95546-1288)
PHONE....................................530 625-4114
Emmit Chase, *CEO*
Dennis Jones, *COO*
EMP: 80
SQ FT: 11,000
SALES: 6.5MM **Privately Held**
SIC: 8093 8399 Specialty outpatient clinics; health systems agency

(P-22055)
KINDRED NURSING CENTERS W LLC
Also Called: Kindred Transitional Care
1359 Pine St, San Francisco (94109-4807)
PHONE....................................415 673-8405
Joseph L Landenwich,
Richard E Chapman,
EMP: 200
SALES (est): 269.4K
SALES (corp-wide): 6B **Privately Held**
SIC: 8093 Rehabilitation center, outpatient treatment
HQ: Kindred Healthcare Operating, Llc
680 S 4th St
Louisville KY 40202
502 596-7300

(P-22056)
KINGS VIEW
Also Called: Mental Hlth Svcs For Kngs Cnty
289 E 8th St, Hanford (93230-3935)
PHONE....................................559 582-9307
Brenda Johnson Hill, *Principal*
EMP: 100
SALES (corp-wide): 26.8MM **Privately Held**
SIC: 8093 Mental health clinic, outpatient
PA: Kings View
7170 N Fincl Dr Ste 110
Fresno CA 93720
559 256-0100

(P-22057)
KINGSVIEW CORP
Also Called: Tuolomne Cnty Bhvrl Hlth
2 S Green St, Sonora (95370-4618)
PHONE....................................209 533-6245
Jack Tanebaum, *Exec Dir*
EMP: 63
SALES (est): 846.5K **Privately Held**
SIC: 8093 Mental health clinic, outpatient

(P-22058)
LEARNING SERVICES CORPORATION
2335 Bear Valley Pkwy, Escondido
(92027-3854)
PHONE....................................760 746-3223
Sharon Brown, *Manager*
EMP: 50
SALES (corp-wide): 17.9MM **Privately Held**
WEB: www.learningservices.com
SIC: 8093 Rehabilitation center, outpatient treatment
PA: Learning Services Corporation
131 Langley Dr Ste B
Lawrenceville GA 30046
470 235-4700

(P-22059)
LEARNING SERVICES CORPORATION
Also Called: Learning Services Northern Cal
10855 De Bruin Way, Gilroy (95020-9315)
PHONE....................................408 848-4379
Kayree Fhreeve, *Director*
EMP: 50

SALES (corp-wide): 17.9MM **Privately Held**
WEB: www.learningservices.com
SIC: 8093 Rehabilitation center, outpatient treatment
PA: Learning Services Corporation
131 Langley Dr Ste B
Lawrenceville GA 30046
470 235-4700

(P-22060)
LINCOLN (PA)
1266 14th St, Oakland (94607-2247)
PHONE....................................510 273-4700
Nancy L Oakley, *COO*
Enrico Hernandez, *CFO*
Rico Hernandez, *CFO*
Allison Becwar, *Principal*
Jessica Rojas, *Program Mgr*
EMP: 75
SQ FT: 40,000
SALES: 17.3MM **Privately Held**
WEB: www.lincolncc.org
SIC: 8093 8361 8049 Mental health clinic, outpatient; orphanage; psychiatric social worker

(P-22061)
LOS ANGELES UNIFIED SCHOOL DST
Also Called: Mental Health Dept
6651 Balboa Blvd, Van Nuys (91406-5586)
PHONE....................................818 997-2640
Gil Palacio, *Director*
EMP: 300
SALES (corp-wide): 4B **Privately Held**
WEB: www.lausd.k12.ca.us
SIC: 8093 Mental health clinic, outpatient
PA: Los Angeles Unified School District
333 S Beaudry Ave Ste 209
Los Angeles CA 90017
213 241-1000

(P-22062)
MADERA CNTY BHVIORAL HLTH SVCS
209 E 7th St, Madera (93638-3780)
P.O. Box 1288 (93639-1288)
PHONE....................................559 673-3508
Dennis Koch, *President*
Steve Duckworth, *Program Mgr*
EMP: 126 **EST:** 2010
SQ FT: 25,000
SALES: 17MM **Privately Held**
SIC: 8093 Specialty outpatient clinics

(P-22063)
MCALISTER INST FOR TRTMNT EDCA (PA)
1400 N Johnson Ave # 101, El Cajon
(92020-1650)
PHONE....................................619 442-0277
Jeanne Mc Alister, *President*
Steve Hubbard, *Vice Pres*
EMP: 130
SQ FT: 9,000
SALES: 17.9MM **Privately Held**
WEB: www.mcalisterinstitute.org
SIC: 8093 Drug clinic, outpatient

(P-22064)
MCALISTER INSTITUTE FOR TREAT
3923 Waring Rd, Oceanside (92056-4457)
PHONE....................................760 726-4451
EMP: 59
SALES (corp-wide): 17.9MM **Privately Held**
SIC: 8093 Drug clinic, outpatient
PA: Mcalister Institute For Treatment & Education, Inc.
1400 N Johnson Ave # 101
El Cajon CA 92020
619 442-0277

(P-22065)
MENDOCINO COAST CLINICS INC
205 South St, Fort Bragg (95437-5540)
PHONE....................................707 964-1251
Paula Cohen, *Exec Dir*
Jeff Warner, *Chairman*
Richard Moon, *Treasurer*
Claudia Boudreau, *Admin Sec*
Stacy Pollina-Millen, *Purchasing*

▲ EMP: 93
SQ FT: 5,000
SALES: 11.7MM **Privately Held**
WEB: www.mendocinocoastclinics.org
SIC: 8093 Family planning & birth control clinics

(P-22066)
MENTAL HEALTH SYSTEMS INC (PA)
Also Called: MHS
9465 Farnham St, San Diego
(92123-1308)
PHONE....................................858 573-2600
Kimberly Bond, *CEO*
Michael Hawkey, *Senior VP*
Ron Stark, *Vice Pres*
Kay Masaryk, *Program Mgr*
Yvette Lebron, *Office Mgr*
EMP: 70
SQ FT: 18,000
SALES (est): 85MM **Privately Held**
WEB: www.mhsinc.org
SIC: 8093 Mental health clinic, outpatient

(P-22067)
MFI RECOVERY CENTER (PA)
5870 Arlington Ave # 103, Riverside
(92504-2037)
PHONE....................................951 683-6596
Craig Lamdon, *Exec Dir*
EMP: 125
SQ FT: 864
SALES: 11MM **Privately Held**
WEB: www.mfirecovery.com
SIC: 8093 8322 Alcohol clinic, outpatient; family counseling services

(P-22068)
NATIONAL THERAPEUTIC SVCS INC (PA)
Also Called: Northbound Treatment Services
3822 Campus Dr Ste 100, Newport Beach
(92660-2636)
PHONE....................................866 311-0003
Michael Neatherton, *President*
Paul Alexander, *COO*
Devon Wayt, *COO*
Ray Pacini, *CFO*
Heather Fotion, *Program Mgr*
EMP: 99
SALES (est): 12.8MM **Privately Held**
SIC: 8093 Alcohol clinic, outpatient

(P-22069)
NATIONL MEDCL ASSN COMP HEALTH
3177 Ocean View Blvd, San Diego
(92113-1432)
PHONE....................................619 231-9300
Shirleen Freeman, *Director*
Jeffrey Morgan, *Pediatrics*
Eliseo Macias, *Director*
EMP: 60
SALES (corp-wide): 3.7MM **Privately Held**
WEB: www.nmasandiego.org
SIC: 8093 Specialty outpatient clinics
PA: National Medical Association Comprehensive Health Center
1601 Precision Park Ln
San Ysidro CA

(P-22070)
NEVADA COUNTY BEHAVIORAL HLTH
500 Crown Point Cir # 120, Grass Valley
(95945-9561)
PHONE....................................530 265-1450
Michael Heggarty, *Director*
Carol Smith, *Admin Asst*
EMP: 50
SQ FT: 22,168
SALES (est): 2.3MM **Privately Held**
SIC: 8093 Mental health clinic, outpatient

(P-22071)
OPEN DOOR COMMUNITY HLTH CTRS
Also Called: Humboldt Open Door Clinic
770 10th St, Arcata (95521-6210)
PHONE....................................707 826-8610
Hermann Spetzler, *Branch Mgr*
EMP: 72 **Privately Held**

PRODUCTS & SVCS

WEB: www.opendoorhealth.com
SIC: 8093 8011 Smoking clinic; offices & clinics of medical doctors
PA: Open Door Community Health Centers
670 9th St Ste 203cfo
Arcata CA 95521

(P-22072)
OPEN DOOR COMMUNITY HLTH CTRS (PA)
670 9th St Ste 203cfo, Arcata (95521-6248)
PHONE....................707 826-8642
Sydney Fisher Larsen, *CEO*
Erik Salholm, *Comms Mgr*
Christina Boone, *Admin Asst*
Laura Gower, *Accountant*
Natasha Wood, *Controller*
EMP: 70
SQ FT: 18,000
SALES (est): 51.7MM **Privately Held**
WEB: www.opendoorhealth.com
SIC: 8093 Smoking clinic

(P-22073)
OPTIONS FAMILY OF SERVICES
5755 Valentina Ave, Atascadero (93422-3532)
PHONE....................805 462-8544
EMP: 50
SQ FT: 576
SALES (corp-wide): 5.6MM **Privately Held**
SIC: 8093
PA: Options Family Of Services, Inc
800 Quintana Rd Ste 2c
Morro Bay CA 93442
805 772-6066

(P-22074)
OPYA INC
1720 S Amphlett Blvd # 110, San Mateo (94402-2702)
PHONE....................650 931-6300
Jonathan Wright, *CEO*
Keiko Ikeda, *COO*
Suchi Deshpande, *Vice Pres*
EMP: 55 **EST:** 2017
SALES (est): 79.7K **Privately Held**
SIC: 8093 8049 7371 Specialty outpatient clinics; speech therapist; computer software development & applications

(P-22075)
ORENDA CENTER
1430 Neotomas Ave, Santa Rosa (95405-7575)
PHONE....................707 565-7450
Diane Madrigal, *Director*
EMP: 60
SALES (est): 873.5K **Privately Held**
SIC: 8093 Rehabilitation center, outpatient treatment

(P-22076)
PACIFIC CLINICS
11721 Telegraph Rd Ste A, Santa Fe Springs (90670-6835)
PHONE....................562 949-8455
Sharon Corey, *Director*
EMP: 65
SALES (corp-wide): 82.2MM **Privately Held**
SIC: 8093 Mental health clinic, outpatient
PA: Pacific Clinics Foundation.
800 S Santa Anita Ave
Arcadia CA 91006
626 254-5000

(P-22077)
PACIFIC FRNSIC PSYCHLGY ASSOC
9261 Folsom Blvd Ste 300, Sacramento (95826-2559)
PHONE....................925 253-3111
Tom Tobin, *CEO*
EMP: 75
SALES (est): 520.7K **Privately Held**
SIC: 8093 Mental health clinic, outpatient

(P-22078)
PARAGON HEALTH & REHAB CT
1090 E Dinuba Ave, Reedley (93654-3577)
PHONE....................559 638-3578
EMP: 50 **EST:** 2005

SALES (est): 2.3MM **Privately Held**
SIC: 8093

(P-22079)
PARENTHOOD OF PLANNED
1140 Sonoma Ave Ste 3, Santa Rosa (95405-4817)
PHONE....................707 527-7656
EMP: 51
SALES (corp-wide): 63.3MM **Privately Held**
SIC: 8093 Family planning & birth control clinics
PA: Planned Parenthood Of San Diego And Riverside Counties
1075 Camino Del Rio S # 100
San Diego CA 92108
619 881-4500

(P-22080)
PARENTHOOD OF PLANNED (PA)
1075 Camino Del Rio S # 100, San Diego (92108-3539)
PHONE....................619 881-4500
Darrah Johnson, *CEO*
Len Dodson, *CFO*
Melvin Galloway, *Exec VP*
Rebecca Karpinski, *Vice Pres*
Cita Walsh, *Vice Pres*
EMP: 100
SQ FT: 24,000
SALES: 63.3MM **Privately Held**
WEB: www.planned.org
SIC: 8093 Family planning clinic; family planning & birth control clinics

(P-22081)
PARENTHOOD OF PLANNED
12900 Frederick St Ste C, Moreno Valley (92553-5266)
PHONE....................951 222-3101
Theresa Gonzales, *Director*
EMP: 61
SALES (corp-wide): 63.3MM **Privately Held**
SIC: 8093 Family planning & birth control clinics
PA: Planned Parenthood Of San Diego And Riverside Counties
1075 Camino Del Rio S # 100
San Diego CA 92108
619 881-4500

(P-22082)
PARENTHOOD OF PLANNED
2935 Bechelli Ln, Redding (96002-1905)
PHONE....................530 351-7100
EMP: 51
SALES (corp-wide): 63.3MM **Privately Held**
SIC: 8093 Family planning clinic
PA: Planned Parenthood Of San Diego And Riverside Counties
1075 Camino Del Rio S # 100
San Diego CA 92108
619 881-4500

(P-22083)
PASADENA CHILD DEV ASSOC INC
620 N Lake Ave, Pasadena (91101-1220)
PHONE....................626 793-7350
Diane Cullinane MD, *Principal*
Claudia Salinas, *Finance Asst*
Julia Scheibmeir, *Director*
EMP: 80
SALES: 4.4MM **Privately Held**
SIC: 8093 Mental health clinic, outpatient

(P-22084)
PATHWAY SOCIETY
102 S 11th St, San Jose (95112-2132)
PHONE....................408 244-1834
Joanne Buckley, *Exec Dir*
EMP: 50
SALES (corp-wide): 8MM **Privately Held**
WEB: www.pathwayinc.com
SIC: 8093 Drug clinic, outpatient; rehabilitation center, outpatient treatment
PA: Pathway Society, Inc.
1659 Scott Blvd Ste 210
Santa Clara CA 95050
408 244-1834

(P-22085)
PEDIATRIC & FAMILY MEDICAL CTR
Also Called: Eisner Pediatric Fmly Med Ctr
1530 S Olive St, Los Angeles (90015-3023)
PHONE....................213 342-3325
Carl Coan, *CEO*
Edward Matthews III, *Ch of Bd*
Kevin Rossi, *Ch of Bd*
Herb Schultz, *President*
Carl Edward Coan, *CEO*
EMP: 160
SQ FT: 21,000
SALES: 25.4MM **Privately Held**
SIC: 8093 Specialty outpatient clinics

(P-22086)
PEDIATRIC PHYSICAL REHAB CLNC
Also Called: Physical/Occupational Therapy
9300 Valley Childrens Pl, Madera (93636-8761)
PHONE....................559 353-6130
Carol Kurushima, *Manager*
EMP: 50 **EST:** 1999
SALES (est): 1.8MM **Privately Held**
SIC: 8093 Rehabilitation center, outpatient treatment

(P-22087)
PEDIATRIC THERAPY NETWORK
1815 W 213th St Ste 100, Torrance (90501-2852)
PHONE....................310 328-0276
Zoe Mailloux, *Exec Dir*
Tom Gosney, *CFO*
Gloria Gonzalez-Karch, *General Mgr*
Kelly Peterson, *CTO*
Kemi Akinwale, *
EMP: 100
SQ FT: 20,000
SALES: 10.7MM **Privately Held**
WEB: www.pediatrictherapy.com
SIC: 8093 Rehabilitation center, outpatient treatment

(P-22088)
PHYSICAL RHBLTATION NETWRK LLC
Also Called: Califrnia Rhblttion Spt Thrapy
1632 Puente Ave, Baldwin Park (91706-5952)
PHONE....................646 430-2300
Alan Vogel, *Principal*
EMP: 123 **Privately Held**
SIC: 8093 Rehabilitation center, outpatient treatment
PA: Physical Rehabilitation Network, Llc
3025 Crte Del Ngal Ste 20
Carlsbad CA 92011

(P-22089)
PLACER COUNTY- ADULT SYS CARE
11533 C Ave, Auburn (95603-2703)
PHONE....................530 886-2974
Maureen F Bauman, *Director*
EMP: 99
SALES (est): 1.1MM **Privately Held**
SIC: 8093 Specialty outpatient clinics

(P-22090)
PLANNED PARENTHOOD FEDERATION
601 W 19th St Ste B, Costa Mesa (92627-5060)
PHONE....................949 548-8830
EMP: 73
SALES (corp-wide): 196.8MM **Privately Held**
SIC: 8093 8011 Family planning clinic; clinic, operated by physicians
PA: Planned Parenthood Federation Of America, Inc.
123 William St Fl 10
New York NY 10038
212 541-7800

(P-22091)
PLANNED PARENTHOOD FEDERATION
555 Capitol Mall Ste 510, Sacramento (95814-4581)
PHONE....................916 446-5247
Ana Sandoval, *Director*
EMP: 63
SALES (corp-wide): 196.8MM **Privately Held**
SIC: 8093 Family planning & birth control clinics
PA: Planned Parenthood Federation Of America, Inc.
123 William St Fl 10
New York NY 10038
212 541-7800

(P-22092)
PLANNED PARENTHOOD LOS ANGELES (PA)
400 W 30th St, Los Angeles (90007-3320)
PHONE....................213 284-3200
Sue Dunlap, *President*
Michael Bernstein, *CFO*
Mark Kimura, *CFO*
Adrianne Black, *Vice Pres*
Barbara Bushnell, *Vice Pres*
EMP: 80 **EST:** 1965
SQ FT: 30,000
SALES: 63.9MM **Privately Held**
WEB: www.plannedparenthood.org
SIC: 8093 Family planning clinic; birth control clinic

(P-22093)
PLANNED PARENTHOOD MAR MONTE (PA)
Also Called: Region Dev & Affairs Off
316 N Main St Ste 100, Salinas (93901-2844)
PHONE....................831 373-1709
Linda Williams, *CEO*
Irene Floyd, *Principal*
Josephine Ramrus, *Admin Sec*
EMP: 63
SALES (est): 2.2MM **Privately Held**
SIC: 8093 Family planning clinic

(P-22094)
PLANNED PARENTHOOD/ORANGE AND (PA)
700 S Tustin St Fl 1, Orange (92866-3425)
PHONE....................714 633-6373
Alexis McGill Johnson, *Chairman*
Cecile Richards, *President*
Jon Dunn, *CEO*
Betha Schnelle, *COO*
Robert Armenta, *Vice Pres*
EMP: 250
SQ FT: 20,000
SALES: 48.9MM **Privately Held**
SIC: 8093 Birth control clinic; family planning & birth control clinics

(P-22095)
PLANNED PRNTHOD SHST-DBLO INC (PA)
Also Called: Planned Parenthood Nthrn Cal
2185 Pacheco St, Concord (94520-2309)
PHONE....................925 676-0300
Heather Estes, *CEO*
Cecile Richards, *President*
Gene Boyett, *Info Tech Dir*
Shelley Sella, *Med Doctor*
Oscar Efigenio, *Director*
EMP: 50
SQ FT: 5,500
SALES (est): 24.5MM **Privately Held**
SIC: 8093 Family planning & birth control clinics

(P-22096)
PLANNED PRNTHOOD CAL CNTL CAST (PA)
Also Called: Planned Prnthood Cal Cntl Cast
518 Garden St, Santa Barbara (93101-1606)
PHONE....................805 963-2445
Cheryl Rollings, *Exec Dir*
Jenna Tosh, *Exec Dir*
EMP: 54
SQ FT: 9,000

SALES: 20.7MM **Privately Held**
SIC: 8093 Birth control clinic

(P-22097)
PLANNED PRNTHOOD MAR MONTE INC
1691 The Alameda, San Jose
(95126-2203)
PHONE..................................408 287-7529
Linda Williams, *CEO*
EMP: 150
SALES (corp-wide): 111.7MM **Privately Held**
SIC: 8093 Family planning clinic
PA: Planned Parenthood Mar Monte, Inc.
1691 The Alameda
San Jose CA 95126
408 287-7532

(P-22098)
PLANNED PRNTHOOD MAR MONTE INC (PA)
1691 The Alameda, San Jose
(95126-2203)
PHONE..................................408 287-7532
Linda T Williams, *President*
Adelina Garcia, *COO*
John Giambruno, *CFO*
Jeanne Ewy, *Vice Pres*
Alison Gaulden, *Vice Pres*
EMP: 58
SQ FT: 41,000
SALES: 111.7MM **Privately Held**
SIC: 8093 Family planning clinic

(P-22099)
PLANNED PRNTHOOD MAR MONTE INC
26302 La Paz Rd 200, Mission Viejo
(92691-5313)
PHONE..................................949 768-3643
EMP: 64
SALES (corp-wide): 111.7MM **Privately Held**
SIC: 8093 8011 Family planning & birth control clinics; clinic, operated by physicians
PA: Planned Parenthood Mar Monte, Inc.
1691 The Alameda
San Jose CA 95126
408 287-7532

(P-22100)
PLEASANTVIEW INDUSTRIES INC
27921 Urbandale Ave, Saugus
(91350-1916)
PHONE..................................661 296-6700
Gerald Howard, *Director*
Del Duyer, *President*
Gerry Howard, *Exec Dir*
EMP: 77
SQ FT: 5,500
SALES: 641.8K **Privately Held**
WEB: www.pleasantviewindustries.org
SIC: 8093 Rehabilitation center, outpatient treatment

(P-22101)
PRINCIPLES INC (PA)
Also Called: Impact DRG Alcohol Trtmnt Ctr
1680 N Fair Oaks Ave, Pasadena
(91103-1642)
P.O. Box 93607 (91109-3607)
PHONE..................................323 681-2575
James M Stillwell, *CEO*
Lois Gonzales, *Controller*
EMP: 51
SQ FT: 40,000
SALES: 10MM **Privately Held**
WEB: www.mcdpartners.com
SIC: 8093 Rehabilitation center, outpatient treatment

(P-22102)
PROVIDENCE SERVICE CORPORATION
1021 4th St, Taft (93268-2433)
PHONE..................................661 765-7025
Courtney Morris, *Branch Mgr*
EMP: 50
SALES (corp-wide): 1.3B **Publicly Held**
SIC: 8093 Mental health clinic, outpatient

PA: Providence Service Corporation
700 Canal St Ste 3
Stamford CT 06902
203 307-2800

(P-22103)
PROVIDENCE SPEECH HEARING CTR
Also Called: Word and Brown Hearing Ctr
1301 W Providence Ave, Orange
(92868-3892)
PHONE..................................714 639-4990
Linda Smith, *CEO*
Bill Ross, *President*
Jack Shradder, *Treasurer*
Margaret A Inman PH, *Founder*
Jerry O'Connor, *Exec VP*
EMP: 50
SQ FT: 15,000
SALES: 12.9MM **Privately Held**
WEB: www.pshc.org
SIC: 8093 Speech defect clinic

(P-22104)
PSYCHIATRIC SOLUTIONS INC
Also Called: B H C Alhambra Hospital
4619 Rosemead Blvd, Rosemead
(91770-1478)
P.O. Box 369 (91770-0369)
PHONE..................................626 286-1191
Margaret Minnick, *Manager*
Debbie Irvin, *Records Dir*
Elio Gonzalez, *Food Svc Dir*
Ray Castillo, *Director*
Jennifer Rousch, *Director*
EMP: 200
SALES (corp-wide): 10.7B **Publicly Held**
WEB: www.intermountainhospital.com
SIC: 8093 8011 8361 8063 Mental health clinic, outpatient; psychiatric clinic; residential care; hospital for the mentally ill
HQ: Psychiatric Solutions, Inc.
6640 Carothers Pkwy # 500
Franklin TN 37067
615 312-5700

(P-22105)
PYRAMID ALTERNATIVES INC (PA)
480 Manor Pl, Pacifica (94044)
PHONE..................................650 355-8787
Linda Malone, *Exec Dir*
Paul Chang, *Exec Dir*
EMP: 50 EST: 1974
SQ FT: 5,000
SALES: 1.4MM **Privately Held**
WEB: www.pyramidalternatives.org
SIC: 8093 8322 Mental health clinic, outpatient; individual & family services; child related social services; family counseling services; general counseling services

(P-22106)
REHABLTATION INST SOUTHERN CAL (PA)
Also Called: Rehabltation Inst Orange Cnty
1800 E La Veta Ave, Orange (92866-2902)
PHONE..................................714 633-7400
Praim S Singh, *Director*
Dana Patton, *Executive Asst*
Bernardo Lahoz III, *Bookkeeper*
Lisa Jenks, *Director*
EMP: 130
SQ FT: 75,000
SALES: 8.3MM **Privately Held**
WEB: www.rio-rehab.com
SIC: 8093 Rehabilitation center, outpatient treatment

(P-22107)
RICHMOND AREA MLT-SERVICES INC
720 Sacramento St, San Francisco
(94108-2535)
PHONE..................................415 392-4453
Kavoos Bassiri, *CEO*
Ken Choi, *CFO*
EMP: 99
SALES (est): 4.9MM **Privately Held**
SIC: 8093 Mental health clinic, outpatient

(P-22108)
RICHMOND AREA MLT-SERVICES INC
1375 Mission St, San Francisco
(94103-2621)
PHONE..................................415 689-5662
Kavoos Bassiri, *CEO*
Kenneth Choi, *CFO*
EMP: 99
SALES (est): 770.4K **Privately Held**
SIC: 8093 Mental health clinic, outpatient

(P-22109)
RICHMOND AREA MLT-SERVICES INC
1282 Market St, San Francisco
(94102-4801)
PHONE..................................415 579-3021
Kenneth Choi, *CFO*
EMP: 61
SALES (corp-wide): 20.8MM **Privately Held**
SIC: 8093 Mental health clinic, outpatient
PA: Richmond Area Multi-Services, Inc.
4355 Geary Blvd
San Francisco CA 94118
415 800-0699

(P-22110)
RICHMOND AREA MLT-SERVICES INC (PA)
4355 Geary Blvd, San Francisco
(94118-3003)
PHONE..................................415 800-0699
Kavoos Bassiri, *CEO*
Lenore Williams, *CFO*
Natalie Quan, *Admin Asst*
Suresh Chacko, *Psychologist*
Ernest Brown, *Manager*
EMP: 76
SQ FT: 8,400
SALES: 20.8MM **Privately Held**
WEB: www.ramsinc.org
SIC: 8093 Mental health clinic, outpatient

(P-22111)
RIO
Also Called: Rehabilitation Inst of Sthrn C
1800 E La Veta Ave, Orange (92866-2902)
PHONE..................................714 633-7400
Glenn Motola, *Exec Dir*
John Berry, *Principal*
EMP: 233 EST: 1964
SQ FT: 3,000
SALES: 8.6MM **Privately Held**
SIC: 8093 8351 Rehabilitation center, outpatient treatment; child day care services

(P-22112)
RIVER OAK CENTER FOR CHILDREN (PA)
5445 Laurel Hills Dr, Sacramento
(95841-3105)
PHONE..................................916 609-5100
Laurie Clothier, *CEO*
EMP: 140
SQ FT: 26,000
SALES: 17.3MM **Privately Held**
SIC: 8093 8699 Mental health clinic, outpatient; charitable organization

(P-22113)
RIVERSIDE-SAN BERNARDINO
11555 1/2 Potrero Rd, Banning
(92220-6946)
PHONE..................................951 849-4761
EMP: 187
SALES (corp-wide): 35.9MM **Privately Held**
SIC: 8093 8011 Specialty outpatient clinics; offices & clinics of medical doctors
PA: Riverside-San Bernardino County Indian Health, Inc.
11980 Mount Vernon Ave
Grand Terrace CA 92313
909 864-1097

(P-22114)
SAFE HARBOR TREATMENT CEN
1040 W 17th St, Costa Mesa (92627-4503)
PHONE..................................949 645-1026
Maggie Grisham, *Director*
Christine Aubele, *Opers Mgr*

EMP: 50
SALES (est): 1.6MM **Privately Held**
SIC: 8093 Alcohol clinic, outpatient

(P-22115)
SALVATION ARMY
1247 S Wilson Way, Stockton
(95205-7096)
PHONE..................................209 466-3871
Dale Brockelman, *Manager*
EMP: 82
SALES (corp-wide): 2.3B **Privately Held**
WEB: www.salvationarmy.usawest.org
SIC: 8093 Rehabilitation center, outpatient treatment
HQ: The Salvation Army
30840 Hawthorne Blvd
Rancho Palos Verdes CA 90275
562 491-8496

(P-22116)
SALVATION ARMY
363 S Doolittle Ave, San Bernardino
(92408-1623)
PHONE..................................909 889-9605
Jack Smith, *Principal*
EMP: 80
SQ FT: 49,540
SALES (corp-wide): 2.3B **Privately Held**
WEB: www.salvationarmy-usaeast.org
SIC: 8093 8331 4225 Rehabilitation center, outpatient treatment; job training & vocational rehabilitation services; general warehousing & storage
HQ: The Salvation Army
30840 Hawthorne Blvd
Rancho Palos Verdes CA 90275
562 491-8496

(P-22117)
SAN FERNANDO CITY OF INC
10605 Balboa Blvd Ste 100, Granada Hills
(91344-6367)
PHONE..................................818 832-2400
Wendi Tovey, *Branch Mgr*
EMP: 100 **Privately Held**
SIC: 8093 9111 Mental health clinic, outpatient; county supervisors' & executives' offices
PA: San Fernando, City Of Inc
117 N Macneil St
San Fernando CA 91340
818 898-1201

(P-22118)
SAN FERNANDO VALLEY COMMUNITY (PA)
16360 Roscoe Blvd Fl 2, Van Nuys
(91406-1219)
PHONE..................................818 901-4830
Ian Hunter PHD, *President*
Emily Chen, *CFO*
Bonnie Roth, *Exec Dir*
Vivian Akomah, *Program Mgr*
Jennifer Calderon, *Program Mgr*
EMP: 450
SQ FT: 13,000
SALES: 40.1MM **Privately Held**
SIC: 8093 Substance abuse clinics (outpatient); mental health clinic, outpatient

(P-22119)
SAN FRANCISCO CITY CLINIC
356 7th St, San Francisco (94103-4030)
PHONE..................................415 487-5500
Jeffrey Klausner, *Director*
Wendy Wolf, *Deputy Dir*
Susan Philip, *Director*
EMP: 80
SQ FT: 2,500
SALES (est): 3.6MM **Privately Held**
WEB: www.cityclinic.net
SIC: 8093 Birth control clinic

(P-22120)
SAN JOAQUIN VALLEY REHABILI (HQ)
7173 N Sharon Ave, Fresno (93720-3329)
PHONE..................................559 436-3600
Edward C Palacios, *Partner*
Shaina Shaikh, *Pharmacy Dir*
Diane Kisling, *Accountant*
Connie Pierce, *Human Res Dir*
Mark Rakis, *Opers Mgr*
EMP: 275

PRODUCTS & SVCS

SALES: 35MM
SALES (corp-wide): 330.4MM **Privately Held**
WEB: www.sjvrehab.com
SIC: 8093 Rehabilitation center, outpatient treatment
PA: Vibra Healthcare, Llc
4600 Lena Dr Ste 100
Mechanicsburg PA 17055
717 591-5700

(P-22121)
SAN MATEO CNTY PUB HLTH CLINIC
380 90th St, Daly City (94015-1807)
PHONE..................................650 301-8600
Cathy Lehmkuhl, *Director*
Denise R Gonzalez, *Internal Med*
EMP: 50
SALES (est): 1.1MM **Privately Held**
WEB: www.sanmateolafco.org
SIC: 8093 Birth control clinic

(P-22122)
SARAH ELIZABETH TREUSDELL
921 W Avenue J Ste C, Lancaster (93534-3443)
PHONE..................................661 949-0131
S E Treusdell, *Principal*
Sarah Elizabeth Treusdell, *Principal*
EMP: 50
SALES (est): 124.3K **Privately Held**
SIC: 8093 Mental health clinic, outpatient

(P-22123)
SCRIPPS HEALTH
Also Called: Scripps Del Mar
3811 Valley Centre Dr, San Diego (92130-3318)
PHONE..................................858 794-0160
Melody Stewart, *Manager*
EMP: 250
SALES (corp-wide): 2.1B **Privately Held**
WEB: www.scripps.org
SIC: 8093 Specialty outpatient clinics
PA: Scripps Health
10140 Campus Point Dr Ax415
San Diego CA 92121
800 727-4777

(P-22124)
SKIN HEALTH EXPERTS MEDIC
Also Called: Kate Summerville
144 S Beverly Dr Ste 500, Beverly Hills (90212-3023)
PHONE..................................310 623-6869
Michelle Taylor, *CEO*
Laura Shaff, *CFO*
EMP: 70 **EST:** 2013
SALES (est): 956.9K **Privately Held**
SIC: 8093 Specialty outpatient clinics

(P-22125)
SMILE HOUSING CORPORATION
800 Quintana Rd Ste 2c, Morro Bay (93442-2300)
P.O. Box 877 (93443-0877)
PHONE..................................805 772-6066
Debbie Bertrando, *CEO*
Jennifer Gaalswyk, *CFO*
EMP: 99 **EST:** 2008
SALES: 99.8K **Privately Held**
SIC: 8093 Specialty outpatient clinics

(P-22126)
SOUTH BAYLO UNIVERSITY
Also Called: South Baylo Acupuncture Clinic
2727 W 6th St, Los Angeles (90057-3111)
PHONE..................................213 387-2414
EMP: 136
SALES (corp-wide): 6.8MM **Privately Held**
SIC: 8093 8221 8049
PA: South Baylo University
1126 N Brookhurst St
Anaheim CA 92801
714 533-1495

(P-22127)
SOUTH CNTL HEATLH & REHAB PROG
Also Called: Barbour & Floyd Medical Assoc
2620 Industry Way, Lynwood (90262-4024)
PHONE..................................310 667-4070
Jack M Barbour, *Principal*
EMP: 53 **Privately Held**

SIC: 8093 Rehabilitation center, outpatient treatment
PA: South Central Health & Rehabilitation Program
2610 Industry Way Ste A
Lynwood CA 90262

(P-22128)
SOUTH CNTL HEATLH & REHAB PROG
Also Called: Scharp's Oasis House
5201 S Vermont Ave, Los Angeles (90037-3527)
PHONE..................................323 751-2677
Jack Barbour, *Director*
EMP: 100 **Privately Held**
SIC: 8093 Mental health clinic, outpatient
PA: South Central Health & Rehabilitation Program
2610 Industry Way Ste A
Lynwood CA 90262

(P-22129)
SOUTHERN CALIFORNIA ALCOHOL AN (PA)
11500 Paramount Blvd, Downey (90241-4530)
PHONE..................................562 923-4545
Lynne Appel, *CEO*
Gary Munger, *Ch of Bd*
Marsie Alford, *CFO*
Judith Edwards, *Treasurer*
Leon Emerson, *Treasurer*
EMP: 60 **EST:** 1972
SALES: 9.3MM **Privately Held**
SIC: 8093 Specialty outpatient clinics

(P-22130)
SPENCER RECOVERY CENTERS INC (PA)
1316 S Coast Hwy, Laguna Beach (92651-3118)
P.O. Box 9296 (92652-7261)
PHONE..................................949 376-3705
Chris Spencer, *President*
Cindy Spencer, *Admin Sec*
EMP: 58
SQ FT: 2,000
SALES (est): 6.2MM **Privately Held**
WEB: www.spencerrecovery.com
SIC: 8093 Alcohol clinic, outpatient; substance abuse clinics (outpatient)

(P-22131)
STAFFREHAB
5000 Birch St, Newport Beach (92660-2127)
PHONE..................................888 835-0894
Sara Palmer, *CEO*
Lindsay Joseph, *CTO*
EMP: 284 **EST:** 2009
SALES (est): 63.2K
SALES (corp-wide): 28.8MM **Privately Held**
SIC: 8093 Rehabilitation center, outpatient treatment
PA: Pediatric Therapy Services, Llc
2586 Trailridge Dr E # 100
Lafayette CO 80026
866 337-5965

(P-22132)
STRATEGIES FOR CHANGE (PA)
4343 Williamsbourgh Dr, Sacramento (95823-2006)
PHONE..................................916 395-3552
Bobby J Davis, *Exec Dir*
B J Davis, *Exec Dir*
Christopher Packey, *Manager*
EMP: 60
SQ FT: 8,000
SALES: 2.8MM **Privately Held**
SIC: 8093 Substance abuse clinics (outpatient)

(P-22133)
SUBACUTE TRTMNT ADOLESCNT REHA (PA)
Also Called: Stars
545 Estudillo Ave, San Leandro (94577-4611)
PHONE..................................510 352-9200
Peter Zucker, *President*

John Weller, *CFO*
Kent Dunlap, *Senior VP*
Tara Morgan, *Human Resources*
EMP: 77
SQ FT: 7,442
SALES: 3.9MM **Privately Held**
SIC: 8093 8051 Mental health clinic, outpatient; substance abuse clinics (outpatient); drug clinic, outpatient; rehabilitation center, outpatient treatment; mental retardation hospital

(P-22134)
SUTTER HEALTH
Also Called: Sutter Auburn Faith Hospital
11775 Education St # 201, Auburn (95602-2453)
PHONE..................................530 888-4500
Mitch Hanna, *CEO*
Yvette Martinez, *Hum Res Coord*
Ingrid Metzler, *Internal Med*
Christina Baker, *Manager*
Catherine Nishikawa, *Manager*
EMP: 650
SQ FT: 7,584
SALES (corp-wide): 12.7B **Privately Held**
WEB: www.sutterhealth.org
SIC: 8093 8062 8011 Rehabilitation center, outpatient treatment; general medical & surgical hospitals; hospital, medical school affiliated with nursing & residency; freestanding emergency medical center
PA: Sutter Health
2200 River Plaza Dr
Sacramento CA 95833
916 733-8800

(P-22135)
TARZANA TREATMENT CENTERS INC
422 W Rancho Vista Blvd C280, Palmdale (93551-3793)
PHONE..................................818 654-3815
Albert Senella, *President*
Phyllis Cohen, *Family Practiti*
EMP: 115
SALES (corp-wide): 49.1MM **Privately Held**
SIC: 8093 Substance abuse clinics (outpatient)
PA: Tarzana Treatment Centers, Inc.
18646 Oxnard St
Tarzana CA 91356
818 996-1051

(P-22136)
TARZANA TREATMENT CENTERS INC (PA)
18646 Oxnard St, Tarzana (91356-1411)
PHONE..................................818 996-1051
Albert Senella, *President*
Sylvia Cadena, *CFO*
Bobbi Sloan, *Corp Secy*
Rochelle Price, *Admin Asst*
Eloy Cruz, *Info Tech Mgr*
EMP: 160
SQ FT: 14,000
SALES: 49.1MM **Privately Held**
WEB: www.tarzanatc.com
SIC: 8093 8322 8063 Mental health clinic, outpatient; individual & family services; psychiatric hospitals

(P-22137)
TARZANA TREATMENT CENTERS INC
Also Called: Tarzana Trtmnt Ctrs LNG Bch O
5190 Atlantic Ave, Lakewood (90805-6510)
PHONE..................................562 428-4111
EMP: 138
SALES (corp-wide): 49.1MM **Privately Held**
SIC: 8093 8299 Substance abuse clinics (outpatient); airline training
PA: Tarzana Treatment Centers, Inc.
18646 Oxnard St
Tarzana CA 91356
818 996-1051

(P-22138)
TARZANA TREATMENT CENTERS INC
2101 Magnolia Ave, Long Beach (90806-4521)
PHONE..................................562 218-1868

Angela Knox, *Branch Mgr*
Devin Smith, *Technician*
EMP: 50
SQ FT: 11,482
SALES (corp-wide): 49.1MM **Privately Held**
WEB: www.tarzanatc.com
SIC: 8093 Substance abuse clinics (outpatient)
PA: Tarzana Treatment Centers, Inc.
18646 Oxnard St
Tarzana CA 91356
818 996-1051

(P-22139)
TARZANA TREATMENT CENTERS INC
Also Called: Tarzana Treatment Ctr
44447 10th St W, Lancaster (93534-3324)
PHONE..................................661 726-2630
Theresa Scott, *Director*
Marcus Nelson, *Info Tech Mgr*
EMP: 70
SALES (corp-wide): 49.1MM **Privately Held**
WEB: www.tarzanatc.com
SIC: 8093 8069 8011 Drug clinic, outpatient; drug addiction rehabilitation hospital; clinic, operated by physicians
PA: Tarzana Treatment Centers, Inc.
18646 Oxnard St
Tarzana CA 91356
818 996-1051

(P-22140)
TELECARE LA STEP DOWN
4335 Atlantic Ave, Long Beach (90807-2803)
PHONE..................................562 216-4900
Mariela Gorosito, *Branch Mgr*
EMP: 50
SALES (est): 483.4K **Privately Held**
SIC: 8093 Mental health clinic, outpatient

(P-22141)
TELECARE LAS POSADAS
1756 S Lewis Rd, Camarillo (93012-8520)
PHONE..................................805 383-3669
Larry Berent, *Principal*
EMP: 60
SALES (est): 141.1K **Privately Held**
SIC: 8093 8082 Mental health clinic, outpatient; home health care services

(P-22142)
TRANSITIONS - MENTAL HLTH ASSN (PA)
Also Called: Slo Transitions
784 High St, San Luis Obispo (93401-5243)
P.O. Box 15408 (93406-5408)
PHONE..................................805 540-6500
Jill B White, *Exec Dir*
Maria Perez, *Partner*
Mark Lamore, *Manager*
EMP: 60
SQ FT: 8,000
SALES: 13.2MM **Privately Held**
WEB: www.t-mha.org
SIC: 8093 Mental health clinic, outpatient

(P-22143)
TRI CITY MENTAL HEALTH CENTER
1900 Royalty Dr, Pomona (91767-3032)
PHONE..................................909 784-3200
Debbie Johnson, *Branch Mgr*
Diana Acosta, *CFO*
Angela Igrisan, *Officer*
Natalie Major, *Officer*
Seeyam Teimoori, *Director*
EMP: 60
SALES (corp-wide): 6.2MM **Privately Held**
SIC: 8093 8322 Mental health clinic, outpatient; individual & family services
PA: Tri City Mental Health Center
2008 N Garey Ave Ste 2c
Pomona CA 91767
909 623-6131

(P-22144)
TRUVIDA RECOVERY
23726 Birtcher Dr, Lake Forest
(92630-1771)
PHONE...................................949 283-4679
Vince Bindi, *Partner*
EMP: 64
SALES (est): 116.2K **Privately Held**
SIC: 8093 Substance abuse clinics (outpatient)

(P-22145)
TULE RIVER INDIAN HLTH CTR INC
380 N Reservation Rd, Porterville
(93257-9673)
P.O. Box 768 (93258-0768)
PHONE...................................559 784-2316
Zahid Sheikh, *CEO*
Casey Carrillo, *CFO*
David Tuttle, *Information Mgr*
Jan L Trigleth, *Physician Asst*
EMP: 65
SQ FT: 15,000
SALES: 10.5MM **Privately Held**
SIC: 8093 Specialty outpatient clinics

(P-22146)
TURN BEHAVIORAL HLTH SVCS INC
Also Called: MHS
2550 W Clinton Ave, Fresno (93705-4201)
PHONE...................................559 264-7521
Kimberly R Bond, *President*
EMP: 52
SALES (corp-wide): 85MM **Privately Held**
SIC: 8093 8011 Mental health clinic, outpatient; medical centers
PA: Mental Health Systems, Inc.
9465 Farnham St
San Diego CA 92123
858 573-2600

(P-22147)
UHS-CORONA INC
Also Called: Corona Regional Medical Center
730 Magnolia Ave, Corona (92879-3117)
PHONE...................................951 736-7200
Pat Sanders, *Director*
David Aguirre, *Marketing Staff*
EMP: 200
SALES (corp-wide): 10.7B **Publicly Held**
SIC: 8093 8062 8069 8051 Rehabilitation center, outpatient treatment; general medical & surgical hospitals; specialty hospitals, except psychiatric; skilled nursing care facilities
HQ: Uhs-Corona, Inc.
800 S Main St
Corona CA 92882
951 737-4343

(P-22148)
UNITED AMERICAN INDIAN INVOLVE (PA)
1125 W 6th St Ste 103, Los Angeles
(90017-1896)
PHONE...................................213 202-3970
Joseph Quintana, *Director*
David L Rambeau, *Exec Dir*
Carrie Johnson PHD, *Director*
EMP: 57 EST: 1974
SQ FT: 26,000
SALES: 7MM **Privately Held**
WEB: www.uaii.org
SIC: 8093 Rehabilitation center, outpatient treatment

(P-22149)
UNITED HEALTH CTRS SAN JOAQUIN (PA)
3875 W Beechwood Ave, Fresno
(93711-0795)
P.O. Box 790, Parlier (93648-0790)
PHONE...................................559 646-6618
Colleen Curtis, *CEO*
Justin Preas, *COO*
Robert Shankerman, *Principal*
EMP: 70
SQ FT: 7,500
SALES: 71MM **Privately Held**
WEB: www.unitedhealthcenters.org
SIC: 8093 Specialty outpatient clinics

(P-22150)
UNITED HEALTH CTRS SAN JOAQUIN
106 E Main St, Fowler (93625-2433)
PHONE...................................559 834-1568
Colleen Curtis, *CEO*
EMP: 57
SALES (corp-wide): 71MM **Privately Held**
SIC: 8093 Mental health clinic, outpatient
PA: United Health Centers Of The San Joaquin Valley
3875 W Beechwood Ave
Fresno CA 93711
559 646-6618

(P-22151)
UNITED HEALTH CTRS SAN JOAQUIN
Also Called: Orange Cove Health Center
445 11th St, Orange Cove (93646-2211)
P.O. Box 427 (93646-0427)
PHONE...................................559 626-4031
Lynee Wilder, *Manager*
Matthew J Easton, *Osteopathy*
EMP: 51
SQ FT: 14,623
SALES (corp-wide): 71MM **Privately Held**
SIC: 8093 Family planning clinic
PA: United Health Centers Of The San Joaquin Valley
3875 W Beechwood Ave
Fresno CA 93711
559 646-6618

(P-22152)
UNIVERSAL CARE INC (PA)
Also Called: Smile Wide Dental
19762 Macarthur Blvd # 100, Irvine
(92612-2425)
PHONE...................................562 424-6200
Howard E Davis, *CEO*
Mark Gunter, *CFO*
Jay Davis, *Vice Pres*
Jeffrey Davis, *Admin Sec*
EMP: 350
SQ FT: 73,000
SALES (est): 23.4MM **Privately Held**
WEB: www.universalcare.com
SIC: 8093 Specialty outpatient clinics

(P-22153)
UPLIFT FAMILY SERVICES
Also Called: Emq Familiesfirst
499 Loma Alta Ave, Los Gatos
(95030-6227)
PHONE...................................408 379-3790
Cynthia Goodman, *Branch Mgr*
EMP: 100
SALES (corp-wide): 93.6MM **Privately Held**
SIC: 8093 8063 8011 Mental health clinic, outpatient; hospital for the mentally ill; offices & clinics of medical doctors
PA: Uplift Family Services
251 Llewellyn Ave
Campbell CA 95008
408 379-3790

(P-22154)
VERDUGO MENTAL HEALTH
1540 E Colorado St, Glendale
(91205-1514)
PHONE...................................818 244-7257
Jeff Smith, *Exec Dir*
Karo Povolitis, *Ch of Bd*
David Igler, *Vice Ch Bd*
Lois Neil, *Vice Pres*
Richard Slavett, *Admin Sec*
EMP: 64 EST: 1957
SALES (est): 2.1MM **Privately Held**
WEB: www.vmhc.org
SIC: 8093 Mental health clinic, outpatient

(P-22155)
VETERINARY PRACTICE ASSOC INC
Also Called: Veterinary Specialty Hospital
10435 Sorrento Valley Rd, San Diego
(92121-1607)
PHONE...................................949 833-9020
Keith P Richter, *CEO*
Gilbert Velasquez, *Administration*
Nathan Batoon, *Opers Mgr*

Christopher S Eich,
EMP: 150
SQ FT: 26,280
SALES: 18MM **Privately Held**
SIC: 8093 Specialty outpatient clinics

(P-22156)
VIBRANTCARE OUTPATIENT REHAB (PA)
2270 Douglas Blvd Ste 216, Roseville
(95661-4239)
PHONE...................................916 782-1212
David Smith, *President*
Roberto Saavedra, *Administration*
Brandon Brown, *Opers Staff*
Kari Kockler, *Opers Staff*
EMP: 65
SALES (est): 28.9MM **Privately Held**
SIC: 8093 Rehabilitation center, outpatient treatment

(P-22157)
VICTOR CMNTY SUPPORT SVCS INC (PA)
1360 E Lassen Ave, Chico (95973-7823)
PHONE...................................530 893-0758
Douglas Scott, *CEO*
Lenny Verser, *CFO*
Rachel Pena, *Exec Dir*
David Monroe, *Controller*
Christina Moore, *Human Res Mgr*
EMP: 402
SQ FT: 4,500
SALES: 37.7MM **Privately Held**
SIC: 8093 Mental health clinic, outpatient

(P-22158)
VISIONS UNLIMITED (PA)
6833 Stockton Blvd # 485, Sacramento
(95823-2372)
PHONE...................................916 394-0800
Roleda Bates, *CEO*
Jennifer Ruiz, *Manager*
EMP: 104
SQ FT: 20,000
SALES: 3.6MM **Privately Held**
WEB: www.vuinc.org
SIC: 8093 Mental health clinic, outpatient

(P-22159)
WELLSPACE HEALTH (PA)
Also Called: Effort, The
1820 J St, Sacramento (95811-3010)
PHONE...................................916 325-5556
Robert Caulk, *CEO*
Jonathan Porteus, *President*
Chue Vang, *Analyst*
Jeremy Meis, *Physician Asst*
Tracey Lattimore, *Director*
EMP: 56
SQ FT: 12,500
SALES (est): 11.2MM **Privately Held**
WEB: www.theeffort.com
SIC: 8093 Mental health clinic, outpatient; alcohol clinic, outpatient; rehabilitation center, outpatient treatment

(P-22160)
WEST OAKLAND HEALTH COUNCIL (PA)
Also Called: WEST OAKLAND HEALTH CENTER
700 Adeline St, Oakland (94607-2608)
PHONE...................................510 835-9610
Benjamin Pettus, *CEO*
EMP: 138
SQ FT: 26,000
SALES: 25.6MM **Privately Held**
SIC: 8093 8021 8011 Mental health clinic, outpatient; drug clinic, outpatient; dental clinic; offices & clinics of medical doctors

(P-22161)
WESTCOAST CHILDRENS CLINIC
3301 E 12th St Ste 259, Oakland
(94601-2940)
PHONE...................................510 269-9030
Stacy Anne Katz, *Exec Dir*
Jeffrey Wands, *CFO*
Edwin Calles, *Admin Asst*
Diane Ramirez, *Project Mgr*
Nick Nguyen, *Research*
EMP: 140

SALES: 14.2MM **Privately Held**
SIC: 8093 Mental health clinic, outpatient

(P-22162)
WESTERN DENTAL SERVICES INC
17660 Lakewood Blvd, Bellflower
(90706-6410)
PHONE...................................562 461-1180
Howard Davis, *Branch Mgr*
EMP: 50
SALES (corp-wide): 271.2MM **Privately Held**
WEB: www.universalcare.com
SIC: 8093 Specialty outpatient clinics
HQ: Western Dental Services, Inc.
530 S Main St Ste 600
Orange CA 92868
714 480-3000

(P-22163)
WOMEN HEALTH CENTER (PA)
1469 Humboldt Rd Ste 200, Chico
(95928-9203)
PHONE...................................530 891-1917
Shauna Heckert, *Exec Dir*
Kimberly Edmunds, *Manager*
EMP: 75 EST: 1974
SALES (est): 1.9MM **Privately Held**
SIC: 8093 Specialty outpatient clinics

(P-22164)
WORKING WITH AUTISM
16530 Ventura Blvd # 310, Encino
(91436-4598)
PHONE...................................818 501-4240
Jennifer Sabin, *Director*
Hilya Delband, *Director*
Christine Allen, *Supervisor*
Adam Di Panni, *Supervisor*
Traci Oberg, *Supervisor*
EMP: 100
SALES (est): 4.9MM **Privately Held**
WEB: www.workingwithautism.com
SIC: 8093 Mental health clinic, outpatient

***

8099 Health & Allied Svcs, NEC

(P-22165)
1LIFE HEALTHCARE INC
Also Called: One Medical Group
1 Embarcadero Ctr # 1900, San Francisco
(94111-3723)
PHONE...................................415 644-5265
Thomas H Lee MD, *President*
Paul Kirincich, *CFO*
Michael Swartzburg, *Vice Pres*
Melissa Costa, *Admin Asst*
Judy Choi, *Technology*
EMP: 98
SALES (est): 11.2MM **Privately Held**
WEB: www.1life.com
SIC: 8099 Medical services organization

(P-22166)
24 HOUR FITNESS USA INC
6345 Commerce Blvd, Rohnert Park
(94928-2403)
PHONE...................................707 536-0048
John-Paul Scirica, *Manager*
EMP: 50
SALES (corp-wide): 480.7MM **Privately Held**
SIC: 8099 7991 Nutrition services; health club
HQ: 24 Hour Fitness Usa, Inc.
12647 Alcosta Blvd # 500
San Ramon CA 94583
925 543-3100

(P-22167)
24 HOUR FITNESS USA INC
1903 W Empire Ave, Burbank
(91504-3433)
PHONE...................................818 531-0257
EMP: 50
SALES (corp-wide): 480.7MM **Privately Held**
SIC: 8099 7991 Nutrition services; physical fitness clubs with training equipment

HQ: 24 Hour Fitness Usa, Inc.
12647 Alcosta Blvd # 500
San Ramon CA 94583
925 543-3100

(P-22168)
24 HOUR FITNESS USA INC
1870 Harbor Blvd Ste 124, Costa Mesa
(92627-5023)
PHONE..............................949 610-0651
EMP: 50
SALES (corp-wide): 480.7MM **Privately Held**
SIC: 8099 7991 Nutrition services; physical fitness clubs with training equipment
HQ: 24 Hour Fitness Usa, Inc.
12647 Alcosta Blvd # 500
San Ramon CA 94583
925 543-3100

(P-22169)
AHMC HEALTHCARE INC
506 W Valley Blvd Ste 300, San Gabriel
(91776-5716)
PHONE..............................626 248-3452
EMP: 1202
SALES (corp-wide): 570.2MM **Privately Held**
SIC: 8099 8062 Blood bank; general medical & surgical hospitals
PA: Ahmc Healthcare Inc.
1000 S Fremont Ave Unit 6
Alhambra CA 91803

(P-22170)
ALIGNMENT HEALTHCARE USA LLC (PA)
1100 W Town And Country R, Orange
(92868-4600)
PHONE..............................844 310-2247
John KAO, CEO
David Jarboe, President
Matt Malin, President
Matthew Malin, President
Scott Powers, President
EMP: 90
SALES (est): 49.6MM **Privately Held**
SIC: 8099 8011 Blood related health services; physical medicine, physician/surgeon

(P-22171)
ALTAMED HEALTH SERVICES CORP
10454 Valley Blvd, El Monte (91731-2444)
PHONE..............................323 889-7847
EMP: 138
SALES (corp-wide): 677.8MM **Privately Held**
SIC: 8099 Childbirth preparation clinic
PA: Altamed Health Services Corporation
2040 Camfield Ave
Commerce CA 90040
323 725-8751

(P-22172)
ALTAMED HEALTH SERVICES CORP
Also Called: Slauson Plaza Med Group
9436 Slauson Ave, Pico Rivera
(90660-4748)
PHONE..............................562 949-8717
Alfredo Nunez, Branch Mgr
EMP: 60
SALES (corp-wide): 677.8MM **Privately Held**
WEB: www.altamed.org
SIC: 8099 8011 Medical services organization; clinic, operated by physicians
PA: Altamed Health Services Corporation
2040 Camfield Ave
Commerce CA 90040
323 725-8751

(P-22173)
AMERICAN HLTHCARE ADM SVCS INC
Also Called: American Health Care
3850 Atherton Rd, Rocklin (95765-3700)
PHONE..............................916 773-7227
Lance Aizen, CEO
EMP: 490
SQ FT: 8,000

SALES (est): 21.3MM **Privately Held**
WEB: www.americanhealthcare.com
SIC: 8099 Medical services organization

(P-22174)
AMERICAN INDIAN HEALTH & SVCS
4141 State St Ste B11, Santa Barbara
(93110-1898)
PHONE..............................805 681-7356
Scott Black, Exec Dir
Martha Vasquez, Admin Asst
EMP: 50
SQ FT: 4,000
SALES: 9.1MM **Privately Held**
SIC: 8099 Health screening service

(P-22175)
AMERICAN NATIONAL RED CROSS
6230 Claremont Ave, Oakland
(94618-1324)
PHONE..............................510 594-5100
Jay Winkenbach, CEO
EMP: 165
SQ FT: 42,714
SALES (corp-wide): 2.6B **Privately Held**
WEB: www.redcross.org
SIC: 8099 Blood related health services
PA: The American National Red Cross
430 17th St Nw
Washington DC 20006
202 737-8300

(P-22176)
AMERICAN NATIONAL RED CROSS
Also Called: American Natl Rd CRS-Bld Svcs
100 Red Cross Cir, Pomona (91768-2580)
PHONE..............................909 859-7006
Joan Manning, General Mgr
Dan D'Angelo, Associate Dir
Janelle Brown, Administration
Kenneth Kay, Director
EMP: 1200
SALES (corp-wide): 2.6B **Privately Held**
WEB: www.redcross.org
SIC: 8099 Blood donor station
PA: The American National Red Cross
430 17th St Nw
Washington DC 20006
202 737-8300

(P-22177)
ANKA BEHAVIORAL HEALTH INC
458 Almond Dr, Lodi (95240-7823)
PHONE..............................209 982-4697
EMP: 104
SALES (corp-wide): 40.4MM **Privately Held**
SIC: 8099 Childbirth preparation clinic
PA: Anka Behavioral Health, Incorporated
3840 Buskirk Ave Ste 300
Pleasant Hill CA 94523
925 825-4700

(P-22178)
ANKA BEHAVIORAL HEALTH INC
Also Called: Casa Fremont
5149 Winston Ct, Fremont (94536-6523)
PHONE..............................510 494-1567
Wayne Thurston, Director
EMP: 104
SALES (corp-wide): 40.4MM **Privately Held**
SIC: 8099 Childbirth preparation clinic
PA: Anka Behavioral Health, Incorporated
3840 Buskirk Ave Ste 300
Pleasant Hill CA 94523
925 825-4700

(P-22179)
APRIA HEALTHCARE LLC
Also Called: Distribution Warehouse
1680 Tide Ct Ste B, Woodland
(95776-6237)
PHONE..............................530 669-6441
Dan Starck, Branch Mgr
EMP: 60 **Privately Held**
WEB: www.respimed.com
SIC: 8099 Blood related health services

HQ: Apria Healthcare Llc
26220 Enterprise Ct
Lake Forest CA 92630
949 639-2000

(P-22180)
APRIA HEALTHCARE LLC
7514 Murray Dr, Stockton (95210-5311)
PHONE..............................209 223-7727
Lawrence Mastrovich, Principal
EMP: 180 **Privately Held**
WEB: www.respimed.com
SIC: 8099 Blood related health services
HQ: Apria Healthcare Llc
26220 Enterprise Ct
Lake Forest CA 92630
949 639-2000

(P-22181)
ARBORMED INC (PA)
725 W Town And Country Rd, Orange
(92868-4703)
PHONE..............................714 689-1500
Charles Morf, President
William Shaw, CFO
Scott Everson, Vice Pres
EMP: 175
SQ FT: 11,000
SALES (est): 3.1MM **Privately Held**
WEB: www.arbormed.com
SIC: 8099 8742 Medical services organization; management consulting services

(P-22182)
ATLAS LIFT TECH INC
210 Porter Dr Ste 300, San Ramon
(94583-1525)
PHONE..............................415 283-1804
Eric Race, President
Robert Zuckswert, COO
Wendy McCollom, CFO
Susan Gallagher, Vice Pres
Giovanni Dominguez, Program Mgr
EMP: 150
SALES (est): 8.7MM **Privately Held**
SIC: 8099 Health screening service

(P-22183)
BAKERSFIELD FAMILY MED GROUP
5601 Auburn St Unit A, Bakersfield
(93306-2977)
PHONE..............................661 846-3605
EMP: 66
SALES (corp-wide): 26.9MM **Privately Held**
SIC: 8099 Childbirth preparation clinic
PA: Bakersfield Family Medical Group, Inc
4580 California Ave
Bakersfield CA 93309
661 327-4411

(P-22184)
BEHAVIORAL HEALTH WORKS INC
1301 E Orangewood Ave, Anaheim
(92805-6807)
PHONE..............................800 249-1266
Robert Douk, CEO
Brenda Bueno, Human Res Mgr
Montgomery Lim, Director
EMP: 99 EST: 2011
SALES (est): 230.7K **Privately Held**
SIC: 8099 Blood related health services

(P-22185)
BIO-MED SERVICES INC
Also Called: Prime Healthcare Services
3300 E Guasti Rd, Ontario (91761-8655)
PHONE..............................909 235-4400
Prem Reddy, CEO
EMP: 85
SALES (est): 869.3K
SALES (corp-wide): 3.4B **Privately Held**
SIC: 8099 Medical services organization
HQ: Prime Healthcare Services Inc
3300 E Guasti Rd Ste 300
Ontario CA 91761

(P-22186)
BIOMAT USA INC (DH)
2410 Lillyvale Ave, Los Angeles
(90032-3514)
PHONE..............................323 225-2221
Gregory Rich, CEO

Shinji Wada, Exec VP
David Bell, Vice Pres
Kim Berger, Associate Dir
Maxim Aloomian, Electrical Engi
◆ EMP: 50
SQ FT: 20,000
SALES (est): 168.1MM
SALES (corp-wide): 741MM **Privately Held**
SIC: 8099 Plasmapherous center; blood bank
HQ: Grifols Shared Services North America, Inc.
2410 Lillyvale Ave
Los Angeles CA 90032
323 225-2221

(P-22187)
BIOMAT USA INC
246 Bernard St, Bakersfield (93305-3541)
PHONE..............................661 863-0621
Gustavo Castellanos, Manager
EMP: 62
SALES (corp-wide): 741MM **Privately Held**
SIC: 8099 Blood bank
HQ: Biomat Usa, Inc.
2410 Lillyvale Ave
Los Angeles CA 90032
323 225-2221

(P-22188)
BLOOD BANK OF REDWOODS (PA)
Also Called: Blood Center of The Pacific
3505 Industrial Dr, Santa Rosa
(95403-2064)
PHONE..............................707 545-1222
Cathy Bryan, Administration
EMP: 110
SQ FT: 13,540
SALES (est): 10.1MM **Privately Held**
WEB: www.bbr.org
SIC: 8099 Blood bank

(P-22189)
BLOOD BANK OF SAN BERNARDINO A (HQ)
Also Called: Lifestream
384 W Orange Show Rd, San Bernardino
(92408-2028)
P.O. Box 1429 (92402-1429)
PHONE..............................909 885-6503
Frederick B Axelrod, CEO
Jim Schraith, Treasurer
Frank Ercoli, Bd of Directors
JP Fletcher, Bd of Directors
Erick Frykman, Bd of Directors
EMP: 240
SQ FT: 50,000
SALES: 66.5MM
SALES (corp-wide): 11.7B **Privately Held**
WEB: www.bbsbrc.org
SIC: 8099 Blood bank; blood donor station
PA: Vitalant
6210 E Oak St
Scottsdale AZ 85257
602 414-3819

(P-22190)
BLOODSOURCE INC (PA)
10536 Peter A Mccuen Blvd, Mather
(95655-4128)
PHONE..............................916 456-1500
Michael J Fuller, CEO
Jim Eldridge, CFO
Dirk Johnson, Vice Pres
Erin Frye, Director
Samantha Sherman, Supervisor
EMP: 325
SQ FT: 105,000
SALES: 85MM **Privately Held**
WEB: www.bloodsource.org
SIC: 8099 Blood bank

(P-22191)
BLOODSOURCE INC
382 E Yosemite Ave, Merced (95340-9100)
PHONE..............................209 724-0428
Jaime Suarez, Manager
EMP: 54
SALES (corp-wide): 85MM **Privately Held**
SIC: 8099 Blood bank

PA: Bloodsource, Inc.
10536 Peter A Mccuen Blvd
Mather CA 95655
916 456-1500

(P-22192)
BLOODSOURCE INC
3099 Fair Oaks Blvd, Sacramento
(95864-5613)
PHONE...................916 488-1701
Whitney Karen, *Branch Mgr*
EMP: 50
SALES (corp-wide): 85MM Privately Held
SIC: 8099 Blood bank
PA: Bloodsource, Inc.
10536 Peter A Mccuen Blvd
Mather CA 95655
916 456-1500

(P-22193)
BROOKSIDE COMMUNITY HEALTH CTR (PA)
Also Called: Mahony, John MD
2023 Vale Rd, San Pablo (94806-3834)
PHONE...................510 215-9092
Joseph Gomes, *President*
Cheryl Johnson, *Exec Dir*
EMP: 86
SALES (est): 7.9MM Privately Held
SIC: 8099 Medical services organization

(P-22194)
CALIFORNIA CRYOBANK INC
Also Called: Califrnia Cryobank Lf Sciences
611 Gateway Blvd Ste 820, South San
Francisco (94080-7029)
PHONE...................650 635-1420
EMP: 300
SALES (corp-wide): 21.4MM Privately Held
SIC: 8099 Blood bank
PA: California Cryobank Llc
11915 La Grange Ave
Los Angeles CA 90025
310 496-5691

(P-22195)
CALIFORNIA CRYOBANK LLC (PA)
11915 La Grange Ave, Los Angeles
(90025-5213)
PHONE...................310 496-5691
Richards Jennings, *CEO*
Pamela Richardson, *President*
Charles A Sims MD, *CEO*
Brian Rizkallah, *CFO*
Kristen Swingle, *Vice Pres*
EMP: 75
SQ FT: 21,300
SALES (est): 21.4MM Privately Held
WEB: www.cryobank.com
SIC: 8099 Sperm bank

(P-22196)
CALIFRNIA FRNSIC MED GROUP INC
2801 Meadow Lark Dr, San Diego
(92123-2709)
PHONE...................858 694-4690
Penny Looper, *General Mgr*
EMP: 70
SALES (corp-wide): 33.7MM Privately Held
WEB: www.cfmg.com
SIC: 8099 9223 Medical services organization; jail, government
PA: California Forensic Medical Group, In-corporated
1283 Murfreesboro Pike # 500
Nashville TN 37217
831 649-8994

(P-22197)
CALIFRNIA FRNSIC MED GROUP INC
Also Called: Cfmg
300 Forni Rd, Kelsey (95667-5400)
PHONE...................530 573-3035
Elaine Huestand, *Manager*
EMP: 88
SALES (corp-wide): 33.7MM Privately Held
WEB: www.cfmg.com
SIC: 8099 Medical services organization

PA: California Forensic Medical Group, In-corporated
1283 Murfreesboro Pike # 500
Nashville TN 37217
831 649-8994

(P-22198)
CALIFRNIA FRNSIC MED GROUP INC
800 S Victoria Ave, Ventura (93009-0001)
PHONE...................805 654-3343
Elaine Hustedt, *Vice Pres*
EMP: 100
SALES (corp-wide): 33.7MM Privately Held
WEB: www.cfmg.com
SIC: 8099 Medical services organization
PA: California Forensic Medical Group, In-corporated
1283 Murfreesboro Pike # 500
Nashville TN 37217
831 649-8994

(P-22199)
CARE 1ST HEALTH PLAN (PA)
601 Potrero Grande Dr # 2, Monterey Park
(91755-7430)
PHONE...................323 889-6638
Maureen Tyson, *President*
Janet Jan, *CFO*
Michael Rowan, *Vice Pres*
Jamie Ueoka, *Vice Pres*
Josie Wong, *Vice Pres*
EMP: 165
SALES (est): 23MM Privately Held
WEB: www.care1st.com
SIC: 8099 Blood related health services

(P-22200)
CENTER TO PROMOTE HEALTHCARE A (PA)
Also Called: SOCIAL INTEREST SOLU-TIONS
1951 Webster St Fl 2, Oakland
(94612-2909)
PHONE...................510 834-1300
John Caterham, *President*
Bhavin Africawala, *Software Dev*
Angie Kiju, *Project Mgr*
Walker Ker, *Manager*
EMP: 58
SQ FT: 6,000
SALES: 26.6MM Privately Held
SIC: 8099 Medical services organization

(P-22201)
CENTRAL CALIFORNIA BLOOD CTR
Also Called: Ccbc Reference Lab
4343 W Herndon Ave, Fresno
(93722-3794)
PHONE...................559 389-5433
EMP: 98
SALES (corp-wide): 21.6MM Privately Held
SIC: 8099 8071
PA: Central California Blood Center
4343 W Herndon Ave
Fresno CA 93722
559 389-5433

(P-22202)
CENTRAL CALIFORNIA BLOOD CTR
8094 N Cedar Ave, Fresno (93720-1817)
PHONE...................559 324-1211
Dean Eller, *Branch Mgr*
EMP: 98
SALES (corp-wide): 20.7MM Privately Held
SIC: 8099 Blood bank
PA: Central California Blood Center
4343 W Herndon Ave
Fresno CA 93722
559 389-5433

(P-22203)
CENTRAL CALIFORNIA BLOOD CTR (PA)
4343 W Herndon Ave, Fresno
(93722-3794)
PHONE...................559 389-5433
Christopher Staub, *President*
Janet Ripley, *CFO*
Monica Rivera, *General Mgr*

Doane Stewart, *Opers Staff*
Betzabel Gonzalez, *Director*
EMP: 180
SQ FT: 53,000
SALES: 20.7MM Privately Held
WEB: www.cencalblood.org
SIC: 8099 Blood bank

(P-22204)
CENTRAL CALIFORNIA FACULTY MED
1085 W Minnesota Ave, Turlock
(95382-0827)
PHONE...................209 620-6937
Jason Elliot, *Branch Mgr*
EMP: 262
SALES (corp-wide): 53.8MM Privately Held
SIC: 8099 Blood related health services
PA: Central California Faculty Medical
Group, Inc.
2625 E Divisadero St
Fresno CA 93721
559 453-5200

(P-22205)
CHICO CSU
400 W 1st St, Chico (95929-0001)
PHONE...................530 898-3917
James Holloway, *Principal*
Sean Black, *Vice Pres*
Patrick McDougall, *Vice Pres*
Chelby Polines, *Vice Pres*
Anne Stephens, *Managing Dir*
EMP: 61
SALES (est): 4MM Privately Held
SIC: 8099 Health & allied services

(P-22206)
CHIRON CORPORATION
4560 Horton St, Emeryville (94608-2916)
PHONE...................510 655-8730
Edward E Penhoet, *President*
EMP: 72
SALES (est): 70.9MM
SALES (corp-wide): 39.5B Privately Held
WEB: www.chiron.com
SIC: 8099 Blood related health services
HQ: Novartis Vaccines And Diagnostics,
Inc.
475 Green Oaks Pkwy
Holly Springs NC 27540
617 871-7000

(P-22207)
CITRUS VLY HLTH PARTNERS INC
1325 N Grand Ave Ste 300, Covina
(91724-4046)
PHONE...................626 732-3100
Carol Eaton, *Principal*
EMP: 1001 Privately Held
SIC: 8099 Blood related health services
PA: Emanate Health Inter-Community Hos-pital
210 W San Bernardino Rd
Covina CA 91723

(P-22208)
CLINICA SIERRA VISTA
1430 Truxtun Ave Ste 300, Bakersfield
(93301-5220)
PHONE...................661 326-6490
Steve Shilling, *Director*
EMP: 50
SALES (corp-wide): 136.6MM Privately Held
SIC: 8099 Childbirth preparation clinic
PA: Clinica Sierra Vista
1430 Truxtun Ave Ste 400
Bakersfield CA 93301
661 635-3050

(P-22209)
COMMUNITY BLOOD BANK INC
70025 Highway 111 Ste 101, Rancho Mi-rage (92270-2935)
PHONE...................760 773-4190
Robert E Albee, *President*
Michelle Shanahan,
EMP: 61 EST: 1972
SQ FT: 8,000
SALES: 80.9K Privately Held
SIC: 8099 Blood bank

(P-22210)
COUNTY OF GLENN
Also Called: Glenn County Health Svcs Agcy
247 N Villa Ave, Willows (95988-2607)
PHONE...................530 934-6582
Scott Gruendl, *Director*
EMP: 100 Privately Held
WEB: www.countyofglen.net
SIC: 8099 9111 Medical services organi-zation; county supervisors' & executives' offices
PA: County Of Glenn
516 W Sycamore St Fl 2
Willows CA 95988
530 934-6410

(P-22211)
COUNTY OF IMPERIAL
Also Called: Public Health Department
935 Broadway Ave, El Centro
(92243-2349)
PHONE...................760 482-4441
Evon Smith, *Director*
Holly Maag, *Lab Dir*
EMP: 134 Privately Held
WEB: www.imperialcounty.net
SIC: 8099 9111 Health screening service; county supervisors' & executives' offices
PA: County Of Imperial
940 W Main St Ste 208
El Centro CA 92243
760 482-4556

(P-22212)
COUNTY OF LOS ANGELES
Also Called: Countywide Childrens Case MGT
600 S Commwl Ave Fl 2 Flr 2, Los Angeles
(90005)
PHONE...................213 739-2360
Bryan Mershon, *Branch Mgr*
EMP: 85 Privately Held
SIC: 8099 Blood related health services
PA: County Of Los Angeles
500 W Temple St Ste 437
Los Angeles CA 90012
213 974-1101

(P-22213)
COUNTY OF LOS ANGELES
Also Called: Compton Family Mhc Fsp
546 W Compton Blvd, Compton
(90220-3011)
PHONE...................310 885-2100
Phillip Mobley, *Manager*
EMP: 85 Privately Held
SIC: 8099 Blood related health services
PA: County Of Los Angeles
500 W Temple St Ste 437
Los Angeles CA 90012
213 974-1101

(P-22214)
COUNTY OF LOS ANGELES
921 E Compton Blvd, Compton
(90221-3303)
PHONE...................310 668-6845
Marvin Southard, *Branch Mgr*
EMP: 85 Privately Held
SIC: 8099 Blood related health services
PA: County Of Los Angeles
500 W Temple St Ste 437
Los Angeles CA 90012
213 974-1101

(P-22215)
COUNTY OF LOS ANGELES
Also Called: Specilzed Foster Care Pasadena
532 E Colorado Blvd Fl 8, Pasadena
(91101-2044)
PHONE...................626 229-3825
Jonathan E Sherin, *Director*
EMP: 85 Privately Held
SIC: 8099 Blood related health services
PA: County Of Los Angeles
500 W Temple St Ste 437
Los Angeles CA 90012
213 974-1101

(P-22216)
COUNTY OF LOS ANGELES
Also Called: Department of Health
3530 Wilshire Blvd Fl 9, Los Angeles
(90010-2344)
PHONE...................213 351-7800
Michelle Parra PHD, *Manager*

PRODUCTS & SVCS

Eloisa Gonzalez, *Director*
EMP: 70 Privately Held
WEB: www.co.la.ca.us
SIC: 8099 9431 Medical services organization; administration of public health programs;
PA: County Of Los Angeles
500 W Temple St Ste 437
Los Angeles CA 90012
213 974-1101

(P-22217)
COUNTY OF LOS ANGELES
Also Called: Los Angeles County Pub Works
5525 Imperial Hwy, South Gate
(90280-7417)
PHONE....................562 861-0316
Phil Doudar, *Manager*
EMP: 100 Privately Held
WEB: www.la.ca.us
SIC: 8099 9111 Blood related health services; executive offices
PA: County Of Los Angeles
500 W Temple St Ste 437
Los Angeles CA 90012
213 974-1101

(P-22218)
COUNTY OF RIVERSIDE DEPARTMENT
554 S Paseo Dorotea, Palm Springs
(92264-1445)
PHONE....................760 320-1048
EMP: 76
SALES (corp-wide): 3.6MM **Privately Held**
SIC: 8099 Childbirth preparation clinic
PA: The County Of Riverside Department Of Public Health Auxiliary
4065 County Circle Dr
Riverside CA 92503
951 358-5000

(P-22219)
COUNTY OF SAN DIEGO
Also Called: Medical Care Services Division
6255 Mission Gorge Rd, San Diego
(92120-3505)
PHONE....................858 505-6423
David Steele, *Principal*
Nicholas Yphantides, *Principal*
Denise Blaine, *Manager*
EMP: 50 EST: 2017
SALES (est): 680.5K **Privately Held**
SIC: 8099 Medical services organization

(P-22220)
COUNTY OF SAN DIEGO
Also Called: Health and Human Services Agcy
6255 Mission Gorge Rd, San Diego
(92120-3505)
PHONE....................858 505-6423
Nicholas Yphantides, *Director*
EMP: 50 EST: 2017
SALES (est): 249.3K **Privately Held**
SIC: 8099 Medical services organization

(P-22221)
COUNTY OF SAN DIEGO
Also Called: Medical Examiner Forensic Ctr
5570 Overland Ave Ste 101, San Diego
(92123-1215)
PHONE....................619 531-4521
Glenn Wagner, *Chief Mktg Ofcr*
EMP: 60 Privately Held
WEB: www.sdlcc.org
SIC: 8099 Medical services organization
PA: County Of San Diego
1600 Pacific Hwy Ste 209
San Diego CA 92101
619 531-5880

(P-22222)
CRC HEALTH GROUP INC (HQ)
20400 Stev Creek Blvd 6 Flr 6, Cupertino
(95014)
PHONE....................877 272-8668
Jerome E Rhodes, *CEO*
Leanne M Stewart, *CFO*
Christopher Gordon, *Bd of Directors*
Philip L Herschman, *Officer*
Teri Rodman, *Vice Pres*
▲ **EMP:** 68
SALES (est): 407MM **Publicly Held**
SIC: 8099 Medical services organization

(P-22223)
DAVID-KLEIS II LLC
Also Called: Palm Grove Healthcare
1665 E Eighth St, Beaumont (92223-2512)
PHONE....................951 845-3125
Madelyn V Smith,
EMP: 86
SALES (est): 492.9K **Privately Held**
SIC: 8099 Health & allied services

(P-22224)
DELTA BLOOD BANK
Also Called: American National Red Cross
1900 W Orangeburg Ave, Modesto
(95350-3740)
PHONE....................209 943-3830
Dr Benjamin Spindler, *Principal*
EMP: 100
SQ FT: 6,239
SALES (corp-wide): 2.6B **Privately Held**
SIC: 8099 7389 Blood bank; personal service agents, brokers & bureaus
HQ: Delta Blood Bank
65 N Commerce St
Stockton CA 95202
800 244-6794

(P-22225)
DELTA BLOOD BANK (HQ)
Also Called: American Natl Red Cross
65 N Commerce St, Stockton
(95202-2318)
P.O. Box 800 (95201-0800)
PHONE....................800 244-6794
Benjamin Spindler, *CEO*
Robert Lawrence, *Ch of Bd*
Alfonso Figueroa, *CFO*
◆ **EMP:** 85
SQ FT: 30,000
SALES: 3.1MM
SALES (corp-wide): 2.6B **Privately Held**
SIC: 8099 Blood bank
PA: The American National Red Cross
430 17th St Nw
Washington DC 20006
202 737-8300

(P-22226)
DIGNITY HEALTH MED FOUNDATION
6615 Valley Hi Dr, Sacramento
(95823-7076)
PHONE....................916 681-6300
Douglas Locke, *Branch Mgr*
Kristina Freas, *Director*
EMP: 76 Privately Held
SIC: 8099 8011 Medical services organization; eyes, ears, nose & throat specialist: physician/surgeon
HQ: Dignity Health Medical Foundation
3400 Data Dr
Rancho Cordova CA 95670

(P-22227)
DIGNITY HEALTH MED FOUNDATION
Also Called: Dignity Health Medical Grp
1667 Dominican Way # 134, Santa Cruz
(95065-1518)
PHONE....................831 475-8834
George Lenzi, *CFO*
EMP: 95 Privately Held
SIC: 8099 Medical rescue squad
HQ: Dignity Health Medical Foundation
3400 Data Dr
Rancho Cordova CA 95670

(P-22228)
DIGNITY HEALTH MED FOUNDATION
Also Called: Dignity Hlth Med Grp-Dominican
9515 Soquel Dr Ste 100, Aptos
(95003-4136)
PHONE....................831 535-1560
Cristina Lingo, *General Mgr*
EMP: 95 Privately Held
SIC: 8099 Medical services organization
HQ: Dignity Health Medical Foundation
3400 Data Dr
Rancho Cordova CA 95670

(P-22229)
DIGNITY HEALTH MED FOUNDATION
Also Called: Dignity Hlth Med Grp-Dominican
3400 Data Dr, Rancho Cordova
(95670-7956)
PHONE....................916 379-2840
Laurie Schwarctz, *President*
EMP: 810
SQ FT: 45,000 **Privately Held**
SIC: 8099 Medical services organization
HQ: Dignity Health Medical Foundation
3400 Data Dr
Rancho Cordova CA 95670
-

(P-22230)
DIGNITY HEALTH MED FOUNDATION
2110 Prfcional Dr Ste 120, Roseville
(95661)
PHONE....................916 787-0404
A Alan White, *Principal*
EMP: 76 Privately Held
SIC: 8099 8071 8011 Medical services organization; medical laboratories; radiologist
HQ: Dignity Health Medical Foundation
3400 Data Dr
Rancho Cordova CA 95670

(P-22231)
DIVERSIFIED CLINICAL SERVICES
4225 E La Palma Ave, Anaheim
(92807-1815)
PHONE....................714 579-8400
James R Sechrist, *Ch of Bd*
EMP: 85
SQ FT: 74,000
SALES (est): 1.1MM **Privately Held**
SIC: 8099 Medical services organization

(P-22232)
DONOR NETWORK WEST (PA)
12667 Alcosta Blvd # 500, San Ramon
(94583-5272)
PHONE....................925 480-3100
Cynthia D Siljestrom, *CEO*
Jackie Manzanedo, *Partner*
Sandra Mejia, *CFO*
Mark Borer, *Vice Pres*
Jt Mason, *Vice Pres*
EMP: 121
SQ FT: 41,039
SALES: 85.5MM **Privately Held**
SIC: 8099 Medical services organization

(P-22233)
DONOR NETWORK WEST
Also Called: Ctdn - Redding
5800 Airport Rd Ste B, Redding
(96002-9359)
PHONE....................510 418-0336
EMP: 78
SALES (corp-wide): 85.5MM **Privately Held**
SIC: 8099 Medical services organization
PA: Donor Network West
12667 Alcosta Blvd # 500
San Ramon CA 94583
925 480-3100

(P-22234)
DUAL DIAGNOSIS TRTMNT CTR INC
Also Called: Sovereign Health
69640 Highway 111, Rancho Mirage
(92270-2868)
PHONE....................949 324-4531
Tonmoy Sharma, *Branch Mgr*
EMP: 178
SALES (corp-wide): 68.5MM **Privately Held**
SIC: 8099 Childbirth preparation clinic
PA: Dual Diagnosis Treatment Center, Inc.
1211 Puerta Del Sol # 200
San Clemente CA 92673
949 276-5553

(P-22235)
EAST BAY FOUNDATION GRAD MED
1411 E 31st St, Oakland (94602-1018)
P.O. Box 309, Concord (94522-0309)
PHONE....................510 437-4197
Theresa Azevedo, *Exec Dir*
Alden Harken, *Ch of Bd*
EMP: 54
SALES: 4.1MM **Privately Held**
SIC: 8099 Medical services organization

(P-22236)
EASTER SEAL SOC SUPERIOR CAL (PA)
Also Called: Easter Seals Main Office
3205 Hurley Way, Sacramento
(95864-3853)
P.O. Box 254867 (95865-4867)
PHONE....................916 485-6711
Gary T Kasai, *President*
Sue Harris, *General Mgr*
EMP: 100 EST: 1934
SQ FT: 28,500
SALES: 12.1MM **Privately Held**
WEB: www.essuperior.org
SIC: 8099 8093 Medical services organization; rehabilitation center, outpatient treatment

(P-22237)
EASY CARE MSO LLC
3900 Kilroy Airport Way # 110, Long Beach
(90806-6809)
PHONE....................562 676-9600
Michelle Bui, *President*
EMP: 227
SALES (est): 244K
SALES (corp-wide): 18.8B **Publicly Held**
SIC: 8099 Medical services organization
PA: Molina Healthcare, Inc.
200 Oceangate Ste 100
Long Beach CA 90802
562 435-3666

(P-22238)
EHEALTHWIRECOM INC
2450 Venture Oaks Way # 100, Sacramento (95833-3292)
PHONE....................916 924-8092
Yousry Mekhamer, *Chairman*
Don Thompson, *Vice Pres*
EMP: 250
SQ FT: 17,000
SALES (est): 2.8MM **Privately Held**
WEB: www.ehealthline.com
SIC: 8099 Health screening service

(P-22239)
ELIZABETH GLASER PEDIA
16130 Ventura Blvd # 250, Encino
(91436-2503)
PHONE....................310 231-0400
Charles Lyons, *Branch Mgr*
Sushant Mukherjee, *Software Dev*
EMP: 875
SALES (corp-wide): 126MM **Privately Held**
SIC: 8099 Medical services organization
PA: Elizabeth Glaser Pediatric Aids Foundation
1140 Conn Ave Nw Ste 200
Washington DC 20036
202 296-9165

(P-22240)
EVOLENT HEALTH INC
1 Kearny St Ste 300, San Francisco
(94108-5549)
PHONE....................571 389-6000
EMP: 400
SALES (corp-wide): 627MM **Publicly Held**
SIC: 8099 Medical services organization
PA: Evolent Health, Inc.
800 N Glebe Rd Ste 500
Arlington VA 22203
571 389-6000

(P-22241)
EXAMONE WORLD WIDE INC
7480 Mission Valley Rd # 101, San Diego
(92108-4433)
PHONE....................619 299-3926
EMP: 100

SALES (corp-wide): 7.5B **Publicly Held**
SIC: **8099** Physical examination service, insurance
HQ: Examone World Wide, Inc.
10101 Renner Blvd
Lenexa KS 66219
913 888-1770

(P-22242)
FACEY MEDICAL FOUNDATION
11211 Sepulveda Blvd, Mission Hills (91345-1115)
PHONE...................818 837-5677
Cathy Hawes, *Branch Mgr*
Cornelia De Licona MD, *Med Doctor*
EMP: 200
SALES (corp-wide): 197.1MM **Privately Held**
SIC: **8099** 8042 8011 Medical services organization; offices & clinics of optometrists; offices & clinics of medical doctors
PA: Facey Medical Foundation
15451 San Fernando Msn
Mission Hills CA 91345
818 365-9531

(P-22243)
FACEY MEDICAL FOUNDATION
Also Called: Facey Medical Group
17909 Soledad Canyon Rd, Santa Clarita (91387-3210)
PHONE...................661 250-5225
Leslie Holland, *Branch Mgr*
Jeanette Pilliner, *Pediatrics*
Khai Kim T Tram, *Director*
EMP: 60
SALES (corp-wide): 197.1MM **Privately Held**
SIC: **8099** 8011 Medical services organization; offices & clinics of medical doctors
PA: Facey Medical Foundation
15451 San Fernando Msn
Mission Hills CA 91345
818 365-9531

(P-22244)
FACEY MEDICAL FOUNDATION
27924 Seco Canyon Rd, Santa Clarita (91350-3870)
PHONE...................661 513-2100
Joan Rhee, *Manager*
EMP: 86
SALES (corp-wide): 197.1MM **Privately Held**
SIC: **8099** Medical services organization
PA: Facey Medical Foundation
15451 San Fernando Msn
Mission Hills CA 91345
818 365-9531

(P-22245)
FACEY MEDICAL FOUNDATION
Also Called: Marshall, Spector MD
1237 E Main St, San Gabriel (91776)
PHONE...................626 576-0800
Ana Ventura, *Manager*
EMP: 86
SALES (corp-wide): 197.1MM **Privately Held**
SIC: **8099** 8011 Medical services organization; pediatrician
PA: Facey Medical Foundation
15451 San Fernando Msn
Mission Hills CA 91345
818 365-9531

(P-22246)
FYEO APPAREL INC
747 E 10th St Unit 303, Los Angeles (90021-2256)
PHONE...................213 278-0435
Alexandra Vince, *CEO*
EMP: 50
SALES (est): 169.3K **Privately Held**
SIC: **8099** 7221 Medical photography & art; photographer, still or video

(P-22247)
GLENVIEW ASSISTED LIVING LLP
1950 Calle Barcelona, Carlsbad (92009-8401)
PHONE...................760 704-6800
Justin Wilson, *Partner*
EMP: 50

SALES (est): 976.9K **Privately Held**
SIC: **8099** 8361 8052 Health & allied services; residential care; intermediate care facilities

(P-22248)
HALO UNLIMTED INC
Also Called: Infant Hring Scrning Spcalists
1867 California Ave # 101, Corona (92881-7281)
P.O. Box 77010 (92877-0100)
PHONE...................714 692-2270
Martha Hawkins, *President*
Nina Murcia, *Area Mgr*
EMP: 54
SQ FT: 7,500
SALES (est): 4.5MM **Privately Held**
SIC: **8099** Hearing testing service

(P-22249)
HARBOR HEALTH SYSTEMS LLC
3501 Jamboree Rd Ste 540, Newport Beach (92660-2950)
PHONE...................949 273-7020
Gregory Moore, *CEO*
James W Dolan, *CEO*
EMP: 67 EST: 2001
SALES (est): 2.7MM **Privately Held**
SIC: **8099** 7372 Blood related health services; business oriented computer software
PA: One Call Medical, Inc.
841 Prudential Dr Ste 900
Jacksonville FL 32207

(P-22250)
HEALTHCARE PARTNERS LLC
1236 N Magnolia Ave, Anaheim (92801-2607)
PHONE...................714 995-1000
Kathy Porter, *Admin Asst*
Shu Wu, *Family Practiti*
EMP: 60 **Publicly Held**
SIC: **8099** 8011 Medical services organization; offices & clinics of medical doctors
HQ: Davita Medical Management, Llc
2175 Park Pl
El Segundo CA 90245

(P-22251)
HEALTHCARE PARTNERS LLC
Also Called: Family Health Program
4910 Airport Plaza Dr, Long Beach (90815-1376)
PHONE...................562 429-2473
Rhonda Luster, *Director*
EMP: 100 **Publicly Held**
SIC: **8099** 8011 Medical services organization; clinic, operated by physicians
HQ: Davita Medical Management, Llc
2175 Park Pl
El Segundo CA 90245

(P-22252)
HEALTHCARE PARTNERS LLC
3501 S Harbor Blvd # 100, Santa Ana (92704-6919)
PHONE...................714 964-6229
Francis Gale, *Manager*
EMP: 50 **Publicly Held**
SIC: **8099** Blood related health services
HQ: Davita Medical Management, Llc
2175 Park Pl
El Segundo CA 90245

(P-22253)
HEMACARE CORPORATION (PA)
8500 Balboa Blvd Ste 130, Northridge (91325-5802)
PHONE...................877 310-0717
Pete Van Der Wal, *President*
Anna Stock, *COO*
Lisa Bacerra, *CFO*
Robert Chilton, *CFO*
Rochelle Martel, *CFO*
EMP: 105 EST: 1978
SQ FT: 19,600

SALES (est): 14.4MM **Publicly Held**
WEB: www.hemacare.com
SIC: **8099** 5122 Blood related health services; blood bank; blood donor station; blood plasma

(P-22254)
HENRY MAYO NEWHALL MEM HOSP
Also Called: Santa Clarita Health Care Ctr
23845 Mcbean Pkwy, Santa Clarita (91355-2001)
PHONE...................661 253-8227
David R Tumilty, *Principal*
EMP: 373
SALES (corp-wide): 320MM **Privately Held**
WEB: www.henrymayo.com
SIC: **8099** Childbirth preparation clinic
PA: Henry Mayo Newhall Memorial Hospital
23845 Mcbean Pkwy
Valencia CA 91355
661 253-8000

(P-22255)
HERITAGE MEDICAL GROUP
12370 Hesperia Rd Ste 6, Victorville (92395-4787)
PHONE...................760 956-1286
Stanley Wohl, *Branch Mgr*
Kelly Bell, *Mktg Coord*
EMP: 237 **Privately Held**
SIC: **8099** Blood related health services
PA: Heritage Medical Group
4580 California Ave
Bakersfield CA

(P-22256)
HORIZONS ADULT DAY HEALTH CARE
1035 Harbison Ave, National City (91950-3919)
PHONE...................619 474-1822
Marina Murashova, *President*
Russ Kraus, *CFO*
EMP: 75
SALES (est): 3MM **Privately Held**
SIC: **8099** Blood related health services

(P-22257)
HOUCHIN BLOOD SERVICES
11515 Bolthouse Dr, Bakersfield (93311-8822)
PHONE...................661 327-8541
EMP: 60
SALES (corp-wide): 8.6MM **Privately Held**
WEB: www.hcbb.org
SIC: **8099**
PA: Houchin Blood Services
11515 Bolthouse Dr
Bakersfield CA 93311
661 323-4222

(P-22258)
INCARE DME
15446 Sherman Way Apt 319, Van Nuys (91406-4254)
PHONE...................818 582-1016
Natasha Larson, *Owner*
EMP: 99
SALES (est): 721.7K **Privately Held**
SIC: **8099** Health & allied services

(P-22259)
INLAND BHAVIORAL HLTH SVCS INC (PA)
1963 N E St, San Bernardino (92405-3919)
PHONE...................909 881-6146
Temetry Ann Lindsey, *President*
Vernon Bragg Jr, *Ch of Bd*
John Wilson, *COO*
Peter Demel, *CFO*
Victoria Olagunju, *Human Res Dir*
EMP: 68 EST: 1978
SQ FT: 13,500
SALES: 9.7MM **Privately Held**
WEB: www.ibhealth.org
SIC: **8099** 8093 Medical services organization; drug clinic, outpatient; alcohol clinic, outpatient

(P-22260)
INNOVATIVE INTEGRATED HLTH INC
2042 Kern St, Fresno (93721-2008)
PHONE...................949 228-5577
Ibrahim Marouf, *Principal*
EMP: 150
SALES (est): 1MM **Privately Held**
SIC: **8099** Health & allied services

(P-22261)
INSTITUTE FOR BHVORAL HLTH INC
1905 Bus Ctr Dr S Ste 100, San Bernardino (92408)
PHONE...................909 289-1041
Azadeh K Jebelli, *President*
EMP: 265
SALES (est): 264.4K **Privately Held**
SIC: **8099** Childbirth preparation clinic

(P-22262)
INTEGRATED BEHAVIORAL HLTH INC
3070 Bristol St Ste 350, Costa Mesa (92626-7825)
P.O. Box 30018, Laguna Niguel (92607-0018)
PHONE...................714 442-4150
Dan Clark, *CEO*
Jonathan Bosanac, *President*
Tom H Yankoff, *Chairman*
David Sockel, *Ch Credit Ofcr*
EMP: 54
SQ FT: 11,000
SALES (est): 5.2MM **Privately Held**
WEB: www.ibhworklife.com
SIC: **8099** Health screening service

(P-22263)
JET HEALTH INC (PA)
20 Fairbanks Ste 175, Irvine (92618-1673)
PHONE...................949 356-6525
Jim Glynn, *President*
EMP: 653
SALES (est): 9.5MM **Privately Held**
SIC: **8099** Medical services organization

(P-22264)
JWCH INSTITUTE INC
14371 Clark Ave, Bellflower (90706-2901)
PHONE...................562 867-7999
Alvaro Ballesteros, *Branch Mgr*
Sheila Eaton,
Gloria Molina, *Manager*
Steve Lopez, *Assistant*
EMP: 78
SALES (corp-wide): 33.9MM **Privately Held**
SIC: **8099** Blood related health services
PA: Jwch Institute, Inc.
5650 Jillson St
Commerce CA 90040
323 477-1171

(P-22265)
KAISER FOUNDATION HOSPITALS
Also Called: Kaiser Foundation Health Plan
2055 Kellogg Ave, Corona (92879-3111)
PHONE...................866 984-7483
Ruth Jasse, *Administration*
EMP: 99
SALES (corp-wide): 76.5B **Privately Held**
WEB: www.kaiser.com
SIC: **8099** Childbirth preparation clinic
HQ: Kaiser Foundation Hospitals Inc
1 Kaiser Plz
Oakland CA 94612
510 271-6611

(P-22266)
KAWEAH DLTA HLTH CARE DST GILD
4945 W Cypress Ave, Visalia (93277-1592)
PHONE...................559 624-3100
Robert Havard, *President*
Mercy Jauregui, *Med Doctor*
EMP: 236
SALES (corp-wide): 537.4MM **Privately Held**
SIC: **8099** Childbirth preparation clinic

PA: Kaweah Delta Health Care District
400 W Mineral King Ave
Visalia CA 93291
559 624-2000

(P-22267)
KAWEAH DLTA HLTH CARE DST GILD
1014 San Juan Ave Ste A, Exeter
(93221-1312)
PHONE..................559 592-7300
EMP: 236
SALES (corp-wide): 537.4MM **Privately Held**
SIC: 8099 Childbirth preparation clinic
PA: Kaweah Delta Health Care District
400 W Mineral King Ave
Visalia CA 93291
559 624-2000

(P-22268)
KIMCO STAFFING SERVICES INC
1801 Oakland Blvd Ste 220, Walnut Creek
(94596-7033)
PHONE..................925 945-1444
EMP: 1190
SALES (corp-wide): 113.7MM **Privately Held**
SIC: 8099 Medical services organization
PA: Kimco Staffing Services, Inc.
17872 Cowan
Irvine CA 92614
949 331-1199

(P-22269)
LEGACY HEALTHCARE CENTER LLC
1570 N Fair Oaks Ave, Pasadena
(91103-1822)
PHONE..................626 798-0558
Raphael Oscherowitz, *Principal*
Dov Jacobs, *Principal*
EMP: 90
SALES (est): 885.1K **Privately Held**
SIC: 8099 Health & allied services

(P-22270)
LIFE LINE SCREENING AMER LTD
2854 Casitas Ave, Altadena (91001-4960)
PHONE..................626 797-9774
EMP: 330 **Privately Held**
SIC: 8099 Health screening service
PA: Life Line Screening Of America Ltd.
6111 Oak Tree Blvd # 301
Independence OH 44131

(P-22271)
LONG BEACH BEHAVIORAL HEALTH U
3200 Long Beach Blvd, Long Beach
(90807-5062)
PHONE..................310 221-6336
Yvonne Lozano, *Principal*
EMP: 60
SALES (est): 210.7K **Privately Held**
SIC: 8099 Health & allied services

(P-22272)
LOS ANGELES CNTY DEV SVC FNDTN
Also Called: FRANK D LANTERMAN RE-GIONAL CEN
3303 Wilshire Blvd # 700, Los Angeles
(90010-1704)
PHONE..................213 383-1300
Dianne Anand, *Exec Dir*
Marie Bueta, *COO*
Patrick Aulicino, *Associate Dir*
Marcus Smith, *Technology*
Karen Chacana, *Human Res Dir*
EMP: 180
SQ FT: 80,000
SALES: 189.6MM **Privately Held**
SIC: 8099 8322 8093 Medical services organization; individual & family services; mental health clinic, outpatient

(P-22273)
MCKESSON PTENT CARE SLTONS INC (HQ)
Also Called: National Rehab
9235 Activity Rd Ste 105, San Diego
(92126-4440)
P.O. Box 1135, Coraopolis PA (15108-6135)
PHONE..................412 507-0077
Heather Edmunds, *President*
John Blood, *Corp Secy*
EMP: 65
SQ FT: 26,500
SALES (est): 9.4MM
SALES (corp-wide): 214.3B **Publicly Held**
SIC: 8099 5047 Medical services organization; medical equipment & supplies
PA: Mckesson Corporation
6555 State Highway 161
Irving TX 75039
972 446-4800

(P-22274)
MEDASEND BIOMEDICAL INC (PA)
1402 Daisy Ave, Long Beach (90813-1521)
PHONE..................800 200-3581
Steve Grand, *CEO*
Stephanie Harrison, *Vice Pres*
EMP: 150
SQ FT: 10,000
SALES: 5MM **Privately Held**
SIC: 8099 4953 Health screening service; hazardous waste collection & disposal

(P-22275)
MERCY FOUNDATION NORTH
2625 Edith Ave Ste E, Redding
(96001-3040)
PHONE..................530 247-3424
Jeanine Hedman, *President*
Alisa Johnson, *Officer*
EMP: 60
SALES: 1.4MM **Privately Held**
SIC: 8099 Medical services organization

(P-22276)
MOLINA HEALTHCARE INC
9275 Sky Park Ct Ste 400, San Diego
(92123-4386)
PHONE..................858 614-1580
Lisa Ferrari, *Manager*
Connie Robertson, *Vice Pres*
Crystal Moran, *Program Mgr*
White Melissa, *Comp Spec*
Raymond Rubio, *Technician*
EMP: 318
SALES (corp-wide): 18.8B **Publicly Held**
SIC: 8099 Blood related health services
PA: Molina Healthcare, Inc.
200 Oceangate Ste 100
Long Beach CA 90802
562 435-3666

(P-22277)
MOLINA HEALTHCARE INC
1 Golden Shore, Long Beach (90802-4202)
PHONE..................562 435-3666
Sriram Bharadwaj, *Branch Mgr*
April Krajewski, *Partner*
Khaled Ghaly, *President*
Robert Gordon, *President*
Rajan Jain, *President*
EMP: 318
SALES (corp-wide): 18.8B **Publicly Held**
SIC: 8099 Blood related health services
PA: Molina Healthcare, Inc.
200 Oceangate Ste 100
Long Beach CA 90802
562 435-3666

(P-22278)
MORRISON MGT SPECIALISTS INC
Also Called: Morrison MGT Specialists
2823 Fresno St, Fresno (93721-1324)
PHONE..................559 459-6449
EMP: 200
SALES (corp-wide): 27.3B **Privately Held**
SIC: 8099
HQ: Morrison Management Specialists, Inc.
5801 Pachtree Dunwoody Rd
Atlanta GA 30350
-

(P-22279)
NATIONAL ORGANIZATION OF
18663 Ventura Blvd, Tarzana (91356-4162)
PHONE..................800 489-0210
Amonra Elohim, *President*
EMP: 150 **EST:** 1999
SALES (est): 9.3MM **Privately Held**
SIC: 8099 Blood related health services

(P-22280)
NATURAL HEALTH TRENDS CORP
609 Deep Valley Dr # 390, Rllng HLS Est
(90274-3629)
PHONE..................310 541-0888
EMP: 60
SALES (corp-wide): 191.9MM **Publicly Held**
SIC: 8099 Blood related health services
PA: Natural Health Trends Corp.
609 Deep Valley Dr # 395
Rllng Hls Est CA 90274
310 541-0888

(P-22281)
NEIGHBORHOOD HEALTHCARE
41840 Enterprise Cir N, Temecula
(92590-5654)
PHONE..................951 225-6400
EMP: 78
SALES (corp-wide): 67.7MM **Privately Held**
SIC: 8099 Childbirth preparation clinic
PA: Neighborhood Healthcare
425 N Date St Ste 203
Escondido CA 92025
760 520-8372

(P-22282)
NEIGHBORHOOD HEALTHCARE
10039 Vine St Ste A, Lakeside
(92040-3122)
PHONE..................619 390-9975
Tracy Ream, *Branch Mgr*
EMP: 78
SALES (corp-wide): 67.7MM **Privately Held**
SIC: 8099 8011 Health screening service; clinic, operated by physicians
PA: Neighborhood Healthcare
425 N Date St Ste 203
Escondido CA 92025
760 520-8372

(P-22283)
NEIGHBORHOOD HEALTHCARE
401 E Valley Pkwy, Escondido
(92025-3317)
PHONE..................760 737-6903
Melissa Bishop, *Family Practiti*
EMP: 117
SALES (corp-wide): 67.7MM **Privately Held**
SIC: 8099 Childbirth preparation clinic
PA: Neighborhood Healthcare
425 N Date St Ste 203
Escondido CA 92025
760 520-8372

(P-22284)
NEXUS HEALTHCARE SOLUTIONS INC
648 N St Andrews Pl, Los Angeles
(90004-1704)
PHONE..................310 448-2693
Akiva Greenfield, *Principal*
EMP: 50
SALES (est): 81.9K **Privately Held**
SIC: 8099 Medical services organization

(P-22285)
NORTHEAST VALLEY HEALTH CORP
7107 Remmet Ave, Canoga Park
(91303-2016)
PHONE..................818 340-3570
Gary Morris, *Branch Mgr*
EMP: 77
SALES (corp-wide): 89.4MM **Privately Held**
SIC: 8099 Blood related health services
PA: Northeast Valley Health Corp
1172 N Maclay Ave
San Fernando CA 91340
818 898-1388

(P-22286)
NORTHEAST VALLEY HEALTH CORP
7223 Fair Ave, Sun Valley (91352-4964)
PHONE..................818 432-4400
Prudence Oey, *Administration*
Marcia Howarth, *Accounting Mgr*
EMP: 92
SALES (corp-wide): 89.4MM **Privately Held**
SIC: 8099 Childbirth preparation clinic
PA: Northeast Valley Health Corp
1172 N Maclay Ave
San Fernando CA 91340
818 898-1388

(P-22287)
NOVA SKILLED HOME HEALTH INC
3300 N San Fernando Blvd, Burbank
(91504-2530)
PHONE..................323 658-6232
Nelson Aguilar, *CEO*
Julita Fraley, *CFO*
Carol Vega, *Administration*
EMP: 136
SALES (est): 38.2K **Privately Held**
SIC: 8099 Health & allied services

(P-22288)
OCCUPNL URGNT CARE HLTH SYST
Also Called: Ouch Systems
750 Riverpoint Dr, West Sacramento
(95605-1625)
PHONE..................916 374-4600
James C Smith, *President*
Joseph Whitters, *CFO*
Dan Brunner, *Exec VP*
EMP: 380
SALES (est): 4.9MM **Privately Held**
WEB: www.ouchsystems.com
SIC: 8099 Medical services organization

(P-22289)
OCEANSIDE HLTHCARE STFFING INC
Also Called: R and R Prof Hlthcare Staffing
2216 El Camino Rela 211, Santa Clarita
(91350)
PHONE..................213 503-5649
Andy Gibbs, *President*
EMP: 140
SALES: 2.2MM **Privately Held**
SIC: 8099 Childbirth preparation clinic

(P-22290)
ONELEGACY (PA)
221 S Figueroa St Ste 500, Los Angeles
(90012-2526)
PHONE..................213 625-0665
Thomas D Mone, *CEO*
Robert Mendez, *President*
Matthew Crump, *Vice Pres*
Thomas Trinh, *Administration*
Martha Cueva, *Accountant*
EMP: 60
SALES: 88.6MM **Privately Held**
SIC: 8099 Organ bank

(P-22291)
ONSITE HEALTH INC (PA)
85 Argonaut Ste 220, Aliso Viejo
(92656-4105)
PHONE..................949 305-2253
Ernest Blackwelder, *CEO*
David Joe, *Principal*
EMP: 69
SALES (est): 400MM **Privately Held**
SIC: 8099 Medical services organization

(P-22292)
ONTARIO MONTCLAR SCH DIST FOOD
1525 S Bon View Ave, Ontario
(91761-4408)
PHONE..................909 930-6360
James Hammon, *Principal*
Sara Maragni, *Director*
EMP: 120
SALES (est): 3.2MM **Privately Held**
SIC: 8099 Nutrition services

(P-22293)
PANCREATIC CANCR ACTN NETWRK I (PA)
Also Called: Pancan
1500 Rosecrans Ave # 200, Manhattan Beach (90266-3763)
PHONE.................................310 725-0025
Julie Fleshman, *President*
Jodi Lipe, *Officer*
Megan Gordon Don, *Vice Pres*
Tak Fujii, *Vice Pres*
Jenny Isaacson, *Vice Pres*
EMP: 130
SALES: 32.6MM **Privately Held**
WEB: www.pancan.com
SIC: 8099 8399 Medical services organization; social service information exchange

(P-22294)
PATHWAYS HOME HEALTH
395 Oyster Point Blvd # 128, South San Francisco (94080-1928)
PHONE.................................650 634-0133
Mary Dias, *Manager*
EMP: 50
SALES (est): 352.3K **Privately Held**
SIC: 8099 Health & allied services

(P-22295)
PERMANENTE MEDICAL GROUP INC (DH)
1950 Franklin St Fl 18th, Oakland (94612-5118)
PHONE.................................866 858-2226
Robert M Pearl, *CEO*
Gerard C Bajada, *CFO*
Pat Conolly, *Exec Dir*
Sue Schepers, *Administration*
Rhoda Wynn, *Med Doctor*
EMP: 500
SQ FT: 10,000
SALES (est): 805.2MM
SALES (corp-wide): 76.5B **Privately Held**
WEB: www.permanente.net
SIC: 8099 Medical services organization
HQ: Kaiser Foundation Hospitals Inc
1 Kaiser Plz
Oakland CA 94612
510 271-6611

(P-22296)
PIT RIVER HEALTH SERVICE INC (PA)
36977 Park Ave, Burney (96013-4067)
PHONE.................................530 335-3651
Glenna Moore, *Exec Dir*
Inder Wadhwa, *Administration*
EMP: 51
SALES: 5.6MM **Privately Held**
SIC: 8099 Medical services organization

(P-22297)
PLASMA COLLECTION CENTERS INC
2410 Lillyvale Ave, Los Angeles (90032-3514)
PHONE.................................323 441-7720
David Bell, *Ch of Bd*
Shinji Wada, *President*
EMP: 200
SALES (est): 2.6MM **Privately Held**
SIC: 8099 Blood bank

(P-22298)
PPONEXT INC
1501 Hughes Way Ste 400, Long Beach (90810-1881)
PHONE.................................888 446-6098
Barbara E Rodin PHD, *President*
EMP: 300 EST: 1999
SALES (est): 2MM
SALES (corp-wide): 5B **Publicly Held**
WEB: www.pponext.com
SIC: 8099 Medical services organization
HQ: Beech Street Corporation
25550 Commercentre Dr # 200
Lake Forest CA 92630
949 672-1000

(P-22299)
PUBLIC HEALTH INSTITUTE
1825 Bell St Ste 203, Sacramento (95825-1020)
PHONE.................................916 285-1231

Arti Parikhpatel, *Branch Mgr*
EMP: 196
SALES (corp-wide): 112.1MM **Privately Held**
SIC: 8099 Blood related health services
PA: Public Health Institute
555 12th St Ste 1050
Oakland CA 94607
510 285-5500

(P-22300)
PUBLIC HLTH FNDATION ENTPS INC
12781 Schabarum Ave, Irwindale (91706-6807)
PHONE.................................626 856-6600
Eliose Jenks, *Branch Mgr*
Kiran Saluja, *Principal*
See Lee, *IT/INT Sup*
Denise Gee, *Manager*
EMP: 154
SALES (corp-wide): 97.5MM **Privately Held**
SIC: 8099 Blood related health services
PA: Public Health Foundation Enterprises, Inc.
13300 Crssrds Pkwy N
City Of Industry CA 91746
800 201-7320

(P-22301)
PUBLIC HLTH FNDATION ENTPS INC
3648 E Olympic Blvd, Los Angeles (90023-3129)
PHONE.................................323 261-6388
EMP: 115
SALES (corp-wide): 97.5MM **Privately Held**
SIC: 8099 Blood related health services
PA: Public Health Foundation Enterprises, Inc.
13300 Crssrds Pkwy N
City Of Industry CA 91746
800 201-7320

(P-22302)
PUBLIC HLTH FNDATION ENTPS INC
8666 Whittier Blvd, Pico Rivera (90660-2655)
PHONE.................................562 801-2323
Nicolle Fevere, *Principal*
EMP: 115
SALES (corp-wide): 97.5MM **Privately Held**
SIC: 8099 Blood related health services
PA: Public Health Foundation Enterprises, Inc.
13300 Crssrds Pkwy N
City Of Industry CA 91746
800 201-7320

(P-22303)
PUBLIC HLTH FNDATION ENTPS INC
1649 W Washington Blvd, Los Angeles (90007-1116)
PHONE.................................323 733-9381
Eloise Jenks, *President*
EMP: 115
SALES (corp-wide): 97.5MM **Privately Held**
SIC: 8099 Blood related health services
PA: Public Health Foundation Enterprises, Inc.
13300 Crssrds Pkwy N
City Of Industry CA 91746
800 201-7320

(P-22304)
PUBLIC HLTH FNDATION ENTPS INC
125 E Anaheim St, Wilmington (90744-4590)
PHONE.................................310 518-2835
EMP: 154
SALES (corp-wide): 97.5MM **Privately Held**
SIC: 8099 Blood related health services
PA: Public Health Foundation Enterprises, Inc.
13300 Crssrds Pkwy N
City Of Industry CA 91746
800 201-7320

(P-22305)
PUBLIC HLTH FNDATION ENTPS INC
Also Called: Wic
12781 Shama Rd, El Monte (91732)
PHONE.................................626 856-6618
Juan Chong, *Branch Mgr*
EMP: 231
SALES (corp-wide): 97.5MM **Privately Held**
SIC: 8099 Blood related health services
PA: Public Health Foundation Enterprises, Inc.
13300 Crssrds Pkwy N
City Of Industry CA 91746
800 201-7320

(P-22306)
QTC MANAGEMENT INC (DH)
924 Overland Ct, San Dimas (91773-1742)
PHONE.................................800 260-1515
Stephanie Hill, *CEO*
Courtney Bush, *Office Mgr*
Buddy Lunati, *Office Mgr*
Armenoohi Zakaria, *Office Mgr*
Ning Lin, *Sr Software Eng*
▼ EMP: 160
SQ FT: 20,000
SALES (est): 61.6MM
SALES (corp-wide): 10.1B **Publicly Held**
SIC: 8099 Medical services organization
HQ: Qtc Holdings Inc.
700 N Frederick Ave
Gaithersburg MD 20879
909 859-2100

(P-22307)
QTC MDCAL GROUP INC A MED CORP
924 Overland Ct, San Dimas (91773-1742)
PHONE.................................800 260-1515
Brant Kim, *CEO*
Joyce Sarreal, *Manager*
EMP: 1000
SALES (est): 601.1K **Privately Held**
SIC: 8099 Physical examination & testing services

(P-22308)
REDDING RANCHERIA
Also Called: Redding Ranch Indian Hlth CL
1441 Liberty St, Redding (96001-0811)
PHONE.................................530 224-2700
Ron Sissan, *Director*
EMP: 65
SALES (corp-wide): 36.5MM **Privately Held**
WEB: www.redding-rancheria.com
SIC: 8099 Medical services organization
PA: Redding Rancheria
2000 Redding Rancheria Rd
Redding CA 96001
530 225-8979

(P-22309)
RESCUE MISSION ALLIANCE
125 S Harrison Ave, Oxnard (93030-6038)
PHONE.................................805 201-4341
Carol Roberg, *Principal*
EMP: 50
SALES (est): 1.2MM
SALES (corp-wide): 26.5MM **Privately Held**
WEB: www.erescuemission.com
SIC: 8099 Health & allied services
PA: Rescue Mission Alliance
315 N A St
Oxnard CA 93030
805 487-1234

(P-22310)
S&F MANAGEMENT COMPANY LLC
Also Called: Windsor Post Acute Care Center
25919 Gading Rd, Hayward (94544-2725)
PHONE.................................310 385-1088
Lee C Samson, *President*
EMP: 904 **Privately Held**
SIC: 8099 Childbirth preparation clinic
PA: S&F Management Company, Llc
9200 W Sunset Blvd # 700
West Hollywood CA 90069

(P-22311)
SAINT AGNES MED PROVIDERS INC
1379 E Herndon Ave, Fresno (93720-3309)
PHONE.................................559 435-2630
David J Cavagnaro MD, *Partner*
EMP: 69
SALES (corp-wide): 4.7MM **Privately Held**
SIC: 8099 Childbirth preparation clinic
PA: Saint Agnes Medical Providers, Inc.
1105 E Spruce Ave Ste 201
Fresno CA 93720
559 450-7200

(P-22312)
SAINT-JOSEPH HOME HEALTH
1525 Mccarthy Blvd # 208, Milpitas (95035-7452)
PHONE.................................408 244-5488
Daryl Velasco, *Principal*
EMP: 50
SALES: 2.3MM **Privately Held**
SIC: 8099 Medical services organization

(P-22313)
SAN BERNARDINO CITY UNF SCHOOL
Also Called: Nutrition Services
1257 Northpark Blvd, San Bernardino (92407-2946)
PHONE.................................909 881-8000
Adrian Robles, *Branch Mgr*
EMP: 65
SALES (corp-wide): 712MM **Privately Held**
WEB: www.sbcusd.k12.ca.us
SIC: 8099 8211 Nutrition services; elementary school
PA: San Bernardino City Unified School District
777 N F St
San Bernardino CA 92410
909 381-1100

(P-22314)
SAN DIEGO BLOOD BANK (PA)
Also Called: San Diego Blood Bnk Foundation
3636 Gtwy Ctr Ave Ste 100, San Diego (92102-4508)
PHONE.................................619 296-6393
Ramona Walker, *CEO*
Richard Dickson, *Vice Pres*
Debbie Yoo, *Executive*
Margie Flowers, *Lab Dir*
Jackie Vella, *Exec Dir*
▲ EMP: 168
SQ FT: 132,000
SALES (est): 37.4MM **Privately Held**
SIC: 8099 8071 Blood bank; medical laboratories

(P-22315)
SAN DIEGO COASTL MED GROUP INC
2201 Mission Ave, Oceanside (92058-2313)
PHONE.................................760 901-5259
Meredith Acosta, *Principal*
Mary Beth Casement, *Pediatrics*
EMP: 126 EST: 2008
SALES (est): 962.3K
SALES (corp-wide): 2.1B **Privately Held**
SIC: 8099 Health & allied services
PA: Scripps Health
10140 Campus Point Dr Ax415
San Diego CA 92121
800 727-4777

(P-22316)
SAN DIEGO FAMILY CARE
4290 Polk Ave, San Diego (92105-1524)
PHONE.................................619 563-0250
EMP: 114
SALES (corp-wide): 21.3MM **Privately Held**
SIC: 8099 Childbirth preparation clinic
PA: San Diego Family Care
6973 Linda Vista Rd
San Diego CA 92111
858 279-0925

(P-22317)
SAN MATEO HEALTH COMMISSION
Also Called: Health Plan of San Mateo
801 Gateway Blvd Ste 100, South San
Francisco (94080-7408)
PHONE.................................650 616-0050
Maya Altman, *CEO*
Ron Robinson, *CFO*
Rion Manning, *Marketing Staff*
Ruth Trask, *Nurse*
Jimmy Holman, *Manager*
EMP: 211
SQ FT: 58,758
SALES (est): 17.2MM **Privately Held**
WEB: www.hpsm.org
SIC: 8099 Physical examination service,
insurance

(P-22318)
SANTA ANA UNIFIED SCHOOL DST
Also Called: Nutririon Services
1749 Carnegie Ave, Santa Ana
(92705-5525)
PHONE.................................714 431-1900
Mark Chavez, *Director*
EMP: 100
SQ FT: 30,295
SALES (corp-wide): 763.5MM **Privately
Held**
WEB: www.santaanaeducation.com
SIC: 8099 Nutrition services
PA: Santa Ana Unified School District Pub-
lic Facilities Corporation
1601 E Chestnut Ave
Santa Ana CA 92701
714 558-5501

(P-22319)
SANTA BARBARA COUNTY OF
Also Called: Public Health Dept
345 Camino Del Remedio, Santa Barbara
(93110-1332)
PHONE.................................805 681-5100
Tekashi Wada, *Director*
EMP: 60 **Privately Held**
WEB: www.sbcountyhr.org
SIC: 8099 9431 Medical services organi-
zation; administration of public health pro-
grams;
PA: County Of Santa Barbara
105 E Anapamu St Rm 406
Santa Barbara CA 93101
805 568-3400

(P-22320)
SANTA CLARA VALLEY MEDICAL CTR
2220 Moorpark Ave, San Jose
(95128-2613)
PHONE.................................408 885-5730
Claribel Balance, *Technology*
EMP: 599 **Privately Held**
SIC: 8099 Childbirth preparation clinic
PA: Santa Clara Valley Medical Center
751 S Bascom Ave
San Jose CA 95128

(P-22321)
SEA VIEW MEDICAL GROUP INC
1901 Solar Dr Ste 265, Oxnard
(93036-2692)
PHONE.................................805 373-5781
Dr Gary Prossfett, *Director*
Dr Yacoob Mall, *Treasurer*
Dr Richard Brand, *Admin Sec*
EMP: 80
SQ FT: 6,000
SALES (est): 1.6MM
SALES (corp-wide): 214.3B **Publicly
Held**
WEB: www.hserve.com
SIC: 8099 Medical services organization
HQ: Change Healthcare Practice Manage-
ment Solutions Group, Inc.
7 Parkway Ctr Ste 400
Pittsburgh PA 15220

(P-22322)
SHARE OUR SELVES CORPORATION
1 Purpose Dr, Lake Forest (92630-8717)
PHONE.................................949 609-8199
EMP: 52
SALES (corp-wide): 16.1MM **Privately
Held**
SIC: 8099 Childbirth preparation clinic
PA: Share Our Selves Corporation
1550 Superior Ave
Costa Mesa CA 92627
949 270-2135

(P-22323)
SIERRA VISTA FAMILY MEDICAL
1227 E Los Angeles Ave, Simi Valley
(93065-2871)
PHONE.................................805 582-4000
EMP: 80 EST: 2009
SALES (est): 2.6MM **Privately Held**
SIC: 8099

(P-22324)
SOBALIVING LLC
22669 Pacific Coast Hwy, Malibu
(90265-5036)
PHONE.................................800 595-3803
Gregory Hannley, *President*
EMP: 50
SALES (est): 4.1MM **Privately Held**
SIC: 8099 Health & allied services

(P-22325)
SOUTH CNTY CMNTY HLTH CTR INC (PA)
Also Called: Ravenswood Family Health Ctr
1885 Bay Rd, East Palo Alto (94303-1312)
PHONE.................................650 330-7407
Wayne Yost, *CFO*
Laila Gulzar, *Officer*
Luisa Buada, *Exec Dir*
Maria Zamora, *IT/INT Sup*
Gralyn Jacques, *Controller*
EMP: 70
SALES: 23.3MM **Privately Held**
SIC: 8099 Medical services organization

(P-22326)
SOUTHERN CAL PRMNNTE MED GROUP
23781 Maquina, Mission Viejo
(92691-2716)
PHONE.................................949 376-8619
EMP: 354
SALES (corp-wide): 3.5B **Privately Held**
SIC: 8099 Blood related health services
PA: Southern California Permanente Med-
ical Group
393 Walnut Dr
Pasadena CA 91107
626 405-5704

(P-22327)
STAR OF CALIFORNIA
299 W Hillcrest Dr, Thousand Oaks
(91360-4264)
PHONE.................................805 379-1401
Doug Moes, *Branch Mgr*
EMP: 56 **Privately Held**
SIC: 8099 Medical services organization
PA: Star Of California, A Professional Psy-
chological Corporation
4880 Market St
Ventura CA 93003
-

(P-22328)
STAR OF CALIFORNIA
8834 Morro Rd, Atascadero (93422-3953)
PHONE.................................805 466-1638
EMP: 189 **Privately Held**
SIC: 8099 Medical services organization
PA: Star Of California, A Professional Psy-
chological Corporation
4880 Market St
Ventura CA 93003
-

(P-22329)
STAR OF CALIFORNIA (PA)
4880 Market St, Ventura (93003-7783)
PHONE.................................805 644-7823
Doug Moes, *President*
Doug Wright, *CFO*

Quy Neel, *Office Admin*
Sarah Bass, *Manager*
Stephanie Chapman, *Manager*
EMP: 110
SQ FT: 6,640
SALES (est): 5.8MM **Privately Held**
SIC: 8099 Medical services organization

(P-22330)
SUTTER HEALTH
2950 Collier Canyon Rd, Livermore
(94551-9224)
PHONE.................................925 371-3800
Ronald D Workman, *Branch Mgr*
EMP: 88
SALES (corp-wide): 12.7B **Privately Held**
SIC: 8099 Blood related health services
PA: Sutter Health
2200 River Plaza Dr
Sacramento CA 95833
916 733-8800

(P-22331)
SUTTER HLTH SCRMNTO SIERRA REG
701 Howe Ave Ste F20, Sacramento
(95825-4681)
PHONE.................................916 733-7080
Mary Ashuckian, *Branch Mgr*
Barbara Berry, *Manager*
EMP: 1265
SALES (corp-wide): 12.7B **Privately Held**
SIC: 8099 Blood related health services
HQ: Sutter Health Sacramento Sierra Re-
gion
2200 River Plaza Dr
Sacramento CA 95833
916 733-8800

(P-22332)
TELEMEDICINE CORP
8920 Wilshire Blvd # 310, Beverly Hills
(90211-2003)
PHONE.................................888 472-2853
David Woroboff, *CEO*
George Willard, *COO*
EMP: 50
SQ FT: 2,000
SALES (est): 400K **Privately Held**
SIC: 8099 Childbirth preparation clinic

(P-22333)
TENDERLOIN HOUSING CLINIC INC
472 Turk St, San Francisco (94102-3330)
PHONE.................................415 771-2427
Randall Shaw, *Branch Mgr*
Rebecca Tang, *Finance*
Colleen Carrigan, *Sales Dir*
EMP: 226 **Privately Held**
SIC: 8099 Blood related health services
PA: Tenderloin Housing Clinic, Inc.
126 Hyde St
San Francisco CA 94102

(P-22334)
UCSD HEALTHCARE
355 Dickinson St 340, San Diego
(92103-2075)
P.O. Box 33268 (92163-3268)
PHONE.................................858 657-7105
Stephen Crawford, *Principal*
EMP: 92
SALES (est): 11.4MM **Privately Held**
SIC: 8099 Health & allied services

(P-22335)
UNIFIED INV PROGRAMS INC (PA)
Also Called: Palm Grove Health Care
2368 Torrance Blvd # 200, Torrance
(90501-2500)
PHONE.................................310 782-1878
Cynthia Schein, *Owner*
Emmanuel B David, *President*
EMP: 70
SALES (est): 1.7MM **Privately Held**
SIC: 8099 8051 Medical services organi-
zation; skilled nursing care facilities

(P-22336)
VITALANT
Also Called: United Blood Services Ventura
4119 Broad St Ste 100, San Luis Obispo
(93401-7965)
PHONE.................................805 543-1077
Vicki Finson, *Exec Dir*
EMP: 90
SALES (est): 11.7B **Privately Held**
SIC: 8099 Blood bank
PA: Vitalant
6210 E Oak St
Scottsdale AZ 85257
602 414-3819

(P-22337)
VITALANT
Also Called: Tri-Counties Blood Bank
4119 Broad St Ste 100, San Luis Obispo
(93401-7965)
PHONE.................................831 751-1993
Vicky Finson, *Director*
EMP: 80
SALES (corp-wide): 11.7B **Privately Held**
SIC: 8099 Blood bank
PA: Vitalant
6210 E Oak St
Scottsdale AZ 85257
602 414-3819

(P-22338)
VITALANT
Also Called: United Blood Svcs Centl Coast
2223 Eastman Ave Ste A, Ventura
(93003-8050)
PHONE.................................805 654-1603
Susan Noone, *Director*
EMP: 60
SALES (corp-wide): 11.7B **Privately Held**
SIC: 8099 Blood bank; blood donor station
PA: Vitalant
6210 E Oak St
Scottsdale AZ 85257
602 414-3819

(P-22339)
VITALANT RESEARCH INSTITUTE
Also Called: Peninsula South Bay
111 Rollins Rd, Millbrae (94030-3114)
PHONE.................................650 697-4034
Tatiana Bobrova, *Director*
EMP: 50
SALES (corp-wide): 59.7MM **Privately
Held**
SIC: 8099 8071 Blood related health serv-
ices; medical laboratories
PA: Vitalant Research Institute
270 Masonic Ave
San Francisco CA 94118
415 567-6400

(P-22340)
VITALANT RESEARCH INSTITUTE (PA)
Also Called: Shasta Blood Center
270 Masonic Ave, San Francisco
(94118-4417)
PHONE.................................415 567-6400
Nora Hirschler, *President*
Maureen O'Dea, *Admin Asst*
Kaishan Huang, *Technical Staff*
Shelly Chung, *Human Res Mgr*
Salima Shaikh, *Asst Director*
EMP: 120
SQ FT: 67,000
SALES: 59.7MM **Privately Held**
SIC: 8099 Blood bank

(P-22341)
VITALANT RESEARCH INSTITUTE
620 Kings Ct Ste 110, Ukiah (95482-5005)
PHONE.................................707 462-1754
EMP: 97
SALES (corp-wide): 59.7MM **Privately
Held**
SIC: 8099 Blood bank
PA: Vitalant Research Institute
270 Masonic Ave
San Francisco CA 94118
415 567-6400

(P-22342)
**VITALANT RESEARCH
INSTITUTE**
Also Called: NAPA Solano Cmnty Blood Ctr
1325 Gateway Blvd Ste C1, Fairfield
(94533-6919)
PHONE..............................707 428-6001
Lana Dyson, *Manager*
EMP: 50
SALES (corp-wide): 59.7MM **Privately
Held**
SIC: **8099** Blood bank
PA: Vitalant Research Institute
270 Masonic Ave
San Francisco CA 94118
415 567-6400

8111 Legal Svcs

(P-22343)
**A BUCHALTER PROFESSIONAL
CORP (PA)**
1000 Wilshire Blvd # 150, Los Angeles
(90017-2457)
PHONE..............................213 891-0700
Adam Bass, *CEO*
Daniel Slate, *Shareholder*
Steven Spector, *Shareholder*
Jeremy Weitz, *Shareholder*
Robert Willner, *Shareholder*
EMP: 209
SQ FT: 84,000
SALES (est): 56.6MM **Privately Held**
SIC: **8111** General practice law office

(P-22344)
**A BUCHALTER PROFESSIONAL
CORP**
18400 Von Karman Ave # 800, Irvine
(92612-1514)
PHONE..............................714 549-5150
Tammy Curtis, *Manager*
David W Bustle, *Info Tech Dir*
EMP: 60
SALES (corp-wide): 56.6MM **Privately
Held**
SIC: **8111** General practice law office
PA: A Buchalter Professional Corporation
1000 Wilshire Blvd # 150
Los Angeles CA 90017
213 891-0700

(P-22345)
**AARON DOWLING
INCORPORATED**
8080 N Palm Ave Ste 300, Fresno
(93711-5797)
P.O. Box 28902 (93729-8902)
PHONE..............................559 432-4500
Larry B Lindenau, *CEO*
Ronald Henderson, *Partner*
Stephanie Borchers, *Shareholder*
Leigh Burnside, *Shareholder*
Mark Kruthers, *Shareholder*
EMP: 80
SQ FT: 16,000
SALES (est): 11.9MM **Privately Held**
SIC: **8111** General practice attorney,
lawyer

(P-22346)
**ADELSON TESTAN BRUNDO
NOVEL (PA)**
31330 Oak Crest Dr, Westlake Village
(91361-4632)
PHONE..............................805 604-1816
Steven Testan, *President*
Lily Shyu, *CFO*
Judy Robertson, *Executive Asst*
Bryan Montalbon, *Info Tech Dir*
Dennis Bonnilla, *Info Tech Mgr*
EMP: 50
SQ FT: 17,900
SALES (est): 57.7MM **Privately Held**
SIC: **8111** Labor & employment law

(P-22347)
AKIN GUMP STRAUSS
2029 Century Park E # 2400, Los Angeles
(90067-3010)
PHONE..............................310 229-1000
David Allen, *Managing Prtnr*
Aj Nadershahi, *CTO*

Zak Franklin,
Robert Humphreys, *Counsel*
Oleg Stolyar, *Counsel*
EMP: 100
SALES (corp-wide): 263MM **Privately
Held**
WEB: www.akingump.com
SIC: **8111** General practice law office
PA: Akin, Gump, Strauss, Hauer, & Feld Llp
2001 K St Nw Ste Ll
Washington DC 20006
202 887-4000

(P-22348)
**AKIN GUMP STRAUSS HAUER
& FEL**
580 California St # 1500, San Francisco
(94104-1000)
PHONE..............................415 765-9500
Karen Kubin, *Branch Mgr*
EMP: 131
SALES (corp-wide): 263MM **Privately
Held**
WEB: www.akingump.net
SIC: **8111** Specialized law offices, attor-
neys
PA: Akin, Gump, Strauss, Hauer, & Feld Llp
2001 K St Nw Ste Ll
Washington DC 20006
202 887-4000

(P-22349)
**ALBERT MCKNZIE A PROF LAW
CORP**
1800 Sutter St Ste 360, Concord
(94520-2590)
PHONE..............................925 689-8000
Bruce Albert, *Branch Mgr*
Mario Jauregui, *Sr Associate*
EMP: 51
SALES (corp-wide): 3.2MM **Privately
Held**
SIC: **8111** Specialized law offices, attor-
neys
PA: Albert & Mackenzie, Llp
28216 Dorothy Dr Ste 200
Agoura Hills CA 91301
818 575-9876

(P-22350)
**ALBERT MCKNZIE A PROF LAW
CORP**
Also Called: ALBERT AND MACKENZIE, A
PROFESSIONAL LAW CORPORATION
16600 Sherman Way, Van Nuys
(91406-3875)
PHONE..............................818 650-6900
EMP: 51
SALES (corp-wide): 3.2MM **Privately
Held**
SIC: **8111** General practice law office
PA: Albert & Mackenzie, Llp
28216 Dorothy Dr Ste 200
Agoura Hills CA 91301
818 575-9876

(P-22351)
ALDRIDGE PITE LLP
4375 Jutland Dr Ste 200, San Diego
(92117-3600)
P.O. Box 17935 (92177-7923)
PHONE..............................858 750-7700
Monica Swenson, *Opers Staff*
Benton Christina C, *Associate*
Lloyd T Workman, *Associate*
EMP: 198
SALES (corp-wide): 61.7MM **Privately
Held**
SIC: **8111** Real estate law
PA: Aldridge Pite Llp
3575 Piedmont Rd Ne 15-500
Atlanta GA 30305
404 994-7400

(P-22352)
ALLEN MATKINS LECK GMBLE
3 Embarcadero Ctr # 1200, San Francisco
(94111-4015)
PHONE..............................415 837-1515
Richard C Mallory, *Partner*
Jerry Neuman, *Partner*
Alexander Nestor, *Counsel*
Kamran Javandel, *Associate*
EMP: 80

SALES (est): 6.1MM
SALES (corp-wide): 64.6MM **Privately
Held**
WEB: www.allenmatkins.com
SIC: **8111** General practice law office
PA: Allen Matkins Leck Gamble Mallory &
Natsis Llp
865 S Figueroa St # 2800
Los Angeles CA 90017
213 622-5555

(P-22353)
**ALLEN MATKINS LECK GMBLE
(PA)**
865 S Figueroa St # 2800, Los Angeles
(90017-2543)
PHONE..............................213 622-5555
David L Osias, *Managing Prtnr*
Keith Paul Bishop, *Partner*
Raymond M Buddie, *Partner*
Jeffrey Chine, *Partner*
John C Condas, *Partner*
EMP: 300
SQ FT: 40,000
SALES (est): 64.6MM **Privately Held**
WEB: www.allenmatkins.com
SIC: **8111** General practice law office; labor
& employment law; corporate, partnership
& business law; real estate law

(P-22354)
ALLEN MATKINS LECK GMBLE
1900 Main St Fl 5, Irvine (92614-7321)
PHONE..............................949 553-1313
Drew Emmel, *Senior Partner*
Ralph Allen, *COO*
Allen Matkins, *General Counsel*
Courtney Davis, *Counsel*
Lindsay Tabaian, *Counsel*
EMP: 100
SALES (est): 8.6MM
SALES (corp-wide): 64.6MM **Privately
Held**
WEB: www.allenmatkins.com
SIC: **8111** General practice law office
PA: Allen Matkins Leck Gamble Mallory &
Natsis Llp
865 S Figueroa St # 2800
Los Angeles CA 90017
213 622-5555

(P-22355)
ALSTON & BIRD LLP
333 S Hope St Ste 1600, Los Angeles
(90071-1410)
PHONE..............................213 626-8830
Wayne Mitchell, *Branch Mgr*
Mark Hahs, *Managing Prtnr*
Karen Schmid, *Vice Pres*
Greg Dennerlein, *Managing Dir*
Julie Hite, *Branch Mgr*
EMP: 165
SALES (corp-wide): 781.8MM **Privately
Held**
SIC: **8111** General practice attorney,
lawyer
PA: Alston & Bird Llp
1201 W Peachtree St Nw # 4000
Atlanta GA 30309
404 881-7000

(P-22356)
ALSTON & BIRD LLP
2815 Townsgate Rd Ste 200, Westlake Vil-
lage (91361-3091)
PHONE..............................202 239-3673
Michael D Bradbury, *Principal*
EMP: 294
SALES (corp-wide): 781.8MM **Privately
Held**
SIC: **8111** General practice attorney,
lawyer
PA: Alston & Bird Llp
1201 W Peachtree St Nw # 4000
Atlanta GA 30309
404 881-7000

(P-22357)
**ALVARADOSMITH A PROF CORP
(PA)**
1 Macarthur Pl Ste 200, Santa Ana
(92707-5941)
PHONE..............................714 852-6800
Ruben A Smith, *CEO*
Jonathan Werner, *Shareholder*
Lydia Rodriguez, *President*

Wendy Roman, *President*
Jacqueline Bustamante, *Admin Sec*
EMP: 110
SALES (est): 16.9MM **Privately Held**
SIC: **8111** General practice law office

(P-22358)
**ANDERSON MCPHARLIN
CONNERS LLP (PA)**
Also Called: AMC&
707 Wilshire Blvd # 4000, Los Angeles
(90017-3501)
PHONE..............................213 688-0080
David T Dibiase, *Partner*
Mark E Aronson, *Partner*
Carleton R Burch, *Partner*
Colleen A Dziel, *Partner*
Jesse S Hernandez, *Partner*
EMP: 59
SQ FT: 23,000
SALES (est): 13.6MM **Privately Held**
WEB: www.amclaw.com
SIC: **8111** General practice attorney,
lawyer

(P-22359)
ARENT FOX LLP
555 W 5th St Ste 4800, Los Angeles
(90013-1065)
PHONE..............................213 629-7400
Robert O'Brien, *Partner*
EMP: 115
SALES (corp-wide): 104.4MM **Privately
Held**
SIC: **8111** General practice attorney,
lawyer
PA: Arent Fox Llp
1717 K St Nw Ste B1
Washington DC 20006
202 857-6000

(P-22360)
ARNOLD & PORTER LLP
3 Embarcadero Ctr Fl 7, San Francisco
(94111-4078)
PHONE..............................818 788-8081
Elizabeth Respess, *Exec Dir*
Deborah G Douglas, *Marketing Staff*
Denis Rice, *Counsel*
Julie A Kent, *Associate*
Emily Wood, *Associate*
EMP: 350
SALES (corp-wide): 296.2MM **Privately
Held**
SIC: **8111** Corporate, partnership & busi-
ness law
PA: Arnold & Porter Kaye Scholer Llp
601 Massachusetts Ave Nw
Washington DC 20001
202 942-5000

(P-22361)
ARNOLD & PORTER PC
3 Embarcadero Ctr Fl 7, San Francisco
(94111-4078)
PHONE..............................415 434-1600
Lawrence Rabkin, *Ch of Bd*
Alina Austin, *President*
Judy Lord, *President*
Sean Howell, *CFO*
Michelle Johnson, *Exec Dir*
▲ EMP: 350
SQ FT: 70,000
SALES (est): 26.5MM **Privately Held**
WEB: www.hrice.com
SIC: **8111** Corporate, partnership & busi-
ness law

(P-22362)
**ARNOLD PORTER KAYE
SCHOLER LLP**
3000 El Camino Real 2-500, Palo Alto
(94306-2125)
PHONE..............................650 319-4500
Aurel Iderstine, *Manager*
EMP: 68
SALES (corp-wide): 296.2MM **Privately
Held**
SIC: **8111** General practice law office
PA: Arnold & Porter Kaye Scholer Llp
601 Massachusetts Ave Nw
Washington DC 20001
202 942-5000

(P-22363)
ARNOLD PORTER KAYE SCHOLER LLP
1999 Avenue Of The Stars # 1600, Los Angeles (90067-4616)
PHONE............................310 788-1000
Aurel Van Iderstine, *Branch Mgr*
Rhonda Trotter, *Managing Prtnr*
Aurel V Iderstine, *Branch Mgr*
Ruth Vega,
Brian Witkowski, *Counsel*
EMP: 128
SALES (corp-wide): 296.2MM **Privately Held**
SIC: 8111 General practice law office
PA: Arnold & Porter Kaye Scholer Llp
601 Massachusetts Ave Nw
Washington DC 20001
202 942-5000

(P-22364)
ARTIANO SHINOFF ABED (PA)
Also Called: Law Offices of James F. Holtz
16935 W Bernardo Dr # 114, San Diego (92127-1634)
PHONE............................619 232-3122
Shari Randall, *Administration*
Robert E Gallagher, *Admin Sec*
James F Holtz,
Robert R Templeton Jr,
EMP: 51
SALES (est): 7.7MM **Privately Held**
WEB: www.stutzlawfirm.com
SIC: 8111 General practice attorney, lawyer

(P-22365)
ATKINSON AND LY RD & RM LW (PA)
Also Called: Atkinson Andelson Loya
12800 Center Court Dr S # 300, Cerritos (90703-9363)
PHONE............................562 653-3200
James C Romo, *CEO*
Adam Newman, *Partner*
Steven Atkinson, *President*
Steven Andelson, *Vice Pres*
Paul Loya, *Principal*
EMP: 150
SALES (est): 38.2MM **Privately Held**
SIC: 8111 General practice attorney, lawyer

(P-22366)
BAKER KEENER & NAHRA
Also Called: Baker Keener & Nahra
633 W 5th Ste 5500, Los Angeles (90071-2014)
PHONE............................213 241-0900
Robert Baker, *Partner*
Patricia Aguayo, *President*
EMP: 50
SQ FT: 18,000
SALES (est): 9.9MM **Privately Held**
WEB: www.bknlawyers.com
SIC: 8111 Malpractice & negligence law

(P-22367)
BAKER & HOSTETLER LLP
11601 Wilshire Blvd Fl 14, Los Angeles (90025-1750)
PHONE............................310 820-8800
John F Cermak Jr, *Partner*
Cathryn Rowley, *Partner*
Hernandez Bernard, *IT/INT Sup*
Bob Lofton,
Teresa R Tracy,
EMP: 76
SALES (corp-wide): 228.4MM **Privately Held**
SIC: 8111 General practice attorney, lawyer; bankruptcy law; labor & employment law; real estate law
PA: Baker & Hostetler Llp
127 Public Sq Ste 2000
Cleveland OH 44114
216 621-0200

(P-22368)
BAKER & MCKENZIE LLP
2 Embarcadero Ctr # 1100, San Francisco (94111-3911)
PHONE............................415 576-3000
Peter Engstrom, *Manager*
Bartley Baer, *Partner*

Edward D Burmeister, *Partner*
Robin Chesler, *Partner*
Peter Denwood, *Partner*
EMP: 120
SALES (corp-wide): 810.6MM **Privately Held**
SIC: 8111 Administrative & government law; corporate, partnership & business law
PA: Baker & Mckenzie Llp
300 E Randolph St # 5000
Chicago IL 60601
312 861-8000

(P-22369)
BAKER & MCKENZIE LLP
660 Hansen Way Ste 1, Palo Alto (94304-1045)
PHONE............................650 856-2400
Peter Engstrom, *Branch Mgr*
Jon Appleton, *Partner*
Bartley Baer, *Partner*
Michael Bumbaca, *Partner*
Robin Chesler, *Partner*
EMP: 60
SALES (corp-wide): 810.6MM **Privately Held**
SIC: 8111 8011 General practice law office; medical centers
PA: Baker & Mckenzie Llp
300 E Randolph St # 5000
Chicago IL 60601
312 861-8000

(P-22370)
BAKER MNOCK JENSEN A PROF CORP
Also Called: Baker Mnock Jnsen Attys At Law
5260 N Palm Ave Ste 421, Fresno (93704-2217)
PHONE............................559 432-5400
Bob Smittcamp, *CEO*
Donald P Fishbach, *Senior Partner*
Douglas B Jensen, *Senior Partner*
Kendall Manock, *Senior Partner*
David Camenson, *Vice Pres*
EMP: 110 EST: 1904
SQ FT: 30,000
SALES (est): 13MM **Privately Held**
WEB: www.bmj-law.com
SIC: 8111 General practice law office

(P-22371)
BALLARD ROSENBERG GOLPER SAV (PA)
15760 Ventura Blvd # 1800, Encino (91436-3000)
PHONE............................818 508-3700
John Golper,
Richard Rosenberg, *Executive*
Karen Thomson, *Admin Sec*
Marlene Aposhian, *Administration*
Elsa Baauelos, *Counsel*
EMP: 51
SQ FT: 21,000
SALES (est): 9.4MM **Privately Held**
WEB: www.brgslaw.com
SIC: 8111 Labor & employment law; general practice attorney, lawyer

(P-22372)
BALLARD SPAHR LLP
2029 Century Park E # 800, Los Angeles (90067-2909)
PHONE............................424 204-4400
Alan Petlak, *Branch Mgr*
Irma Williams, *Marketing Mgr*
Olabisi Okubadejo, *Counsel*
EMP: 76
SALES (corp-wide): 224.2MM **Privately Held**
SIC: 8111 General practice attorney, lawyer
PA: Ballard Spahr Llp
1735 Market St Fl 51
Philadelphia PA 19103
215 665-8500

(P-22373)
BARGER & WOLEN LLP
275 Battery St Ste 480, San Francisco (94111-3309)
PHONE............................415 434-2800
Linda Kiel, *Branch Mgr*
Margarita Fernandez, *President*
EMP: 50

SALES (corp-wide): 19.3MM **Privately Held**
WEB: www.bargerwolen.com
SIC: 8111 General practice attorney, lawyer
PA: Barger & Wolen Llp
633 W 5th St Ste 5000
Los Angeles CA
213 680-2800

(P-22374)
BARNES & THORNBURG LLP
2029 Century Park E # 300, Los Angeles (90067-2904)
PHONE............................310 284-3880
Paul J Laurin, *Partner*
Andrea Augustine, *Admin Sec*
Jonathan J Boustani, *Litigation*
Gloria Jan, *Counsel*
EMP: 113
SALES (corp-wide): 167.8MM **Privately Held**
SIC: 8111 General practice law office
PA: Barnes & Thornburg Llp
11 S Meridian St Ste 1313
Indianapolis IN 46204
317 236-1313

(P-22375)
BARRETT BUSINESS SERVICES INC
Also Called: B B S I
8880 Rio San Diego Dr # 800, San Diego (92108-1634)
PHONE............................858 314-1100
Milan Todorovic, *Branch Mgr*
EMP: 5003
SALES (corp-wide): 940.7MM **Publicly Held**
SIC: 8111 Legal services
PA: Barrett Business Services Inc
8100 Ne Parkway Dr # 200
Vancouver WA 98662
360 828-0700

(P-22376)
BARRY BISHOP
6001 Shellmound St # 875, Emeryville (94608-1957)
PHONE............................510 596-0888
Nelson C Barry Sr, *President*
Carol Healey, *Shareholder*
Nelson C Barry III, *Vice Pres*
Jeffrey N Haney, *Vice Pres*
Fredric W Trester, *Vice Pres*
EMP: 60 EST: 1917
SQ FT: 14,000
SALES (est): 7.1MM **Privately Held**
WEB: www.bbhhr.com
SIC: 8111 General practice law office

(P-22377)
BARTHOLOMEW BARRY & ASSOCIATES
701 N Brand Blvd Ste 800, Glendale (91203-3279)
PHONE............................818 543-4000
EMP: 73
SALES (est): 3.7MM **Privately Held**
SIC: 8111

(P-22378)
BARTKO ZANKEL TARRANT & MIL
1 Embarcadero Ctr Ste 800, San Francisco (94111-3629)
PHONE............................415 956-1900
Richard T Tarrant, *President*
Martin I Zankel, *Chairman*
Charles Miller, *Vice Pres*
May Tolentino, *Executive*
John Bartko, *Principal*
EMP: 80 EST: 1975
SQ FT: 18,000
SALES (est): 11.3MM **Privately Held**
WEB: www.bztm.com
SIC: 8111 Corporate, partnership & business law; real estate law; bankruptcy law

(P-22379)
BERDING & WEIL LLP (PA)
2175 N Calif Blvd Ste 500, Walnut Creek (94596-7336)
PHONE............................925 838-2090
Tyler Berding, *Partner*

Roanne Jolicoeur, *Chief Mktg Ofcr*
David M Austin,
Cori L Barton,
Scott W Barton,
EMP: 75
SQ FT: 20,000
SALES (est): 17MM **Privately Held**
WEB: www.bwclassaction.com
SIC: 8111 General practice law office

(P-22380)
BERGER KAHN (PA)
Also Called: Simon and Gladstone A Prof
1 Park Plz Ste 340, Irvine (92614-2511)
PHONE............................949 474-1880
Craig Simon, *Owner*
Ron Alberts, *Partner*
Jason Wallach, *Partner*
Mike Aiken, *Principal*
Arthur I Willner, *Principal*
▲ EMP: 70 EST: 1928
SQ FT: 22,250
SALES (est): 17.3MM **Privately Held**
WEB: www.bergerkahn.com
SIC: 8111 General practice attorney, lawyer

(P-22381)
BERGER KAHN
10085 Crrl Cnyn Rd Ste 21, San Diego (92131)
PHONE............................858 547-0075
Craig S Simon, *Manager*
Julia Mouser,
Carol Schaner,
Ashley Rodriguez, *Legal Staff*
EMP: 50
SALES (corp-wide): 17.3MM **Privately Held**
WEB: www.bergerkahn.com
SIC: 8111 General practice attorney, lawyer
PA: Berger Kahn
1 Park Plz Ste 340
Irvine CA 92614
949 474-1880

(P-22382)
BERRY & BERRY LAW FIRM
475 14th St Ste 550, Oakland (94612-1938)
PHONE............................510 250-0200
Phillip S Berry, *President*
EMP: 75
SALES (est): 8.7MM **Privately Held**
SIC: 8111 General practice attorney, lawyer

(P-22383)
BEST BEST & KRIEGER LLP (PA)
Also Called: BB&k
3390 University Ave # 500, Riverside (92501-3369)
P.O. Box 1028 (92502-1028)
PHONE............................951 686-1450
Eric L Garner, *Partner*
Jason M Ackerman, *Partner*
Franklin C Adams, *Partner*
Franklin Adams, *Partner*
Clark Alsop, *Partner*
EMP: 188 EST: 1891
SQ FT: 57,000
SALES (est): 63.7MM **Privately Held**
WEB: www.bbklaw.com
SIC: 8111 General practice attorney, lawyer

(P-22384)
BEST BEST & KRIEGER LLP
18101 Von Karman Ave # 1000, Irvine (92612-0164)
PHONE............................949 263-2600
Monica Elmar, *Branch Mgr*
EMP: 50
SALES (corp-wide): 63.7MM **Privately Held**
SIC: 8111 General practice attorney, lawyer
PA: Best Best & Krieger Llp
3390 University Ave # 500
Riverside CA 92501
951 686-1450

(P-22385)
BET TZEDEK
3250 Wilshire Blvd Fl 13, Los Angeles
(90010-1601)
PHONE...............................323 939-0506
Jessie Kornberg, *President*
Jordan Aiken, *Partner*
Stanley Kandel, *Partner*
Michael D Seplow, *Partner*
David Lash, *President*
EMP: 51
SALES: 9MM **Privately Held**
SIC: 8111 Legal aid service

(P-22386)
BHATNAGAR LAW OFFICE
84 W Santa Clara St # 560, San Jose
(95113-1812)
PHONE...............................408 564-8051
Nikhil Bhatnagar, *Owner*
EMP: 50
SALES (est): 199.5K **Privately Held**
SIC: 8111 Legal services

(P-22387)
**BIRD MRLLA BXER WLPERT A
PROF**
1875 Century Park E Fl 23, Los Angeles
(90067-2337)
PHONE...............................310 201-2100
Vincent Marella, *Partner*
Terry Bird, *Partner*
Joel Boxer, *Partner*
Dorothy Wolpert, *Partner*
Sandy Palmieri, *President*
EMP: 60
SALES: 6MM **Privately Held**
WEB: www.bmbwlaw.com
SIC: 8111 General practice law office

(P-22388)
BLANK ROME LLP
2029 Century Park E Fl 6, Los Angeles
(90067-2901)
PHONE...............................424 239-3400
William Small, *Branch Mgr*
Justina Byers, *Associate*
Maria Carnicella, *Associate*
Richard Chou, *Associate*
Philip Guffy, *Associate*
EMP: 91
SALES (corp-wide): 152.9MM **Privately
Held**
SIC: 8111 General practice attorney,
lawyer
PA: Blank Rome Llp
1 Logan Sq
Philadelphia PA 19103
215 569-5500

(P-22389)
**BLOOM DAVID LAW OFFICES
OF**
3530 Wilshire Blvd # 1300, Los Angeles
(90010-2318)
PHONE...............................323 938-5248
David Bloom, *Owner*
EMP: 50
SALES (est): 2.8MM **Privately Held**
SIC: 8111 General practice attorney,
lawyer

(P-22390)
**BLOOM HERGOTT DIEMER
COOK LLC**
Also Called: Bloom, Jacob A
150 S Rodeo Dr Fl 3, Beverly Hills
(90212-2410)
PHONE...............................310 859-6800
Jacob A Bloom, *Partner*
Lawrence H Graves, *Partner*
Candice S Hansen, *Partner*
Allen Hergott, *Partner*
Tina J Kahn, *Partner*
EMP: 52
SALES (est): 6.6MM **Privately Held**
SIC: 8111 General practice law office

(P-22391)
BMC GROUP INC
Also Called: Bankruptcy Management Cons
300 N Cntntl Blvd Ste 570, El Segundo
(90245)
PHONE...............................310 321-5555
Shawn Allen, *President*

EMP: 100 **Privately Held**
SIC: 8111 Bankruptcy referee
PA: The Bmc Group Inc
3732 W 120th St
Hawthorne CA 90250

(P-22392)
BOHM LAW GROUP INC (PA)
4600 Northgate Blvd # 210, Sacramento
(95834-1133)
PHONE...............................916 927-5574
Lawrance Bohm, *CEO*
EMP: 50
SALES (est): 5.7MM **Privately Held**
SIC: 8111 General practice law office

(P-22393)
**BONNE BRIDGE MUELL
OKEEF & (PA)**
3699 Wilsh Boule Fl 10 Flr 10, Los Angeles
(90010)
PHONE...............................213 480-1900
David J O'Keefe, *President*
George Peterson, *Corp Secy*
James D Nichols, *Vice Pres*
Vivian Chin, *Executive Asst*
Bruce Blakely, *Finance*
EMP: 100
SQ FT: 48,000
SALES (est): 20.3MM **Privately Held**
SIC: 8111 General practice attorney,
lawyer

(P-22394)
**BOORNAZIAN JENSEN &
GARTHE A**
555 12th St, Oakland (94607-4046)
PHONE...............................510 834-4350
David Garthe, *Principal*
Denise Agan, *President*
Brenda Bruessard, *President*
Leslie Hassberg, *President*
Charles Eisner, *CFO*
EMP: 60
SQ FT: 18,500
SALES (est): 7.7MM **Privately Held**
WEB: www.bjg.com
SIC: 8111 General practice attorney,
lawyer

(P-22395)
BOWLES & VERNA
2121 N Calif Blvd Ste 875, Walnut Creek
(94596-7335)
PHONE...............................925 935-3300
Richard Bowles, *Partner*
Richard Ergo, *Partner*
Kp Dean Harper, *Partner*
Mary Sullivan, *Partner*
Michael Verna, *Partner*
EMP: 50
SQ FT: 15,000
SALES (est): 6.7MM **Privately Held**
WEB: www.bv-law.com
SIC: 8111 General practice attorney,
lawyer

(P-22396)
BOWMAN AND BROOKE LLP
Also Called: Bowman & Brooke-Attys
970 W 190th St Ste 700, Torrance
(90502-1091)
PHONE...............................310 768-3068
Mark Berry, *Manager*
Stacy Eikenberry, *Admin Sec*
Deanna Louviere-Hernan, *Admin Sec*
Sweety Ray, *Admin Sec*
Lisa Sullivan, *Admin Sec*
EMP: 84
SALES (corp-wide): 55.7MM **Privately
Held**
WEB: www.bowmanandbrooke.com
SIC: 8111 Specialized law offices, attor-
neys
PA: Bowman And Brooke Llp
150 S 5th St Ste 3000
Minneapolis MN 55402
612 339-8682

(P-22397)
**BRADFORD & BARTHEL LLP
(PA)**
2518 River Plaza Dr, Sacramento
(95833-3673)
PHONE...............................916 569-0790
Donald R Barthel, *Partner*
Georgia Inclan, *President*
Kimberly Reynolds, *President*
Mia Hipkins, *Office Mgr*
Yolanda Cordero, *Admin Sec*
EMP: 150
SALES: 37MM **Privately Held**
SIC: 8111 General practice law office

(P-22398)
**BRADY VORWERCK RYDR &
CSPNO (PA)**
19200 Von Karman Ave, Irvine
(92612-8553)
PHONE...............................480 456-9888
James Brady, *CEO*
Robert Ryder, *Principal*
Gregg Vorwerck, *Principal*
EMP: 75
SALES (est): 8.9MM **Privately Held**
SIC: 8111 Legal services

(P-22399)
BRAYTON PURCELL APC (PA)
222 Rush Landing Rd, Novato
(94945-2469)
P.O. Box 6169 (94948-6169)
PHONE...............................415 898-1555
Alan Richard Brayton, *CEO*
Tom Gremmels, *CFO*
Laura Elkurdi, *Legal Staff*
James Ghilotti, *Manager*
Ellen Snyder, *Clerk*
EMP: 250
SQ FT: 40,000
SALES (est): 32MM **Privately Held**
WEB: www.asbestosnetwork.com
SIC: 8111 General practice attorney,
lawyer

(P-22400)
**BREMER WHYTE BROWN
OMEARA LLP (PA)**
Also Called: Bremer Whyte Brown Omeara
20320 Sw Birch St Ste 200, Newport Beach
(92660-1791)
PHONE...............................949 221-1000
Keith Bremer, *Partner*
Nicole Whyte, *Partner*
John Toohey, *Managing Prtnr*
Shawn Reutter, *President*
Brenda Newkirk, *General Mgr*
EMP: 50
SQ FT: 6,000
SALES: 16.7MM **Privately Held**
SIC: 8111 General practice attorney,
lawyer

(P-22401)
**BRYAN CAVE LIGHTON PAISNER
LLP**
333 Market St Fl 25, San Francisco
(94105-2126)
PHONE...............................415 675-3400
Alicia Kuhn, *Manager*
Terri Parafina, *President*
Mary McHugh, *Manager*
Donald A Cole, *Associate*
David A Harford, *Associate*
EMP: 50
SALES (corp-wide): 386.2MM **Privately
Held**
SIC: 8111 General practice attorney,
lawyer
PA: Bryan Cave Leighton Paisner Llp
1 Metropolitan Sq 211n
Saint Louis MO 63102
314 259-2000

(P-22402)
**BRYAN CAVE LIGHTON PAISNER
LLP**
3161 Michelson Dr # 1500, Irvine
(92612-4400)
PHONE...............................949 223-7000
Ren Hayhurst, *Manager*
Ren Hayhurft, *Partner*
EMP: 56

SALES (corp-wide): 386.2MM **Privately
Held**
SIC: 8111 General practice attorney,
lawyer
PA: Bryan Cave Leighton Paisner Llp
1 Metropolitan Sq 211n
Saint Louis MO 63102
314 259-2000

(P-22403)
**BRYAN CAVE LIGHTON PAISNER
LLP**
120 Broadway Ste 300, Santa Monica
(90401-2386)
PHONE...............................310 576-2100
Louise Caplan, *President*
Ronald N Jacobi, *Counsel*
Robert G Lancaster, *Counsel*
Nancy Neiman, *Manager*
EMP: 130
SALES (corp-wide): 386.2MM **Privately
Held**
SIC: 8111 General practice attorney,
lawyer
PA: Bryan Cave Leighton Paisner Llp
1 Metropolitan Sq 211n
Saint Louis MO 63102
314 259-2000

(P-22404)
**BURKE WILLIAMS & SORENSEN
LLP (PA)**
444 S Flower St Ste 2400, Los Angeles
(90071-2953)
PHONE...............................213 236-0600
John J Welsh, *Managing Prtnr*
James T Bradshaw Jr, *Partner*
Harold Bridges, *Partner*
Steven J Dawson, *Partner*
Leland C Dolley, *Partner*
EMP: 90
SQ FT: 51,000
SALES (est): 22.4MM **Privately Held**
WEB: www.bwslaw.com
SIC: 8111 General practice attorney,
lawyer

(P-22405)
**BURNHAM BROWN A PROF
CORP**
Also Called: Burnham & Brown
1901 Harrison St Ste 1100, Oakland
(94612-3648)
P.O. Box 119 (94604-0119)
PHONE...............................510 444-6800
Gregory D Brown, *President*
Thomas Downey, *Partner*
Michael Johnson, *Partner*
John Verber, *Managing Prtnr*
Linda Andrew-Marshall, *President*
EMP: 120
SQ FT: 50,000
SALES (est): 16.7MM **Privately Held**
WEB: www.burnhambrown.com
SIC: 8111 General practice law office

(P-22406)
C T CORPORATION SYSTEM
2875 Michelle Ste 100, Irvine (92606-1024)
PHONE...............................925 287-9801
Despina Shields, *Regional Mgr*
EMP: 60
SALES (corp-wide): 4.8B **Privately Held**
WEB: www.ctadvantage.com
SIC: 8111 5999 7375 Legal services; tele-
phone equipment & systems; information
retrieval services
HQ: C T Corporation System
28 Liberty St Fl 42
New York NY 10005
212 894-8940

(P-22407)
CALL & JENSEN APC
610 Nwport Ctr Dr Ste 700, Newport Beach
(92660)
PHONE...............................949 717-3000
Wayne W Call, *President*
Jon Jensen, *Administration*
Carrie Daly, *Legal Staff*
Janelle Lford, *Legal Staff*
Tina Ramirez, *Director*
EMP: 50
SALES (est): 7.7MM **Privately Held**
SIC: 8111 General practice attorney,
lawyer

PRODUCTS & SVCS

(P-22408)
CAROTHERS DSNTE FRDNBERGER LLP (PA)
2600 Michelson Dr Ste 800, Irvine (92612-6522)
PHONE................................949 622-1661
Christopher Carlton, *General Mgr*
Marianne C Koepf, *Partner*
Anthony B Lewis, *Partner*
Christopher M Robertson, *Partner*
Mark S Spring, *Partner*
EMP: 64
SALES (est): 11.1MM **Privately Held**
SIC: 8111 Specialized law offices, attorneys

(P-22409)
CARR & FERRELL
120 Constitution Dr, Menlo Park (94025-1107)
PHONE................................650 812-3400
Wininger Aaron, *Principal*
Dale Withers, *Admin Asst*
Stuart Clark, *Marketing Staff*
Joel Samson, *Patent Law*
Michael Tuman, *Patent Law*
EMP: 72 EST: 2010
SALES (est): 3.1MM **Privately Held**
SIC: 8111 Specialized law offices, attorneys

(P-22410)
CARR & FERRELL LLP (PA)
120 Constitution Dr, Menlo Park (94025-1107)
PHONE................................650 812-3400
Barry Carr, *General Ptnr*
Jill E Fishbein, *Partner*
Jefferson F Scher, *Partner*
Kenneth B Wilson, *Partner*
Robert Yorio, *Partner*
EMP: 68
SALES (est): 9.5MM **Privately Held**
WEB: www.carr-ferrell.com
SIC: 8111 General practice attorney, lawyer; corporate, partnership & business law; patent, trademark & copyright law; labor & employment law

(P-22411)
CARR MC CLELLAN INGERSOLL THOM (PA)
Also Called: Carr, McClellan
216 Park Rd, Burlingame (94010-4200)
P.O. Box 513 (94011-0513)
PHONE................................650 342-9600
Mark A Cassanego, *President*
Tracy Francis, *President*
Vanessa Hodam, *President*
Steven D Anderson, *CFO*
Krista Mencarelli, *Exec Dir*
EMP: 65
SQ FT: 19,000
SALES (est): 10.7MM **Privately Held**
WEB: www.cmithlaw.com
SIC: 8111 General practice attorney, lawyer

(P-22412)
CARROLL BURDICK MC DONOUGH LLP (PA)
275 Battery St Ste 2600, San Francisco (94111-3358)
PHONE................................415 989-5900
Angela Bradstreet, *Partner*
Marcelino Nogueiro, *Analyst*
Kelly Sanderson, *Legal Staff*
Carmen Tapia, *Legal Staff*
G David Godwin,
EMP: 185
SQ FT: 50,000
SALES (est): 15.2MM **Privately Held**
WEB: www.cbmlaw.com
SIC: 8111 General practice attorney, lawyer

(P-22413)
CARSON KURTZMAN CONSULTANTS (DH)
Also Called: K C C
2335 Alaska Ave, El Segundo (90245-4808)
PHONE................................310 823-9000
Jon A Orr,
James Le Transitions, *Exec VP*

Evan Gershbein, *Vice Pres*
Justin Hughes, *Vice Pres*
CA Novato, *Vice Pres*
EMP: 180
SQ FT: 46,000
SALES (est): 19.3MM **Privately Held**
WEB: www.kccllc.com
SIC: 8111 Specialized legal services

(P-22414)
CHILDRENS LAW CENTER CAL (PA)
101 Centre Plaza Dr, Monterey Park (91754-2155)
PHONE................................323 980-8700
Leslie Starr Heimov, *CEO*
EMP: 122
SALES (est): 40.1MM **Privately Held**
SIC: 8111 Legal aid service

(P-22415)
CHODOROW DE CASTRO WEST
10960 Wilshire Blvd # 1400, Los Angeles (90024-3717)
PHONE................................310 478-2541
Hugo Decastro, *President*
Buddy Epstein,
Henry Reitzenstein,
Michael Abrams, *Counsel*
EMP: 65
SQ FT: 19,400
SALES (est): 10.2MM **Privately Held**
WEB: www.dwclaw.com
SIC: 8111 General practice law office

(P-22416)
CITY & COUNTY OF SAN FRANCISCO
Also Called: City Attorney
1 Carlton B Goodlett Pl # 234, San Francisco (94102-4604)
PHONE................................415 554-4700
Dennis Herrera, *Principal*
EMP: 250 **Privately Held**
SIC: 8111 9222 General practice attorney, lawyer; legal counsel & prosecution; ;
PA: City & County Of San Francisco
1 Dr Carlton B Goodlett P
San Francisco CA 94102
415 554-7500

(P-22417)
CITY & COUNTY OF SAN FRANCISCO
Also Called: District Attorney's Office
850 Bryant St Ste 600, San Francisco (94103-4613)
PHONE................................415 553-1752
Kamala Harris, *Manager*
EMP: 130 **Privately Held**
SIC: 8111 9222 Legal services; legal counsel & prosecution; ;
PA: City & County Of San Francisco
1 Dr Carlton B Goodlett P
San Francisco CA 94102
415 554-7500

(P-22418)
CITY OF LONG BEACH
Also Called: Long Beach Cty Flt Svc Ofc
2600 Temple Ave, Long Beach (90806-2209)
PHONE................................562 570-5423
Dennis Hill, *Principal*
EMP: 67 **Privately Held**
WEB: www.polb.com
SIC: 8111 Legal services
PA: City Of Long Beach
411 W Ocean Blvd
Long Beach CA 90802
562 570-6450

(P-22419)
CITY OF LONG BEACH
Also Called: City Attorneys Office
333 W Ocean Blvd Lbby, Long Beach (90802-4689)
PHONE................................562 570-6919
Karen Brandt, *Manager*
EMP: 67 **Privately Held**
WEB: www.polb.com
SIC: 8111 9111 General practice attorney, lawyer; mayors' offices

PA: City Of Long Beach
411 W Ocean Blvd
Long Beach CA 90802
562 570-6450

(P-22420)
CITY OF LOS ANGELES
Also Called: General Svcs Cy Los Angeles
111 E 1st St Ste 404, Los Angeles (90012-4115)
PHONE................................213 473-6872
Len Appledaum, *Chief Acct*
Tony Royster, *General Mgr*
Ken Chang, *Administration*
Louis Carr, *CIO*
Ruby Cheung, *Programmer Anys*
EMP: 200 **Privately Held**
WEB: www.lacity.org
SIC: 8111 Legal services
PA: City Of Los Angeles
200 N Spring St Ste 303
Los Angeles CA 90012
213 978-0600

(P-22421)
CITY OF LOS ANGELES
Also Called: City Attorney
200 N Main St Ste 800, Los Angeles (90012-4133)
PHONE................................213 978-8100
Mike Feuer, *General Mgr*
Carl Sampson, *Director*
Frank Mateljan, *Manager*
EMP: 800 **Privately Held**
WEB: www.lacity.org
SIC: 8111 9222 Legal services; legal counsel & prosecution;
PA: City Of Los Angeles
200 N Spring St Ste 303
Los Angeles CA 90012
213 978-0600

(P-22422)
CLIFFORD & BROWN A PROF CORP
1430 Truxtun Ave Ste 900, Bakersfield (93301-5226)
PHONE................................661 322-6023
Steven Clifford, *President*
Michael O'Dell, *Executive*
Kathy Smith, *Executive*
Jim Brown, *Principal*
Bob Harding, *Admin Sec*
EMP: 51
SQ FT: 100,000
SALES: 2.5MM **Privately Held**
WEB: www.clifford-law.com
SIC: 8111 General practice law office

(P-22423)
CLYDE & CO US LLP
101 2nd St Fl 24, San Francisco (94105-3665)
PHONE................................415 365-9800
Rhonda Jenkins, *Principal*
Chriszayda Escobar, *Office Admin*
Patrick Postolka, *Admin Sec*
Paul Cirone, *Technology*
Yvonne Catig, *Legal Staff*
EMP: 55
SALES (corp-wide): 773.4MM **Privately Held**
SIC: 8111 General practice attorney, lawyer
HQ: Clyde & Co Us Llp
405 Lexington Ave
New York NY 10174

(P-22424)
COLEMAN CHAVEZ & ASSOC LLP
1731 E Roseville Pkwy # 200, Roseville (95661-6453)
PHONE................................916 787-2310
Chad Coleman, *Partner*
Agnieszka Bielecka, *Associate*
Eugene Vinitsky, *Associate*
EMP: 75
SALES (est): 5.7MM **Privately Held**
SIC: 8111 General practice law office

(P-22425)
COLLINS CLLINS MUIR STWART LLP
1100 El Centro St Frnt, South Pasadena (91030-5213)
PHONE................................626 243-1100
John Collins, *Partner*
Samuel J Muir, *Partner*
Brian Stewart, *Partner*
Laurey Carpenter, *President*
Chelsea Reyes, *President*
EMP: 50
SQ FT: 20,000
SALES (est): 7.5MM **Privately Held**
SIC: 8111 General practice attorney, lawyer

(P-22426)
COMMUNITY ACTION PARTNERSHIP
1152 E Grand Ave, Arroyo Grande (93420-2583)
PHONE................................805 489-4026
Raye Flemming, *Branch Mgr*
EMP: 245
SALES (corp-wide): 79.1MM **Privately Held**
SIC: 8111 General practice law office
PA: Community Action Partnership Of San Luis Obispo County, Inc.
1030 Southwood Dr
San Luis Obispo CA 93401
805 544-4355

(P-22427)
COMPEX LEGAL SERVICES INC (PA)
325 Maple Ave, Torrance (90503-2602)
PHONE................................310 782-1801
Arvind Korde, *CEO*
Nitin Mehta, *Chairman*
Anthony Bazurto, *Exec VP*
Humilad Pasimio, *Vice Pres*
Rajesh Rangaswamy, *Vice Pres*
EMP: 120
SQ FT: 47,740
SALES (est): 84.7MM **Privately Held**
WEB: www.compexlegal.com
SIC: 8111 7338 7334 Specialized legal services; secretarial & court reporting; photocopying & duplicating services

(P-22428)
COOKSEY TOOLEN GAGE DUFFY (PA)
535 Anton Blvd Fl 10, Costa Mesa (92626-1947)
PHONE................................714 431-1100
David Cooksey, *President*
Robert L Toolen, *Vice Pres*
Richard C Buck,
Kim Patterson Gage,
Griffith H Hayes,
EMP: 54
SALES (est): 14.1MM **Privately Held**
WEB: www.cookseylaw.com
SIC: 8111 General practice law office

(P-22429)
COOLEY LLP
Also Called: Cooley Godward Kronish
101 California St Fl 5, San Francisco (94111-5800)
PHONE................................415 693-2000
Lee Benton, *Partner*
Whitty Somvichian, *Partner*
Brendan J Murphy, *Litigation*
Jessica Lopez, *Legal Staff*
Eric Haber, *Counsel*
EMP: 100
SALES (corp-wide): 168.9MM **Privately Held**
WEB: www.cooley.com
SIC: 8111 Specialized law offices, attorneys
PA: Cooley Llp
3175 Hanover St
Palo Alto CA 94304
650 843-5000

(P-22430)
COOLEY LLP (PA)
3175 Hanover St, Palo Alto (94304-1130)
PHONE................................650 843-5000
Joe Conroy, *Managing Prtnr*

Tom Reicher -, *Partner*
Kenneth J Adelson, *Partner*
Mike Attanasio, *Partner*
Andrew Basile, *Partner*
EMP: 300
SALES (est): 168.9MM **Privately Held**
WEB: www.cooley.com
SIC: 8111 Corporate, partnership & business law

(P-22431)
COOLEY LLP
4 Palo Alto Sq, Palo Alto (94306)
PHONE.................................650 843-5124
Chris Johnston, *Branch Mgr*
Mercedes Milana, *President*
Iris Wong, *President*
Kathleen Howard, *Admin Sec*
EMP: 143
SALES (corp-wide): 168.9MM **Privately Held**
SIC: 8111 General practice attorney, lawyer
PA: Cooley Llp
   3175 Hanover St
   Palo Alto CA 94304
   650 843-5000

(P-22432)
COOLEY LLP
4401 Eastgate Mall, San Diego
(92121-1909)
PHONE.................................858 550-6000
Fred Muto, *Partner*
Christopher J Kearns, *Partner*
Lisa St John, *Personnel Exec*
Leo Norton, *Associate*
EMP: 150
SALES (corp-wide): 168.9MM **Privately Held**
WEB: www.cooley.com
SIC: 8111 General practice law office
PA: Cooley Llp
   3175 Hanover St
   Palo Alto CA 94304
   650 843-5000

(P-22433)
COOPER WHITE & COOPER LLP (PA)
201 California St Fl 17, San Francisco
(94111-5002)
PHONE.................................415 433-1900
Mark P Schreiber, *Partner*
Walter Hansell, *Partner*
Keith Howard, *Partner*
Peter Sibley, *Partner*
Jed Solomon, *Partner*
EMP: 150
SQ FT: 44,000
SALES (est): 18.5MM **Privately Held**
WEB: www.cwclaw.com
SIC: 8111 General practice attorney, lawyer

(P-22434)
COUNTY OF FRESNO
Also Called: Superior Court Unit
1130 O St, Fresno (93724-2201)
PHONE.................................559 600-3420
Rick Chavez, *Manager*
Jeffrey Hamilton,
EMP: 96 **Privately Held**
WEB: www.first5fresno.org
SIC: 8111 9199 Divorce & family law;
PA: County Of Fresno
   2420 Mariposa St
   Fresno CA 93721
   559 600-1710

(P-22435)
COUNTY OF FRESNO
Also Called: Public Defender's Office
2220 Tulare St Ste 300, Fresno
(93721-2130)
PHONE.................................559 600-3546
Kenneth Taniguchi, *Branch Mgr*
EMP: 96 **Privately Held**
WEB: www.first5fresno.org
SIC: 8111 9222 Specialized law offices, attorneys; public defenders' offices;
PA: County Of Fresno
   2420 Mariposa St
   Fresno CA 93721
   559 600-1710

(P-22436)
COUNTY OF KERN
1215 Truxtun Ave Fl 4, Bakersfield
(93301-4619)
PHONE.................................661 868-2000
William Fawns, *Branch Mgr*
EMP: 95 **Privately Held**
SIC: 8111 Legal services
PA: County Of Kern
   1115 Truxtun Ave Rm 505
   Bakersfield CA 93301
   661 868-3690

(P-22437)
COUNTY OF LOS ANGELES
Also Called: Public Defenders Office
1601 Eastlake Ave Ste 4, Los Angeles
(90033-1009)
PHONE.................................323 226-8998
Ron Brown, *Principal*
EMP: 214 **Privately Held**
SIC: 8111 Legal services
PA: County Of Los Angeles
   500 W Temple St Ste 437
   Los Angeles CA 90012
   213 974-1101

(P-22438)
COUNTY OF LOS ANGELES
300 S Park Ave Ste 770, Pomona
(91766-1557)
PHONE.................................909 620-3330
EMP: 214 **Privately Held**
SIC: 8111 General practice attorney, lawyer
PA: County Of Los Angeles
   500 W Temple St Ste 437
   Los Angeles CA 90012
   213 974-1101

(P-22439)
COUNTY OF LOS ANGELES
Also Called: District Attorney
200 W Compton Blvd # 700, Compton
(90220-6676)
PHONE.................................310 603-7483
Julie Sulman, *Manager*
EMP: 110 **Privately Held**
WEB: www.co.la.ca.us
SIC: 8111 9222 Legal services; District Attorneys' offices;
PA: County Of Los Angeles
   500 W Temple St Ste 437
   Los Angeles CA 90012
   213 974-1101

(P-22440)
COUNTY OF LOS ANGELES
Also Called: Public Defender Administration
210 W Temple St Fl 19, Los Angeles
(90012-3231)
PHONE.................................213 974-2811
Ronald Brown, *Branch Mgr*
EMP: 200 **Privately Held**
WEB: www.co.la.ca.us
SIC: 8111 9222 Legal services; public defenders' offices;
PA: County Of Los Angeles
   500 W Temple St Ste 437
   Los Angeles CA 90012
   213 974-1101

(P-22441)
COUNTY OF LOS ANGELES
Also Called: Public Defender
200 W Compton Blvd Fl 8, Compton
(90220-6676)
PHONE.................................310 603-7271
John Brock, *Manager*
EMP: 214 **Privately Held**
WEB: www.co.la.ca.us
SIC: 8111 9222 Legal services; public defenders' offices;
PA: County Of Los Angeles
   500 W Temple St Ste 437
   Los Angeles CA 90012
   213 974-1101

(P-22442)
COUNTY OF LOS ANGELES
Also Called: Court House
20221 Hamilton Ave, Torrance
(90502-1321)
PHONE.................................310 222-3552
Charles Mandel, *Branch Mgr*
EMP: 214 **Privately Held**

SIC: 8111 General practice attorney, lawyer
PA: County Of Los Angeles
   500 W Temple St Ste 437
   Los Angeles CA 90012
   213 974-1101

(P-22443)
COUNTY OF LOS ANGELES
Also Called: District Attorney
6230 Sylmar Ave Ste 201, Van Nuys
(91401-2731)
PHONE.................................818 374-2406
Nancy Lidamore, *Director*
EMP: 60 **Privately Held**
WEB: www.co.la.ca.us
SIC: 8111 9222 General practice attorney, lawyer; District Attorneys' offices;
PA: County Of Los Angeles
   500 W Temple St Ste 437
   Los Angeles CA 90012
   213 974-1101

(P-22444)
COUNTY OF ORANGE
Also Called: Public Defender
1440 N Harbor Blvd # 400, Fullerton
(92835-4127)
PHONE.................................714 626-3700
Sharon Petrosino, *Manager*
EMP: 50 **Privately Held**
SIC: 8111 9222 Legal services; public defenders' offices;
PA: County Of Orange
   333 W Santa Ana Blvd 3f
   Santa Ana CA 92701
   714 834-6200

(P-22445)
COUNTY OF RIVERSIDE
Also Called: Public Defender- Main Office
4075 Main St, Riverside (92501-3701)
PHONE.................................951 955-6000
Gary Windom, *Administration*
Ron Mallari, *Information Mgr*
EMP: 200 **Privately Held**
SIC: 8111 9222 Legal services; public defenders' offices;
PA: County Of Riverside
   4080 Lemon St Fl 11
   Riverside CA 92501
   951 955-1110

(P-22446)
COUNTY OF SAN DIEGO
District Attorney
330 W Broadway Ste 1020, San Diego
(92101-3827)
PHONE.................................619 531-4040
Steven Silva, *Admin Sec*
Anne Calle, *Officer*
Tanya Sierra, *Officer*
Nathan Cunningham, *Technician*
Wilson Tang, *Technology*
EMP: 93 **Privately Held**
WEB: www.sdlcc.org
SIC: 8111 9222 Specialized legal services; District Attorneys' offices
PA: County Of San Diego
   1600 Pacific Hwy Ste 209
   San Diego CA 92101
   619 531-5880

(P-22447)
COUNTY OF SHASTA
Also Called: Dist Attorney's Office
1355 West St, Redding (96001-1652)
PHONE.................................530 245-6300
Gerald Benito, *Principal*
EMP: 85 **Privately Held**
WEB: www.rsdnmp.org
SIC: 8111 Legal services
PA: County Of Shasta
   1450 Court St Ste 308a
   Redding CA 96001
   530 225-5561

(P-22448)
COUNTY OF SONOMA
Also Called: District Attorney
600 Administration Dr 212j, Santa Rosa
(95403-2825)
PHONE.................................707 565-2209
Jill R Ravitch, *Branch Mgr*
Desiree Henley, *VP Bus Dvlpt*
EMP: 120 **Privately Held**

WEB: www.sonomacompost.com
SIC: 8111 9111 Legal services; county supervisors' & executives' offices
PA: County Of Sonoma
   585 Fiscal Dr 100
   Santa Rosa CA 95403
   707 565-2431

(P-22449)
COVINGTON & BURLING LLP
333 Twin Dolphin Dr # 700, Redwood City
(94065-1418)
PHONE.................................650 632-4700
Kurt G Calia, *Manager*
Andrew Regan, *Associate*
EMP: 115
SALES (corp-wide): 210.8MM **Privately Held**
SIC: 8111 General practice law office
PA: Covington & Burling Llp
   1 City Ctr 850 10th St Nw
   Washington DC 20001
   202 662-6000

(P-22450)
COVINGTON & BURLING LLP
415 Mission St Ste 700, San Francisco
(94105-2597)
PHONE.................................415 591-6000
Jim Snipes, *Partner*
George M Chester Jr, *Partner*
David Jolley,
Wendy L Feng, *Counsel*
Tess Hamilton, *Associate*
EMP: 50
SALES (corp-wide): 210.8MM **Privately Held**
SIC: 8111 General practice law office
PA: Covington & Burling Llp
   1 City Ctr 850 10th St Nw
   Washington DC 20001
   202 662-6000

(P-22451)
COVINGTON & BURLING LLP
1999 Avenue Of The Stars # 3500, Los Angeles (90067-4643)
PHONE.................................424 332-4800
Michelle Liffman, *Manager*
Sharon Taft, *Admin Sec*
Jerome Ackerman,
Jeffrey Kiburtz, *Counsel*
Amy Coleman, *Manager*
EMP: 311
SALES (corp-wide): 210.8MM **Privately Held**
SIC: 8111 General practice law office
PA: Covington & Burling Llp
   1 City Ctr 850 10th St Nw
   Washington DC 20001
   202 662-6000

(P-22452)
COX CASTLE & NICHOLSON LLP (PA)
Also Called: Cox Castle
2029 Century Park E # 2100, Los Angeles
(90067-3007)
PHONE.................................310 284-2200
Gary A Glick, *Partner*
Lindsey H Barr, *Partner*
Robin L Bennett, *Partner*
Kenneth B Bley, *Partner*
Erica A Bose, *Partner*
EMP: 165
SQ FT: 60,000
SALES (est): 79.3MM **Privately Held**
SIC: 8111 General practice attorney, lawyer

(P-22453)
CROWELL & MORING LLP
275 Battery St Ste 2200, San Francisco
(94111-3337)
PHONE.................................415 986-2800
Dawn Tonya, *Branch Mgr*
Joanne Richardson, *President*
Cristina Solorio, *President*
Tessie Spagna, *Admin Sec*
Anita Stephen, *Administration*
EMP: 60
SALES (corp-wide): 400MM **Privately Held**
SIC: 8111 Specialized law offices, attorneys

PRODUCTS & SVCS

PA: Crowell & Moring Llp
1001 Pennsylvania Ave Nw # 10
Washington DC 20004
202 624-2500

(P-22454)
CROWELL & MORING LLP
3 Park Plz Ste 2000, Irvine (92614-2591)
PHONE.............................949 263-8400
Daniel Sasse, *Manager*
Charles De Jager, *Counsel*
William Helvestine, *Counsel*
A Jeschke, *Counsel*
Tali B Kindred, *Counsel*
EMP: 50
SALES (corp-wide): 400MM **Privately Held**
WEB: www.crowell.com
SIC: 8111 Specialized law offices, attorneys
PA: Crowell & Moring Llp
1001 Pennsylvania Ave Nw # 10
Washington DC 20004
202 624-2500

(P-22455)
CUNEO BLACK WARD MISSLER A LAW
Also Called: Cuneo, Black, Ward & Missler
700 University Ave # 110, Sacramento
(95825-6722)
P.O. Box 276650 (95827-6650)
PHONE.............................916 363-8822
John Black, *President*
James Missler, *Shareholder*
Alan Jong, *CFO*
Jan Bueno, *Admin Asst*
Alex Harary, *Associate*
EMP: 50
SQ FT: 13,000
SALES (est): 5.4MM **Privately Held**
WEB: www.cbwmlaw.com
SIC: 8111 General practice attorney, lawyer

(P-22456)
CURTIS LEGAL GROUP A PROFESSI
1300 K St Fl 2, Modesto (95354-0928)
P.O. Box 3030 (95353-3030)
PHONE.............................209 521-1800
Ralph S Curtis, *Partner*
Connie Gonzalez, *Controller*
Paul Scheele, *Litigation*
EMP: 50
SQ FT: 18,000
SALES (est): 6MM **Privately Held**
SIC: 8111 General practice law office

(P-22457)
DALEY & HEFT ATTORNEYS
462 Stevens Ave Ste 201, Solana Beach
(92075-2099)
PHONE.............................858 755-5666
Dennis W Daley, *Partner*
Robert Brockman Jr, *Partner*
Mitchell D Dean, *Partner*
Robert Heft, *Partner*
Neal Meyers, *Partner*
EMP: 50
SALES (est): 7.6MM **Privately Held**
WEB: www.daleyheft.com
SIC: 8111 General practice attorney, lawyer

(P-22458)
DAMRELL NELSON SCHRIMP PALL
Also Called: Schrimp, Roger Attorney
703 W F St, Oakdale (95361-3736)
PHONE.............................209 848-3500
Roger Schrimp, *Branch Mgr*
EMP: 50
SALES (corp-wide): 4.5MM **Privately Held**
SIC: 8111 General practice law office
PA: Damrell, Nelson, Schrimp, Pallios, Pacher, Silva Pc
1601 I St Ste 500
Modesto CA 95354
209 526-3500

(P-22459)
DANIEL ROBERT KNOWLTON
68368 Madrid Rd, Cathedral City
(92234-4836)
PHONE.............................760 265-5293
Daniel R Knowlton, *Owner*
EMP: 73 **EST:** 2010
SALES (est): 182.5K **Privately Held**
SIC: 8111 Legal services

(P-22460)
DANNING GILL DAMND KOLLITZ LLP
1900 Avenue Of The Stars # 11, Los Angeles (90067-4301)
PHONE.............................310 277-0077
David A Gill, *Partner*
Richard K Diamond, *Partner*
Howard Kollitz, *Partner*
David M Poitras, *Partner*
Eric P Israel PC, *Partner*
EMP: 70
SALES (est): 8.7MM **Privately Held**
WEB: www.dgdk.com
SIC: 8111 General practice law office

(P-22461)
DANNIS WLVER KLLEY A PROF CORP (PA)
275 Battery St Ste 1150, San Francisco
(94111-3333)
PHONE.............................415 543-4111
Gregory Dannis, *President*
A'Ree Hewitt, *President*
David Miller, *Vice Pres*
Chelsea Murphy, *Counsel*
Nestor Lagumen,
EMP: 70
SQ FT: 14,000
SALES (est): 8.6MM **Privately Held**
WEB: www.mbdlaw.com
SIC: 8111 General practice attorney, lawyer

(P-22462)
DAVID DARROCH
300 Lakeside Dr Fl 24, Oakland
(94612-3534)
PHONE.............................510 835-9100
H James Wulfsberg, *Ch of Bd*
Charles W Reese, *President*
Wulfsberg Colvig, *Producer*
EMP: 60
SQ FT: 34,000
SALES (est): 4.5MM **Privately Held**
WEB: www.wulfslaw.com
SIC: 8111 General practice attorney, lawyer

(P-22463)
DAVIS WRIGHT TREMAINE LLP
505 Montgomery St Ste 800, San Francisco
(94111-6533)
PHONE.............................415 276-6500
Jeff Gray, *Partner*
Gerald Hinkley, *Partner*
Michael Labianca, *Partner*
Paul Leboffe, *Partner*
Gregory Miller, *Partner*
EMP: 75
SALES (corp-wide): 294.7MM **Privately Held**
WEB: www.dwt.com
SIC: 8111 General practice attorney, lawyer
PA: Davis Wright Tremaine Llp
920 5th Ave Ste 3300
Seattle WA 98104
206 622-3150

(P-22464)
DAVIS WRIGHT TREMAINE LLP
865 S Figueroa St # 2400, Los Angeles
(90017-2566)
PHONE.............................213 633-6800
Mary Haas, *Partner*
EMP: 90
SALES (corp-wide): 294.7MM **Privately Held**
WEB: www.dwt.com
SIC: 8111 General practice law office
PA: Davis Wright Tremaine Llp
920 5th Ave Ste 3300
Seattle WA 98104
206 622-3150

(P-22465)
DECHERT LLP
650 Town Center Dr # 700, Costa Mesa
(92626-7122)
PHONE.............................949 442-6000
Robert Roberton, *Mng Member*
Jane Portillo, *President*
EMP: 210
SALES (corp-wide): 97.7MM **Privately Held**
SIC: 8111 General practice law office
PA: Dechert Llp
2929 Arch St Ste 400
Philadelphia PA 19104
202 261-3300

(P-22466)
DECHERT LLP
1 Bush St Ste 1600, San Francisco
(94104-4422)
PHONE.............................415 262-4500
John Randal, *Office Mgr*
Jason Rozes, *Partner*
Virgen M Laureano, *Admin Sec*
Deborah A Rizzo, *Admin Sec*
Martill Seymour, *Admin Sec*
EMP: 50
SALES (corp-wide): 97.7MM **Privately Held**
SIC: 8111 8748 General practice law office; business consulting
PA: Dechert Llp
2929 Arch St Ste 400
Philadelphia PA 19104
202 261-3300

(P-22467)
DEMLER ARMSTRONG & ROWLAND LLP
4500 E Pacific Cst Hwy # 400, Long Beach
(90804-3293)
PHONE.............................562 597-0029
Robert Armstrong, *Partner*
Sean Beatty, *Partner*
Edison Demler, *Partner*
Terry Rowland, *Partner*
Waseem Dulloo, *Associate*
EMP: 50
SQ FT: 13,500
SALES (est): 7.7MM **Privately Held**
WEB: www.darlaw.com
SIC: 8111 General practice attorney, lawyer

(P-22468)
DENTONS US LLP
1530 Page Mill Rd Ste 200, Palo Alto
(94304-1140)
PHONE.............................650 798-0300
Joe Borski, *Director*
EMP: 65
SALES (corp-wide): 340.8MM **Privately Held**
SIC: 8111 General practice attorney, lawyer
PA: Dentons Us Llp
233 S Wacker Dr Ste 5900
Chicago IL 60606
312 876-8000

(P-22469)
DENTONS US LLP
4675 Macarthur Ct # 1250, Newport Beach
(92660-8803)
PHONE.............................949 732-3700
Roger Rushing, *Owner*
Phyllis Young, *Admin Sec*
EMP: 104
SALES (corp-wide): 340.8MM **Privately Held**
SIC: 8111 Specialized law offices, attorneys
PA: Dentons Us Llp
233 S Wacker Dr Ste 5900
Chicago IL 60606
312 876-8000

(P-22470)
DENTONS US LLP
750 B St Ste 3300, San Diego
(92101-8188)
PHONE.............................619 595-5400
Douglas Farry, *Director*
Barbara Ippolito, *Manager*
EMP: 51

SALES (corp-wide): 340.8MM **Privately Held**
WEB: www.mckennalong.com
SIC: 8111 Specialized law offices, attorneys
PA: Dentons Us Llp
233 S Wacker Dr Ste 5900
Chicago IL 60606
312 876-8000

(P-22471)
DENTONS US LLP
4655 Executive Dr Ste 700, San Diego
(92121-3128)
PHONE.............................619 236-1414
EMP: 350
SALES (corp-wide): 340.8MM **Privately Held**
SIC: 8111 General practice law office
PA: Dentons Us Llp
233 S Wacker Dr Ste 5900
Chicago IL 60606
312 876-8000

(P-22472)
DENTONS US LLP
1 Market Plz Fl 24, San Francisco
(94105-1102)
PHONE.............................415 882-5000
Paul Glad, *Branch Mgr*
Rose Gartland, *Admin Sec*
Slava Madrit, *Info Tech Dir*
D W Kallstrom,
Mark Mackler,
EMP: 120
SALES (corp-wide): 340.8MM **Privately Held**
WEB: www.sonnenschein.com
SIC: 8111 General practice law office
PA: Dentons Us Llp
233 S Wacker Dr Ste 5900
Chicago IL 60606
312 876-8000

(P-22473)
DENTONS US LLP
Also Called: A Dentons Innovation Wirthlin
601 S Figueroa St # 2500, Los Angeles
(90017-5704)
PHONE.............................213 623-9300
Edwin Reeser, *General Mgr*
Michael Lubic, *Partner*
John Walker, *Partner*
Glenda Spratt, *Admin Sec*
Paterson Lee,
EMP: 150
SALES (corp-wide): 340.8MM **Privately Held**
WEB: www.sonnenschein.com
SIC: 8111 General practice attorney, lawyer
PA: Dentons Us Llp
233 S Wacker Dr Ste 5900
Chicago IL 60606
312 876-8000

(P-22474)
DENTONS US LLP
300 S Grand Ave Fl 14, Los Angeles
(90071-3124)
PHONE.............................213 688-1000
Janice Moor, *Administration*
Jayme Long, *Products*
Michael T Kavanaugh, *Manager*
EMP: 104
SALES (corp-wide): 340.8MM **Privately Held**
SIC: 8111 General practice attorney, lawyer
PA: Dentons Us Llp
233 S Wacker Dr Ste 5900
Chicago IL 60606
312 876-8000

(P-22475)
DIEPENBROCK ELKIN LLP
500 Capitol Mall Ste 650, Sacramento
(95814-4739)
PHONE.............................916 492-5000
Bradley Elkin, *President*
Michael V Brady, *Shareholder*
Michael Brady, *Chairman*
Mark Harrison, *Vice Pres*
Serena Albaeck, *Admin Sec*
EMP: 56
SQ FT: 20,000

SALES: 15MM **Privately Held**
WEB: www.diepenbrock.com
SIC: 8111 General practice law office

(P-22476)
DIETZ GLMOR CHAZEN A PROF CORP (PA)
7071 Convoy Ct Ste 300, San Diego
(92111-1023)
PHONE..................................858 565-0269
William Dietz, *Principal*
Avery G Chazen, *Principal*
Michael Dofflemyre, *Principal*
Mark R Gilmor, *Principal*
Paul D Leveque,
EMP: 55
SALES (est) 12.5MM **Privately Held**
SIC: 8111 Specialized law offices, attorneys

(P-22477)
DISABILITY GROUP INC
1014 23rd St, Santa Monica (90403-4520)
PHONE..................................310 829-5100
Ronald D Miller, *President*
EMP: 258
SALES (est): 15.2MM **Privately Held**
SIC: 8111 Specialized law offices, attorneys

(P-22478)
DISABILITY RIGHTS CALIFORNIA
350 S Bixel St, Los Angeles (90017-1418)
PHONE..................................213 213-8000
Kathy Blakemore, *President*
EMP: 76
SALES (corp-wide): 23.7MM **Privately Held**
SIC: 8111 Legal services
PA: Disability Rights California
1831 K St
Sacramento CA 95811
916 488-9950

(P-22479)
DISABILITY RIGHTS CALIFORNIA (PA)
Also Called: D R C
1831 K St, Sacramento (95811-4114)
PHONE..................................916 488-9950
Izetta Jackson, *President*
Herb Anderson, *CFO*
Diana Lynn Nelson, *CFO*
Catherine Blakemore, *Exec Dir*
Diana Honig, *Admin Sec*
EMP: 55
SQ FT: 8,500
SALES (est): 23.7MM **Privately Held**
SIC: 8111 Legal services

(P-22480)
DISCOVERREADY LLC
27200 Tourney Rd Ste 450, Valencia
(91355-4992)
PHONE..................................661 284-6401
Phil Richard, *Branch Mgr*
Kiefer Lance, *Vice Pres*
Jeff Knight, *Software Dev*
Melissa Parker, *Engineer*
EMP: 70
SALES (corp-wide): 36.6MM **Privately Held**
SIC: 8111 Legal services
HQ: Discoverready Llc
200 S College St Fl 10
Charlotte NC 28202
980 939-7516

(P-22481)
DLA PIPER LLP (US)
550 S Hope St Ste 2400, Los Angeles
(90071-2618)
PHONE..................................213 330-7700
Betty Shumener, *Principal*
Janet Celly, *Officer*
Kimberly Bachman, *Admin Sec*
Stephanie Cooley, *Marketing Mgr*
Thomas Pilkerton, *Sr Associate*
EMP: 305 **Privately Held**
SIC: 8111 Corporate, partnership & business law

HQ: Dla Piper Llp (Us)
6225 Smith Ave Ste 200
Baltimore MD 21209
410 580-3000

(P-22482)
DLA PIPER LLP (US)
2000 University Ave # 100, East Palo Alto
(94303-2215)
PHONE..................................650 833-2000
Francis Burch Jr, *CEO*
Carol Buss,
Elisabeth Eisner,
Michelle Harbottle,
Stacy Snowman,
EMP: 300 **Privately Held**
SIC: 8111 General practice attorney, lawyer
HQ: Dla Piper Llp (Us)
6225 Smith Ave Ste 200
Baltimore MD 21209
410 580-3000

(P-22483)
DLA PIPER LLP (US)
2000 Avenue Of The Stars 400n, Los Angeles (90067-4735)
PHONE..................................310 595-3000
Ronnie Decesare, *Branch Mgr*
Nicole C King, *Associate*
EMP: 100 **Privately Held**
SIC: 8111 General practice attorney, lawyer
HQ: Dla Piper Llp (Us)
6225 Smith Ave Ste 200
Baltimore MD 21209
410 580-3000

(P-22484)
DLA PIPER LLP (US)
2000 University Ave # 100, East Palo Alto
(94303-2215)
PHONE..................................650 833-2000
Rusty Conner, *Partner*
Eugene T Liipfert,
EMP: 400 **Privately Held**
SIC: 8111 General practice law office
HQ: Dla Piper Llp (Us)
6225 Smith Ave Ste 200
Baltimore MD 21209
410 580-3000

(P-22485)
DLA PIPER LLP (US)
4365 Executive Dr # 1100, San Diego
(92121-2133)
PHONE..................................858 677-1400
Gary O'Malley, *Partner*
Lynn Moon, *Comp Tech*
Amy Giannamore, *Counsel*
Carla Hoffman, *Sr Project Mgr*
Matthew A Holian, *Associate*
EMP: 100 **Privately Held**
SIC: 8111 General practice attorney, lawyer
HQ: Dla Piper Llp (Us)
6225 Smith Ave Ste 200
Baltimore MD 21209
410 580-3000

(P-22486)
DOMINGUEZ FIRM INC
Also Called: Law Offices Juan J. Dominguez
3250 Wilshire Blvd # 1200, Los Angeles
(90010-1577)
PHONE..................................213 388-7788
Juan J Dominguez, *President*
EMP: 100
SQ FT: 5,000
SALES (est): 7.6MM **Privately Held**
WEB: www.juanjdominguez.com
SIC: 8111 General practice attorney, lawyer; general practice law office

(P-22487)
DONAHUE GALLAGER WOODS LLP (PA)
1999 Harrison St Ste 2500, Oakland
(94612-4705)
PHONE..................................415 381-4161
Lawrence K Rockwell, *Partner*
George J Barron, *Partner*
John J Coppinger, *Partner*
Michael J Dalton, *Partner*
Eric W Doney, *Partner*
EMP: 75 **EST:** 1918

SQ FT: 20,827
SALES (est): 7MM **Privately Held**
WEB: www.donahue.com
SIC: 8111 General practice attorney, lawyer

(P-22488)
DOWNEY BRAND LLP (PA)
621 Capitol Mall Fl 18, Sacramento
(95814-4731)
PHONE..................................916 444-1000
Dale A Stern, *Managing Prtnr*
David R E Aladjem, *Partner*
Rhonda Cate Canby, *Partner*
Julie A Carter, *Partner*
Thomas N Cooper, *Partner*
EMP: 207 **EST:** 1926
SALES (est): 33.3MM **Privately Held**
WEB: www.dbsr.com
SIC: 8111 General practice attorney, lawyer

(P-22489)
DREYER BBICH BCCOLA CLLHAM LLP
20 Bicentennial Cir, Sacramento
(95826-2802)
PHONE..................................916 379-3500
Roger A Dreyer, *Managing Prtnr*
Joseph J Babich, *Partner*
Robert A Buccola, *Partner*
William Callaham, *Partner*
Debbie Hunter, *Office Mgr*
EMP: 70
SQ FT: 5,000
SALES (est): 7.7MM **Privately Held**
WEB: www.dbbc.com
SIC: 8111 General practice attorney, lawyer

(P-22490)
DRINKER BIDDLE & REATH LLP
1800 Century Park E # 1400, Los Angeles
(90067-1517)
PHONE..................................310 229-1282
Adam Thurston, *Vice Pres*
Summer Conley, *Counsel*
Eileen Somers, *Associate*
EMP: 170
SALES (corp-wide): 262.2MM **Privately Held**
SIC: 8111 Corporate, partnership & business law
PA: Drinker, Biddle & Reath Llp
1 Logan Sq Ste 2000
Philadelphia PA 19103
215 988-2700

(P-22491)
DRINKER BIDDLE & REATH LLP
4 Embarcadero Ctr Lbby, San Francisco
(94111-4174)
PHONE..................................415 591-7500
Debra Krueger, *Principal*
EMP: 170
SALES (corp-wide): 262.2MM **Privately Held**
SIC: 8111 Specialized law offices, attorneys
PA: Drinker, Biddle & Reath Llp
1 Logan Sq Ste 2000
Philadelphia PA 19103
215 988-2700

(P-22492)
DUANE MORRIS LLP
1 Market Plz Ste 2200, San Francisco
(94105-1127)
PHONE..................................415 957-3000
Leslye Olson, *Manager*
Glenn Manishin, *Partner*
Beth Coffey, *Admin Sec*
Allegra Jones, *Legal Staff*
Geoffrey Heaton, *Associate*
EMP: 150
SALES (corp-wide): 235.3MM **Privately Held**
WEB: www.duanemorris.com
SIC: 8111 General practice attorney, lawyer
PA: Duane Morris Llp
30 S 17th St Fl 5
Philadelphia PA 19103
215 979-1000

(P-22493)
DUCKOR SPRADLING METZGER
101 W Broadway Ste 1700, San Diego
(92101-8289)
PHONE..................................619 209-3000
Michael J Duckor, *President*
Scott Metzger, *Shareholder*
Jill Osmars, *Shareholder*
Gary J Spradling, *Vice Ch Bd*
Carol McCabe, *Administration*
EMP: 70
SQ FT: 25,000
SALES (est): 8.5MM **Privately Held**
WEB: www.dsm-law.com
SIC: 8111 General practice law office

(P-22494)
DYKEMA GOSSETT PLLC
333 S Grand Ave Ste 2100, Los Angeles
(90071-1525)
PHONE..................................213 457-1800
Caroline Acossano, *Manager*
Karen Forrand, *Admin Asst*
Dianne Mueller, *Admin Asst*
Jason Grinnell, *Counsel*
Brian Newman, *Counsel*
EMP: 60
SALES (corp-wide): 135.6MM **Privately Held**
SIC: 8111 General practice law office
PA: Dykema Gossett P.L.L.C.
400 Renaissance Ctr
Detroit MI 48243
313 568-6800

(P-22495)
EILEEN NOTTOLI
Also Called: Allen Matkins
3 Embarcadero Ctr # 1200, San Francisco
(94111-4003)
PHONE..................................415 837-1515
EMP: 75 **EST:** 2013
SALES (est): 1.7MM **Privately Held**
SIC: 8111

(P-22496)
ENGSTROM LIPSCOMB AND LACK A (PA)
10100 Santa Monica Blvd # 1200, Los Angeles (90067-4113)
PHONE..................................310 552-3800
Paul Engstrom, *President*
Lee G Lipscomb, *Vice Pres*
Walter J Lack, *Admin Sec*
EMP: 70
SQ FT: 22,000
SALES (est): 13.6MM **Privately Held**
WEB: www.elllaw.com
SIC: 8111 General practice law office

(P-22497)
EPSTEIN BECKER & GREEN PC
1875 Century Park E # 500, Los Angeles
(90067-2337)
PHONE..................................310 556-8861
Sandy Siciliano, *Manager*
Joy Ingoglia, *Admin Sec*
James Flynn, *General Counsel*
Alan B Dickson,
John Darbyshire, *Manager*
EMP: 60
SALES (corp-wide): 117MM **Privately Held**
SIC: 8111 General practice attorney, lawyer
PA: Epstein Becker & Green, P.C.
875 3rd Ave
New York NY 10022
212 351-4500

(P-22498)
FEDERAL DFENDERS SAN DIEGO INC (PA)
225 Broadway Ste 900, San Diego
(92101-5030)
PHONE..................................619 234-8467
Jami Ferrara, *CEO*
Lou Soldinger, *CFO*
Shereen J Charlick, *Principal*
Mario Conte, *Exec Dir*
Linda Acosta, *CTO*
EMP: 75
SALES: 23.1MM **Privately Held**
SIC: 8111 General practice law office

PRODUCTS & SVCS

(P-22499)
FENWICK & WEST LLP (PA)
801 California St, Mountain View
(94041-1990)
PHONE................................650 988-8500
Gordon K Davidson, *General Ptnr*
Greg Hopewell, *General Ptnr*
Michael R Blum, *Partner*
Darren E Donnelly, *Partner*
Dan Dorosin, *Partner*
EMP: 375 EST: 1971
SALES (est): 72MM **Privately Held**
SIC: 8111 General practice attorney,
lawyer; patent, trademark & copyright law;
taxation law

(P-22500)
FENWICK & WEST LLP
555 California St # 1200, San Francisco
(94104-1515)
PHONE................................415 875-2300
Kacey Leonis, *Office Mgr*
EMP: 120
SALES (corp-wide): 72MM **Privately
Held**
SIC: 8111 General practice attorney,
lawyer; patent, trademark & copyright law;
taxation law
PA: Fenwick & West Llp
801 California St
Mountain View CA 94041
650 988-8500

(P-22501)
**FIRM A CHUGH PROFESSIONAL
CORP**
15925 Carmenita Rd, Cerritos
(90703-2206)
PHONE................................562 229-1220
Navneet Singh Chugh, *Principal*
Jagminder Matharu, *Office Admin*
Sarah Williams, *Admin Asst*
Jyoti Jhaveri, *IT/INT Sup*
Nikita Amin, *Accountant*
EMP: 73 EST: 2011
SALES (est): 10.5MM **Privately Held**
SIC: 8111 General practice law office

(P-22502)
**FIRM A CHUGH PROFESSIONAL
CORP**
1600 Duane Ave, Santa Clara
(95054-3442)
PHONE................................408 970-0100
Navneet Chugh, *Manager*
EMP: 50
SALES (corp-wide): 18.3MM **Privately
Held**
WEB: www.chugh.com
SIC: 8111 General practice law office
PA: Chugh Firm, The A Professional Corpo-
ration
15925 Carmenita Rd
Cerritos CA 90703
562 229-1220

(P-22503)
**FIRST LEGAL SUPPORT SVCS
LLC (PA)**
1517 Beverly Blvd, Los Angeles
(90026-5704)
PHONE................................213 250-1111
Elisha Gilboa, *Mng Member*
Nia Troup, *Vice Pres*
Brian Malouf, *Regional Mgr*
Aida Lopez, *Area Mgr*
Miguel Meza, *IT/INT Sup*
EMP: 54
SQ FT: 3,000
SALES (est): 15.1MM **Privately Held**
WEB: www.firstlegalsupport.com
SIC: 8111 Legal aid service

(P-22504)
FISH & RICHARDSON PC
500 Arguello St Ste 500 # 500, Redwood
City (94063-1568)
PHONE................................650 839-5070
Peter Devlin, *President*
Lori Cox, *President*
Cecilia Acosta, *Admin Sec*
Melissa Alexander, *Admin Sec*
Cheryl Sherwood, *Admin Sec*
EMP: 100

SALES (corp-wide): 88.5MM **Privately
Held**
WEB: www.fr.com
SIC: 8111 General practice attorney,
lawyer
PA: Fish & Richardson P.C.
1 Marina Park Dr Ste 1700
Boston MA 02210
617 542-5070

(P-22505)
FISH & RICHARDSON PC
12390 El Camino Real, San Diego
(92130-3162)
PHONE................................858 678-5070
Cindy Winters, *Financial Exec*
Susan Rodriguez, *Admin Asst*
Jenifer Potter, *Project Mgr*
Rudy Cobian, *Technology*
Steven McCracken, *General Counsel*
EMP: 150
SALES (corp-wide): 88.5MM **Privately
Held**
WEB: www.fr.com
SIC: 8111 General practice law office
PA: Fish & Richardson P.C.
1 Marina Park Dr Ste 1700
Boston MA 02210
617 542-5070

(P-22506)
FISHER & PHILLIPS LLP
2050 Main St Ste 1000, Irvine
(92614-8240)
PHONE................................949 851-2424
James McDonald, *Partner*
John L Zenoe, *Counsel*
Mike Ulrich, *Manager*
EMP: 53
SALES (corp-wide): 171.2MM **Privately
Held**
WEB: www.laborlawyers.com
SIC: 8111 General practice attorney,
lawyer; general practice law office
PA: Fisher & Phillips Llp
1075 Peachtree St Ne # 3500
Atlanta GA 30309
404 231-1400

(P-22507)
**FITZGRALD ABBOTT
BEARDSLEY LLP**
1221 Broadway Fl 21, Oakland
(94612-1837)
P.O. Box 12867 (94604-2867)
PHONE................................510 451-3300
Michael S Word, *Managing Prtnr*
Susan Von,
EMP: 71
SQ FT: 20,000
SALES (est): 9MM **Privately Held**
WEB: www.fablaw.com
SIC: 8111 General practice law office

(P-22508)
**FLOYD SKEREN & KELLY LLP
(PA)**
Also Called: FS&k
101 Moody Ct Ste 200, Thousand Oaks
(91360-6068)
PHONE................................818 206-9222
Thomas M Skeren Jr, *President*
Aimee Haverlah, *Admin Sec*
Tim Jurich, *Administration*
Rosalie Garcia, *Legal Staff*
Mary Sinacori, *Legal Staff*
EMP: 74
SALES (est): 24.2MM **Privately Held**
SIC: 8111 General practice law office

(P-22509)
FOLEY & LARDNER LLP
975 Page Mill Rd, Palo Alto (94304-1013)
PHONE................................650 856-3700
Susan Lamont, *Manager*
Katy Koski, *Partner*
Brenda Allen-Johnson, *President*
Jane Barr, *President*
Monique Blakey, *President*
EMP: 121
SALES (corp-wide): 368.4MM **Privately
Held**
SIC: 8111 General practice attorney,
lawyer

PA: Foley & Lardner Llp
777 E Wisconsin Ave # 3800
Milwaukee WI 53202
414 271-2400

(P-22510)
FOLEY & LARDNER LLP
555 California St # 1700, San Francisco
(94104-1503)
PHONE................................415 434-4484
Eileen Ridley, *Managing Prtnr*
Nancy Geenen, *Partner*
EMP: 80
SQ FT: 3,000
SALES (corp-wide): 368.4MM **Privately
Held**
WEB: www.foley.com
SIC: 8111 General practice attorney,
lawyer
PA: Foley & Lardner Llp
777 E Wisconsin Ave # 3800
Milwaukee WI 53202
414 271-2400

(P-22511)
FOLEY & LARDNER LLP
555 S Flower St Ste 3300, Los Angeles
(90071-2418)
PHONE................................213 972-4500
Sergiy Sivochek, *Branch Mgr*
Deborah Felianco, *Executive*
Richard Torres, *Technical Staff*
Kevin Pray, *Litigation*
Michael K Chung, *Associate*
EMP: 125
SALES (corp-wide): 368.4MM **Privately
Held**
SIC: 8111 General practice attorney,
lawyer
PA: Foley & Lardner Llp
777 E Wisconsin Ave # 3800
Milwaukee WI 53202
414 271-2400

(P-22512)
FOLEY & LARDNER LLP
3579 Vly Cntre Dr Ste 300, San Diego
(92130)
PHONE................................858 847-6700
Greg Moser, *Partner*
Robert Ward, *Associate*
EMP: 70
SALES (corp-wide): 368.4MM **Privately
Held**
WEB: www.foley.com
SIC: 8111 General practice attorney,
lawyer
PA: Foley & Lardner Llp
777 E Wisconsin Ave # 3800
Milwaukee WI 53202
414 271-2400

(P-22513)
FONDA & FRAZER LLP (PA)
1925 Century Park E # 1360, Los Angeles
(90067-2710)
PHONE................................310 553-3320
Peter M Fonda, *Partner*
Pamela A Benben, *Partner*
Todd E Croutch, *Partner*
Stephen C Fraser, *Partner*
Alexander M Watson, *Partner*
EMP: 60
SQ FT: 11,000
SALES (est): 3.3MM **Privately Held**
WEB: www.fondafraserlaw.com
SIC: 8111 Criminal law

(P-22514)
FORD MOTOR COMPANY
3 Glen Bell Way Ste 200, Irvine
(92618-3392)
PHONE................................949 341-5800
Michael O'Driscoll, *President*
Scott Gerald, *Business Anlyst*
Ulrich John, *Sales Staff*
EMP: 450
SALES (corp-wide): 160.3B **Publicly
Held**
WEB: www.ford.com
SIC: 8111 7549 Corporate, partnership &
business law; automotive customizing
services, non-factory basis

PA: Ford Motor Company
1 American Rd
Dearborn MI 48126
313 322-3000

(P-22515)
FOX ROTHSCHILD LLP
1 Sansome St Ste 2850, San Francisco
(94104-4426)
PHONE................................415 539-3336
Raquel L Sefton, *Branch Mgr*
EMP: 70
SALES (corp-wide): 188.8MM **Privately
Held**
SIC: 8111 Divorce & family law
PA: Fox Rothschild Llp
2000 Market St Fl 20
Philadelphia PA 19103
215 299-2000

(P-22516)
FRAGOMEN DEL REY BERNSE
11238 El Camino Real # 100, San Diego
(92130-2653)
PHONE................................858 793-1600
Gary Mor, *Partner*
EMP: 60
SALES (corp-wide): 245.3MM **Privately
Held**
SIC: 8111 General practice law office
PA: Fragomen, Del Rey, Bernsen & Loewy,
Llp
90 Matawan Rd
Matawan NJ 07747
732 862-5000

(P-22517)
FRAGOMEN DEL REY BERNSE
11150 W Olympic Blvd # 1000, Los Angeles
(90064-1827)
PHONE................................310 820-3322
Peter Loewy, *Principal*
Shelly Song, *Associate*
EMP: 50
SALES (corp-wide): 245.3MM **Privately
Held**
SIC: 8111 General practice law office
PA: Fragomen, Del Rey, Bernsen & Loewy,
Llp
90 Matawan Rd
Matawan NJ 07747
732 862-5000

(P-22518)
FRAGOMEN DEL REY BERNSE
18401 Von Karman Ave # 255, Irvine
(92612-1596)
PHONE................................949 660-3504
EMP: 81
SALES (corp-wide): 248.2MM **Privately
Held**
SIC: 8111
PA: Fragomen, Del Rey, Bernsen & Loewy,
Llp
90 Matawan Rd
Matawan NJ 07747
732 862-5000

(P-22519)
FRAGOMEN DEL REY BERNSE
2121 Tasman Dr, Santa Clara
(95054-1027)
PHONE................................408 919-0600
Cynthia Lang, *Branch Mgr*
Ali Ramezanzadeh, *Associate*
Da N Rowan, *Associate*
EMP: 81
SALES (corp-wide): 245.3MM **Privately
Held**
SIC: 8111 General practice law office
PA: Fragomen, Del Rey, Bernsen & Loewy,
Llp
90 Matawan Rd
Matawan NJ 07747
732 862-5000

(P-22520)
**FRANCISCO EMILIO ASSOC
LAW OFF**
17532 Von Karman Ave, Irvine
(92614-6279)
PHONE................................949 474-2222
Emilio Francisco, *President*
EMP: 100

SALES (est): 3.7MM **Privately Held**
SIC: 8111 General practice attorney, lawyer

(P-22521)
FRANDZEL SHARE ROBINS BLOOM LC
1000 Wilshire Blvd # 1900, Los Angeles (90017-2457)
PHONE...................................323 852-1000
Steve N Bloom, *President*
Thomas Robins, *Vice Pres*
Damon Rubin, *Research Analys*
EMP: 55
SQ FT: 40,000
SALES (est): 7.7MM **Privately Held**
WEB: www.frandzel.com
SIC: 8111 General practice attorney, lawyer; general practice law office

(P-22522)
FREEMAN FREEMAN & SMILEY (PA)
Also Called: Freeman Freeman & Smiley LLP
1888 Century Park E Fl 19, Los Angeles (90067-1723)
PHONE...................................310 398-6100
Bruce M Smiley, *Principal*
Elyse Henry, *President*
Stephen Lowe, *Officer*
Fred J Marcus, *Principal*
Glenn T Sherman, *Principal*
EMP: 94
SQ FT: 25,000
SALES (est): 17.3MM **Privately Held**
WEB: www.ffslaw.com
SIC: 8111 General practice law office; general practice attorney, lawyer

(P-22523)
FULWIDER AND PATTON LLP
6100 Center Dr Ste 1200, Los Angeles (90045-9203)
PHONE...................................310 824-5555
Richard A Bardin, *Managing Prtnr*
Scott Hansen, *Partner*
Katherine McDaniel, *Partner*
David Pitman, *Partner*
Scott Brashear, *Accounting Mgr*
EMP: 100
SQ FT: 48,000
SALES (est): 13MM **Privately Held**
SIC: 8111 General practice law office

(P-22524)
GALLOWAY LUCCHESE EVERSON
2300 Contra Costa Blvd, Walnut Creek (94596)
PHONE...................................925 930-9090
G Patrick Galloway, *President*
David Lucchese, *Senior Partner*
David R Lucchese, *Vice Pres*
Jeannette Avila, *Legal Staff*
Carrie Hughes, *Legal Staff*
EMP: 50
SQ FT: 13,700
SALES (est): 5.5MM **Privately Held**
WEB: www.glattys.com
SIC: 8111 General practice law office

(P-22525)
GANG TYRE RAMER & BROWN INC
Also Called: Shandon Properties
132 S Rodeo Dr Ste 306, Beverly Hills (90212-2414)
PHONE...................................310 777-7158
Norman R Tyre, *President*
Donald S Passman, *Treasurer*
Bruce M Ramer, *Vice Pres*
Hermione K Brown, *Admin Sec*
Nancy Boxwell,
EMP: 50 EST: 1943
SALES: 12.8K **Privately Held**
SIC: 8111 General practice attorney, lawyer

(P-22526)
GAW VAN MALE SMITH MYERS
1411 Oliver Rd Ste 300, Fairfield (94534-3433)
PHONE...................................707 425-1250
Scott Reynolds, *Manager*
EMP: 62

SALES (corp-wide): 9.4MM **Privately Held**
WEB: www.gvmsmm.com
SIC: 8111 General practice attorney, lawyer
PA: Gaw, Van Male, Smith, Myers & Miroglio A Professional Corp
1000 Main St Ste 300
Napa CA 94559
707 469-7100

(P-22527)
GIBBS GIDEN LOCHER
1880 Century Park E # 1200, Los Angeles (90067-1621)
PHONE...................................310 552-3400
Richard J Wittbrodt, *Principal*
Barbara R Gadbois, *Partner*
Lannette M Pabon, *Chief Mktg Ofcr*
Kenneth C Gibbs, *Principal*
Joseph M Giden, *Principal*
EMP: 70
SQ FT: 27,000
SALES (est): 10.7MM **Privately Held**
WEB: www.gglt.com
SIC: 8111 General practice attorney, lawyer

(P-22528)
GIBSON DUNN & CRUTCHER LLP
1881 Page Mill Rd, Palo Alto (94304-1146)
PHONE...................................650 849-5300
Russel Hansel, *Managing Prtnr*
Paul J Collins, *Partner*
H Mark Lyon, *Partner*
Dave Goodell, *Info Tech Mgr*
Sean Twomey, *Associate*
EMP: 60
SALES (corp-wide): 276.8MM **Privately Held**
WEB: www.gibsondunn.com
SIC: 8111 General practice law office
PA: Gibson, Dunn & Crutcher Llp
333 S Grand Ave Ste 4600
Los Angeles CA 90071
213 229-7000

(P-22529)
GIBSON DUNN & CRUTCHER LLP
3161 Michelson Dr # 1200, Irvine (92612-4412)
PHONE...................................949 451-3800
Karen Kubani, *Branch Mgr*
Alba Cabriales, *Admin Sec*
Donna Luca, *Admin Sec*
Candie Trainor, *Admin Sec*
Misty Lenahan, *Administration*
EMP: 200
SALES (corp-wide): 276.8MM **Privately Held**
WEB: www.gibsondunn.com
SIC: 8111 General practice law office
PA: Gibson, Dunn & Crutcher Llp
333 S Grand Ave Ste 4600
Los Angeles CA 90071
213 229-7000

(P-22530)
GIBSON DUNN & CRUTCHER LLP (PA)
333 S Grand Ave Ste 4600, Los Angeles (90071-1512)
PHONE...................................213 229-7000
Kenneth M Doran, *Managing Prtnr*
John Behrendt, *Senior Partner*
Nicholas Aleksander, *Partner*
Peter Alexiadis, *Partner*
Lisa A Alfaro, *Partner*
EMP: 500
SQ FT: 250,000
SALES (est): 276.8MM **Privately Held**
WEB: www.gibsondunn.com
SIC: 8111 General practice law office

(P-22531)
GIBSON DUNN & CRUTCHER LLP
2029 Century Park E # 4000, Los Angeles (90067-3026)
PHONE...................................310 552-8500
Julie Denton, *General Mgr*
William Stinehart Jr, *Partner*
EMP: 65

SALES (corp-wide): 276.8MM **Privately Held**
WEB: www.gibsondunn.com
SIC: 8111 General practice law office
PA: Gibson, Dunn & Crutcher Llp
333 S Grand Ave Ste 4600
Los Angeles CA 90071
213 229-7000

(P-22532)
GIBSON DUNN & CRUTCHER LLP
555 Mission St Ste 3000, San Francisco (94105-0921)
PHONE...................................415 393-8200
Mike Saad, *Manager*
Kathrin Sears, *Partner*
Michael Saad, *CFO*
Philip Gordon, *Training Spec*
Nerney Dan, *Legal Staff*
EMP: 101
SALES (corp-wide): 276.8MM **Privately Held**
WEB: www.gibsondunn.com
SIC: 8111 General practice law office
PA: Gibson, Dunn & Crutcher Llp
333 S Grand Ave Ste 4600
Los Angeles CA 90071
213 229-7000

(P-22533)
GILBERT LLP
655 Montgomery St Ste 700, San Francisco (94111-2689)
PHONE...................................415 646-4002
EMP: 63
SALES (corp-wide): 9.7MM **Privately Held**
SIC: 8111 General practice attorney, lawyer
PA: Gilbert, Llp
1100 New York Ave Nw # 700
Washington DC 20005
202 216-9199

(P-22534)
GILBERT KLLY CRWLEY JNNETT LLP (PA)
550 S Hope St Ste 2200, Los Angeles (90071-2631)
PHONE...................................213 615-7000
Jon H Tisdale, *Managing Prtnr*
Paul Bigley, *Partner*
Timothy Kenna, *Partner*
Arthur J Mc Keon III, *Partner*
Lisa Braham, *President*
EMP: 75
SQ FT: 30,000
SALES (est): 12.9MM **Privately Held**
WEB: www.gilbertkelly.com
SIC: 8111 General practice law office

(P-22535)
GIPSON HOFFMAN & PANCIONE A
1901 Avenue Of The Stars # 1100, Los Angeles (90067-6002)
PHONE...................................310 556-4660
Lawrence R Barnett, *President*
Richard P Solomon, *Partner*
Kenneth I Sidle, *Partner*
Robert E Gipson, *Vice Pres*
Robert H Steinberg, *Vice Pres*
EMP: 70
SQ FT: 27,000
SALES (est): 9.3MM **Privately Held**
WEB: www.ghplaw.com
SIC: 8111 General practice attorney, lawyer; corporate, partnership & business law; bankruptcy law

(P-22536)
GIRARDI & KEESE (PA)
1126 Wilshire Blvd, Los Angeles (90017-1904)
PHONE...................................213 977-0211
Thomas V Girardi, *Partner*
Robert M Keese, *Partner*
Elizabeth Escobedo, *President*
Shelby Fujioka, *President*
Kim Cory, *Admin Sec*
EMP: 100
SQ FT: 5,000

SALES (corp-wide): 276.8MM **Privately Held**
WEB: www.gibsondunn.com
SIC: 8111 General practice law office
PA: Gibson, Dunn & Crutcher Llp
333 S Grand Ave Ste 4600
Los Angeles CA 90071
213 229-7000

(P-22537)
GLASER WEIL FINK JACOBS (PA)
10250 Constellation Blvd # 1900, Los Angeles (90067-6229)
PHONE...................................310 553-3000
Terry Christensen, *Managing Prtnr*
Patricia L Glaser, *Partner*
John Mason, *Partner*
Richard Volpert, *Partner*
George Wall, *Partner*
EMP: 160
SQ FT: 76,000
SALES (est): 34.4MM **Privately Held**
SIC: 8111 General practice law office

(P-22538)
GLASPY & GLASPY A PROF CORP
100 Pringle Ave Ste 750, Walnut Creek (94596-7330)
P.O. Box 8104 (94596-8104)
PHONE...................................408 279-8844
David M Glaspy, *President*
Thomas C Glaspy, *Vice Pres*
Carlos K Poza, *Nurse*
Stephanie Payne, *Manager*
EMP: 50
SALES (est): 4.1MM **Privately Held**
WEB: www.glaspy.com
SIC: 8111 Corporate, partnership & business law

(P-22539)
GLOBAL USA GREEN CARD
201 Spear St Ste 1100, San Francisco (94105-6164)
PHONE...................................415 915-4151
Eran Druker, *VP Opers*
EMP: 60 EST: 2016
SALES (est): 1MM **Privately Held**
SIC: 8111 Immigration & naturalization law

(P-22540)
GOODWIN PROCTER LLP
601 S Figueroa St # 4100, Los Angeles (90017-5710)
PHONE...................................213 426-2500
Dean Pappas, *Managing Prtnr*
EMP: 60
SALES (corp-wide): 306.7MM **Privately Held**
SIC: 8111 General practice attorney, lawyer
PA: Goodwin Procter Llp
100 Northern Ave
Boston MA 02210
617 570-1000

(P-22541)
GORDON EDELSTEIN KREPACK GR
Also Called: Gordon Edelstein & Krepack
3580 Wilshire Blvd # 1800, Los Angeles (90010-2530)
PHONE...................................213 739-7000
Roger L Gordon, *Partner*
Mark Edelstein, *Partner*
Richard Felton, *Partner*
Irwin Goldstein, *Partner*
Larry Goldstein, *Partner*
EMP: 50
SALES (est): 8.7MM **Privately Held**
WEB: www.geklaw.com
SIC: 8111 General practice attorney, lawyer

(P-22542)
GORDON REES SCULLY MANSUKHANI
655 University Ave # 200, Sacramento (95825-6707)
PHONE...................................916 830-6900
Kathleen M Rhoads, *Managing Prtnr*
Veronica Whitaker, *Admin Sec*
Allison Jones, *Counsel*
Kara Keister, *Counsel*
Jennifer Lynch, *Associate*
EMP: 94

(PA)=Parent Co (HQ)=Headquarters (DH)=Div Headquarters
✪ = New Business established in last 2 years

2019 Directory of California
Wholesalers and Services Companies

953

PRODUCTS & SVCS

SALES (corp-wide): 204.2MM **Privately Held**
SIC: **8111** Specialized law offices, attorneys
PA: Gordon Rees Scully Mansukhani, Llp.
   275 Battery St Ste 2000
   San Francisco CA 94111
   415 986-5900

(P-22543)
GORDON REES SCULLY MANSUKHANI
2211 Michelson Dr Ste 400, Irvine (92612-1390)
PHONE.....................949 255-6950
Douglas Smith, *Office Mgr*
Sandra Avants, *President*
Tara Martin, *Counsel*
EMP: 80
SALES (corp-wide): 204.2MM **Privately Held**
SIC: **8111** Specialized law offices, attorneys
PA: Gordon Rees Scully Mansukhani, Llp.
   275 Battery St Ste 2000
   San Francisco CA 94111
   415 986-5900

(P-22544)
GORDON REES SCULLY MANSUKHANI (PA)
275 Battery St Ste 2000, San Francisco (94111-3361)
PHONE.....................415 986-5900
Dion N Cominos, *Partner*
Marie Holvick, *Partner*
Jorge J Perez, *Partner*
Stephen E Ronk, *Partner*
Marc Thirkell, *Partner*
EMP: 325
SQ FT: 57,500
SALES (est): 204.2MM **Privately Held**
WEB: www.gordonrees.com
SIC: **8111** Corporate, partnership & business law

(P-22545)
GORDON REES SCULLY MANSUKHANI
633 W 5th St Fl 52, Los Angeles (90071-2086)
PHONE.....................213 576-5000
Scott Sirlin, *Owner*
Dina Cordero, *President*
Wendy Fletcher, *President*
Mila Owen, *President*
Frank Gonzalez, *Executive Asst*
EMP: 79
SALES (corp-wide): 204.2MM **Privately Held**
SIC: **8111** Specialized law offices, attorneys
PA: Gordon Rees Scully Mansukhani, Llp.
   275 Battery St Ste 2000
   San Francisco CA 94111
   415 986-5900

(P-22546)
GORDON REES SCULLY MANSUKHANI
101 W Broadway Ste 1600, San Diego (92101-8217)
PHONE.....................619 696-6700
Gary Zacher, *Managing Prtnr*
Susan Orona, *Marketing Staff*
James E Hawley, *Associate*
Eugene Roymisher, *Associate*
EMP: 100
SQ FT: 7,000
SALES (corp-wide): 204.2MM **Privately Held**
WEB: www.gordonrees.com
SIC: **8111** Specialized law offices, attorneys
PA: Gordon Rees Scully Mansukhani, Llp.
   275 Battery St Ste 2000
   San Francisco CA 94111
   415 986-5900

(P-22547)
GORDON REES SCULLY MANSUKHANI
101 W Broadway Ste 2000, San Diego (92101-8221)
PHONE.....................415 986-5900

Craig Hill, *Manager*
Elisa Martinez, *Admin Sec*
Kimberly Kaye, *Legal Staff*
EMP: 90
SALES (corp-wide): 204.2MM **Privately Held**
WEB: www.gordonrees.com
SIC: **8111** Specialized law offices, attorneys
PA: Gordon Rees Scully Mansukhani, Llp.
   275 Battery St Ste 2000
   San Francisco CA 94111
   415 986-5900

(P-22548)
GREEN GLUSK FIELD CLAMA & MACH
1900 Avenue Of The Stars 21f, Los Angeles (90067-4301)
PHONE.....................310 553-3610
Jonathan R Fitzgarrald, *Principal*
ARI B Brumer, *Partner*
Ricardo P Cestero, *Partner*
Stephen Claman, *Partner*
Bert Fields, *Partner*
EMP: 200
SQ FT: 80,000
SALES (est): 32.1MM **Privately Held**
SIC: **8111** General practice attorney, lawyer

(P-22549)
GREENBERG TRAURIG LLP
4 Embarcadero Ctr # 3000, San Francisco (94111-5983)
PHONE.....................415 655-1300
Evan S Nadel, *Branch Mgr*
Howard Holderness, *Shareholder*
Leslie Katz, *Shareholder*
Brad Marsh, *Shareholder*
Randy Single, *Shareholder*
EMP: 98
SALES (corp-wide): 376.8MM **Privately Held**
SIC: **8111** General practice attorney, lawyer
HQ: Greenberg Traurig, Llp
   1 Intl Pl Ste 2000
   Boston MA 02110

(P-22550)
GREENBERG TRAURIG LLP
1840 Century Park E # 1900, Los Angeles (90067-2121)
PHONE.....................310 586-7708
Richard Rowan, *Branch Mgr*
Karin Bohmholdt, *Shareholder*
Jeffrey Joyner, *Shareholder*
John McBride, *Shareholder*
Edward Schultz, *Shareholder*
EMP: 76
SALES (corp-wide): 376.8MM **Privately Held**
SIC: **8111** General practice attorney, lawyer
HQ: Greenberg Traurig, Llp
   1 Intl Pl Ste 2000
   Boston MA 02110

(P-22551)
GREENBERG TRAURIG LLP
1900 University Ave Fl 5, East Palo Alto (94303-2283)
PHONE.....................650 328-8500
Lance Joseph, *Branch Mgr*
Charles Birenbaum, *Shareholder*
Vivek Chavan, *Shareholder*
Cindy Hamilton, *Shareholder*
Jason Lindsay, *Shareholder*
EMP: 73
SALES (corp-wide): 376.8MM **Privately Held**
SIC: **8111** General practice attorney, lawyer
HQ: Greenberg Traurig, Llp
   1 Intl Pl Ste 2000
   Boston MA 02110

(P-22552)
GREENBERG TRAURIG LLP
3161 Michelson Dr # 1000, Irvine (92612-4410)
PHONE.....................949 732-6500

Ray Lee, *Managing Prtnr*
Daniel Donahue, *Shareholder*
Bruce Fischer, *Shareholder*
Dillon Colucci, *Associate*
EMP: 70
SALES (corp-wide): 376.8MM **Privately Held**
SIC: **8111** General practice attorney, lawyer
HQ: Greenberg Traurig, Llp
   1 Intl Pl Ste 2000
   Boston MA 02110

(P-22553)
GREENE RDVSKY MALONEY SHARE LP
4 Embarcadero Ctr # 4000, San Francisco (94111-4100)
PHONE.....................415 981-1400
Mark Hennigh, *Managing Prtnr*
Richard Green, *Senior Partner*
James Abrams, *Partner*
Thomas Feldstein, *Partner*
James Fotenos, *Partner*
EMP: 69
SQ FT: 18,800
SALES (est): 7.6MM **Privately Held**
WEB: www.grmslaw.com
SIC: **8111** Specialized law offices, attorneys; corporate, partnership & business law; real estate law; taxation law

(P-22554)
GRESHAM SAVAGE NOLAN & TILDEN (PA)
550 E Hospitality Ln # 300, San Bernardino (92408-4205)
PHONE.....................619 794-0050
Mark A Ostoich, *President*
Bob Ritter, *Partner*
Christie Bowman, *President*
Tom Jacobsen, *COO*
Robert Ritter, *CFO*
EMP: 53
SQ FT: 16,500
SALES (est): 11.8MM **Privately Held**
SIC: **8111** General practice law office

(P-22555)
GUNDERSON DETTMER STOUGH VILLE (PA)
550 Allerton St, Redwood City (94063-1524)
PHONE.....................650 321-2400
Robert Gunderson, *Partner*
Colin Chapman, *Partner*
Dan O Connor, *Partner*
Joshua Cook, *Partner*
Scott Dettmer, *Partner*
EMP: 125
SALES (est): 28.1MM **Privately Held**
WEB: www.gdsvfh.com
SIC: **8111** General practice law office

(P-22556)
HAHN & HAHN LLP
301 E Colo Blvd Ste 900, Pasadena (91101)
PHONE.....................626 796-9123
Karl Swaidan, *Managing Prtnr*
Gene E Gregg Jr, *Partner*
R Scott Jenkins, *Partner*
Kristianne Kerns, *Partner*
Natasha Zaharov, *Partner*
EMP: 80
SQ FT: 15,175
SALES (est): 9.7MM **Privately Held**
WEB: www.hahnlawyers.com
SIC: **8111** General practice attorney, lawyer

(P-22557)
HAIGHT BROWN & BONESTEEL LLP (PA)
555 S Flower St Ste 4500, Los Angeles (90071-2441)
PHONE.....................213 542-8000
S Christian Stouder, *Managing Prtnr*
Carolyn Harper, *CFO*
Yamile Soto, *Human Resources*
William Baumgaertner, *Sales Mgr*
Sean Swayze, *Marketing Staff*
EMP: 80
SQ FT: 36,265

SALES (est): 25.4MM **Privately Held**
WEB: www.hbblaw.com
SIC: **8111** General practice law office

(P-22558)
HANNA BROPHY MAC LEAN MC ALE (PA)
1956 Webster St Ste 450, Oakland (94612-2930)
PHONE.....................510 839-1180
Leslie Tuxhorn, *Managing Prtnr*
John Armanino, *Senior Partner*
Joseph Nisim, *Partner*
Barbara Wood, *Partner*
Edmund Leonard, *Exec VP*
EMP: 50
SQ FT: 10,000
SALES (est): 48.2MM **Privately Held**
WEB: www.hannabrophy.com
SIC: **8111** General practice law office

(P-22559)
HANSON BRIDGETT LLP
500 Capitol Mall Ste 1500, Sacramento (95814-4740)
PHONE.....................916 442-3333
Linda Hall, *Admin Sec*
Catherine Velasco, *Analyst*
EMP: 50
SALES (corp-wide): 60.6MM **Privately Held**
SIC: **8111** General practice attorney, lawyer
PA: Hanson Bridgett Llp
   425 Market St Fl 26
   San Francisco CA 94105
   415 543-2055

(P-22560)
HANSON BRIDGETT LLP (PA)
425 Market St Fl 26, San Francisco (94105-5401)
PHONE.....................415 543-2055
Andrew G Giacomini, *Partner*
Lawrence Cirelli, *Partner*
Theodore A Hellman, *Partner*
Frank Lopez, *Partner*
Mary McEachron, *Partner*
EMP: 311
SQ FT: 79,120
SALES (est): 60.6MM **Privately Held**
WEB: www.hansonbridgett.com
SIC: **8111** General practice attorney, lawyer

(P-22561)
HARRIS STOCKWELL (PA)
3580 Wilshire Blvd Fl 19, Los Angeles (90010-2532)
PHONE.....................310 277-6669
Steven I Harris, *CEO*
Richard M Widom, *Vice Pres*
Christine McKenna, *Admin Sec*
Patricia A Olive, *Admin Sec*
Norma Orozco, *Admin Sec*
EMP: 50 EST: 1970
SALES (est): 20MM **Privately Held**
SIC: **8111** General practice attorney, lawyer

(P-22562)
HART KING COLDREN A PROF CORP
4 Hutton Cntre Dr Ste 900, Santa Ana (92707)
PHONE.....................714 432-8700
Robert S Coldren, *President*
Bill Hart, *Managing Prtnr*
Gary R King, *Treasurer*
William R Hart, *Admin Sec*
William Hart, *CTO*
EMP: 60
SQ FT: 20,000
SALES (est): 9.2MM **Privately Held**
WEB: www.hkclaw.com
SIC: **8111** General practice attorney, lawyer

(P-22563)
HASSARD BONNINGTON LLP (PA)
Also Called: HB
275 Battery St Ste 1600, San Francisco (94111-3993)
PHONE.....................415 288-9800

James M Goodman, *General Ptnr*
Phillip F Ward, *Partner*
Eliza Busch, *Legal Staff*
Renee Richards, *Counsel*
EMP: 80
SALES (est): 11.6MM **Privately Held**
WEB: www.hassard.com
SIC: 8111 General practice law office

(P-22564)
HAYNES AND BOONE LLP
525 University Ave # 400, Palo Alto
(94301-1903)
PHONE..................650 687-8800
Laurie Armstrong, *Manager*
Gary Edwards, *Partner*
Eric Deutsch, *Director*
EMP: 91
SALES (corp-wide): 212.2MM **Privately Held**
SIC: 8111 General practice attorney, lawyer
PA: Haynes And Boone, Llp
   2323 Victory Ave Ste 700
   Dallas TX 75219
   214 651-5000

(P-22565)
HEIGHT BROWN AND BONESTEEL
555 S Flower St Ste 4500, Los Angeles
(90071-2441)
PHONE..................213 241-0900
Christian Stouder, *Managing Prtnr*
EMP: 60
SALES (est): 1.8MM **Privately Held**
SIC: 8111 Legal services

(P-22566)
HEMAR ROUSSO & HEALD L L P
Also Called: Hemar & Rousso Attys At Law
15910 Ventura Blvd # 1201, Encino
(91436-2829)
PHONE..................818 501-3800
Richard P Hemar, *Managing Prtnr*
Daniel E Heald, *Partner*
Martin J Rousso, *Partner*
Tammy Dunn, *President*
Michele Kilroy, *Legal Staff*
EMP: 50
SQ FT: 10,000
SALES (est): 5.4MM **Privately Held**
WEB: www.hemar-rousso.com
SIC: 8111 General practice law office

(P-22567)
HENDERSON FINNEGAN FARABOW
3300 Hillview Ave Fl 2, Palo Alto
(94304-1251)
PHONE..................650 849-6600
Amy Duxbury, *Manager*
Patrick Maher, *Technical Staff*
George Hutchinson, *Asst Treas*
Sabrina Greenawald, *Marketing Staff*
Jeff Danley, *Publications*
EMP: 70
SALES (corp-wide): 141.5MM **Privately Held**
SIC: 8111 General practice attorney, lawyer
PA: Finnegan, Henderson, Farabow, Garrett & Dunner, L.L.P.
   901 New York Ave Nw # 1150
   Washington DC 20001
   202 408-4000

(P-22568)
HIGGS FLETCHER & MACK LLP
Also Called: Goproto
401 W A St Ste 2600, San Diego
(92101-7913)
PHONE..................619 236-1551
John Morrell, *General Ptnr*
Anna F Roppo, *Partner*
Phillip C Samouis, *Partner*
Lisa Berry, *Admin Sec*
Iuliano Maria, *Admin Sec*
EMP: 150
SQ FT: 45,000
SALES (est): 26MM **Privately Held**
WEB: www.higgslaw.com
SIC: 8111 General practice attorney, lawyer

(P-22569)
HILL FARRER & BURRILL
Also Called: One California Plaza
300 S Grand Ave Fl 37, Los Angeles
(90071-3147)
PHONE..................213 620-0460
Scott Gilmore, *Partner*
Steven W Bacon, *Partner*
Julia L Birkel, *Partner*
William M Bitting, *Partner*
Michael S Blanton, *Partner*
EMP: 100
SQ FT: 32,000
SALES (est): 16MM **Privately Held**
WEB: www.hillfarrer.com
SIC: 8111 General practice law office

(P-22570)
HINSHAW & CULBERTSON LLP
633 W 5th St Ste 4700, Los Angeles
(90071-2043)
PHONE..................213 680-2800
Jenny Bernal, *Administration*
EMP: 60
SALES (corp-wide): 200MM **Privately Held**
SIC: 8111 General practice attorney, lawyer
PA: Hinshaw & Culbertson Llp
   151 N Franklin St # 2500
   Chicago IL 60606
   312 704-3000

(P-22571)
HIRSCHFELD KRAEMER LLP (PA)
505 Montgomery St Fl 13, San Francisco
(94111-2551)
PHONE..................415 835-9000
Richard Curiale, *Partner*
EMP: 50
SALES (est): 6.4MM **Privately Held**
WEB: www.employmentlawalliance.com
SIC: 8111 General practice law office

(P-22572)
HOLLAND & KNIGHT LLP
400 S Hope St Ste 800, Los Angeles
(90071-2809)
PHONE..................213 896-2400
Maita Prout, *Manager*
Rishi Maragh, *Technology*
Arnold D Kahn, *Counsel*
Nicholas Melzer, *Counsel*
James W Michalski, *Counsel*
EMP: 100
SALES (corp-wide): 100MM **Privately Held**
WEB: www.hollandandknight.com
SIC: 8111 General practice attorney, lawyer
PA: Holland & Knight Llp
   524 Grand Regency Blvd
   Brandon FL 33510
   813 901-4200

(P-22573)
HOLLAND & KNIGHT LLP
Also Called: Haight Gdnr Holland & Knight
50 California St Ste 2800, San Francisco
(94111-4726)
PHONE..................415 743-6900
Erik Dale, *Manager*
Leona McFarlane, *Assistant*
Joshua S Miller, *Assistant*
Jennifer A Modrich, *Assistant*
Judith Nemsick, *Assistant*
EMP: 50
SALES (corp-wide): 100MM **Privately Held**
WEB: www.hollandandknight.com
SIC: 8111 General practice attorney, lawyer
PA: Holland & Knight Llp
   524 Grand Regency Blvd
   Brandon FL 33510
   813 901-4200

(P-22574)
HOLLINS SCHECHTER A PROF CORP
1851 E 1st St Ste 600, Santa Ana
(92705-4049)
PHONE..................714 558-9119
Andrew S Hollins, *President*

Bruce L Schechter, *Vice Pres*
Jennifer Tusko, *Finance Dir*
EMP: 60 **EST:** 1978
SQ FT: 15,000
SALES (est): 4.3MM **Privately Held**
WEB: www.hollins-law.com
SIC: 8111 General practice attorney, lawyer

(P-22575)
HOPKINS & CARLEY A LAW CORP (PA)
70 S 1st St, San Jose (95113-2406)
P.O. Box 1469 (95109-1469)
PHONE..................408 286-9800
William S Klein, *Principal*
Jennifer Johnson, *Shareholder*
Lloyd Schmidt, *Shareholder*
Candice Allen, *President*
Edwina Feguis, *President*
EMP: 100 **EST:** 1968
SQ FT: 33,000
SALES (est): 19.6MM **Privately Held**
WEB: www.hopkinscarley.com
SIC: 8111 Corporate, partnership & business law; divorce & family law; environmental law; real estate law

(P-22576)
HUESTON HENNIGAN LLP
523 W 6th St Ste 400, Los Angeles
(90014-1208)
PHONE..................213 788-4340
Marshall A Camp, *Partner*
Douglas J Dixon, *Partner*
Alexander C D Giza, *Partner*
Brian J Hennigan, *Partner*
John C Hueston, *Partner*
EMP: 80
SQ FT: 25,000
SALES (est): 387.6K **Privately Held**
SIC: 8111 General practice attorney, lawyer

(P-22577)
HUNT ORTMANN PALFFY NIEVES
301 N Lake Ave Fl 7, Pasadena
(91101-5118)
PHONE..................626 440-5200
Dale A Ortmann, *Co-Founder*
John Darling, *Shareholder*
Thomas Palffy, *Treasurer*
Laurence Lubka, *Principal*
Omel Nieves, *Principal*
EMP: 50
SQ FT: 18,000
SALES (est): 7.7MM **Privately Held**
SIC: 8111 General practice law office

(P-22578)
HUNTON ANDREWS KURTH LLP
50 California St Ste 1700, San Francisco
(94111-4604)
PHONE..................415 975-3700
Fraser McAlpine, *Partner*
EMP: 94
SALES (corp-wide): 348.8MM **Privately Held**
SIC: 8111 General practice attorney, lawyer
PA: Hunton Andrews Kurth Llp
   951 E Byrd St Ste 200
   Richmond VA 23219
   804 788-8200

(P-22579)
HUNTON ANDREWS KURTH LLP
550 S Hope St Ste 2000, Los Angeles
(90071-2631)
PHONE..................213 532-2000
Wally Martinez, *Managing Prtnr*
Julio Matamoros, *Info Tech Mgr*
Diana Biason, *Associate*
Matthew Bobb, *Associate*
Stephanie Der, *Associate*
EMP: 91
SALES (corp-wide): 348.8MM **Privately Held**
SIC: 8111 General practice attorney, lawyer
PA: Hunton Andrews Kurth Llp
   951 E Byrd St Ste 200
   Richmond VA 23219
   804 788-8200

(P-22580)
IMMERSION MEDICAL INC
50 Rio Robles, San Jose (95134-1806)
PHONE..................408 467-1900
Shum Mukherjee, *CFO*
Sandhya Jain, *Marketing Staff*
EMP: 85 **EST:** 1995
SALES (est): 5.1MM **Publicly Held**
WEB: www.immersion.com
SIC: 8111 5047 Patent, trademark & copyright law; instruments, surgical & medical
PA: Immersion Corporation
   50 Rio Robles
   San Jose CA 95134

(P-22581)
IRELL & MANELLA LLP (PA)
1800 Avenue Of The Stars # 900, Los Angeles (90067-4276)
PHONE..................310 277-1010
Elliot Brown, *Managing Prtnr*
Morgan Chu, *Partner*
Gregory Klein, *Partner*
David Siegel, *Partner*
Steven Zelman, *CFO*
EMP: 400
SQ FT: 154,000
SALES: 34.6K **Privately Held**
WEB: www.irell.com
SIC: 8111 General practice law office

(P-22582)
IRELL & MANELLA LLP
840 Nwport Ctr Dr Ste 400, Newport Beach
(92660)
PHONE..................949 760-0991
Nancy Adams, *Manager*
Daniel Lefler, *Partner*
Sherman Richard,
Robert W Stedman,
EMP: 100
SALES (corp-wide): 34.6K **Privately Held**
WEB: www.irell.com
SIC: 8111 General practice attorney, lawyer
PA: Irell & Manella Llp
   1800 Avenue Of The Stars # 900
   Los Angeles CA 90067
   310 277-1010

(P-22583)
IRON LAW INC (PA)
663 S Rancho Santa Fe Rd, San Marcos
(92078-3973)
PHONE..................844 476-6529
Jesse Wagner, *CEO*
EMP: 80 **EST:** 2015
SQ FT: 500
SALES (est): 4.5MM **Privately Held**
SIC: 8111 General practice law office

(P-22584)
IVIE MCNEILL WYATT A PROF LAW
444 S Flower St Ste 1800, Los Angeles
(90071-2919)
PHONE..................213 489-0028
Robert H Mc Neill Jr, *President*
Rickey Ivie, *Vice Pres*
Keith Wyatt, *Admin Sec*
Sam Chilakos, *Counsel*
Marie Maurice, *Associate*
EMP: 50
SALES (est): 7.1MM **Privately Held**
WEB: www.imwlaw.com
SIC: 8111 General practice attorney, lawyer

(P-22585)
JACKOWAY TYREMAN WERTHEIMER AU
1925 Century Park E Fl 2, Los Angeles
(90067-2701)
PHONE..................310 553-0305
Barry Hirsch, *President*
Eric Weissler, *Shareholder*
Leonard Cox, *CFO*
EMP: 100 **EST:** 1976
SQ FT: 3,000
SALES (est): 13.3MM **Privately Held**
SIC: 8111 General practice law office

PRODUCTS & SVCS

(P-22586)
JACKSON DEMARCO TIDUS PETER (PA)
2030 Main St Ste 1200, Irvine
(92614-7256)
P.O. Box 19703 (92623-9703)
PHONE..............................949 752-8585
M Alim Malik, *CEO*
James Demarco, *President*
Thomas D Peckenpaugh, *President*
Ruth Mijuskovic, *CEO*
Andrea Herting, *Office Admin*
EMP: 82
SQ FT: 23,000
SALES (est): 12.6MM **Privately Held**
SIC: 8111 General practice law office

(P-22587)
JACKSON LEWIS PC
50 California St Ste 900, San Francisco
(94111-4615)
PHONE..............................415 394-9400
Gloria Kennard, *Office Admin*
Lauretta Adams, *Admin Sec*
John Bartkowiak, *Legal Staff*
Rebecca T Benhuri, *Associate*
Dylan B Carp, *Associate*
EMP: 50
SALES (corp-wide): 250.5MM **Privately Held**
WEB: www.jacksonlewis.com
SIC: 8111 General practice law office
PA: Jackson Lewis Pc
1133 Weschester Ave
West Harrison NY 10604
914 872-8060

(P-22588)
JACKSON LEWIS PC
725 S Figueroa St # 2500, Los Angeles
(90017-5408)
PHONE..............................213 689-0404
Wendy Sweet, *Manager*
Karina Ramirez, *Admin Sec*
Josh Sable,
Scott Price, *Manager*
Yvonne D Arvanitis, *Associate*
EMP: 100
SQ FT: 2,000
SALES (corp-wide): 250.5MM **Privately Held**
WEB: www.jacksonlewis.com
SIC: 8111 General practice law office
PA: Jackson Lewis Pc
1133 Weschester Ave
West Harrison NY 10604
914 872-8060

(P-22589)
JEFFER MNGELS BTLR MTCHELL LLP (PA)
Also Called: Jmbm
1900 Avenue Of The Stars, Los Angeles
(90067-4301)
PHONE..............................310 203-8080
Bruce P Jeffer, *Managing Prtnr*
James R Butler Jr, *Partner*
Dan E Chambers, *Partner*
Randy Harris, *Partner*
Jennifer A Irrgang, *Partner*
EMP: 230
SALES (est): 47.3MM **Privately Held**
WEB: www.jmbm.com
SIC: 8111 General practice attorney, lawyer

(P-22590)
JEFFER MNGELS BTLR MTCHELL LLP
2 Embarcadero Ctr Fl 5, San Francisco
(94111-3813)
PHONE..............................415 398-8080
Richard Rogan, *Manager*
Scott Castro, *Partner*
Nicolas De Lancie, *Partner*
Nicolas Delancie, *Partner*
Michael Hassen, *Partner*
EMP: 65
SALES (corp-wide): 47.3MM **Privately Held**
WEB: www.jmbm.com
SIC: 8111 General practice attorney, lawyer

PA: Jeffer, Mangels, Butler & Mitchell, Llp
1900 Avenue Of The Stars
Los Angeles CA 90067
310 203-8080

(P-22591)
JOHN F DMINGUE ATTORNEY AT LAW
10 Almaden Blvd Ste 1100, San Jose
(95113-2270)
PHONE..............................408 591-5180
John F Domingue, *Owner*
EMP: 150
SALES (est): 2.7MM **Privately Held**
SIC: 8111 Labor & employment law; general practice law office

(P-22592)
JOHNSON LA FOLLETTE
2677 N Main St Ste 901, Santa Ana
(92705-6632)
PHONE..............................714 558-7008
Dennis Ames, *Managing Prtnr*
Odell Steven,
Scott Foley, *Associate*
EMP: 65
SALES (corp-wide): 17.9MM **Privately Held**
WEB: www.ljdfa.com
SIC: 8111 General practice law office
PA: La Follette, Johnson, De Haas,
865 S Figueroa St # 3200
Los Angeles CA 90017
213 426-3600

(P-22593)
JONES DAY LIMITED PARTNERSHIP
4655 Executive Dr # 1500, San Diego
(92121-3134)
PHONE..............................858 314-1200
Karen P Hewitt, *Partner*
Michael Staab, *Office Admin*
Jayne McCullough, *Admin Sec*
Brooke Schultz, *Associate*
EMP: 60
SALES (corp-wide): 675.1MM **Privately Held**
SIC: 8111 General practice attorney, lawyer
PA: Jones Day Limited Partnership
901 Lakeside Ave E Ste 2
Cleveland OH 44114
216 586-3939

(P-22594)
JONES DAY LIMITED PARTNERSHIP
555 California St # 2600, San Francisco
(94104-1602)
PHONE..............................415 626-3939
Aaron L Agenboard, *Partner*
Jason McDonell, *Partner*
Jennifer Seraphine, *Partner*
Paul Kuo, *Counsel*
David Morris, *Counsel*
EMP: 100
SQ FT: 45,000
SALES (corp-wide): 675.1MM **Privately Held**
SIC: 8111 General practice law office
PA: Jones Day Limited Partnership
901 Lakeside Ave E Ste 2
Cleveland OH 44114
216 586-3939

(P-22595)
JONES DAY LIMITED PARTNERSHIP
3161 Michelson Dr Ste 800, Irvine
(92612-4408)
PHONE..............................949 851-3939
R J Grabowski, *General Mgr*
Thomas R Malcolm, *Partner*
Cher Schuerman, *Admin Sec*
Jeffrey Kirzner,
Dulcie D Brand, *Manager*
EMP: 85
SQ FT: 22,500
SALES (corp-wide): 675.1MM **Privately Held**
SIC: 8111 General practice attorney, lawyer

PA: Jones Day Limited Partnership
901 Lakeside Ave E Ste 2
Cleveland OH 44114
216 586-3939

(P-22596)
JONES DAY LIMITED PARTNERSHIP
1755 Embarcadero Rd, Palo Alto
(94303-3340)
PHONE..............................650 739-3939
Brian G Selden, *Partner*
Behrooz Shariati, *Partner*
Neal Stephens, *Partner*
Bob Clarkson, *Managing Prtnr*
Julie Gleaves, *Admin Sec*
EMP: 100
SALES (corp-wide): 675.1MM **Privately Held**
SIC: 8111 General practice attorney, lawyer
PA: Jones Day Limited Partnership
901 Lakeside Ave E Ste 2
Cleveland OH 44114
216 586-3939

(P-22597)
JOSEPH C SANSONE COMPANY (PA)
Also Called: Tobin Lucks
21300 Victory Blvd # 300, Woodland Hills
(91367-2525)
P.O. Box 4502 (91365-4502)
PHONE..............................818 226-3400
Irvin Lucks, *Partner*
Edwin Lucks, *Partner*
Donald Tobin, *Partner*
Wayne Myers, *Controller*
Rose White, *Legal Staff*
EMP: 97
SALES (est): 23.5MM **Privately Held**
SIC: 8111 General practice law office

(P-22598)
K&L GATES LLP
55 2nd St Ste 1700, San Francisco
(94105-3493)
PHONE..............................415 882-8200
Bob Schweda, *Manager*
Polly A Dinkel, *Partner*
Maryam Baz, *IT/INT Sup*
EMP: 70
SALES (corp-wide): 446.4MM **Privately Held**
WEB: www.klxtra.com
SIC: 8111 General practice attorney, lawyer
PA: K&L Gates Llp
210 6th Ave Ste 1100
Pittsburgh PA 15222
412 355-6500

(P-22599)
K&L GATES LLP
10100 Santa Monica Blvd # 700, Los Angeles (90067-4003)
PHONE..............................310 552-5000
Karen Doyle, *Manager*
Jeryl A Bowers, *Partner*
Frederick J Ufkes, *Partner*
Arlene Zamora, *Admin Sec*
Derek Christopher, *Analyst*
EMP: 50
SALES (corp-wide): 446.4MM **Privately Held**
WEB: www.klxtra.com
SIC: 8111 General practice law office
PA: K&L Gates Llp
210 6th Ave Ste 1100
Pittsburgh PA 15222
412 355-6500

(P-22600)
KASDAN SMNDS RILEY VAUGHAN LLP (PA)
19900 Macarthur Blvd # 850, Irvine
(92612-8422)
PHONE..............................949 851-9000
Kenneth Kasdan, *Partner*
EMP: 56
SQ FT: 20,000
SALES (est): 11.1MM **Privately Held**
SIC: 8111 General practice law office

(P-22601)
KATTEN MUCHIN ROSENMAN LLP
515 S Flower St, Los Angeles
(90071-2201)
PHONE..............................310 788-4498
Susan Taylor, *Branch Mgr*
EMP: 175
SALES (corp-wide): 220.7MM **Privately Held**
SIC: 8111 General practice law office
PA: Katten Muchin Rosenman Llp
525 W Monroe St
Chicago IL 60661
312 902-5200

(P-22602)
KATTEN MUCHIN ROSENMAN LLP
1999 Harrison St Ste 700, Oakland
(94612-4704)
PHONE..............................415 360-5444
Shannon Broome, *Branch Mgr*
EMP: 175
SALES (corp-wide): 220.7MM **Privately Held**
SIC: 8111 General practice law office
PA: Katten Muchin Rosenman Llp
525 W Monroe St
Chicago IL 60661
312 902-5200

(P-22603)
KATTEN MUCHIN ROSENMAN LLP
2029 Century Park E # 2600, Los Angeles
(90067-3012)
PHONE..............................310 788-4400
Tanya Russell, *Branch Mgr*
Kristopher Ring, *Partner*
EMP: 150
SALES (corp-wide): 220.7MM **Privately Held**
WEB: www.kattenlaw.com
SIC: 8111 General practice law office
PA: Katten Muchin Rosenman Llp
525 W Monroe St
Chicago IL 60661
312 902-5200

(P-22604)
KAWELA ONE LLC
3000 El Camino Real, Palo Alto
(94306-2100)
PHONE..............................650 843-5000
Cooley Godward, *Principal*
EMP: 71
SALES (est): 6.7MM **Privately Held**
SIC: 8111 Specialized law offices, attorneys

(P-22605)
KAZAN MCCLAIN SATTERLEY &
55 Harrison St Ste 400, Oakland
(94607-3858)
PHONE..............................877 995-6372
Steven Kazan, *Partner*
Justin Bosl, *Partner*
Denyse Clancy, *Partner*
Gordon Greenwood, *Partner*
John Langdoc, *Partner*
EMP: 108
SALES (est): 11.6MM **Privately Held**
SIC: 8111 General practice law office

(P-22606)
KEESAL YOUNG LOGAN A PROF CORP (PA)
400 Oceangate Ste 1400, Long Beach
(90802-4325)
PHONE..............................562 436-2000
Samuel A Keesal Jr, *CEO*
Lisa Beazley, *Shareholder*
Chris Stecher, *Shareholder*
Robert Stemler, *Shareholder*
J Stephen Young, *Corp Secy*
EMP: 90
SQ FT: 65,000
SALES (est): 931.4K **Privately Held**
WEB: www.kyl.com
SIC: 8111 General practice law office

(P-22607)
KEKER VAN NEST & PETERS LLP
633 Battery St Bsmt 91, San Francisco (94111-1899)
PHONE.....................415 391-5400
John W Keker,
Susan Cole, *President*
DOT D Fox, *President*
Patty Lemos, *President*
Laure Mandin, *President*
EMP: 100
SQ FT: 70,000
SALES (est): 22.5MM **Privately Held**
WEB: www.kvn.com
SIC: 8111 Criminal law; specialized law offices, attorneys

(P-22608)
KELLEY DRYE & WARREN LLP
10100 Santa Monica Blvd, Los Angeles (90067-4003)
PHONE.....................310 712-6100
Ken Kow, *Branch Mgr*
EMP: 210
SALES (corp-wide): 183.8MM **Privately Held**
SIC: 8111 General practice law office
PA: Kelley Drye & Warren Llp
101 Park Ave Fl 30
New York NY 10178
212 808-7800

(P-22609)
KILPATRICK TWNSEND STCKTON LLP
2175 N California Blvd, Walnut Creek (94596-3579)
PHONE.....................925 472-5000
Harold Williams, *Branch Mgr*
Angelo Acevedo, *Technology*
EMP: 103
SALES (corp-wide): 261.1MM **Privately Held**
SIC: 8111 General practice attorney, lawyer
PA: Kilpatrick Townsend & Stockton Llp
1100 Peachtree St Ne
Atlanta GA 30309
404 815-6500

(P-22610)
KIMBALL TIREY & ST JOHN LLP (PA)
7676 Hazard Center Dr # 900, San Diego (92108-4515)
PHONE.....................619 234-1690
Theodore C Kimball, *Partner*
Maria Wampler, *President*
Leslie Mason, *Principal*
EMP: 70
SQ FT: 6,000
SALES (est): 22MM **Privately Held**
SIC: 8111 General practice attorney, lawyer

(P-22611)
KING HLMES PTERNO SORIANO LLP
1900 Avenue Of The Stars, Los Angeles (90067-4301)
PHONE.....................310 282-8989
Howard King, *Partner*
Peter Paterno, *Partner*
Lori Soriano, *Partner*
Aurora Gomez, *President*
EMP: 50
SALES (est): 7.9MM **Privately Held**
WEB: www.khpblaw.com
SIC: 8111 General practice attorney, lawyer

(P-22612)
KING & SPALDING LLP
101 2nd St Ste 2300, San Francisco (94105-3664)
PHONE.....................415 318-1200
Donald Zimmer, *Partner*
George Morris, *Counsel*
Steven Park, *Sr Associate*
Anthony Rutella, *Manager*
Anisha Sud, *Associate*
EMP: 296

SALES (corp-wide): 341.3MM **Privately Held**
SIC: 8111 General practice law office
PA: King & Spalding Llp
1180 Peachtree St
Atlanta GA 30309
404 572-4600

(P-22613)
KIRKLAND & ELLIS LLP
555 California St # 2700, San Francisco (94104-1603)
PHONE.....................415 439-1400
Caroline Recht, *Manager*
Josephine Isvoranu, *President*
Bao Nguyen, *Executive*
Diana Atherton, *Admin Sec*
Samantha Benson, *Admin Sec*
EMP: 200
SALES (corp-wide): 456.1MM **Privately Held**
WEB: www.kirkland.com
SIC: 8111 General practice attorney, lawyer
PA: Kirkland & Ellis Llp
300 N La Salle Dr # 2400
Chicago IL 60654
312 862-2000

(P-22614)
KLEIN DENATALE GOLDNER ET AL (PA)
Also Called: Klein Denatale Goldner Cooper
4550 California Ave Fl 2, Bakersfield (93309-7012)
P.O. Box 11172 (93389-1172)
PHONE.....................661 401-7755
Anthony J Klein, *Partner*
Anthony Klein, *Senior Partner*
Jennifer A Adams, *Partner*
Hagop T Bedoyan, *Partner*
David J Cooper, *Partner*
EMP: 69
SQ FT: 25,000
SALES (est): 15.7MM **Privately Held**
SIC: 8111 General practice law office

(P-22615)
KLEIN-TESTAN-BRUNDO
1851 E 1st St Ste 100, Santa Ana (92705-4036)
PHONE.....................714 245-8888
Jeffrey Adelson, *Partner*
EMP: 50
SALES (est): 282.2K **Privately Held**
SIC: 8111 Labor & employment law

(P-22616)
KMEA (PA)
2423 Hoover Ave, National City (91950-6619)
PHONE.....................619 399-5900
R Chuck Forrest III, *President*
Lou Anne Vogler, *Director*
EMP: 60
SALES: 13.6MM **Privately Held**
WEB: www.kmea.net
SIC: 8111 8741 8711 Environmental law; administrative management; engineering services

(P-22617)
KNOBBE MARTENS OLSON BEAR LLP (PA)
2040 Main St Fl 14, Irvine (92614-8214)
PHONE.....................949 760-0404
Steven J Nataupsky, *Managing Prtnr*
Michelle Armond, *Partner*
William B Bunker, *Partner*
Drew S Hamilton, *Partner*
Ned Israelsen, *Partner*
EMP: 350
SQ FT: 120,000
SALES (est): 120.4MM **Privately Held**
WEB: www.knobbe.com
SIC: 8111 General practice law office

(P-22618)
KNOBBE MARTENS OLSON BEAR LLP
12790 El Camino Real # 100, San Diego (92130-2008)
PHONE.....................858 707-4000
Wesly Pettus, *Branch Mgr*
John Riedel, *Purchasing*

Heungsoo Choi, *Associate*
Ryan S Furtado, *Associate*
Peter Law, *Associate*
EMP: 100
SALES (corp-wide): 120.4MM **Privately Held**
WEB: www.knobbe.com
SIC: 8111 Patent, trademark & copyright law
PA: Knobbe Martens Olson & Bear, Llp
2040 Main St Fl 14
Irvine CA 92614
949 760-0404

(P-22619)
KNOX ATTORNEY SERVICE INC (PA)
Also Called: Knox Services
2250 4th Ave Ste 200, San Diego (92101-2124)
PHONE.....................619 233-9700
Steve Knox, *President*
Robert Porambo, *CFO*
Danny Marin, *Office Mgr*
Dave Rekalske, *Info Tech Mgr*
Sue Sornsin, *Accounting Mgr*
EMP: 227 **EST:** 1973
SQ FT: 165,929
SALES (est): 39.3MM **Privately Held**
WEB: www.knoxservices.com
SIC: 8111 Legal aid service

(P-22620)
KO HOLDINGS LLC
220 Newport Center Dr, Newport Beach (92660-7506)
PHONE.....................949 629-3044
John C Kelly,
EMP: 51
SALES (est): 775.7K **Privately Held**
SIC: 8111 Legal services

(P-22621)
KOELLER NBKER CRLSON HLUCK LLP (PA)
3 Park Plz Ste 1500, Irvine (92614-8558)
P.O. Box 19799 (92623-9799)
PHONE.....................949 864-3400
Keith Koeller, *Managing Prtnr*
Bob Carlson, *Managing Prtnr*
William Haluck, *Managing Prtnr*
Bill Nebeker, *Managing Prtnr*
Erin Moore, *Office Mgr*
EMP: 170
SALES (est): 21.8MM **Privately Held**
SIC: 8111 General practice law office

(P-22622)
KRONICK MOSKOVITZ TIEDEMANN (PA)
400 Capitol Mall Fl 27, Sacramento (95814-4416)
PHONE.....................916 321-4500
Robert Murphy, *Chairman*
Michael A Grob, *President*
Bruce A Scheidt, *CEO*
Rick Fowler, *COO*
Kren A Sluiter, *CFO*
EMP: 93
SQ FT: 35,781
SALES (est): 20.8MM **Privately Held**
WEB: www.kmtg.com
SIC: 8111 General practice law office

(P-22623)
LA FOLLETTE JOHNSON DE HAAS (PA)
865 S Figueroa St # 3200, Los Angeles (90017-5431)
PHONE.....................213 426-3600
Daren T Johnson, *President*
Jim Wallace, *Managing Prtnr*
Mark Stewart, *Shareholder*
Barry Vogel, *Shareholder*
Dennis Ames, *Treasurer*
EMP: 105
SALES (est): 17.9MM **Privately Held**
WEB: www.ljdfa.com
SIC: 8111 General practice law office

(P-22624)
LADAS & PARRY LLP
4525 Wilshire Blvd # 240, Los Angeles (90010-3846)
PHONE.....................323 934-2300

Richard P Berg, *Partner*
Louis Pezzullo, *Executive*
Shannon Miller, *Legal Staff*
Richard Berg, *Counsel*
Mavis Galleson, *Manager*
EMP: 50
SALES (corp-wide): 25.1MM **Privately Held**
WEB: www.ladas.com
SIC: 8111 General practice law office
PA: Ladas & Parry Llp
1040 Ave Of The Amrcs 5
New York NY 10018

(P-22625)
LANG RICHERT & PATCH
Also Called: Attorneys At Law
5200 N Palm Ave Ste 401, Fresno (93704-2227)
P.O. Box 40012 (93755-4012)
PHONE.....................559 228-6700
Val W Saldana, *President*
Robert Patch, *President*
Douglas Griffin, *CFO*
Rene La Streto II, *Vice Pres*
Victoria Salisch, *Admin Sec*
EMP: 50 **EST:** 1962
SQ FT: 17,500
SALES (est): 7.1MM **Privately Held**
WEB: www.lrplaw.net
SIC: 8111 General practice law office

(P-22626)
LATHAM & WATKINS LLP
140 Scott Dr, Menlo Park (94025-1008)
PHONE.....................650 328-4600
Ora Fisher, *Branch Mgr*
Dean Baxtresser, *Associate*
Mark Bekheit, *Associate*
Gabriel Bell, *Associate*
Jessica J Chen, *Associate*
EMP: 180
SALES (corp-wide): 549.8MM **Privately Held**
WEB: www.lw.com
SIC: 8111 Corporate, partnership & business law
PA: Latham & Watkins Llp
355 S Grand Ave Ste 1000
Los Angeles CA 90071
213 485-1234

(P-22627)
LATHAM & WATKINS LLP
1722 Skyhill Way, Santa Ana (92705-2585)
PHONE.....................714 755-8288
Perry Viscouty, *Partner*
Nicole Jackson, *Admin Sec*
Darlene Julian, *Admin Sec*
Amanda Poore, *Admin Sec*
Amanda Stipe, *Business Mgr*
EMP: 323
SALES (corp-wide): 549.8MM **Privately Held**
SIC: 8111 General practice attorney, lawyer
PA: Latham & Watkins Llp
355 S Grand Ave Ste 1000
Los Angeles CA 90071
213 485-1234

(P-22628)
LATHAM & WATKINS LLP
12670 High Bluff Dr # 100, San Diego (92130-3086)
PHONE.....................858 523-5400
Bruce Shepard, *Partner*
Cynthia H Cwik-Martin, *Partner*
Pat Beebe, *Admin Sec*
Debra Dveris, *Admin Sec*
Samantha Seikkula, *Admin Sec*
EMP: 180
SALES (corp-wide): 549.8MM **Privately Held**
WEB: www.lw.com
SIC: 8111 General practice attorney, lawyer
PA: Latham & Watkins Llp
355 S Grand Ave Ste 1000
Los Angeles CA 90071
213 485-1234

(P-22629)
LATHAM & WATKINS LLP
111 Univrsal Hllywd 257, Universal City
(91608-1054)
PHONE..........................818 753-5000
EMP: 323
SALES (corp-wide): 549.8MM **Privately Held**
SIC: 8111 General practice attorney, lawyer
PA: Latham & Watkins Llp
355 S Grand Ave Ste 1000
Los Angeles CA 90071
213 485-1234

(P-22630)
LATHAM & WATKINS LLP (PA)
355 S Grand Ave Ste 1000, Los Angeles
(90071-3419)
PHONE..........................213 485-1234
Robert Dell, *Managing Prtnr*
Christopher J Allen, *Partner*
James P Beaubien, *Partner*
Joseph A Bevash, *Partner*
Jos Luis Blanco, *Partner*
EMP: 570 EST: 1934
SALES (est): 549.8MM **Privately Held**
WEB: www.lw.com
SIC: 8111 General practice attorney, lawyer

(P-22631)
LATHAM & WATKINS LLP
555 W 5th St Ste 800, Los Angeles
(90013-1021)
PHONE..........................213 891-7108
Carol Mindzak, *President*
Patricia Chase, *Admin Sec*
Marie D'Egidio, *Admin Sec*
Candy Willard, *Admin Sec*
Corwin Wills, *Admin Asst*
EMP: 81
SALES (corp-wide): 549.8MM **Privately Held**
SIC: 8111 General practice attorney, lawyer
PA: Latham & Watkins Llp
355 S Grand Ave Ste 1000
Los Angeles CA 90071
213 485-1234

(P-22632)
LATHAM & WATKINS LLP
650 Town Center Dr # 2000, Costa Mesa
(92626-7135)
PHONE..........................714 540-1235
Shayne Kennedy, *Managing Prtnr*
Scott Shean, *Managing Prtnr*
Mary Newman, *President*
Bror Andringa, *Info Tech Mgr*
Roland Lee, *Software Dev*
EMP: 175
SALES (corp-wide): 549.8MM **Privately Held**
WEB: www.lw.com
SIC: 8111 General practice attorney, lawyer
PA: Latham & Watkins Llp
355 S Grand Ave Ste 1000
Los Angeles CA 90071
213 485-1234

(P-22633)
LATHAM & WATKINS LLP
520 S Grand Ave Ste 200, Los Angeles
(90071-2655)
PHONE..........................213 891-1200
Leanne Black, *Director*
Rene Mendoza, *Admin Asst*
Anthony Ojeda, *Administration*
Farhan Aziz, *Auditing Mgr*
John D Watson Jr, *Clerk*
EMP: 200
SALES (corp-wide): 549.8MM **Privately Held**
SIC: 8111 Specialized legal services
PA: Latham & Watkins Llp
355 S Grand Ave Ste 1000
Los Angeles CA 90071
213 485-1234

(P-22634)
LATHAM & WATKINS LLP
505 Montgomery St # 1900, San Francisco
(94111-2562)
PHONE..........................415 391-0600

Scott Haber, *Managing Prtnr*
Meghan Esparza, *Opers Staff*
Frank Lee, *Librarian*
Jens Hillen,
John Kenny,
EMP: 240
SALES (corp-wide): 549.8MM **Privately Held**
WEB: www.lw.com
SIC: 8111 General practice attorney, lawyer
PA: Latham & Watkins Llp
355 S Grand Ave Ste 1000
Los Angeles CA 90071
213 485-1234

(P-22635)
LATHROP & GAGE LLP
1888 Century Park E # 1000, Los Angeles
(90067-1714)
PHONE..........................310 789-4600
John Schaffer, *Branch Mgr*
EMP: 70
SALES (corp-wide): 90.3MM **Privately Held**
SIC: 8111 General practice law office; general practice attorney, lawyer
PA: Lathrop & Gage Llp
2345 Grand Blvd Ste 2200
Kansas City MO 64108
816 292-2000

(P-22636)
LAUGHLIN FALBO LEVY MORESI LLP (PA)
1001 Galaxy Way Ste 200, Concord
(94520-5735)
PHONE..........................510 628-0496
John Geyer, *Managing Prtnr*
John Bennett Jr, *Partner*
Phillip J Klein, *Partner*
James Wesolowski, *Partner*
Kevin Calegari, *Managing Prtnr*
EMP: 76
SALES (est): 31.1MM **Privately Held**
SIC: 8111 General practice law office

(P-22637)
LAW OFFICES BERGLUND & JOHNSON (PA)
Also Called: Berglund & Johnson Law Office
21550 Oxnard St Ste 900, Woodland Hills
(91367-7144)
PHONE..........................951 276-4783
David W Berglund, *Partner*
Daniel W Johnson, *Partner*
EMP: 56
SALES (est): 4MM **Privately Held**
WEB: www.bjslawfirm.com
SIC: 8111 General practice law office

(P-22638)
LAW OFFICES OF THOMAS W
14286 Danielson St # 103, Poway
(92064-8819)
P.O. Box 503230, San Diego (92150-3230)
PHONE..........................858 883-2000
Thomas W Rutledge, *President*
Allison R Rutledge, *Exec VP*
Laurie Rauh, *Supervisor*
EMP: 135
SQ FT: 6,000
SALES (est): 12.8MM **Privately Held**
SIC: 8111 General practice law office

(P-22639)
LEE HONG DEGERMAN KANG
3501 Jamboree Rd Ste 6000, Newport
Beach (92660-2960)
PHONE..........................949 250-9954
Melissa Well, *Principal*
EMP: 60
SALES (corp-wide): 6.8MM **Privately Held**
SIC: 8111 Specialized law offices, attorneys
PA: Lee, Hong, Degerman, Kang &
Waimey, A Professional Corporation
660 S Figueroa St # 2300
Los Angeles CA 90017
213 623-2221

(P-22640)
LEGAL RECOVERY LAW OFFICES INC
5030 Camino De La Siesta # 340, San
Diego (92108-3118)
P.O. Box 84060 (92138-4060)
PHONE..........................619 275-4001
Mark Walsh, *President*
Andrew Rundquist, *Admin Sec*
EMP: 70
SQ FT: 2,500
SALES (est): 9.1MM **Privately Held**
WEB: www.lrlo.com
SIC: 8111 General practice law office

(P-22641)
LEGAL SOLUTIONS HOLDINGS INC
Also Called: Getmedlegal
955 Overland Ct Ste 200, San Dimas
(91773-1747)
PHONE..........................800 244-3495
Greg Webber, *CEO*
Kenneth Gleockler, *CFO*
Keahi Kakugawa, *Principal*
EMP: 237
SALES: 29.3MM **Privately Held**
SIC: 8111 Legal services

(P-22642)
LEGALMATCHCOM (PA)
395 Oyster Point Blvd, South San Francisco (94080-1928)
PHONE..........................415 946-0800
Randy Wells, *CEO*
Eric Briese, *CFO*
Neil Fradkin, *CTO*
Kurt Jerdon, *Controller*
Neal Carmichael, *VP Sales*
EMP: 50
SQ FT: 25,000
SALES (est): 6.3MM **Privately Held**
WEB: www.legalmatch.com
SIC: 8111 General practice attorney, lawyer

(P-22643)
LEGALZOOMCOM INC (DH)
101 N Brand Blvd Fl 11, Glendale
(91203-2638)
PHONE..........................323 962-8600
Daniel Wernikoff, *CEO*
Robert Shapiro, *Shareholder*
Brian Liu, *Ch of Bd*
Frank Monestere, *President*
Laura Goldberg, *Chief Mktg Ofcr*
EMP: 300
SQ FT: 17,000
SALES (est): 14.4MM
SALES (corp-wide): 34.6MM **Privately Held**
WEB: www.legalzoom.com
SIC: 8111 Legal services
HQ: Permira Advisers Llc
320 Park Ave Fl 28
New York NY 10022
212 386-7480

(P-22644)
LEVIN AND SIMES
353 Sacramento St # 2000, San Francisco
(94111-3620)
PHONE..........................415 426-3000
William A Levin, *Mng Member*
Martha-Alice Berman, *Principal*
EMP: 50
SQ FT: 10,000
SALES (est): 4.7MM **Privately Held**
SIC: 8111 Labor & employment law

(P-22645)
LEWIS BRSBOIS BSGARD SMITH LLP
28765 Single Oak Dr Ste 1, Temecula
(92590-3661)
PHONE..........................951 252-6150
Robert F Lewis, *Managing Prtnr*
EMP: 97
SALES (corp-wide): 284.9MM **Privately Held**
SIC: 8111 General practice law office
PA: Lewis Brisbois Bisgaard & Smith Llp
633 W 5th St Ste 4000
Los Angeles CA 90071
213 250-1800

(P-22646)
LEWIS BRSBOIS BSGARD SMITH LLP (PA)
633 W 5th St Ste 4000, Los Angeles
(90071-2074)
PHONE..........................213 250-1800
Robert F Lewis, *Managing Prtnr*
Josh Aicklen, *Partner*
Christopher P Bisgaard, *Partner*
Roy M Brisbois, *Partner*
Heather Jensen, *Partner*
EMP: 650
SQ FT: 80,000
SALES (est): 284.9MM **Privately Held**
WEB: www.lbbslaw.com
SIC: 8111 General practice law office

(P-22647)
LEWIS BRSBOIS BSGARD SMITH LLP
701 B St Ste 1900, San Diego
(92101-8198)
PHONE..........................619 233-1006
Susan O' Brien, *Systems Mgr*
Missy Palka, *President*
Martha Villavicenzio, *President*
Susan Obrien, *Officer*
Robert G Bernstein, *Principal*
EMP: 100
SALES (corp-wide): 284.9MM **Privately Held**
WEB: www.lbbslaw.com
SIC: 8111 General practice law office
PA: Lewis Brisbois Bisgaard & Smith Llp
633 W 5th St Ste 4000
Los Angeles CA 90071
213 250-1800

(P-22648)
LEWIS BRSBOIS BSGARD SMITH LLP
333 Bush St, San Francisco (94104-2806)
PHONE..........................415 362-2580
Cindy Aiello, *Manager*
Kathryn L Anderson, *Partner*
Jeffrey Bairey, *Partner*
Donald E Brier, *Partner*
Peter Dixon, *Partner*
EMP: 150
SALES (corp-wide): 284.9MM **Privately Held**
WEB: www.lbbslaw.com
SIC: 8111 General practice law office
PA: Lewis Brisbois Bisgaard & Smith Llp
633 W 5th St Ste 4000
Los Angeles CA 90071
213 250-1800

(P-22649)
LEWIS BRSBOIS BSGARD SMITH LLP
650 E Hospitality Ln # 600, San Bernardino
(92408-3535)
PHONE..........................909 387-1130
John Lowenthal, *Manager*
EMP: 50
SQ FT: 6,203
SALES (corp-wide): 284.9MM **Privately Held**
WEB: www.lbbslaw.com
SIC: 8111 General practice law office
PA: Lewis Brisbois Bisgaard & Smith Llp
633 W 5th St Ste 4000
Los Angeles CA 90071
213 250-1800

(P-22650)
LEWIS MARENSTEIN WICKE SHERWIN
20750 Ventura Blvd # 400, Woodland Hills
(91364-2390)
PHONE..........................818 703-6000
Michael B Lewis, *Partner*
Alan B Marenstein, *Partner*
Robert Sherwin, *Partner*
Thomas Wicke, *Partner*
Kal Borisov, *Info Tech Mgr*
EMP: 50 EST: 1971
SQ FT: 15,000
SALES (est): 5.9MM **Privately Held**
WEB: www.lmwslaw.com
SIC: 8111 General practice law office

(P-22651)
LFK LAW
9595 Wilshire Blvd # 900, Beverly Hills
(90212-2512)
PHONE....................310 300-8464
Louis Fkmontcho, *CFO*
Justin Weaver, *VP Engrg*
EMP: 55
SALES (est): 870.2K **Privately Held**
SIC: 8111 Legal services

(P-22652)
LIEFF CABRASER HEIMANN &
(PA)
275 Battery St Ste 2800, San Francisco
(94111-3314)
PHONE....................415 788-0245
Robert L Lieff, *Partner*
Kenneth S Byrd, *Partner*
Elizabeth J Cabraser, *Partner*
James M Finberg, *Partner*
Richard M Heimann, *Partner*
EMP: 120
SQ FT: 42,592
SALES (est): 22.8MM **Privately Held**
SIC: 8111 Antitrust & trade regulation law;
environmental law; labor & employment
law; securities law

(P-22653)
LINER LLP
Also Called: Liner Law
1100 Glendon Ave 14th, Los Angeles
(90024-3503)
PHONE....................310 500-3500
Stuart A Liner, *Managing Prtnr*
Mitchell C Regenstreif, *Partner*
Najwa Batarse, *Human Res Mgr*
Cheryleigh Bullock, *Legal Staff*
Matthew Nichols, *Associate*
EMP: 104 **EST:** 1996
SQ FT: 21,000
SALES (est): 580.1K **Privately Held**
SIC: 8111 Real estate law
HQ: Dla Piper Llp (Us)
6225 Smith Ave Ste 200
Baltimore MD 21209
410 580-3000

(P-22654)
LITTLER MENDELSON PC (PA)
333 Bush St Fl 34, San Francisco
(94104-2874)
P.O. Box 45547 (94145-0547)
PHONE....................415 433-1940
Thomas J Bender, *CEO*
Mindy Caterine, *Shareholder*
Juan Varela, *Shareholder*
Robert Millman, *Ch of Bd*
Marko Mrkonich, *President*
EMP: 500
SQ FT: 85,000
SALES (est): 311.2MM **Privately Held**
SIC: 8111 General practice law office

(P-22655)
LLP DOWNEY BRAND
621 Capitol Mall Fl 18, Sacramento
(95814-4731)
PHONE....................775 329-5900
Jeffrey Hartman, *Owner*
EMP: 77
SALES (corp-wide): 33.3MM **Privately
Held**
SIC: 8111 General practice attorney,
lawyer
PA: Downey Brand Llp
621 Capitol Mall Fl 18
Sacramento CA 95814
916 444-1000

(P-22656)
LLP DOWNEY BRAND
455 Market St Ste 1500, San Francisco
(94105-2443)
PHONE....................415 848-4800
EMP: 77
SALES (corp-wide): 33.3MM **Privately
Held**
SIC: 8111 General practice attorney,
lawyer
PA: Downey Brand Llp
621 Capitol Mall Fl 18
Sacramento CA 95814
916 444-1000

(P-22657)
LLP LOCKE LORD
101 Montgomery St # 1950, San Francisco
(94104-4154)
PHONE....................415 318-8800
Matthew Blackburn, *Branch Mgr*
EMP: 161
SALES (corp-wide): 193.3MM **Privately
Held**
SIC: 8111 General practice attorney,
lawyer
PA: Locke Lord Llp
2200 Ross Ave Ste 2800
Dallas TX 75201
214 740-8000

(P-22658)
LLP LOCKE LORD
660 Nwport Ctr Dr Ste 900, Newport Beach
(92660)
PHONE....................949 423-2100
Jon-Paul Lapointe, *Branch Mgr*
EMP: 87
SALES (corp-wide): 193.3MM **Privately
Held**
SIC: 8111 General practice law office
PA: Locke Lord Llp
2200 Ross Ave Ste 2800
Dallas TX 75201
214 740-8000

(P-22659)
LLP MAYER BROWN
2 Palo Alto Sq Ste 300, Palo Alto (94306)
PHONE....................650 331-2000
Martin Collins, *Branch Mgr*
Michele Quinnette, *Admin Sec*
EMP: 679
SALES (corp-wide): 707.3MM **Privately
Held**
SIC: 8111 General practice attorney,
lawyer
PA: Mayer Brown Llp
71 S Wacker Dr Ste 1000
Chicago IL 60606
312 782-0600

(P-22660)
LLP MAYER BROWN
Also Called: Mayer Brown & Platt
350 S Grand Ave Ste 2500, Los Angeles
(90071-3486)
PHONE....................213 229-9500
Jim Tancula, *Manager*
David B Bolstad, *Partner*
Pierre Vogelenzang, *Partner*
Brian Neale, *Info Tech Mgr*
David Chow, *Network Mgr*
EMP: 130
SALES (corp-wide): 707.3MM **Privately
Held**
SIC: 8111 General practice attorney,
lawyer
PA: Mayer Brown Llp
71 S Wacker Dr Ste 1000
Chicago IL 60606
312 782-0600

(P-22661)
LLP ROBINS KAPLAN
2049 Century Park E # 3400, Los Angeles
(90067-3208)
PHONE....................310 552-0130
Roman Silberfeld, *Manager*
EMP: 78
SALES (corp-wide): 117.5MM **Privately
Held**
WEB: www.rkmc.com
SIC: 8111 General practice attorney,
lawyer
PA: Llp Robins Kaplan
800 Lasalle Ave Ste 2800
Minneapolis MN 55402
612 349-8500

(P-22662)
LOEB & LOEB LLP (PA)
10100 Santa Monica Blvd # 2200, Los An-
geles (90067-4120)
PHONE....................310 282-2000
Barry I Slotnick, *Chairman*
Douglas N Masters, *Partner*
Mickey Mayerson, *Partner*
David S Schaefer, *Partner*
Stan Johnson, *Chairman*
EMP: 134

SALES (est): 51MM **Privately Held**
WEB: www.loeb.com
SIC: 8111 General practice attorney,
lawyer

(P-22663)
LONG & LEVIT LLP
465 California St Ste 500, San Francisco
(94104-1814)
PHONE....................415 397-2222
Joseph McMonigle, *Managing Prtnr*
Jessica R Macgregor, *Partner*
Luzia Ebnoether, *Executive*
James Locker, *Office Mgr*
Kate Kimberlin, *Counsel*
EMP: 50
SQ FT: 48,500
SALES (est): 8.2MM **Privately Held**
WEB: www.longlevit.com
SIC: 8111 Corporate, partnership & busi-
ness law; taxation law; environmental law

(P-22664)
LORBER GREENFIELD &
POLITO LLP (PA)
13985 Stowe Dr, Poway (92064-6887)
PHONE....................858 486-6757
Bruce Lorber, *Partner*
Joyia Greenfield, *Partner*
Cherrie Harris, *Partner*
Jill Ann Herman, *Partner*
Thomas Olsen, *Partner*
EMP: 62 **EST:** 1980
SQ FT: 20,000
SALES (est): 19.4MM **Privately Held**
SIC: 8111 General practice law office

(P-22665)
LOUIE ALMEIDA & SETTLER
(PA)
303 N Glenoaks Blvd # 400, Burbank
(91502-1116)
PHONE....................818 461-9559
David Stettler, *Senior Partner*
Donald Leiber, *Partner*
EMP: 54
SALES (est): 4.8MM **Privately Held**
SIC: 8111 General practice law office

(P-22666)
LOW BALL & LYNCH A PROF
CORP (PA)
505 Montgomery St Fl 7, San Francisco
(94111-6522)
PHONE....................415 981-6630
Steven D Werth, *President*
Sonja Blomquist, *Partner*
Thomas Losavio, *Shareholder*
Linda Meyer, *Shareholder*
Christine Reed, *Shareholder*
EMP: 72
SQ FT: 20,000
SALES (est): 10.3MM **Privately Held**
SIC: 8111 General practice law office

(P-22667)
LOWENSTEIN SANDLER LLP
390 Lytton Ave, Palo Alto (94301-1432)
PHONE....................650 433-5800
Rahul Shekher, *Associate*
Chandra K Shih, *Associate*
EMP: 50
SALES (corp-wide): 119.8MM **Privately
Held**
SIC: 8111 General practice law office
PA: Lowenstein Sandler Llp
1 Lowenstein Dr
Roseland NJ 07068
973 597-2500

(P-22668)
LOZANO SMITH LLP
7404 N Spalding Ave, Fresno
(93720-3370)
PHONE....................559 431-5600
Carlita C Romero, *Exec Dir*
Gena Morettini, *Office Mgr*
Angelique Toro, *Office Mgr*
Mariela Cantoriano, *Admin Sec*
Kip Pinette, *Admin Sec*
EMP: 167
SALES: 30K **Privately Held**
SIC: 8111 Specialized law offices, attor-
neys

(P-22669)
LOZANO SMITH A PROF CORP
(PA)
7404 N Spalding Ave, Fresno
(93720-3370)
PHONE....................559 431-5600
Gregory A Wedner, *CEO*
Tina Cobabe, *President*
Lou Lozano, *President*
Krista Steiner, *President*
Peter Fagen, *Treasurer*
EMP: 54
SALES (est): 19.1MM **Privately Held**
SIC: 8111 Corporate, partnership & busi-
ness law

(P-22670)
LYNBERG & WATKINS A PROF
CORP (PA)
Also Called: Lynberg & Watkins Attys At Law
1150 S Olive St Fl 18, Los Angeles
(90015-3989)
PHONE....................213 624-8700
Norman J Watkins, *President*
Charles A Lynberg, *President*
Randall J Peters, *CEO*
Daisy Beach, *Legal Staff*
Sierra Fruhn, *Assistant*
EMP: 50
SQ FT: 32,108
SALES (est): 13.8MM **Privately Held**
WEB: www.lynberg.com
SIC: 8111 General practice law office

(P-22671)
LYNCH GILARDI & GRUMMER
LLP
170 Columbus Ave Fl 5, San Francisco
(94133-5128)
P.O. Box 143 (94104-0143)
PHONE....................415 397-2800
Robert Lynch, *Managing Prtnr*
Dwane Grummer, *Managing Prtnr*
William A Bogdan,
James E Sell,
Kenneth F Vierra Jr,
EMP: 50
SQ FT: 4,000
SALES (est): 5.7MM **Privately Held**
WEB: www.lgglaw.com
SIC: 8111 Malpractice & negligence law;
product liability law; corporate, partner-
ship & business law

(P-22672)
MALCOLM & CISNEROS A LAW
CORP
Also Called: Malcolm Cisneros
2112 Business Center Dr # 100, Irvine
(92612-7136)
PHONE....................949 252-1039
William Malcolm, *CEO*
Roman Cisneros, *COO*
Arturo Cisneros, *CFO*
EMP: 110
SALES (est): 16.3MM **Privately Held**
WEB: www.malcolmcisneros.com
SIC: 8111 General practice law office

(P-22673)
MANATT PHELPS & PHILLIPS
LLP
695 Town Center Dr # 1400, Costa Mesa
(92626-7223)
PHONE....................714 371-2500
Shierley Hands, *Manager*
Tracey Dunn, *President*
Stella Dagostino, *Supervisor*
EMP: 50
SALES (corp-wide): 146.5MM **Privately
Held**
WEB: www.manatt.com
SIC: 8111 General practice attorney,
lawyer
PA: Manatt, Phelps & Phillips, Llp
11355 W Olympic Blvd Fl 2
Los Angeles CA 90064
310 312-4000

P
R
O
D
U
C
T
S

&

S
V
C
S

(P-22674)
MANNING KASS ELLROD RAM TRESTR (PA)
801 S Figueroa St Fl 15, Los Angeles
(90017-5504)
PHONE..........................213 624-6900
Steven D Manning, *Managing Prtnr*
Steve Manning, *Managing Prtnr*
Martha Alfaro, *Admin Sec*
Adriana Alvarado, *Admin Sec*
Demetrius Roman, *Info Tech Mgr*
EMP: 150
SALES (est): 32.2MM **Privately Held**
WEB: www.mmker.com
SIC: 8111 General practice attorney, lawyer

(P-22675)
MATHENY SARS LINKERT JAIME LLP
3638 American River Dr, Sacramento
(95864-5901)
PHONE..........................916 978-3434
Richard S Linkert, *Partner*
Matthew C Jamie, *Partner*
Douglas A Sears, *Partner*
Rick Linkert, *Managing Prtnr*
Liz Pitzer, *Human Res Mgr*
EMP: 52
SQ FT: 12,000
SALES (est): 5.7MM **Privately Held**
WEB: www.msll.com
SIC: 8111 General practice law office

(P-22676)
MAYNARD COOPER & GALE PC
600 Montgomery St # 2600, San Francisco
(94111-2728)
PHONE..........................415 704-7433
Mila Dunn, *Corp Counsel*
Tara L Blake, *Associate*
Alexandra Drury, *Associate*
EMP: 117
SALES (corp-wide): 52.1MM **Privately Held**
SIC: 8111 Specialized law offices, attorneys; general practice attorney, lawyer
PA: Maynard, Cooper & Gale, P.C.
    1901 6th Ave N Ste 2400
    Birmingham AL 35203
    205 254-1000

(P-22677)
MC NAMARA DODGE NEY BEATT (PA)
3480 Buskirk Ave Ste 250, Pleasant Hill
(94523-7310)
PHONE..........................925 939-5330
Richard Dodge, *General Ptnr*
Thomas G Beatty, *Partner*
Guy Borges, *Partner*
Roger Brothers, *Partner*
Michael J Ney, *Partner*
EMP: 70 EST: 1965
SQ FT: 9,500
SALES (est): 8.6MM **Privately Held**
WEB: www.mcnamaralaw.com
SIC: 8111 Specialized law offices, attorneys; malpractice & negligence law

(P-22678)
MCCORMICK BARSTOW SHEPPRD WAYT (PA)
Also Called: McCormick Barstow
7647 N Fresno St, Fresno (93720-2578)
P.O. Box 28912 (93729-8912)
PHONE..........................559 433-1300
Jeffrey M Reid, *Managing Prtnr*
Kenneth Cochrane, *Senior Partner*
Kenneth A Baldwin, *Partner*
Michael F Ball, *Partner*
Todd W Baxter, *Partner*
EMP: 89
SQ FT: 67,000
SALES (est): 35MM **Privately Held**
WEB: www.mbswc.com
SIC: 8111 Antitrust & trade regulation law; corporate, partnership & business law; bankruptcy law

(P-22679)
MCDERMOTT WILL & EMERY LLP
2049 Century Park E # 3200, Los Angeles
(90067-3206)
PHONE..........................310 277-4110
Joan Schulman, *Partner*
Richard K Simon,
Kate Hammond, *Associate*
George Houhanisin, *Associate*
Anna Park, *Associate*
EMP: 140
SALES (corp-wide): 1.1B **Privately Held**
WEB: www.europe.mwe.com
SIC: 8111 General practice law office
PA: Mcdermott Will & Emery Llp
    444 W Lake St Ste 4000
    Chicago IL 60606
    312 372-2000

(P-22680)
MCDERMOTT WILL & EMERY LLP
18565 Jamboree Rd Ste 250, Irvine
(92612-2565)
PHONE..........................949 757-7165
Vicki Lowenstein, *Systems Mgr*
Carol Hanna, *Admin Sec*
Todd Mobley,
EMP: 70
SALES (corp-wide): 1.1B **Privately Held**
WEB: www.europe.mwe.com
SIC: 8111 General practice law office
PA: Mcdermott Will & Emery Llp
    444 W Lake St Ste 4000
    Chicago IL 60606
    312 372-2000

(P-22681)
MCGUIREWOODS LLP
1800 Century Park E Fl 8, Los Angeles
(90067-1501)
PHONE..........................310 315-8200
Richard Grant, *Managing Prtnr*
Thomas Becket, *Vice Pres*
Barbara Cooper, *Admin Sec*
Leslie M Werlin Jr, *Manager*
Shannon Jones, *Receptionist*
EMP: 92
SALES (corp-wide): 253.3MM **Privately Held**
SIC: 8111 General practice attorney, lawyer
PA: Mcguirewoods Llp
    800 E Canal St
    Richmond VA 23219
    804 775-1000

(P-22682)
MCKOOL SMITH HENNIGAN
300 S Grand Ave Ste 2900, Los Angeles
(90071-3139)
PHONE..........................213 694-1200
J Michael Hennigan, *Partner*
Bruce Bennett, *Partner*
James W Mercer, *Partner*
Bruce Mac Leod,
EMP: 90
SQ FT: 35,000
SALES (est): 12.4MM **Privately Held**
WEB: www.hbdlawyers.com
SIC: 8111 General practice attorney, lawyer

(P-22683)
MCMANIS FAULKNER A PROF CORP
50 W San Fernando St # 1000, San Jose
(95113-2415)
PHONE..........................408 279-8700
James McManis, *President*
Sharon Kirsch, *President*
Carlos Nunez, *President*
William Faulkner, *Admin Sec*
Vanessa Jacobsen, *Administration*
EMP: 50
SALES (est): 7.9MM **Privately Held**
WEB: www.mfmlaw.com
SIC: 8111 General practice attorney, lawyer

(P-22684)
MED-LEGAL LLC
4401 Atlantic Ave, Long Beach
(90807-2218)
PHONE..........................626 653-5160
Victor Landero, *COO*
EMP: 116
SALES (corp-wide): 14MM **Privately Held**
SIC: 8111 Legal aid service
PA: Med-Legal, Llc
    955 Overland Ct Ste 200
    San Dimas CA 91773
    626 653-5160

(P-22685)
MELMET STEVEN J LAW OFC
2912 Daimler St, Santa Ana (92705-5811)
PHONE..........................949 263-1000
Steven J Melmet, *President*
Nancy Salzman,
EMP: 70
SALES: 10MM **Privately Held**
WEB: www.melmetlaw.com
SIC: 8111 6531 General practice law office; debt collection law; escrow agent, real estate

(P-22686)
MEYERS NAVE RIBACK SILVER & (PA)
555 12th St Ste 1500, Oakland
(94607-4095)
PHONE..........................510 351-4300
David W Skinner, *CEO*
Jo Barrington, *President*
Terry Bremer, *President*
Sandra Chao, *President*
Anabelle Cotapos, *President*
EMP: 107
SQ FT: 28,678
SALES (est): 19.3MM
SALES (corp-wide): 21.2MM **Privately Held**
WEB: www.meyersnave.com
SIC: 8111 Specialized law offices, attorneys

(P-22687)
MICHAEL SULLIVAN & ASSOC LLP
400 Continental Blvd # 250, El Segundo
(90245-5076)
P.O. Box 85059, San Diego (92186-5059)
PHONE..........................310 337-4480
Michael W Sullivan, *Partner*
Karen Joseph, *Legal Staff*
Zaneta Crayton, *Manager*
Alexander Green, *Associate*
EMP: 147
SALES: 22.6MM **Privately Held**
SIC: 8111 General practice attorney, lawyer

(P-22688)
MILBANK TWEED HDLEY MCCLOY LLP
Also Called: Milbank Global Securities
2029 Century Park E # 3300, Los Angeles
(90067-3019)
PHONE..........................424 386-4000
David C Frauman, *Director*
Dino T Barajas,
EMP: 120
SQ FT: 40,000
SALES (corp-wide): 144.8MM **Privately Held**
WEB: www.mthm.net
SIC: 8111 Corporate, partnership & business law
PA: Milbank Llp
    55 Hudson Yards
    New York NY 10001
    212 530-5000

(P-22689)
MILLER STARR & REGALIA A PRO (PA)
1331 N Calif Blvd Ste 500, Walnut Creek
(94596-4599)
P.O. Box 8177 (94596-8177)
PHONE..........................925 935-9400
Anthony M Leones, *CEO*
Richard Carlson, *Principal*
Elisa Trees, *Legal Staff*

Marika Rothfeld, *Associate*
EMP: 90
SQ FT: 30,000
SALES (est): 12.7MM **Privately Held**
WEB: www.msandr.com
SIC: 8111 General practice law office

(P-22690)
MILLER & ASSOCIATES LLP
2530 Wilshire Blvd Fl 1, Santa Monica
(90403-4664)
PHONE..........................310 315-1100
Ronald Miller, *Partner*
W Ashington Ttorney,
Angela Lumzy Jones,
EMP: 60
SALES: 11.1MM **Privately Held**
WEB: www.criminallawyer.net
SIC: 8111 General practice attorney, lawyer

(P-22691)
MINAMI TAMAKI LLP
360 Post St Fl 8, San Francisco
(94108-4911)
PHONE..........................415 788-9000
Dale Minami, *Co-Owner*
Minette Kwok, *Partner*
Jack Lee, *Partner*
Donald K Tamaki, *Partner*
Brad Yamauchi, *Partner*
EMP: 50
SQ FT: 4,500
SALES: 10MM **Privately Held**
WEB: www.mltsf.com
SIC: 8111 General practice attorney, lawyer

(P-22692)
MINTZ LEVIN COHN FERRIS GL
3580 Carmel Mountain Rd # 300, San Diego (92130-6768)
PHONE..........................858 314-1500
Gurneet Singh, *Technology*
Jake Anderson, *Opers Mgr*
Meg O'Donnell, *Corp Comm Staff*
Kenneth Jenkins,
Anthony Nash,
EMP: 100
SALES (corp-wide): 199.9MM **Privately Held**
SIC: 8111 General practice law office
PA: Mintz, Levin, Cohn, Ferris, Glovsky And Popeo, P.C.
    1 Financial Ctr Fl 40
    Boston MA 02111
    617 348-4951

(P-22693)
MITCHELL SILBERBERG KNUPP LLP (PA)
2049 Century Park E Fl 18, Los Angeles
(90067-3101)
PHONE..........................310 312-2000
Jeffrey K Eisen, *Principal*
Larry C Drapkin, *Partner*
Steven M Schneider, *Partner*
Thomas P Lambert, *Managing Prtnr*
Kevin E Gaut, *COO*
EMP: 110
SALES: 27.7K **Privately Held**
WEB: www.msk.com
SIC: 8111 General practice law office; real estate law; taxation law; labor & employment law

(P-22694)
ML PRIOR INC
955 Berrand Ct Ste 200, San Dimas
(91773)
PHONE..........................626 653-5160
Stephen Schneider, *President*
Warren Schneider, *CEO*
Victor Landero, *COO*
Kenneth Gleockler, *CFO*
Kenny Gleockler, *CFO*
EMP: 135
SQ FT: 31,770
SALES (est): 13.1MM **Privately Held**
SIC: 8111 Legal services

(P-22695)
MOADDEL LAW FIRM APC
3435 Wilshire Blvd # 2430, Los Angeles
(90010-2010)
PHONE..................323 999-5099
Daniel Moaddel, *President*
EMP: 50
SALES (est): 215.7K **Privately Held**
SIC: 8111 General practice law office

(P-22696)
MOORE LAW GROUP A PROF CORP
3710 S Susan St Ste 210, Santa Ana
(92704-6956)
P.O. Box 25145 (92799-5145)
PHONE..................714 431-2000
Harvey Moore, *President*
Donnie Pangburn, *Treasurer*
Angela Dawson, *Info Tech Mgr*
Connie Kopp, *Manager*
EMP: 65 EST: 2008
SALES (est): 8.4MM **Privately Held**
SIC: 8111 General practice law office

(P-22697)
MORGAN LEWIS & BOCKIUS LLP
1 Market St Ste 500, San Francisco
(94105-1306)
PHONE..................415 393-2000
Donn Pickett, *Partner*
Dale Barnes, *Partner*
Michael Begert, *Partner*
Charles Crompton, *Partner*
Anne Deibert, *Partner*
EMP: 696 EST: 1880
SALES (est): 77.6MM
SALES (corp-wide): 444MM **Privately Held**
SIC: 8111 General practice law office
PA: Morgan, Lewis & Bockius Llp
1701 Market St Ste Con
Philadelphia PA 19103
215 963-5000

(P-22698)
MORGAN LEWIS & BOCKIUS LLP
1400 Page Mill Rd, Palo Alto (94304-1177)
PHONE..................650 843-4000
Thomas Kellerman, *Partner*
Alexandre Bailly, *Partner*
Kathleen Gregory, *President*
Rizzel Milanes, *Personnel Assit*
Teresa Hillstrom, *Facilities Mgr*
EMP: 75
SALES (corp-wide): 444MM **Privately Held**
WEB: www.envinfo.com
SIC: 8111 General practice law office
PA: Morgan, Lewis & Bockius Llp
1701 Market St Ste Con
Philadelphia PA 19103
215 963-5000

(P-22699)
MORGAN LEWIS & BOCKIUS LLP
600 Anton Blvd Ste 1800, Costa Mesa
(92626-7653)
PHONE..................949 399-7000
Anne M Brafford, *Branch Mgr*
Randy Wood, *Associate*
EMP: 181
SALES (corp-wide): 444MM **Privately Held**
SIC: 8111 General practice law office
PA: Morgan, Lewis & Bockius Llp
1701 Market St Ste Con
Philadelphia PA 19103
215 963-5000

(P-22700)
MORGAN LEWIS & BOCKIUS LLP
300 S Grand Ave Ste 2200, Los Angeles
(90071-3132)
PHONE..................213 612-2500
John F Hartigan, *Managing Prtnr*
J Jack, *Partner*
Michael Jack, *Partner*
Gary C Moss, *Partner*
Lydia Ramirez, *President*
EMP: 200

SALES (corp-wide): 444MM **Privately Held**
WEB: www.envinfo.com
SIC: 8111 General practice law office
PA: Morgan, Lewis & Bockius Llp
1701 Market St Ste Con
Philadelphia PA 19103
215 963-5000

(P-22701)
MORGAN LEWIS & BOCKIUS LLP
1 Market Plz Lbby 1 # 1, San Francisco
(94105-1002)
PHONE..................415 442-1000
Erika Smith, *Officer*
EMP: 300
SALES (corp-wide): 444MM **Privately Held**
SIC: 8111 General practice law office
PA: Morgan, Lewis & Bockius Llp
1701 Market St Ste Con
Philadelphia PA 19103
215 963-5000

(P-22702)
MORGAN LEWIS & BOCKIUS LLP
300 S Grand Ave Ste 2200, Los Angeles
(90071-3132)
PHONE..................213 612-2500
Joseph Duffy, *Managing Prtnr*
Richard J Riordan, *Counsel*
Emily Calmeyer, *Associate*
Jason W Capps, *Associate*
Jeremy Esterkin, *Associate*
EMP: 110
SALES (corp-wide): 444MM **Privately Held**
SIC: 8111 General practice law office
PA: Morgan, Lewis & Bockius Llp
1701 Market St Ste Con
Philadelphia PA 19103
215 963-5000

(P-22703)
MORRIS POLICH & PURDY LLP (PA)
1055 W 7th St Ste 2400, Los Angeles
(90017-2550)
PHONE..................213 891-9100
Theodore D Levin, *Partner*
Jeff Barron, *Partner*
William M Betley, *Partner*
Anthony Brazil, *Partner*
James Chantland, *Partner*
EMP: 100
SQ FT: 40,000
SALES (est): 27.7MM **Privately Held**
WEB: www.mpplaw.com
SIC: 8111 General practice attorney, lawyer

(P-22704)
MORRISON & FOERSTER LLP
Also Called: Morrison & Foerster - Library
755 Page Mill Rd Ste A100, Palo Alto
(94304-1061)
PHONE..................650 813-5600
Alan Cope Johnston, *Managing Prtnr*
Michael Carlson, *Partner*
Gerald Dodson, *Partner*
Tyler M Dylan, *Partner*
Suzanne S Graeser, *Partner*
EMP: 277
SALES (corp-wide): 810MM **Privately Held**
SIC: 8111 General practice law office
PA: Morrison & Foerster Llp
425 Market St Fl 30
San Francisco CA 94105
415 268-7000

(P-22705)
MORRISON & FOERSTER LLP
707 Wilshire Blvd # 6000, Los Angeles
(90017-3501)
PHONE..................213 892-5200
Gregory Koltun, *Managing Prtnr*
John W Alden Jr, *Partner*
Mark T Gillett, *Partner*
Dan Marmalefsky, *Partner*
Mark McDonald, *Partner*
EMP: 250

SALES (corp-wide): 444MM **Privately Held**
WEB: www.envinfo.com
SIC: 8111 General practice attorney, lawyer
PA: Morrison & Foerster Llp
1701 Market St Ste Con
Philadelphia PA 19103
215 963-5000

(P-22706)
MORRISON & FOERSTER LLP (PA)
Also Called: Mofo
425 Market St Fl 30, San Francisco
(94105-2482)
PHONE..................415 268-7000
Larren Nashelsky, *Chairman*
Jay Baris, *Partner*
Tien-Yo Chao, *Partner*
Paul T Friedman, *Partner*
Greg Giammittorio, *Partner*
EMP: 400 EST: 2000
SALES (est): 810MM **Privately Held**
SIC: 8111 General practice attorney, lawyer

(P-22707)
MORRISON & FOERSTER LLP
12531 High Bluff Dr # 100, San Diego
(92130-3014)
PHONE..................858 720-5100
Mark Zebrowski, *Managing Prtnr*
Rajka K Hayden, *Regional Mgr*
Marc Sharp, *Research*
Jean Horrall, *Technology*
Melissa Ruth, *Marketing Staff*
EMP: 125
SALES (corp-wide): 810MM **Privately Held**
SIC: 8111 General practice attorney, lawyer
PA: Morrison & Foerster Llp
425 Market St Fl 30
San Francisco CA 94105
415 268-7000

(P-22708)
MORRISON & FOERSTER LLP
Also Called: Marketing Department
425 Market St Fl 32, San Francisco
(94105-2467)
PHONE..................415 268-7178
Roland Brandel, *Branch Mgr*
EMP: 143
SALES (corp-wide): 810MM **Privately Held**
SIC: 8111 General practice attorney, lawyer
PA: Morrison & Foerster Llp
425 Market St Fl 30
San Francisco CA 94105
415 268-7000

(P-22709)
MORRISON & FOERSTER LLP
425 Market St Fl 32, San Francisco
(94105-2467)
P.O. Box 8130, Walnut Creek (94596)
PHONE..................925 295-3300
David A Gold, *Managing Prtnr*
R Clark Morrison, *Partner*
EMP: 50
SALES (corp-wide): 810MM **Privately Held**
SIC: 8111 General practice attorney, lawyer
PA: Morrison & Foerster Llp
425 Market St Fl 30
San Francisco CA 94105
415 268-7000

(P-22710)
MULLEN & HENZELL LLP
112 E Victoria St, Santa Barbara
(93101-2068)
P.O. Box 789 (93102-0789)
PHONE..................805 966-1501
Dennis W Reilly, *Mng Member*
Megan Phillips, *President*
Cheryl Tedesco, *President*
Terry Atterbury, *Executive*
Susan Villegas, *Executive*
EMP: 50 EST: 1931
SQ FT: 15,000

SALES (est): 7.3MM **Privately Held**
WEB: www.mullenlaw.com
SIC: 8111 Real estate law; will, estate & trust law; general practice attorney, lawyer

(P-22711)
MUNGER TOLLES & OLSON LLP
350 S Grand Ave Fl 50, Los Angeles
(90071-3426)
PHONE..................213 683-9100
Sandra Seville-Jones, *Partner*
Thomas B Edwards, *Exec Dir*
EMP: 108
SALES (est): 30.4MM **Privately Held**
SIC: 8111 Corporate, partnership & business law; specialized law offices, attorneys

(P-22712)
MUNGER TOLLES OLSON FOUNDATION (PA)
350 S Grand Ave Fl 50, Los Angeles
(90071-3426)
PHONE..................213 683-9100
O'Malley M Miller, *CEO*
Robert Johnson, *President*
Larry Kleinberg, *CFO*
Mark Helm, *Vice Pres*
Steven B Weisburd, *Vice Pres*
EMP: 470 EST: 1962
SQ FT: 100,000
SALES (est): 44.5MM **Privately Held**
WEB: www.mto.com
SIC: 8111 General practice attorney, lawyer

(P-22713)
MUNGER TOLLES OLSON FOUNDATION
560 Mission St Fl 27, San Francisco
(94105-3089)
PHONE..................415 512-4000
Kim Coates, *Branch Mgr*
EMP: 50
SALES (est): 5.8MM
SALES (corp-wide): 44.5MM **Privately Held**
WEB: www.mto.com
SIC: 8111 General practice attorney, lawyer
PA: Munger Tolles & Olson Foundation
350 S Grand Ave Fl 50
Los Angeles CA 90071
213 683-9100

(P-22714)
MURCHISON & CUMMING LLP (PA)
Also Called: M & C
801 S Grand Ave Ste 900, Los Angeles
(90017-4624)
PHONE..................213 623-7400
Friedrich W Seitz, *Partner*
Edmund G Farrell, *Senior Partner*
Guy R Gruppie, *Senior Partner*
Guy Gruppie, *Senior Partner*
Jean M Lawler, *Senior Partner*
EMP: 100
SQ FT: 30,000
SALES (est): 20.1MM **Privately Held**
WEB: www.murchison-cumming.com
SIC: 8111 General practice law office

(P-22715)
MURPHY (PA)
88 Kearny St Fl 10, San Francisco
(94108-5524)
PHONE..................415 788-1900
Michael P Bradley, *President*
James Murphy, *Shareholder*
Gena James, *President*
Gregory A Bastian, *Vice Pres*
John H Feeney, *Vice Pres*
EMP: 53 EST: 1978
SALES (est): 18.5MM **Privately Held**
WEB: www.mpbf.com
SIC: 8111 General practice law office

(P-22716)
MURTAUGH MYER NLSON TRGLIA LLP
2603 Main St Ste 900, Irvine (92614-4270)
P.O. Box 19627 (92623-9627)
PHONE..........................949 794-4000
Michael J Nelson, *Managing Prtnr*
Harry A Halkowich, *Partner*
Mark S Himmelstein, *Partner*
Robert T Lemen, *Partner*
James A Murphy IV, *Partner*
EMP: 60
SALES (est): 7MM **Privately Held**
WEB: www.mmnt.com
SIC: 8111 General practice law office

(P-22717)
MUSICK PEELER & GARRETT LLP (PA)
624 S Grand Ave Ste 2000, Los Angeles (90017-3321)
PHONE..........................213 629-7600
R Joseph De Briyn, *Managing Prtnr*
Peter J Diedrich, *Partner*
Susan Field, *Partner*
Edward Landrey, *Partner*
Wayne Littlefied, *Partner*
EMP: 168
SQ FT: 100,000
SALES (est): 38.2MM **Privately Held**
WEB: www.mpgweb.com
SIC: 8111 General practice law office; taxation law; corporate, partnership & business law; labor & employment law

(P-22718)
NATIONWIDE LEGAL LLC (PA)
Also Called: Headquarters
1609 James M Wood Blvd, Los Angeles (90015-1005)
P.O. Box 15012 (90015-0012)
PHONE..........................213 249-9999
Tony Davoodi, *CEO*
Joe Caamal, *COO*
Louis Nelson, *Exec VP*
Michael Lazcano, *Senior VP*
Mary Bukovskis, *Executive*
EMP: 64
SALES (est): 37.8MM **Privately Held**
SIC: 8111 General practice attorney, lawyer

(P-22719)
NED E DUNPHY
4550 California Ave Fl 2, Bakersfield (93309-7012)
P.O. Box 11172 (93389-1172)
PHONE..........................661 395-1000
Ned E Dunphy, *Partner*
EMP: 56
SALES (est): 1.9MM **Privately Held**
SIC: 8111 General practice attorney, lawyer

(P-22720)
NEIL DYMOTT FRANK MCFALL
Also Called: Neil Dymott Perkins Brown
110 W A St, San Diego (92101-3711)
PHONE..........................619 238-1712
Michael I Neil, *President*
Teresa Anderson, *President*
Robert Frank, *Vice Pres*
Hannah Dubois, *Admin Sec*
Sandra Slewa, *Admin Sec*
EMP: 108
SQ FT: 15,000
SALES (est): 11.9MM **Privately Held**
WEB: www.neil-dymott.com
SIC: 8111 General practice law office

(P-22721)
NEWMEYER & DILLION LLP (PA)
895 Dove St Fl 5, Newport Beach (92660-2999)
PHONE..........................949 854-7000
Gregory L Dillion, *Partner*
John A O Hara, *Partner*
Jon J Janecek, *Partner*
Thomas F Newmeyer, *Partner*
Diane McCullough, *President*
EMP: 115
SQ FT: 52,000
SALES: 35.7MM **Privately Held**
WEB: www.newmeyeranddillion.com
SIC: 8111 General practice law office

(P-22722)
NICOLE PTTRSON CRT RPRTING LLC
545 E Alluvial Ave # 109, Fresno (93720-2826)
PHONE..........................559 400-2407
Nicole Patterso, *President*
Nicole Patterson, *President*
EMP: 50
SALES (est): 1.7MM **Privately Held**
SIC: 8111 7338 Legal services; court reporting service

(P-22723)
NIXON PEABODY LLP
1 Embarcadero Ctr # 3200, San Francisco (94111-3628)
PHONE..........................415 984-8200
Gina Hrens, *Manager*
Mike Philippi, *Partner*
Staci Riordan, *Partner*
Rosie Mangin, *President*
Karen Burde, *Admin Sec*
EMP: 150
SALES (corp-wide): 236.3MM **Privately Held**
SIC: 8111 Specialized law offices, attorneys; antitrust & trade regulation law; environmental law; labor & employment law
PA: Nixon Peabody Llp
     1300 Clinton Sq
     Rochester NY 14604
     585 263-1000

(P-22724)
NIXON PEABODY LLP
555 W 5th St Fl 30, Los Angeles (90013-1048)
PHONE..........................213 629-6000
Steph Levy, *Managing Prtnr*
Christina Fletes, *Associate*
Eric R Ideta, *Associate*
Gretchen Sherwood, *Associate*
Irene Tatevosyan, *Associate*
EMP: 85
SALES (corp-wide): 236.3MM **Privately Held**
SIC: 8111 General practice attorney, lawyer
PA: Nixon Peabody Llp
     1300 Clinton Sq
     Rochester NY 14604
     585 263-1000

(P-22725)
NOLAND HAMERLY ETIENNE (PA)
333 Salinas St, Salinas (93901-2751)
PHONE..........................831 372-7525
Myron Etienne, *President*
Lloyd W Lowerly Jr, *Shareholder*
Mike Masuda, *Shareholder*
Werner Meyenberg, *Shareholder*
Terry O' Connor, *Shareholder*
EMP: 50
SQ FT: 10,000
SALES (est): 3.6MM **Privately Held**
WEB: www.nheh.com
SIC: 8111 General practice law office

(P-22726)
NORDMAN CORMANY HAIR & COMPTON
1000 Town Center Dr Fl 6, Oxnard (93036-1132)
P.O. Box 9100 (93031-9100)
PHONE..........................805 485-1000
Tammian Cook, *CEO*
Marc L Charney, *Partner*
Robert L Compton, *Partner*
Glenn J Dickinson, *Partner*
Randall H George, *Partner*
EMP: 115
SQ FT: 35,000
SALES (est): 10.6MM **Privately Held**
WEB: www.nchc.com
SIC: 8111 General practice law office

(P-22727)
NOSSAMAN LLP (PA)
777 S Figueroa St # 3400, Los Angeles (90017-5834)
PHONE..........................213 612-7800
E George Joseph, *Managing Prtnr*
Kelly Pepper, *COO*

Christopher Flaherty, *Officer*
Kim Lahs, *Officer*
Paige McDaniel, *Office Admin*
EMP: 74
SQ FT: 20,000
SALES (est): 50.1MM **Privately Held**
WEB: www.nossaman.com
SIC: 8111 General practice attorney, lawyer

(P-22728)
NOSSAMAN LLP
1925 Palomar Oaks Way # 220, Carlsbad (92008-6526)
PHONE..........................760 918-0500
EMP: 74
SALES (corp-wide): 50.1MM **Privately Held**
SIC: 8111 General practice attorney, lawyer
PA: Nossaman Llp
     777 S Figueroa St # 3400
     Los Angeles CA 90017
     213 612-7800

(P-22729)
NOSSAMAN LLP
Also Called: Bagley, William T
50 California St Ste 3400, San Francisco (94111-4799)
PHONE..........................415 398-3600
Susan Eres, *Manager*
Michelle Hart, *Mktg Dir*
Barney Allison, *Partner*
Martin A Mattes,
EMP: 50
SALES (corp-wide): 50.1MM **Privately Held**
WEB: www.nossaman.com
SIC: 8111 General practice attorney, lawyer
PA: Nossaman Llp
     777 S Figueroa St # 3400
     Los Angeles CA 90017
     213 612-7800

(P-22730)
NOSSAMAN LLP
18101 Von Karman Ave # 1800, Irvine (92612-0177)
PHONE..........................949 833-7800
George Joseph, *Partner*
Gregory W Sanders, *Partner*
Kathryn Bell-Taylor, *Admin Sec*
Robin Golder, *Admin Sec*
EMP: 50
SALES (corp-wide): 50.1MM **Privately Held**
WEB: www.nossaman.com
SIC: 8111 General practice attorney, lawyer
PA: Nossaman Llp
     777 S Figueroa St # 3400
     Los Angeles CA 90017
     213 612-7800

(P-22731)
OGLETREE DEAKINS NASH SMOAK
1 Market St Ste 1300, San Francisco (94105-1497)
PHONE..........................415 442-4810
Patrick Sum, *Chairman*
Jack Sholkoff, *Shareholder*
Eileen Lewis, *Legal Staff*
Sharon Moser, *Manager*
EMP: 77
SALES (corp-wide): 257.1MM **Privately Held**
SIC: 8111 General practice law office
PA: Ogletree, Deakins, Nash, Smoak & Stewart, P.C.
     300 N Main St Ste 500
     Greenville SC 29601
     864 271-1300

(P-22732)
OMELVENY & MYERS LLP (PA)
400 S Hope St Fl 19, Los Angeles (90071-2831)
PHONE..........................213 430-6000
Arthur B Culvahouse Jr, *Mng Member*
John Motley, *Managing Prtnr*
Burton N Rosenberg, *Principal*
Michelle Egan, *Managing Dir*
Paula E Ambrosini, *Practice Mgr*

EMP: 850 **EST:** 1885
SQ FT: 250,000
SALES (est): 279.1MM **Privately Held**
SIC: 8111 General practice law office

(P-22733)
OMELVENY & MYERS LLP
610 Nwport Ctr Dr Fl 17 Flr 17, Newport Beach (92660)
PHONE..........................949 760-9600
Elizabeth L McKeen, *Manager*
Terrence R Allen, *Partner*
Martha Cocker, *Nurse*
Richard Jones,
Nikole Kingston, *Counsel*
EMP: 130
SALES (corp-wide): 279.1MM **Privately Held**
SIC: 8111 General practice law office
PA: O'melveny & Myers Llp
     400 S Hope St Fl 19
     Los Angeles CA 90071
     213 430-6000

(P-22734)
OMELVENY & MYERS LLP
1999 Avenue Of The Stars # 600, Los Angeles (90067-6035)
PHONE..........................310 553-6700
Jodi Yamada, *Manager*
EMP: 225
SALES (corp-wide): 279.1MM **Privately Held**
SIC: 8111 General practice attorney, lawyer; general practice law office
PA: O'melveny & Myers Llp
     400 S Hope St Fl 19
     Los Angeles CA 90071
     213 430-6000

(P-22735)
OMELVENY & MYERS LLP
2765 Sand Hill Rd, Menlo Park (94025-7098)
PHONE..........................650 473-2600
Tina Schinick, *Branch Mgr*
EMP: 201
SALES (corp-wide): 279.1MM **Privately Held**
SIC: 8111 General practice law office
PA: O'melveny & Myers Llp
     400 S Hope St Fl 19
     Los Angeles CA 90071
     213 430-6000

(P-22736)
OMELVENY & MYERS LLP
2 Embarcadero Ctr Fl 28, San Francisco (94111-3823)
PHONE..........................415 984-8700
Luann Simmons, *Manager*
Debra Belaga, *Partner*
William Franklin Birchfield, *Partner*
Claire Philipott,
EMP: 175
SALES (corp-wide): 279.1MM **Privately Held**
SIC: 8111 General practice law office
PA: O'melveny & Myers Llp
     400 S Hope St Fl 19
     Los Angeles CA 90071
     213 430-6000

(P-22737)
ORRICK HRRINGTON SUTCLIFFE LLP (PA)
405 Howard St, San Francisco (94105-2625)
PHONE..........................415 773-5700
Ralph H Baxter Jr, *CEO*
Pascal Agboyibor, *Partner*
Martin Bartlam, *Partner*
Peter A Bicks, *Partner*
Benedikt Burger, *Partner*
EMP: 148
SQ FT: 146,000
SALES (est): 365MM **Privately Held**
WEB: www.orrick.com
SIC: 8111 General practice law office

(P-22738)
ORRICK HRRINGTON SUTCLIFFE LLP
1000 Marsh Rd, Menlo Park (94025-1015)
PHONE..........................650 614-7400
Don Keller, *Branch Mgr*

Stacey Donlon, *Executive*
Parvine Wadia, *Executive*
Laura Gao, *Project Mgr*
Mark Neary, *Technical Staff*
EMP: 160
SALES (corp-wide): 365MM **Privately Held**
SIC: 8111 General practice attorney, lawyer
PA: Orrick, Herrington & Sutcliffe, Llp
    405 Howard St
    San Francisco CA 94105
    415 773-5700

(P-22739)
ORRICK HRRINGTON SUTCLIFFE LLP
1020 Marsh Rd, Menlo Park (94025-1015)
PHONE.................................650 614-7454
Barbara Whiteley, *Branch Mgr*
Peter Cohen, *Partner*
Christopher R Ottenweller,
EMP: 152
SALES (corp-wide): 365MM **Privately Held**
WEB: www.orrick.com
SIC: 8111 General practice attorney, lawyer
PA: Orrick, Herrington & Sutcliffe, Llp
    405 Howard St
    San Francisco CA 94105
    415 773-5700

(P-22740)
ORRICK HRRINGTON SUTCLIFFE LLP
777 S Figueroa St # 3200, Los Angeles (90017-5800)
PHONE.................................213 629-2020
Delores Hamilton, *Branch Mgr*
Daniel Tyukody Jr, *Partner*
Jerry J Walsh, *Partner*
Ramon Galvan,
Antonio Martini,
EMP: 118
SALES (corp-wide): 365MM **Privately Held**
WEB: www.orrick.com
SIC: 8111 General practice attorney, lawyer
PA: Orrick, Herrington & Sutcliffe, Llp
    405 Howard St
    San Francisco CA 94105
    415 773-5700

(P-22741)
ORRICK HRRINGTON SUTCLIFFE LLP
400 Capitol Mall Ste 3000, Sacramento (95814-4497)
PHONE.................................916 447-9200
Betty Neal,
Virginia Magan, *Partner*
John Myers,
EMP: 67
SQ FT: 19,336
SALES (corp-wide): 365MM **Privately Held**
SIC: 8111 General practice attorney, lawyer
PA: Orrick, Herrington & Sutcliffe, Llp
    405 Howard St
    San Francisco CA 94105
    415 773-5700

(P-22742)
PACHULSKI STANG ZEHL JONES LLP (PA)
Also Called: Pszyjw
10100 Santa Monica Blvd # 1100, Los Angeles (90067-4003)
PHONE.................................310 277-6910
Richard M Pachulski, *President*
Diane Potts, *President*
Tanya Thompson, *President*
Dean A Ziehl, *Vice Pres*
Lincoln Sneed, *Office Mgr*
EMP: 90
SQ FT: 21,000
SALES (est): 37.2MM **Privately Held**
WEB: www.pszyj.com
SIC: 8111 General practice law office

(P-22743)
PACIFIC LEGAL FOUNDATION (PA)
930 G St, Sacramento (95814-1802)
PHONE.................................916 419-7111
Robert K Best, *President*
John C Harris, *Ch of Bd*
Robin L Rivett, *President*
Chad Wilcox, *COO*
John Cameron, *Officer*
EMP: 50
SQ FT: 14,000
SALES: 13.3MM **Privately Held**
SIC: 8111 General practice law office

(P-22744)
PALUMBO LAWYERS LLP (PA)
15635 Alton Pkwy Ste 300, Irvine (92618-7332)
PHONE.................................949 442-0300
Diane O Palumbo, *Partner*
Jay Bergstrom, *Partner*
Julia Bergstrom, *Partner*
Diane Palumbo, *Managing Prtnr*
Melissa Forbes, *Office Mgr*
EMP: 54
SQ FT: 13,258
SALES (est): 7.5MM **Privately Held**
WEB: www.palumbolawyers.com
SIC: 8111 General practice attorney, lawyer

(P-22745)
PARASEC INCORPORATED (PA)
2804 Gateway Oaks Dr # 100, Sacramento (95833-4346)
P.O. Box 160568 (95816-0568)
PHONE.................................916 576-7000
Matthew Marzucco, *President*
Barbara Geiger, *Vice Pres*
Jocelyn Heredia, *Executive*
Yassriah Bullard, *Technician*
Abigale Peterson, *Technician*
▲ **EMP:** 53
SQ FT: 24,000
SALES (est): 18.3MM **Privately Held**
WEB: www.parasec.com
SIC: 8111 Specialized legal services

(P-22746)
PARKER MILLIKEN CLARK OHAR
555 S Flower St Fl 30, Los Angeles (90071-2440)
PHONE.................................818 784-8087
Larry Ivanjack, *President*
Brent Cheney, *Shareholder*
Gary Meyer, *Shareholder*
Richard D Robbins, *President*
William M Reid, *CFO*
EMP: 70 **EST:** 1914
SQ FT: 25,000
SALES (est): 9.1MM **Privately Held**
WEB: www.pmcos.com
SIC: 8111 General practice law office

(P-22747)
PARKER STANBURY LLP (PA)
444 S Flower St Ste 1900, Los Angeles (90071-2909)
PHONE.................................619 528-1259
Robert Lo Presti, *Partner*
Graham J Baldwin, *Partner*
John D Barrett Jr, *Partner*
John W Dannhausen, *Partner*
Douglas M Degrade, *Partner*
EMP: 60 **EST:** 1922
SQ FT: 17,152
SALES (est): 11.4MM **Privately Held**
WEB: www.parkstan.com
SIC: 8111 General practice law office

(P-22748)
PATENAUDE & FELIX A PROF CORP (PA)
4545 Murphy Canyon Rd # 3, San Diego (92123-4363)
PHONE.................................858 244-7600
Raymond Patenaude, *Partner*
Patrick Felix, *Partner*
Neal Prasad, *COO*
Jeff Dillon, *CFO*
EMP: 57
SQ FT: 30,000

SALES (est): 20.4MM **Privately Held**
WEB: www.pandf.us
SIC: 8111 General practice attorney, lawyer

(P-22749)
PATTERSON RITNER LOCKWOOD (PA)
620 N Brand Blvd Fl 3, Glendale (91203-4221)
P.O. Box 361, Pacific Palisades (90272-0361)
PHONE.................................818 241-8001
William F Ritner, *Partner*
Harold H Gartner III, *Partner*
John A Jurich, *Partner*
Clyde E Lockwood, *Partner*
James McGahan, *Partner*
EMP: 90
SQ FT: 16,000
SALES (est): 5.5MM **Privately Held**
WEB: www.pattersonritner.com
SIC: 8111 General practice law office

(P-22750)
PAUL HASTINGS LLP
695 Town Ctr, Santa Ana (92704)
PHONE.................................714 668-6200
Marilyn Radley, *Partner*
Josh Christensen, *Associate*
Beatrice Difino, *Associate*
Edward George, *Associate*
Jora Guo, *Associate*
EMP: 100
SALES (corp-wide): 332MM **Privately Held**
SIC: 8111 General practice law office
PA: Paul Hastings Llp
    515 S Flower St Fl 25
    Los Angeles CA 90071
    213 683-6000

(P-22751)
PAUL HASTINGS LLP
695 Town Center Dr # 120, Costa Mesa (92626-7216)
PHONE.................................714 668-6200
Marilyn Radley, *Managing Prtnr*
Douglas A Schaaf, *Partner*
Peter J Tennyson, *Partner*
Stephen D Coke,
EMP: 200
SALES (corp-wide): 332MM **Privately Held**
SIC: 8111 General practice attorney, lawyer
PA: Paul Hastings Llp
    515 S Flower St Fl 25
    Los Angeles CA 90071
    213 683-6000

(P-22752)
PAUL HASTINGS LLP (PA)
515 S Flower St Fl 25, Los Angeles (90071-2228)
PHONE.................................213 683-6000
Greg Nitzkowski, *Mng Member*
George W Abele, *Partner*
Jesse H Austin, *Partner*
Dino T Barajas, *Partner*
Tollie Besson, *Partner*
EMP: 148
SQ FT: 209,000
SALES (est): 332MM **Privately Held**
SIC: 8111 General practice law office

(P-22753)
PAUL HASTINGS LLP
4747 Executive Dr # 1200, San Diego (92121-3114)
PHONE.................................858 458-3000
Craig Price, *Administration*
Anita Patel, *Executive*
Todd Schneider, *Executive*
Lisa Vermeulen, *Legal Staff*
Patty Rhoads, *Assistant*
EMP: 100
SALES (corp-wide): 332MM **Privately Held**
SIC: 8111 General practice law office
PA: Paul Hastings Llp
    515 S Flower St Fl 25
    Los Angeles CA 90071
    213 683-6000

(P-22754)
PAUL HASTINGS LLP
101 California St Fl 48, San Francisco (94111-5871)
PHONE.................................415 856-7000
Dennis Dehrens, *Administration*
Lane D Barrasso, *Associate*
EMP: 168
SALES (corp-wide): 332MM **Privately Held**
SIC: 8111 General practice law office
PA: Paul Hastings Llp
    515 S Flower St Fl 25
    Los Angeles CA 90071
    213 683-6000

(P-22755)
PAUL HASTINGS LLP
1117 California Ave, Palo Alto (94304-1106)
PHONE.................................650 320-1800
Paul Janofsky, *Branch Mgr*
Joseph J Rumper, *Associate*
EMP: 179
SALES (corp-wide): 332MM **Privately Held**
SIC: 8111 General practice attorney, lawyer
PA: Paul Hastings Llp
    515 S Flower St Fl 25
    Los Angeles CA 90071
    213 683-6000

(P-22756)
PAYNE & FEARS LLP (PA)
4 Park Plz Ste 1100, Irvine (92614-8550)
PHONE.................................949 851-1101
James L Payne, *Partner*
Jeffrey Brown, *Partner*
Daniel Fears, *Partner*
Eric Fohlgren, *Partner*
Karen Frankudakis, *Partner*
EMP: 68
SQ FT: 22,000
SALES (est): 18.3MM **Privately Held**
SIC: 8111 Corporate, partnership & business law; labor & employment law

(P-22757)
PEARLMAN BORSKA & WAX LLP (PA)
15910 Ventura Blvd Fl 18, Encino (91436-2819)
PHONE.................................818 501-4343
Barry S Pearlman, *Partner*
Elliot F Borska, *Partner*
Dean Brown, *Partner*
Steven H Wax, *Partner*
EMP: 60
SQ FT: 4,000
SALES: 13.3MM **Privately Held**
WEB: www.4pbw.com
SIC: 8111 General practice law office

(P-22758)
PERKINS COIE LLP
3150 Porter Dr, Palo Alto (94304-1212)
PHONE.................................415 725-1313
Edward West, *Manager*
Kate Smith, *Litigation*
Miguel Bombach, *Counsel*
EMP: 70
SALES (corp-wide): 299.6MM **Privately Held**
WEB: www.perkinscoie.com
SIC: 8111 General practice attorney, lawyer
PA: Perkins Coie Llp
    1201 3rd Ave Ste 4900
    Seattle WA 98101
    206 359-8000

(P-22759)
PERKINS COIE LLP
1620 26th St Ste 600s, Santa Monica (90404-4013)
PHONE.................................310 788-9900
Sally Cano, *Manager*
Mark E Birnbaum, *Partner*
Donald E Karl,
EMP: 75
SALES (corp-wide): 299.6MM **Privately Held**
WEB: www.perkinscoie.com
SIC: 8111 General practice attorney, lawyer

PRODUCTS & SVCS

PA: Perkins Coie Llp
1201 3rd Ave Ste 4900
Seattle WA 98101
206 359-8000

(P-22760)
PERKINS COIE LLP
505 Howard St Ste 1000, San Francisco
(94105-3222)
PHONE....................................415 344-7000
John Rossiter, *Principal*
Wing Liang, *Counsel*
Christina McCullough, *Counsel*
Julie Schwartz, *Counsel*
David Dedyo, *Director*
EMP: 50
SALES (corp-wide): 299.6MM **Privately
Held**
WEB: www.perkinscoie.com
SIC: 8111 General practice attorney,
lawyer
PA: Perkins Coie Llp
1201 3rd Ave Ste 4900
Seattle WA 98101
206 359-8000

(P-22761)
PERONA LANGER BECK A PROF CORP
300 E San Antonio Dr, Long Beach
(90807-2002)
PHONE....................................562 426-6155
James T Perona, *President*
Todd Harrison, *Managing Prtnr*
Major A Langer, *CFO*
Ronald Beck, *Admin Sec*
EMP: 100 EST: 1966
SQ FT: 18,000
SALES (est): 10.3MM **Privately Held**
WEB: www.fightforyou.com
SIC: 8111 General practice law office

(P-22762)
PETTI KOHN INGRASSIA & L PR CO
11622 El Camino Real, San Diego
(92130-2049)
PHONE....................................310 649-5772
Andrew N Kohn, *President*
John Durant, *COO*
Thomas S Ingrassia, *CFO*
Douglas Pettit, *Vice Pres*
Susan Oltraver, *Accountant*
EMP: 66
SALES (est): 7.3MM **Privately Held**
SIC: 8111 General practice law office

(P-22763)
PHILLIPS & ASSOC LAW OFFS PC
1300 Clay St Ste 600, Oakland
(94612-1427)
PHONE....................................510 464-8040
P Knudsen, *Branch Mgr*
EMP: 76 **Privately Held**
SIC: 8111 General practice law office
PA: Phillips & Associates Law Offices Pc
3101 N Central Ave # 1500
Phoenix AZ 85012

(P-22764)
PILLSBURY WINTHROP SHAW
4 Embarcadero Ctr Fl 22, San Francisco
(94111-5998)
PHONE....................................415 983-1000
Jeffrey M Vesely, *General Ptnr*
Terri Chytrowski, *Comms Dir*
Maria Stanfield, *Administration*
James Bailey, *Engineer*
Martha Leong, *Production*
EMP: 194
SALES (corp-wide): 265.5MM **Privately
Held**
SIC: 8111 General practice law office
PA: Pillsbury Winthrop Shaw Pittman Llp
31 W 52nd St Fl 26
New York NY 10019
212 858-1000

(P-22765)
PILLSBURY WINTHROP SHAW
725 S Figueroa St # 2900, Los Angeles
(90017-5429)
PHONE....................................213 488-7100

Melissa Burton, *Administration*
Yoshiko Ono-Palacios, *Executive Asst*
Catherine D Meyer,
EMP: 150
SALES (corp-wide): 265.5MM **Privately
Held**
SIC: 8111 General practice law office
PA: Pillsbury Winthrop Shaw Pittman Llp
31 W 52nd St Fl 26
New York NY 10019
212 858-1000

(P-22766)
PILLSBURY WINTHROP SHAW
29 Eucalyptus Rd, Berkeley (94705-2801)
PHONE....................................415 983-1865
Thomas Loran, *Branch Mgr*
EMP: 143
SALES (corp-wide): 265.5MM **Privately
Held**
SIC: 8111 General practice law office
PA: Pillsbury Winthrop Shaw Pittman Llp
31 W 52nd St Fl 26
New York NY 10019
212 858-1000

(P-22767)
PILLSBURY WINTHROP SHAW
12255 El Camino Real # 300, San Diego
(92130-4087)
PHONE....................................858 509-4000
Sue Hodges, *Branch Mgr*
EMP: 100
SALES (corp-wide): 265.5MM **Privately
Held**
SIC: 8111 General practice law office
PA: Pillsbury Winthrop Shaw Pittman Llp
31 W 52nd St Fl 26
New York NY 10019
212 858-1000

(P-22768)
PILLSBURY WINTHROP SHAW
50 Fremont St Ste 522, San Francisco
(94105-2232)
P.O. Box 7880 (94120-7880)
PHONE....................................415 983-1075
Jeffrey M Vesely, *Partner*
Catherine Schmitz, *Partner*
Richard W Odgers, *CPA*
Carol Maffin, *Human Res Dir*
EMP: 300
SALES (corp-wide): 265.5MM **Privately
Held**
SIC: 8111 General practice law office
PA: Pillsbury Winthrop Shaw Pittman Llp
31 W 52nd St Fl 26
New York NY 10019
212 858-1000

(P-22769)
PILLSBURY WINTHROP SHAW
2550 Hanover St, Palo Alto (94304-1115)
PHONE....................................650 233-4500
Kathie Pieri, *Manager*
David Jakopin, *Partner*
Hall Trish, *President*
Nora Godby, *Admin Sec*
Scott Kline, *Counsel*
EMP: 200
SALES (corp-wide): 265.5MM **Privately
Held**
SIC: 8111 General practice law office
PA: Pillsbury Winthrop Shaw Pittman Llp
31 W 52nd St Fl 26
New York NY 10019
212 858-1000

(P-22770)
PIRCHER NICHOLS & MEEKS (PA)
1925 Century Park E # 1700, Los Angeles
(90067-2740)
PHONE....................................310 201-0132
Gary Laughlin, *Senior Partner*
Jan Cawley, *President*
Belinda Lambert, *President*
Akasha Lee, *President*
Natasha Palmer, *President*
EMP: 95
SQ FT: 35,000
SALES (est): 17.1MM **Privately Held**
WEB: www.pircher.com
SIC: 8111 General practice attorney,
lawyer

(P-22771)
POLLARD CRNERT CRWFORD STEVENS
35 N Lake Ave Ste 500, Pasadena
(91101-4195)
PHONE....................................626 793-4440
Michael Pollard, *Principal*
Janice Okanishi, *Legal Staff*
EMP: 50
SALES (est): 4MM **Privately Held**
SIC: 8111 General practice attorney,
lawyer

(P-22772)
POLSINELLI PC
Also Called: Polsinelli LLP
2049 Century Park E, Los Angeles
(90067-3101)
PHONE....................................310 556-1801
Norma Ayala, *Administration*
Lisa Quateman, *Partner*
EMP: 70
SALES (corp-wide): 227.6MM **Privately
Held**
SIC: 8111 General practice attorney,
lawyer
PA: Polsinelli Pc
900 W 48th Pl Ste 900 # 900
Kansas City MO 64112
816 753-1000

(P-22773)
PRICE ASSOCIATES
Also Called: Price, Stuart
15760 Ventura Blvd # 1100, Encino
(91436-3044)
PHONE....................................818 995-9216
Stuart Price, *Owner*
Karen Tahler, *Opers Staff*
EMP: 50
SALES (est): 2.7MM **Privately Held**
SIC: 8111 General practice law office

(P-22774)
PRICE LAW GROUP A PROF CORP (PA)
15760 Ventura Blvd # 1100, Encino
(91436-3044)
PHONE....................................818 995-4540
Stuart M Price, *President*
EMP: 115
SQ FT: 15,000
SALES (est): 13.3MM **Privately Held**
SIC: 8111 Bankruptcy law; debt collection
law

(P-22775)
PRICE POSTEL AND PARMA LLP
200 E Carrillo St Ste 400, Santa Barbara
(93101-2190)
P.O. Box 99 (93102-0099)
PHONE....................................805 962-0011
Terry J Schwartz, *Partner*
Lonni Meanley Collins, *Partner*
James H Hurley Jr, *Partner*
Shereef Moharram, *Partner*
Gerald S Thede, *Partner*
EMP: 60
SQ FT: 5,000
SALES (est): 8.6MM **Privately Held**
WEB: www.ppplaw.com
SIC: 8111 General practice law office

(P-22776)
PRINDLE DECKER & AMARO LLP (PA)
310 Golden Shore Fl 4, Long Beach
(90802-4232)
PHONE....................................562 436-3946
R Joseph Decker, *Partner*
Michael Amaro, *Partner*
Kenneth Prindle, *Partner*
Greg Fox, *Technology*
Cathy Diehl, *Associate*
EMP: 85
SALES (est): 8.7MM **Privately Held**
SIC: 8111 General practice attorney,
lawyer

(P-22777)
PRISON INDUSTRY AUTHORITY-PIA
1 Kings Way, Avenal (93204-9708)
PHONE....................................559 386-6060
Annette Coopwood, *Officer*

Roxanne Schilling, *Officer*
Christa Golinski, *Administration*
Tess Hernandez, *Administration*
EMP: 60
SALES (est): 8MM **Privately Held**
SIC: 8111 Legal services

(P-22778)
PROBER & RAPHAEL A LAW CORP
Also Called: Prober & Raphael, ALC
20750 Ventura Blvd # 100, Woodland Hills
(91364-2338)
P.O. Box 4365 (91365-4365)
PHONE....................................818 227-0100
Dean R Prober, *President*
Lee S Raphael, *Principal*
Barbara Scott, *Admin Sec*
Verzhine Khachatryan, *Accountant*
Joe Peloso, *Human Resources*
EMP: 70
SALES (est): 8.3MM **Privately Held**
SIC: 8111 General practice law office

(P-22779)
PROSKAUER ROSE LLP
Also Called: Scott J Witlin Atty
2049 Century Park E # 3200, Los Angeles
(90067-3206)
PHONE....................................310 557-2900
Alan Jaffe, *President*
EMP: 60
SALES (corp-wide): 258MM **Privately
Held**
SIC: 8111 General practice attorney,
lawyer
PA: Proskauer Rose Llp
11 Times Sq Fl 17
New York NY 10036
212 969-3000

(P-22780)
PUBLIC COUNSEL
610 S Ardmore Ave, Los Angeles
(90005-2322)
PHONE....................................213 385-2977
Margaret Morrow, *President*
Madaline Kleiner, *Ch of Bd*
Benjamin Harville, *Counsel*
David Bubis, *Director*
Erika Luna, *Receptionist*
EMP: 94 EST: 1970
SQ FT: 12,000
SALES: 14.1MM **Privately Held**
SIC: 8111 Specialized law offices, attor-
neys

(P-22781)
QUINN EMANUEL URQUHART
50 California St Ste 2200, San Francisco
(94111-4788)
PHONE....................................415 875-6600
Charles K Verhoeven, *Managing Prtnr*
Kirill Parinov, *Managing Prtnr*
Lupe Espinoza, *Admin Sec*
Eric Gebhardt, *Administration*
EMP: 50
SALES (corp-wide): 179.3MM **Privately
Held**
SIC: 8111 Specialized law offices, attor-
neys
PA: Quinn Emanuel Urquhart & Sullivan,
Llp
865 S Figueroa St Fl 10
Los Angeles CA 90017
213 443-3000

(P-22782)
QUINN EMANUEL URQUHART
555 Twin Dolphin Dr Fl 5, Redwood City
(94065-2129)
PHONE....................................650 801-5000
Claude M Stern, *Managing Prtnr*
Chad Okada, *IT/INT Sup*
Meghan E Bordonaro, *Associate*
Claire Hausman, *Associate*
David E Myre, *Associate*
EMP: 80
SALES (corp-wide): 179.3MM **Privately
Held**
SIC: 8111 General practice attorney,
lawyer

PA: Quinn Emanuel Urquhart & Sullivan, Llp
865 S Figueroa St Fl 10
Los Angeles CA 90017
213 443-3000

(P-22783)
QUINN EMANUEL URQUHART (PA)
865 S Figueroa St Fl 10, Los Angeles (90017-5003)
PHONE..................................213 443-3000
John B Quinn, *Partner*
Anthony Alden, *Partner*
Wayne Alexander, *Partner*
Steven Anderson, *Partner*
Peter Armenio, *Partner*
EMP: 366
SALES (est): 179.3MM **Privately Held**
SIC: 8111 General practice law office

(P-22784)
RAINES LAW GROUP LLP
9720 Wilshire Blvd Fl 5, Beverly Hills (90212-2014)
PHONE..................................310 440-4100
Andrew Raines, *General Ptnr*
Robert Pardo, *Partner*
Megan Bulow, *Accounting Mgr*
EMP: 50
SALES (est): 1.2MM **Privately Held**
SIC: 8111 General practice law office

(P-22785)
REED SMITH LLP
2 Embarcadero Ctr Fl 20, San Francisco (94111-3922)
PHONE..................................415 659-5964
Janette Davis, *Manager*
Suzie A Savage, *Sr Associate*
EMP: 70
SALES (corp-wide): 306.8MM **Privately Held**
SIC: 8111 General practice law office
PA: Reed Smith Llp
225 5th Ave Ste 1200
Pittsburgh PA 15222
412 288-3131

(P-22786)
REED SMITH LLP
355 S Grand Ave Ste 2900, Los Angeles (90071-1514)
PHONE..................................213 457-8000
Peter Kennedy, *Partner*
Patty Carr, *President*
Socorro Dominguez, *President*
Charlie Koster, *President*
Sonia Martinez, *President*
EMP: 158
SALES (corp-wide): 306.8MM **Privately Held**
WEB: www.reedsmith.com
SIC: 8111 General practice attorney, lawyer
PA: Reed Smith Llp
225 5th Ave Ste 1200
Pittsburgh PA 15222
412 288-3131

(P-22787)
REED SMITH LLP
101 2nd St Ste 1800, San Francisco (94105-3659)
PHONE..................................415 543-8700
Bettie B Epstein, *Partner*
James Schad, *Analyst*
Kevin Hara, *Associate*
Jeffery Rieger, *Associate*
Farah Tabibkhoei, *Associate*
EMP: 158
SALES (corp-wide): 306.8MM **Privately Held**
WEB: www.reedsmith.com
SIC: 8111 General practice attorney, lawyer
PA: Reed Smith Llp
225 5th Ave Ste 1200
Pittsburgh PA 15222
412 288-3131

(P-22788)
REED SMITH LLP
2 Embarcadero Ctr Fl 21, San Francisco (94111-3995)
PHONE..................................415 543-8700

David A Thompson, *Partner*
Gloria Sandoval, *President*
EMP: 143
SALES (corp-wide): 306.8MM **Privately Held**
WEB: www.reedsmith.com
SIC: 8111 General practice attorney, lawyer
PA: Reed Smith Llp
225 5th Ave Ste 1200
Pittsburgh PA 15222
412 288-3131

(P-22789)
REID & HELLY
3880 Lemon St Fl 5, Riverside (92501-3667)
P.O. Box 1300 (92502-1300)
PHONE..................................951 682-1771
Michael Kerbs, *Partner*
Dan McKinney, *Admin Sec*
EMP: 60
SALES (est): 3.4MM **Privately Held**
SIC: 8111 General practice law office

(P-22790)
RICHARDS WATSON & GERSHON PC (PA)
Also Called: RW&g
355 S Grand Ave Fl 40, Los Angeles (90071-1560)
PHONE..................................213 626-8484
Laurence S Wiener, *CEO*
Bruce Galloway, *Shareholder*
Jim G Grayson, *Shareholder*
Jim Grayson, *Shareholder*
Susan Cribbs, *President*
EMP: 125
SQ FT: 45,000
SALES (est): 17.3MM **Privately Held**
WEB: www.rwglaw.com
SIC: 8111 General practice law office

(P-22791)
ROBBINS GELLER RUDMAN DOWD LLP (PA)
655 W Broadway Ste 1900, San Diego (92101-8498)
PHONE..................................619 231-1058
Michael J Dowd, *Partner*
Jonathan E Behar, *Partner*
Christopher M Burke, *Partner*
James Deguelle, *Partner*
Amber L Eck, *Partner*
EMP: 300
SQ FT: 135,000
SALES (est): 64.7MM **Privately Held**
WEB: www.lcsr.com
SIC: 8111 Corporate, partnership & business law; specialized law offices, attorneys

(P-22792)
ROBINSN CLGNE RSN SHPR DVS INC
620 Nwport Ctr Dr Ste 700, San Diego (92101)
PHONE..................................619 338-4060
Mark P Robinson, *Principal*
Allan F Davis,
EMP: 60
SALES (corp-wide): 8.5MM **Privately Held**
SIC: 8111 General practice attorney, lawyer
PA: Robinson Calcagnie Robinson Shapiro Davis, Inc.
19 Corporate Plaza Dr
Newport Beach CA 92660
949 720-1288

(P-22793)
ROBINSON AND WOOD INC
Also Called: Bautista, Jennifer L
160 W Santa Clara St # 1000, San Jose (95113-1000)
PHONE..................................408 298-7120
Archie Robinson, *President*
Hugh Lennon, *Corp Secy*
Joseph Balestrieri, *Vice Pres*
Arthur Casey, *Vice Pres*
Thomas Fellows, *Vice Pres*
EMP: 60 EST: 1962
SQ FT: 23,000

SALES (est): 7.5MM **Privately Held**
WEB: www.robinsonwood.com
SIC: 8111 General practice law office

(P-22794)
RONALD J LEMIEUX ASSOC LAW OFF
4195 N Viking Way Ste E, Long Beach (90808-1470)
PHONE..................................562 375-0095
Ronald J Lemieux, *President*
EMP: 60
SALES (est): 5.1MM **Privately Held**
SIC: 8111 Specialized law offices, attorneys

(P-22795)
ROPERS MAJESKI KOHN BENTLEY (PA)
Also Called: Ropers Majeski Kohn & Bentley
1001 Marshall St Fl 3, Redwood City (94063-2054)
PHONE..................................650 364-8200
Jesshill E Love, *CEO*
Anthony CHI-Hung, *Partner*
Anthony Grande, *Partner*
Geoffrey Heineman, *Partner*
Eugene J Majeski, *Partner*
EMP: 81
SQ FT: 69,000
SALES (est): 51.6MM **Privately Held**
WEB: www.ropers.com
SIC: 8111 General practice law office

(P-22796)
ROPES & GRAY LLP
3 Embarcadero Ctr Ste 300, San Francisco (94111-4006)
PHONE..................................415 315-6300
Adam Trott, *Branch Mgr*
Aimee Davis, *Admin Sec*
Jeff Murray, *Engineer*
Haley N Bavasi, *Associate*
Adam Leamon, *Associate*
EMP: 410
SALES (corp-wide): 345.3MM **Privately Held**
SIC: 8111 General practice law office
PA: Ropes & Gray Llp
Prudential Tower 800 Boys
Boston MA 02199
617 951-7000

(P-22797)
ROPES & GRAY LLP
1900 University Ave # 600, East Palo Alto (94303-2299)
PHONE..................................650 617-4000
Kitty Dowgert, *Branch Mgr*
Eric Wright, *Partner*
Jennifer Wisnia, *Practice Mgr*
Darlene Mroz, *Executive Asst*
Patti Rapozo, *Admin Sec*
EMP: 63
SALES (corp-wide): 345.3MM **Privately Held**
SIC: 8111 General practice law office
PA: Ropes & Gray Llp
Prudential Tower 800 Boys
Boston MA 02199
617 951-7000

(P-22798)
ROSSI HAMERSLOUGH REISHCHL &
1960 The Alameda Ste 200, San Jose (95126-1451)
PHONE..................................408 244-4570
Sam Chuck, *President*
Colleen Eastman, *Dean*
Carmen Mendez, *Legal Staff*
EMP: 54
SALES (est): 4.6MM **Privately Held**
SIC: 8111 General practice law office

(P-22799)
RUTAN & TUCKER LLP (PA)
611 Anton Blvd Ste 1400, Costa Mesa (92626-1931)
P.O. Box 1950 (92628-1950)
PHONE..................................714 641-5100
Richard Boden, *Mng Member*
William F Meehan, *Partner*
Tony Malkani, *Officer*
Josette Cann, *Managing Dir*

Nancy Bush, *Admin Sec*
EMP: 275
SQ FT: 90,000
SALES: 82MM **Privately Held**
WEB: www.rutan.com
SIC: 8111 General practice law office

(P-22800)
SALTZBURG RAY & BERGMAN LLP
12121 Wilshire Blvd # 600, Los Angeles (90025-1123)
PHONE..................................310 481-6700
David Ray, *Partner*
Alan Bergman, *Partner*
Genise Reiter, *Partner*
Henley Saltzburg, *Partner*
Aaron Rosenberg, *President*
EMP: 124
SQ FT: 15,000
SALES (est): 12.9MM **Privately Held**
WEB: www.srblaw.com
SIC: 8111 7389 General practice attorney, lawyer; courier or messenger service

(P-22801)
SAN BERNARDINO CALIFORNIA CITY (PA)
290 N D St, San Bernardino (92401-1734)
PHONE..................................909 384-7272
R Carey Davis, *Mayor*
Palupe Iosefa, *Treasurer*
David Kennedy, *Treasurer*
Emil Kokesh, *Bd of Directors*
Dixon Mutadzakupa, *Officer*
EMP: 352
SALES (est): 193MM **Privately Held**
SIC: 8111 Administrative & government law

(P-22802)
SAN DIEGO CAR ACCIDENT LAWYERS
Maple St, San Diego (92104)
PHONE..................................858 201-4178
Harry Keller, *Principal*
EMP: 50
SALES (est): 705.2K **Privately Held**
SIC: 8111 Legal services

(P-22803)
SANTA BARBARA COUNTY OF
Also Called: District Attorney
312 E Cook St Ste D, Santa Maria (93454-5162)
PHONE..................................805 346-7540
Joyce Bedley, *Principal*
EMP: 50 **Privately Held**
WEB: www.sbcountyhr.org
SIC: 8111 9222 General practice attorney, lawyer; District Attorneys' offices;
PA: County Of Santa Barbara
105 E Anapamu St Rm 406
Santa Barbara CA 93101
805 568-3400

(P-22804)
SANTA CLARA COUNTY OF
Also Called: District Attroney's Office
3180 Newberry Dr Ste 150, San Jose (95118-1566)
PHONE..................................408 792-2704
George Doorley, *Manager*
EMP: 600 **Privately Held**
WEB: www.countyairports.org
SIC: 8111 Legal services
PA: County Of Santa Clara
3180 Newberry Dr Ste 150
San Jose CA 95118
408 299-5105

(P-22805)
SCOTT A PORTER PROF CORP
350 University Ave # 200, Sacramento (95825-6581)
P.O. Box 255428 (95865-5428)
PHONE..................................916 929-1481
Sherrie Cork, *Office Mgr*
Tom Bailey, *Partner*
Tim Blaine, *Partner*
Craig Caldwell, *Partner*
Carl Calnero, *Partner*
EMP: 85
SQ FT: 22,000

SALES (est): 12.9MM **Privately Held**
WEB: www.pswdlaw.com
SIC: 8111 General practice attorney, lawyer; general practice law office

(P-22806)
SEAN P OCONNOR
Also Called: D'Angelo, Michael L
1900 Main St Ste 700, Irvine (92614-7328)
PHONE..............................949 851-7323
Michael L D'Angelo, *Principal*
EMP: 80
SALES (est): 2.4MM **Privately Held**
SIC: 8111 General practice attorney, lawyer

(P-22807)
SELTZER CAPLAN MCMAHON (PA)
750 B St Ste 2100, San Diego (92101-8177)
PHONE..............................619 685-3003
Robert Caplan, *President*
Dennis Wickham, *Partner*
James Dawe, *CFO*
Neal P Panish, *Treasurer*
Gerald L Mc Mahon, *Senior VP*
EMP: 173
SQ FT: 78,000
SALES (est): 21.5MM **Privately Held**
WEB: www.scmv.com
SIC: 8111 General practice law office

(P-22808)
SEVERSON & WERSON A PROF CORP
1 Embarcadero Ctr Fl 26, San Francisco (94111-3745)
PHONE..............................415 398-3344
James B Werson, *Ch of Bd*
Donald Read, *Partner*
Sylvia Coleman, *President*
Emily Rhea, *President*
Robert L Lofts, *CFO*
EMP: 100
SQ FT: 40,000
SALES (est): 19.3MM **Privately Held**
WEB: www.severson.com
SIC: 8111 Labor & employment law; corporate, partnership & business law

(P-22809)
SEYFARTH SHAW LLP
601 S Figueroa St # 3300, Los Angeles (90017-5793)
P.O. Box 17961 (90017-0961)
PHONE..............................213 270-9600
Arthur Wood IV, *Branch Mgr*
Timothy Fisher, *Associate*
Christine Kim, *Associate*
Navid More, *Associate*
EMP: 125
SALES (corp-wide): 266MM **Privately Held**
SIC: 8111 General practice law office
PA: Seyfarth Shaw Llp
    233 S Wacker Dr Ste 8000
    Chicago IL 60606
    312 460-5000

(P-22810)
SEYFARTH SHAW LLP
2029 Century Park E # 3400, Los Angeles (90067-3020)
PHONE..............................310 277-7200
Sandy Abrahamian, *Branch Mgr*
Susie Diaz, *Office Admin*
Rachel Victor, *Admin Sec*
Gayle Vinson, *Admin Sec*
Sarah Guigliano, *Marketing Staff*
EMP: 200
SALES (corp-wide): 266MM **Privately Held**
WEB: www.seyfarth.com
SIC: 8111 General practice law office
PA: Seyfarth Shaw Llp
    233 S Wacker Dr Ste 8000
    Chicago IL 60606
    312 460-5000

(P-22811)
SEYFARTH SHAW LLP
560 Mission St Fl 31, San Francisco (94105-2930)
PHONE..............................415 397-2823
William Dritsas, *Principal*

Lauren Abria, *Admin Asst*
Constance Hughes, *Admin Asst*
Patricia H Cullison, *Admin Asst*
Michael Stevens, *Sr Associate*
EMP: 100
SALES (corp-wide): 266MM **Privately Held**
WEB: www.seyfarth.com
SIC: 8111 General practice law office
PA: Seyfarth Shaw Llp
    233 S Wacker Dr Ste 8000
    Chicago IL 60606
    312 460-5000

(P-22812)
SHARTSIS FRIESE LLP
1 Maritime Plz Fl 18, San Francisco (94111-3508)
PHONE..............................415 421-6500
Arthur J Shartsis, *Partner*
Derek Boswell, *Partner*
John P Broadhurst, *Partner*
Zesara Chan, *Partner*
Frank Cialone, *Partner*
EMP: 120
SQ FT: 47,709
SALES (est): 19.4MM **Privately Held**
WEB: www.sflaw.com
SIC: 8111 Patent, trademark & copyright law; taxation law; will, estate & trust law; real estate law

(P-22813)
SHEKINAH INC
7755 Center Ave Ste 1000, Huntington Beach (92647-3090)
PHONE..............................714 475-5460
Cecilia Trent, *President*
James Trent, *CFO*
David Vasquez Sr, *Vice Pres*
Dana Kowprowski, *Director*
Lynn Kafer, *Manager*
EMP: 50
SQ FT: 2,400
SALES (est): 1.9MM **Privately Held**
SIC: 8111 Debt collection law

(P-22814)
SHEPPARD MULLIN RICHTER (PA)
Also Called: Sheppard Mullin
333 S Hope St Fl 43, Los Angeles (90071-1422)
PHONE..............................213 620-1780
Guy N Halgren, *Partner*
Charles Barker, *Partner*
Robert Beall, *Partner*
Lawrence Braun, *Partner*
Justine M Casey, *Partner*
EMP: 370
SQ FT: 52,820
SALES (est): 207.6MM **Privately Held**
WEB: www.smrh.com
SIC: 8111 General practice law office

(P-22815)
SHEPPARD MULLIN RICHTER
12275 El Camino R Ste 200, San Diego (92130)
PHONE..............................619 338-6500
EMP: 84
SALES (corp-wide): 200.4MM **Privately Held**
SIC: 8111
PA: Sheppard, Mullin, Richter & Hampton, Llp
    333 S Hope St Fl 43
    Los Angeles CA 90071
    202 218-0000

(P-22816)
SHEPPARD MULLIN RICHTER
4 Embarcadero Ctr # 1700, San Francisco (94111-4106)
PHONE..............................415 434-9100
Aline Pearl, *Office Admin*
A John Murphy, *Partner*
Thomas Nevins, *Partner*
Richard J Simmons, *Partner*
Robert Uram, *Partner*
EMP: 62
SALES (corp-wide): 207.6MM **Privately Held**
SIC: 8111 Corporate, partnership & business law; general practice law office

PA: Sheppard, Mullin, Richter & Hampton, Llp
    333 S Hope St Fl 43
    Los Angeles CA 90071
    213 620-1780

(P-22817)
SHEPPARD MULLIN RICHTER
1901 Avenue Of The Stars # 1600, Los Angeles (90067-6055)
PHONE..............................310 228-3700
Sherry Wilson, *Administration*
Cristina Ongsing, *Admin Sec*
Brian Kay, *Technical Staff*
Vivian Katapodis, *Legal Staff*
Gloria Schmidt, *Legal Staff*
EMP: 61
SALES (corp-wide): 207.6MM **Privately Held**
SIC: 8111 General practice law office
PA: Sheppard, Mullin, Richter & Hampton, Llp
    333 S Hope St Fl 43
    Los Angeles CA 90071
    213 620-1780

(P-22818)
SHEPPARD MULLIN RICHTER
650 Town Center Dr Fl 10, Costa Mesa (92626-1993)
PHONE..............................714 513-5100
Sheila Cantrell, *Office Admin*
Finley Taylor, *Partner*
Carole Dubienny, *President*
Tina Hammer, *President*
Robert Philibosian, *Counsel*
EMP: 100
SALES (corp-wide): 207.6MM **Privately Held**
SIC: 8111 General practice law office
PA: Sheppard, Mullin, Richter & Hampton, Llp
    333 S Hope St Fl 43
    Los Angeles CA 90071
    213 620-1780

(P-22819)
SHERIFFS OFFICES
Also Called: Inyo Sheriff Office
550 S Clay St, Independence (93526)
PHONE..............................760 878-0383
Dan Lucas, *Principal*
William Lutze, *Principal*
EMP: 60 **EST:** 2001
SALES (est): 2.5MM **Privately Held**
SIC: 8111 General practice law office

(P-22820)
SHOOK HARDY & BACON LLP
1 Montgomery St Ste 2700, San Francisco (94104-5527)
PHONE..............................415 544-1900
Shannon Spangler, *Managing Prtnr*
Andrew Chang, *Associate*
EMP: 60
SALES (corp-wide): 310MM **Privately Held**
WEB: www.shb.com
SIC: 8111 General practice law office
PA: Shook, Hardy & Bacon L.L.P.
    2555 Grand Blvd
    Kansas City MO 64108
    816 474-6550

(P-22821)
SIDEMAN & BANCROFT LLP
1 Embarcadero Ctr Ste 860, San Francisco (94111-3645)
PHONE..............................415 392-1960
Jeffrey Hallam, *General Ptnr*
Kelly P McCarthy, *Partner*
Hilary Pierce, *Partner*
Mary Eslava, *President*
Janice Graves, *President*
EMP: 95
SALES (est): 17.3MM **Privately Held**
SIC: 8111 General practice law office

(P-22822)
SIDLEY AUSTIN LLP
1001 Page Mill Rd Bldg 1, Palo Alto (94304-1006)
PHONE..............................650 565-7000
Dorce Zimmermann, *Branch Mgr*
Nathan Greenblatt, *Patent Law*
Christopher P Masterson, *Associate*

Dorna Moini, *Associate*
EMP: 85
SALES (corp-wide): 413.2MM **Privately Held**
SIC: 8111 General practice attorney, lawyer
PA: Sidley Austin Llp
    1 S Dearborn St Ste 900
    Chicago IL 60603
    312 853-7000

(P-22823)
SILVER FREDMAN A PROF LAW CORP
2029 Century Park E # 1900, Los Angeles (90067-2901)
PHONE..............................310 556-2356
Perry Silver, *President*
Andrew B Kaplan, *Partner*
Beth Schroeder, *Managing Prtnr*
Neil Freedman, *Admin Sec*
EMP: 50
SQ FT: 21,500
SALES (est): 3.4MM **Privately Held**
WEB: www.silver-freedman.com
SIC: 8111 General practice law office

(P-22824)
SIMPSON DELMORE AND GREENE LLP (PA)
600 W Broadway Ste 400, San Diego (92101-3352)
PHONE..............................619 515-1194
Paul Delmore, *Partner*
Terence Greene, *Partner*
John Simpson, *Partner*
EMP: 50
SQ FT: 20,000
SALES (est): 5.3MM **Privately Held**
WEB: www.sdgllp.com
SIC: 8111 General practice law office

(P-22825)
SIMPSON THACHER & BARTLETT LLP
2475 Hanover St, Palo Alto (94304-1155)
PHONE..............................650 251-5000
Richard Capelouto, *Manager*
Teresa Firoozye, *Admin Asst*
Misael Amador, *Technology*
Dena Acevedo, *Associate*
John Bennett, *Associate*
EMP: 120
SALES (corp-wide): 908.1K **Privately Held**
WEB: www.stblaw.com
SIC: 8111 Corporate, partnership & business law
PA: Simpson Thacher & Bartlett Llp
    425 Lexington Ave Fl 15
    New York NY 10017
    212 455-2000

(P-22826)
SKADDEN ARPS SLATE MEAGHER & F
300 S Grand Ave Ste 3400, Los Angeles (90071-3137)
PHONE..............................213 687-5000
Rand S April, *Partner*
Meryl K Chae, *Partner*
Kristine Dunn, *Partner*
Brian J McCarthy, *Partner*
Jeffrey Mishkin, *Exec VP*
EMP: 250
SALES (corp-wide): 461.9MM **Privately Held**
SIC: 8111 General practice attorney, lawyer
PA: Skadden, Arps, Slate, Meagher & Flom Llp
    4 Times Sq Fl 24
    New York NY 10036
    212 735-3000

(P-22827)
SMS TRANSPORTATION
18516 S Broadway, Gardena (90248-4615)
PHONE..............................310 527-9200
John W Harris, *Principal*
Jennifer Wiltz, *COO*
EMP: 100
SALES (est): 8MM **Privately Held**
SIC: 8111 Legal services

(P-22828)
SNELL & WILMER LLP
600 Anton Blvd Ste 1400, Costa Mesa
(92626-7689)
PHONE....................714 427-7000
Andrea Bryant, *Principal*
Alexander L Conti, *Partner*
Frank Cronin, *Partner*
Christy D Joseph, *Partner*
William S O'Hare, *Officer*
EMP: 160
SQ FT: 3,000
SALES (corp-wide): 95.9MM **Privately Held**
SIC: 8111 General practice law office; specialized law offices, attorneys
PA: Snell & Wilmer L.L.P.
400 E Van Buren St Fl 10
Phoenix AZ 85004
602 382-6000

(P-22829)
SOBEL ROSS H LAW OFFICES
Also Called: Sobel, Ross Howell
1875 Century Park E # 2000, Los Angeles
(90067-2545)
PHONE....................310 788-8995
Ross H Sobel, *Owner*
EMP: 50
SALES (est): 2.1MM **Privately Held**
SIC: 8111 Criminal law

(P-22830)
SOLOMON WARD SDNWURM SMITH LLP
401 B St Ste 1200, San Diego
(92101-4295)
PHONE....................619 231-0303
Herbert Solomon, *Partner*
Lawrence Kaplan, *Partner*
Richard E McCarthy, *Partner*
Richard L Seidenwurm, *Partner*
Jeffrey H Silberman, *Partner*
EMP: 60
SQ FT: 17,000
SALES (est): 8.8MM **Privately Held**
WEB: www.swsslaw.com
SIC: 8111 General practice attorney, lawyer

(P-22831)
SQUIRE PATTON BOGGS (US) LLP
555 S Flower St Ste 3100, Los Angeles
(90071-2255)
PHONE....................213 624-2500
Chris M Amantea, *Manager*
Scott Kane, *Partner*
Brandi Hann, *Office Admin*
Marilyn Stimson, *Executive Asst*
Pamela Wedemeyer, *Research*
EMP: 60
SALES (corp-wide): 297.2MM **Privately Held**
WEB: www.squiresandersdempsey.com
SIC: 8111 General practice law office
PA: Squire Patton Boggs (Us) Llp
4900 Key Tower
Cleveland OH 44114
216 479-8500

(P-22832)
SQUIRE PATTON BOGGS (US) LLP
275 Battery St Ste 2600, San Francisco
(94111-3356)
PHONE....................415 954-0334
Thomas H Woofter, *Manager*
Keri Li, *Business Mgr*
Tom Zarcone, *Marketing Staff*
Louise Boyce, *Counsel*
Catherine Romanchek, *Sr Associate*
EMP: 120
SALES (corp-wide): 297.2MM **Privately Held**
WEB: www.squiresandersdempsey.com
SIC: 8111 General practice law office
PA: Squire Patton Boggs (Us) Llp
4900 Key Tower
Cleveland OH 44114
216 479-8500

(P-22833)
STEELE CIS LLC
1 Sansome St Ste 3500, San Francisco
(94104-4436)
PHONE....................415 692-5000
Ken Kurtz, *President*
Mehak Waraich, *Project Mgr*
Rojer Du, *Analyst*
Andrew Glikman, *Manager*
EMP: 350
SALES (est): 27MM **Privately Held**
SIC: 8111 Legal services

(P-22834)
STEIN & LUBIN LLP
600 Montgomery St Fl 14, San Francisco
(94111-2716)
PHONE....................415 981-0550
Mark Lubin, *Partner*
Robert S Stein, *Partner*
Eyleen Nadolny, *President*
Sabrina Stewart, *President*
Betsy Glover, *Executive*
EMP: 50
SALES (est): 7.7MM **Privately Held**
WEB: www.steinlubin.com
SIC: 8111 General practice law office

(P-22835)
STEPTOE & JOHNSON LLP
633 W 5th St Fl 7, Los Angeles
(90071-3503)
PHONE....................213 439-9400
Leslie Graine, *Administration*
Elena Hernandez, *Executive Asst*
Phyllis Lee, *Executive Asst*
Shannon Ramme, *Executive Asst*
Aja Clark, *Admin Sec*
EMP: 50
SALES (corp-wide): 356MM **Privately Held**
WEB: www.steptoe.com
SIC: 8111 General practice law office
PA: Steptoe & Johnson Llp
1330 Connecticut Ave Nw
Washington DC 20036
202 429-3000

(P-22836)
STRADLING YOCCA CARLSON & RAUT (PA)
660 Newport Center Dr # 1600, Newport
Beach (92660-6458)
PHONE....................949 725-4000
John F Cannon, *Principal*
Bruce Feuchter, *Partner*
Sean Absher, *Shareholder*
Sarah Brooks, *Shareholder*
Allison Burns, *Shareholder*
EMP: 200 EST: 1975
SQ FT: 64,000
SALES (est): 40.6MM **Privately Held**
WEB: www.sycr.com
SIC: 8111 General practice law office

(P-22837)
STRADLING YOCCA CARLSON & RAUT
500 Capitol Mall, Sacramento
(95814-4737)
PHONE....................916 449-2350
Kevin Civale, *Manager*
Richard Goodman,
EMP: 108
SALES (corp-wide): 40.6MM **Privately Held**
SIC: 8111 General practice law office
PA: Stradling Yocca Carlson & Rauth A Professional Corp
660 Newport Center Dr # 1600
Newport Beach CA 92660
949 725-4000

(P-22838)
STRETTO (PA)
Also Called: B M S
5 Peters Canyon Rd # 200, Irvine
(92606-1791)
PHONE....................949 222-1212
Steve Moore, *CEO*
David Beltran, *Officer*
Melinda Teter, *Vice Pres*
Carl Liberato, *Prgrmr*
Aditya Kaseebhatla, *Engineer*
EMP: 72

SALES (est): 25.9MM **Privately Held**
SIC: 8111 Bankruptcy referee

(P-22839)
STROOCK & STROOCK & LAVAN LLP
2029 Century Park E # 1800, Los Angeles
(90067-3086)
PHONE....................310 556-5800
Diane Cohen, *Branch Mgr*
Howard Lavin, *Partner*
Bruce Schneider, *General Counsel*
EMP: 150
SALES (corp-wide): 102.3MM **Privately Held**
SIC: 8111 General practice attorney, lawyer
PA: Stroock & Stroock & Lavan Llp
180 Maiden Ln Fl 17
New York NY 10038
212 806-5400

(P-22840)
STUTMAN TRSTER GLATT PROF CORP
Also Called: Stutman Treister Glatt Prof Co
1901 Avenue Of The, Los Angeles (90067)
PHONE....................310 228-5600
Scott H Yun, *CEO*
Charles D Axelrod, *Vice Pres*
Michael H Goldstein, *Vice Pres*
Robert A Greenfield, *Vice Pres*
Robert Greenfield, *Vice Pres*
EMP: 75
SQ FT: 40,000
SALES (est): 512K **Privately Held**
WEB: www.stutman.com
SIC: 8111 General practice law office

(P-22841)
SULLIVAN & CROMWELL LLP
1888 Century Park E # 2100, Los Angeles
(90067-1725)
PHONE....................310 712-6600
Laura Henry, *Manager*
Adam S Paris, *Partner*
Alison S Ressler, *Partner*
Michael H Steinberg, *Partner*
Liana Tucker, *President*
EMP: 65
SALES (corp-wide): 321.4MM **Privately Held**
SIC: 8111 Specialized law offices, attorneys
PA: Sullivan & Cromwell Llp
125 Broad St Fl 35
New York NY 10004
212 558-4000

(P-22842)
SYNNEXXUS LLC
20251 Sw Acacia St # 200, Newport Beach
(92660-1716)
PHONE....................714 933-4500
Frank Nese, *Mng Member*
EMP: 50
SALES (est): 3MM **Privately Held**
SIC: 8111 Legal services

(P-22843)
TERIS-BAY AREA LLC
2455 Faber Pl Ste 200, Palo Alto
(94303-3316)
PHONE....................650 213-9922
Stefan Wikstrom, *CEO*
Kip Hauser, *COO*
Darisa Hill, *Controller*
EMP: 99
SALES (est): 3.8MM **Privately Held**
SIC: 8111 Legal services

(P-22844)
THARPE & HOWELL (PA)
15250 Ventura Blvd Fl 9, Sherman Oaks
(91403-3221)
PHONE....................818 205-9955
John Maile, *Managing Prtnr*
Robert M Freedman, *Senior Partner*
Todd R Howell, *Partner*
Timothy D Lake, *Partner*
Christopher S Maile, *Partner*
EMP: 78
SQ FT: 13,500
SALES (est): 11.6MM **Privately Held**
WEB: www.tharpe-howell.com
SIC: 8111 General practice law office

(P-22845)
THOMPSON & COLEGATE LLP
3610 14th St Lowr, Riverside (92501-3852)
P.O. Box 1299 (92502-1299)
PHONE....................951 682-5550
John W Marshall, *Partner*
John A Boyd, *Partner*
Donald G Grant, *Partner*
J E Holmes III, *Partner*
Michael J Marlatt, *Partner*
EMP: 50 EST: 1920
SQ FT: 28,500
SALES: 4.9MM **Privately Held**
WEB: www.tclaw.net
SIC: 8111 General practice attorney, lawyer

(P-22846)
THOMPSON COBURN LLP
2029 Century Park E # 1900, Los Angeles
(90067-3005)
PHONE....................310 282-2500
EMP: 304
SALES (corp-wide): 139.2MM **Privately Held**
SIC: 8111 General practice attorney, lawyer
PA: Thompson Coburn Llp
505 N 7th St Ste 2700
Saint Louis MO 63101
314 552-6000

(P-22847)
THORSNES BARTOLOTTA & MCGUIRE
2550 5th Ave Ste 1100, San Diego
(92103-6694)
PHONE....................619 236-9363
Mickey McGuire, *Partner*
Vincent Bartolotta, *Partner*
Mitchell Golub, *Partner*
Darel Mazzerlla, *Partner*
Kevin Quinn, *Partner*
EMP: 67
SQ FT: 20,000
SALES (est): 10MM **Privately Held**
WEB: www.tbmlawyers.com
SIC: 8111 Specialized law offices, attorneys

(P-22848)
TRESSLER LLP
2 Park Plz Ste 1050, Irvine (92614-8521)
PHONE....................949 336-1200
Katherine Liner, *Owner*
EMP: 69
SALES (corp-wide): 41.6MM **Privately Held**
SIC: 8111 Specialized law offices, attorneys
PA: Tressler Llp
233 S Wacker Dr Ste 6100
Chicago IL 60606
312 627-4000

(P-22849)
TROPE AND TROPE LLP
Also Called: Trope & Trope
12121 Wilshire Blvd # 801, Los Angeles
(90025-1164)
PHONE....................323 879-2726
Sorrell Trope, *Partner*
EMP: 57
SALES (est): 7.7MM **Privately Held**
SIC: 8111 Divorce & family law

(P-22850)
TROUTMAN SANDERS LLP
11682 El Camino Real # 400, San Diego
(92130-2092)
PHONE....................858 509-6000
Michael J Whitton, *Branch Mgr*
Sheri Clifton, *Office Admin*
Bruce Crawford, *Analyst*
Roy Bell, *Counsel*
EMP: 88
SALES (corp-wide): 273.1MM **Privately Held**
SIC: 8111 General practice attorney, lawyer
PA: Troutman Sanders Llp
600 Peachtree St Ne Ste 3
Atlanta GA 30308
404 885-3000

PRODUCTS & SVCS

(P-22851)
TROUTMAN SANDERS LLP
580 California St # 1100, San Francisco
(94104-1000)
PHONE.....................415 477-5700
Paige Fitzgerald, *Counsel*
Shannon Varner, *Counsel*
Timothy Heaton, *Counsel*
Christopher Araujo, *Associate*
Kimberly Hargrove, *Associate*
EMP: 82
SALES (corp-wide): 273.1MM **Privately Held**
SIC: 8111 General practice attorney, lawyer
PA: Troutman Sanders Llp
  600 Peachtree St Ne Ste 3
  Atlanta GA 30308
  404 885-3000

(P-22852)
TROYGOULD PC
1801 Century Park E # 1600, Los Angeles (90067-2367)
PHONE.....................310 553-4441
Sanford J Hillsberg, *Principal*
Diane Gordon, *Exec Dir*
Keith Brownley, *Technology*
Tanya Simon, *Legal Staff*
Martin Goldblum,
EMP: 80 EST: 1970
SQ FT: 24,000
SALES (est): 13MM **Privately Held**
WEB: www.troygould.com
SIC: 8111 General practice attorney, lawyer

(P-22853)
TUCKER ELLIS LLP
1000 Wilshire Blvd # 1800, Los Angeles (90017-2457)
PHONE.....................213 430-3400
William Weech, *Administration*
Karen Scheel, *President*
Bill Weech, *Executive*
Rebecca Gutierrez, *Associate*
EMP: 54
SALES (corp-wide): 54MM **Privately Held**
WEB: www.tuckerellis.com
SIC: 8111 General practice attorney, lawyer
PA: Tucker Ellis Llp
  950 Main Ave Ste 1100
  Cleveland OH 44113
  216 592-5000

(P-22854)
TYLER PALMIERI WIENER
1900 Main St Ste 700, Irvine (92614-7328)
P.O. Box 19712 (92623-9712)
PHONE.....................949 851-9400
James E Wilhelm, *Partner*
Mike Greene, *Partner*
Robert Ihrke, *Partner*
David Parr, *Partner*
L Richard Rawls, *Partner*
EMP: 100
SQ FT: 34,000
SALES (est): 16.6MM **Privately Held**
SIC: 8111 General practice law office

(P-22855)
UNISOURCE DISCOVERY LLC (PA)
625 The City Dr S Ste 303, Orange (92868-4984)
PHONE.....................888 248-0020
Steven Cerasale,
April Padron, *Manager*
EMP: 60
SALES (est): 8.3MM **Privately Held**
WEB: www.unisourcediscovery.com
SIC: 8111 Legal services

(P-22856)
UNITED STATES ATTORNEYS
300 N Los Angeles St Lbby, Los Angeles (90012-3336)
PHONE.....................213 894-2400
Leon Wheidman, *Chief*
EMP: 101 **Publicly Held**
WEB: www.mvpdallas.com
SIC: 8111 9222 Legal services; United States attorneys' offices;

HQ: United States Attorneys, Executive Office For
  175 N St Ne Fl 6
  Washington DC 20002

(P-22857)
VEATCH CARLSON GROGAN & NELSON
1055 Wilshire Blvd Fl 11, Los Angeles (90017-2431)
PHONE.....................213 381-2861
Jim Galloway, *Partner*
David Failer, *Partner*
Juana Guevara, *President*
Jim Nelson, *Litigation*
EMP: 50
SALES (est): 6.2MM **Privately Held**
WEB: www.veatchfirm.com
SIC: 8111 General practice law office

(P-22858)
VINSON & ELKINS LLP
1841 Page Mill Rd Fl 2, Palo Alto (94304-1255)
PHONE.....................650 617-8400
Rose Sullivan, *Assistant*
EMP: 198
SALES (corp-wide): 420.7MM **Privately Held**
SIC: 8111 General practice attorney, lawyer
PA: Vinson & Elkins L.L.P.
  1001 Fannin St Ste 2500
  Houston TX 77002
  713 758-2222

(P-22859)
WADE & LOWE A PROF CORP (PA)
3200 Inland Empire Blvd # 160, Ontario (91764-5575)
PHONE.....................909 483-6700
Richard W Miller, *CEO*
Curtis Metzgar, *Partner*
William R Lowe, *President*
Randolph W Even, *Treasurer*
Edwin Brown, *Vice Pres*
▲ EMP: 100 EST: 1976
SQ FT: 7,000
SALES (est): 8.4MM **Privately Held**
WEB: www.evencrandall.com
SIC: 8111 General practice attorney, lawyer

(P-22860)
WALKUP MELODIA KELLY
Also Called: Walkup Law Office
650 California St Fl 26, San Francisco (94108-2615)
PHONE.....................415 981-7210
Paul W Melodia, *President*
Kirsten Benzien, *President*
Lily Connors, *President*
Kevin Domecus, *Treasurer*
Jefferey Holl, *Vice Pres*
EMP: 50
SQ FT: 30,000
SALES (est): 8.1MM **Privately Held**
WEB: www.walkuplawoffice.com
SIC: 8111 Labor & employment law; malpractice & negligence law

(P-22861)
WALSWRTH FRNKLIN BEVINS MCCALL (PA)
Also Called: Walsworth Franklin & Bevins
1 City Blvd W Ste 500, Orange (92868-3677)
PHONE.....................714 634-2522
Jeffrey P Walsworth, *Partner*
Ronald H Bevins Jr, *Partner*
Ian P Dillon, *Partner*
Ferdie F Franklin, *Partner*
Daniel R Jacobs, *Partner*
EMP: 75
SQ FT: 2,800
SALES (est): 13.3MM **Privately Held**
SIC: 8111 General practice law office

(P-22862)
WARREN DRYE KELLEY
10100 Santa Monica Blvd # 1050, Los Angeles (90067-4003)
PHONE.....................310 712-6100

Andrew White, *Managing Prtnr*
Michael O'Cannor, *Managing Prtnr*
EMP: 60
SALES (est): 5.8MM **Privately Held**
SIC: 8111 General practice law office

(P-22863)
WASSERMAN COMDEN & CASSELMAN (PA)
5567 Reseda Blvd Ste 330, Tarzana (91356-2699)
P.O. Box 7033 (91357-7033)
PHONE.....................323 872-0995
Steve Wasserman, *Partner*
David B Casselman, *Partner*
Leonard J Comden, *Partner*
Clifford H Pearson, *Partner*
Pamela Scott-Belinfant, *Manager*
EMP: 96
SQ FT: 15,000
SALES (est): 11.2MM **Privately Held**
WEB: www.wcclaw.com
SIC: 8111 General practice law office

(P-22864)
WEIL GOTSHAL & MANGES LLP
201 Redwood Shors Pkwy, Redwood City (94065)
PHONE.....................650 802-3000
Craig Adas, *Managing Prtnr*
Rod J Howard, *Partner*
Kyle C Krpata, *Partner*
Curtis L MO, *Partner*
Edward R Reines, *Partner*
EMP: 180
SALES (corp-wide): 322.7MM **Privately Held**
WEB: www.weil.com
SIC: 8111 General practice law office
PA: Weil, Gotshal & Manges Llp
  767 5th Ave Fl Conc1
  New York NY 10153
  212 310-8000

(P-22865)
WEINBERG ROGER & RESENFELD (PA)
1001 Marina Village Pkwy # 200, Alameda (94501-6480)
PHONE.....................510 337-1001
Stewart Weinberg, *President*
David Rosenfeld, *Shareholder*
Tony Ruiz, *Shareholder*
Lara Hull, *President*
Andrea Laiacona, *Admin Sec*
EMP: 69 EST: 1964
SQ FT: 12,000
SALES (est): 9.5MM **Privately Held**
WEB: www.unioncounsel.net
SIC: 8111 General practice law office

(P-22866)
WEINTRAUB TOBIN CHEDIAK
9665 Wilshire Blvd # 900, Beverly Hills (90212-2315)
PHONE.....................310 858-7888
Marvin Gelfand, *Partner*
EMP: 50 **Privately Held**
SIC: 8111 General practice law office
PA: Weintraub Tobin Chediak Coleman Grodin Law Corporation
  400 Capitol Mall Fl 11
  Sacramento CA 95814

(P-22867)
WEINTRAUB TOBIN CHEDIAK (PA)
400 Capitol Mall Fl 11, Sacramento (95814-4434)
PHONE.....................916 558-6000
Michael Kvarme, *CEO*
Geoffrey Burroughs, *Partner*
Dale C Campbelll, *Partner*
Christopher Chediak, *Partner*
Peggy A Dalton, *Partner*
EMP: 50
SQ FT: 44,900
SALES (est): 20.8MM **Privately Held**
WEB: www.weintraub.com
SIC: 8111 General practice law office

(P-22868)
WEITZ & LUXENBERG PC
1880 Century Park E # 700, Los Angeles (90067-1618)
PHONE.....................310 247-0921
Collin Garcia, *Administration*
Mark Bratt,
EMP: 68
SALES (corp-wide): 69.1MM **Privately Held**
SIC: 8111 General practice attorney, lawyer
PA: Weitz & Luxenberg, P.C.
  700 Broadway Lbby A
  New York NY 10003
  212 558-5500

(P-22869)
WENDEL ROSEN LLP (PA)
1111 Broadway Ste 2400, Oakland (94607-4028)
PHONE.....................510 834-6600
Howard Lance, *Managing Prtnr*
Mark S Bostic, *Partner*
Elizabeth Burke-Dreyfuss, *Partner*
Joan M Cambray, *Partner*
Michael D Cooper, *Partner*
EMP: 110
SQ FT: 40,000
SALES (est): 14MM **Privately Held**
WEB: www.wendel.com
SIC: 8111 General practice attorney, lawyer

(P-22870)
WILMER CUTLER PICK HALE DORR
350 S Grand Ave Ste 2100, Los Angeles (90071-3409)
PHONE.....................213 443-5300
Mark Flanagan, *Partner*
David C Marcus, *Partner*
Sarah Zarrabi, *Associate*
EMP: 247
SALES (corp-wide): 250.3MM **Privately Held**
SIC: 8111 Specialized law offices, attorneys
PA: Wilmer Cutler Pickering Hale And Dorr Llp
  1875 Pennsylvania Ave Nw
  Washington DC 20006
  202 663-6000

(P-22871)
WILSON ELSER MOSKOWITZ
555 S Flower St Ste 2900, Los Angeles (90071-2407)
PHONE.....................213 443-5100
Patrick M Kelly, *Manager*
Martin K Deniston, *Partner*
David Simantob, *Partner*
Delia Guerrero, *Admin Sec*
James Donovan, *Human Res Dir*
EMP: 62
SALES (corp-wide): 307MM **Privately Held**
SIC: 8111 General practice law office
PA: Wilson, Elser, Moskowitz, Edelman & Dicker Llp
  150 E 42nd St Fl 23
  New York NY 10017
  212 490-3000

(P-22872)
WILSON SONSINI GOODRICH & ROSA
12235 El Camino Real # 200, San Diego (92130-3002)
PHONE.....................858 350-2300
Tina Drews, *Office Mgr*
Monica Huettl, *President*
Trina Slama, *Executive Asst*
Steve Warner, *Marketing Staff*
Misty Elam, *Patent Law*
EMP: 120
SALES (corp-wide): 156.6MM **Privately Held**
SIC: 8111 General practice attorney, lawyer
PA: Wilson Sonsini Goodrich & Rosati, Professional Corporation
  650 Page Mill Rd
  Palo Alto CA 94304
  650 493-9300

(P-22873)
WILSON SONSINI GOODRICH & ROSA
633 W 5th St Ste 1540, Los Angeles (90071-3543)
PHONE..................................650 353-6352
Edward Poplawski,
Yongdan LI, *Associate*
EMP: 272
SALES (corp-wide): 156.6MM **Privately Held**
SIC: 8111 Specialized law offices, attorneys
PA: Wilson Sonsini Goodrich & Rosati, Professional Corporation
650 Page Mill Rd
Palo Alto CA 94304
650 493-9300

(P-22874)
WILSON SONSINI GOODRICH & ROSA (PA)
650 Page Mill Rd, Palo Alto (94304-1001)
PHONE..................................650 493-9300
Steven E Bochner, *CEO*
Bradford Obrien, *General Ptnr*
James Clessuras, *Partner*
Jack Sheridan, *Partner*
Effie Toshav, *Partner*
EMP: 1100
SQ FT: 184,000
SALES (est): 156.6MM **Privately Held**
WEB: www.rsklaw.com
SIC: 8111 Corporate, partnership & business law

(P-22875)
WILSON SONSINI GOODRICH & ROSA
1 Market Plz Fl 33, San Francisco (94105-1196)
PHONE..................................415 947-2000
Peter Mostow, *Partner*
Usha Smerdon,
Lauren Lichtblau, *Associate*
EMP: 60
SALES (corp-wide): 156.6MM **Privately Held**
WEB: www.rsklaw.com
SIC: 8111 Corporate, partnership & business law
PA: Wilson Sonsini Goodrich & Rosati, Professional Corporation
650 Page Mill Rd
Palo Alto CA 94304
650 493-9300

(P-22876)
WILSON TURNER KOSMO LLP
402 W Broadway Ste 1600, San Diego (92101-8522)
PHONE..................................619 236-9600
Claudette G Wilson, *Partner*
Frederick W Kosmo Jr, *Partner*
Barbara Boxer,
Wilson Kosmo,
EMP: 54
SALES: 11.4MM **Privately Held**
WEB: www.wilsonturnerkosmo.com/
SIC: 8111 General practice law office

(P-22877)
WINGERT GREBING BRUBAKER & JUS
600 W Broadway Ste 1200, San Diego (92101-3314)
PHONE..................................619 232-8151
Stephen Grebing, *Partner*
Michael Anello, *Partner*
Alan Brubaker, *Partner*
James Goodwin, *Partner*
Charles Grebing, *Partner*
EMP: 100
SALES (est): 11.2MM **Privately Held**
WEB: www.wingertlaw.com
SIC: 8111 General practice attorney, lawyer

(P-22878)
WINSTON & STRAWN LLP
Also Called: Silicon Valley Office
275 Middlefield Rd # 205, Menlo Park (94025-3597)
PHONE..................................650 858-6500
Tom Fitzgerald, *Partner*

EMP: 411
SALES (corp-wide): 296.6MM **Privately Held**
SIC: 8111 Patent, trademark & copyright law
PA: Winston & Strawn Llp
35 W Wacker Dr Ste 4200
Chicago IL 60601
312 558-5600

(P-22879)
WOLF FIRM A LAW CORPORATION
2955 Main St Ste 200, Irvine (92614-2528)
PHONE..................................949 720-9200
Alan S Wolf, *President*
Jenny Giacopelli, *Partner*
Krys Fuller, *COO*
Brenda Britten, *Trustee*
Darlene Clark, *Officer*
EMP: 60 EST: 1993
SALES (est): 8.8MM **Privately Held**
WEB: www.wolffirm.com
SIC: 8111 General practice law office; specialized law offices, attorneys

(P-22880)
WOMBLE BOND DICKINSON (US) LLP
1841 Page Mill Rd Fl 2, Palo Alto (94304-1255)
PHONE..................................408 720-8300
Karen Wilson, *Director*
Bill Holbrow, *Partner*
Gregory Caldwell, *Managing Prtnr*
Michael Goode, *Facilities Mgr*
Bradley J Bereznak,
EMP: 120
SALES (corp-wide): 239.4MM **Privately Held**
WEB: www.bstz.com
SIC: 8111 General practice attorney, lawyer
PA: Womble Bond Dickinson (Us) Llp
1 W 4th St
Winston Salem NC 27101
336 721-3600

(P-22881)
WOOD SMITH HENNING BERMAN LLP (PA)
Also Called: WSH&b
10960 Wilshire Blvd Fl 18, Los Angeles (90024-3804)
PHONE..................................310 481-7600
David Wood, *Partner*
Steven Henning, *Partner*
Kevin Smith, *Partner*
Stewart Reid, *Managing Prtnr*
Susan Montalvo, *Office Mgr*
EMP: 50
SQ FT: 24,500
SALES (est): 48MM **Privately Held**
WEB: www.wshblaw.com
SIC: 8111 General practice law office

(P-22882)
WOODRUFF SPRADLIN & SMART
555 Anton Blvd Ste 1200, Costa Mesa (92626-7670)
PHONE..................................714 558-7000
Ken Smart, *President*
Joseph Forbath, *Shareholder*
Bradley Hogin, *Shareholder*
Thomas L Woodruff, *Treasurer*
Lois E Jeffrey, *Vice Pres*
EMP: 62
SALES (est): 10.3MM **Privately Held**
WEB: www.wss-law.com
SIC: 8111 General practice attorney, lawyer

(P-22883)
WRIGHT FINLAY & ZAK LLP
4665 Macarthur Ct Ste 200, Newport Beach (92660-1811)
PHONE..................................949 477-5050
Robin P Wright, *Managing Prtnr*
Robert Finley, *Partner*
Dana Nitz, *Partner*
Jonathan Zak, *Partner*
Gretchen Grant, *Admin Sec*
EMP: 60

SALES (est): 10.6MM **Privately Held**
WEB: www.wrightlegal.net
SIC: 8111 Corporate, partnership & business law

(P-22884)
YUKEVICH / CVANAUGH A LAW CORP (PA)
355 S Grand Ave Fl 15, Los Angeles (90071-3180)
PHONE..................................213 362-7777
James J Yukevich, *Managing Prtnr*
Alexander Calfo, *Principal*
Todd Cavanaugh, *Principal*
Vivian Powers, *Administration*
EMP: 65
SALES (est): 10.8MM **Privately Held**
WEB: www.asonnettlaw.com
SIC: 8111 General practice law office

(P-22885)
ZELLE LLP
44 Montgomery St Ste 3400, San Francisco (94104-4807)
PHONE..................................415 693-0700
Dan Mason, *Manager*
EMP: 50
SALES (est): 2.4MM **Privately Held**
SALES (corp-wide): 23.3MM **Privately Held**
WEB: www.zelle.com
SIC: 8111 General practice attorney, lawyer
PA: Zelle Llp
500 Washington Ave S # 4000
Minneapolis MN 55415
612 339-2020

(P-22886)
ZIEVE BRODNAX & STEELE LLP (PA)
30 Corporate Park Ste 450, Irvine (92606-3401)
PHONE..................................714 848-7920
Les Zieve, *Principal*
Mark Kayton, *Principal*
Paul Kim, *Project Mgr*
Katherine Kellams, *Opers Mgr*
Crystal Gonzalez, *Legal Staff*
EMP: 105
SQ FT: 1,000
SALES (est): 2.4MM **Privately Held**
SIC: 8111 General practice law office

(P-22887)
ZIFFREN B B F G-L S&C FND
1801 Century Park W, Los Angeles (90067-6409)
PHONE..................................310 552-3388
Kenneth Ziffren, *Owner*
John G Branca, *Principal*
Harry M Brittenham, *Principal*
Steven Burkow, *Principal*
David Byrnes, *Principal*
EMP: 103
SQ FT: 33,000
SALES (est): 16.4MM **Privately Held**
WEB: www.ziffrenlaw.com
SIC: 8111 General practice law office

(P-22888)
ZWICKER & ASSOCIATES PC
1320 Willow Paca Rd 730, Concord (94520)
PHONE..................................925 689-7070
Dawn Valverde, *Human Res Mgr*
EMP: 225
SALES (corp-wide): 94.2MM **Privately Held**
SIC: 8111 General practice attorney, lawyer
PA: Zwicker & Associates, P.C.
80 Minuteman Rd
Andover MA 01810
978 686-2255

8322 Individual & Family Social Svcs

(P-22889)
A PLUS SENIOR CARE INC
4701 Arrow Hwy, Montclair (91763-1229)
PHONE..................................909 989-2563
Gahta Lutfi, *Owner*

EMP: 50
SALES (est): 370.9K **Privately Held**
SIC: 8322 Senior citizens' center or association

(P-22890)
A TOUCH OF KINDNESS
353 1/2 N La Brea Ave, Los Angeles (90036-2517)
P.O. Box 481270 (90048-9761)
PHONE..................................323 997-6500
Yona Landau, *Director*
EMP: 75
SALES (est): 1.1MM **Privately Held**
WEB: www.atouchofkindness.com
SIC: 8322 Public welfare center

(P-22891)
ABILITIES UNITED (PA)
525 E Charleston Rd, Palo Alto (94306-4247)
PHONE..................................650 494-0550
Charlie Weidanz, *CEO*
Jane Machin, *CFO*
Soheila Razban, *Vice Pres*
Misty Accristo, *Program Mgr*
Tim Harper, *Admin Sec*
EMP: 85
SQ FT: 4,000
SALES: 6.4MM **Privately Held**
WEB: www.c-a-r.org
SIC: 8322 8361 Multi-service center; residential care

(P-22892)
ABILITYFIRST
Also Called: LL Frank Work Center
3812 S Grand Ave, Los Angeles (90037-1336)
PHONE..................................213 748-7309
Fennie Washington, *Director*
EMP: 80
SQ FT: 15,854
SALES (corp-wide): 14.3MM **Privately Held**
WEB: www.abilityfirst.org
SIC: 8322 8093 Association for the handicapped; rehabilitation center, outpatient treatment
PA: Abilityfirst
1300 E Green St
Pasadena CA 91106
626 396-1010

(P-22893)
ABODE SERVICES (PA)
40849 Fremont Blvd, Fremont (94538-4306)
PHONE..................................510 657-7409
Louis Chicoine, *Exec Dir*
Sophora Acheson, *Social Dir*
Janine Evans, *Social Dir*
Dario Loeb, *Info Tech Mgr*
Cindy Rancatore, *Project Mgr*
EMP: 70
SALES: 30MM **Privately Held**
WEB: www.tricityhomeless.org
SIC: 8322 Social service center

(P-22894)
ABRAZAR INC
Also Called: ABRAZAR ELDERLY ASSISTANCE
7101 Wyoming St, Westminster (92683-3811)
PHONE..................................714 893-3581
Gloria Reyes, *CEO*
Mario Ortega, *COO*
EMP: 80
SALES: 8.2MM **Privately Held**
WEB: www.abrazarinc.com
SIC: 8322 Social service center

(P-22895)
ADMINSTRTIVE OFFICE OF US CRTS
Also Called: United States Fdral Prbatn
280 S 1st St, San Jose (95113-3002)
PHONE..................................408 535-5200
Sue Rossi, *Office Mgr*
EMP: 69 **Publicly Held**
WEB: www.ao.uscourts.gov
SIC: 8322 Probation office

HQ: The United States Courts Administrative Office Of
1 Columbus Cir Ne
Washington DC 20544
202 502-3800

(P-22896)
ADMINSTRTIVE OFFICE OF US CRTS
Also Called: United States Probation Office
101 W Broadway Ste 700, San Diego
(92101-8208)
PHONE...................................619 557-6650
Kennith O Young, *Director*
EMP: 200 **Publicly Held**
WEB: www.ao.uscourts.gov
SIC: **8322** 9211 Individual & family services; courts;
HQ: The United States Courts Administrative Office Of
1 Columbus Cir Ne
Washington DC 20544
202 502-3800

(P-22897)
AFRICAN AMERICAN UNITY CENTER
Also Called: A A U C
944 W 53rd St, Los Angeles (90037-3643)
PHONE...................................323 789-7300
Charisse Bermond, *Exec Dir*
Will Harris, *Principal*
Elondra Jackson, *Principal*
EMP: 62
SALES: 683.8K **Privately Held**
SIC: **8322** 8331 Social service center; job training & vocational rehabilitation services

(P-22898)
AGE CONCERNS INC
2650 Camino Del Rio N # 203, San Diego
(92108-1621)
PHONE...................................619 544-1622
Ed Petrivelli, *Exec Dir*
Laura Spitler-Hansen, *President*
EMP: 295
SQ FT: 2,700
SALES (est): 1.9MM
SALES (corp-wide): 50.6MM **Privately Held**
SIC: **8322** 8082 7361 Geriatric social service; home health care services; nurses' registry
PA: Livhome, Inc.
5670 Wilshire Blvd # 500
Los Angeles CA 90036
800 807-5854

(P-22899)
AIDS PROJECT LOS ANGELES (PA)
Also Called: Aids Project La
611 S Kingsley Dr, Los Angeles
(90005-2319)
PHONE...................................213 201-1600
Craig E Thompson, *CEO*
Robyn Goldman, *CFO*
EMP: 90
SALES: 10.3MM **Privately Held**
SIC: **8322** Social service center

(P-22900)
AIDS SVCS FNDATION ORANGE CNTY
Also Called: A.S. Foundation-Orange County
17982 Sky Park Cir Ste J, Irvine
(92614-6482)
PHONE...................................949 809-5700
Alan Witchey, *Exec Dir*
EMP: 66
SQ FT: 16,051
SALES: 8.9MM **Privately Held**
SIC: **8322** 8011 Social service center; clinic, operated by physicians

(P-22901)
ALAMEDA CNTY CMNTY FD BNK INC
7900 Edgewater Dr, Oakland (94621-2004)
P.O. Box 2599 (94614-0599)
PHONE...................................510 635-3663
Suzan Bateson, *President*
EMP: 70
SQ FT: 118,000

SALES: 75.6MM **Privately Held**
WEB: www.accfb.org
SIC: **8322** Social service center

(P-22902)
ALDEA INC
470 Chadbourne Rd Ste F, Fairfield
(94534-9620)
PHONE...................................925 577-3102
EMP: 65
SALES (corp-wide): 11.1MM **Privately Held**
SIC: **8322** Individual & family services
PA: Aldea, Inc.
1546 1st St
Napa CA 94559
707 224-8266

(P-22903)
ALL CARE SERVICES INC
17671 Irvine Blvd Ste 110, Tustin
(92780-3128)
PHONE...................................714 669-1148
Lynn Stevens, *Director*
Kenneth E Stevens, *Administration*
EMP: 100
SALES: 2.5MM **Privately Held**
WEB: www.allcareservices.com
SIC: **8322** Old age assistance

(P-22904)
ALTA CAL REGIONAL CTR INC
950 Tharp Rd Ste 202, Yuba City
(95993-8345)
PHONE...................................530 674-3070
Terry Rhoades, *Manager*
EMP: 300
SALES (corp-wide): 383.5MM **Privately Held**
WEB: www.altaregional.org
SIC: **8322** 8699 General counseling services; charitable organization
PA: Alta California Regional Center, Inc.
2241 Harvard St Ste 100
Sacramento CA 95815
916 978-6400

(P-22905)
ALTA LOMA ASSISTED LIVING LLC
Also Called: Sunlit Gardens
9428 19th St, Murrieta (92562)
PHONE...................................909 481-2600
Ernest Hix, *Mng Member*
Sharon Hix,
EMP: 66
SALES (est): 1.3MM **Privately Held**
SIC: **8322** Old age assistance

(P-22906)
ALZHEIMERS GREATER LOS ANGELES
4221 Wilshire Blvd # 400, Los Angeles
(90010-3512)
PHONE...................................323 938-3379
Heather Cooper Ortner, *President*
Debra Cherry, *Exec VP*
Kara Bonela, *Vice Pres*
John Seiber, *Vice Pres*
Martha Chavez, *Accountant*
EMP: 58
SALES: 5.5MM **Privately Held**
SIC: **8322** Geriatric social service

(P-22907)
AMERICAN CARE GIVERS WESTWOOD
947 Tiverton Ave Ste 533, Los Angeles
(90024-3012)
PHONE...................................310 208-8005
Vicky London, *President*
Denise London, *CFO*
David London, *Vice Pres*
EMP: 60
SALES (est): 1.1MM **Privately Held**
WEB: www.americancaregivers.com
SIC: **8322** Geriatric social service

(P-22908)
AMERICAN NATIONAL RED CROSS
601 N Golden Circle Dr, Santa Ana
(92705-3902)
P.O. Box 11364 (92711-1364)
PHONE...................................714 481-5300

Stanley Perdue, *Branch Mgr*
EMP: 50
SQ FT: 30,092
SALES (corp-wide): 2.6B **Privately Held**
WEB: www.redcross.org
SIC: **8322** Social service center
PA: The American National Red Cross
430 17th St Nw
Washington DC 20006
202 737-8300

(P-22909)
AMERICAN NATIONAL RED CROSS
Also Called: American Nat Red Cross - Blood
85 2nd St Ste 800, San Francisco
(94105-3466)
PHONE...................................415 427-8134
Harold Brooks, *Manager*
EMP: 120
SALES (corp-wide): 2.6B **Privately Held**
WEB: www.redcross.org
SIC: **8322** Social service center
PA: The American National Red Cross
430 17th St Nw
Washington DC 20006
202 737-8300

(P-22910)
AMERICAN NATIONAL RED CROSS
Also Called: American Red Cross
1300 Alberta Way, Concord (94521-3705)
PHONE...................................925 603-7400
Harold Brooks, *Principal*
EMP: 50
SQ FT: 4,765
SALES (corp-wide): 2.6B **Privately Held**
SIC: **8322** Individual & family services
PA: The American National Red Cross
430 17th St Nw
Washington DC 20006
202 737-8300

(P-22911)
AMERICAN NATIONAL RED CROSS
11355 Ohio Ave, Los Angeles
(90025-3266)
PHONE...................................310 445-9900
Enrique Rivera, *Office Mgr*
Brian Kilb, *Partner*
EMP: 100
SALES (corp-wide): 2.6B **Privately Held**
WEB: www.redcross.org
SIC: **8322** Individual & family services
PA: The American National Red Cross
430 17th St Nw
Washington DC 20006
202 737-8300

(P-22912)
AMERICAN NATIONAL RED CROSS
3950 Calle Fortunada, San Diego
(92123-1827)
PHONE...................................858 309-1200
Dodie Rotherham, *CEO*
EMP: 90
SALES (corp-wide): 2.6B **Privately Held**
WEB: www.redcross.org
SIC: **8322** Social service center
PA: The American National Red Cross
430 17th St Nw
Washington DC 20006
202 737-8300

(P-22913)
AMERICAN RED CROSS LA CHAPTER (PA)
1320 Newton St, Los Angeles
(90021-2724)
PHONE...................................310 445-9900
Roger Dixon, *CEO*
Kirk Richard Hyde, *Ch of Bd*
Scott J Olmsted, *Ch of Bd*
Michelle McCarthy, *CFO*
Thomas E Stephenson, *CFO*
EMP: 150
SALES (est): 15.1MM **Privately Held**
SIC: **8322** Social service center

(P-22914)
AMERICAN RED CROSS SAN DIEGO (PA)
3950 Calle Fortunada, San Diego
(92123-1827)
PHONE...................................858 309-1200
Joe Craver, *CEO*
Ashley Schmeltzer, *Officer*
Lara Kiefer, *Exec Dir*
Amy Meister, *Exec Dir*
Kim Kentolall, *Executive Asst*
EMP: 200
SALES (est): 6.9MM **Privately Held**
SIC: **8322** Individual & family services

(P-22915)
AMERICAN WHT MSSN IN STHRN
7212 Orangethorpe Ave 7a, Buena Park
(90621-3341)
P.O. Box 1400, Cypress (90630-6400)
PHONE...................................714 522-4599
Young Lee, *Owner*
EMP: 100
SALES (est): 1MM **Privately Held**
SIC: **8322** Temporary relief service

(P-22916)
ANTELOPE VALLEY FOUNDATION
Also Called: DAYSTAR FOUNDATION
646 W Lancaster Blvd # 109, Lancaster
(93534-3154)
PHONE...................................661 945-7290
Steven Sultan, *President*
Dorothy Edgar, *CEO*
Linda Harris, *Sales Executive*
EMP: 50
SQ FT: 11,000
SALES: 2MM **Privately Held**
SIC: **8322** 5999 Individual & family services; technical aids for the handicapped

(P-22917)
ANTELOPE VLY DOM VLNCE COUNCIL (PA)
Also Called: VALLEY OASIS SHELTER
43434 Sahuayo St, Lancaster
(93535-4659)
P.O. Box 2980 (93539-2980)
PHONE...................................661 723-7772
Carol Crabson, *Exec Dir*
Darryl Kniss, *CFO*
Toni Severino, *Accountant*
EMP: 52
SQ FT: 16,500
SALES: 10.9MM **Privately Held**
SIC: **8322** 8361 Individual & family services; halfway group home, persons with social or personal problems

(P-22918)
ARC - IMPERIAL VALLEY (PA)
298 E Ross Ave, El Centro (92243-9303)
P.O. Box 1828 (92244-1828)
PHONE...................................760 352-0180
Arturo Santos, *CEO*
Poli Flores, *President*
Art Santos, *Exec Dir*
Martha Carrillo, *General Mgr*
Sherri Gutierrez, *Admin Sec*
EMP: 60
SQ FT: 22,000
SALES: 10.8MM **Privately Held**
SIC: **8322** 4729 8361 Adult day care center; carpool/vanpool arrangement; home for the mentally handicapped

(P-22919)
ARC OF ALAMEDA COUNTY (PA)
14700 Doolittle Dr, San Leandro
(94577-6619)
PHONE...................................510 357-3569
Ron Luter, *Exec Dir*
Frank Alvarado, *President*
Sandie Craven, *Admin Sec*
Angie Tam, *Technology*
Francis Zamora, *Production*
▲ EMP: 135 EST: 1969
SQ FT: 66,000
SALES: 4MM **Privately Held**
WEB: www.tiw-alameda.com
SIC: **8322** Association for the handicapped

(P-22920)
ARC OF BUTTE COUNTY (PA)
2030 Park Ave, Chico (95928-6701)
P.O. Box 3697 (95927-3697)
PHONE..............................530 891-5865
Courtney Casey, *CEO*
Michael McGinnis, *CEO*
Jean Campbell, *Treasurer*
Nelson Corwin, *Associate Dir*
Tom Leonardi, *Associate Dir*
EMP: 200
SQ FT: 12,268
SALES: 7.5MM **Privately Held**
WEB: www.arcbutte.org
SIC: 8322 Individual & family services

(P-22921)
ARC STARLIGHT CENTER
Also Called: ARC of San Diego
1280 Nolan Ave, Chula Vista (91911-3738)
PHONE..............................619 427-7524
Terri Thorn, *Director*
EMP: 70
SALES (est): 1.6MM **Privately Held**
SIC: 8322 Social services for the handi-
capped

(P-22922)
ARGONAUT KENSINGTON ASSOCIATES
Also Called: Kensington Place
1580 Geary Rd Ofc, Walnut Creek
(94597-2786)
PHONE..............................925 943-1121
Richard Fordiani, *Partner*
James Houston, *Partner*
EMP: 60
SALES (est): 2.9MM **Privately Held**
SIC: 8322 Senior citizens' center or associ-
ation

(P-22923)
ARMENIAN AMERCN CUNCIL ON AGING
Also Called: Armenn-Mrican Council On
Aging
407 E Colorado St, Glendale (91205-1604)
PHONE..............................818 241-8690
Mardiros Edgarian, *Director*
Minas Dersarkissian, *Treasurer*
EMP: 50
SQ FT: 5,600
SALES: 47.7K **Privately Held**
SIC: 8322 Senior citizens' center or associ-
ation

(P-22924)
ARROYO DEVELOPMENTAL SERVICES
1839 Potrero Grande Dr, Monterey Park
(91755-5847)
PHONE..............................626 307-2240
Robert Wark, *President*
Duran Archie, *Program Dir*
George Barnes, *Supervisor*
EMP: 60
SQ FT: 1,232
SALES (est): 1.5MM **Privately Held**
SIC: 8322 Individual & family services

(P-22925)
ARTS AND SERVICES FOR DISABLED
3626 E Pacific Coast Hwy, Long Beach
(90804-2015)
PHONE..............................562 377-0302
Kay Hagen, *Director*
EMP: 50
SALES: 2.6MM **Privately Held**
SIC: 8322 Association for the handicapped

(P-22926)
ASANA INTEGRATED MEDICAL GROUP
6200 Canoga Ave Ste 350, Woodland Hills
(91367-7782)
PHONE..............................888 212-7545
Nitin Nanda, *Principal*
EMP: 95
SALES (est): 2.3MM
SALES (corp-wide): 287.4MM **Privately
Held**
SIC: 8322 General counseling services

HQ: Ipc Healthcare, Inc.
4605 Lankershim Blvd
North Hollywood CA 91602
888 447-2362

(P-22927)
ASIAN AMERCN RECOVERY SVCS INC (PA)
1115 Mission Rd 2, South San Francisco
(94080-1302)
PHONE..............................650 243-4888
Tony Doug, *Exec Dir*
EMP: 160
SALES (est): 6MM **Privately Held**
WEB: www.aars-inc.org
SIC: 8322 8069 General counseling serv-
ices; substance abuse counseling; drug
addiction rehabilitation hospital

(P-22928)
ASIAN COMMUNITY CENTER OF SAC (PA)
Also Called: ACC SENIOR SERVICES
7334 Park City Dr, Sacramento
(95831-3865)
PHONE..............................916 394-6399
William Yee, *President*
King Gee, *CFO*
Jean Shiomoto, *Vice Pres*
Judi Keen, *Admin Sec*
Tony Waterford, *Human Res Dir*
EMP: 150
SALES: 23.2MM **Privately Held**
WEB: www.accsv.org
SIC: 8322 8059 Community center; nurs-
ing home, except skilled & intermediate
care facility

(P-22929)
ASPEN YOUTH INC
17777 Center Court Dr N # 300, Cerritos
(90703-9320)
PHONE..............................562 567-5507
Elliot A Sainer, *Exec Dir*
EMP: 69
SALES (est): 471.8K **Publicly Held**
SIC: 8322 Individual & family services
HQ: Aspen Education Group, Inc.
17777 Center Court Dr N # 300
Cerritos CA 90703
562 467-5500

(P-22930)
ASPIRANET
151 E Canal Dr, Turlock (95380-3901)
PHONE..............................209 669-2582
Sharon Salaiz, *Manager*
Anne Gable, *Consultant*
EMP: 61
SALES (corp-wide): 59MM **Privately
Held**
SIC: 8322 Adoption services
PA: Aspiranet
400 Oyster Point Blvd # 501
South San Francisco CA 94080
650 866-4080

(P-22931)
ASPIRANET
Also Called: Excell Center, The
2513 Youngstown Rd, Turlock
(95380-9707)
PHONE..............................209 667-0327
Christopher Essary, *Principal*
EMP: 60
SALES (corp-wide): 59MM **Privately
Held**
WEB: www.verosantes.com
SIC: 8322 8361 Child related social serv-
ices; residential care
PA: Aspiranet
400 Oyster Point Blvd # 501
South San Francisco CA 94080
650 866-4080

(P-22932)
ASSOCIATED STUDENTS INC (PA)
Also Called: ASSICIATED STUDENTS
University Un Bldg 65, San Luis Obispo
(93407)
PHONE..............................805 756-1281
Richard Johnson, *Director*
Dwayne Brummett, *Business Mgr*
EMP: 70

SQ FT: 110,000
SALES: 12.7MM **Privately Held**
SIC: 8322 8221 Multi-service center; col-
leges universities & professional schools

(P-22933)
AUTISM OTRACH SOUTHERN CAL LLC
3110 Cmino Del Rio S 30, San Diego
(92108)
PHONE..............................619 795-9925
Abigail R Bun, *Mng Member*
Abigail Bunt, *Principal*
Patrick Bunt, *Opers Dir*
Elizabeth Jordan, *Director*
EMP: 75
SALES: 4MM **Privately Held**
SIC: 8322 Individual & family services

(P-22934)
AVENIDAS (PA)
Also Called: AVENIDAS SENIOR HEALTH
DAY HEA
4000 Middlefield Rd Ste I, Palo Alto
(94303-4761)
PHONE..............................650 289-5400
Lisa Hendrickson, *President*
Sue Campbell, *Treasurer*
Morien Breen, *Vice Pres*
Mary Hohensee, *Vice Pres*
Annette Bialson, *Admin Sec*
EMP: 60
SQ FT: 25,000
SALES: 12.6MM **Privately Held**
WEB: www.avenidas.org
SIC: 8322 Senior citizens' center or associ-
ation

(P-22935)
BAY AREA COMMUNITY SVCS INC (PA)
Also Called: East Bay Transitional Homes
390 40th St, Oakland (94609-2633)
PHONE..............................510 613-0330
Jamie Almanza, *CEO*
David Stoloff, *Chairman*
Amanda Callow, *Program Mgr*
Asha Koshy, *Program Mgr*
Chris Llorente, *Program Mgr*
EMP: 50
SQ FT: 1,000
SALES: 1MM **Privately Held**
WEB: www.bayareacs.org
SIC: 8322 Senior citizens' center or associ-
ation

(P-22936)
BAY AREA SENIOR SERVICES INC
Also Called: Peninsula Regent, The
1 Baldwin Ave Ofc, San Mateo
(94401-3837)
PHONE..............................650 579-5500
M Mannstab, *Exec Dir*
EMP: 140
SALES (corp-wide): 30.6MM **Privately
Held**
WEB: www.peninsularegent.com
SIC: 8322 Senior citizens' center or associ-
ation
HQ: Bay Area Senior Services Inc
1 Hawthorne St Ste 400
San Francisco CA 94105
415 989-1111

(P-22937)
BEACON HEALTH OPTIONS INC
10805 Holder St Ste 300, Cypress
(90630-5147)
PHONE..............................714 763-2405
Steve Rockowitz, *Principal*
EMP: 111
SALES (corp-wide): 482.1MM **Privately
Held**
SIC: 8322 Individual & family services
HQ: Beacon Health Options, Inc.
200 State St Ste 302
Boston MA 02109
757 459-5100

(P-22938)
BEHAVIORAL HEALTH SERVICES INC (PA)
15519 Crenshaw Blvd, Gardena
(90249-4525)
PHONE..............................310 679-9031
Henry Van Oudheudsen, *CEO*
Lawrence T Gentile, *President*
Andy Worrell, *CFO*
Ballue Michael, *Officer*
Juan Pena, *Opers Mgr*
EMP: 50
SQ FT: 35,000
SALES: 21MM **Privately Held**
SIC: 8322 Substance abuse counseling;
alcoholism counseling, nontreatment;
drug abuse counselor, nontreatment; sen-
ior citizens' center or association

(P-22939)
BEHAVIORAL HEALTH SERVICES INC
Also Called: Redgate Memorial Hospital
1775 Chestnut Ave, Long Beach
(90813-1674)
PHONE..............................562 599-4194
Robert Worrell, *Director*
EMP: 65
SQ FT: 21,780
SALES (corp-wide): 21MM **Privately
Held**
SIC: 8322 8069 Substance abuse coun-
seling; alcoholism rehabilitation hospital
PA: Behavioral Health Services, Inc.
15519 Crenshaw Blvd
Gardena CA 90249
310 679-9031

(P-22940)
BEHAVIORAL HEALTH SERVICES INC
Also Called: American Recovery Center
2180 Valley Blvd, Pomona (91768-3325)
PHONE..............................909 865-2336
Booker Blebsoe, *Administration*
Rory Moore, *Hlthcr Dir*
Son Hong J Le, *Director*
EMP: 100
SQ FT: 40,868
SALES (corp-wide): 21MM **Privately
Held**
SIC: 8322 8093 8361 Drug abuse coun-
selor, nontreatment; specialty outpatient
clinics; residential care
PA: Behavioral Health Services, Inc.
15519 Crenshaw Blvd
Gardena CA 90249
310 679-9031

(P-22941)
BEHAVIORAL LEARNING CENTER INC
28245 Avenue Crocker # 220, Valencia
(91355-0940)
PHONE..............................661 254-7086
Jody Stiegemeyer, *President*
Danielle Sheehy, *Admin Sec*
Kim Loth, *Administration*
EMP: 99 **EST:** 2007
SQ FT: 4,000
SALES (est): 4.1MM **Privately Held**
SIC: 8322 Child related social services

(P-22942)
BEHAVORAL AUTISM THERAPIES LLC (PA)
2930 Inland Empire Blvd, Ontario
(91764-4802)
PHONE..............................909 483-5000
Mia Humphreys, *Mng Member*
Larry Humphreys,
Psyd Natalie Garcia Bcb, *Director*
Natalie Garcia, *Director*
Joanna Herrera, *Supervisor*
EMP: 247 **EST:** 2013
SQ FT: 2,000
SALES (est): 5.6MM **Privately Held**
SIC: 8322 Individual & family services

PRODUCTS & SVCS

(P-22943)
BERNARD OSHER MARIN JEWISH COM
Also Called: J C C
200 N San Pedro Rd, San Rafael (94903-4213)
PHONE..................415 444-8000
Marty Friedman, *President*
George Mann, *CFO*
Mark Goodman, *Treasurer*
Deborah Stadtner, *Vice Pres*
Karen Young, *Vice Pres*
EMP: 200
SQ FT: 90,000
SALES: 12.7MM **Privately Held**
SIC: 8322 Community center

(P-22944)
BETTER WAY SERVICES
5329 Office Center Ct # 100, Bakersfield (93309-7425)
PHONE..................661 326-6444
Jim Kirkendole, *President*
EMP: 100 EST: 2000
SQ FT: 4,000
SALES: (est) 3MM **Privately Held**
SIC: 8322 Individual & family services

(P-22945)
BIRTH CHOICE OF SAN MARCO
277 S Rancho Santa Fe Rd, San Marcos (92078-2343)
PHONE..................760 744-1313
Rose Mary Brown, *Director*
EMP: 60
SALES: 368.4K **Privately Held**
SIC: 8322 Individual & family services

(P-22946)
BLC RESIDENTIAL CARE INC
1455 W 112th St, Los Angeles (90047-4926)
PHONE..................310 722-7541
Brenda Chandler, *President*
EMP: 80 EST: 2004
SALES: (est) 2.1MM **Privately Held**
SIC: 8322 Adult day care center

(P-22947)
BONITA HOUSE INC
6333 Telg Ave Ste 102, Oakland (94609)
PHONE..................510 923-0180
Rick Crispino, *Exec Dir*
Lorna Jones, *Exec Dir*
Lori Magistrado, *General Mgr*
Steve Alimonti, *Opers Mgr*
Allegra Count, *Opers Mgr*
EMP: 76
SQ FT: 4,000
SALES: 7.8MM **Privately Held**
SIC: 8322 Association for the handicapped

(P-22948)
BRAILLE INSTITUTE AMERICA INC (PA)
741 N Vermont Ave, Los Angeles (90029-3594)
PHONE..................323 663-1111
Lester M Sussman, *Ch of Bd*
Peter Mindnich, *President*
Les Stocker, *President*
Reza Rahman, *CFO*
Rezaur Rahman, *Vice Pres*
EMP: 208 EST: 1919
SQ FT: 167,079
SALES: 34MM **Privately Held**
SIC: 8322 8231 2731 2759 Individual & family services; specialized libraries; textbooks: publishing & printing; commercial printing

(P-22949)
BREAKOUT PRISON OUTREACH
Also Called: California Youth Outreach
1560 Berger Dr, San Jose (95112-2703)
P.O. Box 8671, Fresno (93747-8671)
PHONE..................408 702-2405
Anthony Ortiz, *President*
Kurt Foreman, *Treasurer*
Sandra Martinez, *Admin Sec*
Mark Riddle, *Accountant*
EMP: 72
SQ FT: 1,800
SALES: (est) 4.5MM **Privately Held**
SIC: 8322 Youth center

(P-22950)
BRIGHTER BEGINNINGS (PA)
3478 Buskirk Ave Ste 105, Pleasant Hill (94523-4345)
PHONE..................510 903-7503
Barbara B McCullough, *CEO*
Liz Nickels, *Director*
EMP: 60
SALES: 5.4MM **Privately Held**
WEB: www.brighter-beginnings.org
SIC: 8322 8011 8093 Individual & family services; primary care medical clinic; mental health clinic, outpatient

(P-22951)
BUCKELEW PROGRAMS (PA)
1401 Los Gamos Dr Ste 240, San Rafael (94903-1835)
PHONE..................415 457-6964
Tamara Player, *CEO*
Alex Tolkach, *Opers Staff*
Teresa Bowman, *Director*
EMP: 150 EST: 1970
SALES: 15MM **Privately Held**
WEB: www.buckelew.org
SIC: 8322 Social services for the handicapped

(P-22952)
CALIFORNIA CHILD CARE RESOURC
Also Called: Infant/Toddler Consort
5232 Claremont Ave, Oakland (94618-1033)
PHONE..................510 658-0381
Betty Cohen, *Exec Dir*
EMP: 50
SALES: (est) 287.8K
SALES: (corp-wide): 3.8MM **Privately Held**
WEB: www.rrnetwork.org
SIC: 8322 Referral service for personal & social problems
PA: California Child Care Resource And Referral Network
1182 Market St Ste 300
San Francisco CA 94102
415 882-0234

(P-22953)
CALIFORNIA CHILDCARE RESOURCE (PA)
1182 Market St Ste 300, San Francisco (94102-4919)
PHONE..................415 882-0234
Linda Asato, *CEO*
Lena Bilik, *Executive Asst*
Linda Eskridge, *VP Mktg*
Cindy Mall, *Director*
Gretchen Schwab, *Assistant*
EMP: 71
SQ FT: 4,000
SALES: 3.8MM **Privately Held**
WEB: www.rrnetwork.org
SIC: 8322 Child related social services; referral service for personal & social problems

(P-22954)
CALIFORNIA PEDIATRIC FMLY SVCS
Also Called: ABLE
326 E Foothill Blvd, Azusa (91702-2515)
PHONE..................626 812-0055
Louise Vanzee PHD, *President*
Faviola Acevedo, *Manager*
EMP: 75
SQ FT: 2,417
SALES: 228.3K **Privately Held**
WEB: www.cal-peds.com
SIC: 8322 Family counseling services

(P-22955)
CAN-DO
Also Called: Compass Actn Netwk Direct Outcm
578 Washington Blvd 39o, Marina Del Rey (90292-5421)
PHONE..................646 228-7049
Eric Klein, *Director*
EMP: 60
SALES: (est) 539.1K **Privately Held**
SIC: 8322 Disaster service

(P-22956)
CARE 4 U LLC
22726 Eccles St, West Hills (91304-3324)
P.O. Box 10297, Canoga Park (91309-1297)
PHONE..................818 593-7911
Ralph Stokes,
Orli Almog,
EMP: 56
SALES: 225K **Privately Held**
SIC: 8322 Social service center

(P-22957)
CAREFIELD SOLANA LLC
201 Lomas Santa Fe Dr, Solana Beach (92075-1299)
PHONE..................858 259-5591
EMP: 50
SALES: (est) 184.5K **Privately Held**
SIC: 8322 Senior citizens' center or association

(P-22958)
CARESCOPE LLC
1455 Response Rd Ste 120, Sacramento (95815-4848)
P.O. Box 2121 (95812-2121)
PHONE..................916 780-1384
Okja Sim,
Frank Sim, *General Mgr*
EMP: 60
SALES: (est) 985.2K **Privately Held**
SIC: 8322 Senior citizens' center or association

(P-22959)
CAREWORKS HEALTH SERVICES
18682 Beach Blvd Ste 225, Huntington Beach (92648-2079)
PHONE..................949 859-4700
Anh Tu Dang, *President*
EMP: 65
SALES: (est) 63.8K **Privately Held**
SIC: 8322 Senior citizens' center or association

(P-22960)
CASA ALLEGRA COMMUNITY SVCS
35 Mitchell Blvd Ste 8, San Rafael (94903-2012)
PHONE..................415 499-1116
Jeanne Santangelo, *Director*
Mia Brown, *Bd of Directors*
EMP: 70
SALES: 4.7MM **Privately Held**
SIC: 8322 Individual & family services

(P-22961)
CASA COLINA INC (PA)
Also Called: Casa Colina Hospital & Ctr
255 E Bonita Ave, Pomona (91767-1933)
PHONE..................909 596-7733
Felice L Loverso, *CEO*
Elizabeth Janairo, *Lab Dir*
Beth Janiro, *Lab Dir*
Nirmal Patel, *Business Dir*
Shawna Sharp, *Ch Nursing Ofcr*
EMP: 800 EST: 1981
SALES: 111.2MM **Privately Held**
SIC: 8322 8011 Rehabilitation services; ambulatory surgical center

(P-22962)
CASA PACIFICA CENTERS (PA)
1722 S Lewis Rd, Camarillo (93012-8520)
PHONE..................805 482-3260
Steven E Elson, *CEO*
Polly Huffer, *Partner*
Felice Ginsberg, *CFO*
Michael Redard, *CFO*
Lynne Gibbons, *Admin Mgr*
EMP: 175
SQ FT: 63,000
SALES: 29.5MM **Privately Held**
WEB: www.casapacifica.org
SIC: 8322 8361 8211 Child related social services; residential care for children; specialty education

(P-22963)
CASPAR COMMUNITY
15051 Caspar Rd, Caspar (95420-0114)
P.O. Box 84 (95420)
PHONE..................707 964-4997
Judy Parbell, *President*
Rochelle Elkan, *Treasurer*
Maryflannery Kaurt, *Treasurer*
Dalen Anderson, *Admin Sec*
EMP: 50
SALES: 151K **Privately Held**
SIC: 8322 Community center

(P-22964)
CATHOLIC CHARITIES DIOCESE (PA)
1106 N El Dorado St, Stockton (95202-1332)
PHONE..................209 444-5900
Elvira Ramirez, *Exec Dir*
Hugo Chiprez, *Executive Asst*
Carmen Thompkins, *Administration*
Robyn Aronna, *Legal Staff*
Rosie Darcy, *Director*
EMP: 100
SQ FT: 3,600
SALES: 4.3MM **Privately Held**
WEB: www.catholiccharitiesstk.org
SIC: 8322 Social service center; old age assistance; association for the handicapped

(P-22965)
CATHOLIC CHARITIES DIOCESE SAN
Also Called: Refugee Resettlement
4575 Mission Gorge Pl A, San Diego (92120-4106)
PHONE..................619 287-9454
Robert Moser, *Director*
EMP: 50
SALES: (corp-wide): 13.2MM **Privately Held**
SIC: 8322 Refugee service
PA: Catholic Charities, Diocese Of San Diego
3888 Paducah Dr
San Diego CA 92117
619 323-2841

(P-22966)
CATHOLIC CHARITIES OF LA INC
21600 Hart St, Canoga Park (91303)
PHONE..................818 883-6015
EMP: 50
SALES: (corp-wide): 29MM **Privately Held**
SIC: 8322
PA: Catholic Charities Of Los Angeles, Inc.
1531 James M Wood Blvd
Los Angeles CA 90015
213 251-3400

(P-22967)
CATHOLIC CHARITIES OF LA INC
1400 James M Wood Blvd, Los Angeles (90015-1210)
P.O. Box 15095 (90015-0095)
PHONE..................213 251-3400
James E Bathker, *Branch Mgr*
EMP: 71
SALES: (corp-wide): 34.2MM **Privately Held**
SIC: 8322 Social service center
PA: Catholic Charities Of Los Angeles, Inc.
1531 James M Wood Blvd
Los Angeles CA 90015
213 251-3400

(P-22968)
CATHOLIC CHARITIES OF SANTA CL (PA)
2625 Zanker Rd Ste 200, San Jose (95134-2130)
PHONE..................408 468-0100
Gregory Kepferle, *CEO*
Susan L Taylor, *Officer*
Lin Velasquez, *Officer*
Milton Cadena, *Program Mgr*
Wanda Hale, *Program Mgr*
EMP: 200
SQ FT: 50,000

SALES: 35.7MM **Privately Held**
SIC: 8322 Social service center

(P-22969)
CATHOLIC CHARITIES OF SANTA CL
303 N Ventura Ave Ste A, Ventura
(93001-1961)
PHONE....................805 643-4694
Robert Batdazian, *Director*
EMP: 60
SALES (corp-wide): 30.6MM **Privately Held**
SIC: 8322 Family counseling services
PA: Catholic Charities Of Santa Clara
County
2625 Zanker Rd Ste 200
San Jose CA 95134
408 468-0100

(P-22970)
CATHOLIC CHARITIES OF THE DIOC (PA)
Also Called: CATHOLIC CHARITIES OF EAST BAY
433 Jefferson St, Oakland (94607-3592)
PHONE....................510 768-3100
Chuck Fernandez, *Exec Dir*
EMP: 90
SQ FT: 10,376
SALES: 6.8MM **Privately Held**
SIC: 8322 8661 Social service center; religious organizations

(P-22971)
CATHOLIC CHRTS CYO ARCHDIOCS
810 Avenue D, San Francisco
(94130-2002)
PHONE....................415 743-0017
Nella Goncalves, *Principal*
EMP: 61
SALES (corp-wide): 39.6MM **Privately Held**
SIC: 8322 Social service center
PA: Catholic Charities Cyo Of The Archdiocese Of San Francisco
990 Eddy St
San Francisco CA 94109
415 972-1200

(P-22972)
CATHOLIC CHRTS CYO ARCHDIOCS
Also Called: Leland House
141 Leland Ave, San Francisco
(94134-2847)
PHONE....................415 405-2000
Jeff Bialik, *Exec Dir*
Jose Cartagena, *Program Mgr*
EMP: 61
SALES (corp-wide): 39.6MM **Privately Held**
SIC: 8322 Child guidance agency
PA: Catholic Charities Cyo Of The Archdiocese Of San Francisco
990 Eddy St
San Francisco CA 94109
415 972-1200

(P-22973)
CATHOLIC CHRTS CYO ARCHDIOCS
1111 Junipero Serra Blvd, San Francisco
(94132-2653)
PHONE....................415 334-5550
Jeffrey Bialik V, *Principal*
Lucia Lopez, *Case Mgr*
EMP: 61
SALES (corp-wide): 39.6MM **Privately Held**
SIC: 8322 Social service center
PA: Catholic Charities Cyo Of The Archdiocese Of San Francisco
990 Eddy St
San Francisco CA 94109
415 972-1200

(P-22974)
CATHOLIC CHRTS CYO ARCHDIOCS
Also Called: Derek Silva Community
20 Franklin St, San Francisco
(94102-6000)
PHONE....................415 553-8700

Theresa Flores, *Principal*
EMP: 61
SALES (corp-wide): 39.6MM **Privately Held**
SIC: 8322 Child guidance agency
PA: Catholic Charities Cyo Of The Archdiocese Of San Francisco
990 Eddy St
San Francisco CA 94109
415 972-1200

(P-22975)
CATHOLIC CHRTS CYO ARCHDIOCS (PA)
990 Eddy St, San Francisco (94109-7713)
PHONE....................415 972-1200
Jeffrey V Bialik, *CEO*
Cailan Franz, *Comms Dir*
Kathie Autumn, *Exec Dir*
Erick Brown, *Program Mgr*
Lauren Muszynski, *Program Mgr*
EMP: 56 **EST:** 1907
SALES: 39.6MM **Privately Held**
SIC: 8322 Child guidance agency; senior citizens' center or association; family service agency; rehabilitation services

(P-22976)
CATHOLIC CHRTS CYO ARCHDIOCS
1 Saint Vincents Dr, San Rafael
(94903-1504)
PHONE....................415 507-2000
Chuck Fernandez, *Branch Mgr*
EMP: 300
SALES (corp-wide): 39.6MM **Privately Held**
SIC: 8322 8641 Child related social services; civic social & fraternal associations
PA: Catholic Charities Cyo Of The Archdiocese Of San Francisco
990 Eddy St
San Francisco CA 94109
415 972-1200

(P-22977)
CENTER CNSLNG EDCTN & CRISIS
Also Called: Valley Community Health Center
4361 Railroad Ave, Pleasanton
(94566-6611)
PHONE....................925 462-1755
Ronald Greenspane, *Exec Dir*
EMP: 73
SALES (est): 866.6K **Privately Held**
SIC: 8322 General counseling services

(P-22978)
CENTER FOR DOMESTIC PEACE
Also Called: Marin Abused Women's Services
734 A St, San Rafael (94901-3923)
PHONE....................415 457-2464
Donna Garske, *Exec Dir*
Kate Kain, *Exec Dir*
Keith Kane, *Exec Dir*
Cyndi Salvisberg Haeu, *Accountant*
Gayle Shearman, *Opers Mgr*
EMP: 50
SALES: 3MM **Privately Held**
WEB: www.maws.org
SIC: 8322 Individual & family services

(P-22979)
CENTER FOR INDVDUAL AND FAM TH
840 W Town And Country Rd, Orange
(92868-4712)
PHONE....................714 558-9266
Jim Masteller, *Director*
EMP: 55
SALES (est): 692.2K **Privately Held**
SIC: 8322 Family (marriage) counseling

(P-22980)
CENTER FOR LEARNING AND
Also Called: Class
424 Peninsula Ave, San Mateo
(94401-1653)
PHONE....................800 538-8365
Denise Pollard, *CEO*
Ross Berman, *Vice Pres*
Natalia Villalba, *Human Res Mgr*
Krista Wynne, *Opers Staff*
EMP: 400

SALES (est): 36.8K **Privately Held**
SIC: 8322 Family counseling services

(P-22981)
CENTER POINT INC (PA)
135 Paul Dr, San Rafael (94903-2023)
PHONE....................415 492-4444
Sushma D Taylor PHD, *President*
Terrell Anderson, *Treasurer*
Marc Hering, *Vice Pres*
H Gaines, *Program Mgr*
Mahesh Venketraman, *Controller*
EMP: 91
SQ FT: 7,750
SALES: 29.9MM **Privately Held**
SIC: 8322 Social service center

(P-22982)
CENTRAL VALLEY AUTISM PROJECT
3425 Coffee Rd Ste C2, Modesto
(95355-1582)
PHONE....................209 521-4791
Gina Pallotta, *Director*
Donna Pearson, *Project Mgr*
Angela Castro, *Opers Staff*
EMP: 80 **EST:** 2000
SALES (est): 3.6MM **Privately Held**
SIC: 8322 Social service center

(P-22983)
CENTRAL VLY CHLD SVCS NETWRK
1911 N Helm Ave, Fresno (93727-1614)
PHONE....................559 456-1100
Jane Martin, *Exec Dir*
Irene Alvarado, *Admin Asst*
Gayle Duffy, *Director*
Marisela Sosa, *Manager*
Ignacio Napoles, *Receptionist*
EMP: 60
SQ FT: 15,000
SALES: 12.5MM **Privately Held**
WEB: www.cvcsn.org
SIC: 8322 Social service center

(P-22984)
CENTRL TERRITRL SALVATION ARMY
10200 Pioneer Rd, Tustin (92782-1417)
PHONE....................714 832-7100
Nigel Cross, *Director*
EMP: 60
SALES (corp-wide): 2.3B **Privately Held**
WEB: www.salarmychicago.org
SIC: 8322 8661 8699 Social service center; religious organizations; charitable organization
HQ: Central Territorial Of The Salvation Army
5550 Prairie Stone Pkwy # 130
Hoffman Estates IL 60192
847 294-2000

(P-22985)
CENTRO DE SALUD DE LA
1420 E Plaza Blvd Ste E4, National City
(91950-3636)
PHONE....................619 477-0165
Marie Mulhall, *Principal*
EMP: 57
SALES (corp-wide): 87.1MM **Privately Held**
SIC: 8322 Individual & family services
PA: Centro De Salud De La Comunidad De San Ysidro, Inc.
4004 Beyer Blvd
San Ysidro CA 92173
619 428-4463

(P-22986)
CHILD & FAMILY CENTER
21545 Centre Pointe Pkwy, Santa Clarita
(91350-2947)
PHONE....................661 259-9439
Joan Aschoff, *CEO*
Denise Jeansonne, *Partner*
Victor Chavira, *Exec VP*
Bert Paras, *Vice Pres*
EMP: 120
SQ FT: 26,581

SALES: 11.4MM **Privately Held**
SIC: 8322 8099 8093 8049 Family counseling services; childbirth preparation clinic; mental health clinic, outpatient; clinical psychologist

(P-22987)
CHILD ABUSE LSTENING MEDIATION
Also Called: C A L M
1236 Chapala St, Santa Barbara
(93101-3116)
PHONE....................805 965-2376
Anna M Kokotovic, *Exec Dir*
Sydney Casler, *Executive Asst*
Mireya Hernandez, *Info Tech Mgr*
Rachel Hopsicker, *Psychologist*
Iona M Tripathi, *Psychiatry*
EMP: 50 **EST:** 1971
SALES: 7MM **Privately Held**
WEB: www.calm4kids.org
SIC: 8322 Crisis intervention center; general counseling services

(P-22988)
CHILD CARE COORDINATING COUNSI
330 Twin Dolphin Dr # 119, Redwood City
(94065-1454)
PHONE....................650 517-1400
Jan Stokley, *Exec Dir*
EMP: 50
SALES: 8.9MM **Privately Held**
WEB: www.thecouncil.net
SIC: 8322 Referral service for personal & social problems

(P-22989)
CHILD CARE RESOURCE CENTER INC (PA)
20001 Prairie St, Chatsworth (91311-6508)
PHONE....................818 717-1000
Michael Olenick, *CEO*
Casey Quinn, *CFO*
Denise Trinh, *CFO*
Ellen Cervantes, *Vice Pres*
Rick Robertss, *Vice Pres*
EMP: 130 **EST:** 1976
SALES: 111.3MM **Privately Held**
SIC: 8322 Child related social services

(P-22990)
CHILD CARE RESOURCE CENTER INC
250 Grand Cypress Ave # 601, Palmdale
(93551-3675)
PHONE....................661 723-3246
Ann Bubont, *Principal*
EMP: 50
SALES (corp-wide): 111.3MM **Privately Held**
SIC: 8322 Child related social services
PA: Child Care Resource Center, Inc.
20001 Prairie St
Chatsworth CA 91311
818 717-1000

(P-22991)
CHILD DEVELOPMENT INSTITUTE
Also Called: CDI
6340 Variel Ave Ste A, Woodland Hills
(91367-2514)
PHONE....................818 888-4559
Joan Samaltese, *Exec Dir*
Wendy Lara, *Executive*
Tessa Graham, *Director*
EMP: 50
SALES: 4.8MM **Privately Held**
WEB: www.childdevelopmentinstitute.org
SIC: 8322 Child related social services

(P-22992)
CHILD DEVELOPMENT RESOURCES OF (PA)
Also Called: C D R
221 Ventura Blvd, Oxnard (93036-0277)
PHONE....................805 485-7878
Jack Hinojosa, *CEO*
Alec Hairabedian, *Controller*
Amneh Qaralleh, *Teacher*
EMP: 200
SQ FT: 67,007

SALES: 36.2MM **Privately Held**
SIC: 8322 8699 Child guidance agency; charitable organization

(P-22993)
CHILDNET YOUTH & FMLY SVCS INC (PA)
4155 Outer Traffic Cir, Long Beach (90804-2111)
P.O. Box 4550 (90804-0550)
PHONE...............................562 498-5500
Kathy L Hughes, *CEO*
Kathy Hughes, *COO*
Ana Barraza, *Exec Dir*
Shirley Herrera, *Office Mgr*
Cherrie Gibbs, *QA Dir*
EMP: 177 **EST:** 1970
SQ FT: 16,073
SALES: 23.8MM **Privately Held**
WEB: www.childnet.net
SIC: 8322 Child related social services

(P-22994)
CHILDRENS ANGELCARE AID INTL
4535 58th St, San Diego (92115-3711)
PHONE...............................619 795-6234
Michael Challgren, *Chairman*
T P Grosser, *President*
Wayne Peimann, *Vice Pres*
EMP: 200
SQ FT: 2,500
SALES: 5.5MM **Privately Held**
SIC: 8322 Individual & family services

(P-22995)
CHILDRENS BUREAU SOUTHERN CAL (PA)
1910 Magnolia Ave, Los Angeles (90007-1220)
PHONE...............................213 342-0100
Alex Morales, *President*
Sona Chandwani, *CFO*
Susan Wirth, *Comms Dir*
Rolando Salvador, *Facilities Mgr*
Jose A Ramos, *Director*
EMP: 107 **EST:** 1904
SQ FT: 43,000
SALES: 30.6MM **Privately Held**
SIC: 8322 Child related social services

(P-22996)
CHILDRENS CRISIS CNTR STANISLS
1244 Fiori Ave, Modesto (95350-5503)
P.O. Box 1062 (95353-1062)
PHONE...............................209 577-4413
Colleen Garcia, *Exec Dir*
Kimberlee Speidel, *Human Res Mgr*
Brenda McDonald, *Director*
EMP: 100 **EST:** 1980
SALES: 3.8MM **Privately Held**
SIC: 8322 Social service center; crisis center

(P-22997)
CHILDRENS CUNCIL SAN FRANCISCO (PA)
445 Church St, San Francisco (94114-1720)
PHONE...............................415 343-3378
Sandee Blechman, *Exec Dir*
Jim Kirk, *Bd of Directors*
Jennifer Brooks, *Officer*
Kim Kruckel, *Exec Dir*
Marlina Chan, *Department Mgr*
EMP: 95
SALES: 85.9MM **Privately Held**
SIC: 8322 8351 Youth center; child day care services

(P-22998)
CHILDRENS INST LOS ANGELES
679 S New Hampshire Ave, Los Angeles (90005-1355)
PHONE...............................213 383-2765
Mary Emmons, *Branch Mgr*
EMP: 650
SALES (corp-wide): 680.1K **Privately Held**
SIC: 8322 Social service center
PA: Children's Institute Of Los Angeles
2121 W Temple St
Los Angeles CA 90026
213 385-5100

(P-22999)
CHILDRENS INSTITUTE INC (PA)
2121 W Temple St, Los Angeles (90026-4915)
PHONE...............................213 385-5100
Martine Singer, *CEO*
Shahram Aminian, *President*
Mark Engel, *CFO*
Todd Sosna, *COO*
Dr Steve Ambrose, *Senior VP*
EMP: 190 **EST:** 1906
SQ FT: 18,000
SALES: 75MM **Privately Held**
SIC: 8322 8699 Child related social services; charitable organization

(P-23000)
CHILDRENS PROTECTIVE SERVICES
5730 Packard Ave, Marysville (95901-7118)
P.O. Box 2320 (95901-0082)
PHONE...............................530 749-6311
EMP: 60
SALES (est): 492.9K **Privately Held**
WEB: www.childrensprotectiveservices.com
SIC: 8322

(P-23001)
CHILDRENS SERVICES
Also Called: Colusa City Office Education
345 5th St Ste A, Colusa (95932-2445)
PHONE...............................530 458-0300
Rick Perym, *Director*
EMP: 90
SALES (est): 4.1MM **Privately Held**
SIC: 8322 Children's aid society

(P-23002)
CHRISTIAN COUNSELING CENTERS
3880 S Bascom Ave Ste 202, San Jose (95124-2675)
PHONE...............................408 559-1115
Margeret Greig, *Director*
EMP: 56
SALES (corp-wide): 2.6MM **Privately Held**
SIC: 8322 General counseling services
PA: Christian Counseling Centers, Inc
1161 Cherry St Ste P
San Carlos CA 94070
650 570-7273

(P-23003)
CITY & COUNTY OF SAN FRANCISCO
Also Called: Adult Probation Department
850 Bryant St Ste 200, San Francisco (94103-4614)
PHONE...............................415 553-1706
Karen Fletcher, *Branch Mgr*
EMP: 150 **Privately Held**
SIC: 8322 9221 Probation office; ;
PA: City & County Of San Francisco
1 Dr Carlton B Goodlett P
San Francisco CA 94102
415 554-7500

(P-23004)
CITY & COUNTY OF SAN FRANCISCO
Also Called: Sheriff's Dept
375 Woodside Ave 1, San Francisco (94127-1221)
PHONE...............................415 753-7561
Janete Shalwitz, *Branch Mgr*
EMP: 93 **Privately Held**
SIC: 8322 9441 Child related social services; administration of social & manpower programs; ;
PA: City & County Of San Francisco
1 Dr Carlton B Goodlett P
San Francisco CA 94102
415 554-7500

(P-23005)
CITY IMPACT INC
555 S A St Ste 175, Oxnard (93030-8115)
P.O. Box 5678 (93031-5678)
PHONE...............................805 983-3636
Betty Alvarez Ham, *President*
Pam Stewart, *Vice Pres*
Tina Quolas, *Bookkeeper*

Maricela Lopez, *Case Mgr*
Hugo Sotomayor, *Assistant*
EMP: 55
SALES: 1.4MM **Privately Held**
WEB: www.cityimpact.com
SIC: 8322 Family (marriage) counseling

(P-23006)
CITY OF BAKERSFIELD
Rabobank Arena Theater & Conve
1001 Truxtun Ave, Bakersfield (93301-4714)
PHONE...............................661 852-7300
John Dorman, *General Mgr*
Jon Dorman, *General Mgr*
Ariel Roberts, *Executive Asst*
Chris Hartzell, *Technology*
Deslund Grimes, *Opers Mgr*
EMP: 110 **Privately Held**
WEB: www.bakersfieldfire.us
SIC: 8322 9111 6512 Community center; mayors' offices; nonresidential building operators
PA: City Of Bakersfield
1600 Truxtun Ave Fl 5th
Bakersfield CA 93301
661 326-3000

(P-23007)
CITY OF BELL
Also Called: Dept of Community Services
6250 Pine Ave, Bell (90201-1219)
PHONE...............................323 773-1596
Annett Peretz, *Director*
EMP: 100 **Privately Held**
SIC: 8322 9111 Community center; mayors' offices
PA: City Of Bell
6330 Pine Ave
Bell CA 90201
323 588-6211

(P-23008)
CITY OF CARSON
Also Called: Carson Community Center
3 Civic Plaza Dr, Carson (90745-2231)
PHONE...............................310 835-0212
Zenora Bellard, *Director*
EMP: 53 **Privately Held**
SIC: 8322 9111 7299 5812 Community center; mayors' offices; banquet hall facilities; caterers
PA: City Of Carson
701 E Carson St
Carson CA 90745
310 830-7600

(P-23009)
CITY OF IRVINE
Also Called: Lakeview Senior Center
20 Lake Rd, Irvine (92604-4567)
PHONE...............................949 724-6900
Ed Kaleikini, *Superintendent*
EMP: 64 **Privately Held**
SIC: 8322 Senior citizens' center or association
PA: City Of Irvine
1 Civic Center Plz
Irvine CA 92606
949 724-6000

(P-23010)
CITY OF LA HABRA
Also Called: Community Services Department
101 W La Habra Blvd, La Habra (90631-5401)
P.O. Box 337 (90633-0337)
PHONE...............................562 905-9708
Sal Failla, *Director*
EMP: 50 **Privately Held**
SIC: 8322 Community center
PA: City Of La Habra
110 E La Habra Blvd
La Habra CA 90631
562 383-4053

(P-23011)
CITY OF MOORPARK
Also Called: Moorpark Active Adult Center
799 Moorpark Ave, Moorpark (93021-1155)
PHONE...............................805 517-6261
Steven Kueny, *CEO*
EMP: 60 **Privately Held**
SIC: 8322 Senior citizens' center or association

PA: City Of Moorpark
799 Moorpark Ave
Moorpark CA 93021
805 517-6200

(P-23012)
CITY OF OAKLAND
Also Called: Health & Human Services Dept
150 Frank H Ogawa Plz # 3332, Oakland (94612-2021)
PHONE...............................510 238-6796
Andrea Youngdahl, *Director*
EMP: 300 **Privately Held**
WEB: www.cityofbuellton.com
SIC: 8322 9441 Individual & family services; administration of social & manpower programs;
PA: City Of Oakland
150 Frank H Ogawa Plz # 3332
Oakland CA 94612
510 238-3280

(P-23013)
CITY OF ORANGE
230 E Chapman Ave, Orange (92866-1506)
PHONE...............................714 744-7264
Bonnie Hagen, *Director*
EMP: 75 **Privately Held**
WEB: www.cityoforange.org
SIC: 8322 9111 Community center; mayors' offices
PA: City Of Orange
300 E Chapman Ave
Orange CA 92866
714 744-5500

(P-23014)
CITY OF OXNARD
Also Called: Senior Services
350 N C St, Oxnard (93030-4646)
PHONE...............................805 385-8019
Jocelyn Peterson, *Director*
EMP: 99 **Privately Held**
WEB: www.oxnardtourism.com
SIC: 8322 9111 Senior citizens' center or association; mayors' offices
PA: City Of Oxnard
300 W 3rd St Uppr Fl4
Oxnard CA 93030
805 385-7803

(P-23015)
CITY OF VACAVILLE
1100 Alamo Dr, Vacaville (95687-5606)
PHONE...............................707 449-6122
Carry Walker, *Manager*
EMP: 80 **Privately Held**
WEB: www.lenaugustine.com
SIC: 8322 Community center
PA: City Of Vacaville
650 Merchant St
Vacaville CA 95688
707 449-5100

(P-23016)
CITY OF WHITTIER
Also Called: Whittier City Community Svcs
7630 Washington Ave, Whittier (90602-1733)
PHONE...............................562 567-9446
Fran Shields, *Director*
Jeff Lopez, *Manager*
EMP: 100 **Privately Held**
WEB: www.whittierpd.org
SIC: 8322 Community center
PA: City Of Whittier
13230 Penn St
Whittier CA 90602
562 567-9999

(P-23017)
CLARE MATRIX (PA)
2644 30th St Ste 100, Santa Monica (90405-3051)
PHONE...............................310 314-6200
Kevin Fahy, *President*
Cathy Walter, *Executive Asst*
EMP: 65
SALES: 7.4MM **Privately Held**
SIC: 8322 Self-help organization

(P-23018)
CLARE FOUNDATION INC
Also Called: Dui Program
1871 9th St, Santa Monica (90404-4501)
PHONE.................................310 314-6200
Nicholas Vrataric, *Exec Dir*
EMP: 60
SALES (corp-wide): 7.4MM **Privately Held**
SIC: 8322 Substance abuse counseling
PA: Clare Matrix
        2644 30th St Ste 100
        Santa Monica CA 90405
        310 314-6200

(P-23019)
CLINICA SIERRA VISTA
3727 N 1st St Ste 106, Fresno
(93726-5628)
PHONE.................................559 457-6900
Stephen W Schilling, *CEO*
EMP: 86
SALES (corp-wide): 136.6MM **Privately Held**
SIC: 8322 Community center
PA: Clinica Sierra Vista
        1430 Truxtun Ave Ste 400
        Bakersfield CA 93301
        661 635-3050

(P-23020)
COACHELLA VLY RESCUE MISSION
Also Called: Cvrm
82873 Via Venecia, Indio (92201-6971)
P.O. Box 10660 (92202-2564)
PHONE.................................760 347-3512
Floyd Rhoades, *Ch of Bd*
Pete Del Rio, *Vice Chairman*
Joseph Hayes, *Treasurer*
Jim Parrish, *Vice Ch Bd*
Darla Burkett, *Exec Dir*
EMP: 50
SQ FT: 43,000
SALES: 7.3MM **Privately Held**
WEB: www.cvrm.org
SIC: 8322 8661 Social service center; non-church religious organizations

(P-23021)
COALITION FOR FAMILY HARMONY
1030 N Ventura Rd, Oxnard (93030-3855)
PHONE.................................805 983-6014
Cherie Douval, *President*
Laura Dunlap, *Admin Asst*
EMP: 75
SQ FT: 20,000
SALES: 2.8MM **Privately Held**
SIC: 8322 Emergency shelters

(P-23022)
COLUSA CNTY SBSTNCE ABUSE SVCS
Also Called: Colusa County Behavioral Hlth
162 E Carson St Ste A, Colusa
(95932-2880)
PHONE.................................530 458-0520
Terrance Rooney, *Director*
Jack Joiner, *Deputy Dir*
Gerardo S Toribio, *Psychiatry*
EMP: 52
SALES (est): 1.4MM **Privately Held**
SIC: 8322 Substance abuse counseling

(P-23023)
COMMONWEAL
451 Mesa Rd, Bolinas (94924)
P.O. Box 316 (94924-0316)
PHONE.................................415 868-0970
Michael Lerner, *President*
Michael Lerner PHD, *President*
Susan Braun, *Director*
Sharyle Patton, *Director*
EMP: 58
SQ FT: 10,800
SALES: 3.4MM **Privately Held**
WEB: www.commonweal.org
SIC: 8322 Social service center; refugee service

(P-23024)
COMMUNITY ACTION AGENCY OF BUT (PA)
181 E Shasta Ave, Chico (95973-0523)
P.O. Box 6369 (95927-6369)
PHONE.................................530 712-2600
Jane Davis, *Ch of Bd*
Thomas Tenorio, *CEO*
Doug Benander, *Treasurer*
EMP: 70
SQ FT: 20,000
SALES: 5.4MM **Privately Held**
WEB: www.buttecaa.com
SIC: 8322 7389 8699 Social service center; ; charitable organization

(P-23025)
COMMUNITY ACTION MARIN (PA)
555 Northgate Dr Ste 201, San Rafael
(94903-3696)
PHONE.................................415 485-1489
Lauren Hill, *Exec Dir*
Sadaf Fakhri, *Administration*
Patricia Cunningham, *Controller*
Heather Bettini, *Director*
Gail Crain, *Manager*
EMP: 280
SQ FT: 3,000
SALES: 16.3MM **Privately Held**
SIC: 8322 Social service center

(P-23026)
COMMUNITY ACTION PARTNERSHI
Also Called: OC FOOD BANK
11870 Monarch St, Garden Grove
(92841-2113)
PHONE.................................714 897-6670
Gregory C Scott, *CEO*
Marleen Morril, *Admin Asst*
Caroline Coleman, *Exec Sec*
Belinda Ong, *Manager*
Judy Chacon, *Supervisor*
EMP: 105
SQ FT: 86,300
SALES: 33.1MM **Privately Held**
WEB: www.capoc.org
SIC: 8322 Individual & family services

(P-23027)
COMMUNITY ACTION PARTNERSHIP
3970 Short St, San Luis Obispo
(93401-7567)
PHONE.................................805 541-4122
EMP: 326
SALES (corp-wide): 79.1MM **Privately Held**
SIC: 8322 Individual & family services
PA: Community Action Partnership Of San
        Luis Obispo County, Inc.
        1030 Southwood Dr
        San Luis Obispo CA 93401
        805 544-4355

(P-23028)
COMMUNITY ACTION PARTNERSHIP (PA)
1030 Southwood Dr, San Luis Obispo
(93401-5813)
PHONE.................................805 544-4355
Anita Robinson, *Ch of Bd*
Frances I Coughlin, *President*
Joan Limov, *CFO*
Rob Garcia, *Treasurer*
Missey Hobson, *Corp Secy*
EMP: 72
SQ FT: 20,000
SALES: 79.1MM **Privately Held**
SIC: 8322 Child related social services

(P-23029)
COMMUNITY ACTION PARTNR KERN
217 W Kern Ave, Mc Farland (93250-1360)
PHONE.................................661 792-1066
EMP: 66
SALES (corp-wide): 63.1MM **Privately Held**
SIC: 8322 Individual & family services

PA: Community Action Partnership Of Kern
        5005 Business Park N
        Bakersfield CA 93309
        661 336-5236

(P-23030)
COMMUNITY ACTION PARTNR KERN (PA)
5005 Business Park N, Bakersfield
(93309-1651)
PHONE.................................661 336-5236
Jeremy Tobias, *Exec Dir*
Letisha Brooks, *Program Mgr*
Glen Ephrom, *Program Mgr*
Angelica Nelson, *Program Mgr*
Sandi Truman, *Program Mgr*
EMP: 50
SQ FT: 14,500
SALES: 63.1MM **Privately Held**
WEB: www.capk.org
SIC: 8322 Social service center; senior citizens' center or association; child guidance agency; public welfare center

(P-23031)
COMMUNITY BRIDGES
Also Called: Golden Age Nutrition Program
114 E 5th St, Watsonville (95076-4309)
PHONE.................................831 724-2024
Valerie Rivera, *Principal*
EMP: 104
SALES (corp-wide): 14.4MM **Privately Held**
WEB: www.cbridges.org
SIC: 8322 Senior citizens' center or association
PA: Community Bridges
        519 Main St
        Watsonville CA 95076
        831 688-8840

(P-23032)
COMMUNITY CARE ADHC INC
Also Called: Consultants For Adhc
9917 Las Tunas Dr, Temple City
(91780-2211)
PHONE.................................626 614-8999
Behrooz Sumekh, *President*
EMP: 60 **EST:** 2001
SALES (est): 2.2MM **Privately Held**
SIC: 8322 Adult day care center

(P-23033)
COMMUNITY CHILD CARE COUNCI AL (PA)
Also Called: 4 C'S
22351 City Center Dr # 200, Hayward
(94541-2822)
PHONE.................................510 582-2182
Renee Herzfeld, *Exec Dir*
EMP: 75
SALES: 21.9MM **Privately Held**
SIC: 8322 Child related social services

(P-23034)
COMMUNITY COLLEGE FOUNDATION
3530 Wilshire Blvd # 610, Los Angeles
(90010-2372)
PHONE.................................213 427-6910
Nanette Fowler, *President*
EMP: 50
SALES (corp-wide): 6MM **Privately Held**
SIC: 8322 Child related social services
PA: Community College Foundation
        1901 Royal Oaks Dr # 100
        Sacramento CA 95815
        916 418-5100

(P-23035)
COMMUNITY CONNECT (PA)
2060 University Ave # 212, Riverside
(92507-5259)
PHONE.................................951 686-4402
Bobbie Neff, *CEO*
Greg Taber, *President*
Ann Macias, *Vice Pres*
Diana Rivera, *Admin Asst*
Grace Slocum, *Director*
EMP: 52
SQ FT: 4,200
SALES: 1.3MM **Privately Held**
SIC: 8322 Multi-service center

(P-23036)
COMMUNITY GATEPATH
Also Called: IMPACT BUSINESS SERVICE
350 Twin Dolphin Dr # 123, Redwood City
(94065-1457)
PHONE.................................650 259-8500
Sheryl Young, *CEO*
Carol Elliott, *Administration*
Erin Montgomery, *Human Res Dir*
Arwa Motiwala,
Cheryl Oku, *Manager*
EMP: 120
SQ FT: 25,000
SALES: 13.6MM **Privately Held**
WEB: www.communitygatepath.com
SIC: 8322 Social services for the handicapped

(P-23037)
COMMUNITY HOUSING OPTIONS
Also Called: CHOICESS
348 E Foothill Blvd, Arcadia (91006-2542)
PHONE.................................626 359-3300
Joseph Donofrio, *Director*
Lydia Del Rio, *Office Mgr*
EMP: 100
SQ FT: 850
SALES: 1.9MM **Privately Held**
WEB: www.choicess.com
SIC: 8322 Social services for the handicapped

(P-23038)
COMMUNITY INTEGRATED WORK PROG
Also Called: Cwip
4623 W Jacquelyn Ave, Fresno
(93722-6413)
PHONE.................................559 276-8564
Louis Leon, *Director*
EMP: 50
SALES (corp-wide): 49.8MM **Privately Held**
SIC: 8322 Individual & family services
PA: Community Integrated Work Program,
        Inc.
        3701 Stocker St Ste 203
        View Park CA 90008
        925 776-1040

(P-23039)
COMMUNITY INTEGRATED WORK PROG
Also Called: Community Intgrted Work
Prgram
1875 Whipple Rd, Hayward (94544-7834)
PHONE.................................510 487-9768
Cathi Vaughns, *Manager*
EMP: 50
SALES (corp-wide): 49.8MM **Privately Held**
SIC: 8322 Individual & family services
PA: Community Integrated Work Program,
        Inc.
        3701 Stocker St Ste 203
        View Park CA 90008
        925 776-1040

(P-23040)
COMMUNITY INTERFACE SERVICES
2621 Roosevelt St Ste 100, Carlsbad
(92008-1660)
PHONE.................................760 729-3866
Rose M Hanson, *President*
Pamela Oakes, *Admin Asst*
EMP: 100
SALES: 10.7MM **Privately Held**
WEB: www.communityinterfaceservices.org
SIC: 8322 Individual & family services

(P-23041)
COMMUNITY LIVING SERVICES LLC
8282 University Ave, La Mesa
(91942-9321)
PHONE.................................619 921-3136
Parvin Pashaee, *Mng Member*
EMP: 50
SALES (est): 1.5MM **Privately Held**
SIC: 8322 Social services for the handicapped

(P-23042)
COMMUNITY SUPPORT OPTIONS INC
1401 Poso Dr, Wasco (93280-2584)
P.O. Box 8018 (93280-8108)
PHONE..............................661 758-5331
John Stockton, *CEO*
Anna Poggi, *President*
Ben Goosen, *Treasurer*
Jose Hernandez, *Vice Pres*
Violet Ratzlass, *Admin Sec*
EMP: 102
SQ FT: 9,000
SALES (est): 5.9MM **Privately Held**
SIC: 8322 Association for the handicapped

(P-23043)
COMMUNTY SLNS FOR CHLDRN FMLS (PA)
9015 Murray Ave Ste 100, Gilroy (95020-3617)
P.O. Box 546, Morgan Hill (95038-0546)
PHONE..............................408 779-2113
Erin O'Brien, *CEO*
Rodney Clark, *Director*
Eman Aziz, *Case Mgr*
Priscilla Chavez, *Case Mgr*
Sylvia Gallegos, *Case Mgr*
EMP: 185
SALES: 26.8MM **Privately Held**
SIC: 8322 Social service center; family counseling services

(P-23044)
COMPASS FAMILY SERVICES
Also Called: Compass Family Shelter
626 Polk St, San Francisco (94102-3328)
PHONE..............................415 644-0504
Erica Kisch, *Exec Dir*
EMP: 80
SALES (corp-wide): 9.2MM **Privately Held**
SIC: 8322 Family (marriage) counseling
PA: Compass Family Services
37 Grove St
San Francisco CA 94102
415 644-0504

(P-23045)
COMPASS FAMILY SERVICES
Also Called: Compass Clara House
111 Page St, San Francisco (94102-5892)
PHONE..............................415 644-0504
Erica Kisch, *Exec Dir*
EMP: 80
SALES (corp-wide): 9.2MM **Privately Held**
SIC: 8322 Individual & family services
PA: Compass Family Services
37 Grove St
San Francisco CA 94102
415 644-0504

(P-23046)
COMPREHENSIVE YOUTH SER
Also Called: C Y S
4545 N West Ave Ste 101, Fresno (93705-0946)
PHONE..............................559 229-3561
Captain Mike Reid, *President*
Kevin Torosian, *Vice Pres*
Jacqueline Smith, *Exec Dir*
Sheryl Noel, *Admin Sec*
EMP: 90
SQ FT: 9,000
SALES: 4.7MM **Privately Held**
WEB: www.cys.com
SIC: 8322 Child related social services

(P-23047)
CONCEPT 7 INC (PA)
Also Called: CONCEPT 7 FAMILY SUPPORT & TRE
13020 Bailey St, Whittier (90601-4203)
PHONE..............................714 966-9734
John Peel, *CEO*
EMP: 57
SQ FT: 3,900
SALES: 5.6MM **Privately Held**
SIC: 8322 Adoption services

(P-23048)
CONCERTO HEALTHCARE INC (PA)
85 Enterprise Ste 200, Aliso Viejo (92656-2614)
PHONE..............................949 537-3400
Alec Cunningham, *CEO*
Chrissie Cooper, *COO*
Dawn Gilbert, *CFO*
Norris Vivatrat, *Chief Mktg Ofcr*
Julie M Webb-Hopkins, *Officer*
EMP: 139 **EST:** 2004
SALES (est): 25.4MM **Privately Held**
SIC: 8322 Adult day care center

(P-23049)
CONSULTNTS IN EDCTL PER SKILLS (PA)
Also Called: Ceps
5825 Auburn Blvd Ste 1, Sacramento (95841-2977)
P.O. Box 417010 (95841-7010)
PHONE..............................916 348-1890
Patricia Vollenweider, *Exec Dir*
Karla Miller,
Robin Burris, *Accounts Mgr*
EMP: 56 **EST:** 1995
SALES: 1.4MM **Privately Held**
SIC: 8322 General counseling services

(P-23050)
CORNELL CORRECTIONS CAL INC (DH)
1811 Knoll Dr, Ventura (93003-7321)
PHONE..............................805 644-8700
David M Cornell, *Ch of Bd*
Tom Jenkens, *President*
Steven W Logan, *President*
Brian E Bergeron, *CFO*
Marvin H Wiebe, *Senior VP*
EMP: 255
SQ FT: 4,100
SALES (est): 5.8MM
SALES (corp-wide): 2.3B **Privately Held**
SIC: 8322 Rehabilitation services

(P-23051)
CORRECTONS RHBLTATION CAL DEPT
Also Called: Parole Unit Office
930 3rd St Ste 100, Eureka (95501-0554)
PHONE..............................707 445-6520
Ray Hilburn, *Manager*
EMP: 73 **Privately Held**
SIC: 8322 Parole office; offender self-help agency
HQ: California Department Of Corrections & Rehabilitation
1515 S St
Sacramento CA 95811

(P-23052)
CORRECTONS RHBLTATION CAL DEPT
Also Called: San Bernardino Parole Unit 14
303 W 5th St, San Bernardino (92401-1306)
PHONE..............................909 806-3516
Michael Passmore, *Administration*
EMP: 60 **Privately Held**
SIC: 8322 Parole office; offender self-help agency; correctional institutions;
HQ: California Department Of Corrections & Rehabilitation
1515 S St
Sacramento CA 95811

(P-23053)
COUNCIL ON AGING - S CALI INC
2 Executive Cir Ste 175, Irvine (92614-6773)
PHONE..............................714 479-0107
Lisa Wright Jenkins, *CEO*
Rim Hussin, *Manager*
Lee Woolery, *Manager*
Sara Yu, *Manager*
EMP: 83
SALES: 4.6MM **Privately Held**
SIC: 8322 Senior citizens' center or association

(P-23054)
COUNCIL ON AGING SVCS FOR SRS (PA)
30 Kawana Springs Rd, Santa Rosa (95404-6309)
PHONE..............................707 525-0143
Shirlee Zane, *Exec Dir*
Mare O'Cannel, *CFO*
Michael Randall, *Treasurer*
Theresa Strickland, *Sr Associate*
Zachary Carroll, *Director*
EMP: 103
SQ FT: 6,500
SALES: 4.5MM **Privately Held**
WEB: www.councilonaging.com
SIC: 8322 Senior citizens' center or association; adult day care center; meal delivery program; social service center

(P-23055)
COUNTRY VILLA RANCHO
39950 Vista Del Sol, Rancho Mirage (92270-3206)
PHONE..............................760 340-0053
Scott Gillis, *Administration*
EMP: 200
SALES (est): 11.4MM **Privately Held**
SIC: 8322 Rehabilitation services

(P-23056)
COUNTRY VILLA SERVICE CORP
3000 N Gate Rd, Seal Beach (90740-2535)
PHONE..............................562 598-2477
Jennifer Rose, *Branch Mgr*
EMP: 82
SALES (corp-wide): 125.3MM **Privately Held**
SIC: 8322 8011 Rehabilitation services; medical centers
PA: Country Villa Service Corp.
2400 E Katella Ave # 800
Anaheim CA 92806
310 574-3733

(P-23057)
COUNTRY VILLA SERVICE CORP
Also Called: Cntry Vlla Merced Hlthcre Cntr
510 W 26th St, Merced (95340-2804)
PHONE..............................209 723-2911
Joel Saltzburg, *CEO*
EMP: 82
SALES (corp-wide): 125.3MM **Privately Held**
SIC: 8322 8051 Rehabilitation services; skilled nursing care facilities
PA: Country Villa Service Corp.
2400 E Katella Ave # 800
Anaheim CA 92806
310 574-3733

(P-23058)
COUNTY MONTEREY SOCIAL SVCS
Also Called: County of Monterey Social Svcs
1281 Broadway Ave, Seaside (93955-4925)
PHONE..............................831 899-8001
Loma Livernois, *Manager*
EMP: 65
SALES (est): 1.4MM **Privately Held**
SIC: 8322 Social service center

(P-23059)
COUNTY OF BUTTE
Also Called: Butte County Probation
42 County Center Dr, Oroville (95965-3335)
PHONE..............................530 538-7661
John Wardell, *Chief*
EMP: 130 **Privately Held**
WEB: www.bcihsspa.org
SIC: 8322 Probation office
PA: County Of Butte
25 County Center Dr # 125
Oroville CA 95965
530 538-7701

(P-23060)
COUNTY OF BUTTE
Also Called: Welfare Administration
202 Mira Loma Dr, Oroville (95965-3500)
P.O. Box 1649 (95965-1649)
PHONE..............................530 538-7572
Cathy Grams, *Director*
EMP: 570 **Privately Held**

WEB: www.bcihsspa.org
SIC: 8322 9111 Individual & family services; county supervisors' & executives' offices
PA: County Of Butte
25 County Center Dr # 125
Oroville CA 95965
530 538-7701

(P-23061)
COUNTY OF BUTTE
Also Called: Welfare Dept Warehouse
205 Mira Loma Dr, Oroville (95965-3582)
P.O. Box 1649 (95965-1649)
PHONE..............................530 538-6802
Art Howe, *Superintendent*
EMP: 500 **Privately Held**
WEB: www.bcihsspa.org
SIC: 8322 9111 Individual & family services; county supervisors' & executives' offices
PA: County Of Butte
25 County Center Dr # 125
Oroville CA 95965
530 538-7701

(P-23062)
COUNTY OF BUTTE
Also Called: Butte County Employment Center
78 Table Mountain Blvd, Oroville (95965-3578)
P.O. Box 1649 (95965-1649)
PHONE..............................530 538-7711
Cathy Grams, *Branch Mgr*
EMP: 570 **Privately Held**
WEB: www.bcihsspa.org
SIC: 8322 9111 Public welfare center; county supervisors' & executives' offices
PA: County Of Butte
25 County Center Dr # 125
Oroville CA 95965
530 538-7701

(P-23063)
COUNTY OF CALAVERAS
Also Called: Road Dept
891 Mountain Ranch Rd, San Andreas (95249-9713)
PHONE..............................209 754-6402
Rob Houghton, *Director*
EMP: 80 **Privately Held**
WEB: www.ccsolidwaste.org
SIC: 8322 Public welfare center
PA: County Of Calaveras
891 Mountain Ranch Rd
San Andreas CA 95249
209 754-6303

(P-23064)
COUNTY OF CONTRA COSTA
50 Douglas Dr Ste 200, Martinez (94553-8500)
PHONE..............................925 313-4000
Lionel Chatman, *Chief*
EMP: 150 **Privately Held**
SIC: 8322 9441 Probation office; parole office; administration of social & manpower programs
PA: County Of Contra Costa
625 Court St Ste 100
Martinez CA 94553
925 957-5280

(P-23065)
COUNTY OF CONTRA COSTA
Also Called: Child Support Svcs
50 Douglas Dr Ste 100, Martinez (94553-8500)
PHONE..............................866 901-3212
Linda Dippel, *Director*
EMP: 200 **Privately Held**
SIC: 8322 9441 Individual & family services;
PA: County Of Contra Costa
625 Court St Ste 100
Martinez CA 94553
925 957-5280

(P-23066)
COUNTY OF EL DORADO
Also Called: Edc Probation
3974 Durock Rd Ste 205, Shingle Springs (95682-8568)
PHONE..............................530 621-5625
Joseph Warchol, *Chief*

EMP: 109 **Privately Held**
WEB: www.filmtahoe.com
SIC: **8322** Probation office
PA: County Of El Dorado
330 Fair Ln
Placerville CA 95667
530 621-5830

(P-23067)
COUNTY OF EL DORADO
Also Called: Department of Social Services
3057 Briw Rd Ste A, Placerville
(95667-5335)
PHONE..................530 642-7130
Glen Helland, *Director*
EMP: 85 **Privately Held**
WEB: www.filmtahoe.com
SIC: **8322** 9111 Individual & family services; executive offices
PA: County Of El Dorado
330 Fair Ln
Placerville CA 95667
530 621-5830

(P-23068)
COUNTY OF FRESNO
Also Called: Probation Department
2212 N Winery Ave Ste 122, Fresno
(93703-2896)
PHONE..................559 600-3800
Rick Chavez, *Manager*
EMP: 59 **Privately Held**
SIC: **8322** 9441 Probation office;
PA: County Of Fresno
2420 Mariposa St
Fresno CA 93721
559 600-1710

(P-23069)
COUNTY OF FRESNO
Also Called: Probation Department
333 W Pontiac Way, Clovis (93612-5613)
P.O. Box 453, Fresno (93709-0453)
PHONE..................559 600-5127
Rick Chavez, *Manager*
Daniel Moore, *Info Tech Mgr*
Angela Perez, *Technology*
EMP: 100 **Privately Held**
WEB: www.first5fresno.org
SIC: **8322** 9441 Probation office.
PA: County Of Fresno
2420 Mariposa St
Fresno CA 93721
559 600-1710

(P-23070)
COUNTY OF FRESNO
Probation Department
3333 E American Ave Ste B, Fresno
(93725-9248)
PHONE..................559 600-3996
Rick Chavez, *Manager*
EMP: 130 **Privately Held**
WEB: www.first5fresno.org
SIC: **8322** 9441 Probation office; administration of social & manpower programs;
PA: County Of Fresno
2420 Mariposa St
Fresno CA 93721
559 600-1710

(P-23071)
COUNTY OF GLENN
525 W Sycamore St Ste A1, Willows
(95988-2748)
P.O. Box 366 (95988-0366)
PHONE..................530 934-6453
Robert Chittenden, *Branch Mgr*
EMP: 97 **Privately Held**
SIC: **8322** Social service center
PA: County Of Glenn
516 W Sycamore St Fl 2
Willows CA 95988
530 934-6410

(P-23072)
COUNTY OF GLENN
Also Called: Glenn County Humn Resorce
Agcy
420 E Laurel St, Willows (95988-3115)
P.O. Box 611 (95988-0611)
PHONE..................530 934-6514
Kim Gaghagen, *Principal*
EMP: 250 **Privately Held**
WEB: www.countyofglen.net

SIC: **8322** 9111 Individual & family services; county supervisors' & executives' offices
PA: County Of Glenn
516 W Sycamore St Fl 2
Willows CA 95988
530 934-6410

(P-23073)
COUNTY OF HUMBOLDT
Also Called: Dept of Social Services
929 Koster St, Eureka (95501-0106)
PHONE..................707 445-6180
John Frank, *Branch Mgr*
EMP: 300 **Privately Held**
SIC: **8322** 9441 Social service center; administration of social & manpower programs;
PA: County Of Humboldt
825 5th St
Eureka CA 95501
707 268-2543

(P-23074)
COUNTY OF IMPERIAL
Also Called: Imperial County Probation Off
324 Applestille Rd, El Centro (92243-9661)
PHONE..................760 336-3581
Micheal Kelly, *Director*
Marisol Del Leon, *Technician*
Debbie Angulo, *Business Mgr*
EMP: 150 **Privately Held**
WEB: www.imperialcounty.net
SIC: **8322** 9111 Individual & family services; county supervisors' & executives' offices
PA: County Of Imperial
940 W Main St Ste 208
El Centro CA 92243
760 482-4556

(P-23075)
COUNTY OF KERN
Also Called: Probation Dept-Juvenile
2005 Ridge Rd, Bakersfield (93305-4123)
P.O. Box 3309 (93385-3309)
PHONE..................661 868-4100
John R Roberts, *Chief*
EMP: 600 **Privately Held**
WEB: www.kccfc.org
SIC: **8322** 9111 Probation office; county supervisors' & executives' offices;
PA: County Of Kern
1115 Truxtun Ave Rm 505
Bakersfield CA 93301
661 868-3690

(P-23076)
COUNTY OF KERN
Also Called: Aging & Adult Services
2014 Calloway Dr, Bakersfield
(93312-2729)
PHONE..................661 392-2010
Grace Bradbury, *Manager*
EMP: 61 **Privately Held**
WEB: www.kccfc.org
SIC: **8322** 9441 Community center; administration of social & manpower programs;
PA: County Of Kern
1115 Truxtun Ave Rm 505
Bakersfield CA 93301
661 868-3690

(P-23077)
COUNTY OF KERN
2001 28th St Ste C, Bakersfield
(93301-1924)
PHONE..................661 336-6800
Lewis Verna, *Exec Dir*
EMP: 61 **Privately Held**
SIC: **8322** Probation office
PA: County Of Kern
1115 Truxtun Ave Rm 505
Bakersfield CA 93301
661 868-3690

(P-23078)
COUNTY OF KERN
Also Called: Aging & Adult Services
5357 Truxtun Ave, Taft (93268)
PHONE..................661 763-1535
Connie Redfield, *Director*
EMP: 61 **Privately Held**
WEB: www.kccfc.org

SIC: **8322** 9441 Senior citizens' center or association; administration of social & manpower programs;
PA: County Of Kern
1115 Truxtun Ave Rm 505
Bakersfield CA 93301
661 868-3690

(P-23079)
COUNTY OF KERN
Also Called: Human Services Dept
1816 Cecil Ave, Delano (93215-1520)
P.O. Box 339 (93216-0339)
PHONE..................661 721-5134
Donalda Salsbery, *Director*
EMP: 60 **Privately Held**
WEB: www.kccfc.org
SIC: **8322** 9441 Public welfare center; administration of social & manpower programs;
PA: County Of Kern
1115 Truxtun Ave Rm 505
Bakersfield CA 93301
661 868-3690

(P-23080)
COUNTY OF KERN
Also Called: Aging & Adult Services
6601 Niles Senior St, Bakersfield (93306)
PHONE..................661 363-8910
Lavita Greenly, *Branch Mgr*
EMP: 61 **Privately Held**
WEB: www.kccfc.org
SIC: **8322** 9441 Senior citizens' center or association; administration of social & manpower programs;
PA: County Of Kern
1115 Truxtun Ave Rm 505
Bakersfield CA 93301
661 868-3690

(P-23081)
COUNTY OF KINGS
Also Called: Kings County Probation Dept.
1424 Forum Dr, Hanford (93230-5900)
PHONE..................559 852-4316
Dorothy Van Den Berg, *Chief*
Jeff Taber, *Director*
EMP: 160 **Privately Held**
WEB: www.countyofkings.com
SIC: **8322** Probation office
PA: County Of Kings
1400 W Lacey Blvd
Hanford CA 93230
559 582-0326

(P-23082)
COUNTY OF LOS ANGELES
Also Called: Probation Department
300 E Walnut St Dept 200, Pasadena
(91101-1584)
PHONE..................626 356-5281
Diana Cunningham, *Principal*
EMP: 135 **Privately Held**
WEB: www.co.la.ca.us
SIC: **8322** 9199 Probation office;
PA: County Of Los Angeles
500 W Temple St Ste 437
Los Angeles CA 90012
213 974-1101

(P-23083)
COUNTY OF LOS ANGELES
Also Called: County Probation
11234 Valley Blvd Ste 103, El Monte
(91731-3239)
PHONE..................626 575-4059
Kwadwo Akosah, *Principal*
EMP: 140 **Privately Held**
SIC: **8322** Probation office
PA: County Of Los Angeles
500 W Temple St Ste 437
Los Angeles CA 90012
213 974-1101

(P-23084)
COUNTY OF LOS ANGELES
Also Called: Probation Department
5300 W Avenue I, Lancaster (93536-8312)
PHONE..................661 940-4181
Willie Doyle, *Director*
EMP: 300 **Privately Held**
WEB: www.co.la.ca.us
SIC: **8322** 9223 Probation office; correctional institutions;

PA: County Of Los Angeles
500 W Temple St Ste 437
Los Angeles CA 90012
213 974-1101

(P-23085)
COUNTY OF LOS ANGELES
Also Called: Child Support Services
5770 S Eastern Ave Fl 4th, Commerce
(90040-2948)
PHONE..................323 889-3405
Steven Golightly, *Manager*
EMP: 300 **Privately Held**
WEB: www.co.la.ca.us
SIC: **8322** 9441 Child related social services; administration of social & manpower programs;
PA: County Of Los Angeles
500 W Temple St Ste 437
Los Angeles CA 90012
213 974-1101

(P-23086)
COUNTY OF LOS ANGELES
Also Called: Children & Family Svcs Dept
10355 Slusher Dr, Santa Fe Springs
(90670-7353)
PHONE..................562 903-5000
Barbara Betlem, *Director*
EMP: 350 **Privately Held**
WEB: www.co.la.ca.us
SIC: **8322** 9441 Child related social services;
PA: County Of Los Angeles
500 W Temple St Ste 437
Los Angeles CA 90012
213 974-1101

(P-23087)
COUNTY OF LOS ANGELES
Also Called: Dept Children and Family Svcs
4060 Watson Plaza Dr, Lakewood
(90712-4033)
PHONE..................562 497-3500
Joy Russell, *Administration*
EMP: 500 **Privately Held**
WEB: www.co.la.ca.us
SIC: **8322** 9111 Children's aid society; executive offices
PA: County Of Los Angeles
500 W Temple St Ste 437
Los Angeles CA 90012
213 974-1101

(P-23088)
COUNTY OF LOS ANGELES
1000 Corp Ctr Dr Ste 200b, Monterey Park
(91754)
PHONE..................323 265-1804
Renee Watkinson, *Branch Mgr*
EMP: 137 **Privately Held**
SIC: **8322** Individual & family services
PA: County Of Los Angeles
500 W Temple St Ste 437
Los Angeles CA 90012
213 974-1101

(P-23089)
COUNTY OF LOS ANGELES
Also Called: Community & Senior Svcs
777 W Jackman St, Lancaster
(93534-2419)
PHONE..................661 948-2320
Nusun Muhamad, *Manager*
EMP: 135 **Privately Held**
WEB: www.co.la.ca.us
SIC: **8322** 9441 Senior citizens' center or association; administration of social & manpower programs;
PA: County Of Los Angeles
500 W Temple St Ste 437
Los Angeles CA 90012
213 974-1101

(P-23090)
COUNTY OF LOS ANGELES
Also Called: Probation Dept
320 W Temple St Ste 1101, Los Angeles
(90012-3289)
PHONE..................213 974-9331
Mike Verilla, *Director*
EMP: 170 **Privately Held**
WEB: www.co.la.ca.us
SIC: **8322** 9223 8093 Probation office; correctional institutions; ; mental health clinic, outpatient

PRODUCTS & SVCS

PA: County Of Los Angeles
500 W Temple St Ste 437
Los Angeles CA 90012
213 974-1101

(P-23091)
COUNTY OF LOS ANGELES
Also Called: La County Probation
8240 Broadway Ave, Whittier (90606-3120)
PHONE..............................562 908-3119
Donna Rose, *Manager*
EMP: 102 **Privately Held**
WEB: www.co.la.ca.us
SIC: **8322** 9111 Probation office; county
supervisors' & executives' offices
PA: County Of Los Angeles
500 W Temple St Ste 437
Los Angeles CA 90012
213 974-1101

(P-23092)
COUNTY OF LOS ANGELES
Also Called: Probation Department
1601 Eastlake Ave, Los Angeles (90033-1009)
PHONE..............................323 226-8511
Taula Heath, *Director*
EMP: 135 **Privately Held**
WEB: www.co.la.ca.us
SIC: **8322** Probation office; parole office
PA: County Of Los Angeles
500 W Temple St Ste 437
Los Angeles CA 90012
213 974-1101

(P-23093)
COUNTY OF LOS ANGELES
Also Called: Children & Family Svcs Dept
425 Shatto Pl, Los Angeles (90020-1712)
PHONE..............................213 351-5600
Jackie Contreras, *Director*
EMP: 100 **Privately Held**
WEB: www.co.la.ca.us
SIC: **8322** 9441 Child related social serv-
ices; administration of social & manpower
programs;
PA: County Of Los Angeles
500 W Temple St Ste 437
Los Angeles CA 90012
213 974-1101

(P-23094)
COUNTY OF LOS ANGELES
5445 Whittier Blvd Fl 400, Los Angeles
(90022-4125)
PHONE..............................323 727-1639
Minhha Ngyuen, *Branch Mgr*
EMP: 140 **Privately Held**
SIC: **8322** Senior citizens' center or associ-
ation
PA: County Of Los Angeles
500 W Temple St Ste 437
Los Angeles CA 90012
213 974-1101

(P-23095)
COUNTY OF LOS ANGELES
Also Called: Department of Social Services
530 12th St Fl 1, Paso Robles
(93446-2201)
PHONE..............................805 237-3110
Michelle Chambers, *Manager*
EMP: 140 **Privately Held**
SIC: **8322** Social service center
PA: County Of Los Angeles
500 W Temple St Ste 437
Los Angeles CA 90012
213 974-1101

(P-23096)
COUNTY OF LOS ANGELES
Also Called: Public Social Services
2707 S Grand Ave, Los Angeles
(90007-3300)
PHONE..............................213 744-5601
Petra Gonzalez, *Director*
EMP: 430 **Privately Held**
WEB: www.co.la.ca.us
SIC: **8322** 9441 Individual & family serv-
ices; administration of social & manpower
programs;
PA: County Of Los Angeles
500 W Temple St Ste 437
Los Angeles CA 90012
213 974-1101

(P-23097)
COUNTY OF LOS ANGELES
Also Called: San Fernando Valley Interfaith
14555 Osborne St Ofc, Van Nuys
(91402-1859)
PHONE..............................818 362-6437
Estella Lyons, *Chairman*
EMP: 135 **Privately Held**
WEB: www.co.la.ca.us
SIC: **8322** 9441 Geriatric social service;
administration of social & manpower pro-
grams;
PA: County Of Los Angeles
500 W Temple St Ste 437
Los Angeles CA 90012
213 974-1101

(P-23098)
COUNTY OF LOS ANGELES
Also Called: Health Services, Dept of
17171 Gale Ave, City of Industry
(91745-1822)
PHONE..............................626 854-4987
Althea Shirley, *Director*
EMP: 200 **Privately Held**
WEB: www.co.la.ca.us
SIC: **8322** 9431 Public welfare center; ad-
ministration of public health programs;
PA: County Of Los Angeles
500 W Temple St Ste 437
Los Angeles CA 90012
213 974-1101

(P-23099)
COUNTY OF LOS ANGELES
Also Called: County Los Angles Prbtion Dept
1660 W Mission Blvd, Pomona
(91766-1200)
PHONE..............................909 469-4500
Lorraine Hubbard-Johns, *Manager*
EMP: 100 **Privately Held**
WEB: www.co.la.ca.us
SIC: **8322** 9223 Probation office; correc-
tional institutions;
PA: County Of Los Angeles
500 W Temple St Ste 437
Los Angeles CA 90012
213 974-1101

(P-23100)
COUNTY OF LOS ANGELES
Also Called: Probation Dept
1725 Main St Rm 125, Santa Monica
(90401-3267)
PHONE..............................310 266-3711
Ernest P Gonzalez, *Branch Mgr*
Curtis McClendon, *Exec Dir*
Glenda Dunn, *Sales Executive*
EMP: 65 **Privately Held**
WEB: www.co.la.ca.us
SIC: **8322** 9223 Probation office; correc-
tional institutions;
PA: County Of Los Angeles
500 W Temple St Ste 437
Los Angeles CA 90012
213 974-1101

(P-23101)
COUNTY OF LOS ANGELES
Also Called: Probation Dept
14414 Delano St, Van Nuys (91401-2703)
PHONE..............................818 374-2000
Ed Johnson, *Director*
EMP: 100 **Privately Held**
WEB: www.co.la.ca.us
SIC: **8322** 9223 Probation office; correc-
tional institutions;
PA: County Of Los Angeles
500 W Temple St Ste 437
Los Angeles CA 90012
213 974-1101

(P-23102)
COUNTY OF LOS ANGELES
Also Called: Mental Health Dept of
330 E Live Oak Ave, Arcadia (91006-5617)
PHONE..............................626 821-5858
Len Tower, *Director*
Marita G Cristobal, *Psychiatry*
John S Wells, *Psychiatry*
EMP: 50 **Privately Held**
WEB: www.co.la.ca.us
SIC: **8322** 9431 Crisis center; mental
health agency administration, govern-
ment;

PA: County Of Los Angeles
500 W Temple St Ste 437
Los Angeles CA 90012
213 974-1101

(P-23103)
COUNTY OF LOS ANGELES
Also Called: Probation Dept
4849 Civic Center Way, Los Angeles
(90022-1679)
PHONE..............................323 780-2185
Debbie Nelson, *Director*
EMP: 80 **Privately Held**
SIC: **8322** 9223 Probation office; correc-
tional institutions;
PA: County Of Los Angeles
500 W Temple St Ste 437
Los Angeles CA 90012
213 974-1101

(P-23104)
COUNTY OF LOS ANGELES
Also Called: Public Social Services
12727 Norwalk Blvd, Norwalk
(90650-3145)
PHONE..............................562 807-7860
Tony Iniguez, *Director*
EMP: 250 **Privately Held**
WEB: www.co.la.ca.us
SIC: **8322** 9441 Individual & family serv-
ices; administration of social & manpower
programs;
PA: County Of Los Angeles
500 W Temple St Ste 437
Los Angeles CA 90012
213 974-1101

(P-23105)
COUNTY OF LOS ANGELES
Also Called: Department Children Fmly Svcs
501 Shatto Pl Ste 301, Los Angeles
(90020-1749)
PHONE..............................213 351-7257
Bill Browning, *Director*
EMP: 700 **Privately Held**
WEB: www.co.la.ca.us
SIC: **8322** 9111 Senior citizens' center or
association; executive offices
PA: County Of Los Angeles
500 W Temple St Ste 437
Los Angeles CA 90012
213 974-1101

(P-23106)
COUNTY OF LOS ANGELES
Also Called: Probation Dept
8526 Grape St, Los Angeles (90001-4134)
PHONE..............................323 586-6469
Mark Garcia, *Director*
EMP: 60 **Privately Held**
WEB: www.co.la.ca.us
SIC: **8322** 9223 Probation office; correc-
tional institutions;
PA: County Of Los Angeles
500 W Temple St Ste 437
Los Angeles CA 90012
213 974-1101

(P-23107)
COUNTY OF LOS ANGELES
Also Called: Probation Dept
200 W Compton Blvd # 300, Compton
(90220-6676)
PHONE..............................310 603-7311
Peggy May, *Director*
EMP: 140 **Privately Held**
WEB: www.co.la.ca.us
SIC: **8322** 9223 Probation office; correc-
tional institutions;
PA: County Of Los Angeles
500 W Temple St Ste 437
Los Angeles CA 90012
213 974-1101

(P-23108)
COUNTY OF LOS ANGELES
Also Called: Probation Dept
199 N Euclid Ave, Pasadena (91101-1757)
PHONE..............................626 356-5281
Steve Yoder, *Director*
EMP: 71 **Privately Held**
WEB: www.co.la.ca.us
SIC: **8322** 9223 Probation office; correc-
tional institutions;

PA: County Of Los Angeles
500 W Temple St Ste 437
Los Angeles CA 90012
213 974-1101

(P-23109)
COUNTY OF LOS ANGELES
Also Called: Dpss
3307 N Glenoaks Blvd, Burbank
(91504-2011)
PHONE..............................818 557-4164
Pamar Amirian, *Manager*
EMP: 135 **Privately Held**
WEB: www.co.la.ca.us
SIC: **8322** Emergency social services
PA: County Of Los Angeles
500 W Temple St Ste 437
Los Angeles CA 90012
213 974-1101

(P-23110)
COUNTY OF LOS ANGELES
200 W Woodward Ave, Alhambra
(91801-3459)
PHONE..............................626 308-5542
Roger Fernandez, *Branch Mgr*
EMP: 135 **Privately Held**
WEB: www.co.la.ca.us
SIC: **8322** 9111 Probation office; county
supervisors' & executives' offices
PA: County Of Los Angeles
500 W Temple St Ste 437
Los Angeles CA 90012
213 974-1101

(P-23111)
COUNTY OF LOS ANGELES
Also Called: Madera County Probation Dept
209 W Yosemite Ave, Madera
(93637-3534)
PHONE..............................559 675-7739
Linda Nash, *Manager*
EMP: 140 **Privately Held**
SIC: **8322** Individual & family services
PA: County Of Los Angeles
500 W Temple St Ste 437
Los Angeles CA 90012
213 974-1101

(P-23112)
COUNTY OF MARIN
Also Called: Marin City Library
164 Donahue St, Sausalito (94965-1250)
PHONE..............................415 332-6158
EMP: 300 **Privately Held**
SIC: **8322** Community center
PA: County Of Marin
3501 Civic Center Dr # 258
San Rafael CA 94903
415 473-6358

(P-23113)
COUNTY OF MARIN
Also Called: Marin County Welfare Dept
120 N Redwood Dr, San Rafael
(94903-1941)
P.O. Box 4160 (94913-4160)
PHONE..............................415 499-6970
Jane Chopson, *Director*
EMP: 300 **Privately Held**
SIC: **8322** 9441 Public welfare center; ad-
ministration of social & manpower pro-
grams;
PA: County Of Marin
3501 Civic Center Dr # 258
San Rafael CA 94903
415 473-6358

(P-23114)
COUNTY OF MENDOCINO
Also Called: Social Services, Department of
737 S State St, Ukiah (95482-5815)
P.O. Box 8508 (95482-8508)
PHONE..............................707 463-2437
Alison Glassey, *Administration*
EMP: 300 **Privately Held**
WEB: www.mcdss.org
SIC: **8322** Individual & family services
PA: County Of Mendocino
501 Low Gap Rd Rm 1010
Ukiah CA 95482
707 463-4441

(P-23115)
COUNTY OF MODOC
Also Called: Department of Social Services
120 N Main St, Alturas (96101-4045)
PHONE...............................530 233-6501
Pauline Cravens, *Branch Mgr*
Sarah K Holshouser, *Exec Dir*
EMP: 52 **Privately Held**
SIC: 8322 Social service center
PA: County Of Modoc
202 W 4th St Ste A
Alturas CA 96101
530 233-6400

(P-23116)
COUNTY OF MODOC
Also Called: Modoc County ADM Svcs
204 S Court St Ste 6, Alturas (96101-4138)
PHONE...............................530 233-6400
Michael Maxwell, *Branch Mgr*
EMP: 99 **Privately Held**
WEB: www.modoccounty.us
SIC: 8322 9111 Individual & family services; county supervisors' & executives' offices
PA: County Of Modoc
202 W 4th St Ste A
Alturas CA 96101
530 233-6400

(P-23117)
COUNTY OF MONTEREY
Department Social & Employment
1000 S Main St Ste 216, Salinas
(93901-2390)
PHONE...............................831 755-8500
Elliot Robinson, *Director*
EMP: 600 **Privately Held**
WEB: www.montereycountyfarmbureau.org
SIC: 8322 9111 Social service center; county supervisors' & executives' offices
PA: County Of Monterey
168 W Alisal St Fl 2
Salinas CA 93901
831 755-5040

(P-23118)
COUNTY OF NAPA
Also Called: NAPA Auto Parts
650 Imperial Way Ste 101, NAPA
(94559-1344)
PHONE...............................707 253-4625
Randy Snowden, *Director*
Jose Pelayo, *Administration*
Ben Guerard, *Technology*
Shanna Murray, *Opers Staff*
Janet Nottley, *Director*
EMP: 450 **Privately Held**
WEB: www.billkeller.com
SIC: 8322 Geriatric social service
PA: County Of Napa
1195 Third St Ste 310
Napa CA 94559
707 253-4421

(P-23119)
COUNTY OF NAPA
Also Called: NAPA County Juvenile Probation
212 Walnut St, NAPA (94559-3703)
PHONE...............................707 253-4361
Mary Butler, *Director*
EMP: 50
SQ FT: 122,839 **Privately Held**
WEB: www.billkeller.com
SIC: 8322 9111 Probation office; county supervisors' & executives' offices
PA: County Of Napa
1195 Third St Ste 310
Napa CA 94559
707 253-4421

(P-23120)
COUNTY OF ORANGE
Also Called: District Attorney
8141 13th St, Westminster (92683-4576)
PHONE...............................714 896-7188
Gary Tackett, *Branch Mgr*
EMP: 56 **Privately Held**
SIC: 8322 9211 Substance abuse counseling; courts
PA: County Of Orange
333 W Santa Ana Blvd 3f
Santa Ana CA 92701
714 834-6200

(P-23121)
COUNTY OF ORANGE
Also Called: Probation Dept
1535 E Orangewood Ave, Anaheim
(92805-6824)
PHONE...............................714 937-4500
Lalaw Reagan, *Manager*
Kim Hubbard,
Stacey McCoy, *Manager*
Lisa Bartlett, *Supervisor*
EMP: 100 **Privately Held**
SIC: 8322 9111 Probation office; executive offices
PA: County Of Orange
333 W Santa Ana Blvd 3f
Santa Ana CA 92701
714 834-6200

(P-23122)
COUNTY OF ORANGE
Also Called: Probation Dept
14180 Beach Blvd Ste 120, Westminster
(92683-4452)
PHONE...............................714 896-7500
Mac Jenkins, *Director*
Ann Spiratos, *Director*
EMP: 58 **Privately Held**
SIC: 8322 9223 Probation office; correctional institutions;
PA: County Of Orange
333 W Santa Ana Blvd 3f
Santa Ana CA 92701
714 834-6200

(P-23123)
COUNTY OF ORANGE
Also Called: Children & Family Serivces
800 N Eckhoff St Bldg 121, Orange
(92868-1008)
P.O. Box 14101 (92863-1501)
PHONE...............................714 704-8000
Michael Riley, *Director*
EMP: 150 **Privately Held**
SIC: 8322 9441 Children's aid society; administration of social & manpower programs;
PA: County Of Orange
333 W Santa Ana Blvd 3f
Santa Ana CA 92701
714 834-6200

(P-23124)
COUNTY OF ORANGE
Also Called: Social Services Agency
2020 W Walnut St, Santa Ana
(92703-4315)
P.O. Box 1943 (92702-1943)
PHONE...............................714 834-8899
Terry Row, *Branch Mgr*
EMP: 56 **Privately Held**
SIC: 8322 9441 Social service center; public welfare administration: non-operating, government;
PA: County Of Orange
333 W Santa Ana Blvd 3f
Santa Ana CA 92701
714 834-6200

(P-23125)
COUNTY OF ORANGE
Also Called: Social Services Agency
341 The City Dr S, Orange (92868-3205)
PHONE...............................714 935-6435
Linda Perring, *Director*
EMP: 56 **Privately Held**
SIC: 8322 9441 Social service center; administration of social & manpower programs;
PA: County Of Orange
333 W Santa Ana Blvd 3f
Santa Ana CA 92701
714 834-6200

(P-23126)
COUNTY OF PLACER
Also Called: Health & Human Services
379 Nevada St, Auburn (95603-3722)
PHONE...............................530 886-1870
Don Ferretti, *Manager*
EMP: 58 **Privately Held**
WEB: www.ssvems.com
SIC: 8322 9441 8231 Senior citizens' center or association; administration of social & manpower programs; ; public library

PA: County Of Placer
2986 Richardson Dr
Auburn CA 95603
530 889-4200

(P-23127)
COUNTY OF PLACER
Also Called: Mental Hlth Sbstnce Abuse Svcs
11512 B Ave, Auburn (95603-2605)
PHONE...............................530 823-4300
Maureen Bauman, *Director*
EMP: 150 **Privately Held**
WEB: www.ssvems.com
SIC: 8322 9431 Substance abuse counseling; mental health agency administration, government;
PA: County Of Placer
2986 Richardson Dr
Auburn CA 95603
530 889-4200

(P-23128)
COUNTY OF PLACER
Also Called: Probation Dept
2929 Richardson Dr Ste B, Auburn
(95603-2615)
PHONE...............................530 889-7900
Stephen G Pecor, *Principal*
EMP: 120 **Privately Held**
WEB: www.ssvems.com
SIC: 8322 9221 Probation office; parole office; police protection
PA: County Of Placer
2986 Richardson Dr
Auburn CA 95603
530 889-4200

(P-23129)
COUNTY OF RIVERSIDE
Also Called: Public Social Service
3178 Hamner Ave, Norco (92860-1936)
PHONE...............................951 272-5400
Sherri Feldt, *Manager*
EMP: 50 **Privately Held**
SIC: 8322 9441 Individual & family services; public welfare administration: non-operating, government;
PA: County Of Riverside
4080 Lemon St Fl 11
Riverside CA 92501
951 955-1110

(P-23130)
COUNTY OF RIVERSIDE
2560 N Perris Blvd Ste N1, Perris
(92571-3251)
PHONE...............................951 443-2262
EMP: 99 **Privately Held**
SIC: 8322 Probation office
PA: County Of Riverside
4080 Lemon St Fl 11
Riverside CA 92501
951 955-1110

(P-23131)
COUNTY OF RIVERSIDE
Also Called: Public Social Services
1400 W Minthorn St, Lake Elsinore
(92530-2808)
PHONE...............................951 245-3060
Mary Thoman, *Principal*
EMP: 99 **Privately Held**
SIC: 8322 9441 Individual & family services; administration of social & manpower programs;
PA: County Of Riverside
4080 Lemon St Fl 11
Riverside CA 92501
951 955-1110

(P-23132)
COUNTY OF RIVERSIDE
43264 Business Park Dr # 102, Temecula
(92590-3646)
PHONE...............................951 600-6500
Virginia Hedberg, *Branch Mgr*
EMP: 99 **Privately Held**
SIC: 8322 Public welfare center
PA: County Of Riverside
4080 Lemon St Fl 11
Riverside CA 92501
951 955-1110

(P-23133)
COUNTY OF RIVERSIDE
Also Called: Economic Development Dept
1325 Spruce St Ste 100, Riverside
(92507-0503)
PHONE...............................951 955-3100
Loren Sims, *Office Mgr*
Heidi Marshall, *Asst Director*
Peggy Sanchez, *Director*
EMP: 106 **Privately Held**
SIC: 8322 9441 Individual & family services; administration of social & manpower programs;
PA: County Of Riverside
4080 Lemon St Fl 11
Riverside CA 92501
951 955-1110

(P-23134)
COUNTY OF RIVERSIDE
4168 12th St, Riverside (92501-3409)
PHONE...............................951 275-8783
Yab Cordinator, *Principal*
EMP: 99 **Privately Held**
SIC: 8322 Youth center
PA: County Of Riverside
4080 Lemon St Fl 11
Riverside CA 92501
951 955-1110

(P-23135)
COUNTY OF RIVERSIDE
Also Called: Office On Aging, ADRC Of River
6296 River Crest Dr Ste K, Riverside
(92507-0738)
P.O. Box 2099 (92516-2099)
PHONE...............................951 697-4699
Edward Walsh, *Director*
EMP: 80 **Privately Held**
SIC: 8322 9441 Geriatric social service; administration of social & manpower programs;
PA: County Of Riverside
4080 Lemon St Fl 11
Riverside CA 92501
951 955-1110

(P-23136)
COUNTY OF RIVERSIDE
Also Called: Riverside Cnty Probation Dept
3960 Orange St Ste 500, Riverside
(92501-3644)
P.O. Box 833 (92502-0833)
PHONE...............................951 955-0905
Michelina lybar, *Supervisor*
Julie Terrell, *Manager*
Kathleen Atkins, *Supervisor*
EMP: 875 **Privately Held**
SIC: 8322 Probation office
PA: County Of Riverside
4080 Lemon St Fl 11
Riverside CA 92501
951 955-1110

(P-23137)
COUNTY OF RIVERSIDE
Also Called: Van Horn Youth Center
10000 County Farm Rd, Riverside
(92503-3508)
PHONE...............................951 358-4415
Pam Cronk, *Principal*
EMP: 99 **Privately Held**
SIC: 8322 9223 Youth center; correctional institutions;
PA: County Of Riverside
4080 Lemon St Fl 11
Riverside CA 92501
951 955-1110

(P-23138)
COUNTY OF SACRAMENTO
Also Called: Health and Human Services
9750 Bus Park Dr Ste 104, Sacramento
(95827-1716)
P.O. Box 5140 (95817-0140)
PHONE...............................916 875-4467
Mindy Yamasaki, *Branch Mgr*
EMP: 135 **Privately Held**
WEB: www.sna.com
SIC: 8322 9441 Old age assistance; administration of social & human resources;
PA: County Of Sacramento
700 H St Ste 7650
Sacramento CA 95814
916 874-5544

P
R
O
D
U
C
T
S

&

S
V
C
S

(P-23139)
COUNTY OF SAN BERNARDINO
Also Called: Human Services Systems
412 W Hospitality Ln Fl 2, San Bernardino
(92415-0913)
PHONE.....................909 891-3300
Mae Harns-Oglesby, *Director*
EMP: 70 **Privately Held**
SIC: **8322** 9441 Adoption services; administration of social & manpower programs;
PA: County Of San Bernardino
385 N Arrowhead Ave
San Bernardino CA 92415
909 387-3841

(P-23140)
COUNTY OF SAN BERNARDINO
Also Called: Probation Dept
8303 Haven Ave, Rancho Cucamonga
(91730-3848)
PHONE.....................909 945-4000
Wes Krause, *Branch Mgr*
EMP: 70 **Privately Held**
SIC: **8322** 9441 Probation office; administration of social & manpower programs;
PA: County Of San Bernardino
385 N Arrowhead Ave
San Bernardino CA 92415
909 387-3841

(P-23141)
COUNTY OF SAN BERNARDINO
Also Called: Aging & Adult Services
17270 Bear Valley Rd # 108, Victorville
(92395-7751)
PHONE.....................760 843-5100
EMP: 51 **Privately Held**
SIC: **8322** 9441
PA: County Of San Bernardino
385 N Arrowhead Ave
San Bernardino CA 92415
909 387-5455

(P-23142)
COUNTY OF SAN BERNARDINO
Also Called: Transitional Assistance Dept
56357 Pima Trl, Yucca Valley (92284-3607)
PHONE.....................760 228-5234
John Michealson, *Director*
EMP: 70 **Privately Held**
SIC: **8322** 9441 Individual & family services; administration of social & manpower programs;
PA: County Of San Bernardino
385 N Arrowhead Ave
San Bernardino CA 92415
909 387-3841

(P-23143)
COUNTY OF SAN DIEGO
Also Called: Health & Human Services
6950 Levant St, San Diego (92111-6010)
PHONE.....................858 694-5141
Debra Zanders-Willis, *Director*
EMP: 82 **Privately Held**
WEB: www.sdlcc.org
SIC: **8322** 9441 Adoption services; administration of social & manpower programs;
PA: County Of San Diego
1600 Pacific Hwy Ste 209
San Diego CA 92101
619 531-5880

(P-23144)
COUNTY OF SAN DIEGO
Also Called: Health & Human Services
130 E Alvarado St, Fallbrook (92028-2048)
PHONE.....................866 262-9881
Carol Schier, *Branch Mgr*
EMP: 82 **Privately Held**
WEB: www.sdlcc.org
SIC: **8322** Parole office
PA: County Of San Diego
1600 Pacific Hwy Ste 209
San Diego CA 92101
619 531-5880

(P-23145)
COUNTY OF SAN DIEGO
Also Called: Health and Human Service Agcy
5560 Overland Ave Ste 310, San Diego
(92123-1204)
PHONE.....................760 967-4621
Kimberly Gallo, *Manager*
Ellen Schmeding, *Principal*
Kristen Smith, *Administration*

EMP: 70 **Privately Held**
WEB: www.sdlcc.org
SIC: **8322** 9441 Individual & family services; administration of social & manpower programs;
PA: County Of San Diego
1600 Pacific Hwy Ste 209
San Diego CA 92101
619 531-5880

(P-23146)
COUNTY OF SAN DIEGO
Also Called: Probation Dept
330 W Broadway Ste 1100, San Diego
(92101-3827)
P.O. Box 23596 (92193-3596)
PHONE.....................619 515-8202
Don Blevins, *Director*
Ana Desntigo, *Counsel*
EMP: 82 **Privately Held**
WEB: www.sdlcc.org
SIC: **8322** 9431 Probation office; parole office; administration of public health programs
PA: County Of San Diego
1600 Pacific Hwy Ste 209
San Diego CA 92101
619 531-5880

(P-23147)
COUNTY OF SAN DIEGO
Also Called: Health & Human Services
1320 Union Plaza Ct, Oceanside
(92054-5659)
PHONE.....................760 754-3456
June Hercog, *Administration*
Ruth Supranovich, *Manager*
EMP: 160 **Privately Held**
WEB: www.sdlcc.org
SIC: **8322** 9441 Parole office;
PA: County Of San Diego
1600 Pacific Hwy Ste 209
San Diego CA 92101
619 531-5880

(P-23148)
COUNTY OF SAN DIEGO
Also Called: County Child Welfare Services
8965 Balboa Ave, San Diego (92123-1507)
PHONE.....................858 616-5989
Nick Macchione, *Director*
EMP: 350 **Privately Held**
WEB: www.sdlcc.org
SIC: **8322** Individual & family services
PA: County Of San Diego
1600 Pacific Hwy Ste 209
San Diego CA 92101
619 531-5880

(P-23149)
COUNTY OF SAN DIEGO
Also Called: Parks & Recreation Dept
8735 Jamacha Blvd, Spring Valley
(91977-5632)
PHONE.....................619 479-1832
Renell Nailon, *Director*
EMP: 75 **Privately Held**
WEB: www.sdlcc.org
SIC: **8322** 9512 Individual & family services; recreational program administration, government;
PA: County Of San Diego
1600 Pacific Hwy Ste 209
San Diego CA 92101
619 531-5880

(P-23150)
COUNTY OF SAN DIEGO
Also Called: Health and Human Services Agcy
3255 Camino Del Rio S, San Diego
(92108-3806)
PHONE.....................619 563-2765
Delia Mateo, *Principal*
EMP: 74 **Privately Held**
SIC: **8322** Individual & family services
PA: County Of San Diego
1600 Pacific Hwy Ste 209
San Diego CA 92101
619 531-5880

(P-23151)
COUNTY OF SAN DIEGO
Also Called: Health and Human Services
4588 Market St, San Diego (92102-4764)
PHONE.....................619 236-8725

Deborah Lester, *Branch Mgr*
EMP: 150 **Privately Held**
WEB: www.sdlcc.org
SIC: **8322** 9431 Individual & family services; administration of public health programs
PA: County Of San Diego
1600 Pacific Hwy Ste 209
San Diego CA 92101
619 531-5880

(P-23152)
COUNTY OF SAN JOAQUIN
Also Called: Dept of Child Support
409 E Market St, Stockton (95202-3007)
PHONE.....................209 468-2601
Judy Grimes, *Branch Mgr*
EMP: 400 **Privately Held**
WEB: www.sjclawlib.org
SIC: **8322** 9441 Child related social services; public welfare administration: non-operating, government
PA: County Of San Joaquin
44 N San Joaquin St # 640
Stockton CA 95202
209 468-3203

(P-23153)
COUNTY OF SAN JOAQUIN
Also Called: San Joaquin County Adult Svcs
24 S Hunter St Ste 201, Stockton
(95202-3231)
PHONE.....................209 468-4100
Dave Newaj, *CEO*
EMP: 78 **Privately Held**
SIC: **8322** Probation office
PA: County Of San Joaquin
44 N San Joaquin St # 640
Stockton CA 95202
209 468-3203

(P-23154)
COUNTY OF SAN JOAQUIN
Also Called: Mary Grahams Childrens Shelter
500 W Hospital Rd, French Camp
(95231-9693)
P.O. Box 201056, Stockton (95201-3006)
PHONE.....................209 468-6966
Brian Woods, *Director*
EMP: 75 **Privately Held**
WEB: www.sjclawlib.org
SIC: **8322** 9512 Child related social services; land conservation agencies
PA: County Of San Joaquin
44 N San Joaquin St # 640
Stockton CA 95202
209 468-3203

(P-23155)
COUNTY OF SAN LUIS OBISPO
Also Called: Department of Social Services
3433 S Higuera St, San Luis Obispo
(93401-7301)
PHONE.....................805 781-5437
Lee Collins, *Director*
EMP: 108 **Privately Held**
SIC: **8322** Child related social services
PA: County Of San Luis Obispo
Government Center Rm. 300
San Luis Obispo CA 93408
805 781-5040

(P-23156)
COUNTY OF SAN LUIS OBISPO
Also Called: Dept of Social Services Dss
3433 S Higuera St, San Luis Obispo
(93401-7301)
P.O. Box 8119 (93403-8119)
PHONE.....................805 781-1864
Leland Collins, *Director*
EMP: 450 **Privately Held**
SIC: **8322** Individual & family services
PA: County Of San Luis Obispo
Government Center Rm. 300
San Luis Obispo CA 93408
805 781-5040

(P-23157)
COUNTY OF SAN MATEO
Also Called: Probation Department
680 Warren St, Redwood City
(94063-1522)
PHONE.....................650 599-7336
Michael J Stauffer, *Manager*
EMP: 130 **Privately Held**
WEB: www.ci.sanmateo.ca.us

SIC: **8322** 9223 Probation office;
PA: County Of San Mateo
400 County Ctr
Redwood City CA 94063
650 363-4123

(P-23158)
COUNTY OF SAN MATEO
Also Called: Probation Department
222 Paul Scannell Dr, San Mateo
(94402-4061)
PHONE.....................650 312-5327
Stuart Forrest, *Chief*
Tracy Shwan, *General Mgr*
EMP: 250 **Privately Held**
WEB: www.ci.sanmateo.ca.us
SIC: **8322** 9223 Probation office; parole office;
PA: County Of San Mateo
400 County Ctr
Redwood City CA 94063
650 363-4123

(P-23159)
COUNTY OF SAN MATEO
Also Called: Probation Department
222 Paul Scannell Dr Fl 2, San Mateo
(94402-4061)
PHONE.....................650 312-8887
Stewart Forest, *Manager*
EMP: 400 **Privately Held**
WEB: www.ci.sanmateo.ca.us
SIC: **8322** 9199 Probation office; general government administration;
PA: County Of San Mateo
400 County Ctr
Redwood City CA 94063
650 363-4123

(P-23160)
COUNTY OF SAN MATEO
Also Called: Probation Department
2277 University Ave, East Palo Alto
(94303-1717)
PHONE.....................650 853-3139
Robert Hoover, *Manager*
EMP: 51 **Privately Held**
WEB: www.ci.sanmateo.ca.us
SIC: **8322** 9223 Probation office; parole office;
PA: County Of San Mateo
400 County Ctr
Redwood City CA 94063
650 363-4123

(P-23161)
COUNTY OF SAN MATEO
Child Support Services Dept
555 County Ctr Fl 2, Redwood City
(94063-1665)
PHONE.....................650 363-1910
Kim Cagno, *Director*
EMP: 80 **Privately Held**
WEB: www.ci.sanmateo.ca.us
SIC: **8322** 9441 Child related social services;
PA: County Of San Mateo
400 County Ctr
Redwood City CA 94063
650 363-4123

(P-23162)
COUNTY OF SAN MATEO
Also Called: Human Services Agency
400 Harbor Blvd Bldg B, Belmont
(94002-4047)
PHONE.....................650 802-6470
Beverly Beasley Johnson, *Manager*
Marnita G Fulle, *Analyst*
EMP: 150 **Privately Held**
WEB: www.ci.sanmateo.ca.us
SIC: **8322** 9441 Adoption services; administration of social & manpower programs;
PA: County Of San Mateo
400 County Ctr
Redwood City CA 94063
650 363-4123

(P-23163)
COUNTY OF SAN MATEO
Also Called: Probation Department
222 Paul Scannell Dr, San Mateo
(94402-4061)
PHONE.....................650 312-8803
John Keene, *Branch Mgr*
EMP: 200 **Privately Held**

WEB: www.ci.sanmateo.ca.us
SIC: 8322 9199 Probation office; general
  government administration;
PA: County Of San Mateo
  400 County Ctr
  Redwood City CA 94063
  650 363-4123

(P-23164)
COUNTY OF SAN MATEO
Also Called: Probation Department
400 County Ctr Fl 5, Redwood City
(94063-1662)
P.O. Box 441 (94064-0441)
PHONE..................................650 363-4244
John Keene, *Chairman*
Jody Dimauro, *Manager*
EMP: 143 **Privately Held**
SIC: 8322 9223 Probation office;
PA: County Of San Mateo
  400 County Ctr
  Redwood City CA 94063
  650 363-4123

(P-23165)
COUNTY OF SHASTA
Also Called: Children's Protective Services
1313 Yuba St, Redding (96001-1012)
PHONE..................................530 225-5554
Dianna Wagner, *Director*
EMP: 75 **Privately Held**
WEB: www.rsdnmp.org
SIC: 8322 Children's aid society
PA: County Of Shasta
  1450 Court St Ste 308a
  Redding CA 96001
  530 225-5561

(P-23166)
COUNTY OF SISKIYOU
Also Called: Human Services Department
818 S Main St, Yreka (96097-3321)
PHONE..................................530 841-2700
Nadine Dellabitta, *Director*
EMP: 60 **Privately Held**
WEB: www.siskiyoucounty.org
SIC: 8322 Individual & family services
PA: County Of Siskiyou
  311 4th St Rm 108
  Yreka CA 96097
  530 841-4100

(P-23167)
COUNTY OF SOLANO
Also Called: Health and Social Services
275 Beck Ave, Fairfield (94533-6804)
PHONE..................................707 784-8400
Patrick Dulerte, *Director*
EMP: 56 **Privately Held**
SIC: 8322 Individual & family services
PA: County Of Solano
  675 Texas St Ste 2600
  Fairfield CA 94533
  707 784-6706

(P-23168)
COUNTY OF SOLANO
Also Called: Solano County Probation Dept
475 Union Ave, Fairfield (94533-6319)
PHONE..................................707 784-7600
Isabelle Voight, *Principal*
Donna Vestal, *Analyst*
Christopher Hansen, *Director*
EMP: 237 **Privately Held**
SIC: 8322 Probation office
PA: County Of Solano
  675 Texas St Ste 2600
  Fairfield CA 94533
  707 784-6706

(P-23169)
COUNTY OF SONOMA
2300 County Center Dr B100, Santa Rosa
(95403-3013)
PHONE..................................707 527-2641
Peter Boomer, *Branch Mgr*
Robert Kambak, *Architect*
EMP: 60 **Privately Held**
WEB: www.sonomacompost.com
SIC: 8322 Child related social services
PA: County Of Sonoma
  585 Fiscal Dr 100
  Santa Rosa CA 95403
  707 565-2431

(P-23170)
COUNTY OF STANISLAUS
Also Called: Community Services
830 Scenic Dr, Modesto (95350-6131)
PHONE..................................209 558-8828
Nancy Fisher, *Superintendent*
EMP: 75 **Privately Held**
WEB: www.co.stanislaus.ca.us
SIC: 8322 Youth self-help agency
PA: County Of Stanislaus
  1010 10th St Ste 5100
  Modesto CA 95354
  209 525-6398

(P-23171)
COUNTY OF STANISLAUS
Also Called: Probation Dept
801 11th St, Modesto (95354-2348)
PHONE..................................209 567-4120
Mike Hamasaki, *Branch Mgr*
EMP: 110 **Privately Held**
SIC: 8322 Probation office
PA: County Of Stanislaus
  1010 10th St Ste 5100
  Modesto CA 95354
  209 525-6398

(P-23172)
COUNTY OF STANISLAUS
108 Campus Way, Modesto (95350-5803)
PHONE..................................209 558-7377
Elaine Emory, *Manager*
EMP: 110 **Privately Held**
SIC: 8322 Individual & family services
PA: County Of Stanislaus
  1010 10th St Ste 5100
  Modesto CA 95354
  209 525-6398

(P-23173)
COUNTY OF STANISLAUS
Also Called: Dcss
251 E Hackett Rd, Modesto (95358-9800)
P.O. Box 4189 (95352-4189)
PHONE..................................209 558-9675
Tamara Thomas, *Branch Mgr*
Marissa De Almeida, *Chief*
EMP: 223 **Privately Held**
WEB: www.modairport.com
SIC: 8322 Family counseling services
PA: County Of Stanislaus
  1010 10th St Ste 5100
  Modesto CA 95354
  209 525-6398

(P-23174)
COUNTY OF STANISLAUS
Also Called: Family Support Division
108 Campus Way, Modesto (95350-5803)
P.O. Box 4189 (95352-4189)
PHONE..................................209 558-2500
Joan Kingman, *Branch Mgr*
EMP: 95 **Privately Held**
WEB: www.co.stanislaus.ca.us
SIC: 8322 Child related social services
PA: County Of Stanislaus
  1010 10th St Ste 5100
  Modesto CA 95354
  209 525-6398

(P-23175)
COUNTY OF TEHAMA
Also Called: Mental Health Services
1860 Walnut St, Red Bluff (96080-3611)
P.O. Box 400 (96080-0400)
PHONE..................................530 527-5631
Valerie Lucero, *Director*
EMP: 200 **Privately Held**
SIC: 8322 9111 Social service center;
  county supervisors' & executives' offices
PA: The County Of Tehama
  727 Oak St
  Red Bluff CA 96080
  530 527-4655

(P-23176)
COUNTY OF TEHAMA
Also Called: Probation
1840 Walnut St, Red Bluff (96080-3611)
P.O. Box 99 (96080-0099)
PHONE..................................530 527-4052
David Finch, *Branch Mgr*
EMP: 70 **Privately Held**
SIC: 8322 9111 Probation office; county
  supervisors' & executives' offices

PA: The County Of Tehama
  727 Oak St
  Red Bluff CA 96080
  530 527-4655

(P-23177)
COUNTY OF TUOLUMNE
Also Called: Welfare Department
20075 Cedar Rd N, Sonora (95370-5900)
P.O. Box 5024 (95370-2024)
PHONE..................................209 533-5711
Kent Skellenger, *Director*
Jema Padavana, *Analyst*
Ann Connolly, *Director*
EMP: 110 **Privately Held**
WEB: www.tuolumne.courts.ca.gov
SIC: 8322 Social service center
PA: County Of Tuolumne
  2 S Green St
  Sonora CA 95370
  209 533-5521

(P-23178)
COUNTY OF VENTURA
Also Called: County Ventura Human Re-
sources
800 S Victoria Ave, Ventura (93009-0003)
PHONE..................................805 654-2561
Jodi Lee Prior, *Branch Mgr*
Jill George, *Treasurer*
Manny Ramos, *Officer*
Clifford Shuey, *Officer*
Leah Velador, *Officer*
EMP: 104 **Privately Held**
WEB: www.vcoe.org
SIC: 8322 9441 Individual & family serv-
  ices; administration of social & human re-
  sources
PA: County Of Ventura
  800 S Victoria Ave
  Ventura CA 93009
  805 654-2644

(P-23179)
COUNTY OF VENTURA
Also Called: Foster Care Licensing & Svc
4651 Telephone Rd Ste 300, Ventura
(93003-8779)
PHONE..................................805 654-3456
Ellen Mastright, *Branch Mgr*
Armand Paez, *Human Res Mgr*
EMP: 90 **Privately Held**
WEB: www.vcoe.org
SIC: 8322 9111 Hotline; executive offices
PA: County Of Ventura
  800 S Victoria Ave
  Ventura CA 93009
  805 654-2644

(P-23180)
COUNTY OF VENTURA
1400 Vanguard Dr Fl 2nd, Oxnard
(93033-2402)
PHONE..................................805 385-8654
Bonita Kraft, *Branch Mgr*
EMP: 104 **Privately Held**
SIC: 8322 Probation office
PA: County Of Ventura
  800 S Victoria Ave
  Ventura CA 93009
  805 654-2644

(P-23181)
COUNTY OF VENTURA
Also Called: Medical Center
3291 Loma Vista Rd, Ventura
(93003-3099)
PHONE..................................805 652-6000
Michael Powers, *Manager*
Ron Sandoval, *Radiology Dir*
Gillian Dorner, *Med Doctor*
EMP: 600 **Privately Held**
WEB: www.vcoe.org
SIC: 8322 9431 Individual & family serv-
  ices; administration of public health pro-
  grams;
PA: County Of Ventura
  800 S Victoria Ave
  Ventura CA 93009
  805 654-2644

(P-23182)
COUNTY OF VENTURA
Also Called: Department Child Support Svcs
5171 Verdugo Way, Camarillo
(93012-8603)
PHONE..................................805 654-5529
Stanley Trom, *Director*
EMP: 273 **Privately Held**
WEB: www.vcoe.org
SIC: 8322 9199 Individual & family serv-
  ices; child health program administration,
  government
PA: County Of Ventura
  800 S Victoria Ave
  Ventura CA 93009
  805 654-2644

(P-23183)
COUNTY OF YUBA
Also Called: Yuba County Probation Dept
215 5th St Ste 154, Marysville
(95901-5737)
PHONE..................................530 749-7550
Jim Arnold, *Director*
EMP: 183 **Privately Held**
SIC: 8322 9199 Probation office;
PA: County Of Yuba
  915 8th St Ste 109
  Marysville CA 95901
  530 749-7575

(P-23184)
**COUNTY SANDIEGO DEPT
CHLDSPPRT**
3666 Krny Vlla Rd Ste 100, San Diego
(92123)
PHONE..................................619 578-6660
Jeff Grissom, *Director*
EMP: 500
SALES (est): 201.2K **Privately Held**
SIC: 8322 Individual & family services

(P-23185)
**COVIA AFFORDABLE
COMMUNITIES**
2185 N Calif Blvd Ste 215, Walnut Creek
(94596-3566)
PHONE..................................925 956-7400
Kevin Gerber, *CEO*
Jonathan Casey, *CFO*
EMP: 105
SALES: 2.1MM **Privately Held**
WEB: www.lyttongardens.org
SIC: 8322 6513 Individual & family serv-
  ices; apartment building operators

(P-23186)
**CRESTWOOD BEHAVIORAL
HLTH INC**
Also Called: 115 Bakersfield Mhrc
6700 Eucalyptus Dr Ste A, Bakersfield
(93306-6076)
PHONE..................................661 363-8127
Ronda Banclive, *Director*
Deleon Delphina, *Exec Dir*
EMP: 75
SALES (corp-wide): 188.6MM **Privately
Held**
WEB: www.crestwoodbehavioralhealth.com
SIC: 8322 8011 Rehabilitation services;
  psychiatric clinic
PA: Crestwood Behavioral Health, Inc.
  520 Capitol Mall Ste 800
  Sacramento CA 95814
  510 651-1244

(P-23187)
CRUCIBLE
1260 7th St, Oakland (94607-2150)
PHONE..................................510 444-0919
Susan Mernit, *Exec Dir*
Michael Sturtz, *Exec Dir*
Steven Young, *Exec Dir*
EMP: 215
SQ FT: 46,980
SALES: 2.9MM **Privately Held**
WEB: www.thecrucible.com
SIC: 8322 8331 Outreach program; skill
  training center

(P-23188)
CRYSTAL STAIRS INC (PA)
5110 W Goldleaf Cir # 150, Los Angeles
(90056-1287)
PHONE..................................323 299-8998

PRODUCTS & SVCS

Jackie B Majors, *CEO*
Dianna Torres, *Ch of Bd*
Dr Karen Hill-Scott, *President*
Javier La Fianza, *COO*
Robert Trujillo, *Treasurer*
EMP: 330
SQ FT: 83,000
SALES: 132.2MM **Privately Held**
WEB: www.crystalstairs.com
SIC: 8322 Social service center

(P-23189)
DACARE INC (PA)
Also Called: Dayout Brawley
643 Main St, Brawley (92227-2547)
PHONE..........................760 344-4654
Elizabeth Machado, *CEO*
EMP: 55 EST: 1996
SALES (est): 3MM **Privately Held**
WEB: www.daycare.com
SIC: 8322 Adult day care center

(P-23190)
DESERT AIDS PROJECT (PA)
Also Called: Get Tested Coachella Valley
1695 N Sunrise Way Bldg 1, Palm Springs
(92262-3702)
P.O. Box 2890 (92263-2890)
PHONE..........................760 323-2118
David Brinkman, *CEO*
Mary Park, *CFO*
Sherry Saenz, *Human Res Mgr*
EMP: 65
SQ FT: 46,050
SALES: 33.6MM **Privately Held**
WEB: www.desertaidsproject.org
SIC: 8322 5932 8011 General counseling
services; used merchandise stores; clinic,
operated by physicians

(P-23191)
DESERTARC
Also Called: DESERT VALLEY INDUSTRIES
73255 Country Club Dr, Palm Desert
(92260-2309)
PHONE..........................760 346-1611
Lori Serfling, *Treasurer*
Robert Anzalone, *President*
Robin Keagen, *CFO*
Robin Keegan, *CFO*
Jay Chesterton, *Treasurer*
EMP: 256 EST: 1959
SQ FT: 12,000
SALES: 14.7MM **Privately Held**
WEB: www.desertarc.org
SIC: 8322 Association for the handi-
capped; social services for the handi-
capped

(P-23192)
DEVELOP DISABILITIES SVC ORG
Also Called: Community Integration Program
2331 Saint Marks Way G1, Sacramento
(95864-0626)
PHONE..........................916 973-1951
Yvonne Soto, *CEO*
Amy Nishimura, *CEO*
Susan Burger, *Deputy Dir*
EMP: 75
SALES (est): 897K **Privately Held**
SIC: 8322 Association for the handi-
capped; social services for the handi-
capped

(P-23193)
DEVELOPMENTAL DISABILITIES (PA)
Also Called: Ddso
5051 47th Ave, Sacramento (95824-4036)
PHONE..........................916 456-5166
Yvonne Soto, *Acting CEO*
Jon Hutchison, *Ch of Bd*
Ann Larson, *Ch of Bd*
Jennifer Bonacorso, *CFO*
Trish Williams, *Sales Executive*
EMP: 99
SQ FT: 36,000
SALES: 4.4MM **Privately Held**
WEB: www.ddso.org
SIC: 8322 Community center

(P-23194)
DIDI HIRSCH PSYCHIATRIC SVC (PA)
Also Called: DIDI HIRSCH COMMUNITY
MENTAL H
4760 Sepulveda Blvd, Culver City
(90230-4820)
PHONE..........................310 390-6612
Michael Wierwille, *Chairman*
Andrew Rubin, *Admin Sec*
John McGann, *VP Finance*
EMP: 150 EST: 1944
SQ FT: 35,000
SALES: 44.5MM **Privately Held**
SIC: 8322 8093 Family counseling serv-
ices; mental health clinic, outpatient

(P-23195)
DISTRICT COUNCIL DC (PA)
Also Called: St Vincent De Paul
2272 San Pablo Ave, Oakland
(94612-1321)
PHONE..........................510 638-7600
Blase Bova, *Exec Dir*
EMP: 100
SQ FT: 40,000
SALES: 7.4MM **Privately Held**
SIC: 8322 Individual & family services

(P-23196)
DIVERSE JOURNEYS INC (PA)
525 S Douglas St Ste 210, El Segundo
(90245-4827)
PHONE..........................310 643-7403
Amanda Gerhart, *President*
Laura Broderrick, *Director*
EMP: 98
SQ FT: 2,000
SALES (est): 3.1MM **Privately Held**
SIC: 8322 Social services for the handi-
capped

(P-23197)
DREW CHILD DEV CORP INC (PA)
1770 E 118th St, Los Angeles
(90059-2518)
PHONE..........................323 249-2950
Michael Jackson, *President*
James Hays, *CEO*
EMP: 150
SALES: 21MM **Privately Held**
SIC: 8322 Child guidance agency

(P-23198)
EAST BAY ASIAN YOUTH CENTER
2025 E 12th St, Oakland (94606-4925)
PHONE..........................510 533-1092
Gianna Tran, *President*
EMP: 50
SALES (corp-wide): 5.1MM **Privately
Held**
WEB: www.ebayc.org
SIC: 8322 Youth center
PA: East Bay Asian Youth Center
2025 E 12th St
Oakland CA 94606
510 533-1092

(P-23199)
EAST L A REMARKABLE CITIZENS (PA)
Also Called: EL ARCA
3839 Selig Pl, Los Angeles (90031-3143)
PHONE..........................323 223-3079
Carlos Madrid, *Exec Dir*
Karina Andrade, *Vice Pres*
John Menchaca, *Vice Pres*
Miriam Alarcon, *Human Resources*
EMP: 85
SQ FT: 23,360
SALES: 5.4MM **Privately Held**
WEB: www.elarca.com
SIC: 8322 Social services for the handi-
capped

(P-23200)
EASTER SEALS CENTRAL CAL
9010 Soquel Dr, Aptos (95003-4082)
PHONE..........................831 684-2166
Bruce Hinman, *President*
EMP: 300
SALES: 3.2MM **Privately Held**
SIC: 8322 Social service center

(P-23201)
EASTERN LOS ANGELES RE (PA)
1000 S Fremont Ave # 40, Alhambra
(91803-8873)
P.O. Box 7916 (91802-7916)
PHONE..........................626 299-4700
Gloria Wong, *Exec Dir*
Felicitas Navera, *Bd of Directors*
Manuel Garcia, *Technology*
Noriko Ikoma, *Technology*
Sophia Tang Hao, *Controller*
EMP: 287
SQ FT: 31,704
SALES: 196.3MM **Privately Held**
WEB: www.elarc.org
SIC: 8322 Association for the handicapped

(P-23202)
EASTERN STAR HOMES CALIFORNIA (PA)
Also Called: EASTERN STAR PROFES-
SIONAL BUIL
16850 Bastanchury Rd, Yorba Linda
(92886-1608)
PHONE..........................714 986-2380
Norma Stillwell, *President*
Danna Willoughby, *President*
EMP: 57
SQ FT: 15,604
SALES: 3.5MM **Privately Held**
SIC: 8322 Geriatric social service

(P-23203)
EGGLESTON YOUTH CENTERS INC (PA)
13001 Ramona Blvd Ste E, Irwindale
(91706-3752)
P.O. Box 638, Baldwin Park (91706-0638)
PHONE..........................626 480-8107
Clarence Brown, *Exec Dir*
April Mitchell, *President*
Don Gutierrez, *Administration*
EMP: 90
SQ FT: 7,616
SALES (est): 8MM **Privately Held**
SIC: 8322 Social service center; youth
center

(P-23204)
EL CAMINO CHILDREN & FMLY SVCS
9900 Lakewood Blvd # 104, Downey
(90240-4038)
PHONE..........................562 364-1258
Jorge Gutierrez, *CEO*
Robert Donin, *Chairman*
John Rojas, *Vice Pres*
David Sanchez, *Admin Sec*
EMP: 50
SQ FT: 3,000
SALES: 68.2K **Privately Held**
WEB: www.eccafs.com
SIC: 8322 Family counseling services

(P-23205)
EL CAMINO HOSPITAL
1503 Grant Rd Ste 120, Mountain View
(94040-3293)
PHONE..........................650 988-7444
Vicki Chryssos, *Exec Dir*
EMP: 172
SALES (corp-wide): 973.3MM **Privately
Held**
SIC: 8322 Social worker
PA: El Camino Hospital
2500 Grant Rd
Mountain View CA 94040
650 940-7000

(P-23206)
EL CONCILIO SAN MATEO CNTY INC
Also Called: HISPANIC CONCILIO OF SAN
MATEO
3180 Middlefield Rd, Redwood City
(94063-3762)
PHONE..........................650 373-1080
Ortensia Lopez, *President*
EMP: 50
SALES: 1.8MM **Privately Held**
WEB: www.el-concilio.com
SIC: 8322 Social service center

(P-23207)
EL NIDO FAMILY CENTERS (PA)
10200 Sepulveda Blvd # 350, Mission Hills
(91345-3318)
PHONE..........................818 830-3646
Liz Herrera, *Director*
Susanne Nagle, *Broker*
EMP: 130
SQ FT: 3,650
SALES (est): 8.6MM
SALES (corp-wide): 8.8MM **Privately
Held**
WEB: www.elnidofamilycenters.org
SIC: 8322 Social service center

(P-23208)
ELDER OPTIONS (PA)
82 Main St, Placerville (95667-5506)
P.O. Box 2113 (95667-2113)
PHONE..........................530 626-6939
Carol Heape, *Owner*
EMP: 50
SALES (est): 2.5MM **Privately Held**
SIC: 8322 Senior citizens' center or associ-
ation; geriatric social service

(P-23209)
ENCOMPASS COMMUNITY SERVICES
Also Called: Headstart
225 Westridge Dr, Watsonville
(95076-4168)
P.O. Box 927 (95077-0927)
PHONE..........................831 724-3885
Gloria Martinez, *Branch Mgr*
EMP: 300
SALES (corp-wide): 29.3MM **Privately
Held**
SIC: 8322 8351 Social service center;
head start center, except in conjunction
with school
PA: Encompass Community Services
380 Encinal St Ste 200
Santa Cruz CA

(P-23210)
EPISCOPAL COMM SVC SAN FRAN (PA)
Also Called: Ecs
165 8th St Fl 3, San Francisco
(94103-2726)
PHONE..........................415 487-3300
Kenneth J Reggio, *Exec Dir*
Sedge Dienst, *President*
Peter Mc Coy, *CEO*
Alan Fox, *Treasurer*
Andrea Clay, *Vice Pres*
EMP: 200
SQ FT: 12,000
SALES: 21.3MM **Privately Held**
WEB: www.ecs-sf.org
SIC: 8322 Emergency shelters

(P-23211)
EPISCOPAL COMMUNITY
Also Called: Ecs South Bay Head Start
1261 Third Ave Ste B, Chula Vista
(91911-3262)
PHONE..........................619 228-2800
Buffy Boyer, *Director*
Gene Merlino, *Director*
EMP: 60
SALES (est): 760.2K **Privately Held**
SIC: 8322 8741 Community center; man-
agement services

(P-23212)
ETNA POLICE ACTIVITIES LEAGUE
448 Main St, Etna (96027)
P.O. Box 460 (96027-0460)
PHONE..........................530 467-3400
Josh Short, *President*
Autumn Kistler, *Director*
EMP: 200
SALES: 12.9K **Privately Held**
SIC: 8322 Community center

(P-23213)
EXCEPTNAL PRENTS UNLIMITED INC
Also Called: E P U
4440 N 1st St, Fresno (93726-2304)
PHONE..........................559 229-2000

Lowell Ens, *CEO*
Kim Majors, *Human Res Dir*
Krista Rose, *Education*
Danny Armenta, *Director*
Daryl Hitchcock, *Director*
EMP: 115
SQ FT: 24,000
SALES: 7.7MM **Privately Held**
WEB: www.exceptionalparents.org
SIC: 8322 Family counseling services

(P-23214)
FAMILY & CHILDREN SERVICES
375 Cambridge Ave, Palo Alto
(94306-1613)
PHONE..................650 326-6576
Jim Welsh, *President*
Cassie Blume, *Executive*
Howard Lagoze, *General Mgr*
Fish Williams, *Finance*
Annette Janczura, *Human Res Dir*
EMP: 100
SQ FT: 6,000
SALES: 9.4MM **Privately Held**
SIC: 8322 Child related social services

(P-23215)
FAMILY ASSESSMENT CNSLNG EDCTN
1651 E 4th St Ste 128, Santa Ana
(92701-5141)
PHONE..................714 447-9024
Mary O Harris, *Branch Mgr*
EMP: 50
SALES (est): 301.7K **Privately Held**
SIC: 8322 Family counseling services;
general counseling services
PA: Family Assessment Counseling Education Services
2601 E Chapman Ave # 114
Fullerton CA 92831

(P-23216)
FAMILY BRIDGES INC
168 11th St, Oakland (94607-4841)
PHONE..................510 839-2270
Corinne Jan, *Exec Dir*
Susanna Ng-Lee, *Vice Pres*
Mary Marshall, *Admin Sec*
Vienna Gao, *Admin Asst*
Amy Yiu, *Administration*
EMP: 126
SQ FT: 5,000
SALES: 6.9MM **Privately Held**
WEB: www.familybridges.net
SIC: 8322 8641 Social service center;
civic social & fraternal associations

(P-23217)
FAMILY CIRCLE INC
Also Called: Oxnard Family Circle Adhc
2100 Outlet Center Dr # 380, Oxnard
(93036-0612)
PHONE..................805 385-4180
Inna Berger, *CEO*
Katy Krul, *CFO*
Dina Treglia, *Accounts Mgr*
EMP: 56
SQ FT: 12,000
SALES: 3.3MM **Privately Held**
WEB: www.familycircle.com
SIC: 8322 Adult day care center

(P-23218)
FAMILY RESOURCE & REFERRAL CTR
509 W Weber Ave Ste 101, Stockton
(95203-3107)
PHONE..................209 948-1553
Fax: 209 948-3554
EMP: 100
SALES (est): 28.6MM **Privately Held**
SIC: 8322

(P-23219)
FAMILY SERVICE AGENCY
Also Called: FSA
101 S B St Ste A, Lompoc (93436-6933)
PHONE..................805 735-4376
Stephanie Wilson, *Co-President*
Lisa Brabo, *Exec Dir*
EMP: 50
SALES (est): 541.3K **Privately Held**
SIC: 8322 8011 Social service center;
health maintenance organization

(P-23220)
FAMILY SERVICES TULARE COUNTY
815 W Oak Ave, Visalia (93291-6033)
PHONE..................559 732-1970
Caity Meader, *Exec Dir*
EMP: 85
SQ FT: 2,000
SALES: 6.2MM **Privately Held**
SIC: 8322 Family counseling services; social service center

(P-23221)
FAMILY SUPPORT SERVICES (PA)
303 Hegenberger Rd # 400, Oakland
(94621-1419)
PHONE..................510 834-2443
Lou Fox, *Director*
EMP: 58
SALES: 5.2MM **Privately Held**
WEB: www.fssba-oak.org
SIC: 8322 Social service center

(P-23222)
FAMILY SVC AGCY SANTA BARBARA
123 W Gutierrez St, Santa Barbara
(93101-3424)
PHONE..................805 965-1001
Denise Cicourel, *Administration*
Lisa Brabo, *Exec Dir*
Nancy A Ranck, *Director*
Georgina Dahill, *Supervisor*
EMP: 100
SALES: 5.3MM **Privately Held**
WEB: www.fsacares.org
SIC: 8322 Family (marriage) counseling

(P-23223)
FAMILY SVCS AGCY MARIN CNTY (PA)
Also Called: Family Service Agency
555 Northgate Dr, San Rafael
(94903-3680)
PHONE..................415 491-5700
Margret Hallett, *Director*
EMP: 82
SALES (est): 2MM **Privately Held**
SIC: 8322 Family (marriage) counseling

(P-23224)
FAR NORTHERN COORDINATING COUN
Also Called: Regional Center
1377 E Lassen Ave, Chico (95973-7824)
PHONE..................530 895-8633
Laura Larson, *Director*
EMP: 75
SALES (corp-wide): 127MM **Privately Held**
SIC: 8322 8399 Social services for the handicapped; health & welfare council
PA: Far Northern Coordinating Council On Developmental Disabilities
1900 Churn Creek Rd # 114
Redding CA 96002
530 222-4791

(P-23225)
FAR NORTHERN COORDINATING COUN (PA)
Also Called: Far Northern Regional Center
1900 Churn Creek Rd # 114, Redding
(96002-0292)
P.O. Box 492418 (96049-2418)
PHONE..................530 222-4791
Laura L Larson, *Exec Dir*
EMP: 100
SALES: 127MM **Privately Held**
SIC: 8322 Association for the handicapped; social services for the handicapped

(P-23226)
FHAR FMLY HSING ADULT RSOURCES
205 W 20th Ave, San Mateo (94403-1302)
PHONE..................650 573-3341
Dave Carson, *President*
Phil Surdel, *Director*
EMP: 90

SALES (est): 1.3MM **Privately Held**
WEB: www.fhar.org
SIC: 8322 Social service center

(P-23227)
FIREFIGHTER CANCER SUPPORT NTW
3460 Fletcher Ave, El Monte (91731-3002)
PHONE..................866 994-3276
Dan Crow, *President*
Jeffrey Howe, *Treasurer*
Curtis Dunn, *Vice Pres*
Steve Fisher, *Vice Pres*
Holden Leon, *Director*
EMP: 50
SALES: 228.2K **Privately Held**
SIC: 8322 Social service center

(P-23228)
FIRST AMERICAN TITLE COMPANY
1 First American Way, Santa Ana
(92707-5913)
PHONE..................714 250-3109
James Boxdell, *Vice Pres*
Marianne Finlinson, *Officer*
Maura Freitas, *Officer*
Mary Moore, *Branch Mgr*
EMP: 6000
SALES (est): 8MM **Privately Held**
SIC: 8322 Settlement house

(P-23229)
FIRST PLACE FOR YOUTH (PA)
426 17th St Ste 100, Oakland
(94612-2814)
PHONE..................510 272-0979
Sam Cobbs, *Exec Dir*
EMP: 50 **EST:** 1999
SALES: 19.2MM **Privately Held**
SIC: 8322 Youth center

(P-23230)
FOUNDATION FOR EARLY CHILDHOOD (PA)
3360 Flair Dr Ste 100, El Monte
(91731-2833)
PHONE..................626 572-5107
Sharyn Muhammad-Beeker, *CEO*
Jaleh Hazian, *Administration*
Cynthia Nishi, *Asst Director*
EMP: 72 **EST:** 1965
SALES: 11.1MM **Privately Held**
SIC: 8322 Child guidance agency

(P-23231)
FRESH LIFELINES FOR YOUTH INC
568 Valley Way, Milpitas (95035-4106)
PHONE..................408 263-2630
Christa Gannon, *CEO*
Meghan Bernstein, *Director*
EMP: 57
SALES (est): 215.8K **Privately Held**
SIC: 8322 Child guidance agency

(P-23232)
FRESNO CNTY ECONOMIC OPPORTUNT
Also Called: Fresno Eoc
1900 Mariposa Mall # 300, Fresno
(93721-2514)
PHONE..................559 263-1000
Bryan Angus, *CEO*
EMP: 1200
SALES (corp-wide): 102.6MM **Privately Held**
SIC: 8322 Social service center
PA: Fresno County Economic Opportunities Commission
1920 Mariposa Mall # 300
Fresno CA 93721
559 263-1010

(P-23233)
FRESNO CNTY ECONOMIC OPPORTUNT (PA)
Also Called: FRESNO EOC
1920 Mariposa Mall # 300, Fresno
(93721-2504)
PHONE..................559 263-1010
Brian Angus, *CEO*
Vongsavanh Mouanoutoua, *President*
Salam Nalia, *CFO*

Marina Magdaleno, *Treasurer*
Naomi Quiring-Mizumot, *Officer*
EMP: 600 **EST:** 1965
SQ FT: 115,312
SALES: 102.6MM **Privately Held**
SIC: 8322 8399 Social service center;
community development groups

(P-23234)
FRESNO CNTY ECONOMIC OPPORTUNT
Also Called: Eoc Resource Development
1920 Mariposa Mall, Fresno (93721-2504)
PHONE..................559 263-1013
Roger Palomino, *Manager*
EMP: 500
SALES (corp-wide): 102.6MM **Privately Held**
SIC: 8322 Individual & family services
PA: Fresno County Economic Opportunities Commission
1920 Mariposa Mall # 300
Fresno CA 93721
559 263-1010

(P-23235)
FRESNO CNTY ECONOMIC OPPORTUNT
3120 W Nielsen Ave # 102, Fresno
(93706-1139)
PHONE..................559 485-3733
George Egewa, *Manager*
EMP: 100
SALES (corp-wide): 102.6MM **Privately Held**
SIC: 8322 Individual & family services
PA: Fresno County Economic Opportunities Commission
1920 Mariposa Mall # 300
Fresno CA 93721
559 263-1010

(P-23236)
FRESNO RESCUE MISSION INC (PA)
263 G St, Fresno (93706-3452)
P.O. Box 470, West Yellowstone MT
(59758-0470)
PHONE..................559 268-0839
Larry Arce, *CEO*
Rob Cravy, *COO*
Sandra Patel, *Vice Pres*
Trish Carruth, *Admin Sec*
Robert Metheney, *Maintence Staff*
EMP: 50
SQ FT: 29,000
SALES: 28.9MM **Privately Held**
WEB: www.fresnorescuemission.org
SIC: 8322 Emergency shelters; child related social services

(P-23237)
FRIENDS OF FAMILY
16861 Parthenia St, Northridge
(91343-4539)
PHONE..................818 988-4430
Susan Kaplan, *Exec Dir*
Wynn Helms, *Exec Dir*
Traci Williams, *Division Mgr*
Norma Rosales, *Education*
Brenda Hillhouse, *Director*
EMP: 50 **EST:** 1972
SQ FT: 5,500
SALES: 2.2MM **Privately Held**
WEB: www.fofca.org
SIC: 8322 Family counseling services

(P-23238)
FRIENDS OUTSIDE
7272 Murray Dr, Stockton (95210-3339)
P.O. Box 4085 (95204-0085)
PHONE..................209 955-0701
Gretchen Newby, *Exec Dir*
EMP: 130
SQ FT: 7,800
SALES (est): 4.2MM **Privately Held**
WEB: www.friendsoutside.org
SIC: 8322 Social service center

(P-23239)
FULL SPECTRUM SERVICES INC
Also Called: Community Actv Rhbltn & Em-
plym
1570 S Railroad Ave, Crescent City
(95531-6821)
P.O. Box 592 (95531-0592)
PHONE..................................707 465-1460
Michael Roach, *President*
EMP: 50
SALES (est): 31.8K **Privately Held**
SIC: 8322 Individual & family services

(P-23240)
FUTURES EXPLORED
Also Called: Nifty Thrift
2380 Salvio St Ste 302, Concord
(94520-2193)
P.O. Box 418 (94522-0418)
PHONE..................................925 332-7183
Will Stanford, *Director*
Dina Gibson, *Principal*
Angelique Goldberg, *Principal*
Heather Hackett, *Principal*
Jenny McKeon, *Principal*
EMP: 60
SQ FT: 1,740
SALES: 12.2MM **Privately Held**
WEB: www.futures-explored.org
SIC: 8322 Association for the handicapped

(P-23241)
G & L PENASQUITOS INC
Also Called: Arbors, The
10584 Rancho Carmel Dr, San Diego
(92128-3629)
PHONE..................................858 538-0802
Gary Penovich, *Exec Dir*
EMP: 65
SQ FT: 48,685
SALES (est): 2.3MM
SALES (corp-wide): 297.8MM **Privately
Held**
WEB: www.glrealty.com
SIC: 8322 Individual & family services
PA: G&L Realty Corp, Llc
439 N Bedford Dr
Beverly Hills CA 90210
310 273-9930

(P-23242)
GIARRETTO INSTITUTE
Also Called: Parents United
232 E Gish Rd, San Jose (95112-4706)
PHONE..................................408 453-7616
Jerry Doyle, *CEO*
EMP: 50
SALES (est): 711K **Privately Held**
SIC: 8322 Individual & family services

(P-23243)
**GOLDEN GATE REGIONAL CTR
INC (PA)**
1355 Market St Ste 220, San Francisco
(94103-1314)
PHONE..................................415 546-9222
Ron Fell, *CEO*
Eric Zigman, *Bd of Directors*
James Shorter, *Exec Dir*
Ophelie Irrilo, *Office Mgr*
Erika Bolden, *Admin Asst*
EMP: 210 EST: 1966
SQ FT: 16,901
SALES: 243MM **Privately Held**
SIC: 8322 Referral service for personal &
social problems; outreach program

(P-23244)
**GOLDEN GATE REGIONAL CTR
INC**
3130 La Selva St Ste 202, San Mateo
(94403-2191)
PHONE..................................650 574-9232
David Beuerman, *General Mgr*
EMP: 65
SALES (corp-wide): 243MM **Privately
Held**
SIC: 8322 Social services for the handi-
capped
PA: Golden Gate Regional Center, Inc.
1355 Market St Ste 220
San Francisco CA 94103
415 546-9222

(P-23245)
GOLDEN LIVING LLC
Also Called: Beverly Healthcare
24100 Monroe Ave, Murrieta (92562-9507)
PHONE..................................951 600-4640
Doug Lendoff, *Manager*
EMP: 100
SALES (corp-wide): 409.2MM **Privately
Held**
WEB: www.nwbeccorp.com
SIC: 8322 Rehabilitation services
PA: Beaver Dam Health Care Center
5220 Tennyson Pkwy # 400
Plano TX 75024
972 372-6300

(P-23246)
GOOD SAMARITAN SHELTER
245 Inger Dr Ste 103b, Santa Maria
(93454-8669)
PHONE..................................805 346-8185
Sylvia Barnard, *Exec Dir*
Kirsten Cahoon, *Manager*
EMP: 60
SQ FT: 2,400
SALES: 5.4MM **Privately Held**
SIC: 8322 Emergency shelters

(P-23247)
GRASSHOPPER HOUSE LLC
Also Called: Passages
6428 Meadows Ct, Malibu (90265-4492)
PHONE..................................310 589-2880
Chris Prentiss,
Pax Prentiss,
EMP: 105
SQ FT: 16,000
SALES (est): 11.6MM **Privately Held**
WEB: www.passagesmalibu.com
SIC: 8322 Rehabilitation services

(P-23248)
**GREATER LOS ANGELES
AGENCY**
2239 Norwalk Ave, Los Angeles (90041)
PHONE..................................323 478-8000
Patricia Hughes, *CEO*
EMP: 70
SALES: 7.1MM **Privately Held**
SIC: 8322 Social service center

(P-23249)
H E L P INC
53 S 6th St, Banning (92220-4809)
P.O. Box 996 (92220-0007)
PHONE..................................951 922-2305
Al Silva, *President*
Bruce Kuhn, *Vice Pres*
Nancy Guthrie, *Admin Sec*
EMP: 85
SQ FT: 3,000
SALES (est): 300.6K **Privately Held**
SIC: 8322 Individual & family services

(P-23250)
**HALLMARK REHABILITATION
GP LLC**
2 Park Plz Ste 225, Irvine (92614-2541)
PHONE..................................949 282-5900
Jose Lynch,
Jimmy Sims,
Mark Whartley,
Laurie Thomas, *Mng Member*
EMP: 1200
SALES (est): 19.7MM **Privately Held**
WEB: www.hallmarkrehabinc.com
SIC: 8322 Rehabilitation services

(P-23251)
HAMILTON FAMILIES
1631 Hayes St, San Francisco
(94117-1326)
PHONE..................................415 409-2100
Rosa Caspaneda, *Director*
Patricia Babiraz, *Administration*
Rosa Castaneda, *Finance*
Jack Fagan, *Deputy Dir*
EMP: 65
SALES: 33MM **Privately Held**
WEB: www.hamiltonfamilycenter.org
SIC: 8322 Emergency shelters

(P-23252)
**HANFORD JOINT UN HIGH SCHL
DST**
Also Called: Hanford Adult School
905 Campus Dr, Hanford (93230-3552)
PHONE..................................559 583-5905
Heather Keran, *Principal*
EMP: 56
SALES (corp-wide): 51MM **Privately
Held**
SIC: 8322 Adult day care center
PA: Hanford Joint Union High School Dis-
trict
823 W Lacey Blvd
Hanford CA 93230
559 583-5901

(P-23253)
**HATHAWAY RESOURCE
CENTER**
5701 S Eastrn Ave Ste 550, Los Angeles
(90040)
PHONE..................................323 837-0838
Many Galledos, *Branch Mgr*
Rosio Bugarin, *Branch Mgr*
EMP: 50
SALES (corp-wide): 2.6MM **Privately
Held**
SIC: 8322 Family counseling services
PA: Hathaway Resource Center
840 N Avenue 66
Los Angeles CA 90042
323 257-9600

(P-23254)
**HEALTH SOUTH TUSTIN REHAB
HOSP**
14851 Yorba St, Tustin (92780-2925)
PHONE..................................714 832-9200
Paula Redman, *Controller*
EMP: 140
SQ FT: 90,000
SALES (est): 2.4MM
SALES (corp-wide): 4.2B **Publicly Held**
WEB: www.healthsouth.com
SIC: 8322 8069 Rehabilitation services;
specialty hospitals, except psychiatric
PA: Encompass Health Corporation
9001 Liberty Pkwy
Birmingham AL 35242
205 967-7116

(P-23255)
HEALTHRIGHT 360
Also Called: Prototypes Women's Center
845 E Arrow Hwy, Pomona (91767-2535)
PHONE..................................909 624-1233
April Wilson, *Vice Pres*
EMP: 100
SALES (corp-wide): 96.1MM **Privately
Held**
SIC: 8322 8069 General counseling serv-
ices; drug addiction rehabilitation hospital
PA: Healthright 360
1563 Mission St Fl 1
San Francisco CA 94103
415 762-3700

(P-23256)
HELP FOR THE HURTING INC
Also Called: Helping Hands Pantry
2205 S Artesia St, San Bernardino
(92408-3906)
P.O. Box 1224, Redlands (92373-0401)
PHONE..................................909 796-4222
Paul Dickau, *Exec Dir*
EMP: 90 EST: 2009
SALES: 1.6MM **Privately Held**
SIC: 8322 Social service center

(P-23257)
**HELP HOSPITALIZED
VETERANS II**
36585 Penfield Ln, Winchester
(92596-9672)
PHONE..................................951 926-4500
Mike Lynch, *Exec Dir*
EMP: 65 EST: 1971
SQ FT: 25,000
SALES: 31MM **Privately Held**
WEB: www.hhv.org
SIC: 8322 Individual & family services

(P-23258)
**HELPLINE YOUTH COUNSELING
(PA)**
14181 Telegraph Rd, Whittier (90604-2554)
PHONE..................................562 273-0722
Deepak Nanda, *Ch of Bd*
Jacques Welche C P A, *Treasurer*
Jeff Farber, *Exec Dir*
Jeffrey Farber, *Exec Dir*
Pam Van Alstyne, *Admin Sec*
EMP: 50
SQ FT: 9,000
SALES: 5.5MM **Privately Held**
WEB: www.vfnet.com
SIC: 8322 Family (marriage) counseling;
social service center

(P-23259)
HIGH ROAD PROGRAM (PA)
250 N Westlake Blvd # 210, Westlake Vil-
lage (91362-3700)
PHONE..................................805 497-8800
Robert T Dorris Jr, *President*
Bill McVay, *CEO*
EMP: 62
SQ FT: 2,000
SALES: 3MM **Privately Held**
WEB: www.highroadprogram.org
SIC: 8322 Social service center

(P-23260)
HOMEBOY INDUSTRIES (PA)
Also Called: HOMEBOY BAKERY
130 Bruno St, Los Angeles (90012-1815)
PHONE..................................323 526-1254
Greg Boyle, *Exec Dir*
John Brady, *Ch of Bd*
Jack Faherty, *CFO*
Dalia Torres, *Admin Sec*
Chris Evenson, *Controller*
EMP: 270
SQ FT: 3,690
SALES: 14.4MM **Privately Held**
SIC: 8322 Rehabilitation services; social
service center

(P-23261)
HOMEBRIDGE INC
Also Called: IHSS CONSORTIUM, THE
1035 Market St Ste L1, San Francisco
(94103-1666)
PHONE..................................415 255-2079
Gay Kaplan, *CEO*
Nenita Sayson, *Executive*
Margaret Baran, *Principal*
Mark Burns, *Principal*
Debra J Dolch, *Principal*
EMP: 500
SALES: 26.4MM **Privately Held**
SIC: 8322 Homemakers' service

(P-23262)
**HOMEFRST SVCS SANTA
CLARA CNTY**
Also Called: EHC LIFEBUILDERS
507 Valley Way, Milpitas (95035-4105)
PHONE..................................408 539-2100
Jennifer Niklaus, *CEO*
Mary Zavala, *Officer*
Sarah Swanson, *Human Res Dir*
Loann Roe, *Director*
Summer-Lee Rodriguez, *Case Mgr*
EMP: 115
SALES: 12.2MM **Privately Held**
SIC: 8322 Individual & family services

(P-23263)
**HOMELESS PRENATAL
PROGRAM**
33 Middle Point Rd, San Francisco (94124)
PHONE..................................415 546-6756
Martha Ryan, *Director*
Aisianti Darmawan, *Accountant*
Sonia Batres, *VP Mktg*
Carla Roberts, *VP Mktg*
Lilli Milton, *Program Dir*
EMP: 50
SALES: 8MM **Privately Held**
WEB: www.homelessprenatal.org
SIC: 8322 Social service center

(P-23264)
HOPE OF VALLEY RESCUE MISSION
11076 Norris Ave Fl 2, Pacoima (91331-2468)
P.O. Box 7609, Mission Hills (91346-7609)
PHONE...................................818 392-0020
Ken Craft, *President*
Michael Klausman, *Ch of Bd*
David Faustina, *COO*
Chris Delaplane, *Treasurer*
Cindy Hubbard, *Finance*
EMP: 54
SQ FT: 22,000
SALES: 5.3MM **Privately Held**
SIC: 8322 Emergency shelters

(P-23265)
HUMAN OPTIONS INC
1901 Newport Blvd Ste 240, Costa Mesa (92627-2294)
PHONE...................................949 757-3635
Maricela Rios, *Branch Mgr*
Jessica Reynaga, *Education*
EMP: 50 **Privately Held**
SIC: 8322 Individual & family services
PA: Human Options, Inc
5540 Trabuco Rd Ste 100
Irvine CA 92620

(P-23266)
HUMAN OPTIONS INC (PA)
5540 Trabuco Rd Ste 100, Irvine (92620-5745)
P.O. Box 53745 (92619-3745)
PHONE...................................949 737-5242
Maricela Rios, *Officer*
Vivian Clecak, *Exec Dir*
Andrew Morales, *Admin Sec*
Krystal Minniefield, *Finance Mgr*
Renalynn Funtanilla, *Pub Rel Mgr*
EMP: 65
SALES: 5.1MM **Privately Held**
SIC: 8322 Family counseling services

(P-23267)
HUMAN SERVICES ASSOCIATION (PA)
6800 Florence Ave, Bell (90201-4957)
PHONE...................................562 806-5400
Susanne Sundberg, *Principal*
Ricardo Mota, *Officer*
Manuel Maiztegui, *Director*
Bre Mathis, *Supervisor*
EMP: 75
SQ FT: 10,000
SALES: 15.8MM **Privately Held**
WEB: www.hsala.org
SIC: 8322 Individual & family services

(P-23268)
HUMBOLDT COMMNTY ACCSS RESRC
Also Called: Baybridge Employment Services
1707 E St Ste 2, Eureka (95501-7621)
PHONE...................................707 443-7077
Ross Jantz, *Principal*
EMP: 56
SALES (corp-wide): 4.2MM **Privately Held**
WEB: www.thestudioonline.org
SIC: 8322 Referral service for personal & social problems
PA: Humboldt Community Access And Resource Center
1707 E St Ste 2
Eureka CA 95501
707 443-7077

(P-23269)
HUMBOLDT SENIOR RESOURCE CTR (PA)
1910 California St, Eureka (95501-2899)
PHONE...................................707 443-9747
Joyce Hayes, *Exec Dir*
Claudia Padilla, *Information Mgr*
Rene Arche, *Corp Comm Staff*
Barbara Walser, *Nutritionist*
Tina Taylor, *Manager*
EMP: 110
SQ FT: 14,000
SALES: 16.1MM **Privately Held**
SIC: 8322 8741 Senior citizens' center or association; management services

(P-23270)
HUNTINGTON PK POLICE LEAGUE
Also Called: HUNTINGTON PARK POLICE DEPARTM
6542 Miles Ave, Huntington Park (90255-4318)
PHONE...................................323 584-6254
Paul Wadley, *President*
EMP: 75
SALES: 6.9K **Privately Held**
SIC: 8322 Outreach program

(P-23271)
IDEAL PROGRAM SERVICES INC
3970 W Martin Luther King, Los Angeles (90008-1732)
PHONE...................................323 296-2255
Omolara Okunubi, *CEO*
Ivan Martinez, *COO*
Lara Okunubi, *Administration*
Tara Mitchell, *Manager*
Nakia Powell, *Manager*
EMP: 71
SQ FT: 8,880
SALES (est): 1.7MM **Privately Held**
WEB: www.idealprogram.com
SIC: 8322 5999 Social services for the handicapped; technical aids for the handicapped

(P-23272)
INCLUSION SERVICES LLC
7255 Greenleaf Ave 20, Whittier (90602-1340)
PHONE...................................562 945-2000
Cesar Torres, *Mng Member*
Molly Aragon, *Human Res Dir*
Flor Ulloa, *Human Res Mgr*
Israel Ibenez, *Mng Member*
Nicole Geames, *Manager*
EMP: 103
SALES (est): 7.1MM **Privately Held**
SIC: 8322 8331 Social services for the handicapped; skill training center

(P-23273)
INDEPENDENT OPTIONS
Also Called: Harbor Village II
2532 Santa Catalina Dr # 104, Costa Mesa (92626-6880)
PHONE...................................714 434-1175
Dennis Mattson, *Owner*
EMP: 100
SALES (est): 1.6MM **Privately Held**
SIC: 8322 8361 Social services for the handicapped; residential care

(P-23274)
INDIVIDUALS NOW
Also Called: SOCIAL ADVOCATES FOR YOUTH
2447 Summerfield Rd, Santa Rosa (95405-7815)
PHONE...................................707 544-3299
Matt Martin, *CEO*
Katrina Thurman, *COO*
Dave Koressel, *CFO*
Cat Cvengros, *Officer*
EMP: 55
SALES: 5.5MM **Privately Held**
SIC: 8322 Child guidance agency; youth center

(P-23275)
INLAND CNTIES REGIONAL CTR INC (PA)
Also Called: Inland Regional Center
1365 S Waterman Ave, San Bernardino (92408-2804)
P.O. Box 19037 (92423-9037)
PHONE...................................909 890-3000
Carol A Fitzgibbons, *CEO*
Carol Fitzgibbons, *Exec Dir*
Mia Gurri, *Program Mgr*
Sandra Fortino, *Admin Sec*
Sharrie Mills, *Med Doctor*
EMP: 104
SQ FT: 82,000
SALES: 502.5MM **Privately Held**
SIC: 8322 Individual & family services

(P-23276)
INLAND VALLEY DRUG & ALCOHOL (PA)
Also Called: ADMINISTRATIVE OFFICES
1260 E Arrow Hwy, Upland (91786-4982)
PHONE...................................909 932-1069
Tina Hughes, *CEO*
Julie Thompson, *Admin Asst*
Laurie Figueroa, *Finance*
EMP: 65
SALES: 6.3MM **Privately Held**
WEB: www.ivdars.org
SIC: 8322 Alcoholism counseling, nontreatment

(P-23277)
INSIDE OUTDOORS FOUNDATION
8755 Santiago Canyon Rd, Silverado (92676-9758)
P.O. Box 9050, Costa Mesa (92628-9050)
PHONE...................................714 708-3885
Manny Kiesser, *President*
EMP: 200
SQ FT: 3,000
SALES: 430.4K **Privately Held**
SIC: 8322 Outreach program

(P-23278)
INSTITUTE ON AGING
Also Called: Irene Swindell's Adult Day Car
3698 California St, San Francisco (94118-1702)
PHONE...................................415 600-2690
Cindy Kauffman, *Administration*
EMP: 111 **Privately Held**
SIC: 8322 Individual & family services
PA: Institute On Aging
3575 Geary Blvd
San Francisco CA 94118

(P-23279)
INSTITUTE ON AGING (PA)
Also Called: ADULT DAY CARE CENTER
3575 Geary Blvd, San Francisco (94118-3212)
PHONE...................................415 750-4101
J Thomas Briody, *President*
Shabana Siegel, *Vice Pres*
Karyn Skultety, *Vice Pres*
Tamari Hedani, *Associate Dir*
Patricia Montgomery, *Executive Asst*
EMP: 100
SQ FT: 10,000
SALES: 38.9MM **Privately Held**
SIC: 8322 Geriatric social service

(P-23280)
INTERCOMMUNITY CHILD
10155 Colima Rd, Whittier (90603-2042)
PHONE...................................562 692-0383
Charlene Dimas, *CEO*
EMP: 70
SALES (est): 655.1K **Privately Held**
SIC: 8322 Child related social services

(P-23281)
INTERFACE COMMUNITY (PA)
Also Called: INTERFACE CHILDREN FAMILY SERV
4001 Mission Oaks Blvd, Camarillo (93012-5121)
PHONE...................................805 485-6114
Charles T Watson, *President*
Fernando Salguero, *CFO*
Dale Stoeber, *CFO*
Terryl Miller, *CFO*
Erik Sternad, *Exec Dir*
EMP: 96
SQ FT: 3,000
SALES: 8.4MM **Privately Held**
WEB: www.icfs.org
SIC: 8322 Family service agency

(P-23282)
INTERFAITH COMMUNITY SVCS INC
550 W Washington Ave B, Escondido (92025-1643)
PHONE...................................760 489-6380
Greg Anglea, *Exec Dir*
Amber Zinsky, *Principal*
Marinea Goodson, *Program Mgr*
Joan Rector, *Rector*

Valerie Brown, *Manager*
EMP: 100
SQ FT: 23,000
SALES: 12.6MM **Privately Held**
WEB: www.interfaithservices.org
SIC: 8322 Social service center

(P-23283)
INTERNATIONAL INST LOS ANGELES (PA)
3845 Selig Pl, Los Angeles (90031-3143)
PHONE...................................323 224-3800
E Stephen Voss, *President*
Susan Eckert, *VP Admin*
Hasmik Ktoian, *Administration*
Lilian Alba, *Director*
Robert Foss, *Director*
EMP: 52 **EST:** 1935
SQ FT: 18,000
SALES: 15.5MM **Privately Held**
WEB: www.iilosangeles.org
SIC: 8322 Family service agency

(P-23284)
INTERNATIONAL MEDICAL CORPS (PA)
12400 Wilshire Blvd # 1500, Los Angeles (90025-1030)
PHONE...................................310 826-7800
Nancy Aossey, *President*
Barry A Porter, *General Ptnr*
Cory Mitchell, *Partner*
Jonathan M Glaser, *Managing Prtnr*
Michael Burns, *Vice Chairman*
EMP: 78
SALES: 131.7MM **Privately Held**
WEB: www.imc-la.com
SIC: 8322 Disaster service

(P-23285)
INTERNTNAL RSCUE COMMITTEE INC
5348 University Ave # 205, San Diego (92105-8025)
PHONE...................................619 641-7510
Roisin Wisneski, *Branch Mgr*
Farah A Banna, *Education*
EMP: 63
SALES (corp-wide): 744.4MM **Privately Held**
SIC: 8322 Social service center
PA: International Rescue Committee, Inc.
122 E 42nd St
New York NY 10168
212 551-3000

(P-23286)
INTERPRSNAL DVLPMNTAL FCLTTORS
Also Called: IDS
891 Worcester Ave Apt 3, Pasadena (91104-4258)
PHONE...................................626 793-8967
Dorothea A Bradley, *CEO*
EMP: 71
SALES (est): 567.8K **Privately Held**
SIC: 8322 Association for the handicapped; meal delivery program

(P-23287)
ISLAMIC RELIEF USA
6131 Orangethorpe Ave # 280, Buena Park (90620-4902)
PHONE...................................714 676-1300
Abed Ayoub, *Branch Mgr*
David Hawa, *Comms Dir*
Mohammad Abdelmagd, *Principal*
Ahmed El-Bendary, *Principal*
Almas Talib, *Principal*
EMP: 70 **Privately Held**
SIC: 8322 Community center
PA: Islamic Relief Usa
3655 Wheeler Ave
Alexandria VA 22304

(P-23288)
J GELT CORPORATION
Also Called: Casa Pacifica Adult Day H
1424 30th St Ste C, San Diego (92154-3417)
PHONE...................................619 424-8181
Luba Vaisman, *President*
Tatyana Cohen, *Assistant VP*
EMP: 50

SQ FT: 15,000
SALES: 3.4MM **Privately Held**
SIC: 8322 Adult day care center

(P-23289)
JACOBS CSHMAN SAN DIEGO FD BNK
9850 Distribution Ave, San Diego (92121-2320)
PHONE.....................................858 527-1419
James Floros, *President*
Casey Castillo, *CFO*
Scody Hage, *Executive*
Stephen Darbeau, *General Mgr*
Denise Agostini, *Executive Asst*
EMP: 50
SALES: 41.2MM **Privately Held**
SIC: 8322 Social service center

(P-23290)
JAMISON CHILDRENS HOME
1010 Shalimar Dr, Bakersfield (93306-5633)
P.O. Box 511 (93302-0511)
PHONE.....................................661 334-3500
Carl Guilford, *Director*
EMP: 60
SALES (est): 721.3K **Privately Held**
SIC: 8322 Individual & family services

(P-23291)
JANUS OF SANTA CRUZ
200 7th Ave Ste 150, Santa Cruz (95062-4669)
PHONE.....................................831 462-1060
Rod Libbey, *Exec Dir*
Rikki Bell, *Supervisor*
EMP: 100 **EST:** 1976
SALES: 7.4MM **Privately Held**
WEB: www.janussc.org
SIC: 8322 Rehabilitation services

(P-23292)
JEWISH COMMUNITY CTR LONG BCH
Also Called: ALPERT JEWISH COMMUNITY CENTRE
3801 E Willow St, Long Beach (90815-1734)
PHONE.....................................562 426-7601
Gordon Lentzner, *President*
Winston Abigail, *CFO*
Eugene Ross, *Treasurer*
Jeff Antonoff, *Exec Dir*
John Reynoso, *Graphic Designe*
EMP: 150
SQ FT: 90,000
SALES: 6.3MM **Privately Held**
SIC: 8322 Community center

(P-23293)
JEWISH FAMILY AND CHLD SVCS
Also Called: Seniors At Home
200 Channing Ave, Palo Alto (94301-2720)
PHONE.....................................650 931-1860
EMP: 84
SALES (corp-wide): 37.8MM **Privately Held**
SIC: 8322 Family service agency
PA: Jewish Family And Children's Services
2150 Post St
San Francisco CA 94115
415 449-1200

(P-23294)
JEWISH FAMILY AND CHLD SVCS (PA)
Also Called: CLEANERIFIC
2150 Post St, San Francisco (94115-3508)
P.O. Box 159004 (94115-9004)
PHONE.....................................415 449-1200
Anita Friedman, *Exec Dir*
Nan Toder, *Partner*
Michael R Zent, *CEO*
Marga Dusedau, *CFO*
Javier Favela, *CFO*
EMP: 80
SALES: 37.8MM **Privately Held**
SIC: 8322 Family service agency

(P-23295)
JEWISH FAMILY AND CHLD SVCS
Also Called: Parents Place
200 Channing Ave, Palo Alto (94301-2720)
PHONE.....................................650 688-3030
Diane Wasson, *Branch Mgr*
Claire H O'Neill, *Manager*
EMP: 253
SALES (corp-wide): 37.8MM **Privately Held**
SIC: 8322 Family service agency
PA: Jewish Family And Children's Services
2150 Post St
San Francisco CA 94115
415 449-1200

(P-23296)
JEWISH FAMILY SVC LOS ANGELES
Also Called: Valley Stre Frnt Jwsh Fmly Svc
12821 Victory Blvd, North Hollywood (91606-3012)
PHONE.....................................818 984-0276
Karen Leaf, *Director*
EMP: 72
SALES (corp-wide): 1.6MM **Privately Held**
WEB: www.jewishla.com
SIC: 8322 5331 Social service center; variety stores
PA: Jewish Family Service Of Los Angeles
3580 Wilshire Blvd
Los Angeles CA 90010
323 761-8800

(P-23297)
JEWISH FAMILY SVC LOS ANGELES
Senior Citizens Center
330 N Fairfax Ave, Los Angeles (90036-2109)
PHONE.....................................323 937-5900
Doreen Klee, *Owner*
EMP: 50
SALES (corp-wide): 1.6MM **Privately Held**
WEB: www.jewishla.com
SIC: 8322 Old age assistance
PA: Jewish Family Service Of Los Angeles
3580 Wilshire Blvd
Los Angeles CA 90010
323 761-8800

(P-23298)
JEWISH FAMILY SVC SAN DIEGO (PA)
8804 Balboa Ave, San Diego (92123-1506)
PHONE.....................................858 637-3000
Michael Hopkins, *CEO*
Felicia Mandelbaum, *President*
Meredith Morgenroth, *Social Dir*
Lea Bush, *Program Mgr*
Elissa Landsman, *Program Mgr*
EMP: 100
SQ FT: 25,000
SALES: 15.8MM **Privately Held**
SIC: 8322 Family (marriage) counseling; family counseling services

(P-23299)
JEWISH FMLY & CMNTY SVCS E BAY (PA)
Also Called: JFCS/EAST BAY
2484 Shattuck Ave Ste 210, Berkeley (94704-2076)
PHONE.....................................510 704-7475
AVI Rose, *Exec Dir*
EMP: 63
SALES: 7.7MM **Privately Held**
SIC: 8322 8049 Senior citizens' center or association; psychologist, psychotherapist & hypnotist

(P-23300)
JON K TAKATA CORPORATION (PA)
Also Called: Restoration Management Company
4142 Point Eden Way, Hayward (94545-3703)
PHONE.....................................510 315-5400
Jon Takata, *President*
EMP: 70

SQ FT: 100,000
SALES (est): 38.1MM **Privately Held**
WEB: www.restorationmanagement.com
SIC: 8322 1799 4959 Disaster service; asbestos removal & encapsulation; environmental cleanup services

(P-23301)
JONI AND FRIENDS (PA)
30009 Ladyface Ct, Agoura (91301-2583)
PHONE.....................................818 707-5664
Joni E Tada, *CEO*
Billy Burnett, *Exec VP*
Douglas Mazza, *Exec VP*
◆ **EMP:** 84
SQ FT: 30,000
SALES: 24.9MM **Privately Held**
SIC: 8322 Association for the handicapped

(P-23302)
KAINOS HOME & TRAINING CTR
Also Called: Kainos Work Activity Ctr
2761 Fair Oaks Ave Ste A, Redwood City (94063-3540)
PHONE.....................................650 361-1355
Christen Rodgers, *Manager*
EMP: 50
SALES (corp-wide): 6.3MM **Privately Held**
WEB: www.kainosusa.org
SIC: 8322 Social services for the handicapped
PA: Kainos Home & Training Center For Developmentally Disabled Adults
3631 Jefferson Ave
Redwood City CA
650 363-2423

(P-23303)
KEDREN COMMUNITY HLTH CTR INC
3800 S Figueroa St, Los Angeles (90037-1206)
PHONE.....................................323 524-0634
John Griffith, *President*
EMP: 153
SALES (corp-wide): 35.8MM **Privately Held**
SIC: 8322 Community center
PA: Kedren Community Health Center, Inc.
4211 Avalon Blvd
Los Angeles CA 90011
323 233-0425

(P-23304)
KINGS COMMUNITY ACTION O (PA)
Also Called: Kcao
1130 N 11th Ave, Hanford (93230-3608)
PHONE.....................................559 582-4386
David Droker, *Exec Dir*
EMP: 77
SQ FT: 15,000
SALES: 17.2MM **Privately Held**
SIC: 8322 8399 Individual & family services; antipoverty board

(P-23305)
KINGS REHABILITATION CENTER (PA)
490 E Hanford Armona Rd, Hanford (93230-6129)
P.O. Box 719 (93232-0719)
PHONE.....................................559 582-9234
Carol Rogers, *Marketing Staff*
Veronica Chavarin, *MIS Staff*
Sherrie Martin, *Manager*
EMP: 57
SQ FT: 13,000
SALES: 8.3MM **Privately Held**
WEB: www.kingsrehab.com
SIC: 8322 8361 Rehabilitation services; rehabilitation center, residential: health care incidental

(P-23306)
KINSHIP CENTER
Also Called: Seneca Family of Agency
18302 Irvine Blvd Ste 300, Tustin (92780-3437)
PHONE.....................................714 979-2365
Josie Romehiod, *Director*
EMP: 100

SALES (corp-wide): 5.4MM **Privately Held**
SIC: 8322 8093 Adoption services; mental health clinic, outpatient
PA: Kinship Center
124 River Rd
Salinas CA 93908
831 455-9965

(P-23307)
KOREAN COMMUNITY SERVICES INC
Also Called: KC SERVICES
8633 Knott Ave, Buena Park (90620-3852)
PHONE.....................................714 527-6561
Ellen Ahn, *Exec Dir*
Kay Ahn, *CFO*
Kwangho Kim, *Managing Dir*
Charlene Choi, *Director*
EMP: 50
SALES: 4.4MM **Privately Held**
SIC: 8322 8069 Social service center; drug addiction rehabilitation hospital

(P-23308)
KOREAN HEALTH EDUCATION (PA)
Also Called: Kheir
3727 W 6th St Ste 210, Los Angeles (90020-5108)
PHONE.....................................213 427-4000
Erin K Pak, *CEO*
Chakma Nadesh, *Technology*
Papehn Navid, *Director*
Damian Kelly, *Manager*
EMP: 60
SQ FT: 800
SALES: 5.6MM **Privately Held**
SIC: 8322 8011 Individual & family services; offices & clinics of medical doctors

(P-23309)
KOREATOWN YOUTH AND CMNTY CTR (PA)
Also Called: KYCC
3727 W 6th St Ste 300, Los Angeles (90020-5108)
PHONE.....................................213 365-7400
John Ho Song, *Exec Dir*
Jessica Estrada, *Office Mgr*
Yun Pak, *Opers Spvr*
Katherine Kim, *Corp Comm Staff*
Ernie Yoshikawa, *Senior Mgr*
EMP: 74
SALES: 8.6MM **Privately Held**
SIC: 8322 8211 8641 Youth center; elementary & secondary schools; environmental protection organization

(P-23310)
LA ASOCIACION NACIONAL PRO PER
Also Called: National Assn For Hispanic
1452 W Temple St Ste 100, Los Angeles (90026-5649)
PHONE.....................................213 202-5900
Zecia Soto, *Principal*
EMP: 350
SALES (est): 1.5MM
SALES (corp-wide): 14.4MM **Privately Held**
SIC: 8322 7361 8611 Social service center; employment agencies; business associations
PA: La Asociacion Nacional Pro Personas Mayores
234 E Colo Blvd Ste 300
Pasadena CA 91101
626 564-1988

(P-23311)
LA ASOCIACION NACIONAL PRO PER (PA)
Also Called: NAT'L ASSN FOR HISPANIC ELDERL
234 E Colo Blvd Ste 300, Pasadena (91101)
PHONE.....................................626 564-1988
Carmela G Lacayo, *President*
Maria Ramirez, *Ch of Bd*
Carole Kracer, *Treasurer*
Therese Grenier, *Admin Sec*
EMP: 1330
SQ FT: 11,000

SALES: 14.4MM **Privately Held**
SIC: 8322 Social service center

(P-23312)
LA FAMILIA COUNSELING CENTER
5523 34th St, Sacramento (95820-4725)
PHONE................................916 452-3601
Rachell R Rios, *Exec Dir*
Marianela Appelgren, *Partner*
Rachel Rios, *Exec Dir*
EMP: 60
SALES: 3.8MM **Privately Held**
WEB: www.lafcc.com
SIC: 8322 Social service center

(P-23313)
LAURAS HOUSE
999 Corporate Dr Ste 225, Mission Viejo
(92694-2156)
PHONE................................949 361-3775
Margaret Bayston, *Exec Dir*
Sandra Condello, *Principal*
EMP: 56
SALES: 3.8MM **Privately Held**
WEB: www.laurashouse.net
SIC: 8322 Crisis center

(P-23314)
LIFE OPTONS VCTNAL RSOURCE CTR (PA)
Also Called: LOVARC
116 N I St, Lompoc (93436-6721)
PHONE................................805 735-3428
William Reardon, *Exec Dir*
Elen Vanderhoof, *CFO*
▲ **EMP:** 130
SQ FT: 2,000
SALES: 6MM **Privately Held**
WEB: www.lovarc.com
SIC: 8322 Social service center

(P-23315)
LIFE STEPS FOUNDATION INC
Also Called: Lsf Central Cal Adult Svcs
1431 Pomeroy Rd, Arroyo Grande
(93420-5943)
PHONE................................805 474-8431
EMP: 225
SALES (corp-wide): 3.9MM **Privately Held**
SIC: 8322 Social service center
PA: Life Steps Foundation, Inc.
5757 W Century Blvd # 880
Los Angeles CA 90045
310 410-8190

(P-23316)
LIFE STEPS FOUNDATION INC
500 E 4th St, Long Beach (90802-2501)
PHONE................................562 436-0751
Kristine Engels, *Director*
Robert Turner, *Manager*
EMP: 70
SALES (corp-wide): 3.9MM **Privately Held**
WEB: www.lifestepsfoundation.org
SIC: 8322 8399 Social service center; community development groups
PA: Life Steps Foundation, Inc.
5757 W Century Blvd # 880
Los Angeles CA 90045
310 410-8190

(P-23317)
LIFE STEPS FOUNDATION INC
1107 Johnson Ave, San Luis Obispo
(93401-3303)
PHONE................................805 549-0150
Virginia Franco, *Manager*
EMP: 80
SALES (corp-wide): 3.9MM **Privately Held**
WEB: www.lifestepsfoundation.org
SIC: 8322 Social service center
PA: Life Steps Foundation, Inc.
5757 W Century Blvd # 880
Los Angeles CA 90045
310 410-8190

(P-23318)
LIFEHOUSE INC (PA)
899 Northgate Dr Ste 500, San Rafael
(94903-3667)
PHONE................................415 472-2373
Nancy Dow Moody, *CEO*

Matthew Tarver-Wahlquis, *Vice Pres*
Liza Padua, *Controller*
Johanna Schleret, *Human Res Mgr*
Rita Castro, *Psychologist*
EMP: 350 **EST:** 1957
SALES: 15.3MM **Privately Held**
WEB: www.lifehouseagency.org
SIC: 8322 8361 Social services for the handicapped; general counseling services; self-help organization; residential care for the handicapped

(P-23319)
LIFEMOVES (PA)
181 Constitution Dr, Menlo Park
(94025-1106)
PHONE................................650 685-5880
Bruce Ives, *President*
Jeff Vanzanten, *Bd of Directors*
Lorena Collins, *Assoc VP*
Scott Flesher, *Vice Pres*
Anne Jarchow, *Vice Pres*
EMP: 50
SALES: 24MM **Privately Held**
SIC: 8322 Social service center

(P-23320)
LIFESTYLES SENIOR HOUSING MAN
Also Called: Meadows Senior Living, The
9325 E Stockton Blvd, Elk Grove
(95624-1282)
PHONE................................916 714-3755
Dan Carsel, *Manager*
EMP: 60 **Privately Held**
SIC: 8322 8052 Geriatric social service; intermediate care facilities
PA: Lifestyles Senior Housing Managers Llc
7600 Ne 41st St Ste 330
Vancouver WA

(P-23321)
LIGHTHOUSE LIVING SERVICES (PA)
3600 Power Inn Rd Ste H, Sacramento
(95826-3826)
P.O. Box 660905 (95866-0905)
PHONE................................916 454-4381
Tabias Cowan, *President*
EMP: 53
SQ FT: 4,500
SALES (est): 2.8MM **Privately Held**
WEB: www.lighthouseils.com
SIC: 8322 Social service center

(P-23322)
LOS ANGELES REGIONAL FOOD BANK
1734 E 41st St, Vernon (90058-1502)
PHONE................................323 234-3030
Michael Flood, *President*
Edward McCarthy, *COO*
Czarina Luna, *CFO*
Marie Ortiz, *Admin Asst*
Weldon Wu, *CIO*
EMP: 120
SQ FT: 100,000
SALES: 90.2MM **Privately Held**
SIC: 8322 Meal delivery program

(P-23323)
LOS ANGELES SEC NATIONAL (PA)
Also Called: Ncjw La
543 N Fairfax Ave, Los Angeles
(90036-1715)
PHONE................................323 651-2930
Hillary Sullivan, *Exec Dir*
Shelli Dodell, *President*
Carrie Jacoves, *Comms Dir*
Nabila Sosa, *Program Mgr*
Greg Buccella, *Store Mgr*
EMP: 50 **EST:** 1909
SALES: 2.2MM **Privately Held**
WEB: www.ncjwla.org
SIC: 8322 Multi-service center

(P-23324)
LOS ANGELES UNIFIED SCHOOL DST
Also Called: Westchester Emerson Cmnty
8810 Emerson Ave, Los Angeles
(90045-3609)
PHONE................................310 258-2000

Patricia Colby, *Principal*
EMP: 150
SALES (corp-wide): 4B **Privately Held**
WEB: www.lausd.k12.ca.us
SIC: 8322 Adult day care center
PA: Los Angeles Unified School District
333 S Beaudry Ave Ste 209
Los Angeles CA 90017
213 241-1000

(P-23325)
LOS ANGELES UNIFIED SCHOOL DST
Also Called: Marine Avenue Adult Center
1468 N Marine Ave, Wilmington
(90744-2046)
PHONE................................310 518-1128
Lanny Nelms, *Principal*
EMP: 109
SALES (corp-wide): 4B **Privately Held**
WEB: www.lausd.k12.ca.us
SIC: 8322 Adult day care center
PA: Los Angeles Unified School District
333 S Beaudry Ave Ste 209
Los Angeles CA 90017
213 241-1000

(P-23326)
LOS ANGLES CHILD GDANCE CLINIC (PA)
3031 S Vermont Ave, Los Angeles
(90007-3033)
PHONE................................323 373-2400
Elizabeth Pfromm, *President*
John R Liebman, *Treasurer*
Joe Loo, *IT/INT Sup*
Monica Chong, *Controller*
Whitney Sturdy, *Psychologist*
EMP: 110
SALES: 18.6MM **Privately Held**
WEB: www.lacgc.net
SIC: 8322 Child guidance agency

(P-23327)
LYDIA C GONZALEZ
1400 Veterans Blvd, Redwood City
(94063-2612)
PHONE................................650 299-4707
EMP: 50
SALES (est): 1.9MM **Privately Held**
SIC: 8322

(P-23328)
MANCHESTER BAND POMO INDIANS
Also Called: Manchester Point Arena
24 Mamie Laiwa Dr, Point Arena (95468)
P.O. Box 623 (95468-0623)
PHONE................................707 882-2788
Christina Dukatz, *CEO*
Nelson Pinola, *Chairman*
EMP: 96
SALES: 1.6MM **Privately Held**
SIC: 8322 Individual & family services

(P-23329)
MARIN SNIOR CRDNTING CNCIL INC
Also Called: Whistlestop
930 Tamalpais Ave, San Rafael
(94901-3325)
PHONE................................415 454-0964
Joe O'Hehir, *CEO*
Linda Compton, *CEO*
Nancy Geisse, *COO*
Ashley Baker, *Officer*
Chris Tokarski, *Finance*
EMP: 94
SQ FT: 12,000
SALES: 12.4MM **Privately Held**
WEB: www.thewhistlestop.org
SIC: 8322 Senior citizens' center or association

(P-23330)
MARTHAS VILLAGE & KITCHEN
83791 Date Ave, Indio (92201-4737)
PHONE................................760 347-4741
Joe Carol, *President*
Matthew Packard, *Vice Pres*
Claudia Castorena, *Director*
Rachelle Flores, *Director*
Gloria Gomez, *Director*
EMP: 65

SALES: 3.8MM **Privately Held**
SIC: 8322 Social service center

(P-23331)
MARTIS CAMP CLUB
7951 Fleur Du Lac Ct, Truckee
(96161-4261)
PHONE................................530 550-6000
Mark Johnson, *President*
Chris Simpson, *Opers Staff*
Kim Kennedy, *Sales Executive*
Jonas Mikals, *Sales Executive*
Tracy Feik, *Sales Staff*
EMP: 300
SQ FT: 80,000
SALES: 17MM **Privately Held**
SIC: 8322 Community center

(P-23332)
MD P FOUNDATION INC
Also Called: MARTIN DE PORRES HOUSE
225 Potrero Ave, San Francisco
(94103-4814)
PHONE................................415 552-0240
Charles Engelstein, *President*
EMP: 200
SQ FT: 7,000
SALES: 261.6K **Privately Held**
WEB: www.mdpfoundation.com
SIC: 8322 Individual & family services

(P-23333)
MEADOWBROOK SENIOR LIVING
5217 Chesebro Rd, Agoura Hills
(91301-2212)
PHONE................................818 991-3544
Isaac Chernoesky, *Director*
EMP: 80
SALES (est): 1MM **Privately Held**
SIC: 8322 Old age assistance

(P-23334)
MEALS ON WHEELS DIABLO REGION (PA)
1300 Civic Dr Fl 1, Walnut Creek
(94596-4398)
PHONE................................925 937-8311
Elaine Clark, *Director*
EMP: 55
SQ FT: 5,500
SALES: 2.6MM **Privately Held**
SIC: 8322 Meal delivery program; family counseling services; geriatric social service; social services for the handicapped

(P-23335)
MEALS ON WHEELS-THE HEALTH TR
1400 Parkmoor Ave Ste 230, San Jose
(95126-3798)
PHONE................................408 961-9870
Gary Allen, *President*
EMP: 50
SALES (est): 997.6K **Privately Held**
SIC: 8322 Meal delivery program

(P-23336)
MEALS ON WHELS SAN FRNCSCO INC
1375 Fairfax Ave, San Francisco
(94124-1735)
PHONE................................415 920-1111
Ashley McCumber, *Exec Dir*
Anne Quaintance, *Principal*
Jim Oswald, *Marketing Staff*
EMP: 50
SQ FT: 19,330
SALES: 22.6MM **Privately Held**
WEB: www.mowsf.org
SIC: 8322 Meal delivery program

(P-23337)
MEALS-ON-WHEELS GRTR SN DIEGO (PA)
Also Called: MEALS ON WHEELS
2254 San Diego Ave # 200, San Diego
(92110-2944)
PHONE................................619 260-6110
Debbie Case, *President*
Darlyne Baddour, *Ch of Bd*
Matt Topper, *CFO*
James Johnson, *Officer*
Pamela Taliaferro, *Opers Staff*
EMP: 84

SQ FT: 3,565
SALES: 9.3MM **Privately Held**
SIC: 8322 Meal delivery program; senior citizens' center or association

(P-23338)
MENTAL HEALTH AMER LOS ANGELES
Also Called: Village Integrated Svc Agcy
456 Elm Ave, Long Beach (90802-2426)
PHONE..................................562 437-6717
Leslie Giambone, *Exec Dir*
Paul Pawlowski, *Psychiatry*
Jenny Bruner, *Med Doctor*
Stan Sorensen, *Manager*
Gerald Thompson, *Asst Mgr*
EMP: 74
SQ FT: 25,129
SALES (corp-wide): 14.2MM **Privately Held**
WEB: www.myfrontdoor.org
SIC: 8322 Social service center
PA: Mental Health America Of Los Angeles
   200 Pine Ave Ste 400
   Long Beach CA 90802
   562 285-1330

(P-23339)
MEXICAN AMRCN OPRTNTY FNDATION (PA)
Also Called: MAOF
401 N Garfield Ave, Montebello (90640-2901)
P.O. Box 4602 (90640-9311)
PHONE..................................323 890-9600
Martin Vasquez Castro, *President*
Carlos J Viramontes, *Principal*
EMP: 100
SQ FT: 25,000
SALES: 73.3MM **Privately Held**
SIC: 8322 Social service center

(P-23340)
MEXICAN AMRCN OPRTNTY FNDATION
Also Called: Maof Commerce
5657 E Washington Blvd, Commerce (90040-1405)
PHONE..................................323 890-1555
Martin Castro, *President*
EMP: 60
SALES (corp-wide): 73.3MM **Privately Held**
SIC: 8322 Social service center
PA: Mexican American Opportunity Foundation
   401 N Garfield Ave
   Montebello CA 90640
   323 890-9600

(P-23341)
MHN GOVERNMENT SERVICES LLC
2370 Kerner Blvd, San Rafael (94901-5613)
PHONE..................................916 294-4941
Billy Maynard, *President*
Lisa Ostergren, *Info Tech Mgr*
EMP: 189
SQ FT: 67,000
SALES (est): 3.8MM **Publicly Held**
WEB: www.mhn.com
SIC: 8322 Individual & family services
HQ: Health Net, Llc
   21650 Oxnard St Fl 25
   Woodland Hills CA 91367
   818 676-6000

(P-23342)
MILESTONES ADULT DEV CTR
1 Florida St, Vallejo (94590-5000)
PHONE..................................707 644-0464
Terry Rowland, *General Mgr*
Steve Mack, *Administration*
John Yates, *Administration*
EMP: 90
SALES (est): 1.3MM **Privately Held**
SIC: 8322 Adult day care center

(P-23343)
MINORITY AIDS PROJECT INC
5147 W Jefferson Blvd, Los Angeles (90016)
PHONE..................................323 936-4949
Victor McKamie, *Exec Dir*

EMP: 55
SQ FT: 3,500
SALES: 1.5MM **Privately Held**
WEB: www.map-usa.org
SIC: 8322 Social service center

(P-23344)
MONO NATION
58288 Road 225, North Fork (93643-9428)
P.O. Box 1377 (93643-1377)
PHONE..................................559 877-2450
Kendrick Sherman, *Principal*
EMP: 65
SALES: 40.2K **Privately Held**
SIC: 8322 Individual & family services

(P-23345)
MUTUAL ASSIST NETWORK DEL PASO (PA)
811 Grand Ave Ste A, Sacramento (95838-3466)
PHONE..................................916 927-7694
Richard Dana, *Exec Dir*
Danielle Lawrence, *Program Dir*
EMP: 50
SALES: 2.5MM **Privately Held**
WEB: www.mutualassistance.org
SIC: 8322 Disaster service

(P-23346)
NATIONAL CENTER ON DEAFNESS
18111 Nordhoff St, Northridge (91330-0001)
PHONE..................................818 677-2054
Meri C Pearson, *Director*
Dean Meri C Pearson, *Pastor*
EMP: 80 EST: 2001
SALES (est): 994.9K **Privately Held**
SIC: 8322 Social services for the handicapped

(P-23347)
NEIGHBORHOOD HOUSE ASSOCIATION (PA)
Also Called: N H A
5660 Copley Dr, San Diego (92111-7902)
PHONE..................................858 715-2642
Rudolph A Johnson III, *CEO*
Joseph Maull, *Officer*
Charlotte Ochiqui, *Officer*
Sheryl White, *Vice Pres*
Elizabeth Ferrusca, *Admin Mgr*
EMP: 500
SQ FT: 60,000
SALES: 86.7MM **Privately Held**
WEB: www.sandiegofoodbank.org
SIC: 8322 Neighborhood center

(P-23348)
NEIGHBORHOOD HOUSE ASSOCIATION
Also Called: Naht Care At
4425 Federal Blvd Ste 24, San Diego (92102-2500)
PHONE..................................619 527-1287
Frank Andrews, *Principal*
EMP: 50
SALES (corp-wide): 86.7MM **Privately Held**
WEB: www.sandiegofoodbank.org
SIC: 8322 Neighborhood center
PA: The Neighborhood House Association
   5660 Copley Dr
   San Diego CA 92111
   858 715-2642

(P-23349)
NEIGHBORHOOD HOUSE ASSOCIATION
Also Called: Neighborhood Hse Assoc Fmily
841 S 41st St, San Diego (92113-1899)
PHONE..................................619 263-7761
Ellen Brown, *Manager*
EMP: 100
SALES (corp-wide): 86.7MM **Privately Held**
WEB: www.sandiegofoodbank.org
SIC: 8322 Neighborhood center; 8399 community development groups
PA: The Neighborhood House Association
   5660 Copley Dr
   San Diego CA 92111
   858 715-2642

(P-23350)
NEW BRIDGE FOUNDATION INC
2323 Hearst Ave, Berkeley (94709-1319)
PHONE..................................510 548-7270
Kosta Markakis, *CEO*
Jenny Knowles, *CFO*
Aisha Ware, *Opers Staff*
EMP: 65
SALES: 5.8MM **Privately Held**
WEB: www.newbridgefoundation.org
SIC: 8322 Rehabilitation services

(P-23351)
NEW DIRECTIONS INC (PA)
Also Called: New Directions For Veterans
11303 Wilshire Blvd, Los Angeles (90025-5069)
P.O. Box 25536 (90025-0536)
PHONE..................................310 914-4045
Edgar H Howell, *CEO*
Usha Murthy, *CFO*
Susan Michael, *Officer*
Tony Reinis, *Exec Dir*
Ren Ross, *Project Mgr*
EMP: 80
SQ FT: 60,000
SALES: 6.6MM **Privately Held**
SIC: 8322 Substance abuse counseling

(P-23352)
NEW ECONOMICS FOR WOMEN (PA)
303 Loma Dr, Los Angeles (90017-1103)
PHONE..................................213 483-2060
Maggie Cervantes, *Exec Dir*
Liz Garcia, *Admin Asst*
Edith Martinez, *Project Mgr*
Michelle Reyes, *Personnel Assit*
Andrea Osorio, *Director*
EMP: 70
SQ FT: 25,000
SALES: 3.7MM **Privately Held**
WEB: www.neweconomicsforwomen.org
SIC: 8322 Settlement house

(P-23353)
NEW HAVEN YOUTH FMLY SVCS INC
P.O. Box 1199 (92085-1199)
PHONE..................................760 630-4060
EMP: 108
SALES (corp-wide): 8.2MM **Privately Held**
SIC: 8322 Family counseling services
PA: New Haven Youth And Family Services, Inc.
   216 W Los Angeles Dr
   Vista CA

(P-23354)
NEW START HOME HEALTH CARE INC
21515 Vanowen St Ste 205, Canoga Park (91303-2715)
PHONE..................................818 665-7898
Mary Williams, *CEO*
John Eckels, *Manager*
EMP: 200
SQ FT: 2,000
SALES: 6.5MM **Privately Held**
SIC: 8322 8082 Social services for the handicapped; home health care services

(P-23355)
NEXCARE COLLABORATIVE (PA)
15477 Ventura Blvd, Sherman Oaks (91403-3006)
PHONE..................................818 907-0322
Pejman Salimpour, *President*
Ralph Salimpour MD, *Corp Secy*
Pedram Salimpour MD, *Exec VP*
Kristin Tonozzi, *Director*
EMP: 50
SQ FT: 15,000
SALES (est): 6.7MM **Privately Held**
WEB: www.carenex.com
SIC: 8322 Child related social services

(P-23356)
NO BARRIERS
479 Mason St Ste 325, Vacaville (95688-4592)
PHONE..................................707 451-1947

Joe Zavala, *President*
Jon McGill, *Manager*
EMP: 75
SALES (est): 619.1K **Privately Held**
SIC: 8322 Social services for the handicapped

(P-23357)
NORTHCOAST CHILDRENS SERVICES
730 Hwy 96, Willow Creek (95573)
P.O. Box 149 (95573-0149)
PHONE..................................530 629-2283
Jamie Mackenzie, *Director*
EMP: 62
SALES (corp-wide): 9.9MM **Privately Held**
SIC: 8322 Individual & family services
PA: Northcoast Children's Services Inc
   1266 9th St
   Arcata CA 95521
   707 822-7206

(P-23358)
NORTHEAST VALLEY HEALTH CORP (PA)
1172 N Maclay Ave, San Fernando (91340-1328)
PHONE..................................818 898-1388
Kimberly Wyard, *CEO*
Vince Avila, *CFO*
Patricia Moraga, *CFO*
Nelson Wong, *Chairman*
Antonio Lugo, *Treasurer*
EMP: 75 EST: 1971
SALES: 89.4MM **Privately Held**
SIC: 8322 Community center

(P-23359)
NORTHERN CALIFORNIA INALLIANCE
411 4th St, Wheatland (95692-9467)
PHONE..................................530 633-9695
Andrea Croom, *Exec Dir*
EMP: 120
SALES (corp-wide): 20.4MM **Privately Held**
SIC: 8322 Association for the handicapped
PA: Northern California Inalliance
   6950 21st Ave
   Sacramento CA 95820
   916 381-1300

(P-23360)
NORTHERN CALIFORNIA INALLIANCE (PA)
6950 21st Ave, Sacramento (95820-5948)
PHONE..................................916 381-1300
Richard Royse, *Exec Dir*
Kavin Black, *Program Dir*
Janine Reed, *Director*
EMP: 190 EST: 1968
SQ FT: 20,000
SALES: 20.4MM **Privately Held**
WEB: www.inallianceinc.com
SIC: 8322 Social service center

(P-23361)
NORTHERN VALLEY CATHOLIC SOCIA
2400 Washington Ave, Redding (96001-2802)
PHONE..................................530 241-0552
Jan Maurer Watkins, *CEO*
Don C Chapman, *CEO*
January Giles, *Program Mgr*
Virgie Limones, *Technician*
Kathy Lytle, *Accountant*
EMP: 151
SALES: 10.2MM **Privately Held**
SIC: 8322 Outreach program

(P-23362)
NUEVO AMNECER LATINO CHLD SVCS (PA)
5400 Pomona Blvd, Los Angeles (90022-1717)
PHONE..................................323 720-9951
Norma Duque-Acosta, *President*
EMP: 65
SQ FT: 2,600
SALES: 11.4MM **Privately Held**
SIC: 8322 Adoption services

(P-23363)
OLDER ADULTS CARE MANAGEMENT (PA)
881 Fremont Ave Ste A2, Los Altos
(94024-5637)
PHONE..................................650 329-1411
Cherry Jackson, *Director*
Jim Wilde, *Supervisor*
EMP: 180
SQ FT: 2,000
SALES (est): 4.4MM **Privately Held**
SIC: 8322 8741 8082 Geriatric social
service; general counseling services;
management services; home health care
services

(P-23364)
ONEGENERATION (PA)
Also Called: Onegeneration Adult Day Health
17400 Victory Blvd, Van Nuys
(91406-5349)
PHONE..................................818 708-6625
Lawrence Gordon, *Exec Dir*
Angela Pennacchio, *Executive Asst*
Adam Tavitian, *Financial Analy*
Erin Collins, *Opers Staff*
Heidi Hamilton, *Asst Director*
EMP: 73
SALES: 6MM **Privately Held**
WEB: www.onegeneration.net
SIC: 8322 Senior citizens' center or association

(P-23365)
OPARC
355 S Lemon Ave Ste J, Walnut
(91789-2739)
PHONE..................................909 598-8055
Tom Randall, *Branch Mgr*
EMP: 53
SALES (corp-wide): 13MM **Privately Held**
SIC: 8322 8051 8049 Association for the
handicapped; mental retardation hospital;
psychologist, psychotherapist & hypnotist
PA: Oparc
9029 Vernon Ave
Montclair CA 91763
909 982-4090

(P-23366)
ORANGE COUNTY CHILD ABUSE
Also Called: Welcome Baby
2390 E Orangewood Ave # 300, Anaheim
(92806-6141)
PHONE..................................714 543-4333
Scott Trotter, *Exec Dir*
Stephanie Enano, *Principal*
EMP: 99
SALES: 7.4MM **Privately Held**
SIC: 8322 Child related social services

(P-23367)
ORANGEWOOD FOUNDATION
1575 E 17th St, Santa Ana (92705-8506)
PHONE..................................714 619-0200
Chris Simonsen, *CEO*
John Luker, *CFO*
Rick Wiepking, *Info Tech Dir*
Linda Levshin, *Info Tech Mgr*
Jami Smith, *Human Res Mgr*
EMP: 85
SQ FT: 22,340
SALES: 12.8MM **Privately Held**
WEB: www.orangewoodfoundation.org
SIC: 8322 Individual & family services

(P-23368)
OSHMAN FAMILY JEWISH CMNTY CTR
3921 Fabian Way, Palo Alto (94303-4606)
PHONE..................................650 223-8700
Alan Sataloff, *Exec Dir*
Haim Hovav, *CFO*
Sally Porush, *Officer*
Paul Raczynski, *Info Tech Dir*
Nicky Hornstein, *Director*
EMP: 200
SALES: 26.8MM **Privately Held**
SIC: 8322 Community center

(P-23369)
OUTREACH & ESCORT INC (PA)
2221 Oakland Rd Ste 200, San Jose
(95131-1415)
P.O. Box 640910 (95164-0910)
PHONE..................................408 678-8585
Katheryn H Heatley, *President*
William Chawarz, *Vice Pres*
Elizabeth Jespersen, *Analyst*
EMP: 79
SQ FT: 20,000
SALES: 9.9MM **Privately Held**
WEB: www.outreach1.org
SIC: 8322 Individual & family services

(P-23370)
PACIFIC ASIAN CONSORTM EMPLYMN
Also Called: Pace Administrator To Work
1055 Wilshire Blvd # 1475, Los Angeles
(90017-2431)
PHONE..................................213 989-3228
Kerry Doi, *Branch Mgr*
EMP: 100
SALES (corp-wide): 22.8MM **Privately Held**
SIC: 8322 Individual & family services
PA: Pacific Asian Consortium In Employment
1055 Wilshire Blvd Ste 14
Los Angeles CA 90017
213 353-3982

(P-23371)
PACIFIC CLINICS FOUNDATION
855 N Orange Grove Blvd, Pasadena
(91103-3333)
PHONE..................................626 796-3453
EMP: 63
SALES (corp-wide): 82.2MM **Privately Held**
SIC: 8322 Youth center
PA: Pacific Clinics Foundation.
800 S Santa Anita Ave
Arcadia CA 91006
626 254-5000

(P-23372)
PAJARO VALLEY PREVNTN & STUDEN
335 E Lake Ave, Watsonville (95076-4826)
PHONE..................................831 728-6445
Jenny Sarmiento, *CEO*
Linda Perez, *Exec Dir*
EMP: 65
SALES: 4.7MM **Privately Held**
SIC: 8322 Alcoholism counseling, nontreatment; drug abuse counselor, nontreatment

(P-23373)
PALOMAR FMLY CUNSELING SVC INC (PA)
1002 E Grand Ave, Escondido
(92025-4605)
PHONE..................................760 741-2660
Albert Trevison, *CEO*
EMP: 100
SALES: 3.6MM **Privately Held**
SIC: 8322 Family counseling services

(P-23374)
PARTNERS ADVCTES FOR RMRKBLE C
Also Called: PARCA
800 Airport Blvd Ste 320, Burlingame
(94010-1919)
PHONE..................................650 312-0730
Diana Conti, *Exec Dir*
Suzanne Hinton, *Human Res Dir*
Joseph Fenerty, *Anesthesiology*
EMP: 86 EST: 1952
SALES: 3.6MM **Privately Held**
WEB: www.parca.org
SIC: 8322 Association for the handicapped

(P-23375)
PARTNERS FOR COMMUNITY ACCESS
708 Gilman St, Berkeley (94710-1333)
PHONE..................................510 558-6700
Rosalee Shubert, *Principal*
EMP: 60

SALES (est): 875.3K **Privately Held**
SIC: 8322 Social service center

(P-23376)
PASADENA CHILD DEVELOPMENT ASS
620 N Lake Ave, Pasadena (91101-1220)
PHONE..................................626 793-7350
Diane Cullinane, *Owner*
Mimi Winer, *Co-Owner*
EMP: 70 EST: 1997
SALES (est): 981.6K **Privately Held**
WEB: www.pasadenachilddevelopment.org
SIC: 8322 Individual & family services

(P-23377)
PATHWAY INC
287 W Orange Show Ln, San Bernardino
(92408-2037)
PHONE..................................909 890-1070
Robert McGuire, *President*
Joyce Hampton, *President*
EMP: 100
SQ FT: 2,300
SALES (est): 3.1MM **Privately Held**
SIC: 8322 5999 Social services for the
handicapped; technical aids for the handicapped

(P-23378)
PATHWAY TO CHOICES INC
751 Belmont Way, Pinole (94564-2661)
PHONE..................................510 724-9044
Juan Velasquez, *President*
EMP: 52
SALES (est): 2.2MM **Privately Held**
SIC: 8322 General counseling services

(P-23379)
PATHWAYS LA (PA)
3325 Wilshire Blvd # 1100, Los Angeles
(90010-1703)
PHONE..................................213 427-2700
Karen Park, *President*
Carla Buck, *Vice Pres*
Les Guttman, *Principal*
Duane Dennis, *Exec Dir*
Matt Youngman, *Technology*
EMP: 50
SQ FT: 24,000
SALES: 21.5MM **Privately Held**
WEB: www.pathwaysla.org
SIC: 8322 Child related social services

(P-23380)
PENINSULA FAMILY SERVICE
Also Called: Leo J Ryan Child Care Ctr
1200 Miller Ave, South San Francisco
(94080-1221)
PHONE..................................650 952-6848
Liliya Sergiyemko, *Branch Mgr*
EMP: 55
SALES (corp-wide): 13.1MM **Privately Held**
WEB: www.familyserviceagency.org
SIC: 8322 8351 Family (marriage) counseling; child day care services
PA: Peninsula Family Service
24 2nd Ave
San Mateo CA 94401
650 403-4300

(P-23381)
PENINSULA JEWISH COMMUNITY CTR
800 Foster City Blvd, Foster City
(94404-2228)
PHONE..................................650 212-7522
Paul Gedulig, *CEO*
EMP: 200
SALES: 17.7MM **Privately Held**
SIC: 8322 Community center

(P-23382)
PENINSULA VOLUNTEERS INC (PA)
Also Called: ROSENER HOUSE
800 Middle Ave, Menlo Park (94025-5198)
PHONE..................................650 326-0665
Peter Olsen, *Exec Dir*
Michelle Knapik, *Exec Dir*
Paige Sweetin, *Program Mgr*
Cathy Duhring, *Executive Asst*
Tina Rees, *Admin Asst*
EMP: 50 EST: 1947

SQ FT: 25,000
SALES: 4.6MM **Privately Held**
WEB: www.penvol.org
SIC: 8322 Adult day care center

(P-23383)
PEOPLE ASSISTING HOMELESS
Also Called: P A T H
340 N Madison Ave, Los Angeles
(90004-3504)
PHONE..................................323 644-2216
Joel John Roberts, *President*
Sandy Oluwek, *Human Res Dir*
EMP: 167
SALES: 35.3MM **Privately Held**
WEB: www.epath.org
SIC: 8322 Social service center

(P-23384)
PEOPLE CONCERN
Safe Haven
1751 Cloverfield Blvd, Santa Monica
(90404-4007)
PHONE..................................310 883-1222
Andrew Schwich, *Director*
EMP: 123
SALES (corp-wide): 13.5MM **Privately Held**
SIC: 8322 Emergency shelters; emergency
social services
PA: The People Concern
2116 Arlington Ave # 100
Los Angeles CA 90018
323 334-9000

(P-23385)
PEOPLE CONCERN
Daybreak
1751 Cloverfield Blvd, Santa Monica
(90404-4007)
PHONE..................................310 450-0650
Anya Booker, *Director*
EMP: 185
SALES (corp-wide): 13.5MM **Privately Held**
SIC: 8322 Community center
PA: The People Concern
2116 Arlington Ave # 100
Los Angeles CA 90018
323 334-9000

(P-23386)
PEOPLE CREATING SUCCESS INC
1607 E Palmdale Blvd H, Palmdale
(93550-7801)
PHONE..................................661 225-9700
Robert Donery, *Branch Mgr*
EMP: 85
SALES (corp-wide): 14.8MM **Privately Held**
SIC: 8322 Individual & family services
PA: People Creating Success, Inc.
2585 Teller Rd
Newbury Park CA 91320
805 375-9222

(P-23387)
PEOPLE CREATING SUCCESS INC
5350 Hollister Ave Ste I, Santa Barbara
(93111-2326)
PHONE..................................805 692-5290
Brian Fay, *Manager*
EMP: 113
SALES (corp-wide): 14.8MM **Privately Held**
SIC: 8322 Social service center
PA: People Creating Success, Inc.
2585 Teller Rd
Newbury Park CA 91320
805 375-9222

(P-23388)
PHFE WIC PROGRAM
12871 Schabarum Ave, Irwindale (91706)
PHONE..................................626 856-6650
Eloise Jenks, *Director*
EMP: 120
SALES (est): 2.8MM **Privately Held**
SIC: 8322 Individual & family services

(P-23389)
PINOLE SENIOR CENTER
2500 Charles St, Pinole (94564-1301)
PHONE..................................510 724-9800

Janette Bilbas, *Director*
EMP: 58
SALES (est): 838.2K **Privately Held**
SIC: 8322 Senior citizens' center or association
PA: City Of Pinole
2131 Pear St
Pinole CA 94564
510 724-9000

(P-23390)
PLAN-IT LIFE INC
5729 Vista Del Caballero, Riverside
(92509-6423)
P.O. Box 2994, Corona (92878-2994)
PHONE..................................951 742-7561
Sheila McLean, *CEO*
Nyron McLean, *CFO*
Carl Sampson MD, *Vice Pres*
EMP: 56
SQ FT: 2,800
SALES: 2.3MM **Privately Held**
SIC: 8322 Substance abuse counseling

(P-23391)
PLUMAS RURAL SERVICES
711 E Main St, Quincy (95971-9722)
PHONE..................................530 283-2725
Michele Pillar, *Exec Dir*
EMP: 90
SQ FT: 6,000
SALES: 5.3MM **Privately Held**
WEB: www.plumasruralservices.org
SIC: 8322 Drug abuse counselor, nontreatment

(P-23392)
POMEROY RCRTION RHBLTATION CTR (PA)
Also Called: R C H
207 Skyline Blvd, San Francisco
(94132-1025)
PHONE..................................415 665-4100
John McCue, *Exec Dir*
Maria Crespin, *Social Dir*
Henry Woo, *Exec Dir*
Loida Dantes, *Accountant*
Celina Lam, *Controller*
EMP: 180
SQ FT: 22,000
SALES: 9.1MM **Privately Held**
WEB: www.janetpomeroy.org
SIC: 8322 Social services for the handicapped

(P-23393)
PRECISION HOME CARE LLC
2365 Iron Point Rd # 270, Folsom
(95630-8712)
PHONE..................................916 749-4051
John Alves, *Mng Member*
Julio Quinones, *COO*
Diane Logan, *Vice Pres*
EMP: 56
SALES (est): 140.1K **Privately Held**
SIC: 8322 8361 Old age assistance; residential care

(P-23394)
PROJECT OPEN HAND (PA)
730 Polk St Fl 3, San Francisco
(94109-7813)
PHONE..................................415 292-3400
Paul Hepfer, *CEO*
Eileen Ward, *Human Res Dir*
EMP: 96
SQ FT: 50,000
SALES: 9.7MM **Privately Held**
WEB: www.openhand.org
SIC: 8322 Meal delivery program

(P-23395)
PROTEUS INC
1816 Cecil Ave, Delano (93215-1520)
PHONE..................................661 721-5800
EMP: 127
SALES (corp-wide): 28.6MM **Privately Held**
SIC: 8322 Social service center
PA: Proteus, Inc.
1830 N Dinuba Blvd
Visalia CA 93291
559 733-5423

(P-23396)
PROTOTYPES CENTERS FOR INNOV
1000 N Alameda St Ste 390, Los Angeles
(90012-1804)
PHONE..................................213 542-3838
Cassandra Loch, *President*
Maryann Fraser, *Exec VP*
Nial Stimson, *Vice Pres*
John Baldrias, *Nurse*
EMP: 250
SQ FT: 8,400
SALES: 20.1MM **Privately Held**
SIC: 8322 General counseling services

(P-23397)
R L SAFETY INC
2157 Cherrystone Dr, San Jose
(95128-1217)
PHONE..................................408 557-0887
Brent Rapport, *President*
Loisa Rapport, *Vice Pres*
EMP: 50
SALES (est): 718.3K **Privately Held**
SIC: 8322 8099 7389 Emergency social services; blood related health services;

(P-23398)
RANCHO LOS AMIGOS NATIONA
Also Called: Information Management Svcs
7601 Imperial Hwy, Downey (90242-3456)
PHONE..................................562 401-7111
EMP: 364 **Privately Held**
SIC: 8322 Individual & family services
PA: Rancho Los Amigos National Rehabilitation Center
7601 Imperial Hwy
Downey CA 90242

(P-23399)
RANCHO LOS AMIGOS NATIONA
Also Called: Professional Staffing Associat
7601 Imperial Hwy, Downey (90242-3456)
PHONE..................................562 401-7111
Consuelo Diaz, *CEO*
EMP: 729 **Privately Held**
WEB: www.co.la.ca.us
SIC: 8322 Individual & family services
PA: Rancho Los Amigos National Rehabilitation Center
7601 Imperial Hwy
Downey CA 90242

(P-23400)
RANCHO LOS AMIGOS NATIONA
12852 Erickson Ave, Downey
(90242-4004)
PHONE..................................562 401-7266
EMP: 273 **Privately Held**
SIC: 8322 Individual & family services
PA: Rancho Los Amigos National Rehabilitation Center
7601 Imperial Hwy
Downey CA 90242

(P-23401)
RANCHO LOS AMIGOS NATIONA (PA)
7601 Imperial Hwy, Downey (90242-3456)
PHONE..................................562 401-7111
Jorge R Orozco, *CEO*
Benjamin Ovando Sr, *COO*
Robin Bayus, *CFO*
Aries Limbaga, *Principal*
Greg Waskul, *Exec Dir*
EMP: 84
SALES (est): 74.1MM **Privately Held**
SIC: 8322 Rehabilitation services

(P-23402)
READING PARTNERS
600 Valley Way, Milpitas (95035-4138)
PHONE..................................408 945-5720
Michael Lombardo, *Exec Dir*
Diana Martin, *Program Mgr*
EMP: 91
SALES (corp-wide): 23.5MM **Privately Held**
SIC: 8322 Individual & family services

PA: Reading Partners
180 Grand Ave Ste 800
Oakland CA 94612
510 444-9800

(P-23403)
REDWOOD COAST REGIONAL (PA)
Also Called: REDWOOD COAST REGIONAL CENTER
1116 Airport Park Blvd, Ukiah (95482-7431)
PHONE..................................707 462-3832
Mike Ring, *Administration*
Pamela Jensen, *Bd of Directors*
Mary Yates, *Bd of Directors*
Kim Orsi, *Admin Sec*
Dina Petterson, *Admin Asst*
EMP: 79
SQ FT: 6,600
SALES: 115.2MM **Privately Held**
WEB: www.redwoodcoastrc.org
SIC: 8322 Social services for the handicapped

(P-23404)
REDWOOD COAST REGIONAL
Also Called: Redwood Coast Regional Center
525 2nd St Ste 300, Eureka (95501-0488)
PHONE..................................707 445-0893
Clay Jones, *Director*
EMP: 50
SALES (est): 1.8MM
SALES (corp-wide): 115.2MM **Privately Held**
WEB: www.redwoodcoastrc.org
SIC: 8322 8699 Social services for the handicapped; personal interest organization
PA: Redwood Coast Developmental Services Corporation
1116 Airport Park Blvd
Ukiah CA 95482
707 462-3832

(P-23405)
REDWOOD COAST SENIORS INC
Also Called: SENIOR NUTRITION
490 N Harold St, Fort Bragg (95437-3331)
PHONE..................................707 964-0443
Joseph Curren, *Exec Dir*
EMP: 60
SALES: 993.8K **Privately Held**
SIC: 8322 Senior citizens' center or association

(P-23406)
REDWOOD COMMUNITY SERVICES (PA)
631 S Orchard Ave, Ukiah (95482-5011)
P.O. Box 2077 (95482-2077)
PHONE..................................707 467-2000
Camille Shraeder, *Exec Dir*
Lynn Sallee, *CFO*
Lancy Armstrong, *Admin Sec*
Danielle Lower, *Opers Mgr*
Lorraine Montano, *Asst Director*
EMP: 165
SALES: 10.8MM **Privately Held**
SIC: 8322 Family service agency

(P-23407)
REGIONAL CENTER OF E BAY INC
500 Davis St Ste 100, San Leandro
(94577-2758)
PHONE..................................510 618-6100
Jim Burton, *Director*
EMP: 150 **EST:** 1975
SQ FT: 26,000
SALES: 311.1MM **Privately Held**
SIC: 8322 Social services for the handicapped

(P-23408)
REHABILITATION CALIFORNIA DEPT
Also Called: Los Angeles South Bay Dst Off
4300 Long Beach Blvd # 200, Long Beach
(90807-2011)
PHONE..................................562 422-8325
Brenda Brent, *Manager*
EMP: 50 **Privately Held**
WEB: www.carehab.org

SIC: 8322 9431 Rehabilitation services; administration of public health programs
HQ: California Department Of Rehabilitation
721 Capitol Mall Fl 6
Sacramento CA 95814

(P-23409)
RESCUE CHILDREN INC
Also Called: CRAYCROFT YOUTH CENTER
335 G St, Fresno (93706-3422)
P.O. Box 1422 (93716-1422)
PHONE..................................559 268-1123
Fax: 559 268-3465
EMP: 50
SALES: 1.3MM **Privately Held**
SIC: 8322

(P-23410)
RESOURCE CONNECTION OF AMADOR (PA)
Also Called: RESOURCE CONNECTION, THE
444 E Saint Charles St, San Andreas
(95249)
P.O. Box 919 (95249-0919)
PHONE..................................209 754-3114
Linda Foster, *Ch of Bd*
Amber Shelton, *Principal*
Kelli Fraguero, *Admin Dir*
Catherine C Bourland, *Director*
EMP: 57
SALES: 8.7MM **Privately Held**
WEB: www.theresourceconnection.net
SIC: 8322 Social service center

(P-23411)
RESOURCE CONNECTION OF AMADOR
Also Called: W I C
430 Sutter Hill Rd, Sutter Creek
(95685-4149)
PHONE..................................209 223-7685
Damian Wolin, *President*
EMP: 63
SALES (corp-wide): 8.7MM **Privately Held**
SIC: 8322 Social service center
PA: The Resource Connection Of Amador And Calaveras Counties Incorporated
444 E Saint Charles St
San Andreas CA 95249
209 754-3114

(P-23412)
RESOURCE RFRRAL CHILD CARE DEV
1225 Gill Ave, Madera (93637-5234)
PHONE..................................559 673-9173
Mary Jane Nabors, *Director*
EMP: 50
SALES (est): 392.2K **Privately Held**
SIC: 8322 Individual & family services

(P-23413)
REUTLINGER COMMUNITY
Also Called: REUTLINGER COMMUNITY FOR JEWIS
4000 Camino Tassajara, Danville
(94506-4711)
PHONE..................................925 964-2062
Jay Zimmer, *CEO*
EMP: 160
SALES: 17.7MM **Privately Held**
WEB: www.rcjl.org
SIC: 8322 Individual & family services

(P-23414)
RICHMOND DST NEIGHBORHOOD CTR (PA)
741 30th Ave, San Francisco (94121-3519)
PHONE..................................415 751-6600
Michelle Cusano, *Exec Dir*
Michelle Menegaz, *Program Mgr*
Bessie Natareno, *Program Mgr*
Mia Tswago, *Program Mgr*
Megan Han, *Human Res Mgr*
EMP: 80
SALES: 4.3MM **Privately Held**
WEB: www.rdnc.org
SIC: 8322 Community center; outreach program

(P-23415)
RICHMOND RESCUE MISSION (PA)
Also Called: BAY AREA RESCUE MISSION
2114 Macdonald Ave, Richmond (94801-3311)
P.O. Box 1112 (94802-0112)
PHONE..............................510 215-4555
John M Anderson, *President*
Debra Anderson, *Vice Pres*
Tim Hammack, *Vice Pres*
Jonathan Russell, *Vice Pres*
Woody Tausend, *Vice Pres*
EMP: 52
SQ FT: 80,000
SALES: 10MM **Privately Held**
SIC: 8322 Emergency shelters

(P-23416)
RIO HONDO EDUCATION CONSORTIUM
Also Called: LEARN
7200 Greenleaf Ave # 300, Whittier (90602-1383)
PHONE..............................562 945-0150
Robert Arellanes, *CEO*
Brenda Carrillo, *COO*
Carolina Arce, *Principal*
Robert Bell, *Principal*
Linda Contreras, *Principal*
EMP: 150
SALES: 3.9MM **Privately Held**
WEB: www.riohondoec.org
SIC: 8322 Individual & family services

(P-23417)
RURAL CMNTY ASSISTANCE CORP (PA)
Also Called: Rcac
3120 Freeboard Dr Ste 201, West Sacramento (95691-5039)
PHONE..............................916 447-2854
Stan Keasling, *CEO*
Kevin McCumber, *CFO*
Chuck Miller, *Loan Officer*
Monette Stevens, *Analyst*
ARI Neumann, *Asst Director*
EMP: 60 EST: 1978
SALES: 24.3MM **Privately Held**
SIC: 8322 6111 Individual & family services; federal & federally sponsored credit agencies

(P-23418)
RUTH BARAJAS
Also Called: Bacr
965 Mission St Ste 520, San Francisco (94103-2959)
PHONE..............................415 977-6949
Ruth Barajas, *Administration*
Andrea Juarez, *Associate Dir*
EMP: 50
SALES (est): 754K **Privately Held**
WEB: www.chalk.org
SIC: 8322 Youth center

(P-23419)
S&F MANAGEMENT COMPANY LLC
Also Called: Windsor Sacramento Estates
501 Jessie Ave, Sacramento (95838-2608)
PHONE..............................916 922-8855
EMP: 1356 **Privately Held**
SIC: 8322 Rehabilitation services
PA: S&F Management Company, Llc
9200 W Sunset Blvd # 700
West Hollywood CA 90069
-

(P-23420)
SACRAMENTO CHINESE COMMUNITY S
420 I St Ste 5, Sacramento (95814-2319)
PHONE..............................916 442-4228
Henry Kloczkowski, *Director*
Choua Yang, *Associate Dir*
Oscar Bermudez, *Program Mgr*
Andrea Cunningham, *Program Mgr*
Maria Gonzalez, *Program Mgr*
EMP: 200
SQ FT: 2,000
SALES: 7.8MM **Privately Held**
SIC: 8322 8699 8611 Social service center; charitable organization; community affairs & services

(P-23421)
SACRAMENTO COUNTY OFF EDUCATN
Also Called: Probation Department
9750 Bus Park Dr Ste 220, Sacramento (95827-1716)
PHONE..............................916 875-0300
Lee Seale, *Director*
EMP: 50 **Privately Held**
WEB: www.sna.com
SIC: 8322 Probation office;
PA: Sacramento County Office Of Education
10474 Mather Blvd
Mather CA 95655
-

(P-23422)
SACRAMENTO LOAVES & FISHES (PA)
1351 N C St Ste 22, Sacramento (95811-0608)
P.O. Box 2161 (95812-2161)
PHONE..............................916 446-0874
Libby Hernandez, *Director*
Noel Kammermann, *Exec Dir*
EMP: 55
SALES: 5.9MM **Privately Held**
SIC: 8322 Social service center

(P-23423)
SALESFORCECOM/FOUNDATION
The Landmark One St The Landma, San Francisco (94105)
PHONE..............................800 667-6389
Marc Benioff, *CEO*
Keith Block, *President*
Suzanne Dibianca, *President*
Rob Acker, *COO*
Kurt Hagen, *CFO*
EMP: 150
SALES (est): 17.5MM **Privately Held**
SIC: 8322 Disaster service; temporary relief service

(P-23424)
SALVATION ARMY
900 James M Wood Blvd, Los Angeles (90015-1356)
PHONE..............................213 553-3273
Paul Bollwahn, *Director*
EMP: 100
SALES (corp-wide): 2.3B **Privately Held**
WEB: www.salvationarmy.usawest.org
SIC: 8322 Individual & family services
HQ: The Salvation Army
30840 Hawthorne Blvd
Rancho Palos Verdes CA 90275
562 491-8496

(P-23425)
SALVATION ARMY
1615 D St, Sacramento (95814-1013)
PHONE..............................916 441-5137
Stephen Arnold, *Branch Mgr*
EMP: 100
SALES (corp-wide): 2.3B **Privately Held**
WEB: www.salvationarmy.usawest.org
SIC: 8322 Individual & family services
HQ: The Salvation Army
30840 Hawthorne Blvd
Rancho Palos Verdes CA 90275
562 491-8496

(P-23426)
SALVATION ARMY (HQ)
30840 Hawthorne Blvd, Rancho Palos Verdes (90275-5300)
P.O. Box 93002, Long Beach (90809-3002)
PHONE..............................562 491-8496
James M Knaggs, *Principal*
Commissioner Carolyn R Knaggs, *President*
Manny Ramirez, *President*
Rachael Fowler, *Comms Mgr*
Kenneth Hodder, *Principal*
▼ EMP: 140
SALES (est): 72.8MM
SALES (corp-wide): 2.3B **Privately Held**
WEB: www.salvationarmy.usawest.org
SIC: 8322 Individual & family services

PA: The Salvation Army National Corporation
615 Slaters Ln
Alexandria VA 22314
703 684-5500

(P-23427)
SALVATION ARMY
2737 W Sunset Blvd, Los Angeles (90026-2181)
PHONE..............................213 484-0772
Ana Aguirre, *Director*
EMP: 50
SALES (corp-wide): 2.3B **Privately Held**
WEB: www.salvationarmy.usawest.org
SIC: 8322 Refugee service
HQ: The Salvation Army
30840 Hawthorne Blvd
Rancho Palos Verdes CA 90275
562 491-8496

(P-23428)
SALVATION ARMY GLDEN STATE DIV (PA)
832 Folsom St Fl 6, San Francisco (94107-1142)
PHONE..............................415 553-3500
Steve Smith, *Principal*
Shawn McDaniel, *Officer*
Tammy Ray, *Officer*
Dennis Trimmer, *Administration*
Ruth Scheline, *Hum Res Coord*
EMP: 80
SALES (est): 7.1MM **Privately Held**
SIC: 8322 8741 Social service center; administrative management

(P-23429)
SAMARITAN VILLAGE INC
7700 Fox Rd, Hughson (95326-9100)
P.O. Box 444, Yuba City (95992-0444)
PHONE..............................209 883-3212
Daniel Aguilar, *CEO*
Victor Savage, *CEO*
EMP: 115
SALES: 60K **Privately Held**
SIC: 8322 Adult day care center

(P-23430)
SAN ANDREAS REGIONAL CENTER (PA)
6203 San Ignacio Ave # 110, San Jose (95119-1371)
P.O. Box 50002 (95150-0002)
PHONE..............................408 374-9960
Mary Lu Gonzalez, *CEO*
Greg Hoffman, *CFO*
Yoshiharu Kuroiwa, *CFO*
Lisa Lopez, *Vice Pres*
Javier Zaldivar, *Exec Dir*
EMP: 174
SQ FT: 29,000
SALES: 408.1MM **Privately Held**
SIC: 8322 Association for the handicapped

(P-23431)
SAN DIEGO LESBIAN GAY BISEXU
Also Called: CENTER, THE
3909 Centre St, San Diego (92103-3410)
P.O. Box 3357 (92163-1357)
PHONE..............................619 692-2077
Delores Jacobs, *Exec Dir*
EMP: 50
SQ FT: 15,490
SALES: 7.7MM **Privately Held**
WEB: www.thecentersd.org
SIC: 8322 Community center

(P-23432)
SAN DIEGO YOUTH SERVICES INC (PA)
Also Called: S D Y S
3255 Wing St Ste 550, San Diego (92110-4641)
P.O. Box 80756 (92138-0756)
PHONE..............................619 221-8600
Walter Philips, *Exec Dir*
Angie Tran, *CFO*
Steven Jella, *Exec Dir*
Walter Phillips, *Exec Dir*
Jan Stankus, *Program Mgr*
EMP: 55
SQ FT: 5,634

SALES: 15MM **Privately Held**
SIC: 8322 Youth center

(P-23433)
SAN DIEGO-IMPERIAL
Also Called: San Diego Regional Ctr For Dev
2727 Hoover Ave, National City (91950-6602)
PHONE..............................619 336-6600
Judy Borchert, *Manager*
Michael Rath, *Program Mgr*
Kim Gaines, *Technology*
EMP: 54
SALES (corp-wide): 2.3MM **Privately Held**
WEB: www.sdrc.org
SIC: 8322 Social service center
PA: San Diego-Imperial Counties Developmental Services, Inc.
4355 Ruffin Rd Ste 220
San Diego CA 92123
858 576-2996

(P-23434)
SAN DIEGO-IMPERIAL COUNTIES DE (PA)
4355 Ruffin Rd Ste 220, San Diego (92123-4308)
PHONE..............................858 576-2996
Carlos Flores, *Exec Dir*
Edward Kenney, *CFO*
Judy Wallace Patton, *Treasurer*
Mark Gates, *Program Mgr*
Darlene Jean, *Program Mgr*
EMP: 474
SQ FT: 62,000
SALES (est): 2.3MM **Privately Held**
WEB: www.sdrc.org
SIC: 8322 Social services for the handicapped

(P-23435)
SAN DIEGO-IMPERIAL COUNTIES DE
Also Called: Developmentally Research Ctr
1370 W Sn Mrcos Blvd # 100, San Marcos (92078-1601)
PHONE..............................760 736-1200
Nina Garrett, *Director*
EMP: 70
SALES (est): 542K
SALES (corp-wide): 2.3MM **Privately Held**
WEB: www.sdrc.org
SIC: 8322 Social services for the handicapped
PA: San Diego-Imperial Counties Developmental Services, Inc.
4355 Ruffin Rd Ste 220
San Diego CA 92123
858 576-2996

(P-23436)
SAN FRANCISCO CITY & COUNTY
Also Called: San Francisco Public Schools
1520 Oakdale Ave, San Francisco (94124-2323)
PHONE..............................415 695-5660
David Hollands, *Branch Mgr*
EMP: 93 **Privately Held**
SIC: 8322 Child related social services
PA: City & County Of San Francisco
1 Dr Carlton B Goodlett P
San Francisco CA 94102
415 554-7500

(P-23437)
SAN FRANCISCO AIDS FOUNDATION (PA)
1035 Market St Ste 400, San Francisco (94103-1665)
PHONE..............................415 487-3000
Joe Hollendoner, *CEO*
Jody Schaffer, *Volunteer Dir*
Rick Andrews, *Owner*
Elizabeth Pesch, *CFO*
Robert Grant, *Chief Mktg Ofcr*
EMP: 100
SQ FT: 45,000
SALES: 29.9MM **Privately Held**
WEB: www.sfaf.org
SIC: 8322 Social service center

PRODUCTS & SVCS

(P-23438)
SAN FRANCISCO CITY & COUNTY
Also Called: Child Support Services
617 Mission St, San Francisco
(94105-3503)
PHONE...............................415 356-2700
Christine Anderson, *Manager*
Laurena Yarbrough, *Officer*
Nancy Crowley, *Comms Dir*
Martha Cohen, *Admin Sec*
Maria Kam, *Admin Sec*
EMP: 93 **Privately Held**
SIC: **8322** 9441 Individual & family services; administration of social & manpower programs; ;
PA: City & County Of San Francisco
1 Dr Carlton B Goodlett P
San Francisco CA 94102
415 554-7500

(P-23439)
SAN FRANCISCO CITY & COUNTY
Also Called: Family Support Bureau
617 Mission St, San Francisco
(94105-3503)
PHONE...............................415 356-2700
EMP: 93 **Privately Held**
SIC: **8322** 9441 Individual & family services; administration of social & manpower programs; ;
PA: City & County Of San Francisco
1 Dr Carlton B Goodlett P
San Francisco CA 94102
415 554-7500

(P-23440)
SAN FRANCISCO FOOD BANK
Also Called: SF-MARIN FOOD BANK
900 Pennsylvania Ave, San Francisco
(94107-3498)
PHONE...............................415 282-1900
Paul Ash, *Exec Dir*
Leslie Bacho, *COO*
Michael Braude, *CFO*
Andy Burns, *Program Mgr*
Maria Stokes, *Marketing Staff*
EMP: 80
SQ FT: 55,000
SALES: 96.3MM **Privately Held**
WEB: www.sffb.org
SIC: **8322** Social service center

(P-23441)
SAN FRANCISCO PARTCLR CNCL SCT
525 5th St, San Francisco (94107-1012)
PHONE...............................415 255-3525
Lisa Handley, *Director*
EMP: 85
SALES (corp-wide): 9.5MM **Privately Held**
SIC: **8322** Individual & family services
PA: The San Francisco Particular Council Of The Society Of St Vincent De Paul
1175 Howard St
San Francisco CA 94103
415 552-2943

(P-23442)
SAN GABRIEL/POMONA VALLEYS
Also Called: SAN GABRIEL/POMONA REGIONAL CE
75 Rancho Camino Dr, Pomona
(91766-4728)
PHONE...............................909 620-7722
R Keith Penman, *Exec Dir*
John Hunt, *CFO*
Carol Tomblin, *Director*
Aaron Christian, *Manager*
EMP: 323
SQ FT: 100,000
SALES: 234.2MM **Privately Held**
SIC: **8322** Social service center

(P-23443)
SAN JOAQUIN CNTY AGING & COMMU
102 S San Joaquin St, Stockton
(95202-3213)
P.O. Box 201056 (95201-3006)
PHONE...............................209 468-9455
Michael Miller, *Director*

Kirsten Yeh, *Analyst*
EMP: 120
SALES: 10MM **Privately Held**
SIC: **8322** Senior citizens' center or association

(P-23444)
SANTA BARBARA COUNTY OF
Also Called: Probation Dept
117 E Carrillo St, Santa Barbara
(93101-2110)
PHONE...............................805 882-3700
Beverly Taylor, *Chief*
EMP: 400 **Privately Held**
WEB: www.sbcounty.org
SIC: **8322** Probation office; parole office
PA: County Of Santa Barbara
105 E Anapamu St Rm 406
Santa Barbara CA 93101
805 568-3400

(P-23445)
SANTA BARBARA COUNTY OF
Also Called: Probation Dept
1410 S Broadway Ste L, Santa Maria
(93454-6971)
PHONE...............................805 614-1550
Brian Carroll, *Branch Mgr*
EMP: 122 **Privately Held**
WEB: www.sbcountyhr.org
SIC: **8322** 9223 Child related social services; parole office; correctional institutions;
PA: County Of Santa Barbara
105 E Anapamu St Rm 406
Santa Barbara CA 93101
805 568-3400

(P-23446)
SANTA BARBARA COUNTY OF
Also Called: Social Services Dept
1100 W Laurel Ave, Lompoc (93436-5155)
PHONE...............................805 737-7080
Beverly Littlejohn, *Director*
EMP: 122 **Privately Held**
WEB: www.sbcountyhr.org
SIC: **8322** 9441 Public welfare center; administration of social & manpower programs;
PA: County Of Santa Barbara
105 E Anapamu St Rm 406
Santa Barbara CA 93101
805 568-3400

(P-23447)
SANTA BARBARA COUNTY OF
Also Called: Probation Dept
429 N San Antonio Rd, Santa Barbara
(93110-1399)
PHONE...............................805 884-1600
Scott Whiteley, *Manager*
EMP: 70 **Privately Held**
WEB: www.sbcountyhr.org
SIC: **8322** 9223 Child related social services; correctional institutions;
PA: County Of Santa Barbara
105 E Anapamu St Rm 406
Santa Barbara CA 93101
805 568-3400

(P-23448)
SANTA BARBARA COUNTY OF
Also Called: Human Resources
4 E Carrillo St, Santa Barbara
(93101-2707)
PHONE...............................866 901-3212
Karin Roser, *Branch Mgr*
EMP: 122 **Privately Held**
WEB: www.sbcountyhr.org
SIC: **8322** 9441 Individual & family services; administration of social & manpower programs;
PA: County Of Santa Barbara
105 E Anapamu St Rm 406
Santa Barbara CA 93101
805 568-3400

(P-23449)
SANTA CLARA COUNTY OF
Also Called: Adult Probation Department
2600 N 1st St, San Jose (95134-2014)
PHONE...............................408 435-2000
Karen Fletcher, *Chief*
EMP: 100 **Privately Held**
SIC: **8322** Probation office

PA: County Of Santa Clara
3180 Newberry Dr Ste 150
San Jose CA 95118
408 299-5105

(P-23450)
SANTA CLARA COUNTY OF
Also Called: Probation Dept
2314 N 1st St, San Jose (95131-1011)
PHONE...............................408 435-2111
EMP: 200 **Privately Held**
WEB: www.countyairports.org
SIC: **8322** 9441 Probation office; parole office; administration of social & manpower programs
PA: County Of Santa Clara
3180 Newberry Dr Ste 150
San Jose CA 95118
408 299-5105

(P-23451)
SANTA CLARITA VLLY CMMTT AGING
Also Called: SANTA CLARITA VALLEY SENIOR CE
22900 Market St, Santa Clarita
(91321-3608)
PHONE...............................661 259-9444
Brad Berens, *Director*
Jeff Pollard, *President*
Greg Kory, *CFO*
Don Kimball, *Vice Pres*
Linda Lieblang, *Exec Dir*
EMP: 65
SQ FT: 10,000
SALES: 11.2MM **Privately Held**
WEB: www.scvseniorcenter.org
SIC: **8322** Senior citizens' center or association

(P-23452)
SANTA ROSA COMMUNITY HLTH CTRS (PA)
3569 Round Barn Cir, Santa Rosa
(95403-5781)
PHONE...............................707 547-2222
Naomi Fuchs, *CEO*
Erin Moilanen, *Program Mgr*
EMP: 110 EST: 1996
SALES: 63.7MM **Privately Held**
WEB: www.swhealthcenter.org
SIC: **8322** Individual & family services

(P-23453)
SANTEE SENIOR RETIREMENT COM
Also Called: Pointe At Lantern Crest, The
400 Lantern Crest Way, Santee
(92071-4633)
PHONE...............................619 955-0901
Kaan Ciftci, *Exec Dir*
EMP: 104 **Privately Held**
SIC: **8322** Senior citizens' center or association
PA: Santee Senior Retirement Communities, Llc
8510 Railroad Ave
Santee CA

(P-23454)
SANTEE SYSTEMS SERVICES II
229 E Gage Ave, Los Angeles
(90003-1533)
PHONE...............................323 445-0044
Veronica Santee, *CEO*
EMP: 99
SALES (est): 699.6K **Privately Held**
SIC: **8322** Child related social services

(P-23455)
SECOND CHANCE INC (PA)
Also Called: NEWARK CRISIS CENTER
6330 Thornton Ave Ste B, Newark
(94560-3734)
P.O. Box 643 (94560-0643)
PHONE...............................510 792-4357
Jimmy Rogers, *Director*
Mark Conville, *Exec Dir*
John Balentine, *Office Mgr*
Ron Erlantson, *CTO*
EMP: 50
SQ FT: 10,000

SALES: 2.7MM **Privately Held**
WEB: www.secondchanceinc.com
SIC: **8322** Crisis intervention center

(P-23456)
SECOND HARVEST FOOD
8014 Marine Way, Irvine (92618-2235)
PHONE...............................949 653-2900
Joe Schoeningh, *Owner*
EMP: 56 EST: 2008
SALES: 53.1MM **Privately Held**
SIC: **8322** Social service center

(P-23457)
SECOND HARVEST SILICON VALLEY (PA)
Also Called: Second Harvest Food Bank
750 Curtner Ave, San Jose (95125-2113)
PHONE...............................408 266-8866
Kathryn Jackson, *CEO*
EMP: 120
SQ FT: 65,000
SALES: 127.6MM **Privately Held**
SIC: **8322** Meal delivery program

(P-23458)
SELF-HELP FOR ELDERLY
777 Stockton St Ste 110, San Francisco
(94108-2372)
PHONE...............................415 391-3843
EMP: 57
SALES (corp-wide): 24.3MM **Privately Held**
SIC: **8322** Senior citizens' center or association
PA: Self-Help For The Elderly
731 Sansome St Ste 100
San Francisco CA 94111
415 677-7600

(P-23459)
SELF-HELP FOR ELDERLY (PA)
Also Called: San Francisco Residential Care
731 Sansome St Ste 100, San Francisco
(94111-1735)
PHONE...............................415 677-7600
Anni Chung, *President*
Janie Kaung, *Vice Chairman*
William Schulte, *Chairman*
Gerald Lee, *Treasurer*
Linda Wang, *Admin Sec*
EMP: 145
SALES: 24.3MM **Privately Held**
WEB: www.selfhelpelderly.org
SIC: **8322** 8361 8082 Senior citizens' center or association; residential care; home health care services

(P-23460)
SELMA PORTUGUESE AZORIAN ASSN
1245 Nebraska Ave, Selma (93662-9738)
P.O. Box 734 (93662-0734)
PHONE...............................559 896-2508
Louis Cardoza, *President*
EMP: 50
SALES: 78.3K **Privately Held**
SIC: **8322** 5813 Community center; drinking places

(P-23461)
SENECA FAMILY OF AGENCIES
Also Called: Seneca Center
40950 Chapel Way, Fremont (94538-4236)
PHONE...............................510 226-6180
Jessica Stryczek, *Principal*
EMP: 100
SALES (corp-wide): 112.1MM **Privately Held**
WEB: www.senecacenter.org
SIC: **8322** 8211 8361 Social service center; elementary & secondary schools; home for the emotionally disturbed
PA: Seneca Family Of Agencies
15942 Foothill Blvd
San Leandro CA 94578
510 317-1444

(P-23462)
SEQUOIA ADRC LP
Also Called: Sequoia Alchol DRG Rcovery Ctr
650 Main St, Redwood City (94063-1922)
PHONE...............................650 364-5504
Barry Rosan, *Exec Dir*
Donald Drotts, *Manager*
EMP: 60

▲ = Import ▼=Export
◆ =Import/Export

SALES (est): 1.6MM **Privately Held**
SIC: 8322 Rehabilitation services

(P-23463)
SEQUOIA SENIOR SOLUTIONS INC
825 S Main St, Lakeport (95453-5510)
PHONE..............................707 263-3070
Stanton C Lawson, *Branch Mgr*
EMP: 87
SALES (corp-wide): 9.5MM **Privately Held**
SIC: 8322 Adult day care center
PA: Sequoia Senior Solutions, Inc.
1372 N Mcdowell Blvd S
Petaluma CA 94954
707 763-6600

(P-23464)
SEQUOIA SENIOR SOLUTIONS INC
205 W Clay St, Ukiah (95482-5452)
PHONE..............................707 621-9235
Stanton C Lawson, *Branch Mgr*
EMP: 87
SALES (corp-wide): 9.5MM **Privately Held**
SIC: 8322 Adult day care center
PA: Sequoia Senior Solutions, Inc.
1372 N Mcdowell Blvd S
Petaluma CA 94954
707 763-6600

(P-23465)
SHELTER INC (PA)
1333 Willow Pass Rd # 206, Concord (94520-7931)
P.O. Box 5368 (94524-0368)
PHONE..............................925 335-0698
John Eckstrom, *CEO*
Karri Edgers, *COO*
Teresa Schow, *Admin Sec*
Ivan Lopez, *Technology*
Leslie Gleason, *Opers Staff*
EMP: 62
SQ FT: 7,000
SALES (est): 11.6MM **Privately Held**
WEB: www.shelterincofccc.org
SIC: 8322 Emergency social services

(P-23466)
SIERRA FOREVER FAMILIES
Also Called: SFF
8928 Volunteer Ln Ste 100, Sacramento (95826-3238)
PHONE..............................916 368-5114
Bob Herne, *Exec Dir*
Amanda Dragon, *Social Worker*
EMP: 68
SALES: 7.1MM **Privately Held**
SIC: 8322 Adoption services

(P-23467)
SOCIAL ADVOCATES FOR Y
4275 El Cajon Blvd # 101, San Diego (92105-1293)
PHONE..............................619 283-9624
Nancy G Hornberger, *CEO*
Sheri Easterly, *Program Mgr*
EMP: 202
SALES (corp-wide): 18.6MM **Privately Held**
SIC: 8322 Social worker
PA: Social Advocates For Youth, San Diego, Inc.
4775 Viewridge Ave
San Diego CA 92123
858 565-4148

(P-23468)
SOCIAL ADVOCATES FOR YOUTH (PA)
105 N Lincoln St, Santa Maria (93458-4319)
PHONE..............................805 928-1707
William Rogers, *Director*
Judy Nishimori, *Director*
EMP: 50
SQ FT: 3,470
SALES: 2.6MM **Privately Held**
SIC: 8322 Children's aid society; family (marriage) counseling

(P-23469)
SOLANO COUNTY MENTAL HEALTH
Also Called: Exodus Recovery
9808 Venice Blvd Ste 700, Culver City (90232-6824)
PHONE..............................707 428-1131
Camille Dullathan, *Director*
EMP: 50
SALES (est): 1.3MM **Privately Held**
SIC: 8322 Emergency social services

(P-23470)
SOURCEWISE
2115 The Alameda, San Jose (95126-1141)
PHONE..............................408 350-3200
Stephen M Schmoll, *Director*
Altamirano Manuel, *COO*
Kimberly Marlar, *CFO*
Crystal Shafiabady, *Director*
EMP: 100
SQ FT: 10,000
SALES: 10.8MM **Privately Held**
WEB: www.scccoa.org
SIC: 8322 Senior citizens' center or association; old age assistance

(P-23471)
SOUTH ASIAN HELP REFERRAL AGCY
Also Called: Sahara
17100 Pioneer Blvd # 260, Artesia (90701-2776)
PHONE..............................562 402-4132
EMP: 50
SALES: 914.4K **Privately Held**
SIC: 8322

(P-23472)
SOUTH BAY COMMUNITY SERVICES
430 F St, Chula Vista (91910-3711)
PHONE..............................619 420-3620
Kathryn Lembo, *Exec Dir*
Helena Sabala, *Director*
EMP: 200
SQ FT: 2,900
SALES: 27.3MM **Privately Held**
WEB:
www.southbaycommunityservices.org
SIC: 8322 Social service center

(P-23473)
SOUTH BAY CTR FOR COUNSELING
Also Called: SOUTH BAY CENTER FOR COMMUNITY
540 N Marine Ave, Wilmington (90744-5528)
PHONE..............................310 414-2090
Colleen Mooney, *Exec Dir*
Gina Lomibao-Budnick, *Info Tech Mgr*
Jones Robert, *Superintendent*
EMP: 90
SALES: 5.4MM **Privately Held**
WEB: www.sbaycenter.com
SIC: 8322 General counseling services

(P-23474)
SOUTH COAST CHILDRENS SOC INC
24950 Redlands Blvd, Loma Linda (92354-4032)
PHONE..............................909 478-3377
EMP: 233
SALES (corp-wide): 30MM **Privately Held**
SIC: 8322 Social service center; rehabilitation services; community center
PA: South Coast Children's Society, Inc.
27261 Las Ramblas Ste 220
Mission Viejo CA 92691
714 966-8650

(P-23475)
SOUTH COAST CHILDRENS SOC INC
11780 Central Ave, Chino (91710-6498)
PHONE..............................909 364-9788
EMP: 135
SALES (corp-wide): 30MM **Privately Held**
SIC: 8322

PA: South Coast Children's Society, Inc.
27261 Las Ramblas Ste 220
Mission Viejo CA 92691
714 966-8650

(P-23476)
SOUTHEAST AREA SOCIAL SERVICES
10400 Pioneer Blvd Ste 8, Santa Fe Springs (90670-3728)
PHONE..............................562 946-2237
Kirk Kain, *Director*
EMP: 50
SALES (est): 255.2K **Privately Held**
SIC: 8322 Social service center

(P-23477)
SOUTHGATE RECREATION & PK DST
Also Called: Rizal Community Center
7320 Florin Mall Dr, Sacramento (95823-3255)
PHONE..............................916 421-7275
Jeremy Yee, *Manager*
EMP: 50
SALES (corp-wide): 7.9MM **Privately Held**
SIC: 8322 Community center
PA: Southgate Recreation & Park District
6000 Orange Ave
Sacramento CA 95823
916 428-1171

(P-23478)
SPANISH TRILS GIRL SCOUT CNCIL
5007 Center St, Chino (91710-3409)
PHONE..............................909 627-2609
Beverly Fowler, *Owner*
EMP: 50
SALES (est): 389.4K **Privately Held**
SIC: 8322 Youth center

(P-23479)
SPECTRUM COMMUNITY SERVICES (PA)
2617 Barrington Ct, Hayward (94545-1100)
PHONE..............................510 881-0300
Lara Calvert, *Exec Dir*
Debora Darden, *CFO*
Kamny Wong, *General Mgr*
Amy Clifford, *Director*
Mark Smith, *Manager*
EMP: 56
SALES: 5MM **Privately Held**
SIC: 8322 Senior citizens' center or association

(P-23480)
SPIRITUAL DIRECTION
164 San Luis Ave, San Bruno (94066-5507)
P.O. Box 1454, Millbrae (94030-5454)
PHONE..............................650 952-9456
Ariosto Coelho, *Owner*
EMP: 50
SALES (est): 447.7K **Privately Held**
WEB: www.spiritualdirection.com
SIC: 8322 General counseling services

(P-23481)
ST ANTHONY FOUNDATION (PA)
150 Golden Gate Ave, San Francisco (94102-3810)
PHONE..............................415 241-2600
John Hardin, *Exec Dir*
Barry J Stenger, *Exec Dir*
Carl Taibl, *Finance*
Jeanne Zarka Brooks, *Director*
EMP: 50
SQ FT: 45,000
SALES (est): 12.7MM **Privately Held**
WEB: www.stanthonysf.com
SIC: 8322 Social service center

(P-23482)
ST BARNBAS SNIOR CTR LOS ANGLE
Also Called: SAINT BARNABAS SENIOR SERVICES
675 S Carondelet St, Los Angeles (90057-3309)
PHONE..............................213 388-4444
Rigo Sabareo, *President*
Nick Dumicreseu, *Treasurer*

Kotick John, *Vice Pres*
Lani Garcia, *Accountant*
Gordon Gibb, *Director*
EMP: 61
SQ FT: 27,000
SALES: 4.9MM **Privately Held**
SIC: 8322 Senior citizens' center or association

(P-23483)
ST JOSEPH CENTER
Also Called: SAINT JOSEPH CENTER VOLUNTEER
204 Hampton Dr, Venice (90291-8633)
PHONE..............................310 396-6468
Felecia Adams, *Vice Pres*
John McGann, *CFO*
VA Lecia Adams Kellum, *Exec Dir*
Tifara Monroe, *Director*
Paul Rubenstein, *Director*
EMP: 85
SQ FT: 32,000
SALES: 24.6MM **Privately Held**
SIC: 8322 8331 8351 Social service center; child related social services; temporary relief service; job training services; vocational rehabilitation agency; child day care services

(P-23484)
ST JOSEPH HOSPICE
Also Called: Saint Joseph Hlth Sys Hospice
200 W Center St Promenade, Anaheim (92805-3960)
PHONE..............................714 712-7100
Linda Glomp, *Director*
Ron Nagano, *CFO*
Maire Blaistell, *Director*
EMP: 80 **EST:** 1994
SQ FT: 3,000
SALES (est): 2.1MM
SALES (corp-wide): 15.2B **Privately Held**
WEB: www.stjosephhospice.com
SIC: 8322 8063 Geriatric social service; psychiatric hospitals
HQ: St Joseph Home Health Network
441 College Ave
Santa Rosa CA 95401
714 712-9500

(P-23485)
ST VNCENT DE PAUL BLTMORE INC
3100 Norris Ave, Sacramento (95821-4023)
PHONE..............................916 485-3482
EMP: 125
SALES (corp-wide): 22.2MM **Privately Held**
SIC: 8322 Social service center
PA: St. Vincent De Paul Of Baltimore, Inc.
2305 N Charles St Ste 300
Baltimore MD 21218
410 662-0500

(P-23486)
STAND FOR FMLIES FREE VOLENCE
3220 Blume Dr, San Pablo (94806-1767)
PHONE..............................510 964-7109
EMP: 61
SALES (corp-wide): 4.8MM **Privately Held**
SIC: 8322 Crisis intervention center
PA: Stand For Families Free Of Violence
1410 Danzig Plz Fl 2
Concord CA 94520
925 676-2845

(P-23487)
STANFORD UNIV MED CTR AUX
Also Called: STANFORD LINEAR ACCELERATOR CE
300 Pasteur Dr, Stanford (94305-2200)
P.O. Box 20410, Palo Alto (94309-0410)
PHONE..............................650 723-6636
Mary Dahlquist, *CEO*
Sarah Clark, *President*
M Allen, *Associate Dir*
P Joanne Cornbleet, *Pathologist*
Robert V Rouse, *Pathologist*
EMP: 400
SALES: 21.4K
SALES (corp-wide): 11.3B **Privately Held**
SIC: 8322 Adult day care center

PA: Leland Stanford Junior University
450 Jane Stanford Way
Stanford CA 94305
650 723-2300

(P-23488)
STANISLAUS COUNTY POLICE
1325 Beverly Dr, Modesto (95351-2313)
PHONE 209 529-9121
Alfredo Guerra, *Exec Dir*
Vicki Bauman, *President*
Bret Silveira, *Deputy Dir*
Celeste Robles, *Assistant*
Thania Jimenez, *Supervisor*
EMP: 144
SALES: 2.3MM **Privately Held**
SIC: 8322 Social service center

(P-23489)
STAR VIEW CHLDRN FMLY SRVCS
1085 W Victoria St, Compton (90220-5817)
PHONE 310 868-5379
Paul Stansbury, *CEO*
Kent Dunlap, *Vice Pres*
Maryjane Gross, *Admin Sec*
Ontson Placide, *Director*
EMP: 99
SALES (est): 2.5MM **Privately Held**
SIC: 8322 Family counseling services

(P-23490)
STARVISTA
610 Elm St Ste 212, San Carlos
(94070-3070)
PHONE 650 591-9623
Michael GRB, *CEO*
Lexie Munevar, *Partner*
Dianette Washer, *CFO*
Alison Proctor, *Treasurer*
Michelle Blakely, *Bd of Directors*
EMP: 118
SQ FT: 7,200
SALES: 13.6MM **Privately Held**
SIC: 8322 Substance abuse counseling

(P-23491)
STEPHOUSE RECOVERY CENTER
Also Called: Step House Recovery
10529 Slater Ave, Fountain Valley
(92708-4841)
PHONE 714 394-3494
George J Vilagut, *CEO*
Eric Peterson, *Marketing Staff*
EMP: 70
SALES: 8MM **Privately Held**
SIC: 8322 General counseling services

(P-23492)
SUN BASKET INC (PA)
1170 Olinder Ct, San Jose (95122-2619)
PHONE 408 669-4418
Adam Zbar, *CEO*
Don Barnett, *COO*
Marc Friend, *CFO*
Jessica Jensen, *Chief Mktg Ofcr*
Mike Wargocki, *General Mgr*
EMP: 200
SALES (est): 76MM **Privately Held**
SIC: 8322 Meal delivery program

(P-23493)
SUNNY CAL ADHC INC
8450 Valley Blvd Ste 121b, Rosemead
(91770-1681)
PHONE 626 307-7772
Tony Leung, *President*
EMP: 60
SALES (est): 1MM **Privately Held**
SIC: 8322 Adult day care center

(P-23494)
SUNRISE FOOD MINISTRY
5901 San Juan Ave, Citrus Heights
(95610-6508)
PHONE 916 965-5431
Fred Chirstensen, *President*
EMP: 60
SALES: 89K **Privately Held**
SIC: 8322 Individual & family services

(P-23495)
SUPPORT FOR FAMILY LLC
Also Called: Apexcare
1333 Howe Ave Ste 206, Sacramento
(95825-3362)
PHONE 877 916-9111
Jason Wu,
EMP: 59
SALES (est): 202.9K **Privately Held**
SIC: 8322 Individual & family services

(P-23496)
SUPREME COURT UNITED STATES
Also Called: US Probation
101 W Broadway Ste 700, San Diego
(92101-8208)
PHONE 619 557-7149
Kenneth Young, *Chief*
EMP: 157 **Publicly Held**
WEB: www.supremecourtus.gov
SIC: 8322 Probation office; offender reha-
bilitation agency
HQ: Supreme Court, United States
1 1st St Ne
Washington DC 20543
202 479-3000

(P-23497)
SUTTER HLTH RHABILITATION SVCS
Also Called: Sutter Medical Ctr Sacramento
2801 L St Fl 3, Sacramento (95816-5615)
P.O. Box 160727 (95816-0727)
PHONE 916 733-3040
Lisa Drewslucero, *Manager*
Yuhwan Hong, *Surg-Orthopdc*
EMP: 70
SALES (est): 7.5MM **Privately Held**
SIC: 8322 Rehabilitation services

(P-23498)
TEEN CHALLENGE NORWESTCAL NEV
Also Called: SOUTHBAY TEEN CHALLENGE
390 Mathew St, Santa Clara (95050-3114)
P.O. Box 24309, San Jose (95154-4309)
PHONE 408 703-2001
Dana Rowe, *Director*
EMP: 100
SALES: 1.3MM **Privately Held**
SIC: 8322 Social service center

(P-23499)
TERKENSHA ASSOCIATES INC
Also Called: NORTH AREA COMMUNITY
MENTAL HE
811 Grand Ave Ste D, Sacramento
(95838-3466)
PHONE 916 922-9868
William Benda, *Director*
William Moss, *President*
EMP: 52 **EST:** 1980
SALES: 3.6MM **Privately Held**
SIC: 8322 General counseling services

(P-23500)
TERRA NOVA COUNSELING (PA)
5750 Sunrise Blvd Ste 100, Citrus Heights
(95610-7639)
PHONE 916 344-0249
Mary Stroube, *Exec Dir*
Bonnie Hinojos, *Office Mgr*
Robin Howard, *Admin Sec*
EMP: 80
SQ FT: 4,789
SALES: 3.3MM **Privately Held**
WEB: www.after.com
SIC: 8322 Alcoholism counseling, nontreat-
ment; drug abuse counselor, nontreat-
ment; family (marriage) counseling; family
counseling services

(P-23501)
TESSIE CLVLAND CMNTY SVCS CORP
Also Called: Tccsc
8019 Compton Ave Ste 219, Los Angeles
(90001-3409)
PHONE 323 586-7333
Forescee Hogan-Rowles, *CEO*
Carolyn Chadwick, *CFO*
Moses Chadwick, *Exec Dir*
Sylvia Ramirez, *General Mgr*
Sheila Sarain, *Technology*

EMP: 100
SALES: 12MM **Privately Held**
WEB: www.tccsc.org
SIC: 8322 Child related social services

(P-23502)
TIFFANYS LIU
9465 Wilshire Blvd, Beverly Hills
(90212-2612)
PHONE 415 644-0846
Liu Tiffanys, *Owner*
EMP: 57
SALES: 6MM **Privately Held**
SIC: 8322 8742 Individual & family serv-
ices; management consulting services

(P-23503)
TLCS INC
650 Howe Ave Ste 400, Sacramento
(95825-4732)
PHONE 916 441-0123
Michael Lazar, *Exec Dir*
EMP: 100
SQ FT: 1,868
SALES: 11.1MM **Privately Held**
SIC: 8322 Social service center

(P-23504)
TOOLWORKS INC
3075 Adeline St Ste 230, Berkeley
(94703-2578)
PHONE 510 649-1322
Steve Crabiel, *Branch Mgr*
EMP: 407
SALES (corp-wide): 16MM **Privately
Held**
SIC: 8322 Individual & family services
PA: Toolworks Inc
25 Kearny St Ste 400
San Francisco CA 94108
415 733-0990

(P-23505)
TOWARD MAXIMUM INDEPENDENCE (PA)
Also Called: T M I
4740 Murphy Canyon Rd # 300, San Diego
(92123-4385)
PHONE 858 467-0600
Kerby Wohlander, *Director*
Rachel Harris, *Exec Dir*
Jill Prieboy, *Division Mgr*
Brent Ramsey, *Division Mgr*
Christina Romero, *Division Mgr*
EMP: 190
SQ FT: 5,700
SALES: 15.6MM **Privately Held**
SIC: 8322 Social services for the handi-
capped

(P-23506)
TPD DELL DIOS
1817 Avenida Del Diablo, Escondido
(92029-3112)
PHONE 760 741-2888
D Williams, *Exec Dir*
Donald Williams, *Exec Dir*
EMP: 50
SALES (est): 650K **Privately Held**
SIC: 8322 Old age assistance

(P-23507)
TRACY INTERFAITH MINISTRIES
311 W Grant Line Rd, Tracy (95376-2547)
P.O. Box 404 (95378-0404)
PHONE 209 836-5424
Darlene Quinn, *Exec Dir*
Lamar Stephenson, *Chairman*
Sleevaraj Pasala, *Assoc Pastor*
David Dutra, *Pastor*
Mikayla Anderson, *Education*
EMP: 65
SALES: 712K **Privately Held**
SIC: 8322 Social service center

(P-23508)
TRAINING TOWARD SELF RELIANCE
Also Called: TTSR
1446 Ethan Way 101, Sacramento
(95825-2214)
PHONE 916 442-8877
Nancy Chance, *Director*
EMP: 50

SALES: 1.2MM **Privately Held**
WEB: www.ttsr.org
SIC: 8322 Social services for the handi-
capped

(P-23509)
TRI COUNTY RESPITE CARE SVC
Also Called: RESPITE SERVICE
1215 Plumas St Ste 1600, Yuba City
(95991-3456)
P.O. Box 1296 (95992-1296)
PHONE 530 755-3500
Diane Rose, *Director*
Joy Scott, *Principal*
EMP: 56
SALES: 1.5MM **Privately Held**
SIC: 8322 Individual & family services

(P-23510)
TRI-COUNTIES ASSOCIATION F (PA)
Also Called: TRI-COUNTIES REGIONAL
CENTER
520 E Montecito St, Santa Barbara
(93103-3278)
PHONE 805 962-7881
Bob Cobbs, *President*
EMP: 240
SQ FT: 16,000
SALES: 293.2MM **Privately Held**
SIC: 8322 Association for the handicapped

(P-23511)
TUPAZ DAY CARE SERVICES INC
3015 Union Ave, San Jose (95124-2006)
PHONE 408 377-1622
Rosario Tupaz, *President*
Beebe Tupaz, *Vice Pres*
EMP: 75
SALES: 2.9MM **Privately Held**
SIC: 8322 Adult day care center

(P-23512)
TURNING POINT CENTRAL CAL INC
Also Called: Visalia Youth Services
711 N Court St, Visalia (93291-3638)
PHONE 559 627-1490
Jose Ochoa, *Branch Mgr*
Jeanette Evaro, *Manager*
EMP: 50
SALES (corp-wide): 56.7MM **Privately
Held**
SIC: 8322 8093 Individual & family serv-
ices; mental health clinic, outpatient
PA: Turning Point Of Central California, Inc.
615 S Atwood St
Visalia CA 93277
559 732-8086

(P-23513)
UCSF AIDS HEALTH PROJECT
1930 Market St, San Francisco
(94102-6228)
PHONE 415 476-6445
Jim Dilley, *President*
Lori Thoemmes, *Director*
EMP: 80 **EST:** 1985
SALES (est): 2.6MM **Privately Held**
SIC: 8322 Social service center

(P-23514)
UNION PAN ASIAN COMMUNITIES (PA)
Also Called: UPAC
1031 25th St, San Diego (92102-2194)
PHONE 619 232-6454
Margaret Iwanaga-Penrose, *Director*
Koji Fukumura, *Vice Chairman*
Margaret Penrose, *Webmaster*
D Dauz, *Mktg Coord*
Angela Chen, *Program Dir*
EMP: 58
SQ FT: 14,000
SALES: 10.9MM **Privately Held**
WEB: www.upacsd.com
SIC: 8322 Social service center

(P-23515)
UNITED CEREBRAL PALSY ASSOC
980 Roosevelt Ste 100, Irvine (92620-3670)
PHONE.....................949 333-6400
Deborah Levy, *President*
EMP: 130
SQ FT: 5,000
SALES: 5.2MM **Privately Held**
SIC: 8322 Association for the handicapped

(P-23516)
UNITED CP/S CHLDRNS FNDN LA
2170 N Westlake Blvd 22, Westlake Village (91362-5122)
PHONE.....................805 494-1141
Steve Bird, *Administration*
EMP: 50
SALES (corp-wide): 24.2MM **Privately Held**
SIC: 8322 Association for the handicapped
PA: United Cerebral Palsy/Spastic Children's Foundation Of Los Angeles And Ventura Counties
6430 Independence Ave
Woodland Hills CA 91367
818 782-2211

(P-23517)
UNITED CP/S CHLDRNS FNDN LA
2628 Brighton Ave, Los Angeles (90018-2752)
PHONE.....................323 737-0303
Nicole Seaton, *Director*
EMP: 71
SALES (corp-wide): 24.2MM **Privately Held**
SIC: 8322 Association for the handicapped
PA: United Cerebral Palsy/Spastic Children's Foundation Of Los Angeles And Ventura Counties
6430 Independence Ave
Woodland Hills CA 91367
818 782-2211

(P-23518)
UNITED CRBRAL PLSY ASSN SAN DE (PA)
8525 Gibbs Dr Ste 209, San Diego (92123-1765)
PHONE.....................858 571-7803
David Carrucci, *Exec Dir*
James O'Leary, *President*
Daniel Alessio, *Treasurer*
David Carucci, *Exec Dir*
Mary Krieger, *Administration*
EMP: 50 **EST:** 1958
SALES: 3.1MM **Privately Held**
WEB: www.readystamps.com
SIC: 8322 Individual & family services

(P-23519)
UNITED WAY OF BAY AREA (PA)
Also Called: UNITED WAY, THE
550 Kearny St Ste 1000, San Francisco (94108-2524)
PHONE.....................415 808-4300
Anne Wilson, *CEO*
Michael Scanlon, *Chairman*
Moses Awe, *Treasurer*
Stanislava Peycheva, *Officer*
Lisa Simons, *Officer*
EMP: 85 **EST:** 1923
SQ FT: 40,000
SALES: 37.2MM **Privately Held**
WEB: www.uwba.org
SIC: 8322 8399 Individual & family services; fund raising organization, non-fee basis

(P-23520)
UNITY CARE GROUP
1400 Parkmoor Ave Ste 115, San Jose (95126-3797)
P.O. Box 730276 (95173-0276)
PHONE.....................408 971-9822
Andre Chapman, *CEO*
Gary Rummelhoff, *CFO*
Linda Phillips, *Principal*
EMP: 70

SALES: 17.9MM **Privately Held**
WEB: www.unitycare.com
SIC: 8322 Youth self-help agency

(P-23521)
UPLIFT FAMILY SERVICES (PA)
Also Called: Emq Familiesfirst
251 Llewellyn Ave, Campbell (95008-1940)
PHONE.....................408 379-3790
Darrell Evora, *CEO*
Rosie Garcia, *Partner*
R Donald McNeil, *Ch of Bd*
Jason D Gurahoo, *CFO*
Kathy McCarthy,
EMP: 60
SQ FT: 65,000
SALES: 93.6MM **Privately Held**
SIC: 8322 Individual & family services

(P-23522)
VALLEY CMNTY COUNSELING SVCS (PA)
6707 Embarcadero Dr, Stockton (95219-3382)
PHONE.....................209 956-4240
David Love, *Exec Dir*
Sue Sutherland, *General Mgr*
Shana Lucchessi, *Bookkeeper*
Bonnie Bramer, *Director*
EMP: 93
SALES: 6.6MM **Privately Held**
SIC: 8322 General counseling services; substance abuse counseling; referral service for personal & social problems

(P-23523)
VALLEY MTN REGIONAL CTR INC (PA)
702 N Aurora St, Stockton (95202-2200)
P.O. Box 692290 (95269-2290)
PHONE.....................209 473-0951
Paul Billodeau, *CEO*
Debra Roth, *CFO*
Robin Dickinson, *Program Mgr*
Wanda Farinelli, *Program Mgr*
Mary Gonzalez, *Program Mgr*
EMP: 160
SQ FT: 63,000
SALES: 159.8MM **Privately Held**
SIC: 8322 Multi-service center

(P-23524)
VENTURA CNTY COUNCIL ON AGING
4917 S Rose Ave, Oxnard (93033-7803)
P.O. Box 2429 (93034-2429)
PHONE.....................805 986-1424
Tom Carlisle, *CEO*
EMP: 60
SQ FT: 15,000
SALES: 46.7K **Privately Held**
SIC: 8322 Senior citizens' center or association

(P-23525)
VINTAGE SENIOR MANAGEMENT INC
2721 W Willow St, Burbank (91505-4544)
PHONE.....................818 954-9500
Brian Flornes, *Branch Mgr*
EMP: 517 **Privately Held**
SIC: 8322 Geriatric social service
PA: Senior Vintage Management Inc
23 Corporate Plaza Dr # 190
Newport Beach CA 92660

(P-23526)
VISALIA UNIFIED SCHOOL DST
Also Called: Office of Nutritional Services
801 N Mooney Blvd, Visalia (93291-3230)
PHONE.....................559 730-7871
Regina Ocampo, *Director*
Angela Sanchez, *Administration*
Diane Townsend, *Teacher*
EMP: 180
SALES (corp-wide): 354.9MM **Privately Held**
SIC: 8322 8621 Individual & family services; health association
PA: Visalia Unified School District
5000 W Cypress Ave
Visalia CA 93277
559 730-7529

(P-23527)
VISTA CARE GROUP LLC (PA)
Also Called: Vista Gardens
1863 Devon Pl, Vista (92084-7624)
PHONE.....................760 295-3900
Avelen Delgado, *Administration*
Harry Crowell, *Chairman*
Joe Balbas,
EMP: 83
SALES (est): 4.7MM **Privately Held**
SIC: 8322 Senior citizens' center or association

(P-23528)
VISTA HILL FOUNDATION
4125 Alpha St, San Diego (92113-4553)
PHONE.....................619 266-0166
EMP: 85
SALES (corp-wide): 28.2MM **Privately Held**
SIC: 8322 8051 Geriatric social service; skilled nursing care facilities
PA: Vista Hill Foundation
8910 Clairemont Mesa Blvd
San Diego CA 92123
585 514-5100

(P-23529)
VOLUNTEERS OF AMER LOS ANGELES
11512 Valerio St, North Hollywood (91605-3976)
PHONE.....................818 764-8722
EMP: 166
SALES (corp-wide): 87.5MM **Privately Held**
SIC: 8322 Social service center
PA: Volunteers Of America Of Los Angeles
3600 Wilshire Blvd # 1500
Los Angeles CA 90010
213 389-1500

(P-23530)
VOLUNTEERS OF AMER LOS ANGELES
10896 Lehigh Ave, Pacoima (91331-2584)
PHONE.....................818 834-9097
Paloma Cisneros, *Manager*
EMP: 133
SALES (corp-wide): 87.5MM **Privately Held**
SIC: 8322 Individual & family services
PA: Volunteers Of America Of Los Angeles
3600 Wilshire Blvd # 1500
Los Angeles CA 90010
213 389-1500

(P-23531)
VOLUNTEERS OF AMER LOS ANGELES
522 N Dangler Ave, Los Angeles (90022-1218)
PHONE.....................323 780-3770
EMP: 133
SALES (corp-wide): 87.5MM **Privately Held**
SIC: 8322 Social service center
PA: Volunteers Of America Of Los Angeles
3600 Wilshire Blvd # 1500
Los Angeles CA 90010
213 389-1500

(P-23532)
VOLUNTEERS OF AMER LOS ANGELES
1760 W Cameron Ave # 104, West Covina (91790-2739)
PHONE.....................626 337-9878
EMP: 133
SALES (corp-wide): 87.5MM **Privately Held**
SIC: 8322 Social service center
PA: Volunteers Of America Of Los Angeles
3600 Wilshire Blvd # 1500
Los Angeles CA 90010
213 389-1500

(P-23533)
VOLUNTEERS OF AMER LOS ANGELES
25141 Avenida Rondel, Valencia (91355-3205)
PHONE.....................661 290-2829
EMP: 100

SALES (corp-wide): 87.5MM **Privately Held**
SIC: 8322 Social service center
PA: Volunteers Of America Of Los Angeles
3600 Wilshire Blvd # 1500
Los Angeles CA 90010
213 389-1500

(P-23534)
VOLUNTEERS OF AMER LOS ANGELES
10819 Plainview Ave, Tujunga (91042-1633)
PHONE.....................818 352-5974
EMP: 166
SALES (corp-wide): 87.5MM **Privately Held**
SIC: 8322 Social service center
PA: Volunteers Of America Of Los Angeles
3600 Wilshire Blvd # 1500
Los Angeles CA 90010
213 389-1500

(P-23535)
VOLUNTEERS OF AMER LOS ANGELES
2100 N Broadway Ste 300, Santa Ana (92706-2624)
PHONE.....................714 426-9834
EMP: 100
SALES (corp-wide): 87.5MM **Privately Held**
SIC: 8322 Individual & family services
PA: Volunteers Of America Of Los Angeles
3600 Wilshire Blvd # 1500
Los Angeles CA 90010
213 389-1500

(P-23536)
VOLUNTEERS OF AMER LOS ANGELES
6724 Tujunga Ave, North Hollywood (91606-1910)
PHONE.....................818 769-3617
EMP: 133
SALES (corp-wide): 87.5MM **Privately Held**
SIC: 8322 Individual & family services
PA: Volunteers Of America Of Los Angeles
3600 Wilshire Blvd # 1500
Los Angeles CA 90010
213 389-1500

(P-23537)
VOLUNTEERS OF AMER LOS ANGELES
Also Called: Maud Booth Family Center
11243 Kittridge St, North Hollywood (91606-2605)
PHONE.....................818 506-0597
Felix Cruz, *Manager*
EMP: 50
SALES (corp-wide): 87.5MM **Privately Held**
WEB: www.voala.org
SIC: 8322 Social service center
PA: Volunteers Of America Of Los Angeles
3600 Wilshire Blvd # 1500
Los Angeles CA 90010
213 389-1500

(P-23538)
VOLUNTEERS OF AMER LOS ANGELES
12550 Van Nuys Blvd, Pacoima (91331-1354)
PHONE.....................818 834-8957
Letecia Aguirre, *Principal*
EMP: 199
SALES (corp-wide): 87.5MM **Privately Held**
WEB: www.voa.org
SIC: 8322 Individual & family services
PA: Volunteers Of America Of Los Angeles
3600 Wilshire Blvd # 1500
Los Angeles CA 90010
213 389-1500

(P-23539)
VOLUNTEERS OF AMERICA GREATER (PA)
3434 Marconi Ave Ste A, Sacramento (95821-6242)
PHONE.....................916 265-3400
Leo McFarland, *CEO*

PRODUCTS & SVCS

Amani Sawires, *COO*
Joel Rusco, *CFO*
Rachele Burton, *Officer*
Rachel Laurie, *Senior VP*
EMP: 90
SALES (est): 20.5MM **Privately Held**
WEB: www.voa.org
SIC: 8322 Social service center

(P-23540)
WATCH RESOURCES INC (PA)
Also Called: T.C.A.H
12801 Cabezut Rd, Sonora (95370-5294)
PHONE..................................209 533-0510
Christine Daily, *Exec Dir*
Jeff Rains, *President*
Eric Carlson, *Treasurer*
Jason Land, *Vice Pres*
Patt Koral, *Admin Sec*
EMP: 55
SQ FT: 7,200
SALES: 3MM **Privately Held**
SIC: 8322 0782 7349 4783 Association
for the handicapped; landscape contractors; janitorial service, contract basis; packing & crating; mailing & messenger services

(P-23541)
WATTS LABOR COMMUNITY ACTION
Also Called: Wlcac
4142 Palmwood Dr Apt 11, Los Angeles (90008-2355)
PHONE..................................323 563-5639
Timothy Watkins, *CEO*
EMP: 190
SALES (corp-wide): 15.3MM **Privately Held**
SIC: 8322 7299 Social service center; handyman service
PA: Watts Labor Community Action Committee
10950 S Central Ave
Los Angeles CA 90059
323 563-5639

(P-23542)
WEINGART CENTER ASSOCIATION
Also Called: Weingart Center For Homeless
566 S San Pedro St, Los Angeles (90013-2102)
PHONE..................................213 622-6359
Kevin Murray, *President*
Warren Loui, *Partner*
Sonny Santa Ines, *CFO*
Eugene Williams, *Admin Mgr*
Peter Getoff, *Director*
EMP: 150
SQ FT: 175,000
SALES: 14.2MM **Privately Held**
SIC: 8322 Emergency social services

(P-23543)
WEST COUNTRA COSTA YOUTH SVCS (PA)
263 S 20th St, Richmond (94804-2709)
PHONE..................................510 412-5647
John Ziesenhenne, *President*
EMP: 55
SALES: 3.2MM **Privately Held**
SIC: 8322 Youth center

(P-23544)
WESTVIEW SERVICES INC
Also Called: Day Star Educational Center
626 W Commonwealth Ave, Fullerton (92832-1725)
PHONE..................................714 879-3980
EMP: 88
SQ FT: 4,419
SALES (corp-wide): 16.6MM **Privately Held**
SIC: 8322 Adult day care center
PA: Westview Services, Inc
10522 Katella Ave
Anaheim CA 92804
714 517-6606

(P-23545)
WHALEN MEDICAL CORPORATION (PA)
Also Called: Mogannam and Whalen Med Corp
1000 S Hope St Ste 101, Los Angeles (90015-4057)
PHONE..................................213 622-6010
Sean P Whalen, *CEO*
Paul Mogannam, *President*
Sean Whalen, *Vice Pres*
Amanda Gundrum, *Human Res Mgr*
Jennifer Reed, *Med Doctor*
EMP: 50
SQ FT: 5,322
SALES (est): 11.7MM **Privately Held**
SIC: 8322 Rehabilitation services

(P-23546)
WILLITS SENIORS INC
1501 Baechtel Rd, Willits (95490-4516)
PHONE..................................707 459-6826
Allyn Noneman, *Director*
EMP: 57
SQ FT: 4,000
SALES: 1MM **Privately Held**
SIC: 8322 Senior citizens' center or association

(P-23547)
WOMENS CENTER-YOUTH FMLY SVCS (PA)
620 N San Joaquin St, Stockton (95202-2030)
PHONE..................................209 941-2611
Joelle Gomez, *CEO*
Elizabeth Bifhay, *Principal*
Kimberly Miller, *Administration*
EMP: 111
SALES: 4.2MM **Privately Held**
SIC: 8322 Child related social services

(P-23548)
YORK HLTHCARE WLLNESS CNTRE LP
6071 York Blvd, Los Angeles (90042-3503)
PHONE..................................323 254-3407
Steve Henry, *Managing Prtnr*
EMP: 99 **EST:** 2012
SALES: 11.6MM **Privately Held**
SIC: 8322 Rehabilitation services

(P-23549)
YOUNG MENS CHRSTN ASSN OF LA
Also Called: Downey YMCA
11531 Downey Ave, Downey (90241-4936)
PHONE..................................562 862-4201
George Saikali, *Exec Dir*
Beth Crawford, *Exec Dir*
EMP: 150
SALES (corp-wide): 105.9MM **Privately Held**
SIC: 8322 7997 Social service center; membership sports & recreation clubs
PA: Young Men's Christian Association Of Metropolitan Los Angeles
625 S New Hampshire Ave
Los Angeles CA 90005
213 380-6448

(P-23550)
YOUTH FOR CHANGE
2400 Washington Ave, Redding (96001-2802)
PHONE..................................530 605-1520
EMP: 68 **Privately Held**
SIC: 8322 Youth center
PA: Youth For Change
5538 Skyway
Paradise CA 95969

(P-23551)
YOUTH FOR CHANGE (PA)
Also Called: Paradise Ridge Fmly Resources
5538 Skyway, Paradise (95969-4932)
P.O. Box 1476 (95967-1476)
PHONE..................................530 877-8187
Dennis Cargile, *Principal*
Janet Goodson, *Partner*
Andy Martinez, *CFO*
Michele Peterson, *Chairman*
Alan White, *Chairman*
EMP: 115

SQ FT: 5,000
SALES: 13.7MM **Privately Held**
SIC: 8322 Youth center

(P-23552)
YOUTH FOR CHANGE
2185 Baldwin Ave, Oroville (95966-5312)
PHONE..................................530 538-8347
Bobby Jones, *Branch Mgr*
EMP: 68 **Privately Held**
SIC: 8322 Youth center
PA: Youth For Change
5538 Skyway
Paradise CA 95969

(P-23553)
YUBA COMMUNITY COLLEGE DST
Also Called: Beale Air Force Base Outreach
2088 N Beale Rd, Marysville (95901-7605)
PHONE..................................530 788-0973
Kristina Page, *Admin Sec*
EMP: 99
SALES (corp-wide): 20.8MM **Privately Held**
SIC: 8322 Outreach program
PA: Yuba Community College District
425 Plumas Blvd Ste 200
Yuba City CA 95991
530 741-8949

(P-23554)
YUE FENG INC
145 S Fairfax Ave, Los Angeles (90036-2166)
PHONE..................................310 253-9795
Cheng Chen, *President*
EMP: 72
SQ FT: 8,500
SALES: 7MM **Privately Held**
SIC: 8322 Individual & family services

(P-23555)
YWCA CONTRA COSTA/SACRAMENTO (PA)
1320 Arnold Dr Ste 170, Martinez (94553-6537)
PHONE..................................925 372-4213
Nancy Atkinson, *CEO*
Pamela Mitchell, *Controller*
Annette Hee Jimenez, *Director*
EMP: 60
SQ FT: 8,000
SALES: 3.2MM **Privately Held**
SIC: 8322 8641 8351 Individual & family services; community membership club; child day care services

---

8331 Job Training & Vocational Rehabilitation Svcs

(P-23556)
ABILITY COUNTS INC (PA)
775 Trademark Cir Ste 101, Corona (92879-2084)
PHONE..................................951 734-6595
Joyce Hearn, *CEO*
EMP: 100
SQ FT: 28,000
SALES (est): 6.7MM **Privately Held**
WEB: www.abilitycounts.org
SIC: 8331 Sheltered workshop

(P-23557)
ABLE INDUSTRIES INC
8929 W Goshen Ave, Visalia (93291-7969)
PHONE..................................559 651-8150
Wende Ayers, *Exec Dir*
Brandi Miller, *Technician*
Kathleen Valencia, *Human Res Dir*
Gerald Ormonde, *Mktg Coord*
Jerry Ormonde, *Mktg Coord*
▲ **EMP:** 52
SQ FT: 75,000
SALES: 4.7MM **Privately Held**
WEB: www.ableindustries.com
SIC: 8331 Community service employment training program; job counseling

(P-23558)
ADVOCACY FOR RESPECT AND CH (PA)
Also Called: Hillside Entps - AR C Long Bch
4519 E Stearns St, Long Beach (90815-2540)
PHONE..................................562 597-7716
Marion Lieberman, *CEO*
EMP: 81
SQ FT: 35,000
SALES: 4.8MM **Privately Held**
SIC: 8331 Sheltered workshop

(P-23559)
ANITA BORG INST FOR WOMEN TECH
1301 Shoreway Rd Ste 425, Belmont (94002-4154)
PHONE..................................650 236-4756
Dr Telle Whitney, *President*
Laurie Greer, *Partner*
Dr Anita Borg, *President*
Cindy Georal, *Vice Pres*
Farideh Eshagh, *VP Finance*
EMP: 67 **EST:** 1998
SALES: 22MM **Privately Held**
SIC: 8331 Job training & vocational rehabilitation services

(P-23560)
APPRENTICE & JOURNEYMEN TRN TR
Also Called: Compton Training Center
7850 Haskell Ave, Van Nuys (91406-1907)
PHONE..................................323 636-9871
Micheal Hazard, *Exec Dir*
EMP: 99
SALES: 13.8MM **Privately Held**
SIC: 8331 Job training services

(P-23561)
ARC FRESNO/MADERA COUNTIES (PA)
4490 E Ashlan Ave, Fresno (93726-2647)
PHONE..................................559 226-6268
Lori Rmirez, *CEO*
Carolyn Wallace, *President*
Mike Takechi, *Treasurer*
Peter Mersino, *Vice Pres*
Alan Lagunoff, *Admin Sec*
EMP: 57
SALES: 11MM **Privately Held**
SIC: 8331 Job training services

(P-23562)
ARC LOS ANGLES ORANGE COUNTIES (PA)
Also Called: SOUTHEAST INDUSTRIES
12049 Woodruff Ave, Downey (90241-5669)
PHONE..................................562 803-1556
Kevin Mac Donald, *Exec Dir*
EMP: 94
SQ FT: 9,800
SALES: 3.8MM **Privately Held**
SIC: 8331 5932 Skill training center; vocational training agency; used merchandise stores

(P-23563)
ARC MID-CITIES INC
14208 Towne Ave, Los Angeles (90061-2653)
PHONE..................................310 329-9272
Lena Cole Dennis, *President*
John Wagner, *Exec Dir*
Bedsog Jugo, *Human Res Mgr*
EMP: 160
SALES (est): 6.6MM **Privately Held**
WEB: www.arcmidcities.org
SIC: 8331 8322 Job training services; individual & family services

(P-23564)
ARC OF ALAMEDA COUNTY
Also Called: Walpert Center
1101 Walpert St, Hayward (94541-6705)
PHONE..................................510 582-8151
Renee Tuddel, *Manager*
EMP: 110
SQ FT: 2,000

SALES (corp-wide): 6.5MM **Privately Held**
WEB: www.tiw-alameda.com
SIC: 8331 Sheltered workshop
PA: The Arc Of Alameda County
14700 Doolittle Dr
San Leandro CA 94577
510 357-3569

(P-23565)
ARC SAN FRANCISCO (PA)
1500 Howard St, San Francisco
(94103-2525)
PHONE...................415 255-7200
Timothy Hornbecker, *Exec Dir*
Kirsten Mellor, *CEO*
Brian Wagman, *CFO*
Ann Relling, *Officer*
Jonathan Zimman, *Officer*
EMP: 156
SQ FT: 30,000
SALES: 10.2MM **Privately Held**
WEB: www.thearcsanfrancisco.org
SIC: 8331 8361 7361 Job training services; vocational rehabilitation agency; home for the mentally handicapped; employment agencies

(P-23566)
ARRIBA JUNTOS (PA)
1850 Mission St, San Francisco
(94103-3502)
PHONE...................415 487-3240
Dalila Ohumada, *Director*
Gladys Garcia, *Manager*
EMP: 62 **EST:** 1965
SQ FT: 10,000
SALES: 7.6MM **Privately Held**
WEB: www.arribajuntos.org
SIC: 8331 Community service employment training program

(P-23567)
ASIAN REHABILITATION SVC INC (PA)
7009 Washington Ave, Whittier
(90602-1416)
PHONE...................562 632-1141
Si Ho, *Exec Dir*
Cherry Habacon, *Executive*
EMP: 62
SQ FT: 28,000
SALES: 2.3MM **Privately Held**
WEB: www.asianrehab.org
SIC: 8331 Vocational rehabilitation agency

(P-23568)
ASSOCIATION FOR RETARDED
Also Called: Arc, The
796 E 6th St, San Bernardino
(92410-4532)
PHONE...................909 884-6484
Kris Oxnevad, *Director*
Kris N Oxnevad, *Director*
EMP: 55 **EST:** 1952
SALES: 963.1K **Privately Held**
WEB: www.schoolofhope.com
SIC: 8331 5399 Job training & vocational rehabilitation services; surplus & salvage goods

(P-23569)
BAKERSFIELD ASSC RRTD CTZNS
2240 S Union Ave, Bakersfield
(93307-4158)
PHONE...................661 834-2272
Jim Baldwin, *President*
EMP: 210
SQ FT: 30,000
SALES (est): 10.8MM **Privately Held**
SIC: 8331 Sheltered workshop; skill training center; work experience center

(P-23570)
BENEFITVISION INC
5550 Topanga Canyon Blvd # 180, Woodland Hills (91367-6478)
PHONE...................818 348-3100
Terry Fuzue, *Branch Mgr*
EMP: 58
SALES (corp-wide): 20MM **Privately Held**
SIC: 8331 Job training & vocational rehabilitation services

PA: Benefitvision, Inc.
4522 Rfd
Long Grove IL 60047
877 737-5526

(P-23571)
BLANCHARDCOACHINGCOM INC
125 State Pl, Escondido (92029-1323)
PHONE...................760 489-5005
Kenneth S Blanchard, *President*
Tom McKee, *CEO*
Randy Redwitz, *CFO*
Andor Czinege, *Managing Dir*
EMP: 300 **EST:** 1979
SALES (est): 6.3MM **Privately Held**
SIC: 8331 Job training & vocational rehabilitation services

(P-23572)
BUFFINI & COMPANY (PA)
6349 Palomar Oaks Ct, Carlsbad
(92011-1428)
PHONE...................760 827-2100
Brian Buffini, *Ch of Bd*
Corinne Archuleta, *Broker*
Suzanne Drace, *Broker*
Elena Vasquez, *Broker*
Lindsey Zimmer, *Broker*
EMP: 182
SALES (est): 18.7MM **Privately Held**
WEB: www.buffiniandcompany.com
SIC: 8331 Job training services

(P-23573)
CALIFORNIA HUMAN DEV CORP (PA)
Also Called: Anthony Soto Emplyment Trning
3315 Airway Dr, Santa Rosa (95403-2005)
PHONE...................707 523-1155
Miguel Mejia, *Chairman*
Christopher Paige, *CEO*
Doris Unsod, *Treasurer*
Hector Brambila, *Admin Sec*
Peter Anderson, *Graphic Designe*
EMP: 140
SQ FT: 15,000
SALES: 12.6MM **Privately Held**
SIC: 8331 7361 8399 7374 Job training services; placement agencies; community development groups; calculating service (computer)

(P-23574)
CAMBLE CENTER
Also Called: Self-Aid Workshop
6512 San Fernando Rd, Glendale
(91201-2109)
PHONE...................818 242-2434
Wendy Jacoby, *President*
EMP: 100 **EST:** 1958
SQ FT: 8,000
SALES: 2.1MM **Privately Held**
SIC: 8331 5947 8322 7389 Job training & vocational rehabilitation services; gift, novelty & souvenir shop; individual & family services; packaging & labeling services; mailing service; recycling, waste materials

(P-23575)
CAREER TRANSITION CENTER
Also Called: Workforce Development Bureau
3447 Atlantic Ave Ste 100, Long Beach
(90807-4513)
PHONE...................562 570-9675
Brian Rogers, *Director*
EMP: 135
SALES (est): 3MM **Privately Held**
SIC: 8331 Job training services

(P-23576)
CENTER FOR EMPLOYMENT TRAINING (PA)
Also Called: C E T
701 Vine St, San Jose (95110-2940)
PHONE...................408 287-7924
Hermelinda Sapien, *CEO*
Asbjorn Osland, *Vice Chairman*
Mohammad Aryanpour, *CFO*
Bob Martinez, *Treasurer*
Greg Adams, *Bd of Directors*
EMP: 70
SQ FT: 120,000

SALES: 27.7MM **Privately Held**
SIC: 8331 9721 Vocational training agency; immigration services, government

(P-23577)
CENTRAL VALLEY OPRTNTY CTR INC (PA)
Also Called: Cvoc
6838 Bridget Ct, Winton (95388)
P.O. Box 1389 (95388-1389)
PHONE...................209 357-0062
Ernie Flores, *Exec Dir*
Ofelia Reynoso, *Persnl Dir*
Tom Davenport, *Instructor*
Don Curiel-Ruth, *Manager*
EMP: 110
SQ FT: 27,000
SALES: 5.9MM **Privately Held**
SIC: 8331 Vocational training agency

(P-23578)
CHINATOWN SERVICE CENTER (PA)
767 N Hill St Ste 200b, Los Angeles
(90012-2365)
PHONE...................213 808-1700
Karen Elizabeth Blakeney, *CEO*
Peter Ng, *President*
Gloria Tang, *Treasurer*
Henry Kwong, *Admin Sec*
Lawrence Lue, *Director*
EMP: 120
SQ FT: 20,000
SALES: 7.5MM **Privately Held**
WEB: www.cscla.org
SIC: 8331 8322 8011 Job counseling; family (marriage) counseling; clinic, operated by physicians

(P-23579)
CHURCH OF JSUS CHRST OF LD STS
Also Called: Deseret Industries
3000 Auburn Blvd Ste B, Sacramento
(95821-1831)
PHONE...................916 482-1480
Jack P McKinney, *Manager*
Jack McKinney, *Manager*
EMP: 100
SALES (corp-wide): 3.5B **Privately Held**
WEB: www.lds.org
SIC: 8331 5932 Sheltered workshop; used merchandise stores
PA: Corporation Of The President Of The Church Of Jesus Christ Of Latter-Day Saints
50 E North Temple
Salt Lake City UT 84150
801 240-1000

(P-23580)
COGNIFIT INC
600 California St Fl 11, San Francisco
(94108-2727)
PHONE...................646 340-1740
Nathanael Eisenberg, *Chairman*
Tommy Sagcoun, *President*
Michal Frenkiel, *Vice Pres*
EMP: 51
SALES (est): 692.8K **Privately Held**
SIC: 8331 7371 Skill training center; computer software development & applications

(P-23581)
COMMUNITY CATALYSTS CALIFORNIA
935 W San Marcos Blvd # 103, San Marcos
(92078-1142)
PHONE...................760 471-3700
EMP: 50 **Privately Held**
SIC: 8331 Job training & vocational rehabilitation services
PA: Community Catalysts Of California
3750 Convoy St Ste 306
San Diego CA 92111

(P-23582)
COMPRHNSIVE TRNING SYSTEMS INC
497 11th St Ste 4, Imperial Beach
(91932-1661)
PHONE...................619 424-6650

Linda Blairforth, *President*
EMP: 50
SQ FT: 8,300
SALES: 51.3K **Privately Held**
WEB: www.ctsjobs.org
SIC: 8331 Job training & vocational rehabilitation services

(P-23583)
CONSERVATION CORPS LONG BEACH
340 Nieto Ave, Long Beach (90814-1845)
PHONE...................562 986-1249
Samara Ashley, *Principal*
Mike Bassett, *CEO*
John Dunay, *CFO*
Dan Knapp, *Exec Dir*
Mario R Beas, *Admin Sec*
EMP: 165
SQ FT: 10,000
SALES: 2.9MM **Privately Held**
WEB: www.cclb-corps.org
SIC: 8331 8322 Community service employment training program; individual & family services

(P-23584)
CONTRA COSTA ARC
Also Called: Commercial Spport Svcs Antioch
2505 W 10th St, Antioch (94509-1374)
PHONE...................925 755-4925
David Duart, *Manager*
EMP: 70
SQ FT: 7,992
SALES (corp-wide): 19.2MM **Privately Held**
WEB: www.ccarealtors.com
SIC: 8331 7389 Skill training center; packaging & labeling services
PA: Contra Costa Arc
1340 Arnold Dr Ste 127
Martinez CA 94553
925 646-4690

(P-23585)
COUNTY OF ALAMEDA
Private Industry Council
24100 Amador St Ste 130, Hayward
(94544-1287)
PHONE...................510 670-5700
Kirill Elistratov, *Manager*
EMP: 50 **Privately Held**
WEB: www.co.alameda.ca.us
SIC: 8331 9411 Job training services; administration of educational programs;
PA: County Of Alameda
1221 Oak St Ste 555
Oakland CA 94612
510 272-6691

(P-23586)
COUNTY OF MERCED
Also Called: Workforce Investment- Admin
1205 W 18th St, Merced (95340-4513)
PHONE...................209 724-2000
Andrea P Baker, *Director*
EMP: 110 **Privately Held**
WEB: www.mercednccp-hcp.net
SIC: 8331 9441 Job training services; administration of social & manpower programs;
PA: County Of Merced
2222 M St
Merced CA 95340
209 385-7511

(P-23587)
COUNTY OF RIVERSIDE
Also Called: Economic Development
3403 10th St Ste 500, Riverside
(92501-3658)
P.O. Box 553 (92502-0553)
PHONE...................951 955-3100
Selicia Slournoy, *Director*
EMP: 97 **Privately Held**
SIC: 8331 9441 Skill training center; administration of social & manpower programs;
PA: County Of Riverside
4080 Lemon St Fl 11
Riverside CA 92501
951 955-1110

(P-23588)
COUNTY OF SAN JOAQUIN
San Joaquin County
56 S Lincoln St, Stockton (95203-3100)
PHONE..............................209 468-3500
EMP: 200 **Privately Held**
SIC: 8331 9111
PA: County Of San Joaquin
44 N San Joaquin St # 640
Stockton CA 95202
209 468-3203

(P-23589)
COUNTY OF STANISLAUS
Also Called: Department Workforce Dev
251 E Hackett Rd Ste 2, Modesto
(95358-9800)
P.O. Box 3389 (95353-3389)
PHONE..............................209 558-2100
Khristy Santos, *Director*
EMP: 150 **Privately Held**
WEB: www.co.stanislaus.ca.us
SIC: 8331 Job training & vocational reha-
bilitation services
PA: County Of Stanislaus
1010 10th St Ste 5100
Modesto CA 95354
209 525-6398

(P-23590)
DEL NORTE WORKFORCE CENTER
Also Called: Real Human Svcs & Workforce
875 5th St Ste 12, Crescent City
(95531-4000)
PHONE..............................707 464-8347
Cindy Salatnay, *Director*
EMP: 50
SALES (est): 409.9K **Privately Held**
SIC: 8331 Job training services

(P-23591)
DEVELOPMENTAL SVCS CAL DEPT
Also Called: Fairview Developmental Center
2501 Harbor Blvd, Costa Mesa
(92626-6143)
PHONE..............................714 957-5151
Bill Wilson, *Exec Dir*
EMP: 1500 **Privately Held**
WEB: www.ldc.dds.ca.gov
SIC: 8331 9431 8361 Job training & vocational rehabilitation services; administration of public health programs; ;
residential care
HQ: California Department Of Developmental Services
1600 9th St
Sacramento CA 95814
916 654-1690

(P-23592)
EDEN AREA REGNL OCCUPATIONAL P
Also Called: Eden Area Rop School
26316 Hesperian Blvd, Hayward
(94545-2458)
PHONE..............................510 293-2900
Cyril Bonanno, *Exec Dir*
EMP: 90
SQ FT: 74,000
SALES (est): 5.9MM **Privately Held**
WEB: www.edenrop.org
SIC: 8331 8249 Vocational training
agency; skill training center; vocational
schools

(P-23593)
EMPLOYMENT & COMMUNITY OPTIONS
5050 Murphy Canyon Rd # 220, San Diego
(92123-4441)
PHONE..............................858 565-9870
Nancy Batterman, *President*
Richard Gutierrez, *CFO*
Lindsay Arvanitis, *Program Mgr*
Michelle Bozman, *Program Mgr*
Nicki Burnworth, *Program Mgr*
EMP: 250
SQ FT: 6,000
SALES: 14.1MM **Privately Held**
SIC: 8331 Job training & vocational reha-
bilitation services

(P-23594)
EXCEPTIONAL CHLD FOUNDATION (PA)
Also Called: PAR SERVICES
5350 Machado Ln, Culver City
(90230-8800)
PHONE..............................310 204-3300
Scott Bowling, *President*
Paul K Zimmerman, *Partner*
Kramer H LLP, *Vice Chairman*
Clark Jensen, *COO*
Denise Orme, *CFO*
EMP: 120 EST: 1946
SQ FT: 45,000
SALES: 26.6MM **Privately Held**
WEB: www.ecf-la.org
SIC: 8331 Vocational training agency; vo-
cational rehabilitation agency

(P-23595)
EXCEPTIONAL CHLD FOUNDATION
Also Called: Par Services
1430 Venice Blvd, Los Angeles
(90006-4818)
PHONE..............................213 748-3556
Nanette Cruz, *Principal*
EMP: 165
SALES (corp-wide): 26.6MM **Privately Held**
SIC: 8331 Job training & vocational reha-
bilitation services
PA: Exceptional Children's Foundation
5350 Machado Ln
Culver City CA 90230
310 204-3300

(P-23596)
FONTANA RESOURCES AT WORK
Also Called: INDUSTRIAL SUPPORT SYS-
TEMS
8608 Live Oak Ave, Fontana (92335-3172)
P.O. Box 848 (92334-0848)
PHONE..............................909 428-3833
Ulric Jones, *CFO*
Sylvia Anderson, *Exec Dir*
Danny Cervera, *Opers-Prdtn-Mfg*
Alexa Uribe, *Manager*
EMP: 140
SQ FT: 22,600
SALES: 1.8MM **Privately Held**
SIC: 8331 3444 Vocational rehabilitation
agency; sheet metalwork

(P-23597)
GLENN CNTY HUMN RESOURCE AGCY
Also Called: Colusa, Glenn, Trinity Communt
420 E Laurel St, Willows (95988-3115)
PHONE..............................530 934-6510
Kim W Gaghagen, *Director*
Betty Skala, *Deputy Dir*
EMP: 130
SALES (est): 2.9MM **Privately Held**
SIC: 8331 8322 Job training services;
emergency social services

(P-23598)
GOODWILL INDS ORANGE CNTY CAL
2910 W Garry Ave, Santa Ana
(92704-6510)
PHONE..............................714 754-7808
EMP: 110
SALES (corp-wide): 126.7MM **Privately Held**
SIC: 8331
PA: Goodwill Industries Of Orange County,
California
410 N Fairview St
Santa Ana CA 92703
714 547-6308

(P-23599)
GOODWILL INDS S CENTL CAL
1115 Olive Dr, Bakersfield (93308-4141)
PHONE..............................661 377-0191
Debbie Stwart, *Principal*
EMP: 50
SALES (corp-wide): 16.4MM **Privately Held**
SIC: 8331 Vocational rehabilitation agency

PA: Goodwill Industries Of South Central
California
4901 Stine Rd
Bakersfield CA 93313
661 837-0595

(P-23600)
GOODWILL INDUSTRS OF SAN FRANC
1270 Oddstad Dr, Redwood City
(94063-2606)
PHONE..............................650 556-9709
EMP: 55
SALES (corp-wide): 36.8MM **Privately Held**
SIC: 8331 Vocational rehabilitation agency
PA: Goodwill Industries Of San Francisco,
San Mateo, And Marin Counties, Inc.
750 Post St
San Francisco CA 94109
415 575-2101

(P-23601)
HOPE SERVICES
744 La Guardia St Ste B, Salinas
(93905-3358)
PHONE..............................831 455-4940
Greg Dinsmore, *Manager*
EMP: 65
SALES (corp-wide): 40.3MM **Privately Held**
SIC: 8331 Vocational rehabilitation agency
PA: Hope Services
30 Las Colinas Ln
San Jose CA 95119
408 284-2850

(P-23602)
HOWARD TRAINING CENTER (PA)
1424 Stonum Rd, Modesto (95351-5197)
PHONE..............................209 538-2431
Claudia K Miller, *Exec Dir*
Angelina Melgoza, *Human Res Mgr*
EMP: 100
SQ FT: 10,000
SALES: 6.3MM **Privately Held**
SIC: 8331 Skill training center

(P-23603)
ICI ENTERPRISES INC
790 E Willow St Ste 150, Long Beach
(90806-2719)
PHONE..............................562 989-7715
Robert Nelson, *Principal*
EMP: 100
SALES: 8MM **Privately Held**
SIC: 8331 Job training services

(P-23604)
INCLUSIVE CMNTY RESOURCES LLC
2855 Telegraph Ave Ste Ll, Berkeley
(94705-1168)
PHONE..............................510 981-8115
Julie Steinbaugh,
Mike Steinbaugh, *Vice Pres*
Michael Steinbaugh,
Shana Ring, *Clerk*
EMP: 120
SQ FT: 4,800
SALES (est): 4.1MM **Privately Held**
SIC: 8331 Community service employment
training program

(P-23605)
INSTITUTE FOR EDUCTL THERAPY
1007 University Ave, Berkeley
(94710-2113)
PHONE..............................831 457-1207
Karen Rotstein, *Exec Dir*
Vicko Cesko, *Technical Staff*
Arianna Rosenthal, *Marketing Staff*
Nori Hudson, *Instructor*
Lori Cottrell, *Manager*
EMP: 50 **Privately Held**
WEB: www.baumancollege.org
SIC: 8331 8249 Vocational training
agency; vocational schools
PA: Institute For Educational Therapy
10151 Main St Ste 128
Penngrove CA 94951

(P-23606)
JEWIS VOCATIONAL & COUNSELING
225 Bush St Ste 400, San Francisco
(94104-4252)
PHONE..............................415 391-3600
Abby Snay, *Exec Dir*
Sadie Robertson, *Partner*
Nicoll Mischel, *COO*
Jamie Austin, *Vice Pres*
Juha Suuraho, *Software Dev*
EMP: 70
SQ FT: 8,000
SALES: 10.8MM **Privately Held**
WEB: www.jvs.org
SIC: 8331 Job counseling; job training
services

(P-23607)
JEWISH VOCATIONAL SERVICES (PA)
Also Called: JVSLA
6505 Wilshire Blvd # 200, Los Angeles
(90048-4957)
PHONE..............................323 761-8888
Vivian B Seigel, *CEO*
Claudia Finkel, *COO*
Olwen Brown, *CFO*
David Walkley, *Vice Pres*
Zoya Kavutskaya, *Info Tech Dir*
EMP: 50
SQ FT: 11,000
SALES: 16.8MM **Privately Held**
SIC: 8331 Vocational rehabilitation agency

(P-23608)
KINGS VIEW
100 Airpark Rd, Atwater (95301-9535)
P.O. Box 774 (95301-0774)
PHONE..............................209 357-0321
Sam Kalember, *Branch Mgr*
EMP: 50
SALES (corp-wide): 26.8MM **Privately Held**
SIC: 8331 Sheltered workshop; work expe-
rience center
PA: Kings View
7170 N Fincl Dr Ste 110
Fresno CA 93720
559 256-0100

(P-23609)
LAW CROSSING (PA)
175 S Lake Ave Unit 200, Pasadena
(91101-2629)
PHONE..............................626 243-1801
A Harrison Barnes, *President*
Sachin Shah, *Programmer Anys*
Mihir Sheth, *Human Res Mgr*
Jade Harvey, *Marketing Staff*
EMP: 65
SALES (est): 1.2MM **Privately Held**
WEB: www.lawcrossing.com
SIC: 8331 Job counseling

(P-23610)
LINCOLN TRAINING CENTER AND RE
2643 Loma Ave, South El Monte
(91733-1478)
PHONE..............................626 442-0621
Judith Angelo, *CEO*
David Nelson, *Vice Chairman*
Eric Brown, *Chairman*
Rosemary Garza, *Vice Pres*
Melissa Rus, *Program Mgr*
EMP: 85
SQ FT: 30,000
SALES: 18.6MM **Privately Held**
WEB: www.lincolntc.com
SIC: 8331 Vocational rehabilitation agency

(P-23611)
LOS ANGELES JOB CORPS
4867 E 61st St Apt C, Maywood
(90270-4436)
PHONE..............................213 748-0135
Fred Williams, *Director*
Fowler Anthony, *Officer*
Ruby Brown, *Director*
EMP: 197
SALES (est): 5.6MM **Privately Held**
SIC: 8331 Job training services

(P-23612)
MARRIOTT FOUNDATION FOR PEOPLE
Also Called: Bridges From School To Work
344 Thomas L Berkley Way, Oakland (94612-3577)
PHONE..................................510 834-4700
Anthea Charles, *Director*
EMP: 80
SALES: 20K **Privately Held**
SIC: 8331 Job training & vocational rehabilitation services

(P-23613)
METROPOLITAN AREA ADVISORY COM (PA)
Also Called: M A A C Project
1355 Third Ave, Chula Vista (91911-4302)
PHONE..................................619 426-3595
Arnulfo Manriquez, *CEO*
Antonio Pizano, *President*
Adolfo Ventura, *COO*
Austin Foye, *CFO*
Claudia Arreola, *Director*
EMP: 100
SQ FT: 820,000
SALES: 44.3MM **Privately Held**
SIC: 8331 8351 8748 Job training services; head start center, except in conjunction with school; energy conservation consultant

(P-23614)
METROPOLITAN AREA ADVISORY COM
Also Called: Maac Project Cwbh
1102 Cesar E Chavez Pkwy, San Diego (92113-2108)
PHONE..................................619 255-7284
Vicky Rodriguez, *Branch Mgr*
EMP: 350
SALES (corp-wide): 44.3MM **Privately Held**
SIC: 8331 Job training services
PA: Metropolitan Area Advisory Committee On Anti-Poverty Of San Diego County, Inc.
1355 Third Ave
Chula Vista CA 91911
619 426-3595

(P-23615)
METROPOLITAN AREA ADVISORY COM
Also Called: Maac Project
1355 Third Ave, Chula Vista (91911-4302)
PHONE..................................619 420-8981
Michael Finneran, *Manager*
EMP: 122
SALES (corp-wide): 44.3MM **Privately Held**
SIC: 8331 8011 Job training services; offices & clinics of medical doctors
PA: Metropolitan Area Advisory Committee On Anti-Poverty Of San Diego County, Inc.
1355 Third Ave
Chula Vista CA 91911
619 426-3595

(P-23616)
MID-CITIES ASSOCIATION INC (PA)
Also Called: Hub-Limited Workshop
14208 Towne Ave, Los Angeles (90061-2653)
PHONE..................................310 537-4510
John Wagoner, *Exec Dir*
EMP: 60
SALES: 7.2MM **Privately Held**
SIC: 8331 Sheltered workshop

(P-23617)
NAPA VALLEY PSI INC
651 Trabajo Ln, NAPA (94559-4258)
P.O. Box 600 (94559-0600)
PHONE..................................707 255-0177
Jeanne Fauquet, *President*
Rick Wood, *General Mgr*
Heather Dawley-Alfaro, *Admin Asst*
Lea Ronald, *Director*
EMP: 80
SQ FT: 43,800

SALES: 735K **Privately Held**
SIC: 8331 2521 2511 Vocational rehabilitation agency; filing cabinets (boxes), office: wood; wood household furniture

(P-23618)
NATIONAL MENTOR INC
Also Called: First Step Ind Living Program
9166 Anaheim Pl Ste 200, Rancho Cucamonga (91730-8547)
PHONE..................................909 483-2505
Gregory Torres, *President*
EMP: 80
SALES (corp-wide): 310.7MM **Privately Held**
SIC: 8331 Job training & vocational rehabilitation services
HQ: National Mentor, Inc.
313 Congress St Fl 5
Boston MA 02210
617 790-4800

(P-23619)
NORTH BAY DEVELOPMENTAL (PA)
Also Called: North Bay Regional Center
10 Executive Ct Ste A, NAPA (94558-6331)
P.O. Box 3360 (94558-0295)
PHONE..................................707 256-1224
Toll Free:.................................888 -
Nancy Gardner, *Exec Dir*
Maureen O'Hare, *Case Mgr*
EMP: 100
SALES: 157.1MM **Privately Held**
WEB: www.nbrc.net
SIC: 8331 8322 Job training services; individual & family services

(P-23620)
OAKLAND PRIVATE INDUSTRY COUNC
268 Grand Ave, Oakland (94610-4724)
PHONE..................................510 768-4400
Gay Plair Cobb, *President*
EMP: 64
SALES: 7.1MM **Privately Held**
SIC: 8331 Community service employment training program; job training services

(P-23621)
OPARC (PA)
Also Called: DIVERSIFIED INDUSTRIES
9029 Vernon Ave, Montclair (91763-2000)
PHONE..................................909 982-4090
Ronald P Wolff, *President*
Nancy Dediemar, *Treasurer*
Donna Norum, *Officer*
Andrea Wells, *Officer*
Sonia Borja, *Vice Pres*
EMP: 50
SQ FT: 350,000
SALES: 13MM **Privately Held**
WEB: www.oparc.org
SIC: 8331 8322 Job training & vocational rehabilitation services; individual & family services

(P-23622)
ORANGE CNTY CONSERVATION CORPS
1853 N Raymond Ave, Anaheim (92801-1117)
PHONE..................................714 451-1301
Dick Dittmar, *President*
Peggy Dougherty, *Treasurer*
Max Carter, *Exec Dir*
EMP: 100
SQ FT: 10,000
SALES: 4.4MM **Privately Held**
SIC: 8331 Job training & vocational rehabilitation services

(P-23623)
OWL COMPANIES (PA)
2465 Campus Dr, Irvine (92612-1502)
PHONE..................................949 797-2000
Gregory J Burden, *CEO*
Gregory Burden, *CFO*
Sylvia Goldstein, *Executive Asst*
Steve Seastrom, *Controller*
Nichole Degidio, *Human Res Mgr*
EMP: 1389
SQ FT: 22,800

SALES (est): 42.7MM **Privately Held**
WEB: www.owlcompanies.com
SIC: 8331 6519 4911 Job training & vocational rehabilitation services; real property lessors; generation, electric power

(P-23624)
OWL EDUCATION AND TRAINING
2465 Campus Dr, Irvine (92612-1502)
PHONE..................................949 797-2000
Gregory J Burden, *President*
Stephen Seastrom, *Corp Secy*
EMP: 1380
SQ FT: 22,800
SALES (est): 4.8MM
SALES (corp-wide): 42.7MM **Privately Held**
WEB: www.owlcompanies.com
SIC: 8331 Job training & vocational rehabilitation services
PA: Owl Companies
2465 Campus Dr
Irvine CA 92612
949 797-2000

(P-23625)
PACIFIC ASIAN CONSORTM EMPLYMN (PA)
Also Called: P A C E
1055 Wilshire Blvd Ste 14, Los Angeles (90017-2431)
PHONE..................................213 353-3982
Kerry N Doi, *Exec Dir*
Antonio Fernandez, *Accountant*
Janet Hernandez, *Personnel Assit*
Myriah Ogas, *Site Mgr*
John Varga, *Education*
EMP: 130 **EST:** 1976
SQ FT: 20,000
SALES: 22.8MM **Privately Held**
SIC: 8331 8322 7361 1521 Community service employment training program; individual & family services; labor contractors (employment agency); new construction, single-family houses

(P-23626)
PATHPOINT
11491 Los Osos Valley Rd, San Luis Obispo (93405-6428)
PHONE..................................805 782-8890
Aline Graham, *Director*
EMP: 100
SALES (corp-wide): 21.2MM **Privately Held**
SIC: 8331 Skill training center; vocational rehabilitation agency
PA: Pathpoint
315 W Haley St Ste 102
Santa Barbara CA 93101
805 966-3310

(P-23627)
POMONA VALLEY WORKSHOP (PA)
4650 Brooks St, Montclair (91763-4797)
PHONE..................................909 624-3555
Karen Jones, *Exec Dir*
Sharon Varga, *Vice Pres*
Mitch Gariador, *Administration*
Carol Martinez, *Director*
EMP: 70
SQ FT: 34,000
SALES: 5.5MM **Privately Held**
SIC: 8331 Job training services

(P-23628)
PRIDE INDUSTRIES
Also Called: Auburn Pride
13080 Earhart Ave, Auburn (95602-9536)
PHONE..................................530 888-0331
Vic Wursten, *Branch Mgr*
Kim Curry, *General Mgr*
Patrick Papia, *Train & Dev Mgr*
Rachel Kelly, *Production*
Michelle McKnight, *Manager*
EMP: 180
SQ FT: 5,000
SALES (corp-wide): 290.6MM **Privately Held**
SIC: 8331 Sheltered workshop
PA: Pride Industries
10030 Foothills Blvd
Roseville CA 95747
916 788-2100

(P-23629)
PRIDE INDUSTRIES
12451 Loma Rica Dr, Grass Valley (95945-9059)
PHONE..................................530 477-1832
Kathy Gardinier, *Branch Mgr*
EMP: 72
SQ FT: 16,290
SALES (corp-wide): 290.6MM **Privately Held**
SIC: 8331 7389 7331 Sheltered workshop; packaging & labeling services; mailing service
PA: Pride Industries
10030 Foothills Blvd
Roseville CA 95747
916 788-2100

(P-23630)
PRIDE INDUSTRIES
3608 Madison Ave Ste 43, North Highlands (95660-5002)
PHONE..................................916 334-5415
Vicki Coyle, *Branch Mgr*
EMP: 57
SQ FT: 2,500
SALES (corp-wide): 290.6MM **Privately Held**
SIC: 8331 Sheltered workshop
PA: Pride Industries
10030 Foothills Blvd
Roseville CA 95747
916 788-2100

(P-23631)
PROGRSSIVE EMPLOYMENT CONCEPTS (PA)
6060 Sunrise Vista Dr # 1875, Citrus Heights (95610-7053)
PHONE..................................916 723-3112
Carole Watilo, *President*
Robert Black, *Treasurer*
Debbie Bates, *Bd of Directors*
Mark Savickas, *Bd of Directors*
Rob Watilo, *Executive*
EMP: 62
SQ FT: 1,500
SALES: 2.6MM **Privately Held**
SIC: 8331 Job training & vocational rehabilitation services

(P-23632)
SACRAMENTO EMPLOYEMENT & TRAIN
Also Called: Set A Head Start Westside
925 Del Paso Blvd Ste 100, Sacramento (95815-3568)
PHONE..................................916 263-3800
Kathy Kossick, *Exec Dir*
EMP: 250 **Privately Held**
SIC: 8331 8351 Job training services; head start center, except in conjunction with school
PA: Sacramento Employment & Training Agency
925 Del Paso Blvd Ste 100
Sacramento CA 95815

(P-23633)
SACRAMENTO EMPLOYEMENT & TRAIN (PA)
Also Called: Seta
925 Del Paso Blvd Ste 100, Sacramento (95815-3568)
PHONE..................................916 263-3800
Kathy Kossick, *Exec Dir*
Lisa Carr, *Manager*
Ralph Giddings, *Manager*
William Walker, *Manager*
Victor Bonanno, *Supervisor*
EMP: 250
SQ FT: 30,000
SALES (est): 19.9MM **Privately Held**
WEB: www.seta.net
SIC: 8331 7361 8351 Job training services; employment agencies; child day care services

(P-23634)
SAN GABRIEL VLY TRAINING CTR (PA)
Also Called: Production Fcilities Unlimited
400 S Covina Blvd, La Puente
(91746-2212)
PHONE..............................626 330-3185
Randy Hyatt, *Exec Dir*
Mary Ryan Indenbaum, *President*
Robert Darragh, *Treasurer*
Shirley Roland, *Admin Sec*
EMP: 55 **EST:** 1962
SQ FT: 6,400
SALES: 5.1MM **Privately Held**
WEB: www.sgvtc.org
SIC: 8331 7389 Vocational rehabilitation agency; packaging & labeling services

(P-23635)
SAN JOSE CONSERVATION CORPS
2650 Senter Rd, San Jose (95111-1121)
PHONE..............................408 283-7171
Bob Hennessy, *CEO*
Natali Mendoza, *Recruiter*
Sal Munoz, *Opers Dir*
Scott Curtis, *Teacher*
Erin Krueger, *Director*
EMP: 150
SQ FT: 1,800
SALES: 7.2MM **Privately Held**
WEB: www.sjccharterschool.org
SIC: 8331 Community service employment training program; job counseling

(P-23636)
SANTA ANITA FAMILY YOUNG
501 S Mountain Ave, Monrovia
(91016-3655)
PHONE..............................626 359-9244
Patrice Reinhand, *Ch of Bd*
Damian Colaluca, *CEO*
EMP: 60 **EST:** 1999
SALES: 1.8MM **Privately Held**
WEB: www.safymca.org
SIC: 8331 Community service employment training program

(P-23637)
SISKIYOU OPPORTUNITY CENTER (PA)
Also Called: YREKA EMPLOYMENT SERVICES
1516 S Mount Shasta Blvd, Mount Shasta
(96067-2700)
P.O. Box 304 (96067-0304)
PHONE..............................530 926-4698
Daniel Chianello, *Director*
Dan Chianello, *Exec Dir*
Laurinda Palmer, *Admin Asst*
Tena Rulofson, *Admin Asst*
Kristina Jackson, *Program Dir*
EMP: 120
SQ FT: 4,820
SALES: 2.2MM **Privately Held**
WEB: www.siskiyouopportunitycenter.org
SIC: 8331 Job counseling

(P-23638)
SKILLS CENTER INC (PA)
220 Lincoln St, Santa Cruz (95060-4351)
PHONE..............................831 421-9900
John Christensen, *President*
EMP: 70
SQ FT: 9,500
SALES (est): 440.9K **Privately Held**
SIC: 8331 Vocational rehabilitation agency

(P-23639)
SOUTH BAY REGL PUBLIC SAFETY T
Also Called: Sbrpstc
560 Bailey Ave, San Jose (95141-1004)
PHONE..............................408 270-6494
Steve Cushing, *President*
Gregg Giusiana, *Vice Pres*
Al J Padron, *Opers Staff*
EMP: 50
SALES (est): 3.1MM **Privately Held**
WEB: www.theacademy.ca.gov
SIC: 8331 Job training services

(P-23640)
SOUTH BAY VOCATIONAL CENTER
Also Called: SOUTH BAY PACKAGING & ASSEMBLY
20706 Main St, Carson (90745-1117)
PHONE..............................424 215-4589
Corey Sylve, *President*
Clare Gray, *Vice Pres*
EMP: 50
SQ FT: 19,000
SALES: 1.8MM **Privately Held**
WEB: www.sbvc1.com
SIC: 8331 Work experience center

(P-23641)
SPECIAL SERVICE FOR GROUPS INC (PA)
Also Called: Special Service For Groups Ssg
905 E 8th St, Los Angeles (90021-1848)
PHONE..............................213 368-1888
Herbert K Hatanaka, *CEO*
Antonio Gutierrez, *Officer*
Donna Wong, *Vice Pres*
Robert Oleinik, *Associate Dir*
Yvonne Suarez, *Program Mgr*
EMP: 625
SALES (est): 60.6MM **Privately Held**
WEB: www.ssgmain.org
SIC: 8331 8093 8399 Vocational rehabilitation agency; mental health clinic, outpatient; advocacy group

(P-23642)
ST MADELEINE SOPHIES CENTER
2119 E Madison Ave, El Cajon
(92019-1111)
PHONE..............................619 442-5129
Debra Turner, *Director*
Martha Diobilda, *Accountant*
Tom Carr, *Director*
John Faulkner, *Case Mgr*
Martin Breceda, *Manager*
EMP: 70
SQ FT: 13,092
SALES: 8.4MM **Privately Held**
WEB: www.stmsc.org
SIC: 8331 Vocational training agency

(P-23643)
STEPPING STN GRWTH CTR FR CHLD
Also Called: Boatworks
311 Macarthur Blvd, San Leandro
(94577-2110)
PHONE..............................510 568-3331
Paula Champagne, *President*
Monte Cohen, *Director*
EMP: 85
SALES: 2.5MM **Privately Held**
WEB: www.steppingstonesgrowth.org
SIC: 8331 8211 8351 Skill training center; private special education school; child day care services

(P-23644)
SUCCESS STRATEGIES INST INC
Also Called: Tom Ferry Your Coach
6 Hutton Cntre Dr Ste 700, Santa Ana
(92707)
PHONE..............................949 721-6808
Thomas Ferry, *President*
Jon Holt, *Consultant*
Cheryl Ingraham, *Consultant*
Ryan Jhono, *Consultant*
Steve Kinney, *Consultant*
EMP: 70
SALES (est): 6.8MM **Privately Held**
WEB: www.yourcoach.com
SIC: 8331 Job training & vocational rehabilitation services

(P-23645)
THE FOR VALLEY RESOURCE CENTER (PA)
1285 N Santa Fe St, Hemet (92543-1823)
PHONE..............................951 766-8659
Lee Trisler, *CEO*
Darlene Noon, *Human Resources*
Valerie Patterson, *Supervisor*
Lucinda Johnson, *Clerk*
EMP: 50

SQ FT: 80,000
SALES: 9MM **Privately Held**
SIC: 8331 2389 Vocational training agency; apparel for handicapped

(P-23646)
THE FOR WORK TRAINING CENTER
1811 Kusel Rd, Oroville (95966-9528)
PHONE..............................530 534-1112
Dave Ennes, *Manager*
EMP: 50
SALES (corp-wide): 10.8MM **Privately Held**
WEB: www.wtcinc.org
SIC: 8331 Vocational rehabilitation agency
PA: Work Training Center For The Handicapped, Inc.
2255 Fair St
Chico CA 95928
530 343-7994

(P-23647)
TOOLWORKS INC (PA)
25 Kearny St Ste 400, San Francisco
(94108-5518)
PHONE..............................415 733-0990
Steve Crabiel, *Exec Dir*
Jan Behr, *COO*
Jonathan McAdams, *Info Tech Mgr*
Mike Oxley, *Project Mgr*
Stefan Lazar, *Human Res Dir*
EMP: 471
SQ FT: 3,500
SALES: 16MM **Privately Held**
WEB: www.toolworks.org
SIC: 8331 Vocational rehabilitation agency

(P-23648)
UCP WORK INC (PA)
Also Called: W O R K
5320 Carpinteria Ave G, Carpinteria
(93013-2107)
PHONE..............................805 566-9000
Kathy Webb, *Exec Dir*
Judy Linares, *Director*
EMP: 60
SQ FT: 2,000
SALES: 9.3MM **Privately Held**
SIC: 8331 Vocational rehabilitation agency; vocational training agency

(P-23649)
UKIAH VLY ASSN FOR HBILITATION (PA)
Also Called: MAYACAMA INDUSTRIES
990 S Dora St, Ukiah (95482-5754)
P.O. Box 689 (95482-0689)
PHONE..............................707 468-8824
Pamela Jensen, *Director*
Janeen Saunders, *Director*
Kris Vipond, *Manager*
EMP: 60
SALES: 2.2MM **Privately Held**
WEB: www.uvah.org
SIC: 8331 8361 Sheltered workshop; residential care

(P-23650)
UNYEWAY INC
11440 Riverside Dr Ste D, Lakeside
(92040-2731)
PHONE..............................619 562-6330
Carrie Hancock, *Branch Mgr*
EMP: 52
SALES (corp-wide): 4.9MM **Privately Held**
SIC: 8331 8322 Skill training center; family counseling services
PA: Unyeway, Inc
2330 Main St Ste E
Ramona CA
-

(P-23651)
URBAN CORPS OF SAN DIEGO
3127 Jefferson St, San Diego
(92110-4422)
P.O. Box 80156 (92138-0156)
PHONE..............................619 235-6884
Sam Duran, *CEO*
Michael Sterns, *Chairman*
Mike Priegel, *Controller*
EMP: 132
SQ FT: 25,000

SALES: 9.7MM **Privately Held**
WEB: www.urbancorpssd.org
SIC: 8331 Work experience center

(P-23652)
VALLEY LIGHT INDUSTRIES INC
5360 Irwindale Ave, Baldwin Park
(91706-2086)
PHONE..............................626 337-6200
Andrew M Altman, *CEO*
Pamela Hayes, *President*
Johnny Camacho, *Technology*
Julie Garcia, *Finance Mgr*
Penny Wiegand, *Director*
EMP: 250
SQ FT: 14,220
SALES: 4.1MM **Privately Held**
WEB: www.valleylightind.org
SIC: 8331 Job training & vocational rehabilitation services

(P-23653)
VOCATIONAL IMPRV PROGRAM INC (PA)
9210 Rochester Ave, Rancho Cucamonga
(91730-5521)
PHONE..............................909 483-5924
Wendy A Rogina, *CEO*
Christopher J McArdle, *Treasurer*
Rick Rogina, *Vice Pres*
M Stephen Cho, *Admin Sec*
EMP: 175
SQ FT: 23,000
SALES: 15.3MM **Privately Held**
WEB: www.vipsolutions.com
SIC: 8331 Vocational rehabilitation agency

(P-23654)
VOCATIONAL VISIONS
26041 Pala, Mission Viejo (92691-2705)
PHONE..............................949 837-7280
Joan McKinney, *CEO*
Kathryn Hebel, *Exec Dir*
EMP: 170 **EST:** 1975
SQ FT: 17,000
SALES: 8MM **Privately Held**
WEB: www.vocationalvisions.org
SIC: 8331 Sheltered workshop

(P-23655)
VTC ENTERPRISES (PA)
2445 A St, Santa Maria (93455-1401)
P.O. Box 1187 (93456-1187)
PHONE..............................805 928-5000
Jason Telander, *CEO*
Dr Mark Malangko, *President*
Lisa Walker, *CFO*
Henry M Grennan, *Treasurer*
Cole Kinney, *Admin Sec*
EMP: 330 **EST:** 1962
SQ FT: 21,093
SALES: 11.2MM **Privately Held**
WEB: www.vtc-sm.org
SIC: 8331 Vocational rehabilitation agency

(P-23656)
WESTVIEW SERVICES INC
Also Called: Starlight Educational Center
9421 Edinger Ave, Westminster
(92683-7426)
PHONE..............................714 418-2090
Lourdis Painter, *Principal*
EMP: 70
SQ FT: 3,775
SALES (corp-wide): 16.6MM **Privately Held**
SIC: 8331 8244 Community service employment training program; business & secretarial schools
PA: Westview Services, Inc
10522 Katella Ave
Anaheim CA 92804
714 517-6606

(P-23657)
WOMENS TRANSITIONAL LIVING CTR
Also Called: WTLC
P.O. Box 916 (92836-0916)
PHONE..............................714 992-1939
Angelique Tsontos, *CEO*
EMP: 50
SALES: 2.9MM **Privately Held**
SIC: 8331 Sheltered workshop

(P-23658)
WORK2FUTURE FOUNDATION
Also Called: Work2fture - Yuth Training Ctr
2072 Lucretia Ave, San Jose (95122-3305)
PHONE..................................408 794-1234
EMP: 242
SALES (corp-wide): 5.1MM **Privately Held**
SIC: 8331 Skill training center
PA: Work2future Foundation
   1601 Foxworthy Ave
   San Jose CA 95118
   408 794-1100

(P-23659)
WORK2FUTURE FOUNDATION
Also Called: North San Jose Job Center
1901 Zanker Rd, San Jose (95112-4217)
PHONE..................................408 216-6202
EMP: 145
SALES (corp-wide): 5.1MM **Privately Held**
SIC: 8331 Job training services
PA: Work2future Foundation
   1601 Foxworthy Ave
   San Jose CA 95118
   408 794-1100

(P-23660)
WORK2FUTURE FOUNDATION
Also Called: Work2future - Gilroy Job Ctr
379 Tomkins Ct, Gilroy (95020-3631)
PHONE..................................408 758-3477
EMP: 145
SALES (corp-wide): 5.1MM **Privately Held**
SIC: 8331 Skill training center
PA: Work2future Foundation
   1601 Foxworthy Ave
   San Jose CA 95118
   408 794-1100

(P-23661)
XQAWESOME INC
20 Mason Ln, Ladera Ranch (92694-0325)
PHONE..................................949 929-9622
Bonnie Jean Bradley, *CEO*
EMP: 183
SALES (est): 1.3MM **Privately Held**
SIC: 8331 8742 7389 Job training services; marketing consulting services;

8351 Child Day Care Svcs

(P-23662)
4 CS COUNCIL
2515 N 1st St, San Jose (95131-1003)
PHONE..................................408 487-0747
Alfredo Villasenor, *Principal*
EMP: 110
SQ FT: 6,100
SALES (est): 4.9MM **Privately Held**
SIC: 8351 Child day care services

(P-23663)
ABC CHILD CARE INC (PA)
Also Called: ABC Child Care Center
29705 Solana Way, Temecula
(92591-3611)
PHONE..................................951 699-5251
Malinda Smith Margiotta, *CEO*
Jennifer Salazar, *CFO*
Brett Tyndale, *CFO*
Shannon Porter, *Asst Director*
Wright Tonya, *Asst Director*
EMP: 70
SQ FT: 20,000
SALES (est): 3.4MM **Privately Held**
WEB: www.abccares.com
SIC: 8351 Preschool center

(P-23664)
ABRAHAM JSHA HSCHL DY SCHL WST
27400 Canwood St, Agoura (91301-2462)
PHONE..................................818 707-2365
Bruce Friedman, *CEO*
Suzan Huntington, *Director*
EMP: 62
SALES: 2MM **Privately Held**
SIC: 8351 Group day care center

(P-23665)
ACHIEVER CHRISTIAN PRE-SCHL &
540 Sands Dr, San Jose (95125-6233)
PHONE..................................408 264-2345
Julie Brown, *Principal*
David Culley, *Director*
EMP: 50
SALES (est): 677.6K **Privately Held**
SIC: 8351 8211 Montessori child development center; private elementary & secondary schools; private elementary school

(P-23666)
ACTION DAY NRSERIES PRMRY PLUS
18720 Bucknall Rd, Saratoga
(95070-4106)
PHONE..................................408 370-0350
Tracy Sarge, *Director*
EMP: 51
SALES (corp-wide): 5.8MM **Privately Held**
WEB: www.actiondayprimaryplus.com
SIC: 8351 Preschool center
PA: Action Day Nurseries & Primary Plus, Inc
   3030 Moorpark Ave Bldg D
   San Jose CA 95128
   408 247-6972

(P-23667)
ACTION DAY NRSERIES PRMRY PLUS
2148 Lincoln Ave, San Jose (95125-3540)
PHONE..................................408 266-8952
Carol Freitas, *Manager*
EMP: 50
SALES (corp-wide): 5.8MM **Privately Held**
WEB: www.actiondayprimaryplus.com
SIC: 8351 Preschool center
PA: Action Day Nurseries & Primary Plus, Inc
   3030 Moorpark Ave Bldg D
   San Jose CA 95128
   408 247-6972

(P-23668)
ADAMS LEARNING CENTER
Also Called: Adams Early Childhood Lrng Ctr
50800 Desert Club Dr, La Quinta
(92253-2982)
PHONE..................................760 777-4260
Maria Moore, *Director*
EMP: 50
SALES (est): 511.9K **Privately Held**
SIC: 8351 Preschool center

(P-23669)
ADESTE PROGRAM COMPANY
1531 James M Wood Blvd, Los Angeles
(90015-1112)
PHONE..................................213 251-3551
Gregory Cox, *Exec Dir*
Elvia Martinez, *Administration*
Armine Lalaine, *Director*
EMP: 400
SALES (est): 2.9MM **Privately Held**
SIC: 8351 Child day care services

(P-23670)
ALA COSTA CENTER PROGRAM FOR (PA)
1300 Rose St, Berkeley (94702-1108)
PHONE..................................510 527-2550
Michael Pereira, *Director*
Ron Halog, *Exec Dir*
Margie Bennett, *Supervisor*
EMP: 52 **EST:** 1973
SALES: 1.7MM **Privately Held**
WEB: www.alacostacenter.org
SIC: 8351 Child day care services

(P-23671)
ALAMEDA FAMILY SERVICES
2325 Clement Ave, Alameda (94501-7063)
PHONE..................................510 629-6300
Irene Kudarauskas, *Exec Dir*
Bruce Kariya, *VP Finance*
Tom Gallagher, *Finance*
Marianne Boudreau, *Human Res Mgr*
Kobi Mar, *Psychologist*
EMP: 100

SALES: 5.8MM **Privately Held**
WEB: www.alamedafs.org
SIC: 8351 8322 Head start center, except in conjunction with school; youth self-help agency; offender rehabilitation agency; child guidance agency; general counseling services

(P-23672)
ALLIES FOR EVERY CHILD INC
5721 W Slauson Ave # 200, Culver City
(90230-6587)
PHONE..................................310 846-4100
Heather Carrigan, *CEO*
EMP: 92
SQ FT: 18,000
SALES: 8.4MM **Privately Held**
SIC: 8351 8322 Child day care services; child related social services

(P-23673)
ASSOCIATED STUDENTS CDC
460 S 8th St, San Jose (95112-3835)
PHONE..................................408 924-6988
Maria Davis, *Director*
Sheryl Vargas, *Exec Dir*
EMP: 60
SALES (est): 628K **Privately Held**
SIC: 8351 Child day care services

(P-23674)
BAY AREA HISPN INST ADVANCMNT
Also Called: CENTRO VIDA
1000 Camelia St, Berkeley (94710-1514)
PHONE..................................510 525-1463
Beatriz Leyva Cutler, *Director*
Beatriz Leyva, *Exec Dir*
Dolores Franco, *Bookkeeper*
Martha Cueva, *Education*
EMP: 66
SQ FT: 1,200
SALES: 1.7MM **Privately Held**
SIC: 8351 8299 Group day care center; preschool center; educational services

(P-23675)
BELMONT OAKS ACADEMY
2200 Carlmont Dr, Belmont (94002-3310)
PHONE..................................650 593-6175
Pamela Clarke, *President*
Joanna Reames, *Director*
EMP: 63
SALES (est): 2.2MM **Privately Held**
SIC: 8351 8211 Preschool center; private elementary school

(P-23676)
BERMUDA DUNES LEARNING CTR INC
42115 Yucca Ln, Bermuda Dunes
(92203-8111)
PHONE..................................760 772-7127
Gayle Clark, *President*
EMP: 50
SALES (est): 1.4MM **Privately Held**
SIC: 8351 Preschool center

(P-23677)
BLIND CHILDRENS LRNG CTR INC
18542 Vanderlip Ave Ste B, Santa Ana
(92705-8201)
P.O. Box 25209 (92799-5209)
PHONE..................................714 573-8888
Kathy Buehler, *Exec Dir*
Denise Grajek, *Administration*
Mindy Weinheimer, *Manager*
Morgan Fields, *Receptionist*
EMP: 50
SQ FT: 18,824
SALES: 2.8MM **Privately Held**
WEB: www.blindkids.org
SIC: 8351 8211 Child day care services; private special education school

(P-23678)
BRIGHT HORIZONS CHLD CTRS LLC
Also Called: Camp Amgen
1 Amgen Center Dr, Thousand Oaks
(91320-1730)
PHONE..................................805 447-6793
Kelly Travis, *Director*
EMP: 170

SALES (corp-wide): 1.9B **Publicly Held**
WEB: www.atlantaga.ncr.com
SIC: 8351 Child day care services
HQ: Bright Horizons Children's Centers Llc
   200 Talcott Ave
   Watertown MA 02472
   617 673-8000

(P-23679)
BRIGHT HORIZONS CHLD CTRS LLC
Also Called: Sisco Family Connection
800 Barber Ln, Milpitas (95035-7926)
PHONE..................................408 853-2196
Janice Inman, *Exec Dir*
Monica McCarthy, *Executive*
EMP: 120
SALES (corp-wide): 1.9B **Publicly Held**
WEB: www.atlantaga.ncr.com
SIC: 8351 Group day care center
HQ: Bright Horizons Children's Centers Llc
   200 Talcott Ave
   Watertown MA 02472
   617 673-8000

(P-23680)
BUSINESS AND SUPPORT SERVICES
Also Called: Browne Child Development Ctr
Santa Jancinto Rd 20286, Oceanside
(92054)
PHONE..................................760 725-2817
Maria Langlie, *Director*
EMP: 50 **Publicly Held**
WEB: www.mccssc.com
SIC: 8351 9711 Child day care services; Marine Corps;
HQ: Business And Support Services
   3044 Catlin Ave
   Quantico VA 22134
   703 432-0109

(P-23681)
CABRILLO COLLEGE CHILDREN CTR
6500 Soquel Dr, Aptos (95003-3198)
PHONE..................................831 479-6352
Erick Hoffman, *Director*
EMP: 70
SALES (est): 555.8K **Privately Held**
SIC: 8351 8221 Child day care services; colleges universities & professional schools

(P-23682)
CALVARY BAPTIST CH LOS GATOS
Also Called: Calvary Infant Care Center
16330 Los Gatos Blvd, Los Gatos
(95032-4520)
PHONE..................................408 356-5126
Bob Thomas, *Principal*
EMP: 80
SALES (corp-wide): 4.5MM **Privately Held**
WEB: www.calvarylosgatos.org
SIC: 8351 Preschool center
PA: Calvary Baptist Church Of Los Gatos
   16330 Los Gatos Blvd # 408
   Los Gatos CA 95032
   408 358-8871

(P-23683)
CALVARY CHURCH SANTA ANA INC
1010 N Tustin Ave, Santa Ana
(92705-3598)
PHONE..................................714 973-4800
Michael Welles, *Pastor*
EMP: 160
SQ FT: 133,000
SALES: 10.9MM **Privately Held**
SIC: 8351 8661 Nursery school; miscellaneous denomination church

(P-23684)
CAROLYN E WYLIE CENTER
4164 Brockton Ave Ste A, Riverside
(92501-3400)
PHONE..................................951 683-5193
Melody Amaral, *CEO*
Lisa M Dryan, *Director*
EMP: 100
SQ FT: 3,000

PRODUCTS & SVCS

SALES: 2.5MM **Privately Held**
SIC: **8351** Child day care services

(P-23685)
CENTRAL STATE PRE-SCHOOL
2310 Aldergrove Ave, Escondido
(92029-1935)
PHONE..................................760 432-2499
Susan Chambers, *Principal*
EMP: 50
SALES (est): 616.5K **Privately Held**
SIC: **8351** Preschool center

(P-23686)
CHALLENGER SCHOOLS
4949 Harwood Rd, San Jose (95124-5209)
PHONE..................................408 723-0111
Josh McKay, *Principal*
Lavaniya Jimenez, *Director*
EMP: 61
SALES (corp-wide): 109.8MM **Privately Held**
SIC: **8351** 8211 Preschool center; private elementary school
PA: Challenger Schools
  9424 S 300 W
  Sandy UT 84070
  801 569-2700

(P-23687)
CHANGING TIDES FAMILY SERVICES (PA)
2259 Myrtle Ave, Eureka (95501-3325)
PHONE..................................707 444-8293
Carol A Hill, *Exec Dir*
Joshua Leong, *Finance Dir*
Jeannie Campbell, *Director*
EMP: 168
SQ FT: 2,500
SALES: 10.9MM **Privately Held**
SIC: **8351** 8322 Head start center, except in conjunction with school; child related social services

(P-23688)
CHILD ACTION INC (PA)
9800 Old Winery Pl, Sacramento
(95827-1700)
PHONE..................................916 369-4460
Lynn Patten, *Exec Dir*
Tracey Strack, *Controller*
Jaci White, *Director*
Dina Dean, *Manager*
EMP: 301
SQ FT: 140,000
SALES: 62.1MM **Privately Held**
SIC: **8351** Head start center, except in conjunction with school

(P-23689)
CHILD CARE RESOURCE CENTER INC
Also Called: Volunteers America Head Start
454 S Kalisher St, San Fernando
(91340-3535)
PHONE..................................818 837-0097
EMP: 312
SALES (corp-wide): 111.3MM **Privately Held**
SIC: **8351** Child day care services
PA: Child Care Resource Center, Inc.
  20001 Prairie St
  Chatsworth CA 91311
  818 717-1000

(P-23690)
CHILD DEVELOPMENT ASSOC INC (PA)
180 Otay Lakes Rd Ste 310, Bonita
(91902-2442)
PHONE..................................619 427-4411
Richard Richardson, *President*
Jorge Hernandez, *Treasurer*
Jolie Buberl, *Director*
EMP: 50
SQ FT: 6,000
SALES: 87.6MM **Privately Held**
WEB: www.cdasandiego.com
SIC: **8351** 8322 Preschool center; child related social services

(P-23691)
CHILD DEVELOPMENT CENTER
309 N Rios Ave, Solana Beach
(92075-1241)
PHONE..................................858 794-7160
Susan Blackwood, *Director*
Jennifer Goldston, *Director*
EMP: 50 EST: 1980
SALES (est): 1.9MM **Privately Held**
SIC: **8351** Child day care services

(P-23692)
CHILD DEVELOPMENT INCORPORATED (PA)
Also Called: Child Development Centers
350 Woodview Ave, Morgan Hill
(95037-8104)
PHONE..................................408 556-7300
Carol Anderson, *CEO*
Alison Michel-Hall, *Prgrmr*
Kristen Raibon, *Program Dir*
EMP: 50
SALES: 28MM **Privately Held**
SIC: **8351** Child day care services

(P-23693)
CHILD DEVELOPMENT INCORPORATED
312 Gibson Rd, Woodland (95695-4765)
PHONE..................................530 666-4822
Diana Sorelle, *Branch Mgr*
EMP: 256
SALES (corp-wide): 28MM **Privately Held**
SIC: **8351** Child day care services
PA: Child Development Incorporated
  350 Woodview Ave
  Morgan Hill CA 95037
  408 556-7300

(P-23694)
CHILD DEVELOPMENT INCORPORATED
Also Called: Turtle Rock Cdc
5151 Amalfi Dr, Irvine (92603-3443)
PHONE..................................949 854-5060
Mindy Ho, *Director*
EMP: 512
SALES (corp-wide): 28MM **Privately Held**
SIC: **8351** Child day care services
PA: Child Development Incorporated
  350 Woodview Ave
  Morgan Hill CA 95037
  408 556-7300

(P-23695)
CHILD EDUCATIONAL CENTER
Also Called: Cec
140 Foothill Blvd, La Canada (91011-3727)
PHONE..................................818 354-3418
Elyssa Nelson, *Director*
EMP: 100
SALES: 8MM **Privately Held**
SIC: **8351** Preschool center

(P-23696)
CHILD FAMILY & CMNTY SVCS INC
32980 Alvarado Niles Rd # 856, Union City
(94587-3186)
PHONE..................................510 796-9512
Karen Deshayes, *Exec Dir*
John Anthony Borsella, *Finance Dir*
Catherine Clennen Seymour, *Business Mgr*
Cynthia Esquivel-Delgado, *Human Res Mgr*
EMP: 140
SQ FT: 20,000
SALES: 15.1MM **Privately Held**
SIC: **8351** Preschool center

(P-23697)
CHILDREN OF RAINBOW INC (PA)
4890 Logan Ave, San Diego (92113-3004)
PHONE..................................619 615-0652
Gale R Walker, *President*
Yanira Molina, *Supervisor*
EMP: 101
SQ FT: 8,500
SALES (est): 3.6MM **Privately Held**
WEB: www.childrenoftherainbow.com
SIC: **8351** Group day care center

(P-23698)
CHILDREN OF THE RAINBOW HEAD
4890 Logan Ave, San Diego (92113-3004)
PHONE..................................619 266-7311
Gale Walker, *Mng Member*
Kursat Misirlioglu,
EMP: 185
SALES: 6.8MM **Privately Held**
SIC: **8351** Child day care services

(P-23699)
CHILDRENS DAY SCHOOL
333 Dolores St, San Francisco
(94110-1006)
PHONE..................................415 861-5432
Rick Ackerly, *Headmaster*
Diane Larrabee, *Bd of Directors*
Jake Fishman, *Executive*
Terry Hall, *Info Tech Dir*
Wilfredo Valle, *Technical Staff*
EMP: 50
SQ FT: 22,050
SALES: 14.7MM **Privately Held**
WEB: www.cds-sf.org
SIC: **8351** 8211 Preschool center; elementary & secondary schools

(P-23700)
CHILDRENS HOSPITAL ORANGE CNTY
500 Superior Ave, Newport Beach
(92663-3657)
PHONE..................................949 631-2062
EMP: 973
SALES (corp-wide): 523.1MM **Privately Held**
SIC: **8351** Child day care services
PA: Children's Hospital Of Orange County
  1201 W La Veta Ave
  Orange CA 92868
  714 997-3000

(P-23701)
CHOICES FOR CHILDREN (PA)
20 Great Oaks Blvd # 200, San Jose
(95119-1368)
PHONE..................................408 297-3295
Vivian Cooper, *Owner*
EMP: 52
SALES (est): 788.7K **Privately Held**
SIC: **8351** Preschool center

(P-23702)
CITY OF PACIFICA-VALLEMAR
170 Santa Maria Ave, Pacifica
(94044-2506)
PHONE..................................650 738-7466
Scott Leslie, *Director*
Steve Rhodes, *Manager*
Steven Rhodes, *Manager*
EMP: 55
SALES (est): 413.5K **Privately Held**
SIC: **8351** Preschool center

(P-23703)
COLLEGE OPERATIONS LLC
1730 S College Ave, Dinuba (93618-2812)
PHONE..................................559 353-0576
Travis Greenwood, *CFO*
EMP: 50
SALES (est): 586.8K **Privately Held**
SIC: **8351** Nursery school

(P-23704)
COLTON JOINT UNIFIED SCHL DST
Also Called: San Salvador Pre-School
471 Agua Mansa Rd, Colton (92324-3325)
PHONE..................................909 876-4240
EMP: 100
SALES (corp-wide): 297.1MM **Privately Held**
SIC: **8351** 8211
PA: Colton Joint Unified School District
  1212 Valencia Dr
  Colton CA 92324
  909 580-5000

(P-23705)
COMMUNITY ACTION PRTNRSHP (PA)
1225 Gill Ave, Madera (93637-5234)
PHONE..................................559 673-9173
Mattie Mendez, *Exec Dir*

Linda L Wright, *CEO*
Donna Tooley, *CFO*
Maria Castellanos, *Area Mgr*
EMP: 200 EST: 1965
SQ FT: 18,000
SALES: 24.8MM **Privately Held**
WEB: www.maderacap.org
SIC: **8351** Head start center, except in conjunction with school

(P-23706)
COMMUNITY CHLD CRE CNCL SONOMA (PA)
Also Called: 4 Cs
131a Stony Cir Ste 300, Santa Rosa
(95401-9507)
PHONE..................................707 522-1413
Mary Ann Doan, *Exec Dir*
Emily Peterson, *Human Res Dir*
EMP: 75
SALES (est): 1.9MM **Privately Held**
WEB: www.sonoma4cs.org
SIC: **8351** Group day care center

(P-23707)
COMMUNITY DEV INST HEAD START
12988 Bowron Rd, Poway (92064-5790)
PHONE..................................858 668-2985
EMP: 60
SALES (corp-wide): 93.8MM **Privately Held**
SIC: **8351** Head start center, except in conjunction with school
PA: Community Development Institute Head Start
  10065 E Harvard Ave # 700
  Denver CO 80231
  720 747-5100

(P-23708)
COMPASS FAMILY SERVICES
Also Called: Compass Children's Center
144 Leavenworth St, San Francisco
(94102-3806)
PHONE..................................415 644-0504
Mary McNamara, *Director*
EMP: 80
SQ FT: 12,143
SALES (corp-wide): 9.2MM **Privately Held**
SIC: **8351** Child day care services
PA: Compass Family Services
  37 Grove St
  San Francisco CA 94102
  415 644-0504

(P-23709)
COMPREHENSIVE CHILD DEV INC
Also Called: Comprehensive Child Dev Ctr
769 W 3rd St, San Pedro (90731-2425)
PHONE..................................310 514-4998
Mona Maamoun, *Director*
EMP: 55
SALES (corp-wide): 11.1MM **Privately Held**
SIC: **8351** Preschool center
PA: Comprehensive Child Development, Inc.
  2545 Pacific Ave
  Long Beach CA 90806
  562 427-8834

(P-23710)
CONEJO VALLEY UNIFIED SCHL DST
Also Called: Conejo Vly Nghborhood For Lrng
100 S Conejo School Rd, Thousand Oaks
(91362)
PHONE..................................805 496-9035
Jeffrey Baarstad PHD, *Superintendent*
EMP: 285
SALES (corp-wide): 225.2MM **Privately Held**
SIC: **8351** Child day care services
PA: Conejo Valley Unified School District
  1400 E Janss Rd
  Thousand Oaks CA 91362
  805 497-9511

(P-23711)
CONTINUING DEVELOPMENT INC (PA)
Also Called: CDI Centers
350 Woodview Ave Ste 100, Morgan Hill
(95037-8105)
PHONE...............................408 556-7300
Doris Fredericks, *President*
Susan Blake, *Admin Sec*
Desiree Ortiz, *Legal Staff*
Angela Lussier, *Director*
EMP: 75
SQ FT: 10,000
SALES: 53MM **Privately Held**
SIC: 8351 8399 Child day care services;
social service information exchange

(P-23712)
COUNTY OF SAN BERNARDINO
Also Called: Preschool Service
662 S Tippecanoe Ave, San Bernardino
(92415-0630)
PHONE...............................909 387-5455
Robyn Johnson, *Manager*
Kathy Turnbull, *Officer*
Adel Nizami, *Administration*
Cindi Tompkins, *Human Res Dir*
Jeff Carter, *Manager*
EMP: 100 **Privately Held**
SIC: 8351 Head start center, except in con-
junction with school
PA: County Of San Bernardino
385 N Arrowhead Ave
San Bernardino CA 92415
909 387-3841

(P-23713)
COUNTY OF SAN BERNARDINO
Also Called: Human Services Systems
250 S Lena Rd, San Bernardino
(92415-0461)
PHONE...............................909 387-2363
Ron Griffin, *Director*
EMP: 67
SQ FT: 934 **Privately Held**
SIC: 8351 9411 8741 Head start center,
except in conjunction with school; pre-
school center; administration of educa-
tional programs; ; management services
PA: County Of San Bernardino
385 N Arrowhead Ave
San Bernardino CA 92415
909 387-3841

(P-23714)
COUNTY OF SAN BERNARDINO
Also Called: Highland Head Start
26887 5th St, Highland (92346-4178)
PHONE...............................909 425-0785
Lisa Simmons, *Branch Mgr*
EMP: 50 **Privately Held**
SIC: 8351 Head start center, except in con-
junction with school
PA: County Of San Bernardino
385 N Arrowhead Ave
San Bernardino CA 92415
909 387-3841

(P-23715)
COUNTY OF SHASTA
Also Called: Monte Vista School
43 Hilltop Dr, Redding (96003-2807)
PHONE...............................530 225-2999
Sharon Simpson, *Principal*
EMP: 50 **Privately Held**
WEB: www.rsdnmp.org
SIC: 8351 Preschool center
PA: County Of Shasta
1450 Court St Ste 308a
Redding CA 96001
530 225-5561

(P-23716)
COUNTY OF VENTURA
Also Called: Ventura Cnty Human Srvce
300 W 9th St, Oxnard (93030-7060)
PHONE...............................805 240-2701
David Weinreich, *Manager*
EMP: 50 **Privately Held**
WEB: www.vcoe.org
SIC: 8351 9431 Child day care services;
child health program administration, gov-
ernment

PA: County Of Ventura
800 S Victoria Ave
Ventura CA 93009
805 654-2644

(P-23717)
DESER SANDS UNIFI SCHOO DISTR
Also Called: Early Childhood Education
47950 Dune Palms Rd, La Quinta
(92253-4000)
PHONE...............................760 777-4200
Debra Loukatos, *Principal*
Adriana Romero, *Executive Asst*
Adelita Whitener, *Purch Dir*
Armstrong Dan, *Athletic Dir*
EMP: 74
SALES (corp-wide): 403.6MM **Privately
Held**
SIC: 8351 Preschool center
PA: Desert Sands Unified School District
School Building Corporation
47950 Dune Palms Rd
La Quinta CA 92253
760 771-8567

(P-23718)
DIANNE ADAIR DAY CARE CENTERS (PA)
1862 Bailey Rd, Concord (94521-1349)
PHONE...............................925 429-3232
Todd Porter, *CEO*
Brian Carbine, *CFO*
Sheila Bergum, *Principal*
EMP: 100
SALES (est): 4.7MM **Privately Held**
SIC: 8351 Group day care center

(P-23719)
DIGNITY HEALTH
2301 Ashe Rd, Bakersfield (93309-4301)
P.O. Box 119 (93302-0119)
PHONE...............................661 832-8300
Sharon Brown, *Director*
EMP: 60 **Privately Held**
WEB: www.chw.edu
SIC: 8351 Child day care services
HQ: Dignity Health
185 Berry St Ste 300
San Francisco CA 94107
415 438-5500

(P-23720)
E CENTER
1506 Starr Dr, Yuba City (95993-2602)
PHONE...............................530 634-1200
Kulraj Samra, *CEO*
Amanda Rhyne, *Administration*
Jim Fuoco, *Controller*
EMP: 150
SQ FT: 4,000
SALES: 21.7MM **Privately Held**
SIC: 8351 Head start center, except in con-
junction with school

(P-23721)
EDUCATION CALIFORNIA DEPT
Also Called: Califrnia Schl For Deaf Frmont
39350 Gallaudet Dr, Fremont (94538-2308)
PHONE...............................510 794-3666
David Eberwein, *Principal*
EMP: 450 **Privately Held**
WEB: www.csb-cde.ca.gov
SIC: 8351 9411 Preschool center;
HQ: California Department Of Education
1430 N St Ste 3217
Sacramento CA 95814

(P-23722)
ENRICHMENT EDUCTL EXPERIENCES
4400 Coldwater Canyon Ave # 300, Studio
City (91604-5053)
PHONE...............................818 989-7509
Nancy Simpson, *President*
EMP: 55
SALES (est): 844.4K **Privately Held**
SIC: 8351 Child day care services

(P-23723)
ENVIRONMENTS FOR LEARNING INC (PA)
Also Called: Montessori On The Lake
24291 Muirlands Blvd, Lake Forest
(92630-3001)
PHONE...............................949 855-5630
Sara Sanin, *President*
EMP: 65
SALES (est): 3.4MM **Privately Held**
SIC: 8351 8211 Montessori child develop-
ment center; preparatory school; private
combined elementary & secondary school

(P-23724)
FAMILY CARE NETWORK INC (PA)
1255 Kendall Rd, San Luis Obispo
(93401-8750)
PHONE...............................805 503-6240
James Robert, *CEO*
Christina Combs, *Admin Asst*
Rolonda Nulton, *Administration*
Ralph Perez, *Info Tech Dir*
Noel Castle, *Technology*
EMP: 175
SQ FT: 2,600
SALES: 14.3MM **Privately Held**
SIC: 8351 Child day care services

(P-23725)
FIRST BAPTIST HEAD START
3890 Railroad Ave, Pittsburg (94565-6540)
PHONE...............................925 473-2000
Arika Spencer-Brown, *Exec Dir*
Ramona Acosta, *Director*
EMP: 87
SALES (est): 2.5MM **Privately Held**
WEB: www.firstbaptistheadstart.org
SIC: 8351 Head start center, except in con-
junction with school

(P-23726)
GALT JOINT UNION SCHOOL DST
Also Called: Fairsite Preschool
902 Caroline Ave, Galt (95632-2003)
PHONE...............................209 745-1546
Donna Whitlock, *Principal*
EMP: 50 **Privately Held**
SIC: 8351 Preschool center
PA: Galt Joint Union School District
1018 C St Ste 210
Galt CA 95632

(P-23727)
GARDEN GROVE UNIFIED SCHL DST
Also Called: Bryant Elementary School
8371 Orangewood Ave, Garden Grove
(92841-1517)
PHONE...............................714 663-6437
Sharon Hazelleaf, *Principal*
Heather Tarango, *Manager*
EMP: 71
SALES (corp-wide): 613MM **Privately
Held**
SIC: 8351 Preschool center
PA: Garden Grove Unified School District
10331 Stanford Ave
Garden Grove CA 92840
714 663-6000

(P-23728)
GLENN COUNTY OFFICE EDUCATION
Also Called: Child & Family Services
676 E Walker St Fl 2, Orland (95963-2203)
PHONE...............................530 865-1145
Tracey Quarne, *Superintendent*
Deana-Marie Berry, *Info Tech Mgr*
EMP: 81
SALES: 4.4MM **Privately Held**
SIC: 8351 8322 Child day care services;
family counseling services

(P-23729)
HARMONIUM INC (PA)
Also Called: CITY ARTS ACADEMY
9245 Activity Rd Ste 200, San Diego
(92126-2383)
PHONE...............................858 684-3080
Rosa Ana Lozada, *CEO*

Melinda Mallie, *CFO*
Rosana Lozada, *Executive Asst*
Rolando Park, *Technology*
Melissa Sande, *Human Res Dir*
EMP: 150
SALES: 7.9MM **Privately Held**
SIC: 8351 Preschool center

(P-23730)
IMMANUEL BAPTIST CRUCH
Also Called: Immanuel Baptist Day School
28355 Baseline St, Highland (92346-5008)
PHONE...............................909 862-6641
Rob Zinn, *Pastor*
Andrew Preslar, *Maintence Staff*
EMP: 65
SALES (est): 2.8MM **Privately Held**
WEB: www.ibchighland.org
SIC: 8351 8661 Preschool center; Baptist
Church

(P-23731)
INGLEWOOD UNIFIED SCHOOL DST
Also Called: Inglewood Child Dev Ctr
401 S Inglewood Ave, Inglewood
(90301-2599)
PHONE...............................310 419-2691
Linda Anderson, *Principal*
EMP: 80
SALES (corp-wide): 146.4MM **Privately
Held**
WEB: www.payne.inglewood.k12.ca.us
SIC: 8351 8211 Child day care services;
public elementary school
PA: Inglewood Unified School District
401 S Inglewood Ave
Inglewood CA 90301
310 419-2700

(P-23732)
INSTITUTE FOR HUMN SOCIAL DEV (PA)
Also Called: SAN MATEO HEAD START PROGRAM
155 Bovet Rd Ste 300, San Mateo
(94402-3142)
PHONE...............................650 871-5613
Amy Liew, *Director*
Mayte Reynoso, *Office Mgr*
Ofelia Alfaro, *Opers Mgr*
Joy Duenas, *Facilities Mgr*
EMP: 61
SQ FT: 6,000
SALES: 11.2MM **Privately Held**
SIC: 8351 Head start center, except in con-
junction with school

(P-23733)
KIDANGO INC (PA)
44000 Old Warm Sprng Blvd, Fremont
(94538-6145)
PHONE...............................510 897-6900
Scott Moore, *CEO*
Nereyra Houle, *CFO*
Kate Breitzman, *Officer*
Andrea Garcia, *Officer*
Jennifer Pare, *Officer*
EMP: 80
SQ FT: 5,000
SALES (est): 26MM **Privately Held**
SIC: 8351 Preschool center; group day
care center

(P-23734)
KIDANGO INC
4700 Calaveras Ave, Fremont
(94538-1124)
PHONE...............................510 494-9601
MAI Ton, *Branch Mgr*
EMP: 187
SALES (corp-wide): 26MM **Privately
Held**
SIC: 8351 Child day care services
PA: Kidango, Inc.
44000 Old Warm Sprng Blvd
Fremont CA 94538
510 897-6900

(P-23735)
KIDS KLUB CARE CENTERS INC (PA)
Also Called: Kids Klub Pasadena
380 S Raymond Ave, Pasadena
(91105-2608)
PHONE....................626 795-2501
Michael Wojciechowski, *President*
Bambi Wojciechowski, *Chairman*
EMP: 60
SQ FT: 7,800
SALES (est): 4.9MM **Privately Held**
SIC: 8351 Preschool center

(P-23736)
KIDS N THINGS INC (PA)
4221 Cochran St, Simi Valley (93063-2349)
PHONE....................805 522-1011
Shirley Blaskl, *President*
Lawrence Blasko, *Treasurer*
EMP: 75
SQ FT: 5,000
SALES (est): 2MM **Privately Held**
SIC: 8351 Nursery school; preschool center

(P-23737)
KINDERCARE EDUCATION LLC
3280 Crow Canyon Rd, San Ramon
(94583-1304)
PHONE....................925 824-0267
Thomas Jamison, *Manager*
EMP: 85
SALES (corp-wide): 1.1B **Privately Held**
WEB: www.knowledgelearning.com
SIC: 8351 Group day care center
PA: Kindercare Education Llc
650 Ne Holladay St # 1400
Portland OR 97232
503 872-1300

(P-23738)
KINDERCARE LEARNING CTRS LLC
Also Called: Belmont Shores Kindercare
5251 E Las Lomas St, Long Beach
(90815-4206)
PHONE....................562 961-8882
Bernice Gonzalez, *Director*
Alicia Syfers, *Exec Dir*
Theresa Kappermeyer, *Director*
Tanea Robinson, *Manager*
Vangie Robles, *Manager*
EMP: 80
SALES (corp-wide): 1.1B **Privately Held**
WEB: www.kindercare.com
SIC: 8351 Group day care center
HQ: Kindercare Learning Centers, Llc
650 Ne Holladay St # 1400
Portland OR 97232
503 872-1300

(P-23739)
LAKE ELSINORE UNIFIED SCHL DST
Also Called: Ortega High School
565 Chaney St, Lake Elsinore
(92530-2722)
PHONE....................951 253-7091
Frieda Brands, *Principal*
David Walda, *Teacher*
EMP: 58
SALES (corp-wide): 283.5MM **Privately Held**
SIC: 8351 Head start center, except in conjunction with school
PA: Lake Elsinore Unified School District
545 Chaney St
Lake Elsinore CA 92530
951 253-7000

(P-23740)
LINDA BEACH COOP PRE-SCHOOL
400 Highland Ave, Piedmont (94611-4043)
PHONE....................510 547-4432
Barbara Ulbrich, *Director*
Parents Co-Op, *Principal*
EMP: 50
SALES: 161.2K **Privately Held**
SIC: 8351 Preschool center

(P-23741)
LINDAMOOD-BELL LRNG PROCESSES (PA)
406 Higuera St Ste 120, San Luis Obispo
(93401-6131)
PHONE....................805 541-3836
Nanci Bell, *President*
Greg Slowinski, *CFO*
Patricia Lindamood, *Treasurer*
Rod Bell, *Officer*
Ellen Lathrop, *Officer*
EMP: 200
SQ FT: 8,000
SALES (est): 39.2MM **Privately Held**
WEB: www.lblp.com
SIC: 8351 8093 Head start center, except in conjunction with school; preschool center; specialty outpatient clinics

(P-23742)
LITTLE CITIZENS SCHOOLS INC
4256 S Western Ave, Los Angeles
(90062-1645)
PHONE....................323 732-1212
Doris Evans, *President*
Roy Evans, *Corp Secy*
EMP: 100
SQ FT: 5,000
SALES (est): 2MM **Privately Held**
SIC: 8351 8211 Preschool center; elementary school

(P-23743)
LONG BEACH DAY NURSERY (PA)
1548 Chestnut Ave, Long Beach
(90813-1623)
PHONE....................562 421-1488
Patrice Wong, *Director*
EMP: 75
SQ FT: 8,000
SALES: 3.1MM **Privately Held**
WEB: www.lbdn.org
SIC: 8351 Nursery school; group day care center

(P-23744)
LONG BEACH DAY NURSERY
3965 N Bellflower Blvd, Long Beach
(90808-1902)
PHONE....................562 421-1488
Margareth McMahon, *Director*
EMP: 50
SALES (est): 537.9K
SALES (corp-wide): 3.1MM **Privately Held**
WEB: www.lbdn.org
SIC: 8351 Preschool center
PA: Long Beach Day Nursery
1548 Chestnut Ave
Long Beach CA 90813
562 421-1488

(P-23745)
LOS ANGELES UNIFIED SCHOOL DST
Also Called: Queen Anne Early Education Ctr
1212 Queen Anne Pl, Los Angeles
(90019-6819)
PHONE....................323 939-7322
Salvador Rodriguez, *Principal*
EMP: 60
SALES (corp-wide): 4B **Privately Held**
WEB: www.lausd.k12.ca.us
SIC: 8351 Preschool center
PA: Los Angeles Unified School District
333 S Beaudry Ave Ste 209
Los Angeles CA 90017
213 241-1000

(P-23746)
LOS ANGLES UNIVERSAL PRESCHOOL
Also Called: Child360
515 S Figueroa St Ste 900, Los Angeles
(90071-3309)
PHONE....................213 416-1200
William Sperling, *CEO*
Elsa Luna, *CFO*
Dawn Kurtz, *Officer*
Clare Shephard, *Officer*
Maria Veloz, *Senior VP*
EMP: 200
SQ FT: 12,000

SALES: 76.2MM **Privately Held**
WEB: www.laup.net
SIC: 8351 Preschool center

(P-23747)
MARIN HORIZON SCHOOL INC
305 Montford Ave, Mill Valley (94941-3370)
PHONE....................415 388-8408
Rosalind Hamar, *Exec Dir*
Scott Satterfield, *Maintenance Dir*
Kelley Gallardo, *Teacher*
Susan Guadagno, *Teacher*
Rochelle Reodica, *Director*
EMP: 50
SQ FT: 20,000
SALES: 11.3MM **Privately Held**
WEB: www.marinhorizon.org
SIC: 8351 8211 Montessori child development center; private elementary school

(P-23748)
MARYVALE DAY CARE CENTER
Also Called: Maryvale Edcatn Fmly Rsrce Ctr
2502 Huntington Dr, Duarte (91010-2221)
PHONE....................626 357-1514
Steve Gunther, *Director*
EMP: 124
SALES (corp-wide): 21.9MM **Privately Held**
SIC: 8351 Preschool center
PA: Maryvale Day Care Center
7600 Graves Ave
Rosemead CA 91770
626 280-6511

(P-23749)
MARYVALE DAY CARE CENTER (PA)
Also Called: MARYVALE EDUCATIONAL DAY CARE
7600 Graves Ave, Rosemead
(91770-3414)
P.O. Box 1039 (91770-1000)
PHONE....................626 280-6511
Steve Gunpher, *President*
Christina Moore, *Vice Pres*
EMP: 76
SALES: 21.9MM **Privately Held**
WEB: www.maryvale-ca.org
SIC: 8351 8361 Child day care services; residential care for children

(P-23750)
MCCUSKER ENTERPRISES INC
Also Called: Kids World Preschool
29879 Santiago Rd, Temecula
(92592-3004)
PHONE....................951 699-9777
John McCusker, *President*
Kris Dean McCusker, *Vice Pres*
EMP: 70 EST: 1976
SQ FT: 6,000
SALES (est): 2.1MM **Privately Held**
SIC: 8351 8211 Preschool center; private elementary school

(P-23751)
MERCIES HOME (PA)
910 S Real Rd, Bakersfield (93309-4132)
PHONE....................661 832-3424
Mercedes Penarejo, *Owner*
EMP: 50
SQ FT: 2,300
SALES (est): 1.7MM **Privately Held**
SIC: 8351 8361 Group day care center; home for the mentally handicapped

(P-23752)
MEXICAN AMRCN OPRTNTY FNDATION
2650 Zoe Ave Fl 3, Huntington Park
(90255-4198)
PHONE....................323 588-7320
Lisa Viveros, *Branch Mgr*
EMP: 50
SALES (corp-wide): 73.3MM **Privately Held**
SIC: 8351 Head start center, except in conjunction with school
PA: Mexican American Opportunity Foundation
401 N Garfield Ave
Montebello CA 90640
323 890-9600

(P-23753)
MONTESSORI LEARNING COMMONS (PA)
Also Called: Elk Grove Montessori School
1123 D St, Sacramento (95814-0809)
PHONE....................916 444-7786
Norman Lorenz, *President*
Edward Condon, *CFO*
EMP: 100
SQ FT: 3,500
SALES (est): 1MM **Privately Held**
SIC: 8351 Montessori child development center

(P-23754)
MOUNTAIN VIEW CHILD CARE INC
Also Called: Totally Kids Spcalty Hlth Care
10716 La Tuna Canyon Rd, Sun Valley
(91352-2130)
PHONE....................818 252-5863
Michelle Nydam, *Branch Mgr*
EMP: 150 **Privately Held**
SIC: 8351 Child day care services
PA: Mountain View Child Care, Inc.
1720 Mountain View Ave
Loma Linda CA 92354

(P-23755)
NEIGHBORHOOD HOUSE ASSOCIATION
4111 Home Ave Ste F, San Diego
(92105-5200)
PHONE....................619 262-8199
Michelle Tylor, *Exec Dir*
EMP: 80
SALES (corp-wide): 86.7MM **Privately Held**
SIC: 8351 Head start center, except in conjunction with school
PA: The Neighborhood House Association
5660 Copley Dr
San Diego CA 92111
858 715-2642

(P-23756)
NORTH BAY CHILDRENS CENTER (PA)
932 C St, Novato (94949-5060)
PHONE....................415 883-6222
Susan Gilmore, *CEO*
Sharon Vaughn, *Human Res Dir*
Debbie Neal, *Director*
Kristen Berg, *Supervisor*
Michelle Fox, *Supervisor*
EMP: 58
SALES: 4.6MM **Privately Held**
WEB: www.nbcc.net
SIC: 8351 Preschool center

(P-23757)
NORTH COAST PRESBYTERIAN CH
1831 S El Camino Real, Encinitas
(92024-4913)
PHONE....................760 753-2535
Daniel Foley, *Business Mgr*
Tami Axtell, *Admin Sec*
Bryan Schafer, *Assoc Pastor*
Hunter Benson, *Pastor*
Donald Seltzer, *Pastor*
EMP: 70
SALES (est): 1.9MM **Privately Held**
WEB: www.ncpcinfo.com
SIC: 8351 8661 Preschool center; Presbyterian Church

(P-23758)
NORTH WEST LEARNING CENTER
3485 W Ashcroft Ave, Fresno (93722-4249)
PHONE....................559 228-3057
Rosemary Avalos, *Director*
Alvis Bytel, *Exec Dir*
EMP: 50
SALES (est): 481.7K **Privately Held**
SIC: 8351 Child day care services

(P-23759)
NURTURING TOTS INC
3784 Winford Dr, Tarzana (91356-5811)
PHONE....................818 996-1602
Eugene Cobuzzi, *Owner*

Linda Cobuzzi, *President*
Debra Dinielli, *President*
EMP: 60
SALES (est): 156.9K **Privately Held**
SIC: 8351 Child day care services

(P-23760)
OFFICE OF CHILD DEVELOPMENT
10800 Farragut Dr, Culver City (90230-4107)
PHONE..................................310 842-4230
Audrey Stephens, *Director*
Audrey Jones, *Director*
Audrey Stevens, *Director*
Maria Luisa Gonzalez, *Assistant*
EMP: 80
SALES (est): 505.5K **Privately Held**
SIC: 8351 Preschool center

(P-23761)
OLIVE KNOLLS CHRISTIAN SCHOOL
6201 Fruitvale Ave, Bakersfield (93308-2706)
PHONE..................................661 393-3566
Wendy Nayes, *Director*
Jabo Baldwin, *Teacher*
Vicki Cecil, *Teacher*
Shirley Friberg, *Director*
Theron Friberg, *Director*
EMP: 60
SALES (est): 1.8MM **Privately Held**
WEB: www.okcs.org
SIC: 8351 8661 Child day care services; religious organizations

(P-23762)
OLYMPUS ADHC INC
Also Called: Olympus Adult Day Hlthcare Ctr
11613 Washington Pl, Los Angeles (90066-5013)
PHONE..................................310 572-7272
Boris Frigman, *President*
EMP: 50
SALES (est): 1MM **Privately Held**
SIC: 8351 Group day care center

(P-23763)
OPTIONS FOR LEARNING
Also Called: State Preschool
2001 Elm St, Alhambra (91803-2905)
PHONE..................................626 308-2411
EMP: 75
SALES (corp-wide): 81.7MM **Privately Held**
SIC: 8351 Group day care center
PA: Options For Learning
    885 S Village Oaks Dr # 12
    Covina CA 91724
    626 967-7848

(P-23764)
ORANGE CNTY SPRNTNDENT SCHOOLS
Also Called: Lindburgh Child Development
220 23rd St, Costa Mesa (92627-1810)
PHONE..................................949 650-2506
Elivira Frescas, *Director*
EMP: 60
SALES (corp-wide): 304MM **Privately Held**
WEB: www.ocprob.com
SIC: 8351 Preschool center
PA: Orange County Superintendent Of Schools
    200 Kalmus Dr
    Costa Mesa CA 92626
    714 966-4000

(P-23765)
ORANGE COUNTY HEAD START (PA)
2501 Pullman St, Santa Ana (92705-5515)
P.O. Box 9269, Fountain Valley (92728-9269)
PHONE..................................714 241-8920
Colleen Versteeg, *Exec Dir*
Loyal Sharp, *Finance Dir*
Monica Portan, *Human Res Mgr*
Talishia Gadlin, *Education*
EMP: 75
SQ FT: 20,000

SALES: 37MM **Privately Held**
SIC: 8351 Head start center, except in conjunction with school

(P-23766)
ORANGE COUNTY HEAD START
9200 W Pacific Pl, Anaheim (92804-6387)
PHONE..................................714 761-4967
Colleen Versteeg, *Director*
EMP: 136
SALES (corp-wide): 37MM **Privately Held**
SIC: 8351 Head start center, except in conjunction with school
PA: Orange County Head Start
    2501 Pullman St
    Santa Ana CA 92705
    714 241-8920

(P-23767)
ORANGE COUNTY HEAD START
Also Called: Ted Fisher Head Start
14422 Hammon Ln, Huntington Beach (92647-2010)
PHONE..................................714 241-8920
Sherry Moyer, *Director*
EMP: 50
SALES (corp-wide): 37MM **Privately Held**
SIC: 8351 Head start center, except in conjunction with school
PA: Orange County Head Start
    2501 Pullman St
    Santa Ana CA 92705
    714 241-8920

(P-23768)
PALCARE INC
945 California Dr, Burlingame (94010-3605)
PHONE..................................650 340-1289
Pettis Perry, *Exec Dir*
EMP: 50
SQ FT: 12,000
SALES: 3.5MM **Privately Held**
WEB: www.palcare.org
SIC: 8351 Preschool center

(P-23769)
PALO ALTO COMMUNITY CHILD CARE
890 Escondido Rd, Stanford (94305-7101)
PHONE..................................650 855-9828
Gary Prehn, *Principal*
EMP: 65
SALES (corp-wide): 9.6MM **Privately Held**
SIC: 8351 Child day care services
PA: Palo Alto Community Child Care Inc
    3990 Ventura Ct
    Palo Alto CA
    650 493-5990

(P-23770)
PARA LOS NINOS
845 E 6th St, Los Angeles (90021-1026)
PHONE..................................213 623-3942
Tim Gray, *CEO*
EMP: 113
SALES (corp-wide): 31.7MM **Privately Held**
SIC: 8351 Preschool center
PA: Para Los Ninos
    5000 Hollywood Blvd
    Los Angeles CA 90027
    213 250-4800

(P-23771)
PENINSULA FAMILY SERVICE (PA)
24 2nd Ave, San Mateo (94401-3828)
PHONE..................................650 403-4300
Judy Swanson, *CEO*
Laurie Wishard, *President*
Ame Croce, *CEO*
Kimberly Hines, *Vice Pres*
Chanel Paulson, *Facilities Mgr*
EMP: 100 **EST:** 1950
SALES: 13.1MM **Privately Held**
WEB: www.familyserviceagency.org
SIC: 8351 8322 Group day care center; family (marriage) counseling

(P-23772)
PENINSULA FAMILY SERVICE
2635 N 1st St, San Jose (95134-2026)
PHONE..................................650 403-4300
EMP: 83
SALES (corp-wide): 13.1MM **Privately Held**
SIC: 8351 Child day care services
PA: Peninsula Family Service
    24 2nd Ave
    San Mateo CA 94401
    650 403-4300

(P-23773)
PEOPLES CARE INC
12215 Telg Rd Ste 208, Santa Fe Springs (90670)
PHONE..................................562 320-0174
Torres Cesaer, *Principal*
EMP: 147
SALES (corp-wide): 39.2MM **Privately Held**
SIC: 8351 Child day care services
PA: People's Care Inc.
    13920 City Center Dr # 230
    Chino Hills CA 91709
    855 773-6753

(P-23774)
PLAZA DE LA RAZA CHILD DEVELOP
225 N Avenue 25, Los Angeles (90031-1794)
PHONE..................................323 224-1788
EMP: 93
SALES (corp-wide): 21MM **Privately Held**
SIC: 8351 Head start center, except in conjunction with school
PA: Plaza De La Raza Child Development Services, Inc.
    13300 Crssrds Pkwy N 44
    La Puente CA 91746
    562 776-1301

(P-23775)
PLAZA DE LA RAZA CHILD DEVELOP
6411 Norwalk Blvd, Whittier (90606-1502)
PHONE..................................562 695-1070
Adriana Gonzalez, *President*
EMP: 93
SALES (corp-wide): 21MM **Privately Held**
SIC: 8351 Head start center, except in conjunction with school
PA: Plaza De La Raza Child Development Services, Inc.
    13300 Crssrds Pkwy N 44
    La Puente CA 91746
    562 776-1301

(P-23776)
PLAZA DE LA RAZA CHILD DEVELOP (PA)
13300 Crssrds Pkwy N 44, La Puente (91746)
PHONE..................................562 776-1301
Anthony Rendon, *Exec Dir*
Mike M Oz, *Vice Chairman*
Jessica Guerra, *Bd of Directors*
Cesar G Hindu, *Bd of Directors*
Veronica Torres, *Bd of Directors*
EMP: 72
SALES: 21MM **Privately Held**
SIC: 8351 Head start center, except in conjunction with school

(P-23777)
PRECIOUS ENTERPRISES INC
Also Called: Clement Preschool
14130 Douglass Ln, Saratoga (95070-5536)
PHONE..................................408 265-2226
Faz Ulla, *Owner*
Shahana Shah, *Co-Owner*
Husna Ulla, *Co-Owner*
Nilu Ulla, *Co-Owner*
EMP: 62
SQ FT: 7,500
SALES (est): 1.1MM **Privately Held**
WEB: www.preschools.indiaedu.com
SIC: 8351 Preschool center

(P-23778)
PRESTIGE PRESCHOOLS INC (PA)
3795 La Crescenta Ave # 200, Glendale (91208-1057)
PHONE..................................818 957-1170
Steven L Bush, *Principal*
EMP: 56 **EST:** 2008
SALES (est): 7.9MM **Privately Held**
SIC: 8351 Preschool center

(P-23779)
QUALITY CHILDRENS SERVICES (PA)
6108 Innovation Way, Carlsbad (92009-1728)
P.O. Box 234203, Encinitas (92023-4203)
PHONE..................................760 942-3433
Amory Ramirez, *President*
EMP: 150
SQ FT: 3,500
SALES: 9.6MM **Privately Held**
SIC: 8351 Group day care center

(P-23780)
SAINT JHNS HLTH CTR FOUNDATION
Also Called: Saint Johns Child Fmly Dev Ctr
2121 Santa Monica Blvd, Santa Monica (90404-2303)
PHONE..................................310 829-5511
Robert Klein, *Principal*
EMP: 70
SQ FT: 26,032
SALES (corp-wide): 2.7B **Privately Held**
SIC: 8351 Child day care services
HQ: Saint John's Health Center Foundation.
    2121 Santa Monica Blvd
    Santa Monica CA 90404
    310 829-5511

(P-23781)
SAN BERNARDINO CITY UNF SCHOOL
Also Called: Allred Child Developement Ctr
303 S K St, San Bernardino (92410-2416)
PHONE..................................909 388-6307
Latashia Kelly, *Director*
EMP: 100
SALES (corp-wide): 712MM **Privately Held**
WEB: www.sbcusd.k12.ca.us
SIC: 8351 Child day care services
PA: San Bernardino City Unified School District
    777 N F St
    San Bernardino CA 92410
    909 381-1100

(P-23782)
SAN DIEGO UNIFIED SCHOOL DST
Also Called: Kennedy Elementary School
445 S 47th St, San Diego (92113-2007)
PHONE..................................619 266-4500
Lillie McMillan, *Principal*
EMP: 80
SALES (corp-wide): 888.1MM **Privately Held**
WEB: www.sdcs.k12.ca.us
SIC: 8351 8211 Child day care services; public elementary school
PA: San Diego Unified School District
    4100 Normal St
    San Diego CA 92103
    619 725-8000

(P-23783)
SANTA CRUZ MONTESSORI SCHOOL
Also Called: Scms
6230 Soquel Dr, Aptos (95003-3118)
PHONE..................................831 476-1646
Kathleen Ann Rideout, *CEO*
EMP: 50
SALES: 6.2MM **Privately Held**
WEB: www.savmait.com
SIC: 8351 8211 Preschool center; private elementary & secondary schools; private elementary school; private junior high school

(PA)=Parent Co (HQ)=Headquarters (DH)=Div Headquarters
✿ = New Business established in last 2 years

2019 Directory of California
Wholesalers and Services Companies

PRODUCTS & SVCS

1005

(P-23784)
SANTA MONICA CITY OF
Also Called: Child Development Office, The
2802 4th St, Santa Monica (90405-4308)
PHONE..........................310 399-5865
Alice Chung, *Director*
EMP: 60 **Privately Held**
WEB: www.santamonicapd.org
SIC: 8351 Child day care services
PA: City Of Santa Monica
1685 Main St
Santa Monica CA 90401
310 458-8411

(P-23785)
SHASTA COUNTY HEAD START
CHILD (PA)
375 Lake Blvd Ste 100, Redding
(96003-2557)
PHONE..........................530 241-1036
Carla Clark, *Exec Dir*
EMP: 50
SQ FT: 5,000
SALES: 12.9MM **Privately Held**
SIC: 8351 Head start center, except in con-
junction with school

(P-23786)
SIERRA CSCADE FMLY
OPPRTNITIES (PA)
Also Called: Head Start
424 N Mill Creek Rd, Quincy (95971-9678)
PHONE..........................530 283-1242
Brenda Poteete, *Director*
EMP: 101
SQ FT: 2,600
SALES: 3.3MM **Privately Held**
SIC: 8351 Head start center, except in con-
junction with school

(P-23787)
SJB CHILD DEVELOPMENT
CENTERS (PA)
Also Called: Sick Child Care Center, The
1400 Parkmoor Ave Ste 220, San Jose
(95126-3798)
PHONE..........................408 538-0200
Victor Hassan, *CEO*
Kent Williams, *Principal*
Mylene Acosta, *Supervisor*
EMP: 110 EST: 1971
SQ FT: 12,840
SALES: 6.1MM **Privately Held**
SIC: 8351 Preschool center

(P-23788)
SOLANO FAMILY & CHLD
COUNCIL
Also Called: SOLANO FAMILY & CHIL-
DREN'S SER
421 Executive Ct N, Fairfield (94534-4019)
PHONE..........................707 863-3950
Kathryn Lago, *Exec Dir*
EMP: 74
SALES: 20.6MM **Privately Held**
WEB: www.solanosfcs.org
SIC: 8351 Child day care services

(P-23789)
SOUTH MARKET CHILD CARE
INC
790 Folsom St, San Francisco
(94107-1276)
PHONE..........................415 820-3500
Noushin Mofakham, *Director*
EMP: 54
SALES (corp-wide): 3.8MM **Privately**
Held
SIC: 8351 Montessori child development
center
PA: South Of Market Child Care, Inc.
790 Folsom St
San Francisco CA 94107
415 820-3500

(P-23790)
ST ANDREWS CHILDREN
CENTER
4400 Barranca Pkwy, Irvine (92604-4739)
PHONE..........................949 651-0198
Carolyn Jones, *Director*
EMP: 50
SALES (est): 1.4MM **Privately Held**
SIC: 8351 Preschool center

(P-23791)
STATE PRESCHOOL
Also Called: Martin Lthr Kng Chldr Ctr
950 El Pueblo Ave, Pittsburg (94565-4116)
PHONE..........................925 473-4380
Karan Latimer, *Director*
Kristin Hills, *Director*
EMP: 50
SALES (est): 354.7K **Privately Held**
SIC: 8351 Preschool center

(P-23792)
STRATFORD SCHOOL INC
220 Kensington Way, Los Gatos
(95032-4028)
PHONE..........................408 371-3020
Esperanza Hernandez, *Principal*
EMP: 53
SALES (corp-wide): 7.9MM **Privately**
Held
SIC: 8351 8211 Preschool center;
preparatory school
PA: Stratford School, Inc.
870 N California Ave
Palo Alto CA 94303
650 493-1151

(P-23793)
STRATFORD SCHOOL INC (PA)
870 N California Ave, Palo Alto
(94303-3631)
PHONE..........................650 493-1151
Matthew Wulfstat, *CEO*
Celia Schiffner, *Controller*
Rasha Barakat, *Teacher*
Todd Bickel, *Teacher*
Erin Blake, *Teacher*
EMP: 50
SALES (est): 7.9MM **Privately Held**
SIC: 8351 8211 Preschool center; private
elementary school

(P-23794)
STUDENTS OF ASSOCIATED
Also Called: Csus Children's Center
6000 J St, Sacramento (95819-2605)
PHONE..........................916 278-6216
Denise Wessels, *Director*
EMP: 80
SALES (corp-wide): 10.1MM **Privately**
Held
SIC: 8351 Child day care services
PA: Associated Students Of California State
University, Sacramento
6000 J St
Sacramento CA
916 278-7917

(P-23795)
TAFT COLLEGE CHILDREN
CENTER
29 Emmons Park Dr, Taft (93268-2317)
PHONE..........................661 763-7850
Genevieve Garcia, *Director*
Leslie Braggo, *Director*
EMP: 50
SALES (est): 853.4K **Privately Held**
SIC: 8351 Child day care services

(P-23796)
THINK TOGETHER
202 E Airport Dr Ste 200, San Bernardino
(92408-3429)
PHONE..........................909 723-1400
EMP: 503
SALES (corp-wide): 47.1MM **Privately**
Held
SIC: 8351 Child day care services
PA: Think Together
2101 E 4th St Ste 200b
Santa Ana CA 92705
714 543-3807

(P-23797)
THINK TOGETHER
800 S Barranca Ave # 120, Covina
(91723-3680)
PHONE..........................626 373-2311
Tom Lopez, *Branch Mgr*
EMP: 704
SALES (corp-wide): 47.1MM **Privately**
Held
SIC: 8351 Child day care services

PA: Think Together
2101 E 4th St Ste 200b
Santa Ana CA 92705
714 543-3807

(P-23798)
THINK TOGETHER
22620 Goldencrest Dr # 104, Moreno Valley
(92553-9032)
PHONE..........................951 571-9944
Taylor Morris, *Senior Mgr*
EMP: 503
SALES (corp-wide): 47.1MM **Privately**
Held
SIC: 8351 Child day care services
PA: Think Together
2101 E 4th St Ste 200b
Santa Ana CA 92705
714 543-3807

(P-23799)
TOM SAWYER CAMPS INC
Also Called: T.S.c
707 W Woodbury Rd Ste F, Altadena
(91001-5386)
PHONE..........................626 794-1156
Sarah Horner Fish, *CEO*
Michael H Horner, *President*
Rick Benfield, *CFO*
Sally Horner, *Vice Pres*
Guy Fish, *Exec Dir*
EMP: 120
SQ FT: 4,000
SALES (est): 5.4MM **Privately Held**
WEB: www.daycampjobs.com
SIC: 8351 Child day care services

(P-23800)
TULARE CNTY CHLD CARE
HOME EDU
7000 W Doe Ave Ste C, Visalia
(93291-8623)
PHONE..........................559 651-0247
Senaida Garcia, *Director*
EMP: 68
SALES (est): 2.6MM **Privately Held**
SIC: 8351 Head start center, except in con-
junction with school

(P-23801)
WE CARE DAY CARE & PRE
SCHOOL
Also Called: West Valley Christian Academy
1790 Sequoia Blvd, Tracy (95376-4329)
PHONE..........................209 832-4072
Tim Smith, *Administration*
EMP: 60 EST: 1996
SALES (est): 1.4MM **Privately Held**
SIC: 8351 Preschool center

(P-23802)
WEST VALLEY FAMILY YMCA
Also Called: Vanalden Ave School
18810 Vanowen St, Reseda (91335-5213)
PHONE..........................818 774-2840
Greg Koubek, *Director*
Stacy Childress, *Principal*
Shane Ruffin, *Principal*
EMP: 125
SALES (est): 2.1MM **Privately Held**
SIC: 8351 8322 Child day care services;
youth center

(P-23803)
WU YEE CHILDRENS SERVICES
880 Clay St, San Francisco (94108-1611)
PHONE..........................415 677-0100
Alyson Suzeuki, *Program Dir*
Fion Chan, *Office Admin*
Yolly Matthews, *Teacher*
Donna Dizon, *Manager*
Jenny Yu, *Manager*
EMP: 68
SALES (corp-wide): 20.4MM **Privately**
Held
WEB: www.wuyee.org
SIC: 8351 8322 Group day care center; in-
dividual & family services
PA: Wu Yee Children's Services
827 Broadway
San Francisco CA 94133
415 230-7504

(P-23804)
YESHIVA RAU ISACSOHN
ACADEMY
Also Called: Yeshivath Torath Emeth Acad-
emy
540 N La Brea Ave, Los Angeles
(90036-2016)
PHONE..........................323 549-3170
Marc Chopp, *Administration*
Charles Abbott, *Ch of Bd*
Morris Weiss, *President*
Rabbi Berish Goldenberg, *Corp Secy*
EMP: 120
SALES (est): 4MM **Privately Held**
SIC: 8351 8211 Preschool center; nursery
school; elementary school

(P-23805)
YOUNG MENS CHRSTN ASSN
OF LA
Also Called: East Valley Family YMCA Dcc
5142 Tujunga Ave, North Hollywood
(91601-3742)
PHONE..........................818 763-5126
Debbie Lozano, *Director*
EMP: 90
SQ FT: 11,260
SALES (corp-wide): 105.9MM **Privately**
Held
SIC: 8351 8322 Group day care center;
youth center
PA: Young Men's Christian Association Of
Metropolitan Los Angeles
625 S New Hampshire Ave
Los Angeles CA 90005
213 380-6448

(P-23806)
YOUNG MNS CHRSTN ASSN OF
E BAY
Also Called: Y M C A
2241 Russell St, Berkeley (94705-1029)
PHONE..........................510 644-6290
Fran Gallati, *President*
EMP: 2381
SALES (corp-wide): 27.5MM **Privately**
Held
SIC: 8351 Child day care services
PA: Young Men's Christian Association Of
The East Bay
2330 Broadway
Oakland CA 94612
510 549-4515

8361 Residential Care

(P-23807)
ABILTY FIRST
3770 E Willow St, Long Beach
(90815-1731)
PHONE..........................562 426-6161
Lori Ganbmi, *President*
EMP: 60
SALES (est): 605K **Privately Held**
SIC: 8361 Residential care

(P-23808)
ADVENT GROUP MINISTRIES
INC
90 Great Oaks Blvd # 108, San Jose
(95119-1314)
PHONE..........................408 281-0708
Jeff Davis, *Ch of Bd*
Mark Miller, *Exec Dir*
EMP: 63
SQ FT: 4,400
SALES: 4.4MM **Privately Held**
WEB: www.adventgm.com
SIC: 8361 Children's home

(P-23809)
AEGIS ASSSTED LIVING PRPTS
LLC
Also Called: Aegis of Fremont
3850 Walnut Ave 228, Fremont
(94538-2263)
PHONE..........................510 739-1515
Dave Peper, *General Mgr*
Barb Wilson, *Nurse*
EMP: 50
SALES (corp-wide): 102MM **Privately**
Held
SIC: 8361 Residential care

HQ: Aegis Assisted Living Properties, Llc
220 Concourse Blvd
Santa Rosa CA 95403
707 535-3200

(P-23810)
AEGIS ASSSTED LIVING PRPTS LLC
Also Called: Aegis At Shadowridge
1440 S Melrose Dr, Oceanside (92056-5394)
PHONE...................................760 806-3600
Gregory Case, *Manager*
EMP: 65
SALES (corp-wide): 102MM **Privately Held**
SIC: **8361** Home for the aged
HQ: Aegis Assisted Living Properties, Llc
220 Concourse Blvd
Santa Rosa CA 95403
707 535-3200

(P-23811)
AEGIS OF CARMICHAEL
4050 Walnut Ave, Carmichael (95608-1600)
PHONE...................................916 972-1313
Dwane Clark, *President*
Jerry Myer, *COO*
EMP: 60 EST: 1999
SALES (est): 2.1MM **Privately Held**
SIC: **8361** Home for the aged

(P-23812)
AEGIS SENIOR COMMUNITIES LLC
Also Called: Aegis of Laguna Niguel
32170 Niguel Rd, Laguna Niguel (92677-4264)
PHONE...................................949 496-8080
Pamela Kerr, *Exec Dir*
Becky Spencer, *Info Tech Mgr*
EMP: 50
SALES (corp-wide): 102MM **Privately Held**
WEB: www.aegisal.com
SIC: **8361** Residential care
PA: Senior Aegis Communities Llc
415 118th Ave Se
Bellevue WA 98005

(P-23813)
AEGIS SENIOR COMMUNITIES LLC
Also Called: Aegis Assisted Living
4050 Walnut Ave, Carmichael (95608-1600)
PHONE...................................916 972-1313
Terry Ervin, *Branch Mgr*
Angie Snyder, *Chief Mktg Ofcr*
Tom Laborde, *Officer*
Sandra Preyale, *Officer*
EMP: 328
SALES (corp-wide): 102MM **Privately Held**
SIC: **8361** Residential care
PA: Senior Aegis Communities Llc
415 118th Ave Se
Bellevue WA 98005

(P-23814)
AGEIS LIVING
Also Called: Aegis of San Francisco
2280 Gellert Blvd, South San Francisco (94080-5411)
PHONE...................................650 952-6100
Wayne Clark, *President*
Charles Stevenson, *Exec Dir*
EMP: 50 EST: 2010
SALES (est): 808.6K **Privately Held**
SIC: **8361** Residential care

(P-23815)
ALLEN SPEES FAMILY HOMES
524 W Roberts Ave, Fresno (93704-1832)
PHONE...................................559 432-3664
Sue Allen, *Partner*
Terry Spees, *Partner*
EMP: 50
SALES (est): 1.3MM **Privately Held**
SIC: **8361** Home for the aged

(P-23816)
ALTCARE CEDAR CREEK LLC
Also Called: Cedar Creek Alzhimers Dementia
868 Ensenada Ave, Berkeley (94707-1850)
PHONE...................................510 527-7282
Terry Carson, *CEO*
Cole Smith,
EMP: 55
SALES (est): 975.3K **Privately Held**
SIC: **8361** Residential care

(P-23817)
AMERICAN BAPTIST HOMES OF WEST
Also Called: San Joaquin Gardens
5555 N Fresno St, Fresno (93710-6006)
PHONE...................................559 439-4770
Keli Swales, *Branch Mgr*
Binder Singh, *Nursing Dir*
EMP: 203
SALES (corp-wide): 21.8MM **Privately Held**
WEB: www.abhow.com
SIC: **8361** 8051 Home for the aged; skilled nursing care facilities
HQ: American Baptist Homes Of The West
6120 Stoneridge Mall Rd # 300
Pleasanton CA 94588
925 924-7100

(P-23818)
AMERICAN BAPTIST HOMES OF WEST
Also Called: Piedmont Gardens
110 41st St Ofc, Oakland (94611-5219)
PHONE...................................510 654-7172
Reginald Nyles, *Branch Mgr*
Timi Tessaro, *Records Dir*
Roxann King, *Education*
Jeremy Thomas, *Food Svc Dir*
Tony Hobbs, *Director*
EMP: 220
SALES (corp-wide): 21.8MM **Privately Held**
WEB: www.abhow.com
SIC: **8361** Home for the aged
HQ: American Baptist Homes Of The West
6120 Stoneridge Mall Rd # 300
Pleasanton CA 94588
925 924-7100

(P-23819)
AMERICAN BAPTIST HOMES OF WEST (HQ)
6120 Stoneridge Mall Rd # 300, Pleasanton (94588-3298)
PHONE...................................925 924-7100
David B Ferguson, *CEO*
Christopher A Vito, *President*
Randy Stamper, *Chairman*
Sloan Bentley, *Senior VP*
Terese Farkas, *Senior VP*
EMP: 60 EST: 1955
SQ FT: 26,000
SALES: 162.1MM
SALES (corp-wide): 21.8MM **Privately Held**
WEB: www.abhow.com
SIC: **8361** Residential care
PA: Humangood
6120 Stoneridge Mall Rd
Pleasanton CA 94588
602 906-4024

(P-23820)
ANGEL VIEW INC
Also Called: Angel View Resale Store
454 N Indian Canyon Dr, Palm Springs (92262-6018)
PHONE...................................760 322-2440
Tracy Powers, *General Mgr*
EMP: 50
SALES (corp-wide): 24.9MM **Privately Held**
SIC: **8361** Rehabilitation center, residential: health care incidental
PA: Angel View, Inc.
12379 Miracle Hill Rd
Desert Hot Springs CA 92234
760 329-6471

(P-23821)
ARC INDUSTRIES
5143 Cochran St Ste 93063, Simi Valley (93063-3064)
PHONE...................................805 520-0399
Larry Rice, *Manager*
EMP: 57
SALES (est): 618.7K **Privately Held**
SIC: **8361** Rehabilitation center, residential: health care incidental

(P-23822)
ARDCORE SENIOR LIVING
Also Called: Canyon Hills Club
525 S Anaheim Hills Rd, Anaheim (92807-4721)
PHONE...................................714 974-2226
J Bert Sprenger, *Manager*
EMP: 70
SALES (est): 1.8MM **Privately Held**
SIC: **8361** 6513 Home for the aged; apartment building operators
PA: Obayashi Corporation
2-15-2, Konan
Minato-Ku TKY 108-0

(P-23823)
ASPIRANET
Also Called: Sunset Neighborhood Beacon Ctr
3925 Noriega St, San Francisco (94122-3935)
PHONE...................................415 759-3690
Ruby LI, *Manager*
Melissa Maher, *Partner*
Jeff Rosenplot, *Comms Dir*
John Gardner, *Admin Sec*
Aaron Leiderman,
EMP: 56
SALES (corp-wide): 59MM **Privately Held**
WEB: www.verosantes.com
SIC: **8361** 8322 Residential care; individual & family services
PA: Aspiranet
400 Oyster Point Blvd # 501
South San Francisco CA 94080
650 866-4080

(P-23824)
ATRIA SENIOR LIVING INC
Also Called: Atria Park Pacific Palisades
15441 W Sunset Blvd, Pacific Palisades (90272-3525)
PHONE...................................310 573-9545
Elisa Brown, *Director*
Krav Maga, *Manager*
EMP: 60
SQ FT: 27,513
SALES (corp-wide): 3.7B **Publicly Held**
WEB: www.sunrise.com
SIC: **8361** Residential care
HQ: Atria Senior Living Inc.
300 E Market St Ste 100
Louisville KY 40202

(P-23825)
ATRIA SENIOR LIVING INC
Also Called: Villa Las Posas
24 Las Posas Rd, Camarillo (93010-2780)
PHONE...................................805 482-9771
Cyntia Drachenberg, *Director*
June Anilao, *Maintenance Dir*
Angela Mafioli, *Hlthcr Dir*
Sarah Dodd, *Director*
Colleen McCutchan, *Director*
EMP: 63
SALES (corp-wide): 3.7B **Publicly Held**
WEB: www.atriacom.com
SIC: **8361** Home for the aged
HQ: Atria Senior Living Inc.
300 E Market St Ste 100
Louisville KY 40202

(P-23826)
ATRIA SENIOR LIVING INC
Also Called: Chateau San Juan
32353 San Juan Creek Rd, San Juan Capistrano (92675-4254)
PHONE...................................949 661-1220
Del Woytek, *Manager*
George Gonzalez, *Food Svc Dir*
Laura Garcia, *Director*

(P-23827)
ATRIA SENIOR LIVING INC
Also Called: Willow Glen Villa
1660 Gaton Dr Ofc, San Jose (95125-4599)
PHONE...................................408 266-1660
Laurie Becker, *Exec Dir*
Jett Cabuena, *Nursing Dir*
EMP: 63
SALES (corp-wide): 3.7B **Publicly Held**
WEB: www.atriacom.com
SIC: **8361** Residential care
HQ: Atria Senior Living Inc.
300 E Market St Ste 100
Louisville KY 40202

(P-23828)
ATRIA SENIOR LIVING INC
Also Called: Tamalpais Creek
853 Tamalpais Ave Ofc, Novato (94947-3052)
PHONE...................................415 892-0944
Jason Englehorn, *Exec Dir*
EMP: 50
SALES (corp-wide): 3.7B **Publicly Held**
WEB: www.atriacom.com
SIC: **8361** Home for the aged
HQ: Atria Senior Living Inc.
300 E Market St Ste 100
Louisville KY 40202

(P-23829)
ATRIA SENIOR LIVING INC
Also Called: El Camino Gardens
2426 Garfield Ave Ofc, Carmichael (95608-5199)
PHONE...................................916 488-5722
Maryann Peterson, *Director*
Ingrid Weber, *Director*
EMP: 70
SALES (corp-wide): 3.7B **Publicly Held**
WEB: www.atriacom.com
SIC: **8361** Residential care
HQ: Atria Senior Living Inc.
300 E Market St Ste 100
Louisville KY 40202

(P-23830)
ATRIA SENIOR LIVING INC
44600 Monterey Ave Ofc, Palm Desert (92260-3328)
PHONE...................................760 341-0890
Jim Dunning, *Exec Dir*
James Dunning, *Director*
EMP: 75
SALES (corp-wide): 3.7B **Publicly Held**
WEB: www.atriacom.com
SIC: **8361** Home for the aged
HQ: Atria Senior Living Inc.
300 E Market St Ste 100
Louisville KY 40202

(P-23831)
AVALON A CERRITOS
11000 New Falcon Way Ofc # 177, Cerritos (90703-1553)
PHONE...................................562 865-9500
Laura Trujillo, *Director*
EMP: 50
SALES (est): 2.5MM **Privately Held**
SIC: **8361** Residential care

(P-23832)
AVALON AT NEWPORT LLC
Also Called: Avalon At Newport Beach
393 Hospital Rd, Newport Beach (92663-3501)
PHONE...................................949 631-3555
Fran Lacas, *Administration*
EMP: 93
SQ FT: 4,562

EMP: 109
SALES (corp-wide): 3.7B **Publicly Held**
WEB: www.atriacom.com
SIC: **8361** Home for the aged
HQ: Atria Senior Living Inc.
300 E Market St Ste 100
Louisville KY 40202

SALES (corp-wide): 4.2MM **Privately Held**
SIC: 8361 Residential care
PA: Avalon At Newport, Llc
23 Corporate Plaza Dr # 190
Newport Beach CA 92660
949 719-4082

(P-23833)
AVALON GOLDEN GATE LLC
Also Called: Vintage Golden Gate
1601 19th Ave Apt 122, San Francisco
(94122-3469)
PHONE...................................415 664-6264
Eric K Davidson, *Principal*
Vicki R Clark,
Brian J Flornes,
EMP: 77
SALES (est): 4.8MM **Privately Held**
SIC: 8361 Home for the aged

(P-23834)
BAKER PLACES INC (PA)
170 9th St, San Francisco (94103-2603)
PHONE...................................415 864-4655
Jonathan Vernick, *President*
Judith Stevenson, *CFO*
John Fostel, *Officer*
Yolanda McDaniel, *Office Mgr*
Brian Couture, *Program Dir*
EMP: 200 **EST:** 1969
SALES: 15MM **Privately Held**
SIC: 8361 Halfway group home, persons
with social or personal problems

(P-23835)
BETHESDA LTHRAN CMMUNITIES INC
5440 W Wren Ave, Visalia (93291-9142)
PHONE...................................559 636-6300
EMP: 57
SALES (corp-wide): 126.8MM **Privately Held**
SIC: 8361 Home for destitute men &
women
PA: Bethesda Lutheran Communities, Inc.
600 Hoffmann Dr
Watertown WI 53094
920 261-3050

(P-23836)
BEYER PARK VILLAS LLC
3529 Forest Glenn Dr, Modesto
(95355-1360)
PHONE...................................209 236-1900
Bill Schilz, *Managing Prtnr*
Clarence Becker,
Donald Cefaloni,
Harold Johnson,
Nicole Rodriguez,
EMP: 75
SQ FT: 59,000
SALES (est): 3.2MM **Privately Held**
SIC: 8361 Home for the aged

(P-23837)
BHO LLC
5801 Sun Lakes Blvd, Banning
(92220-6507)
PHONE...................................951 845-2220
Terry Raisio,
EMP: 50
SALES (est): 973K **Privately Held**
SIC: 8361 Geriatric residential care

(P-23838)
BOYS REPUBLIC (PA)
Also Called: Girls Republic
1907 Boys Republic Dr, Chino Hills
(91709-5447)
PHONE...................................909 902-6690
Dennis Slattery, *CEO*
Timothy J Kay, *President*
Robert Key, *Vice Pres*
Jeff Seymour, *Vice Pres*
Nadine Bosen, *Admin Sec*
EMP: 150
SQ FT: 173,000
SALES: 13.2MM **Privately Held**
SIC: 8361 Group foster home

(P-23839)
BRETHREN HILLCREST HOMES
2705 Mountain View Dr Ofc, La Verne
(91750-4398)
PHONE...................................909 593-4917

Matthew Neeley, *President*
Barbara Feliciano, *CFO*
Mathew Neeley, *Vice Pres*
Scott Frederick, *Human Res Dir*
Mike Townsend, *Mktg Dir*
EMP: 230
SQ FT: 34,000
SALES: 26.7MM **Privately Held**
WEB: www.livingathillcrest.org
SIC: 8361 8059 8051 Rest home, with
health care incidental; nursing home, ex-
cept skilled & intermediate care facility;
extended care facility

(P-23840)
BRITTANY HOUSE LLC
5401 E Centralia St, Long Beach
(90808-1452)
PHONE...................................562 421-4717
Colleen Rosatti, *Exec Dir*
EMP: 100
SQ FT: 43,018
SALES (est): 3.2MM
SALES (corp-wide): 35.4MM **Privately Held**
WEB: www.healthcaregrp.com
SIC: 8361 Home for the aged
PA: Activcare Living, Inc.
10603 Rancho Bernardo Rd
San Diego CA 92127
858 565-4424

(P-23841)
BROOKDALE LVING CMMUNITIES INC
Also Called: Atrium of San Jose
1009 Blossom River Way, San Jose
(95123-6304)
PHONE...................................408 445-7770
Michele Merritt, *Exec Dir*
Cynthia King, *Vice Pres*
EMP: 110
SALES (corp-wide): 4.5B **Publicly Held**
WEB: www.parkplace-spokane.com
SIC: 8361 Geriatric residential care
HQ: Brookdale Living Communities, Inc.
515 N State St Ste 1750
Chicago IL 60654

(P-23842)
BURLINGAME SENIOR CARE LLC
Also Called: Burlingame Skilled Nursing
1100 Trousdale Dr, Burlingame
(94010-3207)
PHONE...................................650 692-3758
Marcus Weenig, *CFO*
EMP: 300
SALES (est): 4.9MM **Privately Held**
SIC: 8361 Residential care

(P-23843)
CAL SOUTHERN PRESBT HOMES
Also Called: White Sands of La Jolla Clinic
7450 Olivetas Ave Ofc, La Jolla
(92037-4900)
PHONE...................................858 454-4201
Wendy Matalon, *Branch Mgr*
EMP: 165
SALES (corp-wide): 101.5MM **Privately Held**
WEB: www.scths.com
SIC: 8361 8051 Home for the aged; skilled
nursing care facilities
PA: Southern California Presbyterian
Homes
516 Burchett St
Glendale CA 91203
818 247-0420

(P-23844)
CAL SOUTHERN PRESBT HOMES
Also Called: Redwood Senior Homes & Svcs
710 W 13th Ave, Escondido (92025-5511)
PHONE...................................760 747-4306
Gary Boriero, *Manager*
EMP: 161
SQ FT: 8,552
SALES (corp-wide): 101.5MM **Privately Held**
WEB: www.scths.com
SIC: 8361 Home for the aged

PA: Southern California Presbyterian
Homes
516 Burchett St
Glendale CA 91203
818 247-0420

(P-23845)
CAL SOUTHERN PRESBT HOMES
Also Called: Redwood Town Court
500 E Valley Pkwy Ofc, Escondido
(92025-3073)
PHONE...................................760 737-5110
Les Curtis, *Manager*
EMP: 89
SALES (corp-wide): 101.5MM **Privately Held**
WEB: www.scths.com
SIC: 8361 Home for the aged
PA: Southern California Presbyterian
Homes
516 Burchett St
Glendale CA 91203
818 247-0420

(P-23846)
CALIFORNIA FRIENDS HOMES
Also Called: QUAKER GARDENS
12151 Dale Ave, Stanton (90680-3889)
PHONE...................................714 530-9100
Randy Brown, *CEO*
Gina Kolb, *Exec Dir*
Glenda Hementiza, *Managing Dir*
EMP: 315
SQ FT: 10,000
SALES: 16.4MM **Privately Held**
WEB: www.quakergardens.com
SIC: 8361 8051 Home for the aged; con-
valescent home with continuous nursing
care

(P-23847)
CALIFORNIA PEO HOME
Also Called: MARGUERITE GARDENS
849 Foothill Blvd Ste 8, La Canada
Flintridge (91011-3368)
PHONE...................................626 300-0400
Bessie Ang, *Principal*
Lenita Castillo, *Nursing Dir*
Johee Lee, *Manager*
Joohee Lee, *Manager*
Debra Mecka, *Manager*
EMP: 95
SQ FT: 77,343
SALES: 761.5K **Privately Held**
SIC: 8361 Home for the aged

(P-23848)
CARE ASSOCIATES INC
Also Called: Helen Evans Home For Children
15125 Gale Ave, Hacienda Heights
(91745-1407)
PHONE...................................626 330-4048
Paula De Lisio, *President*
EMP: 60 **EST:** 1998
SQ FT: 9,698
SALES: 2.7MM **Privately Held**
SIC: 8361 Children's home; home for the
mentally retarded

(P-23849)
CARLTON SENIOR LIVING INC
380 Branham Ln Ofc Ofc, San Jose
(95136-4302)
PHONE...................................408 972-1400
Mandi Farrell, *Director*
EMP: 111
SALES (corp-wide): 29.6MM **Privately Held**
SIC: 8361 Residential care
PA: Senior Carlton Living Inc
4005 Port Chicago Hwy # 120
Concord CA 94520
925 338-2434

(P-23850)
CARLTON SENIOR LIVING INC
1075 Fulton Ave, Sacramento
(95825-4275)
PHONE...................................916 971-4800
Timothy Macdonald, *Branch Mgr*
EMP: 111

SALES (corp-wide): 29.6MM **Privately Held**
SIC: 8361 8052 8051 Residential care; intermediate care facilities; skilled nursing
care facilities
PA: Senior Carlton Living Inc
4005 Port Chicago Hwy # 120
Concord CA 94520
925 338-2434

(P-23851)
CARSON SENIOR ASSISTED LIVING
345 E Carson St, Carson (90745-2709)
PHONE...................................310 830-4010
Fax: 310 830-0264
EMP: 75
SALES (est): 3.3MM **Privately Held**
SIC: 8361

(P-23852)
CASA DE AMPARO (PA)
325 Buena Creek Rd, San Marcos
(92069-9679)
PHONE...................................760 754-5500
Sharon Delphenich, *Exec Dir*
Debbie Slattery, *Treasurer*
Mary Alice Cedrone, *Controller*
Lili Chen, *Controller*
Tamara Fleck-Myers, *Director*
EMP: 74
SQ FT: 25,000
SALES: 9.7MM **Privately Held**
WEB: www.casadeamparo.org
SIC: 8361 8351 Residential care; child
day care services

(P-23853)
CASA DE LAS CAMPANAS INC (PA)
18655 W Bernardo Dr, San Diego
(92127-3099)
PHONE...................................858 451-9152
Jill Sorenson, *Exec Dir*
Kathy Frederick, *Vice Chairman*
David Johnson, *CFO*
Robert L Reeves, *Chairman*
Maria Rivera, *Officer*
EMP: 107
SQ FT: 709,627
SALES: 38.9MM **Privately Held**
SIC: 8361 8052 8051 6513 Home for the
aged; intermediate care facilities; skilled
nursing care facilities; apartment building
operators

(P-23854)
CASA-PACIFICA INC
Also Called: Freedom Properties
2200 W Acacia Ave Ofc, Hemet
(92545-3737)
PHONE...................................951 658-3369
Mary Ann Casino, *Director*
EMP: 300
SALES (corp-wide): 18.7MM **Privately Held**
WEB: www.fmcwest.com
SIC: 8361 8059 Geriatric residential care;
rest home, with health care
PA: Casa-Pacifica, Inc
23442 El Toro Rd
San Juan Capistrano CA 92675
949 489-0430

(P-23855)
CASA-PACIFICA INC
Also Called: Freedom Properties Village
2400 W Acacia Ave, Hemet (92545-3743)
PHONE...................................951 766-5116
Valeria Machain, *General Mgr*
Maricela Zambrano, *Records Dir*
EMP: 100
SALES (corp-wide): 18.7MM **Privately Held**
WEB: www.fmcwest.com
SIC: 8361 8052 8051 6513 Home for the
aged; intermediate care facilities; skilled
nursing care facilities; apartment building
operators
PA: Casa-Pacifica, Inc
23442 El Toro Rd
San Juan Capistrano CA 92675
949 489-0430

(P-23856)
CASABLANCA ALZHEIMERS RESID
Also Called: Casablanca Alzheimer's Care
158 Rockaway Rd, Oak View (93022-9306)
PHONE..................................805 649-5143
Nilson Froula, *President*
Laurie Froula, *Partner*
EMP: 60
SQ FT: 12,000
SALES (est): 2.8MM **Privately Held**
SIC: 8361 Rest home, with health care incidental

(P-23857)
CENTINELA VALLEY CARE CENTER
950 S Flower St, Inglewood (90301-4186)
PHONE..................................310 674-3216
William A Nelson, *President*
EMP: 200
SALES (est): 5MM **Privately Held**
SIC: 8361 8059 Home for the aged; convalescent home

(P-23858)
CENTRAL CAL NIKKEI FOUNDATION
Also Called: VINTAGE GARDENS
540 S Peach Ave, Fresno (93727-3957)
PHONE..................................559 237-4006
Melvin K Renge, *President*
Louis Gebbia, *Exec Dir*
EMP: 52 **EST:** 1989
SALES: 2.9MM **Privately Held**
SIC: 8361 Residential care

(P-23859)
CHAMBERLAINS CHILDREN CTR INC
1850 Cienega Rd, Hollister (95023-5516)
P.O. Box 1269 (95024-1269)
PHONE..................................831 636-2121
Robert Freiri, *Exec Dir*
Sarah Garvin, *Office Mgr*
EMP: 60
SALES: 2.9MM **Privately Held**
WEB: www.chamberlaincc.org
SIC: 8361 Residential care for children

(P-23860)
CHARLEE FAMILY CARE
136 E Sixth St, Beaumont (92223-2146)
PHONE..................................951 845-3588
Richard E Rios, *Principal*
EMP: 79
SALES (est): 3.4MM **Privately Held**
SIC: 8361 Residential care

(P-23861)
CHILDHELP INC
Also Called: Child Help Head Start Center
14700 Manzanita Rd, Beaumont
(92223-3026)
P.O. Box 247 (92223-0247)
PHONE..................................951 845-6737
Klara Pakozdi, *Manager*
Diana Correa, *Exec Dir*
EMP: 165
SALES (corp-wide): 36.6MM **Privately Held**
WEB: www.childhelpusa.com
SIC: 8361 Children's home
PA: Childhelp, Inc.
4350 E Camelback Rd F250
Phoenix AZ 85018
480 922-8212

(P-23862)
CHILDNET YOUTH & FMLY SVCS INC
Also Called: Behavioral Health Svcs Dept
5150 E Pacific Cst Hwy # 100, Long Beach
(90804-3312)
PHONE..................................562 492-9983
Cathy Hughes, *CEO*
EMP: 65
SALES (corp-wide): 23.8MM **Privately Held**
WEB: www.childnet.net
SIC: 8361 8322 Juvenile correctional facilities; family counseling services

PA: Childnet Youth And Family Services, Inc.
4155 Outer Traffic Cir
Long Beach CA 90804
562 498-5500

(P-23863)
CHILDRENS HOME OF STOCKTON
430 N Pilgrim St, Stockton (95205-4428)
PHONE..................................209 466-0853
Michael Dutra, *Principal*
EMP: 90
SQ FT: 10,000
SALES: 8.3MM **Privately Held**
WEB: www.chsstk.com
SIC: 8361 8211 Children's home; private combined elementary & secondary school

(P-23864)
CHILDRENS HOMES SOUTHERN CAL (PA)
22455 Victory Blvd, West Hills
(91307-3729)
PHONE..................................818 592-2960
J Marquez, *Exec Dir*
Jorge Marquez, *Exec Dir*
Michelle Villacorte, *Director*
EMP: 50
SALES: 4MM **Privately Held**
SIC: 8361 Home for the emotionally disturbed

(P-23865)
CHILDRENS RECVG HM SACRAMENTO
3555 Auburn Blvd, Sacramento
(95821-2071)
PHONE..................................916 482-2370
David Ballard, *CEO*
Rich Bryan, *CFO*
Patricia Santiago, *Manager*
Stephanie Kvasager, *Supervisor*
EMP: 160
SQ FT: 26,000
SALES: 10.5MM **Privately Held**
WEB: www.crhkids.org
SIC: 8361 Children's home

(P-23866)
CHURCH OF VLY RTRMENT HMES INC
Also Called: VALLEY VILLAGE
390 N Winchester Blvd, Santa Clara
(95050-6563)
PHONE..................................408 241-7750
Martha Ayala, *President*
EMP: 52
SALES: 5.2MM **Privately Held**
SIC: 8361 Home for the aged

(P-23867)
CLAREMONT HOUSE INCORPORATED
Also Called: Claremont Retirement MGT
4500 Gilbert St, Oakland (94611-4657)
PHONE..................................510 658-9266
Douglas R Gill, *President*
Justin Gill, *Exec Dir*
EMP: 75
SALES: 6MM **Privately Held**
SIC: 8361 Home for the aged

(P-23868)
CLIFF VIEW TERRACE INC
Also Called: Mission Terrace
623 W Junipero St, Santa Barbara
(93105-4213)
PHONE..................................805 682-7443
Eve Murphy, *Manager*
EMP: 100
SALES (corp-wide): 13MM **Privately Held**
SIC: 8361 8051 Home for the aged; convalescent home with continuous nursing care
PA: Cliff View Terrace Inc
1020 Cliff Dr
Santa Barbara CA 93109
805 963-7556

(P-23869)
COLLWOOD TER STELLAR CARE INC
4518 54th St, San Diego (92115-3527)
PHONE..................................619 287-2920
Chris Cho, *President*
Barbara Moore, *Business Dir*
Annelie Damasco, *Director*
Rachel Robinson, *Director*
Amelia Fowler, *Receptionist*
EMP: 90
SALES (est): 4.1MM **Privately Held**
SIC: 8361 Residential care

(P-23870)
COMMUNITY HOUSING INC
Also Called: Lytton Garden II
437 Webster St, Palo Alto (94301-1242)
PHONE..................................650 328-3300
Gery Yearout, *President*
Jonathan Casey, *Vice Pres*
EMP: 50
SALES (est): 7.3MM **Privately Held**
SIC: 8361 Home for the aged

(P-23871)
CONGREGATION OF POOR SISTERS
Also Called: Nazareth House
2121 N 1st St, Fresno (93703-2301)
PHONE..................................559 237-3444
Sister Rose, *Director*
Kevin Nguyen, *Director*
EMP: 84
SQ FT: 58,644
SALES (corp-wide): 4.2MM **Privately Held**
SIC: 8361 Home for the aged
PA: Nazareth House
169-175 Hammersmith Road
London W6 8D
-

(P-23872)
CONTRA COSTA ARC
Also Called: Commercial Support Services
1420 Regatta Blvd, Richmond
(94804-4579)
PHONE..................................510 233-7303
Betty Jo Dubois, *Director*
EMP: 90
SALES (corp-wide): 19.2MM **Privately Held**
WEB: www.ccarealtors.com
SIC: 8361 Home for the mentally retarded
PA: Contra Costa Arc
1340 Arnold Dr Ste 127
Martinez CA 94553
925 646-4690

(P-23873)
CORECARE I I I
Also Called: Morningside of Fullerton
800 Morningside Dr, Fullerton
(92835-3597)
PHONE..................................714 256-8000
Carl Wilkins, *Administration*
EMP: 130
SQ FT: 24,000
SALES (est): 6.9MM **Privately Held**
WEB: www.msfpv.com
SIC: 8361 8052 Home for the aged; intermediate care facilities

(P-23874)
COUNSELING AND RESEARCH ASSOC (PA)
Also Called: MASADA HOMES
108 W Victoria St, Gardena (90248-3523)
P.O. Box 47001 (90247-6801)
PHONE..................................310 715-2020
George Igi, *Exec Dir*
Bernard Smith, *COO*
Staci Boehle, *Program Dir*
John McCullough, *Director*
Patrick Imamura, *Case Mgr*
EMP: 220
SQ FT: 2,500
SALES: 15.9MM **Privately Held**
SIC: 8361 Children's home

(P-23875)
COUNSELING AND RESEARCH ASSOC
Also Called: Masada Homes Foster Fmly Agcy
314 E Avenue K4, Lancaster (93535-4689)
PHONE..................................661 726-5500
Rick Colman, *Branch Mgr*
EMP: 74
SALES (corp-wide): 15.9MM **Privately Held**
SIC: 8361 Children's home
PA: Counseling And Research Associates
108 W Victoria St
Gardena CA 90248
310 715-2020

(P-23876)
COUNTY OF LOS ANGELES
1605 Eastlake Ave, Los Angeles
(90033-1009)
PHONE..................................323 226-8611
Richard Shumsky, *Manager*
Nazo Wahab, *Psychologist*
EMP: 62 **Privately Held**
WEB: www.co.la.ca.us
SIC: 8361 9111 Juvenile correctional facilities; executive offices
PA: County Of Los Angeles
500 W Temple St Ste 437
Los Angeles CA 90012
213 974-1101

(P-23877)
COUNTY OF LOS ANGELES
Also Called: San Fernando Juvenile Hall
16350 Filbert St, Sylmar (91342-1002)
PHONE..................................818 364-2011
Dan Torres, *Superintendent*
EMP: 69 **Privately Held**
WEB: www.co.la.ca.us
SIC: 8361 9223 8093 Juvenile correctional home; correctional institutions; mental health clinic, outpatient
PA: County Of Los Angeles
500 W Temple St Ste 437
Los Angeles CA 90012
213 974-1101

(P-23878)
COUNTY OF LOS ANGELES
4024 Durfee Ave Rm 225, El Monte
(91732-2510)
PHONE..................................626 455-4700
Michael Mills, *Manager*
EMP: 62 **Privately Held**
WEB: www.co.la.ca.us
SIC: 8361 9111 Juvenile correctional home; county supervisors' & executives' offices
PA: County Of Los Angeles
500 W Temple St Ste 437
Los Angeles CA 90012
213 974-1101

(P-23879)
COUNTY OF RIVERSIDE
Also Called: Juvenile Hall
47 665 Oasis St, Indio (92201)
PHONE..................................760 863-7600
Rick Quinata, *Director*
EMP: 100 **Privately Held**
SIC: 8361 9441 Juvenile correctional home; administration of social & manpower programs;
PA: County Of Riverside
4080 Lemon St Fl 11
Riverside CA 92501
951 955-1110

(P-23880)
COUNTY OF SAN BERNARDINO
Also Called: Children Services
860 E Gilbert St, San Bernardino
(92415-0002)
PHONE..................................909 387-0535
Allyson Williams, *Manager*
EMP: 60 **Privately Held**
SIC: 8361 9441 Juvenile correctional facilities; rest home, with health care incidental; administration of social & manpower programs
PA: County Of San Bernardino
385 N Arrowhead Ave
San Bernardino CA 92415
909 387-3841

(P-23881)
COUNTY OF STANISLAUS
Stanislaus Cnty Probation Dept
2215 Blue Gum Ave, Modesto
(95358-1052)
PHONE..............................209 525-5400
Linda Duffy, *Director*
Vicki Martin, *Mktg Dir*
Leslie Buckley, *Nurse*
Debra Boggs, *Consultant*
EMP: 250 **Privately Held**
WEB: www.co.stanislaus.ca.us
SIC: 8361 Juvenile correctional facilities
PA: County Of Stanislaus
1010 10th St Ste 5100
Modesto CA 95354
209 525-6398

(P-23882)
COURTYARDS AT PINE CREEK INC
1081 Mohr Ln, Concord (94518-3757)
PHONE..............................925 798-3900
Patricia Mead, *Exec Dir*
Kirt Hamburg, *President*
EMP: 50
SALES (est): 2.2MM **Privately Held**
SIC: 8361 Residential care

(P-23883)
COVENANT HOUSE CALIFORNIA
Also Called: Chc
1325 N Western Ave, Los Angeles
(90027-5615)
PHONE..............................323 461-3131
Luz Juan, *CEO*
AMI Rowland, *COO*
David Weaver, *CFO*
Jillian Robinson, *Officer*
Alana Weinroth, *Officer*
EMP: 150
SQ FT: 16,000
SALES: 10.3MM **Privately Held**
WEB: www.covenanthousecalifornia.net
SIC: 8361 Children's home

(P-23884)
COVENANT RTIREMENT COMMUNITIES
Also Called: Covenant Village of Turlock
2125 N Olive Ave Ofc, Turlock
(95382-1947)
PHONE..............................209 632-9976
Dwayne Gabrielson, *Administration*
EMP: 130
SALES (corp-wide): 4.3MM **Privately Held**
SIC: 8361 8052 8051 Rest home, with health care incidental; intermediate care facilities; skilled nursing care facilities
HQ: Covenant Retirement Communities
5700 Old Orchard Rd # 100
Skokie IL 60077

(P-23885)
COVIA COMMUNITIES
Also Called: St Paul's Towers
100 Bay Pl Ofc, Oakland (94610-4422)
PHONE..............................510 835-4700
Christopher Iechien, *Exec Dir*
Tristan Piper, *Hlthcr Dir*
Rob Anzilotti, *Director*
EMP: 180
SALES (corp-wide): 146.5MM **Privately Held**
SIC: 8361 8052 8051 Home for the aged; intermediate care facilities; skilled nursing care facilities
PA: Covia Communities
2185 N Calif Blvd Ste 215
Walnut Creek CA 94596
925 956-7400

(P-23886)
COVIA COMMUNITIES
Also Called: Canterbury Woods
651 Sinex Ave, Pacific Grove (93950-4253)
PHONE..............................831 373-3111
Norma Brenbella, *Director*
Stella McNish, *Human Res Dir*
Rowena Perez, *Education*
Tammy Brooks, *Hlthcr Dir*
Geozen Snaer, *Director*

EMP: 90
SALES (corp-wide): 146.5MM **Privately Held**
SIC: 8361 Home for the aged
PA: Covia Communities
2185 N Calif Blvd Ste 215
Walnut Creek CA 94596
925 956-7400

(P-23887)
COVIA COMMUNITIES
Also Called: Spring Lake Village
5555 Montgomery Dr, Santa Rosa
(95409-8846)
P.O. Box 1105, Boyes Hot Springs (95416-1105)
PHONE..............................707 538-8400
Sharon York, *Exec Dir*
Renee Hayward, *Social Dir*
Sharon Eldridge, *Administration*
EMP: 300
SALES (corp-wide): 146.5MM **Privately Held**
SIC: 8361 6531 8052 8051 Home for the aged; real estate managers; intermediate care facilities; skilled nursing care facilities
PA: Covia Communities
2185 N Calif Blvd Ste 215
Walnut Creek CA 94596
925 956-7400

(P-23888)
COVIA COMMUNITIES
Also Called: San Francisco Towers
1661 Pine St Apt 911, San Francisco
(94109-0410)
PHONE..............................415 776-0500
Donna Teandler, *Branch Mgr*
EMP: 139
SALES (corp-wide): 146.5MM **Privately Held**
SIC: 8361 8052 8051 Home for the aged; intermediate care facilities; skilled nursing care facilities
PA: Covia Communities
2185 N Calif Blvd Ste 215
Walnut Creek CA 94596
925 956-7400

(P-23889)
CRASH INC
1081 Camino Del Ri, San Diego (92108)
PHONE..............................619 297-5131
Bill Dawson, *Exec Dir*
Maria Resendez, *Principal*
Mary Himmelberger, *Exec Dir*
EMP: 53
SALES: 2.8MM **Privately Held**
SIC: 8361 8322 Rehabilitation center, residential: health care incidental; general counseling services

(P-23890)
CREATIVE ALTERNATIVES
2855 Geer Rd Ste A, Turlock (95382-1133)
PHONE..............................209 668-9361
Stephanie Biddle, *CEO*
EMP: 220
SQ FT: 40,000
SALES: 16MM **Privately Held**
SIC: 8361 8211 8322 Children's home; private special education school; child related social services

(P-23891)
CREATIVE LIVING OPTIONS INC
2945 Ramco St Ste 120, West Sacramento
(95691-5998)
PHONE..............................916 372-2102
Joan Schmidt, *CEO*
Mary Anne Delaney, *Finance Dir*
EMP: 115
SALES: 3.3MM **Privately Held**
WEB: www.creativelivingoptions.com
SIC: 8361 Home for the physically handicapped

(P-23892)
CRESTWOOD BEHAVIORAL HLTH INC
Also Called: 107 San Jose Mhrc
1425 Fruitdale Ave, San Jose
(95128-3234)
PHONE..............................408 275-1067
John Suggs, *Director*

EMP: 85
SALES (corp-wide): 188.6MM **Privately Held**
WEB: www.dreamcatch.us
SIC: 8361 8063 7389 Halfway group home, persons with social or personal problems; psychiatric hospitals; personal service agents, brokers & bureaus
PA: Crestwood Behavioral Health, Inc.
520 Capitol Mall Ste 800
Sacramento CA 95814
510 651-1244

(P-23893)
CRESTWOOD BEHAVIORAL HLTH INC
Also Called: 120 Fremont Snf
3062 Churn Creek Rd, Redding
(96002-2124)
PHONE..............................530 221-0976
Nicoletta Groff, *Administration*
EMP: 80
SQ FT: 15,000
SALES (corp-wide): 188.6MM **Privately Held**
WEB: www.dreamcatch.us
SIC: 8361 8051 Halfway group home, persons with social or personal problems; skilled nursing care facilities
PA: Crestwood Behavioral Health, Inc.
520 Capitol Mall Ste 800
Sacramento CA 95814
510 651-1244

(P-23894)
CRESTWOOD BEHAVIORAL HLTH INC
Also Called: 134 Alameda Snf
4303 Stevenson Blvd, Fremont
(94538-2645)
PHONE..............................510 651-1244
Leeann Labrie, *Administration*
EMP: 150
SQ FT: 33,790
SALES (corp-wide): 188.6MM **Privately Held**
WEB: www.dreamcatch.us
SIC: 8361 8069 Halfway group home, persons with social or personal problems; specialty hospitals, except psychiatric
PA: Crestwood Behavioral Health, Inc.
520 Capitol Mall Ste 800
Sacramento CA 95814
510 651-1244

(P-23895)
CRESTWOOD BEHAVIORAL HLTH INC
Also Called: 152 Vallejo Rcfe
115 Oddstad Dr, Vallejo (94589-2520)
PHONE..............................707 552-0215
Minda Bunnggay, *Manager*
Rebecca Best, *Director*
EMP: 150
SALES (corp-wide): 188.6MM **Privately Held**
WEB: www.dreamcatch.us
SIC: 8361 8063 8051 Halfway group home, persons with social or personal problems; psychiatric hospitals; skilled nursing care facilities
PA: Crestwood Behavioral Health, Inc.
520 Capitol Mall Ste 800
Sacramento CA 95814
510 651-1244

(P-23896)
CRESTWOOD BEHAVIORAL HLTH INC
Also Called: 120 Fremont Snf
2171 Mowry Ave, Fremont (94538-1717)
PHONE..............................510 793-8383
Janet Timble, *Superintendent*
EMP: 100
SQ FT: 10,000
SALES (corp-wide): 188.6MM **Privately Held**
WEB: www.dreamcatch.us
SIC: 8361 8063 8052 8069 Halfway group home, persons with social or personal problems; psychiatric hospitals; intermediate care facilities; specialty hospitals, except psychiatric

PA: Crestwood Behavioral Health, Inc.
520 Capitol Mall Ste 800
Sacramento CA 95814
510 651-1244

(P-23897)
CRI-HELP INC (PA)
Also Called: CRI HELP DRUG REHABILITATION
11027 Burbank Blvd, North Hollywood
(91601-2431)
P.O. Box 899 (91603-0899)
PHONE..............................818 985-8323
Jack Bernstein, *President*
Victoria Wyner, *Executive*
Kim Long, *Program Mgr*
Shirley Salguero, *Project Mgr*
Pat Franco, *Controller*
EMP: 101
SQ FT: 40,000
SALES: 8MM **Privately Held**
WEB: www.cri-help.org
SIC: 8361 8069 Rehabilitation center, residential: health care incidental; drug addiction rehabilitation hospital

(P-23898)
CROWN COVE SENIOR CARE CMNTY
3901 E Coast Hwy Ofc, Corona Del Mar
(92625-5504)
PHONE..............................949 760-2800
Sanford Fleschman, *Exec Dir*
EMP: 70
SALES (est): 2.7MM **Privately Held**
SIC: 8361 Residential care

(P-23899)
DAVID AND MARGARET HOME INC
Also Called: DAVID & MARGARET YOUTH AND FAM
1350 3rd St, La Verne (91750-5299)
PHONE..............................909 596-5921
Arun Tolia, *President*
Cindy Walkenbach, *President*
Timothy Evans, *Treasurer*
Sabina Sullivan, *Vice Pres*
Linda Thomas, *Executive*
EMP: 240
SQ FT: 40,000
SALES: 17.8MM **Privately Held**
WEB: www.dmhome.org
SIC: 8361 8322 Home for the emotionally disturbed; individual & family services

(P-23900)
DAYBREAK CARE CENTER (PA)
9040 Sunland Blvd, Sun Valley
(91352-2049)
PHONE..............................818 504-6154
Robert Nydam, *President*
Linda Nydam, *CFO*
EMP: 50
SALES (est): 5.2MM **Privately Held**
SIC: 8361 Residential care for the handicapped

(P-23901)
DELANCEY STREET FOUNDATION (PA)
Also Called: Delancey Street Coach Service
600 The Embarcadero, San Francisco
(94107-2116)
PHONE..............................415 957-9800
Mimi Silbert, *President*
Jerry Raymond, *Treasurer*
EMP: 400 **EST:** 1971
SQ FT: 325,000
SALES (est): 50.8MM **Privately Held**
SIC: 8361 5199 8322 4212 Rehabilitation center, residential: health care incidental; advertising specialties; individual & family services; moving services; eating places; caterers

(P-23902)
DESERT MANOR CARE CENTER LP
8515 Cholla Ave, Yucca Valley
(92284-4247)
PHONE..............................760 365-0717
Rich Thomas, *CFO*
Sylvia Sanchez-Figueroa, *Administration*
Lisa Ingram, *Controller*

EMP: 70 EST: 2008
SALES: 3.4MM **Privately Held**
SIC: **8361** 8059 8051 Home for the aged; nursing home, except skilled & intermediate care facility; skilled nursing care facilities

(P-23903)
DEVELOPMENTAL SVCS CONTINUUM
7944 Golden Ave, Lemon Grove (91945-1810)
PHONE..........................619 460-7333
Elaine Lewis, *President*
Cecelia Ramsey, *Exec Dir*
Diane Spurgeon, *Director*
EMP: 75
SALES: 2.9MM **Privately Held**
SIC: **8361** Group foster home

(P-23904)
DIVERSIFIED HEALTH SVCS DEL
Also Called: Terraces At Par Marino
2585 E Washington Blvd, Pasadena (91107-1446)
PHONE..........................626 798-6753
Maru Cohen, *Director*
Christina Watanabe, *Exec Dir*
EMP: 50
SALES (corp-wide): 5.3MM **Privately Held**
SIC: **8361** 8059 Home for the aged; convalescent home
PA: Diversified Health Services (Del)
136 Washington Ave
Richmond CA 94801
510 231-6200

(P-23905)
DOMINICAN HOSPITAL FOUNDATION
Also Called: Dominican Rehab Services
610 Frederick St, Santa Cruz (95062-2203)
PHONE..........................831 457-7057
Debbie Hite, *Branch Mgr*
EMP: 200 **Privately Held**
SIC: **8361** 8093 Rehabilitation center, residential: health care incidental; rehabilitation center, outpatient treatment
HQ: Dominican Hospital Foundation
1555 Soquel Dr
Santa Cruz CA 95065
831 462-7700

(P-23906)
DREAM HOME CARE INC
3939 Atlantic Ave Ste 213, Long Beach (90807-3535)
PHONE..........................562 595-9021
Cora Manalang, *CEO*
Reynaldo David, *COO*
Hazel Manalang, *CFO*
Maricris Ocampo, *Admin Asst*
EMP: 60
SALES: 2.4MM **Privately Held**
SIC: **8361** Group foster home

(P-23907)
DREAMCTCHERS EMPWERMENT NETWRK (PA)
Also Called: CRESTWOOD BEHAVIORAL HEALTH
7590 Shoreline Dr Ste B, Stockton (95219-5455)
P.O. Box 7877 (95267-0877)
PHONE..........................209 478-5291
George Lytal, *President*
Lori Blackburn, *Treasurer*
EMP: 590 EST: 1970
SQ FT: 1,500
SALES: 1.4MM **Privately Held**
WEB: www.dreamcatch.us
SIC: **8361** Halfway group home, persons with social or personal problems

(P-23908)
DREAMCTCHERS EMPWERMENT NETWRK
Also Called: Rosewood Convalescent Hospital
1911 Oak Park Blvd, Pleasant Hill (94523-4601)
PHONE..........................925 935-6630
Maggie Yousess, *Administration*
EMP: 111

SALES (corp-wide): 1.4MM **Privately Held**
WEB: www.dreamcatch.us
SIC: **8361** 8059 8051 Halfway group home, persons with social or personal problems; skilled nursing care facilities; convalescent home
PA: Dreamcatchers Empowerment Network
7590 Shoreline Dr Ste B
Stockton CA 95219
209 478-5291

(P-23909)
DREAMCTCHERS EMPWERMENT NETWRK
Elmhaven Convelescent Hospital
6940 Pacific Ave, Stockton (95207-2602)
PHONE..........................209 477-4817
Mike Blaufus, *Principal*
EMP: 100
SALES (corp-wide): 1.4MM **Privately Held**
WEB: www.dreamcatch.us
SIC: **8361** 8051 8052 Halfway group home, persons with social or personal problems; skilled nursing care facilities; intermediate care facilities
PA: Dreamcatchers Empowerment Network
7590 Shoreline Dr Ste B
Stockton CA 95219
209 478-5291

(P-23910)
E & S RSIDENTIAL CARE SVCS LLC
6083 N Marks Ave, Fresno (93711-1600)
PHONE..........................559 275-3555
Stephanie Hendricks, *Mng Member*
Eddie Gilbert, *Mng Member*
EMP: 100
SALES (est): 8.1MM **Privately Held**
SIC: **8361** Residential care for the handicapped

(P-23911)
E R I T INC (PA)
251 Airport Rd, Oceanside (92058-1201)
PHONE..........................760 433-6024
Cheryl Kilmer, *Exec Dir*
Debbie Horne, *Software Dev*
Lisa Hightower-Kibbe, *Instructor*
Melody Swan, *Nurse*
William E Mara, *Asst Director*
EMP: 85
SQ FT: 15,000
SALES: 17.1MM **Privately Held**
WEB: www.teriinc.org
SIC: **8361** Home for the mentally retarded

(P-23912)
E R I T INC
Also Called: Our Way
251 Airport Rd, Oceanside (92058-1201)
PHONE..........................760 721-1706
Cheryl Kilmer, *Principal*
EMP: 250
SALES (corp-wide): 17.1MM **Privately Held**
WEB: www.teriinc.org
SIC: **8361** Home for the mentally retarded
PA: E R I T Inc
251 Airport Rd
Oceanside CA 92058
760 433-6024

(P-23913)
EDGEWOOD CTR FOR CHILDRENS (PA)
1801 Vicente St, San Francisco (94116-2923)
PHONE..........................415 681-3211
Lynn Dolce, *CEO*
Julia Timmons, *Partner*
Justine Underhill, *Officer*
Jill Anderson, *Exec Dir*
William Brimmer, *Program Mgr*
EMP: 320 EST: 1850
SQ FT: 100,000
SALES: 30.5MM **Privately Held**
WEB: www.edgewoodcenter.org
SIC: **8361** 8211 8322 8093 Home for the emotionally disturbed; specialty education; child related social services; specialty outpatient clinics

(P-23914)
EES RESIDENTIAL GROUP HOMES
5369 Camden Ave Ste 280, San Jose (95124-5856)
PHONE..........................408 265-8780
Richard Shanley, *Exec Dir*
Edward Eldefonso, *Ch of Bd*
Jennifer Mihojevich, *Program Mgr*
EMP: 55
SALES: 1.3MM **Privately Held**
SIC: **8361** 8322 Juvenile correctional facilities; child related social services

(P-23915)
ELDER CARE ALLIANCE CAMARILLO
Also Called: ALMA VIA OF CAMARILLO
1301 Marina Village Pkwy # 210, Alameda (94501-1049)
PHONE..........................510 769-2700
Jesse Jantzen, *CEO*
Jerry Cooper, *Director*
EMP: 60
SALES: 5.7MM **Privately Held**
SIC: **8361** Home for the aged

(P-23916)
ENCOMPASS HEALTH CORPORATION
Also Called: HealthSouth
5001 Commerce Dr, Bakersfield (93309-0648)
PHONE..........................661 323-5500
Rosa Arriola, *Manager*
EMP: 200
SALES (corp-wide): 4.2B **Publicly Held**
WEB: www.healthsouth.com
SIC: **8361** 8069 Rehabilitation center, residential: health care incidental; specialty hospitals, except psychiatric
PA: Encompass Health Corporation
9001 Liberty Pkwy
Birmingham AL 35242
205 967-7116

(P-23917)
EPISCOPAL SENIOR COMMUNITIES
Also Called: Los Gatos Meadows
110 Wood Rd Ofc, Los Gatos (95030-6799)
PHONE..........................408 354-0211
Tina Heany, *Exec Dir*
Cheryl Wilson, *Office Mgr*
Annie Tseng, *Food Svc Dir*
Alex Gerasimov, *Director*
EMP: 120
SALES (corp-wide): 146.5MM **Privately Held**
SIC: **8361** Home for the aged
PA: Covia Communities
2185 N Calif Blvd Ste 215
Walnut Creek CA 94596
925 956-7400

(P-23918)
ESKATON LODGE
22 Cadillac Dr Apt 301, Sacramento (95825-5413)
PHONE..........................916 789-0326
Vicky Cross, *Director*
Stephanie Watson, *Principal*
EMP: 50
SALES (est): 1.4MM **Privately Held**
SIC: **8361** Home for the aged

(P-23919)
ESKATON PROPERTIES INC
Eskaton Manzanita Manor
5318 Manzanita Ave, Carmichael (95608-0512)
PHONE..........................916 331-8513
Denie Crum, *Administration*
EMP: 100
SALES (corp-wide): 102.2MM **Privately Held**
SIC: **8361** Residential care
PA: Eskaton Properties Incorporated
5105 Manzanita Ave Ste A
Carmichael CA 95608
916 334-0810

(P-23920)
ESKATON PROPERTIES INC
Also Called: Eskaton Village Roseville
1650 Eskaton Loop, Roseville (95747-5180)
PHONE..........................916 334-0810
Vicki Cross, *Manager*
Daisy Absalon,
EMP: 60
SALES (corp-wide): 102.2MM **Privately Held**
SIC: **8361** Home for the aged
PA: Eskaton Properties Incorporated
5105 Manzanita Ave Ste A
Carmichael CA 95608
916 334-0810

(P-23921)
ESKATON PROPERTIES INC
Also Called: Eskaton Village Charmichael
3939 Walnut Ave Unit 399, Carmichael (95608-7333)
PHONE..........................916 974-2000
Betsy Donovan, *Exec Dir*
EMP: 200
SALES (corp-wide): 102.2MM **Privately Held**
SIC: **8361** Home for the aged
PA: Eskaton Properties Incorporated
5105 Manzanita Ave Ste A
Carmichael CA 95608
916 334-0810

(P-23922)
EVANGELICAL COVENANT CHURCH
Also Called: Mount Miguel Covenant Village
325 Kempton St, Spring Valley (91977-5810)
PHONE..........................619 931-1114
Thad Rothrock, *Manager*
EMP: 100 **Privately Held**
WEB: www.npcts.edu
SIC: **8361** Rest home, with health care incidental
HQ: The Evangelical Covenant Church
8303 W Higgins Rd Fl 1
Chicago IL 60631
773 907-3303

(P-23923)
EVANGELICAL COVENANT CHURCH
Also Called: Samarkand Retirement Community
2550 Treasure Dr, Santa Barbara (93105-4148)
PHONE..........................805 687-0701
Kenneth D Noreen, *Administration*
EMP: 200 **Privately Held**
WEB: www.npcts.edu
SIC: **8361** 8059 Home for the aged; rest home, with health care
HQ: The Evangelical Covenant Church
8303 W Higgins Rd Fl 1
Chicago IL 60631
773 907-3303

(P-23924)
EVOLVE GROWTH INITIATIVES LLC
Also Called: Evolve Treatment Centers
820 Moraga Dr, Los Angeles (90049-1632)
PHONE..........................424 281-5000
Menachem Baron, *CEO*
EMP: 50
SQ FT: 1,700
SALES (est): 1MM **Privately Held**
SIC: **8361** 8093 Rehabilitation center, residential: health care incidental; mental health clinic, outpatient

(P-23925)
FELLOWSHIP HOMES INC
Also Called: Casa De Modesto
1745 Eldena Way, Modesto (95350-3568)
PHONE..........................209 529-4950
Carolyn Amaral, *Exec Dir*
Curt Willems, *Exec Dir*
Vijay Sharma, *Comptroller*
Joel Merriam, *Opers Staff*
EMP: 150
SALES: 7.9MM **Privately Held**
SIC: **8361** Residential care

(P-23926)
FERREES GROUP HOME INC
878 Highland Home Rd, Banning
(92220-1244)
PHONE..................................951 849-1927
Philip Anthony Ferrees, *Director*
EMP: 60
SALES: 1.5MM **Privately Held**
SIC: 8361 Group foster home

(P-23927)
FIVE ACRES-THE BOYS & GIRLS &
760 Mountain View St, Altadena
(91001-4996)
PHONE..................................626 798-6793
Chanel W Boutakidis, *CEO*
Daniel Braun, *CFO*
Robert A Ketch, *Exec Dir*
Kim Hutchigs, *Admin Sec*
Michael Strawn, *Info Tech Dir*
EMP: 419 EST: 1888
SQ FT: 70,000
SALES (est): 24.8MM **Privately Held**
SIC: 8361 8322 8211 Children's home;
public welfare center; public combined el-
ementary & secondary school

(P-23928)
FLORENCE CRITTENTON SERVICES
Also Called: CRITTENTON SERVICES FOR
CHILDR
801 E Chapman Ave Ste 203, Fullerton
(92831-3846)
P.O. Box 9 (92836-0009)
PHONE..................................714 680-9000
Joyce Capelle, *CEO*
Denise Cunningham, *Officer*
Martha Jasso, *Comms Dir*
Michelle Standfield, *QA Dir*
Lisa Curley, *Personnel Assit*
EMP: 320
SALES: 35.5MM **Privately Held**
SIC: 8361 Residential care for children;
home for the emotionally disturbed

(P-23929)
FORD STREET PROJECT INC
139 Ford St, Ukiah (95482-4011)
PHONE..................................707 462-1934
Jacque Williams, *President*
Jackie Williams, *Exec Dir*
Clover Martin, *General Mgr*
EMP: 50
SALES: 3.4MM **Privately Held**
WEB: www.fordstreet.org
SIC: 8361 Rehabilitation center, residen-
tial: health care incidental

(P-23930)
FOREMOST OPERATIONS LLC
Also Called: Foremost Terrace Room
17581 Sultana St, Hesperia (92345-6552)
PHONE..................................760 244-5579
Ben Vangala, *Owner*
Leonard M Crites, *President*
EMP: 50
SALES (est): 1.7MM **Privately Held**
SIC: 8361 6531 Residential care; rental
agent, real estate

(P-23931)
FOUNTAINWOOD RESIDENTIAL CARE
8773 Oak Ave, Orangevale (95662-2410)
PHONE..................................916 988-2200
Robert Spince, *President*
Kenneth Davis, *Food Svc Dir*
EMP: 80
SALES (est): 3MM **Privately Held**
WEB: www.fountainwood.org
SIC: 8361 8059 Home for the aged; con-
valescent home

(P-23932)
FREDERICKA MANOR
183 Third Ave, Chula Vista (91910-1822)
PHONE..................................619 422-9271
Robert Anderson, *Principal*
Minette Advento, *Data Proc Exec*
Gloria Delrio, *Hum Res Coord*
Kimberly Prendergast, *Pub Rel Dir*
Heather Rager, *Director*
EMP: 60

SALES (est): 4.4MM **Privately Held**
SIC: 8361 6513 Home for the aged; apartment building operators

(P-23933)
FRONT PORCH COMMUNITIES
Also Called: Villa Gardens
842 E Villa St, Pasadena (91101-1259)
PHONE..................................626 796-8162
Jeff Sianko, *CEO*
Kathleen Vanderveen, *Executive*
Ripsime Dzhanikyan, *Social Dir*
Lavern Villarba, *Education*
Carme Nidoy, *Food Svc Dir*
EMP: 192
SALES (corp-wide): 165.1MM **Privately Held**
SIC: 8361 Home for the aged
PA: Front Porch Communities And Services
- Casa De Manana, Llc
800 N Brand Blvd Fl 19
Glendale CA 91203
818 729-8100

(P-23934)
FRONT PORCH COMMUNITIES
Also Called: Carlsbad By The Sea
2855 Carlsbad Blvd, Carlsbad
(92008-2902)
PHONE..................................760 729-4983
Tim Wetzel, *Manager*
Heidi Kvitli, *Director*
EMP: 150
SALES (corp-wide): 165.1MM **Privately Held**
SIC: 8361 Home for the aged
PA: Front Porch Communities And Services
- Casa De Manana, Llc
800 N Brand Blvd Fl 19
Glendale CA 91203
818 729-8100

(P-23935)
FUTURO INFANTIL HISPANO FFA
2227 E Garvey Ave N, West Covina
(91791-1500)
PHONE..................................626 339-1824
Oma Velasco-Rodrigues, *President*
Jose Tejeda, *Finance Mgr*
EMP: 50
SALES: 5.5MM **Privately Held**
SIC: 8361 Group foster home

(P-23936)
GATE THREE HEALTHCARE LLC
Also Called: Palm Ter Hlth Care Rhblitation
24962 Calle Aragon, Laguna Hills
(92637-3883)
PHONE..................................949 770-3348
Soon Burnam,
EMP: 120
SALES: 13.4MM
SALES (corp-wide): 2B **Publicly Held**
SIC: 8361 Rehabilitation center, residen-
tial: health care incidental
PA: The Ensign Group Inc
27101 Puerta Real Ste 450
Mission Viejo CA 92691
949 487-9500

(P-23937)
GATEWAY CTR OF MONTEREY CNTY (PA)
850 Congress Ave, Pacific Grove
(93950-4811)
PHONE..................................831 372-8002
Kathleen Adanson, *President*
Duane Burnell, *Exec Dir*
Anjeanette Nunez, *Program Mgr*
Rosie Dias, *Admin Asst*
Priscila Rivera, *Admin Asst*
EMP: 65
SQ FT: 33,000
SALES: 4.5MM **Privately Held**
WEB: www.gatewaycenter.org
SIC: 8361 Home for the mentally handi-
capped

(P-23938)
GOLDEN LIVING LLC
Also Called: Beverly Healthcare
5555 Prospect Rd Ofc, San Jose
(95129-4897)
PHONE..................................408 255-5555
Ron Anderson, *Manager*
EMP: 50

SALES (corp-wide): 409.2MM **Privately Held**
WEB: www.nwbeccorp.com
SIC: 8361 Geriatric residential care
PA: Beaver Dam Health Care Center
5220 Tennyson Pkwy # 400
Plano TX 75024
972 372-6300

(P-23939)
GOLDEN POND LP
Also Called: Golden Pond Retirement Cmnty
3415 Mayhew Rd Ofc, Sacramento
(95827-3107)
PHONE..................................916 369-8967
Doug Gill, *Partner*
Paul Mason, *Partner*
Dana McManus, *Partner*
Brian Walgenbach, *Partner*
Lorine Racardos, *Director*
EMP: 50
SALES (est): 3.2MM **Privately Held**
SIC: 8361 6513 Home for the aged; apart-
ment building operators

(P-23940)
GOOD SHEPHERD LUTHERAN HM OF W (PA)
Also Called: Good Shepherd Communities
119 N Main St, Porterville (93257-3713)
PHONE..................................559 791-2000
David Geske, *CEO*
EMP: 60
SQ FT: 6,000
SALES (est): 15.9MM **Privately Held**
SIC: 8361 Residential care for the handi-
capped

(P-23941)
GRASS VALLEY LLC
Also Called: Quail Ridge Senior Living
150 Sutton Way Ofc, Grass Valley
(95945-4104)
PHONE..................................530 272-1055
Mark E Nicol,
Pari Manouchehri, *Exec Dir*
Lacy Ward,
Mark Chiolis, *Director*
EMP: 60
SALES (est): 2.5MM **Privately Held**
WEB: www.quailridgeseniorliving.com
SIC: 8361 Geriatric residential care

(P-23942)
GREENRIDGE SENIOR CARE
2150 Pyramid Dr, El Sobrante
(94803-3220)
PHONE..................................510 758-9600
Linda Joseph, *Director*
EMP: 110
SALES: 7.7MM **Privately Held**
SIC: 8361 Geriatric residential care; home
for the aged

(P-23943)
HALL WINDSOR
1415 James M Wood Blvd, Los Angeles
(90015-1209)
PHONE..................................213 383-1547
Michael Bolong, *Owner*
Windsor Hall, *Owner*
EMP: 80 EST: 2000
SALES (est): 1.5MM **Privately Held**
WEB: www.windsorhall.com
SIC: 8361 Residential care

(P-23944)
HAMBURGER HOME (PA)
Also Called: Aviva Center
7120 Franklin Ave, Los Angeles
(90046-3002)
PHONE..................................323 876-0550
Regina Bette, *President*
Thomas Bernal, *CFO*
EMP: 90 EST: 1915
SQ FT: 25,000
SALES: 18.8MM **Privately Held**
SIC: 8361 Children's home

(P-23945)
HAMBURGER HOME
5900 Sepulvda Blvd # 104, Van Nuys
(91411-2511)
PHONE..................................818 980-3200
Jamerson Jeffrey, *Branch Mgr*
EMP: 103

SALES (corp-wide): 18.8MM **Privately Held**
SIC: 8361 Children's home
PA: Hamburger Home
7120 Franklin Ave
Los Angeles CA 90046
323 876-0550

(P-23946)
HANK FISHER PROPERTIES INC
Also Called: Chateau On Capitol Avenue, The
2701 Capitol Ave, Sacramento
(95816-6036)
PHONE..................................916 447-4444
Nancy Fisher, *Branch Mgr*
EMP: 108
SALES (corp-wide): 17.5MM **Privately Held**
SIC: 8361 Geriatric residential care
PA: Hank Fisher Properties, Inc.
641 Fulton Ave Ste 200
Sacramento CA 95825
916 485-1441

(P-23947)
HARBOR HEALTH CARE INC
16917 Clark Ave, Bellflower (90706-5703)
PHONE..................................562 866-7054
Cheryl Hutchins, *President*
EMP: 200
SALES (est): 9.7MM **Privately Held**
WEB: www.harborhealthcare.org
SIC: 8361 Home for the mentally handi-
capped

(P-23948)
HARVEST MANAGEMENT SUB LLC
Also Called: Las Brisas
1299 Briarwood Dr, San Luis Obispo
(93401-5965)
PHONE..................................805 543-0187
David Dolan, *Branch Mgr*
Ron Jackson, *Manager*
EMP: 4604
SALES (corp-wide): 468.2MM **Privately Held**
SIC: 8361 Rest home, with health care in-
cidental
PA: Harvest Management Sub Llc
631 W Morse Blvd Ste 100
Winter Park FL 32789
503 370-7070

(P-23949)
HATHAWAY-SYCAMORES CHLD FAM SV
840 N Avenue 66, Los Angeles
(90042-1508)
PHONE..................................323 257-9600
Jim Cheney, *President*
EMP: 54
SALES (corp-wide): 51.8MM **Privately Held**
SIC: 8361 8093 Home for the emotionally
disturbed; mental health clinic, outpatient
PA: Hathaway-Sycamores Child And Family
Services
100 W Walnut St Ste 375
Pasadena CA 91124
626 395-7100

(P-23950)
HATHAWAY-SYCAMORES CHLD FAM SV
3741 Stocker St Ste 101, View Park
(90008-5150)
PHONE..................................323 733-0322
Debbie Manners, *Branch Mgr*
EMP: 60
SALES (corp-wide): 51.8MM **Privately Held**
SIC: 8361 Home for the emotionally dis-
turbed
PA: Hathaway-Sycamores Child And Family
Services
100 W Walnut St
Pasadena CA 91124
626 844-1677

(P-23951)
HATHAWAY-SYCAMORES CHLD FAM SV (PA)
100 W Walnut St Ste 375, Pasadena (91124-0001)
PHONE..................................626 395-7100
Michael Galper, *Ch of Bd*
Tracy Hall, *Partner*
Sandra Tudor, *Partner*
Stephanie Arsnow, *President*
William Martone, *President*
EMP: 65
SQ FT: 75,175
SALES: 51.8MM **Privately Held**
SIC: 8361 8093 Home for the emotionally disturbed; mental health clinic, outpatient

(P-23952)
HAYNES FAMILY PROGRAMS INC
Also Called: Leroy Haynes Center
233 Baseline Rd, La Verne (91750-2353)
P.O. Box 400 (91750-0400)
PHONE..................................909 593-2581
Daniel Maydeck, *President*
Tony Williams, *CFO*
Frank Linebaugh, *Senior VP*
Amy Humphrey, *Vice Pres*
Kristine Gutierrez, *Human Res Mgr*
EMP: 225
SQ FT: 72,466
SALES: 19.1MM **Privately Held**
WEB: www.leroyhaynes.org
SIC: 8361 8211 8099 Boys' Towns; specialty education; medical services organization

(P-23953)
HEALTHCARE GROUP
Also Called: Grossmont Grdns Rtrement Cmnty
5480 Marengo Ave Ste 619, La Mesa (91942-2408)
PHONE..................................619 463-0281
Mary Shepherd, *Exec Dir*
EMP: 235
SQ FT: 5,000
SALES (est): 9.3MM **Privately Held**
SIC: 8361 8052 8051 Residential care; intermediate care facilities; skilled nursing care facilities

(P-23954)
HEALTHVIEW INC (PA)
Also Called: Harbor View House
921 S Beacon St, San Pedro (90731-3740)
P.O. Box 1860 (90733-1860)
PHONE..................................310 547-3341
Jeff Smith, *CEO*
Susan Major, *Principal*
EMP: 135
SQ FT: 110,000
SALES: 5MM **Privately Held**
WEB: www.hvi.com
SIC: 8361 8052 Home for the mentally handicapped; rehabilitation center, residential: health care incidental; home for the mentally retarded, with health care

(P-23955)
HEALTHVIEW INC
Also Called: Lifecare Health
12750 Center Court Dr S # 410, Cerritos (90703-8581)
PHONE..................................562 468-0136
Denise Stanton, *Branch Mgr*
EMP: 50
SALES (est): 474.7K
SALES (corp-wide): 5MM **Privately Held**
WEB: www.hvi.com
SIC: 8361 8082 Home for the mentally handicapped; home health care services
PA: Healthview, Inc.
921 S Beacon St
San Pedro CA 90731
310 547-3341

(P-23956)
HELPING HEARTS FOUNDATION INC
3050 Fite Cir Ste 108, Sacramento (95827-1808)
PHONE..................................916 368-7200
James Borgmeyer, *President*
EMP: 55

SALES: 1.2MM **Privately Held**
SIC: 8361 Residential care

(P-23957)
HILLSIDES
940 Avenue 64, Pasadena (91105-2711)
PHONE..................................323 254-2274
Joseph M Costa, *CEO*
EMP: 460 **EST:** 1913
SQ FT: 18,217
SALES: 43.6MM **Privately Held**
SIC: 8361 Home for the emotionally disturbed

(P-23958)
HILLVIEW ACRES
Also Called: Hillview Acres Childrens Home
23091 Mill Creek Dr, Laguna Hills (92653-1258)
PHONE..................................714 694-2828
Noah McMahon, *Chairman*
Ronald Storm, *President*
Eric Carter, *Corp Secy*
EMP: 75 **EST:** 1929
SQ FT: 39,989
SALES: 3.5MM **Privately Held**
WEB: www.hillview.org
SIC: 8361 Children's home

(P-23959)
HOLLENBECK PALMS
Also Called: Hollenbeck Home For The Aged
24431 Lyons Ave Apt 336, Newhall (91321-2360)
PHONE..................................323 263-6195
William G Heideman Jr, *President*
Morris Shockley, *Vice Pres*
John Shively, *Chief Engr*
Johnny Young, *Controller*
Peggy Heideman, *Pub Rel Dir*
EMP: 170
SALES: 17.7MM **Privately Held**
WEB: www.hollenbeckhome.com
SIC: 8361 Halfway group home, persons with social or personal problems

(P-23960)
HOME GUIDING HANDS CORPORATION (PA)
1908 Friendship Dr Ste A, El Cajon (92020-1154)
PHONE..................................619 938-2850
Mark Klaus, *CEO*
Jan Adams, *CFO*
Edward Hershey, *Vice Pres*
Laurie J Purcell, *Vice Pres*
Carol A Fitzgibbons, *Exec Dir*
EMP: 266
SALES (est): 17.4MM **Privately Held**
WEB: www.guidinghands.org
SIC: 8361 8052 Residential care for the handicapped; intermediate care facilities

(P-23961)
HOPE HSE FOR MLTPLE HNDICAPPED (PA)
Also Called: SCHMITT HOUSE
4215 Peck Rd, El Monte (91732-2198)
PHONE..................................626 443-1313
D Bernstein, *Exec Dir*
David Bernstein, *Exec Dir*
Dorothy Gonzalez, *Exec Dir*
Patty Fraijo, *Comptroller*
EMP: 150
SQ FT: 15,000
SALES: 6.2MM **Privately Held**
SIC: 8361 Residential care for the handicapped; rest home, with health care incidental

(P-23962)
HR MISSION COMMONS FC 5183
10 Terracina Blvd, Redlands (92373-4808)
PHONE..................................909 793-8691
Patty Van Dyk, *Principal*
EMP: 88
SALES (est): 3.1MM **Privately Held**
SIC: 8361 Residential care

(P-23963)
INDEPENDENT OPTIONS INC
8555 Aero Dr Ste 205, San Diego (92123-1745)
PHONE..................................858 598-5260
EMP: 127

SALES (corp-wide): 16MM **Privately Held**
SIC: 8361 Home for the mentally handicapped
PA: Independent Options, Inc
391 Corporate Terrace Cir # 102
Corona CA 92879
951 279-2585

(P-23964)
KIDS FIRST FOUNDATION
1025 Service Pl Ste 103, Vista (92084-7271)
PHONE..................................760 631-7550
Ihab Shahawi, *CEO*
EMP: 165
SALES: 6.7MM **Privately Held**
SIC: 8361 Residential care

(P-23965)
KIDS FIRST FOUNDATION
993 S Santa Fe Ave Ste C, Vista (92083-6995)
PHONE..................................760 631-7550
Ihab Shahawi, *CEO*
EMP: 99
SALES (est): 1.7MM **Privately Held**
SIC: 8361 Residential care

(P-23966)
KNOLLS WEST ENTERPRISE
Also Called: Knolls West Residential Care
16890 Green Tree Blvd, Victorville (92395-5618)
PHONE..................................760 245-0107
Larry Bechtold, *Partner*
Fred Bechtold, *Partner*
Gary Bechtold, *Partner*
EMP: 100
SQ FT: 44,000
SALES (est): 4.5MM
SALES (corp-wide): 6.5MM **Privately Held**
WEB: www.desertknollsconvhospital.com
SIC: 8361 Geriatric residential care
PA: Knolls Convalescent Hospital Inc
16890 Green Tree Blvd
Victorville CA 92395
760 245-5361

(P-23967)
LA HABRA VILLA
220 Newport Center Dr # 11, Newport Beach (92660-7506)
PHONE..................................714 529-1697
David Tsoong, *Partner*
Herbert Tarlow MD, *Partner*
EMP: 54
SQ FT: 100,000
SALES (est): 2.7MM **Privately Held**
SIC: 8361 Home for the aged

(P-23968)
LAMP INC
Also Called: Lamp Community
2116 Arlington Ave Lbby, Los Angeles (90018-1365)
PHONE..................................213 488-9559
Donna Gallup, *CEO*
Kim Carson, *Finance Dir*
Brooke Robie, *Cust Mgr*
EMP: 110
SQ FT: 4,500
SALES: 11.6MM **Privately Held**
SIC: 8361 Residential care for the handicapped

(P-23969)
LASSEN HSE ASSISTED LIVING LLC
705 Luther Rd, Red Bluff (96080-4265)
PHONE..................................530 529-2900
Eric Jacobsen,
EMP: 50
SALES: 1.2MM **Privately Held**
SIC: 8361 Home for the aged

(P-23970)
LE BLEU CHATEAU INC
Also Called: Bleu Chateau Assisted Living
1900 Grismer Ave, Burbank (91504-4405)
PHONE..................................818 843-3141
Adam Zenou, *President*
Robert Rosenberg, *Vice Pres*
EMP: 50

SALES (est): 1.5MM **Privately Held**
WEB: www.lebleuchateau.com
SIC: 8361 Home for the aged

(P-23971)
LEISURE CARE LLC
Also Called: Nohl Ranch Inn
380 S Anaheim Hills Rd, Anaheim (92807-4026)
PHONE..................................714 974-1616
Wanda Reynolds, *Branch Mgr*
EMP: 50
SQ FT: 82,222
SALES (corp-wide): 112.4K **Privately Held**
WEB: www.leisurecare.com
SIC: 8361 8051 Residential care; skilled nursing care facilities
HQ: Leisure Care, Llc
999 3rd Ave Ste 4550
Seattle WA 98104
206 436-7827

(P-23972)
LEISURE CARE LLC
Also Called: Fairwinds Woodward Park
9525 N Fort Washington Rd, Fresno (93730-0662)
PHONE..................................559 434-1237
Coint Folwer, *Branch Mgr*
Alice Quijano, *Executive*
EMP: 100
SALES (corp-wide): 112.4K **Privately Held**
WEB: www.leisurecare.com
SIC: 8361 Residential care
HQ: Leisure Care, Llc
999 3rd Ave Ste 4550
Seattle WA 98104
206 436-7827

(P-23973)
LINCOLN CHILD CENTER INC
Also Called: Hope Contra Costa
51 Marina Blvd, Pittsburg (94565-2068)
PHONE..................................925 521-1270
Allison Staulcup, *Principal*
EMP: 104
SALES (corp-wide): 17.3MM **Privately Held**
SIC: 8361 Home for the mentally handicapped
PA: Lincoln
1266 14th St
Oakland CA 94607
510 273-4700

(P-23974)
LITTLE PEOPLES
39514 Brookside Ave, Cherry Valley (92223-4602)
P.O. Box 248, Beaumont (92223-0248)
PHONE..................................951 849-1959
EMP: 60
SALES: 2.8MM **Privately Held**
WEB: www.littlepeoples.com
SIC: 8361

(P-23975)
LITTLE SISTERS OF POOR
Also Called: ST ANNE'S HOME
300 Lake St, San Francisco (94118-1397)
PHONE..................................415 751-6510
Patricia Metzgar, *President*
Steve Lewey, *Human Res Dir*
EMP: 107
SQ FT: 110,000
SALES: 6.8MM **Privately Held**
SIC: 8361 8661 Home for the aged; religious organizations

(P-23976)
LONGWOOD MANAGEMENT CORP
Also Called: Parkers Retirement Residence
9925 La Alameda Ave, Fountain Valley (92708-3548)
PHONE..................................714 962-5531
Stephanie Radu, *Manager*
EMP: 65
SALES (corp-wide): 170MM **Privately Held**
SIC: 8361 8059 Residential care; rest home, with health care

PA: Longwood Management Corp.
4032 Wilshire Blvd Fl 6
Los Angeles CA 90010
213 389-6900

(P-23977)
LOS ANGELES MISSION INC (PA)
303 E 5th St, Los Angeles (90013-1505)
P.O. Box 55900 (90055-0630)
PHONE..............................213 629-1227
Herb Smith, *President*
Steve Kennedy, *CFO*
EMP: 77
SQ FT: 155,000
SALES: 13.7MM **Privately Held**
SIC: 8361 Home for destitute men & women; rehabilitation center, residential: health care incidental

(P-23978)
LOS ANGELES ORPHAN ASYLUM INC
7600 Graves Ave, Rosemead (91770-3414)
PHONE..............................323 283-9311
Sister Linda A Cahill, *Director*
EMP: 122
SQ FT: 25,000
SALES: 5.4MM **Privately Held**
SIC: 8361 Orphanage

(P-23979)
LOS ANGELES ORPHANS HOME SOC (HQ)
815 N El Centro Ave, Los Angeles (90038-3805)
PHONE..............................323 463-2119
Darrell Evora, *President*
Jennifer Wong, *Program Mgr*
Alma Gomez, *Administration*
EMP: 192
SQ FT: 45,000
SALES (est): 2.9MM
SALES (corp-wide): 93.6MM **Privately Held**
SIC: 8361 Residential care for children
PA: Uplift Family Services
251 Llewellyn Ave
Campbell CA 95008
408 379-3790

(P-23980)
LOS ANGELES RESIDENTIAL COMM F
29890 Bouquet Canyon Rd, Santa Clarita (91390-5111)
PHONE..............................661 296-8636
Kathy Sturky, *Exec Dir*
Larry Sallows, *CFO*
Maureen Medeiros, *Office Mgr*
EMP: 85
SQ FT: 5,000
SALES (est): 2.4MM **Privately Held**
WEB: www.larcfoundation.org
SIC: 8361 8322 8051 Home for the mentally handicapped; individual & family services; skilled nursing care facilities

(P-23981)
LOS PRIETOS BOYS CAMP
3900 Paradise Rd, Santa Barbara (93105-9734)
PHONE..............................805 692-1750
Patricia Stewart, *Director*
EMP: 60
SALES (est): 930.1K **Privately Held**
SIC: 8361 Juvenile correctional facilities

(P-23982)
LOYALTON AT RANCHO SOLANO
3350 Cherry Hills Ct Ofc, Fairfield (94534-7885)
PHONE..............................707 425-3588
Kimberly Kent, *Exec Dir*
Dorothy King, *Manager*
EMP: 60
SALES (est): 1.6MM **Privately Held**
SIC: 8361 Residential care

(P-23983)
MAGNOLIA OF MILLBRAE INC
201 Chadbourne Ave, Millbrae (94030-2570)
PHONE..............................650 697-7700
Vincent Muzzi, *President*
EMP: 93 **EST:** 1986
SALES (est): 5.8MM **Privately Held**
WEB: www.themagnolia.com
SIC: 8361 Home for the aged

(P-23984)
MARY AND FRIENDS
1101 Farrington Dr, La Habra (90631-2510)
PHONE..............................562 691-1575
Eric Rico, *CEO*
Christine Rico, *President*
EMP: 120
SALES (est): 3MM **Privately Held**
SIC: 8361 Residential care for the handicapped

(P-23985)
MARYVALE
7600 Graves Ave, Rosemead (91770-3414)
P.O. Box 1039 (91770-1000)
PHONE..............................626 280-6510
Steve Gunter, *CEO*
EMP: 53 **EST:** 2011
SALES: 22.8MM **Privately Held**
SIC: 8361 8322 Residential care for children; public welfare center

(P-23986)
MASONIC HOMES OF CALIFORNIA (PA)
1111 California St, San Francisco (94108-2252)
PHONE..............................415 776-7000
David R Doan, *President*
Timothy A Wood, *CFO*
Dave Doan, *Treasurer*
Allan Casalou, *Vice Pres*
Andrew Uehling, *Vice Pres*
EMP: 375
SQ FT: 8,000
SALES: 54.8MM **Privately Held**
WEB: www.mhcuc.org
SIC: 8361 Children's home

(P-23987)
MASONIC HOMES OF CALIFORNIA
Also Called: Masonic Home For Adults
34400 Mission Blvd, Union City (94587-3604)
PHONE..............................510 441-3700
Gilbert Smart, *Branch Mgr*
Yolanda Wasniewski, *Controller*
EMP: 350
SALES (corp-wide): 54.8MM **Privately Held**
WEB: www.mhcuc.org
SIC: 8361 8051 Rest home, with health care incidental; skilled nursing care facilities
PA: Masonic Homes Of California Inc
1111 California St
San Francisco CA 94108
415 776-7000

(P-23988)
MASONIC HOMES OF CALIFORNIA
3823 N Reeder Ave, Covina (91724)
PHONE..............................626 251-2200
John Howle, *Manager*
EMP: 100
SALES (corp-wide): 54.8MM **Privately Held**
WEB: www.mhcuc.org
SIC: 8361 Children's home
PA: Masonic Homes Of California Inc
1111 California St
San Francisco CA 94108
415 776-7000

(P-23989)
MCKINLEY CHILDRENS CENTER INC (PA)
762 Cypress St, San Dimas (91773-3505)
PHONE..............................909 599-1227
Anil Vadatary, *CEO*
Michael Frazer, *CFO*

George King, *CFO*
Chris Murray, *Officer*
Julio Arizaga, *Administration*
EMP: 190
SQ FT: 8,055
SALES: 19.3MM **Privately Held**
WEB: www.mckinleycc.org
SIC: 8361 8211 Boys' Towns; private elementary & secondary schools

(P-23990)
MEADOWBROOK CONVALESCENT HOSP
461 E Johnston Ave, Hemet (92543-7195)
PHONE..............................951 658-2293
Bridgette Grimaldi, *President*
EMP: 78 **EST:** 1955
SALES: 2.8MM **Privately Held**
SIC: 8361 8051 Rest home, with health care incidental; convalescent home with continuous nursing care

(P-23991)
MEADOWBROOK VILLAGE CHRISTIAN
100 Holland Gln, Escondido (92026-1354)
PHONE..............................760 746-2500
Jacob Bronwer, *President*
Sarah Rogh, *Manager*
EMP: 109
SALES: 4.8MM **Privately Held**
SIC: 8361 Home for the aged

(P-23992)
MERCEDES DIAZ HOMES INC
7239 Washington Ave # 100, Whittier (90602-1432)
PHONE..............................562 945-4576
Mercedes Diaz, *President*
Ramon Diaz, *Vice Pres*
EMP: 60
SALES (est): 10.4MM **Privately Held**
SIC: 8361 Residential care

(P-23993)
MERCY RETIREMENT AND CARE CTR
3431 Foothill Blvd, Oakland (94601-3199)
PHONE..............................510 534-8540
Jesse Jantzen, *CEO*
Asha Kooliyadan, *Records Dir*
Tamara Schmutzler, *Director*
EMP: 160
SQ FT: 125,000
SALES: 23.9MM **Privately Held**
SIC: 8361 8051 Home for the aged; skilled nursing care facilities

(P-23994)
MGH CORPORATION
Also Called: Mitchells Group Home
1202 W 101st St, Los Angeles (90044-1802)
PHONE..............................323 754-1408
Hazel Mitchell, *President*
Stephnie Weathersby, *Vice Pres*
EMP: 50
SALES (est): 3MM **Privately Held**
SIC: 8361 Geriatric residential care

(P-23995)
MISSION HILLS POST ACUTE CARE
Also Called: Cloisters Mssion Hills Hosp HM
3680 Reynard Way, San Diego (92103-3847)
PHONE..............................619 297-4484
Kennon S Shea, *President*
Matt Scott, *Administration*
Daniel Bressler, *Director*
Cindy Martinez, *Director*
EMP: 92
SQ FT: 16,920
SALES (est): 5.2MM **Privately Held**
SIC: 8361 8051 Rehabilitation center, residential: health care incidental; skilled nursing care facilities

(P-23996)
MISSION HILLS SENIOR LIVING
34560 Bob Hope Dr, Rancho Mirage (92270-1727)
PHONE..............................760 770-7737
Roland Gandy, *Exec Dir*
EMP: 62

SALES (est): 1.2MM **Privately Held**
SIC: 8361 Geriatric residential care

(P-23997)
MISSION VILLA LLC
995 E Market St, Daly City (94014-2168)
PHONE..............................650 756-1995
Jeannie Lawler, *Director*
EMP: 50
SALES (est): 2.2MM **Privately Held**
WEB: www.missionvillage.org
SIC: 8361 Home for the aged

(P-23998)
MISSION VLLA ALZHMERS RSIDENCE
3333 S Bascom Ave, Campbell (95008-7005)
PHONE..............................408 559-8301
Jeanie Lalor, *Administration*
EMP: 50
SQ FT: 14,535
SALES (est): 1MM **Privately Held**
SIC: 8361 Home for the aged

(P-23999)
MONARCH PLACE PIEDMONT LLC
4500 Gilbert St, Oakland (94611-4657)
PHONE..............................510 658-9266
Frank J Haffner II, *Mng Member*
EMP: 125
SALES (est): 3.7MM **Privately Held**
SIC: 8361 Home for the aged

(P-24000)
MONTE NIDO HOLDINGS LLC
Also Called: Monte Nido & Affiliates
514 Live Oak Circle Dr, Calabasas (91302-2139)
PHONE..............................818 457-9958
EMP: 184
SALES (corp-wide): 60MM **Privately Held**
SIC: 8361 Residential care
PA: Monte Nido Holdings, Llc
6100 Sw 76th St
South Miami FL 33143
310 457-9958

(P-24001)
MONTE VISTA GROVE HOMES
2889 San Pasqual St, Pasadena (91107-5364)
PHONE..............................626 796-6135
M Helen Baatz, *Exec Dir*
Kim Houser, *CFO*
Noelle Gonzales, *Admin Asst*
Barbara Stevens, *Accountant*
Donna Shepard, *Human Resources*
EMP: 85
SQ FT: 12,000
SALES: 9.3MM **Privately Held**
SIC: 8361 Home for the aged

(P-24002)
MOTHER LODE REHABILIT
Also Called: MORE WORKSHOP
415 Placerville Dr Ste J, Placerville (95667-4046)
PHONE..............................530 622-4848
Susie Davies, *Exec Dir*
Kelli Nuttall, *Director*
EMP: 150
SALES: 3.1MM **Privately Held**
SIC: 8361 8322 Rehabilitation center, residential: health care incidental; individual & family services

(P-24003)
NEW WAY LLC
1130 Burnett Ave Ste G, Concord (94520-5610)
PHONE..............................925 688-1520
Lupe Henry, *Mng Member*
EMP: 50
SALES (est): 2.6MM **Privately Held**
SIC: 8361 Residential care for the handicapped

(P-24004)
NINOS LATINO UNIDOS FSA
10016 Pioneer Blvd # 123, Santa Fe Springs (90670-3245)
PHONE..............................562 801-5454

Fahir Milian, *President*
Gurith Torres, *Corp Secy*
Luis I Mendes, *Administration*
EMP: 60
SALES: 6.8MM **Privately Held**
WEB: www.nlu.org
SIC: 8361 8322 Group foster home; individual & family services

(P-24005)
NOIA RESIDENTIAL SERVICES INC
606 E Belmont Ave Ste 101, Fresno (93701-1527)
PHONE..................................559 485-5555
Lucia Noia, *CEO*
Bonda Aranas, *Controller*
EMP: 96
SQ FT: 9,767
SALES (est): 3.7MM **Privately Held**
SIC: 8361 Home for destitute men & women

(P-24006)
NORTHERN CA RETIREDD OFCRS
Also Called: PARADISE VALLEY ESTATES
2600 Estates Dr, Fairfield (94533-9711)
PHONE..................................707 432-1200
James G Mertz, *CEO*
Debra Murphy, *CFO*
Robin Murray, *Social Dir*
Neil Calhoun,
Charity S Blackford, *Accountant*
EMP: 225
SALES: 24.9MM **Privately Held**
WEB: www.pvestates.com
SIC: 8361 Home for the aged

(P-24007)
NORTHERN CAL ADPTIVE LVING CTR (PA)
Also Called: NCALC
2725 Esplanade, Chico (95973-1183)
PHONE..................................530 894-2726
Susan Kolar, *Exec Dir*
Donald Pierce, *Manager*
EMP: 105
SQ FT: 1,200
SALES: 1.9MM **Privately Held**
SIC: 8361 Residential care for the handicapped

(P-24008)
NORTHERN CAL YUTH FMLY PRGRAMS (PA)
2577 California Park Dr, Chico (95928-4166)
PHONE..................................530 893-2316
Eric James, *Asst Director*
Ralph Ward, *Director*
EMP: 86
SQ FT: 6,000
SALES: 7MM **Privately Held**
SIC: 8361 Residential care

(P-24009)
NURSECORE MANAGEMENT SVCS LLC
1010 S Broadway, Santa Maria (93454-6600)
PHONE..................................805 938-7660
Veronica Aburto, *Branch Mgr*
EMP: 700 **Privately Held**
SIC: 8361 8082 8049 7361 Residential care; home health care services; nurses & other medical assistants; nurses' registry
PA: Nursecore Management Services, Llc
2201 Brookhollow Plaza Dr # 450
Arlington TX 76006

(P-24010)
ODD FELLOW-REBEKAH CHLD HM CAL (PA)
Also Called: Rebekah Children's Services
290 I O O F Ave, Gilroy (95020-5204)
PHONE..................................408 846-2100
Nancy Johnson, *CEO*
Christophe Rebboah, *CEO*
Charmian Hadlock, *Bd of Directors*
Alejandra Arreola, *Program Mgr*
Sue Nasser, *Administration*
EMP: 173

SQ FT: 46,000
SALES: 19MM **Privately Held**
SIC: 8361 8093 Home for the emotionally disturbed; mental health clinic, outpatient

(P-24011)
ODD FELLOW-REBEKAH CHLD HM CAL
Also Called: Rebekah Children's Services
1260 S Main St Ste 101, Salinas (93901-2292)
PHONE..................................831 775-0348
Jorge Montes, *Branch Mgr*
David Vasquez, *Partner*
EMP: 72
SALES (corp-wide): 19MM **Privately Held**
SIC: 8361 8093 Home for the emotionally disturbed; mental health clinic, outpatient
PA: Odd Fellow-Rebekah Children's Home Of California
290 I O O F Ave
Gilroy CA 95020
408 846-2100

(P-24012)
ODD FELLOWS HOME CALIFORNIA
Also Called: Saratoga Retirement Community
14500 Fruitvale Ave # 3000, Saratoga (95070-6169)
PHONE..................................408 741-7100
Cathy Schumacher, *Administration*
Erandy Gonzalez, *Office Mgr*
Marina Smetyukh, *Business Mgr*
Carla Guglielmelli, *Director*
EMP: 275 **EST:** 1853
SALES: 48.7MM **Privately Held**
SIC: 8361 8051 Home for the aged; skilled nursing care facilities

(P-24013)
OLIVE CREST
73700 Dinah Shore Dr # 101, Palm Desert (92211-0815)
PHONE..................................760 341-8507
Angela Allenn, *Branch Mgr*
EMP: 77
SALES (corp-wide): 49.3MM **Privately Held**
SIC: 8361 Group foster home
PA: Olive Crest
2130 E 4th St Ste 200
Santa Ana CA 92705
714 543-5437

(P-24014)
OLIVE CREST
Also Called: Olive Crest Op
917 Pine Ave, Long Beach (90813-4325)
PHONE..................................562 216-8841
Donald Verleur, *Branch Mgr*
EMP: 77
SALES (corp-wide): 49.3MM **Privately Held**
SIC: 8361 Home for the emotionally disturbed
PA: Olive Crest
2130 E 4th St Ste 200
Santa Ana CA 92705
714 543-5437

(P-24015)
OLIVE CREST (PA)
2130 E 4th St Ste 200, Santa Ana (92705-3818)
PHONE..................................714 543-5437
Donald A Verleur, *CEO*
Monica Aceves, *Partner*
Matthew Boughton, *Partner*
Leilani Brown, *Partner*
Dailene Coad, *Partner*
EMP: 300
SQ FT: 40,000
SALES: 55.5MM **Privately Held**
WEB: www.olivecrest.net
SIC: 8361 8322 Home for the emotionally disturbed; individual & family services

(P-24016)
OMNITRANS INC
Also Called: Omnitrans Access
234 S I St, San Bernardino (92410-2408)
PHONE..................................909 383-1680
Brian Niemann, *Principal*
EMP: 337

SALES (corp-wide): 13.3MM **Privately Held**
SIC: 8361 Home for the physically handicapped
PA: Omnitrans, Inc.
1700 W 5th St
San Bernardino CA 92411
909 379-7100

(P-24017)
P MONTEREY LP
Also Called: Park Lane, The
47 Via Cimarron, Monterey (93940-4332)
PHONE..................................831 250-6159
Deepak Israni, *Principal*
EMP: 70
SALES (est): 2.9MM **Privately Held**
SIC: 8361 Residential care

(P-24018)
PACIFIC LODGE YOUTH SERVICES
Also Called: Pacific Lodge Boy's Home
4900 Serrania Ave, Woodland Hills (91364-3301)
P.O. Box 308 (91365-0308)
PHONE..................................818 347-1577
Leslie King, *Ch of Bd*
Lisa Alegria, *CEO*
Ed Lappeus, *Opers Mgr*
Hazel Benavides, *Cust Mgr*
Sami Raboubi, *Director*
EMP: 110
SQ FT: 22,634
SALES: 4.9MM **Privately Held**
WEB: www.plys.org
SIC: 8361 Residential care

(P-24019)
PACIFIC RETIREMENT SVCS INC
Also Called: University Retirement Cmnty
1515 Shasta Dr Ofc, Davis (95616-6695)
PHONE..................................530 753-1450
Mark Blazer, *Exec Dir*
Judi Del Ponte, *Marketing Staff*
Laura Tomasello, *Sales Staff*
Tim Silver, *Director*
EMP: 170 **Privately Held**
WEB: www.prsmedia.com
SIC: 8361 Home for the aged
PA: Pacific Retirement Services, Inc.
1 W Main St Ste 303
Medford OR 97501

(P-24020)
PALADIN EASTSIDE SERVICES INC
111 S Grfield Ave Ste 101, Montebello (90640)
PHONE..................................323 890-0180
Octavio Delgado, *President*
Lolita David, *CFO*
EMP: 100
SQ FT: 1,800
SALES (est): 3.6MM **Privately Held**
SIC: 8361 Residential care

(P-24021)
PALM GRDNS RSDNTIAL CARE FCLTY
240 Palm Ave, Woodland (95695-2844)
PHONE..................................530 661-0574
Sue Farrow, *President*
EMP: 50
SALES (est): 2.8MM **Privately Held**
SIC: 8361 8322 Geriatric residential care; individual & family services

(P-24022)
PALO ALTO COMMONS
4075 El Camino Way, Palo Alto (94306-4005)
PHONE..................................650 320-8626
William Reller, *Partner*
Carolyn Reller, *Partner*
EMP: 85
SQ FT: 80,000
SALES (est): 6MM **Privately Held**
WEB: www.paloaltocommons.com
SIC: 8361 8052 Home for the aged; intermediate care facilities

(P-24023)
PASADENA CHLD TRAINING SOC
Also Called: Sycamores School
2933 El Nido Dr, Altadena (91001-4529)
PHONE..................................626 798-0853
William P Martone, *Exec Dir*
EMP: 192
SQ FT: 24,658
SALES (corp-wide): 12.8MM **Privately Held**
WEB: www.sycamores.com
SIC: 8361 8322 Home for the emotionally disturbed; individual & family services
PA: Pasadena Children's Training Society
210 S De Lacey Ave # 110
Pasadena CA 91105
626 395-7100

(P-24024)
PEOPLE SERVICES INC (PA)
Also Called: KONOCTI TRANSPORTATION SERVICE
4195 Lakeshore Blvd, Lakeport (95453-6411)
PHONE..................................707 263-3810
F Ilene Dumont, *Exec Dir*
EMP: 88
SQ FT: 13,125
SALES: 4.1MM **Privately Held**
WEB: www.peopleservices.org
SIC: 8361 Self-help group home

(P-24025)
PEPPERMINT RIDGE (PA)
825 Magnolia Ave, Corona (92879-3129)
PHONE..................................951 273-7320
Danette McCarnes, *Exec Dir*
EMP: 83
SQ FT: 25,000
SALES: 7.5MM **Privately Held**
WEB: www.peppermintridge.org
SIC: 8361 8322 Residential care for the handicapped; individual & family services

(P-24026)
PHOENIX HOUSE ORANGE COUNTY
1207 E Fruit St, Santa Ana (92701-4296)
PHONE..................................714 953-9373
Pouria Abbassi, *CEO*
Elena Ksendzov, *CFO*
Stephen Donowitz, *Vice Pres*
EMP: 67
SALES (est): 2MM
SALES (corp-wide): 14.7MM **Privately Held**
SIC: 8361 Rehabilitation center, residential: health care incidental
PA: Phoenix Houses Of California, Inc
11600 Eldridge Ave
Sylmar CA 91342
818 896-1121

(P-24027)
PHOENIX HOUSES LOS ANGELES INC
Also Called: PHOENIX HSE FNDTN, INC. & AF
11600 Eldridge Ave, Lake View Terrace (91342-6506)
PHONE..................................818 686-3000
Winifred Wechsler, *President*
EMP: 99
SALES: 11.3MM
SALES (corp-wide): 14.7MM **Privately Held**
SIC: 8361 Rehabilitation center, residential: health care incidental
PA: Phoenix Houses Of California, Inc
11600 Eldridge Ave
Sylmar CA 91342
818 896-1121

(P-24028)
POOR SISTERS OF NAZARETH OF SA
Also Called: Nazareth House
6333 Rancho Mission Rd, San Diego (92108-2001)
PHONE..................................619 563-0480
Sister Margaret Spence, *Administration*
Barbara-Anne Crowley, *Exec Dir*
EMP: 75

SALES (est): 5.1MM **Privately Held**
WEB: www.nazarethhouse.com
SIC: 8361 8051 Home for the aged; skilled nursing care facilities

(P-24029)
PRIMROSE ALZHEIMERS LIVING (PA)
726 College Ave, Santa Rosa (95404-4107)
PHONE..................707 568-4355
John Wotring, *President*
EMP: 50
SALES (est): 4.6MM **Privately Held**
WEB: www.primrosealz.com
SIC: 8361 Home for the aged

(P-24030)
PRIMROSE ALZHEIMERS LIVING
2080 Guerneville Rd, Santa Rosa (95403-4117)
PHONE..................707 578-8360
John J Wortring, *Manager*
Jack Burton, *Food Svc Dir*
EMP: 50
SALES (est): 1.1MM
SALES (corp-wide): 4.6MM **Privately Held**
WEB: www.primrosealz.com
SIC: 8361 Home for the aged
PA: Primrose Alzheimer's Living Inc
726 College Ave
Santa Rosa CA 95404
707 568-4355

(P-24031)
PRIMROSE ALZHEIMERS LIVING
Also Called: Primrose Sacramento
7707 Rush River Dr, Sacramento (95831-5229)
PHONE..................916 392-3510
John Wotring, *Exec Dir*
EMP: 65
SALES (corp-wide): 4.6MM **Privately Held**
WEB: www.primrosealz.com
SIC: 8361 8099 Home for the aged; medical services organization
PA: Primrose Alzheimer's Living Inc
726 College Ave
Santa Rosa CA 95404
707 568-4355

(P-24032)
PROGRESS HOUSE INC (PA)
2844 Coloma St Ste A&B, Placerville (95667-4406)
P.O. Box 1666 (95667-1666)
PHONE..................530 626-9240
Barbara Vermilyea, *Exec Dir*
Kristina Harris, *Program Mgr*
EMP: 55
SQ FT: 6,184
SALES (est): 2.5MM **Privately Held**
WEB: www.progresshouseinc.org
SIC: 8361 Rehabilitation center, residential: health care incidental

(P-24033)
PROMESA BEHAVIORAL HEALTH
2815 G St, Merced (95340-2133)
PHONE..................209 725-3114
Lisa Weigant, *Branch Mgr*
EMP: 51 **Privately Held**
SIC: 8361 Group foster home
PA: Promesa Behavioral Health
7120 N Marks Ave
Fresno CA 93711

(P-24034)
PROMESA BEHAVIORAL HEALTH (PA)
7120 N Marks Ave, Fresno (93711-0268)
PHONE..................559 439-5437
Lisa Weigant, *CEO*
EMP: 150
SALES: 8.7MM **Privately Held**
SIC: 8361 Residential care

(P-24035)
PROVIDENT CARE INC
1025 14th St, Modesto (95354-1001)
P.O. Box 3558 (95352-3558)
PHONE..................209 578-1210
Robin Conley, *President*
Cheryl Seals, *Manager*
Cathi Terry, *Supervisor*
▲ **EMP:** 167
SQ FT: 4,571
SALES (est): 2.2MM **Privately Held**
SIC: 8361 Home for the aged

(P-24036)
PSYNERGY PROGRAMS INC
18225 Hale Ave, Morgan Hill (95037-3547)
PHONE..................408 776-0422
Christopher Zubaite, *President*
Michael S Weinstein, *CFO*
L Jean Edwards, *Ch Credit Ofcr*
EMP: 55
SALES (est): 5.3MM **Privately Held**
SIC: 8361 Residential care

(P-24037)
RAISER SENIOR SERVICES LLC
Also Called: Stratford
601 Laurel Ave Apt 903, San Mateo (94401-4164)
PHONE..................650 342-4106
Jennifer Raiser, *President*
Phillip Raiser, *Vice Pres*
EMP: 75
SQ FT: 184,000
SALES (est): 2.5MM **Privately Held**
SIC: 8361 Rest home, with health care incidental

(P-24038)
RANCHO DE SUS NINOS INC
Also Called: His Kids Ranch
P.O. Box 360 (91963-0360)
PHONE..................619 661-9232
Steve Horner, *Director*
EMP: 60
SALES: 2MM **Privately Held**
SIC: 8361 Orphanage

(P-24039)
RANCHO SAN ANTONIO BOYS HM INC (PA)
21000 Plummer St, Chatsworth (91311-4903)
PHONE..................818 882-6400
Brother John Crowe, *CEO*
Nicholas Rizzo, *Finance Dir*
Brandy Reid, *Social Worker*
EMP: 105 **EST:** 1933
SALES: 2.3MM **Privately Held**
SIC: 8361 Boys' Towns

(P-24040)
RANCHO SAN ANTONIO RETIREMENT
Also Called: Forum At Rancho San Antonio
23500 Cristo Rey Dr, Cupertino (95014-6503)
PHONE..................650 265-2637
Ken Fullmore, *Exec Dir*
EMP: 302
SALES (est): 17.9MM **Privately Held**
SIC: 8361 8051 Rest home, with health care incidental; skilled nursing care facilities

(P-24041)
REDWOOD ELDERLINK SCPH
Also Called: Redwood Elderlink & Homelink
710 W 13th Ave, Escondido (92025-5511)
PHONE..................760 480-1030
Kurt Norden, *Director*
Dan Johnson, *President*
Tom Vedvick, *Chairman*
Fran Hillebrecht, *Treasurer*
Doug Best, *Admin Sec*
EMP: 450
SQ FT: 200,000
SALES: 6.5MM
SALES (corp-wide): 101.5MM **Privately Held**
WEB: www.redwoodelderlink.com
SIC: 8361 8742 Home for the aged; compensation & benefits planning consultant

PA: Southern California Presbyterian Homes
516 Burchett St
Glendale CA 91203
818 247-0420

(P-24042)
REGENCY PARK SENIOR LIVING INC
Also Called: Regency Park Oak Knoll
255 S Oak Knoll Ave, Pasadena (91101-2992)
PHONE..................626 396-4911
Fax: 626 584-5719
EMP: 62
SALES (corp-wide): 10.6MM **Privately Held**
SIC: 8361
PA: Regency Park Senior Living, Inc.
150 S Los Robles Ave # 480
Pasadena CA 91101
626 773-8800

(P-24043)
REGENT ASSISTED LIVING INC
Also Called: Regent Senior Living W Covina
150 S Grand Ave Ofc, West Covina (91791-2355)
PHONE..................626 332-3344
Lorena Arechiga, *Manager*
EMP: 60 **Privately Held**
WEB: www.regentassistedliving.com
SIC: 8361 Residential care
PA: Regent Assisted Living, Inc.
121 Sw Morrison St # 950
Portland OR 97204

(P-24044)
REGENT ASSISTED LIVING INC
Also Called: Regent At Laurel Springs
8100 Westwold Dr Ofc, Bakersfield (93311-3471)
PHONE..................661 663-8400
Janice Calco, *Manager*
EMP: 50 **Privately Held**
WEB: www.regentassistedliving.com
SIC: 8361 Residential care
PA: Regent Assisted Living, Inc.
121 Sw Morrison St # 950
Portland OR 97204

(P-24045)
REGENT ASSISTED LIVING INC
Also Called: Regent Court
2325 St Pauls Way, Modesto (95355-3309)
PHONE..................209 491-0800
Karen Schemper, *Manager*
EMP: 53 **Privately Held**
WEB: www.regentassistedliving.com
SIC: 8361 Residential care
PA: Regent Assisted Living, Inc.
121 Sw Morrison St # 950
Portland OR 97204

(P-24046)
REGENT ASSISTED LIVING INC
Also Called: Sunshine Villa Assisted Living
80 Front St, Santa Cruz (95060-5098)
PHONE..................831 459-8400
Deann Daniel, *Manager*
EMP: 80 **Privately Held**
WEB: www.regentassistedliving.com
SIC: 8361 8052 Geriatric residential care; intermediate care facilities
PA: Regent Assisted Living, Inc.
121 Sw Morrison St # 950
Portland OR 97204

(P-24047)
REGENT ASSISTED LIVING INC
Also Called: Orchard Park
675 W Alluvial Ave Ofc, Clovis (93611-4403)
PHONE..................559 325-8400
Debbie Aramian, *Manager*
EMP: 80 **Privately Held**
WEB: www.regentassistedliving.com
SIC: 8361 8052 Residential care; intermediate care facilities

PA: Regent Assisted Living, Inc.
121 Sw Morrison St # 950
Portland OR 97204

(P-24048)
REMI VISTA INC (PA)
2701 Park Marina Dr, Redding (96001-2805)
P.O. Box 494100 (96049-4100)
PHONE..................530 245-5805
John Tillery, *CEO*
Glenda York, *Manager*
EMP: 190
SQ FT: 4,000
SALES: 12.6MM **Privately Held**
WEB: www.remivistainc.org
SIC: 8361 8322 Residential care for the handicapped; child related social services

(P-24049)
RETIREMENT HOUSING FOUNDATION
Also Called: Auburn Ravine Terrace
750 Auburn Ravine Rd, Auburn (95603-3820)
PHONE..................530 823-6131
Robert Mauer, *General Mgr*
Beth Murphy, *Social Dir*
Jenny Applegate, *Marketing Staff*
EMP: 104
SQ FT: 9,756
SALES (corp-wide): 39.7MM **Privately Held**
WEB: www.bixbyknollstowers.com
SIC: 8361 Residential care
PA: Retirement Housing Foundation Inc
911 N Studebaker Rd # 100
Long Beach CA 90815
562 257-5100

(P-24050)
RETIREMENT LF CARE COMMUNITIES
Also Called: Carlton Plaza of Fremont
3800 Walnut Ave Apt 401, Fremont (94538-2273)
PHONE..................510 505-0555
Stephanie Brice, *Exec Dir*
EMP: 64
SQ FT: 104,000
SALES (est): 2.5MM **Privately Held**
SIC: 8361 6513 Home for the aged; retirement hotel operation

(P-24051)
RHF PLYMOUTH TOWER
3401 Lemon St Ofc, Riverside (92501-2817)
PHONE..................951 248-0456
Wes Jones, *Administration*
EMP: 65
SALES (est): 2.4MM **Privately Held**
WEB: www.bixbyknollstowers.com
SIC: 8361 Residential care

(P-24052)
RITE OF PASS ATHL TRAI CENT
10400 Fricot City Rd, San Andreas (95249-9642)
PHONE..................209 736-4500
Ken Dukek, *Manager*
Ingrid Mann, *Human Res Mgr*
Deborah Mayfield, *Human Res Mgr*
Harriet Caruso, *Education*
EMP: 103 **Privately Held**
SIC: 8361 Residential care for children
PA: Rite Of Passage Adolescent Treatment Centers And Schools, Inc.
2560 Business Pkwy Ste B
Minden NV 89423

(P-24053)
ROBERT C HAMILTON
Also Called: Bel Vista Convalescent Hosp
1760 N Fair Oaks Ave, Pasadena (91103-1617)
PHONE..................626 794-4103
Robert C Hamilton, *Owner*
Ann Hamilton, *Owner*
EMP: 70
SQ FT: 2,230
SALES (est): 767.5K **Privately Held**
SIC: 8361 Children's boarding home

(P-24054)
ROSEMARY CHILDRENS SERVICES (PA)
36 S Kinneloa Ave 200, Pasadena (91107-3853)
PHONE......................626 844-3033
Greg Wessels, *Exec Dir*
Sungo Wang, *President*
Lynn Lu, *Vice Pres*
Veronica Fuentes, *Admin Sec*
Lesley Evangelista, *Finance Dir*
EMP: 150
SQ FT: 9,000
SALES: 13.6MM **Privately Held**
WEB: www.rosemarychildren.org
SIC: 8361 Home for the emotionally disturbed

(P-24055)
SACRAMENTO CHILDRENS HOME
1217 Del Paso Blvd Ste B, Sacramento (95815-3660)
PHONE......................916 927-5059
Roy Alexander, *CEO*
EMP: 62
SALES (corp-wide): 14.9MM **Privately Held**
SIC: 8361 Children's home
PA: Sacramento Childrens Home
2750 Sutterville Rd
Sacramento CA 95820
916 452-3981

(P-24056)
SACRAMENTO CHILDRENS HOME (PA)
2750 Sutterville Rd, Sacramento (95820-1093)
PHONE......................916 452-3981
Roy Alexander, *CEO*
Colleen Calandra, *CFO*
Julia Chubb, *CFO*
Glenn Carson, *Program Mgr*
Annette Jumper, *General Mgr*
EMP: 125
SQ FT: 15,500
SALES: 14.9MM **Privately Held**
WEB: www.donatetocharity.com
SIC: 8361 Children's home

(P-24057)
SAFE REFUGE
Also Called: SOBRIETY HOUSE
1041 Redondo Ave, Long Beach (90804-3928)
PHONE......................562 987-5722
Kathryn Romo, *Exec Dir*
Cathy Romo, *Administration*
EMP: 80
SQ FT: 2,300
SALES: 7.1MM **Privately Held**
WEB: www.safinc.org
SIC: 8361 Rehabilitation center, residential: health care incidental

(P-24058)
SAINT JOSEPH HOME CARE NETWORK
1165 Montgomery Dr, Santa Rosa (95405-4801)
PHONE......................707 206-9124
Shirley Sleeker, *Administration*
Robert Stanley, *Manager*
EMP: 80
SALES: 11.3MM **Privately Held**
SIC: 8361 Home for the aged

(P-24059)
SALEM CHRISTIAN HOMES INC (PA)
6921 Edison Ave Ste A, Chino (91710-9058)
PHONE......................909 614-0575
Roderick McLeish, *Principal*
Bert V Dam, *Treasurer*
Ray Hommes, *Admin Sec*
EMP: 150 **EST:** 1960
SQ FT: 31,400
SALES: 7.9MM **Privately Held**
WEB: www.salemchristianhomes.org
SIC: 8361 Home for the mentally handicapped; home for the physically handicapped

(P-24060)
SALVATION ARMY
2799 Health Center Dr, San Diego (92123-2708)
PHONE......................858 279-1100
James Knaggs, *President*
Kenneth Hodder, *Principal*
Terry Hughes, *Principal*
EMP: 79
SALES (est): 2MM **Privately Held**
SIC: 8361 8322 Self-help group home; emergency shelters

(P-24061)
SALVATION ARMY
154 Oshaughnessy Blvd, San Francisco (94127-1700)
PHONE......................415 643-8000
Larry Nakashima, *Principal*
EMP: 100
SALES (corp-wide): 2.3B **Privately Held**
WEB: www.salvationarmy.usawest.org
SIC: 8361 Rehabilitation center, residential: health care incidental
HQ: The Salvation Army
30840 Hawthorne Blvd
Rancho Palos Verdes CA 90275
562 491-8496

(P-24062)
SAN CLEMENTE VILLAS BY SEA
660 Camino De Los Mares, San Clemente (92673-1800)
PHONE......................949 489-3400
Paul J Brazeau,
Maria Nemeth, *Sales Executive*
Paul Brazeau, *Marketing Mgr*
EMP: 80
SALES (est): 4.8MM **Privately Held**
SIC: 8361 Home for the aged

(P-24063)
SAN FRANCISCO LADIES PROTECTI
Also Called: Heritage, The
3400 Laguna St, San Francisco (94123-2271)
PHONE......................415 931-3136
Marla Hastings, *Administration*
Doug Kaplan, *Social Dir*
Joseph Conroy, *Controller*
EMP: 100 **EST:** 1853
SQ FT: 15,000
SALES: 15.8MM **Privately Held**
SIC: 8361 Home for the aged

(P-24064)
SAN GABRIEL CHILDRENS CTR INC
4740 N Grand Ave, Covina (91724-2005)
PHONE......................626 859-2089
Peter Rincon, *Manager*
EMP: 70 **Privately Held**
WEB: www.sangabrielchild.com
SIC: 8361 8322 Children's home; crisis intervention center
PA: San Gabriel Children's Center, Inc.
2200 E Route 66 Ste 100
Glendora CA 91740

(P-24065)
SANTA CLARA COUNTY OF
Also Called: Probation Dept-Juvenile Div
19050 Malaguerra Ave, Morgan Hill (95037-9032)
PHONE......................408 201-7600
Nick Berchard, *Manager*
EMP: 70 **Privately Held**
WEB: www.countyairports.org
SIC: 8361 9223 Juvenile correctional home; correctional institutions;
PA: County Of Santa Clara
3180 Newberry Dr Ste 150
San Jose CA 95118
408 299-5105

(P-24066)
SEASONS
200 W Whittier Blvd, La Habra (90631-3877)
PHONE......................562 691-1200
Phil Smith, *Director*
Sherry Burmmer, *Director*
EMP: 80

SALES (est): 3.1MM **Privately Held**
SIC: 8361 Residential care

(P-24067)
SEAVIEW HLTHCRE & REHAB CTR LL
6400 Purdue Dr, Eureka (95503-7095)
PHONE......................707 443-5668
Ted Chigaros, *Vice Pres*
EMP: 99
SALES (est): 3.2MM **Privately Held**
WEB: www.seaviewfoundation.org
SIC: 8361 Rehabilitation center, residential: health care incidental

(P-24068)
SENIOR CARE INC
4960 Mills St, La Mesa (91942-9310)
PHONE......................619 928-5644
Carol Parkin, *Food Svc Dir*
EMP: 113 **Privately Held**
SIC: 8361 Residential care
PA: Senior Care, Inc.
700 N Hurstbourne Pkwy # 200
Louisville KY 40222

(P-24069)
SENIOR CARE INC
3423 Channel Way, San Diego (92110-5104)
PHONE......................619 817-8855
Floyd C Weathers, *Owner*
EMP: 113 **Privately Held**
SIC: 8361 Residential care
PA: Senior Care, Inc.
700 N Hurstbourne Pkwy # 200
Louisville KY 40222

(P-24070)
SENIOR KEIRO HEALTH CARE
Also Called: Japanese Retirement Home
325 S Boyle Ave, Los Angeles (90033-3812)
PHONE......................323 263-9651
Shawn Miyake, *CEO*
George Aratani, *President*
Rev David Shigekawa, *Treasurer*
Christina Tatsugawa, *Corp Comm Staff*
EMP: 90
SQ FT: 50,000
SALES: 7.7MM **Privately Held**
SIC: 8361 Home for the aged

(P-24071)
SENIOR RESOURCE GROUP LLC
Also Called: La Vida Del Mar Associates
850 Del Mar Downs Rd # 338, Solana Beach (92075-2725)
PHONE......................858 519-0890
Terry Oquest, *Manager*
EMP: 50
SALES (corp-wide): 103.5MM **Privately Held**
WEB: www.srgseniorliving.com
SIC: 8361 Residential care
PA: Senior Resource Group, Llc
500 Stevens Ave Ste 100
Solana Beach CA 92075
858 792-9300

(P-24072)
SHALEV SENIOR LIVING
6245 Matilija Ave, Van Nuys (91401-2923)
PHONE......................818 780-4808
Mia Levi, *Principal*
EMP: 50
SALES (est): 1.1MM **Privately Held**
SIC: 8361 Geriatric residential care

(P-24073)
SIERRA OAKS SENIOR LIVING
1520 Collyer Dr, Redding (96003-9535)
PHONE......................530 241-5100
Sue Becker, *Director*
Carla Jones, *Food Svc Dir*
EMP: 60
SALES (est): 2MM **Privately Held**
SIC: 8361 Home for the aged

(P-24074)
SILVERADO SENIOR LIVING INC
Also Called: Tustin Hcnda Memory Care Cmnty
240 E 3rd St, Tustin (92780-3623)
PHONE......................657 888-5752
EMP: 58
SALES (corp-wide): 180.3MM **Privately Held**
SIC: 8361 Residential care
PA: Senior Silverado Living Inc
6400 Oak Cyn Ste 200
Irvine CA 92618
949 240-7200

(P-24075)
SILVERADO SENIOR LIVING HOLDIN
6400 Oak Cyn Ste 200, Irvine (92618-5233)
PHONE......................949 240-7200
Loren B Shook, *CEO*
EMP: 4000
SALES (est): 5.9MM **Privately Held**
SIC: 8361 Home for the aged

(P-24076)
SIPPI ANNE RIVERSIDE RANCH LLP
Also Called: Anne Sppi Clnic Riverside Rnch
18200 Highway 178, Bakersfield (93306-9510)
PHONE......................661 871-9697
Michael Rosberg, *Owner*
Suzaane Rajlal, *Administration*
EMP: 50
SALES (est): 2MM **Privately Held**
SIC: 8361 Residential care

(P-24077)
SISTERS OF NZARETH LOS ANGELES
3333 Manning Ave, Los Angeles (90064-4804)
PHONE......................310 839-2361
Margarette Brody, *Administration*
EMP: 100
SQ FT: 62,558
SALES: 5.9MM **Privately Held**
WEB: www.nazarethhousela.org
SIC: 8361 Home for the aged

(P-24078)
SKY PARK GARDENS ASSISTED
5510 Sky Pkwy Ofc, Sacramento (95823-2282)
PHONE......................916 422-5650
Habib Bokhari, *Owner*
EMP: 55
SALES (est): 1.3MM **Privately Held**
SIC: 8361 Home for the aged

(P-24079)
SOCIAL VOCATIONAL SERVICES INC
1401 Fulton St Ste 510, Fresno (93721-1644)
PHONE......................559 443-7119
EMP: 74
SALES (corp-wide): 93.5MM **Privately Held**
SIC: 8361 Rehabilitation center, residential: health care incidental
PA: Social Vocational Services, Inc.
3555 Torrance Blvd
Torrance CA 90503
310 944-3303

(P-24080)
SOLHEIM LUTHERAN HOME
2236 Merton Ave, Los Angeles (90041-1915)
PHONE......................323 257-7518
James Graunke, *Principal*
Antonio Davila, *CFO*
Norma Heaton, *Exec Dir*
Sherry Wait, *Nursing Dir*
EMP: 185 **EST:** 1923
SQ FT: 82,591
SALES: 14.6MM **Privately Held**
WEB: www.solheimlh.org
SIC: 8361 Home for the aged

(P-24081)
SONORA RETIREMENT CENTER INC
Also Called: Skyline Place
12877 Sylva Ln Ofc, Sonora (95370-6965)
PHONE................................209 588-0373
Mark Weisner, *President*
EMP: 50
SQ FT: 56,000
SALES (est): 2.9MM **Privately Held**
SIC: 8361 Home for the aged

(P-24082)
SOUTH BAY BRIGHT FUTURE INC (PA)
Also Called: YOUTH DEVELOPMENT CENTER
24404 Vermont Ave Ste 206, Harbor City (90710-2323)
PHONE................................310 891-0096
William M Hill, *CEO*
EMP: 67
SQ FT: 3,000
SALES: 3.4MM **Privately Held**
SIC: 8361 8322 Group foster home; child related social services

(P-24083)
ST ANNES MATERNITY HOME
155 N Occidental Blvd, Los Angeles (90026-4641)
PHONE................................213 381-2931
Tony Walker, *President*
EMP: 158
SQ FT: 100,000
SALES: 24.5MM **Privately Held**
SIC: 8361 Rehabilitation center, residential: health care incidental

(P-24084)
ST PAULS EPISCOPAL HOME INC
2635 2nd Ave Ofc, San Diego (92103-6597)
PHONE................................619 239-2097
EMP: 53
SALES (corp-wide): 19.1MM **Privately Held**
SIC: 8361 Home for the aged
PA: St. Paul's Episcopal Home, Inc.
328 Maple St
San Diego CA 92103
619 239-6900

(P-24085)
ST PAULS EPISCOPAL HOME INC
Saint Pauls Health Care Center
235 Nutmeg St, San Diego (92103-6201)
PHONE................................619 239-8687
Ben Geske, *Manager*
EMP: 65
SQ FT: 1,100
SALES (corp-wide): 19.1MM **Privately Held**
SIC: 8361 8051 Rest home, with health care incidental; skilled nursing care facilities
PA: St. Paul's Episcopal Home, Inc.
328 Maple St
San Diego CA 92103
619 239-6900

(P-24086)
ST PAULS EPISCOPAL HOME INC
Also Called: St Paul's Villa
2700 E 4th St, National City (91950-3006)
PHONE................................619 232-2996
Cheryl Wilson, *Director*
EMP: 65
SALES (corp-wide): 19.1MM **Privately Held**
SIC: 8361 Home for the aged
PA: St. Paul's Episcopal Home, Inc.
328 Maple St
San Diego CA 92103
619 239-6900

(P-24087)
STOCKTON CONGREGATIONAL HOME
Also Called: PLYMOUTH SQUARE
1319 N Madison St Ofc, Stockton (95202-1001)
PHONE................................209 466-4341
Peter Peabody, *Vice Pres*
Stuart Hartman, *Principal*
EMP: 84
SALES: 4MM **Privately Held**
SIC: 8361 Home for the aged

(P-24088)
SUMMER HOUSE INC (PA)
206 5th St, Woodland (95695-3505)
P.O. Box 1724 (95776-1724)
PHONE................................530 662-8493
Erin Plankryan, *Exec Dir*
Dale Campbell, *Exec Dir*
EMP: 54
SQ FT: 6,500
SALES: 1.6MM **Privately Held**
SIC: 8361 8059 8322 Residential care for the handicapped; home for the mentally retarded; home for the mentally retarded, exc. skilled or intermediate; social services for the handicapped

(P-24089)
SUMMERVILLE AT HAZEL CREEK LLC
Also Called: Hazel Creek Assisted Living
6125 Hazel Ave, Orangevale (95662-4558)
PHONE................................916 988-7901
Lonnie Irvine, *President*
EMP: 1283
SALES (est): 14.1MM
SALES (corp-wide): 4.5B **Publicly Held**
SIC: 8361 Home for the aged
HQ: Emeritus Corporation
3131 Elliott Ave Ste 500
Milwaukee WI 53214
-

(P-24090)
SUMMITVIEW CHILD TREATMENT CTR
5036 Sunrey Rd, Placerville (95667-9529)
PHONE................................530 644-2412
Carla Wills, *Exec Dir*
Paul Sunseri, *Director*
EMP: 50
SQ FT: 1,480
SALES (est): 5.2MM **Privately Held**
SIC: 8361 Halfway group home, persons with social or personal problems

(P-24091)
SUNHARBOR MANAGEMENT LLC
Also Called: The Valley Inn
708 E 5th St, Holtville (92250-1514)
PHONE................................760 356-1262
Gary Rust,
Fred Harder,
John Harder,
Elaine Rust,
Bruce Thorne,
EMP: 50
SALES (est): 1.2MM **Privately Held**
SIC: 8361 Residential care

(P-24092)
SUNNY ROSE GLEN LLC
29620 Bradley Rd, Sun City (92586-6521)
PHONE................................951 679-3355
Karen Roper, *Exec Dir*
Mike Adams, *President*
EMP: 55
SALES (est): 1.4MM **Privately Held**
SIC: 8361 Home for the aged

(P-24093)
SUNNYSIDE GARDENS
1025 Carson Dr, Sunnyvale (94086-5800)
PHONE................................408 730-4070
Anna Ready, *Director*
Jann Acevedo, *Manager*
EMP: 72
SALES (est): 2.4MM **Privately Held**
SIC: 8361 Geriatric residential care

(P-24094)
TERRACES RETIREMENT COMMUNITY
Also Called: Lodge Inn and Health Center
2850 Sierra Sunrise Ter, Chico (95928-8401)
PHONE................................530 894-1010
Cheryl Haury, *CEO*
Cerel Havority, *President*
Heidi Hukill, *CFO*
Grace Mejia, *Principal*
EMP: 166
SQ FT: 1,000
SALES (est): 2.7MM **Privately Held**
WEB: www.theterraceschico.com
SIC: 8361 Home for the aged; skilled nursing care facilities

(P-24095)
THE REDWOODS A CMNTY SENIORS
Also Called: REDWOODS, THE
40 Camino Alto Ofc, Mill Valley (94941-2997)
PHONE................................415 383-2741
Barbara Solomon, *CEO*
Susan Badger, *COO*
Alan Kern, *CFO*
Ron Bruno, *Human Resources*
EMP: 140
SQ FT: 140,000
SALES: 19.8MM **Privately Held**
WEB: www.redwoodsoft.com
SIC: 8361 Home for the aged

(P-24096)
TIERRA DEL SOL FOUNDATION (PA)
9919 Sunland Blvd, Sunland (91040-1599)
PHONE................................818 352-1419
Steve Miller, *Exec Dir*
Anne M Rosenstein, *CFO*
Cathy Galarneau, *Bd of Directors*
James Chavez, *Program Mgr*
Kevin Lehmann, *Program Mgr*
EMP: 95
SQ FT: 20,000
SALES: 16.6MM **Privately Held**
WEB: www.tierradelsol.org
SIC: 8361 8211 8322 Home for the mentally handicapped; home for the physically handicapped; public special education school; individual & family services

(P-24097)
TRINITY YOUTH SERVICES (PA)
201 N Indian Hill Blvd # 201, Claremont (91711-4668)
P.O. Box 1210 (91711-1210)
PHONE................................909 980-4755
John Neiuber, *CEO*
Aris Alexandre, *President*
Nathan Mitakides, *President*
Fr Paul O'Callaghan, *Treasurer*
Gary Vrinos, *Vice Pres*
EMP: 60
SQ FT: 7,600
SALES: 19.2MM **Privately Held**
WEB: www.trinitycfs.org
SIC: 8361 Halfway home for delinquents & offenders

(P-24098)
TURNING POINT CMNTY PROGRAMS
Also Called: Turning Point I S A
4600 47th Ave Ste 111, Sacramento (95824-3923)
PHONE................................916 393-1222
Andre Lavaly, *Branch Mgr*
Russell F Lim, *Psychiatry*
Sadie Schen, *Program Dir*
Ron Gilbert, *Director*
EMP: 72
SALES (corp-wide): 33MM **Privately Held**
SIC: 8361 Residential care
PA: Turning Point Community Programs
10850 Gold Center Dr # 325
Rancho Cordova CA 95670
916 364-8395

(P-24099)
UNITED CP/S CHLDRNS FNDN LA
11051 Old Snta Susna Pass, Chatsworth (91311-1206)
PHONE................................818 998-8755
Rick Macdonough, *Administration*
Paula Hill, *Director*
EMP: 135
SQ FT: 20,019
SALES (corp-wide): 24.2MM **Privately Held**
SIC: 8361 8322 Rehabilitation center, residential: health care incidental; individual & family services
PA: United Cerebral Palsy/Spastic Children's Foundation Of Los Angeles And Ventura Counties
6430 Independence Ave
Woodland Hills CA 91367
818 782-2211

(P-24100)
VALLEY MTN REGIONAL CTR INC
1620 Cummins Dr, Modesto (95358-6414)
PHONE................................209 529-2626
Richard Jacobs, *Branch Mgr*
EMP: 70
SALES (corp-wide): 159.8MM **Privately Held**
SIC: 8361 Residential care for the handicapped
PA: Valley Mountain Regional Center, Inc.
702 N Aurora St
Stockton CA 95202
209 473-0951

(P-24101)
VALLEY PINTE NURSING REHAB CTR
20090 Stanton Ave, Castro Valley (94546-5203)
PHONE................................510 538-8464
Daniel Wittman, *Administration*
EMP: 50
SQ FT: 7,500
SALES: 5MM **Privately Held**
SIC: 8361 Rehabilitation center, residential: health care incidental

(P-24102)
VALLEY TEEN RANCH
2610 W Shaw Ln Ste 105, Fresno (93711-2775)
PHONE................................559 437-1144
Connie Clendenan, *Exec Dir*
Legion Escobar, *Tech/Comp Coord*
Jennifer Moore, *Social Worker*
Carlos Vigil, *Social Worker*
Margarita Estrada, *Cust Mgr*
EMP: 76
SQ FT: 9,996
SALES: 4.3MM **Privately Held**
WEB: www.valleyteenranch.org
SIC: 8361 8322 Group foster home; individual & family services

(P-24103)
VALLEY VILLAGE (PA)
20830 Sherman Way, Winnetka (91306-2707)
PHONE................................818 587-9450
Debra Donovan, *CEO*
Vania Rodriguez, *Human Res Mgr*
Joyce Brady, *Director*
Jenny D Freese, *Director*
Rebecca Holik, *Director*
EMP: 75 **EST:** 1973
SQ FT: 14,000
SALES: 19.2MM **Privately Held**
WEB: www.vvc.org
SIC: 8361 Home for the mentally retarded

(P-24104)
VASINDAS AROUND THE CLOCK CARE
Also Called: AROUND THE CLOCK HOME CARE
5251 Office Park Dr # 403, Bakersfield (93309-0695)
PHONE................................661 395-5820
Mary Vasinda, *President*
John Vasinda, *Vice Pres*
Norma Alvarado, *Sales Executive*

Cassandra Ortiz, *Program Dir*
EMP: 50 **EST:** 1996
SALES: 11.1MM **Privately Held**
SIC: 8361 Geriatric residential care

(P-24105)
VICTOR TREATMENT CENTERS INC
Also Called: Willow Creek Treatment Center
341 Irwin Ln, Santa Rosa (95401-5603)
PHONE...................707 360-1509
Gala Goodwin, *Branch Mgr*
EMP: 130
SQ FT: 3,060
SALES (corp-wide): 25MM **Privately Held**
WEB: www.victor.org
SIC: 8361 Home for the emotionally disturbed
PA: Victor Treatment Centers, Inc.
1360 E Lassen Ave
Chico CA 95973
530 893-0758

(P-24106)
VILLAGE AT GRANITE BAY
8550 Barton Rd, Granite Bay (95746-8843)
PHONE...................916 789-0326
EMP: 68
SALES (est): 579K **Privately Held**
SIC: 8361

(P-24107)
VILLAGE AT NORTHRIDGE
9222 Corbin Ave, Northridge (91324-2409)
PHONE...................818 514-4497
EMP: 167
SALES (est): 1.4MM
SALES (corp-wide): 103.5MM **Privately Held**
SIC: 8361 Home for the aged
PA: Senior Resource Group, Llc
500 Stevens Ave Ste 100
Solana Beach CA 92075
858 792-9300

(P-24108)
VILLAS DE CARLSBAD LTD A CALI (PA)
Also Called: Las Villas De Carlsbad
9619 Chesapeake Dr # 103, San Diego (92123-1368)
PHONE...................858 565-4424
Jack Rowe, *Partner*
William M Chance, *Partner*
Ronald J McElliott, *Partner*
Daniel A Moriarty, *Partner*
EMP: 120
SQ FT: 3,200
SALES (est): 2.6MM **Privately Held**
SIC: 8361 Home for the aged

(P-24109)
VILLAS DE CARLSBAD LTD A CALI
Also Called: Las Villas De Carlsbad
3500 Lake Blvd, Oceanside (92056-4600)
PHONE...................760 434-7116
Jack Rowe, *Owner*
EMP: 50
SALES (est): 1.8MM
SALES (corp-wide): 2.6MM **Privately Held**
SIC: 8361 Home for the aged
PA: Villas De Carlsbad Ltd, A California
Limited Partnership
9619 Chesapeake Dr # 103
San Diego CA 92123
858 565-4424

(P-24110)
VISTA DEL MAR CHILD FMLY SVCS
1533 Euclid St, Santa Monica (90404-3306)
PHONE...................310 836-1223
Louis Josephson, *Branch Mgr*
David Locken, *Director*
EMP: 413
SALES (corp-wide): 45.5MM **Privately Held**
SIC: 8361 Home for the mentally handicapped

PA: Vista Del Mar Child And Family Services
3200 Motor Ave
Los Angeles CA 90034
310 836-1223

(P-24111)
WATERS EDGE LODGE
801 Island Dr Apt 267, Alameda (94502-6765)
PHONE...................510 769-6264
Christian Zimmerman, *Partner*
John Zimmerman, *Partner*
EMP: 50
SALES (est): 2.9MM **Privately Held**
WEB: www.watersedgelodge.com
SIC: 8361 Home for the aged

(P-24112)
WESTCARE CALIFORNIA INC (HQ)
1900 N Gateway Blvd 100, Fresno (93727-1622)
P.O. Box 12107 (93776-2107)
PHONE...................559 251-4800
Richard Steinberg, *President*
Jenifer Nolan, *President*
Shawn Jenkins, *Vice Pres*
Maurice Lee, *Vice Pres*
Tina Stiles, *Controller*
EMP: 52
SALES (est): 10.9MM
SALES (corp-wide): 10.1MM **Privately Held**
SIC: 8361 8093 Rehabilitation center, residential; health care incidental; specialty outpatient clinics
PA: Westcare Foundation, Inc.
1711 Whitney Mesa Dr # 100
Henderson NV 89014
702 385-3330

(P-24113)
WESTERN LIVING CONCEPTS INC (PA)
Also Called: Timber Ridge At Eureka
2740 Timber Ridge Ln Ofc, Eureka (95503-4867)
PHONE...................707 443-3000
Erica Farnum, *Exec Dir*
Cheryl Lyons, *Director*
Andrew Roberts, *Director*
EMP: 50
SALES (est): 3.3MM **Privately Held**
SIC: 8361 Home for the aged

(P-24114)
WESTLIVING MANAGEMENT LLC (PA)
5800 Armada Dr Ste 100, Carlsbad (92008-4611)
PHONE...................760 602-5850
John Rimbach,
Patrick Collins, *Vice Pres*
Kimberly Holmes, *Vice Pres*
Ramona Powell, *Vice Pres*
Bhakti Vora, *Accountant*
EMP: 51
SALES (est): 3.7MM **Privately Held**
SIC: 8361 Geriatric residential care

(P-24115)
WESTMONT LIVING INC
Also Called: Terraces Of Roseville, The
707 Sunrise Ave, Roseville (95661-4524)
PHONE...................916 786-3277
Andrew Plant, *President*
Jacob Weintraub, *Project Mgr*
Alejandra Hernandez, *Accountant*
Jodi Ross, *Director*
EMP: 318
SALES (corp-wide): 41MM **Privately Held**
SIC: 8361 Home for the aged
PA: Westmont Living, Inc.
7660 Fay Ave Ste N
La Jolla CA 92037
858 456-1233

(P-24116)
WESTMONT LIVING INC (PA)
7660 Fay Ave Ste N, La Jolla (92037-4875)
PHONE...................858 456-1233
Michael O Rourke, *CEO*
Andrew Plant, *President*

Leo McKinley, *CFO*
George Grivanos, *Accountant*
Morgan Hill, *Maintence Staff*
EMP: 142
SALES (est): 41MM **Privately Held**
SIC: 8361 Home for the aged

(P-24117)
WHITE RABBIT PARTNERS INC
9000 W Sunset Blvd, West Hollywood (90069-5801)
PHONE...................310 975-1450
Andrew William Spanswick, *CEO*
EMP: 150 **EST:** 2009
SALES (est): 3.8MM **Privately Held**
SIC: 8361 Residential care

(P-24118)
WILLOW SPRNGS ALZHMRS SPCL CR
191 Churn Creek Rd, Redding (96003-3044)
PHONE...................530 242-0654
Jerry Erwin, *Partner*
EMP: 50
SALES (est): 2.1MM **Privately Held**
SIC: 8361 8099 Rehabilitation center, residential: health care incidental; blood related health services

(P-24119)
WILSHIRE HEALTH AND CMNTY SVCS
Also Called: Heritage House
903 Carmen Dr, Camarillo (93010-4527)
PHONE...................805 484-2777
Heather Frankel, *Director*
EMP: 60
SALES (corp-wide): 13MM **Privately Held**
SIC: 8361 Home for the aged
PA: Wilshire Health And Community Services, Inc.
285 South St Ste J
San Luis Obispo CA 93401
805 547-7025

(P-24120)
YOUTH HOMES INCORPORATED (PA)
3480 Buskirk Ave Ste 210, Pleasant Hill (94523-4304)
P.O. Box 5759, Walnut Creek (94596-1759)
PHONE...................925 933-2627
Stuart McCoullough, *Exec Dir*
Donna Heimbruch, *Admin Asst*
Maria Lewis, *Administration*
Shaina Van Pelt, *Project Mgr*
Audrey Tormey, *Human Res Dir*
EMP: 65 **EST:** 1965
SQ FT: 5,000
SALES: 8.2MM **Privately Held**
WEB: www.youthhomes.org
SIC: 8361 8011 8322 Home for the emotionally disturbed; psychiatrist; family counseling services

(P-24121)
YOUTH HOMES INCORPORATED
Also Called: Anderson House
1159 Everett Ct, Concord (94518-1714)
P.O. Box 5759, Walnut Creek (94596-1759)
PHONE...................925 933-2627
Stuart McCoullough, *Exec Dir*
Yuliya Korentsvit, *Manager*
Lucas Dangler, *Supervisor*
EMP: 55
SALES (corp-wide): 8.2MM **Privately Held**
WEB: www.youthhomes.org
SIC: 8361 Home for the emotionally disturbed
PA: Youth Homes Incorporated
3480 Buskirk Ave Ste 210
Pleasant Hill CA 94523
925 933-2627

8399 Social Services, NEC

(P-24122)
A COMMUNITY FOR PEACE
6060 Sunrise Vista Dr # 2340, Citrus Heights (95610-7057)
PHONE...................916 728-5613
Carole Ching, *President*
EMP: 51
SALES: 836.8K **Privately Held**
SIC: 8399 Advocacy group

(P-24123)
ADVANCED MEDICAL PLACEMENT
Also Called: Leadhealthstaff
18425 Burbank Blvd # 508, Tarzana (91356-6692)
PHONE...................818 996-9812
Labanyendu Pattanaik, *President*
Chris Speer, *Info Tech Dir*
Todd Suk, *Info Tech Dir*
Chalinee Menchaya, *Payroll Mgr*
Todd Sukpatratham, *Manager*
EMP: 120
SQ FT: 1,400
SALES: 2MM **Privately Held**
SIC: 8399 Health systems agency

(P-24124)
ALTA HEALTHCARE SYSTEM LLC
Also Called: Van Nuys Community Hospital
14433 Emelita St, Van Nuys (91401-4213)
PHONE...................818 787-1511
Tony Lozano, *Branch Mgr*
Marjan Azimi, *Business Dir*
Laura Difusco, *Director*
EMP: 250
SALES (corp-wide): 1.2B **Privately Held**
SIC: 8399 8063 Health systems agency; psychiatric hospitals
HQ: Alta Healthcare System Llc
4081 E Olympic Blvd
Los Angeles CA 90023
323 267-0477

(P-24125)
ALTA HEALTHCARE SYSTEM LLC (HQ)
4081 E Olympic Blvd, Los Angeles (90023-3330)
PHONE...................323 267-0477
David Topper, *Mng Member*
Bruce Grimshaw, *Vice Pres*
Sam Lee,
Leslia Gomez, *Director*
EMP: 250
SALES (est): 20.5MM
SALES (corp-wide): 1.2B **Privately Held**
SIC: 8399 Health systems agency
PA: Prospect Medical Holdings, Inc.
3415 S Sepulveda Blvd # 9
Los Angeles CA 90034
310 943-4500

(P-24126)
AMADOR TLMNE CMNTY ACTION AGCY (PA)
Also Called: Atcaa
10590 State Highway 88, Jackson (95642-9470)
PHONE...................209 296-2785
Shelly Hance, *Exec Dir*
Patty Cunningham, *Deputy Dir*
EMP: 150
SALES (est): 11MM **Privately Held**
SIC: 8399 Community action agency

(P-24127)
AMADOR TLMNE CMNTY ACTION AGCY
Also Called: Aatcaa Headstart
427 Highway 49, Sonora (95370-5666)
PHONE...................209 533-1397
Shelly Hance, *Exec Dir*
EMP: 50
SALES (est): 1.3MM
SALES (corp-wide): 11MM **Privately Held**
SIC: 8399 Community action agency

PRODUCTS & SVCS

PA: Amador Tuolumne Community Action
Agency
10590 State Highway 88
Jackson CA 95642
209 296-2785

(P-24128)
AMADOR-TOLUMNE CMNTY RESOURCES
Also Called: ATCR
10590 State Highway 88, Jackson
(95642-9470)
PHONE..................................209 223-1485
Shelly Hance, *Exec Dir*
EMP: 99
SALES: 356.1K **Privately Held**
SIC: 8399 Community action agency

(P-24129)
AMERICAN CANCER SOC CAL DIV
Also Called: Discovery Shop
1103 Branham Ln, San Jose (95118-3702)
PHONE..................................408 265-5535
Wendy Huge, *Branch Mgr*
EMP: 50
SALES (corp-wide): 38.8MM **Privately
Held**
SIC: 8399 Social service information ex-
change
PA: American Cancer Society California Di-
vision, Inc
1001 Marina Village Pkwy
Alameda CA 94501
510 893-7900

(P-24130)
ARC OF SAN DIEGO (PA)
Also Called: ARC Enterprises
3030 Market St, San Diego (92102-3230)
PHONE..................................619 685-1175
David W Schneider, *CEO*
Anthony J Desalis, *COO*
Chad Lyle, *CFO*
Jennifer Bates Navarra, *Vice Pres*
Rich Coppa, *Principal*
▲ EMP: 200
SQ FT: 55,093
SALES: 33.9MM **Privately Held**
WEB: www.arc-sd.com
SIC: 8399 8351 8361 8322 Advocacy
group; child day care services; home for
the mentally retarded; individual & family
services

(P-24131)
ARC OF SAN DIEGO
Also Called: ARC - SD E Cnty Training Ctrs
1855 John Towers Ave, El Cajon
(92020-1116)
PHONE..................................619 448-2415
Millie Oveross, *Manager*
EMP: 175
SALES (corp-wide): 33.9MM **Privately
Held**
WEB: www.arc-sd.com
SIC: 8399 8361 Advocacy group; home for
the physically handicapped
PA: The Arc Of San Diego
3030 Market St
San Diego CA 92102
619 685-1175

(P-24132)
ASIAN PCF HLTH CARE VENTR INC (PA)
4216 Fountain Ave, Los Angeles
(90029-2256)
PHONE..................................323 644-3880
Kazue Shibata, *CEO*
Andrew MA, *Associate Dir*
Lorali Delos Reyes, *Principal*
M Ymorinaga, *CTO*
Natasha Salcedo, *Info Tech Mgr*
EMP: 104
SQ FT: 1,800
SALES: 16.2MM **Privately Held**
WEB: www.realyc.com
SIC: 8399 Health systems agency

(P-24133)
ASSISTANCE LEAGUE OF REDLANDS
Also Called: ASSISTANCE LEAGUE THRIFT
SHOP
506 W Colton Ave, Redlands (92374-3054)
PHONE..................................909 792-2675
Madelene Handy, *President*
Sandy Arsenault, *Treasurer*
Beth Goodrich, *Manager*
EMP: 150
SALES: 559.1K **Privately Held**
WEB: www.assistanceleague.org
SIC: 8399 5932 Advocacy group; clothing,
secondhand

(P-24134)
ASSISTNCE LEAG OF FTHILL CMMNT
Also Called: SAN ANTONIO COMMUNITY
HOSPITAL
8555 Archibald Ave 8593, Rancho Cuca-
monga (91730-4633)
P.O. Box 927, Upland (91785-0927)
PHONE..................................909 987-2813
Esther Mott, *Treasurer*
Sandy Kimball, *Treasurer*
Linda Melmeth, *Director*
EMP: 167
SQ FT: 10,000
SALES: 538.8K **Privately Held**
SIC: 8399 Fund raising organization, non-
fee basis

(P-24135)
ASSOCIATED STUDENTS UCLA (PA)
Also Called: Ucla Bookstore
308 Westwood Plz, Los Angeles
(90095-8355)
PHONE..................................310 825-4321
Robert Williams, *Principal*
Randy Jenkins, *Sr Corp Ofcr*
Alfred Osborne, *Trustee*
Tom Phelan, *Officer*
Emily Hughes, *Executive*
EMP: 500
SQ FT: 200,000
SALES: 42.7MM **Privately Held**
SIC: 8399 5942 Council for social agency;
book stores

(P-24136)
ASSOCIATED STUDENTS UCLA
924 Westwood Blvd, Los Angeles
(90024-2910)
PHONE..................................310 794-0242
Roseanna P Malone, *Branch Mgr*
Sofia Liou, *Pathologist*
Rebecca Bavolek, *Emerg Med Spec*
Alexandra Dyer, *Emerg Med Spec*
Brandon Endo, *Emerg Med Spec*
EMP: 139
SALES (corp-wide): 42.7MM **Privately
Held**
SIC: 8399 Council for social agency
PA: Associated Students U.C.L.A.
308 Westwood Plz
Los Angeles CA 90095
310 825-4321

(P-24137)
BASIC OCCPATIONAL TRAINING CTR
Also Called: Basic Occpational Training Ctr
1323 Jet Way, Perris (92571-7466)
PHONE..................................951 657-8028
Richard Yodites, *President*
Mitzies Yodites, *Exec Dir*
Matthew Bauer, *Opers Staff*
Alycya Bazan, *Manager*
Brienna Santangelo, *Assistant*
EMP: 154 EST: 1994
SQ FT: 12,000
SALES: 6.5MM **Privately Held**
SIC: 8399 Community development groups

(P-24138)
BEACH CITIES HEALTH DISTRICT
1200 Del Amo St, Redondo Beach
(90277-3050)
PHONE..................................310 374-3426
Tom Bakaly, *CEO*
Monica Suua, *CFO*

Charlnisha Garnett, *Accountant*
Catherine Bem, *Corp Comm Staff*
EMP: 108
SALES (est): 9.5MM **Privately Held**
SIC: 8399 Health systems agency

(P-24139)
CALIFORNIA ENDOWMENT (PA)
1000 N Alameda St, Los Angeles
(90012-1804)
PHONE..................................213 928-8800
Robert K Ross, *President*
Dan C Deleon, *CFO*
Cecilia Echeverr A, *Officer*
Ray Colmenar, *Officer*
Sarah Reyes, *Officer*
EMP: 80
SQ FT: 110,000
SALES (est): 181MM **Privately Held**
SIC: 8399 Fund raising organization, non-
fee basis

(P-24140)
CALIFORNIA RURAL INDIAN HEALTH
1020 Sun Down Way, Roseville
(95661-4473)
PHONE..................................916 437-0104
James Crouch, *Exec Dir*
Jason C Lopez, *CFO*
Ronald Moody, *CFO*
Laura Rambeau-Lawson, *Treasurer*
Glenda Nelson, *Admin Sec*
EMP: 80
SQ FT: 18,627
SALES: 53.6MM **Privately Held**
WEB: www.crihb.org
SIC: 8399 Health & welfare council

(P-24141)
CALIFRNIA ATISM FOUNDATION INC (PA)
4075 Lakeside Dr, Richmond (94806-1937)
PHONE..................................510 758-0433
John Rockefeller, *Principal*
John D Rockefeller, *CEO*
Don Johnson, *CFO*
Valisha Fullard, *Vice Pres*
Xiaoming Lou, *Principal*
EMP: 250
SQ FT: 4,400
SALES: 7.3MM **Privately Held**
SIC: 8399 Community development groups

(P-24142)
CANCER FEDERATION INC (PA)
711 W Ramsey St, Banning (92220-4941)
P.O. Box 1298 (92220-0009)
PHONE..................................951 849-4325
John Steinbacher, *Trust Officer*
Karen Alene, *Administration*
EMP: 200
SALES: 349.4K **Privately Held**
WEB: www.cancerfed.com
SIC: 8399 8011 Social service information
exchange; offices & clinics of medical
doctors

(P-24143)
CAPC INC
Also Called: COMMUNITY ADVOCATE FOR
PEOPLE'
7200 Greenleaf Ave # 170, Whittier
(90602-1391)
PHONE..................................562 693-8826
Carolyn Reggio, *Exec Dir*
Paul Velasco, *President*
Cheryl Turner, *Treasurer*
Maria Segovia, *Admin Sec*
Jeanette Demirjian, *Director*
EMP: 150
SALES: 3.9MM **Privately Held**
SIC: 8399 Advocacy group

(P-24144)
CEMENT MASON HEALTH & WELFARE
220 Campus Ln, Suisun City (94534-1497)
PHONE..................................707 864-3300
Marvin Johnson, *Manager*
EMP: 100
SQ FT: 43,000

SALES: 25.7MM **Privately Held**
WEB: www.norcalcementmasons.org
SIC: 8399 6282 Fund raising organization,
non-fee basis; investment advice

(P-24145)
CITY OF POMONA
Also Called: Welfare Dept
2040 W Holt Ave Fl 2, Pomona
(91768-3307)
PHONE..................................909 397-5506
John Minato, *Director*
EMP: 400
SQ FT: 3,455 **Privately Held**
SIC: 8399 Social service information ex-
change
PA: Pomona, City Of (Inc)
585 E Holt Ave
Pomona CA 91766
909 620-2051

(P-24146)
CMP WELLNESS LLC
1732 Aviation Blvd 317, Redondo Beach
(90278-2810)
PHONE..................................323 697-8808
Luis Soto,
Hayde Gutierrez,
EMP: 62
SALES (est): 93.6K
SALES (corp-wide): 148.9MM **Publicly
Held**
SIC: 8399 Health systems agency
PA: Kushco Holdings, Inc.
11958 Monarch St
Garden Grove CA 92841
714 243-4311

(P-24147)
COLUSA INDIAN CMNTY COUNCIL
Also Called: Colusa Casino
3740 Highway 45, Colusa (95932-4030)
PHONE..................................530 458-6572
Laurie Costa, *Director*
Tammy Harris, *Human Res Mgr*
Doyle Smotherman, *Opers Staff*
Cathy Wells, *Opers Staff*
EMP: 650 **Privately Held**
WEB: www.colusacasino.com
SIC: 8399 7991 Community development
groups; health club
PA: Colusa Indian Community Council
3730 State Highway 45 B
Colusa CA 95932
530 458-8231

(P-24148)
COMMUNICATION SVC FOR DEAF INC
Also Called: Community Services For Deaf
81 W March Ln, Stockton (95207-5723)
PHONE..................................209 475-5000
Rhasan Waser, *Manager*
EMP: 50
SALES (corp-wide): 31.5MM **Privately
Held**
WEB: www.relaysd.com
SIC: 8399 Social service information ex-
change
PA: Communication Service For The Deaf,
Inc.
2028 E B White 240-5250
Austin TX 78741
844 222-0002

(P-24149)
COMMUNITY ACTION COMMSN SANTA
4545 10th St, Guadalupe (93434-1421)
PHONE..................................805 343-0615
Fran Forman, *Exec Dir*
EMP: 122
SALES (corp-wide): 23.4MM **Privately
Held**
SIC: 8399 Community action agency
PA: Community Action Commission Of
Santa Barbara County
5638 Hollister Ave # 230
Goleta CA 93117
805 964-8857

(P-24150)
COMMUNITY ACTION COMMSN SANTA
1890 Sandalwood Dr, Santa Maria (93455-2846)
PHONE..................................805 614-0786
Mary Flores, *Branch Mgr*
Miriam Angel, *Manager*
EMP: 400
SALES (corp-wide): 23.4MM **Privately Held**
WEB: www.cacsb.com
SIC: 8399 8322 Community action agency; individual & family services
PA: Community Action Commission Of Santa Barbara County
5638 Hollister Ave # 230
Goleta CA 93117
805 964-8857

(P-24151)
COMMUNITY ACTION COMMSN SANTA (PA)
Also Called: C A C
5638 Hollister Ave # 230, Goleta (93117-3474)
PHONE..................................805 964-8857
Fran Forman, *President*
Cesar Arroyo, *Program Mgr*
Elizabeth Fry, *General Mgr*
Irene Mau, *Admin Sec*
Mark Navarro, *Accountant*
EMP: 50
SALES: 23.4MM **Privately Held**
WEB: www.cacsb.com
SIC: 8399 Community action agency

(P-24152)
COMMUNITY ACTION COMMSN SANTA
201 W Chapel St, Santa Maria (93458-4303)
PHONE..................................805 922-2243
Maggie Espinosa, *Manager*
EMP: 60
SALES (corp-wide): 23.4MM **Privately Held**
WEB: www.cacsb.com
SIC: 8399 Community action agency
PA: Community Action Commission Of Santa Barbara County
5638 Hollister Ave # 230
Goleta CA 93117
805 964-8857

(P-24153)
COMMUNITY ACTION PARTNR KERN
7998 Alicante Ave, Lamont (93241-1744)
PHONE..................................661 845-3901
Maryann Mooney, *Manager*
EMP: 88
SALES (corp-wide): 63.1MM **Privately Held**
SIC: 8399 Community action agency
PA: Community Action Partnership Of Kern
5005 Business Park N
Bakersfield CA 93309
661 336-5236

(P-24154)
COMMUNITY ACTION PARTNR KERN
Also Called: Sunrise Villa Ctr Head Start
1600 Poplar Ave, Wasco (93280-3405)
PHONE..................................661 758-0129
Yolanda Gonzales, *Director*
EMP: 88
SALES (corp-wide): 63.1MM **Privately Held**
SIC: 8399 Community action agency
PA: Community Action Partnership Of Kern
5005 Business Park N
Bakersfield CA 93309
661 336-5236

(P-24155)
COMMUNITY ACTION PARTNR KERN
2400 Truxtun Ave, Bakersfield (93301-3405)
PHONE..................................661 336-0317
EMP: 66

SALES (corp-wide): 63.1MM **Privately Held**
SIC: 8399 8351 Community action agency; preschool center
PA: Community Action Partnership Of Kern
5005 Business Park N
Bakersfield CA 93309
661 336-5236

(P-24156)
COMMUNITY ACTION PARTNR KERN
814 N Norma St, Ridgecrest (93555-3509)
PHONE..................................760 371-1469
Maria Harley, *Branch Mgr*
EMP: 110
SALES (corp-wide): 63.1MM **Privately Held**
SIC: 8399 8351 Community action agency; child day care services
PA: Community Action Partnership Of Kern
5005 Business Park N
Bakersfield CA 93309
661 336-5236

(P-24157)
COMMUNITY ACTION PARTNR KERN
4404 Pioneer Dr, Bakersfield (93306-5730)
PHONE..................................661 366-5953
Marie Galaviz, *Branch Mgr*
EMP: 66
SALES (corp-wide): 63.1MM **Privately Held**
SIC: 8399 Community action agency
PA: Community Action Partnership Of Kern
5005 Business Park N
Bakersfield CA 93309
661 336-5236

(P-24158)
COMMUNITY ACTION PRTNSHIP SB C
Also Called: Capsbc
696 S Tippecanoe Ave, San Bernardino (92408-2607)
PHONE..................................909 723-1500
Patricia L Nickols, *CEO*
Joanne Gilbert, *Ch of Bd*
Socorro Enriquez, *Vice Chairman*
Richard Schmidt, *CFO*
Ammie Hines, *Treasurer*
EMP: 88
SALES: 24.2MM **Privately Held**
SIC: 8399 8699 Community action agency; charitable organization

(P-24159)
COMMUNITY PARTNERS (PA)
1000 N Alameda St Ste 240, Los Angeles (90012-1804)
PHONE..................................213 346-3200
Paul Vandeventer, *President*
Gary Erickson, *Ch of Bd*
Janet Elliott, *CFO*
Eric V Ibarra, *Exec Dir*
Arpine Shakhbandaryan, *Program Mgr*
EMP: 75
SALES: 41.7MM **Privately Held**
WEB: www.communitypartners.org
SIC: 8399 Social service information exchange

(P-24160)
COUNTY OF DEL NORTE
Also Called: Health and Human Service
880 Northcrest Dr, Crescent City (95531-2313)
PHONE..................................707 464-3191
Gary Blatnick, *Director*
Jocelyn Woodral, *Supervisor*
EMP: 120 **Privately Held**
SIC: 8399 Health systems agency
PA: County Of Del Norte
981 H St Ste 200
Crescent City CA 95531
707 464-7204

(P-24161)
COUNTY OF KERN
Also Called: Human Services Dept
100 E California Ave, Bakersfield (93307-1031)
P.O. Box 511 (93302-0511)
PHONE..................................661 631-6346

Kathleen Irvine, *Director*
EMP: 800 **Privately Held**
WEB: www.kccfc.org
SIC: 8399 9199 Health & welfare council; general government administration
PA: County Of Kern
1115 Truxtun Ave Rm 505
Bakersfield CA 93301
661 868-3690

(P-24162)
COUNTY OF LOS ANGELES
Also Called: Department Public Social Svcs
8130 Atlantic Ave, Cudahy (90201-5804)
PHONE..................................323 560-5001
Lilia Erviti, *Director*
EMP: 220 **Privately Held**
SIC: 8399 Community development groups
PA: County Of Los Angeles
500 W Temple St Ste 437
Los Angeles CA 90012
213 974-1101

(P-24163)
COUNTY OF MONTEREY
Also Called: Health Department
1270 Natividad Rd, Salinas (93906-3144)
PHONE..................................831 755-4500
Len Foster, *Manager*
EMP: 50 **Privately Held**
WEB: www.montereycountyfarmbureau.org
SIC: 8399 9111 Health & welfare council; county supervisors' & executives' offices
PA: County Of Monterey
168 W Alisal St Fl 2
Salinas CA 93901
831 755-5040

(P-24164)
COUNTY OF RIVERSIDE
Also Called: Community Health Agency
4065 County Circle Dr, Riverside (92503-3410)
P.O. Box 7600 (92513-7600)
PHONE..................................951 358-5306
Gary Feldman, *Director*
EMP: 400 **Privately Held**
SIC: 8399 9511 Health systems agency;
PA: County Of Riverside
4080 Lemon St Fl 11
Riverside CA 92501
951 955-1110

(P-24165)
COUNTY OF SAN JOAQUIN
Also Called: Neighborhood Preservation Div
1810 E Hazelton Ave, Stockton (95205-6232)
PHONE..................................209 468-3021
Carrie Sullivan, *Director*
EMP: 60 **Privately Held**
WEB: www.sjclawlib.org
SIC: 8399 9441 Community development groups; public welfare administration: non-operating, government
PA: County Of San Joaquin
44 N San Joaquin St # 640
Stockton CA 95202
209 468-3203

(P-24166)
COUNTY OF STANISLAUS
Also Called: Behavioral Hlth Recovery Svcs
800 Scenic Dr, Modesto (95350-6131)
PHONE..................................209 525-6225
Denise C Hunt, *Director*
EMP: 99 **Privately Held**
WEB: www.co.stanislaus.ca.us
SIC: 8399 Health & welfare council
PA: County Of Stanislaus
1010 10th St Ste 5100
Modesto CA 95354
209 525-6398

(P-24167)
DESERT AREA RESOURCES TRAINING
Also Called: Early Childhood Services
201 E Ridgecrest Blvd, Ridgecrest (93555-3919)
PHONE..................................760 375-8494
Fax: 760 375-1288
EMP: 70
SALES (est): 619.4K **Privately Held**
SIC: 8399

(P-24168)
DREW HEALTH FOUNDATION
1191 Runnymede St, East Palo Alto (94303-1331)
P.O. Box 50997, Palo Alto (94303-0678)
PHONE..................................650 328-1619
Myrtle Walker, *President*
Ora Johnson, *Manager*
EMP: 50
SQ FT: 84,000
SALES: 226.7K **Privately Held**
SIC: 8399 Health & welfare council; health systems agency

(P-24169)
EAST BAY COMMUNITY FOUNDATION
Also Called: E B C F
200 Frank H Ogawa Plz, Oakland (94612-2005)
PHONE..................................510 836-3223
Nichole Taylor, *President*
Karen Stevenson, *President*
EMP: 55
SQ FT: 15,500
SALES: 133.1MM **Privately Held**
WEB: www.eastbaycf.org
SIC: 8399 Community development groups

(P-24170)
EASTER SEALS SOUTHERN CAL INC
710 W Broadway, Glendale (91204-1010)
PHONE..................................818 551-0128
Gloria Acosta, *Director*
EMP: 80
SALES (corp-wide): 179.7MM **Privately Held**
WEB: www.essc.org
SIC: 8399 8322 Fund raising organization, non-fee basis; individual & family services
PA: Easter Seals Southern California, Inc.
1063 Mcgaw Ave Ste 100
Irvine CA 92614
714 834-1111

(P-24171)
EASTER SEALS SOUTHERN CAL INC
Also Called: Easter Seal Society
340 E Avenue I Ste 101, Lancaster (93535-1941)
PHONE..................................661 723-3414
Paula Pompa-Craven, *Director*
EMP: 50
SALES (corp-wide): 179.7MM **Privately Held**
WEB: www.essc.org
SIC: 8399 8322 Fund raising organization, non-fee basis; individual & family services
PA: Easter Seals Southern California, Inc.
1063 Mcgaw Ave Ste 100
Irvine CA 92614
714 834-1111

(P-24172)
EL SEGUNDO EDUCTL FOUNDATION
641 Sheldon St, El Segundo (90245-3036)
PHONE..................................310 615-2650
Duane Conover, *President*
Alex Abad, *Vice Chairman*
Geoff Yantz, *Superintendent*
EMP: 300
SALES: 2MM **Privately Held**
SIC: 8399 Fund raising organization, non-fee basis

(P-24173)
ESSENTIAL ACCESS HEALTH (PA)
Also Called: Cfhc
3600 Wilshire Blvd # 600, Los Angeles (90010-2603)
PHONE..................................213 386-5614
Julie Rabinovitz, *President*
Nomsa Khalfani, *Senior VP*
Ron Frezieres, *Vice Pres*
Amy Moy, *Vice Pres*
Brenda Flores, *Executive*
EMP: 81 EST: 1968
SQ FT: 18,000

PRODUCTS & SVCS

SALES: 26.4MM Privately Held
SIC: 8399 8011 8099 Fund raising organization, non-fee basis; primary care medical clinic; medical services organization

(P-24174)
ETHIOPIAN WORLD FEDERATION
422 E 41st St, Los Angeles (90011-2906)
PHONE..................323 844-1826
Enoch Nack, *Principal*
EMP: 50
SALES (est): 991.9K **Privately Held**
SIC: 8399 Social services

(P-24175)
FRIENDS FITZGERALD MAR RESERVE
Also Called: F F M L R
200 Nevada Ave, Moss Beach (94038)
P.O. Box 669 (94038-0669)
PHONE..................650 728-3584
Mary Wolfe, *Admin Sec*
Mary Delong, *President*
EMP: 70
SALES (est): 718.4K **Privately Held**
WEB: www.fitzgeraldreserve.org
SIC: 8399 Social service information exchange

(P-24176)
FRIENDS OF THE LOS ANGELES
8405 Beverly Blvd, Los Angeles (90048-3401)
PHONE..................323 653-0440
EMP: 200
SALES: 2.2MM **Privately Held**
SIC: 8399

(P-24177)
GREATER LOS ANGELES ZOO ASSN
Also Called: Glaza
5333 Zoo Dr, Los Angeles (90027-1451)
PHONE..................323 644-4200
Connie M Morgan, *President*
Jeb Bonner, *CFO*
Robert N Ruth, *Treasurer*
Eugenia Vasels, *Vice Pres*
Genie Vasels, *Vice Pres*
EMP: 100
SQ FT: 8,200
SALES: 16.8MM **Privately Held**
SIC: 8399 7999 Fund raising organization, non-fee basis; concession operator

(P-24178)
HABITAT FOR HUMANITY OF GREATE
8739 Artesia Blvd, Bellflower (90706-6330)
PHONE..................310 323-4663
Erin Garrity Rank, *President*
Mark Van Lue, *COO*
Gia Stokes, *CFO*
Veronica Garcia, *Vice Pres*
Alison Treleaven J, *Vice Pres*
EMP: 50
SALES: 23.2MM **Privately Held**
WEB: www.habitatla.org
SIC: 8399 Community development groups

(P-24179)
HARBOR DEVELOPMENTAL DISABILIT
Also Called: Harbor Regional Center
21231 Hawthorne Blvd, Torrance (90503-5501)
P.O. Box 2930 (90509-2930)
PHONE..................310 540-1711
Judy Wada, *CFO*
Patricia Monico, *Exec Dir*
Liz Cohen-Zeboulon, *Program Mgr*
Steven Hankow, *Program Mgr*
Tonantzin Martinez, *Program Mgr*
EMP: 225
SQ FT: 60,000
SALES: 221.6MM **Privately Held**
SIC: 8399 Council for social agency

(P-24180)
HEALTH ADVOCATES LLC
21540 Plummer St Ste B, Chatsworth (91311-0888)
PHONE..................818 995-9500
Al Leibovic, *Mng Member*

William Russell, *CFO*
Nuria Morales, *Human Res Mgr*
Sally Elizondo, *Training Spec*
Camila Cruz, *Legal Staff*
EMP: 371
SQ FT: 40,900
SALES (est): 14.6MM **Privately Held**
SIC: 8399 Advocacy group

(P-24181)
HOSPITAL ASSN SOUTHERN CAL (PA)
Also Called: Hasc
515 S Figueroa St # 1300, Los Angeles (90071-3301)
PHONE..................213 347-2002
Jim Barber, *CEO*
Roger Seaver, *Ch of Bd*
Isela Rivas, *President*
Scott Toomey, *CFO*
Martin Gallegos, *Senior VP*
EMP: 58
SQ FT: 30,000
SALES (est): 9.1MM **Privately Held**
WEB: www.reddinet.com
SIC: 8399 Advocacy group

(P-24182)
INTERNATIONAL FDN FOR KOREA UN
3435 Wilshire Blvd # 480, Los Angeles (90010-1918)
PHONE..................213 550-2182
Willie Wang-Pyo Seung, *CEO*
EMP: 300 **EST:** 2016
SALES: 538.9K **Privately Held**
SIC: 8399 Advocacy group

(P-24183)
INYO MONO ADVCTS FR CMMNTY ACT (PA)
Also Called: I M A C A
137 E South St, Bishop (93514-3545)
P.O. Box 845 (93515-0845)
PHONE..................760 873-8557
Lynn Bethel, *Exec Dir*
Charles Broten, *Exec Dir*
Daniela Velazquez, *Admin Asst*
Michael Ocarroll, *Controller*
Queenie Barnard, *Director*
EMP: 70
SALES: 3.2MM **Privately Held**
WEB: www.imaca.net
SIC: 8399 Community action agency

(P-24184)
JAPANESE CMNTY YOUTH COUNCIL (PA)
Also Called: CHIBI CHAN PRESCHOOL
2012 Pine St, San Francisco (94115-2899)
PHONE..................415 202-7905
John Osaki, *Exec Dir*
Patricia Justafort, *Associate Dir*
Lisa MA, *Associate Dir*
Emily Thayer, *Analyst*
Phily Truong, *Opers Staff*
EMP: 75
SQ FT: 4,000
SALES: 12.8MM **Privately Held**
SIC: 8399 Community development groups

(P-24185)
JEWISH COMMUNITY FEDRTN SAN FR (PA)
121 Steuart St Fl 7, San Francisco (94105-1280)
PHONE..................415 777-0411
Jennifer Gorvitz, *CEO*
Holden Lee, *CFO*
Bill Powers, *CFO*
Hallie Baron, *Associate Dir*
Joey Blatt, *Program Mgr*
EMP: 70
SQ FT: 50,000
SALES: 147.2MM **Privately Held**
SIC: 8399 Fund raising organization, non-fee basis

(P-24186)
KCRW FOUNDATION INC
Also Called: KCRW FM RADIO
1900 Pico Blvd, Santa Monica (90405-1628)
PHONE..................310 450-5183
Jennifer Ferro, *CEO*

Herbert Roney, *Treasurer*
Tom Wertheimer, *Treasurer*
Alex Couri, *Officer*
Warren Olney, *Social Dir*
EMP: 51
SQ FT: 4,000
SALES: 21.1MM **Privately Held**
SIC: 8399 Fund raising organization, non-fee basis

(P-24187)
KERN REGIONAL CENTER (PA)
3200 N Sillect Ave, Bakersfield (93308-6333)
P.O. Box 2536 (93303-2536)
PHONE..................661 327-8531
Michal Clark, *Exec Dir*
Duane Law, *CEO*
Jerry Bowman, *CFO*
John Gusman, *CFO*
Sheryl Rodriguez, *Vice Pres*
EMP: 178 **EST:** 1971
SQ FT: 33,000
SALES: 169.9MM **Privately Held**
SIC: 8399 Social service information exchange

(P-24188)
KEYSTONE NPS LLC (DH)
Also Called: Keystone Schools-Ramona
11980 Mount Vernon Ave, Grand Terrace (92313-5172)
PHONE..................909 633-6354
Alfredo Alvarado, *Principal*
Don Whitfield, *CFO*
Martha Petrey, *Exec VP*
EMP: 100
SALES (est): 14.8MM
SALES (corp-wide): 10.7B **Publicly Held**
SIC: 8399 Advocacy group
HQ: Children's Comprehensive Services, Inc.
3401 West End Ave Ste 400
Nashville TN 37203
615 250-0000

(P-24189)
KIPP FOUNDATION
135 Main St Ste 1700, San Francisco (94105-1850)
PHONE..................415 399-1556
Richard Barth, *CEO*
Jack Chorowsky, *COO*
Tarun Bhatia, *CFO*
Tina Sachs, *CFO*
Steve Small, *CFO*
EMP: 110
SQ FT: 10,000
SALES: 77.1MM **Privately Held**
SIC: 8399 Fund raising organization, non-fee basis

(P-24190)
LAKE ARROWHEAD CMNTY SVCS DST
6727 Arrowhead Lake Rd, Hesperia (92345-9343)
P.O. Box 700, Lake Arrowhead (92352-0700)
PHONE..................909 337-6395
Bob Bobki, *Branch Mgr*
Shanna Christopherson, *IT/INT Sup*
EMP: 50
SALES (corp-wide): 13.9MM **Privately Held**
WEB: www.lakearrowheadcsd.com
SIC: 8399 Advocacy group
PA: Lake Arrowhead Community Services District
28200 Highway 189
Lake Arrowhead CA 92352
909 336-1359

(P-24191)
LAWRENCE FAMILY JEWISH COMMU (PA)
4126 Executive Dr, La Jolla (92037-1348)
PHONE..................858 362-1144
Craig Schluss, *President*
David Wax, *President*
Nancy Johnson, *CFO*
Katharine Wardle, *CFO*
Nate Stein, *Exec Dir*
EMP: 250 **EST:** 1945

SALES: 11.6MM **Privately Held**
WEB: www.lfjcc.com
SIC: 8399 8351 Community development groups; child day care services

(P-24192)
LIFESPAN INC
Also Called: Lifespan Care Management Agcy
600 Frederick St, Santa Cruz (95062-2203)
PHONE..................831 469-4900
Pamela Goodman, *President*
Pam Goodman, *President*
EMP: 90
SALES (est): 3.3MM **Privately Held**
WEB: www.lifespancare.com
SIC: 8399 8082 Health systems agency; home health care services

(P-24193)
LONG BEACH CMNTY ACTION PARTNR
Also Called: Long Beach Cap
117 W Victoria St, Long Beach (90805-2162)
PHONE..................562 216-4600
Darrick Simpson, *Exec Dir*
Janet McCarthy, *Ch of Bd*
Mary Sramek, *Treasurer*
Marisa Semense, *Officer*
Baty Amit, *Principal*
EMP: 110
SQ FT: 10,000
SALES: 5.8MM **Privately Held**
WEB: www.lbcaa.com
SIC: 8399 Antipoverty board; community action agency

(P-24194)
LOS ANGELES LGBT CENTER (PA)
Also Called: L.A. Gay & Lesbian Center
1625 Schrader Blvd, Los Angeles (90028-6213)
P.O. Box 2988 (90078-2988)
PHONE..................323 993-7618
Lorri L Jean, *CEO*
Michael Holtzman, *CFO*
Jim Key, *Chief Mktg Ofcr*
Simon Costello, *Associate Dir*
Susan Holt, *Program Mgr*
EMP: 148
SQ FT: 45,000
SALES: 91.6MM **Privately Held**
WEB: www.lagaycenter.org
SIC: 8399 Community development groups

(P-24195)
MCKINLEY HOME FOUNDATION
762 Cypress St, San Dimas (91773-3505)
PHONE..................909 599-1227
Victor Liotta, *President*
Mario Gallegos, *Officer*
EMP: 100
SQ FT: 8,055
SALES: 1.7MM **Privately Held**
SIC: 8399 6519 Fund raising organization, non-fee basis; landholding office

(P-24196)
MIRAMNTE HIGH SCHL PARENTS CLB
750 Moraga Way, Orinda (94563-4330)
P.O. Box 171 (94563-0171)
PHONE..................925 280-3965
Raul Zamora, *Principal*
Catherine Corn, *President*
Dr Craig Dennis, *Treasurer*
Dixie Mohan, *Vice Pres*
Mark Uhrenholt, *Principal*
EMP: 130
SALES: 453.4K **Privately Held**
SIC: 8399 Fund raising organization, non-fee basis

(P-24197)
MOMENTUM FOR MENTAL HEALTH
Also Called: Maccarthy House
2001 The Alameda, San Jose (95126-1136)
PHONE..................408 261-7777
Paul S Taylor, *CEO*
Melinda Golden, *CFO*
Richard Jennings, *Human Res Dir*

Mary Angel, *Property Mgr*
EMP: 100
SALES (corp-wide): 36.8MM **Privately Held**
WEB: www.alliance4care.org
SIC: 8399 8093 8322 Health systems agency; specialty outpatient clinics; individual & family services
PA: Momentum For Mental Health
438 N White Rd
San Jose CA 95127
408 254-6828

(P-24198)
MORALE WELFARE RECREATION FUND
4260 Gigling Rd, Seaside (93955)
PHONE...............................831 242-6631
Bob Emanuel, *President*
EMP: 200
SALES (est): 1.5MM **Privately Held**
SIC: 8399 Fund raising organization, non-fee basis

(P-24199)
MT HAMILTON GRANGE
2840 Aborn Rd, San Jose (95135-2001)
P.O. Box 731060 (95173-1060)
PHONE...............................408 513-5528
Douglas Krause, *Principal*
EMP: 100
SALES: 74.3K **Privately Held**
SIC: 8399 Fund raising organization, non-fee basis

(P-24200)
NATIONAL MENTOR INC
Also Called: California Mentor
2131 Mars Ct, Bakersfield (93308-6830)
PHONE...............................661 387-1000
EMP: 50
SALES (corp-wide): 310.7MM **Privately Held**
SIC: 8399 Social service information exchange
HQ: National Mentor, Inc.
313 Congress St Fl 5
Boston MA 02210
617 790-4800

(P-24201)
NEW ADVANCES FOR PEOPLE DISABI
Also Called: Center For Achievement Center
1120 21st St, Bakersfield (93301-4613)
PHONE...............................661 327-0188
Linda Waninger, *Manager*
EMP: 60
SALES (corp-wide): 7.3MM **Privately Held**
SIC: 8399 Community development groups
PA: New Advances For People With Disabilities
2601 F St
Bakersfield CA 93301
661 395-1361

(P-24202)
NEXT DOOR SLTONS TO DOM VLENCE
234 E Gish Rd Ste 200, San Jose (95112-4724)
PHONE...............................408 279-2962
Kathleen Krenek, *Exec Dir*
Wayne Mascia, *President*
Susan McInnis, *Finance*
Colsaria Henderson, *Director*
Beth Williams, *Director*
EMP: 80
SQ FT: 4,100
SALES: 2.9MM **Privately Held**
WEB: www.nextdoor.org
SIC: 8399 8322 Advocacy group; social change association; individual & family services

(P-24203)
NORTHERN CALIFORNIA INSTITUTE
Also Called: Ncire
4150 Clement St, San Francisco (94121-1563)
PHONE...............................415 750-6954
Robert Obana, *Exec Dir*
EMP: 300

SQ FT: 1,650
SALES: 37MM **Privately Held**
SIC: 8399 8741 Fund raising organization, non-fee basis; management services

(P-24204)
OCPW
Also Called: Oc Public Works
601 N Ross St, Santa Ana (92701)
PHONE...............................714 955-0255
Shane L Silsby, *Principal*
Frank Kim, *Principal*
WEI Zhu, *Research*
EMP: 940 **EST:** 2009
SALES (est): 566.7K **Privately Held**
SIC: 8399 Social services

(P-24205)
ON THE MOVE
780 Lincoln Ave, NAPA (94558-5110)
PHONE...............................707 251-9432
Leslie Medine, *Exec Dir*
Diana Gordon, *CFO*
Alissa Gentille, *Exec Dir*
EMP: 50
SALES: 4.1MM **Privately Held**
SIC: 8399 Social services

(P-24206)
PENNY LANE CENTERS (PA)
15305 Rayen St, North Hills (91343-5117)
P.O. Box 2548 (91393-2548)
PHONE...............................818 892-3423
Arthur Barr, *President*
Marisol Aguilar, *Partner*
Ivelise Markovits, *Exec Dir*
Lee Overson, *General Mgr*
Kassie Steward, *Office Mgr*
EMP: 275
SQ FT: 7,000
SALES: 56.2MM **Privately Held**
WEB: www.pennylane.org
SIC: 8399 Social service information exchange

(P-24207)
PENNY LANE CENTERS
Valley High School
15317 Rayen St, North Hills (91343-5198)
PHONE...............................818 892-3423
Shawn Welch, *Principal*
EMP: 170
SALES (corp-wide): 56.2MM **Privately Held**
WEB: www.pennylane.org
SIC: 8399 Social service information exchange
PA: Penny Lane Centers
15305 Rayen St
North Hills CA 91343
818 892-3423

(P-24208)
PENNY LANE CENTERS
10330 Pioneer Blvd # 290, Santa Fe Springs (90670-8279)
PHONE...............................562 903-4135
Lily Amezqua, *Manager*
EMP: 170
SALES (corp-wide): 56.2MM **Privately Held**
SIC: 8399 Social service information exchange
PA: Penny Lane Centers
15305 Rayen St
North Hills CA 91343
818 892-3423

(P-24209)
PENNY LANE CENTERS
15331 Rayen St, North Hills (91343)
PHONE...............................818 892-3423
Ivelise Markovits, *Branch Mgr*
EMP: 170
SALES (corp-wide): 56.2MM **Privately Held**
WEB: www.pennylane.org
SIC: 8399 Social service information exchange
PA: Penny Lane Centers
15305 Rayen St
North Hills CA 91343
818 892-3423

(P-24210)
PENNY LANE CENTERS
15302 Rayen St, North Hills (91343-5118)
PHONE...............................818 892-1112
Evy Markovits, *Manager*
EMP: 170
SALES (corp-wide): 56.2MM **Privately Held**
SIC: 8399 Social service information exchange
PA: Penny Lane Centers
15305 Rayen St
North Hills CA 91343
818 892-3423

(P-24211)
PENNY LANE CENTERS
15256 Acre St, North Hills (91343-5256)
PHONE...............................818 892-3423
EMP: 170
SALES (corp-wide): 56.2MM **Privately Held**
SIC: 8399 Social service information exchange
PA: Penny Lane Centers
15305 Rayen St
North Hills CA 91343
818 892-3423

(P-24212)
PENNY LANE CENTERS
1020 E Palmdale Blvd, Palmdale (93550-4756)
PHONE...............................818 892-3423
Rosana Fianza, *Opers Staff*
EMP: 170
SALES (corp-wide): 56.2MM **Privately Held**
SIC: 8399 Social service information exchange
PA: Penny Lane Centers
15305 Rayen St
North Hills CA 91343
818 892-3423

(P-24213)
PENNY LANE CENTERS
2450 S Atl Blvd Ste 101, Commerce (90040)
PHONE...............................323 318-9960
Rosana La Fianza, *Branch Mgr*
EMP: 170
SALES (corp-wide): 56.2MM **Privately Held**
SIC: 8399 Health & welfare council
PA: Penny Lane Centers
15305 Rayen St
North Hills CA 91343
818 892-3423

(P-24214)
PENNY LANE CENTERS
43520 Division St, Lancaster (93535-4089)
PHONE...............................661 274-0770
James Ocon, *President*
Yojanne Blanco, *Social Worker*
Lara Hoffman, *Supervisor*
EMP: 170
SALES (corp-wide): 56.2MM **Privately Held**
SIC: 8399 Social service information exchange
PA: Penny Lane Centers
15305 Rayen St
North Hills CA 91343
818 892-3423

(P-24215)
PRC
170 9th St, San Francisco (94103-2603)
PHONE...............................415 777-0333
Brett Andrews, *Exec Dir*
Demetri Moshoyannis, *Managing Dir*
Jim Wegman, *Info Tech Dir*
Joe Tuohy, *Director*
Pat Riley, *Manager*
EMP: 53
SQ FT: 7,000
SALES: 9.2MM **Privately Held**
WEB: www.positiveresource.org
SIC: 8399 8322 Council for social agency; individual & family services

(P-24216)
QUALITY GROUP HOMES INC (PA)
Also Called: QUALITY FOSTER CARE
4928 E Clinton Way # 108, Fresno (93727-1526)
PHONE...............................559 255-8519
Mae Johnson, *Exec Dir*
Ted Johnson, *Officer*
Pavel Petlinsky, *Principal*
Laura Romero, *Human Res Dir*
Johnson Mae, *Personnel Assit*
EMP: 200
SALES: 7.7MM **Privately Held**
SIC: 8399 Community development groups

(P-24217)
REACH OUT WEST END
1126 W Foothill Blvd # 250, Upland (91786-3786)
PHONE...............................909 982-8641
Diana Fox, *Director*
EMP: 60
SQ FT: 12,232
SALES: 3.6MM **Privately Held**
SIC: 8399 Social change association

(P-24218)
REACHING FOR INDEPENDENCE INC
609 14th St, Fortuna (95540-2464)
PHONE...............................707 725-9010
J Pockett, *Exec Dir*
Matt Eberhart, *Chairman*
Robert Frawley, *Exec Dir*
Jeff Pockett, *Exec Dir*
Jeffrey Pockett, *Exec Dir*
EMP: 66 **EST:** 2008
SALES: 1.8MM **Privately Held**
SIC: 8399 Community development groups

(P-24219)
RIO HONDO COMMUNITY DEV CORP
11706 Ramona Blvd Ste 107, El Monte (91732-2300)
PHONE...............................626 401-2784
Donna L Duncan, *President*
EMP: 57
SALES: 384.3K **Privately Held**
SIC: 8399 Community development groups

(P-24220)
ROMAN CTHLIC BSHP OF SNTA ROSA
987 Airway Ct, Santa Rosa (95403-2048)
P.O. Box 4900 (95402-4900)
PHONE...............................707 528-8712
Len Marabella, *Branch Mgr*
Marla A Gullickson CP, *Treasurer*
Angie Moeller, *Principal*
EMP: 110
SALES (corp-wide): 8.8MM **Privately Held**
SIC: 8399 Social service information exchange
PA: Roman Catholic Bishop Of Santa Rosa, The
985 Airway Ct
Santa Rosa CA 95403
707 545-7610

(P-24221)
SAFE HARBOR INTL RELIEF
30615 Avnida De Las Flres, Rancho Santa Margari (92688)
P.O. Box 80820, Rcho STA Marg (92688-0820)
PHONE...............................949 858-6786
Gary Kusunoki, *CEO*
David Kruckenberg, *Principal*
EMP: 50
SALES: 146K **Privately Held**
SIC: 8399 Social services

(P-24222)
SAINT JUSTIN EDUCATION FU
Also Called: IN TOUCH LEADERSHIP PROJECT
2415 Shoredale Ave, Los Angeles (90031-1120)
P.O. Box 27790 (90027-0790)
PHONE...............................323 221-3400
Gary Krauss, *CEO*
Laura Sardagna, *Business Mgr*

PRODUCTS & SVCS

EMP: 51 EST: 1992
SALES: 444.2K Privately Held
SIC: 8399 Fund raising organization, non-fee basis

(P-24223)
SAN DIEGO RESCUE MISSION INC (PA)
Also Called: City Rescue Mission
299 17th St, San Diego (92101-7665)
P.O. Box 80427 (92138-0427)
PHONE..................................619 819-1880
Herb Johnson, *CEO*
C Greg Helton, *Vice Pres*
Shari Finney Houser, *Vice Pres*
John Suderman, *Vice Pres*
Warren Perrin, *Technology*
EMP: 92
SALES: 17.7MM Privately Held
WEB: www.sdrescue.org
SIC: 8399 5932 8322 Social change association; used merchandise stores; emergency shelters

(P-24224)
SAN FRNNDO VLY INTRFITH CUNCIL
8956 Vanalden Ave, Northridge (91324-3753)
PHONE..................................818 885-5220
EMP: 102
SALES (corp-wide): 4.1MM Privately Held
SIC: 8399 Council for social agency
PA: San Fernando Valley Interfaith Council, Inc
4505 Las Virgenes Rd
Calabasas CA 91302
818 880-4842

(P-24225)
SILICON VLY EDUCATN FOUNDATION
1400 Parkmoor Ave Ste 200, San Jose (95126-3798)
PHONE..................................408 790-9400
Muhammed Chaudhry, *CEO*
Sandy Sanders, *Partner*
Manny Barbara, *Vice Pres*
James R Otieno, *Vice Pres*
Magana Rigo, *Marketing Mgr*
EMP: 1000
SALES: 2.6MM Privately Held
WEB: www.fmsd.k12.ca.us
SIC: 8399 Fund raising organization, non-fee basis

(P-24226)
SIX RIVERS PLANNED PARENTHOOD
3225 Timber Fall Ct, Eureka (95503-4892)
P.O. Box 97, Cutten (95534-0097)
PHONE..................................707 442-5700
Denise Danden Boss, *CEO*
EMP: 75
SQ FT: 3,900
SALES: 3.6MM Privately Held
SIC: 8399 8322 Community development groups; individual & family services

(P-24227)
SOUTH CENTRAL LOS (PA)
Also Called: SCLARC
2500 S Western Ave, Los Angeles (90018-2609)
PHONE..................................213 744-7000
Dexter Henderson, *CEO*
Sandra Casado, *Director*
EMP: 235
SQ FT: 110,470
SALES: 262.6MM Privately Held
WEB: www.sclarc.org
SIC: 8399 Health & welfare council

(P-24228)
SOUTHLAND INTEGRATED SVCS INC (PA)
Also Called: VIETNAMESE COMMUNITY OF ORANGE
1618 W 1st St, Santa Ana (92703-3614)
PHONE..................................714 558-6009
Tricia Nguyen, *CEO*
EMP: 70

SALES: 6.7MM Privately Held
WEB: www.vietnam-minnesota.org
SIC: 8399 8322 8351 8011 Community development groups; senior citizens' center or association; social service center; preschool center; primary care medical clinic; mental health clinic, outpatient

(P-24229)
SPECIAL SERVICE FOR GROUPS INC
Also Called: Occupational Therapy Training
19401 S Vt Ave Ste A200, Torrance (90502-4418)
PHONE..................................310 323-6887
Sarah Bream, *Branch Mgr*
EMP: 60
SALES (corp-wide): 60.6MM Privately Held
SIC: 8399 8322 Community action agency; individual & family services
PA: Special Service For Groups, Inc.
905 E 8th St
Los Angeles CA 90021
213 368-1888

(P-24230)
SPECIAL SERVICE FOR GROUPS INC
470 E 3rd St Ste D, Los Angeles (90013-1630)
PHONE..................................213 620-5713
EMP: 65
SALES (est): 424.5K
SALES (corp-wide): 60.6MM Privately Held
SIC: 8399 Community action agency
PA: Special Service For Groups, Inc.
905 E 8th St
Los Angeles CA 90021
213 368-1888

(P-24231)
STANFORD YOUTH SOLUTIONS (PA)
Also Called: STANFORD & LATHROP MEMORIAL HO
8912 Volunteer Ln, Sacramento (95826-3221)
PHONE..................................916 344-0199
Jovina Neves, *CFO*
EMP: 85
SQ FT: 30,000
SALES: 11.5MM Privately Held
SIC: 8399 Community development groups

(P-24232)
TEMPLO CALVARIO CMNTY DEV CORP
2501 W 5th St, Santa Ana (92703-1816)
PHONE..................................714 543-3711
Eleazar De Leon, *President*
Linda Decker, *Admin Sec*
EMP: 60
SQ FT: 9,000
SALES: 5.2MM Privately Held
SIC: 8399 Community action agency

(P-24233)
TIDES INC (PA)
Also Called: Tides Shared Spaces
1014 Torney Ave Ste 1, San Francisco (94129-1756)
P.O. Box 29198 (94129-0198)
PHONE..................................415 561-6400
Melissa Bradley, *CEO*
Nick Hodges, *COO*
China Brotsky, *Vice Pres*
EMP: 110
SQ FT: 180,000
SALES (est): 2.9MM Privately Held
SIC: 8399 Community development groups

(P-24234)
TIDES NETWORK
The Prsdio 1014 Trney Ave, San Francisco (94129)
P.O. Box 29198 (94129-0198)
PHONE..................................415 561-6400
Gary Schwartz, *CEO*
Judith Hill, *CFO*
Kim Sarnecki, *Director*
EMP: 80
SALES: 18.4MM Privately Held
SIC: 8399 Community development groups

(P-24235)
UNITED CRBRL PLSY OF CNTRL CA (PA)
Also Called: U C P-UNITED CEREBAL PALSY ASS
4224 N Cedar Ave, Fresno (93726-3731)
PHONE..................................559 221-8272
Mark Lanier, *President*
Carol Kloninger, *Vice Pres*
Jamie Marrash, *Exec Dir*
Pat Murphy, *Exec Dir*
Bonnie Peterson, *Admin Sec*
EMP: 50
SQ FT: 15,000
SALES: 5.3MM Privately Held
WEB: www.mcvalleycup.com
SIC: 8399 Fund raising organization, non-fee basis

(P-24236)
UNITED WAY INC (PA)
Also Called: UNITED WAY OF GREATER LOS ANGE
1150 S Olive St Ste T500, Los Angeles (90015-2482)
PHONE..................................213 808-6220
Caroline W Nahas, *Ch of Bd*
Elise Buik, *President*
Claire Kitayama, *Officer*
Michael Nailat, *Officer*
Les Brockhurst, *Vice Pres*
▲ EMP: 95
SQ FT: 40,000
SALES: 46.7MM Privately Held
WEB: www.unitedwayla.org
SIC: 8399 Fund raising organization, non-fee basis; United Fund councils; health & welfare council

(P-24237)
VALLEY CAN
921 11th St Ste 220, Sacramento (95814-2842)
PHONE..................................916 273-4890
Carla Musser, *President*
EMP: 50
SALES: 2.2MM Privately Held
SIC: 8399 Advocacy group

(P-24238)
VALLEY RSRCE CTR FOR RETARDED
Also Called: Exceed
1285 N Santa Fe St, Hemet (92543-1823)
PHONE..................................951 766-8659
Lee Trisler, *Exec Dir*
EMP: 99
SALES (est): 464.6K Privately Held
SIC: 8399 Community development groups

(P-24239)
WATSON CARTON
4178 Ross Ave, San Jose (95124-3728)
PHONE..................................408 979-9618
Peter Frietman, *CEO*
EMP: 63
SALES (est): 693.7K Privately Held
SIC: 8399 Community development groups

(P-24240)
WEST VALLEY AREA SQUAD CLUB
5825 De Soto Ave, Woodland Hills (91367-5202)
PHONE..................................818 888-0980
Brian Denike, *President*
Oscar Loza, *Officer*
Daniel Olivas, *Officer*
Orrin Heitmann, *Vice Pres*
Eric L Anderson, *Technology*
EMP: 104
SALES (est): 1.3MM Privately Held
SIC: 8399 Fund raising organization, non-fee basis

(P-24241)
WESTSIDE JEWISH CMNTY CTR INC (PA)
5870 W Olympic Blvd, Los Angeles (90036-4657)
PHONE..................................323 938-2531
Brian Greene, *Exec Dir*
Oscar Yglesias, *Facilities Dir*
Rachel Flader, *Teacher*
Erin Goldstrom, *Nurse*

ARI Cohen, *Director*
EMP: 600
SQ FT: 150,000
SALES: 3.6MM Privately Held
SIC: 8399 8641 8322 Community development groups; civic social & fraternal associations; individual & family services

(P-24242)
WESTSIDE LODGE
120 Page St, San Francisco (94102-5811)
PHONE..................................415 864-1515
Jonathan Dernick, *President*
EMP: 50
SALES (est): 369.5K Privately Held
SIC: 8399 Community development groups

(P-24243)
X PRIZE FOUNDATION INC
800 Crprate Pinte Ste 350, Culver City (90230)
PHONE..................................310 741-4880
Robert Weiss, *President*
Paul Rappoort, *COO*
Francis B Land, *Vice Pres*
Jyotika Virmani, *Technical Staff*
Annie Nguyen, *Sr Associate*
EMP: 50
SQ FT: 17,705
SALES: 39.4MM Privately Held
SIC: 8399 Fund raising organization, non-fee basis

(P-24244)
YUBA CITY UNIFIED SCHOOL
Also Called: Ycusd
750 N Palora Ave, Yuba City (95991-3627)
PHONE..................................530 822-7601
Steven Scriven, *President*
Lonetta Riley, *Vice Pres*
Kelle Nelson, *Branch Mgr*
Robert Shemwell, *General Mgr*
Cathy Watkins, *Admin Sec*
EMP: 2000
SALES (est): 23.2MM Privately Held
SIC: 8399 Fund raising organization, non-fee basis

8412 Museums & Art Galleries

(P-24245)
ANAHEIM ARTS COUNCIL
5239 E Glen Arbor Ln, Anaheim (92807-3615)
PHONE..................................714 868-6094
Charlotte Brady, *Owner*
EMP: 200 EST: 1977
SALES (est): 52.5K Privately Held
WEB: www.anaheimartscouncil.com
SIC: 8412 Museum

(P-24246)
ARMAND HAMMER MUSEUM
10899 Wilshire Blvd, Los Angeles (90024-4343)
PHONE..................................310 443-7000
Ann Philbin, *Director*
Marr Mitch, *Senior Mgr*
Susan Edwards, *Director*
Lindsay Martin, *Director*
Hannah Howe, *Manager*
▲ EMP: 101
SQ FT: 20,000
SALES: 51.1MM Privately Held
SIC: 8412 Museum

(P-24247)
ASIAN ART MUSEUM FOUND SAN FRA
Also Called: Asian Art Meusuem of SF
200 Larkin St, San Francisco (94102-4734)
PHONE..................................415 581-3500
Anthony Sun, *CEO*
Akiko Yamazaki, *President*
Timothy F Kahn, *Treasurer*
Nancy Sackson,
Robert L Duffy, *Vice Pres*
▲ EMP: 140
SALES (est): 31.4MM Privately Held
SIC: 8412 Museum

(P-24248)
AUTRY MUSEUM OF AMERICAN WEST
4700 Western Heritage Way, Los Angeles (90027-1462)
PHONE.................................323 667-2000
Richard West, *Principal*
Robert Caragher, *Vice Pres*
Maren Dougherty, *Vice Pres*
Susan Harlow, *Vice Pres*
EMP: 140
SQ FT: 144,000
SALES: 33.9MM **Privately Held**
SIC: 8412 5947 5812 6512 Museum; gift shop; cafeteria; theater building, owner-ship & operation

(P-24249)
CALIFRNIA SCNCE CTR FOUNDATION
700 Exposition Park Dr, Los Angeles (90037-1254)
PHONE.................................213 744-2545
Jeffrey N Rudolph, *President*
Cynthia Pygin, *CFO*
Dennis Jenkins, *Project Dir*
Erica Guzman, *Accountant*
EMP: 260
SALES (est): 37.7MM **Privately Held**
WEB: www.casciencectr.com
SIC: 8412 7832 5947 Museum; motion picture theaters, except drive-in; gifts & novelties

(P-24250)
CHARLES W BOWERS MUSEUM CORP
2002 N Main St, Santa Ana (92706-2731)
PHONE.................................714 567-3600
Peter C Keller, *President*
Paul Dowdle, *Vice Pres*
Jennifer Alvarado, *Director*
Jennifer Peterson, *Director*
Pauline Rusterholtz, *Manager*
▲ **EMP:** 72
SALES: 6.2MM **Privately Held**
SIC: 8412 Museum

(P-24251)
CHILDRENS CREATIVITY MUSEUM
221 4th St, San Francisco (94103-3116)
PHONE.................................415 820-3320
Adrienne Pon, *CEO*
MAI MAI Wythes, *Chairman*
John Gonzalez, *Treasurer*
Carol Tang, *Executive*
Michael Nobleza, *Exec Dir*
EMP: 65
SALES: 2.3MM **Privately Held**
WEB: www.zeum.com
SIC: 8412 5947 Museum; gift shop

(P-24252)
CHILDRENS MUSEUM OF DESERT
Also Called: CHILDREN'S DISCOVERY MUSEUM
71701 Gerald Ford Dr, Rancho Mirage (92270-1934)
PHONE.................................760 321-0602
Betty Barker, *Chairman*
Lee Vanderbeck, *Director*
EMP: 50
SQ FT: 18,000
SALES: 915.3K **Privately Held**
WEB: www.cdmod.org
SIC: 8412 Museum

(P-24253)
CITY & COUNTY OF SAN FRANCISCO
Also Called: Asian Art Museum
200 Larkin St, San Francisco (94102-4734)
PHONE.................................415 581-3500
Emily Sano, *Director*
Szuhan Chen, *Partner*
Nancy Brennan, *Officer*
Kevin Conley, *Info Tech Dir*
Alex Herreria, *Network Mgr*
EMP: 60 **Privately Held**
SIC: 8412 9199 Museum; general govern-ment administration; ;

PA: City & County Of San Francisco
1 Dr Carlton B Goodlett P
San Francisco CA 94102
415 554-7500

(P-24254)
CITY OF FREMONT
Also Called: Ardenwood Farm
34600 Ardenwood Blvd, Fremont (94555-3645)
P.O. Box 5006 (94537-5006)
PHONE.................................510 791-4196
Randy Hees, *Manager*
EMP: 105
SQ FT: 72,576 **Privately Held**
WEB: www.ci.fremont.ca.us
SIC: 8412 9111 Historical society; mayors' offices
PA: City Of Fremont
3300 Capitol Ave
Fremont CA 94538
510 284-4000

(P-24255)
CITY OF LOS ANGELES
Also Called: Parks & Recreation Dept
2800 E Observatory Ave, Los Angeles (90027-1255)
PHONE.................................213 473-0800
Edwin C Krupp, *Director*
EMP: 200 **Privately Held**
WEB: www.lacity.org
SIC: 8412 9532 Museum; urban & com-munity development
PA: City Of Los Angeles
200 N Spring St Ste 303
Los Angeles CA 90012
213 978-0600

(P-24256)
COMPUTER HISTORY MUSEUM
1401 N Shoreline Blvd, Mountain View (94043-1311)
PHONE.................................650 810-1010
John C Hollar, *President*
Laurie Yoler, *Trustee*
George Holmes, *Vice Pres*
Michelle Mertz, *Vice Pres*
Kirsten Tashev, *Vice Pres*
▲ **EMP:** 52
SQ FT: 111,670
SALES: 13.1MM **Privately Held**
SIC: 8412 Museum

(P-24257)
CORPORTION OF FINE ARTS MSEUMS
Also Called: Palace of The Legion Honor
50 Hagiwara Tea Garden Dr, San Francisco (94118-4502)
PHONE.................................415 750-3600
John Duchanan, *Manager*
EMP: 200 **Privately Held**
SIC: 8412 Museum
PA: Corporation Of The Fine Arts Museums
50 Hagiwara Tea Garden Dr
San Francisco CA 94118

(P-24258)
CORPORTION OF FINE ARTS MSEUMS
Also Called: M H Deyoung Memorial
50 Golden Gate Pk Hgiwara, San Francisco (94118)
PHONE.................................415 750-3600
EMP: 125 **Privately Held**
SIC: 8412 Museum
PA: Corporation Of The Fine Arts Museums
50 Hagiwara Tea Garden Dr
San Francisco CA 94118

(P-24259)
CORPORTION OF FINE ARTS MSEUMS (PA)
Also Called: Deyoung Museum
50 Hagiwara Tea Garden Dr, San Francisco (94118-4502)
PHONE.................................415 750-3600
Michelle Gutierrez, *Officer*
Cynthia Inaba, *CFO*
Nelson Favenir, *Officer*
Darwin Wong, *Officer*
Ken Garcia, *Comms Dir*

▲ **EMP:** 132
SQ FT: 300,000
SALES: 64.5MM **Privately Held**
SIC: 8412 Museum

(P-24260)
COUNTY OF LOS ANGELES
Also Called: Administration
5905 Wilshire Blvd, Los Angeles (90036-4504)
PHONE.................................323 857-6000
Andrea L Rich, *President*
EMP: 100 **Privately Held**
WEB: www.co.la.ca.us
SIC: 8412 9411 Art gallery, noncommer-cial; administration of educational pro-grams;
PA: County Of Los Angeles
500 W Temple St Ste 437
Los Angeles CA 90012
213 974-1101

(P-24261)
DESERT ARTS CENTER
Also Called: Dac
550 N Palm Canyon Dr, Palm Springs (92262-5526)
P.O. Box 2813 (92263-2813)
PHONE.................................760 323-7973
Adele Hill, *President*
EMP: 90
SALES: 160.6K **Privately Held**
SIC: 8412 Museum

(P-24262)
DUBLIN HSTRCAL PRSRVATION ASSN
7172 Regional St Pmb 316, Dublin (94568-2324)
PHONE.................................925 785-2898
Steven Minniear, *President*
EMP: 100
SALES: 6K **Privately Held**
SIC: 8412 Museum

(P-24263)
EASTERN CALIFORNIA MUSEUM (PA)
155 N Grant St, Independence (93526)
PHONE.................................760 878-0292
Margaret Mairs, *Ch of Bd*
Leah Kirk, *Treasurer*
Del Hubbs, *Vice Ch Bd*
William Michaels, *Director*
EMP: 350
SQ FT: 3,200
SALES (est): 1.6MM **Privately Held**
SIC: 8412 Museum

(P-24264)
ETIWANDA HISTORICAL SOCIETY
7150 Etiwanda Ave, Rancho Cucamonga (91739-9758)
P.O. Box 63 (91739-0063)
PHONE.................................909 899-8432
Jan Sutton, *President*
EMP: 99
SALES (est): 3.9MM **Privately Held**
SIC: 8412 Historical society

(P-24265)
EXPLORATORIUM
17 Pier Ste 100, San Francisco (94111-1455)
PHONE.................................415 528-4462
Chris Flink, *Exec Dir*
Roberta Katz, *Ch of Bd*
Laura Zander, *COO*
Ron Hipschman, *Administration*
David Torgersen, *Prgrmr*
▲ **EMP:** 401
SQ FT: 200,000
SALES: 65.1MM **Privately Held**
WEB: www.exploratorium.org
SIC: 8412 Museum

(P-24266)
HISTORICAL SOC CENTINELA VLY
7634 Midfield Ave, Los Angeles (90045-3234)
PHONE.................................310 649-6272
Leonard Utter, *President*
Claydine Burt, *Vice Pres*

EMP: 300
SALES (est): 1.8MM **Privately Held**
SIC: 8412 Historical society

(P-24267)
KIDSPACE A PRTICIPATORY MUSEUM
480 N Arroyo Blvd, Pasadena (91103-3269)
PHONE.................................626 449-9144
Jane Popovich, *President*
Mark McKinley, *Treasurer*
Chris Morphy, *Vice Pres*
Stephen H Baumann, *Exec Dir*
Nam Jack, *Admin Sec*
EMP: 83
SALES: 4.4MM **Privately Held**
WEB: www.kidspacemuseum.org
SIC: 8412 Museum

(P-24268)
LINDSAY WILDLIFE MUSEUM
1931 1st Ave, Walnut Creek (94597-2540)
PHONE.................................925 935-1978
Kramer Klabau, *President*
John Kikuchi, *President*
Loren Behr, *Exec Dir*
Dana Eder, *Opers Mgr*
Elisabeth Nardi, *Marketing Staff*
EMP: 90
SQ FT: 28,000
SALES: 2.2MM **Privately Held**
WEB: www.wildlife-museum.org
SIC: 8412 Museum

(P-24269)
LONG BCH MUSEUM ART FOUNDATION
2300 E Ocean Blvd, Long Beach (90803-2442)
PHONE.................................562 439-2119
Ronald B Nelson, *Director*
Ron Nelson, *Exec Dir*
Laurie Webb, *Admin Asst*
Lisa Marsh, *Education*
Harold B Nelson, *Director*
▲ **EMP:** 62
SQ FT: 24,000
SALES: 1.4MM **Privately Held**
WEB: www.lbma.org
SIC: 8412 Museum

(P-24270)
LOS ANGELES CNTY MSEUM OF ART
Also Called: Lacma
5905 Wilshire Blvd, Los Angeles (90036-4504)
PHONE.................................323 857-6000
Michael Govan, *CEO*
Ann Rowland, *CFO*
Alison Edelstein, *Officer*
Mark Mitchell, *Officer*
Rachel Zelaya, *Officer*
▲ **EMP:** 94
SALES (est): 9MM **Privately Held**
SIC: 8412 Museum

(P-24271)
MEXICAN HERITG CTR GALLERY INC
111 S Sutter St, Stockton (95202-3220)
P.O. Box 77985 (95267-1285)
PHONE.................................209 969-9306
Gracie Madrid, *President*
EMP: 75
SQ FT: 6,799
SALES: 41.4K **Privately Held**
SIC: 8412 Museums & art galleries

(P-24272)
MUSEUM ASSOCIATES
Also Called: LA COUNTY MUSEUM OF ART
5905 Wilshire Blvd, Los Angeles (90036-4504)
PHONE.................................323 857-6172
Michael Gavin, *CEO*
Ernesto Portillo, *Social Dir*
Alicia Saenz, *Education*
Veronica Alvarez, *Director*
Kim CHI-Young, *Manager*
EMP: 400
SALES: 278.1MM **Privately Held**
SIC: 8412 Museum

(P-24273)
MUSEUM CNTMPRARY ART SAN DIEGO
Also Called: MCASD
1100 Kettner Blvd, San Diego
(92101-3306)
PHONE.................................858 454-3541
Hugh M Davies, *CEO*
Kathlene J Gusel, *Admin Asst*
Anneka Van Dongen, *Accountant*
Jill Dawsey, *Associate*
▼ EMP: 70 EST: 1941
SQ FT: 45,200
SALES: 18.1MM **Privately Held**
SIC: 8412 Museum

(P-24274)
MUSEUM OF CONTEMPORARY ART (PA)
250 S Grand Ave, Los Angeles
(90012-3021)
PHONE.................................213 626-6222
Charles Young, *CEO*
Jeffrey Deitch, *CEO*
Michael Harrison, *CFO*
Kate Motonaga, *Officer*
Grace KAO, *Executive Asst*
▲ EMP: 150
SQ FT: 100,000
SALES (est): 39.7MM **Privately Held**
SIC: 8412 Museum

(P-24275)
MUSEUM OF LATIN AMERICAN ART
628 Alamitos Ave, Long Beach
(90802-1513)
PHONE.................................562 437-1689
Robert M Gumbiner, *Chairman*
Jessica Salazar, *President*
Mike Deovlet, *Corp Secy*
Gina Adams, *Vice Pres*
Tim Buckingham, *Accounting Mgr*
▲ EMP: 50
SQ FT: 30,000
SALES: 2.2MM **Privately Held**
SIC: 8412 Arts or science center; museum

(P-24276)
NATURAL HISTORY MUSEUM OF LOS
900 Exposition Blvd, Los Angeles
(90007-4057)
PHONE.................................213 763-3442
EMP: 300
SALES: 54MM **Privately Held**
SIC: 8412

(P-24277)
NEW CHILDRENS MUSEUM
200 W Island Ave, San Diego
(92101-6850)
PHONE.................................619 233-8792
Judy Forrester, *CEO*
Gabby Gracida, *Marketing Staff*
Lilli-Mari Andresen, *Director*
Hannah Berger, *Director*
Kerri Fox, *Director*
EMP: 90
SQ FT: 50,000
SALES (est): 3.8MM **Privately Held**
SIC: 8412 Museum

(P-24278)
NORTON SIMON MUSEUM
411 W Colorado Blvd, Pasadena
(91105-1825)
PHONE.................................626 449-6840
Ronald H Dykhuizen, *Principal*
Jennifer J Simon, *Ch of Bd*
Walter W Timoshuk, *Treasurer*
Robert Walker, *Vice Pres*
Jennifer Johnson, *Graphic Designe*
▲ EMP: 100
SQ FT: 70,000
SALES: 9.4MM **Privately Held**
WEB: www.nortonsimon.org
SIC: 8412 Museum

(P-24279)
OAKLAND MUSEUM OF CALIFORNIA
1000 Oak St, Oakland (94607-4892)
PHONE.................................510 318-8400

Lori Fogarty, *CEO*
Lori G Fogarty, *CEO*
Johanna Jones, *Associate Dir*
Cynthia Taylor, *Associate Dir*
Scot Jaffe, *Facilities Dir*
EMP: 100
SQ FT: 150,000
SALES: 23.5MM **Privately Held**
SIC: 8412 Historical society; museum

(P-24280)
PALM SPRINGS ART MUSEUM INC
101 N Museum Dr, Palm Springs
(92262-5659)
P.O. Box 2310 (92263-2310)
PHONE.................................760 322-4800
Donna Macmillan, *Ch of Bd*
Stanley Rosen, *Bd of Directors*
Betty Rinnig, *Associate Dir*
Elizabeth Armstrong, *Exec Dir*
Michael Hinkle, *IT/INT Sup*
▲ EMP: 96
SQ FT: 75,000
SALES: 10.5MM **Privately Held**
WEB: www.psmuseum.org
SIC: 8412 Museum

(P-24281)
PARKS AND RECREATION CAL DEPT
Also Called: Malibu Lagoon Museum
23200 Pacific Coast Hwy, Malibu
(90265-4937)
P.O. Box 291 (90265-0291)
PHONE.................................310 456-8432
Sandra Mitchell, *Branch Mgr*
EMP: 80 **Privately Held**
WEB: www.californiastatepark.com
SIC: 8412 9512 Museum; land, mineral & wildlife conservation;
HQ: California Department Of Parks And Recreation
1416 9th St Ste 1041
Sacramento CA 95814
800 777-0369

(P-24282)
REUBEN H FLEET SCIENCE CENTER
1875 El Prado, San Diego (92101-1625)
P.O. Box 33303 (92163-3303)
PHONE.................................619 238-1233
Gary Thomas Phillips, *CEO*
Craig A Blower, *COO*
Jeffrey Kirsch, *Exec Dir*
Michelle Hewitt, *Controller*
Julie Schardin, *Director*
EMP: 105
SQ FT: 93,500
SALES: 7.7MM **Privately Held**
WEB: www.rhfleet.org
SIC: 8412 Museum

(P-24283)
RONALD REAGAN PRESIDENTIAL
Also Called: Ronald Reagan Presdntl Library
40 Presidential Dr # 200, Simi Valley
(93065-0600)
PHONE.................................805 522-2977
Glenn Baker, *CFO*
Mike Shahin, *Treasurer*
Ronald Reagan, *Vice Pres*
John Heubusch, *Exec Dir*
Katherine Hicks, *Executive Asst*
EMP: 70
SQ FT: 225,000
SALES: 34.9MM **Privately Held**
WEB: www.reaganfoundation.org
SIC: 8412 8231 5947 8399 Museum; public library; gifts & novelties; community development groups; fund raising organization, non-fee basis

(P-24284)
SAN DEGO SOC OF NTURAL HISTORY
Also Called: San Dego Ntural History Museum
1788 El Prado, San Diego (92101-1624)
P.O. Box 121390 (92112-1390)
PHONE.................................619 232-3821
Michael W Hager, *CEO*
George Gonyer, *COO*

Susan Loveall, *Vice Pres*
Paul Murphey, *Research*
Christine Griffith, *Education*
▲ EMP: 70 EST: 1874
SQ FT: 60,000
SALES: 14.5MM **Privately Held**
WEB: www.sdnhm.org
SIC: 8412 5047 Museum; dental equipment & supplies

(P-24285)
SAN DIEGO AEROSPACE MUSEUM
335 Kenney St, El Cajon (92020-1249)
PHONE.................................619 258-1221
Jeff Eads, *Manager*
French Francis, *Advisor*
EMP: 60
SALES (est): 491.8K **Privately Held**
WEB: www.sdasm.org
SIC: 8412 Museum

(P-24286)
SAN DIEGO ARCFT CARIER MUSEUM
910 N Harbor Dr, San Diego (92101-5811)
PHONE.................................619 544-9600
Theresa Randall, *President*
EMP: 150
SALES: 21.9MM **Privately Held**
WEB: www.midway.org
SIC: 8412 Museum

(P-24287)
SAN FRANCISCO MERITIME N H P
Fort Myson Ctr Bldg E265, San Francisco
(94123)
PHONE.................................415 561-7000
Craig Kenkel, *Superintendent*
EMP: 80
SALES (est): 535K **Privately Held**
SIC: 8412 Museum

(P-24288)
SAN FRNCSCO MRTIME NAT PK ASSN (PA)
Fort Mason Fl 2 Bldg E, San Francisco
(94123)
P.O. Box 470310 (94147-0310)
PHONE.................................415 561-6662
John Tregenza, *CEO*
EMP: 50
SQ FT: 2,500
SALES: 2.5MM **Privately Held**
WEB: www.sanbrunosuper8.com
SIC: 8412 8299 8699 Museum; educational services; charitable organization

(P-24289)
SAN JOSE CHLD DISCOVERY MUSEUM
180 Woz Way, San Jose (95110-2722)
PHONE.................................408 298-5437
William Sullivan, *CEO*
Cheryl Blumenthal, *Director*
Patricia Narciso, *Director*
Jessica Torres, *Director*
Marisa Rojas, *Receptionist*
EMP: 85
SQ FT: 52,000
SALES: 8.9MM **Privately Held**
SIC: 8412 Museum

(P-24290)
SAN JOSE MUSEUM OF ART ASSN
110 S Market St, San Jose (95113-2383)
PHONE.................................408 271-6840
Daniel Keegan, *Director*
Karen Rapp, *Officer*
Jessica Yee, *Exec Dir*
Paulina Vu, *Manager*
Claire Tsai, *Assistant*
▲ EMP: 70 EST: 1969
SQ FT: 80,000
SALES: 5.1MM **Privately Held**
WEB: www.sjmusart.org
SIC: 8412 5942 5947 Museum; book stores; gift shop

(P-24291)
SANTA BARBARA MUSEUM
2559 Puesta Del Sol, Santa Barbara
(93105-2936)
PHONE.................................805 682-4711
Luke Swetland, *CEO*
Diane Wondowloski, *CFO*
Carolyn Chandler, *Vice Pres*
Elisabeth Fowler, *Vice Pres*
Janet Sands, *Vice Pres*
EMP: 95 EST: 1916
SALES: 10.4MM **Privately Held**
WEB: www.sbnature.org
SIC: 8412 Museum

(P-24292)
SANTA BARBARA MUSEUM OF ART (PA)
Also Called: Fine Arts Museum
1130 State St, Santa Barbara
(93101-2746)
PHONE.................................805 963-4364
Larry J Feinberg, *CEO*
James Owen, *President*
Diane Wondolowski, *President*
Larry Feinberg, *CEO*
James Hutchinson, *CFO*
▲ EMP: 60
SQ FT: 50,000
SALES: 6.6MM **Privately Held**
WEB: www.sbmuseart.org
SIC: 8412 Museum

(P-24293)
SKIRBALL CULTURAL CENTER
2701 N Sepulveda Blvd, Los Angeles
(90049-6833)
PHONE.................................310 440-4500
Uri D Herscher, *President*
Monyia Jackson, *Human Res Dir*
Beto Gonzalez, *Associate*
▲ EMP: 150
SQ FT: 65,000
SALES (est): 25.4MM **Privately Held**
SIC: 8412 Museum

(P-24294)
STANSBURY HM PRESERVATION ASSN
307 W 5th St, Chico (95928-5505)
P.O. Box 3262 (95927-3262)
PHONE.................................530 895-3848
EMP: 50
SQ FT: 3,500
SALES (est): 786.2K **Privately Held**
SIC: 8412

(P-24295)
TECH MUSEUM OF INNOVATION (PA)
201 S Market St, San Jose (95113-2008)
PHONE.................................408 795-6116
Peter Friess, *CEO*
Christopher Digiorgio, *Ch of Bd*
Tim Ritchie, *President*
Naresh Kapahi, *CFO*
Matthew Sapp, *Treasurer*
◆ EMP: 88
SQ FT: 130,000
SALES: 19.9MM **Privately Held**
SIC: 8412 Arts or science center; museum

(P-24296)
TECH MUSEUM OF INNOVATION
145 W San Carlos St, San Jose
(95113-2006)
PHONE.................................408 795-6168
Bill Bailor, *Director*
Pete Adams, *Manager*
EMP: 76
SALES (corp-wide): 19.9MM **Privately Held**
SIC: 8412 Arts or science center
PA: The Tech Museum Of Innovation
201 S Market St
San Jose CA 95113
408 795-6116

(P-24297)
THE FOR CALIFO CENTE
340 N Escondido Blvd, Escondido
(92025-2600)
PHONE.................................760 839-4138
Vicky Basehore, *President*
EMP: 185

SALES: 5.7MM **Privately Held**
WEB: www.artcenter.org
SIC: 8412 5999 Arts or science center; art dealers

(P-24298)
TURTLE BAY EXPLORATION PARK
1335 Arboretum Dr Ste A, Redding (96003-3628)
PHONE....................530 243-4282
John C Peterson, *President*
Judy Lalouche, *Vice Pres*
Jessica Bullington, *Store Mgr*
Nicholas Williams, *Facilities Mgr*
Jan Dehate, *Education*
EMP: 50
SALES: 7MM **Privately Held**
SIC: 8412 Museum

(P-24299)
WALT DISNEY FAMILY MUSEUM
104 Montgomery St, San Francisco (94129-1718)
PHONE....................415 345-6800
Ronald W Miller, *President*
Jennifer Miller-Goff, *Corp Secy*
Joanna Miller, *Vice Pres*
Kirsten Komoroske, *Exec Dir*
Alice Carter, *Managing Dir*
EMP: 60
SALES: 12.1MM **Privately Held**
SIC: 8412 Museum

8422 Arboreta, Botanical & Zoological Gardens

(P-24300)
AQUARIUM OF PACIFIC
310 Golden Shore Ste 300, Long Beach (90802-4240)
PHONE....................562 590-3100
Jerry R Schubel, *Branch Mgr*
EMP: 56 **Privately Held**
SIC: 8422 Aquarium
PA: Aquarium Of The Pacific
100 Aquarium Way
Long Beach CA 90802

(P-24301)
AQUARIUM OF PACIFIC (PA)
100 Aquarium Way, Long Beach (90802-8126)
PHONE....................562 590-3100
Jerry R Schubel, *President*
Anthony Brown, *CFO*
Cecile Fisher, *Vice Pres*
Perry Hampton, *Vice Pres*
Erica Noriega, *Social Dir*
▲ **EMP:** 220
SQ FT: 10,000
SALES: 39.4MM **Privately Held**
SIC: 8422 Aquarium

(P-24302)
BAYORG
Also Called: AQUARIUM OF THE BAY, THE
Embarcadero At Beach St, San Francisco (94133)
PHONE....................415 623-5300
John Frawley, *President*
Bobbi Evans, *CFO*
EMP: 99
SALES: 11.5MM **Privately Held**
SIC: 8422 Aquarium

(P-24303)
BIRCH AQUARIUM AT SCRIPPS
Also Called: Scripps Aquarium
2300 Expedition Way, La Jolla (92037)
PHONE....................858 534-4109
Nigella Hillgarth, *Director*
Evelyn Rose, *Analyst*
Patrick Helbling, *Opers Dir*
EMP: 50
SALES (est): 2MM **Privately Held**
SIC: 8422 8412 Aquarium; museum

(P-24304)
CALIFORNIA ACADEMY SCIENCES (PA)
55 Music Concourse Dr, San Francisco (94118-4503)
PHONE....................415 379-8000
John Hafernik, *President*
Rebecca Schuett, *Partner*
Alison Brown, *CFO*
Stephanie Stone, *Officer*
Mindee Kashiwagi, *Associate Dir*
EMP: 635 **EST:** 1853
SQ FT: 410,000
SALES: 83.5MM **Privately Held**
SIC: 8422 2721 8412 Aquarium; periodicals; publishing only; museums & art galleries

(P-24305)
CITY OF SAN JOSE
Also Called: Visitor Services & Facilities
1300 Senter Rd, San Jose (95112-2520)
PHONE....................408 794-6400
Randy Adams, *Supervisor*
EMP: 60 **Privately Held**
WEB: www.csjfinance.org
SIC: 8422 9512 Zoological garden, noncommercial; recreational program administration, government;
PA: City Of San Jose
200 E Santa Clara St
San Jose CA 95113
408 535-3500

(P-24306)
CONSERVATION SOCIETY CAL
Also Called: Oakland Zoo In Knowland Park
9777 Golf Links Rd, Oakland (94605-4925)
P.O. Box 5238 (94605-0238)
PHONE....................510 632-9525
Joel J Parrott, *CEO*
Steven E Kane, *Ch of Bd*
William L Marchant, *Admin Sec*
EMP: 85
SQ FT: 1,000
SALES (est): 21.4MM **Privately Held**
SIC: 8422 Arboreta & botanical or zoological gardens

(P-24307)
FILOLI CENTER
Also Called: FILOLI GARDEN SHOP
86 Canada Rd, Woodside (94062-4144)
PHONE....................650 364-8300
Cynthia D'Agosta, *CEO*
Pamela Smith, *President*
Julie Lovell, *Social Dir*
Robert Walker, *Principal*
Chantelle Gomez, *Graphic Designe*
EMP: 60
SQ FT: 1,000
SALES: 7.9MM **Privately Held**
SIC: 8422 Botanical garden

(P-24308)
FRESNOS CHAFFEE ZOO CORP
894 W Belmont Ave, Fresno (93728-2807)
PHONE....................559 498-5910
Scott Barton, *CEO*
Brian Goldman, *CFO*
Richard Rick Treatch Edd, *CFO*
Ciara Castellanoz, *Marketing Mgr*
Pam Wheelen, *Manager*
◆ **EMP:** 121
SALES: 15.4MM **Privately Held**
WEB: www.fresnochaffeezoo.com
SIC: 8422 Animal & reptile exhibit

(P-24309)
LIVING DESERT
47900 Portola Ave, Palm Desert (92260-6156)
PHONE....................760 346-5694
Allen Monroe, *CEO*
Terrie Correll, *COO*
Bill Powers, *Bd of Directors*
Kathy Lambert, *Officer*
Edward Thayer, *Officer*
EMP: 124
SQ FT: 1,700
SALES: 18.9MM **Privately Held**
WEB: www.livingdesert.org
SIC: 8422 5947 Aquariums & zoological gardens; botanical garden; gift shop

(P-24310)
LOS ANGLES ARBRETUM FOUNDATION
301 N Baldwin Ave, Arcadia (91007-2697)
PHONE....................626 821-3222
Richard Schulhof, *CEO*
EMP: 65
SALES: 2.3MM **Privately Held**
SIC: 8422 Arboretum

(P-24311)
MONTALVO ASSOCIATION
Also Called: Montalvo Arts Center
15400 Montalvo Rd, Saratoga (95070-6327)
P.O. Box 158 (95071-0158)
PHONE....................408 961-5800
Angela McConnell, *CEO*
Laura Amador, *Education*
EMP: 65
SQ FT: 13,000
SALES (est): 4.4MM **Privately Held**
WEB: www.villamontalvo.org
SIC: 8422 8412 Arboretum; art gallery, noncommercial

(P-24312)
MONTEREY BAY AQAR FOUNDATION (PA)
886 Cannery Row, Monterey (93940-1023)
PHONE....................831 648-4800
Peter Bing, *Ch of Bd*
Susan Wagner, *Volunteer Dir*
Julie E Packard, *CEO*
Edward Prohaska, *CFO*
Scott Chapman, *Officer*
EMP: 380
SQ FT: 326,000
SALES (est): 85.1MM **Privately Held**
WEB: www.montereyaquarium.org
SIC: 8422 Aquarium

(P-24313)
RANCHO SANTA ANA BOTANIC GRDN
1500 N College Ave, Claremont (91711-3157)
PHONE....................909 625-8767
Clement Hamilton, *Exec Dir*
Richard Grant, *Chairman*
Sonja Evensen, *Vice Pres*
Lucinda McDade, *Exec Dir*
Naomi Fraga, *Prgrmr*
EMP: 52
SQ FT: 30,000
SALES: 3.9MM **Privately Held**
WEB: www.rsabg.org
SIC: 8422 Botanical garden

(P-24314)
SACRAMENTO ZOOLOGICAL SOCIETY
3930 W Land Park Dr, Sacramento (95822-1123)
PHONE....................916 808-5888
Mary Healy, *Exec Dir*
EMP: 50
SALES: 7MM **Privately Held**
WEB: www.saczoo.com
SIC: 8422 Arboreta & botanical or zoological gardens

(P-24315)
SANTA BRBARA ZLGCAL FOUNDATION
500 Ninos Dr, Santa Barbara (93103-3759)
PHONE....................805 962-1673
Yul Vanek, *CEO*
Fred Clough, *President*
Nancy McToldridge, *COO*
Carol Bedford, *CFO*
Eldon Shiffman, *Treasurer*
▲ **EMP:** 130
SQ FT: 1,200
SALES: 11.6MM **Privately Held**
WEB: www.santabarbarazoo.org
SIC: 8422 Zoological garden, noncommercial

(P-24316)
ZOOLOGICAL SOCIETY SAN DIEGO (PA)
Also Called: World Famous San Diego Zoo
2920 Zoo Dr, San Diego (92101-1646)
P.O. Box 120551 (92112-0551)
PHONE....................619 231-1515
Douglas G Myers, *Exec Dir*
Paula S Brock, *CFO*
Frank Alexander, *Treasurer*
Don Leiker, *Vice Pres*
Kelly Craig, *Associate Dir*
◆ **EMP:** 1500
SALES: 342.1MM **Privately Held**
WEB: www.sdzoo.com
SIC: 8422 5812 5947 Aquarium; eating places; gift shop

(P-24317)
ZOOLOGICAL SOCIETY SAN DIEGO
Also Called: San Diego Wild Animal Park
15500 San Pasqual Vly Rd, Escondido (92027-7017)
PHONE....................760 747-8702
Robert McClure, *Manager*
EMP: 800
SALES (corp-wide): 342.1MM **Privately Held**
WEB: www.sdzoo.com
SIC: 8422 7999 Animal & reptile exhibit; tourist attraction, commercial
PA: Zoological Society Of San Diego
2920 Zoo Dr
San Diego CA 92101
619 231-1515

(P-24318)
ZOOLOGICAL SOCIETY SAN DIEGO
Also Called: San Diego Zoo
2920 Zoo Dr, San Diego (92101-1646)
P.O. Box 120551 (92112-0551)
PHONE....................619 744-3325
Richard Farrar, *Director*
Sara Graef, *Executive Asst*
Elaine Chafe, *Manager*
Jennifer Dunlap, *Manager*
EMP: 1200
SALES (corp-wide): 342.1MM **Privately Held**
WEB: www.sdzoo.com
SIC: 8422 Arboreta & botanical or zoological gardens
PA: Zoological Society Of San Diego
2920 Zoo Dr
San Diego CA 92101
619 231-1515

8611 Business Associations

(P-24319)
AEROVIRONMENT INC
85 Moreland Rd, Simi Valley (93065-1662)
PHONE....................805 581-2187
John Grabowsky, *Branch Mgr*
EMP: 150
SALES (corp-wide): 314.2MM **Publicly Held**
WEB: www.avinc.com
SIC: 8611 Manufacturers' institute
PA: Aerovironment, Inc.
900 Innovators Way
Simi Valley CA 93065
805 581-2187

(P-24320)
ALL STATE ASSOCIATION INC
11487 San Fernando Rd, San Fernando (91340-3406)
PHONE....................877 425-2558
Steve Avetyan, *CEO*
Alfred Megrabyan, *President*
Armen Karibyan, *COO*
Talina Ghazarian, *Manager*
EMP: 250
SALES (est): 108MM **Privately Held**
SIC: 8611 Trade associations

P R O D U C T S & S V C S

(P-24321)
ALMOND BOARD OF CALIFORNIA
1150 9th St Ste 1500, Modesto (95354-0845)
PHONE..................................209 549-8262
Richard Waycott, *CEO*
Karen Lapsley, *Officer*
Harbinder Maan, *Associate Dir*
Julie Adams, *Director*
Jenny Heap, *Manager*
EMP: 50
SQ FT: 10,000
SALES: 73MM **Privately Held**
WEB: www.almondboard.com
SIC: 8611 Trade associations

(P-24322)
ASOCIACON DE BOMBEROS DEL ESTA
1100 Calle Del Cerro 52d, San Clemente (92672-6022)
PHONE..................................949 355-4249
Marco Olmos, *Principal*
EMP: 99
SALES (est): 812.4K **Privately Held**
SIC: 8611 Business associations

(P-24323)
BAY MEADOWS RACING ASSOCIATION
2600 S Delaware St, San Mateo (94403-1904)
P.O. Box 1490 (94401-0872)
PHONE..................................650 573-4500
Fax: 650 573-4677
EMP: 200
SALES (est): 4.5MM **Privately Held**
WEB: www.baymeadows.com
SIC: 8611

(P-24324)
BERES CONSULTING
Also Called: PCA
470 S Bentley Ave, Los Angeles (90049-3513)
P.O. Box 252008 (90025-8908)
PHONE..................................310 476-9941
John Gleason, *President*
EMP: 80
SALES (est): 1.5MM **Privately Held**
SIC: 8611 Trade associations

(P-24325)
C A H H S
1215 K St Ste 800, Sacramento (95814-3946)
PHONE..................................916 552-7507
Duane Dauner, *President*
EMP: 65
SALES (est): 597.7K **Privately Held**
WEB: www.calhospital.org
SIC: 8611 Trade associations

(P-24326)
CALIFORNIA ASSN REALTORS INC (PA)
525 S Virgil Ave, Los Angeles (90020-1403)
PHONE..................................213 739-8200
Joel S Singer, *CEO*
Lefrancis Arnold, *CEO*
Joel S Singer, *CEO*
Don Flyn, *CFO*
Don Faught, *Treasurer*
EMP: 110 **EST:** 1907
SQ FT: 52,000
SALES: 33.4MM **Privately Held**
SIC: 8611 8742 Real Estate Board; real estate consultant

(P-24327)
CALIFORNIA CERTIFIED ORGANIC
Also Called: CCOF CERTIFICATION SERVICES
2155 Delaware Ave Ste 150, Santa Cruz (95060-5732)
PHONE..................................831 423-2263
Cathy Calfo, *Exec Dir*
James Marquez, *Info Tech Dir*
Veronica Romero, *Personnel Assit*
Maria Lopez, *Sales Staff*
Jessica Parr, *Asst Director*

EMP: 58
SALES: 3.3MM **Privately Held**
SIC: 8611 Trade associations

(P-24328)
CALIFORNIA CHAMBER COMMERCE (PA)
Also Called: Cal Chamber
1215 K St Ste 1400, Sacramento (95814-3953)
P.O. Box 1736 (95812-1736)
PHONE..................................916 444-6670
Allan Zaremberg, *President*
Lawrence M Dicke, *CFO*
Jeanne Cain, *Exec VP*
Dave Kilby, *Exec VP*
Russell Lahodny, *Vice Pres*
EMP: 65
SQ FT: 26,000
SALES: 24.6MM **Privately Held**
WEB: www.calchamber.com
SIC: 8611 Chamber of Commerce

(P-24329)
CALIFORNIA CHAMBER COMMERCE
920 Riverside Pkwy Ste 30, West Sacramento (95605-1529)
PHONE..................................916 928-3594
Allan Zaremberg, *President*
EMP: 65
SALES (corp-wide): 24.6MM **Privately Held**
WEB: www.calchamber.com
SIC: 8611 Chamber of Commerce
PA: California Chamber Of Commerce
1215 K St Ste 1400
Sacramento CA 95814
916 444-6670

(P-24330)
CALIFORNIA GOLF ASSOCIATION
3200 Lopez Rd, Pebble Beach (93953-2900)
PHONE..................................831 625-4653
Bob Scarpitto, *President*
EMP: 55
SALES: 175.9K **Privately Held**
SIC: 8611 Merchants' association

(P-24331)
CITY ORANGE POLICE ASSN INC
1107 N Batavia St, Orange (92867-4615)
P.O. Box 906 (92856-6906)
PHONE..................................714 457-5340
John Mancini, *President*
EMP: 216
SALES: 435.5K **Privately Held**
SIC: 8611 Business associations

(P-24332)
CWS UTILITY SERVICES CORP
1720 N 1st St, San Jose (95112-4508)
PHONE..................................408 367-8200
Robert W Foye, *Principal*
EMP: 398
SALES (est): 6.5MM
SALES (corp-wide): 666.8MM **Publicly Held**
WEB: www.calwater.com
SIC: 8611 Public utility association
PA: California Water Service Group
1720 N 1st St
San Jose CA 95112
408 367-8200

(P-24333)
DOWNTOWN SAN DIEGO PARTNR INC (PA)
401 B St Ste 100, San Diego (92101-4224)
PHONE..................................619 234-0201
Chris Mitchell, *President*
Christina Chadwick, *Vice Pres*
John Hanley, *Vice Pres*
Lindsay Thomas, *Vice Pres*
Alonso Vivas, *Exec Dir*
EMP: 56
SQ FT: 3,500
SALES: 10MM **Privately Held**
WEB: www.downtown-digital.com
SIC: 8611 Business associations

(P-24334)
DOWNTOWN SAN DIEGO PARTNR INC
1111 6th Ave Ste 101, San Diego (92101-5230)
PHONE..................................619 234-8900
Ryan Loofbourrow, *Manager*
EMP: 55
SQ FT: 10,480
SALES (corp-wide): 10MM **Privately Held**
WEB: www.downtown-digital.com
SIC: 8611 Business associations
PA: Downtown San Diego Partnership, Inc.
401 B St Ste 100
San Diego CA 92101
619 234-0201

(P-24335)
ELECTRA OWNERS ASSOC
700 W E St, San Diego (92101-5984)
PHONE..................................619 236-3310
J E Martin, *Principal*
EMP: 150
SALES (est): 5.4MM
SALES (corp-wide): 95.6MM **Privately Held**
SIC: 8611 Business associations
PA: Action Property Management, Inc.
2603 Main St Ste 500
Irvine CA 92614
949 450-0202

(P-24336)
ELK GROVE ADULT CMNTY TRAINING
8810 Elk Grove Blvd, Elk Grove (95624-1811)
PHONE..................................916 431-3162
Larry Sherrill, *CEO*
Rebecca Brubaker, *Exec Dir*
Gary Lawson, *Exec Dir*
EMP: 54
SALES: 3.7MM **Privately Held**
WEB: www.egact.org
SIC: 8611 Community affairs & services

(P-24337)
EPSILON SYSTEMS SOLUTIONS INC
2101 Haffley Ave A, National City (91950-6416)
PHONE..................................619 474-3252
Robert Duran, *Branch Mgr*
James Blasko, *Vice Pres*
Kathy Woody, *Director*
EMP: 50
SALES (corp-wide): 110MM **Privately Held**
SIC: 8611 Shipping & steamship company association
PA: Epsilon Systems Solutions, Inc.
9242 Lightwave Ave # 100
San Diego CA 92123
619 702-1700

(P-24338)
FIRE AND POLICE
4645 E Anaheim St, Long Beach (90804-3122)
PHONE..................................562 961-0066
Patrick Ahern, *CEO*
Kevin Davis, *Director*
EMP: 50
SALES (est): 935.6K **Privately Held**
SIC: 8611 Community affairs & services

(P-24339)
FOUNDTION FOR CAL CMNTY CLLGES (PA)
1102 Q St Ste 4800, Sacramento (95811-6539)
PHONE..................................916 325-4300
Keetha Mills, *CEO*
John O'Sullivan, *CFO*
Mark Carlock, *Vice Pres*
Melissa Conner, *Vice Pres*
Joseph Quintana, *Vice Pres*
EMP: 250
SQ FT: 10,000
SALES: 38.5MM **Privately Held**
SIC: 8611 Business associations

(P-24340)
GOLDEN BEAR REST ASSN LLC
760 2nd St, San Francisco (94107-2012)
PHONE..................................415 227-8660
Peter W Osborne, *Mng Member*
Peter Osbourne,
EMP: 50
SALES (est): 1.5MM **Privately Held**
SIC: 8611 Merchants' association

(P-24341)
HAPPY CAMP CHAMBER COMMERCE
35 Davis Rd, Happy Camp (96039)
PHONE..................................530 493-2900
James Buchner, *President*
Rosemary Boren, *Treasurer*
Roberta Cullum, *Vice Pres*
EMP: 50
SALES (est): 836K **Privately Held**
SIC: 8611 Chamber of Commerce

(P-24342)
IAPMO RESEARCH AND TESTING INC (HQ)
5001 E Philadelphia St, Ontario (91761-2816)
PHONE..................................909 472-4100
G P Russ Chaney, *Exec Dir*
Jin Luo, *Exec VP*
Russ Chaney, *Executive*
Shahin Moinian, *Surgery Dir*
Neil Bogatz, *General Counsel*
▲ **EMP:** 57 **EST:** 1994
SALES: 39.8MM
SALES (corp-wide): 8.8MM **Privately Held**
SIC: 8611 Contractors' association
PA: International Association Of Plumbing And Mechanical Officials, A Non-Profit Corporation
4755 E Philadelphia St
Ontario CA 91761
909 472-4100

(P-24343)
INDIAN HEALTH COUNCIL INC (PA)
50100 Golsh Rd, Valley Center (92082-5338)
P.O. Box 406, Pauma Valley (92061-0406)
PHONE..................................760 749-1410
Orvin Hanson, *CEO*
Gina Rothermel, *Officer*
Donna Calac-Dusek, *Assoc VP*
Robert Schostag, *Pharmacy Dir*
Natasha Kitchen, *Admin Asst*
EMP: 82
SALES: 22.5MM **Privately Held**
SIC: 8611 Business associations

(P-24344)
INTERNATIONAL ASSOC OF PLMBNG (PA)
Also Called: IAPMO
4755 E Philadelphia St, Ontario (91761-2810)
PHONE..................................909 472-4100
GP Russ Chaney, *CEO*
Gary Hile, *Corp Secy*
Lee Mercer, *Exec VP*
Richard Beck, *Vice Pres*
John Hadi, *Vice Pres*
▲ **EMP:** 56 **EST:** 1926
SQ FT: 65,000
SALES: 8.8MM **Privately Held**
SIC: 8611 Contractors' association

(P-24345)
L W ROTH INSURANCE AGENCY
Also Called: National Association For Self
6060 Sunrise Vista Dr, Citrus Heights (95610-7053)
PHONE..................................916 721-6273
L W Roth, *Owner*
EMP: 100 **EST:** 1981
SALES (est): 1MM **Privately Held**
SIC: 8611 Regulatory associations

(P-24346)
LASSENS ALI LEADS CLUB (PA)
Also Called: Lassen's, Ali Success System
2644 Madison St, Carlsbad (92008-1721)
P.O. Box 278, Cardiff By The Sea (92007-0278)
PHONE..........................760 434-3761
Lisa Bentson, *Owner*
EMP: 56
SQ FT: 2,200
SALES (est): 1MM **Privately Held**
WEB: www.leadsclub.com
SIC: 8611 Trade associations

(P-24347)
LOS ANGLES AREA CHMBER CMMERCE
350 S Bixel St, Los Angeles (90017-1418)
PHONE..........................213 580-7500
Maria S Salinas, *President*
Benjamin Stilp, *CFO*
Cristina Torres, *Accounting Mgr*
La A Chamber,
Brian Boyle, *Senior Mgr*
EMP: 85
SALES: 7.2MM **Privately Held**
SIC: 8611 Chamber of Commerce

(P-24348)
MENS APPAREL GUILD IN CAL INC
Also Called: Magic International
2901 28th St Ste 100, Santa Monica (90405-2975)
PHONE..........................310 857-7500
Joe Loggia, *President*
Jeff Stevenson, *Exec Dir*
Mike Ausec, *Sales Staff*
Belinda Pina, *Sales Staff*
Arielle Mandell, *Mktg Coord*
EMP: 100 **EST:** 1932
SALES (est): 2.7MM
SALES (corp-wide): 1.3B **Privately Held**
WEB: www.magiconline.com
SIC: 8611 Manufacturers' institute
HQ: Advanstar Communications Inc.
2501 Colorado Ave Ste 280
Santa Monica CA 90404
310 857-7500

(P-24349)
MERCHANT VALLEY CORPORATION
1808 Avondale Dr, Roseville (95747-8390)
PHONE..........................916 786-7227
Mahmood Merchant, *Principal*
EMP: 125
SALES (est): 5.1MM **Privately Held**
SIC: 8611 Merchants' association

(P-24350)
MERCY HOUSE LIVING CENTERS
Also Called: Mercy Hse Trnstnal Living Ctrs
807 N Garfield St, Santa Ana (92701-3821)
P.O. Box 1905 (92702-1905)
PHONE..........................714 836-7188
Larry Haynes, *Exec Dir*
Carrie Delaurie, *Director*
EMP: 170
SQ FT: 19,000
SALES: 6.7MM **Privately Held**
WEB: www.mercyhouse.net
SIC: 8611 Community affairs & services

(P-24351)
MOTION PICTURE ASSN AMER INC (PA)
15301 Ventura Blvd Bldg E, Sherman Oaks (91403-5885)
PHONE..........................818 995-6600
Christopher J Dodd, *CEO*
Steven Fabrizio, *Exec VP*
Emily Lenzner, *Exec VP*
Jim C Williams, *Senior VP*
Tom Zigo, *Comms Dir*
EMP: 120 **EST:** 1922
SQ FT: 74,000
SALES (est): 25.6MM **Privately Held**
SIC: 8611 6512 Trade associations; commercial & industrial building operation

(P-24352)
NATIONAL ASSN MUS MRCHANTS INC
Also Called: Namm
5790 Armada Dr, Carlsbad (92008-4608)
PHONE..........................760 438-8001
Joe Lamond, *President*
Larry Manley, *CFO*
Larry Morton, *Treasurer*
Wendell Wong, *Executive*
Carolyn Grant, *Exec Dir*
EMP: 62
SQ FT: 38,000
SALES: 24.4MM **Privately Held**
WEB: www.namm.com
SIC: 8611 Trade associations

(P-24353)
NORTHERN MONO CHAMBER COMMERCE
115281 Us Highway 395, Topaz (96133-9127)
PHONE..........................530 208-6078
Pam Hamick, *President*
Dianne Evans, *Corp Secy*
Mary Dayhoff, *Vice Pres*
Susan Robbins, *Admin Sec*
EMP: 50
SALES (est): 1.7MM **Privately Held**
SIC: 8611 Chamber of Commerce

(P-24354)
PGANDE
10901 E Highway 120, Manteca (95336-8920)
PHONE..........................209 942-1745
R Nick Jordan, *Principal*
EMP: 50
SALES (est): 569K **Privately Held**
SIC: 8611 Public utility association

(P-24355)
PRINTING INDS ASSN SUTHERN CAL
5800 S Eastrn Ave Ste 400, Commerce (90040)
P.O. Box 910936, Los Angeles (90091-0936)
PHONE..........................323 728-9500
Robert Lindgren, *President*
EMP: 75
SQ FT: 14,000
SALES: 2.8MM **Privately Held**
SIC: 8611 Merchants' association

(P-24356)
PROJECT CONCERN INTERNATIONAL (PA)
Also Called: PCI
5151 Murphy Canyon Rd # 320, San Diego (92123-4339)
PHONE..........................858 279-9690
Carrie Hessler-Radelet, *President*
Mark O Donnell, *COO*
Kote Lomidze, *CFO*
Lauren Galvin, *Officer*
Janine Schooley, *Senior VP*
EMP: 79
SQ FT: 12,000
SALES: 69.3MM **Privately Held**
WEB: www.projectconcern.org
SIC: 8611 Business associations

(P-24357)
PUBLIC POLICY INSTITUTE CAL (PA)
Also Called: Ppic
500 Washington St Ste 600, San Francisco (94111-2907)
PHONE..........................415 291-4400
David Lyon, *President*
Robert E Obana, *CFO*
Andy Grose, *Principal*
Marla Gladney-Smallwo, *Admin Asst*
Theresa Dang, *Administration*
EMP: 73
SQ FT: 105,044
SALES: 12.7MM **Privately Held**
WEB: www.ppic.org
SIC: 8611 8732 Business associations; commercial nonphysical research

(P-24358)
SACRAMENTO HARNESS ASSOCIATION
1600 Exposition Blvd, Sacramento (95815-5104)
PHONE..........................916 239-4040
Ralph Scurfield, *President*
Chris Schick, *Manager*
EMP: 90
SALES (est): 1.3MM **Privately Held**
WEB: www.sacharness.com
SIC: 8611 Merchants' association

(P-24359)
SAN BERNARDINO CALIFORNIA CITY
Also Called: City Hall Pblc Wrks Eng Dpt
300 N D St Fl 3, San Bernardino (92418-0001)
PHONE..........................909 384-5111
James Funt, *Manager*
EMP: 70
SALES (corp-wide): 193MM **Privately Held**
SIC: 8611 Chamber of Commerce
PA: California City Of San Bernardino
290 N D St
San Bernardino CA 92401
909 384-7272

(P-24360)
SAN DIEGO ASSN GOVERNMENTS (PA)
Also Called: Regional Transportation Comm
401 B St Ste 800, San Diego (92101-4231)
PHONE..........................619 699-1900
Jack Dale, *Chairman*
Joann Sheridan, *Executive*
Don Higginson, *Principal*
Jim Janney, *Principal*
Gary L Gallegos, *Exec Dir*
EMP: 320
SQ FT: 20,000
SALES: 222.5MM **Privately Held**
WEB: www.gonctd.com
SIC: 8611 Business associations

(P-24361)
SAN JOSE SILICON VALLEY CHAM
Also Called: CHAMBERPAC
101 W Santa Clara St, San Jose (95113-1760)
PHONE..........................408 291-5250
Patricia Dando, *President*
EMP: 55 **EST:** 1874
SALES: 2.2MM **Privately Held**
SIC: 8611 Chamber of Commerce

(P-24362)
SATICOY LEMON ASSOCIATION
600 E 3rd St, Oxnard (93030-6001)
P.O. Box 46, Santa Paula (93061-0046)
PHONE..........................805 654-6543
Kevin Colvard, *Plant Mgr*
EMP: 130
SALES (corp-wide): 171MM **Privately Held**
SIC: 8611 Growers' associations
PA: Saticoy Lemon Association
103 N Peck Rd
Santa Paula CA 93060
805 654-6500

(P-24363)
SEMI (PA)
673 S Milpitas Blvd, Milpitas (95035-5473)
PHONE..........................408 943-6900
Ajit Manocha, *President*
Bertrand Loy, *Ch of Bd*
Eric Tien, *President*
Richard Salsman, *CFO*
Mary G Puma, *Treasurer*
EMP: 133 **EST:** 1970
SALES: 41.7MM **Privately Held**
WEB: www.semi.org
SIC: 8611 Trade associations

(P-24364)
SISTERS OF SOUL (SOS) YOUTH
937 Via Lata Ste 400, Colton (92324-3958)
PHONE..........................909 533-4889
Angela Beal, *CEO*
EMP: 55
SQ FT: 2,800
SALES: 200K **Privately Held**
SIC: 8611 8322 Community affairs & services; general counseling services

(P-24365)
SOUTHERN CALIFORNIA GOLF ASSN (PA)
3740 Cahuenga Blvd, North Hollywood (91604-3502)
P.O. Box 7186 (91615-0186)
PHONE..........................818 980-3630
Ken Bien, *President*
Keenan Barber, *Treasurer*
Al Frank, *Vice Pres*
Jonathan Coe, *Comms Mgr*
Tom Lindgren, *Principal*
EMP: 72
SQ FT: 15,000
SALES: 7.7MM **Privately Held**
WEB: www.scga.org
SIC: 8611 7992 Trade associations; public golf courses

(P-24366)
SOUTHLAND RGONAL ASSN REALTORS (PA)
7232 Balboa Blvd, Van Nuys (91406-2701)
PHONE..........................818 786-2110
James Link, *Exec VP*
Steve White, *President*
Tim Johnson, *COO*
Chuck Nickerson, *Vice Pres*
Brian Paul, *Vice Pres*
EMP: 75
SQ FT: 25,000
SALES (est): 69.4K **Privately Held**
WEB: www.srar.com
SIC: 8611 Real Estate Board

(P-24367)
SPECIALTY EQUIPMENT MKT ASSN (PA)
Also Called: Sema
1575 Valley Vista Dr, Diamond Bar (91765-3914)
PHONE..........................909 396-0289
Christopher J Kersting, *President*
EMP: 70 **EST:** 1963
SQ FT: 23,000
SALES: 40.5MM **Privately Held**
WEB: www.enjoythedrive.com
SIC: 8611 Trade associations

(P-24368)
SURPLUS LINE ASSOCIATION CAL
12667 Alcosta Blvd # 450, San Ramon (94583-4427)
PHONE..........................415 434-4900
Ted Pierce, *Exec Dir*
Patricia McAuley, *Data Proc Staff*
Sandhya Dhital, *Education*
Joy Laughery, *Director*
EMP: 65
SQ FT: 8,400
SALES: 11.9MM **Privately Held**
SIC: 8611 Trade associations

(P-24369)
UNITED AGRIBUSINESS LEAGUE (PA)
Also Called: U A L
54 Corporate Park, Irvine (92606-5105)
PHONE..........................800 223-4590
William C Goodrich, *President*
Kirti Mutatkar, *CFO*
Clare M Einsmann, *Exec VP*
EMP: 50
SQ FT: 14,099
SALES: 45.2MM **Privately Held**
WEB: www.ual.org
SIC: 8611 Growers' associations

(P-24370)
US LINES LLC (DH)
3501 Jamboree Rd Ste 300, Newport Beach (92660-2936)
PHONE..........................714 751-3333
Ed Aldridge, *President*
Thomas Aldridge, *Vice Pres*
Timothy Dillon, *Vice Pres*
Lita Woodruff, *Administration*
EMP: 75

PRODUCTS & SVCS

SALES (est): 34.9MM
SALES (corp-wide): 20.8MM **Privately Held**
WEB: www.uslines.com
SIC: 8611 Shipping & steamship company association
HQ: Cma Cgm
Jacques Saade
Marseille 2e Arrondissement 13002
491 915-247

(P-24371)
WATER RESOURCES CONTROL BD CAL
Also Called: San Diego Region
2375 Northside Dr Ste 100, San Diego (92108-2700)
PHONE............................619 521-3010
David Gibson, *Exec Dir*
EMP: 90 **Privately Held**
WEB: www.rb3.swrcb.ca.gov
SIC: 8611 Regulatory associations
HQ: Water Resources Control Board, California
1001 I St
Sacramento CA 95814

(P-24372)
WESTERN GROWERS ASSOCIATION (PA)
Also Called: W G A
15525 Sand Canyon Ave, Irvine (92618-3114)
P.O. Box 57089 (92619-7089)
PHONE............................949 863-1000
Tom A Nassif, *CEO*
Steve Patricio, *Ch of Bd*
Matt McInerney, *Exec VP*
Dave Puglia, *Senior VP*
Ward Kennedy, *Vice Pres*
EMP: 150
SQ FT: 35,000
SALES: 7.9MM **Privately Held**
WEB: www.wga.com
SIC: 8611 8111 Growers' associations; legal services

8621 Professional Membership Organizations

(P-24373)
ACADEMY MPIC ARTS & SCIENCES (PA)
8949 Wilshire Blvd, Beverly Hills (90211-1907)
PHONE............................310 247-3000
Dawn Hudson, *CEO*
Andrew Horn, *CFO*
Andy Horn, *CFO*
Bruce Davis, *Exec Dir*
Yolanda Enamorado, *Managing Dir*
EMP: 100
SQ FT: 35,000
SALES: 123.6MM **Privately Held**
SIC: 8621 7819 8611 Professional membership organizations; services allied to motion pictures; business associations

(P-24374)
ACADEMY TV ARTS SCNCES FNDTION
Also Called: Television Academy
5220 Lankershim Blvd, North Hollywood (91601-3109)
PHONE............................818 754-2800
Maury McImtyre, *President*
EMP: 60
SALES (est): 4.7MM **Privately Held**
SIC: 8621 Professional membership organizations

(P-24375)
AMERICAN ACADEMY OF OPTHALMLGY (PA)
655 Beach St Fl 1, San Francisco (94109-1346)
P.O. Box 7424 (94120-7424)
PHONE............................415 561-8500
David W Parke II, *CEO*
Keith Carter, *President*
Lawrence Mendenhall, *COO*
Jill Boyett, *CFO*

Vicky Loni, *CFO*
EMP: 160
SQ FT: 66,000
SALES: 60MM **Privately Held**
WEB: www.aao.org
SIC: 8621 Medical field-related associations

(P-24376)
AMERICAN HEART ASSOCIATION INC
Also Called: Western States Affiliate
816 S Figueroa St, Los Angeles (90017-2516)
PHONE............................213 291-7000
Cass Wheeler, *Branch Mgr*
EMP: 50
SALES (corp-wide): 460.7MM **Privately Held**
WEB: www.americanheart.org
SIC: 8621 Professional membership organizations
PA: American Heart Association, Inc.
7272 Greenville Ave
Dallas TX 75231
214 373-6300

(P-24377)
ARMED FORCES OFFICIALS ASSN
14532 Penasquitos Dr, San Diego (92129-1606)
PHONE............................858 672-1438
Paul Bardsley, *Treasurer*
Robert Cauffman, *President*
Robery Kauffman, *President*
Clarence Langston, *Vice Pres*
Donald Robinson, *Admin Sec*
EMP: 50
SALES (est): 1.3MM **Privately Held**
SIC: 8621 Education & teacher association

(P-24378)
ARTISTS OF RIVER TOWN
56 Highlands Blvd, Oroville (95966-3643)
PHONE............................530 534-7690
Dawn Bozine, *President*
Carmen Hironimus, *President*
Bee Boyd, *Treasurer*
Karen Comvey, *Admin Sec*
EMP: 76
SALES (est): 4.5MM **Privately Held**
WEB: www.global411.net
SIC: 8621 Professional membership organizations

(P-24379)
ASSOCIATED GENERAL CONTRACT
Also Called: A G C
6212 Ferris Sq, San Diego (92121-3205)
PHONE............................858 558-0739
Jim Ryan, *Exec VP*
Brad Barnum, *Vice Pres*
Pete Saucedo, *Exec Dir*
Marcy Knopman, *Executive Asst*
Glen Schaffer, *Marketing Staff*
EMP: 53
SQ FT: 4,000
SALES (est): 3.6MM **Privately Held**
SIC: 8621 Professional membership organizations

(P-24380)
BAR ASSCATION OF SAN FRANCISCO (PA)
301 Battery St Fl 3, San Francisco (94111-3237)
PHONE............................415 982-1600
James Donato, *President*
Jonathan Bond, *CFO*
Dan Burkhardt, *Exec Dir*
Samantha Silver, *Admin Asst*
Debi Ham, *Administration*
EMP: 120
SQ FT: 23,600
SALES: 7.2MM **Privately Held**
SIC: 8621 Bar association

(P-24381)
BEVERLY HILLS POLC OFCRS ASSOC
464 N Rexford Dr, Beverly Hills (90210-4873)
PHONE............................310 288-1755

Joe Chirillo, *President*
EMP: 100
SALES: 399.5K **Privately Held**
SIC: 8621 8742 Professional membership organizations; management consulting services

(P-24382)
CALIFORNIA ASSOCIATION O (PA)
Also Called: CALIFORNIA HOSPITAL ASSOCIATIO
1215 K St Ste 800, Sacramento (95814-3946)
PHONE............................916 443-7401
Carmela Coyle, *President*
Jennifer Davenport, *President*
Lois M Suder, *COO*
Lois Suder, *COO*
Dietmar Grellmann, *Senior VP*
EMP: 74
SQ FT: 30,000
SALES: 35.7MM **Privately Held**
SIC: 8621 8011 Health association; group health association

(P-24383)
CALIFORNIA DENTAL ASSOCIATION (PA)
1201 K St Fl 14, Sacramento (95814-3925)
PHONE............................916 443-0505
Peter A Dubois, *CEO*
Dennis Kalebjian, *President*
Carol Summerhayes, *President*
Cynthia Schneider, *CFO*
Carrie Gordon, *Officer*
EMP: 120
SQ FT: 28,932
SALES: 21.4MM **Privately Held**
WEB: www.sbvcds.org
SIC: 8621 Dental association

(P-24384)
CALIFORNIA HEALTH BENEFIT EXCH
Also Called: California Health Insur Exch
1601 Exposition Blvd, Sacramento (95815-5103)
PHONE............................916 228-8210
Peter V Lee, *CEO*
Desi Malone, *Manager*
Desiree Hayhurst Malone, *Manager*
Joyce McGhie, *Manager*
EMP: 99
SALES (est): 12.8MM **Privately Held**
SIC: 8621 Health association

(P-24385)
CALIFORNIA MEDICAL ASSOCIATION (PA)
Also Called: C M A
1201 K St Ste 800, Sacramento (95814-3933)
PHONE............................916 444-5532
Dustin Corcoren, *CEO*
Lance Lewis, *COO*
Nick Birtcil, *Vice Pres*
Lishaun Francis, *Associate Dir*
Jennifer Williams, *Executive Asst*
EMP: 77 **EST:** 1856
SALES: 18.3MM **Privately Held**
WEB: www.cmanet.org
SIC: 8621 Medical field-related associations

(P-24386)
CALIFORNIA NURSES ASSOCIATION (PA)
Also Called: NATIONAL NURSES UNITED
155 Grand Ave Ste 115, Oakland (94612-3758)
PHONE............................510 273-2200
Rose Anne Demoro, *CEO*
Deborah Burger, *President*
Nikki Dones, *Admin Sec*
Kamila Tanaka, *Personnel Assit*
Mike Griffing, *Director*
EMP: 100
SQ FT: 36,000
SALES: 28.1MM **Privately Held**
WEB: www.calnurse.org
SIC: 8621 Nursing association

(P-24387)
CALIFORNIA SCHOOL BOARDS ASSN
Also Called: Csba
3251 Beacon Blvd, West Sacramento (95691-3531)
PHONE............................800 266-3382
Vernon M Billy, *CEO*
Cindy Marks, *President*
Stephen Pogemiller, *CFO*
Jesus Holguin, *Vice Pres*
Scott Plotkin, *Exec Dir*
EMP: 100
SQ FT: 15,000
SALES (est): 15MM **Privately Held**
WEB: www.csba.org
SIC: 8621 Education & teacher association

(P-24388)
CALIFORNIA TEACHERS ASSN
222 Judy Dr, Kelsey (95667-3325)
P.O. Box 1624, Placerville (95667-1624)
PHONE............................530 622-8013
George Sabato, *Admin Sec*
EMP: 65
SALES (corp-wide): 187.1MM **Privately Held**
WEB: www.cntaonline.org
SIC: 8621 Education & teacher association
PA: California Teachers Association
1705 Murchison Dr
Burlingame CA 94010
650 697-1400

(P-24389)
CALIFORNIA TEACHERS ASSN (PA)
1705 Murchison Dr, Burlingame (94010-4583)
P.O. Box 921 (94011-0921)
PHONE............................650 697-1400
Carolyn Doggett, *Exec Dir*
Gail Holmes, *Regional Mgr*
Quinnetta Gill, *Admin Sec*
Gina Domenici, *Research*
Gregory Gee, *Technical Staff*
EMP: 210
SALES: 187.1MM **Privately Held**
WEB: www.cntaonline.org
SIC: 8621 8631 Education & teacher association; labor unions & similar labor organizations

(P-24390)
CALIFRNIA CPA EDCATN FUNDATION
1800 Gateway Dr Ste 200, San Mateo (94404-4072)
PHONE............................800 922-5272
Anthony Pugliese, *CEO*
Vinit Shrawagi, *Technical Staff*
EMP: 60 **EST:** 1966
SQ FT: 8,071
SALES: 11MM **Privately Held**
SIC: 8621 Professional membership organizations

(P-24391)
CAMBODIAN ASSOCIATION AMERICA (PA)
2390 Pacific Ave, Long Beach (90806-3051)
PHONE............................562 988-1863
Kimthai Kuoch, *Director*
Kim Ovalle, *Financial Analy*
Marinett Lishka, *Accountant*
Kimthai Kaoch, *Marketing Staff*
EMP: 50
SALES: 3MM **Privately Held**
WEB: www.cambodian.org
SIC: 8621 Professional membership organizations

(P-24392)
CAPITAL INVSTMNTS VNTURES CORP (PA)
Also Called: Civco
30151 Tomas, Rcho STA Marg (92688-2125)
PHONE............................949 858-0647
Drew Richardson, *President*
Brian Cronin, *Ch of Bd*
Gary Prenovost, *CFO*
Marjorie Kelso, *Human Resources*
EMP: 195

SQ FT: 95,000
SALES (est): 33.2MM
SALES (corp-wide): 30MM **Privately Held**
SIC: 8621 4724 Professional membership organizations; travel agencies

(P-24393)
CITY & COUNTY OF SAN FRANCISCO
Public Works Dept Bureau Arch
30 Van Ness Ave Ste 4100, San Francisco (94102-6034)
PHONE...................................415 557-4713
Gary Hoy, *Principal*
EMP: 75 **Privately Held**
SIC: 8621 9199 Architect association; general government administration; ;
PA: City & County Of San Francisco
　　1 Dr Carlton B Goodlett P
　　San Francisco CA 94102
　　415 554-7500

(P-24394)
CITY OF IRVINE
Also Called: Irvine Police Department
1 Civic Center Plz, Irvine (92606-5208)
PHONE...................................949 724-7101
David Maggard, *President*
EMP: 73 **Privately Held**
SIC: 8621 Professional membership organizations
PA: City Of Irvine
　　1 Civic Center Plz
　　Irvine CA 92606
　　949 724-6000

(P-24395)
COMMUNITY CLINICS HLTH NETWRK
Also Called: HEALTH CENTER PARTNERS OF SOUT
3710 Ruffin Rd, San Diego (92123-1812)
PHONE...................................619 542-4300
Henry Tuttle, *CEO*
Fran Cote, *Controller*
Deborah McEntee, *Human Resources*
EMP: 50
SALES: 5.3MM
SALES (corp-wide): 45.6MM **Privately Held**
SIC: 8621 Medical field-related associations
PA: Council Of Community Clinics
　　3710 Ruffin Rd
　　San Diego CA 92123
　　619 542-4300

(P-24396)
COOPERTIVE AMRCN PHYSCIANS INC (PA)
Also Called: Cap-Mpt
333 S Hope St Fl 8, Los Angeles (90071-3001)
PHONE...................................213 473-8600
James Weidner, *CEO*
Cindy Belcher, *COO*
John Donaldson, *CFO*
Russ Lemley, *Officer*
Hammon P Acuna, *Senior VP*
EMP: 100
SALES (est): 16.8MM **Privately Held**
WEB: www.cap-mpt.com
SIC: 8621 Medical field-related associations

(P-24397)
COUNTY LAKE HEALTH SERVICES
Also Called: Public Health Di
922 Bevins Ct, Lakeport (95453-9754)
PHONE...................................707 263-1090
Denise Pomeroy, *Director*
Karen Tait, *Officer*
Carla Ritz, *Exec Dir*
Linda Cathcart, *General Mgr*
Geoff Hasz, *Info Tech Dir*
EMP: 90 EST: 1950
SALES (est): 2.5MM **Privately Held**
SIC: 8621 Health association

(P-24398)
COUNTY OF FRESNO
Also Called: Assessor-Recorder's Office
2281 Tulare St Ste 201, Fresno (93721-2139)
P.O. Box 1146 (93715-1146)
PHONE...................................559 600-3534
Paul Dictos, *Manager*
EMP: 166 **Privately Held**
WEB: www.first5fresno.org
SIC: 8621 9441 Accounting association;
PA: County Of Fresno
　　2420 Mariposa St
　　Fresno CA 93721
　　559 600-1710

(P-24399)
COUNTY OF LOS ANGELES
313 N Figueroa St Fl 9, Los Angeles (90012-2602)
PHONE...................................213 240-8412
Thomas L Garthwaite, *Branch Mgr*
Aguilar Aida, *Admin Asst*
Kathleen Dinsmore, *Manager*
EMP: 863 **Privately Held**
WEB: www.co.la.ca.us
SIC: 8621 9431 Professional membership organizations; prenatal (maternity) health program administration, govt.
PA: County Of Los Angeles
　　500 W Temple St Ste 437
　　Los Angeles CA 90012
　　213 974-1101

(P-24400)
DUBLIN UNIFIED SCHOOL DISTRICT
Also Called: Kolb Elementary School
3150 Palermo Way, Dublin (94568-7326)
PHONE...................................925 415-2407
Lymm Medici, *Principal*
Matthew Martin, *Teacher*
EMP: 185
SALES (corp-wide): 162.6MM **Privately Held**
SIC: 8621 Education & teacher association
PA: Dublin Unified School District
　　7471 Larkdale Ave
　　Dublin CA 94568
　　925 828-2551

(P-24401)
GLEN BEVERLY LABORATORIES INC
Also Called: Inc J-Network
7777 Center Ave Ste 500, Huntington Beach (92647-3099)
PHONE...................................714 848-5777
Akira Kodama, *CEO*
Jackie Yashiro, *Office Mgr*
EMP: 60
SALES (est): 2.4MM **Privately Held**
SIC: 8621 Professional membership organizations

(P-24402)
HEALTH TRUST (PA)
3180 Newberry Dr Ste 200, San Jose (95118-1566)
PHONE...................................408 513-8700
Frederick J Ferrer, *CEO*
Robert Humphreys, *Partner*
Mary Patterson, *Partner*
Gary Allen, *President*
Todd Hansen J D, *COO*
EMP: 150 EST: 1960
SALES: 28MM **Privately Held**
SIC: 8621 8299 Health association; educational services

(P-24403)
INDYNE
300 W Point Ave, El Granada (94018)
PHONE...................................805 606-0664
C Donald Bishop, *President*
Bob Miller, *CFO*
EMP: 99
SALES (est): 950K **Privately Held**
SIC: 8621 Professional membership organizations

(P-24404)
INTERNAL MDCINE RSDNCY AFFAIRS
Also Called: EC Davis Health Services
4150 V St Ste 3116, Sacramento (95817-1460)
PHONE...................................916 734-7080
Kristi Threlkeld, *Manager*
Mark Henderson, *Director*
EMP: 85
SALES (est): 5.8MM **Privately Held**
SIC: 8621 Health association

(P-24405)
INTERNATIONAL CODE COUNCIL INC
Also Called: Los Angeles Regional Office
3060 Saturn St Ste 100, Brea (92821-1732)
PHONE...................................562 699-0541
Mark Johnson, *Branch Mgr*
Lawrence Lukasik, *IT/INT Sup*
Dianna Hallmark, *Marketing Staff*
Chris Ochoa, *Manager*
Cheryl Ellis, *Clerk*
EMP: 56
SALES (corp-wide): 34.9MM **Privately Held**
WEB: www.icccampus.com
SIC: 8621 Professional membership organizations
PA: International Code Council, Inc.
　　500 New Jersey Ave Nw # 6
　　Washington DC 20001
　　202 370-1800

(P-24406)
JEWISH FAMILY SVC LOS ANGELES (PA)
Also Called: JEWISH FREE LOAN ASSOCIATION
3580 Wilshire Blvd, Los Angeles (90010-2501)
PHONE...................................323 761-8800
Paul Castro, *CEO*
Tran Maggard, *CFO*
Rachel Grose, *Exec Dir*
Brandon Levin, *Admin Sec*
Meri Barkinskaya, *Info Tech Dir*
EMP: 50
SQ FT: 7,600
SALES: 1.6MM **Privately Held**
WEB: www.jewishla.com
SIC: 8621 Professional membership organizations

(P-24407)
LEIGHTON GROUP INC
75450 Gerald Ford Dr, Palm Desert (92211-6022)
PHONE...................................760 776-4192
EMP: 103
SALES (corp-wide): 29.2MM **Privately Held**
SIC: 8621 Professional membership organizations
PA: Leighton Group, Inc.
　　17781 Cowan
　　Irvine CA 92614
　　949 477-4040

(P-24408)
LEXISNEXIS COURTLINK INC
2101 K St, Sacramento (95816-4920)
PHONE...................................425 974-5000
Michele Vivona, *President*
EMP: 160
SQ FT: 40,000
SALES (est): 3.8MM
SALES (corp-wide): 9.6B **Privately Held**
SIC: 8621 Professional membership organizations
HQ: Relx Inc.
　　230 Park Ave Ste 700
　　New York NY 10169
　　212 309-8100

(P-24409)
LOS ANGELES COUNTY BAR ASSN (PA)
Also Called: Los Angeles Lawyer Magazine
1055 W 7th St Ste 2700, Los Angeles (90017-2553)
P.O. Box 55020 (90055-2020)
PHONE...................................213 627-2727

Paul R Kiesel, *President*
Kevin Mahoney, *Bd of Directors*
Sally Suchil, *Exec Dir*
Ron Deaton, *General Mgr*
Henry Martinez, *General Mgr*
EMP: 85 EST: 1878
SQ FT: 25,000
SALES (est): 11.7MM **Privately Held**
WEB: www.lacba.org
SIC: 8621 Bar association

(P-24410)
MARIANNE FROSTIG CENTER (PA)
971 N Altadena Dr, Pasadena (91107-1870)
PHONE...................................626 791-1255
Bennett Ross PHD, *CEO*
Dean Conklin, *Exec Dir*
Rick Benavides, *Data Admn*
Giovanni Delgado, *Finance*
Kaye Sergaent, *Finance*
EMP: 50 EST: 1948
SQ FT: 33,000
SALES: 4.6MM **Privately Held**
WEB: www.frostig.org
SIC: 8621 Education & teacher association

(P-24411)
MEDIMPACT HLTHCARE SYSTEMS INC (HQ)
10181 Scripps Gateway Ct, San Diego (92131-5152)
PHONE...................................858 566-2727
Frederick Howe, *Ch of Bd*
Jeanine Mc Bride, *Vice Pres*
Brian Swett, *Vice Pres*
Louis C Tripoli, *Vice Pres*
Jason Twombly, *Vice Pres*
EMP: 595
SQ FT: 100,000
SALES: 16MM **Privately Held**
WEB: www.medegram.com
SIC: 8621 Medical field-related associations

(P-24412)
NATIONAL NOTARY ASSOCIATION
Also Called: Nna Services
9350 De Soto Ave, Chatsworth (91311-4926)
PHONE...................................818 739-4071
Milton G Valera, *Chairman*
Thomas A Heymann, *CEO*
Robert Clarke, *CFO*
Deborah M Thaw, *Exec VP*
Bill Anderson, *Vice Pres*
EMP: 204
SQ FT: 55,000
SALES (est): 32MM **Privately Held**
SIC: 8621 Professional membership organizations

(P-24413)
NNA SERVICES
9350 De Soto Ave, Chatsworth (91311-4926)
PHONE...................................818 739-4071
Thomas Heymann, *CEO*
Robert Clarke, *CFO*
Milt Valera, *Chairman*
Steven Bastian, *Vice Pres*
EMP: 205
SQ FT: 55,000
SALES (est): 1.4MM **Privately Held**
SIC: 8621 Professional membership organizations

(P-24414)
NORWALK LA MIRADA UNIF
Also Called: Association of CA Schl Admnstr
15135 Escalona Rd, La Mirada (90638-4601)
PHONE...................................714 521-0970
Bonita Cadra-Lytle, *Branch Mgr*
EMP: 61
SALES (corp-wide): 262.2MM **Privately Held**
SIC: 8621 Professional membership organizations
PA: Norwalk La Mirada Unified School District
　　12820 Pioneer Blvd
　　Norwalk CA 90650
　　562 868-0431

(P-24415)
ORANGE CNTY ASSN FOR MNTAL HLT (PA)
Also Called: Mental Health Assn Orange Cnty
1971 E 4th St Ste 130, Santa Ana
(92705-3917)
PHONE....................714 547-7559
Margaret Riley, *President*
EMP: 57
SALES: 7.7MM **Privately Held**
WEB: www.mhaoc.org
SIC: 8621 Professional membership organizations

(P-24416)
ORANGE COUNTY HEALTH AUTH
505 City Pkwy W, Orange (92868-2924)
PHONE....................714 246-8500
Richard Chambers, *CEO*
EMP: 432
SQ FT: 200,000
SALES (est): 92.6MM **Privately Held**
SIC: 8621 Professional membership organizations

(P-24417)
ORANGE COUNTY HEALTH CARE AGCY
405 W 5th St Ste 700, Santa Ana
(92701-4534)
PHONE....................714 568-5683
Jenny Qian, *Principal*
EMP: 99
SALES (est): 10.3MM **Privately Held**
SIC: 8621 Health association

(P-24418)
PADI AMERICAS INC
30151 Tomas, Rcho STA Marg
(92688-2125)
P.O. Box 7005 (92688-7005)
PHONE....................949 858-7234
Drew Richardson, *Principal*
Gary Prenovost, *Officer*
Yvonne Sumner, *Officer*
Shane Blaser, *Vice Pres*
Al Hornsby, *Vice Pres*
◆ EMP: 200
SQ FT: 96,000
SALES (est): 28.2MM
SALES (corp-wide): 30MM **Privately Held**
WEB: www.padi.com
SIC: 8621 Education & teacher association
HQ: Padi Holdco, Inc.
30151 Tomas
Rcho Sta Marg CA 92688
949 858-7234

(P-24419)
PLACER CO BAR ASSOCIATION (PA)
P.O. Box 4598 (95604-4598)
PHONE....................916 557-9181
David G Cohen, *Principal*
EMP: 284
SALES (est): 43.2K **Privately Held**
SIC: 8621 Bar association

(P-24420)
POMONA COMMUNITY HEALTH CENTER
Also Called: PARKTREE COMMUNITY HEALTH CENT
1450 E Holt Ave, Pomona (91767-5822)
PHONE....................909 630-7927
Ellen Silver, *CEO*
EMP: 60
SALES: 7.1MM **Privately Held**
SIC: 8621 Health association

(P-24421)
REGAL MEDICAL GROUP INC (PA)
Also Called: Heritage California Aco
8510 Balboa Blvd Ste 275, Northridge
(91325-5809)
PHONE....................818 654-3400
Richard N Merkin, *CEO*
Malara Justin, *Comp Tech*
EMP: 80

SALES (est): 27.5MM **Privately Held**
SIC: 8621 Medical field-related associations

(P-24422)
SALU BEAUTY INC
Also Called: Salu.net
11344 Coloma Rd Ste 725, Gold River
(95670-4464)
PHONE....................916 475-1400
Jim O Steeb, *President*
Steve Brown, *COO*
John V Crisan, *CFO*
Nikki Lynn, *Vice Pres*
Jim Fisher, *Exec Dir*
EMP: 55
SALES (est): 8.1MM
SALES (corp-wide): 1.1B **Privately Held**
SIC: 8621 5961 Health association; general merchandise, mail order
HQ: The Hut.Com Limited
Meridian House
Northwich CW9 7
845 094-9889

(P-24423)
SAN FRANCISCO HEALTH AUTHORITY (PA)
Also Called: Hsf Programme
50 Beale St Fl 12, San Francisco
(94105-1823)
P.O. Box 194247 (94119-4247)
PHONE....................415 615-4407
John Grgurina Jr, *CEO*
Philip Hartman, *President*
James Glauber, *Chief Mktg Ofcr*
Peggy McCrea, *Officer*
Sumi Sousa, *Officer*
EMP: 99
SQ FT: 26,000
SALES (est): 27.1MM **Privately Held**
WEB: www.sfhp.org
SIC: 8621 Health association

(P-24424)
SHARP COMMUNITY MEDICAL GROUP
Also Called: Scmg
8695 Spectrum Center Blvd, San Diego
(92123-1489)
PHONE....................858 499-4525
Kenneth Roth, *President*
Michael Caramat, *Database Admin*
Eden Keh, *Business Mgr*
Manuel Deleon, *Analyst*
EMP: 200
SALES (est): 7.8MM
SALES (corp-wide): 3.4B **Privately Held**
WEB: www.scmg.com
SIC: 8621 Professional membership organizations
PA: Sharp Healthcare
8695 Spectrum Center Blvd
San Diego CA 92123
858 499-4000

(P-24425)
ST BALDRICKS FOUNDATION INC (PA)
1333 S Mayflower Ave, Monrovia
(91016-4066)
PHONE....................626 792-8247
Charles M Chamness, *Ch of Bd*
Jennifer McCabe, *Officer*
Kathleen Ruddy, *Exec Dir*
Matthew Wallace, *IT/INT Sup*
Danette Ocaranza, *Human Res Dir*
EMP: 60
SALES: 35.9MM **Privately Held**
SIC: 8621 Health association

(P-24426)
ST VINCENT SENIOR CITIZN NUTR (PA)
2131 W 3rd St, Los Angeles (90057-1901)
PHONE....................213 484-7775
Sister A Marie Quinn, *President*
Alice Marie Quinn, *President*
EMP: 71
SALES: 7.1MM **Privately Held**
SIC: 8621 Professional membership organizations

(P-24427)
STATE BAR OF CALIFORNIA (PA)
180 Howard St Fl Grnd, San Francisco
(94105-6155)
PHONE....................415 538-2000
Bill Hebert, *President*
Peggy Van Horn, *CFO*
Leah Wilson, *Exec Dir*
Ana Castillo, *Admin Asst*
Resty Buenavidez, *Info Tech Dir*
EMP: 296
SQ FT: 72,000
SALES (est): 79.1MM **Privately Held**
SIC: 8621 Bar association

(P-24428)
TRI-COUNTIES ASSOCIATION F
1234 Fairway Dr A, Santa Maria
(93455-1406)
PHONE....................805 922-4640
EMP: 136
SALES (corp-wide): 293.2MM **Privately Held**
SIC: 8621 Professional membership organizations
PA: Tri-Counties Association For The Developmentally Disabled, Inc.
520 E Montecito St
Santa Barbara CA 93103
805 962-7881

(P-24429)
TRUCK UNDERWRITERS ASSOCIATION (DH)
4680 Wilshire Blvd, Los Angeles
(90010-3807)
PHONE....................323 932-3200
Leonard H Gelfand, *President*
Gerald Faulwell, *Vice Pres*
Martin Feinstein, *Vice Pres*
Jason Katz, *Vice Pres*
John Lynch, *Vice Pres*
EMP: 1767
SALES (est): 78.2MM
SALES (corp-wide): 48.2B **Privately Held**
SIC: 8621 Professional membership organizations
HQ: Farmers Group, Inc.
6301 Owensmouth Ave
Woodland Hills CA 91367
323 932-3200

(P-24430)
UNITED CEREBRAL PALSY ASSOC (PA)
Also Called: Cerebral Palsy Assn San Joaqui
333 W Benjamin Holt Dr # 1, Stockton
(95207-3906)
PHONE....................209 956-0290
Ray All, *Exec Dir*
EMP: 175
SQ FT: 15,000
SALES (est): 5.6MM **Privately Held**
WEB: www.ucpsj.org
SIC: 8621 Professional membership organizations

(P-24431)
UPWORK GLOBAL INC
2625 Augustine Dr Ste 601, Santa Clara
(95054-2956)
PHONE....................650 316-7500
Stephane Kasriel, *CEO*
Brian Kinion, *CFO*
Brian Levey, *Officer*
Hayden Brown, *Vice Pres*
Stratis Karamanlakis, *CTO*
EMP: 50
SQ FT: 16,000
SALES (est): 6.6MM
SALES (corp-wide): 253.3MM **Publicly Held**
SIC: 8621 7371 2741 Professional membership organizations; computer software development & applications; miscellaneous publishing
PA: Upwork Inc.
2625 Augustine Dr Ste 601
Santa Clara CA 95054
650 316-7500

(P-24432)
VISITING NURSE & HOSPICE CARE (PA)
Also Called: VISITING NURSE & HOSPICE CARE
509 E Montecito St # 200, Santa Barbara
(93103-3293)
PHONE....................805 965-5555
Lynda Tanner, *CEO*
Michelle Martinich, *Chairman*
Mary Pritchard, *Treasurer*
Rick Keith, *Exec Dir*
Neil Levinson, *Admin Sec*
EMP: 130
SQ FT: 13,765
SALES: 24.6MM **Privately Held**
WEB: www.sbvna.org
SIC: 8621 Nursing association

(P-24433)
VISTA HILL FOUNDATION (PA)
8910 Clairemont Mesa Blvd, San Diego
(92123-1104)
PHONE....................585 514-5100
Robert Dean, *President*
Belle Nunley, *Vice Pres*
Christina Gomez, *Program Mgr*
Bob Miller, *Info Tech Dir*
Shirley Fett, *Nurse Practr*
EMP: 50
SQ FT: 16,802
SALES: 28.2MM **Privately Held**
SIC: 8621 8741 Medical field-related associations; management services

---

8631 Labor Unions & Similar Organizations

(P-24434)
ALPHA CONNECTION GROUP HOME
Also Called: ALPHA CONNECTION YOUTH FAMILY
22675 Anoka Rd, Apple Valley
(92308-5436)
PHONE....................760 247-6370
Juanita Wilson, *President*
Barron Wilson, *Vice Pres*
EMP: 70
SALES: 2.8MM **Privately Held**
SIC: 8631 Labor unions & similar labor organizations

(P-24435)
ASSOCIATIONS OF UNITED NURSES (PA)
Also Called: UNAC/UHCP
955 Overland Ct Ste 150, San Dimas
(91773-1740)
PHONE....................909 599-8622
Ken Deitz, *President*
Jettie Deden-Castillo, *Treasurer*
Denise Duncan, *Vice Pres*
Charmaine Morales, *Admin Sec*
Max Carbuccia, *Director*
EMP: 63
SALES: 4.2MM **Privately Held**
SIC: 8631 Employees' association

(P-24436)
BUENA PARK POLICE ASSOCIATION
6650 Beach Blvd, Buena Park
(90621-2905)
P.O. Box 579 (90621-0579)
PHONE....................714 562-3901
Sgt Steven Martinez, *President*
Thomas Carney, *Officer*
Sgt Frank Nunes, *Vice Pres*
Jose Castrellon, *Database Admin*
EMP: 90
SALES: 107.9K **Privately Held**
SIC: 8631 Employees' association

(P-24437)
CALIFORNIA CORRECTNL PEACE OFC (PA)
Also Called: CCPOA
755 Riverpoint Dr, West Sacramento
(95605-1673)
PHONE....................916 372-6060
Chuck Alexander, *President*
James Martin, *Treasurer*

Charles Alexander, *Vice Pres*
Perry Speth, *Admin Sec*
Katrina Salazar, *Controller*
EMP: 60
SQ FT: 32,000
SALES: 30.4MM **Privately Held**
WEB: www.ccpoa.org
SIC: 8631 8111 Labor union; legal services

(P-24438)
CALIFORNIA SCHL EMPLOYEES ASSN (PA)
Also Called: Csea
2045 Lundy Ave, San Jose (95131-1865)
PHONE......................408 473-1000
Steve Brashear, *CFO*
Kathryn Cho, *Admin Asst*
Angela Martin, *Admin Asst*
Brian Schroeder, *Director*
EMP: 180
SQ FT: 65,000
SALES: 65.6MM **Privately Held**
WEB: www.csea.com
SIC: 8631 Labor union

(P-24439)
CALIFRNIA STATE EMPLOYEES ASSN (PA)
Also Called: CSEA
1108 O St Ste 405, Sacramento
(95814-5746)
PHONE......................916 444-8134
Dave Hart, *President*
Debbie Cotton, *CFO*
Dave Okunura, *Treasurer*
Alex Velasco, *Technician*
Michael Carr, *Controller*
EMP: 270
SQ FT: 30,000
SALES: 5.3MM **Privately Held**
SIC: 8631 Labor unions & similar labor organizations

(P-24440)
COUNTY OF LOS ANGELES
Also Called: Carson Gang Diversion Team
21356 Avalon Blvd, Carson (90745-2213)
PHONE......................310 847-4018
EMP: 226 **Privately Held**
SIC: 8631
PA: County Of Los Angeles
500 W Temple St Ste 375
Los Angeles CA 90012
213 974-1101

(P-24441)
HAYWARD POLICE OFFICERS ASSN
300 W Winton Ave, Hayward (94544-1137)
PHONE......................510 293-7207
Julie Kirkland, *Principal*
EMP: 75
SALES: 404.9K **Privately Held**
SIC: 8631 Labor union

(P-24442)
INTERNATIONAL ALLIANCE THEA
Also Called: Local 442
P.O. Box 413 (93102-0413)
PHONE......................805 898-0442
Gary Hilton, *Principal*
EMP: 60
SALES (est): 75.9K **Privately Held**
SIC: 8631 Labor union

(P-24443)
INTERNATIONAL ASSOC OF MACHINI
Also Called: NFFE-IAM 2152
1303 S Highway 95, Needles (92363-4217)
PHONE......................760 326-7048
Elaine Downing, *President*
Remijio Chavez, *Vice Pres*
EMP: 50
SALES: 68.2K **Privately Held**
SIC: 8631 Labor union

(P-24444)
INTERNATIONAL BRTHRHD OF ELCTR (PA)
Also Called: AFL-CIO #1245
30 Orange Tree Cir, Vacaville
(95687-3105)
PHONE......................707 452-2700
Ed Mallory, *President*
James McCulley, *Vice Pres*
Michael J Davis,
Kathy Tindall,
EMP: 68
SALES: 34.8MM **Privately Held**
WEB: www.ibew1245.com
SIC: 8631 Labor union

(P-24445)
INTERNATIONAL LONGSHOREMENS
Also Called: LONGSHOREMEN'S & WAREHOUSEMENS
22 N Union St, Stockton (95205-4915)
PHONE......................209 464-1827
Marc Cuavas, *President*
Dennis Brueckner, *President*
Lee Flood, *Vice Pres*
Frank Aeonis, *Admin Sec*
EMP: 81 **EST:** 1934
SQ FT: 1,000
SALES: 218.6K **Privately Held**
SIC: 8631 Trade union; labor union

(P-24446)
INTERNATIONAL UNION OF OPERATI
1620 S Loop Rd, Alameda (94502-7085)
PHONE......................510 748-7400
M Kling, *Manager*
EMP: 200
SALES (est): 45.3MM **Privately Held**
SIC: 8631 Labor unions & similar labor organizations

(P-24447)
INTERNTIONAL UN OPER ENGINEERS
Local 12
150 Corson St, Pasadena (91103-3839)
P.O. Box 7109 (91109-7209)
PHONE......................626 792-2519
William C Waggoner, *Manager*
EMP: 50
SQ FT: 32,534
SALES (corp-wide): 52.1MM **Privately Held**
WEB: www.iuoestateunit12.org
SIC: 8631 Labor union
PA: International Union Of Operating Engineers
1121 L St Ste 401
Sacramento CA 95814
916 444-6880

(P-24448)
INTERNTIONAL UN OPER ENGINEERS (PA)
1121 L St Ste 401, Sacramento
(95814-3969)
PHONE......................916 444-6880
Tim Neep, *Director*
EMP: 67 **EST:** 2014
SALES (est): 52.1MM **Privately Held**
WEB: www.iuoestateunit12.org
SIC: 8631 Labor union

(P-24449)
IUOE STTONARY ENGINEERS LCL 39
Also Called: Iuoe Local 39
1620 N Market Blvd, Sacramento
(95834-1958)
PHONE......................916 928-0399
Tony De Marco, *President*
Jim Maple, *Training Dir*
EMP: 50
SALES (est): 295.6K **Privately Held**
SIC: 8631 Labor union

(P-24450)
LABORERS FUNDS ADMINISTRATIVE (PA)
Also Called: Laborers Trust Funds Nthrn Cal
220 Campus Ln, Fairfield (94534-1498)
PHONE......................707 864-2800

Edward Smith, *Admin Sec*
EMP: 100
SQ FT: 43,000
SALES (est): 16.4MM **Privately Held**
SIC: 8631 Labor unions & similar labor organizations

(P-24451)
LOS ANGLES CNTY EMPLOYEES ASSN
Also Called: Service Employee Intl Un
1545 Wilshire Blvd, Los Angeles
(90017-4501)
PHONE......................213 368-8660
Annelle Grajeda, *President*
Kathleen Austria, *Treasurer*
Bob Schoonover, *Vice Pres*
Annette Jeffrief, *Admin Sec*
EMP: 60
SQ FT: 40,000
SALES: 6.9MM **Privately Held**
WEB: www.local660.org
SIC: 8631 Labor union

(P-24452)
MILLMENS LOCAL 1496
6190 N Cecelia Ave, Fresno (93722-3204)
PHONE......................559 275-8676
Norman Avila, *President*
EMP: 50
SALES (est): 720.6K **Privately Held**
SIC: 8631 Labor union

(P-24453)
NATIONAL ASSN LTR CARRIERS
Also Called: National Assn Ltr Crrers BR 52
4251 S Higuera St, San Luis Obispo
(93401-7700)
PHONE......................805 543-7329
Edward L Somogyi, *Branch Mgr*
EMP: 300
SALES (corp-wide): 1.1B **Privately Held**
SIC: 8631 Labor union
PA: National Association Of Letter Carriers
100 Indana Ave Nw Ste 709
Washington DC 20001
202 393-4695

(P-24454)
NATIONAL ASSN LTR CARRIERS
2310 Mason St Fl 4, San Francisco
(94133-1800)
PHONE......................415 362-0214
John Beaumont, *Manager*
EMP: 300
SALES (corp-wide): 1.1B **Privately Held**
WEB: www.nalc.org
SIC: 8631 Labor union
PA: National Association Of Letter Carriers
100 Indana Ave Nw Ste 709
Washington DC 20001
202 393-4695

(P-24455)
PACIFIC CST MAR FIREMAN OILERS (PA)
Also Called: MARINE FIREMENS UNION
240 2nd St Fl 2, San Francisco
(94105-3113)
PHONE......................415 362-4592
Anthony Poplawski, *President*
William O'Brien, *Vice Pres*
Karen Mohr, *Controller*
EMP: 70
SQ FT: 1,000
SALES: 1.2MM **Privately Held**
WEB: www.mfoww.org
SIC: 8631 Labor union

(P-24456)
PORT OF LONG BCH EMPLOYEES CLB
4801 Airport Plaza Dr, Long Beach
(90815-1263)
P.O. Box 570 (90801-0570)
PHONE......................562 590-4102
Paul McArthy, *CEO*
Richard Steinke, *Director*
EMP: 400
SALES (est): 40.2MM **Privately Held**
SIC: 8631 4499 Employees' association; marine salvaging & surveying services

(P-24457)
SAG-AFTRA FOUNDATION
5757 Wilshire Blvd Ph 1, Los Angeles
(90036-3681)
PHONE......................323 549-6708
Cyd Wilson, *Exec Dir*
Aric Shuford, *Administration*
Rochelle Rose, *Prgrmr*
Franz Reynold, *Project Dir*
Marlena Campbell, *Accounting Mgr*
EMP: 50
SALES (est): 8MM **Privately Held**
SIC: 8631 Labor union

(P-24458)
SAN BRNRDINO PUB EMPLYEES ASSN
Also Called: SBPEA
433 N Sierra Way, San Bernardino
(92410-4831)
P.O. Box 432 (92402-0432)
PHONE......................909 386-1260
Paula Ready, *President*
Gina Jordan, *Trustee*
Marcie Larkin, *Trustee*
EMP: 50
SQ FT: 20,000
SALES: 6.3MM **Privately Held**
WEB: www.sbpea.com
SIC: 8631 Employees' association

(P-24459)
SAN DIEGO COUNTY EMPLOYEES RET
2275 Rio Bonito Way # 100, San Diego
(92108-1685)
PHONE......................619 515-6800
Brian White, *CEO*
Dianne Jacob, *Bd of Directors*
Mario Correa, *Officer*
James Lery,
Mary Montgomery,
EMP: 90
SALES (est): 7.3MM **Privately Held**
SIC: 8631 Employees' association

(P-24460)
SEIU LOCAL 1021
447 29th St, Oakland (94609-3510)
P.O. Box 2077 (94604-2077)
PHONE......................510 350-9811
Damita Davis-Howard, *Director*
EMP: 165
SALES: 51.7MM **Privately Held**
SIC: 8631 Labor unions & similar labor organizations

(P-24461)
SEIU LOCAL 2015
2910 Beverly Blvd, Los Angeles
(90057-1012)
PHONE......................213 985-0384
Laphonza Butler, *President*
Dereck Smith, *COO*
Malcolm Glover, *Controller*
Amanda Steele, *Director*
EMP: 210
SALES: 76.9MM **Privately Held**
SIC: 8631 Labor union

(P-24462)
SEIU LOCAL 721
1545 Wilshire Blvd # 100, Los Angeles
(90017-4510)
PHONE......................213 368-8660
Annelle Grajeda, *Owner*
EMP: 55
SALES (est): 5.2MM **Privately Held**
SIC: 8631 Labor unions & similar labor organizations

(P-24463)
SEIU UNITED HEALTHCARE WORKERS (PA)
560 Thomas L Berkley Way, Oakland
(94612-1602)
PHONE......................510 251-1250
Dave Regan, *President*
Lee Farrell, *President*
Edgard Tajina, *CFO*
Eliseo Medina, *Trustee*
Debbie M Schneider, *Trustee*
EMP: 140
SQ FT: 33,000

PRODUCTS & SVCS

SALES: 107.3MM **Privately Held**
WEB: www.seiu-uhw.org
SIC: 8631 Labor union

(P-24464)
SEIU UNITED HEALTHCARE WORKERS
Also Called: Seiu Uhw-West
5480 Ferguson Dr, Commerce
(90022-5119)
PHONE..............................323 734-8399
Liza Leyva, *Director*
EMP: 50
SALES (corp-wide): 107.3MM **Privately Held**
SIC: 8631 Labor union
PA: Seiu United Healthcare Workers-West
Local 2005
560 Thomas L Berkley Way
Oakland CA 94612
510 251-1250

(P-24465)
SERVICE WORKERS LOCAL 715 (PA)
Also Called: Service Employees Intl Union
2302 Zanker Rd, San Jose (95131-1115)
PHONE..............................408 678-3300
Rosemary Romo, *President*
Stephen Harris, *Pediatrics*
Kristina Sermersheim, *Exec Sec*
EMP: 60
SQ FT: 1,000
SALES: 2.1MM **Privately Held**
WEB: www.seiu715.org
SIC: 8631 8621 Labor union; professional
membership organizations

(P-24466)
SUGAR WORKERS LOCAL 1
641 Loring Ave, Crockett (94525-1233)
PHONE..............................510 787-1676
Ed Cummings, *President*
Surinder M Bhanot, *President*
EMP: 330
SQ FT: 5,000
SALES: 237.8K **Privately Held**
SIC: 8631 Labor union

(P-24467)
TEMPORARY STAFFING UNION
19800 Macarthur Blvd, Irvine (92612-2421)
PHONE..............................714 728-5186
Veronica Lake, *CEO*
Fe Santos, *President*
EMP: 4000
SQ FT: 1,500
SALES: 100K **Privately Held**
SIC: 8631 Labor union

(P-24468)
TURLOCK IRRIGATION DISTRICT (PA)
333 E Canal Dr, Turlock (95380-3946)
P.O. Box 949 (95381-0949)
PHONE..............................209 883-8222
Joe Alamo, *President*
Calvin Curtin, *Officer*
Michael Frantz, *Admin Sec*
Janis-Dylan Scott, *Admin Sec*
Willie Manuel, *Planning*
EMP: 250
SQ FT: 20,000
SALES (est): 54.8MM **Privately Held**
WEB: www.tid.com
SIC: 8631 Employees' association

(P-24469)
UNITED FARM WORKERS AMERICA (PA)
29700 Wdford Tehachapi Rd, Keene
(93531)
P.O. Box 62 (93531-0062)
PHONE..............................661 822-5571
Arturo Rodriguez, *President*
Liz Villarino, *CFO*
Tanis Ybarra, *Corp Secy*
Irv Hershenbaum, *Vice Pres*
Eric Miller, *Project Mgr*
EMP: 110
SQ FT: 5,000
SALES: 7.2MM **Privately Held**
WEB: www.ufw.org
SIC: 8631 Labor union

(P-24470)
UNITED FOOD AND COMMERCIAL (PA)
Also Called: Ufcw Local 770
630 Shatto Pl Ste 300, Los Angeles
(90005-1372)
P.O. Box 770 (90078-0770)
PHONE..............................213 487-7070
Ricardo F Icaza, *President*
Rodney Diamond, *Corp Secy*
Cheryl Butler, *Vice Pres*
Lisa Lee, *Comms Mgr*
Johnny Fung, *Controller*
EMP: 60
SALES (est): 17.1MM **Privately Held**
SIC: 8631 Labor union

(P-24471)
UNITED TEACHERS-LOS ANGELES
Also Called: U T L A
3303 Wilshire Blvd Fl 10, Los Angeles
(90010-1794)
PHONE..............................213 487-5560
Aj Duffy, *President*
David Goldburg, *Treasurer*
Joshua Pechthalt, *Vice Pres*
Ana Valencia, *Vice Pres*
Betty Forrester, *Admin Sec*
EMP: 72
SQ FT: 144,000
SALES: 40.9MM **Privately Held**
WEB: www.utla.net
SIC: 8631 Collective bargaining unit

(P-24472)
WRITERS GUILD AMERICA WEST INC
7000 W 3rd St, Los Angeles (90048-4321)
PHONE..............................323 951-4000
David Young, *CEO*
Theresa F Savino, *COO*
Elias Davis, *Corp Secy*
Sally Burmester, *Officer*
Kymberly Jackson, *Senior VP*
EMP: 160 EST: 1954
SQ FT: 67,000
SALES: 32.3MM **Privately Held**
WEB: www.wga.org
SIC: 8631 Labor union

8641 Civic, Social & Fraternal Associations

(P-24473)
ACTION PROPERTY MANAGEMENT INC
530 S Hewitt St, Los Angeles (90013-2286)
PHONE..............................800 400-2284
Mary Moore, *Branch Mgr*
EMP: 120
SALES (corp-wide): 95.6MM **Privately Held**
SIC: 8641 Homeowners' association
PA: Action Property Management, Inc.
2603 Main St Ste 500
Irvine CA 92614
949 450-0202

(P-24474)
AMERICAN LEGION AMBULANCE SVC
Also Called: American Legion Hall
11350 American Legion Dr, Sutter Creek
(95685)
P.O. Box 100 (95685-0100)
PHONE..............................209 223-2963
Al Lennox, *General Mgr*
EMP: 70
SQ FT: 800
SALES: 8.2MM **Privately Held**
SIC: 8641 Veterans' organization

(P-24475)
ARTHRTIS FUNDATION PCF REG INC
800 W 6th St Ste 1250, Los Angeles
(90017-2721)
PHONE..............................323 954-5760
EMP: 50
SALES: 12.5MM **Privately Held**
SIC: 8641

(P-24476)
ASSOCIATED STUDENTS CALIFORNIA
Also Called: A S I
1212 N Bellflower Blvd # 220, Long Beach
(90815-4148)
PHONE..............................562 985-4994
Richard Haller, *Exec Dir*
EMP: 260 EST: 1956
SQ FT: 184,000
SALES: 15.1MM **Privately Held**
SIC: 8641 University club

(P-24477)
ASSOCIATED STUDENTS STANFORD (PA)
Also Called: A S S U
201 Tresidder Un, Stanford (94305)
PHONE..............................650 723-4331
Linda Whitcomb, *Director*
Alice Willoughby, *Principal*
Sarah Holcomb, *Program Mgr*
EMP: 63
SALES: 1.4MM **Privately Held**
SIC: 8641 University club

(P-24478)
BALANCE4KIDS
4500 Soquel Dr, Soquel (95073-2122)
PHONE..............................831 464-8669
Victoria George, *Director*
Shannon Crane, *Treasurer*
Mary Willis, *Director*
EMP: 92
SALES: 3.5MM **Privately Held**
SIC: 8641 Youth organizations

(P-24479)
BAYVIEW HUNTERS POINT Y M C A
Also Called: YMCA
1601 Lane St, San Francisco (94124-2732)
PHONE..............................415 822-7728
Cheryl Smith-Thornton, *Exec Dir*
EMP: 64
SALES (est): 2.5MM **Privately Held**
SIC: 8641 7991 8351 7032 Youth organizations; physical fitness facilities; child day care services; youth camps; individual & family services

(P-24480)
BEAR VALLEY SPRINGS ASSN
29541 Rollingoak Dr, Tehachapi
(93561-7133)
PHONE..............................661 821-5537
Todd Lander, *President*
Terry Quinn, *President*
Larry Thompson, *Treasurer*
Tim Hawkins, *Vice Pres*
EMP: 200
SQ FT: 2,000
SALES: 7.1MM **Privately Held**
WEB: www.bearinfo.com
SIC: 8641 Homeowners' association

(P-24481)
BERRYESSA UNION SCHOOL DST
Also Called: Pta CA Cngrss of Prnts
1100 Summerdale Dr, San Jose
(95132-2934)
PHONE..............................408 923-1960
Pamela Calara, *Teacher*
Brenda Quetano, *Consultant*
Patty McDonald, *Superintendent*
EMP: 52
SALES (corp-wide): 85.9MM **Privately Held**
SIC: 8641 Parent-teachers' association
PA: Berryessa Union School District
1376 Piedmont Rd
San Jose CA 95132
408 923-1800

(P-24482)
BODEGA HARBOUR HOMEOWNERS ASSN
Also Called: Bodega Harbour Golf Links
21301 Heron Dr, Bodega Bay
(94923-9401)
P.O. Box 368 (94923-0368)
PHONE..............................707 875-3519
Judith A Steeves, *Admin Mgr*

Ken Felker, *Controller*
Mary Angelo, *Exec Sec*
Tj Smith, *Manager*
EMP: 65
SQ FT: 10,000
SALES (est): 3MM **Privately Held**
SIC: 8641 5812 5813 7997 Homeowners' association; American restaurant; bars & lounges; yacht club, membership

(P-24483)
BOHEMIAN CLUB (PA)
Also Called: BOHEMIAN GROVE
624 Taylor St, San Francisco (94102-1075)
PHONE..............................415 885-2440
Robert L Spence, *CEO*
Matt Ogerio, *General Mgr*
Bert Botta, *Research*
Kevin Sullivan, *Research*
Deena Soulon, *Finance*
EMP: 105 EST: 1872
SQ FT: 20,000
SALES: 9.3MM **Privately Held**
WEB: www.bc-owl.org
SIC: 8641 Social club, membership

(P-24484)
BOYS & GIRLS CLUB OF TRACY (PA)
753 W Lowell Ave, Tracy (95376-2935)
PHONE..............................209 832-2582
Kelly Wilson, *President*
EMP: 50
SQ FT: 15,000
SALES: 1.9MM **Privately Held**
SIC: 8641 Boy Scout organization; youth organizations

(P-24485)
BOYS & GIRLS CLUB SILICON VLY
518 Valley Way, Milpitas (95035-4106)
PHONE..............................408 957-9685
Dana Fraticelli, *Director*
Jaime Chavez, *Treasurer*
Kelly Sandoval, *Exec Dir*
Shannon Penrose, *Opers-Prdtn-Mfg*
Anna Ho, *Director*
EMP: 51
SALES: 3.5MM **Privately Held**
WEB: www.bgclub.org
SIC: 8641 Youth organizations

(P-24486)
BOYS & GIRLS CLUB SIMI VLY INC
2850 Lemon Dr, Simi Valley (93063-2193)
PHONE..............................805 527-4437
Linda White, *CEO*
Chuck Theobald, *Info Tech Dir*
Beth Welden, *Finance*
James Lucas, *Opers Mgr*
Sandee Covone, *Asst Director*
EMP: 50
SALES: 2.6MM **Privately Held**
WEB: www.bgcsimi.com
SIC: 8641 Youth organizations

(P-24487)
BOYS & GIRLS CLUBS OF N VLY
601 Wall St, Chico (95928-5626)
PHONE..............................530 899-0335
Rashell Brobst, *Exec VP*
Lisa Spiegler, *Director*
EMP: 80
SQ FT: 14,000
SALES: 2.5MM **Privately Held**
SIC: 8641 Boy Scout organization; youth organizations

(P-24488)
BOYS & GIRLS CLUBS SOUTH CNTY
847 Encina Ave, Imperial Beach
(91932-2135)
P.O. Box 520 (91933-0520)
PHONE..............................619 424-2266
Ken Blinsman, *President*
Aaron Ruiz, *Program Dir*
EMP: 100
SALES: 2.9MM **Privately Held**
SIC: 8641 5812 Youth organizations; eating places

(P-24489)
BOYS AND GIRLS CLUBS OF THE LA (PA)
Also Called: BOYS & GIRLS CLUB OF SAN PEDRO
1200 S Cabrillo Ave, San Pedro (90731-4011)
PHONE..................310 833-1322
Mike Lansing, *Director*
Robert Nizich, *President*
Dennis Lane, *Treasurer*
Joseph Rich, *Vice Pres*
John Robinson, *Vice Pres*
EMP: 59
SQ FT: 26,083
SALES: 7.7MM **Privately Held**
WEB: www.bgclaharbor.org
SIC: 8641 Youth organizations

(P-24490)
BOYS AND GIRLS CLUBS OF THE LA
Also Called: Dana Middle Schl Bys Girls CLB
1501 S Cabrillo Ave, San Pedro (90731-4617)
PHONE..................310 833-1322
Mike Lansing, *Branch Mgr*
EMP: 99
SALES (corp-wide): 7.7MM **Privately Held**
SIC: 8641 Youth organizations
PA: Boys And Girls Clubs Of The Angeles Harbor
1200 S Cabrillo Ave
San Pedro CA 90731
310 833-1322

(P-24491)
BOYS AND GIRLS CLUBS OF THE LA
Also Called: Wilmington Schll Bys & Grls CL
1700 Gulf Ave, Wilmington (90744-1311)
PHONE..................310 833-1322
Mike Lansing, *Branch Mgr*
EMP: 99
SALES (corp-wide): 7.7MM **Privately Held**
SIC: 8641 Youth organizations
PA: Boys And Girls Clubs Of The Los Angeles Harbor
1200 S Cabrillo Ave
San Pedro CA 90731
310 833-1322

(P-24492)
BOYS CLUB OF FALLBROOK INC
Also Called: Boys & Girls Clubs North Cnty
445 E Ivy St, Fallbrook (92028-2122)
P.O. Box 2665 (92088-2665)
PHONE..................760 728-5871
Allison Barclay, *CEO*
EMP: 65
SALES: 1.4MM **Privately Held**
WEB: www.bgcnorthcounty.com
SIC: 8641 Youth organizations

(P-24493)
BOYS GIRLS CLB HUNTINGTON VLY (PA)
16582 Brookhurst St, Fountain Valley (92708-2353)
PHONE..................714 531-2582
Tanya Hoxsie, *President*
Kim Nguyen, *Finance*
Sharanjit Dhaliwal, *Program Dir*
Diana Kacic, *Program Dir*
Diana Martinez, *Program Dir*
EMP: 89
SALES: 7.2MM **Privately Held**
SIC: 8641 Youth organizations

(P-24494)
BOYS GIRLS CLUBS MONTEREY CNTY (PA)
1332 La Salle Ave, Seaside (93955-3219)
P.O. Box 97 (93955-0097)
PHONE..................831 394-5171
Donna Ferraro, *President*
Don Jordan, *Bd of Directors*
Ron Johnson, *Vice Pres*
Jennifer Ugaz, *Admin Asst*
Florence Gilliam, *Human Res Dir*
EMP: 60

SQ FT: 24,000
SALES: 4.6MM **Privately Held**
WEB: www.bgcmc.org
SIC: 8641 Youth organizations

(P-24495)
BOYS GIRLS CLUBS OF KERN CNTY
Also Called: Boy's & Girls Club Bakersfield
801 Niles St, Bakersfield (93305-4419)
PHONE..................661 325-3730
Zane Smith, *Exec Dir*
Ed Kuhn, *President*
Murry Tragish, *President*
Craig Stickler, *Treasurer*
Bill Campbell, *Vice Pres*
EMP: 100
SALES: 5.8MM **Privately Held**
SIC: 8641 8322 Boy Scout organization; individual & family services

(P-24496)
BOYS GIRLS CLUBS SONOMA-MARIN
1400 N Dutton Ave Ste 24, Santa Rosa (95401-4644)
PHONE..................707 528-7977
Jennifer Weiss, *Exec Dir*
Dawn Holman, *Administration*
Margaret Forbes, *Business Mgr*
Shannon Baron, *Director*
EMP: 187
SALES: 9.1MM **Privately Held**
SIC: 8641 Youth organizations

(P-24497)
BOYS GRLS CLB SNTA MONICA INC
Also Called: BOYS & GIRLS CLUBS OF SANTA MO
1220 Lincoln Blvd, Santa Monica (90401-1704)
PHONE..................310 361-8500
Aaron Young, *Director*
Diane Bell, *VP Admin*
Virginia Kato, *General Mgr*
Cat Smith, *Executive Asst*
Jesse Satterfield, *Athletic Dir*
EMP: 83
SQ FT: 6,000
SALES: 4.2MM **Privately Held**
WEB: www.smbgc.org
SIC: 8641 7997 Youth organizations; membership sports & recreation clubs

(P-24498)
BOYS GRLS CLUBS GRDN GROVE INC
Also Called: Girls and Boys Club Grdn Grove
13645 Clinton St, Garden Grove (92843-4110)
PHONE..................714 537-8833
Evelyn Matua, *Branch Mgr*
EMP: 169
SALES (corp-wide): 11.5MM **Privately Held**
SIC: 8641 Youth organizations
PA: Boys & Girls Clubs Of Garden Grove, Inc.
10540 Chapman Ave
Garden Grove CA 92840
714 530-0430

(P-24499)
BOYS GRLS CLUBS OF SAN DEGUITO (PA)
Also Called: BOYS & GIRLS CLUBS OF SAN DIEG
533 Lomas Santa Fe Dr, Solana Beach (92075-1323)
PHONE..................858 755-9371
Alex Barrera, *President*
James Watkins, *Vice Chairman*
Andy Brosche, *COO*
Rose Mary Eller, *Treasurer*
Eric Nelte, *Executive Asst*
EMP: 100 **EST:** 1966
SQ FT: 25,000
SALES: 6.5MM **Privately Held**
WEB: www.bgcsdto.org
SIC: 8641 Youth organizations

(P-24500)
BOYS GRLS CLUBS OF SQUOIAS INC
215 W Tulare Ave, Visalia (93277-4813)
PHONE..................559 592-4074
Joe Engelbrecht, *Exec Dir*
Jerry Petty, *Info Tech Dir*
Carri Chambers, *Opers Staff*
Leticia Betancourt, *Director*
Dodds Lynn, *Director*
EMP: 62
SALES (est): 2.2MM **Privately Held**
SIC: 8641 Youth organizations

(P-24501)
BOYSCOUT OF AMERICA
Also Called: BOY SCOUTS OF AMERICA
10 Highland Way, Piedmont (94611-4095)
PHONE..................510 547-4493
Josephine Hazelett, *Exec Dir*
EMP: 78
SALES: 630.3K **Privately Held**
WEB: www.piedmontbsa.org
SIC: 8641 Boy Scout organization

(P-24502)
BRIDGES CLUB AT RANCHO SA
18550 Seven Bridges Rd, Rancho Santa Fe (92091-0216)
P.O. Box 1322 (92067-1322)
PHONE..................858 759-7200
Tom Martin, *President*
EMP: 140
SALES: 4MM **Privately Held**
SIC: 8641 Social club, membership

(P-24503)
BUNKER HILL CLUB INC
Also Called: City Club On Bunker Hill
555 S Flower St Ste 5100, Los Angeles (90071-2400)
PHONE..................213 620-9662
Isaias Ledesma, *Manager*
EMP: 72
SQ FT: 16,874
SALES (est): 1.5MM
SALES (corp-wide): 841.1MM **Privately Held**
WEB: www.remington-gc.com
SIC: 8641 Bars & restaurants, members only
HQ: Clubcorp Usa, Inc.
3030 Lyndon B Johnson Fwy
Dallas TX 75234
972 243-6191

(P-24504)
CALI CALMECAC LANGUAGE ACADEMY
9491 Starr Rd, Windsor (95492-9460)
PHONE..................707 837-7747
Jeanne Acuna, *Principal*
Sharon Ferrer, *Vice Pres*
Marisol Hernandez, *Teacher*
Gabriela Mendoza-Torres, *Teacher*
Lidia Teruel-Albert, *Assistant*
EMP: 60
SALES: 117.5K **Privately Held**
SIC: 8641 8211 Parent-teachers' association; elementary & secondary schools

(P-24505)
CALIFORNIA ALUMNI ASSOCIATION (PA)
1 Alumni House, Berkeley (94720-7520)
PHONE..................510 900-8225
Robert Tuck Coop, *Exec Dir*
Phil Culisse, *CFO*
Joanna Juarez, *Bd of Directors*
Matt Terwilliger, *Officer*
Joanna Aguiar, *Asst Director*
EMP: 50 **EST:** 1873
SQ FT: 16,000
SALES: 15.2MM **Privately Held**
SIC: 8641 Alumni association

(P-24506)
CALIFORNIA CLUB
538 S Flower St, Los Angeles (90071-2548)
PHONE..................213 622-1391
Robert C Baker, *CEO*
Jann McCord, *Director*
Angel Tecun, *Manager*
Philippa Gutridge, *Asst Mgr*

EMP: 185 **EST:** 1888
SALES: 15.5MM **Privately Held**
SIC: 8641 7041 Business persons club; bars & restaurants, members only; residence club, organization

(P-24507)
CALIFRNIA LEAG CNSRVTION VTERS (PA)
350 Frank H Ogawa Plz # 1100, Oakland (94612-2006)
PHONE..................510 271-0900
Sarah Rose, *Director*
Mike Young, *Admin Asst*
EMP: 55 **EST:** 1971
SQ FT: 3,500
SALES: 1.5MM **Privately Held**
SIC: 8641 Environmental protection organization

(P-24508)
CAMP FIRE USA LONG BEACH CNCL
7070 E Carson St, Long Beach (90808-2353)
PHONE..................562 421-2725
Shirlee Jackert, *Administration*
Angela Schoreder, *Executive*
Georgia Stewart, *Director*
EMP: 50
SALES: 1.9MM **Privately Held**
WEB: www.campfirelb.org
SIC: 8641 Youth organizations

(P-24509)
CAMP ROYANEH BOY SCOUT
P.O. Box 39 (95421-0039)
PHONE..................707 632-5291
Stanley Andrew, *Principal*
Jim Schiechl, *Director*
EMP: 60
SALES (est): 644.7K **Privately Held**
SIC: 8641 Boy Scout organization

(P-24510)
CANYON LK PROPERTY OWNERS ASSN
31512 Railroad Canyon Rd, Canyon Lake (92587-9400)
PHONE..................951 244-6841
Carl Armburst, *President*
Marty Gibson, *Treasurer*
Clint Warrell, *General Mgr*
Ron Phipps, *Controller*
Eric Kazakoff, *Opers Staff*
EMP: 84 **EST:** 1968
SQ FT: 18,000
SALES (est): 7.4MM **Privately Held**
SIC: 8641 Homeowners' association

(P-24511)
CARLSBAD INN VACTN CONDO OWNRS
3001 Carlsbad Blvd, Carlsbad (92008-2964)
PHONE..................760 434-7542
David Brown, *President*
Joe Spirito, *President*
Tim Stripe, *Co-President*
Randall Chapin, *General Mgr*
Eric Segal, *Director*
EMP: 68
SQ FT: 130,000
SALES: 3.5MM **Privately Held**
WEB: www.carlsbadinn.com
SIC: 8641 Homeowners' association

(P-24512)
CENTRAL UNIFIED SCHOOL DST
Also Called: Pta Calfrnia Congress of
6240 W Palo Alto Ave, Fresno (93722-2001)
PHONE..................559 276-3185
Tim Swain, *Principal*
EMP: 60
SALES (corp-wide): 199.6MM **Privately Held**
SIC: 8641 Parent-teachers' association
PA: Central Unified School District
4605 N Polk Ave
Fresno CA 93722
559 274-4700

(P-24513)
CENTRAL VLY YNG MNS CHRN ASSOC
Also Called: Central Valley YMCA
4045 N Fresno St Ste 101, Fresno
(93726-4099)
PHONE..................................559 225-9191
Jeff Teliha, *President*
EMP: 50 EST: 1886
SQ FT: 50,000
SALES: 371.5K Privately Held
SIC: 8641 7991 8351 7032 Youth organizations; physical fitness facilities; child day care services; youth camps; individual & family services

(P-24514)
CHANNEL ISLANDS YOUNG MENS CH
Also Called: Lompoc Family YMCA
201 W College Ave, Lompoc (93436-4415)
PHONE..................................805 736-3483
Dan Powell, *Branch Mgr*
EMP: 51
SALES (corp-wide): 18.6MM Privately Held
WEB: www.ciymca.org
SIC: 8641 7991 8351 7032 Youth organizations; physical fitness facilities; child day care services; youth camps; individual & family services
PA: Channel Islands Young Men's Christian Association
105 E Carrillo St
Santa Barbara CA 93101
805 569-1103

(P-24515)
CHANNEL ISLANDS YOUNG MENS CH
Also Called: Camarillo Family YMCA
3111 Village Park Dr, Camarillo (93012)
PHONE..................................805 484-0423
Marge Castellano, *Director*
EMP: 85
SALES (corp-wide): 18.6MM Privately Held
WEB: www.ciymca.org
SIC: 8641 7991 8351 7032 Youth organizations; physical fitness facilities; child day care services; youth camps; individual & family services
PA: Channel Islands Young Men's Christian Association
105 E Carrillo St
Santa Barbara CA 93101
805 569-1103

(P-24516)
CHANNEL ISLANDS YOUNG MENS CH
Also Called: Santa Barbara Family YMCA
36 Hitchcock Way, Santa Barbara
(93105-3102)
PHONE..................................805 687-7727
Tim Hardy, *Branch Mgr*
Gary Sarcione, *Facilities Dir*
EMP: 139
SALES (corp-wide): 18.6MM Privately Held
WEB: www.ciymca.org
SIC: 8641 7991 8351 7032 Youth organizations; physical fitness facilities; child day care services; youth camps; individual & family services
PA: Channel Islands Young Men's Christian Association
105 E Carrillo St
Santa Barbara CA 93101
805 569-1103

(P-24517)
CHANNEL ISLANDS YOUNG MENS CH
Also Called: Montecito Family YMCA
591 Santa Rosa Ln, Santa Barbara
(93108-2145)
PHONE..................................805 969-3288
Yvonne Rubio, *Director*
EMP: 73

SALES (corp-wide): 18.6MM Privately Held
WEB: www.ciymca.org
SIC: 8641 7991 8351 7032 Youth organizations; physical fitness facilities; child day care services; youth camps; individual & family services
PA: Channel Islands Young Men's Christian Association
105 E Carrillo St
Santa Barbara CA 93101
805 569-1103

(P-24518)
CHANNEL ISLANDS YOUNG MENS CH
Also Called: Ventura Family YMCA
3760 Telegraph Rd, Ventura (93003-3421)
PHONE..................................805 484-0423
Sarah Abrams, *Director*
Amy Bailey, *Director*
EMP: 144
SALES (corp-wide): 18.6MM Privately Held
WEB: www.ciymca.org
SIC: 8641 7991 8351 7032 Youth organizations; physical fitness facilities; child day care services; youth camps; individual & family services
PA: Channel Islands Young Men's Christian Association
105 E Carrillo St
Santa Barbara CA 93101
805 569-1103

(P-24519)
CHANNEL ISLANDS YOUNG MENS CH
Also Called: Stuart C. Gildred Family YMCA
900 N Refugio Rd, Santa Ynez
(93460-9314)
PHONE..................................805 686-2037
Paula Parisotto, *Branch Mgr*
Marcus Kocmur, *Vice Chairman*
EMP: 80
SALES (corp-wide): 18.6MM Privately Held
WEB: www.ciymca.org
SIC: 8641 7991 8351 7032 Youth organizations; physical fitness facilities; child day care services; youth camps; individual & family services
PA: Channel Islands Young Men's Christian Association
105 E Carrillo St
Santa Barbara CA 93101
805 569-1103

(P-24520)
CHATEAU LAKE SAN MARCOS HOMEOW
1502 Circa Del Lago, San Marcos
(92078-7201)
PHONE..................................760 471-0083
Chris Arvanitis, *President*
EMP: 75
SQ FT: 240,000
SALES: 3MM Privately Held
SIC: 8641 Homeowners' association

(P-24521)
CHICO STATE ENTERPRISES
25 Main St Unit 203, Chico (95928-5388)
PHONE..................................530 898-6811
Jessica Bourne, *Exec Dir*
EMP: 2000
SQ FT: 15,000
SALES (est): 45.1MM Privately Held
SIC: 8641 Civic social & fraternal associations

(P-24522)
CHINESE CNSLD BENEVOLENT ASSN
843 Stockton St, San Francisco
(94108-2120)
PHONE..................................415 982-6000
Thomas Ng, *Exec Dir*
EMP: 55
SALES: 43.2K Privately Held
SIC: 8641 Community membership club

(P-24523)
CHINO VALLEY UNIFIED SCHL DST
Also Called: 802 Newman Elem Pta Congress
4150 Walnut Ave, Chino (91710-2105)
PHONE..................................909 627-9758
EMP: 53
SALES (corp-wide): 346.1MM Privately Held
SIC: 8641 Parent-teachers' association
PA: Chino Valley Unified School District
5130 Riverside Dr
Chino CA 91710
909 628-1201

(P-24524)
CHINO VALLEY UNIFIED SCHL DST
Also Called: Pta CA Cngress of Parnts Eagle
13435 Eagle Canyon Dr, Chino Hills
(91709-1281)
PHONE..................................909 590-2707
EMP: 53
SALES (corp-wide): 346.1MM Privately Held
SIC: 8641 Parent-teachers' association
PA: Chino Valley Unified School District
5130 Riverside Dr
Chino CA 91710
909 628-1201

(P-24525)
COMMUNITY ACTION BRD OF SNT CR
406 Main St Ste 202, Watsonville
(95076-4639)
PHONE..................................831 724-0206
Elena Dela Garza, *Director*
Helen Ewan, *CEO*
EMP: 50
SALES (corp-wide): 3MM Privately Held
SIC: 8641 Civic social & fraternal associations
PA: Community Action Board Of Santa Cruz County Inc
406 Main St Ste 207
Watsonville CA 95076
831 763-2147

(P-24526)
CONTEMPRARY HSTRICAL VHCL ASSN
430 Oak View Dr, Vacaville (95688-4224)
PHONE..................................707 448-7266
Eric V Beeby, *Principal*
Eric Beeby, *Principal*
EMP: 90
SALES (est): 579K Privately Held
SIC: 8641 Civic social & fraternal associations

(P-24527)
COUNTY OF SHASTA
Also Called: Shasta Cattle Women
19897 Gas Point Rd, Cottonwood
(96022-9115)
P.O. Box 1491 (96022-1491)
PHONE..................................530 347-6276
Diane Montagner, *President*
EMP: 80 Privately Held
WEB: www.rsdnmp.org
SIC: 8641 Civic social & fraternal associations
PA: County Of Shasta
1450 Court St Ste 308a
Redding CA 96001
530 225-5561

(P-24528)
COWELL HOMEOWNERS ASSOCIATION (PA)
Also Called: Walnut Country
4498 Lawson Ct, Concord (94521-4410)
PHONE..................................925 825-0250
Rhinan Harris, *General Mgr*
Michael Demeo, *President*
EMP: 64 EST: 1972
SQ FT: 2,300
SALES (est): 1.1MM Privately Held
WEB: www.walnutcountry.com
SIC: 8641 8351 Homeowners' association; child day care services

(P-24529)
CRENSHAW YMCA
3820 Santa Rosalia Dr, Los Angeles
(90008-2516)
PHONE..................................323 290-9113
EMP: 70
SALES: 2MM Privately Held
SIC: 8641 7991 8351 7032

(P-24530)
CRESCENTA-CANADA YMCA (PA)
Also Called: YMCA Crescenta-Canada
1930 Foothill Blvd, La Canada
(91011-1933)
PHONE..................................818 790-0123
Larry Hall, *CEO*
Ken Gorvetzian, *Ch of Bd*
Hillary Schenk, *Director*
EMP: 280 EST: 1953
SALES (est): 5.2MM Privately Held
SIC: 8641 7991 8351 7032 Youth organizations; physical fitness facilities; child day care services; youth camps; individual & family services

(P-24531)
CRESCENTA-CANADA YMCA
Also Called: Learning Tree Pre-School
6840 Foothill Blvd, Tujunga (91042-2711)
PHONE..................................818 352-3255
Kathi Brink, *Branch Mgr*
EMP: 50
SALES (est): 355.8K
SALES (corp-wide): 5.2MM Privately Held
SIC: 8641 7991 8351 7032 Youth organizations; physical fitness facilities; child day care services; youth camps; individual & family services
PA: Crescenta-Canada Ymca
1930 Foothill Blvd
La Canada CA 91011
818 790-0123

(P-24532)
CYPRESS COLLEGE FOUNDATION
9200 Valley View Ave, Whittier (90603)
PHONE..................................714 484-7128
Raul Alvarez, *Principal*
EMP: 62
SALES: 723K Privately Held
SIC: 8641 Civic social & fraternal associations

(P-24533)
CYPRESS EDUCATION FOUNDATION
9470 Moody St, Cypress (90630-2919)
PHONE..................................714 220-6900
William D Eller, *CEO*
EMP: 51
SALES: 547.6K Privately Held
WEB: www.cypressmonterey.com
SIC: 8641 Educator's association

(P-24534)
D A V INDUSTRIES
1049 Elkelton Blvd, Spring Valley
(91977-4720)
PHONE..................................619 337-9244
William D Mudd, *President*
Donald Pouliot, *CFO*
Bernard Bandish, *Vice Pres*
Melvin Whitmer, *General Mgr*
EMP: 100
SQ FT: 8,000
SALES: 8.8MM Privately Held
WEB: www.davindustries.com
SIC: 8641 5932 Veterans' organization; clothing, secondhand

(P-24535)
DESERT PRNCESS HOMEOWNERS ASSN
Also Called: Desert Princess Hoa
28555 Landau Blvd, Cathedral City
(92234-3508)
PHONE..................................760 322-1907
Mario Gonzales, *CEO*
Tom Adamo, *President*
Marilyn J White, *CEO*
Mark McLaughlin, *Treasurer*
EMP: 100

SQ FT: 3,000
SALES (est): 4.3MM **Privately Held**
WEB: www.desertprincesscc.com
SIC: **8641** Homeowners' association

(P-24536)
DON JUAN AVILA ELEMENTARY PTA
26278 Wood Canyon Dr, Aliso Viejo
(92656-8060)
PHONE..............................949 349-9452
Dennie Samuels, *Principal*
EMP: 69
SALES: 210.5K **Privately Held**
SIC: **8641** Parent-teachers' association

(P-24537)
DUCKS UNLIMITED INC
Also Called: Western Regional Office
3074 Gold Canal Dr, Rancho Cordova
(95670-6116)
PHONE..............................916 852-2000
Rudy Rosses, *Director*
Camacho Maria, *Admin Asst*
Keith Wesley, *Technician*
Garrett Coussens, *Director*
Tim Fehringer, *Director*
EMP: 50
SALES (corp-wide): 60MM **Privately Held**
WEB: www.ducks.org
SIC: **8641** Environmental protection organization
PA: Ducks Unlimited, Inc.
1 Waterfowl Way
Memphis TN 38120
901 758-3825

(P-24538)
EAST PALO ALTO Y M C A
550 Bell St, East Palo Alto (94303-1701)
PHONE..............................650 328-9622
Robert Huges, *Director*
EMP: 50 EST: 1994
SALES (est): 292.5K **Privately Held**
SIC: **8641** 7991 8351 7032 Youth organizations; physical fitness facilities; child day care services; youth camps; individual & family services

(P-24539)
EMBARCADERO HOMES ASSN INC
4623 Quail Lakes Dr, Stockton
(95207-5258)
PHONE..............................954 776-2611
Kathy Dharnidharka, *President*
Charles Klass, *Treasurer*
Edmund Weiss, *Bd of Directors*
Cheri Margie, *Vice Pres*
Donna Zuckerman, *Admin Sec*
EMP: 73
SALES (est): 703.4K **Privately Held**
SIC: **8641** Homeowners' association

(P-24540)
EMERSON ELEMENTARY
720 E Cypress Ave, Burbank (91501-1812)
PHONE..............................818 558-5419
Linda Acuff, *Principal*
EMP: 65
SALES: 31.8K **Privately Held**
SIC: **8641** Parent-teachers' association

(P-24541)
EXCEPTIONAL CHLD FOUNDATION
11124 Fairbanks Way, Culver City
(90230-4945)
PHONE..............................310 915-6606
Scott Bowling, *Branch Mgr*
EMP: 165
SALES (corp-wide): 26.6MM **Privately Held**
SIC: **8641** Civic social & fraternal associations
PA: Exceptional Children's Foundation
5350 Machado Ln
Culver City CA 90230
310 204-3300

(P-24542)
FORT WASHINGTON PARENT ASSOC
Also Called: FT. WASHINGTON ELEM.
960 E Teague Ave, Fresno (93720-1704)
PHONE..............................559 327-6600
Melanie Hashimoto, *Principal*
EMP: 55
SALES: 40K **Privately Held**
SIC: **8641** Parent-teachers' association

(P-24543)
FOUNDATION LEAD GROUP LLC
Also Called: Doctor Genius
2121 Alton Pkwy Ste 150, Irvine
(92606-4957)
PHONE..............................877 477-2311
Christopher M Lopez, *Mng Member*
Joseph Alcaraz,
EMP: 66 EST: 2009
SALES: 6MM **Privately Held**
SIC: **8641** Civic social & fraternal associations

(P-24544)
FOUNDTION FOR HISPANIC EDUCATN (PA)
14271 Story Rd, San Jose (95127-3823)
P.O. Box 730453 (95173-0453)
PHONE.................(408 585-5022
Edward Alvarez, *CEO*
John Ramirez, *Vice Pres*
Terri McCluskey, *Executive Asst*
Cynthia Tapia, *Accountant*
Nancy Bergner, *Controller*
EMP: 65 EST: 2011
SQ FT: 60
SALES: 15.5MM **Privately Held**
SIC: **8641** Civic social & fraternal associations

(P-24545)
FRIENDS SANTA CRUZ STATE PARKS
1543 Pacific Ave Ste 206, Santa Cruz
(95060-3962)
PHONE..............................831 429-1840
Bonny Hawley, *Exec Dir*
EMP: 80
SALES: 6.6MM **Privately Held**
SIC: **8641** Environmental protection organization

(P-24546)
GENERAL GEORGE W SLINEY BASHA
Also Called: China Brma India Veterans Assn
4839 Rio Vista Ave, San Jose
(95129-1009)
PHONE..............................408 296-3423
Robert E Burke, *Treasurer*
EMP: 75
SALES (est): 2.8MM **Privately Held**
SIC: **8641** Veterans' organization

(P-24547)
GEOSYNTEC CONSULTANTS INC
2100 Main St Ste 150, Huntington Beach
(92648-2460)
PHONE..............................714 969-0800
Bert Palmer, *Manager*
Erin Lacosta, *Technician*
Julia Ryan, *Engineer*
Eric Suchomel PHD Pe, *Engineer*
Susan Bright, *Manager*
EMP: 55
SALES (corp-wide): 204.7MM **Privately Held**
SIC: **8641** 8711 Environmental protection organization; engineering services
PA: Geosyntec Consultants, Inc.
900 Broken Sound Pkwy Nw
Boca Raton FL 33487
561 995-0900

(P-24548)
GIRL SCOUTS HEART CENTRAL CAL
6601 Elvas Ave, Sacramento (95819-4339)
PHONE..............................916 452-9181
Linda Farley, *CEO*
Kerry Koyasako, *Vice Pres*
Sarah Sanford, *Director*

Sue Schoneman, *Manager*
EMP: 127
SALES: 9.6MM **Privately Held**
SIC: **8641** Girl Scout organization

(P-24549)
GIRL SCOUTS NORTHERN CAL (PA)
1650 Harbor Bay Pkwy # 100, Alameda
(94502-3012)
PHONE..............................510 562-8470
Marina Park, *CEO*
Robin Macgillivray, *President*
Bruce Morrow, *COO*
Diana Bell, *Vice Pres*
Ellen Richey, *Vice Pres*
EMP: 70
SQ FT: 17,000
SALES: 19.6MM **Privately Held**
SIC: **8641** Girl Scout organization

(P-24550)
GIRL SCTS SN DIEGO-IMPRL CNCL (PA)
1231 Upas St, San Diego (92103-5127)
PHONE..............................619 610-0751
Jo Dee C Jacob, *CEO*
Michael Diddock, *Controller*
Danielle Russell, *Sales Mgr*
Tanya Robinson, *Sales Staff*
Alison Bushan, *Director*
▼ EMP: 95
SQ FT: 7,926
SALES: 12.3MM **Privately Held**
SIC: **8641** Girl Scout organization

(P-24551)
GIRL SCUTS GREATER LOS ANGELES (PA)
1150 S Olive St Fl 6, Los Angeles
(90015-2846)
PHONE..............................626 677-2200
Lise Luttgens, *CEO*
Sylvia Rosenberger, *COO*
EMP: 155
SALES: 20.9MM **Privately Held**
WEB: www.gsmwvc.org
SIC: **8641** Girl Scout organization

(P-24552)
GIRL SCUTS SAN GRGONIO COUNCIL (PA)
1751 Plum Ln, Redlands (92374-4505)
PHONE..............................909 307-6555
Cynthia Harnisch-Breunig, *CEO*
EMP: 60
SALES: 8.2MM **Privately Held**
SIC: **8641** Girl Scout organization

(P-24553)
GLENWOOD VILLAGE CMNTY ASSN
Also Called: Seabreeze Management Comp
26840 Aliso Viejo Pkwy # 100, Aliso Viejo
(92656-2624)
PHONE..............................949 855-1800
Susan Larson, *President*
Annette Chong, *Manager*
EMP: 55
SALES (est): 482K **Privately Held**
SIC: **8641** Homeowners' association

(P-24554)
GOLD HILL GRANGE NO 326
1514 5th St, Lincoln (95648-1511)
PHONE..............................916 645-3605
Ron Smith, *Director*
EMP: 75
SALES (est): 687.4K **Privately Held**
SIC: **8641** Fraternal associations

(P-24555)
GOLDEN HL ELEMENTARY SCHL PTA
732 Barris Dr, Fullerton (92832-1002)
PHONE..............................714 447-7715
Robert Johnson, *Principal*
EMP: 50
SALES (est): 591.4K **Privately Held**
SIC: **8641** Parent-teachers' association

(P-24556)
GOLDEN RAIN FOUNDATION
800 Rockview Dr, Walnut Creek
(94595-3002)
PHONE..............................925 988-7800
Warren Thurlow Salmons, *Branch Mgr*
Nancy Bunch, *Opers Staff*
EMP: 282
SQ FT: 24,100
SALES (corp-wide): 23.8MM **Privately Held**
WEB: www.rossmoornews.com
SIC: **8641** Homeowners' association
PA: Golden Rain Foundation Of Walnut Creek
1001 Golden Rain Rd
Walnut Creek CA 94595
925 988-7700

(P-24557)
GORDON BETTY MOORE FOUNDATION
1661 Page Mill Rd, Palo Alto (94304-1209)
PHONE..............................650 213-3000
Steve McCormick, *President*
Beth Berselli, *Officer*
Adam Jones, *Officer*
Julie Lawrence, *Officer*
Heather Wright, *Officer*
EMP: 89
SALES (est): 4.4MM **Privately Held**
SIC: **8641** Civic social & fraternal associations

(P-24558)
GREATER LOS ANG (PA)
2333 Scout Way, Los Angeles
(90026-4912)
PHONE..............................213 413-4400
Cash Sutton, *President*
EMP: 67
SALES (est): 5.9MM **Privately Held**
SIC: **8641** Boy Scout organization

(P-24559)
GROSSMONT-CUYAMACA COMMUNITY
Also Called: GCCCD AUXILIARY
8800 Grossmont College Dr, El Cajon
(92020-1765)
PHONE..............................619 644-7684
Stanley Schroeder, *Exec Dir*
Sue Rearic, *CFO*
Stan Schroeder, *Exec Dir*
Waters Shari, *Manager*
EMP: 86
SQ FT: 1,000
SALES: 21.8MM **Privately Held**
SIC: **8641** Educator's association

(P-24560)
HACIENDA INVLVED PARENTS STAFF
Also Called: Hips
1290 Kimberly Dr, San Jose (95118-1536)
PHONE..............................408 535-6259
Anna Lily, *CEO*
Melissa Mohammed, *Principal*
EMP: 55
SALES: 272.2K **Privately Held**
SIC: **8641** Parent-teachers' association

(P-24561)
HEMET UNIFIED SCHOOL DISTRICT
Also Called: Pta California Congress of
41535 Mayberry Ave, Hemet (92544-6389)
PHONE..............................951 765-2550
Darin Clark, *Info Tech Mgr*
EMP: 189
SALES (corp-wide): 301.8MM **Privately Held**
SIC: **8641** Parent-teachers' association
PA: Hemet Unified School District
1791 W Acacia Ave
Hemet CA 92545
951 765-5100

(P-24562)
HENTREL GREATHOUSE FOUNDATION
127 S 1st Ave, Barstow (92311-2827)
PHONE..............................302 513-4056
David Taylor, *President*

EMP: 68
SQ FT: 15,000
SALES (est): 81.8K **Privately Held**
SIC: 8641 Civic social & fraternal associations

(P-24563)
HIDDEN VALLEY LAKE ASSOCIATION (PA)
Also Called: Hidden Valley Golf Course
18174 Hidden Valley Rd, Hidden Valley Lake (95467-8690)
PHONE.............................707 987-3146
Wililam E Waite, *CEO*
EMP: 71
SQ FT: 1,000
SALES (est): 6.7MM **Privately Held**
WEB: www.hvla.com
SIC: 8641 7997 5813 Homeowners' association; golf club, membership; swimming club, membership; bar (drinking places)

(P-24564)
HORIZONS 4 CONDOMINIUMS INC
Also Called: Horizon For Hmwners Asscations
·2113 Meridan Blvd, Mammoth Lakes (93546)
P.O. Box 175 (93546-0175)
PHONE.............................760 934-6779
Fax: 760 934-4224
EMP: 92
SALES (est): 1.1MM **Privately Held**
SIC: 8641

(P-24565)
INSTITUTE FOR WILDLIFE STUDIES (PA)
835 3rd St, Eureka (95501-0511)
P.O. Box 1104, Arcata (95518-1104)
PHONE.............................707 822-4258
David K Garcelon, *President*
Doug Page, *Project Leader*
EMP: 50
SQ FT: 2,300
SALES: 3.5MM **Privately Held**
WEB: www.iws.org
SIC: 8641 Environmental protection organization

(P-24566)
JAMES MONROE SCHOOL PTO
42100 Yucca Ln, Bermuda Dunes (92203-8100)
PHONE.............................760 772-4130
Mike Kent, *Principal*
EMP: 50
SALES: 74.6K **Privately Held**
SIC: 8641 Parent-teachers' association

(P-24567)
JEFFERSON CALIFORNIA CONGRESS
6225 El Camino Real, Carlsbad (92009-1604)
PHONE.............................760 331-5500
Chad Lund, *Principal*
EMP: 65
SALES: 88.7K **Privately Held**
SIC: 8641 Parent-teachers' association

(P-24568)
JEWISH CMNTY FNDN OF (PA)
6505 Wilshire Blvd, Los Angeles (90048-4906)
PHONE.............................323 761-8700
Richard V Sandler, *Ch of Bd*
J Sanderson, *President*
Jack Klein, *COO*
Ivan Wolkind, *COO*
Leslie E Bider, *Chairman*
EMP: 150
SQ FT: 100,000
SALES: 47.7MM **Privately Held**
SIC: 8641 8661 Community membership club; religious organizations

(P-24569)
JONATHAN CLUB (PA)
545 S Figueroa St, Los Angeles (90071-1793)
PHONE.............................213 624-0881
Gregory J Dumas, *President*
Randolph P Sinnott, *CEO*

Emma Ivester, *CFO*
Plato Skouras, *CFO*
Tico Baloyan, *Comms Dir*
EMP: 300 **EST:** 1895
SQ FT: 230,276
SALES: 39.4MM **Privately Held**
WEB: www.jc.org
SIC: 8641 Social club, membership

(P-24570)
KIWANIS INTERNATIONAL INC
Also Called: North Modesto Kiwanis Club
3201 Canterbury Ct, Modesto (95350-1419)
PHONE.............................209 578-1448
Robert Dunbar, *Principal*
EMP: 80
SALES (corp-wide): 23.6MM **Privately Held**
WEB: www.kfne.org
SIC: 8641 Civic associations
PA: Kiwanis International, Inc.
3636 Woodview Trce
Indianapolis IN 46268
317 875-8755

(P-24571)
KNIGHTS OF COLUMBUS
871 Founders Ln, Milpitas (95035-3345)
PHONE.............................408 262-6609
Wm Poehlman Jr, *Owner*
EMP: 80
SALES (est): 361.1K **Privately Held**
SIC: 8641 Fraternal associations

(P-24572)
KNIGHTS OF COLUMBUS
1344 Magnolia Dr, Santa Paula (93060-1112)
PHONE.............................805 525-7810
Frank Arpuelles, *President*
EMP: 150
SALES (corp-wide): 2.3B **Privately Held**
WEB: www.kofc.org
SIC: 8641 Fraternal associations
PA: Knights Of Columbus
1 Columbus Plz Ste 1700
New Haven CT 06510
203 752-4000

(P-24573)
LA MESA LIONS CLUB
4387 Summit Dr, La Mesa (91941-7842)
P.O. Box 1441 (91944-1441)
PHONE.............................619 469-9988
Howard C Linke, *Admin Sec*
EMP: 60
SALES: 34K **Privately Held**
SIC: 8641 Civic associations

(P-24574)
LA PUERTA
560 4th Ave, San Diego (92101-6905)
PHONE.............................619 696-3466
Darren Morre, *Owner*
Darren Moore, *Owner*
EMP: 50
SALES (est): 973.7K **Privately Held**
SIC: 8641 Bars & restaurants, members only

(P-24575)
LACOLINA JR HIGH CA CONGRESS O
4025 Foothill Rd, Santa Barbara (93110-1209)
PHONE.............................805 967-4506
Cristine Gallagher, *President*
EMP: 55
SALES: 40.2K **Privately Held**
SIC: 8641 Civic social & fraternal associations

(P-24576)
LAKE FOREST LI MASTER HOMEOWN
Also Called: SUN & SAIL CLUB
24752 Toledo Ln, Lake Forest (92630-2318)
PHONE.............................949 586-0860
Sonny Morper, *President*
Jim Richert, *President*
Ted Brackez, *Principal*
Terri Graham, *Principal*
Ken Hedge, *Principal*
EMP: 80 **EST:** 1971

SQ FT: 9,000
SALES: 4.3MM **Privately Held**
WEB: www.lf2.org
SIC: 8641 Homeowners' association

(P-24577)
LAKE MISSION VIEJO ASSOCIATION
22555 Olympiad Rd, Mission Viejo (92692-1118)
PHONE.............................949 770-1313
Fred Mellenbruch, *President*
Sid Wittenberg, *Treasurer*
Jane Chadburn, *Vice Pres*
Sen Jeff Miklaus, *Vice Pres*
Wayne Dunn, *Admin Sec*
EMP: 90
SQ FT: 7,400
SALES: 7.7MM **Privately Held**
WEB: www.lakemissionviejo.org
SIC: 8641 Homeowners' association

(P-24578)
LAKE OF THE PINES ASSOCIATION
Also Called: LAKE OF THE PINES HOMEOWNERS
11665 Lakeshore N, Auburn (95602-8325)
PHONE.............................530 268-1141
Edwin Vitrano, *General Mgr*
Sislei Goldsmith, *Accountant*
Donna Lowenthal, *Controller*
EMP: 50
SALES: 7.2MM **Privately Held**
WEB: www.lop.org
SIC: 8641 Homeowners' association

(P-24579)
LAKE WILDWOOD ASSOCIATION
Also Called: Lake Wildwood Golf Course.
11255 Cottontail Way, Penn Valley (95946-9409)
PHONE.............................530 432-1152
Tom Cross, *CEO*
Dustin Wright, *Food Svc Dir*
William Haushalter, *Director*
EMP: 120
SQ FT: 10,000
SALES: 9.1MM **Privately Held**
SIC: 8641 7997 Homeowners' association; golf club, membership

(P-24580)
LEGION CORPORATION
106 Sanchez St, San Francisco (94114-1367)
PHONE.............................415 829-7307
Joseph Shelley, *Branch Mgr*
EMP: 60
SALES (corp-wide): 5.4MM **Privately Held**
SIC: 8641 Veterans' organization
PA: Legion Corporation
784 Geary St
San Francisco CA 94109
800 750-0062

(P-24581)
LEISURE VILLAGE ASSOCIATION
200 Leisure Village Dr, Camarillo (93012-6802)
PHONE.............................805 484-2861
Robert Scheaffer, *General Mgr*
EMP: 100
SQ FT: 6,000
SALES (est): 3.5MM **Privately Held**
SIC: 8641 Homeowners' association

(P-24582)
LELAND STANFORD JUNIOR UNIV
Also Called: Stanford Alumni Association
326 Galvez St, Stanford (94305-6105)
PHONE.............................650 723-2021
Howard Wolf, *Branch Mgr*
Subhan Ali, *Bd of Directors*
Karen McKinley, *Senior Mgr*
Blair Critchlow, *Director*
Anne Kircher, *Manager*
EMP: 250
SALES (corp-wide): 11.3B **Privately Held**
SIC: 8641 8221 Alumni association; university

PA: Leland Stanford Junior University
450 Jane Stanford Way
Stanford CA 94305
650 723-2300

(P-24583)
LINDA VERDE SCHOOL
Also Called: Pta California Congress of
44924 5th St E, Lancaster (93535-2688)
PHONE.............................661 942-0431
Storm Lydon, *Principal*
EMP: 50
SALES (est): 642.6K **Privately Held**
SIC: 8641 Parent-teachers' association

(P-24584)
LOMA LINDA VET ASSOCIATION FOR
Also Called: L L V A R E
710 Brookside Ave Ste 2, Redlands (92373-5181)
P.O. Box 10849, San Bernardino (92423-0849)
PHONE.............................909 583-6250
Alan Jacobson, *President*
David Buxbaum, *Treasurer*
Gayle Rundberg, *Exec Dir*
Robert Miller, *Admin Sec*
EMP: 60
SQ FT: 44,000
SALES: 3.8MM **Privately Held**
WEB: www.llvare.org
SIC: 8641 Veterans' organization

(P-24585)
LOMA RIVIERA COMMUNITY ASSN
9610 Waples St, San Diego (92121-2955)
PHONE.............................619 224-1313
Dale Bredon, *President*
Anne Wagner, *President*
EMP: 100
SQ FT: 300
SALES (est): 3.7MM **Privately Held**
SIC: 8641 Homeowners' association

(P-24586)
LOS ANGELES AIRPORT PEACE OFFC
Also Called: LAAPOA
6080 Center Dr Fl 6, Los Angeles (90045-9205)
PHONE.............................310 242-5218
Marshall E McClain, *President*
Rodney Rouzan, *Treasurer*
Andrei Soto, *Treasurer*
Julius Levy, *Vice Pres*
Rupert Staine, *Admin Sec*
EMP: 425
SQ FT: 500
SALES: 990.6K **Privately Held**
SIC: 8641 Civic social & fraternal associations

(P-24587)
LOS ANGELES UNIFIED SCHOOL DST
Also Called: YMCA Metro La-52nd St School
816 W 51st St, Los Angeles (90037-3603)
PHONE.............................323 753-3175
Beverly Crosby, *Principal*
Katie Gaspard, *Principal*
EMP: 200
SALES (corp-wide): 4B **Privately Held**
WEB: www.lausd.k12.ca.us
SIC: 8641 7991 8351 7032 Youth organizations; physical fitness facilities; child day care services; youth camps; individual & family services
PA: Los Angeles Unified School District
333 S Beaudry Ave Ste 209
Los Angeles CA 90017
213 241-1000

(P-24588)
LOS ANGELES UNIFIED SCHOOL DST
Also Called: Tulsa Street Pta CA Cngrss of
10900 Hayvenhurst Ave, Granada Hills (91344-5121)
PHONE.............................818 363-5061
EMP: 105
SALES (corp-wide): 4B **Privately Held**
SIC: 8641 Parent-teachers' association

PA: Los Angeles Unified School District
333 S Beaudry Ave Ste 209
Los Angeles CA 90017
213 241-1000

(P-24589)
MADE IN USA FOUNDATION INC
11950 San Vicente Blvd # 220, Los Angeles
(90049-5013)
PHONE..................................310 623-3872
Joel Joseph, *President*
EMP: 50
SALES (est): 1.1MM **Privately Held**
SIC: 8641 Civic social & fraternal associations

(P-24590)
MARAVILLA FOUNDATION (PA)
5729 Union Pacific Ave, Commerce
(90022-5134)
PHONE..................................323 721-4162
Alex M Sotomayor, *CEO*
Tristen Sotomayor, *COO*
George Ross, *CFO*
Deo Tinana, *CFO*
Paul Lopez, *Chairman*
EMP: 56
SQ FT: 30,000
SALES: 10.7MM **Privately Held**
SIC: 8641 Civic associations

(P-24591)
MARINES MEMORIAL ASSOCIATION
Also Called: MARINES' MEMORIAL CLUB & HOTEL
609 Sutter St, San Francisco (94102-1081)
PHONE..................................415 673-6672
James M Myatt, *President*
Ruby Wu, *CFO*
William Kelly, *Treasurer*
Roxanne Goodfellow, *Executive*
Bethany Meyer, *Executive*
EMP: 148 **EST:** 1946
SQ FT: 160,062
SALES: 15.4MM **Privately Held**
WEB: www.marineclub.com
SIC: 8641 7011 5921 5813 Veterans' organization; hotels; liquor stores; bar (drinking places); eating places

(P-24592)
MIDNIGHT MISSION (PA)
601 S San Pedro St, Los Angeles
(90014-2415)
PHONE..................................213 624-9258
R Stephen Doan, *Chairman*
Larry Adamson, *President*
Lori Neville, *COO*
Charles Cross, *CFO*
Glenn D Woody, *CFO*
EMP: 69 **EST:** 1914
SQ FT: 11,550
SALES: 2.8MM **Privately Held**
WEB: www.midnightmission.org
SIC: 8641 8322 Civic social & fraternal associations; individual & family services

(P-24593)
MILKEN FAMILY FOUNDATION
1250 4th St Fl 1, Santa Monica
(90401-1418)
PHONE..................................310 570-4800
Lowell J Milken, *President*
Susan Fox, *CFO*
Mariano Guzm N, *Trustee*
Bonnie Somers, *Vice Pres*
Sonia Lowman, *Comms Dir*
EMP: 200
SALES: 27.8MM **Privately Held**
WEB: www.mff.org
SIC: 8641 Civic social & fraternal associations

(P-24594)
MONTECITO FIRE PROTECTION DST
595 San Ysidro Rd, Santa Barbara
(93108-2124)
PHONE..................................805 969-7762
Chip Hickman, *Fire Chief*
Todd Edwards, *Chief*
Kevin Wallace, *Fire Chief*
EMP: 50

SALES (est): 2.1MM **Privately Held**
SIC: 8641 9224 Civic social & fraternal associations; fire protection

(P-24595)
MOORE FOUNDATIONS INC
7046 Darby Ave, Reseda (91335-4401)
PHONE..................................818 698-4737
Ryan Moore, *CEO*
EMP: 50
SALES (est): 46.8K **Privately Held**
SIC: 8641 Civic social & fraternal associations

(P-24596)
MOOSE INTERNATIONAL INC
Also Called: Moose Family Center 545
2470 El Rancho Dr, Santa Cruz
(95060-1106)
P.O. Box 66292, Scotts Valley (95067-6292)
PHONE..................................831 438-1817
Perry James, *Administration*
EMP: 208
SQ FT: 2,800
SALES (corp-wide): 48.4MM **Privately Held**
WEB: www.thalist.com
SIC: 8641 Fraternal associations
PA: Moose International, Incorporated
155 S International Dr
Mooseheart IL 60539
630 859-2000

(P-24597)
MORNINGSIDE COMMUNITY ASSN
82 Mayfair Dr, Rancho Mirage
(92270-2562)
PHONE..................................760 328-3323
M Abdelnour, *General Mgr*
Michelle Abdelnour, *General Mgr*
EMP: 73
SQ FT: 3,500
SALES (est): 2.5MM **Privately Held**
SIC: 8641 Homeowners' association

(P-24598)
MRCA FIRE DIVISION
1670 Las Virgenes Cyn Rd, Calabasas
(91302-1920)
PHONE..................................818 880-4752
Ken Nelson, *COO*
Jakub Slovacek, *Officer*
EMP: 50
SALES (est): 467K **Privately Held**
SIC: 8641 Environmental protection organization

(P-24599)
MXB BATTERY OPERATIONS LP
Also Called: Battery The
717 Battery St, San Francisco
(94111-1515)
PHONE..................................415 230-8000
Steven Flowers, *Exec Dir*
Stacy Horne, *Vice Pres*
Colleen Curlin, *Manager*
EMP: 100
SALES (corp-wide): 1.3MM **Privately Held**
SIC: 8641 Social club, membership
PA: Mxb Battery Operations, Lp
387 Tehama St
San Francisco CA 94103
415 896-9200

(P-24600)
NAPA SUNRISE ROTARY CLUB INC
Also Called: ROTARY CLUB OF NAPA SUNRISE OF
P.O. Box 5324 (94581-0324)
PHONE..................................707 257-9564
William Jabin, *Treasurer*
EMP: 80
SALES: 166.6K **Privately Held**
SIC: 8641 Community membership club

(P-24601)
NATURAL RSRCES DEF COUNCIL INC
1314 2nd St, Santa Monica (90401-1103)
PHONE..................................310 434-2300
Frances Beinecke, *Exec Dir*

Rene Leni, *Office Admin*
Taryn Heimer, *Analyst*
Gayle Petersen, *Manager*
Aline Goganian, *Assistant*
EMP: 70
SQ FT: 10,558
SALES (corp-wide): 155.1MM **Privately Held**
WEB: www.savebiogems.org
SIC: 8641 Environmental protection organization
PA: Natural Resources Defense Council Inc.
40 W 20th St
New York NY 10011
212 727-2700

(P-24602)
OAKLAND UNIFIED SCHOOL DST
Also Called: E Morris Cox Elementary School
9860 Sunnyside St, Oakland (94603-2750)
PHONE..................................510 729-7775
Enikia F Mothel, *Principal*
EMP: 100
SALES (corp-wide): 677MM **Privately Held**
WEB: www.ousd.k12.ca.us
SIC: 8641 8211 Parent-teachers' association; public elementary school
PA: Oakland Unified School District
1000 Broadway Ste 300
Oakland CA 94607
510 434-7790

(P-24603)
OAKLEY UNION SCHOOL DISTRICT
Also Called: Pta Calif Congress of Parents
1100 Ohara Ave, Oakley (94561-3502)
PHONE..................................925 625-5060
Colleen Crestwell, *President*
EMP: 68
SALES (corp-wide): 58.8MM **Privately Held**
SIC: 8641 Parent-teachers' association
PA: Oakley Union School District
91 Mercedes Ln
Oakley CA 94561
925 625-5057

(P-24604)
OLYMPIC CLUB (PA)
524 Post St, San Francisco (94102-1295)
PHONE..................................415 345-5100
John M Jack, *CEO*
Andrew Collins, *Vice Pres*
Traci Mysliwiec, *Comms Mgr*
Jay Bedsworth, *Principal*
Patrick Merritt, *General Mgr*
EMP: 200
SQ FT: 160,000
SALES: 48.3MM **Privately Held**
WEB: www.ocrugby.com
SIC: 8641 7997 5812 Civic social & fraternal associations; golf club, membership; health food restaurant

(P-24605)
OLYMPIC CLUB
Also Called: Lakeside Clubhouse
599 Skyline Dr, Daly City (94015-4611)
PHONE..................................415 404-4300
EMP: 103
SALES (corp-wide): 48.3MM **Privately Held**
SIC: 8641 5812 Civic social & fraternal associations; health food restaurant
PA: The Olympic Club
524 Post St
San Francisco CA 94102
415 345-5100

(P-24606)
ORANGE COUNTY CNCL BSA (PA)
1211 E Dyer Rd Ste 100, Santa Ana
(92705-5670)
PHONE..................................714 546-4990
Les Baron, *President*
Robert Neal, *Ch of Bd*
Jeffrie A Herrmann, *President*
Larry Behm, *Principal*
EMP: 65

SALES: 9.1MM **Privately Held**
WEB: www.ocbsa.com
SIC: 8641 Boy Scout organization

(P-24607)
ORTEGA ELEMENTARY PTO
1283 Terra Nova Blvd, Pacifica
(94044-4341)
PHONE..................................650 738-6670
Jannel Jones, *President*
EMP: 75
SALES (est): 189.2K **Privately Held**
SIC: 8641 Parent-teachers' association

(P-24608)
PACIFIC UNION CLUB
1000 California St, San Francisco
(94108-2280)
PHONE..................................415 775-1234
Thomas Gaston, *General Mgr*
EMP: 62
SQ FT: 54,000
SALES: 10.2MM **Privately Held**
WEB: www.pacificunionclub.com
SIC: 8641 Social club, membership

(P-24609)
PALISADES OPTIMIST FOUNDATION
15312 Whitfield Ave, Pacific Palisades
(90272-2547)
PHONE..................................310 454-4111
Harold Vicau, *Treasurer*
EMP: 71
SALES (est): 2.1MM **Privately Held**
SIC: 8641 Social associations

(P-24610)
PALM DESERT GREENS ASSOCIATION
73750 Country Club Dr, Palm Desert
(92260-8663)
PHONE..................................760 346-8005
Roberta Hollingsworth, *General Mgr*
Ken Dobson, *President*
Mal Sinclair, *Treasurer*
Barbara Houcek, *Executive*
Roberta Reynolds, *General Mgr*
EMP: 75 **EST:** 1971
SQ FT: 12,400
SALES: 7MM **Privately Held**
SIC: 8641 Homeowners' association

(P-24611)
PALO ALTO FAMILY Y M C A
3412 Ross Rd, Palo Alto (94303-4411)
PHONE..................................650 856-9622
Scott Glissmeyer, *Manager*
John Logan, *CEO*
EMP: 50
SALES (est): 589.3K **Privately Held**
SIC: 8641 7991 8351 7032 Youth organizations; physical fitness facilities; child day care services; youth camps; individual & family services

(P-24612)
PARENTHOOD OF PLANNED
1650 Valencia St, San Francisco
(94110-5013)
PHONE..................................415 821-1282
EMP: 51
SALES (corp-wide): 63.3MM **Privately Held**
SIC: 8641 8322 8093 8049 Civic social & fraternal associations; referral service for personal & social problems; family planning clinic; acupuncturist
PA: Planned Parenthood Of San Diego And Riverside Counties
1075 Camino Del Rio S # 100
San Diego CA 92108
619 881-4500

(P-24613)
PENINSULA COMMUNITY FOUNDATION
Also Called: Center For Ventr Philanthropy
1700 S El Camino Real # 300, San Mateo
(94402-3047)
PHONE..................................650 358-9369
Sterling K Speirn, *President*
George Chong, *Controller*
Rebecca Levine, *Director*
Patricia Supriana, *Director*

Katie Kibbee, *Associate*
EMP: 55
SQ FT: 16,800
SALES: 200MM **Privately Held**
SIC: 8641 Civic social & fraternal associations

(P-24614)
PESCADERO CONSERVATION ALLIANCE
4100 Cabrillo Hwy, Pescadero (94060-9724)
P.O. Box 873 (94060-0873)
PHONE..................650 879-1441
John Wade, *Associate*
Randy Bennett, *President*
Jack Olsen, *Admin Sec*
Bert Fewss, *Director*
EMP: 50
SALES: 13.2K **Privately Held**
WEB: www.gazos.org
SIC: 8641 Environmental protection organization

(P-24615)
PINE MOUNTAIN LAKE ASSOCIATION (PA)
19228 Pine Mountain Dr, Groveland (95321-9581)
PHONE..................209 962-4080
Brian Sweeney, *President*
Dana Chavarria, *Treasurer*
Ian Morcott, *Vice Pres*
Joe Powell, *General Mgr*
Jerry Dickson, *Admin Sec*
EMP: 130
SQ FT: 20,000
SALES: 9.8MM **Privately Held**
SIC: 8641 Homeowners' association

(P-24616)
PROGRESS FOUNDATION
52 Dore St, San Francisco (94103-3828)
PHONE..................415 553-3100
Steven Fields, *Exec Dir*
EMP: 57
SALES (corp-wide): 20.8MM **Privately Held**
SIC: 8641 Civic social & fraternal associations
PA: Progress Foundation
368 Fell St
San Francisco CA 94102
415 861-0828

(P-24617)
PTA CA CNGRSS OF PARNTS TCHRS
3030 N Hesperian St, Santa Ana (92706-1151)
PHONE..................714 836-2700
Kim Podd, *Exec Dir*
EMP: 95
SALES (est): 349.6K **Privately Held**
SIC: 8641 Parent-teachers' association

(P-24618)
PTA CA CONG PRENTS EMPEROR SCH
6415 N Muscatel Ave, San Gabriel (91775-1845)
PHONE..................626 548-5084
Kathy Perini, *Principal*
EMP: 70
SALES: 61.1K **Privately Held**
SIC: 8641 Parent-teachers' association

(P-24619)
PTA CA CONG PRENTS KELLEY SCHL
4885 Kelly Dr, Carlsbad (92008-3734)
PHONE..................760 331-5800
Tressie Armstrong, *Principal*
EMP: 50
SALES: 114K **Privately Held**
SIC: 8641 Parent-teachers' association

(P-24620)
PTA CA CONGRESS OF PARENTS
Also Called: Serrania Charter Elementary
5014 Serrania Ave, Woodland Hills (91364-3303)
PHONE..................818 340-6700

Theresa C Wedaa, *Principal*
Luis Alvoredo, *Principal*
EMP: 50
SALES (est): 112.2K **Privately Held**
SIC: 8641 Parent-teachers' association

(P-24621)
PTA CALIFORNIA CONG P A S ELEM
5280 Irene Way, Livermore (94550-3508)
PHONE..................925 606-4700
Denise Mathanson, *Principal*
EMP: 50
SALES (est): 77.9K **Privately Held**
SIC: 8641 Parent-teachers' association

(P-24622)
PTA CALIFORNIA CONGRESS OF PAR
Also Called: Annie R Mitchell Elementary
2121 E Laura Ave, Visalia (93292-1407)
PHONE..................559 622-3195
Loreta Bryant, *Principal*
EMP: 50
SALES (est): 513.7K **Privately Held**
SIC: 8641 Parent-teachers' association

(P-24623)
PTA CALIFORNIA CONGRESS OF PAR
21514 Halldale Ave, Torrance (90501-3016)
PHONE..................310 328-3100
Deborah Evers-Allen, *Principal*
EMP: 80
SALES (est): 358.3K **Privately Held**
SIC: 8641 Parent-teachers' association

(P-24624)
PTAC CARMEL VALLEY MID SCHOOL
3800 Mykonos Ln, San Diego (92130-3572)
PHONE..................858 481-8221
Laurie Brady, *Principal*
Adam Camacho, *Asst Principal*
EMP: 85
SALES (est): 77K **Privately Held**
SIC: 8641 Parent-teachers' association

(P-24625)
PTAC DON L RHEE ELEM SCH R PTA
90 Laird Dr, Moraga (94556-1407)
PHONE..................925 376-4441
Elaine Frank, *Principal*
EMP: 60
SALES (est): 172.3K **Privately Held**
SIC: 8641 Parent-teachers' association

(P-24626)
PTAC RAIL RANCH ELEM SCHOOL
25030 Via Santee, Murrieta (92563-5020)
PHONE..................951 696-1404
Hunter Wethers, *Principal*
EMP: 60
SALES: 22.8K **Privately Held**
SIC: 8641 Parent-teachers' association

(P-24627)
PUBLIC HLTH FNDATION ENTPS INC
277 S Atlantic Blvd, Los Angeles (90022-1734)
PHONE..................323 263-0262
Laurie Hill, *Principal*
EMP: 115
SALES (corp-wide): 97.5MM **Privately Held**
SIC: 8641 Civic social & fraternal associations
PA: Public Health Foundation Enterprises, Inc.
13300 Crssrds Pkwy N
City Of Industry CA 91746
800 201-7320

(P-24628)
PUBLIC HLTH FNDATION ENTPS INC
Also Called: Wic
1640 W Carson St Ste G, Torrance (90501-3877)
PHONE..................310 320-5215
EMP: 115
SALES (corp-wide): 97.5MM **Privately Held**
SIC: 8641 Civic social & fraternal associations
PA: Public Health Foundation Enterprises, Inc.
13300 Crssrds Pkwy N
City Of Industry CA 91746
800 201-7320

(P-24629)
PUBLIC HLTH FNDATION ENTPS INC (PA)
Also Called: Heluna Health
13300 Crssrds Pkwy N, City of Industry (91746)
PHONE..................800 201-7320
Blain Cutler, *President*
Devecchio Finley, *Vice Chairman*
Gerald D Jensen, *President*
Michael R Gomez, *CEO*
Karen L Angel, *Treasurer*
EMP: 168
SQ FT: 25,000
SALES: 97.5MM **Privately Held**
SIC: 8641 Civic social & fraternal associations

(P-24630)
READING AND BEYOND
4670 E Butler Ave, Fresno (93702-4608)
PHONE..................559 840-1068
Luis Santana, *President*
Arasely Rosas, *Program Mgr*
Alicia Pearce, *Executive Asst*
Nikki Newsome, *Director*
EMP: 74
SALES: 6.7MM **Privately Held**
SIC: 8641 Youth organizations

(P-24631)
RECREATIONAL ASSN CORCORAN
Also Called: RAC
900 Dairy Ave, Corcoran (93212-2114)
P.O. Box 176 (93212-0176)
PHONE..................559 992-5171
S S Brown, *Exec Dir*
Jim Razor, *President*
EMP: 63
SALES (est): 208.4K **Privately Held**
SIC: 8641 8699 Recreation association; charitable organization

(P-24632)
ROSARY ACADEMY PARENT COUNCIL
1340 N Acacia Ave, Fullerton (92831-1202)
PHONE..................714 879-6302
Patty Weller, *President*
EMP: 72
SALES (est): 3.1MM **Privately Held**
SIC: 8641 Parent-teachers' association

(P-24633)
ROTARY INTERNATIONAL
Also Called: Rotary Club
9839 Meadowlark Way, Palo Cedro (96073-8750)
PHONE..................530 547-5272
EMP: 62
SALES (corp-wide): 355.9MM **Privately Held**
SIC: 8641
PA: Rotary International
1 Rotary Ctr
Evanston IL 60201
847 866-3000

(P-24634)
RRUFF-ROCKLIN RESIDENTS UNITE
3031 St, Rocklin (95765)
PHONE..................415 806-2778
Victoria Curtis, *Principal*
EMP: 50 **EST:** 2014

SALES (est): 234.3K **Privately Held**
SIC: 8641 Veterans' organization

(P-24635)
SAA SIERRA PROGRAMS LLC
Also Called: Stanford Sierra Camp & Lodge
130 Fallen Leaf Rd, South Lake Tahoe (96150-6165)
P.O. Box 10618 (96158-3618)
PHONE..................530 541-1244
David Bunnett, *Director*
Antja Thompson, *Asst Director*
Nancy Marzocco, *Director*
EMP: 90
SALES (est): 1.7MM
SALES (corp-wide): 11.3B **Privately Held**
SIC: 8641 Civic associations
PA: Leland Stanford Junior University
450 Jane Stanford Way
Stanford CA 94305
650 723-2300

(P-24636)
SACRAMENTO CY UNIFIED SCHL DST (PA)
5735 47th Ave, Sacramento (95824-4528)
P.O. Box 246870 (95824-6870)
PHONE..................916 643-7400
Jose Banda, *Superintendent*
Tom Barrinson, *CFO*
Jeff Weiss, *Advisor*
EMP: 300 **EST:** 1854
SQ FT: 45,000
SALES: 635.5MM **Privately Held**
WEB: www.sachigh.org
SIC: 8641 Veterans' organization; environmental protection organization; Boy Scout organization

(P-24637)
SACROMENTO EDUCTN READNG LIONS
10461 Old Plza Vlle 130, Sacramento (95827)
PHONE..................916 228-2219
Alice Furry, *Director*
EMP: 50
SALES (est): 786.9K **Privately Held**
SIC: 8641 Civic associations

(P-24638)
SALESIAN BOYS AND GIRLS CLUB
680 Filbert St, San Francisco (94133-2805)
PHONE..................415 397-3068
Russell Gumina, *Exec Dir*
Randal Demartini, *Asst Director*
EMP: 79
SALES: 2.4MM **Privately Held**
SIC: 8641 Youth organizations

(P-24639)
SAN DIEGO COUNTRY ESTATES ASSN
Also Called: San Vicente Inn & Golf Club
24157 San Vicente Rd, Ramona (92065-4166)
PHONE..................760 789-3788
Jim Piva, *President*
Dusty Brown, *Treasurer*
Maureen Rabehl, *Executive*
Juli Elliott, *Finance Mgr*
Crystal Carle, *Accountant*
EMP: 147
SQ FT: 14,000
SALES (est): 11.6MM **Privately Held**
WEB: www.sdcea.net
SIC: 8641 7997 7992 7011 Homeowners' association; membership sports & recreation clubs; tennis club, membership; golf club, membership; boating & swimming clubs; public golf courses; vacation lodges; restaurant, family: independent; bar (drinking places)

(P-24640)
SAN FRANCISCO BAY AREA COUNCL
1001 Davis St, San Leandro (94577-1514)
PHONE..................510 577-9000
Kenneth Mehlhorn, *CEO*
Scott Evans, *Director*
Trish Ferenz, *Director*
EMP: 56 **EST:** 2008

SALES: 5.2MM **Privately Held**
SIC: 8641 Boy Scout organization

(P-24641)
SAN LUIS OBISPO COUNTY YMCA (PA)
1020 Southwood Dr, San Luis Obispo (93401-5813)
PHONE.....................805 543-8235
Monica Grant, *Exec Dir*
Lori Paris, *Human Res Dir*
Jennifer Vialpando, *Director*
EMP: 90
SQ FT: 2,500
SALES: 3.4MM **Privately Held**
WEB: www.sloymca.org
SIC: 8641 7991 8351 7032 Youth organizations; physical fitness facilities; child day care services; youth camps; individual & family services

(P-24642)
SAN MARCOS KIDS HELPNG KIDS FN
Also Called: Kid Helping Kids
4750 Hollister Ave, Santa Barbara (93110-1921)
PHONE.....................800 659-6411
James Devries, *President*
Isabel Huerta, *COO*
Dillon Stave, *Chief Mktg Ofcr*
Alexander Fell, *Director*
Chris Newton, *Director*
EMP: 147 EST: 2002
SALES: 229.5K **Privately Held**
SIC: 8641 Youth organizations

(P-24643)
SAN PABLO LODGE 43
342 Georgia St, Vallejo (94590-5907)
PHONE.....................707 642-1391
Al Hieb, *President*
EMP: 80
SALES (est): 976.5K **Privately Held**
SIC: 8641 Civic associations

(P-24644)
SAN YSIDRO SCHOOL DISTRICT
Also Called: Pta CA Congrss of Prnts
222 Avenida De La Madrid, San Ysidro (92173-1508)
PHONE.....................619 428-4424
Jose Torres, *Branch Mgr*
EMP: 61
SALES (corp-wide): 71.5MM **Privately Held**
SIC: 8641 Parent-teachers' association
PA: San Ysidro School District
4350 Otay Mesa Rd
San Ysidro CA 92173
619 428-9778

(P-24645)
SANTA ANA POLICE OFFICERS ASSN
1607 N Sycamore St, Santa Ana (92701-2352)
PHONE.....................714 836-1211
Mark R Nichols, *President*
Berg Alan, *Officer*
Brenda Vega, *Case Mgr*
EMP: 600
SQ FT: 10,157
SALES: 121.1K **Privately Held**
SIC: 8641 Civic social & fraternal associations

(P-24646)
SANTA CLARA VNGARD BOOSTER CLB
1795 Space Park Dr, Santa Clara (95054-3436)
PHONE.....................408 727-5532
Jeff Fiedler, *CEO*
Marc Hebert, *President*
Richard Lesher, *Treasurer*
Marie Bienkowski, *Vice Pres*
Linda Garbarino, *Admin Sec*
EMP: 50 EST: 1967
SQ FT: 21,000
SALES: 4.2MM **Privately Held**
WEB: www.scvanguard.com
SIC: 8641 Youth organizations

(P-24647)
SANTA MARIA VALLEY YMCA
3400 Skyway Dr, Santa Maria (93455-2504)
PHONE.....................805 937-8521
Shannon Seifert, *Director*
Cathy Mendez, *Volunteer Dir*
Dave Wright, *Treasurer*
Kevin James, *Admin Sec*
Andrea Gallardo, *Director*
EMP: 120
SQ FT: 22,000
SALES: 2.7MM **Privately Held**
WEB: www.smvymca.org
SIC: 8641 7991 8351 7032 Youth organizations; physical fitness facilities; child day care services; youth camps; individual & family services

(P-24648)
SANTA MNICA MNTINS TRILS CNCIL
24735 Mulholland Hwy, Woodland Hills (91302-2327)
P.O. Box 345, Agoura Hills (91376-0345)
PHONE.....................818 222-4531
Ruth Gerson, *President*
Anita Sneddon, *Treasurer*
Linda Palmer, *Vice Pres*
Georgia Farinella, *Admin Sec*
EMP: 100
SALES (est): 1.1MM **Privately Held**
WEB: www.smmtc.org
SIC: 8641 Environmental protection organization

(P-24649)
SANTA MONICA FAMILY YMCA
1332 6th St, Santa Monica (90401-1604)
P.O. Box 1160 (90406-1160)
PHONE.....................310 451-7387
Tara Pomposini, *Director*
Ana-Marie Schaefer, *Officer*
M Scotty, *CTO*
EMP: 80
SQ FT: 157,000
SALES: 5MM **Privately Held**
WEB: www.ymcasm.org
SIC: 8641 8351 8322 Youth organizations; recreation association; child day care services; individual & family services

(P-24650)
SANTEE SCHOOL DISTRICT
Also Called: Hill Creek Schl Ptsa Pta CA
9665 Jeremy St, Santee (92071-2836)
PHONE.....................619 956-5000
EMP: 57
SALES (corp-wide): 79MM **Privately Held**
SIC: 8641 Parent-teachers' association
PA: Santee School District
9625 Cuyamaca St
Santee CA 92071
619 258-2300

(P-24651)
SAVE OUR SUNOL
2934 Kilkare Rd, Sunol (94586-9428)
P.O. Box 501 (94586-0501)
PHONE.....................925 862-2263
Patricia Stillman, *President*
Lois Throop, *Treasurer*
Neil Davies, *Vice Pres*
Andrew Turnvull, *Admin Sec*
EMP: 100
SALES (est): 942.9K **Privately Held**
WEB: www.sunol.net
SIC: 8641 Environmental protection organization

(P-24652)
SCIOTS TRACT ASSOCIATION
937 Chestnut Ln, Davis (95616-2411)
PHONE.....................530 753-5219
Robert Monty, *Vice Pres*
Beverly Monty, *Admin Sec*
EMP: 80
SALES (est): 802.2K **Privately Held**
SIC: 8641 Social club, membership

(P-24653)
SCORPION ATHC BOOSTER CLB INC
300 E Esplanade Dr # 250, Oxnard (93036-1238)
PHONE.....................805 482-2005
Bob Graham, *CEO*
Martin Marietta, *Treasurer*
EMP: 50 EST: 2011
SALES: 280.1K **Privately Held**
SIC: 8641 Booster club

(P-24654)
SCRIPPS HEALTH
10010 Campus Point Dr, San Diego (92121-1518)
PHONE.....................858 678-6966
Chris Van Gorder, *President*
Jaimie Bottorf, *Human Resources*
EMP: 157
SALES (corp-wide): 2.1B **Privately Held**
SIC: 8641 Civic social & fraternal associations
PA: Scripps Health
10140 Campus Point Dr Ax415
San Diego CA 92121
800 727-4777

(P-24655)
SCRIPPS HEALTH
9850 Genesee Ave Ste 900, La Jolla (92037-1220)
PHONE.....................858 452-1279
EMP: 188
SALES (corp-wide): 2.1B **Privately Held**
SIC: 8641 Civic social & fraternal associations
PA: Scripps Health
10140 Campus Point Dr Ax415
San Diego CA 92121
800 727-4777

(P-24656)
SELF HELP ENTERPRISES (PA)
Also Called: S H E
8445 W Elowin Ct, Visalia (93291-9262)
P.O. Box 6520 (93290-6520)
PHONE.....................559 651-1000
Thomas Collishaw, *President*
Kathy Long-Tence, *CFO*
EMP: 75
SQ FT: 15,000
SALES: 27.9MM **Privately Held**
SIC: 8641 Dwelling-related associations

(P-24657)
SIERRA CLUB (PA)
Also Called: SIERRA CLUB BOOKS
2101 Webster St Ste 1300, Oakland (94612-3546)
PHONE.....................415 977-5500
Robin Mann, *President*
Trey Pollard, *President*
Jennifer Trahan, *COO*
Donna Buell, *Treasurer*
Allison Chin, *Treasurer*
EMP: 175 EST: 1892
SQ FT: 43,500
SALES: 141.3MM **Privately Held**
WEB: www.youngboglelaw.com
SIC: 8641 8399 Environmental protection organization; advocacy group

(P-24658)
SIERRA MASONIC ASSOCIATION
Also Called: Sierra Lodge 788
2166 Hwy 49, Oakhurst (93644)
P.O. Box 805 (93644-0805)
PHONE.....................559 683-7713
William Bastian, *Admin Sec*
EMP: 78
SALES (est): 724.8K **Privately Held**
SIC: 8641 Civic associations

(P-24659)
SIGNAL HEALTH POLICE DEPT
2745 Walnut Ave, Signal Hill (90755-1831)
PHONE.....................562 989-7200
Christopher Nunley, *Chief*
EMP: 50
SALES (est): 45.5K **Privately Held**
SIC: 8641 Civic social & fraternal associations

(P-24660)
SILICON VLY CMNTY FOUNDATION
Also Called: Svcf
2440 W El Cmino Real Ste, Mountain View (94040)
PHONE.....................650 450-5400
Nicole Taylor, *President*
Emmett Carson, *CEO*
Vera Bennett, *CFO*
Marla Betsch, *Officer*
Chuck Brown, *Officer*
EMP: 120 EST: 2006
SALES (est): 11MM **Privately Held**
SIC: 8641 Civic social & fraternal associations

(P-24661)
SILICON VLY MNTREY BAY CNCIL I (PA)
970 W Julian St, San Jose (95126-2719)
PHONE.....................408 279-2086
Jason Stein, *Exec Dir*
EMP: 68
SQ FT: 10,000
SALES: 9.5MM **Privately Held**
WEB: www.sccc-scouting.org
SIC: 8641 5699 5941 Boy Scout organization; uniforms; camping & backpacking equipment

(P-24662)
SILVER LAKES ASSOCIATION
Also Called: Homeowners Association
15273 Orchard Hill Ln, Helendale (92342-7824)
P.O. Box 179 (92342-0179)
PHONE.....................760 245-1606
Michael Bennett, *General Mgr*
Mike Keith, *Officer*
Britainy Hijoe, *Administration*
Elizabeth Hernandez, *Controller*
Mellisa Smith, *Human Res Mgr*
EMP: 90
SQ FT: 3,000
SALES (est): 5MM **Privately Held**
WEB: www.silverlakesassociation.com
SIC: 8641 Homeowners' association

(P-24663)
SONOMA VALLEY WOMANS CLUB
574 1st St E, Sonoma (95476-6753)
PHONE.....................707 938-8313
Carmella A Greco, *Principal*
EMP: 70
SQ FT: 3,216
SALES: 56.8K **Privately Held**
SIC: 8641 Civic associations

(P-24664)
SPYGLASS HILL COMMUNITY ASSN
39 Argonaut Ste 100, Aliso Viejo (92656-4152)
P.O. Box 57063, Irvine (92619-7063)
PHONE.....................949 855-1800
Susan Larson, *President*
EMP: 50
SALES: 497.4K **Privately Held**
SIC: 8641 Homeowners' association

(P-24665)
SUN CITY PALM DSERT CMNTY ASSN (PA)
Also Called: Palm Desert Community Assn
38180 Del Webb Blvd, Palm Desert (92211-1256)
PHONE.....................760 200-2100
Helen McEnerney, *President*
Flor Limon, *Human Res Mgr*
Vanessa Schussler, *Opers Staff*
EMP: 80
SQ FT: 4,000
SALES (est): 7.7MM **Privately Held**
SIC: 8641 7992 7997 Dwelling-related associations; public golf courses; country club, membership

PRODUCTS & SVCS

(P-24666)
SUN LAKES CNTRY CLUB HMEOWNRS
850 Country Club Dr, Banning
(92220-5306)
PHONE..................................951 845-2135
Tim Taylor, *Manager*
EMP: 100
SALES: 23.3K **Privately Held**
SIC: 8641 Homeowners' association

(P-24667)
SUTTER CLUB INC
1220 9th St, Sacramento (95814-4897)
PHONE..................................916 442-0456
Tom Narozonick, *General Mgr*
EMP: 75
SQ FT: 45,000
SALES: 4.1MM **Privately Held**
WEB: www.sutterclub.com
SIC: 8641 Social club, membership

(P-24668)
SUTTER HEALTH
1301 Mission St, Santa Cruz (95060-3530)
PHONE..................................831 458-6310
Roger A Larsen, *President*
Brian Alexander, *Officer*
Anna R Matelski, *Executive Asst*
Andrew Kim, *Admin Sec*
Diana Riley, *Admin Sec*
EMP: 147
SALES (corp-wide): 12.7B **Privately Held**
SIC: 8641 Civic social & fraternal associations
PA: Sutter Health
2200 River Plaza Dr
Sacramento CA 95833
916 733-8800

(P-24669)
SUTTER HEALTH
2950 Research Park Dr, Soquel
(95073-2000)
PHONE..................................831 458-6272
Paul Krause, *Otolaryngology*
Scott Imahara, *Plastic Surgeon*
EMP: 353
SALES (corp-wide): 12.7B **Privately Held**
SIC: 8641 Civic social & fraternal associations
PA: Sutter Health
2200 River Plaza Dr
Sacramento CA 95833
916 733-8800

(P-24670)
SUTTER HEALTH
520 W I St, Los Banos (93635-3419)
PHONE..................................209 827-4866
Lena Reza, *Office Mgr*
Alex Gutierrez, *Opers Staff*
EMP: 147
SALES (corp-wide): 12.7B **Privately Held**
SIC: 8641 Civic social & fraternal associations
PA: Sutter Health
2200 River Plaza Dr
Sacramento CA 95833
916 733-8800

(P-24671)
SUTTER HEALTH
Also Called: Gyneclgic Onclogy Plvic Srgery
360 Dardanelli Ln Ste 2d, Los Gatos
(95032-1421)
PHONE..................................408 523-3900
EMP: 163
SALES (corp-wide): 12.7B **Privately Held**
SIC: 8641 Civic social & fraternal associations
PA: Sutter Health
2200 River Plaza Dr
Sacramento CA 95833
916 733-8800

(P-24672)
SUTTER HEALTH
2880 Soquel Ave, Santa Cruz
(95062-1423)
PHONE..................................831 458-5500
Kathleen McNupp, *Branch Mgr*
Julie Gillham,
Arthur Vedder, *Director*
EMP: 174

SALES (corp-wide): 12.7B **Privately Held**
SIC: 8641 Civic social & fraternal associations
PA: Sutter Health
2200 River Plaza Dr
Sacramento CA 95833
916 733-8800

(P-24673)
SUTTER HEALTH
1025 Atlantic Ave Ste 100, Alameda
(94501-1187)
PHONE..................................916 286-6665
EMP: 177
SALES (corp-wide): 12.7B **Privately Held**
SIC: 8641 Civic social & fraternal associations
PA: Sutter Health
2200 River Plaza Dr
Sacramento CA 95833
916 733-8800

(P-24674)
SUTTER REGIONAL MED FOUNDATION
127 Hospital Dr Ste 102, Vallejo
(94589-2500)
PHONE..................................707 551-3616
Bobbi Underhill, *Principal*
EMP: 70
SALES (corp-wide): 28.5MM **Privately Held**
SIC: 8641 Civic social & fraternal associations
PA: Sutter Regional Medical Foundation Inc
2702 Low Ct
Fairfield CA 94534
707 427-4900

(P-24675)
TABLE COMMUNITY FOUDATION
3201 W Benjamin Holt Dr, Stockton
(95219-3741)
PHONE..................................209 951-1753
Tyronne Gross Jr, *President*
EMP: 92
SALES (est): 361.7K **Privately Held**
SIC: 8641 Youth organizations

(P-24676)
TAHOE DONNER ASSOCIATION
12790 Northwoods Blvd, Truckee
(96161-6334)
PHONE..................................530 587-9437
Leighanne Gachowski, *Vice Pres*
David Gravell, *General Mgr*
Bettye Carmichael, *Admin Sec*
Annie Rosenfeldt, *Human Res Mgr*
EMP: 109
SALES (corp-wide): 18.1MM **Privately Held**
SIC: 8641 Homeowners' association
PA: Tahoe Donner Association
11509 Northwoods Blvd
Truckee CA 96161
530 587-9400

(P-24677)
TAMARACK BCH CONDO OWNERS ASSN
3200 Carlsbad Blvd, Carlsbad
(92008-3101)
PHONE..................................760 729-3500
Connie Bloem, *President*
EMP: 50
SQ FT: 2,000
SALES (est): 857K **Privately Held**
SIC: 8641 Homeowner's association

(P-24678)
TECHSOUP GLOBAL (PA)
Also Called: Tech Soup
435 Brannan St Ste 100, San Francisco
(94107-1780)
PHONE..................................800 659-3579
Rebecca Masisak, *CEO*
James Hebert, *CFO*
Marnie Webb, *Co-CEO*
Daniel Ben-Horin, *Principal*
Joe Tate, *Admin Asst*
EMP: 114
SALES: 30.5MM **Privately Held**
WEB: www.techsoup.org
SIC: 8641 Social associations

(P-24679)
TEMPLE CITY YOUTH DEV FUND
6415 N Muscatel Ave, San Gabriel
(91775-1845)
PHONE..................................626 548-5085
Kathy Perini, *Principal*
EMP: 68
SALES (est): 758.1K **Privately Held**
SIC: 8641 Youth organizations

(P-24680)
THEAT AND ARTS FOUND OF SAN DI
Also Called: LA JOLLA PLAYHOUSE
2910 La Jolla Village Dr, La Jolla
(92093-5100)
P.O. Box 12039 (92039-2039)
PHONE..................................858 623-3366
Jeffrey Ressler, *Chairman*
Steven Libman, *President*
Michael L Eagle, *CEO*
Lynelle Lynch, *Chairman*
Tim Scott, *Chairman*
EMP: 250
SQ FT: 1,440
SALES: 21.8MM **Privately Held**
WEB: www.lajollaplayhouse.com
SIC: 8641 7922 Civic associations; theatrical producers & services

(P-24681)
TIERRA DEL ORO GIRL SCOUT CNSL
6601 Elvas Ave, Sacramento (95819-4339)
PHONE..................................916 452-9174
Pamela Saltenberger, *Exec Dir*
EMP: 84
SQ FT: 12,200
SALES: 8.1MM **Privately Held**
WEB: www.tdogs.org
SIC: 8641 Girl Scout organization

(P-24682)
TWAIN HARTE HORSEMEN
23580 View Ln, Columbia (95310)
P.O. Box 1326, Twain Harte (95383-1326)
PHONE..................................209 586-4841
EMP: 80
SALES: 12.3K **Privately Held**
SIC: 8641 Civic social & fraternal associations

(P-24683)
UNITED STATES MARINES YOUTH FD
90 La Venta Dr, Santa Barbara
(93110-1716)
PHONE..................................805 967-7990
EMP: 54
SALES (corp-wide): 105.9K **Privately Held**
WEB: www.usmc.mil
SIC: 8641 Veterans' organization
PA: Marine Corps League
3619 Jefferson Davis Hwy # 115
Stafford VA 22554
703 207-9588

(P-24684)
UNIVERSITY STDNT UN CAL STATE
18111 Nordhoff St, Northridge
(91330-0001)
PHONE..................................818 677-2251
Debra Hammond, *Exec Dir*
Stephen Thomas, *CFO*
Charity Chia, *Officer*
Joseph Illuminate, *Associate Dir*
Scottie Schorn, *Associate Dir*
EMP: 450
SQ FT: 350,000
SALES: 17.2MM **Privately Held**
SIC: 8641 Civic social & fraternal associations

(P-24685)
VALLEY HUNT CLUB
520 S Orange Grove Blvd, Pasadena
(91105-1799)
PHONE..................................626 793-7134
David Mole, *CEO*
Donald F Crumrine, *COO*
Katherine Hughes, *Accountant*
Bill Roemer, *Controller*
Tayde Lomas, *Human Res Dir*

EMP: 85
SQ FT: 40,000
SALES: 8.8MM **Privately Held**
WEB: www.valleyhuntclub.com
SIC: 8641 Social club, membership

(P-24686)
VENTURA COUNTY FIRE DEPARTMENT
165 Durley Ave, Camarillo (93010-8586)
PHONE..................................805 389-9710
Mark Lorensen, *Chief*
Pamela Mack, *Human Res Mgr*
EMP: 50
SALES (est): 1.6MM **Privately Held**
SIC: 8641 Civic social & fraternal associations

(P-24687)
VENTURA COUNTY OFFICE EDUCATN
1379 Oakridge Ct, Thousand Oaks
(91362-1923)
PHONE..................................805 495-7037
EMP: 77 **Privately Held**
SIC: 8641
PA: Ventura County Office Of Education
5189 Verdugo Way
Camarillo CA 93012
805 383-1900

(P-24688)
VETERANS MEDICAL RESEARCH FUND
3350 La Jolla Village Dr, San Diego
(92161-0002)
PHONE..................................858 642-3080
Kerstin B Lynam, *CEO*
Barabara Dovenbarger, *CFO*
EMP: 250
SALES: 19.9MM **Privately Held**
WEB: www.vapop.ucsd.edu
SIC: 8641 Civic social & fraternal associations

(P-24689)
VFW POST 6476
1789 N 8th St, Colton (92324-1303)
PHONE..................................909 754-3828
Joe Quioz, *Principal*
EMP: 130
SALES (est): 540K **Privately Held**
SIC: 8641 Veterans' organization

(P-24690)
VICTOR VALLEY MOOSE LODGE NO
10230 E Ave, Hesperia (92345-7615)
P.O. Box 402277 (92340-2277)
PHONE..................................760 244-1808
Douglas Padua, *President*
EMP: 140
SQ FT: 9,500
SALES (est): 185.9K **Privately Held**
SIC: 8641 7041 Civic associations; fraternities & sororities

(P-24691)
VIETNAM VETERANS OF SAN DIEGO (PA)
Also Called: Veterans Village of San Diego
4141 Pacific Hwy, San Diego (92110-2030)
PHONE..................................619 497-0142
Phil Landis, *President*
Andre Simpson, *COO*
Harry Guess, *CFO*
EMP: 65
SQ FT: 35,719
SALES: 10.6MM **Privately Held**
WEB: www.vvsd.net
SIC: 8641 Veterans' organization

(P-24692)
VIETNMS-MRCAN YUTH ALANCE CORP
Also Called: Vaya
7968 Arjons Dr Ste 109, San Diego
(92126-6362)
P.O. Box 711912 (92171-1912)
PHONE..................................619 320-8292
Hien Nguyen, *President*
EMP: 50

SALES: 101K **Privately Held**
SIC: **8641** Civic social & fraternal associations

(P-24693)
VILLA BALBOA COMMUNITY ASSOC
22 Mauchly, Irvine (92618-2306)
P.O. Box 4708 (92616-4708)
PHONE..949 450-1515
Janice Walley, *President*
EMP: 65
SALES (est): 797.3K **Privately Held**
SIC: **8641** Homeowners' association

(P-24694)
VILLA MARIN HOMEOWNERS ASSN
Also Called: Villa Mrin Rtrement Residences
100 Thorndale Dr, San Rafael
(94903-4599)
PHONE..415 499-8711
Danel Walker, *CEO*
Dan Walker, *CEO*
EMP: 170
SQ FT: 500,000
SALES: 11.7MM **Privately Held**
SIC: **8641** 8051 8059 Homeowners' association; skilled nursing care facilities; personal care home, with health care

(P-24695)
VINTAGE CLUB MASTER ASSN INC
75001 Vintage Dr W, Indian Wells
(92210-7304)
PHONE..760 340-0500
Art Allen, *Exec Dir*
Red Scott, *President*
EMP: 60
SALES: 3MM **Privately Held**
SIC: **8641** Homeowners' association

(P-24696)
WEST END YUNG MNS CHRISTN ASSN
Also Called: Ontario/Montclair YMCA
1257 E D St, Ontario (91764)
P.O. Box 3220 (91761-0922)
PHONE..909 477-2780
Dianna Lee-Mitchell, *Director*
EMP: 80
SALES (corp-wide): 3.5MM **Privately Held**
WEB: www.westendymca.org
SIC: **8641** 7991 8351 7032 Youth organizations; physical fitness facilities; child day care services; youth camps; individual & family services
PA: West End Young Men's Christian Association Inc
    1150 E Foothill Blvd
    Upland CA 91786
    909 481-0722

(P-24697)
WJC TRAPP ELEMENTARY PTA
2750 N Riverside Ave, Rialto (92377-3983)
PHONE..909 820-7914
Danielle Osoenduagwik, *Principal*
EMP: 50
SALES (est): 565.4K **Privately Held**
SIC: **8641** Parent-teachers' association

(P-24698)
WOODBRIDGE VILLAGE ASSOCIATION
31 Creek Rd, Irvine (92604-4793)
PHONE..949 786-1800
Kevin Chudy, *Exec Dir*
Bertha Rivera, *Admin Sec*
Ray Serna, *Corp Comm Staff*
Santiago Arteaga, *Maintence Staff*
Anne Sheldon,
EMP: 65
SQ FT: 15,000
SALES: 10.2MM **Privately Held**
WEB: www.wva.org
SIC: **8641** Homeowners' association

(P-24699)
WOODLAND SWIM TEAM BOSTERS CLB
155 West St, Woodland (95695-3162)
P.O. Box 763 (95776-0763)
PHONE..530 662-9783
EMP: 60
SALES: 125.2K **Privately Held**
SIC: **8641**

(P-24700)
Y W C A OF SONOMA COUNTY
Also Called: YWCA
811 3rd St Ste 100, Santa Rosa
(95404-4541)
P.O. Box 3506 (95402-3506)
PHONE..707 546-9922
Madeline O'Connell, *Exec Dir*
Julie Lafranchi, *General Mgr*
Jennifer Lake, *General Mgr*
Wendy Adams, *Director*
Doreen Lorinczi, *Director*
EMP: 50
SALES: 2.1MM **Privately Held**
SIC: **8641** 7991 8351 7032 Youth organizations; physical fitness facilities; child day care services; youth camps; individual & family services

(P-24701)
YMCA OF EAST VALLEY (PA)
500 E Citrus Ave, Redlands (92373-5285)
PHONE..909 798-9622
Darwin Barnett, *CEO*
Ken Stein, *CEO*
Kevin Pearson, *COO*
Doug Thorne, *CFO*
Perry Mecate, *Vice Pres*
EMP: 125 EST: 1887
SQ FT: 100,000
SALES: 12.9MM **Privately Held**
WEB: www.ymcaofredlands.com
SIC: **8641** Youth organizations

(P-24702)
YMCA OF EAST VALLEY
Also Called: San Bernardino Family YMCA
808 E 21st St, San Bernardino
(92404-4874)
PHONE..909 881-9622
Bill Blank, *Director*
Darrell Black, *Director*
EMP: 50
SALES (corp-wide): 12.9MM **Privately Held**
WEB: www.ymcaofredlands.com
SIC: **8641** 7991 8351 7032 Youth organizations; physical fitness facilities; child day care services; youth camps; individual & family services
PA: Ymca Of The East Valley
    500 E Citrus Ave
    Redlands CA 92373
    909 798-9622

(P-24703)
YMCA OF EAST VALLEY
7793 Central Ave, Highland (92346-4106)
PHONE..909 425-9622
Ursula Walsh, *Branch Mgr*
EMP: 50
SALES (corp-wide): 12.9MM **Privately Held**
WEB: www.ymcaofredlands.com
SIC: **8641** 7991 8351 7032 Youth organizations; physical fitness facilities; child day care services; youth camps; individual & family services
PA: Ymca Of The East Valley
    500 E Citrus Ave
    Redlands CA 92373
    909 798-9622

(P-24704)
YMCA OF NORTH ORANGE COUNTY
Also Called: North Orange Cnty Fmly Y M C A
2000 Youth Way, Fullerton (92835-3878)
PHONE..714 879-9622
Jim Lapak, *Exec Dir*
Clare McKenna, *Director*
Claire Akenna, *Manager*
EMP: 85
SQ FT: 10,000

SALES (est): 1.1MM **Privately Held**
SIC: **8641** 7991 8351 7032 Youth organizations; physical fitness facilities; child day care services; youth camps; individual & family services

(P-24705)
YMCA OF SAN DIEGO COUNTY
Also Called: Y M C A Childcare Resource Ser
1310 Union Plaza Ct # 200, Oceanside
(92054-5604)
PHONE..760 754-6042
Job Moraido, *Branch Mgr*
EMP: 76
SALES (corp-wide): 170.6MM **Privately Held**
WEB: www.ymcacrs.org
SIC: **8641** 7991 8351 7032 Youth organizations; physical fitness facilities; child day care services; youth camps; individual & family services
PA: Ymca Of San Diego County
    3708 Ruffin Rd
    San Diego CA 92123
    858 292-9622

(P-24706)
YMCA OF SAN DIEGO COUNTY
Also Called: La Jolla YMCA
8355 Cliffridge Ave, La Jolla (92037-2107)
PHONE..858 453-3483
Sam Wurtzbacher, *Director*
EMP: 200
SALES (corp-wide): 170.6MM **Privately Held**
WEB: www.ymcacrs.org
SIC: **8641** 8351 7997 Youth organizations; child day care services; membership sports & recreation clubs
PA: Ymca Of San Diego County
    3708 Ruffin Rd
    San Diego CA 92123
    858 292-9622

(P-24707)
YMCA OF SAN DIEGO COUNTY (PA)
Also Called: Y, THE
3708 Ruffin Rd, San Diego (92123-1812)
PHONE..858 292-9622
Baron Herdelin Doherty, *CEO*
Charmaine Carter, *CFO*
John Merritt, *Senior VP*
Shelly McTighe-Rippeng, *Vice Pres*
Ronald Lelakes, *Exec Dir*
EMP: 116
SQ FT: 19,600
SALES: 170.6MM **Privately Held**
WEB: www.ymcacrs.org
SIC: **8641** Youth organizations

(P-24708)
YMCA OF SAN DIEGO COUNTY
Also Called: Pelomar Family YMCA
1050 N Broadway, Escondido
(92026-3044)
PHONE..760 745-7490
Alfredo Velasco, *Manager*
EMP: 500
SALES (corp-wide): 170.6MM **Privately Held**
WEB: www.ymcacrs.org
SIC: **8641** 7991 8351 7032 Youth organizations; physical fitness facilities; child day care services; youth camps; individual & family services
PA: Ymca Of San Diego County
    3708 Ruffin Rd
    San Diego CA 92123
    858 292-9622

(P-24709)
YMCA OF SAN DIEGO COUNTY
8881 Dallas St, La Mesa (91942-3297)
PHONE..619 464-1323
Steve Rowe, *Exec Dir*
EMP: 76
SALES (corp-wide): 170.6MM **Privately Held**
WEB: www.ymcacrs.org
SIC: **8641** 7991 8351 7032 Youth organizations; physical fitness facilities; child day care services; youth camps; individual & family services

PA: Ymca Of San Diego County
    3708 Ruffin Rd
    San Diego CA 92123
    858 292-9622

(P-24710)
YMCA OF SAN DIEGO COUNTY
Also Called: Magdalena Ecke Family YMCA
200 Saxony Rd, Encinitas (92024-2720)
PHONE..858 292-4034
Susan J Cocke, *Branch Mgr*
EMP: 76
SALES (corp-wide): 170.6MM **Privately Held**
WEB: www.ymcacrs.org
SIC: **8641** 8351 8322 7997 Youth organizations; child day care services; youth center; membership sports & recreation clubs
PA: Ymca Of San Diego County
    3708 Ruffin Rd
    San Diego CA 92123
    858 292-9622

(P-24711)
YMCA OF SAN DIEGO COUNTY
Also Called: YMCA Youth & Family Services
2927 Meade Ave, San Diego (92116-4251)
PHONE..619 281-8313
Cesar Marcano, *Exec Dir*
EMP: 72
SALES (corp-wide): 170.6MM **Privately Held**
SIC: **8641** 7991 8351 7032 Youth organizations; physical fitness facilities; child day care services; youth camps; individual & family services
PA: Ymca Of San Diego County
    3708 Ruffin Rd
    San Diego CA 92123
    858 292-9622

(P-24712)
YMCA OF SAN DIEGO COUNTY
Also Called: Peninsula Family YMCA Sunshine
2150 Beryl St Ste 18, San Diego
(92109-3617)
PHONE..619 226-8888
Andrea Sanchez, *Director*
EMP: 75
SQ FT: 3,500
SALES (corp-wide): 170.6MM **Privately Held**
WEB: www.ymcacrs.org
SIC: **8641** 8322 Youth organizations; individual & family services
PA: Ymca Of San Diego County
    3708 Ruffin Rd
    San Diego CA 92123
    858 292-9622

(P-24713)
YMCA OF SAN DIEGO COUNTY
Also Called: YMCA Child Care Resource Svcs
3333 Camino Del Rio S # 120, San Diego
(92108-3836)
PHONE..619 521-3055
Debbie Macdonald, *Director*
EMP: 180
SALES (corp-wide): 170.6MM **Privately Held**
WEB: www.ymcacrs.org
SIC: **8641** 7991 8351 7032 Youth organizations; physical fitness facilities; child day care services; youth camps; individual & family services
PA: Ymca Of San Diego County
    3708 Ruffin Rd
    San Diego CA 92123
    858 292-9622

(P-24714)
YMCA OF SAN DIEGO COUNTY
Also Called: YMCA Overnight Camp
4761 Pine Hills Rd, Julian (92036)
P.O. Box 2440 (92036-2440)
PHONE..760 765-0642
Thomas Madeyski, *Exec Dir*
EMP: 50

PRODUCTS & SVCS

SALES (corp-wide): 170.6MM **Privately Held**
WEB: www.ymcacrs.org
SIC: **8641** 7991 8351 7032 Youth organizations; physical fitness facilities; child day care services; youth camps; individual & family services
PA: Ymca Of San Diego County
　　3708 Ruffin Rd
　　San Diego CA 92123
　　858 292-9622

(P-24715)
YMCA OF SAN DIEGO COUNTY
Also Called: Mission Valley YMCA
5505 Friars Rd, San Diego (92110-2682)
PHONE..................................619 298-3576
Dick Webster, *Manager*
EMP: 200
SALES (corp-wide): 170.6MM **Privately Held**
WEB: www.ymcacrs.org
SIC: **8641** 7997 Youth organizations; membership sports & recreation clubs
PA: Ymca Of San Diego County
　　3708 Ruffin Rd
　　San Diego CA 92123
　　858 292-9622

(P-24716)
YMCA OF SAN DIEGO COUNTY
Also Called: Cameron Family YMCA
10123 Riverwalk Dr, Santee (92071-5295)
PHONE..................................619 449-9622
Steve Rowe, *Branch Mgr*
EMP: 100
SQ FT: 32,970
SALES (corp-wide): 170.6MM **Privately Held**
WEB: www.ymcacrs.org
SIC: **8641** 8322 Youth organizations; individual & family services
PA: Ymca Of San Diego County
　　3708 Ruffin Rd
　　San Diego CA 92123
　　858 292-9622

(P-24717)
YMCA OF SAN DIEGO COUNTY
Also Called: Joe & Mary Mottino YMCA
4701 Mesa Dr, Oceanside (92056-6568)
PHONE..................................760 758-0808
Jeff Guzzardo, *Branch Mgr*
Kate Winzenburg, *Sales Executive*
Gary Wegener, *Director*
Brent Ayers, *Manager*
EMP: 100
SALES (corp-wide): 170.6MM **Privately Held**
WEB: www.ymcacrs.org
SIC: **8641** 8322 Youth organizations; individual & family services
PA: Ymca Of San Diego County
　　3708 Ruffin Rd
　　San Diego CA 92123
　　858 292-9622

(P-24718)
YMCA OF SAN DIEGO COUNTY
Also Called: Santa Margarita YMCA Garrison
333 Garrison St, Oceanside (92054-4700)
PHONE..................................760 757-8270
Margie Oliver, *Branch Mgr*
EMP: 76
SALES (corp-wide): 170.6MM **Privately Held**
WEB: www.ymcacrs.org
SIC: **8641** 7991 8351 7032 Youth organizations; physical fitness facilities; child day care services; youth camps; individual & family services
PA: Ymca Of San Diego County
　　3708 Ruffin Rd
　　San Diego CA 92123
　　858 292-9622

(P-24719)
YMCA OF SAN JOAQUIN COUNTY
2105 W March Ln Ste 1, Stockton (95207-6422)
PHONE..................................209 472-9622
Dan Chapman, *CEO*
Julia Verduzco, *Finance Dir*
Sam Prak, *Finance*
Isela Robles, *Manager*

EMP: 70
SQ FT: 2,000
SALES: 3MM **Privately Held**
WEB: www.ymcasjc.org
SIC: **8641** Social club, membership; youth organizations

(P-24720)
YMCA OF SILICON VALLEY (PA)
80 Saratoga Ave, Santa Clara (95051-7303)
PHONE..................................408 351-6400
Kathy Riggins, *President*
Tom Nelson, *COO*
Ed Barrantes, *CFO*
Karla Jessup, *Officer*
Judy Hayner, *Exec VP*
EMP: 60 EST: 1867
SQ FT: 5,000
SALES: 74.7MM **Privately Held**
WEB: www.scvymca.org
SIC: **8641** 7991 8351 7032 Youth organizations; physical fitness facilities; child day care services; youth camps; individual & family services

(P-24721)
YMCA OF SILICON VALLEY
1922 The Alameda Ste 300, San Jose (95126-1430)
PHONE..................................650 493-9622
EMP: 300
SALES (corp-wide): 74.7MM **Privately Held**
SIC: **8641** 7991 8351 7032 Youth organizations; physical fitness facilities; child day care services; youth camps; individual & family services
PA: Ymca Of Silicon Valley
　　80 Saratoga Ave
　　Santa Clara CA 95051
　　408 351-6400

(P-24722)
YMCA OF SILICON VALLEY
Also Called: Central Branch YMCA
1717 The Alameda, San Jose (95126-1794)
PHONE..................................408 298-1717
Barbara Cardinez, *Manager*
Sarah Shea, *Director*
EMP: 150
SQ FT: 52,715
SALES (corp-wide): 74.7MM **Privately Held**
WEB: www.scvymca.org
SIC: **8641** 8351 8322 7997 Youth organizations; child day care services; individual & family services; membership sports & recreation clubs; physical fitness facilities
PA: Ymca Of Silicon Valley
　　80 Saratoga Ave
　　Santa Clara CA 95051
　　408 351-6400

(P-24723)
YMCA OF SILICON VALLEY
Also Called: El Camino YMCA
2400 Grant Rd, Mountain View (94040-4324)
PHONE..................................650 969-9622
Elaine Glissmeyer, *Director*
EMP: 300
SALES (corp-wide): 74.7MM **Privately Held**
SIC: **8641** 7991 8351 7032 Youth organizations; physical fitness facilities; child day care services; youth camps; individual & family services
PA: Ymca Of Silicon Valley
　　80 Saratoga Ave
　　Santa Clara CA 95051
　　408 351-6400

(P-24724)
YMCA OF SILICON VALLEY
Also Called: YMCA of Santa Clara Valley
5632 Santa Teresa Blvd, San Jose (95123-2698)
PHONE..................................408 226-9622
Rick Valdez, *Exec Dir*
EMP: 60

SALES (corp-wide): 74.7MM **Privately Held**
WEB: www.scvymca.org
SIC: **8641** 7991 8351 7032 Youth organizations; physical fitness facilities; child day care services; youth camps; individual & family services
PA: Ymca Of Silicon Valley
　　80 Saratoga Ave
　　Santa Clara CA 95051
　　408 351-6400

(P-24725)
YMCA OF THE MID-PENINSULA INC
1922 The Alameda Ste 300, San Jose (95126-1430)
PHONE..................................650 493-9622
Kathy Riggins, *CEO*
Elizabeth Jordan, *COO*
Ron Fior, *Treasurer*
Jim Sandstrom, *Admin Sec*
EMP: 300
SQ FT: 6,000
SALES (est): 1.2MM **Privately Held**
SIC: **8641** 7991 8351 7032 Youth organizations; physical fitness facilities; child day care services; youth camps; individual & family services

(P-24726)
YOSEMITE LAKES OWNERS ASSN
30250 Yosemite Springs Pk, Coarsegold (93614-9369)
PHONE..................................559 658-7466
Steve Payne, *General Mgr*
John Nino, *Info Tech Mgr*
EMP: 70 EST: 1970
SQ FT: 10,000
SALES (est): 2.8MM **Privately Held**
WEB: www.yloa.org
SIC: **8641** Homeowners' association

(P-24727)
YOUNG MENS CHRISTIAN (PA)
Also Called: YMCA
321 E Magnolia Blvd, Burbank (91502-1132)
PHONE..................................818 845-8551
JC Holt, *CEO*
Brandon Mullins, *Director*
EMP: 174 EST: 1924
SQ FT: 47,000
SALES: 5.9MM **Privately Held**
SIC: **8641** 7991 8351 7032 Youth organizations; physical fitness facilities; child day care services; youth camps; individual & family services

(P-24728)
YOUNG MENS CHRISTIAN ASSNSF
Also Called: Presido YMCA
63 Funston Ave, San Francisco (94129-1110)
PHONE..................................415 447-9622
Robert Sindelar, *Exec Dir*
Sean Dries, *Director*
EMP: 86
SALES (corp-wide): 82.8MM **Privately Held**
SIC: **8641** 7999 Youth organizations; tennis services & professionals
PA: Young Men's Christian Association Of San Francisco
　　50 California St Ste 650
　　San Francisco CA 94111
　　415 777-9622

(P-24729)
YOUNG MENS CHRISTIAN ASSNSF
Also Called: YMCA Youth & Family Service
1115 3rd St, San Rafael (94901-3017)
PHONE..................................415 459-9622
Don Carney, *Exec Dir*
EMP: 200
SALES (corp-wide): 82.8MM **Privately Held**
SIC: **8641** 7991 8351 7032 Youth organizations; physical fitness facilities; child day care services; youth camps; individual & family services

PA: Young Men's Christian Association Of San Francisco
　　50 California St Ste 650
　　San Francisco CA 94111
　　415 777-9622

(P-24730)
YOUNG MENS CHRISTIAN ASSO
4031 N Moorpark Rd, Thousand Oaks (91360-2660)
PHONE..................................805 523-7613
Kelly Dulek, *Director*
EMP: 100
SALES (corp-wide): 10.2MM **Privately Held**
SIC: **8641** 7997 8351 Youth organizations; membership sports & recreation clubs; child day care services
PA: Young Men's Christian Association Of Southeast Ventura County
　　31105 E Thusand Oaks Blvd
　　Thousand Oaks CA 91362
　　805 497-3081

(P-24731)
YOUNG MENS CHRISTIAN ASSOC (PA)
Also Called: ANAHEIM FAMILY YMCA
240 S Euclid St, Anaheim (92802-1047)
PHONE..................................714 635-9622
Rick Martens, *CEO*
Joan Cirafic, *CFO*
John Guustaferro, *Vice Pres*
Debbie Jauch, *Vice Pres*
Lizeth Casasola, *Hum Res Coord*
EMP: 450 EST: 1911
SQ FT: 9,000
SALES: 10.8MM **Privately Held**
SIC: **8641** Youth organizations; recreation association

(P-24732)
YOUNG MENS CHRISTIAN ASSOC SF
Also Called: Argonne YMCA After School
680 18th Ave, San Francisco (94121-3823)
PHONE..................................415 831-4093
Robin Sharp, *Manager*
EMP: 86
SALES (corp-wide): 82.8MM **Privately Held**
SIC: **8641** 7991 8351 7032 Youth organizations; physical fitness facilities; child day care services; youth camps; individual & family services
PA: Young Men's Christian Association Of San Francisco
　　50 California St Ste 650
　　San Francisco CA 94111
　　415 777-9622

(P-24733)
YOUNG MENS CHRISTIAN ASSOC SF
Also Called: Presidio Community YMCA
57 Post St, San Francisco (94104-5003)
PHONE..................................415 447-9602
EMP: 86
SALES (corp-wide): 82.8MM **Privately Held**
SIC: **8641** 7999 Youth organizations; swimming instruction
PA: Young Men's Christian Association Of San Francisco
　　50 California St Ste 650
　　San Francisco CA 94111
　　415 777-9622

(P-24734)
YOUNG MENS CHRISTIAN ASSOC SF
Also Called: Peninsula YMCA
1877 S Grant St, San Mateo (94402-2647)
PHONE..................................650 286-9622
Rachel Del Monte, *Manager*
Patrizia Guiotto, *Principal*
EMP: 200
SALES (corp-wide): 82.8MM **Privately Held**
SIC: **8641** 7991 8351 Youth organizations; physical fitness facilities; child day care services

PA: Young Men's Christian Association Of
San Francisco
50 California St Ste 650
San Francisco CA 94111
415 777-9622

(P-24735)
YOUNG MENS CHRISTIAN ASSOC SF (PA)
Also Called: YMCA of San Francisco
50 California St Ste 650, San Francisco
(94111-4607)
PHONE....................415 777-9622
Charles M Collins, *President*
Kathy Cheng, *CFO*
Rachel Del Monte, *Branch Mgr*
Linda Griffith, *Admin Sec*
Maria Catalina Reyes, *Controller*
▲ EMP: 50
SQ FT: 10,000
SALES (corp-wide): 82.8MM **Privately Held**
SIC: **8641** 7991 8351 7032 Youth organizations; physical fitness facilities; child day care services; youth camps; individual & family services

(P-24736)
YOUNG MENS CHRISTIAN ASSOC SF
Also Called: Richmond District YMCA
360 18th Ave, San Francisco (94121-2317)
PHONE....................415 666-9622
Tiffany Patterson, *Branch Mgr*
EMP: 80
SALES (corp-wide): 82.8MM **Privately Held**
SIC: **8641** 7991 8351 7032 Youth organizations; physical fitness facilities; child day care services; youth camps; individual & family services
PA: Young Men's Christian Association Of
San Francisco
50 California St Ste 650
San Francisco CA 94111
415 777-9622

(P-24737)
YOUNG MENS CHRISTIAN ASSOC SF
Also Called: YMCA
169 Steuart St, San Francisco
(94105-1206)
PHONE....................415 957-9622
Larry Bush, *Branch Mgr*
EMP: 100
SQ FT: 54,186
SALES (corp-wide): 82.8MM **Privately Held**
SIC: **8641** 7991 8351 7032 Youth organizations; physical fitness facilities; child day care services; youth camps; individual & family services
PA: Young Men's Christian Association Of
San Francisco
50 California St Ste 650
San Francisco CA 94111
415 777-9622

(P-24738)
YOUNG MENS CHRISTIAN ASSOC SF
Also Called: Shih Yu-Lang Central YMCA
246 Eddy St, San Francisco (94102-2716)
PHONE....................415 885-0460
Carmela Gold, *Exec Dir*
EMP: 100
SALES (corp-wide): 82.8MM **Privately Held**
SIC: **8641** 7997 8322 7999 Youth organizations; membership sports & recreation clubs; senior citizens' center or association; swimming instruction; aerobic dance & exercise classes; hotels
PA: Young Men's Christian Association Of
San Francisco
50 California St Ste 650
San Francisco CA 94111
415 777-9622

(P-24739)
YOUNG MENS CHRISTIAN ASSOC SF
3 Hamilton Landing # 140, Novato
(94949-8248)
PHONE....................415 883-9622

EMP: 88
SALES (corp-wide): 82.8MM **Privately Held**
SIC: **8641** 7991 8351 7032
PA: Young Men's Christian Association Of
San Francisco
50 California St Ste 650
San Francisco CA 94111
415 777-9622

(P-24740)
YOUNG MENS CHRISTIAN ASSOC SF
Also Called: Ymcasf
1500 Los Gamos Dr, San Rafael
(94903-1841)
PHONE....................415 492-9622
Luann Jackman, *Exec Dir*
EMP: 300
SALES (corp-wide): 82.8MM **Privately Held**
SIC: **8641** 8351 7991 Community membership club; child day care services; physical fitness facilities
PA: Young Men's Christian Association Of
San Francisco
50 California St Ste 650
San Francisco CA 94111
415 777-9622

(P-24741)
YOUNG MENS CHRISTIAN ASSOCIAT
Also Called: Downtown Community Dev YMCA
525 E 7th St, Long Beach (90813-4559)
PHONE....................562 624-2376
EMP: 99
SALES: 3.3MM **Privately Held**
SIC: **8641** 7991 8351 7032

(P-24742)
YOUNG MENS CHRSTN ASSC GR L B
Also Called: Lakewood Y M C A Gymnastics
4116 South St, Lakewood (90712-1005)
PHONE....................562 272-4884
Rick Carlson, *Branch Mgr*
EMP: 89
SALES (corp-wide): 20MM **Privately Held**
WEB: www.lbymca.org
SIC: **8641** 7991 8351 7032 Youth organizations; physical fitness facilities; child day care services; youth camps; individual & family services
PA: Young Men's Christian Association Of
Greater Long Beach
3605 Lngbach Blvd Ste 210
Long Beach CA 90807
562 279-1700

(P-24743)
YOUNG MENS CHRSTN ASSC GR L B
Also Called: Los Altos YMCA
1720 N Bellflower Blvd, Long Beach
(90815-4011)
PHONE....................562 596-3394
Sierra Lahera, *Director*
Brandi Collato, *Director*
EMP: 500
SQ FT: 9,740
SALES (corp-wide): 20MM **Privately Held**
WEB: www.lbymca.org
SIC: **8641** 7991 8351 7032 Youth organizations; physical fitness facilities; child day care services; youth camps; individual & family services
PA: Young Men's Christian Association Of
Greater Long Beach
3605 Lngbach Blvd Ste 210
Long Beach CA 90807
562 279-1700

(P-24744)
YOUNG MENS CHRSTN ASSC GR L B
Also Called: Y M C A Los Cerritos
15530 Woodruff Ave, Bellflower
(90706-4014)
PHONE....................562 925-1292
Michele Janssen, *Director*
EMP: 80

SQ FT: 6,190
SALES (corp-wide): 20MM **Privately Held**
WEB: www.lbymca.org
SIC: **8641** 8351 Community membership club; child day care services
PA: Young Men's Christian Association Of
Greater Long Beach
3605 Lngbach Blvd Ste 210
Long Beach CA 90807
562 279-1700

(P-24745)
YOUNG MENS CHRSTN ASSC GR L B
Also Called: Weingart-Lakewood Family YMCA
5835 Carson St, Lakewood (90713-3056)
PHONE....................562 425-7431
Chanelle Collo, *Director*
EMP: 125
SALES (corp-wide): 20MM **Privately Held**
WEB: www.lbymca.org
SIC: **8641** 7991 8351 7032 Youth organizations; physical fitness facilities; child day care services; youth camps; individual & family services
PA: Young Men's Christian Association Of
Greater Long Beach
3605 Lngbach Blvd Ste 210
Long Beach CA 90807
562 279-1700

(P-24746)
YOUNG MENS CHRSTN ASSC GR L B
Also Called: Fairfield Family YMCA
4949 Atlantic Ave, Long Beach
(90805-6505)
PHONE....................562 423-0491
Ricky Grober, *Director*
EMP: 60
SALES (corp-wide): 20MM **Privately Held**
WEB: www.lbymca.org
SIC: **8641** 8351 8322 Youth organizations; child day care services; youth center
PA: Young Men's Christian Association Of
Greater Long Beach
3605 Lngbach Blvd Ste 210
Long Beach CA 90807
562 279-1700

(P-24747)
YOUNG MENS CHRSTN ASSC GR L B
Also Called: YMCA Glb Grant
4949 Atlantic Ave, Long Beach
(90805-6505)
PHONE....................562 423-0491
Katherine Tarlecky, *Director*
EMP: 89
SALES (corp-wide): 20MM **Privately Held**
WEB: www.lbymca.org
SIC: **8641** 8351 Youth organizations; child day care services
PA: Young Men's Christian Association Of
Greater Long Beach
3605 Lngbach Blvd Ste 210
Long Beach CA 90807
562 279-1700

(P-24748)
YOUNG MENS CHRSTN ASSC GR L B
Also Called: Y M C A The
6125 Coke Ave, Long Beach (90805-3925)
PHONE....................562 633-0106
Lyle Yballe, *Branch Mgr*
EMP: 89
SALES (corp-wide): 20MM **Privately Held**
WEB: www.lbymca.org
SIC: **8641** 7999 8351 Youth organizations; recreation center; group day care center
PA: Young Men's Christian Association Of
Greater Long Beach
3605 Lngbach Blvd Ste 210
Long Beach CA 90807
562 279-1700

(P-24749)
YOUNG MENS CHRSTN ASSN OF LA
Also Called: Mid-Valley Y M C A
6901 Lennox Ave, Van Nuys (91405-4002)
PHONE....................818 989-3800
Wendy Sunders, *Exec Dir*
EMP: 50
SQ FT: 37,223
SALES (corp-wide): 105.9MM **Privately Held**
SIC: **8641** 7991 8351 7032 Youth organizations; physical fitness facilities; child day care services; youth camps; individual & family services
PA: Young Men's Christian Association Of
Metropolitan Los Angeles
625 S New Hampshire Ave
Los Angeles CA 90005
213 380-6448

(P-24750)
YOUNG MENS CHRSTN ASSN OF LA
Also Called: South Pasadena San Marino YMCA
1605 Garfield Ave, South Pasadena
(91030-4968)
PHONE....................626 799-9119
Sue Marasco, *Director*
EMP: 65
SQ FT: 23,031
SALES (corp-wide): 105.9MM **Privately Held**
SIC: **8641** 7991 8351 7032 Youth organizations; physical fitness facilities; child day care services; youth camps; individual & family services
PA: Young Men's Christian Association Of
Metropolitan Los Angeles
625 S New Hampshire Ave
Los Angeles CA 90005
213 380-6448

(P-24751)
YOUNG MENS CHRSTN ASSN OF LA
Also Called: YMCA of Westchester
8015 S Sepulveda Blvd, Los Angeles
(90045-2940)
PHONE....................310 216-9036
Patricia De Frelice, *Exec Dir*
EMP: 50
SALES (corp-wide): 105.9MM **Privately Held**
SIC: **8641** 8322 Youth organizations; individual & family services
PA: Young Men's Christian Association Of
Metropolitan Los Angeles
625 S New Hampshire Ave
Los Angeles CA 90005
213 380-6448

(P-24752)
YOUNG MENS CHRSTN ASSN OF LA
Also Called: YMCA Metro La Summit Park
26147 Mcbean Pkwy, Valencia
(91355-2015)
PHONE....................661 253-3593
Brian Thorn, *Exec Dir*
EMP: 130
SQ FT: 13,124
SALES (corp-wide): 105.9MM **Privately Held**
SIC: **8641** 7991 8351 7032 Youth organizations; physical fitness facilities; child day care services; youth camps; individual & family services
PA: Young Men's Christian Association Of
Metropolitan Los Angeles
625 S New Hampshire Ave
Los Angeles CA 90005
213 380-6448

(P-24753)
YOUNG MENS CHRSTN ASSN OF LA
Also Called: National Fitness Testing
1553 N Shrader Blvd, Los Angeles (90028)
PHONE....................323 467-4161
Rosa Najera, *Branch Mgr*
Jenny Chiu, *Vice Pres*
Daria Price, *Vice Pres*
EMP: 150

SALES (corp-wide): 105.9MM **Privately Held**
SIC: 8641 Youth organizations
PA: Young Men's Christian Association Of Metropolitan Los Angeles
625 S New Hampshire Ave
Los Angeles CA 90005
213 380-6448

(P-24754)
YOUNG MENS CHRSTN ASSN OF LA
Also Called: Downey Family Y M C A
11531 Downey Ave, Downey (90241-4936)
PHONE..................562 862-4201
George Saikali, *Director*
EMP: 100
SALES (corp-wide): 105.9MM **Privately Held**
SIC: 8641 7991 8351 7032 Youth organizations; physical fitness facilities; child day care services; youth camps; individual & family services
PA: Young Men's Christian Association Of Metropolitan Los Angeles
625 S New Hampshire Ave
Los Angeles CA 90005
213 380-6448

(P-24755)
YOUNG MENS CHRSTN ASSN OF LA
Also Called: Ketchum YMCA
401 S Hope St, Los Angeles (90071-1903)
PHONE..................213 624-2348
Laurie Goganzer, *Director*
EMP: 100
SALES (corp-wide): 105.9MM **Privately Held**
SIC: 8641 8322 Youth organizations; youth center
PA: Young Men's Christian Association Of Metropolitan Los Angeles
625 S New Hampshire Ave
Los Angeles CA 90005
213 380-6448

(P-24756)
YOUNG MENS CHRSTN ASSN OF LA
Also Called: Young Mens Christian Assn
1605 Garfield Ave, South Pasadena (91030-4968)
PHONE..................323 682-2147
Sue Marasco, *Manager*
EMP: 75
SALES (corp-wide): 105.9MM **Privately Held**
SIC: 8641 7991 8351 7032 Youth organizations; physical fitness facilities; child day care services; youth camps; individual & family services
PA: Young Men's Christian Association Of Metropolitan Los Angeles
625 S New Hampshire Ave
Los Angeles CA 90005
213 380-6448

(P-24757)
YOUNG MENS CHRSTN ASSN ORANGE
2300 University Dr, Newport Beach (92660-3313)
PHONE..................949 642-9990
Joy Hyde, *General Mgr*
EMP: 65
SQ FT: 17,976
SALES (corp-wide): 36.3MM **Privately Held**
WEB: www.ymcaoc.com
SIC: 8641 7991 Youth organizations; physical fitness facilities
PA: Young Men's Christian Association Of Orange County
13821 Newport Ave Ste 200
Tustin CA 92780
714 549-9622

(P-24758)
YOUNG MENS CHRSTN ASSN ORANGE
Also Called: YMCA
2000 Youth Way, Fullerton (92835-3812)
PHONE..................714 879-9622
Clare McKenna, *Director*

EMP: 60
SALES (corp-wide): 36.3MM **Privately Held**
WEB: www.ymcaoc.com
SIC: 8641 8322 7991 Youth organizations; individual & family services; athletic club & gymnasiums, membership
PA: Young Men's Christian Association Of Orange County
13821 Newport Ave Ste 200
Tustin CA 92780
714 549-9622

(P-24759)
YOUNG MENS CHRSTN ASSN ORANGE
Also Called: Saddle Back Valley YMCA
27341 Trabuco Cir, Mission Viejo (92692-1939)
PHONE..................949 859-9622
Mary J Goodrick, *Exec Dir*
EMP: 100
SALES (corp-wide): 36.3MM **Privately Held**
WEB: www.ymcaoc.com
SIC: 8641 7991 8351 7032 Youth organizations; physical fitness facilities; child day care services; youth camps; individual & family services
PA: Young Men's Christian Association Of Orange County
13821 Newport Ave Ste 200
Tustin CA 92780
714 549-9622

(P-24760)
YOUNG MENS CHRSTN ASSOC GNDL
Also Called: Glendale YMCA Swim School
140 N Louise St, Glendale (91206-4226)
PHONE..................818 484-8256
Tom Tyler, *CEO*
Catherine Gharapetian, *Director*
Norberto Montalvan, *Director*
Ryan Nekota, *Director*
EMP: 86 **EST:** 1924
SQ FT: 15,000
SALES: 3.8MM **Privately Held**
WEB: www.glenymca.org
SIC: 8641 Youth organizations

(P-24761)
YOUNG MNS CHRSTN ASSN MTRO LOS (PA)
Also Called: YMCA
625 S New Hampshire Ave, Los Angeles (90005-1342)
PHONE..................213 380-6448
Alan Hostrup, *President*
W J Ellison, *Ch of Bd*
Mark Dengler, *COO*
Dan Cooper, *CFO*
Jennifer Chan, *Vice Pres*
EMP: 70
SQ FT: 16,000
SALES: 105.9MM **Privately Held**
SIC: 8641 Youth organizations

(P-24762)
YOUNG MNS CHRSTN ASSN OF E BAY
Also Called: Urban Services YMCA
3265 Market St, Oakland (94608-4332)
PHONE..................510 654-9622
Chris Chatmon, *Exec Dir*
EMP: 72
SALES (corp-wide): 27.5MM **Privately Held**
SIC: 8641 7991 8351 7032 Youth organizations; physical fitness facilities; child day care services; youth camps; individual & family services
PA: Young Men's Christian Association Of The East Bay
2330 Broadway
Oakland CA 94612
510 549-4515

(P-24763)
YOUNG MNS CHRSTN ASSN OF E BAY
350 Civic Dr, Pleasant Hill (94523-1921)
PHONE..................925 687-8900
M Saenz, *Exec Dir*
Noel Panganiban, *Director*

EMP: 62
SALES (corp-wide): 27.5MM **Privately Held**
SIC: 8641 Youth organizations
PA: Young Men's Christian Association Of The East Bay
2330 Broadway
Oakland CA 94612
510 549-4515

(P-24764)
YOUNG MNS CHRSTN ASSN OF E BAY
Also Called: Berkeley Albany YMCA
1705 Thornwood Dr, Concord (94521-1915)
PHONE..................925 609-7971
EMP: 1584
SALES (corp-wide): 27.5MM **Privately Held**
SIC: 8641 Youth organizations
PA: Young Men's Christian Association Of The East Bay
2330 Broadway
Oakland CA 94612
510 549-4515

(P-24765)
YOUNG MNS CHRSTN ASSN OF E BAY
Also Called: YMCA of East Bay
2350 Broadway, Oakland (94612-2415)
PHONE..................510 451-8039
Fran Gallati, *President*
David Leung, *Director*
EMP: 852
SALES (corp-wide): 27.5MM **Privately Held**
SIC: 8641 7991 8351 7032 Youth organizations; physical fitness facilities; child day care services; youth camps; individual & family services
PA: Young Men's Christian Association Of The East Bay
2330 Broadway
Oakland CA 94612
510 549-4515

(P-24766)
YOUNG MNS CHRSTN ASSN OF E BAY
Also Called: Emery Marina
4727 San Pablo Ave, Emeryville (94608-3035)
PHONE..................510 601-8674
Henry Der, *Branch Mgr*
EMP: 68
SALES (corp-wide): 27.5MM **Privately Held**
SIC: 8641 7991 8351 7032 Youth organizations; physical fitness facilities; child day care services; youth camps; individual & family services
PA: Young Men's Christian Association Of The East Bay
2330 Broadway
Oakland CA 94612
510 549-4515

(P-24767)
YOUNG MNS CHRSTN ASSN OF E BAY
Also Called: Y M C A Metro Clinic
2111 Mrtn Lthr King Jr Wa, Berkeley (94704-1108)
PHONE..................510 486-8400
Larry Bush, *Manager*
EMP: 63
SALES (corp-wide): 27.5MM **Privately Held**
SIC: 8641 7991 8351 7032 Youth organizations; physical fitness facilities; child day care services; youth camps; individual & family services
PA: Young Men's Christian Association Of The East Bay
2330 Broadway
Oakland CA 94612
510 549-4515

(P-24768)
YOUNG MNS CHRSTN ASSN OF E BAY
Also Called: YMCA Head Start
2009 10th St, Berkeley (94710-2119)
PHONE..................510 848-9092
Pamela Shaw, *Director*
EMP: 70
SALES (corp-wide): 27.5MM **Privately Held**
SIC: 8641 7991 8351 7032 Youth organizations; physical fitness facilities; child day care services; youth camps; individual & family services
PA: Young Men's Christian Association Of The East Bay
2330 Broadway
Oakland CA 94612
510 549-4515

(P-24769)
YOUNG MNS CHRSTN ASSN OF E BAY
Also Called: Downtown Berkeley YMCA
2001 Allston Way, Berkeley (94704-1417)
PHONE..................510 848-9622
Fran Gallati, *Exec Dir*
Sebastian De Rosa, *Director*
Kristine Nachand, *Director*
EMP: 130
SQ FT: 70,135
SALES (corp-wide): 27.5MM **Privately Held**
SIC: 8641 7991 8351 7032 Youth organizations; physical fitness facilities; child day care services; youth camps; individual & family services
PA: Young Men's Christian Association Of The East Bay
2330 Broadway
Oakland CA 94612
510 549-4515

(P-24770)
YOUNG MNS CHRSTN ASSN OF E BAY
Also Called: YMCA Pre School Hillview
3800 Clark Rd, Richmond (94803-3145)
PHONE..................510 223-7070
EMP: 743
SALES (corp-wide): 27.5MM **Privately Held**
SIC: 8641 Youth organizations
PA: Young Men's Christian Association Of The East Bay
2330 Broadway
Oakland CA 94612
510 549-4515

(P-24771)
YOUNG MNS CHRSTN ASSN OF E BAY
Also Called: Kids' Club YMCA Oxford School
1130 Oxford St, Berkeley (94707-2624)
PHONE..................510 526-2146
Stephanie Hochman, *Branch Mgr*
EMP: 63
SALES (corp-wide): 27.5MM **Privately Held**
SIC: 8641 7991 8351 7032 Youth organizations; physical fitness facilities; child day care services; youth camps; individual & family services
PA: Young Men's Christian Association Of The East Bay
2330 Broadway
Oakland CA 94612
510 549-4515

(P-24772)
YOUNG MNS CHRSTN ASSN OF E BAY
Also Called: Coronado YMCA
263 S 20th St, Richmond (94804-2709)
PHONE..................510 412-5647
Don Lau, *Branch Mgr*
EMP: 325
SQ FT: 16,338
SALES (corp-wide): 27.5MM **Privately Held**
SIC: 8641 Youth organizations; recreation association

PA: Young Men's Christian Association Of
The East Bay
2330 Broadway
Oakland
510 549-4515

(P-24773)
**YOUNG MNS CHRSTN ASSN OF
E BAY**
Also Called: Hilltop Family YMCA
4300 Lakeside Dr, Richmond (94806-5717)
PHONE....................................510 222-9622
Linda Cook, *Branch Mgr*
EMP: 125
SALES (corp-wide): 27.5MM **Privately
Held**
SIC: 8641 Youth organizations; recreation
association
PA: Young Men's Christian Association Of
The East Bay
2330 Broadway
Oakland CA 94612
510 549-4515

(P-24774)
**YOUNG MNS CHRSTN ASSN OF
E BAY**
2001 Allston Way, Berkeley (94704-1417)
PHONE....................................510 848-6800
Peter Gerharz, *Branch Mgr*
Tracy Rogers, *Diabetes*
EMP: 62
SALES (corp-wide): 27.5MM **Privately
Held**
SIC: 8641 7991 8351 7032 Youth organi-
zations; physical fitness facilities; child
day care services; youth camps; individ-
ual & family services
PA: Young Men's Christian Association Of
The East Bay
2330 Broadway
Oakland CA 94612
510 549-4515

(P-24775)
**YOUNG MNS CHRSTN ASSN OF
E BAY**
1422 San Pablo Ave, Berkeley
(94702-1024)
PHONE....................................510 559-2090
Larry Bush, *Branch Mgr*
EMP: 68
SALES (corp-wide): 27.5MM **Privately
Held**
SIC: 8641 8322 8351 Youth organiza-
tions; individual & family services; head
start center, except in conjunction with
school
PA: Young Men's Christian Association Of
The East Bay
2330 Broadway
Oakland CA 94612
510 549-4515

(P-24776)
**YOUNG WOMENS CHRISTIAN
ASSOC**
2501 W Vernon Ave, Los Angeles
(90008-3927)
PHONE....................................323 295-4280
EMP: 182
SALES (corp-wide): 29.3MM **Privately
Held**
SIC: 8641 Youth organizations
PA: Young Women's Christian Association
Of Greater Los Angeles, California
1020 S Olive St Fl 7
Los Angeles CA 90015
213 365-2991

(P-24777)
**YOUNG WOMENS CHRISTIAN
ASSOCI**
Also Called: YWCA SILICON VALLEY
375 S 3rd St, San Jose (95112-3649)
PHONE....................................408 295-4011
Keri Procunier McLain, *President*
Tanis Crosby, *CEO*
Lorraine Michelle, *Officer*
Sue Barnes, *Principal*
Adriana Caldera, *Principal*
EMP: 83

SALES: 8.2MM **Privately Held**
WEB: www.ywca-sv.org
SIC: 8641 8322 Community membership
club; individual & family services

8651 Political Organizations

(P-24778)
COUNTY OF ORANGE
Also Called: Registrar of Voters
1300 S Grand Ave Ste C, Santa Ana
(92705-4402)
P.O. Box 11298 (92711-1298)
PHONE....................................714 567-7422
Neal Kelly, *Director*
EMP: 50 **Privately Held**
SIC: 8651 9199 Political campaign organi-
zation; general government administra-
tion;
PA: County Of Orange
333 W Santa Ana Blvd 3f
Santa Ana CA 92701
714 834-6200

(P-24779)
**LEAGUE OF WMEN VOTERS
WHITTIER**
10011 Melgar Dr, Whittier (90603-1458)
PHONE....................................562 947-5818
Margo Reeg, *Treasurer*
EMP: 50
SALES (est): 1.3MM **Privately Held**
SIC: 8651 Political organizations

(P-24780)
PEACE ACTION WEST (PA)
2201 Broadway Ste 321, Oakland
(94612-3044)
PHONE....................................510 830-3600
Eric See, *Finance Dir*
Jon Rainwater, *Exec Dir*
Jonathan Rainwater, *Exec Dir*
Gabriel Showers, *Asst Director*
EMP: 50
SQ FT: 1,600
SALES: 999.6K **Privately Held**
SIC: 8651 Political action committee

**8699 Membership
Organizations, NEC**

(P-24781)
AAUW ACTION FUND INC
P.O. Box 1239 (94401-0816)
PHONE....................................650 574-9160
Lowla Ghompson, *President*
EMP: 100
SALES (corp-wide): 226.2K **Privately
Held**
SIC: 8699 Charitable organization
PA: Aauw Action Fund, Inc.
1310 L St Nw Ste 1000
Washington DC 20005
202 785-7700

(P-24782)
**AFFINITY DEVELOPMENT
GROUP INC**
Also Called: A D G
10251 Vista Sorrento Pkwy # 300, San
Diego (92121-3774)
PHONE....................................858 643-9324
Jeff Skeen, *President*
Gary Drean, *COO*
Greg Siebenthal, *CFO*
Rick Borg, *Exec VP*
Jay Woodcock, *Vice Pres*
EMP: 120
SQ FT: 46,000
SALES (est): 13.1MM **Privately Held**
WEB: www.affinitydev.com
SIC: 8699 Automobile owners' association

(P-24783)
**AGUA CLNTE BAND CHILLA
INDIANS (PA)**
5401 Dinah Shore Dr, Palm Springs
(92264-5970)
PHONE....................................760 699-6800
Jeff L Grubbe, *Chairman*

Vincent Gonzales III, *Corp Secy*
Larry N Olinger, *Principal*
Stone Robin, *Exec Dir*
Marc Payan, *General Mgr*
EMP: 157
SALES (est): 202.5MM **Privately Held**
SIC: 8699 6552 7999 Reading rooms &
other cultural organizations; subdividers &
developers; tour & guide services

(P-24784)
**ALL SOUTH BAY CENTRAL
OFFICE**
1411 Marcelina Ave, Torrance
(90501-3210)
PHONE....................................310 618-1180
Liza Ferguson, *Manager*
EMP: 80 EST: 2000
SALES: 85K **Privately Held**
WEB: www.southbayaa.org
SIC: 8699 Charitable organization

(P-24785)
ALLBRIGHT GROUP LA LLC
8474 Melrose Pl, Los Angeles (90069)
PHONE....................................310 402-3570
Azzi Kashani,
EMP: 50
SALES (est): 144.2K **Privately Held**
SIC: 8699 Membership organizations

(P-24786)
ALLIANCE FC
Also Called: INLAND EMPIRE SURF SOC-
CER CLUB
3496 Little League Dr, San Bernardino
(92407)
P.O. Box 90211 (92427-1211)
PHONE....................................909 784-0005
Bryan Young, *President*
Taisha Wick, *Treasurer*
Brian Jensen, *Vice Pres*
Rodney Nelson, *Vice Pres*
Donna Hurst, *Admin Sec*
EMP: 50
SALES: 1.5MM **Privately Held**
SIC: 8699 Personal interest organization

(P-24787)
**ALLIANCE FOR SAFETY &
JUSTICE**
1700 Broadway Fl 7th, Oakland
(94612-2116)
PHONE....................................209 507-6882
Joel Bashevkinn, *Principal*
Paul Amador, *Info Tech Dir*
EMP: 56
SALES (est): 153.9K **Privately Held**
SIC: 8699 Charitable organization

(P-24788)
**ALLIANCE MEMBER SERVICES
INC**
333 Front St Ste 200, Santa Cruz
(95060-4533)
P.O. Box 8507 (95061-8507)
PHONE....................................831 459-0980
Pamela Davis, *President*
EMP: 63
SQ FT: 25,000
SALES: 15.2MM **Privately Held**
SIC: 8699 Charitable organization

(P-24789)
**AMERICAN AUTOMOBILE
ASSCTN**
Also Called: AAA
1982 Pleasant Valley Ave A, Oakland
(94611-4250)
P.O. Box 23392 (94623-0392)
PHONE....................................510 350-2042
Annette Kwan, *Branch Mgr*
EMP: 191
SALES (corp-wide): 907.9MM **Privately
Held**
SIC: 8699 6331 6311 Automobile owners'
association; automobile insurance; life in-
surance carriers
PA: American Automobile Association Of
Northern California, Nevada & Utah
1900 Powell St Ste 1200
Emeryville CA 94608
800 922-8228

(P-24790)
**AMERICAN AUTOMOBILE
ASSCTN**
Also Called: Csaa Travel Agency
3116 W March Ln Ste 100, Stockton
(95219-2374)
PHONE....................................209 952-4100
Jim Owens, *Manager*
EMP: 50
SALES (corp-wide): 907.9MM **Privately
Held**
WEB: www.californiastateautomobileasso-
ciation.c
SIC: 8699 Automobile owners' association
PA: American Automobile Association Of
Northern California, Nevada & Utah
1900 Powell St Ste 1200
Emeryville CA 94608
800 922-8228

(P-24791)
**ASSOCIATED STUDENTS SAN
DIEGO (PA)**
Also Called: MISSION BAY AQUATIC CEN-
TER
5500 Campanile Dr, San Diego
(92182-0001)
PHONE....................................619 594-0234
Christina Brown, *Exec Dir*
EMP: 1120
SALES: 30.1MM **Privately Held**
SIC: 8699 Automobile owners' association

(P-24792)
**AUTOMOBILE CLUB SOUTHERN
CAL**
Also Called: AAA
15503 Ventura Blvd # 150, Encino
(91436-3115)
PHONE....................................818 997-6230
Jim Okun, *Branch Mgr*
EMP: 50
SALES (corp-wide): 7.2B **Privately Held**
SIC: 8699 4724 6331 Automobile owners'
association; travel agencies; fire, marine
& casualty insurance
PA: Automobile Club Of Southern California
2601 S Figueroa St
Los Angeles CA 90007
213 741-3686

(P-24793)
**AUTOMOBILE CLUB SOUTHERN
CAL**
Also Called: AAA
23001 Hawthorne Blvd, Torrance
(90505-3702)
P.O. Box 4298 (90510-4298)
PHONE....................................310 325-3111
Bud Hudson, *Branch Mgr*
Gloria Gutierrez, *Admin Sec*
Debbie Burge, *Supervisor*
EMP: 60
SQ FT: 34,720
SALES (corp-wide): 7.2B **Privately Held**
SIC: 8699 Automobile owners' association
PA: Automobile Club Of Southern California
2601 S Figueroa St
Los Angeles CA 90007
213 741-3686

(P-24794)
**AUTOMOBILE CLUB SOUTHERN
CAL**
Also Called: AAA
1501 S Victoria Ave, Ventura (93003-6539)
P.O. Box 3618 (93006-3618)
PHONE....................................805 644-7171
Sigmund Grant, *Manager*
EMP: 70
SALES (corp-wide): 7.2B **Privately Held**
SIC: 8699 4724 6331 Automobile owners'
association; travel agencies; fire, marine
& casualty insurance
PA: Automobile Club Of Southern California
2601 S Figueroa St
Los Angeles CA 90007
213 741-3686

PRODUCTS & SVCS

(P-24795)
AUTOMOBILE CLUB SOUTHERN CAL
Also Called: AAA
1301s S Grand Ave, Glendora
(91740-5040)
PHONE..................................626 963-8531
Connie Stelzer, *Manager*
EMP: 50
SQ FT: 8,261
SALES (corp-wide): 7.2B **Privately Held**
SIC: 8699 Automobile owners' association
PA: Automobile Club Of Southern California
2601 S Figueroa St
Los Angeles CA 90007
213 741-3686

(P-24796)
AUTOMOBILE CLUB SOUTHERN CAL
Also Called: AAA
1500 Commercial Way, Bakersfield
(93309-0625)
PHONE..................................661 327-4661
Jeff Goldsmith, *Branch Mgr*
EMP: 50
SALES (corp-wide): 7.2B **Privately Held**
SIC: 8699 Automobile owners' association
PA: Automobile Club Of Southern California
2601 S Figueroa St
Los Angeles CA 90007
213 741-3686

(P-24797)
AUTOMOBILE CLUB SOUTHERN CAL
Also Called: AAA
9440 Reseda Blvd, Northridge
(91324-6014)
PHONE..................................818 993-1616
Freedom Homes, *Branch Mgr*
EMP: 54
SQ FT: 15,624
SALES (corp-wide): 7.2B **Privately Held**
SIC: 8699 Automobile owners' association
PA: Automobile Club Of Southern California
2601 S Figueroa St
Los Angeles CA 90007
213 741-3686

(P-24798)
AUTOMOBILE CLUB SOUTHERN CAL
Also Called: AAA
22708 Victory Blvd, Woodland Hills
(91367-1697)
PHONE..................................818 883-2660
Glenn Lumley, *Branch Mgr*
EMP: 50
SQ FT: 15,624
SALES (corp-wide): 7.2B **Privately Held**
SIC: 8699 4724 6331 Automobile owners' association; travel agencies; fire, marine & casualty insurance
PA: Automobile Club Of Southern California
2601 S Figueroa St
Los Angeles CA 90007
213 741-3686

(P-24799)
AUTOMOBILE CLUB SOUTHERN CAL
3700 Central Ave, Riverside (92506-2421)
P.O. Box 2217 (92516-2217)
PHONE..................................951 684-4250
Richard Meyer, *Branch Mgr*
EMP: 80
SALES (corp-wide): 7.2B **Privately Held**
SIC: 8699 Automobile owners' association
PA: Automobile Club Of Southern California
2601 S Figueroa St
Los Angeles CA 90007
213 741-3686

(P-24800)
AUTOMOBILE CLUB SOUTHERN CAL
Also Called: A A A Automobile Club So Cal
25181 Paseo De Alicia, Laguna Hills
(92653-4614)
PHONE..................................949 951-1400
Cindy Raymond, *Manager*
Heather Felix, *Regional Mgr*
EMP: 50

SQ FT: 13,948
SALES (corp-wide): 7.2B **Privately Held**
SIC: 8699 Automobile owners' association
PA: Automobile Club Of Southern California
2601 S Figueroa St
Los Angeles CA 90007
213 741-3686

(P-24801)
AUTOMOBILE CLUB SOUTHERN CAL
2488 Foothill Blvd Ste A, La Verne
(91750-3062)
PHONE..................................909 392-1444
Bob Barron, *Manager*
EMP: 108
SALES (corp-wide): 7.2B **Privately Held**
SIC: 8699 Automobile owners' association
PA: Automobile Club Of Southern California
2601 S Figueroa St
Los Angeles CA 90007
213 741-3686

(P-24802)
AUTOMOBILE CLUB SOUTHERN CAL
19201 Bear Valley Rd C, Apple Valley
(92308-2704)
PHONE..................................760 247-4110
EMP: 108
SALES (corp-wide): 7.2B **Privately Held**
SIC: 8699 Automobile owners' association
PA: Automobile Club Of Southern California
2601 S Figueroa St
Los Angeles CA 90007
213 741-3686

(P-24803)
AUTOMOBILE CLUB SOUTHERN CAL
Also Called: AAA
8765 Fletcher Pkwy, La Mesa
(91942-3200)
PHONE..................................619 464-7001
Marria Porter, *Manager*
EMP: 75
SQ FT: 42,441
SALES (corp-wide): 7.2B **Privately Held**
SIC: 8699 Automobile owners' association
PA: Automobile Club Of Southern California
2601 S Figueroa St
Los Angeles CA 90007
213 741-3686

(P-24804)
AUTOMOTIVE SERVICE COUNCIL
10813 Airport Dr, El Cajon (92020-1202)
PHONE..................................800 810-4272
Steve Vanlandingham, *President*
EMP: 90
SALES: 42.4K **Privately Held**
SIC: 8699 Automobile owners' association

(P-24805)
BAYVIEW HUNTERS POINT FOUNDATI (PA)
Also Called: BVHP
150 Executive Park Blvd, San Francisco
(94134-3303)
PHONE..................................415 468-5100
Jacob K Moody, *Exec Dir*
Lillian Shine, *Deputy Dir*
EMP: 81
SQ FT: 3,700
SALES: 5.6MM **Privately Held**
SIC: 8699 8641 Animal humane society; youth organizations

(P-24806)
BEAD SOCIETY
Also Called: Bead Society , The
1454 Valley High Ave, Thousand Oaks
(91362-1906)
P.O. Box 1456, Culver City (90232-1456)
PHONE..................................805 495-2550
Adel Boehm-Mabe, *President*
Adel B Mabe, *President*
Joan Eppen, *CFO*
EMP: 250
SALES: 36.9K **Privately Held**
SIC: 8699 Personal interest organization

(P-24807)
BERKELEY CLINIC AUXILLARY
Also Called: TURNABOUT SHOP
10052 San Pablo Ave, El Cerrito
(94530-3927)
PHONE..................................510 525-7844
Barbara Coleman, *President*
Vl Galardo, *President*
Peggy Eanaman, *Chairman*
Kay Jevons, *Chairman*
Dorothy Zwoyer, *Treasurer*
EMP: 60
SQ FT: 1,800
SALES: 84.4K **Privately Held**
SIC: 8699 5932 Charitable organization; used merchandise stores

(P-24808)
BEST FRIENDS ANIMAL SOCIETY
15321 Brand Blvd, Mission Hills
(91345-1438)
PHONE..................................818 643-3989
Marc Peralta, *Manager*
EMP: 360
SALES (corp-wide): 87.1MM **Privately Held**
SIC: 8699 Animal humane society
PA: Best Friends Animal Society
5001 Angel Canyon Rd
Kanab UT 84741
435 644-2001

(P-24809)
BRIARPATCH COOP NEV CNTY INC
Also Called: Briarpatch Coop-Community Mkt
290 Sierra College Dr, Grass Valley
(95945-5762)
PHONE..................................530 272-5333
Christopher Maher, *CEO*
Kat Bass-Pederson, *Admin Asst*
Brett Torgrimson, *Info Tech Mgr*
Kiyoko Wilcox, *Accounting Mgr*
Gwen Birk, *Opers Staff*
EMP: 180 **EST:** 1976
SALES (est): 11.8MM **Privately Held**
WEB: www.briarpatchcoop.com
SIC: 8699 Food co-operative

(P-24810)
CAL POLY POMONA FOUNDATION INC (PA)
3801 W Temple Ave Bldg 55, Pomona
(91768-2557)
PHONE..................................909 869-2950
J Michael Ortiz, *Chairman*
David Karacozoff, *CEO*
Jonna Lewis, *CFO*
Dr Whinney Dong, *Corp Secy*
Dennis Miller, *Officer*
EMP: 2200
SQ FT: 27,000
SALES (est): 76.1MM **Privately Held**
WEB: www.kelloggwest.com
SIC: 8699 Charitable organization

(P-24811)
CALIF STAT UNIV FRES FOUN
5370 N Chestnut Ave, Fresno (93725)
PHONE..................................559 278-0850
Linda Alatorre, *Branch Mgr*
Lynn Hemink, *Finance*
David Doleoske, *Director*
EMP: 229
SALES (corp-wide): 76.9MM **Privately Held**
WEB: www.auxiliary.com
SIC: 8699 Amateur sports promotion
PA: California State University, Fresno Foundation
4910 N Chestnut Ave
Fresno CA 93726
559 278-0850

(P-24812)
CALIFRNIA YUTH SOCCER ASSN INC
Also Called: CAL NORTH
1040 Serpentine Ln # 206, Pleasanton
(94566-4754)
PHONE..................................925 426-5437
Kenyatta Scott, *Chairman*
Ilona Montoya, *CFO*
Doug Couden, *Treasurer*

Lela Huenergardt, *Commissioner*
Craig Sannebeck, *Commissioner*
EMP: 87
SALES: 4.3MM **Privately Held**
WEB: www.cysanorth.org
SIC: 8699 Personal interest organization

(P-24813)
CARE 2
203 Redwood Shores Pkwy # 230, Redwood City (94065-6106)
PHONE..................................650 622-0860
Randy Paynter, *Principal*
Ginger Hanssen, *Editor*
EMP: 56
SALES (est): 1.1MM **Privately Held**
SIC: 8699 Charitable organization

(P-24814)
CARLSBAD FIREFIGHTERS ASSN
2560 Orion Way, Carlsbad (92010-7240)
P.O. Box 945 (92018-0945)
PHONE..................................760 729-3730
Josh Clark, *President*
EMP: 80
SALES (est): 252.9K **Privately Held**
SIC: 8699 Charitable organization

(P-24815)
CASAS - COMPREHENSIVE
5151 Murphy Canyon Rd # 220, San Diego
(92123-4440)
PHONE..................................858 292-2900
Robert S Muir, *Director*
Jennifer Suarez, *Social Dir*
Anthony Castle, *Software Dev*
Andy Fons, *Controller*
EMP: 55
SALES: 5.7MM **Privately Held**
SIC: 8699 Charitable organization

(P-24816)
CATHEDRAL CENTER OF ST PAUL
Also Called: Cathedral Bookstore
840 Echo Park Ave, Los Angeles
(90026-4209)
PHONE..................................213 482-2040
Bishop Jon Bruno,
Peter Mann, *Treasurer*
Janet Wild, *Admin Sec*
EMP: 75 **EST:** 1898
SALES (est): 1.4MM **Privately Held**
WEB: www.cathedralbookstore.com
SIC: 8699 5942 Charitable organization; books, religious

(P-24817)
CCNA VONS ATHLETES FOR LIFE
Also Called: AFL
10670 6th St Ste 113, Rancho Cucamonga
(91730-5912)
PHONE..................................805 453-2499
Greg Bell, *President*
EMP: 60
SALES (est): 235.4K **Privately Held**
SIC: 8699 7389 Athletic organizations; fund raising organizations

(P-24818)
CITY IMPACT
230 Jones St Fl 1, San Francisco
(94102-2619)
PHONE..................................415 292-1770
Christian Huang, *Exec Dir*
Ryan Hsu, *Opers Dir*
Samuel Pushpa, *Manager*
Alex Quock, *Manager*
EMP: 50
SALES (est): 203.6K **Privately Held**
SIC: 8699 Charitable organization

(P-24819)
CITY OF LOS ANGELES
Also Called: Department of Cultural Affairs
201 N Figueroa St # 1400, Los Angeles
(90012-2623)
PHONE..................................213 202-5500
Karen Constine, *General Mgr*
EMP: 64 **Privately Held**
WEB: www.lacity.org

SIC: **8699** 9512 Literary, film or cultural club; recreational program administration, government
PA: City Of Los Angeles
200 N Spring St Ste 303
Los Angeles CA 90012
213 978-0600

(P-24820)
COMMUNITY CLLBRTIVE CHRTR SCHL
Also Called: Excel Academy Charter
1200 Quail St Ste 175, Newport Beach (92660-2707)
PHONE..................................949 387-7822
Heidi Gasca, *Director*
EMP: 90
SALES (est): 222.4K **Privately Held**
SIC: 8699 Charitable organization

(P-24821)
COUNTY OF MONTEREY
Also Called: Monterey County Sheriffs Dept
1414 Natividad Rd, Salinas (93906-3102)
PHONE..................................831 755-3700
Mike Kanalakis, *Sheriff*
EMP: 474 **Privately Held**
WEB: www.montereycountyfarmbureau.org
SIC: 8699 Personal interest organization
PA: County Of Monterey
168 W Alisal St Fl 2
Salinas CA 93901
831 755-5040

(P-24822)
COUNTY OF RIVERSIDE DEPARTMENT (PA)
4065 County Circle Dr, Riverside (92503-3410)
P.O. Box 7600 (92513-7600)
PHONE..................................951 358-5000
Susan Harrington, *Director*
Socorro Manzanilla, *Administration*
EMP: 99
SALES (est): 3.6MM **Privately Held**
WEB: www.rivcoph.org
SIC: 8699 Charitable organization

(P-24823)
CROCKER ART MUSEUM ASSOCIATION
Also Called: CROCKER ART MUSEUM
216 O St, Sacramento (95814-5324)
PHONE..................................916 808-7000
Lial Jones, *CEO*
Reggae Brown, *Bd of Directors*
Scott Shields, *Associate Dir*
Michele Roberts, *Marketing Staff*
Erin Dorn, *Education*
EMP: 66 **EST:** 1875
SQ FT: 150,000
SALES: 22MM **Privately Held**
WEB: www.crockerartmuseum.org
SIC: 8699 5942 8412 Art council; book stores; museum

(P-24824)
DEATH VALLEY 49ERS INC
1442 Carson Ave, Clovis (93611-6906)
P.O. Box 997, Kernville (93238-0997)
PHONE..................................559 297-5691
Bill Pool, *President*
Edtytat Pool, *Treasurer*
Richard Gering, *Vice Pres*
Marv Jensen, *Vice Pres*
EMP: 80 **EST:** 1949
SALES: 78.9K **Privately Held**
WEB: www.deathvalley49ers.org
SIC: 8699 Charitable organization

(P-24825)
DELTA RESCUE INC
P.O. Box 9, Glendale (91209-0009)
PHONE..................................661 269-4010
Leo Grillo, *President*
EMP: 60
SALES (est): 1.1MM **Privately Held**
SIC: 8699 Animal humane society

(P-24826)
DFA OF CALIFORNIA
6100 Wilson Landing Rd, Chico (95973-8902)
PHONE..................................530 345-5077
Marie Cowan, *Branch Mgr*

EMP: 186
SALES (corp-wide): 9.7MM **Privately Held**
SIC: 8699 Athletic organizations
PA: Dfa Of California
710 Striker Ave
Sacramento CA 95834
916 561-5900

(P-24827)
EARTH ISLAND INSTITUTE INC
2150 Allston Way Ste 460, Berkeley (94704-1375)
PHONE..................................510 859-9100
Michael Mitrani, *CEO*
John A Knox, *Principal*
David Phillips, *Exec Dir*
Mona Shomali, *Director*
EMP: 76
SQ FT: 4,400
SALES: 11.2MM **Privately Held**
WEB: www.earthisland.org
SIC: 8699 8748 8641 Charitable organization; business consulting; environmental protection organization

(P-24828)
EMPLOYMENT TRAINING ACADEMY
4045 Coronado Ave, Stockton (95204-2311)
PHONE..................................209 475-1529
Stacie J Rodriguez, *Administration*
EMP: 50
SALES (est): 232.2K **Privately Held**
SIC: 8699 Charitable organization

(P-24829)
F50 LEAGUE LLC
Also Called: Sailgp
475 Sansome St Fl 12, San Francisco (94111-3169)
PHONE..................................415 939-4076
Andrew Thompson, *CFO*
EMP: 50
SALES (est): 80MM **Privately Held**
SIC: 8699 Personal interest organization

(P-24830)
FAMILY SERVICES
807 W Oak Ave, Visalia (93291-6033)
PHONE..................................559 741-7310
Kaitey Meader, *Director*
Caity Meader, *Exec Dir*
Heather Reed, *Hum Res Coord*
Susan Munter, *Deputy Dir*
EMP: 50
SALES (est): 1.9MM **Privately Held**
SIC: 8699 Charitable organization

(P-24831)
FARMS OF AMADOR
12200b Airport Rd, Jackson (95642-9527)
P.O. Box 1543 (95642-1543)
PHONE..................................209 257-0112
Sean Kriletich, *Principal*
EMP: 99
SALES (est): 1.3MM **Privately Held**
SIC: 8699 Membership organizations

(P-24832)
FREMONT CANDLE LIGHTERS
Also Called: CANDLE LIGHTERS THE
39261 Fremont Hub, Fremont (94538)
P.O. Box 174 (94537-0174)
PHONE..................................510 796-0595
Claire Douglas, *President*
EMP: 110
SALES: 68.2K **Privately Held**
SIC: 8699 Charitable organization

(P-24833)
GIRLS ROCK SB
1522b Eucalyptus Hill Rd, Santa Barbara (93103-2811)
PHONE..................................805 861-8128
Jen Baron, *Exec Dir*
Kelsey Maloney, *Administration*
EMP: 70
SALES: 330K **Privately Held**
SIC: 8699 8299 Charitable organization; music school

(P-24834)
GOODWILL INDS SAN DIEGO CNTY
3841 Plaza Dr Ste 902, Oceanside (92056-4649)
PHONE..................................760 806-7670
Tim Hurley, *Manager*
EMP: 232
SALES (corp-wide): 55.4MM **Privately Held**
SIC: 8699 8331 5932 Charitable organization; vocational rehabilitation agency; used merchandise stores
PA: Goodwill Industries Of San Diego County
3663 Rosecrans St
San Diego CA 92110
619 225-2200

(P-24835)
HALO
4916 Chism Way, Antioch (94531-8148)
P.O. Box 2011 (94531-2011)
PHONE..................................925 473-4642
Karen Kops, *President*
Linda Mills, *Admin Sec*
EMP: 50
SALES (est): 624.8K **Privately Held**
SIC: 8699 Animal humane society

(P-24836)
HELEN WOODWARD ANIMAL CENTER (PA)
6461 El Apajo, Rancho Santa Fe (92067)
PHONE..................................858 756-4117
Michael A Arms, *President*
Bryce Rhoades, *Ch of Bd*
Marcie Grube, *Admin Asst*
Renee Simmons, *Finance Mgr*
Janelle Bloomberg, *Asst Controller*
EMP: 100
SQ FT: 45,000
SALES: 13MM **Privately Held**
WEB: www.sddac.com
SIC: 8699 Animal humane society

(P-24837)
HEWLETT WLLIAM FLORA FNDATION
Also Called: HEWLETT FOUNDATION
2121 Sand Hill Rd, Menlo Park (94025-6909)
PHONE..................................650 234-4500
Paul Brest, *President*
Amy Arbreton, *Officer*
Jean Bordewich, *Officer*
Neha Singh Gohil, *Officer*
Jessica Halverson, *Officer*
EMP: 60
SALES: 317.4MM **Privately Held**
SIC: 8699 Charitable organization

(P-24838)
HOPLAND BAND POMO INDIANS INC (PA)
3000 Shanel Rd, Hopland (95449-9809)
PHONE..................................707 472-2100
Romen Carrillo, *President*
Rachel Whetstone, *CFO*
EMP: 84
SQ FT: 3,800
SALES (est): 17.8MM **Privately Held**
WEB: www.hoplandtribe.com
SIC: 8699 Personal interest organization

(P-24839)
HUMANE SOCIETY SILICON VALLEY
Also Called: PET POURRI
901 Ames Ave, Milpitas (95035-6326)
PHONE..................................408 262-2133
Carol Novello, *CEO*
Christine B Arnold, *Exec Dir*
Candice Balmaceda, *VP Finance*
EMP: 80
SQ FT: 3,000
SALES: 13.4MM **Privately Held**
SIC: 8699 Animal humane society

(P-24840)
INLAND EMPIRE CHAPTER-ASSN OF
4200 Concours Ste 360, Ontario (91764-4982)
PHONE..................................512 478-9000
EMP: 82
SALES: 4.1K **Privately Held**
SIC: 8699

(P-24841)
INLAND VALLEY BUSINESS AND COM
Also Called: IVBCF
40335 Winchester Rd, Temecula (92591-5500)
PHONE..................................951 378-5316
Steve Matley, *President*
Steve Matly, *President*
Dena Lansford, *Treasurer*
Wendy Johnson, *Bd of Directors*
Hans R Monod De Froideville, *Vice Pres*
EMP: 80
SALES: 31.3K **Privately Held**
SIC: 8699 Charitable organization

(P-24842)
IRVINE COMPANY LLC
Also Called: Oak Creek Golf Club
1 Golf Club Dr, Irvine (92618-5210)
PHONE..................................949 653-5300
John McCook, *Manager*
John Mc Cook, *Director*
Lorrie De Bellis, *Manager*
EMP: 70
SALES (corp-wide): 2B **Privately Held**
WEB: www.irvineco.com
SIC: 8699 Professional golf association
PA: The Irvine Company Llc
550 Newport Center Dr # 160
Newport Beach CA 92660
949 720-2000

(P-24843)
LAUGH FACTORY INC
151 S Pine Ave, Long Beach (90802-4536)
PHONE..................................562 495-2844
Ivy Schember, *General Mgr*
EMP: 101
SALES (corp-wide): 10MM **Privately Held**
SIC: 8699 5813 Athletic organizations; night clubs
PA: Laugh Factory, Inc.
8001 W Sunset Blvd
Los Angeles CA 90046
323 848-2800

(P-24844)
LAVA BEDS NATIONAL MONUMENTS
Also Called: U S GOVERNMENT
1 Indian Wells Hqtrs, Tulelake (96134-8216)
P.O. Box 1240 (96134-1240)
PHONE..................................530 667-2282
Fax: 530 667-3299
EMP: 50 **EST:** 1963
SALES: 55.2K **Publicly Held**
SIC: 8699 8412
PA: Government Of The United States
1600 Pennsylvania Ave Nw
Washington DC 20500
202 456-1414

(P-24845)
LOS ANGELES MEM COLISEUM COMM
Also Called: La Sports Arena
3911 S Figueroa St, Los Angeles (90037-1207)
PHONE..................................213 747-7111
Don Knabe, *President*
Gregory Hellmold, *CFO*
John Sandbrook, *Administration*
EMP: 500
SQ FT: 2,000
SALES (est): 13.4MM **Privately Held**
SIC: 8699 Athletic organizations

(P-24846)
LOS ANGELES POLICE COMMAND
100 W 1st St, Los Angeles (90012-4112)
P.O. Box 53188 (90053-0188)
PHONE........................877 275-5273
Deborah A Gonzales, *Principal*
EMP: 296
SALES: 258K **Privately Held**
SIC: 8699 Charitable organization

(P-24847)
MARIN HUMANE SOCIETY
171 Bel Marin Keys Blvd, Novato
(94949-6183)
PHONE........................415 883-4621
Suzanne Golt, *Exec Dir*
Anne Oliver, *Volunteer Dir*
John Reese, *COO*
Marilyn Castellblanch, *CFO*
Dave Stapp, *Officer*
EMP: 91
SQ FT: 42,500
SALES: 9.2MM **Privately Held**
WEB: www.marinhumanesociety.com
SIC: 8699 Animal humane society

(P-24848)
MENLO PARK-ATHERTON EDUCATION (PA)
181 Encinal Ave, Atherton (94027-3102)
P.O. Box 584, Menlo Park (94026-0584)
PHONE........................650 325-0100
Ghysels Maurice, *Superintendent*
EMP: 59
SALES: 4.3MM **Privately Held**
SIC: 8699 Charitable organization

(P-24849)
MISSION HOSPICE & HM CARE INC (PA)
1670 S Amphlett Blvd # 300, San Mateo
(94402-2534)
PHONE........................650 554-1000
Dwight Wilson, *Exec Dir*
Alex Ignacio, *Info Tech Dir*
Michael Sucher, *Technology*
George Sheil Tichy, *Corp Comm Staff*
Michael Westley, *Med Doctor*
EMP: 200
SALES: 25MM **Privately Held**
WEB: www.missionhospice.org
SIC: 8699 Charitable organization

(P-24850)
NATIONAL COUNCIL NEGRO WOMEN
Also Called: Golden Gate Section
784 Cole St, San Francisco (94117-3912)
PHONE........................415 564-4153
Catherine J Bradford, *President*
EMP: 99
SALES: 25K **Privately Held**
WEB: www.co.rappahannock.comm-
rev.state.va.us
SIC: 8699 Membership organizations

(P-24851)
NATUREBRIDGE
1033 Fort Cronkhite, Sausalito
(94965-2609)
PHONE........................415 332-5771
EMP: 68 **Privately Held**
SIC: 8699 Charitable organization
PA: Naturebridge
28 Geary St Ste 650
San Francisco CA 94108
-

(P-24852)
ONEOC (PA)
Also Called: VOLUNTEER CENTER OR-
ANGE COUNTY
1901 E 4th St Ste 100, Santa Ana
(92705-3918)
PHONE........................714 953-5757
Daniel McQuaid, *President*
Tim Strauch, *COO*
Cindy Braun, *Project Mgr*
Victoria Torres, *Training Dir*
Abby Edmunds, *Manager*
EMP: 79 **EST**: 1958
SQ FT: 7,500

SALES: 11.5MM **Privately Held**
WEB: www.volunteercenter.org
SIC: 8699 8399 Charitable organization;
community development groups

(P-24853)
ORCUTT LIONS CLUB
126 S Broadway St, Orcutt (93455-4607)
PHONE........................805 937-0158
Tom Hughes, *Chairman*
EMP: 56
SQ FT: 2,880
SALES (est): 39.9K **Privately Held**
SIC: 8699 8641 5813 Personal interest
organization; civic associations; drinking
places

(P-24854)
ORGANZTION AMRCN KDALY EDCTORS
10801 National Blvd # 590, Los Angeles
(90064-4139)
PHONE........................310 441-3555
Roger D Chittum Esq, *Principal*
EMP: 50
SALES: 755.1K **Privately Held**
SIC: 8699 Charitable organization

(P-24855)
PASADENA HUMANE SOCIETY
361 S Raymond Ave, Pasadena
(91105-2687)
PHONE........................626 792-7151
Steven R Mc Nall, *President*
Elizabeth Campo, *Vice Pres*
Kristina Lamas, *Vice Pres*
Ricky Whitman, *Vice Pres*
Jonathan Budisantoso, *Information Mgr*
EMP: 70
SQ FT: 26,000
SALES: 12.7MM **Privately Held**
WEB: www.phsspca.org
SIC: 8699 0752 Animal humane society;
animal specialty services

(P-24856)
PETS UNLIMITED
2343 Fillmore St, San Francisco
(94115-1812)
PHONE........................415 563-6700
Suzanne Troxel, *President*
Brandyn Denico, *COO*
Theresa L Smith, *CFO*
Sally Wortman, *Vice Pres*
Nan Vinton-Zimmerma, *Executive*
EMP: 110
SALES (est): 7.7MM **Privately Held**
WEB: www.petsunlimited.org
SIC: 8699 Animal humane society

(P-24857)
POINT REYES BIRD OBSERVATOR
Also Called: Point Blue Cnservation Science
3820 Cypress Dr Ste 11, Petaluma
(94954-6964)
P.O. Box 69, Bolinas (94924-0069)
PHONE........................415 868-0371
Allie Cohen, *CEO*
Pete McCormick, *Opers Staff*
Wendell Gilgert, *Director*
Emily Allen, *Manager*
Stacey Atchley, *Manager*
EMP: 86 **EST**: 2011
SQ FT: 20,000
SALES (est): 3MM **Privately Held**
SIC: 8699 Charitable organization

(P-24858)
RACELEGAL COM
Also Called: CENTER FOR INJURY PRE-
VENTION
315 Fourth Ave, Chula Vista (91910-3801)
P.O. Box 600943, San Diego (92160-0943)
PHONE........................619 265-8159
Charles Chris, *Chairman*
EMP: 50
SALES: 289.5K **Privately Held**
WEB: www.racelegal.com
SIC: 8699 Charitable organization

(P-24859)
RESCUE MISSION ALLIANCE (PA)
Also Called: MISSION BARGAIN CENTER
315 N A St, Oxnard (93030-4901)
P.O. Box 5545 (93031-5545)
PHONE........................805 487-1234
Gary Gray, *President*
David Chittenden, *CFO*
Jim Ownes, *Chairman*
Andy Stay, *Treasurer*
Scott West, *Bd of Directors*
EMP: 77
SQ FT: 30,000
SALES: 26.5MM **Privately Held**
WEB: www.erescuemission.com
SIC: 8699 Charitable organization

(P-24860)
SALVATION ARMY
8538 Bennett Ave, Fontana (92335-3810)
PHONE........................323 263-1206
Dr Douglas Loisel, *Director*
EMP: 50
SALES (corp-wide): 2.3B **Privately Held**
WEB: www.salvationarmy.usawest.org
SIC: 8699 Charitable organization
HQ: The Salvation Army
30840 Hawthorne Blvd
Rancho Palos Verdes CA 90275
562 491-8496

(P-24861)
SAN DIEGO HUMANE SOC & SPCA
5500 Gaines St, San Diego (92110-2572)
PHONE........................619 299-7012
Gary L Weitzman, *President*
Kim Shannon, *COO*
Kelly Riseley, *CFO*
Renee Harris, *Exec VP*
Shelly Stuart, *Vice Pres*
EMP: 65
SQ FT: 44,500
SALES: 25.8MM **Privately Held**
WEB: www.sdhumane.org
SIC: 8699 Animal humane society

(P-24862)
SAN FRANCISCO BAY AR TRAN ASSN
915 San Antonio Ave, Alameda
(94501-3959)
PHONE........................510 501-5318
Jahan Byrne, *President*
Monte Boscovich, *Treasurer*
EMP: 150
SALES: 85.5K **Privately Held**
SIC: 8699 7389 Athletic organizations;
fund raising organizations

(P-24863)
SAN JOAQUIN VALLEY INTERGRP
Also Called: Sjvi
6048 E Cimarron Ave, Fresno
(93727-6810)
P.O. Box 8302 (93747-8302)
PHONE........................559 856-0559
Marjorie J Donovan, *Ch of Bd*
EMP: 50
SALES (est): 258.4K **Privately Held**
SIC: 8699 Charitable organization

(P-24864)
SANKARA EYE FOUNDATION USA
1900 Mccarthy Blvd # 302, Milpitas
(95035-7440)
PHONE........................408 456-0555
Krishan Murlidharan, *Chairman*
Anil Lal, *Bd of Directors*
EMP: 50 **EST**: 1998
SALES: 6.2MM **Privately Held**
WEB: www.giftofvision.org
SIC: 8699 7929 Personal interest organi-
zation; entertainers & entertainment
groups

(P-24865)
SANTA MONICA BAY WOMENS CLUB
1210 4th St, Santa Monica (90401-1304)
PHONE........................310 395-1308

Darlene Bahr, *President*
EMP: 50
SQ FT: 12,226
SALES: 329.8K **Privately Held**
SIC: 8699 6732 Charitable organization;
trusts: educational, religious, etc.

(P-24866)
SJSU FOUNDATION
210 N 4th St Ste 300, San Jose
(95112-5569)
PHONE........................408 924-1410
Mary Sidney, *COO*
EMP: 750
SALES (est): 6.9MM **Privately Held**
WEB: www.foundation.sjsu.edu
SIC: 8699 Charitable organization

(P-24867)
SKOLL FOUNDATION
250 University Ave Lbby, Palo Alto
(94301-1725)
PHONE........................650 331-1031
Donald H Gips, *CEO*
Richard Fahey, *COO*
Sally Farhat, *Officer*
Elizabeth Diebold, *Principal*
Lindsey Fishleder, *Program Mgr*
EMP: 50
SALES: 13.9MM **Privately Held**
SIC: 8699 Charitable organization

(P-24868)
SOCIETY FOR SAN FRANCISCO
201 Alabama St, San Francisco
(94103-4217)
PHONE........................415 554-3000
Katherine Brown, *Ch of Bd*
Jane McHugh-Smith, *President*
David Tateosian, *Treasurer*
Eric Roberts, *Vice Ch Bd*
EMP: 200 **EST**: 1868
SQ FT: 57,000
SALES: 34.5MM **Privately Held**
WEB: www.sfspca.org
SIC: 8699 Animal humane society

(P-24869)
SOCIETY FOR THE PREVENTION OF (PA)
Also Called: Spca La
5026 W Jefferson Blvd, Los Angeles
(90016-3925)
PHONE........................888 772-2521
Madeline Bernstein, *President*
Caitlin Lavin, *Manager*
Jessica Wolf, *Asst Mgr*
EMP: 70
SQ FT: 5,000
SALES: 7.4MM **Privately Held**
SIC: 8699 0742 Animal humane society;
veterinary services, specialties

(P-24870)
SOCIETY OF ST VINCENT (PA)
2272 San Pablo Ave, Oakland
(94612-1321)
PHONE........................510 638-7600
Blase Bova, *Exec Dir*
Ron Dean, *Principal*
EMP: 80
SALES: 7.8MM **Privately Held**
SIC: 8699 Charitable organization

(P-24871)
SOCIETY OF ST VINCENT DE (PA)
Also Called: St Vincent De Paul of La
210 N Avenue 21, Los Angeles
(90031-1713)
PHONE........................323 226-9645
David Garcia, *Exec Dir*
Lessy Benedith, *Officer*
Susana Santana, *Exec Dir*
Anthony Terrazas, *Sales Executive*
Frank Jacinto, *Program Dir*
EMP: 77
SQ FT: 108,000
SALES (est): 11.4MM **Privately Held**
SIC: 8699 Charitable organization

(P-24872)
SOROPTOMIST INTL TAHOE SIERRA
3050 Lake Tahoe Blvd, South Lake Tahoe (96150-7810)
P.O. Box 18727 (96151-8727)
PHONE....................................530 573-1657
Lydia Rogers, *President*
EMP: 50
SALES: 71.1K **Privately Held**
SIC: 8699 Charitable organization

(P-24873)
SOUTH BAY HISTORICAL RR SOC
1005 Railroad Ave, Santa Clara (95050-4319)
PHONE....................................408 243-3969
Robert Dolci, *President*
EMP: 50
SALES: 82.4K **Privately Held**
WEB: www.sbhrs.org
SIC: 8699 8412 Personal interest organization; museum

(P-24874)
SOUTHERN CAL BLLDOG RESCUE INC
2219 N Spurgeon St, Santa Ana (92706-2962)
PHONE....................................714 381-7691
Gilbertt Van Der Marliere, *President*
EMP: 50 **EST:** 2008
SALES: 300K **Privately Held**
SIC: 8699 Animal humane society

(P-24875)
ST VINCENT DE PAUL VLG INC
Also Called: Joan Kroc Center
28225 Driza, Mission Viejo (92692-1305)
PHONE....................................619 233-8500
Richard Swain, *Principal*
EMP: 150 **Privately Held**
WEB: www.neighbor.org
SIC: 8699 Charitable organization
PA: St. Vincent De Paul Village, Inc.
1501 Imperial Ave
San Diego CA 92101

(P-24876)
STUDENT UN SAN JOSE STATE UNIV
Also Called: Student Union Building
211 S. 9th Street, San Jose (95192-0001)
PHONE....................................408 924-6405
Terry Gregory, *Manager*
EMP: 60
SALES (corp-wide): 8.3MM **Privately Held**
SIC: 8699 Personal interest organization
PA: Student Union Of San Jose State University
1 Washington Sq
San Jose CA
408 924-6315

(P-24877)
THE DAVID LCILE PCKARD FNDTION
300 2nd St, Los Altos (94022-3694)
PHONE....................................650 917-7167
Carol S Larson, *President*
Cole Wilbur, *Trustee*
Lana Dakan, *Officer*
Chad English, *Officer*
Jean Ries, *Officer*
▲ **EMP:** 85
SALES: 283MM **Privately Held**
SIC: 8699 Personal interest organization

(P-24878)
THE FOR SACRAMENTO SOCIETY
Also Called: SSPCA
6201 Florin Perkins Rd, Sacramento (95828-1012)
PHONE....................................916 383-7387
Maryann Subbotin, *Director*
Giselle Chan,
Dan Marple, *Manager*
Kristi Maryman, *Manager*
EMP: 76
SQ FT: 40,000

SALES: 8.6MM **Privately Held**
WEB: www.sspca.org
SIC: 8699 Animal humane society

(P-24879)
TORRANCE AMATEUR RDO ASSN INC
Also Called: Tara
2162 248th St, Lomita (90717-1608)
PHONE....................................310 245-0989
Charles Galbasin, *Principal*
Kenneth Edwards, *Principal*
Bruce Fauver, *Principal*
Shelly Fauver, *Principal*
Kathleen Galbasin, *Principal*
EMP: 50
SALES (est): 193K **Privately Held**
SIC: 8699 Membership organizations

(P-24880)
UNITED STTES BOWL CONGRESS INC
12895 Arbor Ln, Red Bluff (96080-9387)
PHONE....................................530 527-9049
Fred Zastrow, *Branch Mgr*
EMP: 51
SALES (corp-wide): 32.9MM **Privately Held**
SIC: 8699 Athletic organizations
PA: United States Bowling Congress, Inc.
621 Six Flags Dr
Arlington TX 76011
817 385-8200

(P-24881)
USA TRAVEL SERVICES LLC
714 Washington Blvd, Marina Del Rey (90292-5543)
PHONE....................................207 899-8803
Julian Brand,
EMP: 800
SALES (est): 1MM **Privately Held**
SIC: 8699 Travel club

(P-24882)
USC SHOAH FNDN INST FOR VISUAL
650 W 35th St Ste 114, Los Angeles (90089-0033)
PHONE....................................213 740-6001
Linda Sturm, *Executive Asst*
Steven Klappholz, *Exec Dir*
Linda Sturmm, *Executive Asst*
EMP: 100
SALES (est): 2.5MM **Privately Held**
WEB: www.vhf.org
SIC: 8699 Historical club

(P-24883)
VICKIE LOBELLO
Also Called: Saint Baldricks Foundation
1333 S Mayflower Ave 40, Simi Valley (93063)
PHONE....................................805 750-2327
Kathleen Ruddy, *CEO*
EMP: 65 **EST:** 2010
SALES (est): 2.3MM **Privately Held**
SIC: 8699 Charitable organization

(P-24884)
VICTORIA PLACE COMMUNITY ASSN
195 N Euclid Ave, Upland (91786-6055)
PHONE....................................909 981-4131
John Melcher, *President*
EMP: 75 **EST:** 2008
SALES (est): 57.8K **Privately Held**
SIC: 8699 Membership organizations

(P-24885)
VISION TO LEARN
11611 San Vicente Blvd # 500, Los Angeles (90049-5106)
PHONE....................................800 485-9196
Ann Hollister, *President*
EMP: 50 **EST:** 2017
SALES: 4.8MM **Privately Held**
SIC: 8699 8399 Charitable organization; advocacy group

(P-24886)
WALNUT VALLEY UNIFIED SCHL DST
Child Care Program
880 S Lemon Ave, Walnut (91789-2931)
PHONE....................................909 595-1261
Josephine Jones, *Director*
Helen Hall, *President*
EMP: 67
SALES (corp-wide): 170.1MM **Privately Held**
SIC: 8699 8351 Charitable organization; child day care services
PA: Walnut Valley Unified School District
880 S Lemon Ave
Walnut CA 91789
909 595-1261

(P-24887)
WIKIMEDIA FOUNDATION INC
1 Montgomery St Ste 1600, San Francisco (94104-5516)
PHONE....................................415 839-6885
Katherine Maher, *Exec Dir*
V Ronique Kessler, *COO*
Jaime Villagomez, *CFO*
Sue Gardner, *Exec Dir*
Lila Tretikov, *Exec Dir*
EMP: 240
SALES: 89.9MM **Privately Held**
SIC: 8699 6732 Charitable organization; trusts: educational, religious, etc.

(P-24888)
WILDLIFE WAYSTATION
14831 Lttle Tjunga Cyn Rd, Sylmar (91342-5906)
PHONE....................................818 899-5201
Martine Colette, *President*
Peggy Summers, *Admin Sec*
Stacey Holman, *Bookkeeper*
Deanna Armbruster, *Director*
Martine D Colette, *Manager*
EMP: 50
SQ FT: 800
SALES: 2.5MM **Privately Held**
WEB: www.wildlifewaystation.org
SIC: 8699 Animal humane society

(P-24889)
WISDOM UNIVERSITY
35 Miller Ave, Mill Valley (94941-1903)
PHONE....................................415 259-7122
Rhonda Britten, *Principal*
EMP: 51
SALES: 659.6K **Privately Held**
SIC: 8699 Charitable organization

(P-24890)
WORLD VISION INTERNATIONAL (HQ)
Also Called: Vision Fund International
800 W Chestnut Ave, Monrovia (91016-3198)
PHONE....................................626 303-8811
Dean Hirsch, *President*
Kevin Jenkins, *President*
Paul Elliott, *COO*
David Baroi, *Officer*
Sabina Kamau, *Officer*
EMP: 196
SQ FT: 94,000
SALES (est): 42.6MM
SALES (corp-wide): 1B **Privately Held**
SIC: 8699 Charitable organization
PA: World Vision Inc.
34834 Weyerhaeuser Way S
Federal Way WA 98001
253 815-1000

(P-24891)
YMCA OF SILICON VALLEY
Also Called: Southwest YMCA
13500 Quito Rd, Saratoga (95070-4749)
PHONE....................................408 370-1877
Maria Drake, *Exec Dir*
Trung Ho, *Program Dir*
EMP: 116
SALES (corp-wide): 74.7MM **Privately Held**
WEB: www.scvymca.org
SIC: 8699 8641 Personal interest organization; youth organizations

PA: Ymca Of Silicon Valley
80 Saratoga Ave
Santa Clara CA 95051
408 351-6400

(P-24892)
YOUR MAN TOURS INC
100 N Pacific Coast Hwy # 1700, El Segundo (90245-5662)
PHONE....................................513 772-4411
Jerrey Fuque, *President*
EMP: 90
SALES (corp-wide): 22.3B **Privately Held**
WEB: www.ymtvacations.com
SIC: 8699 Travel club
HQ: Your Man Tours Merger, Inc.
100 N Pacific Coast Hwy # 1700
El Segundo CA 90245
310 649-3820

8711 Engineering Services

(P-24893)
7 LAYERS INC
15 Musick, Irvine (92618-1638)
PHONE....................................949 716-6512
Hans Jrgen Meckelburg, *CEO*
Fernando Rodriguez, *COO*
John Fairchild, *Web Dvlpr*
Grace Hsieh, *Project Mgr*
Deven Inamdar, *Senior Engr*
EMP: 59 **EST:** 1999
SQ FT: 20,000
SALES (est): 15.1MM
SALES (corp-wide): 280.5MM **Privately Held**
WEB: www.7layers.com
SIC: 8711 Consulting engineer
HQ: 7layers Gmbh
Borsigstr. 11
Ratingen 40880
210 274-90

(P-24894)
A P H TECHNOLOGICAL CONSULTING
2500 E Colo Blvd Ste 300, Pasadena (91107)
PHONE....................................626 796-0331
Steve Rodgers, *President*
EMP: 50 **EST:** 1974
SQ FT: 5,000
SALES (est): 2.5MM **Privately Held**
SIC: 8711 Consulting engineer

(P-24895)
A URSGI-BMDC JOINT VENTURE
4225 Executive Sq # 1600, La Jolla (92037-9122)
PHONE....................................858 812-9292
Martin Koffel, *CEO*
Burns McDonnell Engineering, *Principal*
EMP: 70
SALES (est): 2.7MM **Privately Held**
SIC: 8711 Engineering services

(P-24896)
A-C ELECTRIC COMPANY
Also Called: Automated Ctrl Technical Svcs
315 30th St, Bakersfield (93301-2511)
P.O. Box 81376 (93380-1376)
PHONE....................................661 633-5368
Dave Morton, *VP Opers*
EMP: 60
SALES (corp-wide): 66.6MM **Privately Held**
SIC: 8711 Engineering services
PA: A-C Electric Company
2921 Hanger Way
Bakersfield CA 93308
661 410-0000

(P-24897)
ABBOOD ZEYAD
Also Called: Nafithat Alsharq
7914 La Mesa Blvd Apt 6, La Mesa (91942-5056)
PHONE....................................619 212-2820
Zeyad Abbood, *Owner*
EMP: 50

SALES (est): 810.9K **Privately Held**
SIC: 8711 0761 1731 1623 Electrical or electronic engineering; crew leaders, farm labor: contracting services; electric power systems contractors; electric power line construction; excavation & grading, building construction

(P-24898)
ABS CONSULTING INC
Also Called: ABS Group
300 Commerce Ste 150, Irvine (92602-1302)
PHONE..................................714 734-4242
Doug Frazier, *CEO*
Peter Yanev, *President*
Jim Johnson, *COO*
George Reitter, *CFO*
EMP: 100
SALES (est): 8MM
SALES (corp-wide): 484.4MM **Privately Held**
SIC: 8711 8742 Consulting engineer; management consulting services
HQ: Abs Group Of Companies, Inc.
1701 City Plaza Dr
Spring TX 77389

(P-24899)
ACCEL BIOTECH LLC
103 Cooper Ct, Los Gatos (95032-7604)
PHONE..................................408 354-1700
Tracy Macneal, *Mng Member*
David Boone, *Project Mgr*
Brady Boone, *Electrical Engi*
Seong Son, *Controller*
Jeff Thomas, *Opers Staff*
EMP: 68
SALES (est): 6.4MM **Privately Held**
SIC: 8711 Mechanical engineering; consulting engineer; electrical or electronic engineering
PA: Ximedica, Llc
55 Dupont Dr
Providence RI 02907

(P-24900)
ACCUNEX INC
Also Called: Accurate Electronics
20700 Lassen St, Chatsworth (91311-4507)
PHONE..................................818 882-5858
Farid Jadali, *President*
Roxana Coronado, *Vice Pres*
Mike Blaustein, *Sales Staff*
▲ **EMP:** 50
SQ FT: 25,000
SALES (est): 11.1MM **Privately Held**
WEB: www.accurate-elec.com
SIC: 8711 3679 Engineering services; electronic circuits

(P-24901)
ACETECH CONSTRUCTION INC
3699 Wilshire Blvd # 655, Los Angeles (90010-2742)
PHONE..................................213 637-4702
Chong Lee, *President*
EMP: 50
SALES: 10MM **Privately Held**
SIC: 8711 Building construction consultant

(P-24902)
ACL CONSTRUCTION COMPANY INC
207 W State St, Ontario (91762-4360)
P.O. Box 1929, Chino Hills (91709-0065)
PHONE..................................909 391-4477
Jonathan Jordan, *President*
EMP: 50
SQ FT: 800
SALES: 5MM **Privately Held**
SIC: 8711 Engineering services

(P-24903)
ACRONICS SYSTEMS INC
2102 Commerce Dr, San Jose (95131-1804)
PHONE..................................408 432-0888
Kim Tran, *CEO*
Long Tran, *Design Engr*
Michael Nguyen, *Project Mgr*
Jessica Tran, *Accounting Mgr*
Vivian Nguyen, *Purch Mgr*

EMP: 110
SQ FT: 16,000
SALES (est): 15.9MM **Privately Held**
WEB: www.acronics.com
SIC: 8711 7373 Electrical or electronic engineering; systems engineering, computer related

(P-24904)
ADAMS STREETER CIVIL ENGINEERS
16755 Von Karman Ave # 150, Irvine (92606-4980)
PHONE..................................949 474-2330
Jan A Adams, *President*
Sue Zarrin, *COO*
Chris Dyer, *CFO*
Randal Streeter, *Vice Pres*
Nick Streeter-Pe, *Vice Pres*
EMP: 57
SALES (est): 5.9MM **Privately Held**
SIC: 8711 Civil engineering

(P-24905)
ADKISON ENGINEERS INC
Also Called: Adkan Engineers
6879 Airport Dr, Riverside (92504-1903)
PHONE..................................951 688-0241
Ed Adkison, *President*
Jerry Snell, *Exec VP*
Chrissa Leach, *Vice Pres*
Yasmir Quintero, *Administration*
Chris Szewczyk, *Technician*
EMP: 52
SALES (est): 8.6MM **Privately Held**
WEB: www.adkan.com
SIC: 8711 8713 Civil engineering; surveying services

(P-24906)
ADTEK ENGINEERING SERVICE
2090 N Tustin Ave Ste 160, Santa Ana (92705-7868)
P.O. Box 325, Tustin (92781-0325)
PHONE..................................800 451-0782
Joel R Spellacy, *President*
EMP: 75 **EST:** 1974
SALES: 8.7MM **Privately Held**
WEB: www.adtekjobs.com
SIC: 8711 7361 Consulting engineer; employment agencies

(P-24907)
ADVANTEDGE TECHNOLOGY INC
271 Market St Ste 15, Port Hueneme (93041-3219)
PHONE..................................805 488-0405
Tim Edward Huggins, *CEO*
Tim Huggins, *Exec Dir*
Bruce Underwood, *Administration*
David Benham, *Senior Engr*
Myron Moore, *Site Mgr*
EMP: 60
SQ FT: 2,000
SALES (est): 14.3MM **Privately Held**
WEB: www.advantedgetechnology.com
SIC: 8711 Engineering services

(P-24908)
AECOM (PA)
1999 Avenue Of The Stars # 2600, Los Angeles (90067-6033)
PHONE..................................213 593-8000
Michael S Burke, *Ch of Bd*
Sean C S Chiao, *President*
EMP: 148
SQ FT: 31,500
SALES: 20.1B **Publicly Held**
SIC: 8711 8712 Engineering services; architectural engineering

(P-24909)
AECOM C&E INC
Also Called: Aecom Environment
1220 Avenida Acaso, Camarillo (93012-8750)
PHONE..................................805 388-3775
Rick Simon, *Manager*
Allan Burdett, *Administration*
Rachel Fish, *Manager*
EMP: 100
SALES (corp-wide): 20.1B **Publicly Held**
SIC: 8711 Consulting engineer

HQ: Aecom C&E, Inc
250 Apollo Dr
Chelmsford MA 01824
978 905-2100

(P-24910)
AECOM E&C HOLDINGS INC (DH)
1999 Avenue Of The Stars, Los Angeles (90067-6022)
PHONE..................................213 593-8000
Robert W Zaist, *CEO*
Gary V Jandegian, *President*
H Thomas Hicks, *CFO*
Judy L Rodgers, *Treasurer*
Joseph Masters, *Vice Pres*
EMP: 87
SALES (est): 4.7B
SALES (corp-wide): 20.1B **Publicly Held**
SIC: 8711 1611 1629 1623 Consulting engineer; general contractor, highway & street construction; dams, waterways, docks & other marine construction; industrial plant construction; power plant construction; pipeline construction; industrial buildings, new construction; bridge construction; tunnel construction; highway construction, elevated
HQ: Urs Holdings, Inc.
600 Montgomery St Fl 25
San Francisco CA 94111
415 774-2700

(P-24911)
AECOM GLOBAL II LLC
1320 S Simpson Cir, Anaheim (92806-5531)
PHONE..................................415 774-2700
Bill Prior, *Branch Mgr*
EMP: 73
SALES (corp-wide): 20.1B **Publicly Held**
SIC: 8711 Engineering services
HQ: Aecom Global Ii, Llc
1999 Avenue Of The Stars
Los Angeles CA 90067
213 593-8100

(P-24912)
AECOM GLOBAL II LLC
130 Robin Hill Rd Ste 100, Goleta (93117-3153)
PHONE..................................805 692-0600
Tim Cohen, *Senior Partner*
Julie Doane Allmon, *Project Mgr*
EMP: 74
SALES (corp-wide): 20.1B **Publicly Held**
SIC: 8711 Consulting engineer
HQ: Aecom Global Ii, Llc
1999 Avenue Of The Stars
Los Angeles CA 90067
213 593-8100

(P-24913)
AECOM GLOBAL II LLC (HQ)
1999 Avenue Of The Stars, Los Angeles (90067-6022)
PHONE..................................213 593-8100
Michael Burke, *Mng Member*
Tommy Bell, *President*
Rick L Randall, *President*
James Angelos, *Vice Pres*
Nancy Henry, *Assistant*
EMP: 65
SALES (est): 9.7B
SALES (corp-wide): 20.1B **Publicly Held**
SIC: 8711 8712 8741 Engineering services; consulting engineer; architectural engineering; construction management
PA: Aecom
1999 Avenue Of The Stars # 2600
Los Angeles CA 90067
213 593-8000

(P-24914)
AECOM GLOBAL II LLC
2870 Gateway Oaks Dr # 150, Sacramento (95833-3577)
PHONE..................................916 679-2000
Sujan Punyamurthuai, *General Mgr*
EMP: 300
SALES (corp-wide): 20.1B **Publicly Held**
SIC: 8711 Consulting engineer
HQ: Aecom Global Ii, Llc
1999 Avenue Of The Stars
Los Angeles CA 90067
213 593-8100

(P-24915)
AECOM GLOBAL II LLC
600 Montgomery St, San Francisco (94111-2702)
PHONE..................................415 774-2700
Thomas Bishop, *Vice Pres*
Lynn Mayo, *Vice Pres*
Al Mock, *Vice Pres*
David Richmond, *Vice Pres*
John Sikora, *Vice Pres*
EMP: 83
SALES (corp-wide): 20.1B **Publicly Held**
SIC: 8711 Engineering services
HQ: Aecom Global Ii, Llc
1999 Avenue Of The Stars
Los Angeles CA 90067
213 593-8100

(P-24916)
AECOM GLOBAL II LLC
74 C St, Herlong (96113-7400)
P.O. Box 30 (96113-0030)
PHONE..................................530 827-2406
Mike Rhodes, *Branch Mgr*
EMP: 73
SALES (corp-wide): 20.1B **Publicly Held**
SIC: 8711 Engineering services
HQ: Aecom Global Ii, Llc
1999 Avenue Of The Stars
Los Angeles CA 90067
213 593-8100

(P-24917)
AECOM GLOBAL II LLC
5168 E Dakota Ave, Fresno (93727-7404)
PHONE..................................559 347-5669
Erik Newlander, *Branch Mgr*
EMP: 105
SALES (corp-wide): 20.1B **Publicly Held**
SIC: 8711 Aviation &/or aeronautical engineering
HQ: Aecom Global Ii, Llc
1999 Avenue Of The Stars
Los Angeles CA 90067
213 593-8100

(P-24918)
AECOM TECHNICAL SERVICES INC
1333 Broadway Ste 800, Oakland (94612-1924)
PHONE..................................510 834-4304
David Dickinson, *President*
EMP: 180
SALES (corp-wide): 20.1B **Publicly Held**
WEB: www.earthtech.com
SIC: 8711 8742 Engineering services; transportation consultant
HQ: Aecom Technical Services, Inc.
300 S Grand Ave Ste 1100
Los Angeles CA 90071
213 593-8000

(P-24919)
AECOM TECHNICAL SERVICES INC
901 Via Piemonte Ste 400, Ontario (91764-6597)
PHONE..................................909 554-5000
Brian Weith, *Manager*
EMP: 65
SQ FT: 15,000
SALES (corp-wide): 20.1B **Publicly Held**
WEB: www.earthtech.com
SIC: 8711 8748 Engineering services; environmental consultant
HQ: Aecom Technical Services, Inc.
300 S Grand Ave Ste 1100
Los Angeles CA 90071
213 593-8000

(P-24920)
AECOM TECHNICAL SERVICES INC
401 W A St Ste 1200, San Diego (92101-7905)
PHONE..................................619 610-7600
Richard Leja, *Manager*
EMP: 60
SALES (corp-wide): 20.1B **Publicly Held**
WEB: www.earthtech.com
SIC: 8711 8748 8641 Consulting engineer; environmental consultant; environmental protection organization

HQ: Aecom Technical Services, Inc.
300 S Grand Ave Ste 1100
Los Angeles CA 90071
213 593-8000

(P-24921)
AECOM TECHNOLOGY CORPORATION
2020 L St Ste 400, Sacramento
(95811-4267)
PHONE..................916 414-5800
Colleen Johnston, *Branch Mgr*
Victor Auvinen, *Vice Pres*
Janet Dallas, *Marketing Mgr*
EMP: 66
SALES (corp-wide): 20.1B **Publicly Held**
SIC: 8711 Consulting engineer
PA: Aecom
1999 Avenue Of The Stars # 2600
Los Angeles CA 90067
213 593-8000

(P-24922)
AECOM-TSE JOINT VENTURE
300 Lakeside Dr Ste 400, Oakland
(94612-3573)
PHONE..................510 285-6639
Simon Kim, *Vice Pres*
Etty Mercurio, *Administration*
Paul Van Der Wel, *Administration*
EMP: 99 **EST:** 2017
SQ FT: 150,000
SALES (est): 1.5MM **Privately Held**
SIC: 8711 Engineering services

(P-24923)
AEROVIRONMENT INC
900 Innovators Way, Simi Valley
(93065-2072)
PHONE..................626 357-9983
EMP: 79
SALES (corp-wide): 314.2MM **Publicly Held**
SIC: 8711 3694 3721 Engineering services; energy conservation engineering; battery charging alternators & generators; gliders (aircraft)
PA: Aerovironment, Inc.
900 Innovators Way
Simi Valley CA 93065
805 581-2187

(P-24924)
AFFORDABLE ENGRG SVCS INC
1455 Frazee Rd Ste 860, San Diego
(92108-4309)
PHONE..................973 890-8915
Jason Kamdar, *Branch Mgr*
EMP: 91
SALES (corp-wide): 39.9MM **Privately Held**
SIC: 8711 Consulting engineer
PA: Affordable Engineering Services, Inc.
1455 Frazee Rd Ste 860
San Diego CA 92108
619 522-9800

(P-24925)
ALAMEDA CORRIDOR ENGRG TEAM
1 Civic Plaza Dr Ste 600, Carson
(90745-7980)
PHONE..................310 816-0460
Rachel Vandenberg, *Admin Mgr*
Moffatt Nichol Engineers, *Partner*
Daniel Mann Johnson and Menden, *Partner*
East Los Angeles Community UNI, *Partner*
EMP: 65
SALES (est): 3.6MM **Privately Held**
WEB: www.trenchteam.com
SIC: 8711 Engineering services

(P-24926)
ALBERT A WEBB ASSOCIATES (PA)
3788 Mccray St, Riverside (92506-2927)
PHONE..................951 686-1070
A Hubert Webb, *Chairman*
Matt Webb, *President*
Todd R Smith, *CFO*
Scott Webb, *CFO*
Roger D Prend Pe, *Senior VP*
EMP: 134
SQ FT: 20,000

SALES (est): 20.1MM **Privately Held**
WEB: www.webbassociates.com
SIC: 8711 Civil engineering

(P-24927)
ALFA TECH CNSLTING ENGNERS INC (PA)
Also Called: Alfa Tech Consulting Entps
1321 Ridder Park Dr 50, San Jose
(95131-2306)
PHONE..................408 487-1200
Jeff Fini, *Ch of Bd*
William Hurley, *Manager*
EMP: 67
SQ FT: 22,000
SALES (est): 24MM **Privately Held**
WEB: www.atcginc.net
SIC: 8711 Consulting engineer

(P-24928)
ALION SCIENCE AND TECH CORP
266 E Scott St, Port Hueneme
(93041-2918)
PHONE..................805 488-8761
Christopher Learned, *Manager*
David Domaguin, *Engineer*
Ritchie Laurie, *Food Svc Dir*
EMP: 57
SQ FT: 1,000
SALES (corp-wide): 700.6MM **Privately Held**
SIC: 8711 8731 Engineering services; commercial physical research; commercial physical research
PA: Alion Science And Technology Corporation
1750 Tysons Blvd Ste 1300
Mc Lean VA 22102
703 918-4480

(P-24929)
ALTA VISTA SOLUTIONS
3260 Blume Dr Ste 500, Richmond
(94806-5715)
PHONE..................510 594-0510
Mazen A Wahbeh, *CEO*
Patrick S Lowry, *President*
EMP: 120
SALES (est): 19.8MM **Privately Held**
SIC: 8711 Consulting engineer

(P-24930)
AMEC FSTER WHELER E C SVCS INC
250 E Rincon St Ste 204, Corona
(92879-1363)
PHONE..................951 273-7400
Thomas Cheahan, *Vice Pres*
EMP: 113
SALES (corp-wide): 10B **Privately Held**
SIC: 8711 Engineering services
HQ: Amec Foster Wheeler E&C Services, Inc.
1979 Lkeside Pkwy Ste 400
Tucker GA 30084

(P-24931)
AMERICAN ELECTRONIC WARFARE AS
16766 Bernardo Center Dr, San Diego
(92128-2545)
PHONE..................858 524-6119
EMP: 63
SALES (corp-wide): 52.2MM **Privately Held**
SIC: 8711 Electrical or electronic engineering
PA: American Electronic Warfare Associates, Incorporated
44427 Airport Rd Ste 200
California MD 20619
301 863-7102

(P-24932)
AMERICAN GNC CORPORATION
888 E Easy St, Simi Valley (93065-1812)
PHONE..................805 582-0582
Dr Ching-Fang Lin, *President*
Emily Melgarejo, *General Mgr*
EMP: 50
SQ FT: 30,000

SALES (est): 5MM **Privately Held**
WEB: www.americangnc.com
SIC: 8711 Engineering services

(P-24933)
AMERICAN TECHNICAL SVCS INC
20384 Via Mantua, Porter Ranch
(91326-4441)
PHONE..................951 372-9664
Alen Petrossian, *President*
EMP: 70
SQ FT: 2,040
SALES (est): 4.5MM **Privately Held**
WEB: www.americantechnicalservices.net
SIC: 8711 Consulting engineer

(P-24934)
AMG HUNTINGTON BEACH LLC
Also Called: Notthoff Engineering
5416 Argosy Ave, Huntington Beach
(92649-1039)
PHONE..................714 894-9802
David L Patterson, *CEO*
J Ross Feeney, *COO*
Robert Taylor, *Exec VP*
Kelley Kaller, *Vice Pres*
John Nicklos, *Vice Pres*
EMP: 50
SALES (est): 11.1MM **Privately Held**
SIC: 8711 Engineering services
HQ: Aerospace Manufacturing Group Inc
5401 Business Dr
Huntington Beach CA 92649
714 894-9802

(P-24935)
ANATEC INTERNATIONAL INC (HQ)
2950 E Birch St, Brea (92821-6246)
PHONE..................949 498-3350
Blaine Curtis, *President*
Tammy Holden, *Vice Pres*
EMP: 60
SQ FT: 12,000
SALES (est): 11MM
SALES (corp-wide): 2.4B **Publicly Held**
WEB: www.anatectexas.com
SIC: 8711 Consulting engineer
PA: Curtiss-Wright Corporation
130 Harbour Place Dr # 300
Davidson NC 28036
704 869-4600

(P-24936)
APEX MACHINE WORKS INC
2118 Wilshire Blvd # 258, Santa Monica
(90403-5704)
PHONE..................310 393-5987
EMP: 100
SALES (est): 3.3MM **Privately Held**
SIC: 8711

(P-24937)
APPLIED COMPANIES
28020 Avenue Stanford, Santa Clarita
(91355-1105)
P.O. Box 802078 (91380-2078)
PHONE..................661 257-0090
Mary Elizabeth Klinger, *CEO*
Joseph Klinger, *Vice Pres*
Nayeem Khawaja, *Program Mgr*
Sheila Garcia, *Clerk*
EMP: 50 **EST:** 1962
SQ FT: 58,000
SALES (est): 10.3MM **Privately Held**
WEB: www.appliedcompanies.net
SIC: 8711 3585 3443 3621 Mechanical engineering; ice making machinery; cylinders, pressure; metal plate; motors & generators

(P-24938)
APPLIED GEOKINETICS
77 Bunsen, Irvine (92618-4218)
PHONE..................949 502-5353
Glenn Tofani, *President*
Felicity Meek, *Treasurer*
Berge Basmadjian, *Executive*
Kevin Lea, *Engineer*
EMP: 65
SALES (est): 9.3MM **Privately Held**
WEB: www.appliedgeokinetics.com
SIC: 8711 Consulting engineer

(P-24939)
APTIM CORP
4005 Port Chicago Hwy, Concord
(94520-1180)
PHONE..................925 288-2011
Karen Cracken, *Branch Mgr*
EMP: 502
SALES (corp-wide): 2.1B **Privately Held**
SIC: 8711 Engineering services
HQ: Aptim Corp.
1780 Hughes Landing Blvd # 1000
The Woodlands TX 77380
832 823-2700

(P-24940)
APTIM CORP
18100 Von Karman Ave, Irvine
(92612-0169)
PHONE..................949 261-6441
Richard Fowler, *Branch Mgr*
EMP: 63
SALES (corp-wide): 2.1B **Privately Held**
SIC: 8711 Pollution control engineering
HQ: Aptim Corp.
1780 Hughes Landing Blvd # 1000
The Woodlands TX 77380
832 823-2700

(P-24941)
AQUATIC DESIGNING INC
4801 West End Rd, Arcata (95521-9242)
PHONE..................707 822-4629
Paula E Crowley, *President*
EMP: 50
SALES (est): 1.3MM **Privately Held**
SIC: 8711 Engineering services

(P-24942)
ARCHITRENDS INC
Also Called: ATI
3860 Blackhawk Rd Ste 160, Danville
(94506-4615)
PHONE..................925 648-8800
Robert Desautels, *President*
Paul Didonato, *Vice Pres*
EMP: 70
SQ FT: 3,500
SALES (est): 4MM **Privately Held**
WEB: www.architrends.com
SIC: 8711 8741 Structural engineering; construction management

(P-24943)
ARIA GROUP INCORPORATED
17395 Daimler St, Irvine (92614-5510)
PHONE..................949 475-2915
Clive Hawkins, *President*
Charles Taylor, *Exec VP*
EMP: 70
SQ FT: 45,489
SALES (est): 12.7MM **Privately Held**
WEB: www.getbedbugs.com
SIC: 8711 Consulting engineer

(P-24944)
ARINC INCORPORATED
4553 Glencoe Ave Ste 100, Marina Del Rey
(90292-7917)
PHONE..................310 301-9040
John Belcher, *CEO*
EMP: 100
SALES (corp-wide): 66.5B **Publicly Held**
SIC: 8711 Aviation &/or aeronautical engineering
HQ: Arinc Incorporated
2551 Riva Rd
Annapolis MD 21401
410 266-4000

(P-24945)
ARMSTRONG MFG & ENGRG INC
12780 Earhart Ave, Auburn (95602-9027)
PHONE..................530 888-6262
Arthur W Armstrong, *President*
Lisa Kodl, *Office Mgr*
▼ **EMP:** 55
SALES: 7MM **Privately Held**
SIC: 8711 5084 Mechanical engineering; industrial machinery & equipment

(P-24946)
ARTIMISA & CO
220 Forest Knoll Ln, Quincy (95971-9350)
P.O. Box 3585 (95971-3585)
PHONE..................................530 283-3700
Chris D Kennedy, *President*
Christian Kennedy, *Officer*
EMP: 54
SALES (est): 2.4MM **Privately Held**
WEB: www.mainecoon.com
SIC: 8711 Engineering services

(P-24947)
ARUP NORTH AMERICA LIMITED
12777 W Jefferson Blvd, Los Angeles
(90066-7048)
PHONE..................................310 578-4182
Tony Panossian, *Branch Mgr*
Karla Martinez, *Administration*
Kevin Caraballo, *IT/INT Sup*
Paris Borovilos, *Engineer*
Moe Goudarzi, *Engineer*
EMP: 101
SALES (corp-wide): 2.1B **Privately Held**
SIC: 8711 Consulting engineer
HQ: Arup North America Limited
560 Mission St Fl 7
San Francisco CA 94105
415 957-9445

(P-24948)
**ARUP NORTH AMERICA LIMITED
(DH)**
560 Mission St Fl 7, San Francisco
(94105-0915)
PHONE..................................415 957-9445
Mahadev Ramen, *President*
Andrew Howard, *Vice Pres*
James Quiter, *Vice Pres*
Gabrielle Gallagher, *Administration*
Eric De Oliveira, *Engineer*
EMP: 200
SALES (est): 95.1MM
SALES (corp-wide): 2.1B **Privately Held**
SIC: 8711 Consulting engineer

(P-24949)
ATA ENGINEERING INC (PA)
13290 Evening Creek Dr S # 250, San
Diego (92128-4695)
PHONE..................................858 480-2000
Mary Baker, *President*
William Cherom, *Treasurer*
Paul A Blelloch, *Vice Pres*
Paul Blelloch, *Vice Pres*
Ralph Brillhart, *Vice Pres*
EMP: 60
SQ FT: 50,215
SALES: 34.5MM **Privately Held**
WEB: www.ata-e.com
SIC: 8711 Consulting engineer

(P-24950)
ATHICON
6310 San Vicente Blvd, Los Angeles
(90048-5426)
PHONE..................................213 454-0662
Victoria Lozada, *Manager*
EMP: 50 EST: 2017 **Privately Held**
SIC: 8711 Engineering services

(P-24951)
ATKINS NORTH AMERICA INC
9275 Sky Park Ct Ste 200, San Diego
(92123-4905)
PHONE..................................858 874-1810
Marc Cavallero, *Branch Mgr*
EMP: 100
SALES (corp-wide): 7.6B **Privately Held**
WEB: www.cargillmt.com
SIC: 8711 Consulting engineer
HQ: Atkins North America, Inc.
4030 W Boy Scout Blvd
Tampa FL 33607
813 282-7275

(P-24952)
**AUGUSTINE CONSULTING INC
(PA)**
24560 Silver Cloud Ct # 102, Monterey
(93940-6560)
PHONE..................................831 920-1754
Cary Christopher Augustine, *CEO*
Henry Kinnison, *President*
Pete Arsenault, *COO*

Mike Gordon, *Program Mgr*
Kristin Augustine, *Admin Sec*
EMP: 98
SALES: 20MM **Privately Held**
SIC: 8711 Engineering services

(P-24953)
AUSENCO PSI LLC (HQ)
5027 Coml Cir Ste Ef, Concord (94520)
PHONE..................................925 939-4420
Ed Meka, *President*
Andrew Fletcher, *Treasurer*
Delbert Boyle, *Senior VP*
Craig Allen, *Admin Sec*
Kenneth Bennert, *Finance Mgr*
EMP: 80
SALES (est): 10MM
SALES (corp-wide): 6.9MM **Privately
Held**
SIC: 8711 Engineering services
PA: Ausenco Usa Inc.
1320 Willow Pass Rd
Concord CA 94520
925 939-4420

(P-24954)
AUSENCO USA INC (PA)
1320 Willow Pass Rd, Concord
(94520-5232)
PHONE..................................925 939-4420
Zimi Meka, *President*
Simon Cmrlec, *President*
Ed Meka, *President*
Craig Allen, *CFO*
Linda Cochrane, *CFO*
EMP: 80
SALES (est): 6.9MM **Privately Held**
SIC: 8711 Consulting engineer

(P-24955)
AUSGAR TECHNOLOGIES INC
10721 Treena St Ste 100, San Diego
(92131-1016)
PHONE..................................855 428-7427
Jonathan Dien, *President*
Eric Lofgren, *CFO*
Karen Dien, *Admin Sec*
Saul Dien,
EMP: 115
SQ FT: 16,000
SALES (est): 18.2MM **Privately Held**
SIC: 8711 7371 7373 7379 Consulting
engineer; custom computer programming
services; computer integrated systems
design; computer related consulting serv-
ices; testing laboratories

(P-24956)
**AZTEC ENGINEERING GROUP
INC**
2151 Michelson Dr Ste 100, Irvine
(92612-1311)
PHONE..................................951 471-6190
Robert L Lemke Jr Pe, *Branch Mgr*
EMP: 61 **Privately Held**
SIC: 8711 Consulting engineer
PA: Aztec Engineering Group, Inc.
4561 E Mcdowell Rd
Phoenix AZ 85008

(P-24957)
B&C TRANSIT INC (PA)
Also Called: B & C
1924 Franklin St Ste 200, Oakland
(94612-2913)
PHONE..................................510 483-3560
Alberto Fernandez, *President*
Tanya Powell, *CFO*
Rashid Sigg, *Exec VP*
Steven Falk, *Vice Pres*
Jerome S Furman, *Vice Pres*
EMP: 70 EST: 1999
SQ FT: 25,000
SALES (est): 19.7MM **Privately Held**
SIC: 8711 Electrical or electronic engineer-
ing

(P-24958)
BARA INFOWARE INC (PA)
Also Called: Bara Construction
4115 Blackhawk Plaza Cir, Danville
(94506-4901)
PHONE..................................925 790-0130
Elina Singh, *President*
Menginder Singh, *Vice Pres*

EMP: 63
SQ FT: 600
SALES: 6.6MM **Privately Held**
SIC: 8711 1542 Engineering services;
custom builders, non-residential

(P-24959)
**BEACON WEST ENERGY
GROUP LLC**
1145 Eugenia Pl Ste 101, Carpinteria
(93013-1970)
PHONE..................................805 816-2790
Larry Huskins, *Mng Member*
Christer Peltonen,
Keith Wenal,
Michael Wracher,
EMP: 55
SQ FT: 5,000
SALES: 3MM **Privately Held**
SIC: 8711 Engineering services

(P-24960)
**BECHTEL GLOBAL ENERGY
INC**
50 Beale St Bsmt 1, San Francisco
(94105-1819)
PHONE..................................415 768-1234
Riley Bechtel, *Ch of Bd*
Peter A Dawson, *Senior VP*
Judith A Miller, *Director*
A Zaccaria, *Director*
EMP: 4013
SALES (est): 75K
SALES (corp-wide): 13.6B **Privately Held**
SIC: 8711 1629 8742 Civil engineering;
industrial plant construction; power plant
construction; construction project man-
agement consultant
HQ: Bechtel Corporation
12011 Sunset Hills Rd # 110
Reston VA 20190
571 392-6300

(P-24961)
BEDON CONSTRUCTION INC
27989 Holland Rd, Menifee (92584-9703)
PHONE..................................951 246-9005
Don Parker, *President*
Marti Manser, *Manager*
Marti Maser, *Manager*
Jerry Mayes, *Superintendent*
EMP: 68
SQ FT: 2,000
SALES (est): 7.9MM **Privately Held**
WEB: www.bedonconstruction.com
SIC: 8711 Construction & civil engineering

(P-24962)
**BIGGS CARDOSA ASSOCIATES
INC (PA)**
865 The Alameda, San Jose (95126-3133)
PHONE..................................408 296-5515
Steven A Biggs, *President*
Mark Cardosa, *Vice Pres*
Jake Delgado, *Department Mgr*
Carrie Bibolet, *Admin Asst*
David Chan, *Project Engr*
EMP: 70
SQ FT: 7,237
SALES (est): 12.8MM **Privately Held**
SIC: 8711 Structural engineering

(P-24963)
BKF ENGINEERS (PA)
255 Shoreline Dr Ste 200, Redwood City
(94065-1428)
PHONE..................................650 482-6300
David Lavelle, *President*
Maureen Nevin, *CFO*
Max Keech, *Treasurer*
Todd Adair, *Vice Pres*
Dave Evans, *Vice Pres*
EMP: 250 EST: 1915
SQ FT: 18,155
SALES (est): 68.1MM **Privately Held**
SIC: 8711 8713 Civil engineering; survey-
ing services

(P-24964)
**BLACK & VEATCH
CORPORATION**
5 Peters Canyon Rd # 300, Irvine
(92606-1793)
PHONE..................................913 458-2000
Steve Foellmi, *Vice Pres*

EMP: 50
SALES (corp-wide): 3.1B **Privately Held**
WEB: www.bv.com
SIC: 8711 Consulting engineer
HQ: Black & Veatch Corporation
11401 Lamar Ave
Overland Park KS 66211
913 458-2000

(P-24965)
BLAIR ENGINEERING INC (PA)
Also Called: Blair, Church & Flynn
451 Clovis Ave Ste 200, Clovis
(93612-1376)
PHONE..................................559 326-1400
David Mowry, *CEO*
Adam Holt, *CFO*
Jeffrey Brians, *Vice Pres*
Karl Kienow, *Vice Pres*
EMP: 95
SQ FT: 15,000
SALES (est): 13.3MM **Privately Held**
WEB: www.bcf-engr.com
SIC: 8711 8713 Civil engineering; consult-
ing engineer; surveying services

(P-24966)
**BMT COMMERCIAL USA INC
(HQ)**
355 W Grand Ave Ste 5, Escondido
(92025-2649)
PHONE..................................760 737-3505
Thomas L Johnson, *President*
Cynthia Ballard, *CFO*
Rod Edwards, *Vice Pres*
R Peter Johnson, *Vice Pres*
Thomas Anderson, *Executive*
▲ EMP: 65
SALES (est): 19.6MM
SALES (corp-wide): 223.9MM **Privately
Held**
WEB: www.scimar.com
SIC: 8711 Marine engineering
PA: Bmt Group Limited
1 Park Road
Teddington MIDDX TW11
208 943-5544

(P-24967)
BOEING COMPANY
329 Bernardo Ave, Mountain View
(94043-5225)
PHONE..................................650 316-3732
Samuel Tricoli, *Manager*
EMP: 500
SALES (corp-wide): 101.1B **Publicly
Held**
SIC: 8711 3812 Engineering services;
radar systems & equipment
PA: The Boeing Company
100 N Riverside Plz
Chicago IL 60606
312 544-2000

(P-24968)
BOEING COMPANY
5800 Woolsey Canyon Rd, West Hills
(91304-1148)
PHONE..................................818 466-8800
Philip Condit, *Branch Mgr*
Joseph Lindquist, *Engineer*
EMP: 50
SALES (corp-wide): 101.1B **Publicly
Held**
SIC: 8711 8748 Engineering services;
safety training service
PA: The Boeing Company
100 N Riverside Plz
Chicago IL 60606
312 544-2000

(P-24969)
BOOZ ALLEN HAMILTON INC
2250 E Imperial Hwy # 540, El Segundo
(90245-3543)
PHONE..................................310 524-1557
Loren Caddick, *Manager*
EMP: 60 **Publicly Held**
WEB: www.arinc.com
SIC: 8711 Engineering services
HQ: Booz Allen Hamilton Inc.
8283 Greensboro Dr # 700
Mc Lean VA 22102
703 902-5000

(P-24970)
BOYLE ENGINEERING CORPORATION
999 W Town And Country Rd, Orange (92868-4713)
P.O. Box 7350, Newport Beach (92658-7350)
PHONE.............................714 543-5274
EMP: 80
SALES (corp-wide): 8.3B **Publicly Held**
SIC: 8711 8712
HQ: Boyle Engineering Corporation
  999 W Town And Country Rd
  Orange CA 92868
  949 476-3300

(P-24971)
BRADY GCE II
2655 Camino, San Diego (92108)
PHONE.............................858 496-0500
Marisol Canales, *Principal*
Richard Brady, *Principal*
EMP: 99 EST: 2013
SQ FT: 20,000
SALES (est): 2.7MM **Privately Held**
SIC: 8711 1542 1623 8744 Civil engineering; commercial & office building, new construction; water & sewer line construction;

(P-24972)
BRINDERSON LP (HQ)
19000 Macarthur Blvd # 800, Irvine (92612-1461)
PHONE.............................714 466-7100
Gary Wilson, *Principal*
Billy Short, *Exec VP*
Kris Aflatooni, *Program Mgr*
Bob Lawvey, *Program Mgr*
Arnold Gonzalez, *Area Mgr*
EMP: 150
SQ FT: 30,000
SALES (est): 388.4MM
SALES (corp-wide): 1.3B **Publicly Held**
SIC: 8711 1629 Engineering services; dams, waterways, docks & other marine construction
PA: Aegion Corporation
  17988 Edison Ave
  Chesterfield MO 63005
  636 530-8000

(P-24973)
BRINDERSON LP
19000 Macarthur Blvd # 800, Irvine (92612-1461)
PHONE.............................714 466-7100
EMP: 60
SALES (est): 2.5MM
SALES (corp-wide): 1.3B **Publicly Held**
SIC: 8711
HQ: Energy & Mining Holding Company Llc
  17988 Edison Ave
  Chesterfield MO 63005
  636 530-8000

(P-24974)
BROSAMER & WALL INC
1777 Oakland Blvd Ste 300, Walnut Creek (94596-4063)
PHONE.............................925 932-7900
Robert Brosamer, *Ch of Bd*
Charles Wall, *Vice Ch Bd*
EMP: 140 EST: 2012
SQ FT: 13,000
SALES: 60.6MM **Privately Held**
SIC: 8711 Engineering services

(P-24975)
BROWN AND CALDWELL (PA)
201 N Civic Dr Ste 115, Walnut Creek (94596-3865)
P.O. Box 8045 (94596-1220)
PHONE.............................925 937-9010
Craig Goehring, *CEO*
Richard D' Amanto, *President*
James Miller, *Vice Ch Bd*
Cindy Paulson, *Officer*
Carey Allen, *Senior VP*
▲ EMP: 131
SQ FT: 24,000
SALES (est): 496.4MM **Privately Held**
SIC: 8711 Civil engineering; sanitary engineers; consulting engineer

(P-24976)
BROWN AND CALDWELL
202 Cousteau Pl Ste 175, Davis (95618-7761)
PHONE.............................530 747-0650
Dave Zuber, *Manager*
William Pevec, *Engineer*
EMP: 80
SQ FT: 4,000
SALES (corp-wide): 496.4MM **Privately Held**
SIC: 8711 Consulting engineer
PA: Brown And Caldwell
  201 N Civic Dr Ste 115
  Walnut Creek CA 94596
  925 937-9010

(P-24977)
BROWN AND CALDWELL
9665 Chesapeake Dr # 201, San Diego (92123-1383)
PHONE.............................858 514-8822
George Khoury, *Vice Pres*
Victor Occiano, *Vice Pres*
Alexander Aquino, *Engineer*
Billy Chu, *Engineer*
Jocelyn Lu, *Engineer*
EMP: 56
SALES (corp-wide): 496.4MM **Privately Held**
SIC: 8711 Civil engineering; sanitary engineers; consulting engineer
PA: Brown And Caldwell
  201 N Civic Dr Ste 115
  Walnut Creek CA 94596
  925 937-9010

(P-24978)
BSK ASSOCIATES
Also Called: B S K Analytical Laboratories
1414 Stanislaus St, Fresno (93706-1623)
PHONE.............................559 497-2888
Jeff Koelelwyn, *Director*
Mike Vartanian, *CFO*
Adam Trevarrow, *Project Mgr*
EMP: 60
SQ FT: 6,316
SALES (corp-wide): 55.3MM **Privately Held**
WEB: www.bskinc.com
SIC: 8711 8734 Professional engineer; testing laboratories
PA: Bsk Associates
  550 W Locust Ave
  Fresno CA 93650
  559 497-2880

(P-24979)
BURNS & MCDONNELL INC
140 S State College Blvd, Brea (92821-5850)
PHONE.............................714 256-1595
Ken Gerling, *Branch Mgr*
Travis McKinney, *Department Mgr*
Kevin Mathey, *Engineer*
Donna Webb, *Manager*
Holly Shores, *Regional*
EMP: 80
SALES (corp-wide): 3.3B **Privately Held**
SIC: 8711 Consulting engineer
PA: Burns & Mcdonnell, Inc.
  9400 Ward Pkwy
  Kansas City MO 64114
  816 333-9400

(P-24980)
C D LYON CONSTRUCTION INC (PA)
380 W Stanley Ave, Ventura (93001-1350)
P.O. Box 1456 (93002-1456)
PHONE.............................805 653-0173
Christopher D Lyon, *CEO*
Debra C Lyon, *Corp Secy*
Vincent Torres, *Opers Mgr*
EMP: 80
SALES (est): 23.5MM **Privately Held**
WEB: www.cdlyon.com
SIC: 8711 Petroleum engineering

(P-24981)
CALIFORNIA ENVMTL SYSTEMS INC
12265 Locksley Ln, Auburn (95602-2055)
PHONE.............................530 820-3693
Carter Pierce, *Principal*
Jeanette Pierce, *Controller*
EMP: 70 EST: 2011
SQ FT: 10,000
SALES: 6MM **Privately Held**
SIC: 8711 Engineering services

(P-24982)
CALIFORNIA MFG TECH CONSULTING
Also Called: Cmtc
690 Knox St Ste 200, Torrance (90502-1323)
PHONE.............................310 263-3060
Robert Wee, *CEO*
Bill Doxakis, *Partner*
James Watson, *President*
Patrick Billiter, *CFO*
James R Watson, *Vice Pres*
EMP: 86
SQ FT: 10,000
SALES: 29.9MM **Privately Held**
SIC: 8711 8742 Consulting engineer; marketing consulting services

(P-24983)
CALNETIX INC (PA)
Also Called: Calnetix Technologies
16323 Shoemaker Ave, Cerritos (90703-2244)
PHONE.............................562 293-1660
Vatche Artinian, *President*
Dennis Strouse, *COO*
Ian Hart, *CFO*
Herman Artinian, *Vice Pres*
Patrick McMullen, *Director*
▲ EMP: 105 EST: 1998
SQ FT: 68,000
SALES: 22MM **Privately Held**
WEB: www.calnetix.com
SIC: 8711 Engineering services

(P-24984)
CALNEV PIPE LINE LLC
1100 W Town And Cntry Rd, Orange (92868-4600)
PHONE.............................714 560-4400
Richard Kinder,
EMP: 200
SALES: 66.3MM **Publicly Held**
WEB: www.kindermorgan.com
SIC: 8711 Energy conservation engineering
HQ: Kinder Morgan Energy Partners, L.P.
  1001 La St Ste 1000
  Houston TX 77002
  713 369-9000

(P-24985)
CAMBRIDGE DESIGN PARTNR INC
228 Hamilton Ave Fl 3, Palo Alto (94301-2583)
PHONE.............................650 387-7812
Matt Schumann, *CEO*
Dominique Freeman, *Admin Sec*
EMP: 85 EST: 2015
SALES (est): 1.6MM **Privately Held**
SIC: 8711 8742 7379 Engineering services; management consulting services; business consultant; business planning & organizing services; marketing consulting services; computer related consulting services; data processing consultant

(P-24986)
CAPITAL ENGINEERING CONS INC (PA)
11020 Sun Center Dr # 100, Rancho Cordova (95670-6287)
PHONE.............................916 851-3500
Lowell E Shields, *President*
Thomas Duval, *Treasurer*
John Lionakis, *Vice Pres*
Bob Barcelon, *Administration*
Mark Reid, *Info Tech Dir*
EMP: 59
SQ FT: 6,800
SALES: 7.6MM **Privately Held**
WEB: www.capital-engineering.com
SIC: 8711 Consulting engineer

(P-24987)
CARLILEMACY INC
15 3rd St, Santa Rosa (95401-6204)
PHONE.............................707 542-6451
David Hanson, *President*
Mark Hale, *Treasurer*
Curtis Nichols, *Vice Pres*
Bruce Jarvis, *Admin Sec*
Curt Nichols, *Engineer*
EMP: 50
SQ FT: 10,000
SALES (est): 6.8MM **Privately Held**
WEB: www.carlilemacy.com
SIC: 8711 Civil engineering

(P-24988)
CARLSON BARBEE & GIBSON INC
2633 Camino Ramon Ste 350, San Ramon (94583-9139)
PHONE.............................925 866-0322
David Carlson, *President*
Grant Gibson, *Vice Pres*
Michael Barbee, *Admin Sec*
Christopher Quibol, *Admin Asst*
Justin Deknoblough, *Project Mgr*
EMP: 100
SQ FT: 6,800
SALES (est): 14.3MM **Privately Held**
WEB: www.cbandg.com
SIC: 8711 Civil engineering

(P-24989)
CAROLLO ENGINEERS INC (PA)
2700 Ygnacio Valley Rd # 300, Walnut Creek (94598-3466)
PHONE.............................925 932-1710
Balakrishnan Narayanan, *President*
Gary Meyerhofer, *Partner*
Rick D Wheadon, *Treasurer*
John Briones, *Assoc VP*
Michael Fleury, *Assoc VP*
EMP: 100
SQ FT: 20,000
SALES (est): 188.6MM **Privately Held**
SIC: 8711 Consulting engineer

(P-24990)
CAROLLO ENGINEERS INC
3100 S Harbor Blvd # 200, Santa Ana (92704-6823)
PHONE.............................714 540-4300
Mary Lee, *Manager*
Ash K Wason, *Partner*
Toby Weissert, *Partner*
C B Hagar, *Principal*
John S Heckler, *Principal*
EMP: 90
SALES (corp-wide): 188.6MM **Privately Held**
SIC: 8711 Consulting engineer
PA: Carollo Engineers, Inc.
  2700 Ygnacio Valley Rd # 300
  Walnut Creek CA 94598
  925 932-1710

(P-24991)
CAROLLO ENGINEERS INC
701 Palomar Airport Rd, Carlsbad (92011-1027)
PHONE.............................858 505-1020
Gary Deis, *Manager*
EMP: 110
SALES (corp-wide): 188.6MM **Privately Held**
SIC: 8711 Consulting engineer
PA: Carollo Engineers, Inc.
  2700 Ygnacio Valley Rd # 300
  Walnut Creek CA 94598
  925 932-1710

(P-24992)
CBS BROADCASTING INC
7800 Beverly Blvd, Los Angeles (90036-2112)
PHONE.............................323 575-2345
Michael Klausman, *Senior VP*
Garen Vandebeek, *Vice Pres*
Al Colini, *Engineer*
Lyn Sereno, *Human Res Mgr*
Bob Blair, *Opers Staff*
EMP: 90
SALES (corp-wide): 25.9B **Publicly Held**
SIC: 8711 Engineering services
HQ: Cbs Broadcasting Inc.
  524 W 57th St
  New York NY 10019
  212 975-4321

PRODUCTS & SVCS

(P-24993)
CDM SMITH INC
46 Discovery Ste 250, Irvine (92618-3133)
PHONE..............................949 752-5452
Steve Brewer, *Manager*
R B Chalmers, *Principal*
EMP: 72
SALES (corp-wide): 1.1B **Privately Held**
WEB: www.cdm.com
SIC: 8711 Consulting engineer
PA: Cdm Smith Inc
　　75 State St Ste 701
　　Boston MA 02109
　　617 452-6000

(P-24994)
CDM SMITH INC
Also Called: Camp Dresser & McKee
703 Palomar Airport Rd # 300, Carlsbad
(92011-1043)
PHONE..............................760 438-7755
Kelly Burn-Roy, *Director*
Keith London, *Principal*
Tony Arce, *General Mgr*
Jason Yoshimura, *Project Mgr*
Thomas Sweet, *Buyer*
EMP: 60
SALES (corp-wide): 1.1B **Privately Held**
WEB: www.cdm.com
SIC: 8711 Consulting engineer
PA: Cdm Smith Inc
　　75 State St Ste 701
　　Boston MA 02109
　　617 452-6000

(P-24995)
CDM SMITH INC
2300 Clayton Rd Ste 950, Concord
(94520-2196)
PHONE..............................617 452-6000
Randall Smith, *Manager*
Paul Meyerhofer, *Vice Pres*
EMP: 80
SALES (corp-wide): 1.1B **Privately Held**
WEB: www.cdm.com
SIC: 8711 Consulting engineer
PA: Cdm Smith Inc
　　75 State St Ste 701
　　Boston MA 02109
　　617 452-6000

(P-24996)
CE2 KLEINFELDER JV
7901 Stoneridge Dr # 315, Pleasanton
(94588-3677)
PHONE..............................925 463-7301
Clyde Wong, *Principal*
EMP: 72
SQ FT: 300
SALES (est): 3.3MM **Privately Held**
SIC: 8711 8748 Consulting engineer; energy conservation engineering; systems analysis & engineering consulting services

(P-24997)
CEM BUILDERS INC
Also Called: Dirtmarket , The
37 S 4th St, Campbell (95008-2943)
PHONE..............................408 395-1490
David Rossi, *CEO*
Lesley Matheson, *President*
Nathan Stanley, *Vice Pres*
EMP: 50
SQ FT: 3,000
SALES: 2MM **Privately Held**
WEB: www.dirtmarket.com
SIC: 8711 5093 Engineering services; scrap & waste materials

(P-24998)
CH2M HILL INC
155 Grand Ave Ste 800, Oakland
(94612-3767)
P.O. Box 12681 (94604-2681)
PHONE..............................510 604-4144
Robert Keyes, *Manager*
Ana Demorest, *Project Mgr*
EMP: 200
SALES (corp-wide): 14.9B **Publicly Held**
SIC: 8711 Consulting engineer; civil engineering
HQ: Ch2m Hill, Inc.
　　9191 S Jamaica St
　　Englewood CO 80112
　　303 771-0900

(P-24999)
CHADUXTT JV
1230 Columbia St Ste 1000, San Diego
(92101-8588)
PHONE..............................619 525-7188
Michael J Wanta, *President*
Ed Philemonof, *Principal*
EMP: 83
SALES (est): 4.5MM **Privately Held**
SIC: 8711 Consulting engineer

(P-25000)
CHEVRON ENERGY TECHNOLOGY CO (HQ)
100 Chevron Way, Richmond
(94801-2016)
PHONE..............................510 242-5059
R William Potter, *Principal*
EMP: 72
SALES (est): 24.9MM
SALES (corp-wide): 166.3B **Publicly Held**
WEB: www.chevrontexaco.com
SIC: 8711 Engineering services
PA: Chevron Corporation
　　6001 Bollinger Canyon Rd
　　San Ramon CA 94583
　　925 842-1000

(P-25001)
CIERRA WIRELESS
2738 Loker Ave W Ste A, Carlsbad
(92010-6629)
PHONE..............................760 476-8700
Jason Collinhower, *President*
EMP: 110
SALES (est): 4.2MM **Privately Held**
WEB: www.sierrawireless.com
SIC: 8711 4813 Engineering services;

(P-25002)
CITY OF DALY CITY
Also Called: Public Works Engineering Div
333 90th St Fl 1, Daly City (94015-1808)
PHONE..............................650 991-8064
John Fuller, *Director*
EMP: 70 **Privately Held**
WEB: www.dalycity.org
SIC: 8711 9111 Engineering services; mayors' offices
PA: City Of Daly City
　　333 90th St
　　Daly City CA 94015
　　650 991-8000

(P-25003)
CITY OF GLENDALE
Also Called: Engineering Public Works
633 E Broadway Ste 205, Glendale
(91206-4310)
PHONE..............................818 548-3945
Lou Le Blanc, *Director*
EMP: 60 **Privately Held**
WEB: www.glendaleca.com
SIC: 8711 9511 Engineering services; air, water & solid waste management;
PA: City Of Glendale
　　141 N Glendale Ave Fl 2
　　Glendale CA 91206
　　818 548-2085

(P-25004)
CITY OF LOS ANGELES
Also Called: Public Works Dept
600 S Spring St Unit 200, Los Angeles
(90014-1979)
PHONE..............................213 978-0259
Deborah Weignard, *Branch Mgr*
EMP: 1000 **Privately Held**
WEB: www.lacity.org
SIC: 8711 9532 Mechanical engineering; electrical or electronic engineering; urban & community development;
PA: City Of Los Angeles
　　200 N Spring St Ste 303
　　Los Angeles CA 90012
　　213 978-0600

(P-25005)
CITY OF LOS ANGELES
6262 Van Nuys Blvd # 451, Van Nuys
(91401-2793)
PHONE..............................818 756-8022
Michael Kantor, *Branch Mgr*
Claudia Rodriguez, *Bd of Directors*
Connie Mesinas, *Clerk*

EMP: 508 **Privately Held**
WEB: www.lacity.org
SIC: 8711 9224 Fire protection engineering; fire protection
PA: City Of Los Angeles
　　200 N Spring St Ste 303
　　Los Angeles CA 90012
　　213 978-0600

(P-25006)
CITY OF VACAVILLE
Also Called: Public Works Office
650 Merchant St, Vacaville (95688-6992)
PHONE..............................707 449-5170
Dale Pfeiffer, *Manager*
EMP: 400 **Privately Held**
WEB: www.lenaugustine.com
SIC: 8711 Engineering services
PA: City Of Vacaville
　　650 Merchant St
　　Vacaville CA 95688
　　707 449-5100

(P-25007)
CITY OF WOODLAND
Also Called: Public Works Department
42929 County Road 24, Woodland
(95776-9111)
PHONE..............................530 661-5961
Gary Wagner, *Director*
EMP: 75 **Privately Held**
WEB: www.ci.woodland.ca.us
SIC: 8711 8748 Engineering services; city planning
PA: City Of Woodland
　　300 1st St
　　Woodland CA 95695
　　530 661-5830

(P-25008)
CLARK RICHARDSON AND BISKUP
Also Called: C.R. B Cnsulting Engineers Inc
3207 Grey Hawk Ct Ste 150, Carlsbad
(92010-6668)
PHONE..............................760 496-3714
EMP: 51
SALES (corp-wide): 128MM **Privately Held**
SIC: 8711 Consulting engineer
PA: Clark, Richardson And Biskup Consulting Engineers, Inc.
　　1251 Nw Briarcliff Pkwy # 500
　　Kansas City MO 64116
　　816 880-9800

(P-25009)
COMPREHENSIVE ENVIRO
1615 Murray Canyon Rd, San Diego
(92108-4314)
PHONE..............................619 294-9400
EMP: 50
SALES (est): 1.5MM **Privately Held**
SIC: 8711

(P-25010)
CONCEPT TECHNOLOGY INC
2941 W Macarthur Blvd # 136, Santa Ana
(92704-6952)
PHONE..............................949 851-6550
EMP: 468
SALES (corp-wide): 21.7MM **Privately Held**
SIC: 8711 Consulting engineer
PA: Concept Technology, Inc.
　　895 Dove St Fl 3
　　Newport Beach CA 92660
　　949 854-7047

(P-25011)
CONDOR EARTH TECHNOLOGIES INC
17857 High School Rd, Jamestown
(95327-9769)
PHONE..............................209 984-4593
Robert John Job, *Branch Mgr*
EMP: 51
SALES (corp-wide): 12.2MM **Privately Held**
WEB: www.condorearth.com
SIC: 8711 8713 Consulting engineer; surveying services
PA: Condor Earth Technologies, Inc.
　　21663 Brian Ln
　　Sonora CA 95370
　　209 532-0361

(P-25012)
CONNEXSYS ENGINEERING INC
1320 Willow Pass Rd # 500, Concord
(94520-5269)
PHONE..............................510 243-2050
Flavio Santini, *CEO*
Franklin L Baker, *COO*
EMP: 50
SQ FT: 10,000
SALES (est): 11.5MM
SALES (corp-wide): 13.1MM **Privately Held**
WEB: www.connexsysinc.com
SIC: 8711 Consulting engineer
PA: Versa Engineering & Technology, Inc.
　　1320 Willow Pass Rd # 500
　　Concord CA 94520
　　925 405-4505

(P-25013)
CONSTRUCTION TSTG & ENGRG INC (PA)
1441 Montiel Rd Ste 115, Escondido
(92026-2239)
PHONE..............................760 746-4955
Thomas Gaeto, *CEO*
Rodney Ballard, *Vice Pres*
Dharmesh Amin, *Branch Mgr*
EMP: 60
SQ FT: 4,800
SALES (est): 21.1MM **Privately Held**
SIC: 8711 Construction & civil engineering

(P-25014)
CONTINENTAL GRAPHICS CORP
Also Called: Continental Data Graphics
4000 N Lakewood Blvd, Long Beach
(90808-1700)
PHONE..............................714 503-4200
Steve Meade, *Manager*
Jose Madrid, *Vice Pres*
Otto Varela, *IT/INT Sup*
Victor Petre, *Technical Staff*
Mohammed Kasbati, *Opers Staff*
EMP: 875
SALES (corp-wide): 101.1B **Publicly Held**
WEB: www.cdgnow.com
SIC: 8711 Engineering services
HQ: Continental Graphics Corporation
　　4060 N Lakewood Blvd
　　Long Beach CA 90808
　　714 503-4200

(P-25015)
COOPER VALI & ASSOCIATES INC (DH)
1850 Gateway Blvd Ste 100, Concord
(94520-8447)
PHONE..............................510 446-8301
Gary Bedey, *CEO*
John Collins, *COO*
Marian Ross, *CFO*
Agnes Weber, *Officer*
Connie Fremier, *Exec VP*
EMP: 80
SQ FT: 3,000
SALES (est): 32.1MM
SALES (corp-wide): 165.4MM **Privately Held**
SIC: 8711 Construction & civil engineering; building construction consultant
HQ: Trc Companies, L.L.C.
　　650 Suffolk St
　　Lowell MA 01854
　　978 970-5600

(P-25016)
CORA CONSTRUCTORS INC
Also Called: General Contractor
75140 Saint Charles Pl A, Palm Desert
(92211-9044)
PHONE..............................760 674-3201
Dennis Stockton, *CEO*
EMP: 50
SQ FT: 2,500
SALES (est): 11.3MM **Privately Held**
WEB: www.coraconstructors.com
SIC: 8711 Building construction consultant

(P-25017)
COUNTY ENGINEERS ASSN CAL
120 Round Ct, Petaluma (94952-4720)
PHONE..............................707 762-3492
EMP: 58

SALES: 353.7K **Privately Held**
SIC: 8711

(P-25018)
COUNTY OF LOS ANGELES
Also Called: Engineering Division
44933 Fern Ave, Lancaster (93534-2461)
PHONE..................................661 723-6088
Bert Perry, *Branch Mgr*
EMP: 130 **Privately Held**
WEB: www.co.la.ca.us
SIC: 8711 9111 Engineering services; executive offices
PA: County Of Los Angeles
500 W Temple St Ste 437
Los Angeles CA 90012
213 974-1101

(P-25019)
COUNTY OF LOS ANGELES
Public Works, Dept of
14747 Ramona Blvd, Baldwin Park (91706-3435)
PHONE..................................626 337-1277
William Wolfer, *Branch Mgr*
EMP: 130 **Privately Held**
WEB: www.co.la.ca.us
SIC: 8711 9199 Engineering services; general government administration;
PA: County Of Los Angeles
500 W Temple St Ste 437
Los Angeles CA 90012
213 974-1101

(P-25020)
COUNTY OF MARIN
Also Called: Department of Public Works
3501 Civic Center Dr, San Rafael (94903-4112)
P.O. Box 4186 (94913-4186)
PHONE..................................415 499-7877
Mehdi Sadjadi, *Director*
EMP: 200 **Privately Held**
SIC: 8711 1611 7349 6552 Civil engineering; highway & street construction; building maintenance services; subdividers & developers; automotive & apparel trimmings
PA: County Of Marin
3501 Civic Center Dr # 258
San Rafael CA 94903
415 473-6358

(P-25021)
COUNTY OF PLACER
Also Called: Public Works Dept
3091 County Center Dr # 290, Auburn (95603-2610)
PHONE..................................530 889-7500
Ken Grehm, *Director*
EMP: 150 **Privately Held**
WEB: www.ssvems.com
SIC: 8711 9511 Structural engineering;
PA: County Of Placer
2986 Richardson Dr
Auburn CA 95603
530 889-4200

(P-25022)
COUNTY OF SAN LUIS OBISPO
Also Called: County Government
Government Center Rm 207, San Luis Obispo (93408-0001)
PHONE..................................805 781-5258
Tim Nanson, *Branch Mgr*
EMP: 170 **Privately Held**
SIC: 8711 Engineering services
PA: County Of San Luis Obispo
Government Center Rm. 300
San Luis Obispo CA 93408
805 781-5040

(P-25023)
CROWN ENERGY SERVICES INC
Also Called: Able Services
611 Gateway Blvd, South San Francisco (94080-7015)
PHONE..................................415 546-6534
EMP: 1791 **Privately Held**
SIC: 8711 Engineering services
PA: Crown Energy Services, Inc.
868 Folsom St
San Francisco CA 94107

(P-25024)
CSG CONSULTANTS INC (PA)
550 Pilgrim Dr, Foster City (94404-1253)
PHONE..................................650 522-2500
Cyrus Kianpour, *CEO*
Dave Gottlieb, *CFO*
Hatem Ahmed, *Vice Pres*
Khoa Duong, *Vice Pres*
Bradley Donohue, *Admin Sec*
EMP: 50
SQ FT: 16,000
SALES: 28.3MM **Privately Held**
SIC: 8711 Consulting engineer

(P-25025)
CURTISS-WRIGHT CONTROLS
28965 Avenue Penn, Santa Clarita (91355-4185)
PHONE..................................661 257-4430
Val Zarov, *Branch Mgr*
EMP: 109
SALES (corp-wide): 2.4B **Publicly Held**
SIC: 8711 Engineering services
HQ: Curtiss-Wright Controls Electronic Systems, Inc.
28965 Avenue Penn
Santa Clarita CA 91355
661 702-1494

(P-25026)
CURTISS-WRIGHT CONTROLS (DH)
28965 Avenue Penn, Santa Clarita (91355-4185)
PHONE..................................661 702-1494
Thomas P Quinly, *CEO*
David Dietz, *President*
Sara Franke, *Manager*
EMP: 172
SQ FT: 18,700
SALES (est): 51.5MM
SALES (corp-wide): 2.4B **Publicly Held**
WEB: www.cwcembedded.com
SIC: 8711 8731 3769 3625 Consulting engineer; commercial physical research; guided missile & space vehicle parts & auxiliary equipment; relays & industrial controls
HQ: Curtiss-Wright Controls, Inc.
15801 Brixham Hill Ave # 200
Charlotte NC 28277
704 869-4600

(P-25027)
D & K ENGINEERING (PA)
15890 Bernardo Center Dr, San Diego (92127-2320)
PHONE..................................858 451-8999
Scott M Dennis, *CEO*
Alex Kunczynski, *President*
Bruce Pinkston, *COO*
Jody Zevenbergen, *CFO*
Bruce Kingston, *Officer*
▲ EMP: 148
SQ FT: 60,000
SALES (est): 170.2MM **Privately Held**
WEB: www.dkengineering.com
SIC: 8711 3824 Acoustical engineering; mechanical & electromechanical counters & devices

(P-25028)
D A WOOD CONSTRUCTION INC
601 Albers Rd, Modesto (95357-1015)
P.O. Box 1810, Empire (95319-1810)
PHONE..................................209 491-4970
Danny Wood, *President*
Kristine Wood, *Admin Sec*
EMP: 56
SQ FT: 960
SALES (est): 9MM **Privately Held**
WEB: www.dawoodinc.com
SIC: 8711 Construction & civil engineering

(P-25029)
DAVID EVANS AND ASSOCIATES INC
4141 Inland Empire Blvd # 250, Ontario (91764-5003)
PHONE..................................909 481-5750
Cliff Simental, *Branch Mgr*
EMP: 50

SALES (corp-wide): 135MM **Privately Held**
WEB: www.deainc.com
SIC: 8711 Civil engineering
PA: David Evans And Associates, Inc.
2100 Sw River Pkwy
Portland OR 97201
503 223-6663

(P-25030)
DAVID EVANS ENTERPRISES INC
201 S Figueroa St Ste 240, Los Angeles (90012-2543)
PHONE..................................213 337-3680
Adriana Klooth, *Engineer*
EMP: 747
SALES (corp-wide): 25.2MM **Privately Held**
SIC: 8711 7389 Consulting engineer; design services
PA: David Evans Enterprises, Inc.
2100 Sw River Pkwy
Portland OR 97201
503 223-6663

(P-25031)
DEGENKOLB ENGINEERS (PA)
375 Beale St Ste 500, San Francisco (94105-2177)
PHONE..................................415 392-6952
Stacy Bartoletti, *CEO*
Chris Poland, *Ch of Bd*
Robert Beggs, *CFO*
David Bonneville, *Principal*
Theresa Turri, *Office Mgr*
EMP: 165
SQ FT: 22,800
SALES (est): 24.6MM **Privately Held**
WEB: www.degenkolb.com
SIC: 8711 Structural engineering; consulting engineer

(P-25032)
DELTA PROJECT MANAGEMENT INC
650 California St Fl 7, San Francisco (94108-2737)
PHONE..................................415 590-3202
Feras Al-Zubaidy, *Chairman*
Scott Kobayashi, *CEO*
Hannah Sherman, *Opers Mgr*
EMP: 60
SQ FT: 1,000
SALES (est): 2.2MM **Privately Held**
SIC: 8711 Consulting engineer

(P-25033)
DENNIS GROUP INC
705 Palomar Airpt Rd # 100, Carlsbad (92011-1060)
PHONE..................................858 847-9633
EMP: 75
SALES (corp-wide): 157.4MM **Privately Held**
SIC: 8711 Engineering services
PA: The Dennis Group Inc.
1537 Main St Fl 2
Springfield MA 01103
413 787-1785

(P-25034)
DEPLOYABLE SPACE SYSTEMS INC
Also Called: D S S
153 Castilian Dr, Goleta (93117-3025)
PHONE..................................805 722-8090
Brian Spence, *President*
Steve White, *Vice Pres*
EMP: 50
SQ FT: 3,000
SALES (est): 2.1MM **Privately Held**
SIC: 8711 Structural engineering

(P-25035)
DEVELOPMENT RESOURCE CONS INC (PA)
160 S Old Springs Rd # 210, Anaheim (92808-1260)
PHONE..................................714 685-6860
Lawrence Gates, *President*
Matthew Hellesen, *Design Engr*
Megan Shamy, *Design Engr*
Wayne Pena, *Project Mgr*
Julie Huang, *Project Engr*

EMP: 90
SQ FT: 12,000
SALES (est): 11.7MM **Privately Held**
SIC: 8711 Civil engineering

(P-25036)
DEX CORPORATION
Also Called: Data Exchange
3600 Via Pescador, Camarillo (93012-5051)
PHONE..................................805 388-1711
Sheldon Malchiconfqs, *CEO*
EMP: 150
SQ FT: 100,000
SALES (est): 6.4MM **Privately Held**
SIC: 8711 5065 Engineering services; electronic parts

(P-25037)
DIVERGENT TECHNOLOGIES INC
19601 Hamilton Ave, Torrance (90502-1309)
PHONE..................................310 339-1186
Kevin Czinger, *President*
Broc Tenhouten, *COO*
Kira Khodskaya, *CFO*
Yong Cho, *Technical Staff*
July Aye, *Engineer*
EMP: 97
SALES (est): 928.5K **Privately Held**
SIC: 8711 Mechanical engineering

(P-25038)
DMS FACILITY SERVICES LLC
5735 Krny Vlla Rd Ste 108, San Diego (92123)
PHONE..................................858 560-4191
John Harris, *Branch Mgr*
EMP: 150 **Privately Held**
WEB: www.dmsfacilityservices.com
SIC: 8711 7349 0781 Engineering services; janitorial service, contract basis; landscape services
PA: Dms Facility Services, Llc
1040 Arroyo Dr
South Pasadena CA 91030

(P-25039)
DOKKEN ENGINEERING (PA)
110 Blue Ravine Rd # 200, Folsom (95630-4711)
PHONE..................................916 858-0642
Richard Dokken, *CEO*
Richard Liptak, *President*
Bradley Dokken, *CFO*
Lynne Castillo, *Executive Asst*
Cathy Chan, *Admin Sec*
EMP: 70
SQ FT: 12,931
SALES: 21.9MM **Privately Held**
WEB: www.dokkenengineering.com
SIC: 8711 8741 Civil engineering; construction management

(P-25040)
DUDEK (PA)
605 3rd St, Encinitas (92024-3513)
PHONE..................................760 942-5147
Frank J Dudek, *Ch of Bd*
Joe Monaco, *President*
Dave Carter, *CFO*
Christine Moore, *CFO*
Shannon Baer, *Planning*
EMP: 100
SQ FT: 50,000
SALES (est): 60.7MM **Privately Held**
SIC: 8711 8748 Civil engineering; environmental consultant

(P-25041)
DZYNE TECHNOLOGIES INC
11 Vanderbilt, Irvine (92618-2011)
PHONE..................................703 454-0704
Thomas Strat, *CEO*
David Sammons, *CFO*
Adam Thurn, *Engineer*
EMP: 50 EST: 2013
SALES (est): 6.4MM **Privately Held**
SIC: 8711 Mechanical engineering; aviation &/or aeronautical engineering

(P-25042)
E2 CONSULTING ENGINEERS INC
1900 Powell St Ste 250, Emeryville (94608-1807)
PHONE.................510 652-1164
Matthew Rindiera, *Office Mgr*
Ricardo Carmona, *Business Anlyst*
EMP: 300
SALES (corp-wide): 40MM **Privately Held**
SIC: 8711 Consulting engineer
PA: E2 Consulting Engineers, Inc.
450 E 17th Ave Unit 200
Denver CO 80203
303 232-9800

(P-25043)
EARTH SYSTEMS SOUTHWEST (HQ)
79811 Country Club Dr B, Bermuda Dunes (92203-1290)
PHONE.................760 345-1588
Mark Spykerman, *President*
Jerol Brown, *Corp Secy*
Scot Stormo, *Senior VP*
Mark Houghton, *Vice Pres*
Lutz Kunze, *Vice Pres*
EMP: 59 **EST:** 1998
SQ FT: 6,750
SALES: 3.2MM
SALES (corp-wide): 20.1MM **Privately Held**
WEB: www.earthsystems.com
SIC: 8711 8734 8748 7389 Engineering services; testing laboratories; soil analysis; environmental consultant; building inspection service
PA: Earth Systems, Inc.
720 Aerovista Pl Ste A
San Luis Obispo CA 93401
805 781-0112

(P-25044)
EARTHQUAKE PROTECTION SYSTEMS
Also Called: E P S
451 Azuar Ave Bldg 759, Vallejo (94592-1148)
PHONE.................707 644-5993
Victor Zayas, *President*
Julie Robinson, *CFO*
Stanley Low, *Vice Pres*
Anoop Mokha, *Vice Pres*
▲ **EMP:** 80
SQ FT: 310,000
SALES: 40MM **Privately Held**
WEB: www.earthquakeprotection.com
SIC: 8711 Engineering services

(P-25045)
EFS WEST
28472 Constellation Rd, Valencia (91355-5081)
PHONE.................661 705-8200
Arthur Babcock, *CEO*
Robert Golden, *President*
Dante Jumanan, *Vice Pres*
Tom Soper, *Vice Pres*
Jay Persaud, *Project Mgr*
EMP: 50
SQ FT: 41,000
SALES (est): 9.7MM **Privately Held**
SIC: 8711 Engineering services

(P-25046)
EICHLEAY INC (PA)
1390 Willow Pass Rd # 600, Concord (94520-5200)
PHONE.................925 689-7000
George F Eichleay Jr, *CEO*
Tom McClure, *Safety Dir*
EMP: 150
SQ FT: 17,000
SALES (est): 48.1MM **Privately Held**
WEB: www.eichleay.com
SIC: 8711 Consulting engineer

(P-25047)
EICHLEAY INC
3780 Kilroy Airport Way # 440, Long Beach (90806-2498)
PHONE.................562 256-8600
Lori M Lofstrom, *Branch Mgr*
EMP: 149

SALES (corp-wide): 48.1MM **Privately Held**
SIC: 8711 Consulting engineer
PA: Eichleay, Inc.
1390 Willow Pass Rd # 600
Concord CA 94520
925 689-7000

(P-25048)
ELECTROSONIC INC (DH)
3320 N San Fernando Blvd, Burbank (91504-2530)
PHONE.................818 333-3600
James Bowie, *President*
Scott Meyer, *CFO*
Chris Conte, *Vice Pres*
Nico Ahlstrom, *Managing Dir*
Nancy Johnson, *Office Mgr*
◆ **EMP:** 150
SALES: 42.7MM
SALES (corp-wide): 2.2K **Privately Held**
WEB: www.mediasonic.com
SIC: 8711 7359 7812 Engineering services; audio-visual equipment & supply rental; audio-visual program production
HQ: Electrosonic Limited
Hawley Mill
Dartford DA2 7
132 222-2211

(P-25049)
EMBEE PROCESSING LLC
Also Called: Embee Processing, Inc.
2136 S Hathaway St, Santa Ana (92705-5248)
PHONE.................714 546-9842
Michael Coburn, *CEO*
Scott Chrisman, *CFO*
Jim Pintarelli, *Vice Pres*
Leslie Zimmer, *Vice Pres*
Mitch Tanner, *General Mgr*
EMP: 385 **EST:** 1947
SQ FT: 100,000
SALES (est): 56.6MM **Privately Held**
WEB: www.embee.com
SIC: 8711 3398 3479 8734 Aviation &/or aeronautical engineering; shot peening (treating steel to reduce fatigue); coating of metals & formed products; metallurgical testing laboratory
HQ: All Metals Processing Of Orange County, Llc
8401 Standustrial St
Stanton CA 90680
714 828-8238

(P-25050)
EMERY SMITH LABORATORIES INC
Also Called: Inspection and Testing
1195 N Tustin Ave, Anaheim (92807-1736)
PHONE.................714 238-6133
Mark Lastufka, *Manager*
EMP: 99
SALES (est): 5.3MM **Privately Held**
SIC: 8711 8071 Engineering services; testing laboratories

(P-25051)
ENCORE SEMI INC
9444 Waples St Ste 150, San Diego (92121-2941)
PHONE.................858 225-4993
Olivier Lauvray, *President*
EMP: 67
SALES (est): 11.2MM **Privately Held**
SIC: 8711 Electrical or electronic engineering

(P-25052)
ENERTIS SOLAR INC
1750 Montgomery St # 127, San Francisco (94111-1000)
PHONE.................415 400-5271
Jose Galindo, *President*
Inaki Herrero, *General Mgr*
EMP: 50
SALES (est): 2.8MM **Privately Held**
SIC: 8711 Consulting engineer

(P-25053)
ENGIE SERVICES US INC (HQ)
500 12th St Ste 300, Oakland (94607-4087)
PHONE.................844 678-3772
John Mahoney, *CEO*

Ryan Blair, *President*
John Sullivan, *CFO*
Mark Emerson, *Chief Mktg Ofcr*
Brad Boerger, *Vice Pres*
EMP: 60
SQ FT: 17,250
SALES (est): 835.4K
SALES (corp-wide): 31.8B **Privately Held**
SIC: 8711 Energy conservation engineering
PA: Engie
1 Place Samuel De Champlain
Courbevoie
144 220-000

(P-25054)
ENGILITY LLC
Also Called: Titan Pulse Sciences Division
2700 Merced St, San Leandro (94577-5602)
PHONE.................510 357-4610
David Price, *Manager*
EMP: 125
SALES (corp-wide): 4.6B **Publicly Held**
SIC: 8711 Consulting engineer
HQ: Engility Llc
4803 Stonecroft Blvd
Chantilly VA 20151
703 708-1400

(P-25055)
ENGILITY LLC
Also Called: Command & Control Systems
3033 Science Park Rd, San Diego (92121-1167)
PHONE.................858 552-9500
Mike Lawson, *Branch Mgr*
EMP: 202
SALES (corp-wide): 4.6B **Publicly Held**
SIC: 8711 Consulting engineer
HQ: Engility Llc
4803 Stonecroft Blvd
Chantilly VA 20151
703 708-1400

(P-25056)
ENGILITY LLC
200 W Los Angeles Ave, Simi Valley (93065-1650)
PHONE.................703 633-8300
Sewanee Johnson, *Branch Mgr*
Anthony Smeraglinolo, *CEO*
EMP: 3937
SALES (corp-wide): 4.6B **Publicly Held**
SIC: 8711 Engineering services
HQ: Engility Llc
4803 Stonecroft Blvd
Chantilly VA 20151
703 708-1400

(P-25057)
ENGINRING SFTWR SYS SLTONS INC (PA)
Also Called: E S 3
550 W C St Ste 1630, San Diego (92101-3569)
PHONE.................619 338-0380
Teri Sgammato, *President*
Doug Wiser, *COO*
Chuck Dahms, *CFO*
Daniele Pelessone, *CFO*
Clint Forrest, *Principal*
EMP: 80
SQ FT: 8,000
SALES (est): 45.9MM **Privately Held**
WEB: www.es3inc.com
SIC: 8711 Engineering services

(P-25058)
ENGLEKIRK INSTITUTIONAL INC (PA)
888 S Figueroa St Ste 180, Los Angeles (90017-5307)
PHONE.................323 733-2640
Tom Sabol, *President*
EMP: 50
SQ FT: 12,000
SALES (est): 6.2MM **Privately Held**
SIC: 8711 Structural engineering

(P-25059)
ENGLEKIRK STRUCTURAL ENGINEERS (PA)
888 S Figueroa St # 1800, Los Angeles (90017-5449)
PHONE.................323 733-6673
Tom Sabol, *President*
Christopher Rosien, *CFO*
EMP: 50
SALES (est): 6.5MM **Privately Held**
SIC: 8711 Structural engineering

(P-25060)
ENVIRONMENTAL CHEMICAL CORP (PA)
Also Called: Ecc
1240 Bayshore Hwy, Burlingame (94010-1805)
PHONE.................650 347-1555
Manjiv S Vohra, *President*
▼ **EMP:** 75
SQ FT: 21,000
SALES (est): 124.1MM **Privately Held**
WEB: www.ecc.net
SIC: 8711 1542 8744 Engineering services; commercial & office building contractors;

(P-25061)
EPRISOLUTIONS INC
Also Called: Epri Csg
3412 Hillview Ave, Palo Alto (94304-1395)
PHONE.................650 855-8900
Philip Curtis, *President*
Roger Ailshie, *Treasurer*
Walter Bak, *Vice Pres*
EMP: 80
SQ FT: 20,000
SALES (est): 8.4MM **Privately Held**
WEB: www.eprictcenter.com
SIC: 8711 Engineering services

(P-25062)
EPSILON MISSION SOLUTIONS INC
9242 Lightwave Ave # 100, San Diego (92123-6402)
PHONE.................619 702-1700
Alan Stewart, *CFO*
Robin Nordberg, *Vice Pres*
EMP: 99
SALES (est): 4.3MM **Privately Held**
SIC: 8711 Electrical or electronic engineering

(P-25063)
EPSILON SYSTEMS SOLUTIONS INC
Also Called: Rugged Engineered Pdts Sector
5482 Complex St Ste 109, San Diego (92123-1125)
PHONE.................619 702-1700
Roy Erickson, *Branch Mgr*
EMP: 115
SALES (corp-wide): 110MM **Privately Held**
SIC: 8711 Electrical or electronic engineering
PA: Epsilon Systems Solutions, Inc.
9242 Lightwave Ave # 100
San Diego CA 92123
619 702-1700

(P-25064)
EPSILON SYSTEMS SOLUTIONS INC (PA)
9242 Lightwave Ave # 100, San Diego (92123-6402)
PHONE.................619 702-1700
Bryan Min, *CEO*
Joe Quinn, *CFO*
Jeff Giglio, *Vice Pres*
Bill Lapsansky, *Vice Pres*
Ralph Staples, *Vice Pres*
EMP: 100
SQ FT: 50,000
SALES: 110MM **Privately Held**
WEB: www.epsilonsystems.com
SIC: 8711 Engineering services

(P-25065)
ERM-WEST INC (DH)
Also Called: Environmental Resources MGT
1277 Treat Blvd Ste 500, Walnut Creek
(94597-7989)
PHONE...................................925 946-0455
Tim Strawn, *President*
Gary Keating, *Senior Partner*
John C Stipa, *Treasurer*
Jonathan Beevers, *Vice Pres*
Alexandra Fraser, *Vice Pres*
EMP: 72
SQ FT: 19,455
SALES: 192.5MM
SALES (corp-wide): 358.4MM **Privately Held**
SIC: 8711 8742 Consulting engineer; management consulting services
HQ: Erm North America, Inc.
75 Valley Stream Pkwy
Malvern PA 19355
484 913-0300

(P-25066)
ES ENGINEERING SERVICES LLC
1 Park Plz Ste 1000, Irvine (92614-8507)
PHONE...................................949 988-3500
EMP: 85
SALES (est): 1.1MM
SALES (corp-wide): 182.7MM **Privately Held**
SIC: 8711 8748 Engineering services; systems analysis & engineering consulting services
PA: Montrose Environmental Group, Inc.
1 Park Plz Ste 1000
Irvine CA 92614
949 988-3500

(P-25067)
EXP US SERVICES INC
5670 Oberlin Dr, San Diego (92121-1721)
PHONE...................................858 597-0555
Paul Gibson, *Branch Mgr*
EMP: 70
SALES (corp-wide): 559.8MM **Privately Held**
SIC: 8711 Consulting engineer
HQ: Exp U.S. Services Inc.
205 N Michigan Ave # 3600
Chicago IL 60601
312 616-0000

(P-25068)
EXPONENT INC (PA)
149 Commonwealth Dr, Menlo Park
(94025-1133)
PHONE...................................650 326-9400
Toll Free:..........................888 -
Catherine Ford Corrigan, *President*
Richard L Schlenker Jr, *CFO*
Sally B Shepard, *Officer*
Robert Caligiuri, *Vice Pres*
John Osteraas, *Vice Pres*
EMP: 148
SQ FT: 153,738
SALES: 379.5MM **Publicly Held**
SIC: 8711 8742 8999 Consulting engineer; management consulting services; scientific consulting

(P-25069)
FARADAY&FUTURE INC
Also Called: Faraday & Future
18455 S Figueroa St, Gardena
(90248-4503)
PHONE...................................424 276-7616
Chaoying Deng, *CEO*
Carsten Breitfeld, *CEO*
Nick Sampson, *Senior VP*
Alan Cherry, *Vice Pres*
Dag Reckhorn, *Vice Pres*
EMP: 1500 EST: 2014
SALES (est): 1.5MM **Privately Held**
SIC: 8711 7389 6282 Engineering services; design, commercial & industrial; investment advisory service

(P-25070)
FBA INC (PA)
1675 Sabre St, Hayward (94545-1013)
PHONE...................................510 265-1888
Waldi Naja, *President*
Chris Bane, *Engineer*
Amir K Kazemi, *Manager*

EMP: 50
SALES (est): 3.2MM **Privately Held**
WEB: www.fbaengineers.com
SIC: 8711 Electrical or electronic engineering

(P-25071)
FEHR & PEERS
101 Pacifica Ste 300, Irvine (92618-7338)
PHONE...................................949 308-6300
Christine Shields, *Branch Mgr*
EMP: 55
SALES (corp-wide): 50MM **Privately Held**
SIC: 8711 Engineering services
PA: Fehr & Peers
100 Pringle Ave Ste 600
Walnut Creek CA 94596
925 977-3200

(P-25072)
FEHR & PEERS (PA)
100 Pringle Ave Ste 600, Walnut Creek
(94596-3582)
PHONE...................................925 977-3200
Matthew Henry, *CEO*
Marion Donnelly, *CFO*
Steven Brown, *Vice Pres*
Alan Telford, *Vice Pres*
EMP: 60
SQ FT: 16,000
SALES (est): 50MM **Privately Held**
SIC: 8711 Consulting engineer

(P-25073)
FICCADENTI WAGGONER & CASTLE S (PA)
16969 Von Karman Ave # 240, Irvine
(92606-4948)
PHONE...................................949 474-0502
Seb Ficcadenti, *President*
Sayola Briney, *Business Dir*
Sayola Elmohtaseb, *Business Dir*
Suzanne Whiting, *Executive Asst*
Maggie De Guzman, *Admin Asst*
EMP: 52
SALES (est): 7.6MM **Privately Held**
WEB: www.fwcse.com
SIC: 8711 Structural engineering

(P-25074)
FLINTCO PACIFIC INC
401 Derek Pl, Roseville (95678-7153)
PHONE...................................916 757-1000
John R Bates, *CEO*
David P Parkes, *President*
EMP: 80
SALES (est): 6.6MM
SALES (corp-wide): 1.5B **Privately Held**
SIC: 8711 Building construction consultant
HQ: Flintco, Llc
1624 W 21st St
Tulsa OK 74107
918 587-8451

(P-25075)
FLUOR CORPORATION
Also Called: Trs Staffing Solutions
3 Polaris Way, Aliso Viejo (92656-5338)
PHONE...................................949 349-2000
Tim Kirk, *Principal*
James Toler, *Vice Pres*
David Parker, *Exec Dir*
Patrick Wong, *Software Dev*
Mike Pena, *Design Engr*
EMP: 99
SALES (corp-wide): 19.1B **Publicly Held**
SIC: 8711 7363 Engineering services; help supply services
PA: Fluor Corporation
6700 Las Colinas Blvd
Irving TX 75039
469 398-7000

(P-25076)
FLUOR ENTERPRISES INC
5600 Cottle Rd, San Jose (95123-3696)
PHONE...................................408 256-0853
Barry Subotkin, *Branch Mgr*
EMP: 60
SALES (corp-wide): 19.1B **Publicly Held**
SIC: 8711 1799 Building construction consultant; decontamination services

HQ: Fluor Enterprises, Inc.
6700 Las Colinas Blvd
Irving TX 75039
469 398-7000

(P-25077)
FLUOR ENTERPRISES INC
9701 Jeronimo Rd, Irvine (92618-2076)
PHONE...................................949 349-2000
Philip J Carroll, *Principal*
Prashant Kumar, *Project Mgr*
Bill Sargent, *Project Mgr*
Richard Dionne, *Manager*
Steve Pitts, *Manager*
EMP: 100
SALES (corp-wide): 19.1B **Publicly Held**
SIC: 8711 Consulting engineer
HQ: Fluor Enterprises, Inc.
6700 Las Colinas Blvd
Irving TX 75039
469 398-7000

(P-25078)
FLUOR ENTERPRISES INC
1 Fluor Daniel Dr, Aliso Viejo (92698-1000)
PHONE...................................469 398-7000
Scott Snyder, *Manager*
Gregory Amparano, *Vice Pres*
Gerald Stone, *Vice Pres*
Larry Grosskreuz, *Info Tech Mgr*
Denny LI, *Engineer*
EMP: 52
SALES (corp-wide): 19.1B **Publicly Held**
SIC: 8711 Engineering services
HQ: Fluor Enterprises, Inc.
6700 Las Colinas Blvd
Irving TX 75039
469 398-7000

(P-25079)
FLUOR PLANT SERVICES INTL INC
Also Called: Fluor Daniel
1 Enterprise, Aliso Viejo (92656-2606)
PHONE...................................949 349-2000
D Michael Steuert, *CFO*
Bennett Hatfield, *COO*
Richard Carano, *Vice Pres*
Edward Godlewski, *Vice Pres*
Stephen Johnson, *Vice Pres*
EMP: 79
SALES (est): 16.5MM
SALES (corp-wide): 19.1B **Publicly Held**
SIC: 8711 Engineering services
PA: Fluor Corporation
6700 Las Colinas Blvd
Irving TX 75039
469 398-7000

(P-25080)
FLUORAMEC LLC (HQ)
1 Enterprise, Aliso Viejo (92656-2606)
PHONE...................................949 349-2000
Michelle Bell, *Director*
EMP: 50
SALES (est): 25.2MM
SALES (corp-wide): 19.1B **Publicly Held**
SIC: 8711 Engineering services
PA: Fluor Corporation
6700 Las Colinas Blvd
Irving TX 75039
469 398-7000

(P-25081)
FORD MOTOR LAND DEV CORP
3 Glen Bell Way Ste 100, Irvine
(92618-3390)
PHONE...................................949 242-6606
Dan Werbin, *Exec Dir*
Tony Varlesi, *Technology*
EMP: 500
SALES (corp-wide): 160.3B **Publicly Held**
WEB: www.fordcreditpr.com
SIC: 8711 Engineering services
HQ: Ford Motor Land Development Corporation
330 Town Center Dr # 1100
Dearborn MI 48126
313 323-3100

(P-25082)
FORWARD SLOPE INCORPORATED
Also Called: Forward Slope.
2020 Camino Del Rio N, San Diego
(92108-1541)
PHONE...................................619 299-4400
Carlos Persichetti, *President*
Kevin Noonan, *Vice Pres*
Andrew Pidduck, *Senior Mgr*
EMP: 80
SALES (est): 12.7MM **Privately Held**
WEB: www.forwardslope.com
SIC: 8711 7371 7389 Consulting engineer; software programming applications; financial services

(P-25083)
FRANK M BOOTH INC (PA)
Also Called: Valley Sheet Metal Co
222 3rd St, Marysville (95901-5948)
P.O. Box 5 (95901-0001)
PHONE...................................530 742-7134
Lawrence R Booth, *President*
Rich Gabel, *CFO*
Richard Gabel, *CFO*
Kathy Kerrisk, *Admin Asst*
Lance Blanchard, *Project Mgr*
EMP: 80
SQ FT: 75,000
SALES: 71.4MM **Privately Held**
WEB: www.frankbooth.com
SIC: 8711 Mechanical engineering

(P-25084)
FTI CONSULTING INC
350 S Grand Ave Ste 3000, Los Angeles
(90071-3424)
PHONE...................................213 689-1200
Stewart Kahn, *President*
Ruth Haile, *Exec Dir*
Jean Callam, *Managing Dir*
Alan Ruffier, *Managing Dir*
Russell Craig, *Marketing Staff*
EMP: 80
SALES (corp-wide): 2B **Publicly Held**
SIC: 8711 8748 8742 Consulting engineer; business consulting; management consulting services
PA: Fti Consulting, Inc.
555 12th St Nw Ste 3
Washington DC 20004
202 312-9100

(P-25085)
FUGRO USA LAND INC
1777 Botelho Dr Ste 262, Walnut Creek
(94596-5132)
PHONE...................................925 256-6070
Edwin Saarloos, *Security Mgr*
Osman El Manchawi, *Manager*
EMP: 50
SALES (corp-wide): 242.1K **Privately Held**
SIC: 8711 Engineering services
HQ: Fugro Usa Land, Inc
6100 Hillcroft St Ste 100
Houston TX 77081
713 369-5400

(P-25086)
FUJITSU ELECTRONICS AMER INC (DH)
Also Called: F E A
1250 E Arques Ave, Sunnyvale
(94085-5401)
PHONE...................................408 737-5600
Shinichi Machida, *President*
Irene Mason, *Assoc VP*
Victor Kan, *Exec VP*
Doug Saylor, *Senior VP*
Geldsetzer Steffen, *Business Mgr*
EMP: 84
SQ FT: 49,000
SALES (est): 18.7MM **Privately Held**
WEB: www.fma.fujitsu.com
SIC: 8711 5065 Engineering services; electronic parts & equipment

(P-25087)
FUSCOE ENGINEERING INC (PA)
16795 Von Karman Ave # 100, Irvine
(92606-4974)
PHONE...................................949 474-1960

Patrick Fuscoe, *President*
EMP: 85
SQ FT: 16,000
SALES (est): 23.8MM **Privately Held**
WEB: www.fuscoe.com
SIC: 8711 Civil engineering

(P-25088)
FUTURE ENERGY CORPORATION
9701 Elk Grove Florin Rd, Elk Grove (95624-2277)
PHONE..............................916 685-4200
Jeffrey Adkins, *Branch Mgr*
EMP: 97
SALES (corp-wide): 28.4MM **Privately Held**
SIC: 8711 Building construction consultant
PA: Future Energy Corporation
8980 Grant Line Rd
Elk Grove CA 95624
800 985-0733

(P-25089)
G2 SOFTWARE SYSTEMS INC
4025 Hancock St Ste 105, San Diego (92110-5167)
PHONE..............................619 222-8025
Georgia D Griffiths, *CEO*
William Long, *CFO*
Michelle Krencik, *Executive*
Todd Jasso, *Admin Sec*
Mark Bertone, *Sr Software Eng*
EMP: 140
SQ FT: 4,000
SALES (est): 34.2MM **Privately Held**
SIC: 8711 Engineering services

(P-25090)
GARCIA JUAREZ CONSTRUCTION INC (PA)
6801 Atlantic Ave, Long Beach (90805-1413)
P.O. Box 309, Brea (92822-0309)
PHONE..............................951 657-3535
Jim Jackson, *CEO*
EMP: 64
SALES (est): 5.1MM **Privately Held**
SIC: 8711 Engineering services

(P-25091)
GARRAD HASSAN AMERICA INC (DH)
Also Called: GL
9665 Chesapeake Dr # 435, San Diego (92123-1378)
PHONE..............................858 836-3370
Carole Barbeau, *CEO*
EMP: 70
SQ FT: 1,380
SALES (est): 13MM **Privately Held**
SIC: 8711 Consulting engineer

(P-25092)
GARRETT J GENTRY GEN ENGRG INC
1297 W 9th St, Upland (91786-5706)
PHONE..............................909 693-3391
Garrett J Gentry, *President*
Bryan Copping, *Admin Sec*
EMP: 85
SALES: 30MM **Privately Held**
SIC: 8711 Acoustical engineering

(P-25093)
GAS TRANSMISSION SYSTEMS INC
Also Called: GTS
130 Amber Grove Dr # 134, Chico (95973-5880)
PHONE..............................530 893-6711
Katie Clapp, *President*
Kathleen B Clapp, *President*
Robert Gross, *Vice Pres*
Scott R Clapp, *Admin Sec*
Scott Cameron, *Project Mgr*
EMP: 220
SQ FT: 4,500
SALES (est): 29.7MM **Privately Held**
WEB: www.gtsinc.us
SIC: 8711 Professional engineer

(P-25094)
GATAN INC (HQ)
5794 W Las Positas Blvd, Pleasanton (94588-4083)
PHONE..............................925 463-0200
Benjamin Wood, *President*
Ed Morrissey, *Treasurer*
Jack Buhsmer, *Vice Pres*
Robert Buchanan, *Principal*
David B Liner, *Admin Sec*
EMP: 55
SQ FT: 30,000
SALES (est): 46.9MM
SALES (corp-wide): 5.1B **Publicly Held**
SIC: 8711 3826 Designing; ship, boat, machine & product; analytical optical instruments
PA: Roper Technologies, Inc.
6901 Prof Pkwy E Ste 200
Sarasota FL 34240
941 556-2601

(P-25095)
GDA TECHNOLOGIES INC (HQ)
25 Metro Dr Fl 3, San Jose (95110-1316)
PHONE..............................408 753-1191
Isaac Sundarajan, *CEO*
Gopa Periyadan, *Exec VP*
Gopakumar K Periyadan, *Vice Pres*
Ravi Thummarukudy, *Vice Pres*
Sandeep Mohan Kumar, *Sales Mgr*
EMP: 100
SALES (est): 24.4MM
SALES (corp-wide): 12.1B **Privately Held**
WEB: www.gdatech.com
SIC: 8711 Electrical or electronic engineering
PA: Larsen And Toubro Limited
L&T Business Park Gate 5, Tc-2, Level 7
Mumbai MH 400 0
226 752-5656

(P-25096)
GEI CONSULTANTS INC
2868 Prospect Park Dr # 400, Rancho Cordova (95670-6065)
PHONE..............................916 631-4500
Frank Leathers, *President*
Emily Keck, *Project Engr*
Richard Anderson, *Engineer*
Jasmine Gerber, *Mktg Coord*
EMP: 55
SALES (corp-wide): 177.3MM **Privately Held**
WEB: www.geiconsultants.com
SIC: 8711 Engineering services
PA: Gei Consultants, Inc.
400 Unicorn Park Dr Ste 8
Woburn MA 01801
781 721-4000

(P-25097)
GENER8 LLC
500 Mercury Dr, Sunnyvale (94085-4018)
PHONE..............................650 940-9898
David Louis Klein, *CEO*
Osborne Zoe, *CFO*
William Bischel, *General Mgr*
Julie Dupre, *Office Mgr*
James Quigley, *Software Engr*
▲ **EMP:** 130
SQ FT: 16,000
SALES (est): 32.9MM **Privately Held**
WEB: www.gener8.net
SIC: 8711 3429 Engineering services; locks or lock sets

(P-25098)
GENERAL DYNAMICS ADVANCED INFO
General Dynamics Adv Info Sys
100 Ferguson Dr, Mountain View (94043-5239)
P.O. Box 7188 (94039)
PHONE..............................650 966-2000
John Stewart, *Branch Mgr*
Rich Riveron, *Program Mgr*
Lawrence Hartsook, *Architect*
EMP: 4000
SALES (corp-wide): 36.1B **Publicly Held**
SIC: 8711 8731 Engineering services; commercial physical research

HQ: General Dynamics Mission Systems, Inc.
12450 Fair Lakes Cir # 200
Fairfax VA 22033
703 263-2800

(P-25099)
GENERAL ELECTRIC COMPANY
2120 Diamond Blvd Ste 100, Concord (94520-5720)
PHONE..............................925 602-5950
Malcolm Jepson, *Principal*
EMP: 100
SALES (corp-wide): 121.6B **Publicly Held**
SIC: 8711 7629 Engineering services; electrical repair shops
PA: General Electric Company
41 Farnsworth St
Boston MA 02210
617 443-3000

(P-25100)
GENERAL SERVICES CAL DEPT
Also Called: Telecommunications Division
601 Sequoia Pacific Blvd, Sacramento (95811-0231)
PHONE..............................916 657-9960
Wendell McCullough, *Branch Mgr*
EMP: 500 **Privately Held**
WEB: www.4c.net
SIC: 8711 9199 Electrical or electronic engineering; general government administration;
HQ: California Department Of General Services
707 3rd St
West Sacramento CA 95605

(P-25101)
GEOCON INCORPORATED
6960 Flanders Dr, San Diego (92121-3992)
PHONE..............................858 558-6900
Michael Chapin, *CEO*
William Lydon, *CFO*
EMP: 54
SALES: 8MM **Privately Held**
SIC: 8711 Consulting engineer

(P-25102)
GEORGE G SHARP INC
1065 Bay Blvd Ste D, Chula Vista (91911-1626)
PHONE..............................619 425-4211
Joseph Aven, *Manager*
Joe Kuftack, *Manager*
EMP: 75
SALES (corp-wide): 32.1MM **Privately Held**
WEB: www.ggsharp.com
SIC: 8711 Consulting engineer
PA: George G. Sharp, Inc.
160 Broadway Rm 800
New York NY 10038
212 732-2800

(P-25103)
GEOSYNTEC CONSULTANTS INC
Also Called: Geo Mmi Engineering
1111 Broadway Ste 600, Oakland (94607-4172)
PHONE..............................510 836-3034
Pat Lucia, *Branch Mgr*
R J Dunn, *Principal*
Patrick Lucia, *Principal*
Holly Van Norman, *Admin Asst*
EMP: 50
SALES (corp-wide): 204.7MM **Privately Held**
SIC: 8711 8748 Consulting engineer; environmental consultant
PA: Geosyntec Consultants, Inc.
900 Broken Sound Pkwy Nw
Boca Raton FL 33487
561 995-0900

(P-25104)
GHD INC
718 3rd St, Eureka (95501-0504)
P.O. Box 1010 (95502-1010)
PHONE..............................707 443-8326
Steve Allen, *Principal*
Jay Walter, *Branch Mgr*
Karen Burgesser, *Benefits Mgr*

EMP: 50 **Privately Held**
SIC: 8711 Engineering services
HQ: Ghd Inc.
4747 N 22nd St Ste 200
Phoenix AZ 85016
602 216-7200

(P-25105)
GHD INC
2235 Mercury Way Ste 150, Santa Rosa (95407-5470)
PHONE..............................707 523-1010
Alex Culick, *Principal*
Lloyd B Darnell II, *Principal*
Peggy Dezurik, *Info Tech Mgr*
Mary Grace Pawson, *Project Mgr*
Margaret Dezurik, *Finance Mgr*
EMP: 100 **Privately Held**
WEB: www.sjoeng.com
SIC: 8711 Consulting engineer
HQ: Ghd Inc.
4747 N 22nd St Ste 200
Phoenix AZ 85016
602 216-7200

(P-25106)
GILBANE FEDERAL (DH)
1655 Grant St Ste 1200, Concord (94520-2790)
PHONE..............................925 946-3100
Sarabjit Singh, *CEO*
Jon Verlinde, *Senior VP*
EMP: 110
SALES (est): 1.3MM
SALES (corp-wide): 5.4B **Privately Held**
WEB: www.itsi.com
SIC: 8711 8748 Building construction consultant; environmental consultant
HQ: Gilbane Building Company
7 Jackson Walkway Ste 2
Providence RI 02903
401 456-5800

(P-25107)
GLENN A RICK ENGRG & DEV CO (PA)
Also Called: Rick Engineering Company
5620 Friars Rd, San Diego (92110-2513)
PHONE..............................619 291-0708
Roger Ball, *Principal*
William B Rick, *President*
Deborah B Ragione, *CFO*
Dennis C Bowling, *Vice Pres*
Paul J Iezzi, *Vice Pres*
EMP: 212 **EST:** 1955
SQ FT: 50,000
SALES (est): 56.6MM **Privately Held**
SIC: 8711 Civil engineering

(P-25108)
GLOBAL SOLUTIONS INTEGRATION
Also Called: Gsico
26632 Towne Centre Dr # 300, Foothill Ranch (92610-2813)
PHONE..............................949 307-1849
Cel Esmundi, *President*
EMP: 75
SQ FT: 3,000
SALES (est): 13.5MM **Privately Held**
SIC: 8711 Engineering services

(P-25109)
GPA TECHNOLOGIES INC
2368 Eastman Ave Ste 8, Ventura (93003-5770)
PHONE..............................805 643-7878
Michael Vaswani, *President*
Christine Hill, *Controller*
Jeremy Johnson, *Supervisor*
EMP: 55
SQ FT: 6,580
SALES (est): 8.6MM **Privately Held**
WEB: www.gpatech.com
SIC: 8711 Consulting engineer

(P-25110)
GRADIENT ENGINEERS INC
Also Called: Leighton & Associates
17781 Cowan Ste 140, Irvine (92614-6009)
PHONE..............................949 477-0555
Terry Brennan, *Chairman*
Kris Lutton, *President*
Fred Schultz, *CFO*
Tom Mills, *Vice Pres*
EMP: 70

SALES (est): 3.5MM
SALES (corp-wide): 29.2MM **Privately Held**
WEB: www.gradientengineers.com
SIC: 8711 8744 Engineering services;
PA: Leighton Group, Inc.
    17781 Cowan
    Irvine CA 92614
    949 477-4040

(P-25111)
GRYPHON MARINE LLC
694 Moss St, Chula Vista (91911-1616)
PHONE..................................619 407-4010
M S Karlovic, *CEO*
Stephen Karlovic, *CEO*
EMP: 50
SALES (corp-wide): 286.4MM **Privately Held**
SIC: 8711 Engineering services
HQ: Gryphon Marine, Llc
    4600 Village Ave
    Norfolk VA 23502
    757 763-6666

(P-25112)
GULFSTREAM AEROSPACE CORP GA
4150 E Donald Douglas Dr, Long Beach
(90808-1725)
PHONE..................................562 420-1818
Barry Russell, *Vice Pres*
Fred Alvarez, *IT/INT Sup*
Will Jarvis, *Technology*
Jayrard Lazo, *Engineer*
John Nguyen, *Engineer*
EMP: 800
SALES (corp-wide): 36.1B **Publicly Held**
WEB: www.gdavservices.net
SIC: 8711 3721 Engineering services; aircraft
HQ: Gulfstream Aerospace Corporation (Georgia)
    500 Gulfstream Rd
    Savannah GA 31408
    912 965-3000

(P-25113)
H M H ENGINEERS
1570 Oakland Rd, San Jose (95131-2430)
P.O. Box 611510 (95161-1510)
PHONE..................................408 487-2200
William J Wagner, *President*
Tom Armstrong, *Vice Pres*
Ryan Fong, *Engineer*
EMP: 54 **EST:** 1976
SALES (est): 7.9MM **Privately Held**
SIC: 8711 8713 Consulting engineer; surveying services

(P-25114)
HARRIS & ASSOCIATES INC
22 Executive Park Ste 200, Irvine
(92614-2704)
PHONE..................................949 655-3900
Jeff Cooper, *Branch Mgr*
Randall Berry, *Engineer*
EMP: 60
SALES (corp-wide): 70MM **Privately Held**
WEB: www.harris-assoc.com
SIC: 8711 8712 Construction & civil engineering; civil engineering; sanitary engineers; architectural engineering
PA: Harris & Associates, Inc.
    1401 Wllw Pca Rd 500
    Concord CA 94520
    925 827-4900

(P-25115)
HARRIS & ASSOCIATES INC (PA)
Also Called: Harris & Associates Cnstr MGT
1401 Wllw Pca Rd 500, Concord (94520)
PHONE..................................925 827-4900
Lisa Larrabee, *CEO*
Carl Harris, *Ch of Bd*
Guy Erickson, *President*
Gary Yagade, *President*
Ehab Gerges, *COO*
▲ **EMP:** 104
SQ FT: 23,000

SALES (est): 70MM **Privately Held**
WEB: www.harris-assoc.com
SIC: 8711 8712 Construction & civil engineering; civil engineering; sanitary engineers; architectural engineering

(P-25116)
HDR ARCHITECTURE INC
Also Called: H D R
350 S Grand Ave Ste 2900, Los Angeles
(90071-3406)
PHONE..................................626 584-1700
Al Korth, *Manager*
EMP: 100
SQ FT: 5,905
SALES (corp-wide): 1.4B **Privately Held**
SIC: 8711 8712 Designing: ship, boat, machine & product; architectural services
HQ: Hdr Architecture, Inc.
    1917 S 67th St
    Omaha NE 68106
    402 399-1000

(P-25117)
HDR ARCHITECTURE INC
201 California St # 1500, San Francisco
(94111-5002)
PHONE..................................415 546-4242
Bill Brinkman, *Director*
EMP: 55
SALES (corp-wide): 1.4B **Privately Held**
SIC: 8711 8712 Designing: ship, boat, machine & product; architectural services
HQ: Hdr Architecture, Inc.
    1917 S 67th St
    Omaha NE 68106
    402 399-1000

(P-25118)
HDR ENGINEERING INC
3230 El Camino Real # 200, Irvine
(92602-1333)
PHONE..................................714 730-2300
William Bennet, *Manager*
EMP: 150
SALES (corp-wide): 1.4B **Privately Held**
SIC: 8711 8742 Engineering services; management consulting services
HQ: Hdr Engineering, Inc.
    1917 S 67th St
    Omaha NE 68106
    402 399-1000

(P-25119)
HDR ENGINEERING INC
401 B St Ste 1110, San Diego
(92101-4271)
PHONE..................................619 231-4865
Melissa Kiscoan, *Branch Mgr*
EMP: 100
SALES (corp-wide): 1.4B **Privately Held**
SIC: 8711 Consulting engineer
HQ: Hdr Engineering, Inc.
    1917 S 67th St
    Omaha NE 68106
    402 399-1000

(P-25120)
HDR ENGINEERING INC
100 Pringle Ave Ste 400, Walnut Creek
(94596-7326)
PHONE..................................925 974-2500
Zuraile Wilson, *Principal*
EMP: 70
SALES (corp-wide): 1.4B **Privately Held**
SIC: 8711 8742 Engineering services; construction project management consultant
HQ: Hdr Engineering, Inc.
    1917 S 67th St
    Omaha NE 68106
    402 399-1000

(P-25121)
HDR ENGINEERING INC
Also Called: Hydro Power Service
2379 Gateway Oaks Dr # 200, Sacramento
(95833-4238)
PHONE..................................916 564-4214
EMP: 74
SALES (corp-wide): 2.3B **Privately Held**
SIC: 8711
HQ: Hdr Engineering, Inc.
    8404 Indian Hills Dr
    Omaha NE 68106
    402 399-1000

(P-25122)
HDR ENGINEERING INC
431 W Baseline Rd, Claremont
(91711-1608)
PHONE..................................909 626-0967
Graham E Bell, *Branch Mgr*
EMP: 56
SALES (corp-wide): 1.4B **Privately Held**
SIC: 8711 Engineering services
HQ: Hdr Engineering, Inc.
    1917 S 67th St
    Omaha NE 68106
    402 399-1000

(P-25123)
HDR/CARDNO ENTRIX JOINT VENTR
2365 Iron Point Rd # 300, Folsom
(95630-8711)
PHONE..................................916 817-4700
Dave Lecureux, *Senior VP*
EMP: 99
SALES (est): 2.6MM **Privately Held**
SIC: 8711 Engineering services

(P-25124)
HENKEL US OPERATIONS CORP
Also Called: Aerospace Material Division
2850 Willow Pass Rd, Bay Point
(94565-3237)
P.O. Box 312 (94565-0031)
PHONE..................................925 458-8086
Rosen Angelov, *Technology*
Tina Miao, *Engineer*
Peter Naye, *Engineer*
Kristin Mendoza, *Analyst*
Kristine Malzahn, *Human Res Mgr*
EMP: 170
SQ FT: 6,325
SALES (corp-wide): 22.7B **Privately Held**
SIC: 8711 Engineering services
HQ: Henkel Us Operations Corporation
    1 Henkel Way
    Rocky Hill CT 06067
    860 571-5100

(P-25125)
HENWOOD ENERGY SERVICES INC (DH)
2379 Gateway Oaks Dr # 110, Sacramento
(95833-4239)
PHONE..................................916 955-6031
Mark Henwood, *President*
David Branchcomb, *Vice Pres*
EMP: 118
SALES (est): 8.4MM
SALES (corp-wide): 36.4B **Privately Held**
WEB: www.globalenergydecisions.com
SIC: 8711 Consulting engineer
HQ: Global Energy Decisions Llc
    1495 Canyon Blvd Ste 100
    Boulder CO 80302
    720 221-5700

(P-25126)
HMS CONSTRUCTION INC (PA)
2885 Scott St, Vista (92081-8547)
PHONE..................................760 727-9808
Michael High, *President*
Ian High, *Vice Pres*
Sharon High, *Admin Sec*
Buck Hubbard, *Project Mgr*
Reynold Kam, *Project Mgr*
EMP: 75
SQ FT: 5,200
SALES (est): 35.9MM **Privately Held**
WEB: www.hmsconstructioninc.com
SIC: 8711 1781 1731 Engineering services; geothermal drilling; electrical work; electronic controls installation; general electrical contractor

(P-25127)
HNTB CORPORATION
601 W 5th St Ste 1000, Los Angeles
(90071-2028)
PHONE..................................213 403-1000
Lanson Nichols, *Vice Pres*
Khalil Saba, *Vice Pres*
Susan Shaffer, *Admin Asst*
Jessica Baker, *Technology*
Trebecca McDonald, *Engineer*
EMP: 56

SALES (corp-wide): 77.5MM **Privately Held**
WEB: www.hntb.com
SIC: 8711 Consulting engineer
HQ: Hntb Corporation
    715 Kirk Dr
    Kansas City MO 64105
    816 472-1201

(P-25128)
HNTB CORPORATION
200 Sandpointe Ave # 200, Santa Ana
(92707-8797)
PHONE..................................714 460-1600
Andres Ocon, *Branch Mgr*
Mark Ramsey, *Assoc VP*
EMP: 57
SALES (corp-wide): 77.5MM **Privately Held**
WEB: www.hntb.com
SIC: 8711 Consulting engineer
HQ: Hntb Corporation
    715 Kirk Dr
    Kansas City MO 64105
    816 472-1201

(P-25129)
HNTB GERWICK WATER SOLUTIONS
200 Sandpointe Ave, Santa Ana
(92707-5751)
PHONE..................................714 460-1600
Larry Davis, *Partner*
Dale Berner, *Partner*
EMP: 150
SALES (est): 3.7MM **Privately Held**
SIC: 8711 8712 Consulting engineer; architectural services

(P-25130)
HOLDREGE KULL CONSULTIMG ENGR
48 Bellarmine Ct Ste 40, Chico
(95928-7261)
PHONE..................................530 894-2487
Tom Hodrege, *President*
EMP: 70
SALES (est): 4.2MM **Privately Held**
SIC: 8711 Consulting engineer

(P-25131)
HOLMES & NARVER INC (HQ)
999 W Town And Country Rd, Orange
(92868-4713)
P.O. Box 6240 (92863-6240)
PHONE..................................714 567-2400
Danny Seal, *CEO*
Raymond Landy, *President*
Dennis Deslatte, *CFO*
Tina Clugston, *Principal*
EMP: 250 **EST:** 1933
SQ FT: 100,000
SALES (est): 18.1MM
SALES (corp-wide): 20.1B **Publicly Held**
SIC: 8711 8742 8741 1542 Engineering services; training & development consultant; construction management; nonresidential construction
PA: Aecom
    1999 Avenue Of The Stars # 2600
    Los Angeles CA 90067
    213 593-8000

(P-25132)
HUNSAKER & ASSOC IRVINE INC (PA)
3 Hughes, Irvine (92618-2021)
PHONE..................................949 583-1010
Richard Hunsaker, *CEO*
Douglas Snyder, *President*
Chuck Cater, *Vice Pres*
Kamal Karam, *Vice Pres*
Doug Staley, *Vice Pres*
EMP: 100
SQ FT: 27,000
SALES (est): 52.1MM **Privately Held**
WEB: www.hunsaker.com
SIC: 8711 8713 Civil engineering; surveying services

(P-25133)
IBI GROUP A CALIFORNIA PARTNR
Also Called: Ibi Group, Los Angeles
315 W 9th St Ste 600, Los Angeles
(90015-4206)
PHONE..............................213 769-0011
Scott Stewart, *CEO*
EMP: 52
SALES (corp-wide): 279.2MM **Privately Held**
SIC: 8711 Engineering services
HQ: Ibi Group, A California Partnership
18401 Von Karman Ave
Irvine CA 92612
949 833-5588

(P-25134)
ICI SERVICES CORPORATION
1000 Town Center Dr # 225, Oxnard
(93036-1155)
PHONE..............................805 988-3210
Vicki Ervin, *Branch Mgr*
EMP: 320
SALES (corp-wide): 76.2MM **Privately Held**
SIC: 8711 Professional engineer
PA: Ici Services Corporation
500 Viking Dr Ste 400
Virginia Beach VA 23452
757 340-6970

(P-25135)
INDUS TECHNOLOGY INC
2243 San Diego Ave # 200, San Diego
(92110-2069)
PHONE..............................619 299-2555
James B Lasswell, *President*
Rebecca Spane, *CFO*
Will Nevilles, *Senior VP*
Ron File, *Vice Pres*
Anthony Lopez, *Vice Pres*
EMP: 230
SQ FT: 12,000
SALES (est): 31.9MM **Privately Held**
WEB: www.industechnology.com
SIC: 8711 Engineering services

(P-25136)
INDUSTRIAL AUTOMTN GROUP LLC
4400 Sisk Rd, Modesto (95356-8729)
PHONE..............................209 579-7527
Brad Stegmann, *President*
Ron Gouveia, *Project Mgr*
Albert Salcedo, *Project Mgr*
Julio Velasco, *Project Mgr*
Rodney Schmidt, *Project Engr*
EMP: 75
SALES (est): 14.5MM **Privately Held**
SIC: 8711 Mechanical engineering

(P-25137)
INFINITE TECHNOLOGIES INC (PA)
1264 Hawks Flight Ct # 210, El Dorado Hills
(95762-9349)
PHONE..............................916 987-3261
John A Runnberg, *CEO*
Jenet Taylor, *Administration*
David Evans, *Prgrmr*
Nicolas Bailey, *Programmer Anys*
Eric Jonsson, *Programmer Anys*
EMP: 68
SQ FT: 3,450
SALES (est): 9MM **Privately Held**
WEB: www.infintech.com
SIC: 8711 7371 7379 Engineering services; custom computer programming services; computer related maintenance services

(P-25138)
INFORMATION SYSTEMS LABS INC (PA)
12900 Brookprinter Pl # 800, Poway
(92064-8802)
PHONE..............................858 535-9680
Richard G Miller, *CEO*
William Gang, *COO*
Peter Kuebler, *CFO*
David Honey, *Vice Pres*
James Meyer, *Vice Pres*
EMP: 50
SQ FT: 31,000

SALES (est): 28.2MM **Privately Held**
WEB: www.islinc.com
SIC: 8711 Electrical or electronic engineering

(P-25139)
INGENIUM TECHNOLOGIES CORP
5665 Oberlin Dr Ste 202, San Diego
(92121-1739)
PHONE..............................858 227-4422
Duane Wingate, *Principal*
EMP: 87
SALES (corp-wide): 20.2MM **Privately Held**
SIC: 8711 Consulting engineer
PA: Ingenium Technologies Corp.
4216 Maray Dr
Rockford IL 61107
815 399-8803

(P-25140)
INNOVATIVE ENGRG SYSTEMS INC (PA)
Also Called: Ies Engineering
8800 Crippen St, Bakersfield (93311-9686)
P.O. Box 20610 (93390-0610)
PHONE..............................661 381-7800
David Wolfer, *President*
Steve Johnson, *Division Mgr*
Amy Pearson, *Division Mgr*
Jordan Stockton, *Division Mgr*
Patricia Kincheloe, *Admin Asst*
EMP: 100
SQ FT: 20,000
SALES (est): 26.3MM **Privately Held**
SIC: 8711 1731 Engineering services; electrical work

(P-25141)
INSPIRIA INC (PA)
Also Called: Audiovisions
25741 Atl Ocn Dr Ste A, Lake Forest
(92630-8864)
PHONE..............................949 206-0606
Mark Hoffenberg, *President*
Katie Forester, *Office Mgr*
John Salow, *Info Tech Mgr*
Todd Leiter, *Prgrmr*
Chris Montreuil, *Analyst*
EMP: 64
SQ FT: 20,000
SALES (est): 14.4MM **Privately Held**
WEB: www.avisions.com
SIC: 8711 Electrical or electronic engineering

(P-25142)
INTERACT PMTI INC (PA)
260 Maple Ct Ste 210, Ventura
(93003-3566)
PHONE..............................805 658-5600
Tom Kennedy, *President*
Graves Clay, *Project Mgr*
Jeff Hall, *Project Mgr*
Val Lerma, *Engineer*
Allen Scoging, *Engineer*
EMP: 62
SQ FT: 6,000
SALES (est): 5.1MM **Privately Held**
WEB: www.interactpmti.com
SIC: 8711 Consulting engineer

(P-25143)
INTERNATIONAL DESIGN SERVICES
2437 Micheltorena St, Los Angeles
(90039-2531)
PHONE..............................323 662-3963
Zigmas Tanaka, *Ch of Bd*
Betty Tanaka, *President*
Steve Murray, *Exec Dir*
EMP: 57
SQ FT: 3,600
SALES (est): 2.8MM **Privately Held**
SIC: 8711 Consulting engineer

(P-25144)
IQA SOLUTIONS INC
4089 E Conant St, Long Beach
(90808-1777)
PHONE..............................562 420-1000
Mohsem H Hashemi, *CEO*
Andrew Stasio, *Vice Pres*
Shohreh Zahabi, *Finance Mgr*

EMP: 62
SQ FT: 8,500
SALES: 6.8MM **Privately Held**
WEB: www.iqasolutions.com
SIC: 8711 Mechanical engineering

(P-25145)
JACOBS ATCS FEMA A JOINT VENTR
155 N Lake Ave Fl 5, Pasadena
(91101-1849)
PHONE..............................571 218-1115
Ed Pogreba, *Vice Pres*
EMP: 99
SALES (est): 1.3MM **Privately Held**
SIC: 8711 8712 8748 8741 Engineering services; architectural services; business consulting; management services

(P-25146)
JACOBS CIVIL INC
1500 Hughes Way Ste B400, Long Beach
(90810-1882)
PHONE..............................310 847-2500
EMP: 78
SALES (corp-wide): 14.9B **Publicly Held**
SIC: 8711 Consulting engineer
HQ: Jacobs Civil Inc.
501 N Broadway Ste 185
Saint Louis MO

(P-25147)
JACOBS ENGINEERING COMPANY
1111 S Arroyo Pkwy, Pasadena
(91105-3254)
P.O. Box 7084 (91109-7084)
PHONE..............................626 449-2171
Noel G Watson, *CEO*
C L Martin, *President*
EMP: 4000 **EST:** 1979
SALES (est): 98.4MM
SALES (corp-wide): 14.9B **Publicly Held**
WEB: www.jacobs.com
SIC: 8711 1629 Engineering services; chemical plant & refinery construction
PA: Jacobs Engineering Group Inc.
1999 Bryan St Ste 1200
Dallas TX 75201
214 583-8500

(P-25148)
JACOBS ENGINEERING GROUP INC
2600 Michelson Dr Ste 500, Irvine
(92612-6506)
PHONE..............................949 224-7585
Dan Grubb, *Branch Mgr*
Jason Blackburn, *Info Tech Dir*
Bryan Bostic, *IT/INT Sup*
Vic Montellano, *Electrical Engi*
Dennis Blackwood, *Engineer*
EMP: 88
SALES (corp-wide): 14.9B **Publicly Held**
WEB: www.iqacobs.com
SIC: 8711 Consulting engineer
PA: Jacobs Engineering Group Inc.
1999 Bryan St Ste 1200
Dallas TX 75201
214 583-8500

(P-25149)
JACOBS ENGINEERING GROUP INC
37528 Morning Cir, Palmdale (93550-2578)
PHONE..............................661 275-5685
EMP: 93
SALES (corp-wide): 14.9B **Publicly Held**
SIC: 8711 Aviation &/or aeronautical engineering
PA: Jacobs Engineering Group Inc.
1999 Bryan St Ste 1200
Dallas TX 75201
214 583-8500

(P-25150)
JACOBS ENGINEERING GROUP INC
2300 Clayton Rd, Concord (94520-2100)
PHONE..............................925 356-3900
EMP: 92
SALES (corp-wide): 12.7B **Publicly Held**
SIC: 8711

PA: Jacobs Engineering Group Inc.
155 N Lake Ave
Pasadena CA 75201
626 578-3500

(P-25151)
JACOBS ENGINEERING GROUP INC
1500 Hughes Way Ste B400, Long Beach
(90810-1882)
PHONE..............................310 847-2500
Susan Davis, *Admin Asst*
Stacy Rojo, *Administration*
Joseph Novak, *Project Mgr*
Clifton Jones, *Project Engr*
Sean Okamoto, *Project Engr*
EMP: 91
SALES (corp-wide): 14.9B **Publicly Held**
SIC: 8711 Consulting engineer
PA: Jacobs Engineering Group Inc.
1999 Bryan St Ste 1200
Dallas TX 75201
214 583-8500

(P-25152)
JACOBS ENGINEERING GROUP INC
3257 E Guasti Rd Ste 130, Ontario
(91761-1237)
PHONE..............................909 974-2700
Chao Chen, *Manager*
Laura Bonson, *Admin Asst*
Javid Sharifi, *Project Engr*
James Hoyt, *Manager*
EMP: 88
SALES (corp-wide): 14.9B **Publicly Held**
SIC: 8711 Consulting engineer
PA: Jacobs Engineering Group Inc.
1999 Bryan St Ste 1200
Dallas TX 75201
214 583-8500

(P-25153)
JACOBS ENGINEERING GROUP INC
1737 N 1st St Ste 300, San Jose
(95112-4585)
PHONE..............................408 436-4936
Chris R Bartos, *Branch Mgr*
EMP: 88
SALES (corp-wide): 14.9B **Publicly Held**
WEB: www.jacobs.com
SIC: 8711 Consulting engineer
PA: Jacobs Engineering Group Inc.
1999 Bryan St Ste 1200
Dallas TX 75201
214 583-8500

(P-25154)
JACOBS ENGINEERING GROUP INC
1000 Wilshire Blvd # 2100, Los Angeles
(90017-2417)
PHONE..............................213 362-4336
Bruce Russell, *Branch Mgr*
Norma Teran, *Admin Asst*
EMP: 250
SALES (corp-wide): 14.9B **Publicly Held**
SIC: 8711 Consulting engineer
PA: Jacobs Engineering Group Inc.
1999 Bryan St Ste 1200
Dallas TX 75201
214 583-8500

(P-25155)
JACOBS ENGINEERING GROUP INC
1111 S Arroyo Pkwy, Pasadena
(91105-3254)
P.O. Box 7084 (91109-7084)
PHONE..............................626 578-3500
George Kunberger Jr, *Exec VP*
Mary Bloom, *Vice Pres*
John Hoehner, *Vice Pres*
Randy Lycans, *Vice Pres*
Tom McDuffie, *Vice Pres*
EMP: 89
SALES (corp-wide): 14.9B **Publicly Held**
SIC: 8711 Engineering services
PA: Jacobs Engineering Group Inc.
1999 Bryan St Ste 1200
Dallas TX 75201
214 583-8500

1062   2019 Directory of California
Wholesalers and Services Companies   ▲ = Import ▼=Export
◆ =Import/Export

(P-25156)
JACOBS ENGINEERING INC (HQ)
155 N Lake Ave, Pasadena (91101-1849)
P.O. Box 7084 (91109-7084)
PHONE.....................626 578-3500
Craig L Martin, *CEO*
Ed Campbell, *Department Mgr*
Russell Morlando, *Sr Software Eng*
Amy Bender, *Info Tech Mgr*
Alicia Collins, *Info Tech Mgr*
EMP: 125
SALES (est): 213.6MM
SALES (corp-wide): 14.9B **Publicly Held**
SIC: 8711 Consulting engineer
PA: Jacobs Engineering Group Inc.
    1999 Bryan St Ste 1200
    Dallas TX 75201
    214 583-8500

(P-25157)
JACOBS INTERNATIONAL LTD INC
155 N Lake Ave, Pasadena (91101-1849)
P.O. Box 7084 (91109-7084)
PHONE.....................626 578-3500
Craig Martin, *President*
John W Prosser Jr, *Treasurer*
Keith Ackley, *Vice Pres*
Don D'Adam, *Vice Pres*
Vinayak Pai, *Vice Pres*
EMP: 300
SQ FT: 120,000
SALES: 85MM
SALES (corp-wide): 10B **Publicly Held**
SIC: 8711 Engineering services
PA: Jacobs Engineering Group Inc.
    1999 Bryan St Ste 1200
    Dallas TX 75201
    214 583-8500

(P-25158)
JACOBS PROJECT MANAGEMENT CO
2600 Michelson Dr Ste 500, Irvine (92612-6506)
PHONE.....................949 224-7695
Les Steinberger, *Manager*
Frank Joyce, *Contract Mgr*
EMP: 99
SALES: 950K
SALES (corp-wide): 14.9B **Publicly Held**
SIC: 8711 Engineering services
PA: Jacobs Engineering Group Inc.
    1999 Bryan St Ste 1200
    Dallas TX 75201
    214 583-8500

(P-25159)
JACOBS PROJECT MANAGEMENT CO
402 W Broadway Ste 1450, San Diego (92101-8544)
PHONE.....................619 687-0110
Craig Martin, *President*
Frank Joyce, *Contract Mgr*
EMP: 66
SALES: 950K
SALES (corp-wide): 14.9B **Publicly Held**
SIC: 8711 Engineering services
PA: Jacobs Engineering Group Inc.
    1999 Bryan St Ste 1200
    Dallas TX 75201
    214 583-8500

(P-25160)
JACOBS TECHNOLOGY INC
1550 N Norma St, Ridgecrest (93555-2556)
PHONE.....................760 446-1549
Penny Hersley, *Manager*
EMP: 150
SALES (corp-wide): 10B **Publicly Held**
SIC: 8711 Aviation &/or aeronautical engineering
HQ: Jacobs Technology Inc.
    600 William Northern Blvd
    Tullahoma TN 37388
    931 455-6400

(P-25161)
JAS PACIFIC
201 N Euclid Ave Ste A, Upland (91786-8308)
P.O. Box 2 (91785-0002)
PHONE.....................909 605-7777
Jason Addison Smith, *CEO*
Addison Smith, *CEO*
Harley J Jenkins, *Manager*
EMP: 110 EST: 1992
SALES (est): 7.7MM **Privately Held**
WEB: www.jaspacific.com
SIC: 8711 Engineering services

(P-25162)
JOHNSON CONTROLS INC
2226 Northpoint Pkwy, Santa Rosa (95407-7398)
PHONE.....................707 546-3042
Glen Nold, *Branch Mgr*
EMP: 82 **Privately Held**
SIC: 8711 7623 Heating & ventilation engineering; air conditioning repair
HQ: Johnson Controls, Inc.
    5757 N Green Bay Ave
    Milwaukee WI 53209
    414 524-1200

(P-25163)
JSL TECHNOLOGIES INC
1451 N Rice Ave Ste A, Oxnard (93030-7991)
PHONE.....................805 985-7700
Joseph T Black III, *President*
Ben Fujikawa, *Vice Pres*
Jed Williams, *Vice Pres*
Debbie Taggesell, *Administration*
Alissa Borsuk, *Hum Res Coord*
EMP: 290
SQ FT: 22,155
SALES: 28MM **Privately Held**
SIC: 8711 Consulting engineer

(P-25164)
JT3 LLC
190 S Wolfe Ave Bldg 1260, Edwards (93524-6501)
PHONE.....................661 277-4900
James Tedeschi, *Manager*
EMP: 900
SALES (corp-wide): 150MM **Privately Held**
WEB: www.jt3.com
SIC: 8711 Engineering services
PA: Jt3, L.L.C.
    821 Grier Dr
    Las Vegas NV 89119
    704 492-2181

(P-25165)
K&B ELECTRIC LLC
Also Called: K&B Engineering
290 Corporate Terrace Cir # 200, Corona (92879-6033)
PHONE.....................951 808-9501
Sandee Gibbs, *General Mgr*
Trey Gibbs,
EMP: 158
SALES (est): 2.6MM **Privately Held**
SIC: 8711 Engineering services

(P-25166)
K&B ENGINEERING
290 Corporate Terrace Cir, Corona (92879-6033)
PHONE.....................951 808-9501
Trey Gibbs, *Owner*
Valerie Corsaut, *Admin Asst*
Connie Moreno, *Admin Asst*
Candice Chavez, *Planning*
Luke Polling, *IT/INT Sup*
EMP: 200
SALES (est): 23.7MM **Privately Held**
SIC: 8711 Civil engineering

(P-25167)
KAISER GROUP HOLDINGS INC
Also Called: Earthtech
2101 Webster St Ste 1000, Oakland (94612-3060)
PHONE.....................510 419-6000
EMP: 90
SALES (corp-wide): 527.4MM **Publicly Held**
SIC: 8711

PA: Kaiser Group Holdings, Inc.
    9300 Lee Hwy
    Fairfax VA 22031
    703 934-3000

(P-25168)
KBRWYLE TECH SOLUTIONS LLC
Honeywell
850 E Main St, Barstow (92311-2347)
PHONE.....................760 255-8322
Tom Millard, *Manager*
EMP: 200 **Publicly Held**
WEB: www.honeywell-tsi.com
SIC: 8711 Pollution control engineering
HQ: Kbrwyle Technology Solutions, Llc
    7000 Columbia Gateway Dr # 100
    Columbia MD 21046
    410 964-7000

(P-25169)
KENNEDY/JENKS CONSULTANTS INC (PA)
Also Called: Kennedy Jenks
303 2nd St Ste 300s, San Francisco (94107-3632)
PHONE.....................415 243-2150
Gary Carlton, *Chairman*
Keith A London, *President*
Patrick J Courtney, *CFO*
Lynn Takaichi, *Chairman*
Don Weiden, *Officer*
EMP: 100
SQ FT: 45,000
SALES (est): 106.3MM **Privately Held**
SIC: 8711 Consulting engineer

(P-25170)
KEVCOMP INC
Also Called: Kevcomp Engineering
4300 Long Beach Blvd # 720, Long Beach (90807-2019)
PHONE.....................562 423-3028
Kevin Ngo, *President*
Mike T Diep, *CEO*
EMP: 80
SQ FT: 1,500
SALES (est): 7.5MM **Privately Held**
WEB: www.kevcomp.com
SIC: 8711 7379 Engineering services; computer related consulting services

(P-25171)
KIMLEY-HORN AND ASSOCIATES INC
401 B St Ste 600, San Diego (92101-4218)
PHONE.....................619 234-9411
James Roberts, *Manager*
Richard Schafer, *Technology*
Kari Nelson, *Analyst*
EMP: 60
SALES (corp-wide): 579.2MM **Privately Held**
WEB: www.itscareers.com
SIC: 8711 Consulting engineer
HQ: Kimley-Horn And Associates, Inc.
    421 Fayetteville St # 600
    Raleigh NC 27601
    919 677-2000

(P-25172)
KINEMETRICS INC (DH)
222 Vista Ave, Pasadena (91107-3295)
PHONE.....................626 795-2220
Tadashi Jimbo, *CEO*
Kimberly Page, *CFO*
Michelle Harrington, *Treasurer*
Melvin Lund, *Exec VP*
Ogie Kuraica, *Vice Pres*
EMP: 59
SQ FT: 50,000
SALES (est): 22.6MM **Privately Held**
WEB: www.kinemetrics.com
SIC: 8711 3829 Engineering services; seismographs

(P-25173)
KLEINFELDER INC (HQ)
550 W C St Ste 1200, San Diego (92101-3532)
P.O. Box 51958, Los Angeles (90051-6258)
PHONE.....................619 831-4600
John Murphy, *CFO*
Lisa Millet, *Exec VP*
Thomas Rodriguez, *Exec VP*

James Cosgrove, *Vice Pres*
Roy Pierce, *Program Mgr*
EMP: 160
SQ FT: 5,000
SALES: 175.4MM
SALES (corp-wide): 249.4MM **Privately Held**
WEB: www.kleinfelder.com
SIC: 8711 8712 Consulting engineer; architectural engineering
PA: The Kleinfelder Group Inc
    550 W C St Ste 1200
    San Diego CA 92101
    619 831-4600

(P-25174)
KLEINFELDER INC
5125 N Gates Ave Ste 102, Fresno (93722-6414)
PHONE.....................559 486-0750
Walt Placata, *Manager*
David Pearson, *Project Engr*
EMP: 60
SALES (corp-wide): 249.4MM **Privately Held**
WEB: www.kleinfelder.com
SIC: 8711 8734 8731 Consulting engineer; testing laboratories; commercial physical research
HQ: Kleinfelder, Inc.
    550 W C St Ste 1200
    San Diego CA 92101
    619 831-4600

(P-25175)
KLEINFELDER INC
6700 Koll Center Pkwy # 120, Pleasanton (94566-7060)
PHONE.....................925 484-1700
Mike Majchrzak, *Manager*
EMP: 60
SALES (corp-wide): 249.4MM **Privately Held**
WEB: www.kleinfelder.com
SIC: 8711 8742 8734 8748 Consulting engineer; management consulting services; testing laboratories; environmental consultant
HQ: Kleinfelder, Inc.
    550 W C St Ste 1200
    San Diego CA 92101
    619 831-4600

(P-25176)
KLEINFELDER INC
2882 Prospect Park Dr # 200, Rancho Cordova (95670-6058)
PHONE.....................916 366-1701
Mark Cannolly, *Manager*
Nancy Walker, *Opers Staff*
Bruce Ross, *Sr Project Mgr*
Ken Sorensen, *Associate*
EMP: 90
SALES (corp-wide): 249.4MM **Privately Held**
WEB: www.kleinfelder.com
SIC: 8711 Consulting engineer
HQ: Kleinfelder, Inc.
    550 W C St Ste 1200
    San Diego CA 92101
    619 831-4600

(P-25177)
KLEINFELDER ASSOCIATES
550 W C St Ste 1200, San Diego (92101-3532)
PHONE.....................619 831-4600
George J Pierson, *President*
Bart Patton, *COO*
John Pilkington, *CFO*
Larry Peterson, *Senior VP*
Russ Carey, *Vice Pres*
EMP: 1500
SALES (est): 61.6MM
SALES (corp-wide): 249.4MM **Privately Held**
SIC: 8711 Consulting engineer
PA: The Kleinfelder Group Inc
    550 W C St Ste 1200
    San Diego CA 92101
    619 831-4600

PRODUCTS & SVCS

(P-25178)
KOCH-ARMSTRONG GENERAL ENGRG
15315 Olde Highway 80, El Cajon (92021-2408)
P.O. Box 1190, Lakeside (92040-0906)
PHONE..............................619 561-2005
Monte J Koch, *CEO*
Christopher Armstrong, *Vice Pres*
Sara Schmidt, *Administration*
EMP: 65 **EST:** 1998
SALES (est): 9.2MM **Privately Held**
WEB: www.koch-armstrong.com
SIC: 8711 Building construction consultant

(P-25179)
KPFF INC
Also Called: K P F F Consulting Engineers
700 S Flower St Ste 2100, Los Angeles (90017-4208)
PHONE..............................310 665-1536
John Gavan, *Manager*
David McGraw, *Engineer*
Alex Piolatto, *Engineer*
Kyle Trudeau, *Engineer*
Samuel Vanhersecke, *Engineer*
EMP: 114
SALES (corp-wide): 182.5MM **Privately Held**
WEB: www.kpff.com
SIC: 8711 Consulting engineer
PA: Kpff, Inc.
1601 5th Ave Ste 1600
Seattle WA 98101
206 622-5822

(P-25180)
KPFF INC
400 Oceangate Ste 500, Long Beach (90802-4392)
PHONE..............................562 437-9100
Todd Graham, *Branch Mgr*
EMP: 71
SALES (corp-wide): 182.5MM **Privately Held**
SIC: 8711 Consulting engineer
PA: Kpff, Inc.
1601 5th Ave Ste 1600
Seattle WA 98101
206 622-5822

(P-25181)
KPFF INC
Also Called: Kpff Consulting Engineers
45 Fremont St Fl 28, San Francisco (94105-2209)
PHONE..............................415 989-1004
Marc Press, *Manager*
Anna Migliaccio, *Design Engr*
Karina Abdon, *Engineer*
Leslie Quiter, *Engineer*
Ron Raphael, *Accounting Mgr*
EMP: 56
SALES (corp-wide): 182.5MM **Privately Held**
WEB: www.kpff.com
SIC: 8711 Consulting engineer
PA: Kpff, Inc.
1601 5th Ave Ste 1600
Seattle WA 98101
206 622-5822

(P-25182)
KSI ENGINEERING INC
6205 District Blvd, Bakersfield (93313-2141)
PHONE..............................661 617-1700
Kevin Small, *President*
Glenda Sue Small, *Corp Secy*
EMP: 50
SQ FT: 7,000
SALES: 6.5MM **Privately Held**
WEB: www.dcck.com
SIC: 8711 Electrical or electronic engineering

(P-25183)
L3 MARIPRO INC
Also Called: L-3 Communications Maripro Inc
1522 Cook Pl, Goleta (93117-3124)
PHONE..............................805 683-3881
Dan Chabot, *Vice Pres*
EMP: 90
SQ FT: 100,000

SALES (est): 4.6MM
SALES (corp-wide): 6.8B **Publicly Held**
WEB: www.nautronix.com
SIC: 8711 Marine engineering
HQ: L3 Technologies, Inc.
600 3rd Ave Fl 34
New York NY 10016
212 697-1111

(P-25184)
LACO ASSOCIATES (PA)
21 W 4th St, Eureka (95501-0216)
P.O. Box 1023 (95502-1023)
PHONE..............................707 443-5054
Leonard Osborne, *President*
David Lindberg, *Vice Pres*
Bradley A Thomas, *Vice Pres*
Christopher Watt, *Vice Pres*
Madison Green, *Admin Mgr*
EMP: 50
SQ FT: 6,000
SALES (est): 8.6MM **Privately Held**
WEB: www.lacoassociates.us
SIC: 8711 8999 0711 Structural engineering; mechanical engineering; building construction consultant; civil engineering; geological consultant; soil testing services

(P-25185)
LANWAVE TECHNOLOGY INC
20111 Stevens Creek Blvd # 260, Cupertino (95014-2399)
PHONE..............................408 253-3883
Kenneth Chan, *President*
Alan Chan, *CFO*
Khan Liu, *Data Proc Staff*
EMP: 53
SQ FT: 3,000
SALES (est): 2.3MM **Privately Held**
WEB: www.lanwave.com
SIC: 8711 Consulting engineer

(P-25186)
LEE & RO INC (PA)
1199 Fullerton Rd, City of Industry (91748-1232)
PHONE..............................626 912-3391
Myong Ro, *CEO*
Gregory Holmes, *CFO*
Dhiru Patel, *Vice Pres*
Charles Ro, *Vice Pres*
Daniel Park, *Info Tech Mgr*
EMP: 50 **EST:** 1979
SQ FT: 19,000
SALES: 9.8MM **Privately Held**
WEB: www.lee-ro.com
SIC: 8711 Civil engineering; mechanical engineering; sanitary engineers

(P-25187)
LEIDOS ENGINEERING LLC
590 W Central Ave Ste I, Brea (92821-3019)
PHONE..............................714 257-6400
Sherif Philobos, *Branch Mgr*
EMP: 54
SALES (corp-wide): 10.1B **Publicly Held**
SIC: 8711 Consulting engineer
HQ: Leidos Engineering, Llc
11951 Freedom Dr
Reston VA 20190
571 526-6000

(P-25188)
LEIDOS ENGINEERING LLC
4161 Campus Point Ct E, San Diego (92121-1513)
PHONE..............................858 826-6000
David Bernal, *Branch Mgr*
Manuel Guzman, *Engineer*
Quintin Mabanta, *Analyst*
Raymond S Bamford, *Director*
EMP: 54
SALES (corp-wide): 10.1B **Publicly Held**
SIC: 8711 Engineering services
HQ: Leidos Engineering, Llc
11951 Freedom Dr
Reston VA 20190
571 526-6000

(P-25189)
LINQUEST CORPORATION (PA)
5140 W Goldleaf Cir # 40, Los Angeles (90056-1299)
PHONE..............................323 924-1600
Timothy Dills, *President*

Leon Biederman, *President*
F Scott Stowe, *COO*
Greg Young, *COO*
Matthew C Lyons, *CFO*
EMP: 200
SQ FT: 20,000
SALES (est): 80.9MM **Privately Held**
WEB: www.linquest.com
SIC: 8711 Aviation &/or aeronautical engineering

(P-25190)
LIONAKIS
20371 Irvine Ave Ste 120, Newport Beach (92660-0119)
PHONE..............................949 955-1919
Jeffrey Gill, *Principal*
EMP: 156
SALES (corp-wide): 45.6MM **Privately Held**
WEB: www.lbdg.com
SIC: 8711 7389 Civil engineering; design, commercial & industrial
PA: Lionakis
1919 19th St
Sacramento CA 95811
916 558-1901

(P-25191)
LIONAKIS (PA)
1919 19th St, Sacramento (95811-6714)
PHONE..............................916 558-1901
Tim Fry, *President*
Andrew Deeble, *CFO*
David Younger, *Vice Pres*
Maynard Feist, *Social Dir*
Dave Younger, *Admin Sec*
EMP: 150 **EST:** 1909
SQ FT: 38,000
SALES (est): 45.6MM **Privately Held**
WEB: www.lbdg.com
SIC: 8711 7389 8712 Engineering services; interior design services; architectural services

(P-25192)
LOCKHEED MARTIN CORPORATION
255 California St Ste 400, San Francisco (94111-4921)
PHONE..............................415 402-0406
Marc Mansour, *Manager*
Dennis Harper, *Administration*
Howard Segal, *Business Anlyst*
Daryl Jones, *Technician*
Steve Heires, *Engineer*
EMP: 232 **Publicly Held**
WEB: www.lockheedmartin.com
SIC: 8711 3721 Aviation &/or aeronautical engineering; aircraft
PA: Lockheed Martin Corporation
6801 Rockledge Dr
Bethesda MD 20817

(P-25193)
LOS ANGELES ENGINEERING INC
633 N Barranca Ave, Covina (91723-1229)
PHONE..............................626 869-1400
Henry Angus O'Brien, *President*
Aaron O'Brien, *COO*
Beth Ballard, *CFO*
EMP: 110
SQ FT: 33,000
SALES: 38.7MM **Privately Held**
WEB: www.laeng.net
SIC: 8711 1622 Construction & civil engineering; bridge, tunnel & elevated highway

(P-25194)
LUND CONSTRUCTION CO
5302 Roseville Rd, North Highlands (95660-5000)
PHONE..............................916 344-5800
Jerry A Lund, *President*
Alta M Lund, *Treasurer*
Jeff Lund, *Vice Pres*
Kevin Lund, *Vice Pres*
Jason Ferro, *Project Mgr*
EMP: 155 **EST:** 1959
SQ FT: 7,500

SALES: 38.5MM **Privately Held**
SIC: 8711 1794 1623 4212 Construction & civil engineering; excavation & grading; building construction; underground utilities contractor; hazardous waste transport

(P-25195)
LUNDSTROM & ASSOCIATES INC
4804 Sunrise Hills Dr, El Cajon (92020-8259)
PHONE..............................619 641-5900
Jeffrey R Lundstrom, *President*
Bill Lundstrom, *Vice Pres*
Sherri Murray, *Director*
EMP: 50
SALES (est): 4.1MM **Privately Held**
SIC: 8711 Civil engineering; consulting engineer

(P-25196)
M-E ENGINEERS INC
600 Wilshire Blvd # 1200, Los Angeles (90017-3200)
PHONE..............................310 842-8700
Akira Hiruma, *General Mgr*
EMP: 65
SALES (corp-wide): 43.6MM **Privately Held**
WEB: www.meengineers.com
SIC: 8711 Consulting engineer
PA: M-E Engineers, Inc.
14143 Denver West Pkwy # 300
Lakewood CO 80401
303 421-6655

(P-25197)
MACDONALD MOTT GROUP INC
3699 Crenshaw Blvd, Los Angeles (90016-4849)
PHONE..............................323 903-4100
EMP: 70
SALES (corp-wide): 507.4MM **Privately Held**
SIC: 8711 Consulting engineer
PA: Macdonald Mott Group Inc
111 Wood Ave S Ste 5
Iselin NJ 08830
973 379-3400

(P-25198)
MACDONALD MOTT GROUP INC
12647 Alcosta Blvd, San Ramon (94583-4439)
PHONE..............................925 469-8010
Tony Purdon, *Branch Mgr*
Melanie Graham, *Executive*
EMP: 75
SALES (corp-wide): 507.4MM **Privately Held**
WEB: www.hatchmott.com
SIC: 8711 Professional engineer
PA: Macdonald Mott Group Inc
111 Wood Ave S Ste 5
Iselin NJ 08830
973 379-3400

(P-25199)
MACDONALD MOTT LLC
3103 N 1st St Bldg B, San Jose (95134-1934)
PHONE..............................408 321-5900
EMP: 64
SALES (corp-wide): 507.4MM **Privately Held**
SIC: 8711 Engineering services
HQ: Macdonald Mott Llc
12647 Alcosta Blvd
San Ramon CA 94583

(P-25200)
MACDONALD MOTT LLC
Also Called: Railroad Technology
180 Promenade Cir Ste 300, Sacramento (95834-2952)
PHONE..............................916 399-0580
Cara Stromm, *Office Mgr*
EMP: 64
SALES (corp-wide): 507.4MM **Privately Held**
SIC: 8711 Consulting engineer
HQ: Macdonald Mott Llc
12647 Alcosta Blvd
San Ramon CA 94583

(P-25201)
MACKAY SMPS CVIL ENGINEERS INC (PA)
5142 Franklin Dr Ste C, Pleasanton (94588-3368)
PHONE...................925 416-1790
James C Ray, *President*
Bob Chan, *Vice Pres*
John F Kuzia, *Admin Sec*
Craig Zoller, *Project Mgr*
Steve Smith, *Engineer*
EMP: 62 EST: 1953
SALES (est): 8.8MM Privately Held
WEB: www.msce.com
SIC: 8711 Civil engineering

(P-25202)
MANGAN INC (PA)
3901 Via Oro Ave, Long Beach (90810-1800)
PHONE....................310 835-8080
Richard D Mangan, *Principal*
Rick Dockrill, *Design Engr*
Matthew Balch, *Project Mgr*
Julie Caldera, *Project Mgr*
James M Janzen, *Project Mgr*
EMP: 90
SQ FT: 15,000
SALES: 49.4MM Privately Held
WEB: www.mangan.com
SIC: 8711 Consulting engineer

(P-25203)
MARQUES PIPELINE INC
7225 26th St, Sacramento (95834)
PHONE....................916 923-3434
Jeremy R Jaeger, *CEO*
Jeremy Jaeger, *President*
Dennis Loosli, *Vice Pres*
Garrett Davis, *Project Engr*
Randy Fein, *Controller*
EMP: 50
SQ FT: 2,000
SALES (est): 12.7MM Privately Held
WEB: www.marquespipeline.com
SIC: 8711 Engineering services

(P-25204)
MARTIN ASSOCIATES GROUP INC (PA)
Also Called: Martin, John A & Associates
950 S Grand Ave Fl 4, Los Angeles (90015-1436)
PHONE....................213 483-6490
John A Martin Jr, *CEO*
Barry Schindler, *Vice Pres*
Ben Rogowski, *Project Engr*
EMP: 63
SQ FT: 70,000
SALES (est): 50.3MM Privately Held
WEB: www.johnmartin.com
SIC: 8711 Structural engineering

(P-25205)
MAZDA RESEARCH & DEV OF N AMER
1421 Reynolds Ave, Irvine (92614-5531)
PHONE....................949 852-8898
Kelvin Hiraishi, *Manager*
EMP: 100
SQ FT: 127,000
SALES (est): 5.7MM Privately Held
WEB: www.mazdamotorsports.com
SIC: 8711 Designing: ship, boat, machine & product
HQ: Mazda Motor Of America, Inc.
200 Spectrum Center Dr
Irvine CA 92618
949 727-1990

(P-25206)
MAZZETTI INC (PA)
Also Called: Mazzetti GBA
220 Montgomery St Ste 650, San Francisco (94104-3491)
PHONE....................415 362-3266
Walt Vernon, *CEO*
Darryl Wandry, *CFO*
Jaclyn McColgan, *Office Admin*
Winna MEI, *Executive Asst*
Theresa Gehbauer, *Administration*
EMP: 50
SQ FT: 17,700

SALES (est): 51MM Privately Held
WEB: www.mazzetti.com
SIC: 8711 Electrical or electronic engineering; mechanical engineering; consulting engineer

(P-25207)
MCMILLEN JACOBS ASSOCIATES INC
3954 Carson Rd, Camino (95709-9347)
PHONE....................530 497-5407
EMP: 96
SALES (corp-wide): 22.2MM Privately Held
SIC: 8711 1629 4911 Construction & civil engineering; civil engineering; structural engineering; dams, waterways, docks & other marine construction; waterway construction; distribution, electric power
PA: Mcmillen Jacobs Associates, Inc.
49 Stevenson St Ste 300
San Francisco CA 94105
415 434-1822

(P-25208)
MDS CONSULTING (PA)
17320 Red Hill Ave # 350, Irvine (92614-5644)
PHONE....................949 251-8821
Stanley C Morse, *Owner*
Jerry R Schultz, *Co-Owner*
Ed Lenth, *Vice Pres*
Dario Bran, *Project Mgr*
Leo Pacis, *Project Mgr*
EMP: 91 EST: 1976
SQ FT: 8,837
SALES (est): 10.5MM Privately Held
WEB: www.mdsconsulting.net
SIC: 8711 Civil engineering

(P-25209)
MGGB INC
Also Called: Alltech Services
10841 Noel St Ste 110, Los Alamitos (90720-6701)
P.O. Box 1065, Sunset Beach (90742-1065)
PHONE....................714 226-0520
Miles D Sleeth, *CEO*
Phil Gentile, *Director*
Dan Jakary, *Director*
EMP: 114
SQ FT: 3,900
SALES (est): 8.5MM Privately Held
SIC: 8711 8748 Pollution control engineering; construction & civil engineering; environmental consultant

(P-25210)
MICHAEL BAKER JR INC
5051 Verdugo Way Ste 300, Camarillo (93012-8683)
PHONE....................805 383-3373
Kurt Bergman, *CEO*
Louis Levner, *Assistant VP*
EMP: 99
SALES (est): 2.8MM Privately Held
SIC: 8711 Civil engineering

(P-25211)
MICHAEL BAKER INTL INC
1 Kaiser Plz Ste 1150, Oakland (94612-3601)
PHONE....................510 879-0950
Mike Conrad, *Branch Mgr*
EMP: 140
SALES (corp-wide): 592.9MM Privately Held
SIC: 8711 Engineering services
HQ: Baker Michael International Inc
500 Grant St Ste 5400
Pittsburgh PA 15219
412 269-6300

(P-25212)
MICHAEL BAKER INTL INC
40810 County Center Dr # 100, Temecula (92591-6053)
PHONE....................951 676-8042
William Green, *Vice Pres*
EMP: 60
SALES (corp-wide): 592.9MM Privately Held
WEB: www.rbf.com
SIC: 8711 8713 Civil engineering; surveying services

HQ: Baker Michael International Inc
5 Hutton Cntre Dr Ste 500
Santa Ana CA 92707
949 472-3505

(P-25213)
MILLENNIUM ENGRG INTEGRATION
350 N Akron Rd, Moffett Field (94035)
P.O. Box 1 (94035-0001)
PHONE....................703 413-7750
Rick Maurer, *Branch Mgr*
EMP: 99
SALES (corp-wide): 138.5MM Privately Held
SIC: 8711 Engineering services
PA: Millennium Engineering And Integration Co.
1400 Crystal Dr Ste 800
Arlington VA 22202
703 413-7750

(P-25214)
MILLSAP DEGNAN & ASSOC INC
4280 Redwood Hwy Ste 10, San Rafael (94903-2600)
PHONE....................415 472-4244
Steve Millsap, *CEO*
Doug Degnan, *President*
Mike Millsap, *Manager*
EMP: 60
SALES (est): 5.6MM Privately Held
WEB: www.millsapdegnan.com
SIC: 8711 1522 1771 Engineering services; residential construction; concrete work

(P-25215)
MISTRAS GROUP INC
Also Called: Mistras Impro
21215 Kratzmeyer Rd A, Bakersfield (93314-9498)
PHONE....................661 829-1192
Jorky Kidwell, *General Mgr*
EMP: 70 Publicly Held
SIC: 8711 Consulting engineer
PA: Mistras Group, Inc.
195 Clarksville Rd Ste 2
Princeton Junction NJ 08550

(P-25216)
MISTRAS GROUP INC
2230 E Artesia Blvd, Long Beach (90855-1739)
PHONE....................562 597-3932
EMP: 58 Publicly Held
SIC: 8711 Engineering services
PA: Mistras Group, Inc.
195 Clarksville Rd Ste 2
Princeton Junction NJ 08550

(P-25217)
MISTRAS GROUP INC
8427 Atlantic Ave, Cudahy (90201-5809)
PHONE....................323 583-1653
Victor Altomare, *General Mgr*
Britni Altomare, *Director*
EMP: 58 Publicly Held
SIC: 8711 Engineering services
PA: Mistras Group, Inc.
195 Clarksville Rd Ste 2
Princeton Junction NJ 08550

(P-25218)
MNS ENGINEERS INC (PA)
201 N Calle Cesar, Santa Barbara (93103)
PHONE....................805 692-6921
James A Salvito, *CEO*
Shawn Kowalewski, *President*
Mark E Reinhardt, *CFO*
Greg Chelini, *Vice Pres*
Gregory A Chelini, *Vice Pres*
EMP: 94 EST: 1962
SQ FT: 7,000
SALES (est): 18.9MM Privately Held
WEB: www.mnsengineers.com
SIC: 8711 8713 Civil engineering; surveying services

(P-25219)
MOBILENET SERVICES INC (PA)
18 Morgan Ste 200, Irvine (92618-2074)
PHONE....................949 951-4444

Richard Grant, *President*
Eugene Powell, *Vice Pres*
Kellie Ohr, *Office Admin*
Sundara M Narasimhan, *Engineer*
Harish Pillai, *Engineer*
EMP: 180
SQ FT: 17,500
SALES (est): 46.9MM Privately Held
WEB: www.mobilenetservices.net
SIC: 8711 4813 Engineering services; telephone communication, except radio

(P-25220)
MOFFATT & NICHOL
2001 N Main St Ste 360, Walnut Creek (94596-7253)
PHONE....................925 944-5411
Robin Rhodes, *Manager*
EMP: 50
SQ FT: 150,000
SALES (corp-wide): 132.2MM Privately Held
SIC: 8711 Civil engineering
PA: Moffatt & Nichol
4225 E Conant St Ste 101
Long Beach CA 90808
562 590-6500

(P-25221)
MOFFATT & NICHOL
555 Anton Blvd Ste 400, Costa Mesa (92626-7811)
PHONE....................657 261-2699
Eric Nichol, *CEO*
EMP: 70
SALES (corp-wide): 132.2MM Privately Held
SIC: 8711 Structural engineering
PA: Moffatt & Nichol
4225 E Conant St Ste 101
Long Beach CA 90808
562 590-6500

(P-25222)
MOFFATT & NICHOL
Also Called: Branch
1300 Clay St, Oakland (94612-1425)
PHONE....................510 645-1238
Rick Rhode, *Branch Mgr*
EMP: 50
SALES (corp-wide): 132.2MM Privately Held
WEB: www.moffattnichol.com
SIC: 8711 Consulting engineer
PA: Moffatt & Nichol
4225 E Conant St Ste 101
Long Beach CA 90808
562 590-6500

(P-25223)
MOFFATT & NICHOL
4225 E Conant St Ste 201, Long Beach (90808-1867)
PHONE....................562 426-9551
Mike McCarthy, *Manager*
Eric Nichol, *CEO*
EMP: 55
SALES (corp-wide): 132.2MM Privately Held
WEB: www.moffattnichol.com
SIC: 8711 Consulting engineer
PA: Moffatt & Nichol
4225 E Conant St Ste 101
Long Beach CA 90808
562 590-6500

(P-25224)
MOOG INC
2581 Leghorn St, Mountain View (94043-1613)
PHONE....................650 210-9000
Christopher Head, *Branch Mgr*
EMP: 57
SALES (corp-wide): 2.9B Publicly Held
SIC: 8711 Engineering services
PA: Moog Inc.
400 Jamison Rd
Elma NY 14059
716 805-2604

(P-25225)
MORTON & PITALO INC (PA)
75 Iron Point Cir Ste 120, Folsom (95630-8813)
PHONE....................916 984-7621
Eddie Kho, *President*

PRODUCTS & SVCS

Vincent Doyle, *CFO*
Gregory J Bardini, *Vice Pres*
Christopher J Gorges, *Vice Pres*
Craig Kendall, *Project Mgr*
EMP: 64
SQ FT: 5,200
SALES (est): 11.7MM **Privately Held**
WEB: www.mpengr.com
SIC: 8711 Civil engineering

(P-25226)
MULTIPOINT WIRELESS LLC
2549 Eastbluff Dr Ste 474, Newport Beach
(92660-3500)
PHONE...................................714 262-4172
Rick Luch, *CEO*
Rob Brownjohn, *CFO*
Ilaha Omar, *Vice Pres*
EMP: 50
SALES (est): 5.9MM **Privately Held**
WEB: www.multipointllc.com
SIC: 8711 Engineering services

(P-25227)
MVE INC (PA)
Also Called: M V E
1117 L St, Modesto (95354-0833)
PHONE...................................209 526-4214
Kirk Delamare, *CEO*
Catherine De La Mare, *Vice Pres*
EMP: 62
SQ FT: 10,000
SALES (est): 8MM **Privately Held**
WEB: www.mve.net
SIC: 8711 8713 Civil engineering; survey-
ing services

(P-25228)
MWH AMERICAS INC
437 2nd St, Solvang (93463-2763)
PHONE...................................805 683-2409
EMP: 77
SALES (corp-wide): 1.5B **Privately Held**
SIC: 8711
HQ: Mwh Americas, Inc.
370 Interlocken Blvd
Broomfield CO 80021
303 410-4000

(P-25229)
MWH AMERICAS INC
M W H Laboratories
750 Royal Oaks Dr Ste 100, Monrovia
(91016-6359)
PHONE...................................626 386-1100
Mona Alteri, *Managing Dir*
EMP: 129
SALES (corp-wide): 3.2B **Privately Held**
WEB: www.mw.com
SIC: 8711 Engineering services
HQ: Mwh Americas, Inc.
370 Interlocken Blvd
Broomfield CO 80021
303 410-4000

(P-25230)
MWH AMERICAS INC
44 Montgomery St Ste 1400, San Francisco
(94104-4717)
PHONE...................................415 430-1800
Janell Cook, *Branch Mgr*
EMP: 74
SALES (corp-wide): 3.2B **Privately Held**
WEB: www.mwh-inc.com
SIC: 8711 Consulting engineer
HQ: Mwh Americas, Inc.
370 Interlocken Blvd
Broomfield CO 80021
303 410-4000

(P-25231)
MWH AMERICAS INC
618 Michillinda Ave # 200, Arcadia
(91007-6342)
PHONE...................................626 796-9141
Ellen Seymour, *Branch Mgr*
Bob Armstrong, *Vice Pres*
Cynthia Collyard, *Vice Pres*
Rodney Dell, *Vice Pres*
Kimberly Kesler-Arnold, *Vice Pres*
EMP: 74
SALES (corp-wide): 3.2B **Privately Held**
SIC: 8711 Consulting engineer

HQ: Mwh Americas, Inc.
370 Interlocken Blvd
Broomfield CO 80021
303 410-4000

(P-25232)
NATIONAL SECURITY TECH LLC
Also Called: Bechtel
161 S Vasco Rd Ste A, Livermore
(94551-5131)
PHONE...................................925 960-2500
Gary Still, *Branch Mgr*
EMP: 80
SALES (corp-wide): 565.3MM **Privately
Held**
SIC: 8711 1629 Civil engineering; indus-
trial plant construction
PA: National Security Technologies, Llc
2621 Losee Rd
North Las Vegas NV 89030
702 295-1000

(P-25233)
**NAVAL FAC ENG CMMD SW
WRKNG CA**
1220 Pacific Hwy, San Diego (92132-5190)
PHONE...................................619 532-1158
Shahraam Plaseied, *Principal*
Capt Darius Banaji, *COO*
Mark Johnson, *Engineer*
Nancy Wright, *Accountant*
EMP: 99
SQ FT: 4,000
SALES (est): 5.9MM **Privately Held**
SIC: 8711 1623 8744 Pollution control en-
gineering; civil engineering; underground
utilities contractor; base maintenance
(providing personnel on continuing basis)

(P-25234)
**NEW ENGLAND SHTMTL
WORKS INC**
2731 S Cherry Ave, Fresno (93706-5423)
P.O. Box 4287 (93744-4287)
PHONE...................................559 268-7375
Michael Hensley, *CEO*
Matt Grabowski, *Sales Mgr*
Tia Eastham, *Clerk*
EMP: 150 **EST:** 1920
SQ FT: 43,000
SALES (est): 35.7MM **Privately Held**
WEB: www.nesmw.com
SIC: 8711 8741 1542 Engineering serv-
ices; construction management; commer-
cial & office building, new construction;
commercial & office buildings, renovation
& repair; hospital construction; school
building construction

(P-25235)
**NMI INDUSTRIAL HOLDINGS
INC**
8503 Weyand Ave, Sacramento
(95828-2610)
PHONE...................................916 635-7030
Majid Rahimian, *President*
Steve Mathias, *COO*
Javad Rahimian, *CFO*
William Woodson, *Info Tech Mgr*
Alex Potts, *Project Engr*
EMP: 90
SALES: 7.9MM **Privately Held**
SIC: 8711 1799 Construction & civil engi-
neering; building site preparation

(P-25236)
NOVARIANT INC (PA)
Also Called: Autofarm
46610 Landing Pkwy, Fremont
(94538-6420)
PHONE...................................510 933-4800
Dave Vaughn, *President*
Mike Manning, *CFO*
Mark Bittner, *Vice Pres*
Dennis Connor, *Vice Pres*
Husam Kal, *Vice Pres*
EMP: 60
SQ FT: 20,000
SALES (est): 21.7MM **Privately Held**
WEB: www.novariant.com
SIC: 8711 Engineering services

(P-25237)
NOVO ENGINEERING INC (PA)
1350 Specialty Dr Ste A, Vista
(92081-8565)
PHONE...................................760 598-6686
Dan Kline, *CEO*
Rajan Ramaswamy, *President*
Dave Peterson, *Vice Pres*
Justin Osborne, *Technician*
Tony Barghini, *Design Engr*
EMP: 60
SQ FT: 18,000
SALES (est): 16.8MM **Privately Held**
WEB: www.novoengineering.com
SIC: 8711 Consulting engineer

(P-25238)
NV5 INC (DH)
Also Called: Nolte Associates
2525 Natomas Park Dr # 300, Sacramento
(95833-2933)
PHONE...................................916 641-9100
Dickerson Wright, *CEO*
Brad Riel, *Vice Pres*
Victor Alaniz, *Engineer*
Nona Espinosa, *Senior Engr*
Chris Weigt, *Analyst*
EMP: 80
SQ FT: 27,000
SALES (est): 68.7MM
SALES (corp-wide): 418MM **Publicly
Held**
WEB: www.nolte.com
SIC: 8711 Civil engineering

(P-25239)
NV5 INC
Also Called: Nolte, George S & Associates
15092 Avenue Of Science # 200, San
Diego (92128-3404)
PHONE...................................858 385-0500
EMP: 200
SALES (corp-wide): 418MM **Publicly
Held**
WEB: www.nolte.com
SIC: 8711 8713 Civil engineering; survey-
ing services
HQ: Nv5, Inc.
2525 Natomas Park Dr # 300
Sacramento CA 95833
916 641-9100

(P-25240)
NV5 INC
2495 Natomas Park Dr # 300, Sacramento
(95833-2935)
PHONE...................................916 641-9100
Steve Hiatt, *Vice Pres*
EMP: 72
SALES (corp-wide): 418MM **Publicly
Held**
WEB: www.nolte.com
SIC: 8711 8713 Civil engineering; survey-
ing services
HQ: Nv5, Inc.
2525 Natomas Park Dr # 300
Sacramento CA 95833
916 641-9100

(P-25241)
OC ENGINEERING
300 N Flower St, Santa Ana (92703-5001)
PHONE...................................714 667-3212
Ignacio G Ochoa, *Principal*
EMP: 99
SALES (est): 3.1MM **Privately Held**
SIC: 8711 Engineering services

(P-25242)
**ONCORE MANUFACTURING LLC
(HQ)**
Also Called: Neo Tech
9340 Owensmouth Ave, Chatsworth
(91311-6915)
PHONE...................................818 734-6500
Sudesh Arora, *President*
Kunal Sharma, *COO*
Laura Siegal, *CFO*
John Lowrey,
David Lane, *CTO*
▲ **EMP:** 700
SALES (est): 174.7MM
SALES (corp-wide): 1.1B **Privately Held**
WEB: www.oncorems.com
SIC: 8711 3672 Electrical or electronic en-
gineering; printed circuit boards

PA: Natel Engineering Company, Llc
9340 Owensmouth Ave
Chatsworth CA 91311
818 495-8617

(P-25243)
OPERATING ENGINEERS LOCA
325 Digital Dr, Morgan Hill (95037-2878)
PHONE...................................408 782-9803
Lisa Kunkel, *Branch Mgr*
EMP: 202
SALES (corp-wide): 220.1K **Privately
Held**
SIC: 8711 Engineering services
PA: Operating Engineers Local Union No. 3
Scholarship Foundation
1620 S Loop Rd
Alameda CA 94502
510 748-7400

(P-25244)
OPTIMUM INC (PA)
17890 Valley Blvd Ste A, Bloomington
(92316-1981)
PHONE...................................909 990-0767
Ivan Iordanov Atanassov, *CEO*
Christopher Giordano, *Vice Pres*
EMP: 50
SALES (est): 11.5MM **Privately Held**
SIC: 8711 1623 Engineering services; un-
derground utilities contractor

(P-25245)
OSI ENGINEERING INC
901 Campisi Way Ste 160, Campbell
(95008-2365)
PHONE...................................408 550-2800
Javier Diaz, *President*
EMP: 120
SALES (est): 749.4K **Privately Held**
SIC: 8711 Consulting engineer

(P-25246)
P & D CONSULTANTS INC (HQ)
999 W Town And Country Rd, Orange
(92868-4713)
P.O. Box 5367 (92863-5367)
PHONE...................................714 835-4447
John L Kinley, *President*
EMP: 50
SQ FT: 23,000
SALES (est): 11.6MM
SALES (corp-wide): 20.1B **Publicly Held**
SIC: 8711 8742 Civil engineering; plan-
ning consultant
PA: Aecom
1999 Avenue Of The Stars # 2600
Los Angeles CA 90067
213 593-8000

(P-25247)
P2S INC
Also Called: P2s Engineering
5000 E Spring St Ste 800, Long Beach
(90815-5247)
PHONE...................................562 497-2999
Kevin L Peterson, *CEO*
Jagjit Singh, *Principal*
Gary Jewell, *IT/INT Sup*
Sunila Eapen, *Design Engr*
Kent Sayler, *Design Engr*
EMP: 209
SQ FT: 42,700
SALES (est): 18.4MM **Privately Held**
WEB: www.p2seng.com
SIC: 8711 8741 Consulting engineer; con-
struction management

(P-25248)
PACIFIC AIRWORKS GROUP LLC
255 S Leland Norton Way, San Bernardino
(92408-0103)
PHONE...................................909 815-7012
Jose L Gonzalez,
Jose Gonzalez,
Dale Stix,
EMP: 84
SQ FT: 15,000
SALES (est): 3.2MM **Privately Held**
SIC: 8711 7699 Aviation &/or aeronautical
engineering; aircraft & heavy equipment
repair services

(P-25249)
PACIFIC CIVIL & STRL CONS LLC
7415 Greenhaven Dr # 100, Sacramento (95831-5167)
PHONE..................................916 421-1000
Fred Huang, *Partner*
EMP: 50
SALES: 5MM **Privately Held**
SIC: 8711 Structural engineering

(P-25250)
PACIFIC HYDROTECH CORPORATION
314 E 3rd St, Perris (92570-2225)
PHONE..................................951 943-8803
J Kirk Harns, *President*
Joselito Guintu, *Vice Pres*
Dale McKay, *Vice Pres*
Bobby Owens, *Vice Pres*
EMP: 135
SQ FT: 1,500
SALES (est): 37.2MM **Privately Held**
WEB: www.pachydro.com
SIC: 8711 Construction & civil engineering

(P-25251)
PACIFICA SERVICES INC
106 S Mentor Ave Ste 200, Pasadena (91106-2931)
PHONE..................................626 405-0131
Ernest M Camacho, *President*
Stephen Caropino, *CFO*
Elena Gonzales, *Vice Pres*
EMP: 84 **EST:** 1979
SQ FT: 15,000
SALES (est): 12.7MM **Privately Held**
WEB: www.pacificaservices.com
SIC: 8711 7629 8741 Civil engineering; electronic equipment repair; construction management

(P-25252)
PAE CONSULTING ENGINEERS INC
48 Golden Gate Ave, San Francisco (94102-3919)
PHONE..................................503 226-2921
Christian Agulles, *Branch Mgr*
EMP: 66
SALES (corp-wide): 56.4MM **Privately Held**
SIC: 8711 Engineering services
PA: Pae Consulting Engineers, Inc.
522 Sw 5th Ave Ste 1500
Portland OR 97204
503 226-2921

(P-25253)
PANASONIC AVIONICS CORPORATION
26211 Enterprise Way, Lake Forest (92630-8402)
PHONE..................................949 472-2376
Paul Margis, *President*
Mark Ngo, *Engineer*
Margaret Wang, *Engineer*
Andy Coles, *Director*
Wendy Shortley, *Director*
EMP: 86 **Privately Held**
SIC: 8711 Aviation &/or aeronautical engineering
HQ: Panasonic Avionics Corporation
26200 Enterprise Way
Lake Forest CA 92630

(P-25254)
PANASONIC AVIONICS CORPORATION (DH)
26200 Enterprise Way, Lake Forest (92630-8400)
PHONE..................................949 672-2000
Paul Margis, *CEO*
Yasu Enokido, *President*
David Chung, *Treasurer*
Kevin Cooper, *Vice Pres*
Neil James, *Exec Dir*
▲ **EMP:** 400
SQ FT: 20,000
SALES (est): 672.2MM **Privately Held**
SIC: 8711 3728 Aviation &/or aeronautical engineering; aircraft parts & equipment

HQ: Panasonic Corporation Of America
2 Riverfront Plz Ste 200
Newark NJ 07102
201 348-7000

(P-25255)
PARSONS ENGRG SCIENCE INC (DH)
100 W Walnut St, Pasadena (91124-0001)
P.O. Box 88954, Chicago IL (60695-1954)
PHONE..................................626 440-2000
Charles Harrington, *CEO*
Mary Ann Hopkins, *President*
Curtis A Bower, *Exec VP*
Nicholas L Presecan, *Senior VP*
Gary L Stone, *Senior VP*
EMP: 500
SALES (est): 174.9MM
SALES (corp-wide): 3.5B **Publicly Held**
SIC: 8711 Consulting engineer
HQ: Parsons Government Services Inc.
100 W Walnut St
Pasadena CA 91124
626 440-2000

(P-25256)
PARSONS GOVERNMENT SVCS INC (HQ)
100 W Walnut St, Pasadena (91124-0001)
PHONE..................................626 440-2000
Charles L Harrington, *Ch of Bd*
Carey A Smith, *President*
Marc Radin, *Senior VP*
Jerry Oliver, *Vice Pres*
Gary L Stone, *Vice Pres*
EMP: 500 **EST:** 1930
SQ FT: 900,000
SALES (est): 715.7MM
SALES (corp-wide): 3.5B **Publicly Held**
SIC: 8711 Consulting engineer
PA: The Parsons Corporation
5875 Trinity Pkwy Ste 300
Centreville VA 20120
703 988-8500

(P-25257)
PARSONS GOVERNMENT SVCS INC
2000 Marina Vista Ave, Martinez (94553-1301)
PHONE..................................925 313-3217
Dean Lunsford, *Manager*
EMP: 75
SALES (corp-wide): 3.5B **Publicly Held**
SIC: 8711 Engineering services
HQ: Parsons Government Services Inc.
100 W Walnut St
Pasadena CA 91124
626 440-2000

(P-25258)
PARSONS GOVERNMENT SVCS INC (HQ)
25531 Commercentre Dr, Lake Forest (92630-8873)
PHONE..................................949 768-8161
Charles L Harrington, *CEO*
Sophie Odonnell, *Vice Pres*
David Schreiman, *VP Finance*
Cindy Marinkovich, *Controller*
Jody L Chiaro, *VP Human Res*
EMP: 53
SALES (est): 105.8MM
SALES (corp-wide): 3.5B **Publicly Held**
WEB: www.sparta.com
SIC: 8711 Engineering services
PA: The Parsons Corporation
5875 Trinity Pkwy Ste 300
Centreville VA 20120
703 988-8500

(P-25259)
PARSONS GOVERNMENT SVCS INC
525 B St Ste 1600, San Diego (92101-4413)
PHONE..................................619 685-0085
Christopher Bush, *Vice Pres*
Carey Smith, *President*
EMP: 301
SALES (corp-wide): 3.5B **Publicly Held**
SIC: 8711 Engineering services

HQ: Parsons Government Services Inc.
100 W Walnut St
Pasadena CA 91124
626 440-2000

(P-25260)
PARSONS SERVICES COMPANY
100 W Walnut St, Pasadena (91124-0001)
PHONE..................................626 440-2000
Geoge L Ball, *Principal*
EMP: 797
SALES (est): 79.7MM **Privately Held**
SIC: 8711 Construction & civil engineering

(P-25261)
PARSONS TECHNICAL SERVICES INC
100 W Walnut St, Pasadena (91124-0001)
PHONE..................................626 440-3998
Mary Ann Hopkins, *President*
EMP: 99
SALES (est): 8.2MM
SALES (corp-wide): 3.5B **Publicly Held**
SIC: 8711 Engineering services
PA: The Parsons Corporation
5875 Trinity Pkwy Ste 300
Centreville VA 20120
703 988-8500

(P-25262)
PARSONS WTR INFRASTRUCTURE INC
100 W Walnut St, Pasadena (91124-0001)
PHONE..................................626 440-7000
Virginia Grebbien, *CEO*
Anthony F Leketa, *President*
Christian Alexander, *Accounts Mgr*
EMP: 1522
SQ FT: 1,220,000
SALES (est): 76.4MM
SALES (corp-wide): 3.5B **Publicly Held**
SIC: 8711 Consulting engineer
PA: The Parsons Corporation
5875 Trinity Pkwy Ste 300
Centreville VA 20120
703 988-8500

(P-25263)
PARTNER ASSESSMENT CORPORATION (PA)
Also Called: Partner Engineering & Science
2154 Torrance Blvd # 200, Torrance (90501-2609)
PHONE..................................800 419-4923
Joseph P Derhake, *President*
Dana Derhake, *Shareholder*
Brad Fountain, *Principal*
Lauren Shafer, *Executive Asst*
Monique Burrola, *Admin Sec*
EMP: 148
SQ FT: 10,000
SALES (est): 92.7MM **Privately Held**
WEB: www.partneresi.com
SIC: 8711 Consulting engineer

(P-25264)
PERRY & SHAW INC
9029 Park Plaza Dr # 104, La Mesa (91942-3450)
PHONE..................................619 390-6500
Michael Shaw, *President*
Harold Perry, *Vice Pres*
EMP: 85 **EST:** 1995
SALES (est): 48.5MM **Privately Held**
WEB: www.perry-shaw.com
SIC: 8711 Engineering services

(P-25265)
PHG ENGINEERING SERVICES LLC
180 N Rverview Dr Ste 165, Anaheim (92808)
PHONE..................................714 283-8288
Francis L Price,
Steve Kosto, *Engineer*
EMP: 100
SALES (est): 1.4MM **Privately Held**
SIC: 8711 Engineering services

(P-25266)
POWER ENGINEERS INCORPORATED
731 E Ball Rd Ste 100, Anaheim (92805-5951)
PHONE..................................714 507-2700

Douglas M Sharpe, *Branch Mgr*
EMP: 51
SALES (corp-wide): 466MM **Privately Held**
SIC: 8711 Engineering services
PA: Power Engineers, Incorporated
3940 Glenbrook Dr
Hailey ID 83333
208 788-3456

(P-25267)
POWER ENGINEERS INCORPORATED
218 Loreto Ct, Martinez (94553-3551)
P.O. Box 2037 (94553-0203)
PHONE..................................925 372-9284
EMP: 52
SALES (corp-wide): 298.6MM **Privately Held**
SIC: 8711
PA: Power Engineers, Incorporated
3940 Glenbrook Dr
Hailey ID 83333
208 788-3456

(P-25268)
PREDICATE LOGIC INC (PA)
6498 Weathers Pl Ste 200, San Diego (92121-3915)
PHONE..................................858 715-0100
Mary J Lawler, *CEO*
Steve Keller, *Vice Pres*
James M Lawler, *Vice Pres*
EMP: 70
SQ FT: 4,126
SALES (est): 8.6MM **Privately Held**
WEB: www.tychometrics.com
SIC: 8711 Engineering services

(P-25269)
PSOMAS
1075 Crkside Rdg Dr # 200, Roseville (95678-3504)
PHONE..................................916 788-8122
Paul Enneking, *Manager*
Tina Andersen, *Vice Pres*
Diana Slater, *Office Admin*
Mike Kristal, *Administration*
Monika Bowden, *Project Mgr*
EMP: 140
SALES (corp-wide): 84.4MM **Privately Held**
SIC: 8711 8713 Civil engineering; surveying services
PA: Psomas
555 S Flower St Ste 4300
Los Angeles CA 90071
213 223-1400

(P-25270)
PTSI MANAGED SERVICES INC
100 W Walnut St, Pasadena (91124-0001)
PHONE..................................626 440-3118
Mary Ann Hopkins, *President*
EMP: 99 **EST:** 1983
SALES (est): 5.7MM **Privately Held**
SIC: 8711 Engineering services

(P-25271)
QUAD KNOPF INC (PA)
901 E Main St, Visalia (93292-6546)
P.O. Box 3699 (93278-3699)
PHONE..................................559 733-0440
Michael Knopf, *President*
Janel Freeman, *CFO*
Amber Adams, *Branch Mgr*
Nathan D Meeks, *Branch Mgr*
Becky Smith, *Executive Asst*
EMP: 50
SQ FT: 12,000
SALES: 16.9MM **Privately Held**
WEB: www.quadknopf.com
SIC: 8711 8712 Civil engineering; consulting engineer; architectural services

(P-25272)
QUARTUS ENGINEERING INC (PA)
9689 Towne Centre Dr, San Diego (92121-1964)
PHONE..................................858 875-6000
Mark Stabb, *Principal*
Doug Botos, *CEO*
Chris Flanigan, *Vice Pres*
Jeff Frantz, *Vice Pres*
Alexander Halterman, *Admin Sec*

PRODUCTS & SVCS

EMP: 70
SQ FT: 3,100
SALES (est): 30.4MM **Privately Held**
WEB: www.quartus.com
SIC: 8711 Mechanical engineering

(P-25273)
R G VANDERWEIL ENGINEERS LLP
3760 Kilroy Airport Way # 230, Long Beach (90806-2443)
PHONE....................562 256-8623
Jeff Duncan, *Principal*
EMP: 110
SALES (corp-wide): 68.8MM **Privately Held**
SIC: 8711 Consulting engineer
PA: R. G. Vanderweil Engineers, Llp
274 Summer St Fl 2
Boston MA 02210
617 423-7423

(P-25274)
R JOY INC
Also Called: Richard Joy Engineering
1584 Wolf Meadows Ln, Portola (96122-7080)
PHONE....................530 832-5760
Richard Joy, *Owner*
EMP: 100
SALES (est): 1.7MM **Privately Held**
SIC: 8711 Engineering services

(P-25275)
R M A GROUP INC (PA)
Also Called: RMA Group
12130 Santa Margarita Ct, Rancho Cucamonga (91730-6138)
PHONE....................909 980-6096
Edward Duane Lyon, *Chairman*
Slawek Dymerski, *President*
Ed Lyon, *President*
Sue Lyon, *Corp Secy*
Brian Haber, *Area Mgr*
EMP: 70
SQ FT: 9,600
SALES (est): 23.9MM **Privately Held**
WEB: www.rmagrp.com
SIC: 8711 Engineering services

(P-25276)
RADIUS PRODUCT DEVELOPMENT INC
6375 San Ignacio Ave, San Jose (95119-1200)
PHONE....................408 361-6000
John Van Akkeren, *President*
EMP: 800
SALES (est): 36.2MM
SALES (corp-wide): 25.2B **Publicly Held**
SIC: 8711 7389 8742 Designing; ship, boat, machine & product; design services; marketing consulting services
HQ: Nypro Inc.
101 Union St
Clinton MA 01510
978 365-8100

(P-25277)
RAILPROS INC (PA)
15265 Alton Pkwy Ste 140, Irvine (92618-2605)
PHONE....................714 734-8765
Eric Hankinson, *President*
Jason Barton, *Vice Pres*
Karen Hankinson, *Vice Pres*
Kyle Hawthorn, *Vice Pres*
Johnny Johnson, *Vice Pres*
EMP: 62 EST: 2000
SQ FT: 1,200
SALES (est): 16MM **Privately Held**
WEB: www.railpros.com
SIC: 8711 Civil engineering

(P-25278)
RAILPROS FIELD SERVICES
1 Ada Ste 200, Irvine (92618-5341)
PHONE....................877 315-0513
Johnny Johnson, *CEO*
Mark A Martin, *Engineer*
Bill Pairman, *Manager*
EMP: 50
SQ FT: 900

SALES (est): 4.9MM
SALES (corp-wide): 16.2MM **Privately Held**
SIC: 8711 Consulting engineer
PA: Railpros Field Services Inc
1705 W Northwest Hwy # 150
Grapevine TX 76051
682 223-6897

(P-25279)
RAMSGATE ENGINEERING INC
2331 Cepheus Ct, Bakersfield (93308-6944)
P.O. Box 20068 (93390-0068)
PHONE....................661 392-0050
Donald C Nelson, *President*
EMP: 95
SALES (est): 12MM **Privately Held**
SIC: 8711 Consulting engineer

(P-25280)
RANGE GENERATION NEXT LLC
Also Called: Rgnext
105 13th St Bldg 6525, Vandenberg Afb (93437-5209)
PHONE....................310 647-9438
Tom Kennedy, *CEO*
Donna Mc Cullough, *Manager*
Donna McCullough, *Manager*
EMP: 99
SQ FT: 100
SALES (est): 3.9MM **Privately Held**
SIC: 8711 Engineering services

(P-25281)
RAYTHEON COMPANY
9985 Pcf Hts Blvd Ste 200, San Diego (92121)
PHONE....................858 455-9741
Penny Lee, *Project Mgr*
Sonya Vitali, *VP Opers*
EMP: 187
SALES (corp-wide): 27B **Publicly Held**
SIC: 8711 8733 5045 Aviation &/or aeronautical engineering; scientific research agency; computer software
PA: Raytheon Company
870 Winter St
Waltham MA 02451
781 522-3000

(P-25282)
RAYTHEON COMPANY
2000 E El Segundo Blvd, El Segundo (90245-4501)
PHONE....................310 647-9438
Donna McCullough, *Branch Mgr*
EMP: 220
SALES (corp-wide): 27B **Publicly Held**
SIC: 8711 Electrical or electronic engineering
PA: Raytheon Company
870 Winter St
Waltham MA 02451
781 522-3000

(P-25283)
REAUME AND ASSOCIATES INC
Also Called: Reaume, E M & Associates
11527 W Washington Blvd, Los Angeles (90066-5913)
PHONE....................310 398-5768
John Wilmer, *President*
Allen John Wilmer, *Vice Pres*
EMP: 80
SQ FT: 1,500
SALES: 1.1MM **Privately Held**
SIC: 8711 Consulting engineer

(P-25284)
RECON REFRACTORY & CNSTR INC
3914 Cherry Ave Ste B, Long Beach (90807-3738)
P.O. Box 93120 (90809-3120)
PHONE....................562 988-7981
Robert Bellamy, *Owner*
EMP: 50
SALES (corp-wide): 25MM **Privately Held**
SIC: 8711 3297 1522 Engineering services; nonclay refractories; residential construction

PA: Recon Refractory & Construction, Inc.
10741 Los Alamitos Blvd
Los Alamitos CA 90720
562 799-7980

(P-25285)
RIALTO BIOENERGY FACILITY LLC
5780 Fleet St Ste 310, Carlsbad (92008-4714)
PHONE....................760 436-8870
Arun Sharma, *Mng Member*
EMP: 250 EST: 2013
SQ FT: 12,937
SALES (est): 6.2MM
SALES (corp-wide): 39.7MM **Privately Held**
SIC: 8711 Energy conservation engineering
PA: Anaergia Inc
4210 South Service Rd
Burlington ON L7L 4
905 766-3333

(P-25286)
RIPCORD INC
30955 Huntwood Ave, Hayward (94544-7005)
PHONE....................408 838-7446
Alex Fielding, *CEO*
Kim Lembo, *Partner*
Kevin Hall, *President*
Ahson Ahmad, *Officer*
Christopher Blake, *Senior VP*
EMP: 60 EST: 2015
SALES (est): 1MM **Privately Held**
SIC: 8711 7374 Engineering services; data processing & preparation

(P-25287)
RIVER CY GEOPROFESSIONALS INC
Also Called: Wallace-Kuhl & Associates
3050 Industrial Blvd, West Sacramento (95691-3470)
PHONE....................916 372-1434
David R Gius, *President*
Andrew Wallace, *CFO*
EMP: 56 EST: 2010
SALES (est): 5.7MM **Privately Held**
SIC: 8711 Engineering services

(P-25288)
ROBERT CONSL ENGLEKIRK STRCTRL (PA)
2116 Arlington Ave Lbby, Los Angeles (90018-1365)
PHONE....................323 733-6673
Robert E Englekirk, *President*
Solveig Jensen, *Treasurer*
EMP: 55 EST: 1969
SQ FT: 12,000
SALES (est): 4.3MM **Privately Held**
SIC: 8711 Structural engineering

(P-25289)
ROQUE DEVELOPMENT AND INV
Also Called: Rdi Engineering
227 E Pomona Blvd Ste B, Monterey Park (91755-7226)
PHONE....................626 427-9077
Hector Mendoza Jr, *CEO*
Jason Roque, *Real Est Agnt*
EMP: 99
SQ FT: 5,000
SALES (est): 6.8MM **Privately Held**
SIC: 8711 Civil engineering

(P-25290)
ROSS F CARROLL INC
8873 Warnerville Rd, Oakdale (95361-9411)
P.O. Box 1308 (95361-1308)
PHONE....................209 848-5959
Sean Carroll, *President*
Sheila M Carroll, *Corp Secy*
EMP: 50
SALES (est): 9.3MM **Privately Held**
WEB: www.rossfcarrollinc.com
SIC: 8711 Engineering services

(P-25291)
RWC ENTERPRISES INC
Also Called: Professional Construction Svcs
9130 Santa Anita Ave, Rancho Cucamonga (91730-6143)
PHONE....................909 373-4100
Robert William Casey, *President*
Lori Casey, *Admin Sec*
Frank Heaton, *Project Mgr*
EMP: 50
SQ FT: 16,000
SALES (est): 7.3MM **Privately Held**
SIC: 8711 0781 Civil engineering; landscape counseling services

(P-25292)
SAALEX CORP (PA)
Also Called: Saalex Solutions
811 Camarillo Springs Rd A, Camarillo (93012-9465)
PHONE....................805 482-1070
Travis Mack, *President*
Dennis Meehan, *Program Mgr*
Kelly Nguyen, *Program Mgr*
Lauren Cook, *Administration*
Schuyler Roberts, *IT/INT Sup*
EMP: 245
SQ FT: 7,000
SALES: 36.5MM **Privately Held**
SIC: 8711 7379 Consulting engineer; computer related consulting services

(P-25293)
SAIFUL/BOUQUET CON STRU ENG (PA)
155 N Lake Ave Fl 6, Pasadena (91101-1849)
PHONE....................626 304-2616
Saiful Islam, *CEO*
Tom Bouquet, *CFO*
Helen Yoon, *Vice Pres*
Y K Low, *Admin Sec*
Tim Townsend, *Info Tech Dir*
EMP: 53 EST: 1997
SQ FT: 25,000
SALES (est): 10.5MM **Privately Held**
WEB: www.sbise.com
SIC: 8711 Structural engineering

(P-25294)
SALAS OBRIEN ENGINEERS INC (PA)
305 S 11th St, San Jose (95112-2218)
PHONE....................408 282-1500
Paul Silva, *CEO*
Ronnie Hilton, *Assoc VP*
Israel Moreno, *Assoc VP*
Chris Cox, *Vice Pres*
Bi Nguyen, *Vice Pres*
▲ **EMP:** 50
SQ FT: 10,000
SALES (est): 45.8MM **Privately Held**
WEB: www.salasobrien.com
SIC: 8711 Consulting engineer

(P-25295)
SAN DIEGO COMPOSITES INC
9220 Activity Rd Ste 100, San Diego (92126-4420)
PHONE....................858 751-0450
Rob Kolozs, *President*
Christine Benzie, *CFO*
Carl Sloan, *Vice Pres*
Ken Mercer, *CTO*
Kevin Harness, *Technician*
EMP: 70
SQ FT: 70,000
SALES: 19MM
SALES (corp-wide): 30.3MM **Privately Held**
WEB: www.sdcomposites.com
SIC: 8711 8734 3761 3764 Consulting engineer; testing laboratories; guided missiles & space vehicles; guided missile & space vehicle propulsion unit parts
PA: Ac&A Enterprises Holdings, Llc
25692 Atlantic Ocean Dr
Lake Forest CA 92630
949 716-3511

(P-25296)
SAN DIEGO SERVICES LLC
Also Called: Paragon Services Engineering
5415 Oberlin Dr, San Diego (92121-1716)
PHONE....................858 654-0102

Rosemary Dymek, *Officer*
Wesley S Dymek, *Principal*
Ken Lindsay, *Chief Engr*
Bertha Valdez, *Controller*
EMP: 150
SQ FT: 2,477
SALES: 11MM **Privately Held**
SIC: 8711 Engineering services

(P-25297)
SAN DIEGO TESTING ENGINEERS
Also Called: Testing Engineers San Diego
7895 Convoy Ct Ste 18, San Diego
(92111-1215)
PHONE....................858 715-5800
Mark Baron, *President*
Dickerson Wright, *CEO*
EMP: 94
SQ FT: 13,000
SALES (est): 5.4MM **Privately Held**
WEB: www.uslaboratories.com
SIC: 8711 8734 8742 Structural engineering; testing laboratories; construction project management consultant

(P-25298)
SC WRIGHT CONSTRUCTION INC
3838 Camino Del Rio Nth S, San Diego
(92108)
P.O. Box 3250, La Mesa (91944-3250)
PHONE....................619 698-6909
Steven C Wright, *President*
Laurie Beckham, *Admin Asst*
Jim Barker, *Human Res Mgr*
Tracie Maxwell, *Opers Staff*
EMP: 400
SALES (est): 28.6MM **Privately Held**
WEB: www.scwright.com
SIC: 8711 Building construction consultant

(P-25299)
SCHILLING ROBOTICS LLC
Also Called: Manufacturing Facility
201 Cousteau Pl, Davis (95618-5412)
PHONE....................530 753-6718
Tyler Schilling, *Manager*
Inez Shipp, *Buyer*
EMP: 100
SALES (corp-wide): 12.6B **Privately Held**
SIC: 8711 3593 Engineering services; fluid power cylinders & actuators
HQ: Schilling Robotics, Llc
260 Cousteau Pl Ste 200
Davis CA 95618
530 753-6718

(P-25300)
SCICON TECHNOLOGIES CORP (PA)
27525 Newhall Ranch Rd # 2, Valencia
(91355-4003)
PHONE....................661 295-8630
Thomas J Bulger, *President*
Bradley Bulger, *Vice Pres*
Marie Bulger, *Admin Sec*
Mitch Greenwood, *Info Tech Mgr*
Daniel Smith, *Senior Engr*
EMP: 65
SQ FT: 25,000
SALES (est): 10.5MM **Privately Held**
WEB: www.scicontech.com
SIC: 8711 3999 Mechanical engineering; models, except toy

(P-25301)
SCICON TECHNOLOGIES CORP
1300 Quail St Ste 208, Newport Beach
(92660-2710)
PHONE....................949 252-1341
Tom Bulger, *Manager*
Matthew Titner, *Manager*
EMP: 60
SALES (corp-wide): 10.5MM **Privately Held**
WEB: www.scicontech.com
SIC: 8711 Engineering services
PA: Scicon Technologies Corp
27525 Newhall Ranch Rd # 2
Valencia CA 91355
661 295-8630

(P-25302)
SEQUOIA CONSULTANTS INC
11588 Sorrento Valley Rd, San Diego
(92121-1336)
PHONE....................858 345-1544
EMP: 62 **Privately Held**
SIC: 8711 8742 8071 Engineering services; quality assurance consultant; testing laboratories
PA: Sequoia Consultants, Inc.
361 W Grove Ave
Orange CA 92865

(P-25303)
SERCO INC
9350 Waxie Way Ste 400, San Diego
(92123-1056)
PHONE....................858 569-8979
Kent Brown, *Branch Mgr*
Brad Hector, *Network Enginr*
Taryn Jones, *Technician*
Olen Hanf, *Purchasing*
Jay Odonnell, *VP Opers*
EMP: 132
SALES (corp-wide): 3.6B **Privately Held**
WEB: www.serco.com
SIC: 8711 Engineering services
HQ: Serco Inc.
12930 Worldgate Dr # 600
Herndon VA 20170

(P-25304)
SHN CONSULTING ENGIN (PA)
Also Called: Shn Cnslting Engnrs-Geologists
812 W Wabash Ave, Eureka (95501-2138)
PHONE....................707 441-8855
Kenneth Jeffrey Nelson, *President*
Mark Chaney, *Regional Mgr*
Anders Rasmussen, *Engineer*
Charles Swanson, *Engineer*
Brenda Sigler, *Human Res Dir*
EMP: 60
SQ FT: 14,000
SALES (est): 14.9MM **Privately Held**
WEB: www.shn-engr.com
SIC: 8711 8999 Consulting engineer; geological consultant

(P-25305)
SIA ENGINEERING (USA) INC
7001 W Imperial Hwy, Los Angeles
(90045-6313)
PHONE....................310 693-7108
Cheng Hian Tan, *CEO*
Chiuyen Tseng, *CFO*
EMP: 51
SALES (est): 9.2MM **Privately Held**
SIC: 8711 Consulting engineer

(P-25306)
SIEMENS AG
Also Called: Siemens Healthineers
685 E Middlefield Rd, Mountain View
(94043-4045)
PHONE....................650 969-9112
◆ **EMP:** 250
SALES (est): 3.3MM **Privately Held**
SIC: 8711 8721 8742 Engineering services; accounting, auditing & bookkeeping; marketing consulting services

(P-25307)
SIERRA LOBO INC
465 N Halstead St Ste 130, Pasadena
(91107-3144)
PHONE....................626 510-6340
EMP: 126 **Privately Held**
SIC: 8711 Engineering services
PA: Sierra Lobo, Inc.
102 Pinnacle Dr
Fremont OH 43420

(P-25308)
SIERRA NEVADA CORPORATION
985 University Ave Ste 4, Los Gatos
(95032-7639)
PHONE....................408 395-2004
Michael Weiland, *Branch Mgr*
Eren Ozmen, *President*
Fatih Ozmen, *CEO*
Luciano Saccani, *Business Dir*
Deborah Sipos, *Technology*
EMP: 123

SALES (corp-wide): 1.9B **Privately Held**
SIC: 8711 Engineering services
PA: Sierra Nevada Corporation
444 Salomon Cir
Sparks NV 89434
775 331-0222

(P-25309)
SIMPSON GUMPERTZ & HEGER INC
100 Pine St Ste 1600, San Francisco
(94111-5202)
PHONE....................415 495-3700
John Sumnchit, *Systems Mgr*
Dr Rene W Luff, *Principal*
Ryan Magner, *Admin Mgr*
Mohamed Talaat, *Engineer*
Christine Diosdado, *Sr Project Mgr*
EMP: 90
SALES (corp-wide): 91.6MM **Privately Held**
WEB: www.sgh.com
SIC: 8711 8741 Consulting engineer; construction management
PA: Simpson Gumpertz & Heger Inc.
480 Totten Pond Rd
Waltham MA 02451
781 907-9000

(P-25310)
SOLOPOINT SOLUTIONS INC
150 Paularino Ave Ste 282, Costa Mesa
(92626-3302)
PHONE....................714 708-3639
Dinh Le, *Branch Mgr*
EMP: 53
SALES (corp-wide): 8.8MM **Privately Held**
SIC: 8711 Consulting engineer
PA: Solopoint Solutions, Inc.
3350 Scott Blvd Bldg 2
Santa Clara CA 95054
408 246-5945

(P-25311)
SOLUTE (PA)
Also Called: Solute Consulting
1660 Hotel Cir N Ste 600, San Diego
(92108-2806)
PHONE....................619 224-2810
John Lyons, *CEO*
Dan Bishop, *Vice Pres*
EMP: 80
SQ FT: 7,000
SALES (est): 15.5MM
SALES (corp-wide): 20MM **Privately Held**
WEB: www.solute.us
SIC: 8711 Civil engineering

(P-25312)
SONIC INDUSTRIES INC
Also Called: Airframer R
20030 Normandie Ave, Torrance
(90502-1210)
PHONE....................310 532-8382
Steven Scott Stil, *CEO*
Sharon Couturiaux, *Marketing Staff*
▲ **EMP:** 150
SQ FT: 65,000
SALES (est): 28.7MM
SALES (corp-wide): 702.5MM **Publicly Held**
SIC: 8711 7699 Machine tool design; aviation propeller & blade repair
HQ: Roller Bearing Company Of America, Inc.
102 Willenbrock Rd
Oxford CT 06478
203 267-7001

(P-25313)
SPEC SERVICES INC
10540 Talbert Ave 100e, Fountain Valley
(92708-6051)
PHONE....................714 963-8077
Kim R Henry, *President*
Chris Smart, *COO*
Dan Letcher, *CFO*
Chuck Lake, *Vice Pres*
Robert Randig, *Planning*
EMP: 190
SQ FT: 16,000
SALES (est): 61.3MM **Privately Held**
WEB: www.specservices.com
SIC: 8711 Consulting engineer

(P-25314)
SPIRAL TECHNOLOGY INC
229 E Avenue K8 Ste 105, Lancaster
(93535-4517)
PHONE....................661 723-3148
Archie L Moore, *President*
Steve McCarter, *Ch of Bd*
Daniel Hare, *COO*
Cynthia Hull, *Finance*
Debra Murphy, *Controller*
EMP: 56
SQ FT: 4,984
SALES (est): 8.9MM **Privately Held**
WEB: www.spiraltechinc.com
SIC: 8711 Industrial engineers

(P-25315)
SSC CONSTRUCTION INC
4195 Chino Hills Pkwy, Chino Hills
(91709-2618)
PHONE....................951 278-1177
Gregory E Larkin, *CEO*
Neil Nehmens, *Senior VP*
EMP: 200
SALES (est): 33.4MM **Privately Held**
WEB: www.sscconstruction.com
SIC: 8711 Engineering services

(P-25316)
SSL ROBOTICS LLC (DH)
Also Called: Mda US Systems LLC
1250 Lincoln Ave Ste 100, Pasadena
(91103-2466)
PHONE....................626 296-1373
Daniel Friedmann,
Mohammad Manki, *Principal*
Chris Thayer, *General Mgr*
Irma Franco, *Sr Project Mgr*
Mike Adams, *Manager*
EMP: 54
SALES (est): 43.7MM
SALES (corp-wide): 2.1B **Publicly Held**
SIC: 8711 8731 Aviation &/or aeronautical engineering; commercial physical research
HQ: Maxar Technologies Ltd
200 Burrard St Suite 1570
Vancouver BC V6C 3
604 974-5275

(P-25317)
SSL ROBOTICS LLC
1250 Lincoln Ave Ste 100, Pasadena
(91103-2466)
PHONE....................626 296-1373
Mohammad Manki, *Branch Mgr*
Rius Billing, *Engineer*
Jill Staats, *HR Admin*
Keith Vanbuskirk, *Deputy Dir*
EMP: 65
SALES (corp-wide): 2.1B **Publicly Held**
SIC: 8711 8731 Aviation &/or aeronautical engineering; commercial physical research
HQ: Ssl Robotics Llc
1250 Lincoln Ave Ste 100
Pasadena CA 91103
626 296-1373

(P-25318)
SSL ROBOTICS LLC
4398 Corporate Center Dr, Los Alamitos
(90720-2537)
PHONE....................626 296-1373
Ted Cheng, *General Mgr*
EMP: 150
SALES (corp-wide): 2.1B **Publicly Held**
SIC: 8711 Aviation &/or aeronautical engineering
HQ: Ssl Robotics Llc
1250 Lincoln Ave Ste 100
Pasadena CA 91103
626 296-1373

(P-25319)
STANTEC ARCH & ENGRG PC
38 Technology Dr Ste 100, Irvine
(92618-5312)
PHONE....................949 923-6000
EMP: 117
SALES (corp-wide): 3.2B **Privately Held**
SIC: 8711 8712 Engineering services; architectural services

PRODUCTS & SVCS

HQ: Stantec Architecture And Engineering
P.C.
311 Summer St
Boston MA 02210

(P-25320)
STANTEC ARCHITECTURE INC
100 California St # 1000, San Francisco
(94111-4505)
PHONE.................................415 882-9500
Michael Gambucci, *CEO*
Lori Van Dermark, *Marketing Staff*
Rachel Ginsberg, *Librarian*
Lynn Befu, *Director*
Robert Shurell, *Manager*
EMP: 96
SALES (corp-wide): 3.2B **Privately Held**
SIC: 8711 8712 Engineering services; ar-
chitectural services
HQ: Stantec Architecture Inc.
224 S Michigan Ave # 1400
Chicago IL 60604
336 714-7413

(P-25321)
**STANTEC CONSULTING SVCS
INC**
1340 Treat Blvd Ste 525, Walnut Creek
(94597-7984)
PHONE.................................925 627-4500
Stacey Robinson, *Office Mgr*
Maria Chryssofos, *Technology*
EMP: 170
SALES (corp-wide): 3.2B **Privately Held**
WEB: www.mw.com
SIC: 8711 Consulting engineer
HQ: Stantec Consulting Services Inc.
475 5th Ave Fl 12
New York NY 10017
212 352-5160

(P-25322)
**STANTEC CONSULTING SVCS
INC**
111 E Victoria St, Santa Barbara
(93101-2018)
PHONE.................................805 963-9532
Lori Van Dermark, *Marketing Staff*
William Lupo, *Manager*
EMP: 55
SALES (corp-wide): 3.2B **Privately Held**
WEB: www.penfieldsmith.com
SIC: 8711 Engineering services
HQ: Stantec Consulting Services Inc.
475 5th Ave Fl 12
New York NY 10017
212 352-5160

(P-25323)
**STANTEC CONSULTING SVCS
INC**
300 N Lake Ave Ste 400, Pasadena
(91101-4169)
PHONE.................................626 796-9141
Paul Boulos, *Branch Mgr*
Lori Van Dermark, *Agent*
EMP: 79
SALES (corp-wide): 3.2B **Privately Held**
WEB: www.mw.com
SIC: 8711 Engineering services
HQ: Stantec Consulting Services Inc.
475 5th Ave Fl 12
New York NY 10017
212 352-5160

(P-25324)
**STANTEC CONSULTING SVCS
INC**
3301 C St Ste 1900, Sacramento
(95816-3394)
PHONE.................................916 924-8844
Mike Watson, *Manager*
Deborah Kintz, *Executive*
Joe Niland, *Principal*
EMP: 50
SALES (corp-wide): 3.2B **Privately Held**
WEB: www.mw.com
SIC: 8711 Consulting engineer
HQ: Stantec Consulting Services Inc.
475 5th Ave Fl 12
New York NY 10017
212 352-5160

(P-25325)
**STANTEC CONSULTING SVCS
INC**
100 California St # 1000, San Francisco
(94111-4505)
PHONE.................................415 882-9500
Nicole Collins, *Manager*
Lori Van Dermark, *Marketing Staff*
Herb Moussa, *Director*
Rebecca Leonardis-Grefski, *Manager*
EMP: 96
SALES (corp-wide): 3.2B **Privately Held**
WEB: www.keithco.com
SIC: 8711 8712 Consulting engineer; ar-
chitectural services
HQ: Stantec Consulting Services Inc.
475 5th Ave Fl 12
New York NY 10017
212 352-5160

(P-25326)
**STRUCTURAL INTEGRITY
ASSOC INC (PA)**
5215 Hellyer Ave Ste 210, San Jose
(95138-1079)
PHONE.................................408 978-8200
Laney H Bisbee, *CEO*
David Stager, *CFO*
Darren Gale, *Vice Pres*
Jonnathan Warwick, *Info Tech Dir*
Celestine De Leon, *Accountant*
EMP: 65
SQ FT: 17,000
SALES: 72MM **Privately Held**
SIC: 8711 Consulting engineer

(P-25327)
**STURGEON SON GRADING &
PAV INC**
Also Called: Sturgeon Services Intl
6516 Cat Canyon Rd, Santa Maria
(93454-9605)
PHONE.................................805 938-0618
Fax: 805 938-0894
EMP: 114
SALES (corp-wide): 56.7MM **Privately
Held**
SIC: 8711 1794
PA: Sturgeon & Son Grading & Paving, Inc.
3511 Gilmore Ave
Bakersfield CA 93308
661 322-4408

(P-25328)
**SYSKA & HENNESSY
ENGINEERS INC**
800 Crprate Pinte Ste 200, Culver City
(90230)
PHONE.................................310 312-0200
Gary A Brennen, *President*
Ann Banning-Wright, *Vice Pres*
Jennifer Crawford, *Principal*
EMP: 99
SALES (est): 8.3MM **Privately Held**
SIC: 8711 Consulting engineer

(P-25329)
**SYSTEMS APPLICATION & TECH
INC**
Also Called: Sa-Tech
1000 Town Center Dr # 110, Oxnard
(93036-1100)
P.O. Box 25, Port Hueneme (93044-0025)
PHONE.................................805 487-7373
Geoff Dezavala, *Senior VP*
EMP: 80
SALES (corp-wide): 67.1MM **Privately
Held**
WEB: www.sa-techinc.com
SIC: 8711 Consulting engineer
PA: Systems Application & Technologies,
Inc.
1101 Merc Ln Ste 200
Largo MD 20774
301 322-8880

(P-25330)
SYZYGY TECHNOLOGIES INC
1272 Calpella Ct, Chula Vista
(91913-1426)
P.O. Box 1422, Solana Beach (92075-
7422)
PHONE.................................619 297-0970
Santos Discar, *President*
EMP: 60

SALES (est): 2.3MM **Privately Held**
SIC: 8711 7371 Engineering services;
computer software development

(P-25331)
T Y LIN INTERNATIONAL (HQ)
345 California St # 2300, San Francisco
(94104-2606)
PHONE.................................415 291-3700
Alvaro J Piedrahita, *President*
EMP: 84
SQ FT: 30,159
SALES (est): 134.7MM
SALES (corp-wide): 160MM **Privately
Held**
WEB: www.tyli.com
SIC: 8711 Consulting engineer
PA: T.Y.Lin International Group, Ltd.
345 California St Fl 23
San Francisco CA 94104
415 291-3700

(P-25332)
TALENTSCALE LLC
31805 Temecula Pkwy 204, Temecula
(92592-8203)
PHONE.................................951 744-0053
Douglas Poldrugo, *President*
Steve Santich, *President*
Richard Nester, *Vice Pres*
Kristin Wolfram, *Administration*
Amy Corothers, *Tech Recruiter*
EMP: 83
SALES (est): 8.7MM
SALES (corp-wide): 67.7MM **Privately
Held**
SIC: 8711 Engineering services
HQ: Scst, Inc.
6280 Riverdale St
San Diego CA 92120
619 280-4321

(P-25333)
TECHNICAL AMERICA INC
301 N Smith Ave, Corona (92880-1742)
PHONE.................................951 272-9540
Jing Xie, *CEO*
EMP: 55
SALES (est): 9.6MM **Privately Held**
SIC: 8711 Engineering services

(P-25334)
TEECOM
1333 Broadway Ste 601, Oakland
(94612-1906)
PHONE.................................510 337-2800
David Marks, *CEO*
Jerry Dreiling, *CFO*
Samuel Fajner, *Vice Pres*
Andrew Gonzales, *Design Engr*
Paul Herget, *Design Engr*
EMP: 87
SQ FT: 12,600
SALES (est): 3.1MM **Privately Held**
WEB: www.teecom.com
SIC: 8711 Consulting engineer

(P-25335)
**TERO TEK INTERNATIONAL INC
(PA)**
1408 S Lexington St, Delano (93215-9783)
P.O. Box 310 (93216-0310)
PHONE.................................661 725-1135
William R Aldrich, *President*
Jerry Doss, *Vice Pres*
Lee E Brown, *Director*
James C Josephson, *Director*
Denise Moore, *Manager*
EMP: 51
SQ FT: 120
SALES: 365.8K **Privately Held**
SIC: 8711 Engineering services

(P-25336)
TETER LLP (PA)
7535 N Palm Ave Ste 201, Fresno
(93711-5504)
PHONE.................................559 437-0887
Glen Teter, *Partner*
Clay Davis, *Partner*
Byron Dietrich, *Partner*
Paul Halajian, *Partner*
Jamie Hickman, *Partner*
EMP: 50

SALES (est): 9.7MM **Privately Held**
WEB: www.tetercon.com
SIC: 8711 8712 Structural engineering; ar-
chitectural services

(P-25337)
TETRA TECH INC
17885 Von Karman Ave # 500, Irvine
(92614-5227)
PHONE.................................949 263-0846
Jack Chicca, *Branch Mgr*
EMP: 85
SALES (corp-wide): 2.9B **Publicly Held**
SIC: 8711 Consulting engineer
PA: Tetra Tech, Inc.
3475 E Foothill Blvd
Pasadena CA 91107
626 351-4664

(P-25338)
TETRA TECH INC
Also Called: Tetra Tech Engrg & Arch Svcs
17885 Von Karman Ave # 500, Irvine
(92614-5227)
PHONE.................................949 809-5000
Steve Tedesco, *Branch Mgr*
EMP: 91
SALES (corp-wide): 2.9B **Publicly Held**
WEB: www.tetratech.com
SIC: 8711 Civil engineering
PA: Tetra Tech, Inc.
3475 E Foothill Blvd
Pasadena CA 91107
626 351-4664

(P-25339)
TETRA TECH BAS INC (HQ)
Also Called: B A S
21700 Copley Dr Ste 200, Diamond Bar
(91765-2219)
PHONE.................................909 860-7777
Bryan A Stirrat, *President*
Ira Snyder, *CFO*
Jeanne Stirrat, *Admin Sec*
Kelly McGregor, *Engineer*
Jose A Velez, *Manager*
EMP: 65
SALES (est): 10.5MM
SALES (corp-wide): 2.9B **Publicly Held**
WEB: www.bas.com
SIC: 8711 Civil engineering; pollution con-
trol engineering
PA: Tetra Tech, Inc.
3475 E Foothill Blvd
Pasadena CA 91107
626 351-4664

(P-25340)
TETRA TECH EC INC
1230 Columbia St Ste 750, San Diego
(92101-8536)
PHONE.................................619 234-8690
Andy Bolt, *Branch Mgr*
EMP: 67
SALES (corp-wide): 2.9B **Publicly Held**
SIC: 8711 Engineering services
HQ: Tetra Tech Ec, Inc.
6 Century Dr Ste 3
Parsippany NJ 07054
973 630-8000

(P-25341)
**TETRA TECH TECHNICAL
SERVICES**
3475 E Foothill Blvd Fl 3, Pasadena
(91107-6024)
PHONE.................................626 351-4664
Dan Batrack, *CEO*
EMP: 244
SALES (est): 14.8MM
SALES (corp-wide): 2.9B **Publicly Held**
WEB: www.tetratech.com
SIC: 8711 Consulting engineer
PA: Tetra Tech, Inc.
3475 E Foothill Blvd
Pasadena CA 91107
626 351-4664

(P-25342)
TGCON INC (HQ)
50 Contractors St, Livermore (94551-4863)
PHONE.................................925 449-5764
William L Gates, *President*
John Copriviza, *President*
Brian L Gates, *COO*
Scott Blaine, *CFO*

Brian Gates, *Exec VP*
EMP: 71
SQ FT: 25,000
SALES (est): 55.2MM
SALES (corp-wide): 203MM **Privately Held**
WEB: www.topgradeconstruction.com
SIC: 8711 Construction & civil engineering
PA: Goodfellow Bros. Llc
135 N Wenatchee Ave
Wenatchee WA 98801
509 662-7111

(P-25343)
THERMAL ENGRG INTL USA INC (HQ)
18000 Studebaker Rd # 400, Cerritos (90703-2691)
PHONE..................323 726-0641
Thomas Richardson, *President*
Brian Antonini, *President*
William Farris, *President*
Andrew Finizio, *President*
Abraham L Yarden, *President*
◆ **EMP:** 70 **EST:** 1919
SQ FT: 18,000
SALES: 75.8MM
SALES (corp-wide): 509MM **Privately Held**
WEB: www.thermalengint.com
SIC: 8711 3443 Professional engineer; air coolers, metal plate; condensers, steam; heat exchangers: coolers (after, inter), condensers, etc.; economizers (boilers)
PA: Babcock Power Inc.
6 Kimball Ln Ste 210
Lynnfield MA 01940
978 646-3300

(P-25344)
THOMAS MARK & COMPANY INC (PA)
2833 Junction Ave Ste 110, San Jose (95134-1920)
PHONE..................408 453-5373
Mike Lohman, *President*
Robert A Himes, *President*
Richard K Tanaka, *Chairman*
Matt Brogan, *Vice Pres*
Sasha Dansky, *Vice Pres*
EMP: 150
SALES (est): 26MM **Privately Held**
WEB: www.markthomas.com
SIC: 8711 8713 Consulting engineer; surveying services

(P-25345)
THORNTON TOMASETTI INC
301 Howard St Ste 1030, San Francisco (94105-6607)
PHONE..................415 365-6900
EMP: 60
SALES (corp-wide): 218.2MM **Privately Held**
SIC: 8711 Structural engineering
PA: Thornton Tomasetti, Inc.
51 Madison Ave Fl 19
New York NY 10010
917 661-7800

(P-25346)
TJ CROSS ENGINEERS INC
200 New Stine Rd Ste 270, Bakersfield (93309-2658)
PHONE..................661 831-8782
Timothy Couch, *Principal*
Kent Halley, *Principal*
Stuart Heisler, *Principal*
Chuck Soderstrom, *Principal*
Lisa Wong, *Principal*
EMP: 130
SQ FT: 22,000
SALES (est): 12.1MM
SALES (corp-wide): 3.5B **Publicly Held**
WEB: www.tjcross.com
SIC: 8711 Consulting engineer
PA: The Parsons Corporation
5875 Trinity Pkwy Ste 300
Centreville VA 20120
703 988-8500

(P-25347)
TMX ENGINEERING LLC
2141 S Standard Ave, Santa Ana (92707-3034)
PHONE..................714 641-5884

Eric Clack,
EMP: 70
SALES (est): 2.4MM **Privately Held**
SIC: 8711 Engineering services

(P-25348)
TOYON RESEARCH CORPORATION (PA)
6800 Cortona Dr, Goleta (93117-3139)
PHONE..................805 968-6787
Joel R Garbarino, *Ch of Bd*
Mark Fennell, *Vice Pres*
Tom Geyer, *Vice Pres*
Michael Grace, *Vice Pres*
Abhejit Rajagopal, *Research*
EMP: 84 **EST:** 1980
SQ FT: 16,000
SALES: 32.7MM **Privately Held**
WEB: www.toyon.com
SIC: 8711 7371 Electrical or electronic engineering; custom computer programming services

(P-25349)
TRANDES CORP
4669 Murphy Canyon Rd # 102, San Diego (92123-4333)
PHONE..................858 522-7021
Scott Iwanowski, *Branch Mgr*
Tess Spaulding, *QC Mgr*
EMP: 50
SALES (corp-wide): 13.7MM **Privately Held**
WEB: www.trandes.com
SIC: 8711 7378 7371 Consulting engineer; computer maintenance & repair; custom computer programming services
PA: Trandes Corp.
1099 Winterson Rd Ste 105
Linthicum Heights MD 21090
301 459-0200

(P-25350)
TRANDES CORP
4297 Pacific Hwy Bldg 2, San Diego (92110-3236)
PHONE..................619 524-2235
Thomas Waddell, *Principal*
EMP: 50
SALES (corp-wide): 13.7MM **Privately Held**
SIC: 8711 Engineering services
PA: Trandes Corp.
1099 Winterson Rd Ste 105
Linthicum Heights MD 21090
301 459-0200

(P-25351)
TRANSTECH ENGINEERS INC (PA)
13367 Benson Ave, Chino (91710-5246)
PHONE..................909 595-8599
Allen Cayir, *President*
EMP: 91
SQ FT: 10,000
SALES (est): 6.8MM **Privately Held**
WEB: www.transteche.com
SIC: 8711 Civil engineering; consulting engineer

(P-25352)
TREADWELL & ROLLO INC (DH)
555 Montgomery St # 1300, San Francisco (94111-2561)
PHONE..................415 955-9040
Philip Ttringale, *Director*
Antonio Mencarini, *Treasurer*
Philip G Smith, *Exec VP*
Maria G Flessas, *Vice Pres*
Maria Flessas, *Vice Pres*
EMP: 50
SQ FT: 12,500
SALES (est): 10.9MM
SALES (corp-wide): 177.9MM **Privately Held**
WEB: www.treadwellrollo.com
SIC: 8711 Consulting engineer
HQ: Langan Engineering And Environmental Services, Inc.
300 Kimball Dr
Parsippany NJ 07054
973 560-4900

(P-25353)
TRIAD HOMES ASSOC
Also Called: Triad-Holmes Associates
873 N Main St Ste 150, Bishop (93514-2479)
PHONE..................760 873-4273
Thomas Platz, *President*
EMP: 60
SQ FT: 800
SALES (est): 5MM
SALES (corp-wide): 5.1MM **Privately Held**
SIC: 8711 8713 6552 Civil engineering; surveying services; subdividers & developers
PA: Holmes Triad Associates
549 Old Mammoth Rd # 202
Mammoth Lakes CA
760 934-7588

(P-25354)
TRUST AUTOMATION INC
143 Suburban Rd Ste 100, San Luis Obispo (93401-1102)
PHONE..................805 544-0761
Ty Safreno, *CEO*
Trudie Safreno, *CFO*
Chuck Kass, *Exec VP*
Vanessa Fridley, *Vice Pres*
Dave Rennie, *Vice Pres*
▲ **EMP:** 65
SQ FT: 100,000
SALES (est): 17.8MM **Privately Held**
WEB: www.trustautomation.com
SIC: 8711 3812 3731 3621 Machine tool design; antennas, radar or communications; submersible marine robots, manned or unmanned; generators for gas-electric or oil-electric vehicles; automation & robotics consultant

(P-25355)
TTG ENGINEERS
222 S Harbor Blvd Ste 800, Anaheim (92805-3715)
PHONE..................714 490-5555
Albert Chiu, *Branch Mgr*
EMP: 55
SALES (corp-wide): 54.8MM **Privately Held**
WEB: www.tmadengineers.com
SIC: 8711 Consulting engineer
PA: Ttg Engineers
300 N Lake Ave Fl 14
Pasadena CA 91101
626 463-2800

(P-25356)
TTG ENGINEERS (PA)
Also Called: Mbe
300 N Lake Ave Fl 14, Pasadena (91101-4164)
PHONE..................626 463-2800
Zareh Astourian, *President*
Stephen Boase, *CFO*
Ed Gharabans, *Vice Pres*
Sunil Patel, *Vice Pres*
Ron Sheldon, *Vice Pres*
EMP: 160
SQ FT: 16,000
SALES (est): 54.8MM **Privately Held**
WEB: www.tmadengineers.com
SIC: 8711 Consulting engineer

(P-25357)
TYLIN INTL GROUP LTD (PA)
345 California St Fl 23, San Francisco (94104-2646)
PHONE..................415 291-3700
Matthew G Cummings, *President*
Maribel Castillo, *Vice Pres*
Veronica Fennie, *Vice Pres*
John Flint, *Vice Pres*
Robert Radley, *Vice Pres*
EMP: 109 **EST:** 1961
SQ FT: 34,000
SALES (est): 160MM **Privately Held**
SIC: 8711 Consulting engineer

(P-25358)
U S ARMY CORPS OF ENGINEERS
1645 Riverbank Rd, West Sacramento (95605-1743)
PHONE..................916 557-7491
EMP: 66 **Publicly Held**

SIC: 8711 9199 Engineering services; general government administration
HQ: U.S. Army Corps Of Engineers
441 G St Nw
Washington DC 20314
202 761-0001

(P-25359)
U S ARMY CORPS OF ENGINEERS
2194 Ascot Ave, Rio Linda (95673-5337)
PHONE..................916 649-0133
EMP: 65 **Publicly Held**
SIC: 8711 9711 Engineering services; Army
HQ: U.S. Army Corps Of Engineers
441 G St Nw
Washington DC 20314
202 761-0001

(P-25360)
U S ARMY CORPS OF ENGINEERS
3900 Roseville Rd, North Highlands (95660-5707)
PHONE..................916 925-7001
Ed Fager, *Branch Mgr*
EMP: 66 **Publicly Held**
SIC: 8711 Engineering services
HQ: U.S. Army Corps Of Engineers
441 G St Nw
Washington DC 20314
202 761-0001

(P-25361)
U S ARMY CORPS OF ENGINEERS
2100 Bridgeway, Sausalito (94965-1753)
PHONE..................415 289-3067
Linda Holm, *Manager*
EMP: 65 **Publicly Held**
SIC: 8711 Engineering services
HQ: U.S. Army Corps Of Engineers
441 G St Nw
Washington DC 20314
202 761-0001

(P-25362)
UCI CONSTRUCTION INC
3900 Fruitvale Ave, Bakersfield (93308-5114)
PHONE..................661 587-0192
David Krugh, *Branch Mgr*
EMP: 98
SALES (corp-wide): 54.3MM **Privately Held**
SIC: 8711 Professional engineer
PA: U.C.I. Construction, Inc.
261 Arthur Rd
Martinez CA 94553
800 245-6750

(P-25363)
UNITED INFRSTRCTURE PRJCTS INC
Also Called: Uiprojects
1041 W 18th St Ste B104, Costa Mesa (92627-4583)
PHONE..................949 310-0092
Wail Sadiq, *General Mgr*
Brian Poyant, *Vice Pres*
Zulfa Sadiq, *Director*
EMP: 99
SALES: 950K **Privately Held**
WEB: www.uiprojects.net
SIC: 8711 1542 Engineering services; custom builders, non-residential

(P-25364)
UNITED TECHNOLOGIES CORP
Also Called: UTC Aerospace Systems
8200 Arlington Ave, Riverside (92503-0428)
PHONE..................951 351-5400
Leland Walley, *Vice Pres*
Shirin Folsom, *General Mgr*
Chris Originales, *IT/INT Sup*
Richard Pekarske, *Research*
Andrew Adan, *Engineer*
EMP: 61

P R O D U C T S & S V C S

SALES (corp-wide): 66.5B **Publicly Held**
WEB: www.bfgoodrich.com
SIC: **8711** 3724 3728 Aviation &/or aeronautical engineering; aircraft engines & engine parts; aircraft landing assemblies & brakes
PA: United Technologies Corporation
10 Farm Springs Rd
Farmington CT 06032
860 728-7000

(P-25365)
UNIVERSAL GENERAL BUILDERS
871 Industrial Rd Ste A, San Carlos (94070-3389)
PHONE.....................650 591-3104
EMP: 99
SALES (est): 2.6MM **Privately Held**
SIC: **8711** Building construction consultant

(P-25366)
UNIVERSAL SPACE LINES INC
Also Called: Usl
1501 Quail St Ste 102, Newport Beach (92660-2739)
PHONE.....................215 328-9130
David Wopschall, *CFO*
Dag Hellstenius, *VP Sales*
EMP: 60
SALES (est): 5.5MM **Privately Held**
SIC: **8711** 8731 Aviation &/or aeronautical engineering; industrial laboratory, except testing

(P-25367)
URS GROUP INC
1333 Broadway, Oakland (94612-1917)
PHONE.....................510 893-3600
Louise Armstrong, *Manager*
Linda Pappas, *Vice Pres*
Robert Michna, *Project Mgr*
Robert K Green, *Engineer*
Carlos C Toledo, *Engineer*
EMP: 200
SALES (corp-wide): 20.1B **Publicly Held**
SIC: **8711** 4953 Engineering services; refuse systems
HQ: Urs Group, Inc.
300 S Grand Ave Ste 1100
Los Angeles CA 90071
213 593-8000

(P-25368)
URS GROUP INC
915 Wilshire Blvd Ste 700, Los Angeles (90017-3436)
P.O. Box 116183, Atlanta GA (30368-6183)
PHONE.....................213 996-2200
Paul Ryan, *Manager*
Carla Willis, *Project Dir*
Andrew Bui, *Project Mgr*
Peter Stumpf, *Senior Engr*
Reyes Mendoza, *Manager*
EMP: 99
SALES (corp-wide): 20.1B **Publicly Held**
SIC: **8711** 8712 8741 Consulting engineer; architectural engineering; construction management
HQ: Urs Group, Inc.
300 S Grand Ave Ste 1100
Los Angeles CA 90071
213 593-8000

(P-25369)
URS GROUP INC
915 Wilshire Blvd Ste 700, Los Angeles (90017-3436)
P.O. Box 116183, Atlanta GA (30368-6183)
PHONE.....................213 996-2200
Shahram Bahbagu, *Branch Mgr*
EMP: 100
SALES (corp-wide): 20.1B **Publicly Held**
SIC: **8711** Engineering services
HQ: Urs Group, Inc.
300 S Grand Ave Ste 1100
Los Angeles CA 90071
213 593-8000

(P-25370)
URS GROUP INC
300 Lakeside Dr Ste 400, Oakland (94612-3573)
PHONE.....................925 446-3800
Sam Capps, *Branch Mgr*
EMP: 69

SALES (corp-wide): 20.1B **Publicly Held**
SIC: **8711** 8712 8741 Consulting engineer; architectural engineering; construction management
HQ: Urs Group, Inc.
300 S Grand Ave Ste 1100
Los Angeles CA 90071
213 593-8000

(P-25371)
URS GROUP INC
130 Robin Hill Rd Ste 100, Santa Barbara (93117-3153)
PHONE.....................805 964-6010
Timothy Cohen, *Manager*
Richard Rosenbaum, *Safety Mgr*
EMP: 80
SQ FT: 29,621
SALES (corp-wide): 20.1B **Publicly Held**
SIC: **8711** Engineering services
HQ: Urs Group, Inc.
300 S Grand Ave Ste 1100
Los Angeles CA 90071
213 593-8000

(P-25372)
URS GROUP INC
100 W San Fernando St # 200, San Jose (95113-2219)
PHONE.....................408 297-9585
William Hadaya, *Branch Mgr*
Len Phillips, *MIS Mgr*
James Hawald, *Project Leader*
Millette Litzinger, *Sr Project Mgr*
EMP: 55
SALES (corp-wide): 20.1B **Publicly Held**
SIC: **8711** Engineering services
HQ: Urs Group, Inc.
300 S Grand Ave Ste 1100
Los Angeles CA 90071
213 593-8000

(P-25373)
URS GROUP INC
2870 Gateway Oaks Dr # 300, Sacramento (95833-3577)
PHONE.....................916 679-2000
Victor Auvinen, *Branch Mgr*
Kevin Spesert, *Executive*
Dwayne Duetscher, *Dept Chairman*
Warren Haven, *Database Admin*
John Clark, *Project Engr*
EMP: 200
SALES (corp-wide): 20.1B **Publicly Held**
SIC: **8711** Engineering services
HQ: Urs Group, Inc.
300 S Grand Ave Ste 1100
Los Angeles CA 90071
213 593-8000

(P-25374)
URS HOLDINGS INC (DH)
600 Montgomery St Fl 25, San Francisco (94111-2724)
PHONE.....................415 774-2700
Thomas W Bishop, *CEO*
Martin M Koffel, *Ch of Bd*
Kim Long, *Admin Asst*
Carol Frieda Brandenburg-Smith, *Asst Sec*
EMP: 470
SALES (est): 5B
SALES (corp-wide): 20.1B **Publicly Held**
SIC: **8711** 7389 6531 8249 Consulting engineer; financial services; real estate agents & managers; aviation school; aircraft maintenance & repair services
HQ: Aecom Global Ii, Llc
1999 Avenue Of The Stars
Los Angeles CA 90067
213 593-8100

(P-25375)
URS-GEI JOINT VENTURE
1333 Broadway Ste 800, Oakland (94612-1924)
PHONE.....................510 874-3051
Said Salah-Mars, *Principal*
EMP: 50
SALES (est): 2.1MM **Privately Held**
SIC: **8711** Engineering services

(P-25376)
US ARMY CORPS OF ENGINEERS
Also Called: U S ARMY CORPS OF ENGINEERS
1325 J St Frnt, Sacramento (95814-2922)
PHONE.....................916 557-7490
Thomas Chapman, *Director*
EMP: 800 **Publicly Held**
WEB: www.sac.usace.army.mil
SIC: **8711** 9711 Engineering services; Army;
HQ: U.S. Army Corps Of Engineers
441 G St Nw
Washington DC 20314
202 761-0001

(P-25377)
US ARMY CORPS OF ENGINEERS
Also Called: U S ARMY CORPS OF ENGINEERS
915 Wilshire Blvd Ste 930, Los Angeles (90017-3489)
PHONE.....................213 452-3967
Col Richard Thompson, *Manager*
Col R Thompson, *Manager*
EMP: 650 **Publicly Held**
WEB: www.sac.usace.army.mil
SIC: **8711** 9711 Engineering services; Army;
HQ: U.S. Army Corps Of Engineers
441 G St Nw
Washington DC 20314
202 761-0001

(P-25378)
VANDORPE CHOU ASSOCIATES INC
Also Called: VCA Engineering
1845 W Orangewood Ave # 210, Orange (92868-2096)
PHONE.....................714 978-9780
Daniel T Van Dorpe, *President*
Neil Evans, *Shareholder*
David Byrnes, *CFO*
Margaret Van Dorpe, *Corp Secy*
Charles Russell, *Vice Pres*
EMP: 50
SQ FT: 3,000
SALES (est): 7.9MM **Privately Held**
WEB: www.vcaengineers.com
SIC: **8711** Civil engineering; structural engineering

(P-25379)
VCA CODE GROUP
1845 W Orangewood Ave # 210, Orange (92868-2096)
PHONE.....................714 363-4700
Dan Van Dope, *President*
Bob Chou, *Vice Pres*
Kathy Ibarra, *Administration*
EMP: 50
SALES (est): 6.5MM **Privately Held**
WEB: www.vcacodegroup.com
SIC: **8711** Engineering services

(P-25380)
VECTOR RESOURCES INC
Also Called: Vector USA
9808 Waples St, San Diego (92121-2921)
PHONE.....................858 546-1014
Debra Treece, *Branch Mgr*
Debra Preece, *General Mgr*
EMP: 50
SALES (corp-wide): 71MM **Privately Held**
SIC: **8711** Consulting engineer
PA: Vector Resources, Inc.
20917 Higgins Ct
Torrance CA 90501
310 436-1000

(P-25381)
VELOCITEL RF INC
2415 Campus Dr Ste 200, Irvine (92612-8530)
PHONE.....................949 809-4999
EMP: 200
SALES (est): 6.1MM
SALES (corp-wide): 648MM **Privately Held**
SIC: **8711**

PA: Velocitel, Inc.
1033 Skokie Blvd Ste 320
Northbrook IL 27616
224 757-0001

(P-25382)
VERSA ENGINEERING & TECH INC (PA)
1320 Willow Pass Rd # 500, Concord (94520-5269)
PHONE.....................925 405-4505
Fred Fong, *President*
Flavio Santini, *Chairman*
Tom Nollie, *Principal*
EMP: 55
SALES (est): 13.1MM **Privately Held**
SIC: **8711** Consulting engineer

(P-25383)
VT MILCOM INC
1660 Logan Ave Ste 2, San Diego (92113-1044)
PHONE.....................619 424-9024
Brian Upthegrove, *Branch Mgr*
Noel Jackson, *Info Tech Mgr*
EMP: 100
SALES (corp-wide): 724.3MM **Privately Held**
WEB: www.milcom-systems.com
SIC: **8711** Engineering services
HQ: Vt Milcom Inc.
448 Viking Dr Ste 350
Virginia Beach VA 23452
757 463-2800

(P-25384)
W M LYLES CO
2810 Unicorn Rd, Bakersfield (93308-6853)
PHONE.....................661 387-1600
Mike Burson, *President*
EMP: 50
SALES (corp-wide): 28.6MM **Privately Held**
WEB: www.wmlyles.com
SIC: **8711** 1623 Engineering services; pipeline construction
HQ: W. M. Lyles Co.
1210 W Olive Ave
Fresno CA 93728
559 441-1900

(P-25385)
WALLACE-KUHL INVESTMENTS LLC (PA)
3050 Industrial Blvd, West Sacramento (95691-3470)
P.O. Box 1137 (95691-1137)
PHONE.....................916 372-1434
Douglas J Kuhl,
Thomas S Wallace,
EMP: 100
SQ FT: 11,300
SALES (est): 9.6MM **Privately Held**
WEB: www.wallace-kuhl.com
SIC: **8711** 8748 Civil engineering; business consulting

(P-25386)
WATLOW ELECTRIC MFG CO
6781 Via Del Oro, San Jose (95119-1360)
PHONE.....................408 776-6646
EMP: 85
SALES (corp-wide): 616.4MM **Privately Held**
SIC: **8711** Engineering services
PA: Watlow Electric Manufacturing Company
12001 Lackland Rd
Saint Louis MO 63146
314 878-4600

(P-25387)
WEST YOST & ASSOCIATES INC (PA)
2020 Res Pk Dr Ste 100, Davis (95618)
PHONE.....................530 756-5905
Charles Duncan, *President*
Bruce West, *President*
Steven R Dalrymple, *Corp Secy*
Jim Yost, *Vice Pres*
EMP: 76
SQ FT: 25,000

SALES (est): 26.7MM **Privately Held**
WEB: www.westyost.com
SIC: 8711 Civil engineering

(P-25388)
WESTWIND ENGINEERING INC
553 N Pcfc Cst Hwy B179, Redondo Beach
(90277)
PHONE..................................310 831-3454
Mary Anne Graves, *CEO*
Carl Graves, *Founder*
EMP: 175 EST: 1992
SQ FT: 2,400
SALES: 13MM **Privately Held**
SIC: 8711 7363 Engineering services;
temporary help service

(P-25389)
WESTWIND ENGINEERING INC
553 N Pcf Coastte B179 B, Redondo Beach
(90277)
PHONE..................................310 831-3454
EMP: 70
SALES (est): 2.7MM **Privately Held**
SIC: 8711

(P-25390)
WILLDAN GROUP INC (PA)
2401 E Katella Ave # 300, Anaheim
(92806-5909)
PHONE..................................800 424-9144
Thomas D Brisbin, *Ch of Bd*
Daniel Chow, *COO*
Stacy B McLaughlin, *CFO*
Tom D Brisbin, *Bd of Directors*
Arne Lovnaseth, *Bd of Directors*
EMP: 107
SQ FT: 18,000
SALES: 272.2MM **Publicly Held**
WEB: www.willdangroup.com
SIC: 8711 8748 Civil engineering; consult-
ing engineer; urban planning & consulting
services

(P-25391)
WILLIAM E HEINSELMAN
3303 Luyung Dr, Rancho Cordova
(95742-6860)
PHONE..................................916 920-0220
William E Heinselman, *Owner*
EMP: 50
SALES: 10MM **Privately Held**
SIC: 8711 Sanitary engineers

(P-25392)
WINZLER & KELLY
2235 Mercury Way Ste 150, Santa Rosa
(95407-5470)
PHONE..................................707 523-1010
Theodore B Whiton, *Sales & Mktg St*
Alex Culick, *Manager*
EMP: 95
SQ FT: 7,000
SALES (corp-wide): 1.2MM **Privately
Held**
WEB: www.sjoeng.com
SIC: 8711 8748 8742 Consulting engi-
neer; environmental consultant; industrial
hygiene consultant
PA: Winzler & Kelly
2235 Mercury Way Ste 150
Santa Rosa CA 95407
707 523-1010

(P-25393)
WOOD ENVIRONMENT &
3560 Hyland Ave 100, Costa Mesa
(92626-1438)
PHONE..................................949 642-0245
Jay River, *President*
EMP: 95
SALES (corp-wide): 10B **Privately Held**
SIC: 8711 Engineering services
HQ: Wood Environment & Infrastructure
Solutions, Inc.
1105 Lakewood Pkwy # 300
Alpharetta GA 30009
770 360-0600

(P-25394)
WOOD ENVIRONMENT &
180 Grand Ave Fl 11, Oakland
(94612-3741)
PHONE..................................510 663-4100
Susan Gallardo, *Branch Mgr*
Lester Feldman, *Vice Pres*

Richard Frappa, *Vice Pres*
Bob Youngs, *Vice Pres*
EMP: 150
SALES (corp-wide): 10B **Privately Held**
SIC: 8711 8999 8744 Consulting engi-
neer; pollution control engineering; earth
science services; facilities support serv-
ices
HQ: Wood Environment & Infrastructure
Solutions, Inc.
1105 Lakewood Pkwy # 300
Alpharetta GA 30009
770 360-0600

(P-25395)
WOOD ENVIRONMENT &
6001 Rickenbacker Rd, Commerce
(90040-3031)
PHONE..................................323 889-5300
Bruce Corkel, *Branch Mgr*
Carmen Mendoza, *General Mgr*
EMP: 85
SQ FT: 30,000
SALES (corp-wide): 10B **Privately Held**
SIC: 8711 8748 Consulting engineer; envi-
ronmental consultant
HQ: Wood Environment & Infrastructure
Solutions, Inc.
1105 Lakewood Pkwy # 300
Alpharetta GA 30009
770 360-0600

(P-25396)
WOOD RODGERS INC (PA)
3301 C St Ste 100b, Sacramento
(95816-3350)
PHONE..................................916 341-7760
Mark Rodgers, *President*
Martin Rodriguez, *Officer*
Steve Balbierz, *Vice Pres*
Gerardo Calvillo, *Vice Pres*
Tim Crush, *Vice Pres*
EMP: 120 EST: 1996
SQ FT: 5,500
SALES (est): 45.7MM **Privately Held**
WEB: www.woodrodgers.com
SIC: 8711 Civil engineering

(P-25397)
WORLEYPARSONS GROUP INC
181 W Huntington Dr 100, Monrovia
(91016-3456)
PHONE..................................626 803-9000
Chris Ashton, *Branch Mgr*
EMP: 253 **Privately Held**
SIC: 8711 Engineering services
HQ: Worley Group Inc.
5995 Rogerdale Rd
Houston TX 77072
832 351-6000

(P-25398)
WORLEYPARSONS GROUP INC
721 Charles E Young Dr S, Los Angeles
(90095-8342)
PHONE..................................610 855-2000
Christopher L Parker, *CEO*
EMP: 329 **Privately Held**
SIC: 8711 Acoustical engineering
HQ: Worley Group Inc.
5995 Rogerdale Rd
Houston TX 77072
832 351-6000

(P-25399)
WORLEYPARSONS GROUP INC
100 W Walnut, Pasadena (91101)
PHONE..................................626 440-7000
Antonio V Dy, *Principal*
Sachin Lahoti, *Engineer*
Russel Metlitzky, *Engineer*
EMP: 253 **Privately Held**
SIC: 8711 8742 Designing: ship, boat, ma-
chine & product; construction project
management consultant
HQ: Worley Group Inc.
5995 Rogerdale Rd
Houston TX 77072
832 351-6000

(P-25400)
WSP USA BUILDINGS INC
425 Market St Fl 17, San Francisco
(94105-2425)
PHONE..................................415 398-3833
Randy J Meyers, *Branch Mgr*

Joseph Delpozzo, *Senior VP*
Patricia McCaffery, *Senior VP*
Isabelle Adjahi, *Vice Pres*
Matthieu L Blanc, *Vice Pres*
EMP: 120
SALES (corp-wide): 20MM **Privately
Held**
WEB: www.flackandkurtz.com
SIC: 8711 8748 Consulting engineer;
telecommunications consultant
HQ: Wsp Usa Buildings Inc.
1 Penn Plz Fl 2
New York NY 10119
212 465-5000

(P-25401)
WSP USA INC
1100 W Town And Cntry 2, Orange
(92868-4600)
PHONE..................................714 973-4880
Charline Talmer, *General Mgr*
Gregory A Kelly, *President*
Mark Briggs, *Vice Pres*
Sarah Bradfield, *Electrical Engi*
Lynn Pham, *Payroll Mgr*
EMP: 100
SALES (corp-wide): 20MM **Privately
Held**
SIC: 8711 Consulting engineer
HQ: Wsp Usa Inc.
1 Penn Plz
New York NY 10119
212 465-5000

(P-25402)
WSP USA INC
444 S Flower St Ste 800, Los Angeles
(90071-2962)
PHONE..................................212 465-5000
Carl Enson, *General Mgr*
Gregory A Kelly, *President*
Isanower Jesiah, *Manager*
EMP: 50
SALES (corp-wide): 20MM **Privately
Held**
SIC: 8711 Consulting engineer
HQ: Wsp Usa Inc.
1 Penn Plz
New York NY 10119
212 465-5000

(P-25403)
WSP USA INC
425 Market St Fl 17, San Francisco
(94105-2425)
PHONE..................................415 243-4600
Stuart Sunshine, *Branch Mgr*
Gregory A Kelly, *President*
Jim Bourgart, *Vice Pres*
Rebecca Kohlstrand, *Vice Pres*
Anges Bishop, *Administration*
EMP: 180
SALES (corp-wide): 20MM **Privately
Held**
SIC: 8711 Consulting engineer
HQ: Wsp Usa Inc.
1 Penn Plz
New York NY 10119
212 465-5000

(P-25404)
WSP USA INC
451 E Vanderbilt Way # 200, San
Bernardino (92408-3614)
PHONE..................................909 888-1106
Danika Bragg, *Branch Mgr*
Gregory A Kelly, *President*
Basem Muallem, *Vice Pres*
EMP: 70
SQ FT: 10,000
SALES (corp-wide): 20MM **Privately
Held**
SIC: 8711 Consulting engineer
HQ: Wsp Usa Inc.
1 Penn Plz
New York NY 10119
212 465-5000

(P-25405)
YUPANA INC
5039 Commercial Cir Ste J, Concord
(94520-1445)
PHONE..................................925 482-0657
Muzaffer Mete Dalan, *CEO*
John McWeeny, *Admin Sec*
Cary Workmon, *Technician*

Manuel Hernandez, *Technical Staff*
Korzay Nayman, *Manager*
EMP: 50
SALES (est): 5.4MM **Privately Held**
SIC: 8711 Engineering services

8712 Architectural Services

(P-25406)
5 DESIGN INC
Also Called: 5design
1024 N Orange Dr Ste 215, Los Angeles
(90038-2348)
PHONE..................................323 308-3558
Stan Hathaway, *President*
Arthur Benedetti Jr, *Vice Pres*
Tim Magill, *Admin Sec*
Karen Brocato, *Accountant*
Lorraine Polanski, *Consultant*
EMP: 76
SALES: 12MM **Privately Held**
WEB: www.5plusdesign.com
SIC: 8712 Architectural engineering

(P-25407)
**A SMWM CALIFORNIA
CORPORATION**
Also Called: Simon Mrtn-Vgue Wnklstein Mris
185 Berry St Ste 5100, San Francisco
(94107-1772)
PHONE..................................415 546-0400
Cathy Simon, *President*
Karen Alschuler, *Chairman*
John Long, *Vice Pres*
Prakash Pinto, *Vice Pres*
Evan Rose, *Vice Pres*
EMP: 60
SQ FT: 16,200
SALES: 10MM **Privately Held**
WEB: www.smwm.com
SIC: 8712 Architectural services

(P-25408)
AECOM
5001 E Commercecenter Dr # 100, Bakers-
field (93309-1655)
PHONE..................................661 266-0802
EMP: 120
SALES (corp-wide): 20.1B **Publicly Held**
SIC: 8712 Architectural engineering
PA: Aecom
1999 Avenue Of The Stars # 2600
Los Angeles CA 90067
213 593-8000

(P-25409)
AECOM SERVICES INC (HQ)
Also Called: Aecom Design
300 S Grand Ave Fl 2, Los Angeles
(90071-3470)
PHONE..................................213 593-8000
Michael S Burke, *CEO*
Raymond Landy, *President*
Jane Chmielinski, *COO*
Deborah Klem, *CFO*
Richard G Newman, *Chairman*
EMP: 250 EST: 1946
SALES (est): 1.7B
SALES (corp-wide): 20.1B **Publicly Held**
WEB: www.dmjmhn.com
SIC: 8712 8741 8711 Architectural serv-
ices; management services; engineering
services
PA: Aecom
1999 Avenue Of The Stars # 2600
Los Angeles CA 90067
213 593-8000

(P-25410)
AEWESTJV
363 5th Ave Ste 202, San Diego
(92101-6965)
PHONE..................................619 233-1023
Ralph Joseph Roesling, *Principal*
EMP: 50
SALES (est): 1.2MM **Privately Held**
SIC: 8712 Architectural engineering

(P-25411)
ALTOON PARTNERS LLP (PA)
Also Called: Altoon Porter
617 W 7th St Ste 400, Los Angeles
(90017-3889)
PHONE..................................213 225-1900
Ronald A Altoon, *Partner*
James Auld, *Partner*
Gary Dempster, *Partner*
William Sebring, *Partner*
Christine Anderson, *Principal*
EMP: 70
SQ FT: 20,000
SALES (est): 8.9MM **Privately Held**
WEB: www.altoonporter.com
SIC: 8712 Architectural engineering

(P-25412)
AMERICAN GENERAL DESIGN
245 S Los Robles Ave # 100, Pasadena
(91101-2820)
PHONE..................................626 304-0800
Patrick Chraghchian, *President*
EMP: 50
SALES (est): 2.8MM **Privately Held**
SIC: 8712 Architectural services

(P-25413)
ARCHITECTS ORANGE
144 N Orange St, Orange (92866-1400)
PHONE..................................714 639-9860
Jack Selman, *Senior Partner*
RC Alley III, *Partner*
Jim Dietze, *Partner*
Darrel Hebenstreit, *Partner*
Hugh Rose, *Partner*
EMP: 200 **EST:** 1973
SQ FT: 10,000
SALES (est): 34.9MM **Privately Held**
WEB: www.architectsorange.com
SIC: 8712 Architectural engineering

(P-25414)
ATC SERVICES INC
999 W Town And Country Rd, Orange
(92868-4713)
PHONE..................................213 593-8100
Richard Erickson, *Manager*
Ray Landy, *President*
EMP: 400
SALES (est): 52.8K
SALES (corp-wide): 20.1B **Publicly Held**
SIC: 8712 Architectural services
PA: Aecom
1999 Avenue Of The Stars # 2600
Los Angeles CA 90067
213 593-8000

(P-25415)
AUSTIN VEUM RBBINS
PRTNERS INC (PA)
501 W Broadway Ste A, San Diego
(92101-3562)
PHONE..................................619 231-1960
Douglas H Austin, *CEO*
Chris Vium, *President*
Doreen Austin, *CFO*
Jeffrey Parshalle, *Vice Pres*
Randy Robbins, *Vice Pres*
EMP: 83
SQ FT: 12,500
SALES (est): 5.3MM **Privately Held**
SIC: 8712 Architectural services

(P-25416)
BAR ARCHITECTS
901 Battery St Ste 300, San Francisco
(94111-1350)
PHONE..................................415 293-5700
Robert Hunter, *President*
Bob Hunter, *CFO*
Earl Wilson, *Principal*
Lisa Dougherty, *Accountant*
Christine Phoen, *Accountant*
EMP: 80
SQ FT: 13,500
SALES (est): 11.3MM **Privately Held**
WEB: www.bararch.com
SIC: 8712 Architectural engineering

(P-25417)
BASSENIAN/LAGONI
ARCHITECTS
2031 Orchard Dr Ste 100, Newport Beach
(92660-0753)
PHONE..................................949 553-9100
Aram Bassenian, *CEO*
Carl Lagoni, *President*
Lee R Rogaliner, *CFO*
Lee Rogaliner, *CFO*
Robert Chavez, *Exec VP*
EMP: 65 **EST:** 1979
SQ FT: 22,800
SALES (est): 10.7MM **Privately Held**
WEB: www.bassenianlagoni.com
SIC: 8712 Architectural engineering

(P-25418)
CALLISON LLC
1453 3rd Street Promenade # 400, Santa
Monica (90401-3428)
PHONE..................................310 394-8460
Mackey Deasy, *Director*
EMP: 205 **Privately Held**
SIC: 8712 Architectural services
PA: Callison Llc
1420 5th Ave Ste 2400
Seattle WA 98101

(P-25419)
CALLISONRTKL INC
818 W 7th St Ste 300, Los Angeles
(90017-3426)
PHONE..................................213 627-7373
EMP: 140
SALES (corp-wide): 2.5B **Privately Held**
SIC: 8712
HQ: Callisonrtkl Inc.
901 S Bond St
Baltimore MD 21231
410 528-8600

(P-25420)
CALLISONRTKL INC
333 S Hope St Ste C200, Los Angeles
(90071-3005)
PHONE..................................213 633-6000
Barbara Proano, *Branch Mgr*
Yuwen Peng, *Assoc VP*
Danielle Simpson, *Assoc VP*
Tan Warren, *Assoc VP*
Daun Amand, *Vice Pres*
EMP: 143
SALES (corp-wide): 6.6MM **Privately
Held**
WEB: www.rtkl.com
SIC: 8712 Architectural engineering
HQ: Callisonrtkl Inc.
901 S Bond St
Baltimore MD 21231
410 537-6000

(P-25421)
CARRIER JOHNSON (PA)
Also Called: Culture
185 W F St Ste 600, San Diego
(92101-4012)
PHONE..................................619 236-9462
Gordon Carrier, *President*
Michael Johnson, *Vice Pres*
Rick Castillo, *Director*
Kari McFall, *Director*
EMP: 68
SALES (est): 13.1MM **Privately Held**
WEB: www.carrierjohnson.com
SIC: 8712 7389 Architectural engineering;
interior design services

(P-25422)
CGL COMPANIES LLC
2260 Del Paso Rd 100, Sacramento
(95834-9671)
PHONE..................................916 678-7890
Robert Glass, *Exec VP*
Jami Godkin, *Vice Pres*
EMP: 70 **EST:** 2017
SALES (est): 1.6MM **Privately Held**
SIC: 8712 Architectural services

(P-25423)
CH2M HILL INC
2485 Natomas Park Dr # 600, Sacramento
(95833-2975)
PHONE..................................916 920-0300
Craig Eldrich, *Branch Mgr*

Matt Negrete, *Exec Dir*
Matt Franck, *Project Mgr*
Jerry Salamy, *Project Mgr*
Chris Serroels, *Project Mgr*
EMP: 50
SALES (corp-wide): 14.9B **Publicly Held**
SIC: 8712 Architectural services
HQ: Ch2m Hill, Inc.
9191 S Jamaica St
Englewood CO 80112
303 771-0900

(P-25424)
CH2M HILL INC
1737 N 1st St Ste 300, San Jose
(95112-4585)
PHONE..................................408 436-4936
Mark Janay, *Finance Other*
James Isles, *Project Mgr*
Steve Long, *Project Mgr*
Olivas Ronald, *Opers Staff*
EMP: 50
SALES (corp-wide): 14.9B **Publicly Held**
SIC: 8712 8711 1622 1611 Architectural
services; engineering services; bridge,
tunnel & elevated highway; highway &
street construction
HQ: Ch2m Hill, Inc.
9191 S Jamaica St
Englewood CO 80112
303 771-0900

(P-25425)
CHONG PARTNERS
ARCHITECHER INC
901 Market St Ste 600, San Francisco
(94103-1740)
PHONE..................................613 995-8210
Gordon H Chong, *President*
David A Englund, *CFO*
EMP: 125
SQ FT: 16,000
SALES (est): 4.2MM **Privately Held**
SIC: 8712 Architectural services

(P-25426)
CITY OF FREMONT
Also Called: Building & Safety Department
39550 Liberty St, Fremont (94538-2211)
P.O. Box 5006 (94537-5006)
PHONE..................................510 494-4460
Neil Hawkins, *General Mgr*
EMP: 150 **Privately Held**
WEB: www.ci.fremont.ca.us
SIC: 8712 Architectural services
PA: City Of Fremont
3300 Capitol Ave
Fremont CA 94538
510 284-4000

(P-25427)
CITY OF LOS ANGELES
Also Called: Architecture Division
1149 S Broadway Ste 800, Los Angeles
(90015-2237)
PHONE..................................213 485-4282
Mahmood Karimzadeh, *Manager*
EMP: 65 **Privately Held**
WEB: www.lacity.org
SIC: 8712 Architectural engineering
PA: City Of Los Angeles
200 N Spring St Ste 303
Los Angeles CA 90012
213 978-0600

(P-25428)
COACT DESIGNWORKS
Also Called: Stafford-King-Wiese Architects
3348 Montclaire St, Sacramento
(95821-3738)
PHONE..................................916 930-5900
Pat Derickson, *President*
Kelly Reynolds, *Vice Pres*
Christopher Garcia, *Education*
John Miller, *Director*
Sachindra Sharma, *Manager*
EMP: 50
SALES (est): 9MM **Privately Held**
WEB: www.skwaia.com
SIC: 8712 Architectural engineering

(P-25429)
CUNINGHAM GROUP ARCH INC
Also Called: Cuningham Group, The
8665 Hayden Pl, Culver City (90232-2901)
PHONE..................................310 895-2200

John Cuiter, *President*
EMP: 50
SALES (corp-wide): 31.7MM **Privately
Held**
WEB: www.cuningham.com
SIC: 8712 Architectural engineering
PA: Cuningham Group Architecture, Inc.
201 Se Main St Ste 325
Minneapolis MN 55414
612 379-3400

(P-25430)
DAHLIN GROUP INC (PA)
5865 Owens Dr, Pleasanton (94588-3942)
PHONE..................................925 251-7200
Nancy K Keenan, *President*
Karl Danielson, *Vice Pres*
Charles Meyer, *Vice Pres*
Harrison Pierson, *Vice Pres*
John Thatch, *Vice Pres*
EMP: 60
SQ FT: 300,000
SALES (est): 17.5MM **Privately Held**
WEB: www.dahlingroup.com
SIC: 8712 Architectural engineering

(P-25431)
DARDEN ARCHITECTS INC
6790 N West Ave Ste 104, Fresno
(93711-4306)
PHONE..................................559 448-8051
Martin Dietz, *President*
EMP: 75 **EST:** 1959
SQ FT: 5,000
SALES (est): 12.6MM **Privately Held**
SIC: 8712 7389 Architectural engineering;
interior designer

(P-25432)
DES ARCHITECTS + ENGINEERS
INC
399 Bradford St Ste 300, Redwood City
(94063-1585)
P.O. Box 3599 (94064-3599)
PHONE..................................650 364-6453
Thomas Gilman, *President*
Stephen D Mincey, *CFO*
Craig Ivancovich, *Corp Secy*
Brandi Reyes, *Executive*
Jessica Langford, *Admin Asst*
EMP: 115
SQ FT: 35,000
SALES (est): 18.4MM **Privately Held**
WEB: www.des-ae.com
SIC: 8712 8711 Architectural engineering;
engineering services

(P-25433)
DG ARCHITECTS INC (PA)
Also Called: Dga Plnning L Arch L Interiors
550 Ellis St, Mountain View (94043-2236)
PHONE..................................650 943-1660
Randall Dowler, *President*
Nancy Escano, *Treasurer*
Tanya Saunders, *Office Admin*
Trey Post, *Planning*
Jon Ohlson, *Technology*
EMP: 78
SQ FT: 15,000
SALES (est): 12.2MM **Privately Held**
WEB: www.dga-mv.com
SIC: 8712 Architectural engineering

(P-25434)
DLR GROUP INC
700 S Flower St Fl 22, Los Angeles
(90017-4209)
PHONE..................................626 796-8230
EMP: 150
SALES (corp-wide): 109.7MM **Privately
Held**
SIC: 8712 Architectural services
HQ: Dlr Group Inc.
700 Suth Flwr St Fl 22 Flr 22
Los Angeles CA 90017
213 800-9400

(P-25435)
DLR GROUP INC (HQ)
700 Suth Flwr St Fl 22 Flr 22, Los Angeles
(90017)
PHONE..................................213 800-9400
Adrian O Cohen, *President*
Dennis Wiederholt, *Treasurer*
Jon P Anderson, *Vice Pres*
Jon Anderson, *Vice Pres*

Brian Arial, *Vice Pres*
EMP: 140 **EST:** 1997
SALES (est): 16.3MM
SALES (corp-wide): 109.7MM **Privately Held**
SIC: 8712 8711 Architectural services; engineering services; mechanical engineering
PA: Dlr Holding Company
6457 Frances St Ste 200
Omaha NE
402 393-4100

(P-25436)
GEHRY PARTNERS LLP
12541 Beatrice St, Los Angeles
(90066-7001)
PHONE..............................310 482-3000
Frank Gehry, *Partner*
Brian Aamoth, *Partner*
John Bowers, *Partner*
Anand Devarajan, *Partner*
Morri Freeman, *Partner*
EMP: 130 **EST:** 2001
SQ FT: 12,100
SALES (est): 13.9MM **Privately Held**
SIC: 8712 Architectural services

(P-25437)
GENERAL SERVICES CAL DEPT
Also Called: Division of State Architect
1515 Clay St Ste 1201, Oakland
(94612-1474)
PHONE..............................510 622-3101
Lee Roy Tam, *Manager*
Diane Elliott, *Manager*
EMP: 60 **Privately Held**
WEB: www.4c.net
SIC: 8712 9199 Architectural services; general government administration;
HQ: California Department Of General Services
707 3rd St
West Sacramento CA 95605

(P-25438)
GENERAL SERVICES CAL DEPT
Also Called: Division of State Architect
700 N Alameda St Ste 500, Los Angeles
(90012-3352)
PHONE..............................213 897-3995
Sharqat Ullah, *Manager*
EMP: 55 **Privately Held**
WEB: www.4c.net
SIC: 8712 9199 Architectural services; general government administration;
HQ: California Department Of General Services
707 3rd St
West Sacramento CA 95605

(P-25439)
GKK CORPORATION
1775 Hancock St Ste 150, San Diego
(92110-2039)
PHONE..............................619 398-0215
EMP: 59 **Privately Held**
SIC: 8712 Architectural engineering
PA: Gkk Corporation
2355 Main St Ste 220
Irvine CA 92614

(P-25440)
GKK CORPORATION (PA)
Also Called: Gkkworks
2355 Main St Ste 220, Irvine (92614-4251)
PHONE..............................949 250-1500
Praful Kulkarni, *President*
David Hunt, *Vice Pres*
Dhannya Joby, *Office Mgr*
Leslie Long, *Office Mgr*
Becca Chikes, *Administration*
EMP: 85
SQ FT: 11,000
SALES: 117.5MM **Privately Held**
SIC: 8712 8711 Architectural engineering; building construction consultant

(P-25441)
GONZALEZ/GOODALE ARCHITECTS
Also Called: Chcg Architects
135 W Green St Ste 200, Pasadena
(91105-4131)
PHONE..............................626 568-1428
Armando L Gonzalez, *Owner*
Ali Barar, *Principal*
Harry Drake, *Principal*
John Ferguson, *Principal*
David Goodale, *Principal*
EMP: 52
SQ FT: 8,000
SALES: 9.8MM **Privately Held**
WEB: www.gonzalezgoodale.com
SIC: 8712 7389 Architectural engineering; interior designer

(P-25442)
GOULD EVANS P C
95 Brady St, San Francisco (94103-1241)
PHONE..............................415 503-1411
Robert M Baum, *Administration*
Bella Vista, *Master*
Steve Brezovec, *Sr Associate*
Carrie Jones, *Sr Associate*
Holly Kan, *Sr Associate*
EMP: 75
SALES (corp-wide): 10.2MM **Privately Held**
SIC: 8712 Architectural engineering
PA: Gould Evans, P C
4200 Pennsylvania Ave # 150
Kansas City MO 64111
816 931-6655

(P-25443)
GRUEN ASSOCIATES
Also Called: Gruen Assoc Archtects Planners
6330 San Vicente Blvd # 200, Los Angeles
(90048-5441)
PHONE..............................323 937-4270
Ki Suh Park, *Partner*
Michael A Enomoto, *Partner*
Larry Schlossberg, *Partner*
Michael Enomoto, *Managing Prtnr*
Karl Swope, *Vice Pres*
EMP: 75 **EST:** 1947
SQ FT: 14,000
SALES (est): 11.5MM **Privately Held**
WEB: www.gruenassociates.com
SIC: 8712 Architectural engineering

(P-25444)
HAMMEL GREEN & ABRAHAMSON INC
Also Called: Hga Architects and Engineers
1200 R St Ste 100, Sacramento
(95811-5807)
PHONE..............................916 787-5100
Brent Forslin, *Director*
Denis Stroup, *Assoc VP*
Lisa Matthiessen, *Director*
Heidi McElroy, *Associate*
EMP: 65
SALES (corp-wide): 142.8MM **Privately Held**
WEB: www.hga.com
SIC: 8712 8711 Architectural engineering; engineering services
PA: Hammel, Green And Abrahamson, Inc.
420 N 5th St Ste 100
Minneapolis MN 55401
612 758-4000

(P-25445)
HARLEY ELLIS DEVEREAUX CORP
417 Montgomery St Ste 400, San Francisco
(94104-1111)
PHONE..............................415 981-2345
Lee Vandekerchove, *President*
EMP: 64
SALES (corp-wide): 43.5MM **Privately Held**
SIC: 8712 Architectural engineering
PA: Harley Ellis Devereaux Corp
26913 Nrthwstrn Hwy 200
Southfield MI 48033
248 262-1500

(P-25446)
HAWKINS BROWN USA INC
2128 Cotner Ave, Los Angeles
(90025-5714)
PHONE..............................310 600-2695
Matthew Ollier, *Principal*
EMP: 276
SALES (est): 7.6MM **Privately Held**
SIC: 8712 Architectural services

(P-25447)
HDR ENVIRONMENTAL OPE
8690 Balboa Ave Ste 200, San Diego
(92123-6507)
PHONE..............................858 712-8400
Dean Gipson, *Branch Mgr*
EMP: 70
SALES (corp-wide): 1.4B **Privately Held**
SIC: 8712 8711 8748 8999 Architectural services; engineering services; business consulting; communication services
HQ: Hdr Environmental, Operations And Construction, Inc.
9781 S Meridian Blvd
Englewood CO 80112

(P-25448)
HELLMUTH OBATA & KASSABAUM INC (DH)
Also Called: H O K
1 Bush St Ste 200, San Francisco
(94104-4404)
PHONE..............................415 243-0555
Patrick Macleamy, *CEO*
William Hellmuth, *President*
Lisa Green, *Treasurer*
Thomas Robson, *Officer*
Steve Riley, *Vice Pres*
EMP: 193
SALES (est): 54.8MM
SALES (corp-wide): 301.6MM **Privately Held**
SIC: 8712 8711 8742 7389 Architectural engineering; engineering services; management consulting services; interior design services; landscape architects

(P-25449)
HELLMUTH OBATA & KASSABAUM INC
9530 Jefferson Blvd, Culver City
(90232-2918)
PHONE..............................310 838-9555
Jeff Mayer, *Manager*
Peter Mosanyi,
EMP: 50
SALES (corp-wide): 301.6MM **Privately Held**
SIC: 8712 8711 Architectural engineering; engineering services
HQ: Hellmuth, Obata & Kassabaum, Inc.
1 Bush St Ste 200
San Francisco CA 94104

(P-25450)
HFS CONCEPTS 4 INC
3229 E Spring St Ste 330, Long Beach
(90806-2486)
PHONE..............................562 424-1720
John Mamer, *President*
Bill Legg, *Vice Pres*
Jeannette Hurley, *Admin Asst*
Thomas Jeffress, *Purch Agent*
Michelle Montoya, *Safety Mgr*
EMP: 50
SQ FT: 11,000
SALES (est): 3.6MM **Privately Held**
SIC: 8712 7389 Architectural services; interior designer

(P-25451)
HKS INC
10880 Wilshire Blvd # 1850, Los Angeles
(90024-4101)
PHONE..............................310 788-7700
Scott Hunter, *Branch Mgr*
Alfredo Rodriguez, *Vice Pres*
Patrick Treadway, *Vice Pres*
Ala Hason, *Director*
Yoosang Ahn, *Associate*
EMP: 70

SALES (corp-wide): 387.6MM **Privately Held**
SIC: 8712 Architectural services
PA: Hks, Inc.
350 N Saint Paul St # 100
Dallas TX 75201
214 969-5599

(P-25452)
HKS ARCHITECTS INC
500 Howard St Fl 4, San Francisco
(94105-3040)
PHONE..............................415 356-3800
Kirk Teske, *COO*
EMP: 50
SALES (est): 197.8K **Privately Held**
SIC: 8712 Architectural services

(P-25453)
HMC GROUP (HQ)
Also Called: HMC Architects
3546 Concours, Ontario (91764-5584)
PHONE..............................909 989-9979
Brian Staton, *CEO*
Tom Cavanagh, *Vice Pres*
Melanie West, *Controller*
▲ **EMP:** 165
SQ FT: 58,000
SALES (est): 51.8MM **Privately Held**
WEB: www.hmcarchitects.com
SIC: 8712 Architectural engineering
PA: Hmc Holdings, Inc.
3546 Concours
Ontario CA 91764
909 989-9979

(P-25454)
HMC GROUP
2930 Inland Empire Blvd # 100, Ontario
(91764-4802)
PHONE..............................909 980-8058
Lauie L McCoy, *Manager*
EMP: 56
SALES (est): 51.8MM **Privately Held**
SIC: 8712 Architectural engineering
HQ: Hmc Group
3546 Concours
Ontario CA 91764
909 989-9979

(P-25455)
HNTB-GERWICK JV
1300 Clay St Fl 7, Oakland (94612-1425)
PHONE..............................510 839-8972
Dale Berner, *Partner*
EMP: 70
SALES (est): 2.7MM **Privately Held**
SIC: 8712 8711 8742 8741 Architectural services; engineering services; business planning & organizing services; construction management

(P-25456)
HOK GROUP INC
1 Bush St Ste 200, San Francisco
(94104-4404)
PHONE..............................415 243-0555
Russ Drinker, *Branch Mgr*
Matthew Staublin, *Director*
EMP: 233
SALES (corp-wide): 301.6MM **Privately Held**
SIC: 8712 8742 8711 Architectural engineering; planning consultant; engineering services
PA: Hok Group, Inc
10 S Broadway Ste 200
Saint Louis MO 63102
314 421-2000

(P-25457)
HOK GROUP INC
9530 Jefferson Blvd, Culver City
(90232-2918)
PHONE..............................310 838-9555
John L Conley, *Branch Mgr*
Sharon Burton, *Principal*
EMP: 150
SALES (corp-wide): 301.6MM **Privately Held**
SIC: 8712 Architectural engineering
PA: Hok Group, Inc
10 S Broadway Ste 200
Saint Louis MO 63102
314 421-2000

PRODUCTS & SVCS

(P-25458)
HORNBERGER WORSTELL ASSOC INC
Also Called: Hornberger, Mark R
170 Maiden Ln Ste 600, San Francisco
(94108-5334)
PHONE...................................415 391-1080
Mark Hornberger, *President*
Francine Larose, *CFO*
Jack Worstell, *Exec VP*
John Davis, *Senior VP*
AIA Miller, *Vice Pres*
EMP: 50
SALES (est): 8MM **Privately Held**
WEB: www.hornbergerworstell.com
SIC: 8712 Architectural engineering

(P-25459)
HOSPITLITY FCSED SOLUTIONS INC
3229 E Spring St Ste 200, Long Beach
(90806-2472)
PHONE...................................562 424-1720
Chien An Lee, *Chairman*
John Mamer, *President*
John W Wong, *CEO*
David Chen, *Vice Pres*
Michelle Mantoya, *Exec Sec*
EMP: 100
SALES (est): 15.6MM **Privately Held**
WEB: www.concepts4inc.com
SIC: 8712 Architectural services

(P-25460)
HUNTSMAN ARCHITECTURAL GROUP (PA)
50 California St Fl 7, San Francisco
(94111-4624)
PHONE...................................415 394-1212
Sascha Wagner, *President*
Linda H Parker, *President*
Susan Williams, *CFO*
Bill Puetz, *Principal*
Sandra Tripp, *Managing Dir*
EMP: 83
SQ FT: 19,000
SALES: 21MM **Privately Held**
WEB: www.huntsmanag.com
SIC: 8712 Architectural engineering

(P-25461)
JACK P SELMAN
144 N Orange St, Orange (92866-1413)
PHONE...................................714 639-9860
Jack P Selman, *Partner*
R C Alley, *Partner*
Ed Cadavona, *Partner*
Jim Dietze, *Partner*
Darrel Hidenstreit, *Partner*
EMP: 80
SQ FT: 800
SALES (est): 4.3MM **Privately Held**
SIC: 8712 Architectural services

(P-25462)
JEFFREY ROME & ASSOCIATES
1715 Port Charles Pl, Newport Beach
(92660-5319)
PHONE...................................949 760-3929
Jeffery Rome, *President*
Matt Bradford, *Project Mgr*
Harold Crouch, *Project Mgr*
Zac Noguera, *Project Mgr*
Randal Williams, *Project Mgr*
EMP: 60 EST: 1991
SALES (est): 3.7MM **Privately Held**
SIC: 8712 Architectural engineering

(P-25463)
JOHNSON FAIN INC
1201 N Broadway, Los Angeles
(90012-1407)
PHONE...................................323 224-6000
William H Fain Jr, *Co-President*
R Scott Johnson, *Co-President*
Sherry Miller, *Admin Sec*
Tom Brakefield, *Technology*
Ray Rangel, *Facilities Mgr*
EMP: 80
SQ FT: 26,000
SALES (est): 11.7MM **Privately Held**
WEB: www.johnsonfain.com
SIC: 8712 7389 Architectural engineering;
interior design services

(P-25464)
KAA DESIGN GROUP INC
4201 Redwood Ave, Los Angeles
(90066-5605)
PHONE...................................310 821-1400
Grant Kirkpatrick, *President*
EMP: 55
SQ FT: 2,520
SALES (est): 6.7MM **Privately Held**
WEB: www.kaa-architects.com
SIC: 8712 Architectural engineering

(P-25465)
KFA LLP
1625 Olympic Blvd, Santa Monica
(90404-3822)
PHONE...................................310 399-7975
Jonathan Watts, *Partner*
Lise Bornstein, *Partner*
Barbara Flammang, *Partner*
Wade Killefer, *Partner*
Matthew Penrod, *Finance Mgr*
EMP: 58 EST: 2016
SALES (est): 1.3MM **Privately Held**
SIC: 8712 Architectural services

(P-25466)
KMD ARCHITECTS (PA)
417 Montgomery St Ste 200, San Francisco
(94104-1107)
PHONE...................................415 398-5191
Paul Ryan Stevens, *CEO*
Robert Matthew, *Ch of Bd*
Kavinder Singh, *President*
Nathan Galloway, *Admin Sec*
Ivan Romero, *Project Mgr*
▲ EMP: 95
SQ FT: 35,000
SALES (est): 22.1MM **Privately Held**
SIC: 8712 Architectural services

(P-25467)
KTGY GROUP INC
1814 Franklin St Ste 400, Oakland
(94612-3461)
PHONE...................................510 463-2097
Tricia Esser, *CEO*
EMP: 50
SALES (corp-wide): 74.7MM **Privately Held**
SIC: 8712 Architectural engineering
PA: Ktgy Group, Inc.
17911 Von Karman Ave # 250
Irvine CA 92614
949 851-2133

(P-25468)
KTGY GROUP INC (PA)
17911 Von Karman Ave # 250, Irvine
(92614-4243)
PHONE...................................949 851-2133
Tricia Esser, *CEO*
Laurel Gillette, *Exec Dir*
Nick Lehnert, *Exec Dir*
Axel Stoltz, *Exec Dir*
Lucciana Piccone, *Office Mgr*
EMP: 70
SQ FT: 21,000
SALES: 74.7MM **Privately Held**
SIC: 8712 Architectural services

(P-25469)
KTGY GROUP INC
12555 W Jefferson Blvd # 100, Los Angeles
(90066-7032)
PHONE...................................310 394-2625
Stan Braden, *Branch Mgr*
EMP: 50
SALES (corp-wide): 74.7MM **Privately Held**
SIC: 8712 Architectural engineering
PA: Ktgy Group, Inc.
17911 Von Karman Ave # 250
Irvine CA 92614
949 851-2133

(P-25470)
LEE BURKHART LIU INC
100 California St Ste 725, San Francisco
(94111-4545)
PHONE...................................415 580-6740
Kenneth Lee, *Principal*
EMP: 55
SALES (corp-wide): 6.5MM **Privately Held**
SIC: 8712 Architectural services

PA: Lee, Burkhart, Liu, Inc
5510 Lincoln Blvd Ste 250
Playa Vista CA 90094
310 829-2249

(P-25471)
LEO A DALY COMPANY
Also Called: Leo Daly Company
550 S Hope St Ste 2700, Los Angeles
(90071-2675)
PHONE...................................213 627-9300
Brian A Kite, *Branch Mgr*
Michael Walden, *Vice Pres*
Edmund Buch, *Architect*
Bruce E Konschuh, *Architect*
John Williams, *Architect*
EMP: 60
SALES (corp-wide): 113.5MM **Privately Held**
SIC: 8712 8742 8711 Architectural engineering; planning consultant; consulting engineer
PA: Leo A. Daly Company
8600 Indian Hills Dr
Omaha NE 68114
808 521-8889

(P-25472)
LEO A DALY COMPANY
Also Called: Leo A Daly Company
2150 River Plaza Dr, Sacramento
(95833-3883)
PHONE...................................916 564-3259
EMP: 63
SALES (corp-wide): 113.5MM **Privately Held**
SIC: 8712 Architectural engineering
PA: Leo A. Daly Company
8600 Indian Hills Dr
Omaha NE 68114
808 521-8889

(P-25473)
LPA INC (PA)
5301 California Ave # 100, Irvine
(92617-3224)
PHONE...................................949 261-1001
Wendy Rogers, *CEO*
Dan Heinfeld, *President*
Charles Pruitt, *CFO*
James Kelly, *Vice Pres*
Bertha Pena, *Office Mgr*
◆ EMP: 180
SQ FT: 33,700
SALES (est): 44.1MM **Privately Held**
WEB: www.lpainc.com
SIC: 8712 8711 0781 Architectural engineering; engineering services; landscape counseling & planning

(P-25474)
LPA INC
60 S Market St Ste 150, San Jose
(95113-2368)
PHONE...................................408 780-7200
EMP: 110
SALES (corp-wide): 44.1MM **Privately Held**
SIC: 8712 Architectural services
PA: Lpa, Inc.
5301 California Ave # 100
Irvine CA 92617
949 261-1001

(P-25475)
LPAS INC
2484 Natomas Park Dr # 100, Sacramento
(95833-2928)
PHONE...................................916 443-0335
Theressa Page, *Owner*
John Brown, *Vice Pres*
Eloisa Baltazar, *Office Admin*
Brady Smith, *IT/INT Sup*
Ken Bauer, *Associate*
EMP: 60 EST: 1975
SQ FT: 12,000
SALES (est): 8MM **Privately Held**
WEB: www.lpasacramento.com
SIC: 8712 Architectural engineering

(P-25476)
M ARTHUR GENSLER JR ASSOC INC
225 W Santa Clara St, San Jose
(95113-1723)
PHONE...................................408 885-8100

Kevin Schaeffer, *Branch Mgr*
EMP: 50
SALES (corp-wide): 1.4B **Privately Held**
SIC: 8712 Architectural engineering
PA: M. Arthur Gensler Jr. & Associates, Inc.
45 Fremont St Ste 1500
San Francisco CA 94105
415 433-3700

(P-25477)
M ARTHUR GENSLER JR ASSOC INC (PA)
45 Fremont St Ste 1500, San Francisco
(94105-2214)
PHONE...................................415 433-3700
Andy Cohen, *Co-CEO*
Robin Klehr Avia, *Ch of Bd*
Walter Hunt, *Vice Chairman*
Linda Havard, *CFO*
Diane Hoskins, *Co-CEO*
EMP: 360
SQ FT: 57,000
SALES: 1.4B **Privately Held**
SIC: 8712 Architectural services

(P-25478)
M ARTHUR GENSLER JR ASSOC INC
2101 Webster St Ste 2000, Oakland
(94612-3032)
PHONE...................................510 625-7400
EMP: 207
SALES (corp-wide): 915.3MM **Privately Held**
SIC: 8712
PA: M. Arthur Gensler Jr. & Associates, Inc.
2 Harrison St Fl 4
San Francisco CA 94105
415 433-3700

(P-25479)
M ARTHUR GENSLER JR ASSOC INC
Also Called: Gensler and Associates
500 S Figueroa St, Los Angeles
(90071-1705)
PHONE...................................213 927-3600
Rob Jernigan, *Branch Mgr*
AIA Froglia, *Project Mgr*
Hans Krake, *Project Mgr*
Adreana Trejo, *Project Mgr*
Jim Young, *Project Mgr*
EMP: 249
SALES (corp-wide): 1.4B **Privately Held**
SIC: 8712 7389 Architectural engineering; design, commercial & industrial
PA: M. Arthur Gensler Jr. & Associates, Inc.
45 Fremont St Ste 1500
San Francisco CA 94105
415 433-3700

(P-25480)
M ARTHUR GENSLER JR ASSOC INC
4675 Macarthur Ct Ste 100, Newport Beach
(92660-8811)
PHONE...................................949 863-9434
Kim Graham, *Branch Mgr*
EMP: 69
SALES (corp-wide): 1.4B **Privately Held**
SIC: 8712 Architectural services
PA: M. Arthur Gensler Jr. & Associates, Inc.
45 Fremont St Ste 1500
San Francisco CA 94105
415 433-3700

(P-25481)
MARMOL RADZINER
12210 Nebraska Ave, Los Angeles
(90025-3620)
PHONE...................................310 826-6222
Ron Radziner, *CEO*
Leo Marmol, *President*
Todd Jerry, *COO*
Colton Cross, *Project Mgr*
Andrew Parks, *Project Mgr*
EMP: 70
SQ FT: 6,500

SALES (est): 13.3MM **Privately Held**
WEB: www.marmol-radziner.com
SIC: 8712 1521 1542 Architectural engineering; general remodeling, single-family houses; new construction, single-family houses; commercial & office building, new construction; commercial & office buildings, renovation & repair

(P-25482)
MARTIN AC PARTNERS INC
444 S Flower St Ste 1200, Los Angeles (90071-2977)
PHONE....................213 683-1900
Robert Newsom, *President*
Christopher C Martin, *CEO*
David C Martin, *Principal*
EMP: 116 EST: 1906
SALES (est): 19.7MM **Privately Held**
SIC: 8712 Architectural services

(P-25483)
MARTIN ATI-AC INC (PA)
Also Called: ATI Architects & Engineers
4750 Willow Rd Ste 250, Pleasanton (94588-2962)
PHONE....................925 648-8800
Paul Didonato, *President*
Ysenia Cooper, *Administration*
Donna Foster, *Administration*
Sara McCorriston, *Marketing Staff*
Phillip Caires, *Director*
EMP: 74
SQ FT: 14,000
SALES (est): 12MM **Privately Held**
WEB: www.atiengineering.com
SIC: 8712 8711 Architectural engineering; structural engineering

(P-25484)
MBH ARCHITECTS INC
960 Atlantic Ave, Alameda (94501-1086)
PHONE....................510 865-8663
Dennis Heath, *President*
Matt Cornelius, *Project Mgr*
Yoga Firmansyah, *Project Mgr*
Nazgol Golban, *Project Mgr*
Joseph Irwin, *Project Mgr*
EMP: 210
SQ FT: 55,000
SALES (est): 40.2MM **Privately Held**
WEB: www.mbharch.com
SIC: 8712 Architectural services

(P-25485)
MORPHOSIS ARCHITECTS
3440 Wesley St, Culver City (90232-2328)
PHONE....................310 453-2247
Thom Mayne, *President*
Blythe Allison Mayne, *Vice Pres*
Robin Williams, *Sales Staff*
EMP: 62 EST: 1975
SQ FT: 10,000
SALES: 14.2MM **Privately Held**
WEB: www.morphosis.net
SIC: 8712 Architectural engineering

(P-25486)
MVE + PARTNERS INC (PA)
1900 Main St Ste 800, Irvine (92614-7318)
PHONE....................949 809-3388
Carl F McLarand, *CEO*
Raymond Albanesi, *Partner*
Lori Ichisaka, *Partner*
Paolo Leon, *Partner*
Geoff Miasnik, *Partner*
EMP: 60
SQ FT: 22,000
SALES (est): 13.3MM **Privately Held**
WEB: www.mve-architects.com
SIC: 8712 Architectural engineering

(P-25487)
NADEL INC (PA)
1990 S Bundy Dr Ste 400, Los Angeles (90025-5243)
PHONE....................310 826-2100
Herbert Nadel, *CEO*
Brent Harrison, *Assoc VP*
Vic Gaygeshian, *Vice Pres*
David Jacobson, *Vice Pres*
Dale Yonkin, *Exec Dir*
EMP: 55
SQ FT: 29,000
SALES (est): 11MM **Privately Held**
SIC: 8712 Architectural engineering

(P-25488)
NBBJ LP
523 W 6th St Ste 300, Los Angeles (90014-1227)
PHONE....................213 243-3333
Brenda Clark, *Manager*
EMP: 50
SALES (corp-wide): 118.9MM **Privately Held**
SIC: 8712 7389 Architectural services; interior design services
PA: Nbbj Lp
223 Yale Ave N
Seattle WA 98109
206 223-5555

(P-25489)
NEWMA GARRIS GILMO + PARTNE I
3100 Bristol St Ste 400, Costa Mesa (92626-7333)
PHONE....................949 756-0818
Kevin Newman, *Chairman*
Donald J Meeks, *President*
Yulis Ayton, *Project Mgr*
Ben Chiu, *Project Mgr*
Jacob Lesic, *Project Mgr*
EMP: 70 EST: 1974
SQ FT: 7,000
SALES (est): 7.7MM **Privately Held**
WEB: www.nggpartners.com
SIC: 8712 Architectural engineering

(P-25490)
NICHOLS MELBURG ROSSETTO ASSOC (PA)
Also Called: Nmr Design
300 Knollcrest Dr, Redding (96002-0104)
PHONE....................530 222-3300
Gene Nichols, *President*
Dan Rossetto, *Treasurer*
Kyle Matti, *Architect*
EMP: 50
SQ FT: 4,000
SALES (est): 8MM **Privately Held**
SIC: 8712 8711 Architectural engineering; structural engineering

(P-25491)
OEL/HHH INC
1833 Victory Blvd, Glendale (91201-2557)
PHONE....................818 246-6050
Fax: 818 240-0430
EMP: 80 EST: 1978
SQ FT: 20,000
SALES (est): 4.5MM **Privately Held**
WEB: www.lhaarchitects.com
SIC: 8712

(P-25492)
RATCLIFF ARCHITECTS
5856 Doyle St, Emeryville (94608-2520)
PHONE....................510 899-6400
Dan Wetherell, *President*
Scott Haney, *COO*
David Dersch, *CFO*
Joseph Nicola, *Business Dir*
Heidi Bilodeau, *CTO*
EMP: 58
SQ FT: 20,000
SALES (est): 11.7MM **Privately Held**
WEB: www.ratcliffarch.com
SIC: 8712 Architectural engineering

(P-25493)
RBB ARCHITECTS INC (PA)
10980 Wilshire Blvd, Los Angeles (90024-3944)
PHONE....................310 479-1473
Joseph A Balbona, *CEO*
Deneys Purcell, *President*
Kevin Boots, *Senior VP*
Arthur E Border, *Senior VP*
Brian Hughson, *Project Mgr*
EMP: 54
SQ FT: 15,837
SALES (est): 9.5MM **Privately Held**
WEB: www.rbbinc.com
SIC: 8712 Architectural engineering

(P-25494)
RDC-S111 INC (PA)
Also Called: Perkowitz & Ruth Architects
111 W Ocean Blvd Ste 21, Long Beach (90802-4653)
PHONE....................562 628-8000
Bradley Williams, *CEO*
Ian Denny, *CFO*
Brian Wolfe, *Admin Sec*
Kirk Keller, *Director*
EMP: 82
SALES (est): 20.5MM **Privately Held**
SIC: 8712 Architectural engineering

(P-25495)
RRM DESIGN GROUP (PA)
3765 S Higuera St Ste 102, San Luis Obispo (93401-1577)
PHONE....................805 439-0442
Victor Montgomery, *Ch of Bd*
John Wilbanks, *President*
Keith Gurnee, *Senior VP*
Erik P Justesen, *Principal*
Pat Blote, *Project Mgr*
EMP: 99
SQ FT: 23,000
SALES (est): 18.4MM **Privately Held**
WEB: www.rrmdesign.com
SIC: 8712 Architectural engineering

(P-25496)
SKIDMORE OWINGS & MERRILL LLP
1 Maritime Plz Fl 5, San Francisco (94111-3408)
PHONE....................415 981-1555
Gene Schnair, *Partner*
John Kriken, *Partner*
Carrie Byles, *Director*
Ellen Lou, *Director*
Kacey Bills, *Manager*
EMP: 240
SALES (corp-wide): 123.1MM **Privately Held**
SIC: 8712 Architectural engineering
PA: Skidmore, Owings & Merrill Llp
224 S Michigan Ave # 1000
Chicago IL 60604
312 554-9090

(P-25497)
SKIDMORE OWINGS & MERRILL LLP
10100 Santa Monica Blvd, Beverly Hills (90210)
PHONE....................310 651-9924
Michael Mann, *Manager*
EMP: 228
SALES (corp-wide): 123.1MM **Privately Held**
SIC: 8712 Architectural engineering
PA: Skidmore, Owings & Merrill Llp
224 S Michigan Ave # 1000
Chicago IL 60604
312 554-9090

(P-25498)
SKIDMORE OWINGS & MERRILL LLP
555 W 5th St Fl 30, Los Angeles (90013-1048)
PHONE....................213 996-8366
Jeffrey McCarthy, *Partner*
Jenny Ahn, *Opers Staff*
EMP: 228
SALES (corp-wide): 123.1MM **Privately Held**
SIC: 8712 Architectural engineering
PA: Skidmore, Owings & Merrill Llp
224 S Michigan Ave # 1000
Chicago IL 60604
312 554-9090

(P-25499)
SMITHGROUP INC
301 Battery St Fl 7, San Francisco (94111-3237)
PHONE....................415 227-0100
EMP: 100
SALES (corp-wide): 201.1MM **Privately Held**
SIC: 8712 Architectural engineering

HQ: Smithgroup, Inc.
1700 New York Ave Nw # 100
Washington DC 20006
602 265-2200

(P-25500)
SMITHGROUP INC
Also Called: Smithgroupjjr
301 Battery St Fl 7, San Francisco (94111-3237)
PHONE....................313 442-8351
Michael Medici, *President*
Kevin Piontkowski, *Treasurer*
EMP: 146
SALES (corp-wide): 201.1MM **Privately Held**
WEB: www.dc.smithgroup.com
SIC: 8712 Architectural engineering
HQ: Smithgroup, Inc.
1700 New York Ave Nw # 100
Washington DC 20006
602 265-2200

(P-25501)
STANTEC ARCHITECTURE INC
38 Technology Dr, Irvine (92618-5310)
PHONE....................949 923-6000
Eric Nielsen, *Vice Pres*
Michelle Clark, *Administration*
Arthur Maytorena, *Administration*
Ryan Chen, *Engineer*
Cherri Stolz, *Human Res Mgr*
EMP: 117
SALES (corp-wide): 3.2B **Privately Held**
SIC: 8712 8711 4111 Architectural services; engineering services; local & suburban transit
HQ: Stantec Architecture Inc.
224 S Michigan Ave # 1400
Chicago IL 60604
336 714-7413

(P-25502)
STANTEC ARCHITECTURE INC
300 N Lake Ave Ste 400, Pasadena (91101-4169)
PHONE....................626 796-9141
Simon Bluestone, *Branch Mgr*
EMP: 88
SALES (corp-wide): 3.2B **Privately Held**
SIC: 8712 Architectural services
HQ: Stantec Architecture Inc.
224 S Michigan Ave # 1400
Chicago IL 60604
336 714-7413

(P-25503)
STANTEC CONSULTING SVCS INC
3875 Atherton Rd, Rocklin (95765-3716)
PHONE....................916 773-8100
Charles Bunker, *Branch Mgr*
Mike Maddux, *Technical Staff*
Conan Monson, *Senior Engr*
Lori Van Dermark, *Marketing Staff*
EMP: 60
SALES (corp-wide): 3.2B **Privately Held**
SIC: 8712 8711 Architectural services; engineering services
HQ: Stantec Consulting Services Inc.
475 5th Ave Fl 12
New York NY 10017
212 352-5160

(P-25504)
STANTEC CONSULTING SVCS INC
38 Technology Dr Ste 100, Irvine (92618-5312)
PHONE....................949 923-6000
Bob Gomes, *Manager*
Wally Spak, *Network Mgr*
Kevin Brandt, *Project Mgr*
Russell Landphere, *Project Mgr*
Jeff Crawford, *Marketing Staff*
EMP: 117
SALES (corp-wide): 3.2B **Privately Held**
WEB: www.keithco.com
SIC: 8712 8711 Architectural services; engineering services
HQ: Stantec Consulting Services Inc.
475 5th Ave Fl 12
New York NY 10017
212 352-5160

(P-25505)
STEINBERG HART (PA)
Also Called: Steinberg Architects
125 S Market St Ste 110, San Jose
(95113-2210)
PHONE..........................408 295-5446
David Hart, *President*
Katia McClain, *Managing Prtnr*
Robert Steinberg, *Ch of Bd*
Isaac Zamora, *CFO*
Ernest Yamana, *Treasurer*
EMP: 91 **EST:** 1953
SQ FT: 14,000
SALES (est): 16.5MM **Privately Held**
WEB: www.tsgarch.com
SIC: 8712 Architectural engineering

(P-25506)
STV ARCHITECTS INC
1055 W 7th St Ste 3150, Los Angeles
(90017-2556)
PHONE..........................213 482-9444
Wagih Andraos, *Manager*
EMP: 60
SALES (corp-wide): 322.3MM **Privately
Held**
WEB: www.stvinc.com
SIC: 8712 8742 8711 Architectural engi-
neering; transportation consultant; con-
sulting engineer
HQ: Stv Architects Inc
205 W Welsh Dr
Douglassville PA 19518
610 385-8200

(P-25507)
**TAYLOR & ASSOC ARCHITECTS
INC (PA)**
Also Called: Taylor Design
17850 Fitch, Irvine (92614-6002)
PHONE..........................949 574-1325
Linda Taylor, *Ch of Bd*
Gary Davidson, *Corp Secy*
Kristy Jordan, *Executive*
Lauren Edwards, *Admin Mgr*
Leslie Martinez, *Administration*
EMP: 50
SQ FT: 12,000
SALES (est): 10.1MM **Privately Held**
WEB: www.taa1.com
SIC: 8712 Architectural services

(P-25508)
URS GROUP INC
2020 L St Ste 400, Sacramento
(95811-4267)
PHONE..........................916 679-2000
Gary Horton, *Manager*
EMP: 64
SALES (corp-wide): 20.1B **Publicly Held**
SIC: 8712 8741 8711 Architectural engi-
neering; construction management; con-
sulting engineer
HQ: Urs Group, Inc.
300 S Grand Ave Ste 1100
Los Angeles CA 90071
213 593-8000

(P-25509)
**WALTER J CONN &
ASSOCIATES**
Also Called: Charleston Company
800 W 6th St Ste 600, Los Angeles
(90017-2709)
PHONE..........................213 683-0500
Walter J Conn, *Partner*
Sally K Conn, *Partner*
EMP: 60
SALES (est): 6.7MM **Privately Held**
WEB: www.charlestoncompany.com
SIC: 8712 Architectural services

(P-25510)
WARE MALCOMB (PA)
110 Edison Pl, Irvine (92618)
PHONE..........................949 660-9128
Lawrence R Armstrong, *CEO*
Tobin Sloane, *CFO*
Jay Todisco, *Exec VP*
Kenneth Wink, *Exec VP*
Matthew Brady, *Vice Pres*
▲ **EMP:** 137
SQ FT: 22,000

SALES: 90.3MM **Privately Held**
SIC: 8712 7336 8711 7389 Architectural
engineering; commercial art & graphic design; civil engineering; interior design
services; design, commercial & industrial

(P-25511)
WD PARTNERS INC
16808 Armstrong Ave # 100, Irvine
(92606-8278)
PHONE..........................949 753-7676
Christopher Doerschlag, *President*
EMP: 50
SALES (est): 2.3MM **Privately Held**
SIC: 8712 Architectural engineering

(P-25512)
WILL PERKINS INC
617 W 7th St Fl 12, Los Angeles
(90017-3807)
PHONE..........................213 270-8400
Gabriella Bullock, *Principal*
Linda Freeman, *Executive*
Phyllis Dubinsky, *Principal*
Shawn Bullock, *Human Res Mgr*
Merv Burnett, *Sr Associate*
EMP: 129
SALES (corp-wide): 606MM **Privately
Held**
SIC: 8712 Architectural services
HQ: Will Perkins Inc
1250 24th St Nw Ste 800
Washington DC 20037
-

(P-25513)
WILL PERKINS INC
2 Bryant St Ste 300, San Francisco
(94105-1641)
PHONE..........................415 856-3000
Russ Drinker, *Branch Mgr*
EMP: 60
SALES (corp-wide): 606MM **Privately
Held**
SIC: 8712 Architectural services
HQ: Will Perkins Inc
1250 24th St Nw Ste 800
Washington DC 20037
-

(P-25514)
**WILLIAM HZMLHLCH
ARCHTECTS INC**
2850 Redhill Ave Ste 200, Santa Ana
(92705-5543)
PHONE..........................949 250-0607
William Hezmalhalch, *CEO*
Dinna Mize, *Vice Pres*
Denise J Ashton, *Planning*
Roland Salazar, *Project Mgr*
Kerry Shynn, *Project Mgr*
EMP: 75
SALES (est): 14MM **Privately Held**
SIC: 8712 Architectural engineering

(P-25515)
**WIMBERLY ALLISON TONG GOO
INC**
Also Called: Watg
300 Spectrum Center Dr # 500, Irvine
(92618-4925)
PHONE..........................949 574-8500
Monica Cuervo, *Managing Dir*
EMP: 100
SQ FT: 63
SALES (corp-wide): 26.9MM **Privately
Held**
SIC: 8712 Architectural services
PA: Wimberly Allison Tong & Goo, Inc.
700 Bishop St Ste 800
Honolulu HI 96813
808 521-8888

(P-25516)
ZIMMER GUNSUL
Also Called: Zimmer Gnsul Frsca Partnr Amer
515 S Flower St Ste 3700, Los Angeles
(90071-2221)
PHONE..........................213 617-1901
Rachel Morris, *Manager*
Yuwei MA, *Info Tech Dir*
Deb Barbour, *Assistant*
Jerry Bryant, *Associate*
Jihyon Kim, *Associate*
EMP: 63

SALES (corp-wide): 67MM **Privately
Held**
SIC: 8712 7389 Architectural services; in-
terior designer
PA: Zimmer Gunsul Frasca Architects Llp
1223 Sw Washington St # 200
Portland OR 97205
503 224-3860

8713 Surveying Services

(P-25517)
**ADVANCED DCUMENT
SOLUTIONS INC (PA)**
24307 Magic Mountain Pkwy, Valencia
(91355-3402)
PHONE..........................661 251-0337
Michael Hawley, *President*
Michael Brown, *CFO*
EMP: 50
SALES (est): 2.9MM **Privately Held**
WEB: www.adocsolution.com
SIC: 8713 5045 ; computer software

(P-25518)
ANDREGG GEOMATICS
11661 Blocker Dr Ste 200, Auburn
(95603-4649)
PHONE..........................530 885-7072
Dennis Meyer, *President*
Mark Bardakjian, *COO*
Christine Johnson, *Admin Sec*
EMP: 65
SALES: 4.5MM **Privately Held**
WEB: www.andregg.com
SIC: 8713 Surveying services

(P-25519)
CANNON CORPORATION (PA)
1050 Southwood Dr, San Luis Obispo
(93401-5813)
PHONE..........................805 544-7407
Michael F Cannon, *CEO*
Bob Stets, *CFO*
John Evans, *Vice Pres*
Daniel Hutchinson, *Vice Pres*
Eric Porkert, *General Mgr*
EMP: 60
SQ FT: 4,200
SALES (est): 17.7MM **Privately Held**
WEB: www.cannoncorp.us
SIC: 8713 8711 1611 Surveying services;
civil engineering; highway & street con-
struction

(P-25520)
F3 AND ASSOCIATES INC (PA)
701 E H St, Benicia (94510-3567)
P.O. Box 5099, Petaluma (94955-5099)
PHONE..........................707 748-4300
Fred Feickert, *President*
Gene Feickert, *Partner*
Sean Finn, *Partner*
Masood Vydyarakath, *Info Tech Mgr*
Todd Tillotson, *Project Mgr*
EMP: 70
SALES: 13MM **Privately Held**
WEB: www.f3-inc.com
SIC: 8713 Surveying services

(P-25521)
HUITT - ZOLLARS INC
2603 Main St Ste 400, Irvine (92614-4250)
PHONE..........................949 988-5815
Mark Harlinger, *Manager*
Robert Sundstrom, *Vice Pres*
EMP: 50
SALES (corp-wide): 72MM **Privately
Held**
WEB: www.huitt-zollars.com
SIC: 8713 8711 Surveying services; con-
sulting engineer
PA: Huitt - Zollars, Inc.
1717 Mckinney Ave # 1400
Dallas TX 75202
214 871-3311

(P-25522)
**KIER & WRIGHT CIVIL
ENGRS&SRVY**
2850 Collier Canyon Rd, Livermore
(94551-9201)
PHONE..........................925 245-8788
Tony McCants, *Manager*

EMP: 50
SALES (corp-wide): 13.1MM **Privately
Held**
WEB: www.kierwright.com
SIC: 8713 8711 Surveying services; civil
engineering
PA: Kier & Wright Civil Engineers & Survey-
ors Inc
3350 Scott Blvd Bldg 22
Santa Clara CA 95054
408 727-6665

(P-25523)
PSOMAS
Also Called: Bonterra Psomas
3 Hutton Cntre Dr Ste 200, Santa Ana
(92707)
PHONE..........................714 751-7373
Ryan McLean, *Manager*
Erlinda Figueroa, *Assistant*
EMP: 125
SALES (corp-wide): 84.4MM **Privately
Held**
SIC: 8713 8711 Surveying services; con-
sulting engineer
PA: Psomas
555 S Flower St Ste 4300
Los Angeles CA 90071
213 223-1400

(P-25524)
PSOMAS
14369 Park Ave Ste 101b, Victorville
(92392-2392)
PHONE..........................760 843-5700
John Thornton, *Vice Pres*
Steve Gregerson, *Vice Pres*
Ken Stram, *Vice Pres*
EMP: 50
SALES (corp-wide): 84.4MM **Privately
Held**
SIC: 8713 8711 Surveying services; con-
struction & civil engineering
PA: Psomas
555 S Flower St Ste 4300
Los Angeles CA 90071
213 223-1400

(P-25525)
PSOMAS (PA)
555 S Flower St Ste 4300, Los Angeles
(90071-2405)
PHONE..........................213 223-1400
Ryan McLean, *President*
Loren Sokolow, *CFO*
Brett Barnett, *Vice Pres*
Matthew Clark, *Vice Pres*
Frank Martin, *Vice Pres*
EMP: 125
SQ FT: 30,000
SALES (est): 84.4MM **Privately Held**
SIC: 8713 8711 Surveying services; engi-
neering services

(P-25526)
SANDIS CIVIL ENGINEERS (PA)
1700 Winchester Blvd, Campbell
(95008-1163)
PHONE..........................408 636-0900
Ken Olcott, *President*
Tony Brubaker, *Treasurer*
Jeff Setera, *Vice Pres*
Behnaz Davis, *Office Mgr*
Nicole Nagatani, *Office Mgr*
EMP: 61 **EST:** 1965
SQ FT: 12,000
SALES (est): 17.9MM **Privately Held**
SIC: 8713 8711 Surveying services; civil
engineering

(P-25527)
**STANTEC ENERGY &
RESOURCES INC (HQ)**
5500 Ming Ave Ste 410, Bakersfield
(93309-4631)
PHONE..........................661 396-3770
Robert Gomes, *President*
Richard Allen, *COO*
Daniel Lefaivre, *Treasurer*
Kirk Morrison, *Exec VP*
Paul Alpern, *Senior VP*
EMP: 182 **EST:** 2015
SALES (est): 15.9MM **Privately Held**
SIC: 8713 Surveying services

PA: Mustang Acquisition Holdings Inc.
475 5th Ave Fl 12
New York NY 10017
301 220-1861

(P-25528)
STANTEC ENERGY & RESOURCES INC
1340 Treat Blvd Ste 525, Walnut Creek
(94597-7984)
PHONE...................................925 627-4508
Gary Grelli, *Branch Mgr*
EMP: 144
SALES (corp-wide): 15.9MM **Privately Held**
SIC: 8713 Surveying services
HQ: Stantec Energy & Resources Inc.
5500 Ming Ave Ste 410
Bakersfield CA 93309
661 396-3770

8721 Accounting, Auditing & Bookkeeping Svcs

(P-25529)
AAA ACCOUNTING SERVICES
2 Enterprise Apt 1211, Aliso Viejo
(92656-7128)
PHONE...................................949 791-7368
Frazier Shayla, *CEO*
EMP: 99
SALES (est): 1.8MM **Privately Held**
SIC: 8721 Auditing services

(P-25530)
ABBOTT STRINGHAM AN
1530 Meridian Ave 2, San Jose
(95125-5350)
PHONE...................................408 377-8700
Morgan Lynch, *President*
Franceen Borrillo, *Principal*
Bill Melton, *Principal*
Todd Robinson, *Principal*
Raymond E Schaeffer, *Principal*
EMP: 60
SALES (est): 6.7MM **Privately Held**
WEB: www.aslcpa.com
SIC: 8721 Accounting services, except auditing; certified public accountant

(P-25531)
ACCOUNTANTS 4 CONTRACT
235 Montgomery St Ste 630, San Francisco
(94104-2922)
PHONE...................................415 781-8644
Daniel M Maisler, *CEO*
EMP: 80
SQ FT: 2,300
SALES (est): 7.2MM **Privately Held**
SIC: 8721 Accounting, auditing & bookkeeping

(P-25532)
ACCRETIVE SOLUTIONS INC (HQ)
17101 Armstrong Ave # 100, Irvine
(92614-5742)
PHONE...................................312 994-4600
Kerry Barrett, *CEO*
Jonathan Rosenthal, *Ch of Bd*
Joann Lilek, *CFO*
Richard A Moran, *Vice Ch Bd*
Mike Reinecke, *Exec VP*
EMP: 1000
SALES (est): 132.3MM **Publicly Held**
SIC: 8721 Accounting, auditing & bookkeeping

(P-25533)
AGRI VALLEY SERVICES
1532 N West Ave, Fresno (93728-1306)
PHONE...................................559 253-0104
Carmalee Kossaras, *Owner*
EMP: 100
SALES (est): 2.7MM **Privately Held**
SIC: 8721 7363 Payroll accounting service; labor resource services

(P-25534)
AMERICAN TAX SOLUTIONS
1055 W 7th St Ste 3050, Los Angeles
(90017-2509)
PHONE...................................323 306-7032
Tyler Bennett, *COO*

Geoff Plourde, *Vice Pres*
EMP: 50
SALES: 570K **Privately Held**
SIC: 8721 Accounting services, except auditing

(P-25535)
ARMANDO C IBARRA CPA
371 E St, Chula Vista (91910-2615)
PHONE...................................619 422-1348
Armando C Ibarra Sr, *President*
Oscar Ibarra, *Corp Secy*
Armando C Ibarra Jr, *Vice Pres*
EMP: 60
SALES (est): 2.2MM **Privately Held**
SIC: 8721 7291 Accounting services, except auditing; tax return preparation services

(P-25536)
ARMANINO LLP
11766 Wilshire Blvd Fl 9, Los Angeles
(90025-6548)
PHONE...................................310 478-4148
Chris Mays, *Director*
EMP: 150
SALES (corp-wide): 80.6MM **Privately Held**
SIC: 8721 Certified public accountant
PA: Armanino Llp
12657 Alcosta Blvd # 500
San Ramon CA 94583
925 790-2600

(P-25537)
ARMANINO LLP (PA)
12657 Alcosta Blvd # 500, San Ramon
(94583-4406)
PHONE...................................925 790-2600
Andy Armanino, *Managing Prtnr*
Linda Antonelli, *Partner*
Bob Bernstein, *Partner*
John Brychel, *Partner*
Tim Hourigan, *Partner*
EMP: 160
SQ FT: 5,500
SALES (est): 80.6MM **Privately Held**
WEB: www.amllp.com
SIC: 8721 8742 Certified public accountant; management consulting services

(P-25538)
BDO USA LLP
1 Bush St, San Francisco (94104-4425)
PHONE...................................415 397-7900
Doug Hart, *Managing Prtnr*
Terry Lloyd, *Partner*
Peter Meeks, *Partner*
Suzanna Musick, *Partner*
Scott Wilkerson, *Manager*
EMP: 150
SQ FT: 1,500
SALES (corp-wide): 1.6B **Privately Held**
WEB: www.bdo.com
SIC: 8721 Certified public accountant
PA: Bdo Usa, Llp
330 N Wabash Ave Ste 3200
Chicago IL 60611
312 240-1236

(P-25539)
BDO USA LLP
3570 Carmel Mountain Rd # 400, San
Diego (92130-6767)
PHONE...................................858 404-9200
Lee Duran, *Managing Prtnr*
Rebekah Gibson, *Admin Asst*
David Pain, *CTO*
Keith Michaelis, *Human Res Mgr*
Kathy Nunez, *Marketing Staff*
EMP: 78
SALES (corp-wide): 1.6B **Privately Held**
SIC: 8721 Certified public accountant
PA: Bdo Usa, Llp
330 N Wabash Ave Ste 3200
Chicago IL 60611
312 240-1236

(P-25540)
BMS PARENT INC (PA)
1220 Dewey Way Ste F, Upland
(91786-1101)
PHONE...................................909 981-2341
John Wallace, *CEO*
Barbara Gillet, *Vice Pres*
EMP: 68

SQ FT: 9,000
SALES (est): 12MM **Privately Held**
WEB: www.bmsreimbursement.com
SIC: 8721 5045 Billing & bookkeeping service; computer software

(P-25541)
BPM LLP (PA)
Also Called: B P M
600 California St Fl 6, San Francisco
(94108-2733)
PHONE...................................415 421-5757
Mark Berger, *Managing Prtnr*
Philip Leibowitz, *Partner*
Marc Berger, *Managing Prtnr*
Jonathan Fayman, *CFO*
Diana Borova, *Officer*
EMP: 55
SALES (est): 18MM **Privately Held**
WEB: www.lsbcpa.com
SIC: 8721 Certified public accountant

(P-25542)
BROWN ARMSTRONG ACCNTANCY CORP
Also Called: Brown Armstrong Cpas
4200 Truxtun Ave Ste 300, Bakersfield
(93309-0668)
PHONE...................................661 324-4971
Andrew J Paulden, *President*
Benjamin P Reyes, *Corp Secy*
Christina M Thornburgh, *Corp Secy*
Burton H Armstrong, *Vice Pres*
Diana H Branthoover, *Vice Pres*
EMP: 65
SQ FT: 30,000
SALES (est): 8MM **Privately Held**
WEB: www.bacpas.com
SIC: 8721 Accounting services, except auditing

(P-25543)
BURR PILGER MAYER
Also Called: BURR PILGER MAYER
110 Stony Point Rd # 210, Santa Rosa
(95401-4189)
PHONE...................................707 544-4078
Carolyn Amster, *Principal*
Joseph C Kitts, *Shareholder*
Carol S O'Hara, *Shareholder*
Janice Oeming, *Marketing Staff*
Minnie Wright, *Director*
EMP: 63
SALES (corp-wide): 45.4MM **Privately Held**
SIC: 8721 Certified public accountant
PA: Burr Pilger Mayer, Inc.
600 California St Fl 6
San Francisco CA 94108
415 421-5757

(P-25544)
BURR PILGER MAYER INC (PA)
600 California St Fl 6, San Francisco
(94108-2733)
PHONE...................................415 421-5757
James Wallace, *CEO*
Inna Merzheritsky, *Shareholder*
Curtis Burr, *Vice Pres*
James Su, *Managing Dir*
Kristen Lee, *Admin Sec*
EMP: 110
SQ FT: 20,824
SALES (est): 45.4MM **Privately Held**
SIC: 8721 Certified public accountant

(P-25545)
BURR PILGER MAYER INC
10 Almaden Blvd Ste 1000, San Jose
(95113-2238)
PHONE...................................408 961-6300
Mark Loveless, *Manager*
Karen Go, *Manager*
EMP: 50
SALES (corp-wide): 45.4MM **Privately Held**
SIC: 8721 Certified public accountant
PA: Burr Pilger Mayer, Inc.
600 California St Fl 6
San Francisco CA 94108
415 421-5757

(P-25546)
BURR PILGER MAYER INC
4200 Bohannon Dr Ste 250, Menlo Park
(94025-1021)
PHONE...................................650 855-6800
Mark Loveless, *Branch Mgr*
Sharon Selleck, *Director*
EMP: 50
SALES (corp-wide): 45.4MM **Privately Held**
SIC: 8721 Certified public accountant
PA: Burr Pilger Mayer, Inc.
600 California St Fl 6
San Francisco CA 94108
415 421-5757

(P-25547)
C D PAYROLL INC
2300 W Empire Ave, Burbank
(91504-3341)
PHONE...................................818 848-1562
Ed Spietel, *President*
Ed Spiegel, *President*
EMP: 60
SQ FT: 12,000
SALES (est): 2.8MM
SALES (corp-wide): 55MM **Privately Held**
SIC: 8721 Payroll accounting service
PA: Cast & Crew Payroll, Llc
2300 W Empire Ave # 500
Burbank CA 91504
818 848-6022

(P-25548)
CALSTARS
915 L St Fl 7, Sacramento (95814-3705)
PHONE...................................916 445-0211
Freda Luan-Dun, *Co-Owner*
Cassandra Lichnock, *COO*
Solange Brooks, *Officer*
Ricardo Duran, *Officer*
Carrie Lo, *Officer*
EMP: 50
SALES (est): 1.3MM **Privately Held**
SIC: 8721 Accounting, auditing & bookkeeping

(P-25549)
CAST & CREW PAYROLL LLC (PA)
Also Called: Cast and Crew Entrmt Svcs
2300 W Empire Ave # 500, Burbank
(91504-5399)
PHONE...................................818 848-6022
Eric Belcher, *President*
Shardell Cavaliere, *President*
Sally Knutson, *CFO*
Lee David, *Vice Pres*
Patterson Andrew, *CTO*
EMP: 195
SQ FT: 12,000
SALES (est): 55MM **Privately Held**
SIC: 8721 Payroll accounting service

(P-25550)
CBIZ MAYOR HOFFMAN MECHAN (PA)
10616 Scripps Summit Ct, San Diego
(92131-3966)
PHONE...................................858 795-2000
Paul Nation, *President*
David Diamond, *Principal*
Robert Gellman, *Principal*
Steve Hermes, *Principal*
Greg Smith, *Principal*
EMP: 93 **EST:** 1976
SALES (est): 4.3MM **Privately Held**
WEB: www.nshd.com
SIC: 8721 8742 Certified public accountant; financial consultant

(P-25551)
CBIZMHM LLC
Also Called: Cks Business Services
5060 California Ave # 800, Bakersfield
(93309-0728)
PHONE...................................661 325-7500
Mark Luttrell, *Mng Member*
Dan Sprayberry, *Vice Pres*
Marie Ebersbacher, *Info Tech Dir*
Mike Jakovich, *IT/INT Sup*
Martin Goni, *Accountant*
EMP: 50

(PA)=Parent Co (HQ)=Headquarters (DH)=Div Headquarters
✪ = New Business established in last 2 years

SALES (est): 3.6MM **Publicly Held**
SIC: 8721 Certified public accountant
PA: Cbiz, Inc.
　　6050 Oak Tree Blvd # 500
　　Cleveland OH 44131
　　-

(P-25552)
CERIDIAN LLC
1515 W 190th St Ste 100, Gardena
(90248-4913)
PHONE...........................310 719-7481
Chris Byers, *Branch Mgr*
Mary Berg, *Executive Asst*
Tiffany Hall, *Recruiter*
John Gei, *Senior Mgr*
Ramona Little, *Accounts Exec*
EMP: 60 **Privately Held**
WEB: www.ceridian.com
SIC: 8721 Payroll accounting service
HQ: Ceridian Llc
　　3311 E Old Shakopee Rd
　　Minneapolis MN 55425
　　952 853-8100

(P-25553)
CERIDIAN TAX SERVICE INC
17390 Brookhurst St # 100, Fountain Valley
(92708-3720)
P.O. Box 20805 (92728-0805)
PHONE...........................714 963-1311
Webster Hill, *General Mgr*
Kevin Jennings, *Software Dev*
Deborah Curras, *Project Mgr*
Joshua Duston, *Engineer*
Jennifer Huebscher, *Analyst*
EMP: 300 **EST:** 1998
SQ FT: 130,000
SALES (est): 20.3MM **Privately Held**
WEB: www.ceridian.com
SIC: 8721 Payroll accounting service
HQ: Ceridian Llc
　　3311 E Old Shakopee Rd
　　Minneapolis MN 55425
　　952 853-8100

(P-25554)
CFGI LLC
600 California St Fl 14, San Francisco
(94108-2709)
PHONE...........................415 670-9041
Greg Lynch, *Manager*
EMP: 128
SALES (corp-wide): 9.7MM **Privately Held**
SIC: 8721 7291 Accounting, auditing &
　bookkeeping; tax return preparation serv-
　ices
PA: Cfgi, Llc
　　99 High St Ste 3001
　　Boston MA 02110
　　617 531-8270

(P-25555)
CITY OF BERKELEY
Also Called: Police Department
2180 Milvia St, Berkeley (94704-1122)
PHONE...........................510 981-6750
Doug Hambleton, *Chief*
EMP: 1500 **Privately Held**
WEB: www.berkeleycamps.com
SIC: 8721 Auditing services
PA: City Of Berkeley
　　2120 Milvia St
　　Berkeley CA 94704
　　510 981-7300

(P-25556)
CLIFTONLARSONALLEN LLP
925 Highland Pointe Dr # 450, Roseville
(95678-5427)
PHONE...........................916 784-7800
EMP: 300
SALES (corp-wide): 755.1MM **Privately Held**
SIC: 8721 Certified public accountant
PA: Cliftonlarsonallen Llp
　　220 S 6th St Ste 300
　　Minneapolis MN 55402
　　612 376-4500

(P-25557)
CLIFTONLARSONALLEN LLP
2210 E Route 66 Ste 100, Glendora
(91740-4676)
PHONE...........................626 857-7300

EMP: 55
SALES (corp-wide): 755.1MM **Privately Held**
SIC: 8721 Certified public accountant
PA: Cliftonlarsonallen Llp
　　220 S 6th St Ste 300
　　Minneapolis MN 55402
　　612 376-4500

(P-25558)
CLIFTONLARSONALLEN LLP
Also Called: Nsbn
1925 Century Park E Fl 16, Los Angeles
(90067-2701)
PHONE...........................310 273-2501
Randy Wells, *Branch Mgr*
EMP: 91
SALES (corp-wide): 755.1MM **Privately Held**
SIC: 8721 Accounting services, except au-
　diting
PA: Cliftonlarsonallen Llp
　　220 S 6th St Ste 300
　　Minneapolis MN 55402
　　612 376-4500

(P-25559)
COHNREZNICK LLP
21600 Oxnard St Ste 700, Woodland Hills
(91367-4900)
PHONE...........................818 205-2600
Cott Sachs, *Office Mgr*
EMP: 59
SALES (corp-wide): 334.6MM **Privately Held**
SIC: 8721 Certified public accountant
PA: Cohnreznick Llp
　　1301 Avenue Of The Americ
　　New York NY 10019
　　212 297-0400

(P-25560)
COHNREZNICK LLP
11755 Wilshire Blvd # 1700, Los Angeles
(90025-1506)
PHONE...........................310 477-3722
EMP: 50
SALES (corp-wide): 334.6MM **Privately Held**
SIC: 8721 Certified public accountant
PA: Cohnreznick Llp
　　1301 Avenue Of The Americ
　　New York NY 10019
　　212 297-0400

(P-25561)
COLLABRUS INC
Also Called: M Squared Consulting
111 Sutter St Ste 900, San Francisco
(94104-4523)
PHONE...........................415 288-1826
Alex Todd, *CEO*
Russel Orelowitz, *CFO*
Rhonelle Deleon, *Opers Staff*
Leon Carmon Rhonelle, *Opers Staff*
EMP: 240
SQ FT: 8,000
SALES (est): 10.1MM
SALES (corp-wide): 77.7MM **Privately Held**
WEB: www.collabrusinc.com
SIC: 8721 Billing & bookkeeping service
HQ: M Squared Consulting, Inc.
　　111 Sutter St Ste 900
　　San Francisco CA 94104
　　415 391-1038

(P-25562)
COMPUTERIZED MGT SVCS INC
Also Called: CMS
4100 Guardian St Ste 205, Simi Valley
(93063-6721)
P.O. Box 190 (93062-0190)
PHONE...........................805 522-5940
J Daryl Favale, *President*
EMP: 100
SQ FT: 7,500
SALES (est): 8.6MM **Privately Held**
SIC: 8721 Billing & bookkeeping service

(P-25563)
CONSIDINE & CONSIDINE AN ACCO
8989 Rio San Diego Dr # 320, San Diego
(92108-1646)
PHONE...........................619 231-1977

Perry S Wright, *CEO*
Timothy Considine, *President*
Jerry Hotz, *Treasurer*
Michael Boardman, *Vice Pres*
Don Bonk, *Vice Pres*
EMP: 80 **EST:** 1946
SQ FT: 20,000
SALES (est): 8.1MM **Privately Held**
WEB: www.cccpa.com
SIC: 8721 Certified public accountant

(P-25564)
COUNTY OF LOS ANGELES
Also Called: Internal Services Department
1100 N Eastern Ave, Los Angeles
(90063-3200)
PHONE...........................323 267-2136
Scott Minnix, *Director*
EMP: 1800 **Privately Held**
SIC: 8721 Accounting, auditing & book-
　keeping
PA: County Of Los Angeles
　　500 W Temple St Ste 437
　　Los Angeles CA 90012
　　213 974-1101

(P-25565)
COUNTY OF SAN BERNARDINO
Also Called: Auditor Controller Department
222 W Hospitality Ln, San Bernardino
(92415-0013)
PHONE...........................909 386-8818
Larry Walker, *Principal*
A B Brand, *Controller*
EMP: 200
SQ FT: 12,700 **Privately Held**
SIC: 8721 9311 Auditing services; finance,
　taxation & monetary policy;
PA: County Of San Bernardino
　　385 N Arrowhead Ave
　　San Bernardino CA 92415
　　909 387-3841

(P-25566)
COUNTY OF VENTURA
Auditor /controller
800 S Victoria Ave 1540, Ventura
(93009-0003)
PHONE...........................805 654-3152
Christine Cohens, *Manager*
EMP: 61 **Privately Held**
WEB: www.vcoe.org
SIC: 8721 9311 Auditing services; con-
　trollers' office, government;
PA: County Of Ventura
　　800 S Victoria Ave
　　Ventura CA 93009
　　805 654-2644

(P-25567)
CROWE LLP
15233 Ventura Blvd Fl 9, Sherman Oaks
(91403-2250)
PHONE...........................818 501-5200
Ray Calvey, *Manager*
Raymond Calvey, *Partner*
Phillip McCarty, *Partner*
Sharon Jones, *Executive*
Mark Taylor, *Executive*
EMP: 120
SALES (corp-wide): 951.8MM **Privately Held**
SIC: 8721 Certified public accountant
PA: Crowe Llp
　　225 W Wacker Dr Ste 2600
　　Chicago IL 60606
　　312 899-7000

(P-25568)
DELOITTE & TOUCHE LLP
555 W 5th St Ste 2700, Los Angeles
(90013-1024)
PHONE...........................213 688-0800
Byron David, *Branch Mgr*
David N Bowen, *Partner*
Venisa Ibarra, *Partner*
Brent Schoenbaum, *Partner*
Gary Smith, *Partner*
EMP: 1000
SALES (corp-wide): 5.5B **Privately Held**
WEB: www.deloitte.com
SIC: 8721 Accounting services, except au-
　diting

HQ: Deloitte & Touche Llp
　　30 Rockefeller Plz # 4350
　　New York NY 10112
　　212 492-4000

(P-25569)
DELOITTE & TOUCHE LLP
655 W Broadway Ste 700, San Diego
(92101-8480)
PHONE...........................619 232-6500
Cathy Jennings, *Manager*
Russell Gold, *Managing Prtnr*
Corey Litteken, *Exec VP*
Michelle Pham, *Technology*
Shibani Dogra, *Auditing Mgr*
EMP: 200
SALES (corp-wide): 5.5B **Privately Held**
WEB: www.deloitte.com
SIC: 8721 7291 Certified public account-
　ant; tax return preparation services
HQ: Deloitte & Touche Llp
　　30 Rockefeller Plz # 4350
　　New York NY 10112
　　212 492-4000

(P-25570)
DELOITTE & TOUCHE LLP
695 Town Center Dr # 1200, Costa Mesa
(92626-7188)
PHONE...........................714 436-7419
Bob Grant, *Director*
Jim Chergey, *Partner*
Jeffrey D Egertson, *Partner*
Vito Francone, *Partner*
Curtis Hildt, *Partner*
EMP: 700
SALES (corp-wide): 5.5B **Privately Held**
WEB: www.deloitte.com
SIC: 8721 7291 Accounting services, ex-
　cept auditing; tax return preparation serv-
　ices
HQ: Deloitte & Touche Llp
　　30 Rockefeller Plz # 4350
　　New York NY 10112
　　212 492-4000

(P-25571)
DELOITTE & TOUCHE LLP
555 Mission St Ste 1400, San Francisco
(94105-0942)
PHONE...........................415 783-4000
Mark Edmonds, *Branch Mgr*
Mike Deverell, *Principal*
David Gully, *Principal*
Mack Schwing, *Principal*
EMP: 350
SALES (corp-wide): 5.5B **Privately Held**
WEB: www.deloitte.com
SIC: 8721 Accounting services, except au-
　diting
HQ: Deloitte & Touche Llp
　　30 Rockefeller Plz # 4350
　　New York NY 10112
　　212 492-4000

(P-25572)
DELOITTE & TOUCHE LLP
225 W Santa Clara St # 600, San Jose
(95113-1728)
PHONE...........................408 704-4000
Jonathan Tharmapalan, *Manager*
EMP: 450
SALES (corp-wide): 5.5B **Privately Held**
WEB: www.deloitte.com
SIC: 8721 8742 6282 Certified public ac-
　countant; management consulting serv-
　ices; investment advice
HQ: Deloitte & Touche Llp
　　30 Rockefeller Plz # 4350
　　New York NY 10112
　　212 492-4000

(P-25573)
DELOITTE & TOUCHE LLP
5250 N Palm Ave Ste 300, Fresno
(93704-2200)
PHONE...........................559 449-6300
Nada Barrett, *Branch Mgr*
Ashok Venugopalan, *Senior Mgr*
Vincent Paganetti, *Consultant*
EMP: 70
SALES (corp-wide): 5.5B **Privately Held**
WEB: www.deloitte.com
SIC: 8721 Certified public accountant

HQ: Deloitte & Touche Llp
30 Rockefeller Plz # 4350
New York NY 10112
212 492-4000

(P-25574)
DELOITTE & TOUCHE LLP
6210 Stoneridge Mall Rd, Pleasanton
(94588-3268)
PHONE.................................415 782-4020
EMP: 244
SALES (corp-wide): 5.5B **Privately Held**
SIC: 8721 Certified public accountant
HQ: Deloitte & Touche Llp
30 Rockefeller Plz # 4350
New York NY 10112
212 492-4000

(P-25575)
DELOITTE & TOUCHE LLP
555 W 5th St Ste 2700, Los Angeles
(90013-1024)
PHONE.................................213 688-0800
EMP: 244
SALES (corp-wide): 12.3B **Privately Held**
SIC: 8721
HQ: Deloitte & Touche Llp
30 Rockefeller Plz # 4350
New York NY 10112
212 492-4000

(P-25576)
DELOITTE TAX LLP
555 Mission St Ste 1400, San Francisco
(94105-0942)
PHONE.................................415 783-4000
Mark Edmunds, *Branch Mgr*
Carolyn Andrews, *Partner*
Edward Harrison, *Partner*
Lyn Nicholson, *Admin Asst*
Amit Agrawal,
EMP: 294
SALES (corp-wide): 5.5B **Privately Held**
SIC: 8721 Auditing services; certified public accountant
HQ: Deloitte Tax Llp
30 Rockefeller Plz
New York NY 10112
212 492-4000

(P-25577)
DELOITTE TAX LLP
225 W Santa Clara St # 600, San Jose
(95113-1728)
PHONE.................................408 704-4000
Garrett Herbert, *Partner*
Wen H Chow, *Admin Asst*
Etosha Raoof, *Admin Asst*
Janet Wong, *Admin Asst*
Colleen Zacher, *Admin Asst*
EMP: 294
SALES (corp-wide): 5.5B **Privately Held**
SIC: 8721 Auditing services; certified public accountant
HQ: Deloitte Tax Llp
30 Rockefeller Plz
New York NY 10112
212 492-4000

(P-25578)
ECONA CORP
1344 Paizay Pl Unit 732, Chula Vista
(91913-3972)
P.O. Box 296, Alpine (91903-0296)
PHONE.................................619 722-6555
Branden B Moss, *CEO*
EMP: 50 **EST:** 2013
SALES (est): 1.8MM **Privately Held**
SIC: 8721 7389 Payroll accounting service;

(P-25579)
EDWARD E STRAINE CPA
1760 Creekside Oaks Dr, Sacramento
(95833-3632)
PHONE.................................916 646-6464
Edward E Straine, *Principal*
EMP: 60
SALES (est): 1.7MM **Privately Held**
SIC: 8721 Certified public accountant

(P-25580)
EGO INC
Also Called: Emergency Groups Office
444 E Huntington Dr # 300, Arcadia
(91006-6203)
PHONE.................................626 447-0296
Andrea Brault, *President*
Del Brault, *President*
Jane Brault, *Treasurer*
James Blakeman, *Senior VP*
Maria Cmco, *Director*
EMP: 150
SQ FT: 8,500
SALES (est): 16.6MM **Privately Held**
SIC: 8721 Billing & bookkeeping service

(P-25581)
EIDE BAILLY LLP
10681 Fthill Blvd Ste 300, Rancho Cucamonga (91730)
PHONE.................................909 466-4410
Dave Stende, *Managing Prtnr*
EMP: 300
SALES (corp-wide): 339.7MM **Privately Held**
SIC: 8721 Certified public accountant
PA: Eide Bailly Llp
4310 17th Ave S
Fargo ND 58103
701 239-8500

(P-25582)
ENTERTAINMENT PARTNERS INC (PA)
2950 N Hollywood Way, Burbank
(91505-1072)
PHONE.................................818 955-6000
Mark Goldstein, *CEO*
Myfa Cirinna, *Exec VP*
Anthony De La Rosa, *Exec VP*
Davida Lara, *Exec VP*
Jennifer Favors, *Vice Pres*
EMP: 295
SQ FT: 38,000
SALES (est): 54.7MM **Privately Held**
WEB: www.epservices.com
SIC: 8721 Payroll accounting service

(P-25583)
ERNST & YOUNG LLP
Also Called: Ey
725 S Figueroa St Ste 200, Los Angeles
(90017-5403)
PHONE.................................213 977-3200
Jeff Kaufman, *Manager*
Kevin Thoeng, *Technology*
Andrew Mokhov, *CPA*
Amy Cerna, *Personnel Assit*
Alex Borden, *Sr Associate*
EMP: 1000
SALES (corp-wide): 4.1B **Privately Held**
WEB: www.ey.com
SIC: 8721 8742 7291 Certified public accountant; auditing services; business consultant; management information systems consultant; tax return preparation services
PA: Ernst & Young Llp
5 Times Sq Fl Conlv1
New York NY 10036
212 773-3000

(P-25584)
ERNST & YOUNG LLP
Also Called: Ey
200 N Pacific Coast Hwy # 2, El Segundo
(90245-4340)
PHONE.................................310 725-1764
Kristen Schmitt, *Branch Mgr*
EMP: 228
SALES (corp-wide): 4.1B **Privately Held**
SIC: 8721 Certified public accountant
PA: Ernst & Young Llp
5 Times Sq Fl Conlv1
New York NY 10036
212 773-3000

(P-25585)
ERNST & YOUNG LLP
Also Called: Ey
560 Mission St Ste 1600, San Francisco
(94105-2990)
PHONE.................................415 894-8000
Michael Strachan, *Manager*
Gregory Martin, *Partner*
James Oneil, *Principal*
Michael Mulkerin, *Analyst*

Stephanie Mendez, *CPA*
EMP: 100
SALES (corp-wide): 4.1B **Privately Held**
WEB: www.ey.com
SIC: 8721 8742 Accounting services, except auditing; management consulting services
PA: Ernst & Young Llp
5 Times Sq Fl Conlv1
New York NY 10036
212 773-3000

(P-25586)
ERNST & YOUNG LLP
Also Called: Ey
1451 California Ave, Palo Alto
(94304-1109)
PHONE.................................650 496-1600
Alex Turco, *Branch Mgr*
EMP: 230
SALES (corp-wide): 4.1B **Privately Held**
SIC: 8721 Certified public accountant
PA: Ernst & Young Llp
5 Times Sq Fl Conlv1
New York NY 10036
212 773-3000

(P-25587)
ERNST & YOUNG LLP
Also Called: Ey
303 Almaden Blvd Ste 1000, San Jose
(95110-2723)
PHONE.................................408 947-5500
Teri Shaffer, *Partner*
Edwin Carrasquillo, *Partner*
Joseph E Hogan, *Partner*
Dave Price, *Partner*
Mark Stefan, *Partner*
EMP: 650
SALES (corp-wide): 4.1B **Privately Held**
WEB: www.ey.com
SIC: 8721 8742 Certified public accountant; auditing services; business consultant; management information systems consultant
PA: Ernst & Young Llp
5 Times Sq Fl Conlv1
New York NY 10036
212 773-3000

(P-25588)
ERNST & YOUNG LLP
Also Called: Ey
4370 La Jolla Village Dr # 500, San Diego
(92122-1251)
PHONE.................................858 535-7200
Michael J Hartnett, *Manager*
Riju Parakh, *Manager*
EMP: 135
SALES (corp-wide): 4.1B **Privately Held**
WEB: www.ey.com
SIC: 8721 8742 7291 Certified public accountant; auditing services; business consultant; management information systems consultant; tax return preparation services
PA: Ernst & Young Llp
5 Times Sq Fl Conlv1
New York NY 10036
212 773-3000

(P-25589)
ERNST & YOUNG LLP
Also Called: Ey
18101 Von Karman Ave # 1700, Irvine
(92612-1012)
PHONE.................................949 794-2300
Linda Minx, *Office Mgr*
Chris Abston, *Partner*
Kathy Dagestino, *Partner*
Mike Denning, *Partner*
John F Fritz, *Partner*
EMP: 450
SALES (corp-wide): 4.1B **Privately Held**
WEB: www.ey.com
SIC: 8721 8742 Certified public accountant; auditing services; business consultant; management information systems consultant
PA: Ernst & Young Llp
5 Times Sq Fl Conlv1
New York NY 10036
212 773-3000

(P-25590)
ERNST & YOUNG LLP
Also Called: Ey
18006 Sky Park Cir # 106, Irvine
(92614-6406)
PHONE.................................949 838-3300
Ted Esau, *Principal*
EMP: 228
SALES (corp-wide): 4.1B **Privately Held**
WEB: www.ey.com
SIC: 8721 Certified public accountant
PA: Ernst & Young Llp
5 Times Sq Fl Conlv1
New York NY 10036
212 773-3000

(P-25591)
ERNST & YOUNG LLP
Also Called: Ey
2931 Townsgate Rd Ste 100, Westlake Village (91361-5874)
PHONE.................................805 778-7000
Brian Ladin, *Branch Mgr*
Glen Day, *Director*
EMP: 80
SALES (corp-wide): 4.1B **Privately Held**
WEB: www.ey.com
SIC: 8721 8742 8748 Certified public accountant; auditing services; business consultant; management information systems consultant; business consulting
PA: Ernst & Young Llp
5 Times Sq Fl Conlv1
New York NY 10036
212 773-3000

(P-25592)
ERNST & YOUNG LLP
Also Called: Ey
275 Shoreline Dr Ste 600, Redwood City
(94065-1493)
PHONE.................................650 802-4500
Donna Frazer, *Branch Mgr*
EMP: 250
SALES (corp-wide): 4.1B **Privately Held**
WEB: www.ey.com
SIC: 8721 8742 Certified public accountant; auditing services; business consultant; management information systems consultant
PA: Ernst & Young Llp
5 Times Sq Fl Conlv1
New York NY 10036
212 773-3000

(P-25593)
ERNST & YOUNG LLP
Also Called: Ey
2901 Douglas Blvd Ste 300, Roseville
(95661-4247)
PHONE.................................916 218-1900
Craig Pickett, *Manager*
EMP: 228
SALES (corp-wide): 4.1B **Privately Held**
WEB: www.ey.com
SIC: 8721 Certified public accountant; auditing services
PA: Ernst & Young Llp
5 Times Sq Fl Conlv1
New York NY 10036
212 773-3000

(P-25594)
ERNST & YOUNG LLP
Also Called: Ey
4301 Hacienda Dr Ste 450, Pleasanton
(94588-2791)
PHONE.................................925 734-6388
Karen Amato, *Manager*
EMP: 228
SALES (corp-wide): 4.1B **Privately Held**
WEB: www.ey.com
SIC: 8721 Certified public accountant; auditing services
PA: Ernst & Young Llp
5 Times Sq Fl Conlv1
New York NY 10036
212 773-3000

(P-25595)
ERNST & YOUNG LLP
560 Mission St Ste 1600, San Francisco
(94105-0911)
PHONE.................................415 894-8000
EMP: 700
SALES (corp-wide): 3B **Privately Held**
SIC: 8721

PRODUCTS & SVCS

PA: Ernst & Young Llp
5 Times Sq Fl Conlv1
New York NY 10036
212 773-3000

(P-25596)
FILM PAYROLL SERVICES INC (PA)
Also Called: Quantos Payroll
500 S Sepulveda Blvd Fl 4, Los Angeles
(90049-3550)
PHONE....................310 440-9600
Gregory Pickert, *CEO*
EMP: 100
SQ FT: 5,000
SALES (est): 7.9MM **Privately Held**
SIC: 8721 Payroll accounting service

(P-25597)
FRANK RIMERMAN & CO LLP
1 Embarcadero Ctr # 2410, San Francisco
(94111-3628)
PHONE....................415 439-1144
Bryan Polster, *Managing Prtnr*
Tony Mancini, *Partner*
Larry Gentry, *CFO*
Kathryn Feller, *Office Mgr*
Robert Hoffman, *CPA*
EMP: 62
SALES (corp-wide): 27.7MM **Privately Held**
SIC: 8721 Certified public accountant
PA: Frank, Rimerman & Co. Llp
1801 Page Mill Rd Ste 100
Palo Alto CA
650 845-8100

(P-25598)
GRANT THORNTON LLP
101 California St # 2700, San Francisco
(94111-5830)
PHONE....................415 986-3900
Jeff Pera, *Manager*
Daniel Allustiarti, *Admin Asst*
Orus Dearman, *Manager*
EMP: 70
SALES (corp-wide): 65.1MM **Privately Held**
WEB: www.gt.com
SIC: 8721 Accounting services, except auditing
HQ: Grant Thornton Llp
171 N Clark St Ste 200
Chicago IL 60601
312 856-0200

(P-25599)
GRANT THORNTON LLP
1000 Wilshire Blvd # 300, Los Angeles
(90017-2457)
PHONE....................213 627-1717
Mark Bagaason, *Manager*
Jim Hayden, *Principal*
Joe A Monti, *Principal*
Jennie Hartman, *Technology*
Lisa Murphy, *Marketing Staff*
EMP: 50
SALES (corp-wide): 65.1MM **Privately Held**
WEB: www.gt.com
SIC: 8721 8742 7291 Accounting services, except auditing; auditing services; management consulting services; tax return preparation services
HQ: Grant Thornton Llp
171 N Clark St Ste 200
Chicago IL 60601
312 856-0200

(P-25600)
GRANT THORNTON LLP
10 Almaden Blvd Ste 800, San Jose
(95113-2016)
PHONE....................408 275-9000
Harry Smith, *Branch Mgr*
Gary J Gemoll, *Managing Prtnr*
Bill Heppner, *Principal*
EMP: 50
SALES (corp-wide): 65.1MM **Privately Held**
WEB: www.gt.com
SIC: 8721 Accounting services, except auditing

HQ: Grant Thornton Llp
171 N Clark St Ste 200
Chicago IL 60601
312 856-0200

(P-25601)
GRANT THORNTON LLP
515 S Flower St Ste 700, Los Angeles
(90071-2209)
PHONE....................213 627-1717
Don Dahl, *Manager*
Kevin La Roche, *Auditor*
EMP: 99
SALES (corp-wide): 65.1MM **Privately Held**
WEB: www.gt.com
SIC: 8721 Certified public accountant
HQ: Grant Thornton Llp
171 N Clark St Ste 200
Chicago IL 60601
312 856-0200

(P-25602)
GRANT THORNTON LLP
12220 El Camino Real, San Diego
(92130-2091)
PHONE....................858 704-8000
Don Williams,
EMP: 113
SALES (corp-wide): 65.1MM **Privately Held**
WEB: www.gt.com
SIC: 8721 Auditing services
HQ: Grant Thornton Llp
171 N Clark St Ste 200
Chicago IL 60601
312 856-0200

(P-25603)
GREEN HASSON & JANKS LLP
10990 Wilshire Blvd Fl 16, Los Angeles
(90024-3925)
PHONE....................310 873-1600
Leon Janks, *Partner*
William Cline, *CFO*
Yvonne Burke, *Officer*
Yvonne Senouci, *Officer*
Melissa Rodriguez, *Executive Asst*
EMP: 120
SQ FT: 22,000
SALES (est): 17.8MM **Privately Held**
WEB: www.ghjadvisors.com
SIC: 8721 Certified public accountant

(P-25604)
GROBSTEIN HORWATH & CO
Also Called: Grobstein, Horwath & Company
15233 Ventura Blvd Fl 9, Van Nuys
(91403-2250)
PHONE....................818 501-5200
Michael Grobstein, *Partner*
David Agler, *Partner*
Michael Fenstein, *Partner*
David Gottlieb, *Partner*
Jerry Levine, *Partner*
EMP: 70 **EST:** 1969
SQ FT: 11,000
SALES (est): 4.1MM **Privately Held**
WEB: www.horwathcal.com
SIC: 8721 Certified public accountant

(P-25605)
GURSEY SCHNEIDER & CO LLC (PA)
1888 Century Park E # 900, Los Angeles
(90067-1735)
PHONE....................310 552-0960
Stephan H Wasserman, *Partner*
Rudy Fuentes, *Admin Asst*
Andrea Murray, *Admin Asst*
Molly Warren, *Admin Asst*
David Cuevas, *Administration*
EMP: 62
SQ FT: 12,000
SALES (est): 17.2MM **Privately Held**
SIC: 8721 Certified public accountant

(P-25606)
HEALTHCARE COST SOLUTIONS INC
Also Called: H C S
1200 Newprt Cntr Dr 190, Newport Beach
(92660)
PHONE....................949 721-2795
Bridget T Gallagher, *CEO*
EMP: 60 **EST:** 1994

SALES (est): 3.3MM **Privately Held**
WEB: www.hcsstat.com
SIC: 8721 8742 Auditing services; hospital & health services consultant

(P-25607)
HMWC CPAS & BUSINESS ADVISORS
Also Called: Yosemite Capital Mangagement
17501 17th St Ste 100, Tustin
(92780-7924)
PHONE....................714 505-9000
Steven Williams, *President*
Marie F Alvarez, *Executive Asst*
Debra Leon, *Executive Asst*
Janet Anderson, *Admin Sec*
Curtis Campbell, *Admin Sec*
EMP: 57 **EST:** 1972
SALES (est): 6.2MM **Privately Held**
SIC: 8721 Certified public accountant

(P-25608)
HOLTHOUSE CARLIN VAN TRIGT LLP
350 W Colo Blvd Fl 5 Flr 5, Pasadena
(91105)
PHONE....................626 243-5100
Kevin Cordano, *Principal*
EMP: 70 **Privately Held**
SIC: 8721 Certified public accountant
PA: Holthouse Carlin Van Trigt Llp
11444 W Olympic Blvd # 11
Los Angeles CA 90064

(P-25609)
HOLTHOUSE CARLIN VAN TRIGT LLP
400 W Ventura Blvd # 250, Camarillo
(93010-9137)
PHONE....................805 374-8555
Kathleen H Jones, *Principal*
Beth Salverson, *Principal*
EMP: 70 **Privately Held**
SIC: 8721 Certified public accountant
PA: Holthouse Carlin Van Trigt Llp
11444 W Olympic Blvd # 11
Los Angeles CA 90064

(P-25610)
HOLTHOUSE CARLIN VAN TRIGT LLP
15760 Ventura Blvd # 1700, Encino
(91436-3028)
PHONE....................818 849-3140
Norman Tamkin, *President*
EMP: 70 **Privately Held**
SIC: 8721 Certified public accountant
PA: Holthouse Carlin Van Trigt Llp
11444 W Olympic Blvd # 11
Los Angeles CA 90064

(P-25611)
HOLTHOUSE CARLIN VAN TRIGT LLP
18565 Jamboree Rd Ste 400, Irvine
(92612-2562)
PHONE....................714 361-7600
Donna Hansen, *Owner*
EMP: 70 **Privately Held**
SIC: 8721 Certified public accountant
PA: Holthouse Carlin Van Trigt Llp
11444 W Olympic Blvd # 11
Los Angeles CA 90064

(P-25612)
HOLTHOUSE CARLIN VAN TRIGT LLP (PA)
11444 W Olympic Blvd # 11, Los Angeles
(90064-1500)
PHONE....................310 477-5551
Philip Holthouse, *Managing Prtnr*
David Bierhorst, *Partner*
James Carlin, *Partner*
Blake Christian, *Partner*
Greg Hutchins, *Partner*
EMP: 110
SALES (est): 44.8MM **Privately Held**
WEB: www.hcvt.com
SIC: 8721 Certified public accountant

(P-25613)
HOOD & STRONG LLP (PA)
275 Battery St Ste 900, San Francisco
(94111-3332)
PHONE....................415 781-0793
Robert Raffo, *Managing Prtnr*
Raul Hernandez, *Partner*
Steve Piuma, *Partner*
William Amon, *Managing Dir*
Christine Stephens, *Executive Asst*
EMP: 75
SQ FT: 13,000
SALES (est): 14.7MM **Privately Held**
WEB: www.hoodstrong.com
SIC: 8721 Certified public accountant

(P-25614)
HUTCHINSON & BLOODGOOD LLP (PA)
550 N Brand Blvd Fl 14, Glendale
(91203-1952)
P.O. Box 1917 (91209-1917)
PHONE....................818 637-5000
Richard Preciado, *Managing Prtnr*
Michael Benneian, *Partner*
Gary Carruthers, *Partner*
Jenny Chen, *Partner*
Juan Daukowski, *Partner*
EMP: 125
SALES (est): 21MM **Privately Held**
WEB: www.hbllp.com
SIC: 8721 Certified public accountant

(P-25615)
I L S WEST INC
17501 17th St Ste 100, Tustin
(92780-7924)
PHONE....................714 505-7530
EMP: 50
SALES (est): 1.5MM **Privately Held**
SIC: 8721

(P-25616)
INDEVIA ACCOUNTING INC
2667 Camino Del Rio S # 101, San Diego
(92108-3763)
PHONE....................858 450-2981
Dev Purkayastha, *President*
Wendy A McGuire, *COO*
EMP: 60
SQ FT: 200
SALES: 1MM **Privately Held**
SIC: 8721 Accounting, auditing & bookkeeping

(P-25617)
INFINEON TECH AMERICAS CORP
Interntnal Rctfr/Ccunting Dept
222 Kansas St, El Segundo (90245-4315)
PHONE....................310 726-8000
Michael McGee, *Manager*
Marc Rougee, *Exec VP*
Alex Garcia, *Vice Pres*
Alvin Guzon, *Vice Pres*
David Poon, *Vice Pres*
EMP: 699
SALES (corp-wide): 8.7B **Privately Held**
WEB: www.irf.com
SIC: 8721 3674 Accounting, auditing & bookkeeping; semiconductors & related devices
HQ: Infineon Technologies Americas Corp.
101 N Pacific Coast Hwy
El Segundo CA 90245
310 726-8000

(P-25618)
INNOVTIVE EMPLYEE SLUTIONS INC
9665 Gran Rdge Dr Ste 420, San Diego
(92123)
PHONE....................858 715-5100
Karla Hertzog, *CEO*
Peter Limone, *CFO*
Darlene Bruder, *Vice Pres*
Tania Fiero, *Vice Pres*
Trevor Foster, *Vice Pres*
EMP: 1500
SQ FT: 6,641
SALES (est): 85.1MM **Privately Held**
WEB: www.innovative-solution.com
SIC: 8721 Payroll accounting service

(P-25619)
INTERPACIFIC GROUP INC
576 Beale St, San Francisco (94105-2019)
PHONE.............................415 442-0711
Dave Smith, *President*
EMP: 1306
SALES (est): 41.8MM **Privately Held**
WEB: www.interpacific-group.com
SIC: 8721 Accounting, auditing & book-keeping

(P-25620)
JMT CHARITABLE FOUNDATION
1 Market Ste 620, San Francisco (94105-5105)
PHONE.............................415 974-6000
John Williamson, *Managing Prtnr*
Jesse Kaplan, *Finance Mgr*
Christopher Emby, *Senior Mgr*
EMP: 70
SALES (corp-wide): 276.3MM **Privately Held**
SIC: 8721 Certified public accountant
PA: Eisneramper Llp
    750 3rd Ave Fl 16
    New York NY 10017
    212 949-8700

(P-25621)
JOSHUA J BODENSTADT CPA A PROF
4225 Executive Sq Ste 900, La Jolla (92037-1485)
PHONE.............................858 642-5050
Joshua J Bodenstadt, *Partner*
EMP: 50
SALES (est): 159.2K **Privately Held**
SIC: 8721 Certified public accountant

(P-25622)
JPMORGAN XIGN CORPORATION
7077 Koll Center Pkwy, Pleasanton (94566-3142)
PHONE.............................925 469-9446
Thomas M Glassanos, *President*
Jerry Ulrich, *Treasurer*
Bill Williamson, *Vice Pres*
EMP: 85
SQ FT: 26,000
SALES (est): 4.7MM
SALES (corp-wide): 131.4B **Publicly Held**
WEB: www.xign.com
SIC: 8721 Billing & bookkeeping service
HQ: Jpmorgan Chase Bank, National Association
    1111 Polaris Pkwy
    Columbus OH 43240
    614 436-3055

(P-25623)
KELLOGG ANDLSON ACCNTANCY CORP (PA)
21700 Oxnard St Ste 800, Woodland Hills (91367-7500)
PHONE.............................818 971-5100
Christian Payne, *CEO*
James F Walters, *President*
William Wall, *Vice Pres*
EMP: 60
SALES (est): 7.9MM **Privately Held**
WEB: www.k-a.com
SIC: 8721 Certified public accountant

(P-25624)
KIECKHAFER SCHIFFER & CO LLP (PA)
6201 Oak Cyn Ste 200, Irvine (92618-5231)
PHONE.............................949 250-3900
Jim Kieckhafer, *Partner*
Scott Schiffer, *Partner*
Hiromi Nishihara, *Manager*
EMP: 50
SALES (est): 9.7MM **Privately Held**
WEB: www.ksandco.com
SIC: 8721 Certified public accountant

(P-25625)
KPMG LLP
9171 Wilshire Blvd # 500, Beverly Hills (90210-5530)
PHONE.............................310 273-2770
Melvin Ozur, *Branch Mgr*

EMP: 50
SALES (corp-wide): 3.3B **Privately Held**
WEB: www.rkco.com
SIC: 8721 Certified public accountant
PA: Kpmg Llp
    345 Park Ave Lowr Ll4
    New York NY 10154
    212 758-9700

(P-25626)
KPMG LLP
4655 Executive Dr # 1100, San Diego (92121-3132)
PHONE.............................858 750-7100
Elizabeth Altman, *Branch Mgr*
Elton E Winston, *Principal*
Mark Eller, *Managing Dir*
Mildred Fernandez, *Sr Associate*
Judith Mantick, *Sr Associate*
EMP: 150
SALES (corp-wide): 3.3B **Privately Held**
SIC: 8721 Certified public accountant
PA: Kpmg Llp
    345 Park Ave Lowr Ll4
    New York NY 10154
    212 758-9700

(P-25627)
KPMG LLP
55 2nd St Ste 1400, San Francisco (94105-4557)
PHONE.............................415 963-5100
Louis P Miramontes, *Managing Prtnr*
Erika Bonner, *Partner*
Barbara Carbone, *Partner*
Alan Chinn, *Partner*
Glenn M Farrell, *Partner*
EMP: 50
SQ FT: 4,325
SALES (corp-wide): 3.3B **Privately Held**
SIC: 8721 Certified public accountant
PA: Kpmg Llp
    345 Park Ave Lowr Ll4
    New York NY 10154
    212 758-9700

(P-25628)
KPMG LLP
550 S Hope St Ste 1500, Los Angeles (90071-2629)
PHONE.............................703 286-8175
Daniel Smith, *Manager*
Gregory Jay, *Partner*
George Mack, *Associate Dir*
David Mesinger, *Exec Dir*
Andrea Roces, *Admin Asst*
EMP: 99
SALES (corp-wide): 3.3B **Privately Held**
SIC: 8721 Certified public accountant
PA: Kpmg Llp
    345 Park Ave Lowr Ll4
    New York NY 10154
    212 758-9700

(P-25629)
KPMG LLP
4464 Jasmine Ave, Culver City (90232-3429)
PHONE.............................212 758-9700
Joseph T Boyle, *Manager*
William Sand, *Director*
EMP: 3000
SALES (corp-wide): 3.3B **Privately Held**
SIC: 8721 Certified public accountant
PA: Kpmg Llp
    345 Park Ave Lowr Ll4
    New York NY 10154
    212 758-9700

(P-25630)
KPMG LLP
2175 N Calif Blvd # 1000, Walnut Creek (94596-3579)
PHONE.............................925 946-1300
Todd Goldman, *Manager*
Anush Nersisyan, *Auditor*
EMP: 50
SALES (corp-wide): 3.3B **Privately Held**
WEB: www.rkco.com
SIC: 8721 Certified public accountant
PA: Kpmg Llp
    345 Park Ave Lowr Ll4
    New York NY 10154
    212 758-9700

(P-25631)
KPMG LLP
500 Capitol Mall Ste 2100, Sacramento (95814-4754)
PHONE.............................916 448-4700
Rich Wise, *Partner*
Paresh Shah, *Director*
Uma Deshmukh, *Manager*
Eric Castillo, *Associate*
Guangyu Lu, *Associate*
EMP: 110
SALES (corp-wide): 3.3B **Privately Held**
SIC: 8721 Certified public accountant
PA: Kpmg Llp
    345 Park Ave Lowr Ll4
    New York NY 10154
    212 758-9700

(P-25632)
KPMG LLP
21700 Oxnard St Ste 1800, Woodland Hills (91367-3659)
PHONE.............................818 227-6900
Mort Erlich, *Manager*
Keith Catlow, *Managing Dir*
Sarah Stoch, *Internal Med*
Rachel Fonseca, *Manager*
EMP: 50
SALES (corp-wide): 3.3B **Privately Held**
SIC: 8721 Certified public accountant
PA: Kpmg Llp
    345 Park Ave Lowr Ll4
    New York NY 10154
    212 758-9700

(P-25633)
KRANZ & ASSOC HOLDINGS LLC
830 Menlo Ave Ste 100, Menlo Park (94025-4734)
PHONE.............................650 854-4400
Deborah Kranz,
Freda Kong, *VP Finance*
Kim Lain, *VP Finance*
Lourdes Rabelo, *VP Finance*
Anna Matveeva, *Director*
EMP: 90
SQ FT: 750
SALES (est): 1.3MM **Privately Held**
SIC: 8721 Accounting services, except auditing

(P-25634)
LAVINE LOFGREN MORRIS ENGELB
4180 La Jolla Village Dr # 300, La Jolla (92037-1402)
PHONE.............................858 455-1200
Von Morris, *Mng Member*
Andy Goodman, *COO*
Donna Luniewski, *Administration*
Derek Kline, *Accountant*
Garrett Steppat, *Accountant*
EMP: 50
SQ FT: 5,000
SALES (est): 6.3MM **Privately Held**
SIC: 8721 Certified public accountant

(P-25635)
LLP MOSS ADAMS
2882 Prospect Park Dr # 300, Rancho Cordova (95670-6059)
PHONE.............................916 503-8100
Robert Ahern, *Branch Mgr*
Ramos Tina, *Executive Asst*
Mary Michela, *Admin Asst*
Christopher Bell, *IT/INT Sup*
Cheyne Thompson, *Accountant*
EMP: 78
SALES (corp-wide): 340.5MM **Privately Held**
SIC: 8721 Certified public accountant
PA: Moss Adams Llp
    999 3rd Ave Ste 2800
    Seattle WA 98104
    206 302-6800

(P-25636)
LLP MOSS ADAMS
21700 Oxnard St Ste 300, Woodland Hills (91367-7561)
PHONE.............................818 577-1822
Gidget Furness, *COO*
Bob Terada, *Office Mgr*
EMP: 78

SALES (corp-wide): 340.5MM **Privately Held**
SIC: 8721 Certified public accountant
PA: Moss Adams Llp
    999 3rd Ave Ste 2800
    Seattle WA 98104
    206 302-6800

(P-25637)
LLP MOSS ADAMS
3121 W March Ln Ste 100, Stockton (95219-2367)
PHONE.............................209 955-6100
David Gellerman, *Principal*
Tracy Paglia, *Director*
Shonda Furr, *Manager*
Adam Hite, *Manager*
Heather Schlenger, *Manager*
EMP: 50
SALES (corp-wide): 340.5MM **Privately Held**
SIC: 8721 Certified public accountant
PA: Moss Adams Llp
    999 3rd Ave Ste 2800
    Seattle WA 98104
    206 302-6800

(P-25638)
LLP MOSS ADAMS
101 2nd St Ste 900, San Francisco (94105-3650)
PHONE.............................415 956-1500
Joy Robinson, *Branch Mgr*
Dan Cheyney, *Partner*
Steven Schechter, *Partner*
Caryl Thorp, *Partner*
Eric Tostenrud, *Partner*
EMP: 140
SALES (corp-wide): 340.5MM **Privately Held**
WEB: www.mossadams.com
SIC: 8721 Certified public accountant
PA: Moss Adams Llp
    999 3rd Ave Ste 2800
    Seattle WA 98104
    206 302-6800

(P-25639)
LLP MOSS ADAMS
635 Campbell Tech Pkwy # 100, Campbell (95008-5071)
PHONE.............................408 369-2400
Vid Lock, *Partner*
Taylor Doss, *Accountant*
Simran Kaur, *Accountant*
Susie Rosas, *Accountant*
Danielle Spence, *Accountant*
EMP: 200
SALES (corp-wide): 340.5MM **Privately Held**
SIC: 8721 Certified public accountant
PA: Moss Adams Llp
    999 3rd Ave Ste 2800
    Seattle WA 98104
    206 302-6800

(P-25640)
LLP MOSS ADAMS
10960 Wilshire Blvd # 1100, Los Angeles (90024-3714)
PHONE.............................310 477-0450
Rod Green, *Partner*
Jim Chevalier, *Partner*
Carmen Swetland, *Executive Asst*
Jessica Saucedo, *Admin Asst*
Sarah Witten, *Admin Asst*
EMP: 150
SALES (corp-wide): 340.5MM **Privately Held**
WEB: www.mossadams.com
SIC: 8721 Certified public accountant
PA: Moss Adams Llp
    999 3rd Ave Ste 2800
    Seattle WA 98104
    206 302-6800

(P-25641)
LLP MOSS ADAMS
1000 Main St, NAPA (94559-2645)
PHONE.............................707 224-4001
Jennifer Rabanal, *Branch Mgr*
EMP: 58
SALES (corp-wide): 340.5MM **Privately Held**
SIC: 8721 Certified public accountant

PRODUCTS & SVCS

PA: Moss Adams Llp
999 3rd Ave Ste 2800
Seattle WA 98104
206 302-6800

(P-25642)
LLP MOSS ADAMS
2040 Main St Ste 900, Irvine (92614-8213)
PHONE...................949 221-4000
Roger Weninger, *Branch Mgr*
Lisa Meirinho, *Admin Asst*
Doug Buurma, *Senior Mgr*
Doris Tan, *Senior Mgr*
William Norris, *Director*
EMP: 50
SALES (corp-wide): 340.5MM **Privately Held**
WEB: www.mossadams.com
SIC: 8721 Certified public accountant
PA: Moss Adams Llp
999 3rd Ave Ste 2800
Seattle WA 98104
206 302-6800

(P-25643)
LLP MOSS ADAMS
4747 Executive Dr # 1300, San Diego (92121-3114)
PHONE...................858 627-1400
Laura Roos, *Partner*
Bruce Knowlton, *Partner*
Eric Rohner, *Partner*
Simone Edwards, *Admin Asst*
Kim Bryant, *Sales Mgr*
EMP: 65
SALES (corp-wide): 340.5MM **Privately Held**
WEB: www.mossadams.com
SIC: 8721 Certified public accountant
PA: Moss Adams Llp
999 3rd Ave Ste 2800
Seattle WA 98104
206 302-6800

(P-25644)
LODGEN LACHER GOLDITCH SARD
16530 Ventura Blvd # 305, Encino (91436-4554)
PHONE...................818 783-0570
Ben Frankel, *Partner*
Patricia Bates, *Partner*
Bernard S Golditch, *Partner*
Dan Howard, *Partner*
Stephen P Lacher, *Partner*
EMP: 50
SQ FT: 12,000
SALES (est): 4.2MM **Privately Held**
WEB: www.fllgsh.com
SIC: 8721 Certified public accountant

(P-25645)
MACIAS GINI & OCONNELL LLP (PA)
3000 S St Ste 300, Sacramento (95816-7014)
PHONE...................916 928-4600
Kenneth A Macias, *Partner*
Ernest Gini, *Partner*
Jim Godsey, *Partner*
Rick Green, *Partner*
Scott Hammon, *Partner*
EMP: 75
SQ FT: 12,000
SALES: 33.4MM **Privately Held**
WEB: www.mgocpa.com
SIC: 8721 Certified public accountant

(P-25646)
MARCUM LLP
303 2nd St Ste 950, San Francisco (94107-1366)
PHONE...................415 543-6900
Jeffrey M Weiner, *Branch Mgr*
EMP: 55
SALES (corp-wide): 212.1MM **Privately Held**
SIC: 8721 Certified public accountant
PA: Marcum Llp
750 3rd Ave Fl 11
New York NY 10017
212 485-5500

(P-25647)
MARCUM LLP
2049 Century Park E # 300, Los Angeles (90067-3105)
PHONE...................310 432-7400
Ron Friedman, *Branch Mgr*
Claudia Herrera, *Office Admin*
Ken Gryske, *Director*
Lori Rock, *Manager*
EMP: 75
SALES (corp-wide): 212.1MM **Privately Held**
SIC: 8721 Accounting services, except auditing
PA: Marcum Llp
750 3rd Ave Fl 11
New York NY 10017
212 485-5500

(P-25648)
MED-DATA INCORPORATED
3741 Douglas Blvd Ste 170, Roseville (95661-4271)
PHONE...................916 771-1362
Bruce Stewart, *Branch Mgr*
Jeff Harper, *CIO*
EMP: 100
SALES (corp-wide): 16.5MM **Privately Held**
SIC: 8721 Accounting services, except auditing
PA: Med-Data, Incorporated
3326 160th Ave Se Ste 440
Bellevue WA 98008
800 261-0048

(P-25649)
MEDAMERICA BILLING SVCS INC (HQ)
Also Called: California Emergency Physician
1601 Cummins Dr Ste D, Modesto (95358-6411)
PHONE...................209 491-7710
Michael F Harrington, *CEO*
Erik Davenport, *Partner*
Jaime Rivas, *Partner*
James V Proffitt, *Officer*
Philip Weiss, *Administration*
EMP: 68
SQ FT: 75,000
SALES (est): 31.5MM
SALES (corp-wide): 500MM **Privately Held**
WEB: www.cep.com
SIC: 8721 Billing & bookkeeping service
PA: Cep America-California
2100 Powell St Ste 920
Emeryville CA 94608
510 350-2700

(P-25650)
MEDEX PRATICE SOLUTIONS INC
4725 Enterprise Way Ste 1, Modesto (95356-8967)
P.O. Box 188, Oakdale (95361-0188)
PHONE...................209 845-1346
Bryan Williamson, *President*
Michael Mc Gann, *Vice Pres*
Robert Jacobs, *Associate*
EMP: 60
SALES (est): 3.2MM **Privately Held**
SIC: 8721 Billing & bookkeeping service

(P-25651)
MSC SERVICE CO
Also Called: Morley Construction
3330 Ocean Park Blvd # 101, Santa Monica (90405-3202)
PHONE...................310 399-1600
Mark Benjamin, *CEO*
Burt Lewitt, *President*
Todd Paris, *CFO*
Jon Sansom, *Marketing Mgr*
EMP: 85
SQ FT: 20,000
SALES (est): 2.8MM
SALES (corp-wide): 168.7MM **Privately Held**
WEB: www.mscservice.com
SIC: 8721 1542 1522 1521 Auditing services; nonresidential construction; residential construction; single-family housing construction

PA: Morley Builders, Inc.
3330 Ocean Park Blvd # 101
Santa Monica CA 90405
310 399-1600

(P-25652)
NOVOGRADAC & COMPANY LLP
246 1st St Ste 500, San Francisco (94105-4699)
PHONE...................415 356-8000
M J Novogradac, *Branch Mgr*
EMP: 50
SALES (corp-wide): 70.8MM **Privately Held**
SIC: 8721 Certified public accountant
PA: Novogradac & Company Llp
1160 Battery St Ste 400e
San Francisco CA 94111
415 356-8000

(P-25653)
OUM & CO LLP (PA)
601 California St # 1800, San Francisco (94108-2823)
PHONE...................415 434-3744
James E Ullakko, *Partner*
Paul Ainslie, *Partner*
Chris S Millias, *Partner*
John Muranishi, *Partner*
Wendy Weiss, *Partner*
EMP: 68 EST: 1976
SQ FT: 7,700
SALES (est): 15.6MM **Privately Held**
WEB: www.oumcpa.com
SIC: 8721 Certified public accountant

(P-25654)
PASADENA BILLING ASSOCIATES
225 S Lake Ave Ste 535, Pasadena (91101-3010)
PHONE...................626 795-6596
Dale W Zeh Jr, *President*
Lauri G Zeh, *Vice Pres*
EMP: 70
SQ FT: 5,000
SALES (est): 3.3MM **Privately Held**
WEB: www.dobilling.com
SIC: 8721 Billing & bookkeeping service

(P-25655)
PAYCHEX INC
9 E River Park Pl E # 210, Fresno (93720-1530)
PHONE...................559 432-1100
Kevin Hardwick, *Branch Mgr*
EMP: 60
SALES (corp-wide): 3.7B **Publicly Held**
WEB: www.paychex.com
SIC: 8721 Payroll accounting service
PA: Paychex, Inc.
911 Panorama Trl S
Rochester NY 14625
585 385-6666

(P-25656)
PAYCHEX INC
2385 Northside Dr Ste 100, San Diego (92108-2716)
PHONE...................858 547-2920
Ed Nunn, *Manager*
EMP: 100
SALES (corp-wide): 3.7B **Publicly Held**
WEB: www.paychex.com
SIC: 8721 8742 7374 Payroll accounting service; management consulting services; data processing & preparation
PA: Paychex, Inc.
911 Panorama Trl S
Rochester NY 14625
585 385-6666

(P-25657)
PAYCHEX INC
1420 Iowa Ave Ste 100, Riverside (92507-0510)
PHONE...................951 682-6100
Karry Zolz, *Manager*
EMP: 50
SALES (corp-wide): 3.7B **Publicly Held**
WEB: www.paychex.com
SIC: 8721 Payroll accounting service
PA: Paychex, Inc.
911 Panorama Trl S
Rochester NY 14625
585 385-6666

(P-25658)
PAYCHEX INC
300 Crprate Pinte Ste 150, Culver City (90230)
PHONE...................310 338-7900
Debbie Woods, *Manager*
Robert Salazar, *Manager*
EMP: 100
SALES (corp-wide): 3.7B **Publicly Held**
WEB: www.paychex.com
SIC: 8721 Payroll accounting service
PA: Paychex, Inc.
911 Panorama Trl S
Rochester NY 14625
585 385-6666

(P-25659)
PERQUEST INC
268 Bush St, San Francisco (94104-3503)
PHONE...................510 740-6300
Thomas Sinton, *President*
Sheldon Perham, *COO*
Cheryl Paterson, *Exec VP*
EMP: 70
SQ FT: 24,000
SALES (est): 2.2MM **Privately Held**
WEB: www.perquest.com
SIC: 8721 Payroll accounting service

(P-25660)
PERRY-SMITH LLP
400 Capitol Mall Ste 1400, Sacramento (95814-4498)
PHONE...................916 441-1000
Gary A Fox, *Managing Prtnr*
David T Becker, *Partner*
Jeffrey A Bertleson, *Partner*
Jeffrey Claire, *Partner*
Sue Cordonnier, *Partner*
EMP: 100
SALES (est): 5.8MM **Privately Held**
WEB: www.perry-smith.com
SIC: 8721 Certified public accountant

(P-25661)
PHYSICIANS CHOICE LLC
21860 Burbank Blvd # 120, Woodland Hills (91367-6477)
P.O. Box 4419 (91365-4419)
PHONE...................818 340-9988
John D Uphold, *President*
Jonathan Sturm, *COO*
Greer Contreras, *Vice Pres*
Clare Nicholson, *Controller*
EMP: 80
SQ FT: 10,000
SALES (est): 6.2MM **Privately Held**
WEB: www.physchoice.com
SIC: 8721 Billing & bookkeeping service

(P-25662)
PRICEWATERHOUSECOOPERS LLP
2020 Main St Ste 400, Irvine (92614-8243)
PHONE...................949 437-5200
Diana Franklin, *Manager*
Jeanine Olson, *Manager*
Lane Straley, *Clerk*
EMP: 260 **Privately Held**
WEB: www.pwcglobal.com
SIC: 8721 Certified public accountant
HQ: Pricewaterhousecoopers Llp
300 Madison Ave Fl 24
New York NY 10017
646 471-4000

(P-25663)
PRICEWATERHOUSECOOPERS LLP
488 Almaden Blvd Ste 1800, San Jose (95110-2768)
PHONE...................408 817-3700
Don McGovern, *Branch Mgr*
Trudy Doucet, *Executive*
Margarita McKinnell, *Managing Dir*
Victoria Huff, *CPA*
Christopher Alabi, *Sr Associate*
EMP: 700 **Privately Held**
WEB: www.pwcglobal.com
SIC: 8721 Certified public accountant
HQ: Pricewaterhousecoopers Llp
300 Madison Ave Fl 24
New York NY 10017
646 471-4000

(P-25664)
PRICEWATERHOUSECOOPERS LLP
5375 Mira Sorrento Pl, San Diego (92121-3809)
PHONE.................................858 677-2400
Christina Nordvall, *Manager*
Mansoor Nazzal, *Auditor*
EMP: 275 **Privately Held**
SIC: 8721 Certified public accountant
HQ: Pricewaterhousecoopers Llp
3200 Madison Ave Fl 24
New York NY 10017
646 471-4000

(P-25665)
PRICEWATERHOUSECOOPERS LLP
400 Capitol Mall Ste 600, Sacramento (95814-4423)
PHONE.................................916 930-8100
Robert Kittredge, *Branch Mgr*
Sandy Acuna, *Administration*
Carrie Schleicher, *Manager*
EMP: 84
SQ FT: 1,000 **Privately Held**
WEB: www.pwcglobal.com
SIC: 8721 Certified public accountant
HQ: Pricewaterhousecoopers Llp
300 Madison Ave Fl 24
New York NY 10017
646 471-4000

(P-25666)
PRICEWATERHOUSECOOPERS LLP
3 Embarcadero Ctr Fl 20, San Francisco (94111-4004)
PHONE.................................415 498-5000
John McCaffery, *Partner*
Steve El Osta, *Associate*
EMP: 275 **Privately Held**
WEB: www.pwcglobal.com
SIC: 8721 Certified public accountant
HQ: Pricewaterhousecoopers Llp
300 Madison Ave Fl 24
New York NY 10017
646 471-4000

(P-25667)
QBI LLC (PA)
Also Called: Qualified Benefits
21031 Ventura Blvd # 1200, Woodland Hills (91364-2229)
PHONE.................................818 594-4900
Nicholas H Stonnington, *Mng Member*
Desiree Fowlks, *Admin Asst*
Matt Furniss, *Sales Staff*
Phuong Jennings, *Sales Staff*
Taylor Johnson, *Sales Staff*
EMP: 90
SALES: 10MM **Privately Held**
SIC: 8721 6411 Payroll accounting service; pension & retirement plan consultants

(P-25668)
RAND MEDICAL BILLING INC
Also Called: Orion - Rand
1633 Erringer Rd Fl 1, Simi Valley (93065-3557)
PHONE.................................805 578-8300
Marvin Retsky, *President*
Patty Artist, *Office Mgr*
EMP: 100
SQ FT: 10,000
SALES (est): 5.5MM
SALES (corp-wide): 76.7MM **Publicly Held**
SIC: 8721 Billing & bookkeeping service
HQ: Orion Healthcorp, Inc.
3200 Wilcrest Dr Ste 550
Houston TX 77042
713 432-1100

(P-25669)
ROSERYAN INC
35473 Dumbarton Ct, Newark (94560-1100)
PHONE.................................510 456-3056
Kathleen M Ryan, *President*
Pat Voll, *Vice Pres*
Stan Fels, *Business Dir*
John Villa, *Administration*
Sophie Yu, *Technical Staff*
EMP: 60

SALES (est): 4.7MM **Privately Held**
WEB: www.roseryan.com
SIC: 8721 Accounting, auditing & bookkeeping

(P-25670)
RSM US LLP
44 Montgomery St Ste 3900, San Francisco (94104-4812)
PHONE.................................415 848-5300
Tim Tiefenthaler, *Managing Prtnr*
Madison Gress Gress, *Technology*
Megan Farrell, *Sr Associate*
Sarah Pang, *Sr Associate*
Katie Schuhow, *Manager*
EMP: 99
SALES (corp-wide): 2.4B **Privately Held**
SIC: 8721 Certified public accountant
PA: Rsm Us Llp
1 S Wacker Dr Ste 800
Chicago IL 60606
312 384-6000

(P-25671)
RSM US LLP
18401 Von Karman Ave # 500, Irvine (92612-1542)
PHONE.................................949 255-6500
Gretchen Valentine, *Managing Prtnr*
Ryan Lemond, *Auditing Mgr*
Marquis Allen, *Business Mgr*
Jon Abee, *Sr Associate*
Victor KAO, *Director*
EMP: 71
SALES (corp-wide): 2.4B **Privately Held**
SIC: 8721 Certified public accountant
PA: Rsm Us Llp
1 S Wacker Dr Ste 800
Chicago IL 60606
312 384-6000

(P-25672)
RSM US LLP
100 W San Fernando St, San Jose (95113-2219)
PHONE.................................408 572-4440
Dennis Young, *Branch Mgr*
EMP: 84
SALES (corp-wide): 2.4B **Privately Held**
SIC: 8721 Certified public accountant
PA: Rsm Us Llp
1 S Wacker Dr Ste 800
Chicago IL 60606
312 384-6000

(P-25673)
SANTA CLARA COUNTY OF
Also Called: Valley Med Ctr Billing Dept
2325 Enborg Ln Fl 4, San Jose (95128-2649)
PHONE.................................408 885-7200
Mary Wells, *Director*
EMP: 150 **Privately Held**
WEB: www.countyairports.org
SIC: 8721 9311 Billing & bookkeeping service; finance, taxation & monetary policy;
PA: County Of Santa Clara
3180 Newberry Dr Ste 150
San Jose CA 95118
408 299-5105

(P-25674)
SANTA CLARA COUNTY OF
Also Called: Santa Clara Vlly Health/Hosptl
751 S Bascom Ave Fl 4, San Jose (95128-2604)
PHONE.................................408 885-7354
Art Gamez, *Branch Mgr*
EMP: 160 **Privately Held**
WEB: www.countyairports.org
SIC: 8721 9431 Billing & bookkeeping service; administration of public health programs;
PA: County Of Santa Clara
3180 Newberry Dr Ste 150
San Jose CA 95118
408 299-5105

(P-25675)
SEILER LLP (PA)
3 Lagoon Dr Ste 400, Redwood City (94065-5157)
P.O. Box 8043 (94063-0943)
PHONE.................................650 365-4646
George Marinos, *Partner*

Mark Berryman, *Partner*
James G B Demartini III, *Partner*
Brian J Dinsmore, *Partner*
Kenneth Everett, *Partner*
EMP: 102
SQ FT: 31,142
SALES (est): 26.1MM **Privately Held**
SIC: 8721 Certified public accountant

(P-25676)
SEILER LLP
220 Montgomery St Ste 300, San Francisco (94104-3436)
PHONE.................................415 392-2123
Brian Jeffs, *Manager*
Arlan Kertz, *Partner*
Amy Miller, *Partner*
Steven Farkas, *Finance Mgr*
Elaine Barham, *Accountant*
EMP: 57
SQ FT: 10,230
SALES (corp-wide): 26.1MM **Privately Held**
SIC: 8721 Accounting services, except auditing
PA: Seiler Llp
3 Lagoon Dr Ste 400
Redwood City CA 94065
650 365-4646

(P-25677)
SEMA INC (PA)
Also Called: Cell Business Equipment
4 Mason Ste A, Irvine (92618-2554)
PHONE.................................949 830-1400
Tarek Abdulhafiz, *President*
Lisa Veltri, *Admin Asst*
Hany Dief, *Project Mgr*
Steve Nixon, *Technology*
Sam Alzreiqi, *Technical Staff*
▲ **EMP:** 94
SQ FT: 18,000
SALES (est): 31.7MM **Privately Held**
WEB: www.kopiers.com
SIC: 8721 5044 Accounting, auditing & bookkeeping; photocopy machines

(P-25678)
SIERRA BOOKKEEPING & TAX SVC
5777 Madison Ave Ste 615, Sacramento (95841-3312)
PHONE.................................916 349-7610
Joannie D Utley, *Principal*
EMP: 60
SALES (est): 1.8MM **Privately Held**
SIC: 8721 Billing & bookkeeping service

(P-25679)
SINGERLEWAK LLP (PA)
10960 Wilshire Blvd, Los Angeles (90024-3702)
PHONE.................................310 477-3924
Jim Pitrat, *Managing Prtnr*
Marc Abrams, *Partner*
David Free, *Partner*
Norman Greenbaum, *Partner*
Janice McKenna, *Partner*
EMP: 120
SQ FT: 24,000
SALES (est): 48.3MM **Privately Held**
WEB: www.singerlewak.com
SIC: 8721 8742 Certified public accountant; business consultant

(P-25680)
SINGERLEWAK LLP
2050 Main St Ste 700, Irvine (92614-8259)
PHONE.................................949 261-8600
David Krajanowski, *Branch Mgr*
EMP: 52
SALES (corp-wide): 48.3MM **Privately Held**
SIC: 8721 8742 Certified public accountant; business consultant
PA: Singerlewak Llp
10960 Wilshire Blvd
Los Angeles CA 90024
310 477-3924

(P-25681)
SINGERLEWAK LLP
21550 Oxnard St Ste 1000, Woodland Hills (91367-7148)
PHONE.................................818 999-3924
Elizabeth Vanderroest, *Branch Mgr*

EMP: 52
SALES (corp-wide): 48.3MM **Privately Held**
SIC: 8721 8742 Certified public accountant; business consultant
PA: Singerlewak Llp
10960 Wilshire Blvd
Los Angeles CA 90024
310 477-3924

(P-25682)
SOREN MCADAM CHRISTIANSON LLP
2068 Orange Tree Ln # 100, Redlands (92374-4555)
P.O. Box 8010 (92375-1210)
PHONE.................................909 798-2222
James L Soren, *Partner*
Gary Christianson, *Partner*
Jason Lewis, *Partner*
Doug McAdam, *Partner*
Douglas R McAdam, *Partner*
EMP: 59
SQ FT: 14,000
SALES (est): 5MM **Privately Held**
WEB: www.smc-cpas.com
SIC: 8721 Certified public accountant

(P-25683)
SQUAR MILNER PETERSON (PA)
Also Called: Squar Milner
18500 Von Karman Ave # 10, Irvine (92612-0504)
PHONE.................................949 222-2999
Steve Milner, *Managing Prtnr*
Scott Burack, *Partner*
Ray Hermanson, *Partner*
Stan Luker, *Partner*
Steve Speier, *Partner*
EMP: 121
SQ FT: 11,500
SALES (est): 42.5MM **Privately Held**
WEB: www.squarmilner.com
SIC: 8721 Certified public accountant; accounting services, except auditing

(P-25684)
SSAE 16 PROFESSIONALS LLP
3419 E Chapman Ave # 334, Orange (92869-3812)
PHONE.................................866 480-9485
Jim Jimenez, *Partner*
John Mason, *Principal*
Gary Pennington, *Principal*
Tim Roncevich, *Principal*
Joe Jimenez, *Director*
EMP: 55
SALES (est): 767K **Privately Held**
SIC: 8721 Certified public accountant

(P-25685)
SURGICAL CARE AFFILIATE
Also Called: TAC Rbo
2450 Venture Oaks Way # 120, Sacramento (95833-3292)
PHONE.................................916 529-4590
EMP: 50 **EST:** 2011
SALES (est): 2.7MM **Privately Held**
SIC: 8721

(P-25686)
TANNER MAINSTAIN BLATT & GLY
10866 Wilshire Blvd Fl 10, Los Angeles (90024-4350)
PHONE.................................310 446-2700
William Tanner, *President*
Steve Blatt, *Vice Pres*
Michael Glynn, *Vice Pres*
Brad Johnson, *Vice Pres*
Elena Chapovsky, *Executive Asst*
EMP: 70
SQ FT: 13,000
SALES: 7MM **Privately Held**
WEB: www.tmbgcpa.com
SIC: 8721 Accounting services, except auditing

(P-25687)
TAXRESOURCES INC (PA)
Also Called: Taxaudit.com
600 Coolidge Dr Ste 300, Folsom (95630-4211)
PHONE.................................877 369-7827

(PA)=Parent Co (HQ)=Headquarters (DH)=Div Headquarters
✪ = New Business established in last 2 years

Mark D Olander, *CEO*
Dave E Du Val, *Vice Pres*
Nancy K Farwell, *Vice Pres*
Jane T Smith, *Vice Pres*
EMP: 120
SQ FT: 3,000
SALES (est): 36MM **Privately Held**
WEB: www.taxaudit.com
SIC: 8721 Certified public accountant

(P-25688)
THE TEAM COMPANIES LLC (PA)
Also Called: Team Services
901 W Alameda Ave Ste 100, Burbank
(91506-2849)
PHONE......................818 558-3261
Justin Kramer, *CEO*
Geoffrey Matus, *Ch of Bd*
An De Vooght, *CFO*
Diane Clarino, *Vice Pres*
Mark Egmon, *Vice Pres*
EMP: 90
SQ FT: 20,000
SALES (est): 1.3B **Privately Held**
WEB: www.teamservices.net
SIC: 8721 Payroll accounting service

(P-25689)
THOMAS WIRIG DOLL & CO CPAS
Also Called: Thomas Doll & Company
165 Lennon Ln Ste 200, Walnut Creek
(94598-2447)
P.O. Box 30307 (94598-9307)
PHONE......................925 939-2500
Brent P Thomas, *President*
Nathan Berrett, *Manager*
Shawn Stifle, *Manager*
EMP: 66
SQ FT: 9,000
SALES (est): 5.6MM **Privately Held**
SIC: 8721 Certified public accountant

(P-25690)
TRI CITY EMERGENCY MED GROUP
5050 Avenida Encinas # 200, Carlsbad
(92008-4383)
P.O. Box 5567, Oceanside (92052-5567)
PHONE......................760 439-1963
Richard P Buruss, *Partner*
Ilene Spector, *Treasurer*
Sue Kruger, *CPA*
Ariana Dillman, *Emerg Med Spec*
EMP: 50
SALES (est): 5.3MM **Privately Held**
SIC: 8721 8011 Billing & bookkeeping
service; physicians' office, including specialists

(P-25691)
US LOAN AUDITORS LLC
7485 Rush Rver Dr Ste 710, Sacramento
(95831)
PHONE......................916 248-8625
Shane Barker, *Mng Member*
EMP: 100 **EST:** 2009
SALES (est): 3.7MM **Privately Held**
SIC: 8721 Accounting, auditing & bookkeeping

(P-25692)
WILLIAMS ADLEY & COMPANY L L P (PA)
7677 Oakport St Ste 1000, Oakland
(94621-1950)
PHONE......................510 893-8114
Robert Griffin, *Partner*
Tom W Williams Jr, *General Ptnr*
Mary Butler, *Partner*
Kola Isiaq, *Partner*
EMP: 80
SQ FT: 6,000
SALES (est): 4.4MM **Privately Held**
SIC: 8721 8742 Certified public accountant; management consulting services

(P-25693)
WINDES INC (PA)
111 W Ocean Blvd Ste 22, Long Beach
(90802-4653)
PHONE......................562 435-1191
John L Dicarlo, *CEO*
James A Cordova, *Partner*
Jim Jimenez, *Partner*

Susan Laputz, *Partner*
Thomas Monaghan, *Partner*
EMP: 100
SQ FT: 26,560
SALES (est): 22.2MM **Privately Held**
WEB: www.windes.com
SIC: 8721 Certified public accountant

8731 Commercial Physical & Biological Research

(P-25694)
ACEA BIOSCIENCES INC
6779 Mesa Ridge Rd # 100, San Diego
(92121-2996)
PHONE......................858 724-0928
Xiao Xu, *President*
Angela Scigliano, *Admin Asst*
Xiaobo Wang, *CTO*
Phil McMullen, *Controller*
Vladi Cherepakhin, *Regl Sales Mgr*
▲ **EMP:** 85
SALES (est): 363K
SALES (corp-wide): 4.9B **Publicly Held**
WEB: www.aceabio.com
SIC: 8731 Medical research, commercial
PA: Agilent Technologies, Inc.
5301 Stevens Creek Blvd
Santa Clara CA 95051
408 345-8886

(P-25695)
ACHATES POWER INC
4060 Sorrento Valley Blvd A, San Diego
(92121-1428)
PHONE......................858 535-9920
David Crompton, *President*
David Johnson, *CEO*
John Koszewnik, *Principal*
Carol Mottershead, *Finance Dir*
Jerome Paye, *Opers Staff*
EMP: 95
SALES (est): 19.3MM **Privately Held**
WEB: www.achatespower.com
SIC: 8731 Commercial physical research

(P-25696)
ACTIVE MOTIF INC (PA)
Also Called: Timelogic
1914 Palomar Oaks Way # 150, Carlsbad
(92008-6509)
PHONE......................760 431-1263
Joseph Fernandez, *CEO*
Theodore Defrank, *President*
Laura Carpenter, *Vice Pres*
Gary Shiels, *Vice Pres*
Steve Stelman, *Info Tech Dir*
EMP: 53
SQ FT: 16,000
SALES (est): 13.2MM **Privately Held**
WEB: www.activemotif.com
SIC: 8731 Biotechnical research, commercial

(P-25697)
ADVANCED CELL DIAGNOSTICS INC
Also Called: Acd
7707 Gateway Blvd Ste 200, Newark
(94560-1268)
PHONE......................510 576-8800
Yuling Luo, *President*
Steve Chen, *COO*
Jessie Qian Wang, *CFO*
Tom Olenic, *Ch Credit Ofcr*
Rob Monroe, *Chief Mktg Ofcr*
EMP: 75
SQ FT: 2,500
SALES (est): 10.3MM
SALES (corp-wide): 714MM **Publicly Held**
WEB: www.genospectra.com
SIC: 8731 2835 Biotechnical research, commercial; microbiology & virology diagnostic products
PA: Bio-Techne Corporation
614 Mckinley Pl Ne
Minneapolis MN 55413
612 379-8854

(P-25698)
ALECTOR LLC (PA)
151 Oyster Point Blvd # 300, South San
Francisco (94080-1841)
PHONE......................415 231-5660
Arnon Rosenthal, *President*
Tillman Gerngross, *Ch of Bd*
Tina Schwabe, *Bd of Directors*
Robert Paul, *Chief Mktg Ofcr*
Sabah Oney, *Vice Pres*
EMP: 61
SALES (est): 27.6MM **Publicly Held**
SIC: 8731 Biotechnical research, commercial

(P-25699)
ALLCELLS LLC
1301 Harbor Bay Pkwy # 200, Alameda
(94502-6528)
PHONE......................510 521-2600
Jie Tong,
Robert Wong, *General Mgr*
John Ng, *Info Tech Mgr*
Erin Kelly, *Development*
Laurie Ho, *Purchasing*
▲ **EMP:** 52
SALES (est): 12.8MM **Privately Held**
WEB: www.allcells.com
SIC: 8731 Biotechnical research, commercial

(P-25700)
ALLIANT TCHSYSTEMS OPRTONS LLC
9401 Corbin Ave, Northridge (91324-2400)
PHONE......................818 887-8195
Ronald Hill, *Principal*
EMP: 400
SALES (est): 126.5MM **Publicly Held**
WEB: www.mrcwdc.com
SIC: 8731 Commercial physical research
HQ: Northrop Grumman Innovation Systems, Inc.
45101 Warp Dr
Dulles VA 20166
703 406-5000

(P-25701)
ALLOGENE THERAPEUTICS INC
210 E Grand Ave, South San Francisco
(94080-4811)
PHONE......................650 457-2700
David Chang, *President*
Arie Belldegrun, *Ch of Bd*
Eric Schmidt, *CFO*
Rafael G Amado, *Chief Mktg Ofcr*
Alison Moore, *CTO*
EMP: 122
SQ FT: 68,000
SALES (est): 3.4MM **Privately Held**
SIC: 8731 2836 Biological research; biological products, except diagnostic

(P-25702)
ALPHA SOURCE INC
10940 Wilshire Blvd Ste 1, Los Angeles
(90024-3915)
PHONE......................424 270-9600
Howard Lewin, *President*
EMP: 50
SQ FT: 40,000
SALES (est): 6.8MM **Privately Held**
WEB: www.alphasource.com
SIC: 8731 Commercial physical research

(P-25703)
ALPHA TEKNOVA INC
2290 Bert Dr, Hollister (95023-2567)
PHONE......................831 637-1100
Thomas Davis, *CEO*
Richard Alan Goozh, *CFO*
Kimberly Gibson, *QC Mgr*
Katie Roye,
Greg Radon, *Manager*
EMP: 75
SQ FT: 34,000
SALES (est): 9.7MM **Privately Held**
WEB: www.teknova.com
SIC: 8731 Biotechnical research, commercial

(P-25704)
ANASPEC INC (HQ)
Also Called: Anaspec Egt Group
34801 Campus Dr, Fremont (94555-3606)
PHONE......................510 791-9560
Philippe Cronet, *President*
Masanobu Sugawara, *President*
Susan Garcia, *Vice Pres*
Anita Hong, *General Mgr*
Lamarr Kelly, *Info Tech Dir*
▲ **EMP:** 50
SALES (est): 14.8MM **Privately Held**
WEB: www.anaspec.com
SIC: 8731 Chemical laboratory, except testing; biotechnical research, commercial

(P-25705)
APPLIED MOLECULAR EVOLUTION (HQ)
10300 Campus Point Dr # 200, San Diego
(92121-1504)
PHONE......................858 597-4990
Thomas Bumol, *President*
EMP: 50
SQ FT: 43,000
SALES (est): 9.1MM
SALES (corp-wide): 24.5B **Publicly Held**
WEB: www.amevolution.com
SIC: 8731 Commercial physical research
PA: Eli Lilly And Company
Lilly Corporate Ctr
Indianapolis IN 46285
317 276-2000

(P-25706)
APPLIED P & CH LABORATORY SOUT
Also Called: APC Lab
13760 Magnolia Ave, Chino (91710-7018)
PHONE......................909 590-1828
Jack Zhang, *President*
Mary Luo, *Corp Secy*
EMP: 60
SQ FT: 30,000
SALES (est): 3.6MM **Privately Held**
WEB: www.apclab.com
SIC: 8731 Environmental research

(P-25707)
APPLIED RESEARCH ASSOC INC
5425 Hollister Ave # 220, Santa Barbara
(93111-3370)
PHONE......................805 962-4810
Joan Rothenberg, *Branch Mgr*
EMP: 61
SALES (corp-wide): 251.9MM **Privately Held**
SIC: 8731 8711 Commercial physical research; consulting engineer
PA: Applied Research Associates, Inc.
4300 San Mateo Blvd Ne
Albuquerque NM 87110
505 883-3636

(P-25708)
AQUATIC SCIENCE CENTER
4911 Central Ave, Richmond (94804-5803)
PHONE......................510 746-7334
Warner Chabot, *Exec Dir*
Jim Kelly, *Exec Dir*
Lorenzo Flores, *Software Dev*
EMP: 50
SALES (est): 1.7MM **Privately Held**
SIC: 8731 Environmental research

(P-25709)
ARAGEN BIOSCIENCE INC
380 Woodview Ave, Morgan Hill
(95037-2823)
PHONE......................408 779-1700
Axel Schleyer, *CEO*
Manmahesh Kantipudi, *Ch of Bd*
Manni Kantipudi, *CEO*
EMP: 50
SALES: 9MM
SALES (corp-wide): 63.9MM **Privately Held**
WEB: www.aragenbio.com
SIC: 8731 Biotechnical research, commercial; medical research, commercial
HQ: Gvk Biosciences Private Limited
1st Floor, Nrm-lv, Plot No.28a,
Hyderabad TS 50007

(P-25710)
ARCUS BIOSCIENCES INC
3928 Point Eden Way, Hayward
(94545-3719)
PHONE..................510 694-6200
Terry Rosen, *Ch of Bd*
Juan Carlos Jaen, *President*
Rekha Hemrajani, *COO*
Eric Hoefer, *Ch Credit Ofcr*
Nigel Walker, *Vice Pres*
EMP: 108
SQ FT: 70,100
SALES: 8.3MM **Privately Held**
SIC: 8731 Biotechnical research, commercial

(P-25711)
ARETE ASSOCIATES (PA)
9301 Corbin Ave Ste 2000, Northridge
(91324-2508)
PHONE..................818 885-2200
David Campion, *Vice Pres*
Christopher Choi, *CFO*
Sallie Di Vincenzo,
Doug Deprospo, *Security Dir*
Yvette Torres, *Office Mgr*
EMP: 125
SQ FT: 170,000
SALES (est): 49.2MM **Privately Held**
WEB: www.arete-dc.com
SIC: 8731 Commercial physical research

(P-25712)
ARIOSA DIAGNOSTICS INC
5945 Optical Ct, San Jose (95138-1400)
PHONE..................408 229-7500
Kenneth Song MD, *CEO*
Dave Mullarkey, *COO*
Thomas Musci MD, *Chief Mktg Ofcr*
Thomas J Musci, *Vice Pres*
Arnold Oliphant, *Security Dir*
EMP: 140
SALES (est): 28.5MM
SALES (corp-wide): 57.2B **Privately Held**
SIC: 8731 Biotechnical research, commercial
HQ: Roche Holdings, Inc.
1 Dna Way
South San Francisco CA 94080
650 225-1000

(P-25713)
ASTERIAS BIOTHERAPEUTICS INC
1010 Atlantic Ave Ste 102, Alameda
(94501-1258)
PHONE..................510 456-3800
Michael H Mulroy, *President*
Jane S Lebkowski, *President*
Katharine E Spink, *COO*
Ryan D Chavez, *CFO*
Stephen Cartt, *Bd of Directors*
EMP: 55
SALES: 4MM **Publicly Held**
SIC: 8731 2836 Biotechnical research, commercial; biological products, except diagnostic
PA: Lineage Cell Therapeutics, Inc.
2173 Salk Ave Ste 200
Carlsbad CA 92008

(P-25714)
ATK SPACE SYSTEMS INC
370 N Halstead St, Pasadena
(91107-3122)
PHONE..................626 351-0205
Joe Tellegrino, *Manager*
EMP: 70 **Publicly Held**
SIC: 8731 3826 8711 Commercial physical research; instruments measuring thermal properties; engineering services
HQ: Atk Space Systems Inc.
11310 Frederick Ave
Beltsville MD 20705
301 595-5500

(P-25715)
AURORA ALGAE INC
3325 Investment Blvd, Hayward
(94545-3808)
PHONE..................510 266-5000
Paul Angelico, *President*
Bill Roeschlein, *CFO*
Lee Covert, *Senior VP*
Matthew Caspari, *Vice Pres*

Guido Radaelli, *Vice Pres*
EMP: 100
SALES (est): 13.6MM **Privately Held**
WEB: www.aurorabiofuels.com
SIC: 8731 Commercial physical research

(P-25716)
AVERY CORP
207 N Goode Ave Fl 6, Glendale
(91203-1364)
PHONE..................626 304-2000
Dean Scarborough, *President*
Camila Clark, *Business Mgr*
EMP: 200
SALES (est): 9.6MM
SALES (corp-wide): 7.1B **Publicly Held**
WEB: www.avery.com
SIC: 8731 Biological research
PA: Avery Dennison Corporation
207 N Goode Ave
Glendale CA 91203
626 304-2000

(P-25717)
AVICENA LLC (PA)
117 E Colo Blvd Ste 510, Pasadena
(91105)
PHONE..................626 344-9665
Sean Brady, *Mng Member*
EMP: 55 EST: 2014
SALES (est): 87.7K **Privately Held**
SIC: 8731 Biotechnical research, commercial

(P-25718)
AVIVA SYSTEMS BIOLOGY CORP (PA)
7700 Ronson Rd Ste 100, San Diego
(92111-1553)
PHONE..................858 552-6979
Lingxun Duan, *President*
Yi-Chun Wang, *COO*
Stephen Hill, *Controller*
Daniel Schwartz, *Manager*
EMP: 55 EST: 2001
SQ FT: 2,600
SALES: 3MM **Privately Held**
WEB: www.avivasysbio.com
SIC: 8731 Biotechnical research, commercial

(P-25719)
AXONICS MODULATION TECH INC
26 Technology Dr, Irvine (92618-2380)
PHONE..................949 396-6322
Raphael Wisniewski, *Ch of Bd*
Danny L Dearen, *President*
Raymond W Cohen, *CEO*
Rinda Sama, *COO*
Karen Noblett, *Chief Mktg Ofcr*
EMP: 72
SQ FT: 25,548
SALES: 707K **Privately Held**
SIC: 8731 Biotechnical research, commercial; commercial physical research; commercial research laboratory

(P-25720)
BIOCEPT INC
5810 Nancy Ridge Dr # 150, San Diego
(92121-2840)
PHONE..................858 320-8200
Michael W Nall, *President*
David F Hale, *Ch of Bd*
Timothy C Kennedy, *CFO*
Lyle J Arnold, *Senior VP*
Michael Terry, *Senior VP*
EMP: 95
SQ FT: 48,000
SALES: 3.2MM **Privately Held**
WEB: www.biocept.com
SIC: 8731 Biotechnical research, commercial

(P-25721)
BIOCLINCA
Also Called: Synarc Reiscdronate
7707 Gateway Blvd Ste 300, Newark
(94560-1160)
PHONE..................503 284-3334
Elfa Griffith, *Director*
EMP: 50

SALES (corp-wide): 56.5MM **Privately Held**
WEB: www.synarc.com
SIC: 8731 Commercial physical research
PA: Bioclinca
7707 Gateway Blvd Fl 3
Newark CA 94560
415 817-8900

(P-25722)
BIOMEDICURE LLC
7940 Silverton Ave # 107, San Diego
(92126-6340)
PHONE..................858 586-1888
Yong Qian,
EMP: 55
SALES: 100K **Privately Held**
SIC: 8731 Biotechnical research, commercial

(P-25723)
BIONETICS CORPORATION
Mercury Consolidated Div
P.O. Box 115, Moffett Field (94035-0115)
PHONE..................650 604-5327
Charles Spectre, *Branch Mgr*
EMP: 50
SALES (corp-wide): 52.2MM **Privately Held**
WEB: www.bionetics.com
SIC: 8731 Commercial research laboratory
PA: The Bionetics Corporation
101 Production Dr Ste 100
Yorktown VA 23693
757 873-0900

(P-25724)
BIOSPACE INC
Also Called: Inbody
13850 Cerritos Corprt Dr C, Cerritos
(90703-2467)
PHONE..................323 932-6503
Ki Chul Cha, *President*
Hak Hee Yun, *CEO*
Calvin Lee, *Regional Mgr*
Daniel Park, *Sales Mgr*
Daniele Ambrose, *Sales Staff*
▲ EMP: 86 EST: 2000
SQ FT: 35,319
SALES (est): 10.8MM **Privately Held**
WEB: www.biospaceamerica.com
SIC: 8731 3821 Energy research; calibration tapes for physical testing machines

(P-25725)
BOEING COMPANY
5753 W Las Positas Blvd, Pleasanton
(94588-4084)
PHONE..................925 398-7664
W James McNerney Jr, *Manager*
EMP: 70
SALES (corp-wide): 101.1B **Publicly Held**
SIC: 8731 8711 3674 3672 Computer (hardware) development; engineering services; semiconductors & related devices; printed circuit boards
PA: The Boeing Company
100 N Riverside Plz
Chicago IL 60606
312 544-2000

(P-25726)
BOLT THREADS INC (PA)
Also Called: Refactored Materials
5858 Horton St Ste 400, Emeryville
(94608-2046)
PHONE..................415 279-5585
Daniel Widmaier, *CEO*
Hitendra Mishra, *Vice Pres*
Julia Walker, *Executive*
Justine Cohen, *Executive Asst*
David Breslauer, *Admin Sec*
EMP: 61
SQ FT: 32,000
SALES (est): 17.6MM **Privately Held**
SIC: 8731 Biotechnical research, commercial

(P-25727)
BPS BIOSCIENCE INC
6042 Cornerstone Ct W B, San Diego
(92121-4746)
PHONE..................858 202-1401
Henry Zhu, *President*
Colin Cowdrey, *General Mgr*

Jill Ruesch, *Administration*
Charlene Chang, *Research*
Kimberly Skuster, *Research*
EMP: 50
SALES (est): 399.2K **Privately Held**
SIC: 8731 Biotechnical research, commercial; biological research

(P-25728)
CALIFORNIA INSTITUTE TECH
360 S Wilson Ave, Pasadena (91106-3268)
PHONE..................626 395-8700
Bill Nunez, *Manager*
EMP: 200
SQ FT: 3,536
SALES (corp-wide): 3.3B **Privately Held**
WEB: www.caltech.edu
SIC: 8731 Biological research
PA: California Institute Of Technology
1200 E California Blvd
Pasadena CA 91125
626 395-6811

(P-25729)
CCINTEGRATION INC (PA)
2060 Corporate Ct, San Jose
(95131-1753)
PHONE..................408 228-1314
Hank C Ta, *President*
Tiffany Wu, *Executive Asst*
Linh Diep, *Technical Staff*
Jared Beckman, *Business Mgr*
Stacey Moore, *Buyer*
EMP: 50
SQ FT: 235,000
SALES (est): 16.2MM **Privately Held**
WEB: www.ccintegration.com
SIC: 8731 7371 Computer (hardware) development; computer software development

(P-25730)
CGI TECHNOLOGIES SOLUTIONS INC
860 Stillwater Rd Ste 210, West Sacramento (95605-1684)
PHONE..................916 281-3200
Aniket Goundaje, *Sr Consultant*
EMP: 50
SALES (corp-wide): 8.8B **Privately Held**
SIC: 8731 Commercial physical research
HQ: Cgi Technologies And Solutions Inc.
11325 Random Hills Rd
Fairfax VA 22030
703 267-8000

(P-25731)
CIR
1745 Celeste Dr, San Mateo (94402-2603)
PHONE..................650 574-6900
Dan Collins, *Owner*
EMP: 105
SQ FT: 13,500
SALES (est): 4.2MM **Privately Held**
WEB: www.cirlabs.com
SIC: 8731 5169 5191 2899 Industrial laboratory, except testing; chemicals & allied products; chemicals, industrial & heavy; pesticides; fertilizer & fertilizer materials; chemical preparations; insecticides & pesticides; phosphatic fertilizers

(P-25732)
COHERUS BIOSCIENCES INC (PA)
333 Twin Dolphin Dr # 600, Redwood City
(94065-1442)
PHONE..................650 649-3530
Dennis M Lanfear, *Ch of Bd*
Vincent Anicetti, *COO*
Jean-Frdric Viret, *CFO*
Alan Herman, *Officer*
Richard Hameister, *Vice Pres*
EMP: 79
SALES: 1.5MM **Publicly Held**
SIC: 8731 2836 Biological research; biological products, except diagnostic

(P-25733)
COLSA CORPORATION
41240 12th St W, Palmdale (93551-1449)
PHONE..................661 273-3859
Tom Berard, *Director*
EMP: 238

PRODUCTS & SVCS

SALES (corp-wide): 336.1MM **Privately Held**
SIC: 8731 Computer (hardware) development
PA: Colsa Corporation
6728 Odyssey Dr Nw
Huntsville AL 35806
256 964-5361

(P-25734)
COMPARENETWORKS INC (PA)
Also Called: Biocompare
395 Oyster Point Blvd # 300, South San Francisco (94080-1931)
PHONE..................................650 873-9031
Brian Cowley, *CEO*
Paul Gatti, *President*
Mike Okimoto, *Officer*
Bo Purtic, *Officer*
Joan Boyce, *Vice Pres*
EMP: 74
SQ FT: 16,152
SALES (est): 9.8MM **Privately Held**
WEB: www.biocompare.com
SIC: 8731 Commercial physical research

(P-25735)
COVANCE INC
10300 Campus Point Dr # 225, San Diego (92121-1515)
PHONE..................................858 352-2300
MO Chaudry, *Manager*
Elizabeth Sarver, *Technician*
Kristi Wade, *Research*
Teresa Lovelace, *Human Resources*
Tricia Cullen, *Recruiter*
EMP: 85 **Publicly Held**
SIC: 8731 Biological research
HQ: Covance Inc.
206 Carnegie Ctr
Princeton NJ 08540
-

(P-25736)
DEPOSITION SCIENCES INC
Also Called: D S I
3300 Coffey Ln, Santa Rosa (95403-1917)
PHONE..................................707 573-6700
Lee Bartolomei, *President*
Thomas Chambers, *Director*
EMP: 96
SQ FT: 8,400
SALES (est): 13.2MM **Publicly Held**
WEB: www.depsci.com
SIC: 8731 3827 Industrial laboratory, except testing; lens coating equipment
PA: Lockheed Martin Corporation
6801 Rockledge Dr
Bethesda MD 20817
-

(P-25737)
DISNEY RESEARCH PITTSBURGH
532 Paula Ave, Glendale (91201-2328)
PHONE..................................412 623-1800
Jessica K Hodgins, *Lab Dir*
EMP: 134
SALES (est): 19.4MM
SALES (corp-wide): 90.2B **Publicly Held**
SIC: 8731 Commercial research laboratory
HQ: Walt Disney Imagineering Research & Development, Inc.
1401 Flower St
Glendale CA 91201
818 544-6500

(P-25738)
DNA TWOPOINTO INC
Also Called: Dna2.0
37950 Central Ct Ste C, Newark (94560-3464)
PHONE..................................650 853-8347
Jeremy Minshull, *CEO*
Sridhar Govindarajan, *Vice Pres*
Claes Gustafsson, *Vice Pres*
Jon Ness, *Vice Pres*
Colleen V Ende, *Admin Asst*
▼ **EMP:** 68
SQ FT: 40,000
SALES (est): 17MM **Privately Held**
WEB: www.dna20.com
SIC: 8731 Biotechnical research, commercial

(P-25739)
DSM BIOMEDICAL INC
Also Called: Polymer Technology Group, The
2810 7th St, Berkeley (94710-2703)
PHONE..................................510 841-8800
Christophe Dardel, *CEO*
EMP: 120
SQ FT: 55,000
SALES (est): 22.7MM
SALES (corp-wide): 10.6B **Privately Held**
WEB: www.polymertech.com
SIC: 8731 2836 Commercial physical research; biological products, except diagnostic
PA: Koninklijke Dsm N.V.
Het Overloon 1
Heerlen 6411
455 788-111

(P-25740)
E-SCEPTRE INC
16800 Gale Ave, City of Industry (91745-1804)
PHONE..................................888 350-8989
Stephen Liu, *President*
Steven Liu, *CEO*
Richard Gallegos, *Exec VP*
EMP: 60
SQ FT: 80,000
SALES (est): 4.2MM **Privately Held**
SIC: 8731 Computer (hardware) development
PA: Sceptre Industries Inc
16800 Gale Ave
City Of Industry CA 91745

(P-25741)
ELAN DRUG DELIVERY INC
Also Called: Elan Drug Technologies
180 Oyster Point Blvd, South San Francisco (94080-1909)
PHONE..................................770 531-8100
David Czekai, *President*
James L Botkin, *Senior VP*
Gary Liversidge, *CTO*
Brock Hostetler, *Financial Analy*
Earvin Liang, *Director*
EMP: 52
SALES (est): 2.5MM **Privately Held**
SIC: 8731 4215 Medical research, commercial; courier services, except by air
PA: Alkermes Public Limited Company
Connacht House
Dublin D04 C

(P-25742)
ELECTRIC POWER RES INST INC (PA)
3420 Hillview Ave, Palo Alto (94304-1382)
P.O. Box 10412 (94303-0813)
PHONE..................................650 855-2000
Michael Howard, *CEO*
Patricia L Kampling, *Ch of Bd*
Gil C Quiniones, *Ch of Bd*
Terry Boston, *President*
Patricia Vincent-Collawn, *Vice Ch Bd*
EMP: 600
SQ FT: 300,000
SALES: 416.6MM **Privately Held**
WEB: www.epri.com
SIC: 8731 Energy research

(P-25743)
EMERALD CLOUD LAB INC
844 Dubuque Ave, South San Francisco (94080-1804)
PHONE..................................650 257-7554
Daniel Jerome Kleinbaum, *Co-CEO*
Brian Frezza, *Co-CEO*
Micah Merrick, *Vice Pres*
EMP: 60 EST: 2009
SALES (est): 3.7MM **Privately Held**
SIC: 8731 Biotechnical research, commercial

(P-25744)
EMERGENT TRAVEL HEALTH INC
3985 Sorrento Valley Blvd A, San Diego (92121-1421)
PHONE..................................858 450-9595
Paul Shabram, *Principal*
EMP: 50

SALES (corp-wide): 782.4MM **Publicly Held**
SIC: 8731 Biotechnical research, commercial
HQ: Emergent Travel Health Inc.
555 Twin Dolphin Dr # 360
Redwood City CA 94065
-

(P-25745)
ENERGY INNOVATIONS INC
130 W Union St, Pasadena (91103-3628)
PHONE..................................626 585-6900
Joseph Budano, *CEO*
Bill Gross, *President*
Marcia Goodstein, *COO*
Greg Chrisney, *CFO*
▲ **EMP:** 200
SALES (est): 13MM **Privately Held**
WEB: www.energyinnovations.com
SIC: 8731 Commercial physical research

(P-25746)
ENVIRONMENTAL SCIENCE ASSOC (PA)
Also Called: ESA
550 Kearny St Ste 800, San Francisco (94108-2512)
PHONE..................................415 896-5900
Leslie Moulton, *President*
Gary Oates, *Senior VP*
EMP: 65
SQ FT: 20,000
SALES: 80K **Privately Held**
WEB: www.esassoc.com
SIC: 8731 8748 Environmental research; environmental consultant

(P-25747)
ENVIRONMENTAL SCIENCE ASSOC
Also Called: Envrionmental Science Assoc
80 S Lake Ave Ste 570, Pasadena (91101-2597)
PHONE..................................626 204-6170
EMP: 284
SALES (corp-wide): 80K **Privately Held**
SIC: 8731 Environmental research
PA: Environmental Science Associates
550 Kearny St Ste 800
San Francisco CA 94108
415 896-5900

(P-25748)
EPITOMICS INC (HQ)
863 Mitten Rd Ste 103, Burlingame (94010-1311)
PHONE..................................650 583-6688
Guo-Liang Yu, *Ch of Bd*
Zhiqiang An, *Officer*
Brad S Lee, *Exec VP*
Taiying Chen, *Vice Pres*
Weimin Zhu, *Vice Pres*
EMP: 55
SALES (est): 13.1MM
SALES (corp-wide): 312.7MM **Privately Held**
WEB: www.epitomics.com
SIC: 8731 Biotechnical research, commercial
PA: Abcam Plc
Discovery Drive
Cambridge CAMBS CB2 0
122 369-6000

(P-25749)
EUROFINS FOOD
Covance Food Solutions
2441 Constitution Dr, Livermore (94551-7573)
PHONE..................................609 452-4440
EMP: 3572
SALES (corp-wide): 75.3MM **Privately Held**
SIC: 8731 Commercial physical research
PA: Eurofins Food Chemistry Testing Us, Inc.
3301 Kinsman Blvd
Madison WI 53704
717 656-2300

(P-25750)
FERRING RESEARCH INSTITUTE INC
4245 Sorrento Valley Blvd, San Diego (92121-1408)
PHONE..................................858 657-1400
Pierre Riviere, *President*
Robert Meadows, *IT/INT Sup*
Jeremiah Joseph, *Research*
EMP: 65
SQ FT: 30,000
SALES (est): 10.1MM
SALES (corp-wide): 1.1B **Privately Held**
SIC: 8731 Biotechnical research, commercial
HQ: Ferring Pharmaceuticals Sa
Chemin De La Vergognausaz 50
Saint-Prex VD
583 010-000

(P-25751)
FIT ELECTRONICS INC (HQ)
Also Called: Foxconn Electronics
500 S Kraemer Blvd # 100, Brea (92821-6728)
PHONE..................................714 988-9388
Mike Unger, *President*
Ralph Gillespie, *CEO*
Florence Wang, *Office Mgr*
Moises De La Cruz, *Sr Software Eng*
Erwin Fei, *Info Tech Dir*
EMP: 133 EST: 1997
SALES (est): 35.6MM **Privately Held**
SIC: 8731 5065 Electronic research; electronic parts

(P-25752)
FUJITSU LABORATORIES AMER INC (DH)
1240 E Arques Ave 345, Sunnyvale (94085-5401)
PHONE..................................408 530-4500
Hiromu Hayashi, *President*
Nobuaki Kawato, *Exec VP*
Hitoshi Matsumoto, *VP Bus Dvlpt*
Masami Yamamoto, *Principal*
Winnie Tsou, *Director*
EMP: 80
SALES (est): 650MM **Privately Held**
WEB: www.fujitsulabs.com
SIC: 8731 Commercial physical research

(P-25753)
GENEOHM SCIENCES INC
11085 N Torrey Pines Rd # 210, La Jolla (92037-1015)
PHONE..................................201 847-5824
Peter Klemm, *President*
Jamie Condy, *President*
EMP: 150
SQ FT: 22,000
SALES (est): 6.1MM
SALES (corp-wide): 15.9B **Publicly Held**
WEB: www.geneohm.com
SIC: 8731 Commercial physical research
PA: Becton, Dickinson And Company
1 Becton Dr
Franklin Lakes NJ 07417
201 847-6800

(P-25754)
GENERAL ATOMICS (HQ)
3550 General Atomics Ct, San Diego (92121-1194)
P.O. Box 85608 (92186-5608)
PHONE..................................858 455-2810
J Neal Blue, *President*
Liam Kelly, *CFO*
Penelope Gladden, *Treasurer*
Anthony Navarra, *Treasurer*
Frank Pace, *Exec VP*
▲ **EMP:** 2015 EST: 1955
SQ FT: 1,000,000
SALES (est): 1.3B **Privately Held**
WEB: www.generalatomics.com
SIC: 8731 Energy research

(P-25755)
GENERAL ATOMICS
16969 Mesamint St, San Diego (92127-2407)
PHONE..................................858 676-7100
Anthony Navarra, *Vice Pres*
Leslie Williams, *Technical Staff*
EMP: 99 **Privately Held**

WEB: www.generalatomics.com
SIC: 8731 Commercial physical research
HQ: General Atomics
    3550 General Atomics Ct
    San Diego CA 92121
    858 455-2810

(P-25756)
GENERAL ATOMICS
Also Called: General Atomics Energy Pdts
4949 Greencraig Ln, San Diego
(92123-1675)
PHONE..........................858 455-4000
Joel Ennis, *General Mgr*
Claudio Pereida, *President*
Stevieann Nance, *Executive Asst*
Emelie Galace, *Admin Asst*
Ke Zeng, *Info Tech Mgr*
EMP: 170 Privately Held
WEB: www.generalatomics.com
SIC: 8731 7371 3823 Commercial physi-
    cal research; custom computer program-
    ming services; industrial instrmnts msrmnt
    display/control process variable
HQ: General Atomics
    3550 General Atomics Ct
    San Diego CA 92121
    858 455-2810

(P-25757)
GENTEX CORPORATION
Also Called: Western Operations
9859 7th St, Rancho Cucamonga
(91730-5244)
PHONE..........................909 481-7667
Robert McCay, *Branch Mgr*
David Downs, *Engineer*
Mark Jenkins, *Engineer*
Martha Leon, *Marketing Staff*
EMP: 90
SALES (corp-wide): 143.3MM Privately
Held
WEB: www.gentex.net
SIC: 8731 3845 3841 Commercial re-
    search laboratory; biological research;
    electromedical equipment; surgical &
    medical instruments
PA: Gentex Corporation
    324 Main St
    Simpson PA 18407
    570 282-3550

(P-25758)
HELIX HOLDINGS I LLC
1 Circle Star Way Fl 2, San Carlos
(94070-6234)
PHONE..........................415 805-3360
Robin Thurston, *CEO*
EMP: 100
SALES (est): 1.3MM Privately Held
SIC: 8731 Biological research

(P-25759)
HELIX OPCO LLC
1 Circle Star Way Fl 2, San Carlos
(94070-6234)
PHONE..........................415 805-3360
Robin Thurston, *CEO*
Nicole Washington, *Manager*
EMP: 169
SQ FT: 103,948
SALES: 2MM Privately Held
SIC: 8731 Biological research

(P-25760)
HII FLEET SUPPORT GROUP
LLC
9444 Balboa Ave Ste 400, San Diego
(92123-4378)
PHONE..........................858 522-6319
Michelle Wurl, *Director*
Linda Davenport, *Vice Pres*
EMP: 289 Publicly Held
SIC: 8731 8711 Commercial physical re-
    search; engineering services
HQ: Hii Fleet Support Group Llc
    5701 Cleveland St
    Virginia Beach VA 23462
    757 463-6666

(P-25761)
HMCLAUSE INC
Also Called: Harris Moran
9241 Mace Blvd, Davis (95618-9614)
PHONE..........................530 747-3235
Lincoln Moehle, *Manager*

EMP: 80
SALES (corp-wide): 194.4MM Privately
Held
WEB: www.harrismoran.com
SIC: 8731 Agricultural research
HQ: Hm.Clause, Inc.
    260 Cousteau Pl Ste 210
    Davis CA 95618
    800 320-4672

(P-25762)
HOWARD HUGHES MEDICAL
INST
Also Called: H H M I
279 Campus Dr Rm B202, Stanford
(94305-5101)
PHONE..........................650 725-8252
EMP: 100
SALES (corp-wide): 2.3B Privately Held
SIC: 8731 6732
PA: Howard Hughes Medical Institute Inc
    4000 Jones Bridge Rd
    Chevy Chase MD 20815
    301 215-8500

(P-25763)
HOWARD HUGHES MEDICAL
INST
1550 4th St Rm 190, San Francisco
(94143-2324)
PHONE..........................415 476-9668
John Flickinger, *Branch Mgr*
Teresa Tucker, *Admin Asst*
EMP: 120
SALES (corp-wide): 1.3B Privately Held
SIC: 8731 Biological research
PA: Howard Hughes Medical Institute Inc
    4000 Jones Bridge Rd
    Chevy Chase MD 20815
    301 215-8500

(P-25764)
IBIS BIOSCIENCES INC
2251 Faraday Ave Ste 150, Carlsbad
(92008-7209)
PHONE..........................760 476-3200
Andrea Wainer, *CEO*
Jayme Laforte, *Administration*
Lee Ann Paaton, *Administration*
EMP: 120
SALES (est): 15.3MM
SALES (corp-wide): 30.5B Publicly Held
SIC: 8731 Biological research
PA: Abbott Laboratories
    100 Abbott Park Rd
    Abbott Park IL 60064
    224 667-6100

(P-25765)
IMPACT ASSESSMENT INC
2166 Avenida De La Playa F, La Jolla
(92037-3238)
PHONE..........................858 459-0142
John S Petterson, *President*
Mario Amanzio, *Business Anlyst*
Jeff Sanchez, *Director*
Deanna Rossi, *Manager*
EMP: 60 EST: 1981
SQ FT: 1,700
SALES (est): 5.6MM Privately Held
WEB: www.impactassessment.net
SIC: 8731 Environmental research; com-
    mercial research laboratory

(P-25766)
INCLIN INC
2655 Campus Dr Ste 100, San Mateo
(94403-2520)
PHONE..........................650 961-3422
Taylor Kilfoil, *CEO*
Dirk Thye, *CEO*
Tony Pantuso, *COO*
Arnold Wong, *CFO*
Anita Das, *Vice Pres*
EMP: 75
SQ FT: 9,800
SALES (est): 8.8MM Privately Held
SIC: 8731 Biotechnical research, commer-
    cial

(P-25767)
INOVA DIAGNOSTICS INC (HQ)
9900 Old Grove Rd, San Diego
(92131-1638)
PHONE..........................858 586-9900
Roger Ingles, *CEO*

Pere Solagagles, *CFO*
Ronda Elliott, *Vice Pres*
Bryan Hoenig, *Vice Pres*
Patricia Swartwood, *Vice Pres*
▲ EMP: 285
SQ FT: 81,000
SALES (est): 75.5MM
SALES (corp-wide): 115.1MM Privately
Held
WEB: www.inovadx.com
SIC: 8731 2835 Medical research, com-
    mercial; in vitro diagnostics
PA: Werfenlife Sa.
    Plaza Europa, 21 - 23
    L'hospitalet De Llobregat 08908
    934 010-444

(P-25768)
INTARCIA THERAPEUTICS INC
Also Called: Hayward Manufacturing
24650 Industrial Blvd, Hayward
(94545-2234)
PHONE..........................510 782-7800
Kurt Graves, *CEO*
Ved Srivastava, *Vice Pres*
Sunita Zalani, *Vice Pres*
Javier Montes, *Associate Dir*
Catherine Scolieri, *Associate Dir*
EMP: 68
SALES (corp-wide): 19.4MM Privately
Held
SIC: 8731 Biotechnical research, commer-
    cial
PA: Intarcia Therapeutics, Inc.
    1 Marina Park Dr Ste 13
    Boston MA 02210
    617 936-2500

(P-25769)
INTERNATIONAL BUS MCHS
CORP
Also Called: IBM
650 Harry Rd, San Jose (95120-6001)
PHONE..........................408 927-1080
Mark Dean, *Vice Pres*
Jim Modak, *Info Tech Dir*
Jeannette Garcia, *Research*
Aaron Carlson, *Opers Staff*
Charles Gonsalves, *Director*
EMP: 500
SALES (corp-wide): 79.5B Publicly Held
WEB: www.ibm.com
SIC: 8731 Commercial research laboratory
PA: International Business Machines Cor-
    poration
    1 New Orchard Rd Ste 1 # 1
    Armonk NY 10504
    914 499-1900

(P-25770)
ISOTIS ORTHOBIOLOGICS INC
2 Goodyear Ste A, Irvine (92618-2052)
PHONE..........................949 595-8710
Keith Valentine, *CEO*
Peter J Arduini, *President*
Andre Verwei, *CFO*
Christian S Schade, *Exec VP*
Nancy Toledo, *Principal*
EMP: 150
SALES (est): 17.8MM Privately Held
SIC: 8731 5047 Biological research; surgi-
    cal equipment & supplies
HQ: Isotis International Sarl
    C/O Fidulem Sa
    Lausanne VD 1005
    216 206-000

(P-25771)
JANSSEN ALZHEIMER
IMMUNOTHERA
700 Gateway Blvd, South San Francisco
(94080-7020)
PHONE..........................650 794-2500
Dr Stefaan Heylen, *President*
Nadine De Leeuw, *Manager*
EMP: 100
SALES (est): 5.6MM
SALES (corp-wide): 81.5B Publicly Held
SIC: 8731 Commercial physical research
HQ: Janssen Research & Development, Llc
    920 Us Highway 202
    Raritan NJ 08869
    908 704-4000

(P-25772)
KAPL INC
1126 N Brookhurst St, Anaheim
(92801-1702)
PHONE..........................714 991-9543
EMP: 254 Privately Held
SIC: 8731 Energy research
PA: Kapl, Inc.
    2401 River Rd
    Schenectady NY 12309

(P-25773)
KIOXIA AMERICA INC
35 Iron Point Cir Ste 100, Folsom
(95630-8588)
PHONE..........................916 986-4707
Robert Reed, *Branch Mgr*
EMP: 50 Privately Held
SIC: 8731 Electronic research
HQ: Kioxia America, Inc.
    2610 Orchard Pkwy
    San Jose CA 95134
    408 526-2400

(P-25774)
KITE PHARMA INC (HQ)
2400 Broadway Ste 100, Santa Monica
(90404-3058)
PHONE..........................310 824-9999
Christi Shaw, *CEO*
Robin L Washington, *President*
Richard L Wang, *CEO*
Devvon Hinds, *Ch Credit Ofcr*
David Chang, *Exec VP*
EMP: 148
SQ FT: 20,000
SALES (est): 22.1MM
SALES (corp-wide): 22.1B Publicly Held
SIC: 8731 2836 Commercial physical re-
    search; biological products, except diag-
    nostic
PA: Gilead Sciences, Inc.
    333 Lakeside Dr
    Foster City CA 94404
    650 574-3000

(P-25775)
L3 APPLIED TECHNOLOGIES
INC
2700 Merced St, San Leandro
(94577-5602)
PHONE..........................510 577-7100
Janet Luna, *Director*
EMP: 109
SALES (corp-wide): 6.8B Publicly Held
SIC: 8731 Commercial physical research
HQ: L3 Applied Technologies, Inc.
    10180 Barnes Canyon Rd
    San Diego CA 92121
    858 404-7824

(P-25776)
LA JOLLA PHARMACEUTICAL
CO (PA)
4550 Towne Centre Ct, San Diego
(92121-1900)
PHONE..........................858 207-4264
George F Tidmarsh, *President*
Kevin C Tang, *Ch of Bd*
Jennifer A Carver, *COO*
Dennis M Mulroy, *CFO*
Darryl Wellinghoff, *Ch Credit Ofcr*
EMP: 130
SQ FT: 83,008
SALES: 10MM Publicly Held
WEB: www.ljpc.com
SIC: 8731 2834 Biotechnical research,
    commercial; pharmaceutical preparations

(P-25777)
LAB-GISTICS LLC
885 Pacific Ave, San Jose (95126-4821)
PHONE..........................650 309-2627
Minh Phan,
EMP: 200
SQ FT: 60,000
SALES: 25MM Privately Held
SIC: 8731 Computer (hardware) develop-
    ment

(P-25778)
LABCYTE INC (DH)
Also Called: Echo
170 Rose Orchard Way # 200, San Jose
(95134-1374)
PHONE...................408 747-2000
Mark F Colbrie, *President*
Richard Ellson, *Officer*
Mathew Bramwell, *Vice Pres*
Michael F Miller, *Vice Pres*
Nick Samaras, *Managing Dir*
EMP: 74
SQ FT: 19,200
SALES (est): 31MM
SALES (corp-wide): 19.8B **Publicly Held**
WEB: www.labcyte.com
SIC: 8731 Commercial physical research
HQ: Beckman Coulter, Inc.
250 S Kraemer Blvd
Brea CA 92821
714 993-5321

(P-25779)
LEIDOS INC
Also Called: Reveal Imaging
2985 Scott St, Vista (92081-8339)
PHONE...................858 826-9090
John Jumper, *CEO*
Marcus Edwards, *Engineer*
Linda Nguyen, *Accountant*
EMP: 130
SALES (corp-wide): 10.1B **Publicly Held**
WEB: www.saic.com
SIC: 8731 3829 3826 Commercial physical research; measuring & controlling devices; analytical instruments
HQ: Leidos, Inc.
11951 Freedom Dr Ste 500
Reston VA 20190
571 526-6000

(P-25780)
LEIDOS INC
4035 Hancock St, San Diego (92110-5105)
PHONE...................858 826-5552
Diane Malito, *Branch Mgr*
EMP: 377
SALES (corp-wide): 10.1B **Publicly Held**
WEB: www.saic.com
SIC: 8731 Commercial physical research
HQ: Leidos, Inc.
11951 Freedom Dr Ste 500
Reston VA 20190
571 526-6000

(P-25781)
LEIDOS INC
1874 S Pacific Coast Hwy, Redondo Beach
(90277-6117)
PHONE...................310 791-9671
Alexander Preston, *Branch Mgr*
EMP: 82
SALES (corp-wide): 10.1B **Publicly Held**
WEB: www.saic.com
SIC: 8731 Commercial physical research
HQ: Leidos, Inc.
11951 Freedom Dr Ste 500
Reston VA 20190
571 526-6000

(P-25782)
LEIDOS INC
9455 Towne Centre Dr # 200, San Diego
(92121-3079)
PHONE...................858 535-4499
Jim Taylor, *Manager*
John Jumper, *CEO*
EMP: 112
SALES (corp-wide): 10.1B **Publicly Held**
WEB: www.saic.com
SIC: 8731 Commercial physical research
HQ: Leidos, Inc.
11951 Freedom Dr Ste 500
Reston VA 20190
571 526-6000

(P-25783)
LEIDOS INC
Also Called: Saic
10260 Campus Point Dr C, San Diego
(92121-1522)
PHONE...................703 676-4300
Jere Drummond, *Director*
Neal Collins, *Vice Pres*
Ed George, *Vice Pres*
Diane S Graham, *Vice Pres*

Jim Holt, *Vice Pres*
EMP: 148
SALES (corp-wide): 10.1B **Publicly Held**
SIC: 8731 Commercial physical research
HQ: Leidos, Inc.
11951 Freedom Dr Ste 500
Reston VA 20190
571 526-6000

(P-25784)
LEIDOS INC
4161 Campus Point Ct, San Diego
(92121-1513)
PHONE...................858 826-9416
Paul Chang, *Manager*
Roger Krone, *CEO*
EMP: 208
SALES (corp-wide): 10.1B **Publicly Held**
WEB: www.saic.com
SIC: 8731 Commercial physical research
HQ: Leidos, Inc.
11951 Freedom Dr Ste 500
Reston VA 20190
571 526-6000

(P-25785)
LEIDOS INC
Saic
590 W Central Ave Ste I, Brea
(92821-3019)
PHONE...................714 257-6400
Fax: 714 257-9886
EMP: 93
SALES (corp-wide): 7B **Publicly Held**
SIC: 8731
HQ: Leidos, Inc.
11951 Freedom Dr Ste 500
Reston VA 20190
571 526-6000

(P-25786)
LEIDOS INC
300 N Pacific Coast Hwy, El Segundo
(90245-4472)
PHONE...................310 524-3134
Ronald Graves, *Manager*
EMP: 182
SALES (corp-wide): 10.1B **Publicly Held**
WEB: www.saic.com
SIC: 8731 Commercial physical research
HQ: Leidos, Inc.
11951 Freedom Dr Ste 500
Reston VA 20190
571 526-6000

(P-25787)
LEIDOS INC
10740 Thornmint Rd, San Diego
(92127-2700)
PHONE...................858 826-6616
Sarita Ambris, *Branch Mgr*
EMP: 93
SALES (corp-wide): 10.1B **Publicly Held**
WEB: www.saic.com
SIC: 8731 Commercial physical research
HQ: Leidos, Inc.
11951 Freedom Dr Ste 500
Reston VA 20190
571 526-6000

(P-25788)
LEIDOS INC
2000 Powell St Ste 1090, Emeryville
(94608-1780)
PHONE...................510 428-2550
EMP: 93
SALES (corp-wide): 10.1B **Publicly Held**
WEB: www.saic.com
SIC: 8731 Commercial physical research; energy research; environmental research; medical research, commercial
HQ: Leidos, Inc.
11951 Freedom Dr Ste 500
Reston VA 20190
571 526-6000

(P-25789)
LEIDOS INC
1299 Prospect St, La Jolla (92037-3623)
PHONE...................858 826-6000
EMP: 350
SALES (corp-wide): 10.1B **Publicly Held**
WEB: www.saic.com
SIC: 8731 Commercial physical research

HQ: Leidos, Inc.
11951 Freedom Dr Ste 500
Reston VA 20190
571 526-6000

(P-25790)
LEIDOS INC
Also Called: National Security
4065 Hancock St, San Diego (92110-5151)
PHONE...................858 826-6000
Gordon Saakamodo, *Manager*
EMP: 93
SALES (corp-wide): 10.1B **Publicly Held**
WEB: www.saic.com
SIC: 8731 Commercial physical research; energy research; environmental research; medical research, commercial
HQ: Leidos, Inc.
11951 Freedom Dr Ste 500
Reston VA 20190
571 526-6000

(P-25791)
LEIDOS INC
10010 Campus Point Dr, San Diego
(92121-1518)
PHONE...................858 826-7129
Joel Colbourn, *Branch Mgr*
EMP: 241
SQ FT: 64,800
SALES (corp-wide): 10.1B **Publicly Held**
WEB: www.saic.com
SIC: 8731 Energy research; environmental research; medical research, commercial
HQ: Leidos, Inc.
11951 Freedom Dr Ste 500
Reston VA 20190
571 526-6000

(P-25792)
LEIDOS INC
Also Called: Saic
505 14th St Ste 900, Oakland
(94612-1468)
PHONE...................510 466-7138
April Pierson, *Manager*
EMP: 93
SALES (corp-wide): 10.1B **Publicly Held**
SIC: 8731 Commercial physical research
HQ: Leidos, Inc.
11951 Freedom Dr Ste 500
Reston VA 20190
571 526-6000

(P-25793)
LEIDOS INC
N Depo Rd Bldg 4530, Fort Irwin (92310)
PHONE...................910 574-4597
Cassidy Smith, *Manager*
EMP: 93
SALES (corp-wide): 10.1B **Publicly Held**
SIC: 8731 Commercial physical research
HQ: Leidos, Inc.
11951 Freedom Dr Ste 500
Reston VA 20190
571 526-6000

(P-25794)
LEIDOS ENGRG & SCIENCES LLC
1330 30th St Ste A, San Diego
(92154-3471)
PHONE...................619 542-3130
Karen Parizeau, *Manager*
James Sleeth, *Principal*
EMP: 95
SALES (corp-wide): 10.1B **Publicly Held**
SIC: 8731 Natural resource research
HQ: Leidos Engineering & Sciences, Llc
700 N Frederick Ave
Gaithersburg MD 20879
301 240-7000

(P-25795)
LIGHTWAVES 2020 INC
1323 Great Mall Dr, Milpitas (95035-8013)
PHONE...................408 503-8888
J J Pan, *Ch of Bd*
Jewel Chang, *Principal*
EMP: 50
SALES (est): 6.2MM **Privately Held**
WEB: www.lightwaves2020.com
SIC: 8731 Electronic research

(P-25796)
MEMBRANE TECHNOLOGY & RES INC
Also Called: M T R
39630 Eureka Dr, Newark (94560-4805)
PHONE...................650 328-2228
Colin Bailey, *Chairman*
Hans Wijmans, *President*
Nicolas Wynn, *COO*
Meryl Rains, *CFO*
Janet Farrant, *Exec VP*
◆ **EMP:** 70
SQ FT: 60,000
SALES (est): 14.5MM **Privately Held**
WEB: www.mtrinc.com
SIC: 8731 3823 Commercial research laboratory; on-stream gas/liquid analysis instruments, industrial

(P-25797)
MEMORIAL HEALTHTEC LABRATORIES
9920 Talbert Ave, Fountain Valley
(92708-5153)
PHONE...................714 962-4677
Marcia Manker, *Manager*
Lori Debold, *Med Doctor*
Kevin Tauris, *Director*
EMP: 875
SALES (corp-wide): 2.4B **Privately Held**
SIC: 8731 Commercial physical research
HQ: Memorial Healthtec Labratories Inc
2865 Atlantic Ave Ste 203
Long Beach CA 90806

(P-25798)
MERCEDES-BENZ RE
4031 Via Oro Ave, Long Beach
(90810-1458)
PHONE...................310 547-6086
John Espeleta, *Branch Mgr*
EMP: 50
SALES (corp-wide): 191.6B **Privately Held**
SIC: 8731 Commercial physical research
HQ: Mercedes-Benz Research & Development North America, Inc.
309 N Pastoria Ave
Sunnyvale CA 94085

(P-25799)
MICROCONSTANTS INC
9050 Camino Santa Fe, San Diego
(92121-3203)
PHONE...................858 652-4600
Gilbert Lam, *President*
Jose Buenviaje, *Vice Pres*
Moira Brown, *Info Tech Mgr*
Fatuma Yusuf, *Technician*
Cynthia Gomez, *Project Mgr*
EMP: 50
SQ FT: 34,000
SALES (est): 8.3MM **Privately Held**
SIC: 8731 Biotechnical research, commercial

(P-25800)
MIDWEST ENVIROMENTAL CONTROL
22430 13th St, Santa Clarita (91321-1104)
PHONE...................661 255-0722
Dale Brouhl, *Owner*
EMP: 50
SALES (est): 1.8MM **Privately Held**
SIC: 8731 Environmental research

(P-25801)
MOTECH AMERICAS LLC
Also Called: GE Energy
1300 Valley Vista Dr # 207, Diamond Bar
(91765-3940)
PHONE...................302 451-7500
Peng Heng Chang, *CEO*
Eric Kuo, *President*
Dr Alan Wu, *President*
EMP: 320
SALES (est): 23.8MM **Privately Held**
SIC: 8731 3674 Energy research; solar cells
PA: Motech Industries Inc.
6f, 248, Pei Shen Rd., Sec. 3,
New Taipei City TAP 22204

(P-25802)
NATIONAL MARINE FISHERIES SVC
Also Called: Southwest Fsheries Science Ctr
8604 La Jolla Shores Dr, La Jolla
(92037-1508)
PHONE.................................858 546-7081
William W Fox, *Director*
Anne Allen, *Admin Asst*
Pamela G Jones, *Manager*
EMP: 150 **Publicly Held**
SIC: 8731 9512 Biological research; land, mineral & wildlife conservation;
HQ: Western Pacific Regional Fishery Management Council
1315 E West Hwy
Silver Spring MD 20910
-

(P-25803)
NEUROPACE INC
455 Bernardo Ave, Mountain View
(94043-5237)
PHONE.................................650 237-2700
Michael Favet, *CEO*
Frank Fischer, *Ch of Bd*
Rebecca Kuhn, *CFO*
Isabella Abati, *Vice Pres*
Debra Smolley, *Vice Pres*
EMP: 90
SQ FT: 37,500
SALES (est): 19.5MM **Privately Held**
WEB: www.neuropace.com
SIC: 8731 Medical research, commercial

(P-25804)
NORTHROP GRUMMAN INNOVATION
9401 Corbin Ave, Northridge (91324-2400)
PHONE.................................818 887-8100
Bill J Zimmer, *Principal*
Cesar Dominguez, *Design Engr*
Mercle Gomez, *Electrical Engi*
David Goren, *Engineer*
EMP: 100 **Publicly Held**
WEB: www.mrcwdc.com
SIC: 8731 Commercial physical research
HQ: Northrop Grumman Innovation Systems, Inc.
45101 Warp Dr
Dulles VA 20166
703 406-5000

(P-25805)
NORTHROP GRUMMAN SYSTEMS CORP
1 Rancho Carmel Dr, San Diego (92128)
PHONE.................................858 592-3000
Rudy Lozano, *Manager*
Ed Radford, *Executive*
Jerry Wheeler, *Admin Asst*
Covey Darin, *Planning*
Majid Azimi, *Design Engr*
EMP: 1300
SQ FT: 211,000 **Publicly Held**
WEB: www.trw.com
SIC: 8731 8711 7373 3812 Commercial physical research; engineering services; computer integrated systems design; search & navigation equipment
HQ: Northrop Grumman Systems Corporation
2980 Fairview Park Dr
Falls Church VA 22042
703 280-2900

(P-25806)
ORBITAL SCIENCES CORPORATION
Also Called: Space Systems Division
2401 E El Segundo Blvd # 200, El Segundo
(90245-4631)
PHONE.................................703 406-5000
Antonio Elias, *Exec VP*
EMP: 500 **Publicly Held**
SIC: 8731 Commercial physical research
HQ: Orbital Sciences Corporation
45101 Warp Dr
Dulles VA 20166
703 406-5000

(P-25807)
OSTENDO TECHNOLOGIES INC (PA)
6185 Paseo Del Norte # 200, Carlsbad
(92011-1152)
PHONE.................................760 710-3003
Hussein S El-Ghoroury, *CEO*
Joaquin Silva, *President*
Dale A McNeill, *Admin Sec*
Armagan Ergun, *Engineer*
Yh Lee, *Engineer*
EMP: 52
SQ FT: 10,000
SALES (est): 24.5MM **Privately Held**
WEB: www.ostendotech.com
SIC: 8731 Electronic research

(P-25808)
PALL FORTEBIO LLC
47661 Fremont Blvd, Fremont
(94538-6577)
PHONE.................................650 322-1360
Joseph D Keegan, *CEO*
Jack H Fuchs, *CFO*
Danfeng Yao, *Research*
Bob Bragg, *Materials Mgr*
David Pennington, *Sales Staff*
EMP: 94
SALES (est): 17.9MM
SALES (corp-wide): 19.8B **Publicly Held**
WEB: www.fortebio.com
SIC: 8731 Biotechnical research, commercial; biological research
HQ: Pall Corporation
25 Harbor Park Dr
Port Washington NY 11050
516 484-5400

(P-25809)
PALO ALTO MEDICAL FOUNDATION
Research Institute
795 El Camino Real, Palo Alto
(94301-2302)
PHONE.................................650 326-8120
EMP: 50
SALES (corp-wide): 12.7B **Privately Held**
SIC: 8731 Medical research, commercial
HQ: Palo Alto Medical Foundation For Health Care, Research And Education (Inc)
795 El Camino Real
Palo Alto CA 94301
650 321-4121

(P-25810)
PALO ALTO RESEARCH CENTER INC
Also Called: Parc
3333 Coyote Hill Rd, Palo Alto
(94304-1314)
PHONE.................................650 812-4000
Tolga Kurtoglu, *CEO*
Mark Bernstein, *President*
John Knights, *President*
John Pauksta, *CFO*
Jonathan R Wolter, *CFO*
EMP: 250
SQ FT: 200,000
SALES (est): 46.4MM
SALES (corp-wide): 405.1MM **Publicly Held**
WEB: www.parc.com
SIC: 8731 Medical research, commercial
HQ: Xerox Corporation
201 Merritt 7
Norwalk CT 06851
203 968-3000

(P-25811)
PANASONIC CORP NORTH AMERICA
Panasonic Research & Dev
10900 N Tantau Ave 200, Cupertino
(95014-0713)
PHONE.................................408 861-3900
Thomas Eccleston, *Branch Mgr*
Carlos Melos, *Sales Staff*
Michael Stelts, *Director*
EMP: 140 **Privately Held**
SIC: 8731 Electronic research

HQ: Panasonic Corporation Of North America
2 Riverfront Plz Ste 200
Newark NJ 07102
201 348-7000

(P-25812)
PAREXEL INTERNATIONAL CORP
1560 E Chevy Chase Dr # 140, Glendale
(91206-4105)
PHONE.................................818 254-7076
Mollie Barrett, *Director*
Stephanie Mendez, *Admin Asst*
Simon Soden, *Info Tech Mgr*
Veronica Gonzalez, *Research*
Anish Vora, *Analyst*
EMP: 200
SALES (corp-wide): 2.4B **Privately Held**
SIC: 8731 Medical research, commercial
HQ: Parexel International Corporation
8 Federal St
Billerica MA 01821
781 487-9900

(P-25813)
PERLEGEN SCIENCES INC
35473 Dumbarton Ct, Newark
(94560-1100)
PHONE.................................650 625-4500
Bradley Margus, *President*
Stephen Fodor, *Ch of Bd*
William W Sims, *CFO*
David R Cox MD, *Officer*
Mark McCamish MD, *Officer*
EMP: 102
SQ FT: 58,000
SALES (est): 5.5MM **Privately Held**
WEB: www.perlegen.com
SIC: 8731 8071 Biotechnical research, commercial; medical laboratories

(P-25814)
PETER H MATTSON & CO INC
343 Hatch Dr, Foster City (94404-1162)
PHONE.................................650 356-2500
Steve Gundrum, *President*
Peter H Mattson, *Chairman*
Patricia Mattson, *Corp Secy*
Barbara Stuckey, *Officer*
Carol Borba, *Vice Pres*
EMP: 70
SQ FT: 20,000
SALES (est): 11.2MM **Privately Held**
WEB: www.prototothink.com
SIC: 8731 Food research

(P-25815)
PHYSICAL OPTICS CORPORATION (PA)
1845 W 205th St, Torrance (90501-1510)
PHONE.................................310 320-3088
Joanna Jannson, *CEO*
Min-Yi Shih, *President*
Gordon Drew, *CFO*
Tomasz Jannson, *Senior VP*
Gajendra Savant, *Senior VP*
◆ **EMP:** 80
SQ FT: 45,000
SALES (est): 82.4MM **Privately Held**
WEB: www.poc.com
SIC: 8731 7299 Commercial research laboratory; information services, consumer

(P-25816)
POLYPEPTIDE LABS SAN DIEGO LLC
9395 Cabot Dr, San Diego (92126-4310)
PHONE.................................858 408-0808
Timothy Culberth,
Christopher Buckley, *Marketing Staff*
Bernadette Scano, *Marketing Staff*
Jon Rasmussen, *Director*
Trishul Shah, *Director*
EMP: 72
SQ FT: 43,000
SALES: 14MM **Privately Held**
WEB: www.neomps.com
SIC: 8731 2834 2833 Biotechnical research, commercial; pharmaceutical preparations; medicinals & botanicals
HQ: Polypeptide Laboratories Inc.
365 Maple Ave
Torrance CA 90503

(P-25817)
PROMAB BIOTECHNOLOGIES INC
2600 Hilltop Dr, San Pablo (94806-1971)
PHONE.................................510 860-4615
Lijun Wu, *President*
Vita Golubovskaya, *Business Dir*
EMP: 80 **EST:** 2001
SALES (est): 2MM **Privately Held**
SIC: 8731 Biotechnical research, commercial

(P-25818)
PROSCIENTO INC
855 Third Ave Ste 3340, Chula Vista
(91911-1350)
PHONE.................................619 427-1300
Marcus Hompesch, *CEO*
Brian Mooney, *COO*
Linda Morrow, *COO*
Markus Hofmann, *CFO*
Christian Weyer, *Officer*
EMP: 170
SQ FT: 20,000
SALES (est): 32.2MM **Privately Held**
WEB: www.profilinstitute.com
SIC: 8731 Biotechnical research, commercial

(P-25819)
PULSE BIOSCIENCES INC
3957 Point Eden Way, Hayward
(94545-3720)
PHONE.................................510 906-4600
Darrin R Uecker, *President*
Robert W Duggan, *Ch of Bd*
Brian B Dow, *CFO*
Kenneth Clark, *Bd of Directors*
Thomas Fogarty, *Bd of Directors*
EMP: 54
SQ FT: 15,700
SALES (est): 10.9MM **Privately Held**
SIC: 8731 Biotechnical research, commercial

(P-25820)
PULSE-LINK INC
2730 Loker Ave W, Carlsbad (92010-6603)
PHONE.................................760 448-4690
John Santhoff, *CEO*
Paul Dillon, *President*
Bruce Watkins, *President*
Scott Davis, *Info Tech Mgr*
Rusty Cashman, *Engineer*
EMP: 75
SQ FT: 33,000
SALES (est): 5.7MM **Privately Held**
WEB: www.pulselink.net
SIC: 8731 Electronic research

(P-25821)
RAVEN BIOTECHNOLOGIES INC
1 Corporate Dr, South San Francisco
(94080-7043)
PHONE.................................650 624-2600
George Schreiner, *CEO*
Michael Kranda, *Ch of Bd*
John B Whelan, *COO*
William R Rohn, *Vice Ch Bd*
Lucille W S Chang, *Vice Pres*
EMP: 66
SQ FT: 68,000
SALES (est): 5.7MM
SALES (corp-wide): 60.1MM **Publicly Held**
WEB: www.ravenbio.com
SIC: 8731 Biotechnical research, commercial; commercial research laboratory
PA: Macrogenics, Inc.
9704 Medical Center Dr
Rockville MD 20850
301 251-5172

(P-25822)
REVOLUTION MEDICINES INC (PA)
700 Saginaw Dr, Redwood City
(94063-4752)
PHONE.................................650 481-6801
Mark Goldsmith, *President*
Stephen Kelsey, *President*
Ryan Martins, *CFO*
Xiaolin Wang, *Senior VP*
Jeff Jasper, *Vice Pres*
EMP: 52

(PA)=Parent Co (HQ)=Headquarters (DH)=Div Headquarters
✪ = New Business established in last 2 years
2019 Directory of California
Wholesalers and Services Companies
1091

P R O D U C T S   &   S V C S

SQ FT: 40,000
SALES (est): 11.2MM **Privately Held**
SIC: 8731 Biotechnical research, commercial

(P-25823)
RIPPLE FOODS PBC
901 Gilman St Ste A, Berkeley
(94710-1467)
PHONE..............................510 269-2563
Adam Lowry, *CEO*
Steve Orcutt, *CFO*
Holly Beatrice, *Office Mgr*
Jolene Mattson, *Engineer*
Amanda Leong, *Controller*
EMP: 82
SQ FT: 10,000
SALES (est): 516.2K **Privately Held**
SIC: 8731 Food research

(P-25824)
RXSIGHT INC
100 Columbia Ste 120, Aliso Viejo
(92656-4114)
PHONE..............................949 521-7830
Ron Kurtz, *President*
Jack Kavanaugh, *Ch of Bd*
Ilya Goldshleger, *President*
Gordon H Busenbark, *CFO*
Eric Weinberg, *Ch Credit Ofcr*
▼ **EMP:** 50
SQ FT: 3,150
SALES (est): 2.3MM **Privately Held**
SIC: 8731 Medical research, commercial

(P-25825)
SAMSUNG RESEARCH
AMERICA INC (DH)
Also Called: Sisa
665 Clyde Ave, Mountain View
(94043-2235)
PHONE..............................408 544-5700
Young Joon Gil, *President*
Doochan Daniel Eum, *CEO*
Oh-Hyun Kwon, *CEO*
K E Jang, *CFO*
Ju-Hwa Yoon, *CFO*
EMP: 50
SQ FT: 32,000
SALES (est): 65.1MM **Privately Held**
WEB: www.cnl-samsung.com
SIC: 8731 7371 Computer (hardware) development; computer software development & applications
HQ: Samsung Electronics America, Inc.
85 Challenger Rd Fl 7
Ridgefield Park NJ 07660
201 229-4000

(P-25826)
SANGAMO THERAPEUTICS INC
(PA)
501 Canal Blvd, Richmond (94804-3559)
PHONE..............................510 970-6000
Alexander D Macrae, *President*
Stephane Boissel, *CFO*
Sung Lee, *CFO*
Stephen Dilly, *Bd of Directors*
Steven Mento, *Bd of Directors*
EMP: 103
SQ FT: 45,600
SALES: 84.4MM **Publicly Held**
WEB: www.sangamo.com
SIC: 8731 Biotechnical research, commercial

(P-25827)
SANSA TECHNOLOGY LLC
6990 Village Pkwy, Dublin (94568-2438)
PHONE..............................866 204-3710
EMP: 50
SALES (est): 2.6MM **Privately Held**
SIC: 8731

(P-25828)
SCIENTIFIC APPLICATIONS &
RES (PA)
Also Called: Sara
6300 Gateway Dr, Cypress (90630-4844)
PHONE..............................714 828-1465
Parviz Parhami, *CEO*
James Wes, *President*
Bill Bickford, *Administration*
Stephen Wilcox, *Software Engr*
Mark Walker, *Design Engr*

EMP: 58
SQ FT: 43,000
SALES: 26MM **Privately Held**
WEB: www.sarainc.com
SIC: 8731 Commercial physical research

(P-25829)
SCRIPPS HEALTH
Scripps Health Research
10666 N Torrey Pines Rd, La Jolla
(92037-1027)
PHONE..............................858 652-5504
Robert Sarnoff, *Branch Mgr*
Richard Neale, *Vice Pres*
EMP: 188
SALES (corp-wide): 2.1B **Privately Held**
SIC: 8731 Medical research, commercial
PA: Scripps Health
10140 Campus Point Dr Ax415
San Diego CA 92121
800 727-4777

(P-25830)
SEMINIS INC
500 Lucy Brown Rd, San Juan Bautista
(95045-9713)
PHONE..............................831 623-4554
Nancy Bergamini, *Manager*
EMP: 60
SALES (corp-wide): 45.3B **Privately Held**
WEB: www.seminis.com
SIC: 8731 Agricultural research
HQ: Seminis, Inc.
2700 Camino Del Sol
Oxnard CA 93030
-

(P-25831)
SEMINIS INC (DH)
2700 Camino Del Sol, Oxnard
(93030-7967)
PHONE..............................805 485-7317
Bruno Ferrari, *President*
Eugenio N Solorzano, *President*
Charles E Green, *Senior VP*
Oscar J Velasco, *Senior VP*
Enrique Lopez, *Vice Pres*
◆ **EMP:** 300
SALES (est): 88.2MM
SALES (corp-wide): 45.3B **Privately Held**
WEB: www.seminis.com
SIC: 8731 8742 2099 Agricultural research; food research; productivity improvement consultant; marketing consulting services; food preparations
HQ: Monsanto Company
800 N Lindbergh Blvd
Saint Louis MO 63167
314 694-1000

(P-25832)
SENOMYX INC
4767 Nexus Center Dr, San Diego
(92121-3051)
PHONE..............................858 646-8300
John Poyhonen, *President*
David Humphrey, *CFO*
Catherine C Lee, *Senior VP*
Sharon Wicker, *Senior VP*
Susan R Melody, *Vice Pres*
EMP: 59
SQ FT: 65,000
SALES: 29.3MM
SALES (corp-wide): 3.7B **Privately Held**
WEB: www.senomyx.com
SIC: 8731 6794 Food research; franchises, selling or licensing
HQ: Firmenich Incorporated
250 Plainsboro Rd
Plainsboro NJ 08536
609 452-1000

(P-25833)
SEQUENOM INC (HQ)
3595 John Hopkins Ct, San Diego
(92121-1121)
PHONE..............................858 202-9000
Dirk Van Den Boom, *President*
Carolyn D Beaver, *CFO*
Daniel S Grosu, *Chief Mktg Ofcr*
Mathias Ehrich, *Officer*
Jeffrey D Linton, *Senior VP*
EMP: 80
SALES (est): 128.2MM **Publicly Held**
WEB: www.sequenom.com
SIC: 8731 Biological research

(P-25834)
SIMBOL INC
Also Called: Simbol Materials
6920 Koll Center Pkwy # 216, Pleasanton
(94566-3156)
PHONE..............................925 226-7400
Luka Erceg, *President*
EMP: 75
SALES (est): 16.4MM **Privately Held**
SIC: 8731 Natural resource research

(P-25835)
SONY BIOTECHNOLOGY INC
1730 N 1st St Fl 2, San Jose (95112-4642)
PHONE..............................408 352-4257
James Graziadei, *CEO*
EMP: 50 **EST:** 2014
SALES (est): 875.4K **Privately Held**
SIC: 8731 Biotechnical research, commercial

(P-25836)
SORRENTO THERAPEUTICS
INC (PA)
4955 Directors Pl, San Diego (92121-3836)
PHONE..............................858 203-4100
Henry Ji, *Ch of Bd*
Jeff Oster, *Partner*
Jiong Shao, *CFO*
Jerome Zeldis, *Chief Mktg Ofcr*
George K Ng, *Officer*
EMP: 132 **EST:** 2006
SQ FT: 43,000
SALES: 21.1MM **Publicly Held**
SIC: 8731 Biotechnical research, commercial; biological research

(P-25837)
SPREADTRUM CMMNCATIONS
USA INC
10180 Telesis Ct Ste 500, San Diego
(92121-2787)
PHONE..............................858 546-0895
Daniel LI, *CFO*
Kang Yi, *President*
Robert Mix, *Technology*
James Cheng, *Senior Mgr*
Alan Lewis, *Director*
EMP: 70 **EST:** 2008
SALES (est): 11.6MM
SALES (corp-wide): 220.2K **Privately Held**
WEB: www.spreadtrum.com
SIC: 8731 Electronic research
HQ: Spreadtrum Communications (Shanghai) Co., Ltd.
Building 1, Exhibition Center, No.2288,
Zuchongzhi Road, China (
Shanghai 20120
212 036-0600

(P-25838)
STELLARTECH RESEARCH
CORP (PA)
560 Cottonwood Dr, Milpitas (95035-7403)
PHONE..............................408 331-3134
Roger A Stern, *President*
Jerome Jackson, *Vice Pres*
Jerry Smith, *Vice Pres*
Vincent Sullivan, *Vice Pres*
Charlie Truong, *Engineer*
EMP: 100
SQ FT: 20,000
SALES (est): 30.3MM **Privately Held**
SIC: 8731 3842 Medical research, commercial; surgical appliances & supplies

(P-25839)
SUN INNOVATIONS INC
43241 Osgood Rd, Fremont (94539-5657)
PHONE..............................510 573-3913
Ted Sun, *President*
George Donna, *Sales Dir*
EMP: 50
SQ FT: 2,200
SALES (est): 2.8MM **Privately Held**
WEB: www.superimaging.com
SIC: 8731 Commercial physical research

(P-25840)
SUN PHARMACEUTICALS INC
Also Called: Research
13718 Sorbonne Ct, San Diego
(92128-4760)
PHONE..............................858 380-8865

Meng Sun, *President*
Zuolin Zhu, *CTO*
EMP: 102
SALES (est): 2.7MM **Privately Held**
SIC: 8731 Biotechnical research, commercial

(P-25841)
SUNSYSTEM TECHNOLOGY LLC
(PA)
2731 Citrus Rd Ste D, Rancho Cordova
(95742-6303)
PHONE..............................916 671-3351
Kurtis Bank, *President*
Greg Sellers, *Vice Pres*
Mehrall Saidi, *VP Finance*
Mark Santos, *Sales Staff*
Gerard Auer, *Director*
EMP: 61 **EST:** 2014
SALES (est): 41.6MM **Privately Held**
SIC: 8731 Commercial physical research

(P-25842)
SYNTERACT INC (DH)
Also Called: Synteracthcr
5909 Sea Otter Pl Ste 100, Carlsbad
(92010-6674)
PHONE..............................760 268-8200
Ellen Morgan, *President*
Karl Deonanan, *CFO*
Keith Kelson, *CFO*
Richard Paul, *Chief Mktg Ofcr*
Russ Holmes, *Exec VP*
EMP: 330
SQ FT: 30,000
SALES (est): 63.1MM
SALES (corp-wide): 64.3MM **Privately Held**
WEB: www.synteract.com
SIC: 8731 Medical research, commercial
HQ: Synteracthcr Corporation
5909 Sea Otter Pl Ste 100
Carlsbad CA 92010
760 268-8200

(P-25843)
SYNTERACTHCR
CORPORATION (HQ)
5909 Sea Otter Pl Ste 100, Carlsbad
(92010-6674)
PHONE..............................760 268-8200
Steve Powell, *CEO*
Keith Kelson, *CFO*
Cheryl Murphy, *Senior VP*
Martine Dehlinger-Kremer, *Vice Pres*
Tyler Schulenberg, *Vice Pres*
EMP: 330
SALES (est): 64.3MM **Privately Held**
SIC: 8731 Commercial physical research
PA: Synteracthcr Holdings Corporation
5909 Sea Otter Pl Ste 100
Carlsbad CA 92010
760 268-8200

(P-25844)
SYNTERACTHCR HOLDINGS
CORP (PA)
5909 Sea Otter Pl Ste 100, Carlsbad
(92010-6674)
PHONE..............................760 268-8200
Steve Powell, *CEO*
Keith Kelson, *CFO*
Frank Santoro, *Chief Mktg Ofcr*
Stewart Bieler, *Officer*
Rudolph Franziska, *Controller*
EMP: 350 **EST:** 2008
SALES (est): 64.3MM **Privately Held**
SIC: 8731 Commercial physical research

(P-25845)
SYNTHETIC GENOMICS INC
(DH)
11149 N Torrey Pines Rd, La Jolla
(92037-1009)
PHONE..............................858 754-2900
Oliver Fetzer, *CEO*
Aristides Patrinos, *President*
Joseph Mahler, *CFO*
Hamilton O Smith, *Security Dir*
James Flatt, *CTO*
EMP: 123
SQ FT: 45,000

SALES (est): 48MM
SALES (corp-wide): 4.9B **Privately Held**
WEB: www.syntheticgenomics.com
SIC: 8731 Biotechnical research, commercial
HQ: Genting Plantations Berhad
10th Floor Wisma Genting
Kuala Lumpur KLP 50250
323 336-408

(P-25846)
TAE TECHNOLOGIES INC (PA)
19631 Pauling, Foothill Ranch
(92610-2607)
P.O. Box 7010, Rcho STA Marg (92688-7010)
PHONE.................................949 830-2117
Michl Binderbauer, *CEO*
Mark J Lewis, *President*
Kurt Knapp, *Design Engr*
Mark Rouillard, *Design Engr*
Bill Thornton, *Design Engr*
EMP: 155
SALES (est): 50.3MM **Privately Held**
SIC: 8731 Energy research

(P-25847)
TAKARA BIO USA INC
Also Called: Clontech
1290 Terra Bella Ave, Mountain View
(94043-1837)
PHONE.................................650 919-7300
Carol Lou, *President*
Leslee McLennan Bonino, *Vice Pres*
Don Henricksen, *Associate Dir*
Michelle Moreno, *Executive Asst*
Joe Antona, *Administration*
EMP: 175
SQ FT: 100,000
SALES: 95.6MM **Privately Held**
WEB: www.clontech.com
SIC: 8731 2836 Biotechnical research, commercial; biological products, except diagnostic
HQ: Takara Bio Inc.
7-4-38, Nojihigashi
Kusatsu SGA 525-0

(P-25848)
TANVEX BIOPHARMA USA INC (PA)
Also Called: L J B
10394 Pacific Center Ct, San Diego
(92121-4340)
PHONE.................................858 210-4100
Allen Chao, *CEO*
CHI-Chuan Chen, *President*
Kohlton Bickford, *Administration*
Weiming Cheng, *Engineer*
Lily Yuan, *Asst Controller*
EMP: 81 **EST:** 2011
SALES (est): 30MM **Privately Held**
SIC: 8731 Biotechnical research, commercial

(P-25849)
TEGILE SYSTEMS INC
7999 Gateway Blvd Ste 120, Newark
(94560-1144)
PHONE.................................510 791-7900
Rohit Kshetrapal, *CEO*
Tim Lewis, *Partner*
Renato Maranon, *President*
James Yu, *President*
Ian Edmundson, *CFO*
EMP: 130
SQ FT: 6,500
SALES (est): 27.2MM **Privately Held**
SIC: 8731 3572 Computer (hardware) development; computer storage devices

(P-25850)
TELEDYNE SCENTIFIC IMAGING LLC
5212 Verdugo Way, Camarillo
(93012-8662)
PHONE.................................805 373-4979
James Beletic, *President*
EMP: 150
SQ FT: 54,295
SALES (corp-wide): 2.9B **Publicly Held**
SIC: 8731 Commercial physical research

HQ: Teledyne Scientific & Imaging, Llc
1049 Camino Dos Rios
Thousand Oaks CA 91360

(P-25851)
TELEDYNE SCENTIFIC IMAGING LLC (HQ)
Also Called: Teledyne Scientific Company
1049 Camino Dos Rios, Thousand Oaks
(91360-2362)
PHONE.................................805 373-4545
Robert Mehrabian, *CEO*
James Beletic, *President*
Berinder Brar, *President*
Aldo Pichelli, *President*
Roxanne Austin, *Bd of Directors*
EMP: 125
SQ FT: 161,000
SALES (est): 78MM
SALES (corp-wide): 2.9B **Publicly Held**
WEB: www.teledyne-si.com
SIC: 8731 8732 8733 Commercial physical research; commercial nonphysical research; noncommercial research organizations
PA: Teledyne Technologies Inc
1049 Camino Dos Rios
Thousand Oaks CA 91360
805 373-4545

(P-25852)
THE EXECUTIVE OFFICE OF
Also Called: Governors Office Plg & RES
1400 10th St Rm 100, Sacramento
(95814-5502)
PHONE.................................916 322-2318
Sean Walsh, *Director*
EMP: 80 **Privately Held**
SIC: 8731 9111 Environmental research; governors' offices;
HQ: Executive Office Of The State Of California
Governors Ofc
Sacramento CA 95814

(P-25853)
TRANSPHORM INC (PA)
115 Castilian Dr, Goleta (93117-3025)
PHONE.................................805 456-1300
Umesh Mishra, *CEO*
Primit Parikh, *COO*
Heber Clement, *Vice Pres*
Guang Wu, *Software Dev*
Ron Birkhahn, *Technology*
EMP: 53
SQ FT: 3,000
SALES (est): 9.2MM **Privately Held**
SIC: 8731 3674 Commercial physical research; semiconductors & related devices

(P-25854)
TRILINK BIOTECHNOLOGIES LLC
10770 Wtridge Cir Ste 200, San Diego
(92121)
PHONE.................................800 863-6801
Richard Hogrefe, *President*
Terry Beck, *Senior VP*
Carlo Alivia, *Purchasing*
Jennifer Bartels, *Prdtn Mgr*
Craig Dobbs, *VP Mktg*
EMP: 159
SQ FT: 40,000
SALES (est): 14.3MM **Privately Held**
WEB: www.trilinkbiotech.com
SIC: 8731 8748 Biotechnical research, commercial; biological research; test development & evaluation service

(P-25855)
TRUESDAIL LABORATORIES INC
3337 Michelson Dr, Irvine (92612-1699)
PHONE.................................714 730-6239
Ed Wilson, *CEO*
John Hill, *President*
Brian K Service, *Chairman*
Francis Rocha, *Info Tech Mgr*
Javier Robles, *Business Mgr*
EMP: 50 **EST:** 1931
SQ FT: 40,000

SALES: 4.8MM **Privately Held**
WEB: www.truesdail.com
SIC: 8731 8734 1711 Commercial physical research; water testing laboratory; plumbing contractors

(P-25856)
TWIST BIOSCIENCE CORPORATION
455 Mssion Bay Blvd S S 5, San Francisco
(94158)
PHONE.................................800 719-0671
Emily M Leproust, *Ch of Bd*
William Banyai, *COO*
James M Thorburn, *CFO*
Martin Kunz, *Senior VP*
Patrick Weiss, *Vice Pres*
EMP: 221
SQ FT: 13,000
SALES: 25.4MM **Privately Held**
SIC: 8731 Biotechnical research, commercial

(P-25857)
UNITED STATES DEPT OF ENERGY
1 Cyclotron Rd, Berkeley (94720-8099)
PHONE.................................510 486-4936
Fax: 510 486-7192
EMP: 2351 **Publicly Held**
SIC: 8731
HQ: United States Dept Of Energy
1000 Independence Ave Sw
Washington DC 20585
202 586-5000

(P-25858)
UNITED STATES DEPT OF ENERGY
Also Called: Lawrence Livermore Nat Lab
7000 East Ave, Livermore (94550-9698)
P.O. Box 808 (94551-0808)
PHONE.................................925 422-1100
Fax: 925 423-3597
EMP: 7000 **Publicly Held**
SIC: 8731 9611
HQ: United States Dept Of Energy
1000 Independence Ave Sw
Washington DC 20585
202 586-5000

(P-25859)
UNITED STATES DEPT OF NAVY
Also Called: Naval Research
937 N Harbor Dr, San Diego (92132-5001)
PHONE.................................619 532-1897
Erickson Gary, *Branch Mgr*
EMP: 50 **Publicly Held**
SIC: 8731 9711 Commercial physical research; Navy;
HQ: United States Department Of The Navy
1200 Navy Pentagon
Washington DC 20350

(P-25860)
UNITED STATES DEPT OF NAVY
Also Called: Naval Research Lab
7 Grace Hopper Ave Stop 2, Monterey
(93943-5598)
PHONE.................................831 656-4613
Phillip Merilees, *Branch Mgr*
EMP: 64 **Publicly Held**
SIC: 8731 9711 Commercial physical research; Navy;
HQ: United States Department Of The Navy
1200 Navy Pentagon
Washington DC 20350

(P-25861)
UNITY BIOTECHNOLOGY INC
3280 Byshore Blvd Ste 100, Brisbane
(94005)
PHONE.................................650 416-1192
Keith R Leonard Jr, *Ch of Bd*
Nathaniel E David, *President*
Robert C Goeltz II, *CFO*
Jamie Dananberg, *Chief Mktg Ofcr*
Daniel G Marquess, *Security Dir*
EMP: 106
SQ FT: 39,000
SALES (est): 1.6MM **Privately Held**
SIC: 8731 Medical research, commercial

(P-25862)
UNIVERSITY CALIFORNIA IRVINE
Also Called: Henry Samueli School Engrg
2220 Engineering Gateway, Irvine
(92697-0001)
PHONE.................................949 824-2819
Dr GP LI, *Director*
Gonzalo Navajas, *Professor*
EMP: 55 **Privately Held**
SIC: 8731 8221 9411 Electronic research; university; administration of educational programs;
HQ: University Of California, Irvine
510 Aldrich Hall
Irvine CA 92697
949 824-8343

(P-25863)
UNIVERSITY SOUTHERN CALIFORNIA
1000 S Fremont Ave Unit 7, Alhambra
(91803-8897)
PHONE.................................626 457-4240
Mary Ann Pentz, *Director*
Wesley Smith, *Engineer*
EMP: 100
SALES (corp-wide): 4.9B **Privately Held**
WEB: www.usc.edu
SIC: 8731 8221 Medical research, commercial; university
PA: University Of Southern California
3720 S Flower St Fl 3
Los Angeles CA 90089
213 740-7762

(P-25864)
US DEPT OF THE AIR FORCE
Also Called: Chem Lab Rkfe
10 E Saturn Dr, Edwards (93524-7201)
PHONE.................................661 275-5410
Joan Larue, *Manager*
EMP: 85 **Publicly Held**
WEB: www.af.mil
SIC: 8731 9711 Chemical laboratory, except testing; Air Force;
HQ: United States Department Of The Air Force
1000 Air Force Pentagon
Washington DC 20330

(P-25865)
USDA FOREST SERVICE
4955 Canyon Crest Dr, Riverside
(92507-6071)
PHONE.................................951 680-1560
Irene Powell, *Administration*
Angela Coleman, *Chief*
EMP: 75 **Publicly Held**
WEB: www.defendtheforests.org
SIC: 8731 9512 Environmental research; land conservation agencies;
HQ: Us Dept Of Agriculture Forest Service
201 14th St Sw
Washington DC 20024

(P-25866)
VERINATA HEALTH INC
Also Called: Illumina-Redwood City
200 Lincoln Centre Dr, Foster City
(94404-1122)
PHONE.................................650 632-1680
Jeff Bird, *CEO*
Vance Vanier, *President*
EMP: 55
SALES (corp-wide): 3.3B **Publicly Held**
WEB: www.livingmicrosystems.com
SIC: 8731 2835 Biotechnical research, commercial; in vitro & in vivo diagnostic substances
PA: Illumina, Inc.
5200 Illumina Way
San Diego CA 92122
858 202-4500

(P-25867)
VERTEX PHRMCTCALS SAN DEGO LLC (HQ)
3215 Merryfield Row, San Diego
(92121-1126)
PHONE.................................858 404-6600
Joshua S Boger,

PRODUCTS & SVCS

Ian F Smith, *Exec VP*
Tracy Bychowski, *Administration*
Huy Nguyen, *Software Dev*
Philip Salzmann, *Design Engr*
EMP: 235
SQ FT: 81,000
SALES (est): 18.5MM
SALES (corp-wide): 3B **Publicly Held**
SIC: 8731 Biotechnical research, commercial
PA: Vertex Pharmaceuticals Incorporated
50 Northern Ave
Boston MA 02210
617 341-6100

(P-25868)
VIA COMMUNICATIONS INC
940 Mission Ct, Fremont (94539-8202)
PHONE...................................510 687-4650
Wen-CHI Chen, *CEO*
Jonathan Chang, *CFO*
EMP: 250
SQ FT: 3,300
SALES (est): 9.1MM **Privately Held**
SIC: 8731 Computer (hardware) development

(P-25869)
VIRIDENT SYSTEMS INC
1745 Tech Dr Ste 700, San Jose (95110)
PHONE...................................408 573-5000
Mike Gustafson, *Senior VP*
Bruce Horn, *CFO*
Mark Delsman, *Vice Pres*
Kumar Ganapathy, *Vice Pres*
Ken Grohe, *Vice Pres*
EMP: 110
SALES (est): 11MM
SALES (corp-wide): 16.5B **Publicly Held**
SIC: 8731 Computer (hardware) development
HQ: Hgst, Inc.
5601 Great Oaks Pkwy
San Jose CA 95119
408 717-6000

(P-25870)
VISBY MEDICAL INC
625 River Oaks Pkwy, San Jose (95134-1907)
PHONE...................................408 650-8878
Adam De La Zerda, *CEO*
EMP: 80
SALES (est): 6.6MM **Privately Held**
SIC: 8731 8734 8733 Natural resource research; commercial research laboratory; engineering laboratory, except testing; testing laboratories; bacteriological research; medical research

(P-25871)
WILLOW GARAGE INC
921 E Charleston Rd, Palo Alto (94303-4903)
PHONE...................................650 322-2584
Scott Wendell Hassan, *CEO*
Steve Cousins, *President*
Laleh Masnavi, *Vice Pres*
Erdal Taskin, *Vice Pres*
Varsha Narkhede, *Software Dev*
EMP: 59
SQ FT: 10,000
SALES (est): 5.8MM **Privately Held**
SIC: 8731 Electronic research

(P-25872)
ZYMERGEN INC (PA)
5980 Horton St Ste 105, Emeryville (94608-2056)
PHONE...................................415 801-8073
Joshua Hoffman, *CEO*
EMP: 91
SALES (est): 598.7K **Privately Held**
SIC: 8731 2833 Biotechnical research, commercial; medicinals & botanicals

(P-25873)
ZYMO RESEARCH CORP (PA)
17062 Murphy Ave, Irvine (92614-5914)
PHONE...................................949 679-1190
Xiyu Jia MD, *President*
LI Zhang, *Shareholder*
Angela Kim, *Admin Sec*
Mitchell Tran, *Web Dvlpr*
Dana Brecklin, *Research*
EMP: 57

SQ FT: 10,000
SALES (est): 17.6MM **Privately Held**
WEB: www.zymoresearch.com
SIC: 8731 Biotechnical research, commercial; medical research, commercial

8732 Commercial Economic, Sociological & Educational Research

(P-25874)
ADDED VALUE LLC (DH)
3400 Cahuenga Blvd W B, Los Angeles (90068-1376)
PHONE...................................323 254-4326
Meggy Taylor, *President*
Dennis Stefani, *Exec VP*
Agathe Laurent, *Vice Pres*
Chuck Doherty, *Technology*
Marc Agostini, *Senior Mgr*
EMP: 190
SQ FT: 9,800
SALES (est): 19.5MM
SALES (corp-wide): 20B **Privately Held**
WEB: www.us.millwardbrown.com
SIC: 8732 Market analysis or research
HQ: Kantar Llc
175 Greenwich St Fl 35
New York NY 10007
212 548-7200

(P-25875)
ADEPT CONSUMER TESTING INC
16130 Ventura Blvd # 200, Encino (91436-2580)
PHONE...................................310 279-4600
Mark Tobias, *President*
EMP: 50
SQ FT: 12,000
SALES (est): 6.4MM **Privately Held**
WEB: www.adeptconsumer.com
SIC: 8732 Market analysis or research

(P-25876)
AMER ZOETROPE RESEARCH LLC
1991 Saint Helena Hwy, Rutherford (94573)
P.O. Box 208 (94573-0208)
PHONE...................................707 963-9230
Jay Shoemaker, *President*
EMP: 150
SALES (est): 3.5MM **Privately Held**
SIC: 8732 Market analysis or research

(P-25877)
BAY ALARM COMPANY
9836 Kitty Ln, Oakland (94603-1070)
PHONE...................................510 452-3211
Delores Nielsen, *Manager*
Bryan Lubbers, *Executive*
Mark Terry, *Human Resources*
Hamid Ahrari, *Sales Staff*
Prince Ankupui, *Representative*
EMP: 81
SALES (corp-wide): 160.9MM **Privately Held**
WEB: www.bayalarm.com
SIC: 8732 1731 7382 5063 Commercial nonphysical research; electrical work; security systems services; electrical apparatus & equipment
PA: Bay Alarm Company
5130 Commercial Cir
Concord CA 94520
925 935-1100

(P-25878)
CAPITOL CORPORATE SERVICES
455 Capitol Mall Ste 217, Sacramento (95814-4405)
PHONE...................................916 444-6787
John H Robinson, *Vice Pres*
Cheryl Roberts, *President*
EMP: 50
SALES (est): 4.7MM **Privately Held**
WEB: www.capitolcorporateservices.com
SIC: 8732 Research services, except laboratory

(P-25879)
CARNEGIE MELLON UNIVERSITY
Also Called: Robotics Institute
4304 Valley Ave Apt G, Pleasanton (94566-5552)
PHONE...................................412 268-3818
Chuck Thope, *Director*
Lu LI, *Software Dev*
Andrew Dornbush, *Research*
Nishant Pol, *Electrical Engi*
Keenan Crane, *Professor*
EMP: 120
SALES (corp-wide): 1.3B **Privately Held**
WEB: www.cmu.edu
SIC: 8732 8221 Educational research; colleges universities & professional schools
PA: Carnegie Mellon University
5000 Forbes Ave
Pittsburgh PA 15213
412 268-2000

(P-25880)
CHASE GROUP LLC
Also Called: Simi Vly Care & Rehabilitation
5270 E Los Angeles Ave, Simi Valley (93063-4137)
PHONE...................................805 522-9155
Phil Chase, *Manager*
Maria Curiel, *Office Mgr*
Floyd Rhoades, *Administration*
EMP: 100
SALES (est): 10.1MM **Privately Held**
SIC: 8732 8742 Research services, except laboratory; management consulting services
PA: The Chase Group Llc
3075 E Thousand Oaks Blvd
Thousand Oaks CA 91362

(P-25881)
CIC RESEARCH INC
8361 Vickers St Ste 308, San Diego (92111-2112)
PHONE...................................858 637-4000
Gordon H Kubota PHD, *President*
Warren L Hull, *Vice Pres*
Joyce G Revlett, *Vice Pres*
Julie Spinazzola, *Office Mgr*
Pam Jaffe, *Research*
EMP: 65 **EST:** 1965
SQ FT: 15,000
SALES: 3.1MM **Privately Held**
WEB: www.cicresearch.com
SIC: 8732 Economic research; market analysis or research

(P-25882)
COHERENT INC
1100 La Avenida St, Mountain View (94043-1452)
PHONE...................................408 764-4000
Richard Pierce, *CEO*
John H N Fisher, *Principal*
Mike Mielke, *Security Dir*
EMP: 82
SQ FT: 42,000
SALES (est): 15.9MM **Privately Held**
WEB: www.raydiance-inc.com
SIC: 8732 3826 3821 Research services, except laboratory; laser scientific & engineering instruments; laser beam alignment devices

(P-25883)
COMPETITIVE EDGE RES COMM INC
1620 5th Ave Ste 825, San Diego (92101-2750)
PHONE...................................619 702-2372
John E Nienstedt, *President*
EMP: 60
SQ FT: 4,000
SALES: 1.5MM **Privately Held**
WEB: www.cerc.net
SIC: 8732 Opinion research

(P-25884)
CORNERSTONE RESEARCH INC
633 W 5th St Fl 31, Los Angeles (90071-2005)
PHONE...................................213 553-2500
Richard Dalbeck, *Vice Pres*

Shane Oka, *Associate*
EMP: 68
SALES (corp-wide): 83.3MM **Privately Held**
SIC: 8732 Market analysis, business & economic research
PA: Cornerstone Research, Inc.
1000 El Camino Real # 250
Menlo Park CA 94025
650 853-1660

(P-25885)
DAS GLOBAL CAPITAL CORP
42 Peninsula Ctr Ste 317, Rlling HLS Est (90274-3506)
PHONE...................................702 967-1688
Cleooarta Y Natt, *CEO*
EMP: 59 **Privately Held**
SIC: 8732 Merger, acquisition & reorganization research
PA: Das Global Capital Corp
1785 E Sahara Ave Ste 490
Las Vegas NV 89104

(P-25886)
DAVIS RESEARCH LLC
23801 Calabasas Rd # 1036, Calabasas (91302-3319)
PHONE...................................818 591-2408
William A Davis III, *Mng Member*
Robert Davis,
EMP: 150
SQ FT: 16,000
SALES (est): 10.6MM **Privately Held**
WEB: www.davisresearch.com
SIC: 8732 Market analysis or research

(P-25887)
DECIPHER INC (HQ)
7 E River Park Pl E # 110, Fresno (93720-1669)
PHONE...................................559 436-6940
Jamin Brazil, *President*
Kristin Luck, *President*
Ian Duffield, *COO*
Jeffrey Bergman, *CFO*
Jayme Plunkett, *Co-CEO*
EMP: 60
SQ FT: 13,000
SALES (est): 11MM
SALES (corp-wide): 50.3MM **Privately Held**
WEB: www.decipherinc.com
SIC: 8732 Economic research
PA: Focusvision Worldwide, Inc.
1266 E Main St Ste 3
Stamford CT 06902
203 355-9020

(P-25888)
DISQO INC
Also Called: Survey Junkie
800 N Brand Blvd Fl 21, Glendale (91203-1245)
PHONE...................................818 459-4330
Armen Adjemian, *CEO*
Drew Kutcharian, *CTO*
EMP: 60
SALES (est): 3.2MM **Privately Held**
SIC: 8732 7375 Market analysis or research; on-line data base information retrieval

(P-25889)
DSG ASSOCIATES INC
15500 Erwin St Ste 4007, Van Nuys (91411-1010)
PHONE...................................800 462-8765
Donna Guido, *CEO*
Mike Guido, *President*
Jennifer Mason, *Opers Staff*
EMP: 50
SQ FT: 6,700
SALES (est): 2.8MM **Privately Held**
WEB: www.dsgai.com
SIC: 8732 Market analysis, business & economic research

(P-25890)
DYNATA LLC
Also Called: Instantly
16501 Ventura Blvd # 300, Encino (91436-2007)
PHONE...................................866 872-4006
Jim Collins, *Exec VP*

EMP: 200 **Privately Held**
SIC: 8732 Market analysis or research;
market analysis, business & economic research; survey service: marketing, location, etc.
HQ: Dynata, Llc
6 Research Dr Ste 200
Shelton CT 06484
203 567-7200

(P-25891)
ECKER CONSUMER RECRUITING INC
Also Called: Ecker & Associates
1303 Melbourne St, Foster City
(94404-3739)
PHONE............................650 871-6800
Leon Ecker, *President*
Bette Rosenthal, *Vice Pres*
EMP: 51
SQ FT: 5,300
SALES (est): 2.5MM **Privately Held**
WEB: www.eckersf.com
SIC: 8732 Opinion research

(P-25892)
ELECTRONIC ENTRMT DESIGN & RES
Also Called: Eedar
2075 Corte Del Nogal B, Carlsbad
(92011-1413)
PHONE............................760 579-7100
Gregory Short, *CEO*
Geoffrey Zatkiin, *President*
Patrick Walker, *Vice Pres*
Ryan Stelzner, *Analyst*
Robert Felix, *Director*
EMP: 53
SQ FT: 11,000
SALES (est): 5.3MM **Privately Held**
WEB: www.eedar.com
SIC: 8732 Market analysis or research

(P-25893)
ELLIOTT BENSON MARKET RESEARCH
1226 H St, Sacramento (95814-1911)
PHONE............................916 325-1670
Jaclyn Benson, *Partner*
EMP: 50
SALES (est): 956.3K **Privately Held**
WEB: www.elliottbenson.com
SIC: 8732 Market analysis or research

(P-25894)
ERNEST GALLO CLINIC & RES CTR
5980 Horton St Ste 370, Emeryville
(94608-2058)
PHONE............................510 985-3856
Raymond L White PHD, *President*
John De Luca, *Chairman*
William Sawyers, *Vice Pres*
EMP: 115
SQ FT: 87,200
SALES (est): 1.4MM **Privately Held**
WEB: www.gallo.ucsf.edu
SIC: 8732 8731 Commercial nonphysical
research; commercial physical research

(P-25895)
FLEISCHMAN FIELD RESEARCH INC
250 Sutter St Fl 2, San Francisco
(94108-4462)
P.O. Box 641620 (94164-1620)
PHONE............................415 398-4140
Molly Fleischman, *President*
Andrew Fleischman, *CEO*
EMP: 130
SALES (est): 6.7MM **Privately Held**
WEB: www.ffrsf.com
SIC: 8732 Market analysis or research

(P-25896)
FRANCE TELECOM RES & DEV LLC
Also Called: Orange Labs
60 Spear St Ste 1100, San Francisco
(94105-1599)
PHONE............................415 284-9765
Elie Girard,
Bruno Mettling, *Exec VP*
Thierry Souche, *Senior VP*
Glenn Maloof, *Vice Pres*

Monique MAI, *Vice Pres*
EMP: 65
SALES (est): 12MM
SALES (corp-wide): 26.4B **Privately Held**
WEB: www.francetelecom.com
SIC: 8732 Market analysis or research
PA: Orange
78 84
Paris 15e Arrondissement 75015
800 023-900

(P-25897)
FRANK N MAGID ASSOCIATES INC
15260 Ventura Blvd # 1840, Sherman Oaks
(91403-5379)
PHONE............................818 263-3300
Brent Magid, *Owner*
EMP: 70 EST: 2001
SALES (est): 3.2MM **Privately Held**
SIC: 8732 Market analysis or research

(P-25898)
FRANK N MAGID ASSOCIATES INC
15260 Vntr Blvd Ste 1840, Sherman Oaks
(91403)
PHONE............................818 263-3300
Frank N Magid, *Branch Mgr*
EMP: 105
SALES (corp-wide): 23.4MM **Privately Held**
SIC: 8732 Market analysis or research
PA: Frank N. Magid Associates, Inc.
5825 Council St Ne
Cedar Rapids IA 52402
319 377-7349

(P-25899)
GARTNER INC
11845 W Olympic Blvd 505w, Los Angeles
(90064-5057)
PHONE............................310 479-2108
Bill Kumagai, *Manager*
EMP: 55
SALES (corp-wide): 3.9B **Publicly Held**
WEB: www.gartner.com
SIC: 8732 Market analysis or research
PA: Gartner, Inc.
56 Top Gallant Rd
Stamford CT 06902
203 316-1111

(P-25900)
GFK CUSTOM RESEARCH LLC
360 Pine St Fl 6, San Francisco
(94104-3226)
PHONE............................415 398-2812
Xiaoyan Zhao, *Branch Mgr*
Eric Wagatha, *Vice Pres*
Tetyana Shvets, *Prgrmr*
Brian Dowdy, *Research*
Leah Smith, *Research*
EMP: 54
SALES (corp-wide): 536.6K **Privately Held**
WEB: www.gfknop.com
SIC: 8732 8713 Market analysis or re-
search; surveying services
HQ: Gfk Custom Research, Llc
200 Liberty St Fl 4
New York NY 10281
212 240-5300

(P-25901)
GFK CUSTOM RESEARCH LLC
879 W 190th St Ste 390, Gardena
(90248-4229)
PHONE............................310 527-2100
Jaroslaw Muszynski, *Technical Staff*
EMP: 112
SALES (corp-wide): 536.6K **Privately Held**
SIC: 8732 Market analysis or research
HQ: Gfk Custom Research, Llc
200 Liberty St Fl 4
New York NY 10281
212 240-5300

(P-25902)
GLASS LEWIS & CO LLC (HQ)
255 California St # 1100, San Francisco
(94111-4927)
PHONE............................415 678-4110
Katherine Rabin, *CEO*
John Wieck, *COO*

Carla Topino, *Assoc VP*
Fergus Curtin, *Vice Pres*
David Eaton, *Vice Pres*
EMP: 60
SALES (est): 19.8MM
SALES (corp-wide): 140B **Privately Held**
WEB: www.glasslewis.com
SIC: 8732 Business analysis
PA: Ontario Teachers' Pension Plan Board
5650 Yonge St Suite 300
North York ON M2M 4
416 228-5900

(P-25903)
GLOBAL INDUSTRY ANALYSTS INC
6150 Hellyer Ave Ste 100, San Jose
(95138-1072)
PHONE............................408 528-9966
Kalakoti S Reddy, *CEO*
EMP: 700
SALES (est): 29.5MM **Privately Held**
WEB: www.sisinfotech.com
SIC: 8732 Market analysis or research

(P-25904)
GREENBERG INC (PA)
1250 53rd St Ste 5, Emeryville
(94608-2965)
PHONE............................510 446-8200
Andrew Greenberg, *President*
Iwan Thomis, *Officer*
Nicola Finnerty, *Vice Pres*
Philip Heuring, *Vice Pres*
Steve Ingledew, *Vice Pres*
EMP: 53
SQ FT: 5,500
SALES (est): 6.1MM **Privately Held**
WEB: www.gqrinc.com
SIC: 8732 Market analysis or research

(P-25905)
HANLEY WOOD MKT INTELLIGENCE (HQ)
Also Called: Meyers Group
555 Anton Blvd Ste 950, Costa Mesa
(92626-7811)
PHONE............................714 540-8500
Jeff Meyers, *CEO*
Karen Meyers, *Managing Prtnr*
Tom Flynn, *President*
EMP: 55
SALES (est): 6.2MM
SALES (corp-wide): 164.8MM **Privately Held**
SIC: 8732 Market analysis or research
PA: Hw Holdco, Llc
1 Thomas Cir Nw Ste 600
Washington DC 20005
202 452-0800

(P-25906)
HIGH DESERT PARTNERSHIP
Also Called: NORTON SCIENCE AND LAN-
GUAGE AC
17500 Mana Rd, Apple Valley
(92307-2181)
PHONE............................760 946-5414
Lisa Lamb, *CEO*
Larri Curtis, *CFO*
Linda Locke, *Executive*
Gordon Soholt, *General Mgr*
Teresa Dowd, *Executive Asst*
EMP: 350
SQ FT: 35,000
SALES (est): 23.2MM **Privately Held**
WEB: www.lcer.org
SIC: 8732 Commercial nonphysical re-
search

(P-25907)
HONDA R&D AMERICAS INC
7514 Reseda Blvd, Reseda (91335-2820)
PHONE............................818 345-7922
David Colby, *Branch Mgr*
EMP: 50 **Privately Held**
WEB: www.hra.com
SIC: 8732 Market analysis or research
HQ: Honda R&D Americas, Inc.
1900 Harpers Way
Torrance CA 90501
310 781-5500

(P-25908)
IBISWORLD INC (DH)
11755 Wilshire Blvd # 1100, Los Angeles
(90025-1506)
PHONE............................800 330-3772
Phil Ruthven, *Principal*
Quinn Callaway, *President*
Justin Ruthven, *President*
Jason Baker, *COO*
Harvey Jones, *COO*
EMP: 74
SALES (est): 18.1MM **Privately Held**
SIC: 8732 Market analysis or research

(P-25909)
INFORMA RESEARCH SERVICES INC (HQ)
26565 Agoura Rd Ste 300, Calabasas
(91302-1942)
PHONE............................818 880-8877
Michael E Adler, *President*
Charles A Miwa, *COO*
Lori Jomsky, *Vice Pres*
Brian Richards, *Vice Pres*
Michelle Grabow, *Research*
EMP: 193
SQ FT: 16,000
SALES (est): 33.4MM
SALES (corp-wide): 3B **Privately Held**
WEB: www.informars.com
SIC: 8732 Market analysis or research
PA: Informa Plc
5 Howick Place
London SW1P
207 017-7483

(P-25910)
INTERVIEWING SERVICE AMER INC
200 S Grfield Ave Ste 302, Alhambra
(91801)
PHONE............................626 979-4140
Kelly Simmoms, *Manager*
EMP: 100
SALES (corp-wide): 25MM **Privately Held**
SIC: 8732 Market analysis or research
PA: Interviewing Service Of America, Llc
15400 Sherman Way Ste 400
Van Nuys CA 91406
818 989-1044

(P-25911)
INTERVIEWING SERVICE AMER LLC (PA)
Also Called: ISA
15400 Sherman Way Ste 400, Van Nuys
(91406-4211)
PHONE............................818 989-1044
Michael Halberstam, *Chairman*
Tony Kretzmer, *President*
Jacqueline Rosales, *COO*
Vicky Agalsoff, *Vice Pres*
John Fitzpatrick, *Vice Pres*
EMP: 250
SQ FT: 20,000
SALES: 25MM **Privately Held**
SIC: 8732 Market analysis or research

(P-25912)
IPSOS OTX CORPORATION (HQ)
300 Crprate Pinte Ste 500, Culver City
(90230)
PHONE............................310 736-3400
Shelley Zalis, *CEO*
Jeff Dean, *CFO*
EMP: 210
SALES (est): 18.2MM
SALES (corp-wide): 719K **Privately Held**
SIC: 8732 Market analysis or research
PA: Ipsos
35 Rue Du Val De Marne
Paris 13e Arrondissement 75013
141 989-000

(P-25913)
IPSOS PUBLIC AFFAIRS INC
3402 N Blackstone Ave, Fresno
(93726-5395)
PHONE............................559 451-2820
Jorge Zelada, *Branch Mgr*
EMP: 111
SALES (corp-wide): 719K **Privately Held**
SIC: 8732 Market analysis or research

PRODUCTS & SVCS

HQ: Ipsos Public Affairs, Inc.
222 S Rverside Plz Fl 4 Flr 4
Chicago IL 60606
312 526-4000

(P-25914)
J PAUL GETTY TRUST
Also Called: Getty Conservation Institute
1200 Getty Center Dr # 400, Los Angeles
(90049-1657)
PHONE.....................310 440-7325
Tim Wayland, *Branch Mgr*
EMP: 70
SALES (corp-wide): 195.5MM **Privately Held**
SIC: 8732 Commercial nonphysical research
PA: The J Paul Getty Trust
1200 Getty Center Dr # 500
Los Angeles CA 90049
310 440-7300

(P-25915)
JD POWER (HQ)
3200 Park Center Dr Fl 13, Costa Mesa
(92626-7154)
PHONE.....................714 621-6200
Dave Habiger, *President*
Joseph Damour, *CFO*
Yuin Choe, *Treasurer*
Bernardo Rodriguez, *Officer*
Thomas King, *Senior VP*
EMP: 100
SQ FT: 45,000
SALES: 350MM
SALES (corp-wide): 5.9MM **Privately Held**
WEB: www.jdpower.com
SIC: 8732 8742 Survey service: marketing, location, etc.; management consulting services

(P-25916)
JD POWER
30870 Russell Ranch Rd, Westlake Village
(91362-7366)
PHONE.....................805 418-8000
Keith Webster, *Vice Pres*
Andrea Lau, *Research*
David Patton, *Manager*
EMP: 280
SALES (corp-wide): 5.9MM **Privately Held**
WEB: www.jdpower.com
SIC: 8732 Market analysis or research
HQ: J.D. Power
3200 Park Center Dr Fl 13
Costa Mesa CA 92626
714 621-6200

(P-25917)
KELTON RESEARCH LLC (PA)
Also Called: Jury Insight
12121 Bluff Creek Dr, Playa Vista
(90094-2994)
PHONE.....................310 479-4040
Tom Bernthal, *President*
Gareth Schweitzer, *Vice Pres*
EMP: 58
SALES (est): 10.8MM **Privately Held**
WEB: www.juryinsight.com
SIC: 8732 Market analysis or research

(P-25918)
LELAND STANFORD JUNIOR UNIV
Stanf CNT Rsch & Ds Prntn
1070 Arastradero Rd # 100, Palo Alto
(94304-1336)
PHONE.....................650 723-6254
Steven Fortmann, *Director*
EMP: 163
SALES (corp-wide): 11.3B **Privately Held**
SIC: 8732 8221 Educational research; university
PA: Leland Stanford Junior University
450 Jane Stanford Way
Stanford CA 94305
650 723-2300

(P-25919)
LELAND STANFORD JUNIOR UNIV
476 Lomita Mall, Palo Alto (94305-4008)
PHONE.....................650 723-7546
EMP: 300

SALES (corp-wide): 11.3B **Privately Held**
SIC: 8732 8221 Educational research; university
PA: Leland Stanford Junior University
450 Jane Stanford Way
Stanford CA 94305
650 723-2300

(P-25920)
LIEBERMAN RES WORLDWIDE LLC (PA)
Also Called: Lrw Group
1900 Avenue Of The Stars, Los Angeles
(90067-4301)
PHONE.....................310 553-0550
David Sackman, *President*
Arnold Fishman, *Ch of Bd*
Amy Young Adkins, *Vice Pres*
Sara Gormley, *Vice Pres*
Nancy Jagou, *Vice Pres*
EMP: 140 **EST:** 1973
SQ FT: 24,560
SALES (est): 41MM **Privately Held**
WEB: www.lrwonline.com
SIC: 8732 Market analysis or research

(P-25921)
LUTH RESEARCH INC (PA)
Also Called: Surveysavvy.com
1365 4th Ave, San Diego (92101-4208)
PHONE.....................619 234-5884
Roseanne Luth, *President*
Charles Rosen, *Exec VP*
Candice Rab, *Vice Pres*
Anthony Siegrist, *Admin Asst*
Khoa Nguyen, *Sr Software Eng*
EMP: 305
SQ FT: 15,000
SALES (est): 51.7MM **Privately Held**
WEB: www.luthresearch.com
SIC: 8732 Market analysis or research

(P-25922)
MARITZCX RESEARCH LLC
3901 Via Oro Ave Ste 200, Long Beach
(90810-1800)
PHONE.....................310 525-1300
Christopher Gerth, *Branch Mgr*
EMP: 526
SALES (corp-wide): 1.3B **Privately Held**
SIC: 8732 Market analysis or research
HQ: Maritzcx Research Llc
1355 N Highway Dr
Fenton MO 63026
636 827-4000

(P-25923)
MCCANN-ERICKSON USA INC
Also Called: McKann World Group
600 Battery St Fl 1, San Francisco
(94111-1834)
PHONE.....................415 262-5600
Mike Parsons, *Branch Mgr*
Ken Krausgill, *Business Mgr*
Henry Wang, *Analyst*
EMP: 200
SALES (corp-wide): 9.7B **Publicly Held**
SIC: 8732 7311 Market analysis or research; advertising agencies
HQ: Mccann-Erickson Usa, Inc.
622 3rd Ave Fl 3
New York NY 10017
646 865-2000

(P-25924)
MICHAEL A MECZKA
5757 W Century Blvd # 120, Los Angeles
(90045-6401)
PHONE.....................310 670-4824
Michael A Meczka, *President*
Dona Browne, *Vice Pres*
EMP: 50
SALES (est): 1.9MM **Privately Held**
WEB: www.mmrcinc.com
SIC: 8732 Market analysis or research

(P-25925)
MILLWARD BROWN LLC
2425 Olympic Blvd 240e, Santa Monica
(90404-4030)
PHONE.....................310 309-3352
Nile Rowan, *Branch Mgr*
Grace Chang, *Account Dir*
EMP: 50
SALES (corp-wide): 20B **Privately Held**
SIC: 8732 Market analysis or research

HQ: Millward Brown, Llc
11 Madison Ave Ste 1200
New York NY 10010
212 548-7200

(P-25926)
MONTEREY COUNTY OFFICE EDUCATN
Technology Information Svcs
901 Blanco Cir, Salinas (93901-4401)
PHONE.....................831 755-0324
Dave Paulson, *CTO*
EMP: 86 **Privately Held**
SIC: 8732 7374 Educational research; computer processing services
PA: Monterey County Office Of Education
901 Blanco Cir
Salinas CA 93901

(P-25927)
NATIONAL ECNOMIC RES ASSOC INC
777 S Figueroa St # 1950, Los Angeles
(90017-5800)
PHONE.....................213 346-3000
Gary Dorman, *VP Mktg*
Richard Murillo, *IT Executive*
Annie Lam, *Consultant*
Paul Wertheim, *Consultant*
EMP: 62
SALES (corp-wide): 14.9B **Publicly Held**
SIC: 8732 Business economic service
HQ: National Economic Research Associates, Inc.
1166 Ave Of The Americas
New York NY 10036
212 345-3000

(P-25928)
NATIONAL OPINION RESEARCH CTR
50 California St Ste 1500, San Francisco
(94111-4612)
PHONE.....................415 315-2000
EMP: 138
SALES (corp-wide): 181.4MM **Privately Held**
SIC: 8732 Research services, except laboratory
PA: National Opinion Research Center
55 E Monroe St Fl 30
Chicago IL 60603
312 759-4266

(P-25929)
NATIONAL OPINION RESEARCH CTR
1250 Borregas Ave, Sunnyvale
(94089-1309)
PHONE.....................415 315-3800
EMP: 64
SALES (corp-wide): 181.4MM **Privately Held**
SIC: 8732 Commercial nonphysical research
PA: National Opinion Research Center
55 E Monroe St Fl 30
Chicago IL 60603
312 759-4266

(P-25930)
NATIONAL RESEARCH GROUP INC
6255 W Sunset Blvd Fl 19, Los Angeles
(90028-7420)
PHONE.....................323 817-2000
Jon Penn, *CEO*
Jeff Hall, *Exec VP*
James McNamara, *Exec VP*
Ray Ydoyaga, *Exec VP*
Brian Theaker, *Director*
EMP: 400
SALES (est): 41.7MM
SALES (corp-wide): 126.1MM **Privately Held**
WEB: www.nrg.com
SIC: 8732 Market analysis or research; business research service
PA: The Stagwell Group Llc
1808 I St Nw Ste 600
Washington DC 20006
202 524-4364

(P-25931)
NIELSEN COMPANY (US) LLC
Also Called: Nielsen Media Research
6255 W Sunset Blvd Fl 20, Los Angeles
(90028-7405)
PHONE.....................323 817-2000
Tom Borys, *Manager*
Dara Spielvogel, *VP Finance*
Marissa Fiordimalva, *Senior Mgr*
Yesenia Nunez, *Client Mgr*
Sandie Mester, *Director*
EMP: 400
SALES (corp-wide): 6.5B **Privately Held**
WEB: www.nielsenmedia.com
SIC: 8732 Market analysis or research
HQ: The Nielsen Company Us Llc
85 Broad St
New York NY 10004

(P-25932)
NIELSEN COMPANY (US) LLC
5375 Mira Sorrento Pl # 400, San Diego
(92121-3809)
PHONE.....................858 677-9542
Teri Jacobson, *Branch Mgr*
Keith Peterson, *COO*
Hugo Borda, *Vice Pres*
Doug Diem, *Vice Pres*
Mark Nelson, *Vice Pres*
EMP: 127
SALES (corp-wide): 6.5B **Privately Held**
SIC: 8732 Market analysis or research
HQ: The Nielsen Company Us Llc
85 Broad St
New York NY 10004

(P-25933)
NIELSEN COMPANY (US) LLC
6255 W Sunset Blvd Fl 19, Los Angeles
(90028-7420)
PHONE.....................323 462-0050
Adam Levy, *Vice Pres*
Aslam Ghori, *Vice Pres*
Chooi Choong, *Executive*
Waqas Ijaz, *Executive*
Modikoe Kabelo, *Executive*
EMP: 80
SALES (corp-wide): 6.5B **Privately Held**
SIC: 8732 Market analysis or research
HQ: The Nielsen Company Us Llc
85 Broad St
New York NY 10004

(P-25934)
NITTO DENKO TECHNICAL CORP
501 Via Del Monte, Oceanside
(92058-1251)
PHONE.....................760 435-7011
Kenji Matsumoto, *President*
EMP: 100
SALES (est): 19.3MM **Privately Held**
WEB: www.nitto.co.jp
SIC: 8732 3089 3462 Research services, except laboratory; automotive parts, plastic; automotive & internal combustion engine forgings
PA: Nitto Denko Corporation
4-20, Ofukacho, Kita-Ku
Osaka OSK 530-0

(P-25935)
NOVOZYMES INC (DH)
Also Called: Novo Nordisk Biotech
1445 Drew Ave, Davis (95618-4880)
PHONE.....................530 757-8100
Peder Holk Nielsen, *CEO*
EMP: 70
SQ FT: 64,000
SALES (est): 20.4MM
SALES (est): 20.1B **Privately Held**
WEB: www.novozymesbiotech.com
SIC: 8732 Commercial nonphysical research
HQ: Novozymes North America, Inc.
77 Perry Chapel Church Rd
Franklinton NC 27525
919 494-2014

(P-25936)
OTR GLOBAL LLC
155 Montgomery St Ste 501, San Francisco
(94104-4110)
PHONE..............................415 675-7660
Otr Global, *Branch Mgr*
EMP: 50 **Privately Held**
SIC: 8732 Market analysis or research
PA: Otr Global Llc
4 Manhattanville Rd # 205
Purchase NY 10577

(P-25937)
PACIFICA KATIE AVENUE LLC
1775 Hancock St Ste 100, San Diego
(92110-2035)
PHONE..............................619 296-9000
Deepak Israni,
Alison Shovlain, *Executive Asst*
EMP: 80
SALES (est): 5.7MM **Privately Held**
SIC: 8732 Merger, acquisition & reorganization research

(P-25938)
PROXIM WIRELESS CORPORATION
2114 Ringwood Ave, San Jose
(95131-1715)
PHONE..............................408 383-7600
David Renauld, *Vice Pres*
EMP: 240
SALES (corp-wide): 31MM **Publicly Held**
SIC: 8732 Research services, except laboratory
PA: Proxim Wireless Corporation
2114 Ringwood Ave
San Jose CA 95131
408 383-7600

(P-25939)
QURI INC
655 Montgomery St Lbby 1, San Francisco
(94111-2638)
PHONE..............................415 413-0100
Justin Behar, *CEO*
John Mecklenburg, *COO*
Mark Cook, *Vice Pres*
Tom Shrader, *Director*
Drew Northcutt, *Accounts Exec*
EMP: 50
SALES (est): 5MM **Privately Held**
SIC: 8732 Market analysis or research

(P-25940)
REDHILL GROUP INC
18010 Sky Park Cir # 275, Irvine
(92614-6439)
PHONE..............................949 752-5900
Judith Fairweather McCourt, *President*
Ryan Mak, *Research Analys*
EMP: 61
SQ FT: 3,500
SALES (est): 6MM **Privately Held**
WEB: www.redhillgroup.com
SIC: 8732 Market analysis or research

(P-25941)
RETAILNEXT INC
845 Market St Ste 450, San Francisco
(94103-1938)
PHONE..............................408 298-2585
EMP: 150
SALES (corp-wide): 56.3MM **Privately Held**
SIC: 8732 Market analysis or research
PA: Retailnext, Inc.
60 S Market St Ste 1000
San Jose CA 95113
408 884-2162

(P-25942)
S K & A INFORMATION SVCS INC (DH)
Also Called: SK&a
2601 Main St Ste 650, Irvine (92614-4228)
PHONE..............................949 476-2051
David Escalante Jr, *President*
Al M Cosentino, *CFO*
Jaqueline Aguilera, *Director*
EMP: 87
SQ FT: 12,000

SALES (est): 7.8MM
SALES (corp-wide): 6.2MM **Privately Held**
WEB: www.skainfo.com
SIC: 8732 Market analysis or research

(P-25943)
SMARTREVENUECOM INC
101 Cooper St Ste 205, Santa Cruz
(95060-4526)
PHONE..............................203 733-9156
John Dranow, *CEO*
EMP: 492
SALES (corp-wide): 46.7MM **Privately Held**
SIC: 8732 Market analysis or research
PA: Smartrevenue.Com, Inc.
60 Twin Ridge Rd
Ridgefield CT 06877
203 733-9156

(P-25944)
SOLEIL COMMUNICATIONS LLC
Also Called: Prodata Research
2655 Camino DI Rio N 11, San Diego
(92108)
PHONE..............................619 624-2888
Michael Gehrig, *Mng Member*
Susan Nelson, *Sales Mgr*
EMP: 70
SALES (est): 4.9MM
SALES (corp-wide): 100.2MM **Privately Held**
SIC: 8732 Market analysis or research
PA: The Welk Group Inc
8860 Lawrence Welk Dr
Escondido CA 92026
760 749-3000

(P-25945)
SPHERE INSTITUTE
500 Airport Blvd Ste 340, Burlingame
(94010-1934)
PHONE..............................650 558-3980
Thomas MA Curdy, *President*
Ellen Banh, *COO*
Greg Boro, *Treasurer*
Tressa Navalta, *Administration*
Evan Yip, *Administration*
EMP: 225
SQ FT: 2,000
SALES (est): 20.8MM **Privately Held**
WEB: www.sphereinstitute.org
SIC: 8732 Market analysis or research

(P-25946)
SUNING CMMERCE R D CTR USA INC
Also Called: Suning USA
845 Page Mill Rd, Palo Alto (94304-1011)
PHONE..............................650 834-9800
Enlong Hou, *CEO*
Jin Ming, *President*
Linglin Niu, *Business Anlyst*
EMP: 60
SQ FT: 9,800
SALES (est): 4.5MM
SALES (corp-wide): 35.2B **Privately Held**
SIC: 8732 Commercial nonphysical research
PA: Suning.Com Co., Ltd.
1-5f, Jinshan Building, No. 8 Shanxi Road
Nanjing 21004

(P-25947)
TECHAISLE LLC
5053 Doyle Rd Ste 105, San Jose
(95129-4228)
PHONE..............................408 253-4416
Anurag Agrawal,
Lavanya Agrawal, *Info Tech Mgr*
EMP: 50
SALES: 172K **Privately Held**
WEB: www.techaisle.com
SIC: 8732 Market analysis or research

(P-25948)
TOSHIBA EDUCATION CENTER
9740 Irvine Blvd, Irvine (92618-1651)
PHONE..............................949 583-3000
Ted Flati, *Principal*
EMP: 55

SALES (est): 5.6MM **Privately Held**
WEB: www.tams.com
SIC: 8732 Educational research
HQ: Canon Medical Systems Usa, Inc.
2441 Michelle Dr
Tustin CA 92780
714 730-5000

(P-25949)
TREDENCE INC (PA)
1900 Camden Ave Ste 66, San Jose
(95124-2948)
PHONE..............................408 819-2336
Subhankar Bhowmick, *CEO*
Sumit Mehra, *President*
Shashank Kumar Dubey, *Vice Pres*
Chirag Jain, *Business Anlyst*
Rakesh Narayanan, *Manager*
EMP: 250 **EST:** 2014
SQ FT: 500
SALES (est): 15.5MM **Privately Held**
SIC: 8732 Market analysis, business & economic research

(P-25950)
TRENDSOURCE INC
Also Called: Examine Your Practice
4891 Pacific Hwy Ste 200, San Diego
(92110-4026)
PHONE..............................619 718-7467
Rodney Moll, *Chairman*
Bob Post, *COO*
Neil A Wykes, *CFO*
EMP: 57
SQ FT: 7,500
SALES (est): 8.4MM **Privately Held**
WEB: www.trendsource.com
SIC: 8732 Market analysis or research

(P-25951)
TROTTA ASSOCIATES
13160 Mindanao Way # 100, Marina Del Rey (90292-7900)
PHONE..............................310 306-6866
Diane Trotta, *CEO*
EMP: 80
SALES (est): 7.7MM **Privately Held**
SIC: 8732 Market analysis or research

(P-25952)
UNIVERSITY CAL RIVERSIDE
Also Called: Uc Riverside RES Economic Dev
1160 University Ave, Riverside
(92507-4545)
PHONE..............................951 827-4801
Stan Fletcher, *Director*
Julie Lakatos, *Officer*
Iqbal Pittalwala, *Officer*
Boe Choi, *Associate Dir*
Gary Kuzas, *Associate Dir*
EMP: 77 **Privately Held**
SIC: 8732 8221 9411 Economic research; university; administration of educational programs;
HQ: University Cal Riverside
900 University Ave
Riverside CA 92521
951 827-1012

(P-25953)
VERANCE CORPORATION
10089 Willow Creek Rd, San Diego
(92131-1697)
PHONE..............................858 202-2800
Linesh Shah, *CEO*
Clifford Friedman, *Ch of Bd*
EMP: 65
SALES (est): 8.6MM **Privately Held**
WEB: www.verance.com
SIC: 8732 Research services, except laboratory

(P-25954)
XDBS CORPORATION
Also Called: Xdbsb2b
3501 Jack Northrop Ave, Hawthorne
(90250-4433)
PHONE..............................302 566-3006
Julie Strong, *CEO*
Kartik Anand, *Chairman*
Nigel Wright, *Vice Pres*
Shivam Agarwal, *Executive*
EMP: 100
SQ FT: 4,000

SALES (est): 3MM **Privately Held**
SIC: 8732 7389 5963 8742 Survey service: marketing, location, etc.; telemarketing services; direct sales, telemarketing; sales (including sales management) consultant

---

8733 Noncommercial Research Organizations

(P-25955)
A 3 BY AIRBUS LLC
601 W California Ave, Sunnyvale
(94086-4831)
PHONE..............................650 815-1881
Mark Cousin, *CEO*
Eduardo Dominguez-Puerta, *COO*
Trusten Allan McArtor,
EMP: 120 **EST:** 2017
SALES (est): 9MM
SALES (corp-wide): 72.9B **Privately Held**
SIC: 8733 Noncommercial research organizations
HQ: Airbus Americas, Inc.
2550 Wasser Ter Ste 9100
Herndon VA 20171
703 834-3400

(P-25956)
AEROSPACE CORPORATION (PA)
2310 E El Segundo Blvd, El Segundo
(90245-4609)
P.O. Box 92957, Los Angeles (90009-2957)
PHONE..............................310 336-5000
Steven Isakowitz, *President*
Ellen M Beatty, *CFO*
Thomas Oconnor, *Treasurer*
Rufus A Fulton, *Trustee*
James F Jusko, *Officer*
EMP: 2313 **EST:** 1960
SQ FT: 1,167,251
SALES: 916.6MM **Privately Held**
SIC: 8733 8711 8731 Scientific research agency; engineering services; commercial physical research

(P-25957)
AFFYMAX RESEARCH INSTITUTE
4001 Miranda Ave, Palo Alto (94304-1218)
PHONE..............................650 812-8700
Gordon Ringold PHD, *CEO*
Lauren Stevens, *President*
Mark Thompson, *CFO*
Helen S Kim, *Officer*
Emily Lee Kelly, *Vice Pres*
EMP: 50
SQ FT: 103,000
SALES (est): 4.1MM **Privately Held**
SIC: 8733 8732 8731 Medical research; commercial nonphysical research; commercial physical research

(P-25958)
AIR FORCE US DEPT OF
Also Called: Aerospace Federally Funded RES
2310 E El Segundo Blvd, El Segundo
(90245-4609)
PHONE..............................310 336-5000
EMP: 391 **Publicly Held**
SIC: 8733 9711 Noncommercial research organizations; Air Force;
HQ: United States Department Of The Air Force
1000 Air Force Pentagon
Washington DC 20330

(P-25959)
AIR FORCE US DEPT OF
Also Called: Project Air Force
1776 Main St, Santa Monica (90401-3208)
PHONE..............................310 393-0411
EMP: 391 **Publicly Held**
SIC: 8733 9711 Noncommercial research organizations; Air Force
HQ: United States Department Of The Air Force
1000 Air Force Pentagon
Washington DC 20330

(P-25960)
AKELA PHARMA INC
11011 Torreyana Rd 100, San Diego
(92121-1104)
PHONE...................512 391-3525
Rudy Emmelot, *President*
Seth E Lemler, *Ch of Bd*
Fr D Ric Dumais, *Vice Pres*
EMP: 50 **EST:** 2008
SALES (est): 2.6MM **Privately Held**
SIC: 8733 Biotechnical research, noncommercial

(P-25961)
AMERICAN CANCER SOC CAL DIV (PA)
1001 Marina Village Pkwy, Alameda
(94501-1091)
PHONE...................510 893-7900
Carolyn F Katzin, *CEO*
Marilyn Broussard, *CFO*
EMP: 100
SQ FT: 47,000
SALES (est): 38.8MM **Privately Held**
SIC: 8733 Noncommercial research organizations

(P-25962)
AMERICAN CANCER SOC CAL DIV
Also Called: Discovery Shop
748 Santa Cruz Ave, Menlo Park
(94025-4514)
PHONE...................650 325-8939
Susan Galbrath, *Manager*
EMP: 66
SALES (corp-wide): 38.8MM **Privately Held**
SIC: 8733 Noncommercial research organizations
PA: American Cancer Society California Division, Inc
1001 Marina Village Pkwy
Alameda CA 94501
510 893-7900

(P-25963)
AMERICAN INSTITUTE OF AERONAUT
3198 E Fox Run Way, San Diego
(92111-7721)
PHONE...................619 545-3736
Keith Glassman, *Principal*
EMP: 99
SALES (est): 3.3MM **Privately Held**
SIC: 8733 Noncommercial research organizations

(P-25964)
AMERICAN INSTITUTE RESEARCH
2151 River Plaza Dr # 320, Sacramento
(95833-3881)
PHONE...................916 286-8800
EMP: 329
SALES (corp-wide): 461.9MM **Privately Held**
SIC: 8733 Noncommercial social research organization
PA: American Institutes For Research In The Behavioral Sciences
1000 Thmas Jfferson St Nw
Washington DC 20007
202 403-5000

(P-25965)
AMGEN PHARMACEUTICALS INC
1 Amgen Center Dr, Thousand Oaks
(91320-1799)
PHONE...................805 447-1000
Gordon Binder, *President*
EMP: 4200
SALES (est): 64.7MM
SALES (corp-wide): 23.7B **Publicly Held**
SIC: 8733 Biotechnical research, noncommercial
PA: Amgen Inc.
1 Amgen Center Dr
Thousand Oaks CA 91320
805 447-1000

(P-25966)
ASIA FOUNDATION (PA)
465 California St Fl 9, San Francisco
(94104-1892)
P.O. Box 193223 (94119-3223)
PHONE...................415 982-4640
David D Arnold, *President*
Suzanne Siskel, *COO*
Ken Krug, *CFO*
Alexandra Matthews, *Officer*
Elizabeth Silva, *Officer*
◆ **EMP:** 90
SQ FT: 17,207
SALES: 106.5MM **Privately Held**
SIC: 8733 Noncommercial research organizations

(P-25967)
ATK SPACE SYSTEMS INC
7130 Miramar Rd Ste 100b, San Diego
(92121-2340)
PHONE...................858 621-5700
Doan La, *Branch Mgr*
EMP: 300 **Publicly Held**
SIC: 8733 Scientific research agency
HQ: Atk Space Systems Inc.
6033 Bandini Blvd
Commerce CA 90040
323 722-0222

(P-25968)
BAY AREA ENVMTL RES INST
Also Called: Baer Institute
Nasa Resrch Park 101, Moffett Field
(94035)
P.O. Box 25 (94035-0025)
PHONE...................707 938-9387
Robert W Bergstrom, *President*
Mark Sittloh, *Exec Dir*
Juan Torres, *Research*
▲ **EMP:** 87
SQ FT: 750
SALES: 18.2MM **Privately Held**
WEB: www.baeri.org
SIC: 8733 Medical research

(P-25969)
BECKMAN RESEARCH INST HOPE
1500 Duarte Rd, Duarte (91010-3012)
PHONE...................626 359-8111
Michael A Friedman, *CEO*
Robert Stone, *President*
Harlan Levine, *CEO*
William Sargeant, *COO*
Terry Blackwood, *CFO*
EMP: 250
SALES: 298.9MM
SALES (corp-wide): 1.3B **Privately Held**
SIC: 8733 Medical research
PA: City Of Hope
1500 Duarte Rd
Duarte CA 91010
626 256-4673

(P-25970)
BERKELEY LIGHTS INC (PA)
5858 Horton St Ste 320, Emeryville
(94608-2183)
PHONE...................510 898-1433
Eric Hobbs, *CEO*
Kevin Chapman, *Officer*
Sandra Finley, *Executive*
Igor Khandros, *Principal*
Dana Medler, *Office Mgr*
EMP: 84
SALES (est): 31.6MM **Privately Held**
SIC: 8733 Research institute

(P-25971)
BRENTWOOD BMDICAL RES INST INC
11301 Wilshire Blvd, Los Angeles
(90073-1003)
P.O. Box 25027 (90025-0027)
PHONE...................310 312-1554
Kenneth Hickman, *CEO*
Thoyd Ellis, *CFO*
EMP: 130
SQ FT: 1,500
SALES: 5.1MM **Privately Held**
SIC: 8733 Medical research

(P-25972)
BUCK INST FOR RES ON AGING (PA)
8001 Redwood Blvd, Novato (94945-1400)
PHONE...................415 209-2000
Eric M Verdin, *President*
Raja Kamal, *Senior VP*
Nancy Derr, *Vice Pres*
Remy Gross III, *Vice Pres*
Ralph O Rear, *Vice Pres*
EMP: 175
SQ FT: 185,000
SALES: 39.8MM **Privately Held**
SIC: 8733 Medical research

(P-25973)
CALIFORNIA CMPLTE CNT CNSUS
400 R St Ste 350, Sacramento
(95811-6213)
PHONE...................916 852-2020
Ditas Katague, *Principal*
EMP: 60
SALES (est): 908.1K **Privately Held**
SIC: 8733 Noncommercial research organizations

(P-25974)
CALIFORNIA INSTITUTE TECH
Also Called: Jet Propulsion Laboratory
4800 Oak Grove Dr, Pasadena
(91109-8001)
PHONE...................818 354-9154
Michael Watkins, *Director*
Karen Piggee, *Principal*
EMP: 6000
SALES (corp-wide): 3.3B **Privately Held**
SIC: 8733 Research institute
PA: California Institute Of Technology
1200 E California Blvd
Pasadena CA 91125
626 395-6811

(P-25975)
CALIFORNIA INSTITUTE TECH
Also Called: Athenaeum
551 S Hill Ave, Pasadena (91106-3443)
PHONE...................626 395-8200
Charles Albers, *Manager*
EMP: 100
SQ FT: 6,870
SALES (corp-wide): 3.3B **Privately Held**
WEB: www.caltech.edu
SIC: 8733 8221 Noncommercial research organizations; colleges universities & professional schools
PA: California Institute Of Technology
1200 E California Blvd
Pasadena CA 91125
626 395-6811

(P-25976)
CALIFRNIA PCF MED CTR FNDATION (PA)
2015 Steiner St, San Francisco
(94115-2627)
P.O. Box 7999 (94120-7999)
PHONE...................415 600-4400
Sloan Barnett, *Ch of Bd*
Doug Nelson, *President*
Vernon L Giang, *CEO*
Karen Jeu, *Vice Pres*
EMP: 58
SALES (est): 7.5MM **Privately Held**
SIC: 8733 Medical research

(P-25977)
CANCER PREVENTION INST CAL (PA)
Also Called: Greater Bay Area Cncer Rgistry
2201 Walnut Ave Ste 300, Fremont
(94538-2334)
PHONE...................510 608-5000
Matt O'Grady, *CEO*
Reed Goertler, *Officer*
Jay Yu, *Vice Pres*
Theresa N Keegan, *Research*
Juan Yang, *Research*
EMP: 115 **EST:** 1974
SQ FT: 33,598
SALES: 13MM **Privately Held**
SIC: 8733 Medical research

(P-25978)
CANJI INC
3525 John Hopkins Ct, San Diego
(92121-1121)
PHONE...................858 597-0177
Steven Chang, *Vice Pres*
Donald R Conklin, *Ch of Bd*
Raul E Cesan, *President*
Joseph C Conners, *Exec VP*
Thomas H Kelly, *Exec VP*
EMP: 78
SQ FT: 48,000
SALES (est): 1.9MM
SALES (corp-wide): 42.2B **Publicly Held**
WEB: www.canji.com
SIC: 8733 Biotechnical research, noncommercial
PA: Merck & Co., Inc.
2000 Galloping Hill Rd
Kenilworth NJ 07033
908 740-4000

(P-25979)
CAPRION PROTEOMICS USA LLC
1455 Adams Dr Ste 2124, Menlo Park
(94025-1438)
P.O. Box 16044, San Francisco (94116-0044)
PHONE...................650 776-3676
Martin Leblanc, *CEO*
Dr Daniel Chelsky, *Principal*
EMP: 50
SALES (est): 4.4MM
SALES (corp-wide): 7.5MM **Privately Held**
SIC: 8733 Scientific research agency
PA: Caprion Proteomique Inc
201 Av Du President-Kennedy Bureau 3900
Montreal QC
514 360-3600

(P-25980)
CARNEGIE INSTITUTION WASH
Also Called: Observatories of The Carnegie
813 Santa Barbara St, Pasadena
(91101-1232)
PHONE...................626 577-1122
Wendy L Freedman, *Director*
Jacob Robertson, *Technician*
Sharon Kelly, *Buyer*
EMP: 100
SQ FT: 24,075
SALES: 13.1MM
SALES (corp-wide): 134.4MM **Privately Held**
WEB: www.gl.ciw.edu
SIC: 8733 7999 Scientific research agency; observation tower operation
PA: Carnegie Institution Of Washington
1530 P St Nw
Washington DC 20005
202 387-6400

(P-25981)
CATHOLIC CHARITIES OF LA INC (PA)
1531 James M Wood Blvd, Los Angeles
(90015-1112)
P.O. Box 15095 (90015-0095)
PHONE...................213 251-3400
Monsignor G Cox, *Exec Dir*
James E Bathker, *CFO*
Lelend Ratleff, *Human Res Dir*
Ryzbel Pack, *Coordinator*
EMP: 55
SQ FT: 18,000
SALES: 34.2MM **Privately Held**
SIC: 8733 8322 Noncommercial research organizations; individual & family services

(P-25982)
CENTER FOR CIVIC EDUCATION (PA)
5115 Douglas Fir Rd Ste J, Calabasas
(91302-2590)
PHONE...................818 591-9321
Charles N Quigley, *Exec Dir*
John Hale, *Associate Dir*
Jerry Brown, *Governor*
Margaret Stimmann, *Government*
Maria Gallo, *Director*
EMP: 60
SQ FT: 16,000

SALES: 5.5MM **Privately Held**
WEB: www.civiced.org
SIC: 8733 8748 Educational research agency; educational consultant

(P-25983)
CENTRAL CALIFORNIA TR
22847 Road 140, Tulare (93274-9367)
PHONE..................................559 686-4973
Marylou Polek, *Prgrmr*
Vic Corkins, *Chairman*
Dean Gillette, *Admin Sec*
EMP: 55
SQ FT: 12,500
SALES (est): 1.6MM **Privately Held**
WEB: www.cctea.org
SIC: 8733 Bacteriological research

(P-25984)
CG2 INC
Also Called: Quantum3d Government Systems
1759 Mccarthy Blvd, Milpitas (95035-7416)
PHONE..................................407 737-8800
EMP: 69
SALES (est): 3.2MM **Privately Held**
SIC: 8733

(P-25985)
CHILDRENS HOSP OKLAND RES INST
5700 Martin Luther, Oakland (94609)
PHONE..................................510 450-7600
Antonie H Paap, *President*
Yashmeen Imroz, *Vice Pres*
Vern Marsh, *Administration*
Bowen Antonio, *Software Engr*
Bert Ferrell, *Research*
EMP: 100
SALES (est): 10.3MM
SALES (corp-wide): 178.6MM **Privately Held**
SIC: 8733 Scientific research agency
PA: Children's Hospital & Research Center At Oakland
747 52nd St
Oakland CA 94609
510 428-3000

(P-25986)
CHILDRENS HOSPITAL LOS ANGELES
Also Called: Saban Research Institute, The
4661 W Sunset Blvd, Los Angeles (90027-6042)
PHONE..................................323 361-2751
Cheryl Saban, *Branch Mgr*
EMP: 450
SALES (corp-wide): 1.3B **Privately Held**
SIC: 8733 Medical research
PA: The Childrens Hospital Los Angeles
4650 W Sunset Blvd
Los Angeles CA 90027
323 660-2450

(P-25987)
CHILDRENS INST LOS ANGELES (PA)
2121 W Temple St, Los Angeles (90026-4915)
PHONE..................................213 385-5100
Bradley Myslinski, *President*
Helen Contreras, *Partner*
Eugene Straub, *Treasurer*
Catherine Atack, *Vice Pres*
Martine Singer, *Vice Pres*
EMP: 1000
SALES: 680.1K **Privately Held**
SIC: 8733 Noncommercial research organizations

(P-25988)
CHILDRENS INSTITUTE INC
1215 W Manchester Ave, Los Angeles (90044-2237)
PHONE..................................323 541-9368
EMP: 67
SALES (corp-wide): 75MM **Privately Held**
SIC: 8733 Noncommercial research organizations
PA: Childrens Institute, Inc.
2121 W Temple St
Los Angeles CA 90026
213 385-5100

(P-25989)
COMPLETE GENOMICS INC
2904 Orchard Pkwy, San Jose (95134-2009)
PHONE..................................650 943-2800
Clifford A Reid PHD, *Ch of Bd*
Ajay Bansal, *CFO*
Keith Raffel, *Ch Credit Ofcr*
Arthur W Homan, *Senior VP*
Ethan Knowlden, *Senior VP*
EMP: 255
SQ FT: 66,000
SALES (est): 66.1MM
SALES (corp-wide): 47.8MM **Privately Held**
SIC: 8733 Biotechnical research, noncommercial
PA: Beijing Genomics Institute At Shenzhen
Comprehensive Building, Beishan Industrial Zone, Yantian Street, Shenzhen 51800

(P-25990)
FAIR TRADE USA
1901 Harrison St Ste 1700, Oakland (94612-3635)
PHONE..................................510 663-5260
Paul Rice, *President*
Dave Rochlin, *COO*
Joan Catherine Braun, *CFO*
Donna Hall, *Executive Asst*
Amy Blyth, *Business Mgr*
EMP: 80
SALES: 19.1MM **Privately Held**
SIC: 8733 Noncommercial social research organization

(P-25991)
GARY MARY W WIRELESS HLTH INST
10350 N Torrey Pines Rd, La Jolla (92037-1018)
PHONE..................................858 412-8600
Donald M Casey Jr, *CEO*
Michael Caponetto, *CFO*
Gary West, *Chairman*
Dr Joseph Smith, *Chief Mktg Ofcr*
Dr Eric Topol, *Chief Mktg Ofcr*
EMP: 50
SALES: 184.6K **Privately Held**
SIC: 8733 Medical research

(P-25992)
HORIZON PHARMACEUTICAL LLC (HQ)
7 Hamilton Landing # 100, Novato (94949-8209)
PHONE..................................415 408-6200
Timothy P Walbert, *President*
Barry J Moze, *COO*
Paul W Hoelscher, *CFO*
Robert F Carey, *Officer*
EMP: 74
SQ FT: 52,319
SALES: 94.2MM **Privately Held**
WEB: www.torreypinestherapeutics.com
SIC: 8733 2834 Medical research; pharmaceutical preparations

(P-25993)
HRL LABORATORIES LLC
Also Called: Hughes Research Laboratories
3011 Malibu Canyon Rd, Malibu (90265-4797)
PHONE..................................310 317-5000
Penrose Albright, *President*
Leslie Momoda, *COO*
Roger Gronwald, *CFO*
Albert Cosand, *Principal*
Robin Celenza, *Executive Asst*
EMP: 500
SQ FT: 250,000
SALES (est): 8.7MM **Privately Held**
WEB: www.hrl.com
SIC: 8733 8731 Research institute; commercial physical research

(P-25994)
HUBBS-SEA WORLD RESEARCH INST (PA)
2595 Ingraham St, San Diego (92109-7902)
PHONE..................................619 226-3870
Donald B Kent, *President*

Bethany Smith, *CFO*
Pamela K Yochem, *Exec VP*
Laura Vega, *Info Tech Mgr*
Megan Stolen, *Research*
EMP: 58
SQ FT: 30,000
SALES: 5MM **Privately Held**
WEB: www.hswri.org
SIC: 8733 Scientific research agency

(P-25995)
HUNTINGTON MED RES INSTITUTES
734 Fairmount Ave, Pasadena (91105-3104)
PHONE..................................626 397-5804
EMP: 60
SALES (est): 3.5MM
SALES (corp-wide): 15.5MM **Privately Held**
SIC: 8733
PA: Huntington Medical Research Institutes
686 S Fair Oaks Ave
Pasadena CA 91105
626 795-4343

(P-25996)
IDUN PHARMACEUTICALS INC
9380 Judicial Dr, San Diego (92121-3830)
PHONE..................................858 622-3000
Martin Mackay, *CEO*
David Shapiro, *Exec VP*
EMP: 50
SQ FT: 43,000
SALES (est): 1.4MM
SALES (corp-wide): 33.5MM **Publicly Held**
SIC: 8733 Medical research
PA: Conatus Pharmaceuticals Inc.
16745 W Bernardo Dr # 200
San Diego CA 92127
858 376-2600

(P-25997)
INTERNTIONAL CMPT SCIENCE INST
Also Called: I C S I
1947 Center St Ste 600, Berkeley (94704-1159)
PHONE..................................510 643-9153
Rebecca Pieraccini, *President*
Crutchfield Orpheus, *Vice Pres*
Maria Quintana, *General Mgr*
Cindy Ngu, *Admin Asst*
Albert Park, *Admin Asst*
EMP: 50
SQ FT: 26,000
SALES: 7.8MM **Privately Held**
SIC: 8733 Research institute

(P-25998)
J CRAIG VENTER INSTITUTE INC (PA)
4120 Capricorn Ln, La Jolla (92037-3498)
PHONE..................................301 795-7000
J Craig Venter, *CEO*
Karen Nelson, *President*
Robert Friedman, *COO*
Harold Davies, *CFO*
Julie G Adelson, *Vice Pres*
EMP: 325
SQ FT: 125,000
SALES: 23.2MM **Privately Held**
WEB: www.jcvi.org
SIC: 8733 8731 Research institute; biological research

(P-25999)
JBS INTERNATIONAL INC
555 Airport Blvd Ste 400, Burlingame (94010-2036)
PHONE..................................650 373-4900
Cynthia Currin, *Principal*
Sergio Aguilar, *Info Tech Mgr*
EMP: 55
SALES (corp-wide): 61.2MM **Privately Held**
SIC: 8733 Medical research
PA: Jbs International, Inc.
5515 Security Ln Ste 800
North Bethesda MD 20852
301 495-1080

(P-26000)
JOHN WAYNE INSTITUTE FOR CTR
2200 Santa Monica Blvd, Santa Monica (90404-2312)
PHONE..................................310 449-5253
Patrick Wayne, *Ch of Bd*
Gary Grubbs, *COO*
EMP: 160
SQ FT: 57,000
SALES: 13.9MM **Privately Held**
SIC: 8733 Research institute

(P-26001)
JWCH INSTITUTE INC
6912 Ajax Ave, Bell (90201-4057)
PHONE..................................323 562-5813
Annabel Munoz, *Manager*
EMP: 62
SALES (corp-wide): 33.9MM **Privately Held**
SIC: 8733 Noncommercial research organizations
PA: Jwch Institute, Inc.
5650 Jillson St
Commerce CA 90040
323 477-1171

(P-26002)
JWCH INSTITUTE INC
12360 Firestone Blvd, Norwalk (90650-4324)
PHONE..................................562 281-0306
Oyamendan Itohan, *COO*
EMP: 78
SALES (corp-wide): 33.9MM **Privately Held**
SIC: 8733 Noncommercial research organizations
PA: Jwch Institute, Inc.
5650 Jillson St
Commerce CA 90040
323 477-1171

(P-26003)
LA JOLLA INST FOR IMMUNOLOGY
Also Called: La Jolla Inst For Allergy & Im
9420 Athena Cir, La Jolla (92037-1387)
PHONE..................................858 752-6500
Mitchell Kronenberg, *President*
Eric Zwisler, *Ch of Bd*
Skip Carpowich, *CFO*
Michael Dollar, *CFO*
Gina Kirchweger, *Officer*
EMP: 400
SQ FT: 87,000
SALES: 61.5MM **Privately Held**
SIC: 8733 8731 Medical research; biotechnical research, commercial

(P-26004)
LAS CUMBRES OBSERVATORY GLOBAL
6740 Cortona Dr Ste 102, Goleta (93117-5575)
PHONE..................................805 880-1600
Wayne Rosing, *President*
Dorothy Largay, *Treasurer*
Michael Falarsky, *Exec VP*
Brian Haworth, *Info Tech Mgr*
EMP: 50
SQ FT: 37,795
SALES: 6.1MM **Privately Held**
WEB: www.lcogt.net
SIC: 8733 Scientific research agency

(P-26005)
LELAND STANFORD JUNIOR UNIV
Blum, John Erthquake Engrg Ctr
Melcode 4020 Bldg 540, Stanford (94305)
PHONE..................................650 723-4150
Greg Dierlein, *Director*
EMP: 70
SALES (corp-wide): 11.3B **Privately Held**
SIC: 8733 8221 Research institute; university
PA: Leland Stanford Junior University
450 Jane Stanford Way
Stanford CA 94305
650 723-2300

(P-26006)
LELAND STANFORD JUNIOR UNIV
Also Called: Ginzton Laboratory
450 Via Palou Mall, Stanford (94305-4014)
PHONE...................................650 723-0107
Marilynn Elverson, *Director*
Rubi Paredes, *Executive Asst*
Ross Colvin, *Administration*
Babak B Mortezai, *Info Tech Mgr*
EMP: 150
SALES (corp-wide): 11.3B **Privately Held**
SIC: 8733 8221 Physical research, non-commercial; university
PA: Leland Stanford Junior University
　　450 Jane Stanford Way
　　Stanford CA 94305
　　650 723-2300

(P-26007)
LELAND STANFORD JUNIOR UNIV
Also Called: Stanford Univ Earth Secinces
397 Panama Mall Ste 360, Stanford (94305-2237)
PHONE...................................650 724-8899
Pamila Matson, *Principal*
EMP: 150
SALES (corp-wide): 11.3B **Privately Held**
SIC: 8733 8731 Scientific research agency; commercial physical research
PA: Leland Stanford Junior University
　　450 Jane Stanford Way
　　Stanford CA 94305
　　650 723-2300

(P-26008)
LELAND STANFORD JUNIOR UNIV
Diagnostic Radiology
1201 Welch Rd, Palo Alto (94305-5102)
PHONE...................................650 723-4733
Robert Herfkens, *Principal*
EMP: 67
SALES (corp-wide): 11.3B **Privately Held**
SIC: 8733 8221 Medical research; university
PA: Leland Stanford Junior University
　　450 Jane Stanford Way
　　Stanford CA 94305
　　650 723-2300

(P-26009)
LUMINAR TECHNOLOGIES INC
1891 Page Mill Rd 200, Palo Alto (94304-1211)
PHONE...................................650 849-8797
Austin Russell, *CEO*
EMP: 92
SALES (corp-wide): 3MM **Privately Held**
SIC: 8733 3647 3519 3812 Noncommercial research organizations; vehicular lighting equipment; radiators, stationary engine; search & navigation equipment; prepackaged software
PA: Luminar Technologies, Inc.
　　12601 Research Pkwy
　　Orlando FL 32826
　　407 900-5259

(P-26010)
MILKEN INSTITUTE
1250 4th St, Santa Monica (90401-1366)
PHONE...................................310 570-4600
Michael L Klowden, *CEO*
Michael Milken, *Ch of Bd*
Richard Ditizio, *President*
John Hunter, *CFO*
Elizabeth Robison, *Vice Pres*
▲ EMP: 50
SALES: 79.8MM **Privately Held**
WEB: www.milkeninstitute.com
SIC: 8733 Economic research, noncommercial

(P-26011)
MIND RESEARCH INSTITUTE
Also Called: Music Intllgnce Neuro Dev Inst
111 Academy Ste 100, Irvine (92617-3046)
PHONE...................................949 345-8700
Brett Woudenberg, *CEO*
Gabrielle Abutom, *Partner*
Andrew R Coulson, *President*
Josephine Garrett, *CFO*
Andrew Coulson, *Officer*

EMP: 160
SALES: 26.5MM **Privately Held**
WEB: www.mindinst.org
SIC: 8733 Medical research

(P-26012)
MONTEREY BAY AQUARIUM RES INST
Also Called: Mbari
7700 Sandholdt Rd, Moss Landing (95039-9644)
PHONE...................................831 775-1700
Christopher A Scholin, *President*
Marcia McNutt, *President*
Danielle Neff, *CFO*
Frank Flores, *Chief Mktg Ofcr*
Kim Reisenbichler, *Officer*
▲ EMP: 220
SQ FT: 17,000
SALES: 58.9MM **Privately Held**
WEB: www.mbari.org
SIC: 8733 Noncommercial research organizations

(P-26013)
NAVIGATE BIOPHARMA SVCS INC
1890 Rutherford Rd, Carlsbad (92008-7344)
PHONE...................................866 992-4939
EMP: 180
SALES (est): 588.9K
SALES (corp-wide): 49.1B **Privately Held**
SIC: 8733
HQ: Novartis Finance Corporation
　　230 Park Ave Fl 21
　　New York NY 07936

(P-26014)
NT SUNSET INC
2220 Livingston St # 201, Oakland (94606-5216)
PHONE...................................510 420-3772
Wilbur Ross, *Ch of Bd*
James Curley, *President*
Mark Brutten, *Senior VP*
Dirk Keunen, *Senior VP*
Kelvin Chen, *Vice Pres*
EMP: 50 EST: 1998
SALES (est): 5.7MM **Privately Held**
WEB: www.nano-tex.com
SIC: 8733 Noncommercial research organizations

(P-26015)
OLIVE VIEW/UCLA EDUCATION &
14445 Olive View Dr, Sylmar (91342-1437)
PHONE...................................818 364-3434
Denise Tritt, *General Mgr*
Lisa Gipti, *Accountant*
EMP: 75
SQ FT: 1,326
SALES: 2MM **Privately Held**
SIC: 8733 Medical research

(P-26016)
PALO ALTO VTERANS INST FOR RES
Also Called: Pavir
3801 Miran Ave Bldg 101a, Palo Alto (94304)
PHONE...................................650 858-3970
Kerstin Lynam, *CEO*
Christy Broadwater, *Administration*
Regan Kyler, *Administration*
Andrew Chang, *Research*
Nathalie Tcholagheu, *Financial Analy*
EMP: 218
SQ FT: 5,500
SALES: 28.2MM **Privately Held**
WEB: www.paire.org
SIC: 8733 Medical research; noncommercial biological research organization; scientific research agency

(P-26017)
PARKINSONS INSTITUTE
2500 Hospital Dr Bldg 10, Mountain View (94040-4106)
P.O. Box 70727, Sunnyvale (94086-0727)
PHONE...................................800 786-2958
Carrolee Barlow, *CEO*
Irwin Helford, *Ch of Bd*

EMP: 85
SQ FT: 40,000
SALES (est): 8.8MM **Privately Held**
WEB: www.parkinsonsinstitute.org
SIC: 8733 8011 Medical research; clinic, operated by physicians

(P-26018)
PFIZER INC
10777 Science Center Dr, San Diego (92121-1111)
PHONE...................................858 622-3000
Karen Katen, *Branch Mgr*
EMP: 1300
SALES (corp-wide): 53.6B **Publicly Held**
WEB: www.pfizer.com
SIC: 8733 Medical research
PA: Pfizer Inc.
　　235 E 42nd St
　　New York NY 10017
　　212 733-2323

(P-26019)
POINT REYES BIRD OBSERVATORY
Also Called: Point Blue Cnservation Science
3820 Cypress Dr Ste 11, Petaluma (94954-6964)
PHONE...................................707 781-2555
Ellie M Cohen, *President*
Kate Howard, *Partner*
Luke Petersen, *Partner*
Corey Shake, *Partner*
Carrie Wendt, *Partner*
EMP: 85
SQ FT: 2,000
SALES: 12.3MM **Privately Held**
SIC: 8733 8748 Noncommercial biological research organization; business consulting

(P-26020)
PREMIER SOURCE LLC
999 Bayhill Dr Fl 3, San Bruno (94066-3070)
PHONE...................................415 349-2010
EMP: 65
SQ FT: 13,000
SALES (est): 3.4MM
SALES (corp-wide): 153.1B **Publicly Held**
SIC: 8733
PA: Amerisourcebergen Corporation
　　1300 Morris Dr Ste 100
　　Chesterbrook PA 19087
　　610 727-7000

(P-26021)
PROTHENA BIOSCIENCES INC
331 Oyster Point Blvd, South San Francisco (94080-1913)
PHONE...................................650 837-8550
Dale Schenk, *CEO*
Ingrid Paulson, *Associate Dir*
A W Homan, *Principal*
Martin Koller MD, *Principal*
Jose Tapia, *Research*
EMP: 50
SALES (est): 9.9MM **Privately Held**
SIC: 8733 Medical research

(P-26022)
PUBLIC HEALTH INSTITUTE (PA)
555 12th St Ste 1050, Oakland (94607-3630)
PHONE...................................510 285-5500
Mary Pittman, *President*
Melange Matthews, *COO*
Bob Wolfson, *COO*
Tamar Dorfman, *CFO*
Matthew Marsom, *Vice Pres*
EMP: 100
SQ FT: 50,000
SALES: 112.1MM **Privately Held**
WEB: www.bmsg.org
SIC: 8733 Scientific research agency; medical research

(P-26023)
RANCHO RESEARCH INSTITUTE
Also Called: Rri
7601 Imperial Hwy, Downey (90242-3456)
P.O. Box 3500 (90242-3500)
PHONE...................................562 401-8111
Julia Laplount, *CEO*
Yaga Szlachcic, *President*

EMP: 175
SQ FT: 15,000
SALES: 6.8MM **Privately Held**
WEB: www.larei.org
SIC: 8733 Educational research agency; scientific research agency

(P-26024)
REGULUS THERAPEUTICS INC
10628 Science Center Dr # 225, San Diego (92121-1124)
PHONE...................................858 202-6300
Stelios Papadopoulos, *Ch of Bd*
Joseph P Hagan, *President*
Daniel Chevallard, *CFO*
Hugh Rosen, *Bd of Directors*
Leslie Winchester, *Facilities Mgr*
EMP: 63 EST: 2008
SQ FT: 59,000
SALES: 72K **Privately Held**
SIC: 8733 Biotechnical research, noncommercial

(P-26025)
RIVERSIDE RESEARCH INSTITUTE
3333 W Coast Hwy Ste 101, Newport Beach (92663-4039)
PHONE...................................949 631-0107
Rosemary Ellis, *Director*
EMP: 50
SALES (corp-wide): 88.1MM **Privately Held**
SIC: 8733 8092 Research institute; kidney dialysis centers
PA: Riverside Research Institute
　　156 William St Fl 9
　　New York NY 10038
　　212 563-4545

(P-26026)
SANFORD BURNHAM PREBYS MEDICAL (PA)
Also Called: SBP
10901 N Torrey Pines Rd, La Jolla (92037-1005)
PHONE...................................858 795-5000
Perry Nisen, *CEO*
Kristiina Vuori, *President*
Gary Chessum, *CFO*
Vada Nobles, *Officer*
Robin Ryan, *Vice Pres*
EMP: 966
SQ FT: 397,000
SALES: 123.7MM **Privately Held**
SIC: 8733 Research institute

(P-26027)
SANTEN INCORPORATED
6401 Hollis St Ste 125, Emeryville (94608-1462)
PHONE...................................415 268-9100
Akihiro Aki Tsujimura, *Principal*
Xavier Avat, *President*
Reza M Haque, *Senior VP*
Peter Sallstig, *Senior VP*
EMP: 100
SQ FT: 46,000
SALES (est): 25.7MM **Privately Held**
WEB: www.santeninc.com
SIC: 8733 8011 8731 Noncommercial biological research organization; offices & clinics of medical doctors; commercial physical research
PA: Santen Pharmaceutical Co., Ltd.
　　4-20, Ofukacho, Kita-Ku
　　Osaka OSK 530-0

(P-26028)
SCRIPPS RESEARCH INSTITUTE
Also Called: Calibr A Division Scripps RES
11119 N Torrey Pines Rd, La Jolla (92037-1046)
PHONE...................................858 242-1000
EMP: 99 **Privately Held**
SIC: 8733 Medical research
PA: The Scripps Research Institute
　　10550 N Torrey Pines Rd
　　La Jolla CA 92037

(P-26029)
SCRIPPS RESEARCH INSTITUTE (PA)
10550 N Torrey Pines Rd, La Jolla (92037-1000)
PHONE.....................858 784-1000
Peter G Schultz, *CEO*
Ronald L Davis, *Ch of Bd*
John D Diekman, *Ch of Bd*
Steve A Kay, *President*
Cary E Thomas, *CFO*
EMP: 148
SALES: 348.5MM **Privately Held**
SIC: 8733 Research institute

(P-26030)
SETI INSTITUTE
Also Called: Seti Institute, The
189 Bernardo Ave Ste 100, Mountain View (94043-5139)
PHONE.....................650 961-6633
Matthew Doan, *President*
Dr John Billingham, *Vice Chairman*
Edna Devor, *CEO*
Shannon Atkinson, *CFO*
Dr Greg Papadopolous, *Chairman*
EMP: 115
SQ FT: 19,737
SALES: 18.9MM **Privately Held**
WEB: www.voyagesthroughtime.org
SIC: 8733 Research institute

(P-26031)
SOUTHERN CALIFORNIA INSTITUTE
Also Called: S C I R E
5901 E 7th St 151, Long Beach (90822-5201)
P.O. Box 15298 (90815-0298)
PHONE.....................562 826-8139
Timothy R Morgan, *President*
Moti Kashyap MD, *Treasurer*
EMP: 80
SALES: 6MM **Privately Held**
WEB: www.scire.com
SIC: 8733 Medical research

(P-26032)
SRI INTERNATIONAL (PA)
333 Ravenswood Ave, Menlo Park (94025-3493)
P.O. Box 2203 (94026-2203)
PHONE.....................650 859-2000
William Jeffrey, *CEO*
Denise Glyn Borders, *President*
Stephen Ciesinski, *President*
Manish Kothari, *President*
Greg Kovacs, *President*
▲ **EMP:** 1430
SQ FT: 1,300,000
SALES: 461.4MM **Privately Held**
WEB: www.sri.com
SIC: 8733 8748 Scientific research agency; noncommercial social research organization; business consulting

(P-26033)
SRI INTERNATIONAL
4111 Broad St Ste 220, San Luis Obispo (93401-8743)
PHONE.....................805 542-9330
EMP: 142
SALES (corp-wide): 550MM **Privately Held**
SIC: 8733
PA: Sri International
333 Ravenswood Ave
Menlo Park CA 94025
650 859-2000

(P-26034)
STANFORD UNIV FRMAN SPGLI INST
616 Jane Stanford Way, Stanford (94305-6008)
PHONE.....................650 723-8681
Michael McFaul, *Director*
David Pagano, *Corp Comm Staff*
EMP: 250
SALES (est): 3.3MM **Privately Held**
SIC: 8733 Research institute

(P-26035)
STUDY US RESEARCH INST INC
1335 N La Brea Ave 2-205, Los Angeles (90028-3905)
PHONE.....................213 840-9575
Tiffany S Bennett, *President*
EMP: 99
SALES: 250K **Privately Held**
SIC: 8733 Noncommercial research organizations

(P-26036)
TAKEDA CALIFORNIA INC
Also Called: Tcal
10410 Science Center Dr, San Diego (92121-1119)
PHONE.....................858 622-8528
Keith Wilson, *President*
Kim Docken, *President*
David Weitz, *Vice Pres*
Cheryl Magdaraog, *Associate Dir*
Gary Lavaliere, *General Mgr*
EMP: 220
SALES (est): 41.9MM **Privately Held**
WEB: www.takedasd.com
SIC: 8733 Biotechnical research, noncommercial
PA: Takeda Pharmaceutical Company Limited
2-1-1, Nihombashihoncho
Chuo-Ku TKY 103-0

(P-26037)
THE NATIONAL FOOD LAB LLC
365 N Canyons Pkwy # 201, Livermore (94551-7703)
PHONE.....................925 828-1440
Austin Sharp, *President*
Jena Roberts, *Vice Pres*
Carolyn Graham,
Mindy Hungerman,
Kevin Waters,
EMP: 150 **EST:** 1991
SQ FT: 21,000
SALES (est): 23.5MM **Privately Held**
WEB: www.thenfl.com
SIC: 8733 Scientific research agency

(P-26038)
TOYOTA RESEARCH INSTITUTE INC
4440 El Camino Real, Los Altos (94022-1003)
PHONE.....................703 231-6680
Krshan Toursohi, *General Mgr*
EMP: 94 **Privately Held**
SIC: 8733 Research institute
HQ: Toyota Research Institute, Inc.
1 Kendall Sq Ste B200
Cambridge MA 02139
857 285-6160

(P-26039)
UNITED STATES DEPT OF ENERGY
Also Called: Lawrence Berkeley National Lab
1 Cyclotron Rd, Berkeley (94720-8099)
PHONE.....................510 486-4000
EMP: 5000 **Publicly Held**
SIC: 8733 9611
HQ: United States Dept Of Energy
1000 Independence Ave Sw
Washington DC 20585
202 586-5000

(P-26040)
UNIVERSITY CAL LOS ANGELES
Ucla Dept of Mdcine Div Gm/Hsr
1100 Glendon Ave Ste 850, Los Angeles (90024-3525)
PHONE.....................310 794-2284
Mark Lucas, *Manager*
Ron Hays, *Professor*
Julie Friedman, *Director*
EMP: 50 **Privately Held**
SIC: 8733 8221 9411 Medical research; university; administration of educational programs;
HQ: University Of California, Los Angeles
405 Hilgard Ave
Los Angeles CA 90095

(P-26041)
UNIVERSITY CAL SAN FRANCISCO
Also Called: Uscf Caps Department Medicine
500 Parnassus Ave, San Francisco (94143-2203)
PHONE.....................415 476-9000
EMP: 87
SALES (corp-wide): 9.5B **Privately Held**
SIC: 8733 8221 9411
HQ: University Of California, San Francisco
505 Parnassus Ave
San Francisco CA 94143
415 476-9000

(P-26042)
UNIVERSITY CALIFORNIA BERKELEY
Also Called: Lawrence Berkeley National Lab
5885 Hollis St, Emeryville (94608-2404)
PHONE.....................510 495-2490
Michael Witherell, *Director*
EMP: 3304
SALES: 8733 8221 9411 Noncommercial research organizations; university; administration of educational programs;
HQ: The University California Berkeley
200 Clfrnia Hall Spc 1500
Berkeley CA 94720
510 642-6000

(P-26043)
VIACYTE INC
3550 General Atomics Ct B2-503, San Diego (92121-1122)
PHONE.....................858 455-3708
Paul K Laikind, *President*
Anthony Gringeri, *Officer*
Allan Robins, *Senior VP*
Howard Foyt, *Vice Pres*
Anne Sandan, *Vice Pres*
EMP: 55
SQ FT: 12,000
SALES (est): 11.2MM **Privately Held**
WEB: www.novocell.com
SIC: 8733 2836 Medical research; biological products, except diagnostic

(P-26044)
WATER RESOURCES CAL DEPT
Division of Flood Management
3310 El Cmino Ave Ste 200, Sacramento (95821)
PHONE.....................916 574-1423
Jean Hostler, *Engineer*
Irma Clevenger, *Manager*
EMP: 100 **Privately Held**
SIC: 8733 Research institute
HQ: California Department Of Water Resources
1416 9th St
Sacramento CA 95814
916 653-9394

(P-26045)
WCCT GLOBAL INC (PA)
5630 Cerritos Ave, Cypress (90630-4738)
PHONE.....................714 668-1500
Bill Taaffe, *CEO*
EMP: 81
SALES (est): 35.5MM **Privately Held**
SIC: 8733 Research institute

(P-26046)
WESTED
300 Lakeside Dr Fl 25th, Oakland (94612-3534)
PHONE.....................510 302-4200
Teresa Johnson, *Branch Mgr*
Marycruz Diaz, *Research*
Eric Haas, *Research*
Joaquin Petersen, *Technology*
Robert Montgomery, *Sr Project Mgr*
EMP: 62
SALES (corp-wide): 99.7MM **Privately Held**
WEB: www.edgateway.net
SIC: 8733 8732 Educational research agency; commercial nonphysical research
PA: Wested
730 Harrison St Ste 500
San Francisco CA 94107
415 565-3000

(P-26047)
WESTED
180 Harbor Dr Ste 112, Sausalito (94965-2845)
PHONE.....................415 289-2300
Peter Mangione, *Branch Mgr*
Juan Bojorquez, *Research*
Valentin Pedroza, *Research*
Kyle Walsh, *Analyst*
Ronia Tan, *Controller*
EMP: 51
SALES (corp-wide): 99.7MM **Privately Held**
WEB: www.edgateway.net
SIC: 8733 8732 Educational research agency; commercial nonphysical research
PA: Wested
730 Harrison St Ste 500
San Francisco CA 94107
415 565-3000

(P-26048)
WESTED (PA)
730 Harrison St Ste 500, San Francisco (94107-1242)
PHONE.....................415 565-3000
Glen H Harvey, *CEO*
Nancy M Riddle, *CFO*
Sandy Baba, *Vice Pres*
Virginia Besser, *Vice Pres*
Sheyanne Johnson, *Executive Asst*
EMP: 115
SQ FT: 85,000
SALES (est): 99.7MM **Privately Held**
WEB: www.edgateway.net
SIC: 8733 Educational research agency

(P-26049)
WHITTIER INST FOR DIABETES
10140 Campus Point Dr, San Diego (92121-1520)
PHONE.....................877 944-8843
Athena Tsimikas, *Exec Dir*
EMP: 80
SALES (est): 3.9MM
SALES (corp-wide): 2.1B **Privately Held**
WEB: www.scripps.org
SIC: 8733 Medical research
PA: Scripps Health
10140 Campus Point Dr Ax415
San Diego CA 92121
800 727-4777

(P-26050)
ZONARE MEDICAL SYSTEMS INC
420 Bernardo Ave, Mountain View (94043-5209)
P.O. Box 760, Alviso (95002-0760)
PHONE.....................650 230-2800
Donald Southard, *CEO*
Timothy A Marcotte, *President*
Steve Edwards, *Vice Pres*
Michael Gabler, *Vice Pres*
Glen W McLaughlin, *Vice Pres*
EMP: 65
SALES (est): 19.1MM **Privately Held**
WEB: www.zonare.com
SIC: 8733 5047 Research institute; hospital equipment & supplies
PA: Mindray Medical International Limited
C/O: Conyers Trust Company (Cayman) Limited
George Town GR CAYMAN

8734 Testing Laboratories

(P-26051)
ACCION LABS US INC
4633 Old Ironsides Dr # 304, Santa Clara (95054-1807)
PHONE.....................408 970-9809
William Flavin, *General Mgr*
Sandesh Sukamaran, *Vice Pres*
Shyam Upadhyay, *Vice Pres*
Nikhil Damwani, *Business Dir*
Anamika Khandelwal, *Sr Software Eng*
EMP: 1465
SALES (corp-wide): 7.3MM **Privately Held**
SIC: 8734 Testing laboratories

PA: Accion Labs Us, Inc.
1225 Wash Pike Ste 401
Bridgeville PA 15017
724 260-5139

(P-26052)

AGRICULTURE AND PRIORITY POLLU (PA)

Also Called: Appl
908 N Temperance Ave, Clovis
(93611-8606)
PHONE..................559 275-2175
Diane Anderson, *President*
Bradford Anderson, *Corp Secy*
Sharon Dehmlow, *General Mgr*
Cynthia Clark, *Project Mgr*
Rene Patterson, *Safety Mgr*
EMP: 50
SQ FT: 8,000
SALES (est): 9.1MM **Privately Held**
SIC: 8734 Pollution testing

(P-26053)

AIRCRAFT XRAY LABORATORIES INC

5216 Pacific Blvd, Huntington Park
(90255-2595)
PHONE..................323 587-4141
Gary G Newton, *CEO*
Justin Guzman, *President*
James Newton, *Vice Pres*
Sandi Spelic, *Principal*
Alex Mazzeo, *CTO*
EMP: 80
SQ FT: 60,000
SALES (est): 11.5MM **Privately Held**
WEB: www.aircraftxray.com
SIC: 8734 7384 3471 Testing laboratories; photograph developing & retouching; plating & polishing

(P-26054)

ALS SERVICES USA CORP

1875 Coronado Ave, Long Beach
(90755-1245)
PHONE..................562 597-3932
Pete Guebara, *Branch Mgr*
EMP: 100 **Privately Held**
SIC: 8734 Testing laboratories
HQ: Als Services Usa, Corp.
10450 Stncliff Rd Ste 210
Houston TX 77099
281 530-5656

(P-26055)

ATLAS TESTING LABORATORIES INC

9820 6th St, Rancho Cucamonga
(91730-5714)
PHONE..................909 373-4130
H Leo Norton, *President*
Karla Hernandez, *Manager*
EMP: 50
SQ FT: 25,000
SALES (est): 7.2MM **Privately Held**
WEB: www.atlastesting.com
SIC: 8734 Metallurgical testing laboratory

(P-26056)

BABCOCK LABORATORIES INC

Also Called: E. S. Babcock & Sons
6100 Quail Valley Ct, Riverside
(92507-0704)
P.O. Box 432 (92502-0432)
PHONE..................951 653-3351
Allison Mackenzie, *CEO*
Nicole Greenwood, *Technician*
Larry Chrystal, *Technical Staff*
Marianna Etcheverria, *Controller*
Alex Chrystal, *Corp Comm Staff*
EMP: 70
SQ FT: 20,000
SALES (est): 14MM **Privately Held**
WEB: www.babcocklabs.com
SIC: 8734 Water testing laboratory; food testing service

(P-26057)

BC LABORATORIES INC

4100 Atlas Ct, Bakersfield (93308-4510)
PHONE..................661 327-4911
Carolyn I Jackson, *President*
Richard Eglin, *Shareholder*
Stuart Buttram, *Lab Dir*
Miranda Sonia, *QA Dir*

Chrissy Herndon, *Project Mgr*
EMP: 93
SQ FT: 18,000
SALES (est): 11.5MM **Privately Held**
WEB: www.bclabs.com
SIC: 8734 Water testing laboratory

(P-26058)

BIOSCREEN TESTING SERVICES INC (DH)

3904 Del Amo Blvd Ste 801, Torrance
(90503-2183)
PHONE..................310 214-0043
Bradford L Rope, *President*
Ranil M Fernando, *Vice Pres*
EMP: 85
SQ FT: 20,000
SALES (est): 25.7MM **Privately Held**
WEB: www.bioscreen.com
SIC: 8734 8731 Testing laboratories; commercial physical research
HQ: Als Group Usa, Corp.
10450 Stncliff Rd Ste 210
Houston TX 77099
281 530-5656

(P-26059)

CATALENT SAN DIEGO INC

7330 Carroll Rd Ste 200, San Diego
(92121-2364)
PHONE..................858 805-6383
Timothy Scott, *President*
Sara Urbas, *Project Mgr*
Jodie Simbolon, *Controller*
Kristl Kosaka, *Materials Mgr*
Jason Everett, *Mfg Staff*
EMP: 120
SQ FT: 6,600
SALES (est): 21.7MM **Publicly Held**
WEB: www.pharmatek.com
SIC: 8734 8731 Testing laboratories; commercial research laboratory
HQ: Catalent Pharma Solutions, Inc.
14 Schoolhouse Rd
Somerset NJ 08873

(P-26060)

CENTRAL COUNTIES

241 Business Park Way, Atwater
(95301-9487)
PHONE..................209 356-0355
Christine Hackler, *Principal*
EMP: 70
SALES (est): 5.5MM **Privately Held**
SIC: 8734 Testing laboratories

(P-26061)

COOPER & JACKSON INC

310 Shaw Rd Ste D, South San Francisco
(94080-6615)
PHONE..................408 437-2750
Kevin Waldron, *President*
Jeanine Waldron, *Vice Pres*
EMP: 200
SQ FT: 52,000
SALES (est): 11.1MM **Privately Held**
SIC: 8734 1521 Testing laboratories; repairing fire damage, single-family houses; single-family home remodeling, additions & repairs

(P-26062)

DACOR HOLDINGS INC

14425 Clark Ave, City of Industry
(91745-1235)
P.O. Box 90070 (91715-0070)
PHONE..................626 626-4461
Michael Joseph, *President*
EMP: 150
SALES (est): 11.4MM **Privately Held**
SIC: 8734 Testing laboratories

(P-26063)

DE PAR INC

Also Called: Associated Laboratories
931 W Barkley Ave, Orange (92868-1208)
PHONE..................714 771-6900
Tito L Parola, *President*
Robert Webber, *Treasurer*
Edward Behare, *Admin Sec*
Kristen Walker, *Project Mgr*
Winston Yu, *Project Mgr*
EMP: 85 EST: 1924
SQ FT: 17,000

SALES (est): 10.5MM **Privately Held**
WEB: www.associatedlabs.com
SIC: 8734 Testing laboratories

(P-26064)

DICKSON TESTING CO INC (DH)

11126 Palmer Ave, South Gate
(90280-7492)
PHONE..................562 862-8378
Robert Lyddon, *President*
Jim Scanell, *Vice Pres*
EMP: 80
SQ FT: 40,000
SALES (est): 15.2MM
SALES (corp-wide): 225.3B **Publicly Held**
WEB: www.dicksontesting.com
SIC: 8734 Metallurgical testing laboratory
HQ: Precision Castparts Corp.
4650 Sw Mcdam Ave Ste 300
Portland OR 97239
503 946-4800

(P-26065)

ELEMENT MTRLS TECH HB INC

18100 S Wilmington Ave, Compton
(90220-5909)
PHONE..................310 632-8500
Chuck Gee, *General Mgr*
Jo Wetz, *CFO*
Cindy Castellanos, *Purchasing*
EMP: 86
SALES (corp-wide): 222K **Privately Held**
WEB: www.stork.com
SIC: 8734 Metallurgical testing laboratory
HQ: Element Materials Technology Huntington Beach Inc.
15062 Bolsa Chica St
Huntington Beach CA 92649
714 892-1961

(P-26066)

ELEMENT MTRLS TECH HB INC (DH)

15062 Bolsa Chica St, Huntington Beach
(92649-1023)
PHONE..................714 892-1961
Charles Noall, *President*
Eelco Niermeijer, *CFO*
Pete Regan, *Chairman*
Jeff Joyce, *Exec VP*
Jo Wetz, *Exec VP*
EMP: 80
SQ FT: 4,500
SALES (est): 39.8MM
SALES (corp-wide): 222K **Privately Held**
WEB: www.stork.com
SIC: 8734 Metallurgical testing laboratory
HQ: Element Materials Technology Group Us Holdings Inc.
15062 Bolsa Chica St
Huntington Beach CA 92649
714 892-1961

(P-26067)

ELLIOTT LABORATORIES INC

41039 Boyce Rd, Fremont (94538-2434)
PHONE..................510 440-9500
Conrad Chu, *Principal*
EMP: 50
SALES (est): 2.3MM **Privately Held**
SIC: 8734 Testing laboratories

(P-26068)

EMAX LABORATORIES INC

1835 W 205th St, Torrance (90501-1510)
PHONE..................310 618-8889
Caspar J Pang, *CEO*
Kam P Yee, *President*
Richard Beauvil, *Officer*
Sing C Pang, *Admin Sec*
Rina Kato, *Project Mgr*
EMP: 50
SQ FT: 14,000
SALES (est): 11.2MM **Privately Held**
WEB: www.emaxlabs.com
SIC: 8734 8748 8731 Pollution testing; environmental consultant; environmental research

(P-26069)

EMERY SMITH LABORATORIES INC

781 E Washington Blvd, Los Angeles
(90021-3043)
PHONE..................213 745-5333

James E Partridge, *CEO*
EMP: 135
SALES (est): 14.7MM **Privately Held**
SIC: 8734 Testing laboratories

(P-26070)

ENVIRONMENTAL HEALTH HAZARD

1515 Clay St Ste 1600, Oakland
(94612-1499)
PHONE..................510 622-3200
EMP: 70 **Privately Held**
WEB: www.oehha.ca.gov
SIC: 8734 9511 Hazardous waste testing; air, water & solid waste management;
HQ: California Office Of Environmental Health Hazard Assessment
1001 I St
Sacramento CA 95814
916 324-7572

(P-26071)

EUROFINS AIR TOXICS LLC

180 Blue Ravine Rd Ste B, Folsom
(95630-4703)
PHONE..................916 985-1000
J Wilson Hershey, *Ch of Bd*
Thomas E Wolgemuth, *Corp Secy*
Bob Mitzel, *VP Bus Dvlpt*
Delia Rangel, *Technician*
Ed Danek, *Analyst*
EMP: 55
SQ FT: 24,000
SALES (est): 8.9MM
SALES (corp-wide): 11.5MM **Privately Held**
WEB: www.airtoxics.com
SIC: 8734 Water testing laboratory
PA: Eurofins Environment Testing Us Holdings, Inc.
2200 Rittenhouse St # 175
Des Moines IA 50321
515 698-5039

(P-26072)

EUROFINS EAG ENGRG SCIENCE LLC (DH)

2710 Walsh Ave, Santa Clara
(95051-0963)
PHONE..................408 588-0050
Stefan Karnavas, *President*
EMP: 100
SALES (est): 2.4MM
SALES (corp-wide): 866.9K **Privately Held**
SIC: 8734 Testing laboratories
HQ: Eurofins Eag Holdings, Inc.
4747 Executive Dr Ste 700
San Diego CA 92121
949 521-6200

(P-26073)

EUROFINS EAG MTLS SCIENCE LLC (DH)

810 Kifer Rd, Sunnyvale (94086-5203)
PHONE..................408 454-4600
Stefan Karnavas, *President*
Arun Kumar, *Vice Pres*
Carey Lewis, *Vice Pres*
EMP: 148
SQ FT: 70,000
SALES (est): 179.3MM
SALES (corp-wide): 866.9K **Privately Held**
WEB: www.eaglabs.com
SIC: 8734 Product testing laboratories
HQ: Eurofins Eag Holdings, Inc.
4747 Executive Dr Ste 700
San Diego CA 92121
949 521-6200

(P-26074)

FORENSIC ANALYTICAL SPC INC (PA)

3777 Depot Rd Ste 409, Hayward
(94545-2761)
PHONE..................510 887-8828
David Kuhane, *President*
John Martinelli, *Branch Mgr*
Nicole Adams, *Administration*
Dan Coltrin, *IT Executive*
Dan Cox, *Data Proc Staff*
EMP: 120
SQ FT: 40,000

SALES (est): 12.3MM **Privately Held**
WEB: www.forensica.com
SIC: 8734 8748 Forensic laboratory; environmental consultant

(P-26075)
GENZYME CORPORATION
2440 S Sepulveda Blvd # 100, Los Angeles (90064-1784)
PHONE..................................310 482-5000
Richard Adleson, *Branch Mgr*
Robert Bellantuoni, *Human Res Dir*
Robert V Pierre, *Pathologist*
EMP: 200 **Privately Held**
WEB: www.genzyme.com
SIC: 8734 8731 Testing laboratories; commercial physical research
HQ: Genzyme Corporation
50 Binney St
Cambridge MA 02142
617 252-7500

(P-26076)
GITLAB INC
4128 24th St, San Francisco (94114-3615)
PHONE..................................408 569-3035
Sytse Sijbrandij, *CEO*
Paul Machle, *CFO*
Todd Barr, *Chief Mktg Ofcr*
Eric Johnson, *Vice Pres*
Scott Williamson, *Vice Pres*
EMP: 670
SALES (est): 778.1K
SALES (corp-wide): 484.2K **Privately Held**
SIC: 8734 7372 Testing laboratories; prepackaged software
PA: Gitlab B.V.
Ondiep 108
Utrecht
625 588-892

(P-26077)
HORIZON WEST INC
Also Called: Oakwood Village
3388 Bell Rd, Auburn (95603-9242)
PHONE..................................530 889-8122
Roubah Moredhesal, *President*
EMP: 55
SALES (corp-wide): 103.9MM **Privately Held**
SIC: 8734 8361 Food testing service; residential care
PA: Horizon West, Inc.
4020 Sierra College Blvd
Rocklin CA 95677
916 624-6230

(P-26078)
IDEXX REFERENCE LABS INC
1370 Reynolds Ave Ste 109, Irvine (92614-5545)
PHONE..................................949 477-2840
Carlos Vasquez, *Manager*
EMP: 50
SALES (corp-wide): 2.2B **Publicly Held**
SIC: 8734 Testing laboratories
HQ: Idexx Reference Laboratories, Inc.
1 Idexx Dr
Westbrook ME 04092
207 556-0300

(P-26079)
IDEXX REFERENCE LABS INC
2825 Kovr Dr, West Sacramento (95605-1600)
PHONE..................................916 372-4200
Lewis Knight, *Branch Mgr*
EMP: 175
SALES (corp-wide): 2.2B **Publicly Held**
SIC: 8734 Testing laboratories
HQ: Idexx Reference Laboratories, Inc.
1 Idexx Dr
Westbrook ME 04092
207 556-0300

(P-26080)
IMAGING HLTHCARE SPCALISTS LLC
6386 Alvarado Ct, San Diego (92120-4905)
PHONE..................................619 229-2299
EMP: 61 **Privately Held**
SIC: 8734 Testing laboratories

PA: Imaging Healthcare Specialists, Llc
150 W Washington St
San Diego CA 92103

(P-26081)
INTERTEK TESTING SVCS NA INC
25800 Commercentre Dr, Lake Forest (92630-8804)
PHONE..................................949 448-4100
EMP: 65
SALES (corp-wide): 3.6B **Privately Held**
SIC: 8734 Testing laboratories
HQ: Intertek Testing Services Na, Inc.
3933 Us Route 11
Cortland NY 13045
607 753-6711

(P-26082)
INTERTEK TESTING SVCS NA INC
25791 Commercentre Dr, Lake Forest (92630-8803)
PHONE..................................949 349-1684
Richard Adams, *Branch Mgr*
EMP: 60
SALES (corp-wide): 3.6B **Privately Held**
SIC: 8734 Testing laboratories
HQ: Intertek Testing Services Na, Inc.
3933 Us Route 11
Cortland NY 13045
607 753-6711

(P-26083)
INTERTEK USA INC
Also Called: Intertek Pharmaceutical Svcs
10420 Wateridge Cir, San Diego (92121-5773)
PHONE..................................858 558-2599
Arron Xu, *Manager*
EMP: 100
SALES (corp-wide): 3.6B **Privately Held**
SIC: 8734 Testing laboratories
HQ: Intertek Usa Inc.
200 Westlke Prk Blvd 40
Houston TX 77079
713 543-3600

(P-26084)
INVITAE CORPORATION (PA)
1400 16th St, San Francisco (94103-5110)
PHONE..................................415 374-7782
Randal W Scott, *Ch of Bd*
Lisa McCauley, *Regional Mgr*
Will Schaeffler, *Regional Mgr*
Gina Shaner, *Regional Mgr*
Erik Malin, *Division Mgr*
EMP: 142
SQ FT: 7,795
SALES: 147.7MM **Publicly Held**
SIC: 8734 Testing laboratories

(P-26085)
IRVINE PHARMACEUTICAL SVCS INC
30262 Crown Valley Pkwy, Laguna Niguel (92677-2364)
PHONE..................................949 439-6677
Assad Kazeminy, *CEO*
▲ **EMP:** 51
SALES (est): 15MM **Privately Held**
WEB: www.irvinepharma.com
SIC: 8734 Testing laboratories

(P-26086)
ISE LABS INC (DH)
46800 Bayside Pkwy, Fremont (94538-6592)
PHONE..................................510 687-2500
Tien Wu, *CEO*
Jeff Thompson, *Vice Pres*
EMP: 200
SQ FT: 69,000
SALES (est): 52.5MM **Privately Held**
WEB: www.iselabs.com
SIC: 8734 3672 Calibration & certification; printed circuit boards

(P-26087)
MALIBU IT LABS LLC
1250 Borregas Ave, Sunnyvale (94089-1309)
PHONE..................................408 650-6100
Brandon Schmoll, *Principal*

Krishna Doddi, *Principal*
EMP: 99
SALES (est): 1.3MM **Privately Held**
SIC: 8734 Testing laboratories

(P-26088)
MCCAMPBELL ANALYTICAL INC
1534 Willow Pass Rd, Pittsburg (94565-1701)
PHONE..................................925 252-9262
Edward Hamilton, *CEO*
Ed Hamilton, *Lab Dir*
Rosa Venegas, *Business Dir*
Blake Brown, *Project Mgr*
Yen Cao, *Project Mgr*
EMP: 63
SQ FT: 12,896
SALES (est): 10.5MM **Privately Held**
WEB: www.mccampbell.com
SIC: 8734 Testing laboratories

(P-26089)
MICHELSON LABORATORIES INC (PA)
6280 Chalet Dr, Commerce (90040-3761)
PHONE..................................562 928-0553
Grant Michelson, *President*
Jack E Michelson, *CEO*
Eva Vasco, *Administration*
Benjamin Garcia, *Info Tech Mgr*
Steve Roesch, *Director*
EMP: 65
SQ FT: 20,000
SALES (est): 12.9MM **Privately Held**
WEB: www.michelsonlab.com
SIC: 8734 Food testing service

(P-26090)
MILLENNIUM HEALTH LLC
16981 Via Tazon Ste F, San Diego (92127-1645)
PHONE..................................877 451-3534
Jennifer Strickland, *CEO*
Eugene I Davis, *Ch of Bd*
Howard Appel, *President*
David Cohen, *COO*
Mark A Winham, *COO*
EMP: 258
SALES (est): 72.8MM **Privately Held**
SIC: 8734 Testing laboratories

(P-26091)
MIRION TECHNOLOGIES GDS INC (HQ)
Also Called: Global Dosimetry Solutions
2652 Mcgaw Ave, Irvine (92614-5840)
PHONE..................................949 419-1000
Thomas Logan, *CEO*
Sander Perle, *President*
James Hippel, *CFO*
Jack Pacheco, *CFO*
Antony Besso, *Exec VP*
EMP: 125
SALES (est): 35.6MM **Privately Held**
WEB: www.mirion.com
SIC: 8734 Radiation dosimetry laboratory

(P-26092)
MISTRAS GROUP INC
6170 Egret Ct, Benicia (94510-1269)
PHONE..................................707 746-5870
Chuck Penley, *General Mgr*
EMP: 50 **Publicly Held**
SIC: 8734 Testing laboratories
PA: Mistras Group, Inc.
195 Clarksville Rd Ste 2
Princeton Junction NJ 08550

(P-26093)
MOORE TWINING ASSOCIATES INC (PA)
2527 Fresno St, Fresno (93721-1804)
PHONE..................................559 268-7021
Harry D Moore, *President*
Ruth E Moore, *Corp Secy*
EMP: 85 **EST:** 1898
SQ FT: 22,500
SALES (est): 18.8MM **Privately Held**
WEB: www.mooretwining.com
SIC: 8734 8711 Testing laboratories; engineering services

(P-26094)
NANOLAB TECHNOLOGIES INC (PA)
Also Called: Fib Lab
1708 Mccarthy Blvd, Milpitas (95035-7454)
PHONE..................................408 433-3320
John P Traub, *President*
Rachelle Baldock, *Administration*
Janeth Figueroa, *Administration*
Stuart Scott, *Administration*
Jiangtao Zhu, *Technology*
EMP: 65
SQ FT: 15,000
SALES (est): 11.9MM **Privately Held**
WEB: www.nanolab1.com
SIC: 8734 Water testing laboratory

(P-26095)
NATIONAL EVERCLEAN SVCS INC
28632 Roadside Dr Ste 275, Agoura Hills (91301-6052)
PHONE..................................877 532-5326
John McShane, *President*
EMP: 100
SQ FT: 2,500
SALES (est): 273K
SALES (corp-wide): 29.7MM **Privately Held**
WEB: www.evercleanservices.com
SIC: 8734 8711 Food testing service; engineering services
PA: Underwriters Laboratories Inc.
333 Pfingsten Rd
Northbrook IL 60062
847 272-8800

(P-26096)
NITTO AVECIA PHARMA SVCS INC (DH)
10 Vanderbilt, Irvine (92618-2010)
PHONE..................................949 951-4425
Raymond Kaczmarek, *President*
EMP: 180
SQ FT: 62,000
SALES (est): 12.7MM **Privately Held**
SIC: 8734 Product testing laboratories

(P-26097)
NORTH AMERCN SCIENCE ASSOC INC
N A M S A
9 Morgan, Irvine (92618-2005)
PHONE..................................949 951-3110
Dennis Nivens, *Vice Pres*
Steven Elliott, *Director*
Mike Costanzo, *Supervisor*
Robert Villani, *Supervisor*
EMP: 60
SQ FT: 40,000
SALES (corp-wide): 122.7MM **Privately Held**
WEB: www.namsa.com
SIC: 8734 8071 8999 Testing laboratories; medical laboratories; chemical consultant
PA: North American Science Associates, Inc.
6750 Wales Rd
Northwood OH 43619
419 666-9455

(P-26098)
NTS TECHNICAL SYSTEMS
3505 E 3rd St, San Bernardino (92408-0201)
P.O. Box 160, Norco (92860-0160)
PHONE..................................909 863-5150
Emily Turner, *General Mgr*
William McGinnis, *CEO*
EMP: 62
SALES (corp-wide): 330.8MM **Privately Held**
WEB: www.wylelabs.com
SIC: 8734 8742 Testing laboratories; quality assurance consultant
HQ: Nts Technical Systems
2125 E Katella Ave # 250
Anaheim CA 92806
714 450-9100

(P-26099)
NTS TECHNICAL SYSTEMS
1536 E Valencia Dr, Fullerton (92831-4734)
PHONE..................................714 879-6110

Mike Shook, *General Mgr*
Marty McCormick, *Department Mgr*
Wayne Kelee, *Senior Engr*
Allan Lario, *Maint Spvr*
Doug Brisky, *Manager*
EMP: 133
SALES (corp-wide): 330.8MM **Privately Held**
WEB: www.ntscorp.com
SIC: **8734** 8711 Radiation laboratories; sanitary engineers
HQ: Nts Technical Systems
    2125 E Katella Ave # 250
    Anaheim CA 92806
    714 450-9100

(P-26100)
NTS TECHNICAL SYSTEMS
20970 Centre Pointe Pkwy, Santa Clarita (91350-2975)
PHONE...............................661 259-8184
Brian Robb, *General Mgr*
Kogen Jeff, *Engineer*
Gregory Smith, *Opers Mgr*
EMP: 57
SALES (corp-wide): 330.8MM **Privately Held**
WEB: www.ntscorp.com
SIC: **8734** 8742 Testing laboratories; quality assurance consultant
HQ: Nts Technical Systems
    2125 E Katella Ave # 250
    Anaheim CA 92806
    714 450-9100

(P-26101)
NTS TECHNICAL SYSTEMS
41039 Boyce Rd, Fremont (94538-2434)
PHONE...............................510 578-3500
Anuj Kumar, *Branch Mgr*
EMP: 50
SALES (corp-wide): 330.8MM **Privately Held**
SIC: **8734** 8742 Testing laboratories; quality assurance consultant
HQ: Nts Technical Systems
    2125 E Katella Ave # 250
    Anaheim CA 92806
    714 450-9100

(P-26102)
PACIFIC TOXICOLOGY LABS
Also Called: Forensic Toxicology Associates
9348 De Soto Ave, Chatsworth (91311-4926)
PHONE...............................818 598-3110
Jeff Lanzolatta, *CEO*
Sue Barbosa, *COO*
Greg Carroll, *CFO*
Neil Patel Carroll, *CFO*
Rana Ostadrahimi, *Vice Pres*
EMP: 75
SQ FT: 19,000
SALES (est): 13MM **Privately Held**
WEB: www.pactox.com
SIC: **8734** Testing laboratories

(P-26103)
PHAMATECH INCORPORATED
15175 Innovation Dr, San Diego (92128-3401)
PHONE...............................858 643-5555
Tuan Pham, *CEO*
Tuan H Pham, *CEO*
EMP: 200
SQ FT: 50,000
SALES (est): 31.2MM **Privately Held**
WEB: www.phamatech.com
SIC: **8734** 5047 Forensic laboratory; medical laboratory equipment

(P-26104)
PSYCHEMEDICS CORPORATION
5750 Hannum Ave Ste 100, Culver City (90230-6666)
PHONE...............................310 216-7776
Michael Schaffer, *Manager*
EMP: 75
SALES (corp-wide): 42.6MM **Publicly Held**
WEB: www.psychemedics.com
SIC: **8734** Testing laboratories
PA: Psychemedics Corporation
    289 Great Rd Ste 200
    Acton MA 01720
    978 206-8220

(P-26105)
SCST INC (HQ)
6280 Riverdale St, San Diego (92120-3308)
PHONE...............................619 280-4321
John Kirschbaum, *President*
Royce Parker, *Vice Pres*
Emil Rudolph, *Vice Pres*
Clint Adkins, *Lab Dir*
Thomas Canady, *Engineer*
EMP: 93
SQ FT: 15,482
SALES (est): 14.8MM
SALES (corp-wide): 67.7MM **Privately Held**
WEB: www.scst.com
SIC: **8734** 8711 Testing laboratories; engineering services
PA: Atlas Technical Consultants Llc
    13215 Bee Cave Pkwy 260
    Austin TX 78738
    866 858-4499

(P-26106)
SGS NORTH AMERICA INC
1759 S Main St Ste 116, Milpitas (95035-6765)
PHONE...............................408 588-0200
James A Gordon, *Director*
EMP: 95
SALES (corp-wide): 6.7B **Privately Held**
SIC: **8734** Water testing laboratory
HQ: Sgs North America Inc.
    201 Route 17
    Rutherford NJ 07070
    201 508-3000

(P-26107)
SIGNET TESTING LABS INC (HQ)
3526 Breakwater Ct, Hayward (94545-3611)
PHONE...............................510 887-8484
Robert V Tadlock, *President*
EMP: 50
SALES (est): 13.5MM **Privately Held**
SIC: **8734** Testing laboratories
PA: United Engineering Resources, Inc.
    498 N 3rd St
    Sacramento CA 95811
    916 375-6700

(P-26108)
SILLIKER LABS GROUP INC
6360 Gateway Dr, Cypress (90630-4844)
PHONE...............................714 226-0000
Vidyha Ganger, *Managing Dir*
Juvy Tan, *Supervisor*
EMP: 50
SALES (est): 5.1MM
SALES (corp-wide): 7.5MM **Privately Held**
SIC: **8734** Product testing laboratories
HQ: Silliker, Inc.
    111 E Wacker Dr Ste 2300
    Chicago IL 60601
    312 938-5151

(P-26109)
TESTAMERICA LABORATORIES INC
17461 Derian Ave Ste 100, Irvine (92614-5845)
PHONE...............................949 261-1022
Fred Haley, *Branch Mgr*
EMP: 177
SALES (corp-wide): 866.9K **Privately Held**
WEB: www.stl-inc.com
SIC: **8734** Water testing laboratory
HQ: Testamerica Laboratories, Inc.
    4101 Shuffel St Nw # 100
    North Canton OH 44720
    800 456-9396

(P-26110)
TESTAMERICA LABORATORIES INC
880 Riverside Pkwy, West Sacramento (95605-1500)
PHONE...............................916 373-5600
Roger Freize, *Manager*
EMP: 100

SALES (corp-wide): 866.9K **Privately Held**
WEB: www.stl-inc.com
SIC: **8734** 8731 2899 Testing laboratories; commercial physical research; chemical preparations
HQ: Testamerica Laboratories, Inc.
    4101 Shuffel St Nw # 100
    North Canton OH 44720
    800 456-9396

(P-26111)
TWINING INC (PA)
Also Called: Twining Laboratories
2883 E Spring St Ste 300, Long Beach (90806-6847)
PHONE...............................562 426-3355
Edward Butch M Twining Jr, *CEO*
Brian Kramer, *President*
Richard S Hazen, *Vice Pres*
Steve Schiffer, *Vice Pres*
Boris Stein, *Vice Pres*
EMP: 94
SQ FT: 13,600
SALES (est): 41.1MM **Privately Held**
WEB: www.twininglabs.com
SIC: **8734** Testing laboratories

(P-26112)
TWINING INC
3310 E Airport Way, Long Beach (90806-2410)
PHONE...............................562 426-3355
Dayna Michaelsen, *Principal*
Bob Hathaway, *CFO*
Paul Soltis, *Technical Staff*
EMP: 66
SALES (corp-wide): 40.1MM **Privately Held**
SIC: **8734** Testing laboratories
PA: Twining, Inc.
    2883 E Spring St Ste 300
    Long Beach CA 90806
    562 426-3355

(P-26113)
UNDERWRITERS LABORATORIES INC
455 E Trimble Rd, San Jose (95131-1230)
PHONE...............................248 427-5300
Eric Swerrie, *Branch Mgr*
Timothy Dahlgren, *Manager*
EMP: 300
SALES (corp-wide): 29.7MM **Privately Held**
WEB: www.ul.com
SIC: **8734** Testing laboratories
PA: Underwriters Laboratories Inc.
    333 Pfingsten Rd
    Northbrook IL 60062
    847 272-8800

(P-26114)
UNDERWRITERS LABORATORIES INC
4510 Riding Club Ct, Hayward (94542-2238)
PHONE...............................408 754-6500
EMP: 180
SALES (corp-wide): 22.6MM **Privately Held**
SIC: **8734**
PA: Underwriters Laboratories Inc.
    333 Pfingsten Rd
    Northbrook IL 60062
    847 272-8800

(P-26115)
UNDERWRITERS LABORATORIES INC
2191 Zanker Rd, San Jose (95131-2109)
PHONE...............................408 493-9910
EMP: 102
SALES (corp-wide): 29.7MM **Privately Held**
SIC: **8734** Product testing laboratory, safety or performance
PA: Underwriters Laboratories Inc.
    333 Pfingsten Rd
    Northbrook IL 60062
    847 272-8800

(P-26116)
UNITED MFG ASSEMBLY INC
44169 Fremont Blvd, Fremont (94538-6044)
PHONE...............................510 490-1065
Yonwen Chou, *President*
May Mah, *Finance*
May Wah, *Controller*
Margie Vo, *Human Res Mgr*
Sandy Gao, *Buyer*
EMP: 95
SALES (est): 13.2MM **Privately Held**
WEB: www.umai.com
SIC: **8734** 3672 Testing laboratories; printed circuit boards

(P-26117)
VALLEY INDUSTRIAL X-RA
3700 Pegasus Dr Ste 100, Bakersfield (93308-6805)
PHONE...............................661 399-8497
Larry Williams, *President*
Terry Campbell, *Vice Pres*
EMP: 200
SQ FT: 18,000
SALES (est): 19.5MM
SALES (corp-wide): 66.8MM **Privately Held**
WEB: www.vxray.com
SIC: **8734** X-ray inspection service, industrial
HQ: Rontgen Technische Dienst B.V.
    Delftweg 144
    Rotterdam 3046
    107 166-000

8741 Management Services

(P-26118)
800 DEGREES LLC
10889 Lindbrook Dr, Los Angeles (90024-3027)
PHONE...............................310 443-1911
Adam Fleischman,
Anthony Carron,
Allen Ravert,
EMP: 50 EST: 2010
SQ FT: 2,900
SALES (est): 4.3MM **Privately Held**
SIC: **8741** Restaurant management

(P-26119)
ACEPEX MANAGEMENT CORPORATION
13401 Yorba Ave, Chino (91710-5055)
PHONE...............................909 591-1999
EMP: 306
SALES (corp-wide): 37.5MM **Privately Held**
SIC: **8741**
PA: Acepex Management Corporation
    10643 Mills Ave
    Montclair CA 91763
    909 625-6900

(P-26120)
ACTIVCARE LIVING INC (PA)
10603 Rancho Bernardo Rd, San Diego (92127-5722)
PHONE...............................858 565-4424
William Major Chance, *CEO*
Todd A Shetter, *COO*
B Renee Barnard, *CFO*
Dkevin Moriarty, *Vice Pres*
Frank A Virgadamo, *Vice Pres*
EMP: 180
SQ FT: 9,000
SALES (est): 35.4MM **Privately Held**
WEB: www.healthcaregrp.com
SIC: **8741** Nursing & personal care facility management

(P-26121)
ACTIVE WELLNESS LLC
600 California St Fl 11, San Francisco (94108-2727)
P.O. Box 2358 (94126-2358)
PHONE...............................415 741-3300
Jill Stevens Kinney, *Chairman*
William Joseph McBride III, *President*
Carey White, *CFO*
Kiley Mutschler, *Program Mgr*
Jon Wilson, *Program Mgr*
EMP: 1100

SQ FT: 1,000
SALES: 40MM **Privately Held**
SIC: 8741 7991 Hospital management; nursing & personal care facility management; health club

(P-26122)
ADVANCED BIOSERVICES LLC (PA)
19255 Vanowen St, Reseda (91335-5070)
PHONE 818 342-0100
Anna Kane,
EMP: 65
SALES (est): 13.9MM **Privately Held**
SIC: 8741 Administrative management

(P-26123)
ADVANCED MEDICAL MGT INC
5000 Arprt Plz Dr Ste 150, Long Beach (90815)
PHONE 562 766-2000
Stephen Hegstrom, *CEO*
Kathy Hegstrom, *President*
Paul Pew, *Exec VP*
Courtney Plank, *Human Res Mgr*
EMP: 60
SALES (est): 8.7MM **Privately Held**
WEB: www.duongnet.com
SIC: 8741 8721 Hospital management; accounting, auditing & bookkeeping

(P-26124)
AEG MANAGEMENT LACC LLC
Also Called: Los Angeles Convention Center
1201 S Figueroa St, Los Angeles (90015-1308)
PHONE 213 741-1151
Brad Gessner, *Senior VP*
Estella M Flores, *Bd of Directors*
Keith Hilsgen, *Vice Pres*
Carisa Malanum, *Vice Pres*
Greg Rosicky, *Vice Pres*
EMP: 220
SALES (est): 20MM
SALES (corp-wide): 30.6MM **Privately Held**
SIC: 8741 Business management
PA: Aeg Facilities, Llc
800 W Olympic Blvd # 305
Los Angeles CA 90015
213 763-7700

(P-26125)
AIR FORCE US DEPT OF
Also Called: 30th Cpts-Financial Management
1031 California Blvd # 11777, Lompoc (93437-6248)
PHONE 805 606-5355
Steve Kam, *Branch Mgr*
EMP: 65 **Publicly Held**
WEB: www.af.mil
SIC: 8741 9711 Management services; Air Force;
HQ: United States Department Of The Air Force
1000 Air Force Pentagon
Washington DC 20330

(P-26126)
AJIT HEALTHCARE INC
316 S Westlake Ave, Los Angeles (90057-4500)
PHONE 213 484-0510
Jasvant N Modi, *President*
EMP: 80
SALES (est): 5.9MM **Privately Held**
SIC: 8741 Nursing & personal care facility management

(P-26127)
ALL SYSTEM PERSONNEL MGMT
16885 W Bernardo Dr # 150, San Diego (92127-1618)
PHONE 858 674-4090
Laurie Gerrard, *Agent*
EMP: 50
SALES (est): 1.1MM **Privately Held**
SIC: 8741 Management services

(P-26128)
ALLEGIS RESIDENTIAL SVCS INC
Also Called: Aspm-Sandiego
9340 Hazard Way Ste B2, San Diego (92123-1228)
PHONE 858 430-5700
Karen Martinez, *CEO*
Steve Howe, *COO*
Jorge Martinez, *CFO*
George Giannini, *Manager*
EMP: 80
SQ FT: 4,000
SALES (est): 1.8MM **Privately Held**
SIC: 8741 Business management
PA: S.H.E. Manages Properties, Inc.
9340 Hazard Way Ste B2
San Diego CA 92123

(P-26129)
ALLZONE MANAGEMENT SVCS INC
Also Called: Allzone Management Solutions
3700 Wilshire Blvd # 979, Los Angeles (90010-3088)
PHONE 213 291-8879
Jonathan Rodrigues, *President*
EMP: 500
SALES (est): 82.8K **Privately Held**
SIC: 8741 Management services

(P-26130)
AMERICAN INTGRTED RSOURCES INC
2341 N Pacific St, Orange (92865-2601)
PHONE 714 921-4100
Thomas C Stevens, *CEO*
Megan Duffy, *Office Mgr*
Ruben Godinez, *Controller*
Arsenio Hernandez, *Opers Mgr*
Tim Christopoulos, *Sr Project Mgr*
EMP: 80
SALES (est): 2MM **Privately Held**
SIC: 8741 Construction management

(P-26131)
AMERICAN MZHOU DNGPO GROUP INC
4520 Maine Ave, Baldwin Park (91706-2671)
PHONE 626 820-9239
Gang Wang, *CEO*
EMP: 100
SALES (est): 636.5K **Privately Held**
SIC: 8741 Restaurant management

(P-26132)
AMERISOURCEBERGEN CORPORATION
1368 Metropolitan Dr, Orange (92868)
P.O. Box 247, Thorofare NJ (08086-0247)
PHONE 610 727-7000
Daniel Ramirez, *Manager*
Lisa Reberiego, *Credit Staff*
Kurt Costa, *Opers Spvr*
Ken Babinat, *Warehouse Mgr*
Brittany Calderon, *Director*
EMP: 180
SALES (corp-wide): 167.9B **Publicly Held**
WEB: www.amerisourcebergen.net
SIC: 8741 Administrative management
PA: Amerisourcebergen Corporation
1300 Morris Dr Ste 100
Chesterbrook PA 19087
610 727-7000

(P-26133)
AMERISOURCEBERGEN CORPORATION
505 City Pkwy W, Orange (92868-2924)
PHONE 714 704-4407
Dan Cauffiel, *Data Proc Staff*
Matthew Neal, *Technical Staff*
Jeff Lester, *Analyst*
Lorelei Newell, *Analyst*
Pier Rhodes, *Analyst*
EMP: 180
SALES (corp-wide): 167.9B **Publicly Held**
SIC: 8741 Administrative management

PA: Amerisourcebergen Corporation
1300 Morris Dr Ste 100
Chesterbrook PA 19087
610 727-7000

(P-26134)
ANAHEIM FIRST FMLY DNTL GROUP
Also Called: Affd
1161 N Euclid St, Anaheim (92801-1938)
PHONE 714 999-5050
Mary Ann De Santiago, *President*
John Delaney DDS, *Vice Pres*
EMP: 54
SALES (est): 4MM **Privately Held**
SIC: 8741 Office management

(P-26135)
APEX GROUP
17101 Superior St, Northridge (91325-1961)
PHONE 818 885-0513
Damon Zumwalt, *President*
Robert Brockway, *Vice Pres*
Bruce George, *Opers Staff*
EMP: 200
SALES (est): 10.9MM **Privately Held**
SIC: 8741 8721 Administrative management; accounting, auditing & bookkeeping

(P-26136)
APPLECARE MEDICAL MGT LLC
18 Centerpointe Dr # 100, La Palma (90623-1028)
P.O. Box 6014, Artesia (90702-6014)
PHONE 714 443-4507
Vinod Jivrajka, *Principal*
Sean Igarta, *Info Tech Dir*
EMP: 108
SALES (est): 13.1MM
SALES (corp-wide): 226.2B **Publicly Held**
SIC: 8741 Nursing & personal care facility management
PA: Unitedhealth Group Incorporated
9900 Bren Rd E Ste 300w
Minnetonka MN 55343
952 936-1300

(P-26137)
ARCHIVES MANAGEMENT CORP (PA)
Also Called: Bay Management
2301 S El Camino Real, San Mateo (94403-2213)
PHONE 650 544-2200
Harlan Shapers, *President*
EMP: 180
SQ FT: 12,000
SALES (est): 16.3MM **Privately Held**
WEB: www.adultsupersource.com
SIC: 8741 8742 Business management; management consulting services

(P-26138)
ARNEL INTERIOR CORP
Also Called: Arnel and Affiliate
949 S Coast Dr Ste 600, Costa Mesa (92626-7734)
PHONE 714 481-5100
George Argyrox, *Ch of Bd*
Dan Russo, *CEO*
Tony Roxtrom, *Vice Pres*
EMP: 300
SQ FT: 4,000
SALES (est): 6.6MM **Privately Held**
SIC: 8741 Construction management

(P-26139)
ARNOLD PALMER GOLF MGT LLC
300 Finley Rd, San Francisco (94129-1196)
P.O. Box 29063 (94129-0063)
PHONE 415 561-4670
EMP: 70
SALES (corp-wide): 48.4MM **Privately Held**
SIC: 8741 7992
HQ: Arnold Palmer Golf Management, Llc
5430 Lbj Fwy Ste 1400
Dallas TX 75240
972 419-1400

(P-26140)
ARTIST SILVA MANAGEMENT LLC (PA)
Also Called: Silva Artist Management,
722 Seward St, Los Angeles (90038-3504)
PHONE 323 856-8222
John Silva,
Gary Gersh,
Michael Meisel, *Manager*
Pete Smith, *Manager*
EMP: 120
SALES (est): 9.1MM **Privately Held**
WEB: www.sammusicbiz.com
SIC: 8741 Business management

(P-26141)
ASHFORD TRS NICKEL LLC
Also Called: Sheraton Sn Diego Htl Msn Vly
1433 Camino Del Rio S, San Diego (92108-3521)
PHONE 619 260-0111
Mike Rice, *Manager*
EMP: 60 **Privately Held**
SIC: 8741 5813 5812 Hotel or motel management; drinking places; eating places
PA: Ashford Trs Nickel, Llc
1345 Treat Blvd
Walnut Creek CA 94597

(P-26142)
ASSET ATHENE MANAGEMENT L P (HQ)
2121 Rosecrans Ave # 5300, El Segundo (90245-4750)
PHONE 310 698-4444
James R Belardi, *CEO*
Mark Suter, *Officer*
Jeff Boland, *Exec VP*
Nancy De Liban, *Exec VP*
Robert Graham, *Exec VP*
EMP: 69
SALES (est): 71.7MM **Publicly Held**
SIC: 8741 Financial management for business

(P-26143)
ASSET MANAGEMENT TR SVCS LLC
Also Called: A Mediation & Resolution Ctr
1455 Frazee Rd Ste 500, San Diego (92108-4350)
PHONE 858 457-2202
Steven K Dony, *Mng Member*
Rochelle O'Donnell Juarez, *Mng Member*
EMP: 72
SALES (est): 2.8MM **Privately Held**
SIC: 8741 Business management

(P-26144)
ATRIA SENIOR LIVING INC
Also Called: Golden
33 Creek Rd Side, Irvine (92604-4792)
PHONE 949 786-5665
Sandra McDaniel, *Manager*
Maureen Salonga, *Nursing Dir*
Myra Aragones, *Director*
EMP: 60
SALES (corp-wide): 3.7B **Publicly Held**
WEB: www.atriacom.com
SIC: 8741 6531 Hotel or motel management; real estate brokers & agents
HQ: Atria Senior Living Inc.
300 E Market St Ste 100
Louisville KY 40202

(P-26145)
AUDIO VISUAL MGT SOLUTIONS
Also Called: AV Management
12812 Garden Grove Blvd M, Garden Grove (92843-2009)
PHONE 714 590-8755
Just Cameron, *Branch Mgr*
Mike Phillips, *Info Tech Mgr*
EMP: 57 **Privately Held**
SIC: 8741 Business management
PA: Audio Visual Management Solutions, Inc
814 6th Ave S
Seattle WA 98134

(P-26146)
AVIATION CONSULTANTS INC
(PA)
Also Called: Epic Jet Centre
945 Airport Dr, San Luis Obispo
(93401-8354)
PHONE..................................805 548-1300
William Borgsmiller, *President*
Nathan Ross, *CFO*
Andrew Robillard, *Vice Pres*
EMP: 62
SQ FT: 6,100
SALES (est): 9.5MM **Privately Held**
WEB: www.aviationconsultants.net
SIC: 8741 7363 Management services;
    pilot service, aviation

(P-26147)
BACCHUS VINEYARD MGT LLC
1720 River Rd, Fulton (95439-8843)
PHONE..................................707 837-8304
James G Alexander, *Mng Member*
EMP: 60
SALES (est): 7.8MM **Privately Held**
SIC: 8741 Business management

(P-26148)
BANK AMERICA NATIONAL
ASSN
73525 El Paseo, Palm Desert
(92260-4341)
PHONE..................................760 636-7500
EMP: 138
SALES (corp-wide): 110.5B **Publicly**
Held
SIC: 8741 6282 6029 6021 Business
    management; investment advice; com-
    mercial banks; national commercial banks
HQ: Bank Of America, National Association
    100 S Tryon St
    Charlotte NC 28202
    704 386-5681

(P-26149)
BANK AMERICA NATIONAL
ASSN
555 Capitol Mall, Sacramento
(95814-4504)
PHONE..................................916 326-3161
Maria Barry, *Branch Mgr*
EMP: 138
SALES (corp-wide): 110.5B **Publicly**
Held
SIC: 8741 6282 6029 6021 Business
    management; investment advice; com-
    mercial banks; national commercial banks
HQ: Bank Of America, National Association
    100 S Tryon St
    Charlotte NC 28202
    704 386-5681

(P-26150)
BARNETT CUSTOMER
MANAGEMENT
3111 N Tustin St, Orange (92865-1750)
PHONE..................................714 747-7908
Timothy Barnett, *President*
EMP: 50
SALES (est): 1.3MM **Privately Held**
SIC: 8741 Management services

(P-26151)
BARRETT BUSINESS SERVICES
INC
1840 Gateway Dr, San Mateo
(94404-4027)
PHONE..................................650 653-7588
EMP: 5003
SALES (corp-wide): 940.7MM **Publicly**
Held
SIC: 8741 Business management
PA: Barrett Business Services Inc
    8100 Ne Parkway Dr # 200
    Vancouver WA 98662
    360 828-0700

(P-26152)
BAY VISTA SENIOR HOUSING
6120 Stoneridge, Pleasanton (94588)
PHONE..................................925 924-7100
Grace Chrisostomo, *Governor*
Linda Coleman, *Governor*
Andrew McDonald, *Governor*
Susan Tolentino, *Governor*

EMP: 156
SALES (est): 1.3MM
SALES (corp-wide): 21.8MM **Privately**
Held
SIC: 8741 Management services
HQ: Humangood Affordable Housing
    6120 Stoneridge Mall Rd # 100
    Pleasanton CA 94588
    925 924-7163

(P-26153)
BECHTEL CAPITAL MGT CORP
50 Beale St, San Francisco (94105-1813)
PHONE..................................415 768-1234
Riley Bechtel, *Chairman*
Brendan Bechtel, *President*
Bill Dudley, *CEO*
Peter Dawson, *CFO*
Anshul Maheshwari, *Treasurer*
EMP: 2000
SQ FT: 600,000
SALES (est): 48.8MM
SALES (corp-wide): 13.6B **Privately Held**
WEB: www.bechtelgroup.com
SIC: 8741 Financial management for busi-
    ness
PA: Bechtel Group, Inc.
    12011 Sunset Hills Rd
    Reston VA 20190
    571 392-6300

(P-26154)
BEECH STREET CORPORATION
(DH)
25550 Commercentre Dr # 200, Lake For-
est (92630-8893)
PHONE..................................949 672-1000
William Fickling Jr, *Chairman*
William Hale, *President*
Jon Bird, *CFO*
Rick Markus, *Exec VP*
Norm Werthwein, *Senior VP*
EMP: 350
SQ FT: 60,000
SALES (est): 18.9MM
SALES (corp-wide): 5B **Publicly Held**
WEB: www.beechstreet.com
SIC: 8741 Administrative management
HQ: Concentra Operating Corporation
    5080 Spectrum Dr Ste 400w
    Addison TX 75001
    972 364-8000

(P-26155)
BERNARDS INC
555 1st St, San Fernando (91340-3051)
PHONE..................................818 898-1521
Jeff Bernards, *CEO*
Doug Bernards, *CEO*
Greg Simons, *Exec VP*
Gregory Simons, *Manager*
EMP: 60
SALES (est): 111.5K **Privately Held**
SIC: 8741 1542 Construction manage-
    ment; commercial & office building con-
    tractors

(P-26156)
BEVERLY HEALTH CARE CORP
(PA)
5445 Everglades St, Ventura (93003-6523)
PHONE..................................805 642-1736
Carol Tradeway, *Director*
Rose Taylor-Calhoun, *CEO*
Philip Drescher, *Principal*
Harry Maynard, *Principal*
Gary Wolfe, *Principal*
EMP: 50
SQ FT: 85,000
SALES (est): 16.9MM **Privately Held**
SIC: 8741 Management services

(P-26157)
BJS RESTAURANT OPERATIONS
CO
7755 Center Ave Ste 300, Huntington
Beach (92647-3084)
PHONE..................................714 500-2440
EMP: 147
SALES (est): 63.8K
SALES (corp-wide): 1.1B **Publicly Held**
SIC: 8741 Restaurant management
PA: Bj's Restaurants, Inc.
    7755 Center Ave Ste 300
    Huntington Beach CA 92647
    714 500-2400

(P-26158)
BML WORKS NA LLC
228 Hamilton Ave Fl 3, Palo Alto
(94301-2583)
PHONE..................................650 268-8305
George Ferrier,
EMP: 52
SALES (est): 2.5MM **Privately Held**
SIC: 8741 Management services

(P-26159)
BPG STORAGE SOLUTIONS INC
2033 N Main St Ste 340, Walnut Creek
(94596-3727)
PHONE..................................562 467-2000
Michael Barker, *President*
EMP: 60
SALES (est): 3.1MM
SALES (corp-wide): 13.5MM **Privately**
Held
WEB: www.barkerpacific.com
SIC: 8741 Management services
PA: Barker Pacific Group, Inc.
    101 Ygnacio Valley Rd # 210
    Walnut Creek CA 94596
    415 884-9977

(P-26160)
BRET BOYLAN PROPERTY MGT
Also Called: Bret Boylan
35 N Alboni Pl Apt 409, Long Beach
(90802-5438)
P.O. Box 14690 (90853-4690)
PHONE..................................562 437-7886
EMP: 50
SQ FT: 300
SALES (est): 2MM **Privately Held**
SIC: 8741

(P-26161)
BROUGHTON HOSPITALITY
GROUP (PA)
2400 E Katella Ave # 300, Anaheim
(92806-5957)
PHONE..................................714 908-4237
Larry Broughton, *President*
Robert Rycroft, *CFO*
Robert Srycrodt, *CFO*
Shawna Shope, *Vice Pres*
Maria Lipan, *Area Mgr*
EMP: 240 EST: 2001
SALES (est): 19.5MM **Privately Held**
WEB: www.broughtonhospitality.com
SIC: 8741 Hotel or motel management

(P-26162)
BUCKINGHAM AFFRDBL
APRTMNTS LP
Also Called: Buckingham Apartments
11911 San Vicente Blvd, Los Angeles
(90049-5086)
PHONE..................................424 273-6162
Adam Cutler, *Vice Pres*
EMP: 60
SALES (est): 1.7MM **Privately Held**
SIC: 8741 Business management

(P-26163)
BUCKLAND VINEYARD
MANAGEMENT
4560 Slodusty Rd, Garden Valley
(95633-9244)
PHONE..................................530 333-1534
Alfred Buckland, *President*
EMP: 65
SALES (est): 3.6MM **Privately Held**
SIC: 8741 Management services

(P-26164)
BUFFALO SPOT MGT GROUP
LLC
7245 Garden Grove Blvd, Garden Grove
(92841-4216)
PHONE..................................949 354-0884
Ivan Flores, *Mng Member*
EMP: 110
SALES (est): 1.2MM **Privately Held**
SIC: 8741 Restaurant management

(P-26165)
BUONA TERRA FARMING CO
INC
2380 A St, Santa Maria (93455-1009)
PHONE..................................805 614-9229

John Belfy, *President*
EMP: 100
SALES (est): 11.6MM **Privately Held**
SIC: 8741 0762 Management services;
    farm management services

(P-26166)
BUTTE BASIN MANAGEMENT
CO
1624 Poole Blvd, Yuba City (95993-2610)
P.O. Box 3775 (95992-3775)
PHONE..................................530 674-2060
Samuel Neves, *President*
Dominic Neves, *Vice Pres*
EMP: 50
SALES (est): 2.5MM **Privately Held**
SIC: 8741 Management services

(P-26167)
C/O UC SAN FRANCISCO (PA)
Also Called: University of CA Office
1111 Franklin St Fl 12, Oakland
(94607-5201)
PHONE..................................858 534-7323
John Fox, *Principal*
Arthur A Castillo, *Officer*
Mounira Kenaani, *Department Mgr*
Adrian C Miu, *Nursing Mgr*
Alicia R Banks, *Admin Asst*
EMP: 148
SALES (est): 49.8MM **Privately Held**
SIC: 8741 Restaurant management

(P-26168)
CAL CARE INC
Also Called: Atherton Healthcare
1275 Crane St, Menlo Park (94025-4212)
PHONE..................................650 325-8600
Chris Green, *Administration*
David Dediachvili, *Office Mgr*
Nana Cocachvili, *Administration*
EMP: 115
SALES (est): 11.2MM **Privately Held**
SIC: 8741 Nursing & personal care facility
    management

(P-26169)
CAL PINNACLE MLTARY
CMMUNITIES
3200 4th Ave Ste 201, San Diego
(92103-5716)
P.O. Box 10034, Fort Irwin (92310-0034)
PHONE..................................619 764-5087
Shawn Sommerville, *Director*
EMP: 55 EST: 2010
SALES (est): 1.4MM **Privately Held**
SIC: 8741 Management services

(P-26170)
CAL POLY CORPORATION
Also Called: Cal Poly Foundation
Bldg 15, San Luis Obispo (93407)
PHONE..................................805 756-1131
Hank A Mumford, *Exec Dir*
EMP: 210
SALES (corp-wide): 46.7MM **Privately**
Held
WEB: www.calpolyarts.org
SIC: 8741 Business management
PA: Cal Poly Corporation
    1 Grand Ave Bldg 15
    San Luis Obispo CA 93407
    805 756-1131

(P-26171)
CALIFORNIA STATE UNIV AUX
SVCS
Also Called: UNIVERSITY BOOKSTORE
5151 State University Dr Ge314, Los Ange-
les (90032-4226)
PHONE..................................323 343-2531
R Dean Calvo, *Exec Dir*
▲ EMP: 600
SQ FT: 108,000
SALES: 39MM **Privately Held**
SIC: 8741 5942 5651 5812 Business
    management; financial management for
    business; college book stores; unisex
    clothing stores; cafeteria

(P-26172)
CAMARILLO HEALTHCARE
CENTER
205 Granada St, Camarillo (93010-7715)
PHONE..................................805 482-9805

Erica Olsen, *Administration*
Angie Chavz, *Administration*
EMP: 194
SALES (est): 3MM
SALES (corp-wide): 2B **Publicly Held**
SIC: 8741 Nursing & personal care facility
management
PA: The Ensign Group Inc
27101 Puerta Real Ste 450
Mission Viejo CA 92691
949 487-9500

(P-26173)
CASTLEBLACK OWNER HOLDINGS LLC
601 James Way, Pismo Beach
(93449-3502)
PHONE..................................805 773-6020
Gordon Jackson, *Manager*
EMP: 50
SALES (corp-wide): 18.7MM **Privately Held**
SIC: 8741 Hotel or motel management
PA: Castleblack Owner Holdings, Llc
399 Park Ave Fl 18
New York NY 10022
212 547-2609

(P-26174)
CATHAY BANK
977 N Broadway Ste 306, Los Angeles
(90012-1786)
PHONE..................................213 687-1300
Dunson K Cheng, *Ch of Bd*
EMP: 354
SALES (corp-wide): 719.6MM **Publicly Held**
SIC: 8741 6021 Management services;
national commercial banks
HQ: Cathay Bank
9650 Flair Dr
El Monte CA 91731
626 279-3698

(P-26175)
CBS TELEVISION DISTRIBUTION (PA)
Also Called: CBS Enterprises
2450 Colo Ave Ste 500e, Santa Monica
(90404)
PHONE..................................310 264-3300
Paul Franklin, *President*
Bruce Pottash, *Exec VP*
Betsy Siciliano, *Senior VP*
Stuart Green, *Opers Spvr*
Peter Molnar, *Director*
EMP: 20000 **EST:** 2010
SQ FT: 20,000
SALES: 13.6B **Privately Held**
SIC: 8741 Management services

(P-26176)
CHAN FAMILY PARTNERSHIP LP
30249 Point Marina Dr, Canyon Lake
(92587-7412)
PHONE..................................626 322-7132
Ann Chan, *Partner*
EMP: 100
SALES: 3MM **Privately Held**
SIC: 8741 Restaurant management

(P-26177)
CHEVRON INVESTOR INC
100 Chevron Way, Richmond
(94801-2016)
PHONE..................................510 242-3000
Mark Logan, *Branch Mgr*
EMP: 100
SALES (corp-wide): 166.3B **Publicly Held**
SIC: 8741 8731 Management services;
commercial physical research
HQ: Chevron Investor Inc
6001 Bollinger Canyon Rd
San Ramon CA 94583
925 842-1000

(P-26178)
CHILIS 898 CORONA
3579 Grand Oaks, Corona (92881-4634)
PHONE..................................951 734-7275
Deann Demarso, *President*
Deann De Marso, *President*
EMP: 90
SALES (est): 3.1MM **Privately Held**
SIC: 8741 Restaurant management

(P-26179)
CHOOSING INDEPENDENCE INC
7615 Louise Ave, Northridge (91325-4523)
PHONE..................................818 257-0323
Christian Richards Jr, *CEO*
EMP: 53
SQ FT: 3,500
SALES: 1.7MM **Privately Held**
SIC: 8741 Nursing & personal care facility
management

(P-26180)
CIK POWER DISTRIBUTORS LLC
240 W Grove Ave, Orange (92865-3204)
PHONE..................................714 938-0297
Chris A Christopher, *Mng Member*
Marc Oslund, *Project Mgr*
Cynthia Inman, *Human Resources*
Sabrinna Waegner, *Human Resources*
Stephen G Carter,
EMP: 53
SALES (est): 11.9MM **Privately Held**
SIC: 8741 Construction management

(P-26181)
CIRCLE WOOD SERVICES INC
3670 W Temple Ave, Pomona
(91768-2588)
PHONE..................................909 784-0733
Don Watson, *President*
EMP: 70 **EST:** 2007
SQ FT: 1,400
SALES (est): 5.9MM **Privately Held**
SIC: 8741 Business management

(P-26182)
CITY & COUNTY OF SAN FRANCISCO
Also Called: Administrative Services
1 Carlton B Goodlett Pl # 234, San Fran-
cisco (94102-4604)
PHONE..................................415 554-4799
Corrine Mehgan, *Mng Officer*
Alvin C Moses, *Manager*
EMP: 100 **Privately Held**
SIC: 8741 9199 Management services;
general government administration; ;
PA: City & County Of San Francisco
1 Dr Carlton B Goodlett P
San Francisco CA 94102
415 554-7500

(P-26183)
CITY OF REDLANDS (PA)
35 Cajon St, Redlands (92373-4746)
P.O. Box 3005 (92373-1505)
PHONE..................................909 798-7531
Jon Harrison,
Tina Kundig, *CFO*
Mike Reynolds, *CFO*
Brad Koontz, *Lab Dir*
Monica Duran, *Admin Asst*
EMP: 100 **EST:** 1888
SQ FT: 200,000
SALES: 79MM **Privately Held**
WEB: www.akspl.org
SIC: 8741 Office management

(P-26184)
CLARIZEN INC
2755 Campus Dr Ste 300, San Mateo
(94403-2538)
PHONE..................................866 502-9813
Boaz Chalamish, *CEO*
EMP: 55
SALES (est): 10.1MM **Privately Held**
SIC: 8741 Management services
PA: Clarizen Ltd
4 Hacharash, Floor 10
Hod Hasharon
979 443-00

(P-26185)
CLOROX SERVICES COMPANY (HQ)
1221 Broadway Fl 13, Oakland
(94612-1837)
PHONE..................................510 271-7000
R A Llenado, *Ch of Bd*
C E Williams, *President*
EMP: 100

SALES (est): 82.9MM
SALES (corp-wide): 6.2B **Publicly Held**
WEB: www.clorox.com
SIC: 8741 Management services
PA: The Clorox Company
1221 Broadway Ste 1300
Oakland CA 94612
510 271-7000

(P-26186)
COLLECTIVE MGT GROUP LLC
8383 Wilshire Blvd # 1050, Beverly Hills
(90211-2425)
PHONE..................................323 655-8585
Michael Green, *CEO*
Jordan Toplitzky, *CFO*
Jordan Berliant,
Gary Binkow,
Reza Izad,
EMP: 110
SQ FT: 15,000
SALES: 50MM **Privately Held**
SIC: 8741 Management services

(P-26187)
COLUSA REGIONAL MEDICAL CENTER
Also Called: Women's Health Center
199 E Webster St Ste 1, Colusa
(95932-2954)
PHONE..................................530 458-5821
David Zwald, *Principal*
Dale Kirby, *COO*
EMP: 180
SQ FT: 48,000
SALES: 21.1MM **Privately Held**
WEB: www.colusamedicalcenter.org
SIC: 8741 8062 Hospital management;
general medical & surgical hospitals

(P-26188)
COMMUNITY HOUSING OPPORT
Also Called: Sterling Asset Management
5030 Bus Center Dr # 260, Fairfield
(94534-6884)
PHONE..................................707 759-6043
Nancy Conk, *Exec Dir*
EMP: 50
SALES (corp-wide): 7.8MM **Privately Held**
WEB: www.chochousing.org
SIC: 8741 Management services
PA: Community Housing Opportunities Cor-
poration
5030 Business Center Dr # 260
Fairfield CA 94534
530 757-4444

(P-26189)
CONSTRUCTION TESTING SERVICES (PA)
2118 Rheem Dr, Pleasanton (94588-2775)
PHONE..................................925 462-5151
Patrick Greenan, *President*
Amanda Frey, *Admin Asst*
Ambrosia Harnois, *Admin Asst*
Yate Chhoun-Le, *Project Mgr*
Brian Joyce, *Project Mgr*
EMP: 50 **EST:** 1994
SQ FT: 5,000
SALES (est): 11.5MM **Privately Held**
WEB: www.cts-1.com
SIC: 8741 Construction management

(P-26190)
COOPER PUGEDA MANAGEMENT INC
Also Called: CPM Services
65 Mccoppin St, San Francisco
(94103-1235)
PHONE..................................415 543-6251
Ismael Pugeda, *President*
Jeff Cooper, *Vice Pres*
Laurane Delfin, *Office Mgr*
Wendy Glassett, *Office Mgr*
Leticia Scott, *Administration*
EMP: 50
SQ FT: 2,500
SALES (est): 7.5MM **Privately Held**
WEB: www.schedulers.com
SIC: 8741 1542 Construction manage-
ment; nonresidential construction

(P-26191)
CORNERSTONE HOTEL MANAGEMENT (DH)
222 Kearny St Ste 200, San Francisco
(94108-4537)
PHONE..................................415 397-5572
Tom La Tour, *President*
J Kirke Wrench, *CFO*
Nir Margalit, *Admin Sec*
EMP: 75
SALES (est): 7.5MM **Privately Held**
SIC: 8741 Management services
HQ: Alexis Hotel Management Inc
222 Kearny St Ste 200
San Francisco CA
415 397-5572

(P-26192)
CORVEL CORPORATION (PA)
2010 Main St Ste 600, Irvine (92614-7272)
PHONE..................................949 851-1473
Michael Combs, *President*
Kenneth S Cragun, *CFO*
Jeffrey Michael, *Bd of Directors*
Diane J Blaha, *Chief Mktg Ofcr*
Michael D Saverien, *Exec VP*
EMP: 148
SQ FT: 13,000
SALES: 595.7MM **Publicly Held**
WEB: www.corvel.com
SIC: 8741 8011 Nursing & personal care
facility management; internal medicine
practitioners; medical insurance associa-
tions

(P-26193)
COST PLUS MANAGEMENT SVCS INC (DH)
Also Called: World Market
1201 Marina Village Pkwy # 1, Alameda
(94501-1087)
P.O. Box 23350, Oakland (94623-2335)
PHONE..................................510 893-7300
Barry J Feld, *CEO*
Jane Baughman, *CFO*
Mike Lodge, *Planning*
◆ **EMP:** 100
SALES: 57MM
SALES (corp-wide): 12B **Publicly Held**
SIC: 8741 Financial management for busi-
ness
HQ: Cost Plus, Inc.
1201 Marina Village Pkwy # 100
Alameda CA 94501
510 893-7300

(P-26194)
COUNTRY VILLA SERVICE CORP
3002 Rowena Ave, Los Angeles
(90039-2005)
PHONE..................................323 666-1544
Stephen Rissman, *President*
EMP: 120
SALES (corp-wide): 125.3MM **Privately Held**
WEB: www.countryvillahealth.com
SIC: 8741 8051 Nursing & personal care
facility management; skilled nursing care
facilities
PA: Country Villa Service Corp.
2400 E Katella Ave # 800
Anaheim CA 92806
310 574-3733

(P-26195)
COUNTRY VILLA SERVICE CORP (PA)
Also Called: Country Villa Health Services
2400 E Katella Ave # 800, Anaheim
(92806-5945)
PHONE..................................310 574-3733
Stephen Reissman, *CEO*
Eldon Teper, *COO*
Eddie Rowles, *CFO*
Diane Reissman, *Exec VP*
Sharon Ginchansky, *Vice Pres*
EMP: 80 **EST:** 1972
SQ FT: 24,000
SALES (est): 125.3MM **Privately Held**
WEB: www.countryvillahealth.com
SIC: 8741 Nursing & personal care facility
management; hospital management

PRODUCTS & SVCS

(P-26196)
COUNTRY VILLA SERVICE CORP
1730 Grand Ave, Long Beach
(90804-2011)
PHONE.................562 597-8817
Nenita Bartolome, *Financial Exec*
EMP: 110
SALES (corp-wide): 125.3MM **Privately Held**
SIC: 8741 Nursing & personal care facility management
PA: Country Villa Service Corp.
2400 E Katella Ave # 800
Anaheim CA 92806
310 574-3733

(P-26197)
COUNTRY VILLA SERVICE CORP
615 W Duarte Rd, Monrovia (91016-4436)
PHONE.................626 358-4547
Sam Chia, *Branch Mgr*
EMP: 110
SALES (corp-wide): 125.3MM **Privately Held**
SIC: 8741 Management services
PA: Country Villa Service Corp.
2400 E Katella Ave # 800
Anaheim CA 92806
310 574-3733

(P-26198)
COUNTRY VILLA SERVICE CORP
Also Called: Country Villa E Convalescent
2415 S Western Ave, Los Angeles
(90018-2608)
PHONE.................323 734-1101
Phadra Johnson, *Manager*
EMP: 120
SALES (corp-wide): 125.3MM **Privately Held**
WEB: www.countryvillahealth.com
SIC: 8741 8051 8011 8059 Nursing & personal care facility management; skilled nursing care facilities; clinic, operated by physicians; convalescent home
PA: Country Villa Service Corp.
2400 E Katella Ave # 800
Anaheim CA 92806
310 574-3733

(P-26199)
COUNTRY VILLA SERVICE CORP
3533 Motor Ave, Los Angeles
(90034-4806)
PHONE.................310 574-3733
EMP: 110
SALES (corp-wide): 125.3MM **Privately Held**
SIC: 8741
PA: Country Villa Service Corp.
2400 E Katella Ave # 800
Anaheim CA 92806
310 574-3733

(P-26200)
COUNTRY VILLA SERVICE CORP
3233 W Pico Blvd, Los Angeles
(90019-3640)
PHONE.................323 734-9122
Mike Demchuck, *Manager*
EMP: 100
SALES (corp-wide): 125.3MM **Privately Held**
WEB: www.countryvillahealth.com
SIC: 8741 8051 Nursing & personal care facility management; skilled nursing care facilities
PA: Country Villa Service Corp.
2400 E Katella Ave # 800
Anaheim CA 92806
310 574-3733

(P-26201)
COUNTRYSIDE INN-CORONA LP
1015 W Colton Ave, Redlands
(92374-2933)
PHONE.................909 335-9024
Donald B Ayres Jr, *Branch Mgr*
EMP: 50
SALES (corp-wide): 33.8MM **Privately Held**
SIC: 8741 Management services
PA: Countryside Inn-Corona, L.P.
1900 Frontage Rd
Corona CA 92882
714 540-6060

(P-26202)
COUNTRYSIDE INN-CORONA LP
12850 Seal Beach Blvd, Seal Beach
(90740-2714)
PHONE.................562 596-8330
Bill Tolen, *Manager*
EMP: 50
SALES (corp-wide): 33.8MM **Privately Held**
WEB: www.ayreshotelsealbeach.com
SIC: 8741 1531 Management services; operative builders
PA: Countryside Inn-Corona, L.P.
1900 Frontage Rd
Corona CA 92882
714 540-6060

(P-26203)
COUNTY OF LOS ANGELES
Also Called: Social Service Dept- Admin
12900 Crssrds Pkwy S 20, City of Industry
(91746)
PHONE.................562 908-8400
Phillip Browning, *Director*
EMP: 400 **Privately Held**
WEB: www.co.la.ca.us
SIC: 8741 9441 Management services;
PA: County Of Los Angeles
500 W Temple St Ste 437
Los Angeles CA 90012
213 974-1101

(P-26204)
COUNTY OF SAN MATEO
Also Called: Human Resources Department
400 County Ctr, Redwood City
(94063-1662)
PHONE.................650 363-4915
Greg Munks, *Sheriff*
Tony Harwood, *Manager*
EMP: 145 **Privately Held**
WEB: www.ci.sanmateo.ca.us
SIC: 8741 9441 Personnel management;
PA: County of San Mateo
400 County Ctr
Redwood City CA 94063
650 363-4123

(P-26205)
COUNTY OF SAN MATEO
Also Called: Human Resources Department
455 County Ctr, Redwood City
(94063-9700)
PHONE.................650 363-4343
Donna Vaillancourt, *Director*
EMP: 50 **Privately Held**
WEB: www.ci.sanmateo.ca.us
SIC: 8741 9441 Personnel management;
PA: County Of San Mateo
400 County Ctr
Redwood City CA 94063
650 363-4123

(P-26206)
CRESTLINE HOTELS & RESORTS LLC
535 S Grand Ave, Los Angeles
(90071-2601)
PHONE.................213 624-0000
Eddie Andre, *General Mgr*
Yi Tan, *Sales Staff*
Potjaman Pigulsawas, *Supervisor*
EMP: 88
SALES (corp-wide): 52.2MM **Privately Held**
SIC: 8741 Hotel or motel management
PA: Crestline Hotels & Resorts, Llc
3950 University Dr # 301
Fairfax VA 22030
571 529-6100

(P-26207)
CRESTLINE HOTELS & RESORTS LLC
1250 Columbus Ave, San Francisco
(94133-1327)
PHONE.................415 775-7555
Amy Arbuckle, *Manager*
EMP: 175
SALES (corp-wide): 52.2MM **Privately Held**
SIC: 8741 Hotel or motel management

PA: Crestline Hotels & Resorts, Llc
3950 University Dr # 301
Fairfax VA 22030
571 529-6100

(P-26208)
CSI FINANCIAL SERVICES LLC
3636 Nobel Dr Ste 250, San Diego
(92122-1042)
PHONE.................858 200-9200
Janet Shanks, *CFO*
Grant Phillips, *Vice Pres*
Christian Coburn, *Director*
Mitch Patridge, *Manager*
Pete Thompson, *Underwriter*
EMP: 50
SQ FT: 4,050
SALES (est): 6.2MM **Privately Held**
WEB: www.csifinancial.com
SIC: 8741 8742 Management services; hospital & health services consultant

(P-26209)
DELTA ELECTRONICS AMERICAS LTD (DH)
46101 Fremont Blvd, Fremont
(94538-6468)
PHONE.................510 668-5100
Ming H Huang, *President*
Sheryl Chen, *CFO*
Joseph Yu, *QC Mgr*
Christopher Yang, *Marketing Staff*
Simon Product, *Director*
◆ EMP: 100
SALES (est): 71.3MM **Privately Held**
WEB: www.delta-corp.com
SIC: 8741 5045 3577 5063 Management services; computer peripheral equipment; computer peripheral equipment; electrical apparatus & equipment; electronic parts & equipment
HQ: Delta America Ltd
46101 Fremont Blvd
Fremont CA 94538
510 668-5100

(P-26210)
DERJJAN ASSOCIATES INC (PA)
2025 Soquel Ave, Santa Cruz
(95062-1323)
PHONE.................831 423-4111
Larry Deghetaldi, *President*
Gary Loveridge, *Ch of Bd*
Wayne Boss, *President*
Lowell M Sprague, *VP Finance*
EMP: 185
SQ FT: 60,000
SALES (est): 11.2MM **Privately Held**
WEB: www.williamrichards.com
SIC: 8741 6512 Administrative management; bank building operation

(P-26211)
DEWOLF REALTY CO INC
4330 California St, San Francisco
(94118-1316)
P.O. Box 591540 (94159-1540)
PHONE.................415 221-2032
William A Talmage, *President*
Marie Wayne, *Corp Secy*
Aaron Sinel, *Vice Pres*
EMP: 60
SALES (est): 6.5MM **Privately Held**
WEB: www.dewolfsf.com
SIC: 8741 6531 Management services; appraiser, real estate; real estate brokers & agents

(P-26212)
DHS CONSULTING LLC
1820 E 1st St Ste 410, Santa Ana
(92705-8311)
PHONE.................714 276-1135
Sudhir Damle, *President*
Eric Slaasted, *Senior VP*
Gary Cooley, *Vice Pres*
Hemalata Damle, *Vice Pres*
Melanie Estes, *Vice Pres*
EMP: 140
SQ FT: 6,000
SALES (est): 12MM
SALES (corp-wide): 13.7MM **Privately Held**
SIC: 8741 Construction management

PA: Crestline Hotels & Resorts, Llc
3950 University Dr # 301
Fairfax VA 22030
571 529-6100

(P-26213)
DIGITAL MEDIA MANAGEMENT LLC
5670 Wilshire Blvd Fl 11, Los Angeles
(90036-5627)
PHONE.................323 378-6505
Luigi Picarazzi, *Mng Member*
Kolleen Figiel, *Office Mgr*
Amelia Hanson, *Office Mgr*
Terri McAlpine, *Human Res Mgr*
Dave Giglio, *Opers Staff*
EMP: 65
SALES (est): 2.6MM **Privately Held**
SIC: 8741 Management services

(P-26214)
DIRECTORATE OF MWR FMD USAG
420 Montgomery St, San Francisco
(94104-1207)
PHONE.................210 466-1376
Christine Brunner, *Manager*
EMP: 99
SALES (est): 1.9MM **Privately Held**
SIC: 8741 Management services

(P-26215)
DOCTORS OF AFFILIATED
600 City Pkwy W Ste 400, Orange
(92868-2900)
PHONE.................714 539-3100
Frank Rubino, *President*
John Ernsberger, *CEO*
Prakesh Bondade, *Chairman*
EMP: 59
SQ FT: 10,000
SALES (est): 6.4MM **Privately Held**
WEB: www.adoc.us
SIC: 8741 Management services

(P-26216)
DONALD LUCKY LLC
Also Called: Babe's Bbq Grill
4029 Westerly Pl Ste 111, Newport Beach
(92660-2329)
PHONE.................949 752-0647
Donald Callender,
EMP: 120 EST: 2001
SALES (est): 5.1MM **Privately Held**
SIC: 8741 Restaurant management

(P-26217)
E3 HEALTHCARE MANAGEMENT LLC
375 Forest Ave, Palo Alto (94301-2521)
PHONE.................650 324-0600
Carole Wilson, *Mng Member*
Karen Jansen, *Director*
EMP: 100
SALES (est): 3.9MM **Privately Held**
SIC: 8741 Hospital management

(P-26218)
ECONNECTIONS INC
75 N Fair Oaks Ave, Pasadena
(91103-3651)
PHONE.................626 307-6200
Robert Rodin, *President*
Henry W Chin, *Exec VP*
EMP: 150
SALES (est): 5.3MM **Privately Held**
WEB: www.econnections.com
SIC: 8741 5065 8742 Management services; electronic parts & equipment; management consulting services

(P-26219)
ENERGY SALVAGE INC
8231 Alpine Ave Ste 3, Sacramento
(95826-4746)
P.O. Box 255009 (95865-5009)
PHONE.................916 737-8640
Michael P Lien, *President*
Lisa Baltodano, *Officer*
Amber P Beck, *Officer*
Norman Lien, *Officer*
Teresa Shumpert, *Officer*
EMP: 50

PA: Anser Advisory, Llc
11095 Knott Ave Ste L
Cypress CA 90630
714 209-7671

SALES (est): 2.1MM **Privately Held**
SIC: **8741 6512** Business management; financial management for business; nonresidential building operators

(P-26220)
EPIC MANAGEMENT LP (PA)
1615 Orange Tree Ln, Redlands
(92374-4501)
P.O. Box 19020, San Bernardino (92423-9020)
PHONE...........................909 799-1818
John D Goodman, *CEO*
Claudeth Cruz, *Info Tech Mgr*
Matthew Steele, *Network Tech*
Chad Easton, *Engineer*
Brian Fraser, *VP Finance*
EMP: 148
SALES (est): 50.3MM **Privately Held**
SIC: **8741** Nursing & personal care facility management

(P-26221)
ET CAPITAL SOLAR PARTNERS USA
4900 Hopyard Rd Ste 2, Pleasanton
(94588-3344)
PHONE...........................925 460-9898
Boris Schubert, *CEO*
Elaine Jones, *President*
EMP: 50
SALES (est): 980.6K **Privately Held**
SIC: **8741 3674** Financial management for business; solar cells
PA: Et Solar Group

(P-26222)
ETHOS MANAGEMENT INC
560 W Main St, Alhambra (91801-3374)
PHONE...........................626 456-3669
Nhac Vy Ngo, *CEO*
EMP: 50
SALES (est): 2.8MM **Privately Held**
SIC: **8741** Management services

(P-26223)
EUGENE BURGER MANAGEMENT CORP
555 Capitol Mall Ste 725, Sacramento
(95814-4515)
PHONE...........................916 443-6637
Eugene Burger, *Principal*
Kelly Moss, *Supervisor*
EMP: 143
SALES (corp-wide): 21.3MM **Privately Held**
SIC: **8741** Business management
PA: Eugene Burger Management Corp
6600 Hunter Dr
Rohnert Park CA 94928
707 584-5123

(P-26224)
EVEREST SILICON VALLEY MGT LP
8200 Gateway Blvd, Newark (94560-8000)
PHONE...........................510 494-8800
Marshall Young, *CEO*
LI Hui Lo, *COO*
EMP: 54
SQ FT: 7,500
SALES: 450K
SALES (corp-wide): 1.2MM **Privately Held**
SIC: **8741** Hotel or motel management
PA: Everest Hotel Group, Llc
2140 S Dupont Hwy
Camden DE 19934
213 272-0088

(P-26225)
EVERGREEN COMPANY INC
847 E Turner Rd, Lodi (95240-0734)
PHONE...........................916 257-5994
Thomas W Bors, *CEO*
EMP: 60
SALES (est): 5.9MM **Privately Held**
SIC: **8741** Business management

(P-26226)
EVOLUTION HOSPITALITY LLC (PA)
1211 Puerta Del Sol # 170, San Clemente
(92673-6353)
PHONE...........................949 325-1350
John Murphy, *President*
Bhavesh Patel, *Senior VP*
Christopher Conrad, *Vice Pres*
Matt Greene, *Vice Pres*
Lynn Kozlowski, *Vice Pres*
EMP: 94 EST: 2010
SALES (est): 179.2MM **Privately Held**
SIC: **8741 7011** Hotel or motel management; hotels & motels

(P-26227)
FACILITY SERVICES PARTNERS
1 University Dr, Aliso Viejo (92656-8081)
PHONE...........................949 480-4090
Malcolm Thomas, *President*
Scott Collins, *Corp Secy*
EMP: 62 EST: 2008
SALES (est): 4MM **Privately Held**
SIC: **8741 7349** Industrial management; building maintenance services

(P-26228)
FALCON AEROSPACE HOLDINGS LLC
Also Called: Wesco Aircraft
27727 Avenue Scott, Valencia
(91355-1219)
PHONE...........................661 775-7200
Randy J Snyder, *Ch of Bd*
Tommy Lee, *Exec VP*
Gary Hundley, *Vice Pres*
Jeff Misakian, *Vice Pres*
James Matthews, *Exec Dir*
EMP: 1250
SALES (est): 41.3MM **Privately Held**
SIC: **8741** Business management

(P-26229)
FBD VANGUARD CONSTRUCTION INC
550 Greenville Rd, Livermore
(94550-9297)
PHONE...........................925 245-1300
Billie Sposeto, *President*
Madison Adkins, *Administration*
Troy Ravazza, *Manager*
EMP: 120
SALES (est): 21MM **Privately Held**
SIC: **8741** Construction management

(P-26230)
FIVE STAR QUALITY CARE INC
Also Called: Palm Springs Health Care Ctr
277 S Sunrise Way, Palm Springs
(92262-6738)
PHONE...........................760 327-8541
Darrin Tharp, *Administration*
EMP: 100 **Publicly Held**
WEB: www.fivestarqualitycare.com
SIC: **8741 8322** Nursing & personal care facility management; rehabilitation services
PA: Five Star Senior Living Inc.
400 Centre St
Newton MA 02458

(P-26231)
FORT JAMES CORPORATION
Also Called: Fort James Communications Pprs
2000 Powell St, Emeryville (94608-1804)
PHONE...........................510 594-4900
Miles Marsh, *Branch Mgr*
EMP: 100
SALES (corp-wide): 40.6B **Privately Held**
WEB: www.fortjames.com
SIC: **8741** Administrative management
HQ: Fort James Corporation
133 Peachtree St Ne
Atlanta GA 30303
404 652-4000

(P-26232)
FORTE ENTERPRISES INC (PA)
Also Called: St Francis Pavillion
99 Escuela Dr, Daly City (94015-4003)
PHONE...........................650 994-3200
Thomas J Nico, *President*

EMP: 240
SQ FT: 14,000
SALES (est): 9.8MM **Privately Held**
SIC: **8741 8721** Nursing & personal care facility management; accounting, auditing & bookkeeping

(P-26233)
FPI MANAGEMENT INC
1107 Luchessi Dr, San Jose (95118-3739)
PHONE...........................408 267-3952
EMP: 248
SALES (corp-wide): 98.4MM **Privately Held**
SIC: **8741 6513** Business management; apartment building operators
PA: Fpi Management, Inc.
800 Iron Point Rd
Folsom CA 95630
916 357-5300

(P-26234)
FRITO-LAY NORTH AMERICA INC
1500 Francisco St, Torrance (90501-1329)
PHONE...........................310 224-5600
Dexter Matt, *General Mgr*
EMP: 200
SQ FT: 75,861
SALES (corp-wide): 64.6B **Publicly Held**
WEB: www.fritolay.com
SIC: **8741 2099 2096** Management services; food preparations; potato chips & similar snacks
HQ: Frito-Lay North America, Inc.
7701 Legacy Dr
Plano TX 75024

(P-26235)
FRONT LINE MGT GROUP INC
1100 Glendon Ave Ste 2000, Los Angeles
(90024-3524)
PHONE...........................310 209-3100
Irving Azoff, *President*
EMP: 90
SALES (est): 3.9MM
SALES (corp-wide): 10.7B **Publicly Held**
SIC: **8741** Management services
HQ: Flmg Holdings Corp.
9348 Civic Center Dr
Beverly Hills CA 90210
310 867-7000

(P-26236)
GAFCON INC (PA)
5960 Cornerstone Ct W # 100, San Diego
(92121-3780)
PHONE...........................858 875-0010
Yehudi Gaffen, *CEO*
Pam Gaffen, *President*
Robin Duveen, *COO*
Casey Sanfilippo, *COO*
Jon Rodriguez, *CFO*
EMP: 60
SQ FT: 14,000
SALES (est): 16.9MM **Privately Held**
SIC: **8741 8111** Construction management; legal services

(P-26237)
GARDNER NEUROLOGIC ORTHOPEDIC
Also Called: Internal Associates Med Group
6167 Bristol Pkwy Ste 200, Culver City
(90230-6649)
PHONE...........................310 649-5824
Elias Munoz, *Principal*
Felina Setiawan, *Payroll Mgr*
EMP: 70
SALES (est): 1.9MM **Privately Held**
SIC: **8741** Management services

(P-26238)
GEO GROUP INC
10400 Rancho Rd, Adelanto (92301-2237)
P.O. Box 6005 (92301-1190)
PHONE...........................760 246-1171
Jerardo Acevedo, *Warden*
EMP: 100
SALES (corp-wide): 2.3B **Privately Held**
WEB: www.thegeogroupinc.com
SIC: **8741** Management services

PA: The Geo Group Inc
4955 Technology Way
Boca Raton FL 33431
561 893-0101

(P-26239)
GEO GROUP INC
Also Called: Golden State Crrctional Fcilty
611 Frontage Rd, Mc Farland
(93250-1075)
P.O. Box 1518 (93250-0118)
PHONE...........................661 792-2731
Wanda Wilson, *Warden*
Paul Laird, *Vice Pres*
EMP: 120
SALES (corp-wide): 2.3B **Privately Held**
WEB: www.thegeogroupinc.com
SIC: **8741** Management services
PA: The Geo Group Inc
4955 Technology Way
Boca Raton FL 33431
561 893-0101

(P-26240)
GILARDI & CO LLC
3301 Kerner Blvd Ste 100, San Rafael
(94901-4896)
PHONE...........................415 461-0410
Bryan Butvick, *CEO*
Daniel Burke, *Exec VP*
Peter Crudo, *Exec VP*
Lara McDermott, *Exec VP*
Kim Wagner, *Exec VP*
EMP: 80
SQ FT: 16,000
SALES (est): 10.5MM **Privately Held**
WEB: www.gilardi.com
SIC: **8741 8111** Management services; legal services
HQ: Kurtzman Carson Consultants, Inc
2335 Alaska Ave
El Segundo CA 90245
310 823-9000

(P-26241)
GILBANE BUILDING COMPANY
Also Called: Gilbane Construction
1798 Tech Dr Ste 120, San Jose (95110)
PHONE...........................408 660-4400
Bob Crowder, *Director*
Cathy Rendon, *Sr Project Mgr*
EMP: 64
SALES (corp-wide): 5.4B **Privately Held**
WEB: www.gilbaneco.com
SIC: **8741 1542** Construction management; commercial & office building, new construction
HQ: Gilbane Building Company
7 Jackson Walkway Ste 2
Providence RI 02903
401 456-5800

(P-26242)
GLOBAL 360 INC
1080 Marina Village Pkwy # 300, Alameda
(94501-6427)
PHONE...........................510 263-4800
Nina Abbott, *Branch Mgr*
Richard Carreon, *Branch Mgr*
Walter Debus, *VP Engrg*
EMP: 65
SALES (corp-wide): 2.2B **Privately Held**
WEB: www.global360.com
SIC: **8741** Management services
PA: Open Text Corporation
275 Frank Tompa Dr
Waterloo ON N2L 0
519 888-7111

(P-26243)
GLOBAL-DINING INC CALIFORNIA
1212 3rd Street Promenade, Santa Monica
(90401-1308)
PHONE...........................310 576-9922
Kozo Hasegawa, *CEO*
EMP: 140
SALES: 6.2MM **Privately Held**
SIC: **8741** Restaurant management
PA: Global-Dining, Inc.
7-1-5, Minamiaoyama
Minato-Ku TKY 107-0

(P-26244)
GOLDMAN AVRAM
Also Called: Nrt
1855 Gateway Blvd Ste 750, Concord
(94520-3290)
PHONE..........................925 275-3000
Avram Goldman, *President*
Jamie Schlicher, *Vice Pres*
Jennifer Vargas, *Accountant*
EMP: 75
SALES (est): 3.3MM **Privately Held**
SIC: 8741 6531 Management services;
real estate brokers & agents

(P-26245)
**GONZALEZ MANAGEMENT CO
INC**
10147 San Fernando Rd, Pacoima
(91331-2617)
PHONE..........................818 485-0596
Luis Gonzalez, *President*
EMP: 65 EST: 2004
SQ FT: 20,000
SALES (est): 6.8MM **Privately Held**
SIC: 8741 Management services

(P-26246)
GRANITE POWER INC
580 W Beach St, Watsonville (95076-5107)
P.O. Box 50085 (95077-5085)
PHONE..........................831 724-1011
James H Roberts, *CEO*
EMP: 300
SALES (est): 2.8MM
SALES (corp-wide): 3.3B **Publicly Held**
SIC: 8741 Construction management
PA: Granite Construction Incorporated
585 W Beach St
Watsonville CA 95076
831 724-1011

(P-26247)
GRANVILLE GLENDALE INC
Also Called: Granville Cafe
807 Americana Way, Glendale
(91210-1509)
PHONE..........................818 550-0472
Jonathan Weiss, *CEO*
Marc Glantz, *CFO*
EMP: 75 EST: 2008
SALES (est): 4.5MM **Privately Held**
SIC: 8741 Restaurant management

(P-26248)
GRIFFIN GROUP LLC (PA)
4 Rebelo Ln Ste D, Novato (94947-3629)
PHONE..........................415 892-4569
Keith Greggor, *CEO*
Crystal Marty, *CFO*
Tony Foglio, *Chairman*
Lynn Lackey, *Vice Pres*
Daniel Covell, *General Mgr*
EMP: 110
SALES (est): 5MM **Privately Held**
SIC: 8741 Business management

(P-26249)
**GRIFFIN SLR MANAGEMENT
INC**
9454 Wilshire Blvd # 700, Beverly Hills
(90212-2931)
PHONE..........................310 270-4031
Sol L Rabin, *President*
Coleen Rabin, *Principal*
EMP: 66
SALES (est): 3.6MM **Privately Held**
SIC: 8741 Management services

(P-26250)
**GRM INFORMATION MGT
SERVICES**
8500 Mercury Ln, Pico Rivera
(90660-3796)
PHONE..........................562 373-9000
Lev Spivak, *Vice Pres*
Jerry Glatt, *Exec VP*
John Buglino, *Marketing Staff*
EMP: 50
SALES (est): 1.8MM **Privately Held**
SIC: 8741 Management services

(P-26251)
**GRM INFORMATION MGT SVCS
INC**
8500 Mercury Ln, Pico Rivera
(90660-3796)
PHONE..........................562 373-9000
Jack Grimdjean, *Manager*
EMP: 54 **Privately Held**
SIC: 8741 Business management
PA: Grm Information Management Serv-
ices, Inc.
215 Coles St
Jersey City NJ 07310

(P-26252)
GSG ASSOCIATES INC
1010 E Union St Ste 203, Pasadena
(91106-1756)
PHONE..........................626 585-1808
Glenda S Garrard, *CEO*
Jay Garrard, *President*
Maureen Stratton, *President*
Helen Young, *Med Doctor*
EMP: 100
SQ FT: 3,800
SALES (est): 9MM **Privately Held**
WEB: www.gsga.net
SIC: 8741 Nursing & personal care facility
management

(P-26253)
HALL MANAGEMENT CORP
Also Called: Land & Personnel Management
759 S Madera Ave, Kerman (93630-1744)
PHONE..........................559 846-7382
Stacy Hampton, *President*
James Randles, *Vice Pres*
EMP: 2000
SQ FT: 5,000
SALES (est): 98.4MM **Privately Held**
SIC: 8741 Personnel management

(P-26254)
**HARBOR-UCLA MED
FOUNDATION INC (PA)**
Also Called: Harbor Ucla Med Foundation
21840 S Norm Ave, Torrance (90502)
PHONE..........................310 222-5015
Chester Choi, *CEO*
EMP: 400
SQ FT: 45,000
SALES: 11.2MM **Privately Held**
WEB: www.harborucla.org
SIC: 8741 Hospital management

(P-26255)
**HEALTHCARE MGT PARTNERS
LLC**
20 Executive Park Ste 155, Irvine
(92614-4733)
PHONE..........................949 263-8620
Claudia Dwyer,
Douglas Cassel,
Chris Kellogg,
Jay Lichman,
Taylor Moorehead,
EMP: 260
SALES (est): 11.6MM **Privately Held**
WEB: www.hmpllc.com
SIC: 8741 8721 Hospital management;
nursing & personal care facility manage-
ment; accounting, auditing & bookkeeping

(P-26256)
**HOSPITAL CMMTTEE FOR THE
LVRMR (DH)**
Also Called: Valley Care Health System, The
5555 W Las Positas Blvd, Pleasanton
(94588-4000)
PHONE..........................925 847-3000
Scott Gregerson, *CEO*
Gina Teeples, *Officer*
Caryn Thornburg, *Officer*
Dennis Ong, *Pharmacy Dir*
Jennifer Berg, *Exec Dir*
EMP: 500
SALES (est): 96.9MM
SALES (corp-wide): 11.3B **Privately Held**
WEB: www.valleycare.com
SIC: 8741 8062 Hospital management;
general medical & surgical hospitals

HQ: Stanford Health Care
300 Pasteur Dr
Stanford CA 94305
650 723-4000

(P-26257)
**HOSPITAL CMMTTEE FOR THE
LVRMR**
Also Called: VALLEYCARE HEALTH SYS-
TEM
1111 E Stanley Blvd, Livermore
(94550-4115)
PHONE..........................925 447-7000
Marcelina L Feit, *CEO*
Gina Teeples, *Officer*
Isabel Chen, *Exec Dir*
Virgil De Leon, *Network Analyst*
Larry Melim, *Engineer*
EMP: 1000
SALES: 272.7MM **Privately Held**
SIC: 8741 Administrative management;
hospital management

(P-26258)
**HOSTMARK INVESTORS LTD
PARTNR**
Also Called: Santa Clara Hilton, The
4949 Great America Pkwy, Santa Clara
(95054-1216)
PHONE..........................408 330-0001
Roy Truitt, *General Mgr*
EMP: 180 **Privately Held**
SIC: 8741 7991 5813 5812 Hotel or
motel management; physical fitness facili-
ties; drinking places; eating places; hotel,
franchised
PA: Hostmark Investors Limited Partnership
1300 E Wdfield Rd Ste 400
Schaumburg IL 60173

(P-26259)
**HOTEL MANAGERS GROUP
LLC**
11590 W Bernardo Ct # 211, San Diego
(92127-1622)
PHONE..........................858 673-1534
Joel Biggs, *Mng Member*
Michele Demayo, *Exec VP*
Michelle Demayo, *Exec VP*
Emad Alwer, *Vice Pres*
Alan Bowles, *Vice Pres*
EMP: 400 EST: 1996
SALES (est): 33.4MM **Privately Held**
WEB: www.hotelmanagersgroup.com
SIC: 8741 7011 7041 Hotel or motel man-
agement; hotels & motels; membership-
basis organization hotels

(P-26260)
HRONOPOULOS
110 W A St Ste 900, San Diego
(92101-3705)
PHONE..........................619 237-6161
Andreas Hronopoulos, *CEO*
George Hronopoulos, *CFO*
Jordan Yerkes, *Info Tech Dir*
Kevin Kachman,
EMP: 50 EST: 2010
SQ FT: 10,000
SALES: 4MM **Privately Held**
SIC: 8741 Business management

(P-26261)
**HUNT CONVENIENCE STORES
LLC**
5750 S Watt Ave, Sacramento
(95829-9349)
P.O. Box 277670 (95827-7670)
PHONE..........................916 383-4868
Joshua M Hunt, *Mng Member*
Daniel Maue, *CFO*
Joshua Hunt, *Mng Member*
EMP: 50 EST: 2014
SQ FT: 3,200
SALES: 5MM **Privately Held**
SIC: 8741 Administrative management

(P-26262)
**IKEA PURCHASING SVCS US
INC**
600 N San Fernando Blvd, Burbank
(91502-1021)
PHONE..........................818 841-3500
Chris Maynard, *Manager*

EMP: 300
SALES (corp-wide): 200.2K **Privately
Held**
SIC: 8741 8721 5712 Administrative man-
agement; accounting, auditing & book-
keeping; furniture stores
HQ: Ikea Purchasing Services (Us) Inc.
7810 Katy Fwy
Houston TX 77024
888 888-4532

(P-26263)
**INNOVATIVE EDUCATION MGT
INC (PA)**
4535 Missouri Flat Rd 1a, Placerville
(95667-6808)
P.O. Box 2252 (95667-2252)
PHONE..........................530 295-3566
Randy Gaschler, *President*
Denise Williams, *Admin Asst*
Katy Mann, *Administration*
Eugene Linger, *Info Tech Dir*
John Wilberger, *Info Tech Mgr*
EMP: 53
SQ FT: 2,000
SALES: 20MM **Privately Held**
SIC: 8741 Management services

(P-26264)
INTELLECTUAL VENTURES LLC
200 California Ave # 200, Palo Alto
(94306-1635)
PHONE..........................650 941-1330
EMP: 280
SALES (corp-wide): 129.4MM **Privately
Held**
SIC: 8741 Management services
PA: Intellectual Ventures, Llc
3150 139th Ave Se Ste 500
Bellevue WA 98005
425 467-2300

(P-26265)
**INTERSTATE HOTELS RESORTS
INC**
4685 Macarthur Ct Ste 480, Newport Beach
(92660-8850)
PHONE..........................949 783-2500
Mark Burden, *Branch Mgr*
EMP: 61 **Privately Held**
SIC: 8741 Hotel or motel management
HQ: Interstate Hotels & Resorts, Inc.
2011 Crystal Dr Ste 1100
Arlington VA 22202
703 387-3100

(P-26266)
**INTERSTATE HOTELS RESORTS
INC**
Also Called: Doral Palm Sprngs Rsrt & Golf
67 967 Vst Chno At Lndau, Palm Springs
(92263)
P.O. Box 1644 (92263-1644)
PHONE..........................760 322-7000
Elie Zod, *Manager*
EMP: 200 **Privately Held**
WEB: www.sheratonokc.com
SIC: 8741 Hotel or motel management
HQ: Interstate Hotels & Resorts, Inc.
2011 Crystal Dr Ste 1100
Arlington VA 22202
703 387-3100

(P-26267)
**INTERSTATE HOTELS RESORTS
INC**
Also Called: Embassy Suites Walnut Creek
1345 Treat Blvd, Walnut Creek
(94597-2173)
PHONE..........................925 934-2500
David Cano, *Manager*
EMP: 130 **Privately Held**
WEB: www.sheratonokc.com
SIC: 8741 Hotel or motel management
HQ: Interstate Hotels & Resorts, Inc.
2011 Crystal Dr Ste 1100
Arlington VA 22202
703 387-3100

(P-26268)
**INTERSTATE HOTELS RESORTS
INC**
Also Called: Claremont Resort
41 Tunnel Rd, Berkeley (94705-2429)
PHONE..........................510 843-3000

Mike Czarcinski, *General Mgr*
EMP: 99 Privately Held
WEB: www.sheratonokc.com
SIC: 8741 Hotel or motel management
HQ: Interstate Hotels & Resorts, Inc.
2011 Crystal Dr Ste 1100
Arlington VA 22202
703 387-3100

(P-26269)
INVESTORS CAPITAL MGT GROUP
Also Called: Cuisine Partners USA
10390 Santa Monica Blvd, Los Angeles
(90025-5058)
PHONE.....................310 553-5175
EMP: 277
SQ FT: 7,800
SALES (est): 11MM **Privately Held**
SIC: 8741

(P-26270)
JC RESORTS LLC
Also Called: Surf Sand Hotel
1555 S Coast Hwy, Laguna Beach
(92651-3226)
PHONE.....................949 376-2779
Blaise Bartell, *Branch Mgr*
Amy McLimore, *Sales Staff*
Joanna Bear, *Director*
EMP: 300 Privately Held
WEB: www.surfsandsandresort.com
SIC: 8741 5813 5812 7011 Hotel or
motel management; drinking places; eat-
ing places; hotels
PA: Jc Resorts Llc
533 Coast Blvd S
La Jolla CA 92037

(P-26271)
JC RESORTS LLC
Also Called: Encinitas Ranch Golf Course
1275 Quail Gardens Dr, Encinitas
(92024-2368)
PHONE.....................760 944-1936
Rod Landville, *Manager*
EMP: 100
SALES (est): 5.2MM **Privately Held**
WEB: www.surfsandsandresort.com
SIC: 8741 7992 Hotel or motel manage-
ment; public golf courses
PA: Jc Resorts Llc
533 Coast Blvd S
La Jolla CA 92037

(P-26272)
JENKINS GALES & MARTINEZ INC
6033 W Century Blvd # 601, Los Angeles
(90045-6414)
PHONE.....................310 645-0561
Earl Gales III, *CEO*
Mark Colopy, *Principal*
Starla Gale, *Principal*
Kaiya Gales, *Principal*
Ryan Gales, *Principal*
EMP: 70
SQ FT: 5,000
SALES: 3.9MM **Privately Held**
WEB: www.jgminc.com
SIC: 8741 8712 7389 8711 Construction
management; architectural engineering;
mapmaking or drafting, including aerial;
construction & civil engineering; manage-
ment consulting services

(P-26273)
JESSE LEE GROUP INC
Also Called: Castro Valley Care Centers
300 Crprate Pinte Ste 550, Culver City
(90230)
PHONE.....................510 351-3700
George Davis, *Manager*
EMP: 91
SALES (corp-wide): 7.6MM **Privately Held**
SIC: 8741 8051 8059 Hospital manage-
ment; skilled nursing care facilities; con-
valescent home
PA: Jesse Lee Group, Inc
5212 Village Creek Dr
Plano TX 75093
972 931-3800

(P-26274)
JESSE LEE GROUP INC
Also Called: New Hope Care Center
2586 Buthmann Ave, Tracy (95376-2165)
PHONE.....................209 832-2273
Ruby Rakow, *President*
EMP: 120
SALES (corp-wide): 7.6MM **Privately Held**
SIC: 8741 8051 Hospital management;
convalescent home with continuous nurs-
ing care
PA: Jesse Lee Group, Inc
5212 Village Creek Dr
Plano TX 75093
972 931-3800

(P-26275)
JIPC MANAGEMENT INC
Also Called: John's Incredible Pizza Co
22342 Avenida Empresa # 220, Rcho STA
Marg (92688-2161)
PHONE.....................949 916-2000
John M Parlet, *President*
Natalie Cervantes, *Admin Asst*
Alice Louie, *Admin Asst*
Kenneth Perkins, *Software Engr*
EMP: 1000
SALES (est): 77.2MM **Privately Held**
SIC: 8741 Restaurant management

(P-26276)
JOIE DE VIVRE HOSPITALITY LLC
Also Called: Maxwell Hotel, The
386 Geary St, San Francisco (94102-1802)
PHONE.....................415 986-2000
Steven Conley, *Manager*
EMP: 60
SALES (corp-wide): 231.8MM **Privately Held**
WEB: www.hotelbijou.com
SIC: 8741 7011 Hotel or motel manage-
ment; motels
PA: Joie De Vivre Hospitality, Llc
1750 Geary Blvd
San Francisco CA 94115
415 835-0300

(P-26277)
JOIE DE VIVRE HOSPITALITY LLC
Also Called: Costanoa
2001 Rossi Rd, Pescadero (94060-9732)
PHONE.....................650 879-1100
Daniel Medellin, *Branch Mgr*
Trevor Bridge, *General Mgr*
EMP: 65
SALES (corp-wide): 231.8MM **Privately Held**
WEB: www.hotelbijou.com
SIC: 8741 Hotel or motel management
PA: Joie De Vivre Hospitality, Llc
1750 Geary Blvd
San Francisco CA 94115
415 835-0300

(P-26278)
JUVENILE JUSTICE DIVISION CAL
Also Called: Ventura Yuth Crrctional Fcilty
3100 Wright Rd, Camarillo (93010-8307)
PHONE.....................805 485-7951
Vivian Craford, *Superintendent*
Gary Collins, *Principal*
EMP: 350 Privately Held
WEB: www.cya.ca.gov
SIC: 8741 9223 Office management;
house of correction, government
HQ: Juvenile Justice Division, California
1515 S St Ste 502s
Sacramento CA 95811

(P-26279)
KA MANAGEMENT INC
5820 Oberlin Dr Ste 201, San Diego
(92121-3743)
PHONE.....................858 404-6080
Kayvon Agahnia, *CEO*
Jill Muller, *Manager*
EMP: 90
SALES: 12MM **Privately Held**
SIC: 8741 Financial management for busi-
ness

(P-26280)
KAISER HLTH PLAN ASSET MGT INC
Also Called: KAISER PERMANENTE
1 Kaiser Plz Ste 1333, Oakland
(94612-3604)
PHONE.....................510 271-5910
Thomas R Meier, *President*
EMP: 50
SALES: 51MM
SALES (corp-wide): 76.5B **Privately Held**
WEB: www.kaiser.com
SIC: 8741 Hospital management
PA: Kaiser Foundation Health Plan, Inc.
1 Kaiser Plz
Oakland CA 94612
510 271-5800

(P-26281)
KAL KRISHNAN CONSULTING SVCS (PA)
800 S Figueroa St # 1210, Los Angeles
(90017-2521)
PHONE.....................510 893-3500
Kalliana R Krishnan, *President*
Dev Krishnan, *President*
Ron Anderson, *Vice Pres*
Craig Goodall, *Vice Pres*
Stan Tomlinson, *Vice Pres*
EMP: 94
SQ FT: 1,000
SALES (est): 11.5MM **Privately Held**
WEB: www.kalkrishnan.com
SIC: 8741 Construction management

(P-26282)
KEIRO SERVICES
Also Called: KEIRO SENIOR HEALTH CARE
420 E 3rd St Ste 1000, Los Angeles
(90013-1648)
PHONE.....................213 873-5700
Shawn Miyake, *CEO*
EMP: 500
SQ FT: 26,000
SALES: 1.4MM **Privately Held**
SIC: 8741 Nursing & personal care facility
management

(P-26283)
KELLEYAMERIT HOLDINGS INC (PA)
Also Called: Kelleyamerit Fleet Services
1331 N Calif Blvd Ste 150, Walnut Creek
(94596-4535)
PHONE.....................877 512-6374
Dan Williams, *CEO*
Amein Punjani, *COO*
Kent Bates, *CFO*
Robin Jilinda, *Accountant*
Robert Brauer, *VP Sales*
EMP: 53
SQ FT: 10,000
SALES: 180MM **Privately Held**
SIC: 8741 Management services

(P-26284)
KERN AROUND CLOCK FOUNDATION
5251 Office Park Dr # 400, Bakersfield
(93309-0667)
PHONE.....................661 324-3221
Mary Vasinda, *President*
John Vasinda, *Vice Pres*
Gena Morales, *Human Res Mgr*
Stacie Dollar, *VP Mktg*
EMP: 50
SALES: 314.3K **Privately Held**
WEB: www.bakersfieldcare.com
SIC: 8741 8322 Business management;
individual & family services

(P-26285)
KFI
1 Sansome St Fl 32, San Francisco
(94104-4436)
PHONE.....................415 956-9812
Gary Burison, *CEO*
Neil Saavedra, *Marketing Staff*
EMP: 50
SALES (est): 1.5MM **Privately Held**
SIC: 8741 Management services

(P-26286)
KINTETSU ENTERPRISES
328 E 1st St, Los Angeles (90012-3902)
PHONE.....................213 687-2000
EMP: 90
SALES: 5MM
SALES (corp-wide): 11.4B **Privately Held**
WEB: www.miyakoinn.com
SIC: 8741 6531
PA: Kintetsu Group Holdings Co., Ltd.
6-1-55, Uehonmachi, Tennoji-Ku
Osaka OSK 543-0
667 753-355

(P-26287)
KISCO SENIOR LIVING LLC
Also Called: Bridgepoint At San Francisco
1601 19th Ave Ofc, San Francisco
(94122-3478)
PHONE.....................415 664-6264
Susan Edwards, *Branch Mgr*
EMP: 66
SALES (corp-wide): 138.2MM **Privately Held**
WEB: www.kiscosl.com
SIC: 8741 Nursing & personal care facility
management
PA: Senior Kisco Living Llc
5790 Fleet St Ste 300
Carlsbad CA 92008
760 804-5900

(P-26288)
KNIT GENERATION GROUP INC
3818 S Broadway, Los Angeles
(90037-1412)
PHONE.....................213 221-5081
Joseph Dania, *Principal*
Manuela Gisel Villagomez, *Principal*
EMP: 65 **EST:** 2013
SALES (est): 4.7MM **Privately Held**
SIC: 8741 Management services

(P-26289)
KOR HOTEL GROUPS INC
530 Pico Blvd, Santa Monica (90405-1223)
PHONE.....................310 309-8066
Micheal D'Amodio, *President*
Nanda Te, *Accounting Mgr*
EMP: 99
SALES (est): 3.3MM **Privately Held**
SIC: 8741 Hotel or motel management

(P-26290)
KRM RISK MANAGEMENT SVCS INC
4270 W Richert Ave # 101, Fresno
(93722-6334)
P.O. Box 9549 (93793-9549)
PHONE.....................559 277-4800
Steve Wigh, *Vice Pres*
EMP: 51 **Privately Held**
WEB: www.krmrisk.com
SIC: 8741 Management services
PA: Krm Risk Management Services, Inc.
4270 W Richert Ave 101
Fresno CA 93722

(P-26291)
KSL II MNGEMENT OPERATIONS LLC
50905 Avenida Bermudas, La Quinta
(92253-8910)
PHONE.....................760 564-8000
Scott Dalecio, *President*
EMP: 60
SALES (est): 5MM **Privately Held**
SIC: 8741 Management services

(P-26292)
LA 1000 SANTA FE LLC
1000 S Santa Fe Ave, Los Angeles
(90021-1741)
PHONE.....................213 205-1000
Byron Icute,
EMP: 210
SALES (est): 2.1MM **Privately Held**
SIC: 8741 Hotel or motel management

(P-26293)
LA JOIE JERRY
Also Called: La Joie Construction
418 Sonora Dr, San Mateo (94402-2342)
PHONE.....................650 375-1808

PRODUCTS & SVCS

Jerry La Joie, *Owner*
EMP: 50
SALES (est): 2.9MM **Privately Held**
SIC: 8741 1542 1521 Construction management; commercial & office building, new construction; new construction, single-family houses

(P-26294)
LA VOIE & SONS CONSTRUCTION
1061 Nichols Ct, Rocklin (95765-1325)
PHONE.................................916 408-6900
EMP: 50
SALES (est): 2.6MM **Privately Held**
SIC: 8741

(P-26295)
LAKE MRRITT HEALTHCARE CTR LLC
309 Macarthur Blvd, Oakland (94610-3233)
PHONE.................................510 227-1806
Edna Cortez, *Administration*
EMP: 80
SALES (est): 7.5MM **Privately Held**
SIC: 8741 Hospital management

(P-26296)
LAKESIDE SYSTEMS INC
Also Called: Lakeside Medical Systems
8510 Balboa Blvd Ste 150, Northridge (91325-5810)
PHONE.................................866 654-3471
Richard Merkin, *CEO*
EMP: 700
SQ FT: 20,000
SALES (est): 31.2MM
SALES (corp-wide): 46.4MM **Privately Held**
SIC: 8741 8742 6411 Management services; management consulting services; insurance agents, brokers & service
PA: Heritage Provider Network Inc
8510 Balboa Blvd Ste 285
Northridge CA 91325
818 654-3461

(P-26297)
LEDCOR MANAGEMENT SERVICES INC
6405 Mira Mesa Blvd Ste 1, San Diego (92121-4147)
PHONE.................................858 527-6400
Dave Lede, *CEO*
EMP: 50
SALES (est): 4.6MM **Privately Held**
SIC: 8741 Business management

(P-26298)
LEDESMA & MEYER DEV INC
9441 Haven Ave, Rancho Cucamonga (91730-5845)
PHONE.................................909 476-0590
Joseph Ledesma, *CEO*
Kris Meyer, *Vice Pres*
EMP: 55
SQ FT: 16,480
SALES (est): 3.3MM **Privately Held**
SIC: 8741 Construction management

(P-26299)
LEGACY PRTNERS RESIDENTIAL INC
5141 California Ave # 100, Irvine (92617-3060)
PHONE.................................949 930-6600
Deborah Dodd, *Branch Mgr*
Erik Hansen, *Manager*
EMP: 359
SALES (corp-wide): 75.3MM **Privately Held**
SIC: 8741 Management services
PA: Legacy Partners Residential, Inc.
950 Tower Ln Ste 900
Foster City CA 94404
650 571-2250

(P-26300)
LEGACY PRTNERS RESIDENTIAL INC (PA)
950 Tower Ln Ste 900, Foster City (94404-2125)
PHONE.................................650 571-2250
C Preston Butcher, *Ch of Bd*

Gary J Rossi, *CFO*
Jonathan Figone, *General Mgr*
Sarah Argudo, *Office Mgr*
Kathy Drossel, *Office Admin*
EMP: 180
SALES (est): 75.3MM **Privately Held**
SIC: 8741 Management services

(P-26301)
LENDLEASE US CONSTRUCTION INC
800 W 6th St Ste 1600, Los Angeles (90017-2719)
PHONE.................................213 430-4660
Mike Concannon, *Branch Mgr*
EMP: 100 **Privately Held**
SIC: 8741 8742 1541 1542 Construction management; construction project management consultant; industrial buildings, new construction; nonresidential construction
HQ: Lendlease (Us) Construction Inc.
200 Park Ave Fl 9
New York NY 10166
212 592-6700

(P-26302)
LEXXIOM INC
7945 Cartilla Ave Ste A, Rancho Cucamonga (91730-3076)
PHONE.................................909 581-7313
Robert Lemelin, *President*
Brian Lemelin, *COO*
Leo Lemelin, *CFO*
EMP: 360
SALES (est): 21.6MM **Privately Held**
WEB: www.thedebtmediator.com
SIC: 8741 Administrative management

(P-26303)
LIBSOURCE LLC
10390 Santa Monica Blvd, Los Angeles (90025-5058)
PHONE.................................323 852-1083
Deborah Schwarz, *CEO*
Robert Corrao, *COO*
James Hurley, *Research*
Mona Suarez, *Research*
EMP: 140
SQ FT: 2,500
SALES: 20MM **Privately Held**
SIC: 8741 Financial management for business

(P-26304)
LION-VALLEN LTD PARTNERSHIP
22 Area Area A Bldg 2234, Camp Pendleton (92055)
P.O. Box 555045 (92055-5045)
PHONE.................................760 385-4885
Dennis Smith, *Sales Staff*
EMP: 50 **Privately Held**
SIC: 8741 Management services
PA: Lion-Vallen Limited Partnership
7200 Poe Ave Ste 400
Dayton OH 45414

(P-26305)
LIVINGSTON MEM VNA HLTH CORP
Also Called: LIVINGSTON MEMORIAL VISITING N
1996 Eastman Ave Ste 101, Ventura (93003-5768)
PHONE.................................805 642-0239
Lanyard K Dial MD, *President*
Charles Hair MD, *Ch of Bd*
Judy Hecox, *President*
Jeffrey Paul, *Treasurer*
EMP: 292
SQ FT: 12,600
SALES: 15.4MM **Privately Held**
WEB: www.lmvna.org
SIC: 8741 8082 Hospital management; nursing & personal care facility management; home health care services

(P-26306)
LZ MANAGEMENT GROUP LLC
720 Paularino Ave, Costa Mesa (92626-2940)
PHONE.................................714 957-4061
EMP: 64

SALES (corp-wide): 16.3MM **Privately Held**
SIC: 8741 Management services
PA: Lz Management Group Llc
3680 Wilshire Blvd # 206
Los Angeles CA 90010
213 383-4800

(P-26307)
MARITIME MANAGEMENT
Also Called: G Moroni Comp
2368 Maritime Dr Ste 100, Elk Grove (95758-3655)
PHONE.................................916 392-3000
Tony Lutsi, *Owner*
Greg Moroni, *Co-Owner*
EMP: 400 **EST:** 1997
SQ FT: 2,000
SALES (est): 13.6MM **Privately Held**
WEB: www.smartmanagement.us
SIC: 8741 8742 Management services; management consulting services

(P-26308)
MAVERICK HOTEL PARTNERS LLC
Also Called: Filament Hospitality
50 California St, San Francisco (94111-4624)
PHONE.................................415 655-9526
Ingrid Summerfield, *Mng Member*
Beth Belanger, *Sr Associate*
Michael Roguly, *Director*
Maureen Rousseau, *Director*
EMP: 300
SALES: 75K **Privately Held**
SIC: 8741 Hotel or motel management

(P-26309)
MAX SPORTSTERS INC
Also Called: Wheeler and Company
10050 N Foothill Blvd # 200, Cupertino (95014-5661)
PHONE.................................408 446-8330
David Wheeler, *President*
EMP: 50
SALES (est): 1.1MM **Privately Held**
SIC: 8741 Restaurant management

(P-26310)
MCKINLEY PLAZA LLC
2401 E Division St, National City (91950-1901)
PHONE.................................619 405-6307
Roshan Gupta,
EMP: 99
SALES: 950K **Privately Held**
SIC: 8741 Hotel or motel management

(P-26311)
MCMILLAN FARM MANAGEMENT
29379 Rancho California R, Temecula (92591-5208)
PHONE.................................951 676-2045
Gary McMillan, *Owner*
Ellen Lesicko, *Controller*
EMP: 150
SALES (est): 14MM **Privately Held**
SIC: 8741 0174 Management services; citrus fruits

(P-26312)
MEDICAL NETWORK INC
Also Called: MBC Systems
1809 E Dyer Rd Ste 311, Santa Ana (92705-5740)
PHONE.................................949 863-0022
David Conrad, *President*
Erica Weinstein, *Executive*
EMP: 80
SQ FT: 3,500
SALES (est): 9.4MM **Privately Held**
WEB: www.mbcsystems.org
SIC: 8741 Hospital management; nursing & personal care facility management

(P-26313)
MENTOR MEDIA (USA) SUP
3768 Milliken Ave Ste A, Eastvale (91752-1037)
PHONE.................................909 930-0800
Kok Khoon Lim, *CEO*
EMP: 80

SALES (est): 15MM
SALES (corp-wide): 6.1B **Privately Held**
SIC: 8741 8742 Business management; business planning & organizing services
HQ: Mentor Media Ltd
47 Jalan Buroh
Singapore 61949
663 133-33

(P-26314)
MGT INDUSTRIES INC
19034 S Vermont Ave, Gardena (90248-4412)
PHONE.................................310 324-3152
EMP: 69
SALES (corp-wide): 51.4MM **Privately Held**
SIC: 8741 Management services
PA: Mgt Industries, Inc.
13889 S Figueroa St
Los Angeles CA 90061
310 516-5900

(P-26315)
MIG MANAGEMENT SERVICES LLC
660 Newport Center Dr, Newport Beach (92660-6401)
PHONE.................................949 474-5800
Paul Merage,
EMP: 80
SALES (est): 3.3MM
SALES (corp-wide): 133.7K **Privately Held**
SIC: 8741 Management services
PA: Mig Capital, Llc
660 Newport Center Dr # 450
Newport Beach CA 92660
949 474-5800

(P-26316)
MIKE ROVNER CONSTRUCTION INC
22600 Lambert St, Lake Forest (92630-6201)
PHONE.................................949 458-1562
Mike Rovner, *Branch Mgr*
EMP: 171 **Privately Held**
SIC: 8741 1522 1521 Construction management; residential construction; single-family housing construction
PA: Mike Rovner Construction, Inc.
5400 Tech Cir
Moorpark CA 93021

(P-26317)
MIMG MEDICAL MANAGEMENT LLC
26522 La Alameda Ste 120, Mission Viejo (92691-6330)
PHONE.................................949 282-1600
EMP: 60
SQ FT: 1,800
SALES (est): 2.6MM **Privately Held**
SIC: 8741

(P-26318)
MONTAGE HEALTH (PA)
23625 Holman Hwy, Monterey (93940-5902)
P.O. Box Hh (93942-6032)
PHONE.................................831 625-4830
Steven Packer MD, *President*
Terril Lowe, *Vice Pres*
Tim Nylen, *Vice Pres*
Cynthia Peck, *Vice Pres*
Laura Zehm, *Vice Pres*
EMP: 1650
SQ FT: 350,000
SALES: 145.4MM **Privately Held**
SIC: 8741 Hospital management

(P-26319)
MORRISON MGT SPECIALISTS INC
Also Called: Morrison Health Care
1150 N Indian Canyon Dr, Palm Springs (92262-4872)
PHONE.................................760 323-6296
Rick Tinsley, *Director*
Karissa Bouchie, *Nutritionist*
EMP: 97

SALES (corp-wide): 29.6B **Privately Held**
SIC: 8741 5812 8742 5813 Management services; eating places; food & beverage consultant; drinking places
HQ: Morrison Management Specialists, Inc.
400 Northridge Rd Ste 600
Sandy Springs GA 30350

(P-26320)
MORRISON MGT SPECIALISTS INC
1531 Esplanade, Chico (95926-3310)
PHONE..................................530 332-7557
EMP: 97
SALES (corp-wide): 29.6B **Privately Held**
WEB: www.iammorrison.com
SIC: 8741 Management services
HQ: Morrison Management Specialists, Inc.
400 Northridge Rd Ste 600
Sandy Springs GA 30350

(P-26321)
MORRISON MGT SPECIALISTS INC
14445 Olive View Dr, Sylmar (91342-1437)
PHONE..................................818 364-4219
Kathy Dagg, *Manager*
EMP: 78
SALES (corp-wide): 29.6B **Privately Held**
WEB: www.iammorrison.com
SIC: 8741 5812 Restaurant management; eating places
HQ: Morrison Management Specialists, Inc.
400 Northridge Rd Ste 600
Sandy Springs GA 30350

(P-26322)
MOSAIC
Also Called: Mosaic Quest
10991 Via Banco, San Diego (92126-7423)
PHONE..................................858 397-2261
Richard Wincor, *Manager*
EMP: 79
SALES (corp-wide): 257.7MM **Privately Held**
SIC: 8741 Management services
PA: Mosaic
4980 S 118th St
Omaha NE 68137
402 896-3884

(P-26323)
MOSHUN GROUP LLC
1968 S Coast Hwy, Laguna Beach (92651-3681)
PHONE..................................855 258-2220
Tammie Galloway,
EMP: 75
SALES: 500K **Privately Held**
SIC: 8741 Management services

(P-26324)
NAVIGANT CYMETRIX CORPORATION
1515 W 190th St Ste 350, Gardena (90248-4910)
PHONE..................................424 201-6300
Jeff Macdonald, *Branch Mgr*
Karen Ladika, *Principal*
EMP: 125
SALES (corp-wide): 743.6MM **Privately Held**
WEB: www.hmsintl.com
SIC: 8741 Management services
HQ: Navigant Cymetrix Corporation
1 Park Plz Ste 1050
Irvine CA 92614
714 361-6800

(P-26325)
NELSON BROS PROPERTY MGT INC
Also Called: Nelson Brothers Property MGT
16b Journey Ste 200, Aliso Viejo (92656-3317)
PHONE..................................949 916-7300
Patrick Nelson, *President*
EMP: 134 EST: 2007
SALES: 6.5MM **Privately Held**
SIC: 8741 Management services

(P-26326)
NETWORK MANAGEMENT GROUP INC (PA)
1100 S Flower St Ste 3110, Los Angeles (90015-2287)
PHONE..................................323 263-2632
John Park, *President*
EMP: 160
SQ FT: 2,039
SALES (est): 9.8MM **Privately Held**
WEB: www.networkm.com
SIC: 8741 8742 Business management; management consulting services

(P-26327)
NETWORK MEDICAL MANAGEMENT INC
1668 S Grfeld Ave Ste 100, Alhambra (91801)
PHONE..................................626 282-0288
Thomas Lam MD, *Co-CEO*
Gary Augusta, *President*
Hing Ang, *COO*
Mihir Shah, *CFO*
Warren Hosseinion MD, *Co-CEO*
EMP: 130
SQ FT: 14,000
SALES (est): 9.3MM **Publicly Held**
WEB: www.nmm.cc
SIC: 8741 Hospital management; nursing & personal care facility management
PA: Apollo Medical Holdings, Inc.
700 N Brand Blvd Ste 1400
Glendale CA 91203

(P-26328)
NEW SOLAR INCORPORATED
1525 Mccarthy Blvd, Milpitas (95035-7451)
PHONE..................................888 886-0103
Charles Ng, *President*
Porter Wong, *Corp Secy*
EMP: 50
SALES (est): 1.8MM **Privately Held**
WEB: www.newsolarinc.com
SIC: 8741 5063 1731 4931 Financial management for business; electrical apparatus & equipment; electrical work; electric & other services combined; solar energy contractor

(P-26329)
NEWPORT GROUP INC (PA)
1350 Treat Blvd Ste 300, Walnut Creek (94597-7959)
PHONE..................................925 328-4540
Greg W Tschider, *CEO*
Nancy Worth, *COO*
Mendel Melzer, *Ch Invest Ofcr*
Martha Sadler, *Exec VP*
Glenna Bayles, *Vice Pres*
EMP: 115
SALES (est): 68.4MM **Privately Held**
SIC: 8741 Administrative management

(P-26330)
NO SHNACKS INC
7480 Harvard Ct, Fontana (92336-3432)
PHONE..................................909 293-8747
Gary Clark, *Owner*
EMP: 50
SALES (est): 1.3MM **Privately Held**
SIC: 8741 Business management

(P-26331)
NORTH AMERICAN CLIENT SVCS INC (PA)
5150 E A Palma Ave 206, Anaheim (92807)
PHONE..................................949 240-2423
John L Sorensen, *Ch of Bd*
Timothy J Paulsen, *CEO*
Tim Paulson, *CFO*
Donald G Laws, *Chairman*
Tiffany Coates, *Officer*
▲ EMP: 175
SALES (est): 62.4MM **Privately Held**
WEB: www.nahci.com
SIC: 8741 Nursing & personal care facility management

(P-26332)
NORTH AMERICAN HEALTH CARE
Also Called: Cottonwood Post-Acute Rehab
625 Cottonwood St, Woodland (95695-3614)
PHONE..................................530 662-9193
Jason Bliss, *Manager*
Donald Laws, *Principal*
EMP: 80
SALES (corp-wide): 62.4MM **Privately Held**
WEB: www.nahci.com
SIC: 8741 8051 Nursing & personal care facility management; skilled nursing care facilities
PA: North American Client Services, Inc.
5150 E A Palma Ave 206
Anaheim CA 92807
949 240-2423

(P-26333)
NORTH AMERICAN MED MGT CAL INC (DH)
3281 E Guasti Rd Fl 7, Ontario (91761-7622)
PHONE..................................909 605-8000
Richard A Shinto MD, *CEO*
Glen Marconcini, *Exec VP*
Mollie Van Hofwegen, *Executive Asst*
Karen Donan, *Financial Analy*
Annette Todd, *Marketing Staff*
EMP: 75
SALES (est): 7.6MM
SALES (corp-wide): 993.9MM **Privately Held**
SIC: 8741 Nursing & personal care facility management

(P-26334)
NORTHSTAR SENIOR LIVING INC
2334 Washington Ave Ste A, Redding (96001-2159)
PHONE..................................530 242-8300
Rick Jensen, *CEO*
Steven Kregel, *COO*
Brian Uhlir, *CFO*
Lucian Luca, *Vice Pres*
EMP: 586
SALES (est): 51.6MM **Privately Held**
SIC: 8741 Nursing & personal care facility management

(P-26335)
ONE INC (PA)
620 Coolidge Dr Ste 200, Folsom (95630-3183)
PHONE..................................866 343-6940
Christopher W Ewing, *President*
Steve Hall, *Vice Pres*
Tom Temple, *Vice Pres*
EMP: 51
SALES (est): 18.4MM **Privately Held**
SIC: 8741 Management services

(P-26336)
ORANGE COUNTY DEPT EDUCATION
Tustin Unified School District
300 S C St, Tustin (92780-3633)
PHONE..................................714 730-7301
Peter Gorman, *Superintendent*
Ben Valencia, *Analyst*
EMP: 1600
SALES (corp-wide): 304MM **Privately Held**
WEB: www.ocprob.com
SIC: 8741 Administrative management
PA: Orange County Superintendent Of Schools
200 Kalmus Dr
Costa Mesa CA 92626
714 966-4000

(P-26337)
OREQ CORPORATION
Also Called: Pool Pals Division
42306 Remington Ave, Temecula (92590-2512)
PHONE..................................951 296-5076
Jess L Hetzner, *CEO*
Ron Hetzner, *Exec VP*
Karey Valenzuela, *Controller*
Shawna Agajanian, *Manager*

▲ EMP: 50
SALES (est): 10.7MM **Privately Held**
WEB: www.oreqcorp.com
SIC: 8741 5941 5091 Business management; water sport equipment; spa equipment & supplies

(P-26338)
OVATIONS FANFARE
Also Called: Fanfare Enterprises
88 Fair Dr, Costa Mesa (92626-6521)
PHONE..................................714 708-1880
Juan Quintero, *Manager*
EMP: 75
SALES (corp-wide): 5.6MM **Privately Held**
SIC: 8741 5812 Management services; caterers
PA: Ovations Fanfare
61 Haas Pavilion
Berkeley CA 94720
510 704-8361

(P-26339)
PACIFIC PARK MANAGEMENT
1300 Fillmore St, San Francisco (94115-4113)
PHONE..................................415 440-4840
EMP: 141 **Privately Held**
SIC: 8741 7521 Business management; indoor parking services
PA: Pacific Park Management Inc
311 California St Ste 310
San Francisco CA 94104

(P-26340)
PACIFIC PARTNERS MGT SVCS INC
Also Called: Pacific Partners MSI
1051 E Hillsdale Blvd, Foster City (94404-1640)
P.O. Box 5860, San Mateo (94402-5860)
PHONE..................................650 358-5804
Lori Vatcher, *CEO*
M L Bonham MD, *President*
EMP: 100
SALES (est): 12.7MM **Publicly Held**
WEB: www.ppmsi.com
SIC: 8741 8748 Business management; business consulting
PA: Hca Healthcare, Inc.
1 Park Plz
Nashville TN 37203

(P-26341)
PACIFIC PROGRAM/DESIGN MANAGEM
100 W Walnut St, Pasadena (91124-0001)
PHONE..................................626 440-2000
Mary Ann Hopkins, *Manager*
Ozzie Gallo, *Controller*
EMP: 99
SALES (est): 49.9K **Privately Held**
SIC: 8741 8711 Business management; engineering services

(P-26342)
PACIFIC VENTURES LTD
Also Called: Jacmar Companies, The
2200 W Valley Blvd, Alhambra (91803-1928)
PHONE..................................626 576-0737
William H Tilley, *CEO*
Jim Dalpozzo, *President*
Randy Hill, *Exec VP*
EMP: 250 EST: 1976
SQ FT: 20,000
SALES (est): 11.4MM **Privately Held**
SIC: 8741 6722 Restaurant management; management investment, open-end

(P-26343)
PACKARD HOSPITALITY GROUP LLC
9555 Chesapeake Dr # 202, San Diego (92123-6301)
PHONE..................................858 277-4305
Michael Goldstein,
Jeremy Pinkerton, *Vice Pres*
Mark Chute, *General Mgr*
Paula Cohen, *Administration*
Steve Carr,
EMP: 120

PRODUCTS & SVCS

SQ FT: 4,000
SALES: 75MM **Privately Held**
SIC: 8741 Hotel or motel management

(P-26344)
PACWEND III INC
Also Called: Wendy's
1308 Kansas Ave Ste 6, Modesto
(95351-1530)
PHONE.................................209 577-6690
Joe Johal, *CEO*
EMP: 100
SALES (est): 3.9MM **Privately Held**
SIC: 8741 Restaurant management

(P-26345)
PAMA MANAGEMENT CO
123 N Inez St Ste 16, Hemet (92543-4169)
PHONE.................................951 929-0340
EMP: 50
SALES (est): 2.4MM **Privately Held**
SIC: 8741

(P-26346)
PARAMUNT MADOWS NURSING CTR LP
Also Called: Affinity Health Care
7039 Alondra Blvd, Paramount
(90723-3925)
PHONE.................................562 531-0990
Carlos Aragon, *Administration*
EMP: 99 **EST:** 2015
SQ FT: 10,000
SALES (est): 2.8MM **Privately Held**
SIC: 8741 Nursing & personal care facility
management

(P-26347)
PARSONS CONSTRUCTORS INC
Also Called: Operations/Risk Group
100 W Walnut St, Pasadena (91124-0001)
PHONE.................................626 440-2000
Chuck Harrington, *CEO*
Joe Zika, *Vice Pres*
James Brookhouser, *Executive*
Robert Camp, *Admin Sec*
EMP: 5315 **EST:** 1978
SALES (est): 98.4MM
SALES (corp-wide): 3.5B **Publicly Held**
SIC: 8741 8711 Management services;
engineering services
PA: The Parsons Corporation
5875 Trinity Pkwy Ste 300
Centreville VA 20120
703 988-8500

(P-26348)
PARTHENON DCS HOLDINGS LLC
4 Embarcadero Ctr, San Francisco
(94111-4106)
PHONE.................................925 960-4800
EMP: 1400
SALES (est): 25.2MM **Privately Held**
SIC: 8741 Financial management for business

(P-26349)
PATHWAY CAPITAL MANAGEMENT LP (PA)
18575 Jamboree Rd Ste 700, Irvine
(92612-2546)
PHONE.................................949 622-1000
Milt M Best,
Vincent Dee, *COO*
Curt Gerlach, *CFO*
Linda Chaffin, *Senior VP*
Gerard Branka, *Vice Pres*
EMP: 100
SQ FT: 13,302
SALES (est): 15.1MM **Privately Held**
WEB: www.pathwaycapital.com
SIC: 8741 6282 Financial management for
business; investment advice

(P-26350)
PEN-CAL ADMINISTRATORS INC
Also Called: P C A
7633 Suthfront Rd Ste 120, Livermore
(94551)
PHONE.................................925 251-3400
Kirk Penland, *CEO*
Steve Schwaderer, *Vice Pres*
Dan Golesh, *Managing Dir*

Judi Olmos, *Office Mgr*
Jon Van Oosbree, *Info Tech Mgr*
EMP: 75
SQ FT: 15,000
SALES (est): 10.3MM
SALES (corp-wide): 8.5B **Publicly Held**
WEB: www.pencal.com
SIC: 8741 Financial management for business
PA: Voya Financial, Inc.
230 Park Ave Fl 14
New York NY 10169
212 309-8200

(P-26351)
PHYSICIAN MANAGEMENT GROUP INC
Also Called: Childrens Specialist San Diego
3860 Calle Fortunada # 210, San Diego
(92123-4800)
PHONE.................................858 309-6300
Fax: 858 309-6298
EMP: 105
SALES (est): 6.5MM **Privately Held**
WEB: www.pmgservices.org
SIC: 8741

(P-26352)
PHYSICIAN WEBLINK OF CAL (HQ)
7 Technology Dr, Irvine (92618-2302)
PHONE.................................949 923-3201
Jay Cohen, *President*
Bartley Asner, *CEO*
Jacob Furgacth, *COO*
Richard Greene, *CFO*
EMP: 165
SQ FT: 25,000
SALES (est): 4.9MM **Privately Held**
SIC: 8741 Business management

(P-26353)
PIONEER HEALTH CARE SERVICES
1640 School St Ste 100, Moraga
(94556-1119)
PHONE.................................925 631-9100
Charles Patterson, *President*
EMP: 200
SQ FT: 2,300
SALES (est): 6.7MM **Privately Held**
WEB: www.pioneerhealthcareservices.com
SIC: 8741 Hospital management; nursing
& personal care facility management

(P-26354)
PK MANAGEMENT LLC
15301 Ventura Blvd # 570, Sherman Oaks
(91403-3102)
PHONE.................................818 808-0600
Robert Krensky, *Mng Member*
Robert Kriensky, *COO*
Tom McGinty, *Vice Pres*
Sandy Simmons, *Property Mgr*
EMP: 500
SALES (est): 21.9MM **Privately Held**
SIC: 8741 Business management

(P-26355)
PRE CON INDUSTRIES INC
Also Called: Premier Drywall
514 Work St, Salinas (93901-4350)
P.O. Box 5728, Santa Maria (93456-5728)
PHONE.................................805 345-3147
John Amburgey, *Branch Mgr*
EMP: 50 **Privately Held**
SIC: 8741 Management services
PA: Pre Con Industries, Inc.
725 Oak St
Santa Maria CA 93454

(P-26356)
PREMIER HLTHCARE SOLUTIONS INC
Also Called: Premier IMS Insurance Services
12225 El Camino Real, San Diego
(92130-2084)
PHONE.................................858 569-8629
Susan Devore, *Branch Mgr*
Allison Golding, *Info Tech Dir*
EMP: 305
SALES (corp-wide): 1.2B **Publicly Held**
SIC: 8741 Management services

HQ: Premier Healthcare Solutions, Inc.
13034 Balntyn Corp Pl
Charlotte NC 28277
704 357-0022

(P-26357)
PRIMARY CARE ASSOD MED GROUP (PA)
1635 Lake San Marcos Dr # 201, San Marcos (92078-4661)
PHONE.................................760 471-7505
Robert Mongeon, *President*
EMP: 70
SALES (est): 6.6MM **Privately Held**
SIC: 8741 Administrative management

(P-26358)
PRIMARY PROVIDER MGT CO INC (PA)
Also Called: Ppmc
2115 Compton Ave Ste 301, Corona
(92881-7272)
PHONE.................................951 280-7700
Robert Dukes, *CEO*
Maureen B Tyson, *President*
Ranji Somaweera, *Controller*
John Avila, *Director*
Adina Guthrie, *Director*
EMP: 195
SQ FT: 23,500
SALES (est): 23MM **Privately Held**
WEB: www.missionmedicalgroup.net
SIC: 8741 Business management

(P-26359)
PRIMED MGT CONSULTING SVCS INC
2409 Camino Ramon, San Ramon
(94583-4285)
P.O. Box 5080 (94583-0980)
PHONE.................................925 327-6710
David Joyner, *CEO*
Steve McDermott, *President*
Tim Richards, *CFO*
Mitra Javidi, *Vice Pres*
Robert Ramsey, *Vice Pres*
EMP: 488
SQ FT: 30,000
SALES (est): 57.8MM
SALES (corp-wide): 504.8MM **Privately Held**
SIC: 8741 8742 Management services;
management consulting services
PA: Hill Physicians Medical Group, Inc.
2409 Camino Ramon
San Ramon CA 94583
800 445-5747

(P-26360)
PRO UNLIMITED INC
1350 Bayshore Hwy Ste 350, Burlingame
(94010-1831)
PHONE.................................650 344-1099
Allie Shlomo, *COO*
Feliks Shvartsburd, *Vice Pres*
Alida Williamson, *Executive Asst*
Corie Maguire, *Financial Analy*
Kimberly Steffen, *Opers Mgr*
EMP: 50 **Privately Held**
SIC: 8741 Financial management for business
PA: Pro Unlimited, Inc.
7777 Glades Rd Ste 208
Boca Raton FL 33434

(P-26361)
PRO-MED HLTH CARE ADMNISTRATOR
4150 Concours Ste 100, Ontario
(91764-5914)
PHONE.................................909 932-1045
Kit Thapar, *CEO*
Jeereddi A Prasad, *President*
EMP: 75
SQ FT: 20,000
SALES (est): 1.7MM **Privately Held**
WEB: www.promedhealth.com
SIC: 8741 Administrative management
PA: Pamona Valley Medical Group Inc
9302 Pttsbrgh Ave Ste 220
Rancho Cucamonga CA 91730

(P-26362)
PROACTIVE BUS SOLUTIONS INC
428 13th St Fl 5, Oakland (94612-2617)
PHONE.................................510 302-0120
Deidrie Towery, *CEO*
Renee Holloman, *VP Bus Dvlpt*
Darren Graham, *Project Leader*
Nicole Lewis, *IT/INT Sup*
Shaun Lange, *Technician*
EMP: 250 **EST:** 1998
SQ FT: 3,000
SALES: 11.3MM **Privately Held**
WEB: www.proactiveok.com
SIC: 8741 8742 Management services;
business consultant

(P-26363)
PROACTIVE RISK MANAGEMENT INC
22617 Hawthorne Blvd, Torrance
(90505-2510)
PHONE.................................213 840-8856
Benoit Grenier, *CEO*
Gina Savoie, *CFO*
EMP: 100
SALES: 15MM **Privately Held**
SIC: 8741 Business management

(P-26364)
PROFESSIONAL GOLF MGT LLC
49155 Vista Estrella, La Quinta
(92253-6343)
P.O. Box 5566 (92248-5565)
PHONE.................................760 564-0804
Raymond Holohan, *Mng Member*
Carol Holohan,
EMP: 70
SALES (est): 5.8MM **Privately Held**
WEB:
www.professionalgolfmanagement.com
SIC: 8741 Management services

(P-26365)
PROJECT MANAGEMENT INSTITUTE
8895 Towne Centre Dr, San Diego
(92122-5542)
PHONE.................................760 458-6198
Tieman Chang, *Vice Pres*
EMP: 99
SALES (est): 249.5K **Privately Held**
SIC: 8741 Office management

(P-26366)
PROSPECT MEDICAL GROUP INC (HQ)
1920 E 17th St Ste 200, Santa Ana
(92705-8626)
PHONE.................................714 796-5900
Jacob Y Terner MD, *President*
Mitchell Lew, *CEO*
EMP: 350
SQ FT: 2,420
SALES (est): 31.6MM
SALES (corp-wide): 1.2B **Privately Held**
WEB: www.prospectcorona.com
SIC: 8741 Hospital management; nursing
& personal care facility management
PA: Prospect Medical Holdings, Inc.
3415 S Sepulveda Blvd # 9
Los Angeles CA 90034
310 943-4500

(P-26367)
PROVIDENCE HEALTH SYSTEM
Little Company Mary Pathology
4101 Torrance Blvd, Torrance
(90503-4607)
PHONE.................................310 303-6970
Angie Bugg, *Branch Mgr*
EMP: 102
SALES (corp-wide): 15.2B **Privately Held**
SIC: 8741 8071 Hospital management;
pathological laboratory
HQ: Providence Health System-Southern
California
1801 Lind Ave Sw
Renton WA 98057
425 525-3355

(P-26368)
PROVIDENT FINANCIAL MANAGEMENT
3130 Wilshire Blvd # 600, Santa Monica (90403-2349)
P.O. Box 4084 (90411-4084)
PHONE.................................310 282-0477
Ivan Axelrod, *Managing Prtnr*
Barry Siegel, *Partner*
Rosa Grimes, *Business Mgr*
Bill Vuylsteke, *Director*
Heidi Zepf-Young, *Director*
EMP: 95
SQ FT: 34,000
SALES (est): 2.7MM **Privately Held**
WEB: www.providentfm.com
SIC: 8741 Financial management for business

(P-26369)
PS24 INC
Also Called: Grove - Design District, The
65 Division St, San Francisco (94103-5215)
PHONE.................................415 834-5105
Kenneth Zankel, *Principal*
Charles Baldwin, *General Mgr*
EMP: 100
SALES: 500K **Privately Held**
SIC: 8741 Restaurant management

(P-26370)
PTR GROUP INC
Also Called: Glad I'M Not Driving.com
652 S Joyce Ave, Rialto (92376-7178)
PHONE.................................951 965-1822
Paul Rodriguez, *President*
EMP: 50
SALES (est): 1.3MM **Privately Held**
SIC: 8741 7389 Business management;

(P-26371)
R & V MANAGEMENT CORPORATION
768 Hollister St, San Diego (92154-1333)
PHONE.................................619 429-3305
EMP: 61
SALES (corp-wide): 34.3MM **Privately Held**
SIC: 8741 Management services
PA: R & V Management Corporation
3444 Camno DI Rio N 202
San Diego CA 92108
619 285-5500

(P-26372)
RADNET MANAGEMENT INC
Also Called: Modesto Imaging Center
157 E Coolidge Ave, Modesto (95350-4504)
PHONE.................................209 524-6800
EMP: 60 **Publicly Held**
WEB: www.radnetmgt.com
SIC: 8741 Management services
HQ: Radnet Management, Inc.
1510 Cotner Ave
Los Angeles CA 90025
310 445-2800

(P-26373)
RADY CHLD HOSPITAL-SAN DIEGO
Also Called: Bernardy Ctr For Medcly Frgled
8022 Birmingham Dr # 22, San Diego (92123-2707)
PHONE.................................858 966-5833
Kathleen Sellick, *Manager*
Kim Looney, *Software Dev*
EMP: 60 **Privately Held**
SIC: 8741 8051 Nursing & personal care facility management; skilled nursing care facilities
HQ: Rady Children's Hospital-San Diego
3020 Childrens Way
San Diego CA 92123
858 576-1700

(P-26374)
RAYMOND GROUP (PA)
Also Called: Orange Cnty George M Raymond N
520 W Walnut Ave, Orange (92868-5008)
PHONE.................................714 771-7670
Travis Winsor, *CEO*
James Watson, *President*

Mary Raymond, *Corp Secy*
Ken Jensma, *Vice Pres*
Tom Obrien, *Vice Pres*
EMP: 140
SQ FT: 20,000
SALES (est): 29.1MM **Privately Held**
SIC: 8741 Construction management

(P-26375)
REIGN ACCESSORIES INC
4000 Redondo Beach Ave, Redondo Beach (90278-1109)
PHONE.................................310 297-6400
Jon Hirschberg, *President*
EMP: 50
SALES (est): 2MM **Privately Held**
WEB: www.rainforestventures.com
SIC: 8741 Business management

(P-26376)
RELIABLE INTERIORS INC
104 S Maple St, Corona (92880-1704)
PHONE.................................951 371-3390
Gerald C Crowther, *President*
William J Klotz, *President*
Glenn L Crowther, *Vice Pres*
Ralph G Prentiss, *Vice Pres*
Lee Scott, *Vice Pres*
EMP: 200
SALES (est): 7.8MM **Privately Held**
SIC: 8741 1742 Construction management; drywall

(P-26377)
RENOVO SOLUTIONS LLC
4 Executive Cir Ste 185, Irvine (92614-6791)
PHONE.................................714 599-7969
Sandy Morford, *CEO*
Haresh Saitiani, *COO*
Fernando Castorena, *CFO*
Donald K Carson, *Vice Pres*
Kevin Vandegriend, *Area Mgr*
EMP: 270
SQ FT: 5,400
SALES (est): 70MM **Privately Held**
SIC: 8741 Hospital management

(P-26378)
RESIDNTIAL ALZHEIMERS CARE INC
9619 Chesapeake Dr # 103, San Diego (92123-1368)
PHONE.................................858 565-4424
William M Chance, *President*
William Chance, *Principal*
EMP: 180
SQ FT: 9,000
SALES (est): 4.5MM **Privately Held**
SIC: 8741 Nursing & personal care facility management

(P-26379)
RESPONSELOGIX INC
3031 Tisch Way Ste 115, San Jose (95128-2582)
PHONE.................................408 220-6505
Lionel Thomas Mohr, *CEO*
EMP: 112
SALES (corp-wide): 24.4MM **Privately Held**
SIC: 8741 Management services
PA: Responselogix, Inc.
6991 E Camelback Rd B300
Scottsdale AZ 85251
408 220-6545

(P-26380)
RHS CORP
Also Called: REDLANDS COMMUNITY HOSPITAL
350 Terracina Blvd, Redlands (92373-4850)
PHONE.................................909 335-5500
James R Holmes, *President*
James Agee, *Urology*
Bruce Meyer, *Med Doctor*
EMP: 1450
SQ FT: 265,000
SALES (est): 416.6K **Privately Held**
SIC: 8741 Hospital management

(P-26381)
RROMEO CORPORATION
535 Anton Blvd Ste 200, Costa Mesa (92626-7680)
PHONE.................................714 640-3800
Richard Putnam, *Branch Mgr*
EMP: 80
SALES (corp-wide): 13.6B **Privately Held**
WEB: www.rref.com
SIC: 8741 6531 Management services; real estate managers
HQ: The Rromeo Corporation
101 California St Fl 24
San Francisco CA 94111
415 781-3300

(P-26382)
RUBY BURMA INVESTMENT LLC
612 El Camino Real, San Carlos (94070-3104)
PHONE.................................650 590-0545
Max Lee, *Mng Member*
Justin Kwok, *Accountant*
EMP: 51
SALES (est): 3.4MM **Privately Held**
SIC: 8741 Restaurant management

(P-26383)
SAN JOSE ARENA MANAGEMENT LLC
44388 Old Warm Sprng Blvd, Fremont (94538-6148)
PHONE.................................510 623-7200
Greg Jamison, *Branch Mgr*
EMP: 128
SALES (corp-wide): 16.8MM **Privately Held**
SIC: 8741 Management services
PA: San Jose Arena Management, Llc
525 W Santa Clara St
San Jose CA 95113
408 287-7070

(P-26384)
SAN JOSE EARTHQUAKES MGT LLC
451 El Cmino Real Ste 220, Santa Clara (95050)
PHONE.................................408 556-7700
Lew Wolff, *Owner*
John Fisher, *Shareholder*
Dave Kaval, *President*
Jared Shawlee, *Vice Pres*
Mark Raney, *Executive*
EMP: 249
SALES: 120.6K **Privately Held**
SIC: 8741 Management services

(P-26385)
SANTA CLARITA HEALTH CARE ASSN (PA)
23845 Mcbean Pkwy, Santa Clarita (91355-2001)
PHONE.................................661 253-8000
Roger Seaver, *President*
Paul Salomon, *COO*
C R Hudson, *CFO*
James D Hicken, *Treasurer*
John Barstis, *Admin Sec*
EMP: 65
SQ FT: 130,000
SALES (est): 18.9MM **Privately Held**
SIC: 8741 Hospital management; nursing & personal care facility management

(P-26386)
SCCH INC
Also Called: Courtyard Care Center
1880 Dawson Ave, Signal Hill (90755-5913)
PHONE.................................562 494-5188
Julie Javier, *Administration*
Spencer Olsen, *Treasurer*
Arnel Mojica, *Office Mgr*
Dennis Guray, *Director*
EMP: 99
SALES (est): 6.9MM **Privately Held**
WEB: www.nahci.com
SIC: 8741 8052 8051 Management services; intermediate care facilities; skilled nursing care facilities

(P-26387)
SCRIPPS CLINIC FOUNDATION
12395 El Camino Real, San Diego (92130-3082)
PHONE.................................858 554-9000
Dr Hugh Greenway, *CEO*
EMP: 1600
SALES (est): 78.2MM
SALES (corp-wide): 2.1B **Privately Held**
WEB: www.scripps.org
SIC: 8741 Management services
PA: Scripps Health
10140 Campus Point Dr Ax415
San Diego CA 92121
800 727-4777

(P-26388)
SEABREEZE MANAGEMENT CO INC (PA)
26840 Aliso Viejo Pkwy # 100, Aliso Viejo (92656-2624)
PHONE.................................949 855-1800
Isaiah S Henry, *CEO*
Brandon Tryon, *Exec VP*
Marybeth Green, *Vice Pres*
Eron Kaylor, *Vice Pres*
Alisa Toalson, *Vice Pres*
EMP: 69
SQ FT: 22,000
SALES (est): 18.1MM **Privately Held**
WEB: www.seabreezemgmt.com
SIC: 8741 Management services

(P-26389)
SEISMIC SOFTWARE INC (PA)
12770 El Cmino Real Ste 3, San Diego (92130)
PHONE.................................855 466-8748
Douglas Winter, *CEO*
Ed Calnan, *President*
John McCauley, *CFO*
John Raguin, *Chief Mktg Ofcr*
Craig Dunham, *Vice Pres*
EMP: 53
SALES (est): 40.2MM **Privately Held**
SIC: 8741 8742 8732 Management services; sales (including sales management) consultant; market analysis, business & economic research

(P-26390)
SETHI MANAGEMENT INC
6100 Innovation Way, Carlsbad (92009-1728)
P.O. Box 235927, Encinitas (92023-5927)
PHONE.................................760 692-5288
Jeetander Sethi, *CEO*
Gaurav Sethi, *Vice Pres*
EMP: 154
SALES: 40MM **Privately Held**
SIC: 8741 Business management

(P-26391)
SILVER CREEK HOME OWNERS
Also Called: Silver Crk Vlly Ctry CLB HM Ow
1935 Dry Creek Rd Ste 203, Campbell (95008-3631)
PHONE.................................408 559-1977
Tim Johnson, *CEO*
Marianne Hudkins, *Principal*
EMP: 50
SALES (est): 3.5MM **Privately Held**
SIC: 8741 Management services

(P-26392)
SIMPSON & SIMPSON
633 W 5th St Ste 3320, Los Angeles (90071-3542)
PHONE.................................213 736-6664
Brainard Simpson, *Principal*
Robert Fleming, *Principal*
Carl P Simpson, *Principal*
Harverth Cameron, *Auditor*
Mark Frishwasser, *Auditor*
EMP: 61
SQ FT: 5,500
SALES (est): 7.4MM **Privately Held**
WEB: www.simpsonandsimpsoncpas.com
SIC: 8741 8721 Financial management for business; accounting, auditing & bookkeeping; certified public accountant

PRODUCTS & SVCS

(P-26393)
SMILE BRANDS GROUP INC (PA)
Also Called: Bright Now Dental
100 Spectrum Center Dr # 1500, Irvine
(92618-4962)
PHONE..................................714 668-1300
Steven C Bilt, *CEO*
Stan Andrakowicz, *President*
Bradley Schmidt, *CFO*
Jody Martin, *Chief Mktg Ofcr*
Victoria Harvey,
EMP: 90
SQ FT: 15,000
SALES (est): 609MM **Privately Held**
WEB: www.brightnow.com
SIC: 8741 8021 Management services;
dental clinics & offices

(P-26394)
**SMITH BROADCASTING GROUP
INC (PA)**
2315 Red Rose Way, Santa Barbara
(93109-1259)
PHONE..................................805 965-0400
Debrah Egar, *Exec Sec*
David A Fitz, *Vice Pres*
EMP: 165 EST: 1985
SALES (est): 15.2MM **Privately Held**
SIC: 8741 8742 Business management;
management consulting services

(P-26395)
**SMITH BROTHERS
RESTAURANT INC**
100 Corson St Lbby, Pasadena
(91103-3854)
PHONE..................................626 577-2400
Robert Smith, *President*
Jason Tirona, *CFO*
Greg Smith, *Admin Sec*
EMP: 55
SALES (est): 5.5MM **Privately Held**
SIC: 8741 8742 8721 Restaurant man-
agement; management consulting serv-
ices; accounting, auditing & bookkeeping

(P-26396)
SNF MANAGEMENT
9200 W Sunset Blvd # 700, West Holly-
wood (90069-3502)
PHONE..................................310 385-1090
Lee Samson, *President*
Ken Cess, *Director*
Josh Gargoles, *Director*
Zev Tyner, *Director*
EMP: 64
SALES (est): 13MM **Privately Held**
SIC: 8741 Management services

(P-26397)
SOC/GENERAL SERVICES/BPM
455 Golden Gate Ave # 2600, San Fran-
cisco (94102-3670)
PHONE..................................415 703-5341
Sam Flores, *General Mgr*
Paul Gates, *Technician*
Bryan Dugger, *Analyst*
Bruce Fong, *Analyst*
Robin Ramirez, *Analyst*
EMP: 60
SALES (est): 3.4MM **Privately Held**
SIC: 8741 Construction management

(P-26398)
SODEXO MANAGEMENT INC
Also Called: Cific Energy Center
851 Howard St, San Francisco
(94103-3009)
PHONE..................................925 325-9657
Jim Wasley, *Branch Mgr*
EMP: 82
SALES (corp-wide): 133.3MM **Privately
Held**
SIC: 8741 Management services
HQ: Sodexo Management Inc.
9801 Washingtonian Blvd
Gaithersburg MD 20878

(P-26399)
SODEXO MANAGEMENT INC
1 University Cir, Turlock (95382-3200)
PHONE..................................209 667-3634
Tom Welton, *Manager*
EMP: 75

SALES (corp-wide): 133.3MM **Privately
Held**
WEB: www.compass-mgmt.com
SIC: 8741 Management services
HQ: Sodexo Management Inc.
9801 Washingtonian Blvd
Gaithersburg MD 20878

(P-26400)
SODEXO OPERATIONS LLC
100 Campus Ctr Bldg 16, Seaside
(93955-8000)
PHONE..................................831 582-3838
Charles Wesley, *General Mgr*
EMP: 100
SALES (corp-wide): 133.3MM **Privately
Held**
SIC: 8741 5812 Restaurant management;
eating places
HQ: Sodexo Operations, Llc
9801 Washingtonian Blvd
Gaithersburg MD 20878
301 987-4000

(P-26401)
SOLPAC CONSTRUCTION INC
Also Called: SOLTEK PACIFIC CONSTRUC-
TION CO
2424 Congress St, San Diego
(92110-2819)
PHONE..................................619 296-6247
Stephen Thompson, *CEO*
Brandon Richie, *President*
Dave Carlin, *COO*
Kevin Cammall, *Vice Pres*
John Myers, *Vice Pres*
EMP: 235
SQ FT: 12,291
SALES: 206.8MM **Privately Held**
SIC: 8741 1542 1611 Construction man-
agement; commercial & office building
contractors; general contractor, highway
& street construction

(P-26402)
**SOUTHERN CALIFORNIA
PHYSICIA**
6760 Top Gun St Ste 100, San Diego
(92121-4152)
PHONE..................................858 824-7000
Joyce Cook, *CEO*
Marcia Aeschaleman, *CFO*
Marcia Aeschleman, *CFO*
Bryan Berman, *CIO*
Patrick Rousseau, *Controller*
EMP: 65 EST: 1996
SQ FT: 17,000
SALES: 8.2MM **Privately Held**
WEB: www.scpmcs.org
SIC: 8741 Administrative management

(P-26403)
SOUTHERN IMPLANTS INC
5 Holland Ste 209, Irvine (92618-2576)
PHONE..................................949 273-8505
Michael Kehoe, *President*
Michael Nealon, *CFO*
Dan Lu, *Mfg Dir*
Tom Binienda, *Regl Sales Mgr*
EMP: 125
SALES (est): 249.9K **Privately Held**
SIC: 8741 Management services

(P-26404)
SRG MANAGEMENT LLC
500 Stevens Ave Ste 100, Solana Beach
(92075-2055)
PHONE..................................858 792-9300
Michael S Grust, *CEO*
EMP: 192
SALES (est): 43K
SALES (corp-wide): 103.5MM **Privately
Held**
SIC: 8741 Business management
HQ: Srg Holdings, Llc
500 Stevens Ave Ste 100
Solana Beach CA 92075
858 792-9300

(P-26405)
SRHT PROPERTY MGMT CO
1317 E 7th St, Los Angeles (90021-1101)
PHONE..................................213 683-0522
Michael Alvidrez, *Director*
EMP: 100 EST: 1994

SALES: 4.6MM **Privately Held**
SIC: 8741 Management services

(P-26406)
**STAN TASHMAN & ASSOCIATES
INC**
8675 Wash Blvd Ste 203, Culver City
(90232-7486)
PHONE..................................310 460-7600
Richard Tashman, *CEO*
Ty Olson, *Vice Pres*
EMP: 650
SQ FT: 14,000
SALES (est): 38.1MM **Privately Held**
WEB: www.tashman.com
SIC: 8741 Management services

(P-26407)
**STANFORD MANAGEMENT
COMPANY**
635 Knight Way, Stanford (94305-7297)
PHONE..................................650 721-2200
Rob Wallace, *CEO*
EMP: 60
SALES (est): 342.4K **Privately Held**
SIC: 8741 Management services

(P-26408)
**STARZZ MANAGEMENT
SERVICES (PA)**
528 Stonehaven Ct, Hayward
(94544-6696)
PHONE..................................510 632-5533
Monica Walton, *President*
Monica Thompkins, *CFO*
Joe Thompkins, *Vice Pres*
Traci Thompkins, *Admin Asst*
EMP: 92
SQ FT: 2,100
SALES (est): 6.1MM **Privately Held**
SIC: 8741 Management services

(P-26409)
STEWARDSHIP COMPANY LLC
1 Rancho San Carlos Rd, Carmel
(93923-7999)
PHONE..................................831 620-6700
Thomas A Gray,
Don W Wilcoxon,
EMP: 200
SQ FT: 2,000
SALES (est): 13MM **Privately Held**
SIC: 8741 Management services

(P-26410)
STRAIGHT LANDER INC
8335 W Sunset Blvd # 320, Los Angeles
(90069-1500)
PHONE..................................323 337-9075
David Yashar, *President*
EMP: 58
SALES (est): 2MM **Privately Held**
SIC: 8741 Business management

(P-26411)
**SULZER TOWER FIELD SVC CAL
INC**
18711 S Broadwick St, Compton
(90220-6427)
PHONE..................................918 447-7676
EMP: 56
SALES (est): 886K
SALES (corp-wide): 3.3B **Privately Held**
SIC: 8741 Management services
HQ: Sulzer Us Holding Inc.
1255 Enclave Pkwy Ste 300
Houston TX 77077
346 207-9660

(P-26412)
**SUN MAR MANAGEMENT
SERVICES**
Also Called: Laurel Convalescent Center
7509 Laurel Ave, Fontana (92336-2315)
PHONE..................................909 822-8066
Blaine Hendrickson, *President*
EMP: 86
SALES (corp-wide): 50.5MM **Privately
Held**
WEB: www.extendedcarehospital.com
SIC: 8741 8051 Management services;
skilled nursing care facilities

PA: Sun Mar Management Services
3050 Saturn St Ste 201
Brea CA 92821
714 577-3880

(P-26413)
**SUN MAR MANAGEMENT
SERVICES**
Also Called: Sun Mar Health Care
3136 Del Mar Ave, Rosemead
(91770-2326)
PHONE..................................626 288-8353
Steve Montelli, *Administration*
EMP: 60
SALES (corp-wide): 50.5MM **Privately
Held**
WEB: www.extendedcarehospital.com
SIC: 8741 8051 Management services;
skilled nursing care facilities
PA: Sun Mar Management Services
3050 Saturn St Ste 201
Brea CA 92821
714 577-3880

(P-26414)
**SUN MAR MANAGEMENT
SERVICES**
Also Called: North Valley Nursing Center
7660 Wyngate St, Tujunga (91042-1736)
PHONE..................................818 352-1454
Katherine Rodriguez, *Manager*
EMP: 100
SALES (corp-wide): 50.5MM **Privately
Held**
WEB: www.extendedcarehospital.com
SIC: 8741 8059 Management services;
convalescent home
PA: Sun Mar Management Services
3050 Saturn St Ste 201
Brea CA 92821
714 577-3880

(P-26415)
**SUNAMERICA INVESTMENTS
INC (DH)**
1 Sun America Ctr Fl 37, Los Angeles
(90067-6103)
PHONE..................................310 772-6000
Eli Broad, *President*
EMP: 80
SQ FT: 76,000
SALES: 2B
SALES (corp-wide): 47.3B **Publicly Held**
WEB: www.opfa.com
SIC: 8741 6211 6282 7311 Administrative
management; financial management for
business; security brokers & dealers; in-
vestment advisory service; advertising
agencies
HQ: Sunamerica Inc.
1 Sun America Ctr Fl 38
Los Angeles CA 90067
310 772-6000

(P-26416)
**SUPERIOR SUPPORT SERVICES
INC**
Also Called: Superior Services
702 Civic Center Dr, Oceanside
(92054-2636)
PHONE..................................559 458-0507
Sheila Guarderas, *President*
EMP: 500
SQ FT: 6,000
SALES: 17MM **Privately Held**
WEB: www.superiorservices.com
SIC: 8741 7349 Restaurant management;
janitorial service, contract basis

(P-26417)
SYLMARK INC (PA)
Also Called: Sylmark Group
7821 Orion Ave Ste 200, Van Nuys
(91406-2032)
PHONE..................................818 217-2000
Peter Spiegel, *President*
Mark Funk, *CFO*
Steven Ober, *Vice Pres*
EMP: 90
SALES (est): 20MM **Privately Held**
SIC: 8741 Management services

(P-26418)
SYNERMED
711 W College St Fl 4, Los Angeles
(90012-3177)
P.O. Box 2002, Monterey Park (91754-0952)
PHONE....................213 626-4556
John Edwards, *President*
Wallis Wong, *Software Engr*
EMP: 65
SALES (est): 5.2MM **Privately Held**
SIC: 8741 Hospital management

(P-26419)
SYNTIRO HEALTHCARE SERVICES (PA)
Also Called: Physician Weblink MGT Svcs
7 Technology Dr, Irvine (92618-2302)
PHONE....................949 923-3438
Breaux Castleman, *CEO*
William S Bernstein, *Partner*
Richard Greene, *CFO*
EMP: 197
SALES (est): 6.4MM **Privately Held**
SIC: 8741 Hospital management; nursing & personal care facility management

(P-26420)
T3W BUSINESS SOLUTIONS INC
3921 Ampudia St, San Diego (92110-2813)
PHONE....................619 298-0888
Lisa Carman, *President*
Holly Andrews, *CFO*
EMP: 65
SQ FT: 2,523
SALES (est): 4.6MM **Privately Held**
SIC: 8741 8713 8711 7371 Business management; surveying services; engineering services; custom computer programming services; data processing & preparation; facilities support services

(P-26421)
TCM GROUP LLC
3130 Inland Empire Blvd, Ontario (91764-6569)
PHONE....................909 527-8580
Rima Tahan, *President*
S Michael Tahan, *Vice Pres*
Carol Larsen, *Administration*
Bryce Nielsen, *Controller*
Ivan Benavidez, *Sr Project Mgr*
EMP: 50
SALES (est): 2.2MM
SALES (corp-wide): 428.6MM **Publicly Held**
SIC: 8741 8742 Construction management; construction project management consultant
PA: Hill International, Inc.
    2005 Market St Ste 1600
    Philadelphia PA 19103
    215 309-7700

(P-26422)
TCV MANAGEMENT 2004 LLC
528 Ramona St, Palo Alto (94301-1709)
PHONE....................650 614-8200
Jay C Hoag, *Manager*
Nathan Sanders, *IT Executive*
EMP: 50
SALES (est): 2.5MM **Privately Held**
SIC: 8741 Management services

(P-26423)
TEXTAINER GROUP HOLDINGS LTD (DH)
650 California St Fl 16, San Francisco (94108-2720)
PHONE....................415 434-0551
John A Maccarone, *CEO*
Kenneth Chow, *Network Enginr*
Charles Reed, *IT/INT Sup*
Joseph Tilelli, *Opers-Prdtn-Mfg*
Cathy Dudley, *Opers Staff*
EMP: 55 **EST:** 1994
SALES (est): 11.8MM **Privately Held**
SIC: 8741 Business management

(P-26424)
TISHMAN CONSTRUCTION CORP CAL
444 S Flower St Ste 2500, Los Angeles (90071-2926)
PHONE....................213 542-6400
John L Tishman, *Ch of Bd*
Larry Schwarzwalder, *Treasurer*
Thomas McCaslin, *Exec VP*
Scott Vrancich, *Superintendent*
EMP: 70
SQ FT: 14,000
SALES (est): 5.9MM
SALES (corp-wide): 20.1B **Publicly Held**
SIC: 8741 Construction management
HQ: Tishman Realty & Construction Co, Inc.
    100 Park Ave Fl 5
    New York NY 10017
    212 708-6800

(P-26425)
TOFASCO OF AMERICA INC (PA)
1661 Fairplex Dr, La Verne (91750-5871)
PHONE....................909 392-8282
Edward Zheng, *President*
Stephen Chan, *CFO*
Xiu Jun Liang, *Vice Pres*
Albert Sheih, *Vice Pres*
Vanessa Chan, *MIS Dir*
EMP: 60
SQ FT: 160,554
SALES: 9MM **Privately Held**
SIC: 8741 Financial management for business

(P-26426)
TOP OF MARKET
Also Called: San Diego Fish Market
750 N Harbor Dr, San Diego (92101-5806)
PHONE....................619 234-4867
Jim Wentler, *Owner*
Alfonso Deanda, *Owner*
Bob Wilson, *Owner*
Fred Ducket, *Partner*
Dan Houte, *Manager*
EMP: 280
SALES (est): 10.1MM **Privately Held**
SIC: 8741 5813 Restaurant management; cocktail lounge

(P-26427)
TRADESMEN INTERNATIONAL LLC
15500 Rockfield Blvd, Irvine (92618-2725)
PHONE....................949 588-3280
Jason Hammer, *Branch Mgr*
EMP: 60 **Privately Held**
SIC: 8741 7361 Construction management; employment agencies
PA: Tradesmen International, Llc
    9760 Shepard Rd
    Macedonia OH 44056

(P-26428)
TRAFFIC MANAGEMENT INC
1244 S Claudina St, Anaheim (92805-6232)
PHONE....................562 264-2353
Christopher Spano, *Principal*
EMP: 53 **Privately Held**
SIC: 8741 Business management
PA: Traffic Management, Inc.
    2435 Lemon Ave
    Signal Hill CA 90755

(P-26429)
TRAFFIC MANAGEMENT INC
8399 Edgewater Dr, Oakland (94621-1401)
PHONE....................415 370-7916
Mark Coleman, *Principal*
Don Tripeny, *Administration*
EMP: 53 **Privately Held**
SIC: 8741 7389 Business management; flagging service (traffic control)
PA: Traffic Management, Inc.
    2435 Lemon Ave
    Signal Hill CA 90755

(P-26430)
TRI-MARINE FISHING MGT LLC
Also Called: Trimarine Fish Group
220 Cannery St, San Pedro (90731-7308)
PHONE....................310 547-1144
Vince Torre, *Manager*
Phil Roberts, *Principal*
Kevin Stark, *Technology*
Renato Curto,
Renato C Member,
EMP: 50
SQ FT: 8,000
SALES (est): 1.8MM **Privately Held**
SIC: 8741 Management services

(P-26431)
TRICOM MANAGEMENT INC
Also Called: United Owners Services
4025 E La Palma Ave # 101, Anaheim (92807-1734)
PHONE....................714 630-2029
Woody Cary, *President*
Marc Landau, *Treasurer*
Fernando Celis, *Vice Pres*
Lisa Martin, *Controller*
Dina Fischer, *Human Resources*
EMP: 200
SQ FT: 9,000
SALES (est): 19.3MM **Privately Held**
SIC: 8741 7389 Management services; time-share condominium exchange

(P-26432)
TRILAR MANAGEMENT GROUP
1025 S Gilbert St, Hemet (92543-7090)
PHONE....................951 925-2021
Susan A York, *Branch Mgr*
EMP: 124
SALES (corp-wide): 9.1MM **Privately Held**
SIC: 8741 Business management
PA: Trilar Management Group
    2101 Camino Vida Roble A
    Carlsbad CA 92011
    760 603-3205

(P-26433)
TRITON MANAGEMENT SERVICES LLC
1000 Aviara Dr Ste 300, Carlsbad (92011-4218)
PHONE....................760 431-9911
Bob Lloyd, *Principal*
EMP: 53
SALES (est): 9.6MM **Privately Held**
SIC: 8741 Management services

(P-26434)
TROON GOLF LLC
Also Called: Indian Wells Golf Resort
44500 Indian Wells Ln, Indian Wells (92210-8746)
PHONE....................760 346-4653
Rich Carter, *General Mgr*
Steven Rosen, *General Mgr*
Paul Bourgeois, *Sales Staff*
Leslie Graham, *Sales Staff*
Beth Widdowson, *Sales Staff*
EMP: 130 **Privately Held**
WEB: www.americangolf.com
SIC: 8741 7997 Management services; country club, membership
PA: Troon Golf, L.L.C.
    15044 N Scottsdale Rd # 300
    Scottsdale AZ 85254

(P-26435)
TWENTY4SEVEN HOTELS CORP
520 Newport Center Dr # 520, Newport Beach (92660-7020)
PHONE....................949 734-6400
David Wani, *CEO*
Drew Hardy, *President*
Leesa Gibbons, *Vice Pres*
Hilary Anderson, *General Mgr*
Kelly Dickson, *General Mgr*
EMP: 500
SQ FT: 15,000
SALES (est): 20.9MM **Privately Held**
SIC: 8741 Hotel or motel management

(P-26436)
UCD MC HOME CARE SERVICES
Also Called: Uc David Home Care Services
3630 Business Dr, Sacramento (95820-2163)
PHONE....................916 734-2458
Glenda Wegner, *Manager*
Kim Jacobs, *Executive*
John McMillan, *Director*
EMP: 200
SALES (est): 8MM **Privately Held**
SIC: 8741 Nursing & personal care facility management

(P-26437)
UNITED BEHAVIORAL HEALTH
3111 Cmino Del Rio N 50, San Diego (92108)
P.O. Box 601370 (92160-1370)
PHONE....................619 641-6800
Chris Janick, *Manager*
EMP: 100
SALES (corp-wide): 226.2B **Publicly Held**
WEB: www.unitedbehavioralhealth.com
SIC: 8741 8322 Nursing & personal care facility management; individual & family services
HQ: United Behavioral Health
    425 Market St Fl 18
    San Francisco CA 94105
    415 547-1403

(P-26438)
UNITED BEHAVIORAL HEALTH (HQ)
425 Market St Fl 18, San Francisco (94105-2532)
PHONE....................415 547-1403
Saul Feldman, *Ch of Bd*
Keith Dickson, *President*
Ann Mc Clanathan, *COO*
Karen Schievelbein, *CFO*
William Goldman Sr, *Exec VP*
EMP: 250
SQ FT: 20,000
SALES (est): 32.7MM
SALES (corp-wide): 226.2B **Publicly Held**
WEB: www.unitedbehavioralhealth.com
SIC: 8741 8742 Management services; management consulting services
PA: Unitedhealth Group Incorporated
    9900 Bren Rd E Ste 300w
    Minnetonka MN 55343
    952 936-1300

(P-26439)
UNITED PARADYNE CORPORATION
P.O. Box 5368 (93150-5368)
PHONE....................805 734-2359
Randy Cobb, *Manager*
EMP: 52 **Privately Held**
SIC: 8741 Management services
PA: United Paradyne Corporation
    2370 Skyway Dr Ste 203
    Santa Maria CA

(P-26440)
US SKILLSERVE INC (PA)
4115 E Broadway Ste A, Long Beach (90803-1532)
PHONE....................562 930-0777
Simcha Mandeldaum, *CEO*
EMP: 1000
SQ FT: 1,000
SALES (est): 74.8MM **Privately Held**
SIC: 8741 Hospital management; nursing & personal care facility management

(P-26441)
USAG ANSBACH FINANCIAL MGT DIV
420 Montgomery St, San Francisco (94104-1207)
PHONE....................210 466-1376
Karen McGrail, *Manager*
EMP: 99
SALES (est): 2.1MM **Privately Held**
SIC: 8741 Management services

PRODUCTS & SVCS

(P-26442)
USAG RHEINLAND PFALZ FINCL MGT
420 Montgomery St, San Francisco (94104-1207)
PHONE....................210 466-1376
Tanja Lee, *Manager*
EMP: 99
SALES (est): 5.4MM **Privately Held**
WEB: www.usajobs.org
SIC: 8741 Management services

(P-26443)
USAG VICENZA ITALY DMWR F M D
420 Montgomery St, San Francisco (94104-1207)
PHONE....................210 466-1376
David Floyd, *Manager*
EMP: 99
SALES (est): 1.6MM **Privately Held**
SIC: 8741 Financial management for business

(P-26444)
USAG WIESBADEN FINCL MGT DIV
420 Montgomery St, San Francisco (94104-1207)
PHONE....................210 466-1376
Sabine Norton, *Manager*
EMP: 99
SALES (est): 5.5MM **Privately Held**
SIC: 8741 Management services

(P-26445)
VALLEY MANAGEMENT SERVICES
Also Called: Valley Power System
425 S Hacienda Blvd, City of Industry (91745-1123)
PHONE....................626 333-1243
H Clark Lee, *Chairman*
EMP: 425
SALES (est): 22.2MM **Privately Held**
SIC: 8741 Business management; administrative management

(P-26446)
VALLEY PHYSICIANS ALLIANCE LLC
9300 Valley Childrens Pl, Madera (93636-8761)
PHONE....................559 538-3000
Michelle Brown, *Director*
Duane Oswald, *President*
EMP: 81
SALES (est): 1.3MM **Privately Held**
SIC: 8741 Management services

(P-26447)
VANIR CONSTRUCTION MGT INC (PA)
4540 Duckhorn Dr Ste 300, Sacramento (95834-2597)
PHONE....................916 444-3700
Dorene C Dominguez, *Ch of Bd*
John Kuprenas, *CEO*
Alex Leon, *CFO*
Ray Nez, *CFO*
Gloria Barrera, *Vice Pres*
EMP: 70
SQ FT: 16,000
SALES (est): 67.1MM **Privately Held**
WEB: www.vanir.com
SIC: 8741 Construction management

(P-26448)
VENDOR DIRECT SOLUTIONS LLC
515 S Figueroa St # 1900, Los Angeles (90071-3336)
PHONE....................213 362-5622
Jules Buenabenta, *Principal*
Jim Young, *Exec VP*
Stephanie Simmons, *Human Resources*
Elysha Puga, *Marketing Staff*
Angel E Nevarez, *General Counsel*
EMP: 250
SQ FT: 1,200
SALES (est): 41.3MM **Privately Held**
SIC: 8741 Business management

(P-26449)
VENTURA MEDICAL MANAGEMENT LLC
2601 E Main St, Ventura (93003-2801)
PHONE....................805 477-6220
Jim Malone,
Deborah Carlson MD,
Kent Coleman PHD,
John Pritchard MD,
EMP: 325
SALES (est): 11.3MM **Privately Held**
SIC: 8741 Hospital management

(P-26450)
VICTUS GROUP INC
2350 W Shaw Ave, Fresno (93711-3401)
PHONE....................559 429-8080
Bob Young Yoon, *CEO*
Braxton Myers, *Vice Pres*
EMP: 176
SALES (est): 2.8MM **Privately Held**
SIC: 8741 Hotel or motel management

(P-26451)
VIVA SOMA LESSEE INC
Also Called: Park Central Ht San Francisco
50 3rd St, San Francisco (94103-3106)
PHONE....................415 974-6400
John Anderson, *Branch Mgr*
Christina Tang, *Human Res Mgr*
Alan Yee, *Facilities Dir*
Heather Knight, *Manager*
EMP: 511 **Privately Held**
SIC: 8741 Hotel or motel management; restaurant management
HQ: Viva Soma Lessee, Inc.
7550 Wisconsin Ave Fl 10
Bethesda MD

(P-26452)
VPM MANAGEMENT INC
2400 Main St Ste 201, Irvine (92614-6271)
PHONE....................949 863-1500
Philip H McNamee, *CEO*
Mark Ellis,
Steve Tomlin,
Scott J Barker, *Mng Member*
Scott Barker, *Mng Member*
EMP: 150
SALES (est): 18.6MM **Privately Held**
SIC: 8741 Management services

(P-26453)
WARNER BROS DISTRIBUTING INC
Warner Bros. Pictures Domestic
4000 Warner Blvd Bldg 154, Burbank (91522-0002)
PHONE....................818 954-6000
Dan Fellman, *Branch Mgr*
Bruce Rosenblum, *Director*
Terry Semel, *Director*
Jorge Ferran, *Manager*
EMP: 122
SALES (corp-wide): 170.7B **Publicly Held**
SIC: 8741 7822 Management services; distribution, exclusive of production: motion picture
HQ: Warner Bros. Distributing Inc.
4000 Warner Blvd
Burbank CA 91522

(P-26454)
WASTEXPERTS INCORPORATED
901 Howe Rd, Martinez (94553-3443)
P.O. Box 2099 (94553-0209)
PHONE....................925 484-1057
David Lentz, *President*
Chris Silvas, *Supervisor*
EMP: 80
SALES (est): 12.4MM **Privately Held**
SIC: 8741 Management services

(P-26455)
WEALTH EDUCATORS INC
5209 Wilshire Blvd, Los Angeles (90036-4311)
PHONE....................310 623-9145
EMP: 112
SQ FT: 1,800

SALES (est): 3.8MM **Privately Held**
SIC: 8741 Financial management for business

(P-26456)
WESCO AIRCRAFT HOLDINGS INC (PA)
24911 Avenue Stanford, Valencia (91355-1281)
PHONE....................661 775-7200
Todd S Renehan, *CEO*
Kerry A Shiba, *CFO*
Declan O Grant, *Exec VP*
Declan Grant, *Exec VP*
Michelle Abbitt, *Administration*
EMP: 91
SALES: 1.5B **Publicly Held**
SIC: 8741 5072 Management services; hardware

(P-26457)
WESTERN MEDICAL MANAGEMENT LLC
3333 Michelson Dr Ste 735, Irvine (92612-7679)
PHONE....................949 260-6575
EMP: 50
SALES (est): 3.9MM **Privately Held**
WEB: www.1wmm.com
SIC: 8741

(P-26458)
WESTERN NATIONAL CONTRACTORS
8 Executive Cir, Irvine (92614-6746)
PHONE....................949 862-6200
Michael Hayde, *CEO*
Randy Avery, *Vice Pres*
John Townsend, *Vice Pres*
Jeffrey R Scott, *Admin Sec*
Larry Johnson, *Director*
EMP: 88
SALES (est): 14.1MM **Privately Held**
SIC: 8741 Construction management

(P-26459)
WESTLAKE DEVELOPMENT GROUP LLC
520 El Camino Real Fl 9, Belmont (94002)
PHONE....................650 579-1010
T M Chang, *Branch Mgr*
EMP: 100
SQ FT: 600
SALES (corp-wide): 12.4MM **Privately Held**
WEB: www.westlake-global.com
SIC: 8741 Administrative management
PA: Westlake Development Group, Llc
520 S El Camino Real # 900
San Mateo CA 94402
650 579-1010

(P-26460)
WESTWIND MANOR RESORT ASSN
15 Mason Ste A, Irvine (92618-2707)
P.O. Box 2529, Frisco TX (75034-0047)
PHONE....................214 618-7200
Jeremy Rosenthal, *Risk Mgmt Dir*
William J Shaw, *President*
EMP: 100
SALES (est): 1.7MM **Publicly Held**
WEB: www.indianpt.com
SIC: 8741 Management services
HQ: Thousand Trails, Inc.
2325 Highway 90
Gautier MS 39553
228 497-3594

(P-26461)
WHISKEY GIRL
702 5th Ave, San Diego (92101-6918)
PHONE....................619 236-1616
Jerry Lopez, *General Mgr*
David Schissman, *Co-Owner*
EMP: 83
SALES (est): 5.7MM **Privately Held**
SIC: 8741 5813 Restaurant management; night clubs
PA: Buffalo Joe's Lp
1620 5th Ave Ste 770
San Diego CA 92101
619 235-6796

(P-26462)
WILLIAM L LYON & ASSOC INC (PA)
Also Called: Lyon Real Estate
3640 American River Dr, Sacramento (95864-5953)
PHONE....................916 978-4200
Larry Knapp, *CEO*
Jean LI, *President*
Patrick M Shea, *CEO*
Tanya Hill-Shareef, *Officer*
William Lyon, *Vice Pres*
EMP: 1062
SQ FT: 5,000
SALES (est): 98.4MM **Privately Held**
WEB: www.lyonre.com
SIC: 8741 Management services

(P-26463)
WORD & BROWN INSURANCE
Also Called: Conexis
721 S Parker St Ste 200, Orange (92868-4772)
PHONE....................714 567-4398
John Word, *President*
Ivonne Roca, *Executive*
Andrew Russell, *Broker*
EMP: 215
SALES (corp-wide): 383.5MM **Privately Held**
SIC: 8741 Administrative management
PA: Word & Brown, Insurance Administrators, Inc.
721 S Parker St Ste 300
Orange CA 92868
714 835-5006

(P-26464)
WORLDSTAGE INC (PA)
1111 Bell Ave Ste A, Tustin (92780-6463)
PHONE....................714 508-1858
Gary Standard, *CEO*
Stan Jacobs, *CFO*
Rodney Miller, *CFO*
Gregg Whitaker, *CFO*
Richard Bevan, *Senior VP*
EMP: 58
SALES (est): 30.3MM **Privately Held**
SIC: 8741 Business management

(P-26465)
WYNDHAM IRVINE ORANGE
17941 Von Karman Ave, Irvine (92614-6253)
PHONE....................949 863-1999
Paul Gibbs, *Principal*
Justin Gammon, *General Mgr*
EMP: 90
SQ FT: 1,000
SALES (est): 15MM **Privately Held**
SIC: 8741 7011 7389 Management services; hotels & motels; hotel & motel reservation service

(P-26466)
XTRA DEPARTMENT INC
12631 Imperial Hwy F106, Santa Fe Springs (90670-4710)
PHONE....................562 462-3800
Richard Anzalone, *President*
EMP: 60
SALES (est): 3.7MM **Privately Held**
WEB: www.xtradepartment.com
SIC: 8741 Business management

(P-26467)
ZAHARONI HOLDINGS
5400 W Rosecrans Ave Lowr, Hawthorne (90250-6686)
PHONE....................310 297-9722
Isaac Zaharoni, *Principal*
Dan Zaharoni, *Treasurer*
Patty Steiman, *Vice Pres*
Gil Zaharoni, *Admin Sec*
EMP: 50
SQ FT: 75,000
SALES: 80MM **Privately Held**
WEB: www.zaharoni.com
SIC: 8741 Financial management for business

8742 Management Consulting Services

(P-26468)
A T KEARNEY INC
555 Mission St Ste 1800, San Francisco
(94105-0924)
PHONE...............................415 490-4000
Charity Reyes, *Office Mgr*
Paul Somerset, *Executive Asst*
EMP: 98
SALES (corp-wide): 1.2B **Privately Held**
SIC: 8742 Business consultant
HQ: A. T. Kearney, Inc.
227 W Monroe St
Chicago IL 60606
312 648-0111

(P-26469)
A WORLD FIT FOR KIDS
678 S La Fayette Park Pl, Los Angeles
(90057-3206)
PHONE...............................213 387-7712
Normandie Nigh, *Exec Dir*
Samantha Sorbo, *Vice Pres*
Martha Cordero, *Program Mgr*
EMP: 110 **EST:** 1993
SQ FT: 4,800
SALES: 1.8MM **Privately Held**
WEB: www.worldfitforkids.org
SIC: 8742 8641 8322 Management con-
sulting services; civic social & fraternal
associations; youth center

(P-26470)
**ACCENTURE FEDERAL
SERVICES LLC**
Also Called: Accenture National SEC Svcs
1615 Murray Canyon Rd # 400, San Diego
(92108-4314)
PHONE...............................619 574-2400
Jim Wangler, *Branch Mgr*
Terrell Deppe, *CTO*
Evan Busch, *Senior Mgr*
Karen A Justman, *Manager*
Shivanand Mali, *Manager*
EMP: 145 **Privately Held**
SIC: 8742 7361 8711 7373 Business
consultant; employment agencies; engi-
neering services; computer integrated
systems design; computer software de-
velopment
HQ: Accenture Federal Services Llc
800 N Glebe Rd Ste 300
Arlington VA 22203
703 947-2000

(P-26471)
ACCENTURE LLP
2141 Rosecrans Ave # 3100, El Segundo
(90245-7518)
PHONE...............................310 726-2700
Joyce Nitz, *Branch Mgr*
Maggie Urbanik, *Executive Asst*
Lynn Gresham, *Admin Sec*
Arun Palani, *Prgrmr*
Ranjit Satishbabu, *Prgrmr*
EMP: 350 **Privately Held**
WEB: www.wavesecurities.com
SIC: 8742 Business consultant
HQ: Accenture Llp
161 N Clark St Ste 1100
Chicago IL 60601
312 693-0161

(P-26472)
ACCENTURE LLP
2 Santa Ana Ct, Belvedere Tiburon
(94920-1620)
PHONE...............................415 537-5860
Bill Moon, *Vice Pres*
Dave Alverado, *Software Dev*
EMP: 208 **Privately Held**
WEB: www.wavesecurities.com
SIC: 8742 Business consultant
HQ: Accenture Llp
161 N Clark St Ste 1100
Chicago IL 60601
312 693-0161

(P-26473)
ACCENTURE LLP
560 Mission St Fl 12, San Francisco
(94105-2927)
PHONE...............................415 537-5000
Christopher S Digiorgio, *Principal*
Dan Carrington, *Partner*
Kirk Kirkpatrick, *Principal*
Courtney Rosen, *Principal*
Diana Bersohn, *Managing Dir*
EMP: 310 **Privately Held**
WEB: www.wavesecurities.com
SIC: 8742 Business consultant
HQ: Accenture Llp
161 N Clark St Ste 1100
Chicago IL 60601
312 693-0161

(P-26474)
ACCENTURE LLP
50 W San Fernando St # 1208, San Jose
(95113-2429)
PHONE...............................408 817-2100
Jackson Wilson, *Manager*
Thomas Stuermer, *Partner*
Michael Redding, *Managing Dir*
Allison Youngdahl, *Analyst*
Gaetan Vandermensbrugg, *Human
Resources*
EMP: 218 **Privately Held**
WEB: www.wavesecurities.com
SIC: 8742 Business consultant
HQ: Accenture Llp
161 N Clark St Ste 1100
Chicago IL 60601
312 693-0161

(P-26475)
ACCENTURE LLP
50 W San Fernando St # 1200, San Jose
(95113-2429)
PHONE...............................650 213-2000
Christopher S Digiorgio, *Manager*
Paul Hasenwinkel, *Principal*
Vincent Hui, *Principal*
Clifford Jury, *Principal*
Carlisle Kirkpatrick, *Principal*
EMP: 175 **Privately Held**
SIC: 8742 8748 Business consultant; busi-
ness consulting
HQ: Accenture Llp
161 N Clark St Ste 1100
Chicago IL 60601
312 693-0161

(P-26476)
ACCENTURE LLP
1610 R St Ste 240, Sacramento
(95811-6685)
PHONE...............................916 557-2200
Christopher S Digiorgio, *Branch Mgr*
Kirk Jacobi, *Executive*
Brian Quick, *Analyst*
John Nichols, *Manager*
EMP: 175 **Privately Held**
WEB: www.wavesecurities.com
SIC: 8742 Business consultant; manage-
ment information systems consultant
HQ: Accenture Llp
161 N Clark St Ste 1100
Chicago IL 60601
312 693-0161

(P-26477)
ACCOUNTNOW INC
2603 Camino Ramon Ste 485, San Ramon
(94583-9131)
P.O. Box 5100, Pasadena (91117-0100)
PHONE...............................925 498-1800
James G Jones, *CEO*
David J Petrini, *CFO*
Paul Rosenfeld, *Chief Mktg Ofcr*
Jenn Cordeiro, *Technology*
Slava Ostrovsky, *Technology*
EMP: 55
SALES (est): 12.3MM
SALES (corp-wide): 1B **Publicly Held**
SIC: 8742 Financial consultant
PA: Green Dot Corporation
3465 E Foothill Blvd # 100
Pasadena CA 91107
626 765-2000

(P-26478)
ADIVO ASSOCIATES LLC
44 Montgomery St Ste 4050, San Francisco
(94104-4824)
PHONE...............................415 992-1449
Maik Klasen, *Managing Dir*
Anna Santos, *Executive*
Lilia Carmen, *Administration*
Jason Bruton, *Consultant*
Clifford Chiu, *Consultant*
EMP: 90
SALES (est): 4.7MM **Privately Held**
SIC: 8742 Business consultant

(P-26479)
**ADVANTAGE SALES & MKTG
LLC (HQ)**
Also Called: Advantage Solutions
18100 Von Karman Ave # 900, Irvine
(92612-7195)
PHONE...............................949 797-2900
Sonny King, *Chairman*
Tanya Domier, *CEO*
Brian Stevens, *COO*
Robert Murray, *Treasurer*
Glen Schutz, *Bd of Directors*
EMP: 250
SALES (est): 1.9B
SALES (corp-wide): 11.4B **Privately Held**
SIC: 8742 8743 8732 Marketing consult-
ing services; sales (including sales man-
agement) consultant; sales promotion;
market analysis or research
PA: Advantage Sales & Marketing Inc.
18100 Von Karman Ave # 900
Irvine CA 92612
949 797-2900

(P-26480)
AECOM C&E INC
Also Called: Aecom Consulting
1999 Avenue Of The Stars, Los Angeles
(90067-6022)
PHONE...............................213 593-8100
Bill Mehol, *Branch Mgr*
Ray Sosa, *President*
George Sholy, *Assoc VP*
Brian Okane, *Exec VP*
Brett Berra, *Vice Pres*
EMP: 200
SALES (corp-wide): 20.1B **Publicly Held**
SIC: 8742 9441 Human resource consult-
ing services; administration of social &
human resources
HQ: Aecom C&E, Inc
250 Apollo Dr
Chelmsford MA 01824
978 905-2100

(P-26481)
**AEG GLOBAL PARTNERSHIPS
LLC**
1100 S Flower St Ste 3200, Los Angeles
(90015-2125)
PHONE...............................213 763-7700
Todd Goldstein, *President*
Brad Gessner, *Vice Pres*
Rob Reed, *Vice Pres*
David Starensier, *Vice Pres*
Mark Wolffe, *Engineer*
EMP: 50
SALES (est): 1.8MM **Privately Held**
SIC: 8742 Management consulting serv-
ices
HQ: Anschutz Entertainment Group, Inc.
800 W Olympic Blvd # 305
Los Angeles CA 90015
213 337-5052

(P-26482)
AEROMEDEVAC INC
1860 Joe Crosson Dr Ste I, El Cajon
(92020-1263)
PHONE...............................619 284-7910
Adam Williams, *President*
John Olson, *CEO*
Raul Mendoza, *Vice Pres*
Jerry Delrio, *Corp Comm Staff*
EMP: 54
SALES (est): 6.3MM **Privately Held**
WEB: www.aeromedevac.com
SIC: 8742 Management consulting serv-
ices

(P-26483)
AGAMA SOLUTIONS INC
39159 Paseo Padre Pkwy # 216, Fremont
(94538-1689)
PHONE...............................510 796-9300
Shivani G Sanan, *CEO*
Tanu Kalra, *President*
Pankaj Kalra, *Vice Pres*
Ashish Sanan, *Vice Pres*
EMP: 175
SQ FT: 9,000
SALES (est): 20.6MM **Privately Held**
SIC: 8742 7371 Management consulting
services; computer software development

(P-26484)
AGR GROUP INC
13902 Harbor Blvd Ste 2c, Garden Grove
(92843-4013)
PHONE...............................714 245-7151
EMP: 750
SQ FT: 15,500
SALES: 16MM **Privately Held**
WEB: www.agrgroupinc.com
SIC: 8742

(P-26485)
AGREEYA SOLUTIONS INC (PA)
605 Coolidge Dr Ste 200, Folsom
(95630-4210)
PHONE...............................916 294-0075
Neerja Khosla, *President*
Sangeeta Khazanchi, *CFO*
Sanjay Khosla, *Vice Pres*
Sandeep Sharma, *Vice Pres*
Ajay Kaul, *Admin Sec*
EMP: 55
SQ FT: 14,000
SALES (est): 40MM **Privately Held**
WEB: www.agreeya.com
SIC: 8742 7371 Management consulting
services; computer software systems
analysis & design, custom

(P-26486)
AKQA INC (HQ)
360 3rd St Ste 500, San Francisco
(94107-2165)
PHONE...............................415 645-9400
Tom Bedecarre, *CEO*
Olivia Albanese, *Executive*
Ananth Varma, *Associate Dir*
Eamonn Dixon, *Creative Dir*
Whitney Jenkins, *Creative Dir*
EMP: 400
SQ FT: 28,000
SALES (est): 80.4MM
SALES (corp-wide): 20B **Privately Held**
WEB: www.akqa.com
SIC: 8742 Marketing consulting services
PA: Wpp Plc
Sea Containers
London SE1 9
207 282-4600

(P-26487)
**ALAN B WHITSON COMPANY
INC**
1507 W Alton Ave, Santa Ana
(92704-7219)
P.O. Box 9229, Newport Beach (92658-
9229)
PHONE...............................949 955-1200
Alan B Whitson, *President*
EMP: 750
SQ FT: 18,000
SALES: 41.4MM **Privately Held**
SIC: 8742 1389 5411 Corporation organ-
izing; servicing oil & gas wells; conven-
ience stores, chain

(P-26488)
ALIGHT (US) LLC
100 Bayview Cir Ste 100 # 100, Newport
Beach (92660-2963)
P.O. Box 6300, Newport (92658-6300)
PHONE...............................949 725-4500
Eric Watkins, *Manager*
Cheukming Ku, *Consultant*
EMP: 200
SALES (corp-wide): 23.4B **Privately Held**
WEB: www.hewitt.com
SIC: 8742 8748 Compensation & benefits
planning consultant; business consulting

PRODUCTS & SVCS

HQ: Alight (Us), Llc
200 E Randolph St Ll3
Chicago IL 60601

(P-26489)
ALTEGRA HEALTH
3415 S Sepulveda Blvd # 900, Los Angeles
(90034-6981)
PHONE....................310 776-4001
EMP: 99
SALES (est): 6.6MM **Privately Held**
SIC: 8742

(P-26490)
ALVAREZ & MARSAL HOLDINGS
LLC
100 Pine St Fl 9, San Francisco
(94111-5111)
PHONE....................415 490-2300
Bill Kosturos, *Manager*
Mark Stott, *Managing Dir*
Matthew Dresser, *Sr Associate*
Branden Wilson, *Sr Associate*
EMP: 180
SALES (corp-wide): 232.2MM **Privately**
Held
SIC: 8742 3523 3448 Financial consult-
ant; farm machinery & equipment; prefab-
ricated metal buildings
HQ: Alvarez & Marsal, Inc.
600 Madison Ave Fl 8
New York NY 10022
212 759-4433

(P-26491)
AMCO FOODS INC
601 E Glenoaks Blvd # 108, Glendale
(91207-1760)
PHONE....................818 247-4716
Bobken Amirian, *President*
Brian Polthow, *CFO*
Nick Amirian, *Corp Secy*
Nareg Amirian, *Principal*
EMP: 475 EST: 1999
SALES: 5.8MM **Privately Held**
SIC: 8742 Business consultant

(P-26492)
AMERICA CONSULTING GROUP
LLC
23 Corporate Plaza Dr # 150, Newport
Beach (92660-7908)
PHONE....................714 390-3105
Alan Ford, *CEO*
EMP: 200
SALES: 5MM **Privately Held**
SIC: 8742 Business consultant

(P-26493)
AMERICAN ALL RISK LOSS ADM
4270 W Richert Ave # 101, Fresno
(93722-6334)
P.O. Box 9783 (93794-9783)
PHONE....................559 277-4960
Steve Wigh, *President*
EMP: 125
SALES (est): 12.6MM **Privately Held**
SIC: 8742 Administrative services consult-
ant

(P-26494)
AMERICAN FINANCIAL
NETWORK INC
14241 Firestone Blvd, La Mirada
(90638-5530)
PHONE....................562 926-2401
Dan Piumpunyalerd, *Branch Mgr*
EMP: 71
SALES (corp-wide): 183.5MM **Privately**
Held
SIC: 8742 7389 6162 Financial consult-
ant; financial services; mortgage bankers
& correspondents
PA: American Financial Network, Inc.
10 Pointe Dr Ste 330
Brea CA 92821
909 606-3905

(P-26495)
AMERICAN FINANCIAL
NETWORK INC
3400 Inland Empire Blvd # 101, Ontario
(91764-5577)
PHONE....................951 582-2655

EMP: 106
SALES (corp-wide): 183.5MM **Privately**
Held
SIC: 8742 7389 6162 Financial consult-
ant; financial services; mortgage bankers
& correspondents
PA: American Financial Network, Inc.
10 Pointe Dr Ste 330
Brea CA 92821
909 606-3905

(P-26496)
AMGREEN SOLUTIONS INC
1367 Venice Blvd Fl 2, Los Angeles
(90006-5519)
PHONE....................213 388-5647
Changhwan Ko, *President*
Michael Kim, *Sales Dir*
Nick Guillen, *Director*
EMP: 50
SALES: 8MM **Privately Held**
SIC: 8742 7389 Management engineering;
water softener service

(P-26497)
AMMUNITION LLC
1500 Sansome St Ste 110, San Francisco
(94111-1015)
PHONE....................415 632-1170
Peter Rack, *Managing Dir*
Nick Barrett, *Vice Pres*
Kyle Macy, *Creative Dir*
Brett Wickens, *Creative Dir*
Robert Kanes, *Program Mgr*
EMP: 51
SQ FT: 5,200
SALES (est): 14.6MM **Privately Held**
SIC: 8742 Industrial consultant

(P-26498)
AMS VENTURES INC
39055 Hastings St Ste 205, Fremont
(94538-1599)
PHONE....................301 980-5087
Stephen Zuppas, *CFO*
EMP: 70
SALES (est): 1.1MM **Privately Held**
SIC: 8742 Marketing consulting services

(P-26499)
AMTROW GROUP INC
8306 Wilshire Blvd 1042, Beverly Hills
(90211-2304)
PHONE....................310 557-0857
Samuel Neiderberg, *President*
Mikhail Aptor, *Vice Pres*
EMP: 86
SQ FT: 1,400
SALES (est): 3.6MM **Privately Held**
SIC: 8742 8741 1542 1522 Industry spe-
cialist consultants; construction manage-
ment; nonresidential construction;
residential construction

(P-26500)
ANDERSON KAYNE INV MGT INC
(PA)
1800 Avenue Of The Stars # 200, Los An-
geles (90067-4204)
PHONE....................310 556-2721
Richard Kayne, *Ch of Bd*
John Anderson, *CEO*
Paul Stapleton, *Treasurer*
Frank Lee, *Officer*
David J Shladovsky, *Admin Sec*
EMP: 55
SQ FT: 20,000
SALES (est): 22.2MM **Privately Held**
SIC: 8742 6211 6726 6282 Financial
consultant; investment firm, general bro-
kerage; investment offices; investment
advice

(P-26501)
ANDERSONPENNA PARTNERS
INC (HQ)
3737 Birch St Ste 250, Newport Beach
(92660-2682)
PHONE....................949 428-1500
Lisa Penna, *President*
Steve Badum, *President*
Angelique M Lucero, *CFO*
David R Anderson, *Exec VP*
Dino D'Emilia, *Vice Pres*
EMP: 75

SALES (est): 8.7MM **Privately Held**
SIC: 8742 8711 Transportation consultant;
engineering services
PA: Ardurra Group Holdings Llc
3012 26th St
Metairie LA 70002
504 454-3866

(P-26502)
ANJANEYAP INC
830 Hillview Ct Ste 140, Milpitas
(95035-4552)
PHONE....................408 922-9690
Sundeep Bhandal, *President*
Taresh Anand, *Vice Pres*
Geetika Gulati, *Technology*
SAI Kumar, *Recruiter*
Akshatha Sreenivas, *Recruiter*
EMP: 53
SQ FT: 4,300
SALES: 37.7MM **Privately Held**
SIC: 8742 Business consultant

(P-26503)
AON CONSULTING INC
2570 N 1st St Ste 500, San Jose
(95131-1018)
PHONE....................408 321-2500
Steve Radford, *Manager*
EMP: 65
SALES (corp-wide): 10.7B **Privately Held**
WEB: www.radford.com
SIC: 8742 Compensation & benefits plan-
ning consultant
HQ: Aon Consulting, Inc.
200 E Randolph St Ll3
Chicago IL 60601

(P-26504)
APA INCORPORATED
405 S Beverly Dr Ste 500, Beverly Hills
(90212-4425)
P.O. Box 45 (90213-0045)
PHONE....................310 888-4200
Kat Cafeler, *President*
Ralph Berge, *Vice Pres*
Christina Campagnola, *Executive Asst*
Matteo Jin, *Executive Asst*
James Gosnell, *Info Tech Mgr*
EMP: 150
SALES (est): 11.4MM **Privately Held**
SIC: 8742 Business consultant

(P-26505)
APERIAN GLOBAL INC (PA)
1 Kaiser Plz Ste 785, Oakland
(94612-3611)
PHONE....................628 222-3773
Ernest Gundling, *President*
Dave Eaton, *President*
Laurette Bennhold-Samaan, *COO*
Theodore Dale, *COO*
David Reilly, *CFO*
EMP: 62
SQ FT: 4,000
SALES (est): 8.1MM **Privately Held**
WEB: www.meridianglobal.com
SIC: 8742 Business consultant

(P-26506)
APN BUSINESS RESOURCES
INC
21418 Osborne St, Canoga Park
(91304-1520)
PHONE....................818 717-9980
Michael Noori, *CEO*
Julio Arreyguy, *Info Tech Mgr*
EMP: 85
SALES: 15MM **Privately Held**
SIC: 8742 8748 Business planning & or-
ganizing services; business consulting

(P-26507)
ARCHETYPE CONSULTING INC
530 Divisadero St Ste 310, San Francisco
(94117-2213)
PHONE....................888 644-8445
EMP: 100
SALES (corp-wide): 10.2MM **Privately**
Held
SIC: 8742 Financial consultant
PA: Archetype Consulting, Inc.
180 Canal St Ste 600
Boston MA 02114
857 350-4369

(P-26508)
ARCO ENVMTL REMEDIATION
LLC
Also Called: Am/PM Food Mart
5472 Orangethorpe Ave, La Palma
(90623-1005)
PHONE....................714 523-5674
Bruce Niemeyer, *President*
EMP: 68 EST: 1996
SALES (est): 2.1MM
SALES (corp-wide): 298.7B **Privately**
Held
WEB: www.bpamoco.com
SIC: 8742 8748 6794 Management con-
sulting services; environmental consult-
ant; franchises, selling or licensing
HQ: Bp Corporation North America Inc.
501 Westlake Park Blvd
Houston TX 77079
281 366-2000

(P-26509)
ASHLEY MANAGEMENT GROUP
300 Spectrum Center Dr # 400, Irvine
(92618-4925)
PHONE....................949 754-3120
Lance Ashley, *President*
EMP: 50
SALES: 5MM **Privately Held**
SIC: 8742 Business consultant

(P-26510)
ASSET MARKETING SYSTEMS
INSU
Also Called: AMS
15050 Ave Of Science # 100, San Diego
(92128-3418)
PHONE....................888 303-8755
Mike Botkin, *CEO*
Dee Costa, *President*
Louise Kinard Erdman, *CFO*
Jeff Stemler, *Exec VP*
Michael H Botkin, *Vice Pres*
EMP: 70
SQ FT: 19,000
SALES (est): 8.6MM **Privately Held**
WEB: www.assetmarketingsystems.net
SIC: 8742 Marketing consulting services

(P-26511)
AUTISM PARTNERSHIP INC
200 Marina Dr C, Seal Beach
(90740-6023)
PHONE....................562 431-9293
Ronald Leaf, *President*
John McEachin, *Admin Sec*
Julie McEachin, *Administration*
Andrea Waks, *Client Mgr*
EMP: 95
SALES (est): 6MM **Privately Held**
WEB: www.autismpartnership.com
SIC: 8742 Hospital & health services con-
sultant

(P-26512)
AVANTI HEALTH SYSTEM LLC
222 N Pacific Coast Hwy # 950, El Se-
gundo (90245-5627)
PHONE....................310 356-0550
Steve Dixon,
Mark Bell, *Mng Member*
Poe Corn, *Mng Member*
James Macpherson, *Mng Member*
EMP: 446 EST: 2008
SALES (est): 49.5MM **Privately Held**
SIC: 8742 Hospital & health services con-
sultant

(P-26513)
AXA ADVISORS LLC
88 Kearny St Fl 20, San Francisco
(94108-5548)
PHONE....................415 276-2100
Daniel W Worthington, *Manager*
Toni LI, *Principal*
EMP: 70
SALES (corp-wide): 12B **Publicly Held**
WEB: www.axacs.com
SIC: 8742 Financial consultant
HQ: Axa Advisors, Llc
1290 Ave Of Amrcs Fl Cnc1
New York NY 10104
212 554-1234

(P-26514)
B A TECHNOLINKS CORPORATION
4677 Old Ironsides Dr # 440, Santa Clara (95054-1826)
PHONE..................................408 940-5921
Kiran Maruvada, *CEO*
Krishna Vemuri, *President*
EMP: 70 EST: 2010
SALES (est): 5.2MM **Privately Held**
SIC: 8742 Business consultant

(P-26515)
BABCOCK & BROWN ELEC MGT LLC
4350 La Jolla Village Dr, San Diego (92122-1243)
PHONE..................................858 587-5820
Sean McLaughlin, *Branch Mgr*
EMP: 151
SALES (corp-wide): 18.1MM **Privately Held**
SIC: 8742 Management consulting services
PA: Babcock & Brown Electronics Management Llc
4 Embarcadero Ctr Ste 700
San Francisco CA

(P-26516)
BAE SYSTEMS TECH SOL SRVC INC
1434 F Ln 58 B, Mojave (93501)
PHONE..................................661 816-3474
Brad Thiele, *Branch Mgr*
EMP: 57
SALES (corp-wide): 21.6B **Privately Held**
SIC: 8742 Quality assurance consultant
HQ: Bae Systems Technology Solutions & Services Inc.
520 Gaither Rd
Rockville MD 20850
703 847-5820

(P-26517)
BAIN & COMPANY INC
1901 Ave Of The Sts 200, Los Angeles (90067)
PHONE..................................310 229-3000
Kevin Badkoubehi, *Branch Mgr*
Debbie Kowalewicz, *Executive Asst*
Hubert Shen, *Sr Associate*
Joon Choi, *Manager*
Kimberly Fitzgerald, *Manager*
EMP: 80
SALES (corp-wide): 493.3MM **Privately Held**
WEB: www.bain.com
SIC: 8742 Business consultant
PA: Bain & Company, Inc.
131 Dartmouth St Ste 901
Boston MA 02116
617 572-2000

(P-26518)
BAIN & COMPANY INC
1 Embarcadero Ctr # 3500, San Francisco (94111-3628)
PHONE..................................415 627-1000
Vernon Altman, *Manager*
Yesenia Pulido, *Executive Asst*
Veronica Shepherd, *Executive Asst*
Melissa Suchy, *Executive Asst*
Jasmine Stewart, *Human Res Mgr*
EMP: 109
SALES (corp-wide): 493.3MM **Privately Held**
WEB: www.bain.com
SIC: 8742 Business consultant
PA: Bain & Company, Inc.
131 Dartmouth St Ste 901
Boston MA 02116
617 572-2000

(P-26519)
BAINBRIDGE INC (PA)
4435 Estgate Mall Ste 130, San Diego (92121)
PHONE..................................858 638-1800
Steven Stucker, *President*
EMP: 61

SALES (est): 6.3MM **Privately Held**
WEB: www.bbridge.com
SIC: 8742 8732 Management consulting services; market analysis or research

(P-26520)
BASELINE CONSULTING GROUP INC
15300 Ventura Blvd # 200, Sherman Oaks (91403-3138)
PHONE..................................818 906-7638
Evan Levy, *President*
Jill Dyche, *Vice Pres*
EMP: 50
SQ FT: 5,000
SALES (est): 3.4MM
SALES (corp-wide): 3B **Privately Held**
WEB: www.baseline-consulting.com
SIC: 8742 Management consulting services
HQ: Dataflux Corporation Llc
100 Sas Campus Dr
Cary NC

(P-26521)
BASKETBALL MARKETING CO INC
Also Called: and 1
101 Enterprise Ste 100, Aliso Viejo (92656-2604)
PHONE..................................610 249-2255
Kevin Wulff, *President*
▲ EMP: 78
SALES (est): 3.7MM
SALES (corp-wide): 2.8B **Publicly Held**
WEB: www.avia.com
SIC: 8742 Management consulting services
HQ: American Sporting Goods Corp
101 Enterprise Ste 200
Aliso Viejo CA 92656
949 267-2800

(P-26522)
BBCERT
510 Hwy 1, Bodega Bay (94923)
P.O. Box 6 (94923-0006)
PHONE..................................480 220-3799
Linda Stout, *President*
EMP: 50
SALES (est): 1MM **Privately Held**
SIC: 8742 Training & development consultant

(P-26523)
BEACON ACCUNTING RESOURCES LLC
1818 Glenwood Ln, Newport Beach (92660-4317)
PHONE..................................949 981-5946
EMP: 50
SALES (est): 1.8MM **Privately Held**
SIC: 8742 Business planning & organizing services

(P-26524)
BEACON RESOURCES LLC
17300 Red Hill Ave, Irvine (92614-5643)
PHONE..................................949 955-1773
Colleen Freeman,
Mike Kelly,
EMP: 50
SALES (est): 3.2MM
SALES (corp-wide): 156.9MM **Privately Held**
SIC: 8742 Business planning & organizing services
HQ: David M. Lewis Company, Llc
21800 Oxnard St Ste 980
Woodland Hills CA 91367

(P-26525)
BEATING WALL STREET INC (PA)
14934 Dickens St Apt 16, Sherman Oaks (91403-3419)
PHONE..................................818 332-9696
Hamed Khorsand, *President*
EMP: 230
SQ FT: 8,000
SALES (est): 7.6MM **Privately Held**
WEB: www.beatingwallstreet.com
SIC: 8742 Financial consultant

(P-26526)
BECKETT ENTERPRISE
Also Called: Selu College
900 Kincaid Ave K8, Inglewood (90302-2021)
PHONE..................................310 686-3817
Tyesha Beckett, *CEO*
EMP: 50 EST: 2017
SALES (est): 924.5K **Privately Held**
SIC: 8742 Corporation organizing

(P-26527)
BENTLEY HEALTH CARE INC
9777 Wilshire Blvd Fl 4, Beverly Hills (90212-1904)
PHONE..................................310 967-3300
Bernard Salick MD, *President*
Barbara Bromley-Williams, *Vice Pres*
EMP: 70
SQ FT: 32,000
SALES (est): 3.4MM **Privately Held**
SIC: 8742 Hospital & health services consultant

(P-26528)
BITE COMMUNICATIONS LLC (HQ)
100 Montgomery St # 1101, San Francisco (94104-4388)
PHONE..................................415 365-0222
Tim Dyson, *Mng Member*
Alisa Macdonnell, *Senior VP*
Will Willis, *Senior VP*
Molly Stein, *Vice Pres*
David Dewhurst, *Mng Member*
EMP: 75
SQ FT: 10,000
SALES (est): 12.6MM
SALES (corp-wide): 342.1MM **Privately Held**
WEB: www.bitepr.com
SIC: 8742 8743 Marketing consulting services; public relations services
PA: Next Fifteen Communications Group Plc
75 Bermondsey Street
London SE1 3
207 908-6444

(P-26529)
BLACKSTONE CONSULTING INC (PA)
11726 San Vicente Blvd # 550, Los Angeles (90049-5089)
PHONE..................................310 826-4389
Ronald Joseph Blackstone, *President*
Gary Meek, *CFO*
Mike Robinson, *Vice Pres*
Alejandra Ordaz, *Administration*
Kyle Ellis, *Human Res Mgr*
EMP: 148
SQ FT: 1,500
SALES (est): 119MM **Privately Held**
WEB: www.blackstone-consulting.com
SIC: 8742 Management consulting services

(P-26530)
BLANCHARD TRAINING AND DEV INC (PA)
Also Called: Ken Blanchard Companies, The
125 State Pl, Escondido (92029-1323)
PHONE..................................760 489-5005
Thomas J McKee, *CEO*
Sergio Barajas, *Partner*
Maritza Dominguez, *Partner*
Judith Donin, *Partner*
Carmen Flores, *Partner*
▼ EMP: 200
SALES (est): 61.2MM **Privately Held**
SIC: 8742 Training & development consultant

(P-26531)
BLB RESOURCES INC (PA)
16845 Von Karman Ave # 100, Irvine (92606-4961)
PHONE..................................949 261-9155
Rod Gaston, *CEO*
Amy Chun, *Controller*
Greg Siesel, *Opers Staff*
Bernard Goree, *Sales Associate*
Cindy Cano, *Manager*
EMP: 105
SQ FT: 20,000

SALES (est): 14.5MM **Privately Held**
SIC: 8742 Management consulting services

(P-26532)
BON APPETIT MANAGEMENT CO
1259 E Colton Ave, Redlands (92374-3755)
PHONE..................................909 748-8970
Bret Martin, *General Mgr*
EMP: 120
SALES (corp-wide): 29.6B **Privately Held**
WEB: www.cafebonappetit.com
SIC: 8742 Administrative services consultant
HQ: Bon Appetit Management Co.
100 Hamilton Ave Ste 400
Palo Alto CA 94301
650 798-8000

(P-26533)
BOOZ ALLEN HAMILTON INC
5220 Pacific Concourse Dr # 390, Los Angeles (90045-6244)
PHONE..................................310 297-2100
Ralph Shrader, *CEO*
Yong Chen, *Engineer*
Amanda Cohen, *Associate*
EMP: 52 **Publicly Held**
SIC: 8742 Management consulting services
HQ: Booz Allen Hamilton Inc.
8283 Greensboro Dr # 700
Mc Lean VA 22102
703 902-5000

(P-26534)
BOOZ ALLEN HAMILTON INC
1615 Murray Canyon Rd # 220, San Diego (92108-4329)
PHONE..................................619 725-6500
Foster Rich, *Vice Pres*
Philip Summerly, *Social Mgr*
Kristy Brierton, *Admin Asst*
Shane Doyle, *Network Enginr*
Derek Handy, *Engineer*
EMP: 52 **Publicly Held**
WEB: www.bah.com
SIC: 8742 Management consulting services
HQ: Booz Allen Hamilton Inc.
8283 Greensboro Dr # 700
Mc Lean VA 22102
703 902-5000

(P-26535)
BOOZ ALLEN HAMILTON INC
555 S Flower St Fl 36, Los Angeles (90071-2300)
PHONE..................................213 620-1900
Wayne Gilles, *Branch Mgr*
EMP: 52 **Publicly Held**
WEB: www.bah.com
SIC: 8742 Management consulting services
HQ: Booz Allen Hamilton Inc.
8283 Greensboro Dr # 700
Mc Lean VA 22102
703 902-5000

(P-26536)
BOSTON CONSULTING GROUP INC
355 S Grand Ave Ste 3300, Los Angeles (90071-1592)
PHONE..................................213 621-2772
Angela Johnson, *Director*
EMP: 70
SALES (corp-wide): 2.6B **Privately Held**
WEB: www.bcg.com
SIC: 8742 Business consultant
PA: Boston Consulting Group
200 Pier 4 Blvd Fl 11
Boston MA 02210
617 973-1200

(P-26537)
BRAD S MILLER
Also Called: Infotech Global Services
220 Montgomery St Ste 310, San Francisco (94104-3436)
PHONE..................................415 986-5400
Brad Miller, *Owner*
EMP: 200

SALES: 8MM **Privately Held**
SIC: 8742 7363 Management information
systems consultant; help supply services

(P-26538)
BRANDREP LLC
16812 Armstrong Ave, Irvine (92606-4916)
PHONE..................................800 405-7119
Banir Ganatra,
Vasile Popovici, *Controller*
Adam Aloul, *Sales Executive*
Sharon Murray, *Sales Mgr*
Aubryanne Cook, *Marketing Staff*
EMP: 50 **EST:** 2013
SALES (est): 6.5MM **Privately Held**
SIC: 8742 Marketing consulting services

(P-26539)
**BRIDGWTER CONSULTING
GROUP INC**
18881 Von Karman Ave, Irvine
(92612-1500)
PHONE..................................949 535-1755
Mark Montgomery, *President*
Skip Vega, *Sr Consultant*
EMP: 90
SQ FT: 1,600
SALES: 13.5MM **Privately Held**
SIC: 8742 7379 Management consulting
services;

(P-26540)
BROKER SOLUTIONS INC (PA)
Also Called: New American Funding
14511 Myford Rd Ste 100, Tustin
(92780-7057)
PHONE..................................800 450-2010
Rick Arvielo, *CEO*
Patricia Arvielo, *President*
Christy Bunce, *COO*
Scott Frommert, *CFO*
EMP: 650
SALES (est): 183.3MM **Privately Held**
SIC: 8742 6162 Financial consultant; bond
& mortgage companies

(P-26541)
BROWN AND STREZA LLP
40 Pacifica Ste 1500, Irvine (92618-7496)
PHONE..................................949 453-2900
Richard Streza, *President*
David Brown, *Vice Pres*
Victoria Hypolite, *Admin Asst*
Michael Offenheiser, *Planning*
Kj Nguyen, *Info Tech Mgr*
EMP: 60
SQ FT: 1,000
SALES (est): 8.6MM **Privately Held**
WEB: www.brownandstreza.com
SIC: 8742 8111 Business planning & or-
ganizing services; general practice attor-
ney, lawyer

(P-26542)
**BUSINESS FOR SCIAL
RSPNSBILITY (PA)**
Also Called: B S R
220 Montgomery St # 1700, San Francisco
(94104-3539)
PHONE..................................415 984-3200
Aron Cramer, *CEO*
EMP: 130
SALES (est): 21.2MM **Privately Held**
WEB: www.bsr.org
SIC: 8742 General management consult-
ant

(P-26543)
BUSINESS INTELLIGENCE
2131 Palomar Airport Rd # 328, Carlsbad
(92011-1466)
P.O. Box 99973, San Diego (92169-1973)
PHONE..................................858 452-8200
Sean Lesher, *Mng Member*
Aaron Blasi, *Vice Pres*
EMP: 50
SQ FT: 700
SALES: 12MM **Privately Held**
SIC: 8742 Management information sys-
tems consultant

(P-26544)
BUSINESSCOM INC
2120 Colorado Ave Fl 3, Santa Monica
(90404-5510)
PHONE..................................310 586-4000

Ryan Peddycord, *CEO*
Brian Barnum, *President*
EMP: 52
SQ FT: 22,000
SALES (est): 4.2MM
SALES (corp-wide): 158.8MM **Privately
Held**
WEB: www.business.com
SIC: 8742 7375 Management consulting
services; information retrieval services
HQ: Business.Com Media, Inc.
1900 Wright Pl Ste 250
Carlsbad CA 92008
888 441-4466

(P-26545)
CALIF INSTITUTE HUMAN SER
1801 E Cotati Ave, Rohnert Park
(94928-3613)
PHONE..................................707 664-2416
Tony Apolloni, *Director*
Vanessa Pedro, *Analyst*
Natalie Williams-Munger, *Director*
Jessica Kegley, *Representative*
EMP: 70 **EST:** 1980
SALES (est): 2.6MM **Privately Held**
SIC: 8742 Human resource consulting
services

(P-26546)
**CALIFRNIA IND SYS OPRATOR
CORP**
110 Blue Ravine Rd, Folsom (95630-4711)
PHONE..................................916 608-7000
Terry Winter, *President*
Heather Kelley, *Manager*
EMP: 150 **Privately Held**
WEB: www.caiso.com
SIC: 8742 Human resource consulting
services
PA: California Independent System Opera-
tor Corporation
250 Outcropping Way
Folsom CA 95630
-

(P-26547)
CAPTAIN MARKETING INC
3577 N Figueroa St, Los Angeles
(90065-2445)
PHONE..................................310 402-9709
EMP: 81
SALES (corp-wide): 8.1MM **Privately
Held**
SIC: 8742 Marketing consulting services
PA: Captain Marketing, Inc.
337 Ne Emerson Ave
Bend OR 97701
888 297-9977

(P-26548)
**CARLETON BOOKER
MARKETING INC**
5042 Wilshire Blvd # 31584, Los Angeles
(90036-4305)
PHONE..................................510 999-1682
Carleton C Booker, *CEO*
EMP: 52
SALES (est): 1.6MM **Privately Held**
SIC: 8742 Marketing consulting services

(P-26549)
CBRE GLOBAL INVESTORS LLC
3501 Jamboree Rd Ste 100, Newport
Beach (92660-2940)
PHONE..................................949 725-8500
Steven Swerdlow, *Principal*
Peter Andrich, *Vice Pres*
Christopher Bates, *Vice Pres*
Jeffrey Calentino, *Vice Pres*
Ian Parker, *Vice Pres*
EMP: 350
SALES (corp-wide): 21.3B **Publicly Held**
SIC: 8742 6531 Management consulting
services; real estate agent, commercial
HQ: Cbre Global Investors, Llc
601 S Figueroa St Ste 49
Los Angeles CA 90017
213 683-4200

(P-26550)
CBRE SERVICES INC
400 S Hope St Ste 25, Los Angeles
(90071-2800)
PHONE..................................213 613-3333
Robert Sulentic, *CEO*

Scott Crawshaw, *Vice Pres*
Debbie Fan, *Vice Pres*
Robert Kinlin, *Vice Pres*
Wade Lord, *Vice Pres*
EMP: 70
SALES (est): 7.5MM
SALES (corp-wide): 21.3B **Publicly Held**
WEB: www.cbrichardellis.com
SIC: 8742 6531 Real estate consultant;
real estate agent, commercial
PA: Cbre Group, Inc.
400 S Hope St Ste 25
Los Angeles CA 90071
213 613-3333

(P-26551)
**CELERITY CONSULTING GROUP
INC (PA)**
2 Gough St Ste 300, San Francisco
(94103-5420)
PHONE..................................415 986-8850
Rachelle Yowell, *CEO*
Christopher Yowell, *President*
Norman Yee, *COO*
Steffani Aranas, *Vice Pres*
Kevin Liu, *Vice Pres*
EMP: 61
SQ FT: 28,000
SALES (est): 14.6MM **Privately Held**
WEB: www.celerityconsulting.net
SIC: 8742 7371 7379 7375 Management
consulting services; management infor-
mation systems consultant; computer
software development & applications;
data processing consultant; on-line data
base information retrieval; data process-
ing service

(P-26552)
CHASE GROUP LLC
Also Called: Center At Parkwest, The
6740 Wilbur Ave, Reseda (91335-5179)
PHONE..................................818 708-3533
Phil Chase, *Branch Mgr*
EMP: 100 **Privately Held**
SIC: 8742 8049 Management consulting
services; nurses & other medical assis-
tants
PA: The Chase Group Llc
3075 E Thousand Oaks Blvd
Thousand Oaks CA 91362

(P-26553)
CHASE GROUP LLC (PA)
3075 E Thousand Oaks Blvd, Thousand
Oaks (91362-3402)
PHONE..................................805 497-7330
Susan Chase,
Elizabeth Casey,
Phillip L Chase,
EMP: 600
SQ FT: 1,200
SALES (est): 55.9MM **Privately Held**
SIC: 8742 General management consult-
ant

(P-26554)
CHATMETER INC
225 Broadway Ste 1700, San Diego
(92101-5015)
PHONE..................................619 795-6262
Collin Holmes, *CEO*
Samuel Dufel, *Software Dev*
Ryan Glovinsky, *Software Dev*
Adrian Lyjak, *Software Dev*
Evan Green, *Opers Mgr*
EMP: 80
SALES (est): 122K **Privately Held**
SIC: 8742 Marketing consulting services

(P-26555)
CHECK DISC LABS
4121 W Vanowen Pl, Burbank
(91505-1131)
PHONE..................................818 847-2255
Jonathan Burk, *General Mgr*
Jeremiah Magan, *Technician*
EMP: 70
SQ FT: 8,000
SALES (est): 3.5MM **Privately Held**
SIC: 8742 Quality assurance consultant

(P-26556)
CITY OF FULLERTON
Maintenance Dept
1580 W Commonwealth Ave, Fullerton
(92833-2728)
PHONE..................................714 738-6897
Robert Savage, *Director*
EMP: 150 **Privately Held**
SIC: 8742 Maintenance management con-
sultant
PA: City Of Fullerton
303 W Commonwealth Ave
Fullerton CA 92832
714 738-6300

(P-26557)
CITY OF IRVINE
Also Called: Dept of Public Works
6427 Oak Cyn, Irvine (92618-5202)
P.O. Box 19575 (92623-9575)
PHONE..................................949 724-7600
Allison Hart, *Manager*
EMP: 70 **Privately Held**
SIC: 8742 9111 8748 7349 Public utilities
consultant; mayors' offices; business con-
sulting; building maintenance services;
lawn & garden services
PA: City Of Irvine
1 Civic Center Plz
Irvine CA 92606
949 724-6000

(P-26558)
CLOUDTRIGGER INC
760 Garden View Ct # 120, Encinitas
(92024-2473)
PHONE..................................858 367-5272
Doug McLean, *Vice Pres*
EMP: 70
SALES (est): 5.3MM **Privately Held**
SIC: 8742 Management consulting serv-
ices

(P-26559)
CMI MANAGEMENT INC
Also Called: Harvey Apartments, The
5640 Santa Monica Blvd # 116, Los Ange-
les (90038-2962)
PHONE..................................323 465-8044
Eric Guefen, *President*
Max Guefen, *Ch of Bd*
EMP: 175
SQ FT: 4,000
SALES (est): 128.6K **Privately Held**
WEB: www.cmimanagement.net
SIC: 8742 Management consulting serv-
ices

(P-26560)
CO-PRODUCTION INTL INC
8716 Sherwood Ter, San Diego
(92154-7718)
PHONE..................................619 429-4344
Enrique Esparza, *President*
Jaime Edgar Esparza, *Corp Secy*
EMP: 2300
SALES: 23MM **Privately Held**
WEB: www.co-production.net
SIC: 8742 Marketing consulting services
PA: Co-Production De Tijuana, S.A. De
C.V.
Blvd. Corredor Tijuana-Rosarito 2000
Tijuana B.C. 22163
-

(P-26561)
CODE FOR AMERICA LABS INC
972 Mission St Fl 5, San Francisco
(94103-2994)
PHONE..................................415 625-9633
Meghan Reilly, *Vice Pres*
Sarat Mayer, *Officer*
Laura Ramos, *Surgery Dir*
Nohl Espenshade, *Office Mgr*
Lou Moore, *CTO*
EMP: 80
SALES: 18.6MM **Privately Held**
SIC: 8742 Marketing consulting services

(P-26562)
**COHEN BROWN MGT GROUP
INC (PA)**
11835 W Olympic Blvd 920e, Los Angeles
(90064-5001)
PHONE..................................310 966-1001
Martin L Cohen, *CEO*

Edward G Brown, *President*
James W Bywater, *Exec VP*
Cohen Herbst, *Vice Pres*
Christopher Phillips, *Vice Pres*
EMP: 60
SQ FT: 5,500
SALES (est): 11.1MM **Privately Held**
WEB: www.cbmg.com
SIC: 8742 Training & development consultant

(P-26563)
COLLEGE TRACK
112 Linden St, Oakland (94607-2538)
PHONE....................510 834-3295
Elissa Salas, *CEO*
Omar Butler, *Exec Dir*
Jonathan Thornton, *Managing Dir*
Maria Rangel, *General Mgr*
Ashika Maharaj, *Office Mgr*
EMP: 191
SALES (est): 12.8MM **Privately Held**
SIC: 8742 School, college, university consultant

(P-26564)
COMPSPEC INC
425 E Colorado St Ste 410, Glendale
(91205-1675)
PHONE....................818 551-4200
Nabil Haddad, *President*
Terri Pina, *Executive*
Shelly Murph, *Marketing Staff*
Shelle Mitchell, *Director*
Stephanie Torres, *Manager*
EMP: 100
SALES (est): 10.9MM **Privately Held**
WEB: www.compspecinc.com
SIC: 8742 7299 Hospital & health services consultant; debt counseling or adjustment service, individuals

(P-26565)
CONFIG CONSULTANTS LLC
Also Called: A5
6800 Koll Center Pkwy # 160, Pleasanton
(94566-7044)
PHONE....................844 226-6344
Vinay Kruttiventi,
EMP: 50
SALES (est): 764.1K **Privately Held**
SIC: 8742 Management consulting services

(P-26566)
COOPERATIVE PERSONNEL SERVICES (PA)
Also Called: CPS Hr Consulting
2450 Del Paso Rd Ste 220, Sacramento
(95834-9664)
PHONE....................916 263-3600
Jerry Greenwell, *CEO*
Tim Howald, *CFO*
Sandy Macdonald-Hopp, *CFO*
Holly Hatada, *Sr Consultant*
Roger Ganse, *Manager*
EMP: 139
SQ FT: 34,000
SALES (est): 31.2MM **Privately Held**
SIC: 8742 Personnel management consultant

(P-26567)
CORPORATE VISIONS INC (PA)
3875 Hopyard Rd Ste 275, Pleasanton
(94588-8527)
PHONE....................415 464-4400
Erik Peterson, *CEO*
Joseph Terry, *President*
Gloria Fan, *CFO*
Mike Finley, *Ch Credit Ofcr*
Whitney Fragoso, *Project Mgr*
EMP: 67 **EST:** 2011
SALES (est): 32.5MM **Privately Held**
SIC: 8742 Marketing consulting services

(P-26568)
CORPORATE VISIONS INC
2705 Avenida De Anita # 29, Carlsbad
(92010-8355)
PHONE....................760 458-0914
Mark Valle, *Principal*
EMP: 77
SALES (corp-wide): 32.5MM **Privately Held**
SIC: 8742 Marketing consulting services

PA: Corporate Visions Inc
3875 Hopyard Rd Ste 275
Pleasanton CA 94588
415 464-4400

(P-26569)
COUNTY OF ALAMEDA
Also Called: Civil Service Commission
1405 Lakeside Dr, Oakland (94612-4306)
PHONE....................510 271-5138
Denise Etonmay, *Director*
Stephen Amano, *Deputy Dir*
Elsie Lum, *Director*
EMP: 60 **Privately Held**
WEB: www.co.alameda.ca.us
SIC: 8742 9441 Human resource consulting services; administration of social & manpower programs
PA: County Of Alameda
1221 Oak St Ste 555
Oakland CA 94612
510 272-6691

(P-26570)
CPE HR INC
9000 W Sunset Blvd # 900, West Hollywood (90069-5801)
PHONE....................310 270-9800
Harold Walt, *CEO*
Faith Branvold, *President*
Grace Drulias, *CFO*
Walt Robinson, *Vice Pres*
Kern Tam, *Human Res Dir*
EMP: 90
SALES (est): 15.8MM **Privately Held**
SIC: 8742 Human resource consulting services

(P-26571)
CPRIME INC (HQ)
107 S B St Ste 200, San Mateo
(94401-3993)
P.O. Box 4777, Foster City (94404-0777)
PHONE....................650 931-1650
Zubin Irani, *CEO*
Shawn Tretter, *Senior Partner*
Ken France, *Vice Pres*
Brandon Huff, *Managing Dir*
Jisha Nambiar, *Technical Staff*
EMP: 57
SALES (est): 22.5MM
SALES (corp-wide): 614.1MM **Privately Held**
SIC: 8742 8331 8748 Business consultant; personnel management consultant; training & development consultant; manpower training; systems engineering consultant, ex. computer or professional
PA: Alten
40 Avenue Andre Morizet
Boulogne-Billancourt 92100
146 056-673

(P-26572)
CREATIVE EVENTS ENTERPRISES
4872 Topanga Canyon Blvd # 406, Woodland Hills (91364-4229)
PHONE....................818 610-7000
Frank Biedka, *President*
Irving Shanske, *Vice Pres*
Arthur Webb, *Vice Pres*
EMP: 170
SALES (est): 7.2MM **Privately Held**
SIC: 8742 7389 7999 Business consultant; convention & show services; picnic ground operation

(P-26573)
CRIME FINDERS INC
710 S Victory Blvd # 205, Burbank
(91502-2498)
PHONE....................877 999-3203
John Akopyan, *CEO*
Vahe Khodabakhshi, *CFO*
Areg Mirzakanian, *Admin Sec*
EMP: 91
SALES: 7MM **Privately Held**
SIC: 8742 Human resource consulting services
PA: Appriss Inc.
9901 Linn Station Rd # 500
Louisville KY 40223

(P-26574)
CROWN GOLF PROPERTIES LP
Also Called: Tustin Ranch Golf Club
12442 Tustin Ranch Rd, Tustin
(92782-1000)
PHONE....................714 730-1611
Steve Plummer, *Manager*
Karen Tucker, *Instructor*
Kyle Herbold, *Supervisor*
EMP: 200
SALES (corp-wide): 92.1MM **Privately Held**
WEB: www.rvrgolf.com
SIC: 8742 7997 7992 Business consultant; membership sports & recreation clubs; public golf courses
PA: Crown Golf Properties, Lp
222 N La Salle St # 2000
Chicago IL 60601
312 395-7701

(P-26575)
CT LIEN SOLUTION
330 N Brand Blvd Ste 700, Glendale
(91203-2336)
PHONE....................818 662-4100
CT Cor System, *Branch Mgr*
EMP: 148
SALES (corp-wide): 4.8B **Privately Held**
SIC: 8742 Management consulting services
HQ: Ct Lien Solutions
2929 Allen Pkwy Ste 3300
Houston TX 77019
713 533-4600

(P-26576)
CUNNINGHAM GROUP INC
5616 Circle View Dr, Bonsall (92003-5301)
PHONE....................303 295-1982
Paul Cunningham, *CEO*
Troy Cunningham, *President*
EMP: 57
SALES (est): 2.8MM **Privately Held**
SIC: 8742 Financial consultant

(P-26577)
CUSTOMER LOYALTY BUILDERS INC
Also Called: Service Quality
1063 Todos Santos, Concord (94522)
PHONE....................888 478-7787
Jeff Kasper, *Officer*
Michael Mendona, *Principal*
EMP: 100
SALES (est): 4.5MM **Privately Held**
SIC: 8742 8211 Marketing consulting services; seminary

(P-26578)
CUSTOMIZED DIST SVCS INC
3355 E Cedar St, Ontario (91761-7632)
PHONE....................909 947-0084
Mark Tuttle, *Branch Mgr*
Melinda Ramirez, *Executive*
EMP: 100
SALES (corp-wide): 91.1MM **Privately Held**
WEB: www.cds3pl.com
SIC: 8742 7319 8741 Transportation consultant; distribution of advertising material or sample services; management services
PA: Customized Distribution Services, Inc.
20 Harry Shupe Blvd
Wharton NJ 07885
973 366-5090

(P-26579)
DEEP FOCUS INC
6922 Hollywood Blvd Fl 10, Hollywood
(90028-6130)
PHONE....................323 790-5340
EMP: 600
SALES (corp-wide): 48MM **Privately Held**
SIC: 8742 8743 Marketing consulting services; promotion service
HQ: Deep Focus, Inc.
261 Madison Ave Fl 4
New York NY 10016
212 792-6800

(P-26580)
DELOITTE CONSULTING LLP
Also Called: Bersin By Deloitte
555 Mission St, San Francisco
(94105-0920)
PHONE....................510 251-4400
Joshua Bersin, *Principal*
Brian Hansen, *Partner*
Julie Hiipakka, *Vice Pres*
Sebnem Tokcan, *Information Mgr*
Webster Claudine, *Marketing Mgr*
EMP: 63
SALES (corp-wide): 5.5B **Privately Held**
SIC: 8742 Financial consultant
HQ: Deloitte Consulting Llp
30 Rockefeller Plz
New York NY 10112
212 492-4000

(P-26581)
DENTISTAT INC
Also Called: Insurance Dentists Amer Idoa
1688 Dell Ave Ste 210, Campbell
(95008-6926)
PHONE....................408 376-0336
Richard H Guenther, *Ch of Bd*
Richard H Guenther DMD, *Ch of Bd*
Bret W Guenther, *President*
Richard L Garwood DDS, *CEO*
Harry J Kaplan, *Corp Secy*
EMP: 65 **EST:** 1968
SQ FT: 7,661
SALES (est): 6.9MM **Privately Held**
WEB: www.dentistat.com
SIC: 8742 8748 Hospital & health services consultant; business consulting

(P-26582)
DEVCOOL INC
5890 Stoneridge Dr # 107, Pleasanton
(94588-5818)
PHONE....................408 372-4313
Sandeep Deokule, *President*
Dipa Rangarajan, *VP Opers*
EMP: 100
SQ FT: 1,400
SALES (est): 782.7K **Privately Held**
SIC: 8742 Management consulting services

(P-26583)
DEVELPMENT DIMENSIONS INTL INC
4160 Dublin Blvd Ste 450, Dublin
(94568-7723)
PHONE....................925 361-4246
Daniel Prachar, *Director*
EMP: 288
SALES (corp-wide): 173.6MM **Privately Held**
SIC: 8742 Training & development consultant
PA: Development Dimensions International, Inc.
1225 Washington Pike
Bridgeville PA 15017
412 257-0600

(P-26584)
DIGITALTHINK INC (DH)
601 Brannan St, San Francisco
(94107-1511)
PHONE....................415 625-4000
Michael W Pope, *President*
Jon Madonna, *Ch of Bd*
Robert J Krolik, *CFO*
Adam D Levy, *Vice Pres*
EMP: 250
SQ FT: 51,000
SALES (est): 15.4MM
SALES (corp-wide): 20B **Publicly Held**
WEB: www.digitalthink.com
SIC: 8742 Marketing consulting services
HQ: Convergys Customer Management Group Inc.
201 E 4th St Bsmt
Cincinnati OH 45202
513 723-6104

(P-26585)
DOWLING ADVISORY GROUP
3579 E Foothill Blvd # 651, Pasadena
(91107-3119)
PHONE....................626 319-1369
James Dowling, *Owner*
EMP: 100

PRODUCTS & SVCS

SALES: 1MM **Privately Held**
SIC: 8742 Business consultant

(P-26586)
DPK CONSULTING
Also Called: Tetra Tech Dpk
605 Market St Ste 800, San Francisco
(94105-3210)
PHONE...........................415 495-7772
Robert W Page, *President*
EMP: 100
SALES (est): 6.5MM
SALES (corp-wide): 2.9B **Publicly Held**
WEB: www.dpkconsulting.com
SIC: 8742 Business consultant
HQ: Ard, Inc.
159 Bank St Ste 300
Burlington VT 05401
802 658-3890

(P-26587)
DRAWBRIDGE INC
479 N Pastoria Ave, Sunnyvale
(94085-4112)
PHONE...........................650 513-2323
Kamakshi Sivaramakrishnan, *CEO*
EMP: 85
SALES (est): 1.5MM
SALES (corp-wide): 125.8B **Publicly
Held**
SIC: 8742 Marketing consulting services
HQ: Linkedin Corporation
1000 W Maude Ave
Sunnyvale CA 94085
650 687-3600

(P-26588)
DUFF & PHELPS LLC
1950 University Ave # 40Q, East Palo Alto
(94303-2250)
PHONE...........................650 798-5500
Greg Franceschi, *Director*
Mike Ramirez, *Sr Associate*
EMP: 65
SALES (corp-wide): 312.4MM **Privately
Held**
SIC: 8742 Financial consultant
PA: Duff & Phelps, Llc
55 E 52nd St Fl 31
New York NY 10055
212 871-2000

(P-26589)
DUFF & PHELPS LLC
350 S Grand Ave Ste 3100, Los Angeles
(90071-3420)
PHONE...........................213 270-2300
EMP: 67
SALES (corp-wide): 97.4MM **Privately
Held**
SIC: 8742
HQ: Duff & Phelps, Llc
55 E 52nd St Fl 31
New York NY 10055
212 871-6777

(P-26590)
EASTERN GOLDFIELDS INC
1660 Hotel Cir N Ste 207, San Diego
(92108-2803)
PHONE...........................619 497-2555
Michael McChesney, *CEO*
EMP: 218
SALES (est): 4.7MM **Privately Held**
SIC: 8742 Management consulting services

(P-26591)
ECORP CONSULTING INC (PA)
2525 Warren Dr, Rocklin (95677-2167)
PHONE...........................916 782-9100
James Stewart, *President*
James D Stewart, *CEO*
Bjorn Gregersen, *CFO*
Peter Balfour, *Vice Pres*
Brant Brechbiel, *Vice Pres*
EMP: 55
SQ FT: 6,950
SALES (est): 17.2MM
SALES (corp-wide): 19MM **Privately
Held**
WEB: www.ecorpconsulting.com
SIC: 8742 8748 Industry specialist con-
sultants; business consulting

(P-26592)
**EDELMAN FINANCIAL ENGINES
LLC (HQ)**
1050 Entp Way Fl 3 Flr 3, Sunnyvale
(94089)
PHONE...........................408 498-6000
Lawrence M Raffone, *President*
John B Bunch, *COO*
John Shoven, *Bd of Directors*
Debra Babbitt, *Officer*
Lewis E Antone Jr, *Exec VP*
EMP: 170 EST: 1996
SQ FT: 80,995
SALES (est): 432.4MM **Privately Held**
WEB: www.financialadvice.com
SIC: 8742 6282 6411 Financial consult-
ant; investment advice; pension & retire-
ment plan consultants
PA: Financial Engines Edelman, L.P.
4000 Legato Rd Fl 9
Fairfax VA 22033
800 706-3916

(P-26593)
EK HEALTH SERVICES INC (PA)
992 S De Anza Blvd Ste 10, San Jose
(95129-2777)
PHONE...........................408 973-0888
Eunhee Kim, *President*
Douglas Benner, *Chief Mktg Ofcr*
Joseph N Desantis, *Vice Pres*
Jake A Reason, *Vice Pres*
Paulo Franca, *CTO*
EMP: 53
SQ FT: 6,500
SALES (est): 12MM **Privately Held**
WEB: www.ekhealth.com
SIC: 8742 Hospital & health services con-
sultant; human resource consulting serv-
ices; personnel management consultant

(P-26594)
ENBIO CORP
150 E Olive Ave Ste 212, Burbank
(91502-1850)
PHONE...........................818 953-9976
Arthur Zenian, *CEO*
Bahman Hemmati, *Technician*
Edgar Acob, *Manager*
◆ EMP: 142
SQ FT: 1,500
SALES: 7.8MM **Privately Held**
SIC: 8742 Hospital & health services con-
sultant

(P-26595)
ENSIGHTEN INC (HQ)
226 Airport Pkwy Ste 390, San Jose
(95110-1026)
PHONE...........................650 249-4712
Josh Manion, *CEO*
Tim Benhart, *Officer*
Ian Woolley, *Officer*
Jacob Favre, *Vice Pres*
James Niehaus, *Vice Pres*
EMP: 65 EST: 2012
SALES (est): 28.3MM **Privately Held**
SIC: 8742 8741 Management consulting
services; management services

(P-26596)
**ENTERPRISE EVENTS GROUP
INC**
950 Northgate Dr Ste 100, San Rafael
(94903-3430)
PHONE...........................415 499-4444
Matt Gillam, *CEO*
Dennis Borowski, *Info Tech Mgr*
Roy Williams, *Info Tech Mgr*
Jared McCluskey, *Business Anlyst*
Jodie Moore, *Project Mgr*
EMP: 150
SQ FT: 18,000
SALES (est): 32.2MM **Privately Held**
WEB: www.eegweb.com
SIC: 8742 8743 Incentive or award pro-
gram consultant; promotion service

(P-26597)
**EPCM PROF SVC PARTNERS
LLC**
2017 Palo Verde Ave, Long Beach
(90815-3300)
PHONE...........................562 936-1000
F P Kallina, *Mng Member*

Frederick Paul Kallina, *Mng Member*
EMP: 52 EST: 2008
SQ FT: 5,000
SALES (est): 1.2MM **Privately Held**
SIC: 8742 Management consulting serv-
ices

(P-26598)
EPIXEL SOLUTIONS ○
1001 Bayhill Dr, San Bruno (94066-3062)
PHONE...........................650 616-4488
Sajin Rajan, *Principal*
EMP: 80 EST: 2019
SALES (est): 1.2MM **Privately Held**
SIC: 8742 Marketing consulting services

(P-26599)
EVERWISE CORPORATION
2 Embarcadero Ctr Fl 8, San Francisco
(94111-3833)
PHONE...........................888 250-6219
EMP: 76
SALES (corp-wide): 7.9MM **Privately
Held**
SIC: 8742 Training & development consult-
ant
PA: Everwise Corporation
18 W 21st St Fl 7
New York NY 10010
646 807-9114

(P-26600)
EXCEL MANAGED CARE DISA
3840 Watt Ave Bldg C, Sacramento
(95821-2640)
PHONE...........................916 944-7185
Brenda Smith, *President*
Steve Smetana, *Vice Pres*
EMP: 125
SQ FT: 3,600
SALES (est): 10.6MM **Publicly Held**
WEB: www.excelmanagedcare.com
SIC: 8742 Hospital & health services con-
sultant
HQ: Genex Services, Llc
440 E Swedesford Rd Ste 1
Wayne PA 19087
610 964-5100

(P-26601)
**EXCELLIGENCE LEARNING
CORP**
Also Called: Discount School Supply
20 Ryan Ranch Rd Ste 200, Monterey
(93940-6439)
P.O. Box 6013, Carol Stream IL (60197-
6013)
PHONE...........................800 482-5846
EMP: 100
SALES (corp-wide): 204.1MM **Privately
Held**
SIC: 8742 Administrative services consult-
ant
PA: Excelligence Learning Corporation
20 Ryan Ranch Rd Ste 200
Monterey CA 93940
831 333-2000

(P-26602)
EXIT REALTY CONSULTANTS
3018 E Service Rd Ste 104, Ceres
(95307-6423)
PHONE...........................209 484-8075
EMP: 120
SALES (corp-wide): 2.1MM **Privately
Held**
SIC: 8742 Management consulting serv-
ices
PA: Exit Realty Consultants
600 E Main St Ste 300
Turlock CA 95380
209 668-2525

(P-26603)
**EXPRESSWORKS
INTERNATIONAL LLC (PA)**
2410 Camino Ramon Ste 167, San Ramon
(94583-4328)
PHONE...........................925 244-0900
John Quereto, *President*
Debby Bernardi, *Info Tech Mgr*
Samantha Leach,
Tony Harter, *Senior Mgr*
Rick Walters, *Sr Consultant*
EMP: 130
SQ FT: 12,000

SALES (est): 9.4MM **Privately Held**
WEB: www.expressworks.com
SIC: 8742 Marketing consulting services

(P-26604)
EXULT INC
121 Innovation Dr Ste 200, Irvine
(92617-3094)
P.O. Box 6300, Newport Beach (92658-
6300)
PHONE...........................949 856-8800
James C Madden, *Ch of Bd*
Jim Aselta, *Partner*
Kevin Campbell, *President*
John Adams, *CFO*
Robert E Ball,
EMP: 2424
SQ FT: 22,000
SALES (est): 78.3MM
SALES (corp-wide): 23.4B **Privately Held**
SIC: 8742 Human resource consulting
services
HQ: Alight (Us), Llc
200 E Randolph St Ll3
Chicago IL 60601

(P-26605)
FDSI LOGISTICS LLC
27680 Avenue Mentry 2, Valencia
(91355-1200)
PHONE...........................818 971-3300
David Kolchins, *Vice Pres*
Dee Weller, *Marketing Staff*
John Hudson, *Director*
EMP: 75
SALES: 13MM
SALES (corp-wide): 145.5B **Publicly
Held**
WEB: www.fdsi.com
SIC: 8742 4731 Transportation consultant;
freight transportation arrangement
PA: Cardinal Health, Inc.
7000 Cardinal Pl
Dublin OH 43017
614 757-5000

(P-26606)
FIMAC INC
26300 La Alameda Ste 200, Mission Viejo
(92691-8306)
PHONE...........................949 359-6100
James T Assali, *CEO*
Scott Heitmann, *COO*
Michael Shea, *CFO*
EMP: 72
SALES (est): 2.3MM **Privately Held**
SIC: 8742 Marketing consulting services

(P-26607)
**FINANCIAL HEALTHCARE
SERVICES**
690 E Green St Ste 300, Pasadena
(91101-2121)
PHONE...........................626 356-7950
Esther Yatman, *President*
Lon Yatman, *Treasurer*
EMP: 50
SQ FT: 10,000
SALES (est): 3.5MM **Privately Held**
WEB: www.uai-unifi.com
SIC: 8742 Administrative services consult-
ant

(P-26608)
**FIRST CAPITOL CONSULTING
INC**
3530 Wilshire Blvd # 1460, Los Angeles
(90010-2334)
PHONE...........................213 382-1115
Robert Sheen, *President*
EMP: 73
SALES (est): 2.8MM **Privately Held**
WEB: www.fccila.net
SIC: 8742 Management consulting serv-
ices

(P-26609)
FIRST PAGE SAGE LLC
2250 Union St, San Francisco
(94123-3900)
PHONE...........................415 624-3526
Evan Bailyn, *Mng Member*
Mikayla Reine, *Executive Asst*
Bradley Bailyn,
EMP: 51

SALES (est): 83.2K **Privately Held**
SIC: **8742** Marketing consulting services

(P-26610)
FISHERIES RESOURCE VLNTR CORPS
109 Stanford Ln, Seal Beach (90740-2533)
PHONE..................................562 596-9261
Thomas J Walsh, *President*
EMP: 113
SALES (est): 133.2K **Privately Held**
SIC: **8742** Business planning & organizing services

(P-26611)
FOOD MANAGEMENT ASSOCIATES INC
22349 La Palma Ave # 115, Yorba Linda (92887-3810)
PHONE..................................714 694-2828
Richard Warmolts, *President*
EMP: 50
SQ FT: 1,800
SALES (est): 7.2MM **Privately Held**
SIC: **8742** Business consultant

(P-26612)
FOSTERING EXECUTIVE LEADERSHIP
4790 Irvine Blvd 105-432, Irvine (92620-1973)
PHONE..................................949 651-6250
Tammy Wong, *President*
Chris Martell, *Opers Staff*
EMP: 99
SALES (est): 4MM **Privately Held**
SIC: **8742** Training & development consultant

(P-26613)
FRANK GATES SERVICE COMPANY
1107 Investment Blvd, El Dorado Hills (95762-5736)
PHONE..................................916 934-0812
Chanteo Kvigne, *Manager*
EMP: 70
SALES (corp-wide): 97.3MM **Privately Held**
WEB: www.fgsc.com
SIC: **8742** Management consulting services
HQ: The Frank Gates Service Company
5000 Bradenton Ave # 100
Dublin OH 43017
614 793-8000

(P-26614)
FREIGHT MANAGEMENT INC
Also Called: F M I
2900 E La Palma Ave, Anaheim (92806-2616)
PHONE..................................714 632-1440
Robert J Walters, *President*
Heidi Calamusa, *Vice Pres*
Tim Ponder, *Vice Pres*
Angela Shackford, *Vice Pres*
EMP: 53
SQ FT: 9,000
SALES (est): 60.6MM **Privately Held**
SIC: **8742** Transportation consultant

(P-26615)
FTI CONSULTING INC
50 California St Ste 1900, San Francisco (94111-4620)
PHONE..................................415 283-4200
Jerry Keeler, *Manager*
Micah Trilling, *Managing Dir*
Michael WEI, *Managing Dir*
Brandon Beal, *Finance*
EMP: 80
SALES (corp-wide): 2B **Publicly Held**
SIC: **8742** Management consulting services
PA: Fti Consulting, Inc.
555 12th St Nw Ste 3
Washington DC 20004
202 312-9100

(P-26616)
FURTHER PRODUCTS INC
431 Cherry Dr, Pasadena (91105-2152)
P.O. Box 1118, South Pasadena (91031-1118)
PHONE..................................323 839-1246
Marchall Dostal, *President*
EMP: 50
SALES (est): 2.4MM **Privately Held**
SIC: **8742** Marketing consulting services

(P-26617)
FUTUREDONTICS INC (HQ)
Also Called: 1-800 Dentist
6060 Center Dr Fl 7, Los Angeles (90045-1596)
PHONE..................................310 215-6400
Michael Turner, *CEO*
Bret McAllister, *CIO*
EMP: 84
SQ FT: 35,000
SALES (est): 34.2MM
SALES (corp-wide): 3.9B **Publicly Held**
WEB: www.futuredontics.com
SIC: **8742** Marketing consulting services
PA: Dentsply Sirona Inc.
221 W Philadelphia St
York PA 17401
717 845-7511

(P-26618)
GALLUP INC
Also Called: Gallup Organization, The
18300 Von Karman Ave, Irvine (92612-1057)
PHONE..................................949 474-2700
Kelly Aylward, *Partner*
Craig Kamins, *Associate*
EMP: 50
SALES (corp-wide): 191.7MM **Privately Held**
SIC: **8742** Marketing consulting services
PA: Gallup, Inc.
901 F St Nw Ste 400
Washington DC 20004
202 715-3030

(P-26619)
GAVIN DE BECKER & ASSOCIATES
11684 Ventura Blvd # 440, Studio City (91604-2699)
PHONE..................................818 760-4213
Gavin De Becker, *President*
Brad Short, *Technician*
Christopher Asmussen, *Analyst*
Daniel Simmons, *Analyst*
Denise Du, *Accountant*
EMP: 180
SQ FT: 1,600
SALES (est): 32.1MM **Privately Held**
SIC: **8742** Business consultant

(P-26620)
GLOBAL MANAGEMENT COMPANY LLC
3150 E Pico Blvd, Los Angeles (90023-3632)
PHONE..................................323 261-8114
Sandra Berg,
EMP: 100
SALES (est): 2.5MM **Privately Held**
SIC: **8742** Management consulting services

(P-26621)
GLOBAL WORK GROUP LLC
Also Called: Global Realty Group
17224 San Fernando, Granada Hills (91344)
PHONE..................................424 220-9994
Geoff Mills, *Mng Member*
Jill Henson, *Treasurer*
EMP: 75
SALES: 30MM **Privately Held**
SIC: **8742** 7389 Materials mgmt. (purchasing, handling, inventory) consultant;

(P-26622)
GOETZMAN GROUP INC (PA)
21700 Oxnard St Ste 1540, Woodland Hills (91367-3644)
PHONE..................................818 595-1112
Greg Goetzman, *President*
EMP: 75

SQ FT: 4,500
SALES (est): 8MM **Privately Held**
WEB: www.goetzmangroup.com
SIC: **8742** Management consulting services; accounting, auditing & bookkeeping

(P-26623)
GORILLA TECH AMERICAS INC
2678 Bishop Dr Ste 290, San Ramon (94583)
PHONE..................................925 365-1161
Carlo Tortora, *President*
EMP: 99
SALES (est): 6MM **Privately Held**
SIC: **8742** Marketing consulting services

(P-26624)
GPS FLYERS
527 Prospect Ave, Hermosa Beach (90254-4940)
PHONE..................................951 588-7777
Patrick Antrim, *Owner*
EMP: 51
SQ FT: 3,000
SALES: 1.1MM **Privately Held**
SIC: **8742** Marketing consulting services

(P-26625)
GRAND VIEW RESEARCH INC
201 Spear St Ste 1100, San Francisco (94105-6164)
PHONE..................................415 349-0058
Brian Haven, *CEO*
Dipti Pachhade, *Executive*
Thomas Philip, *Executive*
Sakshi Bedi, *Research*
Poorva Chaudhari, *Research*
EMP: 50
SALES (est): 4MM **Privately Held**
SIC: **8742** Marketing consulting services

(P-26626)
GRAPHIC ORB INC
8687 Melrose Ave Ste 8, West Hollywood (90069-5746)
PHONE..................................310 967-2350
John Thompson, *President*
Denis Adair, *Vice Pres*
EMP: 64 EST: 1970
SQ FT: 35,000
SALES (est): 4.3MM **Privately Held**
WEB: www.graphicorb.com
SIC: **8742** Marketing consulting services

(P-26627)
GREAT DESTINATIONS INC
25510 Commercentre Dr, Lake Forest (92630-8855)
PHONE..................................949 667-9401
Andrew Gennuso, *President*
Nishant Machado, *Vice Pres*
Sarahi Maldonado, *Office Mgr*
EMP: 95
SQ FT: 3,000
SALES: 9MM **Publicly Held**
SIC: **8742** Marketing consulting services
PA: Marriott Vacations Worldwide Corporation
6649 Westwood Blvd
Orlando FL 32821

(P-26628)
GREENSPIRE LLC
Also Called: Greenspire Construction
3130 Wilshire Blvd # 200, Santa Monica (90403-2352)
PHONE..................................310 477-7686
David Murray, *CEO*
Andy Baker, *President*
Robert Beihl, *CFO*
Tyler Harikawa, *Manager*
EMP: 50
SQ FT: 4,000
SALES (est): 1.7MM **Privately Held**
SIC: **8742** 7389 Marketing consulting services;

(P-26629)
HAMILTON PARTNERS
1301 Shoreway Rd Ste 250, Burlingame (94010)
PHONE..................................650 347-8800
John Hamilton, *President*
EMP: 55

SALES (est): 293.1K **Privately Held**
SIC: **8742** Training & development consultant

(P-26630)
HARRIS MYCFO INC
2200 Geng Rd Ste 100, Palo Alto (94303-3358)
PHONE..................................480 348-7725
Michael Montogomery, *President*
John Benevides, *President*
Craig Rawlins, *President*
Ross Kari, *CFO*
Phyllis Kempt, *Executive*
EMP: 90
SALES (est): 16.2MM **Privately Held**
SIC: **8742** Financial consultant

(P-26631)
HDR ENGINEERING INC
591 Camno De La Reina 3, San Diego (92108)
PHONE..................................858 712-8400
Bill Bennett, *Branch Mgr*
EMP: 50
SALES (corp-wide): 1.4B **Privately Held**
SIC: **8742** 8711 Management consulting services; engineering services
HQ: Hdr Engineering, Inc.
1917 S 67th St
Omaha NE 68106
402 399-1000

(P-26632)
HDR ENGINEERING INC
350 S Grand Ave Ste 2900, Los Angeles (90071-3406)
PHONE..................................626 584-1700
Al Korth, *Manager*
EMP: 130
SALES (corp-wide): 1.4B **Privately Held**
SIC: **8742** 8711 Management consulting services; engineering services
HQ: Hdr Engineering, Inc.
1917 S 67th St
Omaha NE 68106
402 399-1000

(P-26633)
HDR ENGINEERING INC
201 California St # 1500, San Francisco (94111-5002)
PHONE..................................415 546-4200
Michael Orr, *Manager*
EMP: 99
SALES (corp-wide): 1.4B **Privately Held**
SIC: **8742** 8711 Management consulting services; engineering services
HQ: Hdr Engineering, Inc.
1917 S 67th St
Omaha NE 68106
402 399-1000

(P-26634)
HDR ENGINEERING INC
2365 Iron Point Rd # 300, Folsom (95630-8711)
PHONE..................................916 817-4700
Brent Felker, *Branch Mgr*
EMP: 86
SALES (corp-wide): 1.4B **Privately Held**
SIC: **8742** Construction project management consultant
HQ: Hdr Engineering, Inc.
1917 S 67th St
Omaha NE 68106
402 399-1000

(P-26635)
HEALTH EDUC ECONOMIC DEVLPMNT
304 Coral Reef Rd, Alameda (94501-5929)
PHONE..................................510 604-6143
Leeda Rashid, *President*
EMP: 99
SALES (est): 2.7MM **Privately Held**
SIC: **8742** Hospital & health services consultant

(P-26636)
HIS MANNA INC
Also Called: Workforce
150 Felker St Ste B, Santa Cruz (95060-2849)
P.O. Box 1527 (95061-1527)
PHONE..................................831 423-5515

P
R
O
D
U
C
T
S

&

S
V
C
S

Gordon Agrella, *President*
Carolyn Agrella, *Vice Pres*
Baisy Alvarez, *Admin Asst*
EMP: 200 **EST:** 1972
SQ FT: 4,200
SALES (est): 12.2MM **Privately Held**
WEB: www.hismanna.com
SIC: 8742 7549 7349 Management consulting services; automotive maintenance services; building maintenance, except repairs

(P-26637)
HORIZON ACTUARIAL SERVICES LLC
5200 Lankershim Blvd, North Hollywood (91601-3155)
PHONE..............................818 691-2000
Larry H Weitzner,
Ron Stonehill, *Associate*
EMP: 92
SALES (corp-wide): 17.9MM **Privately Held**
SIC: 8742 Compensation & benefits planning consultant
PA: Horizon Actuarial Services Llc
8601 Georgia Ave Ste 700
Silver Spring MD 20910
240 247-4600

(P-26638)
HORNBLOWER YACHTS INC
2825 5th Ave, San Diego (92103-6326)
PHONE..............................619 234-8687
Jim Unger, *Branch Mgr*
EMP: 160
SALES (corp-wide): 125.4MM **Privately Held**
WEB: www.hornbloweryachts.com
SIC: 8742 7999 7389 7299 Restaurant & food services consultants; pleasure boat rental; convention & show services; wedding chapel, privately operated
PA: Hornblower Yachts, Llc
On The Embarcadero Pier 3 St Pier
San Francisco CA 94111
415 788-8866

(P-26639)
HUMETRIX INC
1155 Camino Del Mar Ste 5, Del Mar (92014-2605)
PHONE..............................858 259-8987
Bettina Experton, *President*
Claudia M Ellison, *Vice Pres*
EMP: 50
SALES (est): 4.3MM **Privately Held**
WEB: www.humetrix.com
SIC: 8742 5047 3841 Hospital & health services consultant; medical & hospital equipment; surgical & medical instruments

(P-26640)
ICF CONSULTING GROUP INC
101 Lucas Valley Rd # 249, San Rafael (94903-1700)
PHONE..............................703 934-3000
Berlin Brett, *Branch Mgr*
EMP: 509
SALES (corp-wide): 1.3B **Publicly Held**
SIC: 8742 Business consultant
HQ: Icf Consulting Group, Inc.
9300 Lee Hwy Ste G130
Fairfax VA 22031
703 934-3000

(P-26641)
ICF JONES & STOKES INC
1 Ada Ste 100, Irvine (92618-5339)
PHONE..............................949 333-6600
David Freytag, *Manager*
EMP: 99
SALES (corp-wide): 1.3B **Publicly Held**
SIC: 8742 8748 Business consultant; business consulting
HQ: Icf Jones & Stokes, Inc
9300 Lee Hwy
Fairfax VA 22031
703 934-3000

(P-26642)
IMPULSA BUS ACCELERATOR LLC
23180 Ravensbury Ave, Los Altos Hills (94024-6428)
PHONE..............................650 924-5010
Leandro Margulis, *Principal*
Fernando Sepulveda,
EMP: 150
SQ FT: 1,000
SALES (est): 4MM **Privately Held**
SIC: 8742 Management consulting services; business consultant

(P-26643)
INDUCTIVE AUTOMATION LLC
90 Blue Ravine Rd, Folsom (95630-4715)
PHONE..............................800 266-7798
Steve Hechtman, *President*
Wendi-Lynn Hechtman, *Vice Pres*
Katharina Jeschke,
Jason Waits, *Principal*
Don Pearson, *Security Dir*
EMP: 100 **EST:** 2011
SALES (est): 313.6K **Privately Held**
SIC: 8742 5734 Automation & robotics consultant; computer software & accessories

(P-26644)
INGENIO LLC
182 Howard St Unit 826, San Francisco (94105-1611)
PHONE..............................415 992-8218
Devina Whitley, *Mng Member*
Natalie Rusnak, *Partner*
EMP: 57
SALES (est): 5.2MM **Privately Held**
SIC: 8742 Management consulting services

(P-26645)
INKLING SYSTEMS INC
343 Sansome St 8, San Francisco (94104-1303)
PHONE..............................415 975-4420
Jeff Carr, *CEO*
Rob Cromwell, *President*
Charles Macinnis, *President*
Matt Macinnis, *Founder*
Kim Desmond, *Vice Pres*
EMP: 66
SALES (est): 11.5MM **Privately Held**
SIC: 8742 Management consulting services
PA: Marlin Equity Partners, Llc
338 Pier Ave
Hermosa Beach CA 90254

(P-26646)
INSPERITY INC
1440 Bridgegate Dr # 200, Diamond Bar (91765-3935)
PHONE..............................909 569-1000
Richard Cleek, *General Mgr*
Matt Hess, *District Mgr*
Cynthia James, *Opers Staff*
Nick Sisca, *Consultant*
Victor Scott, *Supervisor*
EMP: 100
SALES (corp-wide): 3.8B **Publicly Held**
WEB: www.administaff.com
SIC: 8742 Human resource consulting services
PA: Insperity, Inc.
19001 Crescent Springs Dr
Kingwood TX 77339
281 358-8986

(P-26647)
INTELISYS INC
1318 Redwood Way Ste 120, Petaluma (94954-6542)
PHONE..............................800 615-8330
Jay Bradley, *President*
EMP: 80 **Publicly Held**
SIC: 8742 Marketing consulting services
HQ: Intelisys, Inc.
6 Logue Ct
Greenville SC 29615
800 944-2432

(P-26648)
INTER CON SECURITY INC
2801 Camino Del Rio S 300h, San Diego (92108-3800)
PHONE..............................619 523-0291
Rick Hernadez, *President*
Gary Mariner, *Officer*
Frederick Serio, *Officer*
Bruce Whitaker, *Officer*
Dean Lavergne, *Security Dir*
EMP: 50
SALES (est): 2.7MM **Privately Held**
WEB: www.interconsecurity.com
SIC: 8742 7381 Industry specialist consultants; security guard service

(P-26649)
INTERNATIONAL BUS MCHS CORP
Also Called: IBM
4000 Executive Pkwy # 300, San Ramon (94583-4257)
PHONE..............................925 277-5000
Lynn Dail, *Branch Mgr*
Troy Reed, *Senior Mgr*
EMP: 186
SALES (corp-wide): 79.5B **Publicly Held**
WEB: www.ibm.com
SIC: 8742 Sales (including sales management) consultant
PA: International Business Machines Corporation
1 New Orchard Rd Ste 1 # 1
Armonk NY 10504
914 499-1900

(P-26650)
INTERNET MARKETING ASSN INC
10 Mar Del Rey, San Clemente (92673-2761)
PHONE..............................949 443-9300
Sinan Kanatsiz, *Principal*
Rachel Reenders, *Exec Dir*
EMP: 65
SALES (est): 4.1MM **Privately Held**
SIC: 8742 Marketing consulting services

(P-26651)
INTERSTATE ELECTRONICS CORP
Also Called: Human Resources
708 E Vermont Ave, Anaheim (92805-5611)
PHONE..............................714 758-0500
EMP: 600
SALES (corp-wide): 6.8B **Publicly Held**
SIC: 8742 Human resource consulting services
HQ: Interstate Electronics Corporation
602 E Vermont Ave
Anaheim CA 92805
714 758-0500

(P-26652)
INTRAVAS INC
Also Called: Review Boost
6300 Yarrow Dr, Carlsbad (92011-1542)
PHONE..............................760 650-4040
Guillermo Rivas, *CEO*
Pamela Dahl, *Accounts Mgr*
EMP: 65
SALES (est): 3.9MM **Privately Held**
SIC: 8742 Marketing consulting services

(P-26653)
ISYS SOLUTIONS INC
2601 Saturn St Ste 302, Brea (92821-6702)
PHONE..............................714 521-7656
Chris Loumakis, *CEO*
Rebekah Bitar, *Nurse*
Carolyn Lowd, *Nurse*
EMP: 69
SALES (est): 9.3MM **Privately Held**
WEB: www.isyscal.com
SIC: 8742 Hospital & health services consultant

(P-26654)
ITA GROUP INC
455 Market St Ste 1450, San Francisco (94105-2442)
PHONE..............................415 277-3200
Deborah Ebsen, *General Mgr*
Mary Fogle, *Program Mgr*

EMP: 119
SALES (corp-wide): 145.9MM **Privately Held**
SIC: 8742 Incentive or award program consultant
PA: Ita Group, Inc
4600 Westown Pkwy Ste 100
West Des Moines IA 50266
515 326-3400

(P-26655)
J P CONSULTING
4690 E 2nd St Ste 3, Benicia (94510-1008)
PHONE..............................707 747-4800
Jody Hoberson, *Co-Owner*
Robert Perkey, *Co-Owner*
EMP: 50
SALES (est): 3.6MM **Privately Held**
SIC: 8742 Management consulting services

(P-26656)
JACK NADEL INC (PA)
Also Called: Jack Nadel International
8701 Bellanca Ave, Los Angeles (90045-4411)
P.O. Box 8342, Pasadena (91109-8342)
PHONE..............................310 815-2600
Craig Nadel, *CEO*
Robert Kritzler, *CFO*
Jack Nadel, *Chairman*
Debbie Abergel, *Senior VP*
Craig Reese, *Senior VP*
EMP: 70 **EST:** 1953
SQ FT: 30,000
SALES (est): 106MM **Privately Held**
WEB: www.nadel.com
SIC: 8742 5199 Incentive or award program consultant; gifts & novelties

(P-26657)
JACOBS PROJECT MANAGEMENT CO
300 Frank H Ogawa Plz, Oakland (94612-2037)
PHONE..............................510 457-2436
Steve Paquette, *Manager*
Frank Joyce, *Contract Mgr*
EMP: 95
SALES (est): 2.5MM
SALES (corp-wide): 14.9B **Publicly Held**
SIC: 8742 Management consulting services
PA: Jacobs Engineering Group Inc.
1999 Bryan St Ste 1200
Dallas TX 75201
214 583-8500

(P-26658)
JACOBUS CONSULTING INC
15375 Barranca Pkwy B202, Irvine (92618-2213)
P.O. Box 50127 (92619-0127)
PHONE..............................949 727-0720
Sandra Jacobs, *President*
Arizdelsy Vega, *Executive Asst*
Kathy Goodwin, *Human Resources*
Andy Chen, *Representative*
EMP: 50
SQ FT: 1,800
SALES (est): 5.2MM **Privately Held**
SIC: 8742 Hospital & health services consultant

(P-26659)
JB UPLAND LTD LIABILITY CO
9087 Arrow Rte Ste 140, Rancho Cucamonga (91730-4431)
PHONE..............................909 944-5456
Mary R McDonagh,
EMP: 50
SALES (est): 2.4MM **Privately Held**
SIC: 8742 Marketing consulting services

(P-26660)
JIMS STEEL SUPPLY LLC
3530 Buck Owens Blvd, Bakersfield (93308-4920)
P.O. Box 191 (93302-0191)
PHONE..............................661 324-6514
Greg Boylan,
EMP: 50 **EST:** 2017
SALES: 15MM **Privately Held**
SIC: 8742 Business consultant

(P-26661)
JNR INC
19900 Macarthur Blvd # 700, Irvine
(92612-8416)
PHONE.....................................949 476-2788
James Jalet III, *CEO*
Desiree Barto, *CEO*
Luann Jalet, *COO*
Greg Moody, *CFO*
Christopher Fitkin, *Software Dev*
EMP: 60
SQ FT: 15,000
SALES (est): 12MM **Privately Held**
WEB: www.jnrinc.com
SIC: 8742 7389 4724 Incentive or award program consultant; convention & show services; tourist agency arranging transport, lodging & car rental

(P-26662)
JOBVITE INC (PA)
1300 S El Camino Real # 400, San Mateo
(94402-2970)
PHONE.....................................650 376-7200
Aman Brar, *CEO*
John Wonkenbach, *CFO*
Kimberley Kasper, *Chief Mktg Ofcr*
Rachel Bitte, *Officer*
Bill Loller, *Officer*
EMP: 78
SALES (est): 22.6MM **Privately Held**
SIC: 8742 Human resource consulting services

(P-26663)
JUMPSTART DIGITAL MKTG INC (DH)
Also Called: Jumpstart Automotive Media
550 Kearny St Ste 500, San Francisco
(94108-2595)
PHONE.....................................415 844-6336
Nick Matarazzo, *CEO*
Denise Rasmussen, *Pub Rel Mgr*
EMP: 80
SQ FT: 3,600
SALES (est): 2.1MM
SALES (corp-wide): 8.3B **Privately Held**
WEB: www.jumpstartdm.com
SIC: 8742 7311 Marketing consulting services; advertising agencies
HQ: Hearst Communications Inc.
300 W 57th St
New York NY 10019
212 649-2000

(P-26664)
K & S TOWING & TRANSPORT
Also Called: K & S Auto, Truck & Tractor
2780 Willow Pass Rd, Bay Point
(94565-6603)
PHONE.....................................925 709-0759
Khurram Shah, *Owner*
EMP: 55
SQ FT: 10,000
SALES: 5.6MM **Privately Held**
WEB: www.kandstowing.com
SIC: 8742 7299 Transportation consultant; personal item care & storage services

(P-26665)
KABLER CONSTRUCTION SVCS INC
467 Miller Ave, Mill Valley (94941-2941)
PHONE.....................................415 888-8812
Sophia Kabler Cowley, *President*
John Kabler, *Vice Pres*
EMP: 50
SALES: 536K **Privately Held**
SIC: 8742 1771 8741 Construction project management consultant; concrete work; construction management

(P-26666)
KENSHOO INC (HQ)
22 4th St Fl 7, San Francisco (94103-3141)
PHONE.....................................877 536-7462
Yoav Izhar-Prato, *CEO*
Timothy Doherty, *Partner*
Ben Watson, *Partner*
Shirley Grill-Rachman, *COO*
Sarit Firon, *CFO*
EMP: 110

SALES (est): 18.6MM
SALES (corp-wide): 651.3K **Privately Held**
SIC: 8742 Marketing consulting services
PA: Kenshoo Ltd
30 Habarzel
Tel Aviv-Jaffa 69710
732 862-507

(P-26667)
KINGS GARDEN LLC
Also Called: Kings Garden Royal Deliveries
3540 N Anza Rd, Palm Springs
(92262-1606)
PHONE.....................................760 275-4969
Lauri Kibby, *Mng Member*
Michael King, *Mng Member*
EMP: 180 **EST:** 2018
SALES (est): 4.8MM **Privately Held**
SIC: 8742 Marketing consulting services

(P-26668)
KORN FERRY (PA)
1900 Avenue Of The Stars # 2600, Los Angeles (90067-4507)
PHONE.....................................310 552-1834
Gary D Burnison, *President*
Ilene Gochman, *Senior Partner*
Michael Lamb, *Senior Partner*
John Atherton, *Partner*
David Barnes, *Partner*
EMP: 136 **EST:** 1969
SALES: 1.9B **Publicly Held**
WEB: www.kornferry.com
SIC: 8742 7361 Management consulting services; executive placement

(P-26669)
LABMED PARTNERS
5000 Birch St, Newport Beach
(92660-2127)
PHONE.....................................949 242-9925
EMP: 50
SALES (est): 1.3MM **Privately Held**
SIC: 8742

(P-26670)
LANCASHIRE GROUP INCORPORATED
Also Called: Tlg
37053 Cherry St Ste 210, Newark
(94560-3782)
P.O. Box 1138 (94560-6138)
PHONE.....................................510 792-9384
Ian McDonnell, *President*
Johnny Lambert, *COO*
John Lambert, *Senior VP*
Elaine Whelan, *Controller*
EMP: 279
SQ FT: 2,400
SALES (est): 25.5MM **Privately Held**
WEB: www.tlg-inc.com
SIC: 8742 Industry specialist consultants

(P-26671)
LBA INC (PA)
Also Called: Layton-Belling & Associates
3347 Michelson Dr Ste 200, Irvine
(92612-0687)
PHONE.....................................949 833-0400
Philip Belling, *CEO*
Steve Layton, *President*
Tom Rutherford, *CFO*
Kim Cart, *Property Mgr*
EMP: 120
SALES (est): 13.5MM **Privately Held**
SIC: 8742 Real estate consultant

(P-26672)
LEAF COMMERCIAL CAPITAL INC
1100 Town & Country Rd, Orange
(92868-4600)
PHONE.....................................866 219-7924
Rich Vohra, *Vice Pres*
EMP: 50 **Publicly Held**
SIC: 8742 Financial consultant
HQ: Leaf Commercial Capital, Inc.
2005 Market St Fl 14
Philadelphia PA 19103
800 819-5556

(P-26673)
LEEKILPATRICK MANAGEMENT INC
Also Called: Management Success
324 S Myrtle Ave, Monrovia (91016-2849)
PHONE.....................................818 500-9631
Bill Kilpatrick, *President*
EMP: 60
SQ FT: 18,200
SALES (est): 6.8MM **Privately Held**
SIC: 8742 7538 Business consultant; general automotive repair shops

(P-26674)
LEGACY MARKETING GROUP (PA)
2090 Marina Ave, Petaluma (94954-6714)
PHONE.....................................707 778-8638
Lynda R Pitts, *CEO*
Preston Pitts, *President*
Chris Eaken, *Vice Pres*
Dayna Wells, *Vice Pres*
Brenda Putnam, *Web Dvlpr*
EMP: 215
SALES (est): 13.9MM **Privately Held**
WEB: www.legacynet.com
SIC: 8742 Marketing consulting services

(P-26675)
LEK CONSULTING LLC
1100 Glendon Ave Ste 2100, Los Angeles
(90024-3592)
PHONE.....................................310 209-9800
Sherice Lenons, *Manager*
Bill Frack, *Vice Pres*
Dan Schechter, *Vice Pres*
Chelsey Kobuch, *Admin Asst*
John Iacoviello, *Director*
EMP: 60 **Privately Held**
WEB: www.lek.com
SIC: 8742 8748 Business consultant; business consulting
PA: L.E.K. Consulting, Llc
75 State St Ste 1901
Boston MA 02109

(P-26676)
LINARDOS ENTERPRISES INC
75 Broadway, San Francisco (94111-1422)
PHONE.....................................415 644-0827
Peter Lionardo, *President*
Ashley Pease, *Office Mgr*
EMP: 58
SQ FT: 800
SALES: 5.7MM **Privately Held**
SIC: 8742 General management consultant

(P-26677)
LOS ANGLES CLIPPERS FOUNDATION
Also Called: Lac Club
1111 S Figueroa St # 1100, Los Angeles
(90015-1300)
PHONE.....................................213 742-7555
Donald Sterling, *President*
EMP: 55
SALES (est): 1.3MM **Privately Held**
SIC: 8742 Sales (including sales management) consultant

(P-26678)
LOTUS INTERWORKS INC
10801 National Blvd # 500, Los Angeles
(90064-4152)
PHONE.....................................310 442-3330
Bhaskarpilai Gopinath, *Ch of Bd*
EMP: 200
SQ FT: 10,000
SALES (est): 13.3MM **Privately Held**
WEB: www.lotusinterworks.com
SIC: 8742 Management consulting services

(P-26679)
LPL HOLDINGS INC (HQ)
4707 Executive Dr, San Diego
(92121-3091)
PHONE.....................................858 450-9606
Mark Casady, *CEO*
Christopher Defrank, *Senior VP*
Jason Crawford, *Vice Pres*
Dewitt Draper, *Vice Pres*
Al Lopez, *Vice Pres*

EMP: 146
SALES (est): 384MM **Publicly Held**
WEB: www.lpl.com
SIC: 8742 Financial consultant; industrial hygiene consultant

(P-26680)
LYNUP CORPORATION
16875 W Bernardo Dr # 110, San Diego
(92127-1670)
PHONE.....................................858 207-4610
Parvin Garbo-Inkumsah, *President*
Aaron J Gaeir, *Vice Pres*
EMP: 60 **EST:** 2010
SALES (est): 5.1MM **Privately Held**
SIC: 8742 Marketing consulting services

(P-26681)
M E NOLLKAMPER INC (PA)
940 Manor Way, Corona (92882-7979)
PHONE.....................................951 737-9300
Milton Nollkamper, *President*
EMP: 50
SALES (est): 3MM **Privately Held**
SIC: 8742 8711 Public utilities consultant; consulting engineer

(P-26682)
M F SALTA CO INC (PA)
Also Called: Atlas Advertising
20 Executive Park Ste 150, Irvine
(92614-4732)
PHONE.....................................562 421-2512
Mike Salta, *President*
James Smith, *Treasurer*
EMP: 70
SALES (est): 3.6MM **Privately Held**
SIC: 8742 Management consulting services

(P-26683)
MAJESTIC TERMINAL SERVICES INC
9568 Archibald Ave # 100, Rancho Cucamonga (91730-5744)
PHONE.....................................909 390-1210
Shirley Chiu, *Vice Pres*
EMP: 86
SALES (corp-wide): 1.4MM **Privately Held**
SIC: 8742 Human resource consulting services
PA: Majestic Terminal Services, Inc.
15127 Main St E Ste 104p
Sumner WA 98390
253 862-1269

(P-26684)
MALCO SERVICES INC
3703 E Melville Way, Anaheim
(92806-2122)
PHONE.....................................714 630-0194
Duane Malone, *President*
Jack Bryant, *CTO*
EMP: 100
SQ FT: 15,831
SALES: 4MM **Privately Held**
SIC: 8742 Maintenance management consultant

(P-26685)
MANAGEMENT TRUST ASSN INC
12607 Hiddencreek Way R, Cerritos
(90703-2146)
PHONE.....................................562 926-3372
Christie Alviso, *Administration*
EMP: 116 **Privately Held**
SIC: 8742 8741 Management consulting services; business management
PA: The Management Trust Association Inc
15661 Red Hill Ave # 201
Tustin CA 92780

(P-26686)
MANSION HOSPITALITY SERVICES
3410 Westover St, McClellan (95652-1005)
PHONE.....................................916 643-6222
Russell A Dazzio, *Chairman*
Roland Moritz, *Corp Secy*
EMP: 60

SALES (est): 2.2MM **Privately Held**
SIC: 8742 Management consulting services

(P-26687)
MAPP DIGITAL US LLC
3655 Nobel Dr Ste 500, San Diego
(92122-1051)
PHONE..............................619 295-1856
Steve Warren, *CEO*
Jonah Sulak, *President*
Claire Long, *CFO*
Eric Hinkle, *Chairman*
Matthew Langie, *Chief Mktg Ofcr*
EMP: 125 EST: 2000
SALES (est): 12.3MM **Privately Held**
WEB: www.bluehornet.com
SIC: 8742 Marketing consulting services
PA: Marlin Equity Partners, Llc
338 Pier Ave
Hermosa Beach CA 90254

(P-26688)
MARCUS BUCKINGHAM COMPANY
8350 Wilshire Blvd # 200, Beverly Hills
(90211-2327)
PHONE..............................323 302-9810
Marcus Buckingham, *CEO*
Christian Gomez, *President*
EMP: 60
SALES (est): 7.9MM
SALES (corp-wide): 14.1B **Publicly Held**
SIC: 8742 Human resource consulting services
PA: Automatic Data Processing, Inc.
1 Adp Blvd Ste 1 # 1
Roseland NJ 07068
973 974-5000

(P-26689)
MARINER LLC
Also Called: Mariner Wealth Advisors
11512 El Camino Real # 370, San Diego
(92130-3025)
PHONE..............................858 795-2100
Paul Executive, *Branch Mgr*
EMP: 125 **Privately Held**
SIC: 8742 Management consulting services
PA: Mariner, Llc
5700 W 112th St Ste 200
Leawood KS 66211

(P-26690)
MARKETBRIDGE CORP
601 Montgomery St Ste 650, San Francisco
(94111-2608)
PHONE..............................240 752-1800
Ashok Nayyar, *Branch Mgr*
EMP: 62 **Privately Held**
SIC: 8742 Marketing consulting services
PA: Marketbridge Corp.
4800 Montgomery Ln # 500
Bethesda MD 20814

(P-26691)
MARKETING PROFESSIONALS INC
5100 E La Palma Ave # 116, Anaheim
(92807-2081)
PHONE..............................714 578-0500
Joseph L Smith, *President*
Cynthia A Simms, *CFO*
George M Schnitzer, *Chairman*
EMP: 350
SQ FT: 900
SALES (est): 16.7MM **Privately Held**
WEB: www.marketingprofessionals.org
SIC: 8742 7319 Marketing consulting services; retail trade consultant; display advertising service

(P-26692)
MARKSYS LLC
3725 Cincinnati Ave # 200, Rocklin
(95765-1220)
PHONE..............................916 745-4883
EMP: 60
SQ FT: 45,000
SALES: 34MM **Privately Held**
SIC: 8742

(P-26693)
MARKSYS HOLDINGS LLC
3725 Cincinnati Ave # 200, Rocklin
(95765-1220)
PHONE..............................916 745-4883
Tabrez Rajani, *Mng Member*
EMP: 60
SQ FT: 45,000
SALES (est): 881.9K **Privately Held**
SIC: 8742 Marketing consulting services

(P-26694)
MATERIALS MARKETING
250 Baker St Ste 100, Costa Mesa
(92626-4574)
PHONE..............................949 729-9881
John Cina, *Manager*
EMP: 100
SALES (est): 4.9MM **Privately Held**
SIC: 8742 Marketing consulting services

(P-26695)
MATT CONSTRUCTION CORPORATION (PA)
9814 Norwalk Blvd Ste 100, Santa Fe Springs (90670-2997)
PHONE..............................562 903-2277
Paul J Matt, *CEO*
Alan B Matt, *Corp Secy*
Michael Fedorchek, *Vice Pres*
James Muenzer, *Vice Pres*
Robert Welch, *Vice Pres*
EMP: 131
SQ FT: 21,000
SALES (est): 47.5MM **Privately Held**
WEB: www.mattconstruction.com
SIC: 8742 Construction project management consultant

(P-26696)
MAXIMUS INC
Also Called: Maximus CA Healthy Family
625 Coolidge Dr Ste 100, Folsom
(95630-3197)
PHONE..............................916 673-2175
John Antifino, *Principal*
Joaquin Moreno,
EMP: 70
SALES (corp-wide): 2.4B **Publicly Held**
WEB: www.maxinc.com
SIC: 8742 Business consultant
PA: Maximus, Inc.
1891 Metro Center Dr
Reston VA 20190
703 251-8500

(P-26697)
MAXWELL PETERSEN ASSOCIATES
Also Called: Dynamic Chiropractic
13950 Milton Ave Ste 200, Westminster
(92683-2939)
PHONE..............................714 230-3150
Donald M Petersen, *President*
Evelyn Petersen, *Payroll Mgr*
EMP: 50
SQ FT: 2,000
SALES (est): 5.4MM **Privately Held**
WEB: www.mpamedia.com
SIC: 8742 Business consultant

(P-26698)
MCB-CJS LLC
5312 Bolsa Ave, Huntington Beach
(92649-1051)
PHONE..............................714 230-3600
Joan Heid, *Partner*
Chet Seto, *Partner*
David Dowell, *Finance*
EMP: 99
SQ FT: 70,000
SALES (est): 2.3MM **Privately Held**
SIC: 8742 Management consulting services

(P-26699)
MCCLELLAN BUSINESS PARK LLC
Also Called: Mp Holdings
3140 Peacekeeper Way, McClellan
(95652-2508)
PHONE..............................916 965-7100
Larry Kelley, *President*
Jay Hecklively, *Exec VP*
Debra Compton, *Senior VP*

Tiffany Garcia, *Senior VP*
Ken Giannotti, *Senior VP*
EMP: 99 EST: 1999
SQ FT: 22,000
SALES (est): 21MM **Privately Held**
WEB: www.mcclellanpark.com
SIC: 8742 Real estate consultant

(P-26700)
MCINTYRE
14680 Wicks Blvd, San Leandro
(94577-6716)
PHONE..............................510 614-5890
Jo Farsight, *Owner*
EMP: 96
SALES (est): 1.2MM **Privately Held**
SIC: 8742 Manufacturing management consultant

(P-26701)
MCKINSEY & COMPANY INC
2000 Avenue Of The Stars # 800, Los Angeles (90067-4714)
PHONE..............................424 249-1000
John Durat, *General Mgr*
Bruce Simpson, *Chief Mktg Ofcr*
Eduardo Hernandez, *Data Proc Staff*
Roger Roberts, *Finance*
Anne Colleran, *Human Res Mgr*
EMP: 50
SALES (corp-wide): 2.7B **Privately Held**
WEB: www.mckinsey.com
SIC: 8742 Marketing consulting services
PA: Mckinsey & Company, Inc.
55 E 52nd St Fl 16
New York NY 10055
212 446-7000

(P-26702)
MCKINSEY & COMPANY INC
555 California St # 4800, San Francisco
(94104-1779)
PHONE..............................415 981-0250
Gary Pinkus, *Manager*
Michael Bloch, *Senior Partner*
Kenneth Bonheure, *Senior Partner*
Tarek Elmasry, *Senior Partner*
Brendan Gaffey, *Senior Partner*
EMP: 300
SALES (corp-wide): 2.7B **Privately Held**
WEB: www.mckinsey.com
SIC: 8742 Marketing consulting services
PA: Mckinsey & Company, Inc.
55 E 52nd St Fl 16
New York NY 10055
212 446-7000

(P-26703)
MCKINSEY & COMPANY INC
3075 Hansen Way Bldg A, Palo Alto
(94304-1025)
PHONE..............................650 494-6262
Jon Duane, *Manager*
Kelly Kramer, *Info Tech Mgr*
Rob Linden, *Director*
Simon London, *Director*
Abhijit Mahindroo, *Consultant*
EMP: 75
SALES (corp-wide): 2.7B **Privately Held**
WEB: www.mckinsey.com
SIC: 8742 Marketing consulting services
PA: Mckinsey & Company, Inc.
55 E 52nd St Fl 16
New York NY 10055
212 446-7000

(P-26704)
MEDICAL MANAGEMENT CONS INC
Also Called: MMC
6046 Cornerstone Ct W, San Diego
(92121-4758)
PHONE..............................858 587-0609
Rahmani, *Manager*
EMP: 4950
SALES (corp-wide): 71.4MM **Privately Held**
WEB: www.mmchr.com
SIC: 8742 Hospital & health services consultant
PA: Medical Management Consultants, Inc.
8150 Beverly Blvd
Los Angeles CA 90048
310 659-3835

(P-26705)
MEDICAL RECEIVABLES SOLUTIONS
Also Called: M R S
101 W American Canyon Rd, American Canyon (94503-1162)
PHONE..............................707 980-6733
Aleshia L Hunter, *President*
EMP: 50
SALES (est): 7.2MM **Privately Held**
SIC: 8742 Business consultant

(P-26706)
MEDICAL SPECIALTIES MANAGERS
Also Called: Medical Specialty Billing
1 City Blvd W Ste 1100, Orange
(92868-3647)
PHONE..............................714 571-5000
Barry Haberman, *President*
Uri Klugman, *CFO*
Randy Brooks, *Vice Pres*
EMP: 115
SQ FT: 29,000
SALES (est): 17.5MM **Privately Held**
WEB: www.msmnet.com
SIC: 8742 8721 Hospital & health services consultant; billing & bookkeeping service

(P-26707)
MEDSPHERE SYSTEMS CORPORATION (PA)
1903 Wright Pl Ste 120, Carlsbad
(92008-6584)
PHONE..............................760 692-3700
Kenneth W Kizer MD MPH, *Ch of Bd*
Ronald L Gue PH D, *President*
Zubin Emsley, *President*
Irv H Lichtenwald, *CEO*
Irv Lichtenwald, *CEO*
EMP: 95
SALES (est): 17.6MM **Privately Held**
WEB: www.medsphere.com
SIC: 8742 Hospital & health services consultant

(P-26708)
MERCER (US) INC
777 S Figueroa St # 2400, Los Angeles
(90017-5800)
PHONE..............................213 346-2200
Nancy McLean, *Manager*
EMP: 200
SALES (corp-wide): 14.9B **Publicly Held**
SIC: 8742 Compensation & benefits planning consultant
HQ: Mercer (Us) Inc.
1166 Ave Of The Americ
New York NY 10036
212 345-7000

(P-26709)
MERCER (US) INC
Also Called: Mercer Health & Benefits
4 Embarcadero Ctr Lbby 4 # 4, San Francisco (94111-4112)
PHONE..............................415 743-8700
Jerry Murphy, *Manager*
Gary W Blank, *Principal*
Kenia Casarreal, *Principal*
Beverly Croydon, *Principal*
Cheryl V Doege, *Principal*
EMP: 250
SALES (corp-wide): 14.9B **Publicly Held**
SIC: 8742 Compensation & benefits planning consultant
HQ: Mercer (Us) Inc.
1166 Ave Of The Americ
New York NY 10036
212 345-7000

(P-26710)
MERCER (US) INC
17901 Von Karman Ave # 1100, Irvine
(92614-6297)
PHONE..............................949 222-1300
Kathy Spear, *Manager*
Heather Cushnie, *Executive Asst*
Anca De Maio, *Director*
Eric Dupont, *Consultant*
EMP: 100
SALES (corp-wide): 14.9B **Publicly Held**
SIC: 8742 Compensation & benefits planning consultant; personnel management consultant

HQ: Mercer (Us) Inc.
1166 Ave Of The Americ
New York NY 10036
212 345-7000

(P-26711)
MERIDIAN KNWLDGE SOLUTIONS LLC (DH)
80 Iron Pont Cir Ste 100, Folsom (95630)
PHONE...................913 985-9625
Jonna Ward, *CEO*
Steve Carpenter, *Vice Pres*
EMP: 90
SQ FT: 32,481
SALES (est): 10.5MM **Privately Held**
WEB: www.meridianksi.com
SIC: 8742 Training & development consult-
ant
HQ: Visionary Integration Professionals, Llc
80 Iron Point Cir Ste 100
Folsom CA 95630
916 985-9625

(P-26712)
MERIT TECHNOLOGIES LLC
Also Called: MTI
10509 Vista Sorrento Pkwy # 420, San
Diego (92121-2743)
PHONE...................858 623-9800
Donald Wang PHD, *Mng Member*
Steeve Higgins,
▲ EMP: 60
SQ FT: 3,500
SALES (est): 4.5MM **Privately Held**
SIC: 8742 3589 1629 Construction proj-
ect management consultant; sewage &
water treatment equipment; water treat-
ment equipment, industrial; waste water &
sewage treatment plant construction

(P-26713)
MESA COUNSELLING
850 E Foothill Blvd, Rialto (92376-5230)
PHONE...................909 421-9301
Sherwin Farr, *General Mgr*
EMP: 50
SALES (est): 1.8MM **Privately Held**
SIC: 8742 Management consulting serv-
ices

(P-26714)
METRON INCORPORATED
12250 El Camino Real # 260, San Diego
(92130-2226)
PHONE...................858 792-8904
EMP: 50
SALES (corp-wide): 39.9MM **Privately
Held**
SIC: 8742 8731 8733 8711
PA: Metron, Incorporated
1818 Library St Ste 600
Reston VA 20190
703 467-5641

(P-26715)
MEYERS RESEARCH LLC
675 Hartz Ave, Danville (94526-3838)
PHONE...................925 362-1028
Stephen Sun, *Consultant*
EMP: 75
SALES (corp-wide): 11.6MM **Privately
Held**
SIC: 8742 Real estate consultant
PA: Meyers Research, Llc
3200 Bristol St Ste 640
Costa Mesa CA 92626
714 619-7800

(P-26716)
**MF SERVICES COMPANY LLC
(HQ)**
4350 Von Karman Ave # 400, Newport
Beach (92660-2007)
PHONE...................949 474-5800
Paul Merage, *Mng Member*
Richard Merage,
EMP: 60
SALES (est): 2.4MM
SALES (corp-wide): 133.7K **Privately
Held**
SIC: 8742 Financial consultant
PA: Mig Capital, Llc
660 Newport Center Dr # 450
Newport Beach CA 92660
949 474-5800

(P-26717)
**MICHAELSON CONNOR & BOUL
(PA)**
5312 Bolsa Ave, Huntington Beach
(92649-1051)
PHONE...................714 230-3600
Joan Heid, *President*
Firmin Boul, *Corp Secy*
Michael Ryan, *Vice Pres*
Pam Santos, *Manager*
EMP: 100
SQ FT: 12,500
SALES (est): 12.9MM **Privately Held**
WEB: www.mcbreo.com
SIC: 8742 Real estate consultant

(P-26718)
**MIDLAND EXPRESS CREDIT
LLC**
2037 W Bullard Ave # 316, Fresno
(93711-1200)
PHONE...................800 961-3904
Walter Daniels, *President*
EMP: 52
SALES (est): 1.4MM **Privately Held**
SIC: 8742 Marketing consulting services

(P-26719)
MILLENNIA HOLDINGS INC
Also Called: Mellennia Holdings
3731 Wilshire Blvd # 618, Los Angeles
(90010-2876)
PHONE...................213 252-1230
Hiroki Tarui, *CEO*
Chugo Rionie, *CFO*
Chie Kawauchi, *Director*
EMP: 60
SALES (est): 8.4MM **Privately Held**
WEB: www.mhiholdings.com
SIC: 8742 Hospital & health services con-
sultant

(P-26720)
MINDLANCE INC
10679 Westview Pkwy Fl 2, San Diego
(92126-2961)
PHONE...................858 433-9298
EMP: 145
SALES (corp-wide): 200.4MM **Privately
Held**
SIC: 8742 Human resource consulting
services
PA: Mindlance Inc.
1095 Morris Ave Unit 101a
Union NJ 07083
201 386-5400

(P-26721)
MLSLISTINGS INC
Also Called: RE Infolink
740 Kifer Rd, Sunnyvale (94086-5121)
PHONE...................408 874-0200
Gerald J Harrison, *President*
Renee Friel, *Office Admin*
Michael Dowdle, *Analyst*
Sara Sullivan, *Analyst*
Al Mendoza, *Broker*
EMP: 58 EST: 2007
SALES: 14MM **Privately Held**
SIC: 8742 Real estate consultant

(P-26722)
MODERN HR INC
9000 W Sunset Blvd # 900, West Holly-
wood (90069-5804)
PHONE...................310 270-9800
Harold Walt, *CEO*
Faith Branvold, *President*
Grace Drulias, *CFO*
EMP: 400
SALES: 1MM **Privately Held**
SIC: 8742 Human resource consulting
services

(P-26723)
MORRIS & WILLNER PARTNERS
Also Called: Mw Partners
201 Sandpointe Ave # 200, Santa Ana
(92707-5749)
PHONE...................949 705-0682
Divya Pyreddy, *CEO*
Keith Lippert, *Partner*
Michael Willner, *Managing Prtnr*
Jeffrey Skarvan, *Vice Pres*
Richard Low, *General Mgr*

EMP: 100
SALES (est): 923.2K **Privately Held**
SIC: 8742 Management consulting serv-
ices

(P-26724)
**MOTOR VEHICLE SOFTWARE
CORP (PA)**
29901 Agoura Rd, Agoura Hills
(91301-2513)
PHONE...................818 706-1949
Donald E Armstrong, *President*
Myrtle Scotland, *Executive*
Don McNamara, *General Mgr*
Kathryn Jewell, *Technical Staff*
Luciana Fincher, *Accounting Mgr*
EMP: 74
SALES (est): 18MM **Privately Held**
SIC: 8742 Management consulting serv-
ices

(P-26725)
MUNISERVICES LLC (DH)
Also Called: Avenu Muniservices
7625 N Palm Ave Ste 108, Fresno
(93711-5785)
PHONE...................800 800-8181
Steve Roberts, *President*
Doug Jensen, *Vice Pres*
Jamie N Xiong, *Executive*
Kelli Parker, *Business Anlyst*
Linda Lecuyer, *Technology*
EMP: 113
SQ FT: 16,000
SALES (est): 15.1MM
SALES (corp-wide): 40.1MM **Privately
Held**
WEB: www.muniservices.com
SIC: 8742 Industry specialist consultants
HQ: Avenu Insights & Analytics, Llc
555 Madison Ave Fl 16
New York NY 10022
757 519-9300

(P-26726)
MV MEDICAL MANAGEMENT
1860 Colo Blvd Ste 200, Los Angeles
(90041)
PHONE...................323 257-7637
Eva Vargas, *President*
Daniel E Vargas Jr, *COO*
Alma Moreno, *Treasurer*
Evy Vargas, *Admin Sec*
EMP: 60
SQ FT: 7,400
SALES (est): 8.9MM **Privately Held**
WEB: www.mvmedical.com
SIC: 8742 Management consulting serv-
ices

(P-26727)
MW2 CONSULTING LLC
981 Manor Way, Los Altos (94024-5622)
PHONE...................408 573-6310
Michael Morris,
Alice Harmon,
Uwe Wienkauf,
EMP: 85
SQ FT: 5,700
SALES (est): 4.7MM **Privately Held**
WEB: www.mw2consulting.com
SIC: 8742 Management consulting serv-
ices

(P-26728)
**N COMPASS INTERNATIONAL
INC**
Also Called: Ncompass International
8223 Santa Monica Blvd, West Hollywood
(90046-5912)
PHONE...................323 785-1700
Donna Direnzo Graves, *CEO*
Kae Erickson, *COO*
Paul Ioakim, *Account Dir*
EMP: 138
SQ FT: 20,000
SALES (est): 28.2MM **Privately Held**
WEB: www.ncompassinternational.com
SIC: 8742 Marketing consulting services

(P-26729)
**NAN MCKAY AND ASSOCIATES
INC**
1810 Gillespie Way # 202, El Cajon
(92020-0920)
PHONE...................619 258-1855
Nan McKay, *President*
John McKay, *CEO*
Raymond Adair, *Vice Pres*
Dorian Jenkins, *Vice Pres*
James McKay, *Vice Pres*
EMP: 58
SQ FT: 14,000
SALES: 30MM **Privately Held**
WEB: www.nanmckay.com
SIC: 8742 7371 2731 Training & develop-
ment consultant; computer software de-
velopment; textbooks: publishing &
printing

(P-26730)
**NATIONAL FNCL SRVCS
CNSRTM LLC**
3161 Los Prados St, San Mateo
(94403-2013)
PHONE...................650 572-2872
EMP: 99
SALES (est): 2.6MM **Privately Held**
SIC: 8742

(P-26731)
NAVIGANT CONSULTING INC
300 S Grand Ave Ste 3850, Los Angeles
(90071-3174)
PHONE...................213 452-4516
Mike Wallace, *Vice Pres*
Rudina Seseri, *Bd of Directors*
Kathleen Walsh, *Bd of Directors*
Jeffrey Yingling, *Bd of Directors*
EMP: 100
SALES (corp-wide): 743.6MM **Privately
Held**
WEB: www.navigantconsulting.com
SIC: 8742 Business consultant
PA: Navigant Consulting, Inc.
150 N Riverside Plz # 2100
Chicago IL 60606
312 573-5600

(P-26732)
NBC CONSULTING INC
Also Called: Pacific Health and Welness
2110 Artesia Blvd Ste 323, Redondo Beach
(90278-3073)
PHONE...................310 798-5000
Neal M Bychek, *President*
Robin Bychek, *CFO*
EMP: 100
SALES: 1MM **Privately Held**
WEB: www.nbcconsulting.com
SIC: 8742 Hospital & health services con-
sultant

(P-26733)
NEARDATA INC
Also Called: Neardata Systems
4502 Dyer St Ste 103, La Crescenta
(91214-2854)
PHONE...................818 249-2469
Samuel S Chilingurian, *President*
Sam Chillingurian, *COO*
EMP: 76
SQ FT: 5,600
SALES (est): 6.5MM **Privately Held**
SIC: 8742 7371 Management consulting
services; computer software development

(P-26734)
NET4SITE LLC
3350 Scott Blvd Bldg 34b, Santa Clara
(95054-3105)
PHONE...................408 427-3004
C K Singla,
Roger Diaz, *Business Dir*
EMP: 78
SQ FT: 3,000
SALES: 10MM **Privately Held**
SIC: 8742 Management information sys-
tems consultant

(P-26735)
NETLINE CORPORATION (PA)
750 University Ave # 200, Los Gatos
(95032-7697)
PHONE...................408 374-4200

Robert S Alvin, *CEO*
Jeff Possiel, *Partner*
Werner Mansfeld, *President*
David Fortino, *Vice Pres*
Jayaram Kalpathy, *Vice Pres*
EMP: 52
SALES (est): 11.4MM **Privately Held**
WEB: www.netline.com
SIC: 8742 Marketing consulting services

(P-26736)
NEWMARK & COMPANY RE INC
Also Called: Newmark Grubb Knight Frank
1551 N Tustin Ave Ste 300, Santa Ana
(92705-8638)
PHONE...................714 667-8252
EMP: 60
SALES (corp-wide): 2B **Publicly Held**
SIC: 8742 6531 Real estate consultant;
real estate agent, commercial; housing
authority operator
HQ: Newmark & Company Real Estate, Inc.
125 Park Ave
New York NY 10017
212 372-2000

(P-26737)
NEXT IMAGE MEDICAL INC (PA)
3390 Carmel Mountain Rd # 150, San
Diego (92121-1055)
PHONE...................858 847-9185
Elizabeth Griggs, *CEO*
EMP: 60
SALES (est): 8.4MM **Privately Held**
SIC: 8742 Business consultant

(P-26738)
NEXT MANAGEMENT LLC
Also Called: Next Management Co
8447 Wilshire Blvd # 301, Beverly Hills
(90211-3226)
PHONE...................323 782-0038
Faith Kates, *President*
EMP: 50
SALES (corp-wide): 12.4MM **Privately
Held**
SIC: 8742 8021 Management consulting
services; offices & clinics of dentists
PA: Next Management, Llc
15 Watts St Fl 6
New York NY 10013
212 925-5100

(P-26739)
NFP PROPERTY & CASUALTY
SVCS
Also Called: Nfp Advisors
2450 Tapo St, Simi Valley (93063-2454)
PHONE...................805 579-1900
Mary Lue, *CEO*
EMP: 50
SALES (est): 115K **Privately Held**
SIC: 8742 Financial consultant

(P-26740)
NI KI CRUZ LLC
5255 Stevens Creek Blvd, Santa Clara
(95051-6664)
PHONE...................408 332-7616
Carlos R Cruz Jr, *Partner*
EMP: 99
SALES (est): 58.9K **Privately Held**
SIC: 8742 Marketing consulting services

(P-26741)
NINES RESTAURANT
Also Called: Bunkers Grille
100 Summerset Dr, Brentwood
(94513-6426)
PHONE...................925 516-3413
James A Shoemaker, *President*
Sally Shoemaker, *Vice Pres*
EMP: 60
SQ FT: 14,000
SALES (est): 4.2MM **Privately Held**
WEB: www.bunkersgrille.com
SIC: 8742 Management consulting serv-
ices

(P-26742)
NPS MARKETING
3381 Sage Rose Ln, Placerville
(95667-5452)
P.O. Box 2392 (95667-2392)
PHONE...................916 941-5510
Scott Becker, *Owner*

EMP: 300
SALES: 2.5MM **Privately Held**
SIC: 8742 7389 Marketing consulting
services;

(P-26743)
OHL LLC
1162 Cherry Ave, San Bruno (94066-2302)
PHONE...................650 872-3399
Deborah Dodds, *Principal*
EMP: 206
SALES (est): 2.3MM
SALES (corp-wide): 4.2MM **Privately
Held**
SIC: 8742 4225 4226 4731 Management
consulting services; general warehousing
& storage; special warehousing & stor-
age; freight transportation arrangement
HQ: Geodis Logistics Llc
7101 Executive Center Dr # 333
Brentwood TN 37027
615 401-6400

(P-26744)
OM FOOD SEJAL ENTERPRISES
INC
449 W Allen Ave Ste 111, San Dimas
(91773-1483)
PHONE...................626 712-3138
Pete J Patel, *CEO*
EMP: 52
SALES (est): 112.8K **Privately Held**
SIC: 8742 Restaurant & food services con-
sultants

(P-26745)
OMEGA 2 ALPHA SERVICES LLC
Also Called: O2a
935 Riverside Ave Ste 23, Paso Robles
(93446-2605)
PHONE...................805 610-2249
Daniel McGee,
Robert Cidemiller, *Mng Member*
EMP: 53 **EST:** 2014
SALES (est): 1.1MM **Privately Held**
SIC: 8742 Construction project manage-
ment consultant

(P-26746)
OMEGA WASTE MANAGEMENT
INC
Also Called: Omega Management Services
957 Colusa St, Corning (96021-2224)
P.O. Box 495 (96021-0495)
PHONE...................530 824-1890
Robert O'Conner, *President*
Karen O'Conner, *Vice Pres*
Dan O'Connor, *Vice Pres*
Karen Oconnor, *Vice Pres*
Laurie Spindler, *Human Res Mgr*
EMP: 68
SQ FT: 6,000
SALES (est): 12.6MM **Privately Held**
WEB: www.omegawastemanagement.com
SIC: 8742 Management consulting serv-
ices

(P-26747)
ONE CALL MEDICAL INC
8501 Fllbrook Ave Ste 100, Canoga Park
(91304)
PHONE...................818 346-8700
Julie Moss, *Manager*
Barbara Hess, *Executive Asst*
EMP: 67 **Privately Held**
SIC: 8742 Compensation & benefits plan-
ning consultant
PA: One Call Medical, Inc.
841 Prudential Dr Ste 900
Jacksonville FL 32207

(P-26748)
ONE10 LLC
180 Montgomery St, San Francisco
(94104-4205)
PHONE...................415 398-3534
EMP: 100
SALES (corp-wide): 1.8B **Privately Held**
SIC: 8742
HQ: One10 Llc
100 N 6th St Ste 700b
Minneapolis MN 55403
763 445-3000

(P-26749)
ONE10 LLC
735 Battery St Fl 1, San Francisco
(94111-1535)
PHONE...................415 844-2200
Fax: 415 844-2248
EMP: 70
SALES (corp-wide): 1.8B **Privately Held**
SIC: 8742
HQ: One10 Llc
100 N 6th St Ste 700b
Minneapolis MN 55403
763 445-3000

(P-26750)
OPERAM INC
1041 N Formosa Ave 500, West Hollywood
(90046-6703)
PHONE...................855 673-7261
Johnny Wong, *Principal*
Samuel Hafer, *Opers Staff*
EMP: 84
SQ FT: 23,000
SALES (est): 65.9K **Privately Held**
SIC: 8742 Marketing consulting services

(P-26751)
OPERATIX INC
111 N Market St Ste 300, San Jose
(95113-1116)
PHONE...................408 332-5796
Graham Curme, *CEO*
Aurelien Mottier, *Vice Pres*
EMP: 65 **EST:** 2013
SALES (est): 3.2MM **Privately Held**
SIC: 8742 Marketing consulting services

(P-26752)
P H S MANAGEMENT GROUP
(PA)
721 N Eckhoff St, Orange (92868-1005)
PHONE...................714 547-7551
Kevin O Lewand, *President*
EMP: 50
SALES (est): 4.7MM **Privately Held**
SIC: 8742 Hospital & health services con-
sultant

(P-26753)
P K B INVESTMENTS INC
Also Called: Home Instead Senior Care
745 E Locust Ave Ste 105, Fresno
(93720-3000)
PHONE...................559 243-1224
David Phillips, *President*
April Cavanaugh, *CFO*
Patrick Cavanaugh, *Admin Sec*
EMP: 140
SALES (est): 1.9MM **Privately Held**
SIC: 8742 8322 Management consulting
services; individual & family services

(P-26754)
PACIFIC COMPOSITE MTLS INC
9655 Gran Rdge Dr Ste 200, San Diego
(92123)
PHONE...................310 956-5357
Takashi Oshima, *CEO*
EMP: 50
SALES (est): 1.1MM **Privately Held**
SIC: 8742 Business consultant

(P-26755)
PACIFIC SECURED EQUITIES
INC
Also Called: Intercare Holdings Insur Svcs
6020 West Oaks Blvd # 100, Rocklin
(95765-5472)
P.O. Box 579, Roseville (95661-0579)
PHONE...................916 677-2500
George W McCleary Jr, *CEO*
Agnes Hoeberling, *COO*
Don Nguyen, *CFO*
Richard Rothman, *Exec VP*
Kathleen Cooper, *Senior VP*
EMP: 300
SQ FT: 21,000
SALES (est): 548.9K **Privately Held**
WEB: www.intercareins.com
SIC: 8742 Administrative services consult-
ant

(P-26756)
PANDORA MARKETING LLC
Also Called: Timeshare Compliance
26970 Aliso Viejo Pkwy # 150, Aliso Viejo
(92656-2683)
PHONE...................800 705-6856
William Wilson,
Irene Dasalla, *Vice Pres*
EMP: 75 **EST:** 2016
SALES (est): 3MM **Privately Held**
SIC: 8742 Marketing consulting services

(P-26757)
PARSONS BRNCKRHOFF
HLDINGS INC
2329 Oakes Dr Ste 200, Sacramento
(95833)
PHONE...................916 567-2500
Michelle Poe, *Technology*
Vickie Wheeler, *Senior Engr*
EMP: 70
SALES (corp-wide): 307MM **Privately
Held**
SIC: 8742 Management consulting serv-
ices
PA: Parsons Brinckerhoff Holdings Inc.
1 Penn Plz
New York NY 10119
212 465-5000

(P-26758)
PARTNERS IN LEADERSHIP
LLC (HQ)
27555 Ynez Rd Ste 300, Temecula
(92591-4678)
PHONE...................951 694-5596
Gordon Treadway, *CEO*
Marcus Nicolls, *Senior Partner*
Brad Burton, *President*
Maury Hiers, *President*
Brant Barton, *CFO*
EMP: 95
SQ FT: 12,000
SALES: 31MM
SALES (corp-wide): 4.3MM **Privately
Held**
WEB: www.ozprinciple.com
SIC: 8742 Business consultant
PA: Partners In Leadership Intermediate
Holdings Llc
27555 Ynez Rd
Temecula CA 92591
951 506-6878

(P-26759)
PARTNERS IN LEADERSHIP
INTERME (PA)
27555 Ynez Rd, Temecula (92591-4687)
PHONE...................951 506-6878
Yvon Wagner, *Director*
Mattson Newell, *Director*
Barbara Beeskow, *Consultant*
EMP: 95
SALES (est): 4.3MM **Privately Held**
SIC: 8742 Business consultant

(P-26760)
PENNYMAC FINANCIAL SVCS
INC
36 Discovery, Irvine (92618-3751)
PHONE...................949 341-0020
Stanford L Kurland, *Ch of Bd*
EMP: 1067
SALES (corp-wide): 1.1B **Publicly Held**
SIC: 8742 Financial consultant
PA: Pennymac Financial Services, Inc.
3043 Townsgate Rd
Westlake Village CA 91361
818 224-7442

(P-26761)
PERKSTREET FINANCIAL INC
1100 La Avenida St Ste A, Mountain View
(94043-1453)
PHONE...................978 801-1177
Laurence Stock, *CFO*
EMP: 50 **EST:** 2008
SALES (est): 4.4MM **Privately Held**
SIC: 8742 Banking & finance consultant

(P-26762)
PERMANENTE FEDERATION LLC
1 Kaiser Plz Fl 27, Oakland (94612-3610)
PHONE......................................510 625-6920
Cal James, *CEO*
Claire Tamo, *CFO*
Nancy Gin, *Exec VP*
Edward Lee, *Exec VP*
EMP: 80 **EST:** 1997
SQ FT: 18,663
SALES (est): 10MM **Privately Held**
SIC: 8742 Management consulting services

(P-26763)
PHENOMENON MKTG & ENTRMT LLC (PA)
5900 Wilshire Blvd Fl 28, Los Angeles (90036-5013)
PHONE......................................323 648-4000
Krishnan Menon, *CEO*
Kat Friis, *Officer*
Theodore Kapusta, *Creative Dir*
Jonathan Runkle, *Creative Dir*
Michael Allen, *Planning*
EMP: 60
SQ FT: 15,289
SALES (est): 20MM **Privately Held**
SIC: 8742 Marketing consulting services

(P-26764)
PRECISE ENTERPRISES LLC
Also Called: Precise Auto Protection
751 W 9th St, Azusa (91702-2340)
PHONE......................................818 599-6450
Harry Pambuckchyan, *Mng Member*
Gina Pambuckchyan,
Sitta Saghoejian,
EMP: 50
SQ FT: 6,500
SALES (est): 3.4MM **Privately Held**
SIC: 8742 Marketing consulting services

(P-26765)
PRESCRIPTION SOLUTIONS
2858 Loker Ave E Ste 100, Carlsbad (92010-6673)
PHONE......................................760 804-2370
Bobby Robert Bliatout, *President*
Richard Swartz, *Vice Pres*
Cindy Brigman, *Executive*
Bhavnesh Patel, *Administration*
Phil Haworth, *Info Tech Mgr*
EMP: 1000
SALES (est): 73.4MM **Privately Held**
SIC: 8742 Hospital & health services consultant

(P-26766)
PREVENTION INSTITUTE
221 Oak St Ste A, Oakland (94607-4595)
PHONE......................................510 444-4133
Larry Cohen, *Exec Dir*
Emily Kemp, *Officer*
Veonna Washington, *Officer*
Jessica Berthold, *Comms Mgr*
Justin Probert, *Admin Mgr*
EMP: 56 **EST:** 2001
SQ FT: 2,612
SALES (est): 6.9MM **Privately Held**
SIC: 8742 Training & development consultant

(P-26767)
PRIME HEALTHCARE SERVICES - SH
4929 Van Nuys Blvd, Sherman Oaks (91403-1702)
PHONE......................................818 981-7111
Prem Reddy, *CEO*
EMP: 900
SALES (est): 38.1K
SALES (corp-wide): 3.4B **Privately Held**
SIC: 8742 Hospital & health services consultant
PA: Prime Healthcare Foundation, Inc.
3300 E Guasti Rd Fl 3
Ontario CA 91761
909 235-4400

(P-26768)
PRIMUS GROUP INC (PA)
Also Called: Primus Labs
2810 Industrial Pkwy, Santa Maria (93455-1812)
PHONE......................................805 922-0055
Robert F Stovicek, *Principal*
Curtis Wilson, *Technology*
Joel Pasco, *Technical Staff*
Jennifer Scurich, *Controller*
Kara Christopher, *Bookkeeper*
EMP: 50
SQ FT: 12,000
SALES (est): 22.1MM **Privately Held**
WEB: www.primuslabs.com
SIC: 8742 8734 8731 Food & beverage consultant; food testing service; commercial physical research

(P-26769)
PRIZE PROZ
1500 S Hellman Ave, Ontario (91761-7634)
PHONE......................................909 509-8600
Dennis Foland, *Owner*
EMP: 50 **EST:** 2011
SALES (est): 214.3K **Privately Held**
SIC: 8742 Incentive or award program consultant

(P-26770)
PROMO SHOP INC (PA)
5420 Mcconnell Ave, Los Angeles (90066-7037)
PHONE......................................310 821-1780
Guillermo Kahan, *President*
Bob Golden, *CFO*
Memo Kahan, *Executive*
Dawn Rogers, *Executive*
Mary Kellerman, *Executive Asst*
◆ **EMP:** 55
SALES (est): 39.6MM **Privately Held**
WEB: www.promoshopinc.com
SIC: 8742 Marketing consulting services

(P-26771)
PROMOTE MEDIA LP
8484 Wilshire Blvd # 630, Beverly Hills (90211-3227)
PHONE......................................323 433-7950
Jeffrey Essebag,
EMP: 60
SALES (est): 881.9K **Privately Held**
SIC: 8742 Marketing consulting services

(P-26772)
PROPHET BRAND STRATEGY (PA)
1 Bush St Fl 7, San Francisco (94104-4413)
PHONE......................................415 677-0909
Michael Dunn, *President*
Kevin Odonnell, *Senior Partner*
Thomas Han, *Partner*
Jesse Purewal, *Partner*
Jonathan Redman, *Partner*
EMP: 50
SQ FT: 1,744
SALES (est): 100MM **Privately Held**
SIC: 8742 Marketing consulting services

(P-26773)
PROTIVITI INC
2613 Camino Ramon, San Ramon (94583-4289)
PHONE......................................925 913-1000
Keith Waddell, *Manager*
Dennis Cronyn, *Associate Dir*
Jared Docter, *Associate Dir*
Steve Cabello, *Managing Dir*
Michael Schultz, *Managing Dir*
EMP: 58
SALES (corp-wide): 5.8B **Publicly Held**
SIC: 8742 8721 Business consultant; accounting, auditing & bookkeeping
HQ: Protiviti Inc.
2884 Sand Hill Rd Ste 200
Menlo Park CA 94025
650 234-6000

(P-26774)
PROTIVITI INC (HQ)
2884 Sand Hill Rd Ste 200, Menlo Park (94025-7072)
PHONE......................................650 234-6000
Joseph A Tarantino, *Principal*
Brian Christensen, *Exec VP*

John Adams, *Associate Dir*
Rick Beyer, *Associate Dir*
Jeremy Coenen, *Associate Dir*
EMP: 100
SALES (est): 277.2MM
SALES (corp-wide): 5.8B **Publicly Held**
SIC: 8742 8721 Industry specialist consultants; auditing services
PA: Robert Half International Inc.
2884 Sand Hill Rd Ste 200
Menlo Park CA 94025
650 234-6000

(P-26775)
PROTIVITI INC
400 S Hope St Ste 900, Los Angeles (90071-2808)
PHONE......................................213 327-1400
Paul Sacks, *Branch Mgr*
EMP: 100
SALES (corp-wide): 5.8B **Publicly Held**
SIC: 8742 Food & beverage consultant
HQ: Protiviti Inc.
2884 Sand Hill Rd Ste 200
Menlo Park CA 94025
650 234-6000

(P-26776)
PROVIDENCE SEMINARS INC
6349 Palomar Oaks Ct, Carlsbad (92011-1428)
PHONE......................................760 827-2100
Russell Carroll, *President*
Paul Thiboutot, *Marketing Mgr*
EMP: 75
SQ FT: 15,000
SALES (est): 2.5MM **Privately Held**
SIC: 8742 Real estate consultant

(P-26777)
PUBLIC CONSULTING GROUP INC
Also Called: Pcg Technology Consulting
2150 River Plaza Dr # 380, Sacramento (95833-4138)
PHONE......................................916 565-8090
Lori Duff, *Manager*
EMP: 60
SALES (corp-wide): 459.1MM **Privately Held**
SIC: 8742 Business consultant
PA: Public Consulting Group, Inc.
148 State St Fl 10
Boston MA 02109
617 426-2026

(P-26778)
PWC STRATEGY& (US) LLC
3 Embarcadero Ctr Fl 20, San Francisco (94111-4004)
PHONE......................................415 498-5000
Ralph W Shrader, *Branch Mgr*
William T Reed, *Principal*
EMP: 200 **Privately Held**
SIC: 8742 Management consulting services
HQ: Pwc Strategy& (Us) Llc
101 Park Ave Fl 18
New York NY 10178

(P-26779)
Q ANALYSTS LLC (PA)
4320 Stevens Creek Blvd # 130, San Jose (95129-1280)
PHONE......................................408 907-8500
Ross Fernandes,
Joe Lawlor, *President*
Ilisa Kim, *Vice Pres*
Jason Knight, *Business Dir*
Christopher Hatton, *Financial Analy*
EMP: 70
SALES (est): 10.4MM **Privately Held**
WEB: www.qanalysts.com
SIC: 8742 7379 Quality assurance consultant; computer related consulting services

(P-26780)
QLM CONSULTING INC
2400 Bridgeway Ste 290, Sausalito (94965-2851)
P.O. Box 982 (94966-0982)
PHONE......................................415 331-9292
Michael McCartney, *CEO*
EMP: 50

SALES (est): 2.1MM **Privately Held**
WEB: www.qlmconsulting.com
SIC: 8742 Construction project management consultant

(P-26781)
QUALITY PLANNING CORPORATION
388 Market St Ste 750, San Francisco (94111-5352)
PHONE......................................415 369-0707
Raj Bhat, *President*
EMP: 54
SALES (est): 5.2MM **Publicly Held**
SIC: 8742 Financial consultant
HQ: Insurance Services Office, Inc.
545 Washington Blvd
Jersey City NJ 07310
201 469-2153

(P-26782)
QY RESEARCH INC
17890 Castleton St, City of Industry (91748-1756)
PHONE......................................626 295-2442
Song Chunming, *President*
Diao Hongwei, *Vice Pres*
Zhang Dong, *Director*
EMP: 61
SALES (est): 1.5MM **Privately Held**
SIC: 8742 Management consulting services

(P-26783)
R3 STRATEGIC SUPPORT GROUP INC
1050 B Ave Ste A, Coronado (92118-3430)
PHONE......................................800 418-2040
Randall Packard, *President*
Clark Nichols, *Principal*
Mark Sanders, *Principal*
Adam Guziewicz, *Program Mgr*
Bart Davis, *Technology*
EMP: 67
SALES (est): 1.2MM **Privately Held**
SIC: 8742 Business consultant

(P-26784)
RAINIER FINANCIAL GROUP LLC
2321 Rosecrans Ave # 4270, El Segundo (90245-4964)
PHONE......................................310 335-9200
Kevin Neustadt, *Managing Prtnr*
EMP: 50
SALES (est): 3.4MM **Privately Held**
SIC: 8742 Financial consultant

(P-26785)
RAY W CHOI
Also Called: Ictp
731 E Ball Rd Ste 100, Anaheim (92805-5951)
PHONE......................................714 783-1000
Ray W Choi, *Owner*
EMP: 92
SQ FT: 10,000
SALES (est): 3.8MM **Privately Held**
SIC: 8742 7379 Training & development consultant; computer related consulting services

(P-26786)
RED PEAK GROUP LLC
23975 Park Sorrento # 410, Calabasas (91302-4031)
PHONE......................................818 222-7762
Michael Birkin, *CEO*
EMP: 90
SALES (est): 4.8MM **Privately Held**
SIC: 8742 Marketing consulting services

(P-26787)
REDSTONE PRINT & MAIL INC
910 Riverside Pkwy Ste 40, West Sacramento (95605-1510)
PHONE......................................916 318-6450
Ledi Cody, *President*
EMP: 60 **EST:** 2015
SALES: 20MM **Privately Held**
SIC: 8742 Marketing consulting services

(P-26788)
RENEW HEALTH GROUP LLC
107 W Lemon Ave, Monrovia (91016-2809)
PHONE.................................310 625-2838
Crystal Solorzano, *CEO*
EMP: 50
SALES (est): 2.6MM **Privately Held**
SIC: 8742 Hospital & health services consultant

(P-26789)
REPUTATION IMPRESSION LLC
9245 Activity Rd Ste 106, San Diego (92126-4442)
PHONE.................................858 633-4500
Scott Spencer, *CEO*
EMP: 85
SALES (est): 7.6MM **Privately Held**
SIC: 8742 Industry specialist consultants

(P-26790)
REPUTATION MANAGEMENT CONS INC
1720 E Garry Ave Ste 103, Santa Ana (92705-5831)
PHONE.................................949 682-7906
Gary P Hagins, *President*
Anthony Asuncion, *Project Mgr*
Adam Reifman, *Opers Dir*
EMP: 65
SQ FT: 4,000
SALES: 9MM **Privately Held**
SIC: 8742 Business consultant

(P-26791)
RESEARCH TRIANGLE INSTITUTE
2150 Shattuck Ave Ste 800, Berkeley (94704-1352)
PHONE.................................510 849-4942
E Wayne Holden, *Branch Mgr*
Jan Van Bruaene, *President*
John Riedesel, *Project Mgr*
Jim Bentley, *Business Mgr*
Christine Heraldo, *Opers Staff*
EMP: 72
SALES (corp-wide): 957.7MM **Privately Held**
SIC: 8742 8732 Management consulting services; educational research
PA: Research Triangle Institute Inc
3040 Cornwallis Rd
Durham NC 27709
919 541-6000

(P-26792)
RESORT PROCOMM INC
9550 Waples St Ste 105, San Diego (92121-2984)
PHONE.................................858 866-6280
Will Dougherty, *President*
EMP: 61
SALES (est): 2.1MM **Privately Held**
SIC: 8742 Marketing consulting services

(P-26793)
RESOURCES CONNECTION INC
Also Called: Resources Global Professionals
695 Town Center Dr # 600, Costa Mesa (92626-1924)
PHONE.................................714 430-6550
Donald Murray, *Principal*
Hiro Ueda, *CPA*
Lisa Takata, *Director*
Mia Griswold, *Manager*
EMP: 86 **Publicly Held**
SIC: 8742 Management consulting services
PA: Resources Connection, Inc.
17101 Armstrong Ave # 100
Irvine CA 92614

(P-26794)
RESOURCES CONNECTION INC (PA)
Also Called: Resources Global Professionals
17101 Armstrong Ave # 100, Irvine (92614-5742)
PHONE.................................714 430-6400
Kate W Duchene, *President*
Donald B Murray, *Ch of Bd*
Jennifer Ryu, *CFO*
Stephen Barker, *Vice Pres*
Scott Gregerson, *Vice Pres*

EMP: 732
SQ FT: 56,200
SALES: 729MM **Publicly Held**
SIC: 8742 7389 8721 Business consultant; business planning & organizing services; financial services; legal & tax services; accounting, auditing & bookkeeping; auditing services

(P-26795)
RHODES RETAIL SERVICES INC
8603 Excelsior Rd, Elk Grove (95624-9661)
PHONE.................................916 714-9233
Chris Rhodes, *President*
Valerie Rhodes, *CFO*
EMP: 90
SQ FT: 1,200
SALES (est): 8.4MM **Privately Held**
WEB: www.rhodesretail.com
SIC: 8742 Merchandising consultant

(P-26796)
RMD GROUP INC
2311 E South St, Long Beach (90805-4424)
PHONE.................................562 866-9288
Ralph Holguin, *President*
Patzy Holguin, *CFO*
Laura Milanes, *Officer*
Caitlin Stafford, *Executive*
Eli Saiz, *General Mgr*
EMP: 300
SALES (est): 35.2MM **Privately Held**
SIC: 8742 Marketing consulting services

(P-26797)
ROBERTSON PIPER MANAGEMENT LLC
963 Fremont Ave, Los Altos (94024-6098)
PHONE.................................650 625-8333
Robertson Piper, *Principal*
EMP: 185
SALES (est): 4.8MM **Privately Held**
SIC: 8742 Management consulting services

(P-26798)
ROCKPORT ADM SVCS LLC (PA)
Also Called: Rockport Healthcare Services
5900 Wilshire Blvd # 1600, Los Angeles (90036-5016)
PHONE.................................323 330-6500
Vincent S Hambright, *CEO*
Brad Gibson, *CFO*
Michael Wasserman, *Chief Mktg Ofcr*
Paulette Jerry, *Payroll Mgr*
Steven Stroll, *Mng Member*
EMP: 75
SQ FT: 4,800
SALES (est): 33MM **Privately Held**
SIC: 8742 Hospital & health services consultant

(P-26799)
ROI COMMUNICATIONS INC (PA)
5274 Scotts Valley Dr # 107, Scotts Valley (95066-3538)
PHONE.................................831 430-0170
Barbara Fagan Smith, *President*
Charlie Wrench, *President*
Sheryl Lewis, *COO*
Claire Berney, *Vice Pres*
Janice Collins, *Vice Pres*
EMP: 50
SALES (est): 8.1MM **Privately Held**
WEB: www.roico.com
SIC: 8742 Marketing consulting services

(P-26800)
RUBY CREEK RESOURCES INC
11835 W Olympic Blvd, Los Angeles (90064-5001)
PHONE.................................212 671-0404
Robert Slavik, *CEO*
EMP: 50
SALES (est): 9MM **Privately Held**
SIC: 8742 Business planning & organizing services

(P-26801)
RUSSON FINANCIAL SERVICES INC
Also Called: New England Financial
19935 Ventura Blvd # 100, Woodland Hills (91364-9605)
PHONE.................................818 999-2800
Tony Russon, *CEO*
EMP: 60
SQ FT: 10,000
SALES (est): 3.6MM **Privately Held**
SIC: 8742 Financial consultant

(P-26802)
S E O P INC
1621 Alton Pkwy Ste 150, Irvine (92606-4875)
PHONE.................................949 682-7906
Gary Hagins, *CEO*
Rhonda Spears, *President*
Kyra Herrick, *Manager*
EMP: 150
SALES (est): 15.3MM **Privately Held**
WEB: www.seop.com
SIC: 8742 Marketing consulting services

(P-26803)
SABAN BRANDS LLC (HQ)
10100 Santa Monica Blvd # 500, Los Angeles (90067-4121)
PHONE.................................310 557-5230
Elie Dekel, *President*
Jack Sorensen, *President*
Janet Scardino, *COO*
William Kehoe, *CFO*
Jocelyn Belloni, *Vice Pres*
EMP: 88
SQ FT: 605,000
SALES (est): 16.5MM
SALES (corp-wide): 55.4MM **Privately Held**
SIC: 8742 General management consultant
PA: Global Reach 18, Inc.
10100 Santa Monica Blvd # 900
Los Angeles CA 90067
310 203-5850

(P-26804)
SACKETT NATIONAL HOLDINGS INC
2605 Camino Del Rio S # 400, San Diego (92108-3706)
PHONE.................................866 834-6242
EMP: 135
SALES (corp-wide): 53.5MM **Privately Held**
SIC: 8742 7389 Management consulting services; financial services
PA: Sackett National Holdings, Inc.
7373 Peak Dr
Las Vegas NV 89128
702 900-1791

(P-26805)
SAVIYNT INC (PA)
1301 E El Segundo Blvd, El Segundo (90245-4303)
PHONE.................................310 641-1664
Amit Saha, *CEO*
Keith Mozena, *Vice Pres*
David Thomson, *Vice Pres*
Charlie Smith, *Executive*
Vipin Tanwar, *Technical Staff*
EMP: 122
SQ FT: 10,000
SALES (est): 23.8MM **Privately Held**
SIC: 8742 Management consulting services

(P-26806)
SEARCH ENGINE OPTIMIZATION INC
5841 Edison Pl Ste 140, Carlsbad (92008-6500)
PHONE.................................760 929-0039
Garry Grant, *CEO*
Krishnan Coughran, *President*
Sergio Stephano, *Vice Pres*
Anthony Asuncion, *Project Mgr*
MO Bazzaz, *Technology*
EMP: 58
SQ FT: 15,000

SALES (est): 4.4MM **Privately Held**
WEB: www.seoinc.com
SIC: 8742 Marketing consulting services

(P-26807)
SEARCH OPTICS LLC (PA)
5770 Oberlin Dr, San Diego (92121-1723)
PHONE.................................858 678-0707
David Ponn, *CEO*
Eduardo Cortez, *President*
David Cox, *President*
Troy Smith, *President*
Jason Stesney, *Treasurer*
EMP: 60
SQ FT: 16,500
SALES (est): 26.3MM **Privately Held**
WEB: www.searchoptics.com
SIC: 8742 Marketing consulting services

(P-26808)
SECOVA INC
3090 Bristol St Ste 200, Costa Mesa (92626-3061)
PHONE.................................714 384-0530
Venkat Tadanki, *President*
V Chandrasekaran, *COO*
Joel Carter, *Senior VP*
Robert G Parke, *Senior VP*
EMP: 186
SQ FT: 7,662
SALES (est): 7.2MM **Privately Held**
WEB: www.secova.com
SIC: 8742 Human resource consulting services
HQ: Secova Eservices, Inc.
3090 Bristol St Ste 200
Costa Mesa CA 92626
714 384-0655

(P-26809)
SECOVA ESERVICES INC (HQ)
3090 Bristol St Ste 200, Costa Mesa (92626-3061)
PHONE.................................714 384-0655
Venkat R Tadanki, *CEO*
Robert G Parke, *Admin Sec*
V Chandrasekaran, *CTO*
Zahid Chaudhry, *Finance*
Murali Krishnan, *Marketing Mgr*
EMP: 84
SQ FT: 6,713
SALES (est): 28.5MM **Privately Held**
WEB: www.ultralink.com
SIC: 8742 Human resource consulting services

(P-26810)
SEQUOIA BNEFITS INSUR SVCS LLC
1850 Gateway Dr Ste 600, San Mateo (94404-4064)
PHONE.................................650 369-0200
Greg Golub, *President*
Sean Martin, *President*
Geoffrey Valentine, *Chairman*
Michele Floriani, *Chief Mktg Ofcr*
Suzette Germano, *Vice Pres*
EMP: 70
SQ FT: 2,000
SALES (est): 11.7MM **Privately Held**
WEB: www.sequoiabenefits.com
SIC: 8742 Compensation & benefits planning consultant

(P-26811)
SEVILLE CONSTRUCTION SVCS INC
199 S Hudson Ave, Pasadena (91101-2917)
PHONE.................................626 204-0800
Jeffrey S Flores, *President*
Bernadette Vargas, *Business Mgr*
EMP: 75
SQ FT: 3,300
SALES (est): 8.7MM **Privately Held**
WEB: www.sevillecs.com
SIC: 8742 Construction project management consultant

(P-26812)
SIERRA SYSTEMS INC (PA)
222 N Pacific Coast Hwy # 1310, El Segundo (90245-5644)
PHONE.................................310 536-6288
Calvin Yonker, *President*
Patricia Kaiser, *COO*

Brian Fees, *CFO*
Chad Helton, *Consultant*
EMP: 200
SALES (est): 13.1MM **Privately Held**
WEB: www.sierrasys.com
SIC: 8742 Management consulting services

(P-26813)
SIGMAWAYS INC
39737 Paseo Padre Pkwy, Fremont
(94538-2996)
PHONE.................510 573-4208
Prakash Sadasivam, *CEO*
Bhuvana Ravikumar, *Technology*
Sudha Kadirvelu, *Human Res Mgr*
EMP: 60
SQ FT: 5,000
SALES (est): 6.6MM **Privately Held**
SIC: 8742 7379 7373 Management consulting services; computer related consulting services; systems software development services

(P-26814)
SIMI RADIOLOGY & IMAGING
Also Called: Computerized Management Svcs
4100 Guardian St Ste 205, Simi Valley
(93063-6721)
P.O. Box 190 (93062-0190)
PHONE.................805 522-5978
Daryl Favale, *Owner*
EMP: 100
SALES (est): 5.2MM **Privately Held**
SIC: 8742 Hospital & health services consultant

(P-26815)
SITESTUFF YARDI SYSTEMS I
(PA)
430 S Fairview Ave, Goleta (93117-3637)
PHONE.................805 966-3666
Steven Sewell, *Principal*
Jennifer Cornell, *Technical Staff*
Sonia Hamilton, *Technical Staff*
Martin Gedny, *Marketing Staff*
Don Richardson, *Director*
EMP: 83
SALES (est): 15.3MM **Privately Held**
SIC: 8742 Real estate consultant

(P-26816)
SITETRACKER INC
150 Grant Ave Ste A, Palo Alto
(94306-5135)
PHONE.................408 838-9419
Giuseppe Incitti, *CEO*
EMP: 62
SALES (est): 3.4MM **Privately Held**
SIC: 8742 8741 Management consulting services; business consultant; management services

(P-26817)
SITRICK BRINCKO GROUP LLC
1840 Century Park E # 800, Los Angeles
(90067-2101)
PHONE.................310 788-2850
Michael Sitrick, *Mng Member*
John Brincko,
EMP: 60
SALES (est): 3.6MM **Publicly Held**
SIC: 8742 8743 Management consulting services; public relations services
PA: Resources Connection, Inc.
17101 Armstrong Ave # 100
Irvine CA 92614

(P-26818)
SKYLIGHT HALTHCARE
SYSTEMS INC
10935 Vista Sorrento Pkwy # 350, San
Diego (92130-2651)
PHONE.................858 523-3700
David J Schofield, *CEO*
Lisa Romano, *Ch Credit Ofcr*
Rich Holbrook, *CTO*
Karen Rosen, *Manager*
EMP: 56
SQ FT: 11,000

SALES (est): 10.5MM
SALES (corp-wide): 57MM **Privately Held**
WEB: www.skylight.com
SIC: 8742 Hospital & health services consultant
PA: Getwellnetwork, Inc.
7700 Old Georgtwn Rd Fl 4
Bethesda MD 20814
240 482-3200

(P-26819)
SKYLINE CONSULTING GROUP
13186 Skyline Blvd, Woodside
(94062-4542)
PHONE.................650 529-3455
Gustavo Rabin, *Owner*
Annie Abrams, *Vice Pres*
Stacy McCarthy, *Principal*
Rod Blomquist, *Manager*
EMP: 119
SALES (est): 5.7MM **Privately Held**
WEB: www.skylineconsulting.com
SIC: 8742 Training & development consultant

(P-26820)
SKYNET USA ASSET MGT INC
17011 Beach Blvd Fl 9th, Huntington Beach
(92647-5946)
PHONE.................702 969-5599
Johnny Thanh Hong, *CEO*
EMP: 50
SALES (est): 764.1K **Privately Held**
SIC: 8742 Financial consultant

(P-26821)
SMARTZIP ANALYTICS INC
6200 Stoneridge Mall Rd, Pleasanton
(94588-3242)
PHONE.................855 661-1064
Tom Glassanos, *President*
Scott Baumgartner, *CFO*
Frank Richards, *Chairman*
Peter Grace, *Exec VP*
Matt Grant, *Executive*
EMP: 77
SALES (est): 12.1MM **Privately Held**
SIC: 8742 Marketing consulting services; real estate consultant

(P-26822)
SMG HOLDINGS INC
Also Called: Palm Springs Convention Center
277 N Avenida Caballeros, Palm Springs
(92262-6440)
PHONE.................760 325-6611
Jim Dunn, *Branch Mgr*
Henry Durbin, *Engineer*
Gabe Rios, *Opers Mgr*
Kim Leeney, *Sales Staff*
Manuel Lucero, *Sales Staff*
EMP: 60
SALES (corp-wide): 23.7B **Privately Held**
WEB: www.smgworld.com
SIC: 8742 7389 Business consultant; convention & show services
HQ: Smg Holdings, Llc
300 Cnshohckn State Rd # 450
Conshohocken PA 19428

(P-26823)
SMITH-EMERY COMPANY (PA)
781 E Washington Blvd, Los Angeles
(90021-3091)
PHONE.................213 745-5312
James Partridge, *Ch of Bd*
James E Partridge, *Ch of Bd*
Ayesha Syeda, *Manager*
Bob Hay, *Supervisor*
EMP: 70 EST: 1904
SQ FT: 35,000
SALES (est): 28.3MM **Privately Held**
WEB: www.smithemery.com
SIC: 8742 Construction project management consultant

(P-26824)
SOAPROJECTS INC (PA)
495 N Whisman Rd Ste 100, Mountain View
(94043-5725)
PHONE.................650 960-9900
Manpreet Grover, *President*
Dineshni Anumala, *Administration*
Antonio Gallegos, *IT/INT Sup*

Vijay Raghavendar, *Technology*
Jose Cadena, *Technical Staff*
EMP: 51
SALES (est): 21.4MM **Privately Held**
SIC: 8742 7379 8721 Financial consultant; computer related consulting services; accounting, auditing & bookkeeping

(P-26825)
SODEXO INC
1812 Verdugo Blvd Fl 1, Glendale
(91208-1407)
PHONE.................818 952-2201
Ron Reed, *Manager*
EMP: 90
SALES (corp-wide): 133.3MM **Privately Held**
SIC: 8742 Hospital & health services consultant
HQ: Sodexo, Inc.
9801 Washingtonian Blvd # 416
Gaithersburg MD 20878
301 987-4000

(P-26826)
SOLO W-2 INC
Also Called: Solo Workforce
3478 Buskirk Ave Ste 1000, Pleasant Hill
(94523-4378)
PHONE.................925 680-0200
James R Ziegler, *President*
Sara M Wilkison, *CFO*
Sandi Buchanan, *Human Res Dir*
Elizabeth Murphy, *Marketing Staff*
EMP: 110 EST: 1997
SQ FT: 800
SALES: 10MM **Privately Held**
WEB: www.pacepros.com
SIC: 8742 8721 Compensation & benefits planning consultant; billing & bookkeeping service

(P-26827)
SQA SERVICES INC
550 Silver Spur Rd # 300, Rllng HLS Est
(90275-3605)
PHONE.................800 333-6180
James C McKay, *CEO*
J Michael McKay, *President*
Gerard Pearce, *Vice Pres*
Karena Chichester, *Administration*
Jason Anderson, *Engineer*
EMP: 267
SQ FT: 8,000
SALES (est): 32.4MM **Privately Held**
WEB: www.sqaservices.com
SIC: 8742 Quality assurance consultant

(P-26828)
STAGE 4 SOLUTIONS
INCORPORATED
19200 Portos Dr, Saratoga (95070-5123)
PHONE.................408 868-9739
Niti Agrawal, *CEO*
EMP: 50
SALES (est): 596.7K **Privately Held**
WEB: www.stage4solutions.com
SIC: 8742 New products & services consultants

(P-26829)
STATE GROUP LLC
Also Called: Seven Hospitality
77 Turnstone, Irvine (92618-1707)
PHONE.................949 612-2879
Matt Pannek,
Michelle Pannek,
EMP: 280
SALES (est): 20.1MM **Privately Held**
SIC: 8742 Restaurant & food services consultants

(P-26830)
STERLING CONSULTING GROUP
LLC
Also Called: Sterling Brand
55 Union St Fl 3, San Francisco
(94111-1244)
PHONE.................415 248-7900
Austin McGhie, *Manager*
Jj Steeley, *Vice Pres*
Corey Allen, *Accountant*
Lisa Grant, *Receptionist*
EMP: 84 **Privately Held**
SIC: 8742 Marketing consulting services

PA: Sterling Consulting Group Llc
75 Varick St Fl 8
New York NY 10013

(P-26831)
STERLING MKTG & FINCL CORP
Also Called: T3 Direct
4660 Spyres Way Ste 1, Modesto
(95356-9801)
PHONE.................209 593-1140
Albert W Dadesho, *President*
Susie Dadesho, *Vice Pres*
EMP: 50
SQ FT: 8,000
SALES (est): 5.5MM **Privately Held**
SIC: 8742 Marketing consulting services

(P-26832)
STRATEGIC BUS INSIGHTS INC
(PA)
333 Ravenswood Ave, Menlo Park
(94025-3453)
PHONE.................650 859-4600
William Guns, *CEO*
William Ralston, *CFO*
Larry Cohen, *Vice Pres*
Chulho Park, *Principal*
Ellen Boykin, *General Mgr*
EMP: 63 EST: 2000
SQ FT: 10,000
SALES (est): 9.5MM **Privately Held**
WEB: www.sricbi.com
SIC: 8742 Marketing consulting services

(P-26833)
STRATEGIC STAFFING SVCS
INC
Also Called: Total Hr Management
35 N Lake Ave Ste 140, Pasadena
(91101-1898)
PHONE.................818 248-0049
James E Harwood, *President*
EMP: 289
SALES (est): 1.8MM
SALES (corp-wide): 230.4MM **Privately Held**
SIC: 8742 Human resource consulting services
PA: Coadvantage Corporation
6407 Parkland Dr
Sarasota FL 34243
941 925-2990

(P-26834)
SULLIVANCURTISMONROE
INSURANCE (PA)
1920 Main St Ste 600, Irvine (92614-7226)
P.O. Box 19763 (92623-9763)
PHONE.................800 427-3253
John Monroe, *CEO*
Mark Eckenweiler, *CFO*
Carol Jenkins, *Officer*
Amanda C Griffin, *Assoc VP*
Jeannine Coronado, *Exec VP*
EMP: 103
SQ FT: 22,000
SALES (est): 34.8MM **Privately Held**
WEB: www.sullicurt.com
SIC: 8742 6411 Management consulting services; insurance brokers

(P-26835)
SUMMIT HR WORLDWIDE INC
Also Called: Echo Staffing
220 Main St Ste 208a, San Jose (95112)
PHONE.................408 884-7100
Priyaranjan Sinha, *Ch of Bd*
EMP: 100
SALES (est): 4.1MM **Privately Held**
SIC: 8742 Human resource consulting services

(P-26836)
SUN PACIFIC MARKETING
COOP INC
33502 Lerdo Hwy, Bakersfield
(93308-9438)
PHONE.................213 612-9957
Berne H Evans III, *Branch Mgr*
EMP: 843
SALES (corp-wide): 336MM **Privately Held**
SIC: 8742 Marketing consulting services

PRODUCTS & SVCS

PA: Sun Pacific Marketing Cooperative, Inc.
1095 E Green St
Pasadena CA 91106
213 612-9957

(P-26837)
SUTTER HEALTH
633 Folsom St Fl 5, San Francisco
(94107-3623)
PHONE.....................415 600-3311
Janet Avalos, *Admin Sec*
Brett Moore, *Asst Admin*
Victor Wong, *Technology*
Betty Kevan, *Analyst*
Meg Walker, *Corp Comm Staff*
EMP: 383
SALES (corp-wide): 12.7B **Privately Held**
SIC: 8742 Business planning & organizing
services
PA: Sutter Health
2200 River Plaza Dr
Sacramento CA 95833
916 733-8800

(P-26838)
SUTTER PHYSICIAN SERVICES (HQ)
10470 Old Placerville Rd, Sacramento
(95827-2539)
P.O. Box 211584, Saint Paul MN (55121-2884)
PHONE.....................916 854-6600
Jeremy Eaves, *CEO*
Mitch Proaps, *Comms Mgr*
EMP: 800
SQ FT: 87,000
SALES (est): 57.9MM
SALES (corp-wide): 12.7B **Privately Held**
WEB: www.sutterconnect.com
SIC: 8742 8741 8721 Hospital & health
services consultant; management infor-
mation systems consultant; management
services; accounting, auditing & book-
keeping
PA: Sutter Health
2200 River Plaza Dr
Sacramento CA 95833
916 733-8800

(P-26839)
SWANDER PACE CAPITAL LLC (PA)
101 Mission St Ste 1900, San Francisco
(94105-1726)
PHONE.....................415 477-8500
Andrew Richards, *CEO*
Heather Fraser, *CFO*
Tyler Matlock, *Vice Pres*
C Stout, *Exec Dir*
Tara Hyland, *Associate*
EMP: 567
SQ FT: 5,000
SALES (est): 36MM **Privately Held**
WEB: www.spcap.com
SIC: 8742 Restaurant & food services con-
sultants

(P-26840)
TECHNOLOGY ASSOCIATES EC INC
3129 Tiger Run Ct Ste 206, Carlsbad
(92010-6512)
PHONE.....................760 765-5275
Walter Oleski, *CEO*
Wilma Gamboa, *Controller*
Linda Stephenson, *Controller*
EMP: 74
SALES (est): 13.7MM **Privately Held**
SIC: 8742 General management consult-
ant

(P-26841)
TECOLOTE RESEARCH INC
2120 E Grand Ave Ste 200, El Segundo
(90245-5024)
PHONE.....................310 640-4700
James Takayesu, *President*
EMP: 114
SALES (corp-wide): 86.7MM **Privately
Held**
WEB: www.tecolote.com
SIC: 8742 8731 Management consulting
services; commercial physical research

PA: Tecolote Research, Inc.
420 S Fairview Ave # 201
Goleta CA 93117
805 571-6366

(P-26842)
TELEGRAPH HILL PARTNERS INVEST (PA)
360 Post St Ste 601, San Francisco
(94108-4909)
PHONE.....................415 765-6980
J Matthew Mackowski, *Chairman*
Rob C Hart Cfa, *Vice Pres*
M Celeste Salvatto, *Administration*
Deval A Lashkari PHD,
Jeanette M Welsh JD,
EMP: 50
SALES (est): 35MM **Privately Held**
SIC: 8742 6799 Management consulting
services; investors

(P-26843)
TELESTAR CONSULTING INC
519 N Alta Dr, Beverly Hills (90210-3501)
PHONE.....................310 748-0008
Karl Angel, *President*
EMP: 50
SALES (est): 2.4MM **Privately Held**
SIC: 8742 Hospital & health services con-
sultant

(P-26844)
TERRACARE ASSOCIATES LLC
921 Arnold Dr, Martinez (94553-4102)
PHONE.....................925 374-0060
Todd Williams, *Principal*
Brent Trujillo, *Vice Pres*
Matt Bulik, *Administration*
EMP: 92 **Privately Held**
SIC: 8742 Management consulting serv-
ices
PA: Terracare Associates, Llc
8201 Southpark Ln Ste 110
Littleton CO 80120

(P-26845)
TETRA TECH INC
1230 Columbia St Ste 1000, San Diego
(92101-8588)
PHONE.....................619 525-7188
Roger Argus, *Branch Mgr*
Lawrence D Romine Jr, *Engineer*
EMP: 68
SALES (corp-wide): 2.9B **Publicly Held**
SIC: 8742 8744 8711 Management con-
sulting services; facilities support serv-
ices; engineering services
PA: Tetra Tech, Inc.
3475 E Foothill Blvd
Pasadena CA 91107
626 351-4664

(P-26846)
THIEL CAPITAL LLC (PA)
9200 W Sunset Blvd # 1110, West Holly-
wood (90069-3616)
PHONE.....................323 990-2030
Peter Thiel,
Margaret Kirchner, *CFO*
Kellie Ammerman, *Vice Pres*
William Eden, *Vice Pres*
Dennis Kuang, *Vice Pres*
EMP: 65
SALES (est): 10.7MM **Privately Held**
SIC: 8742 Financial consultant

(P-26847)
THRESHOLD DIGITAL RESEARCH LAB
1649 11th St, Santa Monica (90404-3707)
PHONE.....................310 452-8885
Larry Kasanoff, *President*
EMP: 50 **EST:** 1996
SALES (est): 2.9MM **Privately Held**
WEB: www.threshold-digital.com
SIC: 8742 Management consulting serv-
ices

(P-26848)
TOP TIER CONSULTING
21550 Oxnard St Fl 3, Woodland Hills
(91367-7105)
PHONE.....................818 338-2121
Brad Armstrong, *Senior Partner*
Gregory Anderson, *Principal*

Christopher Downey, *Principal*
EMP: 70
SQ FT: 2,000
SALES: 19MM **Privately Held**
SIC: 8742 7379 Management consulting
services; computer related consulting
services

(P-26849)
TOPDOWN CONSULTING INC
530 Divisadero St Ste 310, San Francisco
(94117-2213)
PHONE.....................888 644-8445
EMP: 80 **EST:** 2000
SALES (est): 8.6MM **Privately Held**
WEB: www.topdownconsulting.com
SIC: 8742

(P-26850)
TRACE3 LLC (PA)
7565 Irvine Center Dr, Irvine (92618-4918)
PHONE.....................949 333-2300
Rich Fennessy, *CEO*
EMP: 100
SQ FT: 10,000
SALES (est): 103.4MM **Privately Held**
WEB: www.trace3.com
SIC: 8742 Sales (including sales manage-
ment) consultant

(P-26851)
TRANSIRIS CORPORATION
555 Airport Blvd Ste 325, Burlingame
(94010-2062)
PHONE.....................650 303-3495
Silvian Centiu, *CEO*
Simona Nan, *Director*
EMP: 75
SALES (est): 6.3MM **Privately Held**
SIC: 8742 Marketing consulting services

(P-26852)
TRANZEAL INC
2107 N 1st St Ste 500, San Jose
(95131-2028)
PHONE.....................408 834-8711
Akhil Khera, *Partner*
Murali Kolli, *COO*
Karan Singh, *Senior Mgr*
Sandeep Sunku, *Manager*
EMP: 50
SQ FT: 2,200
SALES (est): 281.6K **Privately Held**
SIC: 8742 Management consulting serv-
ices

(P-26853)
TRIAGE CONSULTING GROUP (PA)
221 Main St Ste 1100, San Francisco
(94105-1927)
PHONE.....................415 512-9400
Brian Neece, *President*
Damon Lewis, *Treasurer*
Tracy Packingham, *Vice Pres*
Melissa Beard, *Program Mgr*
Joyce Balistreri, *Office Mgr*
EMP: 280
SQ FT: 21,665
SALES: 98MM **Privately Held**
WEB: www.triageconsulting.com
SIC: 8742 8748 Hospital & health services
consultant; business consulting

(P-26854)
TRIPLE RING TECHNOLOGIES INC
39655 Eureka Dr, Newark (94560-4806)
PHONE.....................510 592-3000
Joseph A Heanue, *CEO*
Marc Whyte, *Ch of Bd*
Peter Clark, *CFO*
Philip Devlin, *Officer*
Barclay Dorman, *Vice Pres*
EMP: 50
SALES (est): 11.7MM **Privately Held**
WEB: www.tripleringtech.com
SIC: 8742 Business consultant

(P-26855)
TSMC NORTH AMERICA (HQ)
2851 Junction Ave, San Jose (95134-1910)
PHONE.....................408 382-8000
Richard B Cassidy II, *CEO*
Peter Bonfield, *Bd of Directors*
Thomas Engibous, *Bd of Directors*

Albert Shih, *Bd of Directors*
Jeff Shih, *Bd of Directors*
EMP: 108
SALES (est): 33.1MM **Privately Held**
SIC: 8742 8711 5065 3674 Marketing
consulting services; consulting engineer;
electronic parts & equipment; semicon-
ductor circuit networks

(P-26856)
UNITED INNOVATION SERVICES INC
1057 Hoskins Ln, San Ramon
(94582-5915)
PHONE.....................510 322-8922
Tingting Du, *CEO*
EMP: 84
SALES (est): 1.4MM **Privately Held**
SIC: 8742 Management consulting serv-
ices

(P-26857)
UNITED TALENT AGENCY LLC
1880 Century Park E # 711, Los Angeles
(90067-1618)
PHONE.....................310 385-2800
Grant Ledger, *Owner*
Alice Hogg, *Vice Pres*
Sharon Morris, *Administration*
Nate Cornelius, *IT/INT Sup*
Bruce Solar, *Technology*
EMP: 259
SALES (corp-wide): 43.3MM **Privately
Held**
SIC: 8742 Management consulting serv-
ices
PA: United Talent Agency, Llc
9336 Civic Center Dr
Beverly Hills CA 90210
310 273-6700

(P-26858)
UPSTREM INC
1253 University Ave # 1003, San Diego
(92103-3389)
PHONE.....................858 229-2979
Jacob Risman, *CEO*
Steven Maman, *President*
EMP: 70
SQ FT: 1,500
SALES: 18MM **Privately Held**
SIC: 8742 Sales (including sales manage-
ment) consultant

(P-26859)
US TOURNAMENT GOLF LTD LBLTY
5464 Topaz St, Rancho Cucamonga
(91701-1317)
P.O. Box 3373 (91729-3373)
PHONE.....................909 987-6695
Robert E Harrington, *Mng Member*
Kevin Quinton, *Sales Staff*
EMP: 50
SQ FT: 1,000
SALES: 5MM **Privately Held**
SIC: 8742 Business planning & organizing
services

(P-26860)
VALUE-CENTERED SOLUTIONS INC
2300 Stanwell Dr Ste A, Concord
(94520-4841)
PHONE.....................925 332-0555
Michael E Parker, *President*
Darral Brown, *CFO*
Bella Survine, *Executive Asst*
Sharmayne Thompson, *Accounting Mgr*
Samiya Hethcock, *Director*
EMP: 50
SQ FT: 7,000
SALES (est): 1.8MM **Privately Held**
SIC: 8742 Management consulting serv-
ices

(P-26861)
VAN ETTEN SUZUMOTO BECKET LLP
1620 26th St Ste 6000n, Santa Monica
(90404-4074)
PHONE.....................310 315-8284
David Van Etten,
EMP: 65

SALES (est): 3.3MM **Privately Held**
SIC: 8742 Management consulting services

(P-26862)
VARIS LLC
3915 Security Park Dr B, Rancho Cordova
(95742-6903)
PHONE..................................916 294-0860
Dean B Wilkie, *Manager*
Lisa Polte, *Vice Pres*
Fran Degregorio, *Auditor*
Kathy Depaolo, *Manager*
Deborah Markestad, *Asst Mgr*
EMP: 70
SALES (est): 3MM
SALES (corp-wide): 10.3MM **Privately Held**
SIC: 8742 Hospital & health services consultant
PA: Varis Llc
9245 Sierra College Blvd
Roseville CA 95661
916 294-0860

(P-26863)
VARIS LLC (PA)
9245 Sierra College Blvd, Roseville
(95661-5919)
PHONE..................................916 294-0860
Joy A Wilkie, *Mng Member*
Dean Wilkie, *General Mgr*
Adriana Velasquez, *Admin Asst*
Marlana Hill, *Administration*
EMP: 110
SQ FT: 5,600
SALES (est): 10.3MM **Privately Held**
WEB: www.varis1.com
SIC: 8742 Hospital & health services consultant

(P-26864)
VAYAN MARKETING GROUP LLC
10877 Wilshire Blvd Fl 12, Los Angeles
(90024-4332)
PHONE..................................310 943-4990
Jesse Lo RE,
Laura Kall,
Michael Medema,
Brad Morrison,
EMP: 50
SQ FT: 7,000
SALES (est): 3.3MM **Privately Held**
WEB: www.vayan.com
SIC: 8742 Marketing consulting services

(P-26865)
VERIFI INC
8391 Beverly Blvd Ste 310, Los Angeles
(90048-2633)
P.O. Box 310 (90078-0310)
PHONE..................................323 655-5789
Matthew G Katz, *CEO*
Sara Craven, *COO*
Ronald B Cushey, *CFO*
Hitesh Anand,
Tony Wootton, *Risk Mgmt Dir*
EMP: 65
SALES (est): 14.1MM **Publicly Held**
SIC: 8742 Quality assurance consultant
PA: Visa Inc.
900 Metro Center Blvd
Foster City CA 94404
-

(P-26866)
VERITAS MEDIA GROUP LLC
1111 Broadway Ste 300, Oakland
(94607-4167)
PHONE..................................510 867-4699
Jason Ballance, *CEO*
Zach Luechauer, *President*
EMP: 50
SALES (est): 3.1MM **Privately Held**
SIC: 8742 7319 Marketing consulting services; media buying service

(P-26867)
VERTICALRESPONSE INC
550 Kearny St Ste 710, San Francisco
(94108-2589)
PHONE..................................866 683-7842
Janine Popick, *President*
David Shiba, *COO*
Arman Pahiavan, *Admin Sec*

Richard Tan, *Administration*
Joanna Vasquez, *Accountant*
EMP: 110 EST: 2001
SALES (est): 19.3MM
SALES (corp-wide): 2B **Publicly Held**
WEB: www.verticalresponse.com
SIC: 8742 Marketing consulting services
PA: Deluxe Corporation
3680 Victoria St N
Shoreview MN 55126
651 483-7111

(P-26868)
VIDHWAN INC (PA)
Also Called: E-Solutions
2 N Market St Ste 400, San Jose
(95113-1213)
PHONE..................................408 289-8200
Priyanka Gupta, *CEO*
Ashish Pandey, *Executive*
Amit Chhetri, *Tech Recruiter*
Anish Kumar, *Tech Recruiter*
Bhupesh Kumar, *Tech Recruiter*
EMP: 150
SQ FT: 2,000
SALES (est): 25.5MM **Privately Held**
SIC: 8742 Human resource consulting services; training & development consultant

(P-26869)
VINCE SOLUTIONS (PA)
3910 Riverbend Ter, Fremont (94555-1505)
PHONE..................................510 432-0852
Ashok Yalamati, *President*
Sridhar Vadlapudi, *Admin Sec*
Srini Sirigina, *CTO*
Venkata Kodali, *Manager*
EMP: 55
SQ FT: 1,600
SALES (est): 2.6MM **Privately Held**
WEB: www.janvisoft.com
SIC: 8742 Administrative services consultant

(P-26870)
VISIO INTEG PROFE LLC (HQ)
Also Called: Visionary Intgrtion Prfssonals
80 Iron Point Cir Ste 100, Folsom
(95630-8592)
PHONE..................................916 985-9625
Jonna A Ward, *CEO*
Patti Bennion, *CFO*
Nishant Agrawal, *Vice Pres*
Steve Carpenter, *Vice Pres*
Howard Klett, *Technology*
EMP: 95
SQ FT: 9,000
SALES: 100MM **Privately Held**
SIC: 8742 7379 Management consulting services; computer related maintenance services

(P-26871)
VISIONSTAR INC
3435 Wilsh Blvd Ste 2120, Los Angeles
(90010)
PHONE..................................213 387-3700
Mark Anav, *CEO*
EMP: 90
SALES (est): 7.4MM **Privately Held**
SIC: 8742 Marketing consulting services

(P-26872)
VISTAGE INTERNATIONAL INC (PA)
Also Called: Executive Committee, The
4840 Eastgate Mall, San Diego
(92121-1977)
PHONE..................................858 523-6800
Rafael Pastor, *Ch of Bd*
Peter J Campbell, *Managing Prtnr*
Alexis Azpeitia, *Ch of Bd*
Richard Carr, *Vice Chairman*
Gaye Van Den Hombergh, *President*
EMP: 115
SALES (est): 37.6MM **Privately Held**
WEB: www.teconline.com
SIC: 8742 Business planning & organizing services

(P-26873)
VISTANCIA MARKETING LLC
Also Called: Shea Homes Ltd Prtnershp
655 Brea Canyon Rd, Walnut
(91789-3078)
PHONE..................................909 594-9500
John Francisshea, *Principal*
EMP: 55
SALES (est): 3.1MM
SALES (corp-wide): 2.2B **Privately Held**
SIC: 8742 Marketing consulting services
HQ: Shea Homes Limited Partnership, A
California Limited Partnership
655 Brea Canyon Rd
Walnut CA 91789

(P-26874)
WAGEWORKS INC (HQ)
1100 Park Pl 4, San Mateo (94403-1599)
PHONE..................................650 577-5200
Edgar Montes, *President*
Ashlie Eatinger, *Info Tech Mgr*
Kristina Saunders, *VP Opers*
Krista Scott, *Site Mgr*
Heidi Bowie, *Manager*
EMP: 113
SQ FT: 37,937
SALES: 472.1MM **Publicly Held**
SIC: 8742 Compensation & benefits planning consultant

(P-26875)
WASSERMAN MEDIA GROUP LLC (PA)
10900 Wilshire Blvd Fl 12, Los Angeles
(90024-6548)
PHONE..................................310 407-0200
Casey Wasserman, *Mng Member*
Dean Christopher, *CFO*
Barry Hyde, *Exec VP*
Greg Lawrence, *Exec VP*
Sam Macnaughton, *Exec VP*
EMP: 115
SQ FT: 40,000
SALES (est): 57.3MM **Privately Held**
SIC: 8742 Marketing consulting services

(P-26876)
WEST COAST AVIATION SVCS LLC (PA)
Also Called: West Coast Charters
19711 Campus Dr Ste 200, Santa Ana
(92707-5203)
PHONE..................................949 852-8340
Gary Standell, *President*
Michael Griba, *IT/INT Sup*
Chris Kramer, *Finance Mgr*
Jon Eruren, *Sales Staff*
Chris Granger, *Director*
EMP: 50
SQ FT: 2,000
SALES (est): 9MM **Privately Held**
WEB: www.westcoastcharters.com
SIC: 8742 5088 Industry specialist consultants; aircraft & parts

(P-26877)
WESTERN HEALTH RESOURCES
440 Greenfield Ave Ste B, Hanford
(93230-3568)
PHONE..................................559 537-2860
Sandy Delarosa, *Director*
EMP: 50
SALES (corp-wide): 59.7MM **Privately Held**
SIC: 8742 Hospital & health services consultant
PA: Western Health Resources
2100 Douglas Blvd
Roseville CA

(P-26878)
WILSHIRE ASSOCIATES INC (PA)
1299 Ocean Ave Ste 700, Santa Monica
(90401-1085)
PHONE..................................310 451-3051
Dennis A Tito, *CEO*
John C Hindman, *President*
Andrew Junkin, *President*
Michael Wauters, *CFO*
Leah Emkin, *Vice Pres*
EMP: 210

SQ FT: 57,530
SALES: 113.2MM **Privately Held**
WEB: www.wilshire.com
SIC: 8742 Financial consultant

(P-26879)
WIPFLI LLP
Also Called: Wipli HFS Consultants
505 14th St Ste 1220, Oakland
(94612-1419)
PHONE..................................510 768-0066
EMP: 100
SALES (corp-wide): 313.6MM **Privately Held**
SIC: 8742 Hospital & health services consultant
PA: Wipfli Llp
10000 W Innovation Dr 250-260
Milwaukee WI 53226
414 431-9300

(P-26880)
WPROMOTE LLC (PA)
2100 E Grand Ave Fl 1, El Segundo
(90245-5150)
PHONE..................................310 421-4844
Michael Mothner, *President*
Marissa Allen, *Vice Pres*
Jamie Farrell, *Vice Pres*
Aimee Abad, *Executive*
Jared Haynes, *Executive*
EMP: 92
SALES: 12.2MM **Privately Held**
WEB: www.wpromote.com
SIC: 8742 Marketing consulting services

(P-26881)
WSP USA INC
16689 Foothill Blvd, Fontana (92335-8414)
PHONE..................................909 427-9166
EMP: 61
SALES (corp-wide): 20MM **Privately Held**
SIC: 8742 Management consulting services
HQ: Wsp Usa Inc.
1 Penn Plz
New York NY 10119
212 465-5000

(P-26882)
WTW DELAWARE HOLDINGS LLC
Also Called: Willis Towers Watson
345 California St Fl 15, San Francisco
(94104-2629)
PHONE..................................415 733-4100
Jacque Leger, *Principal*
Tapio Boles, *Sr Consultant*
Rick Beal, *Manager*
Calvin Chou, *Consultant*
EMP: 125 **Privately Held**
WEB: www.watsonwyatt.com
SIC: 8742 8999 7371 6411 Compensation & benefits planning consultant; human resource consulting services; actuarial consultant; computer software systems analysis & design, custom; computer software development; pension & retirement plan consultants
HQ: Wtw Delaware Holdings Llc
800 N Glebe Rd
Arlington VA 22203

(P-26883)
WTW DELAWARE HOLDINGS LLC
Also Called: Willis Towers Watson
10955 Vista Sorrento Pkwy # 300, San Diego (92130-8699)
PHONE..................................858 523-5500
Mike Perez, *Network Enginr*
Rick Fischer, *Senior Engr*
EMP: 80 **Privately Held**
WEB: www.watsonwyatt.com
SIC: 8742 Management consulting services
HQ: Wtw Delaware Holdings Llc
800 N Glebe Rd
Arlington VA 22203

PRODUCTS & SVCS

(P-26884)
XAD INC
189 Bernardo Ave Ste 100, Mountain View (94043-5139)
PHONE.............................650 386-6867
EMP: 204
SALES (corp-wide): 37.9MM **Privately Held**
SIC: 8742 Marketing consulting services
PA: Xad, Inc.
　　1 World Trade Ctr Fl 60
　　New York NY 10007
　　888 234-7893

(P-26885)
YODLEE INC (HQ)
3600 Bridge Pkwy Ste 200, Redwood City (94065-6139)
PHONE.............................650 980-3600
Anil Arora, *President*
Mike Armsby, *CFO*
Bill Parsons, *Ch Credit Ofcr*
David Lee, *Chief Mktg Ofcr*
Katy Gibson, *Vice Pres*
▲ EMP: 146 EST: 1999
SQ FT: 35,000
SALES (est): 80.1MM
SALES (corp-wide): 812.3MM **Publicly Held**
SIC: 8742 Banking & finance consultant
PA: Envestnet, Inc.
　　35 E Wacker Dr Ste 2400
　　Chicago IL 60601
　　312 827-2800

(P-26886)
YOUAPPI INC
2 Embarcadero Ctr # 2310, San Francisco (94111-3823)
PHONE.............................646 854-3390
EMP: 70 EST: 2011
SALES (est): 176.4K **Privately Held**
SIC: 8742 7313

(P-26887)
ZIPLINE INTERNATIONAL INC
529 Railroad Ave, South San Francisco (94080-3450)
PHONE.............................415 993-0604
Keller Rinaudo, *CEO*
Keenan Wyrobek, *CTO*
Marina Yang, *Director*
EMP: 150 EST: 2012
SALES (est): 25.1MM **Privately Held**
SIC: 8742 Automation & robotics consultant

(P-26888)
ZIPRECRUITER INC
604 Arizona Ave, Santa Monica (90401-1610)
PHONE.............................800 557-9015
Ian Howard Siegel, *CEO*
Anthony McDaniel, *Executive*
Conorie Richmond, *Executive*
Monika Shah, *Surgery Dir*
Craig Glendenning, *Administration*
EMP: 600
SQ FT: 1,800
SALES (est): 10.7MM **Privately Held**
SIC: 8742 Human resource consulting services

(P-26889)
ZS ASSOCIATES INC
2535 W Hillcrest Dr # 100, Thousand Oaks (91320-2457)
PHONE.............................805 413-5900
EMP: 62
SALES (corp-wide): 317.9MM **Privately Held**
SIC: 8742 Marketing consulting services
PA: Zs Associates, Inc.
　　1560 Sherman Ave Ste 800
　　Evanston IL 60201
　　847 492-3600

(P-26890)
ZS ASSOCIATES INC
4365 Executive Dr # 1530, San Diego (92121-2129)
PHONE.............................858 677-2200
EMP: 62

SALES (corp-wide): 317.9MM **Privately Held**
SIC: 8742 7378 Marketing consulting services; computer maintenance & repair
PA: Zs Associates, Inc.
　　1560 Sherman Ave Ste 800
　　Evanston IL 60201
　　847 492-3600

8743 Public Relations Svcs

(P-26891)
ACCESS PUBLIC RELATIONS LLC
Also Called: Access Brand Communications
720 California St Fl 5, San Francisco (94108-2453)
PHONE.............................415 904-7070
Susan Butenhoff,
Danielle Caff, *Senior VP*
Matt Afflixio,
Jennifer Sims-Fellner,
EMP: 64
SQ FT: 17,000
SALES (est): 8.7MM
SALES (corp-wide): 15.2B **Publicly Held**
WEB: www.accesspr.com
SIC: 8743 Public relations & publicity
HQ: Ketchum Incorporated
　　1285 Avenue Of The Americ
　　New York NY 10019
　　646 935-3900

(P-26892)
ARYAKA NETWORKS INC (PA)
1800 Gateway Dr Ste 200, San Mateo (94404-4072)
PHONE.............................408 273-8420
Matt Carter, *CEO*
Kimberly McRobert, *Partner*
Homa Popal, *Partner*
Shane Quivey, *Partner*
Shawn Farshchi, *President*
EMP: 105
SALES (est): 34.9MM **Privately Held**
SIC: 8743 Sales promotion

(P-26893)
AT&T CORP
50 Fremont St, San Francisco (94105-2276)
PHONE.............................415 442-5900
Dennis Williams, *Branch Mgr*
Fassil Fenikile, *General Mgr*
Daniel Breece, *Technician*
David Katzeff, *Technical Staff*
Donna Hudak, *Analyst*
EMP: 150
SALES (corp-wide): 170.7B **Publicly Held**
WEB: www.att.com
SIC: 8743 Sales promotion
HQ: At&t Corp.
　　1 At&t Way
　　Bedminster NJ 07921
　　800 403-3302

(P-26894)
B T B EVENTS INC
Also Called: California Special Events
10950 Virginia Cir, Fountain Valley (92708-7010)
PHONE.............................714 415-3313
Christopher P Chapin, *CEO*
Robert G Traxel, *President*
Roger Janke, *Vice Pres*
John P Regas, *VP Opers*
EMP: 75
SALES (est): 12.9MM **Privately Held**
SIC: 8743 8742 7359 6512 Sales promotion; public relations & publicity; sales (including sales management) consultant; equipment rental & leasing; nonresidential building operators

(P-26895)
BAKER WINOKUR
Also Called: Bwrpr
9100 Wilshire Blvd 500w, Beverly Hills (90212-3426)
PHONE.............................310 248-6169
M Sorel, *President*
Courtney Sybesma, *Accounts Exec*
EMP: 70 EST: 1979

SALES: 10MM **Privately Held**
WEB: www.bwrpr.com
SIC: 8743 Public relations & publicity

(P-26896)
BEHR PROCESS SALES COMPANY
3000 S Main St Apt 84e, Santa Ana (92707-4225)
P.O. Box 1287 (92702-1287)
PHONE.............................714 545-7101
Kevin Jaffe, *Partner*
John V Croul, *Partner*
Scott Richards, *Vice Pres*
EMP: 150
SQ FT: 54,000
SALES (est): 9.8MM **Privately Held**
SIC: 8743 2851 5198 Sales promotion; varnishes; paints & paint additives; stains; varnish, oil or wax; lacquer: bases, dopes, thinner; paints, varnishes & supplies

(P-26897)
BENDER/HELPER IMPACT INC (PA)
11500 W Olympic Blvd # 655, Los Angeles (90064-1524)
PHONE.............................310 473-4147
Lee Helper, *President*
Dean Bender, *Vice Pres*
Adam Krell, *Executive*
Ranese Southerland, *Office Mgr*
Nicki Dennis, *Executive Asst*
EMP: 55
SQ FT: 9,314
SALES (est): 6.5MM **Privately Held**
WEB: www.bhimpact.com
SIC: 8743 Public relations & publicity

(P-26898)
BNI ENTERPRISES INC
Also Called: B N I
545 College Commerce Way, Upland (91786-4377)
PHONE.............................909 305-1818
Ivan Misner, *Chairman*
EMP: 600
SQ FT: 33,000
SALES (est): 73.5MM **Privately Held**
WEB: www.bni.com
SIC: 8743 Promotion service

(P-26899)
BWR PUBLIC RELATIONS
Also Called: Baker Winokur Ryder
9100 Wilshire Blvd 500w, Beverly Hills (90212-3415)
PHONE.............................310 248-6100
Larry Winokur, *President*
Neal Cohen, *Officer*
Lynda Dorf, *Vice Pres*
Paul Gillis, *Info Tech Mgr*
Adri Palmieri, *Pub Rel Mgr*
EMP: 67
SALES (est): 2.2MM **Privately Held**
SIC: 8743 Public relations & publicity

(P-26900)
CALIBRE INTERNATIONAL LLC (PA)
Also Called: High Caliber Line
6250 N Irwindale Ave, Irwindale (91702-3208)
PHONE.............................626 969-4660
Daniel Oas,
Kenan Ozcan, *CFO*
Tiffiany Fontenot, *Executive*
Catherine Oas,
Jessica Contreras, *Representative*
◆ EMP: 165
SQ FT: 100,000
SALES: 28MM **Privately Held**
WEB: www.calibr.com
SIC: 8743 2759 Promotion service; promotional printing

(P-26901)
CAROLINE PROMOTIONS INC
809 S Adams St Apt 7, Glendale (91205-4424)
PHONE.............................818 507-7666
Caroline Jovenich, *President*
EMP: 55
SQ FT: 600

SALES (est): 3.4MM **Privately Held**
WEB: www.carolinepromotions.com
SIC: 8743 Sales promotion

(P-26902)
CATALINA EVENTS INC
2605 184th St, Redondo Beach (90278-4508)
PHONE.............................310 925-6986
John Ellis, *CEO*
EMP: 50
SALES (est): 843.2K **Privately Held**
SIC: 8743 Promotion service

(P-26903)
CITY OF CORONA
400 S Vicentia Ave, Corona (92882-2187)
PHONE.............................951 279-3647
Kit Field, *Branch Mgr*
EMP: 250 **Privately Held**
SIC: 8743 Public relations services
PA: City Of Corona
　　400 S Vicentia Ave
　　Corona CA 92882
　　951 736-2372

(P-26904)
CMP FILM & DESIGN BURBANK LLC
Also Called: Mocean
2717 W Olive Ave, Burbank (91505-4532)
PHONE.............................818 729-0800
Craig Murray, *Mng Member*
EMP: 65
SQ FT: 12,000
SALES (est): 4.1MM **Privately Held**
SIC: 8743 7812 Promotion service; video tape production

(P-26905)
COMPETITOR GROUP EVENTS INC
5452 Oberlin Dr, San Diego (92121-1715)
PHONE.............................858 450-6510
Tim Murphy, *President*
EMP: 50
SQ FT: 12,500
SALES (est): 3.6MM
SALES (corp-wide): 127MM **Privately Held**
WEB: www.eliteracing.com
SIC: 8743 Promotion service
HQ: Competitor Group, Inc.
　　6420 Sequence Dr
　　San Diego CA 92121

(P-26906)
DANIEL J EDELMAN INC
Also Called: Edelman Public Relations
525 Market St, San Francisco (94105-2708)
PHONE.............................415 222-9944
Jay Porter, *General Mgr*
Emily Chan, *Vice Pres*
EMP: 99
SALES (corp-wide): 441.1MM **Privately Held**
SIC: 8743 Public relations & publicity
HQ: Daniel J. Edelman, Inc.
　　200 E Randolph St Fl 63
　　Chicago IL 60601
　　312 240-3000

(P-26907)
DANIEL J EDELMAN INC
Also Called: Edelman Public Relations
5670 Wilshire Blvd # 2500, Los Angeles (90036-5679)
PHONE.............................323 857-9100
Gail Becker, *Principal*
Fion Lee, *Hum Res Coord*
EMP: 65
SALES (corp-wide): 441.1MM **Privately Held**
SIC: 8743 7313 Public relations & publicity; electronic media advertising representatives; printed media advertising representatives
HQ: Daniel J. Edelman, Inc.
　　200 E Randolph St Fl 63
　　Chicago IL 60601
　　312 240-3000

(P-26908)
FENTON COMMUNICATIONS INC
182 2nd St Ste 400, San Francisco
(94105-3801)
PHONE.............................415 255-1946
Parker Blackman, *Manager*
EMP: 50
SALES (corp-wide): 13.8MM **Privately Held**
WEB: www.dhs.gov
SIC: 8743 Public relations & publicity
PA: Fenton Communications, Inc.
1010 Vermont Ave Nw # 1100
Washington DC 20005
202 822-5200

(P-26909)
FLEISHMAN-HILLARD INC
720 California St Fl 6, San Francisco
(94108-2478)
PHONE.............................415 318-4000
Tim O'Keeffe, *General Mgr*
Kate Whitney, *Executive*
EMP: 50
SALES (corp-wide): 15.2B **Publicly Held**
WEB: www.fleishmanhillard.com
SIC: 8743 Public relations & publicity
HQ: Fleishman-Hillard Inc.
200 N Broadway
Saint Louis MO 63102
314 982-1700

(P-26910)
HAVAS FORMULA LLC
1215 Cushman Ave, San Diego
(92110-3904)
PHONE.............................619 234-0345
Michael A Olguin, *President*
Katie Lippman, *Assoc VP*
Alexis McCance, *Senior VP*
Mia West, *Vice Pres*
Cristina Calderon, *Executive*
EMP: 100
SQ FT: 2,700
SALES (est): 16MM
SALES (corp-wide): 78.1MM **Privately Held**
WEB: www.formulapr.com
SIC: 8743 Public relations & publicity; transit advertising services
HQ: Havas
29 30
Puteaux 92800
158 478-000

(P-26911)
HILL & KNOWLTON STRATEGIES LLC
Blanc & Otus
60 Green St, San Francisco (94111-1435)
PHONE.............................415 281-7120
Quinn Daly, *General Mgr*
Barbara Edler, *Vice Pres*
Laurie White, *Vice Pres*
Chelsea Murillo, *Executive*
Keven Elliott, *General Mgr*
EMP: 55
SALES (corp-wide): 20B **Privately Held**
SIC: 8743 Public relations & publicity
HQ: Hill And Knowlton Strategies, Llc
466 Lexington Ave Frnt 4
New York NY 10017
212 885-0300

(P-26912)
HOFFMAN AGENCY (PA)
325 S 1st St Ste 300, San Jose
(95113-2830)
PHONE.............................408 286-2611
Lou Hoffman, *CEO*
Steve Burkhart, *Manager*
EMP: 53
SQ FT: 23,000
SALES (est): 4.9MM **Privately Held**
WEB: www.hoffman.com
SIC: 8743 Public relations & publicity

(P-26913)
KETCHUM INCORPORATED
12777 W Jefferson Blvd # 120, Los Angeles
(90066-7038)
PHONE.............................310 437-2600
Melissa Kinch, *Director*
Matthew Dernoga, *Research*

Stacy Kika, *Accounts Exec*
EMP: 60
SALES (corp-wide): 15.2B **Publicly Held**
SIC: 8743 7311 Public relations & publicity; advertising agencies
HQ: Ketchum Incorporated
1285 Avenue Of The Americ
New York NY 10019
646 935-3900

(P-26914)
KETCHUM INCORPORATED
1050 Battery St, San Francisco
(94111-1286)
PHONE.............................415 984-6100
Melissa Kinch, *Director*
Christopher Albert, *Vice Pres*
David Allan, *Vice Pres*
Maud Broda, *Vice Pres*
Bob Conrad, *Vice Pres*
EMP: 75
SALES (corp-wide): 15.2B **Publicly Held**
WEB: www.imsfastpak.com
SIC: 8743 Public relations & publicity
HQ: Ketchum Incorporated
1285 Avenue Of The Americ
New York NY 10019
646 935-3900

(P-26915)
LEAGUE OF CALIFORNIA CITIES (PA)
Also Called: Western City Magazine
1400 K St Fl 4, Sacramento (95814-3916)
PHONE.............................916 658-8200
Carolyn Coleman, *Exec Dir*
Norman Coppinger, *CFO*
Janet Reynolds, *Admin Sec*
Kimberly Brady, *Admin Asst*
John McElligott, *Info Tech Mgr*
EMP: 65
SQ FT: 32,000
SALES: 300.6K **Privately Held**
WEB: www.cacities.org
SIC: 8743 2721 Lobbyist; magazines: publishing only, not printed on site

(P-26916)
LEWIS PR INC (DH)
111 Sutter St Ste 850, San Francisco
(94104-4506)
PHONE.............................415 432-2400
Chris Lewis, *CEO*
James Oehlcke, *CFO*
Andres Wittermann, *Exec VP*
Heather Bliss, *Senior VP*
Jen Dobrzelecki, *Senior VP*
EMP: 53
SALES (est): 15.2MM
SALES (corp-wide): 65.4MM **Privately Held**
SIC: 8743 Public relations & publicity
HQ: Lewis Communications Limited
22 Floor, Millbank Tower
London SW1P
207 802-2626

(P-26917)
LIPPIN GROUP INC (PA)
6100 Wilshire Blvd # 400, Los Angeles
(90048-5109)
PHONE.............................323 965-1990
Richard B Lippin, *President*
Don Ciaramella, *President*
Shelly Saarella, *CFO*
Kevin Broderick, *Vice Pres*
Katie Fuchs, *Vice Pres*
EMP: 50
SQ FT: 8,000
SALES (est): 6.6MM **Privately Held**
SIC: 8743 Public relations & publicity

(P-26918)
MAGIC WORKFORCE SOLUTIONS LLC
9100 Wilsh Blvd Ste 700e, Beverly Hills
(90212)
PHONE.............................310 246-6153
Earvin Johnson, *CEO*
Eric Holoman, *President*
Kawanna Brown, *COO*
EMP: 4539 EST: 2007
SALES (est): 3.4MM
SALES (corp-wide): 506.6MM **Privately Held**
SIC: 8743 Promotion service

PA: Magic Johnson Enterprises, Inc.
9100 Wilshire Blvd 700e
Beverly Hills CA 90212
310 247-2033

(P-26919)
MURPHY OBRIEN INC
11444 W Olympic Blvd # 600, Los Angeles
(90064-1549)
PHONE.............................310 453-2539
Karen Murphy O'Brien, *CEO*
EMP: 55
SQ FT: 7,159
SALES (est): 4.6MM **Privately Held**
WEB: www.murphyobrien.com
SIC: 8743 Public relations & publicity

(P-26920)
OGILVY PUB RLTONS WRLDWIDE INC
1530 J St, Sacramento (95814-2052)
PHONE.............................916 231-7700
Suanne Buggy, *Vice Pres*
EMP: 74
SALES (corp-wide): 20B **Privately Held**
SIC: 8743 Public relations & publicity
HQ: Ogilvy Public Relations Worldwide Inc.
636 11th Ave
New York NY 10036
212 880-5200

(P-26921)
OUTCAST AGENCY LLC
100 Montgomery St # 1202, San Francisco
(94104-4388)
PHONE.............................415 392-8282
Tim Dyson,
Alex Constantinople, *Partner*
Catalina McFadin, *CEO*
Meg Dincecco, *Vice Pres*
Nicki Dugan, *Vice Pres*
EMP: 120
SALES (est): 11.6MM **Privately Held**
SIC: 8743 Public relations services

(P-26922)
PMK-BNC INC (PA)
1840 Century Park E # 1400, Los Angeles
(90067-2115)
PHONE.............................310 854-0455
Michael Nyman, *CEO*
John Lundy, *CFO*
Michael Donkis, *Exec VP*
Doug Piwinski, *Exec VP*
Maryann Watson, *Exec VP*
EMP: 130
SQ FT: 4,000
SALES (est): 29.1MM **Privately Held**
SIC: 8743 Public relations & publicity

(P-26923)
PMK-BNC INC
8687 Melrose Ave Fl 8th, Los Angeles
(90069-5746)
PHONE.............................310 854-4800
Eunice Ko, *Branch Mgr*
EMP: 50
SALES (corp-wide): 29.1MM **Privately Held**
SIC: 8743 Public relations & publicity
PA: Pmk-Bnc, Inc.
1840 Century Park E # 1400
Los Angeles CA 90067
310 854-0455

(P-26924)
RPMC INC (PA)
Also Called: R P M C Travel
23975 Park Sorrento # 410, Calabasas
(91302-4031)
PHONE.............................818 222-7762
Robert Olshever, *President*
Kelly Weinberg, *Exec VP*
Murray Schwartz, *Vice Pres*
Melinda Messing, *Project Mgr*
Angelica Diaz, *Senior Mgr*
EMP: 95
SQ FT: 10,000
SALES (est): 11.3MM **Privately Held**
SIC: 8743 8742 Promotion service; marketing consulting services

(P-26925)
WEBER SHANDWICK
600 Battery St Fl 1, San Francisco
(94111-1820)
PHONE.............................415 262-5600
Luca Penati, *Vice Pres*
Will Ludlam, *President*
David Hirota, *Vice Pres*
Traci Mogil, *Vice Pres*
Erin Patton, *Vice Pres*
EMP: 60 EST: 2008
SALES (est): 717.8K **Privately Held**
SIC: 8743 Public relations services

8744 Facilities Support Mgmt Svcs

(P-26926)
ACEPEX MANAGEMENT CORPORATION
10643 Mills Ave, Montclair (91763-4612)
PHONE.............................909 625-6900
Henry C Rhee, *CEO*
Nancy Escobar, *Executive Asst*
Drew Hansen, *IT/INT Sup*
Helen Ward, *Project Mgr*
Thomas Rhee, *Opers Mgr*
EMP: 150
SQ FT: 7,000
SALES: 22.8MM **Privately Held**
WEB: www.acepex.com
SIC: 8744 Base maintenance (providing personnel on continuing basis)

(P-26927)
ADVANCED CLEANUP TECH INC (PA)
4548 Wesley Ln, Bakersfield (93308-9625)
P.O. Box 5270, Compton (90224-5270)
PHONE.............................310 763-1423
Ruben Garcia, *CEO*
EMP: 120
SALES (est): 26.2MM **Privately Held**
WEB: www.actird.com
SIC: 8744

(P-26928)
AGUATIERRA ASSOCIATES INC (PA)
Also Called: Weiss Associates
2000 Powell St Ste 555, Emeryville
(94608-1838)
PHONE.............................510 450-6000
Michael D Dresen, *President*
Richard B Weiss, *CFO*
Scott Bourne, *Vice Pres*
Bob Devany, *Vice Pres*
Robert Devany, *Vice Pres*
EMP: 55
SQ FT: 13,000
SALES (est): 6.2MM **Privately Held**
SIC: 8744 4959 8748 Facilities support services; environmental cleanup services; environmental consultant

(P-26929)
AMERICAN INTEGRATED SVCS INC (PA)
1502 E Opp St, Wilmington (90744-3927)
P.O. Box 92316, Long Beach (90809-2316)
PHONE.............................310 522-1168
Paul David Herrera, *President*
Gerald Adkerson, *Vice Pres*
Razmik Gozalians, *Vice Pres*
Gary Runnells, *Vice Pres*
Sandi Schafer, *Vice Pres*
EMP: 50
SQ FT: 77,000
SALES (est): 29.8MM **Privately Held**
WEB: www.americanintegrated.com
SIC: 8744

(P-26930)
AMERITAC INC (PA)
640 Logan Ln, Danville (94526-1512)
P.O. Box 279 (94526-0279)
PHONE.............................925 743-8398
Isiah Harris, *President*
Lawrence Stevens, *Vice Pres*
EMP: 80
SQ FT: 2,024

SALES: 5.3MM **Privately Held**
WEB: www.ameritac.net
SIC: 8744 Base maintenance (providing personnel on continuing basis)

(P-26931)
ARGUS MANAGEMENT COMPANY LLC
Also Called: Argus Medical Management
5150 E Pacific Coast Hwy # 500, Long Beach (90804-3328)
PHONE.....................562 299-5200
Robert C Boullon,
Peter Ferrera,
Robert Lugliani,
Mansoor Shah,
EMP: 300
SQ FT: 2,500
SALES (est): 19.1MM **Privately Held**
WEB: www.argusmso.com
SIC: 8744 Facilities support services

(P-26932)
CAPE ENVIRONMENTAL MGT INC
18012 Cowan Ste 150, Irvine (92614-6817)
PHONE.....................949 236-3000
Amir Matin, *Manager*
EMP: 265
SALES (corp-wide): 243.8MM **Privately Held**
SIC: 8744
PA: Cape Environmental Management Inc.
500 Pinnacle Ct Ste 100
Norcross GA 30071
770 908-7200

(P-26933)
CASA DSCANSO CONVALESCENT HOSP
Also Called: Huntington Child Care Center
4515 Huntington Dr S, Los Angeles (90032-1940)
PHONE.....................323 225-5991
Jack Gindi, *President*
EMP: 107
SALES (est): 5.6MM **Privately Held**
SIC: 8744 Facilities support services

(P-26934)
CITY OF BREA
Also Called: Maintenance Dept
1 Civic Center Cir Fl 3, Brea (92821-5758)
PHONE.....................714 990-7650
Bill Higgins, *Director*
EMP: 57 **Privately Held**
WEB: www.cityofbrea.net
SIC: 8744 Base maintenance (providing personnel on continuing basis)
PA: City Of Brea
1 Civic Center Cir Fl 3
Brea CA 92821
714 990-7600

(P-26935)
CITY OF WOODLAND
Also Called: Public Works Department
655 N Pioneer Ave, Woodland (95776-6112)
PHONE.....................530 661-5962
Greg Mayer, *Director*
EMP: 200 **Privately Held**
WEB: www.ci.woodland.ca.us
SIC: 8744 Base maintenance (providing personnel on continuing basis)
PA: City Of Woodland
300 1st St
Woodland CA 95695
530 661-5830

(P-26936)
CORECIVIC INC
Also Called: San Diego Correctional Fcilty
446 Alta Rd, San Diego (92158-0001)
P.O. Box 439049, San Ysidro (92143-9049)
PHONE.....................619 661-9119
Rupert Rivera, *Manager*
EMP: 243
SALES (corp-wide): 1.8B **Publicly Held**
WEB: www.correctionscorp.com
SIC: 8744 Correctional facility
PA: Corecivic, Inc.
5501 Virginia Way Ste 110
Brentwood TN 37027
615 263-3000

(P-26937)
CORECIVIC INC
Also Called: California Cy Correctional Ctr
22844 Virginia Blvd, California City (93505)
P.O. Box 2590 (93504-0590)
PHONE.....................760 373-1764
Charles Gilkey, *Warden*
EMP: 150
SALES (corp-wide): 1.8B **Publicly Held**
WEB: www.correctionscorp.com
SIC: 8744 Correctional facility
PA: Corecivic, Inc.
5501 Virginia Way Ste 110
Brentwood TN 37027
615 263-3000

(P-26938)
CORNELL COMPANIES INC
759 Lakeview Ave, San Francisco (94112-2203)
PHONE.....................415 346-9769
EMP: 92
SALES (corp-wide): 2.3B **Privately Held**
SIC: 8744 Correctional facility
HQ: Cornell Companies, Inc.
4955 Technology Way
Boca Raton FL 33431

(P-26939)
CORRECTIONAL SERVICES CORP LLC
7805 Arjons Dr, San Diego (92126-4368)
PHONE.....................858 566-9816
EMP: 51
SALES (corp-wide): 2.3B **Privately Held**
SIC: 8744 Correctional facility
HQ: Correctional Services Corporation, Llc
621 Nw 53rd St Ste 700
Boca Raton FL 33487

(P-26940)
COUNTY OF MONTEREY
Also Called: County Jail
1410 Natividad Rd, Salinas (93906-3102)
PHONE.....................831 755-3782
John Davidson, *Principal*
EMP: 179 **Privately Held**
WEB: www.montereycountyfarmbureau.org
SIC: 8744 Jails, privately operated
PA: County Of Monterey
168 W Alisal St Fl 2
Salinas CA 93901
831 755-5040

(P-26941)
COUNTY OF SACRAMENTO
Also Called: Sheriff's Dept
12500 Bruceville Rd, Elk Grove (95757-9784)
PHONE.....................916 874-1927
James Babcock, *Branch Mgr*
EMP: 250 **Privately Held**
WEB: www.sna.com
SIC: 8744 9223 Correctional facility; correctional institutions;
PA: County Of Sacramento
700 H St Ste 7650
Sacramento CA 95814
916 874-5544

(P-26942)
CVE NB CONTRACTING GROUP INC
Also Called: Central Valley Environmental
135 Utility Ct A, Rohnert Park (94928-1616)
PHONE.....................707 584-1900
Tim Williamson, *CEO*
Glenn Accornero, *COO*
EMP: 50 EST: 2015
SQ FT: 4,700
SALES: 12.5MM **Privately Held**
SIC: 8744

(P-26943)
GEO GROUP INC
Also Called: Taft Correctional Institution
1500 Cadet Rd, Taft (93268-4800)
P.O. Box 7000 (93268-7000)
PHONE.....................661 763-2510
Michael Denop, *Warden*
Jon Swatsburg, *Vice Pres*
Christopher St Jean, *Business Mgr*

EMP: 387
SALES (corp-wide): 2.3B **Privately Held**
WEB: www.thegeogroupinc.com
SIC: 8744 Correctional facility
PA: The Geo Group Inc
4955 Technology Way
Boca Raton FL 33431
561 893-0101

(P-26944)
GERWEND ENTERPRISES INC
Also Called: Integrity Management Entps
2952 Market St, San Diego (92102-3241)
PHONE.....................619 254-5018
Carlos Buzon, *President*
Tony Pizarro, *Vice Pres*
EMP: 150
SQ FT: 4,000
SALES (est): 6.9MM **Privately Held**
SIC: 8744 Facilities support services

(P-26945)
GILBANE AECOM JV
1655 Grant St Fl 12, Concord (94520-2600)
PHONE.....................925 946-3100
Eric Banks, *Manager*
Tab Tsukuda, *Government*
Harvey Coppage, *Manager*
Natalia Rahkman, *Manager*
Matt Tierney, *Manager*
EMP: 54 EST: 2016
SALES (est): 1.2MM
SIC: 8744 Facilities support services
HQ: Gilbane Federal
1655 Grant St Ste 1200
Concord CA 94520

(P-26946)
HUMAN POTENTIAL CONS LLC
500 E Carson Plaza Dr # 127, Carson (90746-3225)
PHONE.....................310 756-1560
Garnett Newcombe, *CEO*
EMP: 63 EST: 1997
SQ FT: 3,500
SALES: 3.5MM **Privately Held**
SIC: 8744 7349 8741 Facilities support services; janitorial service, contract basis; personnel management

(P-26947)
IAP WORLD SERVICES INC
567 Dugan South Akron Rd, Mountain View (94035)
PHONE.....................650 604-0451
Travis Durano, *Project Mgr*
EMP: 68
SALES (corp-wide): 648.3MM **Privately Held**
WEB: www.jcwsi.com
SIC: 8744 Facilities support services
HQ: Iap World Services, Inc.
7315 N Atlantic Ave
Cape Canaveral FL 32920
321 784-7100

(P-26948)
IAP WORLD SERVICES INC
510 S Loop 1st St Bldg T, Fort Irwin (92310)
PHONE.....................760 380-6772
Jeffrey D Williamson, *Manager*
EMP: 290
SALES (corp-wide): 648.3MM **Privately Held**
WEB: www.jcwsi.com
SIC: 8744 Facilities support services
HQ: Iap World Services, Inc.
7315 N Atlantic Ave
Cape Canaveral FL 32920
321 784-7100

(P-26949)
INDYNE INC
1036 California Blvd # 11013, Vandenberg Afb (93437)
PHONE.....................805 606-7225
Kenneth A Cinal, *Branch Mgr*
David Miller, *Principal*
EMP: 700

SALES (corp-wide): 241.8MM **Privately Held**
WEB: www.indyneinc.com
SIC: 8744 Base maintenance (providing personnel on continuing basis)
PA: Indyne, Inc.
21351 Gentry Dr Ste 205
Sterling VA 20166
703 903-6900

(P-26950)
INNOVATIVE CNSTR SOLUTIONS
575 Anton Blvd Ste 850, Costa Mesa (92626-7023)
PHONE.....................714 893-6366
Hirad Emadi, *President*
Greg Sherman, *Vice Pres*
John R White, *Vice Pres*
Keith Dorsa, *General Mgr*
Monique Stefanovic, *Office Mgr*
EMP: 105
SQ FT: 2,000
SALES (est): 20.9MM **Privately Held**
SIC: 8744 1795 ; demolition, buildings & other structures

(P-26951)
JLS ENVIRONMENTAL SERVICES INC
3460 Swetzer Rd, Loomis (95650-7624)
PHONE.....................916 660-1525
Larry Walker, *President*
John G Sheehan, *CEO*
David Locke, *CFO*
Heath Lesher, *Sr Project Mgr*
EMP: 70
SALES (est): 8.4MM **Privately Held**
WEB: www.jls-inc.com
SIC: 8744 8999 ; earth science services

(P-26952)
LEXICON CONSULTING INC (PA)
420 S Magnolia Ave, El Cajon (92020-5213)
PHONE.....................619 792-1530
Jamie J Latshaw, *President*
Bruce Greene, *CFO*
EMP: 60
SQ FT: 2,000
SALES (est): 7.3MM **Privately Held**
WEB: www.lexiconinc.com
SIC: 8744 7363 8322 8331 Base maintenance (providing personnel on continuing basis); medical help service; individual & family services; job training & vocational rehabilitation services

(P-26953)
OLYMPUS BUILDING SERVICES INC
441 La Moree Rd, San Marcos (92078-5017)
PHONE.....................760 750-4629
Anthony Hipple, *Branch Mgr*
EMP: 1090
SALES (corp-wide): 23MM **Privately Held**
SIC: 8744 Facilities support services
PA: Olympus Building Services Inc
1430 E Missouri Ave B205
Phoenix AZ 85014
480 284-8018

(P-26954)
SERVICON SYSTEMS INC (PA)
Also Called: Pacifica Consulting Services
3965 Landmark St, Culver City (90232-2399)
PHONE.....................310 204-5040
Michael Mahdesian, *Chairman*
Laurie Sewell, *President*
Maritza Aguilar, *CFO*
Richard Conti, *Officer*
Robert Harrelson, *Officer*
EMP: 1500
SQ FT: 11,500
SALES (est): 98.4MM **Privately Held**
WEB: www.janitorial.com
SIC: 8744 7349 1771 Facilities support services; building maintenance services; flooring contractor

(P-26955)
SMG
Also Called: Smg Stockton
3445 S El Dorado St, Stockton (95206)
PHONE..................209 937-7433
Kandra Clark, *General Mgr*
EMP: 400
SQ FT: 25,000
SALES (est): 4.9MM
SALES (corp-wide): 23.7B **Privately Held**
SIC: 8744 Facilities support services
HQ: Smg Holdings, Llc
300 Cnshohckn State Rd # 450
Conshohocken PA 19428
-

(P-26956)
SWISS PORT CORP
Also Called: Swissport
11001 Aviation Blvd, Los Angeles
(90045-6123)
PHONE..................310 417-0258
Armin Unternaehrer, *Vice Pres*
Esperanza Cortes, *Manager*
EMP: 500
SALES (est): 33.6MM **Privately Held**
SIC: 8744 4581 Facilities support serv-
ices; airports, flying fields & services

(P-26957)
TECHFLOW INC (PA)
9889 Willow Creek Rd, San Diego
(92131-1119)
PHONE..................858 412-8000
Robert Baum, *CEO*
Mark Carter, *President*
Lorie Atoe, *CFO*
Stephen Bivona, *Vice Pres*
Kenneth Enke, *Vice Pres*
EMP: 104
SQ FT: 19,000
SALES (est): 42.5MM **Privately Held**
WEB: www.techflow.com
SIC: 8744 8711 8748 Facilities support
services; engineering services; systems
analysis & engineering consulting serv-
ices

(P-26958)
VANGUARD RESOURCES CORP
13816 Fontanelle Pl, San Diego
(92128-4755)
P.O. Box 420355 (92142-0355)
PHONE..................858 336-7147
Nicole Murray, *President*
EMP: 60
SALES (est): 2MM **Privately Held**
WEB: www.vanguardresourcescorp.com
SIC: 8744 Facilities support services

(P-26959)
WEST COAST STORM INC (PA)
9701 Wilshire Blvd # 1000, Beverly Hills
(90212-2020)
PHONE..................909 890-5700
Michelle Padilla, *President*
Renata Salo, *CFO*
Rafael Padilla, *Vice Pres*
EMP: 50
SQ FT: 48,000
SALES (est): 6.7MM **Privately Held**
WEB: www.wcstorm.net
SIC: 8744

(P-26960)
WORKCARE INC
300 S Harbor Blvd Ste 600, Anaheim
(92805-3718)
PHONE..................714 978-7488
Dr Peter P Greaney, *CEO*
Bill Nixon, *CFO*
William E Nixon, *CFO*
Scott Gordon, *Vice Pres*
Cynthia Perry-Scott, *Vice Pres*
EMP: 181
SQ FT: 11,000
SALES (est): 26.7MM **Privately Held**
WEB: www.workcare.com
SIC: 8744 8011 Facilities support services;
offices & clinics of medical doctors

(P-26961)
ZERO WASTE SOLUTIONS INC
1850 Gateway Blvd # 1030, Concord
(94520-3279)
P.O. Box 5097 (94524-0097)
PHONE..................925 270-3339
Shavila Singh, *CEO*
Shavlia Fangh, *Mktg Coord*
EMP: 200
SQ FT: 3,000
SALES (est): 25.7MM **Privately Held**
WEB: www.zerowastesolutions.com
SIC: 8744 Facilities support services

8748 Business Consulting Svcs, NEC

(P-26962)
500 STARTUPS INCUBATOR LLC
814 Mission St Ste 600, San Francisco
(94103-3025)
PHONE..................415 974-6343
EMP: 108
SALES (est): 12.1MM **Privately Held**
SIC: 8748 Business consulting

(P-26963)
8020 CONSULTING LLC
6303 Owensmouth Ave Fl 10, Woodland
Hills (91367-2262)
PHONE..................818 523-3201
David Lewis, *Mng Member*
Shawn Spears, *COO*
Kelly Swartzel, *COO*
Teresa Alicer, *Finance Dir*
Henry Badalyan, *Finance*
EMP: 50
SALES: 15MM **Privately Held**
SIC: 8748 Business consulting

(P-26964)
ABSG CONSULTING INC
505 14th St Ste 900, Oakland
(94612-1468)
PHONE..................510 508-6289
William Keogh, *Branch Mgr*
EMP: 50
SALES (corp-wide): 484.4MM **Privately
Held**
WEB: www.absconsulting.com
SIC: 8748 Safety training service; systems
analysis & engineering consulting serv-
ices; testing services
HQ: Absg Consulting Inc.
1701 City Plaza Dr
Spring TX 77389
281 673-2800

(P-26965)
ABSG CONSULTING INC
300 Commerce Ste 150, Irvine
(92602-1302)
PHONE..................714 734-4242
Melinda Arjonilla, *Branch Mgr*
EMP: 68
SALES (corp-wide): 484.4MM **Privately
Held**
WEB: www.absconsulting.com
SIC: 8748 Safety training service; testing
services; systems analysis & engineering
consulting services
HQ: Absg Consulting Inc.
1701 City Plaza Dr
Spring TX 77389
281 673-2800

(P-26966)
AC SQUARE INC
4590 Qantas Ln, Stockton (95206-3903)
PHONE..................650 293-2730
EMP: 239
SALES (corp-wide): 43.7MM **Privately
Held**
SIC: 8748
PA: Ac Square, Inc.
371 Foster City Blvd
Foster City CA 94404
650 293-2730

(P-26967)
ACC-GWG LLC
Also Called: American Commodity Co.
6133 Abel Rd, Williams (95987-5816)
P.O. Box 236 (95987-0236)
PHONE..................530 473-2827
Chris Crutchfield, *President*
Bob Watts, *Vice Pres*
Nicole Montna Van Vleck, *Admin Sec*
Paul Crutchfield,
Al Montna,
EMP: 60
SALES (est): 5.6MM **Privately Held**
SIC: 8748 Agricultural consultant

(P-26968)
ACRT PACIFIC LLC
3443 Deer Park Dr Ste B, Stockton
(95219-2306)
PHONE..................330 945-7500
Brad S Schroeder,
Alan Rothenbuecher,
EMP: 450
SALES: 50MM **Privately Held**
SIC: 8748 Business consulting

(P-26969)
AE & ASSOCIATES LLC
506 Queensland Cir, Corona (92879-1381)
PHONE..................951 278-3477
Arnold Ardevela,
Mark Ardevela, *Opers Staff*
Ester Ardevela,
EMP: 60 **EST:** 1999
SQ FT: 3,755
SALES (est): 750K **Privately Held**
SIC: 8748 Business consulting

(P-26970)
AECOM GLOBAL II LLC
2870 Gateway Oaks Dr # 300, Sacramento
(95833-3577)
PHONE..................916 679-8700
Victor Auvinen, *Branch Mgr*
EMP: 185
SQ FT: 12,000
SALES (corp-wide): 20.1B **Publicly Held**
SIC: 8748 Environmental consultant
HQ: Aecom Global Ii, Llc
1999 Avenue Of The Stars
Los Angeles CA 90067
213 593-8100

(P-26971)
AECOM GLOBAL II LLC
915 Wilshire Blvd Ste 800, Los Angeles
(90017-3488)
PHONE..................213 996-2200
Dave Wu, *Branch Mgr*
Farrah Farzaneh, *Project Mgr*
EMP: 200
SALES (corp-wide): 20.1B **Publicly Held**
SIC: 8748 Systems analysis & engineering
consulting services
HQ: Aecom Global Ii, Llc
1999 Avenue Of The Stars
Los Angeles CA 90067
213 593-8100

(P-26972)
AECOM GLOBAL II LLC
310 Golden Shore Ste 100, Long Beach
(90802-4240)
PHONE..................310 343-6977
Edward Andrechak, *Branch Mgr*
EMP: 65
SALES (corp-wide): 20.1B **Publicly Held**
SIC: 8748 Environmental consultant
HQ: Aecom Global Ii, Llc
1999 Avenue Of The Stars
Los Angeles CA 90067
213 593-8100

(P-26973)
AECOM TECHNICAL SERVICES INC (HQ)
300 S Grand Ave Ste 1100, Los Angeles
(90071-3173)
PHONE..................213 593-8000
Timothy H Keener, *CEO*
Michael Whitmire, *Executive*
▲ **EMP:** 100 **EST:** 1970
SQ FT: 43,000

SALES (est): 1B
SALES (corp-wide): 20.1B **Publicly Held**
WEB: www.earthtech.com
SIC: 8748 4953 8742 8711 Environmental consultant; refuse systems; industry
specialist consultants; engineering services
PA: Aecom
1999 Avenue Of The Stars # 2600
Los Angeles CA 90067
213 593-8000

(P-26974)
AECOM USA INC
515 S Figueroa St Ste 400, Los Angeles
(90071-3323)
PHONE..................213 330-7200
EMP: 104
SALES (corp-wide): 20.1B **Publicly Held**
SIC: 8748 Business consulting
HQ: Aecom Usa, Inc.
605 3rd Ave
New York NY 10158
212 973-2900

(P-26975)
AECOM USA INC
100 W San Fernando St, San Jose
(95113-2219)
PHONE..................408 392-0670
EMP: 104
SALES (corp-wide): 17.4B **Publicly Held**
SIC: 8748
HQ: Aecom Usa, Inc.
605 3rd Ave
New York NY 10158
212 973-2900

(P-26976)
AECOM USA INC
300 S Grand Ave Ste 1100, Los Angeles
(90071-3173)
PHONE..................213 593-8000
Tom Joldersma, *CFO*
EMP: 500
SALES (corp-wide): 20.1B **Publicly Held**
SIC: 8748 Business consulting
HQ: Aecom Usa, Inc.
605 3rd Ave
New York NY 10158
212 973-2900

(P-26977)
AECOM USA INC
999 W Town And Country Rd, Orange
(92868-4713)
PHONE..................714 567-2501
Bruce Toro, *Manager*
EMP: 60
SALES (corp-wide): 20.1B **Publicly Held**
SIC: 8748 Business consulting
HQ: Aecom Usa, Inc.
605 3rd Ave
New York NY 10158
212 973-2900

(P-26978)
AHTNA-CDM SMITH JV
3200 El Camino Real, Irvine (92602-1378)
PHONE..................714 824-3471
Craig O'Rourke, *Partner*
John Czapor, *Partner*
Matt Tisher, *CFO*
EMP: 89
SALES (est): 2.7MM **Privately Held**
SIC: 8748 1794 8711 1611 Environmen-
tal consultant; excavation & grading,
building construction; building construc-
tion consultant; highway & street con-
struction

(P-26979)
ALIANTEL INC
1940 W Corporate Way, Anaheim
(92801-5373)
PHONE..................714 829-1650
Suresh Sachdeva, *CEO*
John Kelly, *Principal*
EMP: 90
SALES (est): 12.9MM **Privately Held**
SIC: 8748 7389 Telecommunications con-
sultant; telephone services

PRODUCTS & SVCS

(P-26980)
ALL ENVIRONMENTAL INC
Also Called: Aei Consultants
1200 Main St Ste D, Irvine (92614-6749)
PHONE..................................949 752-9300
Craig Hertz, *Owner*
EMP: 76 **Privately Held**
SIC: 8748 Environmental consultant
PA: All Environmental, Inc.
2500 Camino Diablo
Walnut Creek CA 94597
-

(P-26981)
ALL ENVIRONMENTAL INC
Also Called: Aei Consultants
2447 Pcf Cast Hwy Ste 101, Hermosa
Beach (90254)
PHONE..................................310 798-4255
Adam Bennett, *Manager*
EMP: 150 **Privately Held**
WEB: www.allenvironmental.com
SIC: 8748 Environmental consultant
PA: All Environmental, Inc.
2500 Camino Diablo
Walnut Creek CA 94597

(P-26982)
**ALL-CITY MANAGEMENT SVCS
INC**
10440 Pioneer Blvd Ste 5, Santa Fe
Springs (90670-8238)
PHONE..................................310 202-8284
Baron Farwell, *CEO*
Martha Holguin, *Area Spvr*
Ron Farwell, *Admin Sec*
EMP: 1800
SQ FT: 3,500
SALES (est): 96.9MM **Privately Held**
SIC: 8748 Traffic consultant

(P-26983)
**ALLIANCES MGT CONSULTING
INC**
544 Hillside Rd, Redwood City
(94062-3345)
PHONE..................................650 780-0466
Charles Anthony Aspinall, *CEO*
EMP: 50
SALES (est): 581K **Privately Held**
SIC: 8748 Business consulting

(P-26984)
**ALLIANT INSURANCE SERVICES
INC (PA)**
1301 Dove St Ste 200, Newport Beach
(92660-2436)
P.O. Box 6450 (92658-6450)
PHONE..................................949 756-0271
Thomas Corbett, *Ch of Bd*
Faith Dolliver, *President*
Greg Zimmer, *President*
Jerold Hall, *COO*
Ilene Anders, *CFO*
EMP: 170
SQ FT: 45,000
SALES (est): 355.5MM **Privately Held**
WEB: www.alliantinsurance.com
SIC: 8748 6411 Business consulting; in-
surance agents

(P-26985)
ALLIED INDUSTRIES INC (PA)
Also Called: Allied Environmental Services
21650 Oxnard St Ste 500, Woodland Hills
(91367-4911)
PHONE..................................800 605-5323
Ernesto Gutierrez, *President*
Fernando Gutierrez, *COO*
EMP: 150
SQ FT: 11,000
SALES (est): 24.7MM **Privately Held**
SIC: 8748 Environmental consultant

(P-26986)
AMATEL INC (PA)
1017 S Mountain Ave, Monrovia
(91016-3642)
PHONE..................................323 801-0199
Joe Nwankwo, *President*
EMP: 50
SQ FT: 5,500

SALES (est): 14.9MM **Privately Held**
WEB: www.amatel.com
SIC: 8748 8711 Telecommunications con-
sultant; engineering services

(P-26987)
AMBREEN ENTERPRISES INC
20370 Via Badalona, Yorba Linda
(92887-3136)
PHONE..................................909 620-1339
EMP: 80 **EST:** 2011
SALES (est): 157.4K **Privately Held**
SIC: 8748

(P-26988)
**AMERICAN NURSING HOME
MGT INC**
Also Called: Briercrest Inglewoodhealthcare
301 Centinela Ave, Inglewood
(90302-3231)
PHONE..................................310 672-1012
Bill Belamger, *Administration*
EMP: 100
SALES (corp-wide): 3MM **Privately Held**
SIC: 8748 8051 Business consulting;
skilled nursing care facilities
PA: American Nursing Home Management,
Inc.
17000 Ventura Blvd # 212
Encino CA

(P-26989)
AMERICAN TECHNOLOGIES INC
8444 Miralani Dr Ste 200, San Diego
(92126-4389)
PHONE..................................858 530-2400
Eric Gotsom, *Branch Mgr*
Stan Schritt, *Sr Project Mgr*
Francisco Navarro, *Supervisor*
EMP: 55
SALES (corp-wide): 287.1MM **Privately
Held**
WEB: www.amer-tech.com
SIC: 8748 Business consulting
PA: American Technologies Inc.
3360 E La Palma Ave
Anaheim CA 92806
714 283-9990

(P-26990)
AMTEL INC
950 S Bascom Ave Ste 2002, San Jose
(95128-3538)
PHONE..................................408 615-0522
Pankaj Gupta, *CEO*
Chet Jackson, *President*
EMP: 50
SALES (est): 8.6MM **Privately Held**
WEB: www.amtelnet.com
SIC: 8748 7371 Telecommunications con-
sultant; computer software development
HQ: Netplus Buyer, Inc.
9707 Key West Ave Ste 202
Rockville MD 20850
800 989-5566

(P-26991)
APX INC (PA)
2001 Gateway Pl Ste 315w, San Jose
(95110-1045)
PHONE..................................408 517-2100
Joseph Varnas, *CEO*
EMP: 50
SALES (est): 18.5MM **Privately Held**
WEB: www.apx.com
SIC: 8748 Energy conservation consultant

(P-26992)
ASHOK THUMMALACHETTY
44721 Aguila Ter, Fremont (94539-6293)
PHONE..................................510 687-9797
Ashok Thummalachetty, *President*
William Lynch, *Vice Pres*
EMP: 115
SQ FT: 3,000
SALES (est): 5.5MM **Privately Held**
WEB: www.fortuna.com
SIC: 8748 7379 1731 Business consult-
ing; computer related consulting services;
electrical work

(P-26993)
ASSURE CONSULTING INC
257 Castro St Ste 205, Mountain View
(94041-1287)
PHONE..................................650 966-1967
Murugesh Ramiah, *Chairman*
Vina Viveck, *President*
EMP: 90
SALES (est): 3.4MM **Privately Held**
WEB: www.assure-usa.com
SIC: 8748 Business consulting

(P-26994)
AT&T CORP
16201 Raymer St, Van Nuys (91406-1210)
PHONE..................................818 997-5998
Laurie Tossie, *Manager*
EMP: 100
SALES (corp-wide): 170.7B **Publicly
Held**
WEB: www.swbell.com
SIC: 8748 Telecommunications consultant
HQ: At&t Corp.
1 At&t Way
Bedminster NJ 07921
800 403-3302

(P-26995)
ATKINS NORTH AMERICA INC
475 Sansome St, San Francisco
(94111-3103)
PHONE..................................916 325-4800
Rod Jeung, *Manager*
EMP: 50
SALES (corp-wide): 7.6B **Privately Held**
WEB: www.cargillemt.com
SIC: 8748 8742 8711 Environmental con-
sultant; planning consultant; consulting
engineer
HQ: Snc-Lavalin Inc
455 Boul Rene-Levesque O
Montreal QC H2Z 1
514 393-1000

(P-26996)
AUCTIVA CORPORATION
360 E 6th St, Chico (95928-5631)
PHONE..................................530 894-7400
Mark A Schwartz, *CEO*
Crystal Estes CPA, *Finance*
Jeff Mengoli, *Counsel*
Michael Davies, *Manager*
EMP: 80
SALES (est): 6.3MM **Privately Held**
WEB: www.theonlineseller.com
SIC: 8748 Business consulting

(P-26997)
AVA THE RABBIT HAVEN INC
Also Called: RABBIT HAVEN THE
1261 S Mary St, Scotts Valley (95067)
P.O. Box 66594 (95067-6594)
PHONE..................................831 600-7479
Heather Bechtel, *Director*
Richard Jacobel, *President*
EMP: 80
SALES: 111.1K **Privately Held**
SIC: 8748 Testing service, educational or
personnel

(P-26998)
**AXIOM GLOBAL
TECHNOLOGIES INC**
220 N Wiget Ln, Walnut Creek
(94598-2404)
PHONE..................................925 393-5800
Mohit Sishu Arora, *CEO*
Priya Arora, *Ch of Bd*
Adam Ireland, *VP Bus Dvlpt*
Arora Kamla, *Executive Asst*
Vikas Bhatia, *Technology*
EMP: 125 **EST:** 2001
SALES (est): 1.8MM **Privately Held**
WEB: www.acg-usa.com
SIC: 8748 Business consulting

(P-26999)
B & L CONSULTING LLC
164 N 2nd Ave 9, Upland (91786-6001)
PHONE..................................682 238-6994
Bayandre Lewis, *Mng Member*
EMP: 63
SQ FT: 5,000
SALES: 5.2MM **Privately Held**
SIC: 8748 Business consulting

(P-27000)
**BARSTOW REDEVELOPMENT
AGENCY**
220 E Mountain View St B, Barstow
(92311-7304)
PHONE..................................760 256-3531
Paul Warrner, *General Mgr*
Michael Lewis, *Treasurer*
Sabrina Ellis, *Officer*
Rich Ross, *Fire Chief*
Tommy Alva, *Director*
EMP: 126
SQ FT: 1,039
SALES (est): 87.9K **Privately Held**
SIC: 8748 Economic consultant

(P-27001)
BAY AREA AIR QUALITY (PA)
375 Beale St Ste 600, San Francisco
(94105-2097)
P.O. Box 420434 (94142-0434)
PHONE..................................415 749-4900
Jack Broadbent, *CEO*
Ricardo Cardenas, *Principal*
Karyn Smith, *Admin Asst*
Davit Baghdasaryan, *Engineer*
Josephine Tam, *Engineer*
EMP: 250
SQ FT: 101,000
SALES (est): 58MM **Privately Held**
WEB: www.baaqmd.gov
SIC: 8748 Environmental consultant

(P-27002)
**BERKELEY RESEARCH GROUP
LLC (PA)**
2200 Powell St Ste 1200, Emeryville
(94608-1833)
PHONE..................................510 285-3300
David Teece, *CEO*
Tri Macdonald, *President*
Marvin Tenenbaum, *President*
David M Johnson, *CFO*
Eric Miller, *Senior VP*
EMP: 148
SALES (est): 214MM **Privately Held**
SIC: 8748 Business consulting

(P-27003)
BMV DIRECT II LP
17190 Bernardo Center Dr, San Diego
(92128-7030)
PHONE..................................858 485-9840
EMP: 59
SALES (est): 1.7MM
SALES (corp-wide): 674.6MM **Privately
Held**
SIC: 8748 Business consulting
HQ: Biomed Realty, L.P.
17190 Bernardo Center Dr
San Diego CA 92128
858 485-9840

(P-27004)
BOCA MESA INCORPORATED
3130 Skyway Dr Ste 701, Santa Maria
(93455-1800)
PHONE..................................805 934-9470
EMP: 69
SALES (est): 4.7MM **Privately Held**
SIC: 8748 7349

(P-27005)
BRANDNET INC
724 Battery St 3, San Francisco
(94111-1559)
PHONE..................................415 216-4152
John Farrar, *President*
Andy Atherton, *COO*
EMP: 60
SALES (est): 5.9MM **Privately Held**
SIC: 8748 Business consulting
HQ: Valassis Communications, Inc.
19975 Victor Pkwy
Livonia MI 48152
734 591-3000

(P-27006)
**BROCADE CMMNCTIONS
SYSTEMS INC**
110 Holger Way, San Jose (95134-1376)
PHONE..................................408 333-4300
EMP: 71
SALES (corp-wide): 13.2B **Privately Held**
SIC: 8748

HQ: Brocade Communications Systems Llc
130 Holger Way
San Jose CA 95134
-

(P-27007)
BUREAU VERITAS NORTH AMER INC
Also Called: Clayton Group Services
1940 E Deere Ave Ste 210, Santa Ana
(92705-5718)
PHONE..................................714 431-4100
Sandi Schafer, *Vice Pres*
Lisa Townsend, *Social Dir*
Matt Konicek, *Human Resources*
EMP: 70
SALES (corp-wide): 280.5MM **Privately Held**
SIC: 8748 Business consulting
HQ: Bureau Veritas North America, Inc.
1601 Sawgrs Corp Pkwy # 400
Sunrise FL 33323
954 236-8100

(P-27008)
BUXTON CONSULTING
5976 W Las Positas Blvd, Pleasanton
(94588-8506)
PHONE..................................925 467-0700
James T Buxton, *President*
Chandra Reddy, *Vice Pres*
EMP: 90
SQ FT: 6,500
SALES (est): 10.3MM **Privately Held**
WEB: www.us-buxton.com
SIC: 8748 Systems engineering consult-
ant, ex. computer or professional

(P-27009)
BY REFERRAL ONLY INC
2035 Corte Del Nogal # 200, Carlsbad
(92011-1445)
PHONE..................................760 707-1300
Joseph F Stumpf, *President*
Jeff Robbins, *Managing Dir*
Jeff Haase, *Controller*
Lori Westbay, *Marketing Mgr*
Nicki Bricker, *Manager*
EMP: 100
SALES (est): 10.1MM **Privately Held**
SIC: 8748 Educational consultant

(P-27010)
CAL SOUTHERN ASSN GOVERNMENTS (PA)
Also Called: S C A G
900 Wilshire Blvd # 1700, Los Angeles
(90017-4701)
PHONE..................................213 236-1800
Hasan Ikhrata, *Exec Dir*
Basil Panas, *CFO*
EMP: 116
SQ FT: 50,000
SALES: 40MM **Privately Held**
SIC: 8748 Urban planning & consulting
services

(P-27011)
CALI HSG FINANCE AGCY
500 Capitol Mall Ste 1400, Sacramento
(95814-4740)
PHONE..................................916 326-8627
Janet Louie, *Manager*
Tom Nann, *Officer*
Amy Golonka, *Administration*
Debbie Romano, *Administration*
Donald Cavier, *Director*
EMP: 99 EST: 2011
SALES (est): 4MM **Privately Held**
SIC: 8748 Urban planning & consulting
services

(P-27012)
CALIFORNIA COML INV GROUP INC
Also Called: Ccig
4530 E Thousand Oaks Blvd # 100, West-
lake Village (91362-3897)
PHONE..................................805 495-8400
Gary Collett, *President*
Louis Mellman, *Vice Pres*
EMP: 50
SALES (est): 5.3MM **Privately Held**
SIC: 8748 Urban planning & consulting
services

(P-27013)
CALIFORNIA DEPT TRANSPORTATION
Also Called: Caltrans District 1
1656 Union St, Eureka (95501-2229)
P.O. Box 3700 (95502-3700)
PHONE..................................707 445-6600
Charlie Fielder, *Director*
Kevin Danel, *Info Tech Mgr*
Tim Day, *IT/INT Sup*
Jose Moreno, *Graphic Designe*
EMP: 500 **Privately Held**
WEB: www.caltip.org
SIC: 8748 4789 9621 Business consult-
ing; railroad maintenance & repair serv-
ices;
HQ: California Dept Of Transportation
1120 N St
Sacramento CA 95814

(P-27014)
CALIFORNIA ENVMTL HLTH ASSN
Also Called: C E H A
2000 A De Las Pulgas 10, San Mateo
(94403)
PHONE..................................650 363-4726
Liberty Cerezo, *Treasurer*
Todd A Frantz, *President*
EMP: 70
SQ FT: 500
SALES (est): 6.1MM **Privately Held**
SIC: 8748 Environmental consultant

(P-27015)
CALIFORNIA TRAFFIC SAFETY INST
Also Called: CTSI
209 E Avenue K8 Ste 210, Lancaster
(93535-4535)
PHONE..................................661 940-1907
Wanda Paulson, *President*
Carrie Pierce, *Vice Pres*
Tiffany Coronado, *Exec Dir*
EMP: 160
SQ FT: 42,000
SALES: 4.8MM **Privately Held**
WEB: www.ctsi-courtnetwork.org
SIC: 8748 Educational consultant

(P-27016)
CAMBRIA SOLUTIONS INC (PA)
1050 20th St Ste 275, Sacramento
(95811-3157)
PHONE..................................916 326-4446
Robert J Rodriguez, *President*
Suzanne Vitale, *Vice Pres*
Gabrielle Saienni, *Executive Asst*
Keith Lauher, *Software Engr*
Tracey Herbert, *Business Anlyst*
EMP: 106
SQ FT: 3,000
SALES: 4MM **Privately Held**
WEB: www.cambriasolutions.com
SIC: 8748 8742 Systems analysis & engi-
neering consulting services; management
consulting services

(P-27017)
CAPITAL OVERSIGHT INC (PA)
2118 Wilshire Blvd, Santa Monica
(90403-5704)
PHONE..................................310 453-8000
Dayne Williams, *CEO*
Matthew Denti, *Vice Pres*
Kenneth Mays, *Vice Pres*
Tamara Stewart, *Vice Pres*
Patricia Sewell, *Admin Sec*
EMP: 328 EST: 2002
SQ FT: 11,000
SALES: 7.7MM **Privately Held**
SIC: 8748 7323 7389 7299 Business
consulting; credit clearinghouse; ; per-
sonal financial services

(P-27018)
CATALINA ENTERPRISE INC
206 Catalina Rd, Fullerton (92835-2506)
PHONE..................................949 637-3091
Stanley Johnson, *CEO*
Easter Johnson, *Vice Pres*
EMP: 52 EST: 2015

SALES (est): 929.7K **Privately Held**
SIC: 8748 Systems engineering consultant, ex. computer or professional

(P-27019)
CAVISSON SYSTEMS INC
5201 Great America Pkwy, Santa Clara
(95054-1122)
PHONE..................................800 701-6125
Anil Kumar, *President*
David Freid, *Vice Pres*
Raj Sajankila, *Vice Pres*
Shakti Jha, *Software Engr*
Jagjeet Kaur, *Software Engr*
EMP: 500
SQ FT: 10,000
SALES: 20MM **Privately Held**
SIC: 8748 Systems analysis & engineering
consulting services

(P-27020)
CBA SITE SERVICES INC
11387 Pyrites Way, Rancho Cordova
(95670-4595)
PHONE..................................925 754-7633
Michael McWhirter, *President*
David Cyr, *Controller*
Ethan McWhirter, *Manager*
EMP: 62
SQ FT: 70,000
SALES (est): 8.8MM **Privately Held**
WEB: www.1cba.com
SIC: 8748 Telecommunications consultant

(P-27021)
CDSNET LLC
Also Called: Fmsinfoserv
6053 W Century Blvd, Los Angeles
(90045-6430)
PHONE..................................310 981-9500
Michael Griffus, *President*
Francis G Homan, *CFO*
Helmut Bredow, *Project Mgr*
EMP: 65
SALES (est): 3.3MM
SALES (corp-wide): 4.2MM **Privately Held**
WEB: www.tectransinc.com
SIC: 8748 Business consulting
HQ: Keolis Transit America, Inc.
6053 W Century Blvd # 900
Los Angeles CA 90045

(P-27022)
CEMTEK ENVIRONMENTAL INC
3041 Orange Ave, Santa Ana (92707-4247)
PHONE..................................714 437-7100
Tyron Smith, *CEO*
EMP: 50
SQ FT: 15,500
SALES: 17.8MM **Privately Held**
WEB: www.cemteks.com
SIC: 8748 Environmental consultant

(P-27023)
CENTER FOR AUTISM RELATED SVCS
5949 Lankershim Blvd, North Hollywood
(91601-1006)
PHONE..................................323 850-7177
Susan Kumaer, *Administration*
Luz Uribe, *Manager*
EMP: 50
SALES (est): 173K **Privately Held**
WEB: www.center4autism.com
SIC: 8748 7361 Educational consultant;
employment agencies

(P-27024)
CENTER FOR SUSTAINABLE ENERGY
3980 Sherman St Ste 170, San Diego
(92110-4314)
PHONE..................................858 244-1177
Michael Akavan, *Chairman*
Mary McGroarty, *Ch of Bd*
Lawrence E Goldenhersh, *President*
Fred Baranowski, *Treasurer*
Heather Shepard, *Director*
EMP: 87
SALES: 179.6MM **Privately Held**
WEB: www.sdenergy.org
SIC: 8748 Environmental consultant

(P-27025)
CETECOM INC
411 Dixon Landing Rd, Milpitas
(95035-2579)
PHONE..................................408 586-6200
Maan Ghanma, *CEO*
Willfried Klassmann, *President*
Heiko Strehlow, *COO*
Clorinda Sammis, *Treasurer*
Dat Hoang, *Technician*
EMP: 85
SQ FT: 48,000
SALES (est): 24.4MM
SALES (corp-wide): 300.2MM **Privately Held**
WEB: www.cetecomusa.com
SIC: 8748 8734 Communications consult-
ing; testing laboratories
HQ: Cetecom Gmbh
Im Teelbruch 116
Essen 45219
205 495-190

(P-27026)
CHAMBERS GROUP INC
17671 Cowan Ste 100, Irvine (92614-6074)
P.O. Box N Centre D, Santa Ana (92707)
PHONE..................................949 261-5414
Sherman Smith, *President*
EMP: 50
SALES (corp-wide): 18.9MM **Privately Held**
WEB: www.chambersgroupinc.com
SIC: 8748 Environmental consultant
PA: Chambers Group, Inc.
5 Hutton Cntre Dr Ste 750
Santa Ana CA 92707
949 261-5414

(P-27027)
CHIKPEA INC
1 Market St Spear Spear Tower, San Fran-
cisco (94127)
PHONE..................................888 342-3828
Adam Kleinberg, *CEO*
Jordan Connor, *Accounts Exec*
EMP: 50
SALES (est): 2.5MM **Privately Held**
SIC: 8748 Telecommunications consultant

(P-27028)
CITADEL ENVIRONMENTAL SVCS INC (PA)
1725 Victory Blvd, Glendale (91201-2833)
PHONE..................................818 246-2707
Loren I Witkin, *President*
EMP: 50
SQ FT: 8,000
SALES (est): 8.5MM **Privately Held**
SIC: 8748 Environmental consultant

(P-27029)
CITY OF MORGAN HILL
Also Called: Public Works Department
100 Edes St, Morgan Hill (95037-5301)
PHONE..................................408 776-7333
Jim Ashcraft, *Director*
EMP: 52 **Privately Held**
WEB: www.mhcommunitycenter.com
SIC: 8748 9111 City planning; mayors' of-
fices
PA: City Of Morgan Hill
17575 Peak Ave
Morgan Hill CA 95037
408 778-6480

(P-27030)
CITY OF NORCO
Also Called: Successor Agency To The Norco
2870 Clark Ave, Norco (92860-1903)
PHONE..................................951 270-5617
Greg Newton, *Mayor*
EMP: 100 **Privately Held**
SIC: 8748 Urban planning & consulting
services
PA: City Of Norco
2870 Clark Ave
Norco CA 92860
951 270-5617

(P-27031)
CITY OF SAN DIEGO
Also Called: Enginrng Capitl Projects Dept
1010 2nd Ave Ste 800, San Diego
(92101-4907)
PHONE..................................619 533-3012

Patti Boekamp, *Deputy Dir*
Brian P Fennessy, *Chief*
EMP: 50 **Privately Held**
WEB: www.eayo.com
SIC: 8748 9621 Traffic consultant; regula-
tion, administration of transportation;
PA: City Of San Diego
202 C St
San Diego CA 92101
619 236-6330

(P-27032)
CLEAN HARBORS ENVMTL
SVCS INC
4101 Industrial Way, Benicia (94510-1211)
PHONE...........................707 747-6699
Kevin Carnahan, *President*
EMP: 100
SALES (corp-wide): 3.3B **Publicly Held**
SIC: 8748 Environmental consultant
HQ: Clean Harbors Environmental Serv-
ices, Inc.
42 Longwater Dr
Norwell MA 02061
781 792-5000

(P-27033)
CLEARESULT CONSULTING INC
Also Called: Peci
1 Sansome St Fl 35, San Francisco
(94104-4436)
PHONE...........................415 848-1250
Karen Healey, *Branch Mgr*
George Kopf, *Advisor*
EMP: 77
SALES (corp-wide): 621.8MM **Privately**
Held
SIC: 8748 Energy conservation consultant
PA: Clearesult Consulting Inc.
4301 Westbank Dr Ste A250
Austin TX 78746
512 327-9200

(P-27034)
CLICKSAFETYCOM INC (HQ)
2185 N Calif Blvd Ste 425, Walnut Creek
(94596-3505)
PHONE...........................800 971-1080
Rick Willett, *CEO*
Blaine Tomimoto, *President*
Brian Tonry, *Exec VP*
Matt Bower, *Vice Pres*
Ron Bruce, *Vice Pres*
EMP: 50
SQ FT: 4,900
SALES (est): 2.9MM
SALES (corp-wide): 49.9MM **Privately**
Held
WEB: www.clicksafety.com
SIC: 8748 Safety training service
PA: Jones & Bartlett Learning, Llc
5 Wall St Fl 3
Burlington MA 01803
978 443-5000

(P-27035)
COASSURE INC
4100 Moorpark Ave Ste 122, San Jose
(95117-1707)
P.O. Box 234, Los Altos (94023-0234)
PHONE...........................408 244-0400
Zaydoon Jawadi, *President*
EMP: 100
SALES (est): 2.9MM **Privately Held**
WEB: www.coassure.com
SIC: 8748 Testing services

(P-27036)
COMMODITY DISTRIBUTION
SERVICE
10035 Painter Ave, Santa Fe Springs
(90670-3015)
PHONE...........................562 777-9969
Dan Nagel, *President*
Mitchell Patton, *CFO*
EMP: 50
SQ FT: 40,000
SALES (est): 2.3MM **Privately Held**
WEB: www.cdscold.com
SIC: 8748 Business consulting

(P-27037)
COMMUNITY HOUSING OPPORT
(PA)
Also Called: C H O C
5030 Business Center Dr # 260, Fairfield
(94534-6884)
PHONE...........................530 757-4444
Manuela Silva, *Exec Dir*
Peter Lundberg, *Vice Pres*
Vincent Nicholas, *Vice Pres*
EMP: 50
SQ FT: 3,000
SALES: 7.8MM **Privately Held**
WEB: www.chochousing.org
SIC: 8748 Urban planning & consulting
services

(P-27038)
COMMUNITY REDEVELOPMENT
AGENCY (PA)
Also Called: C R A
448 S Hill St Ste 1200, Los Angeles
(90013-1153)
PHONE...........................213 977-1600
Cecilia V Estolano, *Administration*
Christine Essel, *CEO*
Craig Bullock, *Officer*
Estevan Valenzuela, *Principal*
Sylvia Amaya, *General Mgr*
EMP: 165 EST: 1948
SQ FT: 80,000
SALES: 7.2MM **Privately Held**
SIC: 8748 Urban planning & consulting
services

(P-27039)
COMPUTACENTER
FUSIONSTORM INC
Also Called: Adexis
2 Bryant St Ste 150, San Francisco
(94105-1641)
PHONE...........................415 623-2626
Daniel Serpico, *Branch Mgr*
Cheryl Claunch, *Partner*
Doug Adams, *Vice Pres*
Justin Griffin, *Vice Pres*
Robert Linsky, *Vice Pres*
EMP: 118
SALES (corp-wide): 5.5B **Privately Held**
SIC: 8748 Systems engineering consult-
ant, ex. computer or professional
HQ: Computacenter Fusionstorm Inc.
124 Grove St Ste 311
Franklin MA 02038
508 520-5000

(P-27040)
CONDOR EARTH
TECHNOLOGIES INC (PA)
21663 Brian Ln, Sonora (95370-9065)
P.O. Box 3905 (95370-3905)
PHONE...........................209 532-0361
Robert John Job, *CEO*
Bob Job, *Vice Pres*
Glenn Nunelley, *Vice Pres*
Carter Redding, *Division Mgr*
Tiffany Harrell, *Admin Asst*
EMP: 110
SQ FT: 9,000
SALES (est): 12.2MM **Privately Held**
WEB: www.condordataserver.com
SIC: 8748 7349 Environmental consultant;
cleaning service, industrial or commercial

(P-27041)
CONSORTM ON REACHNG
EXCELLNCE
Also Called: Core
3112 Cedar Ravine Rd, Placerville
(95667-6506)
PHONE...........................510 540-4200
Linda Diamond, *CEO*
Bill Honig, *President*
Mark Simmons, *Officer*
Dale Webster, *Ch Acad Ofcr*
EMP: 50
SALES (est): 4MM **Privately Held**
WEB: www.corelearn.com
SIC: 8748 Educational consultant

(P-27042)
CORNERSTONE CNSULTING
TECH INC
241 5th St, San Francisco (94103-4102)
PHONE...........................415 705-7800
Wayne Perry, *CEO*
Charles Jones, *Officer*
EMP: 50
SQ FT: 1,400
SALES (est): 4.4MM **Privately Held**
WEB: www.cornerstoneconcilium.com
SIC: 8748 8742 7379 Educational con-
sultant; management consulting services;
computer related consulting services

(P-27043)
CORNERSTONE RESEARCH
INC (PA)
1000 El Camino Real # 250, Menlo Park
(94025-4315)
PHONE...........................650 853-1660
Cynthia Zollinger, *Chairman*
Michael E Burton, *President*
Susan M Wittner, *Chief Mktg Ofcr*
Alexander Aganin, *Senior VP*
Catherine Galley, *Senior VP*
EMP: 100
SQ FT: 40,000
SALES (est): 83.3MM **Privately Held**
WEB: www.cornerstone.com
SIC: 8748 7389 Economic consultant; fi-
nancial services

(P-27044)
CORNERSTONE RESEARCH
INC
2 Embarcadero Ctr Fl 20, San Francisco
(94111-3922)
PHONE...........................415 229-8100
Cynthia Zollinger, *CEO*
Dina Older Aguilar, *Vice Pres*
EMP: 52
SALES (corp-wide): 83.3MM **Privately**
Held
SIC: 8748 Economic consultant
PA: Cornerstone Research, Inc.
1000 El Camino Real # 250
Menlo Park CA 94025
650 853-1660

(P-27045)
COUNTY OF SAN DIEGO
Human Resources Dept
1600 Pacific Hwy Ste 207, San Diego
(92101-2422)
PHONE...........................619 236-2191
Janice Horning, *Branch Mgr*
EMP: 150 **Privately Held**
WEB: www.sdlcc.org
SIC: 8748 9441 Employee programs ad-
ministration; administration of social &
human resources
PA: County Of San Diego
1600 Pacific Hwy Ste 209
San Diego CA 92101
619 531-5880

(P-27046)
DATA RECOGNITION
CORPORATION
Also Called: C T B
20 Ryan Ranch Rd, Monterey
(93940-6439)
PHONE...........................831 393-0700
Mike Limbach, *Vice Pres*
Shankar Ramachandran, *Program Mgr*
Ricardo Mercado, *Director*
Robert Rodriguez, *Supervisor*
EMP: 50
SALES (corp-wide): 255.5MM **Privately**
Held
SIC: 8748 Business consulting
PA: Data Recognition Corporation
13490 Bass Lake Rd
Maple Grove MN 55311
763 268-2000

(P-27047)
DECISION TOOLBOX INC
5319 University Dr 521, Irvine
(92612-2965)
PHONE...........................562 377-5600
Kim Shepherd, *President*
Rina Altaras, *Partner*
Kris Cable, *Partner*

Gene Gordon, *Partner*
Michael Hadity, *Partner*
EMP: 85
SQ FT: 300
SALES (est): 7.4MM **Privately Held**
SIC: 8748 Business consulting

(P-27048)
DESTINATION SCIENCE LLC
953 N Elm St, Orange (92867-5454)
PHONE...........................714 289-9100
Heena Desai,
Sharon Fogg,
Kathy Heraghty,
▲ **EMP:** 150
SQ FT: 5,000
SALES (est): 1MM **Privately Held**
WEB: www.destinationscience.org
SIC: 8748 Educational consultant

(P-27049)
DISRUPTIVE VISIONS LLC
27271 Las Ramblas Ste 300, Mission Viejo
(92691-8042)
PHONE...........................949 502-3800
Marc Anthony, *Mng Member*
EMP: 60
SALES (est): 781.7K **Privately Held**
SIC: 8748 Telecommunications consultant

(P-27050)
DIVERSIFIED RE PACKAGING
CORP
1118 S La Cienega Blvd, Los Angeles
(90035-2519)
PHONE...........................310 855-1946
Jeffrie Green, *President*
EMP: 700
SALES (est): 13.5MM **Privately Held**
SIC: 8748 Business consulting

(P-27051)
DNV GL ENERGY INSIGHTS USA
INC
Also Called: K E M A
155 Grand Ave Ste 500, Oakland
(94612-3747)
PHONE...........................510 891-0446
Rich Barnes, *Branch Mgr*
David Cesio, *Business Dir*
William Vail, *Administration*
Michael Rufo, *Director*
Cynthia Hester, *Manager*
EMP: 50
SALES (corp-wide): 2.3B **Privately Held**
SIC: 8748 Energy conservation consultant
HQ: Dnv Gl Energy Insights Usa, Inc.
1400 Ravello Rd
Katy TX 77449
281 396-1000

(P-27052)
EAG HOLDINGS LLC
2710 Walsh Ave, Santa Clara
(95051-0963)
PHONE...........................408 530-3500
Siddhartha Kadia, *CEO*
Temel Buyuklimanli, *Vice Pres*
Karol Putyera, *Vice Pres*
Larry Wang, *Vice Pres*
David Palmer, *Business Dir*
EMP: 700
SQ FT: 70,000
SALES (est): 18.8MM **Privately Held**
SIC: 8748 Business consulting

(P-27053)
ECHELON SECURITY INC
1604 Kerley Dr, San Jose (95112-4815)
PHONE...........................408 436-8844
Steve Brown, *President*
Ian Phan, *Software Dev*
Rich Blomseth, *Director*
EMP: 67
SQ FT: 2,000
SALES (est): 5.1MM **Privately Held**
SIC: 8748 7381 Business consulting;
guard services; security guard service

(P-27054)
ECO BAY SERVICES INC
1501 Minnesota St, San Francisco
(94107-3521)
PHONE...........................415 643-7777
Trent Scott Michels, *CEO*
Saul Bravo, *Opers Staff*

Genaro Nuno, *Contractor*
Gregory Sadler, *Superintendent*
EMP: 65 **EST:** 2007
SQ FT: 80,000
SALES: 40.2MM **Privately Held**
SIC: 8748 Environmental consultant

(P-27055)
ECONOMIC DEV CORP OF LA COUNTY
Also Called: Laedc
444 S Flower St Ste 3700, Los Angeles
(90071-2972)
PHONE..............................213 622-4300
William C Allen, *President*
Jill Yoshimi, *President*
David A Flaks, *COO*
Susan D Stel, *CFO*
Jose Gomez, *Exec VP*
EMP: 50 **EST:** 1981
SQ FT: 18,000
SALES: 6.8MM **Privately Held**
WEB: www.laedc.org
SIC: 8748 Business consulting

(P-27056)
EDGE MORTGAGE ADVISORY CO LLC
2125 E Katella Ave # 350, Anaheim
(92806-6072)
PHONE..............................714 564-5800
Robin Auerbach, *President*
Doug Speaker, *Senior VP*
Lorie Boutboul, *Hum Res Coord*
EMP: 88
SALES (est): 9.7MM **Privately Held**
SIC: 8748 Business consulting

(P-27057)
ELS
Also Called: Els Architecture
2040 Addison St, Berkeley (94704-1104)
PHONE..............................510 549-2929
Barry Elbasani, *President*
Janette Gross, *Treasurer*
Carol Shen, *Admin Sec*
George Omura, *Technology*
Diana Banh, *Corp Comm Staff*
EMP: 65 **EST:** 1967
SQ FT: 12,000
SALES (est): 7.4MM **Privately Held**
WEB: www.elsarch.com
SIC: 8748 8712 Urban planning & consulting services; architectural services

(P-27058)
EMERGENT VENTURES INTL INC
1156 Clement St, San Francisco
(94118-2115)
PHONE..............................415 655-6617
Ashutosh Pandey, *President*
Thomas Rosenberg, *Vice Pres*
EMP: 99
SALES (est): 2.9MM **Privately Held**
SIC: 8748 Energy conservation consultant

(P-27059)
END TO END ANALYTICS LLC
2595 E Byshore Rd Ste 150, Palo Alto
(94303)
PHONE..............................650 331-9659
Robert Hall,
Ej Tavella, *Vice Pres*
Colin Kessinger,
Gustavo Ferreira, *Consultant*
Angie King, *Consultant*
EMP: 60
SQ FT: 6,000
SALES (est): 12MM **Privately Held**
SIC: 8748 Systems analysis & engineering consulting services

(P-27060)
ENERGY EXPERTS INTERNATIONAL
7111 N Fresno St Ste 260, Fresno
(93720-2959)
PHONE..............................559 449-1124
EMP: 117
SALES (corp-wide): 1.1MM **Privately Held**
SIC: 8748 8742 Energy conservation consultant; management consulting services

PA: Energy Experts International
555 Twin Dolphin Dr # 150
Redwood City CA 94065
650 593-4261

(P-27061)
ENTANGLED VENTURES LLC (PA)
Also Called: Entangled Group
55 2nd St Ste 2500, San Francisco
(94105-4559)
PHONE..............................415 795-2767
Paul Freedman, *CEO*
Nick Lammerschlag, *President*
Paul Sheppard, *CFO*
Kim Umemoto, *Director*
EMP: 58
SALES (est): 6.6MM **Privately Held**
SIC: 8748 8742 Educational consultant; school, college, university consultant

(P-27062)
ENTERPRISE SOLUTIONS INC
2855 Kifer Rd, Santa Clara (95051-0814)
PHONE..............................408 727-3627
Lucy Phang, *CFO*
Savio Pais, *Vice Pres*
Pradeep Shrivastava, *IT/INT Sup*
Zishan Ali, *Engineer*
Nitin Nerkar, *VP Sales*
EMP: 191 **Privately Held**
SIC: 8748 Systems engineering consultant, ex. computer or professional
PA: Enterprise Solutions, Inc.
500 E Diehl Rd Ste 130
Naperville IL 60563

(P-27063)
ENVENT CORPORATION (PA)
3220 E 29th St, Long Beach (90806-2321)
PHONE..............................562 997-9465
Steve Sellinger, *President*
Laikyn Hilborn, *Admin Asst*
Sharon Reyes, *Admin Asst*
Jazmin Fields, *Administration*
Greg Gardner, *Administration*
EMP: 118
SQ FT: 6,400
SALES: 33.3MM **Privately Held**
WEB: www.enventcorporation.com
SIC: 8748 Environmental consultant

(P-27064)
ENVIRONMENTAL RESOLUTIONS INC
Also Called: Cardno Eri
25371 Commercentre Dr # 250, Lake Forest (92630-8867)
PHONE..............................949 457-8950
Steve M Zigan, *CEO*
Robert L Kroeger, *Vice Pres*
Mike Madden, *Info Tech Mgr*
EMP: 300
SQ FT: 14,100
SALES (est): 411.2K **Privately Held**
WEB: www.eri-us.com
SIC: 8748 8744 Environmental consultant;
HQ: Cardno Usa, Inc.
10004 Park Meadows Dr # 300
Lone Tree CO 80124

(P-27065)
ES ENGINEERING INC
1 Park Plz Ste 1000, Irvine (92614-8507)
PHONE..............................714 919-6500
Niu Jinghui, *President*
Bernie Sheff, *Vice Pres*
Daniel Waineo, *Sr Project Mgr*
EMP: 60
SQ FT: 2,300
SALES: 25MM **Privately Held**
SIC: 8748 Environmental consultant

(P-27066)
EUROGENTEC NORTH AMERICA INC
34801 Campus Dr, Fremont (94555-3606)
PHONE..............................510 791-9560
Jean-Pierre Delwart, *President*
EMP: 115
SQ FT: 11,000

SALES (est): 3MM **Privately Held**
WEB: www.eurogentec.com
SIC: 8748 Business consulting
HQ: Kaneka Eurogentec
Rue Du Bois Saint-Jean 5
Seraing 4102
437 274-00

(P-27067)
EXPERIAN MKTG SOLUTIONS LLC
475 Anton Blvd, Costa Mesa (92626-7037)
PHONE..............................714 830-7000
Kevin Dean, *President*
EMP: 501
SQ FT: 4,000
SALES (est): 5.5MM **Privately Held**
SIC: 8748 Business consulting

(P-27068)
EXPRESS COMPANIES INC
Also Called: American Cpr Training
565 Westlake St Ste 100, Encinitas
(92024-3784)
PHONE..............................760 944-1048
Matthew Henry, *President*
EMP: 50
SQ FT: 2,500
SALES (est): 1.2MM **Privately Held**
WEB: www.americancpr.com
SIC: 8748 Safety training service

(P-27069)
FAIR ISAAC CORPORATION (PA)
181 Metro Dr Ste 700, San Jose
(95110-1346)
PHONE..............................408 535-1500
William J Lansing, *CEO*
Leslie Charney, *Partner*
Jennifer Faaborg, *Partner*
Stephen O'Malley, *Partner*
Chris Smith, *Partner*
▲ **EMP:** 366 **EST:** 1956
SQ FT: 55,000
SALES: 1B **Publicly Held**
WEB: www.fairisaac.com
SIC: 8748 7389 7372 Business consulting; financial services; business oriented computer software

(P-27070)
FAITH COM INC (PA)
Also Called: Fci Management
13850 Cerritos, Cerritos (90703)
PHONE..............................562 719-9300
Patricia Watts, *President*
Donald Gregg, *COO*
EMP: 60
SQ FT: 7,000
SALES (est): 7.5MM **Privately Held**
WEB: www.fcimgt.com
SIC: 8748 Energy conservation consultant

(P-27071)
FAME ASSISTANCE CORPORATION
2270 S Harvard Blvd, Los Angeles
(90018-2142)
PHONE..............................323 373-7720
Denise Hunter, *President*
EMP: 75
SQ FT: 33,748
SALES: 2.8MM **Privately Held**
SIC: 8748 Business consulting

(P-27072)
FAMILY AND CHILDREN SERVICES
950 W Julian St, San Jose (95126-2719)
PHONE..............................408 292-9353
Diana Nemen, *CEO*
Cristina Trujillo, *Admin Asst*
Julie Daul, *Director*
Howard Lagoze, *Director*
Viet P Le, *Director*
EMP: 70
SQ FT: 9,500
SALES (est): 4.6MM **Privately Held**
SIC: 8748 Business consulting

(P-27073)
FORENSIC ANALYTICAL
Also Called: Facs
3111 Camino Dl Rio N 43, San Diego
(92108)
PHONE..............................858 859-3322
EMP: 69 **Privately Held**
SIC: 8748 Environmental consultant
PA: Forensic Analytical Consulting Services, Inc.
21228 Cabot Blvd
Hayward CA 94545

(P-27074)
FOX TRANSPORTATION INC (PA)
8610 Helms Ave, Rancho Cucamonga
(91730-4520)
P.O. Box 3119 (91729-3119)
PHONE..............................909 291-4646
Michael K Fox, *CEO*
Mary Anne Fox, *Shareholder*
Chad Shearer, *President*
Mary Fox, *CFO*
David Langrehr, *Senior VP*
EMP: 60
SALES (est): 21.8MM **Privately Held**
SIC: 8748 4213 Business consulting; trucking, except local

(P-27075)
FRIENDEMIC LLC
3944 Murphy Canyon Rd, San Diego
(92123-4498)
PHONE..............................855 880-6337
Crystal Montusar, *Branch Mgr*
EMP: 61
SALES (corp-wide): 1.9MM **Privately Held**
SIC: 8748 Publishing consultant
PA: Friendemic, Llc
1165 E Wilmington Ave # 290
Salt Lake City UT 84106
801 415-9314

(P-27076)
FRYS ELECTRONICS INC
4100 Northgate Blvd, Sacramento
(95834-1240)
PHONE..............................916 286-5800
Mark Ashby, *Branch Mgr*
EMP: 300
SALES (corp-wide): 26.9MM **Privately Held**
WEB: www.frys.com
SIC: 8748 5731 Business consulting; radio, television & electronic stores
PA: Fry's Electronics, Inc.
600 E Brokaw Rd
San Jose CA 95112
408 487-4500

(P-27077)
FUSE PROJECT LLC
1401 16th St, San Francisco (94103-5109)
PHONE..............................415 908-1492
Yves Behar, *President*
Helen Fu Thomas, *Ch of Bd*
Mitch Pergola, *COO*
Christina Park, *Program Mgr*
Vanessa Humes, *Executive Asst*
EMP: 60
SQ FT: 22,000
SALES (est): 3.8MM **Privately Held**
WEB: www.fuseproject.com
SIC: 8748 Business consulting

(P-27078)
GABE INC
300 Spectrum, Irvine (92618)
P.O. Box 8675, Newport Beach (92658-8675)
PHONE..............................949 679-2727
Gabe Gabriel, *Ch of Bd*
Sassine Shahine, *President*
EMP: 55
SQ FT: 1,000
SALES (est): 1.8MM **Privately Held**
SIC: 8748 Business consulting

(P-27079)
GENPACT LLC
3300 Hillview Ave, Palo Alto (94304-1203)
PHONE..............................203 690-9308
Sanjay Srivastava, *Principal*

EMP: 50 **Privately Held**
SIC: 8748 Business consulting
HQ: Genpact Llc
1155 Ave Of The Americas
New York NY 10036
212 896-6600

(P-27080)
GEOCON CONSULTANTS INC (PA)
6960 Flanders Dr, San Diego (92121-3992)
PHONE..................858 558-6900
Michael Chapin, *CEO*
John Hoobs, *Vice Pres*
Neal Berliner, *Principal*
John Juhrend, *Principal*
EMP: 85
SQ FT: 10,000
SALES (est): 25.7MM **Privately Held**
WEB: www.geoconinc.com
SIC: 8748 8711 Environmental consultant;
engineering services

(P-27081)
GLASSFAB TEMPERING SVCS INC (PA)
Also Called: Glass Fab Tempering Sv
1448 Mariani Ct, Tracy (95376-2825)
PHONE..................209 229-1060
Jagmohan Singh, *CEO*
Surinderpal Bains, *President*
Usha Mhay, *CFO*
EMP: 60
SQ FT: 60,000
SALES (est): 11.5MM **Privately Held**
SIC: 8748 Business consulting

(P-27082)
GLOBAL INFOTECH CORPORATION
2890 Zanker Rd Ste 202, San Jose
(95134-2118)
PHONE..................408 567-0600
Atul Sharma, *President*
Gabriel Gambill, *Vice Pres*
Nitin Prasad, *Vice Pres*
Rhea Kapoor, *Tech Recruiter*
Rajesh Motwani, *Engineer*
EMP: 550 EST: 1995
SQ FT: 3,000
SALES: 46.1MM **Privately Held**
WEB: www.global-infotech.com
SIC: 8748 Systems analysis & engineering
consulting services

(P-27083)
GOLDEN GATE CAPITOL
1 Embarcadero Ctr # 3900, San Francisco
(94111-3628)
PHONE..................415 983-2700
Jacob Mizrahi, *Principal*
EMP: 500
SALES (est): 10.9MM **Privately Held**
SIC: 8748 Business consulting

(P-27084)
GORDON E BTTY I MORE FUNDATION
1661 Page Mill Rd, Palo Alto (94304-1209)
PHONE..................650 213-3000
Lewis W Coleman, *President*
Denise Strack, *Ch Invest Ofcr*
Chris McCrum,
Linda Baron, *Executive Asst*
EMP: 75
SALES: 451.9MM **Privately Held**
WEB: www.moorefoundation.org
SIC: 8748 Economic consultant

(P-27085)
H & F GRAIN FARMS LLC
1181 S Wolff Rd, Oxnard (93033-2105)
PHONE..................805 754-4449
Robert Boelts,
EMP: 70
SALES: 4.5MM **Privately Held**
SIC: 8748 0191 Agricultural consultant;
general farms, primarily crop

(P-27086)
HABITAT RSTRATION SCIENCES INC
Also Called: Restoration Resources Hrs
3888 Cincinnati Ave, Rocklin (95765-1312)
PHONE..................916 408-2990

Mark Girard, *President*
EMP: 50
SALES (est): 2.7MM
SALES (corp-wide): 11MM **Privately Held**
SIC: 8748 Environmental consultant
PA: Habitat Restoration Sciences, Inc.
1217 Distribution Way
Vista CA 92081
760 479-4210

(P-27087)
HARRIS & SLOAN CONSULTING
2295 Gateway Oaks Dr # 165, Sacramento
(95833-4211)
PHONE..................916 921-2800
Timothy Sloan, *President*
Alyssa Gutierrez, *Design Engr*
EMP: 50
SALES (est): 1.9MM **Privately Held**
WEB: www.hscgi.com
SIC: 8748 Business consulting

(P-27088)
HERE FILMS
10990 Wilshire Blvd, Los Angeles
(90024-3913)
PHONE..................310 806-4288
EMP: 50
SALES (est): 1.2MM **Privately Held**
SIC: 8748

(P-27089)
HETROSYS LLC
3858 Carrera Ct, San Jose (95148-3716)
PHONE..................408 270-0240
Harpreet Soni, *Mng Member*
EMP: 56
SQ FT: 2,800
SALES: 3.1MM **Privately Held**
SIC: 8748 7389 Telecommunications con-
sultant;

(P-27090)
HINTTECH INC
505 Montgomery St Fl 11, San Francisco
(94111-2585)
PHONE..................415 874-3200
Egbert Hendricks, *President*
EMP: 120
SALES: 17MM **Privately Held**
SIC: 8748 Business consulting

(P-27091)
HUMBOLDT STATE UNIVERSITY SPON
Also Called: HSU FOUNDATION
1 Harpst St, Arcata (95521-8299)
P.O. Box 1185 (95518-1185)
PHONE..................707 826-4189
Steven Karp, *Exec Dir*
Walter Duffy, *Manager*
Michelle Moreno, *Associate*
EMP: 100
SALES: 28MM **Privately Held**
WEB: www.hsujacks.com
SIC: 8748 Educational consultant

(P-27092)
INFOSOFT INC
7891 Westwood Dr Ste 113, Gilroy
(95020-4786)
PHONE..................408 659-4326
Ashish Chopra, *President*
Raj Chopra, *Vice Pres*
Jasmine Banu, *Recruiter*
Amit Kumar, *Recruiter*
Ashley Puri, *Recruiter*
EMP: 80
SALES (est): 272.3K **Privately Held**
SIC: 8748 7361 Systems engineering con-
sultant, ex. computer or professional;
placement agencies

(P-27093)
INSIGNIA ENVIRONMENTAL
258 High St, Palo Alto (94301-1040)
PHONE..................650 321-6787
Anne Marie McGraw, *President*
Alex McGraw, *Vice Pres*
EMP: 65
SQ FT: 11,000
SALES: 16.2MM **Privately Held**
WEB: www.opusenvironmental.com
SIC: 8748 Environmental consultant

(P-27094)
INSTITUTE FOR MULTICULTURAL
121 W Lexington Dr, Glendale
(91203-2203)
PHONE..................818 240-4311
Tara Pir, *Manager*
Nima Nouri, *Psychologist*
EMP: 69 **Privately Held**
SIC: 8748 Educational consultant
PA: Institute For Multicultural Counseling
And Educational Services Inc.
3580 Wilshire Blvd # 2000
Los Angeles CA 90010

(P-27095)
INTEGRTED SPPORT SOLUTIONS INC (PA)
Also Called: Rd Solutions
4283 Empress Ave, Encino (91436-3504)
PHONE..................818 787-2116
Steve Eisner, *President*
Nashwa Eisner, *Admin Sec*
EMP: 386
SQ FT: 2,000
SALES: 17MM **Privately Held**
SIC: 8748 Systems engineering consult-
ant, ex. computer or professional

(P-27096)
INTERNATIONAL MGT SYSTEMS
Also Called: IMS
4640 Admiralty Way # 500, Marina Del Rey
(90292-6621)
PHONE..................310 822-2022
Harry M Thorpe Jr, *President*
EMP: 90
SQ FT: 6,000
SALES (est): 3.9MM **Privately Held**
WEB: www.imssvs.com
SIC: 8748 7374 Systems engineering con-
sultant, ex. computer or professional; data
processing & preparation

(P-27097)
INTRINSIK ENVMTL SCIENCES INC
1608 Pacific Ave Ste 201, Venice
(90291-5112)
PHONE..................310 392-6462
EMP: 67
SALES (corp-wide): 3.5MM **Privately Held**
SIC: 8748
PA: Intrinsik Environmental Sciences Inc
6605 Hurontario St Suite 605
Mississauga ON L5T 0
905 364-7800

(P-27098)
ITC SRVICE GROUP ACQSITION LLC (DH)
Also Called: I T C
7777 Greenback Ln Ste 201, Citrus Heights
(95610-5800)
PHONE..................877 370-4482
Jody Gallagher, *President*
EMP: 50 EST: 1999
SQ FT: 11,843
SALES (est): 97.6MM **Privately Held**
WEB: www.callitc.com
SIC: 8748 Telecommunications consultant
HQ: Afl Network Services, Inc.
170 Ridgeview Center Dr
Duncan SC 29334
864 433-0333

(P-27099)
JACOBS CONSULTANCY INC
555 Airport Blvd Ste 300, Burlingame
(94010-2036)
PHONE..................650 579-7722
Nick Davidson, *Branch Mgr*
EMP: 85
SALES (corp-wide): 10B **Publicly Held**
WEB: www.jacobsconsultancy.com
SIC: 8748 8742 Business consulting;
management consulting services
HQ: Jacobs Consultancy Inc.
5995 Rogerdale Rd
Houston TX 77072
832 351-6000

(P-27100)
JAG PROFESSIONAL SERVICES INC
2008 Walnut Ave, Manhattan Beach
(90266-2841)
P.O. Box 3007, El Segundo (90245-8107)
PHONE..................310 945-5648
Judith Hinkley, *CEO*
EMP: 126
SQ FT: 1,000
SALES (est): 10MM **Privately Held**
WEB: www.jagprof.com
SIC: 8748 Business consulting

(P-27101)
JDR ENGINEERING CONS INC
30422 Via Lindosa, Laguna Niguel
(92677-2351)
PHONE..................949 495-2063
Dionisio E Rodriguez, *Branch Mgr*
EMP: 102
SALES (corp-wide): 5.2MM **Privately
Held**
SIC: 8748 Business consulting
PA: Jdr Engineering Consultants, Inc.
3122 Maple St
Santa Ana CA 92707
714 751-7084

(P-27102)
JK CONSULTANTS
160 Station Way Unit 102, Arroyo Grande
(93421-5008)
PHONE..................209 532-7772
Fred Khachi, *President*
Elaine Khachi, *Exec VP*
Hanna Don, *Exec Dir*
Lorraine Pinto, *Administration*
EMP: 50
SQ FT: 3,000
SALES: 25MM **Privately Held**
WEB: www.jksuccess.com
SIC: 8748 8742 Business consulting;
management consulting services

(P-27103)
JULIO GONZALEZ
1417 S Fairfax Ave Apt 4, Los Angeles
(90019-3736)
PHONE..................310 310-4055
Julio Gonzalez, *Owner*
EMP: 99
SALES: 950K **Privately Held**
SIC: 8748 Business consulting

(P-27104)
JUSTICE CALIFORNIA DEPARTMENT
Also Called: Testing and Selection
1300 I St Ste 720, Sacramento
(95814-2958)
PHONE..................916 324-5039
Richard Busman, *Branch Mgr*
Jeanne Wolfe,
EMP: 1000 **Privately Held**
WEB: www.doj.state.wi.us
SIC: 8748 9222 Testing services; systems
engineering consultant, ex. computer or
professional; legal counsel & prosecution;
HQ: California Department Of Justice
1300 I St Ste 1142
Sacramento CA 95814

(P-27105)
KATZ MEDIA GROUP INC
5700 Wilshire Blvd # 200, Los Angeles
(90036-4485)
PHONE..................323 966-5000
K Thornton, *Manager*
Pat Nejad, *Manager*
EMP: 85 **Publicly Held**
WEB: www.ctvsales.com
SIC: 8748 Business consulting
HQ: Katz Media Group, Inc.
125 W 55th St Fl 11
New York NY 10019

(P-27106)
KEYSTONE STRATEGY LLC
150 Spear St Ste 1750, San Francisco
(94105-1541)
PHONE..................877 419-2623
Henry Liu, *Principal*

Sue Porter, *Office Mgr*
EMP: 80 Privately Held
SIC: **8748** Business consulting
PA: Keystone Strategy, Llc
150 Cambridgepark Dr # 704
Cambridge MA 02140

(P-27107)
KLEINFELDER INC
3880 Lemon St Ste 300, Riverside
(92501-3301)
PHONE...........................951 801-3681
John Lohman, *Manager*
EMP: 55
SALES (corp-wide): 249.4MM Privately Held
WEB: www.kleinfelder.com
SIC: **8748** 7389 Environmental consultant; systems engineering consultant, ex. computer or professional; air pollution measuring service
HQ: Kleinfelder, Inc.
550 W C St Ste 1200
San Diego CA 92101
619 831-4600

(P-27108)
KLH CONSULTING INC
2324 Bethards Dr, Santa Rosa
(95405-8537)
PHONE...........................707 575-9986
Soni Lampert, *CEO*
Hub Lampert, *CFO*
Melanie Muir, *Manager*
EMP: 55 EST: 1978
SALES (est): 9.1MM Privately Held
WEB: www.klhconsulting.com
SIC: **8748** 7371 7372 Systems engineering consultant, ex. computer or professional; custom computer programming services; business oriented computer software

(P-27109)
KRAZAN & ASSOCIATES (PA)
215 W Dakota Ave, Clovis (93612-5608)
PHONE...........................559 348-2200
Dean L Alexander, *President*
Dean Alexander, *COO*
Jodi Ragsdale, *CFO*
Emilo Vargas, *CFO*
Thomas P Krazan, *Chairman*
EMP: 68
SQ FT: 21,000
SALES: 19MM Privately Held
WEB: www.krazan.com
SIC: **8748** 8734 8742 Environmental consultant; product testing laboratory, safety or performance; management engineering

(P-27110)
KROS-WISE
435 E Carmel St, San Marcos
(92078-4362)
PHONE...........................619 607-2899
Lily Aragon, *President*
EMP: 150
SALES (est): 6.3MM Privately Held
WEB: www.kroswise.com
SIC: **8748** Business consulting

(P-27111)
L S A ASSOCIATES INC (PA)
20 Executive Park Ste 200, Irvine
(92614-4739)
PHONE...........................949 553-0666
Les Card, *CEO*
Rob McCann, *President*
James Baum, *CFO*
Rosie Evans, *Vice Pres*
Marco Perez, *Regional Mgr*
EMP: 110
SQ FT: 22,000
SALES (est): 50MM Privately Held
WEB: www.lsa-assoc.com
SIC: **8748** Environmental consultant

(P-27112)
LAND DESIGN CONSULTANTS INC
2700 E Foothill Blvd # 200, Pasadena
(91107-3443)
PHONE...........................626 578-7000
Robert Sims, *President*

Larry Mar, *CFO*
Steve Hunter, *Vice Pres*
Jimmy Lee, *Planning*
EMP: 70
SALES: 9.6MM Privately Held
WEB: www.ldcla.com
SIC: **8748** 8711 8713 Urban planning & consulting services; environmental consultant; civil engineering; surveying services

(P-27113)
LAYNE CHRISTENSEN COMPANY
Colog Div
1717 W Park Ave, Redlands (92373-8049)
PHONE...........................909 390-2833
David Singleton, *General Mgr*
Steve Gillman, *Opers Staff*
EMP: 140
SALES (corp-wide): 3.3B Publicly Held
WEB: www.laynechristensen.com
SIC: **8748** 7699 5084 Environmental consultant; pumps & pumping equipment repair; pumps & pumping equipment
HQ: Layne Christensen Company
1800 Hughes Landing Blvd
The Woodlands TX 77380
281 475-2600

(P-27114)
LEAF COMMUNICATIONS INC
1000 Calle Cordillera, San Clemente
(92673-6235)
PHONE...........................949 388-0192
Dan Leaf, *President*
Lisa Leaf, *Vice Pres*
EMP: 60
SALES (est): 532.4K Privately Held
SIC: **8748** 1623 Communications consulting; telecommunications consultant; transmitting tower (telecommunication) construction

(P-27115)
LEED INTERNATIONAL LLC
1583 Shanghai Cir, San Jose (95131-2411)
PHONE...........................650 861-7883
Hong Zhang, *Chairman*
EMP: 50
SALES (est): 594.2K Privately Held
SIC: **8748** 5961 Business consulting; catalog & mail-order houses

(P-27116)
LEIGHTON AND ASSOCIATES INC (PA)
17781 Cowan, Irvine (92614-6009)
PHONE...........................949 250-1421
Terry Brennan, *President*
Iraj Poormand, *Vice Pres*
Kris Lutton, *Office Mgr*
Deborah Delaney, *Executive Asst*
Vivian Cheng, *Project Engr*
EMP: 70
SQ FT: 30,000
SALES (est): 14.7MM Privately Held
SIC: **8748** 8711 Environmental consultant; engineering services

(P-27117)
LESLEY FOUNDATION
701 Arnold Way Bldg A, Half Moon Bay
(94019-2199)
PHONE...........................650 726-4888
Catherine Evans, *Exec Dir*
EMP: 73
SALES: 8.3MM Privately Held
SIC: **8748** Urban planning & consulting services

(P-27118)
LEVEL FOUR BUSINESS MGT LLC
11812 San Vicente Blvd # 400, Los Angeles
(90049-6625)
PHONE...........................310 914-1600
Mark Friedman, *Mng Member*
Todd Fertig, *Managing Dir*
Charles Clancy, *Business Mgr*
Jeremy Marcusc, *Business Mgr*
Natalia Marootian, *Business Mgr*
EMP: 50
SALES (est): 1.5MM Privately Held
SIC: **8748** Business consulting

(P-27119)
LIVEVOX INC (PA)
655 Montgomery St # 1190, San Francisco
(94111-2647)
PHONE...........................415 671-6000
Louis Summe, *CEO*
Larry Siegel, *CFO*
Michael Leraris, *CFO*
David Dantonio, *Vice Pres*
Linda Esperance, *Vice Pres*
EMP: 85
SALES (est): 34MM Privately Held
WEB: www.tfhinc.net
SIC: **8748** Telecommunications consultant

(P-27120)
LUMETRA HEALTHCARE SOLUTIONS
44 Montgomery St Ste 810, San Francisco
(94104-4620)
PHONE...........................415 677-2000
Patricia Daniel, *CEO*
Lewy Roth, *Office Mgr*
Consuela Bejan, *Executive Asst*
Annie Auyeung, *Accountant*
Danielle Smith, *Recruiter*
EMP: 50
SALES: 4.5MM Privately Held
WEB: www.lumetra.com
SIC: **8748** Business consulting

(P-27121)
LUSIVE DECOR
Also Called: Luxe Light and Home
3400 Medford St, Los Angeles
(90063-2530)
PHONE...........................323 227-9207
Jason Kai Cooper, *CEO*
John Carbajal, *Foreman/Supr*
Nathan Bignell, *Assistant*
EMP: 50 EST: 2006
SALES (est): 8.6MM Privately Held
SIC: **8748** 3646 Lighting consultant; ceiling systems, luminous

(P-27122)
LYLE COMPANY
3140 Gold Camp Dr Ste 30, Rancho Cordova (95670-6192)
P.O. Box 2255 (95741-2255)
PHONE...........................916 266-7000
Lanny G Lyle, *Ch of Bd*
Thu Nguyen, *CFO*
Reuben Mendoza, *Software Dev*
Matt Johnson, *Director*
Robert Dunnett, *Manager*
EMP: 60
SALES (est): 5.7MM Privately Held
WEB: www.lyleco.com
SIC: **8748** Business consulting

(P-27123)
MANAGEMENT TECH CONSULTING LLC
7738 Skyhill Dr, Los Angeles (90068-1232)
PHONE...........................323 851-5008
Darryl Henderson, *CEO*
EMP: 65
SQ FT: 2,800
SALES (est): 3.7MM Privately Held
SIC: **8748** Business consulting

(P-27124)
MANTECH SYSTEMS ENGRG CORP
8328 Clairemont Mesa Blvd # 100, San Diego (92111-1328)
PHONE...........................858 292-9000
Brad Geiger, *Systems Mgr*
EMP: 70
SALES (corp-wide): 1.9B Publicly Held
SIC: **8748** Business consulting
HQ: Mantech Systems Engineering Corporation
12015 Lee Jackson Hwy # 110
Fairfax VA 22033
703 218-6000

(P-27125)
MARLIN ALLIANCE INC
3990 Old Town Ave Ste A, San Diego
(92110-2930)
PHONE...........................619 450-1717
Robin Lipka, *CEO*
Helen Lipka, *President*

EMP: 55
SALES: 750K Privately Held
WEB: www.themarlinalliance.com
SIC: **8748** Business consulting

(P-27126)
MAXIM PLANNING GROUP
1214 E Colorado Blvd, Pasadena
(91106-1899)
PHONE...........................818 425-4343
Steve Vivanco, *Owner*
EMP: 60
SALES (est): 3MM Privately Held
SIC: **8748** Business consulting

(P-27127)
MCWONG ENVMTL & ENRGY GROUP
1921 Arena Blvd, Sacramento
(95834-3770)
PHONE...........................916 371-8080
Margaret Wong, *President*
EMP: 50 EST: 2001
SQ FT: 7,800
SALES: 16MM Privately Held
WEB: www.mcwonginc.com
SIC: **8748** Energy conservation consultant; environmental consultant

(P-27128)
MENKE & ASSOCIATES INC (PA)
1 Kaiser Plz Ste 505, Oakland
(94612-3611)
PHONE...........................415 362-5200
John Menke, *President*
W Kyle Coltman, *CEO*
Trevor Gilmore, *CFO*
Nancy Menke, *Admin Sec*
John Givens, *Director*
EMP: 55
SQ FT: 12,500
SALES: 9MM Privately Held
WEB: www.menke.com
SIC: **8748** Employee programs administration

(P-27129)
MICHAEL BAKER INTL INC
2729 Prospect Park Dr # 220, Rancho Cordova (95670-6291)
PHONE...........................916 361-8384
Phil Carter, *Manager*
Kurt Bergman, *CEO*
EMP: 99
SALES (corp-wide): 592.9MM Privately Held
SIC: **8748** Business consulting
HQ: Baker Michael International Inc
500 Grant St Ste 5400
Pittsburgh PA 15219
412 269-6300

(P-27130)
MICHAEL BAKER INTL INC
9755 Clairemont Mesa Blvd, San Diego
(92124-1333)
PHONE...........................858 453-3602
Phil Carter, *Manager*
EMP: 75
SALES (corp-wide): 592.9MM Privately Held
WEB: www.rbf.com
SIC: **8748** Business consulting
HQ: Baker Michael International Inc
500 Grant St Ste 5400
Pittsburgh PA 15219
412 269-6300

(P-27131)
MICHAEL BAKER INTL INC
3300 E Guasti Rd Ste 100, Ontario
(91761-8656)
PHONE...........................909 974-4900
Ron Craig, *Manager*
EMP: 50
SALES (corp-wide): 592.9MM Privately Held
SIC: **8748** Business consulting
HQ: Baker Michael International Inc
5 Hutton Cntre Dr Ste 500
Santa Ana CA 92707
949 472-3505

PRODUCTS & SVCS

(P-27132)
MIND DRAGON INC
36002 Pansy St, Winchester (92596-8735)
PHONE..............................877 367-6060
Jefferson Nunn, *President*
Fern Rudin, *CFO*
Jim Alexander, *Vice Pres*
Alan Gerson, *Vice Pres*
EMP: 50
SQ FT: 1,700
SALES: 600K **Privately Held**
WEB: www.mindragon.com
SIC: 8748 Business consulting

(P-27133)
MIRAMED GLOBAL SERVICES INC
Also Called: On Call Consulting
199 E Thsand Oaks Blvd, Thousand Oaks (91360)
PHONE..............................805 277-1017
Ron Manzani, *Branch Mgr*
EMP: 579 **Privately Held**
SIC: 8748 Business consulting
PA: Miramed Global Services, Inc.
    255 W Michigan Ave
    Jackson MI 49201

(P-27134)
MONTE VSTA MEM SCHLRSHIP ASSOC
2 School Way, Watsonville (95076-9716)
PHONE..............................831 722-8178
Stephen Sharp, *Administration*
EMP: 50
SALES (est): 3MM **Privately Held**
SIC: 8748 Business consulting

(P-27135)
MONTROSE ENVIRONMENTAL CORP
2825 Verne Roberts Cir, Antioch (94509-7902)
PHONE..............................925 680-4300
WEI Marcus Tan, *Principal*
EMP: 281 **Privately Held**
SIC: 8748 Environmental consultant
PA: Montrose Environmental Corporation
    1 Park Plz Ste 1000
    Irvine CA 92614
    -

(P-27136)
MONTROSE ENVMTL GROUP INC (PA)
1 Park Plz Ste 1000, Irvine (92614-8507)
PHONE..............................949 988-3500
Vijay Manthripragada, *CEO*
Jose Revuelta, *Officer*
Peter Zemek, *Senior VP*
Ryan Brokamp, *Vice Pres*
Jeremy Clark, *Vice Pres*
EMP: 64
SALES (est): 182.7MM **Privately Held**
SIC: 8748 Environmental consultant

(P-27137)
MONTROSE ENVMTL GROUP INC
1631 E Saint Andrew Pl, Santa Ana (92705-4932)
PHONE..............................714 332-8646
EMP: 573
SALES (corp-wide): 182.7MM **Privately Held**
SIC: 8748 Environmental consultant
PA: Montrose Environmental Group, Inc.
    1 Park Plz Ste 1000
    Irvine CA 92614
    949 988-3500

(P-27138)
MONTROSE WATER AND SUSTAINABIL
Also Called: Mwss
1 Park Plz Ste 1000, Irvine (92614-8507)
PHONE..............................949 988-3500
Vijay Manthripragada, *President*
Allan Dicks, *Treasurer*
Jose Revuelta, *Vice Pres*
Nasym Afsari, *Admin Sec*
EMP: 90

SALES (est): 1MM
SALES (corp-wide): 182.7MM **Privately Held**
SIC: 8748 8744 Environmental consultant;
PA: Montrose Environmental Group, Inc.
    1 Park Plz Ste 1000
    Irvine CA 92614
    949 988-3500

(P-27139)
MOORE IACOFANO GOLTSMAN INC (PA)
Also Called: M I G
800 Hearst Ave, Berkeley (94710-2018)
PHONE..............................510 845-7549
Susan M Goltsman, *President*
Donna Sonoda, *Business Dir*
Adele Torreano, *Business Dir*
Priscilla Hoge, *Executive Asst*
Randy Speer, *Executive Asst*
EMP: 63
SQ FT: 6,000
SALES (est): 19.5MM **Privately Held**
WEB: www.migcom.com
SIC: 8748 Environmental consultant

(P-27140)
MOUNTAIN TOP COMM SVCS LLC
1902 Orange Tree Ln, Redlands (92374-2888)
PHONE..............................909 798-4400
Diodore Pesquera,
Joseph Jacobson,
Justin Mata,
EMP: 50 EST: 2011
SQ FT: 4,025
SALES (est): 368.5K **Privately Held**
SIC: 8748 Telecommunications consultant

(P-27141)
MSLA MANAGEMENT LLC
1294 E Colorado Blvd, Pasadena (91106-1901)
PHONE..............................626 824-6020
Michael Lambert, *CEO*
Sahniah Siciarz-Lambert, *President*
Robert Worth Oberrender, *Treasurer*
Thomas Shaun McGlinch, *Asst Treas*
Paul Timothy Runice, *Asst Treas*
EMP: 173
SALES (est): 1.9MM
SALES (corp-wide): 226.2B **Publicly Held**
SIC: 8748 Business consulting
HQ: Logistics Health, Inc.
    328 Front St S
    La Crosse WI 54601
    866 284-8788

(P-27142)
NATIONAL INSURANCE HOUSING
Also Called: National Insurance Associates
265 Santa Helena Ste 210, Solana Beach (92075-1546)
PHONE..............................800 550-1911
Susan Swan, *Executive*
EMP: 99
SALES (est): 3.2MM **Privately Held**
SIC: 8748 Urban planning & consulting services

(P-27143)
NATIONAL SAFETY SERVICES
3400 Avenue Of The Arts, Costa Mesa (92626-1927)
PHONE..............................714 679-9118
EMP: 50
SALES (est): 2.7MM **Privately Held**
SIC: 8748 8999

(P-27144)
NEWTON SOFTED INC
Also Called: Pm2net
2807 Mcgaw Ave, Irvine (92614-5835)
PHONE..............................949 396-6192
Carson Synh, *CEO*
Joel Morrison, *Project Mgr*
EMP: 50
SALES (est): 2MM **Privately Held**
SIC: 8748 7379 Systems analysis & engineering consulting services; computer related consulting services

(P-27145)
NEXANT INC (PA)
101 2nd St Ste 1000, San Francisco (94105-3651)
PHONE..............................415 369-1000
John Gustafson, *CEO*
Arjun Gupta, *Chairman*
Preston Miller, *Bd of Directors*
Eric Bober, *Vice Pres*
Joseph Bright, *Vice Pres*
EMP: 80
SQ FT: 17,462
SALES (est): 126.2MM **Privately Held**
WEB: www.nexant.com
SIC: 8748 Energy conservation consultant

(P-27146)
NINYO & MOORE GEOTECHNICAL (PA)
5710 Ruffin Rd, San Diego (92123-1013)
PHONE..............................858 576-1000
Avram Ninyo, *CEO*
Madan Chirumalla, *Admin Sec*
Angelique Frederick, *Admin Asst*
Tiffany Hooper, *Admin Asst*
Lauren Schuhmacher, *Admin Asst*
EMP: 80
SQ FT: 24,000
SALES (est): 56MM **Privately Held**
SIC: 8748 Environmental consultant

(P-27147)
NINYO & MOORE GEOTECHNICAL
475 Goddard Ste 200, Irvine (92618-4622)
PHONE..............................949 753-7070
Carol Price, *Manager*
Ruth Dolecki, *Administration*
Scott Kurtz, *Project Engr*
Jared Recla, *Sr Project Mgr*
EMP: 65
SALES (corp-wide): 56MM **Privately Held**
SIC: 8748 8711 8734 Environmental consultant; pollution control engineering; soil analysis
PA: Ninyo & Moore Geotechnical & Environmental Sciences Consultants
    5710 Ruffin Rd
    San Diego CA 92123
    858 576-1000

(P-27148)
NMS DATA INC
Also Called: Neilson Marketing Services
23172 Plaza Pointe Dr # 205, Laguna Hills (92653-1477)
PHONE..............................949 472-2700
Lawrence Neilson, *CEO*
Jeffrey Neilson, *President*
Jolie Eritano, *Accountant*
Annie George, *VP Mktg*
Paul Neilson, *VP Sales*
EMP: 50
SQ FT: 9,500
SALES: 5MM **Privately Held**
SIC: 8748 Business consulting

(P-27149)
NORTH LA COUNTY REGIONAL CTR (PA)
15400 Sherman Way Ste 170, Van Nuys (91406-4272)
PHONE..............................818 778-1900
George Stevens, *Exec Dir*
EMP: 350
SQ FT: 57,000
SALES: 462.1MM **Privately Held**
SIC: 8748 Test development & evaluation service

(P-27150)
NORTH LA COUNTY REGIONAL CTR
Also Called: Regional Center For Devlpmtnly
43210 Gingham Ave Ste 6, Lancaster (93535-4512)
PHONE..............................661 945-6761
Joan Daniels, *Manager*
EMP: 70
SALES (corp-wide): 462.1MM **Privately Held**
SIC: 8748 Test development & evaluation service

PA: North La County Regional Center Inc
    15400 Sherman Way Ste 170
    Van Nuys CA 91406
    818 778-1900

(P-27151)
NUGGET MARKET INC
7101 Elk Grove Blvd, Elk Grove (95758-9535)
PHONE..............................916 226-2626
John Sullivan, *Manager*
Mary Muller, *Executive*
EMP: 86
SALES (corp-wide): 311.5MM **Privately Held**
SIC: 8748 5411 Business consulting; grocery stores
PA: Nugget Market Inc.
    168 Court St
    Woodland CA 95695
    530 669-3300

(P-27152)
O C JONES & SONS INC
155 Filbert St Ste 209, Oakland (94607-2524)
PHONE..............................510 663-6911
Carla Radosta, *Branch Mgr*
Victor Babbitt, *Project Mgr*
EMP: 100
SALES (corp-wide): 78.5MM **Privately Held**
SIC: 8748 Business consulting
PA: O. C. Jones & Sons, Inc.
    1520 4th St
    Berkeley CA 94710
    510 526-3424

(P-27153)
OCEAN PARK COMMUNITY CENTER
Turning Point
1447 16th St, Santa Monica (90404-2715)
PHONE..............................310 828-6717
Patricia Bauman, *Director*
EMP: 123
SALES (corp-wide): 13.5MM **Privately Held**
SIC: 8748 Urban planning & consulting services
PA: The People Concern
    2116 Arlington Ave # 100
    Los Angeles CA 90018
    323 334-9000

(P-27154)
OFFICE OF THE LEGISLATIVE COUN
Also Called: Legislative Counsel Tstg Off
925 L St Ste 900, Sacramento (95814-3702)
PHONE..............................916 445-3796
Alison Raymer, *Manager*
EMP: 1000 **Privately Held**
WEB: www.lc.ca.gov
SIC: 8748 9121 Testing services; legislative bodies;
HQ: Office Of The Legislative Counsel
    State Cpitol Bldg Rm 3021
    Sacramento CA 95814

(P-27155)
ONE DIVERSIFIED LLC
3275 Edward Ave, Santa Clara (95054-2340)
PHONE..............................408 969-1972
EMP: 91
SALES (corp-wide): 739.2MM **Privately Held**
SIC: 8748 7373 Systems analysis & engineering consulting services; systems integration services
PA: One Diversified, Llc
    2975 Northwoods Pkwy
    Peachtree Corners GA 30071
    770 447-1001

(P-27156)
ONSITE CONSULTING LLC
5042 Wilshire Blvd # 135, Los Angeles (90036-4305)
PHONE..............................323 401-3190
James D Sinclair, *Mng Member*
EMP: 65

SALES: 9.5MM **Privately Held**
SIC: 8748 Business consulting

(P-27157)
OPALLIOS INC
4633 Old Ironsides Dr # 315, Santa Clara
(95054-1846)
PHONE..............................408 769-4594
Omcar Paradkar, *Principal*
EMP: 50
SALES (est): 2MM **Privately Held**
SIC: 8748 Business consulting

(P-27158)
OPENPOPCOM INC (PA)
5422 Beach Blvd, Buena Park
(90621-1234)
PHONE..............................714 249-7044
Sun Jong Baek, *President*
EMP: 75
SALES (est): 4.5MM **Privately Held**
SIC: 8748 Telecommunications consultant

(P-27159)
ORANGE SILICON VALLEY
60 Spear St Ste 1100, San Francisco
(94105-1599)
PHONE..............................415 243-1500
EMP: 60 EST: 2012
SALES (est): 3.6MM **Privately Held**
SIC: 8748

(P-27160)
OUTSOURCE TESTING INC
Also Called: Ostcs
1278 Center Court Dr, Covina
(91724-3601)
PHONE..............................909 592-8898
Brian Steven Pinkus, *President*
Marie Messina-Soares, *Vice Pres*
Cody Johnston, *Software Engr*
Rafael Garcia, *Technician*
Christian Delarosa, *Technical Staff*
EMP: 75
SQ FT: 8,000
SALES (est): 5.6MM **Privately Held**
WEB: www.outsourcetesting.com
SIC: 8748 Testing services

(P-27161)
P8GE CONSULTING INC
Also Called: Fame Hardwood Floors
8406 Beverly Blvd, Los Angeles
(90048-3402)
PHONE..............................310 666-2301
Pedram Youav Nazarian, *CEO*
EMP: 50
SQ FT: 1,500
SALES: 10MM **Privately Held**
SIC: 8748 Business consulting

(P-27162)
PACIFIC COMMUNICATIONS ASSOC
761 2nd St, Brentwood (94513-1352)
P.O. Box 1147 (94513-3147)
PHONE..............................925 634-1203
Peter Petrovich, *President*
Fred Valverde, *CFO*
Rhonda Petrovich, *Vice Pres*
Mark Isidoro, *VP Opers*
EMP: 50
SQ FT: 600
SALES (est): 2.7MM **Privately Held**
WEB: www.pacific-communications.com
SIC: 8748 Communications consulting

(P-27163)
PACIRA CRYOTECH INC
Also Called: Myoscience, Inc.
46400 Fremont Blvd, Fremont
(94538-6469)
PHONE..............................800 442-0989
Timothy Still, *President*
Brian Farley, *Ch of Bd*
Peter Osborne, *CFO*
Jessica Appelgren, *Comms Dir*
James Berger, *Info Tech Mgr*
EMP: 50
SALES (est): 9.1MM **Publicly Held**
SIC: 8748 Business consulting
PA: Pacira Pharmaceuticals, Inc.
5 Sylvan Way Ste 300
Parsippany NJ 07054

(P-27164)
PARAGON PARTNERS LTD (PA)
5660 Katella Ave Ste 100, Cypress
(90630-5058)
PHONE..............................714 379-3376
Neilia A La Valle, *President*
Joel Sewell, *Vice Pres*
Cuong Nguyen, *Project Mgr*
Peter Rhoad, *Project Mgr*
Mohini Modi, *Technical Staff*
EMP: 65
SQ FT: 10,000
SALES (est): 18.6MM **Privately Held**
WEB: www.paragon-partners.com
SIC: 8748 Business consulting

(P-27165)
PARTNERS RISK SPECIALISTS
6136 Mission Gorge Rd # 125, San Diego
(92120-3494)
PHONE..............................619 326-0840
Jona Barnes, *Principal*
EMP: 50
SALES (est): 2.1MM **Privately Held**
SIC: 8748 Business consulting

(P-27166)
PATRIOT COMMUNICATIONS LLC (PA)
Also Called: Benefit Resources Group
3415 S Sepulveda Blvd # 800, Los Angeles
(90034-6060)
PHONE..............................888 833-4711
Doug Livingston,
Kyra Gagnon, *CFO*
Robyn Campbell, *Exec VP*
John Bruther, *Info Tech Dir*
Dio King, *Software Engr*
EMP: 52 EST: 1990
SQ FT: 15,000
SALES (est): 13MM **Privately Held**
WEB: www.patriotllc.com
SIC: 8748 Telecommunications consultant

(P-27167)
PEOPLES SELF-HELP HOUSING CORP
Also Called: Los Adobes De Maria
1026 W Boone St, Santa Maria
(93458-5499)
PHONE..............................805 349-9341
John Fowler, *Director*
EMP: 65
SALES (corp-wide): 10MM **Privately Held**
SIC: 8748 Urban planning & consulting services
PA: Peoples' Self-Help Housing Corporation
3533 Empleo St
San Luis Obispo CA 93401
805 781-3088

(P-27168)
PINNACLE ELECTRICAL SVCS INC
Also Called: Pinnacle Networking Services
730 Fairmont Ave Ste 100, Glendale
(91203-1079)
PHONE..............................818 241-6009
Avo Amirian, *CEO*
Joe Lucurst, *President*
David Herrera, *Project Mgr*
EMP: 56
SQ FT: 2,500
SALES (est): 3.1MM **Privately Held**
SIC: 8748 Telecommunications consultant

(P-27169)
POLARIS RESEARCH & DEVELOPMENT
390 4th St Fl 1, San Francisco
(94107-1289)
PHONE..............................415 777-3229
Mike Jang, *Vice Pres*
Ernie Fazio, *President*
Rosa Osman, *CFO*
Richard Shoemake, *CFO*
Carol McGruder, *Director*
EMP: 70
SQ FT: 10,000
SALES (est): 3.9MM **Privately Held**
SIC: 8748 Environmental consultant

(P-27170)
PONDER ENVIRONMENTAL SVCS INC (PA)
4563 E 2nd St, Benicia (94510-1032)
P.O. Box 1427 (94510-4427)
PHONE..............................707 748-7775
Jim Ponder, *President*
Sam Hoang, *Controller*
Sharon Taylor, *Safety Dir*
Fred Mitchell, *Sales Mgr*
EMP: 60
SQ FT: 15,000
SALES (est): 17.9MM **Privately Held**
WEB:
www.ponderenvironmentalservices.com
SIC: 8748 Environmental consultant

(P-27171)
PREMIER EXEC SOLUTIONS INC
269 S Beverly Dr Ste 981, Beverly Hills
(90212-3851)
PHONE..............................310 989-9925
Manny Salazar, *President*
EMP: 50
SALES (est): 1.9MM **Privately Held**
SIC: 8748 Business consulting

(P-27172)
PROFIT RECOVERY PARTNERS LLC
Also Called: P R P
2995 Red Hill Ave Ste 200, Costa Mesa
(92626-5984)
PHONE..............................949 851-2777
Donald Steiner, *President*
Jeremy Linehan, *President*
Marty Bozarth, *COO*
Paul J Bottiaux, *CFO*
Edward Lyon, *CFO*
EMP: 75
SQ FT: 260,000
SALES (est): 12.9MM **Privately Held**
WEB: www.prpllc.com
SIC: 8748 Business consulting

(P-27173)
PROJECT CONSULTING SPECIALISTS
425 N Whisman Rd Ste 600, Mountain View
(94043-5733)
PHONE..............................650 265-2400
Brendan McIntyre, *President*
EMP: 50
SQ FT: 2,200
SALES (est): 5.7MM **Privately Held**
SIC: 8748 Systems engineering consultant, ex. computer or professional

(P-27174)
PROJECT DESIGN CONSULTANTS
701 B St Ste 800, San Diego (92101-8162)
PHONE..............................619 235-6471
Gregory M Shields, *CEO*
William R Dick, *President*
Gary Hus, *Vice Pres*
Chris Morrow, *Vice Pres*
Debby Reece, *Vice Pres*
EMP: 100
SQ FT: 22,000
SALES (est): 9.8MM **Privately Held**
WEB: www.projectdesign.com
SIC: 8748 8711 8713 Urban planning & consulting services; civil engineering; surveying services

(P-27175)
PS ARTS
Also Called: CROSSROADS COMMUNITY FOUNDATIO
6701 Center Dr W Ste 550, Los Angeles
(90045-1556)
PHONE..............................310 586-1017
Kristin Paglia, *Exec Dir*
Amy Shario, *Exec Dir*
Allison Schaub, *Manager*
EMP: 50
SALES: 3.4MM **Privately Held**
WEB: www.psarts.org
SIC: 8748 Educational consultant

(P-27176)
Q-FREE AMERICA INC
5962 La Place Ct 150, Carlsbad
(92008-8807)
PHONE..............................855 737-3387
Greg Parzych, *CEO*
EMP: 54 EST: 2012
SQ FT: 4,200
SALES (est): 609.2K
SALES (corp-wide): 104.8MM **Privately Held**
SIC: 8748 Systems engineering consultant, ex. computer or professional
PA: Q-Free Asa
Strindfjordvegen 1
Ranheim 7053
738 265-00

(P-27177)
QUADRIX INFORMATION TECH INC
Also Called: Quadrixit
10736 Jefferson Blvd # 132, Culver City
(90230-4933)
PHONE..............................424 603-2140
Joseph Gutwirth, *CEO*
Naida Gutwirth, *COO*
Dennis Rojas, *Exec VP*
EMP: 50 EST: 2010
SALES (est): 2.1MM **Privately Held**
SIC: 8748 7379 Systems engineering consultant, ex. computer or professional; computer related consulting services

(P-27178)
QUALITYLOGIC INC (PA)
2245 1st St Ste 103, Simi Valley
(93065-0904)
PHONE..............................805 531-9030
Dave Jollota, *CEO*
Gary James, *CEO*
Steve Butterfield, *Principal*
Bill Campbell, *Principal*
James Mater, *Principal*
EMP: 120
SALES: 10MM **Privately Held**
WEB: www.qualitylogic.com
SIC: 8748 7372 Testing services; application computer software

(P-27179)
QUOVA INC
401 Castro St Fl 3, Mountain View
(94041-2089)
PHONE..............................650 965-2898
Marie Alexander, *President*
Gary P Jackson, *COO*
Jean-Louis Casabonne, *CFO*
EMP: 60
SQ FT: 10,000
SALES (est): 4.1MM
SALES (corp-wide): 1B **Privately Held**
WEB: www.quova.com
SIC: 8748 Business consulting
HQ: Neustar, Inc.
21575 Ridgetop Cir
Sterling VA 20166
571 434-5400

(P-27180)
RAHI SYSTEMS INC (PA)
48303 Fremont Blvd, Fremont
(94538-6580)
PHONE..............................510 651-2205
Tarun Raisoni, *Principal*
Ajay Kakde, *Software Dev*
Kathryn Zhang, *Business Mgr*
Manoj Karande, *Analyst*
Vivian Qi, *Opers Mgr*
EMP: 107
SALES (est): 19MM **Privately Held**
SIC: 8748 Telecommunications consultant

(P-27181)
RAMBOLL ENVIRON US CORPORATION
2200 Powell St Ste 700, Emeryville
(94608-1877)
PHONE..............................510 655-7400
Douglas Daugherty, *Manager*
EMP: 70
SALES (corp-wide): 314.9MM **Privately Held**
WEB: www.environcorp.com
SIC: 8748 Environmental consultant

PRODUCTS & SVCS

HQ: Ramboll Us Corporation
4350 Fairfax Dr Ste 300
Arlington VA 22203
703 516-2300

(P-27182)
RAMBOLL ENVIRON US CORPORATION
Also Called: Ramboll Environment & Health
5 Park Plz Ste 500, Irvine (92614-8525)
PHONE..............................949 261-5151
George Linkletter, *Manager*
EMP: 65
SALES (corp-wide): 314.9MM **Privately Held**
WEB: www.environcorp.com
SIC: 8748 8711 Environmental consultant; pollution control engineering
HQ: Ramboll Us Corporation
4350 Fairfax Dr Ste 300
Arlington VA 22203
703 516-2300

(P-27183)
RANGE GENERATION NEXT LLC
Also Called: Rgnext
Pillar Point Air Sta, El Granada (94018)
PHONE..............................310 647-9438
Tom Kennedy, *CEO*
Donna Mc Cullough, *Manager*
EMP: 50
SQ FT: 100
SALES (est): 2.5MM **Privately Held**
SIC: 8748 Systems analysis or design

(P-27184)
RAPID PRODUCT DEV GROUP INC
300 W Grand Ave, Escondido (92025-2659)
PHONE..............................760 703-5770
Tony Moran, *CEO*
EMP: 110
SALES (est): 5.9MM **Privately Held**
WEB: www.rpdg.com
SIC: 8748 Business consulting

(P-27185)
RECON ENVIRONMENTAL INC (PA)
1927 5th Ave Ste 200, San Diego (92101-2357)
PHONE..............................619 308-9333
Charles Bull, *Ch of Bd*
Robert Macaller, *President*
Diane Pearson Bull, *CFO*
Paul Fromer, *Vice Pres*
Roberta Herdes, *Vice Pres*
EMP: 100
SQ FT: 18,500
SALES (est): 24.1MM **Privately Held**
WEB: www.recon-us.com
SIC: 8748 Environmental consultant

(P-27186)
REDEVELOPMENT AGENCY OF THE CI
Also Called: SUISUN REDEVELOPMENT AGENCY
701 Civic Center Blvd, Suisun City (94585-2617)
PHONE..............................707 421-7309
Suzanne Bragdon, *Manager*
Jason Garben, *Director*
EMP: 68
SALES: 12.6MM **Privately Held**
SIC: 8748 Urban planning & consulting services

(P-27187)
REGENESIS BIOREMEDIATION PDTS (PA)
1011 Calle Sombra, San Clemente (92673-4204)
PHONE..............................949 366-8000
Scott B Wilson, *President*
Gavin Herbert Jr, *Chairman*
Rick Gillespie, *Vice Pres*
Tricia Rodewald, *Vice Pres*
Craig Sandefur, *Vice Pres*
EMP: 50
SQ FT: 15,000
SALES: 24.3MM **Privately Held**
SIC: 8748 Environmental consultant

(P-27188)
RESEARCH MANAGEMENT CONS INC (PA)
Also Called: Rmci
816 Camarillo Springs Rd J, Camarillo (93012-9441)
PHONE..............................805 987-5538
Raydean Acevedo, *President*
Cynthia Burns, *CFO*
Beth Wilt, *Web Proj Mgr*
EMP: 97
SQ FT: 2,700
SALES: 15.5MM **Privately Held**
SIC: 8748 8711 Environmental consultant; systems engineering consultant, ex. computer or professional; engineering services

(P-27189)
RESOLUTION ECONOMICS GROUP LLC (PA)
1925 Century Park E Fl 15, Los Angeles (90067-2701)
PHONE..............................310 275-9137
Trevor Sturges, *CFO*
Ali Leeman, *Managing Prtnr*
Scarlett Sidley, *Accounting Mgr*
EMP: 54 **EST:** 2011
SALES (est): 2.8MM **Privately Held**
SIC: 8748 Economic consultant

(P-27190)
RETAIL SERVICES & SYSTEMS INC
2765 E Bidwell St, Folsom (95630-6405)
PHONE..............................916 984-6923
EMP: 75
SALES (corp-wide): 873.4MM **Privately Held**
SIC: 8748 5921 Business consulting; wine
PA: Retail Services & Systems, Inc.
6600 Rockledge Dr Ste 150
Bethesda MD 20817
301 795-1000

(P-27191)
RETAIL SERVICES & SYSTEMS INC
394 N Moorpark Rd, Thousand Oaks (91360-4303)
PHONE..............................805 494-0108
Bill Mazal, *Branch Mgr*
EMP: 75
SALES (corp-wide): 873.4MM **Privately Held**
SIC: 8748 5921 Business consulting; wine
PA: Retail Services & Systems, Inc.
6600 Rockledge Dr Ste 150
Bethesda MD 20817
301 795-1000

(P-27192)
RINCON CONSULTANTS INC
255 W Fallbrook Ave # 103, Fresno (93711-6151)
PHONE..............................559 228-9925
Marcus Jones, *President*
EMP: 233 **Privately Held**
SIC: 8748 8999 Environmental consultant; scientific consulting
PA: Rincon Consultants, Inc.
180 N Ashwood Ave
Ventura CA 93003

(P-27193)
ROSE INTERNATIONAL INC
4000 Executive Pkwy # 150, San Ramon (94583-4314)
PHONE..............................636 812-4000
Mary Coats, *Branch Mgr*
EMP: 200 **Privately Held**
SIC: 8748 7371 7363 7361 Systems engineering consultant, ex. computer or professional; computer software development; help supply services; employment agencies
PA: Rose International, Inc.
16401 Swingley Ridge Rd
Chesterfield MO 63017

(P-27194)
ROSE INTERNATIONAL INC
18952 Macarthur Blvd # 440, Irvine (92612-1402)
PHONE..............................636 812-4000
Jonnie Gray, *Branch Mgr*
EMP: 50 **Privately Held**
SIC: 8748 7371 7363 7361 Systems engineering consultant, ex. computer or professional; computer software development; help supply services; employment agencies
PA: Rose International, Inc.
16401 Swingley Ridge Rd
Chesterfield MO 63017

(P-27195)
ROUGHAN ASSOCIATES AT LINC
465 N Halstead St Ste 120, Pasadena (91107-3144)
PHONE..............................626 351-0991
Jan Roughan, *President*
EMP: 50
SALES (est): 3.4MM **Privately Held**
SIC: 8748 Business consulting

(P-27196)
ROUX ASSOCIATES INC
5150 E Pacific Coast Hwy # 450, Long Beach (90804-3328)
PHONE..............................562 446-8600
Wai Kwan, *President*
EMP: 51
SALES (corp-wide): 85MM **Privately Held**
SIC: 8748 Environmental consultant
PA: Roux Associates, Inc.
209 Shafter St
Islandia NY 11749
631 232-2600

(P-27197)
S R I C B I
333 Ravenswood Ave, Menlo Park (94025-3453)
PHONE..............................650 859-4865
William Guns, *President*
William Rolston, *CFO*
EMP: 70
SALES: 9MM **Privately Held**
SIC: 8748 Business consulting

(P-27198)
SA PHOTONICS INC
120 Knowles Dr, Los Gatos (95032-1828)
PHONE..............................408 560-3500
James Coward, *President*
Andrea Singewald, *CFO*
Mustafa Veziroglu, *Vice Pres*
Michael Browne, *General Mgr*
Leonard Magelky, *Office Mgr*
EMP: 51
SQ FT: 30,000
SALES (est): 7.5MM **Privately Held**
WEB: www.saphotonics.com
SIC: 8748 Business consulting

(P-27199)
SACRAMNTO MTRO A QULTY MGT DST
777 12th St Ste 300, Sacramento (95814-1928)
PHONE..............................916 874-4800
Larry Greene, *Exec Dir*
Joanne Chan, *Engineer*
Joseph Hurley, *Analyst*
Pamela Rader, *Accountant*
Olga Castillon, *Personnel*
EMP: 84 **EST:** 2012
SALES (est): 12.1MM **Privately Held**
SIC: 8748 Environmental consultant

(P-27200)
SAN DIEGO COMMUNITY HSING CORP
230 Catania St, San Diego (92113-1864)
PHONE..............................619 527-4633
Garl Vaughn, *CEO*
John Piper, *CFO*
EMP: 250
SQ FT: 2,200

SALES: 1.2MM **Privately Held**
SIC: 8748 Urban planning & consulting services

(P-27201)
SAN JOAQUIN VAL UNI AIR POL (PA)
Also Called: Valley Air District
1990 E Gettysburg Ave, Fresno (93726-0244)
PHONE..............................559 230-6000
Seyed Sadredin, *Exec Dir*
Ryan Buchanan, *Accountant*
Ryan Kincaid, *Accountant*
Chenecua Dixon, *Human Res Dir*
Fred Cruz, *Purch Dir*
EMP: 200
SQ FT: 60,000
SALES (est): 24.7MM **Privately Held**
SIC: 8748 Environmental consultant

(P-27202)
SAN JOAQUIN VAL UNI AIR POL
Also Called: Southern Regional Office
2700 M St Ste 275, Bakersfield (93301-2373)
PHONE..............................209 497-1000
Linda Phillips, *Manager*
EMP: 56 **Privately Held**
SIC: 8748 Environmental consultant
PA: San Joaquin Valley Unified Air Pollution Control District
1990 E Gettysburg Ave
Fresno CA 93726

(P-27203)
SAN JOAQUIN VALLEY A P C D
Also Called: Air Polution Control District
1990 E Gettysburg Ave, Fresno (93726-0244)
PHONE..............................559 230-6000
David L Crow, *Director*
Steve Shaw, *Executive*
Adriana Myovich, *Teacher*
EMP: 100
SALES (est): 6.7MM **Privately Held**
SIC: 8748 Environmental consultant

(P-27204)
SAN JOSE REDEVELOPMENT AGENCY
200 E Santa Clara St 14th, San Jose (95113-1903)
PHONE..............................408 535-8500
Harry Mavrogenes, *Exec Dir*
Julie Amato, *Officer*
John Wise, *Deputy Dir*
EMP: 140
SQ FT: 10,045
SALES: 234.5MM **Privately Held**
WEB: www.sjredevelopment.org
SIC: 8748 Urban planning & consulting services
PA: City Of San Jose
200 E Santa Clara St
San Jose CA 95113
408 535-3500

(P-27205)
SEALASKA ENVMTL SVCS LLC
3838 Camino Del Rio N # 240, San Diego (92108-1741)
PHONE..............................619 564-8329
Derik Frederiksen,
EMP: 65
SALES (est): 3MM
SALES (corp-wide): 429.3MM **Privately Held**
SIC: 8748 4959 Environmental consultant; environmental cleanup services
PA: Sealaska Corporation
1 Sealaska Plz Ste 400
Juneau AK 99801
907 586-1512

(P-27206)
SENSITY SYSTEMS INC (HQ)
1237 E Arques Ave, Sunnyvale (94085-4701)
PHONE..............................408 841-4200
Hugh Martin, *CEO*
Sean Harrington, *COO*
Phil Rehkemper, *CFO*
Scott Shipman,
Geoff Arnold, *CTO*

▲ = Import ▼=Export
◆ =Import/Export

EMP: 58
SALES (est): 15.4MM
SALES (corp-wide): 130.8B **Publicly Held**
SIC: 8748 Lighting consultant
PA: Verizon Communications Inc.
1095 Ave Of The Americas
New York NY 10036
212 395-1000

(P-27207)
SHIFTPIXY INC
1 Venture Ste 150, Irvine (92618-7411)
PHONE...................................949 207-7184
Scott W Absher, *President*
Domonic J Carney, *CFO*
Kirk Flagg, *Ch Credit Ofcr*
EMP: 55
SQ FT: 8,500
SALES: 34.9MM **Privately Held**
SIC: 8748 Employee programs administration

(P-27208)
SIGNATURE CONSULTANTS LLC
8560 W Sunset Blvd, Los Angeles (90069-2311)
PHONE...................................310 229-5731
Nicholas Ryan, *Manager*
EMP: 87 **Privately Held**
SIC: 8748 Business consulting
PA: Signature Consultants Llc
200 W Cypress Creek Rd # 400
Fort Lauderdale FL 33309

(P-27209)
SILICON VALLEY EXEC NETWRK
1336 Nelson Way, Sunnyvale (94087-3135)
PHONE...................................408 746-5803
Brian Reynard, *CEO*
EMP: 901
SALES (est): 16.4MM **Privately Held**
SIC: 8748 Business consulting

(P-27210)
SILV COMMUNICATION INC
3460 Wilshire Blvd # 1100, Los Angeles (90010-2206)
PHONE...................................213 381-7999
John Shaikh, *President*
Sk Golam Ahia, *Vice Pres*
EMP: 56
SQ FT: 7,500
SALES: 8MM **Privately Held**
SIC: 8748 Telecommunications consultant

(P-27211)
SMART SOFTWARE TSTG SOLUTIONS
2450 Peralta Blvd Ste 202, Fremont (94536-3826)
PHONE...................................833 778-7872
Pankaj Goel, *CEO*
Amit Kumar, *Officer*
EMP: 60 EST: 2016
SALES (est): 985K **Privately Held**
SIC: 8748 7371 Testing services; computer software development & applications

(P-27212)
SOLUGENIX CORPORATION (PA)
601 Valencia Ave, Brea (92823-6358)
PHONE...................................866 749-7658
Shashi Jasthi, *CEO*
Damola Akinola, *Vice Pres*
Marnie Barnhart, *Associate Dir*
Crystal A Kolosick, *Executive Asst*
Alicia Hilke, *Admin Asst*
EMP: 50
SQ FT: 1,600
SALES (est): 43.9MM **Privately Held**
WEB: www.solugenix.com
SIC: 8748 Telecommunications consultant

(P-27213)
SOLVE HEALTHCARE CORPORATION (PA)
1300 Bristol St N Ste 285, Newport Beach (92660-8902)
PHONE...................................949 891-0300
Sheel Mehta, *President*
Sajjad Khan, *Officer*
Paula Dehncke, *Consultant*

EMP: 75
SALES (est): 4.2MM **Privately Held**
SIC: 8748 Business consulting

(P-27214)
SONOMA TECHNOLOGY INC
1450 N Mcdowell Blvd, Petaluma (94954-6515)
PHONE...................................707 665-9900
Lyle R Chinkin, *President*
Paul T Roberts, *Exec VP*
Timothy S Dye, *Senior VP*
Hilary H Hafner, *Senior VP*
Jerry Anderson, *Vice Pres*
EMP: 65
SQ FT: 29,011
SALES: 9.9MM **Privately Held**
WEB: www.sonomatech.com
SIC: 8748 Environmental consultant

(P-27215)
SOURCE 44 LLC
Also Called: Source Intelligence
1921 Palomar Oaks Way # 205, Carlsbad (92008-6523)
PHONE...................................877 916-6337
Jess F Kraus, *CEO*
Matt Thorn, *COO*
Dan Dague, *Officer*
Alex Eng, *Officer*
Jennifer Kraus, *Officer*
EMP: 111
SALES (est): 9.9MM **Privately Held**
SIC: 8748 7371 Business consulting; computer software development

(P-27216)
SOUTH CAPITOL COTTAGE
15054 Daisy Rd, Adelanto (92301-4824)
PHONE...................................951 662-3026
Carol James, *Exec Dir*
Felica Taylor, *President*
Dorothy Shorter, *CFO*
Emma Nash, *Exec VP*
Theodore Nash, *Vice Pres*
EMP: 80
SALES: 450K **Privately Held**
SIC: 8748 Urban planning & consulting services

(P-27217)
SOUTH COAST AIR QULTY MGT DST (PA)
Also Called: A Q M D
21865 Copley Dr, Diamond Bar (91765-4178)
P.O. Box 4940 (91765-0940)
PHONE...................................909 396-2000
Raymond E Robinson, *CEO*
Marcia Crane, *President*
Rebecca Garcia, *President*
Michael O'Kelly, *Officer*
Barbara Baird, *Principal*
EMP: 780 EST: 1955
SQ FT: 350
SALES: 331.1MM **Privately Held**
SIC: 8748 Environmental consultant

(P-27218)
SOUTHEAST FRESNO RAD LP
1331 Fulton St, Fresno (93721-1630)
PHONE...................................559 443-8400
Preston Prince, *CEO*
EMP: 225
SALES (est): 90.4K **Privately Held**
SIC: 8748 Urban planning & consulting services

(P-27219)
SPRINGBOARD SOLUTIONS LLC
Also Called: CREDIT.ORG
4351 Latham St, Riverside (92501-1749)
PHONE...................................951 779-7739
Todd Emerson, *Principal*
Al Nemerofsky, *Administration*
EMP: 150
SALES: 15.9MM
SALES (corp-wide): 19.4MM **Privately Held**
SIC: 8748 Business consulting
PA: Springboard Nonprofit Consumer Credit Management, Inc.
4351 Latham St
Riverside CA 92501
951 781-0114

(P-27220)
SUCCESSOR TO SAN FRANCISCO
Also Called: Office Cmnty Inv Infrstructure
1 S Van Ness Ave Fl 5, San Francisco (94103-5416)
PHONE...................................415 749-2400
Marcia Rosen, *Principal*
Tiffany Bohee, *Exec Dir*
Amit Talwar, *Accountant*
EMP: 99
SALES (est): 5.5MM **Privately Held**
SIC: 8748 Economic consultant

(P-27221)
SWCA INCORPORATED
Also Called: Swca Environmental Consultants
51 W Dayton St Ste 100, Pasadena (91105-2025)
PHONE...................................626 240-0587
Cara Corsetti, *Branch Mgr*
EMP: 89
SALES (corp-wide): 146.4MM **Privately Held**
WEB: www.swca.com
SIC: 8748 8733 Environmental consultant; archeological expeditions
PA: Swca, Incorporated
20 E Thomas Rd Ste 1700
Phoenix AZ 85012
602 274-3831

(P-27222)
SYNAGRO WEST LLC
1499 Bayshore Hwy Ste 111, Burlingame (94010-1723)
PHONE...................................650 652-6531
EMP: 99
SALES: 950K
SALES (corp-wide): 43.6K **Privately Held**
SIC: 8748
HQ: Synagro Technologies, Inc.
435 Williams Ct Ste 100
Baltimore MD 21220

(P-27223)
SYPARTNERS LLC (HQ)
475 Brannan St Ste 100, San Francisco (94107-5419)
PHONE...................................415 536-6600
Susan Schuman, *CEO*
Mickey Stretton, *Creative Dir*
Jessica Harris, *Program Mgr*
Jessica Reeske, *Admin Asst*
Dzigbodi Djugba, *Administration*
EMP: 73
SALES (est): 21.6MM **Privately Held**
WEB: www.sypartners.com
SIC: 8748 Business consulting

(P-27224)
SYSTEMS EXPERIENCE INC
6033 W Century Blvd # 820, Los Angeles (90045-6424)
PHONE...................................310 215-9000
Richard L Jivery, *President*
EMP: 65
SQ FT: 3,600
SALES (est): 4.3MM **Privately Held**
SIC: 8748 Business consulting

(P-27225)
T-FORCE INC (PA)
4695 Macarthur Ct, Newport Beach (92660-1882)
PHONE...................................949 208-1527
Raid Al-Khawaldeh, *President*
EMP: 98
SALES (est): 8.1MM **Privately Held**
WEB: www.t-force.com
SIC: 8748 7379 Telecommunications consultant;

(P-27226)
TAHOE TRCKE UNFD SCH DIS FINCN
Also Called: Truckee High School
11725 Donner Past Rd, Truckee (96160)
PHONE...................................530 582-7630
John Carlson, *Principal*
Trent Kirschner, *Teacher*
EMP: 73

SALES (est): 3.6MM
SALES (corp-wide): 63.1MM **Privately Held**
WEB: www.ttusd.k12.ca.us
SIC: 8748 8211 Business consulting; public senior high school
PA: Tahoe Truckee Unified School District Financing Corporation
11603 Donner Pass Rd
Truckee CA 96161
530 582-2500

(P-27227)
TASSER TECHNOLOGIES INC
43252 Christy St, Fremont (94538-3171)
PHONE...................................408 364-0373
Vijaya G Arunachalam, *CEO*
Greg Matheny, *Director*
EMP: 60
SALES (est): 43.6K **Privately Held**
WEB: www.tasser.com
SIC: 8748 Business consulting

(P-27228)
TEAM RISK MGT STRATEGIES LLC
Also Called: Trust Employee ADM & MGT
3131 Camino Del Rio N # 650, San Diego (92108-5751)
PHONE...................................877 767-8728
Terence J Keating, *President*
Arthur D Candland, *CFO*
Cheryl Doss, *Vice Pres*
EMP: 2500
SALES (est): 98.4MM **Privately Held**
SIC: 8748 Employee programs administration

(P-27229)
TEKWORKS INC
13000 Gregg St Ste B, Poway (92064-7151)
PHONE...................................858 668-1705
William E Bourgeois, *CEO*
Michael Barber, *CFO*
Joshua Montana, *Exec VP*
Dale Bourgeois, *Vice Pres*
Ryan Hardesty, *Vice Pres*
EMP: 210
SQ FT: 22,000
SALES: 50MM
SALES (corp-wide): 13.1MM **Privately Held**
WEB: www.tekworkscomm.com
SIC: 8748 Telecommunications consultant
PA: Paladin Technologies Inc
3001 Wayburne Dr Suite 201
Burnaby BC V5G 4
604 787-8700

(P-27230)
TELECOM TECHNOLOGY SVCS INC
Also Called: Tts
7901 Stoneridge Dr # 500, Pleasanton (94588-3969)
PHONE...................................925 224-7812
Shuky Sheffer, *President*
EMP: 130
SQ FT: 7,102
SALES (est): 18.3MM **Privately Held**
WEB: www.ttswireless.com
SIC: 8748 Telecommunications consultant
HQ: Amdocs, Inc.
1390 Tmberlake Manor Pkwy
Chesterfield MO 63017
314 212-7000

(P-27231)
TEMPEST TELECOM SOLUTIONS LLC (PA)
136 W Canon Perdido St # 100, Santa Barbara (93101-3242)
PHONE...................................805 879-4800
Jessica Firestone, *CEO*
Dan Firestone, *COO*
Julie Lubin, *CFO*
Richard Smith, *Vice Pres*
EMP: 60
SQ FT: 9,000
SALES (est): 42.4MM **Privately Held**
WEB: www.tempesttelecom.com
SIC: 8748 Systems analysis & engineering consulting services; telecommunications consultant

PRODUCTS & SVCS

(P-27232)
TETRA TECH INC
3201 Airpark Dr Ste 108, Santa Maria
(93455-1834)
PHONE.....................805 739-2600
Jeff Matthew, *Branch Mgr*
EMP: 63
SALES (corp-wide): 2.9B **Publicly Held**
WEB: www.tetratech.com
SIC: 8748 Environmental consultant
PA: Tetra Tech, Inc.
3475 E Foothill Blvd
Pasadena CA 91107
626 351-4664

(P-27233)
TETRA TECH EC INC
2969 Prospect Park Dr # 100, Rancho Cordova (95670-6187)
PHONE.....................916 852-8300
Anh Nghiem, *Manager*
EMP: 1000
SALES (corp-wide): 2.9B **Publicly Held**
SIC: 8748 Environmental consultant
HQ: Tetra Tech Ec, Inc.
6 Century Dr Ste 3
Parsippany NJ 07054
973 630-8000

(P-27234)
TETRA TECH NUS INC
3475 E Foothill Blvd, Pasadena
(91107-6024)
PHONE.....................412 921-7090
Dan L Batrack, *CEO*
Steven M Burdick, *Exec VP*
John Trepanowski, *Vice Pres*
Ronald Chu, *Principal*
Janet Mandel, *Director*
EMP: 100
SALES (est): 5.4MM
SALES (corp-wide): 2.9B **Publicly Held**
WEB: www.ttnus.com
SIC: 8748 Environmental consultant
PA: Tetra Tech, Inc.
3475 E Foothill Blvd
Pasadena CA 91107
626 351-4664

(P-27235)
TM FINANCIAL FORENSICS LLC (PA)
2 Embarcadero Ctr # 2510, San Francisco (94111-3823)
PHONE.....................415 692-6350
Paul Meyer, *President*
Elizabeth Dean, *Vice Pres*
Rob Dwyer, *Vice Pres*
Bill Gladden, *Vice Pres*
Robert Groves, *Vice Pres*
EMP: 50 **EST:** 2009
SALES (est): 10.4MM **Privately Held**
SIC: 8748 Communications consulting

(P-27236)
TOTAL EDUCATION SOLUTIONS INC (PA)
625 Fair Oaks Ave Ste 300, South Pasadena (91030-5805)
PHONE.....................323 341-5580
Nancy Lavelle, *President*
Piero Stillitano, *CFO*
Jeanne Bauer, *CIO*
Jeremiah Clark, *Info Tech Mgr*
Lacey Chan, *Marketing Staff*
EMP: 50 **EST:** 1997
SALES (est): 44.8MM **Privately Held**
SIC: 8748 Educational consultant

(P-27237)
TRC SOLUTIONS INC (DH)
Also Called: Alton Geoscience
9685 Research Dr Ste 100, Irvine
(92618-4657)
PHONE.....................949 753-0101
Christopher P Vincze, *Ch of Bd*
Thomas W Bennet Jr, *CFO*
EMP: 125
SQ FT: 47,000
SALES (est): 31MM
SALES (corp-wide): 165.4MM **Privately Held**
WEB: www.trcsolutions.com
SIC: 8748 8711 Environmental consultant; engineering services

HQ: Trc Companies, L.L.C.
650 Suffolk St
Lowell MA 01854
978 970-5600

(P-27238)
TRILLIANT INCORPORATED
1100 Island Dr Ste 201, Redwood City (94065-5187)
PHONE.....................650 204-5050
Andy White, *President*
Salim Khan, *COO*
Bob Habig, *CFO*
Slupo Lupo, *Vice Pres*
Betty Heidler, *Executive Asst*
EMP: 93
SALES (est): 17.6MM **Privately Held**
SIC: 8748 Environmental consultant

(P-27239)
TRIMARK ASSOCIATES INC
2365 Iron Point Rd # 100, Folsom
(95630-8714)
PHONE.....................916 357-5970
Mark J Morosky, *President*
Dean Schoeder, *COO*
Bob Wood, *CTO*
Mario Marquez, *Info Tech Dir*
Bhumi Patel, *Software Dev*
EMP: 53 **EST:** 2000
SQ FT: 108,000
SALES (est): 10.7MM **Privately Held**
WEB: www.trimarkmdma.com
SIC: 8748 Energy conservation consultant

(P-27240)
TRUST FOR CNSRVTION INNOVATION
Also Called: MULTIPLIER
405 14th St Ste 164, Oakland
(94612-2705)
PHONE.....................415 421-3774
Mellissa Clack, *President*
Jill K Johnson, *Principal*
Laura Deaton, *Exec Dir*
EMP: 70
SALES: 18.2MM **Privately Held**
WEB: www.cea.sfex.com
SIC: 8748 Environmental consultant

(P-27241)
UNIVERSAL NETWORK DEV CORP (PA)
Also Called: Undc
2555 3rd St Ste 112, Sacramento
(95818-1100)
PHONE.....................916 475-1200
Cinthia Larkin Kazee, *President*
EMP: 97
SQ FT: 1,600
SALES (est): 11.4MM **Privately Held**
WEB: www.undc.com
SIC: 8748 8711 Communications consulting; telecommunications consultant; professional engineer

(P-27242)
VALLEJO FLOOD AND WASTE
450 Ryder St, Vallejo (94590-7217)
PHONE.....................707 644-8949
Melissa Morton, *CEO*
Mary A Morris, *CFO*
Holly M Charlety, *Admin Sec*
Jason Kaduk, *Info Tech Mgr*
Morris Mary, *Finance Dir*
EMP: 86
SQ FT: 10,000
SALES: 32.5MM **Privately Held**
WEB: www.vsfcd.com
SIC: 8748 Environmental consultant; traffic consultant; economic consultant

(P-27243)
VERIDIAM ALLIED SWISS
4645 North Ave, Oceanside (92056-3593)
PHONE.....................760 941-1702
Thomas Cresante, *Owner*
EMP: 54
SALES (est): 3.7MM
SALES (corp-wide): 79.8MM **Privately Held**
WEB: www.veridiam.com
SIC: 8748 Business consulting

HQ: Veridiam, Inc.
1717 N Cuyamaca St
El Cajon CA 92020
619 448-1000

(P-27244)
VETERANS AFFAIRS CAL DEPT
Also Called: Veterans Affairs Testing Off
1227 O St Ste 105, Sacramento
(95814-5891)
PHONE.....................916 653-2535
Karen Escobar, *Director*
EMP: 347 **Privately Held**
WEB: www.californiachronicle.com
SIC: 8748 9451 Testing services; administration of veterans' affairs;
HQ: California Department Of Veterans Affairs
1227 O St Ste 105
Sacramento CA 95814
800 952-5626

(P-27245)
VETERANS EZ INFO INC
1901 1st Ave Ste 192, San Diego
(92101-2356)
PHONE.....................866 839-1329
James Miner, *Ch of Bd*
Phonprapha Miner, *Senior VP*
Stephen Brouillard, *VP Opers*
EMP: 138
SQ FT: 1,200
SALES: 24MM **Privately Held**
SIC: 8748 7371 7373 Business consulting; computer software development; software programming applications; computer systems analysis & design

(P-27246)
VILLA REAL INC
421 S El Dorado St Ste D1, Stockton
(95203-3459)
P.O. Box 447 (95201-0447)
PHONE.....................209 460-5069
Greg Arnaudo, *Ch of Bd*
EMP: 100
SALES: 41.9K **Privately Held**
SIC: 8748 Urban planning & consulting services

(P-27247)
VIMO INC (PA)
Also Called: Getinsured.com
1305 Terra Bella Ave, Mountain View
(94043-1851)
PHONE.....................650 618-4600
Srinivasan Krishnan, *CEO*
Paul Neutz, *President*
Shankar Srinivasan, *COO*
Krzysztof Kujawa, *Vice Pres*
Scott Osler, *Vice Pres*
EMP: 84
SQ FT: 20,000
SALES (est): 27.3MM **Privately Held**
WEB: www.vimo.com
SIC: 8748 6411 7371 7373 Business consulting; insurance brokers; computer software development & applications; systems software development services

(P-27248)
VINCULUMS SERVICES INC
10 Pasteur Ste 100, Irvine (92618-3823)
PHONE.....................949 783-3552
Paul Foster, *CEO*
Brian Woodward, *COO*
Norm Alexander, *CFO*
Bart Van Aardenne, *Chairman*
Cindy Holbrook, *Program Mgr*
EMP: 220 **EST:** 2005
SQ FT: 8,000
SALES (est): 39.1MM **Privately Held**
SIC: 8748 Telecommunications consultant

(P-27249)
VOICE SMART NETWORKS LLC
10920 Via Frontera # 410, San Diego
(92127-1729)
PHONE.....................619 857-4638
Mark Wadnizak, *CEO*
Brian Suerth, *President*
EMP: 50 **EST:** 2012
SALES (est): 617.7K **Privately Held**
SIC: 8748 Telecommunications consultant

(P-27250)
VOLT TELECOM GROUP INC
Also Called: Volt Telecom Group
218 Helicopter Cir, Corona (92880-2531)
PHONE.....................800 548-6602
Frank Dalessio, *CEO*
EMP: 50
SALES (corp-wide): 1B **Publicly Held**
SIC: 8748 Telecommunications consultant
HQ: Volt Telecommunications Group, Inc.
560 Lexington Ave
New York NY 10022
212 704-2400

(P-27251)
VOLT TELECOM GROUP INC
Also Called: Volt Telecom Group
218 Helicopter Cir, Corona (92880-2531)
PHONE.....................951 493-8900
Frank D'Alessio, *CEO*
Kingsley N Nelson, *Principal*
EMP: 250
SALES (corp-wide): 1B **Publicly Held**
SIC: 8748 Telecommunications consultant
HQ: Volt Telecommunications Group, Inc.
560 Lexington Ave
New York NY 10022
212 704-2400

(P-27252)
VOX NETWORK SOLUTIONS INC
8000 Marina Blvd Ste 130, Brisbane
(94005-1882)
PHONE.....................650 989-1000
Scott Landis, *Ch of Bd*
Todd Harcarik, *Executive*
Tonja Marcus, *Executive*
Matthew Slye, *Executive*
Ramon Cuenco, *Technology*
EMP: 150
SQ FT: 3,904
SALES: 44.9MM **Privately Held**
WEB: www.voxnetworksolutions.com
SIC: 8748 3661 Telecommunications consultant; switching equipment, telephone; telephone central office equipment, dial or manual; telephone sets, all types except cellular radio

(P-27253)
VSC SPORTS INC
Also Called: Yorba Bena Ice Skting Bowl Ctr
750 Folsom St, San Francisco
(94107-1276)
PHONE.....................415 820-3525
Michael Paikin, *Owner*
EMP: 60
SALES (corp-wide): 4.8MM **Privately Held**
WEB: www.vscsports.com
SIC: 8748 Business consulting
PA: Vsc Sports Inc
14909 Magnolia Blvd # 202
Sherman Oaks CA 91403
818 994-3229

(P-27254)
W CORPORATION
Also Called: Vantage Company
1643 W Orange Grove Ave, Orange
(92868-1116)
PHONE.....................714 532-8800
Kenneth Watkins, *President*
Marvin Anderson, *CFO*
Tony Watterson, *General Mgr*
EMP: 120 **EST:** 2001
SALES: 24.5MM **Privately Held**
SIC: 8748 1542 1522 Telecommunications consultant; commercial & office building, new construction; residential construction

(P-27255)
WARNER BROS CONSUMER PDTS INC (DH)
4001 W Olive Ave, Burbank (91505-4272)
PHONE.....................818 954-7980
Brad Globe, *President*
Dan Romanelli, *President*
Randy Blotky, *Senior VP*
Ana De Castro, *Senior VP*
John Schulman, *Admin Sec*
▲ **EMP:** 112

SALES (est): 19.2MM
SALES (corp-wide): 170.7B **Publicly Held**
SIC: 8748 5961 Business consulting; novelty merchandise, mail order
HQ: Warner Bros. Entertainment Inc.
    4000 Warner Blvd
    Burbank CA 91522
    818 954-6000

(P-27256)
WEISSCOMM GROUP LTD (PA)
Also Called: Wcg World
50 Francisco St Ste 400, San Francisco
(94133-2114)
PHONE...............................415 362-5018
James Weiss, *CEO*
Mary Corcoran, *President*
Chris Deri, *President*
Jennifer Gottlieb, *President*
Diane Weiser, *President*
EMP: 75
SQ FT: 16,000
SALES (est): 117.2MM **Privately Held**
WEB: www.wcgworld.com
SIC: 8748 Communications consulting

(P-27257)
WESTON SOLUTIONS INC
5817 Dryden Pl Ste 101, Carlsbad
(92008-5576)
PHONE...............................760 795-6900
Lisa Marie Kay, *Branch Mgr*
EMP: 65
SALES (corp-wide): 631.4MM **Privately Held**
WEB: www.rfweston.com
SIC: 8748 Environmental consultant
HQ: Weston Solutions, Inc.
    1400 Weston Way
    West Chester PA 19380
    610 701-3000

(P-27258)
WILLIAM S HART PONY & SOFTBALL
Also Called: Wm S Hart Pony & Softball
23437 Valencia Blvd, Valencia
(91355-1702)
PHONE...............................661 254-9780
Dave Scripture, *President*
Mike Clare, *Treasurer*
Ken Underwood, *Exec VP*
EMP: 55
SALES (est): 2.3MM **Privately Held**
SIC: 8748 Environmental consultant

(P-27259)
WRIGHT BROADBAND GROUP INC
4413 La Jolla Village Dr, San Diego
(92122-1264)
PHONE...............................858 362-0380
Leroy Wright, *President*
EMP: 75
SQ FT: 3,000
SALES: 7MM **Privately Held**
SIC: 8748 Telecommunications consultant

(P-27260)
X3 MANAGEMENT SERVICES INC
2128 Auto Park Way, Escondido
(92029-1344)
PHONE...............................760 597-9336
David G Cranford, *CEO*
Arlette Zuniga, *CFO*
Bonnie Pierce, *Controller*
John Dykes, *Opers Staff*
Anthony Kachinsky, *Manager*
EMP: 72
SALES (est): 6.3MM **Privately Held**
SIC: 8748 1731 1531 1541 Telecommunications consultant; electrical work; fiber optic cable installation; operative builders; industrial buildings & warehouses; solar energy contractor

(P-27261)
YCG LLC
Also Called: You Consulting Group
566 Shanas Ln, Encinitas (92024-2435)
P.O. Box 231423 (92023-1423)
PHONE...............................760 230-8016
David Hackett, *Mng Member*

Dr Zannah Hackett,
EMP: 52 EST: 2007
SALES: 250K **Privately Held**
SIC: 8748 Business consulting

(P-27262)
YUCAIPA COMPANIES LLC (PA)
9130 W Sunset Blvd, Los Angeles
(90069-3110)
PHONE...............................310 789-7200
Ronald W Burkle, *Mng Member*
Scott Stedman,
EMP: 150
SALES (est): 1.4B **Privately Held**
SIC: 8748 6719 6726 Business consulting; investment holding companies, except banks; investment offices

---

8999 Services Not Elsewhere Classified

(P-27263)
ACTIVE LAWYERS REFERRAL SVC
9301 Wilshire Blvd # 508, Beverly Hills
(90210-5424)
PHONE...............................310 247-0425
Paul Mehdizadeh, *President*
Vincent Mehdizadeh, *Manager*
EMP: 60
SALES (est): 1.1MM **Privately Held**
SIC: 8999 7299 Information bureau; information services, consumer

(P-27264)
AEROSPACE & MARINE INTL
6910 Santa Teresa Blvd, San Jose
(95119-1339)
PHONE...............................408 360-0440
George Carlsgaard, *President*
James Carlsgaard, *CFO*
Paul Xander, *Sr Software Eng*
EMP: 50
SALES (est): 1.7MM **Privately Held**
WEB: www.amiwx.com
SIC: 8999 Weather related services

(P-27265)
ANKA BEHAVIORAL HEALTH INC
2507 Evelyn Ave, Rosemead (91770-3070)
PHONE...............................626 573-5902
EMP: 78
SALES (corp-wide): 40.4MM **Privately Held**
SIC: 8999 Actuarial consultant
PA: Anka Behavioral Health, Incorporated
    3840 Buskirk Ave Ste 300
    Pleasant Hill CA 94523
    925 825-4700

(P-27266)
ASSOCIATED STUDENTS INC
Also Called: Associated Students, Inc.
1 Grand Ave, San Luis Obispo
(93407-9000)
PHONE...............................805 756-1281
Richard Johnson, *Exec Dir*
EMP: 68
SALES (corp-wide): 12.7MM **Privately Held**
SIC: 8999 Artists & artists' studios
PA: Associated Students Inc Of California Polytechnic State University At San Luis Obispo
    University Un Bldg 65
    San Luis Obispo CA 93407
    805 756-1281

(P-27267)
AT&T CORP
1188 W Evelyn Ave, Sunnyvale
(94086-5742)
PHONE...............................650 960-2313
EMP: 68
SALES (corp-wide): 170.7B **Publicly Held**
SIC: 8999 Communication services
HQ: At&T Corp.
    1 At&T Way
    Bedminster NJ 07921
    800 403-3302

(P-27268)
BUCK GLOBAL LLC
1801 Century Park E # 500, Los Angeles
(90067-2302)
PHONE...............................310 282-8232
Harold Love, *Branch Mgr*
Maureen Farrell, *Sales Executive*
EMP: 55
SALES (corp-wide): 540MM **Privately Held**
SIC: 8999 8742 6282 2741 Actuarial consultant; compensation & benefits planning consultant; investment advice; technical papers: publishing only, not printed on site
PA: Buck Global, Llc
    420 Lexington Ave Rm 2220
    New York NY 10170
    212 330-1000

(P-27269)
CALIFORNIA TAHOE CONSERVANCY
1061 3rd St, South Lake Tahoe
(96150-3475)
PHONE...............................530 542-5580
Patrick Wright, *Exec Dir*
Russell Maloney, *Principal*
David Gregorich, *Administration*
EMP: 50
SALES (est): 1.9MM **Privately Held**
SIC: 8999 Natural resource preservation service
HQ: California Natural Resources Agency
    1416 9th St Ste 1311
    Sacramento CA 95814

(P-27270)
CONSERVATION LIQUIDATION
100 Pine St Fl 12, San Francisco
(94111-5114)
PHONE...............................415 676-5000
David Wilson, *CEO*
EMP: 75
SALES (est): 2.7MM **Privately Held**
SIC: 8999 Natural resource preservation service

(P-27271)
COUNTY OF SAN MATEO
Also Called: Information Services Dept
455 County Ctr Fl 3, Redwood City
(94063-9728)
PHONE...............................650 363-4548
Jon Walton, *CIO*
Eric Fan, *Manager*
EMP: 150 **Privately Held**
WEB: www.ci.sanmateo.ca.us
SIC: 8999 9199 Information bureau;
PA: County Of San Mateo
    400 County Ctr
    Redwood City CA 94063
    650 363-4123

(P-27272)
DATA TRACE INFO SVCS LLC (HQ)
4 First American Way, Santa Ana
(92707-5913)
PHONE...............................714 250-6700
Mike Henney Sr,
Gwen Sorensen, *Vice Pres*
Ray Adair, *Info Tech Dir*
Andrea Henney, *Project Mgr*
Jennifer Hooper, *Technology*
EMP: 100
SALES (est): 8.9MM **Publicly Held**
SIC: 8999 Information bureau

(P-27273)
ESSENSE
Also Called: Maxus USA
6300 Wilshire Blvd # 720, Los Angeles
(90048-5204)
PHONE...............................323 202-4650
EMP: 582
SALES (est): 83.6K
SALES (corp-wide): 20B **Privately Held**
SIC: 8999 Communication services
HQ: Maxus Communications Llc
    498 Fashion Ave
    New York NY 10018
    212 297-8300

(P-27274)
FORT MASON CENTER
2 Marina Blvd Bldg A, San Francisco
(94123-1284)
PHONE...............................415 345-7500
Caroline Werth, *President*
Pat Nester, *CFO*
Rich Hillis, *Exec Dir*
Lisa Phillips, *Office Mgr*
Mauricio Ramirez, *Technician*
EMP: 56
SQ FT: 300,000
SALES: 13.8MM **Privately Held**
WEB: www.fortmason.org
SIC: 8999 Art related services

(P-27275)
GLOBAL BUILDING SERVICES INC
17618 Murphy Pkwy, Lathrop (95330-8629)
PHONE...............................209 858-9501
EMP: 515
SALES (corp-wide): 29.9MM **Privately Held**
SIC: 8999 Actuarial consultant
PA: Global Building Services, Inc.
    27433 Tourney Rd Ste 280
    Valencia CA 91355
    800 675-6643

(P-27276)
GOLDEN GATE NAT PRKS CNSRVANCY
1 Presidio Ave, San Francisco
(94115-1017)
PHONE...............................415 440-4068
EMP: 162
SALES (corp-wide): 78.8MM **Privately Held**
SIC: 8999 Natural resource preservation service
PA: Golden Gate National Parks Conservancy
    Fort Mason Bldg 201
    San Francisco CA 94123
    415 561-3000

(P-27277)
GOLDEN GATE NAT PRKS CNSRVANCY
Also Called: Golden Gate Nat Prks Cnsrvancy
1600 Los Gamos Dr, San Rafael
(94903-1806)
PHONE...............................415 785-4787
EMP: 54
SALES (corp-wide): 78.8MM **Privately Held**
SIC: 8999 Natural resource preservation service
PA: Golden Gate National Parks Conservancy
    Fort Mason Bldg 201
    San Francisco CA 94123
    415 561-3000

(P-27278)
GOLDEN GATE NAT PRKS CNSRVANCY (PA)
Fort Mason Bldg 201, San Francisco
(94123)
PHONE...............................415 561-3000
Greg Moore, *CEO*
Diane Ochi, *Project Mgr*
Chris Knapp, *Accountant*
Elena Torres, *HR Admin*
Honore Pedigo, *Opers Staff*
▲ EMP: 70
SQ FT: 5,000
SALES: 78.8MM **Privately Held**
WEB: www.parksconservancy.org
SIC: 8999 Natural resource preservation service

(P-27279)
HEALTHCARE SERVICES GROUP INC
5199 E Pacific Coast Hwy # 402, Long Beach (90804-3309)
PHONE...............................562 494-7939
Mike Hammond, *Principal*
Caroline Galoostian, *District Mgr*
EMP: 5008
SALES (corp-wide): 2B **Publicly Held**
SIC: 8999 Artists & artists' studios

PA: Healthcare Services Group Inc
3220 Tillman Dr Ste 300
Bensalem PA 19020
215 639-4274

(P-27280)
IDEAL BRANDS INC
16060 Ventura Blvd, Encino (91436-2761)
PHONE..................................213 489-5557
Danny BEK, *CEO*
Djamshid Berhrad, *President*
▲ EMP: 50
SALES (est): 2.1MM **Privately Held**
WEB: www.idealbrands.com
SIC: 8999 Personal services

(P-27281)
INDYME SOLUTIONS LLC
8295 Aero Pl Ste 260, San Diego
(92123-2029)
PHONE..................................858 268-0717
Joe Joseph Eudano, *CEO*
James Doss, *CFO*
Philip Joostens, *Vice Pres*
Bill Kepner, *Vice Pres*
EMP: 50
SQ FT: 18,000
SALES (est): 3.2MM **Privately Held**
SIC: 8999 Communication services

(P-27282)
INTERIM INC
Also Called: Interim Services
339 Pajaro St Ste B, Salinas (93901-3400)
PHONE..................................831 754-3838
Fred Harris, *Branch Mgr*
EMP: 122
SALES (corp-wide): 12.5MM **Privately Held**
SIC: 8999 Personal services
PA: Interim, Inc.
604 Pearl St Frnt
Monterey CA 93940
831 649-4399

(P-27283)
J RIVERA ASSOCIATES INC
Also Called: 4 Su Salud Medical Contact Ctr
139 S Guild Ave, Lodi (95240-0867)
PHONE..................................415 617-5660
Jose R Rivera MPH, *CEO*
EMP: 92
SQ FT: 5,000
SALES: 2MM **Privately Held**
SIC: 8999 Communication services

(P-27284)
JAQUI FOUNDATION INC
675 Hegenberger Rd # 209, Oakland
(94621-1973)
P.O. Box 4938 (94605-6938)
PHONE..................................510 562-4721
Robert L Porter Jr, *CEO*
Dorothy M Jones, *Treasurer*
Dawson Andrews, *Admin Sec*
EMP: 50
SQ FT: 600
SALES: 1.5MM **Privately Held**
WEB: www.jaquifoundation.org
SIC: 8999 Personal services

(P-27285)
KCI ENVIRONMENTAL INC
207 Suburban Rd Ste 6, San Luis Obispo
(93401-7559)
P.O. Box 3307 (93403-3307)
PHONE..................................805 543-3311
Curt Boutwell, *President*
Jim Gorter, *General Mgr*
Kim Nunez, *Controller*
EMP: 50
SALES (est): 2.8MM **Privately Held**
WEB: www.kcienv.com
SIC: 8999 Earth science services

(P-27286)
KINGS RIVER CONSERVATION DST
4886 E Jensen Ave, Fresno (93725-1899)
PHONE..................................559 237-5567
Mark McKean, *President*
Brent Graham, *Vice Pres*
Paul Peschel, *General Mgr*
Soua Lee, *Analyst*
EMP: 64
SQ FT: 8,500

SALES (est): 6.7MM **Privately Held**
WEB: www.krcd.org
SIC: 8999 Natural resource preservation
service

(P-27287)
M4 WIND SERVICES INC
4020 Long Beach Blvd Fl 2, Long Beach
(90807-2683)
PHONE..................................562 981-7797
Myles Baker, *President*
Scott Young, *Manager*
EMP: 99
SALES (est): 1.4MM **Privately Held**
SIC: 8999 Artists & artists' studios

(P-27288)
MALKA COMMUNICATIONS GROUP INC
15260 Ventura Blvd # 1200, Sherman Oaks
(91403-5307)
PHONE..................................818 239-4431
Nataly Malka, *CEO*
Robert Malka, *COO*
EMP: 50
SQ FT: 1,900
SALES (est): 1.3MM **Privately Held**
SIC: 8999 Communication services

(P-27289)
MCCLATCHY COMPANY
2100 Q St, Sacramento (95816-6816)
PHONE..................................916 321-1941
EMP: 10000
SALES (est): 72.8K **Privately Held**
SIC: 8999

(P-27290)
MGM AND UA SERVICES COMPANY
245 N Beverly Dr, Beverly Hills
(90210-5319)
PHONE..................................310 449-3000
Gary Barber, *President*
Lauren Peterson, *Production*
Mandy Mamlet, *Director*
Nicole Westling, *Director*
Lisa McGuire, *Representative*
EMP: 560
SALES: 76.3K
SALES (corp-wide): 1.1B **Privately Held**
SIC: 8999 Artists & artists' studios
HQ: Metro-Goldwyn-Mayer, Inc.
245 N Beverly Dr
Beverly Hills CA 90210

(P-27291)
MIDPENINSUL RGNL OPN SP
330 Distel Cir, Los Altos (94022-1404)
PHONE..................................650 691-1200
Craig Britton, *President*
Owen Sterzl, *Technician*
EMP: 65
SQ FT: 12,000
SALES: 52.4MM **Privately Held**
SIC: 8999 Natural resource preservation
service

(P-27292)
MILLIMAN INC
650 California St Fl 21, San Francisco
(94108-2602)
PHONE..................................415 403-1333
Steve White, *Manager*
Jim Walbridge, *Principal*
Rich Wright, *General Mgr*
Gale I Yarymowicz, *Office Mgr*
Melissa Honl, *Admin Asst*
EMP: 50
SALES (corp-wide): 1.1B **Privately Held**
WEB: www.millimanglobal.com
SIC: 8999 6411 Actuarial consultant;
ratemaking organizations, insurance
PA: Milliman, Inc.
1301 5th Ave Ste 3800
Seattle WA 98101
206 624-7940

(P-27293)
NOBELBIZ INC
5759 Fleet St Ste 210, Carlsbad
(92008-4710)
PHONE..................................760 405-0105
Steven Bederman, *President*
Richard L Fahfouz, *President*

Peter Novak, *Vice Pres*
Micaiah Poleate, *Analyst*
Costin Preda, *Purch Agent*
EMP: 50
SALES (est): 5MM **Privately Held**
SIC: 8999 Communication services

(P-27294)
OPTIMA NETWORK SERVICES INC (DH)
15345 Fairfield Ranch Rd # 225, Chino Hills
(91709-8859)
PHONE..................................305 599-1800
Robert E Apple, *CEO*
Michael Mosel, *President*
EMP: 75
SQ FT: 6,475
SALES (est): 7.9MM
SALES (corp-wide): 6.9B **Publicly Held**
WEB: www.optimanet.net
SIC: 8999 Communication services
HQ: Mastec North America, Inc.
800 S Douglas Rd Ste 1200
Coral Gables FL 33134
305 599-1800

(P-27295)
ORACLE CORP
17901 Von Karman Ave # 800, Irvine
(92614-5241)
PHONE..................................650 506-7000
EMP: 567
SALES (est): 27.1MM **Privately Held**
SIC: 8999

(P-27296)
ORANGEPEOPLE LLC
300 Spectrum Center Dr, Irvine
(92618-4925)
PHONE..................................949 535-1308
Raghav Putrevu, *President*
Natasha Myers, *Vice Pres*
Constantinos Metropoulos, *Executive*
Damon LI, *IT/INT Sup*
EMP: 76
SQ FT: 8,000
SALES (est): 12MM **Privately Held**
SIC: 8999 7374 7371 8742 Cloud seed-
ing; data processing service; computer
software development; construction proj-
ect management consultant

(P-27297)
OVERSEAS SERVICE CORPORATION
Also Called: Ocean Service
8221 Arjons Dr Ste B2, San Diego
(92126-6319)
PHONE..................................858 408-0751
Paul Hogan, *President*
EMP: 232
SALES (corp-wide): 46.6MM **Privately Held**
SIC: 8999 Actuarial consultant
PA: Overseas Service Corporation
1100 Northpoint Pkwy # 200
West Palm Beach FL 33407
561 683-4090

(P-27298)
PANGEA CORPORATION
34145 Pacific Coast Hwy, Dana Point
(92629-2808)
PHONE..................................949 443-0666
John Schulte, *CEO*
John Besmehn, *CEO*
Cheryl Ann Wong, *Director*
EMP: 50
SALES (est): 1.2MM **Privately Held**
WEB: www.pangeacorp.com
SIC: 8999 8742 7336 8743 Advertising
copy writing; writing for publication; new
products & services consultants; creative
services to advertisers, except writers;
graphic arts & related design; public relations services; video tape production;
audio-visual program production

(P-27299)
PARADIGM INFORMATION SERVICES
10755 F Scrps Pwy Pkwy424, San Diego
(92131)
PHONE..................................858 693-6115
Elizabeth Bentz, *CEO*

Richard Scheiner, *President*
Gwen Scheiner, *Corp Secy*
EMP: 75
SALES (est): 2.3MM **Privately Held**
WEB: www.paradigmplacements.com
SIC: 8999 8711 7336 7371 Technical
writing; consulting engineer; electrical or
electronic engineering; graphic arts & re-
lated design; computer software develop-
ment & applications; educational services

(P-27300)
PLACER COUNTY ADM SVCS
2962 Richardson Dr, Auburn (95603-2640)
PHONE..................................530 886-5401
Jerry Gamaz, *Director*
EMP: 126
SALES (est): 5.1MM **Privately Held**
SIC: 8999 9199 Information bureau; gen-
eral government administration

(P-27301)
PRIDE INDUSTRIES
1281 National Dr, Sacramento
(95834-1902)
PHONE..................................916 649-9499
Allan Ruzick, *Branch Mgr*
Gary Schlauch, *General Mgr*
Kendal Phipps, *Analyst*
Mike Barnbaum, *Training Spec*
Cinda Smith, *Case Mgr*
EMP: 220
SALES (corp-wide): 290.6MM **Privately Held**
SIC: 8999 Personal services
PA: Pride Industries
10030 Foothills Blvd
Roseville CA 95747
916 788-2100

(P-27302)
RADAR MEDICAL SYSTEMS INC
1510 Cotner Ave, Los Angeles
(90025-3303)
PHONE..................................440 337-9521
Florence Present, *Principal*
EMP: 79 EST: 2015
SALES (est): 65.3K **Publicly Held**
SIC: 8999 Communication services
HQ: Radnet Managed Imaging Services,
Inc.
1510 Cotner Ave
Los Angeles CA 90025
310 445-2800

(P-27303)
RAMBOLL US CORPORATION
Also Called: Ramboll Environ
5 Park Plz Ste 500, Irvine (92614-8525)
PHONE..................................949 798-3604
Anne Pena, *Manager*
Safaa Dergham, *Senior Mgr*
Jeffrey Micha Forde, *Senior Mgr*
Steve Luis, *Senior Mgr*
EMP: 50
SALES (corp-wide): 314.9MM **Privately Held**
SIC: 8999 8748 Earth science services;
environmental consultant
HQ: Ramboll Us Corporation
4350 Fairfax Dr Ste 300
Arlington VA 22203
703 516-2300

(P-27304)
RIVERSIDE COUNTY FLOOD CONTROL
1995 Market St, Riverside (92501-1719)
PHONE..................................951 955-1200
Jason Uhley, *Principal*
Aldous Tsang, *Admin Sec*
Joe Barcenas, *Technician*
Mekbib Degaga, *Engineer*
Stuart McKibbin, *Engineer*
EMP: 210
SALES: 79.4MM **Privately Held**
SIC: 8999 Natural resource preservation
service

(P-27305)
SIGNATURE CONSULTANTS LLC
44 Montgomery St Ste 1450, San Francisco
(94104-4701)
PHONE..................................415 544-7510
EMP: 217 **Privately Held**
SIC: 8999 Scientific consulting

PA: Signature Consultants Llc
200 W Cypress Creek Rd # 400
Fort Lauderdale FL 33309

(P-27306)
STORMGEO (DH)
Also Called: Applied Weather Technology Inc
140 Kifer Ct, Sunnyvale (94086-5120)
PHONE................................408 731-8600
Robert Haydn Jones, *CEO*
Haydn Jones, *President*
William Lapworth, *CFO*
Richard Brown, *Vice Pres*
Neill Moseley, *General Mgr*
EMP: 166
SQ FT: 19,000
SALES (est): 21.2MM
SALES (corp-wide): 2.6MM **Privately Held**
SIC: 8999 Weather forecasting

(P-27307)
SYMPHONY COMM SVCS LLC (PA)
1117 California Ave, Palo Alto (94304-1106)
PHONE................................650 733-6660
Eran Barack,
Fred Stemmelin, *President*
Eran Barak, *COO*
Frederic Stemmelin, *VP Bus Dvlpt*
Jenny Lam, *Executive Asst*
EMP: 52
SALES (est): 7.7MM **Privately Held**
SIC: 8999 Communication services

(P-27308)
UNIVERSAL CYLINDER EXCH INC
692 N Cypress St Ste B, Orange (92867-6665)
P.O. Box 6147 (92863-6147)
PHONE................................714 744-1036
Pamela A Ogier, *President*
EMP: 85
SALES (est): 1.6MM **Privately Held**
SIC: 8999 Natural resource preservation service

(P-27309)
VICTOR CMNTY SUPPORT SVCS INC
900 E Main St Ste 201, Grass Valley (95945-5853)
PHONE................................530 273-2244
Rachel Pena, *Exec Dir*
EMP: 205
SALES (corp-wide): 37.7MM **Privately Held**
SIC: 8999 Artists & artists' studios
PA: Victor Community Support Services, Inc.
1360 E Lassen Ave
Chico CA 95973
530 893-0758

(P-27310)
WESTVIEW SERVICES INC
11728 Magnolia Ave Ste D, Riverside (92503-4970)
PHONE................................951 343-2356
Greg Drann, *Branch Mgr*
Shannon Lavalley, *Program Mgr*
EMP: 88
SALES (corp-wide): 16.6MM **Privately Held**
SIC: 8999 Artists & artists' studios
PA: Westview Services, Inc
10522 Katella Ave
Anaheim CA 92804
714 517-6606

(P-27311)
WOODMONT REAL ESTATE SVCS LP
3883 Airway Dr, Santa Rosa (95403-1670)
PHONE................................707 569-0582
Ron Granville, *Branch Mgr*
Donette Moix, *Property Mgr*
EMP: 279 **Privately Held**
SIC: 8999 Artists & artists' studios
PA: Woodmont Real Estate Services, L.P.
1050 Ralston Ave
Belmont CA 94002

(P-27312)
WU YEE CHILDRENS SERVICES
Also Called: Wu Yee Child Care Center
831 Broadway, San Francisco (94133-4218)
PHONE................................415 677-0100
Alyson Suzeuki, *Program Dir*
EMP: 68
SALES (corp-wide): 20.4MM **Privately Held**
SIC: 8999 Artists & artists' studios
PA: Wu Yee Children's Services
827 Broadway
San Francisco CA 94133
415 230-7504

(P-27313)
ZOE HOLDING COMPANY INC
44 Montgomery St, San Francisco (94104-4602)
PHONE................................415 421-4900
John Unick, *Branch Mgr*
EMP: 131
SALES (corp-wide): 62.1MM **Privately Held**
SIC: 8999 Artists & artists' studios
PA: Zoe Holding Company, Inc.
7025 N Scottsdale Rd # 200
Scottsdale AZ 85253
602 508-1883

PRODUCTS & SVCS

ALPHABETIC SECTION

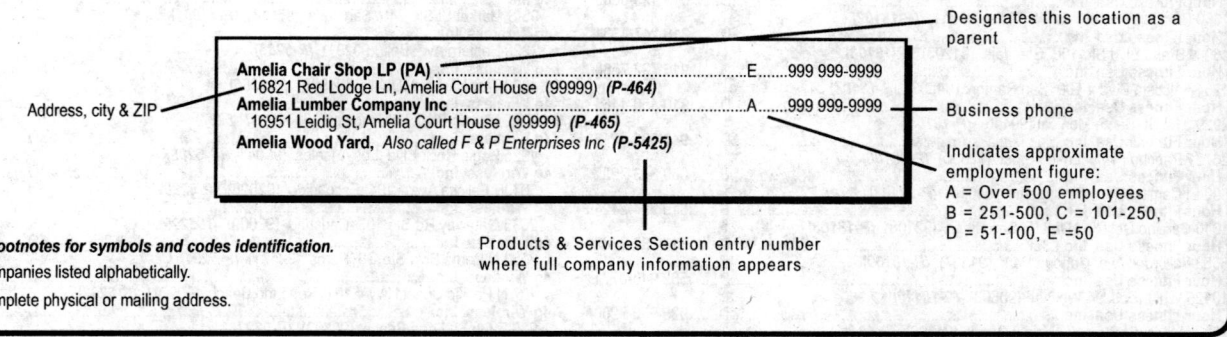

(a) Tool Shed Inc (PA) ....D......831 477-7133
    3700 Soquel Ave Santa Cruz (95062) *(P-14119)*
0EPI, Carmichael *Also called Eskaton Properties Inc* *(P-19896)*
1-800 Dentist, Los Angeles *Also called Futuredontics Inc* *(P-26617)*
1-800 Radiator & A/C (PA) ....D......707 747-7400
    4401 Park Rd Benicia (94510) *(P-6416)*
1-800-Radiator, Benicia *Also called 1-800 Radiator & A/C* *(P-6416)*
1-Carasight Surveillance, San Diego *Also called Inseego North America LLC* *(P-15615)*
1000 Aguajito Op Co LLC ....D......831 373-6141
    1000 Aguajito Rd Monterey (93940) *(P-11972)*
1000 Executive Parkway LLC ....C......530 533-7335
    1000 Executive Pkwy Oroville (95966) *(P-19703)*
106 Sacramento Mhrc, Sacramento *Also called Crestwood Behavioral Hlth Inc* *(P-21402)*
10632 Bolsa Avenue LP ....D......949 673-1221
    500 Nwport Ctr Dr Ste 200 Newport Beach (92660) *(P-10676)*
107 San Jose Mhrc, San Jose *Also called Crestwood Behavioral Hlth Inc* *(P-23892)*
10up Inc ....D......888 571-7130
    2765 Carradale Dr Roseville (95661) *(P-15548)*
11 Main Inc ....C......530 892-9191
    527 Flume St Chico (95928) *(P-5283)*
1105 Media Inc ....C......949 265-1520
    2121 Alton Pkwy Ste 240 Irvine (92606) *(P-5773)*
111 Vallejo IMD, Vallejo *Also called Crestwood Behavioral Hlth Inc* *(P-21406)*
1111 6th Ave LLC ....D......312 283-3683
    1111 6th Ave Ste 102 San Diego (92101) *(P-16585)*
112 Modesto Snf, Modesto *Also called Crestwood Behavioral Hlth Inc* *(P-21401)*
1125 Sir Francis Drake Bouleva ....D......415 456-9680
    1125 Sir Francis Drake Bl Kentfield (94904) *(P-20728)*
1130 W La Palma Ave Inc ....D......562 930-0777
    4115 E Broadway Long Beach (90803) *(P-19704)*
1135 N Leisure Ct Inc ....C......714 772-1353
    1135 N Leisure Ct Anaheim (92801) *(P-19705)*
115 Bakersfield Mhrc, Bakersfield *Also called Crestwood Behavioral Hlth Inc* *(P-23186)*
120 Fremont Snf, Redding *Also called Crestwood Behavioral Hlth Inc* *(P-23893)*
120 Fremont Snf, Fremont *Also called Crestwood Behavioral Hlth Inc* *(P-23896)*
120 South Los Angeles Street H ....D......213 629-1200
    120 S Los Angeles St Los Angeles (90012) *(P-11973)*
123 Home Care, Los Angeles *Also called Confido LLC* *(P-21722)*
123ewireless, Rcho STA Marg *Also called Sarco Inc* *(P-7338)*
1260 Bb Property LLC ....B......805 969-2261
    1260 Channel Dr Santa Barbara (93108) *(P-11974)*
1334 Partners LP ....D......310 546-5656
    1330 Park View Ave Manhattan Beach (90266) *(P-18344)*
134 Alameda Snf, Fremont *Also called Crestwood Behavioral Hlth Inc* *(P-23894)*
137 Bakersfield Bridge, Bakersfield *Also called Crestwood Behavioral Hlth Inc* *(P-21467)*
1370 Realty Corp ....C......818 817-0092
    14545 Friar St Ste 101 Van Nuys (91411) *(P-10884)*
144 Pleasant Hill The Pathway, Pleasant Hill *Also called Crestwood Behavioral Hlth
Inc* *(P-21408)*
145 Fresno Bridge, Fresno *Also called Crestwood Behavioral Hlth Inc* *(P-21404)*
14766 Wash Ave Operations LLC ....A......510 352-2211
    14766 Washington Ave San Leandro (94578) *(P-20472)*
152 Vallejo Rcfe, Vallejo *Also called Crestwood Behavioral Hlth Inc* *(P-23895)*
1524 Abbot Kinney LLC ....D......310 907-6517
    1746 Abbot Kinney Blvd Venice (90291) *(P-10885)*
153 American River PHF, Carmichael *Also called Crestwood Behavioral Hlth Inc* *(P-21407)*
15th & L Investors LLC ....D......916 267-6805
    1121 15th St Sacramento (95814) *(P-11975)*
1651 Tiburon Hotel LLC ....D......401 946-4600
    1651 Tiburon Blvd Belvedere Tiburon (94920) *(P-11976)*
1658 Camden LLC ....E......818 769-1944
    12147 Riverside Dr North Hollywood (91607) *(P-10677)*
16700 Roscoe Associates LLC ....D......818 989-2300
    16700 Roscoe Blvd Van Nuys (91406) *(P-18345)*
1755 Efm 1 LLC ....C......323 231-4174
    1755 Kings Way Los Angeles (90069) *(P-10886)*
1800-R-Ado, Los Angeles *Also called Wilshire Consumer Credit* *(P-9473)*
180la LLC ....C......310 382-1400
    12555 W Jefferson Blvd # 200 Los Angeles (90066) *(P-13463)*
1835 Columbia Street LP ....D......619 564-3993
    1835 Columbia St San Diego (92101) *(P-11977)*
19 Entertainment Worldwide LLC ....D......310 777-1940
    401 Wilshire Blvd Lbby Santa Monica (90401) *(P-17957)*

19 Management, Santa Monica *Also called 19 Entertainment Worldwide LLC* *(P-17957)*
1906 Lodge, Coronado *Also called Four Sisters Inns* *(P-12280)*
1928 Jewelry Company, Burbank *Also called Mel Bernie and Company Inc* *(P-7790)*
1k Studios, Burbank *Also called One K Studios LLC* *(P-13794)*
1life Healthcare Inc ....D......415 644-5265
    1 Embarcadero Ctr # 1900 San Francisco (94111) *(P-22165)*
Integer LLC ....E......424 320-2977
    1437 7th St Ste 400 Santa Monica (90401) *(P-13394)*
1on1 LLC ....E......310 448-5376
    12015 Waterfront Dr # 261 Playa Vista (90094) *(P-15219)*
1st Class Event Services, Long Beach *Also called Cloudstaff LLC* *(P-14247)*
1st Class Laundry Services, Union City *Also called Specialized Laundry Svcs Inc* *(P-13311)*
1st Interstate Bank Building, Oakland *Also called San Francisco Bay Area Rapid* *(P-3585)*
1st Light Energy Inc (PA) ....E......209 824-5500
    1869 Moffat Blvd Manteca (95336) *(P-3367)*
1st Team Real Estate, Tustin *Also called First Team RE - Orange Cnty* *(P-11151)*
1st United Services Credit Un (PA) ....D......800 649-0193
    5901 Gibraltar Dr Pleasanton (94588) *(P-9379)*
20/20 Plumbing & Heating Inc (PA) ....D......951 396-2020
    7343 Orangewood Dr Ste B Riverside (92504) *(P-2005)*
20/20 Plumbing & Heating Inc ....C......760 535-3101
    325 Market Pl Escondido (92029) *(P-2006)*
2100 Trust LLC (PA) ....C......877 469-7344
    625 N Grand Ave Santa Ana (92701) *(P-11775)*
211 La County, San Gabriel *Also called Information & Referral Fed Los* *(P-13431)*
21st Century Health Club (PA) ....D......707 795-0400
    680a E Cotati Ave Cotati (94931) *(P-21942)*
21st Century Insurance Company (HQ) ....A......877 310-5687
    6301 Owensmouth Ave Woodland Hills (91367) *(P-10238)*
21st Century Lf & Hlth Co Inc (PA) ....D......818 887-4436
    21600 Oxnard St Ste 1500 Woodland Hills (91367) *(P-9894)*
21st Century Super Stars., Rcho STA Marg *Also called C-21 Super Stars* *(P-10956)*
2253 Apparel Inc (PA) ....D......323 837-9800
    1708 Aeros Way Montebello (90640) *(P-8052)*
22nd Century Technologies Inc ....C......866 537-9191
    6203 San Ignacio Ave San Jose (95119) *(P-14599)*
2300 West El Secundo LP ....D......310 769-6669
    11916 Eucalyptus Ave Hawthorne (90250) *(P-10887)*
23627 Calabasas Road LLC ....D......818 222-5300
    23627 Calabasas Rd Calabasas (91302) *(P-11978)*
23andme Inc ....C......510 381-7237
    349 Oyster Point Blvd # 100 South San Francisco (94080) *(P-15840)*
23andme Inc (PA) ....C......650 961-7152
    223 N Mathilda Ave Sunnyvale (94086) *(P-15841)*
24 7ai Inc (PA) ....C......650 385-2247
    2001 All Programable # 200 San Jose (95124) *(P-15931)*
24 Hour Elevator Inc ....D......858 279-8900
    4837 Mercury St San Diego (92111) *(P-17478)*
24 Hour Fitness Usa Inc ....E......916 984-1924
    1006 Riley St Folsom (95630) *(P-18091)*
24 Hour Fitness Usa Inc ....E......707 536-0048
    6345 Commerce Blvd Rohnert Park (94928) *(P-22166)*
24 Hour Fitness Usa Inc ....E......510 795-6666
    39300 Paseo Padre Pkwy Fremont (94538) *(P-18092)*
24 Hour Fitness Usa Inc ....E......818 531-0257
    1903 W Empire Ave Burbank (91504) *(P-22167)*
24 Hour Fitness Usa Inc ....E......949 610-0651
    1870 Harbor Blvd Ste 124 Costa Mesa (92627) *(P-22168)*
24 Hour Fitness Usa Inc ....D......760 918-4790
    5964 La Place Ct Carlsbad (92008) *(P-18093)*
24 Hour Fitness Usa Inc ....D......760 602-5001
    1265 Laurel Tree Ln # 100 Carlsbad (92011) *(P-18094)*
24 Hour Fitness Usa Inc ....D......310 553-7600
    9911 W Pico Blvd Ste A Los Angeles (90035) *(P-18095)*
24 Hour Fitness Usa Inc ....D......626 795-7121
    525 E Colorado Blvd Bsmt Pasadena (91101) *(P-18096)*
24 Hour Fitness Usa Inc ....D......909 944-1000
    11787 Foothill Blvd Rancho Cucamonga (91730) *(P-18097)*
24 Hour Fitness Usa Inc ....E......310 652-7440
    8612 Santa Monica Blvd West Hollywood (90069) *(P-18098)*
24 Hour Fitness Usa Inc ....D......949 650-3600
    555 W 19th St Costa Mesa (92627) *(P-18099)*
24 Hour Fitness Usa Inc (HQ) ....C......925 543-3100
    12647 Alcosta Blvd # 500 San Ramon (94583) *(P-18100)*

Employee Codes: A=Over 500 employees, B=251-500
C=101-250, D=51-100, E=50

2020 Directory of California
Wholesalers and Services Companies

© Mergent Inc. 1-800-342-5647

1155

24 Hour Fitness Usa Inc.....E.....714 525-9924
1430 N Lemon St Anaheim (92801) ***(P-18101)***
24 Hour Fitness Usa Inc.....D.....619 425-6600
1660 Broadway Ste 19 Chula Vista (91911) ***(P-18102)***
24 Hour Fitness Usa Inc.....D.....818 247-4334
450 N Brand Blvd Ste 100 Glendale (91203) ***(P-18103)***
24 Hour Fitness Usa Inc.....D.....916 722-7588
12647 Alcosta Blvd # 500 San Ramon (94583) ***(P-18104)***
24 Hour Fitness Usa Inc.....D.....310 450-4464
2929 31st St Santa Monica (90405) ***(P-18105)***
24 Hour Fitness Usa Inc.....D.....949 830-4213
26781 Rancho Pkwy Lake Forest (92630) ***(P-18106)***
24 Hour Fitness Usa Inc.....E.....650 343-7922
500 El Camino Real Burlingame (94010) ***(P-18107)***
24 Hour Fitness Usa Inc.....E.....619 294-2424
1640 Camino Del Rio N # 315 San Diego (92108) ***(P-18108)***
24 Hour Fitness Usa Inc.....D.....818 887-2582
6653 Fallbrook Ave Canoga Park (91307) ***(P-18109)***
24 Hour Fitness Usa Inc.....D.....562 943-3771
10125 Whittwood Dr Whittier (90603) ***(P-18110)***
24 Hour Fitness Usa Inc.....D.....925 930-7900
2033 N Main St Ste 110 Walnut Creek (94596) ***(P-18111)***
24 Hour Fitness Usa Inc.....E.....650 941-2268
550 Showers Dr Ste 1 Mountain View (94040) ***(P-18112)***
24 Hour Fitness Usa Inc.....E.....858 538-4400
10025 Carmel Mountain Rd San Diego (92129) ***(P-18113)***
24 Hour Fitness Usa Inc.....D.....510 264-3275
24727 Amador St Hayward (94544) ***(P-18114)***
24 Hour Fitness Worldwide Inc (PA).....D.....925 543-3100
12647 Alcosta Blvd # 500 San Ramon (94583) ***(P-18115)***
24 Hour Fitness Worldwide Inc.....E.....310 374-4524
1601 Pcf Cast Hwy Ste 100 Hermosa Beach (90254) ***(P-18116)***
24 Hour In Motion Fitness, Chico *Also called B A M I Inc* ***(P-18119)***
24-7 Caregivers Registry Inc.....C.....800 687-8066
6800 Owensmouth Ave # 420 Canoga Park (91303) ***(P-21616)***
24-Hour Med Staffing Svcs LLC.....C.....909 895-8960
21700 Copley Dr Ste 270 Diamond Bar (91765) ***(P-14212)***
24hr Homecare LLC (PA).....D.....310 906-3683
300 N Pacific Coast Hwy # 1065 El Segundo (90245) ***(P-21617)***
2807 Dev LLC.....D.....510 319-7820
2188 Edinburg Ave Cardiff (92007) ***(P-14600)***
29 Palms Enterprises Corp.....A.....760 775-5566
46200 Harrison Pl Coachella (92236) ***(P-18613)***
2dream Inc.....D.....650 943-2366
5729 Sonoma Dr Ste Z Pleasanton (94566) ***(P-16586)***
2h Construction Inc.....D.....562 424-5567
2653 Walnut Ave Signal Hill (90755) ***(P-1393)***
2nd Floor Main Street Concepts.....E.....714 969-9000
126 Main St Ste 201 Huntington Beach (92648) ***(P-10678)***
2ndgear LLC (HQ).....C.....714 702-1023
611 Anton Blvd Ste 700 Costa Mesa (92626) ***(P-15907)***
2wire Inc (HQ).....C.....408 235-5500
2450 Walsh Ave Santa Clara (95051) ***(P-5284)***
3-Way Farms (PA).....E.....831 722-0748
428 Browns Valley Rd Watsonville (95076) ***(P-227)***
3067 Orange Avenue LLC.....C.....714 827-2440
3067 W Orange Ave Anaheim (92804) ***(P-19706)***
30th Cpts-Financial Management, Lompoc *Also called Air Force US Dept of* ***(P-26125)***
314e Corporation (PA).....C.....510 371-6736
6701 Koll Center Pkwy # 340 Pleasanton (94566) ***(P-14601)***
32nd District-Orange Cnty Fair, Costa Mesa *Also called Food & Agriculture Cal Dept* ***(P-18699)***
365 Delivery Inc.....D.....818 815-5005
440 E Huntington Dr # 300 Arcadia (91006) ***(P-3834)***
3900 West Lane Bowl Inc.....E.....209 466-6100
3900 West Ln Stockton (95204) ***(P-18020)***
3d Infotech (PA).....E.....949 988-0200
7 Hubble Irvine (92618) ***(P-15549)***
3dna Corp (PA).....D.....213 394-4623
520 S Grand Ave Fl 2 Los Angeles (90071) ***(P-14602)***
3k Technologies LLC.....C.....408 716-5900
1114 Cadillac Ct Milpitas (95035) ***(P-14603)***
3M Company.....C.....909 974-3004
5151 E Philadelphia St Ontario (91761) ***(P-4361)***
3vr Security Inc.....D.....415 513-4577
814 Mission St Fl 4 San Francisco (94103) ***(P-16485)***
4 C'S, Hayward *Also called Community Child Care Counci Al* ***(P-23033)***
4 Cs, Santa Rosa *Also called Community Chld Cre Cncl Sonoma* ***(P-23706)***
4 CS Council.....C.....408 487-0747
2515 N 1st St San Jose (95131) ***(P-23662)***
4 Earth Farms Inc (PA).....D.....323 201-5800
5555 E Olympic Blvd Commerce (90022) ***(P-8426)***
4 Su Salud Medical Contact Ctr, Lodi *Also called J Rivera Associates Inc* ***(P-27283)***
4 Wheel Parts Performance Ctrs, Compton *Also called Tap Worldwide LLC* ***(P-6474)***
40 Hours Staffing, San Jose *Also called 40 Hrs Inc* ***(P-14213)***
40 Hrs Inc.....A.....408 414-0158
1669 Flanigan Dr San Jose (95121) ***(P-14213)***
417 Stockton St LLC.....D.....323 327-9656
1180 S Beverly Dr Ste 508 Los Angeles (90035) ***(P-11979)***
425 North Point Street LLC.....D.....800 648-4626
101 California St Ste 950 San Francisco (94111) ***(P-11980)***
4290 El Camino Properties LP.....C.....650 857-0787
4290 El Camino Real Palo Alto (94306) ***(P-11981)***
42nd Street Moon.....E.....415 255-8207
601 Van Ness Ave San Francisco (94102) ***(P-17882)***
48123 CA Investors LLC.....C.....831 667-2331
48123 Highway 1 Big Sur (93920) ***(P-11982)***
495 Geary LLC.....C.....415 775-4700
495 Geary St San Francisco (94102) ***(P-11983)***
4as Trucking.....E.....424 308-9563
20604 Belshaw Ave Carson (90746) ***(P-3835)***
4d Inc.....C.....408 557-4600
95 S Market St Ste 240 San Jose (95113) ***(P-14604)***
4g Wireless Inc.....D.....562 928-2972
7220 Eastern Ave Bell (90201) ***(P-5285)***
4g Wireless Inc.....D.....925 307-8990
4620 Tassajara Rd Dublin (94568) ***(P-5286)***
4g Wireless Inc.....D.....310 429-9048
8342 Lincoln Blvd Los Angeles (90045) ***(P-5287)***
4g Wireless Inc.....D.....323 679-9991
4925 Eagle Rock Blvd Los Angeles (90041) ***(P-5288)***
4g Wireless Inc.....D.....760 705-7133
501 W Felicita Ave # 104 Escondido (92025) ***(P-5289)***
4g Wireless Inc.....D.....760 828-2543
2635 Gateway Rd Ste 103 Carlsbad (92009) ***(P-5290)***
4g Wireless Inc.....D.....951 210-7980
2560 N Perris Blvd Ste G8 Perris (92571) ***(P-5291)***
4g Wireless Inc.....D.....310 376-2299
407 N Pacific Coast Hwy # 101 Redondo Beach (90277) ***(P-5292)***
4g Wireless Inc.....D.....562 432-7744
285 E 5th St Long Beach (90802) ***(P-5293)***
4g Wireless Inc (PA).....C.....949 748-6100
8871 Research Dr Irvine (92618) ***(P-5148)***
4inkjets.com, Long Beach *Also called Ld Products Inc* ***(P-6860)***
5 Arches LLC.....D.....949 387-8092
19800 Macarthur Blvd Irvine (92612) ***(P-9611)***
5 Day Business Forms Mfg Inc (PA).....D.....213 623-3577
2910 E La Cresta Ave Anaheim (92806) ***(P-7849)***
5 Day Business Forms Mfg Inc.....D.....714 632-8674
2921 E La Cresta Ave Anaheim (92806) ***(P-7850)***
5 Design Inc.....D.....323 308-3558
1024 N Orange Dr Ste 215 Los Angeles (90038) ***(P-25406)***
5 Diamond Protection Inc.....D.....949 466-1367
2901 W Macarthur Blvd Santa Ana (92704) ***(P-10558)***
5 Nine Group Inc.....C.....805 880-2948
1125 Lindero Canyon Rd Westlake Village (91362) ***(P-14605)***
500 Startups Incubator LLC.....C.....415 974-6343
814 Mission St Ste 600 San Francisco (94103) ***(P-26962)***
500 Startups Management Co LLC.....C.....650 743-4738
444 Castro St Ste 1200 Mountain View (94041) ***(P-11882)***
51 Minds Entertainment LLC.....D.....323 466-9200
5200 Lankershim Blvd # 200 North Hollywood (91601) ***(P-17958)***
51st St & 8th Ave Corp.....A.....619 424-4000
4000 Coronado Bay Rd Coronado (92118) ***(P-11984)***
550 Flower St Operations LLC.....C.....213 892-8080
550 S Flower St Los Angeles (90071) ***(P-11985)***
5design, Los Angeles *Also called 5 Design Inc* ***(P-25406)***
5th & Sunset Productions, Los Angeles *Also called Fifth & Sunset Enterprises LLC* ***(P-14159)***
5th Avenue Partners LLC.....B.....619 515-3000
1047 5th Ave San Diego (92101) ***(P-11986)***
6417 Selma Hotel LLC.....C.....323 844-6417
6417 Selma Ave Los Angeles (90028) ***(P-11987)***
6500 Hllister Ave Partners LLC.....D.....805 722-1362
6500 Hollister Ave Goleta (93117) ***(P-10559)***
6wind Usa Inc.....D.....408 816-1366
2445 Augustine Dr Ste 150 Santa Clara (95054) ***(P-14606)***
7 Diamonds Clothing, Tustin *Also called M & S Trading Inc* ***(P-8039)***
7 Layers Inc.....D.....949 716-6512
15 Musick Irvine (92618) ***(P-24893)***
711 Hope LP.....C.....213 365-5000
3470 Wilshire Blvd # 700 Los Angeles (90010) ***(P-10866)***
72andsunny LLC.....C.....310 215-9009
12101 Bluff Creek Dr Playa Vista (90094) ***(P-13464)***
7410 Woodman Avenue LLC.....D.....805 496-4336
22837 Ventura Blvd # 201 Woodland Hills (91364) ***(P-10679)***
76, San Diego *Also called Cosco Fire Protection Inc* ***(P-2105)***
7days Inc.....C.....424 255-5872
3503 Jack Northrop Ave Hawthorne (90250) ***(P-7222)***
7th Avenue Center LLC.....D.....831 476-1700
1171 7th Ave Santa Cruz (95062) ***(P-21378)***
7th Standard Ranch Company.....B.....661 399-0416
33374 Lerdo Hwy Bakersfield (93308) ***(P-115)***
800 Degrees LLC.....E.....310 443-1911
10889 Lindbrook Dr Los Angeles (90024) ***(P-26118)***
802 Newman Elem Pta Congress, Chino *Also called Chino Valley Unified Schl Dst* ***(P-24523)***
8020 Consulting LLC.....E.....818 523-3201
6303 Owensmouth Ave Fl 10 Woodland Hills (91367) ***(P-26963)***
8110 Aero Holding LLC.....C.....858 277-8888
8110 Aero Dr San Diego (92123) ***(P-11988)***
834 W Arrow Highway LP.....D.....213 355-1024
4032 Wilshire Blvd # 600 Los Angeles (90010) ***(P-20409)***
8520 Western Ave Inc.....C.....714 828-8222
10811 Kiowa Rd Apt 2a Apple Valley (92308) ***(P-20473)***
8x8 Inc (PA).....C.....408 727-1885
2125 Onel Dr San Jose (95131) ***(P-5294)***
901 West Olympic Blvd LP.....C.....347 992-5707
901 W Olympic Blvd Los Angeles (90015) ***(P-11989)***
95cs/Scxc Comp, Edwards *Also called US Dept of the Air Force* ***(P-5807)***
99 Cents Only Stores LLC (HQ).....B.....323 980-8145
4000 Union Pacific Ave Commerce (90023) ***(P-4362)***
9th Medical Group, Marysville *Also called US Dept of the Air Force* ***(P-21346)***
A & A Home Care Services.....D.....760 416-6769
7756 Cntry Clb Dr Bldg A Palm Springs (92263) ***(P-21618)***
A & A Mechanical Contractors.....D.....408 225-1321
2943 Daylight Way San Jose (95111) ***(P-2007)***
A & B Construction, Berkeley *Also called Andrew M Jordan Inc* ***(P-3303)***
A & C Convatescent Hospital, Millbrae *Also called A & C Health Care Services Inc* ***(P-18788)***

A & C Health Care Services Inc ....C 650 689-5784
33 Mateo Ave Millbrae (94030) ***(P-18788)***
A & D Fire Protection Inc ....D 619 258-7697
7130 Convoy Ct San Diego (92111) ***(P-2008)***
A & D Hauling Services Inc ....D 310 514-8969
13337 South St Cerritos (90703) ***(P-3836)***
A & G Grove Service ....D 760 728-5447
32731 Mesa Lilac Rd Escondido (92026) ***(P-445)***
A & H Communications Inc ....C 949 250-4555
1791 Reynolds Ave Irvine (92614) ***(P-1827)***
A & I Color Laboratory, Burbank *Also called Jake Hey Incorporated* ***(P-16580)***
A & I Transportation, Watsonville *Also called A & I Trucking Inc* ***(P-3837)***
A & I Trucking Inc (PA) ....E 831 763-7805
123 Lee Rd Ste E Watsonville (95076) ***(P-3837)***
A & P Towing-Metropro Rd Svcs, Santa Ana *Also called Metropro Road Services Inc* ***(P-17421)***
A & R Electric, Fullerton *Also called Swinford Electric Inc* ***(P-2663)***
A & R Wholesale Distrs Inc ....D 714 777-7742
1765 W Penhall Way Anaheim (92801) ***(P-8337)***
A & S Technologies, Northridge *Also called Ikano Communications Inc* ***(P-15778)***
A & W Maintenance ....D 310 619-8694
7573 Cibola Trl Yucca Valley (92284) ***(P-1069)***
A 3 By Airbus LLC ....C 650 815-1881
601 W California Ave Sunnyvale (94086) ***(P-25955)***
A A A Automobile Club So Cal, Los Angeles *Also called Automobile Club Southern Cal* ***(P-10288)***
A A A Automobile Club So Cal, Laguna Hills *Also called Automobile Club Southern Cal* ***(P-24800)***
A A A Five Star Adventures ....E 760 320-1500
611 S Palm Canyon Dr Palm Springs (92264) ***(P-18346)***
A A A Furnace AC Co ....D 408 293-4717
1712 Stone Ave Ste 1 San Jose (95125) ***(P-2009)***
A A A Furnace Company, San Jose *Also called Rando AAA Hvac Inc* ***(P-2247)***
A A A Packing and Shipping Inc ....E 626 310-7787
2000 E 49th St Vernon (90058) ***(P-3838)***
A A Gonzalez Inc ....D 818 367-2242
13264 Ralston Ave Sylmar (91342) ***(P-2738)***
A A U C, Los Angeles *Also called African American Unity Center* ***(P-22897)***
A B C D Associates ....C 916 363-4843
10410 Coloma Rd Rancho Cordova (95670) ***(P-19707)***
A B S, City of Industry *Also called Magnell Associate Inc* ***(P-6864)***
A B S Auto Auctions, Corona *Also called Auto Buyline Systems Inc* ***(P-6385)***
A Better Life Together Inc ....D 619 741-1548
3322 Sweetwater Springs B Spring Valley (91977) ***(P-21619)***
A Buchalter Professional Corp (PA) ....C 213 891-0700
1000 Wilshire Blvd # 150 Los Angeles (90017) ***(P-22343)***
A Buchalter Professional Corp ....D 714 549-5150
18400 Von Karman Ave # 800 Irvine (92612) ***(P-22344)***
A C F, Covina *Also called Acf Components & Fasteners Inc* ***(P-7373)***
A C G, Laguna Hills *Also called American Capital Group Inc* ***(P-9497)***
A C I Communications, Calabasas *Also called Able Cable Inc* ***(P-17452)***
A C M, Santa Ana *Also called Advanced Clnroom McRclean Corp* ***(P-13852)***
A C N, City of Industry *Also called America Chung Nam LLC* ***(P-7748)***
A C Rentals LLC ....E 858 271-8571
8540 Production Ave Ste A San Diego (92121) ***(P-2010)***
A C S Security, Los Angeles *Also called ACS Security Industries Inc* ***(P-16487)***
A C T Box Office, San Francisco *Also called American Conservatory* ***(P-17887)***
A Caos Medical Corporation ....D 800 362-2731
2655 Camino Del R San Diego (92108) ***(P-21620)***
A Caregiver LLC ....E 951 676-4190
31520 Rr Cyn Rd Ste A Canyon Lake (92587) ***(P-21621)***
A Colmenero Plastering Inc ....D 559 435-3606
1710 W San Madele Ave Fresno (93711) ***(P-2739)***
A Comcast, Modesto *Also called Comcast Corporation* ***(P-5683)***
A Community For Peace ....D 916 728-5613
6060 Sunrise Vista Dr # 2340 Citrus Heights (95610) ***(P-24122)***
A Community of Friends ....D 213 480-0809
3701 Wilshire Blvd # 700 Los Angeles (90010) ***(P-10680)***
A Complete Drywall Co, San Rafael *Also called Michael B Mayock Inc* ***(P-2822)***
A Cori Partnership ....D 818 368-2802
10626 Balboa Blvd Granada Hills (91344) ***(P-20474)***
A Csg-Nova Joint Venture ....D 916 371-7303
3960 Industrial Blvd # 500 West Sacramento (95691) ***(P-1654)***
A D Bilich Inc ....E 925 820-5557
11 Crow Canyon Ct Ste 100 San Ramon (94583) ***(P-9513)***
A D G, San Diego *Also called Affinity Development Group Inc* ***(P-24782)***
A D S, Los Angeles *Also called Advanced Digital Services Inc* ***(P-17569)***
A Dentons Innovation Wirthlin, Los Angeles *Also called Dentons US LLP* ***(P-22473)***
A Development Stage Company, San Francisco *Also called Brience Inc* ***(P-14687)***
A E W/Careage Ops, Bakersfield *Also called Glenwood Gardens* ***(P-19944)***
A F C, Rancho Dominguez *Also called Advanced Fresh Concepts Corp* ***(P-11823)***
A F Evans Company Inc ....D 925 937-1700
1700 Tice Valley Blvd Ofc Walnut Creek (94595) ***(P-16587)***
A F Gilmore Company ....D 323 939-1191
6301 W 3rd St Los Angeles (90036) ***(P-10888)***
A F V W Health Center ....B 951 697-2025
17050 Arnold Dr Ofc Riverside (92518) ***(P-19708)***
A Filml Inc ....D 213 977-8600
6255 W Sunset Blvd Fl 12 Los Angeles (90028) ***(P-17722)***
A G A, Fremont *Also called Homelegance Inc* ***(P-6517)***
A G C, San Diego *Also called Associated General Contract* ***(P-24379)***
A G Hacienda Incorporated ....B 661 792-2418
32794 Sherwood Ave Mc Farland (93250) ***(P-3839)***
A G Paceman Inc ....D 650 592-7282
1100 Industrial Rd Ste 11 San Carlos (94070) ***(P-10867)***
A G Spanos Management Inc ....E 209 478-7954
10100 Trinity Pkwy Fl 5 Stockton (95219) ***(P-10889)***
A Growing Concern Landscapes ....D 714 843-5137
17382 Gothard St Huntington Beach (92647) ***(P-694)***
A I T Development Corp ....D 818 407-5533
21021 Devonshire St # 205 Chatsworth (91311) ***(P-1070)***
A Is For Apple Inc ....C 877 991-0009
1485 Saratoga Ave Ste 200 San Jose (95129) ***(P-19652)***
A Its Laugh Productions Inc ....D 818 848-8787
914 N Victory Blvd Burbank (91502) ***(P-17565)***
A J Esprit ....E 619 223-8171
5102 N Harbor Dr San Diego (92106) ***(P-11990)***
A J Excavation Inc ....C 559 408-5908
514 N Brawley Ave Fresno (93706) ***(P-3302)***
A J Parent Company Inc (PA) ....D 714 521-1100
6910 Aragon Cir Ste 6 Buena Park (90620) ***(P-16588)***
A J R Trucking Inc ....D 562 989-9555
915 Monterey Rd Glendale (91206) ***(P-3840)***
A L Gilbert Company ....D 209 537-0766
4431 Jessup Rd Keyes (95328) ***(P-8675)***
A L S Industries Inc ....E 310 532-9262
1942 Artesia Blvd Torrance (90504) ***(P-7724)***
A Lighting By Design, Anaheim *Also called Albd Electric and Cable* ***(P-2416)***
A M I Encn-Trzana Rgnal Med Ce, Tarzana *Also called AMI-Hti Tarzana Encino Joint V* ***(P-20747)***
A M Ortega Construction Inc ....D 951 360-1352
58 Kellogg St Ventura (93001) ***(P-1071)***
A M Ortega Construction Inc (PA) ....C 619 390-1988
10125 Channel Rd Lakeside (92040) ***(P-2408)***
A M R, Irwindale *Also called American Med* ***(P-3623)***
A M S Partnership (PA) ....D 310 312-6698
1517 S Sepulveda Blvd Los Angeles (90025) ***(P-11537)***
A Mediation & Resolution Ctr, San Diego *Also called Asset Management Tr Svcs LLC* ***(P-26143)***
A Meissners Hhld & Indus Svc ....D 916 920-2121
2417 Cormorant Way Sacramento (95815) ***(P-7513)***
A Mobile Development ....C 415 350-4532
4500 Great America Pkwy Santa Clara (95054) ***(P-14607)***
A O Reed & Co ....B 858 565-4131
4777 Ruffner St San Diego (92111) ***(P-2011)***
A P Express Worldwide, Irwindale *Also called AP Express LLC* ***(P-4892)***
A P H Technological Consulting ....E 626 796-0331
2500 E Colo Blvd Ste 300 Pasadena (91107) ***(P-24894)***
A P I Property Management, Newport Beach *Also called Amarik Properties Inc* ***(P-10912)***
A P R Consulting Inc ....A 714 544-3696
17852 17th St Ste 206 Tustin (92780) ***(P-15932)***
A P R Inc ....C 805 379-3400
100 E Thsnd Oaks Blvd Thousand Oaks (91360) ***(P-14462)***
A Plus Senior Care Inc ....E 909 989-2563
4701 Arrow Hwy Montclair (91763) ***(P-22889)***
A Q M D, Diamond Bar *Also called South Coast Air Qulty MGT Dst* ***(P-27217)***
A R C Fastener Supply, Corona *Also called ARC Fastener Supply & Mfg* ***(P-7616)***
A R Wilson Quarry & Asp Plant, Aromas *Also called Granite Rock Co* ***(P-6688)***
A Ruiz Cnstr Co & Assoc Inc ....E 415 647-4010
1601 Cortland Ave San Francisco (94110) ***(P-1394)***
A S A P Professional Services ....D 800 303-2727
3301 Loreto Dr San Ramon (94583) ***(P-14214)***
A S E C International Inc ....A 803 939-4809
11400 W Olympic Blvd Los Angeles (90064) ***(P-15718)***
A S I, Long Beach *Also called Associated Students California* ***(P-24476)***
A S I, Fremont *Also called Asi Computer Technologies Inc* ***(P-6798)***
A S I Corporation ....C 714 526-5533
1308 N Patt St Anaheim (92801) ***(P-13465)***
A S S U, Stanford *Also called Associated Students Stanford* ***(P-24477)***
A Smwm California Corporation ....D 415 546-0400
185 Berry St Ste 5100 San Francisco (94107) ***(P-25407)***
A T Associates Inc ....E 510 649-6670
2223 Ashby Ave Berkeley (94705) ***(P-20475)***
A T Associates Inc ....D 510 261-8564
2919 Fruitvale Ave Oakland (94602) ***(P-20476)***
A T Associates Inc (PA) ....D 925 808-6540
535 School St Pittsburg (94565) ***(P-20477)***
A T Kearney Inc ....D 415 490-4000
555 Mission St Ste 1800 San Francisco (94105) ***(P-26468)***
A T S, Los Angeles *Also called Authorized Taxi Cab* ***(P-16497)***
A Taxi Cab, Newport Beach *Also called A White and Yellow Cab Inc* ***(P-3742)***
A Teichert & Son Inc (HQ) ....C 916 484-3011
3500 American River Dr Sacramento (95864) ***(P-6668)***
A Tool Shed Equipment Rentals, Santa Cruz *Also called (a) Tool Shed Inc* ***(P-14119)***
A Touch of Kindness ....D 323 997-6500
353 1/2 N La Brea Ave Los Angeles (90036) ***(P-22890)***
A Transportation, Tarzana *Also called Airey Enterprises LLC* ***(P-7688)***
A Ursgi-Bmdc Joint Venture ....D 858 812-9292
4225 Executive Sq # 1600 La Jolla (92037) ***(P-24895)***
A V Nursing Care Center, Lancaster *Also called Antelope Vly Retirement HM Inc* ***(P-20491)***
A W Properties West LLC ....D 858 832-1462
16236 San Dieguito Rd # 310 Rancho Santa Fe (92091) ***(P-1072)***
A White and Yellow Cab Inc ....C 714 258-1000
2082 Se Bristol St # 212 Newport Beach (92660) ***(P-3742)***
A Wireless, Lakeport *Also called ABC Phones North Carolina Inc* ***(P-5149)***
A World Fit For Kids ....C 213 387-7712
678 S La Fayette Park Pl Los Angeles (90057) ***(P-26469)***
A Yafa Pen Company ....E 818 704-8888
21306 Gault St Canoga Park (91303) ***(P-7851)***
A&E Television Networks LLC ....C 310 201-6015
2049 Century Park E # 800 Los Angeles (90067) ***(P-5664)***

Employee Codes: A=Over 500 employees, B=251-500
C=101-250, D=51-100, E=50
2020 Directory of California
Wholesalers and Services Companies
© Mergent Inc. 1-800-342-5647
1157

A&M Rinforcing Specialists Inc.....E.....619 334-6608
10520 Kenney St Ste A Santee (92071) ***(P-3248)***
A&S Floors, Benicia *Also called Anthony Trevino* ***(P-2994)***
A-1 Delivery Co.....D.....909 444-1220
1777 S Vintage Ave Ontario (91761) ***(P-3841)***
A-1 Electric Service Co Inc.....E.....310 204-1077
4204 Sepulveda Blvd Culver City (90230) ***(P-2409)***
A-1 Elite Painting Inc.....E.....760 365-6702
56409 Yuma Trl Yucca Valley (92284) ***(P-2328)***
A-1 Event & Party Rentals.....D.....626 967-0500
251 E Front St Covina (91723) ***(P-13395)***
A-1 Hospice Care Inc.....D.....818 237-2700
217 E Alameda Ave Ste 306 Burbank (91502) ***(P-21622)***
A-1 Party Rentals, Covina *Also called Cwf Inc* ***(P-14151)***
A-1 Pomona Linen, Paramount *Also called Braun Linen Service Inc* ***(P-13211)***
A-Able Inc (PA).....D.....323 658-5779
17801 Ventura Blvd Encino (91316) ***(P-13807)***
A-C Electric Company (PA).....E.....661 410-0000
2921 Hanger Way Bakersfield (93308) ***(P-2410)***
A-C Electric Company.....D.....661 633-5368
315 30th St Bakersfield (93301) ***(P-24896)***
A-Check America Inc (PA).....C.....951 750-1501
1501 Research Park Dr Riverside (92507) ***(P-13705)***
A-Check America, Member Act 1, Riverside *Also called A-Check America Inc* ***(P-13705)***
A-Mark Precious Metals Inc (PA).....D.....310 587-1477
2121 Rosecrans Ave # 6300 El Segundo (90245) ***(P-7779)***
A-Para Transit Corp.....C.....510 562-5500
1400 Doolittle Dr San Leandro (94577) ***(P-3518)***
A-Star Staffing Inc.....C.....619 574-7600
3636 Camino Del Rio N # 102 San Diego (92108) ***(P-14215)***
A-Throne Co Inc.....D.....562 981-1197
1850 E 33rd St Long Beach (90807) ***(P-14120)***
A-Z Bus Sales Inc (PA).....D.....951 781-7188
1900 S Riverside Ave Colton (92324) ***(P-6376)***
A.S. Foundation-Orange County, Irvine *Also called Aids Svcs Fndation Orange Cnty* ***(P-22900)***
A1 Building Management Inc.....C.....714 447-3800
2461 E Orangethorpe Ave # 200 Fullerton (92831) ***(P-13837)***
A1 Event & Party Rentals, Covina *Also called A-1 Event & Party Rentals* ***(P-13395)***
A1 Protective Services Inc.....D.....415 467-7200
5 Thomas Mellon Cir San Francisco (94134) ***(P-16167)***
A1 Protective Services LLC.....E.....916 421-3000
7000 Franklin Blvd # 665 Sacramento (95823) ***(P-16168)***
A10 Networks Inc (PA).....C.....408 325-8668
3 W Plumeria Dr San Jose (95134) ***(P-15550)***
A5, Pleasanton *Also called Config Consultants LLC* ***(P-26565)***
AA Autmtive Personnel Svcs Inc.....C.....310 914-3012
2251 Federal Ave Los Angeles (90064) ***(P-17404)***
Aa/Acme Locksmiths Inc.....D.....510 483-6584
1660 Factor Ave San Leandro (94577) ***(P-2411)***
AAA, Oakland *Also called American Automobile Assctn* ***(P-24789)***
AAA, Encino *Also called Automobile Club Southern Cal* ***(P-24792)***
AAA, Torrance *Also called Automobile Club Southern Cal* ***(P-24793)***
AAA, Ventura *Also called Automobile Club Southern Cal* ***(P-24794)***
AAA, Glendora *Also called Automobile Club Southern Cal* ***(P-24795)***
AAA, Bakersfield *Also called Automobile Club Southern Cal* ***(P-24796)***
AAA, Northridge *Also called Automobile Club Southern Cal* ***(P-24797)***
AAA, Woodland Hills *Also called Automobile Club Southern Cal* ***(P-24798)***
AAA, Capitola *Also called CA Ste Atom Assoc Intr-Ins Bur* ***(P-17413)***
AAA, Redwood City *Also called California State Automobile* ***(P-10080)***
AAA, Mountain View *Also called CA Ste Atom Assoc Intr-Ins Bur* ***(P-10304)***
AAA, La Mesa *Also called Automobile Club Southern Cal* ***(P-24803)***
AAA - Auto CLB Southern Cal, Rancho Cucamonga *Also called Automobile Club Southern Cal* ***(P-10287)***
AAA Accounting Services.....D.....949 791-7368
2 Enterprise Apt 1211 Aliso Viejo (92656) ***(P-25529)***
AAA Auto Club, Costa Mesa *Also called Automobile Club Southern Cal* ***(P-10290)***
AAA Drain Patrol.....E.....916 348-3098
3437 Myrtle Ave Ste 440 North Highlands (95660) ***(P-2012)***
AAA Elctrcal Cmmunications Inc (PA).....C.....800 892-4784
25007 Anza Dr Valencia (91355) ***(P-2412)***
AAA Fire Protection Service, Union City *Also called AAA Restaurant Fire Ctrl Inc* ***(P-16589)***
AAA Network Solutions Inc.....D.....714 484-2711
8401 Page St Buena Park (90621) ***(P-2413)***
AAA Property Services, Valencia *Also called AAA Elctrcal Cmmunications Inc* ***(P-2412)***
AAA Restaurant Fire Ctrl Inc.....D.....510 786-9555
30113 Union City Blvd Union City (94587) ***(P-16589)***
AAA Restoration Inc.....E.....951 471-5828
29850 2nd St Lake Elsinore (92532) ***(P-3368)***
AAA Signs Inc.....D.....916 568-3456
2020 Railroad Dr Sacramento (95815) ***(P-17316)***
AAA Travel.....E.....650 572-5600
1650 S Delaware St San Mateo (94402) ***(P-10065)***
Aaaaa Rent-A-Space, Castro Valley *Also called Ras Management Inc* ***(P-4489)***
Aaaza Inc.....D.....213 380-8333
3250 Wilshire Blvd # 1901 Los Angeles (90010) ***(P-13466)***
Aadlen Brothers Auto Wrecking (PA).....D.....323 875-1400
11590 Tuxford St Sun Valley (91352) ***(P-7745)***
Aah Hudson LP.....A.....626 794-9179
1255 N Hudson Ave Pasadena (91104) ***(P-10681)***
Aall Care In Home Services, San Diego *Also called Faith Jones & Associates Inc* ***(P-21740)***
AAM, Anaheim *Also called Anaheim Arena Management LLC* ***(P-18046)***
Aamcom LLC.....E.....310 318-8100
800 N Pacific Coast Hwy Redondo Beach (90277) ***(P-5295)***
AAR Manufacturing Inc.....D.....916 830-7011
5307 Luce Ave Bldg 243e McClellan (95652) ***(P-17450)***
AAR Manufacturing Inc.....D.....800 422-2213
5239 Luce Ave Bldg 243d McClellan (95652) ***(P-17451)***
Aardex Inc.....D.....805 928-7600
1550 E Main St Santa Maria (93454) ***(P-1395)***
Aardvark Staffing Inc.....E.....916 774-7115
3017 Douglas Blvd Fl 3 Roseville (95661) ***(P-14463)***
Aarki Inc (PA).....E.....408 382-1180
530 Lakeside Dr Ste 260 Sunnyvale (94085) ***(P-14608)***
Aaron Dowling Incorporated.....D.....559 432-4500
8080 N Palm Ave Ste 300 Fresno (93711) ***(P-22345)***
Aaron Thomas Company Inc (PA).....C.....714 894-4468
7421 Chapman Ave Garden Grove (92841) ***(P-16590)***
Aat Kings Tours USA Inc.....D.....714 456-0505
801 E Katella Ave Fl 3 Anaheim (92805) ***(P-4845)***
Aat Torrey Reserve 6 LLC.....D.....858 350-2600
11455 El Cmino Real Ste 2 San Diego (92130) ***(P-10560)***
Aatcaa Headstart, Sonora *Also called Amador Tlmne Cmnty Action Agcy* ***(P-24127)***
Aauw Action Fund Inc.....D.....650 574-9160
P.O. Box 1239 San Mateo (94401) ***(P-24781)***
Aaxis Pacific, Lomita *Also called Aaxis Pharmaceuticals Inc* ***(P-6934)***
Aaxis Pharmaceuticals Inc.....C.....424 263-5294
1835 262nd St Lomita (90717) ***(P-6934)***
AB Cellular Holding LLC.....A.....562 468-6846
1452 Edinger Ave Tustin (92780) ***(P-5296)***
AB Closing Corporation.....D.....707 766-1777
1304 Southpoint Blvd Petaluma (94954) ***(P-14216)***
Ab/SW 70 S Lake Owner LLC.....E.....650 571-2200
70 S Lake Ave Pasadena (91101) ***(P-10868)***
Aba Holdings LLC.....C.....858 565-4131
4777 Ruffner St San Diego (92111) ***(P-11640)***
Abacus Business Capital Inc.....E.....909 594-8080
738 Epperson Dr City of Industry (91748) ***(P-8144)***
Abacus Data Systems Inc (HQ).....D.....858 452-4280
9171 Towne Centre Dr # 200 San Diego (92122) ***(P-14609)***
Abacus Service Corporation.....B.....916 288-8948
1725 23rd St Sacramento (95816) ***(P-14610)***
Abacusnext, San Diego *Also called Abacus Data Systems Inc* ***(P-14609)***
ABB Enterprise Software Inc.....C.....415 527-2850
60 Spear St San Francisco (94105) ***(P-15220)***
ABB Optical Group, Alameda *Also called Abb/Con-Cise Optical Group LLC* ***(P-7020)***
Abb/Con-Cise Optical Group LLC.....D.....800 852-8089
1750 N Loop Rd Ste 150 Alameda (94502) ***(P-7019)***
Abb/Con-Cise Optical Group LLC.....D.....510 483-9400
1750 N Loop Rd Ste 150 Alameda (94502) ***(P-7020)***
Abba Bail Bonds (PA).....E.....213 680-1400
900 Avila St Ste 2 Los Angeles (90012) ***(P-16591)***
Abbey Management Company LLC.....D.....562 243-2100
330 Golden Shore Ste 300 Long Beach (90802) ***(P-11641)***
Abbey of New Clairvaux (PA).....D.....530 839-2161
26240 7th St Vina (96092) ***(P-198)***
Abbey Ranch, Vina *Also called Abbey of New Clairvaux* ***(P-198)***
Abbey-Properties LLC (PA).....D.....562 435-2100
12447 Lewis St Ste 203 Garden Grove (92840) ***(P-10561)***
Abbood Zeyad.....E.....619 212-2820
7914 La Mesa Blvd Apt 6 La Mesa (91942) ***(P-24897)***
Abbott Stringham An.....D.....408 377-8700
1530 Meridian Ave 2 San Jose (95125) ***(P-25530)***
Abbyson Living Corp.....B.....805 465-5500
26500 Agoura Rd Ste 102 Calabasas (91302) ***(P-6498)***
Abbyy USA Software House Inc (HQ).....C.....408 457-9777
890 Hillview Ct Ste 300 Milpitas (95035) ***(P-14611)***
Abc Inc.....B.....818 863-7801
500 Circle Seven Dr Glendale (91201) ***(P-5575)***
ABC 30, Fresno *Also called Kfsn Television LLC* ***(P-5618)***
ABC Bus Inc.....D.....714 444-5888
1485 Dale Way Costa Mesa (92626) ***(P-6377)***
ABC Bus Inc.....D.....650 368-3364
3508 Haven Ave Redwood City (94063) ***(P-6378)***
ABC Cable Networks Group.....C.....415 954-7911
900 Front St San Francisco (94111) ***(P-5576)***
ABC Cable Networks Group.....C.....818 560-4365
698 S Buena Vista St Burbank (91521) ***(P-17782)***
ABC Cable Networks Group (HQ).....C.....818 460-7477
500 S Buena Vista St Burbank (91521) ***(P-5505)***
ABC Cable Networks Group.....C.....323 860-5900
6834 Hollywood Blvd Los Angeles (90028) ***(P-5506)***
ABC Child Care Center, Temecula *Also called ABC Child Care Inc* ***(P-23663)***
ABC Child Care Inc (PA).....D.....951 699-5251
29705 Solana Way Temecula (92591) ***(P-23663)***
ABC Corona, Corona *Also called Amerisourcebergen Drug Corp* ***(P-7919)***
ABC Family Worldwide Inc (HQ).....B.....818 560-1000
500 S Buena Vista St Burbank (91521) ***(P-17566)***
ABC Home Health Care Llc.....C.....858 455-5000
5090 Shoreham Pl Ste 209 San Diego (92122) ***(P-21623)***
ABC Phones North Carolina Inc.....D.....707 263-3959
1029 11th St Lakeport (95453) ***(P-5149)***
ABC Sacramento Striker, Sacramento *Also called Amerisourcebergen Drug Corp* ***(P-7918)***
ABC School Equipment Inc.....D.....951 817-2200
1451 E 6th St Corona (92879) ***(P-7026)***
ABC Security Service Inc (PA).....C.....510 436-0666
1840 Embarcadero Oakland (94606) ***(P-16169)***
ABC Signature Studios Inc.....D.....818 569-7500
500 S Buena Vista St Burbank (91521) ***(P-5577)***
ABC Valencia, Valencia *Also called Amerisourcebergen Drug Corp* ***(P-7917)***
Abc7 Broadcast Center, San Francisco *Also called Kgo Television Inc* ***(P-5620)***
Abco Insulation, Azusa *Also called Oj Insulation LP* ***(P-2831)***
Abcsp LLC.....C.....855 470-2273
1406 Blue Oaks Blvd Roseville (95747) ***(P-21624)***

Mergent e-mail: customerrelations@mergent.com
1158
2020 Directory of California
Wholesalers and Services Companies
(P-0000) Products & Services Section entry number
(PA)=Parent Co (HQ)=Headquarters (DH)=Div Headquarters

Abd Insurance & Fincl Svcs Inc (PA) ....D......650 488-8565
3 Waters Park Dr Ste 100 San Mateo (94403) *(P-10239)*
Abe-El Produce ....B......559 528-3030
42143 Road 120 Orosi (93647) *(P-32)*
ABF Freight System Inc ....E......408 435-8550
2135 Otoole Ave San Jose (95131) *(P-3956)*
ABF Freight System Inc ....D......323 773-2580
8001 Telegraph Rd Pico Rivera (90660) *(P-3957)*
ABF Freight System Inc ....D......510 533-8575
4575 Tidewater Ave Oakland (94601) *(P-3958)*
ABF Freight System Inc ....E......714 974-2485
1601 N Batavia St Orange (92867) *(P-3959)*
ABF Freight System Inc ....D......916 428-3531
3250 47th Ave Sacramento (95824) *(P-3960)*
ABF Freight System Inc ....C......909 355-9805
10744 Almond Ave Fontana (92337) *(P-3961)*
Abhe & Svoboda Inc ....D......619 659-1320
880 Tavern Rd Alpine (91901) *(P-1396)*
ABI Attorneys Service Inc (PA) ....D......909 793-0613
2015 W Park Ave Redlands (92373) *(P-13745)*
ABI Document Support Svcs LLC ....E......909 793-0613
11010 White Rock Rd # 160 Rancho Cordova (95670) *(P-16592)*
ABI Document Support Svcs LLC ....D......909 793-0613
10459 Mountain View Ave E Loma Linda (92354) *(P-16593)*
ABI VIP Attorney Service, Redlands *Also called ABI Attorneys Service Inc* *(P-13745)*
Abilities United (PA) ....D......650 494-0550
525 E Charleston Rd Palo Alto (94306) *(P-22891)*
Ability Counts Inc (PA) ....D......951 734-6595
775 Trademark Cir Ste 101 Corona (92879) *(P-23556)*
Abilityfirst ....D......213 748-7309
3812 S Grand Ave Los Angeles (90037) *(P-22892)*
Abilty First ....D......562 426-6161
3770 E Willow St Long Beach (90815) *(P-23807)*
ABLE, Azusa *Also called California Pediatric Fmly Svcs* *(P-22954)*
Able Building Maintenance, Santa Ana *Also called Crown Building Maintenance Co* *(P-13902)*
Able Building Maintenance, Los Angeles *Also called Crown Building Maintenance Co* *(P-13905)*
Able Cable Inc (PA) ....C......818 223-3600
5115 Douglas Fir Rd Ste A Calabasas (91302) *(P-17452)*
Able Engineering Services, Los Angeles *Also called Crown Energy Services Inc* *(P-13906)*
Able Exterminators Inc ....D......408 251-6500
68 N Sunset Ave San Jose (95116) *(P-13808)*
Able Hands Inc ....D......626 965-2233
18780 Amar Rd Ste 207 Walnut (91789) *(P-21625)*
Able Industries Inc ....D......559 651-8150
8929 W Goshen Ave Visalia (93291) *(P-23557)*
Able Patrol & Guard, San Diego *Also called Locator Services Inc* *(P-16342)*
Able Services, South San Francisco *Also called Crown Energy Services Inc* *(P-25023)*
Ablitt's Fine Cleaners, Santa Barbara *Also called Santa Barbara Fabricare Inc* *(P-13258)*
ABM Aviation Inc ....B......650 872-5400
601 Gateway Blvd Ste 1145 South San Francisco (94080) *(P-4748)*
ABM Distributors Inc ....D......310 401-0434
811 W 7th St Ste 1040 Los Angeles (90017) *(P-17567)*
ABM Elctrcal Ltg Solutions Inc ....D......408 399-3030
6940 Koll Center Pkwy # 100 Pleasanton (94566) *(P-13838)*
ABM Elctrcal Ltg Solutions Inc (HQ) ....D......866 226-2838
14201 Franklin Ave Tustin (92780) *(P-13839)*
ABM Engineering, Oakland *Also called ABM Facility Services Inc* *(P-13840)*
ABM Facility Services Inc (HQ) ....D......510 251-0381
1266 14th St Ste 103 Oakland (94607) *(P-13840)*
ABM Industries Incorporated ....E......323 720-4020
5300 S Eastrn Ave Ste 110 Los Angeles (90040) *(P-13841)*
ABM Janitorial Services Inc ....A......213 384-0600
3580 Wilshire Blvd # 1130 Los Angeles (90010) *(P-9648)*
ABM Janitorial Services Inc ....D......559 651-1612
1335 N Plaza Dr Ste C Visalia (93291) *(P-13842)*
ABM Janitorial Services Inc ....B......925 924-0270
6671 Owens Dr Pleasanton (94588) *(P-13843)*
ABM Janitorial Services Inc ....B......916 374-1739
830 Riverside Pkwy Ste 40 West Sacramento (95605) *(P-13844)*
ABM Janitorial Services Inc ....C......909 987-3700
11955 Jack Benny Dr # 104 Rancho Cucamonga (91739) *(P-13845)*
ABM Janitorial Services Inc ....C......209 983-3923
2385 Arch Airport Rd # 100 Stockton (95206) *(P-13846)*
ABM Office Solutions Inc ....D......909 527-8145
9550 Hermosa Ave Rancho Cucamonga (91730) *(P-6499)*
ABM Securities, Los Angeles *Also called ABM Janitorial Services Inc* *(P-9648)*
Abode Communities ....D......213 629-2702
1149 S Hill St Fl 7 Los Angeles (90015) *(P-10890)*
Abode Services (PA) ....D......510 657-7409
40849 Fremont Blvd Fremont (94538) *(P-22893)*
Above Hlth HM Care Sltions LLC ....D......714 585-2185
960 S Peregrine Pl Anaheim (92806) *(P-21626)*
Abp Liquidating Corp ....E......650 871-7689
299 Lawrence Ave South San Francisco (94080) *(P-8427)*
Abraham Jsha Hschl Dy Schl Wst ....D......818 707-2365
27400 Canwood St Agoura (91301) *(P-23664)*
Abrazar Inc ....D......714 893-3581
7101 Wyoming St Westminster (92683) *(P-22894)*
ABRAZAR ELDERLY ASSISTANCE, Westminster *Also called Abrazar Inc* *(P-22894)*
ABS Capital Partners III LP ....D......415 617-2800
101 California St Fl 24 San Francisco (94111) *(P-11883)*
ABS Computer Technologies, Whittier *Also called Magnell Associate Inc* *(P-4446)*
ABS Computer Technologies, City of Industry *Also called Magnell Associate Inc* *(P-6865)*
ABS Consulting Inc ....D......714 734-4242
300 Commerce Ste 150 Irvine (92602) *(P-24898)*
ABS Group, Irvine *Also called ABS Consulting Inc* *(P-24898)*

Abs-American Building Supply, Sacramento *Also called American Building Supply Inc* *(P-6602)*
ABS-Cbn International (HQ) ....C......800 527-2820
2001 Junipero Serra Blvd # 200 Daly City (94014) *(P-5665)*
Absg Consulting Inc ....E......510 508-6289
505 14th St Ste 900 Oakland (94612) *(P-26964)*
Absg Consulting Inc ....D......714 734-4242
300 Commerce Ste 150 Irvine (92602) *(P-26965)*
Abshear Landscape Development ....E......916 660-1617
3171b Rippey Rd Loomis (95650) *(P-695)*
Abso ....C......800 943-2589
101 Creekside Ridge Ct # 2 Roseville (95678) *(P-14217)*
Absolutdata Technologies Inc ....D......510 748-9922
1320 Harbor Bay Pkwy # 170 Alameda (94502) *(P-16594)*
Absolute Exhibits Inc (PA) ....D......714 685-2800
1382 Valencia Ave Ste H Tustin (92780) *(P-16595)*
Absolute Return Portfolio ....A......800 800-7646
700 Newport Center Dr Newport Beach (92660) *(P-11706)*
Absolute Roofing CA, Fresno *Also called Absolute Urethane* *(P-3021)*
Absolute Towing-Hollenbeck Div ....E......323 225-9294
4760 Valley Blvd Los Angeles (90032) *(P-17405)*
Absolute Urethane ....E......877 471-3626
6614 S Elm Ave Fresno (93706) *(P-3021)*
Abstract, San Francisco *Also called Elastic Projects Inc* *(P-14780)*
Abtech Support, Carlsbad *Also called Abtech Technologies Inc* *(P-15933)*
Abtech Technologies Inc ....D......760 827-5100
2042 Corte Del Nogal D Carlsbad (92011) *(P-15933)*
Abx Engineering Inc ....D......650 552-2300
875 Stanton Rd Burlingame (94010) *(P-7223)*
Abzooba Inc ....C......650 453-8760
1551 Mccarthy Blvd # 204 Milpitas (95035) *(P-14612)*
AC Enterprises, Hayward *Also called Andrew Chekene Enterprises Inc* *(P-1079)*
AC Hotel Beverly Hills, Los Angeles *Also called Candleberry Properties LP* *(P-12110)*
AC Hotel San Jose Sunnyvale CU, Sunnyvale *Also called K3 Dev LLC* *(P-12496)*
AC Square Inc ....C......650 293-2730
4590 Qantas Ln Stockton (95206) *(P-26966)*
AC TRANSIT, Oakland *Also called Alameda-Contra Costa Trnst Dst* *(P-3523)*
Academy Foundation (HQ) ....D......310 247-3000
8949 Wilshire Blvd Beverly Hills (90211) *(P-17723)*
Academy Mpic Arts & Sciences (PA) ....D......310 247-3000
8949 Wilshire Blvd Beverly Hills (90211) *(P-24373)*
Academy Swim Club ....D......661 702-8585
28079 Smyth Dr Valencia (91355) *(P-18347)*
Academy TV Arts Scnces Fndtion ....D......818 754-2800
5220 Lankershim Blvd North Hollywood (91601) *(P-24374)*
Acalvio Technologies Inc ....D......408 931-6160
2520 Mission College Blvd # 110 Santa Clara (95054) *(P-16486)*
ACC SENIOR SERVICES, Sacramento *Also called Asian Community Center of Sac* *(P-22928)*
ACC West Coast, Benicia *Also called American Civil Const* *(P-1661)*
ACC-Gwg LLC ....D......530 473-2827
6133 Abel Rd Williams (95987) *(P-26967)*
Accel Biotech LLC ....D......408 354-1700
103 Cooper Ct Los Gatos (95032) *(P-24899)*
Accela Inc (PA) ....C......925 659-3200
2633 Camino Ramon Ste 500 San Ramon (94583) *(P-15221)*
Accelerated Envmtl Svcs Inc ....D......661 765-4003
23601 Taft Hwy Bakersfield (93311) *(P-13847)*
Accelerize Inc ....D......949 515-2166
204 Riverside Ave Newport Beach (92663) *(P-9858)*
Accelon Inc ....E......925 216-5735
2410 Camino Ramon Ste 194 San Ramon (94583) *(P-14218)*
Accent Service Company Inc ....D......877 611-0131
2001 Lemnos Dr Costa Mesa (92626) *(P-13848)*
Accentcare Inc ....A......858 576-7410
5050 Mrphy Knyan Rd St200 San Diego (92123) *(P-21627)*
Accentcare HM Hlth Scrmnto Inc ....D......916 852-5888
2880 Sunrise Blvd Ste 218 Rancho Cordova (95742) *(P-21628)*
Accentcare Home Health ....E......760 352-4022
2344 S 2nd St Ste A El Centro (92243) *(P-21629)*
Accentcare Home Health Cal Inc ....D......925 356-6066
2300 Contra Costa Blvd # 125 Pleasant Hill (94523) *(P-21630)*
Accentcare Home Health Cal Inc ....E......818 528-8855
15455 San Fernando Ste Mission Hills (91345) *(P-21631)*
Accentcare Home Health Cal Inc ....D......909 605-7000
1455 Auto Center Dr # 200 Ontario (91761) *(P-21632)*
Accentcare Home Health Cal Inc ....C......858 576-7410
5050 Murphy Canyon Rd # 200 San Diego (92123) *(P-21633)*
Accentcare Home Health Cal Inc ....D......949 250-0133
3636 Birch St Ste 195 Newport Beach (92660) *(P-21634)*
Accenture Federal Services LLC ....C......619 574-2400
1615 Murray Canyon Rd # 400 San Diego (92108) *(P-26470)*
Accenture LLP ....B......310 726-2700
2141 Rosecrans Ave # 3100 El Segundo (90245) *(P-26471)*
Accenture LLP ....C......415 537-5860
2 Santa Ana Ct Belvedere Tiburon (94920) *(P-26472)*
Accenture LLP ....B......415 537-5000
560 Mission St Fl 12 San Francisco (94105) *(P-26473)*
Accenture LLP ....C......408 817-2100
50 W San Fernando St # 1208 San Jose (95113) *(P-26474)*
Accenture LLP ....C......650 213-2000
50 W San Fernando St # 1200 San Jose (95113) *(P-26475)*
Accenture LLP ....C......916 557-2200
1610 R St Ste 240 Sacramento (95811) *(P-26476)*
Accenture National SEC Svcs, San Diego *Also called Accenture Federal Services LLC* *(P-26470)*
Access Biologicals LLC ....D......760 931-8444
995 Park Center Dr Vista (92081) *(P-7913)*

A
L
P
H
A
B
E
T
I
C

Access Brand Communications, San Francisco *Also called Access Public Relations LLC* ***(P-26891)***
Access Business Group Intl LLC.......C.......800 879-2732
6500 Beach Blvd Buena Park (90621) ***(P-16596)***
Access Dental Centers, Orange *Also called Access Dental Plan* ***(P-19600)***
Access Dental Plan (PA).......D.......916 922-5000
530 S Main St Orange (92868) ***(P-19600)***
Access Finance Inc.......E.......310 826-4000
3415 S Sepulveda Blvd # 400 Los Angeles (90034) ***(P-16597)***
Access Hollywood.......C.......818 840-4444
3000 W Alameda Ave Burbank (91523) ***(P-5578)***
Access Hollywood LLC.......D.......818 684-7000
100 Universal City Plz Universal City (91608) ***(P-17568)***
Access Info Holdings LLC.......A.......909 459-1417
2021 E Locust Ct Ontario (91761) ***(P-15842)***
Access Info MGT Shred Svcs LLC.......C.......925 461-5352
6818 Patterson Pass Rd A Livermore (94550) ***(P-4553)***
Access Info MGT Shred Svcs LLC.......D.......925 461-5352
4501 Pell Dr Sacramento (95838) ***(P-4554)***
Access Nurses Inc.......D.......858 458-4400
5935 Cornerstone Ct W San Diego (92121) ***(P-14219)***
Access Pacific Inc.......E.......626 792-0616
2835 Sierra Grande St Pasadena (91107) ***(P-1397)***
Access Paratransit, El Monte *Also called Access Services* ***(P-3519)***
Access Public Relations LLC.......D.......415 904-7070
720 California St Fl 5 San Francisco (94108) ***(P-26891)***
Access Services.......D.......213 270-6000
3449 Santa Anita Ave El Monte (91731) ***(P-3519)***
Access Spclty Animal Hospitals.......D.......310 558-6100
9599 Jefferson Blvd Culver City (90232) ***(P-568)***
Access Systems Americas Inc.......A.......408 400-3000
3965 Freedom Cir Ste 200 Santa Clara (95054) ***(P-14613)***
Access To Loans For Learning.......E.......310 979-4700
1230 Rosecrans Ave # 560 Manhattan Beach (90266) ***(P-9612)***
Accessory Power, Westlake Village *Also called AP Global Inc* ***(P-7230)***
Accidental Fire & Casualty, Lancaster *Also called Wilshire Insurance Company* ***(P-10549)***
Accion Labs Us Inc.......A.......408 970-9809
4633 Old Ironsides Dr # 304 Santa Clara (95054) ***(P-26051)***
Acco Engineered Systems Inc.......D.......323 727-7765
3421 S Malt Ave Commerce (90040) ***(P-17440)***
Acco Engineered Systems Inc.......C.......510 346-4300
1133 Aladdin Ave San Leandro (94577) ***(P-2013)***
Acco Engineered Systems Inc.......E.......323 201-0931
6446 E Washington Blvd Commerce (90040) ***(P-16598)***
Accor Bus & Leisure N Amer LLC.......C.......650 598-9000
223 Twin Dolphin Dr Redwood City (94065) ***(P-11991)***
Accor Corp.......C.......310 278-5444
8555 Beverly Blvd Los Angeles (90048) ***(P-11992)***
Accor Services US LLC.......B.......310 319-3122
101 Wilshire Blvd Santa Monica (90401) ***(P-11993)***
Accor Services US LLC (HQ).......A.......415 772-5000
950 Mason St San Francisco (94108) ***(P-11994)***
Account Control Technology Inc.......E.......661 395-5702
5500 Ming Ave Ste 185 Bakersfield (93309) ***(P-13668)***
Accountable Health Staff Inc.......B.......916 286-7667
7777 Greenback Ln Ste 205 Citrus Heights (95610) ***(P-14220)***
Accountants 4 Contract.......D.......415 781-8644
235 Montgomery St Ste 630 San Francisco (94104) ***(P-25531)***
Accountemps, San Francisco *Also called Robert Half International Inc* ***(P-14396)***
Accountemps, Menlo Park *Also called Robert Half International Inc* ***(P-14398)***
Accountnow Inc.......D.......925 498-1800
2603 Camino Ramon Ste 485 San Ramon (94583) ***(P-26477)***
Accounts Payable Department, Ontario *Also called Technicolor HM Entrmt Svcs Inc* ***(P-17772)***
Accounts Payable Dept, Fountain Valley *Also called Orange County Water District* ***(P-6098)***
Accredited Nursing Care, Pasadena *Also called Accredited Nursing Services* ***(P-19709)***
Accredited Nursing Care, Woodland Hills *Also called Dunn & Berger Inc* ***(P-21732)***
Accredited Nursing Care, Costa Mesa *Also called Accredited Nursing Services* ***(P-21635)***
Accredited Nursing Services.......D.......626 573-1234
80 S Lake Ave Ste 630 Pasadena (91101) ***(P-19709)***
Accredited Nursing Services.......D.......714 973-1234
950 S Coast Dr Ste 215 Costa Mesa (92626) ***(P-21635)***
Accretive Solutions Inc (HQ).......A.......312 994-4600
17101 Armstrong Ave # 100 Irvine (92614) ***(P-25532)***
Acct Holdings LLC.......A.......916 971-1981
5949 Fair Oaks Blvd Carmichael (95608) ***(P-16599)***
Accu, Glendora *Also called Americas Christian Credit Un* ***(P-9382)***
Accu-Count Inventory Svcs Inc.......D.......805 231-6310
1024 N Citrus Ave Covina (91722) ***(P-16600)***
Accumen Inc (PA).......D.......858 777-8160
5414 Oberlin Dr Ste 200 San Diego (92121) ***(P-21636)***
Accunex Inc.......E.......818 882-5858
20700 Lassen St Chatsworth (91311) ***(P-24900)***
Accurate Background LLC (PA).......B.......800 784-3911
7515 Irvine Center Dr Irvine (92618) ***(P-15843)***
Accurate Courier Services Inc.......D.......310 481-3937
11022 Santa Monica Blvd # 360 Los Angeles (90025) ***(P-3842)***
Accurate Delivery Systems Inc.......D.......951 823-8870
173 Resource Dr Bloomington (92316) ***(P-3843)***
Accurate Electronics, Chatsworth *Also called Accunex Inc* ***(P-24900)***
Accurate Express, Los Angeles *Also called Accurate Services Inc* ***(P-9418)***
Accurate Firestop Inc.......C.......510 886-1169
1057 Serpentine Ln Ste A Pleasanton (94566) ***(P-16601)***
Accurate Services Inc.......C.......323 906-1000
3429 Glendale Blvd Los Angeles (90039) ***(P-9418)***
Accutherm Air Heating & Coolg, Garden Grove *Also called Accutherm Refrigeraton Inc* ***(P-2014)***
Accutherm Refrigeraton Inc.......D.......714 766-7800
11264 Monarch St Ste A Garden Grove (92841) ***(P-2014)***
Acd, Newark *Also called Advanced Cell Diagnostics Inc* ***(P-25697)***
Ace Beverage Co.......D.......323 266-6238
550 S Mission Rd Los Angeles (90033) ***(P-8743)***
Ace Cash Express Inc.......C.......951 509-3506
6302 Van Buren Blvd Riverside (92503) ***(P-9419)***
Ace Duraflo Pipe Restoration, Santa Ana *Also called Pipe Restoration Inc* ***(P-2231)***
Ace Fence Company, La Puente *Also called Apw Construction Inc* ***(P-1814)***
Ace Financial Services Inc.......D.......510 790-4600
39300 Civic Center Dr # 290 Fremont (94538) ***(P-10240)***
Ace Floor Co Inc.......D.......866 522-4500
5155 Goldman Ave Moorpark (93021) ***(P-2993)***
Ace Hardware, Fresno *Also called Fresno Plumbing & Heating Inc* ***(P-2142)***
Ace Hardware, Bishop *Also called High Country Lumber Inc* ***(P-6626)***
Ace Hardware Corporation.......B.......916 435-4567
3305 Industrial Ave Rocklin (95765) ***(P-4363)***
Ace Heating and AC, Porterville *Also called Raul V Acevedo* ***(P-944)***
Ace High Entertainnment LLC.......E.......916 243-5515
125 Sconce Way Sacramento (95838) ***(P-18045)***
Ace Industrial Supply Inc (PA).......D.......818 252-1981
7535 N San Fernando Rd Burbank (91505) ***(P-1073)***
Ace Parking Management Inc.......D.......510 589-2313
1901 Harrison St Ste 102 Oakland (94612) ***(P-17234)***
Ace Parking Management Inc.......C.......858 552-0237
4352 La Jolla Village Dr San Diego (92122) ***(P-17235)***
Ace Parking Management Inc.......D.......510 272-9788
2101 Webster St Oakland (94612) ***(P-17236)***
Ace Parking Management Inc.......C.......510 251-0509
1330 Broadway Ste 915 Oakland (94612) ***(P-17237)***
Ace Parking Management Inc.......C.......949 727-1470
71 Fortune Dr Ste 916 Irvine (92618) ***(P-17238)***
Ace Parking Management Inc (PA).......E.......619 233-6624
645 Ash St San Diego (92101) ***(P-17239)***
Ace Parking Management Inc.......D.......408 437-2185
2050 Gateway Pl San Jose (95110) ***(P-17240)***
Ace Parking Management Inc.......D.......415 421-8800
350 Bush St San Francisco (94104) ***(P-17241)***
Ace Parking Management Inc.......D.......714 845-8000
21500 Pacific Coast Hwy Huntington Beach (92648) ***(P-17242)***
Ace Parking Management Inc.......D.......619 232-1234
1 Market Pl San Diego (92101) ***(P-17243)***
Ace Property & Casualty, Fremont *Also called Ace Financial Services Inc* ***(P-10240)***
Ace Relocation Systems Inc (PA).......D.......858 677-5500
5608 Eastgate Dr San Diego (92121) ***(P-3844)***
Ace Relocation Systems Inc.......E.......310 632-2800
189 W Victoria St Long Beach (90805) ***(P-3845)***
Ace Tomato Company Inc.......D.......209 982-0734
777 N Pershing Ave Ste 1a Stockton (95203) ***(P-33)***
Ace USA.......D.......510 790-4695
39300 Civic Center Dr # 290 Fremont (94538) ***(P-10241)***
Acea Biosciences Inc.......D.......858 724-0928
6779 Mesa Ridge Rd # 100 San Diego (92121) ***(P-25694)***
Acemi Nursery Inc.......D.......559 842-7766
3626 N Howard Ave Kerman (93630) ***(P-183)***
Acepex Management Corporation.......B.......909 591-1999
13401 Yorba Ave Chino (91710) ***(P-26119)***
Acepex Management Corporation.......C.......909 625-6900
10643 Mills Ave Montclair (91763) ***(P-26926)***
Acer America Corporation (HQ).......D.......408 533-7700
333 W San Carlos St San Jose (95110) ***(P-15934)***
Acera, Oakland *Also called Alameda County Employees Retir* ***(P-10206)***
Acetech Construction Inc.......E.......213 637-4702
3699 Wilshire Blvd # 655 Los Angeles (90010) ***(P-24901)***
Aceteck Roofing Co Inc.......E.......323 231-6060
5830 Woodlawn Ave Los Angeles (90003) ***(P-3022)***
Acetld Solar.......C.......800 241-6030
425 National Ave Ste 199 Mountain View (94043) ***(P-2015)***
Aceva Technologies Inc.......C.......650 227-5500
1810 Gateway Dr Ste 360 San Mateo (94404) ***(P-13706)***
Acf Components & Fasteners Inc.......D.......949 833-0506
742 Arrow Grand Cir Covina (91722) ***(P-7373)***
Ach Mechanical Contractors Inc.......D.......909 307-2850
411 Business Center Ct Redlands (92373) ***(P-2016)***
Achates Power Inc.......D.......858 535-9920
4060 Sorrento Valley Blvd A San Diego (92121) ***(P-25695)***
Achates Security, Salinas *Also called J Waters Inc* ***(P-16330)***
Achem Industry America Inc (PA).......D.......562 802-0998
4250 N Harbor Blvd Fullerton (92835) ***(P-7613)***
Achiever Christian Pre-Schl &.......E.......408 264-2345
540 Sands Dr San Jose (95125) ***(P-23665)***
Achievo Corporation (PA).......D.......925 498-8864
1400 Terra Bella Ave E Mountain View (94043) ***(P-14614)***
Aci International (PA).......D.......310 889-3400
844 Moraga Dr Los Angeles (90049) ***(P-8118)***
ACI Construction Company Inc.......E.......909 391-4477
207 W State St Ontario (91762) ***(P-24902)***
Acm Technologies Inc (PA).......D.......951 738-9898
2535 Research Dr Corona (92882) ***(P-6737)***
Acme Building Maintenance Co (HQ).......D.......408 263-5911
941 Catherine St Alviso (95002) ***(P-13849)***
Acme Furniture Industry Inc (PA).......D.......626 964-3456
18895 Arenth Ave City of Industry (91748) ***(P-6500)***
Acme Metals & Steel Supply, Gardena *Also called Acme Metals LLC* ***(P-7038)***
Acme Metals & Steel Supply.......D.......310 329-2263
14930 S San Pedro St Gardena (90248) ***(P-7037)***
Acme Metals LLC.......D.......310 329-2263
14930 S San Pedro St Gardena (90248) ***(P-7038)***
Acme Staffing, El Centro *Also called I N C Builders Inc* ***(P-14512)***

Mergent e-mail: customerrelations@mergent.com 2020 Directory of California (P-0000) Products & Services Section entry number
1160 Wholesalers and Services Companies (PA)=Parent Co (HQ)=Headquarters (DH)=Div Headquarters

Acme Trading, City of Industry *Also called Acme Furniture Industry Inc* ***(P-6500)***
Acmpc California 3 LLC.....C.....559 591-6140
38773 Rd 48 Lindsay (93247) ***(P-184)***
Acom Solutions Inc (PA).....E.....562 424-7899
2850 E 29th St Long Beach (90806) ***(P-15551)***
Acon Laboratories Inc (PA).....D.....858 875-8000
10125 Mesa Rim Rd San Diego (92121) ***(P-6935)***
Acosta Inc.....C.....714 988-1500
915 W Imperial Hwy # 200 Brea (92821) ***(P-8145)***
Acosta Inc.....D.....925 600-3500
5735 W Las Positas Blvd # 300 Pleasanton (94588) ***(P-8146)***
Acosta Sales & Marketing, Brea *Also called Acosta Inc* ***(P-8145)***
Acoustical Contractor, Thousand Oaks *Also called S A Cali-U Acoustics Inc* ***(P-2855)***
Acrobat Staffing, San Diego *Also called SE Scher Corporation* ***(P-14414)***
Acrobat Staffing, Rocklin *Also called SE Scher Corporation* ***(P-14415)***
Acronics Systems Inc.....C.....408 432-0888
2102 Commerce Dr San Jose (95131) ***(P-24903)***
Across Systems Inc.....D.....877 922-7677
100 N Brand Blvd Ste 100 Glendale (91203) ***(P-6785)***
Acrt Pacific LLC.....B.....330 945-7500
3443 Deer Park Dr Ste B Stockton (95219) ***(P-26968)***
ACS, Huntington Beach *Also called Applied Computer Solutions* ***(P-14644)***
ACS Communications Inc.....E.....310 767-2145
680 Knox St Ste 150 Torrance (90502) ***(P-2414)***
ACS Security Industries Inc.....D.....310 475-9016
1964 Westwood Blvd # 235 Los Angeles (90025) ***(P-16487)***
Acss, Beaumont *Also called Anderson Chrnesky Strl Stl Inc* ***(P-3250)***
Act 1 Group Inc (PA).....D.....310 532-1529
1999 W 190th St Torrance (90504) ***(P-14221)***
Act 1 Personnel Services, Torrance *Also called All In One Inc* ***(P-14223)***
Act Associates, Folsom *Also called Matthew Burns* ***(P-1537)***
Act Fulfillment Inc.....C.....909 930-9083
3155 Universe Dr Mira Loma (91752) ***(P-4364)***
Act Home Health Inc.....D.....714 560-0800
12431 Lewis St Ste 101 Garden Grove (92840) ***(P-21637)***
ACT Lighting Inc.....A.....818 707-0884
2313 N Valley St Burbank (91505) ***(P-7115)***
Actian Corporation (PA).....D.....650 587-5500
2300 Geng Rd Ste 150 Palo Alto (94303) ***(P-15552)***
Action Day Nrseries Prmry Plus.....D.....408 370-0350
18720 Bucknall Rd Saratoga (95070) ***(P-23666)***
Action Day Nrseries Prmry Plus.....E.....408 266-8952
2148 Lincoln Ave San Jose (95125) ***(P-23667)***
Action Force Security.....E.....310 715-6053
1212 W Gardena Blvd Ste C Gardena (90247) ***(P-16170)***
Action Home Nursing Services.....D.....530 756-2600
561 Torero Way El Dorado Hills (95762) ***(P-21638)***
Action Messenger Service, Los Angeles *Also called Peach Inc* ***(P-4277)***
Action Property Management Inc.....C.....800 400-2284
530 S Hewitt St Los Angeles (90013) ***(P-24473)***
Action Property Management Inc (PA).....D.....949 450-0202
2603 Main St Ste 500 Irvine (92614) ***(P-10850)***
Action Roofing, Santa Barbara *Also called JM Roofing Company Inc* ***(P-3066)***
Action Sales, Monterey Park *Also called JC Foodservice Inc* ***(P-6926)***
Action Sports Retailer.....D.....949 226-5744
31910 Del Obispo St # 200 San Juan Capistrano (92675) ***(P-16602)***
Activcare Living Inc (PA).....C.....858 565-4424
10603 Rancho Bernardo Rd San Diego (92127) ***(P-26120)***
Active Lawyers Referral Svc.....D.....310 247-0425
9301 Wilshire Blvd # 508 Beverly Hills (90210) ***(P-27263)***
Active Motif Inc (PA).....D.....760 431-1263
1914 Palomar Oaks Way # 150 Carlsbad (92008) ***(P-25696)***
Active Wellness LLC.....A.....415 741-3300
600 California St Fl 11 San Francisco (94108) ***(P-26121)***
Activehours Inc.....C.....650 272-4083
260 Sheridan Ave Ste 300 Palo Alto (94306) ***(P-16603)***
Actividentity Corporation.....C.....510 574-0100
6623 Dumbarton Cir Fremont (94555) ***(P-15719)***
Activision Blizzard Inc.....C.....415 881-9100
4 Hamilton Landing Novato (94949) ***(P-15222)***
Activision Blizzard Inc.....C.....310 581-4700
3420 Ocean Park Blvd # 2000 Santa Monica (90405) ***(P-14615)***
Activision Blizzard Inc (PA).....B.....310 255-2000
3100 Ocean Park Blvd Santa Monica (90405) ***(P-15223)***
Activision Blizzard Inc.....D.....949 955-1380
3 Blizzard Irvine (92618) ***(P-15224)***
Activision Blizzard Inc.....C.....310 431-4000
653 W Fallbrook Ave # 104 Fresno (93711) ***(P-4365)***
Activision Publishing Inc (HQ).....A.....310 255-2000
3100 Ocean Park Blvd Santa Monica (90405) ***(P-15225)***
Actone Executive Search, Torrance *Also called Act 1 Group Inc* ***(P-14221)***
Actual Reality Pictures Inc.....E.....818 325-8800
16030 Ventura Blvd # 380 Encino (91436) ***(P-10891)***
Acumen LLC.....C.....650 558-8882
500 Airport Blvd Ste 100 Burlingame (94010) ***(P-15553)***
ACWD, Fremont *Also called Alameda County Water District* ***(P-6014)***
Acxiom Corporation.....E.....714 636-3093
8801 Elmer Ln Garden Grove (92841) ***(P-15844)***
Acxiom Corporation.....D.....650 356-3400
100 Redwood Shores Pkwy Redwood City (94065) ***(P-15845)***
Ad Force Private Security, Stockton *Also called California Guard Inc* ***(P-16222)***
Ad Results Media LLC.....D.....858 480-5223
111 C St Encinitas (92024) ***(P-13611)***
Adams & Barnes Inc.....E.....626 358-1858
433 W Foothill Blvd Monrovia (91016) ***(P-10892)***
Adams Early Childhood Lrng Ctr, La Quinta *Also called Adams Learning Center* ***(P-23668)***
Adams Learning Center.....E.....760 777-4260
50800 Desert Club Dr La Quinta (92253) ***(P-23668)***
Adams Pool Specialties, Sacramento *Also called Dave Gross Enterprises Inc* ***(P-3397)***
Adams Steel, Anaheim *Also called Self Serve Auto Dismantlers* ***(P-6281)***
Adams Streeter Civil Engineers.....D.....949 474-2330
16755 Von Karman Ave # 150 Irvine (92606) ***(P-24904)***
Adaptamed LLC.....C.....877 478-7773
6699 Alvarado Rd Ste 2301 San Diego (92120) ***(P-14616)***
Adaptive Insghts LLC A Workday (HQ).....C.....650 528-7500
2300 Geng Rd Ste 100 Palo Alto (94303) ***(P-15226)***
Adaptive Spectrum and Signal A.....D.....650 264-2667
333 Twin Dolphin Dr # 300 Redwood City (94065) ***(P-5297)***
Adara Inc (PA).....D.....408 876-6360
1070 E Meadow Cir Palo Alto (94303) ***(P-13467)***
Adco Container Company.....E.....818 998-2565
9959 Canoga Ave Chatsworth (91311) ***(P-7614)***
Adcolony Inc.....D.....650 625-1262
11400 W Olympic Blvd # 1200 Los Angeles (90064) ***(P-14617)***
Adcom Interactive Media Inc.....D.....800 296-7104
901 W Alameda Ave Ste 102 Burbank (91506) ***(P-15935)***
Add2net Inc (PA).....E.....714 521-8150
931 E La Habra Blvd La Habra (90631) ***(P-15936)***
Added Value LLC (HQ).....C.....323 254-4326
3400 Cahuenga Blvd W B Los Angeles (90068) ***(P-25874)***
Addepar Inc (PA).....D.....855 464-6268
303 Bryant St Mountain View (94041) ***(P-14618)***
Addiction RES & Trtmnt Inc.....D.....415 928-7800
433 Turk St San Francisco (94102) ***(P-21943)***
Addison-Penzak Jewish Communit.....C.....408 358-3636
14855 Oka Rd Ste 201 Los Gatos (95032) ***(P-18117)***
Addus Healthcare Inc.....D.....209 526-8451
817 Coffee Rd Ste B1 Modesto (95355) ***(P-21639)***
Addus Healthcare Inc.....E.....530 566-0405
196 Cohasset Rd Ste 200 Chico (95926) ***(P-21640)***
Addus Healthcare Inc.....B.....650 638-7943
1730 S Amphlett Blvd San Mateo (94402) ***(P-21641)***
Addus Healthcare Inc.....D.....530 247-0858
2851 Park Marina Dr # 150 Redding (96001) ***(P-19653)***
Adee Plumbing and Heating Inc (PA).....D.....323 296-8787
5457 Crenshaw Blvd Los Angeles (90043) ***(P-2017)***
Adelphia, Fullerton *Also called Spectrum MGT Holdg Co LLC* ***(P-5746)***
Adelson Testan Brundo Novel (PA).....E.....805 604-1816
31330 Oak Crest Dr Westlake Village (91361) ***(P-22346)***
Ademco Inc.....E.....714 283-0110
1635 N Batavia St Orange (92867) ***(P-7116)***
Ademco Inc.....D.....408 986-8200
487 Mathew St Santa Clara (95050) ***(P-7117)***
Adept Consumer Testing Inc.....E.....310 279-4600
16130 Ventura Blvd # 200 Encino (91436) ***(P-25875)***
Adept Fasteners Inc (PA).....D.....661 257-6600
28709 Industry Dr Valencia (91355) ***(P-7374)***
Aderholt Specialty Company Inc.....D.....209 526-2000
1020 15th St Ste 9 Modesto (95354) ***(P-2740)***
Adesa Auction, Sacramento *Also called Adesa Corporation LLC* ***(P-6379)***
Adesa Corporation LLC.....C.....916 388-8899
8649 Kiefer Blvd Sacramento (95826) ***(P-6379)***
Adesa Corporation LLC.....E.....951 361-9400
11625 Nino Way Jurupa Valley (91752) ***(P-6380)***
Adesa Corporation LLC.....C.....619 661-5565
2175 Cactus Rd San Diego (92154) ***(P-6381)***
Adesso Inc.....C.....909 839-2929
160 Commerce Way Walnut (91789) ***(P-6786)***
Adeste Program Company.....B.....213 251-3551
1531 James M Wood Blvd Los Angeles (90015) ***(P-23669)***
Adexa Inc (PA).....E.....310 642-2100
5777 W Century Blvd # 1100 Los Angeles (90045) ***(P-15227)***
Adexis, San Francisco *Also called Computacenter Fusionstorm Inc* ***(P-27039)***
Adg Corporation.....E.....415 864-4090
1871 Market St San Francisco (94103) ***(P-11884)***
Adhei Enterprises Inc.....E.....818 788-7680
4627 Lemona Ave Sherman Oaks (91403) ***(P-13850)***
ADI, San Bernardino *Also called Aviation & Defense Inc* ***(P-4754)***
ADI Global Distribution, Orange *Also called Ademco Inc* ***(P-7116)***
ADI Global Distribution, Santa Clara *Also called Ademco Inc* ***(P-7117)***
Adicio Inc.....D.....760 602-9502
5857 Owens Ave Ste 300 Carlsbad (92008) ***(P-5298)***
Adir International LLC.....C.....213 639-7716
4444 Ayers Ave Vernon (90058) ***(P-1327)***
Adir International LLC.....D.....213 386-4412
4444-46 Ayers Ave Los Angeles (90023) ***(P-4366)***
Adivo Associates LLC.....D.....415 992-1449
44 Montgomery St Ste 4050 San Francisco (94104) ***(P-26478)***
Adj Products LLC (PA).....C.....323 582-2650
6122 S Eastern Ave Commerce (90040) ***(P-7118)***
Adkan Engineers, Riverside *Also called Adkison Engineers Inc* ***(P-24905)***
Adkison Engineers Inc.....D.....951 688-0241
6879 Airport Dr Riverside (92504) ***(P-24905)***
Adler Dev LLC.....D.....707 229-3162
2554 Front St Apt 3 San Diego (92103) ***(P-14619)***
Adlink Cable Advertising LLC.....C.....310 477-3994
11150 Santa Monica Blvd # 100 Los Angeles (90025) ***(P-13468)***
ADM Furniture Inc.....D.....310 762-2800
11680 Wright Rd Lynwood (90262) ***(P-6501)***
Admedia, Burbank *Also called Adcom Interactive Media Inc* ***(P-15935)***
Admhs, Santa Barbara *Also called County of Santa Barbara Alcoho* ***(P-22008)***
Admin, Bakersfield *Also called County of Kern* ***(P-18923)***
Administration, Fullerton *Also called St Jude Hospital* ***(P-21233)***
Administration, Los Angeles *Also called County of Los Angeles* ***(P-24260)***
Administration of Public Works, Martinez *Also called County of Contra Costa* ***(P-1688)***
Administrative Office, Redding *Also called Mercy HM Svcs A Cal Ltd Partnr* ***(P-21040)***

Employee Codes: A=Over 500 employees, B=251-500
C=101-250, D=51-100, E=50
2020 Directory of California
Wholesalers and Services Companies
© Mergent Inc. 1-800-342-5647
1161

ADMINISTRATIVE OFFICES, Upland *Also called Inland Valley Drug & Alcohol* ***(P-23276)***
Administrative Services, San Francisco *Also called City & County of San Francisco* ***(P-26182)***
Administrative Services SD..........E.......619 398-2314
3473 Kurtz St San Diego (92110) ***(P-3743)***
Administrative Svcs Coop Inc..........C.......310 715-1968
2129 W Rosecrans Ave Gardena (90249) ***(P-3744)***
Administrative Systems Inc..........D.......916 563-1121
1651 Response Rd Ste 350 Sacramento (95815) ***(P-16604)***
Adminstrtive Office of US Crts..........D.......408 535-5200
280 S 1st St San Jose (95113) ***(P-22895)***
Adminstrtive Office of US Crts..........C.......619 557-6650
101 W Broadway Ste 700 San Diego (92101) ***(P-22896)***
Adminsure Inc..........C.......909 718-1200
3380 Shelby St Ontario (91764) ***(P-10242)***
Admiral Home Health Inc..........D.......562 421-0777
4010 Watson Plaza Dr # 140 Lakewood (90712) ***(P-21642)***
Admiral Security Services Inc..........B.......888 471-1128
2151 Salvio St Ste 260 Concord (94520) ***(P-16488)***
Admiralty Partners Inc..........D.......310 471-3772
1170 Somera Rd Los Angeles (90077) ***(P-11885)***
Adobe Animal Hospital Inc..........D.......650 948-9661
4470 El Camino Real Los Altos (94022) ***(P-569)***
Adobe Inc..........A.......415 832-2000
601 And 625 Townsend St San Francisco (94103) ***(P-15228)***
Adobe Inc (PA)..........A.......408 536-6000
345 Park Ave San Jose (95110) ***(P-15229)***
Adobe Packing Company (PA)..........C.......831 753-6195
367 W Market St Salinas (93901) ***(P-462)***
Adolph Gasser Inc..........C.......415 495-3852
4340 Redwood Hwy Ste 227 San Rafael (94903) ***(P-6729)***
Adolph Gasser Photography, San Rafael *Also called Adolph Gasser Inc* ***(P-6729)***
Adopt-A-Beach, Costa Mesa *Also called Adopt-A-Highway Maintenance* ***(P-1655)***
Adopt-A-Highway Maintenance..........C.......800 200-0003
3158 Red Hill Ave Ste 200 Costa Mesa (92626) ***(P-1655)***
Adorno Construction Inc..........D.......408 369-8675
520 Westchester Dr Ste A Campbell (95008) ***(P-3109)***
ADP, Buena Park *Also called Automatic Data Processing Inc* ***(P-15721)***
ADP, Rancho Cucamonga *Also called Automatic Data Processing Inc* ***(P-15722)***
ADP, Camarillo *Also called Automatic Data Processing Inc* ***(P-15723)***
ADP, San Francisco *Also called Automatic Data Processing Inc* ***(P-15724)***
ADP, San Dimas *Also called Automatic Data Processing Inc* ***(P-15725)***
ADP, Redwood City *Also called Automatic Data Processing Inc* ***(P-15726)***
ADP, Novato *Also called Automatic Data Processing Inc* ***(P-15727)***
ADP, Irvine *Also called Automatic Data Processing Inc* ***(P-15728)***
ADP, Milpitas *Also called Automatic Data Processing Inc* ***(P-15729)***
ADP, La Palma *Also called Automatic Data Processing Inc* ***(P-15730)***
ADP, San Dimas *Also called Automatic Data Processing Inc* ***(P-15731)***
ADP, Los Angeles *Also called Automatic Data Processing Inc* ***(P-15732)***
ADP, San Diego *Also called Automatic Data Processing Inc* ***(P-15733)***
Adrianas Insurance Svcs Inc (PA)..........D.......909 291-4040
9445 Charles Smith Ave Rancho Cucamonga (91730) ***(P-10243)***
Adrienne Mattos Swim Schl Inc (PA)..........E.......866 633-4147
2203 Mariner Square Loop Alameda (94501) ***(P-18614)***
ADS, Bloomington *Also called Accurate Delivery Systems Inc* ***(P-3843)***
ADS Techonlogy, Walnut *Also called Adesso Inc* ***(P-6786)***
ADT Security Corporation..........E.......925 251-9088
2150 John Glenn Dr # 100 Concord (94520) ***(P-16489)***
Adtek Engineering Service..........D.......800 451-0782
2090 N Tustin Ave Ste 160 Santa Ana (92705) ***(P-24906)***
Adult & Childrens Dental Group, South Gate *Also called Scott Jacks DDS Inc* ***(P-19631)***
ADULT DAY CARE CENTER, San Francisco *Also called Institute On Aging* ***(P-23279)***
Adult Mddlhlth Otptient Clinic, Fairfield *Also called County of Solano* ***(P-20422)***
Adult Probation Department, San Francisco *Also called City & County of San Francisco* ***(P-23003)***
Adult Probation Department, San Jose *Also called Santa Clara County of* ***(P-23449)***
Advance Beverage Co Inc..........D.......661 833-3783
5200 District Blvd Bakersfield (93313) ***(P-8744)***
Advance Building Maintenance..........B.......310 247-0077
9601 Wilshire Blvd Gl25 Beverly Hills (90210) ***(P-13851)***
Advance Disposal Company, Hesperia *Also called Best Way Disposal Co Inc* ***(P-6160)***
Advance Health Solutions LLC..........D.......858 876-0136
7825 Fay Ave Ste 200 La Jolla (92037) ***(P-21643)***
Advance Services Inc..........A.......408 767-2797
8021 Kern Ave Gilroy (95020) ***(P-17469)***
Advance Staffing Inc..........B.......408 205-6154
2060 Walsh Ave Ste 101 Santa Clara (95050) ***(P-14464)***
Advanced Acoustics..........E.......925 299-0515
3430 Golden Gate Way Lafayette (94549) ***(P-2741)***
Advanced Bioservices LLC (PA)..........D.......818 342-0100
19255 Vanowen St Reseda (91335) ***(P-26122)***
Advanced Cable Technologies..........E.......818 262-6484
13400 Saticoy St Ste 30 North Hollywood (91605) ***(P-1828)***
Advanced Cell Diagnostics Inc..........D.......510 576-8800
7707 Gateway Blvd Ste 200 Newark (94560) ***(P-25697)***
Advanced Cleanup Tech Inc (PA)..........C.......310 763-1423
4548 Wesley Ln Bakersfield (93308) ***(P-26927)***
Advanced Clnroom McRclean Corp..........C.......714 751-1152
3250 S Susan St Ste A Santa Ana (92704) ***(P-13852)***
Advanced Commercial Corporatio..........C.......760 431-8500
5900 Pasteur Ct Ste 200 Carlsbad (92008) ***(P-11707)***
Advanced Critical Care Emerge..........D.......818 887-2262
18601 Hatteras St Apt 326 Tarzana (91356) ***(P-570)***
Advanced Dcument Solutions Inc (PA)..........E.......661 251-0337
24307 Magic Mountain Pkwy Valencia (91355) ***(P-25517)***
Advanced Digital Services Inc (PA)..........D.......323 962-8585
948 N Cahuenga Blvd Los Angeles (90038) ***(P-17569)***
Advanced Electronic Solutions, Irvine *Also called Patric Communications Inc* ***(P-2582)***
Advanced Environmental Inc..........E.......909 356-9025
13579 Whittram Ave Fontana (92335) ***(P-3846)***
Advanced Fabrication Tech, Hayward *Also called R2g Enterprises Inc* ***(P-3093)***
Advanced Fresh Concepts Corp (PA)..........D.......310 604-3630
19205 S Laurel Park Rd Rancho Dominguez (90220) ***(P-11823)***
Advanced HM Hlth & Hospice Inc..........D.......916 978-0744
4354 Auburn Blvd Sacramento (95841) ***(P-19601)***
Advanced Home Health Inc..........D.......916 978-0744
4354 Auburn Blvd Sacramento (95841) ***(P-21644)***
Advanced Home House, Sacramento *Also called Advanced HM Hlth & Hospice Inc* ***(P-19601)***
Advanced Image Direct, Fullerton *Also called Real Estate Image Inc* ***(P-13738)***
Advanced Industrial Cmpt Inc (PA)..........D.......909 895-8989
21808 Garcia Ln City of Industry (91789) ***(P-6787)***
Advanced Industrial Services, Bakersfield *Also called CL Knox Inc* ***(P-1016)***
Advanced Industrial Svcs Cal, Paramount *Also called Advanced Industrial Svcs Inc* ***(P-2329)***
Advanced Industrial Svcs Inc..........D.......562 940-8305
7831 Alondra Blvd Paramount (90723) ***(P-2329)***
Advanced Ipm..........E.......916 759-1570
205 Kenroy Ln Roseville (95678) ***(P-962)***
Advanced Logistics MGT Inc..........E.......310 638-0715
19067 S Reyes Ave Compton (90221) ***(P-3962)***
Advanced Medical Imaging, Fresno *Also called Community Medical Centers* ***(P-20802)***
Advanced Medical MGT Inc..........D.......562 766-2000
5000 Arprt Plz Dr Ste 150 Long Beach (90815) ***(P-26123)***
Advanced Medical Placement..........C.......818 996-9812
18425 Burbank Blvd # 508 Tarzana (91356) ***(P-24123)***
Advanced Medical Reviews LLC..........D.......310 575-0900
600 Crprate Pinte Ste 300 Culver City (90230) ***(P-14465)***
Advanced Mnlythic Ceramics Inc..........C.......818 364-9800
15191 Bledsoe St Sylmar (91342) ***(P-7224)***
Advanced Mp Technology LLC (HQ)..........C.......800 492-3113
1010 Calle Sombra San Clemente (92673) ***(P-7225)***
Advanced Office, Irvine *Also called Integrus LLC* ***(P-6751)***
Advanced Rehabilitation Tech..........D.......858 621-5959
7950 Dunbrook Rd San Diego (92126) ***(P-6936)***
Advanced Resources, Fontana *Also called Advanced Environmental Inc* ***(P-3846)***
Advanced Rsrvation Systems Inc..........D.......619 501-7000
2445 Truxtun Rd Ste 205 San Diego (92106) ***(P-15937)***
Advanced Software Design Inc..........D.......925 975-0691
1371 Oakland Blvd Ste 100 Walnut Creek (94596) ***(P-14620)***
Advanced Software Dynamics, Walnut Creek *Also called Advanced Software Design Inc* ***(P-14620)***
Advanced Sterlization..........D.......909 350-6987
13135 Napa St Fontana (92335) ***(P-4367)***
Advanced Test Eqp Rentals, San Diego *Also called Advanced Test Equipment Corp* ***(P-14121)***
Advanced Test Equipment Corp..........D.......858 558-6500
10401 Roselle St San Diego (92121) ***(P-14121)***
Advanced Trans Grp, Compton *Also called Advanced Logistics MGT Inc* ***(P-3962)***
Advanced Veterinary Care Ctr..........D.......310 542-8018
15926 Hawthorne Blvd Lawndale (90260) ***(P-571)***
Advantage Framing Solutions..........E.......530 742-7660
1965 N Beale Rd Marysville (95901) ***(P-1398)***
Advantage Ground Trnsp, Costa Mesa *Also called Advantage Ground Trnsp Corp* ***(P-3617)***
Advantage Ground Trnsp Corp..........D.......714 557-2465
2960 Airway Ave Ste B102 Costa Mesa (92626) ***(P-3617)***
Advantage Mailing LLC (PA)..........C.......714 538-3881
1600 N Kraemer Blvd Anaheim (92806) ***(P-13717)***
Advantage Mailing Service, Anaheim *Also called Advantage Mailing LLC* ***(P-13717)***
Advantage Media Services Inc..........C.......661 705-7588
28220 Industry Dr Valencia (91355) ***(P-4368)***
Advantage Plumbing Group Inc..........D.......714 898-6020
3331 Orangewood Ave Los Alamitos (90720) ***(P-2018)***
Advantage Pntg Solutions Inc..........D.......951 739-9204
14734 Yorba Ct Chino (91710) ***(P-2330)***
Advantage Produce Inc..........E.......213 627-2777
1511 Bay St Los Angeles (90021) ***(P-8428)***
Advantage Sales & Marketing..........C.......925 463-5600
5064 Franklin Dr Pleasanton (94588) ***(P-8147)***
Advantage Sales & Mktg Inc..........C.......310 321-6869
200 N Pacific Coast Hwy # 1000 El Segundo (90245) ***(P-8148)***
Advantage Sales & Mktg Inc (PA)..........C.......949 797-2900
18100 Von Karman Ave # 900 Irvine (92612) ***(P-8149)***
Advantage Sales & Mktg LLC..........D.......925 463-5600
6700 Koll Center Pkwy # 300 Pleasanton (94566) ***(P-8150)***
Advantage Sales & Mktg LLC (HQ)..........C.......949 797-2900
18100 Von Karman Ave # 900 Irvine (92612) ***(P-26479)***
Advantage Solutions, Irvine *Also called Advantage Sales & Mktg Inc* ***(P-8149)***
Advantage Solutions, Irvine *Also called Advantage Sales & Mktg LLC* ***(P-26479)***
Advantage Waypoint LLC..........D.......717 424-4973
2642 Michelle Dr Tustin (92780) ***(P-8151)***
Advantage Workforce Svcs LLC..........C.......415 212-6464
39 Stillman St San Francisco (94107) ***(P-14466)***
Advantage-Crown Sls & Mktg LLC (HQ)..........A.......714 780-3000
1400 S Douglass Rd # 200 Anaheim (92806) ***(P-8152)***
Advantech Corporation (HQ)..........C.......408 519-3800
380 Fairview Way Milpitas (95035) ***(P-6788)***
Advantedge Technology Inc..........D.......805 488-0405
271 Market St Ste 15 Port Hueneme (93041) ***(P-24907)***
Advantis Global Inc (PA)..........C.......415 850-1500
20 Sunnyside Ave Ste E Mill Valley (94941) ***(P-15938)***
Advent Group Ministries Inc..........D.......408 281-0708
90 Great Oaks Blvd # 108 San Jose (95119) ***(P-23808)***
Advent Resources Inc..........D.......310 241-1500
235 W 7th St San Pedro (90731) ***(P-15230)***

Mergent e-mail: customerrelations@mergent.com
1162
2020 Directory of California
Wholesalers and Services Companies
(P-0000) Products & Services Section entry number
(PA)=Parent Co (HQ)=Headquarters (DH)=Div Headquarters

ALPHABETIC SECTION Aerospace & Marine Intl

Advent Securities Investments (PA) ....E....562 920-5467
9631 Alondra Blvd Ste 202 Bellflower (90706) **(P-9649)**
Advent Software Inc (HQ) ....C....415 543-7696
600 Townsend St Fl 5 San Francisco (94103) **(P-14621)**
ADVENTIST HEALTH, Hanford *Also called Hanford Community Hospital* **(P-20898)**
Adventist Health Clearlake (HQ) ....B....707 994-6486
15630 18th Ave Clearlake (95422) **(P-20729)**
Adventist Health Cmnty. Care, Dinuba *Also called Adventist Health System* **(P-18789)**
Adventist Health Homecare Svcs, Glendale *Also called Glendale Adventist Medical Ctr* **(P-21747)**
Adventist Health Lodi Memorial, Lodi *Also called Lodi Memorial Hosp Assn Inc* **(P-21008)**
Adventist Health Selma ....B....559 891-1000
1141 Rose Ave Selma (93662) **(P-20730)**
Adventist Health Sonora (HQ) ....A....209 532-5000
1000 Greenley Rd Sonora (95370) **(P-20731)**
Adventist Health System ....A....559 595-9890
250 W El Monte Way Dinuba (93618) **(P-18789)**
Adventist Health System/West ....C....707 995-4888
14880 Olympic Dr Clearlake (95422) **(P-18790)**
Adventist Health System/West ....E....818 409-8540
381 Merrill Ave Glendale (91206) **(P-20732)**
Adventist Health System/West ....D....530 872-3378
6626 Clark Rd Ste P Paradise (95969) **(P-20733)**
Adventist Health System/West ....E....707 995-4500
15230 Lakeshore Dr Clearlake (95422) **(P-20734)**
Adventist Health System/West ....B....707 994-6486
18th Ave Hwy 53 Clearlake (95422) **(P-18791)**
Adventist Health Tulare, Tulare *Also called Tulare Regional Medical Center* **(P-21316)**
Adventist Hlth Med Foundation, Glendale *Also called Adventist Health System/West* **(P-20732)**
Adventist Media Center Inc (PA) ....D....805 955-7777
11291 Pierce St Riverside (92505) **(P-17883)**
Adventres Rlling Cross-Country ....C....415 332-5075
242 Redwd Hwy Frntge 1 Mill Valley (94941) **(P-13140)**
Adventure City Inc ....D....714 821-3311
1238 S Beach Blvd Anaheim (92804) **(P-18615)**
Adventure Connection Inc ....D....530 626-7385
986 Lotus Rd Lotus (95651) **(P-18616)**
Adventureplex ....E....310 546-7708
1701 Marine Ave Manhattan Beach (90266) **(P-18118)**
Adventures Cross-Country, Mill Valley *Also called Adventres Rlling Cross-Country* **(P-13140)**
Adventures In Hospitality Inc ....D....760 356-2806
633 W Canal St Calexico (92231) **(P-18348)**
Advertising, Santa Ana *Also called Dgwb Ventures LLC* **(P-13496)**
Advertising Consultants Inc (PA) ....C....310 233-2750
330 Golden Shore Ste 410 Long Beach (90802) **(P-13642)**
Advertising Department, Long Beach *Also called Comcast Corporation* **(P-5691)**
Advintist Hlth Clearlake Hosp ....B....707 994-6486
18th Ave & Hwy 53 Clearlake (95422) **(P-20735)**
Advisorsquare, Culver City *Also called Liveoffice LLC* **(P-15390)**
Advocacy For Respect and Ch (PA) ....D....562 597-7716
4519 E Stearns St Long Beach (90815) **(P-23558)**
Ae & Associates LLC ....D....951 278-3477
506 Queensland Cir Corona (92879) **(P-26969)**
Aecom ....C....661 266-0802
5001 E Commercecenter Dr # 100 Bakersfield (93309) **(P-25408)**
Aecom (PA) ....C....213 593-8000
1999 Avenue Of The Stars # 2600 Los Angeles (90067) **(P-24908)**
Aecom C&E Inc ....D....805 388-3775
1220 Avenida Acaso Camarillo (93012) **(P-24909)**
Aecom C&E Inc ....C....213 593-8100
1999 Avenue Of The Stars Los Angeles (90067) **(P-26480)**
Aecom Consulting, Los Angeles *Also called Aecom C&E Inc* **(P-26480)**
Aecom Design, Los Angeles *Also called Aecom Services Inc* **(P-25409)**
Aecom E&C Holdings Inc (HQ) ....D....213 593-8000
1999 Avenue Of The Stars Los Angeles (90067) **(P-24910)**
Aecom Energy & Cnstr Inc (HQ) ....C....213 593-8100
1999 Avenue Of The Stars Los Angeles (90067) **(P-1812)**
Aecom Energy & Cnstr Inc ....B....858 481-9502
2850 Carmel Valley Rd Del Mar (92014) **(P-1656)**
Aecom Environment, Camarillo *Also called Aecom C&E Inc* **(P-24909)**
Aecom Global II LLC ....D....415 774-2700
1320 S Simpson Cir Anaheim (92806) **(P-24911)**
Aecom Global II LLC ....D....805 692-0600
130 Robin Hill Rd Ste 100 Goleta (93117) **(P-24912)**
Aecom Global II LLC (HQ) ....D....213 593-8100
1999 Avenue Of The Stars Los Angeles (90067) **(P-24913)**
Aecom Global II LLC ....B....916 679-2000
2870 Gateway Oaks Dr # 150 Sacramento (95833) **(P-24914)**
Aecom Global II LLC ....C....916 679-8700
2870 Gateway Oaks Dr # 300 Sacramento (95833) **(P-26970)**
Aecom Global II LLC ....D....415 774-2700
600 Montgomery St San Francisco (94111) **(P-24915)**
Aecom Global II LLC ....D....530 827-2406
74 C St Herlong (96113) **(P-24916)**
Aecom Global II LLC ....C....559 347-5669
5168 E Dakota Ave Fresno (93727) **(P-24917)**
Aecom Global II LLC ....C....213 996-2200
915 Wilshire Blvd Ste 800 Los Angeles (90017) **(P-26971)**
Aecom Global II LLC ....D....310 343-6977
310 Golden Shore Ste 100 Long Beach (90802) **(P-26972)**
Aecom Services Inc (HQ) ....C....213 593-8000
300 S Grand Ave Fl 2 Los Angeles (90071) **(P-25409)**
Aecom Technical Services Inc (HQ) ....D....213 593-8000
300 S Grand Ave Ste 1100 Los Angeles (90071) **(P-26973)**
Aecom Technical Services Inc ....C....510 834-4304
1333 Broadway Ste 800 Oakland (94612) **(P-24918)**
Aecom Technical Services Inc ....D....909 554-5000
901 Via Piemonte Ste 400 Ontario (91764) **(P-24919)**
Aecom Technical Services Inc ....D....619 610-7600
401 W A St Ste 1200 San Diego (92101) **(P-24920)**
Aecom Technology Corporation ....D....916 414-5800
2020 L St Ste 400 Sacramento (95811) **(P-24921)**
Aecom Usa Inc ....C....213 330-7200
515 S Figueroa St Ste 400 Los Angeles (90071) **(P-26974)**
Aecom Usa Inc ....C....408 392-0670
100 W San Fernando St San Jose (95113) **(P-26975)**
Aecom Usa Inc ....B....213 593-8000
300 S Grand Ave Ste 1100 Los Angeles (90071) **(P-26976)**
Aecom Usa Inc ....D....714 567-2501
999 W Town And Country Rd Orange (92868) **(P-26977)**
Aecom-TSE Joint Venture ....D....510 285-6639
300 Lakeside Dr Ste 400 Oakland (94612) **(P-24922)**
AEG Global Partnerships LLC ....E....213 763-7700
1100 S Flower St Ste 3200 Los Angeles (90015) **(P-26481)**
AEG Management Lacc LLC ....C....213 741-1151
1201 S Figueroa St Los Angeles (90015) **(P-26124)**
AEG Presents LLC (HQ) ....C....323 930-5700
425 W 11th St Los Angeles (90015) **(P-17884)**
AEG Worldwide, Los Angeles *Also called Anschutz Entrmt Group Inc* **(P-17959)**
Aegis Ambulance Service Inc (PA) ....D....626 685-9410
1151 S Boyle Ave Los Angeles (90023) **(P-3618)**
Aegis Assisted Living, Aptos *Also called Aegis Senior Communities LLC* **(P-21647)**
Aegis Assisted Living, Carmichael *Also called Aegis Senior Communities LLC* **(P-23813)**
Aegis Asssted Living Prpts LLC ....E....510 739-1515
3850 Walnut Ave 228 Fremont (94538) **(P-23809)**
Aegis Asssted Living Prpts LLC ....D....760 806-3600
1440 S Melrose Dr Oceanside (92056) **(P-23810)**
Aegis At Shadowridge, Oceanside *Also called Aegis Asssted Living Prpts LLC* **(P-23810)**
Aegis Enterprises Inc ....D....925 417-5550
500 Boulder Ct Ste A Pleasanton (94566) **(P-2019)**
Aegis Fire Systems, Pleasanton *Also called Aegis Enterprises Inc* **(P-2019)**
Aegis Gardens, Fremont *Also called Aegis Senior Communities LLC* **(P-21645)**
Aegis Living, Pleasant Hill *Also called Aegis Senior Communities LLC* **(P-21646)**
AEgis of Carmichael ....D....916 972-1313
4050 Walnut Ave Carmichael (95608) **(P-23811)**
Aegis of Fremont, Fremont *Also called Aegis Asssted Living Prpts LLC* **(P-23809)**
Aegis of Granada Hills, Granada Hills *Also called Aegis Senior Communities LLC* **(P-21648)**
Aegis of Laguna Niguel, Laguna Niguel *Also called Aegis Senior Communities LLC* **(P-23812)**
Aegis of San Francisco, South San Francisco *Also called Ageis Living* **(P-23814)**
Aegis Senior Communities LLC ....E....510 739-0909
36281 Fremont Blvd Fremont (94536) **(P-21645)**
Aegis Senior Communities LLC ....D....925 588-7030
1660 Oak Park Blvd Pleasant Hill (94523) **(P-21646)**
Aegis Senior Communities LLC ....E....831 684-2700
125 Heather Ter Aptos (95003) **(P-21647)**
Aegis Senior Communities LLC ....E....949 496-8080
32170 Niguel Rd Laguna Niguel (92677) **(P-23812)**
Aegis Senior Communities LLC ....B....916 972-1313
4050 Walnut Ave Carmichael (95608) **(P-23813)**
Aegis Senior Communities LLC ....D....818 363-3373
10801 Lindley Ave Granada Hills (91344) **(P-21648)**
Aegis Software Inc ....E....858 551-1652
5580 La Jolla Blvd # 436 La Jolla (92037) **(P-13643)**
Aegis Treatment Centers LLC (PA) ....D....818 206-0360
7246 Remmet Ave Canoga Park (91303) **(P-21944)**
Aei Consultants, Irvine *Also called All Environmental Inc* **(P-26980)**
Aei Consultants, Hermosa Beach *Also called All Environmental Inc* **(P-26981)**
Aem Corporation, Camarillo *Also called Applied Engineering MGT Corp* **(P-14645)**
AEP Span Inc ....D....916 372-0933
2110 Enterprise Blvd West Sacramento (95691) **(P-3023)**
Aer Electronics Inc (PA) ....D....510 300-0500
42744 Boscell Rd Fremont (94538) **(P-6143)**
Aer Technologies Inc ....B....714 871-7357
650 Columbia St Brea (92821) **(P-17479)**
Aera Energy LLC (HQ) ....A....661 665-5000
10000 Ming Ave Bakersfield (93311) **(P-993)**
Aera Energy LLC ....D....661 665-3200
29235 Highway 33 Maricopa (93252) **(P-994)**
Aera Energy South Midway, Maricopa *Also called Aera Energy LLC* **(P-994)**
Aera Technology Inc (PA) ....D....408 524-2222
707 California St Mountain View (94041) **(P-14622)**
Aerelectronics, Fremont *Also called Aer Electronics Inc* **(P-6143)**
Aerial Applicators, Biggs *Also called Chuck Jones Flying Service* **(P-435)**
Aeris Communications Inc (PA) ....D....408 557-1900
2099 Gateway Pl Ste 600 San Jose (95110) **(P-5299)**
Aero Port Services Inc (PA) ....D....310 623-8230
216 W Florence Ave Inglewood (90301) **(P-16490)**
Aero Technologies Inc ....E....415 314-7479
555 Mission St San Francisco (94105) **(P-3520)**
Aero-Engines Inc ....D....323 663-3961
2641 Roseview Ave Los Angeles (90065) **(P-17480)**
Aeroflot Rssina Internatl Arln, Beverly Hills *Also called Aeroflot Russian Airlines* **(P-4641)**
Aeroflot Russian Airlines ....D....323 272-4861
8383 Wilshire Blvd # 648 Beverly Hills (90211) **(P-4641)**
Aerohive Networks Inc (HQ) ....C....408 510-6100
1011 Mccarthy Blvd Milpitas (95035) **(P-15554)**
Aeromedevac Inc ....D....619 284-7910
1860 Joe Crosson Dr Ste I El Cajon (92020) **(P-26482)**
Aeronautical Radio Inc ....D....925 294-8400
6011 Industrial Way Livermore (94551) **(P-5150)**
Aerospace & Marine Intl ....E....408 360-0440
6910 Santa Teresa Blvd San Jose (95119) **(P-27264)**

ALPHABETIC

Employee Codes: A=Over 500 employees, B=251-500
C=101-250, D=51-100, E=50
2020 Directory of California
Wholesalers and Services Companies
© Mergent Inc. 1-800-342-5647
1163

Aerospace Corporation (PA)...A...310 336-5000
2310 E El Segundo Blvd El Segundo (90245) ***(P-25956)***
Aerospace Federally Funded RES, El Segundo *Also called Air Force US Dept of* ***(P-25958)***
Aerospace Material Division, Bay Point *Also called Henkel US Operations Corp* ***(P-25124)***
Aerotransporte De Carge Union...B...310 649-0069
5625 W Imperial Hwy Los Angeles (90045) ***(P-4642)***
Aerounion, Los Angeles *Also called Aerotransporte De Carge Union* ***(P-4642)***
Aerovironment Inc...D...626 357-9983
900 Innovators Way Simi Valley (93065) ***(P-24923)***
Aerovironment Inc...C...805 581-2187
85 Moreland Rd Simi Valley (93065) ***(P-24319)***
AES, Chico *Also called Alternative Energy Systems Inc* ***(P-2036)***
AES Alamitos LLC...D...562 493-7891
690 N Studebaker Rd Long Beach (90803) ***(P-5810)***
AES Huntington Beach LLC...E...714 374-1476
21730 Newland St Huntington Beach (92646) ***(P-5811)***
AES Networks, San Jose *Also called Vormetric Inc* ***(P-16155)***
AES Southland LLC...D...562 430-8685
690 N Studebaker Rd Long Beach (90803) ***(P-5812)***
Aesthetic Maintenance Corp...E...213 353-1525
1625 Palo Alto St Ste 301 Los Angeles (90026) ***(P-13853)***
Aestiva Software Inc...E...310 697-0338
3551 Voyager St Ste 201 Torrance (90503) ***(P-14623)***
Aetna Health California Inc...D...415 645-8200
1 Embarcadero Ctr 300 San Francisco (94111) ***(P-9916)***
Aetna Health California Inc (HQ)...C...925 543-9223
515 S Flower St Los Angeles (90071) ***(P-9917)***
Aevex Flight Operations, Solana Beach *Also called Merlin Global Services LLC* ***(P-4746)***
Aewestjv...E...619 233-1023
363 5th Ave Ste 202 San Diego (92101) ***(P-25410)***
AF Software Holdings Inc...B...888 317-3395
1825 S Grant St Ste 900 San Mateo (94402) ***(P-11642)***
AF Software Parent Inc...B...888 317-3395
1825 S Grant St Ste 900 San Mateo (94402) ***(P-11643)***
AFA Constrctn Grp/Cal Inc JV...D...707 446-7996
2040 Peabody Rd Ste 400 Vacaville (95687) ***(P-1399)***
Afc Distribution Corp...E...310 604-3630
19205 S Laurel Park Rd Rancho Dominguez (90220) ***(P-8153)***
Afex, Woodland Hills *Also called Associated Foreign Exch Inc* ***(P-9421)***
Affd, Anaheim *Also called Anaheim First Fmly Dntl Group* ***(P-26134)***
Affiliated Communications Inc...E...805 650-4949
3601 Calle Tecate Ste 200 Camarillo (93012) ***(P-16605)***
Affiliated Temporary Help...B...323 771-1383
4359 Florence Ave Bell (90201) ***(P-14467)***
Affinity Auto Programs Inc...D...858 643-9324
10251 Vista Cerento Pkwy San Diego (92121) ***(P-16606)***
Affinity Development Group Inc...C...858 643-9324
10251 Vista Sorrento Pkwy # 300 San Diego (92121) ***(P-24782)***
Affinity Group, Ventura *Also called Agi Holding Corp* ***(P-18349)***
Affinity Health Care, Paramount *Also called Paramunt Madows Nursing Ctr LP* ***(P-26346)***
Affordable Engrg Svcs Inc...D...973 890-8915
1455 Frazee Rd Ste 860 San Diego (92108) ***(P-24924)***
Affordable Hsing Key Partners...D...805 736-3423
815 W Ocean Ave Lompoc (93436) ***(P-10893)***
Affordable Installations, Nevada City *Also called Patrick Dean Bryan* ***(P-3450)***
Affymax Research Institute...E...650 812-8700
4001 Miranda Ave Palo Alto (94304) ***(P-25957)***
AFL, Rancho Cucamonga *Also called Ccna Vons Athletes For Life* ***(P-24817)***
AFL-CIO #1245, Vacaville *Also called International Brthrhd of Elctr* ***(P-24444)***
Afm & Sag-Aftra Intellectual...D...818 255-7980
4705 Laurel Canyon Blvd # 400 Valley Village (91607) ***(P-16607)***
African American Unity Center...D...323 789-7300
944 W 53rd St Los Angeles (90037) ***(P-22897)***
After-Party2 Inc...D...310 535-3660
2310 E Imperial Hwy El Segundo (90245) ***(P-14122)***
Aftershock La Studios Inc...D...650 450-9660
3633 Lenawee Ave Ste 100 Los Angeles (90016) ***(P-14624)***
AG Adriano Goldschmied Inc (PA)...D...323 357-1111
2741 Seminole Ave South Gate (90280) ***(P-8017)***
AG Air Conditioning & Htg Inc...E...818 988-5388
14620 Keswick St Van Nuys (91405) ***(P-2020)***
AG Facilities Operations LLC...A...323 651-1808
6380 Wilshire Blvd # 800 Los Angeles (90048) ***(P-20478)***
AG Heating and AC, Van Nuys *Also called AG Air Conditioning & Htg Inc* ***(P-2020)***
AG Jeans, South Gate *Also called AG Adriano Goldschmied Inc* ***(P-8017)***
AG Redlands LLC...C...909 793-2678
700 E Highland Ave Redlands (92374) ***(P-20479)***
AG Rx (PA)...D...805 487-0696
751 S Rose Ave Oxnard (93030) ***(P-8833)***
Ag-Wise Enterprises Inc (PA)...C...661 325-1567
5100 California Ave # 209 Bakersfield (93309) ***(P-651)***
Agama Solutions Inc...C...510 796-9300
39159 Paseo Padre Pkwy # 216 Fremont (94538) ***(P-26483)***
Agamerica Fcb (PA)...D...651 282-8800
3636 American River Dr # 100 Sacramento (95864) ***(P-9443)***
Agape In Home Care Inc...E...661 835-0364
4800 District Blvd Ste A Bakersfield (93313) ***(P-21649)***
Age Advantage HM Care Svcs...D...619 449-5900
5480 Baltimore Dr Ste 214 La Mesa (91942) ***(P-21650)***
Age Concerns Inc...B...619 544-1622
2650 Camino Del Rio N # 203 San Diego (92108) ***(P-22898)***
Ageis Living...E...650 952-6100
2280 Gellert Blvd South San Francisco (94080) ***(P-23814)***
Agemark Corporation (PA)...D...925 257-4671
25 Avenida De Orinda Orinda (94563) ***(P-19710)***
Agency For Performing Arts Inc (PA)...D...310 557-9049
405 S Beverly Dr Ste 500 Beverly Hills (90212) ***(P-17885)***
Agencycom LLC...B...415 817-3800
5353 Grosvenor Blvd Los Angeles (90066) ***(P-15231)***
Agendia Inc...C...949 540-6300
22 Morgan Irvine (92618) ***(P-21945)***
Aggregate West Coast, Thermal *Also called West Coast Aggregate Supply* ***(P-1059)***
Agi Holding Corp (PA)...D...805 667-4100
2575 Vista Del Mar Dr Ventura (93001) ***(P-18349)***
Agile Sourcing Partners Inc...C...951 279-4154
2385 Railroad St Corona (92880) ***(P-6005)***
Agilent Technologies Inc...C...805 566-6655
6392 Via Real Carpinteria (93013) ***(P-7914)***
Agility Holdings Inc (HQ)...D...714 617-6300
310 Commerce Ste 250 Irvine (92602) ***(P-4879)***
Agility Logistics, Irvine *Also called Agility Holdings Inc* ***(P-4879)***
Agility Logistics Corp...D...310 507-6700
21906 Arnold Center Rd Carson (90810) ***(P-4880)***
Agilon Health Inc...D...562 256-3800
1 World Trade Ctr Long Beach (90831) ***(P-9918)***
Agilysys Inc...C...805 692-6339
5383 Hollister Ave # 120 Santa Barbara (93111) ***(P-6789)***
Agilysys Inc...E...702 759-4879
1900 Powell St Ste 230 Emeryville (94608) ***(P-6790)***
Aging & Adult Services, Bakersfield *Also called County of Kern* ***(P-23076)***
Aging & Adult Services, Taft *Also called County of Kern* ***(P-23078)***
Aging & Adult Services, Bakersfield *Also called County of Kern* ***(P-23080)***
Aging & Adult Services, Victorville *Also called County of San Bernardino* ***(P-23141)***
Agire Mortgage Corporation...E...714 564-5821
2125 E Katella Ave # 350 Anaheim (92806) ***(P-9514)***
Agostini and Associates Inc...E...925 691-7300
1470 Civic Ct Ste 1760 Concord (94520) ***(P-14468)***
Agostini Health Care Staffing, Concord *Also called Agostini and Associates Inc* ***(P-14468)***
Agoura Hills Renaissance Hotel, Agoura Hills *Also called Davidson Hotel Partners Lp* ***(P-12201)***
AGR Group Inc...A...714 245-7151
13902 Harbor Blvd Ste 2c Garden Grove (92843) ***(P-26484)***
Agreeya Solutions Inc (PA)...D...916 294-0075
605 Coolidge Dr Ste 200 Folsom (95630) ***(P-26485)***
Agreserves Inc...D...530 343-5365
6100 Wilson Landing Rd Chico (95973) ***(P-170)***
Agri Valley Services...D...559 253-0104
1532 N West Ave Fresno (93728) ***(P-25533)***
Agri-Feed Industries, Imperial *Also called Western Meat Processors Inc* ***(P-381)***
Agri-Mix Transport Inc...C...661 833-6280
1400 S Union Ave Ste 110 Bakersfield (93307) ***(P-3847)***
Agri-World Cooperative...E...559 673-1306
31545 Donald Ave Madera (93636) ***(P-652)***
Agrian Inc (PA)...D...559 437-5700
352 W Spruce Ave Clovis (93611) ***(P-15939)***
Agrichem, Fowler *Also called Kandarian Agri Enterprises* ***(P-138)***
Agriculture and Priority Pollu (PA)...E...559 275-2175
908 N Temperance Ave Clovis (93611) ***(P-26052)***
Agriholding Inc (PA)...D...559 738-5880
3330 S Fairway St Visalia (93277) ***(P-4881)***
Agriland Holding Inc...D...559 665-2100
23400 Road 24 Chowchilla (93610) ***(P-218)***
Agritec International Ltd...E...626 812-7200
5820 Martin Rd Irwindale (91706) ***(P-7796)***
Agro-Jal Farms Inc...D...805 928-2682
257 Kathleen Ct Santa Maria (93458) ***(P-463)***
Agsource Services LLC...E...559 735-9700
222 N Garden St Ste 400 Visalia (93291) ***(P-610)***
Agua Caliente Casino & Resort, Rancho Mirage *Also called Agua Clnte Band Chilla Indians* ***(P-11995)***
Agua Caliente Development Auth...D...760 699-6800
5401 Dinah Shore Dr Palm Springs (92264) ***(P-10894)***
Agua Clnte Band Chilla Indians...A...760 321-2000
32250 Bob Hope Dr Rancho Mirage (92270) ***(P-11995)***
Agua Clnte Band Chilla Indians (PA)...C...760 699-6800
5401 Dinah Shore Dr Palm Springs (92264) ***(P-24783)***
Agua Clnte Band Chilla Indians...A...800 854-1279
401 E Amado Rd Palm Springs (92262) ***(P-11996)***
Aguatierra Associates Inc (PA)...D...510 450-6000
2000 Powell St Ste 555 Emeryville (94608) ***(P-26928)***
Aha Shoes Inc...D...805 434-9891
72 S Main St Ste A Templeton (93465) ***(P-8119)***
Ahg Inc...B...703 596-0111
340 S Lemon Ave 6633 Walnut (91789) ***(P-13382)***
Ahm Gemch Inc...C...626 579-7777
1701 Santa Anita Ave El Monte (91733) ***(P-20736)***
Ahmc, Anaheim *Also called Anaheim Regional Medical Ctr* ***(P-18813)***
Ahmc Garfield Medical Ctr LP...C...626 573-2222
525 N Garfield Ave Monterey Park (91754) ***(P-19711)***
Ahmc Healthcare Inc...A...626 248-3452
506 W Valley Blvd Ste 300 San Gabriel (91776) ***(P-22169)***
Ahmc Healthcare Inc...A...626 579-7777
1701 Santa Anita Ave South El Monte (91733) ***(P-20737)***
Ahmc Whittier Hosp Med Ctr LP...A...562 945-3561
9080 Colima Rd Whittier (90605) ***(P-20738)***
Ahr Professionals, Lake Forest *Also called Validus Group Inc* ***(P-14448)***
Ahrens Landscape & Maintenance, Sacramento *Also called Jma Investments Ltd* ***(P-839)***
Ahtna Government Services Corp...D...916 372-2000
3100 Beacon Blvd West Sacramento (95691) ***(P-1400)***
Ahtna-CDM JV...E...714 824-3470
3200 El Camino Real Irvine (92602) ***(P-1328)***
Ahtna-CDM Smith JV...D...714 824-3471
3200 El Camino Real Irvine (92602) ***(P-26978)***
AIA Holdings Inc (PA)...D...818 222-4999
26560 Agoura Rd Ste 100 Calabasas (91302) ***(P-10157)***

Aic Inc USA, City of Industry *Also called Advanced Industrial Cmpt Inc* ***(P-6787)***
Aicent Inc......C......408 324-1316
900 E Hamilton Ave # 600 Campbell (95008) ***(P-15940)***
Aichinger International Inc......D......310 375-1533
5423 Littlebow Rd Pls Vrds Pnsl (90275) ***(P-6382)***
Aico, Pico Rivera *Also called Amini Innovation Corp* ***(P-6503)***
AID FOR AIDS, Los Angeles *Also called Alliance For Housing & Healing* ***(P-20410)***
AIDS PROJECT LA, Los Angeles *Also called Apla Health & Wellness* ***(P-18821)***
Aids Project La, Los Angeles *Also called Aids Project Los Angeles* ***(P-22899)***
Aids Project Los Angeles (PA)......D......213 201-1600
611 S Kingsley Dr Los Angeles (90005) ***(P-22899)***
Aids Svcs Fndation Orange Cnty......D......949 809-5700
17982 Sky Park Cir Ste J Irvine (92614) ***(P-22900)***
AIG, San Francisco *Also called American Gen Lf Insur Co Del* ***(P-9860)***
AIG Direct Insurance Svcs Inc......B......858 309-3000
9640 Gran Rdge Dr Ste 200 San Diego (92123) ***(P-10244)***
AIG Private Client Group, San Diego *Also called American Intl Group Inc* ***(P-10250)***
Aimloan.com, A Direct Lender, San Diego *Also called American Internet Mortgage Inc* ***(P-9519)***
Air Control Systems Inc......E......909 786-4230
1940 S Grove Ave Ontario (91761) ***(P-2021)***
Air Express Intl USA Inc......E......858 578-9602
6800 Gateway Park Dr San Diego (92154) ***(P-4882)***
Air Force US Dept of......D......805 606-5355
1031 California Blvd # 11777 Lompoc (93437) ***(P-26125)***
Air Force US Dept of......B......310 336-5000
2310 E El Segundo Blvd El Segundo (90245) ***(P-25958)***
Air Force US Dept of......B......310 393-0411
1776 Main St Santa Monica (90401) ***(P-25959)***
Air Force Village West Inc......B......951 697-2000
17050 Arnold Dr Riverside (92518) ***(P-19712)***
Air France (air Nationale)......D......415 877-0179
San Francisco Intl A San Francisco (94125) ***(P-4643)***
Air Lease Corporation (PA)......D......310 553-0555
2000 Avenue Of The Stars 1000n Los Angeles (90067) ***(P-14123)***
Air Mechanical Inc......D......714 995-3947
608 S Vicki Ln Anaheim (92804) ***(P-2022)***
Air New Zealand Limited......D......310 648-7000
222 N Pacific Coast Hwy # 900 El Segundo (90245) ***(P-4644)***
Air Polution Control District, Fresno *Also called San Joaquin Valley A P C D* ***(P-27203)***
Air Rutter International LLC......E......855 359-2576
3501 N Lakewood Blvd Long Beach (90808) ***(P-4737)***
Air Systems Inc......A......408 280-1666
940 Remillard Ct Frnt San Jose (95122) ***(P-2023)***
Air Systems Service & Cnstr......C......916 368-0336
10381 Old Placerville Rd # 100 Sacramento (95827) ***(P-2024)***
Air Tiger Express (usa) Inc......E......626 965-8647
17000 Gale Ave City of Industry (91745) ***(P-4883)***
Air Treatment Corporation (PA)......D......909 869-7975
640 N Puente St Brea (92821) ***(P-7443)***
Air-Sea Forwarders Inc (PA)......D......310 216-1616
9009 S La Cienega Blvd Inglewood (90301) ***(P-4884)***
Air-TEC, Carson *Also called Clay Dunn Enterprises Inc* ***(P-2097)***
Airbnb Inc (PA)......A......415 800-5959
888 Brannan St San Francisco (94103) ***(P-13167)***
Airco Mechanical Inc (PA)......C......916 381-4523
8210 Demetre Ave Sacramento (95828) ***(P-2025)***
Airco Mechanical Inc......C......415 982-4726
401 13th St San Francisco (94130) ***(P-2026)***
Aircraft Xray Laboratories Inc......D......323 587-4141
5216 Pacific Blvd Huntington Park (90255) ***(P-26053)***
Airdrome Orchards Inc (PA)......E......408 297-6461
111 E Alma Ave San Jose (95112) ***(P-185)***
Aire-Rite AC & Rfrgn Inc......D......714 895-2338
15122 Bolsa Chica St Huntington Beach (92649) ***(P-2027)***
Airemasters Air Conditioning, Santa Fe Springs *Also called Scorpio Enterprises* ***(P-2267)***
Airespring Inc......D......818 786-8990
7800 Woodley Ave Van Nuys (91406) ***(P-5300)***
Airey Enterprises LLC......C......818 530-3362
5530 Corbin Ave Ste 325 Tarzana (91356) ***(P-7688)***
Airfield Maintenance, Sacramento *Also called County of Sacramento* ***(P-13898)***
Airframer R, Torrance *Also called Sonic Industries Inc* ***(P-25312)***
Airgas Inc......B......530 241-1544
653 N Market St Redding (96003) ***(P-7514)***
Airgas Inc......C......858 279-8200
9010 Clairemont Mesa Blvd San Diego (92123) ***(P-7515)***
Airgas Safety Inc......D......562 699-5239
2355 Workman Mill Rd City of Industry (90601) ***(P-7516)***
Airgas Usa LLC......C......858 279-8200
9010 Clairemont Mesa Blvd San Diego (92123) ***(P-8687)***
Airgas Usa LLC......D......323 568-2244
11711 S Alameda St Los Angeles (90059) ***(P-7517)***
Airgas Usa LLC......E......510 659-0162
5121 Brandin Ct Fremont (94538) ***(P-7518)***
Airgas Usa LLC......D......408 998-6380
441 Hobson St San Jose (95110) ***(P-7519)***
Airline Coach Service, Burlingame *Also called Jeremiah Phillips LLC* ***(P-3899)***
Airline Coach Service Inc (PA)......D......650 697-7733
863 Malcolm Rd Burlingame (94010) ***(P-3521)***
Airport Cinemas 12, Santa Rosa *Also called North American Cinemas Inc* ***(P-17851)***
Airport Club......C......707 528-2582
432 Aviation Blvd Santa Rosa (95403) ***(P-18350)***
Airport Commisions......A......650 821-5000
San Francisco Intl Arprt San Francisco (94128) ***(P-4749)***
Airport Connection Inc......C......805 389-8196
95 Dawson Dr Camarillo (93012) ***(P-3522)***
Airport Health Club, Santa Rosa *Also called Airport Club* ***(P-18350)***
Airport Parking Service Inc......D......650 875-6655
1000 San Mateo Ave San Bruno (94066) ***(P-17244)***
Airports Dept, Sacramento *Also called County of Sacramento* ***(P-4766)***
Airpush Inc......C......877 944-2490
11400 W Olympic Blvd Los Angeles (90064) ***(P-13469)***
Airx Utility Surveyors Inc (PA)......D......760 480-2347
2534 E El Nrte Pkwy Ste C Escondido (92027) ***(P-1829)***
Ais - Auto Insur Specialists, Long Beach *Also called Auto Ins Spcialists-Long Beach* ***(P-10285)***
Ais Construction Company......D......805 928-9467
713 Rincon Hill Rd Santa Maria (93455) ***(P-1401)***
Ais, Associated Insurance Svc, Tustin *Also called Apollo Agencies Inc* ***(P-10269)***
Alsha Academy......D......310 908-1962
706 S Pershing Ave Stockton (95203) ***(P-13135)***
Ait Worldwide Logistics Inc......D......310 538-4383
19901 Hamilton Ave Ste D Torrance (90502) ***(P-4885)***
AJ Kirkwood & Associates Inc......C......714 505-1977
4300 N Harbor Blvd Fullerton (92835) ***(P-2415)***
AJ Oster West LLC......D......714 692-1000
22833 La Palma Ave Yorba Linda (92887) ***(P-7039)***
Ajax Portable Services......E......831 384-5000
11240 Commercial Pkwy Castroville (95012) ***(P-14124)***
Ajc Sandblasting Inc......D......562 436-3606
932 Schley Ave Wilmington (90744) ***(P-3369)***
Ajit Healthcare Inc......D......213 484-0510
316 S Westlake Ave Los Angeles (90057) ***(P-26126)***
AJM Packaging Corporation......D......619 448-4007
1160 Vernon Way El Cajon (92020) ***(P-8947)***
Ajo, Yorba Linda *Also called AJ Oster West LLC* ***(P-7039)***
Ajr Trucking Inc......C......562 989-9555
435 E Weber Ave Compton (90222) ***(P-3848)***
AJW Restoration Services LLC......E......858 429-5641
7445 Raytheon Rd San Diego (92111) ***(P-1402)***
AK Constructors Inc......D......951 280-0269
1751 Jenks Dr Corona (92880) ***(P-1403)***
AK Electrical Services, Corona *Also called AK Constructors Inc* ***(P-1403)***
Akela Pharma Inc......E......512 391-3525
11011 Torreyana Rd 100 San Diego (92121) ***(P-25960)***
Akin Gump Strauss......D......310 229-1000
2029 Century Park E # 2400 Los Angeles (90067) ***(P-22347)***
Akin Gump Strauss Hauer & Fel......C......415 765-9500
580 California St # 1500 San Francisco (94104) ***(P-22348)***
Akland Healthcare Wellness Ctr, Oakland *Also called Oakland Healthcare & Wellness* ***(P-20167)***
Akqa Inc (HQ)......B......415 645-9400
360 3rd St Ste 500 San Francisco (94107) ***(P-26486)***
Al Anwa USA Incorporated......C......310 301-2000
4200 Admiralty Way Marina Del Rey (90292) ***(P-11997)***
Al Barcellos Et......E......209 826-2636
17599 Ward Rd Los Banos (93635) ***(P-10)***
Al-Tar Services Inc......D......866 522-3499
823 Kifer Rd Sunnyvale (94086) ***(P-17481)***
Ala Costa Center Program For (PA)......D......510 527-2550
1300 Rose St Berkeley (94702) ***(P-23670)***
Alabbasi, Perris *Also called Mamco Inc* ***(P-1751)***
Aladdin Bail Bonds, Carlsbad *Also called Two Jinn Inc* ***(P-17112)***
Aladdin Sonora Motor Inn......E......209 533-4971
14260 Mono Way Sonora (95370) ***(P-11998)***
Alaidandrew Corporation......D......661 334-2200
1205 8th St Bakersfield (93304) ***(P-20480)***
Alain Pinel Realtors......D......831 622-1040
Junipero Between 5 & 6 # 56 Carmel (93921) ***(P-10895)***
Alain Pinel Realtors Inc......D......415 814-6690
2001 Union St Ste 200 San Francisco (94123) ***(P-10896)***
Alain Pinel Realtors Inc......D......415 755-1111
626 Tamalpais Dr Corte Madera (94925) ***(P-10897)***
Alain Pinel Realtors Inc......D......650 548-1111
520 S El Camino Real # 100 San Mateo (94402) ***(P-10898)***
Alain Pinel Realtors Inc......D......408 358-1111
750 University Ave # 150 Los Gatos (95032) ***(P-10899)***
Alain Pinel Realtors Inc......D......707 636-3800
2911 Cleveland Ave Santa Rosa (95403) ***(P-10900)***
Alain Pinel Realtors Inc......D......925 251-1111
900 Main St Ste 101 Pleasanton (94566) ***(P-10901)***
Alain Pinel Realtors Inc......D......650 375-1111
1440 Chapin Ave Ste 200 Burlingame (94010) ***(P-10902)***
Alain Pinel Realtors Inc......C......650 323-1111
578 University Ave Palo Alto (94301) ***(P-10903)***
Alain Pinel Realtors Inc......D......650 941-1111
167 S San Antonio Rd # 1 Los Altos (94022) ***(P-10904)***
Alain Pinel Realtors Inc......D......650 462-1111
1550 El Camino Real # 100 Menlo Park (94025) ***(P-10905)***
Alakor Healthcare LLC......C......626 408-9800
323 S Heliotrope Ave Monrovia (91016) ***(P-20739)***
Alameda Alliance For Health......C......510 747-4555
1240 S Loop Rd Alameda (94502) ***(P-9919)***
Alameda Bureau Elec Imprv Corp (HQ)......D......510 748-3902
2000 Grand St Alameda (94501) ***(P-5813)***
Alameda Care Center, Burbank *Also called Artesia Healthcare Inc* ***(P-19725)***
Alameda Care Center, Alameda *Also called Shoreline S Intermediate Care* ***(P-20453)***
Alameda Chapel of The Chimes, Hayward *Also called Chapel of Chimes* ***(P-11624)***
Alameda Cnty Cmnty Fd Bnk Inc......D......510 635-3663
7900 Edgewater Dr Oakland (94621) ***(P-22901)***
Alameda Corridor Engrg Team......D......310 816-0460
1 Civic Plaza Dr Ste 600 Carson (90745) ***(P-24925)***
Alameda County AG Fair Assn......D......925 426-7600
4501 Pleasanton Ave Pleasanton (94566) ***(P-18617)***

ALPHABETIC

Employee Codes: A=Over 500 employees, B=251-500
C=101-250, D=51-100, E=50
2020 Directory of California
Wholesalers and Services Companies
© Mergent Inc. 1-800-342-5647
1165

Alameda County Employees Retir ....D.......510 628-3000
475 14th St Ste 1000 Oakland (94612) ***(P-10206)***
ALAMEDA COUNTY FAIR, Pleasanton *Also called Alameda County AG Fair Assn* ***(P-18617)***
Alameda County Industries Inc ....E.......510 357-7282
610 Aladdin Ave San Leandro (94577) ***(P-6144)***
Alameda County Water District (PA) ....C.......510 668-4200
43885 S Grimmer Blvd Fremont (94538) ***(P-6014)***
Alameda Family Services ....D.......510 629-6300
2325 Clement Ave Alameda (94501) ***(P-23671)***
Alameda Halthcare Wellness Ctr, Alameda *Also called Alameda Hlthcare & Wellnss Ctr* ***(P-19713)***
Alameda Health System (PA) ....D.......510 437-4800
1411 E 31st St Oakland (94602) ***(P-20740)***
Alameda Hlthcare & Wellnss Ctr ....D.......510 523-8857
430 Willow St Alameda (94501) ***(P-19713)***
Alameda Hospital, Alameda *Also called City Alameda Health Care Corp* ***(P-20792)***
Alameda Municipal Power, Alameda *Also called Alameda Bureau Elec Imprv Corp* ***(P-5813)***
Alameda Produce Market LLC ....D.......213 221-3400
761 Terminal St Ste 2 Los Angeles (90021) ***(P-10906)***
Alameda, County Medical Center, San Leandro *Also called County of Alameda* ***(P-18922)***
Alameda-Contra Costa Trnst Dst (PA) ....A.......510 891-4777
1600 Franklin St Oakland (94612) ***(P-3523)***
Alameda-Contra Costa Trnst Dst ....C.......510 577-8816
10626 International Blvd Oakland (94603) ***(P-3826)***
Alamitos Blmont Rhblttion Hosp, Long Beach *Also called Alamitos-Belmont Rehab Inc* ***(P-19714)***
Alamitos Convalescent Hospital, Los Alamitos *Also called Goodman Group Inc* ***(P-19976)***
Alamitos Enterprises LLC (PA) ....D.......562 596-1827
3311 Katella Ave Los Alamitos (90720) ***(P-17406)***
Alamitos W Convalescent Hosp, Los Alamitos *Also called Katella Properties* ***(P-20040)***
Alamitos-Belmont Rehab Inc ....C.......562 434-8421
3901 E 4th St Long Beach (90814) ***(P-19714)***
Alamo Medical Group, Alamo *Also called John Muir Physician Network* ***(P-19034)***
Alamo Rent A Car, Inglewood *Also called Alamo Rental (us) Inc* ***(P-17194)***
Alamo Rent A Car, Newport Beach *Also called Alamo Rental (us) Inc* ***(P-17195)***
Alamo Rental (us) Inc ....D.......310 649-2242
9020 Aviation Blvd Inglewood (90301) ***(P-17194)***
Alamo Rental (us) Inc ....E.......949 852-0403
4500 Campus Dr Ste 300 Newport Beach (92660) ***(P-17195)***
Alan B Whitson Company Inc ....A.......949 955-1200
1507 W Alton Ave Santa Ana (92704) ***(P-26487)***
Alan Smith Pool Plastering Inc ....D.......714 628-9494
227 W Carleton Ave Orange (92867) ***(P-2742)***
Alaska Airlines Inc ....D.......800 426-0333
1800 W Airport Dr Han Hangar Ontario (91761) ***(P-4645)***
Alaska Airlines Inc ....C.......310 925-2409
600 World Way Los Angeles (90045) ***(P-4646)***
Alaska Airlines Inc ....D.......510 577-5813
1 Alan Shepard Way Oakland (94621) ***(P-4647)***
Alaska Diesel Electric ....C.......626 934-6211
425 S Hacienda Blvd City of Industry (91745) ***(P-17352)***
Albany Inventory Services ....E.......818 986-5705
11490 Burbank Blvd Ste 1 North Hollywood (91601) ***(P-16608)***
Albd Electric and Cable ....D.......949 440-1216
995 E Discovery Ln Anaheim (92801) ***(P-2416)***
Albert A Webb Associates (PA) ....C.......951 686-1070
3788 Mccray St Riverside (92506) ***(P-24926)***
ALBERT AND MACKENZIE, A PROFESSIONAL LAW CORPORATION, Van Nuys *Also called Albert McKnzie A Prof Law Corp* ***(P-22350)***
Albert D Seeno Cnstr Co Inc ....D.......925 671-7711
4021 Port Chicago Hwy Concord (94520) ***(P-1287)***
Albert McKnzie A Prof Law Corp ....D.......925 689-8000
1800 Sutter St Ste 360 Concord (94520) ***(P-22349)***
Albert McKnzie A Prof Law Corp ....D.......818 650-6900
16600 Sherman Way Van Nuys (91406) ***(P-22350)***
Albertson's Distribution Ctr, Irvine *Also called Albertsons LLC* ***(P-4371)***
Albertsons Brea Dist Ctr, Brea *Also called Albertsons LLC* ***(P-4370)***
Albertsons Dist Ctr 8760, La Habra *Also called Albertsons LLC* ***(P-4369)***
Albertsons LLC ....D.......714 578-4670
777 S Harbor Blvd La Habra (90631) ***(P-4369)***
Albertsons LLC ....A.......714 990-8200
200 N Puente St Brea (92821) ***(P-4370)***
Albertsons LLC ....B.......949 855-2465
9300 Toledo Way Irvine (92618) ***(P-4371)***
Albion River Inn Incorporated ....D.......707 937-1919
3790 N Highway 1 Albion (95410) ***(P-11999)***
Albireo Energy, Poway *Also called Electronic Control Systems LLC* ***(P-2485)***
Alca Trax Sea Foods, Santa Rosa *Also called North Coast Fisheries LLC* ***(P-8374)***
Alcal Glass Systems Inc ....D.......916 929-3100
946 N Market Blvd Sacramento (95834) ***(P-3289)***
Alcal Specialty Contg Inc (HQ) ....D.......916 929-3100
946 N Market Blvd Sacramento (95834) ***(P-3024)***
Alcatraz Cruises LLC ....C.......415 981-7625
Hornb Alcat Landi Pier 33 St Pier San Francisco (94111) ***(P-4846)***
Alchemy Communications Inc ....D.......310 568-0700
6171 W Century Blvd Los Angeles (90045) ***(P-5774)***
Alco Iron & Metal Co (PA) ....D.......510 562-1107
2140 Davis St San Leandro (94577) ***(P-7746)***
Alcohol DRG Program Yolo Cnty ....E.......530 666-8650
137 N Cottonwood St Ste 1 Woodland (95695) ***(P-21946)***
Alcone Marketing Group Inc (HQ) ....D.......949 595-5322
4 Studebaker Irvine (92618) ***(P-13470)***
Alcorn Fence Company (PA) ....C.......818 983-0650
9901 Glenoaks Blvd Sun Valley (91352) ***(P-3370)***
Aldea Inc ....D.......925 577-3102
470 Chadbourne Rd Ste F Fairfield (94534) ***(P-22902)***
Aldersly Retirement Center ....D.......415 453-9271
326 Mission Ave San Rafael (94901) ***(P-10682)***
ALDERSLY RETIREMENT COMMUNITY, San Rafael *Also called Aldersly Retirement Center* ***(P-10682)***
ALDERSON CONVALESCENT HOSPITAL, Woodland *Also called United Health Systems Inc* ***(P-20341)***
Alderwood Inc ....D.......626 289-4439
115 Bridge St San Gabriel (91775) ***(P-20481)***
Alderwoods (delaware) Inc ....E.......209 883-0411
900 Santa Fe Ave Hughson (95326) ***(P-11623)***
Aldoc Inc ....D.......714 836-8477
910 E Orangefair Ln Anaheim (92801) ***(P-2028)***
Aldon Ter Convalsent Hosptial, Los Angeles *Also called Longwood Management Corp* ***(P-20620)***
Aldridge Pite LLP ....C.......858 750-7700
4375 Jutland Dr Ste 200 San Diego (92117) ***(P-22351)***
Alector LLC (PA) ....D.......415 231-5660
151 Oyster Point Blvd # 300 South San Francisco (94080) ***(P-25698)***
Alegrecare Inc ....B.......415 974-3530
1375 Sutter St Ste 110 San Francisco (94109) ***(P-21651)***
Alejandro Medina, San Bernardino *Also called Medina Concrete Construction* ***(P-3181)***
Alemeda County Industries LLC ....D.......510 357-7282
610 Aladdin Ave San Leandro (94577) ***(P-6145)***
Alerion Aviation, Long Beach *Also called Air Rutter International LLC* ***(P-4737)***
Alert Communications, Camarillo *Also called Affiliated Communications Inc* ***(P-16605)***
Alert Insulation Company Inc ....D.......626 961-9113
15913 Old Valley Blvd A La Puente (91744) ***(P-2743)***
Alertenterprise Inc ....C.......510 440-0840
4350 Starboard Dr Fremont (94538) ***(P-15232)***
Alex Moving & Storage, Camarillo *Also called Uribe Trucking Inc* ***(P-4238)***
Alexander Becker Carpets, Los Angeles *Also called Becker Interiors Ltd* ***(P-6545)***
Alexander Delu ....D.......209 334-6660
15175 N Devries Rd Lodi (95242) ***(P-116)***
Alexander Properties Company ....E.......925 866-0100
2600 Camino Ramon Ste 201 San Ramon (94583) ***(P-10562)***
Alexander Valley Healthcare, Cloverdale *Also called Coppertower Family Medical Ctr* ***(P-21988)***
Alexander's Grand Salon & Spa, Anaheim *Also called Alexanders Grand Salon* ***(P-13331)***
Alexanders Grand Salon ....D.......714 282-6438
5579 E Santa Ana Cyn Rd Anaheim (92807) ***(P-13331)***
Alexandria Care Center LLC ....C.......323 660-1800
1515 N Alexandria Ave Los Angeles (90027) ***(P-20482)***
Alexandria Clayton ....E.......530 262-5961
2051 Hilltop Dr Ste A16c Redding (96002) ***(P-15555)***
Alfa Tech Cnslting Engners Inc (PA) ....D.......408 487-1200
1321 Ridder Park Dr 50 San Jose (95131) ***(P-24927)***
Alfa Tech Consulting Entps, San Jose *Also called Alfa Tech Cnslting Engners Inc* ***(P-24927)***
Alfreds Pictures Frames Inc ....E.......714 434-4838
1580 Sunflower Ave Costa Mesa (92626) ***(P-16609)***
Alg Inc ....C.......858 945-1312
215 S Highway 101 Ste 111 Solana Beach (92075) ***(P-14125)***
Algos Inc A Medical Corp (PA) ....D.......626 696-1400
224 N Fair Oaks Ave Pasadena (91103) ***(P-21947)***
Alhambra Convalescent Hosp LLC ....D.......925 228-2020
331 Ilene St Martinez (94553) ***(P-19715)***
Alhambra Healthcare & Wellness ....D.......626 282-3151
415 S Garfield Ave Alhambra (91801) ***(P-19716)***
Alhambra Hospital Med Ctr LP ....C.......626 570-1606
100 S Raymond Ave Alhambra (91801) ***(P-20741)***
Aliantel Inc ....D.......714 829-1650
1940 W Corporate Way Anaheim (92801) ***(P-26979)***
Alicia Arroyo Inc ....C.......831 675-2850
800 Johnson Cyn Rd 4 Gonzales (93926) ***(P-611)***
Alienvault LLC (HQ) ....D.......650 713-3333
1100 Park Pl Ste 300 San Mateo (94403) ***(P-15233)***
Alight (us) LLC ....C.......949 725-4500
100 Bayview Cir Ste 100 # 100 Newport Beach (92660) ***(P-26488)***
Alignment Health Plan ....D.......323 728-7232
1100 W Town & Country Orange (92868) ***(P-9920)***
Alignment Healthcare USA LLC (PA) ....D.......844 310-2247
1100 W Town And Country R Orange (92868) ***(P-22170)***
Alion Science and Tech Corp ....D.......805 488-8761
266 E Scott St Port Hueneme (93041) ***(P-24928)***
Alisal Guest Ranch, Solvang *Also called Alisal Properties* ***(P-13141)***
Alisal Health Center, Salinas *Also called County of Monterey* ***(P-18930)***
Alisal Properties (PA) ....C.......805 688-6411
1054 Alisal Rd Solvang (93463) ***(P-13141)***
Alisam Oxnard Operating ....C.......310 877-7179
212 26th St Ste 246 Santa Monica (90402) ***(P-10563)***
Aliso Air Conditioning & Htg, Rancho Santa Margari *Also called Jct Company LLC* ***(P-2164)***
Aliso Creek Inn and Golf Crse, Laguna Beach *Also called Laguna Bch Golf Bnglow Vlg LLC* ***(P-18259)***
Aliso Mechanical Incorporated ....C.......949 544-1601
29736 A De Las Bandera Rancho Santa Margari (92688) ***(P-2029)***
Aliso Viejo Country Club, Aliso Viejo *Also called Aliso Viejo Golf Club Inc* ***(P-18351)***
Aliso Viejo Golf Club Inc ....C.......949 598-9200
33 Santa Barbara Dr Aliso Viejo (92656) ***(P-18351)***
Aliso Viejo Medical Offices, Aliso Viejo *Also called Kaiser Foundation Hospitals* ***(P-19037)***
All Action Security Inc ....D.......800 482-7371
20501 Ventura Blvd # 275 Woodland Hills (91364) ***(P-16171)***
All American Agrigate, Corona *Also called All American Asphalt* ***(P-1657)***
All American Asphalt (PA) ....D.......951 736-7600
400 E 6th St Corona (92879) ***(P-1657)***
All American Asphalt ....C.......951 736-7617
1776 All American Way Corona (92879) ***(P-1658)***
All American Asphalt ....C.......951 736-7617
1776 All American Way Corona (92879) ***(P-1659)***

Mergent e-mail: customerrelations@mergent.com
1166
2020 Directory of California
Wholesalers and Services Companies
(P-0000) Products & Services Section entry number
(PA)=Parent Co (HQ)=Headquarters (DH)=Div Headquarters

All American Decorative Con, Irvine *Also called Home Franchise Concepts LLC* ***(P-3161)***
All American Service & Sups......D......951 736-3880
1776 All American Way Corona (92879) ***(P-17482)***
All Area Plumbing Inc......C......323 939-9990
5742 Venice Blvd Los Angeles (90019) ***(P-2030)***
All California Mortgage Inc (PA)......D......415 925-5225
17 E Sr Frncis Drke Bl200 Larkspur (94939) ***(P-9515)***
All Care Industries Inc......D......562 623-4009
16747 1/2 Parkside Ave Cerritos (90703) ***(P-13854)***
All Care Medical Group Inc......D......408 278-3550
31 Crescent St Huntington Park (90255) ***(P-18792)***
All Care Services Inc......D......714 669-1148
17671 Irvine Blvd Ste 110 Tustin (92780) ***(P-22903)***
All Commercial Landscape Svc......E......559 453-1670
5213 E Pine Ave Fresno (93727) ***(P-770)***
All Control Cleaning Inc......D......805 987-4210
124 N Aviador St Ste 1 Camarillo (93010) ***(P-13855)***
All Counties Courier Inc......C......714 599-9300
1642 Kaiser Ave Irvine (92614) ***(P-4246)***
All Direct Mail Services Inc......C......818 833-7773
5091 4th St Baldwin Park (91706) ***(P-13718)***
All Environmental Inc......D......949 752-9300
1200 Main St Ste D Irvine (92614) ***(P-26980)***
All Environmental Inc......C......310 798-4255
2447 Pcf Cast Hwy Ste 101 Hermosa Beach (90254) ***(P-26981)***
All Fab Prcsion Sheetmetal Inc......D......408 279-1099
1015 Timothy Dr San Jose (95133) ***(P-3025)***
All For You Home Care, Sacramento *Also called Careability Health Svcs Corp* ***(P-21698)***
All Hallows Garden Apartments, San Francisco *Also called All Hallows Preservation LP* ***(P-10683)***
All Hallows Preservation LP......A......415 285-3909
54 Navy Rd San Francisco (94124) ***(P-10683)***
All Health Services Corp (PA)......D......559 583-9101
206 W 8th St Hanford (93230) ***(P-14222)***
All Hnds Crwash Dtail Ctr Lube......D......949 716-3600
22952 Pacific Park Dr Aliso Viejo (92656) ***(P-17359)***
All In One Inc......C......310 538-3374
1999 W 190th St Torrance (90504) ***(P-14223)***
All In One Complete Bldg Svcs, Vacaville *Also called Mark Garcia* ***(P-13973)***
All Motorists Insurance Agency......C......818 880-9070
5230 Las Virgenes Rd # 100 Calabasas (91302) ***(P-10245)***
All Nation Security Svcs Inc (PA)......C......213 769-4510
3701 Wilshire Blvd # 530 Los Angeles (90010) ***(P-16172)***
All Phase Business Supplies......E......310 631-1900
1920 E Gladwick St Compton (90220) ***(P-7852)***
All Pro Drywall......E......530 722-5182
22148 Buckeye Pl Cottonwood (96022) ***(P-2744)***
All Saintsidence Opco LLC......D......510 481-3200
1652 Mono Ave San Leandro (94578) ***(P-19717)***
All Seasons Framing Corp......E......714 634-2324
644 N Eckhoff St Orange (92868) ***(P-2914)***
All Seasons Homecare......D......408 378-0900
2160 The Alameda Ste C San Jose (95126) ***(P-21652)***
All Snts Sbcute Trnstonal Care, San Leandro *Also called All Saintsidence Opco LLC* ***(P-19717)***
All South Bay Central Office......D......310 618-1180
1411 Marcelina Ave Torrance (90501) ***(P-24784)***
All Star Automotive Products......D......626 960-5164
4257 Auction Ave Ste N Baldwin Park (91706) ***(P-6417)***
All Star Glass Inc (PA)......E......619 275-3343
1845 Morena Blvd San Diego (92110) ***(P-17319)***
All Star Maintenance Inc......D......858 259-0900
12250 El Camino Real # 300 San Diego (92130) ***(P-3371)***
All Star Seed (PA)......D......760 482-9400
2015 Silsbee Rd El Centro (92243) ***(P-464)***
All State Association Inc......C......877 425-2558
11487 San Fernando Rd San Fernando (91340) ***(P-24320)***
All System Personnel Mgmt......E......858 674-4090
16885 W Bernardo Dr # 150 San Diego (92127) ***(P-26127)***
All Taxi Electronics, San Francisco *Also called Yellow Cab Cooperative Inc* ***(P-3756)***
All Tmperatures Controlled Inc......D......818 882-1478
9720 Topanga Canyon Pl Chatsworth (91311) ***(P-2031)***
All Types of Baseboard, San Diego *Also called Juan Lopez* ***(P-1146)***
All Valley Home Care, San Diego *Also called All Valley Home Hlth Care Inc* ***(P-21653)***
All Valley Home Hlth Care Inc......D......619 276-8001
3665 Ruffin Rd Ste 103 San Diego (92123) ***(P-21653)***
All Valley Washer Service Inc......D......818 787-1100
15008 Delano St Van Nuys (91411) ***(P-13244)***
All West Coachlines, Sacramento *Also called Cusa AWC LLC* ***(P-3529)***
All-City Management Svcs Inc......A......310 202-8284
10440 Pioneer Blvd Ste 5 Santa Fe Springs (90670) ***(P-26982)***
All-Guard Alarm Systems Inc (PA)......D......800 255-4273
1306 Stealth St Livermore (94551) ***(P-2417)***
All-Phase Electric Supply, Burbank *Also called Consolidated Elec Distrs Inc* ***(P-7138)***
All-Points Petroleum LLC......D......707 745-1116
640 Noyes Ct Benicia (94510) ***(P-8717)***
All-Pro Bail Bonds Inc (PA)......D......858 481-1200
512 Via De La Valle # 302 Solana Beach (92075) ***(P-16610)***
All-Pro Bail Bonds Inc......D......760 941-4100
530 Hacienda Dr Ste 104d Vista (92081) ***(P-16611)***
All-Pro Remodeling......D......714 288-1314
706 N Tustin St Orange (92867) ***(P-1074)***
Allan Automatic Sprinkler Corp......D......714 993-9500
3233 Enterprise St Brea (92821) ***(P-2032)***
Allan Company, Baldwin Park *Also called Cedarwood-Young Company* ***(P-6178)***
Allan Company, Baldwin Park *Also called Cedarwood-Young Company* ***(P-7754)***
Allaquaria LLC......D......310 645-1107
5420 W 104th St Los Angeles (90045) ***(P-8948)***
Allbright Group La LLC......E......310 402-3570
8474 Melrose Pl Los Angeles (90069) ***(P-24785)***
Allcells LLC......D......510 521-2600
1301 Harbor Bay Pkwy # 200 Alameda (94502) ***(P-25699)***
Alldata LLC......D......916 684-5200
9650 W Taron Dr Ste 100 Elk Grove (95757) ***(P-15234)***
Alldayeveryday Productions LLC......E......323 556-6200
2028 E 7th St Los Angeles (90021) ***(P-17570)***
Alldragon International Inc......E......408 410-6248
4285 Payne Ave 10028 San Jose (95117) ***(P-14625)***
Alldrin Brothers Inc......E......855 667-4231
584 Hi Tech Pkwy Oakdale (95361) ***(P-465)***
Alldrin Brothers Almonds, Oakdale *Also called Alldrin Brothers Inc* ***(P-465)***
Allegis Group Inc......C......650 425-6950
1 Waters Park Dr San Mateo (94403) ***(P-14469)***
Allegis Residential Svcs Inc......D......858 430-5700
9340 Hazard Way Ste B2 San Diego (92123) ***(P-26128)***
Allegretto Vineyard Resort, Paso Robles *Also called Ayres - Paso Robles LP* ***(P-12029)***
Allen Spees Family Homes......E......559 432-3664
524 W Roberts Ave Fresno (93704) ***(P-23815)***
Allen Construction Inc......E......818 879-5334
31356 Via Colinas Ste 107 Westlake Village (91362) ***(P-2915)***
Allen Development Partners LLC (PA)......D......559 732-5425
125 Sbridge 100 Visalia (93291) ***(P-11538)***
Allen Drywall & Associates......D......650 579-0664
380 Lang Rd Burlingame (94010) ***(P-2745)***
Allen Edwards Beauty Salon (PA)......D......818 981-7711
16101 Ventura Blvd # 155 Encino (91436) ***(P-13332)***
Allen L Bender Inc......C......916 372-2190
6625 Quail Crossing Ln Granite Bay (95746) ***(P-1404)***
Allen Lund Company LLC (HQ)......D......818 790-8412
4529 Angeles Crest Hwy # 300 La Canada Flintridge (91011) ***(P-4886)***
Allen Lund Company LLC......D......650 358-9454
1875 S Grant St Ste 110 San Mateo (94402) ***(P-4887)***
Allen Lund Corporation (PA)......E......818 790-8412
4529 Angeles Crest Hwy La Canada Flintridge (91011) ***(P-4888)***
Allen Matkins, San Francisco *Also called Eileen Nottoli* ***(P-22495)***
Allen Matkins Leck Gmble......D......415 837-1515
3 Embarcadero Ctr # 1200 San Francisco (94111) ***(P-22352)***
Allen Matkins Leck Gmble (PA)......B......213 622-5555
865 S Figueroa St # 2800 Los Angeles (90017) ***(P-22353)***
Allen Matkins Leck Gmble......D......949 553-1313
1900 Main St Fl 5 Irvine (92614) ***(P-22354)***
Allen Medical Group Inc......E......818 698-8444
14416 Victory Blvd # 211 Van Nuys (91401) ***(P-18793)***
Allen Transportation Co, Sacramento *Also called Amador Stage Lines Inc* ***(P-3768)***
Allfast Fastening Systems LLC......D......626 968-9388
15200 Don Julian Rd City of Industry (91745) ***(P-7375)***
Alliance Bay Funding Inc......D......510 742-6600
37600 Central Ct Ste 264 Newark (94560) ***(P-10907)***
Alliance Capital Markets, Tustin *Also called Alliance Funding Group* ***(P-17724)***
Alliance Construction, Costa Mesa *Also called Empire Leasing Inc* ***(P-2930)***
Alliance Credit Union (PA)......D......408 445-3386
3315 Almaden Expy Ste 55 San Jose (95118) ***(P-9291)***
Alliance Fc......E......909 784-0005
3496 Little League Dr San Bernardino (92407) ***(P-24786)***
Alliance For Housing & Healing (PA)......D......323 344-4885
825 Colorado Blvd Ste 100 Los Angeles (90041) ***(P-20410)***
Alliance For Safety & Justice......D......209 507-6882
1700 Broadway Fl 7th Oakland (94612) ***(P-24787)***
Alliance Funding Group......D......800 978-8817
17542 17th St Ste 200 Tustin (92780) ***(P-17724)***
Alliance Ground Intl LLC......D......310 646-2446
6181 W Imperial Hwy Los Angeles (90045) ***(P-4750)***
Alliance Ground Intl LLC......D......650 821-0855
648 Rest Field Rd San Francisco (94128) ***(P-4751)***
Alliance Healthcare Svcs Inc (HQ)......C......949 242-5300
18201 Von Karman Ave Irvine (92612) ***(P-21504)***
Alliance Home Care Management, Walnut Creek *Also called Alliance Hospital Services* ***(P-21655)***
Alliance Hospital Services......E......650 697-6900
100 S San Mateo Dr San Mateo (94401) ***(P-21654)***
Alliance Hospital Services (PA)......B......925 304-1107
309 Lennon Ln Ste 200 Walnut Creek (94598) ***(P-21655)***
Alliance Information Technolog (PA)......D......925 462-9787
7041 Koll Center Pkwy # 140 Pleasanton (94566) ***(P-14626)***
Alliance Medical Center Inc......D......707 431-8234
1381 University St Healdsburg (95448) ***(P-18794)***
Alliance Member Services Inc......D......831 459-0980
333 Front St Ste 200 Santa Cruz (95060) ***(P-24788)***
Alliance Nrsing Rhbltation Ctr, El Monte *Also called Georgia Atkison Snf LLC* ***(P-19939)***
Alliance Rdwods Cnfrnce Grunds......D......707 874-3507
6250 Bohemian Hwy Occidental (95465) ***(P-13142)***
Alliance Rvrside Hsptality LLC......E......949 229-3168
21520 Yorba Linda Blvd Yorba Linda (92887) ***(P-12000)***
Alliance Title, Glendale *Also called Wfg National Title Insur Co* ***(P-10205)***
Alliance Wall Systems Inc......E......530 740-7800
4638 Skyway Dr Marysville (95901) ***(P-2746)***
Alliancebernstein LP......D......310 286-6000
1999 Ave Of The Sts 215 Los Angeles (90067) ***(P-11708)***
Allianceit, Pleasanton *Also called Alliance Information Technolog* ***(P-14626)***
Alliances MGT Consulting Inc......E......650 780-0466
544 Hillside Rd Redwood City (94062) ***(P-26983)***
Alliant Asset MGT Co LLC (PA)......D......818 668-2805
21600 Oxnard St Ste 1200 Woodland Hills (91367) ***(P-10908)***
Alliant Educational Foundation......C......559 456-2777
5130 E Clinton Way Fresno (93727) ***(P-21948)***
Alliant Insurance Services Inc (PA)......C......949 756-0271
1301 Dove St Ste 200 Newport Beach (92660) ***(P-26984)***

A L P H A B E T I C

Employee Codes: A=Over 500 employees, B=251-500
C=101-250, D=51-100, E=50

2020 Directory of California
Wholesalers and Services Companies

© Mergent Inc. 1-800-342-5647
1167

Alliant Tchsystems Oprtons LLC ....B......818 887-8195
9401 Corbin Ave Northridge (91324) ***(P-25700)***
Allianz Global Corporate &, Petaluma *Also called Allianz Technology America Inc* ***(P-15941)***
Allianz Globl Corp & Specialty, Burbank *Also called Allianz Underwriters Insur Co* ***(P-10068)***
Allianz Globl Risks US Insur (HQ) ....C......818 260-7500
2350 W Empire Ave Burbank (91504) ***(P-10066)***
Allianz Globl Risks US Insur ....B......415 899-3758
1465 N Mcdowell Blvd Petaluma (94954) ***(P-10067)***
Allianz Insurance Company, Burbank *Also called Allianz Globl Risks US Insur* ***(P-10066)***
Allianz Insurance Company, Petaluma *Also called Allianz Globl Risks US Insur* ***(P-10067)***
Allianz Reinsurance Amer Inc ....D......415 899-2000
1465 N Mcdowell Blvd Petaluma (94954) ***(P-9895)***
Allianz Technology America Inc ....C......415 899-2713
1465 N Mcdowell Blvd Petaluma (94954) ***(P-15941)***
Allianz Underwriters Insur Co ....D......818 260-7500
2350 W Empire Ave Ste 200 Burbank (91504) ***(P-10068)***
Allied Anesthesia Med Group ....D......951 830-9816
400 N Tustin Ave Santa Ana (92705) ***(P-18795)***
Allied Artists International, City of Industry *Also called Allied Entertainment Group Inc* ***(P-17571)***
Allied Auto Store, Fremont *Also called Serrato-Mcdermott Inc* ***(P-6468)***
Allied Avocados & Citrus Inc ....D......805 625-7155
1203 S Sespe St Fillmore (93015) ***(P-466)***
Allied Beverage LLC ....B......818 493-6400
13235 Golden State Rd Sylmar (91342) ***(P-7460)***
Allied Building Products Corp ....E......714 647-9792
1201 E Mcfadden Ave Santa Ana (92705) ***(P-6706)***
Allied Building Products Corp ....E......909 796-6926
456 Industrial Rd San Bernardino (92408) ***(P-6601)***
Allied Building Products Corp ....E......707 584-7599
4159 Santa Rosa Ave Santa Rosa (95407) ***(P-6707)***
Allied Building Products Corp ....D......323 721-9011
1620 S Maple Ave Montebello (90640) ***(P-6708)***
Allied Company Holdings Inc (PA) ....B......818 493-6400
13235 Golden State Rd Sylmar (91342) ***(P-8745)***
Allied Digital Services LLC (HQ) ....C......310 431-2375
680 Knox St Ste 200 Torrance (90502) ***(P-15897)***
Allied Electric Motor Svc Inc (PA) ....D......559 486-4222
4690 E Jensen Ave Fresno (93725) ***(P-7119)***
Allied Entertainment Group Inc (PA) ....A......626 330-0600
273 W Allen Ave City of Industry (91746) ***(P-17571)***
Allied Environmental Services, Woodland Hills *Also called Allied Industries Inc* ***(P-26985)***
Allied Farming Company, Exeter *Also called Sun Pacific Farming Coop Inc* ***(P-683)***
Allied Fire Protection ....C......510 533-5516
555 High St Oakland (94601) ***(P-2033)***
Allied Framers Inc ....C......707 452-7050
4990 Allison Pkwy Vacaville (95688) ***(P-2916)***
Allied Gardens Towing Inc (HQ) ....D......619 563-4060
9150 Chesapeake Dr # 240 San Diego (92123) ***(P-17407)***
Allied High Tech Products Inc ....D......310 635-2466
2376 E Pacifica Pl Rancho Dominguez (90220) ***(P-7615)***
Allied Industries Inc (PA) ....C......800 605-5323
21650 Oxnard St Ste 500 Woodland Hills (91367) ***(P-26985)***
Allied International, Valencia *Also called AWI Acquisition Company* ***(P-7384)***
Allied Intl San Franisco, Hayward *Also called Nor-Cal Moving Services* ***(P-4220)***
Allied Landscape Svcs S Inc ....D......408 310-8476
5542 Monterey Hwy Ste 277 San Jose (95138) ***(P-696)***
Allied Lube Texas LP (PA) ....D......949 486-4008
4440 Von Karman Ave # 100 Newport Beach (92660) ***(P-17408)***
Allied Medical Service of Cal ....E......415 931-1400
2570 Bush St San Francisco (94115) ***(P-3619)***
Allied Prof Nursing Care ....D......909 949-1066
2345 W Fthlls Blvd Ste 14 Upland (91786) ***(P-21656)***
Allied Protection Services Inc ....D......310 330-8314
19164 Van Ness Ave Torrance (90501) ***(P-16173)***
Allied Risk Management Inc ....D......661 305-0455
2010 W Avenue K 395 Lancaster (93536) ***(P-16174)***
Allied Steel Co Inc ....D......951 241-7000
1027 Palmyrita Ave Riverside (92507) ***(P-3249)***
Allied Swift, Oceanside *Also called Allied Swiss Limited* ***(P-10564)***
Allied Swiss Limited ....C......760 941-1702
2636 Vista Pacific Dr Oceanside (92056) ***(P-10564)***
Allied Universal, Santa Ana *Also called Universal Services America LP* ***(P-16472)***
Allied Universal Event Svcs, Fullerton *Also called Staff Pro Inc* ***(P-16565)***
Allied Universal Security Svcs, Santa Ana *Also called Universal Protection Svc LP* ***(P-16470)***
Alliedbarton Security Svcs LLC ....C......626 213-3100
765 The City Dr S Ste 150 Orange (92868) ***(P-16175)***
Alliedbarton Security Svcs LLC ....C......310 324-1219
637 E Albertoni St # 202 Carson (90746) ***(P-16176)***
Alliedbarton Security Svcs LLC ....C......916 489-8280
8950 Cal Center Dr # 150 Sacramento (95826) ***(P-16177)***
Alliedbarton Security Svcs LLC ....D......805 983-1204
300 E Esplanade Dr # 1510 Oxnard (93036) ***(P-16178)***
Alliedbarton Security Svcs LLC ....B......562 906-4800
10330 Pioneer Blvd # 235 Santa Fe Springs (90670) ***(P-16179)***
Alliedbarton Security Svcs LLC ....B......510 839-4041
1600 Riviera Ave Ste 375 Walnut Creek (94596) ***(P-16180)***
Alliedbarton Security Svcs LLC ....B......408 954-8274
2540 N 1st St Ste 101 San Jose (95131) ***(P-16181)***
Alliedbarton Security Svcs LLC ....B......858 874-8200
7670 Opportunity Rd # 210 San Diego (92111) ***(P-16182)***
Alliedbarton Security Svcs LLC ....B......800 418-6423
3701 Wilshire Blvd # 600 Los Angeles (90010) ***(P-16183)***
Alliedbarton Security Svcs LLC ....C......714 260-0805
765 The City Dr S Ste 105 Orange (92868) ***(P-16184)***
Allies For Every Child Inc ....D......310 846-4100
5721 W Slauson Ave # 200 Culver City (90230) ***(P-23672)***
Allison, Amanda Dvm, Elk Grove *Also called Bradshaw Veterinary Clinic* ***(P-574)***
Allmark Inc (PA) ....D......909 989-7556
10070 Arrow Rte Rancho Cucamonga (91730) ***(P-10909)***
Allogene Therapeutics Inc ....C......650 457-2700
210 E Grand Ave South San Francisco (94080) ***(P-25701)***
Alloy Construction Inc ....D......661 203-2592
701 Gardner Field Rd Taft (93268) ***(P-1937)***
Allpro Industry Solutions LLC ....E......661 854-3613
7850 White Ln Bakersfield (93309) ***(P-4889)***
Allred Child Developement Ctr, San Bernardino *Also called San Bernardino City Unf School* ***(P-23781)***
Allsafe Selfstorage, Danville *Also called Cubix Construction Company* ***(P-1344)***
Allsale Electric Inc ....D......818 715-0181
9240 Jordan Ave Chatsworth (91311) ***(P-7120)***
Allstar Commercial Cleaning ....E......858 715-0500
8583 Aero Dr Apt 1039 San Diego (92123) ***(P-13856)***
Allstar Home Services, Rancho Cucamonga *Also called Infinity Svc Group Inc A Cal C* ***(P-2157)***
Allstate, Corona *Also called Acm Technologies Inc* ***(P-6737)***
Allstate, Torrance *Also called Janet Hilton* ***(P-10396)***
Allstate Communications, Agoura Hills *Also called Allstate Technologies Inc* ***(P-5301)***
Allstate Communications ASC, Chatsworth *Also called US Interstate Distrg Inc* ***(P-5484)***
Allstate Construction Co ....E......310 652-6942
1364 Londonderry Pl Los Angeles (90069) ***(P-1075)***
Allstate Imaging Inc (PA) ....D......818 678-4550
21621 Nordhoff St Chatsworth (91311) ***(P-6738)***
Allstate Insurance Company ....A......909 612-5504
21950 Copley Dr Ste 130 Diamond Bar (91765) ***(P-10069)***
Allstate Research and Plg Ctr ....D......650 833-6200
4200 Bohannon Dr Ste 200 Menlo Park (94025) ***(P-10246)***
Allstate Technologies Inc (PA) ....D......818 889-7600
5699 Kanan Rd Ste 455 Agoura Hills (91301) ***(P-5301)***
Alltech Services, Los Alamitos *Also called Mggb Inc* ***(P-25209)***
Alltek Company U S A Inc ....E......714 375-9785
18281 Gothard St Ste 102 Huntington Beach (92648) ***(P-7520)***
Alltoss, Glendale *Also called Durini Luis Carlos Estrada* ***(P-16756)***
Alltrade Tools LLC ....E......310 522-9008
6122 Katella Ave Cypress (90630) ***(P-7376)***
Allworth Financial LP ....D......888 577-2489
135 Camino Dorado Ste 1 NAPA (94558) ***(P-9782)***
Allzone Management Solutions, Los Angeles *Also called Allzone Management Svcs Inc* ***(P-26129)***
Allzone Management Svcs Inc ....B......213 291-8879
3700 Wilshire Blvd # 979 Los Angeles (90010) ***(P-26129)***
ALMA VIA OF CAMARILLO, Alameda *Also called Elder Care Alliance Camarillo* ***(P-23915)***
Almaden Golf & Country Club ....D......408 323-4812
6663 Hampton Dr San Jose (95120) ***(P-18352)***
Almaden Health & Rehab Ctr, San Jose *Also called Mariner Health Care Inc* ***(P-20119)***
Almaden Valley Athletic Club ....D......408 445-4900
5400 Camden Ave San Jose (95124) ***(P-18353)***
Almavia of San Francisco ....D......415 337-1339
1 Thomas More Way San Francisco (94132) ***(P-19718)***
Almond Board of California ....E......209 549-8262
1150 9th St Ste 1500 Modesto (95354) ***(P-24321)***
Aloft El Sgnd-Los Angles Arprt, El Segundo *Also called Rubicon B Hacienda LLC* ***(P-12853)***
Aloft Ontario-Rancho Cucamonga ....D......909 484-2018
10480 4th St Rancho Cucamonga (91730) ***(P-12001)***
Aloft Sfo, Millbrae *Also called Millbrae Wcp Hotel II LLC* ***(P-12618)***
Alogent Holdings Inc ....D......760 410-9000
5868 Owens Ave Ste 200 Carlsbad (92008) ***(P-14627)***
Alois LLC ....C......215 297-4492
548 Market St Ste 47970 San Francisco (94104) ***(P-14224)***
Alois Staffing, San Francisco *Also called Alois LLC* ***(P-14224)***
Alom Technologies Corporation (PA) ....C......510 360-3600
48105 Warm Springs Blvd Fremont (94539) ***(P-16612)***
Alondra Golf Course Inc ....D......310 217-9915
16400 Prairie Ave Lawndale (90260) ***(P-18215)***
Alorica Customer Care Inc ....A......619 298-7103
8885 Rio San Diego Dr San Diego (92108) ***(P-16613)***
Alorica Inc (PA) ....D......949 527-4600
5161 California Ave # 100 Irvine (92617) ***(P-15720)***
Alpert & Alpert Iron & Met Inc ....E......562 624-8833
2350 W 16th St Long Beach (90813) ***(P-7040)***
ALPERT JEWISH COMMUNITY CENTRE, Long Beach *Also called Jewish Community Ctr Long Bch* ***(P-23292)***
Alpha Connection Group Home ....D......760 247-6370
22675 Anoka Rd Apple Valley (92308) ***(P-24434)***
ALPHA CONNECTION YOUTH FAMILY, Apple Valley *Also called Alpha Connection Group Home* ***(P-24434)***
Alpha Mechanical Inc ....D......858 278-3500
4990 Greencraig Ln Ste A San Diego (92123) ***(P-2034)***
Alpha Mechanical Inc (PA) ....D......858 278-3500
4885 Greencraig Ln San Diego (92123) ***(P-2035)***
Alpha Net Consulting LLC ....D......408 330-0896
3080 Olcott St Ste C235 Santa Clara (95054) ***(P-14628)***
Alpha Professional Resources, Thousand Oaks *Also called A P R Inc* ***(P-14462)***
Alpha Soft Support LLC ....D......857 219-5505
8605 Santa Monica Blvd West Hollywood (90069) ***(P-14629)***
Alpha Source Inc ....E......424 270-9600
10940 Wilshire Blvd Ste 1 Los Angeles (90024) ***(P-25702)***
Alpha Swimming Pool & Spa ....D......714 879-4667
2600 Athena Pl Fullerton (92833) ***(P-16614)***
Alpha Systems Fire Protection ....E......323 227-0700
7356 Fulton Ave North Hollywood (91605) ***(P-7797)***
Alpha Teknova Inc ....D......831 637-1100
2290 Bert Dr Hollister (95023) ***(P-25703)***
Alpha-Winfield Contractors Inc ....D......510 652-4712
1096 Yerba Buena Ave Emeryville (94608) ***(P-1076)***

Alphabet Inc (PA)...D.......650 253-0000
1600 Amphitheatre Pkwy Mountain View (94043) ***(P-14630)***
Alphaeon Corporation (HQ)...D.......949 284-4555
17901 Von Karman Ave # 150 Irvine (92614) ***(P-6937)***
Alpine Camp Conference Ctr Inc...D.......909 337-6287
415 Clubhouse Dr Blue Jay (92317) ***(P-18618)***
Alpine Carpets, Culver City *Also called Alpine Interiors Corporation* ***(P-6540)***
Alpine Convalescent Center Inc...D.......619 659-3120
2120 Alpine Blvd Alpine (91901) ***(P-21949)***
Alpine Electronics America Inc...C.......310 783-7391
2012 Abalone Ave Ste D Torrance (90501) ***(P-7197)***
Alpine Inn Restaurant, Torrance *Also called Alpine Village* ***(P-10565)***
Alpine Interiors Corporation (PA)...D.......310 390-7639
3961 Sepulveda Blvd # 205 Culver City (90230) ***(P-6540)***
Alpine Meadows Ski Area...E.......530 583-4232
2600 Alpine Meadows Rd Alpine Meadows (96146) ***(P-12002)***
Alpine Meadows Ski Resort, Alpine Meadows *Also called Alpine Meadows Ski Area* ***(P-12002)***
Alpine Special Treatment Ctr, Alpine *Also called Alpine Convalescent Center Inc* ***(P-21949)***
Alpine Village...C.......310 327-4384
833 Torrance Blvd Ste 1a Torrance (90502) ***(P-10565)***
Alquest Technologies Inc...D.......909 592-8708
1760 Yeager Ave La Verne (91750) ***(P-15909)***
Als Services Usa Corp...D.......562 597-3932
1875 Coronado Ave Long Beach (90755) ***(P-26054)***
Alsana, Thousand Oaks *Also called Castlewood Treatment Ctr LLC* ***(P-21969)***
Alsco - Geyer Irrigation Inc...D.......530 476-2253
700 5th St Arbuckle (95912) ***(P-7497)***
Alsco Inc...D.......510 237-9634
1009 Factory St Richmond (94801) ***(P-13186)***
Alsco Inc...C.......323 465-5111
900 N Highland Ave Los Angeles (90038) ***(P-13187)***
Alsco Inc...D.......805 650-6578
2215 Palma Dr Ventura (93003) ***(P-13188)***
Alsco Inc...C.......619 234-7291
705 W Grape St San Diego (92101) ***(P-13189)***
Alsco Inc...D.......415 648-9266
1575 Indiana St San Francisco (94107) ***(P-13190)***
Alsco Inc...D.......714 774-4165
1750 S Zeyn St Anaheim (92802) ***(P-13191)***
Alsco Inc...D.......707 523-3311
3311 Industrial Dr Santa Rosa (95403) ***(P-13192)***
Alsco Inc...C.......408 279-2345
2275 Junction Ave San Jose (95131) ***(P-13193)***
Alsco Inc...D.......916 454-5545
3391 Lanatt St Sacramento (95819) ***(P-13194)***
Alston & Bird LLP...C.......213 626-8830
333 S Hope St Ste 1600 Los Angeles (90071) ***(P-22355)***
Alston & Bird LLP...B.......202 239-3673
2815 Townsgate Rd Ste 200 Westlake Village (91361) ***(P-22356)***
Alston Construction Co Inc (PA)...D.......916 340-2400
8775 Folsom Blvd Ste 201 Sacramento (95826) ***(P-1405)***
Alstyle AP & Activewear MGT Co (HQ)...A.......714 765-0400
1501 E Cerritos Ave Anaheim (92805) ***(P-8053)***
Alta Bates Summit Medical Ctr, Berkeley *Also called Surgery Center of Alta Bates* ***(P-21244)***
Alta Btes Cmprhnsive Cncer Ctr, Berkeley *Also called Surgery Center of Alta Bates* ***(P-19462)***
Alta Cal Regional Ctr Inc...B.......530 674-3070
950 Tharp Rd Ste 202 Yuba City (95993) ***(P-22904)***
Alta Care Center LLC...C.......714 530-6322
13075 Blackbird St Garden Grove (92843) ***(P-20483)***
Alta Drywall, Ramona *Also called Innovative Drywall Systems Inc* ***(P-2798)***
Alta Equipment Leasing Company...D.......415 875-1000
50 California St Fl 24 San Francisco (94111) ***(P-14126)***
Alta Healthcare System LLC...C.......818 787-1511
14433 Emelita St Van Nuys (91401) ***(P-24124)***
Alta Healthcare System LLC (HQ)...C.......323 267-0477
4081 E Olympic Blvd Los Angeles (90023) ***(P-24125)***
Alta Hollywood Community Hsptl...C.......818 787-1511
14433 Emelita St Van Nuys (91401) ***(P-21379)***
Alta Hospitals System LLC...C.......323 267-0477
4081 E Olympic Blvd Los Angeles (90023) ***(P-20742)***
Alta Hospitals System LLC...A.......714 619-7700
14662 Newport Ave Tustin (92780) ***(P-20743)***
Alta Hospitals System LLC (HQ)...C.......310 943-4500
3415 S Sepulveda Blvd # 900 Los Angeles (90034) ***(P-20744)***
Alta Loma Assisted Living LLC...D.......909 481-2600
9428 19th St Murrieta (92562) ***(P-22905)***
ALTA ONE FCU, Ridgecrest *Also called Altaone Federal Credit Union* ***(P-9292)***
Alta Resources Corp...D.......800 424-9378
975 W Imperial Hwy # 200 Brea (92821) ***(P-16615)***
Alta Sierra Country Club Inc...E.......530 273-2041
11897 Tammy Way Grass Valley (95949) ***(P-18354)***
Alta Vista Country Club LLC...D.......714 524-1591
777 Alta Vista St Placentia (92870) ***(P-18355)***
Alta Vista Healthcare and Well...C.......951 688-8200
9020 Garfield St Riverside (92503) ***(P-18796)***
Alta Vista Healthcare Center, Riverside *Also called Kindred Healthcare Operating* ***(P-20609)***
Alta Vista Solutions...C.......510 594-0510
3260 Blume Dr Ste 500 Richmond (94806) ***(P-24929)***
Alta-Dena Certified Dairy LLC...D.......858 292-6930
4656 Cardin St San Diego (92111) ***(P-8308)***
Altaba Inc...C.......408 349-5080
3420 Central Expy Santa Clara (95051) ***(P-5302)***
Altadena Town and Country Club...D.......626 345-9088
2290 Country Club Dr Altadena (91001) ***(P-18356)***
Altaf Zahid Engineering Svcs...E.......760 481-9072
42051 Orange Blossom Dr Temecula (92591) ***(P-16616)***
Altamed Health Services Corp...D.......323 980-4466
5427 Whittier Blvd Los Angeles (90022) ***(P-18797)***
Altamed Health Services Corp...C.......714 635-0593
1820 W Lincoln Ave Anaheim (92801) ***(P-18798)***
Altamed Health Services Corp...D.......626 214-1480
535 S 2nd Ave Covina (91723) ***(P-9896)***
Altamed Health Services Corp...C.......323 276-0267
268 Bloom St Los Angeles (90012) ***(P-18799)***
Altamed Health Services Corp...C.......323 889-7847
10454 Valley Blvd El Monte (91731) ***(P-22171)***
Altamed Health Services Corp (PA)...C.......323 725-8751
2040 Camfield Ave Commerce (90040) ***(P-18800)***
Altamed Health Services Corp...D.......562 949-8717
9436 Slauson Ave Pico Rivera (90660) ***(P-22172)***
Altamed Health Services Corp...E.......323 980-4000
5425 Pomona Blvd Los Angeles (90022) ***(P-18801)***
Altamed Health Services Corp...B.......714 780-5690
1814 W Lincoln Ave Anaheim (92801) ***(P-18802)***
Altametrics LLC...C.......800 676-1281
3191 Red Hill Ave Ste 100 Costa Mesa (92626) ***(P-6791)***
Altamont Infrastructure Co...D.......925 245-5500
6185 Industrial Way Livermore (94551) ***(P-5814)***
Altaone Federal Credit Union (PA)...C.......760 371-7000
701 S China Lake Blvd Ridgecrest (93555) ***(P-9292)***
Altcare Cedar Creek LLC...D.......510 527-7282
868 Ensenada Ave Berkeley (94707) ***(P-23816)***
Altec Products Inc (PA)...D.......949 727-1248
23422 Mill Creek Dr # 225 Laguna Hills (92653) ***(P-16617)***
Altech Services Inc...B.......888 725-8324
400 Continental Blvd Fl 6 El Segundo (90245) ***(P-14470)***
Altegra Health...D.......310 776-4001
3415 S Sepulveda Blvd # 900 Los Angeles (90034) ***(P-26489)***
Alten Construction Inc...D.......510 234-4200
1141 Marina Way S Richmond (94804) ***(P-1077)***
Altenheim Inc...D.......510 530-4013
1720 Macarthur Blvd Oakland (94602) ***(P-10684)***
Altera Real Estate...B.......949 547-7351
33522 Niguel Rd Ste 200 Dana Point (92629) ***(P-10910)***
Alternative Energy Systems Inc...D.......530 345-6980
13620 State Highway 99 N Chico (95973) ***(P-2036)***
Altium LLC...D.......800 544-4186
4275 Executive Sq Ste 825 La Jolla (92037) ***(P-15235)***
Altman Plants, Vista *Also called Altman Specialty Plants LLC* ***(P-8880)***
Altman Specialty Plants LLC (PA)...A.......800 348-4881
3742 Blue Bird Canyon Rd Vista (92084) ***(P-8880)***
Alton Geoscience, Irvine *Also called TRC Solutions Inc* ***(P-27237)***
Alton Irvine Inc...D.......949 428-4141
2052 Alton Pkwy Irvine (92606) ***(P-6502)***
Alton Management Corporation (PA)...D.......510 663-0177
7532 Macarthur Blvd Oakland (94605) ***(P-10911)***
Altoon Partners LLP (PA)...D.......213 225-1900
617 W 7th St Ste 400 Los Angeles (90017) ***(P-25411)***
Altoon Porter, Los Angeles *Also called Altoon Partners LLP* ***(P-25411)***
Altour International Inc...C.......310 571-6000
12100 W Olympic Blvd # 300 Los Angeles (90064) ***(P-4812)***
Altour International Inc (PA)...D.......310 571-6000
12100 W Olympic Blvd # 300 Los Angeles (90064) ***(P-4813)***
Altour Travel Master, Los Angeles *Also called Altour International Inc* ***(P-4812)***
Altran, Santa Clara *Also called Aricent NA Inc* ***(P-14653)***
Altura Centers For Health...D.......559 686-9097
1201 N Cherry St Tulare (93274) ***(P-18803)***
Altura Comm Solutions LLC (HQ)...D.......714 948-8400
1540 S Lewis St Anaheim (92805) ***(P-7226)***
Altura Comm Solutions LLC...D.......650 513-5100
1840 Gateway Dr Ste 100 San Mateo (94404) ***(P-7227)***
Altura Credit Union (PA)...D.......888 883-7228
2847 Campus Pkwy Riverside (92507) ***(P-9380)***
Alumatec Inc...D.......818 609-7460
18411 Sherman Way Reseda (91335) ***(P-995)***
Aluminum Precision Pdts Inc (PA)...A.......714 546-8125
3333 W Warner Ave Santa Ana (92704) ***(P-7041)***
Alvarado Hospital LLC (HQ)...D.......619 287-3270
6655 Alvarado Rd San Diego (92120) ***(P-20745)***
Alvarado Parkway Institute, La Mesa *Also called Helix Healthcare Inc* ***(P-21412)***
Alvaradosmith A Prof Corp (PA)...C.......714 852-6800
1 Macarthur Pl Ste 200 Santa Ana (92707) ***(P-22357)***
Alvarez & Marsal Holdings LLC...C.......415 490-2300
100 Pine St Fl 9 San Francisco (94111) ***(P-26490)***
Alvarion Inc (HQ)...E.......650 314-2500
555 N Mathilda Ave # 210 Sunnyvale (94085) ***(P-7228)***
Alves, Robert L, Selma *Also called Robert Alves Farms Inc* ***(P-157)***
Alvizia Landscape Co LLC...C.......619 661-6557
2520 Cactus Rd San Diego (92154) ***(P-771)***
Always Best, City of Industry *Also called Rongcheng Trading LLC* ***(P-8419)***
Always Best Care Senior Svcs, Roseville *Also called Abcsp LLC* ***(P-21624)***
Always Home Nursing Svc Inc...C.......916 989-6420
7777 Greenback Ln Ste 208 Citrus Heights (95610) ***(P-21657)***
Always There Live In Care LLC...D.......888 606-8880
7121 Magnolia Ave Riverside (92504) ***(P-21658)***
Alzheimer's Living Center, Fresno *Also called Community Medical Centers* ***(P-20801)***
Alzheimers Care Since 1983...E.......714 641-0959
3730 S Greenville St Santa Ana (92704) ***(P-21659)***
Alzheimers Greater Los Angeles...D.......323 938-3379
4221 Wilshire Blvd # 400 Los Angeles (90010) ***(P-22906)***
AM Products Inc...E.......714 662-4454
1661 Palm St Santa Ana (92701) ***(P-7042)***
Am-PM Sewer & Drain Cleaning, San Diego *Also called Bill Howe Plumbing Inc* ***(P-2075)***
Am-TEC Security, Chino *Also called Am-TEC Total Security Inc* ***(P-16491)***

ALPHABETIC

Employee Codes: A=Over 500 employees, B=251-500
C=101-250, D=51-100, E=50
2020 Directory of California
Wholesalers and Services Companies
© Mergent Inc. 1-800-342-5647
1169

Am-TEC Total Security Inc (PA)..........D.......909 573-4678
4075 Schaefer Ave Chino (91710) ***(P-16491)***
Am/PM Food Mart, La Palma *Also called Arco Envmtl Remediation LLC* ***(P-26508)***
Amada America Inc (HQ)..........D.......714 739-2111
7025 Firestone Blvd Buena Park (90621) ***(P-7521)***
Amada Capital Corporation..........D.......714 739-2111
7025 Firestone Blvd Buena Park (90621) ***(P-14127)***
Amada Enterprises Inc..........C.......323 757-1881
12619 Avalon Blvd Los Angeles (90061) ***(P-19719)***
Amador Development, Azusa *Also called David L Amador Inc* ***(P-3138)***
Amador Stage Lines Inc..........D.......916 444-7880
1331 C St Sacramento (95814) ***(P-3768)***
Amador Tlmne Cmnty Action Agcy (PA)..........C.......209 296-2785
10590 State Highway 88 Jackson (95642) ***(P-24126)***
Amador Tlmne Cmnty Action Agcy..........E.......209 533-1397
427 Highway 49 Sonora (95370) ***(P-24127)***
Amador Water Agency..........D.......209 223-3018
12800 Ridge Rd Sutter Creek (95685) ***(P-6015)***
Amador-Tolumne Cmnty Resources..........D.......209 223-1485
10590 State Highway 88 Jackson (95642) ***(P-24128)***
Amanecer Cmnty Counseling Svc..........D.......213 481-7464
1200 Wilshire Blvd # 200 Los Angeles (90017) ***(P-21950)***
Amar Transportation Inc (PA)..........C.......831 728-8209
144 W Lake Ave Ste C Watsonville (95076) ***(P-3963)***
AMARAL RANCHES, Chualar *Also called C & G Farms Inc* ***(P-40)***
Amarik Properties Inc (PA)..........D.......714 505-5200
1400 Bristol St N Ste 220 Newport Beach (92660) ***(P-10912)***
Amatel Inc (PA)..........E.......323 801-0199
1017 S Mountain Ave Monrovia (91016) ***(P-26986)***
Amato Industries Incorporated..........D.......650 697-5548
1550 Gilbreth Rd Burlingame (94010) ***(P-3620)***
Amaturo Sonoma Media Group LLC..........D.......707 543-0126
1410 Neotomas Ave Ste 200 Santa Rosa (95405) ***(P-5507)***
Amawaterways LLC (PA)..........C.......800 626-0126
26010 Mureau Rd Calabasas (91302) ***(P-5090)***
Amax Computer, Fremont *Also called Amax Engineering Corporation* ***(P-6792)***
Amax Engineering Corporation (PA)..........C.......510 651-8886
1565 Reliance Way Fremont (94539) ***(P-6792)***
Ambassador Gaming Inc..........C.......714 969-8730
660 Newport Center Dr # 1050 Newport Beach (92660) ***(P-18619)***
Amber Financial Group LLC (PA)..........C.......858 487-7209
11415 W Bernardo Ct San Diego (92127) ***(P-9516)***
Amber Holdings Inc..........A.......415 765-6500
150 California St San Francisco (94111) ***(P-14631)***
Amber Mortgage, San Diego *Also called Amber Financial Group LLC* ***(P-9516)***
Amberfin Limited..........E.......818 768-8948
7590 N Glenoaks Blvd # 101 Burbank (91504) ***(P-6793)***
Ambiance Transportation LLC..........D.......818 955-5757
13782 Foothill Blvd D Sylmar (91342) ***(P-5108)***
Ambiente Enterprises Inc..........C.......760 674-1905
73726 Alessandro Dr # 203 Palm Desert (92260) ***(P-21660)***
Amblin/Reliance Holding Co LLC..........D.......818 733-6272
100 Universal City Plz Universal City (91608) ***(P-17572)***
Ambreen Enterprises Inc..........D.......909 620-1339
20370 Via Badalona Yorba Linda (92887) ***(P-26987)***
Ambrose Recreation & Park Dst..........D.......925 458-1601
3105 Willow Pass Rd Bay Point (94565) ***(P-18620)***
Ambry Genetics Corporation (HQ)..........D.......949 900-5500
15 Argonaut Aliso Viejo (92656) ***(P-21505)***
Ambulnz Co LLC..........D.......877 311-5555
1151 S Boyle Ave Los Angeles (90023) ***(P-11644)***
Ambulnz Health LLC..........B.......877 311-5555
12531 Vanowen St North Hollywood (91605) ***(P-3621)***
AMC, Burbank *Also called American Multi-Cinema Inc* ***(P-17802)***
AMC, San Diego *Also called American Multi-Cinema Inc* ***(P-17803)***
AMC, Monterey Park *Also called American Multi-Cinema Inc* ***(P-17804)***
AMC, Fair Oaks *Also called Sunset Pet Hospital Inc* ***(P-585)***
AMC, Covina *Also called American Multi-Cinema Inc* ***(P-17805)***
AMC, Torrance *Also called American Multi-Cinema Inc* ***(P-17806)***
AMC, Anaheim *Also called American Multi-Cinema Inc* ***(P-17807)***
AMC, Orange *Also called American Multi-Cinema Inc* ***(P-17808)***
AMC, Fullerton *Also called American Multi-Cinema Inc* ***(P-17809)***
AMC, Pasadena *Also called American Multi-Cinema Inc* ***(P-17810)***
AMC, Norwalk *Also called American Multi-Cinema Inc* ***(P-17811)***
AMC, Huntington Beach *Also called House Seven Gables RE Inc* ***(P-11193)***
AMC, Sylmar *Also called Advanced Mnlythic Ceramics Inc* ***(P-7224)***
AMC, Los Angeles *Also called Aesthetic Maintenance Corp* ***(P-13853)***
AMC, Los Angeles *Also called American Multi-Cinema Inc* ***(P-17812)***
AMC, San Diego *Also called American Multi-Cinema Inc* ***(P-17813)***
AMC, City of Industry *Also called American Multi-Cinema Inc* ***(P-17814)***
AMC, Montebello *Also called American Multi-Cinema Inc* ***(P-17815)***
AMC Entertainment Inc..........E.......909 476-1288
4549 Mills Cir Ontario (91764) ***(P-17801)***
AMC&, Los Angeles *Also called Anderson McPharlin Conners LLP* ***(P-22358)***
Amcal Communities Inc..........E.......818 706-0694
30141 Agoura Rd Ste 100 Agoura Hills (91301) ***(P-11539)***
Amcap Fund Inc..........B.......213 486-9200
333 S Hope St Ste Levb Los Angeles (90071) ***(P-11709)***
Amco Foods Inc..........B.......818 247-4716
601 E Glenoaks Blvd # 108 Glendale (91207) ***(P-26491)***
Amcom Food Service, City of Industry *Also called Klm Management Company* ***(P-8318)***
AMD Trading Company Inc..........C.......415 391-0601
1021 Stockton St San Francisco (94108) ***(P-8949)***
Amdal In-Home Care Inc (PA)..........E.......559 686-6611
147 N K St Tulare (93274) ***(P-20484)***
Amdal In-Home Care Inc..........D.......559 227-1701
3410 Mccall Ave Ste 107 Selma (93662) ***(P-20485)***
Amdocs Inc..........B.......916 934-7000
1104 Investment Blvd El Dorado Hills (95762) ***(P-14632)***
Amdocs Bcs Inc..........B.......916 934-7000
1104 Investment Blvd El Dorado Hills (95762) ***(P-14633)***
Amdx Laboratory Sciences, San Diego *Also called Progenity Inc* ***(P-21569)***
Amec Fster Wheler E C Svcs Inc..........C.......951 273-7400
250 E Rincon St Ste 204 Corona (92879) ***(P-24930)***
Amen Clinics Inc A Med Corp (PA)..........C.......888 564-2700
3150 Bristol St Ste 400 Costa Mesa (92626) ***(P-18804)***
Amen Clinics Inc A Med Corp..........E.......650 416-7830
350 N Wiget Ln Ste 105 Walnut Creek (94598) ***(P-18805)***
Amer Zoetrope Research LLC..........C.......707 963-9230
1991 Saint Helana Hwy Rutherford (94573) ***(P-25876)***
Ameri-Kleen..........B.......831 722-8888
313 W Beach St Watsonville (95076) ***(P-13857)***
Ameri-Kleen..........C.......805 546-0706
1023 E Grand Ave Arroyo Grande (93420) ***(P-13858)***
Ameri-Kleen Building Services, Watsonville *Also called Ameri-Kleen* ***(P-13857)***
Ameri-Kleen Building Services, Arroyo Grande *Also called Ameri-Kleen* ***(P-13858)***
Ameri-West Medical Associates, La Habra *Also called Jayasinghe Medical Group Inc* ***(P-19031)***
America Chung Nam (group) (PA)..........C.......909 839-8383
1163 Fairway Dr City of Industry (91789) ***(P-7747)***
America Chung Nam LLC (HQ)..........C.......909 839-8383
1163 Fairway Dr Fl 3 City of Industry (91789) ***(P-7748)***
America Consulting Group LLC..........C.......714 390-3105
23 Corporate Plaza Dr # 150 Newport Beach (92660) ***(P-26492)***
America Drean Realty, Santa Cruz *Also called David Lyng & Associates Inc* ***(P-11086)***
America Shredding..........D.......702 262-3607
6565 Smith Ave Newark (94560) ***(P-16618)***
America West Airlines Inc..........C.......619 231-7340
3835 N Harbor Dr Ste 128 San Diego (92101) ***(P-4648)***
America West Airlines Inc..........D.......949 852-5471
18601 Airport Way Ste 238 Santa Ana (92707) ***(P-4649)***
American AC Distrs LLC..........D.......407 850-0147
16900 Chestnut St City of Industry (91748) ***(P-2037)***
American Academy of Opthalmlgy (PA)..........C.......415 561-8500
655 Beach St Fl 1 San Francisco (94109) ***(P-24375)***
American Ace International Co..........D.......626 937-6116
313 Newquist Pl Ste A City of Industry (91745) ***(P-8154)***
American Ace Intl Trdg Co, City of Industry *Also called American Ace International Co* ***(P-8154)***
American Advisors Group (PA)..........E.......866 948-0003
3800 W Chapman Ave Fl 3 Orange (92868) ***(P-9783)***
American Agcredit Flca (PA)..........D.......707 545-1200
400 Aviation Blvd Ste 100 Santa Rosa (95403) ***(P-9496)***
American Air, Visalia *Also called American Incorporated* ***(P-2039)***
American Airlines Inc..........D.......408 291-3800
2077 Airport Blvd Ste 103 San Jose (95110) ***(P-4650)***
American Airlines Inc..........B.......650 877-6000
International Airport San Francisco (94128) ***(P-4651)***
American Airlines Inc..........C.......310 215-7054
5950 Avion Dr Los Angeles (90045) ***(P-4652)***
American Airlines Inc..........C.......949 852-5470
18601 Airport Way Ste 213 Santa Ana (92707) ***(P-4653)***
American Airlines Inc..........C.......213 935-6045
7000 World Way W Los Angeles (90045) ***(P-4654)***
American Airlines Inc..........E.......619 574-0615
3707 N Harbor Dr Ste 103 San Diego (92101) ***(P-4655)***
American Airlines Inc..........C.......310 646-3013
7183 World Way W Los Angeles (90045) ***(P-4656)***
American Airlines Inc..........D.......805 988-0407
3100 Wright Rd Camarillo (93010) ***(P-4657)***
American Airlines Group Inc..........A.......310 251-9184
3543 Carlisle St Perris (92571) ***(P-4658)***
American All Risk Loss Adm..........C.......559 277-4960
4270 W Richert Ave # 101 Fresno (93722) ***(P-26493)***
American Ambulance, Fresno *Also called K W P H Enterprises* ***(P-3690)***
American Asp Repr Rsrfcing Inc (PA)..........D.......510 723-0280
24200 Clawiter Rd Hayward (94545) ***(P-3110)***
American Asphalt South Inc..........D.......909 427-8276
14436 Santa Ana Ave Fontana (92337) ***(P-1660)***
American Assets Trust Inc (PA)..........D.......858 350-2600
11455 El Cmino Real Ste 2 San Diego (92130) ***(P-11840)***
American Automobile..........D.......925 279-2300
3055 Oak Rd Walnut Creek (94597) ***(P-10247)***
American Automobile Assctn..........C.......510 350-2042
1982 Pleasant Valley Ave A Oakland (94611) ***(P-24789)***
American Automobile Assctn..........C.......707 566-4000
1501 Farmers Ln Santa Rosa (95405) ***(P-10070)***
American Automobile Assctn..........E.......209 952-4100
3116 W March Ln Ste 100 Stockton (95219) ***(P-24790)***
American Automobile Associatio..........B.......510 596-3669
1277 Treat Blvd Ste 1000 Walnut Creek (94597) ***(P-10071)***
American Baptist Homes of West, Redlands *Also called American Baptist Homes of West* ***(P-10685)***
American Baptist Homes of West..........C.......909 335-3077
460 E Fern Ave Redlands (92373) ***(P-10685)***
American Baptist Homes of West..........C.......559 439-4770
5555 N Fresno St Fresno (93710) ***(P-23817)***
American Baptist Homes of West..........C.......510 654-7172
110 41st St Ofc Oakland (94611) ***(P-23818)***
American Baptist Homes of West..........C.......661 834-0620
1401 New Stine Rd Bakersfield (93309) ***(P-20486)***
American Baptist Homes of West..........C.......909 793-1233
900 Salem Dr Redlands (92373) ***(P-20487)***

Mergent e-mail: customerrelations@mergent.com
1170
2020 Directory of California
Wholesalers and Services Companies
(P-0000) Products & Services Section entry number
(PA)=Parent Co (HQ)=Headquarters (DH)=Div Headquarters

American Baptist Homes of West (HQ) ....D....925 924-7100
6120 Stoneridge Mall Rd # 300 Pleasanton (94588) ***(P-23819)***
American Baptist Homes of West ....C....650 948-8291
373 Pine Ln Los Altos (94022) ***(P-20488)***
American Baptist Homes of West ....C....408 357-1100
800 Blossom Hill Rd Ofc Los Gatos (95032) ***(P-20489)***
American Beef Packers Inc ....C....909 628-4888
13677 Yorba Ave Chino (91710) ***(P-599)***
American Bldg Maint Co of Ill ....E....510 573-1618
44870 Osgood Rd Fremont (94539) ***(P-13859)***
American Bldg Maint Co-West (HQ) ....C....415 733-4000
75 Broadway Ste 111 San Francisco (94111) ***(P-13860)***
American Bolt & Screw Mfg Corp (PA) ....D....909 390-0522
14650 Miller Ave Ste 200 Fontana (92336) ***(P-7377)***
American Brdge/Fluor Entps Inc ....D....510 808-4623
1390 Willow Pass Rd Concord (94520) ***(P-1813)***
American Building Maint Co NY ....A....415 733-4000
101 California St San Francisco (94111) ***(P-13861)***
American Building Maintenance, Los Angeles *Also called Century Plaza Garage* ***(P-17250)***
American Building Service Inc ....D....510 483-5120
4578 Crow Canyon Pl Castro Valley (94552) ***(P-13862)***
American Building Supply Inc (HQ) ....C....916 503-4100
8360 Elder Creek Rd Sacramento (95828) ***(P-6602)***
American Building Supply Inc ....D....209 941-8852
1488 Tillie Lewis Dr Stockton (95206) ***(P-6603)***
American Business Bank ....D....909 919-2040
3633 Inland Empire Blvd # 720 Ontario (91764) ***(P-9027)***
American Cancer Soc Cal Div (PA) ....D....510 893-7900
1001 Marina Village Pkwy Alameda (94501) ***(P-25961)***
American Cancer Soc Cal Div ....E....408 265-5535
1103 Branham Ln San Jose (95118) ***(P-24129)***
American Cancer Soc Cal Div ....D....650 325-8939
748 Santa Cruz Ave Menlo Park (94025) ***(P-25962)***
American Capital Group Inc ....D....949 271-5800
23382 Mill Creek Dr # 115 Laguna Hills (92653) ***(P-9497)***
American Care Givers Westwood ....D....310 208-8005
947 Tiverton Ave Ste 533 Los Angeles (90024) ***(P-22907)***
American Carequest Inc (PA) ....D....415 885-3324
819 Cowan Rd Ste C Burlingame (94010) ***(P-21661)***
American Century Inv MGT Inc ....C....650 965-8300
1665 Charleston Rd Mountain View (94043) ***(P-9784)***
American Century Investments, Mountain View *Also called American Century Inv MGT Inc* ***(P-9784)***
American Chemical & Sanitary, Brea *Also called American Sanitary Supply Inc* ***(P-7664)***
American Civil Const ....D....707 746-8028
2990 Bay Vista Ct Ste D Benicia (94510) ***(P-1661)***
American Civil Constrs LLC ....C....707 746-8028
3701 Mallard Dr Benicia (94510) ***(P-1938)***
American Commodity Co., Williams *Also called ACC-Gwg LLC* ***(P-26967)***
American Companies, Pico Rivera *Also called Three Sons Inc* ***(P-8421)***
American Concrete ....D....760 471-9907
1125 Linda Vista Dr Ste 1 San Marcos (92078) ***(P-3111)***
American Concrete Cutting Inc ....D....714 547-7181
620 N Poinsettia St Santa Ana (92701) ***(P-3335)***
American Conservatory ....D....415 749-2228
415 Geary St San Francisco (94102) ***(P-17886)***
American Conservatory ....D....415 749-2228
405 Geary St San Francisco (94102) ***(P-17887)***
American Contractors Inc ....D....714 282-5700
404 W Blueridge Ave Orange (92865) ***(P-2038)***
American Contrs Indemnity Co (HQ) ....C....213 330-1309
801 S Figueroa St Ste 700 Los Angeles (90017) ***(P-10158)***
American Corporate SEC Inc (PA) ....D....562 216-7440
1 World Trade Ctr # 1240 Long Beach (90831) ***(P-16185)***
American Corporation ....D....310 274-1800
315 N Doheny Dr Beverly Hills (90211) ***(P-6494)***
American Cpr Training, Encinitas *Also called Express Companies Inc* ***(P-27068)***
American Crane Rental Inc ....D....209 838-8815
17800 Comconex Rd Manteca (95336) ***(P-14092)***
American Crclation Innovations, Long Beach *Also called Advertising Consultants Inc* ***(P-13642)***
American Cstm Private SEC Inc ....D....209 369-1200
446 E Vine St Ste A Stockton (95202) ***(P-16186)***
American De Rosa Lamparts LLC (PA) ....D....800 777-4440
1945 S Tubeway Ave Commerce (90040) ***(P-7121)***
American Deck Systems, San Diego *Also called Magnesite Specialties Inc* ***(P-3013)***
American Dj Group of Companies, Commerce *Also called D J American Supply Inc* ***(P-7804)***
American Dmlton/Concrete Cutng, Santa Ana *Also called American Concrete Cutting Inc* ***(P-3335)***
American Dntl Partners of Cal ....C....951 689-5031
7251 Magnolia Ave Riverside (92504) ***(P-19602)***
American Eagle Protctve Svcs ....D....310 412-0019
425 W Kelso St Inglewood (90301) ***(P-16187)***
American Eagle Protective Svcs, Inglewood *Also called American Eagle Protctve Svcs* ***(P-16187)***
American Eagle Services Inc ....D....574 859-2055
1320 Arrow Hwy La Verne (91750) ***(P-14471)***
American Electric Supply Inc (PA) ....D....951 734-7910
361 S Maple St Corona (92880) ***(P-7122)***
American Electrical Svcs Inc ....C....831 638-1737
501 San Benito St Fl 3 Hollister (95023) ***(P-2418)***
American Electronic Warfare As ....D....858 524-6119
16766 Bernardo Center Dr San Diego (92128) ***(P-24931)***
American Engrg Contrs Inc ....C....209 229-1591
25445 S Schulte Rd Tracy (95377) ***(P-2419)***
American Etc Inc ....B....650 873-5353
1140 San Mateo Ave South San Francisco (94080) ***(P-13177)***
American Express Travel ....D....949 453-7123
15353 Barranca Pkwy Irvine (92618) ***(P-4814)***
American Farms LLC ....D....831 424-1815
1107 Harkins Rd Salinas (93901) ***(P-20)***
American Faucet Coatings Corp ....E....760 598-5895
3280 Corporate Vw Vista (92081) ***(P-6541)***
American Fencing, Fresno *Also called A J Excavation Inc* ***(P-3302)***
American Fidelity Assurance Co ....D....559 230-2107
3649 W Beechwood Ave # 103 Fresno (93711) ***(P-10248)***
American Financial Network Inc ....D....562 926-2401
14241 Firestone Blvd La Mirada (90638) ***(P-26494)***
American Financial Network Inc ....D....562 861-1414
8505 Florence Ave Downey (90240) ***(P-9785)***
American Financial Network Inc ....C....951 582-2655
3400 Inland Empire Blvd # 101 Ontario (91764) ***(P-26495)***
American Financial Network Inc ....D....909 287-7585
14748 Pipeline Ave Ste A Chino Hills (91709) ***(P-9786)***
American Financial Network Inc (PA) ....C....909 606-3905
10 Pointe Dr Ste 330 Brea (92821) ***(P-9517)***
American Financial Network Inc ....D....925 705-7710
2125 Oak Grove Rd Walnut Creek (94598) ***(P-9787)***
American First Credit Union (PA) ....D....562 691-1112
700 N Harbor Blvd La Habra (90631) ***(P-9381)***
American Fish and Seafood, Los Angeles *Also called Prospect Enterprises Inc* ***(P-8385)***
American Force Private SEC Inc ....D....909 384-9820
1585 S D St Ste 208 San Bernardino (92408) ***(P-16188)***
American Freightways LP ....D....866 326-5902
10845 Rancho Bernardo Rd # 100 San Diego (92127) ***(P-3964)***
American Funding ....D....408 269-4238
5369 Camden Ave Ste 240 San Jose (95124) ***(P-9613)***
American Funds Distrs Inc (HQ) ....C....213 486-9200
333 S Hope St Ste Levb Los Angeles (90071) ***(P-11710)***
American Funds Service Company ....E....949 975-5000
6455 Irvine Center Dr Irvine (92618) ***(P-9859)***
American Future Tech Corp ....C....888 462-3899
529 Baldwin Park Blvd City of Industry (91746) ***(P-6794)***
American Gen Lf Insur Co Del ....B....415 836-2700
1 Montgomery St Fl 25 San Francisco (94104) ***(P-9860)***
American General Design ....E....626 304-0800
245 S Los Robles Ave # 100 Pasadena (91101) ***(P-25412)***
American General Life Insur ....D....650 994-6679
455 Hickey Blvd Ste 500 Daly City (94015) ***(P-10249)***
American GNC Corporation ....E....805 582-0582
888 E Easy St Simi Valley (93065) ***(P-24932)***
American Golf Construction, Canoga Park *Also called American Landscape Inc* ***(P-697)***
American Golf Corporation ....C....858 755-6768
1505 Lomas Santa Fe Dr Solana Beach (92075) ***(P-18357)***
American Golf Corporation ....D....805 495-5407
4155 Erbes Rd Thousand Oaks (91360) ***(P-18358)***
American Golf Corporation ....C....949 786-1224
1 Ethel Coplen Way Irvine (92612) ***(P-18359)***
American Golf Corporation (HQ) ....C....310 664-4000
909 N Pacific Coast Hwy El Segundo (90245) ***(P-18360)***
American Golf Corporation ....E....562 421-0550
3101 Carson St Lakewood (90712) ***(P-18216)***
American Golf Corporation ....E....209 477-4653
6301 W Eight Mile Rd Stockton (95219) ***(P-18361)***
American Golf Corporation ....D....714 779-2461
19400 Mountain View Ave Yorba Linda (92886) ***(P-18362)***
American Golf Corporation ....E....562 494-4424
5001 Deukmejian Dr Long Beach (90804) ***(P-18217)***
American Golf Corporation ....D....702 431-2191
68311 Paseo Real Cathedral City (92234) ***(P-18363)***
American Golf Corporation ....E....760 737-9762
17166 Stonerdg Cntry Clb Poway (92064) ***(P-18364)***
American Golf Corporation ....D....805 343-1214
1490 Golf Course Ln Nipomo (93444) ***(P-18365)***
American Golf Corporation ....D....714 536-8866
6501 Palm Ave Huntington Beach (92648) ***(P-18366)***
American Golf Corporation ....D....909 861-5757
22751 Golden Springs Dr Diamond Bar (91765) ***(P-18367)***
American Golf Corporation ....D....925 672-9737
1001 Peacock Creek Dr Clayton (94517) ***(P-18368)***
American Golf Corporation ....E....408 262-8813
1500 Country Club Dr Milpitas (95035) ***(P-18369)***
American Golf Corporation ....D....760 757-2100
3202 Vista Way Oceanside (92056) ***(P-18370)***
American Golf Corporation ....D....310 377-7370
7000 Los Verdes Dr Ste 1 Rancho Palos Verdes (90275) ***(P-18371)***
American Golf Corporation ....D....714 846-1364
16782 Graham St Huntington Beach (92649) ***(P-18372)***
American Golf Corporation ....D....831 688-3213
610 Clubhouse Dr Rear Aptos (95003) ***(P-18373)***
American Golf Corporation ....E....760 568-9311
41500 Monterey Ave Palm Desert (92260) ***(P-18374)***
American Golf Corporation ....D....562 943-7123
15501 Alicante Rd La Mirada (90638) ***(P-18375)***
American Golf Corporation ....E....805 522-0803
5031 Alamo St Simi Valley (93063) ***(P-18376)***
American Golf Corporation ....D....805 527-9663
301 Wood Ranch Pkwy Simi Valley (93065) ***(P-18218)***
American Golf Corporation ....D....714 672-6800
1440 E Bastanchury Rd Fullerton (92835) ***(P-18219)***
American Guard Services Inc (PA) ....B....310 645-6200
1125 W 190th St Gardena (90248) ***(P-16189)***
American Health Care, Rocklin *Also called American Hlthcare ADM Svcs Inc* ***(P-22173)***
American Health Connection ....A....424 226-0420
8484 Wilshire Blvd # 501 Beverly Hills (90211) ***(P-16619)***
American Health Services LLC ....C....661 254-6630
26460 Summit Cir Santa Clarita (91350) ***(P-18806)***

ALPHABETIC

Employee Codes: A=Over 500 employees, B=251-500
C=101-250, D=51-100, E=50
2020 Directory of California
Wholesalers and Services Companies
© Mergent Inc. 1-800-342-5647
1171

American Heart Association Inc....E....213 291-7000
816 S Figueroa St Los Angeles (90017) ***(P-24376)***
American Hlthcare ADM Svcs Inc....B....916 773-7227
3850 Atherton Rd Rocklin (95765) ***(P-22173)***
American Home Alarms Inc....C....888 531-5065
128 E Huntington Dr Ste B Arcadia (91006) ***(P-2420)***
American Home Assurance Co....B....213 689-3500
777 S Figueroa St Ste 300 Los Angeles (90017) ***(P-10072)***
American Homes Trust....D....619 694-7821
450 Camino Hermoso San Marcos (92078) ***(P-11841)***
American Honda, Eastvale *Also called Meiko America Inc* ***(P-4449)***
American Honda Finance Corp (HQ)....C....310 972-2239
20800 Madrona Ave Torrance (90503) ***(P-9452)***
American Honda Finance Corp....D....714 816-8110
10801 Walker St Ste 140 Cypress (90630) ***(P-9453)***
American Honda Motor Co Inc (HQ)....A....310 783-2000
1919 Torrance Blvd Torrance (90501) ***(P-6383)***
American Hospital Mgt Corp (PA)....B....707 822-3621
3800 Janes Rd Arcata (95521) ***(P-20746)***
American Hritg Protection Svcs, Winnetka *Also called Memon Aamir* ***(P-16350)***
American Incorporated....B....559 651-1776
1345 N American St Visalia (93291) ***(P-2039)***
American Indian Health & Svcs....E....805 681-7356
4141 State St Ste B11 Santa Barbara (93110) ***(P-22174)***
American Institute of Aeronaut....D....619 545-3736
3198 E Fox Run Way San Diego (92111) ***(P-25963)***
American Institute Research....B....916 286-8800
2151 River Plaza Dr # 320 Sacramento (95833) ***(P-25964)***
American Insurance Company Inc....A....415 899-2000
1465 N Mcdowell Blvd Petaluma (94954) ***(P-10073)***
American Integrated Svcs Inc (PA)....E....310 522-1168
1502 E Opp St Wilmington (90744) ***(P-26929)***
American Interbanc Mrtg LLC....E....714 957-9430
4 Park Plz Ste 650 Irvine (92614) ***(P-9518)***
American Internet Mortgage Inc....C....888 411-4246
4121 Camino Del Rio S San Diego (92108) ***(P-9519)***
American Intgrted Rsources Inc....D....714 921-4100
2341 N Pacific St Orange (92865) ***(P-26130)***
American Intl Group Inc....B....213 689-3500
777 S Figueroa St # 1800 Los Angeles (90017) ***(P-10227)***
American Intl Group Inc....C....619 682-4058
9350 Waxie Way Ste 300 San Diego (92123) ***(P-10250)***
American Janitor Services, Thousand Oaks *Also called American Services and Products* ***(P-13863)***
American Kal Enterprises Inc (PA)....D....626 338-7308
4265 Puente Ave Baldwin Park (91706) ***(P-7378)***
American Landscape Inc....C....818 999-2041
7013 Owensmouth Ave Canoga Park (91303) ***(P-697)***
American Landscape Management....E....805 647-5077
1607 Los Angeles Ave I Ventura (93004) ***(P-772)***
American Landscape Management (PA)....B....818 999-2041
7013 Owensmouth Ave Canoga Park (91303) ***(P-698)***
American Leak Detection Inc....E....714 836-8477
910 E Orangefair Ln Anaheim (92801) ***(P-2040)***
American Legal Copy-Or LLC....D....415 777-4449
98 Battery St Ste 220 San Francisco (94111) ***(P-13746)***
American Legion Ambulance Svc....D....209 223-2963
11350 American Legion Dr Sutter Creek (95685) ***(P-24474)***
American Legion Hall, Sutter Creek *Also called American Legion Ambulance Svc* ***(P-24474)***
American Liberty Capital Corp....C....949 623-0288
19000 Macarthur Blvd # 400 Irvine (92612) ***(P-9614)***
American Liberty Funding, Irvine *Also called American Liberty Capital Corp* ***(P-9614)***
American Marketing Systems Inc....D....800 747-7784
2800 Van Ness Ave San Francisco (94109) ***(P-10913)***
American Med....C....909 793-7676
600 Iowa St Redlands (92373) ***(P-3622)***
American Med....B....626 633-4600
5257 Vincent Ave Irwindale (91706) ***(P-3623)***
American Med....C....650 235-1333
1510 Rollins Rd Burlingame (94010) ***(P-3624)***
American Med....C....510 895-7600
7575 Southfront Rd Livermore (94551) ***(P-3625)***
American Med....C....909 948-1714
7925 Center Ave Rancho Cucamonga (91730) ***(P-3626)***
American Med Resp Amblnc Svc....D....707 536-0400
930 S A St Santa Rosa (95404) ***(P-3627)***
American Med Rspnse Sthern Cal....A....661 945-9310
1055 W Avenue J Lancaster (93534) ***(P-3628)***
American Medical Response, Palm Springs *Also called Springs Ambulance Service Inc* ***(P-3726)***
American Medical Response....C....925 454-6000
2400 Bisso Ln Concord (94520) ***(P-3629)***
American Medical Response....B....916 563-0600
1041 Fee Dr Sacramento (95815) ***(P-3630)***
American Medical Response....D....415 922-9400
1300 Illinois St San Francisco (94107) ***(P-3631)***
American Medical Response....D....831 423-7030
116 Hubbard St Santa Cruz (95060) ***(P-3632)***
American Medical Response (HQ)....D....951 782-5200
879 Marlborough Ave Riverside (92507) ***(P-3633)***
American Medical Response....D....650 235-1333
1510 Rollins Rd Burlingame (94010) ***(P-3634)***
American Medical Response Inc....C....925 602-1300
2400 Bisso Ln Concord (94520) ***(P-3635)***
American Medical Response Inc....C....209 567-4030
1420 Lander Ave Turlock (95380) ***(P-3636)***
American Medical Response Inc....C....858 492-3500
3465 Camino Del Rio S # 410 San Diego (92108) ***(P-3637)***
American Medical Response Inc....C....805 688-6550
240 E Highway 246 Ste 300 Buellton (93427) ***(P-3638)***
American Medical Response Inc....C....760 883-5000
1111 Montalvo Way Palm Springs (92262) ***(P-3639)***
American Medical Response Inc....C....831 718-9555
4548 A St Marina (93933) ***(P-3640)***
American Medical Response Inc....C....951 765-3900
208 E Devonshire Ave A Hemet (92543) ***(P-3641)***
American Medical Response Inc....C....831 636-9391
1870 Hillcrest Rd Hollister (95023) ***(P-3642)***
American Medical Response Inc....E....530 887-9440
13146 Lincoln Way Auburn (95603) ***(P-3643)***
American Medical Response Inc....C....415 794-9204
13992 Catalina St San Leandro (94577) ***(P-3644)***
American Medical Response West....B....209 948-5136
3755 West Ln Stockton (95204) ***(P-3645)***
American Medical Tech Inc....D....949 553-0359
17595 Cartwright Rd Irvine (92614) ***(P-6938)***
American Medical Technologies, Irvine *Also called Gordian Medical Inc* ***(P-6968)***
American Merchant Center Inc....D....818 947-1700
6819 Sepulveda Blvd # 311 Van Nuys (91405) ***(P-9474)***
American Metal & Iron Inc....D....408 452-0777
2377 Tulip Rd San Jose (95128) ***(P-7749)***
American Metals Corporation (HQ)....C....916 371-7700
1499 Parkway Blvd West Sacramento (95691) ***(P-7043)***
American Mobile Healthcare, San Diego *Also called Amn Healthcare Services Inc* ***(P-19654)***
American Multi-Cinema Inc....D....818 953-4020
125 E Palm Ave Burbank (91502) ***(P-17802)***
American Multi-Cinema Inc....E....619 296-0370
7037 Friars Rd San Diego (92108) ***(P-17803)***
American Multi-Cinema Inc....D....626 407-0240
450 N Atlantic Blvd Monterey Park (91754) ***(P-17804)***
American Multi-Cinema Inc....D....626 974-8624
1414 N Azusa Ave Covina (91722) ***(P-17805)***
American Multi-Cinema Inc....C....310 326-5011
2591 Airport Dr Torrance (90505) ***(P-17806)***
American Multi-Cinema Inc....E....714 630-2410
1565 S Disneyland Dr Frnt Anaheim (92802) ***(P-17807)***
American Multi-Cinema Inc....D....714 769-4288
20 City Blvd W Ste E1 Orange (92868) ***(P-17808)***
American Multi-Cinema Inc....E....714 992-6961
1001 S Lemon St Ste A Fullerton (92832) ***(P-17809)***
American Multi-Cinema Inc....E....626 585-8900
42 Miller Aly Pasadena (91103) ***(P-17810)***
American Multi-Cinema Inc....E....562 864-6206
12300 Civic Center Dr Norwalk (90650) ***(P-17811)***
American Multi-Cinema Inc....E....310 228-5500
10250 Snta Mnca Bld Los Angeles (90067) ***(P-17812)***
American Multi-Cinema Inc....D....619 296-2737
1640 Cmino Del Rio N 20 San Diego (92108) ***(P-17813)***
American Multi-Cinema Inc....D....626 810-7949
1560 S Azusa Ave City of Industry (91748) ***(P-17814)***
American Multi-Cinema Inc....E....323 722-4583
1475 N Montebello Blvd Montebello (90640) ***(P-17815)***
American Multimedia TV USA....D....626 466-1038
530 S Lake Ave Unit 368 Pasadena (91101) ***(P-5579)***
American Mutual Fund Inc....C....213 486-9200
333 S Hope St Fl 51 Los Angeles (90071) ***(P-11711)***
American Mzhou Dngpo Group Inc....D....626 820-9239
4520 Maine Ave Baldwin Park (91706) ***(P-26131)***
American Nat Red Cross - Blood, San Francisco *Also called American National Red Cross* ***(P-22909)***
American National Red Cross, Modesto *Also called Delta Blood Bank* ***(P-22224)***
American National Red Cross....C....510 594-5100
6230 Claremont Ave Oakland (94618) ***(P-22175)***
American National Red Cross....E....714 481-5300
601 N Golden Circle Dr Santa Ana (92705) ***(P-22908)***
American National Red Cross....C....415 427-8134
85 2nd St Ste 800 San Francisco (94105) ***(P-22909)***
American National Red Cross....E....925 603-7400
1300 Alberta Way Concord (94521) ***(P-22910)***
American National Red Cross....A....909 859-7006
100 Red Cross Cir Pomona (91768) ***(P-22176)***
American National Red Cross....D....310 445-9900
11355 Ohio Ave Los Angeles (90025) ***(P-22911)***
American National Red Cross....D....858 309-1200
3950 Calle Fortunada San Diego (92123) ***(P-22912)***
American Natl Rd CRS-Bld Svcs, Pomona *Also called American National Red Cross* ***(P-22176)***
American Natl Red Cross, Stockton *Also called Delta Blood Bank* ***(P-22225)***
American Nursing Home MGT Inc....D....310 672-1012
301 Centinela Ave Inglewood (90302) ***(P-26988)***
American Nwland Communities LP (PA)....E....858 455-7503
9820 Towne Centre Dr # 100 San Diego (92121) ***(P-11540)***
American Pacific Mortgage Corp....E....415 891-8706
300 Tamal Plz Ste 250 Corte Madera (94925) ***(P-9520)***
American Pacific Mortgage Corp (PA)....C....916 960-1325
3000 Lava Ridge Ct # 200 Roseville (95661) ***(P-9521)***
American Paper & Plastics Inc....C....626 444-0000
550 S 7th Ave City of Industry (91746) ***(P-7870)***
American Paper & Provisions, City of Industry *Also called American Paper & Plastics Inc* ***(P-7870)***
American Patriot Security....D....916 706-2449
10293 Rockingham Dr # 104 Sacramento (95827) ***(P-16190)***
American Paving Co....E....559 268-9886
315 N Thorne Ave Fresno (93706) ***(P-1662)***
American Plus Bank (PA)....E....626 821-9188
630 W Duarte Rd Arcadia (91007) ***(P-9028)***

American Portwell Tech Inc (PA)..........D.......510 403-3399
44200 Christy St Fremont (94538) ***(P-6795)***
American Power SEC Svc Inc..........D.......866 974-9994
1451 Rimpau Ave Ste 207 Corona (92879) ***(P-16191)***
American President Lines LLC..........D.......510 272-3990
1579 Middle Harbor Rd Oakland (94607) ***(P-4890)***
American Private Duty Inc..........D.......818 386-6358
13111 Ventura Blvd # 100 Studio City (91604) ***(P-21662)***
American Prof Ambulance Corp..........C.......818 996-2200
16945 Sherman Way Van Nuys (91406) ***(P-3646)***
American Property Management..........C.......925 463-8000
7050 Johnson Dr Pleasanton (94588) ***(P-12003)***
American Protection Group Inc (PA)..........C.......818 279-2433
8551 Vesper Ave Panorama City (91402) ***(P-16192)***
American Prprty-Mnagement Corp..........C.......619 232-3121
326 Broadway San Diego (92101) ***(P-12004)***
American Realty, San Jose *Also called American Funding* ***(P-9613)***
American Realty Advisors..........D.......818 545-1152
515 S Flower St Ste 4900 Los Angeles (90071) ***(P-11842)***
American Realty Centre Inc..........D.......323 666-6111
120 S Glendale Ave Glendale (91205) ***(P-10914)***
American Recovery Center, Pomona *Also called Behavioral Health Services Inc* ***(P-22940)***
American Recovery Service, El Dorado Hills *Also called Patrick K Willis Company Inc* ***(P-16987)***
American Red Cross, Concord *Also called American National Red Cross* ***(P-22910)***
American Red Cross La Chapter (PA)..........C.......310 445-9900
1320 Newton St Los Angeles (90021) ***(P-22913)***
American Red Cross San Diego (PA)..........C.......858 309-1200
3950 Calle Fortunada San Diego (92123) ***(P-22914)***
American Reprographics Co LLC..........D.......213 745-3145
934 Venice Blvd Los Angeles (90015) ***(P-13747)***
American Reprographics Co LLC..........D.......916 443-1322
1322 V St Sacramento (95818) ***(P-13748)***
American Reprographics Co LLC..........D.......626 289-5021
616 Monterey Pass Rd Monterey Park (91754) ***(P-13749)***
American Reprographics Co LLC..........D.......408 295-5770
821 Martin Ave Santa Clara (95050) ***(P-13750)***
American Reprographics Co LLC..........C.......714 751-2680
345 Clinton St Costa Mesa (92626) ***(P-13751)***
American Reprographics Co LLC..........D.......951 686-0530
4295 Main St Riverside (92501) ***(P-13752)***
American Residential Svcs LLC..........D.......858 457-5547
9895 Olson Dr Ste A San Diego (92121) ***(P-2041)***
American Residential Svcs LLC..........E.......310 808-0279
15707 S Main St Gardena (90248) ***(P-2042)***
American Residential Svcs LLC..........D.......858 292-4452
P.O. Box 1592 El Cajon (92022) ***(P-2043)***
American Residential Svcs LLC..........D.......650 856-1612
1965 Kyle Park Ct San Jose (95125) ***(P-2044)***
American Residential Svcs LLC..........D.......951 341-9371
1520 W Linden St Riverside (92507) ***(P-2045)***
American Residential Svcs LLC..........D.......510 729-6227
1618 Doolittle Dr San Leandro (94577) ***(P-2046)***
American Residential Svcs LLC..........D.......510 657-7601
29196 Simms Ct Hayward (94544) ***(P-2047)***
American Residential Svcs LLC..........D.......408 435-3810
2305 Paragon Dr San Jose (95131) ***(P-17483)***
American Residential Svcs LLC..........D.......714 634-1826
740 N Hariton St Orange (92868) ***(P-2048)***
American Residential Svcs LLC..........D.......818 833-6677
12507 San Fernando Rd Sylmar (91342) ***(P-2049)***
American Restoration Services, Hayward *Also called American Technologies Inc* ***(P-3373)***
American Restoration Services, Simi Valley *Also called American Technologies Inc* ***(P-3375)***
American Retirement Corp..........C.......310 399-3227
2107 Ocean Ave Santa Monica (90405) ***(P-19720)***
American River Care, Carmichael *Also called Sunbridge Brittany Rehab Centr* ***(P-20281)***
American Sanitary Supply Inc..........E.......714 632-3010
592 Explorer St Brea (92821) ***(P-7664)***
American Security Force Inc..........C.......323 722-8585
5400 E Olympic Blvd # 225 Commerce (90022) ***(P-16193)***
American Service Industries..........D.......323 779-4000
2930 W Imperial Hwy # 332 Inglewood (90303) ***(P-16492)***
American Services and Products..........D.......805 375-2858
949 Camino Dos Rios Thousand Oaks (91360) ***(P-13863)***
American Sign, Van Nuys *Also called Dee Sign Co* ***(P-16742)***
American Solar Solution Inc..........D.......877 946-8855
14701 Albers St Sherman Oaks (91411) ***(P-1078)***
American Spclty Hlth Group Inc..........B.......858 754-2000
10221 Wateridge Cir # 201 San Diego (92121) ***(P-21663)***
American Specialty Health Inc (PA)..........C.......858 754-2000
10221 Wateridge Cir # 201 San Diego (92121) ***(P-10251)***
American State Water Company, San Dimas *Also called Golden State Water Company* ***(P-6065)***
American Synergy Asbestos Remo..........D.......510 444-2333
28436 Satellite St Hayward (94545) ***(P-3372)***
American Tax Solutions..........E.......323 306-7032
1055 W 7th St Ste 3050 Los Angeles (90017) ***(P-25534)***
American Technical Svcs Inc..........D.......951 372-9664
20384 Via Mantua Porter Ranch (91326) ***(P-24933)***
American Technologies Inc..........D.......510 429-5000
25000 Industrial Blvd Hayward (94545) ***(P-3373)***
American Technologies Inc (PA)..........C.......714 283-9990
3360 E La Palma Ave Anaheim (92806) ***(P-3374)***
American Technologies Inc..........E.......818 700-5060
2688 Westhills Ct Simi Valley (93065) ***(P-3375)***
American Technologies Inc..........D.......858 530-2400
8444 Miralani Dr Ste 200 San Diego (92126) ***(P-26989)***
American Textile Maint Co..........E.......213 749-4433
1705 Hooper Ave Los Angeles (90021) ***(P-13195)***
American Textile Maint Co..........D.......562 438-7656
3001 E Anaheim St Long Beach (90804) ***(P-13196)***
American Textile Maint Co..........D.......562 438-1126
3001 E Anaheim St Long Beach (90804) ***(P-13197)***
American Textile Maint Co..........C.......323 735-1661
1664 W Washington Blvd Los Angeles (90007) ***(P-13198)***
American Textile Maint Co..........C.......562 424-1607
2201 E Carson St Long Beach (90807) ***(P-13271)***
American Tile Brick Veneer Inc..........E.......562 595-9293
1389 E 28th St Signal Hill (90755) ***(P-2882)***
American Tire Distributors..........E.......408 435-3340
645 Dado St San Jose (95131) ***(P-6483)***
American Transport Inc..........D.......714 567-8000
3910 Prospect Ave Ste A Yorba Linda (92886) ***(P-9522)***
American Travel Solutions LLC..........D.......818 359-6514
26707 Agoura Rd Ste 204 Calabasas (91302) ***(P-4815)***
American Two-Way, North Hollywood *Also called Emergency Technologies Inc* ***(P-16511)***
American Untd HM Care Crp-Priv, Studio City *Also called American Private Duty Inc* ***(P-21662)***
American Vanguard Corporation..........C.......323 264-3910
4100 E Washington Blvd Commerce (90023) ***(P-8688)***
American Vision Windows Inc..........C.......805 582-1833
2125 N Madera Rd Ste A Simi Valley (93065) ***(P-17484)***
American Voice Mail Inc (PA)..........E.......310 478-4949
11150 W Olympic Blvd # 975 Los Angeles (90064) ***(P-5151)***
American Water Works Co Inc..........D.......916 568-4236
4701 Beloit Dr Sacramento (95838) ***(P-6016)***
American West Worldwide Ex Inc..........E.......805 926-2800
511 Zaca Ln Ste 120 San Luis Obispo (93401) ***(P-3965)***
American West Worldwide Ex Inc (PA)..........D.......800 788-4534
51 Zaca Ln Ste 120 San Luis Obispo (93401) ***(P-4193)***
American Wht Mssn In Sthrn..........D.......714 522-4599
7212 Orangethorpe Ave 7a Buena Park (90621) ***(P-22915)***
American Wrecking Inc..........D.......626 350-8303
2459 Lee Ave South El Monte (91733) ***(P-3336)***
American Zettler Inc (HQ)..........D.......949 831-5000
75 Columbia Aliso Viejo (92656) ***(P-7229)***
American-1 Airtight SEC Co..........E.......714 997-0605
2510 N Grand Ave Ste 207 Santa Ana (92705) ***(P-16194)***
Americantours Intl LLC (HQ)..........C.......310 641-9953
6053 W Century Blvd Los Angeles (90045) ***(P-4816)***
Americare Ambulance Service, Huntington Beach *Also called Americare Medservices Inc* ***(P-3647)***
Americare Hlth Retirement Inc..........D.......760 744-4484
1550 Security Pl Ofc San Marcos (92078) ***(P-10566)***
Americare Medservices Inc..........C.......310 632-1141
6524 Fremont Cir Huntington Beach (92648) ***(P-3647)***
Americas Christian Credit Un (PA)..........D.......626 208-5400
2100 E Route 66 Ste 100 Glendora (91740) ***(P-9382)***
Americas Finest Carpet Company, Chula Vista *Also called Home Carpet Investment Inc* ***(P-3005)***
Americas Flood Services Inc..........D.......916 636-9460
3350 Country Club Dr # 201 Cameron Park (95682) ***(P-10252)***
Americas Lemonade Stand Inc..........C.......707 745-1274
5100 Park Rd Benicia (94510) ***(P-16620)***
Americas Printer.com, Buena Park *Also called A J Parent Company Inc* ***(P-16588)***
Americash..........E.......714 994-7554
3080 Bristol St Ste 300 Costa Mesa (92626) ***(P-9523)***
Americold Logistics LLC..........A.......714 993-3533
2750 Orbiter St Brea (92821) ***(P-4336)***
Americold Logistics LLC..........D.......678 441-1468
1415 N Raymond Ave Anaheim (92801) ***(P-4337)***
Americold Logistics LLC..........E.......831 424-1537
950 S Sanborn Rd Salinas (93901) ***(P-4338)***
Americold Logistics LLC..........E.......909 390-4950
700 Malaga St Ontario (91761) ***(P-4339)***
Americold Logistics LLC..........D.......323 581-0025
3420 E Vernon Ave Vernon (90058) ***(P-4340)***
Americold Realty, Ontario *Also called Americold Logistics LLC* ***(P-4339)***
Americor Funding Inc..........C.......866 333-8686
18200 Von Karman Ave # 600 Irvine (92612) ***(P-13396)***
Ameriflight LLC..........D.......510 569-6000
21889 Skywest Dr Hayward (94541) ***(P-4659)***
Amerifreight Inc..........A.......909 839-2600
218 Machlin Ct Walnut (91789) ***(P-4372)***
AmeriGas Propane LP..........D.......916 852-7400
11030 White Rock Rd # 100 Rancho Cordova (95670) ***(P-8718)***
Amerine Systems Incorporated..........E.......209 847-5968
10866 Cleveland Ave Oakdale (95361) ***(P-699)***
Ameripath Mortgage Corporation..........C.......949 753-9211
6410 Oak Cyn Ste 200 Irvine (92618) ***(P-9524)***
Ameripride Services Inc..........D.......805 239-9449
109 Calle Propano Ste C Paso Robles (93446) ***(P-13199)***
Ameripride Services Inc..........E.......530 242-0564
3750 Eastside Rd Redding (96001) ***(P-13200)***
Ameripride Services Inc..........C.......661 324-7941
335 Washington St Bakersfield (93307) ***(P-13201)***
Ameripride Services Inc..........D.......559 266-0627
1050 W Whites Bridge Ave Fresno (93706) ***(P-13272)***
Ameripride Services Inc..........E.......209 982-0020
4206 S B St Stockton (95206) ***(P-13202)***
Ameripride Services Inc..........E.......714 385-8991
2230 W Chapman Ave Orange (92868) ***(P-13203)***
Ameripride Services Inc..........E.......800 748-6178
3701 Collins Ave Ste 5b Richmond (94806) ***(P-13204)***
Ameripride Services Inc..........E.......800 882-5326
1356 Dayton St Ste R Salinas (93901) ***(P-13205)***
Ameripride Unifom Svcs, Bakersfield *Also called Ameripride Services Inc* ***(P-13201)***
Ameripride Uniform Services, Fresno *Also called Ameripride Services Inc* ***(P-13272)***

ALPHABETIC

Employee Codes: A=Over 500 employees, B=251-500
C=101-250, D=51-100, E=50
2020 Directory of California
Wholesalers and Services Companies
© Mergent Inc. 1-800-342-5647
1173

Ameriquest Capital Corporation (PA) ....B....714 564-0600
1100 W Twn Cntry Rd R Orange (92868) ***(P-9615)***
Amerisourcebergen Corporation ....C....714 704-4407
500 N State College Blvd # 900 Orange (92868) ***(P-7915)***
Amerisourcebergen Corporation ....C....610 727-7000
1368 Metropolitan Dr Orange (92868) ***(P-26132)***
Amerisourcebergen Corporation ....C....951 493-2339
215 Deininger Cir Corona (92880) ***(P-7916)***
Amerisourcebergen Corporation ....C....714 704-4407
505 City Pkwy W Orange (92868) ***(P-26133)***
Amerisourcebergen Drug Corp ....C....661 257-6400
24903 Avenue Kearny Valencia (91355) ***(P-7917)***
Amerisourcebergen Drug Corp ....C....916 830-4500
1325 Striker Ave Sacramento (95834) ***(P-7918)***
Amerisourcebergen Drug Corp ....C....951 371-2000
1851 California Ave Corona (92881) ***(P-7919)***
Amerisuites, Ontario *Also called Todays Vi LLC* ***(P-13029)***
Amerit Fleet Solutions Inc (HQ) ....D....877 512-6374
1331 N Calif Blvd Ste 150 Walnut Creek (94596) ***(P-17409)***
Ameritac Inc (PA) ....D....925 743-8398
640 Logan Ln Danville (94526) ***(P-26930)***
Ameritech Mortgage, Walnut Creek *Also called Izt Mortgage Inc* ***(P-9629)***
Ameriwest Industries Inc ....E....909 930-1898
2910 S Archibald Ave A Ontario (91761) ***(P-7379)***
AMF Bowling Centers Inc ....E....323 728-9161
1201 W Beverly Blvd Montebello (90640) ***(P-18021)***
AMF Bowling Centers Inc ....E....661 324-4966
1819 30th St Bakersfield (93301) ***(P-18022)***
AMF Bowling Centers Inc ....E....949 770-0055
22771 Centre Dr Lake Forest (92630) ***(P-18023)***
AMG Construction Group ....D....800 310-2609
1103 W Gardena Blvd # 201 Gardena (90248) ***(P-1663)***
AMG Huntington Beach LLC ....E....714 894-9802
5416 Argosy Ave Huntington Beach (92649) ***(P-24934)***
Amgen Distribution Inc ....D....760 989-4424
1244 Valley View Rd # 119 Glendale (91202) ***(P-3966)***
Amgen Pharmaceuticals Inc ....A....805 447-1000
1 Amgen Center Dr Thousand Oaks (91320) ***(P-25965)***
Amgreen Solar & Electric Inc ....E....213 388-5647
1367 Venice Blvd Los Angeles (90006) ***(P-2050)***
Amgreen Solutions Inc ....E....213 388-5647
1367 Venice Blvd Fl 2 Los Angeles (90006) ***(P-26496)***
Amgreen-Karena Ht Partnr Ltd (PA) ....D....818 707-9494
5743 Corsa Ave Ste 200 Westlake Village (91362) ***(P-12005)***
Amh Portfolio One LLC ....C....480 921-4600
30601 Agoura Rd Ste 200 Agoura Hills (91301) ***(P-11843)***
AMI Manufacturing, Sacramento *Also called Airco Mechanical Inc* ***(P-2025)***
AMI-Hti Tarzana Encino Joint V ....A....818 881-0800
18321 Clark St Tarzana (91356) ***(P-20747)***
Amica Mutual Insurance Company ....D....877 972-6422
3200 Park Center Dr # 650 Costa Mesa (92626) ***(P-10253)***
Amini Innovation Corp ....C....562 222-2500
8725 Rex Rd Pico Rivera (90660) ***(P-6503)***
Amir Ahmad MD ....D....805 545-8100
628 California Blvd Ste D San Luis Obispo (93401) ***(P-18807)***
Amisub (irvine Regional Hospi) ....A....949 916-7556
1400 S Douglass Rd # 250 Anaheim (92806) ***(P-20748)***
Amisub of California Inc (HQ) ....A....818 881-0800
18321 Clark St Tarzana (91356) ***(P-20749)***
Amk Foodservices Inc ....C....805 544-7600
830 Capitolio Way San Luis Obispo (93401) ***(P-8155)***
Amkotron Inc ....D....562 921-3330
12620 Hiddencreek Way Cerritos (90703) ***(P-15910)***
Ammunition LLC ....D....415 632-1170
1500 Sansome St Ste 110 San Francisco (94111) ***(P-26497)***
Amn Healthcare Inc (HQ) ....C....858 792-0711
12400 High Bluff Dr San Diego (92130) ***(P-18808)***
Amn Healthcare Services Inc ....A....858 792-0711
12400 High Bluff Dr # 100 San Diego (92130) ***(P-19654)***
Amn Healthcare Services Inc (PA) ....C....866 871-8519
12400 High Bluff Dr San Diego (92130) ***(P-14225)***
Amobee Inc (HQ) ....C....650 353-4399
901 Marshall St 200 Redwood City (94063) ***(P-13471)***
Amoeba Music Inc ....D....415 831-1200
1855 Haight St San Francisco (94117) ***(P-16621)***
Amour Vert Inc ....D....650 388-4284
1278 Minnesota St Ste A San Francisco (94107) ***(P-8054)***
AMP Technologies LLC ....C....877 442-2824
445 Melrose Ct San Ramon (94582) ***(P-14634)***
Ampam Parks Mechanical Inc ....A....310 835-1532
17036 Avalon Blvd Carson (90746) ***(P-2051)***
Ampco Contracting Inc ....C....949 955-2255
1420 S Allec St Anaheim (92805) ***(P-6338)***
Ampla Health (PA) ....C....530 674-4261
935 Market St Yuba City (95991) ***(P-19603)***
Ampla Health ....D....530 342-4395
680 Cohasset Rd Chico (95926) ***(P-18809)***
Ampla Health ....D....530 743-4614
4941 Olivehurst Ave Olivehurst (95961) ***(P-18810)***
Amplify Education Inc ....D....562 209-7875
1032 Irving St Ste 445 San Francisco (94122) ***(P-14635)***
Ampronix Inc ....D....949 273-8000
15 Whatney Irvine (92618) ***(P-6939)***
AMR, Los Angeles *Also called American Airlines Inc* ***(P-4652)***
AMR Eagle, San Diego *Also called Envoy Air Inc* ***(P-4663)***
AMS, San Diego *Also called Asset Marketing Systems Insu* ***(P-26510)***
AMS, San Bernardino *Also called Allied Building Products Corp* ***(P-6601)***
AMS, Montebello *Also called Allied Building Products Corp* ***(P-6708)***
AMS - Exotic LLC ....D....213 612-5888
720 S Alameda St Los Angeles (90021) ***(P-8429)***
AMS American Mech Svcs MD Inc ....D....714 888-6820
2116 E Walnut Ave Fullerton (92831) ***(P-2052)***
AMS Bekins Van Lines, Burlingame *Also called AMS Relocation Incorporated* ***(P-4194)***
AMS Electric Inc ....D....925 961-1600
6905 Sierra Ct Ste A Dublin (94568) ***(P-2421)***
AMS Fulfillment, Valencia *Also called Advantage Media Services Inc* ***(P-4368)***
AMS Paving Inc (PA) ....E....909 357-0711
11060 Rose Ave Fontana (92337) ***(P-1664)***
AMS Relocation Incorporated ....D....650 697-3530
1873 Rollins Rd Burlingame (94010) ***(P-4194)***
AMS Ventures Inc ....D....301 980-5087
39055 Hastings St Ste 205 Fremont (94538) ***(P-26498)***
Amsi Real Estate Services, San Francisco *Also called American Marketing Systems Inc* ***(P-10913)***
Amsnet Inc (PA) ....E....925 245-6100
502 Commerce Way Livermore (94551) ***(P-15556)***
Amsurg, Torrance *Also called Torrance Surgery Center LP* ***(P-19507)***
Amsurg, San Diego *Also called Mission Valley Hts Surgery Ctr* ***(P-19201)***
Amsurg, Glendale *Also called Glendale Eye Medical Group* ***(P-18997)***
Amtel Inc ....E....408 615-0522
950 S Bascom Ave Ste 2002 San Jose (95128) ***(P-26990)***
Amtrak, San Diego *Also called National Railroad Pass Corp* ***(P-3503)***
Amtrav, Calabasas *Also called American Travel Solutions LLC* ***(P-4815)***
Amtrow Group Inc ....D....310 557-0857
8306 Wilshire Blvd 1042 Beverly Hills (90211) ***(P-26499)***
Amtv USA, Pasadena *Also called American Multimedia TV USA* ***(P-5579)***
Amvac Chemical, Commerce *Also called American Vanguard Corporation* ***(P-8688)***
Amwins Insurance Brkg Cal LLC (HQ) ....D....818 772-1774
21550 Oxnard St Ste 1100 Woodland Hills (91367) ***(P-10254)***
Amyris Inc ....D....510 597-4839
5850 Hollis St Emeryville (94608) ***(P-16622)***
Amyris Fuels LLC ....C....510 450-0761
5885 Hollis St Ste 100 Emeryville (94608) ***(P-8719)***
Amzn Mobile LLC ....B....925 348-4580
525 Market St Fl 19 San Francisco (94105) ***(P-14636)***
An Open Check, Costa Mesa *Also called North American Acceptance Corp* ***(P-9470)***
Ana Nacapa Surgical Associates, Ventura *Also called Ventura County Medical Center* ***(P-19552)***
Ana Trading Corp USA (HQ) ....D....310 542-2500
3625 Del Amo Blvd Ste 300 Torrance (90503) ***(P-7522)***
Anabella Hotel The, Anaheim *Also called Fjs Inc* ***(P-12268)***
Anaheim Arena, Anaheim *Also called City of Anaheim* ***(P-10578)***
Anaheim Arena Management LLC ....A....714 704-2400
2695 E Katella Ave Anaheim (92806) ***(P-18046)***
Anaheim Arts Council ....C....714 868-6094
5239 E Glen Arbor Ln Anaheim (92807) ***(P-24245)***
Anaheim Ca LLC ....D....714 634-4500
100 The City Dr S Orange (92868) ***(P-12006)***
Anaheim Crest Nursing Center, Anaheim *Also called 3067 Orange Avenue LLC* ***(P-19706)***
Anaheim Ducks Hockey Club LLC ....D....714 940-2900
2101 E Coast Hwy Fl 3 Corona Del Mar (92625) ***(P-18047)***
Anaheim Ducks Hockey Club LLC (PA) ....D....714 940-2900
2695 E Katella Ave Anaheim (92806) ***(P-18048)***
ANAHEIM FAMILY YMCA, Anaheim *Also called Young Mens Christian Assoc* ***(P-24731)***
Anaheim First Fmly Dntl Group ....D....714 999-5050
1161 N Euclid St Anaheim (92801) ***(P-26134)***
Anaheim Gateway Sport Club, Anaheim *Also called 24 Hour Fitness Usa Inc* ***(P-18101)***
Anaheim General Hospital, Los Angeles *Also called Pacific Health Corporation* ***(P-21072)***
Anaheim Global Medical Center ....B....714 533-6220
1025 S Anaheim Blvd Anaheim (92805) ***(P-20750)***
Anaheim Harbor Medical Group (PA) ....C....714 533-4511
710 N Euclid St Anaheim (92801) ***(P-18811)***
Anaheim Hills Auto Body Inc ....D....714 632-8266
3500 E La Palma Ave Anaheim (92806) ***(P-17280)***
Anaheim Hills Medical Offices, Anaheim *Also called Kaiser Foundation Hospitals* ***(P-19054)***
Anaheim Hotel LLC ....C....714 750-1811
1855 S Harbor Blvd Anaheim (92802) ***(P-12007)***
Anaheim Ice ....D....714 535-7465
300 W Lincoln Ave Anaheim (92805) ***(P-18621)***
Anaheim Kraemer Medical Offs, Anaheim *Also called Kaiser Foundation Hospitals* ***(P-19056)***
Anaheim Majestic Garden Hotel, Anaheim *Also called Ken Real Estate Lease Ltd* ***(P-12502)***
Anaheim Medical Center ....D....714 774-1450
1111 W La Palma Ave Anaheim (92801) ***(P-18812)***
Anaheim Park Hotel ....C....714 992-1700
222 W Houston Ave Fullerton (92832) ***(P-12008)***
Anaheim Park Inn and Camelot ....D....714 635-7275
1520 S Harbor Blvd Anaheim (92802) ***(P-12009)***
Anaheim Plaza Hotel & Suites, Anaheim *Also called Anaheim Plaza Hotel Inc* ***(P-12010)***
Anaheim Plaza Hotel Inc ....C....714 772-5900
1700 S Harbor Blvd Anaheim (92802) ***(P-12010)***
Anaheim Regional Medical Ctr ....A....714 774-1450
1111 W La Palma Ave Anaheim (92801) ***(P-20751)***
Anaheim Regional Medical Ctr ....B....714 999-3847
1211 W La Palma Ave Anaheim (92801) ***(P-18813)***
Anaheim Regional Medical Ctr (PA) ....D....714 774-1450
1111 W La Palma Ave Anaheim (92801) ***(P-21447)***
Anaheim V A Clinic, Anaheim *Also called Veterans Health Administration* ***(P-19576)***
Anaheim/Orange Cnty Visitor Bu (PA) ....D....714 765-8888
2099 S State College Blvd Anaheim (92806) ***(P-16623)***
Anaheim/Orange Hilton Suites, Orange *Also called Hit Portfolio II Trs LLC* ***(P-12369)***
Analytic US Market Neutral Off ....D....213 688-3015
555 W 5th St Fl 50 Los Angeles (90013) ***(P-9650)***
Anand Software Inc ....D....209 287-1708
4719 Quail Lakes Dr Stockton (95207) ***(P-14637)***

Mergent e-mail: customerrelations@mergent.com
1174
2020 Directory of California
Wholesalers and Services Companies
(P-0000) Products & Services Section entry number
(PA)=Parent Co (HQ)=Headquarters (DH)=Div Headquarters

ALPHABETIC SECTION
Anning-Johnson Company

Anaplan Inc (PA) ....C....415 742-8199
50 Hawthorne St San Francisco (94105) ***(P-15942)***
Anaspec Inc (HQ) ....E....510 791-9560
34801 Campus Dr Fremont (94555) ***(P-25704)***
Anaspec Egt Group, Fremont *Also called Anaspec Inc* ***(P-25704)***
Anatec International Inc (HQ) ....D....949 498-3350
2950 E Birch St Brea (92821) ***(P-24935)***
Anberry Rehabilitation Hosp, Atwater *Also called Tjd LLC* ***(P-20700)***
Ancca Corporation ....D....949 553-0084
7 Goddard Irvine (92618) ***(P-2747)***
Anchor General Insurance Agcy ....C....858 527-3600
10256 Meanley Dr San Diego (92131) ***(P-10255)***
Anchor J Dairy, Stevinson *Also called James J Stevinson A Corp* ***(P-396)***
Anchor Loans LP ....C....310 395-0010
5230 Las Virgenes Rd # 105 Calabasas (91302) ***(P-11844)***
Anchor Nationwide Loans, Calabasas *Also called Anchor Loans LP* ***(P-11844)***
Ancon Marine ....D....310 952-8160
2209 Zeus Ct Bakersfield (93308) ***(P-17485)***
and 1, Aliso Viejo *Also called Basketball Marketing Co Inc* ***(P-26521)***
and Syndicated Productions Inc ....D....818 308-5200
3500 W Olive Ave Ste 1000 Burbank (91505) ***(P-17573)***
Andaz Sandiego, San Diego *Also called Hyatt Corporation* ***(P-12444)***
Andersen & Sons Shelling Inc ....D....530 839-2236
4530 Rowles Rd Vina (96092) ***(P-467)***
Andersen Nut Company ....E....209 854-6820
3050 S Hunt Rd Gustine (95322) ***(P-468)***
Andersen Tax LLC ....C....213 593-2300
400 Suth Hope St Ste 2000 Los Angeles (90071) ***(P-13383)***
Andersncttonwood Disposal Svcs ....D....530 824-4700
3281 State Highway 99w S Corning (96021) ***(P-3849)***
Anderson Rowe & Buckley Inc ....C....415 282-1625
2833 3rd St San Francisco (94107) ***(P-2053)***
Anderson & Howard Electric Inc ....C....949 250-4555
1791 Reynolds Ave Irvine (92614) ***(P-2422)***
Anderson & Martella Inc ....E....925 934-3831
1200 Mt Diablo Blvd # 400 Walnut Creek (94596) ***(P-3357)***
Anderson Air Conditioning LP ....D....714 998-6850
2100 E Walnut Ave Fullerton (92831) ***(P-2054)***
Anderson Associates Staffing (PA) ....C....323 930-3170
8200 Wilshire Blvd # 200 Beverly Hills (90211) ***(P-14472)***
Anderson Chrnesky Strl Stl Inc ....D....951 769-5700
353 Risco Cir Beaumont (92223) ***(P-3250)***
Anderson Direct Marketing, Poway *Also called T G T Enterprises Inc* ***(P-13741)***
Anderson Hay & Grain Co Inc ....C....509 925-9818
915 E Colon St Wilmington (90744) ***(P-8676)***
Anderson Homes, Lodi *Also called Lodi Development Inc* ***(P-11571)***
Anderson House, Concord *Also called Youth Homes Incorporated* ***(P-24121)***
Anderson Howard, Irvine *Also called Anderson & Howard Electric Inc* ***(P-2422)***
Anderson Kayne Capital ....B....800 231-7414
1800 Avenue Of The Los Angeles (90067) ***(P-9788)***
Anderson Kayne Inv MGT Inc (PA) ....D....310 556-2721
1800 Avenue Of The Stars # 200 Los Angeles (90067) ***(P-26500)***
Anderson Lumber, North Highlands *Also called Pacific Coast Supply LLC* ***(P-6640)***
Anderson McPharlin Conners LLP (PA) ....D....213 688-0080
707 Wilshire Blvd # 4000 Los Angeles (90017) ***(P-22358)***
Anderson News LLC ....D....714 892-7766
15172 Goldenwest Cir Westminster (92683) ***(P-8866)***
Anderson PCF Engrg Cnstr Inc ....D....408 970-9900
1390 Norman Ave Santa Clara (95054) ***(P-1939)***
Anderson Plbg Htg A Condition, El Cajon *Also called Walter Anderson Plumbing Inc* ***(P-2315)***
Anderson Pump Company ....D....559 665-4477
24719 Robertson Blvd Chowchilla (93610) ***(P-6017)***
Andersonpenna Partners Inc (HQ) ....D....949 428-1500
3737 Birch St Ste 250 Newport Beach (92660) ***(P-26501)***
Andover Maintenance Inc ....D....626 254-1651
45 La Porte St Arcadia (91006) ***(P-13864)***
Andregg Geomatics ....D....530 885-7072
11661 Blocker Dr Ste 200 Auburn (95603) ***(P-25518)***
Andreini & Company (PA) ....D....650 573-1111
220 W 20th Ave San Mateo (94403) ***(P-10256)***
Andrew and Williamson Sales Co (PA) ....D....619 661-6000
9940 Marconi Dr San Diego (92154) ***(P-8430)***
Andrew Chekene Enterprises Inc ....C....650 588-1001
21965 Meekland Ave Hayward (94541) ***(P-1079)***
Andrew L Youngquist Cnstr Inc ....D....949 862-5611
3187 Red Hill Ave Ste 200 Costa Mesa (92626) ***(P-1406)***
Andrew Lauren Company Inc ....C....949 861-4222
15225 Alton Pkwy Unit 300 Irvine (92618) ***(P-16624)***
Andrew M Golden MD ....D....619 528-5342
4647 Zion Ave San Diego (92120) ***(P-18814)***
Andrew M Jordan Inc ....D....510 999-6000
1350 4th St Berkeley (94710) ***(P-3303)***
Andrew Williamson Fresh Prod, San Diego *Also called Andrew and Williamson Sales Co* ***(P-8430)***
Andrews Electronics, Santa Clarita *Also called Partsearch Technologies Inc* ***(P-7318)***
Andrews International Inc ....C....818 260-9586
455 N Moss St Burbank (91502) ***(P-16195)***
Andrews International Inc ....C....805 409-4160
3396 Willow Ln Thousand Oaks (91361) ***(P-16196)***
Andrews International Inc (PA) ....A....818 487-4060
455 N Moss St Burbank (91502) ***(P-16197)***
Andrews International Inc ....C....626 407-2290
706 E Arrow Hwy Covina (91722) ***(P-16198)***
Andrian Inc ....E....408 434-0730
1935 Lundy Ave San Jose (95131) ***(P-3376)***
Andrighetto Produce Inc ....D....650 588-0930
155 Terminal Ct Stalls 15 Stalls South San Francisco (94083) ***(P-3377)***

Anduril Industries Inc (PA) ....D....949 891-1607
2722 Michelson Dr Ste 150 Irvine (92612) ***(P-16493)***
Andwin Corporation (PA) ....C....818 999-2828
167 W Cochran St Simi Valley (93065) ***(P-7871)***
Andwin Scientific, Simi Valley *Also called Andwin Corporation* ***(P-7871)***
Andy Boy, Salinas *Also called DArrigo Broscoof California* ***(P-46)***
Andy Gump Inc ....D....818 255-0650
11551 Hart St North Hollywood (91605) ***(P-14128)***
Ane Productions Inc ....D....818 972-0777
3500 W Olive Ave Ste 1000 Burbank (91505) ***(P-17574)***
Anesthesia Business Cons Inc ....D....925 951-1366
1600 Riviera Ave Ste 420 Walnut Creek (94596) ***(P-18815)***
Anesthesia Consultants of Cont, Walnut Creek *Also called Anesthesia Business Cons Inc* ***(P-18815)***
Anesthesia Service Med Group ....E....858 277-4767
3626 Ruffin Rd San Diego (92123) ***(P-18816)***
Anfinson Lumber Sales Inc (PA) ....D....951 681-4707
13041 Union Ave Fontana (92337) ***(P-6604)***
Angel Care Home Health Inc ....E....818 248-8811
2600 Foothill Blvd # 103 La Crescenta (91214) ***(P-21664)***
Angel Island Co, Red Bluff *Also called Concessionaires Urban Park* ***(P-18670)***
Angel View Inc ....E....760 322-2440
454 N Indian Canyon Dr Palm Springs (92262) ***(P-23820)***
Angel View Resale Store, Palm Springs *Also called Angel View Inc* ***(P-23820)***
Angeles Home Health Care Inc ....C....213 487-5131
3701 Wilshire Blvd # 900 Los Angeles (90010) ***(P-21665)***
Angeles Los Equestrian Center ....C....818 840-9063
480 W Riverside Dr Burbank (91506) ***(P-18622)***
Angelika Film Center and Cafe, San Diego *Also called Reading International Inc* ***(P-17859)***
Angels Baseball LP (PA) ....A....714 940-2000
2000 E Gene Autry Way Anaheim (92806) ***(P-18049)***
Angels In Motion LLC ....D....909 590-9102
4091 Riverside Dr Ste 111 Chino (91710) ***(P-21666)***
Angels Nursing Center, Los Angeles *Also called Gva Enterprises Inc* ***(P-20586)***
Angels Nursing Center, Los Angeles *Also called Gva Enterprises Inc* ***(P-19988)***
Angelus Western Ppr Fibers Inc ....D....213 623-9221
2474 Porter St Los Angeles (90021) ***(P-7750)***
Angioscore Inc ....C....510 933-7900
5055 Brandin Ct Fremont (94538) ***(P-6940)***
Anheuser-Busch LLC ....B....707 429-7595
3101 Busch Dr Fairfield (94534) ***(P-7523)***
Anheuser-Busch LLC ....C....951 782-3935
1400 Marlborough Ave Riverside (92507) ***(P-8746)***
Anheuser-Busch LLC ....C....310 761-4600
20499 S Reeves Ave Carson (90810) ***(P-8747)***
Anheuser-Busch LLC ....C....949 263-9270
18952 Macarthur Blvd Irvine (92612) ***(P-8748)***
Animal Care Center ....D....707 584-4343
6470 Redwood Dr Rohnert Park (94928) ***(P-572)***
Animoto LLC ....D....415 987-3139
333 Kearny St Fl 6 San Francisco (94108) ***(P-14638)***
Anita Borg Inst For Women Tech ....D....650 236-4756
1301 Shoreway Rd Ste 425 Belmont (94002) ***(P-23559)***
Anitsa Inc ....C....213 237-0533
6032 Shull St Bell Gardens (90201) ***(P-13178)***
Anixter Inc ....D....916 563-7560
855 National Dr Ste 103 Sacramento (95834) ***(P-7123)***
Anixter Inc ....D....800 854-2088
7140 Opportunity Rd San Diego (92111) ***(P-16494)***
Anixter Inc ....D....510 477-2400
30061 Ahern Ave Union City (94587) ***(P-7124)***
Anixter Inc ....E....925 469-8500
5000 Franklin Dr 200 Pleasanton (94588) ***(P-7125)***
Anjana Software Solutions Inc ....D....805 583-0121
1445 E Los Angeles Ave 301t Simi Valley (93065) ***(P-14639)***
Anjaneyap Inc ....D....408 922-9690
830 Hillview Ct Ste 140 Milpitas (95035) ***(P-26502)***
Anka Behavioral Health Inc ....D....626 573-5902
2507 Evelyn Ave Rosemead (91770) ***(P-27265)***
Anka Behavioral Health Inc ....C....209 982-4697
458 Almond Dr Lodi (95240) ***(P-22177)***
Anka Behavioral Health Inc ....C....951 929-2744
2100 State St Hemet (92543) ***(P-10257)***
Anka Behavioral Health Inc ....C....510 494-1567
5149 Winston Ct Fremont (94536) ***(P-22178)***
Anka Behavioral Health Inc (PA) ....C....925 825-4700
3840 Buskirk Ave Ste 300 Pleasant Hill (94523) ***(P-21951)***
Anka Behavioral Health Inc ....C....909 622-8217
942 Barbara Ln Pomona (91767) ***(P-21952)***
Anna Corporation ....E....951 736-6037
2078 2nd St Norco (92860) ***(P-2331)***
Annabel Investment Company ....D....925 866-0100
2600 Camino Ramon Ste 201 San Ramon (94583) ***(P-11541)***
Annandale Golf Club ....C....626 796-6125
1 N San Rafael Ave Pasadena (91105) ***(P-18377)***
Anne M Kent MD ....D....949 650-7100
500 Superior Ave Ste 310 Newport Beach (92663) ***(P-18817)***
Anne Sppi Clnic Riverside Rnch, Bakersfield *Also called Sippi Anne Riverside Ranch LLP* ***(P-24076)***
Annenberg Foundation Trust (PA) ....D....760 202-2222
37977 Bob Hope Dr Rancho Mirage (92270) ***(P-11776)***
Annie App Inc (HQ) ....D....844 277-2664
23 Geary St Ste 3 San Francisco (94108) ***(P-14640)***
Annie R Mitchell Elementary, Visalia *Also called Pta California Congress of Par* ***(P-24622)***
Annies Homegrown Inc ....D....510 558-7500
1610 5th St Berkeley (94710) ***(P-8542)***
Anning-Johnson Company ....C....510 670-0100
22955 Kidder St Hayward (94545) ***(P-2748)***

ALPHABETIC

Employee Codes: A=Over 500 employees, B=251-500
C=101-250, D=51-100, E=50
2020 Directory of California
Wholesalers and Services Companies
© Mergent Inc. 1-800-342-5647
1175

Anning-Johnson Company ....E....626 369-7131
13250 Temple Ave City of Industry (91746) ***(P-2749)***
Anomali Incorporated ....D....408 800-4050
808 Winslow St Redwood City (94063) ***(P-14641)***
Anonymous Content LLC (PA) ....D....310 558-6000
3532 Hayden Ave Culver City (90232) ***(P-17575)***
Anova Food LLC ....D....813 902-9003
280 10th Ave San Diego (92101) ***(P-8361)***
Anritsu Americas Sales Company ....A....408 778-2000
490 Jarvis Dr Morgan Hill (95037) ***(P-7524)***
Ans World Service Inc ....D....714 441-2400
2751 E Chapman Ave # 204 Fullerton (92831) ***(P-5109)***
Ansafone Contact Centers, Santa Ana *Also called Ephonamationcom Inc* ***(P-16767)***
Anschutz Entrmt Group Inc (HQ) ....C....213 337-5052
800 W Olympic Blvd # 305 Los Angeles (90015) ***(P-17959)***
Anschutz Film Group ....A....310 887-1000
1888 Century Park E # 1400 Los Angeles (90067) ***(P-2750)***
Anschutz So Calif Sports Compl ....C....310 630-2000
18400 Avalon Blvd Ste 100 Carson (90746) ***(P-18050)***
Ansira Partners Inc ....D....818 461-6100
5000 Van Nuys Blvd Sherman Oaks (91403) ***(P-16625)***
Answer Financial Inc (HQ) ....C....818 644-4000
15910 Ventura Blvd Fl 6 Encino (91436) ***(P-16626)***
Antelope Valley Country Club ....C....661 947-3142
39800 Country Club Dr Palmdale (93551) ***(P-18378)***
Antelope Valley Foundation ....E....661 945-7290
646 W Lancaster Blvd # 109 Lancaster (93534) ***(P-22916)***
Antelope Valley Health Center, Lancaster *Also called County of Los Angeles* ***(P-22000)***
Antelope Valley Healthcare Dst, Lancaster *Also called Antelope Valley Hospital Inc* ***(P-20752)***
Antelope Valley Hospital, Lancaster *Also called Kaiser Foundation Hospitals* ***(P-20949)***
Antelope Valley Hospital Inc ....D....661 949-1550
1601 W Avenue J Ste 201 Lancaster (93534) ***(P-18818)***
Antelope Valley Hospital Inc ....C....661 726-6180
1600 W Avenue J Lancaster (93534) ***(P-18819)***
Antelope Valley Hospital Inc (PA) ....A....661 949-5000
1600 W Avenue J Lancaster (93534) ***(P-20752)***
Antelope Valley Mall ....D....661 266-9150
1233 W Rancho Vista Blvd # 405 Palmdale (93551) ***(P-10567)***
Antelope Valley Medical Group ....E....661 945-2783
44469 10th St W Lancaster (93534) ***(P-18820)***
Antelope Valley Recycling ....D....661 945-5944
1200 W City Ranch Rd Palmdale (93551) ***(P-6146)***
Antelope Vly Convalecent Hosp, Lancaster *Also called Antelope Vly Retirement HM Inc* ***(P-20490)***
Antelope Vly Dom Vlnce Council (PA) ....D....661 723-7772
43434 Sahuayo St Lancaster (93535) ***(P-22917)***
Antelope Vly Retirement HM Inc ....B....661 948-7501
44445 15th St W Lancaster (93534) ***(P-20490)***
Antelope Vly Retirement HM Inc ....C....661 949-5524
44567 15th St W Lancaster (93534) ***(P-20491)***
Antelope Vly Schl Trnsp Agcy ....C....661 945-3621
670 W Avenue L8 Lancaster (93534) ***(P-3785)***
Anthem Inc ....B....805 231-0994
4236 Silverado Dr Thousand Oaks (91360) ***(P-9921)***
Anthem Inc ....A....562 622-2869
4553 La Tienda Rd Westlake Village (91362) ***(P-9922)***
Anthem Inc ....B....805 560-3520
1101 Anacapa St Ste 300 Santa Barbara (93101) ***(P-9897)***
Anthony Botelho ....D....831 623-4228
382 Olympia Ave San Juan Bautista (95045) ***(P-199)***
Anthony Harvesting Inc ....C....831 385-6460
401 S Vanderhurst Ave King City (93930) ***(P-446)***
Anthony Lambe ....D....559 268-0709
1521 W Nielsen Ave Ste 69 Fresno (93706) ***(P-6418)***
Anthony P Garofalo A Dental ....D....619 440-0071
742 Broadway El Cajon (92021) ***(P-19604)***
Anthony Soto Emplyment Trining, Santa Rosa *Also called California Human Dev Corp* ***(P-23573)***
Anthony Trevino ....D....707 747-4776
938 Adams St Ste A Benicia (94510) ***(P-2994)***
Anthony Vineyards Inc (PA) ....E....661 858-6211
5512 Valpredo Ave Bakersfield (93307) ***(P-117)***
Anthonys Fish Grotto ....D....619 713-1853
9530 Murray Dr La Mesa (91942) ***(P-8362)***
Antioch Convalescent Hospital, Antioch *Also called Norcal Care Centers Inc* ***(P-20641)***
Antioch Public Golf Corp ....D....925 706-4220
4800 Golf Course Rd Antioch (94531) ***(P-18220)***
Antioch Rotary Club ....E....925 757-1800
324 G St Antioch (94509) ***(P-18379)***
Anvil Builders Inc ....C....415 285-5000
1475 Donner Ave San Francisco (94124) ***(P-1665)***
Anvil Iron, Gardena *Also called Anvil Steel Corporation* ***(P-3251)***
Anvil Steel Corporation ....D....310 329-5811
134 W 168th St Gardena (90248) ***(P-3251)***
Anza A Calabasas Hotel, The, Calabasas *Also called 23627 Calabasas Road LLC* ***(P-11978)***
Ao Freight Corporation (PA) ....E....310 419-8833
419 N Oak St Inglewood (90302) ***(P-4891)***
AOC Technologies Inc ....B....925 875-0808
5960 Inglewood Dr Pleasanton (94588) ***(P-7044)***
AON, Los Angeles *Also called Schirmer Fire Protection Eng* ***(P-10483)***
AON Benfield Fac Inc ....C....415 486-6900
199 Fremont St Fl 15 San Francisco (94105) ***(P-9898)***
AON Consulting Inc ....D....408 321-2500
2570 N 1st St Ste 500 San Jose (95131) ***(P-26503)***
AON Consulting Inc ....D....818 506-4300
707 Wilshire Blvd # 2500 Los Angeles (90017) ***(P-10258)***
AON Consulting Inc ....D....800 558-0655
3461 Fair Oaks Blvd Sacramento (95864) ***(P-10259)***
AON Consulting Inc ....D....562 345-4700
21900 Burbank Blvd # 101 Woodland Hills (91367) ***(P-10260)***
AON Consulting Inc ....D....800 283-1667
851 Van Ness Ave Fl 2 San Francisco (94109) ***(P-10261)***
AON Consulting Inc ....D....800 815-1823
160 Via Verde Ste 200 San Dimas (91773) ***(P-10262)***
AON Consulting Inc ....C....415 486-6226
199 Fremont St Fl 11 San Francisco (94105) ***(P-10263)***
AON Consulting Inc ....D....562 496-2888
5000 E Spring St Ste 100 Long Beach (90815) ***(P-10264)***
AON Consulting Inc ....D....626 683-5200
255 S Lake Ave Ste 900 Pasadena (91101) ***(P-10265)***
AON Consulting & Insur Svcs ....D....415 486-7500
199 Fremont St Fl 14 San Francisco (94105) ***(P-10266)***
AON Risk Svcs Companies Inc ....D....213 630-3200
707 Wilshire Blvd # 2600 Los Angeles (90017) ***(P-10267)***
Aopen America Incorporated ....D....408 586-1200
2150 N 1st St Ste 300 San Jose (95131) ***(P-6796)***
AP Express LLC ....D....562 236-2250
5301a Rivergrade Rd Irwindale (91706) ***(P-4892)***
AP Express International LLC ....D....562 236-2250
8500 Rex Rd Pico Rivera (90660) ***(P-5110)***
AP Global Inc ....D....818 707-3167
31352 Via Colinas Ste 101 Westlake Village (91362) ***(P-7230)***
AP Tech, Fremont *Also called American Portwell Tech Inc* ***(P-6795)***
APA Incorporated ....C....310 888-4200
405 S Beverly Dr Ste 500 Beverly Hills (90212) ***(P-26504)***
APC Lab, Chino *Also called Applied P & Ch Laboratory Sout* ***(P-25706)***
Apeiro, Oceanside *Also called Shieldx Networks Inc* ***(P-15092)***
Aperian Global Inc (PA) ....D....628 222-3773
1 Kaiser Plz Ste 785 Oakland (94612) ***(P-26505)***
Apex Bulk Commodities Inc ....D....909 854-9991
14080 Slover Ave Fontana (92337) ***(P-9777)***
Apex Communications, Fremont *Also called Netversant - Silicon Vly Inc* ***(P-2566)***
Apex Computer Systems Inc ....D....562 926-6820
13875 Cerritos Corprt Dr A Cerritos (90703) ***(P-15911)***
Apex Group ....C....818 885-0513
17101 Superior St Northridge (91325) ***(P-26135)***
Apex Healthcare Med Ctr Inc (PA) ....D....951 765-0700
2390 E Florida Ave # 201 Hemet (92544) ***(P-19655)***
Apex Logistics Intl Inc (PA) ....D....310 665-0288
18554 S Susana Rd Compton (90221) ***(P-4893)***
Apex Machine Works Inc ....D....310 393-5987
2118 Wilshire Blvd # 258 Santa Monica (90403) ***(P-24936)***
Apex Mechanical Systems Inc ....D....858 536-8700
7440 Trade St Ste A San Diego (92121) ***(P-2055)***
Apex Medical Group Lab, Hemet *Also called Apex Healthcare Med Ctr Inc* ***(P-19655)***
Apex Parks Group LLC (PA) ....C....949 349-8461
18575 Jamboree Rd Ste 600 Irvine (92612) ***(P-18322)***
Apex Parks Group LLC ....D....210 341-6663
27061 Aliso Creek Rd # 100 Aliso Viejo (92656) ***(P-18623)***
Apex USA, Compton *Also called Apex Logistics Intl Inc* ***(P-4893)***
Apexcare, Sacramento *Also called Support For Family LLC* ***(P-23495)***
Apexcare Inc (PA) ....A....916 924-9111
1418 Howe Ave Ste B Sacramento (95825) ***(P-21667)***
Apfeld & Neal Insurance Svcs ....E....714 821-7041
11022 Winners Cir Ste 100 Los Alamitos (90720) ***(P-10268)***
Apg, Panorama City *Also called American Protection Group Inc* ***(P-16192)***
Apic Hotels Group LLC (HQ) ....C....415 692-1502
5 Thomas Mellon Cir # 305 San Francisco (94134) ***(P-12011)***
Apical Industries Inc ....D....760 724-5300
3030 Enterprise Ct Ste A Vista (92081) ***(P-7689)***
Apigee Corporation ....B....408 343-7300
1600 Amphitheatre Pkwy Mountain View (94043) ***(P-14642)***
APL Logistics Ltd ....C....310 548-8700
180 E Ocean Blvd Ste 800 Long Beach (90802) ***(P-4582)***
Apla Health & Wellness ....D....213 201-1546
611 S Kingsley Dr Los Angeles (90005) ***(P-18821)***
APM Terminals Pacific LLC ....E....310 221-4000
2500 Navy Way Pier 400 San Pedro (90731) ***(P-4894)***
APM Terminals Pacific LLC (HQ) ....C....704 571-2768
2500 Navy Way San Pedro (90731) ***(P-4609)***
APM Terminals Pacific Ltd ....B....510 992-6430
5801 Christie Ave Emeryville (94608) ***(P-4895)***
Apn Business Resources Inc ....D....818 717-9980
21418 Osborne St Canoga Park (91304) ***(P-26506)***
Apn Software Services Inc (PA) ....D....510 623-5050
39899 Balentine Dr # 385 Newark (94560) ***(P-15943)***
Apollo Agencies Inc (PA) ....D....714 832-2100
700 W 1st St Ste 2 Tustin (92780) ***(P-10269)***
Apollo Couriers Inc (PA) ....D....310 337-0377
1039 W Hillcrest Blvd Inglewood (90301) ***(P-4247)***
Apollo Cpr, Pico Rivera *Also called Ionics Altrpure Wtr Crparation* ***(P-8589)***
Apollo Div Ionics Ultrapure, San Jose *Also called Suez Wts Systems Usa Inc* ***(P-7439)***
Apollo Electric ....D....714 256-8414
330 N Basse Ln Brea (92821) ***(P-2423)***
App Wholesale LLC ....B....323 980-3746
3686 E Olympic Blvd Los Angeles (90023) ***(P-8543)***
Appdirect Inc (PA) ....D....415 852-3924
650 California St Fl 25 San Francisco (94108) ***(P-15236)***
Appdynamics Inc (HQ) ....C....415 442-8400
303 2nd St Fl 8 San Francisco (94107) ***(P-15237)***
Appellation Tours Inc ....E....707 938-9390
21707 8th St E Sonoma (95476) ***(P-4847)***
Appery LLC ....D....925 602-5504
1340 Treat Blvd Ste 375 Walnut Creek (94597) ***(P-14643)***

Appetize Technologies Inc...C...877 559-4225
6601 Center Dr W Ste 700 Los Angeles (90045) ***(P-15238)***
Appfolio Inc (PA)...C...805 364-6093
50 Castilian Dr Ste 101 Goleta (93117) ***(P-15239)***
Appfolio Inc...A...866 648-1536
9201 Spectrum San Diego (92123) ***(P-15240)***
Appl, Clovis *Also called Agriculture and Priority Pollu* ***(P-26052)***
Apple Eght Hospitality MGT Inc...D...714 827-1010
5865 Katella Ave Cypress (90630) ***(P-12012)***
Apple Hospitality Reit Inc...D...916 568-5400
2540 Venture Oaks Way Sacramento (95833) ***(P-12013)***
Apple Inns Inc...E...510 895-1311
68 Monarch Bay Dr San Leandro (94577) ***(P-12014)***
Apple Nine Hospitality MGT...D...858 573-0700
8651 Spectrum Center Blvd San Diego (92123) ***(P-12015)***
Apple One Employment, Glendale *Also called Howroyd-Wright Emplymnt Agcy* ***(P-14301)***
Apple Store Glendale Galleria, Glendale *Also called Glendale Associates Ltd* ***(P-10598)***
Apple Valley Care & Rehab, Sebastopol *Also called Apple Vly Cnvalescent Hosp Inc* ***(P-19721)***
Apple Valley Care Center, Apple Valley *Also called Front Porch Communities & Svcs* ***(P-19929)***
Apple Valley Golf Club...C...760 242-3653
15200 Rancherias Rd Apple Valley (92307) ***(P-18380)***
Apple Valley Golf Course, Apple Valley *Also called Apple Valley Golf Club* ***(P-18380)***
Apple Vlley/ Vctrvlle Cnsrtium...D...760 240-7000
14955 Dale Evans Pkwy Apple Valley (92307) ***(P-13397)***
Apple Vly Cnvalescent Hosp Inc...C...707 823-7675
1035 Gravenstein Hwy N Sebastopol (95472) ***(P-19721)***
Applebee Leasing Inc...D...818 612-6218
4 Maidstone Dr Newport Beach (92660) ***(P-16627)***
Applecare Medical MGT LLC...C...714 443-4507
18 Centerpointe Dr # 100 La Palma (90623) ***(P-26136)***
Appleone Employment Services, Glendale *Also called Howroyd-Wright Emplymnt Agcy* ***(P-14302)***
Applewood Care Center...E...916 446-2506
1090 Rio Ln Sacramento (95822) ***(P-19722)***
APPLEWOOD OPERATING, Redding *Also called Copper Ridge Care Center* ***(P-19814)***
Appliance Recycling Ctrs Amer...D...310 223-2800
1920 S Acacia Ave Compton (90220) ***(P-6147)***
Applied Companies...E...661 257-0090
28020 Avenue Stanford Santa Clarita (91355) ***(P-24937)***
Applied Companies RE LLC...E...661 257-0090
28020 Avenue Stanford Valencia (91355) ***(P-10568)***
Applied Computer Solutions (HQ)...D...714 861-2200
15461 Springdale St Huntington Beach (92649) ***(P-14644)***
Applied Engineering MGT Corp...C...805 484-1909
760 Paseo Camarillo # 101 Camarillo (93010) ***(P-14645)***
Applied Geokinetics...D...949 502-5353
77 Bunsen Irvine (92618) ***(P-24938)***
Applied Language Solutions LLC...C...800 579-5010
1250 W Sunflower La Habra (90631) ***(P-16628)***
Applied Materials, Roseville *Also called Cokeva Inc* ***(P-15913)***
Applied Molecular Evolution (HQ)...E...858 597-4990
10300 Campus Point Dr # 200 San Diego (92121) ***(P-25705)***
Applied P & Ch Laboratory Sout...D...909 590-1828
13760 Magnolia Ave Chino (91710) ***(P-25706)***
Applied Research Assoc Inc...D...805 962-4810
5425 Hollister Ave # 220 Santa Barbara (93111) ***(P-25707)***
Applied Underwriters Inc...E...415 656-5000
950 Tower Ln Ste 1400 Foster City (94404) ***(P-10270)***
Applied Weather Technology Inc, Sunnyvale *Also called Stormgeo* ***(P-27306)***
Appraisal Trend, Encino *Also called Valuation Concepts LLC* ***(P-11498)***
Appraiser Loft LLC...E...858 832-8334
3027 Townsgate Rd Ste 140 Westlake Village (91361) ***(P-10915)***
Apprentice & Journeymen Traini...D...818 464-4579
7850 Haskell Ave Van Nuys (91406) ***(P-2056)***
Apprentice & Journeymen Trn Tr...D...323 636-9871
7850 Haskell Ave Van Nuys (91406) ***(P-23560)***
Appsflyer Ltd...D...415 636-9430
111 New Montgomery St San Francisco (94105) ***(P-13612)***
Apptivo Inc...C...650 906-1034
34364 Eucalyptus Ter Fremont (94555) ***(P-14646)***
Apria Healthcare Group Inc (PA)...B...949 639-2000
26220 Enterprise Ct Lake Forest (92630) ***(P-21668)***
Apria Healthcare LLC...D...530 669-6441
1680 Tide Ct Ste B Woodland (95776) ***(P-22179)***
Apria Healthcare LLC...C...209 223-7727
7514 Murray Dr Stockton (95210) ***(P-22180)***
Apria Healthcare LLC...D...650 588-9744
480 Carlton Ct South San Francisco (94080) ***(P-6941)***
Apria Healthcare LLC...C...805 278-6700
2150 Trabajo Dr Ste B Oxnard (93030) ***(P-14085)***
Apria Healthcare LLC...D...858 653-6800
10090 Willow Creek Rd San Diego (92131) ***(P-14086)***
Apria Healthcare LLC...C...530 677-2713
1450 Expo Pkwy Ste D Sacramento (95815) ***(P-6942)***
Apria Healthcare LLC (HQ)...B...949 639-2000
26220 Enterprise Ct Lake Forest (92630) ***(P-6943)***
Apria Healthcare LLC...D...925 827-8800
2510 Dean Lesher Dr Ste D Concord (94520) ***(P-6944)***
Apria Healthcare LLC...D...949 639-2163
1931 Lundy Ave San Jose (95131) ***(P-14087)***
Apria Healthcare LLC...D...707 543-0979
3636 N Laughlin Rd # 190 Santa Rosa (95403) ***(P-14088)***
Apria Healthcare LLC...D...951 320-1100
815 Marlborough Ave # 200 Riverside (92507) ***(P-21669)***
Apria Healthcare LLC...D...510 346-4000
2476 Verna Ct San Leandro (94577) ***(P-21670)***
Apriso Corporation...C...562 951-8000
301 E Ocean Blvd Ste 1200 Long Beach (90802) ***(P-15557)***
Apteligent Inc...D...415 371-1402
1100 La Avenida St Ste A Mountain View (94043) ***(P-15241)***
Aptim Corp...A...925 288-2011
4005 Port Chicago Hwy Concord (94520) ***(P-24939)***
Aptim Corp...D...949 261-6441
18100 Von Karman Ave Irvine (92612) ***(P-24940)***
Aptiv Digital LLC...D...818 295-6789
2160 Gold St San Jose (95002) ***(P-15242)***
Aptos Berry Farms Inc...D...831 726-3256
730 S A St Oxnard (93030) ***(P-86)***
Apttus Corporation (PA)...C...650 445-7700
1400 Fashion Island Blvd # 100 San Mateo (94404) ***(P-15558)***
Apu Inc (PA)...D...661 948-2880
14939 Oxnard St Van Nuys (91411) ***(P-6419)***
Apumac LLC...C...888 248-7775
6404 Wilshire Blvd # 106 Los Angeles (90048) ***(P-7231)***
Apumac.com, Los Angeles *Also called Apumac LLC* ***(P-7231)***
Apw Construction Inc (PA)...D...626 820-0812
727 Glendora Ave La Puente (91744) ***(P-1814)***
Apw Construction Inc...D...626 855-1720
15135 Salt Lake Ave City of Industry (91746) ***(P-3378)***
Apw International Inc...C...310 884-5003
1073 E Artesia Blvd Carson (90746) ***(P-6420)***
Apw Knox-Seeman Warehouse Inc (HQ)...D...310 604-4373
1073 E Artesia Blvd Carson (90746) ***(P-6421)***
Apx Inc (PA)...E...408 517-2100
2001 Gateway Pl Ste 315w San Jose (95110) ***(P-26991)***
Aqua Gunite Inc...E...408 271-2782
5830 S Naylor Rd Livermore (94551) ***(P-3379)***
Aqua-Serv Engineers Inc (HQ)...D...951 681-9696
13560 Colombard Ct Fontana (92337) ***(P-8689)***
Aquaclean Janitorial...D...858 537-9090
9403 Compass Point Dr S San Diego (92126) ***(P-13865)***
Aqualine Piping Inc...D...408 745-7100
2108 Bering Dr Ste C San Jose (95131) ***(P-2057)***
Aquarium of Pacific...D...562 590-3100
310 Golden Shore Ste 300 Long Beach (90802) ***(P-24300)***
Aquarium of Pacific (PA)...C...562 590-3100
100 Aquarium Way Long Beach (90802) ***(P-24301)***
AQUARIUM OF THE BAY, THE, San Francisco *Also called Bayorg* ***(P-24302)***
Aquatic Designing Inc...E...707 822-4629
4801 West End Rd Arcata (95521) ***(P-24941)***
Aquatic Science Center...E...510 746-7334
4911 Central Ave Richmond (94804) ***(P-25708)***
Aquinas Corporation...C...408 248-7100
3580 Payne Ave San Jose (95117) ***(P-19723)***
Aquirecorps Norwalk Auto Auctn...C...562 864-7464
12405 Rosecrans Ave Norwalk (90650) ***(P-6384)***
AR Preservation LP...D...415 776-2151
201 Eddy St San Francisco (94102) ***(P-10686)***
AR Wilson Quarry, Aromas *Also called Granite Rock Co* ***(P-1055)***
Arable Corporation...D...650 331-1401
530 University Ave Palo Alto (94301) ***(P-14647)***
Araco Enterprises LLC...B...818 767-0675
9189 De Garmo Ave Sun Valley (91352) ***(P-6148)***
Aragen Bioscience Inc...E...408 779-1700
380 Woodview Ave Morgan Hill (95037) ***(P-25709)***
Aragon Commercial Ldscpg Inc...C...408 998-0600
2305 S Vasco Rd Livermore (94550) ***(P-773)***
Aragon Construction Inc...D...909 621-2200
5440 Arrow Hwy Montclair (91763) ***(P-1407)***
Arakelian Enterprises Inc...B...626 336-3636
15045 Salt Lake Ave City of Industry (91746) ***(P-6149)***
Arakelian Enterprises Inc...C...951 342-3300
687 Iowa Ave Riverside (92507) ***(P-6150)***
Arakelian Enterprises Inc (PA)...C...626 336-3636
14048 Valley Blvd City of Industry (91746) ***(P-6151)***
Aramark Facility Services LLC...C...213 740-8968
941 W 35th St Los Angeles (90007) ***(P-13866)***
Aramark Facility Services LLC...E...714 372-0683
5301 Bolsa Ave Bldg 10 Huntington Beach (92647) ***(P-13867)***
Aramark Services Inc...C...831 372-8016
800 Asilomar Blvd Pacific Grove (93950) ***(P-12016)***
Aramark Services Inc...D...323 587-7661
1405 E 58th Pl Los Angeles (90001) ***(P-13318)***
Aramark Services Inc...D...310 635-5000
17044 Montanero Ave Ste 4 Carson (90746) ***(P-16629)***
Aramark Spt & Entrmt Group LLC...C...408 999-5735
525 W Santa Clara St San Jose (95113) ***(P-17960)***
Aramark Spt & Entrmt Group LLC...C...213 740-1224
3400 S Figueroa St Los Angeles (90007) ***(P-17961)***
Aramark Spt & Entrmt Group LLC...C...831 648-9809
886 Cannery Row Monterey (93940) ***(P-17962)***
Aramark Spt & Entrmt Group LLC...D...408 748-7030
5001 Great America Pkwy Santa Clara (95054) ***(P-17963)***
Aramark Unf & Career AP LLC...D...209 368-9785
1617 Jim Way Modesto (95358) ***(P-13273)***
Aramark Unf & Career AP LLC...D...818 973-3700
115 N First St Burbank (91502) ***(P-13274)***
Aramark Unf & Career AP LLC...B...916 286-4100
1419 National Dr Sacramento (95834) ***(P-13275)***
Aramark Unf & Career AP LLC (HQ)...C...818 973-3700
115 N First St Ste 203 Burbank (91502) ***(P-13276)***
Aramark Unf & Career AP LLC...D...408 243-9824
855 Mckendrie St San Jose (95126) ***(P-13206)***
Aramark Unf & Career AP LLC...D...530 241-6433
755 Butte St Redding (96001) ***(P-13277)***

Employee Codes: A=Over 500 employees, B=251-500
C=101-250, D=51-100, E=50
2020 Directory of California
Wholesalers and Services Companies
© Mergent Inc. 1-800-342-5647
1177

Aramark Unf & Career AP LLC ....D....323 774-4216
15525 Garfield Ave Paramount (90723) ***(P-13207)***
Aramark Unf & Career AP LLC ....C....510 835-9285
330 Chestnut St Oakland (94607) ***(P-13278)***
Aramark Unf & Career AP LLC ....C....323 266-0555
4422 Dunham St Los Angeles (90023) ***(P-13279)***
Aramark Unf & Career AP LLC ....D....714 545-4877
3101 W Adams St Santa Ana (92704) ***(P-13280)***
Aramark Unf & Career AP LLC ....C....559 291-6631
3333 N Sabre Dr Fresno (93727) ***(P-13208)***
Aramark Unf & Career AP LLC ....D....510 487-1855
31148 San Antonio St Hayward (94544) ***(P-13281)***
Aramark Unf & Career AP LLC ....D....925 827-3782
5000 Forni Dr Concord (94520) ***(P-13282)***
Aramark Unf & Career AP LLC ....D....951 274-9622
1135 Hall Ave Riverside (92509) ***(P-13283)***
Aramark Unf & Career AP LLC ....C....858 550-5200
5665 Eastgage Dr San Diego (92121) ***(P-13209)***
Aramark Unf & Career AP LLC ....D....818 364-8272
15372 Cobalt St Sylmar (91342) ***(P-13284)***
Aramark Unf & Career AP LLC ....D....650 244-9332
440 N Canal St South San Francisco (94080) ***(P-13285)***
Aramark Unf & Career AP LLC ....C....415 244-8332
440 Carolina St San Francisco (94107) ***(P-13210)***
Aramark Uniform Services ....D....916 286-4100
1419 National Dr Sacramento (95834) ***(P-13286)***
Ararat Home of Los Angeles ....C....818 837-1800
15099 Mission Hills Rd Mission Hills (91345) ***(P-20492)***
Ararat Nursing Facility, Mission Hills *Also called Ararat Home of Los Angeles* ***(P-20492)***
Arb Inc (HQ) ....C....949 598-9242
26000 Commercentre Dr Lake Forest (92630) ***(P-1940)***
Arb Inc ....E....925 432-3649
1875 Loveridge Rd Pittsburg (94565) ***(P-4373)***
Arb Inc ....E....415 206-1015
50 Quint St San Francisco (94124) ***(P-1408)***
Arbitech LLC ....D....949 376-6650
64 Fairbanks Irvine (92618) ***(P-6797)***
Arbor Employment & Training, Canoga Park *Also called Canoga Park Worksource Center* ***(P-14241)***
Arbor Medical Group Inc (PA) ....D....805 614-7591
1502 Marilyn Way Santa Maria (93454) ***(P-18822)***
Arbor Vly Nrsing Rhblttion Ctr, Modesto *Also called Kissito Health Case Inc* ***(P-20057)***
Arbormed Inc (PA) ....C....714 689-1500
725 W Town And Country Rd Orange (92868) ***(P-22181)***
Arbors, The, San Diego *Also called G & L Penasquitos Inc* ***(P-23241)***
Arborwell Inc (PA) ....D....510 881-4260
2337 American Ave Hayward (94545) ***(P-931)***
ARC, Torrance *Also called Good Sports Plus Ltd* ***(P-14838)***
ARC - Imperial Valley (PA) ....D....760 352-0180
298 E Ross Ave El Centro (92243) ***(P-22918)***
ARC - Imperial Valley ....D....760 768-1944
340 E 1st St Calexico (92231) ***(P-21953)***
ARC - SD E Cnty Training Ctrs, El Cajon *Also called ARC of San Diego* ***(P-24131)***
ARC Community Enrichment, Ojai *Also called ARC of Ventura County Inc* ***(P-21954)***
ARC Document Solutions Inc ....C....818 242-6555
655 N Central Ave Glendale (91203) ***(P-13753)***
ARC Document Solutions Inc ....D....626 333-7005
1207 John Reed Ct Ste A City of Industry (91745) ***(P-13754)***
ARC Document Solutions Inc ....E....415 495-8700
945 Bryant St Ste 1000 San Francisco (94103) ***(P-13755)***
ARC Document Solutions Inc ....C....818 908-0222
15019 Califa St Van Nuys (91411) ***(P-13756)***
ARC Enterprises, San Diego *Also called ARC of San Diego* ***(P-24130)***
ARC Fastener Supply & Mfg ....D....909 481-8171
2104 Wembley Ln Corona (92881) ***(P-7616)***
ARC Fresno/Madera Counties (PA) ....D....559 226-6268
4490 E Ashlan Ave Fresno (93726) ***(P-23561)***
ARC Imaging Resources, Monterey Park *Also called American Reprographics Co LLC* ***(P-13749)***
ARC Industries ....D....805 520-0399
5143 Cochran St Ste 93063 Simi Valley (93063) ***(P-23821)***
ARC Los Angeles Orange Counties (PA) ....D....562 803-1556
12049 Woodruff Ave Downey (90241) ***(P-23562)***
ARC Mid-Cities Inc ....C....310 329-9272
14208 Towne Ave Los Angeles (90061) ***(P-23563)***
ARC of Alameda County (PA) ....C....510 357-3569
14700 Doolittle Dr San Leandro (94577) ***(P-22919)***
ARC of Alameda County ....C....510 582-8151
1101 Walpert St Hayward (94541) ***(P-23564)***
ARC of Butte County (PA) ....C....530 891-5865
2030 Park Ave Chico (95928) ***(P-22920)***
ARC of San Diego, Chula Vista *Also called ARC Starlight Center* ***(P-22921)***
ARC of San Diego (PA) ....C....619 685-1175
3030 Market St San Diego (92102) ***(P-24130)***
ARC of San Diego ....C....619 448-2415
1855 John Towers Ave El Cajon (92020) ***(P-24131)***
ARC of Ventura County Inc ....D....805 650-8611
210 Canada St Ojai (93023) ***(P-21954)***
ARC of Ventura County Inc ....C....805 644-0880
4277 Transport St Ste F Ventura (93003) ***(P-21955)***
ARC San Francisco (PA) ....C....415 255-7200
1500 Howard St San Francisco (94103) ***(P-23565)***
ARC Starlight Center ....D....619 427-7524
1280 Nolan Ave Chula Vista (91911) ***(P-22921)***
Arc, The, San Bernardino *Also called Association For Retarded* ***(P-23568)***
Arca Los Angeles, Compton *Also called Appliance Recycling Ctrs Amer* ***(P-6147)***
Arcadia Convalescent Hosp Inc (PA) ....C....323 681-1504
1601 S Baldwin Ave Arcadia (91007) ***(P-20493)***
Arcadia Gardens MGT Corp ....D....626 574-8571
720 W Camino Real Ave Arcadia (91007) ***(P-20411)***
Arcadia Health Care Center, Arcadia *Also called Arcadia Convalescent Hosp Inc* ***(P-20493)***
Arcadia Healthcare, Redding *Also called Northern California Hlth Care* ***(P-21820)***
Arcadia Management Service Co ....E....408 286-4440
5185 Cherry Ave Ste 10 San Jose (95118) ***(P-10916)***
Arcadia Services Inc ....D....248 352-7530
4340 Redwood Hwy Ste 123 San Rafael (94903) ***(P-14473)***
Arcadia Transit Inc ....E....818 252-0630
7955 San Fernando Rd Sun Valley (91352) ***(P-3524)***
Arcana Corporation ....E....805 882-1305
118 Nopalitos Way Santa Barbara (93103) ***(P-16630)***
Arch Bay Holdings LLC ....D....949 679-2400
327 W Maple Ave Monrovia (91016) ***(P-11645)***
Arch Health Partners Inc (HQ) ....D....858 675-3100
15611 Pomerado Rd Ste 575 Poway (92064) ***(P-20753)***
Arch Telecom Inc (PA) ....D....714 312-2724
1940 W Corporate Way Anaheim (92801) ***(P-5152)***
Archer Western Contractors LLC ....D....858 715-7200
9915 Mira Mesa Blvd # 230 San Diego (92131) ***(P-1409)***
Archer-Daniels-Midland Company ....D....559 233-6262
3390 S Chestnut Ave Fresno (93725) ***(P-8544)***
Archetype Consulting Inc ....D....888 644-8445
530 Divisadero St Ste 310 San Francisco (94117) ***(P-26507)***
Architects Orange ....C....714 639-9860
144 N Orange St Orange (92866) ***(P-25413)***
Architectural Coatings Inc ....E....714 701-1360
1565 E Edinger Ave Santa Ana (92705) ***(P-2332)***
Architectural GL & Alum Co Inc (PA) ....C....925 583-2460
6400 Brisa St Livermore (94550) ***(P-7045)***
Architecture Division, Los Angeles *Also called City of Los Angeles* ***(P-25427)***
Architrends Inc ....D....925 648-8800
3860 Blackhawk Rd Ste 160 Danville (94506) ***(P-24942)***
Archives Management Corp (PA) ....C....650 544-2200
2301 S El Camino Real San Mateo (94403) ***(P-26137)***
Arclight Cinema Company ....D....818 501-0753
15301 Ventura Blvd Bldg A Sherman Oaks (91403) ***(P-17816)***
Arclight Cinema Company ....C....323 464-1465
120 N Robertson Blvd Fl 3 Los Angeles (90048) ***(P-17817)***
Arco Envmtl Remediation LLC ....D....714 523-5674
5472 Orangethorpe Ave La Palma (90623) ***(P-26508)***
Arco Olympic Training Center, Chula Vista *Also called United Sttes Olympic Committee* ***(P-18081)***
Arconic Fastening Systems, Torrance *Also called Arconic Global Fas & Rings Inc* ***(P-7619)***
Arconic Fastening Systems, Simi Valley *Also called Arconic Global Fas & Rings Inc* ***(P-7620)***
Arconic Fastening Systems, Fullerton *Also called Arconic Global Fas & Rings Inc* ***(P-7621)***
Arconic Fastening Systems, Torrance *Also called Arconic Global Fas & Rings Inc* ***(P-7622)***
Arconic Fastening Systems, Tracy *Also called Arconic Global Fas & Rings Inc* ***(P-7380)***
Arconic Fastening Systems, Torrance *Also called Arconic Global Fas & Rings Inc* ***(P-7623)***
Arconic Fstening Systems Rings, City of Industry *Also called Arconic Global Fas & Rings Inc* ***(P-7617)***
Arconic Fstening Systems Rings, Torrance *Also called Arconic Global Fas & Rings Inc* ***(P-7618)***
Arconic Global Fas & Rings Inc ....B....626 968-3831
135 N Unruh Ave City of Industry (91744) ***(P-7617)***
Arconic Global Fas & Rings Inc ....D....310 784-0700
3000 Lomita Blvd Torrance (90505) ***(P-7618)***
Arconic Global Fas & Rings Inc ....B....310 530-2220
3014 Lomita Blvd Torrance (90505) ***(P-7619)***
Arconic Global Fas & Rings Inc (HQ) ....C....805 527-3600
3990a Heritage Oak Ct Simi Valley (93063) ***(P-7620)***
Arconic Global Fas & Rings Inc ....D....714 871-1550
800 S State College Blvd Fullerton (92831) ***(P-7621)***
Arconic Global Fas & Rings Inc ....E....310 530-2220
3000 Lomita Blvd Torrance (90505) ***(P-7622)***
Arconic Global Fas & Rings Inc ....D....209 839-3005
1925 N Macarthur Dr # 200 Tracy (95376) ***(P-7380)***
Arconic Global Fas & Rings Inc ....A....310 530-2220
3018 Lomita Blvd Torrance (90505) ***(P-7623)***
Arconix USA, Camarillo *Also called Arconix/Usa Inc* ***(P-7232)***
Arconix/Usa Inc ....D....805 388-2525
880 Avenida Acaso Ste 100 Camarillo (93012) ***(P-7232)***
Arcs Commercial Mortgage Co LP (HQ) ....C....818 676-3274
26901 Agoura Rd Ste 200 Calabasas (91301) ***(P-9525)***
Arcsoft Inc (PA) ....D....510 440-9901
46605 Fremont Blvd Fremont (94538) ***(P-14648)***
Arctouch LLC ....C....415 944-2000
1001 Front St San Francisco (94111) ***(P-14649)***
Arcules Inc ....D....949 439-0053
17875 Von Karman Ave # 450 Irvine (92614) ***(P-14650)***
Arcus Biosciences Inc ....C....510 694-6200
3928 Point Eden Way Hayward (94545) ***(P-25710)***
Ardcore Senior Living ....D....714 974-2226
525 S Anaheim Hills Rd Anaheim (92807) ***(P-23822)***
Arden Health & Rehab Ctr, Sacramento *Also called Mariner Health Care Inc* ***(P-20124)***
Arden Hills Country Club Inc ....D....916 482-6111
1220 Arden Hills Ln Sacramento (95864) ***(P-18381)***
Arden Realty Inc (HQ) ....D....310 966-2600
11601 Wilshire Blvd Fl 5 Los Angeles (90025) ***(P-10569)***
Arden-Mayfair Inc ....E....310 638-2842
6191 Peachtree St Commerce (90040) ***(P-4374)***
Ardenwood Farm, Fremont *Also called City of Fremont* ***(P-24254)***
Ardmore Home Design Inc (PA) ....E....626 333-1177
768 Turnbull Canyon Rd City of Industry (91745) ***(P-6542)***
Ardwin Freight, Burbank *Also called Ardwin Inc* ***(P-3967)***
Ardwin Inc ....C....818 767-7777
2940 N Hollywood Way Burbank (91505) ***(P-3967)***

Mergent e-mail: customerrelations@mergent.com
1178
2020 Directory of California
Wholesalers and Services Companies
(P-0000) Products & Services Section entry number
(PA)=Parent Co (HQ)=Headquarters (DH)=Div Headquarters

Are- Maryland No 31 LLC ....E....626 578-0777
385 E Colo Blvd Ste 299 Pasadena (91101) ***(P-10570)***
Area Distributing Co, San Jose *Also called J T R Company Inc* ***(P-7953)***
Area Distributing Company, San Jose *Also called J T R Company Inc* ***(P-4436)***
Area Housing Authority (PA)....E....805 480-9991
1400 W Hillcrest Dr Newbury Park (91320) ***(P-10917)***
Arena Painting Contractors Inc....D....310 316-2446
525 E Alondra Blvd Gardena (90248) ***(P-2333)***
Arena Solutions Inc (PA)....D....650 513-3500
989 E Hillsdale Blvd # 250 Foster City (94404) ***(P-14651)***
Arena Solutions Inc....E....978 988-3800
989 E Hillsdale Blvd # 250 Foster City (94404) ***(P-15243)***
Arena Stuart Rentals Inc....C....408 856-3232
454 S Abbott Ave Milpitas (95035) ***(P-14129)***
Arent Fox LLP....C....213 629-7400
555 W 5th St Ste 4800 Los Angeles (90013) ***(P-22359)***
Ares Management Corporation (PA)....D....310 201-4100
2000 Avenue Of The Stars # 12 Los Angeles (90067) ***(P-11712)***
Ares Management LLC (HQ)....D....310 201-4100
2000 Avenue Of The Stars # 12 Los Angeles (90067) ***(P-11713)***
Ares Management LLC....C....310 201-4100
1999 Ave Of Stars Fl 37 Los Angeles (90067) ***(P-11714)***
Arete Associates (PA)....C....818 885-2200
9301 Corbin Ave Ste 2000 Northridge (91324) ***(P-25711)***
Arete Hotels LLC....D....209 602-7952
2229 Den Helder Dr Modesto (95356) ***(P-12017)***
AREY JONES EDUCATIONAL SOLUTIO, San Diego *Also called Broadway Typewriter Co Inc* ***(P-6810)***
Argent Hotel, The, San Francisco *Also called L-O Soma Hotel Inc* ***(P-12526)***
Argent Management Co LLC....D....949 777-4070
2392 Morse Ave Irvine (92614) ***(P-10918)***
Argon Enterprises Inc....D....310 349-8777
13658 Hawthorne Blvd Hawthorne (90250) ***(P-10919)***
Argonaut Constructors....C....707 542-4862
360 Sutton Pl Santa Rosa (95407) ***(P-1666)***
Argonaut Hotel....C....415 563-0800
495 Jefferson St San Francisco (94109) ***(P-12018)***
Argonaut Kensington Associates....D....925 943-1121
1580 Geary Rd Ofc Walnut Creek (94597) ***(P-22922)***
Argonne YMCA After School, San Francisco *Also called Young Mens Christian Assoc SF* ***(P-24732)***
Argus Management Company LLC....B....562 299-5200
5150 E Pacific Coast Hwy # 500 Long Beach (90804) ***(P-26931)***
Argus Medical Management, Long Beach *Also called Argus Management Company LLC* ***(P-26931)***
Aria Group Incorporated....D....949 475-2915
17395 Daimler St Irvine (92614) ***(P-24943)***
Aria Systems Inc (PA)....D....415 852-7250
100 Pine St Ste 2450 San Francisco (94111) ***(P-14652)***
Ariba Inc (HQ)....C....650 849-4000
3420 Hillview Ave Bldg 3 Palo Alto (94304) ***(P-15244)***
Aricent NA Inc (HQ)....D....408 324-1800
3979 Freedom Cir Ste 950 Santa Clara (95054) ***(P-14653)***
Aricent Technologies, Santa Clara *Also called Aricent US Inc* ***(P-14654)***
Aricent US Inc (HQ)....E....408 329-7400
3979 Freedom Cir Ste 950 Santa Clara (95054) ***(P-14654)***
Aries Filterworks....E....323 262-1600
13850 Van Ness Ave Gardena (90249) ***(P-7624)***
ARINC Incorporated....D....310 301-9040
4553 Glencoe Ave Ste 100 Marina Del Rey (90292) ***(P-24944)***
Arinwine Arcft Maint Svcs LLC....D....310 338-0063
6201 W Imperial Hwy Los Angeles (90045) ***(P-4752)***
Ariosa Diagnostics Inc....C....408 229-7500
5945 Optical Ct San Jose (95138) ***(P-25712)***
Arise LLC....D....559 485-0881
1033 Van Ness Ave Fresno (93721) ***(P-18624)***
Arise Construction Inc....D....559 449-8989
5390 E Pine Ave Fresno (93727) ***(P-2058)***
Arise Solar, Fresno *Also called Arise Construction Inc* ***(P-2058)***
Arizona and 21st Corp....D....310 829-5377
2021 Arizona Ave Santa Monica (90404) ***(P-20494)***
Arizona Channel Isla....D....480 788-0755
300 W 9th St Oxnard (93030) ***(P-18625)***
Arizona Pipeline Company (PA)....B....760 244-8212
17372 Lilac St Hesperia (92345) ***(P-1830)***
Arizona Pipeline Company....C....951 270-3100
1745 Sampson Ave Corona (92879) ***(P-1831)***
Arizona Tile LLC....D....714 978-6403
1620 S Lewis St Anaheim (92805) ***(P-6669)***
Arkebauer Properties, Irvine *Also called Western National Properties* ***(P-1284)***
Arklin Brothers Hauling, Palmdale *Also called Antelope Valley Recycling* ***(P-6146)***
Arlene Keller MD....E....415 923-3598
2100 Webster St Ste 423 San Francisco (94115) ***(P-18823)***
ARLINGTON GARDENS CARE CENTER, Riverside *Also called Honey Flower Holdings LLC* ***(P-20019)***
Armada Trucking Group Inc....D....800 620-8592
225 Hermosa Ave Unit 202 Long Beach (90802) ***(P-3850)***
Armand Hammer Museum....C....310 443-7000
10899 Wilshire Blvd Los Angeles (90024) ***(P-24246)***
Armando C Ibarra CPA....D....619 422-1348
371 E St Chula Vista (91910) ***(P-25535)***
Armando Gonzalez Contracting....B....661 792-3785
32380 Elmo Hwy Mc Farland (93250) ***(P-612)***
Armanino LLP....C....310 478-4148
11766 Wilshire Blvd Fl 9 Los Angeles (90025) ***(P-25536)***
Armanino LLP (PA)....C....925 790-2600
12657 Alcosta Blvd # 500 San Ramon (94583) ***(P-25537)***
Armc, Colton *Also called Arrowhead Regional Medical Ctr* ***(P-20754)***
Armed Courier Service, Santa Clara *Also called Dan Connolly Inc* ***(P-16252)***
Armed Forces Officials Assn....E....858 672-1438
14532 Penasquitos Dr San Diego (92129) ***(P-24377)***
Armenian Amrcn Cuncil On Aging....E....818 241-8690
407 E Colorado St Glendale (91205) ***(P-22923)***
Armenn-Mrican Council On Aging, Glendale *Also called Armenian Amrcn Cuncil On Aging* ***(P-22923)***
Arminak & Associates LLC....D....626 358-4804
4832 Azusa Canyon Rd A Irwindale (91706) ***(P-8950)***
Armstrong Construction Co, Emeryville *Also called Armstrong Installation Service* ***(P-2334)***
Armstrong Installation Service....D....408 777-1234
4575 San Pablo Ave Emeryville (94608) ***(P-2334)***
Armstrong Mfg & Engrg Inc....D....530 888-6262
12780 Earhart Ave Auburn (95602) ***(P-24945)***
Arnaudo Bros Transport Inc (PA)....D....209 835-0406
16505 S Tracy Blvd Tracy (95304) ***(P-301)***
Arnaudo Bros Trucking, Tracy *Also called Arnaudo Bros Transport Inc* ***(P-301)***
Arnel and Affliate, Costa Mesa *Also called Arnel Interior Corp* ***(P-26138)***
Arnel Development Company....D....760 599-6111
3146 Tiger Run Ct Ste 108 Carlsbad (92010) ***(P-1226)***
Arnel Interior Corp....B....714 481-5100
949 S Coast Dr Ste 600 Costa Mesa (92626) ***(P-26138)***
Arnies Supplies Service Ltd....D....323 263-1696
1501 N Ditman Ave Los Angeles (90063) ***(P-17486)***
Arnold & Porter LLP....B....818 788-8081
3 Embarcadero Ctr Fl 7 San Francisco (94111) ***(P-22360)***
Arnold & Porter PC....B....415 434-1600
3 Embarcadero Ctr Fl 7 San Francisco (94111) ***(P-22361)***
Arnold Palmer Golf MGT LLC....D....415 561-4670
300 Finley Rd San Francisco (94129) ***(P-26139)***
Arnold Porter Kaye Scholer LLP....D....650 319-4500
3000 El Camino Real 2-500 Palo Alto (94306) ***(P-22362)***
Arnold Porter Kaye Scholer LLP....C....310 788-1000
1999 Avenue Of The Stars # 1600 Los Angeles (90067) ***(P-22363)***
Arntz Builders Inc....E....415 382-1188
431 Payran St Ste A Petaluma (94952) ***(P-1329)***
Aroma Spa & Sports LLC....D....213 387-2111
3680 Wilshire Blvd # 301 Los Angeles (90010) ***(P-18626)***
Aroma Wilshire Center, Los Angeles *Also called Hanil Development Inc* ***(P-11629)***
Aroma Wilshire Center, Los Angeles *Also called Aroma Spa & Sports LLC* ***(P-18626)***
AROUND THE CLOCK HOME CARE, Bakersfield *Also called Vasindas Around The Clock Care* ***(P-24104)***
Arraycon LLC (PA)....E....916 925-0201
1143 Blumenfeld Dr # 200 Sacramento (95815) ***(P-2059)***
Arreolas Complete Ldscp Svc, Sacramento *Also called Arreolas Complete Ldscp Svc* ***(P-774)***
Arreolas Complete Ldscp Svc....E....916 387-6777
8671 Morrison Creek Dr # 100 Sacramento (95828) ***(P-774)***
Arriaga Usa Inc....D....818 982-9559
11831 Vose St North Hollywood (91605) ***(P-2883)***
Arriaga Usa Inc (PA)....D....818 982-9559
12000 Sherman Way North Hollywood (91605) ***(P-6670)***
Arriba Juntos (PA)....D....415 487-3240
1850 Mission St San Francisco (94103) ***(P-23566)***
Arrow Bell, Woodland Hills *Also called Arrow Electronics Inc* ***(P-7233)***
Arrow Disposal Services Inc....E....626 336-2255
14332 Valley Blvd La Puente (91746) ***(P-6152)***
Arrow Electronics Inc....D....818 932-1022
20935 Warner Center Ln A Woodland Hills (91367) ***(P-7233)***
Arrow Tools Fas & Saw Inc....E....818 780-1464
7635 Burnet Ave Van Nuys (91405) ***(P-7381)***
Arrow USA....D....951 845-6144
1105 Highland Ct Beaumont (92223) ***(P-7665)***
Arrow Wire & Cable Inc (PA)....E....909 282-1940
13911 Yorba Ave Chino (91710) ***(P-7126)***
Arrowhead Central Credit Union (PA)....B....866 212-4333
8686 Haven Ave Rancho Cucamonga (91730) ***(P-9293)***
Arrowhead Convalescent Home....D....909 886-4731
4343 N Sierra Way San Bernardino (92407) ***(P-19724)***
Arrowhead Gen Insur Agcy Inc (HQ)....C....619 881-8600
701 B St Ste 2100 San Diego (92101) ***(P-10074)***
Arrowhead Home, San Bernardino *Also called Arrowhead Convalescent Home* ***(P-19724)***
Arrowhead Management Company (HQ)....D....619 881-8733
701 B St Ste 2100 San Diego (92101) ***(P-10271)***
Arrowhead Regional Medical Ctr....A....909 580-1000
400 N Pepper Ave Colton (92324) ***(P-20754)***
Arrowhead Water, Orange *Also called Nestle Waters North Amer Inc* ***(P-8615)***
Arroyo & Coates Inc....D....415 445-7800
425 California St # 2000 San Francisco (94104) ***(P-10920)***
Arroyo Developmental Services....D....626 307-2240
1839 Potrero Grande Dr Monterey Park (91755) ***(P-22924)***
Arroyo Grande Care Center, Arroyo Grande *Also called Compass Health Inc* ***(P-20532)***
Arroyo Grande Community Hosp, Arroyo Grande *Also called Dignity Health* ***(P-20836)***
Arroyo Insurance Services Inc (PA)....D....626 799-9532
440 E Huntington Dr # 100 Arcadia (91006) ***(P-10272)***
Arroyo Labor Contracting Svc, Gonzales *Also called Alicia Arroyo Inc* ***(P-611)***
Arroyo Seco Medical Group (PA)....D....626 795-7556
301 S Fair Oaks Ave # 300 Pasadena (91105) ***(P-18824)***
ARS, Whittier *Also called Assocted Reproduction Svcs Inc* ***(P-13757)***
ARS National Services Inc (PA)....C....800 456-5053
201 W Grand Ave Escondido (92025) ***(P-13669)***
ARS West LLC....D....760 480-6631
780 W El Norte Pkwy Escondido (92026) ***(P-17410)***
Art & Logic Inc....D....818 500-1933
87 N Raymond Ave Pasadena (91103) ***(P-15559)***
Art Piccadilly Shaw LLC....D....559 375-7760
5115 E Mckinley Ave Fresno (93727) ***(P-12019)***

ALPHABETIC

Employee Codes: A=Over 500 employees, B=251-500
C=101-250, D=51-100, E=50
2020 Directory of California
Wholesalers and Services Companies
© Mergent Inc. 1-800-342-5647
1179

Art Piccadilly Shaw LLC.......C.......559 224-4200
4961 N Cedar Ave Fresno (93726) *(P-12020)*

Art Supply Enterprises Inc (PA).......C.......510 428-9011
1375 Ocean Ave Emeryville (94608) *(P-8951)*

Artesia Christian Home Inc.......C.......562 865-5218
11614 183rd St Artesia (90701) *(P-20495)*

Artesia Healthcare Inc.......D.......818 843-1771
925 W Alameda Ave Burbank (91506) *(P-19725)*

Arthrtis Fundation PCF Reg Inc.......E.......323 954-5760
800 W 6th St Ste 1250 Los Angeles (90017) *(P-24475)*

Arthur J Gallagher & Co.......E.......949 349-9800
18201 Von Karman Ave # 200 Irvine (92612) *(P-10273)*

Arthur J Gallagher & Co.......C.......818 539-2300
505 N Brand Blvd Ste 600 Glendale (91203) *(P-10274)*

Arthur J Gallagher & Co.......D.......559 733-1181
500 N Santa Fe St Visalia (93292) *(P-10275)*

Arthur J Gallagher & Co.......D.......800 217-9800
1825 Chicago Ave Ste 240 Riverside (92507) *(P-10276)*

Arthur J Gallagher & Co.......C.......415 546-9300
1 Market Spear Tower San Francisco (94105) *(P-10277)*

Arthur J Gallagher & Co.......D.......559 436-0833
7910 N Ingram Ave Ste 201 Fresno (93711) *(P-10278)*

Arthur J Gallagher & Co.......E.......925 299-1112
3697 Mt Diablo Blvd # 300 Lafayette (94549) *(P-10279)*

Arthur Kunde & Sons Inc.......E.......707 833-5501
9825 Sonoma Hwy Kenwood (95452) *(P-653)*

Arthur Loussararian MD, Mission Viejo *Also called Mission Internal Med Group Inc (P-19197)*

Arthur Schawlow Center, Chico *Also called California Vocations Inc (P-20523)*

Artiano Shinoff Abed (PA).......D.......619 232-3122
16935 W Bernardo Dr # 114 San Diego (92127) *(P-22364)*

Artic Mechanical Inc (PA).......D.......909 980-2539
10440 Trademark St Rancho Cucamonga (91730) *(P-2060)*

Artichoke Joe's Casino, San Bruno *Also called Artichoke Joes Inc (P-18627)*

Artichoke Joes Inc.......B.......650 589-8812
659 Huntington Ave San Bruno (94066) *(P-18627)*

Articouture Inc.......E.......626 336-7299
1265 S Johnson Dr City of Industry (91745) *(P-8018)*

Artimex Iron Company Inc.......C.......619 444-3155
315 Cypress Ln El Cajon (92020) *(P-3252)*

Artimisa & Co.......D.......530 283-3700
220 Forest Knoll Ln Quincy (95971) *(P-24946)*

Artisan Bakers.......D.......707 939-1765
21684 8th St E Ste 400 Sonoma (95476) *(P-8545)*

Artisan Entertainment Inc.......A.......310 449-9200
2700 Colorado Ave Ste 200 Santa Monica (90404) *(P-17576)*

Artisan Pictures Inc.......C.......310 449-9200
2700 Colorado Ave Fl 2 Santa Monica (90404) *(P-7798)*

Artisan Sotheby's Intl. Realty, Santa Rosa *Also called Realogy Holdings Corp (P-11403)*

Artist Silva Management LLC (PA).......C.......323 856-8222
722 Seward St Los Angeles (90038) *(P-26140)*

Artistic Entrmt Svcs LLC.......D.......626 334-9388
120 N Aspan Ave Azusa (91702) *(P-17964)*

Artistic Maintenance Inc.......D.......909 390-5156
603 S Milliken Ave Ste A Ontario (91761) *(P-775)*

Artistic Maintenance Inc.......C.......949 733-8690
16092 Construction Cir E Irvine (92606) *(P-776)*

Artists of River Town.......D.......530 534-7690
56 Highlands Blvd Oroville (95966) *(P-24378)*

Artists Studio Gallery.......D.......424 206-9902
5504 Crestridge Rd Rancho Palos Verdes (90275) *(P-18628)*

Artizen Incorporated.......C.......650 261-9400
101 Golf Course Dr # 300 Rohnert Park (94928) *(P-14655)*

Artlogic, Pasadena *Also called Art & Logic Inc (P-15559)*

Arts and Services For Disabled.......E.......562 377-0302
3626 E Pacific Coast Hwy Long Beach (90804) *(P-22925)*

Artwear Inc.......E.......310 217-1393
13621 S Main St Los Angeles (90061) *(P-8019)*

Arup North America Limited.......C.......310 578-4182
12777 W Jefferson Blvd Los Angeles (90066) *(P-24947)*

Arup North America Limited (HQ).......C.......415 957-9445
560 Mission St Fl 7 San Francisco (94105) *(P-24948)*

Arvin-Edison Water Storage Dst (PA).......E.......661 854-5573
20401 E Bear Mtn Blvd Arvin (93203) *(P-6361)*

Arya Design Group, Los Angeles *Also called Arya Group Inc (P-1080)*

Arya Group Inc.......E.......310 446-7000
10490 Santa Monica Blvd Los Angeles (90025) *(P-1080)*

Arya Ice Cream Distrg Co Inc.......D.......323 234-2994
914 E 31st St Los Angeles (90011) *(P-8309)*

Aryaka Networks Inc (PA).......C.......408 273-8420
1800 Gateway Dr Ste 200 San Mateo (94404) *(P-26892)*

Aryzta LLC.......E.......209 469-4920
920 Shaw Rd Stockton (95215) *(P-8546)*

Asai, Glendale *Also called Automated Systems America Inc (P-17487)*

Asana Inc (PA).......D.......415 525-3888
1550 Bryant St Ste 200 San Francisco (94103) *(P-15944)*

Asana Integrated Medical Group.......D.......888 212-7545
6200 Canoga Ave Ste 350 Woodland Hills (91367) *(P-22926)*

ASAP Professional Services, San Ramon *Also called A S A P Professional Services (P-14214)*

Asbestos Instant Response Inc.......D.......323 733-0508
3517 W Washington Blvd Los Angeles (90018) *(P-3380)*

Asbury Environmental Services (PA).......D.......310 886-3400
1300 S Santa Fe Ave Compton (90221) *(P-3851)*

Asbury Pk Nrsing Rhbltion Ctr.......C.......916 649-2000
2257 Fair Oaks Blvd Sacramento (95825) *(P-20496)*

Asbury Transportation Co.......D.......661 327-2271
2144 Mohawk St Bakersfield (93308) *(P-3968)*

ASC Building Products, West Sacramento *Also called ASC Profiles LLC (P-7046)*

ASC Profiles LLC (HQ).......D.......916 376-2800
2110 Enterprise Blvd West Sacramento (95691) *(P-7046)*

Ascend Clinical LLC (PA).......D.......800 800-5655
1400 Industrial Way Redwood City (94063) *(P-21506)*

Ascend Distribution, City of Industry *Also called Eforcity Corp - Nfm (P-7260)*

Ascendantfx Capital USA Inc.......D.......201 633-4667
3478 Buskirk Ave Ste 1000 Pleasant Hill (94523) *(P-9420)*

Ascendify Corporation.......E.......415 528-5503
221 Main St Ste 1350 San Francisco (94105) *(P-14656)*

Ascent Services Group Inc.......B.......925 627-4900
1001 Galaxy Way Ste 408 Concord (94520) *(P-14474)*

Ascon Recycling Co.......C.......760 948-1538
17671 Bear Valley Rd Hesperia (92345) *(P-6153)*

Ascot Hotel LP.......C.......310 476-6411
170 N Church Ln Los Angeles (90049) *(P-12021)*

Asec Group, Los Angeles *Also called A S E C International Inc (P-15718)*

Asgn Incorporated (PA).......C.......818 878-7900
26745 Malibu Hills Rd Calabasas (91301) *(P-14226)*

Ash Holdings LLC.......D.......909 793-2609
1620 W Fern Ave Redlands (92373) *(P-19726)*

Ashbury Market Inc.......D.......650 952-8889
179 Starlite St South San Francisco (94080) *(P-8547)*

Ashford Trs Nickel LLC (PA).......D.......925 934-2500
1345 Treat Blvd Walnut Creek (94597) *(P-12022)*

Ashford Trs Nickel LLC.......D.......619 260-0111
1433 Camino Del Rio S San Diego (92108) *(P-26141)*

Ashland LLC.......D.......310 223-3505
20915 S Wilmington Ave Carson (90810) *(P-8690)*

Ashland Performance Materials, Carson *Also called Ashland LLC (P-8690)*

Ashley Home Care Services LLC.......E.......323 286-2831
200 Spectrum Center Dr # 300 Irvine (92618) *(P-21671)*

Ashley Lane Cherry Orchards LP.......E.......209 546-0426
500 N Jack Tone Rd Stockton (95215) *(P-200)*

Ashley Ltc Inc.......D.......707 528-2100
446 Arrowood Dr Santa Rosa (95407) *(P-19727)*

Ashley Management Group.......E.......949 754-3120
300 Spectrum Center Dr # 400 Irvine (92618) *(P-26509)*

Ashok Thummalachetty.......C.......510 687-9797
44721 Aguila Ter Fremont (94539) *(P-26992)*

Ashunya Inc.......D.......714 385-1900
642 N Eckhoff St Orange (92868) *(P-14657)*

Ashwood Construction Inc.......E.......559 253-7240
5755 E Kings Canyon Rd # 110 Fresno (93727) *(P-1227)*

Asi Computer Technologies Inc (PA).......C.......510 226-8000
48289 Fremont Blvd Fremont (94538) *(P-6798)*

ASI Hastings Inc.......C.......619 590-9300
4870 Vewridge Ave Ste 200 San Diego (92123) *(P-2061)*

Asi Heating, Air and Solar, San Diego *Also called ASI Hastings Inc (P-2061)*

Asia Foundation (PA).......D.......415 982-4640
465 California St Fl 9 San Francisco (94104) *(P-25966)*

Asia Pacific Capital.......D.......213 628-8800
345 Suth Fgroa St Ste 100 Los Angeles (90071) *(P-11750)*

Asiainfo-Linkage Inc.......A.......408 970-9788
5201 Great America Pkwy # 356 Santa Clara (95054) *(P-5303)*

Asian Amercn Recovery Svcs Inc (PA).......C.......650 243-4888
1115 Mission Rd 2 South San Francisco (94080) *(P-22927)*

Asian Amercn Recovery Svcs Inc.......C.......408 271-3900
1340 Tully Rd Ste 304 San Jose (95122) *(P-21448)*

Asian Art Meusuem of SF, San Francisco *Also called Asian Art Museum Found San Fra (P-24247)*

Asian Art Museum, San Francisco *Also called City & County of San Francisco (P-24253)*

Asian Art Museum Found San Fra.......C.......415 581-3500
200 Larkin St San Francisco (94102) *(P-24247)*

Asian Cmnty Mental Hlth Svcs, Oakland *Also called Asian Community Mental Hlth Bd (P-21956)*

Asian Community Center of Sac (PA).......C.......916 394-6399
7334 Park City Dr Sacramento (95831) *(P-22928)*

Asian Community Mental Hlth Bd.......D.......510 869-6000
310 8th St Ste 303 Oakland (94607) *(P-21956)*

Asian Health Services.......D.......510 986-0601
270 13th St Oakland (94612) *(P-18825)*

Asian Health Services (PA).......C.......510 986-6800
101 8th St Oakland (94607) *(P-18826)*

Asian PCF Hlth Care Ventr Inc (PA).......C.......323 644-3880
4216 Fountain Ave Los Angeles (90029) *(P-24132)*

Asian Rehabilitation Svc Inc (PA).......D.......562 632-1141
7009 Washington Ave Whittier (90602) *(P-23567)*

Asics America Corporation (HQ).......C.......949 453-8888
80 Technology Dr Irvine (92618) *(P-8120)*

Asics Tiger, Irvine *Also called Asics America Corporation (P-8120)*

Asig, Ontario *Also called Menzies Aviation (texas) Inc (P-4781)*

Asilomar Conference Center, Pacific Grove *Also called Pacific Grove Aslmar Oper Corp (P-12688)*

Asist Inc.......D.......559 251-7701
1974 N Gateway Blvd # 102 Fresno (93727) *(P-21672)*

Asistencia Villa, Redlands *Also called Redlands Cmnty Hosp Foundation (P-20667)*

Asistencia Villa Rehab & Care, Redlands *Also called Silverscreen Healthcare Inc (P-20688)*

Ask.com, Oakland *Also called IAC Search & Media Inc (P-15868)*

Asmg, San Diego *Also called Anesthesia Service Med Group (P-18816)*

Asociacon De Bomberos Del Esta.......D.......949 355-4249
1100 Calle Del Cerro 52d San Clemente (92672) *(P-24322)*

Aspect Software Inc.......E.......408 595-5002
101 Academy Ste 130 Irvine (92617) *(P-15245)*

Aspects Furniture Mfg Inc.......C.......909 606-5806
15830 El Prado Rd Ste A Chino (91708) *(P-6504)*

Aspen Apts I.......D.......415 673-5879
165 Eddy St San Francisco (94102) *(P-10687)*

Aspen Grove Apartments LLC .... D 408 848-6400
450 E 8th St Gilroy (95020) *(P-10688)*
Aspen Healthcare Corporation (PA) .... D 562 888-6371
17100 Pioneer Blvd # 310 Artesia (90701) *(P-21673)*
Aspen Youth Inc .... D 562 567-5507
17777 Center Court Dr N # 300 Cerritos (90703) *(P-22929)*
Asphalt Management Inc .... E 562 630-6811
7243 Somerset Blvd Paramount (90723) *(P-3112)*
Aspiranet .... D 415 759-3690
3925 Noriega St San Francisco (94122) *(P-23823)*
Aspiranet .... D 209 669-2582
151 E Canal Dr Turlock (95380) *(P-22930)*
Aspiranet .... D 209 667-0327
2513 Youngstown Rd Turlock (95380) *(P-22931)*
Aspiriant LLC .... E 415 371-7800
50 California St Ste 2600 San Francisco (94111) *(P-16631)*
Asplundh Tree Expert Co .... D 805 964-9216
6100 Francis Botello Rd C Goleta (93117) *(P-932)*
Asplundh Tree Expert LLC .... D 805 641-0528
2055 N Ventura Ave Ventura (93001) *(P-933)*
Asplundh Tree Expert LLC .... C 714 893-2405
6101 Gateway Dr Cypress (90630) *(P-934)*
Aspm-Sandiego, San Diego Also called Allegis Residential Svcs Inc *(P-26128)*
Asr, San Juan Capistrano Also called Action Sports Retailer *(P-16602)*
Asr Constructors Inc .... B 951 779-6580
33891 Mission Trl Wildomar (92595) *(P-1410)*
Asrc Industrial Services LLC (HQ) .... D 707 644-7455
2300 Clayton Rd Ste 1050 Concord (94520) *(P-14475)*
Assa Abloy Rsdential Group Inc (HQ) .... C 626 961-0413
15250 Stafford St City of Industry (91744) *(P-7382)*
Assa Abloy Rsdential Group Inc .... B 626 369-4718
600 Balwin Park Blvd City of Industry (91746) *(P-7383)*
Assertive Security Services & .... A 818 888-2405
20501 Ventura Blvd # 150 Woodland Hills (91364) *(P-16495)*
Assessor-Recorder's Office, Fresno Also called County of Fresno *(P-24398)*
Asset Athene Management L P (HQ) .... D 310 698-4444
2121 Rosecrans Ave # 5300 El Segundo (90245) *(P-26142)*
Asset Management Tr Svcs LLC .... D 858 457-2202
1455 Frazee Rd Ste 500 San Diego (92108) *(P-26143)*
Asset Marketing Systems Insu .... D 888 303-8755
15050 Ave Of Science # 100 San Diego (92128) *(P-26510)*
ASset Private Security Inc .... D 831 809-9779
36 Quail Run Cir Ste O Salinas (93907) *(P-16199)*
Assetmark Inc (HQ) .... E 925 521-1040
1655 Grant St Ste 1000 Concord (94520) *(P-9789)*
Assetmark Fincl Holdings Inc .... A 925 521-2200
1655 Grant St 10 Concord (94520) *(P-9790)*
Assi Security (PA) .... D 949 955-0244
1370 Reynolds Ave Ste 201 Irvine (92614) *(P-2424)*
ASSICIATED STUDENTS, San Luis Obispo Also called Associated Students Inc *(P-22932)*
Assign Corporation .... C 818 247-7100
200 N Maryland Ave # 204 Glendale (91206) *(P-15945)*
Assist 65 Plus .... E 323 557-4426
111 W 7th St Ste 211 Los Angeles (90014) *(P-16632)*
Assista Hlthcare Prfssnals LLC .... C 650 393-4293
2006 Pioneer Ct San Mateo (94403) *(P-21674)*
Assistance In Home Care, Garden Grove Also called Our Watch *(P-21832)*
Assistance League of Redlands .... C 909 792-2675
506 W Colton Ave Redlands (92374) *(P-24133)*
ASSISTANCE LEAGUE THRIFT SHOP, Redlands Also called Assistance League of Redlands *(P-24133)*
Assisted Home Care, Northridge Also called Assisted Home Recovery Inc *(P-14227)*
Assisted Home Care, Thousand Oaks Also called Staff Assistance Inc *(P-14427)*
Assisted Home Recovery Inc .... D 626 915-5595
1900 W Garvey Ave S # 210 West Covina (91790) *(P-21675)*
Assisted Home Recovery Inc (PA) .... C 818 894-8117
8550 Balboa Blvd Lbby Northridge (91325) *(P-14227)*
Assistnce Leag of Fthill Cmmnt .... C 909 987-2813
8555 Archibald Ave 8593 Rancho Cucamonga (91730) *(P-24134)*
Assita In-Home Care, San Mateo Also called Assista Hlthcare Prfssnals LLC *(P-21674)*
Associate Mechanical Contrs .... D 760 294-3517
622 S Vinewood St Escondido (92029) *(P-2062)*
Associated Bond, Calabasas Also called AIA Holdings Inc *(P-10157)*
Associated Entrmt Releasing (PA) .... E 323 934-7044
4401 Wilshire Blvd Los Angeles (90010) *(P-17577)*
Associated Feed & Supply Co (PA) .... C 209 667-2708
5213 W Main St Turlock (95380) *(P-8834)*
Associated Foreign Exch Inc (HQ) .... D 888 307-2339
21045 Califa St Woodland Hills (91367) *(P-9421)*
Associated General Contract .... D 858 558-0739
6212 Ferris Sq San Diego (92121) *(P-24379)*
Associated Group, Commerce Also called Associated Landscape *(P-16633)*
Associated Indemnity Corp .... A 415 899-2000
1465 N Mcdowell Blvd # 100 Petaluma (94954) *(P-9861)*
Associated Intl Insur Co, Woodland Hills Also called Markel Corp *(P-10413)*
Associated Koi Clubs America .... D 949 650-5225
P.O. Box 10879 Costa Mesa (92627) *(P-18382)*
Associated Laboratories, Orange Also called De Par Inc *(P-26063)*
Associated Landscape .... D 714 558-6100
2420 S Eastern Ave Commerce (90040) *(P-16633)*
Associated Pension Cons Inc (PA) .... D 530 343-4233
2035 Forest Ave Chico (95928) *(P-10280)*
Associated Press .... D 213 626-1200
221 S Figueroa St Ste 300 Los Angeles (90012) *(P-16570)*
Associated Realtors .... D 949 813-1888
27411 Viana Mission Viejo (92692) *(P-10921)*
Associated Students California .... B 562 985-4994
1212 N Bellflower Blvd # 220 Long Beach (90815) *(P-24476)*

Associated Students Cdc .... D 408 924-6988
460 S 8th St San Jose (95112) *(P-23673)*
Associated Students Inc .... E 760 750-4990
333 S Twin Oaks Valley Rd San Marcos (92096) *(P-13168)*
Associated Students Inc (PA) .... D 805 756-1281
University Un Bldg 65 San Luis Obispo (93407) *(P-22932)*
Associated Students Inc .... D 805 756-1281
1 Grand Ave San Luis Obispo (93407) *(P-27266)*
Associated Students San Diego (PA) .... A 619 594-0234
5500 Campanile Dr San Diego (92182) *(P-24791)*
Associated Students Stanford (PA) .... D 650 723-4331
201 Tresidder Un Stanford (94305) *(P-24477)*
Associated Students Uc Irvine, Irvine Also called Student Government Associat *(P-4837)*
Associated Students UCLA (PA) .... B 310 825-4321
308 Westwood Plz Los Angeles (90095) *(P-24135)*
Associated Students UCLA .... C 310 794-0242
924 Westwood Blvd Los Angeles (90024) *(P-24136)*
Associated Students UCLA .... A 310 825-9451
650 Chrls Yng S Rm 23 120 Los Angeles (90095) *(P-18827)*
Associated Students, Inc., San Luis Obispo Also called Associated Students Inc *(P-27266)*
Associated Television Intl, Los Angeles Also called Associated Entrmt Releasing *(P-17577)*
Association For Retarded .... D 909 884-6484
796 E 6th St San Bernardino (92410) *(P-23568)*
Association of CA Schl Admnstr, La Mirada Also called Norwalk La Mirada Unif *(P-24414)*
Associations of United Nurses (PA) .... D 909 599-8622
955 Overland Ct Ste 150 San Dimas (91773) *(P-24435)*
Assocted Fgn Exch Holdings Inc (PA) .... D 818 386-2702
21045 Califa St Woodland Hills (91367) *(P-9422)*
Assocted Gstrntrlogy Med Group (PA) .... D 714 778-1300
1211 W La Palma Ave Anaheim (92801) *(P-18828)*
Assocted Reproduction Svcs Inc .... C 562 696-1181
13925 Whittier Blvd Whittier (90605) *(P-13757)*
Assocted Third Pty Admnstrtors .... C 619 358-8140
2831 Camino Del Rio S San Diego (92108) *(P-10207)*
Assurant Inc .... B 714 571-3900
2677 N Main St Ste 600 Santa Ana (92705) *(P-10281)*
Assure Consulting Inc .... D 650 966-1967
257 Castro St Ste 205 Mountain View (94041) *(P-26993)*
Assure Detective Agency, Corona Also called Chief Protective Services Inc *(P-16229)*
Assuredpartners Inc .... D 916 443-0200
1455 Response Rd Ste 260 Sacramento (95815) *(P-10282)*
AST Sportswear Inc .... B 714 223-2030
P.O. Box 17219 Anaheim (92817) *(P-13719)*
Asterias Biotherapeutics Inc .... D 510 456-3800
1010 Atlantic Ave Ste 102 Alameda (94501) *(P-25713)*
Astoria Convalescent Hospital .... C 818 367-5881
14040 Astoria St Sylmar (91342) *(P-19728)*
Astoria Nursing & Rehab Center, Sylmar Also called Astoria Convalescent Hospital *(P-19728)*
Astro Realty Inc .... D 562 924-3381
11305 183rd St Cerritos (90703) *(P-10922)*
Asus Computer International .... C 510 739-3777
48720 Kato Rd Fremont (94538) *(P-6799)*
Asylum, The, Glendale Also called Global Asylum Incorporated *(P-17612)*
At & T Wireless Service, Tustin Also called AB Cellular Holding LLC *(P-5296)*
At Home Caregivers, Novato Also called Bear Flag Marketing Corp *(P-21681)*
At Your Home Familycare .... C 858 625-0406
6540 Lusk Blvd Ste C266 San Diego (92121) *(P-13398)*
At Your Svc Htg & Coolg LLC .... D 602 550-6946
333 H St Ste 5000 Chula Vista (91910) *(P-1411)*
AT&T, Artesia Also called New Cingular Wireless Svcs Inc *(P-5264)*
AT&T Corp .... D 714 965-4685
10035 Adams Ave Huntington Beach (92646) *(P-5153)*
AT&T Corp .... D 925 603-9476
2390 Monument Blvd Pleasant Hill (94523) *(P-5154)*
AT&T Corp .... D 415 970-8520
2410 Mission St San Francisco (94110) *(P-5155)*
AT&T Corp .... D 619 448-1798
50 Town Center Pkwy Santee (92071) *(P-5156)*
AT&T Corp .... A 415 442-2600
795 Folsom St San Francisco (94107) *(P-5304)*
AT&T Corp .... D 714 258-8290
2219 Park Ave Ste 8a Tustin (92782) *(P-5157)*
AT&T Corp .... D 909 646-9644
12379 S Mainstreet Rancho Cucamonga (91739) *(P-5158)*
AT&T Corp .... D 909 930-6508
2508 S Grove Ave Ontario (91761) *(P-5159)*
AT&T Corp .... D 626 912-0600
830 W Arrow Hwy San Dimas (91773) *(P-5160)*
AT&T Corp .... D 310 225-3028
20810 Avalon Blvd Carson (90746) *(P-5161)*
AT&T Corp .... D 949 364-4052
27762 Antonio Pkwy Ste L3 Ladera Ranch (92694) *(P-5162)*
AT&T Corp .... D 310 303-3888
1100 Pacific Coast Hwy # 5 Hermosa Beach (90254) *(P-5163)*
AT&T Corp .... D 323 589-7045
6833 Pacific Blvd Huntington Park (90255) *(P-5164)*
AT&T Corp .... D 949 559-1457
6328 Irvine Blvd Irvine (92620) *(P-5165)*
AT&T Corp .... D 310 473-3649
2333 S Sepulveda Blvd Los Angeles (90064) *(P-5166)*
AT&T Corp .... D 626 396-0100
83 E Colorado Blvd Pasadena (91105) *(P-5167)*
AT&T Corp .... D 805 562-0121
7060 Market Place Dr Goleta (93117) *(P-5168)*
AT&T Corp .... D 310 547-0400
980 N Western Ave Ste H San Pedro (90732) *(P-5169)*
AT&T Corp .... D 661 297-1720
26453 Bouquet Canyon Rd Santa Clarita (91350) *(P-5170)*

**A
L
P
H
A
B
E
T
I
C**

Employee Codes: A=Over 500 employees, B=251-500
C=101-250, D=51-100, E=50

2020 Directory of California
Wholesalers and Services Companies

© Mergent Inc. 1-800-342-5647
1181

AT&T Corp ....D....714 284-3818
217 N Lemon St Rm 205 Anaheim (92805) ***(P-5171)***
AT&T Corp ....D....661 799-0800
24935 Pico Canyon Rd Stevenson Ranch (91381) ***(P-5172)***
AT&T Corp ....D....951 275-8801
3977 Chicago Ave Riverside (92507) ***(P-5173)***
AT&T Corp ....D....323 568-2006
4332 Tweedy Blvd South Gate (90280) ***(P-5174)***
AT&T Corp ....D....925 356-6204
2745 Cloverdale Ave Concord (94518) ***(P-5305)***
AT&T Corp ....D....530 891-2025
3750 Morrow Ln Chico (95928) ***(P-5175)***
AT&T Corp ....D....805 445-6562
1955 E Daily Dr Camarillo (93010) ***(P-5176)***
AT&T Corp ....D....530 822-2700
1054 Harter Pkwy Ste 9 Yuba City (95993) ***(P-5177)***
AT&T Corp ....D....760 752-3273
133 S Las Posas Rd # 141 San Marcos (92078) ***(P-5178)***
AT&T Corp ....D....213 787-0055
624 S Grand Ave Ste 2940 Los Angeles (90017) ***(P-5306)***
AT&T Corp ....D....415 721-1470
835 4th St San Rafael (94901) ***(P-5179)***
AT&T Corp ....D....831 465-6771
1855 41st Ave Capitola (95010) ***(P-5180)***
AT&T Corp ....D....805 583-9483
1263 Simi Town Center Way Simi Valley (93065) ***(P-5181)***
AT&T Corp ....D....858 693-0815
8225 Mira Mesa Blvd San Diego (92126) ***(P-5182)***
AT&T Corp ....D....530 661-7724
1810 E Main St Woodland (95776) ***(P-5183)***
AT&T Corp ....D....818 374-6458
6920 Van Nuys Blvd Rm 100 Van Nuys (91405) ***(P-5307)***
AT&T Corp ....D....818 373-6896
14709 Vanoan St Van Nuys (91405) ***(P-5308)***
AT&T Corp ....D....650 960-2313
1188 W Evelyn Ave Sunnyvale (94086) ***(P-27267)***
AT&T Corp ....D....650 780-1005
1121 Jefferson Ave Rm 222 Redwood City (94063) ***(P-5309)***
AT&T Corp ....C....415 394-3000
2600 Camino Ramon San Ramon (94583) ***(P-5310)***
AT&T Corp ....D....323 874-7000
7100 Santa Monica Blvd # 125 West Hollywood (90046) ***(P-5184)***
AT&T Corp ....D....925 327-7100
134 Sunset Dr San Ramon (94583) ***(P-5185)***
AT&T Corp ....D....408 729-8400
1705 Story Rd San Jose (95122) ***(P-5186)***
AT&T Corp ....D....408 871-3870
1546 Saratoga Ave San Jose (95129) ***(P-5311)***
AT&T Corp ....D....949 622-8240
17675 Harvard Ave Ste B Irvine (92614) ***(P-5187)***
AT&T Corp ....D....818 506-9118
6000 Lankershim Blvd North Hollywood (91606) ***(P-5312)***
AT&T Corp ....B....925 560-5011
5130 Hacienda Dr Fl 1 Dublin (94568) ***(P-16634)***
AT&T Corp ....D....310 659-7600
998 S Robertson Blvd # 103 Los Angeles (90035) ***(P-5188)***
AT&T Corp ....D....818 997-5998
16201 Raymer St Van Nuys (91406) ***(P-26994)***
AT&T Corp ....A....925 823-5388
2600 Camino Ramon 2w856 San Ramon (94583) ***(P-5313)***
AT&T Corp ....D....714 666-5504
3925 E Coronado St Anaheim (92807) ***(P-5314)***
AT&T Corp ....C....415 442-5900
50 Fremont St San Francisco (94105) ***(P-26893)***
AT&T Corp ....B....916 830-5000
4130 S Market Ct Sacramento (95834) ***(P-5315)***
AT&T Corp ....D....559 294-5431
3375 Peach Ave Clovis (93612) ***(P-5316)***
AT&T Corp ....D....909 381-7729
455 W 2nd St San Bernardino (92401) ***(P-5317)***
AT&T Corp ....D....408 980-2004
3025 Raymond St Santa Clara (95054) ***(P-5318)***
AT&T Corp ....D....510 965-9714
2105 Macdonald Ave Richmond (94801) ***(P-5189)***
AT&T Corp ....D....831 642-0100
400 Del Monte Ctr Monterey (93940) ***(P-5190)***
AT&T Corp ....D....562 923-3032
8420 Firestone Blvd Downey (90241) ***(P-5191)***
AT&T Corp ....D....415 276-0039
625 Ellis St Ste 205 Mountain View (94043) ***(P-5319)***
AT&T Corp ....D....213 787-0055
700 S Flower St Ste 810 Los Angeles (90017) ***(P-5320)***
AT&T Corp ....D....925 776-1200
2701 Verne Roberts Cir Antioch (94509) ***(P-5192)***
AT&T Datacomm LLC ....E....714 675-9752
16755 Von Karman Ave # 120 Irvine (92606) ***(P-5321)***
AT&T Services Inc ....C....619 515-5100
101 Broadway San Diego (92101) ***(P-5322)***
AT&T Services Inc ....C....661 398-2000
4300 Ming Ave Bakersfield (93309) ***(P-5323)***
AT&T Services Inc ....D....925 901-9318
2 Circle E Ranch Pl San Ramon (94583) ***(P-5193)***
AT&T Services Inc ....D....831 394-2690
161 Calle Del Oaks Monterey (93940) ***(P-5194)***
AT&T Services Inc ....C....415 545-9051
610 Brannan St San Francisco (94107) ***(P-5324)***
AT&T Services Inc ....C....209 223-0012
303 Church St Jackson (95642) ***(P-5325)***
AT&T Services Inc ....C....559 454-3579
5555 E Olive Ave Ste A315 Fresno (93727) ***(P-5195)***
AT&T Services Inc ....B....661 327-6030
50101 Office Park Dr Bakersfield (93304) ***(P-5326)***
AT&T Services Inc ....C....210 886-4922
200 W Center Street Prome Anaheim (92805) ***(P-5327)***
AT&T Services Inc ....C....858 886-2762
7337 Trade St Rm 3600 San Diego (92121) ***(P-5328)***
AT&T Services Inc ....C....714 259-4441
1834 W Victoria Ave Anaheim (92804) ***(P-5329)***
AT&T Services Inc ....C....951 369-2282
3580 Warm St Riverside (92501) ***(P-5330)***
AT&T Services Inc ....C....805 237-9503
908 28th St Paso Robles (93446) ***(P-5331)***
AT&T Services Inc ....D....831 649-2029
787 Munras Ave Monterey (93940) ***(P-5332)***
AT&T Services Inc ....C....650 960-2255
360 Pioneer Way Mountain View (94041) ***(P-5333)***
AT&T Services Inc ....C....916 972-2248
3464 El Camino Ave Sacramento (95821) ***(P-5334)***
AT&T Services Inc ....A....213 975-4089
1010 Wilshire Blvd Los Angeles (90017) ***(P-5335)***
AT&T Services Inc ....D....415 545-9058
666 Folsom St Rm 1132 San Francisco (94107) ***(P-5336)***
AT&T Services Inc ....B....510 836-6889
1270 Arroyo Way Walnut Creek (94596) ***(P-5337)***
AT&T Services Inc ....C....916 638-6096
2615 Mercantile Dr Rancho Cordova (95742) ***(P-5338)***
AT&T Services Inc ....C....707 545-5000
2125 Occidental Rd Santa Rosa (95401) ***(P-5339)***
AT&T Services Inc ....C....650 579-5266
1480 Burlingame Ave Burlingame (94010) ***(P-5340)***
AT&T Services Inc ....B....707 428-2512
1122 Western St Fairfield (94533) ***(P-5341)***
AT&T Services Inc ....E....213 741-3111
1900 S Grand Ave Rm 100 Los Angeles (90007) ***(P-5342)***
AT&T Services Inc ....C....408 554-3335
485 S Monroe St 13a San Jose (95128) ***(P-5343)***
AT&T Services Inc ....B....415 394-3000
140 New Montgomery St San Francisco (94105) ***(P-5344)***
AT&T Services Inc ....C....760 489-3519
146 S Broadway Escondido (92025) ***(P-5345)***
AT&T Services Inc ....D....714 992-3359
8925 Orangethorpe Ave Buena Park (90621) ***(P-5346)***
AT&T Services Inc ....D....925 671-1902
1714 Colfax St Ste 300 Concord (94520) ***(P-5347)***
AT&T Services Inc ....C....415 774-1957
2345 Pine St San Francisco (94115) ***(P-5348)***
AT&T Services Inc ....C....510 732-0830
7701 Artesia Blvd Buena Park (90621) ***(P-5349)***
AT&T Services Inc ....D....916 453-6267
1821 24th St Rm 122 Sacramento (95816) ***(P-5350)***
AT&T Services Inc ....C....760 722-7261
2727 Oceanside Blvd Oceanside (92054) ***(P-5351)***
AT&T Services Inc ....C....916 972-2423
3707 Kings Way Sacramento (95821) ***(P-5352)***
AT&T Services Inc ....B....925 671-1059
1033 Shary Cir Ste A Concord (94518) ***(P-5353)***
AT&T Services Inc ....B....858 495-3907
7650 Convoy Ct Ste 106 San Diego (92111) ***(P-5354)***
AT&T Services Inc ....B....760 489-3187
950 W Washington Ave Escondido (92025) ***(P-5355)***
AT&T Services Inc ....B....925 943-4383
1755 Locust St Fl 2 Walnut Creek (94596) ***(P-5356)***
AT&T Services Inc ....B....323 468-6813
1429 N Gower St Los Angeles (90028) ***(P-5357)***
AT&T Services Inc ....C....510 645-7684
504 C 1550 Oakland (94612) ***(P-5358)***
AT&T Services Inc ....B....626 308-8582
501 S Marengo Ave Alhambra (91803) ***(P-5359)***
AT&T Services Inc ....C....415 823-0993
2600 Camino Ramon Rm 1-E San Ramon (94583) ***(P-5360)***
AT&T Services Inc ....D....408 973-7504
5285 Doyle Rd Rm 3 San Jose (95129) ***(P-5361)***
AT&T Services Inc ....C....916 376-2006
3900 Channel Dr West Sacramento (95691) ***(P-5196)***
Ata Engineering Inc (PA) ....D....858 480-2000
13290 Evening Creek Dr S # 250 San Diego (92128) ***(P-24949)***
Atac (PA) ....D....408 736-2822
2770 De La Cruz Blvd Santa Clara (95050) ***(P-15560)***
Atascadero Hotel Partners LLC ....D....805 462-3500
900 El Camino Real Atascadero (93422) ***(P-12023)***
Atascadero State Hospital, Atascadero *Also called Califrnia Dept State Hospitals* ***(P-21391)***
Atc Services Inc ....B....213 593-8100
999 W Town And Country Rd Orange (92868) ***(P-25414)***
Atcaa, Jackson *Also called Amador Tlmne Cmnty Action Agcy* ***(P-24126)***
Atchesons Express Inc ....E....714 808-9199
1590 S Archibald Ave Ontario (91761) ***(P-3852)***
ATCR, Jackson *Also called Amador-Tolumne Cmnty Resources* ***(P-24128)***
Atech Logistics Inc ....C....707 526-1910
7 College Ave Santa Rosa (95401) ***(P-4896)***
Atech Warehousing & Dist Inc (PA) ....D....707 526-1910
7 College Ave Santa Rosa (95401) ***(P-3969)***
Atel Capital Group (PA) ....D....800 543-2835
600 Montgomery St Fl 9 San Francisco (94111) ***(P-9498)***
Atel Corporation ....D....415 989-8800
600 Montgomery St Ste 900 San Francisco (94111) ***(P-16635)***
Aten Technology Inc ....D....949 428-1111
15365 Barranca Pkwy Irvine (92618) ***(P-6800)***
Athenaeum, Pasadena *Also called California Institute Tech* ***(P-25975)***
Athens Administrators, Concord *Also called Athens Insurance Service Inc* ***(P-10283)***

Mergent e-mail: customerrelations@mergent.com
1182
2020 Directory of California
Wholesalers and Services Companies
(P-0000) Products & Services Section entry number
(PA)=Parent Co (HQ)=Headquarters (DH)=Div Headquarters

Athens Disposal Company Inc (PA)....B....626 336-3636
14048 Valley Blvd La Puente (91746) ***(P-6154)***
Athens Environmental Services, Sun Valley *Also called Araco Enterprises LLC* ***(P-6148)***
Athens Insurance, Concord *Also called James C Jenkins Insur Svc Inc* ***(P-10394)***
Athens Insurance Service Inc....C....925 826-1000
2552 Stanwell Dr Ste 100 Concord (94520) ***(P-10283)***
Athens Services, City of Industry *Also called Arakelian Enterprises Inc* ***(P-6149)***
Athens Services, City of Industry *Also called Arakelian Enterprises Inc* ***(P-6151)***
Atherton Baptist Homes....C....626 863-1710
214 S Atlantic Blvd Alhambra (91801) ***(P-19729)***
Atherton Healthcare, Menlo Park *Also called Cal Care Inc* ***(P-26168)***
Athicon....E....213 454-0662
6310 San Vicente Blvd Los Angeles (90048) ***(P-24950)***
Athletic Department, Stockton *Also called University of Pacific* ***(P-18776)***
Athletics Investment Group LLC (PA)....C....510 638-4900
7000 Coliseum Way Ste 3 Oakland (94621) ***(P-18051)***
Athoc Inc (HQ)....D....925 242-5660
3001 Bishop Dr Ste 400 San Ramon (94583) ***(P-15246)***
ATI, Danville *Also called Architrends Inc* ***(P-24942)***
ATI, Anaheim *Also called American Technologies Inc* ***(P-3374)***
ATI Architects & Engineers, Pleasanton *Also called Martin ATI-AC Inc* ***(P-25483)***
ATI Machinery Inc....E....559 884-2471
21436 S Lassen Ave Five Points (93624) ***(P-7498)***
Atk Audiotek....D....661 705-3700
28238 Avenue Crocker Valencia (91355) ***(P-2425)***
Atk Services, Valencia *Also called Atk Audiotek* ***(P-2425)***
Atk Space Systems Inc....D....626 351-0205
370 N Halstead St Pasadena (91107) ***(P-25714)***
Atk Space Systems Inc....B....858 621-5700
7130 Miramar Rd Ste 100b San Diego (92121) ***(P-25967)***
Atkins North America Inc....D....858 874-1810
9275 Sky Park Ct Ste 200 San Diego (92123) ***(P-24951)***
Atkins North America Inc....E....916 325-4800
475 Sansome St San Francisco (94111) ***(P-26995)***
Atkinson And Ly Rd & Rm Lw (PA)....C....562 653-3200
12800 Center Court Dr S # 300 Cerritos (90703) ***(P-22365)***
Atkinson Andelson Loya, Cerritos *Also called Atkinson And Ly Rd & Rm Lw* ***(P-22365)***
Atkinson Construction Inc....B....303 410-2540
18201 Von Karman Ave # 800 Irvine (92612) ***(P-1667)***
Atkinson-Baker Inc (PA)....C....818 551-7300
500 N Brand Blvd Fl 3 Glendale (91203) ***(P-13802)***
Atlanta Seafoods LLC....D....626 626-4900
10501 Valley Blvd # 1820 El Monte (91731) ***(P-8363)***
Atlantic Aviation Svc....E....408 297-7552
1250 Aviation Ave Hngr E2 San Jose (95110) ***(P-4753)***
Atlantic Express of California, Long Beach *Also called Atlantic Express Trnsp* ***(P-3648)***
Atlantic Express Trnsp....C....562 997-6868
2450 Long Beach Blvd Long Beach (90806) ***(P-3648)***
Atlantic Mem Healthcare Assoc (PA)....C....562 424-8101
2750 Atlantic Ave Long Beach (90806) ***(P-19730)***
ATLANTIC MEMORIAL HEALTHCARE C, Long Beach *Also called Atlantic Mem Healthcare Assoc* ***(P-19730)***
Atlantic Optical Co Inc....D....818 407-1890
9747 Independence Ave Chatsworth (91311) ***(P-7021)***
Atlas Advertising, Irvine *Also called M F Salta Co Inc* ***(P-26682)***
Atlas Construction Supply Inc (PA)....D....858 277-2100
4640 Brinnell St San Diego (92111) ***(P-6671)***
Atlas Database Software Corp (PA)....D....818 340-7080
26679 Agoura Rd Ste 200 Calabasas (91302) ***(P-14658)***
Atlas Development, Calabasas *Also called Atlas Database Software Corp* ***(P-14658)***
Atlas Digital LLC (PA)....D....323 762-2626
170 S Flower St Burbank (91502) ***(P-17578)***
Atlas Disposal Industries LLC....D....916 455-2800
3000 Power Inn Rd Sacramento (95826) ***(P-6155)***
Atlas Entertainment Inc....E....310 786-4900
9200 W Sunset Blvd Ste 10 West Hollywood (90069) ***(P-17579)***
Atlas General Insur Svcs LLC....C....858 529-6700
4365 Executive Dr Ste 400 San Diego (92121) ***(P-10284)***
Atlas Heating, San Jose *Also called American Residential Svcs LLC* ***(P-2044)***
Atlas Hospitality Group....D....949 622-3400
1901 Main St Ste 175 Irvine (92614) ***(P-10923)***
Atlas Lift Tech Inc....C....415 283-1804
210 Porter Dr Ste 300 San Ramon (94583) ***(P-22182)***
Atlas Mover Services, Rancho Dominguez *Also called Mover Services Inc* ***(P-3437)***
Atlas Security & Patrol Inc....E....510 791-7380
39465 Paseo Padre Pkwy # 2800 Fremont (94538) ***(P-16200)***
Atlas Security Inc....E....323 876-1401
11862 Balboa Blvd Ste 395 Granada Hills (91344) ***(P-16496)***
Atlas Testing Laboratories Inc....E....909 373-4130
9820 6th St Rancho Cucamonga (91730) ***(P-26055)***
Atlas/Eastern Van Lines, Pomona *Also called W Why W Enterprises Inc* ***(P-4243)***
Atlassian Inc (HQ)....C....415 701-1110
350 Bush St Ste 13 San Francisco (94104) ***(P-15247)***
Atlaz Inc....D....415 671-6142
10721 Fair Oaks Blvd Fair Oaks (95628) ***(P-14659)***
Atm Consultants, Claremont *Also called Atmc Incorporated* ***(P-2426)***
Atmc Incorporated (PA)....D....909 390-0470
725 W Baseline Rd Claremont (91711) ***(P-2426)***
Atrenta Inc (HQ)....D....408 453-3333
690 E Middlefield Rd Mountain View (94043) ***(P-14660)***
Atria Grand Oaks, Lake Forest *Also called Atria Senior Living Inc* ***(P-10690)***
Atria Park Pacific Palisades, Pacific Palisades *Also called Atria Senior Living Inc* ***(P-23824)***
Atria Senior Living Inc....D....310 573-9545
15441 W Sunset Blvd Pacific Palisades (90272) ***(P-23824)***
Atria Senior Living Inc....D....805 482-9771
24 Las Posas Rd Camarillo (93010) ***(P-23825)***
Atria Senior Living Inc....C....949 661-1220
32353 San Juan Creek Rd San Juan Capistrano (92675) ***(P-23826)***
Atria Senior Living Inc....D....925 938-6611
1400 Montego Walnut Creek (94598) ***(P-10689)***
Atria Senior Living Inc....D....408 266-1660
1660 Gaton Dr Ofc San Jose (95125) ***(P-23827)***
Atria Senior Living Inc....D....916 786-7200
100 Sterling Ct Ofc Roseville (95661) ***(P-14476)***
Atria Senior Living Inc....D....805 370-5400
22032 Arrowhead Ln Lake Forest (92630) ***(P-10690)***
Atria Senior Living Inc....E....415 892-0944
853 Tamalpais Ave Ofc Novato (94947) ***(P-23828)***
Atria Senior Living Inc....D....949 786-5665
33 Creek Rd Side Irvine (92604) ***(P-26144)***
Atria Senior Living Inc....D....916 488-5722
2426 Garfield Ave Ofc Carmichael (95608) ***(P-23829)***
Atria Senior Living Inc....D....760 341-0890
44600 Monterey Ave Ofc Palm Desert (92260) ***(P-23830)***
Atrium Capital Corp....A....650 233-7878
3000 Sand Hill Rd 2-130 Menlo Park (94025) ***(P-11886)***
Atrium Door & Win Co Ariz Inc....B....714 693-0601
5455 E La Palma Ave Ste A Anaheim (92807) ***(P-6605)***
Atrium Finance I LP....C....916 446-0100
300 J St Sacramento (95814) ***(P-12024)***
Atrium Hotel, Irvine *Also called Golden Hotels Ltd Partnership* ***(P-12299)***
Atrium of San Jose, San Jose *Also called Brookdale Lving Cmmunities Inc* ***(P-23841)***
Atrium Plaza LLC....C....650 653-6000
1770 S Amphlett Blvd San Mateo (94402) ***(P-12025)***
Atsugi Kokusai Kanko USA Inc....D....951 924-4444
28095 John F Kennedy Dr Moreno Valley (92555) ***(P-18383)***
Attendant Care Referrals Inc....D....310 399-2904
2801 Ocean Park Blvd # 192 Santa Monica (90405) ***(P-21676)***
Attn Inc....C....323 413-2878
729 Seward St Los Angeles (90038) ***(P-13613)***
Attom Data Solutions, Irvine *Also called Renwood Realtytrac LLC* ***(P-15882)***
Attorney Recovery Systems Inc (PA)....D....818 774-1420
18757 Burbank Blvd # 300 Tarzana (91356) ***(P-13670)***
Attorneys At Law, Fresno *Also called Lang Richert & Patch* ***(P-22625)***
Atypon Systems LLC (PA)....D....408 988-1240
5201 Great America Pkwy # 215 Santa Clara (95054) ***(P-15248)***
Auberge Du Soleil, Rutherford *Also called Terre Du Soleil Ltd* ***(P-13020)***
Auburn Constructors LLC....D....916 924-0344
730 W Stadium Ln Sacramento (95834) ***(P-1941)***
Auburn Gardens Care Center, Auburn *Also called Madera Convalescent Hospital* ***(P-20097)***
Auburn Oaks Care Center....D....650 949-7777
3400 Bell Rd Auburn (95603) ***(P-19731)***
Auburn Old Town Gallery....D....530 887-9150
218 Washington St Ste A Auburn (95603) ***(P-18629)***
Auburn Placer Disposal Service....D....530 885-3735
12305 Shale Ridge Ln Auburn (95602) ***(P-6156)***
Auburn Pride, Auburn *Also called Pride Industries* ***(P-23628)***
Auburn Ravine Terrace, Auburn *Also called Retirement Housing Foundation* ***(P-24049)***
AUBURN RAVINE TERRACE, Auburn *Also called Congrgtnal Ch Retirement Cmnty* ***(P-19813)***
Auburn-Placer Recycling Center, Auburn *Also called Auburn Placer Disposal Service* ***(P-6156)***
Auchante Inc....D....562 231-1880
6730 Florence Ave Bell Gardens (90201) ***(P-10924)***
Auctioncom Inc....C....800 499-6199
1 Mauchly Ste 27 Irvine (92618) ***(P-10925)***
Auctioncom LLC....C....949 609-5376
3050 S Del St Ste 201 San Mateo (94403) ***(P-10926)***
Auctioncom LLC....D....949 609-5376
3501 Jamboree Rd Ste 5000 Newport Beach (92660) ***(P-10927)***
Auctioncom LLC (PA)....D....949 859-2777
1 Mauchly Irvine (92618) ***(P-10928)***
Auctiva Corporation....D....530 894-7400
360 E 6th St Chico (95928) ***(P-26996)***
Audaexplore, San Diego *Also called Audatex North America Inc* ***(P-15249)***
Audatex North America Inc (HQ)....C....858 946-1900
15030 Ave Of San Diego (92128) ***(P-15249)***
Audio Visual MGT Solutions....D....714 590-8755
12812 Garden Grove Blvd M Garden Grove (92843) ***(P-26145)***
Audioquest, Irvine *Also called Quest Group* ***(P-7828)***
Audiovisions, Lake Forest *Also called Inspiria Inc* ***(P-25141)***
Auditboard Inc (PA)....E....877 769-5444
12800 Center Court Dr S # 100 Cerritos (90703) ***(P-14661)***
Auditor Controller Department, San Bernardino *Also called County of San Bernardino* ***(P-25565)***
Audrey Adams MD....E....408 354-2114
718 University Ave # 211 Los Gatos (95032) ***(P-18829)***
Audrey's Boutique, Carlsbad *Also called Omni La Costa Resort & Spa LLC* ***(P-12675)***
Augustine Consulting Inc (PA)....D....831 920-1754
24560 Silver Cloud Ct # 102 Monterey (93940) ***(P-24952)***
Augustine Ideas, Roseville *Also called D Augustine & Associates* ***(P-13484)***
Aura Financial Corporation....D....415 391-2431
303 2nd St Ste N550 San Francisco (94107) ***(P-16636)***
Aurora Algae Inc....D....510 266-5000
3325 Investment Blvd Hayward (94545) ***(P-25715)***
Aurora Behavioral Health....D....707 800-7700
1287 Fulton Rd Santa Rosa (95401) ***(P-21380)***
Aurora Behavioral Health Care....C....858 487-3200
11878 Avenue Of Industry San Diego (92128) ***(P-21381)***
Aurora Behavioral Hlth Care, San Diego *Also called Aurora Healthcare Inc* ***(P-20755)***
Aurora Healthcare Inc....E....858 487-3200
11878 Avenue Of Industry San Diego (92128) ***(P-20755)***
Aurora Las Encinas LLC....C....626 795-9901
2900 E Del Mar Blvd Pasadena (91107) ***(P-21382)***

ALPHABETIC

Employee Codes: A=Over 500 employees, B=251-500
C=101-250, D=51-100, E=50
2020 Directory of California
Wholesalers and Services Companies
© Mergent Inc. 1-800-342-5647
1183

Aurora Las Encinas Hospital, Pasadena *Also called Aurora Las Encinas LLC* ***(P-21382)***
Aurora Resurgence Fund LP....A....310 551-0101
10877 Wilshire Blvd # 2100 Los Angeles (90024) ***(P-11715)***
Aurora World Inc....C....562 205-1222
8820 Mercury Ln Pico Rivera (90660) ***(P-7725)***
Aus Decking Inc....D....916 373-5320
2999 Promenade St Ste 100 West Sacramento (95691) ***(P-3113)***
Ausenco PSI LLC (HQ)....D....925 939-4420
5027 Coml Cir Ste Ef Concord (94520) ***(P-24953)***
Ausenco USA Inc (PA)....D....925 939-4420
1320 Willow Pass Rd Concord (94520) ***(P-24954)***
Ausgar Technologies Inc....C....855 428-7427
10721 Treena St Ste 100 San Diego (92131) ***(P-24955)***
Austin Veum Rbbins Prtners Inc (PA)....D....619 231-1960
501 W Broadway Ste A San Diego (92101) ***(P-25415)***
Authority Tax Services LLC....D....213 486-5135
777 S Figueroa St # 1900 Los Angeles (90017) ***(P-16637)***
Authorized Taxi Cab....D....323 776-5324
6150 W 96th St Los Angeles (90045) ***(P-16497)***
Autism Otrach Southern Cal LLC....D....619 795-9925
3110 Cmino Del Rio S 30 San Diego (92108) ***(P-22933)***
Autism Partnership Inc....D....562 431-9293
200 Marina Dr C Seal Beach (90740) ***(P-26511)***
Auto Body Management Inc....E....818 888-7654
7654 Tampa Ave Reseda (91335) ***(P-17281)***
Auto Buyline Systems Inc (PA)....E....951 271-8999
341 Corporate Terrace Cir Corona (92879) ***(P-6385)***
Auto Club Enterprises (PA)....A....714 850-5111
3333 Fairview Rd Msa451 Costa Mesa (92626) ***(P-9899)***
Auto Club Enterprises....B....310 914-8500
8761 Santa Monica Blvd West Hollywood (90069) ***(P-9900)***
Auto Club Speedway, Fontana *Also called California Speedway Corp* ***(P-18082)***
Auto Expressions LLC....D....310 639-0666
505 E Euclid Ave Compton (90222) ***(P-6422)***
Auto Ins Spcialists-Long Beach....D....562 496-2888
5000 E Spring St Ste 100 Long Beach (90815) ***(P-10285)***
Auto Insurance Specialists LLC (HQ)....C....562 345-6247
17785 Center Court Dr N # 110 Cerritos (90703) ***(P-10286)***
Auto Parts Group, Rancho Cordova *Also called Pick Pull Auto Dismantling Inc* ***(P-6496)***
Auto Parts Warehouse Inc (PA)....E....800 913-6119
16941 Keegan Ave Carson (90746) ***(P-6423)***
Auto Pride, Anaheim *Also called Cal-State Auto Parts Inc* ***(P-6428)***
Auto Town Inc....D....209 473-2513
2150 E Hammer Ln Stockton (95210) ***(P-17322)***
Auto World Car Wash LLC....A....408 345-6532
15951 Los Gatos Blvd Los Gatos (95032) ***(P-17360)***
Autobody Depot, San Diego *Also called Tcp Global Corporation* ***(P-8946)***
Autocrib Inc....C....714 274-0400
2882 Dow Ave Tustin (92780) ***(P-16638)***
Autodesk Inc....D....415 356-0700
1 Market St San Francisco (94105) ***(P-15250)***
Autodesk Inc (PA)....B....415 507-5000
111 Mcinnis Pkwy San Rafael (94903) ***(P-15251)***
Autodesk Inc....C....415 507-5000
3950 Civic Center Dr San Rafael (94903) ***(P-15252)***
Autofarm, Fremont *Also called Novariant Inc* ***(P-25236)***
Automate Parking Inc....D....310 674-3396
8405 Pershing Dr Ste 301 Playa Del Rey (90293) ***(P-17245)***
Automated Ctrl Technical Svcs, Bakersfield *Also called A-C Electric Company* ***(P-24896)***
Automated Systems America Inc....D....877 500-0002
101 N Brand Blvd Ste 1230 Glendale (91203) ***(P-17487)***
Automatic Data Processing Inc....C....714 690-7000
7000 Village Dr Ste 200 Buena Park (90621) ***(P-15721)***
Automatic Data Processing Inc....C....800 225-5237
9445 Fairway View Pl # 200 Rancho Cucamonga (91730) ***(P-15722)***
Automatic Data Processing Inc....C....805 383-8630
5153 Camino Ruiz Ste 100 Camarillo (93012) ***(P-15723)***
Automatic Data Processing Inc....E....800 225-5237
600 California St Fl 11 San Francisco (94108) ***(P-15724)***
Automatic Data Processing Inc....C....909 592-6411
620 W Covina Blvd San Dimas (91773) ***(P-15725)***
Automatic Data Processing Inc....C....800 225-5237
720 Bay Rd Redwood City (94063) ***(P-15726)***
Automatic Data Processing Inc....C....415 899-7300
505 San Marin Dr Ste A110 Novato (94945) ***(P-15727)***
Automatic Data Processing Inc....C....949 751-0360
3972 Barranca Pkwy J610 Irvine (92606) ***(P-15728)***
Automatic Data Processing Inc....B....408 876-6600
820 N Mccarthy Blvd # 120 Milpitas (95035) ***(P-15729)***
Automatic Data Processing Inc....D....714 994-2000
5355 Orangethorpe Ave La Palma (90623) ***(P-15730)***
Automatic Data Processing Inc....C....800 225-5237
400 W Covina Blvd San Dimas (91773) ***(P-15731)***
Automatic Data Processing Inc....D....800 225-5237
600 Crprate Pinte Ste 450 Los Angeles (90230) ***(P-15732)***
Automatic Data Processing Inc....D....619 293-4800
1450 Frazee Rd Ste 601 San Diego (92108) ***(P-15733)***
Automatic Leasing Inc....B....559 233-2444
260 Fulton St Fresno (93721) ***(P-13245)***
Automation Anywhere Inc (PA)....D....888 484-3535
633 River Oaks Pkwy San Jose (95134) ***(P-6801)***
Automation Engrg Systems Inc....D....858 967-8650
10815 Rancho Bernardo Rd San Diego (92127) ***(P-15561)***
Automattic Inc....D....877 273-3049
60 29th St Ste 343 San Francisco (94110) ***(P-5362)***
Automobile Club Southern Cal....B....909 477-8600
6787 Carnelian St Ste A Rancho Cucamonga (91701) ***(P-10287)***
Automobile Club Southern Cal (PA)....C....213 741-3686
2601 S Figueroa St Los Angeles (90007) ***(P-10288)***
Automobile Club Southern Cal....E....818 997-6230
15503 Ventura Blvd # 150 Encino (91436) ***(P-24792)***
Automobile Club Southern Cal....B....213 741-3686
33323 Fairview R Ste Msa Costa Mesa (92626) ***(P-10289)***
Automobile Club Southern Cal....D....310 325-3111
23001 Hawthorne Blvd Torrance (90505) ***(P-24793)***
Automobile Club Southern Cal....D....805 644-7171
1501 S Victoria Ave Ventura (93003) ***(P-24794)***
Automobile Club Southern Cal....E....626 963-8531
1301s S Grand Ave Glendora (91740) ***(P-24795)***
Automobile Club Southern Cal....E....661 327-4661
1500 Commercial Way Bakersfield (93309) ***(P-24796)***
Automobile Club Southern Cal....D....818 993-1616
9440 Reseda Blvd Northridge (91324) ***(P-24797)***
Automobile Club Southern Cal....E....818 883-2660
22708 Victory Blvd Woodland Hills (91367) ***(P-24798)***
Automobile Club Southern Cal....D....951 684-4250
3700 Central Ave Riverside (92506) ***(P-24799)***
Automobile Club Southern Cal....E....949 951-1400
25181 Paseo De Alicia Laguna Hills (92653) ***(P-24800)***
Automobile Club Southern Cal....C....714 885-1343
3333 Fairview Rd Costa Mesa (92626) ***(P-10290)***
Automobile Club Southern Cal....C....909 392-1444
2488 Foothill Blvd Ste A La Verne (91750) ***(P-24801)***
Automobile Club Southern Cal....C....760 247-4110
19201 Bear Valley Rd C Apple Valley (92308) ***(P-24802)***
Automobile Club Southern Cal....C....909 980-0233
10540 Fthill Blvd Ste 100 Rancho Cucamonga (91730) ***(P-10291)***
Automobile Club Southern Cal....C....858 481-7181
2666 Del Mar Heights Rd Del Mar (92014) ***(P-10292)***
Automobile Club Southern Cal....D....619 464-7001
8765 Fletcher Pkwy La Mesa (91942) ***(P-24803)***
Automotive Service Council....D....800 810-4272
10813 Airport Dr El Cajon (92020) ***(P-24804)***
Automotive Services Division, Ontario *Also called Securitas SEC Svcs USA Inc* ***(P-16413)***
Automotive Services Division, Northridge *Also called Securitas SEC Svcs USA Inc* ***(P-16432)***
Automotive Tstg & Dev Svcs Inc (PA)....C....909 390-1100
400 Etiwanda Ave Ontario (91761) ***(P-17411)***
Automted Cntrls Technical Svcs, Bakersfield *Also called A-C Electric Company* ***(P-2410)***
Autonomic LLC (PA)....D....650 823-1806
745 Emerson St Palo Alto (94301) ***(P-14662)***
Autonomy Interwoven, Sunnyvale *Also called Entco LLC* ***(P-15320)***
Autoweb Inc (PA)....C....949 225-4500
18872 Macarthur Blvd Irvine (92612) ***(P-15846)***
Autry Museum of American West....C....323 667-2000
4700 Western Heritage Way Los Angeles (90027) ***(P-24248)***
Autumn Hills Convalescent Home, Glendale *Also called Mariner Health Care Inc* ***(P-20113)***
Auxiliary of Mission....D....949 364-1400
27700 Medical Center Rd Mission Viejo (92691) ***(P-20756)***
AV Brands Inc....E....410 884-9463
635 Broadway Ste 2 Sonoma (95476) ***(P-8796)***
AV Management, Garden Grove *Also called Audio Visual MGT Solutions* ***(P-26145)***
AV Occupational Medicine, Lancaster *Also called Daniel O Mongiano MD A PR* ***(P-18939)***
Ava Enterprises Inc....E....805 988-0192
3451 Lunar Ct Oxnard (93030) ***(P-7198)***
Ava The Rabbit Haven Inc....D....831 600-7479
1261 S Mary St Scotts Valley (95067) ***(P-26997)***
Avac, San Jose *Also called Almaden Valley Athletic Club* ***(P-18353)***
Avadyne Health, San Diego *Also called H & R Accounts Inc* ***(P-14850)***
Avalon A Cerritos....E....562 865-9500
11000 New Falcon Way Ofc # 177 Cerritos (90703) ***(P-23831)***
Avalon At Newport, Newport Beach *Also called Ventage Senior Housing* ***(P-10834)***
Avalon At Newport LLC....D....949 631-3555
393 Hospital Rd Newport Beach (92663) ***(P-23832)***
Avalon At Newport Beach, Newport Beach *Also called Avalon At Newport LLC* ***(P-23832)***
Avalon At Penasquitos Hills, Irvine *Also called Avalonbay Communities Inc* ***(P-10929)***
Avalon Building Maintenance (PA)....C....714 693-2407
3148 E La Palma Ave Ste A Anaheim (92806) ***(P-13868)***
Avalon Care Cen....D....209 723-1056
3170 M St Merced (95348) ***(P-19732)***
Avalon Care Center....C....209 754-3823
900 Mountain Ranch Rd San Andreas (95249) ***(P-19733)***
Avalon Care Center - Merced....D....209 722-6231
3169 M St Merced (95348) ***(P-19734)***
Avalon Care Center - Modesto....D....209 526-1775
1900 Coffee Rd Modesto (95355) ***(P-19735)***
Avalon Care Ctr - Chwchlla LLC....D....559 665-4826
1010 Ventura Ave Chowchilla (93610) ***(P-19736)***
Avalon Care Ctr - Madera LLC....D....559 673-9278
1700 Howard Rd Madera (93637) ***(P-19737)***
Avalon Care Ctr - Modesto LLC....D....209 529-0516
515 E Orangeburg Ave Modesto (95350) ***(P-19738)***
Avalon Care Ctr - Newman LLC....D....209 862-2862
709 N St Newman (95360) ***(P-19739)***
Avalon Care Ctr - Sonora LLC....C....209 533-2500
19929 Greenley Rd Sonora (95370) ***(P-19740)***
Avalon Golden Gate LLC....D....415 664-6264
1601 19th Ave Apt 122 San Francisco (94122) ***(P-23833)***
Avalon Health Care - Madera, Madera *Also called Avalon Care Ctr - Madera LLC* ***(P-19737)***
AVALON HEALTH CARE GROUP, Sonora *Also called Avalon Care Ctr - Sonora LLC* ***(P-19740)***
Avalon Hotel, Beverly Hills *Also called Honeymoon Real Estate LP* ***(P-12381)***
Avalon Staffing, Westlake Village *Also called Jackie Hoofring* ***(P-14315)***
Avalon Staffing LLC....D....925 626-7138
550 Harvest Park Dr Ste B Brentwood (94513) ***(P-14228)***
Avalon Transportation Co, Culver City *Also called Virgin Fish Inc* ***(P-3735)***

Mergent e-mail: customerrelations@mergent.com
1184
2020 Directory of California
Wholesalers and Services Companies
(P-0000) Products & Services Section entry number
(PA)=Parent Co (HQ)=Headquarters (DH)=Div Headquarters

Avalonbay Communities Inc..........E.......949 955-6200
2050 Main St Ste 1200 Irvine (92614) ***(P-10929)***
Avanquest North America LLC (HQ)..........D.......818 591-9600
23801 Calabasas Rd # 2005 Calabasas (91302) ***(P-6802)***
Avanti Agency Corporation..........B.......714 935-0900
282 S Anita Dr Orange (92868) ***(P-16639)***
Avanti Health System LLC..........B.......310 356-0550
222 N Pacific Coast Hwy # 950 El Segundo (90245) ***(P-26512)***
Avantica Technologies, Mountain View *Also called Group Avantica Inc* ***(P-14846)***
Avantra Financial, Arcadia *Also called Avantra Real Estate Services* ***(P-10930)***
Avantra Real Estate Services..........E.......626 357-7028
148 E Fthill Blvd Ste 100 Arcadia (91006) ***(P-10930)***
Avar Construction Inc..........D.......510 354-2000
47375 Fremont Blvd Fremont (94538) ***(P-1668)***
Avar Construction Systems Inc (PA)..........E.......510 354-2000
47375 Fremont Blvd Fremont (94538) ***(P-1815)***
Avaya Inc (HQ)..........C.......908 953-6000
4655 Great America Pkwy Santa Clara (95054) ***(P-16640)***
Avaya Inc..........C.......949 225-5678
18201 Von Karman Ave # 600 Irvine (92612) ***(P-5363)***
Ave Maria Convalescent Hosp..........D.......831 373-1216
1249 Josselyn Canyon Rd Monterey (93940) ***(P-19741)***
Ave Maria Senior Living, Monterey *Also called Ave Maria Convalescent Hosp* ***(P-19741)***
Avenidas (PA)..........D.......650 289-5400
4000 Middlefield Rd Ste I Palo Alto (94303) ***(P-22934)***
AVENIDAS SENIOR HEALTH DAY HEA, Palo Alto *Also called Avenidas* ***(P-22934)***
Aveniu Brands, Sonoma *Also called AV Brands Inc* ***(P-8796)***
Avente Inc..........E.......844 385-1556
200 Spectrum Dr Ste 300 Irvine (92618) ***(P-15946)***
Avenu Muniservices, Fresno *Also called Muniservices LLC* ***(P-26725)***
Avenue of Arts Wyndham Hotel, Costa Mesa *Also called Rosanna Inc* ***(P-12839)***
Avenuesocial Inc..........C.......510 275-4485
440 N Wolfe Rd Sunnyvale (94085) ***(P-14663)***
Aver Information Inc..........E.......408 263-3828
668 Mission Ct Fremont (94539) ***(P-6803)***
Avery Corp..........C.......626 304-2000
207 N Goode Ave Fl 6 Glendale (91203) ***(P-25716)***
Aveva Software LLC (HQ)..........B.......949 727-3200
26561 Rancho Pkwy S Lake Forest (92630) ***(P-15562)***
AVI Systems Inc..........B.......415 915-2070
44150 S Grimmer Blvd Fremont (94538) ***(P-7234)***
Avia Tech LLC..........D.......858 777-5000
7220 Trade St Ste 300 San Diego (92121) ***(P-13472)***
Aviar Golf Club, Carlsbad *Also called Four Seasons Resort Aviara* ***(P-18248)***
Aviara Fsrc Associates Limited..........A.......760 603-6800
7100 Aviara Resort Dr Carlsbad (92011) ***(P-12026)***
Aviara Resort Associates (HQ)..........D.......760 448-1234
7100 Aviara Resort Dr Carlsbad (92011) ***(P-12027)***
Aviation & Defense Inc..........C.......909 382-3487
255 S Leland Norton Way San Bernardino (92408) ***(P-4754)***
Aviation Consultants Inc (PA)..........D.......805 548-1300
945 Airport Dr San Luis Obispo (93401) ***(P-26146)***
Aviation Maintenance Group Inc..........D.......714 469-0515
8352 Kimball Ave Hngr 3 Chino (91708) ***(P-4755)***
Aviation Safeguards, Los Angeles *Also called Command Security Corporation* ***(P-16237)***
Aviation Safeguards, San Jose *Also called Command Security Corporation* ***(P-16238)***
Avicena LLC (PA)..........D.......626 344-9665
117 E Colo Blvd Ste 510 Pasadena (91105) ***(P-25717)***
Avid Bioservices, Tustin *Also called Pphm Inc* ***(P-7977)***
Avida Caregivers Inc..........A.......323 498-1500
11500 W Olympic Blvd # 400 Los Angeles (90064) ***(P-21677)***
Avis Budget Car Rentals, San Leandro *Also called Avis Rent A Car System Inc* ***(P-17197)***
Avis Rent A Car System Inc..........D.......909 974-2192
3450 E Airport Dr Ste 500 Ontario (91761) ***(P-17196)***
Avis Rent A Car System Inc..........C.......510 562-8828
390 Doolittle Dr San Leandro (94577) ***(P-17197)***
Avis Rent A Car System Inc..........D.......510 577-6360
1 Airport Dr Oakland (94621) ***(P-17198)***
Avis Rent A Car System Inc..........C.......916 922-5601
6520 Mcnair Cir Sacramento (95837) ***(P-17199)***
Avis Rent A Car System Inc..........D.......650 616-0150
513 Eccles Ave Ste A South San Francisco (94080) ***(P-17200)***
Avis Rent A Car System Inc..........D.......818 566-3001
4209 W Vanowen Pl Burbank (91505) ***(P-17201)***
Avis Rent A Car Systems, Sacramento *Also called Avis Rent A Car System Inc* ***(P-17199)***
Avita Medical Americas LLC..........D.......661 367-9170
28159 Ave Stnford Ste 220 Valencia (91355) ***(P-6945)***
Avitas Systems Inc..........D.......650 233-3900
2882 Sand Hill Rd Ste 240 Menlo Park (94025) ***(P-16641)***
Aviva Center, Los Angeles *Also called Hamburger Home* ***(P-23944)***
Aviva Systems Biology Corp (PA)..........D.......858 552-6979
7700 Ronson Rd Ste 100 San Diego (92111) ***(P-25718)***
Avnet Inc..........D.......949 789-4100
220 Commerce Ste 100 Irvine (92602) ***(P-7235)***
Avnet Inc..........D.......818 594-8310
20951 Burbank Blvd Ste A Woodland Hills (91367) ***(P-7236)***
Avnet Inc..........D.......408 501-3925
2580 Junction Ave San Jose (95134) ***(P-7237)***
Avnet Inc..........B.......760 946-5030
1400 Montefino Ave # 110 Diamond Bar (91765) ***(P-7238)***
Avnet Inc..........B.......858 385-7500
13500 Evening Creek Dr N # 400 San Diego (92128) ***(P-7239)***
Avnet Computers, Irvine *Also called Avnet Inc* ***(P-7235)***
Avnet Computers, Woodland Hills *Also called Avnet Inc* ***(P-7236)***
Avnet Computers, San Jose *Also called Avnet Inc* ***(P-7237)***
Avnet Computers, San Diego *Also called Avnet Inc* ***(P-7239)***
Avoca Productions Inc..........D.......310 244-4000
10202 Washington Blvd Culver City (90232) ***(P-17580)***
Avocado Post Acute, El Cajon *Also called Eldorado Care Center LP* ***(P-19875)***
Avongard Products USa Ltd..........E.......310 319-2300
12855 Runway Rd Apt 1208 Playa Vista (90094) ***(P-17725)***
Aware Point, San Diego *Also called Awarepoint Corporation* ***(P-14664)***
Awarepoint Corporation (PA)..........D.......858 345-5000
600 W Broadway Ste 250 San Diego (92101) ***(P-14664)***
Awe, San Diego *Also called Herring Networks Inc* ***(P-5612)***
AWH Burbank Hotel LLC..........C.......813 843-6000
2500 N Hollywood Way Burbank (91505) ***(P-12028)***
AWI Acquisition Company (PA)..........D.......818 364-2333
28955 Ave Sherman Valencia (91355) ***(P-7384)***
AWR, San Dimas *Also called Golden State Water Company* ***(P-6064)***
Awt Construction Group Inc..........D.......707 746-7500
4740 E 2nd St Ste 22 Benicia (94510) ***(P-1081)***
Axa Advisors LLC..........D.......213 251-1600
3435 Wilshire Blvd # 2500 Los Angeles (90010) ***(P-9791)***
Axa Advisors LLC..........D.......415 276-2100
88 Kearny St Fl 20 San Francisco (94108) ***(P-26513)***
Axa Advisors LLC..........D.......619 239-0018
701 B St Ste 1500 San Diego (92101) ***(P-9862)***
Axa Equitable Life Insur Co..........D.......858 552-1234
3777 La Jolla Village Dr San Diego (92122) ***(P-10293)***
Axaio Industries LLC..........E.......323 504-1074
538 S Oxford Ave Apt 302 Los Angeles (90020) ***(P-5364)***
Axcient Inc (HQ)..........D.......650 314-7300
1161 San Antonio Rd Mountain View (94043) ***(P-14665)***
Axelacare Holdings Inc..........A.......714 522-8802
12604 Hiddencreek Way C Cerritos (90703) ***(P-21678)***
Axiom Global Technologies Inc..........C.......925 393-5800
220 N Wiget Ln Walnut Creek (94598) ***(P-26998)***
Axiom Home Warranty LLC..........C.......844 562-9466
2015 Manhattan B Redondo Beach (90278) ***(P-10159)***
Axiom Memory Solutions Inc..........D.......949 581-1450
16 Goodyear Ste 120 Irvine (92618) ***(P-6804)***
Axis, Culver City *Also called Rick Solomon Enterprises Inc* ***(P-8046)***
Axis Community Health Inc..........D.......925 462-1755
4361 Railroad Ave Pleasanton (94566) ***(P-21957)***
Axis Construction, Hayward *Also called Axis Services Inc* ***(P-1228)***
Axis Services Inc..........C.......510 732-6111
2544 Barrington Ct Hayward (94545) ***(P-1228)***
Axminster Medical Group Inc (PA)..........D.......310 670-3255
8540 S Sepulveda Blvd # 818 Los Angeles (90045) ***(P-18830)***
Axonics Modulation Tech Inc..........D.......949 396-6322
26 Technology Dr Irvine (92618) ***(P-25719)***
Axos Clearing LLC (HQ)..........A.......858 350-6200
4350 La Jolla Village Dr San Diego (92122) ***(P-9423)***
Aya Healthcare Inc (PA)..........C.......858 458-4410
5930 Cornerstone Ct W # 300 San Diego (92121) ***(P-14477)***
Ayala Corporation..........C.......559 867-5700
21510 S Chteau Fresno Ave Riverdale (93656) ***(P-14229)***
Ayala Drywall..........E.......805 487-3392
2600 Alexander St Oxnard (93033) ***(P-2751)***
Ayala Farms, Riverdale *Also called Ayala Corporation* ***(P-14229)***
Ayco Company LP..........C.......949 955-1544
17885 Von Karman Ave # 300 Irvine (92614) ***(P-9792)***
Aylesva Inc..........C.......562 688-0592
14537 Garfield Ave Paramount (90723) ***(P-8121)***
Ayoob & Peery Plumbing Co Inc..........D.......415 550-0975
975 Indiana St San Francisco (94107) ***(P-2063)***
Ayres - Paso Robles LP..........C.......714 850-0409
2700 Buena Vista Dr Paso Robles (93446) ***(P-12029)***
Ayres Group (PA)..........D.......714 540-6060
355 Bristol St Costa Mesa (92626) ***(P-12030)***
Ayres Hotel Laguna Woods, Laguna Woods *Also called Countryside Inn-Corona LP* ***(P-12172)***
Ayzenberg Group Inc..........D.......626 584-4070
49 E Walnut St Pasadena (91103) ***(P-13473)***
AZ Countertops Inc..........E.......909 983-5386
1445 S Hudson Ave Ontario (91761) ***(P-3381)***
AZ West, Compton *Also called Az/CFS West Inc* ***(P-4555)***
Az/CFS West Inc..........D.......310 898-2090
250 W Manville St Compton (90220) ***(P-4555)***
Azalea & Rose Co..........E.......909 949-2442
1420 N Campus Ave Upland (91786) ***(P-228)***
Azalea Holdings LLC..........D.......916 452-3592
3700 H St Sacramento (95816) ***(P-20757)***
Azcona Harvesting LLC..........C.......831 674-2526
44 El Camino Real Unit A Greenfield (93927) ***(P-447)***
Azimc Investments Inc..........C.......818 678-1200
8901 Canoga Ave Canoga Park (91304) ***(P-6424)***
Aztec Engineering Group Inc..........D.......951 471-6190
2151 Michelson Dr Ste 100 Irvine (92612) ***(P-24956)***
Aztec Harvesting..........A.......760 922-7348
1075 N Broadway Blythe (92225) ***(P-613)***
Aztec Landscaping Inc (PA)..........C.......619 464-3303
7980 Lemon Grove Way Lemon Grove (91945) ***(P-777)***
Aztec Sheet Metal Inc..........D.......619 937-0005
11222 Woodside Ave N Santee (92071) ***(P-3026)***
Aztlan Graphics, Chico *Also called Gonzales Park LLC* ***(P-8031)***
Azubu North America Inc..........E.......310 759-9529
15303 Ventura Blvd # 900 Sherman Oaks (91403) ***(P-7726)***
Azul Systems Inc (PA)..........D.......650 230-6500
385 Moffett Park Dr # 115 Sunnyvale (94089) ***(P-15253)***
Azumio Inc (PA)..........C.......719 310-3774
230 California Ave # 212 Palo Alto (94306) ***(P-14666)***
Azure Acres, Sebastopol *Also called Camp Recovery Centers LP* ***(P-21453)***
B & B Concrete, Santa Clara *Also called Robert A Bothman Inc* ***(P-3209)***
B & B Nurseries Inc..........C.......951 352-8383
9505 Cleveland Ave Riverside (92503) ***(P-8881)***

A
L
P
H
A
B
E
T
I
C

Employee Codes: A=Over 500 employees, B=251-500
C=101-250, D=51-100, E=50
2020 Directory of California
Wholesalers and Services Companies
© Mergent Inc. 1-800-342-5647
1185

B & B Plastics Recyclers Inc (PA) ....D....909 829-3606
3040 N Locust Ave Rialto (92377) ***(P-7751)***
B & B Specialties Inc ....D....714 985-3075
4321 E La Palma Ave Anaheim (92807) ***(P-7385)***
B & B Specialty Metals, Bakersfield *Also called B & B Surplus Inc* ***(P-7047)***
B & B Surplus Inc (PA) ....D....661 589-0381
7020 Rosedale Hwy Bakersfield (93308) ***(P-7047)***
B & C, Oakland *Also called B&C Transit Inc* ***(P-24957)***
B & E Convalescent Center Inc (PA) ....D....562 923-9449
11627 Telg Rd Ste 200 Santa Fe Springs (90670) ***(P-20497)***
B & E Farms Inc ....E....714 893-8166
9112 Mcfadden Ave Westminster (92683) ***(P-87)***
B & L Consulting LLC ....D....682 238-6994
164 N 2nd Ave 9 Upland (91786) ***(P-26999)***
B & M Contractors Inc ....D....805 581-5480
4473 Cochran St Simi Valley (93063) ***(P-3114)***
B & M Racing, Santa Rosa *Also called Driven Performance Brands Inc* ***(P-6434)***
B & R Farm Labor Contractor ....C....805 524-1346
422 Mockingbird Ln Fillmore (93015) ***(P-14230)***
B A M I Inc ....E....530 343-5678
1293 E 1st Ave Chico (95926) ***(P-18119)***
B A S, Diamond Bar *Also called Tetra Tech Bas Inc* ***(P-25339)***
B A Technolinks Corporation ....D....408 940-5921
4677 Old Ironsides Dr # 440 Santa Clara (95054) ***(P-26514)***
B B & K Fund Services Inc ....E....650 571-5800
950 Tower Ln Ste 1900 Foster City (94404) ***(P-9651)***
B B & K Holdings (PA) ....E....650 571-5800
950 Tower Ln Ste 1900 Foster City (94404) ***(P-9793)***
B B & T Management Corp ....C....916 428-8060
1453 Blair Ave Sacramento (95822) ***(P-6606)***
B B G Management Group (PA) ....D....909 797-9581
12164 California St Yucaipa (92399) ***(P-8338)***
B B S I, San Diego *Also called Barrett Business Services Inc* ***(P-22375)***
B Braun Medical Inc ....A....909 906-7575
1151 Mildred St Ste B Ontario (91761) ***(P-6946)***
B C C S Inc (PA) ....D....408 379-5500
1711 Dell Ave Campbell (95008) ***(P-1412)***
B C Life & Health Insurance Co ....D....818 703-2345
21555 Oxnard St Woodland Hills (91367) ***(P-9901)***
B C Rentals LLC (HQ) ....D....714 974-1190
638 W Southern Ave Orange (92865) ***(P-7525)***
B C S, Canoga Park *Also called Buyers Consultation Svc Inc* ***(P-7243)***
B E Giovannetti & Sons (PA) ....E....530 662-1729
403 Court St Woodland (95695) ***(P-1)***
B F C Inc ....C....415 495-3085
675 Davis St San Francisco (94111) ***(P-2427)***
B F Management ....D....323 931-7776
117 N Fuller Ave Los Angeles (90036) ***(P-10931)***
B H C Alhambra Hospital, Rosemead *Also called Psychiatric Solutions Inc* ***(P-22104)***
B H Premier Inc (PA) ....D....310 286-3074
1141 S Beverly Dr Fl 3 Los Angeles (90035) ***(P-21679)***
B H R Operations LLC ....D....408 321-9500
777 Bellew Dr Milpitas (95035) ***(P-12031)***
B I A, Emeryville *Also called Behavioral Intervention Assn* ***(P-14480)***
B Jacqueline and Assoc Inc ....B....626 844-1400
1192 N Lake Ave Pasadena (91104) ***(P-14667)***
B L S Limousine Service, Los Angeles *Also called Bls Lmsine Svc Los Angeles Inc* ***(P-3654)***
B M D, Galt *Also called Building Material Distrs Inc* ***(P-6610)***
B M S, Irvine *Also called Stretto* ***(P-22838)***
B N E U S A, City of Industry *Also called Ettv America Corp* ***(P-5719)***
B N I, Upland *Also called Bni Enterprises Inc* ***(P-26898)***
B P M, San Francisco *Also called Bpm LLP* ***(P-25541)***
B R Funsten & Co ....D....209 825-5375
105 Lndustrial Park Manteca (95337) ***(P-6543)***
B R Funsten & Co ....D....707 863-8300
5200 Watt Ct Ste B Fairfield (94534) ***(P-6544)***
B Riley Financial Inc (PA) ....C....818 884-3737
21255 Burbank Blvd # 400 Woodland Hills (91367) ***(P-16642)***
B S A Partners ....D....714 523-2800
14419 Firestone Blvd La Mirada (90638) ***(P-12032)***
B S Hand & Sons Inc ....E....818 983-1155
4450 Shopping Ln Simi Valley (93063) ***(P-3115)***
B S I Holdings Inc ....A....831 622-1840
100 Clock Tower Pl # 200 Carmel (93923) ***(P-2752)***
B S K Analytical Laboratories, Fresno *Also called BSK Associates* ***(P-24978)***
B S R, San Francisco *Also called Business For Scial Rspnsbility* ***(P-26542)***
B T & T Travel Inc ....D....559 237-9410
2609 E Mckinley Ave Ste N Fresno (93703) ***(P-4817)***
B T B Events Inc ....D....714 415-3313
10950 Virginia Cir Fountain Valley (92708) ***(P-26894)***
B T Mancini Co Inc (PA) ....B....408 942-7900
876 S Milpitas Blvd Milpitas (95035) ***(P-2995)***
B T W, West Sacramento *Also called Bytheways Manufacturing Inc* ***(P-6549)***
B Z Plumbing Company Inc ....C....916 645-1600
1901 Aviation Blvd Lincoln (95648) ***(P-2064)***
B&B Industrial Services Inc (PA) ....D....909 428-3167
14549 Manzanita Dr Fontana (92335) ***(P-2703)***
B&C Transit Inc (PA) ....D....510 483-3560
1924 Franklin St Ste 200 Oakland (94612) ***(P-24957)***
B-Per Electronic Inc ....D....626 912-0600
1600 N Brwy Santa Ana (92706) ***(P-5197)***
B-Spring Valley LLC ....D....619 797-3991
9009 Campo Rd Spring Valley (91977) ***(P-19742)***
B.T. Mancini Company, Milpitas *Also called B T Mancini Co Inc* ***(P-2995)***
B2b Payroll Services, Cypress *Also called B2b Staffing Services Inc* ***(P-14478)***
B2b Staffing Services Inc ....B....714 243-4104
4501 Cerritos Ave Ste 201 Cypress (90630) ***(P-14478)***

Ba Leasing & Capital Corp (HQ) ....C....415 765-1804
555 California St Fl 4 San Francisco (94104) ***(P-14130)***
Baart Behavioral Hlth Svcs Inc ....D....415 928-7800
433 Turk St San Francisco (94102) ***(P-21958)***
Baart Community Healthcare ....D....415 928-7800
433 Turk St San Francisco (94102) ***(P-21959)***
Baaz Global, San Francisco *Also called Baaz Inc* ***(P-14668)***
Baaz Inc ....D....408 621-6912
1 Hallidie Plz Ste 200 San Francisco (94102) ***(P-14668)***
Babcock & Brown Elec MGT LLC ....C....858 587-5820
4350 La Jolla Village Dr San Diego (92122) ***(P-26515)***
Babcock Laboratories Inc ....D....951 653-3351
6100 Quail Valley Ct Riverside (92507) ***(P-26056)***
Babe's Bbq Grill, Newport Beach *Also called Donald Lucky LLC* ***(P-26216)***
Baby Trend Inc (HQ) ....D....909 773-0018
13048 Valley Blvd Fontana (92335) ***(P-8055)***
Babyfirst Americas LLC ....D....310 442-9853
10390 Santa Monica Blvd Los Angeles (90025) ***(P-14669)***
Bacchus Vineyard MGT LLC ....D....707 837-8304
1720 River Rd Fulton (95439) ***(P-26147)***
Bacci Glinn Physcl Therapy Inc ....E....559 733-2478
5533 W Hillsdale Ave A Visalia (93291) ***(P-19656)***
Bachelor Productions Inc ....D....310 567-9249
2121 Avenue Of The Stars Los Angeles (90067) ***(P-17581)***
Back Street Fitness Inc ....E....707 254-7200
3175 California Blvd NAPA (94558) ***(P-18120)***
Backproject Corporation ....D....408 730-1111
170 N Wolfe Rd Sunnyvale (94086) ***(P-6947)***
Backroads (PA) ....D....510 527-1555
801 Cedar St Berkeley (94710) ***(P-4848)***
Backweb Technologies Inc ....E....408 933-1700
2727 Walsh Ave Ste 102 Santa Clara (95051) ***(P-6805)***
Baco Realty Corporation ....D....916 974-9898
6310 Stockton Blvd Sacramento (95824) ***(P-16201)***
Baco Realty Corporation ....D....925 275-0100
2071 Camino Ramon San Ramon (94583) ***(P-4375)***
Bacome Insurance Agency, Fresno *Also called James G Parker Insurance Assoc* ***(P-10395)***
Bacon's Multivision, Oakland *Also called Multivision Inc* ***(P-16934)***
Bacr, San Francisco *Also called Ruth Barajas* ***(P-23418)***
Bad Boys Bail Bonds Inc (PA) ....D....408 298-3333
595 Park Ave Ste 200 San Jose (95110) ***(P-16643)***
Badalian Enterprises Inc ....D....714 635-4082
1540 S Harbor Blvd Anaheim (92802) ***(P-12033)***
Badger Farming Company Inc ....D....559 592-5520
150 W Pine St Exeter (93221) ***(P-186)***
Bae Sys Sierra Detroit Allison (HQ) ....D....510 635-8991
1755 Adams Ave San Leandro (94577) ***(P-17323)***
Bae Systems Tech Sol Srvc Inc ....D....661 816-3474
1434 F Ln 58 B Mojave (93501) ***(P-26516)***
Baechler Investigative Svcs ....D....619 464-5600
1935 N Marshall Ave Ste C El Cajon (92020) ***(P-16202)***
Baer Institute, Moffett Field *Also called Bay Area Envmtl Res Inst* ***(P-25968)***
Bagatelos Glass Systems Inc (PA) ....D....916 364-3600
2750 Redding Ave Sacramento (95820) ***(P-3290)***
Bagatlos Archtctral GL Systems, Sacramento *Also called Bagatelos Glass Systems Inc* ***(P-3290)***
Baghouse and Indus Shtmtl Svcs, Corona *Also called MS Industrial Shtmtl Inc* ***(P-3079)***
Bagley, William T, San Francisco *Also called Nossaman LLP* ***(P-22729)***
Bahia Resort Hotels, San Diego *Also called Bh Partn A Calif Limit Partne* ***(P-12067)***
Bahia Sternwheelers Inc ....E....858 539-7720
998 W Mission Bay Dr San Diego (92109) ***(P-4597)***
Baidu USA LLC ....C....669 224-6400
1195 Bordeaux Dr Sunnyvale (94089) ***(P-15947)***
Bail Hotline Bail Bonds, Riverside *Also called Dmcg Inc* ***(P-16747)***
Bailard, Foster City *Also called B B & K Holdings* ***(P-9793)***
Bailard Inc (HQ) ....E....650 571-5800
950 Tower Ln Ste 1900 Foster City (94404) ***(P-9794)***
Bailey & Dutton (PA) ....D....925 838-1460
3200 Dnville Blvd Ste 200 Alamo (94507) ***(P-1082)***
Bailey, Rollin C MD, Lompoc *Also called Valley Medical Group of Lompoc* ***(P-19542)***
Bain & Company Inc ....D....310 229-3000
1901 Ave Of The Sts 200 Los Angeles (90067) ***(P-26517)***
Bain & Company Inc ....C....415 627-1000
1 Embarcadero Ctr # 3500 San Francisco (94111) ***(P-26518)***
Bainbridge Inc (PA) ....D....858 638-1800
4435 Estgate Mall Ste 130 San Diego (92121) ***(P-26519)***
Baird-Neece Packing Corp ....C....559 784-3393
60 S E St Porterville (93257) ***(P-469)***
Baja Construction Co Inc (PA) ....D....925 229-0732
223 Foster St Martinez (94553) ***(P-3253)***
Baja Freight Forwarders Inc (PA) ....D....619 671-3100
8662 Siempre Viva Rd San Diego (92154) ***(P-4897)***
Baja Life Online Partners ....E....949 376-4619
P.O. Box 4917 Laguna Beach (92652) ***(P-14670)***
Bakbone Software Inc (HQ) ....D....858 450-9009
9540 Towne Centre Dr # 100 San Diego (92121) ***(P-14671)***
Baker Keener & Nahra ....E....213 241-0900
633 W 5th St Ste 5500 Los Angeles (90071) ***(P-22366)***
Baker & Hostetler LLP ....D....310 820-8800
11601 Wilshire Blvd Fl 14 Los Angeles (90025) ***(P-22367)***
Baker & McKenzie LLP ....C....415 576-3000
2 Embarcadero Ctr # 1100 San Francisco (94111) ***(P-22368)***
Baker & McKenzie LLP ....D....650 856-2400
660 Hansen Way Ste 1 Palo Alto (94304) ***(P-22369)***
Baker & Taylor LLC ....C....858 457-2500
10350 Barnes Canyon Rd # 100 San Diego (92121) ***(P-8867)***
Baker Distributing Company LLC ....D....760 708-4201
241 Market Pl Escondido (92029) ***(P-7444)***

Baker Hghes Olfld Oprtions LLC....D....714 893-8511
5421 Argosy Ave Huntington Beach (92649) ***(P-1008)***
Baker Hghes Olfld Oprtions LLC....E....661 834-9654
5700 Doolittle Ave Shafter (93263) ***(P-1009)***
Baker Hughes A GE Company LLC....D....714 893-8511
5421 Argosy Ave Huntington Beach (92649) ***(P-1010)***
Baker Hughes A GE Company LLC....D....661 387-1010
1127 Carrier Parkway Ave Bakersfield (93308) ***(P-1011)***
Baker Hughes A GE Company LLC....D....800 229-7447
5145 Boylan St Bakersfield (93308) ***(P-1012)***
Baker Keener & Nahra, Los Angeles *Also called Baker Keener & Nahra* ***(P-22366)***
Baker Mnock Jensen A Prof Corp....C....559 432-5400
5260 N Palm Ave Ste 421 Fresno (93704) ***(P-22370)***
Baker Mnock Jnsen Attys At Law, Fresno *Also called Baker Mnock Jensen A Prof Corp* ***(P-22370)***
Baker Petrolite LLC....D....661 325-4138
5125 Boylan St Bakersfield (93308) ***(P-1013)***
Baker Places Inc....C....415 503-3137
101 Gough St San Francisco (94102) ***(P-21960)***
Baker Places Inc (PA)....C....415 864-4655
170 9th St San Francisco (94103) ***(P-23834)***
Baker Winokur....D....310 248-6169
9100 Wilshire Blvd 500w Beverly Hills (90212) ***(P-26895)***
Baker Winokur Ryder, Beverly Hills *Also called Bwr Public Relations* ***(P-26899)***
Bakersfield Assc Rrtd Ctzns....C....661 834-2272
2240 S Union Ave Bakersfield (93307) ***(P-23569)***
Bakersfield Community Based, Bakersfield *Also called Veterans Health Administration* ***(P-19577)***
Bakersfield Country Club....D....661 871-4000
4200 Country Club Dr Bakersfield (93306) ***(P-18384)***
Bakersfield District Office, Bakersfield *Also called State Compensation Insur Fund* ***(P-10131)***
Bakersfield Family Med Group....D....661 846-3605
5601 Auburn St Unit A Bakersfield (93306) ***(P-22183)***
Bakersfield Healthcare....D....661 872-2121
2211 Mount Vernon Ave Bakersfield (93306) ***(P-19743)***
Bakersfield Heart Hospital, Bakersfield *Also called Heart Hospital of Bk LLC* ***(P-20907)***
Bakersfield Kitchen & Bath....D....661 836-2284
3529 Pegasus Dr Bakersfield (93308) ***(P-2065)***
Bakersfield Memorial Hospital....A....661 327-1792
420 34th St Bakersfield (93301) ***(P-20758)***
Bakersfield Symphony Orch....D....661 323-7928
1328 34th St Ste A Bakersfield (93301) ***(P-17965)***
Bakersfield Vet Center, Bakersfield *Also called Veterans Health Administration* ***(P-19579)***
Bakery Ex Southern Cal LLC....D....714 446-9470
1910 W Malvern Ave Fullerton (92833) ***(P-8548)***
Bakkavor Foods Usa Inc (HQ)....B....704 522-1977
18201 Central Ave Carson (90746) ***(P-8549)***
Balance Staffing, San Jose *Also called Staffing Solutions Inc* ***(P-14429)***
Balance4kids....D....831 464-8669
4500 Soquel Dr Soquel (95073) ***(P-24478)***
Balboa Bay Club Inc (HQ)....B....949 645-5000
1221 W Coast Hwy Ste 145 Newport Beach (92663) ***(P-18385)***
Balboa Bay Club and Resort, Newport Beach *Also called International Bay Clubs LLC* ***(P-18469)***
Balboa Capital Corporation (PA)....C....949 756-0800
575 Anton Blvd Fl 12 Costa Mesa (92626) ***(P-9454)***
Balboa Enterprises Inc....C....650 961-6161
2530 Solace Pl Mountain View (94040) ***(P-19744)***
Balboa Plaza Admin Offices, Granada Hills *Also called Kaiser Foundation Hospitals* ***(P-19073)***
Balboa Yacht Club....E....949 673-3515
1801 Bayside Dr Corona Del Mar (92625) ***(P-18386)***
Bald Eagle Security Svcs Inc....D....619 230-0022
3626 Main St San Diego (92113) ***(P-16203)***
Baldwin Hospitality LLC....D....626 962-6000
14635 Baldwin Ave Baldwin Park (91706) ***(P-12034)***
Balfour Beatty Cnstr LLC....C....510 903-2060
2335 Broadway Ste 300 Oakland (94612) ***(P-1413)***
Balfour Beatty Cnstr LLC....D....858 635-7400
10620 Treena St Ste 300 San Diego (92131) ***(P-1414)***
Bali Construction Inc....D....626 442-8003
9852 Joe Vargas Way South El Monte (91733) ***(P-1832)***
Ballard Clothing Design, Los Angeles *Also called W Scott Bllard Dsign Arch Inc* ***(P-17157)***
Ballard Rosenberg Golper Sav (PA)....D....818 508-3700
15760 Ventura Blvd # 1800 Encino (91436) ***(P-22371)***
Ballard Spahr LLP....D....424 204-4400
2029 Century Park E # 800 Los Angeles (90067) ***(P-22372)***
Balletto Ranch Inc (PA)....D....707 568-2455
5700 Occidental Rd Santa Rosa (95401) ***(P-34)***
Balliet Bros Construction Corp....E....650 871-9000
390 Swift Ave Ste 14 South San Francisco (94080) ***(P-1415)***
Baloian Farm, Fresno *Also called Baloian Packing Co Inc* ***(P-35)***
Baloian Farms, Fresno *Also called Baloian Packing Co Inc* ***(P-36)***
Baloian Packing Co Inc (PA)....D....559 485-9200
446 N Blythe Ave Fresno (93706) ***(P-35)***
Baloian Packing Co Inc....D....559 441-7043
3138 W Whites Bridge Ave Fresno (93706) ***(P-36)***
Balt USA LLC....D....949 788-1443
29 Parker Ste 100 Irvine (92618) ***(P-6948)***
Baltazar Construction Inc....E....626 339-8620
236 E Arrow Hwy Covina (91722) ***(P-3116)***
Bam Advisor Services LLC....D....800 366-7266
10 Almaden Blvd Fl 15 San Jose (95113) ***(P-9795)***
Bamboo Pipeline Inc....E....925 862-1904
9959 Calaveras Rd Sunol (94586) ***(P-8882)***
Bamko Inc....C....310 470-5859
11620 Wilshire Blvd # 610 Los Angeles (90025) ***(P-13606)***
Bana Home Loan Servicing....A....213 345-7975
31303 Agoura Rd Westlake Village (91361) ***(P-9029)***
Banamex USA, Los Angeles *Also called Busa Servicing Inc* ***(P-9176)***
Banamex USA Bancorp (HQ)....C....310 203-3440
2029 Century Park E Fl 42 Los Angeles (90067) ***(P-11637)***
Banc America Lsg & Capitl LLC (HQ)....C....415 765-7349
555 California St Fl 4 San Francisco (94104) ***(P-9499)***
Banc California National Assn (HQ)....D....877 770-2262
3 Macarthur Pl Santa Ana (92707) ***(P-9030)***
Banc California National Assn....E....310 286-0710
10100 Santa Monica Blvd Los Angeles (90067) ***(P-9248)***
Banc of California Inc (PA)....C....855 361-2262
3 Macarthur Pl Ste 100 Santa Ana (92707) ***(P-9031)***
Bandai Namco Entrmt Amer Inc (HQ)....C....408 235-2000
2051 Mission College Blvd Santa Clara (95054) ***(P-7727)***
Baney Corporation....D....530 899-9090
2035 Business Ln Chico (95928) ***(P-12035)***
Bangkit (usa) Inc....D....626 672-0888
10511 Valley Blvd El Monte (91731) ***(P-7853)***
Bangs Avenue Medical Offices, Modesto *Also called Kaiser Foundation Hospitals* ***(P-19083)***
Banister Electrical Inc....D....925 778-7801
2532 Verne Roberts Cir Antioch (94509) ***(P-2428)***
Bank America National Assn....D....559 445-7731
5292 N Palm Ave Fresno (93704) ***(P-9032)***
Bank America National Assn....E....800 432-1000
1525 Market St San Francisco (94103) ***(P-9033)***
Bank America National Assn....D....805 520-5100
400 National Way Simi Valley (93065) ***(P-9475)***
Bank America National Assn....C....415 913-5891
345 Montgomery St San Francisco (94104) ***(P-9034)***
Bank America National Assn....D....530 891-7019
400 Broadway St Chico (95928) ***(P-9035)***
Bank America National Assn....D....800 432-1000
345 N Brand Blvd Glendale (91203) ***(P-9036)***
Bank America National Assn....E....562 624-4330
6351 E Spring St Long Beach (90808) ***(P-9037)***
Bank America National Assn....D....818 898-3033
120 S Brand Blvd San Fernando (91340) ***(P-9038)***
Bank America National Assn....E....800 432-1000
212 E Main St Visalia (93291) ***(P-9039)***
Bank America National Assn....C....760 636-7500
73525 El Paseo Palm Desert (92260) ***(P-26148)***
Bank America National Assn....D....310 384-4562
550 S Hill St Ste 101 Los Angeles (90013) ***(P-9040)***
Bank America National Assn....C....916 326-3161
555 Capitol Mall Sacramento (95814) ***(P-26149)***
Bank America National Assn....E....714 973-8495
13220 Harbor Blvd Garden Grove (92843) ***(P-9041)***
Bank America National Assn....D....949 474-8801
275 Valencia Ave Brea (92823) ***(P-9042)***
Bank America National Assn....E....951 929-8614
1687 E Florida Ave Hemet (92544) ***(P-9043)***
Bank America National Assn....D....800 432-1000
1450 W Redondo Beach Blvd Gardena (90247) ***(P-9044)***
Bank America National Assn....D....818 577-2000
5901 Canoga Ave Woodland Hills (91367) ***(P-9045)***
Bank America National Assn....D....909 393-3002
4100 Chino Hills Pkwy Chino Hills (91709) ***(P-9046)***
Bank America National Assn....D....951 676-4114
27489 Ynez Rd Temecula (92591) ***(P-9047)***
Bank Leumi Le, Los Angeles *Also called Bank Leumi USA* ***(P-9048)***
Bank Leumi USA....D....323 966-4700
555 W 5th St Fl 33 Los Angeles (90013) ***(P-9048)***
Bank of America, San Francisco *Also called Bankamerica Financial Inc* ***(P-9476)***
Bank of Commerce Mortgage, San Ramon *Also called Commerce Home Mortgage Inc* ***(P-9620)***
Bank of Hope....E....213 389-5550
550 S Western Ave Los Angeles (90020) ***(P-9163)***
Bank of Hope (HQ)....C....213 639-1700
3200 Wilshire Blvd # 1400 Los Angeles (90010) ***(P-9049)***
Bank of Marin....D....415 472-2265
4460 Redwood Hwy Ste 1 San Rafael (94903) ***(P-9164)***
Bank of Marin Bancorp (PA)....C....415 763-4520
504 Redwood Blvd Ste 100 Novato (94947) ***(P-9165)***
Bank of New York Mellon Corp....D....415 399-4450
100 Pine St Ste 3200 San Francisco (94111) ***(P-16644)***
Bank of Orient (HQ)....D....415 338-0668
100 Pine St Ste 600 San Francisco (94111) ***(P-9166)***
Bank of Sierra, San Luis Obispo *Also called Bank of Sierra* ***(P-9050)***
Bank of Sierra....D....805 541-0400
500 Marsh St San Luis Obispo (93401) ***(P-9050)***
Bank of Sierra (HQ)....C....559 782-4300
90 N Main St Porterville (93257) ***(P-9167)***
Bank of Stockton (HQ)....C....209 929-1600
301 E Miner Ave Stockton (95202) ***(P-9168)***
BANK OF THE WEST (HQ)....A....415 765-4800
180 Montgomery St # 1400 San Francisco (94104) ***(P-9169)***
Bank of Tokyo, Los Angeles *Also called Mufg Bank Ltd* ***(P-9268)***
Bank of Tokyo Ltd....A....213 488-3700
445 S Figueroa St # 2700 Los Angeles (90071) ***(P-9249)***
Bankamerica Financial Inc....A....415 622-3521
315 Montgomery St San Francisco (94104) ***(P-9476)***
Bankcard Services, Torrance *Also called Credit Card Services Inc* ***(P-16728)***
Bankcard Services (PA)....C....213 365-1122
21281 S Western Ave Torrance (90501) ***(P-16645)***
Bankcard USA Merchant Srvc....D....818 597-7000
5701 Lindero Canyon Rd Westlake Village (91362) ***(P-6739)***
Bankers Diversified Mortgage, Yorba Linda *Also called American Transport Inc* ***(P-9522)***
Bankruptcy Management Cons, El Segundo *Also called BMC Group Inc* ***(P-22391)***

Employee Codes: A=Over 500 employees, B=251-500
C=101-250, D=51-100, E=50
2020 Directory of California
Wholesalers and Services Companies
© Mergent Inc. 1-800-342-5647
1187

Banner Bank.....D.......916 685-6546
9340 E Stockton Blvd Elk Grove (95624) *(P-9051)*
Banner Bank.....E.......619 243-7900
1350 Rosecrans St San Diego (92106) *(P-9170)*
Banner Health.....C.......530 251-3147
1800 Spring Ridge Dr Susanville (96130) *(P-20759)*
Banner Lassen Medical Center.....C.......530 252-2000
1800 Spring Ridge Dr Susanville (96130) *(P-20760)*
Banquet Facilities.....E.......951 360-2081
6000 Camino Real Riverside (92509) *(P-13399)*
Banyan Solutions Inc.....D.......650 766-9338
2809 Blue Oak Ct Brentwood (94513) *(P-14479)*
Banyan Transcription, Brentwood *Also called Banyan Solutions Inc (P-14479)*
Bapko Metal Inc.....D.......714 639-9380
180 S Anita Dr Orange (92868) *(P-3254)*
Bar Architects.....D.......415 293-5700
901 Battery St Ste 300 San Francisco (94111) *(P-25416)*
Bar Asscation of San Francisco (PA).....C.......415 982-1600
301 Battery St Fl 3 San Francisco (94111) *(P-24380)*
Bara Construction, Danville *Also called Bara Infoware Inc (P-24958)*
Bara Infoware Inc (PA).....D.......925 790-0130
4115 Blackhawk Plaza Cir Danville (94506) *(P-24958)*
Barazani Outdoors Inc.....D.......818 701-6977
14101 Valleyheart Dr # 104 Sherman Oaks (91423) *(P-700)*
Barazani Pave Stone Inc.....C.......818 701-6977
14546 Hamlin St Ste 201 Van Nuys (91411) *(P-2704)*
Barbaccia Properties.....D.......408 225-1010
165 Blossom Hill Rd San Jose (95123) *(P-10862)*
Barbara Worth Resort, Calexico *Also called Adventures In Hospitality Inc (P-18348)*
Barbour & Floyd Medical Assoc, Lynwood *Also called South Cntl Heatlh & Rehab Prog (P-22127)*
Barcelo Enterprises Inc.....D.......760 728-3444
4400 Macarthur Blvd # 980 Newport Beach (92660) *(P-229)*
Barcelon Associates MGT Corp.....C.......925 627-7000
590 Lennon Ln Ste 110 Walnut Creek (94598) *(P-10932)*
Barclays Capital Inc.....D.......650 289-6000
155 Linfield Dr Menlo Park (94025) *(P-11887)*
Barclays Capital Inc.....D.......310 481-4100
10250 Santa Monica Blvd # 24 Los Angeles (90067) *(P-9652)*
Barcott Frank A SEC Invstgtons.....C.......714 891-8556
6446 San Andres Ave Cypress (90630) *(P-16204)*
Barcott SEC & Investigations, Cypress *Also called Barcott Frank A SEC Invstgtons (P-16204)*
Bardex Corporation.....D.......805 964-7747
6338 Lindmar Dr Goleta (93117) *(P-7526)*
Bare Elegance, Monrovia *Also called Imperial Project Inc (P-17981)*
Bargain Wholesale, Commerce *Also called 99 Cents Only Stores LLC (P-4362)*
Barger & Wolen LLP.....E.......415 434-2800
275 Battery St Ste 480 San Francisco (94111) *(P-22373)*
Barkers Food Machinery, Irwindale *Also called Service Solutions Group LLC (P-17463)*
Barlow Group (PA).....C.......213 250-4200
2000 Stadium Way Los Angeles (90026) *(P-21449)*
Barlow Respiratory Hospital (PA).....C.......213 250-4200
2000 Stadium Way Los Angeles (90026) *(P-21450)*
BARLOW RESPITORY HOSPITAL, Los Angeles *Also called Barlow Group (P-21449)*
Barnard Bessac Joint Venture.....D.......650 212-8957
395 Shoreway Rd Redwood City (94065) *(P-1942)*
Barnes & Thornburg LLP.....C.......310 284-3880
2029 Century Park E # 300 Los Angeles (90067) *(P-22374)*
Barnes and Berger.....E.......760 922-6136
1091 S Intake Blvd Blythe (92225) *(P-448)*
Barnett Customer Management.....E.......714 747-7908
3111 N Tustin St Orange (92865) *(P-26150)*
Barnum & Celillo Electric Inc (PA).....D.......916 646-4661
135 Main Ave Ste A Sacramento (95838) *(P-2429)*
Baron Pool Plst Sthern Cal Inc.....D.......909 792-8891
495 Industrial Rd San Bernardino (92408) *(P-3382)*
Barona Creek Golf Club.....D.......619 387-7018
1932 Wildcat Canyon Rd Lakeside (92040) *(P-18221)*
Barona Resort & Casino.....A.......619 443-2300
1932 Wildcat Canyon Rd Lakeside (92040) *(P-12036)*
Baronhr LLC.....C.......909 517-3800
13085 Central Ave Ste 4 Chino (91710) *(P-14231)*
Barr Engineering Inc.....D.......562 944-1722
12612 Clark St Santa Fe Springs (90670) *(P-2066)*
Barra LLC (HQ).....B.......510 548-5442
2100 Milvia St Berkeley (94704) *(P-15254)*
Barracuda Networks Inc (HQ).....C.......408 342-5400
3175 Winchester Blvd Campbell (95008) *(P-15255)*
Barranca Medical Offices, Irvine *Also called Kaiser Foundation Hospitals (P-20932)*
Barrel Ten Quarter Circle Inc.....B.......707 265-4000
33 Harlow Ct NAPA (94558) *(P-8797)*
Barrett Business Services Inc.....A.......858 314-1100
8880 Rio San Diego Dr # 800 San Diego (92108) *(P-22375)*
Barrett Business Services Inc.....A.......909 890-3633
862 E Hospitality Ln San Bernardino (92408) *(P-14232)*
Barrett Business Services Inc.....A.......650 653-7588
1840 Gateway Dr San Mateo (94404) *(P-26151)*
Barrett SF.....E.......415 986-2960
250 Sutter St Ste 200 San Francisco (94108) *(P-13474)*
Barrick Gold Corporation.....D.......707 995-6070
26775 Morgan Valley Rd Lower Lake (95457) *(P-968)*
Barry Bishop.....D.......510 596-0888
6001 Shellmound St # 875 Emeryville (94608) *(P-22376)*
Barry McPherson Inc.....C.......425 343-5000
1932 E Deere Ave Ste 240 Santa Ana (92705) *(P-10294)*
Barrys Security Services Inc (PA).....C.......951 789-7575
16739 Van Buren Blvd Riverside (92504) *(P-16205)*
Barrys Security Services Inc.....C.......562 493-7007
5480 Katella Ave Ste 203 Los Alamitos (90720) *(P-16206)*
Barstow Community Hospital, Barstow *Also called Hospital of Barstow Inc (P-20913)*
Barstow Redevelopment Agency.....C.......760 256-3531
220 E Mountain View St B Barstow (92311) *(P-27000)*
Bart, Oakland *Also called San Frncsco Bay Area Rpid Trns (P-3593)*
Bartco Lighting Inc.....D.......714 230-3200
5761 Research Dr Huntington Beach (92649) *(P-7127)*
Bartell Hotels.....D.......619 291-6700
1960 Harbor Island Dr San Diego (92101) *(P-12037)*
Bartell Hotels.....C.......619 224-3411
2303 Shelter Island Dr San Diego (92106) *(P-12038)*
Bartell Hotels.....C.......619 222-6440
1710 W Mission Bay Dr San Diego (92109) *(P-12039)*
Bartell Hotels.....E.......858 581-3500
610 Diamond St San Diego (92109) *(P-12040)*
Bartell Hotels.....D.......619 222-0561
2051 Shelter Island Dr San Diego (92106) *(P-12041)*
Bartell Hotels.....D.......858 453-5500
3299 Holiday Ct La Jolla (92037) *(P-12042)*
Bartholomew Barry & Associates.....D.......818 543-4000
701 N Brand Blvd Ste 800 Glendale (91203) *(P-22377)*
Bartko Zankel Tarrant & Mil.....D.......415 956-1900
1 Embarcadero Ctr Ste 800 San Francisco (94111) *(P-22378)*
Bartley Optical, Irwindale *Also called Essilor Laboratories Amer Inc (P-7022)*
Barton Hospital.....A.......530 543-5685
2170 South Ave South Lake Tahoe (96150) *(P-20761)*
Baseline Consulting Group Inc.....E.......818 906-7638
15300 Ventura Blvd # 200 Sherman Oaks (91403) *(P-26520)*
Basic Occpational Training Ctr, Perris *Also called Basic Occpational Training Ctr (P-24137)*
Basic Occpational Training Ctr.....C.......951 657-8028
1323 Jet Way Perris (92571) *(P-24137)*
Basic Resources Inc (PA).....E.......209 521-9771
928 12th St Ste 700 Modesto (95354) *(P-1669)*
Basis Worldwide.....E.......424 261-2354
1557 7th St Santa Monica (90401) *(P-13475)*
Bask Jewelry Inc.....D.......831 479-8849
2607 S Main St Soquel (95073) *(P-7780)*
Basket Basics, Carson *Also called Kole Imports (P-8982)*
Basketball Marketing Co Inc.....D.......610 249-2255
101 Enterprise Ste 100 Aliso Viejo (92656) *(P-26521)*
Basquez Tiburcio Health Center.....C.......510 471-5907
33255 9th St Union City (94587) *(P-21961)*
Bass Tickets, Concord *Also called Bay Area Seating Service Inc (P-18630)*
Bassard Convalescent & Med Hm (PA).....D.......510 537-6700
3269 D St Hayward (94541) *(P-20498)*
Bassard Convalscent Home, Hayward *Also called Bassard Convalescent & Med Hm (P-20498)*
Bassenian/Lagoni Architects.....D.......949 553-9100
2031 Orchard Dr Ste 100 Newport Beach (92660) *(P-25417)*
Basslake LLC.....D.......559 642-3121
39255 Marina Dr Bass Lake (93604) *(P-12043)*
Bassmnt, Newport Beach *Also called Downtown SD Ventures LLC (P-18683)*
Bastille Networks Inc.....E.......800 530-3341
499 Lake Ave Santa Cruz (95062) *(P-14672)*
Batchmaster Software, Irvine *Also called Eworkplace Solutions Inc (P-6835)*
Bates Display & Packaging, Chino Hills *Also called Bates Sample Case Company Inc (P-16646)*
Bates Sample Case Company Inc.....D.......951 371-4922
5995 W Park Dr Chino Hills (91709) *(P-16646)*
Battery Agency, Hollywood *Also called Battery Marketing Inc (P-13476)*
Battery Assist, Los Angeles *Also called Club Assist US LLC (P-6430)*
Battery Marketing Inc.....D.......323 467-7267
6515 W Sunset Blvd # 200 Hollywood (90028) *(P-13476)*
Battery The, San Francisco *Also called Mxb Battery Operations LP (P-24599)*
Batth Farms, Caruthers *Also called Charanjit Singh Batth (P-171)*
Bauer Hockey Inc.....B.......818 782-6445
3500 Willow Ln Thousand Oaks (91361) *(P-7704)*
Bauers Intelligent Trnsp Inc (PA).....C.......415 522-1212
50 Pier San Francisco (94158) *(P-3649)*
Bautista, Jennifer L, San Jose *Also called Robinson and Wood Inc (P-22793)*
Bavaria Holdings Inc.....A.......415 418-2900
1 Letterman Dr Bldg C San Francisco (94129) *(P-11646)*
Bavarian Lion Company Cal (PA).....C.......707 545-8530
2777 4th St Santa Rosa (95405) *(P-12044)*
BAVC, San Francisco *Also called Bay Area Video Coalition Inc (P-17726)*
Baxter Healthcare Corporation.....A.......805 372-3000
1 Baxter Way Ste 100 Westlake Village (91362) *(P-7920)*
Bay Advanced Tech 0045, Newark *Also called Bay Advanced Technologies LLC (P-7527)*
Bay Advanced Technologies LLC.....D.......510 857-0900
8100 Central Ave Newark (94560) *(P-7527)*
Bay Alarm Company (PA).....D.......925 935-1100
5130 Commercial Cir Concord (94520) *(P-2430)*
Bay Alarm Company.....D.......510 452-3211
9836 Kitty Ln Oakland (94603) *(P-25877)*
Bay Area Air Quality (PA).....C.......415 749-4900
375 Beale St Ste 600 San Francisco (94105) *(P-27001)*
Bay Area At Home, Belmont *Also called Silverado Senior Living Inc (P-20681)*
Bay Area Beverage, Richmond *Also called T F Louderback Inc (P-8793)*
Bay Area Beverage Co.....C.......510 965-6120
700 National Ct Richmond (94804) *(P-8798)*
Bay Area Cnstr Framers Inc.....C.......925 454-8514
1150 W Center St Ste 105 Manteca (95337) *(P-2917)*
Bay Area Community Med Group, Los Angeles *Also called Santa Monica Bay Physicians He (P-19371)*
Bay Area Community Svcs Inc (PA).....E.......510 613-0330
390 40th St Oakland (94609) *(P-22935)*
Bay Area Community Svcs Inc.....C.......510 537-1688
22505 Woodroe Ave Hayward (94541) *(P-10851)*

Bay Area Concrete LLC..........D.......510 294-0220
24701 Clawiter Rd Hayward (94545) *(P-6157)*
Bay Area Distributing Coinc..........E.......510 232-8554
1061 Factory St Richmond (94801) *(P-8749)*
Bay Area Envmtl Res Inst..........D.......707 938-9387
Nasa Resrch Park 101 Moffett Field (94035) *(P-25968)*
Bay Area Garment, Hayward *Also called Early Transportation Services (P-4007)*
Bay Area Hispn Inst Advancmnt..........D.......510 525-1463
1000 Camelia St Berkeley (94710) *(P-23674)*
Bay Area Installations Inc (PA)..........D.......510 895-8196
2481 Verna Ct San Leandro (94577) *(P-3383)*
Bay Area Kenworth, San Leandro *Also called Ssmb Pacific Holding Co Inc (P-6409)*
Bay Area News Group E Bay LLC (HQ)..........D.......925 302-1683
6270 Houston Pl Ste A Dublin (94568) *(P-13644)*
Bay Area Pdatric Med Group Inc (PA)..........D.......650 992-4200
901 Campus Dr Ste 111 Daly City (94015) *(P-18831)*
BAY AREA RESCUE MISSION, Richmond *Also called Richmond Rescue Mission (P-23415)*
Bay Area Seating Service Inc..........B.......925 671-4000
1855 Gateway Blvd Ste 630 Concord (94520) *(P-18630)*
Bay Area Senior Services Inc..........C.......650 579-5500
1 Baldwin Ave Ofc San Mateo (94401) *(P-22936)*
Bay Area Surgical MGT LLC..........E.......408 297-3432
2110 Forest Ave Fl 2 San Jose (95128) *(P-18832)*
Bay Area Techworkers (PA)..........D.......925 359-2200
2000 Crow Canyon Pl # 150 San Ramon (94583) *(P-14233)*
Bay Area Video Coalition Inc..........D.......415 861-3282
2727 Mariposa St Fl 2 San Francisco (94110) *(P-17726)*
Bay Area/Diablo Petroleum Co (HQ)..........C.......925 228-2222
1340 Arnold Dr Ste 231 Martinez (94553) *(P-8720)*
Bay Area/Diablo Petroleum Co..........C.......925 228-2222
1800 Sutter St Concord (94520) *(P-8721)*
Bay Bread LLC..........D.......415 440-0356
2325 Pine St San Francisco (94115) *(P-8550)*
Bay Brokerage Inc..........E.......650 413-1721
17 Woodleaf Ave Redwood City (94061) *(P-8156)*
Bay Cities Crane & Rigging Inc (PA)..........E.......510 232-7222
457 Parr Blvd Richmond (94801) *(P-14131)*
Bay Cities Pav & Grading Inc..........C.......925 687-6666
1450 Civic Ct Bldg B Concord (94520) *(P-3304)*
Bay City Equipment Inds Inc..........D.......619 938-8200
13625 Danielson St Poway (92064) *(P-7128)*
Bay City Flower Co (PA)..........B.......650 726-5535
2265 Cabrillo Hwy S Half Moon Bay (94019) *(P-8883)*
Bay City Flower Co..........C.......650 712-8147
1450 Cabrillo Hwy S Half Moon Bay (94019) *(P-230)*
Bay City Mechanical Inc..........C.......510 233-7000
4124 Lakeside Dr Richmond (94806) *(P-2067)*
Bay City Television Inc (PA)..........D.......858 279-6666
8253 Ronson Rd San Diego (92111) *(P-5580)*
Bay Club Golden Gateway LLC..........E.......415 616-8800
370 Drumm St San Francisco (94111) *(P-18387)*
Bay Club Golden Gateway Inc, San Francisco *Also called Bay Club Golden Gateway LLC (P-18387)*
Bay Club Holdings III LLC..........D.......415 433-2936
370 Drumm St San Francisco (94111) *(P-18631)*
Bay Club Hotel and Marina A C..........D.......619 224-8888
2131 Shelter Island Dr San Diego (92106) *(P-12045)*
Bay Club Marin, Corte Madera *Also called Bay Clubs Inc (P-18388)*
Bay Clubs Inc..........D.......415 945-3000
220 Corte Madera Town Ctr Corte Madera (94925) *(P-18388)*
Bay Clubs Inc..........D.......408 738-2582
3250 Central Expy Santa Clara (95051) *(P-18121)*
Bay Clubs Inc..........D.......818 884-5034
22235 Sherman Way Canoga Park (91303) *(P-18389)*
Bay Clubs Inc..........D.......650 593-1112
200 Redwood Shr Pkwy Redwood City (94065) *(P-18122)*
Bay Counties Waste Svcs Inc..........D.......408 565-9900
3355 Thomas Rd Santa Clara (95054) *(P-6158)*
Bay Equity Home Loans, Sausalito *Also called Bay Equity LLC (P-9526)*
Bay Equity LLC (PA)..........D.......415 632-5150
28 Liberty Ship Way # 2800 Sausalito (94965) *(P-9526)*
Bay Federal Credit Union (PA)..........C.......831 479-6000
3333 Clares St Capitola (95010) *(P-9294)*
Bay Grove Capital Group LLC (PA)..........E.......415 229-7953
801 Montgomery St Fl 5 San Francisco (94133) *(P-11716)*
Bay Imaging Cons Med Group Inc (PA)..........D.......925 296-7150
175 Lennon Ln Ste 100 Walnut Creek (94598) *(P-18833)*
Bay Management, San Mateo *Also called Archives Management Corp (P-26137)*
Bay Marine & Indus Sup LLC..........E.......510 337-9122
2900 Main St Alameda (94501) *(P-7799)*
Bay Meadows Racing Association..........C.......650 573-4500
2600 S Delaware St San Mateo (94403) *(P-24323)*
Bay Medic Transportation Inc..........D.......800 689-9511
959 Detroit Ave Concord (94518) *(P-3650)*
Bay Medical Management LLC..........C.......925 296-7150
2125 Oak Grove Rd Ste 200 Walnut Creek (94598) *(P-18834)*
Bay Photo Inc..........C.......831 475-6090
2959 Park Ave Ste A Soquel (95073) *(P-13327)*
Bay Point Healthcare Center, Hayward *Also called Kissito Health Care Inc (P-21799)*
Bay Standard Inc..........D.......925 634-1181
24485 Marsh Creek Rd Brentwood (94513) *(P-7625)*
Bay Valley Medical Group Inc (PA)..........D.......510 785-5000
319 Diablo Rd Ste 105 Danville (94526) *(P-18835)*
Bay View Rhbilitation Hosp LLC..........D.......510 521-5600
516 Willow St Alameda (94501) *(P-19745)*
Bay Vista Senior Housing..........C.......925 924-7100
6120 Stoneridge Pleasanton (94588) *(P-26152)*
Bay West Shwplace Invstors LLC (PA)..........D.......415 490-5800
2 Henry Adams St Ste 450 San Francisco (94103) *(P-10571)*
Bayberry Inc (PA)..........D.......707 252-5587
1700 2nd St Ste 350 NAPA (94559) *(P-20412)*
Baybridge Employment Services, Eureka *Also called Humboldt Commnty Accss Resrc (P-23268)*
Bayco Financial Corporation (PA)..........D.......310 378-8181
24050 Madison St Ste 101 Torrance (90505) *(P-10933)*
Bayer Protective Services Inc..........C.......916 486-5800
3436 Amrcn Rver Dr Ste 10 Sacramento (95864) *(P-16498)*
Baymarr Constructors Inc..........D.......661 395-1676
6950 Mcdivitt Dr Bakersfield (93313) *(P-3117)*
Baynote Inc..........D.......866 921-0919
75 E Santa Clara St # 600 San Jose (95113) *(P-6806)*
Bayonet/Blackhorse Golf Course, Seaside *Also called Bsl Golf Corp (P-18225)*
Bayorg..........D.......415 623-5300
Embarcadero At Beach St San Francisco (94133) *(P-24302)*
Bayou Cinemas LP..........C.......213 235-2244
500 Citadel Dr Ste 300 Commerce (90040) *(P-17818)*
Baypoint Trading, San Francisco *Also called Btig LLC (P-9656)*
Bayscape Management Inc..........D.......408 288-2940
1350 Pacific Ave Alviso (95002) *(P-701)*
Bayshore Ambulance Inc (PA)..........D.......650 525-9700
370 Hatch Dr Foster City (94404) *(P-3651)*
Bayshore Healthcare Inc..........C.......805 544-5100
3033 Augusta St San Luis Obispo (93401) *(P-19746)*
Bayside Care Center, Morro Bay *Also called Compass Health Inc (P-20531)*
Bayside Insulation & Cnstr..........D.......925 288-8960
1635 Challenge Dr Concord (94520) *(P-1416)*
Bayside Interiors Inc (PA)..........C.......510 438-9171
3220 Darby Cmn Fremont (94539) *(P-2753)*
Bayside Medical Group, San Ramon *Also called Lucile Salter Packard Chil (P-19170)*
Bayspring Medical Group A Pro..........E.......415 674-2600
1199 Bush St Ste 500 San Francisco (94109) *(P-18836)*
Bayview Engrg & Cnstr Co Inc..........D.......916 939-8986
5040 Rbert J Mathews Pkwy El Dorado Hills (95762) *(P-2068)*
Bayview Hospital and Mental..........C.......619 426-6311
330 Moss St Chula Vista (91911) *(P-21383)*
Bayview Hunters Point Foundati (PA)..........D.......415 468-5100
150 Executive Park Blvd San Francisco (94134) *(P-24805)*
Bayview Hunters Point Y M C A..........D.......415 822-7728
1601 Lane St San Francisco (94124) *(P-24479)*
Bayview Preservation LP..........A.......415 285-7344
5 Commer Ct San Francisco (94124) *(P-10691)*
Bayview Properties Inc (PA)..........D.......831 394-3321
2600 Sand Dunes Dr Monterey (93940) *(P-12046)*
Bayview Properties Inc..........D.......831 655-7650
2600 Sand Dunes Dr Monterey (93940) *(P-12047)*
Bayview Properties Inc..........D.......831 624-1841
3665 Rio Rd Carmel (93923) *(P-12048)*
Baywood Court (PA)..........C.......510 733-2102
21966 Dolores St Castro Valley (94546) *(P-21680)*
Baywood Court Retirement Ctr, Castro Valley *Also called Baywood Court (P-21680)*
Bazan Mario AG Services & Vine..........D.......707 945-0718
1984 Yountville Cross Rd Yountville (94599) *(P-118)*
Bazan Mrio Vinyrd Mgmt AG Svcs, Yountville *Also called Bazan Mario AG Services & Vine (P-118)*
Bazic Product, El Monte *Also called Bangkit (usa) Inc (P-7853)*
BB&k, Riverside *Also called Best Best & Krieger LLP (P-22383)*
Bbam Arcft Holdings 137 Labuan..........D.......415 267-1600
50 California St Fl 14 San Francisco (94111) *(P-14132)*
Bbam Arcft Holdings 139 Labuan, San Francisco *Also called Bbam US LP (P-9653)*
Bbam US LP..........B.......415 267-1600
50 California St Fl 14 San Francisco (94111) *(P-9653)*
Bbccsd, Big Bear City *Also called Big Bear City Cmnty Svcs Dst (P-6128)*
Bbcert..........E.......480 220-3799
510 Hwy 1 Bodega Bay (94923) *(P-26522)*
BBDO Worldwide Inc..........D.......415 808-6200
600 California St Fl 8 San Francisco (94108) *(P-13477)*
Bbk Performance Inc..........D.......951 296-1771
27440 Bostik Ct Temecula (92590) *(P-6425)*
Bbva USA..........B.......951 279-7071
195 W Ontario Ave Corona (92882) *(P-9171)*
Bbva USA..........B.......951 672-4829
27851 Bradley Rd Ste 125 Sun City (92586) *(P-9052)*
Bbva USA..........B.......209 239-1381
201 N Main St Manteca (95336) *(P-9172)*
Bbva USA..........B.......209 473-6925
2427 W Hammer Ln Stockton (95209) *(P-9173)*
Bbva USA..........B.......209 939-3288
2562 Pacific Ave Stockton (95204) *(P-9174)*
Bc Contractors, Gonzales *Also called Bulmaro Castro Contractors (P-14235)*
Bc Laboratories Inc..........D.......661 327-4911
4100 Atlas Ct Bakersfield (93308) *(P-26057)*
Bc Traffic Specialists, Orange *Also called B C Rentals LLC (P-7525)*
Bc2 Environmental, Orange *Also called Beks Acquisition Inc (P-3241)*
Bcbg Max Azria Group LLC..........D.......323 589-2224
2761 Fruitland Ave Vernon (90058) *(P-8056)*
Bcbg Max Azria Group, LLC, Vernon *Also called Runway Liquidation LLC (P-8107)*
Bcci Builders, San Francisco *Also called Bcci Construction Company (P-1417)*
Bcci Construction Company (HQ)..........C.......415 817-5100
1160 Battery St Ste 250 San Francisco (94111) *(P-1417)*
BCII, North Hills *Also called Brentwood Cmmncations Intl Inc (P-17584)*
BCM Construction Company Inc..........E.......530 342-1722
2990 California 32 Chico (95973) *(P-1330)*
BCM Customer Service..........D.......858 679-5757
12155 Kirkham Rd Poway (92064) *(P-2069)*
Bcp Systems Inc..........D.......714 202-3900
1560 S Sinclair St Anaheim (92806) *(P-15912)*

Employee Codes: A=Over 500 employees, B=251-500
C=101-250, D=51-100, E=50
2020 Directory of California
Wholesalers and Services Companies
© Mergent Inc. 1-800-342-5647
1189

Bctc Corporation D 323 888-9388
5500 E Olympic Blvd Ste B Commerce (90022) ***(P-8057)***

Bdc Distribution Center, Redlands *Also called Becton Dickinson and Company* ***(P-6949)***

Bdl Prosthetics, Irvine *Also called James R Glidewell Dental* ***(P-21611)***

Bdo Usa LLP C 415 397-7900
1 Bush St San Francisco (94104) ***(P-25538)***

Bdo Usa LLP D 858 404-9200
3570 Carmel Mountain Rd # 400 San Diego (92130) ***(P-25539)***

Bdp Bowl Inc E 650 878-0300
900 King Plz Daly City (94015) ***(P-18024)***

BDR Industries Inc (PA) D 661 940-8554
820 E Avenue L12 Lancaster (93535) ***(P-5666)***

BDS Marketing LLC (HQ) C 800 234-4237
10 Holland Irvine (92618) ***(P-13478)***

BDS Plumbing Inc D 925 939-1004
2125 Youngs Ct Walnut Creek (94596) ***(P-2070)***

Be Wise Ranch, Escondido *Also called William Brammer* ***(P-8540)***

Bea Systems Inc (HQ) A 650 506-7000
2315 N 1st St San Jose (95131) ***(P-14673)***

Beach & Tennis Club, Pebble Beach *Also called Lone Cypress Company LLC* ***(P-18490)***

Beach and La Mirada Car Wash E 714 994-1099
5231 Beach Blvd Buena Park (90621) ***(P-17361)***

Beach Bunny Swimwear, Costa Mesa *Also called Bunny Beach Swimwear Inc* ***(P-8060)***

Beach Cities 16 Cinemas, El Segundo *Also called Pacific Theaters Inc* ***(P-17853)***

Beach Cities Health District C 310 374-3426
1200 Del Amo St Redondo Beach (90277) ***(P-24138)***

Beach Cities Invest & Protctn B 310 322-4724
2500 Via Cabrillo Marina San Pedro (90731) ***(P-16207)***

Beach Cities Memory Care Cmnty, Redondo Beach *Also called Silverado Senior Living Inc* ***(P-20260)***

Beach Club D 310 395-3254
201 Palisades Beach Rd Santa Monica (90402) ***(P-18390)***

Beach House Ht - Half Moon Bay, Half Moon Bay *Also called Pacific Beach House LLC* ***(P-12685)***

Beach Motel Partners Ltd D 800 755-0222
28 W Cabrillo Blvd Santa Barbara (93101) ***(P-12049)***

Beachbody LLC (PA) B 310 883-9000
3301 Exposition Blvd Fl 3 Santa Monica (90404) ***(P-13614)***

Beachside Nursing Center, Huntington Beach *Also called Sea Breeze Health Care Inc* ***(P-20245)***

Beachsports Inc E 310 372-2202
600 N Catalina Ave Redondo Beach (90277) ***(P-13143)***

Beacon Accunting Resources LLC E 949 981-5946
1818 Glenwood Ln Newport Beach (92660) ***(P-26523)***

Beacon Health Options Inc C 714 763-2405
10805 Holder St Ste 300 Cypress (90630) ***(P-22937)***

Beacon Healthcare Services D 949 650-9750
1501 E 16th St Newport Beach (92663) ***(P-21384)***

Beacon Resources LLC E 949 955-1773
17300 Red Hill Ave Irvine (92614) ***(P-26524)***

Beacon Roofing Supply Inc D 408 293-5947
200 San Jose Ave San Jose (95125) ***(P-6709)***

Beacon Roofing Supply Inc D 818 768-4661
8501 Telfair Ave Sun Valley (91352) ***(P-7626)***

Beacon Sales Acquisition Inc C 714 288-1974
1201 E Mcfadden Ave Santa Ana (92705) ***(P-6710)***

Beacon West Energy Group LLC D 805 816-2790
1145 Eugenia Pl Ste 101 Carpinteria (93013) ***(P-24959)***

Bead Society C 805 495-2550
1454 Valley High Ave Thousand Oaks (91362) ***(P-24806)***

Bead Society , The, Thousand Oaks *Also called Bead Society* ***(P-24806)***

Beador Construction Co Inc D 951 674-7352
26320 Lester Cir Corona (92883) ***(P-1670)***

Beale Air Force Base Outreach, Marysville *Also called Yuba Community College Dst* ***(P-23553)***

Beam "easy Living" Center, Grass Valley *Also called Beam Vacuums California Inc* ***(P-2431)***

Beam Vacuums California Inc E 916 564-3279
422 Henderson St Grass Valley (95945) ***(P-2431)***

Bear Creek Golf & Country Club, Murrieta *Also called Bear Creek Golf Club Inc* ***(P-18391)***

Bear Creek Golf Club Inc D 951 677-8621
22640 Bear Creek Dr N Murrieta (92562) ***(P-18391)***

Bear Creek Manor E 209 723-4674
2929 M St Merced (95348) ***(P-10692)***

Bear Creek Partners LLC D 951 677-8621
22640 Bear Creek Dr N Murrieta (92562) ***(P-18392)***

Bear Flag Marketing Corp C 415 899-8466
7599 Redwood Blvd Ste 200 Novato (94945) ***(P-21681)***

Bear Nash Productions D 310 428-5167
521 E Sycamore Ave El Segundo (90245) ***(P-17727)***

Bear River Casino B 707 733-9644
11 Bear Paws Way Loleta (95551) ***(P-12050)***

Bear River Casino Hotel, Loleta *Also called Bear River Casino* ***(P-12050)***

Bear Stearns, Del Mar *Also called JP Morgan Securities LLC* ***(P-9704)***

Bear Stearns Companies LLC A 949 856-8300
1833 Alton Pkwy Irvine (92606) ***(P-9527)***

Bear Stern Residential Mrtg, Irvine *Also called Bear Stearns Companies LLC* ***(P-9527)***

Bear Trucking Inc D 909 799-1616
19768 Kendall Dr San Bernardino (92407) ***(P-4195)***

Bear Valley Mountain Resort, Bear Valley *Also called Bear Valley Ski Co* ***(P-18632)***

Bear Valley Ski Co B 209 753-2301
2280 State Rte 207 Bear Valley (95223) ***(P-18632)***

Bear Valley Springs Assn C 661 821-5537
29541 Rollingoak Dr Tehachapi (93561) ***(P-24480)***

Bear Vly Cmnty Healthcare Dst (PA) C 909 866-6501
41870 Garstin Dr Big Bear Lake (92315) ***(P-20762)***

Bear Vly Fbrcators Stl Sup Inc D 760 247-5381
10700 Civic Center Dr 100c Rancho Cucamonga (91730) ***(P-1331)***

Beard Land & Investment Co (PA) C 209 524-4631
530 11th St Modesto (95354) ***(P-11542)***

Bearing Engineers Inc (PA) D 949 586-7442
27 Argonaut Aliso Viejo (92656) ***(P-7627)***

Beating Wall Street Inc (PA) C 818 332-9696
14934 Dickens St Apt 16 Sherman Oaks (91403) ***(P-26525)***

Beats Music LLC D 415 590-5104
235 2nd St San Francisco (94105) ***(P-15256)***

Beau Wine Tours, Sonoma *Also called Appellation Tours Inc* ***(P-4847)***

Beauchamp Distributing Company D 310 639-5320
1911 S Santa Fe Ave Compton (90221) ***(P-8750)***

Beaumont Unified School Dst A 951 845-3010
1001 Cougar Way Beaumont (92223) ***(P-3786)***

Beautitudes Beauty Supply LLC D 800 830-6076
7850 White Ln Ste E Bakersfield (93309) ***(P-7666)***

Beauty 21 Cosmetics Inc C 909 945-2220
2021 S Archibald Ave Ontario (91761) ***(P-7921)***

Beauty Barrage LLC C 949 771-3399
4340 Von Karman Ave # 200 Newport Beach (92660) ***(P-13333)***

Beauty Bazar Inc D 650 326-8522
36 Stanford Shopping Ctr Palo Alto (94304) ***(P-13334)***

Beauty Recognized LP D 310 278-7646
224 Via Rodeo Dr Beverly Hills (90210) ***(P-13335)***

Beautycounter, Santa Monica *Also called Counter Brands LLC* ***(P-7939)***

Beaver Dam Health Care Center D 707 255-6060
705 Trancas St NAPA (94558) ***(P-20499)***

Beaver Dam Health Care Center D 209 529-0516
515 E Orangeburg Ave Modesto (95350) ***(P-20500)***

Beaver Dam Health Care Center D 626 962-3368
850 S Sunkist Ave West Covina (91790) ***(P-19747)***

Beaver Dam Health Care Center D 559 638-3577
1090 E Dinuba Ave Reedley (93654) ***(P-19748)***

Beaver Medical Clinic Inc (PA) C 909 793-3311
1615 Orange Tree Ln Redlands (92374) ***(P-18837)***

Beazer Homes Holdings Corp D 714 285-2900
1800 E Imperial Hwy # 140 Brea (92821) ***(P-1083)***

Beazer Pre-Owned Rental Homes, Agoura Hills *Also called Amh Portfolio One LLC* ***(P-11843)***

Becho Inc D 818 362-8391
15901 Olden St Sylmar (91342) ***(P-1671)***

Bechtel, Livermore *Also called National Security Tech LLC* ***(P-25232)***

Bechtel Capital MGT Corp A 415 768-1234
50 Beale St San Francisco (94105) ***(P-26153)***

Bechtel Global Energy Inc A 415 768-1234
50 Beale St Bsmt 1 San Francisco (94105) ***(P-24960)***

Beck Group, The, Beverly Hills *Also called Beck International Inc* ***(P-1332)***

Beck International Inc B 310 281-2980
9641 Sunset Blvd Beverly Hills (90210) ***(P-1332)***

Becker Interiors Ltd E 323 469-1938
5552 Hollywood Blvd Los Angeles (90028) ***(P-6545)***

Beckett Enterprise E 310 686-3817
900 Kincaid Ave K8 Inglewood (90302) ***(P-26526)***

Beckman Research Inst Hope C 626 359-8111
1500 Duarte Rd Duarte (91010) ***(P-25969)***

Becton Dickinson and Company D 909 748-7300
2200 W San Bernardino Ave Redlands (92374) ***(P-6949)***

Bedon Construction Inc D 951 246-9005
27989 Holland Rd Menifee (92584) ***(P-24961)***

Bedrock Company D 951 273-1931
2970 Myers St Riverside (92503) ***(P-3118)***

Bedrosian Farms Inc E 559 834-5981
8333 S Sunnyside Ave Fowler (93625) ***(P-119)***

Bedrosian's Tile & Marble, Anaheim *Also called Paragon Industries Inc* ***(P-6694)***

Beech Street Corporation (HQ) B 949 672-1000
25550 Commercentre Dr # 200 Lake Forest (92630) ***(P-26154)***

Beethoven Holdings Inc C 559 733-4100
400 E Main St Ste 110 Visalia (93291) ***(P-10934)***

Begroup (PA) D 818 638-4563
516 Burchett St Glendale (91203) ***(P-20501)***

Begroup D 626 359-9371
1763 Royal Oaks Dr Ofc Duarte (91010) ***(P-19749)***

Behavioral H Bakersfield C 661 398-1800
5201 White Ln Bakersfield (93309) ***(P-21385)***

Behavioral Health, Lancaster *Also called Kaiser Foundation Hospitals* ***(P-19078)***

Behavioral Health Resources C 951 275-8400
5900 Brockton Ave Riverside (92506) ***(P-21386)***

Behavioral Health Services, Mount Shasta *Also called County of Siskiyou* ***(P-22009)***

Behavioral Health Services Inc (PA) E 310 679-9031
15519 Crenshaw Blvd Gardena (90249) ***(P-22938)***

Behavioral Health Services Inc D 562 599-4194
1775 Chestnut Ave Long Beach (90813) ***(P-22939)***

Behavioral Health Services Inc D 909 865-2336
2180 Valley Blvd Pomona (91768) ***(P-22940)***

Behavioral Health Svcs Dept, Long Beach *Also called Childnet Youth & Fmly Svcs Inc* ***(P-23862)***

Behavioral Health Works Inc D 800 249-1266
1301 E Orangewood Ave Anaheim (92805) ***(P-22184)***

Behavioral Hlth Recovery Svcs, Modesto *Also called County of Stanislaus* ***(P-24166)***

Behavioral Intervention Assn E 510 652-7445
2354 Powell St A Emeryville (94608) ***(P-14480)***

Behavioral Learning Center Inc D 661 254-7086
28245 Avenue Crocker # 220 Valencia (91355) ***(P-22941)***

Behavioral Medicine Center, Redlands *Also called Loma Linda University Med Ctr* ***(P-21013)***

Behavoral Autism Therapies LLC (PA) C 909 483-5000
2930 Inland Empire Blvd Ontario (91764) ***(P-22942)***

Behr Process Sales Company C 714 545-7101
3000 S Main St Apt 84e Santa Ana (92707) ***(P-26896)***

Behringer Harvard Wilshire Blv..............D.....310 475-8711
  10740 Wilshire Blvd Los Angeles (90024) *(P-12051)*
Being Fit Fitness Centers, San Diego *Also called Being Fit Inc (P-18123)*
Being Fit Inc (PA)..............D.....858 549-3456
  8292 Mira Mesa Blvd San Diego (92126) *(P-18123)*
Being Fit Inc..............D.....858 483-9294
  4971 Clairemont Dr Ste A San Diego (92117) *(P-18124)*
Beitler & Associates Inc (PA)..............C.....310 820-2955
  825 S Barrington Ave Los Angeles (90049) *(P-10935)*
Beitler Commercial Realty Svcs, Los Angeles *Also called Beitler & Associates Inc (P-10935)*
Bejac Corporation (PA)..............D.....714 528-6224
  569 S Van Buren St Placentia (92870) *(P-7528)*
Bekins Moving & Storage, Santa Fe Springs *Also called Bekins Moving Solutions Inc (P-4196)*
Bekins Moving Solutions Inc (PA)..............D.....562 356-9460
  12610 Shoemaker Ave Santa Fe Springs (90670) *(P-4196)*
Beks Acquisition Inc..............E.....714 744-2990
  1150 W Trenton Ave Orange (92867) *(P-3241)*
Bel Air Lighting Inc (PA)..............C.....818 768-5511
  28104 Witherspoon Pkwy Valencia (91355) *(P-7129)*
Bel Esprit Builders Inc..............E.....949 709-3500
  23112 Alcalde Dr Ste A Laguna Hills (92653) *(P-1418)*
Bel Vista Convalescent Hosp, Pasadena *Also called Robert C Hamilton (P-24053)*
Bel-Air Bay Club Ltd..............C.....310 230-4700
  16801 Pacific Coast Hwy Pacific Palisades (90272) *(P-18393)*
Bel-Air Country Club..............C.....310 472-9563
  10768 Bellagio Rd Los Angeles (90077) *(P-18394)*
Belcampo Group Inc..............D.....530 842-5200
  329 N Phillipe Ln Yreka (96097) *(P-13400)*
Belcampo Group Inc (PA)..............D.....510 250-7810
  65 Webster St Oakland (94607) *(P-421)*
Belcampo Meat, Yreka *Also called Belcampo Group Inc (P-13400)*
Belinda, Vernon *Also called New Pride Corporation (P-8100)*
Belkin Components, Playa Vista *Also called Belkin International Inc (P-7240)*
Belkin International Inc (HQ)..............B.....310 751-5100
  12045 Waterfront Dr Playa Vista (90094) *(P-7240)*
Bell Gardens Bicycle Club Inc..............A.....562 806-4646
  888 Bicycle Casino Dr Bell Gardens (90201) *(P-18633)*
Bell Pipe & Supply Co..............E.....714 772-3200
  215 E Ball Rd Anaheim (92805) *(P-7628)*
Bell Private Security Inc..............D.....714 964-9381
  18030 Brookhurst St Fountain Valley (92708) *(P-16208)*
Bell Products Inc..............D.....707 255-1811
  722 Soscol Ave NAPA (94559) *(P-2071)*
Bella Terra Carwash, Huntington Beach *Also called Russell Fisher Partnership (P-17395)*
Bella Terra Technologies Inc..............D.....650 316-6660
  1600 Amphitheatre Pkwy Mountain View (94043) *(P-5775)*
Bella Vista Healthcare Center..............D.....909 985-2731
  933 E Deodar St Ontario (91764) *(P-19750)*
Bella Vsta Trnstional Care Ctr, San Luis Obispo *Also called Bayshore Healthcare Inc (P-19746)*
Bellis Steel Company Inc (PA)..............D.....818 886-5601
  8740 Vanalden Ave Northridge (91324) *(P-3255)*
Belmont Athletic Club..............D.....562 438-3816
  4918 E 2nd St Long Beach (90803) *(P-18395)*
Belmont Bruns Construction Inc..............D.....408 977-1708
  1125 Mabury Rd San Jose (95133) *(P-1419)*
BELMONT CONVALESCENT HOSPITAL, Long Beach *Also called Country Villa Blmnt Hght Hlth (P-20533)*
Belmont Corporation..............D.....530 542-1101
  901 Park Ave South Lake Tahoe (96150) *(P-12052)*
Belmont Oaks Academy..............D.....650 593-6175
  2200 Carlmont Dr Belmont (94002) *(P-23675)*
Belmont Shores Kindercare, Long Beach *Also called Kindercare Learning Ctrs LLC (P-23738)*
Belmont Village LP..............D.....408 720-8498
  1039 E El Camino Real Sunnyvale (94087) *(P-10693)*
Belmont Village LP..............D.....858 486-5020
  13075 Evening Creek Dr S San Diego (92128) *(P-20502)*
Belmont Village LP..............D.....818 972-2405
  455 E Angeleno Ave Burbank (91501) *(P-10694)*
Belmont Village LP..............D.....310 377-9977
  5701 Crestridge Rd Rancho Palos Verdes (90275) *(P-10695)*
Belmont Village LP..............E.....323 874-7711
  2051 N Highland Ave Los Angeles (90068) *(P-10696)*
Belmont Village At Sabre Sprng, San Diego *Also called Belmont Village LP (P-20502)*
Belmont Village of Hollywood, Los Angeles *Also called Belmont Village LP (P-10696)*
Belmont Village of Sunnyvale, Sunnyvale *Also called Belmont Village LP (P-10693)*
Belvedere Hotel Partnership..............B.....310 551-2888
  9882 Santa Monica Blvd Beverly Hills (90212) *(P-12053)*
Belvedere Partnership..............D.....310 551-2888
  9882 Santa Monica Blvd Beverly Hills (90212) *(P-12054)*
Belville Enterprises Inc..............D.....858 652-6960
  6225 Nancy Ridge Dr San Diego (92121) *(P-18838)*
Bemus Landscape Inc..............B.....714 557-7910
  1225 Puerta Del Sol # 500 San Clemente (92673) *(P-1943)*
Ben Bennett Inc (PA)..............C.....949 209-9712
  3419 Via Lido 646 Newport Beach (92663) *(P-20503)*
Ben Bollinger Productions Inc..............D.....909 626-3296
  455 W Foothill Blvd Claremont (91711) *(P-17888)*
Ben F Smith Inc..............D.....858 271-4320
  8655 Miramar Pl Ste B San Diego (92121) *(P-3119)*
Ben Myerson Candy Co Inc (PA)..............B.....800 331-2829
  6550 E Washington Blvd Commerce (90040) *(P-8799)*
Ben Myerson Candy Co Inc..............D.....510 236-2233
  3463 Collins Ave Richmond (94806) *(P-8800)*
Benchmark Landscape Inc..............C.....858 513-7190
  12575 Stowe Dr Poway (92064) *(P-778)*

Benchmark-Tech Corporation..............C.....831 475-5600
  1 Chaminade Ln Santa Cruz (95065) *(P-16647)*
Benchmaster Furniture LLC..............B.....714 414-0240
  1481 N Hundley St Anaheim (92806) *(P-6505)*
Benco Dental Supply Co..............D.....714 424-0977
  3590 Harbor Gtwy N Costa Mesa (92626) *(P-6950)*
Bender Miles Construction, San Bernardino *Also called Michael Reyes (P-1543)*
Bender/Helper Impact Inc (PA)..............D.....310 473-4147
  11500 W Olympic Blvd # 655 Los Angeles (90064) *(P-26897)*
Beneficent Technology Inc..............E.....650 644-3400
  480 California Ave # 201 Palo Alto (94306) *(P-16648)*
Beneficial Administration, Irvine *Also called Pension Administrators Inc (P-13734)*
Beneficial State Bank (HQ)..............D.....510 550-8420
  1438 Webster St Ste 100 Oakland (94612) *(P-9175)*
Benefit & Risk Management Svcs..............C.....916 467-1200
  80 Iron Point Cir Ste 200 Folsom (95630) *(P-10295)*
Benefit Planning, Marina Del Rey *Also called Veba Administrators Inc (P-10541)*
Benefit Resources Group, Los Angeles *Also called Patriot Communications LLC (P-27166)*
Benefitvision Inc..............D.....818 348-3100
  5550 Topanga Canyon Blvd # 180 Woodland Hills (91367) *(P-23570)*
Benetech, Palo Alto *Also called Beneficent Technology Inc (P-16648)*
Benetech Inc (PA)..............D.....916 484-6811
  3841 N Freeway Blvd # 185 Sacramento (95834) *(P-10296)*
Benetech Inc..............E.....916 484-6811
  4420 Auburn Blvd Fl 2 Sacramento (95841) *(P-10297)*
Benetrac, San Diego *Also called Paychex Benefit Tech Inc (P-5455)*
Benettis Italia Inc..............D.....310 537-8036
  3037 E Maria St Compton (90221) *(P-6506)*
Benex LLC..............D.....310 675-6200
  169 Saxony Rd Ste 111 Encinitas (92024) *(P-7667)*
Benicia Plumbing Inc..............D.....707 745-2930
  265 W Channel Rd Benicia (94510) *(P-2072)*
Benjamin Kurzban Son Cntrl Inc..............E.....347 227-3425
  24533 Stagg St West Hills (91304) *(P-1288)*
Bennathon Corp (PA)..............D.....916 405-2100
  10278 Iron Rock Way Elk Grove (95624) *(P-1420)*
Bennett Enterprises A CA..............D.....310 534-3543
  25889 Belle Porte Ave Harbor City (90710) *(P-702)*
Bennett Landscape, Harbor City *Also called Bennett Enterprises A CA (P-702)*
Benq America Corp (HQ)..............D.....714 559-4900
  3200 Park Center Dr # 150 Costa Mesa (92626) *(P-6807)*
Bens Asphalt & Maint Co Inc..............E.....951 248-1103
  2537 Rubidoux Blvd Riverside (92509) *(P-1672)*
Bent Tree Nursing Center Inc..............D.....760 945-3033
  247 E Bobier Dr Vista (92084) *(P-19751)*
Bentley Health Care Inc..............D.....310 967-3300
  9777 Wilshire Blvd Fl 4 Beverly Hills (90212) *(P-26527)*
Bentley Systems Incorporated..............D.....925 933-2525
  1600 Riviera Ave Ste 300 Walnut Creek (94596) *(P-14674)*
Bentley-Simonson Inc..............D.....805 650-2794
  1746 S Victoria Ave Ste F Ventura (93003) *(P-976)*
Bento Box Entertainment LLC..............B.....818 333-7700
  5161 Lankershim Blvd North Hollywood (91601) *(P-17582)*
Benz - One Complete Operation, Tehachapi *Also called Pjbs Holdings Inc (P-6233)*
Berding & Weil LLP (PA)..............D.....925 838-2090
  2175 N Calif Blvd Ste 500 Walnut Creek (94596) *(P-22379)*
Beres Consulting..............D.....310 476-9941
  470 S Bentley Ave Los Angeles (90049) *(P-24324)*
Beresford Arms, The, San Francisco *Also called Beresford Corporation (P-12055)*
Beresford Corp..............C.....415 981-7386
  582 Market St Ste 912 San Francisco (94104) *(P-187)*
Beresford Corporation..............D.....415 673-9900
  635 Sutter St San Francisco (94102) *(P-12055)*
Berg Lacquer Co (PA)..............E.....323 261-8114
  3150 E Pico Blvd Los Angeles (90023) *(P-8944)*
Bergelectric Corp (PA)..............D.....760 638-2374
  3182 Lionshead Ave Carlsbad (92010) *(P-2432)*
Bergelectric Corp..............A.....760 746-1003
  650 Opper St Escondido (92029) *(P-2433)*
Bergelectric Corp..............D.....916 636-1880
  11333 Sunrise Park Dr Rancho Cordova (95742) *(P-2434)*
Bergelectric Corp..............D.....949 250-7005
  1935 Deere Ave Irvine (92606) *(P-2435)*
Bergen Brunswig Drug Company..............A.....714 385-4000
  4000 W Metropolitan Dr # 200 Orange (92868) *(P-7922)*
Bergensons Property Svcs Inc..............A.....760 631-5111
  3605 Ocean Ranch Blvd # 200 Oceanside (92056) *(P-13869)*
Berger Kahn (PA)..............D.....949 474-1880
  1 Park Plz Ste 340 Irvine (92614) *(P-22380)*
Berger Kahn..............E.....858 547-0075
  10085 Crrl Cnyn Rd Ste 21 San Diego (92131) *(P-22381)*
Berglund & Johnson Law Office, Woodland Hills *Also called Law Offices Berglund & Johnson (P-22637)*
Bergman Kprs LLC (PA)..............C.....714 924-7000
  2850 Saturn St Ste 100 Brea (92821) *(P-1421)*
Berkeley 75 Hsing Partners LP..............E.....510 705-1488
  1936 University Ave # 130 Berkeley (94704) *(P-10936)*
Berkeley Albany YMCA, Concord *Also called Young MNS Chrstn Assn of E Bay (P-24764)*
Berkeley Cement Inc..............D.....510 525-8175
  1200 6th St Berkeley (94710) *(P-3120)*
Berkeley Clinic Auxullary..............D.....510 525-7844
  10052 San Pablo Ave El Cerrito (94530) *(P-24807)*
Berkeley Country Club..............D.....510 233-7550
  7901 Cutting Blvd El Cerrito (94530) *(P-18396)*
Berkeley Electronic Press, Berkeley *Also called Internet-Journals LLC (P-16037)*
Berkeley Lights Inc (PA)..............D.....510 898-1433
  5858 Horton St Ste 320 Emeryville (94608) *(P-25970)*
Berkeley Pines Care Center, Berkeley *Also called A T Associates Inc (P-20475)*

Employee Codes: A=Over 500 employees, B=251-500
C=101-250, D=51-100, E=50

2020 Directory of California
Wholesalers and Services Companies

© Mergent Inc. 1-800-342-5647

1191

Berkeley Research Group LLC (PA).....C.....510 285-3300
2200 Powell St Ste 1200 Emeryville (94608) ***(P-27002)***
Berkeley Student Coop Inc.....D.....510 848-1936
2424 Ridge Rd Berkeley (94709) ***(P-13169)***
Berkeley Symphony Orchestra.....E.....510 841-2800
1942 University Ave # 207 Berkeley (94704) ***(P-17966)***
Berkeley Unified School Dst.....E.....510 644-6182
1314 7th St Berkeley (94710) ***(P-3787)***
Berkley East Convalescent Hosp, Santa Monica *Also called Arizona and 21st Corp* ***(P-20494)***
Berkley Vly Cnvlscent Hosp Inc.....C.....818 786-0020
6600 Sepulveda Blvd Van Nuys (91411) ***(P-19752)***
Berkshire Hathaway, Lancaster *Also called V Troth Inc* ***(P-11497)***
Berkshire Hathaway Homestates (HQ).....C.....415 433-1650
1 California St Ste 600 San Francisco (94111) ***(P-10298)***
Berkshire Hathaway Homestates.....D.....619 686-8424
2020 Camino Del Rio N San Diego (92108) ***(P-10299)***
Berkshire Hattaway Home Servcs.....D.....626 913-2808
16404 Colima Rd Hacienda Heights (91745) ***(P-10937)***
Berkshire Mortgage Fin Corp.....D.....949 754-6300
7575 Irvine Center Dr # 200 Irvine (92618) ***(P-9528)***
Bermuda Dunes Country Club.....E.....760 360-2481
42765 Adams St Bermuda Dunes (92203) ***(P-18397)***
Bermuda Dunes Learning Ctr Inc.....E.....760 772-7127
42115 Yucca Ln Bermuda Dunes (92203) ***(P-23676)***
Bernard Osher Marin Jewish Com.....C.....415 444-8000
200 N San Pedro Rd San Rafael (94903) ***(P-22943)***
Bernardo Hts Healthcare Inc.....D.....858 673-0101
11895 Avenue Of Industry San Diego (92128) ***(P-20504)***
Bernards Builders Inc.....B.....818 898-1521
555 1st St San Fernando (91340) ***(P-1229)***
Bernards Inc.....D.....818 898-1521
555 1st St San Fernando (91340) ***(P-26155)***
Bernardy Ctr For Medcly Frgled, San Diego *Also called Rady Chld Hospital-San Diego* ***(P-26373)***
Bernel Inc.....C.....714 778-6070
501 W Southern Ave Orange (92865) ***(P-2073)***
Berro Management.....D.....562 432-3444
3950 Parmnt Blvd Ste 115 Lakewood (90712) ***(P-10938)***
Berry & Berry Inc (PA).....D.....559 674-2491
413 W Yosemite Ave # 106 Madera (93637) ***(P-1084)***
Berry & Berry Law Firm.....D.....510 250-0200
475 14th St Ste 550 Oakland (94612) ***(P-22382)***
Berry Construction, Madera *Also called Berry & Berry Inc* ***(P-1084)***
Berry Petroleum Company LLC (HQ).....D.....661 616-3900
5201 Truxtun Ave Ste 100 Bakersfield (93309) ***(P-977)***
Berry Seed & Feed, Keyes *Also called A L Gilbert Company* ***(P-8675)***
Berryessa Union School Dst.....D.....408 923-1960
1100 Summerdale Dr San Jose (95132) ***(P-24481)***
Berryman Health Inc.....D.....707 462-8864
1349 S Dora St Ukiah (95482) ***(P-20505)***
Bershtel Enterprises LLC (PA).....C.....626 301-9214
2745 Huntington Dr Duarte (91010) ***(P-16649)***
Bersin By Deloitte, San Francisco *Also called Deloitte Consulting LLP* ***(P-26580)***
Bert E Jessup Transportation.....D.....408 848-3390
641 Old Gilroy St Gilroy (95020) ***(P-3970)***
Bertolottis Ceres Disposal.....D.....209 537-8000
231 Flamingo Rd Ceres (95307) ***(P-6159)***
Bertram Capital Management LLC.....B.....650 358-5000
950 Tower Ln Ste 1000 Foster City (94404) ***(P-11888)***
Bess Testlab Inc.....E.....408 988-0101
2461 Tripaldi Way Hayward (94545) ***(P-1833)***
Best Best & Krieger LLP (PA).....C.....951 686-1450
3390 University Ave # 500 Riverside (92501) ***(P-22383)***
Best Best & Krieger LLP.....E.....949 263-2600
18101 Von Karman Ave # 1000 Irvine (92612) ***(P-22384)***
BEST Consulting Inc.....E.....916 448-2050
8795 Folsom Blvd Ste 103 Sacramento (95826) ***(P-20413)***
Best Contracting Services Inc.....D.....510 886-7240
4301 Bettencourt Way Union City (94587) ***(P-3027)***
Best Financial, The, Signal Hill *Also called First American Team Realty Inc* ***(P-11140)***
Best Friends Animal Society.....B.....818 643-3989
15321 Brand Blvd Mission Hills (91345) ***(P-24808)***
Best Interiors Inc (PA).....C.....714 490-7999
2100 E Via Burton Anaheim (92806) ***(P-2754)***
Best Life and Health Insur Co.....D.....949 253-4080
17701 Mitchell N Irvine (92614) ***(P-9863)***
Best Overnight Express, Irwindale *Also called Best Overnite Express Inc* ***(P-3971)***
Best Overnite Express Inc (PA).....C.....626 256-6340
406 Live Oak Ave Irwindale (91706) ***(P-3971)***
Best Tours & Travel, Fresno *Also called B T & T Travel Inc* ***(P-4817)***
Best Valet Parking Corporation.....D.....800 708-2538
12792 Valley View St # 201 Garden Grove (92845) ***(P-13401)***
Best Way Disposal Co Inc.....D.....760 244-9773
17105 Mesa St Hesperia (92345) ***(P-6160)***
Best Western, San Simeon *Also called Cavalier Inn Incorporated* ***(P-12126)***
Best Western, Monterey *Also called Bayview Properties Inc* ***(P-12047)***
Best Western, South Lake Tahoe *Also called Belmont Corporation* ***(P-12052)***
Best Western, Santa Barbara *Also called Encina Pepper Tree Joint Ventr* ***(P-12250)***
Best Western, Aptos *Also called Seacliff Inn Inc* ***(P-12897)***
Best Western, San Diego *Also called Tic World-Wide Corp* ***(P-13026)***
Best Western, Victorville *Also called L & S Investment Co Inc* ***(P-12524)***
Best Western, South San Francisco *Also called Grosvenor Properties Ltd* ***(P-12322)***
Best Western, Carpinteria *Also called Carpinteria Motor Inn Inc* ***(P-12119)***
Best Western Amador Inn, Jackson *Also called Sita Ram LLC* ***(P-12931)***
Best Western Bayshore Inn.....E.....707 268-8005
3500 Broadway Eureka (95503) ***(P-12056)***
Best Western Bayside Inn, San Diego *Also called T I C Hotels Inc* ***(P-13012)***
Best Western Golden Sails Ht, Torrance *Also called Long Beach Golden Sails Inc* ***(P-12562)***
Best Western Half Moon Bay, Half Moon Bay *Also called Pacifica Hotel Company* ***(P-12702)***
Best Western Hilltop Inn.....E.....530 221-6100
2300 Hilltop Dr Redding (96002) ***(P-12057)***
Best Western Hotel Tomo.....E.....415 921-4000
1800 Sutter St San Francisco (94115) ***(P-12058)***
Best Western International Inc.....D.....559 592-8118
805 S Kaweah Ave Exeter (93221) ***(P-12059)***
Best Western Island Palms, San Diego *Also called Bartell Hotels* ***(P-12041)***
Best Western Park Place, Anaheim *Also called Best Western Stovalls Inn* ***(P-12061)***
Best Western Pasada At Harbor, San Diego *Also called Tesi Investment Company LLC* ***(P-13021)***
Best Western Plus-Heritage Inn.....E.....209 474-3301
111 E March Ln Stockton (95207) ***(P-12060)***
Best Western Stockton Inn, Stockton *Also called Westland Hotel Corporation* ***(P-13090)***
Best Western Stovalls Inn.....E.....714 776-4800
1544 S Harbor Blvd Anaheim (92802) ***(P-12061)***
Best Western Stovalls Inn (PA).....C.....714 956-4430
1110 W Katella Ave Anaheim (92802) ***(P-12062)***
Best Western, The Beach Resort, Monterey *Also called Bayview Properties Inc* ***(P-12046)***
Best Wstn Carmel Mission Inn, Carmel *Also called Trevi Partners A Calif LP* ***(P-13040)***
Best Wstn El Rancho Inn Suites, Millbrae *Also called El Rancho Motel Inc* ***(P-12244)***
Best Wstn Half Moon Bay Lodge, Half Moon Bay *Also called Half Moon Bay Lodge* ***(P-12328)***
Best Wstn Plus Clnga Inn Sites, Coalinga *Also called Merchant Valley Corp* ***(P-12608)***
Best-Way Distributing Co, Sylmar *Also called Allied Company Holdings Inc* ***(P-8745)***
Bestitcom Inc (PA).....D.....602 667-5613
1464 Madera Rd Simi Valley (93065) ***(P-15948)***
Beston Development.....D.....619 232-6315
1055 1st Ave San Diego (92101) ***(P-12063)***
Bestway Delivery, Van Nuys *Also called Mercury Messenger Service Inc* ***(P-16917)***
Bestway Recycling Company Inc (PA).....D.....323 588-8157
2268 Firestone Blvd Los Angeles (90002) ***(P-7752)***
Bet Tzedek.....D.....323 939-0506
3250 Wilshire Blvd Fl 13 Los Angeles (90010) ***(P-22385)***
Beta Healthcare Group (PA).....D.....925 838-6070
1443 Danville Blvd Alamo (94507) ***(P-10160)***
Bethel Lutheran Home Inc.....D.....559 896-4900
2280 Dockery Ave Selma (93662) ***(P-20506)***
Bethel Retirement Community.....D.....209 577-1901
2345 Scenic Dr Modesto (95355) ***(P-20507)***
Bethesda Lthran Cmmunities Inc.....D.....559 636-6300
5440 W Wren Ave Visalia (93291) ***(P-23835)***
Bettendorf Enterprises Inc.....D.....530 365-1937
20943 Bettendorf Way Anderson (96007) ***(P-3972)***
Bettendorf Trucking, Anderson *Also called Bettendorf Enterprises Inc* ***(P-3972)***
Better Homes and Gardens Mason.....D.....925 776-2740
5887 Lone Tree Way Ste A Antioch (94531) ***(P-10939)***
Better Mens Clothes, Los Angeles *Also called Hirsh Inc* ***(P-1026)***
Better Way Services.....D.....661 326-6444
5329 Office Center Ct # 100 Bakersfield (93309) ***(P-22944)***
Betterworks Systems Inc.....D.....650 656-9013
999 Main St Redwood City (94063) ***(P-15257)***
Betty Ford Center (HQ).....C.....760 773-4100
39000 Bob Hope Dr Rancho Mirage (92270) ***(P-21451)***
Betty Jimenez, Brawley *Also called Clinicas De Slud Del Peblo Inc* ***(P-18907)***
Beutler Heating & AC, Fairfield *Also called Villara Corporation* ***(P-3106)***
Beutler Heating & AC, Manteca *Also called Villara Corporation* ***(P-2313)***
Beverly, Fresno *Also called Golden Living LLC* ***(P-19948)***
Beverly, Fowler *Also called Golden Living LLC* ***(P-19949)***
Beverly, Beverly Hills *Also called Bhrac LLC* ***(P-17202)***
Beverly, Ridgecrest *Also called Golden Living LLC* ***(P-21751)***
Beverly Blvd Leaseco LLC.....D.....310 278-5444
8555 Beverly Blvd Los Angeles (90048) ***(P-12064)***
Beverly Center, Los Angeles *Also called La Cienega Associates* ***(P-11241)***
Beverly Community Hosp Assn.....B.....323 889-2452
101 E Beverly Blvd # 104 Montebello (90640) ***(P-20763)***
Beverly Community Hosp Assn (PA).....C.....323 726-1222
309 W Beverly Blvd Montebello (90640) ***(P-20764)***
Beverly Community Hosp Assn.....A.....323 725-1519
1920 W Whittier Blvd Montebello (90640) ***(P-20765)***
Beverly Health Care Corp (PA).....E.....805 642-1736
5445 Everglades St Ventura (93003) ***(P-26156)***
Beverly Healthcare, Panorama City *Also called Golden Living LLC* ***(P-20571)***
Beverly Healthcare, Costa Mesa *Also called Golden Living LLC* ***(P-19950)***
Beverly Healthcare, Montrose *Also called Golden Living LLC* ***(P-20572)***
Beverly Healthcare, San Francisco *Also called Golden Living LLC* ***(P-19953)***
Beverly Healthcare, Sonora *Also called Golden Living LLC* ***(P-20573)***
Beverly Healthcare, Modesto *Also called Beaver Dam Health Care Center* ***(P-20500)***
Beverly Healthcare, Los Gatos *Also called Golden Living LLC* ***(P-19954)***
Beverly Healthcare, Seal Beach *Also called Golden Living LLC* ***(P-20574)***
Beverly Healthcare, Oxnard *Also called Golden Living LLC* ***(P-19956)***
Beverly Healthcare, Ventura *Also called Golden Living LLC* ***(P-19957)***
Beverly Healthcare, Lodi *Also called Golden Living LLC* ***(P-19958)***
Beverly Healthcare, West Covina *Also called Beaver Dam Health Care Center* ***(P-19747)***
Beverly Healthcare, Madera *Also called Golden Living LLC* ***(P-20575)***
Beverly Healthcare, Capistrano Beach *Also called Golden Living LLC* ***(P-19962)***
Beverly Healthcare, Murrieta *Also called Golden Living LLC* ***(P-23245)***
Beverly Healthcare, Fresno *Also called Golden Living LLC* ***(P-19965)***
Beverly Healthcare, San Jose *Also called Golden Living LLC* ***(P-23938)***
Beverly Healthcare, Modesto *Also called Golden Living LLC* ***(P-19966)***
Beverly Healthcare, Los Gatos *Also called Golden Living LLC* ***(P-19967)***

Beverly Healthcare, Chico *Also called Golden Living LLC* ***(P-19970)***
Beverly Healthcare, Merced *Also called Golden Living LLC* ***(P-20579)***
Beverly Healthcare, Newman *Also called Golden Living LLC* ***(P-19971)***
Beverly Hills Active Club, Los Angeles *Also called 24 Hour Fitness Usa Inc* ***(P-18095)***
Beverly Hills Country Club ....C....310 836-4400
3084 Motor Ave Los Angeles (90064) ***(P-11543)***
Beverly Hills Hotel, Beverly Hills *Also called Sajahtera Inc* ***(P-12865)***
Beverly Hills Lingual Inst ....E....323 651-5000
8383 Wilshire Blvd # 250 Beverly Hills (90211) ***(P-16650)***
Beverly Hills Luxury Hotel LLC ....B....310 274-9999
1801 Century Park E # 1200 Los Angeles (90067) ***(P-12065)***
Beverly Hills Luxury Interiors, Los Angeles *Also called Kenneth Brdwick Intr Dsgns Inc* ***(P-16868)***
Beverly Hills Plaza Hotel, Los Angeles *Also called Donald T Sterling Corporation* ***(P-12225)***
Beverly Hills Polc Ofcrs Assoc ....D....310 288-1755
464 N Rexford Dr Beverly Hills (90210) ***(P-24381)***
BEVERLY HOSPITAL, Montebello *Also called Beverly Community Hosp Assn* ***(P-20764)***
Beverly Pl Memory Care Cmnty, Los Angeles *Also called Silverado Senior Living Inc* ***(P-20687)***
Beverly Radiology Med Group (PA) ....C....310 975-1500
465 N Roxbury Dr Ste 101 Beverly Hills (90210) ***(P-18839)***
Beverly Sunstone Hills LLC ....D....310 228-4100
1177 S Beverly Dr Los Angeles (90035) ***(P-12066)***
Beverly West Health Care Inc ....D....323 938-2451
1020 S Fairfax Ave Los Angeles (90019) ***(P-19753)***
Beverlywood Realty Inc ....E....310 836-8322
2800 S Robertson Blvd Los Angeles (90034) ***(P-10940)***
Bex Portfolio LLC ....D....650 494-3700
925 E Meadow Dr Palo Alto (94303) ***(P-16651)***
Beyer Park Villas LLC ....D....209 236-1900
3529 Forest Glenn Dr Modesto (95355) ***(P-23836)***
BFI Waste Services LLC ....D....559 275-1551
5501 N Golden State Blvd Fresno (93722) ***(P-6161)***
BFI Waste Systems N Amer Inc ....D....805 965-5248
800 Cacique St Santa Barbara (93103) ***(P-6162)***
BFI Waste Systems N Amer Inc ....D....831 775-3850
271 Rianda St Salinas (93901) ***(P-6163)***
BFI Waste Systems N Amer Inc ....D....510 657-1350
42600 Boyce Rd Fremont (94538) ***(P-6164)***
Bfp Fire Protection Inc ....D....831 461-1100
17 Janis Way Scotts Valley (95066) ***(P-2074)***
Bgrs Relocation Inc (HQ) ....D....949 794-7900
3333 Michelson Dr # 1000 Irvine (92612) ***(P-11824)***
Bh Partn A Calif Limit Partne (PA) ....B....858 539-7635
998 W Mission Bay Dr San Diego (92109) ***(P-12067)***
Bh Partn A Calif Limit Partne ....D....858 453-4420
11480 N Torrey Pines Rd A La Jolla (92037) ***(P-12068)***
Bhandal Bros Inc ....E....831 728-2691
2490 San Juan Rd Hollister (95023) ***(P-3973)***
Bhandal Bros Trucking Inc ....D....831 728-2691
2490 San Juan Rd Hollister (95023) ***(P-3974)***
Bhatnagar Law Office ....E....408 564-8051
84 W Santa Clara St # 560 San Jose (95113) ***(P-22386)***
Bho LLC ....E....951 845-2220
5801 Sun Lakes Blvd Banning (92220) ***(P-23837)***
Bhr Trs Tahoe LLC ....C....530 562-3045
13031 Ritz Carlton Truckee (96161) ***(P-12069)***
Bhrac LLC ....D....310 862-1933
9777 Wilshire Blvd # 517 Beverly Hills (90212) ***(P-17202)***
Bi Warehousing Inc ....E....530 671-8787
1490 Bridge St Yuba City (95993) ***(P-6426)***
Bi-County Ambulance Service ....E....530 674-2780
1700 Poole Blvd Yuba City (95993) ***(P-3652)***
BI-RITE FOODSERVICE DISTRIBUTO, Brisbane *Also called Bi-Rite Restaurant Sup Co Inc* ***(P-8157)***
Bi-Rite Restaurant Sup Co Inc ....B....415 656-0187
123 S Hill Dr Brisbane (94005) ***(P-8157)***
Biagi Bros Inc ....C....909 390-6910
3655 E Airport Dr Ontario (91761) ***(P-3975)***
Biagi Bros Inc ....D....707 745-8115
650 Stone Rd Benicia (94510) ***(P-3976)***
Biagi Brothers Bezzerides Co, Benicia *Also called Biagi Bros Inc* ***(P-3976)***
Bianchi Ag Services Inc ....D....530 923-7675
3056 Colusa Hwy Yuba City (95993) ***(P-654)***
Biarca Inc (PA) ....D....408 564-4465
333 W San Carlos St # 600 San Jose (95110) ***(P-15949)***
Bicara Ltd ....B....310 316-6222
318 Avenue I Ste 65 Redondo Beach (90277) ***(P-8400)***
Bickmore and Associates Inc (HQ) ....D....916 244-1100
1750 Creekside Oaks Dr # 200 Sacramento (95833) ***(P-10300)***
Bickmore Risk Svcs Consulting, Sacramento *Also called Bickmore and Associates Inc* ***(P-10300)***
Bicycle Casino LP ....A....562 806-4646
888 Bicycle Casino Dr Bell Gardens (90201) ***(P-12070)***
Bicycle Club Casino, Bell Gardens *Also called Bell Gardens Bicycle Club Inc* ***(P-18633)***
Bicycle Hotel and Casino, Bell Gardens *Also called Bicycle Casino LP* ***(P-12070)***
Bidmail, Tustin *Also called Internet Blueprint Inc* ***(P-14885)***
Bienvenidos Community Hlth Ctr, Los Angeles *Also called Via Care Cmnty Hlth Ctr Inc* ***(P-19581)***
Big 5 Corp ....B....951 774-1600
6125 Sycamore Canyon Blvd Riverside (92507) ***(P-4376)***
Big 5 Sporting Goods, Riverside *Also called Big 5 Corp* ***(P-4376)***
Big 5 Sporting Goods Corp ....B....323 755-2663
11310 Crenshaw Blvd Inglewood (90303) ***(P-18634)***
Big Bear City Cmnty Svcs Dst (PA) ....D....909 585-2565
139 E Big Bear Blvd Big Bear City (92314) ***(P-6128)***
Big Canyon Country Club ....C....949 644-5404
1 Big Canyon Dr Newport Beach (92660) ***(P-18398)***
Big Four Restaurant, San Francisco *Also called Nob Hill Properties Inc* ***(P-12647)***
Big Health Inc ....D....415 867-3473
461 Bush St Ste 200 San Francisco (94108) ***(P-20414)***
Big Joe California North Inc (PA) ....C....510 785-6900
25932 Eden Landing Rd Hayward (94545) ***(P-7529)***
Big Joe Handling Systems, Hayward *Also called Big Joe California North Inc* ***(P-7529)***
Big League Dreams Jurupa LLC ....D....951 685-6900
10550 Cntu Gllano Rnch Rd Jurupa Valley (91752) ***(P-18052)***
Big Lgue Drams Chino Hills LLC ....D....909 287-6900
16333 Fairfield Ranch Rd Chino Hills (91709) ***(P-18053)***
Big Lgue Dreams Consulting LLC ....C....619 846-8855
2155 Trumble Rd Perris (92571) ***(P-18054)***
Big Lgue Dreams Consulting LLC ....C....760 324-5600
33700 Date Palm Dr Cathedral City (92234) ***(P-13144)***
Big Lgue Dreams Consulting LLC ....C....530 223-1177
20155 Viking Way Redding (96003) ***(P-18399)***
Big Lgue Dreams Consulting LLC ....C....626 839-1100
2100 S Azusa Ave West Covina (91792) ***(P-18055)***
Big River Lodge, Mendocino *Also called Big River Ltd-Design* ***(P-12071)***
Big River Ltd-Design ....D....707 937-5615
44850 Comptche Ukiah Rd Mendocino (95460) ***(P-12071)***
Big Sandy Rancheria, Auberry *Also called Mono Wind Casino* ***(P-12625)***
Big Sky Country Club LLC ....D....805 522-4653
3301 Lost Canyons Dr Simi Valley (93063) ***(P-18222)***
Big Star, South Gate *Also called Koos Manufacturing Inc* ***(P-16874)***
Big Switch Networks Inc (PA) ....D....650 322-6510
3111 Coronado Dr Bldg A Santa Clara (95054) ***(P-15258)***
Big Valley Mortgage, Roseville *Also called American Pacific Mortgage Corp* ***(P-9521)***
Big3 Basketball LLC ....D....213 417-2013
644 S Figueroa St Los Angeles (90017) ***(P-18056)***
Biggest Lser Ftnes Rdge Malibu, Malibu *Also called Fitness Ridge Malibu LLC* ***(P-12267)***
Biggie Crane and Ritting, San Leandro *Also called Galena Equipment Rental LLC* ***(P-14096)***
Biggs Cardosa Associates Inc (PA) ....D....408 296-5515
865 The Alameda San Jose (95126) ***(P-24962)***
Bigham Taylor Roofing Corp ....D....510 886-0197
22721 Alice St Hayward (94541) ***(P-3028)***
Bighorn Golf Club ....C....760 773-2468
255 Palowet Dr Palm Desert (92260) ***(P-18400)***
Bigrentz Inc ....D....855 999-5438
1063 Mcgaw Ave Ste 200 Irvine (92614) ***(P-14093)***
Bigrentz.com, Irvine *Also called Bigrentz Inc* ***(P-14093)***
Bill Brown Construction Co ....D....408 297-3738
242 Phelan Ave San Jose (95112) ***(P-1230)***
Bill Brown Construction Co ....D....408 297-3738
242 Phelan Ave San Jose (95112) ***(P-1085)***
Bill Howe Plumbing Inc ....D....800 245-5469
9085 Aero Dr Ste B San Diego (92123) ***(P-2075)***
Bill Nelson GEC, Fresno *Also called Bill Nlson Gen Engrg Cnstr Inc* ***(P-1834)***
Bill Nlson Gen Engrg Cnstr Inc ....D....559 439-1756
7600 N Ingram Ave Ste 126 Fresno (93711) ***(P-1834)***
Bill Papich Construction Inc ....E....805 489-9420
398 Sunrise Ter Arroyo Grande (93420) ***(P-1944)***
Bill Wilson Center (PA) ....D....408 243-0222
3490 The Alameda Santa Clara (95050) ***(P-10301)***
Billabong U S A, Huntington Beach *Also called Burleigh Point Ltd* ***(P-10952)***
Billcom Inc ....C....650 353-3301
1810 Embarcadero Rd Palo Alto (94303) ***(P-15259)***
Billing Services Plus DBA Apex ....D....415 604-3515
70 Dorman Ave San Francisco (94124) ***(P-13870)***
Bilt-Well Roofing & Mtl Co, Los Angeles *Also called Sbb Roofing Inc* ***(P-3097)***
Biltmore Hotel ....C....408 988-8411
2151 Laurelwood Rd Santa Clara (95054) ***(P-12072)***
Biltwell Roofing, Los Angeles *Also called R F R Corporation* ***(P-11595)***
Binding Site Inc (PA) ....D....858 453-9177
6730 Mesa Ridge Rd Ste B San Diego (92121) ***(P-6951)***
Binex Line Corp (PA) ....D....310 416-8600
19515 S Vermont Ave Torrance (90502) ***(P-4898)***
Bio Industries Inc ....E....530 529-3290
2060 Montgomery Rd Red Bluff (96080) ***(P-432)***
Bio-Mdcal Applications Cal Inc ....D....562 920-2070
10116 Rosecrans Ave Bellflower (90706) ***(P-21913)***
Bio-Mdcal Applications Cal Inc ....E....626 457-9002
1801 W Valley Blvd # 102 Alhambra (91803) ***(P-21914)***
Bio-Mdcal Applications Cal Inc ....D....951 343-7700
3470 La Sierra Ave Ste E Riverside (92503) ***(P-21915)***
Bio-Mdical Applications Rl Inc ....D....559 221-6311
3636 N 1st St Ste 144 Fresno (93726) ***(P-21916)***
Bio-Med Services Inc ....D....909 235-4400
3300 E Guasti Rd Ontario (91761) ***(P-22185)***
Bio-Reference Laboratories Inc ....C....408 341-8600
2605 Winchester Blvd Campbell (95008) ***(P-21507)***
Biocept Inc ....D....858 320-8200
5810 Nancy Ridge Dr # 150 San Diego (92121) ***(P-25720)***
Bioclinca (PA) ....C....415 817-8900
7707 Gateway Blvd Fl 3 Newark (94560) ***(P-14675)***
Bioclinca ....E....503 284-3334
7707 Gateway Blvd Ste 300 Newark (94560) ***(P-25721)***
Biocompare, South San Francisco *Also called Comparenetworks Inc* ***(P-25734)***
Biomat Usa Inc (HQ) ....E....323 225-2221
2410 Lillyvale Ave Los Angeles (90032) ***(P-22186)***
Biomat Usa Inc ....D....661 863-0621
246 Bernard St Bakersfield (93305) ***(P-22187)***
Biomed Realty LP (HQ) ....E....858 485-9840
17190 Bernardo Center Dr San Diego (92128) ***(P-11845)***
Biomed Realty Trust Inc ....D....510 505-0932
7677 Gateway Blvd Ste 100 Newark (94560) ***(P-10941)***

A L P H A B E T I C

Employee Codes: A=Over 500 employees, B=251-500
C=101-250, D=51-100, E=50
2020 Directory of California
Wholesalers and Services Companies
© Mergent Inc. 1-800-342-5647
1193

Biomedicure LLC ......D......858 586-1888
7940 Silverton Ave # 107 San Diego (92126) ***(P-25722)***
Bionetics Corporation ......E......650 604-5327
P.O. Box 115 Moffett Field (94035) ***(P-25723)***
Bioscreen Testing Services Inc (HQ) ......D......310 214-0043
3904 Del Amo Blvd Ste 801 Torrance (90503) ***(P-26058)***
Biosite Inc ......D......510 683-9063
9975 Summers Ridge Rd San Diego (92121) ***(P-6952)***
Biospace Inc ......D......323 932-6503
13850 Cerritos Corprt Dr C Cerritos (90703) ***(P-25724)***
Biotheranostics Inc (PA) ......D......877 886-6739
9640 Towne Centre Dr # 200 San Diego (92121) ***(P-21508)***
Birch Aquarium At Scripps ......E......858 534-4109
2300 Expedition Way La Jolla (92037) ***(P-24303)***
Birch Ptrick Convalescent Cntr, Chula Vista *Also called Sharp Healthcare* ***(P-20252)***
Bird Mrlla Bxer Wlpert A Prof ......D......310 201-2100
1875 Century Park E Fl 23 Los Angeles (90067) ***(P-22387)***
Bird Rides Inc (PA) ......D......866 205-2442
406 Broadway Ste 369 Santa Monica (90401) ***(P-14676)***
Birkenstock Usa Lp (HQ) ......D......415 884-3200
8171 Redwood Blvd Novato (94945) ***(P-8122)***
Birnam Wood Golf Club (PA) ......D......805 969-2223
1941 E Valley Rd Santa Barbara (93108) ***(P-18401)***
Birst Inc ......B......415 766-4800
45 Fremont St Ste 1800 San Francisco (94105) ***(P-14677)***
Birtcher Andrson Investors LLC ......E......949 545-0526
31910 Del Obispo St # 100 San Juan Capistrano (92675) ***(P-11889)***
Birtcher/Aetna Laguna Hills ......D......949 458-2311
24903 Moulton Pkwy Ofc Laguna Hills (92653) ***(P-10697)***
Birth Choice of San Marco ......D......760 744-1313
277 S Rancho Santa Fe Rd San Marcos (92078) ***(P-22945)***
Bishop Paiute Gaming Corp ......C......760 872-6005
2742 N Sierra Hwy Bishop (93514) ***(P-12073)***
Bishop Ranch Veterinary Center (PA) ......D......925 743-9300
2000 Bishop Dr San Ramon (94583) ***(P-573)***
Bishop Waste Disposal Inc ......E......760 872-6561
100 Snland Reservation Rd Bishop (93514) ***(P-6165)***
Bissell Bros Bldg Maint Servic, Rancho Cordova *Also called Bissell Brothers Janitorial* ***(P-13871)***
Bissell Brothers Janitorial ......D......916 635-1852
3207 Luyung Dr Rancho Cordova (95742) ***(P-13871)***
Bitalign Inc ......D......415 395-9525
201 Post St Fl 11 San Francisco (94108) ***(P-14678)***
Bite Communications LLC (HQ) ......D......415 365-0222
100 Montgomery St # 1101 San Francisco (94104) ***(P-26528)***
Bitech-Ace A Joint Venture ......D......714 521-1477
7371 Walnut Ave Buena Park (90620) ***(P-3121)***
Bitfone Corporation (PA) ......E......949 234-7000
32451 Golden Lantern # 301 Laguna Niguel (92677) ***(P-14679)***
Bitglass Inc (PA) ......D......408 337-0190
675 Campbell Tech Pkwy # 225 Campbell (95008) ***(P-14680)***
Bitgravity, Burlingame *Also called Tata Communications Amer Inc* ***(P-17080)***
Bittorrent Inc ......E......408 641-4219
612 Howard St Ste 400 San Francisco (94105) ***(P-14681)***
Bizcom Electronics Inc (HQ) ......C......408 262-7877
1171 Montague Expy Milpitas (95035) ***(P-6808)***
Bizmatics Inc (PA) ......C......408 873-3030
4010 Moorpark Ave Ste 222 San Jose (95117) ***(P-15260)***
Bizringer Inc ......D......949 396-0162
1221 E Dyer Rd Ste 250 Santa Ana (92705) ***(P-5365)***
Bjj Company LLC (PA) ......D......209 941-8361
1040 W Kettleman Ln Lodi (95240) ***(P-3977)***
BJs Restaurant Operations Co ......C......714 500-2440
7755 Center Ave Ste 300 Huntington Beach (92647) ***(P-26157)***
BJs Restaurants Inc ......C......209 526-8850
3401 Dale Rd Ste 840 Modesto (95356) ***(P-7781)***
Bkf Engineers (PA) ......C......650 482-6300
255 Shoreline Dr Ste 200 Redwood City (94065) ***(P-24963)***
BKK Corporation (PA) ......D......626 965-0911
2210 S Azusa Ave West Covina (91792) ***(P-6166)***
BKM Officeworks, San Diego *Also called Wmk Office San Diego LLC* ***(P-6539)***
Blach Construction Company (PA) ......D......408 244-7100
2244 Blach Pl Ste 100 San Jose (95131) ***(P-1333)***
Black & Veatch Corporation ......E......913 458-2000
5 Peters Canyon Rd # 300 Irvine (92606) ***(P-24964)***
Black & White TV Inc ......E......310 855-1040
8756 Dorrington Ave West Hollywood (90048) ***(P-17434)***
Black Bear Security Services ......C......415 559-5159
2016 Oakdale Ave Ste B San Francisco (94124) ***(P-16209)***
Black Box Network Services, Los Angeles *Also called Scottel Voice & Data Inc* ***(P-17461)***
Black Diamond Electric Inc ......D......925 777-3440
2595 W 10th St Antioch (94509) ***(P-2436)***
Black Dog Farms of California ......C......760 356-2951
530 W 6th St Holtville (92250) ***(P-37)***
Black Dot Wireless LLC ......D......949 502-3800
27271 Las Ramblas Ste 300 Mission Viejo (92691) ***(P-5198)***
Black Excellence, Los Angeles *Also called Netflix Productions LLC* ***(P-17639)***
Black Gold Golf Club ......D......714 961-0060
1 Black Gold Dr Yorba Linda (92886) ***(P-18223)***
Black Jack Farms, Santa Maria *Also called Blackjack Farms De La Costa CN* ***(P-302)***
Black Knght RE Data Sltons LLC (HQ) ......A......626 808-9000
121 Theory Ste 100 Irvine (92617) ***(P-10942)***
Black Knight Data & Analytics, Irvine *Also called Black Knght RE Data Sltons LLC* ***(P-10942)***
Black Lake Golf Course, Nipomo *Also called American Golf Corporation* ***(P-18365)***
Black Meadow Landing ......D......760 663-4901
156100 Black Meadow Rd Parker Dam (92267) ***(P-12074)***
Black Oak Casino ......D......209 928-9300
19400 Tuolumne Rd N Tuolumne (95379) ***(P-18635)***
Black Tie Transportation LLC ......C......925 847-0747
7080 Commerce Dr Pleasanton (94588) ***(P-3653)***
Blackbaud Internet Solutions, San Diego *Also called Kintera Inc* ***(P-15379)***
Blackbeard's Family Fun Center, Fresno *Also called GLad Entertainment Inc* ***(P-18702)***
Blackberry Corporation (HQ) ......D......972 650-6126
3001 Bishop Dr San Ramon (94583) ***(P-15261)***
Blackhawk Country Club ......C......925 736-6500
599 Blackhawk Club Dr Danville (94506) ***(P-18402)***
Blackhawk Network Inc (HQ) ......A......925 226-9990
6220 Stoneridge Mall Rd Pleasanton (94588) ***(P-9424)***
Blackhawk Network Holdings Inc (HQ) ......B......925 226-9990
6220 Stoneridge Mall Rd Pleasanton (94588) ***(P-9425)***
Blackjack Farms De La Costa CN ......C......805 347-1333
2385 A St Santa Maria (93455) ***(P-302)***
Blackline Inc (PA) ......D......818 223-9008
21300 Victory Blvd Fl 12 Woodland Hills (91367) ***(P-14682)***
Blackline Systems Inc (HQ) ......C......877 777-7750
21300 Victory Blvd Fl 12 Woodland Hills (91367) ***(P-15262)***
Blackrock Funds III ......D......415 597-2000
400 Howard St San Francisco (94105) ***(P-11717)***
Blackrock Global Investors ......A......415 670-2000
400 Howard St San Francisco (94105) ***(P-9796)***
Blackrock Holdco 2 Inc ......D......415 678-2000
50 California St Ste 200 San Francisco (94111) ***(P-10943)***
Blackrock Instnl Tr Nat Assn (HQ) ......A......415 597-2000
400 Howard St San Francisco (94105) ***(P-11718)***
Blackrock Logistics Inc ......C......909 259-5357
14601 Slover Ave Fontana (92337) ***(P-4899)***
Blackstone Consulting Inc (PA) ......C......310 826-4389
11726 San Vicente Blvd # 550 Los Angeles (90049) ***(P-26529)***
Blackstone Technology Group (PA) ......D......415 837-1400
33 New Montgomery St # 850 San Francisco (94105) ***(P-9654)***
Blades of Glory, Universal City *Also called Dw Studios Productions LLC* ***(P-17603)***
Bladium Inc (PA) ......C......510 814-4999
800 W Tower Ave Bldg 40 Alameda (94501) ***(P-18125)***
Bladium Sports Clubs, Alameda *Also called Bladium Inc* ***(P-18125)***
Blaine Convention Services Inc ......A......714 522-8270
114 S Berry St Brea (92821) ***(P-16652)***
Blair Engineering Inc (PA) ......D......559 326-1400
451 Clovis Ave Ste 200 Clovis (93612) ***(P-24965)***
Blair Television Inc ......D......714 537-5923
11111 Santa Monica Blvd # 1900 Los Angeles (90025) ***(P-17583)***
Blair TV Communication, Los Angeles *Also called Blair Television Inc* ***(P-17583)***
Blair, Church & Flynn, Clovis *Also called Blair Engineering Inc* ***(P-24965)***
Blake H Brown Inc (HQ) ......D......310 764-0110
1300 W Artesia Blvd Compton (90220) ***(P-7530)***
Blanchard Training and Dev Inc (PA) ......C......760 489-5005
125 State Pl Escondido (92029) ***(P-26530)***
Blanchardcoachingcom Inc ......B......760 489-5005
125 State Pl Escondido (92029) ***(P-23571)***
Blank Rome LLP ......D......424 239-3400
2029 Century Park E Fl 6 Los Angeles (90067) ***(P-22388)***
Blare's Air & Ground Services, Lemoore *Also called R & D Leasing Inc* ***(P-14193)***
Blayne Pacelli ......D......310 383-6281
12345 Ventura Blvd Ste A Studio City (91604) ***(P-10944)***
Blazer Wilkinson LP ......B......831 455-3700
19040 Portola Dr Salinas (93908) ***(P-8431)***
Blazona Concrete Cnstr Inc ......D......916 375-8337
525 Harbor Blvd Ste 10 West Sacramento (95691) ***(P-1422)***
Blb Resources Inc (PA) ......C......949 261-9155
16845 Von Karman Ave # 100 Irvine (92606) ***(P-26531)***
Blc Residential Care Inc ......D......310 722-7541
1455 W 112th St Los Angeles (90047) ***(P-22946)***
Bleacher Report Inc ......D......415 777-5505
609 Mission St San Francisco (94105) ***(P-15734)***
Bleacher Report Inc ......C......415 777-5505
153 Kearny St Fl 2 San Francisco (94108) ***(P-17783)***
Bledsoe Masonry Inc ......D......951 360-6140
4680 Felspar St Ste A Riverside (92509) ***(P-2705)***
Bleu Chateau Assisted Living, Burbank *Also called Le Bleu Chateau Inc* ***(P-23970)***
Blh Construction Company ......C......818 905-3837
21031 Ventura Blvd # 200 Woodland Hills (91364) ***(P-1231)***
Blind Childrens Lrng Ctr Inc ......E......714 573-8888
18542 Vanderlip Ave Ste B Santa Ana (92705) ***(P-23677)***
Blize Healthcare Cal Inc ......D......800 343-2549
750 Alfred Nobel Dr # 202 Hercules (94547) ***(P-21682)***
Blizzard Entertainment Inc (HQ) ......D......949 955-1380
1 Blizzard Irvine (92618) ***(P-15263)***
Blocka Construction Inc ......D......510 657-3686
4455 Enterprise St Fremont (94538) ***(P-2076)***
Blockade Medical, Irvine *Also called Balt USA LLC* ***(P-6948)***
Blockr.io, San Francisco *Also called Coinbase Inc* ***(P-9426)***
Blois Construction Inc ......C......805 485-0011
3201 Sturgis Rd Oxnard (93030) ***(P-1835)***
Blomberg Window, Sacramento *Also called B B & T Management Corp* ***(P-6606)***
Blood Bank of Redwoods (PA) ......C......707 545-1222
3505 Industrial Dr Santa Rosa (95403) ***(P-22188)***
Blood Bank of San Bernardino A (HQ) ......C......909 885-6503
384 W Orange Show Rd San Bernardino (92408) ***(P-22189)***
Blood Center of The Pacific, Santa Rosa *Also called Blood Bank of Redwoods* ***(P-22188)***
Bloodsource Inc (PA) ......B......916 456-1500
10536 Peter A Mccuen Blvd Mather (95655) ***(P-22190)***
Bloodsource Inc ......D......209 724-0428
382 E Yosemite Ave Merced (95340) ***(P-22191)***
Bloodsource Inc ......E......916 488-1701
3099 Fair Oaks Blvd Sacramento (95864) ***(P-22192)***
Bloom David Law Offices of ......E......323 938-5248
3530 Wilshire Blvd # 1300 Los Angeles (90010) ***(P-22389)***

Mergent e-mail: customerrelations@mergent.com
1194
2020 Directory of California
Wholesalers and Services Companies
(P-0000) Products & Services Section entry number
(PA)=Parent Co (HQ)=Headquarters (DH)=Div Headquarters

Bloom Hergott Diemer Cook LLC..................D.......310 859-6800
150 S Rodeo Dr Fl 3 Beverly Hills (90212) ***(P-22390)***
Bloom, Jacob A, Beverly Hills *Also called Bloom Hergott Diemer Cook LLC* ***(P-22390)***
Bloomberg LP..................D.......415 912-2960
345 California St Fl 35 San Francisco (94104) ***(P-16571)***
Blossom Valley Cnstr Inc..................D.......408 993-0766
1125 Mabury Rd San Jose (95133) ***(P-779)***
Blower-Dempsay Corporation (PA)..................C.......714 481-3800
4042 W Garry Ave Santa Ana (92704) ***(P-8952)***
Bls Lmsine Svc Los Angeles Inc..................B.......323 644-7166
2860 Fletcher Dr Los Angeles (90039) ***(P-3654)***
BLT & Associates Inc..................C.......323 860-4000
6430 W Sunset Blvd # 800 Los Angeles (90028) ***(P-13772)***
Blue and Gold Fleet..................D.......415 705-8200
Marine Terminal Pier 41 St Pier San Francisco (94133) ***(P-4598)***
Blue Box Opco LLC (HQ)..................D.......800 840-4916
10025 Mesa Rim Rd San Diego (92121) ***(P-7728)***
Blue Bus Tours LLC..................C.......415 353-5310
50 Quint St San Francisco (94124) ***(P-18636)***
Blue Casa Communications Inc..................E.......805 966-1669
114 E Haley St Ste A Santa Barbara (93101) ***(P-5366)***
Blue Chip Inventory Service..................D.......818 461-1765
14852 Ventura Blvd # 112 Sherman Oaks (91403) ***(P-16653)***
Blue Chip Mayflower, Hawthorne *Also called Blue Chip Moving and Stor Inc* ***(P-3978)***
Blue Chip Moving and Stor Inc..................D.......323 463-6888
13525 Crenshaw Blvd Hawthorne (90250) ***(P-3978)***
Blue Chip Stamps..................A.......626 585-6700
301 E Colo Blvd Ste 300 Pasadena (91101) ***(P-7048)***
Blue Coat LLC..................A.......408 220-2200
350 Ellis St Mountain View (94043) ***(P-15264)***
Blue Coat Systems LLC (HQ)..................D.......650 527-8000
350 Ellis St Mountain View (94043) ***(P-15265)***
Blue Cross & Blue Shield Mich..................C.......323 782-3046
6300 Wilshire Blvd # 970 Los Angeles (90048) ***(P-9923)***
Blue Cross of California (HQ)..................C.......805 557-6050
4553 La Tienda Rd Westlake Village (91362) ***(P-9924)***
Blue Devils Lessee LLC..................C.......310 399-9344
530 Pico Blvd Santa Monica (90405) ***(P-12075)***
Blue Diamond Growers..................C.......209 545-6221
4800 Sisk Rd Modesto (95356) ***(P-470)***
Blue Diamond Materials, Brea *Also called Sully-Miller Contracting Co* ***(P-1795)***
Blue Eagle Contracting Inc..................D.......530 272-0287
113 Presley Way Ste 8 Grass Valley (95945) ***(P-3853)***
Blue Freight, Tarzana *Also called Blue Sky Services Inc* ***(P-4900)***
Blue Harbor, Aliso Viejo *Also called By Wind Inc* ***(P-14695)***
Blue Jeans Network Inc (PA)..................D.......408 550-2828
3098 Olsen Dr San Jose (95128) ***(P-5776)***
Blue Lagoon Textile Inc..................E.......213 590-4545
737 Crocker St Los Angeles (90021) ***(P-16654)***
Blue Lake Casino..................E.......707 668-5101
777 Casino Way Blue Lk Blue Lake Blue Lake (95525) ***(P-12076)***
Blue Mountain Air, Vacaville *Also called Blue Mountain Cnstr Svcs Inc* ***(P-2077)***
Blue Mountain Cnstr Svcs Inc..................C.......800 889-2085
707 Aldridge Rd Ste B Vacaville (95688) ***(P-2077)***
Blue Planet International Inc..................E.......323 526-9999
2945 E 12th St Los Angeles (90023) ***(P-8058)***
Blue River Seafood Inc..................E.......510 300-6800
25447 Industrial Blvd Hayward (94545) ***(P-8364)***
Blue Sheild of California, Walnut Creek *Also called California Physicians Service* ***(P-9926)***
Blue Shield of California, San Francisco *Also called California Physicians Service* ***(P-9927)***
Blue Shield of California, El Dorado Hills *Also called California Physicians Service* ***(P-9929)***
Blue Shield of California, El Segundo *Also called California Physicians Service* ***(P-9930)***
Blue Shield of California, Woodland Hills *Also called California Physicians Service* ***(P-9931)***
Blue Skies Landscape Maint, Encinitas *Also called Cielo Azul Inc* ***(P-786)***
Blue Sky Services Inc..................D.......818 609-8779
5530 Corbin Ave Ste 220 Tarzana (91356) ***(P-4900)***
Bluebeam Inc (PA)..................C.......626 788-4100
443 S Raymond Ave Pasadena (91105) ***(P-14683)***
Bluebridge Professional Svcs..................D.......909 625-6151
420 W Baseline Rd Ste D Claremont (91711) ***(P-21683)***
Bluegill Solar, Moreno Valley *Also called Bluegill Technologies LLC* ***(P-16499)***
Bluegill Technologies LLC..................D.......877 765-2770
11884 Welby Pl Ste 101 Moreno Valley (92557) ***(P-16499)***
Blueline Construction, Rancho Cordova *Also called Ron Nurss Inc* ***(P-3210)***
Bluevine Capital Inc..................D.......888 216-9619
401 Warren St Ste 300 Redwood City (94063) ***(P-9477)***
Bluewater Envmtl Svcs Inc..................D.......510 346-8800
2075 Williams St San Leandro (94577) ***(P-3384)***
Blufocus Inc..................D.......818 294-7695
2233 N Ontario St Ste 100 Burbank (91504) ***(P-14684)***
Blumenthal Distributing Inc (PA)..................C.......909 930-2000
1901 S Archibald Ave Ontario (91761) ***(P-6507)***
Blx Group Inc..................D.......760 776-6622
71534 Sahara Rd Rancho Mirage (92270) ***(P-231)***
Blx Group LLC..................D.......213 612-2400
777 S Figueroa St # 3200 Los Angeles (90017) ***(P-9797)***
Blx Group LLC (PA)..................D.......213 612-2200
777 S Figueroa St Ste 800 Los Angeles (90017) ***(P-16655)***
Blythe Nursing Care Center..................D.......760 922-8176
285 W Chanslor Way Blythe (92225) ***(P-20508)***
Blytheco LLC..................E.......813 854-3388
23161 Mill Creek Dr # 200 Laguna Hills (92653) ***(P-15950)***
BMA Long Beach, Long Beach *Also called Fresenius Med Care Long Beach* ***(P-21923)***
BMA San Gabriel, Alhambra *Also called Bio-Mdcal Applications Cal Inc* ***(P-21914)***
Bmb 1 LLC..................D.......951 272-6200
495 E Rincon St Ste 211 Corona (92879) ***(P-20509)***
BMC Group Inc..................D.......310 321-5555
300 N Cntntl Blvd Ste 570 El Segundo (90245) ***(P-22391)***
BMC Stock Holdings Inc..................B.......916 481-5030
4300 Jetway Ct North Highlands (95660) ***(P-6607)***
Bml Works Na LLC..................D.......650 268-8305
228 Hamilton Ave Fl 3 Palo Alto (94301) ***(P-26158)***
Bmp, Glendale *Also called Bunim-Murray Productions* ***(P-17586)***
Bmr 21 Erie St LLC..................D.......858 485-9840
17190 Bernardo Center Dr San Diego (92128) ***(P-10945)***
Bmr Apps Inc..................D.......954 651-1412
548 Market St San Francisco (94104) ***(P-15951)***
Bms Parent Inc (PA)..................D.......909 981-2341
1220 Dewey Way Ste F Upland (91786) ***(P-25540)***
Bmt Commercial Usa Inc (HQ)..................D.......760 737-3505
355 W Grand Ave Ste 5 Escondido (92025) ***(P-24966)***
Bmv Direct II LP..................D.......858 485-9840
17190 Bernardo Center Dr San Diego (92128) ***(P-27003)***
BNC Real Estate (PA)..................B.......858 481-3000
990 Highland Dr Ste 203 Solana Beach (92075) ***(P-10946)***
Bni Enterprises Inc..................A.......909 305-1818
545 College Commerce Way Upland (91786) ***(P-26898)***
Bnn, Los Angeles *Also called Breitbart News Network LLC* ***(P-13615)***
Bnsf Railway Company..................C.......909 386-4148
740 Carnegie Dr San Bernardino (92408) ***(P-3496)***
Bnsf Railway Company..................C.......760 255-7803
200 N Avenue H Barstow (92311) ***(P-3497)***
Bnsf Railway Company..................C.......323 869-3002
6300 Sheila St Commerce (90040) ***(P-3498)***
Bnsf Railway Company..................C.......323 267-4133
3770 E Washington Blvd Vernon (90058) ***(P-3499)***
Bny Mellon Asset Servicing, San Francisco *Also called Bank of New York Mellon Corp* ***(P-16644)***
Boatworks, San Leandro *Also called Stepping Stn Grwth Ctr Fr Chld* ***(P-23643)***
Bob Dillon Construction Inc..................C.......805 495-2607
856 Calle Margarita Thousand Oaks (91360) ***(P-2918)***
Bob Hope Health Center, Woodland Hills *Also called Motion Picture and TV Fund* ***(P-21050)***
Bob Hubbard Horse Trnsp Inc (PA)..................E.......951 369-3770
3730 S Riverside Ave Colton (92324) ***(P-3854)***
Boca Mesa Incorporated..................D.......805 934-9470
3130 Skyway Dr Ste 701 Santa Maria (93455) ***(P-27004)***
Bockmon & Woody Elc Co Inc..................C.......209 464-4878
1528 El Pinal Dr Stockton (95205) ***(P-2437)***
Bodega Bay Associates..................D.......650 330-8888
1100 Alma St Ste 106 Menlo Park (94025) ***(P-12077)***
Bodega Bay Lodge, Bodega Bay *Also called NAPA Valley Lodge LP* ***(P-12638)***
Bodega Bay Lodge, Menlo Park *Also called Bodega Bay Associates* ***(P-12077)***
Bodega Harbour Golf Links, Bodega Bay *Also called Bodega Harbour Homeowners Assn* ***(P-24482)***
Bodega Harbour Homeowners Assn..................D.......707 875-3519
21301 Heron Dr Bodega Bay (94923) ***(P-24482)***
Bodhtree Solutions Inc..................C.......844 409-0510
74 W Neal St Ste 100 Pleasanton (94566) ***(P-15952)***
Body Beautiful Car Wash Inc..................D.......858 748-4400
13236 Poway Rd Poway (92064) ***(P-17362)***
Body Transformations, Lodi *Also called R DS For Healthcare* ***(P-19690)***
Boeing Company..................D.......805 606-6340
Slc 2 Bldg 1628 San Luis Obispo (93401) ***(P-4756)***
Boeing Company..................B.......650 316-3732
329 Bernardo Ave Mountain View (94043) ***(P-24967)***
Boeing Company..................D.......925 398-7664
5753 W Las Positas Blvd Pleasanton (94588) ***(P-25725)***
Boeing Company..................E.......818 466-8800
5800 Woolsey Canyon Rd West Hills (91304) ***(P-24968)***
Boeing Distribution Svcs Inc..................C.......310 900-1300
1351 Charles Willard St Carson (90746) ***(P-7690)***
Boeing Satellite Systems..................D.......310 326-3100
200 N Pacific Coast Hwy El Segundo (90245) ***(P-7691)***
Boething Treeland Farms Inc..................A.......650 851-4770
2923 Alpine Rd Portola Valley (94028) ***(P-952)***
Boething Treeland Farms Inc (PA)..................D.......818 883-1222
23475 Long Valley Rd Woodland Hills (91367) ***(P-953)***
Boething Treeland Farms Inc..................C.......209 727-3741
20601 E Kettleman Ln Lodi (95240) ***(P-954)***
Boething Treeland Nursery, Lodi *Also called Boething Treeland Farms Inc* ***(P-954)***
Bogart Construction Inc..................D.......949 453-1400
9980 Irvine Center Dr # 200 Irvine (92618) ***(P-1423)***
Bohemian Club (PA)..................C.......415 885-2440
624 Taylor St San Francisco (94102) ***(P-24483)***
BOHEMIAN GROVE, San Francisco *Also called Bohemian Club* ***(P-24483)***
Bohm Law Group Inc (PA)..................E.......916 927-5574
4600 Northgate Blvd # 210 Sacramento (95834) ***(P-22392)***
Boiling Point Rest Sca Inc..................B.......626 551-5181
13668 Valley Blvd Unit C2 City of Industry (91746) ***(P-14234)***
Bolin Builders Inc..................E.......209 772-9721
3848 Berkesey Ln Valley Springs (95252) ***(P-1086)***
Bollingers Candelight Pavilion, Claremont *Also called Ben Bollinger Productions Inc* ***(P-17888)***
Bolsa Medical Group, Westminster *Also called Co D L Pham MD* ***(P-18908)***
Bolt Threads Inc (PA)..................D.......415 279-5585
5858 Horton St Ste 400 Emeryville (94608) ***(P-25726)***
Bolthouse Farms..................A.......661 366-7205
3200 E Brundage Ln Bakersfield (93304) ***(P-38)***
Bomel Construction Co Inc..................C.......760 431-6360
701 Palomar Airport Rd # 270 Carlsbad (92011) ***(P-1334)***
Bomel Construction Co Inc (PA)..................D.......714 921-1660
96 Corporate Park Ste 100 Irvine (92606) ***(P-1424)***
Bon Appetit Management Co..................C.......909 748-8970
1259 E Colton Ave Redlands (92374) ***(P-26532)***
Bonanza Plumbing Inc (PA)..................D.......951 360-8262
2259 Hamner Ave Norco (92860) ***(P-2078)***

ALPHABETIC

Employee Codes: A=Over 500 employees, B=251-500
C=101-250, D=51-100, E=50
2020 Directory of California
Wholesalers and Services Companies
© Mergent Inc. 1-800-342-5647
1195

Bonanza Productions Inc....A....818 954-4212
4000 Warner Blvd Burbank (91522) ***(P-17967)***
Bonded Carpet, San Diego *Also called Bonded Inc* ***(P-13262)***
Bonded Inc (PA)....D....858 576-8400
7831 Ostrow St San Diego (92111) ***(P-13262)***
Bondi-Nderson Assoc Insur Brks, Santa Rosa *Also called Northwest Insurance Agency* ***(P-10442)***
Boneso Brothers Cnstr Inc....D....805 227-4450
2758 Concrete Ct Paso Robles (93446) ***(P-2079)***
Bongmi Inc....E....415 823-8595
68 Harriet St Unit 3 San Francisco (94103) ***(P-6953)***
Bonhams Bttrflds Actneers Corp (HQ)....C....415 861-7500
220 San Bruno Ave San Francisco (94103) ***(P-16656)***
Bonhams Corporation....C....415 861-7500
220 San Bruno Ave San Francisco (94103) ***(P-16657)***
Bonita Golf Club, Bonita *Also called Crockett & Coinc* ***(P-18237)***
Bonita House Inc....D....510 923-0180
6333 Telg Ave Ste 102 Oakland (94609) ***(P-22947)***
Bonita Medical Offices, Bonita *Also called Kaiser Foundation Hospitals* ***(P-20972)***
Bonne Bridge Muell Okeef & (PA)....D....213 480-1900
3699 Wilsh Boule Fl 10 Flr 10 Los Angeles (90010) ***(P-22393)***
Bonneville International Corp....E....323 634-1800
5900 Wilshire Blvd # 1900 Los Angeles (90036) ***(P-5508)***
Bonneville International Corp....E....415 777-0965
201 3rd St Fl 12 San Francisco (94103) ***(P-5509)***
Bonnie Brae Cnvlscent Hosp Inc (PA)....D....213 483-8144
420 S Bonnie Brae St Los Angeles (90057) ***(P-20510)***
Bontadelli Inc....D....831 423-8572
2611 Mission St Santa Cruz (95060) ***(P-8432)***
Bonterra Psomas, Santa Ana *Also called Psomas* ***(P-25523)***
Boom-Boom Jeans, Los Angeles *Also called Blue Planet International Inc* ***(P-8058)***
Boomers, Newport Beach *Also called Festival Fun Parks LLC* ***(P-18692)***
Boomers, Vista *Also called Festival Fun Parks LLC* ***(P-18694)***
Boornazian Jensen & Garthe A....D....510 834-4350
555 12th St Oakland (94607) ***(P-22394)***
Booth Ranches LLC....D....559 626-4472
440 Anchor Ave Orange Cove (93646) ***(P-424)***
Booz Allen Hamilton Inc....D....310 297-2100
5220 Pacific Concourse Dr # 390 Los Angeles (90045) ***(P-26533)***
Booz Allen Hamilton Inc....D....619 725-6500
1615 Murray Canyon Rd # 220 San Diego (92108) ***(P-26534)***
Booz Allen Hamilton Inc....D....310 524-1557
2250 E Imperial Hwy # 540 El Segundo (90245) ***(P-24969)***
Booz Allen Hamilton Inc....D....213 620-1900
555 S Flower St Fl 36 Los Angeles (90071) ***(P-26535)***
Boral Industries, Oceanside *Also called Boral Roofing LLC* ***(P-3029)***
Boral Roofing LLC....C....760 967-0827
3093 Industry St Ste A Oceanside (92054) ***(P-3029)***
Borbon Incorporated....C....714 994-0170
2560 W Woodland Dr Anaheim (92801) ***(P-2335)***
Border Valley Trading Ltd....D....760 344-6700
604 Mead Rd Brawley (92227) ***(P-8835)***
Border Valley Trading Ltd....D....760 344-6700
604 Mead Rd Brawley (92227) ***(P-8836)***
Boreal Ridge Corporation....C....530 426-1012
19749 Boreal Ridge Rd Soda Springs (95728) ***(P-12078)***
Boreal Ski Area, Soda Springs *Also called Boreal Ridge Corporation* ***(P-12078)***
Boretech Resrce Recovry Engine....E....209 373-2588
5546 Vintage Cir Stockton (95219) ***(P-7531)***
Boretech Rsurce Recovery Engrg, Stockton *Also called Boretech Resrce Recovry Engine* ***(P-7531)***
Borg Redwood Fences, Livermore *Also called Selex Inc* ***(P-3465)***
Borgens & Borgens Inc....D....209 547-2980
141 E Acacia St Ste D Stockton (95202) ***(P-16210)***
Borjon Iscander....C....209 245-6289
18586 Highway 49 Plymouth (95669) ***(P-614)***
Borland Software Corporation....D....650 286-1900
951 Mariners Isl Blvd # 460 San Mateo (94404) ***(P-15266)***
Borrego Cmnty Hlth Foundation....C....760 466-1080
1121 E Washington Ave Escondido (92025) ***(P-18840)***
Borrego Cmnty Hlth Foundation....C....760 765-1223
2721 Washington St Julian (92036) ***(P-18841)***
Borrego Cmnty Hlth Foundation (PA)....C....760 767-5051
4343 Yaqui Pass Rd Borrego Springs (92004) ***(P-18842)***
Borrego Medical Center, Borrego Springs *Also called Borrego Cmnty Hlth Foundation* ***(P-18842)***
Borrmann Metal Center (PA)....D....818 846-7171
110 W Olive Ave Burbank (91502) ***(P-7049)***
Borunda Private SEC Patrol Inc....E....559 299-2662
1308 Clovis Ave Clovis (93612) ***(P-16211)***
Boshart Automotive Tstg Svcs....D....909 466-1602
1840 S Carlos Ave 15 Ontario (91761) ***(P-16658)***
Boskovich Farms Inc (PA)....C....805 487-2299
711 Diaz Ave Oxnard (93030) ***(P-471)***
Boskovich Farms Inc....B....805 987-1443
4224 Pleasant Valley Rd Camarillo (93012) ***(P-39)***
Bosman Dairy LLC....C....559 752-7018
6802 Avenue 120 A Tipton (93272) ***(P-385)***
Boss Audio Systems, Oxnard *Also called Ava Enterprises Inc* ***(P-7198)***
Bossa Nova Robotics Inc (HQ)....C....415 234-5136
610 22nd St Ste 250 San Francisco (94107) ***(P-7800)***
Boston Brick & Stone Inc....E....626 269-2622
2005 Lincoln Ave Pasadena (91103) ***(P-2706)***
Boston Consulting Group Inc....D....213 621-2772
355 S Grand Ave Ste 3300 Los Angeles (90071) ***(P-26536)***
Boston Properties Ltd Partnr....D....415 772-0700
4 Embarcadero Ctr Lbby 1 San Francisco (94111) ***(P-11544)***
Bostonia Medical Offices, El Cajon *Also called Kaiser Foundation Hospitals* ***(P-20956)***
Botanica Landscapes, Yuba City *Also called United Landscape Resource Inc* ***(P-920)***
Bottomley Distributing Co Inc....D....408 945-0660
755 Yosemite Dr Milpitas (95035) ***(P-8751)***
Boulder Active Club, Carlsbad *Also called 24 Hour Fitness Usa Inc* ***(P-18094)***
Boulder Creek Post Acute, Poway *Also called Pomerado Operations LLC* ***(P-20205)***
Boulevard Entertainment Inc....C....818 840-6969
903 S Lake St Ste 202 Burbank (91502) ***(P-16659)***
Boutique Air Inc (PA)....D....415 449-0505
5 3rd St Ste 925 San Francisco (94103) ***(P-4738)***
Bowie Enterprises....D....559 732-2988
1920 S Mooney Blvd Visalia (93277) ***(P-17363)***
Bowie Enterprises (PA)....D....559 227-6221
4411 N Blackstone Ave Fresno (93726) ***(P-17364)***
Bowie Enterprises....D....559 292-6565
801 W Shaw Ave Clovis (93612) ***(P-17365)***
Bowie Enterprises....D....559 227-3400
4411 N Blackstone Ave Fresno (93726) ***(P-17412)***
Bowlero Corp....D....626 339-1286
1060 W San Bernardino Rd Covina (91722) ***(P-18025)***
Bowlero Corp....D....626 960-3636
675 S Glendora Ave West Covina (91790) ***(P-18026)***
Bowlero Corp....E....909 945-9392
7930 Haven Ave Ste 101 Rancho Cucamonga (91730) ***(P-18027)***
Bowlero Corp....E....951 698-2202
40440 California Oaks Rd Murrieta (92562) ***(P-18028)***
Bowles & Verna....E....925 935-3300
2121 N Calif Blvd Ste 875 Walnut Creek (94596) ***(P-22395)***
Bowles Farming Co Inc....E....209 827-3000
11609 Hereford Rd Los Banos (93635) ***(P-303)***
Bowman & Brooke-Attys, Torrance *Also called Bowman and Brooke LLP* ***(P-22396)***
Bowman and Brooke LLP....D....310 768-3068
970 W 190th St Ste 700 Torrance (90502) ***(P-22396)***
Bowman Pipeline Contractors, Bakersfield *Also called Southwest Contractors* ***(P-1914)***
Bowsmith Inc (PA)....D....559 592-9485
131 2nd St Exeter (93221) ***(P-13287)***
Box Inc (PA)....C....877 729-4269
900 Jefferson Ave Redwood City (94063) ***(P-15267)***
Box Bros Corp....E....310 394-8660
825 Wilshire Blvd Santa Monica (90401) ***(P-16660)***
BOY SCOUTS OF AMERICA, Piedmont *Also called Boyscout of America* ***(P-24501)***
Boy's & Girls Club Bakersfield, Bakersfield *Also called Boys Girls Clubs of Kern Cnty* ***(P-24495)***
Boyd & Associates....D....805 988-8298
445 E Esplanade Dr # 210 Oxnard (93036) ***(P-16212)***
Boyd & Associates (PA)....C....818 752-1888
2191 E Thompson Blvd Ventura (93001) ***(P-16213)***
Boyd & Associates....C....714 835-5423
3151 Airway Ave Ste K105 Costa Mesa (92626) ***(P-16214)***
Boyd Corporation....C....714 777-5995
4990 E Hunter Ave Anaheim (92807) ***(P-7629)***
Boyett Construction Inc (PA)....D....510 264-9100
2404 Tripaldi Way Hayward (94545) ***(P-2755)***
Boykin Mgt Co Ltd Lblty Co....E....619 299-6633
3888 Greenwood St San Diego (92110) ***(P-12079)***
Boykin Mgt Co Ltd Lblty Co....B....510 548-7920
200 Marina Blvd Berkeley (94710) ***(P-12080)***
Boyle Engineering Corporation....D....714 543-5274
999 W Town And Country Rd Orange (92868) ***(P-24970)***
Boys & Girls CLB of Peninsula....D....650 322-6255
401 Pierce Rd Menlo Park (94025) ***(P-18403)***
BOYS & GIRLS CLUB OF SAN PEDRO, San Pedro *Also called Boys and Girls Clubs of The La* ***(P-24489)***
Boys & Girls Club of Tracy (PA)....E....209 832-2582
753 W Lowell Ave Tracy (95376) ***(P-24484)***
Boys & Girls Club Silicon Vly....D....408 957-9685
518 Valley Way Milpitas (95035) ***(P-24485)***
Boys & Girls Club Simi Vly Inc....E....805 527-4437
2850 Lemon Dr Simi Valley (93063) ***(P-24486)***
Boys & Girls Clubs North Cnty, Fallbrook *Also called Boys Club of Fallbrook Inc* ***(P-24492)***
Boys & Girls Clubs of N Vly....D....530 899-0335
601 Wall St Chico (95928) ***(P-24487)***
BOYS & GIRLS CLUBS OF SAN DIEG, Solana Beach *Also called Boys Grls Clubs of San Deguito* ***(P-24499)***
BOYS & GIRLS CLUBS OF SANTA MO, Santa Monica *Also called Boys Grls CLB Snta Monica Inc* ***(P-24497)***
Boys & Girls Clubs South Cnty....D....619 424-2266
847 Encina Ave Imperial Beach (91932) ***(P-24488)***
Boys and Girls Club....E....818 225-8406
22450 Mulholland Hwy Calabasas (91302) ***(P-18404)***
Boys and Girls Clubs of The La (PA)....D....310 833-1322
1200 S Cabrillo Ave San Pedro (90731) ***(P-24489)***
Boys and Girls Clubs of The La....D....310 833-1322
1501 S Cabrillo Ave San Pedro (90731) ***(P-24490)***
Boys and Girls Clubs of The La....D....310 833-1322
1700 Gulf Ave Wilmington (90744) ***(P-24491)***
Boys Club of Fallbrook Inc....D....760 728-5871
445 E Ivy St Fallbrook (92028) ***(P-24492)***
Boys Girls CLB Huntington Vly (PA)....D....714 531-2582
16582 Brookhurst St Fountain Valley (92708) ***(P-24493)***
Boys Girls Clubs Monterey Cnty (PA)....D....831 394-5171
1332 La Salle Ave Seaside (93955) ***(P-24494)***
Boys Girls Clubs of Kern Cnty....D....661 325-3730
801 Niles St Bakersfield (93305) ***(P-24495)***
Boys Girls Clubs Sonoma-Marin....C....707 528-7977
1400 N Dutton Ave Ste 24 Santa Rosa (95401) ***(P-24496)***
Boys Grls CLB Snta Monica Inc....D....310 361-8500
1220 Lincoln Blvd Santa Monica (90401) ***(P-24497)***

Mergent e-mail: customerrelations@mergent.com
1196
2020 Directory of California
Wholesalers and Services Companies
(P-0000) Products & Services Section entry number
(PA)=Parent Co (HQ)=Headquarters (DH)=Div Headquarters

Boys Grls Clubs Grdn Grove Inc ....C....714 537-8833
13645 Clinton St Garden Grove (92843) ***(P-24498)***
Boys Grls Clubs of San Deguito (PA) ....D....858 755-9371
533 Lomas Santa Fe Dr Solana Beach (92075) ***(P-24499)***
Boys Grls Clubs of Squoias Inc ....D....559 592-4074
215 W Tulare Ave Visalia (93277) ***(P-24500)***
Boys Republic (PA) ....C....909 902-6690
1907 Boys Republic Dr Chino Hills (91709) ***(P-23838)***
Boyscout of America ....D....510 547-4493
10 Highland Way Piedmont (94611) ***(P-24501)***
BP Industries Incorporated ....D....909 481-0227
5300 E Concours St Ontario (91764) ***(P-6546)***
BP Products W Coast Refinery, Carson *Also called BP West Coast Products LLC* ***(P-8713)***
BP West Coast Products LLC ....B....310 816-8787
22600 Wilmington Ave Carson (90745) ***(P-978)***
BP West Coast Products LLC ....B....510 231-4724
1306 Canal Blvd Richmond (94804) ***(P-979)***
BP West Coast Products LLC ....C....310 549-6204
1801 E Sepulveda Blvd Carson (90745) ***(P-8713)***
Bpaz Holdings 18 LLC ....D....972 354-6250
1 Sansome St Fl 15 San Francisco (94104) ***(P-11647)***
Bpaz Holdings 2 LLC ....E....972 354-6250
1 Sansome St Ste 1500 San Francisco (94104) ***(P-10947)***
Bpaz Holdings 6 LLC ....D....415 295-8080
1 Sansome St Ste 1500 San Francisco (94104) ***(P-11648)***
Bpg Storage Solutions Inc ....D....562 467-2000
2033 N Main St Ste 340 Walnut Creek (94596) ***(P-26159)***
Bpm LLP (PA) ....D....415 421-5757
600 California St Fl 6 San Francisco (94108) ***(P-25541)***
Bpo Management Services Inc (PA) ....D....714 972-2670
8175 E Kaiser Blvd 100 Anaheim (92808) ***(P-14685)***
Bpr Properties Berkeley LLC ....C....650 424-1400
953 Industrial Ave # 100 Palo Alto (94303) ***(P-10572)***
Bps Bioscience Inc ....E....858 202-1401
6042 Cornerstone Ct W B San Diego (92121) ***(P-25727)***
Bps Supply Group (PA) ....D....661 589-9141
3301 Zachary Ave Shafter (93263) ***(P-7050)***
BQE Software Inc ....D....310 602-4020
3825 Del Amo Blvd Trrance Torrance Torrance (90503) ***(P-15268)***
BR Funsten, Manteca *Also called B R Funsten & Co* ***(P-6543)***
Bracket Global LLC ....D....415 293-1340
88 Stevenson St San Francisco (94105) ***(P-14686)***
Brad Rambo & Associates Inc (PA) ....D....949 366-9911
1341 Calle Avanzado San Clemente (92673) ***(P-8020)***
Brad S Miller ....C....415 986-5400
220 Montgomery St Ste 310 San Francisco (94104) ***(P-26537)***
Brad Watkins Masonry Inc ....D....818 360-3796
10315 Woodley Ave Ste 130 Granada Hills (91344) ***(P-2707)***
Braddock & Logan Group II LP ....C....925 736-4000
4155 Blackhawk Plaza Cir # 201 Danville (94506) ***(P-11545)***
Braddock & Logan Inc ....D....925 229-1747
3600 Pine St Apt 3600 # 3600 Martinez (94553) ***(P-10698)***
Braddock & Logan Services Inc ....C....925 736-4000
4155 Blackhawk Plaza Cir # 201 Danville (94506) ***(P-1425)***
Braden Partners LP A Calif ....D....661 632-1979
7500 District Blvd Bakersfield (93313) ***(P-6954)***
Braden Partners LP A Calif (HQ) ....D....415 893-1518
1304 Sthpint Blvd Ste 130 Petaluma (94954) ***(P-21684)***
Bradford & Barthel LLP (PA) ....C....916 569-0790
2518 River Plaza Dr Sacramento (95833) ***(P-22397)***
Bradford Messenger Service ....D....559 252-0775
4955 E Andersen Ave # 118 Fresno (93727) ***(P-16661)***
Bradley Grdns Convalescent Ctr, San Jacinto *Also called Healthcare MGT Systems Inc* ***(P-20008)***
Bradshaw Home, Rancho Cucamonga *Also called Bradshaw International Inc* ***(P-6547)***
Bradshaw International Inc (HQ) ....B....909 476-3884
9409 Buffalo Ave Rancho Cucamonga (91730) ***(P-6547)***
Bradshaw Veterinary Clinic ....D....916 685-2494
9609 Bradshaw Rd Elk Grove (95624) ***(P-574)***
Brady Vorwerck Rydr & Cspno (PA) ....D....480 456-9888
19200 Von Karman Ave Irvine (92612) ***(P-22398)***
Brady Company/Central Cal ....C....831 633-3315
13540 Blackie Rd Castroville (95012) ***(P-2756)***
Brady Company/Los Angeles Inc ....D....714 533-9850
1010 N Olive St Anaheim (92801) ***(P-2757)***
Brady Company/San Diego Inc ....B....619 462-2600
8100 Center St La Mesa (91942) ***(P-2758)***
Brady Gce II ....D....858 496-0500
2655 Camino San Diego (92108) ***(P-24971)***
Brady Socal Incorporated ....D....619 462-2600
8100 Center St La Mesa (91942) ***(P-2759)***
Braemar Country Club Inc ....C....323 873-6880
4001 Reseda Blvd Tarzana (91356) ***(P-18405)***
Braemar Partnership ....B....858 488-1081
3999 Mission Blvd San Diego (92109) ***(P-12081)***
Brafton Incorporated ....D....617 206-3040
220 Montgomery St Ste 917 San Francisco (94104) ***(P-5367)***
Bragg Crane & Rigging, Richmond *Also called Bay Cities Crane & Rigging Inc* ***(P-14131)***
Bragg Crane & Rigging, Long Beach *Also called Bragg Investment Company Inc* ***(P-16662)***
Bragg Investment Company Inc (PA) ....A....562 984-2400
6251 N Paramount Blvd Long Beach (90805) ***(P-16662)***
Braille Institute America Inc (PA) ....C....323 663-1111
741 N Vermont Ave Los Angeles (90029) ***(P-22948)***
Bramasol Inc ....D....408 831-0046
3979 Freedom Cir Ste 620 Santa Clara (95054) ***(P-6809)***
Branch, Oakland *Also called Moffatt & Nichol* ***(P-25222)***
Brand Flower Farms Inc (PA) ....C....805 684-5531
5300 Foothill Rd Carpinteria (93013) ***(P-8884)***
Brand Precision, Benicia *Also called Clean Hrbors Es Indus Svcs Inc* ***(P-17491)***
Brand Scaffold Service, Richmond *Also called Brand Services LLC* ***(P-3385)***
Brand Services Inc ....E....707 603-3400
535 Watt Dr Fairfield (94534) ***(P-7466)***
Brand Services LLC ....D....510 231-9640
940 Hensley St Richmond (94801) ***(P-3385)***
Brand Services of California, Fairfield *Also called Brand Services Inc* ***(P-7466)***
Branded Entrmt Netwrk Inc (PA) ....C....310 342-1500
15250 Ventura Blvd # 300 Sherman Oaks (91403) ***(P-13769)***
Brandel Manor, Turlock *Also called Emanuel Medical Center Inc* ***(P-20867)***
Brandes Inv Partners Inc (PA) ....C....858 755-0239
11988 Charmaine Way Ste 6 San Diego (92131) ***(P-11719)***
Brandnet Inc ....D....415 216-4152
724 Battery St 3 San Francisco (94111) ***(P-27005)***
Brandrep LLC ....E....800 405-7119
16812 Armstrong Ave Irvine (92606) ***(P-26538)***
Brandt Cattle, Brawley *Also called Brandt Co Inc* ***(P-375)***
Brandt Cattle, Calipatria *Also called Brandt Co Inc* ***(P-376)***
Brandt Co Inc (PA) ....D....760 344-3430
299 W Main St Brawley (92227) ***(P-375)***
Brandt Co Inc ....D....760 348-2295
7015 Brandt Rd Calipatria (92233) ***(P-376)***
Brandvia Alliance Inc (PA) ....C....408 955-0500
2159 Bering Dr San Jose (95131) ***(P-8953)***
Branlyn Prominence Inc ....C....760 843-5655
13334 Amargosa Rd Victorville (92392) ***(P-21685)***
Branlyn Prominence Inc (PA) ....D....909 476-9030
9213 Archibald Ave Rancho Cucamonga (91730) ***(P-21686)***
Brannon Inc ....C....805 621-5000
1340 W Betteravia Rd Santa Maria (93455) ***(P-1335)***
Braswell Col Care Redlands CA ....C....909 792-6050
1618 Laurel Ave Redlands (92373) ***(P-20511)***
Braswells Villa Monte Vista ....C....858 487-6242
12696 Monte Vista Rd Poway (92064) ***(P-20512)***
Braswells Yucaipa Valley C ....D....909 795-2476
35253 Avenue H Yucaipa (92399) ***(P-19754)***
Braun Electric Company Inc (HQ) ....E....661 633-1451
3000 E Belle Ter Bakersfield (93307) ***(P-2438)***
Braun Electric Company Inc ....C....661 763-1531
111 Main St Taft (93268) ***(P-2439)***
Braun Linen Service Inc (PA) ....C....909 623-2678
16514 Garfield Ave Paramount (90723) ***(P-13211)***
Braun Linen Service Inc ....D....909 623-2678
396 La Mesa St Pomona (91766) ***(P-13179)***
Bravante Produce, Reedley *Also called Cal Packing & Storage LP* ***(P-4341)***
Bravo Tech Inc ....E....714 230-8333
14600 Industry Cir La Mirada (90638) ***(P-5199)***
Brayton Purcell APC (PA) ....C....415 898-1555
222 Rush Landing Rd Novato (94945) ***(P-22399)***
Bre Diamond Hotel LLC ....C....650 712-7000
1 Miramontes Point Rd Half Moon Bay (94019) ***(P-12082)***
Bre El Segundo Property Owner, El Segundo *Also called Bshh II LLC* ***(P-12096)***
Bre Select Hotels Oper LLC ....D....408 719-1313
30 Ranch Dr Milpitas (95035) ***(P-12083)***
Bre/Japantown Owner LLC ....D....415 922-3200
1625 Post St San Francisco (94115) ***(P-12084)***
Brea Dialysis Center, Brea *Also called Renal Treatment Ctrs - Cal Inc* ***(P-21932)***
Break Floor Productions LLC (PA) ....E....818 432-1234
5446 Satsuma Ave North Hollywood (91601) ***(P-17889)***
Break Media, Beverly Hills *Also called Nextpoint Inc* ***(P-5448)***
Breakout Prison Outreach ....D....408 702-2405
1560 Berger Dr San Jose (95112) ***(P-22949)***
Breast Diagnostic Center ....E....310 517-4709
3275 Skypark Dr Ste A Torrance (90505) ***(P-18843)***
Breast Imaging Center, Sacramento *Also called Sutter Health* ***(P-19481)***
Breeders Choice Pet Foods, Irwindale *Also called Central Garden & Pet Company* ***(P-8958)***
Brehm Communities (PA) ....D....760 448-2420
1935 Camino Vida Roble # 200 Carlsbad (92008) ***(P-1087)***
Brehm Communities (PA) ....D....760 448-2420
1825 Aston Ave Ste B Carlsbad (92008) ***(P-1088)***
Breitbart News Network LLC ....D....424 371-0585
149 S Barrington Ste 735 Los Angeles (90049) ***(P-13615)***
Breitburn GP LLC ....A....213 225-5900
707 Wilshire Blvd # 4600 Los Angeles (90017) ***(P-980)***
Bremer Whyte Brown Omeara, Newport Beach *Also called Bremer Whyte Brown Omeara LLP* ***(P-22400)***
Bremer Whyte Brown Omeara LLP (PA) ....E....949 221-1000
20320 Sw Birch St Ste 200 Newport Beach (92660) ***(P-22400)***
Brendan Tours (PA) ....C....818 428-6000
5551 Katella Ave Cypress (90630) ***(P-4818)***
Brendan Worldwide Vacations, Cypress *Also called Brendan Tours* ***(P-4818)***
Brenden Theatre Corporation ....D....707 469-0180
531 Davis St Vacaville (95688) ***(P-17819)***
Brenden Theatre Corporation ....D....209 491-7770
1021 10th St Frnt Modesto (95354) ***(P-17820)***
Brenden Theatre Corporation (PA) ....C....925 677-0462
1985 Willow Pass Rd Ste C Concord (94520) ***(P-17821)***
Brennan Electric Inc ....C....909 772-2263
460 S Stoddard Ave Ste 3 San Bernardino (92401) ***(P-2440)***
Brenntag Pacific Inc (HQ) ....C....562 903-9626
10747 Patterson Pl Santa Fe Springs (90670) ***(P-8691)***
Brentwood Bmdical RES Inst Inc ....C....310 312-1554
11301 Wilshire Blvd Los Angeles (90073) ***(P-25971)***
Brentwood Cmmncations Intl Inc ....E....818 333-3680
16135 Roscoe Blvd North Hills (91343) ***(P-17584)***
Brentwood Country Club ....C....310 451-8011
590 S Burlingame Ave Los Angeles (90049) ***(P-18406)***
Brentwood Health Care Center, Santa Monica *Also called Coastal Health Care Inc* ***(P-19807)***

Employee Codes: A=Over 500 employees, B=251-500
C=101-250, D=51-100, E=50
2020 Directory of California
Wholesalers and Services Companies
© Mergent Inc. 1-800-342-5647
1197

Brentwood Medical Tech Corp..........D.......800 624-8950
1125 W 190th St Gardena (90248) ***(P-6955)***
Brentwood Skill Nursng & Rehab..........D.......530 527-2046
1795 Walnut St Red Bluff (96080) ***(P-20513)***
Brentwood Sklled Nursng Rhbltn, Red Bluff *Also called Brentwood Skill Nursng & Rehab* ***(P-20513)***
Brer Affiliates LLC (HQ)..........C.......949 794-7900
18500 Von Karman Ave # 400 Irvine (92612) ***(P-11825)***
Bret Boylan, Long Beach *Also called Bret Boylan Property Mgt* ***(P-26160)***
Bret Boylan Property Mgt..........E.......562 437-7886
35 N Alboni Pl Apt 409 Long Beach (90802) ***(P-26160)***
Brethren Inc..........E.......714 836-4800
1170 E Fruit St Santa Ana (92701) ***(P-7801)***
Brethren Hillcrest Homes..........C.......909 593-4917
2705 Mountain View Dr Ofc La Verne (91750) ***(P-23839)***
Breville Usa Inc..........E.......310 755-3000
19400 S Western Ave Torrance (90501) ***(P-6548)***
Brewer Crane & Rigging, Lakeside *Also called LLC Brewer Crane* ***(P-14101)***
Brewster Marble Co Inc..........E.......818 834-2195
20801 Dearborn St Chatsworth (91311) ***(P-2884)***
Brewsters Automotive Inc..........D.......714 528-4683
17357 Los Angeles St Yorba Linda (92886) ***(P-17324)***
Briar Golf LP..........D.......760 328-6571
68311 Paseo Real Cathedral City (92234) ***(P-18224)***
Briarcrest Nursing Center Inc..........C.......562 927-2641
5648 Gotham St Bell (90201) ***(P-19755)***
Briarpatch Coop Nev Cnty Inc..........C.......530 272-5333
290 Sierra College Dr Grass Valley (95945) ***(P-24809)***
Briarpatch Coop-Community Mkt, Grass Valley *Also called Briarpatch Coop Nev Cnty Inc* ***(P-24809)***
Briarwood Health Care Inc..........E.......916 383-2741
5901 Lemon Hill Ave Sacramento (95824) ***(P-20514)***
Brickley Construction Co Inc..........E.......909 888-2010
957 Reece St San Bernardino (92411) ***(P-3386)***
Brickley Environmental, San Bernardino *Also called Brickley Construction Co Inc* ***(P-3386)***
Bricsnet FM America Inc..........D.......202 756-1840
1820 Harvest Rd Pleasanton (94566) ***(P-15953)***
Bridalink Store, Redding *Also called Knot Wedding Wire* ***(P-5432)***
Bridge Bank, San Jose *Also called Western Alliance Bank* ***(P-9247)***
Bridge Bay Resort & Marina..........D.......530 275-3021
10300 Bridge Bay Rd Redding (96003) ***(P-12085)***
Bridge Group Hh Inc..........C.......858 455-5000
5090 Shoreham Pl Ste 209 San Diego (92122) ***(P-11649)***
Bridge Housing Acquisition..........D.......415 989-1111
1 Hawthorne St Ste 400 San Francisco (94105) ***(P-10573)***
Bridge Housing Corporation (PA)..........D.......415 989-1111
600 California St Fl 9 San Francisco (94108) ***(P-11546)***
Bridge Partners Inc (PA)..........D.......925 256-9448
1850 Mt Diablo Blvd Walnut Creek (94596) ***(P-12086)***
Bridgepoint At San Francisco, San Francisco *Also called Kisco Senior Living LLC* ***(P-26287)***
Bridges At Gale Ranch LLC..........D.......925 735-4253
9000 S Gale Ridge Rd San Ramon (94582) ***(P-18407)***
Bridges At Sn Pdro Pnnsla Hspt..........D.......310 514-5359
1300 W 7th St Fl 4 San Pedro (90732) ***(P-21962)***
Bridges Club At Rancho SA..........C.......858 759-7200
18550 Seven Bridges Rd Rancho Santa Fe (92091) ***(P-24502)***
Bridges From School To Work, Oakland *Also called Marriott Foundation For People* ***(P-23612)***
Bridges Golf Club, The, San Ramon *Also called Bridges At Gale Ranch LLC* ***(P-18407)***
Bridgford Foods, Anaheim *Also called A S I Corporation* ***(P-13465)***
Bridgford Marketing Company (HQ)..........D.......714 526-5533
1308 N Patt St Anaheim (92801) ***(P-8401)***
Bridgwter Consulting Group Inc..........D.......949 535-1755
18881 Von Karman Ave Irvine (92612) ***(P-26539)***
Brieck Restoration Inc..........E.......858 679-9928
13750 Danielson St Poway (92064) ***(P-1089)***
Brience Inc (HQ)..........D.......415 974-5300
128 Spear St Fl 3 San Francisco (94105) ***(P-14687)***
Brier Oak On Sunset LLC..........C.......323 663-3951
5154 W Sunset Blvd Los Angeles (90027) ***(P-20515)***
Brier Oak On Sunset Rehab, Los Angeles *Also called Skilled Healthcare LLC* ***(P-20263)***
BRIER OAK ON SUNSET REHAB CENTER, Los Angeles *Also called Brier Oak On Sunset LLC* ***(P-20515)***
Briercrest Inglewoodhealthcare, Inglewood *Also called American Nursing Home MGT Inc* ***(P-26988)***
Briggs Electric Inc (PA)..........D.......714 544-2500
14381 Franklin Ave Tustin (92780) ***(P-2441)***
Bright Bristol Street LLC..........D.......714 557-3000
3131 Bristol St Costa Mesa (92626) ***(P-12087)***
Bright Event Rentals LLC (PA)..........C.......310 202-0011
1640 W 190th St Torrance (90501) ***(P-14133)***
Bright Event Rentals LLC..........A.......858 496-9700
7069 Consolidated Way San Diego (92121) ***(P-14134)***
Bright Event Rentals LLC..........C.......310 202-0011
22674 Broadway Ste A Sonoma (95476) ***(P-14135)***
Bright Expectations Inc..........E.......951 360-2070
8175 Limonite Ave Ste C Riverside (92509) ***(P-21687)***
Bright Health Physicians (PA)..........C.......562 947-8478
15725 Whittier Blvd # 500 Whittier (90603) ***(P-18844)***
Bright Horizons Chld Ctrs LLC..........C.......805 447-6793
1 Amgen Center Dr Thousand Oaks (91320) ***(P-23678)***
Bright Horizons Chld Ctrs LLC..........C.......408 853-2196
800 Barber Ln Milpitas (95035) ***(P-23679)***
Bright House Networks LLC..........D.......661 634-2200
4450 California Ave Ste A Bakersfield (93309) ***(P-5667)***
Bright Now Dental, Irvine *Also called Smile Brands Group Inc* ***(P-26393)***
Bright Pharmaceutical Services..........D.......818 981-9100
4570 Van Nuys Blvd Sherman Oaks (91403) ***(P-7923)***
Brightcloud Inc..........C.......858 652-4803
4370 La Jolla Village Dr # 820 San Diego (92122) ***(P-16500)***
Brightcurrent Inc..........D.......877 896-3306
426 17th St Ste 700 Oakland (94612) ***(P-16663)***
Brightedge Technologies Inc (PA)..........C.......800 578-8023
989 E Hillsdale Blvd Foster City (94404) ***(P-14688)***
Brighter Beginnings (PA)..........D.......510 903-7503
3478 Buskirk Ave Ste 105 Pleasant Hill (94523) ***(P-22950)***
Brighterion Inc..........D.......415 986-5600
123 Mission St Ste 1700 San Francisco (94105) ***(P-14689)***
Brightertech Incorporated..........E.......310 909-4940
510 Strtford Ct Unit 204a Del Mar (92014) ***(P-5368)***
BRIGHTON, Modesto *Also called Del Rio Golf & Country Club* ***(P-18442)***
Brighton Convalescent Center..........D.......626 798-9124
1836 N Fair Oaks Ave Pasadena (91103) ***(P-20516)***
Brighton Gardens Inc..........D.......858 259-2222
13101 Hartfield Ave San Diego (92130) ***(P-19756)***
Brighton Gardens of Camarillo, Camarillo *Also called Sunrise Senior Living LLC* ***(P-20324)***
Brighton Gardens of Sunrise, Palm Desert *Also called Sunrise Senior Living Inc* ***(P-20290)***
Brighton Health Alliance (PA)..........D.......619 461-0376
8322 Clairemont Mesa Blvd San Diego (92111) ***(P-19757)***
Brighton Place East Inc..........D.......619 461-3222
8625 Lamar St Spring Valley (91977) ***(P-19758)***
Brighton Place of San Diego, San Diego *Also called Brighton Health Alliance* ***(P-19757)***
Brighton Place San Diego..........C.......619 263-2166
1350 Euclid Ave San Diego (92105) ***(P-19759)***
BRIGHTON PLACE SPRING VALLEY, Spring Valley *Also called B-Spring Valley LLC* ***(P-19742)***
Brightscope, San Diego *Also called Strategic Insights Inc* ***(P-15510)***
Brightview Companies LLC..........C.......209 993-9277
2447 Stagecoach Rd Stockton (95215) ***(P-703)***
Brightview Companies LLC..........C.......626 574-3940
201 Longden Ave Irwindale (91706) ***(P-704)***
Brightview Companies LLC (HQ)..........C.......818 223-8500
27001 Agoura Rd Ste 350 Calabasas (91301) ***(P-1945)***
Brightview Golf Maint Inc..........E.......805 968-6400
405 Glen Annie Rd Santa Barbara (93117) ***(P-1946)***
Brightview Golf Maint Inc (HQ)..........D.......818 223-8500
24151 Ventura Blvd Calabasas (91302) ***(P-1947)***
Brightview Landscape Dev Inc (HQ)..........E.......818 223-8500
24151 Ventura Blvd Calabasas (91302) ***(P-705)***
Brightview Landscape Dev Inc..........B.......858 458-9900
8450 Miramar Pl San Diego (92121) ***(P-1948)***
Brightview Landscape Dev Inc..........D.......818 838-4700
13691 Vaughn St San Fernando (91340) ***(P-2080)***
Brightview Landscape Dev Inc..........B.......714 546-7975
11555 Cley Rver Cir Ste A Fountain Valley (92708) ***(P-2081)***
Brightview Landscape Dev Inc..........D.......714 546-7843
1960 S Yale St Santa Ana (92704) ***(P-706)***
Brightview Landscape Svcs Inc..........E.......510 487-4826
20551b Corsair Blvd Hayward (94545) ***(P-707)***
Brightview Landscape Svcs Inc..........C.......858 458-1900
8500 Miramar Pl San Diego (92121) ***(P-708)***
Brightview Landscape Svcs Inc..........D.......925 957-8831
4677 Pacheco Blvd Martinez (94553) ***(P-709)***
Brightview Landscape Svcs Inc..........D.......714 546-7843
1960 S Yale St Santa Ana (92704) ***(P-710)***
Brightview Landscape Svcs Inc..........D.......916 381-2800
5745 Alder Ave Sacramento (95828) ***(P-711)***
Brightview Landscape Svcs Inc..........D.......925 924-8900
7039 Commerce Cir Ste B Pleasanton (94588) ***(P-712)***
Brightview Landscape Svcs Inc..........C.......310 327-8700
17813 S Main St Ste 105 Gardena (90248) ***(P-713)***
Brightview Landscapes LLC..........D.......760 438-3551
2420 Cougar Dr Carlsbad (92010) ***(P-714)***
Brightview Landscapes LLC..........D.......619 644-8584
9090 Birch St Spring Valley (91977) ***(P-715)***
Brightview Tree Company..........C.......818 951-5500
9500 Foothill Blvd Sunland (91040) ***(P-955)***
Brightview Tree Company..........C.......714 546-7975
3200 W Telegraph Rd Fillmore (93015) ***(P-956)***
Brightview Tree Company..........D.......925 862-2485
8501 Calaveras Rd Sunol (94586) ***(P-957)***
Brightview Tree Company..........D.......209 886-5511
28915 E Funck Rd Farmington (95230) ***(P-716)***
Brilliance Investment LLC..........D.......510 568-1880
8350 Edes Ave Oakland (94621) ***(P-12088)***
Brillio LLC..........A.......800 317-0575
5201 Great America Pkwy # 100 Santa Clara (95054) ***(P-14690)***
Brillstein Entrmt Partners LLC (PA)..........B.......310 205-5100
9150 Wilshire Blvd # 350 Beverly Hills (90212) ***(P-17585)***
Brillstein Grey Entertainment, Beverly Hills *Also called Brillstein Entrmt Partners LLC* ***(P-17585)***
Brinderson LP (HQ)..........C.......714 466-7100
19000 Macarthur Blvd # 800 Irvine (92612) ***(P-24972)***
Brinderson LP..........D.......714 466-7100
19000 Macarthur Blvd # 800 Irvine (92612) ***(P-24973)***
Brinks Incorporated..........C.......818 503-8630
1120 Venice Blvd Los Angeles (90015) ***(P-16215)***
Brinks Incorporated..........C.......916 452-5279
8178 Alpine Ave Unit A Sacramento (95826) ***(P-16216)***
Brinks Incorporated..........C.......619 263-6615
4520 Federal Blvd Ste A San Diego (92102) ***(P-16217)***
Brinks Incorporated..........D.......408 436-7717
1630 Old Bayshore Hwy San Jose (95112) ***(P-16218)***
Brinks Incorporated..........E.......323 262-2646
1821 S Soto St Los Angeles (90023) ***(P-16219)***

Mergent e-mail: customerrelations@mergent.com
1198
2020 Directory of California
Wholesalers and Services Companies
(P-0000) Products & Services Section entry number
(PA)=Parent Co (HQ)=Headquarters (DH)=Div Headquarters

Brisam Lax (de) LLC ....D....310 649-5151
9901 S La Cienega Blvd Los Angeles (90045) *(P-12089)*
Brisbane Mechanical, Brisbane *Also called F W Spencer & Son Inc (P-2133)*
Bristlecone Incorporated ....A....650 386-4000
10 Almaden Blvd Ste 600 San Jose (95113) *(P-14691)*
Bristol Hotel ....D....619 232-6141
1055 1st Ave San Diego (92101) *(P-12090)*
Bristol Park Medical Group, Fountain Valley *Also called St Jude Hospital Yorba Linda (P-19448)*
Bristol, The, San Diego *Also called Beston Development (P-12063)*
Brita Products Company ....D....510 271-7000
1221 Broadway Ste 290 Oakland (94612) *(P-7413)*
Brite Media LLC ....C....818 826-5790
16027 Ventura Blvd # 210 Encino (91436) *(P-13616)*
Brite Promotions, Encino *Also called Brite Media LLC (P-13616)*
Briteworks Inc ....D....626 337-0099
620 N Commercial Ave Covina (91723) *(P-13872)*
Brithinee Electric ....D....909 825-7971
620 S Rancho Ave Colton (92324) *(P-7130)*
British American Communication ....D....818 943-6111
7965 Foothill Blvd Sunland (91040) *(P-5668)*
Brittany House LLC ....D....562 421-4717
5401 E Centralia St Long Beach (90808) *(P-23840)*
Brittney House ....D....562 421-4717
5401 E Centralia St Long Beach (90808) *(P-21688)*
Britz Fertilizers Inc ....D....559 884-2421
21817 S Frsno Coalinga Rd Five Points (93624) *(P-8837)*
Brix Group Inc (PA) ....D....559 457-4700
838 N Laverne Ave Fresno (93727) *(P-7241)*
Broadcast Co of Americas LLC (PA) ....D....858 453-0658
6160 Cornerstone Ct E # 100 San Diego (92121) *(P-5510)*
Broadmoor Hotel (PA) ....C....415 776-7034
1499 Sutter St San Francisco (94109) *(P-12091)*
Broadmoor Hotel ....D....415 673-8445
1465 65th St Apt 274 Emeryville (94608) *(P-12092)*
Broadmoor Hotel ....D....415 673-2511
1000 Sutter St San Francisco (94109) *(P-12093)*
Broadrach Cpitl Prtners Fund I ....A....650 331-2500
248 Homer Ave Palo Alto (94301) *(P-11720)*
Broadreach Capitl Partners LLC ....A....310 691-5760
6430 W Sunset Blvd # 504 Los Angeles (90028) *(P-11890)*
Broadreach Capitl Partners LLC (PA) ....A....650 331-2500
855 El Camino Real # 350 Palo Alto (94301) *(P-9655)*
Broadreach Capitl Partners LLC ....A....415 354-4640
235 Montgomery St # 1018 San Francisco (94104) *(P-11891)*
Broadsoft Contact Center Inc ....E....408 338-0900
930 Hamlin Ct Sunnyvale (94089) *(P-14692)*
Broadspire Inc ....D....213 785-8043
19425 Soled Canyo Rd Ste Santa Clarita (91351) *(P-5369)*
Broadstone Raquet Club, Folsom *Also called Spare-Time Inc (P-18580)*
Broadstreet Power, Van Nuys *Also called Broadstreet Solar Inc (P-2082)*
Broadstreet Solar Inc ....E....818 206-1464
16112 Hart St Van Nuys (91406) *(P-2082)*
Broadview Inc ....E....323 221-9174
4570 Griffin Ave Los Angeles (90031) *(P-19760)*
Broadvision Inc (PA) ....D....650 331-1000
460 Seaport Ct Ste 102 Redwood City (94063) *(P-15269)*
Broadway By Bay ....C....650 579-5565
853 Industrial Rd Ste H San Carlos (94070) *(P-17890)*
Broadway Manor Care Center, Glendale *Also called Longwood Management Corp (P-20618)*
Broadway Mech - Contrs Inc ....C....510 746-4000
873 81st Ave Oakland (94621) *(P-2083)*
Broadway Sacramento (PA) ....C....916 446-5880
1510 J St Ste 200 Sacramento (95814) *(P-17891)*
Broadway Typewriter Co Inc ....D....800 998-9199
1055 6th Ave Ste 101 San Diego (92101) *(P-6810)*
Brocade Cmmnctions Systems Inc ....D....408 333-4300
110 Holger Way San Jose (95134) *(P-27006)*
Brocchini Farms Inc ....E....209 599-4229
27011 S Austin Rd Ripon (95366) *(P-120)*
Brock LLC (PA) ....D....925 371-2184
333 N Canyons Pkwy # 221 Livermore (94551) *(P-4901)*
Brock Transportation, Livermore *Also called Brock LLC (P-4901)*
Broder Bros Co ....D....559 233-9900
3443 E Central Ave Fresno (93725) *(P-8021)*
Broderick Gen Engineering Inc ....E....707 996-7809
21750 8th St E Ste B Sonoma (95476) *(P-1673)*
Brokaw Nursery LLC ....D....805 647-2262
5501 Elizabeth Rd Ventura (93004) *(P-232)*
Broker Solutions Inc ....D....800 450-2010
233 Milford Dr Corona Del Mar (92625) *(P-9529)*
Broker Solutions Inc (PA) ....A....800 450-2010
14511 Myford Rd Ste 100 Tustin (92780) *(P-26540)*
Brokerage Lgstics Slutions Inc ....D....619 671-0276
1659 Gailes Blvd Ste 101 San Diego (92154) *(P-4902)*
Brook Furniture Clearance Ctr, Hayward *Also called Brook Furniture Rental Inc (P-14136)*
Brook Furniture Rental Inc ....E....510 487-4440
30985 Santana St Hayward (94544) *(P-14136)*
Brook Side Development, Stockton *Also called Groupe Development Associates (P-11566)*
Brookdale Brea ....E....714 706-9968
285 W Central Ave Brea (92821) *(P-10699)*
Brookdale Clairemont, San Diego *Also called Emeritus Corporation (P-19878)*
Brookdale Elk Grove, Elk Grove *Also called Brookdale Senior Living Inc (P-19762)*
Brookdale Folsom, Folsom *Also called Brookdale Senior Living Inc (P-19763)*
Brookdale Lving Cmmunities Inc ....C....408 445-7770
1009 Blossom River Way San Jose (95123) *(P-23841)*
Brookdale Lving Cmmunities Inc ....D....650 366-3900
485 Woodside Rd Ofc Redwood City (94061) *(P-19761)*
Brookdale Redwood City, Redwood City *Also called Brookdale Lving Cmmunities Inc (P-19761)*
Brookdale Senior Living Commun ....D....909 796-5421
25585 Van Leuven St Loma Linda (92354) *(P-10700)*
Brookdale Senior Living Inc ....D....916 683-1881
6727 Laguna Park Dr Elk Grove (95758) *(P-19762)*
Brookdale Senior Living Inc ....D....760 346-7772
72750 Country Club Dr Rancho Mirage (92270) *(P-20517)*
Brookdale Senior Living Inc ....D....916 983-9300
780 Harrington Way Folsom (95630) *(P-19763)*
Brookdale Senior Living Inc ....D....951 744-9861
1001 N Lyon Ave Hemet (92545) *(P-20518)*
Brookdale Sunwest, Hemet *Also called Brookdale Senior Living Inc (P-20518)*
Brooker Associates ....D....949 559-4877
16372 Cnstr Cir E 5 Irvine (92618) *(P-935)*
Brookfeld Bay Area Hldings LLC ....D....925 743-8000
500 La Gonda Way Ste 100 Danville (94526) *(P-11547)*
Brookfeld Sthland Holdings LLC ....C....714 427-6868
3200 Park Center Dr # 1000 Costa Mesa (92626) *(P-1090)*
Brookfield 1996 California, Del Mar *Also called Brookfield Homes of California (P-1091)*
Brookfield Dtla Fund Office ....D....626 792-2727
191 N Los Robles Ave Pasadena (91101) *(P-12094)*
Brookfield Dtla Fund Office ....D....213 626-3300
355 S Grand Ave Ste 3300 Los Angeles (90071) *(P-11846)*
Brookfield Homes, Danville *Also called Brookfeld Bay Area Hldings LLC (P-11547)*
Brookfield Homes of California ....E....858 481-8500
12865 Pointe Del Mar Way # 200 Del Mar (92014) *(P-1091)*
Brookfield Properties, Los Angeles *Also called Trz Holdings II Inc (P-11492)*
Brookfield Relocation Inc., Irvine *Also called Bgrs Relocation Inc (P-11824)*
Brookfield Residential, Costa Mesa *Also called Brookfeld Sthland Holdings LLC (P-1090)*
Brookside Community Health Ctr (PA) ....D....510 215-9092
2023 Vale Rd San Pablo (94806) *(P-22193)*
Brookside Country Club ....D....209 956-6200
3603 Saint Andrews Dr Stockton (95219) *(P-18408)*
Brookside Golf Course, Pasadena *Also called City of Pasadena (P-18232)*
Brooktrails Lodge LLC ....D....707 459-1596
24675 Birch St Willits (95490) *(P-12095)*
Brosamer & Wall Inc ....C....925 932-7900
1777 Oakland Blvd Ste 300 Walnut Creek (94596) *(P-24974)*
Brosamer & Wall LLC ....E....925 932-7900
1777 Oakland Blvd Ste 300 Walnut Creek (94596) *(P-10948)*
Broughton Hospitality Group (PA) ....C....714 908-4237
2400 E Katella Ave # 300 Anaheim (92806) *(P-26161)*
Broward Builders Inc ....D....530 666-5635
1200 E Kentucky Ave Woodland (95776) *(P-1426)*
Brower Mechanical Inc ....D....530 749-0808
4060 Alvis Ct Rocklin (95677) *(P-17441)*
Brown & Toland Medical Group ....C....415 752-8038
3905 Sacramento St # 301 San Francisco (94118) *(P-18845)*
Brown and Caldwell (PA) ....C....925 937-9010
201 N Civic Dr Ste 115 Walnut Creek (94596) *(P-24975)*
Brown and Caldwell ....D....530 747-0650
202 Cousteau Pl Ste 175 Davis (95618) *(P-24976)*
Brown and Caldwell ....D....858 514-8822
9665 Chesapeake Dr # 201 San Diego (92123) *(P-24977)*
Brown and Streza LLP ....D....949 453-2900
40 Pacifica Ste 1500 Irvine (92618) *(P-26541)*
Brown Armstrong Accntancy Corp ....D....661 324-4971
4200 Truxtun Ave Ste 300 Bakersfield (93309) *(P-25542)*
Brown Armstrong Cpas, Bakersfield *Also called Brown Armstrong Accntancy Corp (P-25542)*
Brown Construction Inc ....D....916 374-8616
1465 Entp Blvd Ste 100 West Sacramento (95691) *(P-1427)*
Brown Tland Physcn Svcs Orgnzt (PA) ....B....415 972-4162
1221 Broadway Ste 700 Oakland (94612) *(P-18846)*
Brownco Construction Co Inc ....D....714 935-9600
1000 E Katella Ave Anaheim (92805) *(P-1428)*
Browne Child Development Ctr, Oceanside *Also called Business and Support Services (P-23680)*
Brownie's Digital Imaging, Sacramento *Also called American Reprographics Co LLC (P-13748)*
Browning Apartments ....E....213 252-8847
1104 Browning Blvd Los Angeles (90037) *(P-10701)*
Browning-Ferris Industries Inc ....C....818 790-5410
9200 Glenoaks Blvd Sun Valley (91352) *(P-6167)*
Browning-Ferris Industries LLC ....D....408 262-1401
1601 Dixon Landing Rd Milpitas (95035) *(P-6168)*
Bruce Olson Construction Inc ....D....530 581-1087
7320 River Rd Tahoe City (96145) *(P-1232)*
Bruck Lighting Systems, Tustin *Also called Ledra Brands Inc (P-6568)*
Brudvik Inc (PA) ....D....760 320-4429
600 S Eugene Rd Palm Springs (92264) *(P-2442)*
BRUDVIK RENTAL DIVISION, Palm Springs *Also called Brudvik Inc (P-2442)*
Bruml Management LLC ....E....800 733-3629
2051 Alpine Way Hayward (94545) *(P-8059)*
Brunswick Cal Oaks Bowl, Murrieta *Also called Bowlero Corp (P-18028)*
Brunswick Corner Partnership ....E....916 649-7500
550 Howe Ave Ste 200 Sacramento (95825) *(P-10949)*
Brunswick Covino Lanes, Covina *Also called Bowlero Corp (P-18025)*
Brunswick Deer Creks Lnes 213, Rancho Cucamonga *Also called Bowlero Corp (P-18027)*
Bryan Cave Lighton Paisner LLP ....E....415 675-3400
333 Market St Fl 25 San Francisco (94105) *(P-22401)*
Bryan Cave Lighton Paisner LLP ....D....949 223-7000
3161 Michelson Dr # 1500 Irvine (92612) *(P-22402)*
Bryan Cave Lighton Paisner LLP ....C....310 576-2100
120 Broadway Ste 300 Santa Monica (90401) *(P-22403)*
Bryant Elementary School, Garden Grove *Also called Garden Grove Unified Schl Dst (P-23727)*

A
L
P
H
A
B
E
T
I
C

Employee Codes: A=Over 500 employees, B=251-500
C=101-250, D=51-100, E=50
2020 Directory of California
Wholesalers and Services Companies
© Mergent Inc. 1-800-342-5647
1199

Bryant Ranch Prepack....E....818 764-7225
1919 N Victory Pl Burbank (91504) ***(P-7924)***
Bryce Canyon Resorts, El Portal *Also called Yosemite Management Group LLC* ***(P-13132)***
Bsgs Five Points, Five Points *Also called Britz Fertilizers Inc* ***(P-8837)***
Bshh II LLC....E....310 356-4587
475 N Pacific Coast Hwy El Segundo (90245) ***(P-12096)***
BSK Associates....D....559 497-2888
1414 Stanislaus St Fresno (93706) ***(P-24978)***
Bsl Golf Corp....C....831 899-7271
1 Mcclure Way Seaside (93955) ***(P-18225)***
Bsm UNI....E....213 626-2557
712 Ceres Ave Los Angeles (90021) ***(P-8365)***
Bsnap LLC....D....657 269-4410
4 Hutton Centre Dr Fl 10 Santa Ana (92707) ***(P-9530)***
Bssp, Sausalito *Also called Butler Shine Stern Prtners LLC* ***(P-13479)***
Bst Enterprises Inc....D....310 638-1222
17801 S Susana Rd Compton (90221) ***(P-6427)***
BT Americas Inc....D....646 487-7400
2160 E Grand Ave El Segundo (90245) ***(P-7242)***
BT Holdings Inc....E....707 279-4317
4150 Soda Bay Rd Kelseyville (95451) ***(P-201)***
Bti Wireless, La Mirada *Also called Bravo Tech Inc* ***(P-5199)***
Btig LLC (PA)....D....415 248-2200
600 Montgomery St Fl 6 San Francisco (94111) ***(P-9656)***
Bubbla Inc....E....818 884-2000
7931 Deering Ave Canoga Park (91304) ***(P-8954)***
Buchanan Fund I LLC....D....949 721-1414
620 Nwport Ctr Dr Ste 850 Newport Beach (92660) ***(P-11892)***
Buchanan Street Partners LP....D....949 721-1414
3501 Jamboree Rd Ste 4200 Newport Beach (92660) ***(P-10950)***
Buck Global LLC....D....310 282-8232
1801 Century Park E # 500 Los Angeles (90067) ***(P-27268)***
Buck Inst For RES On Aging (PA)....C....415 209-2000
8001 Redwood Blvd Novato (94945) ***(P-25972)***
Buckelew Programs (PA)....C....415 457-6964
1401 Los Gamos Dr Ste 240 San Rafael (94903) ***(P-22951)***
Buckeye Fire Equipment Company....B....510 483-1815
2416 Teagarden St San Leandro (94577) ***(P-7532)***
Buckingham Affrdbl Aprtmnts LP....D....424 273-6162
11911 San Vicente Blvd Los Angeles (90049) ***(P-26162)***
Buckingham Apartments, Los Angeles *Also called Buckingham Affrdbl Aprtmnts LP* ***(P-26162)***
Buckingham Property Management....D....559 322-1105
12609 Moffatt Ln Fresno (93730) ***(P-13402)***
Buckland Vineyard Management....D....530 333-1534
4560 Slodusty Rd Garden Valley (95633) ***(P-26163)***
Buckles-Smith Electric Company (PA)....D....408 280-7777
540 Martin Ave Santa Clara (95050) ***(P-7533)***
Budget Electric, Tracy *Also called American Engrg Contrs Inc* ***(P-2419)***
Budget Electrical Contrs Inc....C....909 381-2646
25051 5th St San Bernardino (92410) ***(P-2443)***
Budget Rent-A-Car, Beverly Hills *Also called Star Lax LLC* ***(P-17223)***
Buds & Son Trucking Inc....D....619 443-4200
12570 Highway 67 Lakeside (92040) ***(P-3855)***
Budway Enterprises Inc (PA)....D....909 463-0500
13600 Napa St Fontana (92335) ***(P-3979)***
Budway Trucking & Warehousing, Fontana *Also called Budway Enterprises Inc* ***(P-3979)***
Buena Park Medical Group Inc (PA)....D....714 994-5290
6301 Beach Blvd Ste 101 Buena Park (90621) ***(P-18847)***
Buena Park Nursing Center, Apple Valley *Also called 8520 Western Ave Inc* ***(P-20473)***
Buena Park Police Association....D....714 562-3901
6650 Beach Blvd Buena Park (90621) ***(P-24436)***
Buena Ventura Care Center Inc (PA)....D....323 268-0106
1016 S Record Ave Los Angeles (90023) ***(P-19764)***
Buena Ventura Care Center Inc....D....818 247-4476
1505 Colby Dr Glendale (91205) ***(P-20519)***
Buena Vista Care Center, Santa Barbara *Also called Covenant Care California LLC* ***(P-19836)***
Buena Vista Care Center Inc....D....714 535-7264
1440 S Euclid St Anaheim (92802) ***(P-19765)***
Buena Vista Food Products Inc (HQ)....C....626 815-8859
823 W 8th St Azusa (91702) ***(P-8551)***
Buena Vista International Inc (HQ)....E....818 560-1000
500 S Buena Vista St Burbank (91521) ***(P-17784)***
Buena Vista Manor, Duarte *Also called Cal Southern Presbt Homes* ***(P-19769)***
Buena Vista Pictures Dist, Burbank *Also called ABC Cable Networks Group* ***(P-17782)***
Buena Vista Television (HQ)....C....818 560-1878
500 S Buena Vista St Burbank (91521) ***(P-16572)***
Buena Vista TV Advg Sls, Burbank *Also called Buena Vista Television* ***(P-16572)***
Buenaventura Medical Group (PA)....B....805 477-6000
888 S Hill Rd Ventura (93003) ***(P-18848)***
Buenaventura Medical Group....D....805 477-6220
2601 E Main St Ste 104 Ventura (93003) ***(P-18849)***
Buffalo Distribution....E....510 475-9810
1624 Pacific St Union City (94587) ***(P-8123)***
Buffalo Spot MGT Group LLC....C....949 354-0884
7245 Garden Grove Blvd Garden Grove (92841) ***(P-26164)***
Buffini & Company (PA)....C....760 827-2100
6349 Palomar Oaks Ct Carlsbad (92011) ***(P-23572)***
Build Group Inc (PA)....C....415 367-9399
457 Minna St Ste 100 San Francisco (94103) ***(P-1429)***
Build Group Inc....D....408 986-8711
1210 Coleman Ave Santa Clara (95050) ***(P-1430)***
Build Sjc, Santa Clara *Also called Build Group Inc* ***(P-1430)***
Buildcom Inc....B....800 375-3403
402 Otterson Dr Ste 100 Chico (95928) ***(P-7414)***
Builders & Tradesmens....D....916 772-9200
6610 Sierra College Blvd Rocklin (95677) ***(P-10302)***
Builders & Tradesmens Insur....D....916 772-9200
6610 Sierra College Blvd Rocklin (95677) ***(P-9864)***
Builders Firstsource Inc....E....619 440-7711
1262 E Main St El Cajon (92021) ***(P-6608)***
Builders Firstsource Inc....E....619 425-6660
3450 Highland Ave National City (91950) ***(P-6609)***
Building & Safety Department, Fremont *Also called City of Fremont* ***(P-25426)***
Building and Property MGT BR, Los Angeles *Also called General Services Cal Dept* ***(P-13936)***
Building Cleaning Systems, Santa Ana *Also called Carrasco Heleo* ***(P-13876)***
Building Elctronic Contrls Inc (PA)....E....909 305-1600
2246 Lindsay Way Glendora (91740) ***(P-2444)***
Building Material Distrs Inc (PA)....C....209 745-3001
225 Elm Ave Galt (95632) ***(P-6610)***
Building Services, San Bernardino *Also called San Bernardino City Unf School* ***(P-14036)***
Building Services/System Inc....D....925 688-1234
2575 Stanwell Dr Concord (94520) ***(P-10574)***
Buildingminds Inc....E....973 397-6510
1200 Seaport Blvd Redwood City (94063) ***(P-14693)***
Buildings Iot Inc (PA)....D....800 800-7126
3451 Vincent Rd Ste C Pleasant Hill (94523) ***(P-7415)***
Bulk Transportation (PA)....D....909 594-2855
415 S Lemon Ave Walnut (91789) ***(P-3980)***
Bullup Inc....E....566 997-2543
4365 Via Scorpresa San Diego (92124) ***(P-14694)***
Bully Pictures Inc (PA)....C....310 395-6500
1220 Cabrillo Ave Venice (90291) ***(P-17892)***
Bulmaro Castro Contractors....C....831 675-2927
349 Belden St Gonzales (93926) ***(P-14235)***
Bungalow 16 Entertainment LLC....E....310 226-7870
8113 Melrose Ave Los Angeles (90046) ***(P-7782)***
Bunge Milling Inc....C....530 666-1691
845 Kentucky Ave Woodland (95695) ***(P-8677)***
Bunim-Murray Productions....C....818 756-5100
1015 Grandview Ave Glendale (91201) ***(P-17586)***
Bunker Hill Club Inc....D....213 620-9662
555 S Flower St Ste 5100 Los Angeles (90071) ***(P-24503)***
Bunkers Grille, Brentwood *Also called Nines Restaurant* ***(P-26741)***
Bunny Beach Swimwear Inc (PA)....D....949 336-6300
555 Anton Blvd Ste 150 Costa Mesa (92626) ***(P-8060)***
Bunzl Distribution Cal LLC (HQ)....D....714 688-1900
3310 E Miraloma Ave Anaheim (92806) ***(P-7872)***
Bunzl Retail Services LLC....D....909 476-2457
8449 Milliken Ave Ste 102 Rancho Cucamonga (91730) ***(P-7873)***
Bunzl Usa Inc....D....314 997-5959
15959 Piuma Ave Cerritos (90703) ***(P-7874)***
Buona Terra Farming Co Inc....D....805 614-9229
2380 A St Santa Maria (93455) ***(P-26165)***
Burbank Airport Mariott Hotel, Burbank *Also called PHF II Burbank LLC* ***(P-12750)***
Burbank Bob Hope Airport, Burbank *Also called Jetblue Airways Corporation* ***(P-4669)***
Burbank Dental Laboratory Inc....C....818 841-2256
2101 Floyd St Burbank (91504) ***(P-21603)***
Burbank Housing Dev Corp....C....707 526-9782
790 Sonoma Ave Santa Rosa (95404) ***(P-11548)***
Burbank Television Entps LLC....C....818 954-6000
4000 Warner Blvd Burbank (91522) ***(P-5581)***
Burbank Water & Power, Burbank *Also called City of Burbank* ***(P-5993)***
Burch Construction Company Inc....E....760 788-9370
405 Maple St Ste C-101 Ramona (92065) ***(P-1431)***
Burdette De Cock Inc....C....310 542-0563
3625 Del Amo Blvd Ste 105 Torrance (90503) ***(P-21689)***
Burdick Painting....D....408 567-1330
705 Nuttman St Santa Clara (95054) ***(P-3387)***
Bureau Veritas North Amer Inc....D....714 431-4100
1940 E Deere Ave Ste 210 Santa Ana (92705) ***(P-27007)***
Burford Family Farming Co LP (PA)....C....559 431-0902
1443 W Sample Ave Fresno (93711) ***(P-304)***
Burford Ranch, Fresno *Also called Burford Family Farming Co LP* ***(P-304)***
Burger Physcl Therapy Svcs Inc (HQ)....C....916 983-5900
1301 E Bidwell St Ste 201 Folsom (95630) ***(P-19657)***
Burger Physcl Thrapy Rhbltion, Folsom *Also called Burger Physcl Therapy Svcs Inc* ***(P-19657)***
Burger Physical Therapy....E....916 983-5900
1301 E Bidwell St Ste 101 Folsom (95630) ***(P-19658)***
Burger Rhblitation Systems Inc....D....916 617-2400
2101 Stone Blvd Ste 175 West Sacramento (95691) ***(P-19659)***
Burger Rhblitation Systems Inc....D....916 863-5785
6614 Mercy Ct Ste C Fair Oaks (95628) ***(P-19660)***
Burger Rhblitation Systems Inc (PA)....C....800 900-8491
1301 E Bidwell St Ste 201 Folsom (95630) ***(P-19661)***
Burke Williams & Sorensen LLP (PA)....D....213 236-0600
444 S Flower St Ste 2400 Los Angeles (90071) ***(P-22404)***
Burkshire Has A Way Home Servc....D....818 501-4800
16810 Ventura Blvd Fl 1 Encino (91436) ***(P-10951)***
Burleigh Point Ltd (HQ)....C....949 428-3200
5600 Argosy Ave Ste 100 Huntington Beach (92649) ***(P-10952)***
Burlingame Country Club....D....650 696-8100
80 New Place Rd Hillsborough (94010) ***(P-18409)***
Burlingame Industries Inc (PA)....D....909 355-7000
3546 N Riverside Ave Rialto (92377) ***(P-13156)***
Burlingame Industries Inc....C....909 887-7038
277 Lytle Creek Rd Lytle Creek (92358) ***(P-13157)***
Burlingame Industries Inc....D....209 464-9001
4555 Mckinley Ave Stockton (95206) ***(P-6711)***
Burlingame Long Term Care, Burlingame *Also called San Mateo Healthcare & Wellnes* ***(P-20236)***
Burlingame Senior Care LLC....B....650 692-3758
1100 Trousdale Dr Burlingame (94010) ***(P-23842)***

Mergent e-mail: customerrelations@mergent.com
1200
2020 Directory of California
Wholesalers and Services Companies
(P-0000) Products & Services Section entry number
(PA)=Parent Co (HQ)=Headquarters (DH)=Div Headquarters

Burlingame Skilled Nursing, Burlingame *Also called Burlingame Senior Care LLC* ***(P-23842)***
Burlington Convalescent Hosp (PA) ....D.......213 381-5585
845 S Burlington Ave Los Angeles (90057) ***(P-19766)***
Burlington Convalescent Hosp ....D.......323 295-7737
3737 Don Felipe Dr Los Angeles (90008) ***(P-19767)***
Burlington Northern, San Bernardino *Also called Bnsf Railway Company* ***(P-3496)***
Burlington Northern, Barstow *Also called Bnsf Railway Company* ***(P-3497)***
Burlington Northern, Commerce *Also called Bnsf Railway Company* ***(P-3498)***
Burlington Northern, Vernon *Also called Bnsf Railway Company* ***(P-3499)***
Burn 60 LLC ....E.......310 476-5656
159 S Barrington Pl Los Angeles (90049) ***(P-18126)***
Burner Sheet Metal LLC (HQ) ....E.......619 938-9727
9749 Cactus St Ste A Lakeside (92040) ***(P-1432)***
Burnham & Brown, Oakland *Also called Burnham Brown A Prof Corp* ***(P-22405)***
Burnham Brown A Prof Corp ....C.......510 444-6800
1901 Harrison St Ste 1100 Oakland (94612) ***(P-22405)***
Burnham Real Estate, San Diego *Also called Christian and Wakefield* ***(P-11014)***
Burns & McDonnell Inc ....D.......714 256-1595
140 S State College Blvd Brea (92821) ***(P-24979)***
Burns and Sons Trucking Inc ....D.......619 460-5394
9210 Olive Dr Spring Valley (91977) ***(P-3856)***
BURR PILGER MAYER, Santa Rosa *Also called Burr Pilger Mayer* ***(P-25543)***
Burr Pilger Mayer ....D.......707 544-4078
110 Stony Point Rd # 210 Santa Rosa (95401) ***(P-25543)***
Burr Pilger Mayer Inc (PA) ....C.......415 421-5757
600 California St Fl 6 San Francisco (94108) ***(P-25544)***
Burr Pilger Mayer Inc ....E.......408 961-6300
10 Almaden Blvd Ste 1000 San Jose (95113) ***(P-25545)***
Burr Pilger Mayer Inc ....E.......650 855-6800
4200 Bohannon Dr Ste 250 Menlo Park (94025) ***(P-25546)***
Burrtec Waste Group Inc ....D.......760 256-2730
2340 W Main St Barstow (92311) ***(P-3857)***
Burrtec Waste Industries Inc (HQ) ....C.......909 429-4200
9890 Cherry Ave Fontana (92335) ***(P-6169)***
Burtch Construction, Bakersfield *Also called Burtch Trucking Inc* ***(P-1674)***
Burtch Trucking Inc ....D.......661 399-1736
18815 Highway 65 Bakersfield (93308) ***(P-1674)***
Burtech Pipeline Incorporated ....D.......760 634-2822
102 2nd St Encinitas (92024) ***(P-1836)***
Burton-Way House Ltd A CA ....C.......805 214-8075
2 Dole Dr Westlake Village (91362) ***(P-12097)***
Burton-Way House Ltd A CA ....C.......310 273-2222
300 S Doheny Dr Los Angeles (90048) ***(P-12098)***
Burton-Way House Ltd A CA (PA) ....E.......310 552-6623
2029 Century Park E # 2200 Los Angeles (90067) ***(P-12099)***
Bus Company, Santa Clarita *Also called Santa Clarita City of* ***(P-3764)***
Busa Servicing Inc (HQ) ....C.......310 203-3400
2029 Century Park E # 4200 Los Angeles (90067) ***(P-9176)***
Bushnell Gardens ....D.......916 791-4199
5255 Douglas Blvd Granite Bay (95746) ***(P-8885)***
Bushnell's Landscape Creations, Granite Bay *Also called Bushnell Gardens* ***(P-8885)***
Business and Support Services ....D.......760 830-6873
P.O. Box 6001 Twentynine Palms (92278) ***(P-18410)***
Business and Support Services ....B.......760 725-5187
Camp Pendleton Mc Base Oceanside (92055) ***(P-19605)***
Business and Support Services ....E.......760 725-2817
Santa Jancinto Rd 20286 Oceanside (92054) ***(P-23680)***
Business and Support Services ....A.......858 577-1061
Mccs Bldg 2273 Elrod Ave San Diego (92145) ***(P-18637)***
Business Connections ....D.......530 527-6229
332 Pine St Red Bluff (96080) ***(P-14236)***
Business Department, Murrieta *Also called Southwest Healthcare Sys Aux* ***(P-21216)***
Business For Scial Rspnsbility (PA) ....C.......415 984-3200
220 Montgomery St # 1700 San Francisco (94104) ***(P-26542)***
Business Furn Solutions Inc (PA) ....D.......408 325-3100
2150 N 1st St Ste 100 San Jose (95131) ***(P-6508)***
Business Intelligence ....E.......858 452-8200
2131 Palomar Airport Rd # 328 Carlsbad (92011) ***(P-26543)***
Business of Finance, San Francisco *Also called Airport Commisions* ***(P-4749)***
Business Services Network ....D.......415 282-8161
1275 Fairfax Ave Ste 103 San Francisco (94124) ***(P-13720)***
Businesscom Inc ....D.......310 586-4000
2120 Colorado Ave Fl 3 Santa Monica (90404) ***(P-26544)***
Butcher's Brand, San Leandro *Also called Webers Quality Meats Inc* ***(P-8423)***
Butler America Holdings Inc (PA) ....A.......805 880-1978
3820 State St Ste B Santa Barbara (93105) ***(P-14237)***
Butler International Inc (PA) ....C.......805 882-2200
3820 State St Ste A Santa Barbara (93105) ***(P-14238)***
Butler Service Group Inc (HQ) ....D.......201 891-5312
3820 State St Ste A Santa Barbara (93105) ***(P-14481)***
Butler Shine Stern Prtners LLC ....C.......415 331-6049
20 Liberty Ship Way Sausalito (94965) ***(P-13479)***
Butte Basin Management Co ....E.......530 674-2060
1624 Poole Blvd Yuba City (95993) ***(P-26166)***
Butte County Employment Center, Oroville *Also called County of Butte* ***(P-23062)***
Butte County Mental Hlth Svcs, Chico *Also called County of Butte* ***(P-21990)***
Butte County Probation, Oroville *Also called County of Butte* ***(P-23059)***
BUTTE HOME HEALTH & HOSPICE, Chico *Also called Butte Home Health Inc* ***(P-21690)***
Butte Home Health Inc ....C.......530 895-0462
10 Constitution Dr Chico (95973) ***(P-21690)***
Butte Primary Care Med Group ....D.......530 877-0762
6585 Clark Rd Ste 200 Paradise (95969) ***(P-18850)***
Butte-Yb-Stter Wtr Qlty Cltion ....D.......530 673-5131
625 Cooper Ave Yuba City (95991) ***(P-4332)***
Butter Paddle ....D.......408 395-1678
33 N Santa Cruz Ave Los Gatos (95030) ***(P-16664)***
Butter Paddle, The, Los Gatos *Also called Butter Paddle* ***(P-16664)***
Butterfield Electric Inc (PA) ....C.......530 666-2116
2101 Freeway Dr Ste A Woodland (95776) ***(P-2445)***
Butterwick Dr Kimberly Jane MD ....D.......858 657-1002
9339 Genesee Ave Ste 300 San Diego (92121) ***(P-18851)***
Button & Turkovich ....D.......530 795-2090
24604 Buckeye Rd Winters (95694) ***(P-305)***
Button Transportation Inc ....C.......707 678-7434
7000 Button Ln Dixon (95620) ***(P-3981)***
Buttonwillow Warehouse Co Inc (HQ) ....D.......661 695-6500
3430 Unicorn Rd Bakersfield (93308) ***(P-8838)***
Buxton Consulting ....D.......925 467-0700
5976 W Las Positas Blvd Pleasanton (94588) ***(P-27008)***
Buy Fresh Produce Inc ....D.......323 796-0127
6636 E 26th St Commerce (90040) ***(P-8433)***
Buyefficient LLC ....D.......949 382-3129
903 Calle Amanecer # 200 San Clemente (92673) ***(P-6922)***
Buyerlink, Walnut Creek *Also called One Planet Ops Inc* ***(P-13553)***
Buyers Consultation Svc Inc (PA) ....D.......818 341-4820
8735 Remmet Ave Canoga Park (91304) ***(P-7243)***
Buzz Oates Management Services ....E.......916 381-3843
555 Capitol Mall Ste 900 Sacramento (95814) ***(P-10953)***
Buzztime Inc ....C.......760 476-1976
2231 Rutherford Rd # 200 Carlsbad (92008) ***(P-5582)***
BV General Inc ....D.......323 651-0043
619 N Fairfax Ave Los Angeles (90036) ***(P-20520)***
BVHP, San Francisco *Also called Bayview Hunters Point Foundati* ***(P-24805)***
Bvk Gaming Inc ....D.......707 644-8853
3466 Broadway St American Canyon (94503) ***(P-18638)***
Bvls, Plymouth *Also called Borjon Iscander* ***(P-614)***
Bvs Entertainment Inc (HQ) ....E.......818 460-6917
500 S Buena Vista St Burbank (91521) ***(P-17587)***
Bwr Public Relations ....D.......310 248-6100
9100 Wilshire Blvd 500w Beverly Hills (90212) ***(P-26899)***
Bwrpr, Beverly Hills *Also called Baker Winokur* ***(P-26895)***
Bws Group Co., La Habra *Also called Ob Usa Inc* ***(P-8784)***
Bx Construction LLC ....D.......951 509-9412
11671 Sterling Ave Ste K Riverside (92503) ***(P-1092)***
By Referral Only Inc ....D.......760 707-1300
2035 Corte Del Nogal # 200 Carlsbad (92011) ***(P-27009)***
By The Blue Sea LLC ....B.......310 458-0030
1 Pico Blvd Santa Monica (90405) ***(P-12100)***
By Wind Inc ....D.......949 385-6219
15 Enterprise Ste 520 Aliso Viejo (92656) ***(P-14695)***
By-The-Bay Investments Inc ....B.......510 793-2581
37000 Fremont Blvd Fremont (94536) ***(P-11893)***
Bycor General Contractors Inc ....D.......858 587-1901
6490 Marindustry Dr Ste A San Diego (92121) ***(P-1433)***
Byers Enterprises Inc ....D.......530 272-7777
11773 Slow Poke Ln Grass Valley (95945) ***(P-3030)***
Byers Leafguard Gutter Systems, Grass Valley *Also called Byers Enterprises Inc* ***(P-3030)***
Bynd LLC ....D.......415 944-2293
100 Montgomery St # 1102 San Francisco (94104) ***(P-14696)***
Byrd Harvest Inc ....B.......805 343-1608
192 Guadalupe St Guadalupe (93434) ***(P-449)***
Byrd Produce, Guadalupe *Also called Byrd Harvest Inc* ***(P-449)***
Byrom-Davey Inc ....E.......858 513-7199
13220 Evnng Crk Dr S # 103 San Diego (92128) ***(P-1949)***
Byron Park, Walnut Creek *Also called A F Evans Company Inc* ***(P-16587)***
Byte Mobile, Santa Clara *Also called Bytemobile Inc* ***(P-5777)***
Bytedance Inc ....D.......844 523-3993
3000 El Camino Real 2-400 Palo Alto (94306) ***(P-14697)***
Bytemobile Inc (HQ) ....B.......408 327-7700
2860 De La Cruz Blvd # 200 Santa Clara (95050) ***(P-5777)***
Bytheways Manufacturing Inc ....B.......916 453-1212
2080 Enterprise Blvd West Sacramento (95691) ***(P-6549)***
Bz - Bee Pollination Inc ....E.......530 787-3044
24204 Rd 23 Esparto (95627) ***(P-433)***
C & B Delivery Services ....D.......909 623-4708
230 Diamond St Laguna Beach (92651) ***(P-4377)***
C & C Boats Inc ....E.......805 445-9456
1861 Baja Vista Way Camarillo (93010) ***(P-4638)***
C & C Construction Inc ....E.......916 434-5280
7941 E Hidden Lakes Dr Granite Bay (95746) ***(P-1434)***
C & C Security Patrol Inc (PA) ....C.......510 713-1260
4615 Enterprise Cmn Fremont (94538) ***(P-16220)***
C & G Farms Inc ....C.......831 679-2978
25453 Iverson Rd Chualar (93925) ***(P-40)***
C & I, Spring Valley *Also called Commercial Indus Roofg Co Inc* ***(P-3039)***
C & L Refrigeration Corp ....C.......800 901-4822
4111 N Palm St Fullerton (92835) ***(P-2084)***
C & M Transfer San Diego Inc ....D.......619 562-6111
8787 Olive Ln Santee (92071) ***(P-4197)***
C & O Painting Inc ....E.......408 279-8011
1500 N 4th St San Jose (95112) ***(P-2336)***
C & R Systems Inc (PA) ....E.......951 270-0255
1835 Capital St Corona (92880) ***(P-2446)***
C & S Draperies Inc ....C.......209 466-5371
4210 Kiernan Ave Modesto (95356) ***(P-13263)***
C & S Wholesale Grocers Inc ....B.......916 383-5275
8301 Fruitridge Rd Sacramento (95826) ***(P-4378)***
C A A, Los Angeles *Also called Creative Artists Agency LLC* ***(P-17904)***
C A C, Goleta *Also called Community Action Commsn Santa* ***(P-24151)***
C A H H S ....D.......916 552-7507
1215 K St Ste 800 Sacramento (95814) ***(P-24325)***
C A Hofmann Construction Inc ....E.......909 484-5888
8923 Laramie Dr Rancho Cucamonga (91737) ***(P-2760)***
C A L M, Santa Barbara *Also called Child Abuse Lstening Mediation* ***(P-22987)***

A L P H A B E T I C

Employee Codes: A=Over 500 employees, B=251-500
C=101-250, D=51-100, E=50
2020 Directory of California
Wholesalers and Services Companies
© Mergent Inc. 1-800-342-5647
1201

C A Rasmussen Inc (PA) ....E....661 367-9040
28548 Livingston Ave Valencia (91355) ***(P-1950)***
C B B Z S Inc ....D....818 908-1900
7015 Valjean Ave Van Nuys (91406) ***(P-2337)***
C B Coast Newport Properties ....D....949 644-1600
840 Nwport Ctr Dr Ste 100 Newport Beach (92660) ***(P-10954)***
C B Richard Ellis Investors, Los Angeles *Also called T C W Realty Fund VI* ***(P-11877)***
C B S Marketwatch, San Francisco *Also called Marketwatch Inc* ***(P-16574)***
C C Connection Inc ....D....925 937-0100
2950 Buskirk Ave Ste 140 Walnut Creek (94597) ***(P-10955)***
C C S, Los Angeles *Also called Creative Channel Services LLC* ***(P-13482)***
C D C, Costa Mesa *Also called Creative Design Cons Inc* ***(P-16726)***
C D I, Sacramento *Also called Creative Design Interiors Inc* ***(P-2997)***
C D Lyon Construction Inc (PA) ....D....805 653-0173
380 W Stanley Ave Ventura (93001) ***(P-24980)***
C D Payroll Inc ....D....818 848-1562
2300 W Empire Ave Burbank (91504) ***(P-25547)***
C D R, Oxnard *Also called Child Development Resources of* ***(P-22992)***
C D R Enterprises Inc ....D....661 940-0344
42302 8th St E Lancaster (93535) ***(P-2761)***
C E B M Inc ....E....909 975-4440
3100 E Cedar St Ste 17 Ontario (91761) ***(P-13873)***
C E D, Orange *Also called County Whl Elc Co Los Angeles* ***(P-7140)***
C E H A, San Mateo *Also called California Envmtl Hlth Assn* ***(P-27014)***
C E I, Oakland *Also called Center For Elders Independence* ***(P-9936)***
C E P ....D....909 580-1456
400 N Pepper Ave Ste 107 Colton (92324) ***(P-18852)***
C E T, Gardena *Also called Charles E Thomas Company Inc* ***(P-1443)***
C E T, San Jose *Also called Center For Employment Training* ***(P-23576)***
C E Toland & Son ....C....707 747-1000
5300 Industrial Way Benicia (94510) ***(P-3388)***
C F I, Los Angeles *Also called Commodity Forwarders Inc* ***(P-4916)***
C F X, Carson *Also called City Fashion Express Inc* ***(P-4914)***
C H I, Modesto *Also called Community Hospice Inc* ***(P-20419)***
C H O C, Fairfield *Also called Community Housing Opport* ***(P-27037)***
C H Reynolds Electric Inc ....B....408 436-9280
1281 Wayne Ave San Jose (95131) ***(P-2447)***
C H Robinson Intl Inc ....D....310 763-6080
680 Knox St Ste 210 Torrance (90502) ***(P-4903)***
C I C C, Covelo *Also called Covelo Indian Community Center* ***(P-11080)***
C I Container Line, Los Angeles *Also called Carmichael International Svc* ***(P-4906)***
C I Design, Lake Forest *Also called Commercial Indus Design Co Inc* ***(P-6814)***
C I G A, Glendale *Also called Califrnia Insur Guarantee Assn* ***(P-10228)***
C I W, Pittsburg *Also called Concord Iron Works Inc* ***(P-7057)***
C J Foods, Los Angeles *Also called CJ America Inc* ***(P-8557)***
C J Health Services Inc ....D....510 793-3000
38650 Mission Blvd Fremont (94536) ***(P-19768)***
C J Vandergeest Ldscp Care Inc ....D....805 650-0726
2476 Palma Dr Ste G Ventura (93003) ***(P-780)***
C L A, Van Nuys *Also called Clay Lacy Aviation Inc* ***(P-4762)***
C L Bryant Inc ....C....209 566-5000
7401 Del Cielo Way Modesto (95356) ***(P-8714)***
C M A, Sacramento *Also called California Medical Association* ***(P-24385)***
C M A Alliance ....E....818 981-0800
16542 Ventura Blvd # 210 Encino (91436) ***(P-10303)***
C M C Steel Fabricators Inc ....C....909 899-9993
12451 Arrow Rte Etiwanda (91739) ***(P-3256)***
C M C Steel Fabricators Inc ....D....909 873-3060
2755 S Willow Ave Bloomington (92316) ***(P-3257)***
C M S Hospitality, Los Angeles *Also called Concession Management Svcs Inc* ***(P-18669)***
C M Service, San Carlos *Also called Commercial Mechanical Svc Inc* ***(P-17445)***
C N B Commercial Banking Ctr, Riverside *Also called City National Bank* ***(P-9089)***
C N L Hotel Del Partners LP ....A....619 522-8299
1500 Orange Ave San Diego (92118) ***(P-12101)***
C O T S Inc (PA) ....D....714 751-5466
6242 Cherry Ave Long Beach (90805) ***(P-3655)***
C Overaa & Co (PA) ....C....510 234-0926
200 Parr Blvd Richmond (94801) ***(P-1336)***
C Overaa & Co ....C....510 235-0540
2555 El Portal Dr San Pablo (94806) ***(P-1337)***
C P Construction Co Inc ....E....909 981-1091
105 N Loma Pl Upland (91786) ***(P-1837)***
C P S Express (HQ) ....D....951 685-1041
3401 Etiwanda Ave B Jurupa Valley (91752) ***(P-3858)***
C P T C, Anaheim *Also called California Private Trnsp Co LP* ***(P-5103)***
C R A, Los Angeles *Also called Community Redevelopment Agency* ***(P-27038)***
C R S Drywall Inc ....D....408 998-4360
135 San Jose Ave San Jose (95125) ***(P-2762)***
C S C, Northridge *Also called Contemporary Services Corp* ***(P-14250)***
C S D P, Irvine *Also called Customer Srvc Dlvry Pltfrm Crp* ***(P-15972)***
C S I, Simi Valley *Also called Cardservice International Inc* ***(P-16676)***
C S I, Santa Fe Springs *Also called Csi Electrical Contractors Inc* ***(P-2467)***
C S I Patrol Services ....D....562 981-8988
3605 Long Beach Blvd # 205 Long Beach (90807) ***(P-16221)***
C S S, Bakersfield *Also called Construction Specialty Svc Inc* ***(P-1847)***
C S Transport Inc ....D....760 666-5661
425 E Heber Rd Ste 200 Heber (92249) ***(P-3859)***
C T B, Monterey *Also called Data Recognition Corporation* ***(P-27046)***
C T Corporation System ....D....925 287-9801
2875 Michelle Ste 100 Irvine (92606) ***(P-22406)***
C T I, Rancho Cucamonga *Also called Collection Technology Inc* ***(P-13677)***
C Team Construction Inc ....D....619 579-6572
1272 Greenfield Dr El Cajon (92021) ***(P-3122)***
C V S Optical Lab Div, Rancho Cordova *Also called Vision Service Plan* ***(P-10063)***
C V WATER DISTRICT, Coachella *Also called Coachella Valley Water Dst* ***(P-6036)***
C W 5, San Diego *Also called Kswb Inc* ***(P-5626)***
C W C, San Leandro *Also called Continental Western Corp* ***(P-7631)***
C W Driver Incorporated (PA) ....D....626 351-8800
468 N Rosemead Blvd Pasadena (91107) ***(P-1435)***
C W Hotels Ltd ....C....310 395-9700
1740 Ocean Ave Santa Monica (90401) ***(P-12102)***
C W S, San Diego *Also called Communction Wirg Spcalists Inc* ***(P-2460)***
C Y S, Fresno *Also called Comprehensive Youth Ser* ***(P-23046)***
C&C Jewelry Mfg Inc ....D....213 623-6800
323 W 8th St Fl 4 Los Angeles (90014) ***(P-7783)***
C&M Relocation Systems, Santee *Also called C & M Transfer San Diego Inc* ***(P-4197)***
C&R Maintance, Oxnard *Also called HE Julien & Associates Inc* ***(P-826)***
C&S Wholesale Grocers Inc ....B....559 442-4700
2797 S Orange Ave Fresno (93725) ***(P-8158)***
C-21 Super Stars ....D....949 389-1600
22342 Avenida Empresa Rcho STA Marg (92688) ***(P-10956)***
C-Air International Inc ....D....310 695-3400
9841 Arprt Blvd Ste 1400 Los Angeles (90045) ***(P-4904)***
C.E.G. Construction, Pico Rivera *Also called Chalmers Corporation* ***(P-1339)***
C.H.M.B., Escondido *Also called California Healthcare* ***(P-10309)***
C.O.M.P.A.S.S., Redding *Also called Care Options Management Plans* ***(P-21693)***
C.R. B Cnsulting Engineers Inc, Carlsbad *Also called Clark Richardson and Biskup* ***(P-25008)***
C/O Longwood Management, Los Angeles *Also called Magnolia Ventures Ltd* ***(P-16905)***
C/O Uc San Francisco ....D....310 794-1841
1245 16th St Ste 225 Santa Monica (90404) ***(P-18853)***
C/O Uc San Francisco (PA) ....C....858 534-7323
1111 Franklin St Fl 12 Oakland (94607) ***(P-26167)***
C2 Financial Corporation ....C....925 938-1300
3000 Citrus Cir Ste 118 Walnut Creek (94598) ***(P-9798)***
C2 Financial Corporation ....C....559 824-2300
978 Burlingame Ave Clovis (93612) ***(P-9799)***
C2 Financial Corporation ....C....858 220-2112
703 Sunset Ct San Diego (92109) ***(P-9800)***
C2 Imaging, Costa Mesa *Also called Crisp Enterprises Inc* ***(P-13759)***
C21 Peak ....C....818 363-1717
11011 Balboa Blvd Granada Hills (91344) ***(P-10957)***
C3 Iot, Redwood City *Also called C3ai Inc* ***(P-15270)***
C3ai Inc (PA) ....C....650 503-2200
1300 Seaport Blvd Ste 500 Redwood City (94063) ***(P-15270)***
C9 Edge Inc ....D....650 561-7855
177 Bovet Rd Ste 520 San Mateo (94402) ***(P-6811)***
Ca Inc ....C....800 225-5224
3965 Freedom Cir Fl 6 Santa Clara (95054) ***(P-15271)***
CA Landscape and Design, Upland *Also called California Ldscp & Design Inc* ***(P-783)***
CA Station Management Inc ....C....909 245-6251
3200 E Guasti Rd Ste 100 Ontario (91761) ***(P-1838)***
CA Ste Atom Assoc Intr-Ins Bur ....A....415 565-2012
150 Van Ness Ave San Francisco (94102) ***(P-10075)***
CA Ste Atom Assoc Intr-Ins Bur ....D....831 824-9128
4400 Capitola Rd Ste 100 Capitola (95010) ***(P-17413)***
CA Ste Atom Assoc Intr-Ins Bur ....D....650 623-3200
900 Miramonte Ave Mountain View (94040) ***(P-10304)***
Caa Sports LLC (HQ) ....D....424 288-2000
2000 Avenue Of The Stars # 100 Los Angeles (90067) ***(P-18057)***
Cabana Hotel, Palo Alto *Also called 4290 El Camino Properties LP* ***(P-11981)***
Cable Car Eyewear, Hollister *Also called Icu Eyewear Inc* ***(P-7818)***
Cableconn Industries Inc ....D....858 571-7111
7198 Convoy Ct San Diego (92111) ***(P-7131)***
Cabrillo College Children Ctr ....D....831 479-6352
6500 Soquel Dr Aptos (95003) ***(P-23681)***
Cabrillo Economic Dev Corp (PA) ....D....805 659-3791
702 County Square Dr # 200 Ventura (93003) ***(P-11549)***
Cabrillo Gen Insur Agcy Inc ....D....858 244-0550
7071 Convoy Ct Ste 201 San Diego (92111) ***(P-10305)***
Cac Studios, Malibu *Also called Creating Arts Company* ***(P-17903)***
Cache Creek Casino Resort ....A....530 796-3118
14455 State Highway 16 Brooks (95606) ***(P-12103)***
Cacho Landscape Maintenance Co ....E....818 365-0773
711 Truman St San Fernando (91340) ***(P-781)***
Caci Inc - Federal ....E....619 881-6000
1455 Frazee Rd Ste 700 San Diego (92108) ***(P-15563)***
Caci Nss Inc ....C....703 841-7800
3201 Airpark Dr Ste 109 Santa Maria (93455) ***(P-6812)***
Cacique Inc ....C....626 961-3399
14923 Proctor Ave La Puente (91746) ***(P-8310)***
Cactus Recycling Inc (PA) ....C....619 661-1283
8710 Avenida Fuente San Diego (92154) ***(P-6170)***
Cadence Design Systems Inc (PA) ....A....408 943-1234
2655 Seely Ave Bldg 5 San Jose (95134) ***(P-15272)***
Cadent Inc ....C....408 470-1000
2560 Orchard Pkwy San Jose (95131) ***(P-15564)***
Cadent Tech Inc (HQ) ....D....408 642-6400
4 N 2nd St Ste 1100 San Jose (95113) ***(P-14698)***
Cadforce Inc ....A....310 876-1800
10811 Wash Blvd Ste 302 Culver City (90232) ***(P-16665)***
Cadnchev Inc ....D....562 944-6422
13603 Foster Rd Santa Fe Springs (90670) ***(P-6495)***
Cadreon LLC ....C....415 262-5900
600 Battery St San Francisco (94111) ***(P-13480)***
Caesar and Seider Insur Svcs (PA) ....D....805 682-2571
40 E Alamar Ave Ste 4 Santa Barbara (93105) ***(P-10306)***
Caesars Entrtnment Oprting Inc ....A....760 751-3100
777 Harrahs Rincon Way Valley Center (92082) ***(P-18639)***
Caffeine Productions ....D....323 860-8111
1040 N Las Palmas Ave Los Angeles (90038) ***(P-17588)***

Cahill Contractors Inc (PA) ....D.......415 986-0600
425 California St # 2200 San Francisco (94104) *(P-1436)*
Cahill Contractors LLC ....D.......415 986-0600
425 California St # 2200 San Francisco (94104) *(P-1437)*
Cahuilla Creek Casino, Anza *Also called Cahuilla Creek Rest & Casino (P-18640)*
Cahuilla Creek Rest & Casino ....C.......951 763-1200
52702 Us Highway 371 Anza (92539) *(P-18640)*
Cai, Corona *Also called Combustion Associates Inc (P-5823)*
Cai Company, Brea *Also called California Automobile Insur Co (P-10076)*
Cai International Inc (PA) ....C.......415 788-0100
1 Market Plz Ste 900 San Francisco (94105) *(P-14137)*
Caine & Weiner Company Inc (PA) ....D.......818 226-6000
5805 Sepulvda Blvd # 400 Van Nuys (91411) *(P-13671)*
Caito Fisheries Inc (PA) ....D.......707 964-6368
19400 Harbor Ave Fort Bragg (95437) *(P-8366)*
Cake Corporation ....D.......650 215-7777
1528 S El Cmino Real Ste San Mateo (94402) *(P-14699)*
Cal Americas Wholesale Florist, Vista *Also called United Floral Exchange Inc (P-8928)*
Cal Bowl Enterprises LLC ....E.......562 421-8448
2500 Carson St Lakewood (90712) *(P-18029)*
Cal Care Inc ....C.......650 325-8600
1275 Crane St Menlo Park (94025) *(P-26168)*
Cal Chamber, Sacramento *Also called California Chamber Commerce (P-24328)*
Cal Citrus Packing Co ....D.......559 562-2536
111 N Mount Vernon Ave Lindsay (93247) *(P-472)*
Cal Coast Financial Inc ....D.......510 683-9850
39355 California St # 101 Fremont (94538) *(P-9616)*
Cal Coast Telecom, San Jose *Also called Radonich Corp (P-2597)*
Cal Coffee Shop, Lakewood *Also called Nationwide Theatres Corp (P-18040)*
Cal Color Growers LLC ....D.......408 778-0835
330 Peebles Ave Morgan Hill (95037) *(P-8886)*
Cal Consoldated Communications ....D.......916 786-6141
211 Lincoln St Roseville (95678) *(P-5370)*
Cal Courts, Eureka *Also called Nor-Wall Inc (P-18516)*
Cal Custom Tile ....D.......559 875-1460
1300 Commerce Way Sanger (93657) *(P-2885)*
Cal Empire Engineering Inc ....E.......626 915-8030
628 E Edna Pl Covina (91723) *(P-3337)*
Cal Facilities Management Co, San Jose *Also called Yang C Park (P-14458)*
Cal Fresco LLC ....C.......714 690-7700
6850 Artesia Blvd Buena Park (90620) *(P-8434)*
Cal Gran Theatres LLC ....E.......805 934-1582
3170 Santa Maria Way Santa Maria (93455) *(P-17822)*
Cal Micro, Ontario *Also called Ruuhwa Dann and Associates Inc (P-6260)*
Cal Mutual Inc ....D.......888 700-4650
2040 S Santa Cruz St # 115 Anaheim (92805) *(P-9531)*
CAL NORTH, Pleasanton *Also called Califrnia Yuth Soccer Assn Inc (P-24812)*
Cal Packing & Storage LP ....D.......559 638-2929
1356 S Buttonwillow Ave Reedley (93654) *(P-4341)*
Cal Pinnacle Mltary Cmmunities ....D.......619 764-5087
3200 4th Ave Ste 201 San Diego (92103) *(P-26169)*
Cal Poly Corporation ....D.......805 756-1587
Cal Poly Bldg 31 San Luis Obispo (93407) *(P-13136)*
Cal Poly Corporation ....C.......805 756-1131
Bldg 15 San Luis Obispo (93407) *(P-26170)*
Cal Poly Foundation, San Luis Obispo *Also called Cal Poly Corporation (P-26170)*
Cal Poly Pomona Foundation Inc (PA) ....A.......909 869-2950
3801 W Temple Ave Bldg 55 Pomona (91768) *(P-24810)*
CAL SHAKES, Berkeley *Also called California Shakespeare Theater (P-17894)*
Cal Sierra Construction Inc ....D.......916 416-7901
5904 Van Alstine Ave 1 Carmichael (95608) *(P-1839)*
Cal Southern Assn Governments (PA) ....C.......213 236-1800
900 Wilshire Blvd # 1700 Los Angeles (90017) *(P-27010)*
Cal Southern Presbt Homes ....C.......949 854-9500
19191 Harvard Ave Ofc Irvine (92612) *(P-10702)*
Cal Southern Presbt Homes ....C.......858 454-4201
7450 Olivetas Ave Ofc La Jolla (92037) *(P-23843)*
Cal Southern Presbt Homes (PA) ....D.......818 247-0420
516 Burchett St Glendale (91203) *(P-10703)*
Cal Southern Presbt Homes ....C.......818 244-7219
1230 E Windsor Rd Ofc Glendale (91205) *(P-10704)*
Cal Southern Presbt Homes ....D.......626 359-8141
802 Buena Vista St Duarte (91010) *(P-19769)*
Cal Southern Presbt Homes ....D.......818 247-0420
516 Burchett St Glendale (91203) *(P-10705)*
Cal Southern Presbt Homes ....C.......626 357-1632
1763 Royal Oaks Dr Ofc Duarte (91010) *(P-10706)*
Cal Southern Presbt Homes ....C.......760 747-4306
710 W 13th Ave Escondido (92025) *(P-23844)*
Cal Southern Presbt Homes ....D.......760 737-5110
500 E Valley Pkwy Ofc Escondido (92025) *(P-23845)*
Cal Southern Services ....D.......626 281-5942
419 Mcgroarty St San Gabriel (91776) *(P-13212)*
Cal Southern Sound Image Inc (PA) ....D.......760 737-3900
2425 Auto Park Way Escondido (92029) *(P-7244)*
Cal Southern United Food ....C.......714 220-2297
6425 Katella Ave Cypress (90630) *(P-10208)*
Cal Strs, West Sacramento *Also called Califor State Teach Retire Sys (P-10209)*
Cal Tech Emplyees Fderal Cr Un (PA) ....D.......818 952-4444
528 Foothill Blvd La Canada Flintridge (91011) *(P-9295)*
Cal Treehouse Almonds LLC ....C.......661 725-6334
2115 Road 144 Delano (93215) *(P-473)*
Cal West Enterprises, San Diego *Also called Wamc Company Inc (P-10842)*
Cal West General Engrg Inc ....E.......619 469-5811
5480 Baltimore Dr Ste 215 La Mesa (91942) *(P-14138)*
Cal West Underground Inc ....D.......951 371-6775
951 6th St Norco (92860) *(P-1951)*
Cal-A-Vie, Vista *Also called Spa Havens LP (P-18199)*
Cal-Coast Healthcare Inc ....D.......415 479-5149
81 Professional Ctr Pkwy San Rafael (94903) *(P-19770)*
Cal-Lift Inc ....D.......562 566-1400
13027 Crossroads Pkwy S La Puente (91746) *(P-7534)*
Cal-Med Ambulance, South El Monte *Also called California Med Response Inc (P-3657)*
Cal-Organic Farms, Lamont *Also called Grimmway Enterprises Inc (P-8487)*
Cal-Pacific Construction Inc ....E.......650 557-1238
1009 Terra Nova Blvd Pacifica (94044) *(P-1438)*
Cal-State Auto Parts Inc (PA) ....C.......714 630-5950
1361 N Red Gum St Anaheim (92806) *(P-6428)*
Cal-State Steel Corporation ....C.......310 632-2772
1801 W Compton Blvd Compton (90220) *(P-3258)*
Cal-Steam, San Francisco *Also called Ferguson Enterprises Inc (P-7419)*
Cal-West Concrete Cutting Inc (PA) ....C.......510 656-0253
3000 Tara Ct Union City (94587) *(P-3123)*
Cal-West Nurseries Inc ....C.......951 270-0667
138 North Dr Norco (92860) *(P-782)*
Cal/Pac Paintings & Coatings ....D.......714 628-1514
608 N Eckhoff St Orange (92868) *(P-2338)*
Calabasas Country Club, Calabasas *Also called Knight-Calabasas LLC (P-18473)*
Calabasas Country Club ....D.......818 222-8111
4515 Park Entrada Calabasas (91302) *(P-18411)*
Calance, Buena Park *Also called Partners Information Tech Inc (P-16077)*
Calatlantic Group Inc ....C.......760 602-6824
5750 Fleet St Ste 200 Carlsbad (92008) *(P-1093)*
Calatlantic Group Inc ....D.......951 898-5500
355 E Rincon St Ste 300 Corona (92879) *(P-1094)*
Calatlantic Group Inc ....E.......925 847-8700
3825 Hopyard Rd Ste 195 Pleasanton (94588) *(P-1289)*
Calatlantic Group Inc ....D.......949 789-1600
15131 Alton Pkwy Ste 300 Irvine (92618) *(P-1095)*
Calatlantic Group Inc ....D.......310 821-9843
13200 Fiji Way Marina Del Rey (90292) *(P-1096)*
Calatlantic Group Inc ....D.......949 789-1600
26 Technology Dr Irvine (92618) *(P-1097)*
Calatlantic Group Inc ....D.......760 931-4414
5740 Fleet St Ste 200 Carlsbad (92008) *(P-1290)*
Calatlantic Homes, Irvine *Also called Calatlantic Group Inc (P-1095)*
Calaveras County Water Dst ....D.......209 754-3543
120 Toma Ct San Andreas (95249) *(P-6018)*
Calavo Foods, Santa Paula *Also called Calavo Growers Inc (P-5091)*
Calavo Growers Inc ....D.......805 525-5511
15765 W Telegraph Rd Santa Paula (93060) *(P-5091)*
Calavo Growers Inc ....E.......951 676-7331
28410 Vincent Moraga Dr Temecula (92590) *(P-8435)*
Calbee North America LLC ....E.......707 427-2500
2600 Maxwell Way Fairfield (94534) *(P-8285)*
Calbond, Rancho Dominguez *Also called Calpipe Industries LLC (P-7052)*
Calcom Energy, Fresno *Also called California Coml Solar Inc (P-2086)*
Calculi Corporation ....E.......408 970-0007
3945 Freedom Cir Santa Clara (95054) *(P-15565)*
Calderon Building Maintenance ....D.......619 269-5940
3822 Sherman St San Diego (92110) *(P-13874)*
Caldwell Banker Inc ....D.......760 941-6888
40 Main St Ste E100 Vista (92083) *(P-10958)*
Caldwell Realty ....D.......562 907-5655
14831 Whittier Blvd # 102 Whittier (90605) *(P-10959)*
Caldwell Ventures LLC ....E.......530 899-0814
1351 E Lassen Ave Ofc Chico (95973) *(P-19771)*
Calenergy LLC ....B.......402 231-1527
7030 Gentry Rd Calipatria (92233) *(P-2448)*
Calex, Northridge *Also called Valley Hospital Medical Center (P-21352)*
Calex Engineering Inc ....D.......661 254-1866
23651 Pine St Newhall (91321) *(P-3305)*
Calhot Illinios LLC ....C.......310 536-9800
5250 W El Segundo Blvd Hawthorne (90250) *(P-12104)*
Calhoun Construction Inc ....C.......916 434-8356
110 Gateway Dr Ste 260 Lincoln (95648) *(P-1098)*
Cali Calmecac Language Academy ....D.......707 837-7747
9491 Starr Rd Windsor (95492) *(P-24504)*
Cali Hsg Finance Agcy ....D.......916 326-8627
500 Capitol Mall Ste 1400 Sacramento (95814) *(P-27011)*
Caliber Bodyworks Texas Inc ....D.......310 392-7662
1100 Colorado Ave Santa Monica (90401) *(P-17282)*
Caliber Bodyworks Texas Inc ....C.......714 436-5010
1399 Logan Ave Costa Mesa (92626) *(P-17283)*
Caliber Bodyworks Texas Inc ....D.......714 665-3905
5 Auto Center Dr Tustin (92782) *(P-17284)*
Caliber Bodyworks Texas Inc ....D.......408 972-0300
3517 Hillcap Ave San Jose (95136) *(P-17285)*
Caliber Bodyworks Texas Inc ....E.......909 598-1113
20601 Valley Blvd Walnut (91789) *(P-17286)*
Caliber Capital Group LLC ....A.......714 507-1998
5900 Katella Ave Ste A101 Cypress (90630) *(P-9801)*
Caliber Collision Centers, Tustin *Also called Caliber Bodyworks Texas Inc (P-17284)*
Caliber Collision Centers, San Jose *Also called Caliber Bodyworks Texas Inc (P-17285)*
Caliber Holdings Corporation ....D.......323 913-4000
3020 Riverside Dr Los Angeles (90039) *(P-17287)*
Caliber Home Loans Inc ....D.......925 417-3491
6600 Koll Center Pkwy Pleasanton (94566) *(P-9532)*
Caliber Home Loans Inc ....B.......707 432-1000
3700 Hilborn Rd Ste 700 Fairfield (94534) *(P-9533)*
Caliber Home Loans Inc ....D.......805 883-6800
1111 Chapala St Santa Barbara (93101) *(P-9534)*
Calibr A Division Scripps RES, La Jolla *Also called Scripps Research Institute (P-26028)*
Calibre International LLC (PA) ....C.......626 969-4660
6250 N Irwindale Ave Irwindale (91702) *(P-26900)*

Employee Codes: A=Over 500 employees, B=251-500
C=101-250, D=51-100, E=50
2020 Directory of California
Wholesalers and Services Companies
© Mergent Inc. 1-800-342-5647
1203

Calibuilder Construction Inc.......E.......408 832-2337
441 N Central Ave Ste 8 Campbell (95008) ***(P-1099)***
Calico Brands Inc.......E.......909 930-5000
2055 S Haven Ave Ontario (91761) ***(P-8955)***
Calico Building Services Inc.......C.......949 380-8707
15550 Rockfield Blvd C Irvine (92618) ***(P-13875)***
Caliente Farms, Delano *Also called M Caratan Inc* ***(P-146)***
Calif Institute Human Ser.......D.......707 664-2416
1801 E Cotati Ave Rohnert Park (94928) ***(P-26545)***
Calif Land Management, South Lake Tahoe *Also called California Land Mgt Svcs Corp* ***(P-13158)***
Calif Stat Univ Fres Foun.......C.......559 278-0850
5370 N Chestnut Ave Fresno (93725) ***(P-24811)***
Califia Farms LLC (PA).......E.......213 694-4667
1321 Palmetto St Los Angeles (90013) ***(P-8311)***
Califia Farms LLC.......D.......661 679-1000
33502 Lerdo Hwy Bakersfield (93308) ***(P-306)***
Califor State Teach Retire Sys (HQ).......C.......800 228-5453
100 Waterfront Pl West Sacramento (95605) ***(P-10209)***
California Academy Sciences (PA).......A.......415 379-8000
55 Music Concourse Dr San Francisco (94118) ***(P-24304)***
California Access Scaffold LLC.......D.......310 324-3388
331 Vineland Ave City of Industry (91746) ***(P-3389)***
California Air Cartage Inc (PA).......D.......619 291-8544
2357 Airlane Rd Ste B San Diego (92101) ***(P-4660)***
California Alumni Association (PA).......E.......510 900-8225
1 Alumni House Berkeley (94720) ***(P-24505)***
California American Water Co.......D.......619 656-2400
880 Kuhn Dr Chula Vista (91914) ***(P-6019)***
California American Water Co.......E.......707 542-1717
4787 Old Redwood Hwy Santa Rosa (95403) ***(P-6020)***
California American Water Co.......E.......916 568-4216
4701 Beloit Dr Sacramento (95838) ***(P-6021)***
California and Nevada IBEW/Nec.......D.......925 828-6322
7041 Koll Center Pkwy # 100 Pleasanton (94566) ***(P-2449)***
California Anesthesia Asso Med.......D.......800 888-2186
400 N Tustin Ave Ste 400 # 400 Santa Ana (92705) ***(P-18854)***
CALIFORNIA ARMENIAN HOME, Fresno *Also called California HM For The Aged Inc* ***(P-20522)***
California Artichoke & Vegetab.......D.......831 633-2144
10855 Ocean Mist Pkwy Castroville (95012) ***(P-474)***
California Assn Realtors Inc (PA).......C.......213 739-8200
525 S Virgil Ave Los Angeles (90020) ***(P-24326)***
California Association O (PA).......D.......916 443-7401
1215 K St Ste 800 Sacramento (95814) ***(P-24382)***
California Automobile Insur Co (HQ).......A.......714 232-8669
555 W Imperial Hwy Brea (92821) ***(P-10076)***
California Baking Company.......B.......619 591-8289
681 Anita St Chula Vista (91911) ***(P-8552)***
California Bank & Trust, Arcadia *Also called Zions Bancorporation Nat Assn* ***(P-9157)***
California Bank & Trust, Albany *Also called Zions Bancorporation Nat Assn* ***(P-9158)***
California Bank & Trust, Rancho Cucamonga *Also called Zions Bancorporation Nat Assn* ***(P-9159)***
California Bank & Trust, San Diego *Also called Zions Bancorporation Nat Assn* ***(P-9161)***
California Bank & Trust, Culver City *Also called Zions Bancorporation Nat Assn* ***(P-9162)***
California Basic, Santa Fe Springs *Also called Mias Fashion Mfg Co Inc* ***(P-8095)***
California Bath Restoration, Santa Ana *Also called Calspec Enterprises Inc* ***(P-3392)***
California Bistro At Fo.......D.......760 603-3700
7100 Aviara Resort Dr Carlsbad (92011) ***(P-12105)***
California Bread Co., Chula Vista *Also called California Baking Company* ***(P-8552)***
California Broadcast Ctr LLC.......C.......310 233-2425
3800 Via Oro Ave Long Beach (90810) ***(P-5669)***
California Business Bureau Inc (PA).......C.......626 303-1515
1711 S Mountain Ave Monrovia (91016) ***(P-13672)***
California Cancer Assctes.......D.......559 447-4949
7130 N Millbrook Ave Fresno (93720) ***(P-18855)***
California Capital Insur Co (PA).......C.......831 233-5500
2300 Garden Rd Monterey (93940) ***(P-10077)***
California Casuality, San Mateo *Also called California Casualty Mgt Co* ***(P-10078)***
California Casualty Mgt Co (HQ).......C.......650 574-4000
1875 S Grant St Ste 800 San Mateo (94402) ***(P-10078)***
California Cereal Products Inc (PA).......D.......510 452-4500
1267 14th St Oakland (94607) ***(P-8678)***
California Certified Organic.......D.......831 423-2263
2155 Delaware Ave Ste 150 Santa Cruz (95060) ***(P-24327)***
California Chamber Commerce (PA).......D.......916 444-6670
1215 K St Ste 1400 Sacramento (95814) ***(P-24328)***
California Chamber Commerce.......D.......916 928-3594
920 Riverside Pkwy Ste 30 West Sacramento (95605) ***(P-24329)***
California Child Care Resourc.......E.......510 658-0381
5232 Claremont Ave Oakland (94618) ***(P-22952)***
California Childcare Resource (PA).......D.......415 882-0234
1182 Market St Ste 300 San Francisco (94102) ***(P-22953)***
California Choice, Orange *Also called Choic Admini Insur Servi* ***(P-10316)***
California Citrus Cooperative.......D.......951 683-4045
859 Center St Riverside (92507) ***(P-188)***
California Clinical Trials.......C.......310 945-1780
3828 Delmas Ter 2 Culver City (90232) ***(P-10307)***
California Closet Co, San Diego *Also called Dehart Inc* ***(P-3398)***
California Closet Co O.......D.......760 773-4784
42210 Cook St Ste E Palm Desert (92211) ***(P-3390)***
California Club.......C.......213 622-1391
538 S Flower St Los Angeles (90071) ***(P-24506)***
California Club Lucky Lady.......E.......619 287-6690
5526 El Cajon Blvd San Diego (92115) ***(P-12106)***
California Cmnty Foundation (PA).......D.......213 413-4130
221 S Figueroa St Ste 400 Los Angeles (90012) ***(P-11764)***
California Cmplte CNT Cnsus.......D.......916 852-2020
400 R St Ste 350 Sacramento (95811) ***(P-25973)***
California Coast Credit Union (PA).......D.......858 495-1600
9201 Spectrum Center Blvd # 300 San Diego (92123) ***(P-9383)***
California Coast Credit Union.......C.......858 495-1600
5890 Pcf Ctr Blvd Frnt San Diego (92121) ***(P-9296)***
California Coast Credit Union.......D.......858 495-1600
8131 Allison Ave La Mesa (91942) ***(P-9297)***
California Comfort Systems USA.......B.......858 564-1100
7740 Kenamar Ct San Diego (92121) ***(P-2085)***
California Coml Inv Group Inc.......E.......805 495-8400
4530 E Thousand Oaks Blvd # 100 Westlake Village (91362) ***(P-27012)***
California Coml Solar Inc.......D.......559 667-9200
9479 N Fort Washington Rd # 105 Fresno (93730) ***(P-2086)***
California Commerce Club Inc.......A.......323 721-2100
6131 Telegraph Rd Commerce (90040) ***(P-12107)***
California Contrs Sups Inc.......D.......818 785-8823
7729 Burnet Ave Van Nuys (91405) ***(P-7467)***
California Convalescent Center, Los Angeles *Also called Bonnie Brae Cnvlscent Hosp Inc* ***(P-20510)***
California Convalescent Hosp.......D.......805 682-1355
2225 De La Vina St Santa Barbara (93105) ***(P-20521)***
California Convalescent Hosptl.......D.......626 793-5114
120 Bellefontaine St Pasadena (91105) ***(P-19772)***
California Correctnl Peace Ofc (PA).......D.......916 372-6060
755 Riverpoint Dr West Sacramento (95605) ***(P-24437)***
California Country Club.......D.......626 333-4571
1509 Workman Mill Rd City of Industry (90601) ***(P-18412)***
California Credit Union.......D.......818 291-5434
11331 Camarillo St North Hollywood (91602) ***(P-9298)***
California Credit Union.......D.......213 975-1254
333 S Beaudry Ave Ste 215 Los Angeles (90017) ***(P-9299)***
California Credit Union (PA).......C.......818 291-6700
701 N Brand Blvd Ste 100 Glendale (91203) ***(P-9384)***
California Credit Union.......D.......310 671-1080
3550 W Century Blvd # 103 Inglewood (90303) ***(P-9300)***
California Credits Group LLC.......E.......626 584-9800
87 N Raymond Ave Ste 526 Pasadena (91103) ***(P-16666)***
California Cryobank Inc.......B.......650 635-1420
611 Gateway Blvd Ste 820 South San Francisco (94080) ***(P-22194)***
California Cryobank LLC (PA).......D.......310 496-5691
11915 La Grange Ave Los Angeles (90025) ***(P-22195)***
California Cy Correctional Ctr, California City *Also called Corecivic Inc* ***(P-26937)***
California Dental Arts LLC.......D.......408 255-1020
20421 Pacifica Dr Cupertino (95014) ***(P-21604)***
California Dental Association (PA).......C.......916 443-0505
1201 K St Fl 14 Sacramento (95814) ***(P-24383)***
California Dept Fish Wildlife.......C.......916 358-2900
1701 Nimbus Rd Ste A Gold River (95670) ***(P-13145)***
California Dept Rehabilitation.......D.......415 904-7100
301 Howard St Ste 900 San Francisco (94105) ***(P-14239)***
California Dept Transportation.......B.......707 445-6600
1656 Union St Eureka (95501) ***(P-27013)***
California Drywall Co (PA).......C.......408 292-7500
2290 S 10th St San Jose (95112) ***(P-2763)***
California Eastern Labs Inc (PA).......D.......408 919-2500
4590 Patrick Henry Dr Santa Clara (95054) ***(P-7245)***
California Emergency Physician, Modesto *Also called Medamerica Billing Svcs Inc* ***(P-25649)***
California Endive Farm, Rio Vista *Also called California Vegetable Spc Inc* ***(P-8438)***
California Endowment (PA).......D.......213 928-8800
1000 N Alameda St Los Angeles (90012) ***(P-24139)***
California Envmtl Hlth Assn.......D.......650 363-4726
2000 A De Las Pulgas 10 San Mateo (94403) ***(P-27014)***
California Envmtl Systems Inc.......D.......530 820-3693
12265 Locksley Ln Auburn (95602) ***(P-24981)***
California Eye Institute.......C.......559 449-5000
Low Vision Dept St Agnes Fresno (93720) ***(P-18856)***
California Fair Plan Assn.......D.......213 487-0111
3435 Wilshire Blvd # 1200 Los Angeles (90010) ***(P-10308)***
California Family Fitness, Elk Grove *Also called California Family Health LLC* ***(P-18127)***
California Family Health LLC.......E.......916 685-3355
8569 Bond Rd Ste 130 Elk Grove (95624) ***(P-18127)***
California Farms Meat Co Inc.......D.......323 581-3663
4401 S Downey Rd Vernon (90058) ***(P-8402)***
California Field Ironwrkrs, San Bernardino *Also called Iron Workers Local 433* ***(P-11788)***
California First National Bank.......D.......949 255-0500
28 Executive Park Ste 200 Irvine (92614) ***(P-9250)***
California Friends Homes.......B.......714 530-9100
12151 Dale Ave Stanton (90680) ***(P-23846)***
California Fruit Exchange LLC (PA).......C.......209 334-2988
6011 E Pine St Lodi (95240) ***(P-8436)***
California Fuji International.......E.......818 889-6680
901 Encinal Canyon Rd Malibu (90265) ***(P-18226)***
California Golden Realty.......A.......408 822-6000
26752 Calaroga Ave Hayward (94545) ***(P-10960)***
California Golf Association.......D.......831 625-4653
3200 Lopez Rd Pebble Beach (93953) ***(P-24330)***
California Govrnmnt Opr Agncy.......A.......800 228-5453
7667 Folsom Blvd Fl 3 Sacramento (95826) ***(P-10210)***
California Guard Inc.......D.......209 465-8420
3108 N Cherryland Ave Stockton (95215) ***(P-16222)***
California Health Benefit Exch.......D.......916 228-8210
1601 Exposition Blvd Sacramento (95815) ***(P-24384)***
California Health Insur Exch, Sacramento *Also called California Health Benefit Exch* ***(P-24384)***
California Healthcare, Van Nuys *Also called Golden Living LLC* ***(P-21750)***
California Healthcare.......C.......760 520-1333
700 La Terraza Blvd # 200 Escondido (92025) ***(P-10309)***

CALIFORNIA HEALTHCARE AND REHA, Van Nuys *Also called Normand/Wlshire Rtrment Ht Inc* ***(P-10785)***
California Hispanic Com ....C.......562 942-9625
9033 Washington Blvd Pico Rivera (90660) ***(P-21452)***
California Hlth Collaborative (PA) ....D.......559 221-6315
1680 W Shaw Ave Fresno (93711) ***(P-16667)***
California HM For The Aged Inc ....C.......559 251-8414
6720 E Kings Canyon Rd Fresno (93727) ***(P-20522)***
CALIFORNIA HOSPITAL ASSOCIATIO, Sacramento *Also called California Association O* ***(P-24382)***
California Hospital Med Ctr, Los Angeles *Also called Dignity Health* ***(P-20840)***
California Human Dev Corp (PA) ....C.......707 523-1155
3315 Airway Dr Santa Rosa (95403) ***(P-23573)***
California Hydronics Corp (PA) ....E.......510 293-1993
2293 Tripaldi Way Hayward (94545) ***(P-7445)***
California Imaging Nework, Los Angeles *Also called Oaks Diagnostics Inc* ***(P-19235)***
California Institute Tech ....A.......818 354-9154
4800 Oak Grove Dr Pasadena (91109) ***(P-25974)***
California Institute Tech ....C.......626 395-8700
360 S Wilson Ave Pasadena (91106) ***(P-25728)***
California Institute Tech ....D.......626 395-8200
551 S Hill Ave Pasadena (91106) ***(P-25975)***
California ISO, Folsom *Also called Califrnia Ind Sys Oprator Corp* ***(P-5815)***
California Kidney Med Group ....C.......805 497-7775
375 Rolling Oaks Dr # 100 Thousand Oaks (91361) ***(P-18857)***
California Lab Sciences LLC ....B.......562 758-6900
10200 Pioneer Blvd # 500 Santa Fe Springs (90670) ***(P-21509)***
California Land Mgt Svcs Corp (PA) ....E.......650 322-1181
675 Gilman St Palo Alto (94301) ***(P-18641)***
California Land Mgt Svcs Corp ....E.......530 544-5994
2165 Fallen Leaf Rd South Lake Tahoe (96150) ***(P-13158)***
California Ldscp & Design Inc ....C.......909 949-1601
273 N Benson Ave Upland (91786) ***(P-783)***
California Lighting Sales Inc (PA) ....D.......626 775-6000
4900 Rivergrade Rd D110 Baldwin Park (91706) ***(P-7132)***
California Limousines ....D.......949 581-7531
9851 Irvine Center Dr Irvine (92618) ***(P-3656)***
California Linen, Pasadena *Also called Dydee Service of Pasedena* ***(P-13321)***
California Linen Service, Pasadena *Also called Dy-Dee Service Pasadena Inc* ***(P-13320)***
California Linen Services Inc ....D.......626 564-4576
40 E California Blvd Pasadena (91105) ***(P-13213)***
California Lmcc/Ibew-Neca, Pleasanton *Also called California and Nevada IBEW/Nec* ***(P-2449)***
California Marine Cleaning Inc (PA) ....C.......619 231-8788
2049 Main St San Diego (92113) ***(P-6171)***
California Maritime Acdmy ....C.......707 654-1000
200 Maritime Academy Dr Vallejo (94590) ***(P-11765)***
California Marketing, San Diego *Also called Mabie Marketing Group Inc* ***(P-16902)***
California Materials Inc ....E.......209 472-7422
3736 S Highway 99 Stockton (95215) ***(P-3860)***
California Mayoreo-Y-Menudeo, Calexico *Also called California Super Market* ***(P-4379)***
California Med Response Inc ....D.......562 968-1818
1557 Santa Anita Ave South El Monte (91733) ***(P-3657)***
California Medical Association (PA) ....D.......916 444-5532
1201 K St Ste 800 Sacramento (95814) ***(P-24385)***
California Mentor, Bakersfield *Also called National Mentor Inc* ***(P-24200)***
California Mfg Tech Consulting ....D.......310 263-3060
690 Knox St Ste 200 Torrance (90502) ***(P-24982)***
California Motorcycle Club ....D.......510 534-6222
742 45th Ave Oakland (94601) ***(P-18413)***
California Nurses Association (PA) ....D.......510 273-2200
155 Grand Ave Ste 115 Oakland (94612) ***(P-24386)***
California Nursing and Rehab ....C.......760 325-2937
2299 N Indian Ave Palm Springs (92262) ***(P-19773)***
California Oak Valley Golf ....E.......951 769-9771
1888 Golf Club Dr Beaumont (92223) ***(P-18227)***
California Odd Fellows (PA) ....D.......707 257-7885
1800 Atrium Pkwy NAPA (94559) ***(P-10707)***
California Odd Fellows ....D.......707 257-7885
1800 Atrium Pkwy NAPA (94559) ***(P-10708)***
California Oregon Broadcasting (HQ) ....D.......530 243-7777
755 Auditorium Dr Redding (96001) ***(P-5583)***
California Overnight, Stockton *Also called Express Messenger Systems Inc* ***(P-4254)***
California Overnight, Anaheim *Also called Express Messenger Systems Inc* ***(P-4255)***
California Overnight, Sacramento *Also called Express Messenger Systems Inc* ***(P-4260)***
California Overnight, San Francisco *Also called Express Messenger Systems Inc* ***(P-4262)***
California Pacific CA ....E.......415 345-0940
2100 Webster St Ste 516 San Francisco (94115) ***(P-18858)***
California Pacific Homes Inc (PA) ....D.......949 833-6000
16530 Bake Pkwy Ste 200 Irvine (92618) ***(P-1291)***
California Pacific Medical Ctr, San Francisco *Also called Sutter Bay Hospitals* ***(P-21246)***
California Pacific Medical Ctr ....D.......415 600-1378
2100 Webster St Ste 115 San Francisco (94115) ***(P-20766)***
California Pajarosa ....D.......831 722-6374
133 Hughes Rd Watsonville (95076) ***(P-233)***
California Pajarosa Floral ....E.......831 722-6374
133 Hughes Rd Watsonville (95076) ***(P-234)***
California Parking Company (PA) ....D.......415 781-4896
768 Sansome St San Francisco (94111) ***(P-10869)***
California Pav Grading Co Inc ....D.......323 372-5920
3253 Verdugo Rd Los Angeles (90065) ***(P-1675)***
California Pavement Maint Inc ....C.......916 381-8033
9390 Elder Creek Rd Sacramento (95829) ***(P-1676)***
California Pediatric Fmly Svcs ....D.......626 812-0055
326 E Foothill Blvd Azusa (91702) ***(P-22954)***
California Peo Home ....D.......626 300-0400
849 Foothill Blvd Ste 8 La Canada Flintridge (91011) ***(P-23847)***
California Physicians Service ....C.......661 631-2277
2020 17th St Bakersfield (93301) ***(P-9925)***
California Physicians Service ....C.......925 927-7419
2066 Camel Ln Apt 24 Walnut Creek (94596) ***(P-9926)***
California Physicians Service (PA) ....A.......415 229-5000
50 Beale St Bsmt 2 San Francisco (94105) ***(P-9927)***
California Physicians Service ....C.......530 351-6115
4700 Bechelli Ln Redding (96002) ***(P-9928)***
California Physicians Service ....B.......916 350-7800
4203 Town Center Blvd El Dorado Hills (95762) ***(P-9929)***
California Physicians Service ....C.......310 744-2668
100 N Pacific Coast Hwy # 2000 El Segundo (90245) ***(P-9930)***
California Physicians Service ....B.......818 598-8000
6300 Canoga Ave Ste A Woodland Hills (91367) ***(P-9931)***
California Pools, Coachella *Also called Teserra* ***(P-3476)***
California Preferred Bldrs Inc ....E.......818 402-3345
20335 Ventura Blvd # 422 Woodland Hills (91364) ***(P-1100)***
California Private Trnsp Co LP ....D.......714 637-9191
180 N Rverview Dr Ste 200 Anaheim (92808) ***(P-5103)***
California Produce, San Juan Bautista *Also called Christopher Ranch LLC* ***(P-8444)***
California Produce Wholsalers ....E.......562 776-5770
6818 Watcher St Commerce (90040) ***(P-8437)***
California Public Emplyees Ret ....C.......916 795-3000
400 P St Ste 1204 Sacramento (95814) ***(P-10211)***
California Public Emplyees Ret (HQ) ....A.......916 795-3000
400 Q St Sacramento (95811) ***(P-10212)***
California Rain Company Inc ....D.......213 623-6061
1213 E 14th St Los Angeles (90021) ***(P-8061)***
California Repertory Company ....E.......562 985-7891
1250 N Bellflower Blvd # 124 Long Beach (90840) ***(P-17893)***
California Resources Corp (PA) ....C.......888 848-4754
27200 Tourney Rd Ste 200 Santa Clarita (91355) ***(P-981)***
California Resources Corp ....D.......562 624-3400
111 W Ocean Blvd Ste 800 Long Beach (90802) ***(P-982)***
California Resources Prod Corp ....D.......805 483-8017
3450 E 5th St Oxnard (93033) ***(P-983)***
California Resources Prod Corp (HQ) ....C.......661 869-8000
900 Old River Rd Bakersfield (93311) ***(P-984)***
California Rural Indian Health ....D.......916 437-0104
1020 Sun Down Way Roseville (95661) ***(P-24140)***
California Safety Agency ....E.......866 996-6990
8932 Katella Ave Ste 108 Anaheim (92804) ***(P-16223)***
California Schl Employees Assn (PA) ....C.......408 473-1000
2045 Lundy Ave San Jose (95131) ***(P-24438)***
California Schl Employees Assn ....B.......626 258-3300
4600 Santa Anita Ave El Monte (91731) ***(P-14482)***
California School Boards Assn ....D.......800 266-3382
3251 Beacon Blvd West Sacramento (95691) ***(P-24387)***
California Schools Veba ....D.......888 276-0250
1843 Hotel Cir S San Diego (92108) ***(P-18859)***
California Search Services, Red Bluff *Also called Business Connections* ***(P-14236)***
California Security Cons ....C.......209 465-8420
3108 N Cherryland Ave Stockton (95215) ***(P-16224)***
California Shakespeare Theater ....C.......510 548-3422
701 Heinz Ave Berkeley (94710) ***(P-17894)***
California Shellfish Co Inc ....B.......707 542-9490
1280 Columbus Ave 300r San Francisco (94133) ***(P-8367)***
California Shtmtl Works Inc ....D.......619 562-7010
1020 N Marshall Ave El Cajon (92020) ***(P-1338)***
California Sierra Express Inc ....C.......916 375-7070
2975 Oates St Ste 30 West Sacramento (95691) ***(P-4905)***
California Silver-Agriculture ....E.......559 562-3795
831 Ash Ave Lindsay (93247) ***(P-963)***
California Skateparks ....C.......909 949-1601
285 N Benson Ave Upland (91786) ***(P-16668)***
California Special Events, Fountain Valley *Also called B T B Events Inc* ***(P-26894)***
California Speedway Corp ....E.......909 429-5000
9300 Cherry Ave Fontana (92335) ***(P-18082)***
California State Automobile (HQ) ....A.......925 287-7600
1276 S California Blvd Walnut Creek (94596) ***(P-10079)***
California State Automobile ....D.......650 572-5600
510a Veterans Blvd Redwood City (94063) ***(P-10080)***
California State Univ Aux Svcs ....A.......323 343-2531
5151 State University Dr Ge314 Los Angeles (90032) ***(P-26171)***
California Steel and Tube LLC ....C.......626 968-5511
16049 Stephens St City of Industry (91745) ***(P-7051)***
California Strl Concepts Inc ....D.......661 257-6903
28358 Constellation Rd # 660 Valencia (91355) ***(P-1439)***
California Sun Centers Inc ....D.......916 789-9767
8265 Sierra College Blvd Roseville (95661) ***(P-13403)***
California Suncare Inc ....D.......310 578-4400
12777 W Jefferson Blvd Los Angeles (90066) ***(P-7925)***
California Super Market ....D.......760 357-3065
363 W 2nd St Calexico (92231) ***(P-4379)***
California Supply Inc (PA) ....D.......310 532-2500
491 E Compton Blvd Gardena (90248) ***(P-7875)***
California Survey Res Svcs ....C.......818 780-2777
19849 Nordhoff St Northridge (91324) ***(P-15735)***
California Tahoe Conservancy ....E.......530 542-5580
1061 3rd St South Lake Tahoe (96150) ***(P-27269)***
California Tan, Los Angeles *Also called California Suncare Inc* ***(P-7925)***
California Teachers Assn ....D.......530 622-8013
222 Judy Dr Kelsey (95667) ***(P-24388)***
California Teachers Assn (PA) ....C.......650 697-1400
1705 Murchison Dr Burlingame (94010) ***(P-24389)***
California Ticketscom Inc ....C.......925 671-4000
1855 Gateway Blvd Ste 630 Concord (94520) ***(P-17895)***
California Ticketscom Inc (HQ) ....D.......714 327-5400
555 Anton Blvd Fl 11 Costa Mesa (92626) ***(P-17896)***
California Tile Installers, San Jose *Also called U S Perma Inc* ***(P-2913)***

California Title Co Nthrn Cal.......C.......909 825-8800
1955 Hunts Ln Ste 102 San Bernardino (92408) ***(P-10168)***
California Title Company.......D.......619 516-5227
2365 Northside Dr Ste 250 San Diego (92108) ***(P-10169)***
California Title Company (PA).......D.......949 582-8709
28202 Cabot Rd Ste 625 Laguna Niguel (92677) ***(P-11530)***
California Traffic Control.......D.......562 595-7575
3333 Cherry Ave Long Beach (90807) ***(P-16669)***
California Traffic Ctrl Svcs, Long Beach *Also called California Traffic Control* ***(P-16669)***
California Traffic Safety Inst.......C.......661 940-1907
209 E Avenue K8 Ste 210 Lancaster (93535) ***(P-27015)***
California Transit Inc.......D.......323 234-8750
1900 S Alameda St Vernon (90058) ***(P-3525)***
California United Mech Inc (PA).......B.......408 232-9000
2185 Oakland Rd San Jose (95131) ***(P-2087)***
California University Long Bch, Long Beach *Also called California Repertory Company* ***(P-17893)***
California Valley Land Co Inc (PA).......D.......559 945-9292
18036 Gale Huron (93234) ***(P-434)***
California Vegetable Spc Inc.......D.......707 374-2111
15 Poppy House Rd Rio Vista (94571) ***(P-8438)***
California Villa, Van Nuys *Also called Longwood Management Corp* ***(P-10760)***
California Vocations Inc.......C.......530 877-0937
564 Rio Lindo Ave Ste 204 Chico (95926) ***(P-20523)***
California Waste Services LLC.......C.......310 538-5998
621 W 152nd St Gardena (90247) ***(P-6172)***
California Waste Solutions Inc.......D.......408 292-0830
1820 10th St Oakland (94607) ***(P-6173)***
California Waste Solutions Inc (PA).......D.......510 832-8111
1005 Timothy Dr San Jose (95133) ***(P-6174)***
California Water Service Co (HQ).......C.......408 367-8200
1720 N 1st St San Jose (95112) ***(P-6022)***
California Water Service Co.......D.......661 396-2400
3725 S H St Bakersfield (93304) ***(P-6023)***
California Water Service Co.......D.......209 547-7900
1505 E Sonora St Stockton (95205) ***(P-6024)***
California Watercress Inc (PA).......D.......805 524-4808
550 E Telegraph Rd Fillmore (93015) ***(P-41)***
California Yacht Club, Marina Del Rey *Also called Laaco Ltd* ***(P-18481)***
California Yacht Marina Inc (PA).......E.......310 534-8436
22905 Lockness Ave Torrance (90501) ***(P-4633)***
California Youth Outreach, San Jose *Also called Breakout Prison Outreach* ***(P-22949)***
California-American Water Co (HQ).......D.......619 446-4760
655 W Broadway Ste 1410 San Diego (92101) ***(P-6025)***
Californian-Pasadena, Pasadena *Also called California Convalescent Hosptl* ***(P-19772)***
Califrnia Atism Foundation Inc (PA).......C.......510 758-0433
4075 Lakeside Dr Richmond (94806) ***(P-24141)***
Califrnia Auto Dalers Exch LLC.......B.......714 996-2400
1320 N Tustin Ave Anaheim (92807) ***(P-6386)***
Califrnia CPA Edcatn Fundation.......D.......800 922-5272
1800 Gateway Dr Ste 200 San Mateo (94404) ***(P-24390)***
Califrnia Crtive Solutions Inc (PA).......D.......858 208-4143
13475 Danielson St # 220 Poway (92064) ***(P-15954)***
Califrnia Cryobank Lf Sciences, South San Francisco *Also called California Cryobank Inc* ***(P-22194)***
Califrnia Cslty Indemnity Exch (PA).......C.......650 574-4000
1900 Almeda De Las Pulgas San Mateo (94403) ***(P-10081)***
Califrnia Dept State Hospitals.......B.......559 935-4300
24511 W Jayne Ave Coalinga (93210) ***(P-21387)***
Califrnia Dept State Hospitals.......A.......714 957-5000
2501 Harbor Blvd Costa Mesa (92626) ***(P-21388)***
Califrnia Dept State Hospitals.......A.......707 253-5000
2100 Napa Vallejo Hwy NAPA (94558) ***(P-21389)***
Califrnia Dept State Hospitals.......A.......909 425-7000
3102 E Highland Ave Patton (92369) ***(P-21390)***
Califrnia Dept State Hospitals.......A.......805 468-2000
10333 El Camino Real Atascadero (93422) ***(P-21391)***
Califrnia Erctors Bay Area Inc.......C.......707 746-1990
4500 California Ct Benicia (94510) ***(P-3259)***
Califrnia Frnsic Med Group Inc.......D.......858 694-4690
2801 Meadow Lark Dr San Diego (92123) ***(P-22196)***
Califrnia Frnsic Med Group Inc.......C.......831 755-3886
1410 Natividad Rd Salinas (93906) ***(P-18860)***
Califrnia Frnsic Med Group Inc.......D.......530 573-3035
300 Forni Rd Kelsey (95667) ***(P-22197)***
Califrnia Frnsic Med Group Inc.......D.......805 654-3343
800 S Victoria Ave Ventura (93009) ***(P-22198)***
Califrnia Frnsic Med Group Inc.......C.......209 525-5670
200 E Hackett Rd Modesto (95358) ***(P-18861)***
Califrnia Golf CLB San Frncsco.......D.......650 588-9021
844 W Orange Ave South San Francisco (94080) ***(P-18414)***
Califrnia High Speed Rail Auth.......D.......916 324-1541
770 L St Ste 620 Sacramento (95814) ***(P-3500)***
Califrnia Hlth Humn Srvcs Agcy.......B.......916 739-7640
3301 S St Sacramento (95816) ***(P-15736)***
Califrnia Hosp Med Ctr Fndtion.......A.......213 748-2411
1401 S Grand Ave Los Angeles (90015) ***(P-20767)***
Califrnia Ind Sys Oprator Corp.......C.......916 608-7000
110 Blue Ravine Rd Folsom (95630) ***(P-26546)***
Califrnia Ind Sys Oprator Corp (PA).......A.......916 351-4400
250 Outcropping Way Folsom (95630) ***(P-5815)***
Califrnia Insur Guarantee Assn.......C.......818 844-4300
101 N Brand Blvd Ste 600 Glendale (91203) ***(P-10228)***
Califrnia Intermodal Assoc Inc (PA).......D.......323 562-7788
6666 E Washington Blvd Commerce (90040) ***(P-3982)***
Califrnia Leag Cnsrvtion Vters (PA).......D.......510 271-0900
350 Frank H Ogawa Plz # 1100 Oakland (94612) ***(P-24507)***
Califrnia Nrsing Rhbltion Ctr, Palm Springs *Also called Cnrc LLC* ***(P-19805)***
Califrnia Nrsing Rhbltion Ctr, Palm Springs *Also called California Nursing and Rehab* ***(P-19773)***
Califrnia PCF Med Ctr Fndation (PA).......D.......415 600-4400
2015 Steiner St San Francisco (94115) ***(P-25976)***
Califrnia Physcn Reimbursement.......D.......530 241-0473
1321 Butte St Apt 202 Redding (96001) ***(P-10310)***
Califrnia Psychtric Trnsitions.......D.......209 667-9304
9234n Hinton Ave Delhi (95315) ***(P-18862)***
Califrnia Rgional Intranet Inc.......D.......858 974-5080
8929 Complex Dr Ste A San Diego (92123) ***(P-5371)***
Califrnia Rhbltion Spt Thrapy, Baldwin Park *Also called Physical Rhbltation Netwrk LLC* ***(P-22088)***
Califrnia Rsrces Elk Hills LLC.......B.......661 412-5000
900 Old River Rd Bakersfield (93311) ***(P-1000)***
Califrnia Rsurces Long Bch Inc.......C.......562 624-3204
111 W Ocean Blvd Ste 800 Long Beach (90802) ***(P-1014)***
Califrnia Schl For Deaf Frmont, Fremont *Also called Education California Dept* ***(P-23721)***
Califrnia Scnce Ctr Foundation.......B.......213 744-2545
700 Exposition Park Dr Los Angeles (90037) ***(P-24249)***
Califrnia Shock Truma A Rescue (PA).......D.......916 921-4000
4933 Bailey Loop McClellan (95652) ***(P-3658)***
Califrnia State Employees Assn (PA).......B.......916 444-8134
1108 O St Ste 405 Sacramento (95814) ***(P-24439)***
Califrnia Tchers Rtirement Sys, Sacramento *Also called California Govrnmnt Opr Agncy* ***(P-10210)***
Califrnia Yuth Soccer Assn Inc.......D.......925 426-5437
1040 Serpentine Ln # 206 Pleasanton (94566) ***(P-24812)***
Califrnia-Nevada Methdst Homes.......D.......510 835-5511
1850 Alice St Ofc Oakland (94612) ***(P-20524)***
Califrnias Gnite Pool Plst Inc.......D.......925 960-9500
510 Greenville Rd Livermore (94550) ***(P-3391)***
Califronia Department of State.......A.......805 468-2501
10333 El Camino Real Atascadero (93422) ***(P-21392)***
Calimesa Operations LLC.......C.......909 795-2421
13542 2nd St Yucaipa (92399) ***(P-19774)***
Calimesa Post Acute, Yucaipa *Also called Calimesa Operations LLC* ***(P-19774)***
Calistoga Spa Hot Springs, Calistoga *Also called Calistoga Spa Inc* ***(P-18128)***
Calistoga Spa Inc.......D.......707 942-6269
1006 Washington St Calistoga (94515) ***(P-18128)***
Calko Transport Company Inc.......D.......310 816-0602
720 E Watson Center Rd Carson (90745) ***(P-4198)***
Call & Jensen APC.......E.......949 717-3000
610 Nwport Ctr Dr Ste 700 Newport Beach (92660) ***(P-22407)***
Call Center Services Intl LLC.......D.......858 427-8500
809 Bowsprit Rd Ste 204 Chula Vista (91914) ***(P-16670)***
Call Source, Westlake Village *Also called Callsource Inc* ***(P-13404)***
Call To Action LLC (PA).......D.......310 996-7200
11601 Wilshire Blvd Fl 23 Los Angeles (90025) ***(P-11894)***
Callan LLC (PA).......C.......415 974-5060
600 Montgomery St Ste 800 San Francisco (94111) ***(P-9802)***
Callan Management Corporation.......B.......818 846-2215
2919 W Burbank Blvd Ste C Burbank (91505) ***(P-16501)***
Callaway Golf Ball Oprtons Inc (HQ).......A.......760 931-1771
2180 Rutherford Rd Carlsbad (92008) ***(P-7705)***
Calleguas Municipal Water Dict.......D.......805 526-9323
2100 E Olsen Rd Thousand Oaks (91360) ***(P-6026)***
Callfire Inc.......D.......213 221-2289
1410 2nd St Ste 200 Santa Monica (90401) ***(P-14700)***
Callidus Software Inc (HQ).......C.......925 251-2200
4140 Dublin Blvd Ste 400 Dublin (94568) ***(P-14701)***
Calliduscloud, Dublin *Also called Callidus Software Inc* ***(P-14701)***
Callison LLC.......C.......310 394-8460
1453 3rd Street Promenade # 400 Santa Monica (90401) ***(P-25418)***
Callisonrtkl Inc.......C.......213 627-7373
818 W 7th St Ste 300 Los Angeles (90017) ***(P-25419)***
Callisonrtkl Inc.......C.......213 633-6000
333 S Hope St Ste C200 Los Angeles (90071) ***(P-25420)***
Callsource Inc (PA).......C.......818 673-4700
5601 Lindero Canyon Rd # 200 Westlake Village (91362) ***(P-13404)***
Calmet Inc (PA).......C.......323 721-8120
7202 Petterson Ln Paramount (90723) ***(P-6175)***
Calmex Engineering Inc.......D.......909 546-1311
2764 S Vista Ave Bloomington (92316) ***(P-3124)***
Calnetix Inc (PA).......C.......562 293-1660
16323 Shoemaker Ave Cerritos (90703) ***(P-24983)***
Calnetix Technologies, Cerritos *Also called Calnetix Inc* ***(P-24983)***
Calnev Pipe Line LLC.......C.......714 560-4400
1100 W Town And Cntry Rd Orange (92868) ***(P-24984)***
Calpella Distribution Center, Calpella *Also called Mendocino Forest Pdts Co LLC* ***(P-6634)***
Calpers, Sacramento *Also called Public Employees Retirement* ***(P-10223)***
Calpers Investment Office, Sacramento *Also called California Public Emplyees Ret* ***(P-10211)***
Calpine Corporation.......E.......530 821-2075
5029 S Township Rd Yuba City (95993) ***(P-5816)***
Calpine Energy Solutions LLC (HQ).......D.......877 273-6772
401 W A St Ste 500 San Diego (92101) ***(P-5992)***
Calpipe Industries LLC (HQ).......C.......562 803-4388
19440 S Dminguez Hills Dr Rancho Dominguez (90220) ***(P-7052)***
Calply, San Diego *Also called L & W Supply Corporation* ***(P-6690)***
Calspec Enterprises Inc (PA).......D.......949 263-0779
1920 E Warner Ave Ste 3p Santa Ana (92705) ***(P-3392)***
Calstar, McClellan *Also called Califrnia Shock Truma A Rescue* ***(P-3658)***
Calstars.......E.......916 445-0211
915 L St Fl 7 Sacramento (95814) ***(P-25548)***
CALTECH EFCU, La Canada Flintridge *Also called Cal Tech Emplyees Fderal Cr Un* ***(P-9295)***
Caltrain, San Carlos *Also called Peninsula Crrdor Jint Pwers Bd* ***(P-3577)***
Caltrans, Fairfield *Also called Transportation California Dept* ***(P-1803)***
Caltrans District 1, Eureka *Also called California Dept Transportation* ***(P-27013)***

Mergent e-mail: customerrelations@mergent.com
1206
2020 Directory of California
Wholesalers and Services Companies
(P-0000) Products & Services Section entry number
(PA)=Parent Co (HQ)=Headquarters (DH)=Div Headquarters

Caltrans Eastern Reg Rd Maint, Whittier *Also called Transportation California Dept* ***(P-1804)***
Caltronics Business Systems, Sacramento *Also called JJR Enterprises Inc* ***(P-17457)***
Calvary Baptist Ch Los Gatos ....D....408 356-5126
16330 Los Gatos Blvd Los Gatos (95032) ***(P-23682)***
Calvary Cemetery, Santa Barbara *Also called Roman Cath Arch of Los Angels* ***(P-13376)***
Calvary Church Santa Ana Inc ....C....714 973-4800
1010 N Tustin Ave Santa Ana (92705) ***(P-23683)***
Calvary Infant Care Center, Los Gatos *Also called Calvary Baptist Ch Los Gatos* ***(P-23682)***
Calvey Incorporated ....D....916 681-4800
8670 Fruitridge Rd # 300 Sacramento (95826) ***(P-7876)***
Calworks Partnr Conference ....E....858 292-2900
5151 Murphy Canyon Rd # 220 San Diego (92123) ***(P-11766)***
CAM Services, Culver City *Also called Common Area Maint Svcs Inc* ***(P-13888)***
Camanche Lake, Ione *Also called Parks and Recreation Cal Dept* ***(P-18735)***
Camanche Northshore Store, Ione *Also called Concessionaires Urban Park* ***(P-18672)***
Camanche Recreation-North, Ione *Also called Concessionaires Urban Park* ***(P-18671)***
Camarena Health ....D....559 664-4000
505 E Almond Ave Madera (93637) ***(P-18863)***
Camarena Health ....D....559 642-6724
49169 Road 426 Oakhurst (93644) ***(P-18864)***
Camarillo Family YMCA, Camarillo *Also called Channel Islands Young Mens Ch* ***(P-24515)***
Camarillo Healthcare Center ....C....805 482-9805
205 Granada St Camarillo (93010) ***(P-26172)***
Camarillo Ranch Foundation ....D....805 389-8182
201 Camarillo Ranch Rd Camarillo (93012) ***(P-16671)***
Camaro Cleaners Corp (PA) ....D....650 343-4296
1515 Wedgewood Dr Hillsborough (94010) ***(P-13253)***
Cambium Business Group Inc (PA) ....C....714 670-1171
6950 Noritsu Ave Buena Park (90620) ***(P-6509)***
Cambium Networks Inc ....C....847 640-3809
2010 N 1st St San Jose (95131) ***(P-5778)***
Camble Center ....D....818 242-2434
6512 San Fernando Rd Glendale (91201) ***(P-23574)***
Cambodian Association America (PA) ....E....562 988-1863
2390 Pacific Ave Long Beach (90806) ***(P-24391)***
Cambria El Segundo Lax, El Segundo *Also called Fc El Segundo LLC* ***(P-12262)***
Cambria Pines Lodge, Cambria *Also called Pacific Cambria Inc* ***(P-12686)***
Cambria Solutions Inc (PA) ....C....916 326-4446
1050 20th St Ste 275 Sacramento (95811) ***(P-27016)***
Cambrian Homecare Inc ....D....760 955-2250
15401 Anacapa Rd Ste 2 Victorville (92392) ***(P-21691)***
Cambridge Design Partnr Inc ....D....650 387-7812
228 Hamilton Ave Fl 3 Palo Alto (94301) ***(P-24985)***
Camellia Gardens Care Center, Pasadena *Also called Camellia Gardens Care Ctr* ***(P-19775)***
Camellia Gardens Care Ctr ....D....626 798-6777
1920 N Fair Oaks Ave Pasadena (91103) ***(P-19775)***
Camelot Park Santa Maria, Santa Maria *Also called Festival Fun Parks LLC* ***(P-18693)***
Cameron Family YMCA, Santee *Also called YMCA of San Diego County* ***(P-24716)***
Cameron International Corp ....D....510 928-1480
1282 Bayview Farm Rd Pinole (94564) ***(P-1015)***
Cameron Intrstate Pipeline LLC ....C....619 696-3110
488 8th Ave San Diego (92101) ***(P-1840)***
Cameron Park Country Club Inc ....D....530 672-9840
3201 Royal Dr Cameron Park (95682) ***(P-18415)***
Cameron Surface Systems, Bakersfield *Also called Cameron West Coast Inc* ***(P-7468)***
Cameron West Coast Inc ....D....661 837-4980
4316 Yeager Way Bakersfield (93313) ***(P-7468)***
Camflor Inc ....C....831 726-1330
2364 Riverside Rd Watsonville (95076) ***(P-8887)***
Camico Mutual Insurance Co (PA) ....D....650 378-6874
1800 Gateway Dr Ste 300 San Mateo (94404) ***(P-10311)***
Caminar ....D....530 343-4421
376 Rio Lindo Ave Chico (95926) ***(P-21963)***
Camino Dialysis Svcs Oak 110, Mountain View *Also called El Camino Hospital* ***(P-21922)***
Camino Real Group LLC ....E....650 964-1700
840 E El Camino Real Mountain View (94040) ***(P-12108)***
Camino Ruiz Suite 235, San Diego *Also called Operation Samahan Inc* ***(P-19247)***
Camp Amgen, Thousand Oaks *Also called Bright Horizons Chld Ctrs LLC* ***(P-23678)***
Camp Bow Wow Franchising Inc ....D....310 571-6500
12401 W Olympic Blvd Los Angeles (90064) ***(P-575)***
Camp Dresser & McKee, Carlsbad *Also called CDM SMITH INC* ***(P-24994)***
Camp Fire USA Long Beach Cncl ....E....562 421-2725
7070 E Carson St Long Beach (90808) ***(P-24508)***
Camp Harmon Easter Seal Soc, Boulder Creek *Also called Easter Seals Inc* ***(P-13147)***
Camp Pendleton Billeting Fund, Camp Pendleton *Also called Marine Corps United States* ***(P-12577)***
Camp Pendleton Hospital, Oceanside *Also called Marine Corps United States* ***(P-21485)***
Camp Recovery Centers LP ....A....707 823-3385
2264 Green Hill Rd Sebastopol (95472) ***(P-21453)***
Camp Recovery Centers LLP ....D....831 438-1868
3192 Glen Canyon Rd Santa Cruz (95066) ***(P-21964)***
Camp Royaneh Boy Scout ....D....707 632-5291
P.O. Box 39 Cazadero (95421) ***(P-24509)***
CAMP WINNARAINBOW, Berkeley *Also called Winnarainbow Inc* ***(P-13155)***
Campaign Monitor USA Inc ....D....888 533-8098
123 Mission St Fl 26 San Francisco (94105) ***(P-14702)***
Campanile II LP ....B....323 939-6813
13721 Ventura Blvd Sherman Oaks (91423) ***(P-8553)***
Campanile Restaurant, Sherman Oaks *Also called Campanile II LP* ***(P-8553)***
Campbell Hhg Hotel Dev LLP ....E....408 626-9590
655 Creekside Way Campbell (95008) ***(P-12109)***
Campion, Catherine A MD, Newport Beach *Also called Newport Fmly Mdcne/A Med Group* ***(P-19218)***
Campo Band Missions Indians ....B....619 938-6000
1800 Golden Acorn Way Campo (91906) ***(P-18316)***
Campos Dmetrio Frm Labor Contr, Woodland *Also called Campos Dmetrio Frm Labor Contr* ***(P-14240)***
Campos Dmetrio Frm Labor Contr ....D....530 662-4143
117 W Main St Ste 19 Woodland (95695) ***(P-14240)***
Campos Family Farms LLC ....D....559 275-3000
4726 W Jacquelyn Ave Fresno (93722) ***(P-307)***
Campton Place Hotel, San Francisco *Also called Southbourne Inc* ***(P-12948)***
Campton Place, A Taj Hotel, San Francisco *Also called Ihms (sf) LLC* ***(P-12455)***
Campus Laundry, Watsonville *Also called Monterey Bay Acadamy Laundry* ***(P-13181)***
Campus Laundry, Watsonville *Also called Oceanside Laundry LLC* ***(P-13249)***
Camserv, Pinole *Also called Cameron International Corp* ***(P-1015)***
Camstar International Inc ....D....909 931-2540
939 W 9th St Upland (91786) ***(P-7386)***
Can-AM Plumbing Inc ....C....925 846-1833
151 Wyoming St Pleasanton (94566) ***(P-2088)***
Can-Do ....D....646 228-7049
578 Washington Blvd 39o Marina Del Rey (90292) ***(P-22955)***
Can-West Directory Distrs, Monterey *Also called Clum Morford Distributing* ***(P-16706)***
Canadian Imperial Bank ....D....949 759-4718
620 Newport Center Dr Newport Beach (92660) ***(P-9053)***
Cancer Federation Inc (PA) ....C....951 849-4325
711 W Ramsey St Banning (92220) ***(P-24142)***
Cancer Prevention Inst Cal (PA) ....C....510 608-5000
2201 Walnut Ave Ste 300 Fremont (94538) ***(P-25977)***
Candle Center The, Sacramento *Also called Therapeutic Pathways Inc* ***(P-19698)***
CANDLE LIGHTERS THE, Fremont *Also called Fremont Candle Lighters* ***(P-24832)***
Candleberry Properties LP ....E....323 852-7000
6399 Wilshire Blvd Los Angeles (90048) ***(P-12110)***
Candlewood Suites, Santa Clara *Also called Hpt Trs Ihg-2 Inc* ***(P-12417)***
Canedy Court Reporting, San Diego *Also called Rett Inc* ***(P-13804)***
Canessa Investments N V ....E....310 273-8543
9434 Cherokee Ln Beverly Hills (90210) ***(P-11895)***
Canew Inc ....C....818 703-5100
22135 Roscoe Blvd West Hills (91304) ***(P-21605)***
Canfab, Corona *Also called Cannon Fabrication Inc* ***(P-3031)***
Canine Cmpnons For Indpendence (PA) ....D....707 577-1700
2965 Dutton Ave Santa Rosa (95407) ***(P-601)***
Canji Inc ....D....858 597-0177
3525 John Hopkins Ct San Diego (92121) ***(P-25978)***
Cannon Cochran MGT Svcs Inc ....D....949 474-6500
18881 Von Karman Ave # 380 Irvine (92612) ***(P-10312)***
Cannon Corporation (PA) ....D....805 544-7407
1050 Southwood Dr San Luis Obispo (93401) ***(P-25519)***
Cannon Fabrication Inc ....D....951 278-1830
182 Granite St Ste 101 Corona (92879) ***(P-3031)***
Canoga Hotel Corporation ....C....818 595-1000
6360 Canoga Ave Woodland Hills (91367) ***(P-12111)***
Canoga Park Fitness LLC ....E....818 884-5034
22235 Sherman Way Canoga Park (91303) ***(P-18129)***
Canoga Park Worksource Center ....E....818 596-4448
21010 Vanowen St Canoga Park (91303) ***(P-14241)***
Canoga Park/West Hills Club, Canoga Park *Also called 24 Hour Fitness Usa Inc* ***(P-18109)***
Canon Bus Solutions-West Inc ....B....310 217-3000
110 W Walnut St Gardena (90248) ***(P-6740)***
Canon Medical Systems USA Inc (HQ) ....B....714 730-5000
2441 Michelle Dr Tustin (92780) ***(P-6956)***
Canon Recruiting Group LLC ....B....661 252-7400
26531 Summit Cir Santa Clarita (91350) ***(P-14483)***
Canon Solutions America Inc ....D....800 323-4827
203 S Waterman Ave El Centro (92243) ***(P-6741)***
Canon Solutions America Inc ....D....760 438-6990
2382 Faraday Ave Ste 250 Carlsbad (92008) ***(P-16672)***
Canon Solutions America Inc ....D....909 390-7400
3237 E Guasti Rd Ste 200 Ontario (91761) ***(P-6742)***
Canon Solutions America Inc ....D....415 743-7300
201 California St Ste 100 San Francisco (94111) ***(P-6743)***
Canon Solutions America Inc ....D....949 753-4200
123 Paularino Ave Costa Mesa (92626) ***(P-6744)***
Canon USA Inc ....B....949 753-4000
15955 Alton Pkwy Irvine (92618) ***(P-6730)***
Canopy Energy, Van Nuys *Also called Energy Enterprises USA Inc* ***(P-2127)***
Cantamar Property MGT Inc ....E....562 862-4470
9550 Firestone Blvd # 105 Downey (90241) ***(P-10961)***
Canteen Vending, Garden Grove *Also called Compass Group Usa Inc* ***(P-14141)***
Canteen Vending - San Diego ....D....619 527-1900
5515 Market St San Diego (92114) ***(P-8339)***
Canterbury Hotel Corp ....C....415 345-3200
750 Sutter St San Francisco (94109) ***(P-12112)***
Canterbury Woods, Pacific Grove *Also called Covia Communities* ***(P-23886)***
Canterbury, The, Pls Vrds Pnsl *Also called Episcopal Communities & Servic* ***(P-19891)***
Canton Food Co Inc ....C....213 688-7707
750 S Alameda St Los Angeles (90021) ***(P-8159)***
Cantor Art Ctr Stanford Univ, Palo Alto *Also called Leland Stanford Junior Univ* ***(P-20999)***
Cantor Fitzgerald L P ....D....310 282-6500
1925 Century Park E # 700 Los Angeles (90067) ***(P-9657)***
Canvas Worldwide LLC ....C....424 303-4300
12015 Bluff Creek Dr Los Angeles (90094) ***(P-13617)***
Canyon Country Medical Offices, Santa Clarita *Also called Kaiser Foundation Hospitals* ***(P-19099)***
Canyon Crest Country Club Inc ....D....951 274-7900
975 Country Club Dr Riverside (92506) ***(P-18416)***
Canyon Crest Mental Hlth Offs, Riverside *Also called Kaiser Foundation Hospitals* ***(P-19091)***
Canyon Hills Club, Anaheim *Also called Ardcore Senior Living* ***(P-23822)***
Canyon Insulation Inc ....D....951 278-9200
645 E Harrison St Ste 100 Corona (92879) ***(P-2764)***
Canyon Lk Property Owners Assn ....D....951 244-6841
31512 Railroad Canyon Rd Canyon Lake (92587) ***(P-24510)***

ALPHABETIC

Employee Codes: A=Over 500 employees, B=251-500
C=101-250, D=51-100, E=50
2020 Directory of California
Wholesalers and Services Companies
© Mergent Inc. 1-800-342-5647
1207

Canyon Manor Residential Treat, Novato *Also called Marin County Sart Program* ***(P-21419)***

Canyon Partners Incorporated (HQ) ....D....310 272-1000
2000 Ave Of The Sts Fl 11 Los Angeles (90067) ***(P-9658)***

Canyon Properties III LLC ....D....818 890-0430
11723 Fenton Ave Sylmar (91342) ***(P-19776)***

Canyon Ridge Hospital Inc ....C....909 590-3700
5353 G St Chino (91710) ***(P-21393)***

Canyon View Capital Inc ....D....831 480-6335
331 Soquel Ave Ste 100 Santa Cruz (95062) ***(P-11847)***

Canyon Way Nursery, Studio City *Also called Wurzel Landscape Maintenance* ***(P-929)***

Cap Diagnostics LLC ....D....714 966-1221
17661 Cowan Irvine (92614) ***(P-21510)***

Cap-Mpt, Los Angeles *Also called Coopertive Amrcn Physcians Inc* ***(P-24396)***

Cap-Mpt (PA) ....C....213 473-8600
333 S Hope St Fl 8 Los Angeles (90071) ***(P-10161)***

Capacity LLC ....C....732 745-7770
19852 Business Pkwy Walnut (91789) ***(P-4556)***

Capay Fruits and Vegetables, West Sacramento *Also called Capay Incorporated* ***(P-8439)***

Capay Incorporated (PA) ....D....530 796-0730
3880 Seaport Blvd West Sacramento (95691) ***(P-8439)***

Capay Organic, West Sacramento *Also called Farm Fresh To You* ***(P-321)***

Capc Inc ....C....562 693-8826
7200 Greenleaf Ave # 170 Whittier (90602) ***(P-24143)***

Capcom Entertainment Inc ....D....650 350-6500
185 Berry St Ste 1200 San Francisco (94107) ***(P-7729)***

Capcom U S A Inc (HQ) ....C....650 350-6500
185 Berry St Ste 1200 San Francisco (94107) ***(P-7730)***

Capcom U.S.a, San Francisco *Also called Capcom Entertainment Inc* ***(P-7729)***

Cape Clear Software Inc ....D....408 879-7365
900 E Hamilton Ave # 100 Campbell (95008) ***(P-14703)***

Cape Environmental MGT Inc ....B....949 236-3000
18012 Cowan Ste 150 Irvine (92614) ***(P-26932)***

Cape Robbin Inc ....E....626 810-8080
1943 W Mission Blvd Pomona (91766) ***(P-8124)***

Capeconnect, Campbell *Also called Cape Clear Software Inc* ***(P-14703)***

Capgemini America Inc ....D....415 796-6777
427 Brannan St San Francisco (94107) ***(P-15955)***

Capistrano Beach Extended ....D....949 496-5786
35410 Del Rey Capistrano Beach (92624) ***(P-19777)***

Capital Athletic Club Inc ....D....916 442-3927
1515 8th St Sacramento (95814) ***(P-18130)***

Capital Beverage Company (PA) ....C....916 371-8164
2500 Del Monte St West Sacramento (95691) ***(P-8752)***

Capital Brands LLC (HQ) ....D....310 996-7200
11601 Wilshire Blvd Fl 23 Los Angeles (90025) ***(P-8554)***

Capital Brands Dist LLC ....D....310 996-7200
11601 Wilshire Blvd Fl 23 Los Angeles (90025) ***(P-11896)***

Capital Builders, Brentwood *Also called V Development Inc* ***(P-1281)***

Capital City Drywall Inc ....D....916 331-9200
6525 32nd St Ste B1 North Highlands (95660) ***(P-2765)***

Capital Commercial Flrg Inc ....E....916 569-1960
3709 Bradview Dr Ste 100 Sacramento (95827) ***(P-2996)***

Capital Commercial Property, Culver City *Also called Property Management Assoc Inc* ***(P-11376)***

Capital Drywall LP ....C....909 599-6818
333 S Grand Ave Ste 4070 Los Angeles (90071) ***(P-2766)***

Capital Engineering Cons Inc (PA) ....D....916 851-3500
11020 Sun Center Dr # 100 Rancho Cordova (95670) ***(P-24986)***

Capital Eye Medical Group ....D....916 241-9378
6620 Coyle Ave Ste 408 Carmichael (95608) ***(P-18865)***

Capital Group Companies Inc ....B....310 996-6238
11100 Santa Monica Blvd # 1500 Los Angeles (90025) ***(P-9803)***

Capital Group Companies Inc (PA) ....A....213 486-9200
333 S Hope St Fl 55 Los Angeles (90071) ***(P-9804)***

Capital Group Companies Inc ....B....213 486-1698
1 Market Plz Ste 1800 San Francisco (94105) ***(P-9805)***

Capital Group Companies Inc ....B....949 975-5000
M1 Irvine (92618) ***(P-9806)***

Capital Group Private Markets, Irvine *Also called Capital Group Companies Inc* ***(P-9806)***

Capital Group, The, Los Angeles *Also called Capital Group Companies Inc* ***(P-9804)***

Capital Guardian Trust Company (HQ) ....D....213 486-9200
333 S Hope St Fl 52 Los Angeles (90071) ***(P-11777)***

Capital Insurance Group, Monterey *Also called California Capital Insur Co* ***(P-10077)***

Capital Invstmnts Vntures Corp (PA) ....C....949 858-0647
30151 Tomas Rcho STA Marg (92688) ***(P-24392)***

Capital Mortgage Services, Ventura *Also called E&S Financial Group Inc* ***(P-9621)***

Capital Network Funding Svcs, Los Angeles *Also called Capnet Financial Services Inc* ***(P-9500)***

Capital Oversight Inc (PA) ....B....310 453-8000
2118 Wilshire Blvd Santa Monica (90403) ***(P-27017)***

Capital Plus Financial Corp ....E....619 744-1900
909 W Laurel St Ste 250 San Diego (92101) ***(P-9535)***

Capital Public Radio Inc ....E....916 278-8900
7055 Folsom Blvd Sacramento (95826) ***(P-5511)***

Capital Research and MGT Co (HQ) ....B....213 486-9200
333 S Hope St Fl 55 Los Angeles (90071) ***(P-9807)***

Capital Research and MGT Co ....D....949 975-5000
6455 Irvine Center Dr Irvine (92618) ***(P-9808)***

Capital Transitional Care, Sacramento *Also called Covenant Care California LLC* ***(P-19835)***

Capitol LLC (PA) ....B....626 445-0402
615 Las Tunas Dr Ste L Arcadia (91007) ***(P-13758)***

Capitol Casino ....C....916 446-0700
411 N 16th St Sacramento (95811) ***(P-18642)***

Capitol Corporate Services ....E....916 444-6787
455 Capitol Mall Ste 217 Sacramento (95814) ***(P-25878)***

Capitol Dgtal Dcment Solutions, Arcadia *Also called Capitol LLC* ***(P-13758)***

Capitol Records LLC ....A....213 462-6252
1750 Vine St Los Angeles (90028) ***(P-16673)***

Capitol Regency LLC ....B....916 443-1234
1209 L St Sacramento (95814) ***(P-12113)***

Capnet Financial Services Inc (PA) ....D....877 980-0558
11901 Santa Monica Blvd Los Angeles (90025) ***(P-9500)***

Caprion Proteomics USA LLC ....E....650 776-3676
1455 Adams Dr Ste 2124 Menlo Park (94025) ***(P-25979)***

Capsbc, San Bernardino *Also called Community Action Prtnship Sb C* ***(P-24158)***

Captain Marketing Inc ....D....310 402-9709
3577 N Figueroa St Los Angeles (90065) ***(P-26547)***

Captiva Software Corporation (HQ) ....D....858 320-1000
10145 Pacific Hts Blvd San Diego (92121) ***(P-15566)***

Captured Sea Inc ....D....714 856-3358
5901 Warner Ave Huntington Beach (92649) ***(P-1440)***

Capurro Farms, Moss Landing *Also called Capurro Marketing LLC* ***(P-8440)***

Capurro Marketing LLC ....D....831 728-1767
2250 Highway 1 Moss Landing (95039) ***(P-8440)***

Car Park Inc ....C....323 462-6060
6541 Hollywood Blvd Hollywood (90028) ***(P-17246)***

Car Spa Inc ....E....951 279-1422
996 Mountain Ave Norco (92860) ***(P-17414)***

Car Wash Partners Inc ....C....661 837-9485
3201 Panama Ln Bakersfield (93313) ***(P-17366)***

Cara Communications Corp ....E....310 442-5600
12233 W Olympic Blvd # 170 Los Angeles (90064) ***(P-17589)***

Carat ....D....415 541-2700
85 2nd St Fl 6 San Francisco (94105) ***(P-13645)***

Carat N Amer Dntsu Ageis Ntwrk ....C....310 255-1000
5800 Bristol Pkwy Fl 5 Culver City (90230) ***(P-13646)***

Caraustar Industries Inc ....C....209 476-7710
2800 W March Ln Ste 480 Stockton (95219) ***(P-6176)***

Carbon 38 Inc ....D....888 723-5838
10000 Wash Blvd Ste 800 Culver City (90232) ***(P-16674)***

Carbon Five, San Francisco *Also called Carbonfive Incorporated* ***(P-14704)***

Carbonfive Incorporated ....D....415 546-0500
585 Howard St Fl 2 San Francisco (94105) ***(P-14704)***

Cardenas Bros Farming Company ....D....805 928-1559
1141 Tama Ln Santa Maria (93455) ***(P-88)***

Cardflex Inc ....D....714 361-1900
2900 Bristol St Bldg F Costa Mesa (92626) ***(P-16675)***

Cardiac Noninvasive Laboratory, Los Angeles *Also called Cedars-Sinai Medical Center* ***(P-18878)***

Cardiac Unit, Anaheim *Also called Anaheim Regional Medical Ctr* ***(P-20751)***

Cardic Arithmias ....E....650 617-8100
770 Welch Rd Ste 100 Palo Alto (94304) ***(P-18866)***

Cardiff Transportation, Palm Desert *Also called Gary Cardiff Enterprises Inc* ***(P-3676)***

Cardinal Health Inc ....D....909 824-1820
793 Via Lata Colton (92324) ***(P-7926)***

Cardinal Health Inc ....D....951 360-2199
1100 Bird Center Dr Palm Springs (92262) ***(P-6957)***

Cardinal Health Inc ....C....916 372-9880
3238 Dwight Rd Elk Grove (95758) ***(P-7927)***

Cardinal Health Inc ....C....530 406-3600
700 Vaughn Rd Dixon (95620) ***(P-7928)***

Cardinal Health Inc ....D....510 232-2030
1007 Canal Blvd Richmond (94804) ***(P-7929)***

Cardinal Health Inc ....D....559 448-0788
7330 N Palm Ave Ste 104 Fresno (93711) ***(P-7930)***

Cardinal Health Inc ....D....530 225-8735
1935 Pine St Redding (96001) ***(P-7931)***

Cardinal Health Inc ....D....909 605-0900
4551 E Philadelphia St Ontario (91761) ***(P-7932)***

Cardinal Health Inc ....C....661 295-6100
27680 Avenue Mentry Valencia (91355) ***(P-7933)***

Cardinal Health 200 LLC ....C....951 686-8900
3750 Torrey View Ct San Diego (92130) ***(P-6958)***

Cardinal Point Captains Inc ....D....760 438-7361
5005 Texas St Ste 104 San Diego (92108) ***(P-14484)***

Cardinal Transportation, Gardena *Also called First Student Inc* ***(P-3814)***

Cardio Pulmonary Services, La Jolla *Also called Professional Health Tech* ***(P-19309)***

Cardiodx Inc ....C....650 475-2788
3945 Freedom Cir Ste 560 Santa Clara (95054) ***(P-21511)***

CARDIOLOGY DEPARTMENT, Los Angeles *Also called Usc Care Medical Group Inc* ***(P-21347)***

Cardiomart Inc ....E....310 572-6724
11715 Avenida Del Sol Northridge (91326) ***(P-6959)***

Cardiovascular Consultants Hea ....D....559 432-4303
1207 E Herndon Ave Fresno (93720) ***(P-18867)***

Cardivsclr Mdcl Grp of Sthrn ....E....310 278-3400
414 N Camden Dr Ste 1100 Beverly Hills (90210) ***(P-18868)***

Cardno Eri, Lake Forest *Also called Environmental Resolutions Inc* ***(P-27064)***

Cardservice International Inc ....A....800 217-4622
4565 Industrial St Ste 7k Simi Valley (93063) ***(P-16676)***

Cardservice International Inc ....D....714 773-1778
1538 W Commonwealth Ave Fullerton (92833) ***(P-16677)***

Care Inc ....E....818 232-7940
15315 Magnolia Blvd # 306 Sherman Oaks (91403) ***(P-20415)***

Care 1st Health Plan (PA) ....C....323 889-6638
601 Potrero Grande Dr # 2 Monterey Park (91755) ***(P-22199)***

Care 2 ....D....650 622-0860
203 Redwood Shores Pkwy # 230 Redwood City (94065) ***(P-24813)***

Care 4 U LLC ....D....818 593-7911
22726 Eccles St West Hills (91304) ***(P-22956)***

Care A Van Transport, Carlsbad *Also called CAV Inc* ***(P-3661)***

Care Ambulance, San Diego *Also called Care Medical Trnsp Inc* ***(P-14485)***

Care Ambulance Service Inc ....A....714 828-7750
8932 Katella Ave Ste 201 Anaheim (92804) ***(P-3659)***

Care Ambulance Service Inc ....B....323 838-0542
515 W Beverly Blvd Montebello (90640) ***(P-3660)***

Care Associates Inc...D.......626 330-4048
15125 Gale Ave Hacienda Heights (91745) *(P-23848)*
Care Choice Health Systems Inc...D.......760 798-4508
338 Via Vera Cruz Ste 120 San Marcos (92078) *(P-20525)*
Care Choice Home Care, San Marcos *Also called Care Choice Health Systems Inc (P-20525)*
Care Medical Trnsp Inc...C.......858 653-4520
9770 Candida St San Diego (92126) *(P-14485)*
Care Options Management Plans...D.......925 551-3227
7000 Village Pkwy Ste A Dublin (94568) *(P-21692)*
Care Options Management Plans (PA)...D.......530 242-8580
1020 Market St Redding (96001) *(P-21693)*
Care Plus Home Care Inc...C.......949 716-2273
22931 Triton Way Ste 133 Laguna Hills (92653) *(P-21694)*
CARE PLUS HOME HEALTH, Laguna Hills *Also called Care Plus Nursing Services Inc (P-21695)*
Care Plus North of San Diego...D.......619 421-0807
2337 Eastridge Loop Chula Vista (91915) *(P-14242)*
Care Plus Nursing Services Inc...C.......949 600-7194
22931 Triton Way Ste 236 Laguna Hills (92653) *(P-21695)*
Care Solution Associates LLC...D.......925 443-1000
179 Contractors Ave Livermore (94551) *(P-21696)*
Care Tech Inc...D.......909 882-2965
4280 Cypress Dr San Bernardino (92407) *(P-19778)*
Care Unlimited Health Systems...D.......626 332-3767
1025 W Arrow Hwy Ste 105 Glendora (91740) *(P-21697)*
Care Wst-Wrner Mtn Nursing Ctr, Alturas *Also called County of Modoc (P-19822)*
Careability Health Svcs Corp...D.......916 479-8554
1329 Howe Ave Ste 100 Sacramento (95825) *(P-21698)*
Careage Inc...E.......408 238-9751
2501 Alvin Ave San Jose (95121) *(P-19779)*
Carecredit LLC...C.......800 300-3046
555 Anton Blvd Ste 700 Costa Mesa (92626) *(P-16678)*
Caredx Inc (PA)...C.......415 287-2300
3260 Bayshore Blvd Brisbane (94005) *(P-21512)*
Career Dev Inst For Excptnl...E.......951 337-3678
1470 Marsh Way Riverside (92501) *(P-11550)*
Career Group Inc (PA)...A.......310 277-8188
10100 Santa Monica Blvd # 900 Los Angeles (90067) *(P-14243)*
Career Transition Center...C.......562 570-9675
3447 Atlantic Ave Ste 100 Long Beach (90807) *(P-23575)*
Carefield Solana LLC...E.......858 259-5591
201 Lomas Santa Fe Dr Solana Beach (92075) *(P-22957)*
Carefusion Solutions LLC (HQ)...A.......858 617-2100
3750 Torrey View Ct San Diego (92130) *(P-6960)*
Caremark Rx Inc...D.......909 822-1164
1851 N Riverside Ave Rialto (92376) *(P-18869)*
Caremark Rx LLC...E.......760 948-6606
15576 Main St Hesperia (92345) *(P-18870)*
Caremark Rx LLC...E.......209 957-7050
800 Douglas Rd Stockton (95207) *(P-18871)*
Caremore Health Plan (HQ)...D.......562 622-2950
12900 Park Plaza Dr # 150 Cerritos (90703) *(P-18872)*
Caremore Insurance Services, Cerritos *Also called Caremore Health Plan (P-18872)*
Caremore Medical Group, Downey *Also called Conrad A Cox (P-18919)*
Caremore Medical Group Inc...B.......562 622-2900
12900 Park Plz Ste 150 Lakewood (90805) *(P-9902)*
Careonsite Inc...D.......562 437-0381
1805 Arnold Dr Martinez (94553) *(P-18873)*
Careonsite Inc (PA)...E.......562 437-0831
1250 Pacific Ave Long Beach (90813) *(P-18874)*
Cares, San Diego *Also called Center For Autsm Rsrch Evltn (P-21971)*
Cares Community Health...C.......916 443-3299
1500 21st St Sacramento (95811) *(P-18875)*
Carescope LLC...D.......916 780-1384
1455 Response Rd Ste 120 Sacramento (95815) *(P-22958)*
Careworks Health Services...D.......949 859-4700
18682 Beach Blvd Ste 225 Huntington Beach (92648) *(P-22959)*
Carfinance Capital LLC...A.......888 227-9555
7525 Irvine Center Dr # 250 Irvine (92618) *(P-11897)*
Cargill Incorporated...C.......510 797-1820
7220 Central Ave Newark (94560) *(P-8692)*
Cargo Service Center, Los Angeles *Also called Swissport Cargo Services LP (P-4796)*
Caribbean South Amercn Council...E.......925 709-3433
12 Ambrose Ave Bay Point (94565) *(P-4819)*
Carinet, San Diego *Also called Califrnia Rgional Intranet Inc (P-5371)*
Caring Cmpanions Referral Agcy, Hemet *Also called Caring Companions Home (P-21699)*
Caring Companions Home...D.......951 765-1441
116 Las Lunas St Hemet (92543) *(P-21699)*
Caritas Management Corporation...D.......415 647-7191
1358 Valencia St San Francisco (94110) *(P-10962)*
Carleton Booker Marketing Inc...D.......510 999-1682
5042 Wilshire Blvd # 31584 Los Angeles (90036) *(P-26548)*
Carlilemacy Inc...E.......707 542-6451
15 3rd St Santa Rosa (95401) *(P-24987)*
Carlisle Construction Mtls Inc...D.......909 591-7425
5635 Schaefer Ave Chino (91710) *(P-6712)*
Carlisle Construction Mtls Inc...D.......707 678-6900
1155 Business Park Dr Dixon (95620) *(P-6713)*
Carlisle Research Corporation...D.......818 785-8677
7100 Hayvenhurst Ave Ph F Van Nuys (91406) *(P-15567)*
Carlsbad By The Sea, Carlsbad *Also called Front Porch Communities (P-23934)*
Carlsbad Firefighters Assn...D.......760 729-3730
2560 Orion Way Carlsbad (92010) *(P-24814)*
Carlsbad Inn Vactn Condo Ownrs...D.......760 434-7542
3001 Carlsbad Blvd Carlsbad (92008) *(P-24511)*
Carlsbad Medical Offices, Carlsbad *Also called Kaiser Foundation Hospitals (P-19131)*
Carlsbad Municipal Water Dst...E.......760 438-2722
5950 El Camino Real Carlsbad (92008) *(P-6027)*
Carlsbad Surgery Center LLC...E.......760 448-2488
6121 Paseo Del Norte # 100 Carlsbad (92011) *(P-21965)*
Carlson, Tustin *Also called Corland Companies (P-11077)*
Carlson Barbee & Gibson Inc...D.......925 866-0322
2633 Camino Ramon Ste 350 San Ramon (94583) *(P-24988)*
Carlton Hotel Properties LP...D.......415 673-0242
1075 Sutter St San Francisco (94109) *(P-12114)*
Carlton Plaza of Fremont, Fremont *Also called Retirement Lf Care Communities (P-24050)*
Carlton Plaza of San Leandro, San Leandro *Also called Carlton Senior Living (P-10963)*
Carlton Senior Living...D.......925 935-1001
175 Cleaveland Rd Pleasant Hill (94523) *(P-21700)*
Carlton Senior Living...D.......510 636-0660
1000 E 14th St San Leandro (94577) *(P-10963)*
Carlton Senior Living Inc...C.......408 972-1400
380 Branham Ln Ofc Ofc San Jose (95136) *(P-23849)*
Carlton Senior Living Inc...E.......916 714-2404
6915 Elk Grove Blvd Elk Grove (95758) *(P-10964)*
Carlton Senior Living Inc...C.......916 971-4800
1075 Fulton Ave Sacramento (95825) *(P-23850)*
Carlton Senior Living Inc...D.......925 935-1660
2770 Pleasant Hill Rd Ofc Concord (94523) *(P-11551)*
Carmel Architectural Sales...D.......714 630-7221
2300 E Katella Ave # 370 Anaheim (92806) *(P-3032)*
Carmel Hills Care Center, Monterey *Also called Pater Digintas Inc (P-20193)*
Carmel Marina, Castroville *Also called USA Waste of California Inc (P-3948)*
Carmel Mission Inn, Carmel *Also called Bayview Properties Inc (P-12048)*
Carmel Mtn Rhab Healthcare Ctr, San Diego *Also called Bernardo Hts Healthcare Inc (P-20504)*
Carmel Partners Inc (PA)...C.......415 273-2900
1000 Sansome St Fl 1 San Francisco (94111) *(P-10965)*
CARMEL VALLEY MANOR, Carmel *Also called Northern CA Cngrgtnl Rtmt (P-20642)*
Carmel Valley Medical Offices, San Diego *Also called Kaiser Foundation Hospitals (P-19093)*
Carmel Valley Packing Inc...C.......831 771-8860
26965 Encinal Rd Salinas (93908) *(P-475)*
Carmel Valley Ranch...C.......831 625-9500
1 Old Ranch Rd Carmel (93923) *(P-12115)*
Carmel Valley Ranch Hotel, Carmel *Also called Carmel Valley Ranch (P-12115)*
Carmel Valley Resort, Carmel *Also called Carmel Vly Mrtg Borrower LLC (P-12116)*
Carmel Village At Clovis, Clovis *Also called Generation Clovis LLC (P-20566)*
Carmel Vly Mrtg Borrower LLC...D.......831 625-9500
1 Old Ranch Rd Carmel (93923) *(P-12116)*
Carmichael Care Inc...C.......916 483-8103
6041 Fair Oaks Blvd Carmichael (95608) *(P-19780)*
Carmichael International Svc (HQ)...D.......213 353-0800
533 Glendale Blvd Ste 102 Los Angeles (90026) *(P-4906)*
Carmichael Recreation & Pk Dst...C.......916 485-5322
5750 Grant Ave Carmichael (95608) *(P-18643)*
Carnahan Occupational Therapy...E.......805 737-1604
116 E College Ave Ste G Lompoc (93436) *(P-21966)*
Carnegie Agency Inc...E.......805 445-1470
2101 Corp Cntr Dr Ste 150 Newbury Park (91320) *(P-10313)*
Carnegie Institution Wash...D.......626 577-1122
813 Santa Barbara St Pasadena (91101) *(P-25980)*
Carnegie Mellon University...C.......412 268-3818
4304 Valley Ave Apt G Pleasanton (94566) *(P-25879)*
Carneros Inn LLC...B.......707 299-4880
4048 Sonoma Hwy NAPA (94559) *(P-12117)*
Carneros Resort and Spa, NAPA *Also called GF Carneros Tenant LLC (P-13348)*
Carol Electric Company Inc...D.......562 431-1870
3822 Cerritos Ave Los Alamitos (90720) *(P-2450)*
Carolina Trucking Inc (PA)...E.......619 661-1554
552 Alta Rd Ste 8 San Diego (92154) *(P-3861)*
Caroline Promotions Inc...D.......818 507-7666
809 S Adams St Apt 7 Glendale (91205) *(P-26901)*
Carollo Engineers Inc (PA)...D.......925 932-1710
2700 Ygnacio Valley Rd # 300 Walnut Creek (94598) *(P-24989)*
Carollo Engineers Inc...D.......714 540-4300
3100 S Harbor Blvd # 200 Santa Ana (92704) *(P-24990)*
Carollo Engineers Inc...C.......858 505-1020
701 Palomar Airport Rd Carlsbad (92011) *(P-24991)*
Carolyn E Wylie Center...D.......951 683-5193
4164 Brockton Ave Ste A Riverside (92501) *(P-23684)*
Carone & Company Inc...D.......925 602-8800
5009 Forni Dr Ste A Concord (94520) *(P-3306)*
Carothers Dsnte Frdnberger LLP (PA)...D.......949 622-1661
2600 Michelson Dr Ste 800 Irvine (92612) *(P-22408)*
Carparts Technologies...C.......949 488-8860
32122 Camn Capistrano # 100 San Juan Capistrano (92675) *(P-15273)*
Carpenter Fnds Admnstrtive Off...D.......510 633-0333
265 Hegenberger Rd # 100 Oakland (94621) *(P-11778)*
Carpenter Fund Manager Gp LLC...C.......949 261-8888
5 Park Plz Ste 950 Irvine (92614) *(P-9054)*
Carpenters Southwest ADM Corp (PA)...D.......213 386-8590
533 S Fremont Ave Los Angeles (90071) *(P-12118)*
Carpet Care By Tri-Star, Northridge *Also called Tri - Star Win Coverings Inc (P-6591)*
Carpet Solutions...E.......310 886-3800
28126 Peacock Ridge Dr # 115 Rancho Palos Verdes (90275) *(P-13264)*
Carpinteria Motor Inn Inc...E.......805 684-0473
4558 Carpinteria Ave Carpinteria (93013) *(P-12119)*
Carquinez Dialysis, Vallejo *Also called Total Renal Care Inc (P-21940)*
Carr & Ferrell...D.......650 812-3400
120 Constitution Dr Menlo Park (94025) *(P-22409)*
Carr & Ferrell LLP (PA)...D.......650 812-3400
120 Constitution Dr Menlo Park (94025) *(P-22410)*
Carr Mc Clellan Ingersoll Thom (PA)...D.......650 342-9600
216 Park Rd Burlingame (94010) *(P-22411)*
Carr, McClellan, Burlingame *Also called Carr Mc Clellan Ingersoll Thom (P-22411)*

A L P H A B E T I C

Employee Codes: A=Over 500 employees, B=251-500
C=101-250, D=51-100, E=50
2020 Directory of California
Wholesalers and Services Companies
© Mergent Inc. 1-800-342-5647
1209

Carrara Marble Co Amer Inc (PA)......D......626 961-6010
15939 Phoenix Dr City of Industry (91745) ***(P-6672)***
Carrasco Heleo......C......714 639-1759
2510 N Grand Ave Ste 102 Santa Ana (92705) ***(P-13876)***
Carriage Inn, Daly City *Also called Reneson Hotels Inc* ***(P-12807)***
Carrier Commercial Service, Sacramento *Also called Carrier Corporation* ***(P-17442)***
Carrier Corporation......B......510 347-2000
600 Mccormick St Ste B San Leandro (94577) ***(P-2089)***
Carrier Corporation......E......916 928-9500
1168 National Dr Ste 60 Sacramento (95834) ***(P-17442)***
Carrier Johnson (PA)......D......619 236-9462
185 W F St Ste 600 San Diego (92101) ***(P-25421)***
Carrington Mrtg Holdings LLC......C......888 267-0584
1600 S Douglass Rd # 110 Anaheim (92806) ***(P-9536)***
Carroll Burdick Mc Donough LLP (PA)......C......415 989-5900
275 Battery St Ste 2600 San Francisco (94111) ***(P-22412)***
Carrollco Inc......E......559 396-3939
3104 N Miami Ave Fresno (93727) ***(P-1101)***
Carrolls LLC......D......800 559-4897
2478 S Golden State Blvd Fresno (93706) ***(P-6484)***
Carson Capital Corp (PA)......D......951 684-9585
42882 Ivy St Murrieta (92562) ***(P-6387)***
Carson Community Center, Carson *Also called City of Carson* ***(P-23008)***
Carson Gang Diversion Team, Carson *Also called County of Los Angeles* ***(P-24440)***
Carson Kurtzman Consultants (HQ)......C......310 823-9000
2335 Alaska Ave El Segundo (90245) ***(P-22413)***
Carson Landscape Industries, Sacramento *Also called Frank Carson Ldscp & Maint Inc* ***(P-812)***
Carson Medical Offices, Gardena *Also called Kaiser Foundation Hospitals* ***(P-19072)***
Carson Operating Company LLC......D......310 830-9200
2 Civic Plaza Dr Carson (90745) ***(P-12120)***
Carson Senior Assisted Living, Carson *Also called Secrom Inc* ***(P-20678)***
Carson Senior Assisted Living......D......310 830-4010
345 E Carson St Carson (90745) ***(P-23851)***
Cartel Marketing Inc......C......818 483-1130
5230 Las Virgenes Rd # 250 Calabasas (91302) ***(P-10314)***
Carters Details Plus, Burbank *Also called Jim & Doug Carters Automotive* ***(P-17259)***
Cartridge Family Inc......C......510 658-0400
1940 Union St Ste 29 Oakland (94607) ***(P-7854)***
Cartridge Family Ink, Oakland *Also called Cartridge Family Inc* ***(P-7854)***
Cartwright Termite & Pest Ctrl......E......760 771-6091
51360 Calle Guatemala La Quinta (92253) ***(P-13809)***
Caruso MGT Ltd A Cal Ltd Prtnr......D......323 900-8100
101 The Grove Dr Los Angeles (90036) ***(P-10966)***
Casa Allegra Community Svcs......D......415 499-1116
35 Mitchell Blvd Ste 8 San Rafael (94903) ***(P-22960)***
Casa Clina Ctrs For Rhbltation, Pomona *Also called Casa Colina Hospital and Cente* ***(P-20768)***
Casa Colin Comprehensive......C......909 596-7733
255 E Bonita Ave Pomona (91767) ***(P-21967)***
Casa Colina Inc (PA)......A......909 596-7733
255 E Bonita Ave Pomona (91767) ***(P-22961)***
Casa Colina Hospital & Ctr, Pomona *Also called Casa Colina Inc* ***(P-22961)***
Casa Colina Hospital and Cente (HQ)......B......909 596-7733
255 E Bonita Ave Pomona (91767) ***(P-20768)***
Casa Coloma Health Care Center, Rancho Cordova *Also called A B C D Associates* ***(P-19707)***
Casa De Amparo (PA)......D......760 754-5500
325 Buena Creek Rd San Marcos (92069) ***(P-23852)***
Casa De Las Campanas Inc (PA)......C......858 451-9152
18655 W Bernardo Dr San Diego (92127) ***(P-23853)***
Casa De Modesto, Modesto *Also called Fellowship Homes Inc* ***(P-23925)***
Casa Dorinda, Santa Barbara *Also called Montecito Retirement Assn* ***(P-20145)***
Casa Dscanso Convalescent Hosp......C......323 225-5991
4515 Huntington Dr S Los Angeles (90032) ***(P-26933)***
Casa Fremont, Fremont *Also called Anka Behavioral Health Inc* ***(P-22178)***
Casa Madrona Hotel and Spa LLC......D......415 332-0502
801 Bridgeway Sausalito (94965) ***(P-12121)***
Casa Munras Garden Hotel, Monterey *Also called Portfolio Hotels & Resorts LLC* ***(P-12764)***
Casa Munras Hotel LLC......D......831 375-2411
700 Munras Ave Monterey (93940) ***(P-12122)***
Casa Pacifica Adult Day H, San Diego *Also called J Gelt Corporation* ***(P-23288)***
Casa Pacifica Centers (PA)......C......805 482-3260
1722 S Lewis Rd Camarillo (93012) ***(P-22962)***
Casa Palmera Care Center, Del Mar *Also called Lee Johnson* ***(P-20612)***
Casa Sandoval LLC......D......510 727-1700
1200 Russell Way Hayward (94541) ***(P-10709)***
Casa-Pacifica Inc......B......951 658-3369
2200 W Acacia Ave Ofc Hemet (92545) ***(P-23854)***
Casa-Pacifica Inc......D......951 766-5116
2400 W Acacia Ave Hemet (92545) ***(P-23855)***
Casablanca Alzheimer's Care, Oak View *Also called Casablanca Alzheimers Resid* ***(P-23856)***
Casablanca Alzheimers Resid......D......805 649-5143
158 Rockaway Rd Oak View (93022) ***(P-23856)***
Casanova Pndrill Pblicidad Inc (PA)......D......949 474-5001
275 Mccormick Ave Ste 1a Costa Mesa (92626) ***(P-13481)***
Casas - Comprehensive......D......858 292-2900
5151 Murphy Canyon Rd # 220 San Diego (92123) ***(P-24815)***
Casas International Brkg Inc (PA)......D......619 661-6162
9355 Airway Rd Ste 4 San Diego (92154) ***(P-4380)***
Casavina Foundation Corp......C......408 238-9751
2501 Alvin Ave San Jose (95121) ***(P-19781)***
Casbn Investment Inc......D......650 991-2800
345 Gellert Blvd Ste A Daly City (94015) ***(P-10967)***
Cascade Logistics, Tracy *Also called Es3 LLC* ***(P-4405)***
Cascade Logistics LLC......D......209 832-4205
857 Stonebridge Dr Tracy (95376) ***(P-4381)***
Casden Builders LLC......E......310 274-5553
9090 Wilshire Blvd Fl 3 Beverly Hills (90211) ***(P-10575)***
Casden Company LLC......D......310 274-5553
9606 Santa Monica Blvd # 3 Beverly Hills (90210) ***(P-11552)***
Case Medical Group, Sacramento *Also called Central Anesthesia Service* ***(P-18881)***
Case Vlott Cattle......E......559 665-7399
20330 Road 4 Chowchilla (93610) ***(P-386)***
Casecentral Inc (HQ)......D......415 989-2300
1055 E Colo Blvd Ste 400 Pasadena (91106) ***(P-16679)***
Casecentral.com, Pasadena *Also called Casecentral Inc* ***(P-16679)***
Casestack LLC (HQ)......D......310 473-8885
3000 Ocean Park Blvd Santa Monica (90405) ***(P-4382)***
Casestack, Inc., Santa Monica *Also called Casestack LLC* ***(P-4382)***
Casewise Systems Inc (HQ)......D......424 284-4101
9465 Wilshire Blvd # 300 Beverly Hills (90212) ***(P-6813)***
Casey Company (PA)......C......562 436-9685
180 E Ocean Blvd Ste 1010 Long Beach (90802) ***(P-8722)***
Casey Securities Inc (PA)......D......415 544-5030
301 Pine St San Francisco (94104) ***(P-9659)***
Cash It Here, Santa Ana *Also called Continental Currency Svcs Inc* ***(P-9428)***
Cashcall Inc......A......949 752-4600
1 City Blvd W Ste 102 Orange (92868) ***(P-9455)***
Cashedge Inc......D......408 541-3900
525 Almanor Ave Ste 150 Sunnyvale (94085) ***(P-16680)***
Casino, Hopland *Also called Hopland Band Pomo Indians Inc* ***(P-18705)***
Casino Morongo......D......951 849-3080
49500 Seminole Dr Cabazon (92230) ***(P-18323)***
Casino San Pablo, San Pablo *Also called Lytton Rancheria* ***(P-18721)***
Casitas Care Center, Granada Hills *Also called A Cori Partnership* ***(P-20474)***
Cask Technologies LLC (PA)......D......888 418-7067
9350 Waxie Way Ste 210 San Diego (92123) ***(P-14705)***
Caspar Community......E......707 964-4997
15051 Caspar Rd Caspar (95420) ***(P-22963)***
Casper Company......C......619 589-6001
3825 Bancroft Dr Spring Valley (91977) ***(P-3125)***
Caspian Commercial Plbg Inc......D......818 649-2500
711 Ivy St Glendale (91204) ***(P-2090)***
Cass Inc (PA)......C......510 893-6476
2730 Peralta St Oakland (94607) ***(P-7753)***
Cass Construction Inc (PA)......C......619 590-0929
1100 Wagner Dr El Cajon (92020) ***(P-1841)***
Cassidy Medical Group Inc (PA)......E......760 630-5487
145 Thunder Dr Vista (92083) ***(P-18876)***
Cassidy Trly Prop MGT Sn Frncs......D......415 781-8100
201 California St Ste 800 San Francisco (94111) ***(P-10968)***
Cast & Crew Payroll LLC (PA)......C......818 848-6022
2300 W Empire Ave # 500 Burbank (91504) ***(P-25549)***
Cast and Crew Entrmt Svcs, Burbank *Also called Cast & Crew Payroll LLC* ***(P-25549)***
Castaic Lk Wtr Agcy Fing Corp......C......661 259-2737
27234 Bouquet Canyon Rd Santa Clarita (91350) ***(P-6028)***
Caster Family Enterprises Inc......C......619 287-8893
4607 Mission Gorge Pl San Diego (92120) ***(P-11898)***
Castlblack Pismo Bch Owner LLC......E......805 773-6020
601 James Way Pismo Beach (93449) ***(P-12123)***
Castle & Cooke California Inc......E......661 664-6500
10000 Stockdale Hwy # 300 Bakersfield (93311) ***(P-6177)***
Castle Dental......E......323 567-1227
4433 Tweedy Blvd South Gate (90280) ***(P-19606)***
Castle Family Health Ctrs Inc (PA)......D......209 381-2000
3605 Hospital Rd Ste H Atwater (95301) ***(P-21968)***
Castle Manor Convalescent Ctr, National City *Also called Castle Manor Inc* ***(P-19782)***
Castle Manor Inc......D......619 791-7900
541 S V Ave National City (91950) ***(P-19782)***
Castleblack Owner Holdings LLC......E......805 773-6020
601 James Way Pismo Beach (93449) ***(P-26173)***
Castlehill Properties Inc (PA)......D......209 472-9800
3240 W March Ln Stockton (95219) ***(P-12124)***
Castlewood Country Club......C......925 846-2871
707 Country Club Cir Pleasanton (94566) ***(P-18417)***
Castlewood Treatment Ctr LLC (PA)......D......805 273-5217
2545 W Hillcrest Dr 205 Thousand Oaks (91320) ***(P-21969)***
Castlight Health Inc (PA)......C......415 829-1400
150 Spear St Ste 400 San Francisco (94105) ***(P-15737)***
Caston Inc......D......909 381-1619
354 S Allen St San Bernardino (92408) ***(P-2767)***
Castro Valley Care Centers, Culver City *Also called Jesse Lee Group Inc* ***(P-26273)***
Castro Valley Health Inc......C......510 690-1930
39 Beta Ct San Ramon (94583) ***(P-21701)***
Caswell Bay Inc......D......925 933-8181
1777 N Calif Blvd Ste 210 Walnut Creek (94596) ***(P-21702)***
CAT Logistics Inc......D......909 390-1920
5491 E Francis St Ontario (91761) ***(P-4383)***
Catalent San Diego Inc......C......858 805-6383
7330 Carroll Rd Ste 200 San Diego (92121) ***(P-26059)***
Catalina Business Entps Inc......E......310 510-1600
635 Crescent Ave Avalon (90704) ***(P-18644)***
Catalina Channel Express Inc (HQ)......B......310 519-7971
385 E Swinford St San Pedro (90731) ***(P-4599)***
Catalina Channel Express Inc......C......562 435-8686
320 Golden Shore Lbby Long Beach (90802) ***(P-4610)***
Catalina Channel Express Inc......C......562 495-3565
385 E Swinford St San Pedro (90731) ***(P-4600)***
Catalina Enterprise Inc......D......949 637-3091
206 Catalina Rd Fullerton (92835) ***(P-27018)***
Catalina Events Inc......E......310 925-6986
2605 184th St Redondo Beach (90278) ***(P-26902)***
Catalina Express, Long Beach *Also called Catalina Channel Express Inc* ***(P-4610)***
Catalina Express, San Pedro *Also called Catalina Channel Express Inc* ***(P-4600)***

Catalina Express Cruises, San Pedro *Also called Catalina Channel Express Inc* ***(P-4599)***
Catalina Glassbottom Boat Inc...D...310 510-2888
1 Cabrillo Mole Avalon (90704) ***(P-4601)***
Catalina Solar 2 LLC...A...888 903-6926
15445 Innovation Dr San Diego (92128) ***(P-5817)***
Catalina Solar Lessee LLC...A...888 903-6926
11585 Willow Springs Rd Rosamond (93560) ***(P-5818)***
Catalyst Development Corp...E...760 228-9653
56925 Yucca Trl Yucca Valley (92284) ***(P-15274)***
Catamaran Resort Hotel, San Diego *Also called Braemar Partnership* ***(P-12081)***
Catamount Broadcasting of Chic (PA)...C...530 893-2424
3460 Silverbell Rd Chico (95973) ***(P-5584)***
Cataphora Inc (PA)...D...650 622-9840
3425 Edison Way Menlo Park (94025) ***(P-14706)***
Catasys Inc (PA)...C...310 444-4300
11601 Wilshire Blvd # 1100 Los Angeles (90025) ***(P-21394)***
Catati Rohnert Park Inc...E...707 792-4531
1400 Magnolia Ave Rohnert Park (94928) ***(P-16681)***
Catchpoint Systems Inc...C...646 727-4557
6080 Center Dr Ste 715 Los Angeles (90045) ***(P-16682)***
Caterpillar, San Diego *Also called Hawthorne Machinery Co* ***(P-17334)***
Caterpillar, Ontario *Also called CAT Logistics Inc* ***(P-4383)***
Caterpillar Authorized Dealer, Riverside *Also called Johnson Machinery Co* ***(P-7481)***
Caterpillar Authorized Dealer, West Sacramento *Also called Holt of California* ***(P-7477)***
Caterpillar Authorized Dealer, City of Industry *Also called Quinn Shepherd Machinery* ***(P-7489)***
Caterpillar Authorized Dealer, Salinas *Also called Quinn Lift Inc* ***(P-7581)***
Caterpillar Authorized Dealer, San Diego *Also called Hawthorne Machinery Co* ***(P-14099)***
Caterpillar Authorized Dealer, Oxnard *Also called Quinn Group Inc* ***(P-7504)***
Caterpillar Authorized Dealer, Imperial *Also called Empire Southwest LLC* ***(P-7470)***
Caterpillar Authorized Dealer, Bakersfield *Also called Quinn Company* ***(P-7485)***
Caterpillar Authorized Dealer, Oxnard *Also called Quinn Company* ***(P-7486)***
Caterpillar Authorized Dealer, Santa Maria *Also called Quinn Company* ***(P-7487)***
Caterpillar Authorized Dealer, Salinas *Also called Quinn Group Inc* ***(P-7488)***
Caterpillar Authorized Dealer, San Diego *Also called Hawthorne Machinery Co* ***(P-7474)***
Cathay Bank (HQ)...C...626 279-3698
9650 Flair Dr El Monte (91731) ***(P-9177)***
Cathay Bank...D...626 588-1911
250 S Atlantic Blvd Monterey Park (91754) ***(P-9178)***
Cathay Bank...B...213 687-1300
977 N Broadway Ste 306 Los Angeles (90012) ***(P-26174)***
Cathay Bank...D...213 896-0098
800 W 6th St Ste 200 Los Angeles (90017) ***(P-9179)***
Cathay Bank...C...626 452-1582
4128 Temple City Blvd Rosemead (91770) ***(P-9180)***
Cathay Pacific Airways Limited...D...310 615-1113
1960 E Grand Ave Ste 540 El Segundo (90245) ***(P-4871)***
Cathedral Bookstore, Los Angeles *Also called Cathedral Center of St Paul* ***(P-24816)***
Cathedral Center of St Paul...D...213 482-2040
840 Echo Park Ave Los Angeles (90026) ***(P-24816)***
Cathedral Cyn Golf Tennis CLB, Cathedral City *Also called Briar Golf LP* ***(P-18224)***
Cathedral Oaks Athletic Club, Goleta *Also called Swell Athletic Club GP* ***(P-18590)***
Cathedral Pioneer Church Homes (PA)...D...916 442-4906
415 P St Ofc Sacramento (95814) ***(P-19783)***
Catholic Charities Diocese (PA)...D...209 444-5900
1106 N El Dorado St Stockton (95202) ***(P-22964)***
Catholic Charities Diocese San...E...619 287-9454
4575 Mission Gorge Pl A San Diego (92120) ***(P-22965)***
CATHOLIC CHARITIES OF EAST BAY, Oakland *Also called Catholic Charities of The Dioc* ***(P-22970)***
Catholic Charities of La Inc (PA)...D...213 251-3400
1531 James M Wood Blvd Los Angeles (90015) ***(P-25981)***
Catholic Charities of La Inc...E...818 883-6015
21600 Hart St Canoga Park (91303) ***(P-22966)***
Catholic Charities of La Inc...D...213 251-3400
1400 James M Wood Blvd Los Angeles (90015) ***(P-22967)***
Catholic Charities of Santa CL (PA)...C...408 468-0100
2625 Zanker Rd Ste 200 San Jose (95134) ***(P-22968)***
Catholic Charities of Santa CL...D...805 643-4694
303 N Ventura Ave Ste A Ventura (93001) ***(P-22969)***
Catholic Charities of The Dioc (PA)...D...510 768-3100
433 Jefferson St Oakland (94607) ***(P-22970)***
Catholic Chrts Cyo Archdiocs...D...415 743-0017
810 Avenue D San Francisco (94130) ***(P-22971)***
Catholic Chrts Cyo Archdiocs...D...415 405-2000
141 Leland Ave San Francisco (94134) ***(P-22972)***
Catholic Chrts Cyo Archdiocs...E...650 757-2110
699 Serramonte Blvd 210 Daly City (94015) ***(P-3788)***
Catholic Chrts Cyo Archdiocs...D...415 334-5550
1111 Junipero Serra Blvd San Francisco (94132) ***(P-22973)***
Catholic Chrts Cyo Archdiocs...D...415 553-8700
20 Franklin St San Francisco (94102) ***(P-22974)***
Catholic Chrts Cyo Archdiocs (PA)...D...415 972-1200
990 Eddy St San Francisco (94109) ***(P-22975)***
Catholic Chrts Cyo Archdiocs...B...415 507-2000
1 Saint Vincents Dr San Rafael (94903) ***(P-22976)***
CATHOLIC YOUTH ORGANIZATION, Daly City *Also called Catholic Chrts Cyo Archdiocs* ***(P-3788)***
Caton Moving & Storage, Alameda *Also called Chipman Corporation* ***(P-3985)***
Cats U S A Pest Control, North Hollywood *Also called Cats USA Inc* ***(P-13810)***
Cats USA Inc...D...818 506-1000
5683 Whitnall Hwy North Hollywood (91601) ***(P-13810)***
Catta Verdera Country Club...D...916 645-7200
1111 Catta Verdera Lincoln (95648) ***(P-18418)***
Cattail Farms Inc...D...916 207-6580
3970 Cr95b Knights Landing (95645) ***(P-4)***
Cattlemens...D...925 447-1224
2882 Kitty Hawk Rd Livermore (94551) ***(P-13405)***
Cattlemens Restaurant, Livermore *Also called Cattlemens* ***(P-13405)***
Cattrac Construction Inc...D...909 355-1146
15030 Slover Ave Fontana (92337) ***(P-1952)***
CAV Inc...D...760 729-5199
5411 Avenida Encinas # 210 Carlsbad (92008) ***(P-3661)***
Cavalier Inn Inc...D...805 927-4688
9415 Hearst Dr San Simeon (93452) ***(P-12125)***
Cavalier Inn Incorporated...D...805 927-6444
250 San Simeon Ave Ste 4c San Simeon (93452) ***(P-12126)***
Cavalier Oceanfront Resort, San Simeon *Also called Cavalier Inn Inc* ***(P-12125)***
Cavallo Point LLC (PA)...D...415 339-4700
601 Murray Cir Sausalito (94965) ***(P-12127)***
Cavendish Kinetics Inc...E...408 627-4504
2960 N 1st St San Jose (95134) ***(P-7246)***
Cavisson Systems Inc...B...800 701-6125
5201 Great America Pkwy Santa Clara (95054) ***(P-27019)***
CB Associates Inc...E...424 777-8214
11659 Haynes St North Hollywood (91606) ***(P-13673)***
CB C&C Properties/Comm Di Inc...D...530 221-7551
2120 Churn Creek Rd Redding (96002) ***(P-10969)***
CB North LLC...A...831 786-1642
480 W Beach St Watsonville (95076) ***(P-308)***
CB Richard Ellis, Los Angeles *Also called Cbre Inc* ***(P-10973)***
CB Richard Ellis RE Svcs LLC...D...213 613-3333
355 S Grand Ave Ste 2700 Los Angeles (90071) ***(P-10970)***
CB Richard Ellis Strategic Par...D...213 614-6862
515 S Flower St Ste 3100 Los Angeles (90071) ***(P-11899)***
CB Richard Ellis Strtgc Prtnrs...D...213 683-4200
515 S Flower St Los Angeles (90071) ***(P-10576)***
Cb-1 Hotel...D...415 633-3838
757 Market St San Francisco (94103) ***(P-12128)***
CBA Site Services Inc...D...925 754-7633
11387 Pyrites Way Rancho Cordova (95670) ***(P-27020)***
Cbabr Inc (PA)...D...951 640-7056
31620 Rr Cyn Rd Ste A Canyon Lake (92587) ***(P-10971)***
Cbest Inc...D...310 445-2378
11620 Wilshire Blvd # 450 Los Angeles (90025) ***(P-21454)***
Cbiz Mayor Hoffman Mechan (PA)...D...858 795-2000
10616 Scripps Summit Ct San Diego (92131) ***(P-25550)***
Cbizmhm LLC...E...661 325-7500
5060 California Ave # 800 Bakersfield (93309) ***(P-25551)***
Cbol Corporation...C...818 704-8200
19850 Plummer St Chatsworth (91311) ***(P-7247)***
Cbre Inc...D...916 446-6800
500 Capitol Mall Ste 2400 Sacramento (95814) ***(P-10972)***
Cbre Inc (HQ)...C...213 613-3333
400 S Hope St Ste 25 Los Angeles (90071) ***(P-10973)***
Cbre Inc...C...714 939-2100
2125 E Katella Ave # 100 Anaheim (92806) ***(P-10974)***
Cbre Inc...B...626 814-7900
4900 Rivergrade Rd A110 Baldwin Park (91706) ***(P-10975)***
Cbre Inc...D...818 907-4600
15303 Ventura Blvd # 200 Van Nuys (91403) ***(P-10976)***
Cbre Inc...D...408 453-7400
225 W Santa Clara St # 1050 San Jose (95113) ***(P-10977)***
Cbre Inc...C...310 363-4900
2221 Rosecrans Ave # 101 El Segundo (90245) ***(P-10978)***
Cbre Inc...D...818 502-6700
234 S Brand Blvd Ste 800 Glendale (91204) ***(P-10979)***
Cbre Inc...D...310 550-2500
1840 Century Park E # 900 Los Angeles (90067) ***(P-10980)***
Cbre Inc...C...858 546-4600
4365 Executive Dr # 1600 San Diego (92121) ***(P-10981)***
Cbre Inc...D...909 418-2000
4141 Inland Empire Blvd # 100 Ontario (91764) ***(P-10982)***
Cbre Capstone, Los Angeles *Also called Cbre Inc* ***(P-10980)***
Cbre Global Investors LLC (HQ)...C...213 683-4200
601 S Figueroa St Ste 49 Los Angeles (90017) ***(P-10983)***
Cbre Global Investors LLC...B...949 725-8500
3501 Jamboree Rd Ste 100 Newport Beach (92660) ***(P-26549)***
Cbre Group Inc (PA)...C...213 613-3333
400 S Hope St Ste 25 Los Angeles (90071) ***(P-10984)***
Cbre Services Inc...D...213 613-3333
400 S Hope St Ste 25 Los Angeles (90071) ***(P-26550)***
Cbre Valuation and Advisory, Los Angeles *Also called CB Richard Ellis RE Svcs LLC* ***(P-10970)***
CBS Broadcasting Inc...B...415 765-0928
855 Battery St San Francisco (94111) ***(P-5585)***
CBS Broadcasting Inc...D...415 765-4097
A65 Bettery St San Francisco (94111) ***(P-5512)***
CBS Broadcasting Inc...B...818 655-2000
4200 Radford Ave Studio City (91604) ***(P-5586)***
CBS Broadcasting Inc...D...323 575-2345
7800 Beverly Blvd Los Angeles (90036) ***(P-24992)***
CBS Corporation...D...323 575-2345
7800 Beverly Blvd Los Angeles (90036) ***(P-5587)***
CBS Corporation...D...415 765-4000
865 Battery St Fl 2/3 San Francisco (94111) ***(P-5513)***
CBS Corporation...D...760 343-5700
31276 Dunham Way Thousand Palms (92276) ***(P-5588)***
CBS Enterprises, Santa Monica *Also called CBS Television Distribution* ***(P-26175)***
CBS Farms LLC...E...831 724-0700
80 Sakata Ln Watsonville (95076) ***(P-89)***
CBS Interactive Inc...C...415 344-1813
2900 W Alameda Ave Burbank (91505) ***(P-13647)***
CBS Interactive Inc (HQ)...A...415 344-2000
235 2nd St San Francisco (94105) ***(P-13648)***

Employee Codes: A=Over 500 employees, B=251-500 C=101-250, D=51-100, E=50
2020 Directory of California Wholesalers and Services Companies
© Mergent Inc. 1-800-342-5647
1211

CBS Maxpreps Inc ....E.......530 676-6440
4364 Town Center Blvd # 320 El Dorado Hills (95762) ***(P-5372)***
CBS Network News, Los Angeles *Also called Merlot Film Productions Inc* ***(P-17633)***
CBS Radio Inc ....C.......559 490-0106
1071 W Shaw Ave Fresno (93711) ***(P-5514)***
CBS Radio Inc ....D.......415 765-4097
865 Battery St Fl 3 San Francisco (94111) ***(P-5515)***
CBS Radio Inc ....D.......909 825-9525
900 E Washington St # 315 Colton (92324) ***(P-5516)***
CBS Radio Inc ....D.......916 923-6800
280 Commerce Cir Sacramento (95815) ***(P-5517)***
CBS Studio Center, Studio City *Also called Radford Studio Center Inc* ***(P-17940)***
CBS Television Distribution (PA) ....A.......310 264-3300
2450 Colo Ave Ste 500e Santa Monica (90404) ***(P-26175)***
Cbsi, San Francisco *Also called CBS Interactive Inc* ***(P-13648)***
Cbsj Financial Corporation ....D.......408 792-4600
1735 N 1st St Ste 250 San Jose (95112) ***(P-13674)***
Cbsrr Inc ....D.......909 336-2131
27206 Hwy 189 Blue Jay (92317) ***(P-10985)***
CC Wellness LLC (HQ) ....D.......661 295-1700
29000 Hancock Pkwy Valencia (91355) ***(P-7934)***
Cc-Palo Alto Inc ....C.......650 853-5000
620 Sand Hill Rd Palo Alto (94304) ***(P-20416)***
Ccare West, Fresno *Also called California Cancer Assctes* ***(P-18855)***
Ccbc Reference Lab, Fresno *Also called Central California Blood Ctr* ***(P-22201)***
CCC Property Holdings LLC ....C.......310 609-1957
500 S Alameda St Compton (90221) ***(P-11650)***
Ccc2931 LLC ....D.......562 590-8591
2401 E Pacific Coast Hwy Wilmington (90744) ***(P-4557)***
Cccc Growth Fund LLC ....D.......626 441-8770
899 El Centro St South Pasadena (91030) ***(P-11900)***
Cch Computax, Torrance *Also called CCH Incorporated* ***(P-15738)***
CCH Incorporated ....B.......310 800-9800
20101 Hamilton Ave # 200 Torrance (90502) ***(P-15738)***
Ccig, Westlake Village *Also called California Coml Inv Group Inc* ***(P-27012)***
Ccintegration Inc (PA) ....E.......408 228-1314
2060 Corporate Ct San Jose (95131) ***(P-25729)***
Ccmsi, Irvine *Also called Cannon Cochran MGT Svcs Inc* ***(P-10312)***
Ccna Vons Athletes For Life ....D.......805 453-2499
10670 6th St Ste 113 Rancho Cucamonga (91730) ***(P-24817)***
CCOF CERTIFICATION SERVICES, Santa Cruz *Also called California Certified Organic* ***(P-24327)***
CCPOA, West Sacramento *Also called California Correctnl Peace Ofc* ***(P-24437)***
CCS, Hayward *Also called Controlled Contamination Svcs* ***(P-13892)***
CCS Global Tech, Poway *Also called Califrnia Crtive Solutions Inc* ***(P-15954)***
Ccts, Santa Ana *Also called Satellite Management Co* ***(P-11439)***
Ccwd, Concord *Also called Contra Costa Water District* ***(P-6039)***
Cdc San Francisco LLC ....D.......415 616-6512
888 Howard St San Francisco (94103) ***(P-12129)***
Cdcr - California Men's Colony, San Luis Obispo *Also called Correctons Rhbltation Cal Dept* ***(P-21989)***
Cdcr Cal Instn For Men Hosp, Chino *Also called Correctons Rhbltation Cal Dept* ***(P-20806)***
CDI, Woodland Hills *Also called Child Development Institute* ***(P-22991)***
CDI Centers, Morgan Hill *Also called Continuing Development Inc* ***(P-23711)***
CDM Constructors Inc ....D.......909 579-3500
9220 Cleveland Ave # 100 Rancho Cucamonga (91730) ***(P-1842)***
CDM SMITH INC ....D.......949 752-5452
46 Discovery Ste 250 Irvine (92618) ***(P-24993)***
CDM SMITH INC ....D.......760 438-7755
703 Palomar Airport Rd # 300 Carlsbad (92011) ***(P-24994)***
CDM SMITH INC ....D.......617 452-6000
2300 Clayton Rd Ste 950 Concord (94520) ***(P-24995)***
Cdnetworks Inc (HQ) ....E.......408 228-3379
1550 Valley Vista Dr # 110 Diamond Bar (91765) ***(P-5373)***
Cds Moving Equipment Inc (PA) ....D.......310 631-1100
375 W Manville St Rancho Dominguez (90220) ***(P-7535)***
Cdsnet LLC ....D.......310 981-9500
6053 W Century Blvd Los Angeles (90045) ***(P-27021)***
Cdsrvs LLC ....D.......714 912-8353
840 W Grove Ave Orange (92865) ***(P-17488)***
Cdw, Anaheim *Also called Consolidated Design West Inc* ***(P-13776)***
CE Allencompany Inc ....E.......562 989-6100
2109 Gundry Ave Long Beach (90755) ***(P-1953)***
Ce2 Kleinfelder JV ....D.......925 463-7301
7901 Stoneridge Dr # 315 Pleasanton (94588) ***(P-24996)***
Cea-Pack Logistics, Cerritos *Also called Cea-Pack Services Inc* ***(P-4248)***
Cea-Pack Services Inc ....C.......562 407-0660
12607 Hiddencreek Way Cerritos (90703) ***(P-4248)***
Cec, La Canada *Also called Child Educational Center* ***(P-23695)***
Cecchini & Cecchini, Brentwood *Also called Robert Cecchini Inc* ***(P-72)***
Cecelia Packing Corporation ....C.......559 626-5000
24780 E South Ave Orange Cove (93646) ***(P-8441)***
Cecico Inc ....D.......323 269-7000
1016 Towne Ave Unit 110 Los Angeles (90021) ***(P-8062)***
Cecico Town, Los Angeles *Also called Cecico Inc* ***(P-8062)***
CECILLA GONZALEZ DE AL HOYA CA, Los Angeles *Also called White Memorial Medical Center* ***(P-21373)***
Cedar Creek Alzhimers Dementia, Berkeley *Also called Altcare Cedar Creek LLC* ***(P-23816)***
CEDAR CREST NURSING & REHABILITATION CENTER, Sunnyvale *Also called Ghc of Sunnyvale LLC* ***(P-20569)***
Cedar Fair LP ....C.......408 988-1776
4701 Great America Pkwy Santa Clara (95054) ***(P-18324)***
Cedar Holdings LLC ....D.......909 862-0611
7534 Palm Ave Highland (92346) ***(P-19784)***
Cedar House Rehabilitation Ctr, Bloomington *Also called Social Science Service Center* ***(P-21495)***
Cedar Management LLC ....D.......310 396-3100
3233 Dnald Douglas Loop S Santa Monica (90405) ***(P-10986)***
Cedar Mountain Post Acute, Yucaipa *Also called Cedar Operations LLC* ***(P-19785)***
Cedar Operations LLC ....C.......909 790-2273
11970 4th St Yucaipa (92399) ***(P-19785)***
Cedar Signature, Santa Monica *Also called Cedar Management LLC* ***(P-10986)***
Cedar Sinai Medical Group, Beverly Hills *Also called Medical Group Bverly Hills Inc* ***(P-19182)***
CEDARS SINAI MEDICAL GROUP, Beverly Hills *Also called Medical Group Bverly Hills Inc* ***(P-19181)***
Cedars-Sinai Medical Center ....C.......310 824-3664
8635 W 3rd St Ste 1195 Los Angeles (90048) ***(P-18877)***
Cedars-Sinai Medical Center ....C.......310 423-3849
127 S San Vicente Blvd # 3417 Los Angeles (90048) ***(P-18878)***
Cedars-Sinai Medical Center ....A.......323 866-8483
8631 W 3rd St Ste 730 Los Angeles (90048) ***(P-18879)***
Cedars-Sinai Medical Center ....C.......310 385-3400
250 N Robertson Blvd # 101 Beverly Hills (90211) ***(P-20769)***
Cedarwood-Young Company (PA) ....C.......626 962-4047
14620 Joanbridge St Baldwin Park (91706) ***(P-6178)***
Cedarwood-Young Company ....D.......626 962-4047
14618 Arrow Hwy Baldwin Park (91706) ***(P-7754)***
Cederlind Farms LP ....D.......209 606-8586
2514 Kenney Ave Winton (95388) ***(P-121)***
Ceed Security Corp ....E.......951 222-2233
1525 3rd St Ste K Riverside (92507) ***(P-16225)***
Cei, San Jose *Also called Cupertino Electric Inc* ***(P-2469)***
Celebrity Casinos Inc ....B.......310 631-3838
123 E Artesia Blvd Compton (90220) ***(P-12130)***
Celebrity Pink USA, Montebello *Also called 2253 Apparel Inc* ***(P-8052)***
Celerity Consulting Group Inc (PA) ....D.......415 986-8850
2 Gough St Ste 300 San Francisco (94103) ***(P-26551)***
Celestica LLC ....B.......909 418-6986
895 S Rockefeller Ave # 102 Ontario (91761) ***(P-7248)***
Celestix Networks Inc ....D.......510 668-0700
215 Fourier Ave Ste 140 Fremont (94539) ***(P-15568)***
Celex Solutions, Brea *Also called Contract Services Group Inc* ***(P-13890)***
Celgene Corporation ....C.......858 677-0034
10300 Campus Point Dr # 100 San Diego (92121) ***(P-7935)***
Celgene Signal Research, San Diego *Also called Celgene Corporation* ***(P-7935)***
Celigo Inc (PA) ....E.......650 579-0210
1820 Gateway Dr Ste 260 San Mateo (94404) ***(P-15275)***
Cell Business Equipment, Irvine *Also called Sema Inc* ***(P-25677)***
Cell Design Labs Inc ....E.......510 398-0501
5858 Horton St Ste 240 Emeryville (94608) ***(P-7936)***
Cell-Crete Corporation ....D.......510 471-7257
995 Zephyr Ave Hayward (94544) ***(P-3126)***
Cellarstone Inc (PA) ....D.......650 242-0008
1650 Borel Pl Ste 100 San Mateo (94402) ***(P-15956)***
Cellco Partnership ....D.......951 769-0985
1484 E Second St Beaumont (92223) ***(P-5200)***
Cellco Partnership ....D.......831 644-0858
1680 Del Monte Ctr Monterey (93940) ***(P-5201)***
Cellco Partnership ....D.......714 921-5130
1500 E Village Way # 2205 Orange (92865) ***(P-5202)***
Cellco Partnership ....D.......925 626-3480
6471 Lone Tree Way Brentwood (94513) ***(P-5203)***
Cellco Partnership ....D.......951 697-3035
2851 Canyon Springs Pkwy Riverside (92507) ***(P-5204)***
Cellco Partnership ....D.......212 395-1000
255 Parkshore Dr Folsom (95630) ***(P-5205)***
Cellco Partnership ....D.......559 454-0803
550 S Clovis Ave Ste 105 Fresno (93727) ***(P-5206)***
Cellco Partnership ....D.......714 427-0733
901 S Coast Dr Ste K120 Costa Mesa (92626) ***(P-5207)***
Cellco Partnership ....D.......951 361-1850
12459 Limonite Ave C-2 Eastvale (91752) ***(P-5208)***
Cellco Partnership ....D.......916 786-6151
1900 Douglas Blvd Ste D Roseville (95661) ***(P-5209)***
Cellco Partnership ....A.......949 286-7000
15505 Sand Canyon Ave Irvine (92618) ***(P-5210)***
Cellco Partnership ....D.......661 827-8728
2701 Ming Ave Spc 100a Bakersfield (93304) ***(P-5211)***
Cellco Partnership ....D.......760 720-8400
1846 Marron Rd Carlsbad (92008) ***(P-5212)***
Cellco Partnership ....D.......562 809-5650
12607 Artesia Blvd Cerritos (90703) ***(P-5213)***
Cellco Partnership ....D.......951 549-6400
2210 Griffin Way Ste 101 Corona (92879) ***(P-5214)***
Cellco Partnership ....D.......510 490-3800
39050 Argonaut Way Fremont (94538) ***(P-5215)***
Cellco Partnership ....D.......818 500-7779
1023 E Colorado St Glendale (91205) ***(P-5216)***
Cellco Partnership ....D.......858 625-7751
10525 Vista Sorrento Pkwy # 150 San Diego (92121) ***(P-5217)***
Cellco Partnership ....D.......805 237-8200
205 Oak Hill Rd Paso Robles (93446) ***(P-5218)***
Cellco Partnership ....D.......818 842-2722
1729 N Victory Pl Burbank (91502) ***(P-5219)***
Cellco Partnership ....D.......408 263-1960
172 Ranch Dr Milpitas (95035) ***(P-5220)***
Cellco Partnership ....D.......415 402-0640
768 Market St San Francisco (94102) ***(P-5221)***
Cellco Partnership ....D.......925 743-9327
18012 Bollinger Canyon Rd San Ramon (94583) ***(P-5222)***
Cellco Partnership ....D.......510 267-0731
3264 Lakeshore Ave Oakland (94610) ***(P-5223)***

Mergent e-mail: customerrelations@mergent.com
1212
2020 Directory of California
Wholesalers and Services Companies
(P-0000) Products & Services Section entry number
(PA)=Parent Co (HQ)=Headquarters (DH)=Div Headquarters

Cellco Partnership....D....213 380-2299
3458 Wilshire Blvd Los Angeles (90010) *(P-5224)*
Cellco Partnership....D....562 401-1045
12006 Lakewood Blvd Downey (90242) *(P-5225)*
Cellco Partnership....D....559 325-1420
1398 Shaw Ave Clovis (93612) *(P-5226)*
Cellco Partnership....D....661 274-2112
39575 Trade Center Dr Palmdale (93551) *(P-5227)*
Cellco Partnership....D....714 847-8799
16120 Beach Blvd Huntington Beach (92647) *(P-5228)*
Cellco Partnership....D....310 659-0775
100 N La Cienega Blvd # 233 Los Angeles (90048) *(P-5229)*
Cellco Partnership....D....209 543-6500
3801 Pelandale Ave Ste B3 Modesto (95356) *(P-5230)*
Cellco Partnership....D....213 738-9771
3785 Wilshire Blvd Los Angeles (90010) *(P-5231)*
Cellco Partnership....D....310 329-9325
20820 Avalon Blvd Carson (90746) *(P-5232)*
Cellco Partnership....D....323 465-0640
1503 Vine St Hollywood (90028) *(P-5233)*
Cellco Partnership....D....415 695-8400
2654 Mission St San Francisco (94110) *(P-5234)*
Cellco Partnership....D....510 324-5740
30935 Courthouse Dr Spc 1 Union City (94587) *(P-5235)*
Cellco Partnership....D....661 286-2399
24201 Valencia Blvd Valencia (91355) *(P-5236)*
Cellco Partnership....D....714 899-4690
6856 Katella Ave Cypress (90630) *(P-5237)*
Cellco Partnership....D....760 337-5508
880 N Imperial Ave El Centro (92243) *(P-5238)*
Cellco Partnership....D....805 955-9035
1555 Simi Town Center Way Simi Valley (93065) *(P-5239)*
Cellco Partnership....D....831 421-0753
110 Cooper St Ste A Santa Cruz (95060) *(P-5240)*
Cellco Partnership....D....909 381-0576
500 Inland Center Dr # 459 San Bernardino (92408) *(P-5241)*
Cellco Partnership....D....916 536-0440
6065 Sunrise Blvd Citrus Heights (95610) *(P-5242)*
Cellco Partnership....D....415 351-1700
1 Daniel Burnham Ct Bsmt San Francisco (94109) *(P-5243)*
Cellco Partnership....D....805 569-2525
2980 State St Santa Barbara (93105) *(P-5244)*
Cellco Partnership....D....707 525-5010
844 4th St Santa Rosa (95404) *(P-5245)*
Cellco Partnership....D....714 449-0715
503 N State College Blvd Fullerton (92831) *(P-5246)*
Cellco Partnership....D....650 323-6127
219 University Ave Palo Alto (94301) *(P-5247)*
Cellco Partnership....D....805 549-6260
994 Mill St Ste 100 San Luis Obispo (93401) *(P-5248)*
Cellco Partnership....D....714 775-0600
3770 W Mcfadden Ave Ste H Santa Ana (92704) *(P-5249)*
Cellco Partnership....D....323 725-9750
5438 Whittier Blvd Commerce (90022) *(P-5250)*
Cellmark Inc (HQ)....D....415 927-1700
88 Rowland Way Ste 300 Novato (94945) *(P-7802)*
Cellmatics....E....760 692-2424
2309 Masters Rd Carlsbad (92008) *(P-15569)*
Cello & Maudru Cnstr Co Inc....E....707 257-0454
2505 Oak St NAPA (94559) *(P-1441)*
Cellular Palace Inc....D....310 278-2007
10435 Santa Monica Blvd F Los Angeles (90025) *(P-7249)*
Celluphone LLC....D....323 727-9131
6119 E Wash Blvd Ste 200 Commerce (90040) *(P-7250)*
Celmol Inc....D....714 259-1000
1611 E Saint Andrew Pl Santa Ana (92705) *(P-8956)*
Cels Enterprises Inc (PA)....D....310 838-2103
3485 S La Cienega Blvd A Los Angeles (90016) *(P-8125)*
Cem - Victorville River Plant, Victorville *Also called Cemex Cnstr Mtls PCF LLC (P-6673)*
Cem Builders Inc....E....408 395-1490
37 S 4th St Campbell (95008) *(P-24997)*
Cemak Trucking Inc (PA)....D....949 253-2800
4621 Teller Ave Ste 130 Newport Beach (92660) *(P-3862)*
Cement Cutting Inc....D....619 296-9592
3610 Hancock St Frnt Frnt San Diego (92110) *(P-3127)*
Cement Mason Health & Welfare....D....707 864-3300
220 Campus Ln Suisun City (94534) *(P-24144)*
Cemex Cnstr Mtls PCF LLC....C....760 381-7600
16888 E St Victorville (92394) *(P-6673)*
Cemtek Environmental Inc....E....714 437-7100
3041 Orange Ave Santa Ana (92707) *(P-27022)*
Cen Cal Plastering Inc....B....209 981-5265
15300 E Wyman Rd Lathrop (95330) *(P-2768)*
Cencal Health, Santa Barbara *Also called Santa Barbara San Luis Obispo (P-9912)*
Centene Chwp....C....760 482-5593
1699 W Main St El Centro (92243) *(P-9932)*
Centene Corporation....D....714 934-3373
7755 Center Ave Huntington Beach (92647) *(P-9933)*
Centene Corporation....D....530 626-5773
550 Main St Placerville (95667) *(P-9934)*
Centene Corporation....C....314 505-6689
12033 Foundation Pl Gold River (95670) *(P-9935)*
Center At Parkwest, The, Reseda *Also called Chase Group Llc (P-26552)*
Center Cnslng Edctn & Crisis....D....925 462-1755
4361 Railroad Ave Pleasanton (94566) *(P-22977)*
Center Coast Home Help Care, Monterey *Also called Visiting Nurse Association (P-21896)*
Center For Achievement Center, Bakersfield *Also called New Advances For People Disabi (P-24201)*
Center For Autism &....E....949 203-8872
106 Discovery Irvine (92618) *(P-21970)*
Center For Autism & (PA)....C....818 345-2345
21600 Oxnard St Ste 1800 Woodland Hills (91367) *(P-19662)*
Center For Autism Related Svcs....E....323 850-7177
5949 Lankershim Blvd North Hollywood (91601) *(P-27023)*
Center For Autsm Rsrch Evltn....C....858 444-8823
10174 Old Grove Rd San Diego (92131) *(P-21971)*
Center For Civic Education (PA)....D....818 591-9321
5115 Douglas Fir Rd Ste J Calabasas (91302) *(P-25982)*
Center For Discovery, Lakewood *Also called Discovery Practice Management (P-18959)*
Center For Domestic Peace....E....415 457-2464
734 A St San Rafael (94901) *(P-22978)*
Center For Dscovery Adoloscent....E....562 425-6404
4136 Ann Arbor Rd Lakewood (90712) *(P-21455)*
Center For Elders Independence....C....510 433-1150
510 17th St Ste 400 Oakland (94612) *(P-9936)*
Center For Employment Training (PA)....D....408 287-7924
701 Vine St San Jose (95110) *(P-23576)*
Center For Indvdual and Fam Th....D....714 558-9266
840 W Town And Country Rd Orange (92868) *(P-22979)*
CENTER FOR INJURY PREVENTION, Chula Vista *Also called Racelegal Com (P-24858)*
Center For Learning and....B....800 538-8365
424 Peninsula Ave San Mateo (94401) *(P-22980)*
Center For Specialized Surgery, Santa Barbara *Also called Gold Coast Surgery Center LLC (P-18998)*
Center For Sustainable Energy....D....858 244-1177
3980 Sherman St Ste 170 San Diego (92110) *(P-27024)*
Center For Ventr Philanthropy, San Mateo *Also called Peninsula Community Foundation (P-24613)*
Center Glass Co No 3....D....619 469-6181
7853 El Cajon Blvd La Mesa (91942) *(P-3291)*
Center Medical Company....E....626 575-7500
12100 Valley Blvd 109a El Monte (91732) *(P-18880)*
Center of Rehabilitation....C....714 826-2330
9021 Knott Ave Buena Park (90620) *(P-19786)*
Center Point Inc (PA)....D....415 492-4444
135 Paul Dr San Rafael (94903) *(P-22981)*
Center Thtre Group Los Angeles (PA)....C....213 972-7344
601 W Temple St Los Angeles (90012) *(P-17897)*
Center To Promote Healthcare A (PA)....D....510 834-1300
1951 Webster St Fl 2 Oakland (94612) *(P-22200)*
CENTER, THE, San Diego *Also called San Diego Lesbian Gay Bisexu (P-23431)*
Centerfield Media Holdings LLC (PA)....D....310 341-4420
12130 Millennium Ste 500 Los Angeles (90094) *(P-5779)*
Centerline Wood Products....D....760 246-4530
10007 Yucca Rd Adelanto (92301) *(P-7803)*
Centerplate, San Francisco *Also called Volume Services Inc (P-18780)*
Centex Homes Inc....C....949 453-0113
27401 Los Altos Ste 400 Mission Viejo (92691) *(P-1102)*
Centex Homes Inc....C....559 733-2717
1840 S Central St Visalia (93277) *(P-1103)*
Centex Homes Inc....C....949 453-0113
250 Commerce Ste 100 Irvine (92602) *(P-1104)*
Centex Homes Central Valley, Visalia *Also called Centex Homes Inc (P-1103)*
Centimark Corporation....E....909 652-9280
1420 S Archibald Ave Ontario (91761) *(P-3033)*
Centimark Corporation....C....510 921-5500
2380 W Winton Ave Hayward (94545) *(P-3034)*
Centimark Roofing Systems, Hayward *Also called Centimark Corporation (P-3034)*
Centinela Frman Rgonal Med Ctr, Marina Del Rey *Also called Cfhs Holdings Inc (P-20771)*
Centinela Frman Rgonal Med Ctr, Marina Del Rey *Also called Cfhs Holdings Inc (P-20772)*
Centinela Frman Rgonal Med Ctr, Inglewood *Also called Cfhs Holdings Inc (P-20773)*
Centinela Hospital Medical Ctr, Inglewood *Also called Prime Healthcare Centinela LLC (P-21108)*
Centinela Skilled Nursing and....D....310 674-3216
950 S Flower St Inglewood (90301) *(P-19787)*
Centinela Skld Nrng Wlns Cntr, Inglewood *Also called West Cntinela Vly Care Ctr Inc (P-20376)*
Centinela Sklld Nrsng & Wllnss....D....310 674-3216
1001 S Osage Ave Inglewood (90301) *(P-19788)*
Centinela Valley Care Center....C....310 674-3216
950 S Flower St Inglewood (90301) *(P-23857)*
Centra Freight Services Inc (PA)....D....650 873-8147
279 Lawrence Ave South San Francisco (94080) *(P-5092)*
Central Anesthesia Service....D....916 481-6800
3315 Watt Ave Sacramento (95821) *(P-18881)*
Central Branch YMCA, San Jose *Also called YMCA of Silicon Valley (P-24722)*
Central Business Solutions Inc....D....510 573-5500
37600 Central Ct Ste 214 Newark (94560) *(P-15957)*
Central Cal Healthcare Sys, Fresno *Also called Veterans Health Administration (P-19559)*
Central Cal Nikkei Foundation....D....559 237-4006
540 S Peach Ave Fresno (93727) *(P-23858)*
Central California Blood Ctr....D....559 389-5433
4343 W Herndon Ave Fresno (93722) *(P-22201)*
Central California Blood Ctr....D....559 324-1211
8094 N Cedar Ave Fresno (93720) *(P-22202)*
Central California Blood Ctr (PA)....C....559 389-5433
4343 W Herndon Ave Fresno (93722) *(P-22203)*
Central California Ear Nose....E....559 432-3724
1351 E Spruce Ave Fresno (93720) *(P-18882)*
Central California Faculty Med....B....209 620-6937
1085 W Minnesota Ave Turlock (95382) *(P-22204)*
Central California Faculty Med (PA)....D....559 453-5200
2625 E Divisadero St Fresno (93721) *(P-18883)*
Central California Tr....D....559 686-4973
22847 Road 140 Tulare (93274) *(P-25983)*
Central Cardiology Med Clinic....C....661 395-0000
2901 Sillect Ave Ste 100 Bakersfield (93308) *(P-18884)*

A L P H A B E T I C

Central Cast Vsting Nurse Assn, Monterey *Also called Central Coast Cmnty Hlth Care* ***(P-21704)***
Central Cleaning Co, Pleasanton *Also called Dan Lofgren* ***(P-13911)***
Central Coast Cmnty Hlth Care..........C.......831 372-6668
5 Lower Ragsdale Dr # 102 Monterey (93940) ***(P-21703)***
Central Coast Cmnty Hlth Care..........B.......831 648-4200
40 Ragsdale Dr Ste 150 Monterey (93940) ***(P-21704)***
Central Coast Cooling LLC..........D.......831 422-7265
1107 Merrill St Salinas (93901) ***(P-4342)***
Central Coast Distributing LLC..........D.......805 922-2108
815 S Blosser Rd Santa Maria (93458) ***(P-8753)***
Central Coast Management, Ventura *Also called Pierpont Inn Inc* ***(P-12754)***
Central Coast Packing, Soledad *Also called Vasquez Brothers Inc* ***(P-557)***
Central Coast Pathology Lab, Bakersfield *Also called Physicians Automated Lab Inc* ***(P-21565)***
Central Coast Vna & Hospice (PA)..........C.......831 372-6668
5 Lower Ragsdle Dr 102 Monterey (93940) ***(P-21705)***
Central Coast Vna & Hospice..........D.......831 758-8243
45 Plaza Cir Salinas (93901) ***(P-21706)***
Central Cold Storage, Castroville *Also called Vps Companies Inc* ***(P-8305)***
Central Contra Costa Sanit..........D.......925 228-9500
5019 Imhoff Pl Martinez (94553) ***(P-6129)***
Central Counties..........D.......209 356-0355
241 Business Park Way Atwater (95301) ***(P-26060)***
Central Courier LLC..........D.......805 654-1145
758 Calle Plano Camarillo (93012) ***(P-3863)***
Central Freight Lines Inc..........D.......800 782-5036
1621 Main Ave Sacramento (95838) ***(P-3983)***
Central Freight Lines Inc..........D.......559 233-5559
4575 S Chestnut Ave Fresno (93725) ***(P-3864)***
Central Garden & Pet Company..........D.......858 695-0743
9235 Activity Rd San Diego (92126) ***(P-8957)***
Central Garden & Pet Company..........D.......626 334-9301
16321 Arrow Hwy Irwindale (91706) ***(P-8958)***
CENTRAL GARDENS CONVALESCENT H, San Francisco *Also called Central Gardens Inc* ***(P-19789)***
Central Gardens Inc..........C.......415 567-2967
1355 Ellis St San Francisco (94115) ***(P-19789)***
Central Indiana Hdwr Co Inc (PA)..........D.......317 558-5700
3512 Seagate Way Ste 190 Oceanside (92056) ***(P-7387)***
Central Medical Offices, Bakersfield *Also called Kaiser Foundation Hospitals* ***(P-19055)***
Central Orange County Svc Ctr, Santa Ana *Also called Southern California Edison Co* ***(P-5937)***
Central Parking Corporation..........D.......510 832-7227
1624 Franklin St Ste 722 Oakland (94612) ***(P-17247)***
Central Parking System Inc..........D.......714 751-2855
3420 Bristol St Ste 225 Costa Mesa (92626) ***(P-17248)***
Central Parking System Inc..........D.......916 441-1074
716 10th St Ste 101 Sacramento (95814) ***(P-17249)***
Central Payment Co LLC..........D.......415 462-8335
2350 Kerner Blvd Ste 300 San Rafael (94901) ***(P-16683)***
Central Purchasing LLC (PA)..........B.......800 444-3353
3491 Mission Oaks Blvd Camarillo (93012) ***(P-7630)***
Central Refill Pharmaceuticals..........D.......562 401-4214
9521 Dalen St Downey (90242) ***(P-7937)***
Central Reinforcing Corp..........D.......909 773-0840
14166 Slover Ave Fontana (92337) ***(P-3260)***
Central Retail Pharmaceuticals, Downey *Also called Central Refill Pharmaceuticals* ***(P-7937)***
Central Roofing Company, Gardena *Also called Claud Townsley Inc* ***(P-3037)***
Central State Pre-School..........E.......760 432-2499
2310 Aldergrove Ave Escondido (92029) ***(P-23685)***
Central Svc Ctr & Exec Offs..........E.......909 307-6555
1751 Plum Ln Redlands (92374) ***(P-16684)***
Central Technologies, Orange *Also called Inductors Inc* ***(P-7283)***
Central Unified School Dst..........D.......559 276-3185
6240 W Palo Alto Ave Fresno (93722) ***(P-24512)***
Central Valley AG Transload, Oakdale *Also called Central Valley AG Trnspt Inc* ***(P-476)***
Central Valley AG Trnspt Inc..........D.......209 544-9246
5509 Langworth Rd Oakdale (95361) ***(P-476)***
Central Valley Autism Project..........D.......209 521-4791
3425 Coffee Rd Ste C2 Modesto (95355) ***(P-22982)***
Central Valley Cheese Inc..........D.......209 664-1080
115 S Kilroy Rd Turlock (95380) ***(P-8312)***
Central Valley Clinic Inc..........E.......408 885-5400
2425 Enborg Ln San Jose (95128) ***(P-21972)***
Central Valley Cmnty Bancorp (PA)..........C.......559 298-1775
7100 N Fincl Dr Ste 101 Fresno (93720) ***(P-9181)***
Central Valley Community Bank..........D.......559 625-8733
120 N Floral St Visalia (93291) ***(P-9182)***
Central Valley Community Bank..........E.......916 985-8700
905 Sutter St Ste 100 Folsom (95630) ***(P-9183)***
Central Valley Community Bank (HQ)..........C.......559 323-3384
600 Pollasky Ave Clovis (93612) ***(P-9184)***
Central Valley Community Bank..........C.......559 298-1775
7100 N Fincl Dr Ste 101 Fresno (93720) ***(P-9185)***
Central Valley Concrete Inc (PA)..........C.......209 723-8846
3823 N State Highway 59 Merced (95348) ***(P-3865)***
Central Valley Environmental, Rohnert Park *Also called Cve Nb Contracting Group Inc* ***(P-26942)***
Central Valley Fund, The, Davis *Also called Cvf Capital Partners Inc* ***(P-11905)***
Central Valley Indian Hlth Inc (PA)..........D.......559 299-2578
2740 Herndon Ave Clovis (93611) ***(P-18885)***
Central Valley Oprtnty Ctr Inc (PA)..........C.......209 357-0062
6838 Bridget Ct Winton (95388) ***(P-23577)***
Central Valley Party Supply..........E.......209 569-0399
3250 Dale Rd Ste I Modesto (95356) ***(P-14139)***
Central Valley Trucking, Merced *Also called Central Valley Concrete Inc* ***(P-3865)***
Central Valley YMCA, Fresno *Also called Central Vly Yng MNS Chrn Assoc* ***(P-24513)***
Central Vly Chld Svcs Netwrk..........D.......559 456-1100
1911 N Helm Ave Fresno (93727) ***(P-22983)***
Central Vly Regional Ctr Inc..........C.......559 738-2200
5441 W Cypress Ave Visalia (93277) ***(P-21973)***
Central Vly Specialty Hosp Inc..........D.......209 248-7700
730 17th St Modesto (95354) ***(P-20770)***
Central Vly Yng MNS Chrn Assoc..........E.......559 225-9191
4045 N Fresno St Ste 101 Fresno (93726) ***(P-24513)***
Centre Care Management Co LLC..........C.......858 613-6255
15611 Pomerado Rd Ste 400 Poway (92064) ***(P-18886)***
Centre For Health Care, Poway *Also called Centre Care Management Co LLC* ***(P-18886)***
Centre For Neuro Skills (PA)..........C.......661 872-3408
5215 Ashe Rd Bakersfield (93313) ***(P-21974)***
Centrelink Ins & Fincl Svcs, Woodland Hills *Also called Centrelink Insur & Fincl Svcs* ***(P-16685)***
Centrelink Insur & Fincl Svcs..........D.......818 587-2001
20750 Ventura Blvd # 300 Woodland Hills (91364) ***(P-16685)***
Centrescapes Inc..........D.......909 392-3303
165 Gentry St Pomona (91767) ***(P-784)***
Centrify Corporation (PA)..........C.......669 444-5200
3300 Tannery Way Santa Clara (95054) ***(P-14707)***
Centrl Territrl Salvation Army..........D.......714 832-7100
10200 Pioneer Rd Tustin (92782) ***(P-22984)***
Centro De Salud De La..........D.......619 477-0165
1420 E Plaza Blvd Ste E4 National City (91950) ***(P-22985)***
Centro De Salud De La Comuni (PA)..........D.......619 428-4463
1601 Precision Park Ln San Diego (92173) ***(P-21975)***
Centro De Salud De La Comuni..........D.......619 336-2300
1136 D Ave National City (91950) ***(P-21976)***
CENTRO VIDA, Berkeley *Also called Bay Area Hispn Inst Advancmnt* ***(P-23674)***
Centurion Group, The, Los Angeles *Also called Mulholland SEC & Patrol Inc* ***(P-16356)***
Centurion Group, The, Los Angeles *Also called Centurion Security Inc* ***(P-16226)***
Centurion Security Inc..........C.......818 755-0202
11454 San Vicente Blvd Los Angeles (90049) ***(P-16226)***
Centurion Security Svcs Inc (PA)..........D.......949 474-0444
20102 Sw Cypress St Newport Beach (92660) ***(P-16227)***
Century 14, Roseville *Also called Century Theatres Inc* ***(P-17871)***
Century 21, Downey *Also called First Family Homes* ***(P-11141)***
Century 21, Inglewood *Also called Smith Coleman Inc* ***(P-11452)***
Century 21, Downey *Also called Steve Roberson* ***(P-11467)***
Century 21, Monrovia *Also called Adams & Barnes Inc* ***(P-10892)***
Century 21, Laguna Woods *Also called Rainbow Realty Corporation* ***(P-11387)***
Century 21, Redlands *Also called Lois Lauer Realty* ***(P-11251)***
Century 21, Porter Ranch *Also called Coast To Coast Realty* ***(P-11020)***
Century 21, Oakdale *Also called Premier Valley Inc A Cal Corp* ***(P-11366)***
Century 21, Fresno *Also called Century Adanalian & Vasquez* ***(P-11007)***
Century 21, Rancho Cucamonga *Also called Excellnce of Inland Empire Inc* ***(P-11120)***
Century 21, Hesperia *Also called Hannaknapp Realty Inc* ***(P-11184)***
Century 21, Fullerton *Also called John G Shipley* ***(P-11222)***
Century 21, San Dimas *Also called National Credit Industries Inc* ***(P-9638)***
Century 21, Bellflower *Also called Leroy Durbin* ***(P-11249)***
Century 21, Cerritos *Also called Astro Realty Inc* ***(P-10922)***
Century 21..........E.......707 429-2121
301 Dickson Hill Rd Ste A Fairfield (94533) ***(P-10987)***
Century 21 A Better Svc Rlty..........D.......562 287-0230
8077 2nd St Fl Fl Downey (90241) ***(P-10988)***
Century 21 A Better Svc Rlty..........D.......562 806-1000
5831 Firestone Blvd Ste J South Gate (90280) ***(P-10989)***
Century 21 Able Inc..........D.......858 450-2100
3202 Governor Dr Ste 100 San Diego (92122) ***(P-10990)***
Century 21 Alpha LLC..........D.......408 369-2000
1630 W Campbell Ave Ste 1 Campbell (95008) ***(P-10991)***
Century 21 Amber Realty Inc..........D.......310 625-4363
21024 Wood Ave Apt A Torrance (90503) ***(P-10992)***
Century 21 Beverlywood Realty..........D.......310 836-8321
2800 S Robertson Blvd Los Angeles (90034) ***(P-10993)***
Century 21 Crest..........D.......818 248-9100
4005 Foothill Blvd La Crescenta (91214) ***(P-10994)***
Century 21 Dstnctive Prpts Inc..........D.......707 678-9211
1450 Ary Ln Ste A Dixon (95620) ***(P-10995)***
Century 21 E, Diamond Bar *Also called E-N Realty II* ***(P-11105)***
Century 21 Excellence..........E.......562 948-4553
5207 Rosemead Blvd Ste 1 Pico Rivera (90660) ***(P-10996)***
Century 21 Exclusive Realtors..........C.......310 373-5252
22831 Hawthorne Blvd Torrance (90505) ***(P-10997)***
Century 21 Experience, Alta Loma *Also called Expreal Inc* ***(P-11121)***
Century 21 Golden Hills, San Jose *Also called Qal Affiliate Inc* ***(P-11385)***
Century 21 Golden Realty (PA)..........D.......626 797-6680
482 N Rosemead Blvd Pasadena (91107) ***(P-10998)***
Century 21 Green Gable RE, Dixon *Also called Century 21 Dstnctive Prpts Inc* ***(P-10995)***
Century 21 Haley & Associates..........D.......916 782-1500
699 Wshington Blvd Ste B5 Roseville (95678) ***(P-10999)***
Century 21 Hill Top Realtors, Simi Valley *Also called First & La Realty Corp* ***(P-11138)***
Century 21 Home Realtors (PA)..........D.......909 591-0158
4110 Edison Ave Ste 210 Chino (91710) ***(P-11000)***
Century 21 Home Realtors..........D.......909 980-8000
8338 Day Creek Blvd # 101 Rancho Cucamonga (91739) ***(P-11001)***
Century 21 King Realtors, Rancho Cucamonga *Also called Century 21 Home Realtors* ***(P-11001)***
Century 21 Landmark Properties..........E.......562 422-0911
1650 Ximeno Ave Ste 120 Long Beach (90804) ***(P-11002)***
Century 21 Les Ryan Realty..........D.......707 577-7777
1057 College Ave Ofc Ste Santa Rosa (95404) ***(P-11003)***

Mergent e-mail: customerrelations@mergent.com
1214
2020 Directory of California
Wholesalers and Services Companies
(P-0000) Products & Services Section entry number
(PA)=Parent Co (HQ)=Headquarters (DH)=Div Headquarters

ALPHABETIC SECTION
CHAMBERPAC, San Jose

Century 21 Ludecke Inc (PA)........D.......626 445-0123
34 E Foothill Blvd Arcadia (91006) ***(P-11004)***
Century 21 Masters........D.......626 732-6184
480 W Rowland St Ste B Covina (91723) ***(P-11005)***
Century 21 Powerhouse Realty, Huntington Park *Also called Powerhouse Realty Inc* ***(P-11363)***
Century 21 Showcase Inc........D.......909 936-9334
7835 Church St Highland (92346) ***(P-11006)***
Century 8, North Hollywood *Also called Century Theatres Inc* ***(P-17873)***
Century Adanalian & Vasquez........D.......559 244-6000
1415 W Shaw Ave Fresno (93711) ***(P-11007)***
Century Bankcard Services........D.......818 700-3100
25129 The Old Rd Ste 222 Stevenson Ranch (91381) ***(P-16686)***
Century City Primary Care........E.......310 553-3189
2080 Century Park E # 1605 Los Angeles (90067) ***(P-18887)***
Century Commercial Service........E.......530 823-1004
12820 Earhart Ave Auburn (95602) ***(P-7133)***
Century Electronics, Newbury Park *Also called Perillo Industries Inc* ***(P-7319)***
Century Finance Incorporated........D.......310 281-3081
2461 Santa Monica Blvd Santa Monica (90404) ***(P-9537)***
Century Hlth Staffing Svcs Inc........C.......661 322-0606
1701 Westwind Dr Ste 101 Bakersfield (93301) ***(P-14244)***
Century Huntington Beach & Xd, Huntington Beach *Also called Cinemark Usa Inc* ***(P-17826)***
Century National, Encino *Also called Kramer-Wilson Company Inc* ***(P-10099)***
Century National Properties (PA)........D.......818 760-0880
12200 Sylvan St Ste 250 North Hollywood (91606) ***(P-12131)***
Century Pk Capitl Partners LLC (PA)........C.......310 867-2210
2101 Rosecrans Ave # 4275 El Segundo (90245) ***(P-11751)***
Century Plaza Garage........C.......310 226-7495
2049 Century Park E Ste D Los Angeles (90067) ***(P-17250)***
Century Properties Owners Assn........E.......310 272-8580
1 W Century Dr Los Angeles (90067) ***(P-11008)***
Century Skill Care........D.......310 672-1012
301 Centinela Ave Inglewood (90302) ***(P-19790)***
Century Skilled Nursing Care, Inglewood *Also called Century Skill Care* ***(P-19790)***
Century Snacks LLC........B.......323 278-9578
5560 E Slauson Ave Commerce (90040) ***(P-8340)***
Century Stadium 21, Sacramento *Also called Cinemark Usa Inc* ***(P-17825)***
Century Theatres Inc........D.......916 797-3466
1555 Eureka Rd Roseville (95661) ***(P-17871)***
Century Theatres Inc........D.......510 758-9626
3200 Klose Way Richmond (94806) ***(P-17872)***
Century Theatres Inc........D.......818 508-1943
12827 Victory Blvd North Hollywood (91606) ***(P-17873)***
Century Vision Developers Inc........E.......925 588-7390
3000 Oak Rd Ste 360 Walnut Creek (94597) ***(P-1442)***
Century West Plumbing, Westlake Village *Also called Sdg Enterprises* ***(P-2268)***
Century Wilshire Hotel, Culver City *Also called Century Wilshire Inc* ***(P-12132)***
Century Wilshire Inc........D.......310 558-9400
9400 Culver Blvd Culver City (90232) ***(P-12132)***
Century, The, Los Angeles *Also called Century Properties Owners Assn* ***(P-11008)***
Century-National Insurance Co (HQ)........B.......818 760-0880
16650 Sherman Way Ste 200 Van Nuys (91406) ***(P-9865)***
Cep America LLC........D.......510 350-2691
2100 Powell St 400 Emeryville (94608) ***(P-18888)***
Ceps, Sacramento *Also called Consultnts In Edctl Per Skills* ***(P-23049)***
Ceramic Decorating Company Inc........E.......323 268-5135
4651 Sheila St Commerce (90040) ***(P-16687)***
Ceramic Tile Art Inc........D.......818 767-9088
11601 Pendleton St Sun Valley (91352) ***(P-2886)***
Cerebral Palsy Assn San Joaqui, Stockton *Also called United Cerebral Palsy Assoc* ***(P-24430)***
Cerebras Systems Inc........C.......650 933-4980
175 S San Antonio Rd # 1 Los Altos (94022) ***(P-15570)***
Cerenzia Foods Inc........D.......909 989-4000
8585 White Oak Ave Rancho Cucamonga (91730) ***(P-8160)***
Ceridian LLC........D.......310 719-7481
1515 W 190th St Ste 100 Gardena (90248) ***(P-25552)***
Ceridian Tax Service Inc........B.......714 963-1311
17390 Brookhurst St # 100 Fountain Valley (92708) ***(P-25553)***
Cerritos Cinemas 10, Artesia *Also called Edwards Theatres Circuit Inc* ***(P-17840)***
Cerritos Medical Office Bldg, Cerritos *Also called Kaiser Foundation Hospitals* ***(P-19060)***
Certainteed Gypsum Inc........E.......949 282-5300
27442 Portola Pkwy # 100 El Toro (92610) ***(P-6611)***
Certapro Painters, San Francisco *Also called Norcal Painters Inc* ***(P-2374)***
Certified Air Conditioning Inc........C.......858 292-5740
12520 High Bluff Dr # 312 San Diego (92130) ***(P-2091)***
Certified Aviation Svcs LLC........D.......310 338-1224
5720 Avion Dr Los Angeles (90045) ***(P-4757)***
Certified Coatings Company........D.......707 639-4414
2320 Cordelia Rd Fairfield (94534) ***(P-2339)***
Certified Frt Logistics Inc (PA)........C.......800 592-5906
1344 White Ct Santa Maria (93458) ***(P-3984)***
Certified Nursing Registry Inc........C.......626 912-1877
2707 E Valley Blvd # 309 West Covina (91792) ***(P-14245)***
Certified Trnsp Svcs Inc........D.......714 835-8676
1038 N Custer St Santa Ana (92701) ***(P-3789)***
Certona Corporation........C.......858 369-3888
10431 Wtridge Cir Ste 200 San Diego (92121) ***(P-5374)***
Cerutti Bros Inc........D.......209 862-2249
26118 Mcclintock Rd Newman (95360) ***(P-42)***
Cesar Chavez Student Center........C.......415 338-7362
1650 Holloway Ave Rm C134 San Francisco (94132) ***(P-10577)***
Cesars Productions........E.......415 821-1156
91 Miguel St San Francisco (94131) ***(P-16688)***
Cessna Scrmnto Ctation Svc Ctr, Sacramento *Also called Textron Aviation Inc* ***(P-4801)***
Cetecom Inc........D.......408 586-6200
411 Dixon Landing Rd Milpitas (95035) ***(P-27025)***
Cetera Financial Group Inc (PA)........C.......866 489-3100
200 N Pacific Coast Hwy # 11 El Segundo (90245) ***(P-16689)***
Ceva Freight LLC........D.......310 972-5500
19600 S Western Ave Torrance (90501) ***(P-4907)***
Ceva Freight LLC........C.......916 379-6000
8670 Younger Creek Dr Sacramento (95828) ***(P-4908)***
Ceva Logistics LLC........B.......310 223-6500
19600 S Western Ave Torrance (90501) ***(P-4909)***
Ceva Logistics US Inc........E.......951 332-3202
11290 Cntu Gllano Rnch Rd Jurupa Valley (91752) ***(P-4910)***
Ceva Ocean Line, Torrance *Also called Ceva Freight LLC* ***(P-4907)***
Ceva Ocean Line, Sacramento *Also called Ceva Freight LLC* ***(P-4908)***
CF Merced La Sierra LLC........D.......209 723-4224
2424 M St Merced (95340) ***(P-19791)***
CF San Rafael LLC........D.......415 479-5161
81 Professional Ctr Pkwy San Rafael (94903) ***(P-19792)***
CF Watsonville LLC........D.......831 724-7505
525 Auto Center Dr Watsonville (95076) ***(P-19793)***
CF Watsonville East LLC........D.......310 574-3733
535 Auto Center Dr Watsonville (95076) ***(P-19794)***
CF Watsonville West LLC........D.......831 724-7505
525 Auto Center Dr Watsonville (95076) ***(P-19795)***
Cfgi LLC........C.......415 670-9041
600 California St Fl 14 San Francisco (94108) ***(P-25554)***
Cfhc, Los Angeles *Also called Essential Access Health* ***(P-24173)***
Cfhs Holdings Inc........A.......310 823-8911
4650 Lincoln Blvd Marina Del Rey (90292) ***(P-20771)***
Cfhs Holdings Inc........A.......310 448-7800
4640 Admiralty Way # 650 Marina Del Rey (90292) ***(P-20772)***
Cfhs Holdings Inc........A.......310 673-4660
555 E Hardy St Inglewood (90301) ***(P-20773)***
Cfmg, Kelsey *Also called Califrnia Frnsic Med Group Inc* ***(P-22197)***
Cfp Designs Inc........D.......661 903-8940
3121 N Sillect Ave # 300 Bakersfield (93308) ***(P-2092)***
Cfp Fire Protection Inc........D.......949 727-3277
153 Technology Dr Ste 200 Irvine (92618) ***(P-2093)***
Cfr Rinkens LLC (PA)........D.......310 639-7725
15501 Texaco Ave Paramount (90723) ***(P-4911)***
CFS Income Tax, Simi Valley *Also called CFS Tax Software* ***(P-15276)***
CFS Tax Software........D.......805 522-1157
1445 E Los Angeles Ave # 214 Simi Valley (93065) ***(P-15276)***
Cg2 Inc........D.......407 737-8800
1759 Mccarthy Blvd Milpitas (95035) ***(P-25984)***
CGB, Gardena *Also called Pulp Studio Incorporated* ***(P-13796)***
Cgi Technologies Solutions Inc........E.......916 281-3200
860 Stillwater Rd Ste 210 West Sacramento (95605) ***(P-25730)***
Cgi Technologies Solutions Inc........D.......510 238-5300
505 14th St Fl 9 Oakland (94612) ***(P-15958)***
Cgl Companies LLC........D.......916 678-7890
2260 Del Paso Rd 100 Sacramento (95834) ***(P-25422)***
Cgp Holdings LLC........D.......760 764-1300
2 Gill Station Coastal Rd Little Lake (93542) ***(P-6359)***
Cgtech (PA)........E.......949 753-1050
9000 Research Dr Irvine (92618) ***(P-15571)***
Cgtech Vericut, Irvine *Also called Cgtech* ***(P-15571)***
Ch Cupertino Owner LLC........C.......408 253-8900
10050 S De Anza Blvd Cupertino (95014) ***(P-12133)***
Ch Market Center Inc........D.......909 628-9100
4200 Chino Health Ste 325 Chino Hills (91709) ***(P-11009)***
Ch Reynolds, San Jose *Also called C H Reynolds Electric Inc* ***(P-2447)***
CH Robinson Freight Svcs Ltd........E.......310 515-7755
680 Knox St Ste 210 Torrance (90502) ***(P-4912)***
Ch2m Hill Inc........E.......916 920-0300
2485 Natomas Park Dr # 600 Sacramento (95833) ***(P-25423)***
Ch2m Hill Inc........C.......510 604-4144
155 Grand Ave Ste 800 Oakland (94612) ***(P-24998)***
Ch2m Hill Inc........E.......408 436-4936
1737 N 1st St Ste 300 San Jose (95112) ***(P-25424)***
Ch2m Hill Constructors Inc........B.......916 920-0212
2485 Natomas Park Dr # 600 Sacramento (95833) ***(P-1843)***
Cha Hollywood Medical Ctr LP (PA)........A.......213 413-3000
1300 N Vermont Ave Los Angeles (90027) ***(P-20774)***
Chad Garrett Investigations, North Hollywood *Also called Protection Specialists* ***(P-16388)***
Chaduxtt JV........D.......619 525-7188
1230 Columbia St Ste 1000 San Diego (92101) ***(P-24999)***
Chadwick Center For Children &........E.......858 966-5814
3020 Childrens Way San Diego (92123) ***(P-18889)***
Chain & Charm Inc........D.......213 683-1039
817 San Julian St Ph 1 Los Angeles (90014) ***(P-7784)***
Chain & Charm Jewelry Mfg, Los Angeles *Also called Chain & Charm Inc* ***(P-7784)***
Challenge Dairy Products Inc........E.......323 724-3130
5741 Smithway St Commerce (90040) ***(P-8313)***
Challenge Dairy Products Inc (HQ)........D.......925 828-6160
6701 Donlon Way Dublin (94568) ***(P-8314)***
Challenger Ent, Anaheim *Also called Challenger Industries Inc* ***(P-7536)***
Challenger Industries Inc........D.......714 630-4344
2971 E White Star Ave Anaheim (92806) ***(P-7536)***
Challenger Schools........D.......408 723-0111
4949 Harwood Rd San Jose (95124) ***(P-23686)***
Challenger Sheet Metal Inc........D.......619 596-8040
9353 Abraham Way Ste A Santee (92071) ***(P-3035)***
Chalmers Corporation........D.......562 948-4850
7901 Crossway Dr Pico Rivera (90660) ***(P-1339)***
Chamberlains Children Ctr Inc........D.......831 636-2121
1850 Cienega Rd Hollister (95023) ***(P-23859)***
CHAMBERPAC, San Jose *Also called San Jose Silicon Valley Cham* ***(P-24361)***

ALPHABETIC

Employee Codes: A=Over 500 employees, B=251-500
C=101-250, D=51-100, E=50
2020 Directory of California
Wholesalers and Services Companies
© Mergent Inc. 1-800-342-5647
1215

Chambers Group Inc ....E.......949 261-5414
17671 Cowan Ste 100 Irvine (92614) ***(P-27026)***
Chaminade At Santa Cruz, Santa Cruz *Also called Chaminade Ltd* ***(P-12134)***
Chaminade Ltd....................C.......831 475-5600
1 Chaminade Ln Santa Cruz (95065) ***(P-12134)***
Chaminade of Santa Cruz, Santa Cruz *Also called Lho Santa Cruz One Lesse Inc* ***(P-12551)***
Chaminade of Santa Cruz, Santa Cruz *Also called Benchmark-Tech Corporation* ***(P-16647)***
Champagne Landscape Nurs Inc....................D.......559 277-8188
3233 N Cornelia Ave Fresno (93722) ***(P-785)***
Champion Electric Inc....................D.......951 276-9619
3950 Garner Rd Riverside (92501) ***(P-2451)***
Champion Investment Corp (PA)....................D.......917 712-7807
12809 Oakfield Way Poway (92064) ***(P-12135)***
Champion Signs Incorporated....................E.......858 751-2900
7835 Wilkerson Ct San Diego (92111) ***(P-13773)***
Champion Transportation Svcs, Pico Rivera *Also called AP Express International LLC* ***(P-5110)***
Championship Golf Services Inc....................C.......951 272-4340
2340 Silver Oak Cir Corona (92882) ***(P-18228)***
Chamson Management Inc....................D.......714 751-2400
7 Hutton Centre Dr Santa Ana (92707) ***(P-12136)***
Chan Family Partnership LP....................D.......626 322-7132
30249 Point Marina Dr Canyon Lake (92587) ***(P-26176)***
Chance Group LLC....................E.......310 343-3766
911 E 106th St Los Angeles (90002) ***(P-8063)***
Chancellor Hlth Care Cal I Inc (PA)....................D.......909 796-0235
25383 Cole St Loma Linda (92354) ***(P-20526)***
Chandler Convalescent Hospital....................D.......818 240-1610
525 S Central Ave Glendale (91204) ***(P-19796)***
Change Healthcare Tech LLC....................C.......559 455-4000
5110 E Clinton Way # 101 Fresno (93727) ***(P-16690)***
Change Hlthcare Operations LLC....................D.......805 777-7773
241 Lombard St Thousand Oaks (91360) ***(P-15739)***
Changeorg Inc....................C.......415 817-1840
383 Rhode Island St # 300 San Francisco (94103) ***(P-15847)***
Changing Tides Family Services (PA)....................C.......707 444-8293
2259 Myrtle Ave Eureka (95501) ***(P-23687)***
Channel 4-NBC 4 Television, Burbank *Also called Access Hollywood* ***(P-5578)***
Channel 40 Inc....................C.......916 454-4422
4655 Fruitridge Rd Sacramento (95820) ***(P-5589)***
Channel Islands Young Mens Ch....................D.......805 736-3483
201 W College Ave Lompoc (93436) ***(P-24514)***
Channel Islands Young Mens Ch....................D.......805 484-0423
3111 Village Park Dr Camarillo (93012) ***(P-24515)***
Channel Islands Young Mens Ch....................C.......805 687-7727
36 Hitchcock Way Santa Barbara (93105) ***(P-24516)***
Channel Islands Young Mens Ch....................D.......805 969-3288
591 Santa Rosa Ln Santa Barbara (93108) ***(P-24517)***
Channel Islands Young Mens Ch....................C.......805 484-0423
3760 Telegraph Rd Ventura (93003) ***(P-24518)***
Channel Islands Young Mens Ch....................D.......805 686-2037
900 N Refugio Rd Santa Ynez (93460) ***(P-24519)***
Channel Islnds Vegetable Farms (PA)....................D.......805 984-1910
595 Victoria Ave Oxnard (93030) ***(P-289)***
Channel Medical Center, Stockton *Also called Community Medical Centers Inc* ***(P-18915)***
Channing House....................D.......650 327-0950
850 Webster St Ofc Palo Alto (94301) ***(P-20527)***
Chap, Pasadena *Also called Community Hlth Alance Pasadena* ***(P-20796)***
Chapa-De Indian Health (PA)....................D.......530 887-2800
11670 Atwood Rd Auburn (95603) ***(P-18890)***
Chaparral Foundation....................D.......510 848-8774
1309 Allston Way Berkeley (94702) ***(P-19797)***
CHAPARRAL HOUSE, Berkeley *Also called Chaparral Foundation* ***(P-19797)***
Chapel Funding Corporation....................C.......949 580-1800
26521 Rancho Pkwy S Lake Forest (92630) ***(P-9538)***
Chapel of Chimes (HQ)....................D.......510 471-3363
32992 Mission Blvd Hayward (94544) ***(P-11624)***
Chapel of Chimes....................D.......650 349-4411
100 Lifemark Rd Redwood City (94062) ***(P-11625)***
Chapman Family Health, Orange *Also called Chapman Global Medical Center* ***(P-20775)***
Chapman Global Medical Center....................B.......714 633-0011
2601 E Chapman Ave Orange (92869) ***(P-20775)***
Chapman Golf Development LLC....................D.......760 564-8723
78505 Avenue 52 La Quinta (92253) ***(P-18419)***
Chapman Hbr Sklled Nrsing Care....................D.......714 971-5517
12232 Chapman Ave Garden Grove (92840) ***(P-19798)***
Chapman/Leonard Studio Eqp Inc (PA)....................C.......323 877-5309
12950 Raymer St North Hollywood (91605) ***(P-17728)***
Chapmn-Hrbor Sklled Nrsing Ctr, Garden Grove *Also called Chapman Hbr Sklled Nrsing Care* ***(P-19798)***
Charanjit Singh Batth....................D.......559 864-9421
5434 W Kamm Ave Caruthers (93609) ***(P-171)***
Chardonnay, NAPA *Also called NAPA Golf Associates LLC* ***(P-18512)***
Chardonnay Golf Club, NAPA *Also called Chardonnay/ Club Shakespeare* ***(P-18420)***
Chardonnay/ Club Shakespeare....................D.......707 257-1900
2555 Jamieson Canyon Rd NAPA (94558) ***(P-18420)***
Chargers Football Company LLC (PA)....................D.......619 280-2121
3333 Susan St Costa Mesa (92626) ***(P-18058)***
Chariot Travelware, Ontario *Also called Damao Luggage Intl Inc* ***(P-7805)***
Charlee Family Care....................D.......951 845-3588
136 E Sixth St Beaumont (92223) ***(P-23860)***
Charles & Cynthia Eberly Inc....................D.......323 937-6468
8383 Wilshire Blvd # 906 Beverly Hills (90211) ***(P-10710)***
Charles Brooks Cmnty Swim Ctr, Woodland *Also called City of Woodland* ***(P-18668)***
Charles Culberson Inc....................C.......650 335-4730
1084 Allen Way Campbell (95008) ***(P-2769)***
Charles Dunn Co Inc....................C.......213 481-1800
800 W 6th St Ste 800 # 800 Los Angeles (90017) ***(P-11010)***
Charles Dunn Raltor State Svcs, Los Angeles *Also called Charles Dunn Co Inc* ***(P-11010)***
Charles Dunn RE Svcs Inc (PA)....................D.......213 270-6200
800 W 6th St Ste 600 Los Angeles (90017) ***(P-11011)***
Charles E Thomas Company Inc (PA)....................D.......310 323-6730
13701 Alma Ave Gardena (90249) ***(P-1443)***
Charles Fenley Enterprises....................E.......209 523-2832
1109 Oakdale Rd Modesto (95355) ***(P-17367)***
Charles Komar & Sons Inc....................B.......951 934-1377
11850 Riverside Dr Jurupa Valley (91752) ***(P-4384)***
Charles M Kamiya and Sons Inc....................D.......310 781-2066
373 Van Ness Ave Ste 200 Torrance (90501) ***(P-10315)***
Charles McMurray Co (PA)....................C.......559 292-5751
2520 N Argyle Ave Fresno (93727) ***(P-7388)***
Charles Pankow Bldrs Ltd A Cal (PA)....................E.......626 304-1190
199 S Los Robles Ave # 300 Pasadena (91101) ***(P-1444)***
Charles Pankow Bldrs Ltd A Cal....................B.......510 893-5170
1111 Broadway Ste 200 Oakland (94607) ***(P-1445)***
Charles Schwab & Co Inc (HQ)....................D.......415 636-7000
211 Main St Fl 17 San Francisco (94105) ***(P-9660)***
Charles Schwab Corporation (PA)....................C.......415 667-7000
211 Main St Fl 17 San Francisco (94105) ***(P-9661)***
Charles Schwab Corporation....................C.......951 587-2840
27580 Ynez Rd Ste A Temecula (92591) ***(P-16691)***
Charles Schwab Corporation....................D.......530 448-8038
10770 Donner Pass Rd # 103 Truckee (96161) ***(P-9662)***
Charles Schwab Corporation....................D.......310 752-9951
826 Wilshire Blvd Santa Monica (90401) ***(P-9663)***
Charles Schwab Corporation....................C.......714 385-6000
1900 Avenue Of The Stars # 101 Los Angeles (90067) ***(P-9664)***
Charles Schwab Corporation....................D.......415 294-3503
1400 Grant Ave Ste 101 Novato (94945) ***(P-9665)***
Charles Schwab Corporation....................E.......858 523-2454
12481 High Bluff Dr # 100 San Diego (92130) ***(P-9666)***
Charles W Bowers Museum Corp....................D.......714 567-3600
2002 N Main St Santa Ana (92706) ***(P-24250)***
Charleston Company, Los Angeles *Also called Walter J Conn & Associates* ***(P-25509)***
Charlie Mitchell Chld Clinic, Madera *Also called Valley Childrens Hospital* ***(P-21350)***
Charlie W Shaeffer Jr MD....................D.......760 346-0642
39000 Bob Hope Dr Rancho Mirage (92270) ***(P-18891)***
Charlies Enterprises....................C.......559 445-8600
1888 S East Ave Fresno (93721) ***(P-4385)***
Charming Trim & Packaging....................A.......415 302-7021
28 Brookside Ct Novato (94947) ***(P-7994)***
Charolais Care V Inc....................D.......415 921-5038
1426 Fillmore St Ste 207 San Francisco (94115) ***(P-21707)***
Charter Behavioral Health Syst....................D.......626 966-1632
1161 E Covina Blvd Covina (91724) ***(P-21395)***
Charter Cmmnctons Oprating LLC....................D.......760 452-8609
12180 Ridgecrest Rd # 102 Victorville (92395) ***(P-5670)***
Charter Cmmnctons Oprating LLC....................B.......310 971-4001
4031 Via Oro Ave Long Beach (90810) ***(P-5671)***
Charter Cmmnctons Oprating LLC....................E.......530 241-7352
5797 Eastside Rd Redding (96001) ***(P-5672)***
Charter Hospice Colton LLC....................C.......909 825-2969
1007 E Cooley Dr Ste 100 Colton (92324) ***(P-20417)***
Charter Oak Hospital, Covina *Also called Charter Behavioral Health Syst* ***(P-21395)***
Charter Realty Group Inc (PA)....................D.......310 826-3174
12400 Wilshire Blvd Los Angeles (90025) ***(P-11012)***
Chase Bros Dairy, Ventura *Also called Hailwood Inc* ***(P-10604)***
Chase Care Center Inc....................C.......323 935-8490
1101 Crenshaw Blvd Los Angeles (90019) ***(P-20528)***
Chase Credit Systems Inc....................D.......818 762-6262
300 E Magnolia Blvd # 502 Burbank (91502) ***(P-14708)***
Chase Group Llc....................D.......818 708-3533
6740 Wilbur Ave Reseda (91335) ***(P-26552)***
Chase Group Llc....................D.......805 522-9155
5270 E Los Angeles Ave Simi Valley (93063) ***(P-25880)***
Chase Group Llc (PA)....................A.......805 497-7330
3075 E Thousand Oaks Blvd Thousand Oaks (91362) ***(P-26553)***
Chase Receivables, Sonoma *Also called Credit Bureau NAPA County Inc* ***(P-13679)***
Chase Suite and Woodfin Hotels, San Diego *Also called Woodfin Suite Hotels LLC* ***(P-13113)***
Chase Suite Hotel Newark, Newark *Also called Hardage Hospitality LLC* ***(P-10606)***
Chaser, Gardena *Also called Houston Salem Inc* ***(P-8077)***
Chateau At River's Edge, Sacramento *Also called Hank Fisher Properties Inc* ***(P-20587)***
Chateau La Jolla Inn....................E.......858 459-4451
233 Prospect St La Jolla (92037) ***(P-12137)***
Chateau Lake San Marcos Homeow....................D.......760 471-0083
1502 Circa Del Lago San Marcos (92078) ***(P-24520)***
Chateau On Capitol Avenue, The, Sacramento *Also called Hank Fisher Properties Inc* ***(P-23946)***
Chateau Pleasant Hill 2, Concord *Also called Carlton Senior Living Inc* ***(P-11551)***
Chateau San Juan, San Juan Capistrano *Also called Atria Senior Living Inc* ***(P-23826)***
Chatham Inc....................E.......800 222-2002
300 Rancheros Dr Ste 360 San Marcos (92069) ***(P-7785)***
Chatmeter Inc....................D.......619 795-6262
225 Broadway Ste 1700 San Diego (92101) ***(P-26554)***
Chatsworth Health & Rehab, Chatsworth *Also called Golden State Health Ctrs Inc* ***(P-20582)***
Chatsworth Park Hlth Care Ctr, Chatsworth *Also called Cpcc Inc* ***(P-20539)***
Chc, Los Angeles *Also called Covenant House California* ***(P-23883)***
Chcg Architects, Pasadena *Also called Gonzalez/Goodale Architects* ***(P-25441)***
Check Disc Labs....................D.......818 847-2255
4121 W Vanowen Pl Burbank (91505) ***(P-26555)***
Check Point Software Tech Inc (HQ)....................C.......650 628-2000
959 Skyway Rd Ste 300 San Carlos (94070) ***(P-15277)***
Checker Cab Co....................D.......818 488-5088
14943 Califa St Van Nuys (91411) ***(P-3745)***

Mergent e-mail: customerrelations@mergent.com
1216
2020 Directory of California
Wholesalers and Services Companies
(P-0000) Products & Services Section entry number
(PA)=Parent Co (HQ)=Headquarters (DH)=Div Headquarters

Cheema Freightlines LLC ....D....209 599-0777
223 W 5th St Ripon (95366) ***(P-4913)***
Cheema Logistics, Ripon *Also called Cheema Freightlines LLC* ***(P-4913)***
Cheema Logistics ....D....559 702-1444
968 Sierra St Ste 130 Kingsburg (93631) ***(P-4591)***
Cheese Plant, Hanford *Also called Marquez Brothers Intl Inc* ***(P-8190)***
Chef Works Inc (PA) ....C....858 643-5600
12325 Kerran St A Poway (92064) ***(P-8022)***
Chefs Warehouse Westcoast LLC (HQ) ....D....626 465-4200
16633 Gale Ave City of Industry (91745) ***(P-8161)***
Chelbay Schuler & Chelbay (PA) ....D....408 288-4400
6800 Santa Teresa Blvd # 100 San Jose (95119) ***(P-10213)***
Chelsio Communications Inc ....C....408 962-3600
209 N Fair Oaks Ave Sunnyvale (94085) ***(P-14709)***
Chem Lab Rkfe, Edwards *Also called US Dept of the Air Force* ***(P-25864)***
Chem Quip Inc ....D....800 821-1678
2551 Land Ave Sacramento (95815) ***(P-7706)***
Chemical Dependency Recovery ....E....916 482-1132
2829 Watt Ave Ste 150 Sacramento (95821) ***(P-8693)***
Chemical Waste Management Inc ....D....559 386-9711
35251 Old Skyline Rd Kettleman City (93239) ***(P-6179)***
Chemtrans, Gardena *Also called Radford Alexander Corporation* ***(P-3929)***
Chen Dvid MD Dgnstc Med Group ....C....626 566-3900
25 N Santa Anita Ave Arcadia (91006) ***(P-6961)***
Cheque Guard Inc ....D....818 563-9335
512 S Verdugo Dr Burbank (91502) ***(P-14710)***
Cher Ae Heights Casino, Trinidad *Also called Cher-Ae Heights Indian Cmnty* ***(P-18645)***
Cher-Ae Heights Indian Cmnty ....C....707 677-3611
27 Scenic Dr Trinidad (95570) ***(P-18645)***
Cherokee Freight Lines, Stockton *Also called Scan-Vino LLC* ***(P-4126)***
Cherry Avenue Auction Inc ....E....559 266-9856
4640 S Cherry Ave Fresno (93706) ***(P-16692)***
Cherry City Electric, City of Industry *Also called Morrow-Meadows Corporation* ***(P-2558)***
Chesapeake Lodging Trust ....D....415 296-2900
333 Battery St Lbby San Francisco (94111) ***(P-12138)***
Chester Avenue Medical Offices, Bakersfield *Also called Kaiser Foundation Hospitals* ***(P-19057)***
Chester Avenue Medical Offs II, Bakersfield *Also called Kaiser Foundation Hospitals* ***(P-19058)***
Chester C Lehmann Co Inc (PA) ....D....408 293-5818
1135 Auzerais Ave San Jose (95126) ***(P-7134)***
Chester Public Utility Dst ....D....530 258-2171
251 Chester Airport Rd Chester (96020) ***(P-6006)***
Chevron, Modesto *Also called Charles Fenley Enterprises* ***(P-17367)***
Chevron, San Jose *Also called Lark Avenue Car Wash* ***(P-17381)***
Chevron, Norco *Also called Car Spa Inc* ***(P-17414)***
Chevron Energy Technology Co (HQ) ....D....510 242-5059
100 Chevron Way Richmond (94801) ***(P-25000)***
Chevron Federal Credit Union (PA) ....D....888 884-4630
500 12th St Ste 200 Oakland (94607) ***(P-9301)***
Chevron Investor Inc ....D....510 242-3000
100 Chevron Way Richmond (94801) ***(P-26177)***
Chevron Mining Inc ....B....760 856-7625
67750 Bailey Rd Mountain Pass (92366) ***(P-972)***
CHG Security Inc ....E....562 284-6260
16431 Grayville Dr La Mirada (90638) ***(P-16228)***
Chhp Management LLC ....D....323 583-1931
2623 E Slauson Ave Huntington Park (90255) ***(P-20776)***
Chiala, George Packing, Morgan Hill *Also called George Chiala Farms Inc* ***(P-55)***
CHIBI CHAN PRESCHOOL, San Francisco *Also called Japanese Cmnty Youth Council* ***(P-24184)***
Chicago Title & Escrow ....E....760 746-3882
316 W Mission Ave Ste 110 Escondido (92025) ***(P-11531)***
Chicago Title and Trust Co ....E....818 548-0222
535 N Brnd Blvrd Fl 3 Flr 3 Glendale (91203) ***(P-10170)***
Chicago Title Company ....C....408 292-4212
675 N 1st St Ste 400 San Jose (95112) ***(P-10171)***
Chicago Title Company ....C....619 230-6340
701 B St Ste 1120 San Diego (92101) ***(P-10172)***
Chicago Title Company ....D....213 488-4375
725 S Figueroa St Ste 200 Los Angeles (90017) ***(P-10173)***
Chicago Title Company ....D....559 451-3700
7330 N Palm Ave Ste 101 Fresno (93711) ***(P-10174)***
Chicago Title Insurance Co ....D....209 952-5500
3127 Transworld Dr # 103 Stockton (95206) ***(P-11532)***
Chicago Title Insurance Co ....E....916 985-0300
105 Lake Forest Way Folsom (95630) ***(P-10175)***
Chicago Title Insurance Co ....B....916 783-7195
925 Highland Pointe Dr # 340 Roseville (95678) ***(P-10176)***
Chicago Title Insurance Co (HQ) ....C....805 565-6900
4050 Calle Real Santa Barbara (93110) ***(P-10177)***
Chicago Title Insurance Co ....D....559 733-3814
120 N Floral St Visalia (93291) ***(P-10178)***
Chick-Fil-A, Long Beach *Also called Howard John* ***(P-12415)***
Chicken of Sea International, El Segundo *Also called Tri-Union Seafoods LLC* ***(P-8397)***
Chicken Ranch Bingo & Casino ....C....209 984-3000
16929 Chicken Ranch Rd Jamestown (95327) ***(P-18646)***
Chico Area Recreation & Pk Dst (PA) ....C....530 895-4711
545 Vallombrosa Ave Chico (95926) ***(P-18647)***
Chico Creek Care Rhabilitation, Chico *Also called Helios Healthcare LLC* ***(P-20012)***
Chico Csu ....D....530 898-3917
400 W 1st St Chico (95929) ***(P-22205)***
Chico Electric Inc ....D....530 891-1933
36 W Eaton Rd Chico (95973) ***(P-2452)***
Chico Family Health Center, Chico *Also called Ampla Health* ***(P-18809)***
Chico Immdate Care Med Ctr Inc (PA) ....E....530 891-1676
376 Vallombrosa Ave Chico (95926) ***(P-18892)***
Chico Paramedic Rescue, Chico *Also called First Rsponder Emrgncy Med Svc* ***(P-3674)***
Chico Produce Inc (PA) ....C....530 893-0596
70 Pepsi Way Durham (95938) ***(P-8442)***
Chico Sports Club, Chico *Also called Jeff Stover Inc* ***(P-18160)***
Chico State Enterprises ....A....530 898-6811
25 Main St Unit 203 Chico (95928) ***(P-24521)***
Chico V A Outpatient Clinic, Chico *Also called Veterans Health Administration* ***(P-19564)***
Children's Hospital Center, Los Angeles *Also called Childrens Hospital Los Angeles* ***(P-21459)***
Chief Engineering Co, Lake Elsinore *Also called Chief Trnsp & Engrg Contrs Inc* ***(P-1677)***
Chief Protective Services Inc ....D....951 738-0881
1344 W 6th St Ste 300 Corona (92882) ***(P-16229)***
Chief Trnsp & Engrg Contrs Inc ....D....951 258-6607
4056 Tamarind Rdg Lake Elsinore (92530) ***(P-1677)***
Chikpea Inc ....E....888 342-3828
1 Market St Spear Spear Tower San Francisco (94127) ***(P-27027)***
Child & Family Center ....C....661 259-9439
21545 Centre Pointe Pkwy Santa Clarita (91350) ***(P-22986)***
Child & Family Services, Orland *Also called Glenn County Office Education* ***(P-23728)***
Child Abuse Lstening Mediation ....E....805 965-2376
1236 Chapala St Santa Barbara (93101) ***(P-22987)***
CHILD ABUSE PREVENTION, Oakland *Also called Family Paths Inc* ***(P-22028)***
Child Action Inc (PA) ....B....916 369-4460
9800 Old Winery Pl Sacramento (95827) ***(P-23688)***
Child and Family Guidance Ctr ....D....661 265-8627
310 E Plmdle Blvd G Palmdale (93550) ***(P-21977)***
Child and Family Guidance Ctr (PA) ....C....818 739-5140
9650 Zelzah Ave Northridge (91325) ***(P-21978)***
Child and Family Guidance Ctr ....E....818 830-0200
8550 Balboa Blvd Ste 150 Northridge (91325) ***(P-21979)***
Child Care Coordinating Counsi ....E....650 517-1400
330 Twin Dolphin Dr # 119 Redwood City (94065) ***(P-22988)***
Child Care Resource Center Inc (PA) ....C....818 717-1000
20001 Prairie St Chatsworth (91311) ***(P-22989)***
Child Care Resource Center Inc ....E....661 723-3246
250 Grand Cypress Ave # 601 Palmdale (93551) ***(P-22990)***
Child Care Resource Center Inc ....B....818 837-0097
454 S Kalisher St San Fernando (91340) ***(P-23689)***
Child Development Assoc Inc (PA) ....E....619 427-4411
180 Otay Lakes Rd Ste 310 Bonita (91902) ***(P-23690)***
Child Development Center ....E....858 794-7160
309 N Rios Ave Solana Beach (92075) ***(P-23691)***
Child Development Centers, Morgan Hill *Also called Child Development Incorporated* ***(P-23692)***
Child Development Incorporated (PA) ....E....408 556-7300
350 Woodview Ave Morgan Hill (95037) ***(P-23692)***
Child Development Incorporated ....B....530 666-4822
312 Gibson Rd Woodland (95695) ***(P-23693)***
Child Development Incorporated ....B....714 842-4064
17341 Jacquelyn Ln Huntington Beach (92647) ***(P-11013)***
Child Development Incorporated ....A....949 854-5060
5151 Amalfi Dr Irvine (92603) ***(P-23694)***
Child Development Institute ....E....818 888-4559
6340 Variel Ave Ste A Woodland Hills (91367) ***(P-22991)***
Child Development Office, The, Santa Monica *Also called Santa Monica City of* ***(P-23784)***
Child Development Resources of (PA) ....C....805 485-7878
221 Ventura Blvd Oxnard (93036) ***(P-22992)***
Child Educational Center ....D....818 354-3418
140 Foothill Blvd La Canada (91011) ***(P-23695)***
Child Family & Cmnty Svcs Inc ....C....510 796-9512
32980 Alvarado Niles Rd # 856 Union City (94587) ***(P-23696)***
Child Help Head Start Center, Beaumont *Also called Childhelp Inc* ***(P-23861)***
Child Support Services, Commerce *Also called County of Los Angeles* ***(P-23085)***
Child Support Services, San Francisco *Also called San Francisco City & County* ***(P-23438)***
Child Support Svcs, Martinez *Also called County of Contra Costa* ***(P-23065)***
Child360, Los Angeles *Also called Los Angles Universal Preschool* ***(P-23746)***
Childcare Careers LLC ....A....650 372-0211
2000 Sierra Point Pkwy # 702 Brisbane (94005) ***(P-14486)***
Childerns Spec of San Deigo, San Diego *Also called Stanley M Kirkpatrick MD* ***(P-19450)***
Childhelp Inc ....C....951 845-6737
14700 Manzanita Rd Beaumont (92223) ***(P-23861)***
Childnet Youth & Fmly Svcs Inc (PA) ....C....562 498-5500
4155 Outer Traffic Cir Long Beach (90804) ***(P-22993)***
Childnet Youth & Fmly Svcs Inc ....D....562 492-9983
5150 E Pacific Cst Hwy # 100 Long Beach (90804) ***(P-23862)***
Children & Family Serivces, Orange *Also called County of Orange* ***(P-23123)***
Children & Family Svcs Dept, Santa Fe Springs *Also called County of Los Angeles* ***(P-23086)***
Children & Family Svcs Dept, Los Angeles *Also called County of Los Angeles* ***(P-23093)***
Children of Rainbow Inc (PA) ....C....619 615-0652
4890 Logan Ave San Diego (92113) ***(P-23697)***
Children of The Rainbow Head ....C....619 266-7311
4890 Logan Ave San Diego (92113) ***(P-23698)***
Children Services, San Bernardino *Also called County of San Bernardino* ***(P-23880)***
CHILDREN'S DISCOVERY MUSEUM, Rancho Mirage *Also called Childrens Museum of Desert* ***(P-24252)***
Children's Health Center, Chico *Also called Enloe Medical Center* ***(P-18974)***
Children's Protective Services, Redding *Also called County of Shasta* ***(P-23165)***
Childrens Angelcare Aid Intl ....C....619 795-6234
4535 58th St San Diego (92115) ***(P-22994)***
Childrens Associated Med Group, San Diego *Also called Childrens Specialist of San D* ***(P-18896)***
Childrens Botique, The, Rancho Cucamonga *Also called Childrens Btq At Stevens Hope* ***(P-8064)***

ALPHABETIC

Employee Codes: A=Over 500 employees, B=251-500
C=101-250, D=51-100, E=50
2020 Directory of California
Wholesalers and Services Companies
© Mergent Inc. 1-800-342-5647
1217

Childrens Btq At Stevens Hope............E.......909 256-0100
10730 Fthill Blvd Ste 170 Rancho Cucamonga (91730) ***(P-8064)***
Childrens Bureau Southern Cal (PA)............C.......213 342-0100
1910 Magnolia Ave Los Angeles (90007) ***(P-22995)***
Childrens Clinic serving Chl............B.......562 264-4638
701 E 28th St Ste 200 Long Beach (90806) ***(P-18893)***
Childrens Creativity Museum............D.......415 820-3320
221 4th St San Francisco (94103) ***(P-24251)***
Childrens Crisis Cntr Stanisls............D.......209 577-4413
1244 Fiori Ave Modesto (95350) ***(P-22996)***
Childrens Cuncil San Francisco (PA)............D.......415 343-3378
445 Church St San Francisco (94114) ***(P-22997)***
Childrens Day School............E.......415 861-5432
333 Dolores St San Francisco (94110) ***(P-23699)***
Childrens Healthcare Cal............A.......714 997-3000
455 S Main St Orange (92868) ***(P-18894)***
Childrens Healthcare Cal (PA)............A.......714 997-3000
1201 W La Veta Ave Orange (92868) ***(P-21456)***
Childrens Home of Stockton............D.......209 466-0853
430 N Pilgrim St Stockton (95205) ***(P-23863)***
Childrens Homes Southern Cal (PA)............E.......818 592-2960
22455 Victory Blvd West Hills (91307) ***(P-23864)***
Childrens Hosp Okland Res Inst............D.......510 450-7600
5700 Martin Luther Oakland (94609) ***(P-25985)***
Childrens Hospital Los Angeles............C.......818 728-4930
5359 Balboa Blvd Encino (91316) ***(P-20777)***
Childrens Hospital Los Angeles............C.......323 361-2153
5000 W Sunset Blvd # 400 Los Angeles (90027) ***(P-20778)***
Childrens Hospital Los Angeles (PA)............D.......323 660-2450
4650 W Sunset Blvd Los Angeles (90027) ***(P-21457)***
Childrens Hospital Los Angeles............C.......626 795-7177
468 E Santa Clara St Arcadia (91006) ***(P-20779)***
Childrens Hospital Los Angeles............C.......310 820-8608
1301 20th St Ste 460 Santa Monica (90404) ***(P-20780)***
Childrens Hospital Los Angeles............B.......323 361-2119
4650 W Sunset Blvd Los Angeles (90027) ***(P-18895)***
Childrens Hospital Los Angeles............C.......323 361-2215
800 N Brand Blvd Glendale (91203) ***(P-21458)***
Childrens Hospital Los Angeles............B.......323 361-2751
4661 W Sunset Blvd Los Angeles (90027) ***(P-25986)***
Childrens Hospital Los Angeles............B.......714 841-4990
7891 Talbert Ave Ste 103 Huntington Beach (92648) ***(P-19607)***
Childrens Hospital Los Angeles............D.......323 660-2450
4650 W Sunset Blvd Los Angeles (90027) ***(P-20781)***
Childrens Hospital Los Angeles............C.......323 361-5702
4661 W Sunset Blvd Los Angeles (90027) ***(P-21459)***
Childrens Hospital Orange Cnty (PA)............D.......714 997-3000
1201 W La Veta Ave Orange (92868) ***(P-21460)***
Childrens Hospital Orange Cnty............A.......949 365-2416
455 S Main St Orange (92868) ***(P-20782)***
Childrens Hospital Orange Cnty............A.......949 631-2062
500 Superior Ave Newport Beach (92663) ***(P-23700)***
Childrens Hospital Orange Cnty............A.......949 387-2586
980 Roosevelt Irvine (92620) ***(P-20783)***
Childrens Hospotal & Research (PA)............A.......510 428-3000
747 52nd St Oakland (94609) ***(P-20784)***
Childrens Inst Los Angeles............A.......213 383-2765
679 S New Hampshire Ave Los Angeles (90005) ***(P-22998)***
Childrens Inst Los Angeles (PA)............A.......213 385-5100
2121 W Temple St Los Angeles (90026) ***(P-25987)***
Childrens Institute Inc............D.......323 541-9368
1215 W Manchester Ave Los Angeles (90044) ***(P-25988)***
Childrens Institute Inc (PA)............C.......213 385-5100
2121 W Temple St Los Angeles (90026) ***(P-22999)***
Childrens Laboratory, Encino *Also called Childrens Hospital Los Angeles* ***(P-20777)***
Childrens Law Center Cal (PA)............C.......323 980-8700
101 Centre Plaza Dr Monterey Park (91754) ***(P-22414)***
Childrens Museum of Desert............E.......760 321-0602
71701 Gerald Ford Dr Rancho Mirage (92270) ***(P-24252)***
Childrens Protective Services............D.......530 749-6311
5730 Packard Ave Marysville (95901) ***(P-23000)***
Childrens Rcvery Ctr Nthrn Cal, Campbell *Also called Subacute Chld Hosp Cal Inc* ***(P-21497)***
Childrens Recvg Hm Sacramento............C.......916 482-2370
3555 Auburn Blvd Sacramento (95821) ***(P-23865)***
Childrens Services............D.......530 458-0300
345 5th St Ste A Colusa (95932) ***(P-23001)***
Childrens Specialist of San D (PA)............B.......858 576-1700
3020 Childrens Way San Diego (92123) ***(P-18896)***
Childrens Specialist San Diego, San Diego *Also called Physician Management Group Inc* ***(P-26351)***
Chilis 898 Corona............D.......951 734-7275
3579 Grand Oaks Corona (92881) ***(P-26178)***
China Airlines Ltd (HQ)............D.......310 646-4233
11201 Aviation Blvd Los Angeles (90045) ***(P-4661)***
China Brma India Veterans Assn, San Jose *Also called General George W Sliney Basha* ***(P-24546)***
China Peak Mountain Resort LLC............D.......559 233-2500
59265 Hwy 168 Lakeshore (93634) ***(P-12139)***
China Pearl, Pacoima *Also called CPI Luxury Group* ***(P-7786)***
China Yngxin Phrmceuticals Inc............A.......626 581-9098
927 Canada Ct City of Industry (91748) ***(P-6962)***
Chinaamerica Film Distributors, San Marino *Also called Tricor Entertainment Inc* ***(P-17685)***
Chinatown Service Center (PA)............C.......213 808-1700
767 N Hill St Ste 200b Los Angeles (90012) ***(P-23578)***
Chinese Cnsld Benevolent Assn............D.......415 982-6000
843 Stockton St San Francisco (94108) ***(P-24522)***
Chinese Hospital Association (PA)............B.......415 982-2400
845 Jackson St San Francisco (94133) ***(P-20785)***
Chinese Laundry Inc............E.......310 945-3299
3485 S La Cienega Blvd Los Angeles (90016) ***(P-8126)***
Chinese Laundry Shoes, Los Angeles *Also called Cels Enterprises Inc* ***(P-8125)***
Chinese Laundry Shoes, Los Angeles *Also called Chinese Laundry Inc* ***(P-8126)***
Chino Grading Inc............D.......909 364-8667
3613 Philadelphia St Chino (91710) ***(P-3307)***
Chino Medical Group Inc............D.......909 591-6446
5475 Walnut Ave Chino (91710) ***(P-18897)***
Chino Valley Healthcare Center............D.......909 628-1245
2351 S Towne Ave Pomona (91766) ***(P-19799)***
CHINO VALLEY MEDICAL CENTER, Chino *Also called Veritas Health Services Inc* ***(P-21355)***
Chino Valley Rock, Ontario *Also called Chino Valley Sawdust Inc* ***(P-6180)***
Chino Valley Sawdust Inc............D.......909 947-5983
13434 S Ontario Ave Ontario (91761) ***(P-6180)***
Chino Valley Unified Schl Dst............D.......909 627-9758
4150 Walnut Ave Chino (91710) ***(P-24523)***
Chino Valley Unified Schl Dst............D.......909 590-2707
13435 Eagle Canyon Dr Chino Hills (91709) ***(P-24524)***
Chino-Pacific Warehouse Corp (PA)............D.......909 545-8100
3601 Jurupa St Ontario (91761) ***(P-4386)***
Chipman Corporation (PA)............E.......510 748-8700
1040 Marina Village Pkwy # 100 Alameda (94501) ***(P-3985)***
Chipman Corporation............D.......510 748-8787
1555 Zephyr Ave Hayward (94544) ***(P-3986)***
Chiquita Brands Intl Inc............D.......213 488-0925
746 Market Ct Los Angeles (90021) ***(P-8443)***
Chiquita Fresh North Amer LLC............B.......954 924-5642
1440 E 3rd St Oxnard (93030) ***(P-219)***
Chirag Hospitality Inc............D.......415 922-0244
2440 Lombard St San Francisco (94123) ***(P-12140)***
Chiro Inc (PA)............D.......909 879-1160
2260 S Vista Ave Bloomington (92316) ***(P-7668)***
Chiron Corporation............D.......510 655-8730
4560 Horton St Emeryville (94608) ***(P-22206)***
Chlb LLC............C.......562 997-2000
2776 Pacific Ave Long Beach (90806) ***(P-21396)***
Choa Hope LLC............E.......712 277-4101
515 W Washington Ave Escondido (92025) ***(P-12141)***
Choc, Orange *Also called Childrens Hospital Orange Cnty* ***(P-21460)***
Choc Health Alliance............D.......714 565-5100
1120 W La Veta Ave # 450 Orange (92868) ***(P-9937)***
Choc Mission, Orange *Also called Childrens Hospital Orange Cnty* ***(P-20782)***
Chodorow De Castro West............D.......310 478-2541
10960 Wilshire Blvd # 1400 Los Angeles (90024) ***(P-22415)***
Choic Admini Insur Servi............B.......714 542-4200
721 S Parker St Ste 200 Orange (92868) ***(P-10316)***
Choice Hotels Intl Inc............D.......661 764-5207
20688 Tracy Ave Buttonwillow (93206) ***(P-12142)***
Choice In Aging (PA)............D.......925 682-6330
490 Golf Club Rd Pleasant Hill (94523) ***(P-21980)***
Choice Internet, Irvine *Also called Cie Digital Labs LLC* ***(P-13649)***
Choice Medical Group Inc............D.......916 483-2885
2322 Butano Dr Ste 205 Sacramento (95825) ***(P-21981)***
Choice Pak Products, Maywood *Also called Jack H Caldwell & Sons Inc* ***(P-8490)***
Choices For Children (PA)............D.......408 297-3295
20 Great Oaks Blvd # 200 San Jose (95119) ***(P-23701)***
CHOICESS, Arcadia *Also called Community Housing Options* ***(P-23037)***
Chong Partners Architecher Inc............C.......613 995-8210
901 Market St Ste 600 San Francisco (94103) ***(P-25425)***
Chooljian & Sons Inc (PA)............D.......559 888-2031
5287 S Del Rey Ave Del Rey (93616) ***(P-477)***
Chooljian Bros Packing Co Inc............E.......559 875-5501
3192 S Indianola Ave Sanger (93657) ***(P-8555)***
Choosing Independence Inc............D.......818 257-0323
7615 Louise Ave Northridge (91325) ***(P-26179)***
Chopra Center For Wellbeing, Carlsbad *Also called Chopra Cntre For Wll-Being LLC* ***(P-18648)***
Chopra Cntre For Wll-Being LLC............D.......760 494-1600
2013 Costa Del Mar Rd Carlsbad (92009) ***(P-18648)***
Choura Events............D.......310 320-6200
540 Hawaii Ave Torrance (90503) ***(P-14140)***
Choura Venue Services............D.......562 426-0555
4101 E Willow St Long Beach (90815) ***(P-13406)***
Choura Vnue Svcs At Carson Ctr, Long Beach *Also called Choura Venue Services* ***(P-13406)***
Chowchilla Conv. Center, Chowchilla *Also called Avalon Care Ctr - Chwchlla LLC* ***(P-19736)***
Chowchilla Medical Center, Chowchilla *Also called Madera Community Hospital* ***(P-21026)***
Chowchilla Mem Hlth Care Dst (PA)............D.......559 665-3781
1104 Ventura Ave Chowchilla (93610) ***(P-19800)***
Chownow Inc............D.......888 707-2469
12181 Bluff Creek Dr # 200 Playa Vista (90094) ***(P-15278)***
Chrisp Company (PA)............C.......510 656-2840
43650 Osgood Rd Fremont (94539) ***(P-1678)***
Christensen & Giannini LLC............D.......831 449-2494
1588 Moffett St Ste B Salinas (93905) ***(P-43)***
Christian and Wakefield (PA)............D.......619 236-1555
110 W A St Ste 900 San Diego (92101) ***(P-11014)***
Christian Church Homes............B.......510 893-2998
251 28th St Oakland (94611) ***(P-11015)***
Christian Community Credit Un (PA)............D.......626 915-7551
255 N Lone Hill Ave San Dimas (91773) ***(P-9385)***
Christian Community Credit Un............D.......800 347-2228
101 S Barranca Ave Covina (91723) ***(P-9386)***
Christian Conference Grounds, Mount Hermon *Also called Mount Hermon Association Inc* ***(P-13151)***
Christian Counseling Centers............D.......408 559-1115
3880 S Bascom Ave Ste 202 San Jose (95124) ***(P-23002)***
Christiansen Amusements Corp............D.......760 735-8542
1725 S Escondido Blvd E Escondido (92025) ***(P-18649)***

Christie Dgtal Systems USA Inc (HQ)..........D.......714 527-7056
10550 Camden Dr Cypress (90630) ***(P-6731)***
Christmas Bonus Fund of The Pl..........D.......213 385-6161
501 Shatto Pl Fl 5 Los Angeles (90020) ***(P-11779)***
Christopher Ranch LLC (PA)..........C.......408 847-1100
305 Bloomfield Ave Gilroy (95020) ***(P-21)***
Christopher Ranch LLC..........D.......831 636-8722
1690 Freitas Rd San Juan Bautista (95045) ***(P-8444)***
Christopher Ransom LLC..........D.......510 345-9144
1300 Clay St Oakland (94612) ***(P-11016)***
Chroma Systems..........D.......714 557-8480
3201 S Susan St Santa Ana (92704) ***(P-13265)***
Chromalloy San Diego Corp..........C.......858 877-2800
7007 Consolidated Way San Diego (92121) ***(P-17489)***
Chrome Deposit Corp..........D.......925 432-4507
900 Loveridge Rd Pittsburg (94565) ***(P-7053)***
Chrome River Technologies Inc (PA)..........D.......323 857-5800
5757 Wilshire Blvd # 270 Los Angeles (90036) ***(P-14711)***
Chronicle Broadcasting Co..........B.......415 561-8000
900 Front St San Francisco (94111) ***(P-5590)***
Chronicle LLC (HQ)..........D.......650 214-5199
250 Mayfield Ave Mountain View (94043) ***(P-16502)***
Chrysler Plymouth Dodge Jeep, Watsonville *Also called Marty Franich Leasing Co* ***(P-17229)***
Chsp Trs Fisherman Wharf LLC..........C.......415 563-1234
555 N Point St San Francisco (94133) ***(P-12143)***
Chsp Trs Los Angeles LLC..........D.......213 624-0000
535 S Grand Ave Los Angeles (90071) ***(P-12144)***
Chubb, Los Angeles *Also called Pacific Indemnity Company* ***(P-10449)***
Chubb, San Francisco *Also called Federal Insurance Company* ***(P-10361)***
Chubb US Holding Inc..........D.......415 547-4400
455 Market St Ste 500 San Francisco (94105) ***(P-10317)***
Chubb US Holding Inc..........C.......619 563-2400
3131 Camino Del Rio N San Diego (92108) ***(P-10318)***
Chubb US Holding Inc..........C.......818 428-3600
9200 Oakdale Ave Chatsworth (91311) ***(P-10319)***
Chuck Jones Flying Service (PA)..........E.......530 868-5798
216 W Hamilton Rd Biggs (95917) ***(P-435)***
Chukchansi Gold Resort Casino..........A.......866 794-6946
711 Lucky Ln Coarsegold (93614) ***(P-12145)***
Chula Vista Active Club, Chula Vista *Also called 24 Hour Fitness Usa Inc* ***(P-18102)***
Chula Vista Veterans Center, Chula Vista *Also called Veterans Health Administration* ***(P-19566)***
Chumash Casino Resort (HQ)..........C.......805 686-0855
3400 E Highway 246 Santa Ynez (93460) ***(P-18650)***
Church & Larsen Inc..........C.......626 303-8741
16103 Avenida Padilla Irwindale (91702) ***(P-2770)***
Church Brothers LLC (PA)..........D.......831 796-1000
19065 Portola Dr Ste C Salinas (93908) ***(P-8445)***
Church of Jsus Chrst of Ld STS..........C.......323 268-7281
2720 E 11th St Los Angeles (90023) ***(P-17471)***
Church of Jsus Chrst of Ld STS..........D.......916 482-1480
3000 Auburn Blvd Ste B Sacramento (95821) ***(P-23579)***
Church of Vly Rtrment Hmes Inc..........D.......408 241-7750
390 N Winchester Blvd Santa Clara (95050) ***(P-23866)***
Churchill Downs Incorporated..........A.......502 638-3879
800 W El Camino Real # 400 Mountain View (94040) ***(P-18083)***
Churchill MGT Group Corp..........E.......877 937-7110
5900 Wilshire Blvd # 400 Los Angeles (90036) ***(P-9809)***
Cibus Global Ltd..........C.......858 450-0008
6455 Nancy Ridge Dr San Diego (92121) ***(P-478)***
CIC Research Inc..........D.......858 637-4000
8361 Vickers St Ste 308 San Diego (92111) ***(P-25881)***
Cicileo Landscapes..........E.......805 967-3939
4565 Hollister Ave Santa Barbara (93110) ***(P-717)***
Cicoil LLC..........D.......661 295-1295
24960 Avenue Tibbitts Valencia (91355) ***(P-7251)***
Cie Digital Labs LLC (PA)..........D.......949 381-6200
19900 Macarthur Blvd # 1000 Irvine (92612) ***(P-13649)***
Cielo Azul Inc..........D.......855 863-8503
1545 Lake Dr Encinitas (92024) ***(P-786)***
Cierra Wireless..........C.......760 476-8700
2738 Loker Ave W Ste A Carlsbad (92010) ***(P-25001)***
Cific Energy Center, San Francisco *Also called Sodexo Management Inc* ***(P-26398)***
Cigna Healthcare Cal Inc..........C.......415 374-2500
1 Front St Ste 1700 San Francisco (94111) ***(P-9938)***
Cigna Healthcare Cal Inc (HQ)..........B.......818 500-6262
400 N Brand Blvd Ste 400 # 400 Glendale (91203) ***(P-9939)***
Cigna Healthcare Cal Inc..........C.......805 230-8300
2801 Townsgate Rd Ste 121 Thousand Oaks (91361) ***(P-9940)***
Cigna Healthcare Cal Inc..........B.......559 738-2000
5300 W Tulare Ave Ste 100 Visalia (93277) ***(P-9941)***
Cik Power Distributors LLC..........D.......714 938-0297
240 W Grove Ave Orange (92865) ***(P-26180)***
Cim Group LP (PA)..........D.......323 860-4900
4700 Wilshire Blvd Ste 1 Los Angeles (90010) ***(P-12146)***
Cim/Oakland City Center LLC..........D.......510 451-4000
1001 Broadway Oakland (94607) ***(P-12147)***
Cimatron Gibbs LLC..........D.......805 523-0004
323 Science Dr Moorpark (93021) ***(P-14712)***
Cinelease Inc (HQ)..........E.......855 441-5500
5375 W San Fernando Rd Los Angeles (90039) ***(P-17729)***
Cinema City Theaters..........E.......714 970-0865
5635 E La Palma Ave Anaheim (92807) ***(P-17823)***
Cinemark Usa Inc..........D.......510 276-9684
15555 E 14th St Ste 600 San Leandro (94578) ***(P-17824)***
Cinemark Usa Inc..........D.......916 922-4241
1590 Ethan Way Sacramento (95825) ***(P-17825)***
Cinemark Usa Inc..........D.......714 373-4573
7777 Edinger Ave Ste 170 Huntington Beach (92647) ***(P-17826)***
Cinemastar Luxury Theaters..........B.......760 945-2500
1949 Avenida Del Oro # 100 Oceanside (92056) ***(P-17827)***
Cinepolis Luxury Cinemas..........D.......323 556-6340
6420 Wilshire Blvd # 900 Los Angeles (90048) ***(P-17828)***
Cinnabar..........C.......818 842-8190
4571 Electronics Pl Los Angeles (90039) ***(P-13774)***
Cinnabar California Inc..........D.......818 842-8190
4571 Electronics Pl Los Angeles (90039) ***(P-13775)***
Cinnabar Hills Golf Club, San Jose *Also called Traditions Golf LLC* ***(P-18308)***
Cinovation Inc..........D.......818 246-3160
6527 San Fernando Rd Glendale (91201) ***(P-17590)***
Cintas Corporation..........D.......714 646-2550
4320 E Miraloma Ave Anaheim (92807) ***(P-2094)***
Cintas Corporation..........D.......925 743-1745
3201 Dnville Blvd Ste 285 Alamo (94507) ***(P-13214)***
Cintas Corporation No 2..........D.......310 635-8713
18050 Central Ave Carson (90746) ***(P-13407)***
Cintas Corporation No 2..........D.......408 292-6700
2188 Del Franco St Ste 70 San Jose (95131) ***(P-13288)***
Cintas Corporation No 2..........D.......714 288-8400
4320 E Miraloma Ave Anaheim (92807) ***(P-8959)***
Cintas Corporation No 3..........D.......661 282-4300
5500 Young St Bakersfield (93311) ***(P-13289)***
Cintas Corporation No 3..........C.......619 239-1001
675 32nd St San Diego (92102) ***(P-13290)***
Cintas Corporation No 3..........D.......562 692-8741
2829 Workman Mill Rd Whittier (90601) ***(P-13215)***
Cintas Corporation No 3..........E.......510 352-6330
777 139th Ave San Leandro (94578) ***(P-13408)***
Cintas Corporation No 3..........C.......562 368-3200
7735 Paramount Blvd Pico Rivera (90660) ***(P-13216)***
Cintas Corporation No 3..........C.......909 930-9096
2150 Proforma Ave Ontario (91761) ***(P-13217)***
Cintas Corporation No 3..........D.......661 310-7400
28334 Industry Dr Valencia (91355) ***(P-13218)***
Cintas Corporation No 3..........D.......510 352-6330
20929 Cabot Blvd Hayward (94545) ***(P-13291)***
Cintas Corporation No 3..........D.......310 725-2850
20100 S Susana Rd Compton (90221) ***(P-13292)***
Cintas Corporation No 3..........C.......916 419-8519
1231 National Dr Sacramento (95834) ***(P-13293)***
Cintas Corporation No 3..........D.......909 390-4912
1851 S Wineville Ave Ontario (91761) ***(P-13294)***
Cintas Corporation No 3..........D.......650 589-4300
220 Demeter St East Palo Alto (94303) ***(P-13295)***
Cintas Fire, Anaheim *Also called Cintas Corporation* ***(P-2094)***
Cintiva Financial Corporation..........D.......877 246-8482
10145 Pacific Hts 800 San Diego (92121) ***(P-9617)***
Ciphercloud Inc (PA)..........D.......408 519-6930
2581 Junction Ave Ste 200 San Jose (95134) ***(P-15279)***
Cir..........C.......650 574-6900
1745 Celeste Dr San Mateo (94402) ***(P-25731)***
Circle K Ranch..........D.......559 834-1571
8640 E Manning Ave Selma (93662) ***(P-122)***
Circle Marina Car Wash Inc..........E.......562 494-4698
4800 E Pacific Coast Hwy Long Beach (90804) ***(P-17368)***
Circle Marina Hand Car Wash, Long Beach *Also called Circle Marina Car Wash Inc* ***(P-17368)***
Circle Wood Services Inc..........D.......909 784-0733
3670 W Temple Ave Pomona (91768) ***(P-26181)***
Circulating Air Inc (PA)..........D.......818 764-0530
7337 Varna Ave North Hollywood (91605) ***(P-2095)***
Cirks Construction Inc..........C.......916 362-5460
3300 Industrial Blvd West Sacramento (95691) ***(P-1446)***
Cirrus Enterprises LLC..........D.......310 204-6159
18027 Bishop Ave Carson (90746) ***(P-8683)***
Cirrus Health II LP..........C.......949 855-0562
24331 El Toro Rd Ste 150 Laguna Hills (92637) ***(P-18898)***
Cirtech Inc..........E.......714 921-0860
250 E Emerson Ave Orange (92865) ***(P-16693)***
CIS Security, Fresno *Also called Geil Enterprises Inc* ***(P-16290)***
Cisco Ironport Systems LLC (HQ)..........B.......650 989-6500
170 W Tasman Dr San Jose (95134) ***(P-15280)***
Cisco Systems Capital Corp (HQ)..........C.......610 386-5870
170 W Tasman Dr San Jose (95134) ***(P-16694)***
Cisco Webex LLC (HQ)..........A.......408 435-7000
170 W Tasman Dr San Jose (95134) ***(P-16695)***
CIT Bank NA..........D.......760 771-3498
78010 Main St La Quinta (92253) ***(P-9055)***
CIT Bank NA..........D.......310 727-5660
1570 Rosecrans Ave Manhattan Beach (90266) ***(P-9056)***
CIT Bank NA..........D.......909 631-2560
3410 Grand Ave Ste A Chino Hills (91709) ***(P-9057)***
CIT Bank NA..........D.......310 475-4594
2920 N Beverly Glen Cir Los Angeles (90077) ***(P-9058)***
CIT Bank NA..........D.......818 502-8400
1111 N Brand Blvd Ste A Glendale (91202) ***(P-9059)***
CIT Bank NA..........D.......310 452-3802
1750 Ocean Park Blvd Santa Monica (90405) ***(P-9060)***
CIT Bank NA..........D.......562 433-0972
3500 E 7th St Long Beach (90804) ***(P-9061)***
CIT Bank NA..........D.......818 817-5320
17050 Ventura Blvd # 100 Encino (91316) ***(P-9062)***
CIT Bank NA..........D.......805 465-1053
1727 E Daily Dr Camarillo (93010) ***(P-9063)***
CIT Bank NA..........D.......310 390-7745
5573 Sepulveda Blvd Culver City (90230) ***(P-9064)***

ALPHABETIC

Employee Codes: A=Over 500 employees, B=251-500
C=101-250, D=51-100, E=50
2020 Directory of California
Wholesalers and Services Companies
© Mergent Inc. 1-800-342-5647
1219

CIT Bank NA......D......310 559-7222
10784 Jefferson Blvd Culver City (90230) ***(P-9065)***
CIT Bank NA......D......310 477-0546
3000 S Sepulveda Blvd Los Angeles (90034) ***(P-9066)***
CIT Bank NA......D......818 525-3760
1001 N San Fernando Blvd Burbank (91504) ***(P-9067)***
CIT Bank NA......D......949 347-7014
27620 Marguerite Pkwy B Mission Viejo (92692) ***(P-9068)***
CIT Bank NA......D......949 675-2890
3700 E Coast Hwy Corona Del Mar (92625) ***(P-9069)***
CIT Bank NA (HQ)......D......626 859-5400
75 N Fair Oaks Ave Ste C Pasadena (91103) ***(P-9070)***
CIT Bank NA......D......805 379-5520
199 E Thousand Oaks Blvd Thousand Oaks (91360) ***(P-9071)***
CIT Bank National Association......D......818 885-9065
20505 Devonshire St Chatsworth (91311) ***(P-9072)***
CIT Bank National Association......D......626 435-2260
220 N Hacienda Blvd City of Industry (91744) ***(P-9073)***
CIT Bank National Association......D......310 394-1640
401 Wilshire Blvd Santa Monica (90401) ***(P-9074)***
CIT Bank National Association......D......310 820-9650
12401 Wilshire Blvd Los Angeles (90025) ***(P-9075)***
CIT Bank National Association......D......310 577-6142
13405 Washington Blvd Marina Del Rey (90292) ***(P-9076)***
CIT Bank National Association......D......310 829-4477
1630 Montana Ave Santa Monica (90403) ***(P-9077)***
CIT Bank National Association......D......323 838-6881
5701 S Eastrn Ave Ste 108 Commerce (90040) ***(P-9078)***
CIT Bank National Association......D......310 265-1656
30019 Hawthorne Blvd Rancho Palos Verdes (90275) ***(P-9079)***
Citadel Environmental Svcs Inc (PA)......E......818 246-2707
1725 Victory Blvd Glendale (91201) ***(P-27028)***
Citadel Roofing & Solar......C......707 446-5500
4980 Allison Pkwy Vacaville (95688) ***(P-3036)***
Citadel Security Inc......C......562 248-2300
5199 E Pcf Cast Hwy 200 Long Beach (90804) ***(P-16230)***
Citibank FSB (HQ)......B......415 627-6000
1 Sansome St San Francisco (94104) ***(P-9278)***
Citibank National Association......C......805 497-7361
3967 E Thousand Oaks Blvd Westlake Village (91362) ***(P-9080)***
Citibank National Association......C......800 627-3999
3580 Tyler St Riverside (92503) ***(P-9081)***
Citibank National Association......C......619 870-0609
2240 Otay Lakes Rd 304-3 Chula Vista (91915) ***(P-9082)***
Citibank National Association......C......415 431-6940
150 Pennsylvania Ave San Francisco (94107) ***(P-9083)***
Citigroup Global Markets Inc......C......213 486-8811
444 S Flower St Fl 35 Los Angeles (90071) ***(P-9667)***
Citigroup Global Markets Inc......D......310 727-9533
2381 Rosecrans Ave # 115 El Segundo (90245) ***(P-9668)***
Citigroup Global Markets Inc......E......916 567-2056
155 Cadillac Dr Fl 1 Sacramento (95825) ***(P-9669)***
Citigroup Global Markets Inc......D......858 597-7777
4350 La Jolla Village Dr San Diego (92122) ***(P-9670)***
Citigroup Global Markets Inc......E......310 540-9511
21250 Hawthorne Blvd # 650 Torrance (90503) ***(P-9671)***
Citigroup Global Markets Inc......D......949 955-7500
1901 Main St Ste 800 Irvine (92614) ***(P-9672)***
Citigroup Global Markets Inc......D......858 456-4900
1225 Prospect St La Jolla (92037) ***(P-9673)***
Citigroup Global Markets Inc......E......559 438-2542
5250 N Palm Ave Ste 321 Fresno (93704) ***(P-9674)***
Citigroup Global Markets Inc......D......310 544-3600
609 Deep Valley Dr # 400 Rllng HLS Est (90274) ***(P-9675)***
Citigroup Global Markets Inc......D......909 625-0781
456 W Foothill Blvd Claremont (91711) ***(P-9676)***
Citigroup Global Markets Inc......C......650 926-7600
2775 Sand Hill Rd Ste 120 Menlo Park (94025) ***(P-9677)***
Citigroup Inc......D......805 557-0930
325 E Hillcrest Dr # 160 Thousand Oaks (91360) ***(P-9084)***
Citigroup Inc......D......909 335-0547
300 E State St Redlands (92373) ***(P-9085)***
Citigroup Inc......D......949 726-5124
3996 Barranca Pkwy # 130 Irvine (92606) ***(P-9086)***
Citigroup Inc......D......619 498-3158
352 H St Chula Vista (91910) ***(P-9087)***
Citigroup Inc......D......415 617-8524
1 Sansome St Fl 27 San Francisco (94104) ***(P-9678)***
Citigroup Inc......D......714 938-0748
840 N Eckhoff St Ste 140 Orange (92868) ***(P-9539)***
Citimortgage Inc......E......925 730-3800
6160 Stoneridge Mall Rd # 150 Pleasanton (94588) ***(P-9679)***
Citivest Inc......D......949 474-0440
4340 Von Karman Ave # 110 Newport Beach (92660) ***(P-11017)***
Citizens Business Bank (HQ)......C......909 980-4030
701 N Haven Ave Ste 350 Ontario (91764) ***(P-9186)***
Citizens Business Bank......D......949 440-5200
1401 Dove St Ste 100 Newport Beach (92660) ***(P-9187)***
Citizens Business Bank......E......626 577-1700
505 E Colorado Blvd Pasadena (91101) ***(P-9188)***
Citizens Business Bank......D......818 843-0707
4100 W Alameda Ave # 101 Burbank (91505) ***(P-9189)***
Citizens Business Bank......D......661 281-0300
1230 17th St Bakersfield (93301) ***(P-9190)***
Citizens Choice Health Plan, Orange *Also called Alignment Health Plan* ***(P-9920)***
Citizens Development Corp (PA)......D......760 744-0120
1105 La Bonita Dr San Marcos (92078) ***(P-18421)***
Citrix Systems Inc......D......408 790-8000
4988 Great America Pkwy Santa Clara (95054) ***(P-15281)***
Citrus Heights Sport Club, San Ramon *Also called 24 Hour Fitness Usa Inc* ***(P-18104)***
Citrus North Venture......D......256 428-2000
6591 Collins Dr Ste E11 Moorpark (93021) ***(P-12148)***
CITRUS VALLEY HOME HEALTH, West Covina *Also called Citrus Valley Hospice* ***(P-19801)***
Citrus Valley Hospice......D......626 859-2263
820 N Phillips Ave West Covina (91791) ***(P-19801)***
Citrus Valley Medical Ctr Inc (PA)......A......626 962-4011
1115 S Sunset Ave West Covina (91790) ***(P-20786)***
Citrus Valley Medical Ctr Inc......A......626 858-8515
140 W College St Covina (91723) ***(P-20787)***
Citrus Valley Medical Ctr Inc......A......626 963-8411
1115 S Sunset Ave West Covina (91790) ***(P-20788)***
Citrus Valley Medical Ctr Inc......A......626 331-7331
210 W San Bernardino Rd Covina (91723) ***(P-20789)***
Citrus Vly Hlth Partners Inc......A......626 962-4011
1115 S Sunset Ave West Covina (91790) ***(P-20790)***
Citrus Vly Hlth Partners Inc......A......626 732-3100
1325 N Grand Ave Ste 300 Covina (91724) ***(P-22207)***
City & County of San Francisco......C......415 553-1706
850 Bryant St Ste 200 San Francisco (94103) ***(P-23003)***
City & County of San Francisco......D......415 621-6600
401 Van Ness Ave Ste 110 San Francisco (94102) ***(P-17898)***
City & County of San Francisco......D......415 621-6600
401 Van Ness Ave Ste 110 San Francisco (94102) ***(P-17899)***
City & County of San Francisco......A......415 551-3000
525 Golden Gate Ave Fl 5 San Francisco (94102) ***(P-6029)***
City & County of San Francisco......D......415 581-3500
200 Larkin St San Francisco (94102) ***(P-24253)***
City & County of San Francisco......A......415 206-8000
1001 Potrero Ave San Francisco (94110) ***(P-20791)***
City & County of San Francisco......D......415 557-4713
30 Van Ness Ave Ste 4100 San Francisco (94102) ***(P-24393)***
City & County of San Francisco......C......415 554-4700
1 Carlton B Goodlett Pl # 234 San Francisco (94102) ***(P-22416)***
City & County of San Francisco......C......415 553-1752
850 Bryant St Ste 600 San Francisco (94103) ***(P-22417)***
City & County of San Francisco......D......415 753-7561
375 Woodside Ave 1 San Francisco (94127) ***(P-23004)***
City & County of San Francisco......D......415 554-4799
1 Carlton B Goodlett Pl # 234 San Francisco (94102) ***(P-26182)***
City Alameda Health Care Corp......A......510 522-3700
2070 Clinton Ave Alameda (94501) ***(P-20792)***
CITY ARTS ACADEMY, San Diego *Also called Harmonium Inc* ***(P-23729)***
City Attorney, Los Angeles *Also called City of Los Angeles* ***(P-22421)***
City Attorney, San Francisco *Also called City & County of San Francisco* ***(P-22416)***
City Attorneys Office, Long Beach *Also called City of Long Beach* ***(P-22419)***
City Center Grill, Oakland *Also called Cim/Oakland City Center LLC* ***(P-12147)***
City Club LLC......D......415 362-2480
155 Sansome St Fl 9 San Francisco (94104) ***(P-18422)***
City Club of San Francisco, San Francisco *Also called City Club LLC* ***(P-18422)***
City Club On Bunker Hill, Los Angeles *Also called Bunker Hill Club Inc* ***(P-24503)***
City Corporation Yard, Delano *Also called City of Delano* ***(P-18230)***
City Fashion Express Inc......D......310 223-1010
2888 E El Presidio St Carson (90810) ***(P-4914)***
City Fibers Inc (PA)......D......323 583-1013
2500 S Santa Fe Ave Vernon (90058) ***(P-7755)***
City Fibers Inc......D......323 583-1013
2525 E 25th St Vernon (90058) ***(P-4387)***
City Hall, Ventura *Also called Ventura Streets Dept* ***(P-1217)***
City Hall Pblc Wrks Eng Dpt, San Bernardino *Also called San Bernardino California City* ***(P-24359)***
City Hanford Public Imprv Corp......D......559 585-2550
900 S 10th Ave Hanford (93230) ***(P-1844)***
City Hope National Medical Ctr......A......626 256-4673
1500 Duarte Rd Duarte (91010) ***(P-20793)***
City II Enterprises Inc......E......408 275-1200
845 Earle Ave San Jose (95126) ***(P-787)***
City Impact......E......415 292-1770
230 Jones St Fl 1 San Francisco (94102) ***(P-24818)***
City Impact Inc......D......805 983-3636
555 S A St Ste 175 Oxnard (93030) ***(P-23005)***
City Leasing & Rentals......C......619 276-6171
2111 Morena Blvd San Diego (92110) ***(P-17227)***
City Long Bch Prkg Enforcement, Long Beach *Also called City of Long Beach* ***(P-6341)***
City Mechanical Inc......D......510 724-9088
724 Alfred Nobel Dr Hercules (94547) ***(P-17443)***
City Mnterey Pk Recreation Ctr, Monterey Park *Also called City of Monterey Park* ***(P-18660)***
City Moving Inc......E......888 794-8808
6319 Colfax Ave North Hollywood (91606) ***(P-4199)***
City National Bank (HQ)......B......310 888-6000
555 S Flower St Fl 21 Los Angeles (90071) ***(P-9088)***
City National Bank......E......951 276-8800
3484 Central Ave Riverside (92506) ***(P-9089)***
City National Bank......D......619 645-6100
225 Broadway Ste 500 San Diego (92101) ***(P-9090)***
City National Bank......C......310 297-6606
2100 Park Pl Ste 150 El Segundo (90245) ***(P-9091)***
City National Investments, San Diego *Also called City National Bank* ***(P-9090)***
City National SEC Svcs Inc......D......310 641-6666
5901 W Century Blvd # 806 Los Angeles (90045) ***(P-16231)***
City of Anaheim......B......714 704-2400
2695 E Katella Ave Anaheim (92806) ***(P-10578)***
City of Antioch......D......925 779-6950
1201 W 4th St Antioch (94509) ***(P-6339)***
City of Arcadia......B......626 574-5435
240 W Huntington Dr Arcadia (91007) ***(P-3526)***
City of Bakersfield......C......661 852-7300
1001 Truxtun Ave Bakersfield (93301) ***(P-23006)***

Mergent e-mail: customerrelations@mergent.com
1220
2020 Directory of California
Wholesalers and Services Companies
(P-0000) Products & Services Section entry number
(PA)=Parent Co (HQ)=Headquarters (DH)=Div Headquarters

ALPHABETIC SECTION City of Riverside

City of Bell........D.......323 773-1596
6250 Pine Ave Bell (90201) ***(P-23007)***
City of Berkeley........A.......510 981-6750
2180 Milvia St Berkeley (94704) ***(P-25555)***
City of Beverly Hills........B.......310 285-2552
342 Foothill Rd Beverly Hills (90210) ***(P-17251)***
City of Brea........D.......714 990-7650
1 Civic Center Cir Fl 3 Brea (92821) ***(P-26934)***
City of Burbank........B.......818 238-3550
164 W Magnolia Blvd Burbank (91502) ***(P-5993)***
City of Burlingame........E.......650 558-7670
1361 N Carolan Ave Burlingame (94010) ***(P-1679)***
City of Carson........D.......310 835-0212
3 Civic Plaza Dr Carson (90745) ***(P-23008)***
City of Chino........D.......909 591-9843
5050 Schaefer Ave Chino (91710) ***(P-6340)***
City of Commerce........B.......323 722-4805
2535 Commerce Way Commerce (90040) ***(P-18651)***
City of Compton........D.......310 635-3484
1108 N Oleander Ave Compton (90222) ***(P-18652)***
City of Concord........B.......925 692-2400
2000 Kirker Pass Rd Concord (94521) ***(P-17900)***
City of Concord........D.......925 686-6262
4050 Port Chicago Hwy Concord (94520) ***(P-18229)***
City of Corona........C.......951 279-3647
400 S Vicentia Ave Corona (92882) ***(P-26903)***
City of Corona........D.......951 736-2266
400 S Vicentia Ave # 210 Corona (92882) ***(P-6007)***
City of Coronado........D.......619 522-7342
1845 Strand Way Coronado (92118) ***(P-18653)***
City of Coronado........D.......619 522-7380
101 B Ave Coronado (92118) ***(P-5994)***
City of Daly City........D.......650 991-8064
333 90th St Fl 1 Daly City (94015) ***(P-25002)***
City of Delano........E.......661 721-3350
725 S Lexington St Delano (93215) ***(P-18230)***
City of Downey........D.......562 861-8211
8435 Firestone Blvd Downey (90241) ***(P-17901)***
City of El Centro........C.......760 337-4505
307 W Brighton Ave El Centro (92243) ***(P-1680)***
City of Encinitas........E.......760 633-2850
160 Calle Magdalena Encinitas (92024) ***(P-1681)***
City of Fairfield........C.......707 428-7435
1000 Webster St Fairfield (94533) ***(P-10579)***
City of Folsom........D.......916 355-7285
48 Natoma St Folsom (95630) ***(P-18654)***
City of Foster City........E.......650 286-3380
650 Shell Blvd Foster City (94404) ***(P-18655)***
City of Fremont........C.......510 791-4196
34600 Ardenwood Blvd Fremont (94555) ***(P-24254)***
City of Fremont........C.......510 494-4460
39550 Liberty St Fremont (94538) ***(P-25426)***
City of Fresno........B.......559 621-7433
2223 G St Fresno (93706) ***(P-3527)***
City of Fresno........C.......559 621-5300
1910 E University Ave Fresno (93703) ***(P-6030)***
City of Fresno........D.......559 445-8200
700 M St Fresno (93721) ***(P-16696)***
City of Fullerton........C.......714 738-6897
1580 W Commonwealth Ave Fullerton (92833) ***(P-26556)***
City of Galt........D.......209 366-7180
660 Chabolla Ave Galt (95632) ***(P-18656)***
City of Gardena........D.......310 324-1475
13999 S Western Ave Gardena (90249) ***(P-3528)***
City of Glendale........D.......818 548-3945
633 E Broadway Ste 205 Glendale (91206) ***(P-25003)***
City of Glendale........D.......818 548-3950
541 W Chevy Chase Dr Glendale (91204) ***(P-18059)***
City of Glendale........B.......818 548-3300
141 N Glendale Ave Fl 2 Glendale (91206) ***(P-5819)***
City of Glendale........E.......818 548-3980
634 Bekins Way Glendale (91201) ***(P-5820)***
City of Glendale........C.......818 548-2011
800 Air Way Glendale (91201) ***(P-6031)***
City of Inglewood........D.......310 412-5370
700 Warren Ln Inglewood (90302) ***(P-18657)***
City of Irvine........D.......949 724-7600
6427 Oak Cyn Irvine (92618) ***(P-26557)***
City of Irvine........D.......949 724-7740
6443 Oak Cyn Irvine (92618) ***(P-18658)***
City of Irvine........D.......949 724-7101
1 Civic Center Plz Irvine (92606) ***(P-24394)***
City of Irvine........D.......949 724-6900
20 Lake Rd Irvine (92604) ***(P-23009)***
City of La Habra........E.......562 905-9708
101 W La Habra Blvd La Habra (90631) ***(P-23010)***
City of La Mesa........E.......619 667-1450
8152 Commercial St La Mesa (91942) ***(P-1682)***
City of Lemoore........E.......559 924-6744
711 W Cinnamon Dr Lemoore (93245) ***(P-6181)***
City of Livermore........E.......925 960-8100
101 W Jack London Blvd Livermore (94551) ***(P-1954)***
City of Lomita........E.......310 325-9830
24373 Walnut St Lomita (90717) ***(P-6032)***
City of Long Beach........C.......562 570-2828
2600 Temple Ave Long Beach (90806) ***(P-17325)***
City of Long Beach........D.......562 570-5423
2600 Temple Ave Long Beach (90806) ***(P-22418)***
City of Long Beach........C.......562 570-2890
2929 E Willow St Long Beach (90806) ***(P-6341)***
City of Long Beach........C.......562 570-2000
2400 E Spring St Long Beach (90806) ***(P-6000)***
City of Long Beach........D.......562 570-2600
4100 E Don Douglas Dr Fl Flr 2 Long Beach (90808) ***(P-4758)***
City of Long Beach........B.......562 436-3636
300 E Ocean Blvd Long Beach (90802) ***(P-16697)***
City of Long Beach........D.......562 570-6919
333 W Ocean Blvd Lbby Long Beach (90802) ***(P-22419)***
City of Long Beach........B.......562 570-6383
411 W Ocean Blvd Long Beach (90802) ***(P-1683)***
City of Long Beach........D.......562 570-2390
1800 E Wardlow Rd Long Beach (90807) ***(P-6033)***
City of Los Angeles........A.......213 978-0259
600 S Spring St Unit 200 Los Angeles (90014) ***(P-25004)***
City of Los Angeles........C.......213 473-6872
111 E 1st St Ste 404 Los Angeles (90012) ***(P-22420)***
City of Los Angeles........B.......310 732-3550
500 Pier A Pl Wilmington (90744) ***(P-3827)***
City of Los Angeles........C.......213 473-0800
2800 E Observatory Ave Los Angeles (90027) ***(P-24255)***
City of Los Angeles........D.......213 485-4282
1149 S Broadway Ste 800 Los Angeles (90015) ***(P-25427)***
City of Los Angeles........A.......818 756-8022
6262 Van Nuys Blvd # 451 Van Nuys (91401) ***(P-25005)***
City of Los Angeles........D.......213 202-5500
201 N Figueroa St # 1400 Los Angeles (90012) ***(P-24819)***
City of Los Angeles........D.......213 847-2799
3330 W 36th St Los Angeles (90018) ***(P-13877)***
City of Los Angeles........C.......310 732-7681
425 S Palos Verdes St San Pedro (90731) ***(P-4611)***
City of Los Angeles........A.......213 978-8100
200 N Main St Ste 800 Los Angeles (90012) ***(P-22421)***
City of Los Angeles........E.......323 467-7193
3200 Canyon Dr Los Angeles (90068) ***(P-13146)***
City of Los Angeles........D.......213 485-4981
2513 E 24th St Vernon (90058) ***(P-3828)***
City of Los Angeles........D.......818 908-5950
16461 Sherman Way Ste 210 Van Nuys (91406) ***(P-4759)***
City of Mill Valley........E.......415 383-1370
180 Camino Alto Mill Valley (94941) ***(P-18659)***
City of Mill Valley........C.......415 388-4033
26 Corte Madera Ave Mill Valley (94941) ***(P-1684)***
City of Monterey Park........D.......626 307-1388
320 W Newmark Ave Fl 1 Monterey Park (91754) ***(P-18660)***
City of Moorpark........D.......805 517-6261
799 Moorpark Ave Moorpark (93021) ***(P-23011)***
City of Morgan Hill........D.......408 776-7333
100 Edes St Morgan Hill (95037) ***(P-27029)***
City of Morro Bay, Morro Bay *Also called Morro Bay Public Works* ***(P-1761)***
City of NAPA........E.......707 255-7631
1151 Pearl St NAPA (94559) ***(P-3757)***
City of Norco........D.......951 270-5632
2870 Clark Ave Norco (92860) ***(P-6034)***
City of Norco........D.......951 270-5617
2870 Clark Ave Norco (92860) ***(P-27030)***
City of Norwalk, Norwalk *Also called Norwalk Transit System* ***(P-3572)***
City of Oakland........B.......510 238-6796
150 Frank H Ogawa Plz # 3332 Oakland (94612) ***(P-23012)***
City of Oakland........E.......510 238-3494
250 Frank H Ogawa Plz # 6300 Oakland (94612) ***(P-18661)***
City of Oakland........E.......510 268-9000
519 18th St Oakland (94612) ***(P-18662)***
City of Orange........D.......714 744-7264
230 E Chapman Ave Orange (92866) ***(P-23013)***
City of Orange........E.......714 744-7272
230 E Chapman Ave Orange (92866) ***(P-18663)***
City of Oxnard........D.......805 385-8019
350 N C St Oxnard (93030) ***(P-23014)***
City of Oxnard........D.......805 385-8136
251 S Hayes Ave Oxnard (93030) ***(P-6035)***
City of Oxnard........D.......805 385-7950
1060 Pacific Ave Oxnard (93030) ***(P-18325)***
City of Oxnard........D.......805 983-4653
2401 W Vineyard Ave Oxnard (93036) ***(P-18231)***
CITY OF OXNARD PERFORMING ARTS, Oxnard *Also called Oxnard Perfrmn Arts & Convtn* ***(P-16975)***
City of Pacifica-Vallemar........D.......650 738-7466
170 Santa Maria Ave Pacifica (94044) ***(P-23702)***
City of Palm Springs........D.......760 318-3800
3400 E Tahquitz Canyon Wa Palm Springs (92262) ***(P-4760)***
City of Palmdale........C.......661 267-5338
39101 3rd St E Palmdale (93550) ***(P-13878)***
City of Palo Alto........D.......650 329-2598
2501 Embarcadero Way Palo Alto (94303) ***(P-16698)***
City of Pasadena........D.......626 744-4311
117 E Colorado Blvd Pasadena (91105) ***(P-13879)***
City of Pasadena........D.......626 543-4708
1133 Rosemont Ave Pasadena (91103) ***(P-18232)***
City of Pomona........B.......909 397-5506
2040 W Holt Ave Fl 2 Pomona (91768) ***(P-24145)***
City of Pomona........C.......909 620-2361
636 W Monterey Ave Pomona (91768) ***(P-6182)***
City of Redlands (PA)........D.......909 798-7531
35 Cajon St Redlands (92373) ***(P-26183)***
City of Redlands........E.......909 798-7525
35 Cajon St Redlands (92373) ***(P-6183)***
City of Richmond........D.......510 620-6788
3230 Macdonald Ave Fl 2 Richmond (94804) ***(P-18664)***
City of Riverside........D.......951 346-4700
3485 Mission Inn Ave Riverside (92501) ***(P-16699)***

ALPHABETIC

Employee Codes: A=Over 500 employees, B=251-500
C=101-250, D=51-100, E=50
2020 Directory of California
Wholesalers and Services Companies
© Mergent Inc. 1-800-342-5647
1221

City of Salinas...D.......831 758-7233
426 Work St Salinas (93901) *(P-13880)*
City of San Diego...E.......619 533-3012
1010 2nd Ave Ste 800 San Diego (92101) *(P-27031)*
City of San Diego...D.......619 533-6518
202 C St Ms37c San Diego (92101) *(P-21461)*
City of San Jose...B.......408 277-5277
408 Almaden Blvd San Jose (95110) *(P-16700)*
City of San Jose...D.......408 794-6400
1300 Senter Rd San Jose (95112) *(P-24305)*
City of San Jose...B.......408 392-3600
1701 Arprt Blvd Ste B1130 San Jose (95110) *(P-4761)*
City of San Jose...C.......408 226-6765
200 Edenvale Ave San Jose (95136) *(P-12149)*
City of San Mateo...D.......650 522-7300
1949 Pacific Blvd San Mateo (94403) *(P-13881)*
City of Santa Clara...D.......408 615-3770
2600 Benton St Santa Clara (95051) *(P-3393)*
City of Santa Clara...E.......408 615-2300
1500 Warburton Ave Santa Clara (95050) *(P-5821)*
City of Santa Clara...C.......408 615-2046
1705 Martin Ave Santa Clara (95050) *(P-5822)*
City of Santa Clra Parks Svc, Santa Clara *Also called City of Santa Clara (P-3393)*
City of South Lake Tahoe...D.......530 542-6056
1180 Rufus Allen Blvd South Lake Tahoe (96150) *(P-18665)*
City of Sunnyvale...D.......408 730-7451
456 W Olive Ave Sunnyvale (94086) *(P-13170)*
City of Sunnyvale...C.......408 730-7510
221 Commercial St Sunnyvale (94085) *(P-16701)*
City of Torrance...D.......310 781-6901
20500 Madrona Ave Torrance (90503) *(P-18666)*
City of Tulare...D.......559 684-4200
3981 S K St Tulare (93274) *(P-6184)*
City of Vacaville...D.......707 449-6122
1100 Alamo Dr Vacaville (95687) *(P-23015)*
City of Vacaville...B.......707 449-5170
650 Merchant St Vacaville (95688) *(P-25006)*
City of Vallejo...B.......707 644-4000
1001 Fairgrounds Dr Vallejo (94589) *(P-18326)*
City of Visalia...D.......559 713-4000
303 E Acequia Ave Visalia (93291) *(P-16702)*
City of Vista...C.......760 940-9283
101 Wave Dr Vista (92083) *(P-18667)*
City of Whittier...D.......562 567-9446
7630 Washington Ave Whittier (90602) *(P-23016)*
City of Woodland...C.......530 661-5878
2001 East St Woodland (95776) *(P-18668)*
City of Woodland...C.......530 661-5962
655 N Pioneer Ave Woodland (95776) *(P-26935)*
City of Woodland...D.......530 661-5961
42929 County Road 24 Woodland (95776) *(P-25007)*
City Orange Police Assn Inc...C.......714 457-5340
1107 N Batavia St Orange (92867) *(P-24331)*
City Park, San Francisco *Also called Imperial Parking (us) LLC (P-17254)*
City Rescue Mission, San Diego *Also called San Diego Rescue Mission Inc (P-24223)*
City Rise Inc (PA)...C.......209 333-0807
1225 S Sacramento St Lodi (95240) *(P-16703)*
City Rise Services, Lodi *Also called City Rise Inc (P-16703)*
City Security Co Inc...D.......626 458-2325
430 S Grfield Ave Ste 401 Alhambra (91801) *(P-16232)*
City Service Contracting Inc (PA)...D.......714 632-6610
920 Lawrence St Placentia (92870) *(P-1685)*
City Service Paving, Placentia *Also called City Service Contracting Inc (P-1685)*
City Towel & Dust Service Inc...E.......707 542-0391
3016 Dutton Ave Santa Rosa (95407) *(P-13219)*
City Wire Cloth, Fontana *Also called Daniel Gerard Worldwide Inc (P-7059)*
Citywide Plumbing Heating...E.......619 231-2022
9825 Carroll Centre Rd San Diego (92126) *(P-2096)*
Civco, Rcho STA Marg *Also called Capital Invstmnts Vntures Corp (P-24392)*
Civic Auditorium, Santa Monica *Also called Santa Monica City of (P-10641)*
CIVIC THEATRE, San Diego *Also called San Diego Theatres Inc (P-10640)*
Civicactions Inc...D.......510 408-7510
3470 Shangri La Rd Lafayette (94549) *(P-15959)*
Civicorps...C.......510 992-7800
6315 San Leandro St Oakland (94621) *(P-6185)*
Civil Service Commission, Oakland *Also called County of Alameda (P-26569)*
Cixta Enterprises Inc...C.......818 346-1665
21208 Sherman Way Canoga Park (91303) *(P-8556)*
CJ America Inc (HQ)...D.......213 427-5566
5700 Wilshire Blvd # 540 Los Angeles (90036) *(P-8557)*
CJ Construction & Dev Inc...D.......760 247-6868
78206 Varner Rd Ste D Palm Desert (92211) *(P-1233)*
CJ Model Home Maintenance Inc...D.......925 485-3280
240 Spring St Pleasanton (94566) *(P-13882)*
CJJ Farming Inc...E.......805 739-1723
125 W Mill St Santa Maria (93458) *(P-90)*
CK Enterprises Inc...D.......760 967-8863
102 Copperwood Way Ste H Oceanside (92058) *(P-16704)*
CK Franchising Inc (HQ)...D.......800 498-8144
1 Park Plz Ste 300 Irvine (92614) *(P-21708)*
Ckl Construction Inc...B.......408 244-7042
967 W Hedding St San Jose (95126) *(P-1234)*
Cks Business Services, Bakersfield *Also called Cbizmhm LLC (P-25551)*
CL Knox Inc...D.......661 837-0477
34933 Imperial St Bakersfield (93308) *(P-1016)*
Claimremedi Inc...D.......707 827-1274
2235 Mercury Way Ste 107 Santa Rosa (95407) *(P-13707)*
Claims Management Inc...C.......916 631-1250
1101 Crksde Rdge Dr 100 Roseville (95678) *(P-10320)*
Clairemont Healthcare...D.......858 278-4750
8060 Frost St San Diego (92123) *(P-19802)*
Clara Baldwin Stocker Home...E.......626 962-7151
527 S Valinda Ave West Covina (91790) *(P-19803)*
Clarbec Inc...E.......707 996-4012
19368 Orange Ave Sonoma (95476) *(P-123)*
Clare Matrix (PA)...D.......310 314-6200
2644 30th St Ste 100 Santa Monica (90405) *(P-23017)*
Clare Foundation Inc...D.......310 314-6200
1871 9th St Santa Monica (90404) *(P-23018)*
Clare Matrix...D.......310 478-6006
1849 Sawtelle Blvd # 670 Los Angeles (90025) *(P-21462)*
Claremont Club, The, Claremont *Also called Claremont Tennis Club (P-18424)*
Claremont Country Club...D.......510 653-6789
5295 Broadway Ter Oakland (94618) *(P-18423)*
Claremont Hotel Club & Spa, Berkeley *Also called Claremont Ht Prpts Ltd Partnr (P-12150)*
Claremont House Incorporated...D.......510 658-9266
4500 Gilbert St Oakland (94611) *(P-23867)*
Claremont Ht Prpts Ltd Partnr...A.......510 843-3000
41 Tunnel Rd Berkeley (94705) *(P-12150)*
Claremont Manor, Claremont *Also called Front Porch Communities (P-20558)*
Claremont Outpatient Clinic, Claremont *Also called Pomona Valley Hospital Med Ctr (P-21103)*
Claremont Resort, Berkeley *Also called Interstate Hotels Resorts Inc (P-26268)*
Claremont Retirement MGT, Oakland *Also called Claremont House Incorporated (P-23867)*
Claremont Star LP...E.......909 482-0124
555 W Foothill Blvd Claremont (91711) *(P-12151)*
Claremont Tennis Club...C.......909 625-9515
1777 Monte Vista Ave Claremont (91711) *(P-18424)*
Clarendon Specialty Fas Inc...D.......714 842-2603
16761 Burke Ln Huntington Beach (92647) *(P-7389)*
Clarient Diagnostic Svcs Inc...B.......888 443-3310
31 Columbia Aliso Viejo (92656) *(P-21513)*
Clarion Construction Inc...E.......909 598-4060
21067 Commerce Point Dr Walnut (91789) *(P-1340)*
Clarion Corporation America (HQ)...D.......310 327-9100
6200 Gateway Dr Cypress (90630) *(P-7199)*
Clarion Hotel, Anaheim *Also called Comfort California Inc (P-12167)*
Clarion Hotel, Ridgecrest *Also called Peekay Investments Prpts LLC (P-12747)*
Clarion Hotel San Jose Airport...D.......408 453-5340
1355 N 4th St San Jose (95112) *(P-12152)*
Claris International Inc (HQ)...C.......408 987-7000
5201 Patrick Henry Dr Santa Clara (95054) *(P-14713)*
Clarizen Inc...D.......866 502-9813
2755 Campus Dr Ste 300 San Mateo (94403) *(P-26184)*
Clark Richardson and Biskup...D.......760 496-3714
3207 Grey Hawk Ct Ste 150 Carlsbad (92010) *(P-25008)*
Clark & Sullivan Builders Inc...C.......916 338-7707
2024 Opportunity Dr # 150 Roseville (95678) *(P-1447)*
Clark - Pacific Corporation (PA)...B.......916 371-0305
1980 S River Rd West Sacramento (95691) *(P-6674)*
Clark Bros Farming Inc...E.......209 392-6144
19772 State Highway 33 Dos Palos (93620) *(P-11)*
Clark Cnstr Group-California...B.......714 754-0764
18201 Von Karman Ave # 800 Irvine (92612) *(P-1341)*
Clark Cnstr Grup-California LP...B.......714 429-9779
18201 Von Karman Ave Irvine (92612) *(P-1448)*
Clark Pacific, West Sacramento *Also called Clark - Pacific Corporation (P-6674)*
Clark Pest Ctrl Stockton Inc (HQ)...D.......209 368-7152
555 N Guild Ave Lodi (95240) *(P-13811)*
Clark Pest Ctrl Stockton Inc...D.......209 524-6384
480 E Service Rd Modesto (95358) *(P-13812)*
Clark Pest Ctrl Stockton Inc...D.......916 925-7000
5822 Roseville Rd Sacramento (95842) *(P-13813)*
Clark Pest Ctrl Stockton Inc...E.......707 446-9748
811 U Banks Vacaville (95688) *(P-13814)*
Clark Pest Ctrl Stockton Inc...E.......209 474-3204
4816 Clowes St Stockton (95210) *(P-13815)*
Clark Pest Ctrl Stockton Inc...D.......925 449-6203
2313 Research Dr Livermore (94550) *(P-13816)*
Clark Pest Ctrl Stockton Inc...E.......916 635-7770
11285 White Rock Rd Rancho Cordova (95742) *(P-13817)*
Clark Plumbing Co, Van Nuys *Also called Valley Clark Plbg & Htg Co Inc (P-2309)*
Clarklift-West Inc...C.......916 381-5674
4750 Illinois Ave Fair Oaks (95628) *(P-7537)*
Claro Pool Services Inc...D.......760 341-3377
42161 Beacon Hl Palm Desert (92211) *(P-3394)*
Class, San Mateo *Also called Center For Learning and (P-22980)*
Class Act Hair & Nail Salon...D.......530 223-3442
2795 Bechelli Ln Redding (96002) *(P-13336)*
Classic, Torrance *Also called I C Class Components Corp (P-7281)*
Classic Bowling Center, Daly City *Also called Bdp Bowl Inc (P-18024)*
Classic Car Wash Inc (PA)...C.......408 371-2414
871 E Hamilton Ave Ste C Campbell (95008) *(P-17369)*
Classic Collision Center 2, Los Angeles *Also called Caliber Holdings Corporation (P-17287)*
Classic Custom Vacations, San Jose *Also called Classic Vacations LLC (P-4850)*
Classic Custom Vacations Inc...C.......800 221-3949
5893 Rue Ferrari San Jose (95138) *(P-4849)*
Classic Distrg & Bev Group Inc...B.......626 934-3700
120 Puente Ave City of Industry (91746) *(P-8754)*
Classic Hardwood Floors, San Diego *Also called Davenport Development Corp (P-2998)*
Classic Installs Inc...D.......951 678-9906
22475 Baxter Rd Wildomar (92595) *(P-3358)*
Classic Park Lane Partnership...D.......831 373-0101
200 Glenwood Cir Ofc Monterey (93940) *(P-10711)*
Classic Parking Inc...A.......408 278-1444
34 S Autumn St San Jose (95110) *(P-17252)*
Classic Party Rentals, Sonoma *Also called CP Opco LLC (P-14144)*

Mergent e-mail: customerrelations@mergent.com
1222
2020 Directory of California
Wholesalers and Services Companies
(P-0000) Products & Services Section entry number
(PA)=Parent Co (HQ)=Headquarters (DH)=Div Headquarters

Classic Party Rentals, San Diego *Also called CP Opco LLC (P-14145)*
Classic Party Rentals, Los Angeles *Also called CP Opco LLC (P-14146)*
Classic Party Rentals, Inglewood *Also called CP Opco LLC (P-13415)*
Classic Party Rentals, Los Angeles *Also called CP Opco LLC (P-14147)*
Classic Party Rentals, Sonoma *Also called CP Opco LLC (P-14148)*
Classic Party Rentals, Carpinteria *Also called CP Opco LLC (P-14149)*
Classic Party Rentals, Santa Ana *Also called CP Opco LLC (P-14150)*
Classic Protection Inc....E....213 742-1238
3208 Royal St Los Angeles (90007) ***(P-16233)***
Classic Riverdale Inc....D....831 373-0101
200 Glenwood Cir Monterey (93940) ***(P-12153)***
Classic Rsdence Mgt Ltd Partnr....D....831 373-0101
200 Glenwood Cir Ofc Monterey (93940) ***(P-12154)***
Classic Soft Trim Inc....D....510 782-4911
3201 Diablo Ave Hayward (94545) ***(P-8960)***
Classic Tile & Mosaic Inc (PA)....D....310 538-9605
14463 S Broadway Gardena (90248) ***(P-6675)***
Classic Vacations LLC....C....800 221-3949
5893 Rue Ferrari San Jose (95138) ***(P-4850)***
Classified Advertising....D....805 564-5200
715 Anacapa St Santa Barbara (93101) ***(P-8868)***
Classmates Media Corporation....B....818 287-3600
21301 Burbank Blvd Woodland Hills (91367) ***(P-13409)***
Claud Townsley Inc....D....310 527-6770
555 W 182nd St Gardena (90248) ***(P-3037)***
Claude Laval Corporation....D....559 255-1601
1365 N Clovis Ave Fresno (93727) ***(P-7538)***
Claudia Richard Inc....D....323 264-3915
4871 S Santa Fe Ave Vernon (90058) ***(P-8065)***
Clauss Construction....D....619 390-4940
9911 Maine Ave Lakeside (92040) ***(P-3338)***
Clay Dunn Enterprises Inc....C....310 549-1698
1606 E Carson St Carson (90745) ***(P-2097)***
Clay Lacy Aviation Inc (PA)....B....818 989-2900
7435 Valjean Ave Van Nuys (91406) ***(P-4762)***
Clay Miranda Trucking Inc....D....559 275-6250
3220 W Belmont Ave Fresno (93722) ***(P-3866)***
Clayton Group Services, Santa Ana *Also called Bureau Veritas North Amer Inc (P-27007)*
CLC Incorporated (PA)....E....916 789-7600
3001 Lava Ridge Ct # 250 Roseville (95661) ***(P-14246)***
Clean Energy....A....949 437-1000
4675 Macarthur Ct Ste 800 Newport Beach (92660) ***(P-5969)***
Clean Energy Fuels Corp (PA)....C....949 437-1000
4675 Macarthur Ct Ste 800 Newport Beach (92660) ***(P-6001)***
Clean Enviroment....D....619 521-0543
4570 Alvarado Canyon Rd C San Diego (92120) ***(P-17490)***
Clean Harbors Envmtl Svcs Inc....D....707 747-6699
4101 Industrial Way Benicia (94510) ***(P-27032)***
Clean Hrbors Es Indus Svcs Inc....D....707 745-1581
4501 California Ct Benicia (94510) ***(P-17491)***
Clean King Laundry Systems Inc....E....818 363-5500
15431 Chatsworth St Mission Hills (91345) ***(P-13246)***
Clean Power Finance Inc....C....899 525-2123
50 Osgood Pl Ste 400 San Francisco (94133) ***(P-17492)***
Clean-A-Rama Maint Svc LLC....D....415 495-5298
526 Columbus Ave Fl 2 San Francisco (94133) ***(P-13883)***
CLEANERIFIC, San Francisco *Also called Jewish Family and Chld Svcs (P-23294)*
Cleaning Services....E....408 778-9251
7828 Monterey St Gilroy (95020) ***(P-17493)***
Cleanrite Inc....D....916 381-1321
5430 Florin Perkins Rd Sacramento (95826) ***(P-13818)***
Cleanstreet....C....310 329-3078
1937 W 169th St Gardena (90247) ***(P-6342)***
Cleantech Environmental, Irwindale *Also called Agritec International Ltd (P-7796)*
Clear Channel Riverside, Riverside *Also called Iheartcommunications Inc (P-5535)*
Clear Credit Capital, Agoura Hills *Also called Quality Home Loans (P-9597)*
Clear World Communications....B....714 445-3900
3100 S Harbor Blvd # 300 Santa Ana (92704) ***(P-5375)***
Clearbalance Holdings LLC....E....858 535-0870
3636 Nobel Dr Ste 250 San Diego (92122) ***(P-11651)***
Clearcapitalcom Inc....C....530 550-2500
10266 Truckee Airport Rd Truckee (96161) ***(P-11018)***
Clearcapitalcom Inc....D....530 582-5011
1410 Rocky Ridge Dr # 250 Roseville (95661) ***(P-11019)***
Clearcaptions LLC....E....866 868-8695
3001 Lava Ridge Ct # 100 Roseville (95661) ***(P-5376)***
Clearesult Consulting Inc....D....415 848-1250
1 Sansome St Fl 35 San Francisco (94104) ***(P-27033)***
Clearlake Capital Group LP (PA)....B....310 400-8800
233 Wilshire Blvd Ste 800 Santa Monica (90401) ***(P-11901)***
Clearlake Family Health Center, Clearlake *Also called Adventist Health System/West (P-20734)*
Clearpath Lending....C....949 502-3577
15635 Alton Pkwy Ste 300 Irvine (92618) ***(P-9618)***
Clearpath Management Group Inc (PA)....B....209 239-8700
1215 W Center St Ste 102 Manteca (95337) ***(P-14487)***
Clearpath Workforce MGT Inc....B....209 239-8700
1215 W Center St Ste 102 Manteca (95337) ***(P-14488)***
Clearslide Inc (HQ)....D....877 360-3366
45 Fremont St Fl 32 San Francisco (94105) ***(P-15282)***
Clearview Capital LLC....A....310 806-9555
12100 Wilshire Blvd # 800 Los Angeles (90025) ***(P-11902)***
Clearwell Systems Inc....C....877 253-2793
350 Ellis St Mountain View (94043) ***(P-15283)***
Clement Chen & Associates, San Mateo *Also called Pacific Hotel Management LLC (P-12690)*
Clement Preschool, Saratoga *Also called Precious Enterprises Inc (P-23777)*
Clement Support Services Inc....D....408 227-1171
1001 Yosemite Dr Milpitas (95035) ***(P-7054)***
Clendenen Vineyard MGT LLC....D....707 473-0881
9235 W Dry Creek Rd Healdsburg (95448) ***(P-124)***
Cleveland Marble LP....E....714 998-3280
219 E Bristol Ln Orange (92865) ***(P-2708)***
Cli, Indio *Also called Commercial Lighting Inds Inc (P-7136)*
Click Labs Inc....A....415 658-5227
315 Montgomery St Fl 8 San Francisco (94104) ***(P-14714)***
Clicksafetycom Inc (HQ)....E....800 971-1080
2185 N Calif Blvd Ste 425 Walnut Creek (94596) ***(P-27034)***
Clif Bar & Company (PA)....C....510 596-6300
1451 66th St Emeryville (94608) ***(P-8558)***
Cliff House Restaurant, Fort Bragg *Also called Tradewinds Lodge (P-13035)*
Cliff View Terrace Inc....D....805 682-7443
623 W Junipero St Santa Barbara (93105) ***(P-23868)***
Clifford & Brown A Prof Corp....D....661 322-6023
1430 Truxtun Ave Ste 900 Bakersfield (93301) ***(P-22422)***
Clift Hotel Four Season, San Francisco *Also called Morgans Hotel Group MGT LLC (P-12633)*
Clift Hotels, San Francisco *Also called 495 Geary LLC (P-11983)*
Cliftonlarsonallen LLP....B....916 784-7800
925 Highland Pointe Dr # 450 Roseville (95678) ***(P-25556)***
Cliftonlarsonallen LLP....D....626 857-7300
2210 E Route 66 Ste 100 Glendora (91740) ***(P-25557)***
Cliftonlarsonallen LLP....D....310 273-2501
1925 Century Park E Fl 16 Los Angeles (90067) ***(P-25558)***
Clima-Tech Inc....D....909 613-5513
1820 Town And Country Dr Norco (92860) ***(P-17444)***
Climate Corporation (HQ)....D....415 363-0500
201 3rd St Ste 1100 San Francisco (94103) ***(P-655)***
Climatec LLC....E....858 391-7000
13715 Stowe Dr Poway (92064) ***(P-2453)***
Clinapps Inc....D....858 866-0228
9530 Towne Centre Dr # 120 San Diego (92121) ***(P-14715)***
Clinic Business, San Diego *Also called Scripps Health (P-19386)*
Clinic Inc....D....323 730-1920
3834 S Western Ave Los Angeles (90062) ***(P-18899)***
Clinica Medica Familiar....D....714 541-0870
517 N Main St Ste 100 Santa Ana (92701) ***(P-18900)***
Clinica Msr Oscar A Romero (PA)....D....213 989-7700
123 S Alvarado St Los Angeles (90057) ***(P-18901)***
Clinica Popular Medical Group....E....213 381-7175
101 S Rossmore Ave Los Angeles (90004) ***(P-18902)***
Clinica Sagrado Corazon....E....714 491-7777
831 S Harbor Blvd Anaheim (92805) ***(P-18903)***
Clinica Sierra Vista....D....559 457-6900
3727 N 1st St Ste 106 Fresno (93726) ***(P-23019)***
Clinica Sierra Vista....E....661 326-6490
1430 Truxtun Ave Ste 300 Bakersfield (93301) ***(P-22208)***
Clinica Sierra Vista (PA)....D....661 635-3050
1430 Truxtun Ave Ste 400 Bakersfield (93301) ***(P-18904)***
Clinica Sierra Vista....D....559 457-5292
1945 N Fine Ave Ste 100 Fresno (93727) ***(P-18905)***
Clinicas De Slud Del Peblo Inc (PA)....D....760 344-9951
1166 K St Brawley (92227) ***(P-18906)***
Clinicas De Slud Del Peblo Inc....D....760 344-6471
900 Main St Brawley (92227) ***(P-18907)***
Clinicas Del Camino Real Inc....D....805 487-5351
650 Meta St Oxnard (93030) ***(P-21982)***
Clinicas Del Camino Real Inc (PA)....C....805 647-6322
200 S Wells Rd Ste 200 # 200 Ventura (93004) ***(P-21983)***
Clinicomp International Inc (PA)....D....858 546-8202
9655 Towne Centre Dr San Diego (92121) ***(P-15572)***
Clinics On Demand Inc....D....310 709-7355
11000 Wilshire Blvd Los Angeles (90024) ***(P-21709)***
Clipper Corporation (PA)....E....310 533-8585
21124 Figueroa St Carson (90745) ***(P-6923)***
Clm Services, Palo Alto *Also called California Land Mgt Svcs Corp (P-18641)*
Clocktower Inn....D....805 652-0141
181 E Santa Clara St Ventura (93001) ***(P-12155)***
Cloisters Mssion Hills Hosp HM, San Diego *Also called Mission Hills Post Acute Care (P-23995)*
Cloisters of La Jolla Inc....D....858 459-4361
7160 Fay Ave La Jolla (92037) ***(P-19804)***
Clontech, Mountain View *Also called Takara Bio Usa Inc (P-25847)*
Clorox Services Company (HQ)....D....510 271-7000
1221 Broadway Fl 13 Oakland (94612) ***(P-26185)***
Closet World Inc....B....626 855-0846
14438 Don Julian Rd City of Industry (91746) ***(P-2919)***
Closet World, The, City of Industry *Also called Home Organizers Inc (P-2941)*
Closingcorp Inc....D....858 551-1500
3111 Camino Del Rio N # 200 San Diego (92108) ***(P-15960)***
Cloud Automation Division, Aliso Viejo *Also called Quest Software Inc (P-15483)*
Cloudera Inc (PA)....C....650 362-0488
395 Page Mill Rd Ste 300 Palo Alto (94306) ***(P-14716)***
Cloudflare Inc (PA)....C....888 993-5273
101 Townsend St San Francisco (94107) ***(P-15284)***
Cloudpeople Global....E....530 591-7028
2485 Notre Dame Blvd Chico (95928) ***(P-14717)***
Cloudradiant Corp (PA)....C....408 256-1527
12 Fuchsia Lake Forest (92630) ***(P-8961)***
Cloudradiant Corp....A....408 256-1527
1111 Di Napoli Dr San Jose (95129) ***(P-8962)***
Cloudstaff LLC (PA)....D....888 551-5339
1165 E San Antonio Dr D Long Beach (90807) ***(P-14247)***
Cloudtech Incorporated....C....213 230-2616
601 S Figueroa St 40501 Los Angeles (90017) ***(P-15961)***

Cloudtrigger Inc....D....858 367-5272
760 Garden View Ct # 120 Encinitas (92024) ***(P-26558)***
Cloudvirga Inc....D....949 662-2944
5291 California Ave # 300 Irvine (92617) ***(P-14718)***
Clover Network Inc....D....650 210-7888
415 N Mathilda Ave Sunnyvale (94085) ***(P-5377)***
Clover Sonoma, Petaluma *Also called Clover-Stornetta Farms Inc* ***(P-8559)***
Clover-Stornetta Farms Inc (PA)....C....707 769-3282
1800 S Mcdowell Blvd Petaluma (94954) ***(P-8559)***
Cloverdale Healthcare Center, Cloverdale *Also called Ensign Cloverdale LLC* ***(P-19880)***
Cloverleaf Bowl, Fremont *Also called Fremont Sports Inc* ***(P-18034)***
Clovis Community Living, Fresno *Also called Community Medical Center* ***(P-20800)***
Clovis Community Medical Ctr, Clovis *Also called Fresno Cmnty Hosp & Med Ctr* ***(P-20881)***
Clovis Custom Drywall Inc....E....559 297-7073
141 Sunnyside Ave Ste 108 Clovis (93611) ***(P-2771)***
Clovis Unified School District....A....559 327-3900
885 Gettysburg Ave Clovis (93612) ***(P-17878)***
Clp Resources Inc....E....415 508-0910
1485 Bay Shore Blvd # 138 San Francisco (94124) ***(P-14489)***
Clp Resources Inc....E....707 569-0200
1260 N Dutton Ave Santa Rosa (95401) ***(P-14490)***
Clp Resources Inc....D....916 788-0300
1000 Sunrise Ave Ste 8a Roseville (95661) ***(P-14491)***
Clp Resources Inc....C....650 261-2100
570 El Cmino Real Ste 170 Redwood City (94063) ***(P-14492)***
Clp Resources Inc....E....415 446-7000
4460 Redwood Hwy Ste 14 San Rafael (94903) ***(P-14493)***
Clp Resources Inc....D....714 300-0510
741 E Ball Rd Ste 100 Anaheim (92805) ***(P-14494)***
Clp Resources Inc....D....818 260-9190
111 N First St Ste 100 Burbank (91502) ***(P-14495)***
Cls Landscape Management Inc....B....909 628-3005
4329 State St Ste A Montclair (91763) ***(P-936)***
Cls Trnsprttion Los Angles LLC (HQ)....C....310 414-8189
600 S Allied Way El Segundo (90245) ***(P-3662)***
Club Assist North America Inc (HQ)....D....213 388-4333
888 W 6th St Ste 300 Los Angeles (90017) ***(P-6429)***
Club Assist US LLC....C....213 388-4333
888 W 6th St Ste 300 Los Angeles (90017) ***(P-6430)***
Club At Los Gatos Inc....D....408 867-5110
14428 Big Basin Way Ste A Saratoga (95070) ***(P-18131)***
Club At Shnndoah Sprng Vlg Inc....E....760 343-3497
32700 Desert Moon Dr Thousand Palms (92276) ***(P-18425)***
Club of Sunrise Country....D....760 328-6549
71601 Country Club Dr Rancho Mirage (92270) ***(P-18426)***
Club One At Petaluma....D....707 766-8080
1201 Redwood Way Petaluma (94954) ***(P-18427)***
Club One Casino Inc....B....559 497-3000
1033 Van Ness Ave Fresno (93721) ***(P-12156)***
Club Quarters San Francisco....D....415 268-3606
424 Clay St San Francisco (94111) ***(P-12157)***
Club Sport of Fremont....C....510 226-8500
46650 Landing Pkwy Fremont (94538) ***(P-16705)***
Clubcorp Usa Inc....C....858 756-2471
5690 Cancha De Golf Rancho Santa Fe (92091) ***(P-18428)***
Clubcorp Usa Inc....E....916 434-9100
1525 Highway 193 Lincoln (95648) ***(P-18233)***
Clubsport of Fremont, Fremont *Also called Leisure Sports Inc* ***(P-18169)***
Clubsport of Pleasanton, Pleasanton *Also called Cs-Pleasanton LLC* ***(P-18439)***
Clubsport San Ramon LLC....C....925 283-4000
4000 Mt Diablo Blvd Lafayette (94549) ***(P-18132)***
Clubsport San Ramon LLC (PA)....B....925 735-1182
350 Bollinger Canyon Ln San Ramon (94582) ***(P-18133)***
Clum Morford Distributing (PA)....D....831 333-1100
20 Ragsdale Dr Ste 100 Monterey (93940) ***(P-16706)***
Clutter Inc (PA)....C....800 805-4023
3526 Hayden Ave Culver City (90232) ***(P-13410)***
Clyde & Co US LLP....D....415 365-9800
101 2nd St Fl 24 San Francisco (94105) ***(P-22423)***
Clyde Miles Cnstr Co Inc....D....925 427-4473
1110 Burnett Ave Ste C Concord (94520) ***(P-1105)***
CM Laundry LLC....D....310 436-6170
14919 S Figueroa St Gardena (90248) ***(P-13319)***
CM Wind Down Topco Inc....D....415 995-6800
750 Battery St Ste 300 San Francisco (94111) ***(P-5518)***
CMA Fire Protection (PA)....D....661 322-9344
4300 Stine Rd Ste 800 Bakersfield (93313) ***(P-2098)***
Cmac Cnstr Refinery & Pipeline, Long Beach *Also called Cmac Construction Company* ***(P-1845)***
Cmac Construction Company....D....562 435-5611
1450 Santa Fe Ave Long Beach (90813) ***(P-1845)***
Cmat, Stockton *Also called California Materials Inc* ***(P-3860)***
Cmb Laboratory, Cypress *Also called Consoldted Med Bo-Analysis Inc* ***(P-21515)***
CMC Rebar Fabricators, Bloomington *Also called C M C Steel Fabricators Inc* ***(P-3257)***
CMC Rebar West, San Diego *Also called CMC Steel Fabricators Inc* ***(P-1342)***
CMC Steel Fabricators Inc (HQ)....E....858 737-7700
3880 Murphy Canyon Rd # 100 San Diego (92123) ***(P-1342)***
CMC Steel Fabricators Inc....D....909 713-1130
5425 Industrial Pkwy San Bernardino (92407) ***(P-7055)***
Cmf Inc....D....714 637-2409
1317 W Grove Ave Orange (92865) ***(P-3038)***
Cmg Financial Services....D....925 983-3073
3160 Crow Canyon Rd # 400 San Ramon (94583) ***(P-16707)***
Cmg Mortgage Inc (PA)....B....619 554-1327
3160 Crow Canyon Rd # 400 San Ramon (94583) ***(P-9619)***
CMI Management Inc....C....323 465-8044
5640 Santa Monica Blvd # 116 Los Angeles (90038) ***(P-26559)***
Cmp Film & Design Burbank LLC....D....818 729-0800
2717 W Olive Ave Burbank (91505) ***(P-26904)***
Cmp Wellness LLC....D....323 697-8808
1732 Aviation Blvd 317 Redondo Beach (90278) ***(P-24146)***
Cmre Financial Services Inc....B....714 528-3200
3075 E Imperial Hwy # 200 Brea (92821) ***(P-13675)***
CMS, Simi Valley *Also called Computerized Mgt Svcs Inc* ***(P-25562)***
CMS Llnl....E....925 422-5584
7000 East Ave Msl090 Livermore (94550) ***(P-17730)***
Cmsc, San Francisco *Also called Costless Maintenance Svcs Co* ***(P-13895)***
Cmtc, Torrance *Also called California Mfg Tech Consulting* ***(P-24982)***
CNA Financial Corporation....C....714 255-2200
1800 E Imperial Hwy # 200 Brea (92821) ***(P-10321)***
CNA Insurance, Brea *Also called CNA Financial Corporation* ***(P-10321)***
CNA Surety Corporation....D....619 682-3550
1455 Frazee Rd Ste 801 San Diego (92108) ***(P-10322)***
Cncml A California Ltd Partnr....D....530 583-1578
1920 Squaw Valley Rd Olympic Valley (96146) ***(P-12158)***
Cnet Express....C....949 357-5475
15134 Indiana Ave Apt 38 Paramount (90723) ***(P-3867)***
Cnet Networks Inc....A....415 344-2000
235 2nd St San Francisco (94105) ***(P-15573)***
Cnet Technology Corporation (HQ)....C....408 392-9966
26291 Prod Ave Ste 205 Hayward (94545) ***(P-7252)***
Cnh Industrial America LLC....E....510 351-2015
1919 Williams St San Leandro (94577) ***(P-7469)***
Cni Thl Ops LLC....D....408 943-0600
1801 Barber Ln Milpitas (95035) ***(P-12159)***
Cni Thl Propco Fe LLC....D....661 325-9700
5101 California Ave Bakersfield (93309) ***(P-12160)***
Cnn America Inc....D....323 993-5000
6430 W Sunset Blvd # 300 Los Angeles (90028) ***(P-5673)***
Cnrc LLC....D....760 325-2937
2299 N Indian Ave Palm Springs (92262) ***(P-19805)***
Cns Logistics Inc....D....562 229-1133
108 W Walnut St Ste 270 Gardena (90248) ***(P-4915)***
Cntry Vlla Merced Hlthcre Cntr, Merced *Also called Country Villa Service Corp* ***(P-23057)***
CNX Media Inc....D....415 229-8300
1 Beach St Ste 300 San Francisco (94133) ***(P-17591)***
Co D L Pham MD....E....714 531-2091
10362 Bolsa Ave Ste 110 Westminster (92683) ***(P-18908)***
Co-Op Network, Rancho Cucamonga *Also called CU Cooperative Systems Inc* ***(P-9430)***
Co-Optimum, Sherman Oaks *Also called Ansira Partners Inc* ***(P-16625)***
Co-Production Intl Inc....A....619 429-4344
8716 Sherwood Ter San Diego (92154) ***(P-26560)***
Co-Sales, Pleasanton *Also called Impact Group LLC* ***(P-8182)***
Coa Inc (PA)....C....562 944-7899
12928 Sandoval St Santa Fe Springs (90670) ***(P-6550)***
Coach Bus Lines, San Francisco *Also called Cusa Fl LLC* ***(P-3773)***
Coach Usa Inc....C....714 978-8855
2001 S Manchester Ave Anaheim (92802) ***(P-3772)***
Coachella Valley Water Dst (PA)....A....760 398-2651
85995 Avenue 52 Coachella (92236) ***(P-6036)***
Coachella Valley Water Dst....C....760 398-2651
75515 Hovley Ln E Palm Desert (92211) ***(P-6037)***
Coachella Valley Water Dst....C....760 398-2651
75 525 Hovley Ln Palm Desert (92260) ***(P-6038)***
Coachella Vly Rescue Mission....E....760 347-3512
82873 Via Venecia Indio (92201) ***(P-23020)***
Coact Designworks....E....916 930-5900
3348 Montclaire St Sacramento (95821) ***(P-25428)***
Coadna Holdings Inc....D....408 736-1100
1020 Stewart Dr Sunnyvale (94085) ***(P-11652)***
Coalinga Dstngished Cmnty Care....D....559 935-5939
834 Maple Rd Coalinga (93210) ***(P-19806)***
Coalinga Regional Medical Cent....C....559 935-6400
1191 Phelps Ave Coalinga (93210) ***(P-20794)***
Coalinga State Hospital, Coalinga *Also called Califrnia Dept State Hospitals* ***(P-21387)***
Coalition For Family Harmony....D....805 983-6014
1030 N Ventura Rd Oxnard (93030) ***(P-23021)***
Coan Construction Co Inc....D....909 868-6812
1481 E Grand Ave Pomona (91766) ***(P-3128)***
Coassure Inc....D....408 244-0400
4100 Moorpark Ave Ste 122 San Jose (95117) ***(P-27035)***
Coast Alum & Architectural Inc (PA)....C....562 946-6061
10628 Fulton Wells Ave Santa Fe Springs (90670) ***(P-7056)***
Coast Building Products, San Jose *Also called Coast Insulation Contrs Inc* ***(P-2772)***
Coast Building Products, Salinas *Also called Superior Contracting Corp* ***(P-2864)***
Coast Capital, San Jose *Also called ECi Corporation A Corp Nev* ***(P-9546)***
Coast Carwash LP....E....562 961-5555
5677 E 7th St Long Beach (90804) ***(P-17370)***
Coast Central Credit Union (PA)....C....707 445-8801
2650 Harrison Ave Eureka (95501) ***(P-9302)***
Coast Citrus Distributors (PA)....D....619 661-7950
7597 Bristow Ct San Diego (92154) ***(P-8446)***
Coast Citrus Distributors....C....213 955-3444
1601 E Olympic Blvd Los Angeles (90021) ***(P-8447)***
Coast Citrus Distributors....E....650 588-0707
131 Terminal Ct 13 South San Francisco (94080) ***(P-8448)***
Coast Counties Peterbilt, San Leandro *Also called Coast Counties Truck & Eqp Co* ***(P-6388)***
Coast Counties Truck & Eqp Co....D....510 568-6933
260 Doolittle Dr San Leandro (94577) ***(P-6388)***
Coast Environmental Inc....D....760 929-9570
2221 Las Palmas Dr Ste J Carlsbad (92011) ***(P-16708)***
Coast Hand Car Wash, Long Beach *Also called Coast Carwash LP* ***(P-17370)***
Coast Insulation Contrs Inc (HQ)....D....386 304-2222
1341 Old Oakland Rd San Jose (95112) ***(P-2772)***

Coast Iron & Steel Co ....E....562 946-4421
12300 Lakeland Rd Santa Fe Springs (90670) ***(P-3261)***
Coast Landscape Management, Alviso *Also called Bayscape Management Inc* ***(P-701)***
Coast Nurseries Inc (PA) ....C....805 386-4253
5870 E Los Angeles Ave Somis (93066) ***(P-235)***
Coast Personnel Services Inc (PA) ....A....408 653-2100
2295 De La Cruz Blvd Santa Clara (95050) ***(P-14248)***
Coast Plaza Doctors Hospital (PA) ....D....562 868-3751
13100 Studebaker Rd Norwalk (90650) ***(P-20795)***
Coast Plaza Hospital, Norwalk *Also called Cph Hospital Management LLC* ***(P-20823)***
Coast Produce Company (PA) ....C....213 955-4900
1791 Bay St Los Angeles (90021) ***(P-8449)***
Coast To Coast Bus Eqp Inc (PA) ....D....949 457-7300
8 Vanderbilt Ste 200 Irvine (92618) ***(P-6745)***
Coast To Coast Realty ....D....818 360-2609
18879 Brasilia Dr Porter Ranch (91326) ***(P-11020)***
Coast To Coast Restoration, Sun Valley *Also called Coast To Coast Water Damage* ***(P-13884)***
Coast To Coast Water Damage ....E....818 255-3323
10881 La Tuna Canyon Rd Sun Valley (91352) ***(P-13884)***
COAST TROPICAL, San Diego *Also called Coast Citrus Distributors* ***(P-8446)***
Coast Tropical, South San Francisco *Also called Coast Citrus Distributors* ***(P-8448)***
Coast Waste Management ....C....760 753-9412
5960 El Camino Real Carlsbad (92008) ***(P-6186)***
Coast2coast Public Safety LLC ....E....833 262-7877
575 Birch Ct Ste J Colton (92324) ***(P-16503)***
Coastal Alliance Holdings Inc ....C....562 370-1000
1650 Ximeno Ave Ste 120 Long Beach (90804) ***(P-11021)***
Coastal Building Services Inc ....B....714 775-2855
718 N Hariton St Orange (92868) ***(P-13885)***
Coastal Closeouts Inc ....D....323 589-7900
100 Oceangate Ste 1200 Long Beach (90802) ***(P-16709)***
Coastal Cmnty Senior Care LLC ....C....562 596-4884
5500 E Atherton St # 216 Long Beach (90815) ***(P-21710)***
Coastal Community College, Westminster *Also called Orange County One Stop Center* ***(P-14346)***
Coastal Community Hospital, Santa Ana *Also called Health Resources Corp* ***(P-20903)***
Coastal Grading and Excavating ....E....805 445-6433
756 Calle Plano Camarillo (93012) ***(P-3308)***
Coastal Harvesting Inc ....B....805 525-6250
503 S Palm Ave Santa Paula (93060) ***(P-615)***
Coastal Health Care Inc ....D....310 828-5596
1321 Franklin St Santa Monica (90404) ***(P-19807)***
Coastal International Inc (PA) ....D....415 339-1700
2832 Walnut Ave Ste B Tustin (92780) ***(P-16710)***
Coastal Intl Cnstr Svcs, Tustin *Also called Coastal International Inc* ***(P-16710)***
Coastal Pacific Fd Distrs Inc (PA) ....C....909 947-2066
1015 Performance Dr Stockton (95206) ***(P-4388)***
Coastal Pacific Fd Distrs Inc ....C....909 947-2066
1520 E Mission Blvd Ste B Ontario (91761) ***(P-4389)***
Coastal Pacific Foods, Ontario *Also called Coastal Pacific Fd Distrs Inc* ***(P-4389)***
Coastal Paving Incorporated ....D....408 988-5559
1295 Norman Ave Santa Clara (95054) ***(P-3129)***
Coastal Radiation Oncology Med ....D....805 494-4483
1240 S Westlake Blvd Westlake Village (91361) ***(P-18909)***
Coastal Rubbish, Sun Valley *Also called Crown Disposal Company Inc* ***(P-6192)***
Coastal Select Insurance Co ....E....707 863-3700
4820 Busineca Ctr Dr 20 Fairfield (94534) ***(P-10323)***
Coastal The, North Hollywood *Also called Coastal Tile Inc* ***(P-2887)***
Coastal Tile Inc ....D....818 988-6134
7403 Greenbush Ave North Hollywood (91605) ***(P-2887)***
Coastal Traffic Systems Inc ....D....714 641-3744
9391 Power Dr Huntington Beach (92646) ***(P-7135)***
Coastal Transport Co Inc ....D....619 584-1055
9950 San Diego Mission Rd F San Diego (92108) ***(P-3868)***
Coastal View Halthcare Ctr LLC ....D....805 642-4101
4904 Telegraph Rd Ventura (93003) ***(P-20529)***
Coaster Company of America, Santa Fe Springs *Also called Coa Inc* ***(P-6550)***
Coasthills Credit Union (PA) ....D....805 733-7600
3880 Constellation Rd Lompoc (93436) ***(P-9387)***
Coastline Cnstr & Awng Co Inc ....D....714 891-9798
5742 Research Dr Huntington Beach (92649) ***(P-1106)***
Coastside Senior Housing Limit ....E....415 355-7100
925 Main St Half Moon Bay (94019) ***(P-11022)***
Cobalt Construction Company ....D....805 577-6222
2259 Ward Ave Ste 200 Simi Valley (93065) ***(P-1235)***
Cobb Property Services, Orange *Also called Cobb Waterblasting Inc* ***(P-13886)***
Cobb Waterblasting Inc ....D....714 769-2622
1145 W Shelley Ct Orange (92868) ***(P-13886)***
Cockrell Electric Inc ....D....760 864-6233
79553 Country Club Dr B Bermuda Dunes (92203) ***(P-2454)***
Codding Construction Co ....E....707 795-3550
1400 Valley House Dr # 100 Rohnert Park (94928) ***(P-1449)***
Code America Inc ....D....562 502-7365
235 E Broadway Ste 960 Long Beach (90802) ***(P-14249)***
Code For America Labs Inc ....D....415 625-9633
972 Mission St Fl 5 San Francisco (94103) ***(P-26561)***
Coelho West Custom Farming ....D....559 884-2566
26979 S Butte Ave Five Points (93624) ***(P-309)***
Cofa Media Group LLC ....D....877 293-2007
5650 El Camino Real Carlsbad (92008) ***(P-5378)***
Coffman Specialties Inc (PA) ....C....858 536-3100
9685 Via Excelencia # 200 San Diego (92126) ***(P-3130)***
Cofiroute Usa LLC ....C....949 754-0198
200 Spectrum Center Dr # 1650 Irvine (92618) ***(P-5104)***
Cogar International Enrgy Corp (PA) ....E....626 494-8157
5286 Industrial Dr Huntington Beach (92649) ***(P-2455)***
Cogent Financial Group ....D....562 985-1388
5199 E Pacific Coast Hwy Long Beach (90804) ***(P-9478)***
Cognifit Inc ....D....646 340-1740
600 California St Fl 11 San Francisco (94108) ***(P-23580)***
Cognitiveclouds Software Inc ....D....415 234-3611
5433 Ontario Cmn Fremont (94555) ***(P-14719)***
Cognix Automation Inc ....E....925 464-8822
3423 Torlano Pl Pleasanton (94566) ***(P-15574)***
Cohen Brown MGT Group Inc (PA) ....D....310 966-1001
11835 W Olympic Blvd 920e Los Angeles (90064) ***(P-26562)***
Cohen Richard Ldscp & Cnstr ....E....949 768-0599
20795 Canada Rd El Toro (92630) ***(P-788)***
Coherent Inc ....D....408 764-4000
1100 La Avenida St Mountain View (94043) ***(P-25882)***
Coherus Biosciences Inc (PA) ....D....650 649-3530
333 Twin Dolphin Dr # 600 Redwood City (94065) ***(P-25732)***
Cohesity Inc (PA) ....B....855 926-4374
300 Park Ave Ste 1700 San Jose (95110) ***(P-16711)***
Cohn Wholesale Fruit & Grocery (PA) ....C....619 528-1113
3511 Camino Del Rio S # 306 San Diego (92108) ***(P-8450)***
Cohnreznick LLP ....D....818 205-2600
21600 Oxnard St Ste 700 Woodland Hills (91367) ***(P-25559)***
Cohnreznick LLP ....E....310 477-3722
11755 Wilshire Blvd # 1700 Los Angeles (90025) ***(P-25560)***
Coinbase Inc (PA) ....D....415 275-2890
548 Market St Ste 23008 San Francisco (94104) ***(P-9426)***
Coinmach Corporation (PA) ....D....818 637-4300
3628 San Fernando Rd Glendale (91204) ***(P-13247)***
Coit Restoration Services, Modesto *Also called C & S Draperies Inc* ***(P-13263)***
Coit Services Inc ....E....949 760-0760
1297 Logan Ave Costa Mesa (92626) ***(P-13254)***
Cokeva Inc ....C....916 462-6001
9000 Foothills Blvd Roseville (95747) ***(P-15913)***
Coldwater Care Center LLC ....D....818 766-6105
12750 Riverside Dr North Hollywood (91607) ***(P-19808)***
Coldwell Banker, West Hollywood *Also called Coldwer Banker Previews* ***(P-11060)***
Coldwell Banker, Davis *Also called Doug Arnold Real Estate Inc* ***(P-11099)***
Coldwell Banker, Pasadena *Also called Nrt Commercial Utah LLC* ***(P-11322)***
Coldwell Banker, Canyon Lake *Also called Cbabr Inc* ***(P-10971)***
Coldwell Banker, Bakersfield *Also called Preferred Brokers Inc* ***(P-11365)***
Coldwell Banker, Valencia *Also called Vista Valencia Group Inc* ***(P-11502)***
Coldwell Banker, Vista *Also called Caldwell Banker Inc* ***(P-10958)***
Coldwell Banker ....D....916 447-5900
730 Alhambra Blvd Ste 150 Sacramento (95816) ***(P-11023)***
Coldwell Banker ....D....650 596-5400
580 El Camino Real San Carlos (94070) ***(P-10324)***
Coldwell Banker ....D....619 460-6600
9332 Fuerte Dr La Mesa (91941) ***(P-11024)***
Coldwell Banker ....D....760 753-5616
740 Garden View Ct # 100 Encinitas (92024) ***(P-11025)***
Coldwell Banker ....D....650 324-4456
1377 El Camino Real Menlo Park (94025) ***(P-11026)***
Coldwell Banker ....E....650 726-1100
248 Main St Ste 200 Half Moon Bay (94019) ***(P-11027)***
Coldwell Banker Amaral & Assoc ....D....925 439-7400
3775 Main St Ste E Oakley (94561) ***(P-11028)***
Coldwell Banker and Associates (PA) ....D....951 304-2900
23823 Clinton Keith Rd # 102 Wildomar (92595) ***(P-9680)***
Coldwell Banker Coastl Aliance, Long Beach *Also called Coastal Alliance Holdings Inc* ***(P-11021)***
Coldwell Banker Hartwig Co, Lancaster *Also called Hartwig Realty Inc* ***(P-11186)***
Coldwell Banker Home Source ....D....760 684-8100
15500 W Sand St Ste 2 Victorville (92392) ***(P-11029)***
Coldwell Banker Inland Brokers, Wildomar *Also called Coldwell Banker and Associates* ***(P-9680)***
Coldwell Banker Premier Prpts ....D....805 565-2200
1498 E Valley Rd Santa Barbara (93108) ***(P-11030)***
Coldwell Banker Prof Group ....D....408 383-1044
2860 Zanker Rd Ste 204 San Jose (95134) ***(P-11031)***
Coldwell Banker Property Shop ....D....805 646-7288
727 W Ojai Ave Ojai (93023) ***(P-11032)***
Coldwell Banker RE Corp ....D....818 995-2424
15490 Ventura Blvd # 100 Sherman Oaks (91403) ***(P-11033)***
Coldwell Banker RE Corp ....E....408 981-7200
1000 Sunset Dr Ste 190 Roseville (95678) ***(P-11034)***
Coldwell Banker RE Corp ....E....909 792-4147
300 E State St Redlands (92373) ***(P-11035)***
Coldwell Banker RE LLC ....D....408 723-3300
1712 Meridian Ave Ste C San Jose (95125) ***(P-11036)***
Coldwell Banker Residential (HQ) ....D....949 837-5700
27742 Vista Del Lago # 1 Mission Viejo (92692) ***(P-11037)***
Coldwell Banker Residential RE, San Jose *Also called Terry Meyer* ***(P-11480)***
Coldwell Banker Residential RE (HQ) ....B....949 367-1800
27271 Las Ramblas Mission Viejo (92691) ***(P-11038)***
Coldwell Banker Residential RE ....D....626 445-5500
15 E Foothill Blvd Arcadia (91006) ***(P-11039)***
Coldwell Banker Sky Ridge Rlty, Blue Jay *Also called Cbsrr Inc* ***(P-10985)***
Coldwell Banker Solano Pacific, Benicia *Also called Solano Pacific Corporation* ***(P-11460)***
Coldwell Banker Town & Country ....D....626 966-3688
345 E Rowland St Covina (91723) ***(P-11040)***
Coldwell Bankers Residential ....D....510 583-5400
21060 Redwood Rd Ste 100 Castro Valley (94546) ***(P-11041)***
Coldwell Bankers Residential (PA) ....D....818 575-2660
604 Lindero Canyon Rd Agoura Hills (91377) ***(P-11042)***
Coldwell Bnkr Residential Brkg ....D....650 558-6800
181 2nd Ave Ste 100 San Mateo (94401) ***(P-11043)***
Coldwell Bnkr Residential Brkg ....D....530 823-7653
500 Auburn Folsom Rd # 300 Auburn (95603) ***(P-11044)***

Employee Codes: A=Over 500 employees, B=251-500
C=101-250, D=51-100, E=50
2020 Directory of California
Wholesalers and Services Companies
© Mergent Inc. 1-800-342-5647
1225

Coldwell Bnkr Residential Brkg (HQ) ....D.......925 275-3000
1855 Gateway Blvd Ste 750 Concord (94520) ***(P-11045)***

Coldwell Bnkr Residential Brkg ....D.......650 558-4200
1427 Chapin Ave Burlingame (94010) ***(P-11046)***

Coldwell Bnkr Residential Brkg ....D.......831 462-9000
2140 41st Ave Ste 100 Capitola (95010) ***(P-11047)***

Coldwell Bnkr Residential Brkg ....D.......310 273-3113
166 N Canon Dr Ste 200 Beverly Hills (90210) ***(P-11048)***

Coldwell Bnkr Residential Brkg ....D.......415 447-8800
1390 Noriega St San Francisco (94122) ***(P-11049)***

Coldwell Bnkr Residential Brkg ....D.......760 325-4500
1081 N Palm Canyon Dr Palm Springs (92262) ***(P-11050)***

Coldwell Bnkr Residential Brkg ....D.......916 966-8200
5034 Sunrise Blvd Fair Oaks (95628) ***(P-11051)***

Coldwell Bnkr Residential Brkg ....E.......714 832-0020
21580 Yorba Linda Blvd Yorba Linda (92887) ***(P-11052)***

Coldwell Bnkr Residential Brkg ....D.......818 222-0023
23647 Calabasas Rd Calabasas (91302) ***(P-11053)***

Coldwell Bnkr Residential Brkg ....D.......760 776-9898
72605 Highway 111 Ste B2 Palm Desert (92260) ***(P-11054)***

Coldwell Bnkr Residential Brkg ....D.......760 771-5454
45000 Club Dr Indian Wells (92210) ***(P-11055)***

Coldwell Bnkr Residential Brkg ....D.......831 420-2628
410 Sims Rd Santa Cruz (95060) ***(P-11056)***

Coldwell Bnkr Residential Brkg ....D.......510 608-7600
3340 Walnut Ave Ste 110 Fremont (94538) ***(P-11057)***

Coldwell Bnkr Rsdential RE LLC ....D.......408 355-1500
410 N Santa Cruz Ave Los Gatos (95030) ***(P-11058)***

Coldwell Bnkr Rsdntial, Newport Beach *Also called C B Coast Newport Properties* ***(P-10954)***

Coldwell Bnkr Rsdntial RE Svcs ....D.......916 933-1155
4370 Town Center Blvd # 270 El Dorado Hills (95762) ***(P-11059)***

Coldwer Banker Previews ....C.......310 278-9470
9069 W Sunset Blvd # 100 West Hollywood (90069) ***(P-11060)***

Cole, Norman Anne, Anaheim *Also called House Seven Gables RE Inc* ***(P-11194)***

Coleman Chavez & Assoc LLP ....D.......916 787-2310
1731 E Roseville Pkwy # 200 Roseville (95661) ***(P-22424)***

Colfin Esh Funding LLC ....C.......310 282-8820
2450 Broadway Fl 6 Santa Monica (90404) ***(P-11721)***

Colich & Sons, Gardena *Also called Colich Sons* ***(P-1846)***

Colich Sons ....C.......323 770-2920
547 W 140th St Gardena (90248) ***(P-1846)***

Collabria Care ....D.......707 258-9080
414 S Jefferson St NAPA (94559) ***(P-21711)***

Collabrus Inc ....C.......415 288-1826
111 Sutter St Ste 900 San Francisco (94104) ***(P-25561)***

Collectech Systems Inc (HQ) ....C.......818 597-7500
2290 Agate Ct 1a Simi Valley (93065) ***(P-13676)***

Collected Group Company LLC ....E.......323 277-3900
5300 S Santa Fe Ave Vernon (90058) ***(P-8066)***

Collection Technology Inc ....D.......800 743-4284
10801 6th St Ste 200 Rancho Cucamonga (91730) ***(P-13677)***

Collective Digital Studio, LLC, Beverly Hills *Also called Studio 71 LP* ***(P-13634)***

Collective Health, San Francisco *Also called Collectivehealth Inc* ***(P-10325)***

Collective MGT Group LLC ....C.......323 655-8585
8383 Wilshire Blvd # 1050 Beverly Hills (90211) ***(P-26186)***

Collectivehealth Inc ....B.......650 376-3804
85 Bluxome St San Francisco (94107) ***(P-10325)***

Collectors Universe Inc (PA) ....D.......949 567-1234
1610 E Saint Andrew Pl Santa Ana (92705) ***(P-17494)***

College Hospital Inc (PA) ....B.......562 924-9581
10802 College Pl Cerritos (90703) ***(P-21397)***

College Hospital Cerritos, Cerritos *Also called College Hospital Inc* ***(P-21397)***

College Medical Center, Long Beach *Also called Chlb LLC* ***(P-21396)***

College Operations LLC ....E.......559 353-0576
1730 S College Ave Dinuba (93618) ***(P-23703)***

College Park Realty Inc (PA) ....C.......562 594-6753
10791 Los Alamitos Blvd Los Alamitos (90720) ***(P-11061)***

College Park Realty Inc ....E.......562 982-0300
2610 Los Coyotes Diagonal Long Beach (90815) ***(P-11062)***

College Track ....C.......510 834-3295
112 Linden St Oakland (94607) ***(P-26563)***

College Vsta Convalescent Hosp, Los Angeles *Also called Notellage Corporation* ***(P-20645)***

Collier Warehouse Inc ....E.......415 920-9720
90 Dorman Ave San Francisco (94124) ***(P-6612)***

Colliers International ....D.......415 788-3100
101 2nd St Ste 1100 San Francisco (94105) ***(P-11063)***

Colliers Intl Prperty Cons Inc ....E.......858 455-1515
4660 La Jolla Village Dr # 100 San Diego (92122) ***(P-11064)***

Colliers Intl Prperty Cons Inc ....D.......916 929-5999
301 University Ave # 100 Sacramento (95825) ***(P-11065)***

Colliers Investment Services, San Jose *Also called Colliers Parrish Intl Inc* ***(P-11066)***

Colliers Parrish Intl Inc ....D.......408 282-3800
225 W Santa Clara St San Jose (95113) ***(P-11066)***

Colliers Parrish Intl Inc ....D.......925 279-1050
1850 Mt Diablo Blvd # 200 Walnut Creek (94596) ***(P-11067)***

Collins Avenue LLC ....E.......323 930-6633
5410 Wilshire Blvd # 800 Los Angeles (90036) ***(P-5591)***

Collins Cllins Muir Stwart LLP ....E.......626 243-1100
1100 El Centro St Frnt South Pasadena (91030) ***(P-22425)***

Collins Electrical Company Inc (PA) ....C.......209 466-3691
3412 Metro Dr Stockton (95215) ***(P-2456)***

Collins Electrical Company Inc ....C.......209 466-3691
1902 Channel Dr West Sacramento (95691) ***(P-2457)***

Collins Electrical Company Inc ....D.......831 384-0114
385 Reservation Rd Marina (93933) ***(P-2458)***

Collwood Ter Stellar Care Inc ....D.......619 287-2920
4518 54th St San Diego (92115) ***(P-23869)***

Colonial Care Center, Long Beach *Also called Longwood Management Corp* ***(P-20623)***

Colonial Gardens Nursing Home, Pico Rivera *Also called Rivera Sanitarium Inc* ***(P-20216)***

Colonial Home Care Svcs Inc ....C.......714 289-7220
326 W Katella Ave Ste F Orange (92867) ***(P-21712)***

COLONIAL MANOR CONVALESCENT HOSPITAL, West Covina *Also called Wicoro Inc* ***(P-20722)***

Colony Advisors, Los Angeles *Also called Colony Management Inc* ***(P-11068)***

Colony Capital Inc (PA) ....E.......310 282-8820
515 S Flower St Fl 44 Los Angeles (90071) ***(P-11848)***

Colony Management Inc ....D.......310 282-8820
1999 Ave Of The Los Angeles (90067) ***(P-11068)***

Colony Palms Hotel LLC ....D.......760 969-1800
572 N Indian Canyon Dr Palm Springs (92262) ***(P-12161)***

Color By Deluxe, Burbank *Also called Deluxe Laboratories Inc* ***(P-17734)***

Color Concepts, Canoga Park *Also called Rte Enterprises Inc* ***(P-2390)***

Color Spot Lodi, Lodi *Also called Sg Personnel LLC* ***(P-279)***

Color Spot Nurseries Inc ....D.......310 549-7470
321 W Sepulveda Blvd Carson (90745) ***(P-8888)***

Colorado River Adventures Inc (PA) ....C.......760 663-3737
2715 Parker Dam Rd Earp (92242) ***(P-13159)***

Colorado River Medical Center, Needles *Also called Legacy Lifepoint Health Inc* ***(P-20998)***

Colorado River Medical Center ....D.......760 326-4531
1401 Bailey Ave Needles (92363) ***(P-18910)***

Colorama Wholesale Nursery, Azusa *Also called Richard Wilson Wellington* ***(P-273)***

Colorescience Inc ....C.......866 426-5673
2141 Palomar Airport Rd R Carlsbad (92011) ***(P-7938)***

Colorexa, Van Nuys *Also called Exandal Corporation* ***(P-8172)***

Colortokens Inc ....E.......408 341-6030
2101 Tasman Dr Ste 201 Santa Clara (95054) ***(P-15285)***

Colosseum Athletics Corp ....D.......310 667-8341
2400 S Wilmington Ave Compton (90220) ***(P-8023)***

Colrich Communities Inc ....D.......858 350-7672
444 W Beech St Ste 300 San Diego (92101) ***(P-11553)***

Cols Inc ....C.......714 720-6100
1611 S Melrose Dr 253&278 Vista (92081) ***(P-3663)***

Colsa Corporation ....C.......661 273-3859
41240 12th St W Palmdale (93551) ***(P-25733)***

Colt Security Services, Palm Desert *Also called Dlo Enterprises Inc* ***(P-16259)***

Colt Services Inc ....D.......858 271-9910
9655 Via Excelencia San Diego (92126) ***(P-13266)***

Colton Joint Unified Schl Dst ....D.......909 876-4240
471 Agua Mansa Rd Colton (92324) ***(P-23704)***

Colton Real Estate Group (PA) ....D.......949 475-4200
515 Cabrillo Park Dr # 305 Santa Ana (92701) ***(P-10870)***

Columbia Hospitality Inc ....C.......831 646-8900
652 Cannery Row Monterey (93940) ***(P-12162)***

Columbia Hospitality Inc ....D.......831 373-5700
300 Pacific St Monterey (93940) ***(P-12163)***

Columbia Hospitality Inc ....E.......831 373-8000
487 Foam St Monterey (93940) ***(P-12164)***

Columbia Hydronics Co., Hayward *Also called California Hydronics Corp* ***(P-7445)***

Columbia Pictures Inds Inc (HQ) ....C.......310 244-4000
10202 Washington Blvd Culver City (90232) ***(P-17592)***

Columbia San Clemente Hospital, San Clemente *Also called HCA Inc* ***(P-20902)***

Columbia Woodlake LLC ....D.......206 728-9063
500 Leisure Ln Sacramento (95815) ***(P-12165)***

Colusa Casino, Colusa *Also called Colusa Indian Cmnty Council* ***(P-24147)***

Colusa Casino Resort, Colusa *Also called New Colusa Indian Bingo* ***(P-18728)***

Colusa City Office Education, Colusa *Also called Childrens Services* ***(P-23001)***

Colusa Cnty Sbstnce Abuse Svcs ....D.......530 458-0520
162 E Carson St Ste A Colusa (95932) ***(P-23022)***

Colusa County Behavioral Hlth, Colusa *Also called Colusa Cnty Sbstnce Abuse Svcs* ***(P-23022)***

Colusa Indian Cmnty Council ....A.......530 458-6572
3740 Highway 45 Colusa (95932) ***(P-24147)***

Colusa Produce Corporation ....D.......530 696-0121
1954 Progress Rd Meridian (95957) ***(P-8560)***

Colusa Regional Medical Center ....C.......530 458-5821
199 E Webster St Ste 1 Colusa (95932) ***(P-26187)***

Colusa, Glenn, Trinity Commun t, Willows *Also called Glenn Cnty Humn Resource Agcy* ***(P-23597)***

Comak Trading Inc A Cal Corp ....D.......323 261-3404
2550 S Soto St Vernon (90058) ***(P-8067)***

Comav Technical Services LLC ....C.......760 530-2400
18438 Readiness St Victorville (92394) ***(P-4763)***

Combustion Associates Inc ....E.......951 272-6999
555 Monica Cir Corona (92880) ***(P-5823)***

Comca Sport Net Bay Area ....C.......415 896-2557
360 3rd St Fl 2 San Francisco (94107) ***(P-5592)***

Comcast Cable, San Jose *Also called Comcast Corporation* ***(P-5687)***

Comcast Cable, Madera *Also called Comcast Corporation* ***(P-5688)***

Comcast Cable, Fresno *Also called Comcast Corporation* ***(P-5689)***

Comcast Cable, NAPA *Also called Comcast Corporation* ***(P-5690)***

Comcast California Ix Inc ....D.......215 286-3345
1111 Andersen Dr San Rafael (94901) ***(P-5674)***

Comcast Cble Cmmunications LLC ....E.......310 216-3500
6320 Arizona Cir Los Angeles (90045) ***(P-5675)***

Comcast Cble Cmmunications LLC ....C.......415 715-0524
1485 Bay Shore Blvd # 125 San Francisco (94124) ***(P-5676)***

Comcast Cble Cmmunications LLC ....C.......559 253-4050
1031 N Plaza Dr Visalia (93291) ***(P-5677)***

Comcast Cble Cmmunications LLC ....C.......310 216-3686
6357 Arizona Cir Los Angeles (90045) ***(P-5678)***

Comcast Corporation ....D.......916 459-2964
2860 Gateway Oaks Dr Sacramento (95833) ***(P-5679)***

Comcast Corporation ....D.......650 689-5392
860 Stanton Rd Burlingame (94010) ***(P-5680)***

Comcast Corporation ....D.......415 665-5507
1 La Avanzada St Rm 111 San Francisco (94131) ***(P-5681)***

Mergent e-mail: customerrelations@mergent.com
1226
2020 Directory of California
Wholesalers and Services Companies
(P-0000) Products & Services Section entry number
(PA)=Parent Co (HQ)=Headquarters (DH)=Div Headquarters

Comcast Corporation.......D.......707 266-7584
166 Watson Ln American Canyon (94503) ***(P-5682)***

Comcast Corporation.......D.......209 222-3656
3801 Pelandale Ave A11 Modesto (95356) ***(P-5683)***

Comcast Corporation.......D.......415 367-4153
221 2nd St Sausalito (94965) ***(P-5684)***

Comcast Corporation.......D.......510 266-3200
23525 Clawiter Rd Hayward (94545) ***(P-5685)***

Comcast Corporation.......D.......951 268-9378
425 Corona Mall Corona (92879) ***(P-5686)***

Comcast Corporation.......D.......408 216-2878
203 N 27th St San Jose (95116) ***(P-5687)***

Comcast Corporation.......D.......559 474-4194
1300 W Yosemite Ave Madera (93637) ***(P-5688)***

Comcast Corporation.......D.......559 718-9917
2414 E Acacia Ave Fresno (93726) ***(P-5689)***

Comcast Corporation.......D.......707 266-7012
810 Randolph St NAPA (94559) ***(P-5690)***

Comcast Corporation.......D.......800 240-3640
5462 E Del Amo Blvd 239 Long Beach (90808) ***(P-5691)***

Comcast Corporation.......D.......925 432-0500
550 Garcia Ave Pittsburg (94565) ***(P-5692)***

Comcast Corporation.......B.......916 830-6790
1750 Creekside Oaks Dr # 100 Sacramento (95833) ***(P-5693)***

Comcast Corporation.......D.......209 955-6521
6505 Tam O Shanter Dr Stockton (95210) ***(P-5694)***

Comcast Corporation.......D.......323 993-8000
900 N Cahuenga Blvd Los Angeles (90038) ***(P-5695)***

Comcast Corporation.......B.......925 271-9794
2001 Diamond Blvd Ste 150 Concord (94520) ***(P-5696)***

Comcast Corporation.......D.......831 657-6095
2455 Henderson Way Monterey (93940) ***(P-5697)***

Comcast of California/Colo.......D.......925 424-0273
3055 Comcast Pl Livermore (94551) ***(P-5251)***

Comcast West Bay Area, San Francisco *Also called Comcast Cble Cmmunications LLC* ***(P-5676)***

Come Land Maint Svc Co Inc.......A.......818 567-2455
1419 N San Fernando Blvd # 250 Burbank (91504) ***(P-13887)***

Comerica Bank.......D.......925 941-1900
1442 N Main St Walnut Creek (94596) ***(P-9092)***

Comerit Inc.......C.......888 556-5990
2201 Francisco Dr # 140283 El Dorado Hills (95762) ***(P-15962)***

Comet Building Maintenance Inc.......D.......415 383-1035
21 Commercial Blvd Ste 12 Novato (94949) ***(P-718)***

Comet Electric Inc.......C.......818 340-0965
21625 Prairie St Chatsworth (91311) ***(P-2459)***

Comfort Air Inc.......D.......209 466-4601
1607 French Camp Tpke Stockton (95206) ***(P-2099)***

Comfort California Inc.......E.......415 928-5000
2775 Van Ness Ave San Francisco (94109) ***(P-12166)***

Comfort California Inc.......D.......714 750-3131
616 W Convention Way Anaheim (92802) ***(P-12167)***

Comfort Inn, San Francisco *Also called Comfort California Inc* ***(P-12166)***

Comfort Inn, South San Francisco *Also called Comfort Suites* ***(P-12168)***

Comfort Inn, San Diego *Also called A J Esprit* ***(P-11990)***

Comfort Keepers, El Cajon *Also called Way Cool Homecare Inc* ***(P-21909)***

Comfort Keepers, Irvine *Also called CK Franchising Inc* ***(P-21708)***

Comfort Keepers, Claremont *Also called Bluebridge Professional Svcs* ***(P-21683)***

Comfort Keepers - 509, Orange *Also called Cornerstone Family Svcs LLC* ***(P-21723)***

Comfort Keepers of Folsom, El Dorado Hills *Also called Fortune Senior Enterprises* ***(P-21743)***

Comfort Suites, Healdsburg *Also called H2 Hotel LLC* ***(P-12327)***

Comfort Suites.......D.......650 589-7100
121 E Grand Ave South San Francisco (94080) ***(P-12168)***

Comfort Systems Usa Inc.......D.......909 390-6677
4189 Santa Ana St Ste D Ontario (91761) ***(P-2100)***

Comglobal Systems Inc (HQ).......D.......619 321-6000
1315 Dell Ave Campbell (95008) ***(P-15575)***

Comity Designs Inc.......D.......415 967-1530
41 Marvin Ave Los Altos (94022) ***(P-15963)***

Command & Control Systems, San Diego *Also called Engility LLC* ***(P-25055)***

Command Delivery Systems Inc (PA).......D.......909 444-1475
20935 Currier Rd Walnut (91789) ***(P-3869)***

Command Guard, Huntington Beach *Also called United Facility Solutions Inc* ***(P-16465)***

Command Guard Services, Torrance *Also called Resource Collection Inc* ***(P-14025)***

Command International SEC Svcs.......D.......818 997-1666
6819 Sepulveda Blvd Van Nuys (91405) ***(P-16234)***

Command Security Corporation.......C.......714 557-9355
8840 Warner Ave Ste 301 Fountain Valley (92708) ***(P-16235)***

Command Security Corporation.......C.......510 623-2355
890 Hillview Ct Ste 100 Milpitas (95035) ***(P-16236)***

Command Security Corporation.......A.......310 981-4530
8929 S Sepulveda Blvd # 300 Los Angeles (90045) ***(P-16237)***

Command Security Corporation.......D.......650 574-0911
1701 Airport Blvd Ste 205 San Jose (95110) ***(P-16238)***

Commerce Casino, Commerce *Also called California Commerce Club Inc* ***(P-12107)***

Commerce Center Theatres.......D.......323 722-5577
950 Goodrich Blvd Commerce (90022) ***(P-17829)***

Commerce Home Mortgage Inc (HQ).......D.......925 830-1500
3130 Crow Canyon Pl # 400 San Ramon (94583) ***(P-9620)***

Commerce Velocity LLC.......E.......949 756-8950
1 Technology Dr Ste J725 Irvine (92618) ***(P-15286)***

Commerce West Insurance Co.......D.......925 730-6400
6130 Stoneridge Mall Rd # 400 Pleasanton (94588) ***(P-10326)***

Commercial Carriers Insur Agcy.......C.......562 404-4900
4 Centerpointe Dr Ste 300 La Palma (90623) ***(P-10082)***

Commercial Casting Co, Fontana *Also called Hartman Industries* ***(P-7070)***

Commercial Coating Company Inc.......D.......323 256-1331
2809 W Avenue 37 Los Angeles (90065) ***(P-1686)***

Commercial Cooling, City of Industry *Also called Par Engineering Inc* ***(P-2228)***

Commercial Door Company Inc.......D.......714 529-2179
1374 E 9th St Pomona (91766) ***(P-2920)***

Commercial Finance & L.......D.......858 866-8525
12626 High Bluff Dr # 370 San Diego (92130) ***(P-9251)***

Commercial Indus Design Co Inc.......D.......949 273-6199
20372 N Sea Cir Lake Forest (92630) ***(P-6814)***

Commercial Indus Roofg Co Inc.......D.......619 465-3737
9239 Olive Dr Spring Valley (91977) ***(P-3039)***

Commercial Inv MGT Group, Los Angeles *Also called Cim Group LP* ***(P-12146)***

Commercial Landscape Svc.......D.......949 660-8655
1821 Reynolds Ave Irvine (92614) ***(P-719)***

Commercial Lighting Inds Inc.......D.......800 755-0155
81161 Indio Blvd Indio (92201) ***(P-7136)***

Commercial Mechanical Svc Inc (PA).......E.......650 610-8440
981 Bing St San Carlos (94070) ***(P-17445)***

Commercial Metals Company.......B.......909 899-9993
12451 Arrow Rte Rancho Cucamonga (91739) ***(P-3262)***

Commercial Paving, Los Angeles *Also called Commercial Coating Company Inc* ***(P-1686)***

Commercial Prgrm Systems Inc (PA).......C.......818 308-8560
4400 Cldwtr Cyn Ave Studio City (91604) ***(P-15964)***

Commercial Property Management (PA).......D.......213 739-2000
3251 W 6th St Ste 109 Los Angeles (90020) ***(P-10712)***

Commercial Protective Svcs Inc.......A.......310 515-5290
3400 E Airport Way Long Beach (90806) ***(P-16239)***

Commercial Rfrgn Spcalists LLC (HQ).......C.......510 784-8990
3480 Arden Rd Hayward (94545) ***(P-2101)***

Commercial Roofing Systems Inc.......D.......626 359-5354
11735 Goldring Rd Arcadia (91006) ***(P-3040)***

Commercial Site Imprvs Inc.......E.......209 785-1920
192 Poker Flat Rd Copperopolis (95228) ***(P-3309)***

Commercial Spport Svcs Antioch, Antioch *Also called Contra Costa ARC* ***(P-23584)***

Commercial Support Services, Richmond *Also called Contra Costa ARC* ***(P-23872)***

Commission Junction LLC (HQ).......D.......805 730-8000
530 E Montecito St Santa Barbara (93103) ***(P-14720)***

Commodity Distribution Service.......E.......562 777-9969
10035 Painter Ave Santa Fe Springs (90670) ***(P-27036)***

Commodity Forwarders Inc (HQ).......C.......310 348-8855
11101 S La Cienega Blvd Los Angeles (90045) ***(P-4916)***

Commodity Resource Envmtl Inc (PA).......D.......818 843-2811
116 E Prospect Ave Burbank (91502) ***(P-6187)***

Commodore Dining Cruises Inc (PA).......D.......510 337-9000
2394 Mariner Square Dr A Alameda (94501) ***(P-4602)***

Commodore Events, Alameda *Also called Commodore Dining Cruises Inc* ***(P-4602)***

Common Area Maint Svcs Inc (PA).......D.......310 390-3552
5664 Selmaraine Dr Culver City (90230) ***(P-13888)***

Common Ground Ldscp MGT Inc.......E.......408 278-9807
1127 Mockingbird Ct San Jose (95120) ***(P-789)***

Commons At Calabasas, The, Los Angeles *Also called Caruso MGT Ltd A Cal Ltd Prtnr* ***(P-10966)***

Commonweal.......D.......415 868-0970
451 Mesa Rd Bolinas (94924) ***(P-23023)***

Commonwealth Central Credit Un (PA).......D.......408 531-3100
5890 Silver Creek Vly Rd San Jose (95138) ***(P-9388)***

Commonwealth Equity Svcs LLP.......D.......949 336-6440
20 Corporate Park Ste 150 Irvine (92606) ***(P-13384)***

Commonwealth Financial Network, Irvine *Also called Commonwealth Equity Svcs LLP* ***(P-13384)***

Commonwealth International.......E.......626 279-9201
968 Durfee Ave South El Monte (91733) ***(P-16240)***

Commonwealth Land Title Co.......D.......949 460-4500
6 Executive Cir Ste 100 Irvine (92614) ***(P-10179)***

Communction Wirg Spcalists Inc.......D.......858 278-4545
8909 Complex Dr Ste F San Diego (92123) ***(P-2460)***

Communicare Health Centers.......C.......530 758-2060
2051 John Jones Rd Davis (95616) ***(P-18911)***

Communication & Info Tech, Sacramento *Also called County of Sacramento* ***(P-15899)***

Communication Svc For Deaf Inc.......E.......209 475-5000
81 W March Ln Stockton (95207) ***(P-24148)***

Communications Supply Corp.......D.......714 670-7711
6251 Knott Ave Buena Park (90620) ***(P-5780)***

Communigate Systems, Richmond *Also called Stalker Software Inc* ***(P-15509)***

Community & Senior Svcs, Lancaster *Also called County of Los Angeles* ***(P-23089)***

Community Action Agency of But (PA).......D.......530 712-2600
181 E Shasta Ave Chico (95973) ***(P-23024)***

Community Action Brd of Snt Cr.......E.......831 724-0206
406 Main St Ste 202 Watsonville (95076) ***(P-24525)***

Community Action Commsn Santa.......C.......805 343-0615
4545 10th St Guadalupe (93434) ***(P-24149)***

Community Action Commsn Santa.......B.......805 614-0786
1890 Sandalwood Dr Santa Maria (93455) ***(P-24150)***

Community Action Commsn Santa (PA).......E.......805 964-8857
5638 Hollister Ave # 230 Goleta (93117) ***(P-24151)***

Community Action Commsn Santa.......D.......805 922-2243
201 W Chapel St Santa Maria (93458) ***(P-24152)***

Community Action Marin (PA).......B.......415 485-1489
555 Northgate Dr Ste 201 San Rafael (94903) ***(P-23025)***

Community Action Marin.......C.......415 459-6330
1108 Tamalpais Ave San Rafael (94901) ***(P-21984)***

Community Action Marine, San Rafael *Also called Community Action Marin* ***(P-21984)***

Community Action Partnershi.......C.......714 897-6670
11870 Monarch St Garden Grove (92841) ***(P-23026)***

Community Action Partnership.......B.......805 541-4122
3970 Short St San Luis Obispo (93401) ***(P-23027)***

Community Action Partnership.......C.......805 489-4026
1152 E Grand Ave Arroyo Grande (93420) ***(P-22426)***

A L P H A B E T I C

Community Action Partnership (PA).......D.......805 544-4355
1030 Southwood Dr San Luis Obispo (93401) ***(P-23028)***
Community Action Partnr Kern.......D.......661 845-3901
7998 Alicante Ave Lamont (93241) ***(P-24153)***
Community Action Partnr Kern.......D.......661 758-0129
1600 Poplar Ave Wasco (93280) ***(P-24154)***
Community Action Partnr Kern.......D.......661 336-0317
2400 Truxtun Ave Bakersfield (93301) ***(P-24155)***
Community Action Partnr Kern.......C.......760 371-1469
814 N Norma St Ridgecrest (93555) ***(P-24156)***
Community Action Partnr Kern.......D.......661 792-1066
217 W Kern Ave Mc Farland (93250) ***(P-23029)***
Community Action Partnr Kern.......D.......661 366-5953
4404 Pioneer Dr Bakersfield (93306) ***(P-24157)***
Community Action Partnr Kern (PA).......E.......661 336-5236
5005 Business Park N Bakersfield (93309) ***(P-23030)***
Community Action Prtnrshp (PA).......C.......559 673-9173
1225 Gill Ave Madera (93637) ***(P-23705)***
Community Action Prtnship Sb C.......D.......909 723-1500
696 S Tippecanoe Ave San Bernardino (92408) ***(P-24158)***
Community Actv Rhbltn & Emplym, Crescent City *Also called Full Spectrum Services Inc* ***(P-23239)***
COMMUNITY ADVOCATE FOR PEOPLE', Whittier *Also called Capc Inc* ***(P-24143)***
Community Blood Bank Inc.......D.......760 773-4190
70025 Highway 111 Ste 101 Rancho Mirage (92270) ***(P-22209)***
Community Bridges.......C.......831 724-2024
114 E 5th St Watsonville (95076) ***(P-23031)***
Community Care & Rehab Ctr LLC.......C.......951 680-6500
4070 Jurupa Ave Riverside (92506) ***(P-19809)***
Community Care Adhc Inc.......D.......626 614-8999
9917 Las Tunas Dr Temple City (91780) ***(P-23032)***
Community Care Center, Duarte *Also called Kf Community Care LLC* ***(P-20605)***
Community Care Inc.......D.......831 645-1434
80 Garden Ct Ste 105 Monterey (93940) ***(P-21713)***
Community Care On Palm, Riverside *Also called South Coast Health Wellness* ***(P-20267)***
Community Care Rhblitation Ctr, Newport Beach *Also called Ben Bennett Inc* ***(P-20503)***
Community Care Rhblitation Ctr, Riverside *Also called Community Care & Rehab Ctr LLC* ***(P-19809)***
Community Catalysts California.......E.......760 471-3700
935 W San Marcos Blvd # 103 San Marcos (92078) ***(P-23581)***
Community Child Care Counci Al (PA).......D.......510 582-2182
22351 City Center Dr # 200 Hayward (94541) ***(P-23033)***
Community Chld Cre Cncl Sonoma (PA).......D.......707 522-1413
131a Stony Cir Ste 300 Santa Rosa (95401) ***(P-23706)***
Community Clinics Hlth Netwrk.......E.......619 542-4300
3710 Ruffin Rd San Diego (92123) ***(P-24395)***
Community Cllbrtive Chrtr Schl.......D.......949 387-7822
1200 Quail St Ste 175 Newport Beach (92660) ***(P-24820)***
Community College Foundation.......E.......213 427-6910
3530 Wilshire Blvd # 610 Los Angeles (90010) ***(P-23034)***
Community Connect (PA).......D.......951 686-4402
2060 University Ave # 212 Riverside (92507) ***(P-23035)***
Community Convalescent Center.......D.......909 621-4751
9620 Fremont Ave Montclair (91763) ***(P-19810)***
Community Convalescent Hospita.......D.......626 963-6091
638 E Colorado Ave Glendora (91740) ***(P-19811)***
Community Dev Inst Head Start.......D.......858 668-2985
12988 Bowron Rd Poway (92064) ***(P-23707)***
Community Facilities Dst No 6, Los Angeles *Also called County of Los Angeles* ***(P-6043)***
Community Family Guidance Ctr (PA).......D.......562 865-6444
10929 South St Ste 208b Cerritos (90703) ***(P-21985)***
Community Gatepath.......C.......650 259-8500
350 Twin Dolphin Dr # 123 Redwood City (94065) ***(P-23036)***
Community Health Agency, Riverside *Also called County of Riverside* ***(P-24164)***
Community Health Agency, Riverside *Also called County of Riverside* ***(P-18933)***
Community Health Agency, Moreno Valley *Also called County of Riverside* ***(P-18934)***
Community Health Center, Bakersfield *Also called Omni Family Health* ***(P-19240)***
Community Health Centers (PA).......D.......805 929-3211
150 Tejas Pl Nipomo (93444) ***(P-18912)***
Community Health Group.......C.......800 224-7766
2420 Fenton St Ste 100 Chula Vista (91914) ***(P-18913)***
Community Health Network LLC.......D.......951 265-8281
25102 Jefferson Ave Ste B Murrieta (92562) ***(P-21714)***
Community Health Netwrk of San, San Francisco *Also called Ocean Park Health Center* ***(P-19236)***
Community Health Plan, Alhambra *Also called County of Los Angeles* ***(P-9942)***
COMMUNITY HEALTH SYSTEM, Fresno *Also called Community Hospitals Centl Cal* ***(P-20798)***
Community Health Systems Inc.......C.......951 571-2300
22675 Alessandro Blvd # 1 Moreno Valley (92553) ***(P-18914)***
Community Hlth Alance Pasadena (PA).......D.......626 398-6300
1855 N Fair Oaks Ave # 200 Pasadena (91103) ***(P-20796)***
Community Home Health Agency, Santa Barbara *Also called Sansum Clinic* ***(P-21859)***
Community Home Partners LLC.......D.......408 985-5252
2384 Pacific Dr Santa Clara (95051) ***(P-20418)***
Community Hosp Huntington Pk, Huntington Park *Also called Chhp Management LLC* ***(P-20776)***
Community Hosp Recovery Ctr, Monterey *Also called Monterey Peninsula Hospital* ***(P-21049)***
Community Hosp San Bernardino (HQ).......B.......909 887-6333
1805 Medical Center Dr San Bernardino (92411) ***(P-20797)***
Community Hospice Inc (PA).......C.......209 578-6300
4368 Spyres Way Modesto (95356) ***(P-20419)***
Community Hospice Inc.......E.......209 578-6380
2201 Euclid Ave Hughson (95326) ***(P-20420)***
Community Hospitals Centl Cal.......C.......559 459-2916
1140 T St Fresno (93721) ***(P-15740)***
Community Hospitals Centl Cal (PA).......A.......559 459-6000
2823 Fresno St Fresno (93721) ***(P-20798)***
Community Hospitals Centl Cal.......A.......559 459-6000
2823 Fresno St Fresno (93721) ***(P-20799)***
Community Housing Inc.......E.......650 328-3300
437 Webster St Palo Alto (94301) ***(P-23870)***
Community Housing Opport (PA).......E.......530 757-4444
5030 Business Center Dr # 260 Fairfield (94534) ***(P-27037)***
Community Housing Opport.......E.......707 759-6043
5030 Bus Center Dr # 260 Fairfield (94534) ***(P-26188)***
Community Housing Options.......D.......626 359-3300
348 E Foothill Blvd Arcadia (91006) ***(P-23037)***
Community Integrated Work Prog.......E.......559 276-8564
4623 W Jacquelyn Ave Fresno (93722) ***(P-23038)***
Community Integrated Work Prog.......E.......510 487-9768
1875 Whipple Rd Hayward (94544) ***(P-23039)***
Community Integration Program, Sacramento *Also called Develop Disabilities Svc Org* ***(P-23192)***
Community Interface Services.......D.......760 729-3866
2621 Roosevelt St Ste 100 Carlsbad (92008) ***(P-23040)***
Community Intgrted Work Prgram, Hayward *Also called Community Integrated Work Prog* ***(P-23039)***
Community Living Services LLC.......E.......619 921-3136
8282 University Ave La Mesa (91942) ***(P-23041)***
Community MBL Diagnostics LLC.......D.......925 516-6851
10936 Bigge St San Leandro (94577) ***(P-21514)***
Community Medical Center.......C.......559 222-7416
3003 N Mariposa St Fresno (93703) ***(P-20800)***
Community Medical Centers.......C.......559 320-2200
668 E Bullard Ave Fresno (93710) ***(P-20801)***
Community Medical Centers.......D.......559 447-4000
6297 N Fresno St Fresno (93710) ***(P-20802)***
Community Medical Centers Inc.......D.......209 944-4700
701 E Channel St Stockton (95202) ***(P-18915)***
Community Medical Centers Inc (PA).......D.......209 373-2800
7210 Murray Dr Stockton (95210) ***(P-21986)***
Community Mem HSP/Sn Benua.......D.......805 652-5072
147 N Brent St Ventura (93003) ***(P-20803)***
Community Memorial Health Sys.......C.......805 646-1401
1306 Maricopa Hwy Ojai (93023) ***(P-20804)***
Community Mental Health Clinic, Greenbrae *Also called County of Marin* ***(P-22001)***
Community Mental Health Svcs, San Luis Obispo *Also called County of San Luis Obispo* ***(P-22006)***
Community Orthopedic Medical.......D.......949 348-4000
26401 Crown Valley Pkwy # 101 Mission Viejo (92691) ***(P-18916)***
Community Partners (PA).......D.......213 346-3200
1000 N Alameda St Ste 240 Los Angeles (90012) ***(P-24159)***
Community Partners Intl.......C.......510 225-9676
2560 9th St Ste 315b Berkeley (94710) ***(P-11767)***
Community Redevelopment Agency (PA).......C.......213 977-1600
448 S Hill St Ste 1200 Los Angeles (90013) ***(P-27038)***
Community Regional Medical Ctr, Fresno *Also called Community Hospitals Centl Cal* ***(P-20799)***
Community Services, Modesto *Also called County of Stanislaus* ***(P-23170)***
Community Services Department, La Habra *Also called City of La Habra* ***(P-23010)***
Community Services For Deaf, Stockton *Also called Communication Svc For Deaf Inc* ***(P-24148)***
Community Support Options Inc.......C.......661 758-5331
1401 Poso Dr Wasco (93280) ***(P-23042)***
Community Therapies.......E.......661 945-7878
19040 Soledad Canyon Rd Santa Clarita (91351) ***(P-19663)***
Community Therapies Baby Steps, Santa Clarita *Also called Community Therapies* ***(P-19663)***
Community Transit Services, El Monte *Also called First Student Inc* ***(P-3533)***
Community West Bank.......D.......805 692-5821
445 Pine Ave Goleta (93117) ***(P-9093)***
Communty Convlscnt Hosp Mntclr, Montclair *Also called US Skillserve Inc* ***(P-20342)***
Communty Slns For Chldrn Fmls (PA).......C.......408 779-2113
9015 Murray Ave Ste 100 Gilroy (95020) ***(P-23043)***
Companion Home Hlth & Hospice.......D.......714 560-8177
2041 W Orangewood Ave B Orange (92868) ***(P-21715)***
Companion Hospice, Orange *Also called Companion Home Hlth & Hospice* ***(P-21715)***
Companion Hospice and.......D.......310 338-1257
6133 Bristol Parkday 11 # 110 Culver City (90230) ***(P-21716)***
Companion Hospice Care LLC.......C.......562 944-2711
8130 Florence Ave Ste 200 Downey (90240) ***(P-21717)***
Companion Hospice LLC.......D.......562 944-2711
8130 Florence Ave Ste 200 Downey (90240) ***(P-21718)***
Company 3 Inc.......D.......310 255-6600
1661 Lincoln Blvd Ste 400 Santa Monica (90404) ***(P-17731)***
Comparenetworks Inc (PA).......D.......650 873-9031
395 Oyster Point Blvd # 300 South San Francisco (94080) ***(P-25734)***
Compass Actn Netwk Dirct Outcm, Marina Del Rey *Also called Can-Do* ***(P-22955)***
Compass Bank, Corona *Also called Bbva USA* ***(P-9171)***
Compass Bank, Sun City *Also called Bbva USA* ***(P-9052)***
Compass Bank, Manteca *Also called Bbva USA* ***(P-9172)***
Compass Bank, Stockton *Also called Bbva USA* ***(P-9173)***
Compass Bank, Stockton *Also called Bbva USA* ***(P-9174)***
Compass Children's Center, San Francisco *Also called Compass Family Services* ***(P-23708)***
Compass Clara House, San Francisco *Also called Compass Family Services* ***(P-23045)***
Compass Family Services.......D.......415 644-0504
144 Leavenworth St San Francisco (94102) ***(P-23708)***
Compass Family Services.......D.......415 644-0504
626 Polk St San Francisco (94102) ***(P-23044)***
Compass Family Services.......D.......415 644-0504
111 Page St San Francisco (94102) ***(P-23045)***

Compass Family Shelter, San Francisco *Also called Compass Family Services (P-23044)*
Compass Group Usa Inc ......C......714 899-2520
12640 Knott St Garden Grove (92841) *(P-14141)*
Compass Health Inc ......D......805 543-0210
1425 Woodside Dr San Luis Obispo (93401) *(P-20530)*
Compass Health Inc ......C......805 772-7372
1405 Teresa Dr Morro Bay (93442) *(P-20531)*
Compass Health Inc ......C......805 489-8137
1212 Farroll Ave Arroyo Grande (93420) *(P-20532)*
Compass Health Inc ......D......805 466-9254
10805 El Camino Real Atascadero (93422) *(P-19812)*
Compass Real Estate LLC ......A......760 979-5609
617 Saxony Pl Ste 101 Encinitas (92024) *(P-11069)*
Compass Real Estate LLC ......B......949 945-8176
204 Via San Remo Newport Beach (92663) *(P-10327)*
Compass Transportation Charter, South San Francisco *Also called Sfo Airporter Inc (P-3603)*
Competent Care HM Hlth Nursing, Costa Mesa *Also called Competent Care Inc (P-21719)*
Competent Care Inc ......D......714 545-4818
2900 Bristol St Ste D107 Costa Mesa (92626) *(P-21719)*
Competitive Edge RES Comm Inc ......D......619 702-2372
1620 5th Ave Ste 825 San Diego (92101) *(P-25883)*
Competitor Group Events Inc ......E......858 450-6510
5452 Oberlin Dr San Diego (92121) *(P-26905)*
Compex Legal Services Inc (PA) ......C......310 782-1801
325 Maple Ave Torrance (90503) *(P-22427)*
Complete Coach Works (HQ) ......B......951 682-2557
1863 Service Ct Riverside (92507) *(P-17415)*
Complete Food Service Inc ......D......951 685-8490
3815 Wabash Dr Jurupa Valley (91752) *(P-8561)*
Complete Genomics Inc ......B......650 943-2800
2904 Orchard Pkwy San Jose (95134) *(P-25989)*
Complete Landscape Care Inc ......D......562 946-4441
13316 Leffingwell Rd Whittier (90605) *(P-790)*
Complete Linen Services, South San Francisco *Also called Complete Linen Svc (P-13220)*
Complete Linen Svc ......D......650 873-1221
290 S Maple Ave South San Francisco (94080) *(P-13220)*
Complete Logistics Company ......C......909 427-9800
13831 Slover Ave Fontana (92337) *(P-3870)*
Complete Millwork Services Inc ......D......408 567-9664
405 Aldo Ave Santa Clara (95054) *(P-6613)*
Complete Office California Inc ......D......714 880-1222
12724 Moore St Cerritos (90703) *(P-6510)*
Complete Relocation Svcs Inc ......D......714 901-7411
7361 Doig Dr Garden Grove (92841) *(P-4200)*
Completely Fresh Foods Inc ......C......323 722-9136
4401 S Downey Rd Vernon (90058) *(P-8562)*
Complex Studios ......E......310 477-1938
2323 Corinth Ave Los Angeles (90064) *(P-16712)*
Complex The, Los Angeles *Also called Complex Studios (P-16712)*
Complianceonline, Palo Alto *Also called Metricstream Inc (P-15405)*
Composite Software LLC (HQ) ......D......800 553-6387
755 Sycamore Dr Milpitas (95035) *(P-15287)*
Comppartners Inc ......D......949 253-3111
333 City Blvd W Ste 1500 Orange (92868) *(P-21720)*
Comprehensive Autism Ctr Inc ......D......951 813-4035
7839 University Ave # 105 La Mesa (91942) *(P-19664)*
Comprehensive Child Dev Ctr, San Pedro *Also called Comprehensive Child Dev Inc (P-23709)*
Comprehensive Child Dev Inc ......D......310 514-4998
769 W 3rd St San Pedro (90731) *(P-23709)*
Comprehensive Cmnty Hlth Ctr ......E......323 344-4144
5059 York Blvd Los Angeles (90042) *(P-18917)*
Comprehensive Community Health (PA) ......E......818 265-2264
801 S Chevy Chase Dr Glendale (91205) *(P-21721)*
Comprehensive Dist Svcs Inc ......C......310 523-1546
18726 S Wstn Ave Ste 300 Gardena (90248) *(P-5111)*
Comprehensive Enviro ......E......619 294-9400
1615 Murray Canyon Rd San Diego (92108) *(P-25009)*
Comprehensive SEC Svcs Inc (PA) ......D......916 683-3605
10535 E Stockton Blvd G Elk Grove (95624) *(P-16241)*
Comprehensive Youth Ser ......D......559 229-3561
4545 N West Ave Ste 101 Fresno (93705) *(P-23046)*
Comprhnsive Trning Systems Inc ......E......619 424-6650
497 11th St Ste 4 Imperial Beach (91932) *(P-23582)*
Comps Inc ......C......858 658-0576
4535 Towne Centre Ct San Diego (92121) *(P-15848)*
Compspec Inc ......D......818 551-4200
425 E Colorado St Ste 410 Glendale (91205) *(P-26564)*
Compton Family Mhc Fsp, Compton *Also called County of Los Angeles (P-22213)*
Compton Hauling, Compton *Also called USA Waste of California Inc (P-6308)*
Compton Service Center, Compton *Also called Southern California Edison Co (P-5942)*
Compton Training Center, Van Nuys *Also called Apprentice & Journeymen Trn Tr (P-23560)*
Compulaw LLC ......E......310 553-3355
200 Crprate Pinte Ste 400 Culver City (90230) *(P-14721)*
Compulink Business Systems Inc (PA) ......D......805 446-2050
1100 Business Center Cir Newbury Park (91320) *(P-15288)*
Compulink Healthcare Solutions, Newbury Park *Also called Compulink Business Systems Inc (P-15288)*
Compulink Management Ctr Inc ......C......562 988-1688
3545 Long Beach Blvd Long Beach (90807) *(P-15289)*
Compumail Information Svcs Inc ......D......925 689-7100
4057 Port Chicago Hwy # 300 Concord (94520) *(P-16713)*
Computacenter Fusionstorm Inc ......C......415 623-2626
2 Bryant St Ste 150 San Francisco (94105) *(P-27039)*
Computer Consulting (PA) ......A......310 568-5000
600 Corporate Pointe # 1010 Culver City (90230) *(P-5379)*
Computer History Museum ......D......650 810-1010
1401 N Shoreline Blvd Mountain View (94043) *(P-24256)*
Computer Proc Unlimited Inc ......D......858 530-0875
9235 Activity Rd Ste 104 San Diego (92126) *(P-14722)*
Computer Programming Dept, Novato *Also called County of Marin (P-15743)*
Computer Resources Group Inc ......C......415 398-3535
275 Battery St Ste 800 San Francisco (94111) *(P-14723)*
Computer Sciences Corporation ......D......510 645-3000
1111 Broadway Fl 13 Oakland (94607) *(P-15965)*
Computer Task Group Inc ......C......408 573-6070
2033 Gateway Pl Fl 5 San Jose (95110) *(P-14724)*
Computer Task Group Inc ......B......800 992-5350
101 Metro Dr Ste 530 San Jose (95110) *(P-14725)*
Computerized Management ......D......805 522-5999
40 W Cochran St Simi Valley (93065) *(P-14496)*
Computerized Management Svcs, Simi Valley *Also called Simi Radiology & Imaging (P-26814)*
Computerized Mgt Svcs Inc ......D......805 522-5940
4100 Guardian St Ste 205 Simi Valley (93063) *(P-25562)*
Computerworks Technologies, Burbank *Also called Global Service Resources Inc (P-14833)*
Computrition Inc (HQ) ......D......818 961-3999
8521 Fllbrook Ave Ste 100 Canoga Park (91304) *(P-14726)*
Compvue Inc ......D......408 892-9909
440 N Wolfe Rd Sunnyvale (94085) *(P-14727)*
Compwest Insurance Company ......C......415 593-5100
100 Pringle Ave Ste 515 Walnut Creek (94596) *(P-10083)*
Comstock Crosser Assoc Dev Inc ......E......310 546-5781
321 12th St Ste 200 Manhattan Beach (90266) *(P-11554)*
Comstock Homes, Manhattan Beach *Also called Comstock Crosser Assoc Dev Inc (P-11554)*
Comtel Pro Media, Burbank *Also called Edgewise Media Services Inc (P-7259)*
Comtel Systems Technology ......D......408 543-5600
1292 Hammerwood Ave Sunnyvale (94089) *(P-2461)*
Con-Way, Blythe *Also called Xpo Logistics Freight Inc (P-4182)*
Con-Way, Lakeport *Also called Xpo Enterprise Services Inc (P-4171)*
Con-Way, Santa Rosa *Also called Xpo Logistics Freight Inc (P-4183)*
Conam Management Corporation (PA) ......C......858 614-7200
3990 Ruffin Rd Ste 100 San Diego (92123) *(P-11070)*
Concentrix Corporation ......D......510 668-3717
44201 Nobel Dr Fremont (94538) *(P-15966)*
Concept 7 Inc (PA) ......D......714 966-9734
13020 Bailey St Whittier (90601) *(P-23047)*
CONCEPT 7 FAMILY SUPPORT & TRE, Whittier *Also called Concept 7 Inc (P-23047)*
Concept Enterprises Inc ......D......626 968-8827
152 S Brent Cir Walnut (91789) *(P-7200)*
Concept Technology Inc ......B......949 851-6550
2941 W Macarthur Blvd # 136 Santa Ana (92704) *(P-25010)*
Concerro Inc (HQ) ......E......858 882-8500
9276 Scranton Rd Ste 400 San Diego (92121) *(P-14728)*
Concert Golf Partners LLC ......A......949 715-0602
1 Coastal Oak Newport Coast (92657) *(P-18234)*
Concerto Healthcare Inc (PA) ......C......949 537-3400
85 Enterprise Ste 200 Aliso Viejo (92656) *(P-23048)*
Concession Management Svcs Inc ......C......310 846-5830
6033 W Century Blvd # 890 Los Angeles (90045) *(P-18669)*
Concessionaires Urban Park (PA) ......B......530 529-1512
2150 Main St Ste 5 Red Bluff (96080) *(P-18670)*
Concessionaires Urban Park ......E......209 763-5121
2000 Camanche Rd Ofc Ofc Ione (95640) *(P-18671)*
Concessionaires Urban Park ......D......209 763-5166
2000 Camanche Rd Ofc Ofc Ione (95640) *(P-18672)*
Concessionaires Urban Park ......D......530 529-1596
34600 Ardenwood Blvd Fremont (94555) *(P-18673)*
Concessionaires Urban Park ......D......530 529-1513
18013 Bollinger Canyon Rd San Ramon (94583) *(P-18674)*
Conco Cement Company, Concord *Also called Gonsalves & Santucci Inc (P-3153)*
Conco Pumping ......D......909 350-0503
13052 Dahlia St Fontana (92337) *(P-3131)*
Concord Foods Inc (PA) ......D......909 975-2000
4601 E Guasti Rd Ontario (91761) *(P-8162)*
Concord Hotel LLC ......D......925 521-3751
45 John Glenn Dr Concord (94520) *(P-12169)*
Concord Iron Works Inc ......E......925 432-0136
1501 Loveridge Rd Ste 15 Pittsburg (94565) *(P-7057)*
Concord Jet Service Inc ......E......925 825-2980
3000 Oak Rd Ste 200 Walnut Creek (94597) *(P-14142)*
Concord Pavillion, Concord *Also called City of Concord (P-17900)*
Concorde Battery Corp ......C......626 813-1234
1125 N Azusa Canyon Rd West Covina (91790) *(P-4390)*
Concourse Hotel At, Los Angeles *Also called Humnit Hotel At Lax LLC (P-12424)*
Concrete Concepts Inc ......D......760 737-5470
2317 Auto Park Way Escondido (92029) *(P-3132)*
Concrete Construction, San Diego *Also called Ben F Smith Inc (P-3119)*
Concrete Contractor, Mission Viejo *Also called Cs Concrete Solutions Inc (P-3136)*
Concrete Holding Co Cal Inc ......B......818 788-4228
15821 Ventura Blvd # 475 Encino (91436) *(P-11653)*
Concrete Images International ......D......858 676-1253
17237 Saint Andrews Dr Poway (92064) *(P-3133)*
Concrete North Inc ......D......209 745-7400
10274 Iron Rock Way Elk Grove (95624) *(P-3134)*
Concrete Tie Industries Inc (PA) ......D......310 628-2328
130 E Oris St Compton (90222) *(P-6676)*
Condon-Johnson & Assoc Inc (PA) ......E......510 636-2100
480 Roland Way Ste 200 Oakland (94621) *(P-3135)*
Condor Earth Technologies Inc ......D......209 984-4593
17857 High School Rd Jamestown (95327) *(P-25011)*
Condor Earth Technologies Inc (PA) ......C......209 532-0361
21663 Brian Ln Sonora (95370) *(P-27040)*

ALPHABETIC

Condor Productions LLC.......D.......310 449-3000
245 N Beverly Dr Beverly Hills (90210) *(P-17732)*
Condor Trading LP.......A.......415 248-2200
600 Montgomery St Fl 6 San Francisco (94111) *(P-11654)*
Conduit Inc.......C.......650 340-1550
180 Sansome St 18 San Francisco (94104) *(P-5380)*
Conduit Lngage Specialists Inc.......D.......859 299-3178
22720 Ventura Blvd # 100 Woodland Hills (91364) *(P-13411)*
Conejo Pacific Technologies.......D.......805 498-5315
1560 Newbury Rd Ste 1 Newbury Park (91320) *(P-1343)*
Conejo Valley Unified Schl Dst.......B.......805 496-9035
100 S Conejo School Rd Thousand Oaks (91362) *(P-23710)*
Conejo Vly Nghborhood For Lrng, Thousand Oaks *Also called Conejo Valley Unified Schl Dst (P-23710)*
Conestoga Hotel.......D.......714 535-0300
1240 S Walnut St Anaheim (92802) *(P-12170)*
Conexis, Orange *Also called Word & Brown Insurance (P-26463)*
Conexis Bneft Admnistrators LP (HQ).......C.......714 835-5006
721 S Parker St Ste 300 Orange (92868) *(P-10328)*
Confi-Chek Inc (PA).......D.......800 718-8997
1915 21st St Sacramento (95811) *(P-15849)*
Confido LLC.......A.......310 361-8558
3407 W 6th St Ste 709 Los Angeles (90020) *(P-21722)*
Confie Seguros Inc (HQ).......C.......714 252-2500
7711 Center Ave Ste 200 Huntington Beach (92647) *(P-10329)*
Confie Seguros Holdings II Co (PA).......C.......714 252-2649
7711 Center Ave Ste 200 Huntington Beach (92647) *(P-10330)*
Config Consultants LLC.......E.......844 226-6344
6800 Koll Center Pkwy # 160 Pleasanton (94566) *(P-26565)*
Confire J P A.......D.......909 356-2375
1743 Miro Way Rialto (92376) *(P-16714)*
Conforti Plumbing Inc.......A.......530 622-0202
6080 Pleasant Valley Rd C El Dorado (95623) *(P-2102)*
Conglobal Industries LLC.......D.......310 518-2850
1711 Alameda St Wilmington (90744) *(P-4558)*
Congregation of Poor Sisters.......D.......559 237-3444
2121 N 1st St Fresno (93703) *(P-23871)*
Congress Med Surgery Ctr LLC.......D.......626 396-8100
800 S Raymond Ave Pasadena (91105) *(P-18918)*
Congrgtnal Ch Retirement Cmnty.......D.......530 823-6131
750 Auburn Ravine Rd Auburn (95603) *(P-19813)*
Connect Computers, Tustin *Also called General Procurement Inc (P-6843)*
Connect Your Home LLC.......D.......949 777-0100
1 Park Plz Ste 600 Irvine (92614) *(P-1450)*
Conner Logistics Inc.......D.......888 939-4637
4057 W Shaw Ave Ste 110 Fresno (93722) *(P-4917)*
Connexity Inc (HQ).......C.......310 571-1235
2120 Colorado Ave Ste 400 Santa Monica (90404) *(P-5381)*
Connexsys Engineering Inc.......E.......510 243-2050
1320 Willow Pass Rd # 500 Concord (94520) *(P-25012)*
Connotate Technologies Inc.......E.......949 270-1916
2601 Main St Ste 830 Irvine (92614) *(P-14729)*
Conrad A Cox.......E.......562 927-0033
9040 Telegraph Rd Downey (90240) *(P-18919)*
Conrad Acceptance Corporation.......E.......760 735-5000
476 W Vermont Ave Escondido (92025) *(P-9479)*
Conrad Credit, Escondido *Also called Conrad Acceptance Corporation (P-9479)*
Conrad Credit Corporation.......E.......760 735-5000
476 W Vermont Ave Escondido (92025) *(P-13678)*
Conrad Imports Inc.......D.......415 626-3303
540 Barneveld Ave Ste H San Francisco (94124) *(P-6551)*
Conrad Lab, The, Lodi *Also called Lodi Memorial Hosp Assn Inc (P-21009)*
Conroy Farms Inc.......B.......805 981-0537
520 Maulhardt Ave Oxnard (93030) *(P-91)*
Consensus Health, Emeryville *Also called Onebody Inc (P-21826)*
Consensus Orthopedics Inc.......D.......916 355-7123
1115 Windfield Way # 100 El Dorado Hills (95762) *(P-6963)*
Conservation Corps Long Beach.......C.......562 986-1249
340 Nieto Ave Long Beach (90814) *(P-23583)*
Conservation Liquidation.......D.......415 676-5000
100 Pine St Fl 12 San Francisco (94111) *(P-27270)*
Conservation Society Cal.......D.......510 632-9525
9777 Golf Links Rd Oakland (94605) *(P-24306)*
Considine & Considine An Acco.......D.......619 231-1977
8989 Rio San Diego Dr # 320 San Diego (92108) *(P-25563)*
Consoldted Fire Protection LLC (HQ).......A.......949 727-3277
153 Technology Dr Ste 200 Irvine (92618) *(P-16715)*
Consoldted Med Bo-Analysis Inc (PA).......D.......714 657-7369
10700 Walker St Cypress (90630) *(P-21515)*
Consoldted Med Bo-Analysis Inc.......D.......714 657-7389
7631 Wyoming St Ste 105a Westminster (92683) *(P-21516)*
Consoldted Med Bo-Analysis Inc.......D.......714 467-0240
12665 Garden Grove Blvd Garden Grove (92843) *(P-21517)*
Consolidated Cleaning Services.......D.......510 663-2585
6353 Westover Dr Oakland (94611) *(P-13889)*
Consolidated Design West Inc.......D.......714 999-1476
1345 S Lewis St Anaheim (92805) *(P-13776)*
Consolidated Elec Distrs Inc.......D.......858 268-1020
5457 Ruffin Rd San Diego (92123) *(P-7137)*
Consolidated Elec Distrs Inc.......D.......626 345-0000
3020 W Empire Ave Burbank (91504) *(P-7138)*
Consolidated Plastics Corp (PA).......D.......909 393-8222
14954 La Palma Dr Chino (91710) *(P-8684)*
Consolidated Reprographics, Costa Mesa *Also called American Reprographics Co LLC (P-13751)*
Consolidated Tribal Health Prj.......D.......707 485-5115
6991 N State St Redwood Valley (95470) *(P-21987)*
Consortium For Community Svcs, Sacramento *Also called Quality Group Homes Inc (P-1178)*
Consortm On Reachng Excellnce.......E.......510 540-4200
3112 Cedar Ravine Rd Placerville (95667) *(P-27041)*
Consorzio, Berkeley *Also called Homegrown Natural Foods Inc (P-8180)*
Constance Dehaan Dvm, Rohnert Park *Also called Animal Care Center (P-572)*
Constellation Newenergy Inc.......D.......213 576-6001
350 S Grand Ave Ste 3800 Los Angeles (90071) *(P-5824)*
Construction, Fresno *Also called Quiring General LLC (P-1572)*
Construction Customer Service.......E.......714 701-1858
1320 N Hancock St Ste A Anaheim (92807) *(P-1107)*
Construction Specialty Svc Inc.......D.......661 864-7573
4550 Buck Owens Blvd Bakersfield (93308) *(P-1847)*
Construction Temps, Signal Hill *Also called Wannajob Inc (P-14593)*
Construction Testing Services (PA).......E.......925 462-5151
2118 Rheem Dr Pleasanton (94588) *(P-26189)*
Construction Tstg & Engrg Inc (PA).......D.......760 746-4955
1441 Montiel Rd Ste 115 Escondido (92026) *(P-25013)*
Consultants For Adhc, Temple City *Also called Community Care Adhc Inc (P-23032)*
Consultnts In Edctl Per Skills (PA).......D.......916 348-1890
5825 Auburn Blvd Ste 1 Sacramento (95841) *(P-23049)*
Consumer Cr Cnsling Svc San Fr (PA).......D.......888 456-2227
1655 Grant St Ste 1300 Concord (94520) *(P-13412)*
Consumer Loan Underlying.......C.......415 767-4105
71 Stevenson St Ste 1000 San Francisco (94105) *(P-11780)*
Consumer Portfolio Svcs Inc.......C.......949 788-5695
19500 Jamboree Rd Irvine (92612) *(P-9456)*
Consumer Portfolio Svcs Inc.......D.......949 753-6800
16355 Laguna Canyon Rd Irvine (92618) *(P-9457)*
Contact Security Inc.......C.......714 572-6760
3000 E Birch St Ste 111 Brea (92821) *(P-16242)*
Contactual Inc.......E.......650 292-4408
810 W Maude Ave Sunnyvale (94085) *(P-15290)*
Contec Microelectronics USA.......D.......949 250-4025
17811 Gillette Ave Fl 1 Irvine (92614) *(P-6815)*
Contec USA, Irvine *Also called Contec Microelectronics USA (P-6815)*
Contemporary Services Corp.......C.......310 320-8418
369 Van Ness Way Ste 702 Torrance (90501) *(P-16504)*
Contemporary Services Corp (PA).......C.......818 885-5150
17101 Superior St Northridge (91325) *(P-14250)*
Contemporary Services Corp.......D.......909 740-3834
4365 E Lowell St Ste A Ontario (91761) *(P-15898)*
Contemporary Services Corp.......C.......559 225-9325
2650 E Shaw Ave Fresno (93710) *(P-16243)*
Contemprary Hstrical Vhcl Assn.......D.......707 448-7266
430 Oak View Dr Vacaville (95688) *(P-24526)*
Conti Life Comm Plea LLC.......D.......925 227-6800
3300 Stoneridge Creek Way Pleasanton (94588) *(P-16716)*
Contiki Holidays, Anaheim *Also called Contiki US Holdings Inc (P-4851)*
Contiki US Holdings Inc.......D.......714 935-0808
801 E Katella Ave Frnt Anaheim (92805) *(P-4851)*
Continental 155 5th Corp.......E.......310 640-1520
2041 Rosecrans Ave # 200 El Segundo (90245) *(P-11071)*
Continental Agency Inc (PA).......D.......909 595-8884
1768 W 2nd St Pomona (91766) *(P-4918)*
Continental Airlines, Los Angeles *Also called United Airlines Inc (P-4690)*
Continental Currency Svcs Inc (HQ).......E.......714 569-0300
1108 E 17th St Santa Ana (92701) *(P-9427)*
Continental Currency Svcs Inc (PA).......D.......714 569-0300
1108 E 17th St Santa Ana (92701) *(P-9428)*
Continental Data Graphics, Long Beach *Also called Continental Graphics Corp (P-13777)*
Continental Data Graphics, Long Beach *Also called Continental Graphics Corp (P-25014)*
Continental Dntl Ceramics Inc.......E.......310 618-8821
1873 Western Way Torrance (90501) *(P-21606)*
Continental Ex Money Order Co, Santa Ana *Also called Continental Currency Svcs Inc (P-9427)*
Continental Exch Solutions Inc.......D.......562 345-2100
7001 Village Dr Ste 200 Buena Park (90621) *(P-16717)*
Continental Exch Solutions Inc (HQ).......C.......714 522-7044
6565 Knott Ave Buena Park (90620) *(P-9429)*
Continental Graphics Corp (HQ).......C.......714 503-4200
4060 N Lakewood Blvd Long Beach (90808) *(P-13777)*
Continental Graphics Corp.......A.......714 503-4200
4000 N Lakewood Blvd Long Beach (90808) *(P-25014)*
Continental Sales Co., Los Angeles *Also called Val-Pro Inc (P-8534)*
Continental Trnsp Svcs, Long Beach *Also called C O T S Inc (P-3655)*
Continental Western Corp (PA).......E.......510 352-3133
2950 Merced St Ste 200 San Leandro (94577) *(P-7631)*
Continuing Development Inc (PA).......D.......408 556-7300
350 Woodview Ave Ste 100 Morgan Hill (95037) *(P-23711)*
Continuing Lf Communities LLC (PA).......D.......760 704-6400
1940 Levante St Carlsbad (92009) *(P-14251)*
Contra Costa ARC.......D.......925 755-4925
2505 W 10th St Antioch (94509) *(P-23584)*
Contra Costa ARC.......D.......510 233-7303
1420 Regatta Blvd Richmond (94804) *(P-23872)*
Contra Costa Country Club.......D.......925 798-7135
801 Golf Club Rd Pleasant Hill (94523) *(P-18429)*
Contra Costa Electric Inc (HQ).......B.......925 229-4250
825 Howe Rd Martinez (94553) *(P-2462)*
Contra Costa Electric Inc.......C.......661 322-4036
3208 Landco Dr Bakersfield (93308) *(P-2463)*
Contra Costa Metal Fabricators, Oakland *Also called Monterey Mechanical Co (P-1977)*
Contra Costa Newspapers Inc.......E.......925 757-2525
1650 Cavallo Rd Antioch (94509) *(P-8869)*
Contra Costa Vet Med Emrgcy CL.......E.......925 798-5830
1145 Turtle Rock Ln Concord (94521) *(P-576)*
Contra Costa Water District (PA).......C.......925 688-8000
1331 Concord Ave Concord (94520) *(P-6039)*

Contra Costa Water District..............D......925 383-2576
3760 Neroly Rd Oakley (94561) *(P-6040)*
Contract Services Group Inc............C......714 582-1800
480 Capricorn St Brea (92821) *(P-13890)*
Contractor Warehouse...................D......562 633-1428
5950 N Paramount Blvd Lakewood (90805) *(P-1451)*
Contractors Cargo Company, Compton Also called CCC Property Holdings LLC *(P-11650)*
Contractors Cargo Company (PA)........C......310 609-1957
500 S Alameda St Compton (90221) *(P-3987)*
Contractors Complete Surety, Wildomar Also called Asr Constructors Inc *(P-1410)*
Contractors Flrg Svc Cal Inc...........C......714 556-6100
300 E Dyer Rd Santa Ana (92707) *(P-6552)*
Contractors Labor Pool of La, Burbank Also called Clp Resources Inc *(P-14495)*
Contractors Rigging & Erectors, Compton Also called Contractors Cargo Company *(P-3987)*
Contrlled Cntmination Svcs LLC.........888 263-9886
11696 Sorrento Valley Rd # 200 San Diego (92121) *(P-13891)*
Control AC Svc Corp....................D......714 777-8600
5200 E La Palma Ave Anaheim (92807) *(P-2103)*
Control Air North Inc..................D......510 441-1800
30655 San Clemente St Hayward (94544) *(P-2104)*
Controlled Contamination Svcs, San Diego Also called Contrlled Cntmination Svcs LLC *(P-13891)*
Controlled Contamination Svcs..........510 728-1106
23595 Cabot Blvd Ste 115 Hayward (94545) *(P-13892)*
Convention Center Booking Off, Richmond Also called City of Richmond *(P-18664)*
Conventions Arts & Entrmt, San Jose Also called City of San Jose *(P-16700)*
Convergint Technologies LLC............E......510 300-2800
5860 W Las Positas Blvd # 7 Pleasanton (94588) *(P-16505)*
Conversant LLC (HQ)...................C......818 575-4500
30699 Russell Ranch Rd # 250 Westlake Village (91362) *(P-15850)*
Converse Inc...........................D......909 625-6655
2150 E Montclair Plaza Ln Montclair (91763) *(P-8127)*
Converse Inc...........................D......310 451-0314
1437-39 3rd St Promenade Santa Monica (90401) *(P-8128)*
Converse Inc...........................D......909 974-5695
4450 E Lowell St Ontario (91761) *(P-8129)*
Conversionpoint Holdings Inc..........888 706-6764
840 Newport Center Dr # 450 Newport Beach (92660) *(P-15291)*
Convo Communications LLC.............925 227-5500
6601 Owens Dr Ste 155 Pleasanton (94588) *(P-5781)*
Convrgd Data Tech Inc.................C......650 461-4488
999 Commercial St Ste 202 Palo Alto (94303) *(P-6816)*
Cook Cabinets Inc.....................D......530 621-0851
6428 Capitol Ave Diamond Springs (95619) *(P-2921)*
Cook King, La Mirada Also called Stainless Stl Fabricators Inc *(P-7596)*
Cook Realty Inc.......................C......916 451-6702
4305 Freeport Blvd Sacramento (95822) *(P-11072)*
Cook Realty Sales, Sacramento Also called Cook Realty Inc *(P-11072)*
Cooksey Toolen Gage Duffy (PA).......714 431-1100
535 Anton Blvd Fl 10 Costa Mesa (92626) *(P-22428)*
Cool Roofing Systems Inc (PA)........D......209 825-0818
1286 Dupont Ct Manteca (95336) *(P-3041)*
Cool Transport, Colton Also called Van Dyk Tank Lines Inc *(P-3952)*
Cooley Godward Kronish, San Francisco Also called Cooley LLP *(P-22429)*
Cooley LLP............................D......415 693-2000
101 California St Fl 5 San Francisco (94111) *(P-22429)*
Cooley LLP (PA).......................B......650 843-5000
3175 Hanover St Palo Alto (94304) *(P-22430)*
Cooley LLP............................C......650 843-5124
4 Palo Alto Sq Palo Alto (94306) *(P-22431)*
Cooley LLP............................C......858 550-6000
4401 Eastgate Mall San Diego (92121) *(P-22432)*
Cooper & Jackson Inc.................E......408 437-2750
310 Shaw Rd Ste D South San Francisco (94080) *(P-26061)*
Cooper Pugeda Management Inc........E......415 543-6251
65 Mccoppin St San Francisco (94103) *(P-26190)*
Cooper Vail & Associates Inc (HQ).....D......510 446-8301
1850 Gateway Blvd Ste 100 Concord (94520) *(P-25015)*
Cooper White & Cooper LLP (PA).......D......415 433-1900
201 California St Fl 17 San Francisco (94111) *(P-22433)*
Cooperative Personnel Services (PA)...C......916 263-3600
2450 Del Paso Rd Ste 220 Sacramento (95834) *(P-26566)*
Coopertive Amrcn Physcians Inc (PA)...D......213 473-8600
333 S Hope St Fl 8 Los Angeles (90071) *(P-24396)*
Coordnted Dlvry Instlltion Inc.........714 501-4040
905 E Katella Ave Anaheim (92805) *(P-3871)*
Copier Source Inc (PA)................D......909 890-4040
650 E Hospitality Ln # 500 San Bernardino (92408) *(P-6746)*
Coppel Corporation....................D......760 357-3707
503 Scaroni Ave Calexico (92231) *(P-6511)*
Copper Crm Inc (PA)..................C......415 231-6360
301 Howard St Ste 600 San Francisco (94105) *(P-15292)*
Copper Eagle Patrol & Security, Santa Clarita Also called S C Security Inc *(P-16398)*
Copper Ridge Care Center.............C......530 222-2273
201 Hartnell Ave Redding (96002) *(P-19814)*
Copper River Country Club LP (PA).....C......559 434-5200
2140 E Clubhouse Dr Fresno (93730) *(P-18430)*
Coppersmith Global Logistics, El Segundo Also called L E Coppersmith Inc *(P-4983)*
Coppertower Family Medical Ctr........E......707 894-4229
100 W 3rd St Cloverdale (95425) *(P-21988)*
Coptic Clinics.........................D......562 900-2692
3803 W Mission Blvd Pomona (91766) *(P-18920)*
Cora Constructors Inc.................E......760 674-3201
75140 Saint Charles Pl A Palm Desert (92211) *(P-25016)*
Corcoran District Hospital.............559 992-3300
1310 Hanna Ave Corcoran (93212) *(P-20805)*
Cordelia Lighting Inc.................C......310 886-3490
20101 S Santa Fe Ave Compton (90221) *(P-7139)*

Cordevalle Golf Club LLC.............C......408 695-4500
1 Cordevalle Club Dr San Martin (95046) *(P-18431)*
Cordial Experience Inc...............D......619 793-9787
402 W Broadway Ste 700 San Diego (92101) *(P-14730)*
Cordilleras Mental Health Ctr, Redwood City Also called Telecare Corporation *(P-21440)*
Cordoba Corporation...................D......213 895-0224
1401 N Broadway Los Angeles (90012) *(P-15576)*
Core, Placerville Also called Consortm On Reachng Excellnce *(P-27041)*
Core Bts Inc...........................C......818 766-2400
5250 Lankershim Blvd North Hollywood (91601) *(P-15967)*
Core Group, The, Milpitas Also called Tcg Builders Inc *(P-1619)*
Core Medstaff, Los Angeles Also called Total Professional Network *(P-14441)*
Core Nutrition LLC....................D......310 640-0500
100 N Pacific Coast Hwy El Segundo (90245) *(P-8563)*
Core Nutrition LLC....................E......310 640-0500
1222 E Grand Ave Ste 102 El Segundo (90245) *(P-8564)*
Core Realty Holdings LLC (PA).........D......949 863-1031
1600 Dove St Ste 450 Newport Beach (92660) *(P-11849)*
Core Realty Holdings MGT Inc..........D......949 863-1031
1600 Dove St Ste 450 Newport Beach (92660) *(P-11073)*
Core-Mark Corona 2...................E......800 622-1206
1550 Magnolia Ave Corona (92879) *(P-8163)*
Core-Mark International Inc............C......661 366-2673
200 Coremark Ct Bakersfield (93307) *(P-8565)*
Core-Mark International Inc............C......661 366-2673
8333 Edison Hwy Bakersfield (93307) *(P-8938)*
Core-Mark International Inc............C......323 583-6531
2311 E 48th St Vernon (90058) *(P-8566)*
Core-Mark International Inc............C......509 535-9768
3970 Pell Cir Sacramento (95838) *(P-8567)*
Core-Mark International Inc............C......510 487-3000
31300 Medallion Dr Hayward (94544) *(P-8568)*
Core-Mark Sacramento 2...............E......866 791-4210
2959 Thomas Pl Ste 150 West Sacramento (95691) *(P-8164)*
Corecare III...........................C......714 256-8000
800 Morningside Dr Fullerton (92835) *(P-23873)*
Corecare V A Cal Ltd Partnr............C......714 256-1000
2525 Brea Blvd Fullerton (92835) *(P-19815)*
Corecivic Inc..........................C......619 661-9119
446 Alta Rd San Diego (92158) *(P-26936)*
Corecivic Inc..........................C......760 373-1764
22844 Virginia Blvd California City (93505) *(P-26937)*
Corelation Inc.........................C......619 876-5074
2305 Historic Decatur Rd # 300 San Diego (92106) *(P-14731)*
Corelogic Inc..........................E......714 250-6400
201 Spear St Fl 4 San Francisco (94105) *(P-11074)*
Corelogic Inc..........................D......916 431-2146
11010 White Rock Rd Rancho Cordova (95670) *(P-13708)*
Corelogic Inc..........................E......714 250-6400
40 Pacifica Ste 900 Irvine (92618) *(P-11075)*
Corelogic Credco LLC (HQ)............C......949 214-1000
40 Pacifica Ste 900 Irvine (92618) *(P-13709)*
Corelogic Dorado, Oakland Also called Dorado Network Systems Corp *(P-15308)*
Corelogic Info Solutions, Rancho Cordova Also called Corelogic Inc *(P-13708)*
Corelynx Inc..........................877 267-3599
11501 Dublin Blvd Ste 200 Dublin (94568) *(P-14732)*
Coreos LLC............................D......888 733-4281
101 New Montgomery St # 5 San Francisco (94105) *(P-14733)*
Coretechs Staffing Inc................D......650 363-7960
50 Woodside Plz Ste 604 Redwood City (94061) *(P-14734)*
Corey Nursery Co Inc (PA)............C......909 621-6886
1650 Monte Vista Ave Claremont (91711) *(P-8889)*
Corinthian Intl Prkg Svcs Inc...........B......408 867-7275
19925 Stevens Creek Blvd B Cupertino (95014) *(P-13413)*
Corinthian Parking Services, Cupertino Also called Corinthian Intl Prkg Svcs Inc *(P-13413)*
Corinthian Realty LLC.................C......510 487-8653
3902 Smith St Union City (94587) *(P-11076)*
Corinthian Title Company Inc...........D......619 299-4800
5030 Camino De La Siesta San Diego (92108) *(P-10180)*
Corizon Health Inc....................C......925 551-6500
5325 Broder Blvd Dublin (94568) *(P-18921)*
Corkys Pest Control Inc...............C......760 432-8801
909 Rancheros Dr San Marcos (92069) *(P-13819)*
Corland Companies (PA)...............D......714 573-7780
17542 17th St Ste 420 Tustin (92780) *(P-11077)*
Cornell Companies Inc................D......415 346-9769
759 Lakeview Ave San Francisco (94112) *(P-26938)*
Cornell Corrections Cal Inc (HQ).......B......805 644-8700
1811 Knoll Dr Ventura (93003) *(P-23050)*
Corner Bakery Store...................E......714 459-1420
1040 W Imperial Hwy Ste A La Habra (90631) *(P-8569)*
Corner Products Company.............800 876-8889
17110 Armstrong Ave Irvine (92614) *(P-7253)*
Cornerstone Cnsulting Tech Inc........E......415 705-7800
241 5th St San Francisco (94103) *(P-27042)*
Cornerstone Family Svcs LLC..........D......714 744-3800
1748 W Katella Ave # 207 Orange (92867) *(P-21723)*
Cornerstone Healthcare Inc............C......805 777-1133
143 Triunfo Canyon Rd # 103 Westlake Village (91361) *(P-21724)*
Cornerstone Hospice Cal LLC..........D......909 872-8100
1461 E Cooley Dr Ste 220 Colton (92324) *(P-21725)*
Cornerstone Hotel Management (HQ)...D......415 397-5572
222 Kearny St Ste 200 San Francisco (94108) *(P-26191)*
Cornerstone Marketing Alliance, Encino Also called C M A Alliance *(P-10303)*
Cornerstone Medical Group...........E......909 890-4353
1881 Commercenter E # 112 San Bernardino (92408) *(P-19646)*
Cornerstone Ondemand Inc (PA).......C......310 752-0200
1601 Cloverf Blvd 620s Santa Monica (90404) *(P-15293)*

Employee Codes: A=Over 500 employees, B=251-500
C=101-250, D=51-100, E=50

2020 Directory of California
Wholesalers and Services Companies

© Mergent Inc. 1-800-342-5647

1231

A L P H A B E T I C

Cornerstone Research Inc ....D....213 553-2500
633 W 5th St Fl 31 Los Angeles (90071) ***(P-25884)***
Cornerstone Research Inc (PA) ....D....650 853-1660
1000 El Camino Real # 250 Menlo Park (94025) ***(P-27043)***
Cornerstone Research Inc ....D....415 229-8100
2 Embarcadero Ctr Fl 20 San Francisco (94111) ***(P-27044)***
Coroc, Bakersfield *Also called Weatherford International LLC* ***(P-1050)***
Corodata Corporation (PA) ....D....858 748-1100
12375 Kerran St Poway (92064) ***(P-4559)***
Corona - College Heights Ora ....B....951 359-6451
8000 Lincoln Ave Riverside (92504) ***(P-479)***
Corona Clipper Inc ....D....951 737-6515
22440 Temescal Canyon Rd # 102 Corona (92883) ***(P-7390)***
Corona Medical Offices, Corona *Also called Kaiser Foundation Hospitals* ***(P-11798)***
Corona Regional Med Ctr Hosp, Corona *Also called Uhs-Corona Inc* ***(P-21321)***
Corona Regional Medical Center, Corona *Also called Uhs-Corona Inc* ***(P-22147)***
Corona Rgional Med Ctr Bus Off, Corona *Also called Quadramed Corporation* ***(P-13696)***
Coronado Financial Corp ....E....619 946-1900
940 Eastlake Pkwy Chula Vista (91914) ***(P-11078)***
Coronado Royale, Coronado *Also called GK Management Co Inc* ***(P-11168)***
Coronado YMCA, Richmond *Also called Young MNS Chrstn Assn of E Bay* ***(P-24772)***
Coronel Construction Inc ....D....661 725-4400
2328 Venice Dr Delano (93215) ***(P-1108)***
Corovan Corporation (PA) ....C....858 762-8100
12302 Kerran St Poway (92064) ***(P-3988)***
Corovan Moving & Storage Co (HQ) ....D....858 748-1100
12302 Kerran St Poway (92064) ***(P-4201)***
Corp., R.g Barry, Fontana *Also called DSV Solutions LLC* ***(P-4931)***
Corpinfo Services, Santa Monica *Also called K-Micro Inc* ***(P-6858)***
Corporate Alnce Strategies Inc ....C....877 777-7487
3410 La Sierra Ave F244 Riverside (92503) ***(P-16506)***
Corporate Building Svcs Inc ....C....213 252-0999
3325 Wilshire Blvd # 1240 Los Angeles (90010) ***(P-13893)***
Corporate Image Maintenance, Santa Ana *Also called Gamboa Service Inc* ***(P-13933)***
Corporate Production Designs ....E....310 937-9663
1427 Goodman Ave Redondo Beach (90278) ***(P-17593)***
Corporate Risk Hldings III Inc ....A....949 428-5839
3349 Michelson Dr Ste 150 Irvine (92612) ***(P-16718)***
Corporate Soul LLC ....B....707 431-7781
433 Hudson St Healdsburg (95448) ***(P-13414)***
Corporate Visions Inc (PA) ....D....415 464-4400
3875 Hopyard Rd Ste 275 Pleasanton (94588) ***(P-26567)***
Corporate Visions Inc ....D....760 458-0914
2705 Avenida De Anita # 29 Carlsbad (92010) ***(P-26568)***
Corporate Yard, San Mateo *Also called City of San Mateo* ***(P-13881)***
Corporate Yard, Hayward *Also called Hayward Area Recreation Pkdist* ***(P-4429)***
Corporation Service Company ....D....302 636-5400
2710 Gateway Oaks Dr Sacramento (95833) ***(P-13894)***
Corportion of Fine Arts Mseums ....C....415 750-3600
50 Hagiwara Tea Garden Dr San Francisco (94118) ***(P-24257)***
Corportion of Fine Arts Mseums ....C....415 750-3600
50 Golden Gate Pk Hgiwara San Francisco (94118) ***(P-24258)***
Corportion of Fine Arts Mseums (PA) ....C....415 750-3600
50 Hagiwara Tea Garden Dr San Francisco (94118) ***(P-24259)***
Corprate Office, Blythe *Also called Blythe Nursing Care Center* ***(P-20508)***
Corptax LLC ....D....818 316-2400
21550 Oxnard St Ste 700 Woodland Hills (91367) ***(P-14735)***
Corral De Tierra Country Club ....D....831 484-1325
81 Corral De Tierra Rd Salinas (93908) ***(P-18432)***
Corral Del Tierra ....D....831 372-6244
81 Corral De Tierra Rd Salinas (93908) ***(P-18433)***
Correctional Services Corp LLC ....D....858 566-9816
7805 Arjons Dr San Diego (92126) ***(P-26939)***
Correctons Rhbltation Cal Dept ....D....707 445-6520
930 3rd St Ste 100 Eureka (95501) ***(P-23051)***
Correctons Rhbltation Cal Dept ....D....909 806-3516
303 W 5th St San Bernardino (92401) ***(P-23052)***
Correctons Rhbltation Cal Dept ....C....909 597-1821
14901 Central Ave Chino (91710) ***(P-20806)***
Correctons Rhbltation Cal Dept ....A....805 547-7900
Hwy 1 N San Luis Obispo (93409) ***(P-21989)***
Correctons Rhbltation Cal Dept ....C....916 358-2319
1920 Alabama Ave Sacramento (95825) ***(P-15741)***
Corridor Capital LLC (PA) ....C....310 442-7000
12400 Walsh Ave Ste 645 Los Angeles (90066) ***(P-11903)***
Corridor Recycling Inc ....D....310 835-3849
22500 S Alameda St Long Beach (90810) ***(P-6188)***
Corru Kraft Buena Pk Div 5058, Buena Park *Also called Orora North America* ***(P-7892)***
Corru Kraft Fullerton Div 5068, Fullerton *Also called Orora Packaging Solutions* ***(P-7898)***
Cort Business Services Corp ....D....562 582-1515
14350 Grfield Ave Ste 500 Paramount (90723) ***(P-14143)***
Cortel Inc ....D....650 703-7217
14621 Arroyo Hondo San Diego (92127) ***(P-5252)***
Corvel Corporation ....C....909 257-3700
10750 4th St Ste 100 Rancho Cucamonga (91730) ***(P-10331)***
Corvel Corporation (PA) ....C....949 851-1473
2010 Main St Ste 600 Irvine (92614) ***(P-26192)***
Corvel Enterprise Comp Inc ....D....949 851-1473
2010 Main St Ste 600 Irvine (92614) ***(P-10332)***
Corventis Inc (PA) ....D....408 790-9300
2033 Gateway Pl Ste 100 San Jose (95110) ***(P-15851)***
Cosco Agencies (los Angeles) (HQ) ....D....213 689-6700
588 Harbor Scenic Way Long Beach (90802) ***(P-4919)***
Cosco Fire Protection Inc ....D....925 455-2751
7455 Longard Rd Livermore (94551) ***(P-2464)***
Cosco Fire Protection Inc ....D....858 444-2000
4990 Greencraig Ln San Diego (92123) ***(P-2105)***
Cosco Fire Protection Inc ....C....714 989-1800
1075 W Lambert Rd Ste D Brea (92821) ***(P-2106)***
Cosco Garvin Fire Protection, Brea *Also called Cosco Fire Protection Inc* ***(P-2106)***
Cosmopro West Inc ....E....714 258-8301
15773 Gateway Cir Tustin (92780) ***(P-21726)***
Coso Operating Company LLC ....D....760 764-1300
2 Gill Station Coso Rd Little Lake (93542) ***(P-5825)***
Cost Plus Management Svcs Inc (HQ) ....D....510 893-7300
1201 Marina Village Pkwy # 1 Alameda (94501) ***(P-26193)***
Costa Mesa Country Club, Costa Mesa *Also called Mesa Verde Partners* ***(P-18268)***
Costa Mesa Marriott Suites, Costa Mesa *Also called Host Hotels & Resorts LP* ***(P-12394)***
Costa Mesa Sport Club, Costa Mesa *Also called 24 Hour Fitness Usa Inc* ***(P-18099)***
Costa Sons ....E....831 678-0799
36817 Foothill Rd Soledad (93960) ***(P-44)***
Costa View Farms ....E....559 675-3131
16800 Road 15 Madera (93637) ***(P-387)***
Costa View Farms Shop, Madera *Also called Costa View Farms* ***(P-387)***
Costanoa, Pescadero *Also called Joie De Vivre Hospitality LLC* ***(P-26277)***
Costanoa, Pescadero *Also called King-Reynolds Ventures LLC* ***(P-16871)***
Costar Group Inc ....C....858 458-4900
8910 University Center Ln # 300 San Diego (92122) ***(P-11079)***
Costco 179, Tracy *Also called Costco Wholesale Corporation* ***(P-4391)***
Costco Auto Program, San Diego *Also called Affinity Auto Programs Inc* ***(P-16606)***
Costco Wholesale Corporation ....B....209 835-5222
25862 Schulte Ct Tracy (95377) ***(P-4391)***
Costco Wholesale Corporation ....B....951 361-3606
11600 Riverside Dr Ste A Jurupa Valley (91752) ***(P-4392)***
Costco Wholesale Corporation ....C....909 823-8270
16505 Sierra Lakes Pkwy Fontana (92336) ***(P-8963)***
Costco Wholesale Depot, Jurupa Valley *Also called Costco Wholesale Corporation* ***(P-4392)***
Costless Maintenance Svcs Co ....D....415 550-8819
3254 19th St San Francisco (94110) ***(P-13895)***
Cosumnes Community Svcs Dst ....B....916 405-7150
9355 E Stockton Blvd Elk Grove (95624) ***(P-18675)***
Coto De Caza Golf Club Inc ....C....949 766-7886
25291 Vista Del Verde Trabuco Canyon (92679) ***(P-18060)***
Coto De Caza Golf Racquet CLB, Trabuco Canyon *Also called Coto De Caza Golf Racquet CLB* ***(P-18434)***
Coto De Caza Golf Racquet CLB ....C....949 858-4100
25291 Vista Del Verde Trabuco Canyon (92679) ***(P-18434)***
Cottage Care Center ....C....805 682-7111
2415 De La Vina St Santa Barbara (93105) ***(P-20807)***
Cottage Health (PA) ....A....805 682-7111
400 W Pueblo St Santa Barbara (93105) ***(P-20808)***
Cottage Health ....C....805 688-6432
2050 Viborg Rd Solvang (93463) ***(P-20809)***
COTTAGE HEALTH SYSTEM, Santa Barbara *Also called Goleta Valley Cottage Hospital* ***(P-20891)***
Cottage Health System ....A....805 967-3411
351 S Patterson Ave Goleta (93111) ***(P-20810)***
Cottage Hospital Childrens Ctr, Santa Barbara *Also called Santa Barbara Cottage Hospital* ***(P-21162)***
Cottonwood Cyn Healthcare Ctr, El Cajon *Also called Plum Healthcare Group LLC* ***(P-20202)***
Cottonwood Post-Acute Rehab, Woodland *Also called North American Health Care* ***(P-26332)***
Couch Distributing Company Inc ....C....831 724-0649
104 Lee Rd Watsonville (95076) ***(P-8755)***
Council On Aging - S Cali Inc ....D....714 479-0107
2 Executive Cir Ste 175 Irvine (92614) ***(P-23053)***
Council On Aging Svcs For SRS (PA) ....C....707 525-0143
30 Kawana Springs Rd Santa Rosa (95404) ***(P-23054)***
Counseling and Research Assoc (PA) ....C....310 715-2020
108 W Victoria St Gardena (90248) ***(P-23874)***
Counseling and Research Assoc ....D....661 726-5500
314 E Avenue K4 Lancaster (93535) ***(P-23875)***
Counsyl, Inc., South San Francisco *Also called Myriad Womens Health Inc* ***(P-21556)***
Counter Brands LLC (PA) ....D....310 828-0111
1733 Ocean Ave Santa Monica (90401) ***(P-7939)***
Country Archer Jerky, San Bernardino *Also called S&E Gourmet Cuts Inc* ***(P-8360)***
Country Builders Inc ....C....925 373-1020
5915 Graham Ct Livermore (94550) ***(P-1236)***
Country Builders Construction, Livermore *Also called Country Builders Inc* ***(P-1236)***
Country Club Lanes, Sacramento *Also called Pinsetters Inc* ***(P-18041)***
COUNTRY CLUB OF RANCHO BERNARD, San Diego *Also called Rancho Bernardo Golf Club* ***(P-18743)***
Country Floors America LLC (PA) ....D....310 657-0510
8735 Melrose Ave Vernon (90058) ***(P-6677)***
Country Floral Supply Inc (PA) ....D....805 520-8026
3802 Weatherly Cir Westlake Village (91361) ***(P-8890)***
Country Furnishings, Westlake Village *Also called Country Floral Supply Inc* ***(P-8890)***
Country Hills Health Care Inc ....C....619 441-8745
1580 Broadway El Cajon (92021) ***(P-19816)***
Country Inn &SUite By Carlson ....E....909 937-6000
231 N Vineyard Ave Ontario (91764) ***(P-12171)***
Country Manor Health Care, Sylmar *Also called Canyon Properties III LLC* ***(P-19776)***
Country Oaks Care Center, Pomona *Also called Country Oaks Partners LLC* ***(P-19818)***
Country Oaks Care Center Inc ....D....805 922-6657
830 E Chapel St Santa Maria (93454) ***(P-19817)***
Country Oaks Partners LLC ....D....909 622-1067
215 W Pearl St Pomona (91768) ***(P-19818)***
Country Suites By Carlson, Fremont *Also called Merrill Gardens* ***(P-10855)***
Country Villa Blmnt Hght Hlth ....D....562 597-8817
1730 Grand Ave Long Beach (90804) ***(P-20533)***
Country Villa E Convalescent, Los Angeles *Also called Country Villa Service Corp* ***(P-26198)***

Mergent e-mail: customerrelations@mergent.com
1232
2020 Directory of California
Wholesalers and Services Companies
(P-0000) Products & Services Section entry number
(PA)=Parent Co (HQ)=Headquarters (DH)=Div Headquarters

Country Villa East LP ....C....323 939-3184
5916 W Pico Blvd Los Angeles (90035) ***(P-20534)***
COUNTRY VILLA GLENDALE HEALTHC, Glendale *Also called Glendale Healthcare Center* ***(P-19942)***
Country Villa Health Services, Anaheim *Also called Country Villa Service Corp* ***(P-26195)***
Country Villa Rancho ....C....760 340-0053
39950 Vista Del Sol Rancho Mirage (92270) ***(P-23055)***
Country Villa Service Corp ....C....323 666-1544
3002 Rowena Ave Los Angeles (90039) ***(P-26194)***
Country Villa Service Corp ....D....562 598-2477
3000 N Gate Rd Seal Beach (90740) ***(P-23056)***
Country Villa Service Corp ....D....209 723-2911
510 W 26th St Merced (95340) ***(P-23057)***
Country Villa Service Corp (PA) ....D....310 574-3733
2400 E Katella Ave # 800 Anaheim (92806) ***(P-26195)***
Country Villa Service Corp ....C....562 597-8817
1730 Grand Ave Long Beach (90804) ***(P-26196)***
Country Villa Service Corp ....D....818 246-5516
1208 S Central Ave Glendale (91204) ***(P-19819)***
Country Villa Service Corp ....C....626 358-4547
615 W Duarte Rd Monrovia (91016) ***(P-26197)***
Country Villa Service Corp ....C....626 285-2165
112 E Broadway San Gabriel (91776) ***(P-20535)***
Country Villa Service Corp ....D....626 445-2421
400 W Huntington Dr Arcadia (91007) ***(P-19820)***
Country Villa Service Corp ....C....323 734-1101
2415 S Western Ave Los Angeles (90018) ***(P-26198)***
Country Villa Service Corp ....D....760 340-0053
39950 Vista Del Sol Rancho Mirage (92270) ***(P-16719)***
Country Villa Service Corp ....C....310 574-3733
3533 Motor Ave Los Angeles (90034) ***(P-26199)***
Country Villa Service Corp ....D....323 734-9122
3233 W Pico Blvd Los Angeles (90019) ***(P-26200)***
Country Villa Service Corp ....D....310 537-2500
3611 E Imperial Hwy Lynwood (90262) ***(P-19821)***
Country Villa Terrace (PA) ....D....323 653-3980
6050 W Pico Blvd Los Angeles (90035) ***(P-20536)***
Country Villa Terrace ....E....323 939-3184
5916 W Pico Blvd Los Angeles (90035) ***(P-20537)***
COUNTRY VILLA WESTWOOD NURSING, Los Angeles *Also called Westwood Healthcare Center LP* ***(P-20384)***
Country Vlla Convalescent Hosp, Los Angeles *Also called Country Villa Terrace* ***(P-20536)***
Country Vlla Nrsing Rhbltation, Los Angeles *Also called Country Villa East LP* ***(P-20534)***
Countryside Inn-Corona LP ....E....909 335-9024
1015 W Colton Ave Redlands (92374) ***(P-26201)***
Countryside Inn-Corona LP ....D....949 588-0131
24341 El Toro Rd Laguna Woods (92637) ***(P-12172)***
Countryside Inn-Corona LP ....E....562 596-8330
12850 Seal Beach Blvd Seal Beach (90740) ***(P-26202)***
Countryside Inn-Corona LP ....D....714 549-0300
325 Bristol St Costa Mesa (92626) ***(P-12173)***
Countryside Mushrooms Inc ....D....408 683-2748
11300 Center Ave Gilroy (95020) ***(P-290)***
Countryside Suites By Ayres, Costa Mesa *Also called Countryside Inn-Corona LP* ***(P-12173)***
Countrywide Capital Mkts LLC (HQ) ....C....818 225-3000
4500 Park Granada Calabasas (91302) ***(P-9540)***
Countrywide Financial Corp (HQ) ....A....818 225-3000
4500 Park Granada Calabasas (91302) ***(P-9541)***
Countrywide Home Loans Inc (HQ) ....A....818 225-3000
225 W Hillcrest Dr Thousand Oaks (91360) ***(P-9542)***
Countrywide Home Loans Inc ....C....818 550-8700
801 N Brand Blvd Ste 750 Glendale (91203) ***(P-9543)***
Countrywide Securities Corp ....B....818 225-3000
4500 Park Granada Calabasas (91302) ***(P-9681)***
County Building Materials Inc ....D....408 274-4920
2927 S King Rd San Jose (95122) ***(P-6614)***
County Child Welfare Services, San Diego *Also called County of San Diego* ***(P-23148)***
County Engineers Assn Cal ....D....707 762-3492
120 Round Ct Petaluma (94952) ***(P-25017)***
County Government, San Luis Obispo *Also called County of San Luis Obispo* ***(P-25022)***
County Jail, Salinas *Also called County of Monterey* ***(P-26940)***
County Lake Health Services ....D....707 263-1090
922 Bevins Ct Lakeport (95453) ***(P-24397)***
County Los Angles Prbtion Dept, Pomona *Also called County of Los Angeles* ***(P-23099)***
County Monterey Social Svcs ....D....831 899-8001
1281 Broadway Ave Seaside (93955) ***(P-23058)***
County of Alameda ....D....510 271-5138
1405 Lakeside Dr Oakland (94612) ***(P-26569)***
County of Alameda ....B....510 670-5455
399 Elmhurst St Hayward (94544) ***(P-1687)***
County of Alameda ....E....510 670-5700
24100 Amador St Ste 130 Hayward (94544) ***(P-23585)***
County of Alameda ....C....510 481-4141
2060 Fairmont Dr San Leandro (94578) ***(P-18922)***
County of Butte ....C....530 538-7661
42 County Center Dr Oroville (95965) ***(P-23059)***
County of Butte ....A....530 538-7572
202 Mira Loma Dr Oroville (95965) ***(P-23060)***
County of Butte ....B....530 538-6802
205 Mira Loma Dr Oroville (95965) ***(P-23061)***
County of Butte ....A....530 538-7711
78 Table Mountain Blvd Oroville (95965) ***(P-23062)***
County of Butte ....B....530 891-2850
107 Parmac Rd Ste 4 Chico (95926) ***(P-21990)***
County of Calaveras ....D....209 754-6402
891 Mountain Ranch Rd San Andreas (95249) ***(P-23063)***
County of Contra Costa ....C....925 313-4000
50 Douglas Dr Ste 200 Martinez (94553) ***(P-23064)***
County of Contra Costa ....C....925 313-2000
255 Glacier Dr Martinez (94553) ***(P-1688)***
County of Contra Costa ....D....925 646-5877
2099 Arnold Industrial Wa Concord (94520) ***(P-13896)***
County of Contra Costa ....C....866 901-3212
50 Douglas Dr Ste 100 Martinez (94553) ***(P-23065)***
County of Contra Costa ....C....925 370-5000
2500 Alhambra Ave Martinez (94553) ***(P-20811)***
County of Contra Costa ....E....925 646-5480
1420 Willow Pass Rd # 140 Concord (94520) ***(P-21991)***
County of Del Norte ....C....707 464-3191
880 Northcrest Dr Crescent City (95531) ***(P-24160)***
County of El Dorado, Placerville *Also called El Dorado County Health Dept* ***(P-18968)***
County of El Dorado ....D....530 626-4141
3940 Hwy 49 Diamond Springs (95619) ***(P-6189)***
County of El Dorado ....D....530 621-6210
935b Spring St Placerville (95667) ***(P-21398)***
County of El Dorado ....D....530 621-5845
3000 Fairlane Ct Ste 2 Placerville (95667) ***(P-13897)***
County of El Dorado ....C....530 621-5625
3974 Durock Rd Ste 205 Shingle Springs (95682) ***(P-23066)***
County of El Dorado ....D....530 642-7130
3057 Briw Rd Ste A Placerville (95667) ***(P-23067)***
County of Fresno ....D....559 600-3420
1130 O St Fresno (93724) ***(P-22434)***
County of Fresno ....D....559 600-3800
2212 N Winery Ave Ste 122 Fresno (93703) ***(P-23068)***
County of Fresno ....D....559 600-5127
333 W Pontiac Way Clovis (93612) ***(P-23069)***
County of Fresno ....D....559 600-3546
2220 Tulare St Ste 300 Fresno (93721) ***(P-22435)***
County of Fresno ....D....559 600-4600
4417 E Inyo St Bldg 333 Fresno (93702) ***(P-21992)***
County of Fresno ....C....559 600-3534
2281 Tulare St Ste 201 Fresno (93721) ***(P-24398)***
County of Fresno ....C....559 600-3996
3333 E American Ave Ste B Fresno (93725) ***(P-23070)***
County of Glenn ....D....530 934-6582
247 N Villa Ave Willows (95988) ***(P-22210)***
County of Glenn ....C....530 934-6530
777 N Colusa St Willows (95988) ***(P-1689)***
County of Glenn ....D....530 934-6453
525 W Sycamore St Ste A1 Willows (95988) ***(P-23071)***
County of Glenn ....C....530 934-6514
420 E Laurel St Willows (95988) ***(P-23072)***
County of Glenn ....D....530 934-6582
242 N Villa Ave Willows (95988) ***(P-21993)***
County of Humboldt ....B....707 445-6180
929 Koster St Eureka (95501) ***(P-23073)***
County of Humboldt ....C....707 476-4054
720 Wood St Eureka (95501) ***(P-21994)***
County of Imperial ....C....760 482-4441
935 Broadway Ave El Centro (92243) ***(P-22211)***
County of Imperial ....D....760 355-1748
304 E 4th St Imperial (92251) ***(P-1690)***
County of Imperial ....C....760 336-3581
324 Applestille Rd El Centro (92243) ***(P-23074)***
County of Imperial ....D....760 482-4120
202 N 8th St El Centro (92243) ***(P-21995)***
County of Kern ....A....661 868-4100
2005 Ridge Rd Bakersfield (93305) ***(P-23075)***
County of Kern ....D....661 392-2010
2014 Calloway Dr Bakersfield (93312) ***(P-23076)***
County of Kern ....D....661 336-6800
2001 28th St Ste C Bakersfield (93301) ***(P-23077)***
County of Kern ....E....661 868-8360
1721 Westwind Dr Bakersfield (93301) ***(P-18923)***
County of Kern ....A....661 326-2054
1700 Mount Vernon Ave Bakersfield (93306) ***(P-20812)***
County of Kern ....D....661 763-1535
5357 Truxtun Ave Taft (93268) ***(P-23078)***
County of Kern ....E....661 763-4246
500 Cascade Pl Taft (93268) ***(P-18676)***
County of Kern ....D....661 721-5134
1816 Cecil Ave Delano (93215) ***(P-23079)***
County of Kern ....A....661 631-6346
100 E California Ave Bakersfield (93307) ***(P-24161)***
County of Kern ....D....661 363-8910
6601 Niles Senior St Bakersfield (93306) ***(P-23080)***
County of Kern ....D....661 868-2000
1215 Truxtun Ave Fl 4 Bakersfield (93301) ***(P-22436)***
County of Kings ....C....559 584-1411
330 Campus Dr Hanford (93230) ***(P-9903)***
County of Kings ....C....559 852-4316
1424 Forum Dr Hanford (93230) ***(P-23081)***
County of Los Angeles ....C....818 364-1555
14445 Olive View Dr 2b Sylmar (91342) ***(P-20813)***
County of Los Angeles ....C....818 837-6969
1212 Pico St San Fernando (91340) ***(P-18924)***
County of Los Angeles ....C....626 356-5281
300 E Walnut St Dept 200 Pasadena (91101) ***(P-23082)***
County of Los Angeles ....D....661 223-8700
30500 Arrastre Canyon Rd Acton (93510) ***(P-21463)***
County of Los Angeles ....C....626 299-5300
1000 S Fremont Ave Unit 4 Alhambra (91803) ***(P-9942)***
County of Los Angeles ....C....626 575-4059
11234 Valley Blvd Ste 103 El Monte (91731) ***(P-23083)***
County of Los Angeles ....D....213 739-2360
600 S Commwl Ave Fl 2 Flr 2 Los Angeles (90005) ***(P-22212)***
County of Los Angeles ....C....213 974-0515
320 W Temple St Fl 9 Los Angeles (90012) ***(P-15852)***

ALPHABETIC

Employee Codes: A=Over 500 employees, B=251-500
C=101-250, D=51-100, E=50
2020 Directory of California
Wholesalers and Services Companies
© Mergent Inc. 1-800-342-5647
1233

County of Los Angeles D 310 885-2100
546 W Compton Blvd Compton (90220) ***(P-22213)***

County of Los Angeles B 661 940-4181
5300 W Avenue I Lancaster (93536) ***(P-23084)***

County of Los Angeles B 310 222-2401
1000 W Carson St Fl 8 Flr 8 Palos Verdes Peninsu (90274) ***(P-20814)***

County of Los Angeles B 323 889-3405
5770 S Eastern Ave Fl 4th Commerce (90040) ***(P-23085)***

County of Los Angeles A 562 401-7088
7601 Imperial Hwy Downey (90242) ***(P-21996)***

County of Los Angeles A 213 974-7284
515 E 6th St Los Angeles (90021) ***(P-21464)***

County of Los Angeles C 310 668-4545
12025 Wilmington Ave Los Angeles (90059) ***(P-20815)***

County of Los Angeles B 562 903-5000
10355 Slusher Dr Santa Fe Springs (90670) ***(P-23086)***

County of Los Angeles B 562 908-8400
12900 Crssrds Pkwy S 20 City of Industry (91746) ***(P-26203)***

County of Los Angeles C 310 222-4220
1000 W Carson St Torrance (90502) ***(P-18925)***

County of Los Angeles B 562 497-3500
4060 Watson Plaza Dr Lakewood (90712) ***(P-23087)***

County of Los Angeles D 323 226-8611
1605 Eastlake Ave Los Angeles (90033) ***(P-23876)***

County of Los Angeles C 323 265-1804
1000 Corp Ctr Dr Ste 200b Monterey Park (91754) ***(P-23088)***

County of Los Angeles C 323 897-6187
5850 S Main St Los Angeles (90003) ***(P-21997)***

County of Los Angeles C 661 948-2320
777 W Jackman St Lancaster (93534) ***(P-23089)***

County of Los Angeles C 323 226-8998
1601 Eastlake Ave Ste 4 Los Angeles (90033) ***(P-22437)***

County of Los Angeles D 818 364-2011
16350 Filbert St Sylmar (91342) ***(P-23877)***

County of Los Angeles D 310 668-6845
921 E Compton Blvd Compton (90221) ***(P-22214)***

County of Los Angeles D 626 229-3825
532 E Colorado Blvd Fl 8 Pasadena (91101) ***(P-22215)***

County of Los Angeles A 213 922-6210
1 Gateway Plz Los Angeles (90012) ***(P-13778)***

County of Los Angeles C 909 620-3330
300 S Park Ave Ste 770 Pomona (91766) ***(P-22438)***

County of Los Angeles A 323 267-2136
1100 N Eastern Ave Los Angeles (90063) ***(P-25564)***

County of Los Angeles C 213 974-9331
320 W Temple St Ste 1101 Los Angeles (90012) ***(P-23090)***

County of Los Angeles A 213 240-8412
313 N Figueroa St Fl 9 Los Angeles (90012) ***(P-24399)***

County of Los Angeles C 562 908-3119
8240 Broadway Ave Whittier (90606) ***(P-23091)***

County of Los Angeles D 323 769-7800
5205 Melrose Ave Los Angeles (90038) ***(P-21998)***

County of Los Angeles C 323 226-8511
1601 Eastlake Ave Los Angeles (90033) ***(P-23092)***

County of Los Angeles A 323 226-3468
1240 N Mission Rd Los Angeles (90033) ***(P-21465)***

County of Los Angeles A 562 462-2094
12400 Imperial Hwy Norwalk (90650) ***(P-15742)***

County of Los Angeles D 213 351-5600
425 Shatto Pl Los Angeles (90020) ***(P-23093)***

County of Los Angeles C 323 727-1639
5445 Whittier Blvd Fl 400 Los Angeles (90022) ***(P-23094)***

County of Los Angeles C 323 560-5001
8130 Atlantic Ave Cudahy (90201) ***(P-24162)***

County of Los Angeles C 805 237-3110
530 12th St Fl 1 Paso Robles (93446) ***(P-23095)***

County of Los Angeles C 661 723-6088
44933 Fern Ave Lancaster (93534) ***(P-25018)***

County of Los Angeles B 213 744-5601
2707 S Grand Ave Los Angeles (90007) ***(P-23096)***

County of Los Angeles D 213 351-7800
3530 Wilshire Blvd Fl 9 Los Angeles (90010) ***(P-22216)***

County of Los Angeles A 562 940-4324
1100 N Eastern Ave Los Angeles (90063) ***(P-14736)***

County of Los Angeles C 323 226-6021
1100 N Mission Rd Rm 236 Los Angeles (90033) ***(P-20816)***

County of Los Angeles D 661 298-3406
27233 Camp Plenty Rd Canyon Country (91351) ***(P-10214)***

County of Los Angeles C 562 945-2581
9402 Greenleaf Ave Whittier (90605) ***(P-3790)***

County of Los Angeles D 310 222-2357
1000 W Crson St Bsmnt 404 Basement Torrance (90502) ***(P-7940)***

County of Los Angeles D 562 861-0316
5525 Imperial Hwy South Gate (90280) ***(P-22217)***

County of Los Angeles D 323 857-6000
5905 Wilshire Blvd Los Angeles (90036) ***(P-24260)***

County of Los Angeles C 818 362-6437
14555 Osborne St Ofc Van Nuys (91402) ***(P-23097)***

County of Los Angeles C 213 367-3176
6801 E 2nd St Long Beach (90803) ***(P-6041)***

County of Los Angeles C 626 854-4987
17171 Gale Ave City of Industry (91745) ***(P-23098)***

County of Los Angeles C 626 337-1277
14747 Ramona Blvd Baldwin Park (91706) ***(P-25019)***

County of Los Angeles D 909 469-4500
1660 W Mission Blvd Pomona (91766) ***(P-23099)***

County of Los Angeles D 310 266-3711
1725 Main St Rm 125 Santa Monica (90401) ***(P-23100)***

County of Los Angeles D 818 374-2000
14414 Delano St Van Nuys (91401) ***(P-23101)***

County of Los Angeles E 626 821-5858
330 E Live Oak Ave Arcadia (91006) ***(P-23102)***

County of Los Angeles E 562 402-0688
17707 Studebaker Rd Artesia (90703) ***(P-21999)***

County of Los Angeles D 323 730-3507
3834 S Western Ave Los Angeles (90062) ***(P-18926)***

County of Los Angeles D 310 518-8800
1325 Broad Ave Wilmington (90744) ***(P-18927)***

County of Los Angeles C 818 896-1903
13300 Van Nuys Blvd Pacoima (91331) ***(P-18928)***

County of Los Angeles C 661 947-7173
38126 Sierra Hwy Palmdale (93550) ***(P-1691)***

County of Los Angeles B 626 458-4000
900 S Fremont Ave Alhambra (91803) ***(P-6042)***

County of Los Angeles C 310 603-7483
200 W Compton Blvd # 700 Compton (90220) ***(P-22439)***

County of Los Angeles D 626 455-4700
4024 Durfee Ave Rm 225 El Monte (91732) ***(P-23878)***

County of Los Angeles C 213 974-2811
210 W Temple St Fl 19 Los Angeles (90012) ***(P-22440)***

County of Los Angeles C 310 603-7271
200 W Compton Blvd Fl 8 Compton (90220) ***(P-22441)***

County of Los Angeles D 323 780-2185
4849 Civic Center Way Los Angeles (90022) ***(P-23103)***

County of Los Angeles C 562 807-7860
12727 Norwalk Blvd Norwalk (90650) ***(P-23104)***

County of Los Angeles C 310 222-3552
20221 Hamilton Ave Torrance (90502) ***(P-22442)***

County of Los Angeles A 213 351-7257
501 Shatto Pl Ste 301 Los Angeles (90020) ***(P-23105)***

County of Los Angeles D 323 586-6469
8526 Grape St Los Angeles (90001) ***(P-23106)***

County of Los Angeles C 310 603-7311
200 W Compton Blvd # 300 Compton (90220) ***(P-23107)***

County of Los Angeles C 626 458-1700
1525 Alcazar St Bldg 1 Los Angeles (90033) ***(P-1692)***

County of Los Angeles D 626 356-5281
199 N Euclid Ave Pasadena (91101) ***(P-23108)***

County of Los Angeles D 818 374-2406
6230 Sylmar Ave Ste 201 Van Nuys (91401) ***(P-22443)***

County of Los Angeles D 661 524-2005
335 E Avenue K6 Ste B Lancaster (93535) ***(P-22000)***

County of Los Angeles C 323 267-2771
1100 N Eastern Ave Los Angeles (90063) ***(P-16720)***

County of Los Angeles C 562 599-9200
2600 Redondo Ave 3 Long Beach (90806) ***(P-18929)***

County of Los Angeles C 818 557-4164
3307 N Glenoaks Blvd Burbank (91504) ***(P-23109)***

County of Los Angeles B 213 473-6100
450 Bauchet St Los Angeles (90012) ***(P-20817)***

County of Los Angeles C 626 308-5542
200 W Woodward Ave Alhambra (91801) ***(P-23110)***

County of Los Angeles C 213 974-4561
441 Bauchet St Los Angeles (90012) ***(P-5112)***

County of Los Angeles C 559 675-7739
209 W Yosemite Ave Madera (93637) ***(P-23111)***

County of Los Angeles C 213 974-8301
500 W Temple St Ste 525 Los Angeles (90012) ***(P-6043)***

County of Los Angeles C 310 847-4018
21356 Avalon Blvd Carson (90745) ***(P-24440)***

County of Madera D 559 675-7811
2037 W Cleveland Ave Madera (93637) ***(P-17416)***

County of Marin B 415 332-6158
164 Donahue St Sausalito (94965) ***(P-23112)***

County of Marin B 415 499-6970
120 N Redwood Dr San Rafael (94903) ***(P-23113)***

County of Marin D 415 499-7060
371 Bel Marin Keys Blvd # 100 Novato (94949) ***(P-15743)***

County of Marin D 415 448-1500
250 Bon Air Rd Greenbrae (94904) ***(P-22001)***

County of Marin C 415 499-7877
3501 Civic Center Dr San Rafael (94903) ***(P-25020)***

County of Medocina Dept of Mnt, Ukiah *Also called County of Mendocino* ***(P-22002)***

County of Mendocino D 707 463-4363
340 Lake Mendocino Dr Ukiah (95482) ***(P-4764)***

County of Mendocino B 707 463-2437
737 S State St Ukiah (95482) ***(P-23114)***

County of Mendocino C 707 463-4363
340 Lake Mendocino Dr Ukiah (95482) ***(P-1693)***

County of Mendocino C 707 463-4396
860a N Bush St Ukiah (95482) ***(P-22002)***

County of Merced C 209 724-2000
1205 W 18th St Merced (95340) ***(P-23586)***

County of Modoc C 530 233-6223
204 S Court St Ste 6 Alturas (96101) ***(P-16721)***

County of Modoc D 530 233-6501
120 N Main St Alturas (96101) ***(P-23115)***

County of Modoc C 530 233-3416
228 W Mcdowell Ave Alturas (96101) ***(P-19822)***

County of Modoc D 530 233-6400
204 S Court St Ste 6 Alturas (96101) ***(P-23116)***

County of Monterey D 831 755-4944
855 E Laurel Dr Ste D Salinas (93905) ***(P-16722)***

County of Monterey D 831 755-5027
240 Church St Ste 116 Salinas (93901) ***(P-16723)***

County of Monterey E 831 755-4500
1270 Natividad Rd Salinas (93906) ***(P-24163)***

County of Monterey A 831 755-4201
1441 Constitution Blvd # 100 Salinas (93906) ***(P-20818)***

County of Monterey E 831 769-8800
559 E Alisal St Ste 201 Salinas (93905) ***(P-18930)***

Mergent e-mail: customerrelations@mergent.com
1234
2020 Directory of California
Wholesalers and Services Companies
(P-0000) Products & Services Section entry number
(PA)=Parent Co (HQ)=Headquarters (DH)=Div Headquarters

ALPHABETIC SECTION County of San Mateo

County of Monterey ....B....831 755-3700
1414 Natividad Rd Salinas (93906) ***(P-24821)***
County of Monterey ....A....831 755-8500
1000 S Main St Ste 216 Salinas (93901) ***(P-23117)***
County of Monterey ....C....831 755-3782
1410 Natividad Rd Salinas (93906) ***(P-26940)***
County of Monterey ....B....831 755-4800
168 W Alisal St Fl 3 Salinas (93901) ***(P-1694)***
County of Monterey Social Svcs, Seaside *Also called County Monterey Social Svcs* ***(P-23058)***
County of NAPA ....B....707 253-4625
650 Imperial Way Ste 101 NAPA (94559) ***(P-23118)***
County of NAPA ....E....707 253-4361
212 Walnut St NAPA (94559) ***(P-23119)***
County of NAPA ....B....707 253-4461
2261 Elm St NAPA (94559) ***(P-22003)***
County of Orange ....D....714 896-7188
8141 13th St Westminster (92683) ***(P-23120)***
County of Orange ....D....714 937-4500
1535 E Orangewood Ave Anaheim (92805) ***(P-23121)***
County of Orange ....D....714 896-7500
14180 Beach Blvd Ste 120 Westminster (92683) ***(P-23122)***
County of Orange ....E....714 834-8385
1729 W 17th St Santa Ana (92706) ***(P-21518)***
County of Orange ....C....949 252-5006
3160 Airway Ave Costa Mesa (92626) ***(P-4765)***
County of Orange ....E....714 626-3700
1440 N Harbor Blvd # 400 Fullerton (92835) ***(P-22444)***
County of Orange ....B....714 834-4000
300 N Sunflower Ste 400 Santa Ana (92703) ***(P-6190)***
County of Orange ....C....714 704-8000
800 N Eckhoff St Bldg 121 Orange (92868) ***(P-23123)***
County of Orange ....E....714 567-7422
1300 S Grand Ave Ste C Santa Ana (92705) ***(P-24778)***
County of Orange ....D....714 834-8899
2020 W Walnut St Santa Ana (92703) ***(P-23124)***
County of Orange ....A....714 834-6021
405 W 5th St Ofc Santa Ana (92701) ***(P-20421)***
County of Orange ....D....714 935-6435
341 The City Dr S Orange (92868) ***(P-23125)***
County of Placer ....D....530 886-1870
379 Nevada St Auburn (95603) ***(P-23126)***
County of Placer ....D....530 889-7215
3091 County Center Dr # 100 Auburn (95603) ***(P-22004)***
County of Placer ....C....530 889-7500
3091 County Center Dr # 290 Auburn (95603) ***(P-25021)***
County of Placer ....C....530 823-4300
11512 B Ave Auburn (95603) ***(P-23127)***
County of Placer ....C....530 889-7900
2929 Richardson Dr Ste B Auburn (95603) ***(P-23128)***
County of Riverside ....C....951 955-6000
4075 Main St Riverside (92501) ***(P-22445)***
County of Riverside ....E....951 272-5400
3178 Hamner Ave Norco (92860) ***(P-23129)***
County of Riverside ....D....951 955-0840
5256 Mission Blvd Riverside (92509) ***(P-18931)***
County of Riverside ....D....951 443-2262
2560 N Perris Blvd Ste N1 Perris (92571) ***(P-23130)***
County of Riverside ....B....951 358-5306
4065 County Circle Dr Riverside (92503) ***(P-24164)***
County of Riverside ....D....951 486-4000
26520 Cactus Ave Moreno Valley (92555) ***(P-18932)***
County of Riverside ....D....951 358-6000
7140 Indiana Ave Riverside (92504) ***(P-18933)***
County of Riverside ....B....951 486-4000
26520 Cactus Ave Moreno Valley (92555) ***(P-18934)***
County of Riverside ....D....951 245-3060
1400 W Minthorn St Lake Elsinore (92530) ***(P-23131)***
County of Riverside ....D....951 600-6500
43264 Business Park Dr # 102 Temecula (92590) ***(P-23132)***
County of Riverside ....C....951 955-3100
1325 Spruce St Ste 100 Riverside (92507) ***(P-23133)***
County of Riverside ....D....760 863-8283
47923 Oasis St Ste A Indio (92201) ***(P-18935)***
County of Riverside ....D....760 863-7600
47 665 Oasis St Indio (92201) ***(P-23879)***
County of Riverside ....D....951 275-8783
4168 12th St Riverside (92501) ***(P-23134)***
County of Riverside ....D....760 863-8247
82503 Us Highway 111 Indio (92201) ***(P-18677)***
County of Riverside ....D....951 697-4699
6296 River Crest Dr Ste K Riverside (92507) ***(P-23135)***
County of Riverside ....E....951 486-7700
6147 River Crest Dr Riverside (92507) ***(P-15968)***
County of Riverside ....A....951 955-0905
3960 Orange St Ste 500 Riverside (92501) ***(P-23136)***
County of Riverside ....D....951 358-4415
10000 County Farm Rd Riverside (92503) ***(P-23137)***
County of Riverside ....B....951 955-4800
3133 Mission Inn Ave Riverside (92507) ***(P-1109)***
County of Riverside ....D....951 955-3100
3403 10th St Ste 500 Riverside (92501) ***(P-23587)***
County of Riverside Department (PA) ....D....951 358-5000
4065 County Circle Dr Riverside (92503) ***(P-24822)***
County of Riverside Department ....D....760 320-1048
554 S Paseo Dorotea Palm Springs (92264) ***(P-22218)***
County of Sacramento ....B....916 874-7752
799 G St Sacramento (95814) ***(P-15899)***
County of Sacramento ....D....916 875-2711
9700 Goethe Rd Ste D Sacramento (95827) ***(P-1816)***
County of Sacramento ....D....916 875-0900
9616 Micron Ave Ste 750 Sacramento (95827) ***(P-19823)***
County of Sacramento ....D....916 874-0746
7207 Earhart Dr Sacramento (95837) ***(P-13898)***
County of Sacramento ....D....916 363-8383
10361 Rockingham Dr # 100 Sacramento (95827) ***(P-18327)***
County of Sacramento ....C....916 874-1927
12500 Bruceville Rd Elk Grove (95757) ***(P-26941)***
County of Sacramento ....B....916 874-0912
6900 Airport Blvd Sacramento (95837) ***(P-4766)***
County of Sacramento ....C....916 875-4467
9750 Bus Park Dr Ste 104 Sacramento (95827) ***(P-23138)***
County of San Bernardino ....D....909 891-3300
412 W Hospitality Ln Fl 2 San Bernardino (92415) ***(P-23139)***
County of San Bernardino ....C....909 580-1000
400 N Pepper Ave Colton (92324) ***(P-21519)***
County of San Bernardino ....D....909 387-5455
662 S Tippecanoe Ave San Bernardino (92415) ***(P-23712)***
County of San Bernardino ....D....909 387-2363
250 S Lena Rd San Bernardino (92415) ***(P-23713)***
County of San Bernardino ....D....909 945-4000
8303 Haven Ave Rancho Cucamonga (91730) ***(P-23140)***
County of San Bernardino ....D....909 387-0535
860 E Gilbert St San Bernardino (92415) ***(P-23880)***
County of San Bernardino ....C....909 386-8818
222 W Hospitality Ln San Bernardino (92415) ***(P-25565)***
County of San Bernardino ....D....760 843-5100
17270 Bear Valley Rd # 108 Victorville (92395) ***(P-23141)***
County of San Bernardino ....D....760 228-5234
56357 Pima Trl Yucca Valley (92284) ***(P-23142)***
County of San Bernardino ....E....909 425-0785
26887 5th St Highland (92346) ***(P-23714)***
County of San Diego ....D....858 694-5141
6950 Levant St San Diego (92111) ***(P-23143)***
County of San Diego ....D....866 262-9881
130 E Alvarado St Fallbrook (92028) ***(P-23144)***
County of San Diego ....D....760 967-4621
5560 Overland Ave Ste 310 San Diego (92123) ***(P-23145)***
County of San Diego ....D....619 515-8202
330 W Broadway Ste 1100 San Diego (92101) ***(P-23146)***
County of San Diego ....D....619 531-4040
330 W Broadway Ste 1020 San Diego (92101) ***(P-22446)***
County of San Diego ....B....619 956-2800
655 Park Center Dr Santee (92071) ***(P-19824)***
County of San Diego ....E....858 505-6423
6255 Mission Gorge Rd San Diego (92120) ***(P-22219)***
County of San Diego ....E....858 505-6423
6255 Mission Gorge Rd San Diego (92120) ***(P-22220)***
County of San Diego ....C....760 754-3456
1320 Union Plaza Ct Oceanside (92054) ***(P-23147)***
County of San Diego ....B....858 616-5989
8965 Balboa Ave San Diego (92123) ***(P-23148)***
County of San Diego ....D....619 479-1832
8735 Jamacha Blvd Spring Valley (91977) ***(P-23149)***
County of San Diego ....C....619 236-2191
1600 Pacific Hwy Ste 207 San Diego (92101) ***(P-27045)***
County of San Diego ....E....858 694-2895
9320 Farnham St San Diego (92123) ***(P-20819)***
County of San Diego ....B....619 692-8200
3853 Rosecrans St San Diego (92110) ***(P-21399)***
County of San Diego ....D....619 563-2765
3255 Camino Del Rio S San Diego (92108) ***(P-23150)***
County of San Diego ....D....619 531-4521
5570 Overland Ave Ste 101 San Diego (92123) ***(P-22221)***
County of San Diego ....C....619 236-8725
4588 Market St San Diego (92102) ***(P-23151)***
County of San Joaquin ....B....209 468-2601
409 E Market St Stockton (95202) ***(P-23152)***
County of San Joaquin ....D....209 468-4100
24 S Hunter St Ste 201 Stockton (95202) ***(P-23153)***
County of San Joaquin ....B....209 468-8750
1212 N California St Stockton (95202) ***(P-22005)***
County of San Joaquin ....D....209 468-3021
1810 E Hazelton Ave Stockton (95205) ***(P-24165)***
County of San Joaquin ....C....209 468-3500
56 S Lincoln St Stockton (95203) ***(P-23588)***
County of San Joaquin ....D....209 468-6966
500 W Hospital Rd French Camp (95231) ***(P-23154)***
County of San Luis Obispo ....C....805 781-5437
3433 S Higuera St San Luis Obispo (93401) ***(P-23155)***
County of San Luis Obispo ....C....805 781-4700
2178 Johnson Ave San Luis Obispo (93401) ***(P-22006)***
County of San Luis Obispo ....B....805 781-1864
3433 S Higuera St San Luis Obispo (93401) ***(P-23156)***
County of San Luis Obispo ....C....805 781-5258
Government Center Rm 207 San Luis Obispo (93408) ***(P-25022)***
County of San Mateo ....C....650 599-7336
680 Warren St Redwood City (94063) ***(P-23157)***
County of San Mateo ....C....650 312-5327
222 Paul Scannell Dr San Mateo (94402) ***(P-23158)***
County of San Mateo ....B....650 312-8887
222 Paul Scannell Dr Fl 2 San Mateo (94402) ***(P-23159)***
County of San Mateo ....C....650 363-4915
400 County Ctr Redwood City (94063) ***(P-26204)***
County of San Mateo ....E....650 363-4343
455 County Ctr Redwood City (94063) ***(P-26205)***
County of San Mateo ....D....650 853-3139
2277 University Ave East Palo Alto (94303) ***(P-23160)***
County of San Mateo ....C....650 363-4548
455 County Ctr Fl 3 Redwood City (94063) ***(P-27271)***

ALPHABETIC

Employee Codes: A=Over 500 employees, B=251-500
C=101-250, D=51-100, E=50
2020 Directory of California
Wholesalers and Services Companies
© Mergent Inc. 1-800-342-5647
1235

County of San Mateo......D......650 363-1910
555 County Ctr Fl 2 Redwood City (94063) ***(P-23161)***
County of San Mateo......C......650 802-6470
400 Harbor Blvd Bldg B Belmont (94002) ***(P-23162)***
County of San Mateo......D......650 372-8540
150 W 20th Ave San Mateo (94403) ***(P-22007)***
County of San Mateo......C......650 312-8803
222 Paul Scannell Dr San Mateo (94402) ***(P-23163)***
County of San Mateo......D......650 363-4020
455 County Ctr Fl 4 Redwood City (94063) ***(P-13160)***
County of San Mateo......C......650 363-4244
400 County Ctr Fl 5 Redwood City (94063) ***(P-23164)***
County of Santa Barbara Alcoho......D......805 681-4093
300 N San Antonio Rd Santa Barbara (93110) ***(P-22008)***
County of Shasta......D......530 225-5000
1400 California St Redding (96001) ***(P-10215)***
County of Shasta......D......530 225-5554
1313 Yuba St Redding (96001) ***(P-23165)***
County of Shasta......D......530 347-6276
19897 Gas Point Rd Cottonwood (96022) ***(P-24527)***
County of Shasta......D......530 245-6300
1355 West St Redding (96001) ***(P-22447)***
County of Shasta......E......530 225-2999
43 Hilltop Dr Redding (96003) ***(P-23715)***
County of Siskiyou......D......530 918-7200
1107 Ream Ave Mount Shasta (96067) ***(P-22009)***
County of Siskiyou......D......530 841-2700
818 S Main St Yreka (96097) ***(P-23166)***
County of Solano......D......707 784-8400
275 Beck Ave Fairfield (94533) ***(P-23167)***
County of Solano......D......707 451-6090
810 Vaca Valley Pkwy # 203 Vacaville (95688) ***(P-6044)***
County of Solano......C......707 784-7600
475 Union Ave Fairfield (94533) ***(P-23168)***
County of Solano......D......707 784-2080
2101 Courage Dr Fairfield (94533) ***(P-20422)***
County of Sonoma......C......707 823-8511
501 Petaluma Ave Sebastopol (95472) ***(P-20820)***
County of Sonoma......D......707 565-4850
2227 Capricorn Way # 207 Santa Rosa (95407) ***(P-21400)***
County of Sonoma......C......707 527-2911
2615 Paulin Dr Santa Rosa (95403) ***(P-15744)***
County of Sonoma......C......707 565-2209
600 Administration Dr 212j Santa Rosa (95403) ***(P-22448)***
County of Sonoma......D......707 527-2641
2300 County Center Dr B100 Santa Rosa (95403) ***(P-23169)***
County of Sonoma......D......707 527-2911
2300 Prof Dr Rear Door B Santa Rosa (95403) ***(P-15745)***
County of Stanislaus......A......209 525-7000
830 Scenic Dr Modesto (95350) ***(P-20821)***
County of Stanislaus......D......209 558-8828
830 Scenic Dr Modesto (95350) ***(P-23170)***
County of Stanislaus......C......209 567-4120
801 11th St Modesto (95354) ***(P-23171)***
County of Stanislaus......C......209 558-7377
108 Campus Way Modesto (95350) ***(P-23172)***
County of Stanislaus......C......209 558-9675
251 E Hackett Rd Modesto (95358) ***(P-23173)***
County of Stanislaus......D......209 525-6225
800 Scenic Dr Modesto (95350) ***(P-24166)***
County of Stanislaus......C......209 525-7423
800 Scenic Dr Bldg B Modesto (95350) ***(P-22010)***
County of Stanislaus......D......209 558-2500
108 Campus Way Modesto (95350) ***(P-23174)***
County of Stanislaus......C......209 558-2100
251 E Hackett Rd Ste 2 Modesto (95358) ***(P-23589)***
County of Stanislaus......C......209 525-5400
2215 Blue Gum Ave Modesto (95358) ***(P-23881)***
County of Sutter......C......530 822-7250
1965 Live Oak Blvd Ste B Yuba City (95991) ***(P-22011)***
County of Tehama......C......530 527-5631
1860 Walnut St Red Bluff (96080) ***(P-23175)***
County of Tehama......D......530 527-4052
1840 Walnut St Red Bluff (96080) ***(P-23176)***
County of Tuolumne......B......209 533-5561
2 S Green St Sonora (95370) ***(P-15746)***
County of Tuolumne......C......209 533-5711
20075 Cedar Rd N Sonora (95370) ***(P-23177)***
County of Ventura......C......805 654-2561
800 S Victoria Ave Ventura (93009) ***(P-23178)***
County of Ventura......D......805 654-3456
4651 Telephone Rd Ste 300 Ventura (93003) ***(P-23179)***
County of Ventura......C......805 385-8654
1400 Vanguard Dr Fl 2nd Oxnard (93033) ***(P-23180)***
County of Ventura......E......805 240-2701
300 W 9th St Oxnard (93030) ***(P-23716)***
County of Ventura......D......805 654-3152
800 S Victoria Ave 1540 Ventura (93009) ***(P-25566)***
County of Ventura......A......805 652-6000
3291 Loma Vista Rd Ventura (93003) ***(P-23181)***
County of Ventura......B......805 654-5529
5171 Verdugo Way Camarillo (93012) ***(P-23182)***
County of Yolo......D......530 666-8630
137 N Cottonwood St # 2400 Woodland (95695) ***(P-22012)***
County of Yuba......D......530 749-5470
915 8th St Ste 123 Marysville (95901) ***(P-11555)***
County of Yuba......C......530 749-7550
215 5th St Ste 154 Marysville (95901) ***(P-23183)***
County Probation, El Monte *Also called County of Los Angeles* ***(P-23083)***
County Sandiego Dept Chldspprt......B......619 578-6660
3666 Krny Vlla Rd Ste 100 San Diego (92123) ***(P-23184)***
County Santtn Dist 2 of La Co (PA)......A......562 699-7411
1955 Workman Mill Rd Whittier (90601) ***(P-6343)***
County Santtn Dist 2 of La Co......B......310 830-2400
24501 Figueroa St Carson (90745) ***(P-6344)***
County Santtn Dist 2 of La Co......D......562 699-5204
2800 Workman Mill Rd Whittier (90601) ***(P-6191)***
County Santtn Dist 2 of La Co......D......310 638-1161
920 S Alameda St Compton (90221) ***(P-6345)***
County Ventura Human Resources, Ventura *Also called County of Ventura* ***(P-23178)***
County Whl Elc Co Los Angeles......D......714 633-3801
560 N Main St Orange (92868) ***(P-7140)***
Countywide Childrens Case MGT, Los Angeles *Also called County of Los Angeles* ***(P-22212)***
Countywide Mech Systems Inc......C......619 449-9900
1400 N Johnson Ave # 114 El Cajon (92020) ***(P-2107)***
Coupa Software Incorporated (PA)......C......650 931-3200
1855 S Grant St San Mateo (94402) ***(P-15294)***
Courseco Inc (PA)......A......707 763-0335
1039b N Mcdowell Blvd Petaluma (94954) ***(P-18235)***
Coursera Inc (PA)......D......650 963-9884
381 E Evelyn Ave Mountain View (94041) ***(P-14737)***
Court House, Torrance *Also called County of Los Angeles* ***(P-22442)***
Court House Athletic Club (PA)......D......530 885-1964
2514 Bell Rd Auburn (95603) ***(P-18134)***
Courtesy Security Inc......D......888 572-5545
37420 Cedar Blvd Ste D Newark (94560) ***(P-16244)***
Courthuse Tours-Docent Council, Santa Barbara *Also called Santa Barbara City of* ***(P-4863)***
Courtland Farming, Courtland *Also called Delta Breeze Farming Inc* ***(P-312)***
Courtney Inc (PA)......D......949 222-2050
16781 Millikan Ave Irvine (92606) ***(P-3395)***
Courtside Club, Los Gatos *Also called Courtside Tennis Club* ***(P-18435)***
Courtside Tennis Club......D......408 395-7111
14675 Winchester Blvd Los Gatos (95032) ***(P-18435)***
Courtyard & Residence Inn La, Los Angeles *Also called 901 West Olympic Blvd LP* ***(P-11989)***
Courtyard By Marr San Diego Ai, San Diego *Also called Liberty Station Hhg Hotel LP* ***(P-12553)***
Courtyard By Marriott, Woodland Hills *Also called Courtyard Management Corp* ***(P-12179)***
Courtyard By Marriott, San Francisco *Also called Marriot Courtyard* ***(P-12578)***
Courtyard By Marriott, Pleasant Hill *Also called Courtyard Management Corp* ***(P-12181)***
Courtyard By Marriott, Monrovia *Also called Sage Hospitality Resources LLC* ***(P-12863)***
Courtyard By Marriott, Pasadena *Also called Rt Pasad Hotel Partners LP* ***(P-12849)***
Courtyard By Marriott, Baldwin Park *Also called Baldwin Hospitality LLC* ***(P-12034)***
Courtyard By Marriott, Rancho Cordova *Also called Courtyard Management Corp* ***(P-12182)***
Courtyard By Marriott, San Diego *Also called San Diego Hotel Lease LLC* ***(P-12871)***
Courtyard By Marriott, El Segundo *Also called Courtyard Management Corp* ***(P-12183)***
Courtyard By Marriott, Richmond *Also called Pacific Hotel Management LLC* ***(P-12692)***
Courtyard By Marriott, Culver City *Also called Force-Oakleaf LP* ***(P-12271)***
Courtyard By Marriott......D......619 291-5720
595 Hotel Cir S San Diego (92108) ***(P-12174)***
Courtyard By Marriott......D......805 786-4200
1605 Calle Joaquin San Luis Obispo (93405) ***(P-12175)***
Courtyard By Marriott......D......415 925-1800
2500 Larkspur Landing Cir Larkspur (94939) ***(P-12176)***
Courtyard By Marriott......D......626 965-1700
1905 S Azusa Ave Hacienda Heights (91745) ***(P-12177)***
Courtyard By Marriott Irvine, Irvine *Also called Courtyard Management Corp* ***(P-12180)***
Courtyard By Marriott S, Sacramento *Also called Gccfc 2005-Gg5 Y St Ltd Partnr* ***(P-12290)***
Courtyard By Marriott San Dieg, San Diego *Also called Courtyard-Central* ***(P-12185)***
Courtyard By Marriott San Jose, Campbell *Also called Campbell Hhg Hotel Dev LLP* ***(P-12109)***
Courtyard By Marriott/Lax......D......310 981-2350
6161 W Century Blvd Los Angeles (90045) ***(P-12178)***
Courtyard By Marroitt Oxnard, Oxnard *Also called Recp Cy Oxnard LLC* ***(P-12794)***
Courtyard By Mrriott Riverside, Yorba Linda *Also called Alliance Rvrside Hsptality LLC* ***(P-12000)***
Courtyard Care Center, Signal Hill *Also called SCCH Inc* ***(P-26386)***
Courtyard Care Center, San Jose *Also called SSC San Jose Operating Co LP* ***(P-20272)***
Courtyard Cypress, Cypress *Also called Apple Eght Hospitality MGT Inc* ***(P-12012)***
Courtyard Healthcare, Davis *Also called Covenant Care Courtyard LLC* ***(P-19843)***
Courtyard Management Corp......D......818 999-2200
21101 Ventura Blvd Woodland Hills (91364) ***(P-12179)***
Courtyard Management Corp......D......949 453-1033
7955 Irvine Center Dr Irvine (92618) ***(P-12180)***
Courtyard Management Corp......E......925 691-1444
2250 Contra Costa Blvd Pleasant Hill (94523) ***(P-12181)***
Courtyard Management Corp......E......916 638-3800
10683 White Rock Rd Rancho Cordova (95670) ***(P-12182)***
Courtyard Management Corp......C......310 322-0700
2000 E Mariposa Ave El Segundo (90245) ***(P-12183)***
Courtyard Marriott Mission Vly, San Diego *Also called Mbp Land LLC* ***(P-12605)***
Courtyard Oxnard......D......805 988-3600
600 E Esplanade Dr Oxnard (93036) ***(P-12184)***
Courtyard Oxnard Ventura, Oxnard *Also called Js Hospitality Group LLC* ***(P-12494)***
Courtyard Plaza......E......818 780-5005
6951 Lennox Ave Van Nuys (91405) ***(P-19825)***
Courtyard Sacramento-Midtown, Sacramento *Also called Cy Sac Operator LLC* ***(P-12198)***
Courtyard San Diego Carlsbad, Carlsbad *Also called Hit Portfolio II NTC Trs LP* ***(P-12368)***
Courtyard San Diego Central, San Diego *Also called Apple Nine Hospitality MGT* ***(P-12015)***
Courtyard San Diego Gaslamp, San Diego *Also called Cy Gaslamp LLC* ***(P-12197)***
Courtyard-Central......D......858 573-0700
8651 Spectrum Center Blvd San Diego (92123) ***(P-12185)***
Courtyards At Pine Creek Inc......E......925 798-3900
1081 Mohr Ln Concord (94518) ***(P-23882)***

Mergent e-mail: customerrelations@mergent.com
1236
2020 Directory of California
Wholesalers and Services Companies
(P-0000) Products & Services Section entry number
(PA)=Parent Co (HQ)=Headquarters (DH)=Div Headquarters

Covad Communications Group Inc (HQ) ....C......408 952-6400
6800 Koll Center Pkwy Pleasanton (94566) *(P-5382)*
Covance Inc ....D......858 352-2300
10300 Campus Point Dr # 225 San Diego (92121) *(P-25735)*
Covanta Delano Inc ....E......661 792-3067
31500 Pond Rd Delano (93215) *(P-5826)*
Cove Builders Inc ....C......714 436-2973
2264 Arroyo Dr Riverside (92506) *(P-1237)*
Cove Electric Inc ....D......760 568-9924
77971 Wildcat Dr Ste F Palm Desert (92211) *(P-2465)*
Covelo Indian Community Center ....D......707 983-8478
Hwy 162 Covelo (95428) *(P-11080)*
Covenant Aviation Security LLC ....A......650 219-3473
1000 Marina Blvd Ste 100 Brisbane (94005) *(P-16245)*
Covenant Care LLC ....D......831 476-0770
1935 Wharf Rd Capitola (95010) *(P-19826)*
Covenant Care California LLC ....C......209 477-5252
9289 Branstetter Pl Stockton (95209) *(P-19827)*
Covenant Care California LLC ....D......415 327-0511
911 Bryant St Palo Alto (94301) *(P-19828)*
Covenant Care California LLC ....D......408 248-3736
410 N Winchester Blvd Santa Clara (95050) *(P-19829)*
Covenant Care California LLC ....D......510 261-2628
2124 57th Ave Oakland (94621) *(P-19830)*
Covenant Care California LLC ....D......562 427-7493
2725 Pacific Ave Long Beach (90806) *(P-19831)*
Covenant Care California LLC ....C......805 488-3696
5225 S J St Oxnard (93033) *(P-19832)*
Covenant Care California LLC ....C......323 589-5941
6425 Miles Ave Huntington Park (90255) *(P-19833)*
Covenant Care California LLC ....C......559 251-8463
577 S Peach Ave Fresno (93727) *(P-19834)*
Covenant Care California LLC ....D......916 391-6011
6821 24th St Sacramento (95822) *(P-19835)*
Covenant Care California LLC ....C......805 964-4871
160 S Patterson Ave Santa Barbara (93111) *(P-19836)*
Covenant Care California LLC ....C......209 632-3821
1111 E Tuolumne Rd Turlock (95382) *(P-19837)*
Covenant Care California LLC ....C......408 842-9311
8170 Murray Ave Gilroy (95020) *(P-19838)*
Covenant Care California LLC (HQ) ....E......949 349-1200
27071 Aliso Creek Rd # 100 Aliso Viejo (92656) *(P-19839)*
Covenant Care California LLC ....E......760 745-1288
1025 W 2nd Ave Escondido (92025) *(P-19840)*
Covenant Care California LLC ....C......209 521-2094
3620 Dale Rd Ste B Modesto (95356) *(P-20538)*
Covenant Care California LLC ....C......714 554-9700
1929 N Fairview St Santa Ana (92706) *(P-19841)*
Covenant Care California LLC ....D......650 964-0543
1949 Grant Rd Mountain View (94040) *(P-20822)*
Covenant Care California LLC ....C......650 941-5255
809 Fremont Ave Los Altos (94024) *(P-19842)*
Covenant Care Courtyard LLC ....D......530 756-1800
1850 E 8th St Davis (95616) *(P-19843)*
Covenant Care Indiana Inc (HQ) ....D......949 349-1200
27071 Aliso Creek Rd # 100 Aliso Viejo (92656) *(P-19844)*
Covenant Care La Jolla LLC ....C......858 453-5810
2552 Torrey Pines Rd # 1 La Jolla (92037) *(P-19845)*
Covenant House California ....C......323 461-3131
1325 N Western Ave Los Angeles (90027) *(P-23883)*
Covenant Industries Inc ....D......951 808-3708
110 Pine Ave Ste 910 Long Beach (90802) *(P-14252)*
Covenant Players (PA) ....C......805 486-7155
1741 Fiske Pl Oxnard (93033) *(P-17902)*
Covenant Rtirement Communities ....C......619 479-4790
325 Kempton St Spring Valley (91977) *(P-19846)*
Covenant Rtirement Communities ....C......209 632-9976
2125 N Olive Ave Ofc Turlock (95382) *(P-23884)*
Covenant Village of Turlock, Turlock *Also called Covenant Rtirement Communities (P-23884)*
Coventry Court Health Center ....C......714 636-2800
2040 S Euclid St Anaheim (92802) *(P-19847)*
Coventry Cove Apartments, Fresno *Also called Buckingham Property Management (P-13402)*
Coveo Software Corp ....D......800 635-5476
415 Mission St Fl 37 San Francisco (94105) *(P-14738)*
Coverity LLC (HQ) ....D......415 321-5200
185 Berry St Ste 6500 San Francisco (94107) *(P-14739)*
Covey Auto Express Inc (PA) ....C......253 826-0461
1444 El Pinal Dr Stockton (95205) *(P-17417)*
Covey, The, Carmel *Also called Quail Lodge Inc (P-12778)*
Covia Affordable Communities ....C......925 956-7400
2185 N Calif Blvd Ste 215 Walnut Creek (94596) *(P-23185)*
Covia Communities ....C......510 835-4700
100 Bay Pl Ofc Oakland (94610) *(P-23885)*
Covia Communities ....D......831 373-3111
651 Sinex Ave Pacific Grove (93950) *(P-23886)*
Covia Communities ....B......707 538-8400
5555 Montgomery Dr Santa Rosa (95409) *(P-23887)*
Covia Communities ....C......415 776-0500
1661 Pine St Apt 911 San Francisco (94109) *(P-23888)*
Covina Bowl Inc ....D......626 339-1286
675 S Glendora Ave West Covina (91790) *(P-18030)*
Covina Rehabilitation Center ....C......626 967-3874
261 W Badillo St Covina (91723) *(P-19848)*
Covina Service Center, San Dimas *Also called Southern California Edison Co (P-5949)*
Covington & Burling LLP ....C......650 632-4700
333 Twin Dolphin Dr # 700 Redwood City (94065) *(P-22449)*

Covington & Burling LLP ....E......415 591-6000
415 Mission St Ste 700 San Francisco (94105) *(P-22450)*
Covington & Burling LLP ....B......424 332-4800
1999 Avenue Of The Stars # 3500 Los Angeles (90067) *(P-22451)*
Cowboy Poetry, Santa Clarita *Also called Santa Clarita City of (P-18755)*
Cowell Homeowners Association (PA) ....D......925 825-0250
4498 Lawson Ct Concord (94521) *(P-24528)*
Cowell Student Health Center, Davis *Also called University California Davis (P-19528)*
Cowell Student Health Service, Stanford *Also called Leland Stanford Junior Univ (P-19156)*
Cox Castle & Nicholson LLP (PA) ....C......310 284-2200
2029 Century Park E # 2100 Los Angeles (90067) *(P-22452)*
Cox Automotive Inc ....A......404 843-5000
10700 Beech Ave Fontana (92337) *(P-6389)*
Cox Automotive Inc ....B......510 786-4500
29900 Auction Ct Hayward (94544) *(P-6390)*
Cox Automotive Inc ....B......951 689-6000
6446 Fremont St Riverside (92504) *(P-6391)*
Cox Automotive Inc ....B......760 754-3600
691 Calle Joven Oceanside (92057) *(P-6392)*
Cox California Telcom LLC ....D......310 377-1800
43 Peninsula Ctr Rllng HLS Est (90274) *(P-5383)*
Cox California Telcom LLC ....C......760 966-0447
1922 Avenida Del Oro Oceanside (92056) *(P-5782)*
Cox Castle, Los Angeles *Also called Cox Castle & Nicholson LLP (P-22452)*
Cox Communications Inc ....C......949 716-2020
140 Columbia Aliso Viejo (92656) *(P-5698)*
Cox Communications Inc ....C......858 715-4500
1535 Euclid Ave San Diego (92105) *(P-5699)*
Cox Communications Inc ....C......949 240-1212
26181 Avenida Aeropuerto San Juan Capistrano (92675) *(P-5384)*
Cox Communications Inc ....D......805 681-6600
3303 State St Santa Barbara (93105) *(P-5385)*
Cox Communications Inc ....C......949 546-1000
6771 Quail Hill Pkwy Irvine (92603) *(P-5700)*
Cox Communications Cal LLC ....B......619 562-9820
1175 N Cuyamaca St El Cajon (92020) *(P-5701)*
Cox Communications Cal LLC ....B......619 262-1122
5159 Federal Blvd San Diego (92105) *(P-5702)*
Cox Communications Cal LLC ....B......619 263-9251
581 Telegraph Canyon Rd Chula Vista (91910) *(P-5703)*
Cox Petroleum Transport, Bakersfield *Also called H F Cox Inc (P-4057)*
Coyote Creek Consulting Inc ....D......408 383-9200
1551 Mccarthy Blvd # 115 Milpitas (95035) *(P-15969)*
Coyote Creek Golf Club ....D......408 463-1400
1 Coyote Creek Golf Dr Morgan Hill (95037) *(P-18236)*
Coyote Hills Golf Course, Fullerton *Also called American Golf Corporation (P-18219)*
CP Opco LLC ....D......707 253-2332
22674 Broadway A Sonoma (95476) *(P-14144)*
CP Opco LLC ....D......858 496-9700
7069 Cnsld Way Ste 300 San Diego (92121) *(P-14145)*
CP Opco LLC ....D......209 524-1966
333 S Grand Ave Ste 4070 Los Angeles (90071) *(P-14146)*
CP Opco LLC (HQ) ....A......310 966-4900
901 W Hillcrest Blvd A Inglewood (90301) *(P-13415)*
CP Opco LLC ....D......310 966-4900
11766 Wilshire Blvd # 380 Los Angeles (90025) *(P-14147)*
CP Opco LLC ....D......650 652-0300
22674 Broadway A Sonoma (95476) *(P-14148)*
CP Opco LLC ....D......805 566-3566
1120 Mark Ave Carpinteria (93013) *(P-14149)*
CP Opco LLC ....D......714 540-6111
3101 S Harbor Blvd Santa Ana (92704) *(P-14150)*
CP Technologies, Irvine *Also called Corner Products Company (P-7253)*
CPC Services Inc ....D......626 852-6200
2025 E Fincl Way Ste 200 Glendora (91741) *(P-6678)*
Cpcc Inc ....D......818 882-3200
10610 Owensmouth Ave Chatsworth (91311) *(P-20539)*
Cpe Hr Inc ....D......310 270-9800
9000 W Sunset Blvd # 900 West Hollywood (90069) *(P-26570)*
Cpe Peo Inc ....D......310 385-1000
9200 W Sunset Blvd West Hollywood (90069) *(P-14497)*
Cph Hospital Management LLC ....A......562 838-3751
13100 Studebaker Rd Norwalk (90650) *(P-20823)*
Cph Monarch Hotel LLC ....A......949 234-3200
1 Monarch Beach Resort Dana Point (92629) *(P-12186)*
CPI Econco Division (HQ) ....D......530 662-7553
1318 Commerce Ave Woodland (95776) *(P-17453)*
CPI International ....D......707 521-6327
5580 Skylane Blvd Santa Rosa (95403) *(P-7027)*
CPI Luxury Group ....D......818 249-9888
10220 Norris Ave Pacoima (91331) *(P-7786)*
CPM Ltd Inc (PA) ....A......619 237-9900
1855 1st Ave Ste 300 San Diego (92101) *(P-14498)*
CPM Services, San Francisco *Also called Cooper Pugeda Management Inc (P-26190)*
Cpmc, San Francisco *Also called Sutter Health (P-21252)*
Cpmc Mission Bernal Campus, San Francisco *Also called Sutter Health (P-19482)*
Cpn Wild Horse Geothermal LLC ....B......707 431-6229
10350 Socrates Mine Rd Middletown (95461) *(P-5827)*
Cpo Commerce LLC ....D......626 585-3600
120 W Bellevue Dr Ste 300 Pasadena (91105) *(P-7391)*
Cprime Inc (HQ) ....D......650 931-1650
107 S B St Ste 200 San Mateo (94401) *(P-26571)*
CPS, Studio City *Also called Commercial Prgrm Systems Inc (P-15964)*
CPS, Burlingame *Also called Kotobuki-Ya Inc (P-3545)*
CPS Hr Consulting, Sacramento *Also called Cooperative Personnel Services (P-26566)*
CPS Security, Long Beach *Also called Commercial Protective Svcs Inc (P-16239)*
CPS Security Solutions Inc (PA) ....D......310 818-1030
3400 E Airport Way Long Beach (90806) *(P-16246)*

Employee Codes: A=Over 500 employees, B=251-500
C=101-250, D=51-100, E=50

2020 Directory of California
Wholesalers and Services Companies

© Mergent Inc. 1-800-342-5647
1237

A
L
P
H
A
B
E
T
I
C

Cpu Medical Management Systems, San Diego *Also called Computer Proc Unlimited Inc* ***(P-14722)***
Cr Drywall, San Jose *Also called C R S Drywall Inc* ***(P-2762)***
Craft Resources Inc ....C.....310 937-3744
220 S Pcifc Cst Hwy 112 Redondo Beach (90277) ***(P-14499)***
Craftman Concrete ....D.....559 298-8864
755 N Peach Ave Ste F11 Clovis (93611) ***(P-1110)***
Craftsman Lath and Plaster Inc ....B.....951 685-9922
8325 63rd St Riverside (92509) ***(P-2922)***
Craftworks Rest Breweries Inc ....C.....415 292-5800
600 Polk St San Francisco (94102) ***(P-16724)***
Craig Realty Group, Newport Beach *Also called Eureka Realty Partners Inc* ***(P-11561)***
Cramer Painting Inc ....E.....909 397-5770
4080 Mission Blvd Montclair (91763) ***(P-2340)***
Crane Acquisition Inc ....D.....415 922-1666
2700 Geary Blvd San Francisco (94118) ***(P-13820)***
Crane Co ....C.....562 426-2531
3201 Walnut Ave Long Beach (90755) ***(P-7632)***
Crane Pest Control, San Francisco *Also called Crane Acquisition Inc* ***(P-13820)***
Craniofacial Department, Loma Linda *Also called Loma Linda University Med Ctr* ***(P-21010)***
Crash Inc ....D.....619 297-5131
1081 Camino Del Ri San Diego (92108) ***(P-23889)***
Crash Inc Short Term I ....E.....619 282-7274
4161 Marlborough Ave San Diego (92105) ***(P-22013)***
CRAYCROFT YOUTH CENTER, Fresno *Also called Rescue Children Inc* ***(P-23409)***
Crazy Gideons, Los Angeles *Also called F O C Electronics Corporation* ***(P-7203)***
CRC Health Corporate ....D.....714 542-3581
2101 E 1st St Santa Ana (92705) ***(P-22014)***
CRC Health Corporate (HQ) ....D.....408 367-0044
20400 Stevens Cupertino (95014) ***(P-22015)***
CRC Health Corporation, Cupertino *Also called CRC Health LLC* ***(P-21466)***
CRC Health Group Inc (HQ) ....D.....877 272-8668
20400 Stev Creek Blvd 6 Flr 6 Cupertino (95014) ***(P-22222)***
CRC Health LLC (HQ) ....D.....877 272-8668
20400 Stevens Creek Blvd # 600 Cupertino (95014) ***(P-21466)***
Crdn of Southern La County, Long Beach *Also called Foasberg Laundry & Clrs Inc* ***(P-13221)***
Cre, Burbank *Also called Commodity Resource Envmtl Inc* ***(P-6187)***
Create Music Group Inc ....D.....310 623-0696
1320 N Wilton Pl Los Angeles (90028) ***(P-16725)***
Creating Arts Company ....E.....310 804-0223
4380 Hillview Dr Malibu (90265) ***(P-17903)***
Creative Alternatives ....C.....209 668-9361
2855 Geer Rd Ste A Turlock (95382) ***(P-23890)***
Creative Artists Agency LLC (PA) ....A.....424 288-2000
2000 Avenue Of The Stars # 100 Los Angeles (90067) ***(P-17904)***
Creative Channel Services LLC (HQ) ....D.....310 482-6500
6601 Center Dr W Ste 400 Los Angeles (90045) ***(P-13482)***
Creative Circle LLC (HQ) ....D.....323 930-2333
5900 Wilshire Blvd # 1100 Los Angeles (90036) ***(P-14253)***
Creative Design Cons Inc (PA) ....D.....714 641-4868
2915 Red Hill Ave G201 Costa Mesa (92626) ***(P-16726)***
Creative Design Interiors Inc (PA) ....D.....916 641-1121
737 Del Paso Rd Sacramento (95834) ***(P-2997)***
Creative Energy Foods Inc ....D.....510 638-8668
9957 Medford Ave Ste 4 Oakland (94603) ***(P-8570)***
Creative Events Enterprises ....C.....818 610-7000
4872 Topanga Canyon Blvd # 406 Woodland Hills (91364) ***(P-26572)***
Creative Gallery, Culver City *Also called Framestore Inc* ***(P-17975)***
Creative Group, The, Los Angeles *Also called Robert Half International Inc* ***(P-14394)***
Creative Group, The, Menlo Park *Also called Robert Half International Inc* ***(P-14399)***
Creative Housing & Svcs LLC ....C.....626 403-5454
605 E Huntington Dr # 207 Monrovia (91016) ***(P-10713)***
Creative Labs Inc (HQ) ....C.....408 428-6600
1901 Mccarthy Blvd Milpitas (95035) ***(P-6817)***
Creative Living Options Inc ....C.....916 372-2102
2945 Ramco St Ste 120 West Sacramento (95691) ***(P-23891)***
Creative Maintenance Systems ....D.....949 852-2871
1340 Reynolds Ave Ste 111 Irvine (92614) ***(P-13899)***
Creative Recreation, Los Angeles *Also called Kommonwealth Inc* ***(P-8136)***
Creative Security Company Inc ....B.....408 295-2600
150 S Autumn St Ste B San Jose (95110) ***(P-16247)***
Creative Technology Group Inc (HQ) ....D.....818 779-2400
14000 Arminta St Panorama City (91402) ***(P-16727)***
Creativebug LLC ....D.....415 325-5926
835 Market St Ste 700 San Francisco (94103) ***(P-14740)***
Credit Bureau NAPA County Inc ....C.....707 940-3000
1247 Broadway Sonoma (95476) ***(P-13679)***
Credit Card Services Inc (PA) ....D.....213 365-1122
21281 S Western Ave Torrance (90501) ***(P-16728)***
Credit Counselor of California, Concord *Also called Consumer Cr Cnsling Svc San Fr* ***(P-13412)***
Credit Karma Inc (PA) ....C.....415 510-5059
760 Market St Ste 500 San Francisco (94102) ***(P-16729)***
Credit Ssse Securities USA LLC ....D.....213 253-2600
10880 Wilshire Blvd Los Angeles (90024) ***(P-9682)***
Credit Suisse (usa) Inc ....D.....415 249-2100
650 California St Fl 31 San Francisco (94108) ***(P-9683)***
Credit Suisse (usa) Inc ....E.....415 678-3940
650 California St Fl 28 San Francisco (94108) ***(P-9684)***
Credit Union Southern Cal (PA) ....D.....562 698-8326
8028 Greenleaf Ave Whittier (90602) ***(P-9303)***
Credit Union Southern Cal ....C.....562 698-8326
8101 E Kaiser Blvd Anaheim (92808) ***(P-9304)***
CREDIT.ORG, Riverside *Also called Springboard Solutions LLC* ***(P-27219)***
Credo Mobile Inc ....D.....415 369-2000
101 Market St Ste 700 San Francisco (94105) ***(P-5386)***
Creedence Lessee LLC ....D.....415 561-1100
425 N Point St San Francisco (94133) ***(P-12187)***

Creekside Cnvalescent Hosp Inc ....C.....707 544-7750
850 Sonoma Ave Santa Rosa (95404) ***(P-19849)***
Creekside Healthcare Ctr ....E.....510 235-5514
1900 Church Ln San Pablo (94806) ***(P-19850)***
Creekside Rehab and Behavioral ....C.....707 524-7030
850 Sonoma Ave Santa Rosa (95404) ***(P-19851)***
Crenshaw Bowling ....E.....310 326-5120
24600 Crenshaw Blvd Torrance (90505) ***(P-18031)***
Crenshaw Nursing, Los Angeles *Also called Longwood Management Corp* ***(P-20092)***
Crenshaw YMCA ....D.....323 290-9113
3820 Santa Rosalia Dr Los Angeles (90008) ***(P-24529)***
Crescent Court Nursing Home ....E.....209 367-7400
1334 S Ham Ln Lodi (95242) ***(P-20540)***
Crescent Cy Convalescent Hosp, Crescent City *Also called North Shore Investment Inc* ***(P-20158)***
Crescent Healthcare Inc (HQ) ....C.....714 520-6300
11980 Telg Rd Ste 100 Santa Fe Springs (90670) ***(P-21727)***
Crescent Solutions, Irvine *Also called Crescent Staffing Inc* ***(P-14741)***
Crescent Staffing Inc (PA) ....C.....949 724-0304
17871 Mitchell N Ste 100 Irvine (92614) ***(P-14741)***
Crescenta-Canada YMCA (PA) ....B.....818 790-0123
1930 Foothill Blvd La Canada (91011) ***(P-24530)***
Crescenta-Canada YMCA ....E.....818 352-3255
6840 Foothill Blvd Tujunga (91042) ***(P-24531)***
Cresse Mark School of Baseball ....D.....714 892-6145
58 Fulmar Ln Aliso Viejo (92656) ***(P-18678)***
Crest Beverage, San Diego *Also called Reyes Holdings LLC* ***(P-9748)***
Crest Beverage Company Inc ....C.....858 452-2300
3840 Via De La Valle Del Mar (92014) ***(P-8756)***
Crest Digital, Laguna Beach *Also called National Film Laboratories* ***(P-17753)***
Crest Financial Corporation (HQ) ....D.....562 733-6500
12641 166th St Cerritos (90703) ***(P-10333)***
Crest R E O & Relocation, La Crescenta *Also called EAM Enterprises Inc* ***(P-11106)***
Crest Steel Corporation ....D.....310 830-2651
6580 General Rd Riverside (92509) ***(P-7058)***
Cresta Loma, Alameda *Also called Telecare Corporation* ***(P-21441)***
Crestline Funding Corporation ....E.....949 863-8600
18851 Pardeen Ave San Diego (92108) ***(P-9544)***
Crestline Hotels & Resorts Inc ....C.....213 629-1200
120 S Los Angeles St 11 Los Angeles (90012) ***(P-12188)***
Crestline Hotels & Resorts LLC ....D.....213 624-0000
535 S Grand Ave Los Angeles (90071) ***(P-26206)***
Crestline Hotels & Resorts LLC ....C.....415 775-7555
1250 Columbus Ave San Francisco (94133) ***(P-26207)***
Crestline Hotels & Resorts LLC ....C.....760 322-6000
888 E Tahquitz Canyon Way Palm Springs (92262) ***(P-12189)***
Crestmont Capital LLC ....C.....800 949-0401
2030 Main St Irvine (92614) ***(P-11904)***
Creston Village, Paso Robles *Also called Emeritus Corporation* ***(P-10721)***
Crestview Cnvalescent Hosp Inc ....C.....909 877-1361
1471 S Riverside Ave Rialto (92376) ***(P-19852)***
CRESTWOOD BEHAVIORAL HEALTH, Stockton *Also called Dreamctchers Empwerment Netwrk* ***(P-23907)***
Crestwood Behavioral Hlth Inc ....C.....209 526-8050
1400 Celeste Dr Modesto (95355) ***(P-21401)***
Crestwood Behavioral Hlth Inc ....D.....408 275-1067
1425 Fruitdale Ave San Jose (95128) ***(P-23892)***
Crestwood Behavioral Hlth Inc ....D.....530 221-0976
3062 Churn Creek Rd Redding (96002) ***(P-23893)***
Crestwood Behavioral Hlth Inc ....C.....510 651-1244
4303 Stevenson Blvd Fremont (94538) ***(P-23894)***
Crestwood Behavioral Hlth Inc ....C.....916 452-1431
2600 Stockton Blvd Sacramento (95817) ***(P-21402)***
Crestwood Behavioral Hlth Inc ....C.....707 552-0215
115 Oddstad Dr Vallejo (94589) ***(P-23895)***
Crestwood Behavioral Hlth Inc ....D.....510 793-8383
2171 Mowry Ave Fremont (94538) ***(P-23896)***
Crestwood Behavioral Hlth Inc ....D.....760 451-4165
624 E Elder St Fallbrook (92028) ***(P-21403)***
Crestwood Behavioral Hlth Inc ....D.....661 363-8127
6700 Eucalyptus Dr Ste A Bakersfield (93306) ***(P-23186)***
Crestwood Behavioral Hlth Inc ....D.....559 445-9094
153 N U St Fresno (93701) ***(P-21404)***
Crestwood Behavioral Hlth Inc ....D.....707 558-1777
2201 Tuolumne St Vallejo (94589) ***(P-21405)***
Crestwood Behavioral Hlth Inc ....D.....707 552-0215
115 Oddstad Dr Vallejo (94589) ***(P-21406)***
Crestwood Behavioral Hlth Inc ....C.....661 363-6711
6744 Eucalyptus Dr Bakersfield (93306) ***(P-21467)***
Crestwood Behavioral Hlth Inc ....D.....916 977-0949
4741 Engle Rd Carmichael (95608) ***(P-21407)***
Crestwood Behavioral Hlth Inc ....D.....925 938-8050
550 Patterson Blvd Pleasant Hill (94523) ***(P-21408)***
Crew Creative Advertising LLC ....C.....310 451-3225
7966 Beverly Blvd Los Angeles (90048) ***(P-13483)***
Crew Inc ....D.....310 608-6860
19618 S Susana Rd Compton (90221) ***(P-3310)***
Crh Management, Newport Beach *Also called Core Realty Holdings MGT Inc* ***(P-11073)***
CRI HELP DRUG REHABILITATION, North Hollywood *Also called Cri-Help Inc* ***(P-23897)***
Cri-Help Inc (PA) ....C.....818 985-8323
11027 Burbank Blvd North Hollywood (91601) ***(P-23897)***
Cricket Communications LLC (HQ) ....D.....858 882-6000
7337 Trade St San Diego (92121) ***(P-5253)***
Cricket Indiana Property Co ....D.....858 587-2648
10307 Pacific Center Ct San Diego (92121) ***(P-5254)***
Cricket Stx, San Diego *Also called Stx Wireless Operations LLC* ***(P-5272)***
Cricket Wireless, San Diego *Also called Cricket Communications LLC* ***(P-5253)***

Mergent e-mail: customerrelations@mergent.com
1238
2020 Directory of California Wholesalers and Services Companies
(P-0000) Products & Services Section entry number
(PA)=Parent Co (HQ)=Headquarters (DH)=Div Headquarters

Crime Finders Inc ....D....877 999-3203
710 S Victory Blvd # 205 Burbank (91502) ***(P-26573)***
Crime Impact Security & Patrol, Los Angeles *Also called Crime Impact Security Patrol* ***(P-16248)***
Crime Impact Security Patrol....D....323 296-6406
3860 Crenshaw Blvd # 223 Los Angeles (90008) ***(P-16248)***
Crimetek Security....B....209 668-6208
3448 N Golden State Blvd Turlock (95382) ***(P-16249)***
Crimson Wine Group Ltd (PA)....C....800 486-0503
2700 Napa Vly Corp Dr B NAPA (94558) ***(P-8801)***
Cripts Health Care....E....858 554-8646
10666 N Torrey Pines Rd La Jolla (92037) ***(P-18936)***
Crisp California Walnuts, Stratford *Also called Crisp Warehouse Inc* ***(P-480)***
Crisp Enterprises Inc (PA)....D....714 668-5955
3180 Pullman St Costa Mesa (92626) ***(P-13759)***
Crisp Warehouse Inc....D....559 947-9221
20500 Main St Stratford (93266) ***(P-480)***
Cristophe Salon, Beverly Hills *Also called Hair Fashion Inc* ***(P-13349)***
Critchfeld Mech Inc Sthern Cal....D....949 390-2900
15391 Springdale St Huntington Beach (92649) ***(P-2108)***
Critchfield Mechanical Inc....B....650 321-7801
4085 Campbell Ave Menlo Park (94025) ***(P-2109)***
CRITTENTON SERVICES FOR CHILDR, Fullerton *Also called Florence Crittenton Services* ***(P-23928)***
Crmc, Coalinga *Also called Coalinga Regional Medical Cent* ***(P-20794)***
CROCKER ART MUSEUM, Sacramento *Also called Crocker Art Museum Association* ***(P-24823)***
Crocker Art Museum Association....D....916 808-7000
216 O St Sacramento (95814) ***(P-24823)***
Crocker Group LLC....D....714 221-5621
1101 E Orangewood Ave Anaheim (92805) ***(P-11081)***
Crockett & Coinc....D....619 267-1103
5540 Sweetwater Rd Bonita (91902) ***(P-18237)***
Crockett Garbage Service, Richmond *Also called Richmond Sanitary Service Inc* ***(P-6354)***
Crocodile Bay Lodge....C....707 559-7990
731 Southpoint Blvd Petaluma (94954) ***(P-13137)***
Crocus Holdings LLC....D....916 782-1238
1161 Cirby Way Roseville (95661) ***(P-19853)***
Crooks, Jerry C MD, Stockton *Also called Stockton Orthpd Med Group Inc* ***(P-19458)***
Crosby National Golf Club LLC....D....858 756-6310
17102 Bing Crosby Blvd Rancho Santa Fe (92067) ***(P-18436)***
Cross Country Healthcare Inc....C....951 786-7683
1700 Iowa Ave Ste 210 Riverside (92507) ***(P-14254)***
Cross Link Inc....D....415 495-3191
Bldg C Pier 50 San Francisco (94158) ***(P-4629)***
Cross Rock, Paso Robles *Also called Pearce Services LLC* ***(P-1902)***
Crosscap Media Services Inc (PA)....D....415 217-8860
311 California St Ste 320 San Francisco (94104) ***(P-14742)***
Crosscheck Inc (PA)....C....707 665-2100
1440 N Mcdowell Blvd Petaluma (94954) ***(P-16730)***
Crosslink Prof Tax Sltions LLC (PA)....D....800 345-4337
16916 S Harlan Rd Lathrop (95330) ***(P-14743)***
Crossmark Inc....D....714 464-6318
2401 E Katella Ave # 625 Anaheim (92806) ***(P-8165)***
Crossmark Inc....B....925 463-3555
3875 Hopyard Rd Ste 250 Pleasanton (94588) ***(P-8166)***
Crossmark Sales & Marketing, Pleasanton *Also called Crossmark Inc* ***(P-8166)***
Crossroad Services Inc....B....714 728-3915
2360 Alvarado St San Leandro (94577) ***(P-8964)***
CROSSROADS COMMUNITY FOUNDATIO, Los Angeles *Also called PS Arts* ***(P-27175)***
Crossroads Diversfd Svcs Inc....D....916 676-2540
7011 Sylvan Rd Ste A Citrus Heights (95610) ***(P-14255)***
Crossroads Facility Svcs Inc....D....916 568-5230
9300 Tech Center Dr # 100 Sacramento (95826) ***(P-13900)***
Crossroads Live Inc....D....818 247-0400
3900 W Alameda Ave Fl 12 Burbank (91505) ***(P-17905)***
Crossroads Medical Offices, City of Industry *Also called Kaiser Foundation Hospitals* ***(P-19063)***
Crowd Management, Fresno *Also called Contemporary Services Corp* ***(P-16243)***
Crowdstrike Inc (HQ)....C....888 512-8906
150 Mathilda Pl Ste 300 Sunnyvale (94086) ***(P-15970)***
Crowdstrike Holdings Inc (PA)....C....888 512-8906
150 Mathilda Pl Ste 300 Sunnyvale (94086) ***(P-15295)***
Crowe LLP....C....818 501-5200
15233 Ventura Blvd Fl 9 Sherman Oaks (91403) ***(P-25567)***
Crowell & Moring LLP....D....415 986-2800
275 Battery St Ste 2200 San Francisco (94111) ***(P-22453)***
Crowell & Moring LLP....E....949 263-8400
3 Park Plz Ste 2000 Irvine (92614) ***(P-22454)***
Crowell, Weedon & Co., Los Angeles *Also called DA Davidson & Co* ***(P-9685)***
Crown Building Maintenance Co....A....916 920-9556
1832 Tribute Rd Ste H Sacramento (95815) ***(P-13901)***
Crown Building Maintenance Co....E....714 434-9494
3300 W Macarthur Blvd Santa Ana (92704) ***(P-13902)***
Crown Building Maintenance Co....B....303 680-3713
235 Pine St Ste 600 San Francisco (94104) ***(P-13903)***
Crown Building Maintenance Co....C....858 560-5785
5482 Complex St Ste 108 San Diego (92123) ***(P-13904)***
Crown Building Maintenance Co....E....213 765-7800
2601 S Figueroa St # 299 Los Angeles (90007) ***(P-13905)***
Crown Cove Senior Care Cmnty....D....949 760-2800
3901 E Coast Hwy Ofc Corona Del Mar (92625) ***(P-23898)***
Crown Disposal Company Inc....C....818 767-0675
9189 De Garmo Ave Sun Valley (91352) ***(P-6192)***
Crown Energy Services Inc....A....415 546-6534
611 Gateway Blvd South San Francisco (94080) ***(P-25023)***
Crown Energy Services Inc....A....213 765-7800
2601 S Figueroa St Fl 1 Los Angeles (90007) ***(P-13906)***
Crown Facility Solutions....E....657 266-0821
3617 W Macarthur Blvd Santa Ana (92704) ***(P-13907)***
Crown Fence Co....D....562 864-5177
12118 Bloomfield Ave Santa Fe Springs (90670) ***(P-3396)***
Crown Golf Properties LP....C....714 730-1611
12442 Tustin Ranch Rd Tustin (92782) ***(P-26574)***
Crown Limousine L.A., Los Angeles *Also called Crown Transportation Inc* ***(P-3664)***
Crown Media United States LLC (HQ)....D....818 755-2400
12700 Ventura Blvd # 100 Studio City (91604) ***(P-5704)***
Crown Plaza, Pleasanton *Also called Six Continents Hotels Inc* ***(P-12937)***
Crown Plaza, Milpitas *Also called B H R Operations LLC* ***(P-12031)***
Crown Plaza La Harbor Hotel, San Pedro *Also called Spf Capital Real Estate LLC* ***(P-12952)***
Crown Plaza Los Angeles, Los Angeles *Also called Ihg Management (maryland) LLC* ***(P-12454)***
Crown Plaza SD....D....619 297-1101
2270 Hotel Cir N San Diego (92108) ***(P-12190)***
Crown Pointe Retirement, Corona *Also called Provident Group Crown Pnte LLC* ***(P-10801)***
Crown Transportation Inc....D....310 737-0888
12300 W Washington Blvd Los Angeles (90066) ***(P-3664)***
Crown Vly Precision Machining, Irwindale *Also called Sinecera Inc* ***(P-17057)***
Crowne Plaza, Irvine *Also called Intercontinental Hotels Group* ***(P-12461)***
Crowne Plaza, Los Angeles *Also called Hpt Trs Ihg-2 Inc* ***(P-12419)***
Crowne Plaza, Redondo Beach *Also called Hpt Trs Ihg-2 Inc* ***(P-12420)***
Crowne Plaza Concord, Concord *Also called Concord Hotel LLC* ***(P-12169)***
Crowne Plaza Costa Mesa, Costa Mesa *Also called Bright Bristol Street LLC* ***(P-12087)***
Crowne Plaza Hotel, Foster City *Also called Founders Management II Corp* ***(P-12274)***
Crowne Plaza Irvine-Orange Cou, Irvine *Also called Intercontinental Hotels Group* ***(P-12469)***
Crowne Plaza Lax LLC....C....310 258-1321
5985 W Century Blvd Los Angeles (90045) ***(P-12191)***
Crowne Plaza Ventura Beach, Ventura *Also called Ventura Hsptality Partners LLC* ***(P-13062)***
Crowne Plz Los Angeles Hbr Ht, San Pedro *Also called Proficient LLC* ***(P-12772)***
Crowne Plz Los Angeles Hbr Ht, Long Beach *Also called Nhca Inc* ***(P-12645)***
Crowne Plz Scramento Northeast, Sacramento *Also called Khanna Entps - II Ltd Partnr* ***(P-12505)***
Crowner Sheet Metal Pdts Inc....E....626 960-4971
14346 Arrow Hwy Baldwin Park (91706) ***(P-3042)***
CRS, Hayward *Also called Commercial Rfrgn Spcalists LLC* ***(P-2101)***
CRST International Inc....C....909 829-1313
10641 Calabash Ave Fontana (92337) ***(P-3989)***
Crstb Partners LLC....C....916 645-7200
3075 Twelve Bridges Dr Lincoln (95648) ***(P-18238)***
Crucible....C....510 444-0919
1260 7th St Oakland (94607) ***(P-23187)***
Cruisers Carwash & Diner, Northridge *Also called M K H Inc* ***(P-17388)***
Crum & Forster, Los Angeles *Also called United States Fire Insur Co* ***(P-10529)***
Crunch LLC....D....323 654-4550
8000 W Sunset Blvd # 220 West Hollywood (90046) ***(P-18135)***
Crunch LLC....D....650 257-8000
1190 Saratoga Ave San Jose (95129) ***(P-18136)***
Crunch LLC....C....415 495-1939
345 Spear St Ste 104 San Francisco (94105) ***(P-18137)***
Crunch Fitness, West Hollywood *Also called Crunch LLC* ***(P-18135)***
Crunch Fitness....D....805 522-5454
19867 Prairie St Ste 200 Chatsworth (91311) ***(P-18138)***
Crunchyroll, San Francisco *Also called Ellation Inc* ***(P-14782)***
Cruz Hoffstetter LLC....D....626 915-5621
519 W Badillo St Covina (91722) ***(P-16731)***
Cruz Modular Inc (PA)....D....714 283-2890
249 W Baywood Ave Ste B Orange (92865) ***(P-4202)***
Cruz Veterinary Hospital....D....831 475-5400
2585 Soquel Dr Santa Cruz (95065) ***(P-577)***
Crystal Aire Country Club Golf....E....661 944-2112
15701 Boca Raton Ave Llano (93544) ***(P-18437)***
Crystal Art of Florida, Vernon *Also called Rggd Inc* ***(P-7830)***
Crystal Casino & Hotel, Compton *Also called Celebrity Casinos Inc* ***(P-12130)***
Crystal Chrysler Plymuth Dodge....D....760 324-9375
36444 Auto Park Dr Cathedral City (92234) ***(P-17326)***
Crystal Creamery, Modesto *Also called Foster Dairy Farms* ***(P-390)***
Crystal Cruises LLC (HQ)....C....310 785-9300
11755 Wilshire Blvd # 900 Los Angeles (90025) ***(P-4595)***
Crystal Dynamics Inc (HQ)....D....650 421-7600
1400a Saport Blvd Ste 300 Redwood City (94063) ***(P-15296)***
Crystal Organic Farms LLC....B....661 845-5200
6900 Mountain View Rd Bakersfield (93307) ***(P-310)***
Crystal Springs Golf Course, Burlingame *Also called Crystal Springs Golf Partners* ***(P-18438)***
Crystal Springs Golf Partners....E....650 342-4188
6650 Golf Course Dr Burlingame (94010) ***(P-18438)***
Crystal Stairs Inc (PA)....B....323 299-8998
5110 W Goldleaf Cir # 150 Los Angeles (90056) ***(P-23188)***
Crystal Valet Parking Inc....D....323 663-7275
4477 Hollywood Blvd 209 Los Angeles (90027) ***(P-13416)***
Crystalaire Country Club, Llano *Also called Crystal Aire Country Club Golf* ***(P-18437)***
Cs Concrete Solutions Inc....D....949 285-3122
47 Goldbriar Way Mission Viejo (92692) ***(P-3136)***
Cs-Pleasanton LLC....B....925 463-2822
7090 Johnson Dr Pleasanton (94588) ***(P-18439)***
Csaa Insur Group Walnut Creek, Irvine *Also called Western United Insurance Co* ***(P-10547)***
Csaa Insurance AAA, Santa Rosa *Also called American Automobile Assctn* ***(P-10070)***
Csaa Insurance Exchange (PA)....D....800 922-8228
3055 Oak Rd Walnut Creek (94597) ***(P-10334)***
Csaa Travel Agency, Walnut Creek *Also called American Automobile Associatio* ***(P-10071)***
Csaa Travel Agency, Stockton *Also called American Automobile Assctn* ***(P-24790)***
Csaa Travel Agency, Walnut Creek *Also called American Automobile* ***(P-10247)***

ALPHABETIC

Employee Codes: A=Over 500 employees, B=251-500
C=101-250, D=51-100, E=50
2020 Directory of California
Wholesalers and Services Companies
© Mergent Inc. 1-800-342-5647
1239

Csac Excess Insurance Auth.....D.....916 850-7300
75 Iron Point Cir Ste 200 Folsom (95630) ***(P-10335)***
Csba, West Sacramento *Also called California School Boards Assn* ***(P-24387)***
CSC Auto Salv Dismantling Inc.....D.....818 532-4624
12207 Branford St Sun Valley (91352) ***(P-4920)***
CSC Covansys Corporation.....C.....510 304-3430
34740 Tuxedo Cmn Fremont (94555) ***(P-14744)***
CSC Serviceworks Holdings Inc.....C.....510 429-0900
32910 Alvarado Niles Rd # 150 Union City (94587) ***(P-13248)***
CSCU, Lompoc *Also called Coasthills Credit Union* ***(P-9387)***
CSEA, Sacramento *Also called Califrnia State Employees Assn* ***(P-24439)***
Csea, San Jose *Also called California Schl Employees Assn* ***(P-24438)***
Csg Consultants Inc (PA).....E.....650 522-2500
550 Pilgrim Dr Foster City (94404) ***(P-25024)***
Csi, Fullerton *Also called Cardservice International Inc* ***(P-16677)***
Csi Cold Storage 4150, Anaheim *Also called US Foods Inc* ***(P-8668)***
Csi Electrical Contractors Inc.....D.....661 723-0869
41769 11th St W Ste B Palmdale (93551) ***(P-2466)***
Csi Electrical Contractors Inc (HQ).....C.....562 946-0700
10623 Fulton Wells Ave Santa Fe Springs (90670) ***(P-2467)***
Csi Financial Services LLC.....E.....858 200-9200
3636 Nobel Dr Ste 250 San Diego (92122) ***(P-26208)***
Csl Solutions, Fair Oaks *Also called Wightman Enterprises Inc* ***(P-14596)***
CSRA LLC.....A.....619 225-2600
4045 Hancock St San Diego (92110) ***(P-15900)***
CSRA Systems & Solutions LLC.....E.....951 735-3300
2727 Hamner Ave Norco (92860) ***(P-15971)***
CSS Holdings Inc.....D.....888 884-9224
7486 La Jolla Blvd La Jolla (92037) ***(P-14745)***
Csu Holding Company.....E.....707 746-0353
531 Stone Rd Benicia (94510) ***(P-11655)***
Csub Nursing Class of 2006.....D.....408 219-5914
9001 Stockdale Hwy Bakersfield (93311) ***(P-16732)***
Csus Children's Center, Sacramento *Also called Students of Associated* ***(P-23794)***
CSX Corporation.....C.....626 336-1377
14863 Clark Ave Hacienda Heights (91745) ***(P-3501)***
CT Lien Solution.....C.....818 662-4100
330 N Brand Blvd Ste 700 Glendale (91203) ***(P-26575)***
Ctc Food International Inc (PA).....E.....650 873-7600
50 W Ohio Ave Richmond (94804) ***(P-8571)***
Ctc Group Inc (HQ).....C.....310 540-0500
21333 Hawthorne Blvd Torrance (90503) ***(P-12192)***
Ctdn - Redding, Redding *Also called Donor Network West* ***(P-22233)***
Ctg, San Jose *Also called Computer Task Group Inc* ***(P-14725)***
Ctm, Gardena *Also called Classic Tile & Mosaic Inc* ***(P-6675)***
Ctour Holiday LLC.....B.....323 261-8811
222 E Huntington Dr # 105 Monrovia (91016) ***(P-18679)***
Ctpartners Exec Search Inc.....D.....949 754-2821
8001 Irvine Center Dr Irvine (92618) ***(P-14256)***
CTSI, Lancaster *Also called California Traffic Safety Inst* ***(P-27015)***
CU Cooperative Systems Inc (PA).....B.....909 948-2500
9692 Haven Ave Rancho Cucamonga (91730) ***(P-9430)***
CU Direct Corporation (PA).....C.....909 481-2300
2855 E Guasti Rd Ste 500 Ontario (91761) ***(P-14746)***
Cubic Corporation.....A.....858 277-6780
9233 Balboa Ave San Diego (92123) ***(P-15577)***
Cubic Defense Systems, San Diego *Also called Cubic Corporation* ***(P-15577)***
Cubix Construction Company (PA).....C.....925 314-0770
5 Meadowbrook Ln Danville (94526) ***(P-1344)***
Cucamonga Valley Water Dst.....D.....909 987-2591
10440 Ashford St Rancho Cucamonga (91730) ***(P-6045)***
Cudahy Medical Offices, Cudahy *Also called Kaiser Foundation Hospitals* ***(P-20957)***
Cudc, Ontario *Also called CU Direct Corporation* ***(P-14746)***
Cuisine Partners USA, Los Angeles *Also called Investors Capital MGT Group* ***(P-26269)***
Culberson Drywall, Campbell *Also called Charles Culberson Inc* ***(P-2769)***
Culinary Hispanic Foods Inc.....A.....619 955-6101
805 Bow St Chula Vista (91914) ***(P-8572)***
Culinary Services America Inc.....E.....323 965-7582
6363 Wilshire Blvd # 305 Los Angeles (90048) ***(P-14500)***
Culinary Staffing Service, Los Angeles *Also called Culinary Services America Inc* ***(P-14500)***
Culture, San Diego *Also called Carrier Johnson* ***(P-25421)***
Culver West Health Center LLC.....D.....310 390-9506
4035 Grand View Blvd Los Angeles (90066) ***(P-20541)***
Culver-Melin Enterprises.....D.....209 726-9182
2150 Wardrobe Ave Merced (95341) ***(P-13908)***
Cummings Transportation, Shafter *Also called Cummings Vacuum Service Inc* ***(P-1017)***
Cummings Vacuum Service Inc.....D.....661 746-1786
19605 Broken Ct Shafter (93263) ***(P-1017)***
Cummings-Violich Inc.....D.....530 894-5494
1750 Dayton Rd Chico (95928) ***(P-656)***
Cummings-Vlich Inc-Orchard MGT, Chico *Also called Cummings-Violich Inc* ***(P-656)***
Cummins Pacific LLC.....B.....510 351-6101
14775 Wicks Blvd San Leandro (94577) ***(P-7539)***
Cumulus Intrmdate Holdings Inc.....D.....310 840-4900
3321 S La Cienega Blvd Los Angeles (90016) ***(P-5519)***
Cumulus Intrmdate Holdings Inc.....C.....209 766-5103
3136 Boeing Way 125 Stockton (95206) ***(P-5520)***
Cumulus Media, San Francisco *Also called CM Wind Down Topco Inc* ***(P-5518)***
Cumulus Networks Inc (PA).....C.....650 383-6700
185 E Dana St Mountain View (94041) ***(P-15297)***
Cuneo Black Ward Missler A Law.....E.....916 363-8822
700 University Ave # 110 Sacramento (95825) ***(P-22455)***
Cuneo, Black, Ward & Missler, Sacramento *Also called Cuneo Black Ward Missler A Law* ***(P-22455)***
Cunha Draying Inc.....D.....209 858-1400
1500 Madruga Rd Lathrop (95330) ***(P-3990)***
Cuningham Group Arch Inc.....E.....310 895-2200
8665 Hayden Pl Culver City (90232) ***(P-25429)***
Cuningham Group, The, Culver City *Also called Cuningham Group Arch Inc* ***(P-25429)***
Cunningham Group Inc.....D.....303 295-1982
5616 Circle View Dr Bonsall (92003) ***(P-26576)***
Cupertino Electric Inc.....A.....408 808-8260
350 Lenore Way Felton (95018) ***(P-2468)***
Cupertino Electric Inc (PA).....B.....408 808-8000
1132 N 7th St San Jose (95112) ***(P-2469)***
Cupertino Electric Inc.....D.....415 970-3400
1740 Cesar Chavez Fl 2 San Francisco (94124) ***(P-2470)***
Cupertino Healthcare.....D.....408 253-9034
22590 Voss Ave Cupertino (95014) ***(P-19854)***
Cupertino Hlthcare Wllness Ctr, Cupertino *Also called Cupertino Healthcare* ***(P-19854)***
Cupertino Inn, Cupertino *Also called Forge-Vidovich Motel Limited* ***(P-12272)***
Cupertino Lessee LLC.....C.....908 253-8900
10050 S De Anza Blvd Cupertino (95014) ***(P-12193)***
Curatel LLC.....B.....213 427-7411
1605 W Olympic Blvd # 600 Los Angeles (90015) ***(P-5387)***
Curran's Disposal, San Bernardino *Also called Empire Disposal LLC* ***(P-6203)***
Current Elliot, Vernon *Also called Dutch LLC* ***(P-8069)***
Current Tv LLC.....C.....415 995-8328
118 King St San Francisco (94107) ***(P-16733)***
Curtco Publishing LLC (PA).....D.....310 589-7700
29160 Heathercliff Rd # 1 Malibu (90265) ***(P-13618)***
Curti Family Inc.....D.....559 688-8323
3235 Avenue 199 Tulare (93274) ***(P-388)***
Curtis Legal Group A Professi.....E.....209 521-1800
1300 K St Fl 2 Modesto (95354) ***(P-22456)***
Curtiss-Wright Controls.....C.....661 257-4430
28965 Avenue Penn Santa Clarita (91355) ***(P-25025)***
Curtiss-Wright Controls (HQ).....C.....661 702-1494
28965 Avenue Penn Santa Clarita (91355) ***(P-25026)***
Curvature LLC (HQ).....B.....800 230-6638
6500 Hollister Ave # 210 Santa Barbara (93117) ***(P-6818)***
Cusa AWC LLC.....E.....916 423-4000
7701 Wilbur Way Sacramento (95828) ***(P-3529)***
Cusa Fl LLC.....C.....415 642-9400
41 Pier San Francisco (94133) ***(P-3773)***
Cusa Gcbs LLC.....D.....619 266-7365
3888 Beech St San Diego (92105) ***(P-4852)***
Cushman & Wakefield Inc.....C.....408 664-5403
800 W El Camino Real Mountain View (94040) ***(P-13909)***
Cushman & Wakefield Inc.....E.....650 347-3700
1350 Bayshore Hwy Ste 900 Burlingame (94010) ***(P-11082)***
Cushman & Wakefield Cal Inc (HQ).....C.....408 275-6730
1 Maritime Plz Ste 900 San Francisco (94111) ***(P-11083)***
Cushman & Wakefield Cal Inc.....E.....949 474-4004
18111 Von Karman Ave # 1000 Irvine (92612) ***(P-11084)***
Custom Alloy Scrap Sales Inc (HQ).....E.....510 893-6476
2730 Peralta St Oakland (94607) ***(P-7756)***
Custom Bilt Holdings LLC.....D.....909 664-1587
15133 Sierra Bonita Ln Chino (91710) ***(P-7540)***
Custom Business Solutions Inc (PA).....D.....949 380-7674
12 Morgan Irvine (92618) ***(P-6747)***
Custom Chrome, Morgan Hill *Also called Dae-IL Usa Inc* ***(P-6431)***
Custom Commercial Dry Clrs Inc (PA).....E.....510 723-1000
3201 Investment Blvd Hayward (94545) ***(P-13255)***
Custom Companies Inc.....D.....310 672-8800
13012 Molette St Santa Fe Springs (90670) ***(P-4921)***
Custom Cooler Inc (HQ).....D.....909 592-1111
420 E Arrow Hwy San Dimas (91773) ***(P-7461)***
Custom Craft Company, Santa Fe Springs *Also called Interntonal Win Treatments Inc* ***(P-6564)***
Custom Design Co Inc.....E.....818 507-5959
20969 Ventura Blvd # 217 Woodland Hills (91364) ***(P-1452)***
Custom Drywall Inc.....D.....408 263-1616
1570 Gladding Ct Milpitas (95035) ***(P-2773)***
Custom Drywall Service, Clovis *Also called Clovis Custom Drywall Inc* ***(P-2771)***
Custom Goods LLC (PA).....E.....310 241-6700
1035 E Watson Center Rd Carson (90745) ***(P-4393)***
Custom Hotel, Los Angeles *Also called Playa Proper Jv LLC* ***(P-12760)***
Custom Hotel LLC.....D.....310 645-0400
8639 Lincoln Blvd Los Angeles (90045) ***(P-12194)***
Custom House Hotel LP.....D.....831 649-4511
2 Portola Plz Monterey (93940) ***(P-12195)***
Custom Lawn Services, Ventura *Also called American Landscape Management* ***(P-772)***
Custom Lawn Services, Canoga Park *Also called American Landscape Management* ***(P-698)***
Custom Metal Fabricators, Orange *Also called Cmf Inc* ***(P-3038)***
Custom Produce Sales (PA).....C.....559 254-5800
13475 E Progress Dr Parlier (93648) ***(P-8451)***
Custom Product Dev Corp.....D.....925 960-0577
4603 Las Positas Rd Ste A Livermore (94551) ***(P-3043)***
Custom Service Systems, Riverside *Also called Ghossain & Truelock Entps Inc* ***(P-13937)***
Custom Tours Inc.....D.....310 274-8819
24003 Ventura Blvd Ste A Calabasas (91302) ***(P-4872)***
Custom Vinyls, Fontana *Also called Patrick Industries Inc* ***(P-6695)***
Customcare Home Hlth Svcs Inc.....D.....916 714-1155
9826 Bond Rd Ste A Elk Grove (95624) ***(P-21728)***
Customer Loan Depot, Foothill Ranch *Also called Loandepotcom LLC* ***(P-9577)***
Customer Loyalty Builders Inc.....D.....888 478-7787
1063 Todos Santos Concord (94522) ***(P-26577)***
Customer Srvc Dlvry Pltfrm Crp.....E.....717 896-8489
15615 Alton Pkwy Ste 310 Irvine (92618) ***(P-15972)***
Customfab Inc.....C.....714 891-9119
7345 Orangewood Ave Garden Grove (92841) ***(P-16734)***
Customized Dist Svcs Inc.....D.....909 947-0084
3355 E Cedar St Ontario (91761) ***(P-26578)***

Mergent e-mail: customerrelations@mergent.com
1240
2020 Directory of California
Wholesalers and Services Companies
(P-0000) Products & Services Section entry number
(PA)=Parent Co (HQ)=Headquarters (DH)=Div Headquarters

Customline Professional ....B 714 996-1333
567 S Melrose St Placentia (92870) ***(P-13779)***

Customzed Svcs Admnstrtors Inc ....C 858 810-2004
4181 Ruffin Rd Ste 150 San Diego (92123) ***(P-10336)***

Cut N Clean Greens, Oxnard *Also called San Miguel Produce Inc* ***(P-74)***

Cutler Group LP ....E 415 645-6745
101 Montgomery St Ste 700 San Francisco (94104) ***(P-16735)***

Cutting Edge Drywall Inc ....E 858 408-0870
7046 Convoy Ct San Diego (92111) ***(P-2774)***

Cutting Edge Protection I ....E 949 307-1596
381 Crosby St Altadena (91001) ***(P-13365)***

Cve Nb Contracting Group Inc ....E 707 584-1900
135 Utility Ct A Rohnert Park (94928) ***(P-26942)***

Cvf Capital Partners Inc ....C 530 757-7004
1590 Drew Ave Ste 110 Davis (95618) ***(P-11905)***

CVH HOME HEALTH SERVICES, San Ramon *Also called Castro Valley Health Inc* ***(P-21701)***

Cvoc, Winton *Also called Central Valley Oprtnty Ctr Inc* ***(P-23577)***

Cvpartners Inc (HQ) ....C 415 543-8600
655 Montgomery St # 1200 San Francisco (94111) ***(P-14257)***

Cvrm, Indio *Also called Coachella Vly Rescue Mission* ***(P-23020)***

Cw Healthcare Inc ....E 510 636-9000
2884 Wakefield Dr Belmont (94002) ***(P-14501)***

Cw Network LLC (PA) ....C 818 977-2500
3300 W Olive Ave Fl 3 Burbank (91505) ***(P-5593)***

CW Welding Service Inc ....D 661 399-5422
761 Majors Ct Bakersfield (93308) ***(P-7787)***

Cwf Inc ....D 626 967-0500
251 E Front St Covina (91723) ***(P-14151)***

Cwgp Limited Partnership ....D 310 395-9700
1740 Ocean Ave Santa Monica (90401) ***(P-12196)***

Cwi, San Francisco *Also called Collier Warehouse Inc* ***(P-6612)***

Cwip, Fresno *Also called Community Integrated Work Prog* ***(P-23038)***

Cwn Management, Mission Viejo *Also called Goldcoast Liquidating LLC* ***(P-1483)***

Cwp Cabinets Inc ....C 760 246-4530
10007 Yucca Rd Adelanto (92301) ***(P-2923)***

Cwpfl Inc ....E 714 564-7900
1682 Langley Ave Irvine (92614) ***(P-16736)***

Cws Apartment Homes LLC (PA) ....B 949 640-4200
14 Corporate Plaza Dr # 210 Newport Beach (92660) ***(P-11085)***

Cws Capital Partners, Newport Beach *Also called Cws Apartment Homes LLC* ***(P-11085)***

Cws Utility Services Corp ....B 408 367-8200
1720 N 1st St San Jose (95112) ***(P-24332)***

Cwtv, Burbank *Also called Cw Network LLC* ***(P-5593)***

Cy Gaslamp LLC ....D 619 544-1004
453 6th Ave San Diego (92101) ***(P-12197)***

Cy Sac Operator LLC ....D 916 455-6800
4422 Y St Sacramento (95817) ***(P-12198)***

Cyara Solutions Corp ....C 650 549-8522
805 Veterans Blvd Ste 105 Redwood City (94063) ***(P-6819)***

Cyber Policy ....C 877 626-9991
1 California St Ste 1100 San Francisco (94111) ***(P-10337)***

Cybercoders Inc ....C 949 885-5151
6591 Irvine Center Dr # 200 Irvine (92618) ***(P-14258)***

Cybercsi Inc ....D 408 727-2900
3511 Thomas Rd Ste 5 Santa Clara (95054) ***(P-6820)***

Cyberdefender Corporation ....B 323 449-0774
617 W 7th St Fl 10 Los Angeles (90017) ***(P-14747)***

Cybernet Entertainment LLC (PA) ....D 415 865-0230
1800 Mission St San Francisco (94103) ***(P-17594)***

Cyberpower Inc ....D 626 813-7730
730 Baldwin Park Blvd City of Industry (91746) ***(P-6821)***

Cyberscientific, Irvine *Also called Cybercoders Inc* ***(P-14258)***

Cybersource Corporation (HQ) ....D 650 432-7350
900 Metro Center Blvd Foster City (94404) ***(P-15747)***

Cybrex Consulting Inc ....D 513 999-2109
4470 W Sunset Blvd Los Angeles (90027) ***(P-15298)***

Cylance Inc (HQ) ....C 949 375-3380
400 Spectrum Center Dr Irvine (92618) ***(P-15299)***

Cyphort Inc ....E 408 841-4665
1133 Innovation Way Sunnyvale (94089) ***(P-6822)***

Cypress College Foundation ....D 714 484-7128
9200 Valley View Ave Whittier (90603) ***(P-24532)***

Cypress Creek Holdings LLC ....D 310 581-6299
3250 Ocean Park Blvd # 355 Santa Monica (90405) ***(P-5828)***

Cypress Creek Renewables LLC ....D 415 306-5300
445 Bush St Fl 7 San Francisco (94108) ***(P-5829)***

Cypress Ctr For Fmly Medicine ....D 562 799-4801
10601 Walker St Ste 250 Cypress (90630) ***(P-18937)***

Cypress Education Foundation ....D 714 220-6900
9470 Moody St Cypress (90630) ***(P-24533)***

Cypress Funeral Services Inc ....C 650 550-8808
1370 El Camino Real Colma (94014) ***(P-13368)***

Cypress Garden At Citrus Hts ....E 916 729-2722
7375 Stock Ranch Rd Citrus Heights (95621) ***(P-20423)***

Cypress Gardens Convalescent H ....C 951 688-3643
9025 Colorado Ave Riverside (92503) ***(P-20542)***

Cypress Halthcare Partners LLC (PA) ....E 831 649-1000
100 Wilson Rd Ste 100 # 100 Monterey (93940) ***(P-18938)***

Cypress Hotel, Cupertino *Also called Ch Cupertino Owner LLC* ***(P-12133)***

Cypress Lawn Funeral Home, Colma *Also called Cypress Funeral Services Inc* ***(P-13368)***

Cypress Ridge Golf Course ....E 805 474-7979
780 Cypress Ridge Pkwy Arroyo Grande (93420) ***(P-18239)***

Cypress Security LLC (PA) ....D 866 345-1277
478 Tehama St San Francisco (94103) ***(P-16250)***

Cypress Security LLC ....D 562 222-4197
9926 Pioneer Blvd Ste 106 Santa Fe Springs (90670) ***(P-16251)***

Czech Commerce Ltd ....D 831 649-4633
3063 Larkin Rd Pebble Beach (93953) ***(P-8694)***

Cznd Inc ....D 323 378-6505
8444 Wilshire Blvd Fl 5 Beverly Hills (90211) ***(P-17968)***

D & C Care Center Inc ....D 626 798-1175
1640 N Fair Oaks Ave Pasadena (91103) ***(P-20543)***

D & D Ready Mix Inc ....D 209 627-7224
5353 Byron Hot Springs Rd Byron (94514) ***(P-6679)***

D & D Wholesale Distrs Inc ....D 626 333-2111
777 Baldwin Park Blvd City of Industry (91746) ***(P-8452)***

D & H Landscaping Inc ....D 510 223-6597
4221 Appian Way El Sobrante (94803) ***(P-791)***

D & J Plumbing Inc ....D 916 922-4888
4341 Winters St Sacramento (95838) ***(P-2110)***

D & J Tile Company Inc ....D 650 632-4000
1045 Terminal Way San Carlos (94070) ***(P-2888)***

D & K Engineering (PA) ....C 858 451-8999
15890 Bernardo Center Dr San Diego (92127) ***(P-25027)***

D & L Produce, Selma *Also called Serimian M S D L Ranch* ***(P-359)***

D & W LLC ....D 310 345-0075
3501 Rindge Ln Redondo Beach (90278) ***(P-12199)***

D - Link, Fountain Valley *Also called D-Link Systems Incorporated* ***(P-6823)***

D A McCosker Construction Co ....E 925 686-1780
3911 Laura Alice Way Concord (94520) ***(P-1695)***

D A V Industries ....D 619 337-9244
1049 Elkelton Blvd Spring Valley (91977) ***(P-24534)***

D A Wood Construction Inc ....D 209 491-4970
601 Albers Rd Modesto (95357) ***(P-25028)***

D and D Concrete Cnstr Inc ....D 619 518-9737
13795 Blaisdell Pl # 201 Poway (92064) ***(P-3137)***

D Augustine & Associates ....D 916 774-9600
3017 Douglas Blvd Ste 200 Roseville (95661) ***(P-13484)***

D B Specialty Farms, Santa Maria *Also called Darensberries LLC* ***(P-92)***

D C Golf A CA Partnership ....E 626 797-3821
1456 E Mendocino St Altadena (91001) ***(P-18240)***

D C M Data Systems, Fremont *Also called Dcm Technologies Inc* ***(P-14755)***

D C N Wireless, Woodland Hills *Also called Digital Communications Network* ***(P-5255)***

D C S, Brea *Also called Diversfied Cmmnctions Svcs Inc* ***(P-5393)***

D C Taylor Co ....E 925 603-1100
5060 Forni Dr Ste B Concord (94520) ***(P-3044)***

D C Vient Inc (PA) ....B 209 578-1224
1556 Cummins Dr Modesto (95358) ***(P-2341)***

D E L T A Rescue, Acton *Also called Dedication & Everlasting Love* ***(P-602)***

D E Shaw Valence LLC ....C 650 926-9460
2735 Sand Hill Rd Ste 105 Menlo Park (94025) ***(P-11906)***

D E X, Camarillo *Also called Data Exchange Corporation* ***(P-6824)***

D F Rios Construction Inc ....D 510 226-7467
45847 Warm Springs Blvd Fremont (94539) ***(P-2924)***

D G A, Los Angeles *Also called Directors Guild America Inc* ***(P-17735)***

D J American Supply Inc ....C 323 582-2650
6122 S Eastern Ave Commerce (90040) ***(P-7804)***

D J Farm Management ....E 661 792-6222
11298 Magnolia Ave Wasco (93280) ***(P-657)***

D K Fortune & Associates Inc ....C 310 391-7266
5240 Sepulveda Blvd Culver City (90230) ***(P-20544)***

D M Electric Inc ....D 909 888-8639
336 S Waterman Ave Ste K San Bernardino (92408) ***(P-2471)***

D M S, Fremont *Also called DMS Facility Services Inc* ***(P-13914)***

D P S Inc ....D 714 564-7900
1682 Langley Ave Irvine (92614) ***(P-2342)***

D R C, Sacramento *Also called Disability Rights California* ***(P-22479)***

D S I, Santa Rosa *Also called Deposition Sciences Inc* ***(P-25736)***

D S P Janitorial Service, Hayward *Also called D S P Service Inc* ***(P-13910)***

D S P Service Inc ....E 510 782-2200
23762 Foley St Ste 3 Hayward (94545) ***(P-13910)***

D S R Inc ....D 805 275-0039
3503 Arundell Cir Ste A Ventura (93003) ***(P-17495)***

D S S, Goleta *Also called Deployable Space Systems Inc* ***(P-25034)***

D S S Company ....E 209 948-0302
655 W Clay St Stockton (95206) ***(P-1849)***

D W Nicholson Corporation (PA) ....C 510 887-0900
24747 Clawiter Rd Hayward (94545) ***(P-2111)***

D W Powell Construction Inc ....E 909 356-8880
8555 Banana Ave Fontana (92335) ***(P-1696)***

D&A Enterprises Inc ....B 510 445-1600
34943 Newark Blvd Newark (94560) ***(P-8167)***

D&B, San Francisco *Also called Dun & Bradstreet Inc* ***(P-13710)***

D&D Equipment Rental LLC ....E 562 903-9333
2596 Mission St Ste 201 San Marino (91108) ***(P-14094)***

D'Amore Healthcare, Huntington Beach *Also called Guardian Health Care Services* ***(P-22036)***

D'Andrea Graphics, Cypress *Also called DAndrea Graphic Corportion* ***(P-13780)***

D'Angelo, Michael L, Irvine *Also called Sean P OConnor* ***(P-22806)***

D'Best Produce, Fresno *Also called De Benedetto Farms Inc* ***(P-172)***

D-Link Systems Incorporated ....C 714 885-6000
17595 Mount Herrmann St Fountain Valley (92708) ***(P-6823)***

D/K Mechanical Contractors Inc ....C 714 970-0180
3870 E Eagle Dr Anaheim (92807) ***(P-2112)***

D2j Inc ....D 323 589-1374
6351 Regent St Ste 100 Huntington Park (90255) ***(P-16737)***

D3 Go, Encino *Also called D3publisher of America Inc* ***(P-15300)***

D3, Deluxe Ondemand, Los Angeles *Also called Deluxe Digital Dist Inc* ***(P-17733)***

D3publisher of America Inc ....D 310 268-0820
15910 Ventura Blvd # 800 Encino (91436) ***(P-15300)***

D7 Roofing Services Inc ....D 916 447-2175
2851 Gold Tailings Ct Rancho Cordova (95670) ***(P-3045)***

DA Davidson & Co ....B 213 620-1850
624 S Grand Ave Ste 2600 Los Angeles (90017) ***(P-9685)***

Employee Codes: A=Over 500 employees, B=251-500 C=101-250, D=51-100, E=50
2020 Directory of California Wholesalers and Services Companies
© Mergent Inc. 1-800-342-5647
1241

Daart Engineering Company Inc ... D ... 909 888-8696
1598 N H St San Bernardino (92405) ***(P-2113)***

Dac, Palm Springs *Also called Desert Arts Center* ***(P-24261)***

Dacare Inc (PA) ... D ... 760 344-4654
643 Main St Brawley (92227) ***(P-23189)***

Dacor ... D ... 626 961-2256
14525 Clark Ave City of Industry (91745) ***(P-17454)***

Dacor Holdings Inc ... C ... 626 626-4461
14425 Clark Ave City of Industry (91745) ***(P-26062)***

Dae-IL Usa Inc ... D ... 559 651-5170
15750 Vineyard Blvd # 100 Morgan Hill (95037) ***(P-6431)***

Dager Corporation (PA) ... D ... 916 989-4229
8004 Flsom Hydre Aburn Rd Folsom (95630) ***(P-13337)***

Dahl-Beck Electric Co ... D ... 510 237-2325
2775 Goodrick Ave Richmond (94801) ***(P-7141)***

Dahlin Group Inc (PA) ... D ... 925 251-7200
5865 Owens Dr Pleasanton (94588) ***(P-25430)***

Daicel Safety Systems ... C ... 805 387-1004
2655 1st St Ste 300 Simi Valley (93065) ***(P-8695)***

Dailey & Associates ... D ... 323 490-3847
8687 Melrose Ave Ste G300 West Hollywood (90069) ***(P-13485)***

Daily Journal Corporation ... E ... 213 229-5500
915 E 1st St Los Angeles (90012) ***(P-13619)***

Dailylook Inc ... D ... 888 888-6645
2445 E 12th St Ste B Los Angeles (90021) ***(P-16738)***

Daiwa Corporation ... D ... 562 375-6800
11137 Warland Dr Cypress (90630) ***(P-7707)***

Daiwa Golf Company Division, Cypress *Also called Daiwa Corporation* ***(P-7707)***

Daiwa House California Inc ... B ... 310 228-5675
1901 Avenue Of The Stars # 264 Los Angeles (90067) ***(P-1111)***

Dal Cais Inc ... D ... 916 381-8080
5101 Florin Perkins Rd Sacramento (95826) ***(P-1453)***

Dal-Tile Corporation ... D ... 949 260-0488
1132 Duryea Ave Irvine (92614) ***(P-6680)***

Dal-Tile Corporation ... D ... 858 571-0283
7484 Raytheon Rd Ste A San Diego (92111) ***(P-2889)***

Dal-Tile Corporation ... D ... 510 357-6197
2303 Merced St San Leandro (94577) ***(P-2890)***

Dal-Tile Corporation ... D ... 909 390-7000
3625 Jurupa St Ontario (91761) ***(P-2891)***

Dal-Tile Corporation ... D ... 209 543-0924
4201 Technology Dr Modesto (95356) ***(P-6681)***

Dalaklis McKeown Entertainment ... D ... 310 545-0120
2517 Crest Dr Manhattan Beach (90266) ***(P-17595)***

Daleo Inc ... D ... 408 846-9621
550 E Luchessa Ave Gilroy (95020) ***(P-1850)***

Daley, Lakeside *Also called Nicholas Grant Corporation* ***(P-1767)***

Daley & Heft Attorneys ... E ... 858 755-5666
462 Stevens Ave Ste 201 Solana Beach (92075) ***(P-22457)***

Daleys Drywall and Taping Inc ... A ... 408 378-9500
960 Camden Ave Campbell (95008) ***(P-2775)***

Dallas Union Hotel Inc ... C ... 626 356-1000
150 Corson St Pasadena (91103) ***(P-11850)***

Dalton Trucking Inc (PA) ... C ... 909 823-0663
13560 Whittram Ave Fontana (92335) ***(P-4394)***

Damao Luggage Intl Inc ... A ... 909 923-6531
1909 S Vineyard Ave Ontario (91761) ***(P-7805)***

Dameron Hospital Association (PA) ... A ... 209 944-5550
525 W Acacia St Stockton (95203) ***(P-20824)***

Damon Electrical ... D ... 818 426-3450
7800 Bobbyboyar Ave West Hills (91304) ***(P-2472)***

Damrell Nelson Schrimp Pall ... E ... 209 848-3500
703 W F St Oakdale (95361) ***(P-22458)***

Dan Avila and Sons ... D ... 209 495-3899
2718 Roberts Rd Ceres (95307) ***(P-45)***

Dan Connolly Inc ... D ... 408 241-0910
855 Civic Center Dr Ste 5 Santa Clara (95050) ***(P-16252)***

Dan Freitas Electric ... D ... 559 686-9572
983 E Levin Ave Tulare (93274) ***(P-2473)***

Dan Lofgren ... D ... 925 846-6632
7707 Forsythia Ct Pleasanton (94588) ***(P-13911)***

Dan R Costa Inc ... C ... 209 234-2004
17239 Louise Ave Escalon (95320) ***(P-311)***

Dana Middle Schl Bys Girls CLB, San Pedro *Also called Boys and Girls Clubs of The La* ***(P-24490)***

Danco Builders ... D ... 707 822-9000
5251 Ericson Way Ste A Arcata (95521) ***(P-1238)***

Danco Communities ... D ... 707 822-9000
5251 Ericson Way Ste A Arcata (95521) ***(P-11556)***

DAndrea Graphic Corportion ... D ... 310 642-0260
6100 Gateway Dr Cypress (90630) ***(P-13780)***

Danell Bros Inc ... D ... 559 582-1251
8265 Hanford Armona Rd Hanford (93230) ***(P-450)***

Danell Custom Harvesting LLC ... C ... 559 582-1251
8265 Hanford Armona Rd Hanford (93230) ***(P-451)***

Danerica Enterprises Inc ... D ... 818 774-1813
23901 Calabasas Rd # 1068 Calabasas (91302) ***(P-13417)***

Dang Quinten ... D ... 626 429-6332
11272 Frankmont Ct El Monte (91732) ***(P-5783)***

Daniel Gerard Worldwide Inc ... D ... 951 361-1111
13055 Jurupa Ave Fontana (92337) ***(P-7059)***

Daniel J Edelman Inc ... D ... 415 222-9944
525 Market St San Francisco (94105) ***(P-26906)***

Daniel J Edelman Inc ... D ... 323 857-9100
5670 Wilshire Blvd # 2500 Los Angeles (90036) ***(P-26907)***

Daniel J Edelman Inc ... D ... 650 762-2800
201 Baldwin Ave San Mateo (94401) ***(P-13620)***

Daniel J Edelman Inc ... D ... 323 857-9100
5900 Wilshire Blvd # 2400 Los Angeles (90036) ***(P-13621)***

Daniel O Mongiano MD A PR ... E ... 661 951-9195
42220 10th St W Ste 109 Lancaster (93534) ***(P-18939)***

Daniel Robert Knowlton ... D ... 760 265-5293
68368 Madrid Rd Cathedral City (92234) ***(P-22459)***

Daniels Western Meat Packers ... D ... 562 948-2254
5217 Industry Ave Pico Rivera (90660) ***(P-8403)***

Danish Care Center, Atascadero *Also called Compass Health Inc* ***(P-19812)***

Danlil Enterprise Inc ... D ... 714 776-7705
1440 S State College Blvd Anaheim (92806) ***(P-13912)***

Danning Gill Damnd Kollitz LLP ... D ... 310 277-0077
1900 Avenue Of The Stars # 11 Los Angeles (90067) ***(P-22460)***

Dannis Wlver Klley A Prof Corp (PA) ... D ... 415 543-4111
275 Battery St Ste 1150 San Francisco (94111) ***(P-22461)***

Danny Mahagna Shapprie ... E ... 760 341-5070
73280 Highway 111 Palm Desert (92260) ***(P-17969)***

Danny Ryan Precision Contg Inc ... D ... 949 642-6664
1818 N Orangethorpe Park Anaheim (92801) ***(P-3339)***

Dansk Enterprises Inc ... D ... 714 751-0347
3419 Via Lido 345 Newport Beach (92663) ***(P-16253)***

Danville Long-Term Care Inc ... D ... 925 837-4566
336 Diablo Rd Danville (94526) ***(P-19855)***

Danville Post Acute Rehab, Danville *Also called Danville Long-Term Care Inc* ***(P-19855)***

Danville Rehsbilitation, Danville *Also called Danville Village Skilled Nursn* ***(P-19856)***

Danville Village Skilled Nursn ... D ... 925 837-4566
336 Diablo Rd Danville (94526) ***(P-19856)***

Dao Medical Group Inc ... D ... 714 899-2000
9191 Westminster Ave # 204 Garden Grove (92844) ***(P-18940)***

Dapcon Inc ... D ... 408 573-7200
877 Commercial St San Jose (95112) ***(P-2343)***

Daps Naval Hosp, Lemoore *Also called United States Dept of Navy* ***(P-21328)***

Daqri LLC (PA) ... D ... 213 375-8830
1201 W 5th St Ste T800 Los Angeles (90017) ***(P-14748)***

Darco Construction, Stanton *Also called Denver D Darling Inc* ***(P-1345)***

Darden Architects Inc ... D ... 559 448-8051
6790 N West Ave Ste 104 Fresno (93711) ***(P-25431)***

Darensberries LLC ... C ... 805 937-8000
714 S Blosser Rd Santa Maria (93458) ***(P-92)***

Darensburg Roghair & Renier ... E ... 760 256-6891
1520 E Main St Barstow (92311) ***(P-12200)***

Darrell L Green Inc ... D ... 559 688-0686
12652 Avenue 240 Tulare (93274) ***(P-4203)***

DArrigo Broscoof California (PA) ... E ... 831 455-4500
21777 Harris Rd Salinas (93908) ***(P-46)***

Dart Aerospace, Vista *Also called Apical Industries Inc* ***(P-7689)***

Dart Entities, Commerce *Also called Dart International A Corp* ***(P-3991)***

Dart International A Corp (HQ) ... C ... 323 264-8746
1430 S Eastman Ave Commerce (90023) ***(P-3991)***

Dart Warehouse Corporation (HQ) ... B ... 323 264-1011
1430 S Eastman Ave Ste 1 Commerce (90023) ***(P-4395)***

Das Global Capital Corp ... D ... 702 967-1688
42 Peninsula Ctr Ste 317 Rllng HLS Est (90274) ***(P-25885)***

Dassault Systemes Americas ... C ... 818 999-2500
6320 Canoga Ave Fl 3 Woodland Hills (91367) ***(P-14749)***

Dassels Petroleum Inc ... E ... 831 636-5100
340 El Camino Real S Salinas (93901) ***(P-8723)***

Data 911, Poway *Also called Hubb Systems LLC* ***(P-15610)***

Data Center, Sacramento *Also called Correctons Rhbltation Cal Dept* ***(P-15741)***

Data Control Corporation ... D ... 916 774-4000
P.O. Box 2069 Granite Bay (95746) ***(P-15578)***

Data Domain LLC ... A ... 408 980-4800
2421 Mission College Blvd Santa Clara (95054) ***(P-15579)***

Data Exchange, Camarillo *Also called Dex Corporation* ***(P-25036)***

Data Exchange Corporation (PA) ... B ... 805 388-1711
3600 Via Pescador Camarillo (93012) ***(P-6824)***

Data Recognition Corporation ... E ... 831 393-0700
20 Ryan Ranch Rd Monterey (93940) ***(P-27046)***

Data Trace Info Svcs LLC (HQ) ... D ... 714 250-6700
4 First American Way Santa Ana (92707) ***(P-27272)***

Data-Image Systems, Rancho Cordova *Also called Ricoh Usa Inc* ***(P-6763)***

Database Marketing Group Inc ... B ... 714 727-0800
5 Peters Canyon Rd # 150 Irvine (92606) ***(P-13721)***

Databricks Inc (PA) ... D ... 415 494-7672
160 Spear St Fl 13 San Francisco (94105) ***(P-14750)***

Datallegro Inc ... D ... 949 680-3000
85 Enterprise Ste 200 Aliso Viejo (92656) ***(P-6825)***

Datameer Inc (PA) ... D ... 650 286-9100
535 Mission St Ste 2602 San Francisco (94105) ***(P-14751)***

Datapark Inc ... D ... 510 483-7275
1631 Neptune Dr San Leandro (94577) ***(P-15580)***

Datasafe Inc (PA) ... E ... 650 875-3800
574 Eccles Ave South San Francisco (94080) ***(P-4560)***

Datasafe Inc ... E ... 650 875-3800
3160 W Bayshore Rd Palo Alto (94303) ***(P-4561)***

Datastax Inc (PA) ... C ... 650 389-6000
3975 Freedom Cir Ste 400 Santa Clara (95054) ***(P-14752)***

Davalan Fresh, Los Angeles *Also called Davalan Sales Inc* ***(P-8453)***

Davalan Sales Inc ... C ... 213 623-2500
1601 E Olympic Blvd # 325 Los Angeles (90021) ***(P-8453)***

Dave Calhoun and Assoc LLC ... C ... 925 688-1234
2575 Stanwell Dr Ste 100 Concord (94520) ***(P-13913)***

Dave Gross Enterprises Inc ... D ... 916 388-2000
7 Wayne Ct Sacramento (95829) ***(P-3397)***

Dave Spurr Excavating Inc ... E ... 805 238-0834
935 Riverside Ave Ste 18 Paso Robles (93446) ***(P-3311)***

Dave Williams Plbg & Elec Inc ... C ... 760 296-1397
75140 Saint Charles Pl C Palm Desert (92211) ***(P-2114)***

Dave Wilson Nursery Inc (PA) ... E ... 209 874-1821
19701 Lake Rd Hickman (95323) ***(P-236)***

Mergent e-mail: customerrelations@mergent.com
1242
2020 Directory of California
Wholesalers and Services Companies
(P-0000) Products & Services Section entry number
(PA)=Parent Co (HQ)=Headquarters (DH)=Div Headquarters

Davenport Development Corp ....E....858 300-3333
8360 Clairemont Mesa Blvd # 111 San Diego (92111) ***(P-2998)***
Davey Tree Surgery Company ....D....530 378-2674
6915 Eastside Rd Ste 94 Anderson (96007) ***(P-937)***
Davey Tree Surgery Company (HQ) ....A....925 443-1723
2617 S Vasco Rd Livermore (94550) ***(P-938)***
Davey Tree Surgery Company ....D....760 975-0225
1914 Mission Rd Ste N Escondido (92029) ***(P-939)***
David & Goliath LLC ....C....310 445-5200
909 N Pacific Coast Hwy # 700 El Segundo (90245) ***(P-13486)***
DAVID & MARGARET YOUTH AND FAM, La Verne *Also called David and Margaret Home Inc* ***(P-23899)***
David and Margaret Home Inc ....C....909 596-5921
1350 3rd St La Verne (91750) ***(P-23899)***
David Civalier MD Inc ....E....530 244-4034
2510 Airpark Dr Ste 104 Redding (96001) ***(P-18941)***
David D Bohannon Organization (PA) ....D....650 345-8222
60 31st Ave San Mateo (94403) ***(P-10580)***
David Darroch ....D....510 835-9100
300 Lakeside Dr Fl 24 Oakland (94612) ***(P-22462)***
David Evans and Associates Inc ....E....909 481-5750
4141 Inland Empire Blvd # 250 Ontario (91764) ***(P-25029)***
David Evans Enterprises Inc ....A....213 337-3680
201 S Figueroa St Ste 240 Los Angeles (90012) ***(P-25030)***
David King Convalescent Hosp ....D....310 451-9706
1340 15th St Santa Monica (90404) ***(P-20545)***
David L Amador Inc ....D....626 334-2011
762 N Loren Ave Azusa (91702) ***(P-3138)***
David Levy Co Inc ....E....562 404-9998
12753 Moore St Cerritos (90703) ***(P-7254)***
David Lyng & Associates Inc ....D....831 429-5700
1041 41st Ave Ste A Santa Cruz (95062) ***(P-11086)***
David Morse & Assoc., Glendale *Also called Dma Claims Inc* ***(P-10343)***
David Ollis Landscape Dev Inc ....E....909 307-1911
450 Kansas St Ste 104 Redlands (92373) ***(P-792)***
David Ross Inc ....D....323 684-7673
1899 N Raymond Ave Pasadena (91103) ***(P-19857)***
David Santos Farming ....D....209 826-1065
720 Jefferson Ave Los Banos (93635) ***(P-16739)***
David Shield Security Inc ....D....310 849-4950
23945 Calabasas Rd # 102 Calabasas (91302) ***(P-16254)***
David W Golen ....D....213 716-0706
20253 Gifford St Winnetka (91306) ***(P-3872)***
David-Kleis II LLC ....D....951 845-3125
1665 E Eighth St Beaumont (92223) ***(P-22223)***
Davidon Five Star Corp ....D....925 945-8000
1600 S Main St Ste 150 Walnut Creek (94596) ***(P-11907)***
Davidon Homes, Walnut Creek *Also called Davidon Five Star Corp* ***(P-11907)***
Davidson Builders, Del Mar *Also called Davidson Communities LLC* ***(P-11557)***
Davidson Communities LLC (PA) ....E....858 259-8500
1302 Camino Del Mar Del Mar (92014) ***(P-11557)***
Davidson Hotel Partners Lp ....C....818 707-1220
30100 Agoura Rd Agoura Hills (91301) ***(P-12201)***
Davie Brown Entertainment Inc ....D....310 979-1980
12777 W Jefferson Blvd # 120 Los Angeles (90066) ***(P-17906)***
Davis Brothers Framing Inc ....C....909 944-4899
8780 Prestige Ct Rancho Cucamonga (91730) ***(P-2925)***
Davis Cmnty Clnic Dntl Program, Davis *Also called Davis Community Clinic* ***(P-18942)***
Davis Community Clinic (PA) ....D....530 758-2060
2040 Sutter Pl Davis (95616) ***(P-18942)***
Davis Framing Inc ....E....619 463-2394
8103 Commercial St La Mesa (91942) ***(P-2926)***
Davis Medical Offices, Davis *Also called Kaiser Foundation Hospitals* ***(P-19117)***
Davis Research LLC ....C....818 591-2408
23801 Calabasas Rd # 1036 Calabasas (91302) ***(P-25886)***
Davis Trucking LLC (PA) ....E....619 229-9997
7345 Mission Gorge Rd H San Diego (92120) ***(P-3873)***
Davis Wright Tremaine LLP ....D....415 276-6500
505 Montgomery St Ste 800 San Francisco (94111) ***(P-22463)***
Davis Wright Tremaine LLP ....D....213 633-6800
865 S Figueroa St # 2400 Los Angeles (90017) ***(P-22464)***
Davis Ziff Publishing Inc ....C....415 551-4800
235 2nd St San Francisco (94105) ***(P-5388)***
Daviselen Advertising Inc (PA) ....C....213 688-7000
865 S Figueroa St # 1200 Los Angeles (90017) ***(P-13487)***
Daviselen Advertising Inc ....D....858 847-0789
420 Stevens Ave Ste 240 Solana Beach (92075) ***(P-13488)***
Davita Dialysis, Irvine *Also called Renal Treatment Ctrs - Cal Inc* ***(P-21933)***
Davita Hesperia Dialysis Ctr, Hesperia *Also called Total Renal Care Inc* ***(P-21941)***
Davita Inc ....B....949 930-4400
15271 Laguna Canyon Rd Irvine (92618) ***(P-21917)***
Davita Inc ....D....310 536-2400
601 Hawaii St El Segundo (90245) ***(P-21918)***
Davita Magan Management Inc (HQ) ....C....626 331-6411
420 W Rowland St Covina (91723) ***(P-18943)***
Davita Magan Management Inc ....D....909 592-9712
330 W Covina Blvd San Dimas (91773) ***(P-18944)***
Davita Medical Management LLC ....D....323 720-1144
2601 Via Campo Montebello (90640) ***(P-18945)***
Davita Medical Management LLC ....D....626 444-0333
3144 Santa Anita Ave # 201 El Monte (91733) ***(P-18946)***
Davita Medical Management LLC (HQ) ....A....310 354-4200
2175 Park Pl El Segundo (90245) ***(P-18947)***
Davlor Company ....D....949 244-9748
12 Oakbrook Trabuco Canyon (92679) ***(P-1454)***
Davlor Constructio Corp, Trabuco Canyon *Also called Davlor Company* ***(P-1454)***
Daw Industries Inc ....E....858 622-4955
6610 Nncy Rdge Dr Ste 100 San Diego (92121) ***(P-7806)***
Dawn Ranch Lodge & Rd Hse Rest ....D....707 869-0656
16467 Hwy 116 Guerneville (95446) ***(P-12202)***
Day Star Educational Center, Fullerton *Also called Westview Services Inc* ***(P-23544)***
Day Star Fixtures ....E....714 838-4613
1802 Riverford Rd Tustin (92780) ***(P-2927)***
Day Wireless Systems, San Diego *Also called U S Mbile Wrless Cmmunications* ***(P-5280)***
Daybreak Care Center (PA) ....E....818 504-6154
9040 Sunland Blvd Sun Valley (91352) ***(P-23900)***
Daybreak Game Company LLC ....B....858 239-0500
15051 Avenue Of Science San Diego (92128) ***(P-14753)***
Daylight Foods Inc ....C....408 284-7300
30200 Whipple Rd Union City (94587) ***(P-8454)***
Daylight Transport LLC (PA) ....D....310 507-8200
1501 Hughes Way Ste 200 Long Beach (90810) ***(P-3992)***
Daymark Properties Realty, San Diego *Also called Daymark Realty Advisors Inc* ***(P-11087)***
Daymark Realty Advisors Inc ....B....714 975-2999
750 B St Ste 2620 San Diego (92101) ***(P-11087)***
Dayout Brawley, Brawley *Also called Dacare Inc* ***(P-23189)***
Days Inn, Glendale *Also called JP Allen Extended Stay* ***(P-12493)***
Days Inn, Oakland *Also called Brilliance Investment LLC* ***(P-12088)***
Days Inn Bakersfield ....C....661 324-6666
818 Real Rd Bakersfield (93309) ***(P-12203)***
DAYSTAR FOUNDATION, Lancaster *Also called Antelope Valley Foundation* ***(P-22916)***
Daytona Surfise, North Hollywood *Also called Century National Properties* ***(P-12131)***
Daz Systems LLC (HQ) ....D....310 640-1300
800 Crprate Pinte Ste 100 Culver City (90230) ***(P-14754)***
Dazian LLC ....D....818 287-3800
10671 Lorne St Sun Valley (91352) ***(P-7995)***
Dazian's, Sun Valley *Also called Dazian LLC* ***(P-7995)***
Db Custom Farming, Bakersfield *Also called Donald Valpredo Farming Inc* ***(P-49)***
DB Roberts Inc ....D....805 988-4882
880 Avenida Acaso Ste 100 Camarillo (93012) ***(P-7255)***
Dbi Beverage Inc ....D....209 524-2477
4140 Brew Master Dr Ceres (95307) ***(P-8757)***
Dbi Beverage Sacramento (HQ) ....D....916 373-5700
3500 Carlin Dr West Sacramento (95691) ***(P-8802)***
Dbi Beverage San Francisco ....C....415 643-9900
245 S Spruce Ave Ste 100 South San Francisco (94080) ***(P-8758)***
Dbi Services Inc ....D....805 523-7114
2775 Hollister St Simi Valley (93065) ***(P-1851)***
DC Transport Inc ....D....916 438-0888
5411 Raley Blvd Sacramento (95838) ***(P-3993)***
Dcg Fulfillment, Ontario *Also called Dirt Cheap Inc* ***(P-721)***
Dcm Data Systems, Fremont *Also called Dcm Limited* ***(P-15973)***
Dcm Limited ....D....510 494-2321
39159 Paseo Padre Pkwy # 303 Fremont (94538) ***(P-15973)***
Dcm Technologies Inc ....D....510 791-2182
39159 Paseo Padre Pkwy # 303 Fremont (94538) ***(P-14755)***
Dcor LLC (PA) ....D....805 535-2000
290 Maple Ct Ste 290 # 290 Ventura (93003) ***(P-1001)***
Dcp Jl Triton Sf LLC ....E....844 808-0290
342 Grant Ave San Francisco (94108) ***(P-12204)***
Dcp Rights LLC ....E....310 255-4600
2900 Olympic Blvd Santa Monica (90404) ***(P-17596)***
DCS, Lathrop *Also called Performant Recovery Inc* ***(P-13693)***
Dcss, Modesto *Also called County of Stanislaus* ***(P-23173)***
Dct, Fontana *Also called Desert Coastal Transport Inc* ***(P-4000)***
DDB Worldwide ....C....310 907-1500
340 Main St Venice (90291) ***(P-13489)***
DDB Worldwide ....C....415 732-3600
600 California St Fl 7 San Francisco (94108) ***(P-13490)***
Ddso, Sacramento *Also called Developmental Disabilities* ***(P-23193)***
De Anza Campland LLC (PA) ....D....858 581-4200
2211 Pacific Beach Dr San Diego (92109) ***(P-13161)***
De Anza Land & Leisure Corp ....E....619 423-2727
2170 Coronado Ave San Diego (92154) ***(P-17830)***
De Anza Square Shopping Center ....D....408 738-4444
1306 S Mary Ave 1370 Sunnyvale (94087) ***(P-1292)***
De Benedetto AG, Chowchilla *Also called J & R Debenedetto Orchards Inc* ***(P-667)***
De Benedetto Farms Inc ....D....559 276-2400
1547 N Marks Ave Fresno (93722) ***(P-172)***
De La Torre Landscape & Maint ....C....951 549-3525
656 Paseo Grande Corona (92882) ***(P-793)***
De Lasalle Institute, NAPA *Also called Retreat & Conference Center* ***(P-13452)***
De Mattei Construction Inc ....D....408 295-7516
1794 The Alameda San Jose (95126) ***(P-1112)***
De Mello Roofing Inc ....D....415 456-0741
45 Jordan St San Rafael (94901) ***(P-3046)***
De Oliviera Concrete Inc ....E....661 252-7522
14111 Soledad Canyon Rd Santa Clarita (91387) ***(P-3139)***
De Par Inc ....D....714 771-6900
931 W Barkley Ave Orange (92868) ***(P-26063)***
Deacon Construction - Cal ....D....916 969-0900
7745 Greenback Ln Ste 250 Citrus Heights (95610) ***(P-1455)***
Deacon Corp ....D....949 222-9060
17880 Fitch Irvine (92614) ***(P-1456)***
Deacon Holdings Inc (PA) ....D....916 969-0900
7745 Greenback Ln Ste 250 Citrus Heights (95610) ***(P-1457)***
Dealersocket Inc (PA) ....D....949 900-0300
100 Avenida La Pata San Clemente (92673) ***(P-14756)***
Dealertrack Collte Manag Servi ....C....916 368-5300
9750 Goethe Rd Sacramento (95827) ***(P-15974)***
Dean Goodman Inc ....D....714 229-8999
10833 Valley View St # 240 Cypress (90630) ***(P-11088)***
Deanco Healthcare LLC ....A....818 787-2222
14850 Roscoe Blvd Panorama City (91402) ***(P-20825)***
Deardorff Family Farm, Oxnard *Also called Deardorff-Jackson Co* ***(P-8455)***

Employee Codes: A=Over 500 employees, B=251-500
C=101-250, D=51-100, E=50
2020 Directory of California
Wholesalers and Services Companies
© Mergent Inc. 1-800-342-5647
1243

Deardorff-Jackson Co ....E....805 487-7801
400 Lombard St Oxnard (93030) *(P-8455)*
Death Valley 49ers Inc ....D....559 297-5691
1442 Carson Ave Clovis (93611) *(P-24824)*
Debisys Inc (PA) ....D....949 699-1401
27442 Portola Pkwy # 150 Foothill Ranch (92610) *(P-9431)*
Debtmerica LLC ....D....714 389-4200
3100 S Harbor Blvd # 250 Santa Ana (92704) *(P-13418)*
Debtmerica Relief, Santa Ana *Also called Debtmerica LLC (P-13418)*
Decathalon Club, San Francisco *Also called Executives Outlet Inc (P-18144)*
Decathlon Club, Santa Clara *Also called Bay Clubs Inc (P-18121)*
Decathlon Club Inc ....C....408 738-2582
3250 Central Expy Santa Clara (95051) *(P-18139)*
Dechert LLP ....C....949 442-6000
650 Town Center Dr # 700 Costa Mesa (92626) *(P-22465)*
Dechert LLP ....E....415 262-4500
1 Bush St Ste 1600 San Francisco (94104) *(P-22466)*
Decimal Inc ....D....855 980-6612
1160 Battery St Ste 350 San Francisco (94111) *(P-16740)*
Decipher Inc (HQ) ....D....559 436-6940
7 E River Park Pl E # 110 Fresno (93720) *(P-25887)*
Decipher Corp ....D....888 975-4540
10355 Science Center Dr San Diego (92121) *(P-21520)*
Decision Minds ....C....408 309-8051
1525 Mccarthy Blvd # 224 Milpitas (95035) *(P-15748)*
Decision Ready Solutions Inc ....E....949 400-1126
400 Spectrum Center Dr # 2050 Irvine (92618) *(P-9545)*
Decision Sciences Intl Corp ....D....858 571-1900
12345 First American Way # 100 Poway (92064) *(P-7256)*
Decision Toolbox Inc ....D....562 377-5600
5319 University Dr 521 Irvine (92612) *(P-27047)*
Decker Elc Co Inc Elec Contrs ....D....650 635-1390
147 Beacon St South San Francisco (94080) *(P-2474)*
Decker Landscaping Inc ....D....916 652-1780
13265 Bill Francis Dr Auburn (95603) *(P-794)*
Decky Co Inc (PA) ....D....310 608-2726
2121 S Wilmington Ave Compton (90220) *(P-8024)*
Declara Inc ....D....650 800-7695
977 Commercial St Palo Alto (94303) *(P-15975)*
Decurion Corporation (PA) ....D....310 659-9432
120 N Robertson Blvd Fl 3 Los Angeles (90048) *(P-17831)*
Dedicated Dental Systems Inc ....D....661 397-5513
9800 S La Cienega Blvd # 800 Inglewood (90301) *(P-19608)*
Dedicated Fleet Systems Inc (PA) ....D....909 590-8209
1350 Philadelphia St Pomona (91766) *(P-3874)*
Dedicated Management Group LLC ....C....209 385-0694
3876 E Childs Ave Merced (95341) *(P-16741)*
Dedicated Media Inc (PA) ....D....310 524-9400
909 N Pacific Coast Hwy # 320 El Segundo (90245) *(P-13491)*
Dedication & Everlasting Love ....D....661 269-4010
6021 Shannon Valley Rd Acton (93510) *(P-602)*
Dee Sign Co ....D....818 904-3400
7950 Woodley Ave Van Nuys (91406) *(P-16742)*
Deem Inc (HQ) ....D....415 590-8300
642 Harrison St Fl 2 San Francisco (94107) *(P-15301)*
Deep Focus Inc ....A....323 790-5340
6922 Hollywood Blvd Fl 10 Hollywood (90028) *(P-26579)*
Deepak Chopra LLC ....E....760 494-1600
7668 El Camino Real # 101 Carlsbad (92009) *(P-18140)*
Deer Park Pharmacy, Saint Helena *Also called St Helena Hospital (P-21220)*
Defined Contribution Trust Fun ....D....213 385-6161
501 Shatto Pl Ste 500 Los Angeles (90020) *(P-11781)*
Defy Media LLC ....D....310 360-4141
8750 Wilshire Blvd # 200 Beverly Hills (90211) *(P-13492)*
Degenkolb Engineers (PA) ....C....415 392-6952
375 Beale St Ste 500 San Francisco (94105) *(P-25031)*
Dehart Inc ....D....858 695-0882
7550 Miramar Rd Ste 300 San Diego (92126) *(P-3398)*
Dejuno Corporation ....D....909 230-6744
6275 Providence Way Eastvale (92880) *(P-8965)*
Dekra-Lite Industries Inc ....D....714 436-0705
3102 W Alton Ave Santa Ana (92704) *(P-16743)*
Del AMO Construction ....D....310 378-6203
23840 Madison St Torrance (90505) *(P-1458)*
Del AMO Diagnostic Center ....E....310 316-2424
5215 Torrance Blvd Torrance (90503) *(P-22016)*
Del AMO Grdns Cnvlscnt Hosp & ....D....310 378-4233
22419 Kent Ave Torrance (90505) *(P-19858)*
Del AMO Hospital Inc ....B....310 530-1151
23700 Camino Del Sol Torrance (90505) *(P-21409)*
Del AMO Insurance Services ....D....310 534-3444
910 Lomita Blvd Ste E Harbor City (90710) *(P-10338)*
Del Contes Landscaping Inc ....D....510 353-6030
41900 Boscell Rd Fremont (94538) *(P-795)*
Del Mar Convalescent Hospital ....D....626 288-8353
3136 Del Mar Ave Rosemead (91770) *(P-20826)*
Del Mar Country Club Inc ....D....858 759-5500
6001 Clubhouse Dr Rancho Santa Fe (92067) *(P-18440)*
Del Mar French Laundry ....E....831 375-9597
508 Del Monte Ave Monterey (93940) *(P-13180)*
Del Mar Holding LLC ....A....313 659-7300
1022 Bay Marina Dr 10 National City (91950) *(P-8404)*
Del Mar Plastering Inc ....D....951 343-5955
7085 Jurupa Ave Ste 2 Riverside (92504) *(P-2776)*
Del Mar Seafoods Inc ....C....805 850-0421
1449 Spinnaker Dr Ventura (93001) *(P-8368)*
Del Mar Thoroughbred Club ....B....858 755-1141
2260 Jimmy Durante Blvd Del Mar (92014) *(P-18084)*
Del Monaco Specialty Foods Inc ....D....408 500-4100
18675 Madrone Pkwy # 150 Morgan Hill (95037) *(P-8168)*
Del Norte Distribution, Oxnard *Also called Seaboard Produce Distrs Inc (P-4501)*
Del Norte Workforce Center ....E....707 464-8347
875 5th St Ste 12 Crescent City (95531) *(P-23590)*
Del Paso Country Club ....C....916 489-3681
3333 Marconi Ave Sacramento (95821) *(P-18441)*
Del Puerto Health Care Dst ....D....209 892-9100
875 E St Patterson (95363) *(P-18948)*
Del Puerto Health Center, Patterson *Also called Del Puerto Health Care Dst (P-18948)*
Del Rey Packing Co, Del Rey *Also called Chooljian & Sons Inc (P-477)*
Del Rey Systems and Tech Inc (PA) ....D....858 874-8992
7844 Convoy Ct San Diego (92111) *(P-15976)*
Del Rio Convalescent, Bell Gardens *Also called Del Rio Sanitarium Inc (P-19860)*
Del Rio Convalescent Center, Whittier *Also called Del Rio Health Care Inc (P-19859)*
Del Rio Golf & Country Club ....C....209 341-2414
801 Stewart Rd Modesto (95356) *(P-18442)*
Del Rio Health Care Inc ....C....562 947-5221
16016 Rio Florida Dr Whittier (90603) *(P-19859)*
Del Rio Sanitarium Inc ....C....562 927-6586
7002 Gage Ave Bell Gardens (90201) *(P-19860)*
Del Rosa Villa Inc ....D....909 885-3261
2018 Del Rosa Ave San Bernardino (92404) *(P-19861)*
Delancey Street Coach Service, San Francisco *Also called Delancey Street Foundation (P-23901)*
Delancey Street Foundation (PA) ....B....415 957-9800
600 The Embarcadero San Francisco (94107) *(P-23901)*
Delano Dst Sklled Nrsing Fclty ....C....661 720-2100
1509 Tokay St Delano (93215) *(P-19862)*
Delano Energy, Delano *Also called Covanta Delano Inc (P-5826)*
Delaware Electro Inds Inc (PA) ....D....818 786-8111
9248 Eton Ave Chatsworth (91311) *(P-7142)*
Delegata Corporation ....D....916 609-5400
2450 Venture Oaks Way # 400 Sacramento (95833) *(P-15581)*
Delicate Productions Inc (PA) ....D....415 484-1174
874 Verdulera St Camarillo (93010) *(P-17907)*
Delimex Holdings Inc ....A....619 210-2700
7878 Airway Rd San Diego (92154) *(P-11656)*
Dell, San Jose *Also called Force10 Networks Inc (P-15593)*
DELL TECHNOLOGIES, San Francisco *Also called Pivotal Software Inc (P-15013)*
Della Maggiore Tile Inc ....D....408 286-3991
87 N 30th St San Jose (95116) *(P-2892)*
Delmart Farms Inc ....D....661 746-2148
30988 Riverside Cntrl Vly Shafter (93263) *(P-125)*
Deloitte & Touche LLP ....A....213 688-0800
555 W 5th St Ste 2700 Los Angeles (90013) *(P-25568)*
Deloitte & Touche LLP ....C....619 232-6500
655 W Broadway Ste 700 San Diego (92101) *(P-25569)*
Deloitte & Touche LLP ....A....714 436-7419
695 Town Center Dr # 1200 Costa Mesa (92626) *(P-25570)*
Deloitte & Touche LLP ....B....415 783-4000
555 Mission St Ste 1400 San Francisco (94105) *(P-25571)*
Deloitte & Touche LLP ....B....408 704-4000
225 W Santa Clara St # 600 San Jose (95113) *(P-25572)*
Deloitte & Touche LLP ....D....559 449-6300
5250 N Palm Ave Ste 300 Fresno (93704) *(P-25573)*
Deloitte & Touche LLP ....C....415 782-4020
6210 Stoneridge Mall Rd Pleasanton (94588) *(P-25574)*
Deloitte & Touche LLP ....C....213 688-0800
555 W 5th St Ste 2700 Los Angeles (90013) *(P-25575)*
Deloitte Consulting LLP ....D....510 251-4400
555 Mission St San Francisco (94105) *(P-26580)*
Deloitte Tax LLP ....B....415 783-4000
555 Mission St Ste 1400 San Francisco (94105) *(P-25576)*
Deloitte Tax LLP ....B....408 704-4000
225 W Santa Clara St # 600 San Jose (95113) *(P-25577)*
Delphi Productions Inc (PA) ....C....510 748-7494
950 W Tower Ave Alameda (94501) *(P-13493)*
Delphix Corp (PA) ....E....650 494-1645
1400 Saport Blvd Ste 200a Redwood City (94063) *(P-15302)*
Delta Air Lines Inc ....D....310 646-9614
5625 W Imperial Hwy Los Angeles (90045) *(P-4922)*
Delta Air Lines Inc ....D....323 417-7374
500 World Way Los Angeles (90045) *(P-4662)*
Delta Airlines, Los Angeles *Also called Delta Air Lines Inc (P-4922)*
Delta Airlines, Los Angeles *Also called Delta Air Lines Inc (P-4662)*
Delta America Ltd (HQ) ....C....510 668-5100
46101 Fremont Blvd Fremont (94538) *(P-7257)*
Delta Blood Bank ....D....209 943-3830
1900 W Orangeburg Ave Modesto (95350) *(P-22224)*
Delta Blood Bank (HQ) ....D....800 244-6794
65 N Commerce St Stockton (95202) *(P-22225)*
Delta Breeze Farming Inc ....C....916 775-2055
11566 State Highway 160 Courtland (95615) *(P-312)*
Delta Computer Consulting ....C....310 541-9440
25550 Hawthorne Blvd # 106 Torrance (90505) *(P-15977)*
Delta Creative Inc ....C....800 423-4135
2690 Pellissier Pl City of Industry (90601) *(P-7731)*
Delta Dental of California ....B....619 683-2549
1450 Frazee Rd Ste 200 San Diego (92108) *(P-9943)*
Delta Dental of California (PA) ....B....415 972-8300
560 Mission St Ste 1300 San Francisco (94105) *(P-9944)*
Delta Dental of California ....A....916 853-7373
11155 International Dr Sacramento (95826) *(P-9945)*
Delta Dental Plan, Sacramento *Also called Delta Dental of California (P-9945)*
Delta Disposal Service Co, Tracy *Also called Tracy Dlta Solid Waste Mgt Inc (P-6292)*
Delta Electronics Americas Ltd (HQ) ....D....510 668-5100
46101 Fremont Blvd Fremont (94538) *(P-26209)*
Delta Floral Distributors Inc ....C....323 751-8116
6810 West Blvd Los Angeles (90043) *(P-8891)*

Mergent e-mail: customerrelations@mergent.com 2020 Directory of California (P-0000) Products & Services Section entry number
1244 Wholesalers and Services Companies (PA)=Parent Co (HQ)=Headquarters (DH)=Div Headquarters

Delta Galil USA Inc ....D....949 296-0380
16912 Von Karman Ave Irvine (92606) ***(P-8068)***
Delta Growers, Stockton *Also called Heritage Land Company Inc* ***(P-247)***
Delta Hawkeye Security Inc ....D....209 957-3333
7400 Shoreline Dr Ste 2 Stockton (95219) ***(P-16255)***
DELTA HEALTH SYSTEMS, Stockton *Also called Wm Michael Stemler Inc* ***(P-10552)***
Delta Max ....E....949 759-8529
23 Curl Dr Corona Del Mar (92625) ***(P-15978)***
Delta Nrsing Rhbilitation Ctr, Visalia *Also called Delta Nrsing Rhbilitation Hosp* ***(P-19863)***
Delta Nrsing Rhbilitation Hosp ....D....559 625-4003
514 N Bridge St Visalia (93291) ***(P-19863)***
Delta One Security Inc ....D....707 425-9346
342 Acacia St Fairfield (94533) ***(P-16256)***
Delta Personnel Services Inc ....D....925 356-3034
1820 Galindo St Ste 3 Concord (94520) ***(P-16257)***
Delta PHI Chapter, Goleta *Also called Gamma PHI Beta Sorority Inc* ***(P-13171)***
Delta Products, Fremont *Also called Delta America Ltd* ***(P-7257)***
Delta Project Management Inc ....D....415 590-3202
650 California St Fl 7 San Francisco (94108) ***(P-25032)***
Delta Protective Services, Stockton *Also called Borgens & Borgens Inc* ***(P-16210)***
Delta Rescue Inc ....D....661 269-4010
P.O. Box 9 Glendale (91209) ***(P-24825)***
Delta Scientific Corporation (PA) ....C....661 575-1100
40355 Delta Ln Palmdale (93551) ***(P-16507)***
Delta Truck Center, French Camp *Also called Fresno Truck Center* ***(P-6396)***
Delta-T Group Inc ....B....619 543-0556
4420 Hotel Circle Ct # 205 San Diego (92108) ***(P-14259)***
Deluxe Auto Carriers Inc ....D....909 746-0900
4788 Brookhollow Cir Jurupa Valley (92509) ***(P-3875)***
Deluxe Digital Dist Inc ....E....818 260-6202
2400 W Empire Ave Ste 200 Los Angeles (90027) ***(P-17733)***
Deluxe Entrmt Svcs Group Inc (PA) ....D....818 565-3600
2400 W Empire Ave Ste 200 Burbank (91504) ***(P-17970)***
Deluxe Laboratories Inc (HQ) ....A....323 462-6171
2400 W Empire Ave Burbank (91504) ***(P-17734)***
Deluxe Media Services ....B....818 526-3700
2130 N Hollywood Way Burbank (91505) ***(P-15749)***
Deluxe Media Services LLC ....A....323 462-6171
1377 N Serrano Ave Los Angeles (90027) ***(P-17597)***
DEMAND MEDIA, Santa Monica *Also called Demand One Media LLC* ***(P-13622)***
Demand One Media LLC (PA) ....C....310 656-6253
1655 26th St Santa Monica (90404) ***(P-13622)***
Demandbase Inc ....B....415 683-2660
680 Folsom St Ste 400 San Francisco (94107) ***(P-15303)***
Demandtec LLC ....B....914 499-1900
1 Franklin Pkwy Bldg 910 San Mateo (94403) ***(P-14757)***
Demaria Landtech ....E....858 481-5500
5631 Palmer Way Ste C Carlsbad (92010) ***(P-796)***
Demaria Landtech Inc ....E....858 481-5500
2789 High Mead Cir Vista (92084) ***(P-797)***
Demcon Concrete Contrs Inc ....D....858 748-5090
13795 Blaisdell Pl # 202 Poway (92064) ***(P-3140)***
Demenno Kerdoon ....C....310 537-7100
2000 N Alameda St Compton (90222) ***(P-1002)***
Demenno-Kerdoon ....B....310 898-3848
1300 S Santa Fe Ave Compton (90221) ***(P-3876)***
Demko Drywall & Demolition Co ....E....619 590-0025
419 S Marshall Ave El Cajon (92020) ***(P-2777)***
Demler Armstrong & Rowland LLP ....E....562 597-0029
4500 E Pacific Cst Hwy # 400 Long Beach (90804) ***(P-22467)***
Demler Egg Ranch ....E....661 758-4577
28198 Gromer Ave Wasco (93280) ***(P-409)***
Demo Deluxe, Yorba Linda *Also called IMG* ***(P-16840)***
Dena Corp ....D....415 375-3170
185 Berry St Ste 3000 San Francisco (94107) ***(P-14758)***
Denios Roseville Farmers ....C....916 782-2704
2013 Opportunity Dr Roseville (95678) ***(P-16744)***
Denken Solutions Inc ....C....949 630-5263
9170 Irvine Center Dr # 200 Irvine (92618) ***(P-14759)***
Dennett Tile & Stone Inc ....E....707 541-3700
4536 Bennett View Dr Santa Rosa (95404) ***(P-2893)***
Dennis & Leen, Los Angeles *Also called EC Group Inc* ***(P-6512)***
Dennis Allen Associates (PA) ....D....805 884-8777
201 N Milpas St Santa Barbara (93103) ***(P-1113)***
Dennis Blazona Construction ....D....916 375-8337
525 Harbor Blvd Ste 10 West Sacramento (95691) ***(P-3141)***
Dennis Group Inc ....D....858 847-9633
705 Palomar Airpt Rd # 100 Carlsbad (92011) ***(P-25033)***
Dennis Hyde Construction Inc ....D....661 393-1077
7112 Darrin Ave Bakersfield (93308) ***(P-1114)***
Dennis M McCoy & Sons Inc ....D....818 874-3872
32107 Lindero Canyon Rd # 212 Westlake Village (91361) ***(P-1697)***
Denova Home Sales Inc ....D....925 852-0545
1500 Willow Pass Ct Concord (94520) ***(P-11089)***
Denova Homes, Concord *Also called Denova Home Sales Inc* ***(P-11089)***
Denso Pdts & Svcs Americas Inc (HQ) ....C....310 834-6352
3900 Via Oro Ave Long Beach (90810) ***(P-6432)***
Dental, San Diego *Also called Veterans Health Administration* ***(P-19637)***
Dental Office, Oxnard *Also called Clinicas Del Camino Real Inc* ***(P-21982)***
Dentalville, Bell *Also called Leonid M Glosman DDS A D* ***(P-19618)***
Dentistat Inc ....D....408 376-0336
1688 Dell Ave Ste 210 Campbell (95008) ***(P-26581)***
Dentists Insurance Company (HQ) ....C....916 443-4567
1201 K St Ste 1600 Sacramento (95814) ***(P-10339)***
Dentons US LLP ....D....650 798-0300
1530 Page Mill Rd Ste 200 Palo Alto (94304) ***(P-22468)***
Dentons US LLP ....C....949 732-3700
4675 Macarthur Ct # 1250 Newport Beach (92660) ***(P-22469)***
Dentons US LLP ....D....619 595-5400
750 B St Ste 3300 San Diego (92101) ***(P-22470)***
Dentons US LLP ....B....619 236-1414
4655 Executive Dr Ste 700 San Diego (92121) ***(P-22471)***
Dentons US LLP ....C....415 882-5000
1 Market Plz Fl 24 San Francisco (94105) ***(P-22472)***
Dentons US LLP ....C....213 623-9300
601 S Figueroa St # 2500 Los Angeles (90017) ***(P-22473)***
Dentons US LLP ....C....213 688-1000
300 S Grand Ave Fl 14 Los Angeles (90071) ***(P-22474)***
Denver D Darling Inc ....D....714 761-8299
8402 Katella Ave Stanton (90680) ***(P-1345)***
Department Behavioral Health, Fresno *Also called County of Fresno* ***(P-21992)***
Department Child Support Svcs, Camarillo *Also called County of Ventura* ***(P-23182)***
Department Children Fmly Svcs, Los Angeles *Also called County of Los Angeles* ***(P-23105)***
Department Health Care Svcs ....D....510 412-3700
850 Marina Bay Pkwy Richmond (94804) ***(P-21521)***
Department of Ane, Sacramento *Also called University California Davis* ***(P-21341)***
Department of Cultural Affairs, Los Angeles *Also called City of Los Angeles* ***(P-24819)***
Department of Health, Los Angeles *Also called County of Los Angeles* ***(P-22216)***
Department of Health Services, Los Angeles *Also called County of Los Angeles* ***(P-21465)***
Department of Health Services, Martinez *Also called County of Contra Costa* ***(P-20811)***
Department of Health Services, Concord *Also called County of Contra Costa* ***(P-21991)***
Department of Mental Health, Los Angeles *Also called County of Los Angeles* ***(P-15852)***
Department of Mental Health, Willows *Also called County of Glenn* ***(P-21993)***
Department of Public Safety, Stanford *Also called Leland Stanford Junior Univ* ***(P-2538)***
Department of Public Works, Alhambra *Also called County of Los Angeles* ***(P-6042)***
Department of Public Works, Mill Valley *Also called City of Mill Valley* ***(P-1684)***
Department of Public Works, San Rafael *Also called County of Marin* ***(P-25020)***
Department of Regional Parks, Sacramento *Also called County of Sacramento* ***(P-18327)***
Department of Social Services, Alturas *Also called County of Modoc* ***(P-23115)***
Department of Social Services, San Luis Obispo *Also called County of San Luis Obispo* ***(P-23155)***
Department of Social Services, Paso Robles *Also called County of Los Angeles* ***(P-23095)***
Department of Social Services, Placerville *Also called County of El Dorado* ***(P-23067)***
Department of Transportation, Ukiah *Also called County of Mendocino* ***(P-4764)***
Department of Urology, San Francisco *Also called University Cal San Francisco* ***(P-21337)***
Department Public Social Svcs, Cudahy *Also called County of Los Angeles* ***(P-24162)***
Department Workforce Dev, Modesto *Also called County of Stanislaus* ***(P-23589)***
Dependable Aircargo Ex Inc ....C....310 537-2000
19201 S Susana Rd Compton (90221) ***(P-4923)***
Dependable Disposal and Recycl, Spring Valley *Also called Burns and Sons Trucking Inc* ***(P-3856)***
Dependable Furniture Mfrs, San Francisco *Also called Van Sark Inc* ***(P-6533)***
Dependable Highway Express Inc ....D....909 923-0065
1351 S Campus Ave Ontario (91761) ***(P-3994)***
Dependable Highway Express Inc ....C....310 522-4111
800 E 230th St Carson (90745) ***(P-3995)***
Dependable Highway Express Inc ....D....209 342-0184
1343 Lone Palm Ave Modesto (95351) ***(P-3996)***
Dependable Highway Express Inc ....E....510 357-2223
3012 Alvarado St San Leandro (94577) ***(P-3997)***
Dependable Highway Express Inc (PA) ....B....323 526-2200
2555 E Olympic Blvd Los Angeles (90023) ***(P-3998)***
Dependable Highway Express Inc ....D....510 357-2223
3199 Alvarado St San Leandro (94577) ***(P-3999)***
Dependable Highway Express Inc ....E....916 374-0782
830 E St West Sacramento (95605) ***(P-3877)***
Dependable Logistics Services, Los Angeles *Also called Dependable Highway Express Inc* ***(P-3998)***
Deployable Space Systems Inc ....E....805 722-8090
153 Castilian Dr Goleta (93117) ***(P-25034)***
Deployment Solutions LLC ....E....317 281-9682
332 Bandini Pl Vista (92083) ***(P-2475)***
Depo Auto Parts, Fontana *Also called Maxzone Vehicle Lighting Corp* ***(P-6452)***
Deposition Sciences Inc ....D....707 573-6700
3300 Coffey Ln Santa Rosa (95403) ***(P-25736)***
Depot, Porterville *Also called Tharp Truck Rental Inc* ***(P-17553)***
Dept Children and Family Svcs, Lakewood *Also called County of Los Angeles* ***(P-23087)***
Dept of Building Inspection, Salinas *Also called County of Monterey* ***(P-16723)***
Dept of Child Support, Stockton *Also called County of San Joaquin* ***(P-23152)***
Dept of Community Services, Bell *Also called City of Bell* ***(P-23007)***
Dept of Maintenance, Antioch *Also called City of Antioch* ***(P-6339)***
Dept of Mental Health, Woodland *Also called County of Yolo* ***(P-22012)***
Dept of Public Works, Irvine *Also called City of Irvine* ***(P-26557)***
Dept of Social Services, Eureka *Also called County of Humboldt* ***(P-23073)***
Dept of Social Services Dss, San Luis Obispo *Also called County of San Luis Obispo* ***(P-23156)***
Der Manouel Insurance Group, Fresno *Also called Hub Intrntional Insur Svcs Inc* ***(P-10384)***
Derek Silva Community, San Francisco *Also called Catholic Chrts Cyo Archdiocs* ***(P-22974)***
Derjjan Associates Inc (PA) ....C....831 423-4111
2025 Soquel Ave Santa Cruz (95062) ***(P-26210)***
Des Architects + Engineers Inc ....C....650 364-6453
399 Bradford St Ste 300 Redwood City (94063) ***(P-25432)***
Deser Sands Unifi Schoo Distr ....D....760 777-4200
47950 Dune Palms Rd La Quinta (92253) ***(P-23717)***
Deseret Farms of California, Chico *Also called Agreserves Inc* ***(P-170)***
Deseret Industries, Sacramento *Also called Church of Jsus Chrst of Ld STS* ***(P-23579)***
Desert Aids Project (PA) ....D....760 323-2118
1695 N Sunrise Way Bldg 1 Palm Springs (92262) ***(P-23190)***
Desert Air Conditioning Inc ....E....760 323-3383
590 S Williams Rd Palm Springs (92264) ***(P-3047)***

Employee Codes: A=Over 500 employees, B=251-500
C=101-250, D=51-100, E=50
2020 Directory of California
Wholesalers and Services Companies
© Mergent Inc. 1-800-342-5647
1245

Desert Area Resources Training ....D.......760 375-8494
201 E Ridgecrest Blvd Ridgecrest (93555) *(P-24167)*
Desert Arts Center ....D.......760 323-7973
550 N Palm Canyon Dr Palm Springs (92262) *(P-24261)*
Desert Cardiology Cons Med G, Rancho Mirage *Also called Desert Cardiology Consultants (P-18949)*
Desert Cardiology Consultants ....D.......760 346-0642
39000 Bob Hope Dr Rancho Mirage (92270) *(P-18949)*
Desert Cities Dialysis, Victorville *Also called Jamboor Medical Corporation (P-21927)*
Desert Cncpts Ldscpg Maint Inc ....C.......760 200-9007
79469 Country Club Dr I Bermuda Dunes (92203) *(P-720)*
Desert Coastal Transport Inc (PA) ....D.......909 357-3395
10686 Banana Ave Fontana (92337) *(P-4000)*
Desert Dental Group, Victorville *Also called Joseph A Foroosh Dental Corp (P-19613)*
Desert Falls Country Club Inc ....D.......760 340-5646
1111 Desert Falls Pkwy Palm Desert (92211) *(P-18443)*
Desert Haven Enterprises Inc ....A.......661 948-8402
43437 Copeland Cir Lancaster (93535) *(P-798)*
DESERT HORIZONS COUNTRY CLUB, Indian Wells *Also called Dhccnp (P-18445)*
Desert Hot Springs Real Proper ....D.......760 329-6000
10805 Palm Dr Desert Hot Springs (92240) *(P-10581)*
Desert Hot Springs Spa Hotel, Desert Hot Springs *Also called Whatever It Takes Inc (P-13093)*
Desert Hot Springs Spa Hotel, Desert Hot Springs *Also called Desert Hot Springs Real Proper (P-10581)*
Desert Knlls Convalescent Hosp, Victorville *Also called Knolls Convalescent Hospital (P-20058)*
Desert Knolls Convalescent, Victorville *Also called Knolls Convalescent Hospital (P-20059)*
Desert Manor Care Center LP ....D.......760 365-0717
8515 Cholla Ave Yucca Valley (92284) *(P-23902)*
Desert Mechanical Inc ....A.......702 873-7333
15870 Olden St Sylmar (91342) *(P-2115)*
Desert Medical Group Inc (PA) ....C.......760 320-8814
275 N El Cielo Rd D-402 Palm Springs (92262) *(P-18950)*
Desert Medical Group Inc ....C.......760 323-8657
275 N El Cielo Rd Ste C Palm Springs (92262) *(P-18951)*
Desert Oaks Apartments, Visalia *Also called Kern 2008 Cmnty Partners LP (P-1257)*
Desert Oasis Healthcare, Palm Springs *Also called Desert Medical Group Inc (P-18950)*
Desert Orthopdc Center A Mdcl (PA) ....D.......760 568-2684
39000 Bob Hope Dr W301 Rancho Mirage (92270) *(P-18952)*
Desert Princess Hoa, Cathedral City *Also called Desert Prncess Homeowners Assn (P-24535)*
Desert Princess Home ....E.......760 322-1655
28555 Landau Blvd Cathedral City (92234) *(P-18444)*
Desert Prncess Homeowners Assn ....D.......760 322-1907
28555 Landau Blvd Cathedral City (92234) *(P-24535)*
Desert Recreation District (PA) ....D.......760 347-3484
45305 Oasis St Indio (92201) *(P-18680)*
Desert Recycling Inc ....E.......760 948-3122
17105 Mesa St Hesperia (92345) *(P-6193)*
Desert Regional Med Ctr Inc (HQ) ....A.......760 323-6511
1150 N Indian Canyon Dr Palm Springs (92262) *(P-20827)*
Desert Regional Med Ctr Inc ....C.......760 323-6640
1695 N Sunrise Way Palm Springs (92262) *(P-21468)*
Desert Resort Management ....D.......760 831-0172
42635 Melanie Pl Ste 103 Palm Desert (92211) *(P-11090)*
Desert Rose Golf Course, Cathedral City *Also called American Golf Corporation (P-18363)*
DESERT SPRINGS HEALTHCARE & WE, Indio *Also called Indio Hlthcare Wllness Ctr LLC (P-20029)*
Desert Springs Hotel ....E.......760 251-3399
10805 Palm Dr Desert Hot Springs (92240) *(P-10582)*
Desert Star Co ....E.......661 259-5848
23119 Drayton St Saugus (91350) *(P-8696)*
Desert Sun Science Center, The, Idyllwild *Also called Guided Discoveries Inc (P-13148)*
Desert Television LLC ....D.......760 343-5700
73185 Highway 111 Ste D Palm Desert (92260) *(P-5594)*
Desert Valley Date Inc ....E.......760 398-0999
86740 Industrial Way Coachella (92236) *(P-481)*
Desert Valley Hospital Inc (HQ) ....D.......760 241-8000
16850 Bear Valley Rd Victorville (92395) *(P-20828)*
DESERT VALLEY INDUSTRIES, Palm Desert *Also called Desertarc (P-23191)*
Desert Valley Med Group Inc (PA) ....B.......760 241-8000
16850 Bear Valley Rd Victorville (92395) *(P-18953)*
Desert View Funeral Home ....E.......760 244-0007
11478 Amargosa Rd Victorville (92392) *(P-13369)*
Desert Water Agency Fing Corp ....D.......760 323-4971
1200 S Gene Autry Trl Palm Springs (92264) *(P-6046)*
Desert Willow Golf Course, Palm Desert *Also called Desert Willow Golf Resort Inc (P-18241)*
Desert Willow Golf Resort Inc ....C.......760 346-0015
38995 Desert Willow Dr Palm Desert (92260) *(P-18241)*
Desertarc ....B.......760 346-1611
73255 Country Club Dr Palm Desert (92260) *(P-23191)*
Design Collection Inc ....D.......323 277-9200
2209 S Santa Fe Ave Los Angeles (90058) *(P-7996)*
Design Machine and Mfg ....E.......559 897-7374
2491 Simpson St Kingsburg (93631) *(P-17496)*
Design Masonry Inc ....D.......661 252-2784
20703 Santa Clara St Canyon Country (91351) *(P-2709)*
Designed MBL Systems Inds Inc ....C.......209 892-6298
800 S State Highway 33 Patterson (95363) *(P-1459)*
Designers LLC (PA) ....D.......209 982-0600
235 Frank West Cir Stockton (95206) *(P-13267)*
Desilva Gates Construction LP ....C.......916 386-9708
7700 College Town Dr # 230 Sacramento (95826) *(P-1698)*
Desilva Gates Construction LP (PA) ....D.......925 361-1380
11555 Dublin Blvd Dublin (94568) *(P-1699)*
Desmond Mail Delivery Service ....D.......323 262-1085
4600 Worth St Los Angeles (90063) *(P-3878)*
Destination Moon LP ....D.......415 675-7777
615 Battery St Fl 6 San Francisco (94111) *(P-13781)*
Destination Residences LLC ....E.......760 346-4647
45750 San Luis Rey Ave Palm Desert (92260) *(P-12205)*
Destination Residences LLC ....B.......858 550-1000
9700 N Torrey Pines Rd La Jolla (92037) *(P-13419)*
Destination Science LLC ....C.......714 289-9100
953 N Elm St Orange (92867) *(P-27048)*
Destination Shuttle Svcs LLC ....C.......310 338-9466
6150 W 96th St Los Angeles (90045) *(P-3530)*
Destination Webcam, La Jolla *Also called Aegis Software Inc (P-13643)*
Destiny Arts Center ....E.......510 597-1619
970 Grace Ave Oakland (94608) *(P-18681)*
Deutsch La Inc ....D.......310 862-3000
5454 Beethoven St Los Angeles (90066) *(P-13494)*
Deutsche Bank National Tr Co (HQ) ....D.......213 620-8200
2000 Avenue Of The Stars Los Angeles (90067) *(P-9444)*
Deutsche Bank National Tr Co ....D.......714 247-6000
1761 E Saint Andrew Pl Santa Ana (92705) *(P-11782)*
Deutsche Bank National Tr Co ....D.......714 247-6054
1761 E Saint Andrew Pl Santa Ana (92705) *(P-9416)*
Deutsche Bank Tr Co Americas ....C.......415 617-4200
101 California St # 4500 San Francisco (94111) *(P-9686)*
Deutsche Inv MGT Americas Inc ....E.......415 648-9408
101 California St # 2400 San Francisco (94111) *(P-9810)*
Devcon Construction Inc (PA) ....B.......408 942-8200
690 Gibraltar Dr Milpitas (95035) *(P-1460)*
Devcool Inc ....D.......408 372-4313
5890 Stoneridge Dr # 107 Pleasanton (94588) *(P-26582)*
Develop Disabilities Svc Org ....D.......916 973-1951
2331 Saint Marks Way G1 Sacramento (95864) *(P-23192)*
Developers Surety Indemnity Co (HQ) ....D.......949 263-3300
17771 Cowan Ste 100 Irvine (92614) *(P-10162)*
Development Exchange, Mountain View *Also called Devxcom Inc (P-5389)*
Development Resource Cons Inc (PA) ....D.......714 685-6860
160 S Old Springs Rd # 210 Anaheim (92808) *(P-25035)*
Development Services, Lancaster *Also called Lancaster Comm Srvcs Fndtn (P-17336)*
Developmental Disabilities (PA) ....D.......916 456-5166
5051 47th Ave Sacramento (95824) *(P-23193)*
Developmental Svcs Cal Dept ....A.......559 782-2222
26501 Avenue 140 Porterville (93257) *(P-19864)*
Developmental Svcs Cal Dept ....A.......714 957-5151
2501 Harbor Blvd Costa Mesa (92626) *(P-23591)*
Developmental Svcs Continuum ....D.......619 460-7333
7944 Golden Ave Lemon Grove (91945) *(P-23903)*
Developmentally Research Ctr, San Marcos *Also called San Diego-Imperial Counties De (P-23435)*
Develpment Dimensions Intl Inc ....B.......925 361-4246
4160 Dublin Blvd Ste 450 Dublin (94568) *(P-26583)*
Devereux California Center, Goleta *Also called Devereux Foundation (P-22017)*
Devereux Center In California, Goleta *Also called Devereux Foundation (P-11783)*
Devereux Foundation ....B.......805 968-2525
7055 Seaway Dr Goleta (93117) *(P-22017)*
Devereux Foundation ....B.......805 968-2525
El Colegio Rd Goleta (93117) *(P-11783)*
Device Anywhere ....D.......650 655-6400
777 Mariners Isl Blvd # 250 San Mateo (94404) *(P-14760)*
Devincenzi Concrete Cnstr ....E.......707 568-4370
3276 Dutton Ave Santa Rosa (95407) *(P-3142)*
Devine & Son Trucking Co Inc (PA) ....C.......559 486-7440
3870 Channel Dr West Sacramento (95691) *(P-4592)*
Devine Intermodal, West Sacramento *Also called Devine & Son Trucking Co Inc (P-4592)*
Devonshire Care Center LLC ....D.......951 925-2571
1350 E Devonshire Ave Hemet (92544) *(P-20546)*
Devxcom Inc ....E.......650 390-6553
310 Villa St Mountain View (94041) *(P-5389)*
Dewhurst & Associates ....D.......858 456-5345
7533 Girard Ave La Jolla (92037) *(P-1115)*
Dewmobile USA Inc ....E.......408 550-2818
2901 Tasman Dr Ste 107 Santa Clara (95054) *(P-14761)*
Dewolf Realty Co Inc ....D.......415 221-2032
4330 California St San Francisco (94118) *(P-26211)*
Dex Corporation ....C.......805 388-1711
3600 Via Pescador Camarillo (93012) *(P-25036)*
Dexyp, Glendale *Also called Yellowpagescom LLC (P-17175)*
Deyoung Museum, San Francisco *Also called Corportion of Fine Arts Mseums (P-24259)*
Dfa of California ....C.......530 345-5077
6100 Wilson Landing Rd Chico (95973) *(P-24826)*
Dfa of California ....D.......209 465-2289
1050 Diamond St Stockton (95205) *(P-16745)*
Dfds International Corporation ....D.......310 414-1516
898 N Pacific Coast Hwy # 6 El Segundo (90245) *(P-4924)*
Dfds Transport US, El Segundo *Also called Dfds International Corporation (P-4924)*
Dfs Flooring Inc (PA) ....D.......818 374-5200
15651 Saticoy St Van Nuys (91406) *(P-2999)*
Dfusion Software Inc ....E.......323 617-5577
5900 Wilshire Blvd # 2550 Los Angeles (90036) *(P-14762)*
Dg Architects Inc (PA) ....D.......650 943-1660
550 Ellis St Mountain View (94043) *(P-25433)*
Dga Plnning L Arch L Interiors, Mountain View *Also called Dg Architects Inc (P-25433)*
Dga Services Inc (PA) ....D.......408 232-4800
1075 Montague Expy Milpitas (95035) *(P-4204)*
Dgwb Inc ....D.......714 881-2300
217 N Main St Ste 200 Santa Ana (92701) *(P-13495)*
Dgwb Advg & Communications, Santa Ana *Also called Dgwb Inc (P-13495)*

Dgwb Ventures LLC.....D.....714 881-2308
217 N Main St Ste 200 Santa Ana (92701) ***(P-13496)***
DH Smith Company Inc.....D.....408 532-7617
6000 Hellyer Ave Ste 150 San Jose (95138) ***(P-2778)***
Dhap Digital Inc.....E.....415 962-4900
235 Montgomery St # 1320 San Francisco (94104) ***(P-14763)***
Dharne & Company.....D.....949 293-5675
19200 Von Karman Ave # 400 Irvine (92612) ***(P-15979)***
Dhccnp.....D.....760 340-4646
44900 Desert Horizons Dr Indian Wells (92210) ***(P-18445)***
Dhe, Ontario *Also called Dependable Highway Express Inc* ***(P-3994)***
Dhe, San Leandro *Also called Dependable Highway Express Inc* ***(P-3999)***
Dhl Express (usa) Inc.....D.....415 826-7338
401 23rd St San Francisco (94107) ***(P-4697)***
Dhl Global Forwarding, San Diego *Also called Air Express Intl USA Inc* ***(P-4882)***
Dhl Supply Chain (usa).....C.....415 531-0596
485 Valley Dr Brisbane (94005) ***(P-4925)***
Dhl Supply Chain (usa).....E.....909 350-6976
9211 Kaiser Way Fontana (92335) ***(P-4396)***
Dhl Supply Chain (usa).....D.....510 784-7360
2391 W Winton Ave Hayward (94545) ***(P-4397)***
Dhs Consulting LLC.....C.....714 276-1135
1820 E 1st St Ste 410 Santa Ana (92705) ***(P-26212)***
Dhs Member Services.....E.....562 595-5151
3833 Atlantic Ave Long Beach (90807) ***(P-19609)***
Dhv Industries Inc.....D.....661 392-8948
3451 Pegasus Dr Bakersfield (93308) ***(P-7633)***
Dhx-Dependable Hawaiian Ex Inc.....C.....510 686-2600
2375 Davis St San Leandro (94577) ***(P-4926)***
Dhx-Dependable Hawaiian Ex Inc (PA).....C.....310 537-2000
19201 S Susana Rd Compton (90221) ***(P-4927)***
Diablo Country Club.....D.....925 837-4221
1700 Club House Rd Diablo (94528) ***(P-18446)***
Diablo Country Club.....E.....925 837-4221
1700 Clubhouse Rd Diablo (94528) ***(P-18447)***
Diablo Grande Ltd Partnership.....D.....209 892-7421
9521 Morton Davis Dr Patterson (95363) ***(P-11558)***
Diablo Landscape Inc.....D.....408 487-9620
1655 Berryessa Rd San Jose (95133) ***(P-799)***
Diablo Realty Inc.....E.....925 933-9300
975 Ygnacio Valley Rd Walnut Creek (94596) ***(P-11091)***
Diablo Valley Rock, Concord *Also called Carone & Company Inc* ***(P-3306)***
Diablo Vly College Foundation (PA).....C.....925 685-1230
321 Golf Club Rd Pleasant Hill (94523) ***(P-16746)***
Diageo North America Inc.....D.....707 939-6200
21468 8th St E Sonoma (95476) ***(P-8803)***
Diageo North America Inc.....D.....949 421-3974
30 Journey Aliso Viejo (92656) ***(P-8804)***
Diagnostic and Interventio.....D.....310 574-0400
13160 Mindanao Way # 150 Marina Del Rey (90292) ***(P-18954)***
Diagnostic Labs & Rdlgy, Burbank *Also called Kan-Di-Ki LLC* ***(P-21545)***
Diagnstic Med Group Sthern Cal, Arcadia *Also called Chen Dvid MD Dgnstc Med Group* ***(P-6961)***
Dial Communications, Camarillo *Also called Dial Security* ***(P-16508)***
Dial Global Digital, Culver City *Also called Triton Media Group LLC* ***(P-5569)***
Dial Security (PA).....C.....805 389-6700
760 W Ventura Blvd Camarillo (93010) ***(P-16508)***
Dialog Semiconductor Inc.....C.....408 327-8800
1515 Wyatt Dr Santa Clara (95054) ***(P-7258)***
Dialysis Centers Ventura Cnty.....D.....805 658-9211
4567 Telephone Rd Ste 101 Ventura (93003) ***(P-21919)***
Dialysis Clinic Inc.....E.....916 453-0803
1771 Stockton Blvd # 200 Sacramento (95816) ***(P-21920)***
Diamond Bar Golf Course, Diamond Bar *Also called American Golf Corporation* ***(P-18367)***
Diamond Bar Medical Offices, Diamond Bar *Also called Kaiser Foundation Hospitals* ***(P-19065)***
Diamond Environmental Svcs LP.....D.....760 744-7191
807 E Mission Rd San Marcos (92069) ***(P-14152)***
Diamond Intl Investment LLC.....D.....559 226-2200
3737 N Blackstone Ave Fresno (93726) ***(P-12206)***
Diamond Mountain Casino.....C.....530 252-1100
900 Skyline Dr Susanville (96130) ***(P-12207)***
Diamond Resorts LLC.....D.....760 866-1800
2800 S Palm Canyon Dr Palm Springs (92264) ***(P-12208)***
Diamond Ridge Corporation.....C.....909 949-0605
121 S Mountain Ave Upland (91786) ***(P-11092)***
Diamond Ridge Healthcare Ctr, Pittsburg *Also called SSC Pittsburg Operating Co LP* ***(P-20691)***
Diamond W Floorcovering, City of Industry *Also called W Diamond Supply Co* ***(P-6599)***
Diamondpeo LLC.....C.....714 728-5186
27442 Calle Arroyo Ste A San Juan Capistrano (92675) ***(P-14260)***
Diamondrock San Dego Tnant LLC.....B.....619 239-4500
400 W Broadway San Diego (92101) ***(P-12209)***
Diana's Beauty Salon, Los Angeles *Also called Dianas Mexican Food Pdts Inc* ***(P-13338)***
Dianas Mexican Food Pdts Inc.....D.....323 758-4845
5841 S Figueroa St Los Angeles (90003) ***(P-13338)***
Diani Building Corp (PA).....D.....805 925-9533
351 N Blosser Rd Santa Maria (93458) ***(P-1461)***
Dianne Adair Day Care Centers (PA).....D.....925 429-3232
1862 Bailey Rd Concord (94521) ***(P-23718)***
Diaz Plastering Inc.....D.....661 244-8228
4900 California Ave 210b Bakersfield (93309) ***(P-2779)***
Diazyme Laboratories Inc.....D.....858 455-4768
12889 Gregg Ct Poway (92064) ***(P-21522)***
Dibuduo Dfendis Insur Brks LLC (PA).....D.....559 432-0222
6873 N West Ave Fresno (93711) ***(P-10340)***
Dicalite Minerals Corp (HQ).....D.....530 335-5451
36994 Summit Lake Rd Burney (96013) ***(P-17497)***
Dicaperl Corporation (HQ).....D.....610 667-6640
23705 Crenshaw Blvd Torrance (90505) ***(P-1065)***
Dick Anderson & Sons Farming.....C.....559 945-2511
15900 W Dorris Ave Huron (93234) ***(P-313)***
Dickinson, Diane MD, Arcata *Also called Northcountry Clinic* ***(P-19225)***
Dickson Testing Co Inc (HQ).....D.....562 862-8378
11126 Palmer Ave South Gate (90280) ***(P-26064)***
DIDI HIRSCH COMMUNITY MENTAL H, Culver City *Also called Didi Hirsch Psychiatric Svc* ***(P-23194)***
Didi Hirsch Psychiatric Svc (PA).....C.....310 390-6612
4760 Sepulveda Blvd Culver City (90230) ***(P-23194)***
Diede Construction Inc.....D.....209 369-8255
12393 N Hwy 99 Lodi (95240) ***(P-1462)***
Diehard Security Solutions Inc.....C.....510 995-8450
1151 Harbor Bay Pkwy # 140 Alameda (94502) ***(P-16258)***
Diepenbrock Elkin LLP.....D.....916 492-5000
500 Capitol Mall Ste 650 Sacramento (95814) ***(P-22475)***
Diesel Parts and Service, Long Beach *Also called Harbor Diesel and Eqp Inc* ***(P-7549)***
Diestel Turkey Ranch.....C.....209 984-0826
14111 High Tech Dr C Jamestown (95327) ***(P-415)***
Diestel Turkey Ranch (PA).....C.....209 532-4950
22200 Lyons Bald Mtn Rd Sonora (95370) ***(P-416)***
Dietrich Post Co Inc.....E.....510 596-0080
945 Bryant St San Francisco (94103) ***(P-7855)***
Dietz Glmor Chazen A Prof Corp (PA).....D.....858 565-0269
7071 Convoy Ct Ste 300 San Diego (92111) ***(P-22476)***
Diez & Leis RE Group Inc.....D.....916 487-4287
5120 Manzanita Ave # 120 Carmichael (95608) ***(P-11093)***
Digex Inc.....E.....408 468-5000
2950 Zanker Rd San Jose (95134) ***(P-5390)***
Digiquest Corp.....E.....951 776-4344
989 Talcey Ter Riverside (92506) ***(P-6826)***
Digital Communications Network (PA).....D.....818 227-3333
6300 Canoga Ave Ste 1625 Woodland Hills (91367) ***(P-5255)***
Digital Domain 30 Inc (PA).....B.....310 314-2800
12641 Beatrice St Los Angeles (90066) ***(P-17598)***
Digital Film Labs, Los Angeles *Also called Point360* ***(P-17758)***
Digital Foundry Inc.....E.....415 789-1600
1707 Tiburon Blvd Belvedere Tiburon (94920) ***(P-15980)***
Digital Guardian Inc.....B.....408 716-4200
2101 Tasman Dr Ste 210 Santa Clara (95054) ***(P-14764)***
Digital Insight Corporation.....C.....818 879-1010
5601 Lindero Canyon Rd # 100 Westlake Village (91362) ***(P-15853)***
Digital Insight Corporation (HQ).....C.....818 879-1010
1300 Seaport Blvd Ste 300 Redwood City (94063) ***(P-15854)***
Digital Keystone Inc.....E.....650 938-7301
21631 Stevns Crk Blvd A Cupertino (95014) ***(P-15582)***
Digital Kitchen LLC.....E.....310 499-9255
3585 Hayden Ave Culver City (90232) ***(P-17599)***
Digital Map Products Inc.....D.....949 333-5111
5201 California Ave # 200 Irvine (92617) ***(P-5784)***
Digital Media Management LLC.....D.....323 378-6505
5670 Wilshire Blvd Fl 11 Los Angeles (90036) ***(P-26213)***
Digital Networks Group Inc.....D.....949 428-6333
20382 Hermana Cir Lake Forest (92630) ***(P-15981)***
Digital Operative Inc.....E.....310 630-0072
404 Camino Del San Diego (92110) ***(P-13497)***
Digital Path Inc.....E.....800 676-7284
1065 Marauder St Chico (95973) ***(P-5391)***
Digital Realty Trust Inc (PA).....C.....415 738-6500
4 Embarcadero Ctr # 3200 San Francisco (94111) ***(P-15982)***
Digital Realty Trust LP (HQ).....A.....415 738-6500
4 Embarcadero Ctr # 3200 San Francisco (94111) ***(P-11851)***
Digitalist USA Ltd.....A.....949 278-1354
128 Spear St Lbby San Francisco (94105) ***(P-15583)***
Digitalmojo Inc.....D.....800 413-5916
3111 Camino Del Rio N # 400 San Diego (92108) ***(P-5392)***
Digitalthink Inc (HQ).....C.....415 625-4000
601 Brannan St San Francisco (94107) ***(P-26584)***
Digitaria, San Diego *Also called Mirum Inc* ***(P-13791)***
Digite Inc.....C.....408 418-3834
21060 Homestead Rd # 220 Cupertino (95014) ***(P-14765)***
Dignity Health.....B.....213 484-7111
2131 W 3rd St Los Angeles (90057) ***(P-20829)***
Dignity Health.....C.....916 983-7400
1650 Creekside Dr Folsom (95630) ***(P-20830)***
Dignity Health.....B.....805 739-3000
1400 E Church St Santa Maria (93454) ***(P-20831)***
Dignity Health.....E.....916 681-1600
7601 Hospital Dr Ste 103 Sacramento (95823) ***(P-20832)***
Dignity Health.....A.....916 537-5151
6501 Coyle Ave Fl 6 Carmichael (95608) ***(P-20833)***
Dignity Health.....B.....805 384-8071
5051 Verdugo Way Ste 100 Camarillo (93012) ***(P-20834)***
Dignity Health.....D.....805 489-4261
1054 E Grand Ave Ste A Arroyo Grande (93420) ***(P-21729)***
Dignity Health.....C.....916 851-2153
3400 Data Dr Rancho Cordova (95670) ***(P-20835)***
Dignity Health.....B.....805 473-7626
345 S Halcyon Rd Arroyo Grande (93420) ***(P-20836)***
Dignity Health.....B.....415 438-5500
1700 Montgomery St # 300 San Francisco (94111) ***(P-20837)***
Dignity Health.....A.....562 491-9000
1050 Linden Ave Long Beach (90813) ***(P-20838)***
Dignity Health (HQ).....C.....415 438-5500
185 Berry St Ste 300 San Francisco (94107) ***(P-20839)***
Dignity Health.....C.....916 667-0000
8120 Timberlake Way # 201 Sacramento (95823) ***(P-18955)***
Dignity Health.....A.....213 748-2411
1401 S Grand Ave Los Angeles (90015) ***(P-20840)***

Employee Codes: A=Over 500 employees, B=251-500
C=101-250, D=51-100, E=50
2020 Directory of California
Wholesalers and Services Companies
© Mergent Inc. 1-800-342-5647
1247

Dignity Health.....A.....916 537-5000
6501 Coyle Ave Carmichael (95608) ***(P-20841)***

Dignity Health.....C.....209 467-6430
1800 N California St Stockton (95204) ***(P-21523)***

Dignity Health.....D.....661 832-8300
2301 Ashe Rd Bakersfield (93309) ***(P-23719)***

Dignity Health.....B.....916 983-7400
1650 Creekside Dr Folsom (95630) ***(P-20842)***

Dignity Health.....C.....530 225-6345
2175 Rosaline Ave Ste A Redding (96001) ***(P-20843)***

Dignity Health.....C.....530 666-8828
20 N Cottonwood St Woodland (95695) ***(P-20844)***

Dignity Health.....A.....831 462-7700
1555 Soquel Dr Santa Cruz (95065) ***(P-20845)***

Dignity Health.....C.....209 754-3521
768 Mountain Ranch Rd San Andreas (95249) ***(P-20846)***

Dignity Health.....C.....916 423-5940
7500 Hospital Dr Sacramento (95823) ***(P-20847)***

Dignity Health.....A.....916 453-4545
4001 J St Sacramento (95819) ***(P-20848)***

Dignity Health.....E.....916 851-3800
3400 Data Dr Rancho Cordova (95670) ***(P-4398)***

Dignity Health.....C.....805 739-3830
124 S College Dr Santa Maria (93454) ***(P-21730)***

Dignity Health.....C.....805 739-3650
1530 Cypress Way Santa Maria (93454) ***(P-19865)***

Dignity Health.....E.....661 663-6767
551 Shanley Ct Bakersfield (93311) ***(P-20849)***

Dignity Health.....D.....916 983-7988
1600 Creekside Dr # 3700 Folsom (95630) ***(P-18956)***

Dignity Health.....C.....805 389-5800
2309 Antonio Ave Camarillo (93010) ***(P-20850)***

Dignity Health.....A.....805 739-3100
505 Plaza Dr Santa Maria (93454) ***(P-20851)***

Dignity Health.....A.....805 988-2500
1600 N Rose Ave Oxnard (93030) ***(P-20852)***

Dignity Health.....A.....415 668-1000
450 Stanyan St San Francisco (94117) ***(P-20853)***

Dignity Health.....E.....209 943-4663
2333 W March Ln Ste B Stockton (95207) ***(P-21731)***

Dignity Health.....C.....661 632-5279
400 Old River Rd Bakersfield (93311) ***(P-20854)***

Dignity Health.....A.....916 453-4453
4001 J St Sacramento (95819) ***(P-21524)***

Dignity Health.....D.....916 536-2420
8350 Auburn Blvd Ste 200 Citrus Heights (95610) ***(P-18957)***

Dignity Health.....B.....661 632-5000
2215 Truxtun Ave Bakersfield (93301) ***(P-20855)***

Dignity Health Med Foundation.....D.....916 681-6300
6615 Valley Hi Dr Sacramento (95823) ***(P-22226)***

Dignity Health Med Foundation.....D.....831 475-8834
1667 Dominican Way # 134 Santa Cruz (95065) ***(P-22227)***

Dignity Health Med Foundation.....D.....831 535-1560
9515 Soquel Dr Ste 100 Aptos (95003) ***(P-22228)***

Dignity Health Med Foundation.....A.....916 379-2840
3400 Data Dr Rancho Cordova (95670) ***(P-22229)***

Dignity Health Med Foundation.....D.....916 787-0404
2110 Prfcional Dr Ste 120 Roseville (95661) ***(P-22230)***

Dignity Health Med Foundation (HQ).....C.....916 379-2840
3400 Data Dr Rancho Cordova (95670) ***(P-20856)***

Dignity Health Medical Grp, Santa Cruz *Also called Dignity Health Med Foundation* ***(P-22227)***

Dignity Hlth Med Grp-Dominican, Aptos *Also called Dignity Health Med Foundation* ***(P-22228)***

Dignity Hlth Med Grp-Dominican, Rancho Cordova *Also called Dignity Health Med Foundation* ***(P-22229)***

Dignity Hlth Med Grp-Dominican, Rancho Cordova *Also called Dignity Health Med Foundation* ***(P-20856)***

Dilbeck Inc (PA).....D.....818 790-6774
1030 Foothill Blvd La Canada (91011) ***(P-11094)***

Dilbeck Inc.....D.....818 248-2248
2943 Foothill Blvd La Crescenta (91214) ***(P-11095)***

Dilbeck Inc.....E.....805 379-1880
850 Hampshire Rd Ste A Westlake Village (91361) ***(P-11096)***

Dilbeck Inc.....D.....626 584-0101
225 E Colorado Blvd Pasadena (91101) ***(P-11097)***

Dilbeck Realtors, La Canada *Also called Dilbeck Inc* ***(P-11094)***

Dilbeck Realtors, Westlake Village *Also called Dilbeck Inc* ***(P-11096)***

Dilbeck Realtors, Pasadena *Also called Dilbeck Inc* ***(P-11097)***

Dimare Company, Newman *Also called Dimare Enterprises Inc* ***(P-47)***

Dimare Enterprises Inc (PA).....C.....209 827-2900
1406 N St Newman (95360) ***(P-47)***

Dimare Fresh.....B.....916 921-6302
4050 Pell Cir Sacramento (95838) ***(P-8456)***

Dimension Data North Amer Inc.....D.....925 226-8378
5000 Hopyard Rd Pleasanton (94588) ***(P-15584)***

Dimension Development Two LLC.....D.....858 485-9250
11611 Bernardo Plaza Ct San Diego (92128) ***(P-12210)***

Dincloud Inc.....D.....310 929-1101
27520 Hawthorne Blvd # 185 Rllng HLS Est (90274) ***(P-15304)***

Dinuba Medical Center, Dinuba *Also called Dinuba Medical Clinic* ***(P-18958)***

Dinuba Medical Clinic (PA).....D.....559 591-1820
271 N L St Dinuba (93618) ***(P-18958)***

Dinyari Construction Inc.....E.....408 289-5400
500 Phelan Ave San Jose (95112) ***(P-1239)***

Diplomat Packaging, Sylmar *Also called Winning Performance Pdts Inc* ***(P-17171)***

Direct Access Insurance Svcs, Grass Valley *Also called Networked Insurance Agents LLC* ***(P-10434)***

Direct Delivery Center, Ontario *Also called Sears Roebuck and Co* ***(P-17543)***

Direct Pack Inc.....D.....626 380-2360
1025 W 8th St Azusa (91702) ***(P-8966)***

Direct Partners Inc (HQ).....D.....310 482-4200
12777 W Jefferson Blvd # 120 Los Angeles (90066) ***(P-13498)***

Direct Technology, Roseville *Also called Directapps Inc* ***(P-15983)***

Directapps Inc (PA).....C.....916 787-2200
3009 Douglas Blvd Ste 300 Roseville (95661) ***(P-15983)***

Directed LLC.....C.....800 876-0800
1 Viper Way Ste 1 # 1 Vista (92081) ***(P-4928)***

Directorate of Mwr Fmd Usag.....D.....210 466-1376
420 Montgomery St San Francisco (94104) ***(P-26214)***

Directors Guild America Inc (PA).....C.....310 289-2000
7920 W Sunset Blvd # 600 Los Angeles (90046) ***(P-17735)***

Directv Inc.....B.....888 388-4249
2230 E Imperial Hwy El Segundo (90245) ***(P-5705)***

Directv LLC.....D.....909 509-4790
1055 E Francis St Ontario (91761) ***(P-5706)***

Directv Enterprises LLC.....A.....310 535-5000
2230 E Imperial Hwy El Segundo (90245) ***(P-5707)***

Directv Group Inc.....C.....707 452-7409
340 Commerce Ave Fairfield (94533) ***(P-5708)***

Directv Group Inc.....C.....510 481-1324
1129 B St San Lorenzo (94580) ***(P-5709)***

Directv Group Holdings LLC (HQ).....C.....310 964-5000
2260 E Imperial Hwy El Segundo (90245) ***(P-5710)***

Directv Group Inc (HQ).....C.....310 964-5000
2260 E Imperial Hwy El Segundo (90245) ***(P-5711)***

Directv International Inc (HQ).....C.....310 964-6460
2230 E Imperial Hwy Fl 10 El Segundo (90245) ***(P-5712)***

Dirt Cheap Inc (PA).....E.....909 230-6330
1060 Wineville Ave Ontario (91764) ***(P-721)***

Dirt Cheap Demolition Inc.....E.....619 426-9598
171 Mace St Ste A4 Chula Vista (91911) ***(P-3340)***

Dirt Farmer & Co Inc.....D.....707 833-2054
9725 Los Guilicos Ave Kenwood (95452) ***(P-126)***

Dirtmarket , The, Campbell *Also called Cem Builders Inc* ***(P-24997)***

Disability Group Inc.....B.....310 829-5100
1014 23rd St Santa Monica (90403) ***(P-22477)***

Disability Insurance, Stockton *Also called E D D 2100* ***(P-9905)***

Disability Rights California.....D.....213 213-8000
350 S Bixel St Los Angeles (90017) ***(P-22478)***

Disability Rights California (PA).....D.....916 488-9950
1831 K St Sacramento (95811) ***(P-22479)***

Disaster Rstrtion Prfssnals In.....D.....310 301-8030
1517 W 130th St Gardena (90249) ***(P-1116)***

Discharge Resource Group.....C.....650 877-8111
400 Oyster Point Blvd # 440 South San Francisco (94080) ***(P-14502)***

Discount Builders Supply.....D.....415 285-2800
1695 Mission St San Francisco (94103) ***(P-6615)***

Discount School Supply, Monterey *Also called Excelligence Learning Corp* ***(P-26601)***

Discount Tire Center, Northridge *Also called Discount Tire Ctr* ***(P-17353)***

Discount Tire Ctr.....D.....818 993-4758
19545 Parthenia St Ste 3 Northridge (91324) ***(P-17353)***

Discoverorg Data LLC.....D.....360 783-6924
Dept La 24789 Pasadena (91185) ***(P-15855)***

Discoverready LLC.....D.....661 284-6401
27200 Tourney Rd Ste 450 Valencia (91355) ***(P-22480)***

Discovery Bay Ctry Club, Byron *Also called New Discovery Inc* ***(P-18514)***

Discovery Bay Golf & Cntry CLB, Byron *Also called New Discovery Inc* ***(P-18276)***

Discovery Communications Inc (PA).....B.....310 975-5906
10100 Santa Monica Blvd Los Angeles (90067) ***(P-5785)***

Discovery Plz Med & Admin Offs, Bakersfield *Also called Kaiser Foundation Hospitals* ***(P-19059)***

Discovery Practice Management.....E.....562 425-6404
4136 Ann Arbor Rd Lakewood (90712) ***(P-18959)***

Discovery Scnce Ctr Ornge Cnty.....C.....866 552-2823
2500 N Main St Santa Ana (92705) ***(P-18328)***

Discovery Shop, San Jose *Also called American Cancer Soc Cal Div* ***(P-24129)***

Discovery Shop, Menlo Park *Also called American Cancer Soc Cal Div* ***(P-25962)***

Dish Factory Inc (PA).....D.....213 687-9500
333 E Valley Blvd Colton (92324) ***(P-7669)***

Dish Network Corporation.....D.....909 381-4767
396 Orange Show Ln San Bernardino (92408) ***(P-5713)***

Dish Network Corporation.....E.....818 334-8740
1297 N Verdugo Rd Glendale (91206) ***(P-5714)***

Dish Network Corporation.....E.....714 424-0503
2602 Halladay St Santa Ana (92705) ***(P-5715)***

Dish Network Service LLC.....E.....858 452-2239
8318 Miramar Mall San Diego (92121) ***(P-5716)***

Dish Systems, Irvine *Also called Connect Your Home LLC* ***(P-1450)***

Disney Construction Inc.....D.....650 689-5149
533 Airport Blvd Ste 120 Burlingame (94010) ***(P-1700)***

Disney Enterprises Inc (HQ).....C.....818 560-1000
500 S Buena Vista St Burbank (91521) ***(P-5521)***

Disney Enterprises Inc.....A.....714 778-6600
1150 W Magic Way Anaheim (92802) ***(P-12211)***

Disney Enterprises Inc.....B.....818 560-3692
3235 S Buena Vista St Burbank (91521) ***(P-17600)***

Disney Enterprises Inc.....B.....714 999-0990
1717 S Disneyland Dr Anaheim (92802) ***(P-12212)***

Disney Incorporated (HQ).....C.....818 560-1000
500 S Buena Vista St Burbank (91521) ***(P-17601)***

Disney Interactive Studios Inc.....C.....818 560-1000
601 Circle Seven Dr Glendale (91201) ***(P-14766)***

Disney Interactive Studios Inc.....C.....818 553-5000
681 W Buena Vista St Burbank (91521) ***(P-14767)***

Disney Interfinance Corp.....B.....818 560-1000
500 S Buena Vista St Burbank (91521) ***(P-17785)***

Mergent e-mail: customerrelations@mergent.com
1248
2020 Directory of California
Wholesalers and Services Companies
(P-0000) Products & Services Section entry number
(PA)=Parent Co (HQ)=Headquarters (DH)=Div Headquarters

Disney Regional Entrmt Inc (HQ)........C.......818 560-1000
500 S Buena Vista St Burbank (91521) *(P-18682)*
Disney Research Pittsburgh........C.......412 623-1800
532 Paula Ave Glendale (91201) *(P-25737)*
Disneyland, Anaheim *Also called Twdc Enterprises 18 Corp (P-13048)*
Disneyland Hotel, Anaheim *Also called WCO Hotels Inc (P-13080)*
Disneyland International........B.......714 956-6746
1580 S Disneyland Dr Anaheim (92802) *(P-12213)*
Disneyland International (HQ)........C.......714 781-4565
1313 S Harbor Blvd Anaheim (92802) *(P-18329)*
Dispatch Commodity Trucking, Fontana *Also called Dispatch Transportation LLC (P-14153)*
Dispatch Office, Oakland *Also called First Transit Inc (P-3537)*
Dispatch Transportation LLC........C.......909 355-5531
14032 Santa Ana Ave Fontana (92337) *(P-14153)*
Dispatch Trucking LLC (PA)........D.......909 355-5531
14032 Santa Ana Ave Fontana (92337) *(P-4929)*
Disqo Inc........D.......818 459-4330
800 N Brand Blvd Fl 21 Glendale (91203) *(P-25888)*
Disruptive Visions LLC........D.......949 502-3800
27271 Las Ramblas Ste 300 Mission Viejo (92691) *(P-27049)*
Dist Attorney's Office, Redding *Also called County of Shasta (P-22447)*
Distel Family Ranch, Sonora *Also called Diestel Turkey Ranch (P-416)*
Distillery Inc........D.......415 505-5446
90 Heron Ct San Quentin (94964) *(P-15305)*
Distinctive Concrete Inc........E.......858 277-9707
9320 Chesapeake Dr # 214 San Diego (92123) *(P-3143)*
Distribution Alternatives Inc........D.......909 673-1000
1990 S Cucamonga Ave Ontario (91761) *(P-4399)*
Distribution Warehouse, Woodland *Also called Apria Healthcare LLC (P-22179)*
District Attorney, Westminster *Also called County of Orange (P-23120)*
District Attorney, Santa Maria *Also called Santa Barbara County of (P-22803)*
District Attorney, Compton *Also called County of Los Angeles (P-22439)*
District Attorney, Santa Rosa *Also called County of Sonoma (P-22448)*
District Attorney, Van Nuys *Also called County of Los Angeles (P-22443)*
District Attorney's Office, San Francisco *Also called City & County of San Francisco (P-22417)*
District Attroney's Office, San Jose *Also called Santa Clara County of (P-22804)*
District Council DC (PA)........D.......510 638-7600
2272 San Pablo Ave Oakland (94612) *(P-23195)*
District Office East, Bakersfield *Also called Panama-Buena Vista Un Schl Dst (P-13999)*
District Warehouse, Placentia *Also called Linda Placentia-Yorba (P-4442)*
Distritution Center, Ontario *Also called Converse Inc (P-8129)*
Diva Systems Corporation........C.......650 779-3000
800 Saginaw Dr Redwood City (94063) *(P-5717)*
Divergent Technologies Inc........D.......310 339-1186
19601 Hamilton Ave Torrance (90502) *(P-25037)*
Diverscape Inc........D.......951 245-1686
21730 Bundy Canyon Rd Wildomar (92595) *(P-800)*
Diverse Journeys Inc (PA)........D.......310 643-7403
525 S Douglas St Ste 210 El Segundo (90245) *(P-23196)*
Diversfied Cmmnctions Svcs Inc........D.......562 696-9660
1260 Pioneer St Brea (92821) *(P-5393)*
Diversified Clinical Services........D.......714 579-8400
4225 E La Palma Ave Anaheim (92807) *(P-22231)*
Diversified Health Svcs Del........E.......626 798-6753
2585 E Washington Blvd Pasadena (91107) *(P-23904)*
Diversified Health Svcs Del (PA)........C.......510 231-6200
136 Washington Ave Richmond (94801) *(P-20547)*
DIVERSIFIED INDUSTRIES, Montclair *Also called Oparc (P-23621)*
Diversified Landscape Co, Wildomar *Also called Diverscape Inc (P-800)*
Diversified Metal Works, Orange *Also called Rika Corporation (P-3282)*
Diversified RE Packaging Corp........A.......310 855-1946
1118 S La Cienega Blvd Los Angeles (90035) *(P-27050)*
Diversified Transport Systems........E.......559 268-2760
3150 S Willow Ave Fresno (93725) *(P-4400)*
Diversified Transportation LLC........D.......310 981-9500
6053 W Century Blvd # 900 Los Angeles (90045) *(P-3531)*
Diversified Trnsp Svcs, Torrance *Also called DTM Services Inc (P-4933)*
Diversified Utility Svcs Inc........B.......661 325-3212
3105 Unicorn Rd Bakersfield (93308) *(P-1852)*
Diversity Bus Solutions Inc........C.......909 395-0243
2515 S Euclid Ave Ontario (91762) *(P-14261)*
Divine Home Care, Alamo *Also called Wild Karma Inc (P-20385)*
Division 1, Los Angeles *Also called Los Angeles County MTA (P-3550)*
Division 7, Venice *Also called Los Angeles County MTA (P-3558)*
Division 8 Inc........E.......619 741-7552
1920 Cordell Ct Ste 105 El Cajon (92020) *(P-3292)*
Division Infectious Diseases, La Jolla *Also called Scripps Clinic Carmel Valley (P-19373)*
Division of Rheumatology, Los Angeles *Also called Childrens Hospital Los Angeles (P-18895)*
Division of State Architect, Oakland *Also called General Services Cal Dept (P-25437)*
Division of State Architect, Los Angeles *Also called General Services Cal Dept (P-25438)*
Division Three Cnstr Svcs........D.......951 609-3043
30620 Plumas St Lake Elsinore (92530) *(P-1463)*
Dix Metals Inc........D.......714 677-0777
14801 Able Ln Ste 101 Huntington Beach (92647) *(P-7060)*
DJ Scheffler Inc (PA)........E.......909 595-2924
2500 Pomona Blvd Pomona (91768) *(P-2710)*
Djont Operations LLC........D.......650 342-4600
150 Anza Blvd Burlingame (94010) *(P-12214)*
Djont/Cmb Ssf Leasing LLC........D.......650 589-3400
250 Gateway Blvd South San Francisco (94080) *(P-12215)*
Dkd Property Management, San Jose *Also called Property Maintenance Company (P-14019)*
Dkn Hotel LLC (PA)........B.......714 427-4320
42 Corporate Park Ste 200 Irvine (92606) *(P-12216)*
Dkn Hotel LLC........D.......714 535-0300
1240 S Walnut St Anaheim (92802) *(P-12217)*
Dl Imaging, Santa Ana *Also called Dekra-Lite Industries Inc (P-16743)*
DL Long Landscaping Inc........D.......909 628-5531
5475 G St Chino (91710) *(P-722)*
Dla Piper LLP (us)........B.......213 330-7700
550 S Hope St Ste 2400 Los Angeles (90071) *(P-22481)*
Dla Piper LLP (us)........B.......650 833-2000
2000 University Ave # 100 East Palo Alto (94303) *(P-22482)*
Dla Piper LLP (us)........D.......310 595-3000
2000 Avenue Of The Stars 400n Los Angeles (90067) *(P-22483)*
Dla Piper LLP (us)........B.......650 833-2000
2000 University Ave # 100 East Palo Alto (94303) *(P-22484)*
Dla Piper LLP (us)........D.......858 677-1400
4365 Executive Dr # 1100 San Diego (92121) *(P-22485)*
Dlb Fire Protection, Bakersfield *Also called Cfp Designs Inc (P-2092)*
Dlc, Cerritos *Also called David Levy Co Inc (P-7254)*
Dlh Davinci LLC........D.......818 703-5100
22135 Roscoe Blvd Ste 101 West Hills (91304) *(P-21607)*
Dlight Design Inc........A.......415 872-6136
2100 Geng Rd Ste 210 Palo Alto (94303) *(P-7143)*
Dlo Enterprises Inc........D.......760 346-8033
41865 Boardwalk Ste 216 Palm Desert (92211) *(P-16259)*
Dlr Group Inc........C.......626 796-8230
700 S Flower St Fl 22 Los Angeles (90017) *(P-25434)*
Dlr Group Inc (HQ)........C.......213 800-9400
700 Suth Flwr St Fl 22 Flr 22 Los Angeles (90017) *(P-25435)*
Dlt Growers Inc........E.......909 947-8198
13131 S Bon View Ave Ontario (91761) *(P-237)*
Dma Claims Inc (PA)........D.......323 342-6800
330 N Brand Blvd Ste 230 Glendale (91203) *(P-10341)*
Dma Claims Inc........D.......800 649-7602
7188 Via Carmela San Jose (95139) *(P-10342)*
Dma Claims Inc........D.......323 342-6800
330 N Brand Blvd Ste 230 Glendale (91203) *(P-10343)*
Dma Claims Services, Glendale *Also called Dma Claims Inc (P-10341)*
Dma Greencare Contracting Inc........E.......714 630-9470
3000 E Coronado St Anaheim (92806) *(P-801)*
DMC Construction Incorporated........D.......831 656-1600
2110 Del Monte Ave Monterey (93940) *(P-1464)*
Dmcg Inc (PA)........E.......951 683-9685
3605 10th St Riverside (92501) *(P-16747)*
Dmf Inc........D.......323 934-7779
1118 E 223rd St Carson (90745) *(P-7144)*
Dmf Lighting, Carson *Also called Dmf Inc (P-7144)*
Dmi, Sylmar *Also called Desert Mechanical Inc (P-2115)*
DMS Facility Services Inc........A.......510 656-9400
3137 Skyway Ct Fremont (94539) *(P-13914)*
DMS Facility Services LLC........C.......858 560-4191
5735 Krny Vlla Rd Ste 108 San Diego (92123) *(P-25038)*
Dna Specialty Inc........D.......310 767-4070
200 W Artesia Blvd Compton (90220) *(P-6433)*
Dna Twopointo Inc........D.......650 853-8347
37950 Central Ct Ste C Newark (94560) *(P-25738)*
Dna2.0, Newark *Also called Dna Twopointo Inc (P-25738)*
DNC Prks Resorts At Tenaya Inc (HQ)........D.......877 247-9241
1122 Highway 41 Fish Camp (93623) *(P-12218)*
DNC Prks Rsrts At Yosemite Inc........A.......209 372-1001
9001 Village Dr Yosemite Ntpk (95389) *(P-12219)*
Dnj Parking, San Francisco *Also called California Parking Company (P-10869)*
Dnow LP........D.......310 900-3900
1111 W Artesia Blvd Compton (90220) *(P-4562)*
Dns Electronics, Sunnyvale *Also called Screen Spe Usa LLC (P-7339)*
Dnv GL Energy Insights USA Inc........E.......510 891-0446
155 Grand Ave Ste 500 Oakland (94612) *(P-27051)*
Dobler & Sons LLC........B.......831 724-6727
174 Struve Rd Moss Landing (95039) *(P-48)*
Docircle Inc........E.......415 484-4221
2544 W Woodland Dr Anaheim (92801) *(P-5394)*
Docker Inc (PA)........D.......800 764-4847
144 Townsend St Ste 100 San Francisco (94107) *(P-14768)*
Dockside Machine & Ship Repair, Wilmington *Also called Marine Technical Services Inc (P-16906)*
Docler Media LLC (HQ)........D.......424 777-3999
8000 Beverly Blvd Los Angeles (90048) *(P-15750)*
Docmagic Inc........D.......800 649-1362
1800 W 213th St Torrance (90501) *(P-16748)*
Doctor Genius, Irvine *Also called Foundation Lead Group LLC (P-24543)*
Doctor On Demand Inc........D.......415 935-4447
275 Battery St Ste 650 San Francisco (94111) *(P-15306)*
Doctors Ambulance Services, Laguna Hills *Also called Herren Enterprises Inc (P-3685)*
Doctors Company Foundation........A.......800 421-2368
185 Greenwood Rd NAPA (94558) *(P-9904)*
Doctors Company Insurance Svcs........B.......707 226-0100
185 Greenwood Rd NAPA (94558) *(P-10163)*
Doctors Hospital Manteca Inc........B.......209 823-3111
1205 E North St Manteca (95336) *(P-21469)*
Doctors Hospital Riverside LLC (PA)........E.......951 354-7404
3865 Jackson St Riverside (92503) *(P-20857)*
Doctors Hospital W Covina Inc........C.......626 338-8481
725 S Orange Ave West Covina (91790) *(P-20858)*
Doctors Management Company (HQ)........C.......707 226-0100
185 Greenwood Rd NAPA (94558) *(P-10344)*
Doctors Med Ctr Modesto Inc (HQ)........D.......209 578-1211
1441 Florida Ave Modesto (95350) *(P-20859)*
Doctors of Affiliated........D.......714 539-3100
600 City Pkwy W Ste 400 Orange (92868) *(P-26215)*

ALPHABETIC

Employee Codes: A=Over 500 employees, B=251-500
C=101-250, D=51-100, E=50
2020 Directory of California
Wholesalers and Services Companies
© Mergent Inc. 1-800-342-5647
1249

Document Proc Solutions Inc (PA) .... D......714 482-2060
590 W Lambert Rd Brea (92821) *(P-15751)*
Document Systems, Torrance *Also called Docmagic Inc (P-16748)*
Document Technologies LLC .... D......415 495-4100
275 Battery St Ste 250 San Francisco (94111) *(P-16749)*
Document Technologies LLC .... D......213 892-9000
350 S Figueroa St Ste 750 Los Angeles (90071) *(P-16750)*
Document Technologies LLC .... D......650 485-2705
3600 W Bayshore Rd Palo Alto (94303) *(P-16751)*
Docusign Inc (PA) .... B......415 489-4940
221 Main St Ste 1550 San Francisco (94105) *(P-15307)*
DOD Constructors A JV .... D......707 265-1100
185 Devlin Rd NAPA (94558) *(P-1955)*
DOD Fueling Constructors A JV .... D......707 265-1100
185 Devlin Rd NAPA (94558) *(P-1956)*
DOD Marine Constructors A JV .... D......707 265-1100
185 Devlin Rd NAPA (94558) *(P-1957)*
Dodge & Cox .... C......415 981-1710
555 California St # 4000 San Francisco (94104) *(P-11722)*
Dodge Ridge Corporation .... B......209 536-5300
1 Dodge Ridge Rd Pinecrest (95364) *(P-12220)*
Dodge Ridge Winter Sports Area, Pinecrest *Also called Dodge Ridge Corporation (P-12220)*
Dokken Engineering (PA) .... D......916 858-0642
110 Blue Ravine Rd # 200 Folsom (95630) *(P-25039)*
Dolan Concrete Construction .... D......408 869-3250
3045 Alfred St Santa Clara (95054) *(P-3144)*
Dolby Labs Licensing Corp .... C......415 558-0200
100 Potrero Ave San Francisco (94103) *(P-11826)*
Dolce Hayes Mansion, San Jose *Also called City of San Jose (P-12149)*
Dolce International / NAPA LLC .... B......707 257-0200
1600 Atlas Peak Rd NAPA (94558) *(P-12221)*
Dole Food Company Inc (PA) .... C......818 874-4000
1 Dole Dr Westlake Village (91362) *(P-220)*
Dole Fresh Fruit Company (HQ) .... B......818 874-4000
1 Dole Dr Westlake Village (91362) *(P-8457)*
Dole Fresh Vegetables Inc .... C......559 945-2591
16199 9th St Huron (93234) *(P-482)*
Dole Fresh Vegetables Inc .... C......831 678-5030
32655 Camphora Rd Soledad (93960) *(P-8458)*
Dole Holding Company LLC .... A......818 879-6600
1 Dole Dr Westlake Village (91362) *(P-221)*
Dole Holdings Inc (PA) .... D......818 879-6600
1 Dole Dr Westlake Village (91362) *(P-8459)*
Doll Fresh Vegestable, Huron *Also called Royal Packing Dcf (P-73)*
Doll House Footwear, City of Industry *Also called J P Original Corp (P-8135)*
Dollar Smart, Oxnard *Also called G P M M Money Centers Inc (P-9437)*
Dolphin Bay Hotel & Residences, Shell Beach *Also called Dolphin Bay Ht & Residence Inc (P-12222)*
Dolphin Bay Ht & Residence Inc .... D......805 773-4300
2727 Shell Beach Rd Shell Beach (93449) *(P-12222)*
Dolphin Hkg Ltd (PA) .... D......310 215-3356
1125 W Hillcrest Blvd Inglewood (90301) *(P-8967)*
Dolphin Imaging MGT Solutions, Chatsworth *Also called Patterson Dental Supply Inc (P-14998)*
Dolphin Imaging Systems LLC .... E......818 435-1368
9200 Oakdale Ave Ste 500 Chatsworth (91311) *(P-14769)*
Dolphin International, Inglewood *Also called Dolphin Hkg Ltd (P-8967)*
Dolphins Cove Resort Ltd .... D......714 980-0830
465 W Orangewood Ave Anaheim (92802) *(P-12223)*
Domaine Carneros Ltd .... D......707 257-0101
1240 Duhig Rd NAPA (94559) *(P-127)*
Domestic Horizons, Beverly Hills *Also called Global Horizons Inc (P-14291)*
Dominguez Firm Inc .... D......213 388-7788
3250 Wilshire Blvd # 1200 Los Angeles (90010) *(P-22486)*
Dominguez Landscape Svcs Inc .... D......916 381-8855
8376 Rovana Cir Sacramento (95828) *(P-802)*
Dominican Hospital Foundation .... C......831 457-7057
610 Frederick St Santa Cruz (95062) *(P-23905)*
Dominican Hospital Foundation (HQ) .... C......831 462-7700
1555 Soquel Dr Santa Cruz (95065) *(P-20860)*
Dominican Oaks Corporation .... D......831 462-6257
3400 Paul Sweet Rd Ofc Santa Cruz (95065) *(P-10714)*
Dominican Rehab Services, Santa Cruz *Also called Dominican Hospital Foundation (P-23905)*
Dominion International Inc .... D......916 683-9545
2305 Longport Ct Elk Grove (95758) *(P-12224)*
Dominos Pizza LLC .... C......909 390-1990
301 S Rockefeller Ave Ontario (91761) *(P-4563)*
Domus Construction & Design .... E......916 381-7500
8864 Fruitridge Rd Sacramento (95826) *(P-1117)*
Don Brandel Plumbing Inc .... E......562 408-0400
15100 Texaco Ave Paramount (90723) *(P-2116)*
Don Gragnani Farms .... D......559 693-4352
12910 S Napa Ave Tranquillity (93668) *(P-314)*
Don Juan Avila Elementary Pta .... D......949 349-9452
26278 Wood Canyon Dr Aliso Viejo (92656) *(P-24536)*
Don Kinzel Construction Inc .... D......661 322-9105
4300 Easton Dr Ste 2 Bakersfield (93309) *(P-2928)*
Don Turner and Associates, Fresno *Also called Turner Security Systems Inc (P-16462)*
Donaghy Sales Inc .... C......559 486-0901
2363 S Cedar Ave Fresno (93725) *(P-8759)*
Donahue Gallager Woods LLP (PA) .... D......415 381-4161
1999 Harrison St Ste 2500 Oakland (94612) *(P-22487)*
Donahue Schrber Rlty Group Inc (PA) .... D......714 545-1400
200 Baker St Ste 100 Costa Mesa (92626) *(P-11098)*
Donahue Schriber Rlty Group LP (PA) .... D......714 545-1400
200 Baker St Ste 100 Costa Mesa (92626) *(P-10583)*

Donahue Schriber Rlty Group LP .... D......714 545-1400
5082 N Palm Ave Fresno (93704) *(P-10584)*
Donahue Schriber Rlty Group LP .... D......714 283-3535
8020 E Santa Ana Cyn Rd Anaheim (92808) *(P-10585)*
Donahue Schriber Rlty Group LP .... D......858 793-5757
12925 El Camino Real J22 San Diego (92130) *(P-10586)*
Donald J Schefflers Cnstr, Azusa *Also called Heidi Corporation (P-1246)*
Donald Lawrence Company, Visalia *Also called Donald Lawrence Fulbright Co (P-1293)*
Donald Lawrence Fulbright Co .... D......559 625-0762
32557 Road 138 Visalia (93292) *(P-1293)*
Donald Lucky LLC .... C......949 752-0647
4029 Westerly Pl Ste 111 Newport Beach (92660) *(P-26216)*
Donald P Dick AC Inc (PA) .... D......559 255-1644
1444 N Whitney Ave Fresno (93703) *(P-2117)*
Donald T Sterling Corporation .... D......310 275-5575
10300 Wilshire Blvd Los Angeles (90024) *(P-12225)*
Donald Valpredo Farming Inc .... D......661 858-2245
2101 Mttler Frontage Rd E Bakersfield (93307) *(P-49)*
Donatello, San Francisco *Also called Shell Vacations LLC (P-12911)*
Dongalen Enterprises Inc (PA) .... E......916 422-3110
330 Commerce Cir Sacramento (95815) *(P-8685)*
Donor Network West (PA) .... C......925 480-3100
12667 Alcosta Blvd # 500 San Ramon (94583) *(P-22232)*
Donor Network West .... D......510 418-0336
5800 Airport Rd Ste B Redding (96002) *(P-22233)*
Donovan Bros Golf LLC .... D......805 531-9300
15187 Tierra Rejada Rd Moorpark (93021) *(P-18242)*
Donovan Golf Courses MGT .... E......714 528-6400
1800 Carbon Canyon Rd Chino (91708) *(P-18243)*
Doose Landscape Incorporated .... D......760 591-4500
785 E Mission Rd San Marcos (92069) *(P-803)*
Dorado Network Systems Corp .... C......650 227-7300
555 12th St Ste 1100 Oakland (94607) *(P-15308)*
Dorado Software Inc .... D......916 673-1100
4805 Golden Foothill Pkwy El Dorado Hills (95762) *(P-14770)*
Doral Palm Sprngs Rsrt & Golf, Palm Springs *Also called Interstate Hotels Resorts Inc (P-26266)*
Doremus & Company .... E......415 273-7800
55 Union St Fl 3 San Francisco (94111) *(P-13499)*
Dorfman Pacific, Stockton *Also called Dorfman-Pacific Co (P-8025)*
Dorfman-Pacific Co (HQ) .... C......209 982-1400
2615 Boeing Way Stockton (95206) *(P-8025)*
Dorothy Johnson Center, Chico *Also called Chico Area Recreation & Pk Dst (P-18647)*
Dos Palos Mem Rur Hlth Clinic, Dos Palos *Also called Dos Palos Memorial Hosp Inc (P-18960)*
Dos Palos Memorial Hosp Inc .... D......209 392-6121
2118 Marguerite St Dos Palos (93620) *(P-18960)*
Dos Pueblos Ranch, Goleta *Also called Schulte Ranches (P-358)*
DOT Foods Inc .... C......209 581-9090
2200 Nickerson Dr Modesto (95358) *(P-8169)*
DOT Leasing Company .... C......949 474-1100
2424 Mcgaw Ave Irvine (92614) *(P-7846)*
DOT Printer Inc .... E......949 752-7730
1801 S Standard Ave Santa Ana (92707) *(P-4401)*
DOT Printer Warehouse, Santa Ana *Also called DOT Printer Inc (P-4401)*
DOT-Line Transportation Inc .... D......877 900-7768
4366 E 26th St Vernon (90058) *(P-4001)*
Double Day Office Services Inc .... E......650 872-6600
340 Shaw Rd South San Francisco (94080) *(P-4205)*
Double Eagle Trnsp Corp .... C......760 956-3770
12135 Scarbrough Ct Oak Hills (92344) *(P-4002)*
Double G Productions Ltd .... D......310 479-0978
11301 W Olympic Blvd # 115 Los Angeles (90064) *(P-17971)*
Double Three Htlirvinespectrum, Irvine *Also called Spectrum Hotel Group LLC (P-12950)*
Double Tree Club Ht San Diego, San Diego *Also called Pbp Hotel LLC (P-11592)*
Double Tree Past Acute, Sacramento *Also called Sacramento Operating Co LP (P-20230)*
Doubledutch Inc (PA) .... D......800 748-9024
350 Rhode Island St # 375 San Francisco (94103) *(P-15309)*
Doubleline Capital LP .... C......213 633-8200
333 S Grand Ave Fl 18 Los Angeles (90071) *(P-16752)*
DoubleTree by Hilton, San Diego *Also called Swvp Del Mar Hotel LLC (P-13008)*
Doubletree By Hilton, San Diego *Also called San Diego Lessee LLC (P-12872)*
Doubletree By Hilton, San Diego *Also called Gringteam Inc (P-12319)*
Doubletree By Hilton Brky Mrna, Berkeley *Also called Westpost Berkeley LLC (P-13091)*
Doubletree By Hilton Carson, Carson *Also called Carson Operating Company LLC (P-12120)*
Doubletree By Hilton Fresno, Fresno *Also called Uniwell Fresno Hotel LLC (P-13054)*
Doubletree By Hilton Hotel .... C......310 322-0999
1985 E Grand Ave El Segundo (90245) *(P-12226)*
Doubletree By Hilton Hotel .... D......619 881-6900
1515 Hotel Cir S San Diego (92108) *(P-12227)*
Doubletree By Hilton La - Com, Commerce *Also called Tpg La Commerce LLC (P-13032)*
Doubletree By Hilton Los Angel, Culver City *Also called Woodbine Lgacy/Playa Owner LLC (P-13112)*
Doubletree By Hilton Ontario, Ontario *Also called Dt Ontrio Ht Prtners Lssee LLC (P-12231)*
Doubletree By Hilton San Jose .... D......408 453-4000
2050 Gateway Pl San Jose (95110) *(P-12228)*
Doubletree Hotel, Commerce *Also called W2005 Wyn Hotels LP (P-13073)*
Doubletree Hotel, San Diego *Also called Gringteam Inc (P-12313)*
Doubletree Hotel, Santa Ana *Also called Chamson Management Inc (P-12136)*
Doubletree Hotel, Anaheim *Also called Doubltree Suites By Hilton LLC (P-12230)*
Doubletree Hotel, San Jose *Also called Gringteam Inc (P-12314)*
Doubletree Hotel, Irvine *Also called Spectrum Hotel Group LLC (P-12951)*
Doubletree Hotel, Santa Ana *Also called Gringteam Inc (P-12316)*
Doubletree Hotel, Sacramento *Also called Gringteam Inc (P-12317)*

Doubletree Hotel, Santa Barbara *Also called Fess Prker-Red Lion Gen Partnr (P-12265)*
Doubletree Hotel, El Segundo *Also called European Hotl Invstrs of CA (P-12257)*
Doubletree Hotel, Torrance *Also called Ctc Group Inc (P-12192)*
Doubletree Hotel, Modesto *Also called Gringteam Inc (P-12318)*
Doubletree Hotel, Claremont *Also called Claremont Star LP (P-12151)*
Doubletree Hotel, Burlingame *Also called Gringteam Inc (P-12320)*
Doubletree Hotel, Santa Monica *Also called Santa Monica Hsr Ltd Partnr (P-12888)*
Doubletree Hotel, Dana Point *Also called Gringteam Inc (P-12321)*
Doubletree Hotel ....D....323 722-8800
888 Montebello Blvd Rosemead (91770) *(P-12229)*
Doubletree Hotel Modesto, Modesto *Also called Modesto Hospitality Lessee LLC (P-12624)*
Doubletree Hotel-Lax, El Segundo *Also called Tri-Star Ccw Management L P (P-13042)*
Doubletree Ht San Diego Dwntwn, San Diego *Also called Harbor View Hotel Ventures LLC (P-12336)*
Doubletree Suites By Hilton SA, Santa Monica *Also called Santa Monica Hotel Owner LLC (P-12887)*
Doubletree Suites Doheny, Dana Point *Also called Ergs Aim Hotel Realty LLC (P-12253)*
Doubltree By Hilton Ht Modesto, Modesto *Also called Modesto Hospitality LLC (P-12623)*
Doubltree By Hlton Ht Bkrsfeld, Bakersfield *Also called Gringteam Inc (P-12315)*
Doubltree By Hlton Scrmento Ht, Sacramento *Also called Wmk Sacramento LLC (P-13111)*
Doubltree Ht Anhim-Orange Cnty, Orange *Also called Anaheim Ca LLC (P-12006)*
Doubltree Suites By Hilton LLC ....C....714 750-3000
2085 S Harbor Blvd Anaheim (92802) *(P-12230)*
Doudell Trucking Company (PA) ....C....408 263-7300
1505 N 4th St San Jose (95112) *(P-4003)*
Doug Arnold Real Estate Inc (PA) ....E....530 758-3080
505 2nd St Davis (95616) *(P-11099)*
Doughpro, Perris *Also called Proprocess Corporation (P-7579)*
Douglas Elliman Real Estate ....E....310 595-3888
150 El Camino Dr Fl 1 Beverly Hills (90212) *(P-11100)*
Douglas Emmett Realty Fund 199 ....D....310 255-7700
808 Wilshire Blvd Ste 200 Santa Monica (90401) *(P-11101)*
Douglas Fir Holdings LLC ....C....714 842-5551
8382 Newman Ave Huntington Beach (92647) *(P-19866)*
Douglas L Myovich Trucking Inc ....D....559 233-8242
1895 W Jefferson Ave Fresno (93706) *(P-3879)*
Douglas Ranch LLC ....E....949 500-7009
33200 E Carmel Valley Rd Carmel Valley (93924) *(P-425)*
Douglas Ross Construction Inc ....D....408 429-7700
900 E Hamilton Ave # 140 Campbell (95008) *(P-1240)*
Douglas Steel Supply Inc (PA) ....D....323 587-7676
4804 Laurel Canyon Blvd Valley Village (91607) *(P-7061)*
Douglas Steel Supply Co., Valley Village *Also called Douglas Steel Supply Inc (P-7061)*
Douglas W Jackson MD ....D....562 424-6666
2760 Atlantic Ave Long Beach (90806) *(P-18961)*
Doumit Communication Inc ....D....916 362-3519
25 Cadillac Dr Ste 134 Sacramento (95825) *(P-1701)*
Dove Ceilings Inc (PA) ....E....949 597-1794
22991 Belquest Dr Lake Forest (92630) *(P-2780)*
Dowling Advisory Group ....D....626 319-1369
3579 E Foothill Blvd # 651 Pasadena (91107) *(P-26585)*
Downey Brand LLP (PA) ....C....916 444-1000
621 Capitol Mall Fl 18 Sacramento (95814) *(P-22488)*
Downey Care Center, Downey *Also called Ensign Group Inc (P-19882)*
Downey Civic Theatre, Downey *Also called City of Downey (P-17901)*
Downey Community Health Center ....C....562 862-6506
8425 Iowa St Downey (90241) *(P-19867)*
Downey Family Y M C A, Downey *Also called Young Mens Chrstn Assn of La (P-24754)*
Downey Orthopedic Med Group, Lawndale *Also called Southwestern Orthpd Med Corp (P-19438)*
Downey Regional Medical Center, Downey *Also called Pih Health Hospital - Whitti (P-21098)*
Downey YMCA, Downey *Also called Young Mens Chrstn Assn of La (P-23549)*
Downs Fuel Transport Inc ....E....951 256-8286
1296 Magnolia Ave Corona (92879) *(P-8724)*
Downtown Berkeley YMCA, Berkeley *Also called Young MNS Chrstn Assn of E Bay (P-24769)*
Downtown Business Fincl Ctr, Bakersfield *Also called Citizens Business Bank (P-9190)*
Downtown Community Dev YMCA, Long Beach *Also called Young Mens Christian Associat (P-24741)*
Downtown Los Angeles Branch, Los Angeles *Also called Israel Discount Bank New York (P-9212)*
Downtown Metro ....E....760 398-3310
1030 6th St Ste 16 Coachella (92236) *(P-5256)*
Downtown San Diego Partnr Inc (PA) ....D....619 234-0201
401 B St Ste 100 San Diego (92101) *(P-24333)*
Downtown San Diego Partnr Inc ....D....619 234-8900
1111 6th Ave Ste 101 San Diego (92101) *(P-24334)*
Downtown SD Ventures LLC ....D....619 231-9200
20162 Sw Birch St Ste 350 Newport Beach (92660) *(P-18683)*
DP Technology Corp (PA) ....D....805 388-6000
1150 Avenida Acaso Camarillo (93012) *(P-14771)*
Dpi Specialty Foods West Inc (HQ) ....C....909 975-1019
601 S Rockefeller Ave Ontario (91761) *(P-8170)*
Dpk Consulting ....D....415 495-7772
605 Market St Ste 800 San Francisco (94105) *(P-26586)*
Dppm Inc ....D....415 695-7707
4040 24th St San Francisco (94114) *(P-11102)*
Dpr Construction Inc (PA) ....A....650 474-1450
1450 Veterans Blvd Redwood City (94063) *(P-1465)*
Dpr Construction A Gen Partnr ....E....408 370-2322
1510 S Winchester Blvd San Jose (95128) *(P-1466)*
Dpr Construction A Gen Partnr ....B....916 568-3434
2480 Natomas Park Dr # 100 Sacramento (95833) *(P-1467)*
Dpr Construction A Gen Partnr ....B....858 646-0757
5010 Shoreham Pl Ste 100 San Diego (92122) *(P-1468)*
Dpr Construction A Gen Partnr ....E....949 955-3771
4665 Macarthur Ct Ste 100 Newport Beach (92660) *(P-1469)*
Dpr Construction A Gen Partnr (HQ) ....A....650 474-1450
1450 Veterans Blvd Redwood City (94063) *(P-1470)*
Dpr Holdings LLC ....E....323 761-9829
4804 Laurel Canyon Blvd Studio City (91607) *(P-11657)*
Dpss, Burbank *Also called County of Los Angeles (P-23109)*
Dr Fresh LLC ....D....714 690-1573
6 Centerpointe Dr Ste 640 La Palma (90623) *(P-7941)*
DR Horton Inc ....E....951 272-9000
2280 Wardlow Cir Ste 100 Corona (92880) *(P-1294)*
Draftfcb, San Francisco *Also called Fcb Worldwide Inc (P-13507)*
Dragados/Flatiron Joint Ventr ....D....559 847-5388
14555 S Peach Ave Selma (93662) *(P-1471)*
Dragon Engineering, Chowchilla *Also called Anderson Pump Company (P-6017)*
Drain Patrol ....D....858 560-1137
7764 Arjons Dr San Diego (92126) *(P-2118)*
Drake Larson Ranchs ....C....760 399-5494
89780 Ave 60 Thermal (92274) *(P-128)*
Drake Terrace, San Rafael *Also called Kisco Senior Living LLC (P-10747)*
Drawbridge Inc ....D....650 513-2323
479 N Pastoria Ave Sunnyvale (94085) *(P-26587)*
Dream Hollywood, Los Angeles *Also called 6417 Selma Hotel LLC (P-11987)*
Dream Home & Investments Rlty, Lomita *Also called Long Beach Investment Group (P-9578)*
Dream Home Care Inc ....D....562 595-9021
3939 Atlantic Ave Ste 213 Long Beach (90807) *(P-23906)*
Dream Home Estates Inc ....E....949 415-4646
2901 W Coast Hwy Ste 200 Newport Beach (92663) *(P-11103)*
Dream Lounge Inc ....A....213 688-7888
11271 Ventura Blvd 456 Studio City (91604) *(P-8026)*
Dream River, Vernon *Also called Shason Inc (P-8012)*
Dreamctchers Empwerment Netwrk (PA) ....A....209 478-5291
7590 Shoreline Dr Ste B Stockton (95219) *(P-23907)*
Dreamctchers Empwerment Netwrk ....C....925 935-6630
1911 Oak Park Blvd Pleasant Hill (94523) *(P-23908)*
Dreamctchers Empwerment Netwrk ....D....209 477-4817
6940 Pacific Ave Stockton (95207) *(P-23909)*
Dreamhost.com, Brea *Also called New Dream Network LLC (P-5446)*
Dreamhost.com, Los Angeles *Also called New Dream Network LLC (P-5447)*
Dreamscape Ldscp & Maint Inc ....E....619 583-4439
7192 Mission Gorge Rd San Diego (92120) *(P-723)*
Dreier's Nursing Care Center, Glendale *Also called Ksm Healthcare Inc (P-20060)*
Dresick Farms Inc (PA) ....D....559 945-2513
19536 Jayne Ave Huron (93234) *(P-50)*
Drew Chain Security Corp ....D....626 457-8626
55 S Raymond Ave Ste 303 Alhambra (91801) *(P-16260)*
Drew Child Dev Corp Inc (PA) ....C....323 249-2950
1770 E 118th St Los Angeles (90059) *(P-23197)*
Drew Health Foundation ....E....650 328-1619
1191 Runnymede St East Palo Alto (94303) *(P-24168)*
Dreyer Bbich Bccola Cllham LLP ....D....916 379-3500
20 Bicentennial Cir Sacramento (95826) *(P-22489)*
Dreyer's Grand Ice Cream, Walnut *Also called Nestle Dreyers Ice Cream Co (P-8320)*
Dreyers Grand Ice Cream Hold (HQ) ....C....510 652-8187
5929 College Ave Oakland (94618) *(P-8315)*
DRG Health Care Staffing, South San Francisco *Also called Discharge Resource Group (P-14502)*
Driftwood Convalescent Hosp, Davis *Also called Mariner Health Care Inc (P-20112)*
Driftwood Dairy Inc ....C....626 444-9591
10724 Lower Azusa Rd El Monte (91731) *(P-8316)*
Driftwood Health Care Ctr, Torrance *Also called Mariner Health Care Inc (P-20104)*
Driftwood Healthcare Center, Hayward *Also called Mariner Health Care Inc (P-20116)*
Drinker Biddle & Reath LLP ....C....310 229-1282
1800 Century Park E # 1400 Los Angeles (90067) *(P-22490)*
Drinker Biddle & Reath LLP ....C....415 591-7500
4 Embarcadero Ctr Lbby San Francisco (94111) *(P-22491)*
Drinks Holdings Inc ....D....310 441-8400
1125 E Broadway 173 Glendale (91205) *(P-8805)*
Driscolls Inc (PA) ....D....831 424-0506
345 Westridge Dr Watsonville (95076) *(P-8460)*
Driscolls Inc ....D....800 871-3333
150 Westridge Dr Watsonville (95076) *(P-8461)*
Driscolls Inc ....E....831 763-5100
1750 San Juan Rd Aromas (95004) *(P-8462)*
Driveai Inc ....C....408 693-0765
365 Ravendale Dr Mountain View (94043) *(P-15310)*
Driven Performance Brands Inc (PA) ....D....707 544-4761
100 Stony Point Rd # 125 Santa Rosa (95401) *(P-6434)*
Driver Spg ....E....855 300-4774
1501 S Harris Ct Anaheim (92806) *(P-16753)*
Drivesavers Inc ....D....415 382-2000
400 Bel Marin Keys Blvd Novato (94949) *(P-15856)*
Drivesavers Data Recovery, Novato *Also called Drivesavers Inc (P-15856)*
Drohan Trade Center, Rancho Cordova *Also called McKesson Corporation (P-7964)*
Droisys Inc ....C....408 329-1761
4657 Hedgewick Ave Fremont (94538) *(P-15984)*
Droisys Inc ....D....407 610-0916
46540 Fremont Blvd # 516 Fremont (94538) *(P-13420)*
Drop Lot Services, San Juan Capistrano *Also called Merit Logistics LLC (P-5125)*
Dropbox Inc (PA) ....C....415 857-6800
1800 Owens St Ste 200 San Francisco (94158) *(P-15311)*
Dropzone Waterpark ....C....951 210-1600
2165 Trumble Rd Perris (92571) *(P-18684)*
Drug & Alcohol Services of ....D....805 781-4275
2180 Johnson Ave Ste A San Luis Obispo (93401) *(P-22018)*
Drug Abuse Alternatives Center ....E....707 571-2233
2403 Prof Dr Ste 103 Santa Rosa (95403) *(P-22019)*

Employee Codes: A=Over 500 employees, B=251-500
C=101-250, D=51-100, E=50
2020 Directory of California
Wholesalers and Services Companies
© Mergent Inc. 1-800-342-5647
1251

Drum Security Service Inc ....D....818 708-7914
4509 Callada Pl Tarzana (91356) ***(P-16261)***
Drummond Medical Group Inc ....C....760 446-4571
900 N Heritage Dr Ste A Ridgecrest (93555) ***(P-18962)***
Druva Inc (HQ) ....D....650 241-3501
800 W California Ave # 100 Sunnyvale (94086) ***(P-15312)***
Dry Creek Lath & Plaster Inc ....D....209 367-8607
27940 Kennefick Rd Galt (95632) ***(P-2781)***
Dryco Construction Inc (PA) ....C....510 438-6500
42745 Boscell Rd Fremont (94538) ***(P-1702)***
Drywall Works Inc ....D....916 383-6667
5451 Whse Way Ste 105 Sacramento (95826) ***(P-2782)***
Ds Lakeshore LP, Costa Mesa *Also called Donahue Schriber Rlty Group LP* ***(P-10583)***
Ds Services of America Inc ....C....626 472-7201
4548 Azusa Canyon Rd Irwindale (91706) ***(P-8573)***
DSC Logistics Inc ....D....909 363-4354
1895 Marigold Ave Redlands (92374) ***(P-4004)***
DSC Logistics LLC ....B....540 377-2302
5690 Industrial Pkwy San Bernardino (92407) ***(P-4930)***
DSC Logistics LLC ....D....909 605-7233
12350 Philadelphia Ave Eastvale (91752) ***(P-3880)***
DSC Logistics Inc ....D....209 362-2232
1565 N Macarthur Dr Tracy (95376) ***(P-4402)***
DSC LOGISTICS, INC., Tracy *Also called DSC Logistics Inc* ***(P-4402)***
Dsca, Long Beach *Also called Denso Pdts & Svcs Americas Inc* ***(P-6432)***
Dsd Trucking Inc (PA) ....D....310 338-3395
2411 Santa Fe Ave Redondo Beach (90278) ***(P-4767)***
Dsg Associates Inc ....E....800 462-8765
15500 Erwin St Ste 4007 Van Nuys (91411) ***(P-25889)***
Dsh Graphics, Yorba Linda *Also called Dsh West Inc* ***(P-13782)***
Dsh West Inc ....D....714 692-8777
5455 Camino De Bryant Yorba Linda (92887) ***(P-13782)***
DSM Biomedical Inc ....C....510 841-8800
2810 7th St Berkeley (94710) ***(P-25739)***
Dss, Calabasas *Also called David Shield Security Inc* ***(P-16254)***
Dst Output California Inc ....D....916 939-4617
5220 Rbert J Mathews Pkwy El Dorado Hills (95762) ***(P-15914)***
DSV Solutions LLC ....C....909 349-6100
13230 San Bernardino Ave Fontana (92335) ***(P-4931)***
DSV Solutions LLC ....D....714 630-0110
3454 E Miraloma Ave Anaheim (92806) ***(P-4932)***
Dt Club Hotel Santa Ana, Santa Ana *Also called Jhc Investment Inc* ***(P-12488)***
Dt Floormasters Inc ....D....510 476-1000
31164 Huntwood Ave Hayward (94544) ***(P-3000)***
Dt Ontrio Ht Prtners Lssee LLC ....B....909 937-0900
222 N Vineyard Ave Ontario (91764) ***(P-12231)***
Dtex Systems Inc ....E....408 418-3786
3055 Olin Ave Ste 2000 San Jose (95128) ***(P-14772)***
Dti Inc ....D....310 635-9002
1628 S Sportsman Dr Compton (90221) ***(P-4005)***
Dti Services Inc (PA) ....D....213 670-1100
601 S Figueroa St # 4300 Los Angeles (90017) ***(P-15985)***
DTM Services Inc (PA) ....D....310 521-1200
19829 Hamilton Ave Torrance (90502) ***(P-4933)***
Dtrs Santa Monica LLC ....B....310 458-6700
1700 Ocean Ave Santa Monica (90401) ***(P-12232)***
Dtrs St Francis LLC ....A....415 397-7000
335 Powell St San Francisco (94102) ***(P-12233)***
Dts, Sacramento *Also called Technology Services Cal Dept* ***(P-16133)***
Dts Inc (HQ) ....C....818 436-1000
5220 Las Virgenes Rd Calabasas (91302) ***(P-17736)***
Dual Diagnosis Trtmnt Ctr Inc ....C....424 289-9031
12832 Short Ave Los Angeles (90066) ***(P-21525)***
Dual Diagnosis Trtmnt Ctr Inc ....C....949 324-4531
69640 Highway 111 Rancho Mirage (92270) ***(P-22234)***
Dual Diagnosis Trtmnt Ctr Inc (PA) ....C....949 276-5553
1211 Puerta Del Sol # 200 San Clemente (92673) ***(P-22020)***
Dual Diagnosis Trtmnt Ctr Inc ....C....424 207-2220
6167 Bristol Pkwy Culver City (90230) ***(P-22021)***
Duane Morris LLP ....C....415 957-3000
1 Market Plz Ste 2200 San Francisco (94105) ***(P-22492)***
Duarte Manor, Los Angeles *Also called Emp III Inc* ***(P-11909)***
Duarte Nursery Inc ....B....209 887-3409
23456 E Flood Rd Linden (95236) ***(P-238)***
Duarte Nursery Inc (PA) ....B....209 531-0351
1555 Baldwin Rd Hughson (95326) ***(P-239)***
Duarte Properties, Hughson *Also called Duarte Nursery Inc* ***(P-239)***
Dublin Hstrcal Prsrvation Assn ....D....925 785-2898
7172 Regional St Pmb 316 Dublin (94568) ***(P-24262)***
Dublin San Ramon Services Dst (PA) ....C....925 875-2276
7051 Dublin Blvd Dublin (94568) ***(P-6047)***
Dublin San Ramon Services Dst ....D....925 846-4565
7399 Johnson Dr Pleasanton (94588) ***(P-6048)***
Dublin Unified School District ....C....925 415-2407
3150 Palermo Way Dublin (94568) ***(P-24400)***
Duckor Spradling Metzger ....D....619 209-3000
101 W Broadway Ste 1700 San Diego (92101) ***(P-22493)***
Duckpunk Productions Inc ....D....310 836-3818
10728 Westminster Ave Los Angeles (90034) ***(P-17602)***
Ducks Unlimited Inc ....E....916 852-2000
3074 Gold Canal Dr Rancho Cordova (95670) ***(P-24537)***
Ducky's Car Wash, San Carlos *Also called Duckys of San Carlos Inc* ***(P-17371)***
Duckys of San Carlos Inc ....E....650 637-1301
1301 Old County Rd San Carlos (94070) ***(P-17371)***
Dudek (PA) ....D....760 942-5147
605 3rd St Encinitas (92024) ***(P-25040)***
Duff & Phelps LLC ....D....650 798-5500
1950 University Ave # 400 East Palo Alto (94303) ***(P-26588)***
Duff & Phelps LLC ....D....213 270-2300
350 S Grand Ave Ste 3100 Los Angeles (90071) ***(P-26589)***
Duff & Phelps LLC ....D....415 693-5300
345 California St # 2100 San Francisco (94104) ***(P-16754)***
Duggan & Associates Inc ....D....323 965-1502
1442 W 135th St Gardena (90249) ***(P-2344)***
Dui Program, Santa Monica *Also called Clare Foundation Inc* ***(P-23018)***
Duke Energy Corporation ....C....949 727-7434
8001 Irvine Center Dr Irvine (92618) ***(P-5830)***
Duke Financial Co Inc ....C....858 694-1215
100 N Rancho Santa Fe Rd # 117 San Marcos (92069) ***(P-13339)***
Duke Pacific Inc ....D....909 591-0191
13950 Monte Vista Ave Chino (91710) ***(P-3048)***
Dulcinea Farms, Los Angeles *Also called Pacific Trellis Fruit LLC* ***(P-8507)***
Dun & Bradstreet Inc ....D....925 216-2493
1 Embarcadero Ctr # 2060 San Francisco (94111) ***(P-13710)***
Dun & Bradstreet Emerging (HQ) ....C....310 456-8271
22761 Pacific Coast Hwy # 226 Malibu (90265) ***(P-16755)***
Dunbar Armored Inc ....D....510 569-7400
629 Whitney St San Leandro (94577) ***(P-16262)***
Dunhill Staffing, San Francisco *Also called Dunhill Worldwide* ***(P-14262)***
Dunhill Worldwide ....A....415 814-6006
101 California St San Francisco (94111) ***(P-14262)***
Dunlap Property Group Inc ....D....714 879-0111
801 E Chapman Ave Ste 233 Fullerton (92831) ***(P-11104)***
Dunn & Berger Inc ....B....818 986-1234
5955 De Soto Ave Ste 160 Woodland Hills (91367) ***(P-21732)***
Duplo USA Corporation (PA) ....D....949 752-8222
3050 Daimler St Santa Ana (92705) ***(P-6748)***
Dura Freight Lines, Walnut *Also called Patina Freight Inc* ***(P-4468)***
Dura Metrics Inc (PA) ....D....707 546-5138
816 Piner Rd Santa Rosa (95403) ***(P-21608)***
Duran Human Capital Partners ....E....408 540-0070
300 Orchard Cy Dr Ste 142 Campbell (95008) ***(P-14263)***
Durham School Services ....D....408 448-0740
3001 Ross Ave Ste 11 San Jose (95124) ***(P-3791)***
Durham School Services L P ....C....310 767-5820
16627 Avalon Blvd Ste B Carson (90746) ***(P-3792)***
Durham School Services L P ....C....408 377-6655
1506 White Oaks Rd Campbell (95008) ***(P-3793)***
Durham School Services L P ....D....805 495-8338
365 E Avnda De Los Alvare Thousand Oaks (91360) ***(P-3794)***
Durham School Services L P ....C....714 542-8989
2818 W 5th St Santa Ana (92703) ***(P-3829)***
Durham School Services L P ....C....510 887-6005
27577 Industrial Blvd A Hayward (94545) ***(P-3795)***
Durham School Services L P ....D....530 273-7282
10701 E Bennett Rd Grass Valley (95945) ***(P-3796)***
Durham School Services L P ....C....925 686-3391
2121 Piedmont Way Pittsburg (94565) ***(P-3797)***
Durham School Services L P ....C....626 573-3769
2713 River Ave Rosemead (91770) ***(P-3798)***
Durini Luis Carlos Estrada ....E....502 474-3112
100 W Broadway Ste 100 # 100 Glendale (91210) ***(P-16756)***
Durkee Drayage Company ....D....510 970-7550
539 Stone Rd Benicia (94510) ***(P-4206)***
Dust Networks Inc ....D....510 400-2900
32990 Alvrdo Niles Rd # 910 Union City (94587) ***(P-5257)***
Dustin Hoke ....D....949 347-8670
999 Corporate Dr Ladera Ranch (92694) ***(P-1703)***
Dutch LLC (HQ) ....C....323 277-3900
5301 S Santa Fe Ave Vernon (90058) ***(P-8069)***
Duthie Electric Service Corp ....E....562 790-1772
2335 E Cherry Indus Cir Long Beach (90805) ***(P-17455)***
Duthie Power Services, Long Beach *Also called Duthie Electric Service Corp* ***(P-17455)***
Dutra Dredging, San Rafael *Also called Dutra Group* ***(P-1959)***
Dutra Dredging Company (HQ) ....D....415 721-2131
2350 Kerner Blvd Ste 200 San Rafael (94901) ***(P-1958)***
Dutra Group (PA) ....D....415 258-6876
2350 Kerner Blvd Ste 200 San Rafael (94901) ***(P-1959)***
Dutra Manson JV ....D....415 258-6876
1000 Point San Pedro Rd San Rafael (94901) ***(P-1960)***
Dutra Materials, San Rafael *Also called San Rafael Rock Quarry Inc* ***(P-1053)***
Dutra Realty, Pleasanton *Also called Mason-Mcduffie Real Estate Inc* ***(P-11280)***
Dv Custom Farming LLC ....D....661 858-2888
2101 Mettler Frontage E Bakersfield (93307) ***(P-315)***
Dva Renal Healthcare Inc ....D....949 588-9211
23141 Plaza Pointe Dr Laguna Hills (92653) ***(P-21921)***
Dw Berry Farms LLC ....B....805 795-8403
3960 N Rose Ave Oxnard (93036) ***(P-316)***
Dw Logistix, Winnetka *Also called David W Golen* ***(P-3872)***
DW Morgan LLC ....D....925 460-2700
4185 Blackhawk Danville (94506) ***(P-4934)***
Dw Studios Productions LLC (PA) ....E....818 733-9631
100 Universal City Plz Universal City (91608) ***(P-17603)***
DWA, Palm Springs *Also called Desert Water Agency Fing Corp* ***(P-6046)***
Dwa Holdings LLC (HQ) ....D....818 695-5000
1000 Flower St Glendale (91201) ***(P-17604)***
Dwa Nova LLC ....D....818 695-5000
1000 Flower St Glendale (91201) ***(P-15313)***
Dwayne Nash Industries Inc ....C....916 253-1900
8825 Washington Blvd # 100 Roseville (95678) ***(P-3049)***
Dwaynes Engineering & Cnstr ....D....661 762-7261
3655 Addie Ave Mc Kittrick (93251) ***(P-1018)***
Dwiw Inc ....E....949 574-7147
700 W 16th St Costa Mesa (92627) ***(P-804)***
Dwn, Hickman *Also called Dave Wilson Nursery Inc* ***(P-236)***
Dx Holdings LLC ....A....323 462-6171
1377 N Serrano Ave Los Angeles (90027) ***(P-17737)***

Dy-Dee Service Pasadena Inc.....D.....626 792-6183
40 E California Blvd Pasadena (91105) ***(P-13320)***
Dya Assoc.....D.....323 364-4270
8335 W Sunset Blvd # 320 Los Angeles (90069) ***(P-11559)***
Dydee Service of Pasedena.....D.....626 240-0115
40 E California Blvd Pasadena (91105) ***(P-13321)***
Dykema Gossett PLLC.....D.....213 457-1800
333 S Grand Ave Ste 2100 Los Angeles (90071) ***(P-22494)***
Dynalectric Company.....C.....805 517-1253
668 Flinn Ave Moorpark (93021) ***(P-2476)***
Dynalectric Company.....B.....858 712-4700
9505 Chesapeake Dr San Diego (92123) ***(P-2477)***
Dynalectric Company.....C.....714 236-2242
4462 Corporate Center Dr Los Alamitos (90720) ***(P-2478)***
Dynalectric Company.....C.....415 487-4700
825 Howe Rd Martinez (94553) ***(P-2479)***
Dynamex Inc.....D.....209 464-7008
4790 Frontier Way Ste A Stockton (95215) ***(P-4249)***
Dynamex Operations West Inc.....E.....714 994-1615
16900 Valley View Ave La Mirada (90638) ***(P-4250)***
Dynamic Auto Images Inc.....B.....714 981-4367
1407 N Batavia St Ste 102 Orange (92867) ***(P-17372)***
Dynamic Chiropractic, Westminster *Also called Maxwell Petersen Associates* ***(P-26697)***
Dynamic Detail, Orange *Also called Dynamic Auto Images Inc* ***(P-17372)***
Dynamic Home Care Service Inc (PA).....C.....818 981-4446
14260 Ventura Blvd # 301 Sherman Oaks (91423) ***(P-21733)***
Dynamic Maintenance Svcs Inc.....D.....925 228-7434
837 Arnold Dr Ste 220 Martinez (94553) ***(P-13915)***
Dynamic Plumbing Commercial.....D.....951 343-1200
5920 Winterhaven Ave Riverside (92504) ***(P-2119)***
Dynamic Staffing Inc (PA).....C.....916 773-3900
920 Reserve Dr Ste 150 Roseville (95678) ***(P-14264)***
Dynamic Worldwide West Inc (PA).....C.....562 407-1000
14141 Alondra Blvd Santa Fe Springs (90670) ***(P-4935)***
Dynamo Aviation Inc.....D.....818 785-9561
16760 Schoenborn St North Hills (91343) ***(P-4768)***
Dynata LLC.....C.....866 872-4006
16501 Ventura Blvd # 300 Encino (91436) ***(P-25890)***
Dyncorp.....C.....619 522-2222
Nas Nrth Is Bldg 1479 San Diego (92135) ***(P-15585)***
Dyncorp International LLC.....D.....817 224-8200
896 Langford Lake Rd Fort Irwin (92310) ***(P-4769)***
Dynegy Marketing & Trade LLC.....D.....831 633-6700
Hwy 1 & Dolan Rd Moss Landing (95039) ***(P-5831)***
Dynegy Moss Landing LLC.....D.....831 633-6618
7301 Highway 1 Moss Landing (95039) ***(P-5832)***
Dyntek Inc (PA).....C.....949 271-6700
5241 California Ave # 150 Irvine (92617) ***(P-15986)***
Dz Trading Ltd.....C.....951 479-5700
12492 Feather Dr Eastvale (91752) ***(P-7807)***
Dzyne Technologies Inc.....E.....703 454-0704
11 Vanderbilt Irvine (92618) ***(P-25041)***
E & B Ntral Resources Mgt Corp (PA).....D.....661 679-1714
1600 Norris Rd Bakersfield (93308) ***(P-985)***
E & C Fashion Inc.....B.....323 262-0099
1420 Esperanza St Los Angeles (90023) ***(P-16757)***
E & E Co Ltd.....A.....530 669-5991
2222 E Beamer St Woodland (95776) ***(P-1118)***
E & E Co Ltd (PA).....C.....510 490-9788
45875 Northport Loop E Fremont (94538) ***(P-6553)***
E & J Gallo Winery.....D.....707 431-5400
11447 Old Redwood Hwy Healdsburg (95448) ***(P-129)***
E & J Gallo Winery.....D.....209 394-6271
5953 Weir Ave Livingston (95334) ***(P-658)***
E & M AG Svc Inc A Cal Corp.....E.....559 627-2724
1118 N Chinowth St Visalia (93291) ***(P-659)***
E & M Concrete Construction.....D.....805 658-2888
2842 Sherwin Ave Ste A Ventura (93003) ***(P-3145)***
E & M Electric and McHy Inc (PA).....E.....707 433-5578
126 Mill St Healdsburg (95448) ***(P-7541)***
E & S International Entps Inc (PA).....C.....818 887-0700
7801 Hayvenhurst Ave Van Nuys (91406) ***(P-7201)***
E & S Rsidential Care Svcs LLC.....D.....559 275-3555
6083 N Marks Ave Fresno (93711) ***(P-23910)***
E & T Foods Inc.....B.....760 843-7730
14827 Seventh St Victorville (92395) ***(P-426)***
E and B Natural Resources.....D.....661 679-1700
1600 Norris Rd Bakersfield (93308) ***(P-1003)***
E B C F, Oakland *Also called East Bay Community Foundation* ***(P-24169)***
E B Stone & Son Inc.....D.....707 426-2500
6111 Lambie Rd Suisun City (94585) ***(P-8839)***
E C R M C, El Centro *Also called El Centro Regional Medical Ctr* ***(P-20864)***
E C Wise Inc (PA).....D.....415 355-9473
1299 4th St Ste 505 San Rafael (94901) ***(P-15752)***
E Center.....C.....530 634-1200
1506 Starr Dr Yuba City (95993) ***(P-23720)***
E D C, Torrance *Also called Electronic Data Care Inc* ***(P-15587)***
E D D 2100.....D.....209 941-6501
3127 Transworld Dr # 150 Stockton (95206) ***(P-9905)***
E E G and E P, Chico *Also called Enloe Medical Center* ***(P-20874)***
E Film Digital Labratories, Los Angeles *Also called Efilm LLC* ***(P-17606)***
E G Ayers Distributing Inc.....E.....707 445-2077
5819 S Broadway St Eureka (95503) ***(P-8171)***
E H Summit Inc (PA).....C.....310 476-6571
11461 W Sunset Blvd Los Angeles (90049) ***(P-12234)***
E H Summit Inc.....D.....310 273-0300
360 N Rodeo Dr Beverly Hills (90210) ***(P-12235)***
E J Harrison & Sons Inc.....C.....805 647-1414
1589 Lirio Ave Ventura (93004) ***(P-6194)***
E J Williams Property MGT.....D.....209 473-4022
5637 N Pershing Ave Ste D Stockton (95207) ***(P-10715)***
E Jordan Brookes Co Inc (PA).....D.....562 968-2100
10634 Shoemaker Ave Santa Fe Springs (90670) ***(P-7062)***
E Jordan Brookes Co., Santa Fe Springs *Also called E Jordan Brookes Co Inc* ***(P-7062)***
E K T Farms, Watsonville *Also called Edward J Kelly* ***(P-318)***
E L Payne Heating Company.....E.....310 275-5331
226 S Lucerne Blvd Los Angeles (90004) ***(P-2120)***
E L S, Los Angeles *Also called J C Entertainment Ltg Svcs Inc* ***(P-17918)***
E M S Trading Inc.....E.....909 581-7800
5161 Richton St Montclair (91763) ***(P-8130)***
E M Tharp Inc (PA).....D.....559 782-5800
15243 Road 192 Porterville (93257) ***(P-6393)***
E Morris Cox Elementary School, Oakland *Also called Oakland Unified School Dst* ***(P-24602)***
E P, Union City *Also called Emerald Packaging Inc* ***(P-8968)***
E P A, Sacramento *Also called Environmental Protection Agcy* ***(P-6348)***
E P S, Vallejo *Also called Earthquake Protection Systems* ***(P-25044)***
E P U, Fresno *Also called Exceptnal Prents Unlimited Inc* ***(P-23213)***
E R G Home Health Provider.....D.....562 403-1070
11700 South St Ste 200 Artesia (90701) ***(P-21734)***
E R I T Inc (PA).....D.....760 433-6024
251 Airport Rd Oceanside (92058) ***(P-23911)***
E R I T Inc.....C.....760 721-1706
251 Airport Rd Oceanside (92058) ***(P-23912)***
E S 3, San Diego *Also called Enginring Sftwr Sys Sltons Inc* ***(P-25057)***
E S Q, Cupertino *Also called Esq Business Services Inc* ***(P-15323)***
E Street Cold Logistics LLC (PA).....E.....310 233-7300
901 E E St Wilmington (90744) ***(P-4343)***
E T Horn Company (PA).....D.....714 523-8050
16050 Canary Ave La Mirada (90638) ***(P-8697)***
E Tradeshowgirlscom.....D.....949 661-4177
1 Ocean Rdg Laguna Niguel (92677) ***(P-16758)***
E W C H Inc.....D.....510 783-4811
1805 West St Hayward (94545) ***(P-19868)***
E W Merritt Farms (PA).....D.....559 784-8916
11188 Road 192 Porterville (93257) ***(P-317)***
E Z Data Inc (HQ).....D.....626 585-3505
251 S Lake Ave Ste 200 Pasadena (91101) ***(P-14773)***
E Z Staffing Inc (PA).....B.....818 845-2500
801 N Brand Blvd Ste 1120 Glendale (91203) ***(P-14265)***
E&M, Healdsburg *Also called E & M Electric and McHy Inc* ***(P-7541)***
E&S Financial Group Inc.....D.....805 644-1621
3140 Telegraph Rd Ste A Ventura (93003) ***(P-9621)***
E-Loan Inc (HQ).....A.....925 847-6200
6230 Stoneridge Mall Rd Pleasanton (94588) ***(P-9622)***
E-N Realty II.....E.....909 597-1736
1081 Grand Ave Diamond Bar (91765) ***(P-11105)***
E-Sceptre Inc.....D.....888 350-8989
16800 Gale Ave City of Industry (91745) ***(P-25740)***
E-Solutions, San Jose *Also called Vidhwan Inc* ***(P-26868)***
E-Times Corporation Ltd.....B.....213 452-6720
601 S Figueroa St # 5000 Los Angeles (90017) ***(P-15857)***
E. S. Babcock & Sons, Riverside *Also called Babcock Laboratories Inc* ***(P-26056)***
E.V. Roberts, Carson *Also called Cirrus Enterprises LLC* ***(P-8683)***
E2 Consulting Engineers Inc.....B.....510 652-1164
1900 Powell St Ste 250 Emeryville (94608) ***(P-25042)***
E2 Corp.....D.....818 904-5660
8121 Van Nuys Blvd # 308 Panorama City (91402) ***(P-15586)***
E2 Solutions, Panorama City *Also called E2 Corp* ***(P-15586)***
E3 Healthcare Management LLC.....D.....650 324-0600
375 Forest Ave Palo Alto (94301) ***(P-26217)***
EA, Redwood City *Also called Electronic Arts Inc* ***(P-15317)***
Ea Consulting Inc.....E.....916 357-6767
1024 Iron Point Rd Folsom (95630) ***(P-15987)***
Ea Mobile Inc.....B.....310 754-7125
5510 Lincoln Blvd Los Angeles (90094) ***(P-5258)***
Eag Holdings LLC.....A.....408 530-3500
2710 Walsh Ave Santa Clara (95051) ***(P-27052)***
Eagle Glen Country Club LLC.....D.....951 272-4653
1800 Eagle Glen Pkwy Corona (92883) ***(P-18244)***
Eagle Glen Golf Club, Corona *Also called Eagle Glen Country Club LLC* ***(P-18244)***
Eagle High Reach Equipment LLC.....D.....619 265-2637
14241 Alondra Blvd La Mirada (90638) ***(P-14154)***
Eagle Intermodel Services, San Bernardino *Also called Eagle Systems Inc* ***(P-4006)***
Eagle Lath & Plaster Inc.....D.....916 925-1435
4350 Warehouse Ct North Highlands (95660) ***(P-1472)***
Eagle Rafting.....C.....760 376-3648
13226 Sierra Way Kernville (93238) ***(P-18685)***
Eagle Resources Inc.....D.....805 922-0000
516 W Boone St Santa Maria (93458) ***(P-14266)***
Eagle Ridge Golf Club, Gilroy *Also called Eagle Ridge Golf Cntry CLB LLC* ***(P-18448)***
Eagle Ridge Golf Cntry CLB LLC.....C.....408 846-4531
2951 Club Dr Gilroy (95020) ***(P-18448)***
Eagle Roofing Products, Rialto *Also called Burlingame Industries Inc* ***(P-13156)***
Eagle Roofing Products, Stockton *Also called Burlingame Industries Inc* ***(P-6711)***
Eagle Security Service Inc.....C.....310 532-1626
12903 S Normandie Ave Gardena (90249) ***(P-16263)***
Eagle Systems Inc.....C.....909 386-4343
1535 W 4th St San Bernardino (92411) ***(P-4006)***
Eagle Systems Intl Inc.....B.....510 259-1700
28436 Satellite St Hayward (94545) ***(P-2121)***
Eagle Vnes Vnyrds Golf CLB LLC.....D.....707 257-4470
580 S Kelly Rd American Canyon (94503) ***(P-18449)***
Eagles Hall, Roseville *Also called Fraternal Order Eagles 1582* ***(P-10591)***
Eah Elena Gardens LP.....B.....415 295-8840
1902 Lakewood Dr San Jose (95132) ***(P-10716)***
Eah Housing, San Rafael *Also called Eah Inc* ***(P-10852)***

ALPHABETIC

Employee Codes: A=Over 500 employees, B=251-500
C=101-250, D=51-100, E=50
2020 Directory of California
Wholesalers and Services Companies
© Mergent Inc. 1-800-342-5647
1253

EAH HOUSING, San Jose *Also called Eah Elena Gardens LP* ***(P-10716)***
Eah Inc (PA).....D.....415 258-1800
22 Pelican Way San Rafael (94901) ***(P-10852)***
EAM Enterprises Inc (PA).....B.....818 248-9100
4005 Foothill Blvd La Crescenta (91214) ***(P-11106)***
Eappraiseit LLC (PA).....D.....800 281-6200
12395 First American Way Poway (92064) ***(P-11107)***
Earl's Organic Produce, San Francisco *Also called Earls Organic* ***(P-8463)***
Earle M Jorgensen Company.....D.....510 487-2700
31100 Wiegman Rd Hayward (94544) ***(P-7063)***
Earle M Jorgensen Company.....D.....323 567-1122
350 S Grand Ave Ste 5100 Los Angeles (90071) ***(P-7064)***
Earls Organic.....D.....415 824-7419
2101 Jerrold Ave Ste 100 San Francisco (94124) ***(P-8463)***
Earlwood LLC.....D.....310 371-1228
20820 Earl St Torrance (90503) ***(P-19869)***
Earlwood Convalescent Hospital, Torrance *Also called Earlwood LLC* ***(P-19869)***
Early Childhood Education, La Quinta *Also called Deser Sands Unifi Schoo Distr* ***(P-23717)***
Early Childhood Services, Ridgecrest *Also called Desert Area Resources Training* ***(P-24167)***
Early Transportation Services.....D.....510 324-1119
30796 San Clemente St Hayward (94544) ***(P-4007)***
Earnin Hq, Palo Alto *Also called Activehours Inc* ***(P-16603)***
Earth Island Institute Inc.....D.....510 859-9100
2150 Allston Way Ste 460 Berkeley (94704) ***(P-24827)***
Earth Systems Southwest (HQ).....D.....760 345-1588
79811 Country Club Dr B Bermuda Dunes (92203) ***(P-25043)***
Earth Technology Corp USA.....A.....213 593-8000
1999 Avenue Of Los Angeles (90067) ***(P-6195)***
Earthbound Farm LLC (HQ).....A.....831 623-7880
1721 San Juan Hwy San Juan Bautista (95045) ***(P-483)***
Earthbound Productions LLC.....D.....504 734-3337
849 N Occidental Blvd Los Angeles (90026) ***(P-17605)***
Earthco, Santa Ana *Also called Morrison Landscape* ***(P-7114)***
Earthquake Protection Systems.....D.....707 644-5993
451 Azuar Ave Bldg 759 Vallejo (94592) ***(P-25044)***
Earthtech, Oakland *Also called Kaiser Group Holdings Inc* ***(P-25167)***
Easia Golf Investment LLC.....D.....760 775-2000
84000 Terra Lago Pkwy Indio (92203) ***(P-11908)***
East Bay Airport Shuttle, San Jose *Also called South Bay Airport Shuttle* ***(P-3608)***
East Bay Airport Shuttle, Pleasant Hill *Also called East Bay Connection Inc* ***(P-3532)***
East Bay Asian Local Dev Corp.....C.....510 267-1917
1825 San Pablo Ave # 200 Oakland (94612) ***(P-10717)***
East Bay Asian Youth Center.....E.....510 533-1092
2025 E 12th St Oakland (94606) ***(P-23198)***
East Bay Clarklift Inc.....D.....559 268-6621
4646 E Jensen Ave Fresno (93725) ***(P-7542)***
East Bay Community Foundation.....D.....510 836-3223
200 Frank H Ogawa Plz Oakland (94612) ***(P-24169)***
East Bay Connection Inc.....E.....925 609-1920
140 Mayhew Way Ste 1002 Pleasant Hill (94523) ***(P-3532)***
East Bay Foundation Grad Med.....D.....510 437-4197
1411 E 31st St Oakland (94602) ***(P-22235)***
East Bay Innovations.....D.....510 618-1580
2450 Washington Ave # 240 San Leandro (94577) ***(P-16759)***
East Bay Municipl Utilty Distr.....C.....866 403-2683
3999 Lakeside Dr Richmond (94806) ***(P-6049)***
East Bay Municipl Utilty Distr.....D.....866 403-2683
2020 Wake Ave Oakland (94607) ***(P-6196)***
East Bay Municipl Utilty Distr (PA).....A.....866 403-2683
375 11th St Oakland (94607) ***(P-6050)***
East Bay Municipl Utilty Distr.....D.....510 287-0760
375 11th St Oakland (94607) ***(P-6051)***
East Bay Municipl Utilty Distr.....D.....866 403-2683
2149 Union St Oakland (94607) ***(P-6052)***
East Bay Nephrology.....E.....510 235-1057
2089 Vale Rd Ste 32 San Pablo (94806) ***(P-18963)***
East Bay Regional Park Dst.....D.....510 881-1833
17930 Lake Chabot Rd Castro Valley (94546) ***(P-18686)***
East Bay Regional Park Public, Castro Valley *Also called East Bay Regional Park Dst* ***(P-18686)***
East Bay Transitional Homes, Oakland *Also called Bay Area Community Svcs Inc* ***(P-22935)***
East Crson Il Hsing Prtners LP.....D.....310 522-9606
401 W Carson St Carson (90745) ***(P-11108)***
East Hall Investors Inc.....D.....530 328-1900
11601 Blocker Dr Ste 200 Auburn (95603) ***(P-11109)***
East L A Remarkable Citizens (PA).....D.....323 223-3079
3839 Selig Pl Los Angeles (90031) ***(P-23199)***
East Lion Corporation.....E.....626 912-1818
318 Brea Canyon Rd Walnut (91789) ***(P-8131)***
East Los Angeles Community Un (PA).....E.....323 721-1655
5400 E Olympic Blvd Fl 3 Commerce (90022) ***(P-9480)***
East Los Angeles Doctors Hosp, Los Angeles *Also called Eladh LP* ***(P-20865)***
East Los Angeles Mental Hlth.....D.....323 725-1337
1436 Goodrich Blvd Commerce (90022) ***(P-22022)***
East Palo Alto Hotel Dev Inc.....C.....650 566-1200
2050 University Ave East Palo Alto (94303) ***(P-12236)***
East Palo Alto Y M C A.....E.....650 328-9622
550 Bell St East Palo Alto (94303) ***(P-24538)***
East San Gbriel Vly Consortium.....D.....626 960-3964
5200 Irwindale Ave # 210 Irwindale (91706) ***(P-3665)***
East Valley Cmnty Hlth Ctr Inc (PA).....D.....626 919-3402
420 S Glendora Ave West Covina (91790) ***(P-22023)***
East Valley Family YMCA Dcc, North Hollywood *Also called Young Mens Chrstn Assn of La* ***(P-23805)***
East Valley Glendora Hosp LLC.....B.....626 852-5000
150 W Route 66 Glendora (91740) ***(P-20861)***
East Valley Hospital Med Ctr, Glendora *Also called East Valley Glendora Hosp LLC* ***(P-20861)***
East Valley Tourist Dev Auth.....A.....760 342-5000
84245 Indio Springs Dr Indio (92203) ***(P-18687)***
East Valley Water District.....D.....909 889-9501
31111 Greenspot Rd Highland (92346) ***(P-6053)***
East West, Cerritos *Also called Global Med Services Inc* ***(P-21748)***
East West Bank (HQ).....B.....626 768-6000
135 N Los Robles Ave # 1 Pasadena (91101) ***(P-9191)***
East West Bank.....C.....415 391-8912
555 Montgomery St Bsmt San Francisco (94111) ***(P-9192)***
East West Bank.....D.....626 280-1688
228 W Garvey Ave Monterey Park (91754) ***(P-9193)***
Easter Seal Soc Superior Cal (PA).....D.....916 485-6711
3205 Hurley Way Sacramento (95864) ***(P-22236)***
Easter Seal Society, Lancaster *Also called Easter Seals Southern Cal Inc* ***(P-24171)***
Easter Seals Inc.....D.....831 338-3383
16403 Highway 9 Boulder Creek (95006) ***(P-13147)***
Easter Seals Central Cal.....B.....831 684-2166
9010 Soquel Dr Aptos (95003) ***(P-23200)***
Easter Seals Main Office, Sacramento *Also called Easter Seal Soc Superior Cal* ***(P-22236)***
Easter Seals Southern Cal Inc.....D.....818 551-0128
710 W Broadway Glendale (91204) ***(P-24170)***
Easter Seals Southern Cal Inc.....E.....661 723-3414
340 E Avenue I Ste 101 Lancaster (93535) ***(P-24171)***
Eastern California Museum (PA).....B.....760 878-0292
155 N Grant St Independence (93526) ***(P-24263)***
Eastern Goldfields Inc.....C.....619 497-2555
1660 Hotel Cir N Ste 207 San Diego (92108) ***(P-26590)***
Eastern Los Angeles RE (PA).....B.....626 299-4700
1000 S Fremont Ave # 40 Alhambra (91803) ***(P-23201)***
Eastern Municipal Water Dst (PA).....B.....951 928-3777
2270 Trumble Rd Perris (92572) ***(P-6054)***
Eastern Municipal Water Dst.....C.....951 657-7469
19750 Evans Rd Perris (92571) ***(P-6055)***
Eastern Plumas Health Care.....D.....530 993-1225
700 3rd St Loyalton (96118) ***(P-19870)***
Eastern Sierra Transit Auth.....E.....760 872-1901
703 Airport Rd Bishop (93514) ***(P-3758)***
Eastern Star Homes California (PA).....D.....714 986-2380
16850 Bastanchury Rd Yorba Linda (92886) ***(P-23202)***
EASTERN STAR PROFESSIONAL BUIL, Yorba Linda *Also called Eastern Star Homes California* ***(P-23202)***
Eastland Executive Office, West Covina *Also called Eastland Tower Partnership* ***(P-10871)***
Eastland Tower Partnership.....E.....626 858-2000
1932 E Garvey Ave S West Covina (91791) ***(P-10871)***
Eastman Music Company (PA).....D.....909 868-1777
2158 Pomona Blvd Pomona (91768) ***(P-7808)***
Eastmans Guitars, Pomona *Also called Eastman Music Company* ***(P-7808)***
Easton Hockey, Thousand Oaks *Also called Bauer Hockey Inc* ***(P-7704)***
Eastrdge Prsonnel of Las Vegas.....D.....415 248-2567
530 Davis St San Francisco (94111) ***(P-14267)***
Eastrdge Prsonnel of Las Vegas (PA).....E.....619 260-2000
2355 Northside Dr Ste 120 San Diego (92108) ***(P-14268)***
Eastridge ADM Staffing, San Diego *Also called Eplica Inc* ***(P-14503)***
Eastridge Infotech, San Diego *Also called Eastrdge Prsonnel of Las Vegas* ***(P-14268)***
Eastridge Workforce Solutions, San Diego *Also called Teg Staffing Inc* ***(P-14436)***
Eastside Group Corporation.....C.....213 368-9777
1830 W Olympic Blvd # 202 Los Angeles (90006) ***(P-16264)***
Eastside Management Co Inc.....C.....209 578-9852
1131 12th St Ste C Modesto (95354) ***(P-660)***
Eastwestproto Inc.....C.....888 535-5728
1120 S Maple Ave Ste 200 Montebello (90640) ***(P-3666)***
Easun Inc.....C.....916 929-8855
2001 Point West Way Sacramento (95815) ***(P-12237)***
Easy Care Mso LLC.....C.....562 676-9600
3900 Kilroy Airport Way # 110 Long Beach (90806) ***(P-22237)***
Easy Fuel, Aliso Viejo *Also called Efuel LLC* ***(P-8726)***
Easy Ride Transportation.....D.....424 999-8830
1820 W Carson St Ste 202 Torrance (90501) ***(P-5113)***
Easypost, San Francisco *Also called Simpler Postage Inc* ***(P-5051)***
Easyturf Inc (HQ).....D.....760 745-7026
2750 La Mirada Dr Vista (92081) ***(P-3399)***
Eaton Aerospace LLC.....B.....818 409-0200
4690 Colorado Blvd Los Angeles (90039) ***(P-7145)***
Eaton Canyon Golf Course, Altadena *Also called D C Golf A CA Partnership* ***(P-18240)***
Eb, Santa Rosa *Also called Exchange Bank* ***(P-9288)***
Ebc Inc (PA).....D.....310 753-6407
219 Manhattan Beach Blvd Manhattan Beach (90266) ***(P-1119)***
Ebi Aggregates, Livermore *Also called Evans Brothers Inc* ***(P-3341)***
EBM Janitorial Services Inc.....D.....805 523-3700
5260 Bonsai Ave Ste E Moorpark (93021) ***(P-13916)***
Ebmud, Richmond *Also called East Bay Municipl Utilty Distr* ***(P-6049)***
Ebmud, Oakland *Also called East Bay Municipl Utilty Distr* ***(P-6196)***
Ebmud, Oakland *Also called East Bay Municipl Utilty Distr* ***(P-6050)***
Ebmud, Oakland *Also called East Bay Municipl Utilty Distr* ***(P-6051)***
Ebmud - Construction and Maint, Oakland *Also called East Bay Municipl Utilty Distr* ***(P-6052)***
Ebs Concrete Inc.....E.....951 279-6869
1320 E 6th St Ste 100 Corona (92879) ***(P-3146)***
Ebs General Engineering Inc.....D.....951 279-6869
1320 E 6th St Ste 100 Corona (92879) ***(P-1704)***
EBSC LP.....D.....510 547-2244
3875 Telegraph Ave Oakland (94609) ***(P-18964)***
EC Davis Health Services, Sacramento *Also called Internal Mdcine Rsdncy Affairs* ***(P-24404)***
EC Group Inc (PA).....D.....310 815-2700
5960 Bowcroft St Los Angeles (90016) ***(P-6512)***
Ecamsecure.....D.....888 246-0556
3400 E Airport Way Long Beach (90806) ***(P-16509)***

ECB Corp (PA)..........C.......714 385-8900
6400 Artesia Blvd Buena Park (90620) ***(P-2122)***

Ecc, Burlingame *Also called Environmental Chemical Corp* ***(P-25060)***

ECCU, Brea *Also called Evangelical Christian Cr Un* ***(P-9393)***

Echelon Security Inc..........D.......408 436-8844
1604 Kerley Dr San Jose (95112) ***(P-27053)***

Echo, San Jose *Also called Labcyte Inc* ***(P-25778)***

Echo Landscape..........D.......510 481-8614
2401 Grant Ave San Lorenzo (94580) ***(P-805)***

Echo Staffing, San Jose *Also called Summit Hr Worldwide Inc* ***(P-26835)***

Echo, A Heatlhstream Company, San Diego *Also called Healthstream Inc* ***(P-15348)***

ECi Corporation A Corp Nev (PA)..........D.......408 941-9268
4300 Stevens Creek Blvd # 275 San Jose (95129) ***(P-9546)***

Ecifm Solutions Inc..........D.......925 830-1925
3160 Crow Canyon Rd # 240 San Ramon (94583) ***(P-15901)***

Ecker & Associates, Foster City *Also called Ecker Consumer Recruiting Inc* ***(P-25891)***

Ecker Consumer Recruiting Inc..........D.......650 871-6800
1303 Melbourne St Foster City (94404) ***(P-25891)***

Eclipse Berry Farms LLC..........D.......310 207-7879
11812 San Vicente Blvd # 250 Los Angeles (90049) ***(P-93)***

Eclipse Solutions Inc..........D.......916 565-8090
2150 River Plaza Dr # 380 Sacramento (95833) ***(P-15988)***

Ecmc-CA, Rancho Cordova *Also called Educational Credit MGT Corp* ***(P-9445)***

Eco Bay Services Inc..........D.......415 643-7777
1501 Minnesota St San Francisco (94107) ***(P-27054)***

Eco Farm Field Inc..........D.......951 676-4047
28790 Las Haciendas St Temecula (92590) ***(P-661)***

Eco Farms Avocados Inc (PA)..........C.......951 694-3013
28790 Las Haciendas St Temecula (92590) ***(P-8464)***

Eco Farms Sales Inc (PA)..........E.......951 694-3013
28790 Las Haciendas St Temecula (92590) ***(P-8465)***

Eco Flow Transportation LLC..........D.......310 816-0260
18735 S Ferris Pl Rancho Dominguez (90220) ***(P-4936)***

Ecola Services Inc..........D.......818 920-7301
15314 Devonshire St Ste F Mission Hills (91345) ***(P-13821)***

Ecology Control Industries..........D.......510 235-1393
255 Parr Blvd Richmond (94801) ***(P-6346)***

Ecompanies LLC..........E.......310 586-4000
2120 Colorado Ave Fl 3 Santa Monica (90404) ***(P-5395)***

Econa Corp..........E.......619 722-6555
1344 Paizay Pl Unit 732 Chula Vista (91913) ***(P-25578)***

Econco Broadcast Service, Woodland *Also called CPI Econco Division* ***(P-17453)***

Econnections Inc..........C.......626 307-6200
75 N Fair Oaks Ave Pasadena (91103) ***(P-26218)***

Econo Air, Brea *Also called Mddr Inc* ***(P-2198)***

Econo Air Conditioning Inc..........E.......714 630-3090
3366 E La Palma Ave Anaheim (92806) ***(P-2123)***

Econo Lodge Inn & Suites, Buttonwillow *Also called Choice Hotels Intl Inc* ***(P-12142)***

Economic Dev Corp of La County..........E.......213 622-4300
444 S Flower St Ste 3700 Los Angeles (90071) ***(P-27055)***

Economic Development, Riverside *Also called County of Riverside* ***(P-23587)***

Economic Development Dept, Riverside *Also called County of Riverside* ***(P-23133)***

Economy Inn..........E.......760 256-5601
1243 E Main St Barstow (92311) ***(P-12238)***

Econosoft Inc..........D.......408 442-3663
2375 Zanker Rd Ste 250 San Jose (95131) ***(P-14774)***

Econtactlive Inc..........D.......209 548-4300
6436 Oakdale Rd Riverbank (95367) ***(P-16760)***

Ecorp Consulting Inc (PA)..........D.......916 782-9100
2525 Warren Dr Rocklin (95677) ***(P-26591)***

Ecotech Rfrgn & Hvac Inc..........D.......888 833-8100
630 S Sunkist St Ste R Anaheim (92806) ***(P-2124)***

Ecrio Inc..........D.......408 973-7290
19925 Stevens Creek Blvd # 100 Cupertino (95014) ***(P-15314)***

Ecs, San Francisco *Also called Episcopal Comm Svc San Fran* ***(P-23210)***

Ecs Refining Inc..........C.......209 774-5000
2222 S Sinclair Ave Stockton (95215) ***(P-6197)***

Ecs South Bay Head Start, Chula Vista *Also called Episcopal Community* ***(P-23211)***

Ecullet Inc..........D.......650 493-7300
1 Vintage Ct Woodside (94062) ***(P-6198)***

Ed Rocha Livestock Trnsp Inc..........D.......209 538-1302
2400 Nickerson Dr Modesto (95358) ***(P-4008)***

ED Safety Services Inc..........C.......209 333-0807
1040 W Kettleman Ln # 388 Lodi (95240) ***(P-1705)***

Ed Staub & Sons Petroleum Inc..........D.......530 233-2610
406 W 8th St Alturas (96101) ***(P-8725)***

Ed Thoming & Sons Inc..........D.......209 835-2792
33600 S Koster Rd Tracy (95304) ***(P-173)***

Edata Solutions Inc..........A.......510 574-5380
39180 Liberty St Ste 125 Fremont (94538) ***(P-15753)***

Edaw Inc..........D.......619 233-1454
401 W A St Ste 1200 San Diego (92101) ***(P-724)***

Edaw Inc..........D.......916 414-5800
2020 L St Ste 400 Sacramento (95811) ***(P-725)***

Edaw Inc (HQ)..........C.......415 955-2800
300 California St Fl 5 San Francisco (94104) ***(P-11560)***

Edc Probation, Shingle Springs *Also called County of El Dorado* ***(P-23066)***

Edc Service Corporation..........D.......909 390-4747
415 N Vineyard Ave # 205 Ontario (91764) ***(P-9432)***

Edco Disposal Corporation Inc (PA)..........C.......619 287-7555
2755 California Ave Signal Hill (90755) ***(P-3881)***

Edco Disposal Corporation Inc..........D.......714 522-3577
6762 Stanton Ave Buena Park (90621) ***(P-6199)***

Edco Drywall Company, Westminster *Also called Edco Drywall Inc* ***(P-2783)***

Edco Drywall Inc..........E.......714 799-9886
7200 Hazard Ave Westminster (92683) ***(P-2783)***

Edco Waste & Recycl Svcs Inc (HQ)..........D.......760 744-2700
224 S Las Posas Rd San Marcos (92078) ***(P-6200)***

Edd Payroll Services, Sacramento *Also called Employment Dev Cal Dept* ***(P-14274)***

Edelman Financial Engines LLC (HQ)..........C.......408 498-6000
1050 Entp Way Fl 3 Flr 3 Sunnyvale (94089) ***(P-26592)***

Edelman Productions, San Francisco *Also called New Paradigm Productions Inc* ***(P-17640)***

Edelman Public Relations, San Francisco *Also called Daniel J Edelman Inc* ***(P-26906)***

Edelman Public Relations, Los Angeles *Also called Daniel J Edelman Inc* ***(P-26907)***

Edelman Public Relations, San Mateo *Also called Daniel J Edelman Inc* ***(P-13620)***

Edelman Public Relations, Los Angeles *Also called Daniel J Edelman Inc* ***(P-13621)***

Eden Area Regnl Occupational P..........D.......510 293-2900
26316 Hesperian Blvd Hayward (94545) ***(P-23592)***

Eden Area Rop School, Hayward *Also called Eden Area Regnl Occupational P* ***(P-23592)***

Eden Housing Inc (PA)..........D.......510 582-1460
22645 Grand St Hayward (94541) ***(P-1241)***

Eden Housing Management Inc (PA)..........E.......510 582-1460
22645 Grand St Hayward (94541) ***(P-11110)***

Eden Labs Med Group Inc..........E.......510 537-1234
20103 Lake Chabot Rd Castro Valley (94546) ***(P-18965)***

Eden Medical Center, Sacramento *Also called Sutter Health* ***(P-21281)***

Eden Villa, Redding *Also called Ku Kyoung* ***(P-20061)***

Eden West Rehabilitation..........D.......510 783-4811
1805 West St Hayward (94545) ***(P-19871)***

Edf Msschstts Spnsor Mmber LLC..........A.......888 903-6926
15445 Innovation Dr San Diego (92128) ***(P-5833)***

Edf Renewable Energy, San Diego *Also called Milo Wind Project LLC* ***(P-5858)***

Edf Renewables Inc (PA)..........C.......858 521-3300
15445 Innovation Dr San Diego (92128) ***(P-5834)***

Edf Renewables Services Inc (HQ)..........D.......858 521-3575
15445 Innovation Dr San Diego (92128) ***(P-17354)***

Edf Rnwbles Asset Holdings Inc..........A.......888 903-6926
15445 Innovation Dr San Diego (92128) ***(P-5835)***

Edge Financial Inc..........E.......323 857-5809
10100 Santa Monica Blvd Los Angeles (90067) ***(P-13385)***

Edge Logistics Services Corp..........A.......424 320-5300
11777 San Vicente Blvd Los Angeles (90049) ***(P-5114)***

Edge Mortgage Advisory Co LLC..........D.......714 564-5800
2125 E Katella Ave # 350 Anaheim (92806) ***(P-27056)***

Edge Systems LLC (PA)..........C.......800 603-4996
2165 E Spring St Long Beach (90806) ***(P-6964)***

Edgebrook Productions Inc..........D.......818 766-6789
10806 Ventura Blvd Studio City (91604) ***(P-17738)***

Edgemine Inc..........C.......323 267-8222
1801 E 50th St Los Angeles (90058) ***(P-8070)***

Edgemoor Hospital..........B.......619 596-5500
655 Park Center Dr Santee (92071) ***(P-21470)***

Edges Electrical Group LLC (HQ)..........D.......408 293-5818
1135 Auzerais Ave San Jose (95126) ***(P-7146)***

Edgewater Convalescent Hosp..........D.......562 434-0974
2625 E 4th St Long Beach (90814) ***(P-19872)***

Edgewater Networks Inc..........D.......408 351-7200
5225 Hellyer Ave Ste 100 San Jose (95138) ***(P-5396)***

Edgewater Plumbing of Benicia..........E.......707 747-9204
576 Hastings Dr Benicia (94510) ***(P-2125)***

Edgewater Skilled Nursing Ctr, Long Beach *Also called Edgewater Convalescent Hosp* ***(P-19872)***

Edgewise Media Services Inc (PA)..........D.......714 919-2020
4518 W Vanowen St Burbank (91505) ***(P-7259)***

Edgewood Center, Azusa *Also called RES-Care California Inc* ***(P-20449)***

Edgewood Ctr For Childrens (PA)..........B.......415 681-3211
1801 Vicente St San Francisco (94116) ***(P-23913)***

Edgewood Partners Insur Ctr..........C.......415 356-3900
1390 Willow Pass Rd # 800 Concord (94520) ***(P-10345)***

Edgewood Partners Insur Ctr (HQ)..........D.......415 356-3900
425 California St # 2400 San Francisco (94104) ***(P-10346)***

Edgewood Properties (PA)..........D.......925 838-2847
3096 Sandstone Rd Alamo (94507) ***(P-10718)***

Edgewood Prtners Insur Ctr Inc..........D.......415 456-4323
1010 B St Ste 423 San Rafael (94901) ***(P-10347)***

Edinger Medical Group Inc (PA)..........C.......714 965-2500
9900 Talbert Ave 302 Fountain Valley (92708) ***(P-18966)***

Edison Capital..........C.......909 594-3789
18101 Von Karman Ave Irvine (92612) ***(P-5836)***

Edison International (PA)..........D.......626 302-2222
2244 Walnut Grove Ave Rosemead (91770) ***(P-5837)***

Edison Mssion Midwest Holdings..........A.......626 302-2222
2244 Walnut Grove Ave Rosemead (91770) ***(P-5838)***

Edith Witt Senior Community, San Francisco *Also called Mercy Hsing California Xxxiv* ***(P-10769)***

Edje-Enterprises..........D.......951 245-7070
520 Crane St Ste B Lake Elsinore (92530) ***(P-3050)***

Edmin Open Systems Inc (PA)..........D.......858 712-9341
5471 Krny Vlla Rd Ste 310 San Diego (92123) ***(P-15989)***

Edmunds Holding Company (PA)..........A.......310 309-6300
2401 Colorado Ave Santa Monica (90404) ***(P-15858)***

Edmunds.com, Santa Monica *Also called Edmunds Holding Company* ***(P-15858)***

Edmundscom Inc (HQ)..........A.......310 309-6300
2401 Colorado Ave Santa Monica (90404) ***(P-13623)***

EDS West LLC..........D.......323 887-7367
6666 E Washington Blvd Commerce (90040) ***(P-3882)***

Education California Dept..........B.......510 794-3666
39350 Gallaudet Dr Fremont (94538) ***(P-23721)***

Educational Credit MGT Corp..........B.......800 367-1590
P.O. Box 419045 Rancho Cordova (95741) ***(P-9445)***

Educational Employees Cr Un (PA)..........C.......559 437-7700
2222 W Shaw Ave Fresno (93711) ***(P-9305)***

Educational Employees Cr Un..........E.......559 587-4460
1460 W 7th St Hanford (93230) ***(P-9389)***

Educational Employees Cr Un..........D.......559 896-0222
3488 W Shaw Ave Fresno (93711) ***(P-9390)***

ALPHABETIC

Employee Codes: A=Over 500 employees, B=251-500
C=101-250, D=51-100, E=50
2020 Directory of California
Wholesalers and Services Companies
© Mergent Inc. 1-800-342-5647
1255

Educational Media Foundation (PA) ......C......916 251-1600
5700 West Oaks Blvd Rocklin (95765) ***(P-5522)***
Edward B Ward & Company Inc (HQ) ......E......415 330-6600
99 S Hill Dr Ste B Brisbane (94005) ***(P-7446)***
Edward E Straine CPA ......D......916 646-6464
1760 Creekside Oaks Dr Sacramento (95833) ***(P-25579)***
Edward J Kelly ......C......831 724-0832
959 Riverside Rd Watsonville (95076) ***(P-318)***
Edward Straling ......E......760 887-3673
2940 Grace Ln Ste C Costa Mesa (92626) ***(P-2480)***
Edward Thomas Companies ......D......714 782-7500
640 W Katella Ave Anaheim (92802) ***(P-12239)***
Edward Thomas Hospitality Corp ......B......310 458-0030
1 Pico Blvd Santa Monica (90405) ***(P-12240)***
Edward Vincent Park, Inglewood *Also called City of Inglewood* ***(P-18657)***
Edwardo Z Garcia ......C......661 854-5414
380 Tucker St Arvin (93203) ***(P-616)***
Edwards Cinemas University, Irvine *Also called Edwards Theatres Circuit Inc* ***(P-17842)***
Edwards Fitness, Edwards *Also called US Dept of Air Force* ***(P-18209)***
Edwards Lifesciences LLC (HQ) ......A......949 250-2500
1 Edwards Way Irvine (92614) ***(P-18967)***
Edwards Technologies Inc ......D......310 536-7070
139 Maryland St El Segundo (90245) ***(P-2481)***
Edwards Theatres Circuit Inc ......D......951 361-1917
8032 Limonite Ave Riverside (92509) ***(P-17832)***
Edwards Theatres Circuit Inc ......D......714 428-0962
901 S Coast Dr Costa Mesa (92626) ***(P-17833)***
Edwards Theatres Circuit Inc ......D......619 660-3460
2951 Jamacha Rd El Cajon (92019) ***(P-17834)***
Edwards Theatres Circuit Inc ......D......949 582-4078
27741 Crown Valley Pkwy # 323 Mission Viejo (92691) ***(P-17835)***
Edwards Theatres Circuit Inc ......D......858 635-7716
10733 Westview Pkwy San Diego (92126) ***(P-17836)***
Edwards Theatres Circuit Inc ......D......714 557-5701
1561 W Sunflower Ave Santa Ana (92704) ***(P-17837)***
Edwards Theatres Circuit Inc (HQ) ......C......949 640-4600
300 Newport Center Dr Newport Beach (92660) ***(P-17838)***
Edwards Theatres Circuit Inc ......D......760 471-3734
1180 W San Marcos Blvd San Marcos (92078) ***(P-17839)***
Edwards Theatres Circuit Inc ......D......562 403-1133
12761 Towne Center Dr Artesia (90703) ***(P-17840)***
Edwards Theatres Circuit Inc ......D......951 296-0144
40750 Winchester Rd Temecula (92591) ***(P-17841)***
Edwards Theatres Circuit Inc ......D......949 854-8811
4245 Campus Dr Irvine (92612) ***(P-17842)***
Edwards Theatres Circuit Inc ......D......805 526-4329
1457 E Los Angeles Ave Simi Valley (93065) ***(P-17843)***
Edwards Theatres Circuit Inc ......D......805 347-1164
1521 S Bradley Rd Santa Maria (93454) ***(P-17844)***
Edwards, Allen Beauty Salon, Encino *Also called Allen Edwards Beauty Salon* ***(P-13332)***
Eeco, Los Angeles *Also called Elevator Equipment Corporation* ***(P-7543)***
Eedar, Carlsbad *Also called Electronic Entrmt Design & RES* ***(P-25892)***
Ees Residential Group Homes ......D......408 265-8780
5369 Camden Ave Ste 280 San Jose (95124) ***(P-23914)***
Effort, The, Sacramento *Also called Wellspace Health* ***(P-22159)***
Efilm LLC ......C......323 463-7041
1144 N Las Palmas Ave Los Angeles (90038) ***(P-17606)***
Eforcity Corp - Nfm ......D......626 442-3168
18525 Railroad St City of Industry (91748) ***(P-7260)***
Efront Financial Solutions Inc ......D......415 653-3239
135 Main St Ste 1330 San Francisco (94105) ***(P-14775)***
Efs West ......E......661 705-8200
28472 Constellation Rd Valencia (91355) ***(P-25045)***
Efuel LLC ......D......949 330-7145
65 Enterprise Fl 3 Aliso Viejo (92656) ***(P-8726)***
Egain Corporation (PA) ......C......408 636-4500
1252 Borregas Ave Sunnyvale (94089) ***(P-15315)***
Eggleston Youth Centers Inc (PA) ......D......626 480-8107
13001 Ramona Blvd Ste E Irwindale (91706) ***(P-23203)***
Egnyte Inc (PA) ......D......650 968-4018
1350 W Middlefield Rd Mountain View (94043) ***(P-14776)***
Ego Inc ......C......626 447-0296
444 E Huntington Dr # 300 Arcadia (91006) ***(P-25580)***
Egomotion Corp (PA) ......E......415 849-4662
321 11th St San Francisco (94103) ***(P-11111)***
Egs Financial Care Inc (HQ) ......B......877 217-4423
5 Park Plz Ste 1100 Irvine (92614) ***(P-13680)***
Eharmony Inc (HQ) ......C......424 258-1199
10900 Wilshire Blvd Fl 17 Los Angeles (90024) ***(P-13421)***
Eharmony.com, Los Angeles *Also called Eharmony Inc* ***(P-13421)***
EHC LIFEBUILDERS, Milpitas *Also called Homefrst Svcs Santa Clara Cnty* ***(P-23262)***
Ehealth Insurance.com, Gold River *Also called Ehealthinsurance Services Inc* ***(P-14777)***
Ehealthinsurance Services Inc (HQ) ......D......650 584-2700
2625 Augustine Dr Ste 201 Santa Clara (95054) ***(P-10348)***
Ehealthinsurance Services Inc ......C......916 608-6101
11919 Foundation Pl # 100 Gold River (95670) ***(P-14777)***
Ehealthwirecom Inc ......C......916 924-8092
2450 Venture Oaks Way # 100 Sacramento (95833) ***(P-22238)***
Ehmcke Sheet Metal Corp ......D......619 477-6484
840 W 19th St National City (91950) ***(P-3051)***
Ehs Medical Group, Monterey Park *Also called Synermed* ***(P-19497)***
Eht Esan LLC ......D......714 632-1221
3100 E Frontera St Anaheim (92806) ***(P-12241)***
Ehy, Santa Barbara *Also called Evans Hardy & Young Inc* ***(P-13504)***
Eichleay Inc (PA) ......C......925 689-7000
1390 Willow Pass Rd # 600 Concord (94520) ***(P-25046)***
Eichleay Inc ......C......562 256-8600
3780 Kilroy Airport Way # 440 Long Beach (90806) ***(P-25047)***
Eide Bailly LLP ......B......909 466-4410
10681 Fthill Blvd Ste 300 Rancho Cucamonga (91730) ***(P-25581)***
Eie Electric, Costa Mesa *Also called Pmd Industries Inc* ***(P-2588)***
Eight Star Commodities, El Centro *Also called All Star Seed* ***(P-464)***
Eight Star Equipment, El Centro *Also called Noblesse Oblige Inc* ***(P-456)***
Eighty Eight, Los Angeles *Also called Ms Bubbles Inc* ***(P-8098)***
Eighty One Enterprise Inc ......E......626 371-1980
9401 Whitmore St El Monte (91731) ***(P-8071)***
Eileen Nottoli ......D......415 837-1515
3 Embarcadero Ctr # 1200 San Francisco (94111) ***(P-22495)***
Eineridge Care Center, Sylmar *Also called Quality Long Term Care Nev Inc* ***(P-20206)***
Einfochips Inc (HQ) ......D......408 496-1882
2025 Gateway Pl Ste 270 San Jose (95110) ***(P-14778)***
Einstein Dental, San Diego *Also called Einstein Industries Inc* ***(P-14779)***
Einstein Industries Inc ......C......858 459-1182
6825 Flanders Dr San Diego (92121) ***(P-14779)***
Eis Group Inc ......C......415 402-2622
731 Sansome St Fl 4 San Francisco (94111) ***(P-15316)***
Eisenberg International Corp (PA) ......D......818 365-8161
9128 Jordan Ave Chatsworth (91311) ***(P-8027)***
Eisenberg Village, Reseda *Also called Los Angles Jewish HM For Aging* ***(P-20095)***
Eisenhower Desert Crdiolgy Ctr, Rancho Mirage *Also called Charlie W Shaeffer Jr MD* ***(P-18891)***
Eisenhower Health, Rancho Mirage *Also called Eisenhower Medical Center* ***(P-20862)***
Eisenhower Medical Center (PA) ......A......760 340-3911
39000 Bob Hope Dr Rancho Mirage (92270) ***(P-20862)***
Eisner Pediatric Fmly Med Ctr, Los Angeles *Also called Pediatric & Family Medical Ctr* ***(P-22085)***
Ejm Kyrene LLC (PA) ......E......310 278-1830
9061 Santa Monica Blvd Los Angeles (90069) ***(P-1295)***
Ejm Property Management, Los Angeles *Also called Ejm Kyrene LLC* ***(P-1295)***
Ek Health Services Inc (PA) ......D......408 973-0888
992 S De Anza Blvd Ste 10 San Jose (95129) ***(P-26593)***
El Al Israel Airlines Ltd ......C......323 852-1252
6404 Wilshire Blvd # 1250 Los Angeles (90048) ***(P-4873)***
EL ARCA, Los Angeles *Also called East L A Remarkable Citizens* ***(P-23199)***
El Aviso Magazine ......B......323 586-9199
4850 Gage Ave Bell (90201) ***(P-8870)***
El Caballero Country Club ......C......818 654-3000
18300 Tarzana Dr Tarzana (91356) ***(P-18450)***
El Cajon Ford, El Cajon *Also called El Cajon Motors* ***(P-17228)***
El Cajon Medical Offices, El Cajon *Also called Kaiser Foundation Hospitals* ***(P-20958)***
El Cajon Motors (PA) ......D......619 579-8888
1595 E Main St El Cajon (92021) ***(P-17228)***
El Cajon Plumbing & Htg Sup Co ......E......619 449-7300
4360 Mensha Pl San Diego (92130) ***(P-7447)***
El Camino Care Center, Carmichael *Also called Helios Healthcare LLC* ***(P-20010)***
El Camino Children & Fmly Svcs ......E......562 364-1258
9900 Lakewood Blvd # 104 Downey (90240) ***(P-23204)***
El Camino Country Club, Oceanside *Also called American Golf Corporation* ***(P-18370)***
El Camino Gardens, Carmichael *Also called Atria Senior Living Inc* ***(P-23829)***
El Camino Hospital ......C......650 988-7444
1503 Grant Rd Ste 120 Mountain View (94040) ***(P-23205)***
El Camino Hospital ......C......650 940-7000
2240 Tully Rd San Jose (95122) ***(P-21526)***
El Camino Hospital ......D......650 940-7310
2505 Hospital Dr Ste 1 Mountain View (94040) ***(P-21922)***
El Camino Hospital ......C......650 988-4825
1737 N 1st St Ste 220 San Jose (95112) ***(P-21471)***
El Camino Hospital Auxiliary ......A......650 940-7214
2500 Grant Rd Mountain View (94040) ***(P-21735)***
El Camino Labor LLC ......D......831 809-9537
815 Broadway St King City (93930) ***(P-617)***
El Camino Mem Pk & Mortuary, San Diego *Also called Stewart Enterprises Inc* ***(P-13380)***
El Camino Mem Pk & Mortuary, San Diego *Also called San Diego Cemetery Assn* ***(P-13378)***
El Camino Rental ......E......760 722-7368
1833 Oceanside Blvd Ste D Oceanside (92054) ***(P-14155)***
El Camino Surgery Center LLC ......D......650 961-1200
15046 Karl Ave Monte Sereno (95030) ***(P-20863)***
El Camino YMCA, Mountain View *Also called YMCA of Silicon Valley* ***(P-24723)***
El Capitan Canyon LLC ......D......805 685-3887
11560 Calle Real Santa Barbara (93117) ***(P-13162)***
El Centro Regional Medical Ctr (PA) ......A......760 339-7100
1415 Ross Ave El Centro (92243) ***(P-20864)***
El Clasificado (PA) ......D......323 837-4095
11205 Imperial Hwy Norwalk (90650) ***(P-13624)***
El Concilio San Mateo Cnty Inc ......E......650 373-1080
3180 Middlefield Rd Redwood City (94063) ***(P-23206)***
El Cordova Hotel ......D......619 435-4131
1351 Orange Ave Coronado (92118) ***(P-12242)***
El Dorado Country Club ......C......760 346-8081
46000 Fairway Dr Indian Wells (92210) ***(P-18451)***
El Dorado County Health Dept ......D......530 621-6100
931 Spring St Placerville (95667) ***(P-18968)***
El Dorado Enterprises Inc ......A......310 719-9800
1000 W Redondo Beach Blvd Gardena (90247) ***(P-12243)***
El Dorado Hills County Wtr Dst ......D......916 933-6623
1050 Wilson Blvd El Dorado Hills (95762) ***(P-6056)***
El Dorado Hills Fire Dept, El Dorado Hills *Also called El Dorado Hills County Wtr Dst* ***(P-6056)***
El Dorado Irrigation District ......B......530 622-4513
2890 Mosquito Rd Placerville (95667) ***(P-6057)***
El Dorado Savings Bank (PA) ......D......530 622-1492
4040 El Dorado Rd Placerville (95667) ***(P-9279)***
El Dorado Water & Shower Svc ......E......530 622-8995
5821 Mother Lode Dr Placerville (95667) ***(P-6058)***

Mergent e-mail: customerrelations@mergent.com
1256
2020 Directory of California
Wholesalers and Services Companies
(P-0000) Products & Services Section entry number
(PA)=Parent Co (HQ)=Headquarters (DH)=Div Headquarters

El Encanto Healthcare & Rehab....C....626 336-1274
555 El Encanto Rd City of Industry (91745) **(P-19873)**
EL ENCANTO HOME HEALTH CARE, City of Industry *Also called El Encanto Healthcare & Rehab* **(P-19873)**
El Guapo Spices and Herbs Pkg, Commerce *Also called El Guapo Spices Inc* **(P-8574)**
El Guapo Spices Inc (PA)....D....213 312-1300
6200 E Slauson Ave Commerce (90040) **(P-8574)**
El Macero Country Club Inc....D....530 753-3363
44571 Clubhouse Dr El Macero (95618) **(P-18452)**
El Mexicano, Montebello *Also called Marquez Brothers Intl Inc* **(P-8189)**
El Monte Community Credit Un....D....626 444-0501
11718 Ramona Blvd El Monte (91732) **(P-9391)**
El Monte Convalescent Hospital....D....626 442-1500
4096 Easy St El Monte (91731) **(P-20548)**
El Monte Rents Inc (HQ)....C....562 404-9300
12818 Firestone Blvd Santa Fe Springs (90670) **(P-17232)**
El Monte Rv, Santa Fe Springs *Also called El Monte Rents Inc* **(P-17232)**
El Nido Family Centers (PA)....C....818 830-3646
10200 Sepulveda Blvd # 350 Mission Hills (91345) **(P-23207)**
El Pas-Los Angles Lmsne Ex Inc....E....213 623-2323
260 E 6th St Los Angeles (90014) **(P-3774)**
El Paseo Limousine, Santa Clara *Also called Worldwide Ground Transportatio* **(P-3741)**
El Pollo Loco Holdings Inc (PA)....C....714 599-5000
3535 Harbor Blvd Ste 100 Costa Mesa (92626) **(P-11827)**
El Prado Golf Course LP....D....909 597-1751
6555 Pine Ave Chino (91708) **(P-18245)**
El Rancho Motel Inc....C....650 588-8500
1100 El Camino Real Millbrae (94030) **(P-12244)**
El Rancho Vista Hlth Care Ctr, Pico Rivera *Also called Mariner Health Care Inc* **(P-20117)**
El Segundo Eductl Foundation....B....310 615-2650
641 Sheldon St El Segundo (90245) **(P-24172)**
El Toro DC, El Toro *Also called Frito-Lay North America Inc* **(P-8352)**
El Toro Water Distr Public Fac (PA)....D....949 837-1662
24251 Los Alisos Blvd Lake Forest (92630) **(P-6059)**
El-Com Cabletek, Garden Grove *Also called Elrob Inc* **(P-7262)**
Eladh LP....D....323 268-5514
4060 Whittier Blvd Los Angeles (90023) **(P-20865)**
Elaine Null....C....415 345-4428
1388 Sutter St Fl 11 San Francisco (94109) **(P-16761)**
Elan Drug Delivery Inc....D....770 531-8100
180 Oyster Point Blvd South San Francisco (94080) **(P-25741)**
Elan Drug Technologies, South San Francisco *Also called Elan Drug Delivery Inc* **(P-25741)**
Elance Inc (HQ)....C....650 316-7500
2625 Augustine Dr Ste 601 Santa Clara (95054) **(P-13500)**
Elastic Projects Inc....D....415 857-1593
255 Golden Gate Ave San Francisco (94102) **(P-14780)**
Elasticsearch Inc (HQ)....D....650 458-2620
800 W El Cmino Real Ste 3 Mountain View (94040) **(P-14781)**
Elavon Inc....A....954 776-7990
1281 9th Ave Unit 706 San Diego (92101) **(P-15859)**
Elavon Inc....B....925 734-8939
4234 Hacienda Dr Ste 250 Pleasanton (94588) **(P-15860)**
Elcor Electric Inc....C....408 986-1320
3310 Bassett St Santa Clara (95054) **(P-2482)**
Elder Care Alliance Camarillo....D....510 769-2700
1301 Marina Village Pkwy # 210 Alameda (94501) **(P-23915)**
Elder Care Alliance San Rafael....D....510 769-2700
1301 Marina Village Pkwy # 210 Alameda (94501) **(P-19874)**
Elder Options (PA)....E....530 626-6939
82 Main St Placerville (95667) **(P-23208)**
Eldorado Care Center LP....B....619 440-1211
510 E Washington Ave El Cajon (92020) **(P-19875)**
Eldorado Community Service Ctr....D....424 227-7971
335 E Manchester Blvd Inglewood (90301) **(P-18969)**
Electra Owners Assoc....C....619 236-3310
700 W E St San Diego (92101) **(P-24335)**
Electric Department, Santa Clara *Also called City of Santa Clara* **(P-5822)**
Electric Motor & Supply Co., Fresno *Also called Electric Motor Shop* **(P-7147)**
Electric Motor Shop....D....559 233-1153
250 Broadway St Fresno (93721) **(P-7147)**
Electric Power RES Inst Inc (PA)....A....650 855-2000
3420 Hillview Ave Palo Alto (94304) **(P-25742)**
Electric Sales Unlimited....E....562 463-8300
9023 Norwalk Blvd Santa Fe Springs (90670) **(P-7148)**
Electric Svc & Sup Co Pasadena....D....626 795-8641
2668 E Foothill Blvd Pasadena (91107) **(P-2483)**
Electric Tech Construction Inc....D....925 849-5324
1910 Mark Ct Ste 130 Concord (94520) **(P-1853)**
Electric USA....E....800 921-1151
480 Aldo Ave Santa Clara (95054) **(P-2484)**
Electrical Distributors Co, San Jose *Also called Chester C Lehmann Co Inc* **(P-7134)**
Electro Rent Corporation (HQ)....C....818 786-2525
8511 Fllbrook Ave Ste 200 West Hills (91304) **(P-14156)**
Electronic Arts Inc (PA)....B....650 628-1500
209 Redwood Shores Pkwy Redwood City (94065) **(P-15317)**
Electronic Commerce LLC....D....800 770-5520
1 City Blvd W Ste 1850 Orange (92868) **(P-9501)**
Electronic Control Systems LLC....C....858 513-1911
12575 Kirkham Ct Ste 1 Poway (92064) **(P-2485)**
Electronic Data Care Inc....D....310 791-2600
23670 Hawthorne Blvd # 208 Torrance (90505) **(P-15587)**
Electronic Entrmt Design & RES....D....760 579-7100
2075 Corte Del Nogal B Carlsbad (92011) **(P-25892)**
Electronic Recyclers....D....253 736-2627
7815 N Palm Ave Ste 140 Fresno (93711) **(P-6201)**
Electronic Recyclers America, Fresno *Also called Electronic Recyclers Intl Inc* **(P-6202)**
Electronic Recyclers Intl Inc (PA)....C....800 374-3473
7815 N Palm Ave Ste 140 Fresno (93711) **(P-6202)**
Electrosonic Inc (HQ)....C....818 333-3600
3320 N San Fernando Blvd Burbank (91504) **(P-25048)**
Elegance Exotic Wood Flooring, Fontana *Also called Elegance Wood Products Inc* **(P-6554)**
Elegance Wood Products Inc....D....909 484-7676
7351 Mcguire Ave Fontana (92336) **(P-6554)**
Elegant Surfaces....D....209 823-9388
3640 Amrcn Rver Dr 150 Sacramento (95864) **(P-6682)**
Eleganza Tiles Inc (PA)....D....714 224-1700
3125 E Coronado St Anaheim (92806) **(P-2894)**
Element Mtrls Tech HB Inc....D....310 632-8500
18100 S Wilmington Ave Compton (90220) **(P-26065)**
Element Mtrls Tech HB Inc (HQ)....D....714 892-1961
15062 Bolsa Chica St Huntington Beach (92649) **(P-26066)**
Elements Behavioral Health Inc (PA)....C....562 741-6470
5000 Arprt Plz Dr Ste 100 Long Beach (90815) **(P-22024)**
Elena Villa Healthcare Center....D....562 868-0591
13226 Studebaker Rd Norwalk (90650) **(P-20549)**
Elevate Addiction Services, Aptos *Also called Enlightcare Inc* **(P-21473)**
Elevate Credit Inc....C....817 928-1500
11710 El Camino Real San Diego (92130) **(P-9458)**
Elevate Property Services LP....E....562 219-2101
19700 Fairchild Ste 150 Irvine (92612) **(P-10872)**
Elevator Equipment Corporation (PA)....D....323 245-0147
4035 Goodwin Ave Los Angeles (90039) **(P-7543)**
Eleven Inc....C....415 707-1111
500 Sansome St Ste 100 San Francisco (94111) **(P-13501)**
Eleven Communications, San Francisco *Also called Eleven Inc* **(P-13501)**
Eleven Western Builders Inc (PA)....C....760 796-6346
2862 Executive Pl Escondido (92029) **(P-1473)**
Elias Elliott Lampasi Fehn (PA)....D....951 689-5031
7251 Magnolia Ave Riverside (92504) **(P-19610)**
Elica Health Centers....D....916 454-2345
3701 J St Ste 201 Sacramento (95816) **(P-18970)**
Elijah Textiles Inc....D....310 666-3443
1251 E Olympic Blvd Los Angeles (90021) **(P-6555)**
Elim Alzheimers & Rehab....D....559 320-2200
668 E Bullard Ave Fresno (93710) **(P-19876)**
Elioco Produce Inc....C....831 424-5450
367 W Market St Ste A Salinas (93901) **(P-618)**
Eliseo Esparza Delgadillo....E....209 745-3937
88 Wildflower Dr Galt (95632) **(P-619)**
Elite, Culver City *Also called West Publishing Corporation* **(P-15713)**
Elite Airways LLC....C....805 496-3334
4607 Lakeview Canyon Rd Westlake Village (91361) **(P-4874)**
Elite Aviation LLC....D....818 988-5387
7501 Hayvenhurst Pl Van Nuys (91406) **(P-4739)**
Elite Craftsman (PA)....C....562 989-3511
2763 Saint Louis Ave Long Beach (90755) **(P-13917)**
Elite Electric....D....951 681-5811
9415 Bellegrave Ave Riverside (92509) **(P-2486)**
Elite Enfrcment SEC Sltons Inc....E....866 354-8308
29970 Technology Dr Murrieta (92563) **(P-16265)**
Elite Information Group Inc (HQ)....B....323 642-5200
5100 W Goldleaf Cir # 100 Los Angeles (90056) **(P-15588)**
Elite Landscaping Inc....C....559 292-7760
2972 Larkin Ave Clovis (93612) **(P-806)**
Elite Maintenance Services Inc....D....619 516-7000
7770 Regents Rd Ste 113 San Diego (92122) **(P-13918)**
Elite Nursing Services Inc....E....714 919-7898
1915 W Orangewood Ave # 110 Orange (92868) **(P-14269)**
Elite Power Inc....D....916 739-1580
6530 Asher Ln Sacramento (95828) **(P-2487)**
Elite Security Services Inc....B....949 222-2203
18006 Sky Park Cir # 205 Irvine (92614) **(P-16266)**
Elite Show Services Inc....A....619 574-1589
2878 Camino Del Rio S # 260 San Diego (92108) **(P-16267)**
Elite Tek Services Inc....D....714 881-5301
131 Mercer Way Costa Mesa (92627) **(P-15990)**
Elite Tile, Livermore *Also called Mthuron Inc* **(P-2903)**
Elitecare Medical Staffing LLC....D....559 438-7700
761 E Locust Ave Ste 103 Fresno (93720) **(P-14270)**
Elitegroup Cmpt Systems Inc....C....510 226-7333
6851 Mowry Ave Newark (94560) **(P-6827)**
Elizabeth Glaser Pedia....A....310 231-0400
16130 Ventura Blvd # 250 Encino (91436) **(P-22239)**
Elizabeth Hospice Inc (PA)....C....760 737-2050
500 La Terraza Blvd # 130 Escondido (92025) **(P-20424)**
Elizabeth Larson....D....415 409-7300
3736 Jackson St San Francisco (94118) **(P-11112)**
Elizabethan Inn Associates LP....D....916 448-1300
1935 Wright St Apt 231 Sacramento (95825) **(P-12245)**
Elk Grove Adult Cmnty Training....D....916 431-3162
8810 Elk Grove Blvd Elk Grove (95624) **(P-24336)**
Elk Grove Montessori School, Sacramento *Also called Montessori Learning Commons* **(P-23753)**
Elk Grove Unified School Dst....C....916 686-7733
8421 Gerber Rd Sacramento (95828) **(P-3799)**
Elk Hills Power LLC....C....661 763-2730
101 Ash St San Diego (92101) **(P-5839)**
Elk Valley Casino Inc....C....707 464-1020
2500 Howland Hill Rd Crescent City (95531) **(P-12246)**
Elkay Plastics Co Inc (PA)....D....323 722-7073
6000 Sheila St Commerce (90040) **(P-7877)**
Elkhorn Berry Farms LLC....D....831 722-2472
262 E Lake Ave Watsonville (95076) **(P-319)**
Elkor Properties, Santa Monica *Also called Roscoe Real Estate Ltd Partnr* **(P-12840)**
Ellation Inc (PA)....D....415 796-3560
835 Market St Ste 700 San Francisco (94103) **(P-14782)**
Ellen Degeneres Show, The, Burbank *Also called Wad Productions Inc* **(P-17703)**

ALPHABETIC

Ellie Fashion Group Inc......D......818 355-3812
1735 Stewart St Fl 2 Santa Monica (90404) ***(P-16762)***
Ellie Mae Inc (HQ)......C......855 224-8572
4420 Rosewood Dr Ste 500 Pleasanton (94588) ***(P-15318)***
Elliott Auto Supply Co Inc......E......800 278-6394
448 W Katella Ave Orange (92867) ***(P-6435)***
Elliott Auto Supply Co Inc......D......310 527-2500
1600 E Orangethorpe Ave Fullerton (92831) ***(P-6436)***
Elliott Benson Market Research......E......916 325-1670
1226 H St Sacramento (95814) ***(P-25893)***
Elliott Laboratories Inc......E......510 440-9500
41039 Boyce Rd Fremont (94538) ***(P-26067)***
Ellis Building Contractors, Manhattan Beach *Also called Ebc Inc* ***(P-1119)***
Ellison Construction-Framing, Brentwood *Also called Ellison Framing Inc* ***(P-2929)***
Ellison Framing Inc......C......925 516-9269
160 Guthrie Ln Ste 13 Brentwood (94513) ***(P-2929)***
Ellison Machinery Co (HQ)......D......562 949-8311
9912 Pioneer Blvd Santa Fe Springs (90670) ***(P-7544)***
Ellison Technologies, Santa Fe Springs *Also called Ellison Machinery Co* ***(P-7544)***
Ellison Technologies Inc......D......562 949-8311
9912 Pioneer Blvd Santa Fe Springs (90670) ***(P-7545)***
Elljay Acoustics Inc......D......714 961-1173
511 Cameron St Placentia (92870) ***(P-2784)***
Elma Electronic Inc......E......209 858-2411
17700 Shideler Pkwy Lathrop (95330) ***(P-7261)***
Elmco Sales Inc (PA)......D......626 855-4831
15070 Proctor Ave City of Industry (91746) ***(P-7416)***
Elmco Stewart, City of Industry *Also called Elmco/Duddy Inc* ***(P-7417)***
Elmco/Duddy Inc (HQ)......E......626 333-9942
15070 Proctor Ave City of Industry (91746) ***(P-7417)***
Elms Convalescent Hospital, Thousand Oaks *Also called Elms Sanitarium Inc* ***(P-19877)***
Elms Sanitarium Inc......D......818 240-6720
3247 Windmist Ave Thousand Oaks (91362) ***(P-19877)***
Elmwood Care Center, Berkeley *Also called Shattuck Health Care Inc* ***(P-20253)***
Elo Touch Solutions Inc (HQ)......C......408 597-8000
670 N Mccarthy Blvd # 100 Milpitas (95035) ***(P-6828)***
Elrob Inc......D......714 230-6100
12691 Monarch St Garden Grove (92841) ***(P-7262)***
Els......D......510 549-2929
2040 Addison St Berkeley (94704) ***(P-27057)***
Els Architecture, Berkeley *Also called Els* ***(P-27057)***
Els Investments......C......916 388-0308
9980 Horn Rd Sacramento (95827) ***(P-726)***
Elsinore Vly Municpl Wtr Dst (PA)......D......951 674-3146
31315 Chaney St Lake Elsinore (92530) ***(P-6060)***
Elvira Sandoval......C......530 473-5718
2154 Hill Rd Williams (95987) ***(P-14271)***
Elysium Jennings LLC......C......661 679-1700
1600 Norris Rd Bakersfield (93308) ***(P-996)***
Elyxir Distributing LLC......C......831 761-6400
270 W Riverside Dr Watsonville (95076) ***(P-8760)***
Em Eagle Purchaser LLC (PA)......A......855 224-8572
4420 Rosewood Dr Ste 500 Pleasanton (94588) ***(P-11658)***
Emagia Corporation......E......408 654-6575
4701 P Henry Dr Bldg 20 Santa Clara (95054) ***(P-16763)***
Emagined Security Inc......E......415 944-2977
2816 San Simeon Way San Carlos (94070) ***(P-16510)***
Emanate Hlth Intr-Cmmnity Hosp (PA)......A......626 331-7331
210 W San Bernardino Rd Covina (91723) ***(P-20866)***
Emanuel Medical Center Inc......C......209 667-5600
1801 N Olive Ave Turlock (95382) ***(P-20867)***
Emanuel Medical Center Inc (HQ)......A......209 667-4200
825 Delbon Ave Turlock (95382) ***(P-20868)***
Emanuel Medical Center Inc......C......209 664-2520
2121 Colorado Ave Ste A Turlock (95382) ***(P-20869)***
Emax Laboratories Inc......E......310 618-8889
1835 W 205th St Torrance (90501) ***(P-26068)***
Embarcadero Homes Assn Inc......D......954 776-2611
4623 Quail Lakes Dr Stockton (95207) ***(P-24539)***
Embarcadero Inn Associates......C......415 495-2100
155 Steuart St San Francisco (94105) ***(P-12247)***
Embarcadero Systems Corp......C......510 749-7400
1601 Harbor Bay Pkwy # 120 Alameda (94502) ***(P-14783)***
Embarcadero, The, San Francisco *Also called Crunch LLC* ***(P-18137)***
Embassador Private Securities......D......415 822-8811
1341 Evans Ave San Francisco (94124) ***(P-9687)***
Embassy Sites-So San Francisco, South San Francisco *Also called Djont/Cmb Ssf Leasing LLC* ***(P-12215)***
Embassy Stes Monterey Bay Htl, Seaside *Also called Tucson Hotels LP* ***(P-13047)***
Embassy Stes San Dego-La Jolla, San Diego *Also called Sunstone Top Gun LLC* ***(P-13004)***
Embassy Suites, Milpitas *Also called Park Hotels & Resorts Inc* ***(P-12712)***
Embassy Suites, Palmdale *Also called Sunstone Hotel Investors LLC* ***(P-12992)***
Embassy Suites, NAPA *Also called Park Hotels & Resorts Inc* ***(P-12718)***
Embassy Suites, NAPA *Also called NAPA Es Leasing LLC* ***(P-12637)***
Embassy Suites, Burlingame *Also called Djont Operations LLC* ***(P-12214)***
Embassy Suites, Covina *Also called Park Hotels & Resorts Inc* ***(P-12722)***
Embassy Suites, Burlingame *Also called Park Hotels & Resorts Inc* ***(P-12725)***
Embassy Suites, Arcadia *Also called Park Hotels & Resorts Inc* ***(P-12726)***
Embassy Suites, Downey *Also called Park Hotels & Resorts Inc* ***(P-12727)***
Embassy Suites, Buena Park *Also called Park Hotels & Resorts Inc* ***(P-12728)***
Embassy Suites, Irvine *Also called Park Hotels & Resorts Inc* ***(P-12731)***
Embassy Suites, Los Angeles *Also called Sunstone Hotel Investors LLC* ***(P-12997)***
Embassy Suites, San Rafael *Also called Hospitality Ventures MGT LLC* ***(P-12383)***
Embassy Suites, Brea *Also called Windsor Capital Group Inc* ***(P-13104)***
Embassy Suites, Temecula *Also called Windsor Capital Group Inc* ***(P-13105)***
Embassy Suites, Anaheim *Also called Park Hotels & Resorts Inc* ***(P-12734)***
Embassy Suites, Santa Ana *Also called Windsor Capital Group Inc* ***(P-13108)***
Embassy Suites, South San Francisco *Also called Park Hotels & Resorts Inc* ***(P-12735)***
Embassy Suites, South Lake Tahoe *Also called Park Hotels & Resorts Inc* ***(P-12736)***
Embassy Suites Anaheim North, Anaheim *Also called Eht Esan LLC* ***(P-12241)***
Embassy Suites Anaheim Orange, Orange *Also called Ergs Aim Hotel Realty LLC* ***(P-12252)***
Embassy Suites Arcadia, Santa Monica *Also called Windsor Capital Group Inc* ***(P-13101)***
Embassy Suites Brea, Brea *Also called Park Hotels & Resorts Inc* ***(P-12713)***
Embassy Suites By Hilton San, San Diego *Also called Sunstone Top Gun Lessee Inc* ***(P-13005)***
Embassy Suites El Paso, Santa Monica *Also called Windsor Capital Group Inc* ***(P-13107)***
Embassy Suites Lompoc, Santa Monica *Also called Windsor Capital Group Inc* ***(P-13102)***
Embassy Suites Management LLC......C......858 453-0400
4550 La Jolla Village Dr San Diego (92122) ***(P-12248)***
Embassy Suites Walnut Creek, Walnut Creek *Also called Interstate Hotels Resorts Inc* ***(P-26267)***
Embassy Suites- Santa Clara, Santa Clara *Also called Msr Hotels & Resorts Inc* ***(P-12636)***
Embassy Suites- Santa Clara, Santa Clara *Also called Santa Clara Tenant Corp* ***(P-12884)***
Embee Processing LLC......B......714 546-9842
2136 S Hathaway St Santa Ana (92705) ***(P-25049)***
Embee Processing, Inc., Santa Ana *Also called Embee Processing LLC* ***(P-25049)***
Embrane Inc......E......408 550-2700
2350 Mission College Blvd # 703 Santa Clara (95054) ***(P-14784)***
Emco High Voltage, Jackson *Also called Xp Power LLC* ***(P-7368)***
Emcor Fclities Svcs N Amer Inc......C......858 712-4700
9505 Chesapeake Dr San Diego (92123) ***(P-2126)***
Emcor Services, Irvine *Also called Mesa Energy Systems Inc* ***(P-2200)***
Emerald Brook LLC......E......760 345-4770
76000 Frank Sinatra Dr Palm Desert (92211) ***(P-13163)***
Emerald Cloud Lab Inc......D......650 257-7554
844 Dubuque Ave South San Francisco (94080) ***(P-25743)***
Emerald Connect LLC (HQ)......D......800 233-2834
15050 Avenue Of Sci 200 San Diego (92128) ***(P-15754)***
Emerald Desert Rv Resort, Palm Desert *Also called Emerald Brook LLC* ***(P-13163)***
Emerald Expositions LLC (HQ)......B......949 226-5700
31910 Del Obispo St # 200 San Juan Capistrano (92675) ***(P-16764)***
Emerald Landscape Services......D......714 844-2200
1041 N Kemp St Anaheim (92801) ***(P-807)***
Emerald Packaging Inc......C......510 429-5700
33050 Western Ave Union City (94587) ***(P-8968)***
Emerald Site Services Inc......D......916 685-7211
9883 Kent St Elk Grove (95624) ***(P-3312)***
Emerald Ter Convalescent Hosp, Los Angeles *Also called Equicare Medical Supply Inc* ***(P-19892)***
Emerald Trans Los Angeles LLC......E......323 277-2500
5756 Alba St Los Angeles (90058) ***(P-3883)***
Emercon Construction Inc (PA)......D......714 630-9615
2906 E Coronado St Anaheim (92806) ***(P-1120)***
Emerge Digital Inc......D......415 839-5055
543 Howard St Lbby San Francisco (94105) ***(P-15991)***
Emerge Digital Group, San Francisco *Also called Emerge Digital Inc* ***(P-15991)***
Emergency Ambulance Service......D......714 990-1331
3200 E Birch St Ste A Brea (92821) ***(P-3667)***
Emergency Groups Office, Arcadia *Also called Ego Inc* ***(P-25580)***
Emergency Med Group of Folsom......D......916 983-7470
1650 Creekside Dr Folsom (95630) ***(P-18971)***
Emergency Medicine Specialist......D......714 543-8911
1010 W La Veta Ave # 755 Orange (92868) ***(P-20870)***
Emergency Physicians Med Group, Citrus Heights *Also called Dignity Health* ***(P-18957)***
Emergency Reporting Systems, El Monte *Also called ERs SEC Alarm Systems Inc* ***(P-7149)***
Emergency Technologies Inc......D......818 765-4421
7345 Varna Ave North Hollywood (91605) ***(P-16511)***
Emergent Medical Associates (PA)......D......310 379-2134
111 N Sepulveda Blvd # 210 Manhattan Beach (90266) ***(P-18972)***
Emergent Travel Health Inc......E......858 450-9595
3985 Sorrento Valley Blvd A San Diego (92121) ***(P-25744)***
Emergent Ventures Intl Inc......D......415 655-6617
1156 Clement St San Francisco (94118) ***(P-27058)***
Emerging Markets Growth Fund, Irvine *Also called American Funds Service Company* ***(P-9859)***
Emerik Hotel Corp......D......213 748-1291
1020 S Figueroa St Los Angeles (90015) ***(P-12249)***
Emeritus At Casa Glendale, Glendale *Also called Emeritus Corporation* ***(P-10720)***
Emeritus At Villa Colima, Walnut *Also called Emeritus Corporation* ***(P-20427)***
Emeritus Corporation......E......858 292-8044
5219 Clairemont Mesa Blvd San Diego (92117) ***(P-19878)***
Emeritus Corporation......E......707 552-3336
2261 Tuolumne St Vallejo (94589) ***(P-20425)***
Emeritus Corporation......E......707 996-7101
800 Oregon St Sonoma (95476) ***(P-20426)***
Emeritus Corporation......E......760 741-3055
1351 E Washington Ave Escondido (92027) ***(P-10719)***
Emeritus Corporation......E......818 246-7457
426 Piedmont Ave Glendale (91206) ***(P-10720)***
Emeritus Corporation......E......909 595-5030
19850 Colima Rd Walnut (91789) ***(P-20427)***
Emeritus Corporation......E......805 239-1313
1919 Creston Rd Ofc Paso Robles (93446) ***(P-10721)***
Emerson Elementary......D......818 558-5419
720 E Cypress Ave Burbank (91501) ***(P-24540)***
Emery Financial Inc (PA)......D......949 219-0640
625 Kings Rd Newport Beach (92663) ***(P-9623)***
Emery Marina, Emeryville *Also called Young MNS Chrstn Assn of E Bay* ***(P-24766)***
Emery Smith Laboratories Inc......C......213 745-5333
781 E Washington Blvd Los Angeles (90021) ***(P-26069)***

Mergent e-mail: customerrelations@mergent.com
1258
2020 Directory of California
Wholesalers and Services Companies
(P-0000) Products & Services Section entry number
(PA)=Parent Co (HQ)=Headquarters (DH)=Div Headquarters

Emery Smith Laboratories Inc......D......714 238-6133
1195 N Tustin Ave Anaheim (92807) **(P-25050)**
Emeter Corporation......C......650 227-7770
4000 E 3rd Ave Ste 400 Foster City (94404) **(P-14785)**
EMI Music Distribution, Los Angeles *Also called Capitol Records LLC* **(P-16673)**
Emida Technologies, Foothill Ranch *Also called Debisys Inc* **(P-9431)**
Eminence Home Health Care Inc......E......818 830-7113
16921 Parthenia St # 301 Northridge (91343) **(P-21736)**
EMJ Hayward, Hayward *Also called Earle M Jorgensen Company* **(P-7063)**
Emmi Inc......D......213 622-7234
631 S Olive St Ste 302 Los Angeles (90014) **(P-7788)**
Emmi Universal Fine Jeweller, Los Angeles *Also called Emmi Inc* **(P-7788)**
Emmis Communications Corp......C......818 238-6705
2600 W Olive Ave Fl 8 Burbank (91505) **(P-5523)**
Emmis Communications Corp......C......626 484-4440
790 E Colorado Blvd Fl 9 Pasadena (91101) **(P-5524)**
Emmis Publishing Corporation......D......323 801-0100
5900 Wilshire Blvd Fl 10 Los Angeles (90036) **(P-8871)**
Emn8, San Diego *Also called Tillster Inc* **(P-16136)**
Emotiv Systems Inc......E......415 503-3601
1770 Post St Ste 350 San Francisco (94115) **(P-18317)**
Emove Express Company......D......650 377-0913
688 Matsonia Dr Foster City (94404) **(P-15755)**
Emovexpress.com, Foster City *Also called Emove Express Company* **(P-15755)**
Emp III Inc......D......323 231-4174
1755 Mrtn Lthr Kng Jr Blv Los Angeles (90058) **(P-11909)**
Empcc Inc......D......714 564-7900
1682 Langley Ave Fl 2 Irvine (92614) **(P-2345)**
Empi Inc......D......714 446-9606
301 E Orangethorpe Ave Anaheim (92801) **(P-6437)**
Empire Building Services Inc......D......714 836-7700
1570 E Edinger Ave Ste D Santa Ana (92705) **(P-13919)**
Empire Chauffeur Service Ltd......D......310 414-8189
600 S Allied Way El Segundo (90245) **(P-3884)**
Empire Cls Worldwide, El Segundo *Also called Cls Trnsprttion Los Angles LLC* **(P-3662)**
Empire Community Painting, Irvine *Also called Empcc Inc* **(P-2345)**
Empire Community Painting, Irvine *Also called D P S Inc* **(P-2342)**
Empire Company LLC......D......951 742-5273
31 Heron Ln Riverside (92507) **(P-6616)**
Empire Demolition Inc......D......909 393-8300
1623 Leeson Ln Corona (92879) **(P-3147)**
Empire Disposal LLC......E......909 797-9125
5455 Industrial Pkwy San Bernardino (92407) **(P-6203)**
Empire Enterprises Inc......C......562 529-2676
8800 Park St Bellflower (90706) **(P-3668)**
Empire Estates Inc......D......909 980-3100
10750 Civic Center Dr # 100 Rancho Cucamonga (91730) **(P-11113)**
Empire Internation, El Segundo *Also called Empire Chauffeur Service Ltd* **(P-3884)**
Empire Leasing Inc......D......949 646-7400
2045 Placentia Ave Ste A Costa Mesa (92627) **(P-2930)**
Empire Oil Co......D......909 877-0226
2756 S Riverside Ave Bloomington (92316) **(P-8727)**
Empire Parking, Bellflower *Also called Empire Enterprises Inc* **(P-3668)**
Empire Realty Associates Inc......D......925 217-5000
380 Diablo Rd Danville (94526) **(P-11114)**
Empire Southwest LLC......B......760 545-6200
3393 Us Highway 86 Imperial (92251) **(P-7470)**
Empire Transportation......B......562 529-2676
8800 Park St Bellflower (90706) **(P-3769)**
Employbridge LLC (HQ)......C......805 882-2200
301 Mentor Dr 210 Santa Barbara (93111) **(P-14272)**
Employee Benefits Security ADM......D......626 229-1000
1055 E Colo Blvd Ste 200 Pasadena (91106) **(P-10216)**
Employee Solutions, Van Nuys *Also called ME and ME Inc* **(P-14528)**
Employment & Community Options......C......858 565-9870
5050 Murphy Canyon Rd # 220 San Diego (92123) **(P-23593)**
Employment Dev Cal Dept......D......805 614-1550
1410 S Broadway Ste E Santa Maria (93454) **(P-14273)**
Employment Dev Cal Dept......A......916 654-7867
751 N St Fl 6 Sacramento (95814) **(P-14274)**
Employment Intake Training Ctr, Los Angeles *Also called Swissport Usa Inc* **(P-4798)**
Employment Training Academy......E......209 475-1529
4045 Coronado Ave Stockton (95204) **(P-24828)**
Employnet Inc......A......831 233-9999
838 S Main St Ste B Salinas (93901) **(P-14275)**
Empoweredexpansions Corp (PA)......D......310 492-5988
714 Westbourne Dr West Hollywood (90069) **(P-13340)**
Empres Financial Services LLC......D......707 643-2793
1527 Springs Rd Vallejo (94591) **(P-19879)**
EMPRES POST ACUTE REHABILITATION, Petaluma *Also called Evergreen At Petaluma LLC* **(P-19903)**
Empresas Del Bosque Inc......B......209 364-6428
51481 W Shields Ave Firebaugh (93622) **(P-320)**
Empress Care Center......D......408 287-0616
1299 S Bascom Ave San Jose (95128) **(P-20550)**
Empyr Incorporated......D......888 664-5669
8910 University Center Ln # 400 San Diego (92122) **(P-13422)**
Emq Familiesfirst, Campbell *Also called Uplift Family Services* **(P-23521)**
Emq Familiesfirst, Los Gatos *Also called Uplift Family Services* **(P-22153)**
EMR Cpr LLC......B......408 471-6804
48511 Warm Springs Blvd # 206 Fremont (94539) **(P-15589)**
Ems Construction Inc......D......858 679-8292
3276 Highland Dr Carlsbad (92008) **(P-1474)**
Emser International LLC (PA)......D......323 650-2000
8431 Santa Monica Blvd Los Angeles (90069) **(P-6683)**
Emser Tile LLC......D......909 974-1600
5300 Shea Center Dr Ontario (91761) **(P-2895)**
Emsoc, Orange *Also called Emergency Medicine Specialist* **(P-20870)**

En Pointe Technologies Sls LLC......C......310 337-6151
1940 E Mariposa Ave El Segundo (90245) **(P-6829)**
Enbio Corp......C......818 953-9976
150 E Olive Ave Ste 212 Burbank (91502) **(P-26594)**
Enbiz International, Lake Forest *Also called Cloudradiant Corp* **(P-8961)**
Enbiz International, San Jose *Also called Cloudradiant Corp* **(P-8962)**
Encina Pepper Tree Joint Ventr (PA)......D......805 687-5511
3850 State St Santa Barbara (93105) **(P-12250)**
Encina Wastewater Authority......D......760 438-3941
6200 Avenida Encinas Carlsbad (92011) **(P-6130)**
Encina Water Pollution Control, Carlsbad *Also called Encina Wastewater Authority* **(P-6130)**
Encinitas Memory Care Cmnty, Encinitas *Also called Silverado Senior Living Inc* **(P-20686)**
Encinitas Ranch Golf Course, Encinitas *Also called JC Resorts LLC* **(P-26271)**
Encino Branch, Encino *Also called Umpqua Bank* **(P-9120)**
Encino Center Car Wash Inc......E......818 788-6300
16300 Ventura Blvd Encino (91436) **(P-17373)**
Encino Hospital Medical Center......B......818 995-5000
16237 Ventura Blvd Encino (91436) **(P-20871)**
Encino Trzana Regional Med Ctr......B......818 995-5000
16237 Ventura Blvd Encino (91436) **(P-20872)**
Encompass Community Services......B......831 724-3885
225 Westridge Dr Watsonville (95076) **(P-23209)**
Encompass Health Corporation......C......714 832-9200
14851 Yorba St Tustin (92780) **(P-22025)**
Encompass Health Corporation......C......661 323-5500
5001 Commerce Dr Bakersfield (93309) **(P-23916)**
Encompass Health Corporation......D......510 547-2244
3875 Telegraph Ave Oakland (94609) **(P-21472)**
Encore Aerospace LLC......D......562 344-1700
1729 Apollo Ct Seal Beach (90740) **(P-3400)**
Encore Capital Group Inc (PA)......D......877 445-4581
3111 Cmino Del Rio N Ste San Diego (92108) **(P-9481)**
Encore Cnsmr Capitl Fund II LP (PA)......D......415 296-9850
111 Pine St Ste 1825 San Francisco (94111) **(P-11910)**
Encore Events Rentals Inc......D......707 431-3500
20 Mill St Healdsburg (95448) **(P-16765)**
Encore Fund LP......D......415 676-4000
555 California St # 2975 San Francisco (94104) **(P-11723)**
Encore Gymnstics Dnce Climbing, Concord *Also called Encore Inc* **(P-18688)**
Encore Inc......E......925 932-1033
999 Bancroft Rd Concord (94518) **(P-18688)**
Encore Semi Inc......D......858 225-4993
9444 Waples St Ste 150 San Diego (92121) **(P-25051)**
Encore Senior Living III LLC......E......951 360-1616
6280 Clay St Riverside (92509) **(P-10722)**
Encore Senior Vlg At Riverside, Riverside *Also called Encore Senior Living III LLC* **(P-10722)**
End To End Analytics LLC......D......650 331-9659
2595 E Byshore Rd Ste 150 Palo Alto (94303) **(P-27059)**
End-Time Message & Support......E......323 756-6252
855 W 125th St Los Angeles (90044) **(P-11911)**
Endemol......D......310 860-9914
9255 W Sunset Blvd # 1100 West Hollywood (90069) **(P-17908)**
Endocrine Sciences Inc......C......818 880-8040
4301 Lost Hills Rd Calabasas (91301) **(P-21527)**
Endorse Corp......A......617 470-8332
60 E 3rd Ave San Mateo (94401) **(P-6830)**
Endurance Lending Network, San Francisco *Also called Funding Circle Usa Inc* **(P-9482)**
Energetic Lath & Plaster, North Highlands *Also called Energetic Pntg & Drywall Inc* **(P-2785)**
Energetic Pntg & Drywall Inc (PA)......C......916 488-8455
2929 Orange Grove Ave North Highlands (95660) **(P-2785)**
Energy Enterprises USA Inc (PA)......D......424 339-0005
6842 Van Nuys Blvd # 800 Van Nuys (91405) **(P-2127)**
Energy Experts International......C......559 449-1124
7111 N Fresno St Ste 260 Fresno (93720) **(P-27060)**
Energy Innovations Inc......C......626 585-6900
130 W Union St Pasadena (91103) **(P-25745)**
Energy Resource Center, Downey *Also called Southern California Gas Co* **(P-5986)**
Energy Salvage Inc......E......916 737-8640
8231 Alpine Ave Ste 3 Sacramento (95826) **(P-26219)**
Energy Store of California Inc......D......916 825-8751
14958 Venado Dr Rancho Murieta (95683) **(P-2128)**
Enerpath Services Inc......D......909 335-1699
1758 Orange Tree Ln Redlands (92374) **(P-2488)**
Enertis Solar Inc......E......415 400-5271
1750 Montgomery St # 127 San Francisco (94111) **(P-25052)**
Enexus Global Inc......D......510 936-4044
39510 Paseo Padre Pkwy # 390 Fremont (94538) **(P-15992)**
Engagio Inc......E......650 265-2264
181 2nd Ave Ste 200 San Mateo (94401) **(P-15319)**
Enganering and Technical Svcs, Santa Maria *Also called Caci Nss Inc* **(P-6812)**
Engie Services US Inc (HQ)......D......844 678-3772
500 12th St Ste 300 Oakland (94607) **(P-25053)**
Engility LLC......C......510 357-4610
2700 Merced St San Leandro (94577) **(P-25054)**
Engility LLC......C......858 552-9500
3033 Science Park Rd San Diego (92121) **(P-25055)**
Engility LLC......A......703 633-8300
200 W Los Angeles Ave Simi Valley (93065) **(P-25056)**
Engineerai Corp......E......650 721-1158
6300 Arizona Cir Los Angeles (90045) **(P-14786)**
Engineered Forest Products LLC......D......925 376-0881
1340 Bollinger Cyn Moraga (94556) **(P-11912)**
Engineered Soil Repairs Inc (PA)......D......408 297-2150
1267 Springbrook Rd Walnut Creek (94597) **(P-2711)**
Engineered Well Svc Intl Inc......C......866 913-6283
3120 Standard St Bakersfield (93308) **(P-1019)**
Engineering Division, Lancaster *Also called County of Los Angeles* **(P-25018)**

ALPHABETIC

Employee Codes: A=Over 500 employees, B=251-500
C=101-250, D=51-100, E=50
2020 Directory of California
Wholesalers and Services Companies
© Mergent Inc. 1-800-342-5647
1259

Engineering Public Works, Glendale *Also called City of Glendale* ***(P-25003)***
Engineering/Remdtn Rsrcs Grp (PA)....D....925 839-2200
4585 Pacheco Blvd Ste 200 Martinez (94553) ***(P-6347)***
Enginring Capitl Projects Dept, San Diego *Also called City of San Diego* ***(P-27031)***
Enginring Sftwr Sys Sltons Inc (PA)....D....619 338-0380
550 W C St Ste 1630 San Diego (92101) ***(P-25057)***
Englekirk Institutional Inc (PA)....E....323 733-2640
888 S Figueroa St Ste 180 Los Angeles (90017) ***(P-25058)***
Englekirk Structural Engineers (PA)....E....323 733-6673
888 S Figueroa St # 1800 Los Angeles (90017) ***(P-25059)***
English Oaks Convalescent....C....209 577-1001
2633 W Rumble Rd Modesto (95350) ***(P-20551)***
English Oaks Convalescent & RE, Modesto *Also called English Oaks Convalescent* ***(P-20551)***
Engstrom Lipscomb and Lack A (PA)....D....310 552-3800
10100 Santa Monica Blvd # 1200 Los Angeles (90067) ***(P-22496)***
Enhanced Landscape MGT Inc....D....805 557-2737
1938 E Thousand Oaks Blvd Thousand Oaks (91362) ***(P-808)***
Enlighticare Inc....D....831 750-3546
138 Victoria Ln Aptos (95003) ***(P-21473)***
Enloe Homecare Services, Chico *Also called Enloe Medical Center* ***(P-21737)***
Enloe Hospt-Phys Thrpy....C....530 891-7300
1444 Magnolia Ave Chico (95926) ***(P-20873)***
Enloe Medical Center....D....530 332-4111
560 Cohasset Rd Chico (95926) ***(P-20874)***
Enloe Medical Center....B....530 332-7522
175 W 5th Ave Chico (95926) ***(P-18973)***
Enloe Medical Center....B....530 332-6050
1390 E Lassen Ave Chico (95973) ***(P-21737)***
Enloe Medical Center....D....530 332-6138
340 W East Ave Chico (95926) ***(P-19665)***
Enloe Medical Center....C....530 332-6400
888 Lakeside Vlg Cmns Chico (95928) ***(P-20875)***
Enloe Medical Center....B....530 332-6000
1515 Sprngfeld Dr Ste 175 Chico (95928) ***(P-18974)***
Enloe Outpatient Center, Chico *Also called Enloe Medical Center* ***(P-20875)***
Enloe Rehabilitation Center, Chico *Also called Enloe Medical Center* ***(P-19665)***
Enns Farms, Kingsburg *Also called Enns Packing Company Inc* ***(P-202)***
Enns Packing Company Inc....E....559 897-7700
1911 Bergren Ct Kingsburg (93631) ***(P-202)***
Enpower Management Corp....E....925 244-1100
2410 Camino Ramon Ste 360 San Ramon (94583) ***(P-5840)***
Enquero Inc....D....408 406-3203
1551 Mccarthy Blvd # 207 Milpitas (95035) ***(P-15590)***
Enrich Financial Inc....D....818 237-2100
18653 Ventura Blvd Tarzana (91356) ***(P-9811)***
Enrichment Eductl Experiences....D....818 989-7509
4400 Coldwater Canyon Ave # 300 Studio City (91604) ***(P-23722)***
Ensighten Inc (HQ)....D....650 249-4712
226 Airport Pkwy Ste 390 San Jose (95110) ***(P-26595)***
Ensign Cloverdale LLC....D....707 894-5201
300 Cherry Creek Rd Cloverdale (95425) ***(P-19880)***
Ensign Group Inc....D....949 642-0387
340 Victoria St Costa Mesa (92627) ***(P-19881)***
Ensign Group Inc....D....562 923-9301
13007 Paramount Blvd Downey (90242) ***(P-19882)***
Ensign Group Inc....C....818 893-6385
9541 Van Nuys Blvd Panorama City (91402) ***(P-19883)***
Ensign Group Inc....C....562 947-7817
10426 Bogardus Ave Whittier (90603) ***(P-19884)***
Ensign Group Inc....C....707 525-1250
3751 Montgomery Dr Santa Rosa (95405) ***(P-19885)***
Ensign Group Inc....D....760 746-0303
201 N Fig St Escondido (92025) ***(P-19886)***
Ensign Group Inc....D....626 607-2400
4800 Delta Ave Rosemead (91770) ***(P-19887)***
Ensign Palm I LLC....D....760 323-2638
2990 E Ramon Rd Palm Springs (92264) ***(P-19888)***
Ensign Services Inc....D....949 487-9500
27101 Puerta Real Ste 450 Mission Viejo (92691) ***(P-19889)***
Ensign Southland LLC....C....949 487-9500
29222 Rancho Viejo Rd # 127 San Juan Capistrano (92675) ***(P-19890)***
Ent Facial Surgery Center, Fresno *Also called Central California Ear Nose* ***(P-18882)***
Entangled Group, San Francisco *Also called Entangled Ventures LLC* ***(P-27061)***
Entangled Ventures LLC (PA)....D....415 795-2767
55 2nd St Ste 2500 San Francisco (94105) ***(P-27061)***
Entco LLC (HQ)....B....312 580-9100
1140 Enterprise Way Sunnyvale (94089) ***(P-15320)***
Entercom Communications Corp....C....916 766-5000
5345 Madison Ave Sacramento (95841) ***(P-5525)***
Entercom Communications Corp....C....610 660-5610
201 3rd St Fl 12 San Francisco (94103) ***(P-5526)***
Entercom Communications Corp....C....916 334-7777
5345 Madison Ave Ste 100 Sacramento (95841) ***(P-5527)***
Enterprise Events Group Inc....C....415 499-4444
950 Northgate Dr Ste 100 San Rafael (94903) ***(P-26596)***
Enterprise Holdings Inc....D....559 261-9221
780 W Pinedale Ave Fresno (93711) ***(P-17203)***
Enterprise Rent A Car....C....949 240-7000
33949 Camino Capistrano San Juan Capistrano (92675) ***(P-17204)***
Enterprise Rent-A-Car....D....760 772-0281
78385 Varner Rd Ste D Palm Desert (92211) ***(P-17205)***
Enterprise Rent-A-Car....D....619 297-0311
2942 Kettner Blvd San Diego (92101) ***(P-17206)***
Enterprise Rent-A-Car (HQ)....D....657 221-4400
333 City Blvd W Ste 1000 Orange (92868) ***(P-17207)***
Enterprise Rent-A-Car....D....949 373-9350
28112 Camino Capistrano Laguna Niguel (92677) ***(P-17208)***
Enterprise Rent-A-Car Compan....D....916 576-3164
6320 Mcnair Cir Sacramento (95837) ***(P-17209)***
Enterprise Rent-A-Car Compan (HQ)....E....916 787-4500
150 N Sunrise Ave Roseville (95661) ***(P-17210)***
Enterprise Roofing Service Inc....D....925 689-8100
2400 Bates Ave Concord (94520) ***(P-3052)***
Enterprise Services LLC....A....916 636-1000
3215 Prospect Park Dr Rancho Cordova (95670) ***(P-15756)***
Enterprise Services LLC....B....619 817-3851
3990 Sherman St San Diego (92110) ***(P-15757)***
Enterprise Services LLC....C....310 331-1074
1 Hornet Way El Segundo (90245) ***(P-15758)***
Enterprise Signal Inc....D....877 256-8303
440 N Wolfe Rd Sunnyvale (94085) ***(P-15321)***
Enterprise Solutions Inc....C....408 727-3627
2855 Kifer Rd Santa Clara (95051) ***(P-27062)***
Enterprise Vineyards....E....707 996-6513
16600 Norrbom Rd Sonoma (95476) ***(P-130)***
Entertainment & Sports Today....D....213 388-9050
2966 Wilshire Blvd Ste C Los Angeles (90010) ***(P-5595)***
Entertainment Partners Inc (PA)....B....818 955-6000
2950 N Hollywood Way Burbank (91505) ***(P-25582)***
Entertinment Studios Media Inc (PA)....D....310 277-3500
1925 Century Park E # 1025 Los Angeles (90067) ***(P-17972)***
Entitlement LLC....E....224 336-2669
1236 Euclid St Santa Monica (90404) ***(P-17973)***
Entravision Radio, Sacramento *Also called Entravsion Communications Corp* ***(P-5599)***
Entravsion Communications Corp....E....831 333-9736
67 Garden Ct Monterey (93940) ***(P-5596)***
Entravsion Communications Corp....D....323 900-6100
5700 Wilshire Blvd # 250 Los Angeles (90036) ***(P-5597)***
Entravsion Communications Corp....D....760 568-3636
72920 Parkview Dr Palm Desert (92260) ***(P-5598)***
Entravsion Communications Corp....E....916 646-4000
1792 Tribute Rd Ste 450 Sacramento (95815) ***(P-5528)***
Entravsion Communications Corp....E....916 648-6029
1792 Tribute Rd Ste 450 Sacramento (95815) ***(P-5599)***
Entravsion Communications Corp (PA)....C....310 447-3870
2425 Olympic Blvd Ste 600 Santa Monica (90404) ***(P-5600)***
Entrepreneur Preferred, Murrieta *Also called Inzunza Real Estate Inc* ***(P-11212)***
Entrepreneurial Capital Corp....C....949 809-3900
4100 Nwport Pl Dr Ste 400 Newport Beach (92660) ***(P-10587)***
Entrepreneurial Hospitality....C....951 346-4700
3485 Mission Inn Ave Riverside (92501) ***(P-16766)***
Envent Corporation (PA)....C....562 997-9465
3220 E 29th St Long Beach (90806) ***(P-27063)***
Enviance Inc (HQ)....D....760 496-0200
5857 Owens Ave Ste 102 Carlsbad (92008) ***(P-14787)***
Enviro Tech Chemical Svcs Inc (PA)....C....209 581-9576
500 Winmoore Way Modesto (95358) ***(P-8698)***
Environment Control, Visalia *Also called Tim Hofer Inc* ***(P-14064)***
Environment Control....E....559 456-9791
3065 N Sunnyside Ave # 101 Fresno (93727) ***(P-13920)***
Environmental Chemical Corp (PA)....D....650 347-1555
1240 Bayshore Hwy Burlingame (94010) ***(P-25060)***
Environmental Construction Inc....D....818 449-8920
21550 Oxnard St Ste 1060 Woodland Hills (91367) ***(P-1475)***
Environmental Health Hazard....D....510 622-3200
1515 Clay St Ste 1600 Oakland (94612) ***(P-26070)***
Environmental Industries, Fillmore *Also called Brightview Tree Company* ***(P-956)***
Environmental Ldscp Solutions, Sacramento *Also called Els Investments* ***(P-726)***
Environmental Protection Agcy....D....916 324-7572
1001 I St Ste 19b Sacramento (95814) ***(P-6348)***
Environmental Resolutions Inc....B....949 457-8950
25371 Commercentre Dr # 250 Lake Forest (92630) ***(P-27064)***
Environmental Resources MGT, Walnut Creek *Also called Erm-West Inc* ***(P-25065)***
Environmental Science Assoc (PA)....D....415 896-5900
550 Kearny St Ste 800 San Francisco (94108) ***(P-25746)***
Environmental Science Assoc....B....626 204-6170
80 S Lake Ave Ste 570 Pasadena (91101) ***(P-25747)***
Environmental Systems Inc (PA)....D....408 980-1711
3353 De La Cruz Blvd Santa Clara (95054) ***(P-2129)***
Environmental Systems Research....D....916 448-2412
1600 K St Ste 4c Sacramento (95814) ***(P-6831)***
Environments For Learning Inc (PA)....D....949 855-5630
24291 Muirlands Blvd Lake Forest (92630) ***(P-23723)***
Environments Plus (PA)....D....866 865-8120
1700 1st St San Fernando (91340) ***(P-3401)***
Envise....D....714 901-5800
12131 Western Ave Garden Grove (92841) ***(P-2130)***
Envivio Inc....C....650 243-2700
535 Mission St Fl 27 San Francisco (94105) ***(P-5397)***
Envoy Inc....D....415 787-7871
410 Townsend St Ste 410 # 410 San Francisco (94107) ***(P-14788)***
Envoy Air Inc....E....619 260-9069
3707 N Harbor Dr Ste 124 San Diego (92101) ***(P-4663)***
Envrionmental Science Assoc, Pasadena *Also called Environmental Science Assoc* ***(P-25747)***
Enxco, San Diego *Also called Edf Renewables Services Inc* ***(P-17354)***
Eoc Resource Development, Fresno *Also called Fresno Cnty Economic Opportunt* ***(P-23234)***
Eon Innovative Technology Inc....C....213 381-0061
10645 W Vanowen St Burbank (91505) ***(P-16512)***
Eon Reality Inc (PA)....E....949 460-2000
39 Parker Ste 100 Irvine (92618) ***(P-6832)***
Ep Wealth Advisors LLC....D....925 283-2201
250 Lafayette Cir Lafayette (94549) ***(P-9812)***
Epak9, El Cajon *Also called Executive Protection Agency K-* ***(P-16270)***
Epcm Prof Svc Partners LLC....D....562 936-1000
2017 Palo Verde Ave Long Beach (90815) ***(P-26597)***

Mergent e-mail: customerrelations@mergent.com
1260
2020 Directory of California
Wholesalers and Services Companies
(P-0000) Products & Services Section entry number
(PA)=Parent Co (HQ)=Headquarters (DH)=Div Headquarters

ALPHABETIC SECTION
Eskaton (PA)

Ephonamationcom Inc ....C....714 560-1000
145 E Columbine Ave Santa Ana (92707) ***(P-16767)***

Epic Insurance, San Francisco *Also called Edgewood Partners Insur Ctr* ***(P-10346)***

Epic Jet Centre, San Luis Obispo *Also called Aviation Consultants Inc* ***(P-26146)***

Epic Management LP (PA) ....C....909 799-1818
1615 Orange Tree Ln Redlands (92374) ***(P-26220)***

Epic Sciences Inc ....D....858 356-6610
9381 Judicial Dr Ste 200 San Diego (92121) ***(P-21528)***

Epic War, Palo Alto *Also called Machine Zone Inc* ***(P-14922)***

Epicenter Live Inc ....C....424 235-4835
4040 Mahaila Ave Unit A San Diego (92122) ***(P-17909)***

Epicentro Advertising Mktg Svc ....E....408 453-0353
2370 Qume Dr Ste B San Jose (95131) ***(P-13502)***

Epicor Software Corporation ....C....925 361-9900
4120 Dublin Blvd Ste 300 Dublin (94568) ***(P-15322)***

Epidendio Construction Inc ....E....707 994-5100
11325 Highway 29 Lower Lake (95457) ***(P-3148)***

Episcopal Comm Svc San Fran (PA) ....C....415 487-3300
165 8th St Fl 3 San Francisco (94103) ***(P-23210)***

Episcopal Communities & Servic ....D....310 544-2204
5801 Crestridge Rd Pls Vrds Pnsl (90275) ***(P-19891)***

Episcopal Community ....D....619 228-2800
1261 Third Ave Ste B Chula Vista (91911) ***(P-23211)***

Episcopal Senior Communities ....C....408 354-0211
110 Wood Rd Ofc Los Gatos (95030) ***(P-23917)***

Epitec Inc ....A....760 650-2515
515 Olive Ave Vista (92083) ***(P-14789)***

Epitome Enterprises LLC ....D....909 625-4728
821 Mary Pl Claremont (91711) ***(P-14790)***

Epitomics Inc (HQ) ....D....650 583-6688
863 Mitten Rd Ste 103 Burlingame (94010) ***(P-25748)***

Epixel Solutions ....D....650 616-4488
1001 Bayhill Dr San Bruno (94066) ***(P-26598)***

Eplica Inc (PA) ....C....619 260-2000
2355 Northside Dr Ste 120 San Diego (92108) ***(P-14503)***

Eplica Corporate Services Inc ....A....619 282-1400
2375 Northside Dr Ste 360 San Diego (92108) ***(P-14276)***

Epochcom LLC ....C....310 664-5700
3110 Main St Ste 220 Santa Monica (90405) ***(P-15759)***

Eppink of California Inc ....E....562 633-1275
11900 Center St South Gate (90280) ***(P-2931)***

Epri Csg, Palo Alto *Also called Eprisolutions Inc* ***(P-25061)***

Eprisolutions Inc ....D....650 855-8900
3412 Hillview Ave Palo Alto (94304) ***(P-25061)***

Eps Corporate Holdings Inc ....D....714 635-3131
1235 S Lewis St Anaheim (92805) ***(P-7418)***

Epsilon Mission Solutions Inc ....D....619 702-1700
9242 Lightwave Ave # 100 San Diego (92123) ***(P-25062)***

Epsilon Systems Solutions Inc ....E....619 474-3252
2101 Haffley Ave A National City (91950) ***(P-24337)***

Epsilon Systems Solutions Inc ....C....619 702-1700
5482 Complex St Ste 109 San Diego (92123) ***(P-25063)***

Epsilon Systems Solutions Inc (PA) ....D....619 702-1700
9242 Lightwave Ave # 100 San Diego (92123) ***(P-25064)***

Epson America Inc ....C....562 290-5855
1650 Glenn Curtiss St Carson (90746) ***(P-4403)***

Epson West, Carson *Also called Epson America Inc* ***(P-4403)***

Epstein Becker & Green PC ....D....310 556-8861
1875 Century Park E # 500 Los Angeles (90067) ***(P-22497)***

Eqal Inc ....C....818 276-6300
5250 Lankershim Blvd # 720 North Hollywood (91601) ***(P-13503)***

Equal Access International ....D....415 561-4884
1212 Market St Ste 200 San Francisco (94102) ***(P-2489)***

Equator LLC (HQ) ....C....310 469-9500
6060 Center Dr Ste 500 Los Angeles (90045) ***(P-14791)***

Equator Business Solutions, Los Angeles *Also called Equator LLC* ***(P-14791)***

Equicare Medical Supply Inc ....D....213 385-1715
1154 S Alvarado St Los Angeles (90006) ***(P-19892)***

Equilar Inc ....C....877 441-6090
1100 Marshall St Redwood City (94063) ***(P-16768)***

Equinix Inc (PA) ....C....650 598-6000
1 Lagoon Dr Ste 400 Redwood City (94065) ***(P-11852)***

Equinix (us) Enterprises Inc (HQ) ....D....650 598-6363
1 Lagoon Dr Redwood City (94065) ***(P-5786)***

Equinox Fitness Club, San Francisco *Also called Equinox Holdings Inc* ***(P-18141)***

Equinox Fitness Club, Irvine *Also called Equinox-76th Street Inc* ***(P-18143)***

Equinox Holdings Inc ....B....415 243-0492
747 Market St San Francisco (94103) ***(P-18141)***

Equinox-76th Street Inc ....D....415 398-0747
301 Pine St San Francisco (94104) ***(P-18142)***

Equinox-76th Street Inc ....D....949 296-1700
19540 Jamboree Rd Irvine (92612) ***(P-18143)***

Equinox-76th Street Inc ....B....949 975-8400
1980 Main St Fl 4 Irvine (92614) ***(P-19666)***

Equistar Irvine Company LLC ....D....949 833-3331
18800 Macarthur Blvd Irvine (92612) ***(P-12251)***

Equitable Life Assurance, San Diego *Also called Axa Equitable Life Insur Co* ***(P-10293)***

Equitable Variable Lf Insur Co ....D....619 239-0018
701 B St Ste 1500 San Diego (92101) ***(P-9866)***

Equity Title Company (HQ) ....D....818 291-4400
801 N Brand Blvd Ste 400 Glendale (91203) ***(P-10181)***

ERA Realty Center ....D....530 295-2900
49 Placerville Dr Placerville (95667) ***(P-11115)***

Erepublic Inc (PA) ....C....916 932-1300
100 Blue Ravine Rd Folsom (95630) ***(P-16769)***

Erewhon Natural Foods Market, Calabasas *Also called Nowher Partners LLC* ***(P-8620)***

Ergomotion Inc ....D....805 979-9400
6790 Navigator Way Goleta (93117) ***(P-6513)***

Ergs Aim Hotel Realty LLC ....D....714 938-1111
400 N State College Blvd Orange (92868) ***(P-12252)***

Ergs Aim Hotel Realty LLC ....D....949 661-1100
34402 Pacific Coast Hwy Dana Point (92624) ***(P-12253)***

Eric D Feldman MD Inc ....E....562 424-6666
2760 Atlantic Ave Long Beach (90806) ***(P-18975)***

Eric Jones Customs Brokerage ....E....310 348-3777
9841 Arprt Blvd Ste 1400 Los Angeles (90045) ***(P-4937)***

Eric Stark Interiors Inc ....D....408 441-6136
2284 Paragon Dr San Jose (95131) ***(P-2786)***

Erickson Construction LP ....C....916 774-1100
8350 Industrial Ave Roseville (95678) ***(P-2932)***

Erickson-Hall Construction Co (PA) ....D....760 796-7700
500 Corporate Dr Escondido (92029) ***(P-1476)***

Ericsson Inc ....A....408 750-5000
2755 Augustine Dr Santa Clara (95054) ***(P-5398)***

Ericsson Inc ....A....408 597-3600
100 Headquarters Dr San Jose (95134) ***(P-15591)***

Erlanger Distribution Ctr Inc ....E....951 784-5147
797 Palmyrita Ave Riverside (92507) ***(P-4404)***

Erlanger Sales, Riverside *Also called Erlanger Distribution Ctr Inc* ***(P-4404)***

Erm-West Inc (HQ) ....D....925 946-0455
1277 Treat Blvd Ste 500 Walnut Creek (94597) ***(P-25065)***

Ernest Gallo Clinic & RES Ctr ....C....510 985-3856
5980 Horton St Ste 370 Emeryville (94608) ***(P-25894)***

Ernest Packaging (PA) ....C....800 233-7788
5777 Smithway St Commerce (90040) ***(P-8969)***

Ernest Packaging Solutions, Sacramento *Also called Calvey Incorporated* ***(P-7876)***

Ernest Paper, Commerce *Also called Ernest Packaging* ***(P-8969)***

Ernie & Sons Scaffolding ....C....925 446-4442
1960 Olivera Rd Concord (94520) ***(P-3402)***

Ernst & Young LLP ....A....213 977-3200
725 S Figueroa St Ste 200 Los Angeles (90017) ***(P-25583)***

Ernst & Young LLP ....C....310 725-1764
200 N Pacific Coast Hwy # 2 El Segundo (90245) ***(P-25584)***

Ernst & Young LLP ....D....415 894-8000
560 Mission St Ste 1600 San Francisco (94105) ***(P-25585)***

Ernst & Young LLP ....C....650 496-1600
1451 California Ave Palo Alto (94304) ***(P-25586)***

Ernst & Young LLP ....A....408 947-5500
303 Almaden Blvd Ste 1000 San Jose (95110) ***(P-25587)***

Ernst & Young LLP ....C....858 535-7200
4370 La Jolla Village Dr # 500 San Diego (92122) ***(P-25588)***

Ernst & Young LLP ....B....949 794-2300
18101 Von Karman Ave # 1700 Irvine (92612) ***(P-25589)***

Ernst & Young LLP ....C....949 838-3300
18006 Sky Park Cir # 106 Irvine (92614) ***(P-25590)***

Ernst & Young LLP ....D....805 778-7000
2931 Townsgate Rd Ste 100 Westlake Village (91361) ***(P-25591)***

Ernst & Young LLP ....C....650 802-4500
275 Shoreline Dr Ste 600 Redwood City (94065) ***(P-25592)***

Ernst & Young LLP ....C....916 218-1900
2901 Douglas Blvd Ste 300 Roseville (95661) ***(P-25593)***

Ernst & Young LLP ....C....925 734-6388
4301 Hacienda Dr Ste 450 Pleasanton (94588) ***(P-25594)***

Ernst & Young LLP ....A....415 894-8000
560 Mission St Ste 1600 San Francisco (94105) ***(P-25595)***

Ero-Tech Corp ....D....415 468-5600
2301 S El Camino Real San Mateo (94403) ***(P-17786)***

Erp Integrated Solutions Inc ....D....562 425-7800
1501 Hughes Way Ste 320 Long Beach (90810) ***(P-14792)***

Errama Trucking Company Inc ....E....818 381-3341
11336 Montgomery Ave Granada Hills (91344) ***(P-4009)***

Errg, Martinez *Also called Engineering/Remdtn Rsrcs Grp* ***(P-6347)***

ERs SEC Alarm Systems Inc ....D....626 579-2525
4538 Santa Anita Ave El Monte (91731) ***(P-7149)***

Erwin Street Medical Offices, Woodland Hills *Also called Kaiser Foundation Hospitals* ***(P-20961)***

Es Engineering Inc ....D....714 919-6500
1 Park Plz Ste 1000 Irvine (92614) ***(P-27065)***

Es Engineering Services LLC ....D....949 988-3500
1 Park Plz Ste 1000 Irvine (92614) ***(P-25066)***

Es3 LLC ....E....209 832-4205
857 Stonebridge Dr Tracy (95376) ***(P-4405)***

ESA, San Francisco *Also called Environmental Science Assoc* ***(P-25746)***

ESA P Prtfolio Oper Lessee LLC ....E....949 851-2711
4881 Birch St Newport Beach (92660) ***(P-12254)***

ESA P Prtfolio Oper Lessee LLC ....D....714 639-8608
1635 W Katella Ave Orange (92867) ***(P-12255)***

ESA Risk Management, San Jose *Also called SCC ESA Dept of Risk Mgmt* ***(P-10482)***

Esaloncom LLC ....D....866 550-2424
1910 E Maple Ave El Segundo (90245) ***(P-13341)***

Esc Entertainment Inc ....C....818 954-1018
4000 Warner Blvd Burbank (91522) ***(P-17739)***

Escalate Inc (HQ) ....B....858 457-3888
10680 Treena St Ste 170 San Diego (92131) ***(P-14793)***

Escalate Retail, San Diego *Also called Escalate Inc* ***(P-14793)***

Escondido Country Club, Poway *Also called American Golf Corporation* ***(P-18364)***

Escondido Medical Offices, Escondido *Also called Kaiser Foundation Hospitals* ***(P-19116)***

Escondido Memory Care Cmnty, Escondido *Also called Silverado Senior Living Inc* ***(P-20685)***

Escondido Veterans Center, Escondido *Also called Veterans Health Administration* ***(P-19567)***

Eset LLC (HQ) ....D....619 876-5400
610 W Ash St Ste 1700 San Diego (92101) ***(P-6833)***

Eset North America, San Diego *Also called Eset LLC* ***(P-6833)***

Eskaton (PA) ....A....916 334-0296
5105 Manzanita Ave Ste D Carmichael (95608) ***(P-10588)***

ALPHABETIC

Eskaton......D......916 852-7900
11390 Coloma Rd Ofc Gold River (95670) *(P-20428)*
Eskaton Center of Greenhaven, Sacramento *Also called Eskaton Properties Inc (P-19895)*
Eskaton Lodge......E......916 789-0326
22 Cadillac Dr Apt 301 Sacramento (95825) *(P-23918)*
Eskaton Properties Inc......A......916 974-2060
3847 Walnut Ave Carmichael (95608) *(P-19893)*
Eskaton Properties Inc......D......916 331-8513
5318 Manzanita Ave Carmichael (95608) *(P-23919)*
Eskaton Properties Inc......D......916 334-0810
1650 Eskaton Loop Roseville (95747) *(P-23920)*
Eskaton Properties Inc......C......916 965-4663
11300 Fair Oaks Blvd Fair Oaks (95628) *(P-19894)*
Eskaton Properties Inc......C......916 393-2550
455 Florin Rd Sacramento (95831) *(P-19895)*
Eskaton Properties Inc (PA)......D......916 334-0810
5105 Manzanita Ave Ste A Carmichael (95608) *(P-19896)*
Eskaton Properties Inc......C......916 974-2000
3939 Walnut Ave Unit 399 Carmichael (95608) *(P-23921)*
Eskaton Village Care Center, Carmichael *Also called Eskaton Properties Inc (P-19893)*
Eskaton Village Charmichael, Carmichael *Also called Eskaton Properties Inc (P-23921)*
Eskaton Village Roseville, Roseville *Also called Eskaton Properties Inc (P-23920)*
Esl, Burbank *Also called Turtle Entertainment America (P-18013)*
Esl Technologies Inc......B......916 677-4500
8875 Washington Blvd B Roseville (95678) *(P-15915)*
Esna Corporation......E......661 206-6010
44300 Lowtree Ave Ste 100 Lancaster (93534) *(P-9624)*
Esolar Inc (HQ)......D......818 303-9500
900 Glenneyre St Laguna Beach (92651) *(P-1961)*
Esoterix Ctr For Clncal Trails, Calabasas *Also called Endocrine Sciences Inc (P-21527)*
ESP Group Ltd......D......626 301-0280
2397 Bateman Ave Duarte (91010) *(P-8072)*
Esparza Enterprises Inc......B......760 344-2031
251 W Main St Ste G&F Brawley (92227) *(P-662)*
Esparza Enterprises Inc......D......661 831-0002
3851 Fruitvale Ave A Bakersfield (93308) *(P-14277)*
Esparza Enterprises Inc......A......760 398-0349
51335 Harrison St Ste 112 Coachella (92236) *(P-14278)*
Esparza Enterprises Inc......A......661 631-0347
500 Workman St Bakersfield (93307) *(P-4010)*
Esparza Enterprises Inc......B......661 631-0347
222 S Union Ave Bakersfield (93307) *(P-14279)*
Espn Inc......B......212 456-7439
800 W Olympic Blvd Los Angeles (90015) *(P-5718)*
Esprit, Camarillo *Also called DP Technology Corp (P-14771)*
Esq Business Services Inc (PA)......D......925 734-9800
20660 Stevens Cupertino (95014) *(P-15323)*
Esquire Landscape Inc......E......858 530-2949
8380 Miralani Dr Ste B San Diego (92126) *(P-809)*
Ess......D......888 303-6424
5227 Dantes View Dr Agoura Hills (91301) *(P-2131)*
Essco, Pasadena *Also called Electric Svc & Sup Co Pasadena (P-2483)*
Essendant Co......C......626 961-0011
918 S Stimson Ave City of Industry (91745) *(P-7856)*
Essendant Co......C......916 344-6707
5440 Stationers Way Sacramento (95842) *(P-7857)*
Essense......A......323 202-4650
6300 Wilshire Blvd # 720 Los Angeles (90048) *(P-27273)*
Essential Access Health (PA)......D......213 386-5614
3600 Wilshire Blvd # 600 Los Angeles (90010) *(P-24173)*
Essential Products Inc......D......650 300-0000
380 Portage Ave Palo Alto (94306) *(P-14794)*
Essex Properties LLC......D......949 798-8100
18012 Sky Park Cir # 200 Irvine (92614) *(P-11116)*
Essex Property Trust Inc......E......323 461-9346
1234 Larrabee St West Hollywood (90069) *(P-11784)*
Essex Property Trust Inc......D......916 381-0345
8795 Folsom Blvd Ste 101 Sacramento (95826) *(P-11853)*
Essex Property Trust Inc (PA)......D......650 655-7800
1100 Park Pl Ste 200 San Mateo (94403) *(P-10723)*
Essilor Laboratories Amer Inc......D......626 969-6181
1300 W Optical Dr Irwindale (91702) *(P-7022)*
Essrig Taylor Constructions, San Diego *Also called Etc Building & Design Inc (P-16770)*
Estate Investment Group, Dublin *Also called New Home Professionals (P-11311)*
Estes Express Lines Inc......C......714 994-3770
14727 Alondra Blvd La Mirada (90638) *(P-4011)*
Estes Express Lines Inc......D......909 427-9850
10736 Cherry Ave Fontana (92337) *(P-4012)*
Estes Express Lines Inc......D......626 333-9090
13327 Temple Ave City of Industry (91746) *(P-4013)*
Estes Express Lines Inc......E......408 286-3894
1634 S 7th St San Jose (95112) *(P-4014)*
Estes Express Lines Inc......D......510 635-0165
1750 Adams Ave San Leandro (94577) *(P-4015)*
Estes Express Lines Inc......D......818 504-4155
9120 San Fernando Rd Sun Valley (91352) *(P-4016)*
Estes Express Lines Inc......D......209 982-1841
7611 S Airport Way Stockton (95206) *(P-4017)*
Estes Express Lines Inc......D......310 549-7306
1531 Blinn Ave Wilmington (90744) *(P-4018)*
Estrella Inc......C......562 925-6418
1340 Highland Ave 12 Duarte (91010) *(P-19897)*
Estrella Communications Inc......D......818 260-5700
3000 W Alameda Ave Burbank (91523) *(P-5601)*
Estuate Inc......D......408 946-0002
830 Hillview Ct Ste 280 Milpitas (95035) *(P-14795)*
Esurance Insurance Svcs Inc (HQ)......C......415 875-4500
650 Davis St San Francisco (94111) *(P-10349)*
Esys Energy Control Company......D......661 833-1902
4520 Stine Rd Ste 7 Bakersfield (93313) *(P-2490)*
Et Capital Solar Partners USA......E......925 460-9898
4900 Hopyard Rd Ste 2 Pleasanton (94588) *(P-26221)*
Et Whitehall Seascape LLC......C......310 581-5533
1910 Ocean Way Santa Monica (90405) *(P-12256)*
Etairos Consulting......E......844 219-7027
6711 Studio Pl Riverside (92509) *(P-15993)*
Etap, Irvine *Also called Operation Technology Inc (P-14983)*
Etc Building & Design Inc (PA)......C......858 554-1150
6805 Nancy Ridge Dr San Diego (92121) *(P-16770)*
Etchandy Farms LLC......D......805 983-4700
4324 E Vineyard Ave Oxnard (93036) *(P-94)*
Etchegaray Farms LLC......E......661 393-0920
32324 Famoso Rd Mc Farland (93250) *(P-384)*
Ethan Conrad Properties Inc (PA)......D......916 779-1000
1300 National Dr Ste 100 Sacramento (95834) *(P-11117)*
Etherwan Systems Inc......D......714 779-3800
2301 E Winston Rd Anaheim (92806) *(P-15994)*
Ethiopian World Federation......E......323 844-1826
422 E 41st St Los Angeles (90011) *(P-24174)*
Ethos Management Inc......E......626 456-3669
560 W Main St Alhambra (91801) *(P-26222)*
Ethosenergy Field Services LLC (HQ)......D......310 639-3523
10455 Slusher Dr Bldg 12 Santa Fe Springs (90670) *(P-1020)*
Etiwanda Historical Society......D......909 899-8432
7150 Etiwanda Ave Rancho Cucamonga (91739) *(P-24264)*
Etiwanda Power Plant, Rancho Cucamonga *Also called NRG California South LP (P-5864)*
Etna Police Activities League......C......530 467-3400
448 Main St Etna (96027) *(P-23212)*
Etouch Systems Corp......A......510 795-4800
6627 Dumbarton Cir Fremont (94555) *(P-15995)*
Etrigue Corporation......E......408 490-2900
6399 San Ignacio Ave # 200 San Jose (95119) *(P-14796)*
Ettv America Corp......D......626 581-8899
18430 San Jose Ave Ste A City of Industry (91748) *(P-5719)*
Euclid Parking, Porterville *Also called Exeter Packers Inc (P-486)*
Eugene Burger Management Corp......C......916 443-6637
555 Capitol Mall Ste 725 Sacramento (95814) *(P-26223)*
Eugene N Townsend......D......619 442-8807
609 S Marshall Ave El Cajon (92020) *(P-17288)*
Eurasia Power LLC......E......805 383-1234
4022 Cmino Ranchero Ste D Camarillo (93012) *(P-7263)*
Eureka District Office, Eureka *Also called State Compensation Insur Fund (P-10142)*
Eureka Realty Partners Inc (PA)......B......949 224-4100
4100 Macarthur Blvd # 200 Newport Beach (92660) *(P-11561)*
Eureka Rehab & Wellness Center......D......707 445-3261
2353 23rd St Eureka (95501) *(P-19898)*
Eurodent Inc......D......818 832-1325
9310 Topanga Canyon Blvd # 200 Chatsworth (91311) *(P-21609)*
Eurodrip USA Inc......D......559 674-2670
1850 W Almond Ave Madera (93637) *(P-7499)*
Eurofins Air Toxics LLC......D......916 985-1000
180 Blue Ravine Rd Ste B Folsom (95630) *(P-26071)*
Eurofins Eag Engrg Science LLC (HQ)......D......408 588-0050
2710 Walsh Ave Santa Clara (95051) *(P-26072)*
Eurofins Eag Mtls Science LLC (HQ)......C......408 454-4600
810 Kifer Rd Sunnyvale (94086) *(P-26073)*
Eurofins Food......A......609 452-4440
2441 Constitution Dr Livermore (94551) *(P-25749)*
Eurogentec North America Inc......C......510 791-9560
34801 Campus Dr Fremont (94555) *(P-27066)*
European Hotl Invstrs of CA......E......310 322-0999
1985 E Grandave El Segundo (90245) *(P-12257)*
European Hotl Invstrs of CA (PA)......D......949 474-7368
2532 Dupont Dr Irvine (92612) *(P-12258)*
European Paving Designs Inc......D......408 283-5230
1474 Berger Dr San Jose (95112) *(P-2346)*
Ev Ray Inc......E......818 346-5381
6400 Variel Ave Woodland Hills (91367) *(P-6556)*
Evangelical Christian Cr Un......C......714 671-5700
955 W Imperial Hwy # 100 Brea (92821) *(P-9392)*
Evangelical Christian Cr Un (PA)......D......714 671-5700
955 W Imperial Hwy # 100 Brea (92821) *(P-9393)*
Evangelical Covenant Church......D......619 931-1114
325 Kempton St Spring Valley (91977) *(P-23922)*
Evangelical Covenant Church......C......805 687-0701
2550 Treasure Dr Santa Barbara (93105) *(P-23923)*
Evans Hardy & Young Inc......E......805 963-5841
829 De La Vina St Ste 100 Santa Barbara (93101) *(P-13504)*
Evans Brothers Inc (PA)......D......925 443-0225
7589 National Dr Livermore (94550) *(P-3341)*
Evans/Sipes Inc (PA)......C......805 644-1242
5720 Ralston St Ste 100 Ventura (93003) *(P-11118)*
Eveg Inc......E......844 221-3359
16540 Aston Irvine (92606) *(P-14797)*
Event Rentals San Diego, San Diego *Also called Bright Event Rentals LLC (P-14134)*
Eventbrite Inc (PA)......B......415 692-7779
155 5th St Fl 7 San Francisco (94103) *(P-15996)*
Ever Win International Corp......E......626 810-8218
17579 Railroad St City of Industry (91748) *(P-7264)*
Everest Consulting Group Inc......D......510 494-8440
39650 Mission Blvd Fremont (94539) *(P-14798)*
Everest Silicon Valley MGT LP......D......510 494-8800
8200 Gateway Blvd Newark (94560) *(P-26224)*
Everest Wtrprfing Rstrtion Inc......D......415 282-9800
1270 Missouri St San Francisco (94107) *(P-13423)*
Everett Mall 01 LLC......E......818 505-6777
12411 Ventura Blvd Studio City (91604) *(P-10873)*

Mergent e-mail: customerrelations@mergent.com
1262
2020 Directory of California
Wholesalers and Services Companies
(P-0000) Products & Services Section entry number
(PA)=Parent Co (HQ)=Headquarters (DH)=Div Headquarters

Evergent Technologies Inc (PA) ....B........408 718-5453
1250 Borregas Ave Sunnyvale (94089) ***(P-14799)***
Evergreen At Chico LLC ....C........530 342-4885
1200 Springfield Dr Chico (95928) ***(P-19899)***
Evergreen At Lakeport LLC (PA) ....D........707 263-6382
1291 Craig Ave Lakeport (95453) ***(P-19900)***
Evergreen At Lakeport LLC ....C........661 871-3133
6212 Tudor Way Bakersfield (93306) ***(P-19901)***
Evergreen At Oroville LLC ....D........530 533-7335
1000 Executive Pkwy Oroville (95966) ***(P-19902)***
Evergreen At Petaluma LLC ....C........707 763-6887
300 Douglas St Petaluma (94952) ***(P-19903)***
Evergreen Cleaning Systems Inc ....E........213 386-3260
3325 Wilshire Blvd # 622 Los Angeles (90010) ***(P-13921)***
Evergreen Company Inc ....D........916 257-5994
847 E Turner Rd Lodi (95240) ***(P-26225)***
Evergreen Dstntion Hldings LLC ....D........209 379-2606
33160 Evergreen Rd Groveland (95321) ***(P-12259)***
EVERGREEN FULLERTON HEALTHCARE, Fullerton *Also called Healthcare Fullerton & Well* ***(P-20007)***
Evergreen Health Care LLC ....D........661 854-4475
323 Campus Dr Arvin (93203) ***(P-19904)***
Evergreen Healthcare Center, Bakersfield *Also called Evergreen At Lakeport LLC* ***(P-19901)***
Evergreen Lkport Halthcare Ctr, Lakeport *Also called Evergreen At Lakeport LLC* ***(P-19900)***
Evergreen Lodge, Groveland *Also called Evergreen Dstntion Hldings LLC* ***(P-12259)***
Evergreen Solar Services, Agoura Hills *Also called Ess* ***(P-2131)***
Evernote Corporation (PA) ....C........650 216-7700
305 Walnut St Redwood City (94063) ***(P-14800)***
Everwise Corporation ....D........888 250-6219
2 Embarcadero Ctr Fl 8 San Francisco (94111) ***(P-26599)***
Evga Corporation (PA) ....E........714 528-4500
408 Saturn St Brea (92821) ***(P-6834)***
Evgo Services LLC ....D........310 954-2900
11835 W Olympic Blvd 900e Los Angeles (90064) ***(P-17418)***
Evidentio Inc (HQ) ....D........855 933-1337
7901 Stoneridge Dr # 150 Pleasanton (94588) ***(P-14801)***
Evidera Archimedes Inc ....D........415 490-0400
450 Sansome St Ste 650 San Francisco (94111) ***(P-10350)***
Evikecom Inc ....D........626 286-0360
2801 W Mission Rd Alhambra (91803) ***(P-7708)***
Evisions Inc (PA) ....D........949 833-1384
440 Exchange Ste 200 Irvine (92602) ***(P-14802)***
Evolent Health Inc ....B........571 389-6000
1 Kearny St Ste 300 San Francisco (94108) ***(P-22240)***
Evolution Fresh Inc (HQ) ....D........800 794-9986
11655 Jersey Blvd Rancho Cucamonga (91730) ***(P-8466)***
Evolution Hospitality LLC (PA) ....D........949 325-1350
1211 Puerta Del Sol # 170 San Clemente (92673) ***(P-26226)***
Evolution Juice, Rancho Cucamonga *Also called Evolution Fresh Inc* ***(P-8466)***
Evolve Growth Initiatives LLC ....E........424 281-5000
820 Moraga Dr Los Angeles (90049) ***(P-23924)***
Evolve Media Holdings LLC (PA) ....C........310 449-1890
5140 W Goldleaf Cir G100 Los Angeles (90056) ***(P-13505)***
Evolve Treatment Centers, Los Angeles *Also called Evolve Growth Initiatives LLC* ***(P-23924)***
Evoq Properties Inc ....D........213 988-8890
1318 E 7th St Ste 200 Los Angeles (90021) ***(P-11119)***
Evotek Inc (PA) ....D........858 362-5083
6150 Lusk Blvd Ste 204 San Diego (92121) ***(P-15997)***
Evotek Solutions, San Diego *Also called Evotek Inc* ***(P-15997)***
Evox Productions LLC (PA) ....D........310 605-1400
2363 E Pacifica Pl 305 Compton (90220) ***(P-14803)***
Evriholder Products LLC (HQ) ....E........714 490-7878
1500 S Lewis St Anaheim (92805) ***(P-6557)***
EW Scripps Company ....C........619 237-1010
4600 Air Way San Diego (92102) ***(P-5602)***
Ewing-Foley Inc (PA) ....E........408 342-1201
10061 Bubb Rd Ste 100 Cupertino (95014) ***(P-7265)***
Eworkplace Solutions Inc ....C........949 583-1646
9861 Irvine Center Dr Irvine (92618) ***(P-6835)***
Exablox Corporation ....D........408 773-8477
1156 Sonora Ct Sunnyvale (94086) ***(P-15861)***
Exactax Inc (PA) ....D........714 284-4802
1100 E Orangethorpe Ave # 100 Anaheim (92801) ***(P-13386)***
Exadel Inc (PA) ....D........925 363-9510
1340 Treat Blvd Walnut Creek (94597) ***(P-15324)***
Exagen Diagnostics Inc ....D........505 272-7966
1221 Liberty Way Ste A Vista (92081) ***(P-21529)***
Examine Your Practice, San Diego *Also called Trendsource Inc* ***(P-25950)***
Examone World Wide Inc ....D........619 299-3926
7480 Mission Valley Rd # 101 San Diego (92108) ***(P-22241)***
Exandal Corporation ....C........818 705-9497
17620 Sherman Way Ste 207 Van Nuys (91406) ***(P-8172)***
Excalibur Well Services Corp (PA) ....D........661 589-5338
22034 Rosedale Hwy Bakersfield (93314) ***(P-997)***
Exceed, Hemet *Also called Valley Rsrce Ctr For Retarded* ***(P-24238)***
Excel Academy Charter, Newport Beach *Also called Community Cllbrtive Chrtr Schl* ***(P-24820)***
Excel Auto Transporting Towing, Jurupa Valley *Also called Deluxe Auto Carriers Inc* ***(P-3875)***
Excel Building Services LLC ....A........925 474-1080
1061 Serpentine Ln Ste H Pleasanton (94566) ***(P-13922)***
Excel Construction Svcs Inc (PA) ....D........714 680-9200
1950 Raymer Ave Fullerton (92833) ***(P-1346)***
Excel Contractors Inc ....D........661 942-6944
348 E Avenue K8 Ste B Lancaster (93535) ***(P-1121)***
Excel Home Health Inc ....E........619 460-6622
5575 Lake Park Way # 220 La Mesa (91942) ***(P-21738)***
Excel Landscape Inc ....C........951 735-9650
710 Rimpau Ave Ste 108 Corona (92879) ***(P-810)***
Excel Managed Care Disa ....C........916 944-7185
3840 Watt Ave Bldg C Sacramento (95821) ***(P-26600)***
Excel Mdular Scaffold Lsg Corp ....A........760 598-0050
2555 Birch St Vista (92081) ***(P-3403)***
Excel Moving Services ....D........800 392-3596
30047 Ahern Ave Union City (94587) ***(P-4207)***
Excel Paving Co, Long Beach *Also called Palp Inc* ***(P-1773)***
Excell Care Ctr, Oakland *Also called Mariner Health Care Inc* ***(P-20120)***
Excell Center, The, Turlock *Also called Aspiranet* ***(P-22931)***
Excell Health Care Center, Oakland *Also called SSC Oakland Excell Oper Co LP* ***(P-20271)***
Excell Staffing & SEC Svcs, El Cajon *Also called Xl Staffing Inc* ***(P-14457)***
Excellence Ventures Inc ....D........323 262-6800
149 S Mednik Ave Los Angeles (90022) ***(P-16771)***
Excellent Building Maintenance, Moorpark *Also called EBM Janitorial Services Inc* ***(P-13916)***
Excelligence Learning Corp ....D........800 482-5846
20 Ryan Ranch Rd Ste 200 Monterey (93940) ***(P-26601)***
Excellnce of Inland Empire Inc ....C........909 758-4311
9568 Archibald Ave # 110 Rancho Cucamonga (91730) ***(P-11120)***
Exceptional Chld Foundation ....C........310 915-6606
11124 Fairbanks Way Culver City (90230) ***(P-24541)***
Exceptional Chld Foundation (PA) ....C........310 204-3300
5350 Machado Ln Culver City (90230) ***(P-23594)***
Exceptional Chld Foundation ....C........213 748-3556
1430 Venice Blvd Los Angeles (90006) ***(P-23595)***
Exceptnal Prents Unlimited Inc ....C........559 229-2000
4440 N 1st St Fresno (93726) ***(P-23213)***
Exchange Bank (PA) ....C........707 524-3000
545 4th St Santa Rosa (95401) ***(P-9288)***
Exchange Bank ....D........707 762-5555
2 E Washington St Petaluma (94952) ***(P-9194)***
Exchange Bank ....B........707 584-7300
6290 Commerce Blvd Rohnert Park (94928) ***(P-9195)***
Exchange La, Sherman Oaks *Also called WERM Investments LLC* ***(P-18019)***
Execusheld Prtection Group LLC ....D........707 439-6351
301 Georgia St Ste 307 Vallejo (94590) ***(P-16268)***
Execushield Inc ....D........415 508-0825
4104 24th St Ste 501 San Francisco (94114) ***(P-16269)***
Executive Briefing Center, Sunnyvale *Also called Juniper Networks Inc* ***(P-15628)***
Executive Committee, The, San Diego *Also called Vistage International Inc* ***(P-26872)***
Executive Financial HM Ln Corp ....E........818 285-5626
12501 Chandler Blvd Valley Village (91607) ***(P-9547)***
Executive Home Loan, Valley Village *Also called Executive Financial HM Ln Corp* ***(P-9547)***
Executive Inn Inc ....D........408 245-5330
1217 Wildwood Ave Sunnyvale (94089) ***(P-12260)***
Executive Landscape Inc ....C........760 731-9036
2131 Huffstatler St Fallbrook (92028) ***(P-727)***
Executive Living Apartments, Stockton *Also called Grupe Properties Co* ***(P-4424)***
Executive Network Entps Inc ....D........310 457-8822
1224 21st St Apt E Santa Monica (90404) ***(P-3669)***
Executive Network Entps Inc (PA) ....D........310 447-2759
13440 Beach Ave Marina Del Rey (90292) ***(P-3670)***
Executive Personnel Services ....B........714 310-9506
17842 Irvine Blvd Ste 236 Tustin (92780) ***(P-14280)***
Executive Protection Agency K- ....E........619 442-5771
1175 N 2nd St Ste 102 El Cajon (92021) ***(P-16270)***
Executives Outlet Inc ....C........415 433-6044
1 Lombard St Lbby San Francisco (94111) ***(P-18144)***
Exel Inc ....D........310 832-3376
788 W 9th St San Pedro (90731) ***(P-4406)***
Exel N Amercn Logistics Inc ....D........209 942-0102
3735 Imperial Way Stockton (95215) ***(P-4344)***
Exel N Amercn Logistics Inc ....D........209 932-2400
4512 Frontier Way Stockton (95215) ***(P-4345)***
Exel Reporters & Interpreters, San Pedro *Also called Exel Inc* ***(P-4406)***
Exeter Engineering Inc ....D........559 592-3161
109 W Pine St Exeter (93221) ***(P-484)***
Exeter Packers Inc (PA) ....A........559 592-5168
1250 E Myer Ave Exeter (93221) ***(P-485)***
Exeter Packers Inc ....C........661 399-0416
33374 Lerdo Hwy Bakersfield (93308) ***(P-4346)***
Exeter Packers Inc ....C........559 784-8820
23744 Avenue 181 Porterville (93257) ***(P-486)***
Exeter-Ivanhoe Citrus Assn ....D........559 592-3141
901 Rocky Hill Dr Exeter (93221) ***(P-487)***
Exigen (usa) Inc (PA) ....A........415 402-2600
345 California St Fl 22 San Francisco (94104) ***(P-14804)***
Exigen Group, San Francisco *Also called Exigen (usa) Inc* ***(P-14804)***
Exis Inc ....E........408 944-4600
1570 The Alameda Ste 150 San Jose (95126) ***(P-7266)***
Exit Realty Consultants ....C........209 484-8075
3018 E Service Rd Ste 104 Ceres (95307) ***(P-26602)***
Exodus Recovery, Culver City *Also called Solano County Mental Health* ***(P-23469)***
Exodus Recovery Inc (PA) ....D........310 945-3350
9808 Venice Blvd Ste 700 Culver City (90232) ***(P-22026)***
Exodus Recovery Ctr At Brotman (PA) ....D........310 253-9494
3828 Delmas Ter Culver City (90232) ***(P-21474)***
Exp US Services Inc ....D........858 597-0555
5670 Oberlin Dr San Diego (92121) ***(P-25067)***
Expak Logistics, Los Angeles *Also called Edge Logistics Services Corp* ***(P-5114)***
Expak Logistics, Los Angeles *Also called Kxp Advantage Services LLC* ***(P-4982)***
Expansive Collections, West Hollywood *Also called Empoweredexpansions Corp* ***(P-13340)***
Expeditors Intl Wash Inc ....E........415 657-3600
425 Valley Dr Brisbane (94005) ***(P-4938)***
Expeditors Intl Wash Inc ....C........919 489-7431
578 Eccles Ave South San Francisco (94080) ***(P-4939)***

A L P H A B E T I C

Expeditors Intl Wash Inc ....D.......310 343-6200
　12200 Wilkie Ave 100 Hawthorne (90250) **(P-4940)**
Expeditors Intl Wash Inc ....D.......619 710-1900
　1470 Expo Way Ste 110 San Diego (92154) **(P-4941)**
Experian Corporation ....A.......714 830-7000
　475 Anton Blvd Santa Ana (92704) **(P-13711)**
Experian Info Solutions Inc (HQ) ....A.......714 830-7000
　475 Anton Blvd Costa Mesa (92626) **(P-13712)**
Experian Info Solutions Inc ....C.......310 343-6700
　841 Apollo St Ste 200 El Segundo (90245) **(P-13713)**
Experian Info Solutions Inc ....C.......949 567-3731
　18500 Von Karman Ave # 400 Irvine (92612) **(P-13714)**
Experian Marketing, El Segundo Also called Experian Info Solutions Inc **(P-13713)**
Experian Mktg Solutions LLC ....A.......714 830-7000
　475 Anton Blvd Costa Mesa (92626) **(P-27067)**
Experience Unlimited, Capitola Also called Profile of Santa Cruz **(P-14366)**
Experienced Home Care Registry ....D.......760 724-0880
　110 Civic Center Dr # 206 Vista (92084) **(P-21739)**
Experts Exch Exprts-Xchangecom, San Luis Obispo Also called Experts Exchange LLC **(P-15998)**
Experts Exchange LLC ....D.......805 787-0603
　2701 Mcmillan Ave Ste 160 San Luis Obispo (93401) **(P-15998)**
Exploratorium ....B.......415 528-4462
　17 Pier Ste 100 San Francisco (94111) **(P-24265)**
Exponent Inc (PA) ....C.......650 326-9400
　149 Commonwealth Dr Menlo Park (94025) **(P-25068)**
Exponential Interactive Inc (HQ) ....D.......510 250-5500
　5858 Horton St Ste 300 Emeryville (94608) **(P-13506)**
Expreal Inc ....D.......909 373-4400
　7168 Archibald Ave # 100 Alta Loma (91701) **(P-11121)**
Exprescom LLC ....D.......619 271-0531
　10145 Via De La Amistad San Diego (92154) **(P-7202)**
Exprescom S.A. De C.V., San Diego Also called Exprescom LLC **(P-7202)**
Express Cable Communication ....D.......951 272-2029
　350 S Maple St Ste L Corona (92880) **(P-5720)**
Express Companies Inc ....E.......760 944-1048
　565 Westlake St Ste 100 Encinitas (92024) **(P-27068)**
Express Contractors Inc ....D.......951 360-6500
　11625 Industry Ave Fontana (92337) **(P-13268)**
Express Group Inc (PA) ....D.......310 474-5999
　10801 National Blvd # 104 Los Angeles (90064) **(P-4251)**
Express Imaging Services Inc ....D.......888 846-8804
　1805 W 208th St Ste 202 Torrance (90501) **(P-4564)**
Express Messenger Systems Inc ....D.......323 725-2100
　5829 Smithway St Commerce (90040) **(P-4252)**
Express Messenger Systems Inc ....D.......209 234-8255
　1627 Industrial Dr Stockton (95206) **(P-4253)**
Express Messenger Systems Inc ....D.......209 234-8255
　555 Zephyr St Stockton (95206) **(P-4254)**
Express Messenger Systems Inc ....D.......949 235-1400
　1240 S Allec St Anaheim (92805) **(P-4255)**
Express Messenger Systems Inc ....D.......800 488-2829
　914 W Boone St Santa Maria (93458) **(P-4256)**
Express Messenger Systems Inc ....C.......818 504-9043
　11085 Olinda St Sun Valley (91352) **(P-4257)**
Express Messenger Systems Inc ....D.......800 359-2959
　375 W Apra St Compton (90220) **(P-4258)**
Express Messenger Systems Inc ....D.......804 334-5000
　9774 Calabash Ave Fontana (92335) **(P-4259)**
Express Messenger Systems Inc ....D.......916 921-6016
　1635 Main Ave Ste 3 Sacramento (95838) **(P-4260)**
Express Messenger Systems Inc ....D.......559 277-4910
　4603 N Brawley Ave # 103 Fresno (93722) **(P-4261)**
Express Messenger Systems Inc ....D.......415 495-7300
　101 Spear St Ste A1 San Francisco (94105) **(P-4262)**
Express Personnel Services ....D.......530 671-9202
　870 W Onstott Frontage Rd E Yuba City (95991) **(P-14281)**
Express System Intermodal Inc ....C.......801 302-6625
　2633 Camino Ramon Ste 400 San Ramon (94583) **(P-4942)**
Expressworks International LLC (PA) ....C.......925 244-0900
　2410 Camino Ramon Ste 167 San Ramon (94583) **(P-26603)**
Extended Care Hosp Westminster ....C.......714 891-2769
　206 Hospital Cir Westminster (92683) **(P-19905)**
Extended Stay America, Newport Beach Also called ESA P Prtfolio Oper Lessee LLC **(P-12254)**
Extended Stay America, Orange Also called ESA P Prtfolio Oper Lessee LLC **(P-12255)**
Exterior Solutions Inc ....D.......310 400-3510
　25752 Simpson Pl Calabasas (91302) **(P-6714)**
Exterran Inc ....D.......626 455-0739
　3449 Santa Anita Ave El Monte (91731) **(P-14095)**
Extra Express (cerritos) Inc ....E.......714 985-6000
　20405 Business Pkwy Walnut (91789) **(P-4943)**
Extreme Networks Inc ....D.......630 288-3665
　3585 Monroe St Santa Clara (95051) **(P-14805)**
Extreme Telecom Inc ....C.......818 902-4821
　9221 Corbin Ave Ste 260 Northridge (91324) **(P-5399)**
Exult Inc ....A.......949 856-8800
　121 Innovation Dr Ste 200 Irvine (92617) **(P-26604)**
Ey, Los Angeles Also called Ernst & Young LLP **(P-25583)**
Ey, El Segundo Also called Ernst & Young LLP **(P-25584)**
Ey, San Francisco Also called Ernst & Young LLP **(P-25585)**
Ey, Palo Alto Also called Ernst & Young LLP **(P-25586)**
Ey, San Jose Also called Ernst & Young LLP **(P-25587)**
Ey, San Diego Also called Ernst & Young LLP **(P-25588)**
Ey, Irvine Also called Ernst & Young LLP **(P-25589)**
Ey, Irvine Also called Ernst & Young LLP **(P-25590)**
Ey, Westlake Village Also called Ernst & Young LLP **(P-25591)**
Ey, Redwood City Also called Ernst & Young LLP **(P-25592)**

Ey, Roseville Also called Ernst & Young LLP **(P-25593)**
Eye Medical Center of Fresno, Fresno Also called Eye Medical Clinic Fresno Inc **(P-18976)**
Eye Medical Clinic Fresno Inc ....D.......559 486-5000
　1360 E Herndon Ave # 301 Fresno (93720) **(P-18976)**
Eye Physican Medical Group, El Cajon Also called Sharp Healthcare **(P-19395)**
Eye Q Vision Care (PA) ....C.......559 486-2000
　7075 N Sharon Ave Fresno (93720) **(P-18977)**
EZ Acceptance Inc ....C.......858 278-8351
　7651 Ronson Rd San Diego (92111) **(P-14157)**
EZ Electric, Roseville Also called Vexillum Inc **(P-5960)**
Ezcaretech USA Inc ....B.......424 558-3191
　21081 S Wstn Ave Ste 130 Torrance (90501) **(P-16772)**
F & F Contracting Inc ....C.......559 276-2418
　4145 W Alamos Ave Fresno (93722) **(P-620)**
F & G Biagi Transportation, Ontario Also called Biagi Bros Inc **(P-3975)**
F & H Construction (PA) ....D.......209 931-3738
　1115 E Lockeford St Lodi (95240) **(P-1477)**
F and A Farms, Stevinson Also called Frank J Gomes Dairy A Califo **(P-391)**
F C I, Anaheim Also called Fci Lender Services Inc **(P-13681)**
F D I C, Roseville Also called Federal Deposit Insurance Corp **(P-10232)**
F E A, Sunnyvale Also called Fujitsu Electronics Amer Inc **(P-25086)**
F E E, Rcho STA Marg Also called Fakouri Electrical Engrg Inc **(P-15916)**
F F M L R, Moss Beach Also called Friends Fitzgerald Mar Reserve **(P-24175)**
F I N, Van Nuys Also called Financial Information Network **(P-14809)**
F J Hoover Plumbing Inc ....D.......951 360-8262
　2259 Hamner Ave Norco (92860) **(P-2132)**
F Korbel & Bros ....C.......707 525-1875
　4384 Becker Blvd Santa Rosa (95403) **(P-4770)**
F M I, Anaheim Also called Freight Management Inc **(P-26614)**
F M T, Carlsbad Also called Fmt Consultants LLC **(P-15999)**
F M Tarbell Co ....D.......951 471-5333
　18295 Collier Ave Lake Elsinore (92530) **(P-11122)**
F M Tarbell Co ....D.......951 677-3565
　39028 Winchester Rd # 101 Murrieta (92563) **(P-11123)**
F M Tarbell Co ....D.......714 772-8990
　321 S State College Blvd Anaheim (92806) **(P-11124)**
F M Tarbell Co ....E.......714 637-7240
　6396 E Santa Ana Cyn Rd Anaheim (92807) **(P-11125)**
F M Tarbell Co (HQ) ....C.......714 972-0988
　1403 N Tustin Ave Ste 380 Santa Ana (92705) **(P-11126)**
F M Tarbell Co ....C.......951 280-6040
　315 Magnolia Ave Corona (92879) **(P-11127)**
F M Tarbell Co ....D.......949 830-6030
　25201 La Paz Rd Laguna Hills (92653) **(P-11128)**
F M Tarbell Co ....D.......951 301-5932
　27701 Scott Rd Ste 103 Menifee (92584) **(P-11129)**
F M Tarbell Co ....C.......951 303-0307
　31685 Temecula Pkwy Ste B Temecula (92592) **(P-11130)**
F M Tarbell Co ....D.......949 559-8451
　4040 Barranca Pkwy # 220 Irvine (92604) **(P-11131)**
F M Tarbell Co ....D.......951 270-1022
　2409 S Vineyard Ave Ste A Ontario (91761) **(P-11132)**
F M Tarbell Co ....E.......760 346-7405
　73700 El Paseo Palm Desert (92260) **(P-11133)**
F M Tarbell Co ....C.......909 982-8881
　1365 E 19th St Ste A Upland (91784) **(P-11134)**
F O C Electronics Corporation ....E.......213 625-5775
　830 Traction Ave Los Angeles (90013) **(P-7203)**
F P I, Shafter Also called Farm Pump & Irrigation Co Inc **(P-7546)**
F R A L P ....D.......714 633-1442
　1702 Fairhaven Ave Santa Ana (92705) **(P-13370)**
F R Ghianni Drywall Cnstr Co, El Cajon Also called F R Ghianni Enterprises Inc **(P-1122)**
F R Ghianni Enterprises Inc ....D.......619 279-1073
　1937 Friendship Dr Ste A El Cajon (92020) **(P-1122)**
F R H I, San Jose Also called Fertility & Reproductive **(P-18987)**
F R T International Inc ....C.......909 390-4892
　2825 Jurupa St Ontario (91761) **(P-4944)**
F R T International Inc (PA) ....C.......310 604-8208
　1700 N Alameda St Compton (90222) **(P-4407)**
F W Spencer & Son Inc ....C.......415 468-5000
　99 S Hill Dr Brisbane (94005) **(P-2133)**
F&E Aircraft Maintenance, Los Angeles Also called Arinwine Arcft Maint Svcs LLC **(P-4752)**
F&E Aircraft Maintenance (PA) ....B.......310 338-0063
　531 Main St El Segundo (90245) **(P-4771)**
F&M Bank, Long Beach Also called Farmers Merchants Bnk Long Bch **(P-9196)**
F-Secure Inc ....E.......888 432-8233
　470 Ramona St Palo Alto (94301) **(P-6836)**
F3 and Associates Inc (PA) ....D.......707 748-4300
　701 E H St Benicia (94510) **(P-25520)**
F50 League LLC ....E.......415 939-4076
　475 Sansome St Fl 12 San Francisco (94111) **(P-24829)**
Faberware Div, Fairfield Also called Meyer Corporation US **(P-6571)**
Fabric Barn ....C.......562 494-3450
　3123 E Anaheim St Long Beach (90804) **(P-7997)**
Fabulous & Company LLC ....E.......818 261-7242
　19553 Enadia Way Reseda (91335) **(P-13342)**
Facebook Inc (PA) ....A.......650 543-4800
　1 Hacker Way Bldg 10 Menlo Park (94025) **(P-15862)**
Facey Medical Foundation ....C.......805 206-2000
　2655 1st St Simi Valley (93065) **(P-19640)**
Facey Medical Foundation ....C.......818 861-7831
　191 S Buena Vista St Burbank (91505) **(P-19641)**
Facey Medical Foundation (PA) ....C.......818 365-9531
　15451 San Fernando Msn Mission Hills (91345) **(P-18978)**
Facey Medical Foundation ....C.......818 837-5677
　11211 Sepulveda Blvd Mission Hills (91345) **(P-22242)**

Facey Medical Foundation ......D 661 250-5225
17909 Soledad Canyon Rd Santa Clarita (91387) ***(P-22243)***

Facey Medical Foundation ......D 661 513-2100
27924 Seco Canyon Rd Santa Clarita (91350) ***(P-22244)***

Facey Medical Foundation ......C 818 365-9531
11165 Sepulveda Blvd Mission Hills (91345) ***(P-18979)***

Facey Medical Foundation ......D 626 576-0800
1237 E Main St San Gabriel (91776) ***(P-22245)***

Facey Medical Group, Santa Clarita *Also called Facey Medical Foundation* ***(P-22243)***

Facial Reconstructive Surg &, East Palo Alto *Also called Facial Reconstructive Surgery* ***(P-18980)***

Facial Reconstructive Surgery ......E 650 328-0511
1900 University Ave 101e East Palo Alto (94303) ***(P-18980)***

Facilities Management, Oakland *Also called Oakland Unified School Dst* ***(P-13994)***

Facilities Operation and Trnsp ......D 209 826-1936
2657 E Pacheco Blvd Los Banos (93635) ***(P-3800)***

Facility Masters Inc (PA) ......B 408 436-9090
1604 Kerley Dr San Jose (95112) ***(P-13923)***

Facility Services Partners ......D 949 480-4090
1 University Dr Aliso Viejo (92656) ***(P-26227)***

Facility Solutions Group Inc ......D 714 993-3966
801 Richfield Rd Placentia (92870) ***(P-7150)***

Facs, San Diego *Also called Forensic Analytical* ***(P-27073)***

Fact Foundation ......D 818 729-8105
303 N Glenoaks Blvd Burbank (91502) ***(P-16773)***

Facter Direct Ltd ......C 323 634-1999
4751 Wilshire Blvd # 140 Los Angeles (90010) ***(P-16774)***

Factory 2-U Import Export Inc ......D 323 587-9900
13034 Delano St Van Nuys (91401) ***(P-8073)***

Factory Motor Parts, Orange *Also called Elliott Auto Supply Co Inc* ***(P-6435)***

Factory Mutual Insurance Co ......C 925 934-2200
1333 N Calif Blvd Ste 200 Walnut Creek (94596) ***(P-10084)***

Factory Mutual Insurance Co ......D 818 227-2200
6320 Canoga Ave Ste 1100 Woodland Hills (91367) ***(P-10085)***

Factory R D ......D 949 900-3460
23192 Verdugo Dr Laguna Hills (92653) ***(P-7028)***

Faculty Physcans Srgeons Llusm ......D 909 558-4000
11370 Anderson St Loma Linda (92354) ***(P-18981)***

Fair Isaac Corporation (PA) ......B 408 535-1500
181 Metro Dr Ste 700 San Jose (95110) ***(P-27069)***

Fair Isaac International Corp (HQ) ......A 415 446-6000
200 Smith Ranch Rd San Rafael (94903) ***(P-15325)***

Fair Trade Corner Inc ......E 530 566-1405
11591 Meridian Rd Chico (95973) ***(P-488)***

Fair Trade USA ......D 510 663-5260
1901 Harrison St Ste 1700 Oakland (94612) ***(P-25990)***

Fairbanks Ranch Cntry CLB Inc ......C 858 259-8811
15150 San Dieguito Rd Rancho Santa Fe (92067) ***(P-18453)***

Fairchild Medical Center, Yreka *Also called Siskiyou Hospital Inc* ***(P-21202)***

Fairfield Community Center, Fairfield *Also called City of Fairfield* ***(P-10579)***

Fairfield Development Inc (PA) ......C 858 457-2123
5510 Morehouse Dr Ste 200 San Diego (92121) ***(P-1242)***

Fairfield Family YMCA, Long Beach *Also called Young Mens Chrstn Assc Gr L B* ***(P-24746)***

Fairfield Healthcare Center, Fairfield *Also called Fairfield Nursing & Rehab Ctr* ***(P-19906)***

Fairfield Inn, San Diego *Also called RPC Old Town Avenue Owner LLC* ***(P-12846)***

Fairfield Inn, El Segundo *Also called Rubicon B Hacienda LLC* ***(P-12852)***

Fairfield Inn, Rancho Cordova *Also called Presidio Hotel Group LLC* ***(P-12771)***

Fairfield Medical Offices, Fairfield *Also called Kaiser Foundation Hospitals* ***(P-19068)***

Fairfield Nursing & Rehab Ctr ......D 707 425-0623
1255 Travis Blvd Fairfield (94533) ***(P-19906)***

Fairfield-Suisun Sewer Dst ......D 707 429-8930
1010 Chadbourne Rd Fairfield (94534) ***(P-6204)***

Fairfight, Pasadena *Also called Myinternetservicescom LLC* ***(P-5442)***

Fairmont Designs, Buena Park *Also called Cambium Business Group Inc* ***(P-6509)***

Fairmont Hotel, San Francisco *Also called Accor Services US LLC* ***(P-11994)***

Fairmont Miramar Hotel, Santa Monica *Also called Ocean Avenue LLC* ***(P-12659)***

Fairmont San Francisco, San Francisco *Also called Mason Street Opco LLC* ***(P-12602)***

Fairmont Snoma Mission Inn Spa, Sonoma *Also called Sonoma Hotel Operator Inc* ***(P-12944)***

Fairplex Enterprises Inc ......D 909 623-3111
1101 W Mckinley Ave Pomona (91768) ***(P-18689)***

Fairplex Rv Park, Pomona *Also called Los Angeles County Fair Assn* ***(P-18720)***

Fairsite Preschool, Galt *Also called Galt Joint Union School Dst* ***(P-23726)***

Fairview Developmental Center, Costa Mesa *Also called Califrnia Dept State Hospitals* ***(P-21388)***

Fairview Developmental Center, Costa Mesa *Also called Developmental Svcs Cal Dept* ***(P-23591)***

Fairwinds Woodward Park, Fresno *Also called Leisure Care LLC* ***(P-23972)***

Fairwinds-West Hills, West Hills *Also called Leisure Care LLC* ***(P-20436)***

Fairwood Apartments, Carmichael *Also called Fairwood Associates Apts* ***(P-10724)***

Fairwood Associates Apts ......D 916 944-0152
8893 Fair Oaks Blvd Ofc Carmichael (95608) ***(P-10724)***

Faith Com Inc (PA) ......D 562 719-9300
13850 Cerritos Cerritos (90703) ***(P-27070)***

Faith Electric LLC ......C 909 767-2682
12350 Hesperia Rd Ste 215 Victorville (92395) ***(P-2491)***

Faith Enterprises Inc ......E 209 835-6034
545 W Beverly Pl Tracy (95376) ***(P-19907)***

Faith Jones & Associates Inc (PA) ......D 619 297-9601
7801 Mission Center Ct # 106 San Diego (92108) ***(P-21740)***

Faith Quality Auto Body Inc ......D 951 698-8215
41130 Nick Ln Murrieta (92562) ***(P-17289)***

Fakouri Electrical Engrg Inc ......D 949 888-2400
30001 Comercio Rcho STA Marg (92688) ***(P-15916)***

Falcon Aerospace Holdings LLC ......A 661 775-7200
27727 Avenue Scott Valencia (91355) ***(P-26228)***

Falcon Auto Repair, Gardena *Also called Raymak Automotive Inc* ***(P-17343)***

Falcon Trading Company (PA) ......C 831 786-7000
423 Salinas Rd Royal Oaks (95076) ***(P-8575)***

Falconwood Inc ......D 619 297-9080
1011 Camino Del Rio S San Diego (92108) ***(P-15917)***

Falken Tire, Rancho Cucamonga *Also called Sumitomo Rubber North Amer Inc* ***(P-6490)***

Falken Tire Holdings Inc ......D 800 723-2553
8656 Haven Ave Rancho Cucamonga (91730) ***(P-6485)***

Falken Tires, Rancho Cucamonga *Also called Falken Tire Holdings Inc* ***(P-6485)***

Fallbrook Fire Protection Dst ......D 760 723-2010
315 E Ivy St Fallbrook (92028) ***(P-16775)***

Fallbrook Healing Center, Fallbrook *Also called Crestwood Behavioral Hlth Inc* ***(P-21403)***

Fallbrook Public Utility Dst ......D 760 728-1125
990 E Mission Rd Fallbrook (92028) ***(P-6061)***

Fallbrook Sklled Nrsing Fcilty ......D 760 728-2330
325 Potter St Fallbrook (92028) ***(P-19908)***

Fallon Land Company Inc ......E 213 880-1279
4 Corporate Plaza Dr # 210 Newport Beach (92660) ***(P-7065)***

Fam LLC ......D 323 888-7755
5553 Bandini Blvd Ste B Bell (90201) ***(P-8028)***

Fam Brands, Bell *Also called Fam LLC* ***(P-8028)***

Famand Inc ......C 707 255-9295
1604 Airport Blvd Santa Rosa (95403) ***(P-2134)***

Fame Assistance Corporation ......D 323 373-7720
2270 S Harvard Blvd Los Angeles (90018) ***(P-27071)***

Fame Hardwood Floors, Los Angeles *Also called P8ge Consulting Inc* ***(P-27161)***

Fame Systems Inc ......E 805 485-0808
301 Hearst Dr Oxnard (93030) ***(P-13924)***

Family & Children Services ......D 650 326-6576
375 Cambridge Ave Palo Alto (94306) ***(P-23214)***

Family and Children Services ......D 408 292-9353
950 W Julian St San Jose (95126) ***(P-27072)***

Family Assessment Cnslng Edctn ......E 714 447-9024
1651 E 4th St Ste 128 Santa Ana (92701) ***(P-23215)***

Family Bridges Inc ......C 510 839-2270
168 11th St Oakland (94607) ***(P-23216)***

Family Care Network Inc (PA) ......C 805 503-6240
1255 Kendall Rd San Luis Obispo (93401) ***(P-23724)***

Family Circle Inc ......D 805 385-4180
2100 Outlet Center Dr # 380 Oxnard (93036) ***(P-23217)***

Family Health Center, Pomona *Also called Keith T Kusunis MD* ***(P-22053)***

Family Health Program, Long Beach *Also called Healthcare Partners LLC* ***(P-22251)***

Family Health Services Clinic, Madera *Also called Madera Community Hospital* ***(P-21025)***

Family Healthcare Network ......C 559 734-1939
501 N Bridge St Visalia (93291) ***(P-19667)***

Family Healthcare Network ......C 559 781-7242
1137 W Poplar Ave Porterville (93257) ***(P-18982)***

Family Healthcare Network ......C 559 582-2013
250 W 5th St Hanford (93230) ***(P-18983)***

Family Healthcare Network ......C 559 798-1877
33025 159th Rd Ivanhoe (93235) ***(P-18984)***

Family Hlth Ctrs San Diego Inc (PA) ......D 619 515-2303
823 Gateway Center Way San Diego (92102) ***(P-22027)***

Family Mdcine Rsidency Program ......D 559 499-6450
155 N Fresno St Ste 326 Fresno (93701) ***(P-20876)***

Family Mrale Wlfare Recreation ......D 760 380-3493
1317 Normandy Dr Fort Irwin (92310) ***(P-18454)***

Family Paths Inc (PA) ......D 510 893-9230
1727 M L King Jr Way Oakland (94612) ***(P-22028)***

Family Plg Assoc Med Group ......D 562 595-5653
2777 Long Beach Blvd # 150 Long Beach (90806) ***(P-16776)***

Family Plg Assoc Med Group (PA) ......D 213 738-7283
3050 E Airport Way Long Beach (90806) ***(P-18985)***

Family Radio, Alameda *Also called Family Stations Inc* ***(P-5529)***

Family Resource & Referral Ctr ......D 209 948-1553
509 W Weber Ave Ste 101 Stockton (95203) ***(P-23218)***

Family Savings Bank, Los Angeles *Also called Oneunited Bank* ***(P-9219)***

Family Service Agency, San Rafael *Also called Family Svcs Agcy Marin Cnty* ***(P-23223)***

Family Service Agency ......E 805 735-4376
101 S B St Ste A Lompoc (93436) ***(P-23219)***

Family Services ......E 559 741-7310
807 W Oak Ave Visalia (93291) ***(P-24830)***

Family Services Tulare County ......D 559 732-1970
815 W Oak Ave Visalia (93291) ***(P-23220)***

Family Stations Inc (PA) ......C 510 568-6200
1350 S Loop Rd Alameda (94502) ***(P-5529)***

Family Stress Center, Northridge *Also called Child and Family Guidance Ctr* ***(P-21979)***

Family Support Bureau, San Francisco *Also called San Francisco City & County* ***(P-23439)***

Family Support Division, Modesto *Also called County of Stanislaus* ***(P-23174)***

Family Support Services (PA) ......D 510 834-2443
303 Hegenberger Rd # 400 Oakland (94621) ***(P-23221)***

Family Svc Agcy San Francisco (PA) ......D 415 474-7310
1500 Franklin St San Francisco (94109) ***(P-14504)***

Family Svc Agcy Santa Barbara ......D 805 965-1001
123 W Gutierrez St Santa Barbara (93101) ***(P-23222)***

Family Svcs Agcy Marin Cnty (PA) ......D 415 491-5700
555 Northgate Dr San Rafael (94903) ***(P-23223)***

Family Tree Produce Inc ......C 714 693-5688
5510 E La Palma Ave Anaheim (92807) ***(P-8467)***

Family Urgent Care Center, Anaheim *Also called Anaheim Harbor Medical Group* ***(P-18811)***

Famma Group Inc (PA) ......D 323 826-9600
4510 Loma Vista Ave Vernon (90058) ***(P-8029)***

Famous Ramona Water Inc ......E 760 789-0174
250 Aqua Ln Ramona (92065) ***(P-8576)***

Famous Software LLC (PA) ......D 559 438-3600
8080 N Palm Ave Ste 210 Fresno (93711) ***(P-14806)***

ALPHABETIC

Employee Codes: A=Over 500 employees, B=251-500
C=101-250, D=51-100, E=50
2020 Directory of California
Wholesalers and Services Companies
© Mergent Inc. 1-800-342-5647
1265

Famous Vineyards LLC...D...661 392-5000
20715 Ave 8 Richgrove (93261) ***(P-8468)***
Fanfare Enterprises, Costa Mesa *Also called Ovations Fanfare* ***(P-26338)***
Fang Inc...D...714 898-7785
12235 Beach Blvd Ste 20h Stanton (90680) ***(P-18986)***
Fantasy Springs Resort Casino, Indio *Also called East Valley Tourist Dev Auth* ***(P-18687)***
Fao ROC Holdings LLC...C...949 900-6501
15 Cushing Irvine (92618) ***(P-7732)***
Fao Schwarz, Irvine *Also called Fao ROC Holdings LLC* ***(P-7732)***
Far East Broadcasting Co Inc...D...562 947-4651
15700 Imperial Hwy La Mirada (90638) ***(P-5530)***
Far East Home Care Inc...C...949 673-3100
3407 W 6th St Ste 710 Los Angeles (90020) ***(P-21741)***
Far Northern Coordinating Coun...D...530 895-8633
1377 E Lassen Ave Chico (95973) ***(P-23224)***
Far Northern Coordinating Coun (PA)...D...530 222-4791
1900 Churn Creek Rd # 114 Redding (96002) ***(P-23225)***
Far Northern Regional Center, Redding *Also called Far Northern Coordinating Coun* ***(P-23225)***
Far West Electric Inc...D...909 684-8661
6094 Keswick Ave Riverside (92506) ***(P-2492)***
Far West Inc...D...559 627-1241
4444 W Meadow Ave Visalia (93277) ***(P-19909)***
Far West Inc...D...323 564-7761
8455 State St South Gate (90280) ***(P-19910)***
Far West Inc...C...559 733-0901
4525 W Tulare Ave Visalia (93277) ***(P-20552)***
Far West Inc...D...909 884-4781
467 E Gilbert St San Bernardino (92404) ***(P-19911)***
Far West Management Corp (PA)...D...949 863-1757
17941 Mitchell S Ste A Irvine (92614) ***(P-11135)***
Faraday & Future, Gardena *Also called FARaday&future Inc* ***(P-25069)***
FARaday&future Inc...A...424 276-7616
18455 S Figueroa St Gardena (90248) ***(P-25069)***
Farallon Capital Partners LP (PA)...C...415 421-2132
1 Maritime Plz Ste 2100 San Francisco (94111) ***(P-11724)***
Fargo Colonial LLC...D...858 454-2181
910 Prospect St La Jolla (92037) ***(P-12261)***
Farm Fresh To You (PA)...C...916 303-7145
3880 Seaport Blvd West Sacramento (95691) ***(P-321)***
Farm Pump & Irrigation Co Inc (PA)...D...661 589-6901
535 N Shafter Ave Shafter (93263) ***(P-7546)***
Farmers Business Network, San Carlos *Also called Fbn Inputs LLC* ***(P-663)***
Farmers Group Inc (HQ)...A...323 932-3200
6301 Owensmouth Ave Woodland Hills (91367) ***(P-10086)***
Farmers Group Inc...D...213 615-2500
700 S Flower St Ste 2800 Los Angeles (90017) ***(P-9867)***
Farmers Group Inc...D...909 839-2020
13950 Ramona Ave Chino (91710) ***(P-10351)***
Farmers Group Inc...E...408 557-1100
429 Llewellyn Ave Campbell (95008) ***(P-10352)***
Farmers Group Inc...D...818 249-3000
550 S Hill St Ste 1309 Los Angeles (90013) ***(P-10353)***
Farmers Group Inc...D...916 727-4600
6518 Antelope Rd Citrus Heights (95621) ***(P-10354)***
Farmers Group Inc...A...805 583-7400
6303 Owensmouth Ave Fl 1 Woodland Hills (91367) ***(P-10355)***
Farmers Insurance, Woodland Hills *Also called Farmers Group Inc* ***(P-10086)***
Farmers Insurance, Los Angeles *Also called Farmers Group Inc* ***(P-9867)***
Farmers Insurance, Chino *Also called Farmers Group Inc* ***(P-10351)***
Farmers Insurance, Campbell *Also called Farmers Group Inc* ***(P-10352)***
Farmers Insurance, Los Angeles *Also called Farmers Group Inc* ***(P-10353)***
Farmers Insurance, Citrus Heights *Also called Farmers Group Inc* ***(P-10354)***
Farmers Insurance, Woodland Hills *Also called Farmers Group Inc* ***(P-10355)***
Farmers Insurance Exchange (HQ)...A...323 932-3200
6301 Owensmouth Ave Woodland Hills (91367) ***(P-10356)***
Farmers Insurance Exchange...B...559 594-4149
411 E Pine St Ste A Exeter (93221) ***(P-10357)***
Farmers Insurance Fed Cred UNI (PA)...D...323 209-6000
4601 Wilshire Blvd # 110 Los Angeles (90010) ***(P-10358)***
Farmers International Inc...E...530 566-1405
1260 Muir Ave Chico (95973) ***(P-174)***
Farmers Merchants Bnk Long Bch (HQ)...C...562 437-0011
302 Pine Ave Long Beach (90802) ***(P-9196)***
Farmers Merchants Bnk Long Bch...C...562 430-4724
1695 Adolfo Lopez Dr Seal Beach (90740) ***(P-9197)***
Farmers Mrchants Bnk Centl Cal...C...916 394-3200
8799 Elk Grove Blvd Elk Grove (95624) ***(P-9198)***
Farmers W Flowers & Bouquets, Carpinteria *Also called Brand Flower Farms Inc* ***(P-8884)***
Farmex Land Management Inc...C...559 875-7181
11156 E Annadale Ave Sanger (93657) ***(P-16777)***
Farms Golf Club Inc...D...858 756-5585
8500 San Andrews Rd Rancho Santa Fe (92067) ***(P-18246)***
Farms of Amador...D...209 257-0112
12200b Airport Rd Jackson (95642) ***(P-24831)***
Farmstead Gourmet, Lodi *Also called California Fruit Exchange LLC* ***(P-8436)***
Faro Logistics, Norwalk *Also called Faro Services Inc* ***(P-4408)***
Faro Services Inc...C...562 483-7799
15625 Shoemaker Ave Norwalk (90650) ***(P-4408)***
Farwest Corrosion Control Co (PA)...C...310 532-9524
12029 Regentview Ave Downey (90241) ***(P-3404)***
Farwest Insulation Contracting...E...310 634-2800
2741 Yates Ave Commerce (90040) ***(P-2787)***
Farwest Trading, Turlock *Also called Associated Feed & Supply Co* ***(P-8834)***
Faschings Car Wash, Arcadia *Also called George Fasching* ***(P-17374)***
Fashion Resources, Los Angeles *Also called Tarrant Apparel Group* ***(P-8114)***
Fashion Wheel, Fresno *Also called Anthony Lambe* ***(P-6418)***

Fashioncraft Floors Inc (PA)...E...714 255-8400
1630 Faraday Ave Carlsbad (92008) ***(P-3001)***
Fashiongo.com, Los Angeles *Also called Nhn Global Inc* ***(P-8102)***
Fast Deer Bus Chrtr Incrprtion...D...323 201-8988
8105 Slauson Ave Montebello (90640) ***(P-3775)***
Fast Lane Container Services, Wilmington *Also called Fast Lane Transportation Inc* ***(P-4019)***
Fast Lane Transportation Inc (PA)...D...562 435-3000
2400 E Pacific Coast Hwy Wilmington (90744) ***(P-4019)***
Fast Pro Inc...D...408 566-0200
2555 Lafayette St Ste 103 Santa Clara (95050) ***(P-6438)***
Fast Undercar, Santa Clara *Also called Fast Pro Inc* ***(P-6438)***
Fast Undercar Stockton, Antioch *Also called Jamm Management LLC* ***(P-6448)***
Fastclick Inc...D...805 689-9839
530 E Montecito St Santa Barbara (93103) ***(P-13650)***
Fastclick.com, Santa Barbara *Also called Fastclick Inc* ***(P-13650)***
Fastech, Buena Park *Also called Fueling and Service Tech Inc* ***(P-7547)***
Fastly Inc (PA)...C...844 432-7859
475 Brannan St Ste 300 San Francisco (94107) ***(P-14807)***
Fastxchange Inc...E...310 827-2445
4640 Admiralty Way # 710 Marina Del Rey (90292) ***(P-15592)***
Fathers of St Charles...C...818 768-6500
10631 Vinedale St Sun Valley (91352) ***(P-10725)***
Faucetdirect.com, Chico *Also called Buildcom Inc* ***(P-7414)***
Fault Line Plumbing...E...925 443-6450
7640 National Dr Livermore (94550) ***(P-2135)***
Fayaka Airways LLC...C...800 771-5489
659 Macarthur Blvd San Leandro (94577) ***(P-4740)***
Faze Clan Inc...D...818 538-5204
1800 Vine St Ste 301 Los Angeles (90028) ***(P-18690)***
FB Corporation...C...626 300-0880
1211 E Valley Blvd Alhambra (91801) ***(P-9094)***
Fba Inc (PA)...E...510 265-1888
1675 Sabre St Hayward (94545) ***(P-25070)***
Fbd Vanguard Construction Inc...C...925 245-1300
550 Greenville Rd Livermore (94550) ***(P-26229)***
Fbn Inputs LLC...D...844 200-3276
388 El Camino Real San Carlos (94070) ***(P-663)***
Fc El Segundo LLC...D...702 439-7945
199 Continental Blvd El Segundo (90245) ***(P-12262)***
Fc Landscape Inc...D...760 347-6600
43216 Madison St Indio (92201) ***(P-728)***
Fc Metropolitan Lofts Inc...D...213 488-0010
949 S Hope St Ste 100 Los Angeles (90015) ***(P-11562)***
Fcb Worldwide Inc...A...415 820-8545
1160 Battery St Ste 250 San Francisco (94111) ***(P-13507)***
Fce Benefit Administrators Inc (PA)...C...650 341-0306
1528 S El Camino Real # 307 San Mateo (94402) ***(P-10359)***
Fci Lender Services Inc...C...800 931-2424
8180 E Kaiser Blvd Anaheim (92808) ***(P-13681)***
Fci Management, Cerritos *Also called Faith Com Inc* ***(P-27070)***
Fcrta, Fresno *Also called Fresno County Rural Trnst Agcy* ***(P-3539)***
Fcs Medical Corporation...D...323 317-9200
1701 E Cesar E Chavez Ave # 230 Los Angeles (90033) ***(P-19642)***
Fcs Software Solutions Limited...D...408 324-1203
2375 Zanker Rd Ste 250 San Jose (95131) ***(P-14808)***
Fcti Inc (PA)...D...310 405-0022
11766 Wilshire Blvd # 1100 Los Angeles (90025) ***(P-9433)***
Fdi Collateral Management, Sacramento *Also called Dealertrack Collte Manag Servi* ***(P-15974)***
FDIC, Los Angeles *Also called Federal Deposit Insurance Corp* ***(P-10231)***
FDIC-San Frncisco Regional Off, San Francisco *Also called Federal Deposit Insurance Corp* ***(P-10230)***
Fdsi Logistics LLC...D...818 971-3300
27680 Avenue Mentry 2 Valencia (91355) ***(P-26605)***
Feather Falls Casino, Oroville *Also called Mooretown Rancheria* ***(P-18320)***
Feather Falls Casino, Oroville *Also called Mooretown Rancheria* ***(P-18724)***
Feather River Home Health, Paradise *Also called Adventist Health System/West* ***(P-20733)***
Feather Rver Recreation Pk Dst...D...530 533-2011
1875 Feather River Blvd Oroville (95965) ***(P-18691)***
Fed Air Security Corporation...D...626 535-2200
210 S De Lacey Ave Pasadena (91105) ***(P-16513)***
Fedelity National Title Co Org...D...818 758-6849
5000 Van Nuys Blvd 500 Sherman Oaks (91403) ***(P-10182)***
Federal Deposit Insurance Corp...C...626 359-7152
1333 S Mayflower Ave # 450 Monrovia (91016) ***(P-10229)***
Federal Deposit Insurance Corp...C...415 546-0160
25 Jessie St Ste 2300 San Francisco (94105) ***(P-10230)***
Federal Deposit Insurance Corp...C...323 545-9260
5150 W Goldleaf Cir # 405 Los Angeles (90056) ***(P-10231)***
Federal Deposit Insurance Corp...C...916 789-8580
1532 Eureka Rd Ste 102 Roseville (95661) ***(P-10232)***
Federal Dfenders San Diego Inc (PA)...D...619 234-8467
225 Broadway Ste 900 San Diego (92101) ***(P-22498)***
Federal Disposal Service, Tustin *Also called Shubin Services Inc* ***(P-6282)***
Federal Express Corporation...D...800 463-3339
3541 Regional Pkwy Petaluma (94954) ***(P-4698)***
Federal Express Corporation...C...800 463-3339
1650 47th St San Diego (92102) ***(P-4699)***
Federal Express Corporation...C...800 463-3339
1330 Fortress St Chico (95973) ***(P-4700)***
Federal Express Corporation...D...800 463-3339
1286 Lawrence Station Rd Sunnyvale (94089) ***(P-4701)***
Federal Express Corporation...C...800 463-3339
12600 Prairie Ave Hawthorne (90250) ***(P-4702)***
Federal Express Corporation...C...800 463-3339
11340 Sherman Way Sun Valley (91352) ***(P-4664)***

Mergent e-mail: customerrelations@mergent.com
1266
2020 Directory of California
Wholesalers and Services Companies
(P-0000) Products & Services Section entry number
(PA)=Parent Co (HQ)=Headquarters (DH)=Div Headquarters

ALPHABETIC SECTION
Fedex Smartpost Inc

Federal Express Corporation ....C....800 463-3339
1500 Nichols Dr Rocklin (95765) ***(P-4665)***
Federal Express Corporation ....D....800 463-3339
2660 Research Park Dr Soquel (95073) ***(P-4263)***
Federal Express Corporation ....C....800 463-3339
2495 Faraday Ave Carlsbad (92010) ***(P-16778)***
Federal Express Corporation ....C....800 463-3339
1081 Fullerton Rd City of Industry (91748) ***(P-4264)***
Federal Express Corporation ....B....800 463-3339
200 N Pacific Coast Hwy # 800 El Segundo (90245) ***(P-16779)***
Federal Express Corporation ....C....800 463-3339
1111 Bird Center Dr Palm Springs (92262) ***(P-4666)***
Federal Express Corporation ....C....510 347-2430
1601 Aurora Dr San Leandro (94577) ***(P-4703)***
Federal Express Corporation ....D....800 463-3339
1650 Sunflower Ave Costa Mesa (92626) ***(P-4704)***
Federal Express Corporation ....D....800 463-3339
3333 S Grand Ave Los Angeles (90007) ***(P-4020)***
Federal Express Corporation ....D....800 463-3339
7275 Johnson Dr Pleasanton (94588) ***(P-16780)***
Federal Express Corporation ....D....800 463-3339
1 Lower Ragsdale Dr # 4 Monterey (93940) ***(P-4705)***
Federal Express Corporation ....C....800 463-3339
710 Dado St San Jose (95131) ***(P-4265)***
Federal Express Corporation ....B....510 382-2344
9190 Edes Ave Oakland (94603) ***(P-4266)***
Federal Express Corporation ....C....510 465-5209
500 12th St Ste 139 Oakland (94607) ***(P-4706)***
Federal Express Corporation ....D....800 463-3339
8455 Pardee Dr Oakland (94621) ***(P-4707)***
Federal Express Corporation ....C....800 463-3339
6775 Woodrum Cir Redding (96002) ***(P-4708)***
Federal Express Corporation ....E....800 463-3339
935 Performance Dr Stockton (95206) ***(P-4709)***
Federal Express Corporation ....D....800 463-3339
9339 Ann St Santa Fe Springs (90670) ***(P-4710)***
Federal Express Corporation ....C....800 463-3339
9510 W Airport Dr Visalia (93277) ***(P-4711)***
Federal Express Corporation ....B....800 463-3339
7000 Barranca Pkwy Irvine (92618) ***(P-16781)***
Federal Express Corporation ....B....800 463-3339
3371 E Francis St Ontario (91761) ***(P-16782)***
Federal Express Corporation ....D....909 390-3237
2060 S Wineville Ave B Ontario (91761) ***(P-4712)***
Federal Express Corporation ....C....800 463-3339
1600 63rd St Emeryville (94608) ***(P-3885)***
Federal Express Corporation ....C....800 463-3339
2500 Kimberly Ave Fullerton (92831) ***(P-4713)***
Federal Express Corporation ....D....800 463-3339
3150 Paseo Mercado Oxnard (93036) ***(P-4714)***
Federal Express Corporation ....D....916 361-5500
8950 Cal Center Dr # 370 Sacramento (95826) ***(P-4715)***
Federal Express Corporation ....C....800 463-3339
2221 W Washington St San Diego (92110) ***(P-4945)***
Federal Express Corporation ....C....800 463-3339
1875 Marin St San Francisco (94124) ***(P-4716)***
Federal Express Corporation ....C....800 463-3339
2451 N Palm Dr Long Beach (90755) ***(P-4717)***
Federal Express Corporation ....C....949 862-4500
2601 Main St Ste 1000 Irvine (92614) ***(P-4667)***
Federal Express Corporation ....C....562 522-4014
1 World Trade Ctr Ste 191 Long Beach (90831) ***(P-4718)***
Federal Hm Ln Bnk San Frncisco (PA) ....B....415 616-1000
333 Bush St Ste 2700 San Francisco (94104) ***(P-9446)***
Federal Insurance Company....D....818 596-6100
21820 Burbank Blvd # 330 Woodland Hills (91367) ***(P-10360)***
Federal Insurance Company....D....415 273-6300
275 Battery St Fl 12 San Francisco (94111) ***(P-10361)***
Federal Rsrve Bnk San Frncisco (HQ)....A....415 974-2000
101 Market St San Francisco (94105) ***(P-9025)***
Federal Rsrve Bnk San Frncisco....A....213 683-2300
950 S Grand Ave Los Angeles (90015) ***(P-9026)***
Federico Beauty Institute....E....916 929-4242
1515 Sports Dr Ste 100 Sacramento (95834) ***(P-13343)***
Federted Indans Grton Rncheria....A....707 588-7100
630 Park Ct Rohnert Park (94928) ***(P-12263)***
Fedex, Petaluma *Also called Federal Express Corporation* ***(P-4698)***
Fedex, San Diego *Also called Federal Express Corporation* ***(P-4699)***
Fedex, Chico *Also called Federal Express Corporation* ***(P-4700)***
Fedex, Sunnyvale *Also called Federal Express Corporation* ***(P-4701)***
Fedex, Hawthorne *Also called Federal Express Corporation* ***(P-4702)***
Fedex, Sun Valley *Also called Federal Express Corporation* ***(P-4664)***
Fedex, Rocklin *Also called Federal Express Corporation* ***(P-4665)***
Fedex, Soquel *Also called Federal Express Corporation* ***(P-4263)***
Fedex, Carlsbad *Also called Federal Express Corporation* ***(P-16778)***
Fedex, City of Industry *Also called Federal Express Corporation* ***(P-4264)***
Fedex, El Segundo *Also called Federal Express Corporation* ***(P-16779)***
Fedex, Palm Springs *Also called Federal Express Corporation* ***(P-4666)***
Fedex, San Leandro *Also called Federal Express Corporation* ***(P-4703)***
Fedex, Costa Mesa *Also called Federal Express Corporation* ***(P-4704)***
Fedex, Los Angeles *Also called Federal Express Corporation* ***(P-4020)***
Fedex, Pleasanton *Also called Federal Express Corporation* ***(P-16780)***
Fedex, Monterey *Also called Federal Express Corporation* ***(P-4705)***
Fedex, San Jose *Also called Federal Express Corporation* ***(P-4265)***
Fedex, Oakland *Also called Federal Express Corporation* ***(P-4266)***
Fedex, Oakland *Also called Federal Express Corporation* ***(P-4706)***
Fedex, Oakland *Also called Federal Express Corporation* ***(P-4707)***
Fedex, Redding *Also called Federal Express Corporation* ***(P-4708)***
Fedex, Stockton *Also called Federal Express Corporation* ***(P-4709)***
Fedex, Santa Fe Springs *Also called Federal Express Corporation* ***(P-4710)***
Fedex, Visalia *Also called Federal Express Corporation* ***(P-4711)***
Fedex, Irvine *Also called Federal Express Corporation* ***(P-16781)***
Fedex, Ontario *Also called Federal Express Corporation* ***(P-16782)***
Fedex, Ontario *Also called Federal Express Corporation* ***(P-4712)***
Fedex, Emeryville *Also called Federal Express Corporation* ***(P-3885)***
Fedex, Fullerton *Also called Federal Express Corporation* ***(P-4713)***
Fedex, Oxnard *Also called Federal Express Corporation* ***(P-4714)***
Fedex, Sacramento *Also called Federal Express Corporation* ***(P-4715)***
Fedex, San Diego *Also called Federal Express Corporation* ***(P-4945)***
Fedex, San Francisco *Also called Federal Express Corporation* ***(P-4716)***
Fedex, Long Beach *Also called Federal Express Corporation* ***(P-4717)***
Fedex, Irvine *Also called Federal Express Corporation* ***(P-4667)***
Fedex, Long Beach *Also called Federal Express Corporation* ***(P-4718)***
Fedex Corporation....E....415 657-0403
50 Cypress Ln Brisbane (94005) ***(P-16783)***
Fedex Freight Corporation....E....714 637-9346
310 W Grove Ave Orange (92865) ***(P-4579)***
Fedex Freight Corporation....C....323 269-9800
4500 Bandini Blvd Vernon (90058) ***(P-4021)***
Fedex Freight Corporation....C....714 996-8720
1379 N Miller St Anaheim (92806) ***(P-4022)***
Fedex Freight Corporation....C....909 887-3970
7250 Cajon Blvd San Bernardino (92407) ***(P-4023)***
Fedex Freight Corporation....D....760 873-8655
193 Willow St Bishop (93514) ***(P-4024)***
Fedex Freight Corporation....D....619 710-0268
2250 Airway Ln San Diego (92154) ***(P-4025)***
Fedex Freight Corporation....B....310 323-5230
15200 S Main St Gardena (90248) ***(P-4026)***
Fedex Freight Corporation....B....800 288-0743
3200 Workman Mill Rd Whittier (90601) ***(P-4580)***
Fedex Freight Corporation....E....408 988-2111
3255 Victor St Santa Clara (95054) ***(P-3886)***
Fedex Freight Corporation....B....510 895-0440
29001 Hopkins St Hayward (94545) ***(P-4027)***
Fedex Freight Corporation....D....818 899-1141
11911 Branford St Sun Valley (91352) ***(P-4028)***
Fedex Freight Corporation....C....209 466-7726
4520 S Highway 99 Stockton (95215) ***(P-4029)***
Fedex Freight Corporation....D....800 706-1687
56 Fairbanks Irvine (92618) ***(P-4030)***
Fedex Freight West Inc....D....650 244-9522
3050 Teagarden St San Leandro (94577) ***(P-4031)***
Fedex Freight West Inc....C....559 266-0732
4570 S Maple Ave Fresno (93725) ***(P-4032)***
Fedex Freight West Inc....B....909 357-3555
11153 Mulberry Ave Fontana (92337) ***(P-4033)***
Fedex Freight West Inc....E....707 778-3191
1230 N Mcdowell Blvd Petaluma (94954) ***(P-4034)***
Fedex Ground Package Sys Inc....E....800 463-3339
1497 George Dr Ste G Redding (96003) ***(P-4035)***
Fedex Ground Package Sys Inc....C....800 463-3339
590 E Orangethorpe Ave Anaheim (92801) ***(P-4036)***
Fedex Ground Package Sys Inc....C....800 463-3339
10132 Airway Rd San Diego (92154) ***(P-4267)***
Fedex Ground Package Sys Inc....D....800 463-3339
1844 S Haster St Anaheim (92802) ***(P-4037)***
Fedex Ground Package Sys Inc....C....800 463-3339
9999 Olson Dr Ste 100 San Diego (92121) ***(P-4719)***
Fedex Ground Package Sys Inc....D....800 463-3339
1 Carousel Ln Unit B Ukiah (95482) ***(P-4038)***
Fedex Ground Package Sys Inc....C....800 463-3339
101 Book Farm Rd Durham (95938) ***(P-4039)***
Fedex Ground Package Sys Inc....C....800 463-3339
1725 Charles Willard St Carson (90746) ***(P-4040)***
Fedex Ground Package Sys Inc....C....800 463-3339
311 Otterson Dr Chico (95928) ***(P-4041)***
Fedex Ground Package Sys Inc....C....800 463-3339
375 Airport Rd Bishop (93514) ***(P-4042)***
Fedex Ground Package Sys Inc....C....800 463-3339
500 Caletti Ave Windsor (95492) ***(P-4043)***
Fedex Ground Package Sys Inc....E....800 463-3339
1070 San Mateo Ave South San Francisco (94080) ***(P-4268)***
Fedex Ground Package Sys Inc....D....800 463-3339
601 Stone Rd Benicia (94510) ***(P-4269)***
Fedex Ground Package Sys Inc....D....800 463-3339
1500 E Wooley Rd Ste B Oxnard (93030) ***(P-4044)***
Fedex Ground Package Sys Inc....B....800 463-3339
696 E Trimble Rd Ste 10 San Jose (95131) ***(P-4045)***
Fedex Ground Package Sys Inc....A....800 463-3339
330 Resource Dr Bloomington (92316) ***(P-4720)***
Fedex Ground Package Sys Inc....D....800 463-3339
300 Manabe Ow Rd Watsonville (95076) ***(P-4046)***
Fedex Ground Package Sys Inc....D....800 463-3339
9175 San Fernando Rd Sun Valley (91352) ***(P-4047)***
Fedex Office & Print Svcs Inc....E....805 379-1552
2799 E Thousand Oaks Blvd Thousand Oaks (91362) ***(P-13760)***
Fedex Office & Print Svcs Inc....D....562 942-1953
8642 Whittier Blvd Pico Rivera (90660) ***(P-4270)***
Fedex Office & Print Svcs Inc....E....310 827-2297
13488 Maxella Ave Marina Del Rey (90292) ***(P-13761)***
Fedex Office & Print Svcs Inc....E....213 892-1700
800 Wilshire Blvd Los Angeles (90017) ***(P-13762)***
Fedex Smartpost Inc....D....323 888-8879
5560 Ferguson Dr Commerce (90022) ***(P-4271)***

ALPHABETIC

Employee Codes: A=Over 500 employees, B=251-500
C=101-250, D=51-100, E=50
2020 Directory of California
Wholesalers and Services Companies
© Mergent Inc. 1-800-342-5647
1267

Fedex Sup Chain Dist Sys Inc ..... E 909 605-9210
1670 Champagne Ave Ontario (91761) ***(P-4409)***
Fehr & Peers ..... D 949 308-6300
101 Pacifica Ste 300 Irvine (92618) ***(P-25071)***
Fehr & Peers (PA) ..... D 925 977-3200
100 Pringle Ave Ste 600 Walnut Creek (94596) ***(P-25072)***
Fei Enterprises Inc ..... E 323 937-0856
633 S La Brea Ave Los Angeles (90036) ***(P-2493)***
Feiwell, Lawrence MD, Los Alamitos *Also called Marinow Harry MD Facs Inc* ***(P-19174)***
Felina Lingerie, Chatsworth *Also called Piege Co* ***(P-8043)***
Fellowship Homes Inc ..... C 209 529-4950
1745 Eldena Way Modesto (95350) ***(P-23925)***
Felson Companies Inc ..... D 510 538-1150
1290 B St Ste 210 Hayward (94541) ***(P-11136)***
Felton Institute, San Francisco *Also called Family Svc Agcy San Francisco* ***(P-14504)***
Fencecorp Inc (HQ) ..... B 951 686-3170
18440 Van Buren Blvd Riverside (92508) ***(P-3405)***
Fenceworks Inc ..... D 714 238-0091
2861 E La Cresta Ave Anaheim (92806) ***(P-3406)***
Fenceworks Inc (PA) ..... C 951 788-5620
870 Main St Riverside (92501) ***(P-3407)***
Fenceworks Inc ..... D 661 265-0082
891 Corporation St Santa Paula (93060) ***(P-3408)***
Fenderscape Inc ..... C 562 988-2228
1446 E Hill St Signal Hill (90755) ***(P-811)***
Fenix Marine Services Ltd ..... C 310 548-8877
614 Terminal Way San Pedro (90731) ***(P-14158)***
Fennel Inc ..... D 951 284-2020
1169 Sherborn St Corona (92879) ***(P-2933)***
Fenton Communications Inc ..... E 415 255-1946
182 2nd St Ste 400 San Francisco (94105) ***(P-26908)***
Fenton Scripps Landing LLC ..... D 858 586-0206
9970 Erma Rd San Diego (92131) ***(P-10726)***
Fenty Beauty LLC ..... C 818 973-2709
425 Market St Fl 19 San Francisco (94105) ***(P-7942)***
Fenwick & West LLP (PA) ..... B 650 988-8500
801 California St Mountain View (94041) ***(P-22499)***
Fenwick & West LLP ..... C 415 875-2300
555 California St # 1200 San Francisco (94104) ***(P-22500)***
Feralloy PDM Steel Service, Stockton *Also called PDM Steel Service Centers* ***(P-7091)***
Fergadis Enterprises, Bell *Also called Perrin Bernard Supowitz LLC* ***(P-8207)***
Ferguson 601, Van Nuys *Also called Ferguson Enterprises Inc* ***(P-7425)***
Ferguson 667, San Diego *Also called Ferguson Enterprises Inc* ***(P-7422)***
Ferguson 677, Westminster *Also called Ferguson Enterprises Inc* ***(P-7424)***
Ferguson Enterprises Inc ..... D 408 441-7276
898 Pennsylvania Ave San Francisco (94107) ***(P-7419)***
Ferguson Enterprises Inc ..... D 626 965-0724
18825 San Jose Ave City of Industry (91748) ***(P-7420)***
Ferguson Enterprises Inc ..... E 559 253-2900
704 N Laverne Ave Fresno (93727) ***(P-7421)***
Ferguson Enterprises Inc ..... D 619 515-0300
3280 Market St San Diego (92102) ***(P-7422)***
Ferguson Enterprises Inc ..... C 909 364-8700
9750 S Town Ave Pomona (91766) ***(P-7423)***
Ferguson Enterprises Inc ..... C 714 893-1936
6421 Industry Way Westminster (92683) ***(P-7424)***
Ferguson Enterprises Inc ..... E 818 786-9720
7651 Woodman Ave Van Nuys (91402) ***(P-7425)***
Ferguson Fire Fabrication Inc (HQ) ..... D 909 517-3085
2750 S Towne Ave Pomona (91766) ***(P-7426)***
Ferguson Salon Management ..... E 760 434-4141
2946 State St Ste F Carlsbad (92008) ***(P-13344)***
Ferguson Salon Management Inc ..... E 760 434-5008
1104 Knowles Ave Carlsbad (92008) ***(P-13345)***
Fern Oaks Frms A Cal Gen Prtnr ..... E 559 684-8220
17001 Avenue 160 Porterville (93257) ***(P-389)***
Fernandes & Sons Gen Contrs ..... D 408 626-9090
2110 S Bascom Ave Ste 201 Campbell (95008) ***(P-14505)***
Fernview Convalescent Hospital ..... D 626 285-3131
126 N San Gabriel Blvd San Gabriel (91775) ***(P-19912)***
Ferrado Garden Court LLC ..... D 650 543-2224
520 Cowper St Ste 100 Palo Alto (94301) ***(P-12264)***
Ferrees Group Home Inc ..... D 951 849-1927
878 Highland Home Rd Banning (92220) ***(P-23926)***
Ferreira Service Inc (PA) ..... D 925 831-9330
3150 Crow Canyon Pl # 230 San Ramon (94583) ***(P-2136)***
Ferring Research Institute Inc ..... D 858 657-1400
4245 Sorrento Valley Blvd San Diego (92121) ***(P-25750)***
Fertility & Reproductive ..... D 408 358-2500
2581 Samaritan Dr Ste 302 San Jose (95124) ***(P-18987)***
Fess Prker-Red Lion Gen Partnr ..... B 805 564-4333
633 E Cabrillo Blvd Santa Barbara (93103) ***(P-12265)***
Festival Fun Parks LLC ..... D 951 785-3000
3500 Polk St Riverside (92505) ***(P-18330)***
Festival Fun Parks LLC ..... C 954 921-1411
4590 Macarthur Blvd # 400 Newport Beach (92660) ***(P-18692)***
Festival Fun Parks LLC ..... C 805 922-1574
2250 Preisker Ln Santa Maria (93458) ***(P-18693)***
Festival Fun Parks LLC ..... A 909 802-2200
111 Raging Waters Dr San Dimas (91773) ***(P-7709)***
Festival Fun Parks LLC ..... D 760 945-9474
1525 W Vista Way Vista (92083) ***(P-18694)***
Festival Fun Parks LLC ..... E 949 261-0404
340 Blomquist St Redwood City (94063) ***(P-18331)***
Festival Fun Parks LLC ..... D 949 559-8336
3405 Michelson Dr Irvine (92612) ***(P-18695)***
Festival of Arts Laguna Beach ..... D 949 494-1145
650 Laguna Canyon Rd Laguna Beach (92651) ***(P-18696)***
Ffd II, San Diego *Also called Fairfield Development Inc* ***(P-1242)***
Fff Enterprises Inc (PA) ..... B 951 296-2500
44000 Winchester Rd Temecula (92590) ***(P-7943)***
Ffna, Foothill Ranch *Also called Frontech N Fujitsu Amer Inc* ***(P-15596)***
Fhar Fmly Hsing Adult Rsources ..... D 650 573-3341
205 W 20th Ave San Mateo (94403) ***(P-23226)***
Fhpa, Gold River *Also called Health Net California Inc* ***(P-9950)***
Fib Lab, Milpitas *Also called Nanolab Technologies Inc* ***(P-26094)***
Fiber Optic Technologies, Torrance *Also called ACS Communications Inc* ***(P-2414)***
Fibertron Corporation ..... D 714 670-7711
6400 Artesia Blvd Buena Park (90620) ***(P-7267)***
Ficcadenti Waggoner & Castle S (PA) ..... D 949 474-0502
16969 Von Karman Ave # 240 Irvine (92606) ***(P-25073)***
Fidelity Home Energy Inc (PA) ..... D 858 220-7784
2235 Polvorosa Ave # 230 San Leandro (94577) ***(P-2137)***
Fidelity Nat HM Warranty Co ..... C 925 356-0194
1850 Gateway Blvd Ste 400 Concord (94520) ***(P-10183)***
Fidelity National Fincl Inc ..... D 949 622-5000
1300 Dove St Ste 310 Newport Beach (92660) ***(P-10362)***
Fidelity Roof Company (PA) ..... D 510 547-6330
1075 40th St Oakland (94608) ***(P-3053)***
Fidelity Security Services Inc ..... C 661 295-5007
25133 Avenue Tibbitts H Valencia (91355) ***(P-16271)***
Fidelity Tax Relief, Irvine *Also called Tax Rise Inc* ***(P-17081)***
Field Foundation ..... E 562 921-3567
15306 Carmenita Rd Santa Fe Springs (90670) ***(P-1021)***
Field Fresh Farms LLC ..... D 831 722-1422
320 Industrial Rd Watsonville (95076) ***(P-8469)***
Fields Construction Services ..... D 925 294-8183
5715 Southfront Rd Ste B1 Livermore (94551) ***(P-13925)***
Fields Win Clg Win Protection, Livermore *Also called Fields Construction Services* ***(P-13925)***
Fieldserver Technologies ..... E 408 262-2299
1991 Tarob Ct Milpitas (95035) ***(P-6002)***
Fieldstone Co, The, San Diego *Also called Fieldstone Communities Inc* ***(P-1123)***
Fieldstone Communities Inc ..... E 858 546-8226
5465 Morehouse Dr Ste 250 San Diego (92121) ***(P-1123)***
Fieldstone Communities Inc (PA) ..... C 949 790-5400
16 Technology Dr Ste 125 Irvine (92618) ***(P-1296)***
Fieno Inc ..... D 760 352-2996
11583 Big Canyon Ln San Diego (92131) ***(P-489)***
Fierce Wombat Games Inc ..... E 408 745-5400
910 E Hamilton Ave Fl 6 Campbell (95008) ***(P-15760)***
Fiesta De Reyes, San Diego *Also called Old Town Fmly Hospitality Corp* ***(P-12667)***
Fifth & Sunset Enterprises LLC ..... D 310 979-0212
12322 Exposition Blvd Los Angeles (90064) ***(P-14159)***
Fifty Peninsula Partners ..... D 650 344-8200
850 N El Camino Real Ofc San Mateo (94401) ***(P-10727)***
Fig Holdings LLC ..... D 209 524-4817
1310 W Granger Ave Modesto (95350) ***(P-19913)***
Figi Acquisition Company LLC ..... C 800 678-3444
3636 Gateway Center Ave San Diego (92102) ***(P-8970)***
Figure Eight Technologies Inc ..... D 415 471-1920
940 Howard St San Francisco (94103) ***(P-15761)***
Fiji Water Company LLC (HQ) ..... E 310 966-5700
11444 W Olympic Blvd # 250 Los Angeles (90064) ***(P-8577)***
Filament Hospitality, San Francisco *Also called Maverick Hotel Partners LLC* ***(P-26308)***
Filemaker, Inc., Santa Clara *Also called Claris International Inc* ***(P-14713)***
Filice Insurance Agency, San Jose *Also called Ron Filice Enterprises Inc* ***(P-10477)***
Fillmore Convalescent Ctr LLC ..... D 805 524-0083
118 B St Fillmore (93015) ***(P-20553)***
Fillmore Marketplace I, San Francisco *Also called Fillmore Marketplace LP* ***(P-11137)***
Fillmore Marketplace LP ..... E 415 921-6514
1223 Webster St San Francisco (94115) ***(P-11137)***
Film Payroll Services Inc (PA) ..... D 310 440-9600
500 S Sepulveda Blvd Fl 4 Los Angeles (90049) ***(P-25596)***
Film Roman Llc ..... C 818 748-4000
6320 Canoga Ave Ste 450 Woodland Hills (91367) ***(P-17607)***
Film Roman LLC ..... C 818 748-4000
6320 Canoga Ave Ste 450 Woodland Hills (91367) ***(P-17608)***
Filml.a, Los Angeles *Also called A Filml Inc* ***(P-17722)***
Filmquest Pictures Corporation ..... C 818 905-1006
15331 Stonewood Ter Sherman Oaks (91403) ***(P-17609)***
Filoli Center ..... D 650 364-8300
86 Canada Rd Woodside (94062) ***(P-24307)***
FILOLI GARDEN SHOP, Woodside *Also called Filoli Center* ***(P-24307)***
Filyn Corporation ..... C 714 632-0225
2950 E La Jolla St Anaheim (92806) ***(P-3671)***
Fimac Inc ..... D 949 359-6100
26300 La Alameda Ste 200 Mission Viejo (92691) ***(P-26606)***
Final Film ..... D 323 467-0700
3620 W Valhalla Dr Burbank (91505) ***(P-13783)***
Finance America LLC (HQ) ..... C 949 440-1000
1901 Main St Ste 150 Irvine (92614) ***(P-9548)***
Finance America Mortgage LLC ..... B 562 478-4664
13200 Crossroads Pkwy N City of Industry (91746) ***(P-9549)***
Financial Credit Network Inc (PA) ..... D 559 733-7550
1300 W Main St Visalia (93291) ***(P-13682)***
Financial Division, Imperial Beach *Also called Jpmorgan Chase Bank Nat Assn* ***(P-9099)***
Financial Healthcare Services ..... E 626 356-7950
690 E Green St Ste 300 Pasadena (91101) ***(P-26607)***
Financial Information Network ..... D 818 782-0331
6656 Valjean Ave Van Nuys (91406) ***(P-14809)***
Financial Pacific Insurance Co ..... D 916 630-5000
3850 Atherton Rd Rocklin (95765) ***(P-10363)***
Financial Partners Credit Un (PA) ..... D 562 904-3000
7800 Imperial Hwy Downey (90242) ***(P-9306)***
Financial Statement Svcs Inc (PA) ..... C 714 436-3326
3300 S Fairview St Santa Ana (92704) ***(P-13722)***

Mergent e-mail: customerrelations@mergent.com
1268
2020 Directory of California
Wholesalers and Services Companies
(P-0000) Products & Services Section entry number
(PA)=Parent Co (HQ)=Headquarters (DH)=Div Headquarters

Financial Technology Ventures, San Francisco *Also called Ftv Management Company LP* ***(P-11727)***
Financial Transaction, Roseville *Also called Safe Credit Union* ***(P-9341)***
Financialforcecom Inc (HQ).......D.......866 743-2220
595 Market St Ste 2700 San Francisco (94105) ***(P-14810)***
Finastra Merchant Services Inc (PA).......D.......415 277-9900
333 Bush St Fl 26 San Francisco (94104) ***(P-9434)***
Fine Arts Museum, Santa Barbara *Also called Santa Barbara Museum of Art* ***(P-24292)***
Fine Chemicals Holdings Corp.......B.......916 357-6880
Hwy 50 Hzel Ave Bldg 0501 Rancho Cordova (95741) ***(P-11659)***
Fine Line Group Inc.......E.......415 777-4070
457 Minna St San Francisco (94103) ***(P-1478)***
Fine Northern Oak, NAPA *Also called Seguin Mreau NAPA Coperage Inc* ***(P-7656)***
Finest Produce, Bellflower *Also called Produce Company* ***(P-8512)***
Finezi Inc.......D.......510 790-4768
31080 Blvd Ste 212 Union City (94587) ***(P-14282)***
Finley Swim Center.......E.......707 543-3760
2060 W College Ave Santa Rosa (95401) ***(P-18697)***
Finn Holding Corporation (PA).......A.......310 712-1850
360 N Crescent Dr Beverly Hills (90210) ***(P-4593)***
Finnco Services Incorporated.......D.......909 355-0707
8241 Beech Ave Fontana (92335) ***(P-14160)***
Fiorano Software Inc.......D.......650 326-1136
230 California Ave # 103 Palo Alto (94306) ***(P-15326)***
Fire and Police.......E.......562 961-0066
4645 E Anaheim St Long Beach (90804) ***(P-24338)***
Fire Insurance Exchange (PA).......A.......323 932-3200
4680 Wilshire Blvd Los Angeles (90010) ***(P-10364)***
Fire Safe Systems Inc.......D.......310 542-0585
1312 Kingsdale Ave Redondo Beach (90278) ***(P-2138)***
Fire Safety First, Santa Ana *Also called Brethren Inc* ***(P-7801)***
Fire Sprinkler Systems Inc (PA).......D.......800 915-3473
705 E Harrison St Ste 200 Corona (92879) ***(P-2139)***
Firearms Academy, Santa Ana *Also called OC Special Events SEC Inc* ***(P-16365)***
Fireeye Inc (PA).......C.......408 321-6300
601 Mccarthy Blvd Milpitas (95035) ***(P-15327)***
Firefighter Cancer Support Ntw.......E.......866 994-3276
3460 Fletcher Ave El Monte (91731) ***(P-23227)***
Firefighters First Credit Un (PA).......C.......323 254-1700
815 Colorado Blvd Los Angeles (90041) ***(P-9307)***
Firemans Fund Insurance Co (HQ).......A.......415 899-2000
1465 N Mcdowell Blvd # 100 Petaluma (94954) ***(P-10087)***
Firemans Fund Insurance Co.......C.......858 492-3019
9275 Sky Park Ct San Diego (92123) ***(P-10088)***
Firemans Fund Insurance Co.......C.......818 953-6533
2350 W Empire Ave Ste 200 Burbank (91504) ***(P-10089)***
Firm A Chugh Professional Corp.......D.......562 229-1220
15925 Carmenita Rd Cerritos (90703) ***(P-22501)***
Firm A Chugh Professional Corp.......E.......408 970-0100
1600 Duane Ave Santa Clara (95054) ***(P-22502)***
Firma Plastic Co Inc.......B.......323 567-7767
9309 Rayo Ave South Gate (90280) ***(P-7757)***
First & La Realty Corp (PA).......D.......805 581-0021
1301 E Los Angeles Ave Simi Valley (93065) ***(P-11138)***
First Alarm.......A.......831 649-1111
1 Lower Ragsdale Dr # 3700 Monterey (93940) ***(P-2494)***
First Alarm (PA).......C.......831 476-1111
1111 Estates Dr Aptos (95003) ***(P-16514)***
First Alarm SEC & Patrol Inc.......A.......209 473-1110
5250 Claremont Ave Stockton (95207) ***(P-16515)***
First Alarm SEC & Patrol Inc.......B.......925 295-1260
1801 Oakland Blvd Ste 315 Walnut Creek (94596) ***(P-16516)***
First Alarm SEC & Patrol Inc.......B.......707 584-1110
1240 Briggs Ave Santa Rosa (95401) ***(P-16517)***
First Alarm SEC & Patrol Inc (PA).......C.......408 866-1111
1731 Tech Dr Ste 800 San Jose (95110) ***(P-16518)***
First Allied Securities Inc (HQ).......D.......619 702-9600
655 W Broadway Fl 11 San Diego (92101) ***(P-9688)***
First Amercn Lenders Advantage, Concord *Also called First American Title Insur Co* ***(P-10192)***
First Amercn Prof RE Svcs Inc (PA).......C.......714 250-1400
200 Commerce Irvine (92602) ***(P-11139)***
First American Card Service.......E.......951 677-8720
25060 Hancock Ave Ste 103 Murrieta (92562) ***(P-16784)***
First American Casualty Insur, Santa Ana *Also called First American Title Insur Co* ***(P-10191)***
First American Financial Corp (PA).......C.......714 250-3000
1 First American Way Santa Ana (92707) ***(P-10184)***
First American Mortgage Svcs.......B.......714 250-4210
3 First American Way Santa Ana (92707) ***(P-10185)***
First American Team Realty Inc (PA).......C.......562 427-7765
2501 Cherry Ave Ste 100 Signal Hill (90755) ***(P-11140)***
First American Title Company.......A.......714 250-3109
1 First American Way Santa Ana (92707) ***(P-23228)***
First American Title Insur Co.......D.......925 356-7000
1001 Galaxy Way Ste 101 Concord (94520) ***(P-11533)***
First American Title Insur Co (HQ).......C.......800 854-3643
1 First American Way Santa Ana (92707) ***(P-10186)***
First American Title Insur Co.......C.......619 238-1776
411 Ivy St San Diego (92101) ***(P-10187)***
First American Title Insur Co.......C.......909 889-0311
1855 W Rdlands Blvd 100 Redlands (92373) ***(P-10188)***
First American Title Insur Co (HQ).......A.......714 250-3109
330 Soquel Ave Santa Cruz (95062) ***(P-10189)***
First American Title Insur Co.......E.......805 543-8900
899 Pacific St San Luis Obispo (93401) ***(P-10190)***
First American Title Insur Co.......C.......714 800-3000
9 First American Way Santa Ana (92707) ***(P-10191)***
First American Title Insur Co.......D.......925 798-2800
1855 Gateway Blvd Ste 700 Concord (94520) ***(P-10192)***
First American Title Insur Co.......A.......714 250-4000
3 First American Way Santa Ana (92707) ***(P-10193)***
First American Trust Company (HQ).......D.......714 560-7856
5 First American Way Santa Ana (92707) ***(P-9813)***
First Avenue Inc.......D.......626 856-2076
5105 Heintz St Baldwin Park (91706) ***(P-3054)***
First Baptist Head Start.......D.......925 473-2000
3890 Railroad Ave Pittsburg (94565) ***(P-23725)***
First California Mrtg Co II.......D.......415 209-0910
1400 N Mcdowell Blvd # 300 Petaluma (94954) ***(P-9550)***
First Call Nursing Svcs Inc.......C.......408 262-1533
1313 N Milpitas Blvd # 154 Milpitas (95035) ***(P-14283)***
First Capitol Consulting Inc.......D.......213 382-1115
3530 Wilshire Blvd # 1460 Los Angeles (90010) ***(P-26608)***
First Choice Bank.......D.......213 617-0082
888 W 6th St Ste 200 Los Angeles (90017) ***(P-9199)***
First Choice Bank (HQ).......D.......562 345-9092
17785 Center Court Dr N # 750 Cerritos (90703) ***(P-9200)***
First City Credit Union (PA).......C.......213 482-3477
717 W Temple St Ste 400 Los Angeles (90012) ***(P-9308)***
First Community Bancorp.......D.......858 756-3023
5900 La Place Ct Ste 200 Carlsbad (92008) ***(P-9095)***
First Data Hardware Svcs Inc.......B.......916 632-7600
8875 Washington Blvd A Roseville (95678) ***(P-9435)***
First Databank Inc.......D.......650 588-5454
701 Gateway Blvd Ste 600 San Francisco (94188) ***(P-15762)***
First Entertainment Credit Un (PA).......D.......323 851-3673
6735 Forest Lawn Dr # 100 Los Angeles (90068) ***(P-9309)***
First Family Homes.......E.......562 862-7373
12027 Paramount Blvd Downey (90242) ***(P-11141)***
First Fire Systems Inc (PA).......D.......310 559-0900
5947 Burchard Ave Los Angeles (90034) ***(P-16519)***
First Foundation Inc.......C.......626 993-1300
301 N Lake Ave Ste 100 Pasadena (91101) ***(P-9252)***
First Group of America, Santa Maria *Also called First Transit* ***(P-3534)***
First Hotels International Inc.......C.......909 884-9364
295 N E St San Bernardino (92401) ***(P-12266)***
First Interstate Security Inc.......C.......818 995-6664
20548 Ventura Blvd # 118 Woodland Hills (91364) ***(P-16272)***
First Legal Support Svcs LLC (PA).......D.......213 250-1111
1517 Beverly Blvd Los Angeles (90026) ***(P-22503)***
First Marin Realty Inc.......D.......415 383-9393
145 Lomita Dr Mill Valley (94941) ***(P-11142)***
First National Bank.......B.......858 756-3023
6110 El Tordo Rancho Santa Fe (92067) ***(P-9096)***
First National Bank (PA).......D.......619 233-5588
401 W A St Ste 200 San Diego (92101) ***(P-11785)***
First Nationwide Mortgage Corp.......C.......818 209-3134
18440 Bermuda St Northridge (91326) ***(P-9625)***
First Northern Bank of Dixon (HQ).......D.......707 678-4422
195 N 1st St Dixon (95620) ***(P-9201)***
First Northern Community, Dixon *Also called First Northern Bank of Dixon* ***(P-9201)***
First Page Sage LLC.......D.......415 624-3526
2250 Union St San Francisco (94123) ***(P-26609)***
First Place For Youth (PA).......E.......510 272-0979
426 17th St Ste 100 Oakland (94612) ***(P-23229)***
First Priority Financial Inc.......B.......707 432-1000
3700 Hilborn Rd Ste 700 Fairfield (94534) ***(P-9551)***
First Regional Bancorp.......B.......310 552-1776
1801 Century Park E # 800 Los Angeles (90067) ***(P-9202)***
First Reprographic, Los Angeles *Also called Lasr Inc* ***(P-13764)***
First Republic Bank.......C.......415 389-0880
750 Redwood Hwy Frontage # 1218 Mill Valley (94941) ***(P-9253)***
First Republic Bank.......D.......415 392-1400
101 Pine St San Francisco (94111) ***(P-9254)***
First Republic Bank.......C.......415 392-3888
44 Montgomery St Ste 110 San Francisco (94104) ***(P-9203)***
First Republic Bank.......C.......650 233-8880
2550 Sand Hill Rd Ste 100 Menlo Park (94025) ***(P-9204)***
First Republic Bank.......C.......213 239-8883
888 S Figueroa St Ste 100 Los Angeles (90017) ***(P-9205)***
First Republic Bank.......C.......925 254-8993
224 Brookwood Rd Orinda (94563) ***(P-9206)***
First Republic Bank.......C.......619 238-9088
1280 4th Ave San Diego (92101) ***(P-9255)***
First Republic Bank.......C.......415 564-8881
653 Irving St San Francisco (94122) ***(P-9256)***
First Republic Bank.......C.......415 487-0888
1355 Market St Ste 140 San Francisco (94103) ***(P-9257)***
First Republic Bank.......C.......415 975-3877
405 Howard St Ste 110 San Francisco (94105) ***(P-9258)***
First Republic Bank.......D.......310 712-1888
1888 Century Park E # 200 Los Angeles (90067) ***(P-9259)***
First Republic Bank (PA).......B.......415 392-1400
111 Pine St Fl 2 San Francisco (94111) ***(P-9260)***
First Republic Bank.......C.......650 470-8888
1215 El Camino Real Menlo Park (94025) ***(P-9207)***
First Responder Ems.......C.......530 897-6345
333 Huss Dr Ste 100 Chico (95928) ***(P-3672)***
First Responder Ems Inc.......D.......530 897-6345
333 Huss Dr Ste 100 Chico (95928) ***(P-3673)***
First Rsponder Emrgncy Med Svc.......C.......530 891-4357
333 Huss Dr Ste 300 Chico (95928) ***(P-3674)***
First Security Services, San Jose *Also called First Alarm SEC & Patrol Inc* ***(P-16518)***
First State, Huntington Beach *Also called First Team RE - Orange Cnty* ***(P-11148)***
First Step Ind Living Program, Rancho Cucamonga *Also called National Mentor Inc* ***(P-23618)***
First Student Inc.......D.......510 237-6677
436 Parr Blvd Richmond (94801) ***(P-3801)***

Employee Codes: A=Over 500 employees, B=251-500
C=101-250, D=51-100, E=50
2020 Directory of California
Wholesalers and Services Companies
© Mergent Inc. 1-800-342-5647
1269

First Student Inc ....D......925 676-1976
2477 Arnold Indus Way Concord (94520) *(P-3802)*
First Student Inc ....D......650 685-8245
991 E Poplar Ave San Mateo (94401) *(P-3803)*
First Student Inc ....C......951 736-3234
300 S Buena Vista Ave Corona (92882) *(P-3830)*
First Student Inc ....D......909 383-1640
234 S I St San Bernardino (92410) *(P-3804)*
First Student Inc ....D......760 320-4659
5006 E Calle San Raphael Palm Springs (92264) *(P-3805)*
First Student Inc ....C......209 466-7737
2005 Navy Dr Stockton (95206) *(P-3806)*
First Student Inc ....D......909 383-7104
844 E 9th St San Bernardino (92410) *(P-3807)*
First Student Inc ....D......626 448-9446
4337 Rowland Ave El Monte (91731) *(P-3533)*
First Student Inc ....B......415 647-9012
2270 Jerrold Ave San Francisco (94124) *(P-3808)*
First Student Inc ....D......818 707-2082
5320 Derry Ave Ste O Agoura Hills (91301) *(P-3809)*
First Student Inc ....D......714 850-7578
3401 W Castor St Santa Ana (92704) *(P-3810)*
First Student Inc ....C......925 754-4878
801 Wilbur Ave Antioch (94509) *(P-3811)*
First Student Inc ....C......818 896-0333
11233 San Fernando Rd San Fernando (91340) *(P-3812)*
First Student Inc ....C......559 661-7433
123 N E St Ste 102 Madera (93638) *(P-3813)*
First Student Inc ....C......310 769-2400
14800 S Avalon Blvd Gardena (90248) *(P-3814)*
First Team RE - Orange Cnty ....D......760 340-9911
74855 Country Club Dr Palm Desert (92260) *(P-11143)*
First Team RE - Orange Cnty ....D......714 223-2143
18180 Yorba Linda Blvd # 501 Yorba Linda (92886) *(P-11144)*
First Team RE - Orange Cnty ....C......562 596-9911
12501 Seal Beach Blvd # 100 Seal Beach (90740) *(P-11145)*
First Team RE - Orange Cnty ....D......949 759-5747
4 Corporate Plaza Dr # 100 Newport Beach (92660) *(P-11146)*
First Team RE - Orange Cnty (PA) ....C......888 236-1943
108 Pacifica Ste 300 Irvine (92618) *(P-11147)*
First Team RE - Orange Cnty ....D......714 965-2244
20100 Brookhurst St Huntington Beach (92646) *(P-11148)*
First Team RE - Orange Cnty ....D......562 346-5088
42 64th Pl Long Beach (90803) *(P-11149)*
First Team RE - Orange Cnty ....C......949 240-7979
32451 Golden Lantern # 210 Laguna Niguel (92677) *(P-11150)*
First Team RE - Orange Cnty ....C......714 544-5456
17240 17th St Tustin (92780) *(P-11151)*
First Team RE - Orange Cnty ....D......714 974-9191
8028 E Santa Ana Cyn Rd Anaheim (92808) *(P-11152)*
First Team RE - Orange Cnty ....C......949 389-0004
26711 Aliso Creek Rd # 200 Aliso Viejo (92656) *(P-11153)*
First Team Walk-In Realty, Irvine *Also called First Team RE - Orange Cnty* *(P-11147)*
First Technology Federal Cr Un (PA) ....D......855 855-8805
2702 Orchard Pkwy San Jose (95134) *(P-9310)*
First Technology Federal Cr Un ....C......855 855-8805
1011 Sunset Blvd Ste 210 Rocklin (95765) *(P-9311)*
First Transit ....D......805 925-5254
1303 Fairway Dr Santa Maria (93455) *(P-3534)*
First Transit Inc ....D......310 515-8270
2400 E Dominguez St Long Beach (90810) *(P-3535)*
First Transit Inc ....D......510 535-9192
411 High St Oakland (94601) *(P-3536)*
First Transit Inc ....D......510 437-8990
407 High St Oakland (94601) *(P-3537)*
First US Community Credit Un (PA) ....D......916 576-5700
580 University Ave # 100 Sacramento (95825) *(P-9312)*
Firstat Nursing Services Inc ....C......619 220-7600
411 Camino Del Rio S # 100 San Diego (92108) *(P-21742)*
Firstcall (PA) ....C......415 781-4300
1 Sansome St Ste 3500 San Francisco (94104) *(P-16273)*
Firstservice Residential (HQ) ....C......949 448-6000
15241 Laguna Canyon Rd Irvine (92618) *(P-11154)*
Firstsight Vision Services Inc (HQ) ....D......909 920-5008
1202 Monte Vista Ave # 17 Upland (91786) *(P-19648)*
Firstsrvice Rsidential Cal Inc (HQ) ....D......909 981-4131
195 N Euclid Ave Upland (91786) *(P-11155)*
Fischer Inc ....D......909 881-2910
1372 W 26th St San Bernardino (92405) *(P-2140)*
Fischer Tile and Marble Inc ....C......916 452-1426
1800 23rd St Sacramento (95816) *(P-2896)*
Fiserv Inc ....D......909 595-9074
19935 E Walnut Dr N City of Industry (91789) *(P-15763)*
Fiserv Inc ....D......909 598-8700
19935 E Walnut Dr N Walnut (91789) *(P-15764)*
Fiserv Inc ....D......408 242-3011
525 Almanor Ave Sunnyvale (94085) *(P-15765)*
Fiserv Inc ....D......805 532-9100
405 Science Dr Moorpark (93021) *(P-15766)*
Fiserv Inc ....D......818 226-4400
8413 Fallbrook Ave West Hills (91304) *(P-15767)*
Fiserv Inc ....D......909 595-9074
19935 E Walnut Dr N Walnut (91789) *(P-15768)*
Fish & Richardson PC ....D......650 839-5070
500 Arguello St Ste 500 # 500 Redwood City (94063) *(P-22504)*
Fish & Richardson PC ....C......858 678-5070
12390 El Camino Real San Diego (92130) *(P-22505)*
Fishel Company ....D......714 668-9268
647 Young St Santa Ana (92705) *(P-1854)*
Fisher & Paykel Healthcare Inc ....C......949 453-4000
173 Technology Dr Ste 100 Irvine (92618) *(P-6965)*
Fisher & Phillips LLP ....D......949 851-2424
2050 Main St Ste 1000 Irvine (92614) *(P-22506)*
Fisher Communications Inc ....D......661 327-7955
1901 Westwind Dr Bakersfield (93301) *(P-5603)*
Fisher Ranch LLC ....D......760 922-4151
10610 Ice Plant Rd Blythe (92225) *(P-490)*
Fisher Scientific Company LLC ....D......909 393-2100
6722 Bickmore Ave Chino (91708) *(P-7029)*
Fisheries Resource Vlntr Corps ....C......562 596-9261
109 Stanford Ln Seal Beach (90740) *(P-26610)*
Fishers Nursery ....D......209 599-3412
24081 S Austin Rd Ripon (95366) *(P-8892)*
Fishman Supply Company ....D......707 763-8161
1345 Industrial Ave Petaluma (94952) *(P-7670)*
Fisk Electric Company ....C......818 884-1166
15870 Olden St Sylmar (91342) *(P-2495)*
Fit Electronics Inc (HQ) ....C......714 988-9388
500 S Kraemer Blvd # 100 Brea (92821) *(P-25751)*
Fitness 2000 Inc ....E......510 791-2481
35145 Newark Blvd Newark (94560) *(P-18145)*
Fitness International LLC ....E......949 421-6082
24491 Alicia Pkwy Mission Viejo (92691) *(P-18146)*
Fitness International LLC ....E......858 550-5912
10535 Heater Ct San Diego (92121) *(P-18147)*
Fitness Ridge Malibu LLC ....D......818 874-1300
277 Latigo Canyon Rd Malibu (90265) *(P-12267)*
Fitz Fresh Inc ....E......831 763-4440
211 Lee Rd Watsonville (95076) *(P-291)*
Fitzgrald Abbott Beardsley LLP ....D......510 451-3300
1221 Broadway Fl 21 Oakland (94612) *(P-22507)*
Five Acres-The Boys & Girls & ....B......626 798-6793
760 Mountain View St Altadena (91001) *(P-23927)*
Five Star Auto Repair and Wash, Rocklin *Also called Jkf Auto Service Inc* *(P-17379)*
Five Star Auto Repr & Car Wash, Rocklin *Also called Jemtown Inc* *(P-17378)*
Five Star Packing LLC ....A......760 356-4103
437 W 5th St Holtville (92250) *(P-621)*
Five Star Parking-San Diego ....C......619 235-4500
3585 Corporate Ct San Diego (92123) *(P-17253)*
Five Star Quality Care Inc ....D......760 327-8541
277 S Sunrise Way Palm Springs (92262) *(P-26230)*
Five Star Quality Care Inc ....C......949 642-8044
466 Flagship Rd Newport Beach (92663) *(P-19914)*
Five Star Quality Care Inc ....B......858 673-6300
16925 Hierba Dr San Diego (92128) *(P-19915)*
Five Star Quality Care Inc ....D......559 446-6226
6075 N Marks Ave Fresno (93711) *(P-19916)*
Five Star Qulty Care-CA II LLC ....C......209 466-2066
537 E Fulton St Stockton (95204) *(P-19917)*
Five Star Qulty Care-CA II LLC ....D......818 997-1841
6835 Hazeltine Ave Van Nuys (91405) *(P-19918)*
Five Star Senior Living Inc ....E......760 479-1818
1350 S El Camino Real Encinitas (92024) *(P-19919)*
Five Star Senior Living Inc ....E......209 951-6500
3530 Deer Park Dr Stockton (95219) *(P-19920)*
Five Star Transportation Inc ....E......310 348-0820
8703 La Tijera Blvd # 102 Los Angeles (90045) *(P-4875)*
Five9 Inc (PA) ....C......925 201-2000
4000 Executive Pkwy # 400 San Ramon (94583) *(P-15328)*
FJ Willert Contracting Co ....C......619 421-1980
1869 Nirvana Ave Chula Vista (91911) *(P-3313)*
Fjs Inc ....C......714 905-1050
888 S Disneyland Dr # 400 Anaheim (92802) *(P-12268)*
Fkc Partners A Cal Ltd Partnr ....E......714 528-9864
180 N Rverview Dr Ste 100 Anaheim (92808) *(P-11156)*
Fkc Properties, Anaheim *Also called Fkc Partners A Cal Ltd Partnr* *(P-11156)*
Flagship Credit Acceptance LLC ....C......949 748-7172
7525 Irvine Center Dr Irvine (92618) *(P-16785)*
Flagship Health Care Center, Newport Beach *Also called Five Star Quality Care Inc* *(P-19914)*
Flagship Healthcare Center, Newport Beach *Also called SSC Newport Beach Oper Co LP* *(P-20270)*
Flagstar Bancorp Inc ....C......714 549-9100
949 S Coast Dr Ste 100 Costa Mesa (92626) *(P-9436)*
Flair Building Maintanance, Santa Clara *Also called Flair Building Services Inc* *(P-13926)*
Flair Building Services Inc ....D......408 987-4040
3470 Edward Ave Santa Clara (95054) *(P-13926)*
Flamingo Resort Hotel, Santa Rosa *Also called Bavarian Lion Company Cal* *(P-12044)*
Flanders Pointe Apts, Tustin *Also called Steadfast Management Co Inc* *(P-10819)*
Flash Point Graphix, Burbank *Also called Final Film* *(P-13783)*
Flat White Economy Inv USA LLC ....C......949 344-5013
5151 Cal Ave Ste 100 Costa Mesa (92626) *(P-6205)*
Flatiron Electric Group Inc ....E......714 228-9631
15335 Fairfield Ranch Rd # 200 Chino Hills (91709) *(P-2496)*
Flatiron West Inc ....C......707 742-6000
2100 Goodyear Rd Benicia (94510) *(P-1817)*
Flatiron West Inc ....D......909 597-8413
16341 Chino Corona Rd Chino (91708) *(P-1818)*
Flawless Vape Wholesale Dist ....D......714 768-7928
1021 E Orangethorpe Ave Anaheim (92801) *(P-8939)*
Fleet Maintenance Dept, Santa Cruz *Also called Santa Cruz Metro Trnst Dst* *(P-3765)*
Fleet Mangement Solutions, Garden Grove *Also called Teletrac Inc* *(P-5803)*
Fleischman Field Research Inc ....C......415 398-4140
250 Sutter St Fl 2 San Francisco (94108) *(P-25895)*
Fleishman-Hillard Inc ....E......415 318-4000
720 California St Fl 6 San Francisco (94108) *(P-26909)*
Flexcare LLC ....A......866 564-3589
990 Reserve Dr Ste 200 Roseville (95678) *(P-14284)*
Flexcare Medical Staffing, Roseville *Also called Flexcare LLC* *(P-14284)*

Mergent e-mail: customerrelations@mergent.com
1270
2020 Directory of California
Wholesalers and Services Companies
(P-0000) Products & Services Section entry number
(PA)=Parent Co (HQ)=Headquarters (DH)=Div Headquarters

Flexilis, San Francisco *Also called Lookout Inc* ***(P-16542)***
Flexport Inc (PA) ....D....415 231-5252
760 Market St Fl 8 San Francisco (94102) ***(P-5115)***
Flextronics Global Services, Milpitas *Also called Flextronics Intl USA Inc* ***(P-5400)***
Flextronics Intl USA Inc ....C....408 576-6769
890 Yosemite Dr Bldg 14 Milpitas (95035) ***(P-5400)***
Flickr Inc ....E....650 265-0396
390 Fremont St San Francisco (94105) ***(P-14811)***
Flintco Pacific Inc ....D....916 757-1000
401 Derek Pl Roseville (95678) ***(P-25074)***
Flir Commercial Systems Inc (HQ) ....B....805 964-9797
6769 Hollister Ave # 100 Goleta (93117) ***(P-7268)***
Flo Health Inc ....D....510 303-9307
541 Jefferson Ave Ste 100 Redwood City (94063) ***(P-14812)***
Floaties Swim School LLC ....D....877 277-7946
13180 Poway Rd Poway (92064) ***(P-18698)***
Floorgate Inc ....D....323 478-2000
3350 N San Fernando Rd Los Angeles (90065) ***(P-3002)***
Floormasters, The, Hayward *Also called Dt Floormasters Inc* ***(P-3000)***
FLOR DO OAKLEY CLUB, Oakley *Also called Flordo Oakley Hall* ***(P-10589)***
Flora Ter Convalescent Hosp, Los Angeles *Also called Country Villa Terrace* ***(P-20537)***
Flora Terra Landscape MGT, San Jose *Also called City II Enterprises Inc* ***(P-787)***
Flordo Oakley Hall ....C....925 625-4076
520 2nd St Oakley (94561) ***(P-10589)***
Florence Crittenton Services ....B....714 680-9000
801 E Chapman Ave Ste 203 Fullerton (92831) ***(P-23928)***
Florence Filter Corporation ....D....310 637-1137
530 W Manville St Compton (90220) ***(P-7448)***
Florence Villa Hotel ....C....415 397-7700
225 Powell St San Francisco (94102) ***(P-12269)***
Florence Villa Hotel LLC ....D....415 397-7700
225 Powell St San Francisco (94102) ***(P-12270)***
Flores Labor Contracting ....B....661 792-3061
501 6th St Mc Farland (93250) ***(P-622)***
Florida Beauty Flora Inc ....C....805 642-1633
6205 Ventura Blvd Ventura (93003) ***(P-13346)***
Florida Conditioning, City of Industry *Also called American AC Distrs LLC* ***(P-2037)***
Floyd Johnston Cnstr Co Inc ....D....559 299-7373
2301 Herndon Ave Clovis (93611) ***(P-1855)***
Floyd Skeren & Kelly LLP (PA) ....D....818 206-9222
101 Moody Ct Ste 200 Thousand Oaks (91360) ***(P-22508)***
Flt Inc ....C....916 355-1500
12747 Folsom Blvd Folsom (95630) ***(P-17327)***
Fluid Inc (HQ) ....D....877 343-3240
1611 Telegraph Ave # 400 Oakland (94612) ***(P-14813)***
Fluor Corporation ....D....949 349-2000
3 Polaris Way Aliso Viejo (92656) ***(P-25075)***
Fluor Daniel, Aliso Viejo *Also called Fluor Plant Services Intl Inc* ***(P-25079)***
Fluor Daniel Construction Co (HQ) ....B....949 349-2000
3 Polaris Way Aliso Viejo (92656) ***(P-1819)***
Fluor Enterprises Inc ....D....408 256-0853
5600 Cottle Rd San Jose (95123) ***(P-25076)***
Fluor Enterprises Inc ....D....949 349-2000
9701 Jeronimo Rd Irvine (92618) ***(P-25077)***
Fluor Enterprises Inc ....D....469 398-7000
1 Fluor Daniel Dr Aliso Viejo (92698) ***(P-25078)***
Fluor Enterprises Inc ....C....949 349-2000
3 Polaris Way Aliso Viejo (92656) ***(P-7471)***
Fluor Facility & Plant Svcs ....C....408 256-1333
124 Blossom Hill Rd Ste H San Jose (95123) ***(P-13927)***
Fluor Industrial Services Inc ....A....949 439-2000
1 Enterprise Aliso Viejo (92656) ***(P-13928)***
Fluor Plant Services Intl Inc ....D....949 349-2000
1 Enterprise Aliso Viejo (92656) ***(P-25079)***
Fluoramec LLC (HQ) ....E....949 349-2000
1 Enterprise Aliso Viejo (92656) ***(P-25080)***
Flurish Inc ....D....855 253-6387
1750 Broadway 300 Oakland (94612) ***(P-9459)***
Flw Inc ....D....714 751-7512
5672 Bolsa Ave Huntington Beach (92649) ***(P-7204)***
Flyers Energy LLC ....B....661 321-9961
4200 Buck Owens Blvd Bakersfield (93308) ***(P-8728)***
Flyers Energy LLC ....C....909 877-2441
571 W Slover Ave Bloomington (92316) ***(P-8729)***
Flynn Properties Inc ....E....415 835-0225
225 Bush St Ste 1470 San Francisco (94104) ***(P-11157)***
FM Global, Walnut Creek *Also called Factory Mutual Insurance Co* ***(P-10084)***
FM Global, Woodland Hills *Also called Factory Mutual Insurance Co* ***(P-10085)***
FMB, Tustin *Also called Foundation Building Mtls Inc* ***(P-6618)***
FMC Dialysis Svcs Bellflower, Bellflower *Also called Bio-Mdcal Applications Cal Inc* ***(P-21913)***
FMC Dialysis Svcs Riverside, Riverside *Also called Bio-Mdcal Applications Cal Inc* ***(P-21915)***
FMC Financial Group (PA) ....D....949 225-9369
4675 Macarthur Ct # 1250 Newport Beach (92660) ***(P-10365)***
Fmg Suite LLC (PA) ....E....888 364-1260
12395 World Trade Dr # 200 San Diego (92128) ***(P-14814)***
Fmr LLC ....C....800 225-6447
1995 University Ave Berkeley (94704) ***(P-9814)***
Fmr LLC ....C....916 784-3649
1220 Rsville Pkwy Ste 100 Roseville (95678) ***(P-9815)***
Fmsinfoserv, Los Angeles *Also called Cdsnet LLC* ***(P-27021)***
Fmt Consultants LLC (PA) ....D....844 369-4593
2310 Camino Vida Roble # 101 Carlsbad (92011) ***(P-15999)***
Fmwr, Fort Irwin *Also called Family Mrale Wlfare Recreation* ***(P-18454)***
Fnc Inc ....D....714 866-1099
40 Pacifica Ste 900 Irvine (92618) ***(P-14815)***
Fns Inc (PA) ....D....661 615-2300
1545 Francisco St Torrance (90501) ***(P-4946)***
FNS Customs Brokers Inc ....E....310 667-4880
18301 S Broadwick St Compton (90220) ***(P-4947)***
Fnti Fidelity Nat Tech Imagin ....E....408 942-1780
2123 Ringwood Ave San Jose (95131) ***(P-16000)***
Foam Co, The, Van Nuys *Also called Grht Inc* ***(P-8977)***
Foam Distributors Incorporated ....D....510 441-8377
31009 San Antonio St Hayward (94544) ***(P-8971)***
Foam Fabrication For Packaging, Hayward *Also called Foam Distributors Incorporated* ***(P-8971)***
Foasberg Laundry & Clrs Inc (PA) ....D....562 426-7345
640 E Wardlow Rd Long Beach (90807) ***(P-13221)***
Focus 360 Inc ....D....949 234-0008
27721 La Paz Rd Ste B Laguna Niguel (92677) ***(P-14816)***
Focus Diagnostics Inc ....B....714 220-1900
11331 Valley View St # 150 Cypress (90630) ***(P-21530)***
Focus Technologies Holding Co ....B....800 838-4548
10703 Progress Way Cypress (90630) ***(P-21531)***
Foddrill Construction Corp ....D....909 591-4095
13831 Roswell Ave Ste H Chino (91710) ***(P-2497)***
Foland Group Inc ....D....909 930-9900
1500 S Hellman Ave Ontario (91761) ***(P-8972)***
Foley & Lardner LLP ....C....650 856-3700
975 Page Mill Rd Palo Alto (94304) ***(P-22509)***
Foley & Lardner LLP ....D....415 434-4484
555 California St # 1700 San Francisco (94104) ***(P-22510)***
Foley & Lardner LLP ....C....213 972-4500
555 S Flower St Ste 3300 Los Angeles (90071) ***(P-22511)***
Foley & Lardner LLP ....D....858 847-6700
3579 Vly Cntre Dr Ste 300 San Diego (92130) ***(P-22512)***
Folio Wine Company LLC (PA) ....C....707 254-9885
550 Gateway Dr Ste 220 NAPA (94558) ***(P-8806)***
Folio Wine Company LLC ....D....707 256-2757
1285 Dealy Ln NAPA (94559) ***(P-8807)***
Folio Wine Company Imports, NAPA *Also called Folio Wine Company LLC* ***(P-8806)***
Folsom Ambulatory Surgery Ctr, Folsom *Also called Kaiser Foundation Hospitals* ***(P-19071)***
Folsom Lake Bank, Folsom *Also called Central Valley Community Bank* ***(P-9183)***
Folsom Lake Toyota, Folsom *Also called Flt Inc* ***(P-17327)***
Folsom Manlove Venture, Sacramento *Also called Oates Buzz Enterprises* ***(P-10629)***
Folsom Recreation Corp ....D....916 983-4411
511 E Bidwell St Folsom (95630) ***(P-18032)***
Folsom Sport Club, Folsom *Also called 24 Hour Fitness Usa Inc* ***(P-18091)***
Fonda & Frazer LLP (PA) ....D....310 553-3320
1925 Century Park E # 1360 Los Angeles (90067) ***(P-22513)***
Fontana Mental Health Offices, Fontana *Also called Kaiser Foundation Hospitals* ***(P-19070)***
Fontana Resources At Work ....C....909 428-3833
8608 Live Oak Ave Fontana (92335) ***(P-23596)***
Fontana Steel, Etiwanda *Also called C M C Steel Fabricators Inc* ***(P-3256)***
Fontana Water Company, El Monte *Also called San Gabriel Valley Water Co* ***(P-6110)***
Food & Agriculture Cal Dept ....D....714 751-3247
88 Fair Dr Costa Mesa (92626) ***(P-18699)***
Food 4 Less, Downey *Also called Ralphs Grocery Company* ***(P-4485)***
Food Express Inc ....E....323 589-1417
5127 Maywood Ave Maywood (90270) ***(P-3887)***
Food Management Associates Inc ....E....714 694-2828
22349 La Palma Ave # 115 Yorba Linda (92887) ***(P-26611)***
Food Sales West Inc (PA) ....D....714 966-2900
235 Baker St Costa Mesa (92626) ***(P-8173)***
Foodcraft Cof Refreshment Svcs, Long Beach *Also called Steuber Corporation* ***(P-6932)***
Foods and Produce, Buena Park *Also called Walong Marketing Inc* ***(P-8673)***
Footh The / Easte Trans Corri ....D....949 754-3400
125 Pacifica Ste 100 Irvine (92618) ***(P-1706)***
Footh-De Anza Commun Colleg Di ....D....650 949-7260
12345 S El Monte Rd # 6202 Los Altos Hills (94022) ***(P-5531)***
Foothill Distributing Co Inc ....C....530 243-3932
1530 Beltline Rd Redding (96003) ***(P-8761)***
Foothill Estates Inc ....D....831 422-7819
400 Griffin St Salinas (93901) ***(P-11563)***
Foothill Federal Credit Union (PA) ....E....626 445-0950
30 S 1st Ave Arcadia (91006) ***(P-9313)***
Foothill Health Center Inc ....C....408 729-4290
2670 S White Rd Ste 200 San Jose (95148) ***(P-18988)***
Foothill Hsptl-Mrris L Jhnston (PA) ....D....626 857-3145
250 S Grand Ave Glendora (91741) ***(P-20877)***
Foothill Oaks Care Center Inc ....D....530 888-6257
3400 Bell Rd Auburn (95603) ***(P-19921)***
Foothill Packing Inc ....B....805 925-7900
2255 S Broadway Santa Maria (93454) ***(P-8174)***
Foothill Presbyterian Hospital, Glendora *Also called Foothill Hsptl-Mrris L Jhnston* ***(P-20877)***
Foothill Ranch Medical Offices, Foothill Ranch *Also called Kaiser Foundation Hospitals* ***(P-19069)***
Foothill Ranch Sport Club, Lake Forest *Also called 24 Hour Fitness Usa Inc* ***(P-18106)***
Foothill Regional Medical Ctr, Tustin *Also called Alta Hospitals System LLC* ***(P-20743)***
Foothill Transit Service Corp (PA) ....D....626 967-3147
100 S Vincent Ave Ste 200 West Covina (91790) ***(P-3538)***
Foothill Waste Reclamation Inc ....D....818 897-5099
12221 Lopez Canyon Rd Sylmar (91342) ***(P-6206)***
Force Electronics, Visalia *Also called Heilind Electronics Inc* ***(P-7276)***
Force Framing Inc ....E....714 970-3888
21520 Yorba Linda Blvd G Yorba Linda (92887) ***(P-2934)***
Force Measurement Systems, Anaheim *Also called Wasser Filtration Inc* ***(P-7608)***
Force-Oakleaf LP ....D....310 484-7000
6333 Bristol Pkwy Culver City (90230) ***(P-12271)***
Force10 Networks Inc ....A....800 289-3355
350 Holger Way San Jose (95134) ***(P-15593)***
Ford Construction Company Inc ....D....209 333-1116
300 W Pine St Lodi (95240) ***(P-1962)***
Ford Graphics, Los Angeles *Also called American Reprographics Co LLC* ***(P-13747)***

Employee Codes: A=Over 500 employees, B=251-500
C=101-250, D=51-100, E=50
2020 Directory of California
Wholesalers and Services Companies
© Mergent Inc. 1-800-342-5647
1271

Ford Motor Company ....C....323 267-6121
812 Union St Montebello (90640) ***(P-4410)***
Ford Motor Company ....C....209 824-6600
1269 Phoenix Dr Manteca (95336) ***(P-6439)***
Ford Motor Company ....D....925 351-6205
4900 Hopyard Rd Ste 220 Pleasanton (94588) ***(P-9460)***
Ford Motor Company ....B....949 341-5800
3 Glen Bell Way Ste 200 Irvine (92618) ***(P-22514)***
Ford Motor Land Dev Corp ....B....949 242-6606
3 Glen Bell Way Ste 100 Irvine (92618) ***(P-25081)***
Ford Plastering Inc ....B....714 921-0624
732 W Grove Ave Orange (92865) ***(P-3149)***
Ford Street Project Inc ....E....707 462-1934
139 Ford St Ukiah (95482) ***(P-23929)***
Foremost Healthcare Centers ....D....760 244-5579
17581 Sultana St Hesperia (92345) ***(P-10728)***
Foremost Operations LLC ....E....760 244-5579
17581 Sultana St Hesperia (92345) ***(P-23930)***
Foremost Terrace Room, Hesperia *Also called Foremost Operations LLC* ***(P-23930)***
Forensic Analytical ....D....858 859-3322
3111 Camino Dl Rio N 43 San Diego (92108) ***(P-27073)***
Forensic Analytical Spc Inc (PA) ....C....510 887-8828
3777 Depot Rd Ste 409 Hayward (94545) ***(P-26074)***
Forensic Toxicology Associates, Chatsworth *Also called Pacific Toxicology Labs* ***(P-26102)***
Forescout Technologies Inc (PA) ....C....408 213-3191
190 W Tasman Dr San Jose (95134) ***(P-14817)***
Forest City Rental Prpts Corp ....D....661 266-9150
1233 W Avenue P Ste 900 Palmdale (93551) ***(P-10590)***
Forest Lawn Memorial & Mortuar, Cypress *Also called Forest Lawn Memorial-Park Assn* ***(P-11626)***
Forest Lawn Memorial-Park Assn ....D....714 828-3131
4471 Lincoln Ave Cypress (90630) ***(P-11626)***
Forest Lawn Memorial-Park Assn ....D....323 254-7251
6300 Forest Lawn Dr Los Angeles (90068) ***(P-11627)***
Forest Lawn Memorial-Park Assn ....D....562 424-1631
1500 E San Antonio Dr Long Beach (90807) ***(P-11628)***
Forest Park Cabana Club ....E....408 244-1884
2911 Pruneridge Ave Santa Clara (95051) ***(P-18455)***
Forest Products Distrs Inc ....D....707 443-7024
1090 W Waterfront Dr Eureka (95501) ***(P-6617)***
Forestry and Fire Protection ....C....530 225-2418
875 Cypress Ave Redding (96001) ***(P-964)***
Forever Firewood Inc (PA) ....E....831 461-0634
46 El Pueblo Rd Ste A Santa Cruz (95066) ***(P-3055)***
Forever Link International Inc ....E....877 839-9899
888 S Azusa Ave City of Industry (91748) ***(P-8132)***
Forex Capital Markets LLC ....D....415 343-4874
201 Mission St Ste 290 San Francisco (94105) ***(P-9689)***
Forge-Vidovich Motel Limited ....D....408 996-7700
10889 N De Anza Blvd Cupertino (95014) ***(P-12272)***
Forgerock Inc (PA) ....D....415 599-1100
201 Mission St Ste 2900 San Francisco (94105) ***(P-6837)***
Forgerock US Inc (HQ) ....D....415 599-1100
201 Mission St San Francisco (94105) ***(P-15329)***
Formation Inc ....D....650 257-2277
35 Stillman St San Francisco (94107) ***(P-15330)***
Formation Systems, San Francisco *Also called Formation Inc* ***(P-15330)***
Formula One Systems Inc (HQ) ....D....562 424-7899
2850 E 29th St Long Beach (90806) ***(P-14818)***
Fornaca Inc (PA) ....C....866 308-9461
2400 National City Blvd National City (91950) ***(P-17290)***
Forrest City Development, Los Angeles *Also called Fc Metropolitan Lofts Inc* ***(P-11562)***
Forsys Inc ....D....408 409-2567
6036 Stevenson Blvd Fremont (94538) ***(P-16001)***
Forsythe Technology LLC ....D....424 217-6500
222 N Pacific Coast Hwy # 1426 El Segundo (90245) ***(P-16002)***
Fort Hill Construction (PA) ....D....323 656-7425
12711 Ventura Blvd # 390 Studio City (91604) ***(P-1124)***
Fort James Communications Pprs, Emeryville *Also called Fort James Corporation* ***(P-26231)***
Fort James Corporation ....D....510 594-4900
2000 Powell St Emeryville (94608) ***(P-26231)***
Fort Mason Center ....D....415 345-7500
2 Marina Blvd Bldg A San Francisco (94123) ***(P-27274)***
Fort Wash Golf & Cntry CLB ....D....559 434-1702
10272 N Millbrook Ave Fresno (93730) ***(P-18456)***
Fort Washington Parent Assoc ....D....559 327-6600
960 E Teague Ave Fresno (93720) ***(P-24542)***
FORT, THE, Fresno *Also called Fort Wash Golf & Cntry CLB* ***(P-18456)***
Forta (PA) ....D....626 446-7027
671 W Naomi Ave Arcadia (91007) ***(P-19668)***
Fortanasce & Associates, Arcadia *Also called Forta* ***(P-19668)***
Forte Enterprises Inc (PA) ....C....650 994-3200
99 Escuela Dr Daly City (94015) ***(P-26232)***
Fortress Holding Group LLC ....D....714 202-8710
5500 E Santa Ana Canyon R Anaheim (92807) ***(P-11660)***
Fortress Investment Group LLC ....D....310 228-3030
10250 Constellation Blvd # 2300 Los Angeles (90067) ***(P-11725)***
Fortress Investment Group LLC ....D....415 284-7400
42 Florida St Flr San Francisco (94103) ***(P-11726)***
Fortress Resources LLC (HQ) ....C....562 633-9951
24200 Main St Carson (90745) ***(P-17328)***
Fortuna Enterprises LP ....B....310 410-4000
5711 W Century Blvd Los Angeles (90045) ***(P-12273)***
Fortune Avenue Foods Inc ....D....909 930-5989
2117 Pointe Ave Ontario (91761) ***(P-8175)***
Fortune Dynamic Inc ....D....909 979-8318
21923 Ferrero City of Industry (91789) ***(P-8133)***
Fortune Senior Enterprises ....D....916 560-9100
3941 Park Dr Ste 20265 El Dorado Hills (95762) ***(P-21743)***
Forty Four Group LLC ....D....949 407-6360
17391 Mount Cliffwood Cir Fountain Valley (92708) ***(P-13508)***
Forty Niners Football Co LLC ....D....408 562-4949
4949 Mrie P Debartolo Way Santa Clara (95054) ***(P-18061)***
Forum At Rancho San Antonio, Cupertino *Also called Rancho San Antonio Retirement* ***(P-24040)***
Forum Enterprises Inc ....E....310 330-7300
333 W Florence Ave Inglewood (90301) ***(P-17974)***
Forum Healthcare Center ....C....650 944-0200
23600 Via Esplendor Cupertino (95014) ***(P-19922)***
Forward Air Inc ....E....415 570-6040
30108 Eigenbrodt Way # 100 Union City (94587) ***(P-4948)***
Forward Management LLC ....D....415 869-6300
101 California St Fl 16 San Francisco (94111) ***(P-9816)***
Forward Slope Incorporated ....D....619 299-4400
2020 Camino Del Rio N San Diego (92108) ***(P-25082)***
Forward Slope., San Diego *Also called Forward Slope Incorporated* ***(P-25082)***
Foshay Electric Coinc ....D....858 277-7676
1555 Laurel Bay Ln San Diego (92154) ***(P-2498)***
Foss Maritime Co Inc ....D....562 435-0171
Berth 35 Pier D Long Beach (90802) ***(P-4630)***
Foss Maritime Company ....D....510 307-4271
1316 Canal Blvd Richmond (94804) ***(P-4583)***
Foss Maritime Company Llc ....C....562 435-0171
Berth 35 Pier D Long Beach (90801) ***(P-4584)***
Foster Care Licensing & Svc, Ventura *Also called County of Ventura* ***(P-23179)***
Foster Dairy Farms (PA) ....A....209 576-3400
529 Kansas Ave Modesto (95351) ***(P-390)***
Foster Dairy Farms ....C....209 874-9605
1472 Hall Rd Hickman (95323) ***(P-17498)***
Foster Dairy Products Distrg (PA) ....A....209 576-3400
529 Kansas Ave Modesto (95351) ***(P-8317)***
Foster Farms, Fresno *Also called Foster Poultry Farms* ***(P-419)***
Foster Farms LLC ....B....559 793-5501
770 N Plano St Porterville (93257) ***(P-410)***
Foster Poultry Farms ....A....559 457-6509
4107 Ave 360 Traver (93673) ***(P-8840)***
Foster Poultry Farms ....A....209 394-7901
843 Davis St Livingston (95334) ***(P-418)***
Foster Poultry Farms ....A....559 442-3771
2960 S Cherry Ave Fresno (93706) ***(P-419)***
Foster Wheeler Energy Svcs Inc ....E....800 500-1993
9645 Scranton Rd Ste 230 San Diego (92121) ***(P-3359)***
Fostering Executive Leadership ....D....949 651-6250
4790 Irvine Blvd 105-432 Irvine (92620) ***(P-26612)***
Foto Kem Film & Video, Burbank *Also called Foto-Kem Industries Inc* ***(P-17740)***
Foto-Kem Industries Inc (PA) ....B....818 846-3102
2801 W Alameda Ave Burbank (91505) ***(P-17740)***
Foto-Kem Industries Inc ....B....818 846-3102
2801 W Olive Ave Burbank (91505) ***(P-17741)***
Fotokem, Burbank *Also called Foto-Kem Industries Inc* ***(P-17741)***
Foundation 9 Entertainment Inc (PA) ....C....949 698-1500
30211 A De Las Bandera200 Rancho Santa Margari (92688) ***(P-15331)***
Foundation Building Mtls Inc (PA) ....D....714 380-3127
2741 Walnut Ave Ste 200 Tustin (92780) ***(P-6618)***
Foundation Constructors Inc (PA) ....D....925 754-6633
81 Big Break Rd Oakley (94561) ***(P-1963)***
Foundation For Dance Education ....D....909 482-1590
9061 Central Ave Montclair (91763) ***(P-17879)***
Foundation For Early Childhood (PA) ....D....626 572-5107
3360 Flair Dr Ste 100 El Monte (91731) ***(P-23230)***
Foundation Laboratory, Pomona *Also called Latara Enterprise Inc* ***(P-21548)***
Foundation Lead Group LLC ....D....877 477-2311
2121 Alton Pkwy Ste 150 Irvine (92606) ***(P-24543)***
Foundation Pile Inc ....D....909 350-1584
8375 Almeria Ave Fontana (92335) ***(P-1964)***
Foundation Repair of CA, Livermore *Also called Smp Construction & Maint Inc* ***(P-1603)***
Foundation Super Skateboard, San Diego *Also called Tum Yeto Inc* ***(P-7722)***
Founders Healthcare LLC ....D....626 683-5401
170 N Daisy Ave Pasadena (91107) ***(P-21744)***
Founders Management II Corp ....B....650 570-5700
1221 Chess Dr Foster City (94404) ***(P-12274)***
Foundstone Inc ....D....949 297-5600
27201 Puerta Real Ste 400 Mission Viejo (92691) ***(P-15332)***
Foundtion For Cal Cmnty Cllges (PA) ....C....916 325-4300
1102 Q St Ste 4800 Sacramento (95811) ***(P-24339)***
Foundtion For Hispanic Educatn (PA) ....D....408 585-5022
14271 Story Rd San Jose (95127) ***(P-24544)***
Fountain, San Francisco *Also called Onboardiq Inc* ***(P-15875)***
Fountain Grove Golf & Athc CLB ....D....707 701-3050
1525 Fountaingrove Pkwy Santa Rosa (95403) ***(P-18247)***
Fountain Valley Body Works M2 ....E....714 751-8812
17481 Newhope St Fountain Valley (92708) ***(P-17291)***
Fountain Valley Regl Hospl ....A....714 966-7200
17100 Euclid St Fountain Valley (92708) ***(P-20878)***
Fountain Valley School Dst ....D....714 668-5882
17330 Mount Herrmann St Fountain Valley (92708) ***(P-13929)***
Fountain View Cnvalescent Hosp, Los Angeles *Also called Genesis Healthcare LLC* ***(P-20567)***
Fountaingrove Inn LLC ....D....707 578-6101
101 Fountaingrove Pkwy Santa Rosa (95403) ***(P-12275)***
Fountains At Sea Bluffs, Dana Point *Also called Sunrise Senior Living Inc* ***(P-20297)***
Fountains At The Carlotta, Palm Desert *Also called Sunrise Senior Living LLC* ***(P-20327)***
Fountains At The Carlotta, The, Palm Desert *Also called Watermark Rtrment Cmmnties Inc* ***(P-20372)***
FOUNTAINS, THE, Yuba City *Also called United Com Serve* ***(P-20340)***
Fountainwood Residential Care ....D....916 988-2200
8773 Oak Ave Orangevale (95662) ***(P-23931)***

Fountngrove Inn Conference Ctr, Santa Rosa *Also called Fountaingrove Inn LLC* ***(P-12275)***
Four CS Service Inc.....D.....559 237-3990
1560 H St Fresno (93721) ***(P-3056)***
Four Medica Inc.....D.....310 348-4100
13160 Mindanao Way # 280 Marina Del Rey (90292) ***(P-5787)***
Four Points Bakersfield, Bakersfield *Also called Cni Thl Propco Fe LLC* ***(P-12160)***
Four Points By Sheraton, San Diego *Also called Pinnacle 1617 LLC* ***(P-12756)***
Four Points By Sheraton.....D.....310 645-4600
9750 Airport Blvd Los Angeles (90045) ***(P-12276)***
Four Points by Sheraton LAX, Los Angeles *Also called Irp Lax Hotel LLC* ***(P-12478)***
Four Points San Diego-Seaworld, San Diego *Also called Greenwood Holdings LLC* ***(P-12312)***
Four Points San Jose Downtown.....E.....408 282-8800
211 S 1st St San Jose (95113) ***(P-12277)***
Four Points San Rafael, San Rafael *Also called San Rafael Hillcrest LLC* ***(P-12881)***
Four Points Sheraton Lax, Los Angeles *Also called Lax Hotel Ventures LLC* ***(P-12541)***
Four Points Sheraton Ventura, Ventura *Also called Harbor Island Hotel Group LP* ***(P-12334)***
Four Seasons Healthcare.....D.....818 985-1814
5335 Laurel Canyon Blvd North Hollywood (91607) ***(P-19923)***
Four Seasons Hotel, Westlake Village *Also called Burton-Way House Ltd A CA* ***(P-12097)***
Four Seasons Hotel, Los Angeles *Also called Burton-Way House Ltd A CA* ***(P-12098)***
Four Seasons Hotel, Los Angeles *Also called Burton-Way House Ltd A CA* ***(P-12099)***
Four Seasons Hotel, San Francisco *Also called Cb-1 Hotel* ***(P-12128)***
Four Seasons Hotel Inc.....A.....415 633-3441
735 Market St Fl 6 San Francisco (94103) ***(P-12278)***
Four Seasons Hotel Inc.....A.....650 566-1200
2050 University Ave East Palo Alto (94303) ***(P-12279)***
Four Seasons Hotel Silicon Vly, East Palo Alto *Also called East Palo Alto Hotel Dev Inc* ***(P-12236)***
Four Seasons Landscaping, Van Nuys *Also called S G D Enterprises* ***(P-902)***
Four Seasons Landscaping, Van Nuys *Also called S D Property Management Inc* ***(P-11434)***
Four Seasons Resort Aviara, Carlsbad *Also called California Bistro At Fo* ***(P-12105)***
Four Seasons Resort Aviara.....D.....760 603-6900
7447 Batiquitos Dr Carlsbad (92011) ***(P-18248)***
Four Sisters Inns.....C.....619 437-1900
1060 Adella Ave Coronado (92118) ***(P-12280)***
Four Ssons Hotel-San Francisco, San Francisco *Also called Four Seasons Hotel Inc* ***(P-12278)***
Four Ssons Rsort Santa Barbara, Santa Barbara *Also called 1260 Bb Property LLC* ***(P-11974)***
Fourth Phase Los Angeles, San Fernando *Also called Prg (california) Inc* ***(P-17655)***
Fourth Street Bowl.....E.....408 453-5555
1441 N 4th St San Jose (95112) ***(P-18033)***
Fourthfloor Fashion Talent, Los Angeles *Also called Career Group Inc* ***(P-14243)***
Fowler Convalescent Hospital.....E.....559 834-2542
1306 E Sumner Ave Fowler (93625) ***(P-20554)***
Fowler Labor Service Inc.....B.....559 834-3723
633 W Fresno St Fowler (93625) ***(P-14285)***
Fowler Packing Company Inc.....C.....559 834-5911
8570 S Cedar Ave Fresno (93725) ***(P-491)***
Fox Inc (HQ).....A.....310 369-1000
2121 Avenue Of The Stars Los Angeles (90067) ***(P-5604)***
Fox Animation Studios Inc.....B.....323 857-8800
5700 Wilshire Blvd # 325 Los Angeles (90036) ***(P-17610)***
Fox Broadcasting Company (HQ).....C.....310 369-1000
10201 W Pico Blvd Los Angeles (90064) ***(P-5605)***
Fox BSB Holdco Inc.....A.....323 224-1500
1000 Vin Scully Ave Los Angeles (90090) ***(P-18062)***
Fox Corporation, Los Angeles *Also called Twentieth Cntury Fox Intl Corp* ***(P-17792)***
Fox Entertainment Television, Los Angeles *Also called Fox Television Stations Inc* ***(P-5607)***
Fox Factory Holding Corp.....A.....619 768-1800
750 Vernon Way Ste 101 El Cajon (92020) ***(P-6440)***
Fox Family Channel, Burbank *Also called International Fmly Entrmt Inc* ***(P-5730)***
Fox Films Entertainment, Los Angeles *Also called Twentieth Cntury Fox Film Corp* ***(P-17690)***
Fox Head Inc (PA).....C.....888 369-7223
16752 Armstrong Ave Irvine (92606) ***(P-8030)***
Fox Latin American Channel LLC.....B.....305 774-4167
10201 W Pico Blvd Los Angeles (90064) ***(P-5721)***
Fox Luggage Inc.....D.....323 588-1688
5353 E Slauson Ave Commerce (90040) ***(P-7809)***
Fox Network Center, Los Angeles *Also called Fox Networks Group Inc* ***(P-5723)***
Fox Networks Group Inc.....C.....310 369-5104
10201 W Pico Blvd Los Angeles (90064) ***(P-5722)***
Fox Networks Group Inc (HQ).....D.....310 369-9369
10201 W Pico Blvd 101 Los Angeles (90064) ***(P-5723)***
Fox Racing, Irvine *Also called Fox Head Inc* ***(P-8030)***
Fox Rent A Car Inc (PA).....E.....310 342-5155
5500 W Century Blvd Los Angeles (90045) ***(P-17211)***
Fox Rothschild LLP.....D.....415 539-3336
1 Sansome St Ste 2850 San Francisco (94104) ***(P-22515)***
Fox Sports Productions Inc.....A.....310 369-1000
10201 W Pico Blvd Los Angeles (90064) ***(P-5606)***
Fox Television Stations Inc (HQ).....B.....310 584-2000
1999 S Bundy Dr Los Angeles (90025) ***(P-5607)***
Fox Transportation Inc (PA).....D.....909 291-4646
8610 Helms Ave Rancho Cucamonga (91730) ***(P-27074)***
Foxconn Electronics, Brea *Also called Fit Electronics Inc* ***(P-25751)***
Foxy, Salinas *Also called Nunes Company Inc* ***(P-8503)***
FP, San Francisco *Also called Francisco Partners LP* ***(P-15594)***
FPI Management Inc.....C.....408 267-3952
1107 Luchessi Dr San Jose (95118) ***(P-26233)***
FPI Management Inc (PA).....E.....916 357-5300
800 Iron Point Rd Folsom (95630) ***(P-11158)***
Fpk Investigaions, Valencia *Also called Fpk Security Inc* ***(P-16274)***
Fpk Security Inc.....B.....661 702-9091
28348 Constellation Rd # 880 Valencia (91355) ***(P-16274)***
Fpl LLC.....D.....805 643-6144
550 San Jon Rd Ventura (93001) ***(P-12281)***
Fragomen Del Rey Bernse.....D.....858 793-1600
11238 El Camino Real # 100 San Diego (92130) ***(P-22516)***
Fragomen Del Rey Bernse.....E.....310 820-3322
11150 W Olympic Blvd # 1000 Los Angeles (90064) ***(P-22517)***
Fragomen Del Rey Bernse.....D.....949 660-3504
18401 Von Karman Ave # 255 Irvine (92612) ***(P-22518)***
Fragomen Del Rey Bernse.....D.....408 919-0600
2121 Tasman Dr Santa Clara (95054) ***(P-22519)***
Framestore Inc (PA).....E.....310 975-7300
8616 National Blvd Culver City (90232) ***(P-17975)***
Framing Associates Inc.....C.....619 336-9991
1320 Coolidge Ave National City (91950) ***(P-1243)***
Framing Fabrics, Los Angeles *Also called Neuberg Nuberg Importers Group* ***(P-6572)***
Fran-Jom Inc.....D.....626 443-3028
5101 Tyler Ave Temple City (91780) ***(P-20555)***
France Telecom RES & Dev LLC.....D.....415 284-9765
60 Spear St Ste 1100 San Francisco (94105) ***(P-25896)***
Franciscan Conv. Hospital, Merced *Also called Avalon Care Center - Merced* ***(P-19734)***
Franciscan Lines Inc.....C.....415 642-9400
41 Pier San Francisco (94133) ***(P-3675)***
Francisco Emilio Assoc Law Off.....D.....949 474-2222
17532 Von Karman Ave Irvine (92614) ***(P-22520)***
Francisco Partners LP (HQ).....D.....415 418-2900
1 Letterman Dr Bldg C San Francisco (94129) ***(P-15594)***
Francisco Partners MGT LP (PA).....E.....415 418-2900
1 Letterman Dr Ste 410 San Francisco (94129) ***(P-11913)***
Franconnect LLC.....C.....760 720-5354
300 Carlsbad Village Dr 302a Carlsbad (92008) ***(P-15595)***
Frandzel Share Robins Bloom Lc.....D.....323 852-1000
1000 Wilshire Blvd # 1900 Los Angeles (90017) ***(P-22521)***
Frank Rimerman & Co LLP.....D.....415 439-1144
1 Embarcadero Ctr # 2410 San Francisco (94111) ***(P-25597)***
Frank C Alegre Trucking Inc (PA).....C.....209 334-2112
5100 W Highway 12 Lodi (95242) ***(P-4048)***
Frank Carson Ldscp & Maint Inc.....C.....916 856-5400
9530 Elder Creek Rd Sacramento (95829) ***(P-812)***
FRANK D LANTERMAN REGIONAL CEN, Los Angeles *Also called Los Angeles Cnty Dev Svc Fndtn* ***(P-22272)***
Frank D Yelian MD PC.....E.....949 788-1133
3500 Barranca Pkwy # 300 Irvine (92606) ***(P-18989)***
Frank Gates Service Company.....D.....916 934-0812
1107 Investment Blvd El Dorado Hills (95762) ***(P-26613)***
Frank Gates Service Company.....D.....800 994-4611
2400 E Katella Ave # 650 Anaheim (92806) ***(P-10090)***
Frank Ghiglione Inc (PA).....C.....510 483-7000
14327 Washington Ave San Leandro (94578) ***(P-3888)***
Frank Ghiglione Inc.....D.....510 483-2063
2972 Alvarado St Ste H San Leandro (94577) ***(P-3889)***
Frank Howard Allen Fincl Corp.....D.....415 456-3000
1016 Irwin St San Rafael (94901) ***(P-11159)***
Frank Howard Allen Real Estate, San Rafael *Also called Frank Howard Allen Fincl Corp* ***(P-11159)***
Frank J Gomes Dairy A Califo.....D.....209 669-7978
5301 Deangelis Rd Stevinson (95374) ***(P-391)***
Frank M Booth Inc (PA).....D.....530 742-7134
222 3rd St Marysville (95901) ***(P-25083)***
Frank N Magid Associates Inc.....D.....818 263-3300
15260 Ventura Blvd # 1840 Sherman Oaks (91403) ***(P-25897)***
Frank N Magid Associates Inc.....C.....818 263-3300
15260 Vntr Blvd Ste 1840 Sherman Oaks (91403) ***(P-25898)***
Frank S Smith Masonry Inc.....D.....909 468-0525
2830 Pomona Blvd Pomona (91768) ***(P-2712)***
Frank Schipper Construction Co.....E.....805 963-4359
610 E Cota St Santa Barbara (93103) ***(P-1479)***
Frank Sciarrino Marble G.....D.....858 695-8030
7505 Trade St San Diego (92121) ***(P-6684)***
Frank Toyata & Scion, National City *Also called Fornaca Inc* ***(P-17290)***
Frank-Lin Distillers Pdts Ltd (PA).....C.....408 259-8900
2455 Huntington Dr Fairfield (94533) ***(P-8808)***
Franke Con J Electric Inc.....D.....209 462-0717
317 N Grant St Stockton (95202) ***(P-2499)***
Franklin Advisers Inc (HQ).....A.....650 312-2000
1 Franklin Pkwy San Mateo (94403) ***(P-9817)***
Franklin Data, Westlake Village *Also called 5 Nine Group Inc* ***(P-14605)***
Franklin Electric Co Inc.....A.....415 467-2693
1129 Brussels St San Francisco (94134) ***(P-2500)***
Franklin Resources Inc (PA).....D.....650 312-2000
1 Franklin Pkwy San Mateo (94403) ***(P-9818)***
Franklin Templeton Investment, Rancho Cordova *Also called Franklin Tmpleton Inv Svcs LLC* ***(P-9690)***
Franklin Templeton Svcs LLC.....A.....650 312-3000
1 Franklin Pkwy San Mateo (94403) ***(P-9819)***
Franklin Tmpleton Inv Svcs LLC.....C.....650 312-2000
3366 Quality Dr Rancho Cordova (95670) ***(P-9820)***
Franklin Tmpleton Inv Svcs LLC.....C.....925 875-2619
5130 Hacienda Dr Fl 4 Dublin (94568) ***(P-9821)***
Franklin Tmpleton Inv Svcs LLC (HQ).....A.....916 463-1500
3344 Quality Dr Rancho Cordova (95670) ***(P-9690)***
Frantz Wholesale Nursery LLC.....C.....209 874-1459
12161 Delaware Rd Hickman (95323) ***(P-240)***
Franza Sanger Winery, Sanger *Also called Wine Group Inc* ***(P-8823)***
Frasco Inc (PA).....D.....818 848-3888
215 W Alameda Ave Burbank (91502) ***(P-16275)***
Frasco Investigative Services, Burbank *Also called Frasco Inc* ***(P-16275)***

A L P H A B E T I C

Employee Codes: A=Over 500 employees, B=251-500
C=101-250, D=51-100, E=50
2020 Directory of California
Wholesalers and Services Companies
© Mergent Inc. 1-800-342-5647
1273

Fraternal Order Eagles 1582....C....916 782-2694
124 Vernon St Roseville (95678) ***(P-10591)***
Frazier Nut Farms Inc....E....209 522-1406
10830 Yosemite Blvd Waterford (95386) ***(P-175)***
Fred H Lundblade Jr....D....707 442-8049
939 Koster St Ste B Eureka (95501) ***(P-10592)***
Fred Leeds Properties....E....310 826-2466
3860 Crenshaw Blvd # 201 Los Angeles (90008) ***(P-11160)***
Fredericka Manor....D....619 422-9271
183 Third Ave Chula Vista (91910) ***(P-23932)***
FREDERICKA MANOR CARE CENTER, Burbank *Also called Fact Foundation* ***(P-16773)***
Fredericka Manor Care Center, Glendale *Also called Front Porch Communities* ***(P-20557)***
Fredericka Manor Care Center, Chula Vista *Also called Front Porch Communities* ***(P-20559)***
Fredericksen Tank Lines Inc (PA)....D....916 371-4960
840 Delta Ln West Sacramento (95691) ***(P-4049)***
Free Conferencing Corporation....C....562 437-1411
4300 E Pacific Coast Hwy Long Beach (90804) ***(P-5401)***
Free Stream Media Corp (PA)....D....415 854-0073
123 Townsend St 5 San Francisco (94107) ***(P-8973)***
Freeconferencecall.com, Long Beach *Also called Free Conferencing Corporation* ***(P-5401)***
Freedom Debt Relief, San Mateo *Also called Freedom Financial Network LLC* ***(P-13424)***
Freedom Financial Network LLC (PA)....D....650 393-6619
1875 S Grant St Ste 400 San Mateo (94402) ***(P-13424)***
Freedom Painting Inc....E....562 696-0785
8822 Calmada Ave Whittier (90605) ***(P-2347)***
Freedom Properties, Hemet *Also called Casa-Pacifica Inc* ***(P-23854)***
Freedom Properties Village, Hemet *Also called Casa-Pacifica Inc* ***(P-23855)***
Freedom Properties-Hemet LLC....C....949 489-0430
27122b Paseo Espada B San Juan Capistrano (92675) ***(P-10593)***
Freedom Staff Leasing Inc....B....310 834-6621
3142 Pacific Coast Hwy Torrance (90505) ***(P-14506)***
Freedom Village Healthcare Ctr....D....949 472-4733
23442 El Toro Rd Bldg 2 Lake Forest (92630) ***(P-19924)***
Freeman Freeman & Smiley (PA)....D....310 398-6100
1888 Century Park E Fl 19 Los Angeles (90067) ***(P-22522)***
Freeman Audio Visual LLC....C....714 254-3400
901 E South St Anaheim (92805) ***(P-14161)***
Freeman Expositions LLC....C....714 254-3400
2170 S Towne Centre Pl Anaheim (92806) ***(P-16786)***
Freeman Expositions LLC....D....650 878-6023
245 S Spruce Ave South San Francisco (94080) ***(P-16787)***
Freeman Freeman & Smiley LLP, Los Angeles *Also called Freeman Freeman & Smiley* ***(P-22522)***
Freemont Health Care Center, Fremont *Also called Mariner Health Care Inc* ***(P-20105)***
Freemont Rideout Health Group....D....530 671-2883
481 Plumas Blvd Ste 105 Yuba City (95991) ***(P-21532)***
Freeport-Mcmoran Oil & Gas LLC....D....661 322-7600
1200 Discovery Dr Ste 500 Bakersfield (93309) ***(P-986)***
Freeway Insurance, Huntington Beach *Also called Confie Seguros Inc* ***(P-10329)***
Freeway Insurance (PA)....C....714 252-2500
7711 Center Ave Ste 200 Huntington Beach (92647) ***(P-10366)***
Freight Management Inc....D....714 632-1440
2900 E La Palma Ave Anaheim (92806) ***(P-26614)***
Freitas Brothers....E....805 343-3134
Hwy 1 Guadalupe (93434) ***(P-51)***
Freixenet Usa Inc....D....707 996-7256
23555 Arnold Dr Sonoma (95476) ***(P-8809)***
Fremantle Media, Burbank *Also called Prdctions N Fremantle Amer Inc* ***(P-17937)***
Fremont Ambltory Srgery Ctr LP....D....510 456-4600
39350 Civic Center Dr Fremont (94538) ***(P-18990)***
Fremont Bank (HQ)....C....510 505-5226
39150 Fremont Blvd Fremont (94538) ***(P-9208)***
Fremont Candle Lighters....C....510 796-0595
39261 Fremont Hub Fremont (94538) ***(P-24832)***
Fremont Group LLC (PA)....E....415 284-8880
199 Fremont St Fl 19 San Francisco (94105) ***(P-9822)***
FREMONT HOSPITAL, Mariposa *Also called John C Fremont Healthcare Dst* ***(P-20918)***
Fremont Hospital....A....530 751-4000
620 J St Marysville (95901) ***(P-20879)***
Fremont Marriott....C....510 413-3700
46100 Landing Pkwy Fremont (94538) ***(P-12282)***
Fremont Medical Center, Marysville *Also called Fremont Hospital* ***(P-20879)***
Fremont Mutual Funds Inc....D....800 548-4539
333 Market St Ste 2600 San Francisco (94105) ***(P-9691)***
Fremont Properties Inc....E....415 284-8500
199 Fremont St Ste 1900 San Francisco (94105) ***(P-10594)***
Fremont Realty Capital LP....D....415 284-8665
199 Fremont St Fl 19 San Francisco (94105) ***(P-10874)***
Fremont Sports Inc....E....510 656-4411
40645 Fremont Blvd Ste 3 Fremont (94538) ***(P-18034)***
Fremont Surgery Center, Fremont *Also called Fremont Ambltory Srgery Ctr LP* ***(P-18990)***
Fremont Unified School Dst....C....510 657-0761
43772 S Grimmer Blvd Fremont (94538) ***(P-13930)***
French Hosp Med Ctr Foundation (HQ)....B....805 543-5353
1911 Johnson Ave San Luis Obispo (93401) ***(P-20880)***
French Park Care Center....C....714 973-1656
600 E Washington Ave Santa Ana (92701) ***(P-19925)***
French Redwood Inc....C....650 598-9000
223 Twin Dolphin Dr Redwood City (94065) ***(P-12283)***
Freschi Air Systems Inc....D....925 827-9761
715 Fulton Shipyard Rd Antioch (94509) ***(P-2141)***
Freschi Service Experts, Antioch *Also called Freschi Air Systems Inc* ***(P-2141)***
Fresenius Med Care Long Beach....E....562 432-4444
440 W Ocean Blvd Long Beach (90802) ***(P-21923)***
Fresenius Medical Care, Fresno *Also called Bio-Mdical Applications Rl Inc* ***(P-21916)***
Fresh Air Environmental Svcs....D....323 913-1965
10675 Rush St South El Monte (91733) ***(P-3409)***
Fresh Farms Inc....E....831 385-3285
700 Airport Rd King City (93930) ***(P-52)***
Fresh Grill LLC....C....714 444-2126
111 E Garry Ave Santa Ana (92707) ***(P-8578)***
Fresh Leaf Farms LLC (HQ)....E....831 422-7405
1250 Hansen St Salinas (93901) ***(P-53)***
Fresh Lifelines For Youth Inc....D....408 263-2630
568 Valley Way Milpitas (95035) ***(P-23231)***
Fresh Origins LLC....B....760 736-4072
570 Quarry Rd San Marcos (92069) ***(P-22)***
Fresh Pick Produce....E....408 315-4612
195 San Pedro Ave Ste D Morgan Hill (95037) ***(P-7810)***
Fresh Start Bakeries, Stockton *Also called Aryzta LLC* ***(P-8546)***
Fresh Venture Farms LLC....D....805 754-4449
1181 S Wolff Rd Oxnard (93033) ***(P-54)***
Freshko Produce Services Inc....C....559 497-7000
2155 E Muscat Ave Fresno (93725) ***(P-8470)***
Freshology Inc....D....818 847-1888
12400 Wilshire Blvd # 1180 Los Angeles (90025) ***(P-8579)***
Freshpoint Inc....C....510 476-5900
30336 Whipple Rd Union City (94587) ***(P-8471)***
Freshpoint Inc....C....626 855-1400
155 N Orange Ave City of Industry (91744) ***(P-8472)***
Freshpoint Central California....C....209 216-0200
5900 N Golden State Blvd Turlock (95382) ***(P-8473)***
Freshpoint Las Vegas, City of Industry *Also called Freshpoint Inc* ***(P-8472)***
Freshpoint Southern Cal Inc....C....626 855-1400
155 N Orange Ave City of Industry (91744) ***(P-8474)***
Freshpoint Southern California, City of Industry *Also called Freshpoint Southern Cal Inc* ***(P-8474)***
Freshway Farms LLC....C....805 349-7170
2165 W Main St Santa Maria (93458) ***(P-95)***
Fresno Airport Hotels LLC....D....559 252-3611
5090 E Clinton Way Fresno (93727) ***(P-12284)***
Fresno Auto Dealers Auction....C....559 268-8051
278 N Marks Ave Fresno (93706) ***(P-6394)***
Fresno Beverage Company Inc....C....559 650-1500
3525 S East Ave Fresno (93725) ***(P-8762)***
Fresno Cmnty Hosp & Med Ctr....D....559 324-4000
2755 Herndon Ave Clovis (93611) ***(P-20881)***
Fresno Cmnty Hosp & Med Ctr (HQ)....A....559 459-3948
2823 Fresno St Fresno (93721) ***(P-20882)***
Fresno Cnty Economic Opportunt....A....559 263-1000
1900 Mariposa Mall # 300 Fresno (93721) ***(P-23232)***
Fresno Cnty Economic Opportunt (PA)....A....559 263-1010
1920 Mariposa Mall # 300 Fresno (93721) ***(P-23233)***
Fresno Cnty Economic Opportunt....B....559 263-1013
1920 Mariposa Mall Fresno (93721) ***(P-23234)***
Fresno Cnty Economic Opportunt....D....559 485-3733
3120 W Nielsen Ave # 102 Fresno (93706) ***(P-23235)***
Fresno Cnty Sprntndent Schools....D....559 644-1000
16644 S Elm Ave Caruthers (93609) ***(P-3815)***
Fresno Convention Center, Fresno *Also called City of Fresno* ***(P-16696)***
Fresno County Private Security....D....559 233-9800
2150 Tulare St Fresno (93721) ***(P-16276)***
Fresno County Rural Trnst Agcy (PA)....D....559 233-6789
2035 Tulare St Fresno (93721) ***(P-3539)***
Fresno District Office, Fresno *Also called State Compensation Insur Fund* ***(P-10136)***
Fresno Eoc, Fresno *Also called Fresno Cnty Economic Opportunt* ***(P-23232)***
FRESNO EOC, Fresno *Also called Fresno Cnty Economic Opportunt* ***(P-23233)***
Fresno Hauling, Fresno *Also called USA Waste of California Inc* ***(P-6306)***
Fresno Hauling, Visalia *Also called USA Waste of California Inc* ***(P-6311)***
Fresno Heart Hospital LLC....B....559 433-8000
15 E Audubon Dr Fresno (93720) ***(P-20883)***
Fresno Heritage Partners....E....559 446-6226
6075 N Marks Ave Fresno (93711) ***(P-19926)***
Fresno Hotel Partners LP....D....559 224-4040
324 E Shaw Ave Fresno (93710) ***(P-12285)***
Fresno Irrigation District....D....559 233-7161
2907 S Maple Ave Fresno (93725) ***(P-6362)***
Fresno Metro Flood Ctrl Dst....D....559 456-3292
5469 E Olive Ave Fresno (93727) ***(P-16788)***
Fresno Plumbing & Heating Inc (PA)....C....559 294-0200
2585 N Larkin Ave Fresno (93727) ***(P-2142)***
Fresno Rescue Mission Inc (PA)....E....559 268-0839
263 G St Fresno (93706) ***(P-23236)***
Fresno Roofing Co Inc....D....559 255-8377
5950 E Olive Ave Fresno (93727) ***(P-3057)***
Fresno Skilled Nursing....D....559 268-5361
1665 M St Fresno (93721) ***(P-19927)***
Fresno Surgery Center LP (PA)....C....559 431-8000
6125 N Fresno St Fresno (93710) ***(P-20884)***
Fresno Surgical Hospital, Fresno *Also called Fresno Surgery Center LP* ***(P-20884)***
Fresno Truck Center....D....559 486-4310
2727 E Central Ave Fresno (93725) ***(P-6395)***
Fresno Truck Center....C....209 983-2400
10182 S Harlan Rd French Camp (95231) ***(P-6396)***
Fresno Unified School District....C....559 457-3074
4600 N Brawley Ave Fresno (93722) ***(P-13931)***
Fresno-Madera Federal Land....D....559 674-2437
305 N I St Madera (93637) ***(P-9447)***
Fresnos Chaffee Zoo Corp....C....559 498-5910
894 W Belmont Ave Fresno (93728) ***(P-24308)***
Freund Baking Co, Hayward *Also called Oakhurst Industries Inc* ***(P-8202)***
Frey Farming & Tpsry Vineyards....D....805 937-1542
2203 Fallen Leaf Dr Santa Maria (93455) ***(P-664)***
Friant Water Users Association....D....559 562-6305
854 N Harvard Ave Lindsay (93247) ***(P-6062)***

Mergent e-mail: customerrelations@mergent.com
1274
2020 Directory of California
Wholesalers and Services Companies
(P-0000) Products & Services Section entry number
(PA)=Parent Co (HQ)=Headquarters (DH)=Div Headquarters

Friant Water Users Authority, Lindsay *Also called Friant Water Users Association (P-6062)*
Frick Paper Company....C....323 726-8200
2164 N Batavia St Orange (92865) *(P-7878)*
Friedas Inc....D....714 826-6100
4465 Corporate Center Dr Los Alamitos (90720) *(P-8475)*
Friedas Specialty Produce, Los Alamitos *Also called Friedas Inc (P-8475)*
Friedman Professional Mgt Co....D....714 842-1426
17752 Beach Blvd Side Huntington Beach (92647) *(P-18991)*
Friendemic LLC....D....855 880-6337
3944 Murphy Canyon Rd San Diego (92123) *(P-27075)*
Friendly Hills Country Club....C....562 698-0331
8500 Villaverde Dr Whittier (90605) *(P-18457)*
Friendly Valley Recrtl Assn....E....661 252-3223
19345 Avenue Of The Oaks Santa Clarita (91321) *(P-18458)*
FRIENDLY VILLAGE COMMUNITY ASS, Santa Clarita *Also called Friendly Valley Recrtl Assn (P-18458)*
Friends Fitzgerald Mar Reserve....D....650 728-3584
200 Nevada Ave Moss Beach (94038) *(P-24175)*
Friends Group Express Inc....D....909 346-6814
14520 Village Dr Apt 1013 Fontana (92337) *(P-4050)*
Friends of Cultural Center Inc....D....760 346-6505
73000 Fred Waring Dr Palm Desert (92260) *(P-17910)*
Friends of Family....E....818 988-4430
16861 Parthenia St Northridge (91343) *(P-23237)*
Friends of Max Rose LLC....D....424 901-1260
1639 11th St Ste 260 Santa Monica (90404) *(P-17611)*
Friends of The Los Angeles....C....323 653-0440
8405 Beverly Blvd Los Angeles (90048) *(P-24176)*
Friends Outside....C....209 955-0701
7272 Murray Dr Stockton (95210) *(P-23238)*
Friends Santa Cruz State Parks....D....831 429-1840
1543 Pacific Ave Ste 206 Santa Cruz (95060) *(P-24545)*
Frito-Lay North America Inc....C....530 671-7854
401 Burns Dr Yuba City (95991) *(P-8341)*
Frito-Lay North America Inc....B....626 855-1300
14600 Proctor Ave City of Industry (91746) *(P-8342)*
Frito-Lay North America Inc....C....310 224-5600
1500 Francisco St Torrance (90501) *(P-26234)*
Frito-Lay North America Inc....C....661 328-6034
28801 Highway 58 Bakersfield (93314) *(P-8343)*
Frito-Lay North America Inc....C....559 226-8153
3630 N Hazel Ave Fresno (93722) *(P-8344)*
Frito-Lay North America Inc....D....661 951-1399
751 W Avenue L8 Lancaster (93534) *(P-8345)*
Frito-Lay North America Inc....D....559 312-8553
1774 Automation Pkwy San Jose (95131) *(P-8346)*
Frito-Lay North America Inc....D....415 467-1860
151 W Hill Pl Brisbane (94005) *(P-8347)*
Frito-Lay North America Inc....C....916 372-5400
3810 Seaport Blvd West Sacramento (95691) *(P-8348)*
Frito-Lay North America Inc....E....661 835-0347
6320 District Blvd Bakersfield (93313) *(P-8349)*
Frito-Lay North America Inc....D....510 769-5000
1450 S Loop Rd Alameda (94502) *(P-8350)*
Frito-Lay North America Inc....D....760 727-6022
1390 Vantage Ct Vista (92081) *(P-8351)*
Frito-Lay North America Inc....D....949 586-4644
26962 Vista Ter El Toro (92630) *(P-8352)*
Frito-Lay North America Inc....D....559 651-1334
8316 W Elowin Ct Visalia (93291) *(P-8353)*
Frito-Lay North America Inc....C....209 544-5424
4029 Leckron Rd Modesto (95357) *(P-8354)*
Frito-Lay North America Inc....E....310 322-5001
1924 E Maple Ave El Segundo (90245) *(P-8355)*
Frize Corporation....D....800 834-2127
16605 Gale Ave City of Industry (91745) *(P-1347)*
Frog Design Inc (HQ)....D....415 442-4804
1130 Howard St San Francisco (94103) *(P-13784)*
Fromer Inc....D....818 341-3896
22225 Acorn St Chatsworth (91311) *(P-1125)*
Front Line MGT Group Inc....D....310 209-3100
1100 Glendon Ave Ste 2000 Los Angeles (90024) *(P-26235)*
Front Porch Inc (PA)....D....209 288-5500
905 Mono Way Sonora (95370) *(P-14819)*
Front Porch Communities....C....626 796-8162
842 E Villa St Pasadena (91101) *(P-23933)*
Front Porch Communities....C....323 661-1128
1055 N Kingsley Dr Los Angeles (90029) *(P-19928)*
Front Porch Communities....C....714 776-7150
1401 W Ball Rd Anaheim (92802) *(P-20556)*
Front Porch Communities....D....858 454-2151
849 Coast Blvd La Jolla (92037) *(P-10729)*
Front Porch Communities (PA)....D....818 729-8100
800 N Brand Blvd Fl 19 Glendale (91203) *(P-20557)*
Front Porch Communities....B....858 274-4110
2567 2nd Ave Unit 312 San Diego (92103) *(P-10730)*
Front Porch Communities....C....760 729-4983
2855 Carlsbad Blvd Carlsbad (92008) *(P-23934)*
Front Porch Communities....C....909 626-1227
650 Harrison Ave Claremont (91711) *(P-20558)*
Front Porch Communities....C....619 427-2777
111 Third Ave Chula Vista (91910) *(P-20559)*
Front Porch Communities & Svcs....D....818 729-8100
303 N Glenoaks Blvd # 1000 Burbank (91502) *(P-20560)*
Front Porch Communities & Svcs....C....562 868-9761
11701 Studebaker Rd Norwalk (90650) *(P-20561)*
Front Porch Communities & Svcs....D....760 240-5051
11959 Apple Valley Rd Apple Valley (92308) *(P-19929)*
Front Prch Cmmunities/Services....C....805 687-0793
3775 Modoc Rd Santa Barbara (93105) *(P-20562)*
Front St Inc....C....831 420-0120
2115 7th Ave Santa Cruz (95062) *(P-20563)*
FRONT ST RESIDENTIAL CARE, Santa Cruz *Also called Front St Inc (P-20563)*
Frontapp Inc....D....415 680-3048
525 Brannan St Ste 300 San Francisco (94107) *(P-15333)*
Frontech N Fujitsu Amer Inc....D....408 982-3697
2933 Bunker Hill Ln # 101 Santa Clara (95054) *(P-14820)*
Frontech N Fujitsu Amer Inc (HQ)....C....949 855-5500
27121 Towne Centre Dr # 100 Foothill Ranch (92610) *(P-15596)*
Frontier California Inc....D....760 342-0500
83793 Dr Carreon Blvd Indio (92201) *(P-5402)*
Frontier California Inc....D....805 925-0000
200 W Church St Santa Maria (93458) *(P-5403)*
Frontier California Inc....C....818 365-0542
510 Park Ave San Fernando (91340) *(P-5404)*
Frontier California Inc....C....209 239-4128
525 E Yosemite Ave Manteca (95336) *(P-5405)*
Frontier California Inc....A....805 372-6000
112 S Lakeview Canyon Rd Westlake Village (91362) *(P-7269)*
Frontier California Inc....D....805 372-6000
1 Wellpoint Way Westlake Village (91362) *(P-5406)*
Frontier California Inc....D....559 592-2100
200 W Firebaugh Ave Exeter (93221) *(P-5407)*
Frontier California Inc....D....559 224-9222
5195 N Blackstone Ave Fresno (93710) *(P-5259)*
Frontier Communities, Ontario *Also called Shii LLC (P-11449)*
Frontier Land Companies....E....209 957-8112
10100 Trinity Pkwy # 420 Stockton (95219) *(P-1126)*
Frontier Logistics Services, Ontario *Also called F R T International Inc (P-4944)*
Frontier Logistics Services, Compton *Also called F R T International Inc (P-4407)*
Frontier Mechanical Inc....D....661 589-6203
6309 Seven Seas Ave Bakersfield (93308) *(P-2143)*
Frontier Plumbing, Bakersfield *Also called Frontier Mechanical Inc (P-2143)*
Frontier Title Co (PA)....E....707 427-5400
1499 Oliver Rd Fairfield (94534) *(P-10194)*
Frontiir Corporation....C....510 996-2071
1586 Parkview Ave Apt 3 San Jose (95130) *(P-5408)*
Frontrs-Frnters Land Companies, Stockton *Also called Frontier Land Companies (P-1126)*
Frontwave Credit Union (PA)....C....760 430-7511
1278 Rocky Point Dr Oceanside (92056) *(P-9314)*
Frsteam By Custom Commercial, Hayward *Also called Custom Commercial Dry Clrs Inc (P-13255)*
Fruit Growers Supply Company....D....909 390-0190
225 S Wineville Ave Ontario (91761) *(P-8476)*
Fruit Guys....D....714 826-2993
4465 Corporate Center Dr Los Alamitos (90720) *(P-8477)*
Fruit Patch Sales LLC....B....559 591-1170
38773 Road 48 Dinuba (93618) *(P-8478)*
Fruitvale Long Term Care LLC....D....510 261-5613
3020 E 15th St Oakland (94601) *(P-19930)*
Fry, Opal W & Son Farming, Bakersfield *Also called Opal Fry and Son (P-69)*
Frys Electronics Inc....B....916 286-5800
4100 Northgate Blvd Sacramento (95834) *(P-27076)*
Frys Electronics Inc....C....310 364-3797
3600 N Sepulveda Blvd Manhattan Beach (90266) *(P-6838)*
FS Commercial Landscape Inc (PA)....D....951 360-7070
5151 Pedley Rd Riverside (92509) *(P-813)*
FS&k, Thousand Oaks *Also called Floyd Skeren & Kelly LLP (P-22508)*
FSA, Lompoc *Also called Family Service Agency (P-23219)*
Fscc, Santa Barbara *Also called Frank Schipper Construction Co (P-1479)*
Fsq Rio Las Palmas Business Tr....D....209 957-4711
877 E March Ln Apt 378 Stockton (95207) *(P-10731)*
Fssi, Santa Ana *Also called Financial Statement Svcs Inc (P-13722)*
Fst Sand & Gravel Inc....E....951 277-8440
21780 Temescal Canyon Rd Corona (92883) *(P-6685)*
Ft USA, Ontario *Also called Inqbrands Inc (P-16030)*
FT. WASHINGTON ELEM., Fresno *Also called Fort Washington Parent Assoc (P-24542)*
Ftdi West Inc....D....909 473-1111
3375 Enterprise Dr Bloomington (92316) *(P-4411)*
Fti Consulting Inc....D....213 689-1200
350 S Grand Ave Ste 3000 Los Angeles (90071) *(P-25084)*
Fti Consulting Inc....D....415 283-4200
50 California St Ste 1900 San Francisco (94111) *(P-26615)*
Fts Global, Visalia *Also called Agriholding Inc (P-4881)*
Ftv Management Company LP....C....415 291-8164
555 California St # 2900 San Francisco (94104) *(P-11727)*
Fuel Cycle Inc (PA)....D....323 556-5400
11859 Wilshire Blvd Fl 4 Los Angeles (90025) *(P-14821)*
Fuel Delivery Services Inc....D....209 751-2185
4895 S Airport Way Stockton (95206) *(P-4051)*
Fuel TV....D....310 444-8564
1440 S Sepulveda Blvd Los Angeles (90025) *(P-5608)*
Fueling and Service Tech Inc....D....714 523-0194
7050 Village Dr Ste D Buena Park (90621) *(P-7547)*
Fuentes Farms Ag Inc....B....209 722-7201
2346 Glen Ave Merced (95340) *(P-14286)*
Fugro USA Land Inc....E....925 256-6070
1777 Botelho Dr Ste 262 Walnut Creek (94596) *(P-25085)*
Fuji Food Products Inc (PA)....D....562 404-2590
14420 Bloomfield Ave Santa Fe Springs (90670) *(P-8580)*
Fuji Food Products Inc....C....619 268-3118
8660 Miramar Rd Ste N San Diego (92126) *(P-8581)*
Fuji Photo Film, Cypress *Also called Fujifilm North America Corp (P-6732)*
Fujifilm North America Corp....C....714 372-4200
6200 Phyllis Dr Cypress (90630) *(P-6732)*
Fujitsu America Inc (HQ)....B....408 746-6000
1250 E Arques Ave Sunnyvale (94085) *(P-15597)*

ALPHABETIC

Fujitsu America Inc...D.......408 746-8419
3113 Knights Bridge Rd San Jose (95132) ***(P-15598)***
Fujitsu America Inc...C.......310 563-7000
2250 E Imperial Hwy # 200 El Segundo (90245) ***(P-15599)***
Fujitsu Computer Pdts Amer Inc (HQ)...B.......800 626-4686
1250 E Arques Ave Sunnyvale (94085) ***(P-6839)***
Fujitsu Electronics Amer Inc (HQ)...D.......408 737-5600
1250 E Arques Ave Sunnyvale (94085) ***(P-25086)***
Fujitsu Glovia Inc (HQ)...C.......310 563-7000
200 Continental Blvd Fl 3 El Segundo (90245) ***(P-14822)***
Fujitsu Laboratories Amer Inc (HQ)...D.......408 530-4500
1240 E Arques Ave 345 Sunnyvale (94085) ***(P-25752)***
Fujitsu Ten Corp of America...C.......310 327-2151
19600 S Vermont Ave Torrance (90502) ***(P-7205)***
Full Circle Wireless Inc...E.......949 783-7979
8900 Research Dr Irvine (92618) ***(P-7270)***
Full Spectrum Services Inc...E.......707 465-1460
1570 S Railroad Ave Crescent City (95531) ***(P-23239)***
Full Throttle Energy Company...C.......323 474-8417
125 E 56th St Los Angeles (90011) ***(P-16789)***
Fullclip USA, Garden Grove *Also called Customfab Inc* ***(P-16734)***
Fullmer Construction...C.......909 947-9467
1725 S Grove Ave Ontario (91761) ***(P-1348)***
Fullscreen Inc (HQ)...D.......310 202-3333
12180 Millennium Ste 100 Playa Vista (90094) ***(P-13509)***
Fulwider and Patton LLP...D.......310 824-5555
6100 Center Dr Ste 1200 Los Angeles (90045) ***(P-22523)***
Fumai Industrial Inc...D.......626 272-1788
735 W Duarte Rd Arcadia (91007) ***(P-7271)***
Fume-A-Pest & Termite Control, Encino *Also called A-Able Inc* ***(P-13807)***
Fund Services Advisors Inc...E.......213 612-2196
777 S Figueroa St # 3200 Los Angeles (90017) ***(P-9823)***
Fundbox Inc...C.......415 509-1343
300 Montgomery St Ste 900 San Francisco (94104) ***(P-9502)***
Funding Circle Usa Inc...D.......855 385-5356
747 Front St Fl 4 San Francisco (94111) ***(P-9482)***
Fungible Inc...D.......669 292-5522
3201 Scott Blvd Santa Clara (95054) ***(P-16790)***
Funny or Die Inc...E.......650 461-3929
1041 N Formosa Ave West Hollywood (90046) ***(P-16003)***
Funtopia Inc...D.......510 246-3098
3700 Brookstone Dr Turlock (95382) ***(P-18700)***
Furnace Creek Ranch & Inn, Death Valley *Also called Xanterra Parks & Resorts Inc* ***(P-13128)***
Furniture America Cal Inc (PA)...D.......909 718-7276
19605 E Walnut Dr N City of Industry (91789) ***(P-6514)***
Furniture America California, City of Industry *Also called Furniture America Cal Inc* ***(P-6514)***
Furniture Trnsp Systems...D.......909 869-1200
3100 Pomona Blvd Pomona (91768) ***(P-4949)***
Further Products Inc...E.......323 839-1246
431 Cherry Dr Pasadena (91105) ***(P-26616)***
Fuscoe Engineering Inc (PA)...D.......949 474-1960
16795 Von Karman Ave # 100 Irvine (92606) ***(P-25087)***
Fuse Project LLC...D.......415 908-1492
1401 16th St San Francisco (94103) ***(P-27077)***
Fusefx LLC...B.......818 237-5052
14823 Califa St Van Nuys (91411) ***(P-17742)***
Fusion Cloud Company LLC (HQ)...D.......925 201-2500
6800 Koll Center Pkwy Pleasanton (94566) ***(P-5409)***
Fusion Mphc Group Inc...C.......408 324-1353
2510 Zanker Rd San Jose (95131) ***(P-5410)***
Fusion Real Estate Network Inc...D.......916 448-3174
1300 National Dr Ste 170 Sacramento (95834) ***(P-11161)***
Fusionone Inc...D.......408 282-1200
55 Almaden Blvd Ste 500 San Jose (95113) ***(P-14823)***
Fusionzone Automotive Inc...E.......888 576-1136
1011 Swarthmore Ave Pacific Palisades (90272) ***(P-16004)***
Future Dial Incorporated...D.......408 245-8880
392 Potrero Ave Sunnyvale (94085) ***(P-16005)***
Future Energy Corporation...D.......760 477-9700
4120 Avenida De La Plata Oceanside (92056) ***(P-2788)***
Future Energy Corporation (PA)...E.......800 985-0733
8980 Grant Line Rd Elk Grove (95624) ***(P-2789)***
Future Energy Corporation...D.......916 685-4200
9701 Elk Grove Florin Rd Elk Grove (95624) ***(P-25088)***
Future Energy Savers, Elk Grove *Also called Future Energy Corporation* ***(P-2789)***
Future Homes International, Moraga *Also called Engineered Forest Products LLC* ***(P-11912)***
Future State...D.......925 956-4200
2101 Webster St Ste 520 Oakland (94612) ***(P-16006)***
Futuredontics Inc (HQ)...D.......310 215-6400
6060 Center Dr Fl 7 Los Angeles (90045) ***(P-26617)***
Futurenet Technologies Corp...C.......909 396-4000
1320 Valley Vista Dr # 202 Diamond Bar (91765) ***(P-14824)***
Futures Explored...D.......925 332-7183
2380 Salvio St Ste 302 Concord (94520) ***(P-23240)***
Futuro Infantil Hispano Ffa...E.......626 339-1824
2227 E Garvey Ave N West Covina (91791) ***(P-23935)***
Fvbw, Fountain Valley *Also called Fountain Valley Body Works M2* ***(P-17291)***
Fx Networks LLC...C.......310 369-1000
10201 W Pico Blvd Los Angeles (90064) ***(P-5724)***
Fyeo Apparel Inc...E.......213 278-0435
747 E 10th St Unit 303 Los Angeles (90021) ***(P-22246)***
G & G Construction Co, Atwater *Also called Gino/Giuseppe Inc* ***(P-3150)***
G & L Penasquitos Inc...D.......858 538-0802
10584 Rancho Carmel Dr San Diego (92128) ***(P-23241)***
G A T X Rail, Colton *Also called GATX Corporation* ***(P-5116)***
G and L Brock Cnstr Co Inc...E.......209 931-3626
4145 Calloway Ct Stockton (95215) ***(P-3314)***

G B & P Citrus Co Inc (PA)...D.......213 312-1380
1601 E Olympic Blvd # 111 Los Angeles (90021) ***(P-10595)***
G B Group Inc (PA)...D.......408 848-8118
8921 Murray Ave Gilroy (95020) ***(P-1244)***
G Brothers Construction Inc...E.......714 590-3070
7070 Patterson Dr Garden Grove (92841) ***(P-2790)***
G D B, San Rafael *Also called Guide Dogs For Blind Inc* ***(P-603)***
G I L C Inc...E.......831 724-1011
585 W Beach St Watsonville (95076) ***(P-1127)***
G J Sullivan Co Inc...D.......213 626-1000
725 S Figueroa St # 1900 Los Angeles (90017) ***(P-10367)***
G K Tool Corp...D.......626 338-7300
4265 Puente Ave Baldwin Park (91706) ***(P-7392)***
G Katen Partners Ltd Lblty Co...A.......424 354-3241
9903 Santa Monica Blvd Beverly Hills (90212) ***(P-4950)***
G M A C-One Source Realty...D.......619 405-6231
898 Jackman St El Cajon (92020) ***(P-11162)***
G M Floral Company...E.......213 489-7055
740 Maple Ave Los Angeles (90014) ***(P-8893)***
G M Floral Supply, Los Angeles *Also called G M Floral Company* ***(P-8893)***
G M I, San Diego *Also called Guard Management Inc* ***(P-16293)***
G M S, Rancho Cucamonga *Also called General Micro Systems Inc* ***(P-6842)***
G Moroni Comp, Elk Grove *Also called Maritime Management* ***(P-26307)***
G P M M Money Centers Inc...E.......619 288-7607
1460 Doris Ave Oxnard (93030) ***(P-9437)***
G P Resources, Compton *Also called General Petroleum Corporation* ***(P-8730)***
G P S, Taft *Also called General Production Svc Cal Inc* ***(P-1857)***
G R Helm Inc...D.......916 933-9697
5050 Robert J Mathews Pkw El Dorado Hills (95762) ***(P-14507)***
G S C Ball, Commerce *Also called Grocers Specialty Company* ***(P-8179)***
G S N, Santa Monica *Also called Game Show Network LLC* ***(P-5725)***
G S R, Pleasanton *Also called Global Software Resources Inc* ***(P-16018)***
G T C, Whittier *Also called General Transistor Corporation* ***(P-7272)***
G W Maintenance Inc (PA)...D.......714 541-2211
1101 E 6th St Santa Ana (92701) ***(P-7634)***
G W Surfaces (PA)...C.......805 642-5004
2432 Palma Dr Ventura (93003) ***(P-3410)***
G&K Services LLC...D.......916 381-5500
5900 Alder Ave Sacramento (95828) ***(P-13296)***
G&K Services LLC...E.......925 427-4401
1229 California Ave Pittsburg (94565) ***(P-13297)***
G/M Business Interiors, San Diego *Also called Goforth & Marti* ***(P-6515)***
G2 Direct and Digital...E.......415 421-1000
612 Howard St Ste 400 San Francisco (94105) ***(P-14825)***
G2 Software Systems Inc...C.......619 222-8025
4025 Hancock St Ste 105 San Diego (92110) ***(P-25089)***
G3 Enterprises, Modesto *Also called United Sttes Intrmdal Svcs LLC* ***(P-5073)***
G3 Enterprises Inc (PA)...C.......209 341-7515
502 E Whitmore Ave Modesto (95358) ***(P-4412)***
G3 Enterprises Inc...D.......209 341-3441
1300 Camino Diablo Rd Byron (94514) ***(P-4951)***
G3 Enterprises Inc...D.......209 341-4045
500 S Santa Rosa Ave Modesto (95354) ***(P-4952)***
G4s Government Services, Anaheim *Also called G4s Justice Services LLC* ***(P-16520)***
G4s Justice Services LLC...C.......800 589-6003
1290 N Hancock St Ste 103 Anaheim (92807) ***(P-16520)***
G4s Secure Solutions (usa)...C.......661 834-3454
4400 Ashe Rd Ste 206 Bakersfield (93313) ***(P-16277)***
G4s Secure Solutions (usa)...B.......323 938-9100
4929 Wilshire Blvd # 601 Los Angeles (90010) ***(P-16278)***
G4s Secure Solutions (usa)...B.......951 341-3000
1450 Iowa Ave Riverside (92507) ***(P-16279)***
G4s Secure Solutions (usa)...C.......925 543-0008
1 Annabel Ln Ste 208 San Ramon (94583) ***(P-16280)***
G4s Secure Solutions USA Inc...C.......619 295-2394
5030 Camino De La Siesta # 404 San Diego (92108) ***(P-16281)***
G4s Secure Solutions USA Inc...C.......415 591-0780
200 Pine St Fl 7 San Francisco (94104) ***(P-16282)***
G4s Secure Solutions USA Inc...C.......714 939-4900
2300 E Katella Ave # 150 Anaheim (92806) ***(P-16283)***
G4s Secure Solutions USA Inc...C.......818 889-1113
5655 Lindero Canyon Rd # 504 Westlake Village (91362) ***(P-16284)***
G5 Global Partners Ix LLC...D.......619 291-6500
2151 Hotel Cir S San Diego (92108) ***(P-12286)***
G7 Productivity Systems...D.......858 675-1095
16885 W Bernardo Dr # 290 San Diego (92127) ***(P-15334)***
GA Services LLC...E.......949 752-6515
1681 Kettering Irvine (92614) ***(P-16007)***
Gabe Inc...D.......949 679-2727
300 Spectrum Irvine (92618) ***(P-27078)***
Gable House Inc...D.......310 378-2265
22501 Hawthorne Blvd Torrance (90505) ***(P-18035)***
Gable House Bowl, Torrance *Also called Gable House Inc* ***(P-18035)***
Gables of Ojai LLC...D.......805 646-1446
701 N Montgomery St Ojai (93023) ***(P-10732)***
Gabriella Foundation...D.......213 365-2491
639 S Commwl Ave Ste B Los Angeles (90005) ***(P-17880)***
Gachina Landscape MGT Inc...B.......650 853-0400
1130 Obrien Dr Menlo Park (94025) ***(P-814)***
GAF Holdings Inc...B.......559 734-3333
1300 E Mineral King Ave Visalia (93292) ***(P-11661)***
GAF Materials, Stockton *Also called Standard Industries Inc* ***(P-6720)***
GAF Materials, Shafter *Also called Standard Industries Inc* ***(P-6721)***
Gafcon Inc (PA)...D.......858 875-0010
5960 Cornerstone Ct W # 100 San Diego (92121) ***(P-26236)***
Gahvejian Enterprises Inc...E.......559 834-5956
2004 S Temperance Ave Fowler (93625) ***(P-7879)***

Mergent e-mail: customerrelations@mergent.com
1276
2020 Directory of California
Wholesalers and Services Companies
(P-0000) Products & Services Section entry number
(PA)=Parent Co (HQ)=Headquarters (DH)=Div Headquarters

Gaia Interactive Inc....C....408 573-8800
2540 N 1st St Ste 101 San Jose (95131) ***(P-5411)***
Gaia Online, San Jose *Also called Gaia Interactive Inc* ***(P-5411)***
Gainsight Inc....B....888 623-8562
400 Concar Dr 3 San Mateo (94402) ***(P-14826)***
Gaithers Family Home....E....559 781-0301
1408 S Newcomb St Porterville (93257) ***(P-20564)***
Gaju Market Corporation....C....213 382-9444
450 S Western Ave Los Angeles (90020) ***(P-8974)***
Galassos Bakery (PA)....C....951 360-1211
10820 San Sevaine Way Jurupa Valley (91752) ***(P-8582)***
Galaxy Building Systems Inc....C....818 340-6557
23978 Craftsman Rd Calabasas (91302) ***(P-13932)***
Gale Lina Inc....D....909 595-8898
230 S 9th Ave City of Industry (91746) ***(P-7944)***
Gale/Triangle, San Pedro *Also called Performance Team Frt Sys Inc* ***(P-4470)***
Galena Equipment Rental LLC....E....510 638-8100
10700 Bigge St San Leandro (94577) ***(P-14096)***
Galice Inc....D....323 731-8200
30140 Tuttle Ct Tehachapi (93561) ***(P-16791)***
Galkos Construction Inc (PA)....D....714 373-8545
15262 Pipeline Ln Huntington Beach (92649) ***(P-13425)***
Gallagher Bassett, Irvine *Also called Arthur J Gallagher & Co* ***(P-10273)***
Gallagher Construction Svcs, San Francisco *Also called Arthur J Gallagher & Co* ***(P-10277)***
Gallagher Pediatric Therapy, Fullerton *Also called Therapy For Kids Inc* ***(P-19699)***
Gallagher Properties Inc (PA)....D....510 261-0466
344 High St Oakland (94601) ***(P-3315)***
Gallaher Construction Inc....E....707 535-3200
220 Concourse Blvd Santa Rosa (95403) ***(P-1128)***
Galleher LLC (PA)....C....562 944-8885
9303 Greenleaf Ave Santa Fe Springs (90670) ***(P-6558)***
Galleria Park Associates LLC....D....415 781-3060
191 Sutter St San Francisco (94104) ***(P-12287)***
Galleria Park Hotel, San Francisco *Also called Galleria Park Associates LLC* ***(P-12287)***
Galli Produce Company....D....408 436-6100
1650 Old Bayshore Hwy San Jose (95112) ***(P-8479)***
Gallo Cattle Co A Ltd Partnr....B....209 394-7984
10561 State Highway 140 Atwater (95301) ***(P-392)***
Gallo Sales Company Inc (HQ)....C....510 476-5000
30825 Wiegman Rd Hayward (94544) ***(P-8810)***
Galloway Lucchese Everson....E....925 930-9090
2300 Contra Costa Blvd Walnut Creek (94596) ***(P-22524)***
Gallup Inc....E....949 474-2700
18300 Von Karman Ave Irvine (92612) ***(P-26618)***
Gallup & Stribling Orchids LLC....E....805 684-1998
3450 Via Real Carpinteria (93013) ***(P-241)***
Gallup and Stribling Holdings, Carpinteria *Also called Gallup & Stribling Orchids LLC* ***(P-241)***
Gallup Organization, The, Irvine *Also called Gallup Inc* ***(P-26618)***
Galt Joint Union School Dst....E....209 745-1546
902 Caroline Ave Galt (95632) ***(P-23726)***
Galt Park Recreation, Galt *Also called City of Galt* ***(P-18656)***
Gama Berry Farms LLC....D....805 483-1000
730 S A St Oxnard (93030) ***(P-96)***
Gama Contracting Services Inc....C....626 442-7200
1835 Floradale Ave South El Monte (91733) ***(P-7472)***
Gamboa Service Inc....D....714 966-5325
2116 S Wright St Santa Ana (92705) ***(P-13933)***
Game Show Network LLC (HQ)....D....310 255-6800
2150 Colorado Ave Ste 100 Santa Monica (90404) ***(P-5725)***
Gamefly Holdings LLC (PA)....C....310 568-8224
6080 Center Dr Ste 800 Los Angeles (90045) ***(P-16008)***
Gamma PHI Beta Sorority Inc....D....805 968-4221
890 Camino Pescadero Goleta (93117) ***(P-13171)***
Gamut Construction Company Inc....D....909 948-0500
9340 Santa Anita Ave # 105 Rancho Cucamonga (91730) ***(P-11914)***
Gang Tyre Ramer & Brown Inc....E....310 777-7158
132 S Rodeo Dr Ste 306 Beverly Hills (90212) ***(P-22525)***
Gar Enterprises (PA)....D....626 574-1175
418 E Live Oak Ave Arcadia (91006) ***(P-6840)***
Garage Door Specialists, Sacramento *Also called Singley Enterprises* ***(P-6657)***
Garcia Juarez Construction Inc (PA)....D....951 657-3535
6801 Atlantic Ave Long Beach (90805) ***(P-25090)***
Garcia Roofing Inc....E....661 325-5736
201 Mount Vernon Ave Bakersfield (93307) ***(P-3058)***
Garda CL Technical Svcs Inc....D....818 362-7011
15640 Roxford St Sylmar (91342) ***(P-16285)***
Garda CL West Inc....E....909 574-2676
372 S Arrowhead Ave San Bernardino (92408) ***(P-16286)***
Garda CL West Inc (HQ)....B....213 383-3611
1612 W Pico Blvd Los Angeles (90015) ***(P-16287)***
Garda CL West Inc....D....800 883-8305
301 N Lake Ave Ste 600 Pasadena (91101) ***(P-16288)***
Garden City Inc....A....408 244-3333
1887 Matrix Blvd San Jose (95110) ***(P-18701)***
Garden City Casino & Rest, San Jose *Also called Garden City Inc* ***(P-18701)***
GARDEN CITY HEALTHCARE CENTER, Modesto *Also called Fig Holdings LLC* ***(P-19913)***
Garden Court Hotel....D....650 322-9000
520 Cowper St Ste 100 Palo Alto (94301) ***(P-12288)***
Garden Crest Convalesce....D....323 663-8281
909 Lucile Ave Los Angeles (90026) ***(P-19931)***
Garden Crest Rtrment Residence, Los Angeles *Also called Garden Crest Convalesce* ***(P-19931)***
Garden Grove Advanced Imaging....B....310 445-2800
1510 Cotner Ave Los Angeles (90025) ***(P-21533)***
Garden Grove Convales....C....714 638-9470
12882 Shackelford Ln Garden Grove (92841) ***(P-20565)***
GARDEN GROVE HOSPITAL, Garden Grove *Also called Kenneth Corp* ***(P-20988)***
Garden Grove Hospital Med Ctr, Garden Grove *Also called Prime Health Care Svcs Grdn Gr* ***(P-21106)***
Garden Grove Unified Schl Dst....D....714 663-6437
8371 Orangewood Ave Garden Grove (92841) ***(P-23727)***
Garden Medical Offices, Downey *Also called Kaiser Foundation Hospitals* ***(P-19067)***
Garden Terrace Health Care Ctr, Vista *Also called Bent Tree Nursing Center Inc* ***(P-19751)***
Garden View Inc....E....626 303-4043
417 E Huntington Dr Monrovia (91016) ***(P-729)***
Garden View Care Center Inc....D....626 962-7095
14475 Garden View Ln Baldwin Park (91706) ***(P-19932)***
Garden, The, Santa Ana *Also called Alzheimers Care Since 1983* ***(P-21659)***
Gardena Convalescent Center, Santa Fe Springs *Also called B & E Convalescent Center Inc* ***(P-20497)***
Gardena Flores Inc....D....310 323-4570
14165 Purche Ave Gardena (90249) ***(P-19933)***
Gardena Hospital LP....A....310 532-4200
1145 W Redondo Beach Blvd Gardena (90247) ***(P-20885)***
Gardena Medical Offices, Gardena *Also called Kaiser Foundation Hospitals* ***(P-20960)***
Gardena Municipal Bus Lines, Gardena *Also called City of Gardena* ***(P-3528)***
Gardeners Guild Inc....C....415 457-0400
2780 Goodrick Ave Richmond (94801) ***(P-815)***
Gardner Family Hlth Netwrk Inc (PA)....E....408 457-7100
160 E Virginia St Ste 100 San Jose (95112) ***(P-18992)***
Gardner Health Services, San Jose *Also called Gardner Family Hlth Netwrk Inc* ***(P-18992)***
Gardner Neurologic Orthopedic....D....310 649-5824
6167 Bristol Pkwy Ste 200 Culver City (90230) ***(P-26237)***
Gardner Pool Company Inc (PA)....D....619 593-8880
801 Gable Way El Cajon (92020) ***(P-3411)***
Gardner Pool Plastering, El Cajon *Also called Gardner Pool Company Inc* ***(P-3411)***
Gardner Trucking Inc (HQ)....B....909 563-5606
1219 E Elm St Ontario (91761) ***(P-4052)***
Garfield Nuerobehavioral Ctr, Oakland *Also called Telecare Corporation* ***(P-21435)***
Garfield Nursing Home Inc....C....510 582-7676
1100 Marina Village Pkwy # 100 Alameda (94501) ***(P-19934)***
Garich Inc (PA)....B....858 453-1331
6050 Santo Rd Ste 200 San Diego (92124) ***(P-14287)***
Garich Inc....A....951 302-4750
504 E Alvarado St Ste 201 Fallbrook (92028) ***(P-14288)***
Garlic Company....C....661 393-4212
18602 S Zerker Rd Shafter (93263) ***(P-23)***
Garment Industry Laundry....C....323 752-8335
710 W 58th St Los Angeles (90037) ***(P-13298)***
Garrad Hassan America Inc (HQ)....D....858 836-3370
9665 Chesapeake Dr # 435 San Diego (92123) ***(P-25091)***
Garrett J Gentry Gen Engrg Inc....D....909 693-3391
1297 W 9th St Upland (91786) ***(P-25092)***
Garrick Motors Inc....C....760 489-2656
559 S Pine St Escondido (92025) ***(P-17329)***
Garris Plastering, Orange *Also called Padilla Construction Company* ***(P-2840)***
Gartner Inc....D....310 479-2108
11845 W Olympic Blvd 505w Los Angeles (90064) ***(P-25899)***
Gary Cardiff Enterprises Inc....D....760 568-1403
75255 Sheryl Ave Palm Desert (92211) ***(P-3676)***
Gary Lask....D....310 825-0631
200 Ucla Medical Plz 4 Los Angeles (90095) ***(P-18993)***
Gary Mary W Wireless Hlth Inst....E....858 412-8600
10350 N Torrey Pines Rd La Jolla (92037) ***(P-25991)***
Gary R Edwards Inc....D....619 299-8700
3930 Utah St Ste C San Diego (92104) ***(P-16792)***
Gary Steel Division, Santa Fe Springs *Also called Kloeckner Metals Corporation* ***(P-7076)***
Garys Construction Inc....C....760 639-4456
2517 Dos Lomas Fallbrook (92028) ***(P-6349)***
GAS COMPANY, THE, Los Angeles *Also called Southern California Gas Co* ***(P-5974)***
Gas Transmission Systems Inc....C....530 893-6711
130 Amber Grove Dr # 134 Chico (95973) ***(P-25093)***
Gaslamp Hotel Management Inc....C....619 234-0977
202 Island Ave San Diego (92101) ***(P-12289)***
Gastroenterology Division....E....415 206-8823
1001 Potrero Ave Ste 1e21 San Francisco (94110) ***(P-18994)***
Gat - Arln Ground Support Inc....C....818 847-9127
2627 N Hollywood Way Burbank (91505) ***(P-4876)***
Gat - Arln Ground Support Inc....B....916 923-2349
6701 Lindbergh Dr Sacramento (95837) ***(P-4772)***
Gatan Inc (HQ)....D....925 463-0200
5794 W Las Positas Blvd Pleasanton (94588) ***(P-25094)***
Gate City Beverage Bear Trckg, San Bernardino *Also called Bear Trucking Inc* ***(P-4195)***
Gate City Beverage Distrs (PA)....B....909 799-0281
2505 Steele Rd San Bernardino (92408) ***(P-8763)***
Gate City Beverage Distrs....B....760 775-5483
31315 Plantation Dr Thousand Palms (92276) ***(P-8764)***
Gate Five Group LLC....E....415 339-9500
200 Gate 5 Rd Ste 116 Sausalito (94965) ***(P-6559)***
Gate of Heaven Cemetery, Los Altos *Also called Roman Cthlic Bishp of San Jose* ***(P-11633)***
Gate Three Healthcare LLC....C....949 770-3348
24962 Calle Aragon Laguna Hills (92637) ***(P-23936)***
Gatehouse Msi LLC....E....562 623-3000
15511 Carmenita Rd Santa Fe Springs (90670) ***(P-2935)***
Gates of Spain Wibel....E....626 441-3078
2545 Mission St Pasadena (91108) ***(P-13347)***
Gateway, Los Angeles *Also called County of Los Angeles* ***(P-13778)***
Gateway Auto Auction Group, Fresno *Also called Gateway Auto Sales & Lsg Inc* ***(P-6397)***
Gateway Auto Sales & Lsg Inc....D....800 921-4336
3260 E Annadale Ave Fresno (93725) ***(P-6397)***
Gateway Ctr of Monterey Cnty (PA)....D....831 372-8002
850 Congress Ave Pacific Grove (93950) ***(P-23937)***
Gateway Home Realty, Brea *Also called American Financial Network Inc* ***(P-9517)***

ALPHABETIC

Employee Codes: A=Over 500 employees, B=251-500
C=101-250, D=51-100, E=50
2020 Directory of California
Wholesalers and Services Companies
© Mergent Inc. 1-800-342-5647
1277

Gateway Landscape Cnstr Inc..........D.......925 875-0000
6735 Sierra Ct Ste A Dublin (94568) *(P-816)*
Gateway Limousine, Burlingame *Also called Amato Industries Incorporated (P-3620)*
Gateway Post Acute, Porterville *Also called Valley Careidence Opco LLC (P-20344)*
Gateway Security Inc..........A.......310 410-0790
5757 W Century Blvd Los Angeles (90045) *(P-16289)*
Gateways Hosp Mental Hlth Ctr..........D.......323 644-2026
340 N Madison Ave Los Angeles (90004) *(P-20886)*
Gateways Hosp Mental Hlth Ctr (PA)..........C.......323 644-2000
1891 Effie St Los Angeles (90026) *(P-21410)*
GATX Corporation..........D.......909 825-3043
20878 Slover St Colton (92324) *(P-5116)*
Gavin De Becker & Associates..........C.......818 760-4213
11684 Ventura Blvd # 440 Studio City (91604) *(P-26619)*
Gaw Van Male Smith Myers..........D.......707 425-1250
1411 Oliver Rd Ste 300 Fairfield (94534) *(P-22526)*
Gb3, Clovis *Also called George Browns Sports Club (P-18148)*
Gbc Concrete Masnry Cnstr Inc..........C.......951 245-2355
561 Birch St Lake Elsinore (92530) *(P-2713)*
GBI Tile & Stone Inc (PA)..........E.......949 567-1880
5900 Skylab Rd Ste 150 Huntington Beach (92647) *(P-6686)*
Gbp Parent Corp (HQ)..........A.......424 254-9774
2321 Rosecrans Ave # 3255 El Segundo (90245) *(P-11662)*
GBS Financial Corp..........D.......310 937-0073
904 Manhattan Ave Ste 3 Manhattan Beach (90266) *(P-16793)*
GBS Linens Inc (PA)..........D.......714 778-6448
305 N Muller St Anaheim (92801) *(P-13222)*
GBS Party Linens, Anaheim *Also called GBS Linens Inc (P-13222)*
GBT Inc..........D.......626 854-9338
17358 Railroad St City of Industry (91748) *(P-6841)*
Gcc, Santa Rosa *Also called Ghilotti Construction Co Inc (P-1965)*
GCCCD AUXILIARY, El Cajon *Also called Grossmont-Cuyamaca Community (P-24559)*
Gccfc 2005-Gg5 Y St Ltd Partnr..........D.......916 455-6800
4422 Y St Sacramento (95817) *(P-12290)*
GCI Construction Inc..........E.......714 957-0233
1031 Calle Recodo Ste D San Clemente (92673) *(P-1707)*
Gcl W, Los Angeles *Also called Garda CL West Inc (P-16287)*
Gcm Holding Corporation..........B.......510 475-0404
1350 Atlantic St Union City (94587) *(P-11663)*
Gco Inc (PA)..........E.......510 786-3333
27750 Industrial Blvd Hayward (94545) *(P-7427)*
Gcti, Los Angeles *Also called Gentlecare Transport Inc (P-3677)*
Gcu Trucking Inc..........D.......209 845-2117
7819 Crane Rd Oakdale (95361) *(P-4053)*
GD Heil Inc..........C.......714 687-9100
1031 Segovia Cir Placentia (92870) *(P-3342)*
GD Nielson Construction Inc..........D.......707 253-8774
147 Camino Oruga NAPA (94558) *(P-1856)*
Gda Technologies Inc (HQ)..........D.......408 753-1191
25 Metro Dr Fl 3 San Jose (95110) *(P-25095)*
Gdf Parent LLC..........D.......714 743-7209
1510 1/2 W 228th St Torrance (90501) *(P-16794)*
Gdr Group Inc..........D.......949 453-8818
3 Park Plz Ste 1700 Irvine (92614) *(P-16009)*
Gdsa-Lincoln Inc (PA)..........D.......916 645-8961
1501 Aviation Blvd Lincoln (95648) *(P-17456)*
GE Aviation Systems LLC..........C.......661 277-7308
295 N Wolfe Ave Bldg 3810 Edwards Afb (93524) *(P-4773)*
GE Digital LLC (HQ)..........D.......925 242-6200
2623 Camino Ramon San Ramon (94583) *(P-15335)*
GE Energy, Diamond Bar *Also called Motech Americas LLC (P-25801)*
Geary Darling Lessee Inc..........C.......415 292-0100
501 Geary St San Francisco (94102) *(P-12291)*
Gebbs Software Intl Inc..........D.......201 227-0088
4640 Admiralty Way Fl 9 Marina Del Rey (90292) *(P-16010)*
Gebruder Weiss Inc..........D.......310 414-9300
19701 Hamilton Ave # 200 Torrance (90502) *(P-4953)*
Geek Squad Inc..........D.......805 278-9555
2300 N Rose Ave Oxnard (93036) *(P-16011)*
Geek Squad Inc..........D.......800 433-5778
120 Imperial Hwy Fullerton (92835) *(P-16012)*
Geek Squad Inc..........D.......800 433-5778
1490 Fitzgerald Dr Pinole (94564) *(P-16013)*
Geek Squad Inc..........D.......714 434-0132
901 S Coast Dr Ste F Costa Mesa (92626) *(P-16014)*
Geek Squad Inc..........D.......714 938-0380
3741 W Chapman Ave Orange (92868) *(P-16015)*
Gehr Development Corporation (HQ)..........D.......323 728-5558
7400 E Slauson Ave Commerce (90040) *(P-10596)*
Gehry Partners LLP..........C.......310 482-3000
12541 Beatrice St Los Angeles (90066) *(P-25436)*
Gehry Technologies Inc (HQ)..........E.......310 862-1200
12181 Bluff Creek Dr # 200 Playa Vista (90094) *(P-14827)*
Gei Consultants Inc..........D.......916 631-4500
2868 Prospect Park Dr # 400 Rancho Cordova (95670) *(P-25096)*
Geico Corporation..........C.......707 448-7172
2033 Arden Way Ste C Sacramento (95825) *(P-10368)*
Geico General Insurance Co..........B.......858 848-8200
14111 Danielson St Poway (92064) *(P-10369)*
Geil Enterprises Inc..........C.......559 495-3000
1945 N Helm Ave Ste 102 Fresno (93727) *(P-16290)*
Gel Pak LLC..........D.......510 576-2220
31398 Huntwood Ave Hayward (94544) *(P-13785)*
Gelfand Rennert & Feldman LLP (PA)..........C.......310 553-1707
1880 Century Park E # 1600 Los Angeles (90067) *(P-16795)*
Gels Logistics Inc..........D.......909 610-2277
20275 Business Pkwy City of Industry (91789) *(P-4954)*
Gem Mortgage, Barstow *Also called Golden Empire Mortgage Inc (P-9553)*
Gem Trans Care, Pasadena *Also called Gem Transitional Care Center (P-19935)*
Gem Transitional Care Center..........D.......626 737-0560
716 S Fair Oaks Ave Pasadena (91105) *(P-19935)*
Gemalto Cogent Inc (HQ)..........D.......626 325-9600
639 N Rosemead Blvd Pasadena (91107) *(P-15600)*
Gemini Moving Specialists, Toluca Lake *Also called James B Branch Inc (P-4067)*
Gemmm Corp..........D.......805 267-2700
587 W Los Angeles Ave Moorpark (93021) *(P-11163)*
Gemmm Corp..........D.......818 522-0740
2211 Memory Ln Westlake Village (91361) *(P-11164)*
Gemmm Corp (PA)..........D.......805 496-0555
2860 E Thousand Oaks Blvd Thousand Oaks (91362) *(P-11165)*
Gemperle Enterprises..........D.......209 667-2651
10218 Lander Ave Turlock (95380) *(P-411)*
Gemperle Farms, Turlock *Also called Gemperle Enterprises (P-411)*
Genco, Ontario *Also called Fedex Sup Chain Dist Sys Inc (P-4409)*
Gene A Garcia Construction..........E.......559 352-6173
1663 E Poppy Hills Dr Fresno (93730) *(P-1129)*
Gene M Accito..........D.......530 674-3179
331 Pelican Pl Yuba City (95993) *(P-24)*
Gene Townsend's Auto Body, El Cajon *Also called Eugene N Townsend (P-17288)*
Gene Watson Construction A CA..........A.......661 763-5254
801 Kern St Taft (93268) *(P-1022)*
Gene Wheeler Farms Inc..........C.......661 951-2100
444 W Avenue H6 Lancaster (93534) *(P-322)*
Gene's Cooperage, El Monte *Also called Pacific Coast Drum Company (P-7646)*
Genea Energy Partners Inc..........D.......714 694-0536
19100 Von Karman Ave # 550 Irvine (92612) *(P-15601)*
Geneohm Sciences Inc..........C.......201 847-5824
11085 N Torrey Pines Rd # 210 La Jolla (92037) *(P-25753)*
Gener8 LLC..........C.......650 940-9898
500 Mercury Dr Sunnyvale (94085) *(P-25097)*
General Acute Care Hospital, Downey *Also called Pih Health Hospital - Downey (P-21096)*
General Acute Care Hospital, Whittier *Also called Pih Health Hospital - Whittier (P-21099)*
General Atomics (HQ)..........A.......858 455-2810
3550 General Atomics Ct San Diego (92121) *(P-25754)*
General Atomics..........D.......858 676-7100
16969 Mesamint St San Diego (92127) *(P-25755)*
General Atomics..........C.......858 455-4000
4949 Greencraig Ln San Diego (92123) *(P-25756)*
General Atomics Energy Pdts, San Diego *Also called General Atomics (P-25756)*
General Brands Packing, Sun Valley *Also called Sugar Foods Corporation (P-17074)*
General Coatings Corporation..........C.......909 204-4150
9349 Feron Blvd Rancho Cucamonga (91730) *(P-2348)*
General Coatings Corporation..........C.......858 587-1277
600 W Freedom Ave Orange (92865) *(P-2349)*
General Coatings Corporation (PA)..........C.......858 587-1277
6711 Nancy Ridge Dr San Diego (92121) *(P-2350)*
General Coatings Corporation..........C.......559 495-4004
1220 E North Ave Fresno (93725) *(P-2351)*
General Contractor, Palm Desert *Also called Cora Constructors Inc (P-25016)*
General Dynamics Advanced Info..........A.......650 966-2000
100 Ferguson Dr Mountain View (94043) *(P-25098)*
General Dynamics Info Tech Inc..........E.......619 881-8989
1615 Murray Canyon Rd # 600 San Diego (92108) *(P-16016)*
General Dynamics Info Tech Inc..........E.......310 662-3202
1700 E Walnut Ave Ste 210 El Segundo (90245) *(P-15918)*
General Electric Company..........B.......909 605-7603
2264 E Avion Ave Ontario (91761) *(P-17499)*
General Electric Company..........C.......650 725-0516
288 Campus Dr Bldg 14105 Stanford (94305) *(P-5841)*
General Electric Company..........C.......916 286-8020
3100 Zinfandel Dr Ste 255 Rancho Cordova (95670) *(P-9483)*
General Electric Company..........D.......925 242-6200
2623 Camino Ramon San Ramon (94583) *(P-15336)*
General Electric Company..........C.......626 359-7988
1303 Bloomdale St Duarte (91010) *(P-15919)*
General Electric Company..........C.......714 434-4111
2995 Red Hill Ave Ste 100 Costa Mesa (92626) *(P-9503)*
General Electric Company..........D.......925 602-5950
2120 Diamond Blvd Ste 100 Concord (94520) *(P-25099)*
General Electric Company..........C.......949 838-3043
17901 Von Karman Ave # 600 Irvine (92614) *(P-9504)*
General Engineering Wstn Inc (PA)..........D.......714 630-3200
1140 N Red Gum St Anaheim (92806) *(P-2144)*
General Environmental..........D.......916 351-0980
11855 White Rock Rd Rancho Cordova (95742) *(P-16796)*
General George W Sliney Basha..........D.......408 296-3423
4839 Rio Vista Ave San Jose (95129) *(P-24546)*
General Home Medical Sup Inc..........D.......805 449-1559
4607 Lakeview Canyon Rd # 584 Westlake Village (91361) *(P-6966)*
General Micro Systems Inc (PA)..........DH.......909 980-4863
8358 Maple Pl Rancho Cucamonga (91730) *(P-6842)*
General Motors LLC..........C.......800 521-7300
9150 Hermosa Ave Rancho Cucamonga (91730) *(P-4413)*
General Motors LLC..........D.......951 361-6302
11900 Cabernet Dr Dr1 Fontana (92337) *(P-4414)*
General Networks Corporation..........D.......818 249-1962
3524 Ocean View Blvd Glendale (91208) *(P-16017)*
General Petroleum Corporation (HQ)..........C.......562 983-7300
19501 S Santa Fe Ave Compton (90221) *(P-8730)*
General Petroleum Corporation..........D.......209 537-1056
237 E Whitmore Ave Modesto (95358) *(P-8715)*
General Pool & Spa Supply Inc (PA)..........D.......916 853-2401
11285 Sunco Dr Rancho Cordova (95742) *(P-7710)*
General Procurement Inc (PA)..........D.......949 679-7960
2601 Walnut Ave Tustin (92780) *(P-6843)*
General Prod A Cal Ltd Partnr (PA)..........C.......916 441-6431
1330 N B St Sacramento (95811) *(P-8480)*
General Produce, Vernon *Also called V & L Produce Inc (P-8533)*

General Production Svc Cal Inc ....C....661 765-5330
1333 Kern St Taft (93268) ***(P-1857)***
General Restaurant Equipment, Los Angeles *Also called South China Sheet Metal Inc* ***(P-2284)***
General Services, Los Angeles *Also called City of Los Angeles* ***(P-13877)***
General Services, Concord *Also called County of Contra Costa* ***(P-13896)***
General Services, Vernon *Also called City of Los Angeles* ***(P-3828)***
General Services Cal Dept ....C....916 845-4942
9645 Butterfield Way # 1503 Sacramento (95827) ***(P-13934)***
General Services Cal Dept ....D....510 622-3101
1515 Clay St Ste 1201 Oakland (94612) ***(P-25437)***
General Services Cal Dept ....D....213 897-3995
700 N Alameda St Ste 500 Los Angeles (90012) ***(P-25438)***
General Services Cal Dept ....B....916 657-9960
601 Sequoia Pacific Blvd Sacramento (95811) ***(P-25100)***
General Services Cal Dept ....D....562 342-7212
4665 Lampson Ave Los Alamitos (90720) ***(P-15769)***
General Services Cal Dept ....A....916 445-4566
1304 O St Ste 301 Sacramento (95814) ***(P-13935)***
General Services Cal Dept ....D....213 897-2241
300 S Spring St Ste 1726 Los Angeles (90013) ***(P-13936)***
General Svcs Cy Los Angeles, Los Angeles *Also called City of Los Angeles* ***(P-22420)***
General Tool Inc ....D....949 261-2322
2025 Alton Pkwy Irvine (92606) ***(P-7635)***
General Transistor Corporation (PA) ....D....310 578-7344
12449 Putnam St Whittier (90602) ***(P-7272)***
General Underground ....C....714 632-8646
701 W Grove Ave Orange (92865) ***(P-2145)***
Generation Clovis LLC ....C....559 297-4900
1650 Shaw Ave Clovis (93611) ***(P-20566)***
Generation Construction Inc ....C....909 923-2077
15650 El Prado Rd Chino (91710) ***(P-1480)***
Generation Contracting & Emerg ....E....858 679-9928
13685 Stowe Dr Ste B Poway (92064) ***(P-1130)***
Generational Properties Inc ....B....323 583-3163
3141 E 44th St Vernon (90058) ***(P-4415)***
Genesis Healthcare Corporation ....D....310 391-8266
3951 East Blvd Los Angeles (90066) ***(P-19936)***
Genesis Healthcare Corporation ....E....909 622-1069
1425 Laurel Ave Pomona (91768) ***(P-19937)***
Genesis Healthcare Corporation ....C....909 628-6024
2335 S Towne Ave Pomona (91766) ***(P-19938)***
Genesis Healthcare LLC ....C....323 461-9961
5310 Fountain Ave Los Angeles (90029) ***(P-20567)***
Genesis Healthcare Partners PC ....C....619 230-0400
2466 1st Ave Ste B San Diego (92101) ***(P-22029)***
Genesis Healthcare Partners PC (PA) ....C....858 810-7200
3444 Kearny Villa Rd San Diego (92123) ***(P-22030)***
Genesis Home Health Inc ....E....805 520-7100
1687 Erringer Rd Ste 202 Simi Valley (93065) ***(P-14508)***
Genesis Logistics Inc ....D....510 476-0790
4013 Whipple Rd Union City (94587) ***(P-4416)***
Genesis Tech Partners LLC ....C....800 950-2647
21540 Plummer St Ste A Chatsworth (91311) ***(P-17500)***
Genesys Telecom Labs, Daly City *Also called Genesys Telecom Labs Inc* ***(P-15337)***
Genesys Telecom Labs Inc (HQ) ....B....650 466-1100
2001 Junipero Serra Blvd Daly City (94014) ***(P-15337)***
Genetic Dsase Screning Program, Richmond *Also called Public Health California Dept* ***(P-19319)***
Genex (HQ) ....C....424 672-9500
800 Corporate Pointe # 100 Culver City (90230) ***(P-14828)***
Gengo Inc ....E....650 585-4390
307 2nd Ave San Mateo (94401) ***(P-16797)***
Genium Inc ....E....415 935-3593
585 Broadway St Redwood City (94063) ***(P-14829)***
Genius Products Inc ....C....310 453-1222
3301 Expo Blvd Ste 100 Santa Monica (90404) ***(P-7811)***
Genmark Automation (HQ) ....D....510 897-3400
46723 Lakeview Blvd Fremont (94538) ***(P-7548)***
Genomedx Biosciences Corp., San Diego *Also called Decipher Corp* ***(P-21520)***
Genomic Health Inc (PA) ....C....650 556-9300
301 Penobscot Dr Redwood City (94063) ***(P-21534)***
Genomic Health Inc ....B....650 269-0545
101 University Ave Palo Alto (94301) ***(P-21535)***
Genomic Health Inc ....B....650 556-9300
101 Galveston Dr Redwood City (94063) ***(P-21536)***
Genoptix Inc (PA) ....C....760 268-6200
2131 Faraday Ave Carlsbad (92008) ***(P-21537)***
Genoptix Inc ....B....760 268-6200
2110 Rutherford Rd Carlsbad (92008) ***(P-21538)***
Genoptix Mdcial Lab A Novartis, Carlsbad *Also called Genoptix Inc* ***(P-21538)***
Genoptix Medical Laboratory, Carlsbad *Also called Genoptix Inc* ***(P-21537)***
Genpact LLC ....E....203 690-9308
3300 Hillview Ave Palo Alto (94304) ***(P-27079)***
Gensler and Associates, Los Angeles *Also called M Arthur Gensler Jr Assoc Inc* ***(P-25479)***
Genstar Capital LP ....A....415 834-2350
4 Embarcadero Ctr # 1500 San Francisco (94111) ***(P-11915)***
Gentek Media Inc ....E....909 476-3818
12246 Colony Ave Chino (91710) ***(P-6844)***
Gentex Corporation ....D....909 481-7667
9859 7th St Rancho Cucamonga (91730) ***(P-25757)***
Gentiva Health Services Inc ....B....858 565-2499
9444 Balboa Ave Ste 290 San Diego (92123) ***(P-21745)***
Gentiva Health Services Inc ....C....805 549-0801
3220 S Higuera St Ste 101 San Luis Obispo (93401) ***(P-21746)***
Gentiva Home Health Care, San Luis Obispo *Also called Gentiva Health Services Inc* ***(P-21746)***
Gentiva Hospice ....C....661 324-1232
5001 E Commercecenter Dr # 140 Bakersfield (93309) ***(P-20429)***
Gentle Giant Studios Inc ....D....818 504-3555
7511 N San Fernando Rd Burbank (91505) ***(P-16798)***
Gentlecare Transport Inc ....D....323 662-8777
3539 Casitas Ave Los Angeles (90039) ***(P-3677)***
Gentry Associates LLC ....D....619 291-0999
525 Spruce St San Diego (92103) ***(P-12292)***
Gentry Group LLC ....E....310 968-5399
555 N Rockingham Ave Los Angeles (90049) ***(P-17976)***
Genuent Usa LLC ....D....916 772-3700
2240 Douglas Blvd Ste 100 Roseville (95661) ***(P-14289)***
Genuine Parts Distributors ....D....562 692-9034
3200 E Guasti Rd Ste 100 Ontario (91761) ***(P-6441)***
Genzyme Corporation ....C....310 482-5000
2440 S Sepulveda Blvd # 100 Los Angeles (90064) ***(P-26075)***
Geo Group Inc ....D....760 246-1171
10400 Rancho Rd Adelanto (92301) ***(P-26238)***
Geo Group Inc ....B....661 763-2510
1500 Cadet Rd Taft (93268) ***(P-26943)***
Geo Group Inc ....C....661 792-2731
611 Frontage Rd Mc Farland (93250) ***(P-26239)***
Geo Mmi Engineering, Oakland *Also called Geosyntec Consultants Inc* ***(P-25103)***
Geo Telecom ....E....949 362-0921
252 Woodcrest Ln Aliso Viejo (92656) ***(P-1858)***
Geocities, Santa Clara *Also called Altaba Inc* ***(P-5302)***
Geocon Consultants Inc (PA) ....D....858 558-6900
6960 Flanders Dr San Diego (92121) ***(P-27080)***
Geocon Incorporated ....D....858 558-6900
6960 Flanders Dr San Diego (92121) ***(P-25101)***
Geodis Logistics LLC ....D....310 604-8185
301 W Walnut St Compton (90220) ***(P-4417)***
Geodis Logistics LLC ....D....909 801-3145
2301 W San Bernardino Ave Redlands (92374) ***(P-4418)***
Geodis Logistics LLC ....D....909 240-6298
1710 W Base Line Rd Rialto (92376) ***(P-4419)***
Geodis Logistics LLC ....D....951 571-2481
3285 De Forest Cir Jurupa Valley (91752) ***(P-4420)***
Geodis Wilson Usa Inc ....C....650 692-9850
229 Littlefield Ave Ste 1 South San Francisco (94080) ***(P-4955)***
Geographic Expeditions Inc ....D....415 922-0448
1008 General Kennedy Ave # 3 San Francisco (94129) ***(P-4820)***
Georg Fischer LLC (HQ) ....D....714 731-8800
9271 Jeronimo Rd Irvine (92618) ***(P-7066)***
Georg Fischer Piping, Irvine *Also called Georg Fischer LLC* ***(P-7066)***
George Brazil Plbg Htg & AC, Culver City *Also called L A Services Inc* ***(P-2176)***
George Brazil Plbg Htg & AC, Santa Ana *Also called Orange County Services Inc* ***(P-2219)***
George Browns Sports Club (PA) ....D....559 297-8656
1155 N Fowler Ave Ste 500 Clovis (93611) ***(P-18148)***
George Chiala Farms Inc ....C....408 778-0562
15500 Hill Rd Morgan Hill (95037) ***(P-55)***
George E Masker Inc ....D....510 568-1206
7699 Edgewater Dr Oakland (94621) ***(P-2352)***
George Fasching ....E....626 446-0654
425 N Santa Anita Ave Arcadia (91006) ***(P-17374)***
George G Sharp Inc ....D....619 425-4211
1065 Bay Blvd Ste D Chula Vista (91911) ***(P-25102)***
George L Mee Memorial Hospital, King City *Also called Southern Mnterey Cnty Mem Hosp* ***(P-21213)***
George M Rajacich MD PC ....E....818 787-2020
14914 Sherman Way Van Nuys (91405) ***(P-18995)***
George M Robinson & Co (PA) ....D....510 632-7017
1461 Atteberry Ln San Jose (95131) ***(P-2146)***
George P Johnson Company ....C....650 226-0600
999 Skyway Rd Ste 300 San Carlos (94070) ***(P-8975)***
George Richard ....D....619 805-6751
P.O. Box 712002 Santee (92072) ***(P-1349)***
Georges Yellow Taxi Cab Co, Santa Rosa *Also called Neese Inc* ***(P-3747)***
Georgia Atkison Snf LLC ....C....626 444-2535
3825 Durfee Ave El Monte (91732) ***(P-19939)***
Georgia-Pacific LLC ....C....559 651-5500
9525 W Nicholas Ct Visalia (93291) ***(P-7880)***
Georgia-Pacific LLC ....B....562 861-6226
9206 Santa Fe Springs Rd Santa Fe Springs (90670) ***(P-7881)***
Georgia-Pacific LLC ....D....562 926-8888
15500 Valley View Ave La Mirada (90638) ***(P-7758)***
Georgian Hotel ....D....310 395-9945
1415 Ocean Ave Santa Monica (90401) ***(P-12293)***
Geosyntec Consultants Inc ....D....714 969-0800
2100 Main St Ste 150 Huntington Beach (92648) ***(P-24547)***
Geosyntec Consultants Inc ....E....510 836-3034
1111 Broadway Ste 600 Oakland (94607) ***(P-25103)***
Geovera Holdings Inc (PA) ....D....707 863-3700
4820 Busineca Ctr Dr 20 Fairfield (94534) ***(P-11664)***
Geovera Specialty Insurance Co ....D....707 863-3700
1455 Oliver Rd Fairfield (94534) ***(P-10370)***
Gerawan Farming Partners Inc ....B....559 787-8780
15749 E Ventura Ave Sanger (93657) ***(P-436)***
Gerber Ambulance Company Inc ....C....310 542-6464
19801 Mariner Ave Torrance (90503) ***(P-3678)***
Gerber Ambulance Service, Torrance *Also called Gerber Ambulance Company Inc* ***(P-3678)***
Geri Care Inc ....D....310 320-0961
21521 S Vermont Ave Torrance (90502) ***(P-19940)***
Geri-Care II Inc ....C....310 328-0812
22035 S Vermont Ave Torrance (90502) ***(P-20568)***
Gersh Agency Inc (PA) ....D....310 274-6611
9465 Wilshire Blvd Fl 6 Beverly Hills (90212) ***(P-17911)***
Gerson Bakar & Associates, Palo Alto *Also called Oak Creek Apartments* ***(P-10787)***

ALPHABETIC

Gerson Baker & Associates......D......650 756-0959
333 Park Plaza Dr Ofc Daly City (94015) ***(P-10733)***
Gerwend Enterprises Inc......C......619 254-5018
2952 Market St San Diego (92102) ***(P-26944)***
Ges, Chula Vista *Also called Global Exprnce Specialists Inc* ***(P-16804)***
Get Heal Inc......D......310 528-4957
528 Palisades Dr Ste 176 Pacific Palisades (90272) ***(P-14509)***
Get Tested Coachella Valley, Palm Springs *Also called Desert Aids Project* ***(P-23190)***
Get-A-Lift Handicap Bus Trnsp, Bakersfield *Also called Golden Empire Transit District* ***(P-3540)***
Getac Inc......D......949 681-2900
15495 Sand Canyon Ave # 300 Irvine (92618) ***(P-6845)***
Getaround Inc (PA)......C......866 438-2768
55 Green St San Francisco (94111) ***(P-17212)***
Getfeedback Inc......D......888 684-8821
123 Mission St Fl 26 San Francisco (94105) ***(P-16799)***
Getinsured.com, Mountain View *Also called Vimo Inc* ***(P-27247)***
Getmedlegal, San Dimas *Also called Legal Solutions Holdings Inc* ***(P-22641)***
Getright Ventures Inc......D......510 402-4816
3675 Rocky Shore Ct Vallejo (94591) ***(P-9626)***
Gettler-Ryan Inc (PA)......D......925 551-7555
6805 Sierra Ct Ste G Dublin (94568) ***(P-3412)***
Getty Conservation Institute, Los Angeles *Also called J Paul Getty Trust* ***(P-25914)***
Getty Images Inc......D......323 202-4200
6300 Wilshire Blvd # 1600 Los Angeles (90048) ***(P-13770)***
Gettyone Image Bank, Los Angeles *Also called Getty Images Inc* ***(P-13770)***
GF Carneros Tenant LLC......E......707 299-4900
4048 Sonoma Hwy NAPA (94559) ***(P-13348)***
Gfk Custom Research LLC......D......415 398-2812
360 Pine St Fl 6 San Francisco (94104) ***(P-25900)***
Gfk Custom Research LLC......C......310 527-2100
879 W 190th St Ste 390 Gardena (90248) ***(P-25901)***
Ggc Administration LLC......A......415 983-2700
1 Embarcadero Ctr Fl 39 San Francisco (94111) ***(P-11665)***
Ggec America Inc......D......714 750-2280
20450 Stevens Creek Blvd # 220 Cupertino (95014) ***(P-7273)***
Ggis Insurance Services Inc......C......818 553-2110
600 N Brand Blvd Ste 300 Glendale (91203) ***(P-10371)***
Ggwh LLC......E......310 786-1700
9440 Santa Monica Blvd # 610 Beverly Hills (90210) ***(P-12294)***
Ghc of Lompoc LLC......C......805 735-4010
1428 W North Ave Lompoc (93436) ***(P-22031)***
Ghc of Sunnyvale LLC......C......408 738-4880
797 E Fremont Ave Sunnyvale (94087) ***(P-20569)***
Ghd Inc......E......707 443-8326
718 3rd St Eureka (95501) ***(P-25104)***
Ghd Inc......D......707 523-1010
2235 Mercury Way Ste 150 Santa Rosa (95407) ***(P-25105)***
Ghg Properties LLC......D......562 945-8511
7320 Greenleaf Ave Whittier (90602) ***(P-12295)***
Ghilotti Bros Inc......B......415 454-7011
525 Jacoby St San Rafael (94901) ***(P-1708)***
Ghilotti Construction Co Inc......C......707 556-9145
600 S Napa Junction Rd American Canyon (94503) ***(P-1709)***
Ghilotti Construction Co Inc (PA)......C......707 585-1221
246 Ghillotti Ave Santa Rosa (95407) ***(P-1965)***
Ghio Seafood Products, La Mesa *Also called Anthonys Fish Grotto* ***(P-8362)***
Ghossain & Truelock Entps Inc......D......951 781-9345
783 Palmyrita Ave Ste A Riverside (92507) ***(P-13937)***
Ghost Management Group LLC......C......949 870-1400
41 Discovery Irvine (92618) ***(P-13625)***
GI GP IV LLC (PA)......E......415 688-4800
188 The Embarcadero # 700 San Francisco (94105) ***(P-9692)***
GI Industries......D......805 522-2150
195 W Los Angeles Ave Simi Valley (93065) ***(P-6207)***
GI Partners, San Francisco *Also called GI GP IV LLC* ***(P-9692)***
Giampolini & Co......C......415 673-1236
1482 67th St Emeryville (94608) ***(P-2353)***
Giampolini/Courtney, Emeryville *Also called Giampolini & Co* ***(P-2353)***
Giannas Baking Company......D......831 633-3700
11165 Commercial Pkwy Castroville (95012) ***(P-8583)***
Giant Bicycle Inc (HQ)......D......805 267-4600
3587 Old Conejo Rd Newbury Park (91320) ***(P-7711)***
Giant Creative Strategy Llc......C......415 655-5200
1700 Montgomery St # 485 San Francisco (94111) ***(P-13510)***
Giant Sportz Paintball Park, Bellflower *Also called Hollywood Sports Park LLC* ***(P-16832)***
Giarretto Institute......E......408 453-7616
232 E Gish Rd San Jose (95112) ***(P-23242)***
Gibbs Giden Locher......D......310 552-3400
1880 Century Park E # 1200 Los Angeles (90067) ***(P-22527)***
Gibbs & Associates, Moorpark *Also called Cimatron Gibbs LLC* ***(P-14712)***
Gibbs International Inc (PA)......C......805 485-0551
2201 Ventura Blvd Oxnard (93036) ***(P-17330)***
Gibbs International Truck Ctrs, Oxnard *Also called Gibbs International Inc* ***(P-17330)***
Gibralter Convalescent Hosp......D......626 443-9425
2720 Nevada Ave El Monte (91733) ***(P-20570)***
Gibson Dunn & Crutcher LLP......D......650 849-5300
1881 Page Mill Rd Palo Alto (94304) ***(P-22528)***
Gibson Dunn & Crutcher LLP......C......949 451-3800
3161 Michelson Dr # 1200 Irvine (92612) ***(P-22529)***
Gibson Dunn & Crutcher LLP (PA)......B......213 229-7000
333 S Grand Ave Ste 4600 Los Angeles (90071) ***(P-22530)***
Gibson Dunn & Crutcher LLP......D......310 552-8500
2029 Century Park E # 4000 Los Angeles (90067) ***(P-22531)***
Gibson Dunn & Crutcher LLP......C......415 393-8200
555 Mission St Ste 3000 San Francisco (94105) ***(P-22532)***
Gibson Overseas Inc......A......323 832-8900
2410 Yates Ave Commerce (90040) ***(P-6560)***
Gic Real Estate Inc (HQ)......D......415 229-1800
1 Bush St Ste 1100 San Francisco (94104) ***(P-11166)***
Gico Management......D......209 599-7131
23073 S Frederick Rd Ripon (95366) ***(P-8356)***
Gieg Chevron LLC......D......831 755-8000
905 Abbott St 945 Salinas (93901) ***(P-17375)***
Gierahn Dry Wall Inc......E......661 257-7900
28490 Westinghouse Pl # 150 Santa Clarita (91355) ***(P-2791)***
Giga Omni Media Inc......D......415 974-6355
1613a Lyon St San Francisco (94115) ***(P-16573)***
Gigabyte Technology, City of Industry *Also called GBT Inc* ***(P-6841)***
Gigamon Inc (HQ)......C......408 831-4000
3300 Olcott St Santa Clara (95054) ***(P-15338)***
Gigster Inc......C......941 888-4447
301 Howard St Ste 2100 San Francisco (94105) ***(P-14830)***
Gigsurf Inc......B......415 894-2445
217 Dore St San Francisco (94103) ***(P-14290)***
Gigya Inc (HQ)......D......650 353-7230
2513 E Char Rd Ste 200 Mountain View (94043) ***(P-14831)***
Gilardi & Co LLC......D......415 461-0410
3301 Kerner Blvd Ste 100 San Rafael (94901) ***(P-26240)***
Gilbane Aecom JV......D......925 946-3100
1655 Grant St Fl 12 Concord (94520) ***(P-26945)***
Gilbane Building Company......D......408 660-4400
1798 Tech Dr Ste 120 San Jose (95110) ***(P-26241)***
Gilbane Building Company......D......408 660-4400
2033 Gateway Pl Ste 450 San Jose (95110) ***(P-1481)***
Gilbane Construction, San Jose *Also called Gilbane Building Company* ***(P-26241)***
Gilbane Federal (HQ)......C......925 946-3100
1655 Grant St Ste 1200 Concord (94520) ***(P-25106)***
Gilbane Smcc LLC......D......925 946-3100
1655 Grant St 12f Concord (94520) ***(P-1482)***
Gilbert LLP......D......415 646-4002
655 Montgomery St Ste 700 San Francisco (94111) ***(P-22533)***
Gilbert Klly Crwley Jnnett LLP (PA)......D......213 615-7000
550 S Hope St Ste 2200 Los Angeles (90071) ***(P-22534)***
Gilbert Service Corp......C......909 393-7575
6725 Kimball Ave Chino (91708) ***(P-4208)***
Gilbert West, Chino *Also called Gilbert Service Corp* ***(P-4208)***
Gilkey Farms Inc......D......559 992-2136
2411 Whitley Ave Corcoran (93212) ***(P-12)***
Gill Transport LLC......B......805 240-1979
1051 Pacific Ave Oxnard (93030) ***(P-4054)***
Gillette Citrus Company......D......559 626-4236
10175 S Anchor Ave Dinuba (93618) ***(P-492)***
Gilliam & Sons Inc......E......661 589-0913
9831 Rosedale Hwy Bakersfield (93312) ***(P-3316)***
Gills Onions LLC......D......805 240-1983
1051 Pacific Ave Oxnard (93030) ***(P-8481)***
Gilroy Gardens Family Theme Pk......C......408 840-7100
3050 Hecker Pass Rd Gilroy (95020) ***(P-18332)***
Gilroy Health & Rehab Ctr, Gilroy *Also called Mariner Health Care Inc* ***(P-20106)***
Gilroy Health Care, Gilroy *Also called Covenant Care California LLC* ***(P-19838)***
Gils Distributing Service......C......213 627-0539
718 E 8th St Los Angeles (90021) ***(P-13651)***
Gilton Resource Recovery......D......209 527-3781
755 S Yosemite Ave Oakdale (95361) ***(P-6208)***
Gilton Solid Waste MGT Inc......C......209 527-3781
755 S Yosemite Ave Oakdale (95361) ***(P-6209)***
Gina B Ltd Inc......D......310 366-7926
1601 W 134th St Gardena (90249) ***(P-6561)***
Gina B Showroom, Gardena *Also called Gina B Ltd Inc* ***(P-6561)***
Gingerio Inc......D......408 455-0574
116 New Montgomery St # 5 San Francisco (94105) ***(P-14832)***
Gino Rinaldi Inc......D......831 761-0195
51 Fremont St Royal Oaks (95076) ***(P-2897)***
Gino/Giuseppe Inc......C......209 358-0556
700 Enterprise Ct Ste A Atwater (95301) ***(P-3150)***
Ginzton Laboratory, Stanford *Also called Leland Stanford Junior Univ* ***(P-26006)***
Giovannetti Equipment Sales, Woodland *Also called Half Moon Fruit & Produce Co* ***(P-5)***
Gipson Hoffman & Pancione A......D......310 556-4660
1901 Avenue Of The Stars # 1100 Los Angeles (90067) ***(P-22535)***
Girardi & Keese (PA)......D......213 977-0211
1126 Wilshire Blvd Los Angeles (90017) ***(P-22536)***
Girardi and Keefe......D......213 489-5330
1126 Wilshire Blvd Los Angeles (90017) ***(P-10597)***
Girl Scouts Heart Central Cal......C......916 452-9181
6601 Elvas Ave Sacramento (95819) ***(P-24548)***
Girl Scouts Northern Cal (PA)......D......510 562-8470
1650 Harbor Bay Pkwy # 100 Alameda (94502) ***(P-24549)***
Girl Scts Sn Diego-Imprl Cncl (PA)......D......619 610-0751
1231 Upas St San Diego (92103) ***(P-24550)***
Girl Scuts Greater Los Angeles (PA)......C......626 677-2200
1150 S Olive St Fl 6 Los Angeles (90015) ***(P-24551)***
Girl Scuts San Grgonio Council (PA)......D......909 307-6555
1751 Plum Ln Redlands (92374) ***(P-24552)***
Girls and Boys Club Grdn Grove, Garden Grove *Also called Boys Grls Clubs Grdn Grove Inc* ***(P-24498)***
Girls Republic, Chino Hills *Also called Boys Republic* ***(P-23838)***
Girls Rock Sb......D......805 861-8128
1522b Eucalyptus Hill Rd Santa Barbara (93103) ***(P-24833)***
Giroux Glass Inc (PA)......C......213 747-7406
850 W Wash Blvd Ste 200 Los Angeles (90015) ***(P-3293)***
Giti Tire (usa) Ltd (HQ)......D......909 527-8800
10404 6th St Rancho Cucamonga (91730) ***(P-6486)***
Gitlab Inc......A......408 569-3035
4128 24th St San Francisco (94114) ***(P-26076)***
Giumarra Bros Fruit Co Inc (PA)......D......213 627-2900
1601 E Olympic Blvd # 408 Los Angeles (90021) ***(P-8482)***

Giumarra Companies, Escondido *Also called Rio Vista Ventures LLC* ***(P-8212)***
Giumarra Company, The, Reedley *Also called Rio Vista Ventures LLC* ***(P-8213)***
Giumarra Farms Inc......D......661 395-7000
11220 Edison Hwy Edison (93220) ***(P-19)***
Giumarra International Berry, Los Angeles *Also called Giumarra Bros Fruit Co Inc* ***(P-8482)***
Giumarra Vineyards Corporation......D......661 395-7071
11220 Edison Hwy Bakersfield (93307) ***(P-131)***
Giumarra Vineyards Corporation (PA)......B......661 395-7000
11220 Edison Hwy Edison (93220) ***(P-132)***
Giusti Farms LLC......E......650 726-9221
1800 Higgins Canyon Rd Half Moon Bay (94019) ***(P-56)***
Givens Farms, Goleta *Also called Givens John* ***(P-57)***
Givens John......D......805 964-4477
1133 N Fairview Ave Goleta (93117) ***(P-57)***
GK Management Co Inc (PA)......C......310 204-2050
5150 Overland Ave Culver City (90230) ***(P-11167)***
GK Management Co Inc......E......619 437-1777
299 Prospect Pl Coronado (92118) ***(P-11168)***
GK Management Co Inc......D......818 705-8834
6540 Wilbur Ave Reseda (91335) ***(P-11169)***
GK Management Co Inc......D......310 836-1812
3975 Overland Ave Culver City (90232) ***(P-10734)***
Gkk Corporation......D......619 398-0215
1775 Hancock St Ste 150 San Diego (92110) ***(P-25439)***
Gkk Corporation (PA)......D......949 250-1500
2355 Main St Ste 220 Irvine (92614) ***(P-25440)***
Gkkworks, Irvine *Also called Gkk Corporation* ***(P-25440)***
Gky Dental Arts Inc (PA)......D......310 214-8007
4212 Artesia Blvd Torrance (90504) ***(P-21610)***
GL, San Diego *Also called Garrad Hassan America Inc* ***(P-25091)***
GL Nemirow Inc......D......818 562-9433
2550 N Hollywood Way Burbank (91505) ***(P-13511)***
Glacier House Franchisee LLC......E......951 455-3644
12960 Day St Moreno Valley (92553) ***(P-12296)***
GLad Entertainment Inc (PA)......D......559 292-9000
4055 N Chestnut Ave Fresno (93726) ***(P-18702)***
Glad I'M Not Driving.com, Rialto *Also called Ptr Group Inc* ***(P-26370)***
Glad-A-Way Gardens Inc......C......805 938-0569
2669 E Clark Ave Santa Maria (93455) ***(P-242)***
Gladiator Security Services, Ontario *Also called Mazar Corp* ***(P-16349)***
Gladiolus Holdings LLC......D......530 622-3400
1040 Marshall Way Placerville (95667) ***(P-19941)***
Glamour Industries Co......D......213 687-8600
100 Wilshire Blvd Ste 700 Santa Monica (90401) ***(P-7671)***
Glare Technology Usa Inc......C......909 437-6999
38340 Innovation Ct Murrieta (92563) ***(P-16800)***
Glaser Weil Fink Jacobs (PA)......C......310 553-3000
10250 Constellation Blvd # 1900 Los Angeles (90067) ***(P-22537)***
Glaspy & Glaspy A Prof Corp......E......408 279-8844
100 Pringle Ave Ste 750 Walnut Creek (94596) ***(P-22538)***
Glass Lewis & Co LLC (HQ)......D......415 678-4110
255 California St # 1100 San Francisco (94111) ***(P-25902)***
Glass Fab Tempering Sv, Tracy *Also called Glassfab Tempering Svcs Inc* ***(P-27081)***
Glass Pak Inc......D......707 207-0400
5825 Old School Rd Pleasanton (94588) ***(P-5093)***
Glassfab Tempering Svcs Inc (PA)......D......209 229-1060
1448 Mariani Ct Tracy (95376) ***(P-27081)***
Glaxosmithkline LLC......E......858 260-5900
3366 N Torrey Pines Ct La Jolla (92037) ***(P-7945)***
Glaza, Los Angeles *Also called Greater Los Angeles Zoo Assn* ***(P-24177)***
Glen Alpine Building Svcs Inc......D......510 582-7400
24685 Oneil Ave Hayward (94544) ***(P-13938)***
Glen Annie Golf Club......D......805 968-6400
405 Glen Annie Rd Goleta (93117) ***(P-18249)***
Glen Beverly Laboratories Inc......D......714 848-5777
7777 Center Ave Ste 500 Huntington Beach (92647) ***(P-24401)***
Glen Ivy Hot Springs......C......714 990-2090
1001 Brea Mall Brea (92821) ***(P-13426)***
Glenborough LLC (PA)......D......650 343-9300
400 S El Camino Real # 1100 San Mateo (94402) ***(P-11170)***
Glendale Adventist Medical Ctr......E......818 409-8379
281 Harvey Dr Unit B Glendale (91206) ***(P-21747)***
Glendale Adventist Medical Ctr (HQ)......A......818 409-8000
1509 Wilson Ter Glendale (91206) ***(P-20887)***
Glendale Associates Ltd......D......818 246-6737
100 W Broadway Ste 100 # 100 Glendale (91210) ***(P-10598)***
Glendale Eye Medical Group......D......818 956-1010
500 N Cntl Ave Ste 400 Glendale (91203) ***(P-18996)***
Glendale Eye Medical Group (PA)......D......818 956-1010
607 N Central Ave Ste 203 Glendale (91203) ***(P-18997)***
Glendale Healthcare Center......D......818 246-5516
1208 S Central Ave Glendale (91204) ***(P-19942)***
Glendale Medical Offices, Glendale *Also called Kaiser Foundation Hospitals* ***(P-19113)***
Glendale Orange St Med Offs, Glendale *Also called Kaiser Foundation Hospitals* ***(P-19074)***
Glendale Super-Sport Club, Glendale *Also called 24 Hour Fitness Usa Inc* ***(P-18103)***
Glendale Water & Power, Glendale *Also called City of Glendale* ***(P-5819)***
Glendale YMCA Swim School, Glendale *Also called Young Mens Chrstn Assoc Gndl* ***(P-24760)***
Glendora Country Club......D......626 335-4051
2400 Country Club Dr Glendora (91741) ***(P-18459)***
Glenn A Rick Engrg & Dev Co (PA)......C......619 291-0708
5620 Friars Rd San Diego (92110) ***(P-25107)***
Glenn Building Services Inc......D......626 398-8000
1148 N Lake Ave Apt 1 Pasadena (91104) ***(P-13939)***
Glenn Cnty Humn Resource Agcy......C......530 934-6510
420 E Laurel St Willows (95988) ***(P-23597)***
Glenn Cnty Plg Pub Works Agcy......D......530 934-6541
777 N Colusa St Willows (95988) ***(P-1710)***
Glenn County Health Svcs Agcy, Willows *Also called County of Glenn* ***(P-22210)***
Glenn County Humn Resorce Agcy, Willows *Also called County of Glenn* ***(P-23072)***
Glenn County Office Education......D......530 865-1145
676 E Walker St Fl 2 Orland (95963) ***(P-23728)***
Glenn E Porter......E......661 615-1500
3955 Coffee Rd Bakersfield (93308) ***(P-10091)***
Glenn Medical Center Inc......D......530 934-4681
1133 W Sycamore St Willows (95988) ***(P-20888)***
Glenn-Colusa Irrigation Dst (PA)......D......530 934-8881
344 E Laurel St Willows (95988) ***(P-6363)***
Glenoaks Convalescent Hosp LP......D......818 240-4300
409 W Glenoaks Blvd Glendale (91202) ***(P-20889)***
Glenrock Group......D......408 323-9900
1000 Old Quarry Rd San Jose (95123) ***(P-18460)***
Glentrans, Glendale *Also called Hemodialysis Inc* ***(P-21924)***
Glenview Assisted Living LLP......E......760 704-6800
1950 Calle Barcelona Carlsbad (92009) ***(P-22247)***
Glenwood Care Center, Oxnard *Also called Glenwood Corporation* ***(P-19943)***
Glenwood Corporation......D......805 983-0305
1300 N C St Oxnard (93030) ***(P-19943)***
Glenwood Gardens......B......661 587-0221
350 Calloway Dr Unit A1 Bakersfield (93312) ***(P-19944)***
Glenwood Village Cmnty Assn......D......949 855-1800
26840 Aliso Viejo Pkwy # 100 Aliso Viejo (92656) ***(P-24553)***
Gless Ranch Inc (PA)......E......951 780-8458
18541 Van Buren Blvd Riverside (92508) ***(P-665)***
Glidewell Laboratories, Newport Beach *Also called James R Glidewell Dental* ***(P-21612)***
Glint Inc......D......650 817-7240
1100 Island Dr Ste 101 Redwood City (94065) ***(P-15770)***
Global 360 Inc......D......510 263-4800
1080 Marina Village Pkwy # 300 Alameda (94501) ***(P-26242)***
Global Accents Inc......C......310 639-2600
19808 Normandie Ave Torrance (90502) ***(P-6562)***
Global Asylum Incorporated......E......323 850-1214
440 W Los Feliz Rd Glendale (91204) ***(P-17612)***
Global Blue Dvbe Inc......D......916 632-2583
5930 Price Ave McClellan (95652) ***(P-15902)***
Global Building Services Inc......A......209 858-9501
17618 Murphy Pkwy Lathrop (95330) ***(P-27275)***
Global Building Services Inc (PA)......A......800 675-6643
27433 Tourney Rd Ste 280 Valencia (91355) ***(P-13940)***
Global Care Travel, San Diego *Also called Customzed Svcs Admnstrtors Inc* ***(P-10336)***
Global Check Service......C......619 449-5150
1524 Graves Ave Ste C El Cajon (92021) ***(P-16801)***
Global Debt Management LLC (PA)......D......949 825-7800
18881 Von Karman Ave # 1500 Irvine (92612) ***(P-16802)***
Global Dev Strategies Inc......D......858 408-1173
9985 Businesspark Ave A San Diego (92131) ***(P-17501)***
Global Domains International......E......760 602-3000
701 Palomar Airport Rd # 300 Carlsbad (92011) ***(P-5412)***
Global Dosimetry Solutions, Irvine *Also called Mirion Technologies Gds Inc* ***(P-26091)***
Global Eagle Entertainment Inc......C......949 608-8700
2941 Alton Pkwy Irvine (92606) ***(P-17613)***
Global Emergency Road Svc LLC......E......818 518-1166
9908 San Fernando Rd Pacoima (91331) ***(P-3679)***
Global Entertainment Inds Inc......D......818 567-0000
2948 N Ontario St Burbank (91504) ***(P-3413)***
Global Exprnce Specialists Inc......D......818 638-5959
500 N Brand Blvd Ste 1860 Glendale (91203) ***(P-16803)***
Global Exprnce Specialists Inc......C......619 498-6300
491 C St Chula Vista (91910) ***(P-16804)***
Global Fibernet, Van Nuys *Also called Airespring Inc* ***(P-5300)***
Global Futures Exch & Trdg Co......D......818 996-0401
303 17th St Santa Monica (90402) ***(P-9778)***
Global Garments, Los Angeles *Also called Design Collection Inc* ***(P-7996)***
Global Holdings Inc......C......818 905-6000
1230 Rosecrans Ave # 660 Manhattan Beach (90266) ***(P-11666)***
Global Horizons Inc......B......310 234-8475
468 N Camden Dr Ste 200 Beverly Hills (90210) ***(P-14291)***
Global Industry Analysts Inc......A......408 528-9966
6150 Hellyer Ave Ste 100 San Jose (95138) ***(P-25903)***
Global Infotech Corporation......A......408 567-0600
2890 Zanker Rd Ste 202 San Jose (95134) ***(P-27082)***
Global Innovation Partner, Los Angeles *Also called Cbre Global Investors LLC* ***(P-10983)***
Global Language Solutions LLC......D......949 798-1400
19800 Macarthur Blvd Irvine (92612) ***(P-16805)***
Global Mail Inc......C......310 735-0800
921 W Artesia Blvd Compton (90220) ***(P-4956)***
Global Management Company LLC......D......323 261-8114
3150 E Pico Blvd Los Angeles (90023) ***(P-26620)***
Global Med Services Inc......A......562 207-6970
11818 South St Ste 201a Cerritos (90703) ***(P-21748)***
Global Network Travel, Glendale *Also called Goway Travel Inc* ***(P-4821)***
Global Nurses Online Inc......D......310 306-2760
5301 Beethoven St Ste 200 Los Angeles (90066) ***(P-14292)***
Global Paratransit Inc......B......310 715-7550
400 W Compton Blvd Gardena (90248) ***(P-3680)***
Global Plastics Inc......C......951 657-5466
145 Malbert St Perris (92570) ***(P-7759)***
Global Power Group Inc (PA)......D......619 579-1221
12060 Woodside Ave Lakeside (92040) ***(P-2501)***
Global Reach 18 Inc (PA)......D......310 203-5850
10100 Santa Monica Blvd # 900 Los Angeles (90067) ***(P-11752)***
Global Realty Group, Granada Hills *Also called Global Work Group LLC* ***(P-26621)***
Global Risk MGT Solutions LLC......C......949 759-8500
660 Nwport Ctr Dr Ste 600 Newport Beach (92660) ***(P-15863)***
Global Service Resources Inc......D......800 679-7658
711 S Victory Blvd Burbank (91502) ***(P-14833)***

Employee Codes: A=Over 500 employees, B=251-500
C=101-250, D=51-100, E=50
2020 Directory of California
Wholesalers and Services Companies
© Mergent Inc. 1-800-342-5647
1281

Global Software Resources Inc (PA).....E.....925 249-2200
4447 Stoneridge Dr Ste 1 Pleasanton (94588) ***(P-16018)***
Global Solutions Integration.....D.....949 307-1849
26632 Towne Centre Dr # 300 Foothill Ranch (92610) ***(P-25108)***
Global Stainless Supply.....B.....310 525-1865
17006 S Figueroa St Gardena (90248) ***(P-7067)***
Global Touchpoints Inc.....D.....916 878-5954
3005 Douglas Blvd Ste 108 Roseville (95661) ***(P-14834)***
Global USA Green Card.....D.....415 915-4151
201 Spear St Ste 1100 San Francisco (94105) ***(P-22539)***
Global Work Group LLC.....D.....424 220-9994
17224 San Fernando Granada Hills (91344) ***(P-26621)***
Global-Dining Inc California.....C.....310 576-9922
1212 3rd Street Promenade Santa Monica (90401) ***(P-26243)***
Globallogic Inc (PA).....C.....408 273-8900
1741 Tech Dr Ste 400 San Jose (95110) ***(P-14835)***
Globalways Inc (PA).....D.....510 580-1974
42808 Christy St Ste 202 Fremont (94538) ***(P-16019)***
Globe Shoes, El Segundo *Also called Osata Enterprises Inc* ***(P-8140)***
Globecast America Incorporated (HQ).....D.....310 845-3900
10525 Washington Blvd Culver City (90232) ***(P-5726)***
Gloria Ferrer, Sonoma *Also called Freixenet Usa Inc* ***(P-8809)***
Glovia Inc.....C.....310 563-7000
2250 E Imperial Hwy # 200 El Segundo (90245) ***(P-14836)***
Glovis America Inc (HQ).....D.....714 435-2960
17305 Von Karman Ave # 200 Irvine (92614) ***(P-4957)***
Glu Mobile Inc (PA).....C.....415 800-6100
875 Howard St Ste 100 San Francisco (94103) ***(P-14837)***
GM Cruise LLC (HQ).....D.....415 335-4097
1201 Bryant St San Francisco (94103) ***(P-3681)***
GMAC Insurance, Ontario *Also called National General Insurance Co* ***(P-10432)***
Gmh Inc.....E.....805 485-1410
561 Kinetic Dr Ste A Oxnard (93030) ***(P-17446)***
GMI Building Services Inc.....C.....858 279-6262
8001 Vickers St San Diego (92111) ***(P-13941)***
Gms Janitorial Services Inc.....D.....858 569-6009
8690 Aero Dr Ste 115 San Diego (92123) ***(P-13942)***
Go Capital, Roseville *Also called Nations First Capital LLC* ***(P-9507)***
Go Get Em Inc.....D.....702 985-5637
45248 Trevor Ave Lancaster (93534) ***(P-16521)***
Go West Holdings LLC.....C.....888 670-0080
795 Folsom St San Francisco (94107) ***(P-16806)***
Go West Tours Inc (PA).....E.....415 837-0154
790 Eddy St San Francisco (94109) ***(P-4853)***
Go-Staff Inc.....A.....760 730-8520
9878 Complex Dr Oceanside (92054) ***(P-14293)***
Go-Staff Inc.....A.....657 242-9350
240 W Lincoln Ave Anaheim (92805) ***(P-14294)***
Go2 Systems Inc.....D.....949 553-0800
18400 Von Karman Ave Fl 9 Irvine (92612) ***(P-15864)***
Go2systems, Irvine *Also called Go2 Systems Inc* ***(P-15864)***
Gobig Inc.....E.....415 513-3029
338 Main St Unit 5c San Francisco (94105) ***(P-15602)***
Godigital Media Group LLC.....D.....310 853-7940
3103 S La Cienega Blvd Los Angeles (90016) ***(P-5788)***
Goetzman Group Inc (PA).....D.....818 595-1112
21700 Oxnard St Ste 1540 Woodland Hills (91367) ***(P-26622)***
Goforth & Marti (PA).....D.....951 684-0870
110 W A St Ste 140 San Diego (92101) ***(P-6515)***
Gogii, Marina Del Rey *Also called Textplus Inc* ***(P-5277)***
Goguardian, Hermosa Beach *Also called Liminex Inc* ***(P-14912)***
Gold Bond Building Products, Richmond *Also called New Ngc Inc* ***(P-7765)***
Gold Coast Broadcasting, Ventura *Also called Kkzz 1590* ***(P-5547)***
Gold Coast Design Inc.....D.....619 574-0111
7667 Vickers St San Diego (92111) ***(P-2354)***
Gold Coast Farms LLC.....E.....559 564-6316
32701 Road 204 Woodlake (93286) ***(P-243)***
Gold Coast Surgery Center LLC.....C.....805 324-4555
2927 De La Vina St Santa Barbara (93105) ***(P-18998)***
Gold Coast Tours, Fullerton *Also called Hot Dogger Tours Inc* ***(P-3777)***
Gold Country Casino, Oroville *Also called Tyme Maidu Tribe-Berry Creek* ***(P-13049)***
Gold Country Health Center Inc (PA).....C.....530 621-1100
4301 Golden Center Dr Placerville (95667) ***(P-19945)***
Gold Country Management Inc.....D.....916 929-3003
1825 Bell St Ste 100 Sacramento (95825) ***(P-11171)***
Gold Cross Ambulance, Los Angeles *Also called Schaefer Ambulance Service Inc* ***(P-3722)***
Gold Derby Media LLC.....D.....310 321-5000
11175 Santa Monica Blvd Los Angeles (90025) ***(P-5532)***
Gold Hill Grange No 326.....D.....916 645-3605
1514 5th St Lincoln (95648) ***(P-24554)***
Gold Parent LP.....A.....310 954-0444
11111 Santa Monica Blvd Los Angeles (90025) ***(P-9693)***
Gold River Racquet Club, Gold River *Also called Spare-Time Inc* ***(P-18582)***
Gold Star Foods Inc (HQ).....C.....909 843-9600
3781 E Airport Dr Ontario (91761) ***(P-8286)***
Gold's Gym, Redondo Beach *Also called Muscle Improvement Inc* ***(P-18178)***
Gold's Gym, Vacaville *Also called Maximum Fitness LLC* ***(P-18175)***
Golda & I Chocolatiers Inc.....D.....949 660-9581
23052 Alicia Pkwy Ste H Mission Viejo (92692) ***(P-8584)***
Goldberg and Solovy Foods Inc, Vernon *Also called Palisades Ranch Inc* ***(P-8203)***
Goldco Direct LLC.....D.....818 343-0186
21215 Burbank Blvd # 600 Woodland Hills (91367) ***(P-7789)***
Goldcoast Liquidating LLC.....C.....949 461-7170
27845 Snta Margarita Pkwy Mission Viejo (92691) ***(P-1483)***
Goldderby.com, Los Angeles *Also called Gold Derby Media LLC* ***(P-5532)***
Golden, Irvine *Also called Atria Senior Living Inc* ***(P-26144)***
Golden 1 Credit Union.....C.....877 465-3361
1282 Stabler Ln Ste 640 Yuba City (95993) ***(P-9394)***
Golden 1 Credit Union (PA).....B.....916 732-2900
8945 Cal Center Dr Sacramento (95826) ***(P-9395)***
Golden 1 Credit Union.....D.....530 251-0205
2942 Main St Susanville (96130) ***(P-9396)***
Golden Acorn Casino & Trvl Ctr, Campo *Also called Campo Band Missions Indians* ***(P-18316)***
Golden Acres Farms.....E.....760 399-1923
87770 62nd Ave Thermal (92274) ***(P-323)***
Golden Age Nutrition Program, Watsonville *Also called Community Bridges* ***(P-23031)***
Golden Bear Rest Assn LLC.....E.....415 227-8660
760 2nd St San Francisco (94107) ***(P-24340)***
Golden Brands, West Sacramento *Also called Harbor Distributing LLC* ***(P-8767)***
Golden Bridge Intl Group.....D.....626 968-8229
727 9th Ave City of Industry (91745) ***(P-4958)***
Golden Coast Cnstr Restoration.....D.....916 955-7461
4811 Chippendale Dr # 301 Sacramento (95841) ***(P-1484)***
Golden Cross Care II Inc.....D.....559 268-3023
1233 A St Fresno (93706) ***(P-19946)***
Golden Cross Care Inc.....C.....626 791-1948
1450 N Fair Oaks Ave Pasadena (91103) ***(P-19947)***
GOLDEN CROSS HEALTH CARE, Pasadena *Also called Golden Cross Care Inc* ***(P-19947)***
Golden Cross Hlth Care Fresno, Fresno *Also called Golden Cross Care II Inc* ***(P-19946)***
Golden Door Properties LLC.....C.....760 744-5777
777 Deer Springs Rd San Marcos (92069) ***(P-12297)***
Golden Eagle Insurance Corp (HQ).....C.....619 744-6000
525 B St Ste 1300 San Diego (92101) ***(P-10092)***
Golden Eagle Moving Svcs Inc.....D.....909 946-7655
1450 N Benson Ave Unit B Upland (91786) ***(P-4421)***
Golden Empire Concrete Pdts.....D.....661 833-4490
8261 Mccutchen Rd Bakersfield (93311) ***(P-3151)***
Golden Empire Convalescent Hos.....C.....530 273-1316
121 Dorsey Dr Grass Valley (95945) ***(P-20890)***
Golden Empire Mortgage Inc.....D.....626 967-3236
664 Shoppers Ln Ste A Covina (91723) ***(P-9552)***
Golden Empire Mortgage Inc.....D.....760 256-3593
420 Barstow Rd Barstow (92311) ***(P-9553)***
Golden Empire Mortgage Inc (PA).....D.....661 328-1600
1200 Discovery Dr Ste 300 Bakersfield (93309) ***(P-9554)***
Golden Empire Mortgage Inc (PA).....D.....661 328-1600
2130 Chester Ave Bakersfield (93301) ***(P-9555)***
Golden Empire Transit District (PA).....C.....661 869-2438
1830 Golden State Ave Bakersfield (93301) ***(P-3540)***
Golden Gate.....D.....415 455-2000
101 E Sir Francis Drake Larkspur (94939) ***(P-5105)***
Golden Gate Brdg Hwy & Transpo (PA).....C.....415 921-5858
Toll Plz San Francisco (94129) ***(P-5106)***
Golden Gate Bridge High.....A.....415 457-3110
1011 Andersen Dr San Rafael (94901) ***(P-5107)***
Golden Gate Capital, San Francisco *Also called Ggc Administration LLC* ***(P-11665)***
Golden Gate Capitol.....B.....415 983-2700
1 Embarcadero Ctr # 3900 San Francisco (94111) ***(P-27083)***
Golden Gate Ferry, Larkspur *Also called Golden Gate* ***(P-5105)***
Golden Gate Fields, Albany *Also called Pacific Racing Association* ***(P-18087)***
Golden Gate Nat Prks Cnsrvancy, San Rafael *Also called Golden Gate Nat Prks Cnsrvancy* ***(P-27277)***
Golden Gate Nat Prks Cnsrvancy.....C.....415 440-4068
1 Presidio Ave San Francisco (94115) ***(P-27276)***
Golden Gate Nat Prks Cnsrvancy.....D.....415 785-4787
1600 Los Gamos Dr San Rafael (94903) ***(P-27277)***
Golden Gate Nat Prks Cnsrvancy (PA).....D.....415 561-3000
Fort Mason Bldg 201 San Francisco (94123) ***(P-27278)***
Golden Gate Regional Ctr Inc (PA).....C.....415 546-9222
1355 Market St Ste 220 San Francisco (94103) ***(P-23243)***
Golden Gate Regional Ctr Inc.....D.....650 574-9232
3130 La Selva St Ste 202 San Mateo (94403) ***(P-23244)***
Golden Gate Scnic Stmship Corp.....E.....415 901-5249
Shed C Pier 45 St Pier San Francisco (94133) ***(P-4603)***
Golden Gate Section, San Francisco *Also called National Council Negro Women* ***(P-24850)***
Golden Gate Transit, San Rafael *Also called Golden Gate Bridge High* ***(P-5107)***
Golden Gtwy Tennis & Swim CLB, San Francisco *Also called Bay Club Holdings III LLC* ***(P-18631)***
Golden Hl Elementary Schl Pta.....E.....714 447-7715
732 Barris Dr Fullerton (92832) ***(P-24555)***
Golden Hotel LLC.....D.....714 739-5600
7762 Beach Blvd Buena Park (90620) ***(P-12298)***
Golden Hotels Ltd Partnership.....C.....949 833-2770
18700 Macarthur Blvd Irvine (92612) ***(P-12299)***
Golden Hour Data Systems Inc.....C.....858 768-2500
10052 Mesa Ridge Ct # 200 San Diego (92121) ***(P-4959)***
Golden International.....A.....213 628-1388
424 S Los Angeles St # 2 Los Angeles (90013) ***(P-11916)***
Golden Living Center - Chateau, Stockton *Also called Golden Living LLC* ***(P-19951)***
Golden Living LLC.....D.....559 237-8377
1715 S Cedar Ave Fresno (93702) ***(P-19948)***
Golden Living LLC.....D.....818 893-6385
9541 Van Nuys Blvd Panorama City (91402) ***(P-20571)***
Golden Living LLC.....D.....559 834-2542
1306 E Sumner Ave Fowler (93625) ***(P-19949)***
Golden Living LLC.....D.....949 642-0387
340 Victoria St Costa Mesa (92627) ***(P-19950)***
Golden Living LLC.....D.....707 546-0471
1221 Rosemarie Ln Stockton (95207) ***(P-19951)***
Golden Living LLC.....D.....818 249-3925
2123 Verdugo Blvd Montrose (91020) ***(P-20572)***
Golden Living LLC.....D.....559 275-4785
925 N Cornelia Ave Fresno (93706) ***(P-19952)***
Golden Living LLC.....D.....209 745-1537
144 F St Galt (95632) ***(P-21749)***

Golden Living LLC.....D.....415 563-0565
1477 Grove St San Francisco (94117) ***(P-19953)***

Golden Living LLC.....C.....209 533-2500
19929 Greenley Rd Sonora (95370) ***(P-20573)***

Golden Living LLC.....D.....408 356-8136
14966 Terreno De Flores Los Gatos (95032) ***(P-19954)***

Golden Living LLC.....D.....562 598-2477
3000 N Gate Rd Seal Beach (90740) ***(P-20574)***

Golden Living LLC.....D.....661 323-2894
3601 San Dimas St Bakersfield (93301) ***(P-19955)***

Golden Living LLC.....D.....805 494-4949
6700 Sepulveda Blvd Van Nuys (91411) ***(P-21750)***

Golden Living LLC.....D.....805 983-0305
1300 N C St Oxnard (93030) ***(P-19956)***

Golden Living LLC.....D.....805 642-1736
5445 Everglades St Ventura (93003) ***(P-19957)***

Golden Living LLC.....D.....209 368-0693
950 S Fairmont Ave Lodi (95240) ***(P-19958)***

Golden Living LLC.....D.....707 546-0471
4650 Hoen Ave Santa Rosa (95405) ***(P-19959)***

Golden Living LLC.....D.....707 763-4109
217 Lakeville St Apt 3 Petaluma (94952) ***(P-19960)***

Golden Living LLC.....D.....559 673-9278
1700 Howard Rd Madera (93637) ***(P-20575)***

Golden Living LLC.....C.....408 923-7232
401 Ridge Vista Ave San Jose (95127) ***(P-19961)***

Golden Living LLC.....D.....949 496-5786
35410 Del Rey Capistrano Beach (92624) ***(P-19962)***

Golden Living LLC.....D.....530 241-6756
1836 Gold St Redding (96001) ***(P-20576)***

Golden Living LLC.....D.....559 222-4807
3510 E Shields Ave Fresno (93726) ***(P-19963)***

Golden Living LLC.....D.....559 486-4433
2715 Fresno St Fresno (93721) ***(P-20577)***

Golden Living LLC.....D.....559 299-2591
111 Barstow Ave Clovis (93612) ***(P-19964)***

Golden Living LLC.....D.....951 600-4640
24100 Monroe Ave Murrieta (92562) ***(P-23245)***

Golden Living LLC.....D.....559 227-5383
3672 N 1st St Fresno (93726) ***(P-19965)***

Golden Living LLC.....E.....408 255-5555
5555 Prospect Rd Ofc San Jose (95129) ***(P-23938)***

Golden Living LLC.....C.....209 548-0318
1900 Coffee Rd Modesto (95355) ***(P-19966)***

Golden Living LLC.....D.....408 356-9151
350 De Soto Dr Los Gatos (95032) ***(P-19967)***

Golden Living LLC.....D.....559 227-4063
3408 E Shields Ave Fresno (93726) ***(P-20578)***

Golden Living LLC.....D.....209 466-3522
2740 N California St Stockton (95204) ***(P-19968)***

Golden Living LLC.....D.....707 938-1096
678 2nd St W Sonoma (95476) ***(P-19969)***

Golden Living LLC.....D.....530 343-6084
188 Cohasset Ln Chico (95926) ***(P-19970)***

Golden Living LLC.....D.....209 722-6231
3169 M St Merced (95348) ***(P-20579)***

Golden Living LLC.....D.....760 446-3591
1131 N China Lake Blvd Ridgecrest (93555) ***(P-21751)***

Golden Living LLC.....D.....559 875-6501
2550 9th St Sanger (93657) ***(P-20580)***

Golden Living LLC.....D.....209 862-2862
709 N St Newman (95360) ***(P-19971)***

Golden Livingcenter, Sonoma *Also called Golden Living LLC* ***(P-19969)***

Golden Livingcenter - Clovis, Clovis *Also called Golden Living LLC* ***(P-19964)***

Golden Livingcenter - Fresno, Fresno *Also called Golden Living LLC* ***(P-20577)***

Golden Livingcenter - Galt, Galt *Also called Golden Living LLC* ***(P-21749)***

Golden Livingcenter - Hylond, Fresno *Also called Golden Living LLC* ***(P-20578)***

Golden Livingcenter - NAPA, NAPA *Also called Beaver Dam Health Care Center* ***(P-20499)***

Golden Livingcenter - Petaluma, Petaluma *Also called Golden Living LLC* ***(P-19960)***

Golden Livingcenter - Portside, Stockton *Also called Golden Living LLC* ***(P-19968)***

Golden Livingcenter - Redding, Redding *Also called Golden Living LLC* ***(P-20576)***

Golden Livingcenter - Reedley, Reedley *Also called Beaver Dam Health Care Center* ***(P-19748)***

Golden Livingcenter - San Jose, San Jose *Also called Golden Living LLC* ***(P-19961)***

Golden Livingcenter - Sanger, Sanger *Also called Golden Living LLC* ***(P-20580)***

Golden Livingctr-Country View, Fresno *Also called Golden Living LLC* ***(P-19952)***

Golden Lvngcenter - Santa Rosa, Santa Rosa *Also called Golden Living LLC* ***(P-19959)***

Golden Lvngcnter - Bakersfield, Bakersfield *Also called Golden Living LLC* ***(P-19955)***

Golden N-Life Diamite Intl Inc (PA).....D.....510 651-0405
3500 Gateway Blvd Fremont (94538) ***(P-7946)***

Golden Peterbilt, Porterville *Also called E M Tharp Inc* ***(P-6393)***

Golden Pond LP.....E.....916 369-8967
3415 Mayhew Rd Ofc Sacramento (95827) ***(P-23939)***

Golden Pond Retirement Cmnty, Sacramento *Also called Golden Pond LP* ***(P-23939)***

Golden Queen Mining Co LLC.....C.....661 824-4300
2818 Silver Queen Rd Mojave (93501) ***(P-969)***

Golden Rain Foundation (PA).....D.....925 988-7700
1001 Golden Rain Rd Walnut Creek (94595) ***(P-11172)***

Golden Rain Foundation.....D.....562 493-9581
1661 Golden Rain Rd Seal Beach (90740) ***(P-18999)***

Golden Rain Foundation.....B.....925 988-7800
800 Rockview Dr Walnut Creek (94595) ***(P-24556)***

Golden State Care Center, Baldwin Park *Also called Golden State Habilitation Conv* ***(P-19972)***

Golden State Collision Centers.....D.....916 772-1666
841 Galleria Blvd Roseville (95678) ***(P-17292)***

Golden State Colonial Convales, North Hollywood *Also called Silverscreen Healthcare Inc* ***(P-20261)***

Golden State Crrctional Fcilty, Mc Farland *Also called Geo Group Inc* ***(P-26239)***

Golden State Drilling Inc.....D.....661 589-0730
3500 Fruitvale Ave Bakersfield (93308) ***(P-998)***

Golden State Fence, Anaheim *Also called Fenceworks Inc* ***(P-3406)***

Golden State Fence, Santa Paula *Also called Fenceworks Inc* ***(P-3408)***

Golden State Fence Co., Riverside *Also called Fenceworks Inc* ***(P-3407)***

Golden State Habilitation Conv (PA).....B.....626 962-3274
1758 Big Dalton Ave Baldwin Park (91706) ***(P-19972)***

Golden State Health Ctrs Inc (PA).....C.....818 385-3200
13347 Ventura Blvd Sherman Oaks (91423) ***(P-19973)***

Golden State Health Ctrs Inc.....C.....626 579-0310
5522 Gracewood Ave Temple City (91780) ***(P-20581)***

Golden State Health Ctrs Inc.....C.....818 882-8233
21820 Craggy View St Chatsworth (91311) ***(P-20582)***

Golden State Health Ctrs Inc.....C.....818 834-5082
12220 Foothill Blvd Sylmar (91342) ***(P-21411)***

Golden State Herbs (PA).....E.....760 342-7117
60125 Polk St Thermal (92274) ***(P-244)***

Golden State Landscaping, Livermore *Also called J Redfern Inc* ***(P-832)***

Golden State Lumber Inc.....C.....209 234-7700
3033 S Airport Way Stockton (95206) ***(P-6619)***

Golden State Medical Sup Inc.....C.....805 477-9866
5187 Camino Ruiz Camarillo (93012) ***(P-6967)***

Golden State Medical Supply.....D.....805 477-8966
5247 Camino Ruiz Camarillo (93012) ***(P-7812)***

Golden State Mutl Lf Insur Co (PA).....D.....713 526-4361
1999 W Adams Blvd Los Angeles (90018) ***(P-9868)***

Golden State Plastering.....D.....559 439-3920
7082 N Harrison Ave Fresno (93650) ***(P-6687)***

Golden State Warriors LLC.....D.....510 986-2200
1011 Broadway Oakland (94607) ***(P-18063)***

Golden State Water Company.....D.....714 535-7711
1920 W Corporate Way Anaheim (92801) ***(P-6063)***

Golden State Water Company (HQ).....C.....909 394-3600
630 E Foothill Blvd San Dimas (91773) ***(P-6064)***

Golden State Water Company.....D.....909 394-3600
630 E Foothill Blvd San Dimas (91773) ***(P-6065)***

Golden State Water Company.....E.....805 583-6400
600 W Los Angeles Ave Simi Valley (93065) ***(P-6066)***

Golden State Water Company.....E.....909 866-4678
42020 Garstin Dr Big Bear Lake (92315) ***(P-5842)***

Golden State West Valley.....C.....818 348-8422
7057 Shoup Ave Canoga Park (91307) ***(P-19974)***

Golden Valley Citrus Inc.....D.....559 568-1768
19875 Meredith Dr Strathmore (93267) ***(P-493)***

Golden Valley Health Centers (PA).....A.....209 383-1848
737 W Childs Ave Merced (95341) ***(P-22032)***

Golden Valley Health Centers.....D.....209 383-5871
797 W Childs Ave Merced (95341) ***(P-22033)***

Golden Vly Occpational Therapy, Oroville *Also called Oroville Hospital* ***(P-19682)***

Golden West Custom WD Shutters.....E.....949 951-0600
20561 Pascal Way Lake Forest (92630) ***(P-7813)***

Golden West Hotel Partnership (PA).....D.....619 233-7594
724 Rincon Dr Aptos (95003) ***(P-12300)***

Golden West Trading Inc.....C.....323 581-3663
4401 S Downey Rd Vernon (90058) ***(P-8405)***

Goldenpark LLC.....D.....562 863-5555
16209 Paramount Blvd # 214 Paramount (90723) ***(P-12301)***

Goldfield Stage Company, El Cajon *Also called McClintock Enterprises Inc* ***(P-3778)***

Goldman Sachs & Co.....C.....415 393-7500
555 California St # 4500 San Francisco (94104) ***(P-9694)***

Goldman Sachs & Co.....C.....310 407-5700
2121 Avenue Stars 2600 Los Angeles (90067) ***(P-9695)***

Goldman Avram.....D.....925 275-3000
1855 Gateway Blvd Ste 750 Concord (94520) ***(P-26244)***

Goldman Sachs, San Francisco *Also called Goldman Sachs & Co* ***(P-9694)***

Goldman Sachs, Los Angeles *Also called Goldman Sachs & Co* ***(P-9695)***

Goldrich & Kest Industries LLC (PA).....A.....310 204-2050
5150 Overland Ave Culver City (90230) ***(P-11564)***

Goldrichkest (PA).....C.....310 204-2050
5150 Overland Ave Culver City (90230) ***(P-11565)***

Goldrush Getaways, Citrus Heights *Also called Travelmasters Inc* ***(P-4841)***

Golds Gym, Northridge *Also called Musclebound Inc* ***(P-18179)***

Golds Gym International Inc.....D.....626 304-1133
39 S Altadena Dr Pasadena (91107) ***(P-18149)***

Goldsmith Construction Co Inc.....E.....562 595-5975
2683 Lime Ave Signal Hill (90755) ***(P-3152)***

Goldstar, Irvine *Also called Spireon Inc* ***(P-4234)***

Goldstar Hlthcr Cntr of Chtswr.....C.....818 882-8233
145 S Fairfax Ave Ste 200 Los Angeles (90036) ***(P-20583)***

Goleta Hhg Hotel Dev LP.....D.....805 562-5996
6878 Hollister Ave Goleta (93117) ***(P-12302)***

Goleta Valley Athletic Club, Goleta *Also called Millenium Athletic Club LLc* ***(P-18176)***

Goleta Valley Cottage Hospital.....B.....805 681-6468
351 S Patterson Ave Santa Barbara (93111) ***(P-20891)***

Golf Club At Boulder Ridge, San Jose *Also called Glenrock Group* ***(P-18460)***

Golf Club At Roddy Ranch, Antioch *Also called Roddy Ranch Pbc LLC* ***(P-18546)***

Golf Club At Terra Lago, The, Indio *Also called Lb Hills Golf Club LLC* ***(P-18261)***

Golf Investment LLC (PA).....D.....949 498-6604
200 Avenida La Pata San Clemente (92673) ***(P-18461)***

Golf Pro Shop, Riverside *Also called Canyon Crest Country Club Inc* ***(P-18416)***

Golf Pro. Shop, Diablo *Also called Diablo Country Club* ***(P-18447)***

Gomez Farm Labor Contg Inc.....D.....760 399-1994
62610 Monroe St Thermal (92274) ***(P-623)***

Gong's Ventures, Sanger *Also called Gongs Market of Sanger Inc* ***(P-10599)***

Employee Codes: A=Over 500 employees, B=251-500
C=101-250, D=51-100, E=50
2020 Directory of California
Wholesalers and Services Companies
© Mergent Inc. 1-800-342-5647
1283

Gongs Market of Sanger Inc (PA) ....E....559 875-5576
1825 Academy Ave Sanger (93657) ***(P-10599)***
Gonsalves & Santucci Inc (PA) ....E....925 685-6799
5141 Commercial Cir Concord (94520) ***(P-3153)***
Gonzales Painting Corp ....D....951 214-6400
14437 Meridian Pkwy Riverside (92518) ***(P-2355)***
Gonzales Park LLC ....C....530 343-8725
495 Ryan Ave Chico (95973) ***(P-8031)***
Gonzales Salvador Labor Contrs ....D....209 745-2223
217 4th St Galt (95632) ***(P-624)***
Gonzalez Barba Enterprises ....E....323 233-7995
1575 E 46th St Los Angeles (90011) ***(P-4960)***
Gonzalez Management Co Inc ....D....818 485-0596
10147 San Fernando Rd Pacoima (91331) ***(P-26245)***
Gonzalez/Goodale Architects ....D....626 568-1428
135 W Green St Ste 200 Pasadena (91105) ***(P-25441)***
Good Deal Insurance Services ....D....626 275-6795
2140 S Hacienda Blvd A Hacienda Heights (91745) ***(P-10372)***
Good Eggs Inc (PA) ....D....415 483-7344
901 Rankin St San Francisco (94124) ***(P-8325)***
Good Neighbor Pharmacy, Fresno *Also called Northwest Medical Group Inc* ***(P-19230)***
Good Samaritan Hospital ....B....661 399-4461
901 Olive Dr Bakersfield (93308) ***(P-20892)***
Good Samaritan Hospital LP (HQ) ....A....408 559-2011
2425 Samaritan Dr San Jose (95124) ***(P-20893)***
Good Samaritan Hospital LP ....C....408 356-4111
15891 Los Gtos Almaden Rd Los Gatos (95032) ***(P-20894)***
Good Samaritan Hospital Aux ....A....213 977-2121
1225 Wilshire Blvd Los Angeles (90017) ***(P-19000)***
GOOD SAMARITAN REHAB AND CARE, Stockton *Also called Stockton Edson Healthcare Corp* ***(P-20695)***
Good Samaritan Shelter ....D....805 346-8185
245 Inger Dr Ste 103b Santa Maria (93454) ***(P-23246)***
Good Shepherd Communities, Porterville *Also called Good Shepherd Lutheran Hm of W* ***(P-23940)***
Good Shepherd Health Care Ce ....D....310 451-4809
1131 Arizona Ave Santa Monica (90401) ***(P-19975)***
Good Shepherd Lutheran Hm of W (PA) ....D....559 791-2000
119 N Main St Porterville (93257) ***(P-23940)***
Good Sports Plus Ltd ....B....310 671-4400
370 Amapola Ave Ste 208 Torrance (90501) ***(P-14838)***
Good Technology Corporation (HQ) ....C....408 352-9102
3001 Bishop Dr Ste 400 San Ramon (94583) ***(P-14839)***
Good Works LLC ....D....626 584-8130
1250 E Walnut St Ste 220 Pasadena (91106) ***(P-21752)***
Goodall's Charter Bus Company, San Diego *Also called Cusa Gcbs LLC* ***(P-4852)***
Goodby Silverstein & Partners, San Francisco *Also called Goodby Slverstein Partners Inc* ***(P-13512)***
Goodby Slverstein Partners Inc ....C....415 392-0669
720 California St San Francisco (94108) ***(P-13512)***
Goodfellow Bros California LLC ....B....925 245-2111
50 Contractors St Livermore (94551) ***(P-1131)***
Goodhire, Redwood City *Also called Inflection Risk Solutions LLC* ***(P-15780)***
Goodland, Goleta *Also called Khp III Goleta LLC* ***(P-12508)***
Goodman Group Inc ....D....562 596-5561
3902 Katella Ave Los Alamitos (90720) ***(P-19976)***
Goodman Manufacturing Co LP ....B....951 304-7402
41670 Reagan Way Murrieta (92562) ***(P-7449)***
Goodman Manufacturing Co LP ....B....858 569-1715
3562 Ruffin Rd San Diego (92123) ***(P-7450)***
Goodman North America LLC ....D....949 407-0100
18201 Von Karman Ave Irvine (92612) ***(P-11173)***
Goodrich Lax A Cal Ltd Partnr ....D....626 254-9988
310 W Longden Ave Arcadia (91007) ***(P-12303)***
Goodridge Usa Inc (HQ) ....D....310 533-1924
529 Van Ness Ave Torrance (90501) ***(P-6442)***
Goodwill Inds Orange Cnty Cal ....C....714 754-7808
2910 W Garry Ave Santa Ana (92704) ***(P-23598)***
Goodwill Inds S Centl Cal ....E....661 377-0191
1115 Olive Dr Bakersfield (93308) ***(P-23599)***
Goodwill Inds San Diego Cnty ....C....760 806-7670
3841 Plaza Dr Ste 902 Oceanside (92056) ***(P-24834)***
Goodwill Industrs of San Franc ....D....650 556-9709
1270 Oddstad Dr Redwood City (94063) ***(P-23600)***
Goodwill of Silicon Valley (PA) ....D....408 998-5774
1080 N 7th St San Jose (95112) ***(P-14510)***
Goodwill Srvng The Ppl of Sthr (PA) ....D....562 435-3411
800 W Pacific Coast Hwy Long Beach (90806) ***(P-16807)***
Goodwin Ammonia Company ....D....714 894-0531
12361 Monarch St Garden Grove (92841) ***(P-4422)***
Goodwin Procter LLP ....D....213 426-2500
601 S Figueroa St # 4100 Los Angeles (90017) ***(P-22540)***
Google Checkout, Mountain View *Also called Google Payment Corp* ***(P-16808)***
Google Fiber Inc (HQ) ....D....650 253-0000
1600 Amphitheatre Pkwy Mountain View (94043) ***(P-5413)***
Google International LLC (HQ) ....D....650 253-0000
1600 Amphitheatre Pkwy Mountain View (94043) ***(P-5414)***
Google LLC (HQ) ....C....650 253-0000
1600 Amphitheatre Pkwy Mountain View (94043) ***(P-14840)***
Google Payment Corp ....E....650 253-0000
1600 Amphitheatre Pkwy Mountain View (94043) ***(P-16808)***
Goproto, San Diego *Also called Higgs Fletcher & Mack Llp* ***(P-22568)***
Gordian Medical Inc ....B....714 556-0200
17595 Cartwright Rd Irvine (92614) ***(P-6968)***
Gordon Edelstein Krepack Gr ....E....213 739-7000
3580 Wilshire Blvd # 1800 Los Angeles (90010) ***(P-22541)***
Gordon & Schwenkmeyer Inc ....D....916 569-1740
1860 Howe Ave Ste 300 Sacramento (95825) ***(P-16809)***
Gordon Betty Moore Foundation ....D....650 213-3000
1661 Page Mill Rd Palo Alto (94304) ***(P-24557)***
Gordon E Btty I More Fundation ....D....650 213-3000
1661 Page Mill Rd Palo Alto (94304) ***(P-27084)***
Gordon Edelstein & Krepack, Los Angeles *Also called Gordon Edelstein Krepack Gr* ***(P-22541)***
Gordon Lane Convalescent Hosp ....D....714 879-7301
1821 E Chapman Ave Fullerton (92831) ***(P-20895)***
Gordon Rees Scully Mansukhani ....D....916 830-6900
655 University Ave # 200 Sacramento (95825) ***(P-22542)***
Gordon Rees Scully Mansukhani ....D....949 255-6950
2211 Michelson Dr Ste 400 Irvine (92612) ***(P-22543)***
Gordon Rees Scully Mansukhani (PA) ....B....415 986-5900
275 Battery St Ste 2000 San Francisco (94111) ***(P-22544)***
Gordon Rees Scully Mansukhani ....D....213 576-5000
633 W 5th St Fl 52 Los Angeles (90071) ***(P-22545)***
Gordon Rees Scully Mansukhani ....D....619 696-6700
101 W Broadway Ste 1600 San Diego (92101) ***(P-22546)***
Gordon Rees Scully Mansukhani ....D....415 986-5900
101 W Broadway Ste 2000 San Diego (92101) ***(P-22547)***
Gores Group LLC (PA) ....D....310 209-3010
9800 Wilshire Blvd Beverly Hills (90212) ***(P-9696)***
Gores Norment Holdings Inc ....C....310 209-3010
10877 Wilshire Blvd # 1805 Los Angeles (90024) ***(P-11667)***
Gorilla Tech Americas Inc ....D....925 365-1161
2678 Bishop Dr Ste 290 San Ramon (94583) ***(P-26623)***
Gothic Ground Management, Valencia *Also called Gothic Landscaping Inc* ***(P-817)***
Gothic Grounds Mgmt, Valencia *Also called Gothic Landscaping Inc* ***(P-730)***
Gothic Landscaping Inc (PA) ....C....661 257-1266
27502 Avenue Scott Valencia (91355) ***(P-817)***
Gothic Landscaping Inc ....B....661 257-5085
27413 Tourney Rd Ste 200 Valencia (91355) ***(P-730)***
Gottstein Contracting Corp ....D....661 322-8934
4114 Armour Ave Bakersfield (93308) ***(P-7473)***
Gould Evans P C ....D....415 503-1411
95 Brady St San Francisco (94103) ***(P-25442)***
Gourmet Foods ....D....510 887-0340
2557 Barrington Ct Hayward (94545) ***(P-8176)***
Gourmet Foods Inc (PA) ....D....310 632-3300
2910 E Harcourt St Compton (90221) ***(P-8177)***
Gourmet India Food Company LLC ....D....562 698-9763
12220 Rivera Rd Ste A Whittier (90606) ***(P-8585)***
Gourmet Specialties Inc ....D....323 587-1734
2120 E 25th St Vernon (90058) ***(P-8483)***
Gourmet Trading Company, Redondo Beach *Also called Nzg Specialties Inc* ***(P-8201)***
Government Technology, Folsom *Also called Erepublic Inc* ***(P-16769)***
Governmentjobscom Inc ....C....310 426-6304
300 Continental Blvd # 565 El Segundo (90245) ***(P-15339)***
Governors Office Plg & RES, Sacramento *Also called The Executive Office of* ***(P-25852)***
Goway Travel Inc ....D....800 810-3687
505 N Brand Blvd Ste 810 Glendale (91203) ***(P-4821)***
GPA Technologies Inc ....D....805 643-7878
2368 Eastman Ave Ste 8 Ventura (93003) ***(P-25109)***
Gps Flyers ....D....951 588-7777
527 Prospect Ave Hermosa Beach (90254) ***(P-26624)***
Gps Painting Wallcovering Inc ....C....714 730-8904
1307 E Saint Gertrude Pl C Santa Ana (92705) ***(P-2356)***
Gr Hardester LLC ....C....707 987-2325
21088 Calistoga Rd Middletown (95461) ***(P-11854)***
Gr8 Care Inc ....D....626 337-7229
14518 Los Angeles St Baldwin Park (91706) ***(P-19977)***
Gracenote Inc (HQ) ....D....510 428-7200
2000 Powell St Ste 1500 Emeryville (94608) ***(P-14841)***
Gradient Engineers Inc ....D....949 477-0555
17781 Cowan Ste 140 Irvine (92614) ***(P-25110)***
Graham Concrete Cnstr Inc ....D....559 292-6571
1323 Dayton Ave Ste 103 Clovis (93612) ***(P-3154)***
Graham Contractors Inc ....E....408 293-9516
860 Lonus St San Jose (95126) ***(P-1711)***
Graham Packaging Company LP ....C....209 572-5187
4500 Finch Rd Modesto (95357) ***(P-8976)***
Graham-Prewett Inc ....E....559 291-3741
2773 N Bus Park Ave # 101 Fresno (93727) ***(P-3059)***
Grainger 732, San Jose *Also called WW Grainger Inc* ***(P-7192)***
Granada Healthcre & Rehab Cntr ....D....707 443-1627
2885 Harris St Eureka (95503) ***(P-19978)***
Granada Hills Care Center, Granada Hills *Also called Granada Hlls Convalescent Hosp* ***(P-19979)***
Granada Hlls Convalescent Hosp ....D....818 891-1745
16123 Chatsworth St Granada Hills (91344) ***(P-19979)***
Granada Hotel, San Francisco *Also called Broadmoor Hotel* ***(P-12093)***
Grancare LLC ....B....510 232-5945
13484 San Pablo Ave San Pablo (94806) ***(P-19980)***
Grancell Village, Reseda *Also called Los Angles Jewish HM For Aging* ***(P-20094)***
Grand Auto Care ....E....626 331-8390
744 N Grand Ave Covina (91724) ***(P-17331)***
Grand Auto Repair, Covina *Also called Grand Auto Care* ***(P-17331)***
Grand Central Station, Livermore *Also called All-Guard Alarm Systems Inc* ***(P-2417)***
Grand Del Mar Resort LP ....A....858 314-2000
5300 Grand Del Mar Ct San Diego (92130) ***(P-12304)***
Grand Events, Modesto *Also called Central Valley Party Supply* ***(P-14139)***
Grand Hotel The, Sunnyvale *Also called Selvi-Vidovich LP* ***(P-12903)***
Grand Hyatt San Francisco, San Francisco *Also called Hyatt Corporation* ***(P-12433)***
Grand Intelligence LLC ....D....408 954-7368
2880 Zanker Rd Ste 203 San Jose (95134) ***(P-14842)***
Grand Pacific Carlsbad Ht LP ....B....760 827-2400
5480 Grand Pacific Dr Carlsbad (92008) ***(P-12305)***

Grand Pacific Resorts Inc.....C.....760 431-8500
5900 Pasteur Ct Ste 200 Carlsbad (92008) ***(P-16810)***
Grand Pacific Resorts Inc (PA).....C.....760 431-8500
5900 Pasteur Ct Ste 200 Carlsbad (92008) ***(P-11174)***
Grand Pacific Resorts Svcs LP.....C.....760 431-8500
5900 Pasteur Ct Ste 200 Carlsbad (92008) ***(P-12306)***
Grand Park Convalescent Hosp.....C.....213 382-7315
2312 W 8th St Los Angeles (90057) ***(P-19981)***
Grand Performances.....D.....213 687-2190
350 S Grand Ave Ste A4 Los Angeles (90071) ***(P-16811)***
Grand Supercenter Inc.....D.....562 318-3451
8550 Chetle Ave Ste B Whittier (90606) ***(P-8178)***
Grand Terrace Care Center.....D.....909 825-5221
12000 Mount Vernon Ave Grand Terrace (92313) ***(P-19982)***
Grand Valley Health Care Ctr.....C.....818 786-3470
13524 Sherman Way Van Nuys (91405) ***(P-19983)***
Grand View Geranium Grdns Inc.....D.....310 217-0490
18307 Central Ave Carson (90746) ***(P-245)***
Grand View Research Inc.....E.....415 349-0058
201 Spear St Ste 1100 San Francisco (94105) ***(P-26625)***
Grand Vista Hotel, Simi Valley *Also called Simi West Inc* ***(P-12928)***
Grandcare Health Services LLC (PA).....C.....866 554-2447
3452 E Foothill Blvd # 700 Pasadena (91107) ***(P-21753)***
Grandcare Home Health Services, Pasadena *Also called Msj Healthcare LLC* ***(P-21816)***
Grande Colonial, La Jolla *Also called Fargo Colonial LLC* ***(P-12261)***
Grandpoint Capital Inc.....C.....213 542-4410
333 S Grand Ave Ste 4250 Los Angeles (90071) ***(P-11638)***
Grani Installation Inc (PA).....D.....714 898-0441
5411 Commercial Dr Huntington Beach (92649) ***(P-1485)***
Granit-Bayashi 2 A Joint Ventr.....D.....831 724-1011
585 W Beach St Watsonville (95076) ***(P-1859)***
Granit-Bayashi 3 A Joint Ventr.....E.....831 724-1011
585 W Beach St Watsonville (95076) ***(P-1712)***
Granite Bay Golf Club.....C.....916 791-5379
9600 Golf Club Dr Granite Bay (95746) ***(P-18462)***
Granite Construction Company (HQ).....C.....831 724-1011
585 W Beach St Watsonville (95076) ***(P-1713)***
Granite Construction Company.....C.....661 399-3361
3005 James Rd Bakersfield (93308) ***(P-1714)***
Granite Construction Company.....B.....760 775-7500
38000 Monroe St Indio (92203) ***(P-1715)***
Granite Construction Company.....C.....805 964-9951
5335 Debbie Rd Santa Barbara (93111) ***(P-1716)***
Granite Construction Company.....D.....916 855-4400
4001 Bradshaw Rd Sacramento (95827) ***(P-1966)***
Granite Construction Company.....D.....661 854-3051
21541 E Bear Mtn Blvd Arvin (93203) ***(P-1717)***
Granite Construction Company.....C.....661 726-4447
213 E Avenue M Lancaster (93535) ***(P-1718)***
Granite Construction Company.....C.....408 327-7000
715 Comstock St Santa Clara (95054) ***(P-1719)***
Granite Construction Company.....C.....559 441-5700
2716 S Granite Ct Fresno (93706) ***(P-1720)***
Granite Construction Inc.....C.....760 337-3030
2095 Us Highway 111 El Centro (92243) ***(P-1721)***
Granite Construction Inc (PA).....C.....831 724-1011
585 W Beach St Watsonville (95076) ***(P-1820)***
Granite Construction Inc.....D.....831 657-1700
5 Justin Ct Monterey (93940) ***(P-1722)***
Granite Construction Inc.....D.....916 855-4495
4291 Bradshaw Rd Sacramento (95827) ***(P-1723)***
Granite Construction Inc.....D.....707 467-4100
1324 S State St Ukiah (95482) ***(P-1724)***
Granite Construction Inc.....D.....831 763-5595
25485 Iverson Rd Gonzales (93926) ***(P-1725)***
Granite Construction Inc.....D.....831 335-3445
1800 Felton Quarry Rd Felton (95018) ***(P-1726)***
Granite Construction Inc.....D.....805 879-0033
999 Mission Rock Rd Santa Paula (93060) ***(P-1132)***
Granite Escrow Services.....D.....310 288-0110
439 N Canon Dr Ste 220 Beverly Hills (90210) ***(P-9438)***
Granite Hills Healthcare.....D.....619 447-1020
1340 E Madison Ave El Cajon (92021) ***(P-19984)***
Granite Power Inc.....B.....831 724-1011
580 W Beach St Watsonville (95076) ***(P-26246)***
Granite Rock Co (PA).....D.....831 768-2000
350 Technology Dr Watsonville (95076) ***(P-1054)***
Granite Rock Co.....C.....831 768-2330
1900 Quarry Rd Aromas (95004) ***(P-1727)***
Granite Rock Co.....C.....831 392-3780
End Of Quarry Rd Aromas (95004) ***(P-6688)***
Granite Rock Co.....D.....831 768-2300
Quarry Rd Aromas (95004) ***(P-1055)***
Granite Rock Co.....B.....650 869-3370
355 Blomquist St Redwood City (94063) ***(P-1728)***
Granite Solutions Groupe Inc.....C.....415 963-3999
235 Montgomery St Ste 430 San Francisco (94104) ***(P-14295)***
Granlbakken Ski Racquet Resort, Tahoe City *Also called Granlibakken Management Co Ltd* ***(P-12307)***
Granlibakken Management Co Ltd.....D.....800 543-3221
725 Granlibakken Rd Tahoe City (96145) ***(P-12307)***
Granlund Candies, Yucaipa *Also called B B G Management Group* ***(P-8338)***
Grant & Weber (PA).....D.....818 878-7700
26610 Agoura Rd Ste 209 Calabasas (91302) ***(P-13683)***
Grant & Weber Travel, Calabasas *Also called Grant & Weber* ***(P-13683)***
Grant Construction Inc.....C.....661 588-4586
7702 Meany Ave Ste 103 Bakersfield (93308) ***(P-2936)***
Grant Thornton LLP.....D.....415 986-3900
101 California St # 2700 San Francisco (94111) ***(P-25598)***
Grant Thornton LLP.....E.....213 627-1717
1000 Wilshire Blvd # 300 Los Angeles (90017) ***(P-25599)***
Grant Thornton LLP.....E.....408 275-9000
10 Almaden Blvd Ste 800 San Jose (95113) ***(P-25600)***
Grant Thornton LLP.....D.....213 627-1717
515 S Flower St Ste 700 Los Angeles (90071) ***(P-25601)***
Grant Thornton LLP.....C.....858 704-8000
12220 El Camino Real San Diego (92130) ***(P-25602)***
Grant-Cuesta Nursing Center, Mountain View *Also called Covenant Care California LLC* ***(P-20822)***
Grants Custom Cabinets.....C.....805 466-9680
7310 Kingsbury Rd Templeton (93465) ***(P-1133)***
Grants Landscape Services Inc.....D.....714 444-1903
3046 Orange Ave Santa Ana (92707) ***(P-818)***
Granville Cafe, Glendale *Also called Granville Glendale Inc* ***(P-26247)***
Granville Glendale Inc.....D.....818 550-0472
807 Americana Way Glendale (91210) ***(P-26247)***
Granville Homes Inc.....D.....559 268-2000
1396 W Herndon Ave # 101 Fresno (93711) ***(P-1134)***
Granville Hotel Corp.....C.....562 863-5555
13111 Sycamore Dr Norwalk (90650) ***(P-12308)***
Graphic Orb Inc.....D.....310 967-2350
8687 Melrose Ave Ste 8 West Hollywood (90069) ***(P-26626)***
Grappa Software Inc.....D.....925 818-4760
1470 Civic Ct Ste 309 Concord (94520) ***(P-14843)***
Grass Valley LLC.....D.....530 272-1055
150 Sutton Way Ofc Grass Valley (95945) ***(P-23941)***
Grasshopper House LLC.....C.....310 589-2880
6428 Meadows Ct Malibu (90265) ***(P-23247)***
Gray Line of San Francisco, San Francisco *Also called San Frncisco Incoming Svcs LLC* ***(P-4862)***
Graybar Electric Company Inc.....C.....909 451-4300
1370 Valley Vista Dr # 100 Diamond Bar (91765) ***(P-7151)***
Graybar Electric Company Inc.....D.....925 557-3000
3089 Whipple Rd Union City (94587) ***(P-7152)***
Graybill Medical Group Inc (PA).....C.....866 228-2236
332 S Juniper St Ste 100 Escondido (92025) ***(P-19001)***
Graycon Inc.....E.....626 961-9640
232 S 8th Ave City of Industry (91746) ***(P-2147)***
Grayline of San Francisco, San Francisco *Also called Blue Bus Tours LLC* ***(P-18636)***
Graymeta Inc.....E.....855 202-2270
350 Via Las Brisas # 230 Newbury Park (91320) ***(P-16020)***
Graypay LLC.....D.....818 387-6735
6345 Balboa Blvd Ste 115 Encino (91316) ***(P-15340)***
Grayson Service Inc.....C.....661 589-5444
1845 Greeley Rd Bakersfield (93314) ***(P-1023)***
Grc Electric Inc.....D.....818 242-9891
675 S Glenwood Pl Burbank (91506) ***(P-2502)***
Great Amercn Seafood Import Co, Carson *Also called Southwind Foods LLC* ***(P-8391)***
Great American Insurance Co.....D.....323 937-8600
5750 Wilshire Blvd 360 Los Angeles (90036) ***(P-10093)***
Great American Insurance Co.....C.....213 430-4300
725 S Figueroa St # 3400 Los Angeles (90017) ***(P-10094)***
Great American Music Hall.....E.....415 885-0750
859 Ofarrell St San Francisco (94109) ***(P-17912)***
Great Amrcn Logistics Dist Inc.....D.....800 381-4527
13565 Larwin Cir Santa Fe Springs (90670) ***(P-4209)***
Great Destinations Inc.....D.....949 667-9401
25510 Commercentre Dr Lake Forest (92630) ***(P-26627)***
Great Lakes E & I/ Inquip JV.....D.....805 687-2007
6558 Lonetree Blvd Rocklin (95765) ***(P-1967)***
Great Scott Tree Service Inc (PA).....C.....714 826-1750
10761 Court Ave Stanton (90680) ***(P-940)***
Great Western Bancorp Inc.....B.....213 622-1895
706 S Hill St Los Angeles (90014) ***(P-9209)***
Great Western Distributing Svc, Los Angeles *Also called Gils Distributing Service* ***(P-13651)***
Great Western Hotels Corp.....E.....760 446-6543
1050 N Norma St Ridgecrest (93555) ***(P-12309)***
Great Wstn Cnvlescent Hosp Inc.....C.....818 248-6856
2635 Honolulu Ave Montrose (91020) ***(P-20584)***
Greater Alarm Company Inc (HQ).....D.....949 474-0555
3750 Schaufele Ave # 200 Long Beach (90808) ***(P-16522)***
Greater Bay Area Cncer Rgistry, Fremont *Also called Cancer Prevention Inst Cal* ***(P-25977)***
GREATER EL MONTE COMMUNITY HOSPITAL, El Monte *Also called Ahm Gemch Inc* ***(P-20736)***
Greater Los Ang (PA).....D.....213 413-4400
2333 Scout Way Los Angeles (90026) ***(P-24558)***
Greater Los Angeles Agency.....D.....323 478-8000
2239 Norwalk Ave Los Angeles (90041) ***(P-23248)***
Greater Los Angeles Zoo Assn.....D.....323 644-4200
5333 Zoo Dr Los Angeles (90027) ***(P-24177)***
Greater Sacramento Sur.....D.....916 929-7229
2288 Auburn Blvd Ste 201 Sacramento (95821) ***(P-22034)***
Greater Sacramento Surgery Ctr, Sacramento *Also called Greater Sacramento Sur* ***(P-22034)***
Greater San Diego AC Co Inc.....C.....619 469-7818
3883 Ruffin Rd Ste C San Diego (92123) ***(P-2148)***
Greater South Bay Area HM Hlth.....E.....310 329-4835
18726 S Wstn Ave Ste 409 Gardena (90248) ***(P-21754)***
Greater South Bay Home Health, Gardena *Also called Greater South Bay Area HM Hlth* ***(P-21754)***
Greater Vallejo Recreation Dst.....C.....707 648-4600
395 Amador St Vallejo (94590) ***(P-18703)***
Greater Valley Medical Group (PA).....B.....818 838-4500
11600 Indian Hills Rd # 300 Mission Hills (91345) ***(P-22035)***
Greatwide Dedicated Transport, Vernon *Also called Greatwide Logistics Svcs LLC* ***(P-4961)***
Greatwide Logistics Svcs LLC.....D.....323 268-7100
4310 Bandini Blvd Vernon (90058) ***(P-4961)***

ALPHABETIC

Employee Codes: A=Over 500 employees, B=251-500
C=101-250, D=51-100, E=50
2020 Directory of California
Wholesalers and Services Companies
© Mergent Inc. 1-800-342-5647
1285

Gree International Inc.....C.....415 409-5200
275 Battery St Ste 1700 San Francisco (94111) ***(P-14844)***
Gree International Entrmt Inc.....C.....415 409-5200
185 Berry St Ste 590 San Francisco (94107) ***(P-14845)***
Green Acres Lodge, Rosemead *Also called Longwood Management Corp* ***(P-20090)***
Green Acres Nursery & Sup LLC.....D.....916 782-2273
604 Sutter St Folsom (95630) ***(P-7500)***
Green Again Ldscpg & Con Inc.....D.....650 368-9304
851 Charter St Redwood City (94063) ***(P-819)***
Green Bits Inc.....D.....408 596-3341
75 E Santa Clara St # 93 San Jose (95113) ***(P-15603)***
Green Convergence (PA).....D.....661 294-9495
28490 Wstnghuse Pl Ste 16 Valencia (91355) ***(P-7428)***
Green Diamond Resource Company.....D.....707 668-4400
900 Riverside Rd Korbel (95550) ***(P-958)***
Green Dot Corporation (PA).....D.....626 765-2000
3465 E Foothill Blvd # 100 Pasadena (91107) ***(P-9461)***
Green Energy Innovations, Santa Fe Springs *Also called Sfadia Inc* ***(P-2641)***
Green Equity Investors III L P.....A.....310 954-0444
11111 Santa Monica Blvd # 2000 Los Angeles (90025) ***(P-11917)***
Green Equity Investors IV LP (PA).....A.....310 954-0444
11111 Santa Monica Blvd Los Angeles (90025) ***(P-11918)***
Green Farms Inc.....B.....858 831-7701
2652 Long Beach Ave Los Angeles (90058) ***(P-8484)***
Green Farms California LLC (PA).....C.....213 747-4411
2652 Long Beach Ave Ste 2 Los Angeles (90058) ***(P-8485)***
Green Glusk Field Clama & Mach.....C.....310 553-3610
1900 Avenue Of The Stars 21f Los Angeles (90067) ***(P-22548)***
Green Guard Services Inc.....D.....619 488-1065
611 Rock Springs Rd Escondido (92025) ***(P-13943)***
Green Hasson & Janks LLP.....C.....310 873-1600
10990 Wilshire Blvd Fl 16 Los Angeles (90024) ***(P-25603)***
Green Hills Retirement Center, Millbrae *Also called Hillsdale Group LP* ***(P-20595)***
Green Hills Software LLC (HQ).....C.....805 965-6044
30 W Sola St Santa Barbara (93101) ***(P-15341)***
Green Planet 21 Inc (PA).....E.....510 873-8777
336 Adeline St Oakland (94607) ***(P-7760)***
Green Ridge Services LLC.....D.....925 245-5500
6185 Industrial Way Livermore (94551) ***(P-5843)***
Green River Golf Corporation.....D.....714 970-8411
5215 Green River Rd Corona (92880) ***(P-18250)***
Green River Golf Course, Corona *Also called Green River Golf Corporation* ***(P-18250)***
Green Scene Landscape Inc.....D.....818 280-0420
21220 Devonshire St # 102 Chatsworth (91311) ***(P-820)***
Green Thumb International Inc.....D.....818 340-6400
21812 Sherman Way Canoga Park (91303) ***(P-8894)***
Green Thumb Nursery, Canoga Park *Also called Super Garden Centers Inc* ***(P-8924)***
Green Thumb Produce Inc.....C.....951 849-4711
2648 W Ramsey St Banning (92220) ***(P-8486)***
Green Tortoise Adventure Trvl.....D.....415 834-1000
494 Broadway San Francisco (94133) ***(P-3776)***
Green Tree Capital LP.....D.....760 245-3461
14173 Green Tree Blvd Victorville (92395) ***(P-12310)***
Green Tree Inn, Victorville *Also called Lee-Victorville Hotel Corp* ***(P-12546)***
Green Tree Inn, Victorville *Also called Green Tree Capital LP* ***(P-12310)***
Green Tree Nursery.....E.....209 874-9100
23979 Lake Rd La Grange (95329) ***(P-8895)***
Green Trucking, Tulare *Also called Darrell L Green Inc* ***(P-4203)***
Green Valley Corporation (PA).....E.....408 287-0246
777 N 1st St Fl 5 San Jose (95112) ***(P-1486)***
Green Valley Country Club.....D.....707 864-1101
35 Country Club Dr Fairfield (94534) ***(P-18463)***
Green Valley Security Inc.....D.....916 797-4058
6049 Douglas Blvd Ste 28 Granite Bay (95746) ***(P-16291)***
Green Valley Trnsp Corp.....E.....209 836-5192
30131 Highway 33 Tracy (95304) ***(P-4055)***
Green Wave Ingredients Inc.....E.....562 207-9770
14821 Northam St La Mirada (90638) ***(P-7947)***
Greenall, Suisun City *Also called E B Stone & Son Inc* ***(P-8839)***
Greenball Corp (PA).....E.....714 782-3060
222 S Harbor Blvd Ste 700 Anaheim (92805) ***(P-6487)***
Greenberg Inc (PA).....D.....510 446-8200
1250 53rd St Ste 5 Emeryville (94608) ***(P-25904)***
Greenberg Traurig LLP.....D.....415 655-1300
4 Embarcadero Ctr # 3000 San Francisco (94111) ***(P-22549)***
Greenberg Traurig LLP.....D.....310 586-7708
1840 Century Park E # 1900 Los Angeles (90067) ***(P-22550)***
Greenberg Traurig LLP.....D.....650 328-8500
1900 University Ave Fl 5 East Palo Alto (94303) ***(P-22551)***
Greenberg Traurig LLP.....D.....949 732-6500
3161 Michelson Dr # 1000 Irvine (92612) ***(P-22552)***
Greenbrea Care Center, Greenbrae *Also called Ocadian Care Centers LLC* ***(P-20170)***
Greenbriar Homes Communities.....D.....510 497-8200
4340 Stevens Creek Blvd # 240 San Jose (95129) ***(P-1297)***
Greenbriar Homes Community, Fremont *Also called Greenbriar Management Company* ***(P-11175)***
Greenbriar Management Company.....D.....510 497-8200
43160 Osgood Rd Fremont (94539) ***(P-11175)***
Greenbrier Lawn Tree Exprt Co.....D.....619 469-8720
3616 Bancroft Dr Spring Valley (91977) ***(P-821)***
Greencycle US Holding Inc.....D.....858 677-0884
4686 Mercury St San Diego (92111) ***(P-11668)***
Greene Rdvsky Maloney Share LP.....D.....415 981-1400
4 Embarcadero Ctr # 4000 San Francisco (94111) ***(P-22553)***
Greenheart Farms Inc (PA).....D.....805 481-2234
902 Zenon Way Arroyo Grande (93420) ***(P-324)***
Greenland US Consulting Inc.....D.....213 362-9300
515 S Figueroa St # 1703 Los Angeles (90071) ***(P-1298)***
Greenlaw Grupe Jr Operating Co, Angels Camp *Also called Motherlode Investors LLC* ***(P-18274)***
Greenleaf Paper Products.....D.....949 348-0048
26431 Crown Valley Pkwy # 150 Mission Viejo (92691) ***(P-7882)***
Greenleaf Produce, Brisbane *Also called Oakville Produce Partners LLC* ***(P-8504)***
Greenpath Recovery Recycl Svcs, Colton *Also called Greenpath Recovery West Inc* ***(P-7761)***
Greenpath Recovery West Inc.....D.....909 954-0686
330 W Citrus St Ste 250 Colton (92324) ***(P-7761)***
Greenridge Senior Care.....C.....510 758-9600
2150 Pyramid Dr El Sobrante (94803) ***(P-23942)***
Greens Group Inc.....C.....949 829-4902
9289 Research Dr Irvine (92618) ***(P-12311)***
Greensoft Technology Inc.....C.....323 254-5961
155 S El Molino Ave # 100 Pasadena (91101) ***(P-15771)***
Greenspire LLC.....E.....310 477-7686
3130 Wilshire Blvd # 200 Santa Monica (90403) ***(P-26628)***
Greenspire Construction, Santa Monica *Also called Greenspire LLC* ***(P-26628)***
Greenteam of San Jose, San Jose *Also called Waste Connections Cal Inc* ***(P-6317)***
Greentree Property MGT Inc.....E.....415 347-8600
1 Bush St Fl 9 San Francisco (94104) ***(P-10600)***
Greenwalds Autobody Frameworks (PA).....D.....619 477-2600
1814 Roosevelt Ave National City (91950) ***(P-17293)***
Greenwaste Recovery Inc.....E.....408 283-4804
565 Charles St San Jose (95112) ***(P-6210)***
Greenwaste Recovery Inc (PA).....D.....408 283-4800
1500 Berger Dr Watsonville (95077) ***(P-6211)***
Greenway Arts Alliance Inc.....D.....323 655-7679
544 N Fairfax Ave Los Angeles (90036) ***(P-17913)***
Greenwood Holdings LLC.....D.....619 299-6633
3888 Greenwood St San Diego (92110) ***(P-12312)***
Grefco Dicaperl, Torrance *Also called Dicaperl Corporation* ***(P-1065)***
Greg H Carpenter Concrete Inc.....E.....209 367-4224
955 N Guild Ave Lodi (95240) ***(P-3155)***
Grega Brooke Sra.....E.....707 938-3362
18501 Riverside Dr Sonoma (95476) ***(P-11176)***
Gregg Dilling and Testing, Martinez *Also called Gregg Drilling & Testing Inc* ***(P-3244)***
Gregg Drilling LLC (PA).....D.....562 427-6899
2726 Walnut Ave Signal Hill (90755) ***(P-3242)***
Gregg Drilling LLC.....D.....925 313-5800
950 Howe Rd Martinez (94553) ***(P-3243)***
Gregg Drilling & Testing Inc.....D.....925 313-5800
950 Howe Rd Martinez (94553) ***(P-3244)***
Gregg Drilling & Testing Inc (PA).....D.....562 427-6899
2726 Walnut Ave Signal Hill (90755) ***(P-3414)***
Gregg Electric Inc.....C.....909 983-1794
608 W Emporia St Ontario (91762) ***(P-2503)***
Greka Inc.....C.....805 347-8700
1791 Sinton Rd Santa Maria (93458) ***(P-973)***
Greka Integrated Inc (PA).....C.....805 347-8700
1700 Sinton Rd Santa Maria (93458) ***(P-1004)***
Greka Oil & Gas, Santa Maria *Also called Hvi Cat Canyon Inc* ***(P-1028)***
Gresham Savage Nolan & Tilden (PA).....D.....619 794-0050
550 E Hospitality Ln # 300 San Bernardino (92408) ***(P-22554)***
Grey Direct-E Marketing, San Francisco *Also called G2 Direct and Digital* ***(P-14825)***
Greybor Medical Transportation.....E.....213 250-4444
119 Belmont Ave Ste 107 Los Angeles (90026) ***(P-3682)***
Greyhound Lines Inc.....C.....559 268-1829
1033 Broadway St Fresno (93721) ***(P-3759)***
Greyhound Lines Inc.....B.....213 629-8400
1716 E 7th St Los Angeles (90021) ***(P-3831)***
Greyhound Lines Inc.....E.....209 466-3568
121 S Center St Stockton (95202) ***(P-4721)***
Greystar Management Svcs LP.....B.....818 596-2180
6320 Canoga Ave Ste 1512 Woodland Hills (91367) ***(P-11177)***
Greystar Management Svcs LP.....A.....949 705-0010
620 Nwport Ctr Dr Fl 15 Flr 15 Newport Beach (92660) ***(P-11178)***
Greystone Homes Inc.....C.....925 242-0811
6121 Bollinger Canyon Rd # 500 San Ramon (94583) ***(P-1135)***
Greystone Plastering Inc.....D.....408 298-5934
1716 Stone Ave Ste B San Jose (95125) ***(P-2792)***
Greystripe Incorporated.....C.....415 644-1702
30699 Russell Ranch Rd # 250 Westlake Village (91362) ***(P-13513)***
Grht Inc.....D.....323 873-6393
14818 Raymer St Van Nuys (91405) ***(P-8977)***
Gridgain Systems Inc (PA).....D.....650 241-2281
1065 E Hillsdale Blvd Foster City (94404) ***(P-15342)***
Gridley Packing Inc.....C.....530 846-3753
1366 Larkin Rd Gridley (95948) ***(P-494)***
Griffin Group LLC (PA).....C.....415 892-4569
4 Rebelo Ln Ste D Novato (94947) ***(P-26248)***
Griffin Slr Management Inc.....D.....310 270-4031
9454 Wilshire Blvd # 700 Beverly Hills (90212) ***(P-26249)***
Griffin Technology LLC (HQ).....D.....949 250-4929
3347 Michelson Dr Ste 100 Irvine (92612) ***(P-7274)***
Griffith Company (PA).....D.....714 984-5500
3050 E Birch St Brea (92821) ***(P-1729)***
Griffith Company.....D.....562 929-1128
12200 Bloomfield Ave Santa Fe Springs (90670) ***(P-1730)***
Griffith Park Healthcare Ctr, Glendale *Also called Griffith Pk Rhbltation Ctr LLC* ***(P-19985)***
Griffith Pk Rhbltation Ctr LLC.....D.....818 845-8507
201 Allen Ave Glendale (91201) ***(P-19985)***
Grifols Biologicals LLC.....B.....323 255-2221
2410 Lillyvale Ave Los Angeles (90032) ***(P-4423)***
Grifols Diagnstc Solutions Inc (HQ).....C.....323 225-2221
2410 Lillyvale Ave Los Angeles (90032) ***(P-21539)***
Grifols Shared Svcs N Amer Inc (HQ).....C.....323 225-2221
2410 Lillyvale Ave Los Angeles (90032) ***(P-7948)***

Mergent e-mail: customerrelations@mergent.com
1286
2020 Directory of California
Wholesalers and Services Companies
(P-0000) Products & Services Section entry number
(PA)=Parent Co (HQ)=Headquarters (DH)=Div Headquarters

Grifols Worldwide Operations ....D....626 435-2600
13111 Temple Ave City of Industry (91746) ***(P-4565)***
Grill On The Alley The Inc ....A....323 856-5530
6801 Hollywood Blvd Los Angeles (90028) ***(P-16812)***
Grill Recording Studio ....D....510 531-4351
4770 San Pablo Ave Ste C Emeryville (94608) ***(P-16813)***
Grimmway Enterprises Inc ....D....661 854-6240
12020 Malaga Rd Arvin (93203) ***(P-1350)***
Grimmway Enterprises Inc ....C....760 344-0204
2171 W Bannister Rd Brawley (92227) ***(P-17332)***
Grimmway Enterprises Inc ....C....661 393-3320
6101 S Zerker Rd Shafter (93263) ***(P-495)***
Grimmway Enterprises Inc ....B....661 854-6250
830 Sycamore Rd Arvin (93203) ***(P-496)***
Grimmway Enterprises Inc ....D....661 854-6200
11412 Malaga Rd Arvin (93203) ***(P-497)***
Grimmway Enterprises Inc ....C....661 845-5200
6900 Mountain View Rd Bakersfield (93307) ***(P-498)***
Grimmway Enterprises Inc ....B....661 399-0844
6301 S Zerker Rd Shafter (93263) ***(P-325)***
Grimmway Enterprises Inc ....B....661 845-3758
12000 Main St Lamont (93241) ***(P-8487)***
Grimmway Farms, Arvin *Also called Grimmway Enterprises Inc* ***(P-497)***
Grimmway Farms, Bakersfield *Also called Grimmway Enterprises Inc* ***(P-498)***
Grimmway Farms ....D....760 356-2513
2105 Anderholt Rd Holtville (92250) ***(P-326)***
Grimmway Frozen Foods, Arvin *Also called Grimmway Enterprises Inc* ***(P-496)***
Gringteam Inc ....C....858 485-4145
14455 Penasquitos Dr San Diego (92129) ***(P-12313)***
Gringteam Inc ....B....408 453-4000
2050 Gateway Pl San Jose (95110) ***(P-12314)***
Gringteam Inc ....C....661 426-7919
3100 Camino Del Rio Ct Bakersfield (93308) ***(P-12315)***
Gringteam Inc ....C....714 825-3333
201 E Macarthur Blvd Santa Ana (92707) ***(P-12316)***
Gringteam Inc ....B....916 929-8855
2001 Point West Way Sacramento (95815) ***(P-12317)***
Gringteam Inc ....B....209 526-6000
1150 9th St Frnt Modesto (95354) ***(P-12318)***
Gringteam Inc ....B....619 297-5466
7450 Hazard Center Dr San Diego (92108) ***(P-12319)***
Gringteam Inc ....C....650 344-5500
835 Airport Blvd Burlingame (94010) ***(P-12320)***
Gringteam Inc ....D....949 661-1100
34402 Pacific Coast Hwy Dana Point (92624) ***(P-12321)***
Grio, San Francisco *Also called Bitalign Inc* ***(P-14678)***
Gripp, Temecula *Also called Bbk Performance Inc* ***(P-6425)***
Griswald Industries, Perris *Also called Griswold Industries* ***(P-7636)***
Griswold Industries ....D....951 657-1718
24100 Water Ave Perris (92570) ***(P-7636)***
Grisworld Real Estate MGT (PA) ....D....858 597-6100
5703 Oberlin Dr Ste 300 San Diego (92121) ***(P-11179)***
Grizzard Cmmncations Group Inc ....D....818 543-1315
2 N Lake Ave Pasadena (91101) ***(P-13514)***
Grm Information MGT Services ....E....562 373-9000
8500 Mercury Ln Pico Rivera (90660) ***(P-26250)***
Grm Information MGT Svcs Inc ....D....562 373-9000
8500 Mercury Ln Pico Rivera (90660) ***(P-26251)***
Grobstein Horwath & Co ....D....818 501-5200
15233 Ventura Blvd Fl 9 Van Nuys (91403) ***(P-25604)***
Grobstein, Horwath & Company, Van Nuys *Also called Grobstein Horwath & Co* ***(P-25604)***
Grocers Specialty Company (HQ) ....E....323 264-5200
5200 Sheila St Commerce (90040) ***(P-8179)***
Grolink Plant Company Inc (PA) ....C....805 984-7958
4107 W Gonzales Rd Oxnard (93036) ***(P-8896)***
Gross Convalescent Hospital ....D....209 334-3760
321 W Turner Rd Lodi (95240) ***(P-19986)***
Grosslight Insurance Inc ....D....310 473-9611
1333 Westwood Blvd Los Angeles (90024) ***(P-10373)***
Grossmont Center Management, La Mesa *Also called Grossmont Shopping Center Co* ***(P-10601)***
Grossmont Grdns Rtrement Cmnty, La Mesa *Also called Healthcare Group* ***(P-23953)***
Grossmont Home Hlth & Hospice, La Mesa *Also called Grossmont Hospital Corporation* ***(P-20896)***
Grossmont Hospital Corporation (HQ) ....A....619 740-6000
5555 Grossmont Center Dr La Mesa (91942) ***(P-19002)***
Grossmont Hospital Corporation ....C....619 667-1900
8881 Fletcher Pkwy # 105 La Mesa (91942) ***(P-20896)***
Grossmont Shopping Center Co ....D....619 465-2900
5500 Grsmnt Ctr Dr # 213 La Mesa (91942) ***(P-10601)***
Grossmont-Cuyamaca Community ....D....619 644-7684
8800 Grossmont College Dr El Cajon (92020) ***(P-24559)***
Grosvenor Properties Ltd ....C....650 873-3200
380 S Airport Blvd South San Francisco (94080) ***(P-12322)***
Grosvenor Visalia Associates ....D....559 651-5000
9000 W Airport Dr Visalia (93277) ***(P-12323)***
Ground Maintenance Services, Thousand Oaks *Also called Kevin Persons Inc* ***(P-736)***
Groundwork Open Source Inc ....D....415 992-4500
23332 Mill Creek Dr # 155 Laguna Hills (92653) ***(P-15865)***
Groundworks Inc ....D....925 513-0300
2145 Elkins Way Ste C Brentwood (94513) ***(P-3156)***
Group Avantica Inc ....B....650 248-9678
2680 Bayshore Pkwy # 416 Mountain View (94043) ***(P-14846)***
Group Delphi, Alameda *Also called Delphi Productions Inc* ***(P-13493)***
Groupe Development Associates ....D....209 473-6000
3255 W March Ln Fl 4 Stockton (95219) ***(P-11566)***
Groupware Technology Inc (PA) ....E....408 540-0090
541 Division St Campbell (95008) ***(P-15604)***
Grove - Design District, The, San Francisco *Also called Ps24 Inc* ***(P-26369)***
Grove Lumber & Bldg Sups Inc (PA) ....C....909 947-0277
1300 S Campus Ave Ontario (91761) ***(P-6620)***
Grover Landscape Services Inc ....D....209 545-4401
6224 Stoddard Rd Modesto (95356) ***(P-246)***
Grow Brains System Inc ....E....310 428-6445
2324 Ocean Park Blvd D Santa Monica (90405) ***(P-7733)***
Grower Direct Nut Company Inc ....E....209 883-4890
2288 Geer Rd Hughson (95326) ***(P-499)***
Growers Company Inc ....D....831 424-3850
21570 Potter Rd Salinas (93908) ***(P-14296)***
Growers Express LLC (PA) ....C....831 757-9951
150 Main St Ste 210 Salinas (93901) ***(P-8488)***
Growers Street Cooling LLC ....D....831 424-2929
1080 Growers St Salinas (93901) ***(P-500)***
Growers Transplanting Inc (HQ) ....D....831 449-3440
360 Espinosa Rd Salinas (93907) ***(P-292)***
Growing Company Inc ....D....916 379-9088
4 Wayne Ct Ste 3 Sacramento (95829) ***(P-822)***
Growith Inc ....D....805 650-6650
1069 Camero Way Fremont (94539) ***(P-17502)***
Grubb Co Inc ....D....510 339-0400
1960 Mountain Blvd Oakland (94611) ***(P-11180)***
Gruen Assoc Archtects Planners, Los Angeles *Also called Gruen Associates* ***(P-25443)***
Gruen Associates ....D....323 937-4270
6330 San Vicente Blvd # 200 Los Angeles (90048) ***(P-25443)***
Grupe Company (PA) ....D....209 473-6000
3255 W March Ln Ste 400 Stockton (95219) ***(P-11181)***
Grupe Dev Companynorthern Cal ....D....209 473-6000
3255 W March Ln Ste 400 Stockton (95219) ***(P-1299)***
Grupe Properties Co ....E....209 956-7885
2944 W Swain Rd Stockton (95219) ***(P-4424)***
Grupoex, La Mirada *Also called Mejico Express Inc* ***(P-4723)***
Gryphon Marine LLC ....E....619 407-4010
694 Moss St Chula Vista (91911) ***(P-25111)***
Gs Brothers Inc (PA) ....C....310 833-1369
2215 N Gaffey St San Pedro (90731) ***(P-823)***
Gs Foods Group ....B....310 806-9780
11755 Wilshire Blvd # 14 Los Angeles (90025) ***(P-11669)***
GS Levine Insurance Svcs Inc ....D....858 481-8692
10505 Sorrento Valley Rd # 200 San Diego (92121) ***(P-10374)***
Gs1 Group Inc ....D....626 510-6384
70 S Lake Ave Ste 945 Pasadena (91101) ***(P-16292)***
Gsa Des Plaines LLC ....D....310 557-5100
10100 Santa Monica Blvd # 2600 Los Angeles (90067) ***(P-11919)***
Gsa Design Inc ....C....818 241-2558
4551 San Fernando Rd # 102 Glendale (91204) ***(P-16814)***
GSC Logistics Inc (PA) ....C....510 844-3700
530 Water St Fl 5 Oakland (94607) ***(P-4210)***
GSe Construction Company Inc (PA) ....C....925 447-0292
6950 Preston Ave Livermore (94551) ***(P-1860)***
Gsg Associates Inc ....D....626 585-1808
1010 E Union St Ste 203 Pasadena (91106) ***(P-26252)***
Gsico, Foothill Ranch *Also called Global Solutions Integration* ***(P-25108)***
Gt Diamond, Irvine *Also called General Tool Inc* ***(P-7635)***
Gt Nexus Inc (HQ) ....D....510 808-2222
1111 Broadway 5f Oakland (94607) ***(P-14847)***
GTE, Santa Monica *Also called Verizon Communications Inc* ***(P-5490)***
GTS, Chico *Also called Gas Transmission Systems Inc* ***(P-25093)***
Gtt Communications (mp) Inc (HQ) ....C....925 201-2500
6700 Koll Center Pkwy Pleasanton (94566) ***(P-5415)***
Gtxcel Inc ....D....800 609-8994
2855 Telg Ave Ste 600 Berkeley (94705) ***(P-14848)***
Guarachi Wine Partners Inc ....D....818 225-5100
22837 Ventura Blvd # 300 Woodland Hills (91364) ***(P-8811)***
Guarantee Real Estate ....E....559 650-6030
756 W Shaw Ave Ste 105 Fresno (93704) ***(P-11182)***
Guarantee Real Estate Corp ....D....559 321-6040
180 W Bullard Ave Ste 101 Clovis (93612) ***(P-11183)***
Guaranteed Rate Inc ....C....760 310-6008
1455 Frazee Rd Ste 500 San Diego (92108) ***(P-9556)***
Guard Force Inc ....E....951 233-0206
6135 Tam O Shanter Dr 2 Stockton (95210) ***(P-16523)***
Guard Force International, Stockton *Also called Guard Force Inc* ***(P-16523)***
Guard Management Inc ....A....858 279-8282
8001 Vickers St San Diego (92111) ***(P-16293)***
Guard Systems District 1, Monterey Park *Also called Guard-Systems Inc* ***(P-16295)***
Guard-Systems Inc ....B....909 947-5400
1910 S Archibald Ave M2 Ontario (91761) ***(P-16294)***
Guard-Systems Inc ....B....323 881-6715
1190 Monterey Pass Rd Monterey Park (91754) ***(P-16295)***
Guardant Health Inc (PA) ....B....855 698-8887
505 Penobscot Dr Redwood City (94063) ***(P-21540)***
Guardco Security Services ....D....209 723-4273
1360 W 18th St Merced (95340) ***(P-16296)***
Guardian Computer Support ....C....925 251-8800
7075 Commerce Cir Ste D Pleasanton (94588) ***(P-15920)***
Guardian Eagle Security Inc ....B....888 990-0002
11400 W Olympic Blvd Fl 2 Los Angeles (90064) ***(P-16297)***
Guardian General Insur Svcs, Glendale *Also called Ggis Insurance Services Inc* ***(P-10371)***
Guardian Health Care Services ....D....714 375-1110
16541 Gothard St Ste 102 Huntington Beach (92647) ***(P-22036)***
Guardian National Inc ....E....800 700-1467
20361 Prairie St Ste 1 Chatsworth (91311) ***(P-16298)***
Guardian National Security, Chatsworth *Also called Guardian National Inc* ***(P-16298)***
Guardian Rehabilitation Hosp ....D....323 930-4815
533 S Fairfax Ave Los Angeles (90036) ***(P-20585)***
Guardian Security Agency, Concord *Also called Delta Personnel Services Inc* ***(P-16257)***

Employee Codes: A=Over 500 employees, B=251-500
C=101-250, D=51-100, E=50
2020 Directory of California
Wholesalers and Services Companies
© Mergent Inc. 1-800-342-5647
1287

Guardians of The Los Angeles......D......310 479-2468
10780 Santa Monica Blvd # 225 Los Angeles (90025) ***(P-19987)***
Guardnow Inc (PA)......E......877 482-7366
18663 Ventura Blvd # 217 Tarzana (91356) ***(P-16299)***
Guardsmark LLC......B......925 484-4412
4713 1st St Ste 215 Pleasanton (94566) ***(P-16300)***
Guardsmark LLC......D......310 522-9603
1225 W 190th St Ste 280 Gardena (90248) ***(P-16301)***
Guardsmark LLC......C......310 287-3103
3000 S Robertson Blvd # 150 Los Angeles (90034) ***(P-16302)***
Guardsmark LLC (HQ)......C......714 619-9700
1551 N Tustin Ave Ste 650 Santa Ana (92705) ***(P-16303)***
Guardsmark LLC......B......415 956-6070
350 Sansome St San Francisco (94104) ***(P-16304)***
Guardsmark LLC......C......818 841-0288
3701 Wilshire Blvd Los Angeles (90010) ***(P-16305)***
Guardsmark LLC......C......510 562-7606
100 Hegenberger Rd # 130 Oakland (94621) ***(P-16306)***
Guardsmark LLC......C......800 238-5878
4970 El Camino Real Los Altos (94022) ***(P-16307)***
Guardsmark LLC......C......661 325-5906
5300 Lennox Ave Ste 102 Bakersfield (93309) ***(P-16308)***
Guardsmark LLC......C......858 499-0025
5095 Murphy Canyon Rd # 301 San Diego (92123) ***(P-16309)***
Guardsmark LLC......C......559 243-1217
600 W Shaw Ave Ste 200 Fresno (93704) ***(P-16310)***
Guardsmark LLC......C......818 841-0288
1200 Wilshire Blvd # 620 Los Angeles (90017) ***(P-16311)***
Guardsmark LLC......C......831 769-8981
30 E San Joaquin St # 204 Salinas (93901) ***(P-16312)***
Guardsmark LLC......C......650 685-2400
533 Airport Blvd Ste 303 Burlingame (94010) ***(P-16313)***
Guardsmark LLC......C......650 652-9130
1601 Bayshore Hwy Ste 350 Burlingame (94010) ***(P-16314)***
Guardsmark LLC......C......818 841-0288
101 S 1st St Ste 408 Burbank (91502) ***(P-16315)***
Guardsmark LLC......B......909 989-5345
2900 Adams St Ste C10a Riverside (92504) ***(P-16316)***
Guava Holdings LLC......E......530 671-0550
1220 Plumas St Yuba City (95991) ***(P-21475)***
Guavus Inc (HQ)......D......650 243-3400
2125 Zanker Rd San Jose (95131) ***(P-15343)***
Guck Ariba......C......650 390-1445
807 Eleventh Ave Sunnyvale (94089) ***(P-15344)***
Gudgel Roofing Inc......E......916 387-6900
5321 84th St Sacramento (95826) ***(P-3060)***
Guerra Nut Shelling Company......D......831 637-4471
190 Hillcrest Rd Hollister (95023) ***(P-501)***
Guesty Inc......C......415 244-0277
340 S Lemon Ave Walnut (91789) ***(P-12324)***
GUGGENHEIM INVESTMENTS, Los Angeles *Also called Fox BSB Holdco Inc* ***(P-18062)***
Guidance Center (PA)......C......562 595-1159
1301 Pine Ave Long Beach (90813) ***(P-22037)***
Guidance Software Inc (HQ)......C......626 229-9191
1055 E Colo Blvd Ste 400 Pasadena (91106) ***(P-15345)***
Guidance Solutions Inc......E......310 754-4000
4134 Del Rey Ave Marina Del Rey (90292) ***(P-15866)***
Guide Dogs For Blind Inc (PA)......C......415 499-4000
350 Los Ranchitos Rd San Rafael (94903) ***(P-603)***
Guidebook Inc (PA)......D......650 319-7233
340 Bryant St Ste 400 San Francisco (94107) ***(P-14849)***
Guided Discoveries Inc......E......951 659-6062
26800 Saunders Meadows Rd Idyllwild (92549) ***(P-13148)***
Guidewire Software Inc (PA)......C......650 357-9100
2850 S Del St Ste 400 San Mateo (94403) ***(P-15346)***
Guild Mortgage Company......E......916 486-6257
3626 Fair Oaks Blvd Sacramento (95864) ***(P-9557)***
Guillen Electric Company Inc......E......909 480-3915
1485 Andrew Dr Ste D Claremont (91711) ***(P-2504)***
Guinn Corporation......D......661 325-6109
6533 Rosedale Hwy Bakersfield (93308) ***(P-3317)***
Guitar Center Holdings Inc......E......818 735-8800
1508 W Casmalia St Rialto (92377) ***(P-4425)***
Guitar Center Store Wcdc, Rialto *Also called Guitar Center Holdings Inc* ***(P-4425)***
Gulf- California Broadcast Co......C......760 773-0342
31276 Dunham Way Thousand Palms (92276) ***(P-5609)***
Gulfstream Aerospace Corp GA......A......562 420-1818
4150 E Donald Douglas Dr Long Beach (90808) ***(P-25112)***
Gumbiner Savett Inc CPA......D......310 828-9798
1723 Cloverfield Blvd Santa Monica (90404) ***(P-10602)***
Gumbiner, Savett, Finkel, Fing, Santa Monica *Also called Gumbiner Savett Inc CPA* ***(P-10602)***
Gunderson Dettmer Stough Ville (PA)......C......650 321-2400
550 Allerton St Redwood City (94063) ***(P-22555)***
Gursey Schneider & Co LLC (PA)......D......310 552-0960
1888 Century Park E # 900 Los Angeles (90067) ***(P-25605)***
Guru Denim LLC (HQ)......C......323 266-3072
1888 Rosecrans Ave Manhattan Beach (90266) ***(P-8074)***
Gustine Mini Storage, Gustine *Also called Andersen Nut Company* ***(P-468)***
Gusto, San Francisco *Also called Zenpayroll Inc* ***(P-15545)***
Guthy-Renker Direct, Santa Monica *Also called Guthy-Renker LLC* ***(P-7815)***
Guthy-Renker LLC (PA)......D......760 773-9022
100 N Pacific Coast Hwy El Segundo (90245) ***(P-7814)***
Guthy-Renker LLC......D......949 454-1400
25892 Towne Centre Dr Foothill Ranch (92610) ***(P-16815)***
Guthy-Renker LLC......D......310 581-6250
3340 Ocean Park Blvd Fl 2 Santa Monica (90405) ***(P-7815)***
Guy George......E......831 728-2410
315 2nd St Ste A Watsonville (95076) ***(P-97)***
Guy Yocom Construction Inc......C......951 284-3456
10712 E Mariposa Rd Stockton (95215) ***(P-3157)***
Guy Yocom Construction Inc (PA)......C......951 284-3456
3299 Horseless Carriage R Norco (92860) ***(P-3158)***
Gva Enterprises Inc (PA)......D......213 484-0510
316 S Westlake Ave Los Angeles (90057) ***(P-20586)***
Gva Enterprises Inc......D......213 484-0784
415 S Union Ave Los Angeles (90017) ***(P-19988)***
Gvs Italy......D......424 382-4343
8616 La Tijera Blvd Los Angeles (90045) ***(P-7068)***
Gyneclgic Onclogy Plvic Srgery, Los Gatos *Also called Sutter Health* ***(P-24671)***
Gypsum Contractors Inc......E......949 340-9100
23785 El Toro Rd Ste 135 Lake Forest (92630) ***(P-2793)***
Gypsum Dry Wall Supply Co......E......408 993-9710
2049 Senter Rd San Jose (95112) ***(P-7816)***
H & D Construction, El Cajon *Also called Steve Duich Inc* ***(P-3223)***
H & D Electric......B......916 332-0794
5237 Walnut Ave Ste 100 Sacramento (95841) ***(P-2505)***
H & F Grain Farms LLC......D......805 754-4449
1181 S Wolff Rd Oxnard (93033) ***(P-27085)***
H & H Transportation LLC......D......951 817-2300
300 El Sobrante Rd Corona (92879) ***(P-4056)***
H & H Truck Terminal, Victorville *Also called Hartwick & Hand Inc* ***(P-3891)***
H & K Abouaf Corporation......D......310 393-1282
9100 S Sepulveda Blvd # 1 Los Angeles (90045) ***(P-21755)***
H & N Fish Co., Vernon *Also called H & N Foods International Inc* ***(P-8369)***
H & N Foods International Inc (HQ)......C......323 586-9300
5580 S Alameda St Vernon (90058) ***(P-8369)***
H & R Accounts Inc......D......619 819-8844
3131 Cmino Del Rio N Ste San Diego (92108) ***(P-14850)***
H & R Block, San Francisco *Also called H&R Block Inc* ***(P-13389)***
H & R Block Inc......D......805 349-9266
401 N Broadway Ste B Santa Maria (93454) ***(P-13387)***
H & R Block Inc......C......707 643-1856
4300 Sonoma Blvd Ste 600 Vallejo (94589) ***(P-13388)***
H & R Gunlund Ranches Inc......C......559 864-8186
3510 W Saginaw Ave Caruthers (93609) ***(P-133)***
H A Bowen Electric Inc......D......510 483-0500
2055 Williams St San Leandro (94577) ***(P-2506)***
H and H Drug Stores Inc......D......209 931-5200
4692 E Waterloo Rd Stockton (95215) ***(P-7817)***
H B J Corporation......D......707 333-7066
5806 Frontier Way Carmichael (95608) ***(P-2794)***
H C C S Inc......D......916 454-5752
4700 Elvas Ave Sacramento (95819) ***(P-19989)***
H C I, Norco *Also called Hci Inc* ***(P-1861)***
H C I, Corona *Also called Hardwood Creations* ***(P-2938)***
H C Olsen Cnstr Co Inc......D......626 359-8900
710 Los Angeles Ave Monrovia (91016) ***(P-1351)***
H C S, Newport Beach *Also called Healthcare Cost Solutions Inc* ***(P-25606)***
H C T Inc......B......619 224-1234
1441 Quivira Rd San Diego (92109) ***(P-12325)***
H D G Associates......C......805 963-0744
1111 E Cabrillo Blvd Santa Barbara (93103) ***(P-12326)***
H D R, Los Angeles *Also called HDR Architecture Inc* ***(P-25116)***
H D S I Managment......E......323 231-1104
3460 S Broadway Los Angeles (90007) ***(P-10603)***
H D Smith LLC......D......310 641-1885
1370 E Victoria St Carson (90746) ***(P-7949)***
H E L P Inc......D......951 922-2305
53 S 6th St Banning (92220) ***(P-23249)***
H F Cox Inc (PA)......D......661 366-3236
118 Cox Transport Way Bakersfield (93307) ***(P-4057)***
H H M I, Stanford *Also called Howard Hughes Medical Inst* ***(P-25762)***
H L Moe Co Inc (PA)......C......818 572-2100
526 Commercial St Glendale (91203) ***(P-2149)***
H M C, Chula Vista *Also called Heartland Meat Company Inc* ***(P-8407)***
H M E, Carlsbad *Also called H M Electronics Inc* ***(P-7275)***
H M Electronics Inc (PA)......B......858 535-6000
2848 Whiptail Loop Carlsbad (92010) ***(P-7275)***
H M H Engineers......D......408 487-2200
1570 Oakland Rd San Jose (95131) ***(P-25113)***
H Naraghi Farms, Escalon *Also called Noralco Inc* ***(P-522)***
H O K, San Francisco *Also called Hellmuth Obata & Kassabaum Inc* ***(P-25448)***
H P Sears Co Inc......D......661 325-5981
2000 18th St Bakersfield (93301) ***(P-13684)***
H Rauvel Inc (PA)......D......310 604-0060
1710 E Sepulveda Blvd Carson (90745) ***(P-4426)***
H T V, Studio City *Also called High Technology Video Inc* ***(P-17743)***
H U S D Maintenance Operation......D......510 784-2666
24400 Amador St Hayward (94544) ***(P-13944)***
H V Welker Co Inc......D......408 263-4400
970 S Milpitas Blvd Milpitas (95035) ***(P-3003)***
H&H Resolution LLC......D......408 362-2293
151 Bernal Rd Ste 6 San Jose (95119) ***(P-13685)***
H&R Block Inc......E......415 441-2666
1745 Van Ness Ave San Francisco (94109) ***(P-13389)***
H.G. Fenton Company, San Diego *Also called Fenton Scripps Landing LLC* ***(P-10726)***
H.U.G. Company, Hayward *Also called Gourmet Foods* ***(P-8176)***
H2 Hotel LLC......D......707 431-2202
219 Healdsburg Ave Healdsburg (95448) ***(P-12327)***
H2 Wellness Incorporated......D......310 362-1888
15414 Milldale Dr Los Angeles (90077) ***(P-15347)***
H2c2 & Associates Inc (PA)......E......510 562-6181
6925 San Leandro St Oakland (94621) ***(P-1487)***
Ha-Le Aloha Convalescent Hosp, Ceres *Also called Mark One Corporation* ***(P-20627)***
Haaker Equipment Company (PA)......D......909 542-0800
2070 N White Ave La Verne (91750) ***(P-6398)***

Mergent e-mail: customerrelations@mergent.com
1288
2020 Directory of California
Wholesalers and Services Companies
(P-0000) Products & Services Section entry number
(PA)=Parent Co (HQ)=Headquarters (DH)=Div Headquarters

Haas Factory Outlet, Anaheim *Also called Machining Time Savers Inc* ***(P-7559)***
Habenicht & Howlett A Corp ...D.......415 824-7040
25 Patterson St San Francisco (94124) ***(P-3294)***
Habitat For Humanity of Greate ...E.......310 323-4663
8739 Artesia Blvd Bellflower (90706) ***(P-24178)***
Habitat Rstration Sciences Inc (PA) ...D.......760 479-4210
1217 Distribution Way Vista (92081) ***(P-824)***
Habitat Rstration Sciences Inc ...E.......916 408-2990
3888 Cincinnati Ave Rocklin (95765) ***(P-27086)***
Hacienda Golf Club ...D.......562 694-1081
718 East Rd La Habra Heights (90631) ***(P-18464)***
Hacienda Health Care, Hanford *Also called Hacienda Rehabilitation & Heal* ***(P-19991)***
Hacienda Invlved Parents Staff ...D.......408 535-6259
1290 Kimberly Dr San Jose (95118) ***(P-24560)***
Hacienda Rehabilitation & Heal (PA) ...C.......714 778-0221
1440 S State College Blvd 2a Anaheim (92806) ***(P-19990)***
Hacienda Rehabilitation & Heal ...C.......559 582-9221
361 E Grangeville Blvd Hanford (93230) ***(P-19991)***
Hackerone Inc (PA) ...B.......415 891-0777
22 4th St Fl 5 San Francisco (94103) ***(P-15772)***
Hackney Electric Inc (PA) ...D.......949 264-4000
23286 Arroyo Vis Rcho STA Marg (92688) ***(P-2507)***
Haggin Oaks Golf Shop, Sacramento *Also called Morton Golf LLC* ***(P-18273)***
Hahn & Hahn LLP ...D.......626 796-9123
301 E Colo Blvd Ste 900 Pasadena (91101) ***(P-22556)***
Haider Spine Ctr Med Group Inc ...E.......951 413-0200
6276 River Crest Dr Ste A Riverside (92507) ***(P-19003)***
Haight Brown & Bonesteel LLP (PA) ...D.......213 542-8000
555 S Flower St Ste 4500 Los Angeles (90071) ***(P-22557)***
Haight Gdnr Holland & Knight, San Francisco *Also called Holland & Knight LLP* ***(P-22573)***
Hailwood Inc ...D.......805 487-4981
5755 Valentine Rd Ste 203 Ventura (93003) ***(P-10604)***
Hair Fashion Inc ...D.......310 274-0851
348 N Beverly Dr Beverly Hills (90210) ***(P-13349)***
Haircutters ...D.......562 690-2217
1230 W Imperial Hwy Ste A La Habra (90631) ***(P-13366)***
Haiyi Hotels Worldwide, San Francisco *Also called Apic Hotels Group LLC* ***(P-12011)***
Hakes Sash & Door Inc ...C.......951 674-2414
31945 Corydon St Lake Elsinore (92530) ***(P-2937)***
Hal Hays Construction Inc (PA) ...C.......951 788-0703
4181 Latham St Riverside (92501) ***(P-1352)***
Hal-Mar-Jac Enterprises ...C.......415 467-1470
1044 Potrero Cir Suisun City (94585) ***(P-16317)***
Halbert Brothers Inc ...D.......626 913-1800
17400 Chestnut St City of Industry (91748) ***(P-4211)***
Haldeman Inc ...E.......323 726-7011
2937 Tanager Ave Commerce (90040) ***(P-2150)***
Half Moon Bay Golf Links, Half Moon Bay *Also called Ocean Links Corporation* ***(P-18278)***
Half Moon Bay Golf Links, Half Moon Bay *Also called Ocean Colony Partners LLC* ***(P-11587)***
Half Moon Bay Lodge ...E.......650 726-9000
2400 Cabrillo Hwy S Half Moon Bay (94019) ***(P-12328)***
Half Moon Fruit & Produce Co (PA) ...D.......530 662-1727
403 Court St Woodland (95695) ***(P-5)***
Half Moon Fruity and Prod Co, Woodland *Also called B E Giovannetti & Sons* ***(P-1)***
Hall AG Enterprises Inc ...C.......559 846-7360
759 S Madera Ave Kerman (93630) ***(P-625)***
Hall AG Services, Kerman *Also called Hall AG Enterprises Inc* ***(P-625)***
Hall Ambulance Service Inc ...D.......661 322-8741
2001 O St O Bakersfield (93301) ***(P-3683)***
Hall Ambulance Service Inc (PA) ...D.......661 322-8741
1001 21st St Bakersfield (93301) ***(P-3684)***
Hall Capital Partners LLC (PA) ...D.......415 288-0544
1 Maritime Plz Fl 5 San Francisco (94111) ***(P-11728)***
Hall Company ...D.......209 364-0070
44328 W Nees Ave Firebaugh (93622) ***(P-327)***
Hall Management Corp ...A.......559 846-7382
759 S Madera Ave Kerman (93630) ***(P-26253)***
Hall Windsor ...D.......213 383-1547
1415 James M Wood Blvd Los Angeles (90015) ***(P-23943)***
Halliburton Company ...D.......661 393-8111
34722 7th Standard Rd Bakersfield (93314) ***(P-1024)***
Hallmark Channel, Studio City *Also called Crown Media United States LLC* ***(P-5704)***
Hallmark Distributing, Indio *Also called Triangle Distributing Co* ***(P-8795)***
Hallmark Rehabilitation GP LLC ...A.......949 282-5900
2 Park Plz Ste 225 Irvine (92614) ***(P-23250)***
Halo ...E.......925 473-4642
4916 Chism Way Antioch (94531) ***(P-24835)***
Halo Unlimted Inc ...D.......714 692-2270
1867 California Ave # 101 Corona (92881) ***(P-22248)***
Halsen Healthcare LLC ...A.......831 724-4741
75 Neilson St Watsonville (95076) ***(P-20897)***
Halstead Partnership ...D.......916 830-8000
2850 Gateway Oaks Dr # 450 Sacramento (95833) ***(P-10605)***
Hamann Construction ...D.......619 440-7424
1000 Pioneer Way El Cajon (92020) ***(P-1353)***
Hamblin's Auto & Body Shop, Riverside *Also called Hamblins Bdy Pnt Frame Sp Inc* ***(P-17333)***
Hamblins Bdy Pnt Frame Sp Inc ...D.......951 689-8440
7590 Cypress Ave Riverside (92503) ***(P-17333)***
Hamburger Home ...D.......213 637-5000
3701 Wilshire Blvd # 900 Los Angeles (90010) ***(P-1136)***
Hamburger Home (PA) ...D.......323 876-0550
7120 Franklin Ave Los Angeles (90046) ***(P-23944)***
Hamburger Home ...C.......818 980-3200
5900 Sepulvda Blvd # 104 Van Nuys (91411) ***(P-23945)***
Hamilton and Dillon Elc Inc ...D.......209 529-6292
1128 Reno Ave Modesto (95351) ***(P-2508)***
Hamilton Brwart Insur Agcy LLC ...D.......909 920-3250
1282 W Arrow Hwy Upland (91786) ***(P-10375)***
Hamilton Families ...D.......415 409-2100
1631 Hayes St San Francisco (94117) ***(P-23251)***
Hamilton Family Ranch ...D.......760 728-1358
2562 Doville Ranch Rd Fallbrook (92028) ***(P-189)***
Hamilton Partners ...D.......650 347-8800
1301 Shoreway Rd Ste 250 Burlingame (94010) ***(P-26629)***
Hamlow Ranches Inc ...E.......209 632-2873
4018 Swanson Rd Denair (95316) ***(P-203)***
Hammel Green & Abrahamson Inc ...D.......916 787-5100
1200 R St Ste 100 Sacramento (95811) ***(P-25444)***
Hammer Down Davila Cnstr ...D.......559 864-2001
2338 W Erie St Caruthers (93609) ***(P-1245)***
Hammonds Ranch Inc ...D.......209 364-6185
47375 W Dakota Ave Firebaugh (93622) ***(P-328)***
Hampstead Lafayette Hotel LLC ...E.......619 296-2101
2223 El Cajon Blvd San Diego (92104) ***(P-12329)***
Hampton Inn, San Diego *Also called Boykin Mgt Co Ltd Lblty Co* ***(P-12079)***
Hampton Inn, Elk Grove *Also called Dominion International Inc* ***(P-12224)***
Hampton Inn, Santa Ana *Also called Pacifica Hiorange LP* ***(P-12697)***
Hampton Inn, Garden Grove *Also called Harbor Suites LLC* ***(P-12335)***
Hampton Inn, Garden Grove *Also called Stonebridge McWhinney LLC* ***(P-12981)***
Hampton Inn, Aliso Viejo *Also called Sunstone Hotel Properties Inc* ***(P-13002)***
Hampton Inn Norco Corona North ...D.......951 279-1111
1530 Hamner Ave Norco (92860) ***(P-12330)***
Hana Commercial Finance Inc ...D.......213 240-1234
1000 Wilshire Blvd Fl 20 Los Angeles (90017) ***(P-9484)***
Hana Financial Inc (PA) ...D.......213 240-1234
1000 Wilshire Blvd Fl 20 Los Angeles (90017) ***(P-14162)***
Hancock Pk Rhblitation Ctr LLC ...C.......323 937-4860
505 N La Brea Ave Los Angeles (90036) ***(P-19992)***
Handlery Hotels Inc ...C.......415 781-7800
351 Geary St San Francisco (94102) ***(P-12331)***
Handlery Hotels Inc ...C.......415 781-4550
950 Hotel Cir N San Diego (92108) ***(P-12332)***
Handlery Union Square Hotel, San Francisco *Also called Handlery Hotels Inc* ***(P-12331)***
Hands-On Mobile Americas Inc (PA) ...E.......415 580-6400
208 Utah St Ste 300 San Francisco (94103) ***(P-15605)***
Handyman Connection ...E.......714 288-0077
1740 W Katella Ave Ste G Orange (92867) ***(P-13427)***
Hanergy Holding America Inc ...B.......650 288-3722
1350 Bayshore Hwy Ste 825 Burlingame (94010) ***(P-5844)***
Hanford Adult School, Hanford *Also called Hanford Joint Un High Schl Dst* ***(P-23252)***
Hanford Community Hospital (HQ) ...A.......559 582-9000
115 Mall Dr Hanford (93230) ***(P-20898)***
Hanford Hotels LLC ...C.......714 210-0400
17542 17th St Ste 450 Tustin (92780) ***(P-12333)***
Hanford Joint Un High Schl Dst ...D.......559 583-5905
905 Campus Dr Hanford (93230) ***(P-23252)***
Hanford Nursing Rehabilitation, Hanford *Also called Mission Medical Entps Inc* ***(P-20141)***
Hanford Truck Repair & Parts, Hanford *Also called Danell Bros Inc* ***(P-450)***
Hangtown Knnel CLB Plcrvlle CA ...D.......530 622-4867
100 Placerville Dr Placerville (95667) ***(P-604)***
Hanil Development Inc ...E.......213 387-0111
3680 Wilshire Blvd B01 Los Angeles (90010) ***(P-11629)***
Hanin Federal Credit Union (PA) ...E.......213 368-9000
3700 Wilshire Blvd # 104 Los Angeles (90010) ***(P-9315)***
Hanjin Global Logistics, Carson *Also called Hanjin Transportation Co Ltd* ***(P-4962)***
Hanjin Shipping Co Ltd ...A.......201 291-4600
301 Hanjin Rd Long Beach (90802) ***(P-4639)***
Hanjin Transportation Co Ltd ...D.......310 522-5030
1111 E Watson Center Rd A Carson (90745) ***(P-4962)***
Hank Fisher Properties Inc ...C.......916 447-4444
2701 Capitol Ave Sacramento (95816) ***(P-23946)***
Hank Fisher Properties Inc ...D.......916 921-1970
641 Feature Dr Apt 233 Sacramento (95825) ***(P-20587)***
Hankey Group, Los Angeles *Also called Nowcom Corporation* ***(P-16065)***
Hanks Inc ...D.......909 350-8365
13866 Slover Ave Fontana (92337) ***(P-3890)***
Hanley Wood Mkt Intelligence (HQ) ...D.......714 540-8500
555 Anton Blvd Ste 950 Costa Mesa (92626) ***(P-25905)***
Hanmi Bank (HQ) ...C.......213 382-2200
3660 Wilshire Blvd Ph A Los Angeles (90010) ***(P-9210)***
Hanna Brophy Mac Lean Mc Ale (PA) ...E.......510 839-1180
1956 Webster St Ste 450 Oakland (94612) ***(P-22558)***
Hannaknapp Realty Inc ...E.......760 244-8557
15311 Bear Valley Rd # 1 Hesperia (92345) ***(P-11184)***
Hannam Chain Super 1 Market, Los Angeles *Also called Hannam Chain USA Inc* ***(P-6924)***
Hannam Chain USA Inc (PA) ...C.......213 382-2922
2740 W Olympic Blvd Los Angeles (90006) ***(P-6924)***
Hanover Builders Inc ...E.......818 706-2279
141 Duesenberg Dr Ste 6 Westlake Village (91362) ***(P-1137)***
Hans Technologies Inc ...D.......510 464-8018
1300 Clay St Ste 600 Oakland (94612) ***(P-1968)***
Hansen Bros Enterprises (PA) ...D.......530 273-3100
11727 La Barr Meadows Rd Grass Valley (95949) ***(P-1056)***
Hansen Equipment Company LLC ...E.......559 992-3111
7124 Whitley Ave Corcoran (93212) ***(P-666)***
Hansen Information Tech, Rancho Cordova *Also called Infor (us) Inc* ***(P-15358)***
Hansen Ranches ...D.......559 992-3111
7124 Whitley Ave Corcoran (93212) ***(P-329)***
Hansol Goldpoint LLC ...D.......714 594-5073
12792 Valley View St # 211 Garden Grove (92845) ***(P-4963)***
Hanson Bridgett LLP ...E.......916 442-3333
500 Capitol Mall Ste 1500 Sacramento (95814) ***(P-22559)***
Hanson Bridgett LLP (PA) ...B.......415 543-2055
425 Market St Fl 26 San Francisco (94105) ***(P-22560)***
Hanson Distributing Company (PA) ...C.......626 224-9800
975 W 8th St Azusa (91702) ***(P-6443)***

Employee Codes: A=Over 500 employees, B=251-500
C=101-250, D=51-100, E=50

2020 Directory of California
Wholesalers and Services Companies

© Mergent Inc. 1-800-342-5647
1289

Hanson McClain Advisors, NAPA *Also called Allworth Financial LP* ***(P-9782)***

Happy Camp Chamber Commerce ... E ... 530 493-2900
35 Davis Rd Happy Camp (96039) ***(P-24341)***

Happy Money, Costa Mesa *Also called Payoff Inc* ***(P-9471)***

Happy Pet Co ... E ... 707 586-8660
5813 Skylane Blvd Windsor (95492) ***(P-578)***

Hara, San Mateo *Also called Tunari Corp Inc* ***(P-15166)***

Haralambos Beverage Company (PA) ... B ... 562 347-4300
2300 Pellissier Pl City of Industry (90601) ***(P-8765)***

Harbin Hot Springs, Middletown *Also called Heart Consciousness Church* ***(P-13172)***

Harbor Bay Club Inc ... D ... 510 521-5414
200 Packet Landing Rd Alameda (94502) ***(P-18150)***

Harbor Building Services ... D ... 310 320-2966
2701 Plaza Del Amo # 706 Torrance (90503) ***(P-13945)***

HARBOR CARE CENTER, Torrance *Also called Geri Care Inc* ***(P-19940)***

Harbor Corporate Park, Santa Ana *Also called Kaiser Foundation Hospitals* ***(P-19098)***

Harbor Department, San Pedro *Also called City of Los Angeles* ***(P-4611)***

Harbor Developmental Disabilit ... C ... 310 540-1711
21231 Hawthorne Blvd Torrance (90503) ***(P-24179)***

Harbor Diesel and Eqp Inc ... D ... 562 591-5665
537 W Anaheim St Long Beach (90813) ***(P-7549)***

Harbor Distributing LLC (HQ) ... C ... 714 933-2400
5901 Bolsa Ave Huntington Beach (92647) ***(P-8766)***

Harbor Distributing LLC ... B ... 916 373-5700
3500 Carlin Dr West Sacramento (95691) ***(P-8767)***

Harbor Distributing LLC ... B ... 310 538-5483
16407 S Main St Gardena (90248) ***(P-8768)***

Harbor Distributing Co, Gardena *Also called Harbor Distributing LLC* ***(P-8768)***

Harbor Freight Tools, Camarillo *Also called Central Purchasing LLC* ***(P-7630)***

Harbor Fuel Dock ... D ... 650 726-4419
1 Johnson Pier Half Moon Bay (94019) ***(P-4634)***

Harbor Glen Care Center ... D ... 626 963-7531
1033 E Arrow Hwy Glendora (91740) ***(P-19993)***

Harbor Health Care Inc ... C ... 562 866-7054
16917 Clark Ave Bellflower (90706) ***(P-23947)***

Harbor Health Systems LLC ... D ... 949 273-7020
3501 Jamboree Rd Ste 540 Newport Beach (92660) ***(P-22249)***

Harbor Industrial Services ... D ... 310 522-1193
211 N Marine Ave Wilmington (90744) ***(P-14097)***

Harbor Island Hotel Group LP ... D ... 805 658-1212
1050 Schooner Dr Ventura (93001) ***(P-12334)***

Harbor Pipe and Steel Inc ... C ... 951 369-3990
1495 Columbia Ave Bldg 10 Riverside (92507) ***(P-7069)***

Harbor Regional Center, Torrance *Also called Harbor Developmental Disabilit* ***(P-24179)***

Harbor Suites LLC ... E ... 714 703-8800
11747 Harbor Blvd Garden Grove (92840) ***(P-12335)***

Harbor Ucla Med Foundation, Torrance *Also called Harbor-Ucla Med Foundation Inc* ***(P-26254)***

Harbor View Community Svcs Ctr, Long Beach *Also called Sunbridge Healthcare LLC* ***(P-20462)***

Harbor View Hotel Ventures LLC ... D ... 619 239-6800
1646 Front St San Diego (92101) ***(P-12336)***

Harbor View Hotels Inc ... D ... 650 340-8500
600 Airport Blvd Burlingame (94010) ***(P-12337)***

Harbor View House, San Pedro *Also called Healthview Inc* ***(P-23954)***

Harbor View Inn, Santa Barbara *Also called Beach Motel Partners Ltd* ***(P-12049)***

Harbor View Rehabilitation Ctr, Long Beach *Also called Sunbridge Harbor View* ***(P-20284)***

Harbor Villa Care Center ... D ... 714 635-8131
861 S Harbor Blvd Anaheim (92805) ***(P-20588)***

Harbor Village II, Costa Mesa *Also called Independent Options* ***(P-23273)***

Harbor's Insurance, Eureka *Also called Shaw & Petersen Insurance Inc* ***(P-10493)***

Harbor-Cla Med Ctr Dept Srgery ... D ... 310 222-2701
1000 W Carson St 25 Torrance (90502) ***(P-20899)***

Harbor-Ucla Med Foundation Inc (PA) ... B ... 310 222-5015
21840 S Norm Ave Torrance (90502) ***(P-26254)***

Hard Rock Hotel, San Diego *Also called T-12 Three LLC* ***(P-13016)***

Hard Rock Hotel Palm Springs, Palm Springs *Also called Kittridge Hotels & Resorts LLC* ***(P-12518)***

Hardage Hospitality LLC ... E ... 510 795-1200
39150 Cedar Blvd Newark (94560) ***(P-10606)***

Hardage Hospitality LLC (PA) ... D ... 858 314-7910
12555 High Bluff Dr # 330 San Diego (92130) ***(P-12338)***

Hardcore Skateparks Inc ... C ... 909 949-1601
285 N Benson Ave Upland (91786) ***(P-18333)***

Hardesty LLC (PA) ... E ... 949 407-6625
19800 Macar Boule Ste 820 Irvine (92612) ***(P-14297)***

Harding & Associates, San Jose *Also called Harding Mktg Cmmunications Inc* ***(P-13786)***

Harding Mktg Cmmunications Inc (PA) ... D ... 408 345-4545
377 S Daniel Way San Jose (95128) ***(P-13786)***

Hardisty Construction Administ ... D ... 619 245-6828
410 W 30th St Ste A National City (91950) ***(P-1488)***

Hardrock Tile & Marble Inc ... D ... 714 282-1766
23151 Verdugo Dr Ste 111 Laguna Hills (92653) ***(P-2714)***

Hardwood Creations (PA) ... D ... 714 674-0527
1560 N Maple St Corona (92880) ***(P-2938)***

Hardy & Harper Inc ... E ... 714 444-1851
32 Rancho Cir Lake Forest (92630) ***(P-1731)***

Hardy Diagnostics (PA) ... B ... 805 346-2766
1430 W Mccoy Ln Santa Maria (93455) ***(P-6969)***

Hardy Window Company (PA) ... C ... 714 996-1807
1639 E Miraloma Ave Placentia (92870) ***(P-6621)***

Harel General Contractors Inc ... E ... 310 558-8304
6015 Washington Blvd Culver City (90232) ***(P-1489)***

Harelson Mechanical Inc ... D ... 916 386-2586
3899 Security Park Dr Rancho Cordova (95742) ***(P-3360)***

Haringa Inc (PA) ... D ... 800 499-9991
14422 Best Ave Santa Fe Springs (90670) ***(P-16816)***

Harkins Theatres Inc ... D ... 909 627-8010
3100 Chino Ave Chino Hills (91709) ***(P-17845)***

Harley Ellis Devereaux Corp ... D ... 415 981-2345
417 Montgomery St Ste 400 San Francisco (94104) ***(P-25445)***

Harman Cnncted Svcs Holdg Corp (HQ) ... D ... 650 623-9400
636 Ellis St Mountain View (94043) ***(P-15606)***

Harmonium Inc (PA) ... C ... 858 684-3080
9245 Activity Rd Ste 200 San Diego (92126) ***(P-23729)***

Harmony Escrow Inc ... D ... 949 474-1134
17100 Gillette Ave Irvine (92614) ***(P-11185)***

Harmony Home Health LLC ... D ... 916 933-9777
2500 Ranch Rd Ste 104 Placerville (95667) ***(P-21756)***

Harmony Homecare, Placerville *Also called Harmony Home Health LLC* ***(P-21756)***

Harold E Nutter Inc (PA) ... D ... 916 334-4343
5930 Rosebud Ln Sacramento (95841) ***(P-2509)***

Harold E Nutter & Son, Sacramento *Also called Harold E Nutter Inc* ***(P-2509)***

Harold Jones Landscape Inc ... E ... 805 582-7443
530 New Los Angeles Ave Moorpark (93021) ***(P-731)***

Harold L Karpman MD, Beverly Hills *Also called Cardivsclr Mdcl Grp of Sthrn* ***(P-18868)***

Harper Construction Co Inc (PA) ... D ... 619 233-7900
2241 Kettner Blvd Ste 300 San Diego (92101) ***(P-1490)***

Harper's Model Homes Services, Davis *Also called Harpers Model Home Maintenance* ***(P-13946)***

Harpers Model Home Maintenance ... D ... 916 335-0282
1949 5th St Ste 108 Davis (95616) ***(P-13946)***

Harpo Entertainment Group, West Hollywood *Also called Harpo Productions Inc* ***(P-17614)***

Harpo Inc ... D ... 312 633-1000
1041 N Formosa Ave West Hollywood (90046) ***(P-17914)***

Harpo Productions Inc ... C ... 312 633-1000
1041 N Formosa Ave West Hollywood (90046) ***(P-17614)***

Harpo Studios, West Hollywood *Also called Harpo Inc* ***(P-17914)***

Harrah's, Valley Center *Also called Caesars Entrtnment Oprting Inc* ***(P-18639)***

Harrahs Resort Southern Cal, Valley Center *Also called Hcal LLC* ***(P-12344)***

Harrington Industrial Plas LLC (HQ) ... D ... 909 597-8641
14480 Yorba Ave Chino (91710) ***(P-7429)***

Harris & Associates Inc ... D ... 949 655-3900
22 Executive Park Ste 200 Irvine (92614) ***(P-25114)***

Harris & Associates Inc (PA) ... C ... 925 827-4900
1401 Wllw Pca Rd 500 Concord (94520) ***(P-25115)***

Harris & Associates Cnstr MGT, Concord *Also called Harris & Associates Inc* ***(P-25115)***

Harris & Ruth Painting Contg (PA) ... D ... 626 960-4004
28408 Lorna Ave West Covina (91790) ***(P-2357)***

Harris & Sloan Consulting ... E ... 916 921-2800
2295 Gateway Oaks Dr # 165 Sacramento (95833) ***(P-27087)***

Harris Construction Co Inc ... C ... 559 251-0301
5286 E Home Ave Fresno (93727) ***(P-1491)***

Harris Direct ... D ... 818 357-2040
21250 Califa St Ste 114 Woodland Hills (91367) ***(P-16817)***

Harris Farm Horse Division, Coalinga *Also called Harris Farms Inc* ***(P-330)***

Harris Farms Inc ... E ... 559 884-2203
27366 W Oakland Ave Coalinga (93210) ***(P-330)***

Harris Farms Inc ... B ... 559 935-0717
24505 W Dorris Ave Coalinga (93210) ***(P-331)***

Harris Farms Inc ... B ... 559 884-2477
23300 W Oakland Ave Coalinga (93210) ***(P-332)***

Harris Freeman & Co Inc (PA) ... B ... 714 765-1190
3110 E Miraloma Ave Anaheim (92806) ***(P-8586)***

Harris L Woods Elec Contr ... D ... 562 945-8751
9214 Norwalk Blvd Santa Fe Springs (90670) ***(P-2510)***

Harris Moran, Davis *Also called Hmclause Inc* ***(P-25761)***

Harris Mycfo Inc ... D ... 480 348-7725
2200 Geng Rd Ste 100 Palo Alto (94303) ***(P-26630)***

Harris Rebar Northern Cal Inc ... C ... 925 373-0733
355 S Vasco Rd Livermore (94550) ***(P-3263)***

Harris Stockwell (PA) ... E ... 310 277-6669
3580 Wilshire Blvd Fl 19 Los Angeles (90010) ***(P-22561)***

Harris Tea Company, Anaheim *Also called Harris Freeman & Co Inc* ***(P-8586)***

Harris Woolf Cal Almonds LLC ... C ... 559 884-2147
26060 Colusa Ave Coalinga (93210) ***(P-502)***

Harrison Drywall Inc ... E ... 415 821-9584
447 10th St San Francisco (94103) ***(P-2795)***

Harrison Inventory Services ... E ... 661 269-9220
37051 Graphic Ave Littlerock (93543) ***(P-6444)***

Harrison Nichols Co Ltd ... C ... 626 337-5020
14080 Slover Ave Fontana (92337) ***(P-4212)***

Harrison, E J & Sons Recycling, Ventura *Also called E J Harrison & Sons Inc* ***(P-6194)***

Harry's Auto Collision, Los Angeles *Also called Harrys Auto Body Inc* ***(P-17294)***

Harrys Auto Body Inc ... D ... 323 933-4600
1013 S La Brea Ave Los Angeles (90019) ***(P-17294)***

Hart Howerton Ltd (PA) ... D ... 415 439-2200
1 Union St Fl 3 San Francisco (94111) ***(P-732)***

Hart King Coldren A Prof Corp ... D ... 714 432-8700
4 Hutton Cntre Dr Ste 900 Santa Ana (92707) ***(P-22562)***

Harte Hanks Inc ... D ... 210 829-9000
2337 W Commonwealth Ave Fullerton (92833) ***(P-4427)***

Harte-Hanks Direct Mail/Califo ... D ... 714 738-5478
2337 W Commonwealth Ave Fullerton (92833) ***(P-13723)***

Hartford Casualty Insurance Co ... A ... 415 836-4800
101 Montgomery St # 2700 San Francisco (94104) ***(P-10095)***

Hartford Fire Insurance Co ... B ... 916 294-1000
12009 Foundation Pl # 100 Gold River (95670) ***(P-10376)***

Hartford Fire Insurance Co ... C ... 213 452-5179
777 S Figueroa St Ste 700 Los Angeles (90017) ***(P-10377)***

Hartman Industries ... D ... 909 428-0114
14933 Whittram Ave Fontana (92335) ***(P-7070)***

Hartmann Studios Inc ... C ... 510 232-5030
1150 Brickyard Cove Rd # 202 Point Richmond (94801) ***(P-16818)***

Mergent e-mail: customerrelations@mergent.com
1290
2020 Directory of California
Wholesalers and Services Companies
(P-0000) Products & Services Section entry number
(PA)=Parent Co (HQ)=Headquarters (DH)=Div Headquarters

Hartwick & Hand Inc (PA)....D....760 245-1666
16953 N D St Victorville (92394) *(P-3891)*
Hartwig Realty Inc (PA)....D....661 948-8424
43912 20th St W Lancaster (93534) *(P-11186)*
Harvard Grand Inv Inc A Cal....D....310 513-7560
2 Civic Plaza Dr Carson (90745) *(P-11920)*
Harvest Facility Holdings LP....D....909 793-8691
10 Terracina Blvd Ofc Redlands (92373) *(P-10735)*
Harvest Food Distributors, National City *Also called Harvest Meat Company Inc (P-8406)*
Harvest Landscape Entps Inc....C....714 693-8100
2339 N Batavia St Orange (92865) *(P-825)*
Harvest Landscape Maintenance, Orange *Also called Harvest Landscape Entps Inc (P-825)*
Harvest Management Sub LLC....A....805 543-0187
1299 Briarwood Dr San Luis Obispo (93401) *(P-23948)*
Harvest Meat Company Inc (HQ)....D....619 477-0185
1022 Bay Marina Dr # 106 National City (91950) *(P-8406)*
Harvest of The Sea, Los Angeles *Also called Ore-Cal Corp (P-8377)*
Harvest Sensations LLC (PA)....D....213 895-6968
3030 E Washington Blvd Los Angeles (90023) *(P-8489)*
Harvest Small Business Fin LLC....D....949 446-8683
24422 Avenida De Carlota Laguna Hills (92653) *(P-9627)*
Harvest Technical Service Inc....C....925 937-4874
1839 Ygnacio Valley Rd # 390 Walnut Creek (94598) *(P-14298)*
Harvest V Citizens Patrol....C....951 926-9763
25098 Avenida Valencia Homeland (92548) *(P-16318)*
Harvey Inc....C....858 769-4000
9455 Ridgehaven Ct # 200 San Diego (92123) *(P-1492)*
Harvey Apartments, The, Los Angeles *Also called CMI Management Inc (P-26559)*
Harvey General Contracting, San Diego *Also called Harvey Inc (P-1492)*
Harveys Industries Inc....D....714 277-4700
724 N Poinsettia St Santa Ana (92701) *(P-8075)*
Hasc, Los Angeles *Also called Hospital Assn Southern Cal (P-24181)*
Haskell Company (inc)....C....925 960-1815
478 Lindbergh Ave Livermore (94551) *(P-1354)*
Hassard Bonnington LLP (PA)....D....415 288-9800
275 Battery St Ste 1600 San Francisco (94111) *(P-22563)*
Hastings Enterprises, San Mateo *Also called HE Inc (P-11188)*
Hat Creek Cnstr & Mtls Inc (PA)....E....530 335-5501
24339 State Highway 89 Burney (96013) *(P-1969)*
Hatchbeauty Products LLC (PA)....D....310 396-7070
10951 W Pico Blvd Ste 300 Los Angeles (90064) *(P-7950)*
Hatfield Inc....E....415 802-8635
5 3rd St Ste 525 San Francisco (94103) *(P-13390)*
Hathaway Dinwiddie Cnstr Co....D....415 986-2718
565 Laurelwood Rd Santa Clara (95054) *(P-1493)*
Hathaway Dinwiddie Cnstr Co....B....415 986-2718
275 Battery St Ste 300 San Francisco (94111) *(P-1494)*
Hathaway Dinwiddie Cnstr Group (PA)....D....415 986-2718
275 Battery St Ste 300 San Francisco (94111) *(P-1495)*
Hathaway Resource Center....E....323 837-0838
5701 S Eastrn Ave Ste 550 Los Angeles (90040) *(P-23253)*
Hathaway-Sycamores Chld Fam Sv....D....323 257-9600
840 N Avenue 66 Los Angeles (90042) *(P-23949)*
Hathaway-Sycamores Chld Fam Sv....D....323 733-0322
3741 Stocker St Ste 101 View Park (90008) *(P-23950)*
Hathaway-Sycamores Chld Fam Sv (PA)....D....626 395-7100
100 W Walnut St Ste 375 Pasadena (91124) *(P-23951)*
Haulaway Storage Cntrs Inc....A....800 826-9040
11292 Western Ave Stanton (90680) *(P-4428)*
Havas Edge LLC (PA)....D....760 929-0041
2386 Faraday Ave Ste 200 Carlsbad (92008) *(P-13515)*
Havas Formula LLC....D....619 234-0345
1215 Cushman Ave San Diego (92110) *(P-26910)*
Havasu Landing Casino (PA)....D....760 858-5380
1 Main St Needles (92363) *(P-12339)*
Hawaii Parent Corp....B....415 263-3660
600 Montgomery St Fl 32 San Francisco (94111) *(P-11753)*
Hawaiian Airlines Inc....D....310 417-1677
200 World Way Ste 9 Los Angeles (90045) *(P-4668)*
Hawaiian Gardens Casino....A....562 860-5887
11871 Carson St Hawaiian Gardens (90716) *(P-12340)*
Hawaiian Hotels & Resorts Inc....D....805 480-0052
2830 Borchard Rd Newbury Park (91320) *(P-12341)*
Hawk Transportation Inc....D....800 709-4295
15238 Arrow Blvd Fontana (92335) *(P-4058)*
Hawker Pacific Aerospace....B....818 765-6201
11240 Sherman Way Sun Valley (91352) *(P-17503)*
Hawkins Brown USA Inc....B....310 600-2695
2128 Cotner Ave Los Angeles (90025) *(P-25446)*
Haworth Inc....D....408 262-6400
931 Cadillac Ct Milpitas (95035) *(P-6516)*
Hawthorn Suites, Anaheim *Also called Sunstone Hotel Investors LLC (P-12996)*
Hawthorne Cat, San Diego *Also called Hawthorne Machinery Co (P-14098)*
Hawthorne Convalescent Center, Hawthorne *Also called Wilshire Hlth & Cmnty Svcs Inc (P-20725)*
Hawthorne Healthcare....D....310 679-9732
11630 Grevillea Ave Hawthorne (90250) *(P-19994)*
Hawthorne Lift Systems, Fontana *Also called Naumann/Hobbs Material (P-7570)*
Hawthorne Lift Systems, San Marcos *Also called Naumann/Hobbs Material (P-7571)*
Hawthorne Machinery Co (PA)....C....858 674-7000
16945 Camino San Bernardo San Diego (92127) *(P-14098)*
Hawthorne Machinery Co (HQ)....D....858 674-7000
16945 Camino San Bernardo San Diego (92127) *(P-14099)*
Hawthorne Machinery Co....D....858 674-7000
16945 Camino San Bernardo San Diego (92127) *(P-17334)*
Hawthorne Machinery Co....D....858 974-6800
8050 Othello Ave San Diego (92111) *(P-7474)*
Hay House Inc (PA)....D....760 431-7695
2776 Loker Ave W Carlsbad (92010) *(P-8872)*
Hay Kuhn Inc....E....760 353-0124
1880 Jeffrey Rd El Centro (92243) *(P-8978)*
Hayday Farms Inc....D....760 922-4713
15500 S Commercial St Blythe (92225) *(P-25)*
Hayes Mansion Conference Ctr....C....408 226-3200
200 Edenvale Ave San Jose (95136) *(P-12342)*
Hayes Welding Inc (PA)....D....760 246-4878
12522 Violet Rd Adelanto (92301) *(P-17473)*
Haynes and Boone LLP....D....650 687-8800
525 University Ave # 400 Palo Alto (94301) *(P-22564)*
Haynes Building Service LLC....C....626 359-6100
16027 Arrow Hwy Ste I Baldwin Park (91706) *(P-13947)*
Haynes Family Programs Inc....C....909 593-2581
233 Baseline Rd La Verne (91750) *(P-23952)*
Hayward Active Club, Hayward *Also called 24 Hour Fitness Usa Inc (P-18114)*
Hayward Area Recreation Pkdist....E....510 317-2300
1401 Golf Course Rd Hayward (94541) *(P-18251)*
Hayward Area Recreation Pkdist....D....510 881-6750
1099 E St Rear Hayward (94541) *(P-4429)*
Hayward Baker Inc....D....805 933-1331
1780 E Lemonwood Dr Santa Paula (93060) *(P-3415)*
Hayward Convalescent Hospital, Hayward *Also called Hillsdale Group LP (P-20596)*
Hayward Hills Health Care Ctr, Hayward *Also called Mariner Health Care Inc (P-20115)*
Hayward Manufacturing, Hayward *Also called Intarcia Therapeutics Inc (P-25768)*
Hayward Police Officers Assn....D....510 293-7207
300 W Winton Ave Hayward (94544) *(P-24441)*
Hayward Sisters Hospital (HQ)....A....510 264-4000
27200 Calaroga Ave Hayward (94545) *(P-20900)*
Hazard Construction Company....D....858 587-3600
6465 Marindustry Dr San Diego (92121) *(P-1821)*
Hazel Creek Assisted Living, Orangevale *Also called Summerville At Hazel Creek LLC (P-24089)*
HAZEL HAWKINS MEMORIAL HOSPITA, Hollister *Also called San Benito Health Care Dst (P-21152)*
Hazens Investment LLC....B....310 642-1111
6101 W Century Blvd Los Angeles (90045) *(P-12343)*
Hazmat Tsdf Inc (PA)....D....909 873-4141
180 W Monte Ave Rialto (92376) *(P-6212)*
HB, San Francisco *Also called Hassard Bonnington LLP (P-22563)*
HB Healthcare Associates LLC....D....714 887-0144
18811 Florida St Huntington Beach (92648) *(P-19995)*
HB Parkco Construction Inc (PA)....B....714 444-1441
3190 Arprt Loop Dr Ste F Costa Mesa (92626) *(P-3159)*
Hba Incorporated....D....714 635-8602
512 E Vermont Ave Anaheim (92805) *(P-2715)*
Hba International, Santa Monica *Also called Hirsch/Bedner Intl Inc (P-16830)*
Hbe Rental, Grass Valley *Also called Hansen Bros Enterprises (P-1056)*
HCA Inc....C....408 729-2801
225 N Jackson Ave San Jose (95116) *(P-20901)*
HCA Inc....C....949 496-1122
654 Camino De Los Mares San Clemente (92673) *(P-20902)*
Hcal LLC....C....760 751-3100
777 S Resort Dr Valley Center (92082) *(P-12344)*
HCC Investors LLC....C....858 759-7200
18550 Seven Bridges Rd Rancho Santa Fe (92091) *(P-18465)*
HCC Surety Group, Los Angeles *Also called American Contrs Indemnity Co (P-10158)*
Hci, Chowchilla *Also called Winnresidential Ltd Partnr (P-10847)*
Hci Inc (HQ)....B....951 520-4200
3166 Hrseless Carriage Rd Norco (92860) *(P-1861)*
Hci Systems Inc (PA)....E....909 628-7773
1354 S Parkside Pl Ontario (91761) *(P-2511)*
Hcl America Inc (HQ)....C....408 733-0480
330 Potrero Ave Sunnyvale (94085) *(P-15903)*
Hcl Finance Inc (PA)....C....408 845-9035
2560 Mission College Blvd Santa Clara (95054) *(P-9558)*
Hcr Manorcare Inc....D....419 252-5743
1575 Bayshore Hwy Ste 200 Burlingame (94010) *(P-19996)*
Hcr Manorcare Med Svcs Fla LLC....C....925 274-1325
1975 Tice Valley Blvd Walnut Creek (94595) *(P-19997)*
Hcr Manorcare Med Svcs Fla LLC....C....714 241-9800
11680 Warner Ave Fountain Valley (92708) *(P-19998)*
Hcr Manorcare Med Svcs Fla LLC....C....916 967-2929
7807 Uplands Way Citrus Heights (95610) *(P-19999)*
Hcr Manorcare Med Svcs Fla LLC....C....951 925-9171
1717 W Stetson Ave Hemet (92545) *(P-20000)*
Hcr Manorcare Med Svcs Fla LLC....D....408 735-7200
1150 Tilton Dr Sunnyvale (94087) *(P-20001)*
Hcr Manorcare Med Svcs Fla LLC....C....925 975-5000
1226 Rossmoor Pkwy Walnut Creek (94595) *(P-20002)*
Hcr Manorcare Med Svcs Fla LLC....D....760 944-0331
944 Regal Rd Encinitas (92024) *(P-20003)*
Hcs Holdco LLC (HQ)....C....949 349-1200
27071 Aliso Creek Rd # 100 Aliso Viejo (92656) *(P-21757)*
Hct Packaging Inc (HQ)....C....310 260-7680
2800 28th St Ste 240 Santa Monica (90405) *(P-16819)*
Hd Supply Inc....D....800 431-3000
101 Rverview Pkwy Ste 100 Santee (92071) *(P-3892)*
Hd Supply Construction Supply....D....707 863-8282
1995 W Cordelia Rd Fairfield (94534) *(P-7393)*
Hd Supply Construction Supply....E....408 428-2000
595 Brennan St San Jose (95131) *(P-7394)*
Hdd Construction, Caruthers *Also called Hammer Down Davila Cnstr (P-1245)*
HDR Architecture Inc....D....626 584-1700
350 S Grand Ave Ste 2900 Los Angeles (90071) *(P-25116)*
HDR Architecture Inc....D....415 546-4242
201 California St # 1500 San Francisco (94111) *(P-25117)*

A L P H A B E T I C

Employee Codes: A=Over 500 employees, B=251-500
C=101-250, D=51-100, E=50
2020 Directory of California
Wholesalers and Services Companies
© Mergent Inc. 1-800-342-5647
1291

HDR Engineering Inc........C.......714 730-2300
3230 El Camino Real # 200 Irvine (92602) ***(P-25118)***
HDR Engineering Inc........D.......619 231-4865
401 B St Ste 1110 San Diego (92101) ***(P-25119)***
HDR Engineering Inc........E.......858 712-8400
591 Camno De La Reina 3 San Diego (92108) ***(P-26631)***
HDR Engineering Inc........C.......626 584-1700
350 S Grand Ave Ste 2900 Los Angeles (90071) ***(P-26632)***
HDR Engineering Inc........D.......925 974-2500
100 Pringle Ave Ste 400 Walnut Creek (94596) ***(P-25120)***
HDR Engineering Inc........D.......415 546-4200
201 California St # 1500 San Francisco (94111) ***(P-26633)***
HDR Engineering Inc........D.......916 564-4214
2379 Gateway Oaks Dr # 200 Sacramento (95833) ***(P-25121)***
HDR Engineering Inc........D.......909 626-0967
431 W Baseline Rd Claremont (91711) ***(P-25122)***
HDR Engineering Inc........D.......916 817-4700
2365 Iron Point Rd # 300 Folsom (95630) ***(P-26634)***
HDR Environmental Ope........D.......858 712-8400
8690 Balboa Ave Ste 200 San Diego (92123) ***(P-25447)***
HDR/Cardno Entrix Joint Ventr........D.......916 817-4700
2365 Iron Point Rd # 300 Folsom (95630) ***(P-25123)***
Hdsi Management Inc (PA)........D.......323 231-1104
3460 S Broadway Los Angeles (90007) ***(P-11187)***
HE Inc........D.......650 794-1128
3 E 3rd Ave San Mateo (94401) ***(P-11188)***
HE Julien & Associates Inc........E.......805 488-8342
2275 E Hueneme Rd Oxnard (93033) ***(P-826)***
Head Start, Quincy *Also called Sierra Cscade Fmly Opprtnities* ***(P-23786)***
Headquarters, Los Angeles *Also called Nationwide Legal LLC* ***(P-22718)***
Headstart, Watsonville *Also called Encompass Community Services* ***(P-23209)***
Headstart Nursery Inc (PA)........D.......408 842-3030
4860 Monterey Rd Gilroy (95020) ***(P-8897)***
Headstrong Corporation........D.......408 732-8700
150 Mathilda Pl Ste 200 Sunnyvale (94086) ***(P-16021)***
Healdsburg Dist Hosp Rehab Svc........D.......707 433-9150
1540 Healdsburg Ave Healdsburg (95448) ***(P-9946)***
Healdsburg District Hospital, Healdsburg *Also called North Sonoma County Hosp Dst* ***(P-21057)***
Health & Human Services, San Diego *Also called County of San Diego* ***(P-23143)***
Health & Human Services, Fallbrook *Also called County of San Diego* ***(P-23144)***
Health & Human Services, Oceanside *Also called County of San Diego* ***(P-23147)***
Health & Human Services, Auburn *Also called County of Placer* ***(P-23126)***
Health & Human Services, Auburn *Also called County of Placer* ***(P-22004)***
Health & Human Services, San Diego *Also called County of San Diego* ***(P-21399)***
Health & Human Services Dept, Oakland *Also called City of Oakland* ***(P-23012)***
Health & Human Services- Aging, Santee *Also called County of San Diego* ***(P-19824)***
Health & Rehabilitation Center........E.......408 377-9275
2065 Los Gatos Almaden Rd San Jose (95124) ***(P-20004)***
Health Advocates LLC........B.......818 995-9500
21540 Plummer St Ste B Chatsworth (91311) ***(P-24180)***
Health and Human Service, Crescent City *Also called County of Del Norte* ***(P-24160)***
Health and Human Service Agcy, San Diego *Also called County of San Diego* ***(P-23145)***
Health and Human Services, Sacramento *Also called County of Sacramento* ***(P-23138)***
Health and Human Services, San Diego *Also called County of San Diego* ***(P-23151)***
Health and Human Services Agcy, San Diego *Also called County of San Diego* ***(P-22220)***
Health and Human Services Agcy, San Diego *Also called County of San Diego* ***(P-23150)***
Health and Social Services, Fairfield *Also called County of Solano* ***(P-23167)***
Health By Design........E.......916 974-3322
3029 La Via Way Sacramento (95825) ***(P-21758)***
Health Care Agency, Santa Ana *Also called County of Orange* ***(P-21518)***
Health Care Developers, Hesperia *Also called Foremost Healthcare Centers* ***(P-10728)***
Health Care Group, San Diego *Also called L C C H Associates Inc* ***(P-20611)***
Health Care Investments Inc........C.......310 323-3194
1140 W Rosecrans Ave Gardena (90247) ***(P-20005)***
Health Care Workers Union (PA)........C.......510 251-1250
560 Thomas L Berkley Way Oakland (94612) ***(P-10607)***
HEALTH CENTER PARTNERS OF SOUT, San Diego *Also called Community Clinics Hlth Netwrk* ***(P-24395)***
Health Comp Administrators (PA)........C.......559 499-2450
621 Santa Fe Ave Fresno (93721) ***(P-10378)***
Health Data Vision Inc (PA)........D.......866 969-3222
425 W Broadway Ste 100 Glendale (91204) ***(P-15773)***
Health Department, Salinas *Also called County of Monterey* ***(P-24163)***
Health Department, NAPA *Also called County of NAPA* ***(P-22003)***
Health Dept, Los Angeles *Also called County of Los Angeles* ***(P-21997)***
Health Educ Economic Devlpmnt........D.......510 604-6143
304 Coral Reef Rd Alameda (94501) ***(P-26635)***
Health Educatn Psychiatry Offs, Los Angeles *Also called Kaiser Foundation Hospitals* ***(P-22050)***
Health Entps Lf Long Plan........B.......818 654-0330
5805 Sepulveda Blvd Van Nuys (91411) ***(P-21759)***
Health Entps Life-Long Plans, Van Nuys *Also called Health Entps Lf Long Plan* ***(P-21759)***
Health Fitness America, Irvine *Also called Equinox-76th Street Inc* ***(P-19666)***
Health Information Partners........C.......949 261-5000
4041 Macarthur Blvd # 360 Newport Beach (92660) ***(P-20589)***
Health Link Medi Van........D.......310 981-9500
6053 W Century Blvd # 900 Los Angeles (90045) ***(P-5117)***
Health Net LLC (HQ)........C.......818 676-6000
21650 Oxnard St Fl 25 Woodland Hills (91367) ***(P-9947)***
Health Net California Inc........C.......818 543-9037
101 N Brand Blvd Ste 1500 Glendale (91203) ***(P-9948)***
Health Net California Inc........B.......510 465-9600
155 Grand Ave Lbby Oakland (94612) ***(P-9949)***
Health Net California Inc........B.......916 935-3520
12033 Foundation Pl Gold River (95670) ***(P-9950)***
Health Net Federal Svcs LLC (HQ)........A.......916 935-5000
2025 Aerojet Rd Rancho Cordova (95742) ***(P-9951)***
Health Plan of San Joaquin........C.......209 942-6300
7751 S Manthey Rd French Camp (95231) ***(P-9952)***
Health Plan of San Mateo, South San Francisco *Also called San Mateo Health Commission* ***(P-22317)***
Health Quest, NAPA *Also called Back Street Fitness Inc* ***(P-18120)***
Health Resources Corp........B.......714 754-5454
2701 S Bristol St Santa Ana (92704) ***(P-20903)***
Health Services Dept, Palos Verdes Peninsu *Also called County of Los Angeles* ***(P-20814)***
Health Services Dept, Los Angeles *Also called County of Los Angeles* ***(P-20816)***
Health Services, Dept of, Acton *Also called County of Los Angeles* ***(P-21463)***
Health Services, Dept of, Downey *Also called County of Los Angeles* ***(P-21996)***
Health Services, Dept of, Los Angeles *Also called County of Los Angeles* ***(P-20815)***
Health Services, Dept of, Los Angeles *Also called County of Los Angeles* ***(P-21998)***
Health Services, Dept of, Torrance *Also called County of Los Angeles* ***(P-7940)***
Health Services, Dept of, City of Industry *Also called County of Los Angeles* ***(P-23098)***
Health Services, Dept of, Los Angeles *Also called County of Los Angeles* ***(P-18926)***
Health Services, Dept of, Wilmington *Also called County of Los Angeles* ***(P-18927)***
Health South Tustin Rehab Hosp........C.......714 832-9200
14851 Yorba St Tustin (92780) ***(P-23254)***
Health System, San Mateo *Also called County of San Mateo* ***(P-22007)***
Health System Medical Network, Beverly Hills *Also called Cedars-Sinai Medical Center* ***(P-20769)***
Health Trust (PA)........C.......408 513-8700
3180 Newberry Dr Ste 200 San Jose (95118) ***(P-24402)***
Health Valley Foods Inc........B.......626 334-3241
16007 Cmino De La Cantera Irwindale (91702) ***(P-8587)***
Healthcare Barton System (PA)........A.......530 541-3420
2170 South Ave South Lake Tahoe (96150) ***(P-20904)***
Healthcare Barton System........E.......530 543-5685
2270 South South Lake Tahoe (96150) ***(P-20905)***
Healthcare California........D.......559 243-9990
6327 N Fresno St Ste 104 Fresno (93710) ***(P-21760)***
Healthcare Centre of Fresno, Fresno *Also called Fresno Skilled Nursing* ***(P-19927)***
Healthcare Centre of Fresno........C.......559 268-5361
1665 M St Fresno (93721) ***(P-21476)***
Healthcare Cost Solutions Inc........D.......949 721-2795
1200 Newprt Cntr Dr 190 Newport Beach (92660) ***(P-25606)***
Healthcare Ctr of Downey LLC........C.......562 869-0978
12023 Lakewood Blvd Downey (90242) ***(P-20006)***
Healthcare Fullerton & Well........C.......714 992-5701
2222 N Harbor Blvd Fullerton (92835) ***(P-20007)***
Healthcare Group, Escondido *Also called Las Villas Del Norte* ***(P-20067)***
Healthcare Group........C.......619 463-0281
5480 Marengo Ave Ste 619 La Mesa (91942) ***(P-23953)***
Healthcare MGT Partners LLC........B.......949 263-8620
20 Executive Park Ste 155 Irvine (92614) ***(P-26255)***
Healthcare MGT Systems Inc........D.......951 654-9347
980 W 7th St San Jacinto (92582) ***(P-20008)***
Healthcare Partners LLC........D.......714 995-1000
1236 N Magnolia Ave Anaheim (92801) ***(P-22250)***
Healthcare Partners LLC........D.......562 304-2100
3932 Long Beach Blvd Long Beach (90807) ***(P-19004)***
Healthcare Partners LLC........D.......562 429-2473
4910 Airport Plaza Dr Long Beach (90815) ***(P-22251)***
Healthcare Partners LLC........B.......562 988-7000
2600 Redondo Ave Ste 405 Long Beach (90806) ***(P-19005)***
Healthcare Partners LLC........E.......714 964-6229
3501 S Harbor Blvd # 100 Santa Ana (92704) ***(P-22252)***
Healthcare Partners Med Group, Long Beach *Also called Healthcare Partners LLC* ***(P-19004)***
Healthcare Partners Med Group, Montebello *Also called Davita Medical Management LLC* ***(P-18945)***
Healthcare Partners Med Group, El Monte *Also called Davita Medical Management LLC* ***(P-18946)***
Healthcare Partners Med Group, El Segundo *Also called Davita Medical Management LLC* ***(P-18947)***
Healthcare Services, French Camp *Also called San Joaquin General Hospital* ***(P-21157)***
Healthcare Services Group Inc........A.......562 494-7939
5199 E Pacific Coast Hwy # 402 Long Beach (90804) ***(P-27279)***
Healthcomp........B.......559 499-2450
621 Santa Fe Ave Fresno (93721) ***(P-10379)***
Healthcomp Administrators, Fresno *Also called Healthcomp* ***(P-10379)***
Healthfirst Medical Group Inc (PA)........E.......562 949-9328
13440 Imperial Hwy Santa Fe Springs (90670) ***(P-22038)***
Healthfusion Holdings Inc (HQ)........D.......858 523-2120
100 N Rios Ave Solana Beach (92075) ***(P-11670)***
Healthmarkets Inc........D.......949 486-0600
3152 Red Hill Ave Ste 200 Costa Mesa (92626) ***(P-10380)***
Healthnet California Inc........D.......562 598-4043
1661 Golden Rain Rd Seal Beach (90740) ***(P-9953)***
Healthnet Seniority Plus, Seal Beach *Also called Healthnet California Inc* ***(P-9953)***
Healthpeak Properties Inc (PA)........D.......949 407-0700
1920 Main St Ste 1200 Irvine (92614) ***(P-11855)***
Healthpocket Inc........D.......800 984-8015
444 Castro St Ste 710 Mountain View (94041) ***(P-9906)***
Healthpointe Medical Group Inc (PA)........D.......714 956-2663
16702 Valley View Ave La Mirada (90638) ***(P-19006)***
Healthquest Laboratories Inc (PA)........D.......714 418-5867
18023 Sky Park Cir Irvine (92614) ***(P-21541)***
Healthright 360........D.......909 624-1233
845 E Arrow Hwy Pomona (91767) ***(P-23255)***

Mergent e-mail: customerrelations@mergent.com
1292
2020 Directory of California
Wholesalers and Services Companies
(P-0000) Products & Services Section entry number
(PA)=Parent Co (HQ)=Headquarters (DH)=Div Headquarters

Healthsmart Management Service ....D....714 947-8600
10855 Bus Ctr Dr Ste C Cypress (90630) *(P-10381)*
Healthsmart Pacific Inc (PA) ....A....562 595-1911
5150 E Pacific Cst Hwy # 200 Long Beach (90804) *(P-20906)*
HealthSouth, Tustin *Also called Encompass Health Corporation (P-22025)*
HealthSouth, Bakersfield *Also called Encompass Health Corporation (P-23916)*
HealthSouth, Oakland *Also called Encompass Health Corporation (P-21472)*
Healthsport Ltd A Ltd Partnr (PA) ....C....707 822-3488
300 Dr Martin Luther Arcata (95521) *(P-18151)*
Healthsport-Arcata, Arcata *Also called Healthsport Ltd A Ltd Partnr (P-18151)*
Healthstream Inc ....C....800 733-8737
9605 Scranton Rd Ste 200 San Diego (92121) *(P-15348)*
Healthview Inc (PA) ....D....310 547-3341
921 S Beacon St San Pedro (90731) *(P-23954)*
Healthview Inc ....E....562 468-0136
12750 Center Court Dr S # 410 Cerritos (90703) *(P-23955)*
Healthy Beginnings French Camp ....D....209 468-6147
500 W Hospital Rd French Camp (95231) *(P-19007)*
Heallth Sanitation Services, Santa Maria *Also called Valley Garbage Rubbish Co Inc (P-6314)*
Hearsay Social Inc (PA) ....D....888 990-3777
185 Berry St Ste 3800 San Francisco (94107) *(P-15349)*
Hearst Communications Inc ....B....805 375-3121
2323 Teller Rd Newbury Park (91320) *(P-5727)*
Hearst Stations Inc ....D....831 758-8888
238 John St Salinas (93901) *(P-5610)*
Heart Consciousness Church (PA) ....C....707 987-2477
18424 Harbin Springs Rd Middletown (95461) *(P-13172)*
Heart Hospital of Bk LLC ....B....661 316-6000
3001 Sillect Ave Bakersfield (93308) *(P-20907)*
Heartflow Inc (PA) ....D....650 241-1221
1400 Seaport Blvd Bldg B Redwood City (94063) *(P-15607)*
Hearthstone Inc ....D....818 385-0005
24151 Ventura Blvd Calabasas (91302) *(P-9824)*
Heartland Express Inc Iowa ....E....319 626-3600
10131 Redwood Ave Fontana (92335) *(P-4059)*
Heartland Meat Company Inc ....D....619 407-3668
3461 Main St Chula Vista (91911) *(P-8407)*
Heartland Payment Systems LLC ....D....650 678-2824
548 Shorebird Cir # 3101 Redwood City (94065) *(P-16820)*
Heartland Payment Systems LLC ....D....909 609-1836
35804 Octopus Ln Wildomar (92595) *(P-16821)*
Heartland Payment Systems LLC ....D....707 338-0510
1007 W College Ave Ste B Santa Rosa (95401) *(P-16822)*
Heartland Payment Systems LLC ....D....424 247-8521
207 S Broadway Redondo Beach (90277) *(P-16823)*
Heartland Payment Systems LLC ....D....925 360-3258
2225 Buena Vista Ave A Walnut Creek (94597) *(P-16824)*
Heartland Payment Systems LLC ....D....916 844-9548
5325 Elkhorn Blvd Sacramento (95842) *(P-16825)*
Heartland Payment Systems Inc ....D....760 324-0133
510 Cerritos Way Cathedral City (92234) *(P-16826)*
Heartland Payment Systems Inc ....D....415 518-4810
1460 Golden Gate Ave # 5 San Francisco (94115) *(P-16827)*
HEARTLAND PAYMENT SYSTEMS, INC., San Francisco *Also called Heartland Payment Systems Inc (P-16827)*
Heat, San Francisco *Also called Hvsf Transition LLC (P-13519)*
Heat Software, Newport Beach *Also called Heat Waves LLC (P-14851)*
Heat Software Intermediate Inc ....B....408 601-2800
2590 N 1st St Ste 360 San Jose (95131) *(P-15350)*
Heat Waves LLC ....C....323 753-8441
4087 Rivoli Newport Beach (92660) *(P-14851)*
Heather Ann Creations, Costa Mesa *Also called Alfreds Pictures Frames Inc (P-16609)*
Heavenly Construction Inc ....D....408 723-4954
370 Umbarger Rd Ste A San Jose (95111) *(P-3416)*
Heavenly Greens, San Jose *Also called Heavenly Construction Inc (P-3416)*
Heaviland Enterprises Inc (PA) ....C....760 598-7065
2180 La Mirada Dr Vista (92081) *(P-827)*
Heavy Load Transfer LLC ....D....310 816-0260
18735 S Ferris Pl Rancho Dominguez (90220) *(P-3893)*
Heavy Metal, Chatsworth *Also called Noble House Home Furn LLC (P-6523)*
Hebrew Home For Aged Disabled ....A....415 334-2500
302 Silver Ave San Francisco (94112) *(P-20009)*
Heffernan Group, San Francisco *Also called Heffernan Insurance Brokers (P-10382)*
Heffernan Insurance Brokers ....E....800 829-9996
180 Howard St Ste 200 San Francisco (94105) *(P-10382)*
HEI Hospitality LLC ....C....818 887-4800
21850 Oxnard St Woodland Hills (91367) *(P-12345)*
HEI Long Beach LLC ....C....562 983-3400
701 W Ocean Blvd Long Beach (90831) *(P-12346)*
HEI Mission Valley LP ....C....619 299-2729
901 Camino Del Rio S San Diego (92108) *(P-12347)*
Heidi Corporation ....D....626 333-6317
727 N Vernon Ave Azusa (91702) *(P-1246)*
Height Brown and Bonesteel ....D....213 241-0900
555 S Flower St Ste 4500 Los Angeles (90071) *(P-22565)*
Heilind Electronics Inc ....D....559 651-0168
700 N Plaza Dr Visalia (93291) *(P-7276)*
Heilwell Gad MD ....D....626 817-4747
625 S Fair Oaks Ave # 280 Pasadena (91105) *(P-19008)*
Heimark Distributing, Santa Fe Springs *Also called Triangle Distributing Co (P-8794)*
Heinaman Contract Glazing Inc (PA) ....E....949 587-0266
26981 Vista Ter Ste E Lake Forest (92630) *(P-3417)*
Helen Evans Home For Children, Hacienda Heights *Also called Care Associates Inc (P-23848)*
Helen Woodward Animal Center (PA) 858 756-4117
6461 El Apajo Rancho Santa Fe (92067) *(P-24836)*

Helinet Aviation Services LLC (PA) ....D....818 902-0229
16303 Waterman Dr Van Nuys (91406) *(P-17615)*
Helios Healthcare LLC ....C....916 482-0465
2540 Carmichael Way Carmichael (95608) *(P-20010)*
Helios Healthcare LLC ....C....831 449-1515
350 Iris Dr Salinas (93906) *(P-20011)*
Helios Healthcare LLC ....C....530 345-1306
587 Rio Lindo Ave Chico (95926) *(P-20012)*
Helios Healthcare LLC ....C....707 644-7401
2200 Tuolumne St Vallejo (94589) *(P-20590)*
Helix Healthcare Inc ....B....619 465-4411
7050 Parkway Dr La Mesa (91942) *(P-21412)*
Helix Holdings I LLC ....D....415 805-3360
1 Circle Star Way Fl 2 San Carlos (94070) *(P-25758)*
Helix Opco LLC ....C....415 805-3360
1 Circle Star Way Fl 2 San Carlos (94070) *(P-25759)*
Helix Water District ....D....619 596-3860
1233 Vernon Way El Cajon (92020) *(P-6067)*
Hellmann Wrldwide Lgistics Inc ....D....310 847-4600
2270 E 220th St Long Beach (90810) *(P-4964)*
Hellmann Wrldwide Lgistics Inc ....E....310 847-4600
2270 E 220th St Carson (90810) *(P-4965)*
Hellmuth Obata & Kassabaum Inc (HQ) ....C....415 243-0555
1 Bush St Ste 200 San Francisco (94104) *(P-25448)*
Hellmuth Obata & Kassabaum Inc ....E....310 838-9555
9530 Jefferson Blvd Culver City (90232) *(P-25449)*
Hellosign, San Francisco *Also called Jn Projects Inc (P-13435)*
Helloworld Travel Svcs USA Inc ....D....310 535-1000
6171 W Century Blvd # 160 Los Angeles (90045) *(P-4822)*
Helm Management Co (PA) ....D....619 589-6222
4668 Nebo Dr Ste A La Mesa (91941) *(P-11189)*
Helm Technical Services, El Dorado Hills *Also called G R Helm Inc (P-14507)*
Helm, The, La Mesa *Also called Helm Management Co (P-11189)*
Helmet House Inc (PA) ....D....800 421-7247
26855 Malibu Hills Rd Calabasas Hills (91301) *(P-8032)*
Help For The Hurting Inc ....D....909 796-4222
2205 S Artesia St San Bernardino (92408) *(P-23256)*
Help Group West (PA) ....C....818 781-0360
13130 Burbank Blvd Sherman Oaks (91401) *(P-22039)*
Help Hospitalized Veterans II ....D....951 926-4500
36585 Penfield Ln Winchester (92596) *(P-23257)*
Help Unlmted Personnel Svc Inc ....C....805 962-4646
1765 Goodyear Ave Ste 203 Ventura (93003) *(P-21761)*
Helping Hands of Westminster, Westminster *Also called Helping Hands Sanctuary of Ida (P-20013)*
Helping Hands Pantry, San Bernardino *Also called Help For The Hurting Inc (P-23256)*
Helping Hands Sanctuary of Ida ....D....714 892-6686
240 Hospital Cir Westminster (92683) *(P-20013)*
Helping Hearts Foundation Inc ....D....916 368-7200
3050 Fite Cir Ste 108 Sacramento (95827) *(P-23956)*
Helpline Youth Counseling (PA) ....E....562 273-0722
14181 Telegraph Rd Whittier (90604) *(P-23258)*
Heluna Health, City of Industry *Also called Public Hlth Fndation Entps Inc (P-24629)*
Hemacare Corporation (PA) ....C....877 310-0717
8500 Balboa Blvd Ste 130 Northridge (91325) *(P-22253)*
Hemar & Rousso Attys At Law, Encino *Also called Hemar Rousso & Heald L L P (P-22566)*
Hemar Rousso & Heald L L P ....E....818 501-3800
15910 Ventura Blvd # 1201 Encino (91436) *(P-22566)*
Hemet Unified School District ....C....951 765-2550
41535 Mayberry Ave Hemet (92544) *(P-24561)*
Hemet Valley Ambulance, Hemet *Also called American Medical Response Inc (P-3641)*
Hemet Valley Imaging Med Group (PA) ....C....951 925-6537
3292 E Florida Ave Ste F Hemet (92544) *(P-19009)*
Hemington Landscape Svcs Inc ....D....530 677-9290
4170 Business Dr Cameron Park (95682) *(P-828)*
Hemodialysis Inc (PA) ....C....818 500-8736
710 W Wilson Ave Glendale (91203) *(P-21924)*
Hemodialysis Inc ....E....818 365-6961
14901 Rinaldi St Ste 100 Mission Hills (91345) *(P-21925)*
Henderson Finnegan Farabow ....D....650 849-6600
3300 Hillview Ave Fl 2 Palo Alto (94304) *(P-22567)*
Hendrickson Truck Lines Inc ....C....916 387-9614
7080 Florin Perkins Rd Sacramento (95828) *(P-4060)*
Hendrickson Trucking Inc ....B....916 387-9614
7080 Florin Perkins Rd Sacramento (95828) *(P-4061)*
Henkel US Operations Corp. ....C....925 458-8086
2850 Willow Pass Rd Bay Point (94565) *(P-25124)*
Henkels & McCoy Inc ....B....909 517-3011
2840 Ficus St Pomona (91766) *(P-1862)*
Henkels & McCoy Inc ....D....909 590-8419
2840 Ficus St Pomona (91766) *(P-1863)*
Henrietta Weill Memorial Child (PA) ....D....661 322-1021
3628 Stockdale Hwy Bakersfield (93309) *(P-22040)*
Henry Avocado Corporation (PA) ....D....760 745-6632
2208 Harmony Grove Rd Escondido (92029) *(P-222)*
Henry Broadcasting Co ....E....415 285-1133
2277 Jerrold Ave San Francisco (94124) *(P-5533)*
Henry Bros Electronics Inc ....D....714 525-4350
1511 E Orangethorpe Ave A Fullerton (92831) *(P-15608)*
Henry Hibino Farms ....D....831 757-3081
106 Rico St Salinas (93907) *(P-58)*
Henry J Kaiser Fmly Foundation (PA) ....C....650 854-9400
185 Berry St Ste 2000 San Francisco (94107) *(P-11768)*
Henry Mayo Diagnostic Imaging, Valencia *Also called Henry Mayo Newhall Mem Hosp (P-19011)*
Henry Mayo Newhall Mem Hlth ....A....661 253-8000
23845 Mcbean Pkwy Valencia (91355) *(P-20908)*
Henry Mayo Newhall Mem Hosp. ....D....661 253-8112
23845 Mcbean Pkwy Valencia (91355) *(P-19010)*

Employee Codes: A=Over 500 employees, B=251-500
C=101-250, D=51-100, E=50

2020 Directory of California
Wholesalers and Services Companies

© Mergent Inc. 1-800-342-5647

1293

Henry Mayo Newhall Mem Hosp...B...661 253-8400
23845 Mcbean Pkwy Valencia (91355) ***(P-19011)***
Henry Mayo Newhall Mem Hosp...B...661 253-8227
23845 Mcbean Pkwy Santa Clarita (91355) ***(P-22254)***
Henry Samueli School Engrg, Irvine *Also called University California Irvine* ***(P-25862)***
Henry Wine Group LLC (HQ)...B...707 745-8500
4301 Industrial Way Benicia (94510) ***(P-8812)***
Henry Wine Group of C.A., The, Benicia *Also called Henry Wine Group LLC* ***(P-8812)***
Henry's Pub, Berkeley *Also called Hotel Durant A Ltd Partnership* ***(P-12406)***
Henrymayo Newhall Mem Hosp, Valencia *Also called Henry Mayo Newhall Mem Hlth* ***(P-20908)***
Hensel Phelps Construction Co...D...858 266-7979
5271 Viewridge Ct Frnt San Diego (92123) ***(P-1496)***
Hensel Phelps Construction Co...C...408 452-1800
226 Airport Pkwy Ste 150 San Jose (95110) ***(P-1497)***
Hensel Phelps Construction Co...D...619 544-6828
9404 Genesee Ave Ste 140 La Jolla (92037) ***(P-1498)***
Hensel Phelps Construction Co...C...949 852-0111
18850 Von Kamon 100 Irvine (92612) ***(P-1499)***
Hensly Event Resources, Brisbane *Also called Michaael S Hensley* ***(P-13439)***
Henson Recording Studio, Los Angeles *Also called Jim Henson Company Inc* ***(P-17620)***
Hentrel Greathouse Foundation...D...302 513-4056
127 S 1st Ave Barstow (92311) ***(P-24562)***
Henwood Energy Services Inc (HQ)...C...916 955-6031
2379 Gateway Oaks Dr # 110 Sacramento (95833) ***(P-25125)***
Heppner Hardwoods Inc...D...626 969-7983
555 W Danlee St Azusa (91702) ***(P-6622)***
Herald Christian Health Center (PA)...D...626 286-8700
8841 Garvey Ave Rosemead (91770) ***(P-19012)***
Herb Thyme Farm Inc...D...603 542-3690
7909 Crossway Dr Pico Rivera (90660) ***(P-26)***
Herbert Malarkey Roofing Co...D...562 806-8000
9301 Garfield Ave South Gate (90280) ***(P-3061)***
Herbs Pool Service Inc...D...415 479-4040
3769 Redwood Hwy San Rafael (94903) ***(P-16828)***
Herc Rentals 9638, Carson *Also called Herc Rentals Inc* ***(P-14164)***
Herc Rentals 9643, Bakersfield *Also called Herc Rentals Inc* ***(P-14165)***
Herc Rentals 9741, Rohnert Park *Also called Herc Rentals Inc* ***(P-14163)***
Herc Rentals 9748, Benicia *Also called Herc Rentals Inc* ***(P-14166)***
Herc Rentals Inc...D...707 586-6491
5500 Commerce Blvd Rohnert Park (94928) ***(P-14163)***
Herc Rentals Inc...E...310 233-5000
22422 S Alameda St Carson (90810) ***(P-14164)***
Herc Rentals Inc...C...661 392-3661
6315 Snow Rd Bakersfield (93308) ***(P-14165)***
Herc Rentals Inc...E...707 747-4444
5251 Industrial Way Benicia (94510) ***(P-14166)***
Herc Rentals Inc...C...510 633-2040
7727 Oakport St Oakland (94621) ***(P-14167)***
Herc Rentals Prosolutions, Oakland *Also called Herc Rentals Inc* ***(P-14167)***
Herca Construction Services, Perris *Also called Herca Telecomm Services Inc* ***(P-7475)***
Herca Telecomm Services Inc...D...951 940-5941
18610 Beck St Perris (92570) ***(P-7475)***
Hercules Capital Inc (PA)...D...650 289-3060
400 Hamilton Ave Ste 310 Palo Alto (94301) ***(P-11921)***
Hercules Fitness...E...510 724-2900
600 Alfred Nobel Dr Hercules (94547) ***(P-18152)***
Here Films...E...310 806-4288
10990 Wilshire Blvd Los Angeles (90024) ***(P-27088)***
Heritage 1 Window and Building...C...916 481-5030
4300 Jetway Ct North Highlands (95660) ***(P-6623)***
Heritage Bank of Commerce (HQ)...C...408 947-6900
150 Almaden Blvd Lbby San Jose (95113) ***(P-9211)***
Heritage California Aco, Northridge *Also called Regal Medical Group Inc* ***(P-24421)***
Heritage Community Credit Un (PA)...E...916 364-1700
10399 Old Placerville Rd Sacramento (95827) ***(P-9316)***
Heritage Community Credit Un...E...916 364-1700
10399 Old Clasaville Rd Rancho Cordova (95670) ***(P-9317)***
Heritage Conalescent Hospital, Sacramento *Also called Horizon West Inc* ***(P-20021)***
Heritage Gardens Hlth Care Ctr, Loma Linda *Also called Heritage Health Care Inc* ***(P-20014)***
Heritage Golf Group Inc...D...661 254-4401
27330 Tourney Rd Valencia (91355) ***(P-18252)***
Heritage Golf Group LLC...D...949 369-6226
990 Avenida Talega San Clemente (92673) ***(P-18253)***
Heritage Health Care, Lancaster *Also called High Desert Med Corp A Med Grp* ***(P-19013)***
Heritage Health Care Inc...C...909 796-0216
25271 Barton Rd Loma Linda (92354) ***(P-20014)***
Heritage House, Camarillo *Also called Wilshire Health and Cmnty Svcs* ***(P-24119)***
Heritage Indemnity Company...D...303 987-5500
23 Pasteur Irvine (92618) ***(P-10096)***
Heritage Inn, Ridgecrest *Also called Great Western Hotels Corp* ***(P-12309)***
Heritage Interests LLC (PA)...D...916 481-5030
4300 Jetway Ct North Highlands (95660) ***(P-2939)***
Heritage Land Company Inc...E...209 444-1700
111 N Zuckerman Rd Stockton (95206) ***(P-247)***
Heritage Landscape Inc...C...818 999-2041
7949 Deering Ave Canoga Park (91304) ***(P-733)***
Heritage Manor Inc...D...626 573-3141
610 N Garfield Ave Monterey Park (91754) ***(P-20015)***
Heritage Medical Group...C...760 956-1286
12370 Hesperia Rd Ste 6 Victorville (92395) ***(P-22255)***
Heritage One Carpentry Inc...C...530 345-6622
2107 Forest Ave Ste 100 Chico (95928) ***(P-6624)***
Heritage One Door & Carpentry, North Highlands *Also called BMC Stock Holdings Inc* ***(P-6607)***
Heritage One Door and Building...D...916 481-5030
4300 Jetway Ct North Highlands (95660) ***(P-6625)***
Heritage Pointe, Mission Viejo *Also called Jewish Home For The Aging of O* ***(P-20037)***
Heritage Psychiatric Health, Oakland *Also called Telecare Corporation* ***(P-21444)***
Heritage Senior Care Inc...D...800 562-2734
15428 Civic Dr Ste 345 Victorville (92392) ***(P-21762)***
Heritage, The, San Francisco *Also called San Francisco Ladies Protecti* ***(P-24063)***
Herman Health Care Center, San Jose *Also called Herman Sanitarium* ***(P-20016)***
Herman Sanitarium...C...408 269-0701
2295 Plummer Ave San Jose (95125) ***(P-20016)***
Herman Weissker Inc (HQ)...C...951 826-8800
1645 Brown Ave Riverside (92509) ***(P-1864)***
Hermitage Hlthcr Mnkn Mnr...C...410 651-0011
400 Circle Dr Angwin (94508) ***(P-20591)***
Hero, San Diego *Also called Renovate America Inc* ***(P-15057)***
Herren Enterprises Inc...D...949 951-1666
23091 Terra Dr Laguna Hills (92653) ***(P-3685)***
Herrero Builders Incorporated (PA)...C...415 824-7675
2100 Oakdale Ave San Francisco (94124) ***(P-1355)***
Herrick Hospital, Berkeley *Also called Surgery Center of Alta Bates* ***(P-19461)***
Herring Broadcasting Company...E...858 270-6900
4757 Morena Blvd San Diego (92117) ***(P-5611)***
Herring Networks Inc...C...858 270-6900
4757 Morena Blvd San Diego (92117) ***(P-5612)***
Hertz Claim Management Corp...D...626 296-4760
2923 Bradley St Ste 190 Pasadena (91107) ***(P-17213)***
Hertz Corporation...E...818 997-0414
2627 N Hollywood Way # 8 Burbank (91505) ***(P-17214)***
Hertz Corporation...D...408 450-6025
1000 Walsh Ave Santa Clara (95050) ***(P-17215)***
Hertz Corporation...D...925 680-0316
30 S Buchanan Cir Pacheco (94553) ***(P-17216)***
Hertz Corporation...D...650 624-6391
177 S Airport Blvd South San Francisco (94080) ***(P-17217)***
Hertz Corporation...D...818 569-6900
3111 N Kenwood St Burbank (91505) ***(P-17218)***
Herzog Contracting Corp...B...619 849-6990
2155 Hancock St San Diego (92110) ***(P-3418)***
HEs Transportation Svcs Inc...E...510 783-6100
3623 Munster St Hayward (94545) ***(P-4966)***
Hetrosys LLC...D...408 270-0240
3858 Carrera Ct San Jose (95148) ***(P-27089)***
Hewitt and Canfield Cnstr Inc...D...805 522-4426
495 E Easy St Ste A Simi Valley (93065) ***(P-2940)***
HEWLETT FOUNDATION, Menlo Park *Also called Hewlett Wlliam Flora Fndation* ***(P-24837)***
Hewlett Packard...A...650 857-1501
3000 Hanover St Palo Alto (94304) ***(P-14852)***
Hewlett Packard Enterprise Co (PA)...C...650 687-5817
6280 America Center Dr San Jose (95002) ***(P-15351)***
Hewlett Wlliam Flora Fndation...D...650 234-4500
2121 Sand Hill Rd Menlo Park (94025) ***(P-24837)***
HFS Concepts 4 Inc...E...562 424-1720
3229 E Spring St Ste 330 Long Beach (90806) ***(P-25450)***
HG Fenton Company...D...619 400-0120
7577 Mission Valley Rd # 200 San Diego (92108) ***(P-10736)***
Hga Architects and Engineers, Sacramento *Also called Hammel Green & Abrahamson Inc* ***(P-25444)***
Hggc LLC (PA)...B...650 321-4910
1950 University Ave # 350 East Palo Alto (94303) ***(P-14853)***
Hgt, Ontario *Also called Hub Group Trucking Inc* ***(P-3895)***
HHC Trs Portsmouth LLC...D...760 322-6000
888 E Tahquitz Canyon Way Palm Springs (92262) ***(P-12348)***
Hhlp San Diego Lessee LLC...D...619 446-3000
530 Broadway San Diego (92101) ***(P-12349)***
HHS Communications Inc...D...909 230-5170
2042 S Grove Ave Ontario (91761) ***(P-2512)***
Hhsa Data Center, Sacramento *Also called Califrnia Hlth Humn Srvcs Agcy* ***(P-15736)***
HI Anaheim LLC...D...714 533-1500
100 W Katella Ave Anaheim (92802) ***(P-12350)***
HI Fresno Hospitality LLC...D...559 233-6650
1055 Van Ness Ave Fresno (93721) ***(P-12351)***
HI Lo Motel, Edgewood *Also called Siskiyou Development Company* ***(P-12930)***
Hi-Desert Medical Center, Yucca Valley *Also called Hi-Desert Mem Hlth Care Dst* ***(P-20909)***
Hi-Desert Mem Hlth Care Dst (PA)...D...760 820-9229
6530 Lcontenpa Rd Ste 100 Yucca Valley (92284) ***(P-20909)***
Hi-TEC Sports Usa Inc (HQ)...D...209 545-1111
5990 Sepulvda Blvd # 600 Van Nuys (91411) ***(P-8134)***
Hibshman Trading Corporation...D...909 581-1800
9843 6th St Ste 103 Rancho Cucamonga (91730) ***(P-8076)***
Hid Global Safe Inc...D...408 453-1008
3590 N 1st St Ste 320 San Jose (95134) ***(P-15609)***
Hidden Valley Golf Course, Hidden Valley Lake *Also called Hidden Valley Lake Association* ***(P-24563)***
Hidden Valley Lake Association (PA)...D...707 987-3146
18174 Hidden Valley Rd Hidden Valley Lake (95467) ***(P-24563)***
Hidden Valley Mvg & Stor Inc (PA)...D...602 252-7800
1218 Pacific Oaks Pl Escondido (92029) ***(P-4213)***
Hidden Villa Ranch, Norco *Also called Luberski Inc* ***(P-8329)***
Hidden Villa Ranch Produce Inc...B...714 680-3447
310 N Harbor Blvd Ste 205 Fullerton (92832) ***(P-8326)***
Hideaway Club...A...760 777-7400
80440 Hideaway Club Ct La Quinta (92253) ***(P-18466)***
Higard Farms LLC...D...831 753-5982
6 Quail Run Cir Salinas (93907) ***(P-333)***
Higgs Fletcher & Mack Llp...C...619 236-1551
401 W A St Ste 2600 San Diego (92101) ***(P-22568)***
High Caliber Line, Irwindale *Also called Calibre International LLC* ***(P-26900)***
High Country Lumber Inc (PA)...E...760 873-5874
444 S Main St Bishop (93514) ***(P-6626)***
High Desert, Victorville *Also called Southern California Edison Co* ***(P-5952)***

Mergent e-mail: customerrelations@mergent.com
1294
2020 Directory of California
Wholesalers and Services Companies
(P-0000) Products & Services Section entry number
(PA)=Parent Co (HQ)=Headquarters (DH)=Div Headquarters

High Desert Med Corp A Med Grp (PA)...C.......661 945-5984
43839 15th St W Lancaster (93534) ***(P-19013)***
High Desert Partnership...B.......760 946-5414
17500 Mana Rd Apple Valley (92307) ***(P-25906)***
High Desert Phoenix...E.......661 547-5630
42980 Staffordshire Dr Lancaster (93534) ***(P-18704)***
High Dsert Ptent Care Svcs LLC...D.......760 956-4150
17095 Main St Hesperia (92345) ***(P-19014)***
High End Development Inc...D.......925 687-2540
665 Stone Rd Benicia (94510) ***(P-3419)***
High Fidelity Inc...D.......415 862-4434
185 Clara St Ste 100 San Francisco (94107) ***(P-14854)***
HIGH HAVEN, Los Angeles *Also called Broadview Inc* ***(P-19760)***
High Performance Wall Systems, Redding *Also called Redding Drywall Systems Inc* ***(P-2847)***
High Plains Ranch LLC (PA)...C.......559 583-1277
2911 Hanford Armona Rd Hanford (93230) ***(P-393)***
High Ridge Brands, La Palma *Also called Dr Fresh LLC* ***(P-7941)***
High Ridge Wind LLC...A.......888 903-6926
15445 Innovation Dr San Diego (92128) ***(P-5845)***
High Road Program (PA)...D.......805 497-8800
250 N Westlake Blvd # 210 Westlake Village (91362) ***(P-23259)***
High St Car Wash Lube & Oil, Oakland *Also called High Street Hand Car Wash Inc* ***(P-17419)***
High Street Hand Car Wash Inc...D.......510 536-4333
569 High St Oakland (94601) ***(P-17419)***
High Summit LLC...E.......925 605-2900
6909 Las Positas Rd Ste D Livermore (94551) ***(P-17355)***
High Technology Video Inc...D.......323 969-8822
10900 Ventura Blvd Studio City (91604) ***(P-17743)***
High Tide and Green Grass Inc...D.......805 981-8722
2401 W Vineyard Ave Oxnard (93036) ***(P-18254)***
HIGH VALLEY LODGE, Sunland *Also called P R N Convalescent Hospital* ***(P-20180)***
High-Light Electric Inc...D.......951 352-9646
6942 Ed Perkic St Riverside (92504) ***(P-2513)***
Highcom Security Services...D.......510 893-7600
1900 Webster St Ste B Oakland (94612) ***(P-16319)***
Highland Care Center Redlands, Redlands *Also called AG Redlands LLC* ***(P-20479)***
Highland Head Start, Highland *Also called County of San Bernardino* ***(P-23714)***
Highland Hosp Hghland Wellness, Oakland *Also called Alameda Health System* ***(P-20740)***
Highland Lumber Sales Inc...D.......714 778-2293
300 E Santa Ana St Anaheim (92805) ***(P-6627)***
HIGHLAND PALMS HEALTHCARE CENT, Highland *Also called Cedar Holdings LLC* ***(P-19784)***
Highland Park Skilled Nursing...D.......323 254-6125
5125 Monte Vista St Los Angeles (90042) ***(P-20017)***
Highlands Inn Inc...C.......831 620-1234
120 Highland Dr Carmel (93923) ***(P-12352)***
Highlands Inn Investors II LP...B.......831 624-3801
120 Highland Dr Carmel (93923) ***(P-12353)***
Highmark Capital Management...D.......800 582-4734
350 California St Fl 22 San Francisco (94104) ***(P-9825)***
Highpoint Productions Inc...D.......818 728-7600
13400 Rverside Dr Ste 300 Sherman Oaks (91423) ***(P-17616)***
Hightail, San Mateo *Also called Open Text Inc* ***(P-14982)***
Hignell Incorporated...D.......530 345-1965
1836 Laburnum Ave Chico (95926) ***(P-10737)***
Hii Fleet Support Group LLC...B.......858 522-6319
9444 Balboa Ave Ste 400 San Diego (92123) ***(P-25760)***
Hikvision USA Inc (HQ)...C.......909 895-0400
18639 Railroad St City of Industry (91748) ***(P-16524)***
Hilary A Brodie MD PHD...D.......916 734-3744
2521 Stockton Blvd 7200 Sacramento (95817) ***(P-19015)***
Hilbers Inc...D.......530 673-2947
770 N Walton Ave Ste 100 Yuba City (95993) ***(P-1500)***
Hilbers Contractors & Engrg, Yuba City *Also called Hilbers Inc* ***(P-1500)***
Hildreth Farm Incorporated...D.......707 462-0648
1520 Rddick Cunningham Rd Ukiah (95482) ***(P-204)***
Hill & Knowlton Strategies LLC...D.......415 281-7120
60 Green St San Francisco (94111) ***(P-26911)***
Hill Brothers Chemical Company (PA)...C.......714 998-8800
1675 N Main St Orange (92867) ***(P-8699)***
Hill Creek Schl Ptsa Pta CA, Santee *Also called Santee School District* ***(P-24650)***
Hill Cress Home, San Bernardino *Also called Care Tech Inc* ***(P-19778)***
Hill Farrer & Burrill...D.......213 620-0460
300 S Grand Ave Fl 37 Los Angeles (90071) ***(P-22569)***
Hill Physicians Med Group Inc (PA)...B.......800 445-5747
2409 Camino Ramon San Ramon (94583) ***(P-19016)***
Hillcrest AC & Shtmtl, Bakersfield *Also called Hillcrest Sheet Metal Inc* ***(P-3062)***
Hillcrest Care Inc...D.......909 882-2965
4280 Cypress Dr San Bernardino (92407) ***(P-20592)***
Hillcrest Cnvalescent Hosp Inc...C.......323 636-3462
3401 Cedar Ave Long Beach (90807) ***(P-20593)***
Hillcrest Contracting Inc...D.......951 273-9600
1467 Circle City Dr Corona (92879) ***(P-1732)***
Hillcrest Country Club...C.......310 553-8911
10000 W Pico Blvd Los Angeles (90064) ***(P-18467)***
Hillcrest Manor Sanitarium, National City *Also called Imaginative Horizons Inc* ***(P-20028)***
Hillcrest Senior Housing Corp...C.......650 757-1737
35 Hillcrest Dr Daly City (94014) ***(P-1247)***
Hillcrest Sheet Metal Inc...D.......661 335-1500
2324 Perseus Ct Bakersfield (93308) ***(P-3062)***
Hilldale Habilitation Center, La Mesa *Also called Razavi Corporation* ***(P-20209)***
Hillendale Home Care, Walnut Creek *Also called Caswell Bay Inc* ***(P-21702)***
Hillhaven Convalescent Hosp, Burlingame *Also called Kindred Healthcare Operating* ***(P-21479)***
Hills Wldg & Engrg Contr Inc...D.......661 746-5400
22038 Stockdale Hwy Bakersfield (93314) ***(P-1025)***
Hillsborough, Modesto *Also called Woodside Group Inc* ***(P-9610)***
Hillsdale Group LP...D.......818 623-2170
12750 Riverside Dr North Hollywood (91607) ***(P-20594)***
Hillsdale Group LP...E.......650 742-9150
1201 Broadway Ofc Millbrae (94030) ***(P-20595)***
Hillsdale Group LP...D.......510 538-3866
1832 B St Hayward (94541) ***(P-20596)***
Hillside Auto Salvage, Riverside *Also called Team Truck Dismantling Inc* ***(P-6497)***
Hillside Care Center, San Rafael *Also called Cal-Coast Healthcare Inc* ***(P-19770)***
Hillside Contractor, Santa Ana *Also called South Coast Stone Paving* ***(P-1791)***
Hillside Entps - AR C Long Bch, Long Beach *Also called Advocacy For Respect and Ch* ***(P-23558)***
Hillside House Inc...D.......805 687-4818
1235 Veronica Springs Rd Santa Barbara (93105) ***(P-20430)***
Hillside Mem Pk & Mortuary, Los Angeles *Also called Temple Israel of Hollywood* ***(P-13381)***
Hillsides...B.......323 254-2274
940 Avenue 64 Pasadena (91105) ***(P-23957)***
Hilltop Family YMCA, Richmond *Also called Young MNS Chrstn Assn of E Bay* ***(P-24773)***
Hilltop Manor, Auburn *Also called Horizon West Healthcare Inc* ***(P-20597)***
Hilltop Ranch Inc...C.......209 874-1875
13890 Looney Rd Ballico (95303) ***(P-503)***
Hilltop Securities Inc...E.......800 765-2200
8350 Wilshire Blvd Beverly Hills (90211) ***(P-9697)***
Hilltop Trading, Ballico *Also called Hilltop Ranch Inc* ***(P-503)***
Hilltown Packing Co Inc...B.......831 784-1931
9 Harris Pl A Salinas (93901) ***(P-504)***
Hillview Acres...D.......714 694-2828
23091 Mill Creek Dr Laguna Hills (92653) ***(P-23958)***
Hillview Acres Childrens Home, Laguna Hills *Also called Hillview Acres* ***(P-23958)***
Hillview Convalescent Hospital...E.......408 779-3633
530 W Dunne Ave Morgan Hill (95037) ***(P-20018)***
Hillview Mental Health Center...D.......818 896-1161
12450 Van Nuys Blvd # 200 Pacoima (91331) ***(P-22041)***
Hilton, Santa Barbara *Also called Park Hotels & Resorts Inc* ***(P-12711)***
Hilton, San Diego *Also called Ww San Diego Harbor Island LLC* ***(P-13119)***
Hilton, San Diego *Also called Park Hotels & Resorts Inc* ***(P-12714)***
Hilton, Sacramento *Also called Shri Sidhi Vinayaka Hotel Inc* ***(P-12923)***
Hilton, Oakland *Also called Park Hotels & Resorts Inc* ***(P-12716)***
Hilton, La Jolla *Also called Park Hotels & Resorts Inc* ***(P-12717)***
Hilton, Pasadena *Also called Park Hotels & Resorts Inc* ***(P-12720)***
Hilton, Milpitas *Also called Bre Select Hotels Oper LLC* ***(P-12083)***
Hilton, Mountain View *Also called Camino Real Group LLC* ***(P-12108)***
Hilton, Anaheim *Also called Makar Anaheim LLC* ***(P-12573)***
Hilton, Beverly Hills *Also called Park Hotels & Resorts Inc* ***(P-12723)***
Hilton, South Lake Tahoe *Also called Park Hotels & Resorts Inc* ***(P-12724)***
Hilton, Ontario *Also called Park Hotels & Resorts Inc* ***(P-12729)***
Hilton, San Gabriel *Also called Park Hotels & Resorts Inc* ***(P-12730)***
Hilton, Redding *Also called Win River Hotel Corporation* ***(P-13096)***
Hilton, Emeryville *Also called Rljhgn Emeryville Lessee LP* ***(P-12835)***
Hilton, Costa Mesa *Also called Park Hotels & Resorts Inc* ***(P-12732)***
Hilton, Long Beach *Also called Merritt Hospitality LLC* ***(P-12611)***
Hilton, San Diego *Also called Lho Mssion Bay Rsie Lessee Inc* ***(P-12550)***
Hilton, Oxnard *Also called T M Mian & Associates Inc* ***(P-13015)***
Hilton, Huntington Beach *Also called Waterfront Hotel LLC* ***(P-13078)***
Hilton, Monterey *Also called Ocean Park Hotels Inc* ***(P-12661)***
Hilton, Los Angeles *Also called Fortuna Enterprises LP* ***(P-12273)***
Hilton, San Jose *Also called West Hotel Partners LP* ***(P-13084)***
Hilton, Santa Clara *Also called Ontario Airport Hotel Corp* ***(P-12677)***
Hilton, Los Angeles *Also called Park Hotels & Resorts Inc* ***(P-12733)***
Hilton, Irvine *Also called Interstate Hotels Resorts Inc* ***(P-12477)***
Hilton, Valencia *Also called Ocean Park Hotels Inc* ***(P-12662)***
Hilton Checkers Los Angeles, Los Angeles *Also called Chsp Trs Los Angeles LLC* ***(P-12144)***
Hilton Concord, Concord *Also called Vwi Concord LLC* ***(P-13068)***
Hilton El Segundo LLC...D.......310 726-0100
2100 E Mariposa Ave El Segundo (90245) ***(P-12354)***
Hilton Garded, San Diego *Also called SD Stadium Hotel LLC* ***(P-12895)***
Hilton Garden Hotel, Foster City *Also called Hilton Garden In San Mateo* ***(P-12355)***
Hilton Garden In San Mateo...D.......650 522-9000
2000 Bridgepointe Pkwy Foster City (94404) ***(P-12355)***
Hilton Garden Inn, San Diego *Also called M4dev LLC* ***(P-12569)***
Hilton Garden Inn...D.......510 346-5533
510 Lewelling Blvd San Leandro (94579) ***(P-12356)***
Hilton Garden Inn Calabasas, Calabasas *Also called T M Mian & Associates Inc* ***(P-13014)***
Hilton Garden Inn Carlsbad Bch, Carlsbad *Also called Interstate Hotels Resorts Inc* ***(P-12473)***
Hilton Garden Inn Emeryville, Emeryville *Also called Rlj Hgn Emeryville Lessee LP* ***(P-12834)***
Hilton Garden Inn Monterey, Monterey *Also called 1000 Aguajito Op Co LLC* ***(P-11972)***
Hilton Garden Inn Palo Alto, Palo Alto *Also called Palmetto Hospitality* ***(P-12708)***
Hilton Garden Inn Pismo, Pismo Beach *Also called Castlblack Pismo Bch Owner LLC* ***(P-12123)***
Hilton Garden Inn Sacremento, Sacramento *Also called Apple Hospitality Reit Inc* ***(P-12013)***
Hilton Garden Inn San, South San Francisco *Also called Larkspur Hsptality Dev MGT LLC* ***(P-12538)***
Hilton Garden Inn Santa, Goleta *Also called Goleta Hhg Hotel Dev LP* ***(P-12302)***
Hilton Garden Inns MGT LLC...C.......760 476-0800
6450 Carlsbad Blvd Carlsbad (92011) ***(P-12357)***
Hilton Garden Inns MGT LLC...D.......310 726-0100
2100 E Mariposa Ave El Segundo (90245) ***(P-12358)***

ALPHABETIC

Employee Codes: A=Over 500 employees, B=251-500
C=101-250, D=51-100, E=50
2020 Directory of California
Wholesalers and Services Companies
© Mergent Inc. 1-800-342-5647
1295

Hilton Garden Inns MGT LLC.....E.....925 292-2000
2801 Constitution Dr Fl 2 Livermore (94551) ***(P-12359)***
Hilton Hotel Long Beach, Long Beach *Also called Lb Funding LLC* ***(P-12543)***
Hilton Hotels, Long Beach *Also called HEI Long Beach LLC* ***(P-12346)***
Hilton Hotels, Ontario *Also called Park Hotels & Resorts Inc* ***(P-12719)***
Hilton Irvine, Irvine *Also called Equistar Irvine Company LLC* ***(P-12251)***
Hilton Los Angles Universal Cy.....B.....818 506-2500
555 Unversal Hollywood Dr Universal City (91608) ***(P-12360)***
Hilton Los Angls/Nversal Cy Ht, Universal City *Also called Sun Hill Properties Inc* ***(P-12984)***
Hilton Port Los Angls-San Pdro, San Pedro *Also called Meristar San Pedro Hilton LLC* ***(P-12609)***
Hilton Resort In Palm Spring, Palm Springs *Also called Walters Family Partnership* ***(P-13074)***
Hilton Resort Palm Springs.....C.....760 320-6868
400 E Tahquitz Canyon Way Palm Springs (92262) ***(P-12361)***
Hilton Sacramento Arden West, Sacramento *Also called Whgca LLC* ***(P-13095)***
Hilton Sacramento Arden West, Sacramento *Also called Interstate Hotels Resorts Inc* ***(P-12476)***
Hilton San Diego Airport/Hrbr, San Diego *Also called Bartell Hotels* ***(P-12037)***
Hilton San Diego/Del Mar, Del Mar *Also called Ws Hdm LLC* ***(P-13116)***
Hilton San Diego/Del Mar, Del Mar *Also called Sunstone Durante LLC* ***(P-12990)***
Hilton San Francisco, Burlingame *Also called Harbor View Hotels Inc* ***(P-12337)***
Hilton San Francisco Fincl Dst.....D.....415 433-6600
750 Kearny St San Francisco (94108) ***(P-12362)***
Hilton San Jose and Towers, Los Angeles *Also called West Hotel Partners LP* ***(P-13083)***
Hilton Santa Clara, Santa Clara *Also called Stanford Hotels Corporation* ***(P-12960)***
Hilton Santa Cruz/Scotts Vly, Scotts Valley *Also called Inn At Scotts Valley LLC* ***(P-12458)***
Hilton Universal Hotel.....D.....818 506-2500
555 Unversal Hollywood Dr Universal City (91608) ***(P-12363)***
Hilton Wdlnd Hlls / Los Angles, Woodland Hills *Also called Canoga Hotel Corporation* ***(P-12111)***
Hilton Woodland Hills & Towers.....C.....818 595-1000
6360 Canoga Ave Woodland Hills (91367) ***(P-12364)***
Hiltonm Grdn Inn Lax El Sgundo, El Segundo *Also called Hilton El Segundo LLC* ***(P-12354)***
Hinds Hospice (PA).....C.....559 674-0407
2490 W Shaw Ave Ste 100a Fresno (93711) ***(P-21763)***
Hinerfeld-Ward Inc.....D.....310 842-7929
8931 Ellis Ave Ste B1 Los Angeles (90034) ***(P-1138)***
Hines Gs Properties Inc.....E.....415 982-6200
101 California St # 1000 San Francisco (94111) ***(P-11567)***
Hines Interests Ltd Partnr.....C.....650 518-6139
1 Hacker Way Bldg 10 Menlo Park (94025) ***(P-11190)***
Hines Nurseries LLC.....D.....602 254-2831
22941 Mill Creek Dr Laguna Hills (92653) ***(P-8898)***
Hino Motors Mfg USA Inc.....C.....951 727-0286
4550 Wineville Ave Jurupa Valley (91752) ***(P-6445)***
Hinode, Woodland *Also called Sunfoods LLC* ***(P-8264)***
Hinshaw & Culbertson LLP.....D.....213 680-2800
633 W 5th St Ste 4700 Los Angeles (90071) ***(P-22570)***
Hinttech Inc.....C.....415 874-3200
505 Montgomery St Fl 11 San Francisco (94111) ***(P-27090)***
Hips, San Jose *Also called Hacienda Invlved Parents Staff* ***(P-24560)***
Hired Inc (PA).....E.....415 813-4987
303 2nd St Ste S600 San Francisco (94107) ***(P-16829)***
Hired Hands Inc.....D.....707 575-4700
2901 Cleveland Ave # 203 Santa Rosa (95403) ***(P-21764)***
Hireforces, San Jose *Also called Incline Incorporated* ***(P-14308)***
Hireright, Irvine *Also called Corporate Risk Hldings III Inc* ***(P-16718)***
Hireright LLC (HQ).....C.....949 428-5800
3349 Michelson Dr Ste 150 Irvine (92612) ***(P-15867)***
Hirsch Electronics LLC.....D.....949 250-8888
1900 Carnegie Ave Ste B Santa Ana (92705) ***(P-7277)***
Hirsch/Bedner Intl Inc (PA).....D.....310 829-9087
3216 Nebraska Ave Santa Monica (90404) ***(P-16830)***
Hirschfeld Kraemer LLP (PA).....E.....415 835-9000
505 Montgomery St Fl 13 San Francisco (94111) ***(P-22571)***
Hirsh Inc.....E.....213 622-9441
860 S Los Angeles St # 900 Los Angeles (90014) ***(P-1026)***
His Kids Ranch, Potrero *Also called Rancho De Sus Ninos Inc* ***(P-24038)***
His Manna Inc.....C.....831 423-5515
150 Felker St Ste B Santa Cruz (95060) ***(P-26636)***
His Passion Inc.....E.....800 760-6389
17195 Newhope St Ste 201 Fountain Valley (92708) ***(P-21765)***
HISPANIC CONCILIO OF SAN MATEO, Redwood City *Also called El Concilio San Mateo Cnty Inc* ***(P-23206)***
Historic Mission Inn Corp.....B.....951 784-0300
3649 Mission Inn Ave Riverside (92501) ***(P-12365)***
Historic Tours of America, San Diego *Also called Old Town Trlley Turs San Diego* ***(P-4858)***
Historic TW Inc.....E.....818 954-3096
106 Disney Productions Burbank (91521) ***(P-17617)***
Historical Properties Inc (PA).....D.....619 230-8417
311 Island Ave San Diego (92101) ***(P-12366)***
Historical Soc Centinela Vly.....B.....310 649-6272
7634 Midfield Ave Los Angeles (90045) ***(P-24266)***
Hit Portfolio I NTC Trs LP.....E.....310 333-0888
2135 E El Segundo Blvd El Segundo (90245) ***(P-12367)***
Hit Portfolio II NTC Trs LP.....E.....760 431-9399
5835 Owens Ave Carlsbad (92008) ***(P-12368)***
Hit Portfolio II Trs LLC.....C.....714 938-1111
400 N State College Blvd Orange (92868) ***(P-12369)***
Hitachi High Tech Amer Inc.....D.....925 218-2800
5960 Inglewood Dr Ste 200 Pleasanton (94588) ***(P-7278)***
Hitachi Vantara Corporation.....C.....858 537-3000
15231 Ave Of Science # 100 San Diego (92128) ***(P-6846)***
Hive Tech Gurus Incorporated.....E.....323 445-1770
510 Strtford Ct Unit 204a Del Mar (92014) ***(P-5416)***
Hkf Inc (PA).....B.....323 225-1318
5983 Smithway St Commerce (90040) ***(P-7451)***
Hks Inc.....D.....310 788-7700
10880 Wilshire Blvd # 1850 Los Angeles (90024) ***(P-25451)***
Hks Architects Inc.....E.....415 356-3800
500 Howard St Fl 4 San Francisco (94105) ***(P-25452)***
Hmbl LLC.....C.....323 656-8090
8400 W Sunset Blvd Ste 3a West Hollywood (90069) ***(P-12370)***
HMC Architects, Ontario *Also called HMC Group* ***(P-25453)***
HMC Group (HQ).....C.....909 989-9979
3546 Concours Ontario (91764) ***(P-25453)***
HMC Group.....D.....909 980-8058
2930 Inland Empire Blvd # 100 Ontario (91764) ***(P-25454)***
Hmclause Inc (HQ).....C.....800 320-4672
260 Cousteau Pl Ste 210 Davis (95618) ***(P-248)***
Hmclause Inc.....D.....530 747-3235
9241 Mace Blvd Davis (95618) ***(P-25761)***
Hmclause Inc.....D.....530 713-5838
42 Glenshire Ln Chico (95973) ***(P-249)***
HMH BUILDERS, Sacramento *Also called Swinerton Builders Hc* ***(P-1614)***
Hmi Associates Inc.....C.....818 887-6800
6800 Owensmouth Ave # 330 Canoga Park (91303) ***(P-16320)***
Hmi Industrial Contractors Inc, Rancho Cordova *Also called Harelson Mechanical Inc* ***(P-3360)***
HMS Agricultural Corporation.....D.....760 347-2335
46247 Arabia St Indio (92201) ***(P-11191)***
HMS Construction Inc (PA).....D.....760 727-9808
2885 Scott St Vista (92081) ***(P-25126)***
Hmt Electric Inc.....D.....858 458-9771
2340 Meyers Ave Escondido (92029) ***(P-2514)***
Hmwc Cpas & Business Advisors.....D.....714 505-9000
17501 17th St Ste 100 Tustin (92780) ***(P-25607)***
Hntb Corporation.....D.....213 403-1000
601 W 5th St Ste 1000 Los Angeles (90071) ***(P-25127)***
Hntb Corporation.....D.....714 460-1600
200 Sandpointe Ave # 200 Santa Ana (92707) ***(P-25128)***
Hntb Gerwick Water Solutions.....C.....714 460-1600
200 Sandpointe Ave Santa Ana (92707) ***(P-25129)***
Hntb-Gerwick JV.....D.....510 839-8972
1300 Clay St Fl 7 Oakland (94612) ***(P-25455)***
Hoag Memorial Hospital Presbt (PA).....A.....949 764-4624
1 Hoag Dr Newport Beach (92663) ***(P-20910)***
Hob Entertainment LLC.....C.....714 778-2583
1350 Disneyland Dr Anaheim (92802) ***(P-17977)***
Hob Entertainment LLC.....C.....323 848-5100
8430 W Sunset Blvd West Hollywood (90069) ***(P-17978)***
Hob Entertainment LLC.....C.....619 299-2583
1055 5th Ave San Diego (92101) ***(P-17979)***
Hob Entertainment LLC (HQ).....C.....323 769-4600
7060 Hollywood Blvd Los Angeles (90028) ***(P-17980)***
Hoban Management, El Cajon *Also called Thomas J Hoban* ***(P-11482)***
Hobbs Herder Advertising.....D.....800 999-6090
419 Main St Huntington Beach (92648) ***(P-13516)***
Hobbs/Herder Training, Huntington Beach *Also called Hobbs Herder Advertising* ***(P-13516)***
Hochiki America Corporation.....C.....714 522-2246
7051 Village Dr Ste 100 Buena Park (90621) ***(P-7153)***
Hodges Electric Inc.....E.....559 298-5533
1239 Hoblitt Ave Clovis (93612) ***(P-2515)***
Hoem & Associates Inc.....D.....650 871-5194
951 Linden Ave South San Francisco (94080) ***(P-3004)***
Hoffman Agency (PA).....D.....408 286-2611
325 S 1st St Ste 300 San Jose (95113) ***(P-26912)***
Hoffman Concrete Company Inc.....E.....951 372-8333
2621 Green Rver Rd Ste 10 Corona (92882) ***(P-3160)***
Hoffman Farms, Tulare *Also called Nielsens Creamery* ***(P-401)***
Hoffman Hospice of The Valley.....D.....661 410-1010
8501 Brimhall Rd Bldg 100 Bakersfield (93312) ***(P-20431)***
Hoffman Southwest Corp.....E.....714 630-0404
1183 N Kraemer Pl Anaheim (92806) ***(P-17504)***
Hoffman Southwest Corp (PA).....D.....949 380-4161
23311 Madero Mission Viejo (92691) ***(P-17505)***
Hoffman Southwest Corp.....D.....909 397-0567
8930 Center Ave Rancho Cucamonga (91730) ***(P-17506)***
Hoffman Texas Inc.....E.....661 257-9200
24971 Avenue Stanford Valencia (91355) ***(P-17507)***
Hok Group Inc.....C.....415 243-0555
1 Bush St Ste 200 San Francisco (94104) ***(P-25456)***
Hok Group Inc.....C.....310 838-9555
9530 Jefferson Blvd Culver City (90232) ***(P-25457)***
Holbrook Construction Inc.....D.....714 523-1150
9814 Norwalk Blvd Ste 200 Santa Fe Springs (90670) ***(P-1501)***
Holdrege Kull Consultimg Engr.....D.....530 894-2487
48 Bellarmine Ct Ste 40 Chico (95928) ***(P-25130)***
Holiday Garden SF Corp.....E.....714 533-3555
1700 S Clementine St Anaheim (92802) ***(P-12371)***
Holiday Garden Wc Corp.....E.....925 932-3332
2730 N Main St Walnut Creek (94597) ***(P-12372)***
Holiday Inn, Los Angeles *Also called Packard Realty Inc* ***(P-12704)***
Holiday Inn, Victorville *Also called Victorvlle Trsure Holdings LLC* ***(P-13064)***
Holiday Inn, La Mirada *Also called Sunstone Hotel Investors LLC* ***(P-12991)***
Holiday Inn, Burbank *Also called JP Allen Extended Stay* ***(P-12492)***
Holiday Inn, Torrance *Also called Six Continents Hotels Inc* ***(P-12932)***
Holiday Inn, Los Angeles *Also called Brisam Lax (de) LLC* ***(P-12089)***
Holiday Inn, Marina Del Rey *Also called Washington Inn LLC* ***(P-13076)***
Holiday Inn, Van Nuys *Also called Six Continents Hotels Inc* ***(P-12933)***
Holiday Inn, San Diego *Also called Sunstone Hotel Investors LLC* ***(P-12994)***

Mergent e-mail: customerrelations@mergent.com
1296
2020 Directory of California
Wholesalers and Services Companies
(P-0000) Products & Services Section entry number
(PA)=Parent Co (HQ)=Headquarters (DH)=Div Headquarters

Holiday Inn, North Hollywood *Also called Rio Vista Development Company* ***(P-12824)***
Holiday Inn, San Francisco *Also called Intercontinental Hotels Group* ***(P-12463)***
Holiday Inn, Los Angeles *Also called Six Continents Hotels Inc* ***(P-12934)***
Holiday Inn, Concord *Also called Montclair Hotels Mb LLC* ***(P-12628)***
Holiday Inn, Stockton *Also called Best Western Plus-Heritage Inn* ***(P-12060)***
Holiday Inn, Oakland *Also called Tucson Hotels LP* ***(P-13044)***
Holiday Inn, Oceanside *Also called Ocean Holiday LP* ***(P-12660)***
Holiday Inn, Torrance *Also called Intercontinental Hotels Group* ***(P-12464)***
Holiday Inn, San Diego *Also called Manas Hospitality LLC* ***(P-12575)***
Holiday Inn, Sacramento *Also called Atrium Finance I LP* ***(P-12024)***
Holiday Inn, Torrance *Also called Six Continents Hotels Inc* ***(P-12935)***
Holiday Inn, San Francisco *Also called Intercontinental Hotels Group* ***(P-12466)***
Holiday Inn, San Diego *Also called Six Continents Hotels Inc* ***(P-12936)***
Holiday Inn, Goleta *Also called Intercontinental Hotels Group* ***(P-12467)***
Holiday Inn, Sacramento *Also called Tucson Hotels LP* ***(P-13045)***
Holiday Inn, Anaheim *Also called Conestoga Hotel* ***(P-12170)***
Holiday Inn, San Diego *Also called Jck Hotels LLC* ***(P-12487)***
Holiday Inn, Moreno Valley *Also called Glacier House Franchisee LLC* ***(P-12296)***
Holiday Inn, San Francisco *Also called Intercontinental Hotels Group* ***(P-12468)***
Holiday Inn, Santa Ana *Also called S W K Properties LLC* ***(P-12857)***
Holiday Inn, Anaheim *Also called Hpt Trs Ihg-2 Inc* ***(P-12418)***
Holiday Inn, Beverly Hills *Also called Ggwh LLC* ***(P-12294)***
Holiday Inn, Long Beach *Also called Yhb Long Beach LLC* ***(P-13130)***
Holiday Inn, West Hollywood *Also called Hmbl LLC* ***(P-12370)***
Holiday Inn, Dublin *Also called Trevi Partners A Calif LP* ***(P-13039)***
Holiday Inn, Valencia *Also called Ocean Park Hotels Mmex LLC* ***(P-12663)***
Holiday Inn, Bakersfield *Also called Newport Hospitality Group Inc* ***(P-12643)***
Holiday Inn, San Diego *Also called Narven Enterprises Inc* ***(P-12639)***
Holiday Inn, San Diego *Also called San Diego Farah Partners* ***(P-12869)***
Holiday Inn, San Diego *Also called Win Time Ltd* ***(P-13097)***
Holiday Inn, Laguna Hills *Also called Laguna Hills Hotel Dev Ventr* ***(P-12532)***
Holiday Inn, Visalia *Also called Grosvenor Visalia Associates* ***(P-12323)***
Holiday Inn, San Francisco *Also called Todays Hotel Corporation* ***(P-13028)***
Holiday Inn, Anaheim *Also called Dkn Hotel LLC* ***(P-12217)***
Holiday Inn, Palmdale *Also called Palmdale Resort Inc* ***(P-12707)***
Holiday Inn, Buena Park *Also called Uniwell Corporation* ***(P-13053)***
Holiday Inn, San Jose *Also called San Jose Airport Hotel LLC* ***(P-12876)***
Holiday Inn, Willows *Also called Kumar Hotels Inc* ***(P-12522)***
Holiday Inn, Diamond Bar *Also called Oak Creek LP* ***(P-12655)***
Holiday Inn, Santa Maria *Also called Santa Maria Hotel Corp* ***(P-12886)***
Holiday Inn, National City *Also called Six Continents Hotels Inc* ***(P-12939)***
Holiday Inn, Sacramento *Also called Tucson Hotels LP* ***(P-13046)***
Holiday Inn, Los Angeles *Also called Remington Hotel Corporation* ***(P-12801)***
Holiday Inn & Suites Annaheim........D.......714 535-0300
1240 S Walnut St Anaheim (92802) ***(P-12373)***
Holiday Inn Ex Walnut Creek, Walnut Creek *Also called Holiday Garden Wc Corp* ***(P-12372)***
Holiday Inn Express Merced........D.......209 383-0333
730 Motel Dr Merced (95341) ***(P-12374)***
Holiday Inn Hotel Torrance........C.......310 781-9100
19800 S Vermont Ave Torrance (90502) ***(P-12375)***
Holiday Inn Resort At Lodge, Big Bear Lake *Also called Pacific Snow Valley Resort LLC* ***(P-12696)***
Holiday Inn Rncho Bernardo LLC........D.......858 485-6530
17065 W Bernardo Dr San Diego (92127) ***(P-12376)***
Holiday Manor Care Center, Upland *Also called Sela Healthcare Inc* ***(P-20247)***
Holiday Meat & Provision Corp........C.......310 674-0541
405 Centinela Ave Inglewood (90302) ***(P-8408)***
Holistic Approach HM Hlth Care, Stockton *Also called Holistic Approach Inc* ***(P-14299)***
Holistic Approach Inc........D.......209 956-7050
4505 Precissi Ln Ste B Stockton (95207) ***(P-14299)***
Holland & Knight LLP........D.......213 896-2400
400 S Hope St Ste 800 Los Angeles (90071) ***(P-22572)***
Holland & Knight LLP........E.......415 743-6900
50 California St Ste 2800 San Francisco (94111) ***(P-22573)***
Holland Flower Market Inc (PA)........D.......213 627-9900
755 Wall St Ste 7g Los Angeles (90014) ***(P-8899)***
Hollandia Dairy Inc (PA)........C.......760 744-3222
622 E Mission Rd San Marcos (92069) ***(P-394)***
Hollenbeck Home For The Aged, Newhall *Also called Hollenbeck Palms* ***(P-23959)***
Hollenbeck Palms........C.......323 263-6195
24431 Lyons Ave Apt 336 Newhall (91321) ***(P-23959)***
Holliday Rock Co Inc (PA)........D.......909 982-1553
1401 N Benson Ave Upland (91786) ***(P-6689)***
Hollingshead Management, Los Angeles *Also called Proland Property Managment LLC* ***(P-11374)***
Hollins Schechter A Prof Corp........D.......714 558-9119
1851 E 1st St Ste 600 Santa Ana (92705) ***(P-22574)***
Hollister Process Service........E.......831 634-1479
341 Tres Pinos Rd Ste 201 Hollister (95023) ***(P-16831)***
Hollyway Cleaners, Los Angeles *Also called Valetor Inc* ***(P-13261)***
Hollywood Cmnty Hosp Hollywood, Los Angeles *Also called Hollywood Community Hospital M* ***(P-20911)***
Hollywood Community Hospital M........C.......323 462-2271
6245 De Longpre Ave Los Angeles (90028) ***(P-20911)***
Hollywood Health System Inc........D.......323 662-3731
4640 Lankershim Blvd # 100 North Hollywood (91602) ***(P-21766)***
Hollywood Hills, Los Angeles *Also called Forest Lawn Memorial-Park Assn* ***(P-11627)***
HOLLYWOOD HOME HEALTH SERVICES, North Hollywood *Also called Hollywood Health System Inc* ***(P-21766)***
Hollywood Medical Center LP........A.......213 413-3000
1300 N Vermont Ave Los Angeles (90027) ***(P-20912)***
Hollywood Mental Health Center........D.......323 769-6100
1224 Vine St Los Angeles (90038) ***(P-22042)***
Hollywood Presbyterian Med Ctr, Los Angeles *Also called Hollywood Medical Center LP* ***(P-20912)***
Hollywood Presbyterian Med Ctr, Los Angeles *Also called Cha Hollywood Medical Ctr LP* ***(P-20774)***
Hollywood Rntals Prod Svcs LLC (PA)........D.......818 407-7800
5300 Melrose Ave Los Angeles (90038) ***(P-17744)***
Hollywood Roosevelt Hotel, Los Angeles *Also called Roosevelt Hotel LLC* ***(P-12837)***
Hollywood Spa Inc........E.......323 464-0445
5636 Vineland Ave North Hollywood (91601) ***(P-18153)***
Hollywood Spa, The, North Hollywood *Also called Hollywood Spa Inc* ***(P-18153)***
Hollywood Sports Park LLC........D.......562 867-9600
9030 Somerset Blvd Bellflower (90706) ***(P-16832)***
Hollywood Standard LLC........C.......323 822-3111
8300 W Sunset Blvd Los Angeles (90069) ***(P-12377)***
Holman Family Counseling Inc (PA)........D.......818 704-1444
8511 Fllbrook Ave Ste 400 West Hills (91304) ***(P-19669)***
Holman Group, The, West Hills *Also called Holman Family Counseling Inc* ***(P-19669)***
Holmes & Narver Inc (HQ)........C.......714 567-2400
999 W Town And Country Rd Orange (92868) ***(P-25131)***
Holmes Body Shop Inc (PA)........D.......626 795-6447
466 Foothill Blvd La Canada Flintridge (91011) ***(P-17295)***
Holt CA, Pleasant Grove *Also called Holt of California* ***(P-7476)***
Holt of California (HQ)........C.......916 991-8200
7310 Pacific Ave Pleasant Grove (95668) ***(P-7476)***
Holt of California........C.......916 373-4100
3850 Channel Dr West Sacramento (95691) ***(P-7477)***
Holt of California........C.......209 462-3660
1234 W Charter Way Stockton (95206) ***(P-7478)***
Holthouse Carlin Van Trigt LLP........D.......626 243-5100
350 W Colo Blvd Fl 5 Flr 5 Pasadena (91105) ***(P-25608)***
Holthouse Carlin Van Trigt LLP........D.......805 374-8555
400 W Ventura Blvd # 250 Camarillo (93010) ***(P-25609)***
Holthouse Carlin Van Trigt LLP........D.......818 849-3140
15760 Ventura Blvd # 1700 Encino (91436) ***(P-25610)***
Holthouse Carlin Van Trigt LLP........D.......714 361-7600
18565 Jamboree Rd Ste 400 Irvine (92612) ***(P-25611)***
Holthouse Carlin Van Trigt LLP (PA)........C.......310 477-5551
11444 W Olympic Blvd # 11 Los Angeles (90064) ***(P-25612)***
Holy Cross Cemetary & Masoleum, Culver City *Also called Roman Cath Arch of Los Angels* ***(P-13375)***
Holy Cross Cemetery, Daly City *Also called Roman Catholic Archdiocese of* ***(P-11632)***
Holzmueller Corporation........E.......415 826-8383
1000 25th St San Francisco (94107) ***(P-14168)***
Holzmueller Productions, San Francisco *Also called Holzmueller Corporation* ***(P-14168)***
Home Away Inc........D.......559 642-3121
54432 Road 432 Bass Lake (93604) ***(P-12378)***
Home Box Office Inc........D.......310 382-3000
2500 Broadway Ste 400 Santa Monica (90404) ***(P-5728)***
Home Building, Corona *Also called Ryland Hmes Inlnd Empire Cstmr* ***(P-1186)***
Home Capital Group........D.......626 331-4213
948 N Grand Ave Covina (91724) ***(P-9559)***
Home Care America-San Marino, Glendora *Also called Home Care of America Inc* ***(P-21767)***
Home Care of America Inc........D.......626 309-7696
101 W Bennett Ave A Glendora (91741) ***(P-21767)***
Home Carpet Investment Inc (PA)........D.......619 262-8040
730 Design Ct Ste 401 Chula Vista (91911) ***(P-3005)***
Home Comfort USA, Anaheim *Also called Ken Starr Inc* ***(P-2171)***
Home Community Lending, Santa Clara *Also called Hcl Finance Inc* ***(P-9558)***
Home Depot USA Inc........C.......951 361-1235
11650 Venture Dr Jurupa Valley (91752) ***(P-4430)***
Home Depot USA Inc........D.......209 858-9243
18300 S Harlan Rd Lathrop (95330) ***(P-4431)***
Home Depot, The, Jurupa Valley *Also called Home Depot USA Inc* ***(P-4430)***
Home Depot, The, Lathrop *Also called Home Depot USA Inc* ***(P-4431)***
Home Entertainment Div, Los Angeles *Also called Fox Inc* ***(P-5604)***
Home Express Delivery Svc LLC........A.......949 715-9844
230 Diamond St Laguna Beach (92651) ***(P-4967)***
Home Franchise Concepts LLC (PA)........D.......949 404-1100
19000 Macarthur Blvd # 100 Irvine (92612) ***(P-3161)***
Home Guiding Hands Corporation (PA)........B.......619 938-2850
1908 Friendship Dr Ste A El Cajon (92020) ***(P-23960)***
Home Health Brownsville, Brownsville *Also called Sutter North Med Foundation* ***(P-19493)***
Home Health Care Management........D.......530 343-0727
1398 Ridgewood Dr Chico (95973) ***(P-21768)***
Home Health Plus, Santa Clara *Also called In Home Health Inc* ***(P-21786)***
Home Health Plus, West Covina *Also called In Home Health Inc* ***(P-21787)***
Home Helpers, Redding *Also called Thom Sharon & G Enterprises* ***(P-21885)***
Home Helpers San Mateo County........D.......650 532-3122
655 Miramontes St Half Moon Bay (94019) ***(P-21769)***
Home Improvement Company Inc........E.......760 744-4840
1585 Creek St San Marcos (92078) ***(P-3420)***
Home Instead Senior Care, San Jose *Also called South Bay Senior Solutions Inc* ***(P-21869)***
Home Instead Senior Care, Fresno *Also called P K B Investments Inc* ***(P-26753)***
Home Instead Senior Care, Vista *Also called Sherpaul Corporation* ***(P-21865)***
Home Instead Senior Care, Moorpark *Also called Joy Senior Inc* ***(P-21792)***
Home Instead Senior Care, Palm Desert *Also called Ambiente Enterprises Inc* ***(P-21660)***
Home Instead Senior Care, Long Beach *Also called Coastal Cmnty Senior Care LLC* ***(P-21710)***
Home Instead Senior Care, Redlands *Also called Safely Home* ***(P-21857)***
Home Instead Senior Care, Torrance *Also called Burdette De Cock Inc* ***(P-21689)***
Home Instead Senior Care, Azusa *Also called Seracada* ***(P-21863)***

ALPHABETIC

Home Instead Senior Care, Santa Barbara *Also called S B C Senior Care Inc (P-21856)*
Home Instead Senior Care, Los Angeles *Also called Tender Home Healthcare Inc (P-21881)*
Home Instead Senior Care, Victorville *Also called Branlyn Prominence Inc (P-21685)*
Home Instead Senior Care, Rancho Cucamonga *Also called Branlyn Prominence Inc (P-21686)*
Home Instead Senior Care.....D.....858 277-3722
9665 Gran Rdge Dr Ste 250 San Diego (92123) ***(P-21770)***
Home Instead Senior Care.....D.....916 920-2273
11160 Sun Center Dr Rancho Cordova (95670) ***(P-21771)***
Home Instead Senior Care.....E.....619 460-6222
5360 Jackson Dr Ste 120 La Mesa (91942) ***(P-21772)***
Home Instead Senior Care.....E.....707 678-2005
405 Court St Woodland (95695) ***(P-21773)***
Home Instead Senior Care.....D.....510 686-9940
26 Carmello Rd Walnut Creek (94597) ***(P-21774)***
Home Instead Senior Care.....E.....949 347-6767
28570 Marguerite Pkwy # 221 Mission Viejo (92692) ***(P-21775)***
Home Organizers Inc.....A.....562 699-9945
3860 Capitol Ave City of Industry (90601) ***(P-2941)***
Home Port Inc.....D.....408 377-4134
5030 Union Ave San Jose (95124) ***(P-10853)***
HOMEBOY BAKERY, Los Angeles *Also called Homeboy Industries (P-23260)*
Homeboy Industries (PA).....B.....323 526-1254
130 Bruno St Los Angeles (90012) ***(P-23260)***
Homebridge Inc.....B.....415 255-2079
1035 Market St Ste L1 San Francisco (94103) ***(P-23261)***
Homebridge Financial Svcs Inc.....A.....818 981-0606
15301 Ventura Blvd Sherman Oaks (91403) ***(P-9560)***
Homefrst Svcs Santa Clara Cnty.....C.....408 539-2100
507 Valley Way Milpitas (95035) ***(P-23262)***
Homegrown Natural Foods Inc.....D.....510 558-7500
1610 5th St Berkeley (94710) ***(P-8180)***
Homeguard Incorporated (PA).....D.....408 993-1900
510 Madera Ave San Jose (95112) ***(P-13822)***
Homeland Housewares LLC.....D.....310 996-7200
11601 Wilshire Blvd Fl 23 Los Angeles (90025) ***(P-7206)***
Homeland Security Services Inc.....B.....714 956-2200
31805 Temecula Pkwy Temecula (92592) ***(P-16525)***
Homelegance Inc.....D.....510 933-6888
48200 Fremont Blvd Fremont (94538) ***(P-6517)***
Homeless Prenatal Program.....E.....415 546-6756
33 Middle Point Rd San Francisco (94124) ***(P-23263)***
Homeowners Association, Helendale *Also called Silver Lakes Association (P-24662)*
Homepointe Property Management, Sacramento *Also called Ram Commercial Enterprises Inc (P-11388)*
Homeq Servicing Corporation (HQ).....A.....916 339-6192
4837 Watt Ave North Highlands (95660) ***(P-9561)***
Homestar Systems Inc.....D.....415 694-6000
251 Post St Ste 302 San Francisco (94108) ***(P-16022)***
Homestead of Fair Oaks, Fair Oaks *Also called Eskaton Properties Inc (P-19894)*
Homestore Apartments & Rentals, Santa Clara *Also called Move Sales Inc (P-13441)*
Hometown Buffet 261, Cerritos *Also called Hometown Buffet Inc (P-13428)*
Hometown Buffet Inc.....D.....562 402-8307
11471 South St Cerritos (90703) ***(P-13428)***
Homewatch Caregivers, Carlsbad *Also called North Coast Home Care Inc (P-21819)*
Homewatch Caregivers, Los Angeles *Also called South Bay Senior Services Inc (P-21868)*
Homewood Care Center, San Jose *Also called Ocadian Care Centers LLC (P-20172)*
Homewood Mountain Resort, Homewood *Also called Homewood Village Resorts LLC (P-12380)*
Homewood Suites, Fairfield *Also called Hotel NAPA II Opco LP (P-12411)*
Homewood Suites Anaheim Resort, Anaheim *Also called Npl Anaheim Investments LLC (P-12653)*
Homewood Suites Hilton Sfo, Brisbane *Also called Sage Hospitality Resources LLC (P-12864)*
Homewood Suites Libery Station, San Diego *Also called Liberty Station Hhg Hotel LP (P-12554)*
Homewood Suites Management LLC.....E.....510 663-2700
1103 Embarcadero Oakland (94606) ***(P-12379)***
Homewood Suites Redondo, Redondo Beach *Also called Trcf Redondo LLC (P-13037)*
Homewood Suites San Diego Hote, San Diego *Also called SD Hotel Circle LLC (P-12894)*
Homewood Village Resorts LLC.....E.....530 525-2992
5145 W Lake Blvd Homewood (96141) ***(P-12380)***
Hon Hai Precision Indust Ltd.....D.....714 988-9388
500 S Kraemer Blvd # 100 Brea (92821) ***(P-6847)***
Hon Hai Precision Industry, San Jose *Also called Nsg Technology Inc (P-17458)*
Honda Financial Services, Torrance *Also called American Honda Finance Corp (P-9452)*
Honda R&D Americas Inc.....E.....818 345-7922
7514 Reseda Blvd Reseda (91335) ***(P-25907)***
Honey Flower Holdings LLC.....C.....951 351-2800
3688 Nye Ave Riverside (92505) ***(P-20019)***
Honey Lake Hospice Inc.....D.....530 257-3137
60 S Lassen St Susanville (96130) ***(P-6970)***
Honey Olivarez Bees Inc.....D.....530 865-0298
6398 County Road 20 Orland (95963) ***(P-422)***
Honeybook Inc.....D.....770 403-9234
539 Bryant St Ste 200 San Francisco (94107) ***(P-14855)***
Honeymoon Real Estate LP.....D.....310 277-5221
9400 W Olympic Blvd Beverly Hills (90212) ***(P-12381)***
Honeyville Inc.....D.....909 980-9500
11600 Dayton Dr Rancho Cucamonga (91730) ***(P-4333)***
Honeywell, Lompoc *Also called Kbrwyle Tech Solutions LLC (P-5792)*
Honeywell Authorized Dealer, Palm Springs *Also called Desert Air Conditioning Inc (P-3047)*
Honeywell Authorized Dealer, Berkeley *Also called L J Kruse Co (P-2177)*
Honeywell Authorized Dealer, Chatsworth *Also called All Tmperatures Controlled Inc (P-2031)*
Honeywell Authorized Dealer, North Hollywood *Also called Circulating Air Inc (P-2095)*
Honeywell Authorized Dealer, Sylmar *Also called Tri-Signal Integration Inc (P-2675)*
Honeywell Authorized Dealer, San Jose *Also called J & J Air Conditioning Inc (P-2159)*
Honeywell Authorized Dealer, Corona *Also called LDI Mechanical Inc (P-2182)*
HONEYWELL AUTHORIZED DEALER, Santa Clara *Also called Environmental Systems Inc (P-2129)*
Honeywell Authorized Dealer, Fresno *Also called Linkus Enterprises LLC (P-1885)*
Honeywell Authorized Dealer, Riverside *Also called 20/20 Plumbing & Heating Inc (P-2005)*
HONEYWELL AUTHORIZED DEALER, Fullerton *Also called C & L Refrigeration Corp (P-2084)*
Honeywell Authorized Dealer, San Diego *Also called Greater San Diego AC Co Inc (P-2148)*
HONEYWELL AUTHORIZED DEALER, San Diego *Also called Pacific Rim Mech Contrs Inc (P-2224)*
Honeywell Authorized Dealer, Rocklin *Also called Brower Mechanical Inc (P-17441)*
Honeywell Authorized Dealer, Hollister *Also called San Benito Htg & Shtmtl Inc (P-2264)*
Honeywell Authorized Dealer, Corona *Also called Multi Mechanical Inc (P-2206)*
Honeywell Authorized Dealer, Yuba City *Also called R B Spencer Inc (P-2244)*
Honeywell Authorized Dealer, Pleasanton *Also called Sunbelt Controls Inc (P-17448)*
Honeywell Authorized Dealer, Paramount *Also called Reliable Energy Management Inc (P-2253)*
Honeywell International Inc.....D.....650 918-3229
1099 Sneath Ln San Bruno (94066) ***(P-6848)***
Honeywell International Inc.....C.....714 796-7500
514 S Lyon St Santa Ana (92701) ***(P-7452)***
Honeywell International Inc.....D.....916 923-7851
1740 Creekside Oaks 150 Sacramento (95833) ***(P-16526)***
Honeywell International Inc.....E.....408 962-2000
1349 Moffett Park Dr Sunnyvale (94089) ***(P-7279)***
Hong Kong & Shanghai Banking.....D.....213 626-2460
770 Wilshire Blvd Ste 800 Los Angeles (90017) ***(P-9414)***
Hong Kong & Shanghai Hotels.....D.....310 551-2888
9882 Santa Monica Blvd Beverly Hills (90212) ***(P-12382)***
Hong Kong Bank, Los Angeles *Also called Hong Kong & Shanghai Banking (P-9414)*
Honk Technologies Inc.....D.....800 979-3162
2251 Barry Ave Los Angeles (90064) ***(P-15774)***
Honolua Bay Holdings LLC.....E.....530 243-6317
2120 Benton Dr Redding (96003) ***(P-11671)***
Honolulu Freight Service (PA).....E.....323 887-6777
1400 Date St Montebello (90640) ***(P-4968)***
Honor Rancho Station, Valencia *Also called Southern California Gas Co (P-5988)*
Hood & Strong LLP (PA).....D.....415 781-0793
275 Battery St Ste 900 San Francisco (94111) ***(P-25613)***
Hoover Institution.....C.....650 723-0603
434 Galvez Mall Stanford (94305) ***(P-16833)***
Hope Contra Costa, Pittsburg *Also called Lincoln Child Center Inc (P-23973)*
Hope Hse For Mltple Hndicapped (PA).....C.....626 443-1313
4215 Peck Rd El Monte (91732) ***(P-23961)***
Hope of Valley Mission.....E.....661 673-5951
19379 Soledad Canyon Rd Santa Clarita (91351) ***(P-22043)***
Hope of Valley Rescue Mission.....D.....818 392-0020
11076 Norris Ave Fl 2 Pacoima (91331) ***(P-23264)***
Hope Services.....D.....831 455-4940
744 La Guardia St Ste B Salinas (93905) ***(P-23601)***
Hopkins & Carley A Law Corp (PA).....D.....408 286-9800
70 S 1st St San Jose (95113) ***(P-22575)***
Hopland Band Pomo Indians Inc.....C.....707 744-1395
13101 Nokomis Rd Hopland (95449) ***(P-18705)***
Hopland Band Pomo Indians Inc (PA).....D.....707 472-2100
3000 Shanel Rd Hopland (95449) ***(P-24838)***
Horiba Americas Holding Inc (HQ).....A.....949 250-4811
9755 Research Dr Irvine (92618) ***(P-11672)***
Horizon Actuarial Services LLC.....D.....818 691-2000
5200 Lankershim Blvd North Hollywood (91601) ***(P-26637)***
Horizon Beverage Company.....D.....800 332-8358
8380 Pardee Dr Oakland (94621) ***(P-8769)***
Horizon Beverage Company LP.....D.....510 465-2212
8380 Pardee Dr Oakland (94621) ***(P-8770)***
Horizon Dental Grp, El Cajon *Also called Anthony P Garofalo A Dental (P-19604)*
Horizon For Hmwners Asscations, Mammoth Lakes *Also called Horizons 4 Condominiums Inc (P-24564)*
Horizon Media Inc.....B.....310 282-0909
1888 Century Park E # 700 Los Angeles (90067) ***(P-13517)***
Horizon Pharmaceutical LLC (HQ).....D.....415 408-6200
7 Hamilton Landing # 100 Novato (94949) ***(P-25992)***
Horizon Solar Power, Hemet *Also called Lpsh Holdings Inc (P-2192)*
Horizon Systems, Sunnyvale *Also called Horizon Technologies Inc (P-6849)*
Horizon Technologies Inc.....C.....408 733-1530
1270 Oakmead Pkwy Ste 115 Sunnyvale (94085) ***(P-6849)***
Horizon West, Monterey *Also called Monterey Pines Sklld Nursg Fac (P-20147)*
Horizon West Inc.....C.....916 488-8601
3529 Walnut Ave Carmichael (95608) ***(P-20020)***
Horizon West Inc.....D.....916 331-4590
5255 Hemlock St Sacramento (95841) ***(P-20021)***
Horizon West Inc.....D.....530 889-8122
3388 Bell Rd Auburn (95603) ***(P-26077)***
Horizon West Healthcare Inc.....C.....916 782-1238
1161 Cirby Way Roseville (95661) ***(P-21477)***
Horizon West Healthcare Inc (HQ).....D.....916 624-6230
4020 Sierra College Blvd # 190 Rocklin (95677) ***(P-20022)***
Horizon West Healthcare Inc.....D.....707 462-1436
1162 S Dora St Ukiah (95482) ***(P-20023)***
Horizon West Healthcare Inc.....C.....530 885-7511
12225 Shale Ridge Ln Auburn (95602) ***(P-20597)***
Horizons 4 Condominiums Inc.....D.....760 934-6779
2113 Meridan Blvd Mammoth Lakes (93546) ***(P-24564)***

Mergent e-mail: customerrelations@mergent.com
1298
2020 Directory of California
Wholesalers and Services Companies
(P-0000) Products & Services Section entry number
(PA)=Parent Co (HQ)=Headquarters (DH)=Div Headquarters

Horizons Adult Day Health Care..........D.......619 474-1822
1035 Harbison Ave National City (91950) ***(P-22256)***
Horn Group Inc..........E.......415 905-4000
101 Montgomery St Fl 15 San Francisco (94104) ***(P-13518)***
Hornberger Worstell Assoc Inc..........E.......415 391-1080
170 Maiden Ln Ste 600 San Francisco (94108) ***(P-25458)***
Hornberger, Mark R, San Francisco *Also called Hornberger Worstell Assoc Inc* ***(P-25458)***
Hornblower Cruises & Event, San Francisco *Also called Hornblower Yachts LLC* ***(P-4823)***
Hornblower Cruises & Events, San Diego *Also called Hornblower Yachts Inc* ***(P-4605)***
Hornblower Group Inc..........B.......415 635-2210
The Embarcadero Pier 3 St Pier San Francisco (94111) ***(P-4604)***
Hornblower Yachts Inc..........C.......619 686-8700
2825 5th Ave San Diego (92103) ***(P-4605)***
Hornblower Yachts Inc..........C.......619 234-8687
2825 5th Ave San Diego (92103) ***(P-26638)***
Hornblower Yachts LLC..........D.......916 446-1185
200 Marina Blvd Berkeley (94710) ***(P-4606)***
Hornblower Yachts LLC (PA)..........C.......415 788-8866
On The Embarcadero Pier 3 St Pier San Francisco (94111) ***(P-4823)***
Horner-Halleher Holding Co (PA)..........C.......562 944-8885
9303 Greenleaf Ave Santa Fe Springs (90670) ***(P-6563)***
Hornitos Telephone Co..........D.......608 831-1000
2896 Bear Vly Hornitos (95325) ***(P-5417)***
Horsemen Inc..........D.......714 847-4243
16911 Algonquin St Huntington Beach (92649) ***(P-16321)***
Hort Tech Inc..........C.......760 360-9000
78355 Darby Rd Bermuda Dunes (92203) ***(P-829)***
Horton Grand Hotel, San Diego *Also called Historical Properties Inc* ***(P-12366)***
Hortonworks Inc (HQ)..........A.......408 916-4121
5470 Great America Pkwy Santa Clara (95054) ***(P-15352)***
Hoshall Corporation..........E.......916 987-1995
6608 Folsom Auburn Rd # 4 Folsom (95630) ***(P-13350)***
Hoshall Designer Group, Folsom *Also called Hoshall Corporation* ***(P-13350)***
Hospice & Home Health of E Bay..........C.......510 632-4390
333 Hegenberger Rd # 700 Oakland (94621) ***(P-21776)***
Hospice and Palliative Care..........D.......925 945-8924
2849 Miranda Ave Alamo (94507) ***(P-20432)***
Hospice By Bay (PA)..........C.......415 927-2273
17 E Sir Francis Drake Bl Larkspur (94939) ***(P-21777)***
Hospice Caring Project, Scotts Valley *Also called Hospice of Santa Cruz County* ***(P-21780)***
Hospice Caring Project, Watsonville *Also called Hospice of Santa Cruz County* ***(P-21781)***
Hospice Cheers..........D.......626 799-2727
625 Fair Oaks Ave Ste 229 South Pasadena (91030) ***(P-21778)***
Hospice of Foothills (PA)..........D.......530 272-5739
11270 Rough And Ready Hwy Grass Valley (95945) ***(P-21779)***
Hospice of Marin, Larkspur *Also called Hospice By Bay* ***(P-21777)***
Hospice of San Joaquin..........D.......209 957-3888
3888 Pacific Ave Stockton (95204) ***(P-20024)***
Hospice of Santa Cruz County (PA)..........C.......831 430-3000
940 Disc Dr Scotts Valley (95066) ***(P-21780)***
Hospice of Santa Cruz County..........D.......831 430-3000
65 Neilson St Ste 121 Watsonville (95076) ***(P-21781)***
Hospice of The East Bay, Alamo *Also called Hospice and Palliative Care* ***(P-20432)***
Hospice of Valley (PA)..........E.......408 947-1233
4850 Union Ave San Jose (95124) ***(P-21782)***
HOSPICE OF VALLEYS, Murrieta *Also called Hospice of Valleys SC* ***(P-20433)***
Hospice of Valleys SC (PA)..........D.......951 200-7800
25240 Hancock Ave Ste 120 Murrieta (92562) ***(P-20433)***
Hospital Assn Southern Cal (PA)..........D.......213 347-2002
515 S Figueroa St # 1300 Los Angeles (90071) ***(P-24181)***
Hospital Business Services Inc..........C.......909 235-4400
3300 E Guasti Rd Ontario (91761) ***(P-16834)***
Hospital Cmmttee For The Lvrmr (HQ)..........B.......925 847-3000
5555 W Las Positas Blvd Pleasanton (94588) ***(P-26256)***
Hospital Cmmttee For The Lvrmr..........A.......925 447-7000
1111 E Stanley Blvd Livermore (94550) ***(P-26257)***
HOSPITAL COPORATION OF AMERICA, San Jose *Also called Good Samaritan Hospital LP* ***(P-20893)***
HOSPITAL COPORATION OF AMERICA, Thousand Oaks *Also called Los Robles Hospital & Med Ctr* ***(P-21023)***
Hospital of Barstow Inc..........C.......760 256-1761
820 E Mountain View St Barstow (92311) ***(P-20913)***
Hospital of Community (HQ)..........A.......831 624-5311
23625 Holman Hwy Monterey (93940) ***(P-21478)***
Hospitality Ventures MGT LLC..........D.......415 499-9222
101 Mcinnis Pkwy San Rafael (94903) ***(P-12383)***
Hospitlity Fcsed Solutions Inc..........D.......562 424-1720
3229 E Spring St Ste 200 Long Beach (90806) ***(P-25459)***
Hospitlity Prch Group Intl LLC (PA)..........C.......925 949-5706
350 N Wiget Ln Ste 210 Walnut Creek (94598) ***(P-16835)***
Host Healthcare Inc..........A.......858 999-3579
4225 Executive Sq # 1500 La Jolla (92037) ***(P-14511)***
Host Hotels & Resorts Inc..........C.......415 775-7555
1250 Columbus Ave San Francisco (94133) ***(P-12384)***
Host Hotels & Resorts Inc..........C.......619 232-1234
1 Market Pl San Diego (92101) ***(P-12385)***
Host Hotels & Resorts LP..........D.......949 640-4000
900 Newport Center Dr Newport Beach (92660) ***(P-12386)***
Host Hotels & Resorts LP..........D.......619 692-3800
8757 Rio San Diego Dr San Diego (92108) ***(P-12387)***
Host Hotels & Resorts LP..........D.......650 347-1234
1333 Bayshore Hwy Burlingame (94010) ***(P-12388)***
Host Hotels & Resorts LP..........D.......760 341-2211
74855 Country Club Dr Palm Desert (92260) ***(P-12389)***
Host Hotels & Resorts LP..........D.......619 291-2900
1380 Harbor Island Dr San Diego (92101) ***(P-12390)***
Host Hotels & Resorts LP..........D.......415 896-1600
55 4th St San Francisco (94103) ***(P-12391)***
Host Hotels & Resorts LP..........D.......650 692-9100
1800 Old Bayshore Hwy Burlingame (94010) ***(P-12392)***
Host Hotels & Resorts LP..........D.......310 823-1700
4375 Admiralty Way Venice (90292) ***(P-12393)***
Host Hotels & Resorts LP..........D.......714 957-1100
500 Anton Blvd Costa Mesa (92626) ***(P-12394)***
Host Hotels & Resorts LP..........D.......949 854-4500
500 Bayview Cir Newport Beach (92660) ***(P-12395)***
Host Hotels & Resorts LP..........D.......310 216-5858
5400 W Century Blvd Los Angeles (90045) ***(P-12396)***
Host Hotels & Resorts LP..........D.......310 546-7511
1400 Park View Ave Manhattan Beach (90266) ***(P-12397)***
Host Hotels & Resorts LP..........D.......310 301-3000
4100 Admiralty Way Marina Del Rey (90292) ***(P-12398)***
Host International Inc..........C.......408 294-1702
1661 Airport Blvd Ste 3e San Jose (95110) ***(P-12399)***
Host International Inc..........C.......619 231-5100
3835 N Harbor Dr San Diego (92101) ***(P-12400)***
Hostmark Investors Ltd Partnr..........C.......408 330-0001
4949 Great America Pkwy Santa Clara (95054) ***(P-26258)***
Hot Dogger Tours Inc..........C.......714 988-4088
223 Imperial Hwy Ste 165 Fullerton (92835) ***(P-3777)***
Hot Line Construction Inc..........B.......925 634-9333
9020 Brentwood Blvd Ste H Brentwood (94513) ***(P-2516)***
Hotbox, Campbell *Also called Streamray Inc* ***(P-18011)***
Hotdoodle.com, Fremont *Also called Metabyte Inc* ***(P-16056)***
Hotel Adventures LLC..........D.......714 730-7717
17662 Irvine Blvd Ste 4 Tustin (92780) ***(P-12401)***
Hotel Angeleno, Los Angeles *Also called Ascot Hotel LP* ***(P-12021)***
Hotel Bel-Air, Los Angeles *Also called Kava Holdings Inc* ***(P-12501)***
Hotel Britton, San Francisco *Also called Reneson Hotels Inc* ***(P-12808)***
Hotel Casa Del Mar, Santa Monica *Also called Et Whitehall Seascape LLC* ***(P-12256)***
Hotel Circle Inn & Suites..........E.......619 851-6800
2201 Hotel Cir S San Diego (92108) ***(P-12402)***
Hotel Circle Property LLC..........B.......619 291-7131
500 Hotel Cir N San Diego (92108) ***(P-12403)***
Hotel De Anza, San Jose *Also called Saratoga Capital Inc* ***(P-12891)***
Hotel Del Coronado LP..........D.......619 522-8011
1500 Orange Ave Coronado (92118) ***(P-12404)***
Hotel Diamond..........E.......530 893-3100
220 W 4th St Chico (95928) ***(P-12405)***
Hotel Durant A Ltd Partnership..........D.......510 845-8981
2600 Durant Ave Berkeley (94704) ***(P-12406)***
Hotel Fullerton Anaheim, The, Fullerton *Also called Huoyen International Inc* ***(P-12426)***
Hotel Griffon, San Francisco *Also called Embarcadero Inn Associates* ***(P-12247)***
Hotel Healdsburg (PA)..........D.......707 431-2800
25 Matheson St Healdsburg (95448) ***(P-12407)***
Hotel Healdsburg..........D.......707 922-5399
317 Healdsburg Ave Healdsburg (95448) ***(P-12408)***
Hotel Indigo Los Angles Dwntwn, Los Angeles *Also called Metropolis Hotel MGT LLC* ***(P-12614)***
Hotel Indigo San Diego, San Diego *Also called Intercontinental Hotels Group* ***(P-12462)***
Hotel Kabuki, San Francisco *Also called Bre/Japantown Owner LLC* ***(P-12084)***
Hotel La Jolla..........D.......858 459-0261
7955 La Jolla Shores Dr La Jolla (92037) ***(P-12409)***
Hotel Mac Restaurant Inc..........E.......510 233-0576
50 Washington Ave Richmond (94801) ***(P-12410)***
Hotel Managers Group Llc..........B.......858 673-1534
11590 W Bernardo Ct # 211 San Diego (92127) ***(P-26259)***
Hotel Marmonte, Santa Barbara *Also called H D G Associates* ***(P-12326)***
Hotel Maya, Long Beach *Also called Queensbay Hotel LLC* ***(P-12780)***
Hotel Menage, Anaheim *Also called Newport Hotel Capital LLC* ***(P-12644)***
Hotel Moneco, San Francisco *Also called Kimpton Hotel & Rest Group LLC* ***(P-12513)***
Hotel NAPA II Opco LP..........E.......707 863-0300
4755 Business Center Dr Fairfield (94534) ***(P-12411)***
Hotel Nikko San Francisco Inc..........B.......415 394-1111
222 Mason St San Francisco (94102) ***(P-12412)***
Hotel On Huntington Beach, Huntington Beach *Also called R C Hotels Inc* ***(P-12782)***
Hotel Pacific, Monterey *Also called Columbia Hospitality Inc* ***(P-12163)***
Hotel Palomar, Los Angeles *Also called Behringer Harvard Wilshire Blv* ***(P-12051)***
Hotel Portofino, Redondo Beach *Also called Portofino Hotel Partners LP* ***(P-12765)***
Hotel Sfitel San Francisco Bay, Redwood City *Also called French Redwood Inc* ***(P-12283)***
Hotel Sofitel, Redwood City *Also called Accor Bus & Leisure N Amer LLC* ***(P-11991)***
Hotel Solamar, San Diego *Also called Souldriver Lessee Inc* ***(P-12946)***
Hotel Tonight Inc (PA)..........D.......800 208-2949
901 Market St Ste 310 San Francisco (94103) ***(P-12413)***
Hotel Triton, San Francisco *Also called Dcp Jl Triton Sf LLC* ***(P-12204)***
Hotel Vitale, San Francisco *Also called Mission Stuart Ht Partners LLC* ***(P-12620)***
Hotel Whitcomb..........D.......415 626-8000
1231 Market St San Francisco (94103) ***(P-12414)***
Hotel Zoe, San Francisco *Also called Creedence Lessee LLC* ***(P-12187)***
Hotline Telecommunications (PA)..........D.......909 593-6575
528 Bethany Cir Claremont (91711) ***(P-2517)***
Hotrollergirl Productions..........D.......530 521-2745
11890 Silver Spur St Ojai (93023) ***(P-18064)***
Hotwire Inc..........C.......415 343-8400
114 Sansome St Ste 400 San Francisco (94104) ***(P-5418)***
Houalla Enterprises Ltd..........D.......949 515-4350
2610 Avon St Newport Beach (92663) ***(P-1502)***
Houchin Blood Services..........D.......661 327-8541
11515 Bolthouse Dr Bakersfield (93311) ***(P-22257)***
Houdini Inc..........C.......714 228-4406
6311 Knott Ave Buena Park (90620) ***(P-4432)***
Houlihan Lokey Inc (PA)..........B.......310 788-5200
10250 Constellation Blvd Los Angeles (90067) ***(P-9826)***

A L P H A B E T I C

Employee Codes: A=Over 500 employees, B=251-500
C=101-250, D=51-100, E=50
2020 Directory of California
Wholesalers and Services Companies
© Mergent Inc. 1-800-342-5647
1299

House of Air LLC ....D....415 345-9675
926 Mason St San Francisco (94129) ***(P-18706)***
House of Blues, Los Angeles *Also called Hob Entertainment LLC* ***(P-17980)***
House Seven Gables RE Inc ....D....714 500-3300
19440 Goldenwest St Huntington Beach (92648) ***(P-11192)***
House Seven Gables RE Inc ....D....714 754-6262
16872 Bolsa Chica St # 100 Huntington Beach (92649) ***(P-11193)***
House Seven Gables RE Inc ....D....714 282-0306
5753 E Santa Ana Canyon P Anaheim (92807) ***(P-11194)***
Housing Athrty of The Cnty of ....D....831 454-9455
2160 41st Ave Capitola (95010) ***(P-11195)***
Housing Division, Sunnyvale *Also called City of Sunnyvale* ***(P-13170)***
Housing Services, San Luis Obispo *Also called Cal Poly Corporation* ***(P-13136)***
Houston Salem Inc ....E....310 719-7004
217 E 157th St Gardena (90248) ***(P-8077)***
Houzz Inc (PA) ....D....650 326-3000
285 Hamilton Ave Fl 4 Palo Alto (94301) ***(P-14856)***
Hovlid Skilled Nursing ....E....530 846-9065
240 Spruce St Gridley (95948) ***(P-20025)***
Howard John ....D....562 425-4232
7681 Carson Blvd Long Beach (90808) ***(P-12415)***
Howard Building Corporation (PA) ....C....213 683-1850
707 Wilshire Blvd # 3750 Los Angeles (90017) ***(P-1503)***
Howard CDM ....E....562 427-4124
3750 Long Beach Blvd Long Beach (90807) ***(P-1139)***
Howard Construction, Long Beach *Also called Howard CDM* ***(P-1139)***
Howard Contracting Inc ....E....562 596-2969
12354 Carson St Hawaiian Gardens (90716) ***(P-3318)***
Howard Fischer Associates Inc ....E....408 374-0580
10020 N De Anza Blvd # 101 Cupertino (95014) ***(P-14300)***
Howard Frank R Memorial Hosp, Willits *Also called Willits Hospital Inc* ***(P-21375)***
Howard Hughes Medical Inst ....D....650 725-8252
279 Campus Dr Rm B202 Stanford (94305) ***(P-25762)***
Howard Hughes Medical Inst ....C....415 476-9668
1550 4th St Rm 190 San Francisco (94143) ***(P-25763)***
Howard Johnson, Anaheim *Also called Northwest Hotel Corporation* ***(P-12652)***
Howard Johnson (PA) ....C....714 776-6120
1380 S Harbor Blvd Anaheim (92802) ***(P-12416)***
Howard Roofing Company Inc ....D....909 622-5598
245 N Mountain View Ave Pomona (91767) ***(P-3063)***
Howard Training Center (PA) ....D....209 538-2431
1424 Stonum Rd Modesto (95351) ***(P-23602)***
Howards Appliances Inc ....D....626 288-4010
5102 Industry Ave Pico Rivera (90660) ***(P-4433)***
Howards Warehouse & Svc Ctr, Pico Rivera *Also called Howards Appliances Inc* ***(P-4433)***
Howe Community Center ....E....916 927-3802
2201 Cottage Way Sacramento (95825) ***(P-18707)***
Howe Electric Construction Inc ....C....559 255-8992
4682 E Olive Ave Fresno (93702) ***(P-2518)***
Howroyd-Wright Emplymnt Agcy (HQ) ....C....818 240-8688
327 W Broadway Glendale (91204) ***(P-14301)***
Howroyd-Wright Emplymnt Agcy ....C....818 240-8688
325 W Broadway Glendale (91204) ***(P-14302)***
Hoyu America Co ....D....714 230-3000
6265 Phyllis Dr Cypress (90630) ***(P-7951)***
HP Communications Inc ....C....951 572-1200
13341 Temescal Canyon Rd Corona (92883) ***(P-1865)***
HP Inc ....B....858 924-5117
16399 W Bernardo Dr # 61 San Diego (92127) ***(P-7280)***
HP Pavillion At San Jose, San Jose *Also called San Jose Sharks LLC* ***(P-18079)***
HP Sears Co., Bakersfield *Also called H P Sears Co Inc* ***(P-13684)***
Hpa-USA, Compton *Also called Hydroprocessing Associates LLC* ***(P-16837)***
Hpe, San Jose *Also called Hewlett Packard Enterprise Co* ***(P-15351)***
Hpg International, Walnut Creek *Also called Hospitlity Prch Group Intl LLC* ***(P-16835)***
HPM Construction LLC ....D....949 474-9170
17911 Mitchell S Irvine (92614) ***(P-1504)***
Hpp Food Services, Wilmington *Also called Icpk Corporation* ***(P-8181)***
Hps Mechanical Inc (PA) ....C....661 397-2121
3100 E Belle Ter Bakersfield (93307) ***(P-2151)***
Hps Plumbing Service Inc ....B....661 324-2121
3100 E Belle Ter Bakersfield (93307) ***(P-1866)***
Hpt Trs Ihg-2 Inc ....D....408 241-9305
481 El Camino Real Santa Clara (95050) ***(P-12417)***
Hpt Trs Ihg-2 Inc ....D....714 748-7777
1915 S Manchester Ave Anaheim (92802) ***(P-12418)***
Hpt Trs Ihg-2 Inc ....D....310 642-7500
5985 W Century Blvd Los Angeles (90045) ***(P-12419)***
Hpt Trs Ihg-2 Inc ....B....310 318-8888
300 N Harbor Dr Redondo Beach (90277) ***(P-12420)***
Hpt Trs Ihg-2 Inc ....E....408 745-1515
900 Hamlin Ct Sunnyvale (94089) ***(P-12421)***
Hr Mission Commons Fc 5183 ....D....909 793-8691
10 Terracina Blvd Redlands (92373) ***(P-23962)***
Hrc Fertility, Pasadena *Also called Huntington Reprodctve Ctr Inc* ***(P-19019)***
Hrd Aero Systems Inc ....D....661 295-0670
25555 Avenue Stanford Valencia (91355) ***(P-17508)***
Hrd Aero Systems Inc (PA) ....C....661 295-0670
25555 Avenue Stanford Valencia (91355) ***(P-17509)***
Hrd Oxygens, Valencia *Also called Hrd Aero Systems Inc* ***(P-17508)***
Hrl Laboratories LLC ....B....310 317-5000
3011 Malibu Canyon Rd Malibu (90265) ***(P-25993)***
Hrn Services, Citrus Heights *Also called Accountable Health Staff Inc* ***(P-14220)***
Hronis Inc A California Corp (PA) ....D....661 725-2503
10443 Hronis Rd Delano (93215) ***(P-190)***
Hronopoulos ....E....619 237-6161
110 W A St Ste 900 San Diego (92101) ***(P-26260)***
Hsbc Bank USA NA, Los Angeles *Also called Hsbc Business Credit (usa)* ***(P-9261)***
Hsbc Business Credit (usa) ....D....213 553-8089
660 S Figueroa St Los Angeles (90017) ***(P-9261)***
Hsbc Finance Corporation ....C....408 796-3600
1420 El Paseo De Saratoga San Jose (95130) ***(P-9262)***
Hsbc Finance Corporation ....A....909 623-3355
931 Corporate Center Dr Pomona (91768) ***(P-9462)***
Hsbc Finance Corporation ....B....818 999-9175
21801 Ventura Bouelvard Woodland Hills (91364) ***(P-9562)***
Hsbc Finance Corporation ....C....213 628-8167
725 N Broadway Los Angeles (90012) ***(P-9263)***
Hsf Programme, San Francisco *Also called San Francisco Health Authority* ***(P-24423)***
Hssc, Santa Rosa *Also called Sonoma County Humane Society* ***(P-607)***
Hst Lessee Boston LLC ....D....619 692-2255
1380 Harbor Island Dr San Diego (92101) ***(P-12422)***
Hst Lessee San Diego LP ....B....619 291-2900
1380 Harbor Island Dr San Diego (92101) ***(P-12423)***
HSU FOUNDATION, Arcata *Also called Humboldt State University Spon* ***(P-27091)***
Htec Group Inc (PA) ....D....650 949-4880
535 Mission St Fl 14 San Francisco (94105) ***(P-14857)***
Huawei Enterprise USA Inc ....D....408 394-4295
20400 Stevens Creek Blvd Cupertino (95014) ***(P-5419)***
Hub Construction Spc Inc (PA) ....E....909 889-0161
379 S I St San Bernardino (92410) ***(P-14169)***
Hub Construction Spc Inc ....E....909 947-4669
1856 S Bon View Ave Ontario (91761) ***(P-7479)***
Hub Construction Sups & Eqp, San Bernardino *Also called Hub Construction Spc Inc* ***(P-14169)***
Hub Group Trucking Inc ....B....909 770-8950
13867 Valley Blvd Fontana (92335) ***(P-3894)***
Hub Group Trucking Inc ....C....951 693-9813
3801 E Guasti Rd Ontario (91761) ***(P-3895)***
Hub Intrntional Insur Svcs Inc ....D....916 974-7800
3636 American River Dr # 200 Sacramento (95864) ***(P-10383)***
Hub Intrntional Insur Svcs Inc ....D....559 447-4600
548 W Cromwell Ave # 101 Fresno (93711) ***(P-10384)***
Hub Intrntional Insur Svcs Inc ....D....805 682-2571
40 E Alamar Ave Santa Barbara (93105) ***(P-10385)***
Hub-Limited Workshop, Los Angeles *Also called Mid-Cities Association Inc* ***(P-23616)***
Hubb Systems LLC ....D....510 865-9100
12305 Crosthwaite Cir Poway (92064) ***(P-15610)***
Hubbard Iron Doors Inc ....E....323 724-6500
7407 Telegraph Rd Montebello (90640) ***(P-7071)***
Hubbell Lighting Inc ....B....619 946-1800
2498 Roll Dr San Diego (92154) ***(P-7154)***
Hubbs-Sea World Research Inst (PA) ....D....619 226-3870
2595 Ingraham St San Diego (92109) ***(P-25994)***
Hudson Gardens, Pasadena *Also called Aah Hudson LP* ***(P-10681)***
Hudson Pacific Properties Inc (PA) ....D....310 445-5700
11601 Wilshire Blvd Fl 6 Los Angeles (90025) ***(P-11856)***
Hudson Ranch Power I LLC ....D....858 509-0150
12250 El Camino Real # 280 San Diego (92130) ***(P-5846)***
Hudson Tchmart Cmmerce Ctr LLC ....D....408 451-4440
5201 Great America Pkwy Santa Clara (95054) ***(P-10608)***
Hueston Hennigan LLP ....D....213 788-4340
523 W 6th St Ste 400 Los Angeles (90014) ***(P-22576)***
Hughes Research Laboratories, Malibu *Also called Hrl Laboratories LLC* ***(P-25993)***
Huitt - Zollars Inc ....E....949 988-5815
2603 Main St Ste 400 Irvine (92614) ***(P-25521)***
Hulk Construction ....D....714 701-9458
4352 Lakeview Ave Yorba Linda (92886) ***(P-3343)***
Hulu LLC ....C....888 631-4858
12312 W Olympic Boulev Los Angeles (90064) ***(P-5420)***
Hulu LLC (HQ) ....C....310 571-4700
2500 Broadway Ste 200 Santa Monica (90404) ***(P-5421)***
Human Options Inc ....E....949 757-3635
1901 Newport Blvd Ste 240 Costa Mesa (92627) ***(P-23265)***
Human Options Inc (PA) ....D....949 737-5242
5540 Trabuco Rd Ste 100 Irvine (92620) ***(P-23266)***
Human Potential Cons LLC ....D....310 756-1560
500 E Carson Plaza Dr # 127 Carson (90746) ***(P-26946)***
Human Resource Solutions, Chico *Also called Roy Carrington Inc* ***(P-14408)***
Human Resources, Anaheim *Also called Interstate Electronics Corp* ***(P-26651)***
Human Resources, Santa Barbara *Also called Santa Barbara County of* ***(P-23448)***
Human Resources Department, Redwood City *Also called County of San Mateo* ***(P-26204)***
Human Resources Department, Redwood City *Also called County of San Mateo* ***(P-26205)***
Human Resources Department, Covina *Also called Citrus Valley Medical Ctr Inc* ***(P-20787)***
Human Services Agency, Belmont *Also called County of San Mateo* ***(P-23162)***
Human Services Association (PA) ....D....562 806-5400
6800 Florence Ave Bell (90201) ***(P-23267)***
Human Services Department, Yreka *Also called County of Siskiyou* ***(P-23166)***
Human Services Dept, Delano *Also called County of Kern* ***(P-23079)***
Human Services Dept, Bakersfield *Also called County of Kern* ***(P-24161)***
Human Services Systems, San Bernardino *Also called County of San Bernardino* ***(P-23139)***
Human Services Systems, San Bernardino *Also called County of San Bernardino* ***(P-23713)***
Human Touch LLC ....D....562 426-8700
4600 E Conant St Long Beach (90808) ***(P-6518)***
Human Touch Home Health ....C....424 247-8165
3629 N Sepulveda Blvd Manhattan Beach (90266) ***(P-21783)***
Humane Society Silicon Valley ....D....408 262-2133
901 Ames Ave Milpitas (95035) ***(P-24839)***
Humangood (PA) ....D....602 906-4024
6120 Stoneridge Mall Rd Pleasanton (94588) ***(P-20598)***
Humanitycom Inc ....E....415 230-0108
50 Osgood Pl Ste 330 San Francisco (94133) ***(P-14858)***
Humboldt Commnty Accss Resrc ....D....707 443-7077
1707 E St Ste 2 Eureka (95501) ***(P-23268)***
Humboldt County Mental Health, Eureka *Also called County of Humboldt* ***(P-21994)***

Humboldt Dev LLC ....D....213 295-2890
2804 Gateway Oaks Dr # 100 Sacramento (95833) *(P-16023)*
Humboldt Dog Obedience Group ....E....707 444-3862
P.O. Box 6733 Eureka (95502) *(P-605)*
Humboldt Open Door Clinic, Arcata *Also called Open Door Community Hlth Ctrs (P-22071)*
Humboldt Redwood Company LLC (HQ) ....B....707 764-4472
125 Main St Scotia (95565) *(P-6628)*
Humboldt Senior Resource Ctr (PA) ....C....707 443-9747
1910 California St Eureka (95501) *(P-23269)*
Humboldt State University Spon ....D....707 826-4189
1 Harpst St Arcata (95521) *(P-27091)*
Humdog, Eureka *Also called Humboldt Dog Obedience Group (P-605)*
Hume Lake Christian Camps Inc ....D....559 305-7770
64144 Hume Lake Rd Ofc Miramonte (93628) *(P-13149)*
Humetrix Inc ....E....858 259-8987
1155 Camino Del Mar Ste 5 Del Mar (92014) *(P-26639)*
Humnit Hotel At Lax LLC ....D....424 702-1234
6225 W Century Blvd Los Angeles (90045) *(P-12424)*
Humphrey Plumbing Inc ....D....209 634-4626
880 S Kilroy Rd Turlock (95380) *(P-2152)*
Humphreys Half Moon Inn, San Diego *Also called Bartell Hotels (P-12038)*
Hunsaker & Assoc Irvine Inc (PA) ....D....949 583-1010
3 Hughes Irvine (92618) *(P-25132)*
Hunt Ortmann Palffy Nieves ....E....626 440-5200
301 N Lake Ave Fl 7 Pasadena (91101) *(P-22577)*
Hunt Convenience Stores LLC ....E....916 383-4868
5750 S Watt Ave Sacramento (95829) *(P-26261)*
Hunt Enterprises Inc ....C....310 325-1496
2270 Sepulveda Blvd # 50 Torrance (90501) *(P-11196)*
Hunter Advertising Mail Co, San Leandro *Also called Kp LLC (P-13727)*
Hunter Easterday Corporation ....C....714 238-3400
1475 N Hundley St Anaheim (92806) *(P-13948)*
Hunter Realty Inc ....C....805 346-8688
2605 S Miller St Ste 101 Santa Maria (93455) *(P-11197)*
Hunting Energy Services Inc ....D....661 633-4272
4900 California Ave 100a Bakersfield (93309) *(P-1027)*
Hunting-Vinson, Bakersfield *Also called Hunting Energy Services Inc (P-1027)*
Huntington Ambltry Surg Ctr ....E....626 229-8999
625 S Fair Oaks Ave Pasadena (91105) *(P-19017)*
Huntington Bch Cnvlescent Hosp ....B....714 847-3515
18811 Florida St Huntington Beach (92648) *(P-20026)*
Huntington Beach Car Wash, Huntington Beach *Also called Russell Fisher Partnership (P-17396)*
Huntington Beach Hospital, Huntington Beach *Also called Prime Hlthcare Hntngton Bch (P-21114)*
Huntington Care LLC ....B....877 405-6990
3452 E Foothill Blvd # 760 Pasadena (91107) *(P-21784)*
Huntington Child Care Center, Los Angeles *Also called Casa Dscanso Convalescent Hosp (P-26933)*
Huntington Extended Care Ctr, Pasadena *Also called Pasadena Hospital Assn Ltd (P-20191)*
Huntington Home Care, Pasadena *Also called Huntington Care LLC (P-21784)*
Huntington Hotel Company ....D....858 756-1131
5951 Linea Del Cielo Rancho Santa Fe (92067) *(P-12425)*
Huntington Med Pathology Group, Pasadena *Also called Pasadena Cyto Pathology Lab (P-21086)*
Huntington Med Res Institutes ....D....626 397-5804
734 Fairmount Ave Pasadena (91105) *(P-25995)*
Huntington Memory Care Cmnty, Alhambra *Also called Silverado Senior Living Inc (P-20684)*
Huntington Otptent Surgery Ctr ....D....626 535-2434
625 S Fair Oaks Ave # 380 Pasadena (91105) *(P-19018)*
Huntington Park Nursing Center, Huntington Park *Also called Covenant Care California LLC (P-19833)*
HUNTINGTON PARK POLICE DEPARTM, Huntington Park *Also called Huntington Pk Police League (P-23270)*
Huntington Pk Police League ....D....323 584-6254
6542 Miles Ave Huntington Park (90255) *(P-23270)*
Huntington Reprodctve Ctr Inc (PA) ....E....626 204-9699
135 S Rosemead Blvd Pasadena (91107) *(P-19019)*
Huntington Rsdntial Rtrment Ht, Torrance *Also called Longwood Management Inc (P-10762)*
Huntington Vly Healthcare Ctr, Huntington Beach *Also called Douglas Fir Holdings LLC (P-19866)*
Huntleigh USA Corporation ....D....619 231-8111
3707 N Harbor Dr A-110 San Diego (92101) *(P-4774)*
Huntley Hotel Santa Monica Bch, Santa Monica *Also called Second Street Corporation (P-12900)*
Hunton Andrews Kurth LLP ....D....415 975-3700
50 California St Ste 1700 San Francisco (94111) *(P-22578)*
Hunton Andrews Kurth LLP ....D....213 532-2000
550 S Hope St Ste 2000 Los Angeles (90071) *(P-22579)*
Huntsman Architectural Group (PA) ....D....415 394-1212
50 California St Fl 7 San Francisco (94111) *(P-25460)*
Huoyen International Inc ....D....714 635-9000
1500 S Raymond Ave Fullerton (92831) *(P-12426)*
Huppe Landscape Company Inc (HQ) ....D....916 784-7666
9350 Viking Pl Roseville (95747) *(P-734)*
Hurley Construction Inc ....D....916 446-7599
1801 I St Ste 200 Sacramento (95811) *(P-1248)*
Huskies Lessee LLC ....B....415 392-7755
450 Powell St San Francisco (94102) *(P-12427)*
Hustle Digital Inc ....E....310 882-2680
12777 W Jefferson Blvd Los Angeles (90066) *(P-16836)*
Hustler Casino, Gardena *Also called El Dorado Enterprises Inc (P-12243)*
Hutchings Court Reporters LLC (PA) ....E....702 314-7200
400 N Tustin Ave Ste 301 Santa Ana (92705) *(P-13803)*
Hutchinson & Bloodgood LLP (PA) ....C....818 637-5000
550 N Brand Blvd Fl 14 Glendale (91203) *(P-25614)*
Hutchison Corporation ....D....310 763-7991
6107 Obispo Ave Long Beach (90805) *(P-2796)*
Huttig Building Products Inc ....D....916 383-3721
8120 Pwr Rdge Rd Bldg 100 Sacramento (95826) *(P-6629)*
Huttig Sash & Door Co, Sacramento *Also called Huttig Building Products Inc (P-6629)*
Huxley Apartments, The, West Hollywood *Also called Essex Property Trust Inc (P-11784)*
Hvantage Technologies Inc ....D....818 661-6301
6700 Fllbrook Ave Ste 222 West Hills (91307) *(P-14859)*
Hvi Cat Canyon Inc ....C....805 621-5800
2617 E Clark Ave Santa Maria (93455) *(P-1028)*
Hvsf Transition LLC ....D....415 477-1999
1100 Sansome St San Francisco (94111) *(P-13519)*
Hwe Mechanical, Bakersfield *Also called Hills Wldg & Engrg Contr Inc (P-1025)*
Hwmm (HQ) ....D....949 581-1144
7 Studebaker Irvine (92618) *(P-8033)*
Hwn Mariposa Associates LLC ....D....310 478-8757
11150 Santa Monica Blvd # 760 Los Angeles (90025) *(P-1300)*
Hy-Lond Hlth Care Cnter-Merced, Merced *Also called Avalon Care Cen (P-19732)*
Hy-Lond Hlth Care Cntr-Modesto, Modesto *Also called Avalon Care Center - Modesto (P-19735)*
Hy-Tech Tile Inc ....C....951 788-0550
1355 Palmyrita Ave Riverside (92507) *(P-3006)*
Hyatt Carmel Highlands, Carmel *Also called Highlands Inn Inc (P-12352)*
Hyatt Coporation As Agent of B ....D....760 603-6851
7100 Aviara Resort Dr Carlsbad (92011) *(P-12428)*
Hyatt Corporation ....C....323 656-1234
8401 W Sunset Blvd Los Angeles (90069) *(P-12429)*
Hyatt Corporation ....B....530 562-3900
4001 Northstar Dr Truckee (96161) *(P-12430)*
Hyatt Corporation ....B....312 750-1234
6225 W Century Blvd Los Angeles (90045) *(P-12431)*
Hyatt Corporation ....B....909 240-9526
3500 Market St Riverside (92501) *(P-12432)*
Hyatt Corporation ....B....415 848-6050
345 Stockton St San Francisco (94108) *(P-12433)*
Hyatt Corporation ....A....415 788-1234
50 Drumm St San Francisco (94111) *(P-12434)*
Hyatt Corporation ....B....925 743-1882
2323 San Ramon Vly Blvd San Ramon (94583) *(P-12435)*
Hyatt Corporation ....B....562 432-0161
200 S Pine Ave Long Beach (90802) *(P-12436)*
Hyatt Corporation ....B....714 750-1234
11999 Harbor Blvd Garden Grove (92840) *(P-12437)*
Hyatt Corporation ....B....831 372-1234
1 Old Golf Course Rd Monterey (93940) *(P-12438)*
Hyatt Corporation ....B....949 975-1234
17900 Jamboree Rd Irvine (92614) *(P-12439)*
Hyatt Corporation ....B....760 341-1000
44600 Indian Wells Ln Indian Wells (92210) *(P-12440)*
Hyatt Corporation ....B....949 729-1234
1107 Jamboree Rd Newport Beach (92660) *(P-12441)*
Hyatt Corporation ....B....408 453-3006
55 E Brokaw Rd San Jose (95112) *(P-12442)*
Hyatt Corporation ....A....415 788-1234
5 Embarcadero Ctr San Francisco (94111) *(P-12443)*
Hyatt Corporation ....C....619 849-1234
600 F St San Diego (92101) *(P-12444)*
Hyatt Equities LLC ....B....408 993-1234
1740 N 1st St San Jose (95112) *(P-12445)*
Hyatt Fisherman's Wharf, San Francisco *Also called Chsp Trs Fisherman Wharf LLC (P-12143)*
Hyatt Grand Champion Resort, Indian Wells *Also called Hyatt Corporation (P-12440)*
Hyatt Hotel, Monterey *Also called Classic Riverdale Inc (P-12153)*
Hyatt Hotel, Carmel *Also called Highlands Inn Investors II LP (P-12353)*
Hyatt Hotel, Los Angeles *Also called Hyatt Corporation (P-12429)*
Hyatt Hotel, San Francisco *Also called Hyatt Corporation (P-12434)*
Hyatt Hotel, Long Beach *Also called Hyatt Corporation (P-12436)*
Hyatt Hotel, San Jose *Also called Hyatt Equities LLC (P-12445)*
Hyatt Hotel, Irvine *Also called Hyatt Corporation (P-12439)*
Hyatt Hotel, Newport Beach *Also called Hyatt Corporation (P-12441)*
Hyatt Hotel, Los Angeles *Also called Jwmcc Limited Partnership (P-12495)*
Hyatt Hotel, Monterey *Also called Classic Rsdence Mgt Ltd Partnr (P-12154)*
Hyatt Hotels Management Corp ....C....661 799-1234
24500 Town Center Dr Valencia (91355) *(P-12446)*
Hyatt Hotels Management Corp ....B....858 552-1234
3777 Lajolla Village Dr San Diego (92122) *(P-12447)*
Hyatt Hotels Management Corp ....C....760 322-9000
285 N Palm Canyon Dr Palm Springs (92262) *(P-12448)*
Hyatt Hotels Management Corp ....B....650 352-1234
4219 El Camino Real Palo Alto (94306) *(P-12449)*
Hyatt Hotels Management Corp ....B....831 372-1234
1 Old Golf Course Rd Monterey (93940) *(P-12450)*
Hyatt House Rancho Cordova, Rancho Cordova *Also called Select Hotels Group LLC (P-12902)*
Hyatt House San Ramon, San Ramon *Also called Hyatt Corporation (P-12435)*
Hyatt Los Angeles Airport, Los Angeles *Also called Hyatt Corporation (P-12431)*
Hyatt Pl Fremont/Silicon Vly, Fremont *Also called Select Hotels Group LLC (P-12901)*
Hyatt Place San Jose Hotel, San Jose *Also called West San Crlos Ht Partners LLC (P-13086)*
Hyatt Regency Mission Bay Spa, San Diego *Also called H C T Inc (P-12325)*
Hyatt Regency Monterey, Monterey *Also called Hyatt Corporation (P-12438)*
Hyatt Regency Orange County, Garden Grove *Also called Hyatt Corporation (P-12437)*
Hyatt Regency Sacramento, Sacramento *Also called Capitol Regency LLC (P-12113)*
Hyatt Regency San Francisco Ht, San Francisco *Also called Hyatt Corporation (P-12443)*

ALPHABETIC

Employee Codes: A=Over 500 employees, B=251-500
C=101-250, D=51-100, E=50
2020 Directory of California
Wholesalers and Services Companies
© Mergent Inc. 1-800-342-5647
1301

Hyatt Regency Santa Clara.....D.....408 200-1234
5101 Great America Pkwy Santa Clara (95054) ***(P-12451)***
Hyatt Rgncy San Frncisco Arprt, Burlingame *Also called Host Hotels & Resorts LP* ***(P-12388)***
Hyatt Vacation Ownership Inc.....D.....310 285-0990
9615 Brighton Way M180 Beverly Hills (90210) ***(P-11198)***
Hyatt Vineyard Creek Ht & Spa, Santa Rosa *Also called Noble Aew Vineyard Creek LLC* ***(P-12648)***
Hyatt Westlake, Westlake Village *Also called Swvp Westlake LLC* ***(P-13009)***
Hyatt Westlake Plaza Hotel, Westlake Village *Also called Sky Court USA Inc* ***(P-12940)***
Hybrid Promotions LLC (PA).....C.....714 952-3866
10711 Walker St Cypress (90630) ***(P-8034)***
Hyde Park Convalescent Hosp.....E.....323 753-1354
6520 West Blvd Los Angeles (90043) ***(P-20027)***
Hydrafacial Company, The, Long Beach *Also called Edge Systems LLC* ***(P-6964)***
Hydratech LLC (HQ).....D.....559 233-0876
1331 S West Ave Fresno (93706) ***(P-17510)***
Hydraulx, Playa Vista *Also called Avongard Products USa Ltd* ***(P-17725)***
Hydro Chem Industrial Services, Pittsburg *Also called Hydrochem LLC* ***(P-13949)***
Hydro Power Service, Sacramento *Also called HDR Engineering Inc* ***(P-25121)***
Hydro Tek Systems Inc.....D.....909 799-9222
2353 Almond Ave Redlands (92374) ***(P-7672)***
Hydro-Pressure Systems, North Hollywood *Also called Woods Maintenance Services Inc* ***(P-3495)***
Hydrochem LLC.....D.....925 432-1749
901 Loveridge Rd 592 Pittsburg (94565) ***(P-13949)***
Hydrochempsc, Torrance *Also called PSC Industrial Outsourcing LP* ***(P-17532)***
Hydrochempsc, San Ardo *Also called PSC Industrial Outsourcing LP* ***(P-3926)***
Hydroprocessing Associates LLC.....E.....310 667-6456
19122 S Santa Fe Ave Compton (90221) ***(P-16837)***
Hydrox Properties Xii LLC.....D.....510 262-7200
3170 Hilltop Mall Rd Richmond (94806) ***(P-10609)***
Hyland Software Inc.....D.....949 242-3100
2355 Main St Ste 100 Irvine (92614) ***(P-14860)***
Hylton Security Inc.....C.....916 442-1000
1015 2nd St Fl 2 Sacramento (95814) ***(P-16322)***
Hypergrid Inc (PA).....D.....650 316-5524
201 San Antonio Cir # 245 Mountain View (94040) ***(P-14861)***
Hyperloop One, Los Angeles *Also called Hyperloop Technologies Inc* ***(P-5118)***
Hyperloop Technologies Inc (PA).....D.....213 800-3270
2159 Bay St Los Angeles (90021) ***(P-5118)***
Hyrecar Inc.....D.....888 688-6769
355 S Grand Ave Ste 1650 Los Angeles (90071) ***(P-3686)***
Hyrian LLC.....C.....212 590-2567
2355 Westwood Blvd Los Angeles (90064) ***(P-14303)***
Hyundai Atver Tlmtics Amer Inc.....D.....949 381-6000
10550 Talbert Ave Fl 2 Fountain Valley (92708) ***(P-14862)***
Hyundai Capital America (HQ).....D.....714 965-3000
3161 Michelson Dr # 1900 Irvine (92612) ***(P-9463)***
Hyundai Finance, Irvine *Also called Hyundai Capital America* ***(P-9463)***
Hyundai Motor America (HQ).....B.....714 965-3000
10550 Talbert Ave Fountain Valley (92708) ***(P-9485)***
Hyve Solutions Corporation (HQ).....A.....855 869-6873
44201 Nobel Dr Fremont (94538) ***(P-15775)***
I A C, Irvine *Also called Irvine APT Communities LP* ***(P-10741)***
I B S, Roseville *Also called Iptor Supply Chain Systems USA* ***(P-14887)***
I C Class Components Corp (PA).....D.....310 539-5500
23605 Telo Ave Torrance (90505) ***(P-7281)***
I C M, Los Angeles *Also called International Creative Mgt Inc* ***(P-17916)***
I C M, Los Angeles *Also called International Creative MGT Inc* ***(P-17917)***
I C S, San Francisco *Also called Integrated Clg Solutions Inc* ***(P-13952)***
I C S I, Berkeley *Also called Interntional Cmpt Science Inst* ***(P-25997)***
I C W, San Diego *Also called Insurance Company of West* ***(P-10098)***
I Cann, Los Angeles *Also called Internet Corp For Assigned Nam* ***(P-15619)***
I Cypress Company (PA).....D.....831 647-7500
1700 17 Mile Dr Pebble Beach (93953) ***(P-12452)***
I D Property Corporation.....C.....213 625-0100
1001 Wilshire Blvd # 100 Los Angeles (90017) ***(P-11199)***
I G F, Long Beach *Also called International Garment Finisher* ***(P-13299)***
I Hot Leads.....D.....714 960-8028
19671 Beach Blvd Ste 204 Huntington Beach (92648) ***(P-15776)***
I I D, Imperial *Also called Imperial Irrigation District* ***(P-5847)***
I L S West Inc.....E.....714 505-7530
17501 17th St Ste 100 Tustin (92780) ***(P-25615)***
I Lan Systems Inc.....D.....626 304-9021
237 S Raymond Ave Alhambra (91801) ***(P-15611)***
I M A C A, Bishop *Also called Inyo Mono Advcts Fr Cmmnty Act* ***(P-24183)***
I M T, Sherman Oaks *Also called Investors MGT Tr RE Group Inc* ***(P-10740)***
I Mean It Creative Inc.....E.....310 287-1000
1643 Buckingham Rd Los Angeles (90019) ***(P-13520)***
I Merit Inc.....A.....504 226-2427
14435c Big Basin Way Saratoga (95070) ***(P-15777)***
I N C Builders Inc.....B.....760 352-4200
1560 Ocotillo Dr Ste L El Centro (92243) ***(P-14512)***
I N G, Compton *Also called Newport Apparel Corporation* ***(P-8101)***
I P I, Los Angeles *Also called Imperial Parking Industries* ***(P-17258)***
I P S, Mentone *Also called International Paving Svcs Inc* ***(P-1733)***
I P S Services Inc.....D.....909 305-0250
627 E Foothill Blvd San Dimas (91773) ***(P-22044)***
I Pwlc Inc.....D.....760 630-0231
408 Olive Ave Vista (92083) ***(P-735)***
I S A Contracting Svcs Inc.....A.....559 659-1080
958 O St Firebaugh (93622) ***(P-452)***
I S D, Los Angeles *Also called IDS Real Estate Group* ***(P-11201)***
I T C, Citrus Heights *Also called Itc Srvice Group Acqsition LLC* ***(P-27098)***
I T P, Burbank *Also called Information Tech Partners Inc* ***(P-16028)***
I T S, Long Beach *Also called International Trnsp Svc* ***(P-4612)***
I Wmi.....B.....562 977-4906
17100 Pioneer Blvd # 230 Artesia (90701) ***(P-1505)***
I2c Inc.....B.....650 593-5400
100 Redwood Shores Pkwy Redwood City (94065) ***(P-6850)***
IA Lodging NAPA Solano Trs LLC.....C.....707 253-8600
3425 Solano Ave NAPA (94558) ***(P-12453)***
Iaa Inc.....D.....818 487-2222
7245 Laurel Canyon Blvd # 5 North Hollywood (91605) ***(P-6399)***
Iaba, Los Angeles *Also called Institute For Applied Behavior* ***(P-19672)***
Iaba, Camarillo *Also called Institute For Applied Behavior* ***(P-19673)***
IAC Publishing LLC.....D.....510 985-7400
555 12th St Ste 300 Oakland (94607) ***(P-5422)***
IAC Search & Media Inc (HQ).....C.....510 985-7400
555 12th St Ste 500 Oakland (94607) ***(P-15868)***
Iap West Inc.....D.....310 667-9720
20036 S Via Baron Rancho Dominguez (90220) ***(P-6446)***
Iap World Services Inc.....D.....650 604-0451
567 Dugan South Akron Rd Mountain View (94035) ***(P-26947)***
Iap World Services Inc.....B.....760 380-6772
510 S Loop 1st St Bldg T Fort Irwin (92310) ***(P-26948)***
IAPMO, Ontario *Also called International Assoc of Plmbng* ***(P-24344)***
Iapmo Research and Testing Inc (HQ).....D.....909 472-4100
5001 E Philadelphia St Ontario (91761) ***(P-24342)***
Iasco (PA).....B.....707 252-3522
1833 Castenada Dr Burlingame (94010) ***(P-14513)***
Ibackup.com, Calabasas *Also called Idrive Inc* ***(P-16024)***
Ibaset Federal Services LLC (PA).....D.....949 598-5200
27442 Portola Pkwy # 300 Foothill Ranch (92610) ***(P-14863)***
Ibftech Inc.....D.....424 217-8010
343 Main St El Segundo (90245) ***(P-14304)***
Ibi Group A California Partnr.....D.....213 769-0011
315 W 9th St Ste 600 Los Angeles (90015) ***(P-25133)***
Ibi Group, Los Angeles, Los Angeles *Also called Ibi Group A California Partnr* ***(P-25133)***
Ibis Biosciences Inc.....C.....760 476-3200
2251 Faraday Ave Ste 150 Carlsbad (92008) ***(P-25764)***
Ibisworld Inc (HQ).....D.....800 330-3772
11755 Wilshire Blvd # 1100 Los Angeles (90025) ***(P-25908)***
IBM, Agoura Hills *Also called International Bus Mchs Corp* ***(P-15618)***
IBM, San Jose *Also called International Bus Mchs Corp* ***(P-14884)***
IBM, San Francisco *Also called International Bus Mchs Corp* ***(P-6752)***
IBM, Santa Clara *Also called International Bus Mchs Corp* ***(P-16034)***
IBM, Costa Mesa *Also called International Bus Mchs Corp* ***(P-16035)***
IBM, Foster City *Also called International Bus Mchs Corp* ***(P-16036)***
IBM, San Jose *Also called International Bus Mchs Corp* ***(P-6753)***
IBM, San Jose *Also called International Bus Mchs Corp* ***(P-25769)***
IBM, San Ramon *Also called International Bus Mchs Corp* ***(P-26649)***
Ibuypower, City of Industry *Also called American Future Tech Corp* ***(P-6794)***
Ic BP III Holdings Xii LLC.....D.....415 549-5054
1 Sansome St Ste 1500 San Francisco (94104) ***(P-11200)***
Ic BP III Holdings Xv LLC.....E.....415 273-4250
1 Sansome St Fl 15 San Francisco (94104) ***(P-10875)***
Ic Compliance LLC (PA).....A.....650 378-4150
1065 E Hillsdale Blvd # 300 Foster City (94404) ***(P-14864)***
Icarus Fuel Services US Corp.....D.....310 417-0124
7251 World Way W Los Angeles (90045) ***(P-4775)***
Icat Logistics Inc.....D.....310 884-5923
11 Wandering Rill Irvine (92603) ***(P-4969)***
ICC, Fontana *Also called Inland Cc Inc* ***(P-3162)***
Ice Center Enterprises LLC.....D.....510 604-8878
10123 N Wolfe Rd Ste 1020 Cupertino (95014) ***(P-18708)***
Ice Center, The, Cupertino *Also called Ice Center Enterprises LLC* ***(P-18708)***
Ice Data Services Inc.....D.....310 664-2500
2901 28th St Ste 300 Santa Monica (90405) ***(P-14865)***
Ice Delivery Systems Inc.....C.....408 640-4625
6920 Santa Teresa Blvd # 206 San Jose (95119) ***(P-3896)***
Ice Specialty Entrmt Inc (PA).....C.....310 899-3889
409 Santa Monica Blvd E Santa Monica (90401) ***(P-18709)***
Ice Station Valencia L L C.....D.....661 775-8686
27745 Smyth Dr Valencia (91355) ***(P-18710)***
Iceoplex, Santa Monica *Also called Ice Specialty Entrmt Inc* ***(P-18709)***
Icf Consulting Group Inc.....A.....703 934-3000
101 Lucas Valley Rd # 249 San Rafael (94903) ***(P-26640)***
Icf Jones & Stokes Inc.....D.....949 333-6600
1 Ada Ste 100 Irvine (92618) ***(P-26641)***
ICI Enterprises Inc.....D.....562 989-7715
790 E Willow St Ste 150 Long Beach (90806) ***(P-23603)***
ICI Services Corporation.....B.....805 988-3210
1000 Town Center Dr # 225 Oxnard (93036) ***(P-25134)***
Ickler Electric Corporation.....E.....858 486-1585
13250 Kirkham Way Poway (92064) ***(P-2519)***
ICO Rally, Palo Alto *Also called Insulation Sources Inc* ***(P-7156)***
Icon Design and Display Inc.....D.....707 284-3400
645 4th St Ste 212 Santa Rosa (95404) ***(P-16838)***
Icon Exposure Inc.....D.....323 933-1666
5450 Wilshire Blvd Los Angeles (90036) ***(P-16578)***
Icon Media Direct Inc (PA).....D.....818 995-6400
5910 Lemona Ave Van Nuys (91411) ***(P-13521)***
Iconic Chronicles Magazine LLC.....D.....707 712-2097
5120 Monetta Ln Sacramento (95835) ***(P-8873)***
Iconic Collective LLC.....D.....877 930-0409
4136 Del Rey Ave Ste 601 Marina Del Rey (90292) ***(P-13522)***
Icpk Corporation.....D.....310 830-8020
1130 W C St Wilmington (90744) ***(P-8181)***
Icrco Inc (PA).....E.....310 921-9559
26 Coromar Dr Goleta (93117) ***(P-6971)***

Mergent e-mail: customerrelations@mergent.com
1302
2020 Directory of California
Wholesalers and Services Companies
(P-0000) Products & Services Section entry number
(PA)=Parent Co (HQ)=Headquarters (DH)=Div Headquarters

Ics Integrated Comm Systems ....D....408 491-6000
6680 Via Del Oro San Jose (95119) ***(P-2520)***
Ics Professional Services Inc ....C....714 868-3900
7755 Center Ave Fl 11 Huntington Beach (92647) ***(P-3007)***
Ics-CA North, Roseville *Also called Industrial Container Services* ***(P-7637)***
Ictp, Anaheim *Also called Ray W Choi* ***(P-26785)***
Icu Eyewear Inc ....D....831 637-9300
1900 Shelton Dr Hollister (95023) ***(P-7818)***
Icw Group Holdings Inc (PA) ....D....858 350-2400
15025 Innovation Dr San Diego (92128) ***(P-10097)***
Icw Valencia LLC ....D....858 350-2600
11455 El Camino Real San Diego (92130) ***(P-10610)***
Icygen LLC ....D....510 540-7122
940 Dwight Way Ste 13b Berkeley (94710) ***(P-15612)***
ID Analytics LLC ....C....858 312-6200
15253 Ave Of Science San Diego (92128) ***(P-16527)***
ID On Demand, Santa Ana *Also called Idondemand Inc* ***(P-15613)***
Idc Technologies Inc (PA) ....D....408 376-0212
920 Hillview Ct Ste 250 Milpitas (95035) ***(P-14305)***
Idea Travel Company ....A....650 948-0207
13145 Byrd Ln Ste 101 Los Altos Hills (94022) ***(P-4824)***
Ideal Brands Inc ....E....213 489-5557
16060 Ventura Blvd Encino (91436) ***(P-27280)***
Ideal Products LLC ....E....818 217-2574
14724 Ventura Blvd Fl 200 Sherman Oaks (91403) ***(P-13429)***
Ideal Program Services Inc ....D....323 296-2255
3970 W Martin Luther King Los Angeles (90008) ***(P-23271)***
Ideal Transit Inc ....E....626 448-2690
13404 Waco St Baldwin Park (91706) ***(P-3541)***
Idealab Holdings LLC (PA) ....A....626 585-6900
130 W Union St Pasadena (91103) ***(P-11922)***
Idec Corporation (HQ) ....D....408 747-0550
1175 Elko Dr Sunnyvale (94089) ***(P-7282)***
Ideo LP (PA) ....C....650 289-3400
780 High St Palo Alto (94301) ***(P-13787)***
Ideo LP ....D....415 615-5000
28 The Embarcadero Annex San Francisco (94105) ***(P-16839)***
Idexx Reference Labs Inc ....E....949 477-2840
1370 Reynolds Ave Ste 109 Irvine (92614) ***(P-26078)***
Idexx Reference Labs Inc ....C....916 372-4200
2825 Kovr Dr West Sacramento (95605) ***(P-26079)***
IDLE ACRES CONVALESCENT HOSPIT, El Monte *Also called Sabu Enterprises Inc* ***(P-20674)***
Idondemand Inc ....B....415 200-4546
1900 Carnegie Ave Ste B Santa Ana (92705) ***(P-15613)***
Idrive Inc ....D....818 594-5972
26115 Mureau Rd Ste A Calabasas (91302) ***(P-16024)***
IDS, Pasadena *Also called Interprsnal Dvlpmntal Fclttors* ***(P-23286)***
IDS Inc ....D....866 297-5757
20300 Ventura Blvd # 200 Woodland Hills (91364) ***(P-4825)***
IDS Real Estate Group (PA) ....D....213 627-9937
515 S Figueroa St Fl 16 Los Angeles (90071) ***(P-11201)***
IDS Technology, Woodland Hills *Also called IDS Inc* ***(P-4825)***
Idun Pharmaceuticals Inc ....E....858 622-3000
9380 Judicial Dr San Diego (92121) ***(P-25996)***
IEC, Commerce *Also called Interstate Electric Co Inc* ***(P-6925)***
Iehp, Rancho Cucamonga *Also called Inland Empire Health Plan* ***(P-9907)***
Ies Engineering, Bakersfield *Also called Innovative Engrg Systems Inc* ***(P-25140)***
Iest Family Farms ....D....559 674-9417
14576 Avenue 14 Madera (93637) ***(P-395)***
If Holding Inc (PA) ....C....559 875-3354
1912 Industrial Way Sanger (93657) ***(P-11673)***
Ifncom Inc (PA) ....D....213 452-1505
5901 W Century Blvd Fl 9 Los Angeles (90045) ***(P-5423)***
Ifwe Inc (HQ) ....D....415 946-1850
848 Battery St San Francisco (94111) ***(P-15353)***
Igenex Inc ....E....650 424-1191
556 Gibraltar Dr Milpitas (95035) ***(P-21542)***
Igenex Reference Laboratory, Milpitas *Also called Igenex Inc* ***(P-21542)***
Ignite Health LLC (PA) ....C....949 861-3200
7535 Irvine Center Dr # 200 Irvine (92618) ***(P-13523)***
Ignition Creative LLC ....D....310 315-6300
12959 Coral Tree Pl Los Angeles (90066) ***(P-17618)***
Igo Medical Group A Med Corp (PA) ....D....858 455-7520
9339 Genesee Ave Ste 220 San Diego (92121) ***(P-19020)***
Iheartcommunications Inc ....B....415 975-5555
340 Townsend St Fl 4 San Francisco (94107) ***(P-5534)***
Iheartcommunications Inc ....D....951 684-1992
2030 Iowa Ave Ste A Riverside (92507) ***(P-5535)***
Iheartcommunications Inc ....D....559 230-4300
83 E Shaw Ave Ste 150 Fresno (93710) ***(P-5536)***
Iheartcommunications Inc ....B....858 522-5547
9660 Gran Rdge Dr Ste 100 San Diego (92123) ***(P-5537)***
Iheartcommunications Inc ....D....858 292-2000
9660 Gran Rdge Dr Ste 200 San Diego (92123) ***(P-5538)***
Iheartcommunications Inc ....D....818 846-0029
3400 W Olive Ave Ste 550 Burbank (91505) ***(P-5539)***
Iheartcommunications Inc ....C....916 929-5325
1545 River Park Dr # 500 Sacramento (95815) ***(P-5540)***
Iheartcommunications Inc ....D....661 942-1268
352 E Avenue K4 Lancaster (93535) ***(P-5541)***
Iheartcommunications Inc ....D....916 929-5325
1440 Ethan Way Sacramento (95825) ***(P-5542)***
Ihg Management (maryland) LLC ....C....310 642-7500
5985 W Century Blvd Los Angeles (90045) ***(P-12454)***
Ihms (sf) LLC ....C....415 781-5555
340 Stockton St San Francisco (94108) ***(P-12455)***
Ihr Grnbuck Rncho Ccmnga Ventr, Rancho Cucamonga *Also called Aloft Ontario-Rancho Cucamonga* ***(P-12001)***
IHSS CONSORTIUM, THE, San Francisco *Also called Homebridge Inc* ***(P-23261)***
Ikano Communications Inc (PA) ....D....801 924-0900
9221 Corbin Ave Ste 260 Northridge (91324) ***(P-15778)***
IKEA Purchasing Svcs US Inc ....B....818 841-3500
600 N San Fernando Blvd Burbank (91502) ***(P-26262)***
Ikes Landscaping & Maintenance ....D....530 758-1698
2700 Tiber Ave Davis (95616) ***(P-830)***
Illumina-Redwood City, Foster City *Also called Verinata Health Inc* ***(P-25866)***
Illuminate Education Inc (PA) ....D....949 656-3133
6531 Irvine Center Dr # 100 Irvine (92618) ***(P-15354)***
Illumio Inc ....C....669 800-5000
920 De Guigne Dr Sunnyvale (94085) ***(P-14866)***
Ilwu Local 46, Port Hueneme *Also called Interntional Longshore Whse Un* ***(P-14312)***
Image 2000 (PA) ....E....818 781-2200
26037 Huntington Ln Valencia (91355) ***(P-17511)***
Image Business Forms, El Segundo *Also called Ibftech Inc* ***(P-14304)***
Image Capture Review, Goleta *Also called Icrco Inc* ***(P-6971)***
Image Entertainment Inc (HQ) ....D....818 407-9100
6320 Canoga Ave Ste 790 Woodland Hills (91367) ***(P-17787)***
Image IV Systems Inc (PA) ....D....323 849-3049
512 S Varney St Burbank (91502) ***(P-6749)***
Image Options ....C....949 586-7665
80 Icon Foothill Ranch (92610) ***(P-13652)***
Image Source, San Bernardino *Also called Copier Source Inc* ***(P-6746)***
Imagescan Inc ....D....626 844-2050
390 S Fair Oaks Ave Pasadena (91105) ***(P-15779)***
Imagestat Corporation ....C....310 392-1100
2950 28th St Santa Monica (90405) ***(P-6851)***
Imageware Systems Inc (PA) ....D....858 673-8600
13500 Evening Creek Dr N # 550 San Diego (92128) ***(P-15355)***
Imaginative Horizons Inc ....D....619 477-1176
1889 National City Blvd National City (91950) ***(P-20028)***
Imaging Hlthcare Spcalists LLC ....D....619 229-2299
6386 Alvarado Ct San Diego (92120) ***(P-26080)***
Imaging Hlthcare Spcalists LLC (PA) ....D....619 295-9729
150 W Washington St San Diego (92103) ***(P-19021)***
Imaging Technologies Group LLC ....E....310 638-2500
5220 Pacific Concourse Dr Los Angeles (90045) ***(P-7858)***
Imax Corporation (HQ) ....D....310 255-5559
12582 Millennium Los Angeles (90094) ***(P-17846)***
Imax Theatre Marketing, Los Angeles *Also called Imax Corporation* ***(P-17846)***
Imca Capital, Los Angeles *Also called Imperial Mridian Companies Inc* ***(P-14170)***
Imerys Filtration Minerals, Lompoc *Also called Imerys Minerals California Inc* ***(P-1063)***
Imerys Filtration Minerals Inc (HQ) ....E....805 562-0200
1732 N 1st St Ste 450 San Jose (95112) ***(P-1066)***
Imerys Minerals California Inc ....B....805 736-1221
2500 Miguelito Canyon Rd Lompoc (93436) ***(P-1063)***
Imerys Minerals California Inc (HQ) ....D....805 736-1221
2500 San Miguelito Rd Lompoc (93436) ***(P-1067)***
IMG (PA) ....E....714 974-1700
4560 Dorinda Rd Yorba Linda (92887) ***(P-16840)***
Immanuel Baptist Cruch ....D....909 862-6641
28355 Baseline St Highland (92346) ***(P-23730)***
Immanuel Baptist Day School, Highland *Also called Immanuel Baptist Cruch* ***(P-23730)***
Immersion Medical Inc ....D....408 467-1900
50 Rio Robles San Jose (95134) ***(P-22580)***
Immigration Voice ....D....408 204-2200
3561 Homestead Rd 375 Santa Clara (95051) ***(P-11786)***
Imobile LLC ....B....209 833-6757
2613 Naglee Rd Tracy (95304) ***(P-5260)***
Imobile LLC ....B....909 599-8822
875 W Arrow Hwy San Dimas (91773) ***(P-5261)***
Impac Mortgage Corp ....B....949 475-3600
19500 Jamboree Rd Ste 100 Irvine (92612) ***(P-9563)***
Impac Mortgage Holdings Inc (PA) ....A....949 475-3600
19500 Jamboree Rd Ste 100 Irvine (92612) ***(P-11857)***
Impac Secured Assets Corp ....D....949 475-3600
19500 Jamboree Rd Irvine (92612) ***(P-11787)***
Impact Assessment Inc ....D....858 459-0142
2166 Avenida De La Playa F La Jolla (92037) ***(P-25765)***
IMPACT BUSINESS SERVICE, Redwood City *Also called Community Gatepath* ***(P-23036)***
Impact Destinations & Events ....E....415 766-4170
1005 Market St Unit 402 San Francisco (94103) ***(P-13430)***
Impact DRG Alcohol Trtmnt Ctr, Pasadena *Also called Principles Inc* ***(P-22101)***
Impact Events, San Francisco *Also called Impact Destinations & Events* ***(P-13430)***
Impact Group LLC ....D....925 327-7322
7133 Koll Center Pkwy # 200 Pleasanton (94566) ***(P-8182)***
Impact Logistics ....E....909 937-9035
1155 S Milliken Ave Ste I Ontario (91761) ***(P-14306)***
Impact Solutions LLC ....E....760 231-0450
3604 Ocean Ranch Blvd Oceanside (92056) ***(P-14307)***
Impec Group Inc (PA) ....D....408 330-9350
3350 Scott Blvd Bldg 8 Santa Clara (95054) ***(P-13950)***
Imperial Capital Group LLC (PA) ....D....310 246-3700
2000 Ave Of The Los Angeles (90067) ***(P-9698)***
Imperial Capital LLC (PA) ....D....310 246-3700
10100 Santa Monica Blvd # 2400 Los Angeles (90067) ***(P-9699)***
Imperial Care Center, Studio City *Also called Longwood Management Corp* ***(P-20621)***
Imperial Cfs Inc ....E....310 768-8188
1000 Francisco St Torrance (90502) ***(P-4566)***
Imperial Convalescent, La Mirada *Also called Life Care Centers America Inc* ***(P-20076)***
Imperial County Behavioral HLT ....E....760 482-2149
2695 S 4th St El Centro (92243) ***(P-22045)***
Imperial County Mental Health, El Centro *Also called County of Imperial* ***(P-21995)***
Imperial County Probation Off, El Centro *Also called County of Imperial* ***(P-23074)***

ALPHABETIC

Employee Codes: A=Over 500 employees, B=251-500
C=101-250, D=51-100, E=50
2020 Directory of California
Wholesalers and Services Companies
© Mergent Inc. 1-800-342-5647
1303

Imperial Crest Healthcare Ctr, Hawthorne *Also called Longwood Management Corp* ***(P-20088)***
Imperial Irrgtion Dst Wtr Dept, Imperial *Also called Imperial Irrigation District* ***(P-6364)***
Imperial Irrigation District (PA)..........A.......800 303-7756
333 E Barioni Blvd Imperial (92251) ***(P-5847)***
Imperial Irrigation District..........B.......760 339-9220
333 E Barioni Blvd Imperial (92251) ***(P-6364)***
Imperial Irrigation District..........C.......760 398-5811
81600 58th Ave La Quinta (92253) ***(P-6008)***
Imperial Irrigation District..........D.......760 339-9800
2151 W Adams Ave El Centro (92243) ***(P-5995)***
Imperial Mridian Companies Inc..........D.......310 447-3460
11901 Santa Monica Blvd # 338 Los Angeles (90025) ***(P-14170)***
Imperial Parking (us) LLC..........A.......415 495-3909
1740 Cesar Chavez Fl 2 San Francisco (94124) ***(P-17254)***
Imperial Parking (us) LLC..........D.......650 871-5423
195 N Access Rd South San Francisco (94080) ***(P-17255)***
Imperial Parking (us) LLC..........E.......650 724-4309
360 Oak Rd Ste 1 Stanford (94305) ***(P-17256)***
Imperial Parking (us) LLC..........E.......510 382-2140
7801 Earhart Rd Oakland (94621) ***(P-17257)***
Imperial Parking Industries (PA)..........D.......323 651-5588
6404 Wilshire Blvd B Los Angeles (90048) ***(P-17258)***
Imperial Pipe & Supply, Shafter *Also called Bps Supply Group* ***(P-7050)***
Imperial Project Inc..........D.......310 671-3263
1947 S Myrtle Ave Monrovia (91016) ***(P-17981)***
Imperva Inc (HQ)..........C.......650 345-9000
3400 Bridge Pkwy Ste 200 Redwood City (94065) ***(P-14867)***
Import Collection (PA)..........D.......818 782-3060
7885 Nelson Rd Panorama City (91402) ***(P-8979)***
Import Direct, Van Nuys *Also called E & S International Entps Inc* ***(P-7201)***
Import Whl Univ Fund Raising, Torrance *Also called Gdf Parent LLC* ***(P-16794)***
Importers Software, Santa Clara *Also called Laxmi Group Inc* ***(P-14908)***
Impulsa Bus Accelerator LLC..........C.......650 924-5010
23180 Ravensbury Ave Los Altos Hills (94024) ***(P-26642)***
IMS, Marina Del Rey *Also called International Mgt Systems* ***(P-27096)***
IMS, Woodland Hills *Also called Innovative Merch Solutions LLC* ***(P-16844)***
IMS Recycling Services Inc (PA)..........D.......619 231-2521
2697 Main St San Diego (92113) ***(P-6213)***
In & Out Car Wash Inc..........E.......619 316-8492
3615 Monte Real Escondido (92029) ***(P-17376)***
In Home Comfort and Care Inc..........D.......714 485-4120
17155 Newhope St Ste O Fountain Valley (92708) ***(P-21785)***
In Home Health, Burlingame *Also called Hcr Manorcare Inc* ***(P-19996)***
In Home Health Inc..........C.......408 986-8160
2005 De La Cruz Blvd # 271 Santa Clara (95050) ***(P-21786)***
In Home Health Inc..........D.......419 254-7841
1000 Lakes Dr Ste 200 West Covina (91790) ***(P-21787)***
In Shape, Victorville *Also called In-Shape Health Clubs LLC* ***(P-18155)***
In Shape Health Clubs, Stockton *Also called In Shape Management Company* ***(P-18154)***
In Shape Management Company..........B.......209 472-2231
6 S El Dorado St Stockton (95202) ***(P-18154)***
IN TOUCH LEADERSHIP PROJECT, Los Angeles *Also called Saint Justin Education Fu* ***(P-24222)***
In-Shape City, Stockton *Also called In-Shape Health Clubs LLC* ***(P-18156)***
In-Shape Health Clubs LLC..........E.......760 381-1200
14601 Valley Center Dr Victorville (92395) ***(P-18155)***
In-Shape Health Clubs LLC (PA)..........E.......209 472-2231
6 S El Dorado St Ste 700 Stockton (95202) ***(P-18156)***
In-Shape Health Clubs LLC..........C.......209 836-2504
101 S Tracy Blvd Tracy (95376) ***(P-18157)***
Inamar, San Diego *Also called Chubb US Holding Inc* ***(P-10318)***
Inbody, Cerritos *Also called Biospace Inc* ***(P-25724)***
Inc J-Network, Huntington Beach *Also called Glen Beverly Laboratories Inc* ***(P-24401)***
Incalus Inc..........E.......510 209-4064
41829 Albrae St Ste 212 Fremont (94538) ***(P-16025)***
Incare Dme..........D.......818 582-1016
15446 Sherman Way Apt 319 Van Nuys (91406) ***(P-22258)***
Inclin Inc..........D.......650 961-3422
2655 Campus Dr Ste 100 San Mateo (94403) ***(P-25766)***
Incline Incorporated..........C.......408 454-1140
560 S Winchester Blvd # 500 San Jose (95128) ***(P-14308)***
Inclusion Services LLC..........C.......562 945-2000
7255 Greenleaf Ave 20 Whittier (90602) ***(P-23272)***
Inclusive Cmnty Resources LLC..........C.......510 981-8115
2855 Telegraph Ave Ste Ll Berkeley (94705) ***(P-23604)***
Incom Mechanical Inc..........D.......707 586-0511
975 Transport Way Ste 5 Petaluma (94954) ***(P-2153)***
Incremento Inc..........D.......213 624-7777
2670 Leonis Blvd Vernon (90058) ***(P-8078)***
Incube Labs LLC (PA)..........D.......408 457-3700
2051 Ringwood Ave San Jose (95131) ***(P-11923)***
Indemnity Company California (HQ)..........D.......949 263-3300
17771 Cowan Ste 100 Irvine (92614) ***(P-10164)***
Independa Inc..........E.......800 815-7829
11455 El Camino Real # 365 San Diego (92130) ***(P-15614)***
Independence At Home Iah, Long Beach *Also called Senior Care* ***(P-10045)***
Independent Construction Co, Concord *Also called D A McCosker Construction Co* ***(P-1695)***
Independent Electric Sup Inc (HQ)..........C.......510 877-9850
2001 Marina Blvd San Leandro (94577) ***(P-7155)***
Independent Electric Vehicles, Vernon *Also called Indiev Inc* ***(P-6400)***
Independent Options..........D.......714 434-1175
2532 Santa Catalina Dr # 104 Costa Mesa (92626) ***(P-23273)***
Independent Options Inc..........C.......858 598-5260
8555 Aero Dr Ste 205 San Diego (92123) ***(P-23963)***
Independent Quality Care Inc..........D.......415 479-1230
40 Professional Ctr Pkwy San Rafael (94903) ***(P-20599)***
Independent Quality Care Inc (PA)..........D.......925 855-0881
3 Crow Canyon Ct San Ramon (94583) ***(P-20600)***
Independent Quality Care Inc..........D.......510 836-3677
2910 Mcclure St Oakland (94609) ***(P-20601)***
Independent Quality Care Inc..........D.......925 284-5544
3721 Mt Diablo Blvd Lafayette (94549) ***(P-20602)***
Independent Roofing Cons, Santa Ana *Also called IRC Technologies Inc* ***(P-3064)***
Independent Trading Company, San Clemente *Also called Brad Rambo & Associates Inc* ***(P-8020)***
Indepndnt Asstd Lvng & Memory, Arcadia *Also called Arcadia Gardens MGT Corp* ***(P-20411)***
Indevia Accounting Inc..........D.......858 450-2981
2667 Camino Del Rio S # 101 San Diego (92108) ***(P-25616)***
Index Fresh Inc (PA)..........D.......909 877-0999
3880 Lemon St Ste 210 Riverside (92501) ***(P-505)***
Indian Health Council Inc (PA)..........D.......760 749-1410
50100 Golsh Rd Valley Center (92082) ***(P-24343)***
Indian Hills Golf Club, Riverside *Also called Banquet Facilities* ***(P-13399)***
Indian Hlth Ctr Snta Clara Vly..........C.......408 445-3400
1333 Meridian Ave San Jose (95125) ***(P-19022)***
Indian River Transport Co..........B.......209 664-0456
8444 W Doe Ave Visalia (93291) ***(P-4062)***
Indian Valley Golf Club Inc..........E.......415 897-1118
3035 Novato Blvd Novato (94947) ***(P-18255)***
Indian Valley Health Care Dist..........D.......530 284-7191
184 Hot Springs Rd Greenville (95947) ***(P-20914)***
Indian Valley Hospital, Greenville *Also called Indian Valley Health Care Dist* ***(P-20914)***
Indian Wells Country Club Inc..........D.......760 345-2561
46000 Club Dr Indian Wells (92210) ***(P-18468)***
Indian Wells Golf Resort, Indian Wells *Also called Troon Golf LLC* ***(P-26434)***
Indian Wells Resort Hotel..........E.......760 345-6466
76661 Us Highway 111 Indian Wells (92210) ***(P-12456)***
Indian Wells Vly Surgery Ctr, Ridgecrest *Also called Drummond Medical Group Inc* ***(P-18962)***
Indiana Adhc, Los Angeles *Also called Altamed Health Services Corp* ***(P-18801)***
Indiev Inc..........D.......323 703-5720
5001 S Soto St Vernon (90058) ***(P-6400)***
Indigo Hospitality Management..........E.......310 787-7795
1817 N Sepulveda Blvd Manhattan Beach (90266) ***(P-12457)***
Indigo Hotels, Manhattan Beach *Also called Indigo Hospitality Management* ***(P-12457)***
Indio Family Care Center, Indio *Also called County of Riverside* ***(P-18935)***
Indio Hlthcare Wllness Ctr LLC..........D.......760 347-6000
82262 Valencia Ave Indio (92201) ***(P-20029)***
Indio Medical Offices, Indio *Also called Kaiser Foundation Hospitals* ***(P-19075)***
Indium Software Inc..........C.......408 501-8844
1250 Oakmead Pkwy Ste 210 Sunnyvale (94085) ***(P-15356)***
Individuals Now..........D.......707 544-3299
2447 Summerfield Rd Santa Rosa (95405) ***(P-23274)***
Indosys Corporation..........C.......408 705-1953
3315 San Felipe Rd Ste 37 San Jose (95135) ***(P-14309)***
Inductive Automation LLC..........D.......800 266-7798
90 Blue Ravine Rd Folsom (95630) ***(P-26643)***
Inductors Inc..........E.......949 623-2460
1740 W Collins Ave Orange (92867) ***(P-7283)***
Indus Corporation..........D.......415 202-1830
1275 Columbus Ave San Francisco (94133) ***(P-14868)***
Indus Light & Magic (vanco) LL..........D.......415 292-4671
1110 Gorgas Ave San Francisco (94129) ***(P-17512)***
Indus Technology Inc..........C.......619 299-2555
2243 San Diego Ave # 200 San Diego (92110) ***(P-25135)***
Industrial Automtn Group LLC..........D.......209 579-7527
4400 Sisk Rd Modesto (95356) ***(P-25136)***
Industrial Coml Systems Inc..........C.......760 300-4094
1165 Joshua Way Vista (92081) ***(P-2154)***
Industrial Container Services..........D.......916 781-2775
749 Galleria Blvd Roseville (95678) ***(P-7637)***
Industrial Electrical Company, Modesto *Also called Modesto Industrial Elec Co Inc* ***(P-2557)***
Industrial Grwth Partners V LP..........C.......415 882-4550
101 Mission St Ste 1500 San Francisco (94105) ***(P-11674)***
Industrial Masonry Inc..........D.......951 284-0251
3299 Horse Carri Rd Ste H Norco (92860) ***(P-2716)***
Industrial Media Inc..........C.......310 777-1940
6007 Sepulveda Blvd Van Nuys (91411) ***(P-17745)***
Industrial Metal Supply Co, Sun Valley *Also called Norman Industrial Mtls Inc* ***(P-7083)***
Industrial Metal Supply Co Eba, San Diego *Also called Norman Industrial Mtls Inc* ***(P-7084)***
Industrial Parts Depot LLC (HQ)..........D.......310 530-1900
23231 Normandie Ave Torrance (90501) ***(P-7550)***
INDUSTRIAL SUPPORT SYSTEMS, Fontana *Also called Fontana Resources At Work* ***(P-23596)***
Industry Events..........E.......310 834-3422
25501 Narbonne Ave Lomita (90717) ***(P-18318)***
Industry Station, City of Industry *Also called Southern California Gas Co* ***(P-5979)***
Indyme Solutions LLC..........E.......858 268-0717
8295 Aero Pl Ste 260 San Diego (92123) ***(P-27281)***
Indyne..........D.......805 606-0664
300 W Point Ave El Granada (94018) ***(P-24403)***
Indyne Inc..........A.......805 606-7225
1036 California Blvd # 11013 Vandenberg Afb (93437) ***(P-26949)***
Inegrated Care Communities, Moreno Valley *Also called Integrted Care Communities Inc* ***(P-20032)***
Ineos Composites Us LLC..........D.......323 767-1300
6608 E 26th St Commerce (90040) ***(P-8700)***
Infant Hring Scrning Spcalists, Corona *Also called Halo Unlimted Inc* ***(P-22248)***
Infant/Toddler Consort, Oakland *Also called California Child Care Resourc* ***(P-22952)***
Infantino, San Diego *Also called Blue Box Opco LLC* ***(P-7728)***
Infertlity Gynclogy Obstetrics, San Diego *Also called Igo Medical Group A Med Corp* ***(P-19020)***

Mergent e-mail: customerrelations@mergent.com
1304
2020 Directory of California
Wholesalers and Services Companies
(P-0000) Products & Services Section entry number
(PA)=Parent Co (HQ)=Headquarters (DH)=Div Headquarters

Infineon Raceway, Sonoma *Also called Speedway Sonoma LLC* **(P-18090)**
Infineon Tech Americas Corp ...A...310 726-8000
222 Kansas St El Segundo (90245) **(P-25617)**
Infinite Global Logistics, San Diego *Also called Carolina Trucking Inc* **(P-3861)**
Infinite Home Health Inc ...D...818 888-7772
22151 Ventura Blvd # 102 Woodland Hills (91364) **(P-21788)**
Infinite Technologies Inc (PA) ...D...916 987-3261
1264 Hawks Flight Ct # 210 El Dorado Hills (95762) **(P-25137)**
Infinity Broadcasting Corp Cal ...D...323 936-5784
5670 Wilshire Blvd # 200 Los Angeles (90036) **(P-5543)**
Infinity Care of East LA ...D...323 261-8108
101 S Fickett St Los Angeles (90033) **(P-20030)**
Infinity Drywall Contg Inc ...D...714 634-2255
225 S Loara St Anaheim (92802) **(P-2797)**
Infinity Energy Inc ...C...916 474-4723
3855 Atherton Rd Rocklin (95765) **(P-2155)**
Infinity Metals Inc ...E...562 697-8826
600 E Lambert Rd La Habra (90631) **(P-7072)**
Infinity Nurses Care Inc ...D...510 713-8892
39159 Paseo Padre Pkwy # 111 Fremont (94538) **(P-14514)**
Infinity Plumbing Designs Inc ...B...951 737-4436
9182 Stellar Ct Corona (92883) **(P-2156)**
Infinity Staffing Service ...B...831 638-0360
710 Kirkpatric Ct Ste B Hollister (95023) **(P-14515)**
Infinity Svc Group Inc A Cal C ...D...909 466-6237
9155 Archibald Ave # 302 Rancho Cucamonga (91730) **(P-2157)**
Inflection Risk Solutions LLC ...E...650 618-9910
555 Twin Dolphin Dr # 63 Redwood City (94065) **(P-15780)**
Influxdata Inc ...C...415 295-1901
799 Market St Ste 400 San Francisco (94103) **(P-14869)**
Info Plus International, San Mateo *Also called Ip International Inc* **(P-16040)**
Infogain Corporation (PA) ...C...408 355-6000
485 Alberto Way Ste 100 Los Gatos (95032) **(P-16026)**
Infogen Labs Inc ...D...818 825-5024
18223 Charlton Ln Porter Ranch (91326) **(P-16027)**
Infogroup Inc ...D...650 389-0700
951 Mariners Island Blvd # 130 San Mateo (94404) **(P-13724)**
Infor (us) Inc ...C...678 319-8000
26250 Entp Way Ste 220 Lake Forest (92630) **(P-15357)**
Infor (us) Inc ...C...916 921-0883
11000 Olson Dr Ste 201 Rancho Cordova (95670) **(P-15358)**
Infor Public Sector Inc (HQ) ...C...916 921-0883
11092 Sun Center Dr Rancho Cordova (95670) **(P-15359)**
Informa Research Services Inc (HQ) ...C...818 880-8877
26565 Agoura Rd Ste 300 Calabasas (91302) **(P-25909)**
Informatica LLC (PA) ...C...650 385-5000
2100 Seaport Blvd Redwood City (94063) **(P-15360)**
Information & Referral Fed Los ...D...626 350-1841
526 W Las Tunas Dr San Gabriel (91776) **(P-13431)**
Information Management Svcs, Downey *Also called Rancho Los Amigos Nationa* **(P-23398)**
Information Services, Santa Cruz *Also called Santa Cruz County of* **(P-15810)**
Information Services Dept, Fresno *Also called Community Hospitals Centl Cal* **(P-15740)**
Information Services Dept, Redwood City *Also called County of San Mateo* **(P-27271)**
Information Systems & Services, Sonora *Also called County of Tuolumne* **(P-15746)**
Information Systems Department, Santa Rosa *Also called County of Sonoma* **(P-15745)**
Information Systems Labs Inc (PA) ...E...858 535-9680
12900 Brookprinter Pl # 800 Poway (92064) **(P-25138)**
Information Tech Partners Inc ...D...800 789-7487
505 N Lake Shore Dr 102 Burbank (91504) **(P-16028)**
Information Technology, Los Angeles *Also called Los Angeles Unified School Dst* **(P-15922)**
Information Technology Agency, Los Angeles *Also called Los Angeles Unified School Dst* **(P-15785)**
Informative Research (PA) ...E...714 638-2855
13030 Euclid St Ste 209 Garden Grove (92843) **(P-13715)**
Infosoft Inc ...D...408 659-4326
7891 Westwood Dr Ste 113 Gilroy (95020) **(P-27092)**
Infotech Global Services, San Francisco *Also called Brad S Miller* **(P-26537)**
Infrascale Inc (PA) ...D...310 878-2621
999 N Pacific Coast Hwy # 100 El Segundo (90245) **(P-6852)**
Ingenio Inc ...C...415 248-4000
182 Howard St 826 San Francisco (94105) **(P-5424)**
Ingenio LLC ...D...415 992-8218
182 Howard St Unit 826 San Francisco (94105) **(P-26644)**
Ingenium Technologies Corp ...D...858 227-4422
5665 Oberlin Dr Ste 202 San Diego (92121) **(P-25139)**
Inglewood Child Dev Ctr, Inglewood *Also called Inglewood Unified School Dst* **(P-23731)**
Inglewood Health Care Center, Inglewood *Also called Mariner Health Care Inc* **(P-20110)**
Inglewood Meadows Kbs LP ...D...310 820-4888
1 S Locust St Inglewood (90301) **(P-10738)**
Inglewood Unified School Dst ...D...310 419-2691
401 S Inglewood Ave Inglewood (90301) **(P-23731)**
Ingram Micro Inc (HQ) ...A...714 566-1000
3351 Michelson Dr Ste 100 Irvine (92612) **(P-6853)**
Ingredientsonline.com, La Mirada *Also called Green Wave Ingredients Inc* **(P-7947)**
Inhouseit Inc ...D...949 660-5655
400 Exchange Ste 100 Irvine (92602) **(P-15921)**
Initek Soft Solutions LLC ...D...209 309-0263
43674 Ellsworth St Fremont (94539) **(P-14870)**
Initial Security, Santa Fe Springs *Also called Alliedbarton Security Svcs LLC* **(P-16179)**
Initiative Food Company, Sanger *Also called If Holding Inc* **(P-11673)**
Inkling Systems Inc ...D...415 975-4420
343 Sansome St 8 San Francisco (94104) **(P-26645)**
Inko Industrial Corporation ...D...408 830-1040
695 Vaqueros Ave Sunnyvale (94085) **(P-15781)**
Inland Bhavioral Hlth Svcs Inc (PA) ...D...909 881-6146
1963 N E St San Bernardino (92405) **(P-22259)**
Inland Business Machines Inc (HQ) ...D...916 928-0770
1326 N Market Blvd Sacramento (95834) **(P-17513)**
Inland Cc Inc ...C...909 355-1318
13820 Slover Ave Fontana (92337) **(P-3162)**
Inland Christian Home Inc ...C...909 395-9322
1950 S Mountain Ave Ofc Ontario (91762) **(P-20031)**
Inland Cnties Regional Ctr Inc (PA) ...C...909 890-3000
1365 S Waterman Ave San Bernardino (92408) **(P-23275)**
Inland Cold Storage, Bloomington *Also called Lineage Logistics Holdings LLC* **(P-4217)**
Inland Empire Chapter-Assn of ...D...512 478-9000
4200 Concours Ste 360 Ontario (91764) **(P-24840)**
Inland Empire Hauling, Corona *Also called USA Waste of California Inc* **(P-6300)**
Inland Empire Health Plan ...B...866 228-4347
805 W 2nd St Ste C San Bernardino (92410) **(P-9954)**
Inland Empire Health Plan (PA) ...A...909 890-2000
10801 6th St Ste 120 Rancho Cucamonga (91730) **(P-9907)**
Inland Empire RE Solutions ...D...909 476-1000
8794 19th St Alta Loma (91701) **(P-11202)**
INLAND EMPIRE SURF SOCCER CLUB, San Bernardino *Also called Alliance Fc* **(P-24786)**
Inland Empire Therapy Provider (PA) ...D...909 985-7905
1150 N Mountain Ave # 214 Upland (91786) **(P-19670)**
Inland Empire Utilities Agency ...D...909 993-1755
12811 6th St Rancho Cucamonga (91739) **(P-6068)**
Inland Empire Utilities Agency (PA) ...D...909 993-1600
6075 Kimball Ave Chino (91708) **(P-6069)**
Inland Empire Utilities Agency ...D...909 993-1600
9400 Cherry Ave Fontana (92335) **(P-6070)**
Inland Empre 66ers Bsebll CLB ...C...909 888-9922
280 S E St San Bernardino (92401) **(P-18065)**
Inland Erosion Control Svcs ...D...951 301-8334
42181 Avenida Alvarado A Temecula (92590) **(P-3319)**
Inland Eye Inst Med Group Inc (PA) ...D...909 825-3425
1900 E Washington St Colton (92324) **(P-19023)**
Inland Hand Therapy & Rehab, Upland *Also called Mountain View Physical Therapy* **(P-19680)**
Inland Hlth Org of So Cal (HQ) ...E...909 335-7171
1980 Orange Tree Ln # 200 Redlands (92374) **(P-19024)**
Inland Inspections Consulting ...E...951 697-1000
7338 Sycamore Canyon Blvd Riverside (92508) **(P-16841)**
Inland Kenworth (us) Inc (HQ) ...C...909 823-9955
9730 Cherry Ave Fontana (92335) **(P-6401)**
INLAND PACIFIC BALLET, Montclair *Also called Foundation For Dance Education* **(P-17879)**
Inland Regional Center, San Bernardino *Also called Inland Cnties Regional Ctr Inc* **(P-23275)**
Inland Star Dist Ctrs Inc (PA) ...D...559 237-2052
3146 S Chestnut Ave Fresno (93725) **(P-4063)**
Inland Valley Business and Com ...D...951 378-5316
40335 Winchester Rd Temecula (92591) **(P-24841)**
Inland Valley Care & Rehab Ctr, Pomona *Also called Inland Valley Partners LLC* **(P-19671)**
Inland Valley Cnstr Co Inc ...D...909 875-2112
18382 Slover Ave Bloomington (92316) **(P-1301)**
Inland Valley Drug & Alcohol (PA) ...D...909 932-1069
1260 E Arrow Hwy Upland (91786) **(P-23276)**
Inland Valley Partners LLC ...C...909 623-7100
250 W Artesia St Pomona (91768) **(P-19671)**
Inland Vly Rgional Med Ctr Inc ...D...951 677-1111
36485 Inland Valley Dr Wildomar (92595) **(P-20915)**
Inland-Metro Services Inc ...D...909 373-6810
1059 W 14th St Upland (91786) **(P-16842)**
Inlog Inc ...D...949 212-3867
6765 Westminster Blvd # 424 Westminster (92683) **(P-4970)**
Inman Spinosa & Buchan Inc ...D...310 519-1080
28901 S Wstn Ave Ste 139 Rancho Palos Verdes (90275) **(P-11203)**
Inmotion Hosting Inc ...E...888 321-4678
360 N Pacific Coast Hwy # 1055 El Segundo (90245) **(P-5425)**
Inn At Rancho Santa Fe, The, Rancho Santa Fe *Also called Huntington Hotel Company* **(P-12425)**
Inn At Scotts Valley LLC ...D...831 440-1000
6001 La Madrona Dr Scotts Valley (95060) **(P-12458)**
Inncal Incorporated (PA) ...D...209 473-4667
1919 Grand Canal Blvd B5 Stockton (95207) **(P-12459)**
Inner Circle Entertainment ...D...415 693-0777
464 Monterey Ave Ste A Los Gatos (95030) **(P-8357)**
Inner Space Constructors Div, Long Beach *Also called Hutchison Corporation* **(P-2796)**
Inner-City Express, San Jose *Also called Ice Delivery Systems Inc* **(P-3896)**
Innerasia Travel Group, San Francisco *Also called Geographic Expeditions Inc* **(P-4820)**
Innocean Wrldwide Americas LLC (HQ) ...D...714 861-5200
180 5th St Ste 200 Huntington Beach (92648) **(P-13524)**
Innopath Software Inc (PA) ...D...408 962-9200
333 W El Camino Real # 290 Sunnyvale (94087) **(P-14871)**
Innova Solutions Inc ...A...408 889-2020
3211 Scott Blvd Ste 202 Santa Clara (95054) **(P-16029)**
Innovasystems Intl LLC ...D...619 955-5890
850 Beech St Unit 1006 San Diego (92101) **(P-14872)**
Innovasystems Intl LLC (PA) ...D...619 756-6500
2385 Northside Dr Ste 300 San Diego (92108) **(P-14873)**
Innovated Packaging Company ...C...510 713-3560
38505 Cherry St Ste C Newark (94560) **(P-16843)**
Innovations Building Svcs LLC ...D...323 787-6068
402 S Orange Ave Apt D Monterey Park (91755) **(P-13951)**
Innovative Artists Talent Agny (PA) ...D...310 656-0400
1505 10th St Santa Monica (90401) **(P-17915)**
Innovative Cnstr Solutions ...C...714 893-6366
575 Anton Blvd Ste 850 Costa Mesa (92626) **(P-26950)**
Innovative Drywall Systems Inc ...D...760 743-0331
19192 Via Cuesta Ramona (92065) **(P-2798)**
Innovative Education MGT Inc (PA) ...D...530 295-3566
4535 Missouri Flat Rd 1a Placerville (95667) **(P-26263)**
Innovative Engrg Systems Inc (PA) ...D...661 381-7800
8800 Crippen St Bakersfield (93311) **(P-25140)**

ALPHABETIC

Employee Codes: A=Over 500 employees, B=251-500
C=101-250, D=51-100, E=50
2020 Directory of California
Wholesalers and Services Companies
© Mergent Inc. 1-800-342-5647
1305

Innovative Integrated Hlth Inc ....C....949 228-5577
2042 Kern St Fresno (93721) ***(P-22260)***
Innovative Medical Solutions ....D....714 505-7070
3002 Dow Ave Ste 110 Tustin (92780) ***(P-17514)***
Innovative Merch Solutions LLC ....C....818 936-7800
21215 Burbank Blvd Woodland Hills (91367) ***(P-16844)***
Innovative Silicon Inc ....D....408 572-8700
4800 Great America Pkwy # 500 Santa Clara (95054) ***(P-16845)***
Innovative Skin Care, Burbank *Also called Science of Skincare LLC* ***(P-7981)***
Innovative Staffing Resources, Tustin *Also called Innovtive Scntfic Slutions Inc* ***(P-14310)***
Innovel Solutions Inc ....D....707 748-1940
521 Stone Rd Benicia (94510) ***(P-4971)***
Innovel Solutions Inc ....A....661 721-5910
1700 Schuster Rd Delano (93215) ***(P-4972)***
Innovel Solutions Inc ....D....909 605-1446
5691 E Philadelphia St # 200 Ontario (91761) ***(P-4973)***
Innovo Azteca Apparel Inc ....D....323 837-3700
5901 S Eastern Ave 104 Commerce (90040) ***(P-7998)***
Innovtive Emplyee Slutions Inc ....A....858 715-5100
9665 Gran Rdge Dr Ste 420 San Diego (92123) ***(P-25618)***
Innovtive Scntfic Slutions Inc ....C....714 508-8620
17581 Irvine Blvd Ste 202 Tustin (92780) ***(P-14310)***
Inns of Monterey, Monterey *Also called Columbia Hospitality Inc* ***(P-12162)***
Innsuites Hotels, San Diego *Also called Hampstead Lafayette Hotel LLC* ***(P-12329)***
Inova Diagnostics Inc (HQ) ....B....858 586-9900
9900 Old Grove Rd San Diego (92131) ***(P-25767)***
Inovative Packaging, Newark *Also called Integrated Pkg & Crating Svcs* ***(P-5094)***
Inoxpa USA Inc ....B....707 585-3900
3721 Santa Rosa Ave B4 Santa Rosa (95407) ***(P-7551)***
Input 1 LLC ....C....818 340-0030
6200 Canoga Ave Ste 400 Woodland Hills (91367) ***(P-9486)***
Inqbrands Inc ....D....909 390-7788
1801 E Holt Blvd Unit 101 Ontario (91761) ***(P-16030)***
Inreach Internet LLC (HQ) ....D....888 467-3224
4635 Georgetown Pl Stockton (95207) ***(P-5426)***
Insco Dico Group , The, Irvine *Also called Developers Surety Indemnity Co* ***(P-10162)***
Inseego North America LLC (HQ) ....D....541 685-9045
9605 Scranton Rd Ste 300 San Diego (92121) ***(P-15615)***
Inside Outdoors Foundation ....C....714 708-3885
8755 Santiago Canyon Rd Silverado (92676) ***(P-23277)***
Inside Source Inc (PA) ....D....650 508-9101
985 Industrial Rd Ste 101 San Carlos (94070) ***(P-6519)***
Inside Source/Young, San Carlos *Also called Inside Source Inc* ***(P-6519)***
Insideview Technologies Inc ....C....415 728-9309
444 De Haro St Ste 210 San Francisco (94107) ***(P-15361)***
Insight Investments LLC (HQ) ....C....714 939-2300
611 Anton Blvd Ste 700 Costa Mesa (92626) ***(P-15908)***
Insignia Environmental ....D....650 321-6787
258 High St Palo Alto (94301) ***(P-27093)***
Insite Digestive Health Care ....D....818 346-9911
7320 Woodlake Ave Ste 310 West Hills (91307) ***(P-19025)***
Insite Digestive Health Care ....D....626 817-2900
225 W Broadway Ste 350 Glendale (91204) ***(P-19026)***
Insite Digestive Health Care ....C....408 471-2222
200 Jose Figueres Ave San Jose (95116) ***(P-19027)***
Insituform Technologies LLC ....E....714 724-2324
19000 Macarthur Blvd # 800 Irvine (92612) ***(P-1867)***
Insomniac Inc ....D....323 874-7020
9441 W Olympic Blvd Beverly Hills (90212) ***(P-17982)***
Insomniac Holdings LLC ....C....310 867-7041
9441 W Olympic Blvd Beverly Hills (90212) ***(P-17983)***
Inspection and Testing, Anaheim *Also called Emery Smith Laboratories Inc* ***(P-25050)***
Inspectorate America Corp ....C....800 424-0099
3401 Jack Northrop Ave Hawthorne (90250) ***(P-16846)***
Insperity Inc ....D....909 569-1000
1440 Bridgegate Dr # 200 Diamond Bar (91765) ***(P-26646)***
Inspira Inc ....D....408 247-9500
4125 Blackford Ave # 255 San Jose (95117) ***(P-14874)***
Inspire Energy Holdings LLC ....C....866 403-2620
3402 Pico Blvd Ste 215 Santa Monica (90405) ***(P-5848)***
Inspiria Inc (PA) ....D....949 206-0606
25741 Atl Ocn Dr Ste A Lake Forest (92630) ***(P-25141)***
Instabug Inc ....D....650 422-9555
855 El Camino Real Palo Alto (94301) ***(P-14875)***
Instacart, San Francisco *Also called Maplebear Inc* ***(P-3909)***
Instant Systems Inc ....D....510 657-8100
447 King Ave Fremont (94536) ***(P-14876)***
Instantly, Encino *Also called Dynata LLC* ***(P-25890)***
Instantsys, Fremont *Also called Instant Systems Inc* ***(P-14876)***
Instart Labs, Palo Alto *Also called Instart Logic Inc* ***(P-14877)***
Instart Logic Inc (PA) ....D....888 418-5044
450 Lambert Ave Palo Alto (94306) ***(P-14877)***
Instill Corporation ....C....650 645-2600
777 Mariners Island Blvd # 400 San Mateo (94404) ***(P-14878)***
Instittional Property Advisors, Calabasas *Also called Marcus Mllchap RE Inv Svcs Inc* ***(P-11273)***
Institute Applied Bhvior Anlis, Tarzana *Also called Institute For Applied Behavior* ***(P-19674)***
Institute For Applied Behavior (PA) ....C....310 649-0499
5777 W Century Blvd # 675 Los Angeles (90045) ***(P-19672)***
Institute For Applied Behavior ....C....805 987-5886
2310 E Ponderosa Dr Ste 1 Camarillo (93010) ***(P-19673)***
Institute For Applied Behavior ....D....818 881-1933
19510 Ventura Blvd # 204 Tarzana (91356) ***(P-19674)***
Institute For Bhvoral Hlth Inc ....B....909 289-1041
1905 Bus Ctr Dr S Ste 100 San Bernardino (92408) ***(P-22261)***
Institute For Eductl Therapy ....E....831 457-1207
1007 University Ave Berkeley (94710) ***(P-23605)***
Institute For Health & Healing ....E....415 600-3503
2300 California St # 101 San Francisco (94115) ***(P-20916)***
Institute For Humn Social Dev (PA) ....D....650 871-5613
155 Bovet Rd Ste 300 San Mateo (94402) ***(P-23732)***
Institute For Multicultural ....D....818 240-4311
121 W Lexington Dr Glendale (91203) ***(P-27094)***
Institute For One World Health ....E....650 392-2510
600 California St Fl 11 San Francisco (94108) ***(P-18158)***
Institute For Wildlife Studies (PA) ....E....707 822-4258
835 3rd St Eureka (95501) ***(P-24565)***
Institute LLC ....E....408 782-7101
14830 Foothill Ave Morgan Hill (95037) ***(P-18256)***
Institute On Aging ....C....510 536-3377
881 Fremont Ave Ste A2 Los Altos (94024) ***(P-20603)***
Institute On Aging ....C....415 600-2690
3698 California St San Francisco (94118) ***(P-23278)***
Institute On Aging (PA) ....D....415 750-4101
3575 Geary Blvd San Francisco (94118) ***(P-23279)***
Institutional Financing Svcs, Benicia *Also called Americas Lemonade Stand Inc* ***(P-16620)***
Insul Acoustics Inc ....C....323 686-2670
1432 Chico Ave El Monte (91733) ***(P-2799)***
Insulation Sources Inc (PA) ....D....650 856-8378
2575 E Bayshore Rd Palo Alto (94303) ***(P-7156)***
Insulectro (PA) ....D....949 587-3200
20362 Windrow Dr Ste 100 Lake Forest (92630) ***(P-7284)***
Insulfoam, Dixon *Also called Carlisle Construction Mtls Inc* ***(P-6713)***
Insurance Company of West (HQ) ....C....858 350-2400
15025 Innovation Dr San Diego (92128) ***(P-10098)***
Insurance Dentists Amer Idoa, Campbell *Also called Dentistat Inc* ***(P-26581)***
Insurance Services Amercn LLC ....D....805 981-2220
300 E Esplanade Dr # 2100 Oxnard (93036) ***(P-10386)***
INSURANCE SERVICES OFFICE INC, San Francisco *Also called Insurance Services Office Inc* ***(P-15869)***
Insurance Services Office Inc ....B....415 874-4361
388 Market St Ste 750 San Francisco (94111) ***(P-15869)***
Insure Express Insurance Svc, Calabasas *Also called Cartel Marketing Inc* ***(P-10314)***
Intapp Inc (HQ) ....C....650 852-0400
200 Portage Ave Palo Alto (94306) ***(P-14879)***
Intarcia Therapeutics Inc ....D....510 782-7800
24650 Industrial Blvd Hayward (94545) ***(P-25768)***
Intech Mechanical Company LLC ....C....916 797-4900
7501 Galilee Rd Roseville (95678) ***(P-2158)***
Integral Development Corp (PA) ....C....650 424-4500
850 Hansen Way Palo Alto (94304) ***(P-15362)***
Integral Engineering, Palo Alto *Also called Integral Development Corp* ***(P-15362)***
Integral Senior Living LLC (PA) ....C....760 547-2863
2333 State St Ste 300 Carlsbad (92008) ***(P-10739)***
Integrated Behavioral Hlth Inc ....D....714 442-4150
3070 Bristol St Ste 350 Costa Mesa (92626) ***(P-22262)***
Integrated Clg Solutions Inc ....E....415 821-6757
3043 Mission St San Francisco (94110) ***(P-13952)***
Integrated Decision Systems ....D....310 954-5530
11150 W Olympic Blvd # 600 Los Angeles (90064) ***(P-15616)***
Integrated Medical Specialists, San Diego *Also called Genesis Healthcare Partners PC* ***(P-22029)***
Integrated Office Tech LLC (PA) ....D....562 236-9200
12150 Mora Dr Ste 2 Santa Fe Springs (90670) ***(P-6750)***
Integrated Parcel Network ....B....714 278-6100
4373 Santa Anita Ave El Monte (91731) ***(P-4272)***
Integrated Pkg & Crating Svcs ....E....510 745-8180
38505 Cherry St Newark (94560) ***(P-5094)***
Integrated Trnsp Svcs Inc ....D....310 553-6060
9740 W Pico Blvd Los Angeles (90035) ***(P-3687)***
Integrits Corporation (PA) ....E....858 300-1600
5205 Kearny Villa Way # 200 San Diego (92123) ***(P-16031)***
Integrity Healthcare Services ....D....760 432-9811
425 W 5th Ave Ste 101 Escondido (92025) ***(P-21789)***
Integrity Management Entps, San Diego *Also called Gerwend Enterprises Inc* ***(P-26944)***
Integrity Management Svcs Inc ....C....805 238-0905
141 W Dana St Ste 100 Nipomo (93444) ***(P-13953)***
Integrity Rebar Placers ....C....951 696-6843
1345 Nandina Ave Perris (92571) ***(P-3264)***
Integro USA Inc ....E....626 795-9000
115 N El Molino Ave Pasadena (91101) ***(P-10387)***
Integrted Care Communities Inc ....E....951 243-3837
11751 Davis St Moreno Valley (92557) ***(P-20032)***
Integrted Spport Solutions Inc (PA) ....B....818 787-2116
4283 Empress Ave Encino (91436) ***(P-27095)***
Integrus LLC ....D....714 547-9500
14370 Myford Rd Ste 100 Irvine (92606) ***(P-6751)***
Intel Media Inc ....B....408 765-0063
2200 Mission College Blvd Santa Clara (95054) ***(P-5729)***
Intelisys Inc ....D....800 615-8330
1318 Redwood Way Ste 120 Petaluma (94954) ***(P-26647)***
Intell Set, Long Beach *Also called Intelsat US LLC* ***(P-5789)***
Intellective, Irvine *Also called Vegatek Corporation* ***(P-15178)***
Intellectual Ventures LLC ....B....650 941-1330
200 California Ave # 200 Palo Alto (94306) ***(P-26264)***
Intellicus Tech Pvt Ltd ....D....408 213-3314
720 University Ave # 130 Los Gatos (95032) ***(P-15617)***
Intelliguard Security Services ....C....510 547-7656
4663 Harbord Dr Oakland (94618) ***(P-16323)***
Intellipro Group Inc ....B....408 200-9891
3120 Scott Blvd 301 Santa Clara (95054) ***(P-16032)***
Intellirisk Management Corp ....E....818 575-5400
31229 Cedar Valley Dr Westlake Village (91362) ***(P-13686)***
Intelliswift Software Inc (PA) ....C....510 490-9240
39600 Balentine Dr # 200 Newark (94560) ***(P-14880)***

Intellisync Corporation (HQ).....D.....650 625-2185
313 Fairchild Dr Mountain View (94043) ***(P-14881)***
Intelpeer Cloud Cmmnctions LLC.....C.....650 525-9200
155 Bovet Rd Ste 405 San Mateo (94402) ***(P-5427)***
Intelsat US LLC.....C.....310 525-5500
1600 Forbes Way Long Beach (90810) ***(P-5789)***
Inter Community Hospital, Covina *Also called Citrus Valley Medical Ctr Inc* ***(P-20789)***
Inter Community Hospital, Covina *Also called Emanate Hlth Intr-Cmmnity Hosp* ***(P-20866)***
Inter Con Security Inc.....E.....619 523-0291
2801 Camino Del Rio S 300h San Diego (92108) ***(P-26648)***
Inter Con Systems, Pasadena *Also called Inter-Con Investigators Inc* ***(P-16324)***
Inter Valley Pool Supply Inc.....D.....626 969-5657
1415 E 3rd St Pomona (91766) ***(P-7712)***
Inter-City Cleaners.....D.....650 875-9200
438 S Airport Blvd South San Francisco (94080) ***(P-13256)***
Inter-Con Investigators Inc.....D.....626 535-2200
210 S De Lacey Ave Pasadena (91105) ***(P-16324)***
Inter-Con Security Systems Inc (PA).....C.....626 535-2200
210 S De Lacey Ave Pasadena (91105) ***(P-16325)***
Inter-Rail Trnspt Nshville LLC.....D.....510 231-2744
861 Wharf St Richmond (94804) ***(P-5119)***
Inter-Rail Trnspt Nshville LLC.....D.....707 746-1695
3800 Industrial Way Benicia (94510) ***(P-5120)***
Inter-State Oil Co (PA).....D.....916 457-6572
8221 Alpine Ave Sacramento (95826) ***(P-8731)***
Inter-Valley Health Plan Inc.....D.....909 623-6333
300 S Park Ave Ste 300 # 300 Pomona (91766) ***(P-9955)***
Inter/Media Advertising, Woodland Hills *Also called Inter/Media Time Buying Corp* ***(P-13525)***
Inter/Media Time Buying Corp (PA).....E.....818 995-1455
22120 Clarendon St # 300 Woodland Hills (91367) ***(P-13525)***
Interact Pmti Inc (PA).....D.....805 658-5600
260 Maple Ct Ste 210 Ventura (93003) ***(P-25142)***
Interactive Med Specialists.....D.....415 472-4204
252 Waterside Cir San Rafael (94903) ***(P-14516)***
Interactive Media Holdings (HQ).....D.....949 861-8888
2722 Michelson Dr Ste 100 Irvine (92612) ***(P-13526)***
Interana Inc.....D.....650 569-1122
100 Redwood Shores Pkwy Redwood City (94065) ***(P-14882)***
Interbake Foods LLC.....D.....213 484-8161
1910 W Temple St Los Angeles (90026) ***(P-8588)***
Intercare Holdings Insur Svcs, Rocklin *Also called Pacific Secured Equities Inc* ***(P-26755)***
Intercare Specialty Risk Ins (PA).....D.....916 757-1200
130 Diamond Creek Pl # 2 Roseville (95747) ***(P-10388)***
Intercare Therapy Inc.....C.....323 866-1880
4221 Wilshire Blvd 300a Los Angeles (90010) ***(P-19675)***
Intercom Inc.....B.....831 920-7088
55 2nd St Ste 400 San Francisco (94105) ***(P-14883)***
Intercommunity Care Centers.....C.....562 427-8915
2626 Grand Ave Long Beach (90815) ***(P-20033)***
Intercommunity Child.....D.....562 692-0383
10155 Colima Rd Whittier (90603) ***(P-23280)***
Intercommunity Dialysis Center, Whittier *Also called Intercommunity Dialysis Svcs* ***(P-21926)***
Intercommunity Dialysis Svcs.....E.....562 696-1841
12455 Washington Blvd Whittier (90602) ***(P-21926)***
Intercontinental Hotels.....C.....415 616-6500
888 Howard St San Francisco (94103) ***(P-12460)***
Intercontinental Hotels Group.....C.....949 863-1999
17941 Von Karman Ave Irvine (92614) ***(P-12461)***
Intercontinental Hotels Group.....D.....619 727-4000
509 9th Ave San Diego (92101) ***(P-12462)***
Intercontinental Hotels Group.....C.....415 626-6103
50 8th St San Francisco (94103) ***(P-12463)***
Intercontinental Hotels Group.....D.....310 781-9100
19800 S Vermont Ave Torrance (90502) ***(P-12464)***
Intercontinental Hotels Group.....C.....415 398-8900
480 Sutter St San Francisco (94108) ***(P-12465)***
Intercontinental Hotels Group.....B.....415 771-9000
495 Bay St San Francisco (94133) ***(P-12466)***
Intercontinental Hotels Group.....D.....805 964-6241
5650 Calle Real Goleta (93117) ***(P-12467)***
Intercontinental Hotels Group.....E.....415 409-4600
550 N Point St San Francisco (94133) ***(P-12468)***
Intercontinental Hotels Group.....D.....949 863-1999
17941 Von Karman Ave Irvine (92614) ***(P-12469)***
Intercontinental Hotels Group.....C.....909 930-5555
2280 S Haven Ave Ontario (91761) ***(P-12470)***
Intercontinental Mark Hopkins, San Francisco *Also called One Nob Hill Associates LLC* ***(P-12676)***
Intercontinental San Francisco, San Francisco *Also called Cdc San Francisco LLC* ***(P-12129)***
Interdent Inc (HQ).....D.....310 765-2400
9800 S La Cienega Blvd # 800 Inglewood (90301) ***(P-19611)***
Interdent Service Corporation (HQ).....E.....310 765-2400
9800 S La Cienega Blvd # 800 Inglewood (90301) ***(P-19612)***
INTERFACE CHILDREN FAMILY SERV, Camarillo *Also called Interface Community* ***(P-23281)***
Interface Community (PA).....D.....805 485-6114
4001 Mission Oaks Blvd Camarillo (93012) ***(P-23281)***
Interface Rehab Inc.....A.....714 646-8300
774 S Placentia Ave # 200 Placentia (92870) ***(P-19676)***
Interfaith Community Svcs Inc.....D.....760 489-6380
550 W Washington Ave B Escondido (92025) ***(P-23282)***
Intergraded Media Systems Ctr, Los Angeles *Also called University Southern California* ***(P-21344)***
Intergro Rehab Service.....D.....714 901-4200
1922 N Broadway Santa Ana (92706) ***(P-19677)***
Interhealth Corp (PA).....A.....562 698-0811
12401 Washington Blvd Whittier (90602) ***(P-20917)***
Interhealth Services Inc (HQ).....D.....562 698-0811
12401 Washington Blvd Whittier (90602) ***(P-21790)***
Interim Inc.....C.....831 754-3838
339 Pajaro St Ste B Salinas (93901) ***(P-27282)***
Interim Assisited Care of Nort.....D.....530 722-1530
373 Smile Pl Redding (96001) ***(P-21791)***
Interim Hlthcare Nthrn Cal Inc (PA).....B.....530 221-1300
1647 Court St Redding (96001) ***(P-14517)***
Interim Services, Bakersfield *Also called Rncmba Inc* ***(P-14558)***
Interim Services, Redding *Also called Interim Assisited Care of Nort* ***(P-21791)***
Interim Services, Salinas *Also called Interim Inc* ***(P-27282)***
Interior Electric Incorporated.....D.....714 771-9098
747 N Main St Orange (92868) ***(P-2521)***
Interior Experts General Bldrs.....D.....909 203-4922
4534 Carter Ct Chino (91710) ***(P-2800)***
Interior Office Solutions Inc (PA).....E.....949 724-9444
17800 Mitchell N Irvine (92614) ***(P-16847)***
Interior Office Solutions Inc.....E.....310 726-9067
444 S Flower St Ste 200 Los Angeles (90071) ***(P-16848)***
Interior Rmoval Specialist Inc.....C.....323 357-6900
8990 Atlantic Ave South Gate (90280) ***(P-3344)***
Interior Specialists Inc (HQ).....D.....760 929-6700
1630 Faraday Ave Carlsbad (92008) ***(P-3008)***
Interior Specialists Inc.....D.....530 885-0632
9300 Hubbard Rd Auburn (95602) ***(P-3009)***
Interiors By Linda.....E.....760 341-9651
49585 Brian Ct La Quinta (92253) ***(P-16849)***
Interket Enterprise, Fremont *Also called Unitek Inc* ***(P-15707)***
Interlab Inc.....E.....619 302-3095
636 Broadway Ste 322 San Diego (92101) ***(P-7030)***
Interlink.....C.....310 734-1499
10940 Wilshire Blvd Los Angeles (90024) ***(P-9505)***
Interlink Company The, Los Angeles *Also called Interlink* ***(P-9505)***
Intermedia Holdings Inc (PA).....D.....650 641-4000
100 Mathilda Pl Ste 600 Sunnyvale (94086) ***(P-16033)***
Internal Associates Med Group, Culver City *Also called Gardner Neurologic Orthopedic* ***(P-26237)***
Internal Mdcine Rsdncy Affairs.....D.....916 734-7080
4150 V St Ste 3116 Sacramento (95817) ***(P-24404)***
Internal Services, Los Angeles *Also called County of Los Angeles* ***(P-14736)***
Internal Services Department, Los Angeles *Also called County of Los Angeles* ***(P-25564)***
Internal Services Dept, Los Angeles *Also called County of Los Angeles* ***(P-16720)***
International Alliance Thea.....D.....805 898-0442
P.O. Box 413 Santa Barbara (93102) ***(P-24442)***
International Almond Exchange.....E.....831 728-4534
144 W Lake Ave Watsonville (95076) ***(P-176)***
International Assoc of Machini.....E.....760 326-7048
1303 S Highway 95 Needles (92363) ***(P-24443)***
International Assoc of Plmbng (PA).....D.....909 472-4100
4755 E Philadelphia St Ontario (91761) ***(P-24344)***
International Bay Clubs LLC (PA).....B.....949 645-5000
1221 W Coast Hwy Ste 145 Newport Beach (92663) ***(P-18469)***
International Brthrhd of Elctr (PA).....D.....707 452-2700
30 Orange Tree Cir Vacaville (95687) ***(P-24444)***
International Bus Mchs Corp.....D.....914 499-1900
30501 Agoura Rd Ste 100 Agoura Hills (91301) ***(P-15618)***
International Bus Mchs Corp.....A.....408 463-2000
555 Bailey Ave San Jose (95141) ***(P-14884)***
International Bus Mchs Corp.....C.....415 545-4747
425 Market St San Francisco (94105) ***(P-6752)***
International Bus Mchs Corp.....A.....408 850-8999
2350 Mission College Blvd Santa Clara (95054) ***(P-16034)***
International Bus Mchs Corp.....B.....714 327-3501
1540 Scenic Ave Costa Mesa (92626) ***(P-16035)***
International Bus Mchs Corp.....B.....800 426-4968
1001 E Hillsdale Blvd Foster City (94404) ***(P-16036)***
International Bus Mchs Corp.....C.....408 452-4800
2077 Gateway Pl San Jose (95110) ***(P-6753)***
International Bus Mchs Corp.....B.....408 927-1080
650 Harry Rd San Jose (95120) ***(P-25769)***
International Bus Mchs Corp.....C.....925 277-5000
4000 Executive Pkwy # 300 San Ramon (94583) ***(P-26649)***
International City Mrtg Inc.....D.....909 944-7361
2990 Inland Empire Blvd # 111 Ontario (91764) ***(P-9628)***
International Code Council Inc.....D.....562 699-0541
3060 Saturn St Ste 100 Brea (92821) ***(P-24405)***
International Creative Mgt Inc (HQ).....C.....310 550-4000
10250 Constellation Blvd Los Angeles (90067) ***(P-17916)***
International Creative MGT Inc.....C.....310 550-4000
10250 Constellation Blvd # 1 Los Angeles (90067) ***(P-17917)***
International Design Services.....D.....323 662-3963
2437 Micheltorena St Los Angeles (90039) ***(P-25143)***
International Fdn For Korea Un.....B.....213 550-2182
3435 Wilshire Blvd # 480 Los Angeles (90010) ***(P-24182)***
International Fmly Entrmt Inc (HQ).....C.....818 560-1000
3800 W Alameda Ave Burbank (91505) ***(P-5730)***
International Garment Finisher.....D.....562 983-7400
2144 W Gaylord St Long Beach (90813) ***(P-13299)***
International Home Mortgage.....D.....562 945-7753
13601 Whittier Blvd # 311 Whittier (90605) ***(P-9564)***
International House.....C.....510 642-9490
2299 Piedmont Ave Ste 535 Berkeley (94720) ***(P-13138)***
INTERNATIONAL HOUSE AT U C BER, Berkeley *Also called International House* ***(P-13138)***
International Indus Pk Inc.....D.....858 623-9000
5440 Morehouse Dr # 4000 San Diego (92121) ***(P-11754)***
International Inst Los Angeles (PA).....D.....323 224-3800
3845 Selig Pl Los Angeles (90031) ***(P-23283)***
International Litigation Svcs.....E.....888 313-4457
65 Enterprise Aliso Viejo (92656) ***(P-6754)***

ALPHABETIC

Employee Codes: A=Over 500 employees, B=251-500 C=101-250, D=51-100, E=50
2020 Directory of California Wholesalers and Services Companies
© Mergent Inc. 1-800-342-5647
1307

International Longshoremens..........D.......209 464-1827
22 N Union St Stockton (95205) ***(P-24445)***
International Marine Pdts Inc (HQ)..........E.......213 893-6123
500 E 7th St Los Angeles (90014) ***(P-8370)***
International Media Group Inc..........D.......310 478-1818
1990 S Bundy Dr Ste 850 Los Angeles (90025) ***(P-5613)***
International Medical Corps (PA)..........D.......310 826-7800
12400 Wilshire Blvd # 1500 Los Angeles (90025) ***(P-23284)***
International Mgt Systems..........D.......310 822-2022
4640 Admiralty Way # 500 Marina Del Rey (90292) ***(P-27096)***
International Missing Persons..........D.......714 827-1947
609 S Broder St Anaheim (92804) ***(P-13432)***
International Paper, Livermore *Also called Veritiv Operating Company* ***(P-7607)***
International Paper, La Mirada *Also called Veritiv Operating Company* ***(P-7906)***
International Paving Svcs Inc..........D.......909 794-2101
1199 Opal Ave Mentone (92359) ***(P-1733)***
International Thermoproducts..........E.......619 562-7001
11015 Mission Park Ct Santee (92071) ***(P-7552)***
International Toy Inc..........E.......949 333-3777
17682 Cowan Ste 100 Irvine (92614) ***(P-7734)***
International Trnsp Svc (HQ)..........C.......562 435-7781
1281 Pier G Way Long Beach (90802) ***(P-4612)***
International Union of Operati..........C.......510 748-7400
1620 S Loop Rd Alameda (94502) ***(P-24446)***
Internationl TV Media Wireless, Bay Point *Also called Caribbean South Amercn Council* ***(P-4819)***
Internet Archive..........C.......415 561-6767
300 Funston Ave San Francisco (94118) ***(P-15870)***
Internet Blueprint Inc..........E.......714 673-6000
1177 Warner Ave Tustin (92780) ***(P-14885)***
Internet Booking Agencycom Inc..........B.......949 673-7707
232 Via Eboli Newport Beach (92663) ***(P-14311)***
Internet Brands Inc (PA)..........C.......310 280-4000
909 N Pacific Coast Hwy # 11 El Segundo (90245) ***(P-15782)***
Internet Corp For Assigned Nam (PA)..........C.......310 823-9358
12025 Waterfront Dr # 300 Los Angeles (90094) ***(P-15619)***
Internet Escrow Services Inc..........D.......888 511-8600
180 Montgomery St Ste 650 San Francisco (94104) ***(P-11204)***
Internet Marketing Assn Inc..........D.......949 443-9300
10 Mar Del Rey San Clemente (92673) ***(P-26650)***
Internet-Journals LLC..........D.......510 665-1200
2100 Milvia St Ste 300 Berkeley (94704) ***(P-16037)***
Interntional Cmpt Science Inst..........E.......510 643-9153
1947 Center St Ste 600 Berkeley (94704) ***(P-25997)***
Interntional Disposal Corp Cal..........D.......408 945-2802
1601 Dixon Landing Rd Milpitas (95035) ***(P-6214)***
Interntional Longshore Whse Un..........D.......805 488-2944
Bldng 608 Port Heneme Hbr Port Hueneme (93041) ***(P-14312)***
Interntional Pet Sups Dist Inc..........D.......858 453-7845
10850 Via Frontera San Diego (92127) ***(P-8980)***
Interntional Un Oper Engineers..........E.......626 792-2519
150 Corson St Pasadena (91103) ***(P-24447)***
Interntional Un Oper Engineers (PA)..........D.......916 444-6880
1121 L St Ste 401 Sacramento (95814) ***(P-24448)***
Interntnal Arospc Coatings Inc..........C.......760 246-1651
13640 Phantom St Victorville (92394) ***(P-2358)***
Interntnal Prnsrance Assoc LLC..........E.......415 223-5548
504 Redwood Blvd Ste 240e Novato (94947) ***(P-10389)***
Interntnal Pvment Slutions Inc..........D.......909 794-2101
1209 Van Buren St Ste 3 Thermal (92274) ***(P-3163)***
Interntnal Rscue Committee Inc..........D.......619 641-7510
5348 University Ave # 205 San Diego (92105) ***(P-23285)***
Interntonal Win Treatments Inc (PA)..........D.......562 236-2120
12301 Hawkins St Santa Fe Springs (90670) ***(P-6564)***
Intero Real Estate Services..........D.......408 848-8400
7652 Monterey St Gilroy (95020) ***(P-11205)***
Intero Real Estate Svcs Inc..........D.......408 741-1600
12900 Saratoga Ave Saratoga (95070) ***(P-11206)***
Intero Real Estate Svcs Inc..........D.......562 861-7242
8255 Firestone Blvd # 200 Downey (90241) ***(P-11207)***
Intero Real Estate Svcs Inc..........D.......510 489-8989
32145 Alvarado Niles Rd # 101 Union City (94587) ***(P-11208)***
Intero Real Estate Svcs Inc..........C.......408 574-5000
5890 Silver Creek Vly Rd San Jose (95138) ***(P-11209)***
Intero Real Estate Svcs Inc..........E.......408 558-3600
1900 Camden Ave San Jose (95124) ***(P-11210)***
Intero Silicon Valley, San Jose *Also called Intero Real Estate Svcs Inc* ***(P-11210)***
Interpac Distribution Center, Woodland *Also called Interpac Technologies Inc* ***(P-16850)***
Interpac Technologies Inc..........D.......530 662-6363
260 N Pioneer Ave Woodland (95776) ***(P-16850)***
Interpacific Group Inc..........A.......415 442-0711
576 Beale St San Francisco (94105) ***(P-25619)***
Interpoltex, Jamul *Also called Poltex Company Inc* ***(P-15021)***
Interprsnal Dvlpmntal Fclttors..........D.......626 793-8967
891 Worcester Ave Apt 3 Pasadena (91104) ***(P-23286)***
Intersil Techwell, Burlingame *Also called Renesas Electronics Amer Inc* ***(P-7334)***
Interstate Btry San Diego Inc..........E.......858 790-8244
9345 Cabot Dr San Diego (92126) ***(P-6447)***
Interstate Con Pmpg Co Inc..........D.......209 983-3092
11180 Vallejo Ct French Camp (95231) ***(P-3164)***
Interstate Electric Co Inc (PA)..........D.......323 724-0420
2240 Yates Ave Commerce (90040) ***(P-6925)***
Interstate Electronics Corp..........A.......714 758-0500
708 E Vermont Ave Anaheim (92805) ***(P-26651)***
Interstate Electronics Corp..........D.......858 552-9500
3033 Science Park Rd San Diego (92121) ***(P-15620)***
Interstate Foods Inc..........C.......310 635-0426
310 S Long Beach Blvd Compton (90221) ***(P-8327)***
Interstate Fuel Systems Inc..........D.......916 457-6572
8221 Alpine Ave Sacramento (95826) ***(P-8732)***
Interstate Hotels Resorts Inc..........D.......949 783-2500
4685 Macarthur Ct Ste 480 Newport Beach (92660) ***(P-26265)***
Interstate Hotels Resorts Inc..........C.......415 362-5500
2500 Mason St San Francisco (94133) ***(P-12471)***
Interstate Hotels Resorts Inc..........C.......213 617-1133
333 S Figueroa St Los Angeles (90071) ***(P-12472)***
Interstate Hotels Resorts Inc..........D.......760 476-0800
6450 Carlsbad Blvd Carlsbad (92011) ***(P-12473)***
Interstate Hotels Resorts Inc..........B.......213 624-1000
404 S Figueroa St 418a Los Angeles (90071) ***(P-12474)***
Interstate Hotels Resorts Inc..........C.......760 322-7000
67 967 Vst Chno At Lndau Palm Springs (92263) ***(P-26266)***
Interstate Hotels Resorts Inc..........C.......925 934-2500
1345 Treat Blvd Walnut Creek (94597) ***(P-26267)***
Interstate Hotels Resorts Inc..........D.......510 843-3000
41 Tunnel Rd Berkeley (94705) ***(P-26268)***
Interstate Hotels Resorts Inc..........C.......510 489-2200
32083 Alvarado Niles Rd Union City (94587) ***(P-12475)***
Interstate Hotels Resorts Inc..........C.......916 922-4700
2200 Harvard St Sacramento (95815) ***(P-12476)***
Interstate Hotels Resorts Inc..........C.......949 833-9999
18800 Macarthur Blvd Irvine (92612) ***(P-12477)***
Interstate Meat & Provision..........D.......323 838-9400
6114 Scott Way Commerce (90040) ***(P-8287)***
Interstate Plastics, Sacramento *Also called Dongalen Enterprises Inc* ***(P-8685)***
Interstate Protective Services..........D.......818 995-6664
20548 Ventura Blvd # 118 Woodland Hills (91364) ***(P-16326)***
Interstate Rhbltation Svcs LLC..........C.......818 244-5656
333 E Glenoaks Blvd # 204 Glendale (91207) ***(P-22046)***
Interstate Truck Center LLC (PA)..........D.......209 944-5821
2110 S Sinclair Ave Stockton (95215) ***(P-6402)***
Intertek Caleb Brett, Signal Hill *Also called Intertek USA Inc* ***(P-16851)***
Intertek Pharmaceutical Svcs, San Diego *Also called Intertek USA Inc* ***(P-26083)***
Intertek Testing Svcs NA Inc..........D.......949 448-4100
25800 Commercentre Dr Lake Forest (92630) ***(P-26081)***
Intertek Testing Svcs NA Inc..........D.......949 349-1684
25791 Commercentre Dr Lake Forest (92630) ***(P-26082)***
Intertek USA Inc..........D.......858 558-2599
10420 Wateridge Cir San Diego (92121) ***(P-26083)***
Intertek USA Inc..........E.......562 494-4999
1941 Freeman Ave Ste A Signal Hill (90755) ***(P-16851)***
Intertrend Communications Inc..........D.......562 733-1888
228 E Broadway Long Beach (90802) ***(P-13527)***
Intertrust Technologies Corp (HQ)..........C.......408 616-1600
920 Stewart Dr Sunnyvale (94085) ***(P-14886)***
Intervalley Pools, Pomona *Also called Inter Valley Pool Supply Inc* ***(P-7712)***
Intervec Phoenix Travel Club..........C.......828 728-5287
1456 Seacoast Dr Unit 4a Imperial Beach (91932) ***(P-18470)***
Interviewing Service Amer Inc..........D.......626 979-4140
200 S Grfield Ave Ste 302 Alhambra (91801) ***(P-25910)***
Interviewing Service Amer LLC (PA)..........C.......818 989-1044
15400 Sherman Way Ste 400 Van Nuys (91406) ***(P-25911)***
Interwall Dev Systems Inc..........D.......949 553-9102
17401 Armstrong Ave Irvine (92614) ***(P-2801)***
Interwest Insurance Svcs LLC (PA)..........C.......916 488-3100
8950 Cal Center Dr # 200 Sacramento (95826) ***(P-10390)***
Interwest Insurance Svcs LLC..........D.......916 784-1008
5 Sierra Gate Plz Fl 2nd Roseville (95678) ***(P-10391)***
Interwest Insurance Svcs LLC..........D.......530 895-1010
1357 E Lassen Ave Ste 100 Chico (95973) ***(P-10392)***
Intex Recreation Corp..........D.......310 549-1846
4001 Via Oro Ave Ste 210 Long Beach (90810) ***(P-6520)***
Intex Recreation Corp (PA)..........D.......310 549-5400
4001 Via Oro Ave Ste 210 Long Beach (90810) ***(P-7713)***
Intex Recreation Corp..........C.......310 549-5400
1665 Hughes Way Long Beach (90810) ***(P-10611)***
Intouch Health, Goleta *Also called Intouch Technologies Inc* ***(P-15363)***
Intouch Technologies Inc (PA)..........C.......805 562-8686
7402 Hollister Ave Goleta (93117) ***(P-15363)***
Intrade Industries Inc (PA)..........D.......559 274-9877
2559 S East Ave Fresno (93706) ***(P-4581)***
Intrado Corporation..........C.......310 481-7878
170 N Church Ln Los Angeles (90049) ***(P-16852)***
Intrado Corporation..........C.......949 294-2801
3063 W Chapman Ave # 2353 Orange (92868) ***(P-16853)***
Intrado Interactive Svcs Corp..........D.......888 527-5225
100 Enterprise Way A-3 Scotts Valley (95066) ***(P-5502)***
Intratek Computer Inc..........C.......949 334-4200
9950 Irvine Center Dr Irvine (92618) ***(P-16038)***
Intravas Inc..........D.......760 650-4040
6300 Yarrow Dr Carlsbad (92011) ***(P-26652)***
Intrepid Healthcare Svcs Inc, North Hollywood *Also called IPC Healthcare Inc* ***(P-19028)***
Intrepid Inv Bankers LLC..........A.......310 478-9000
11755 Wilshire Blvd # 2200 Los Angeles (90025) ***(P-9700)***
Intrinsik Envmtl Sciences Inc..........D.......310 392-6462
1608 Pacific Ave Ste 201 Venice (90291) ***(P-27097)***
Intuit Financial Services, Redwood City *Also called Digital Insight Corporation* ***(P-15854)***
Intuit Inc (PA)..........D.......650 944-6000
2700 Coast Ave Mountain View (94043) ***(P-15364)***
Intuit Inc..........C.......650 944-6000
2700 Coast Ave Bldg 7 Mountain View (94043) ***(P-15365)***
Intuit Inc..........C.......650 944-6000
2535 Garcia Ave Mountain View (94043) ***(P-15366)***
Intuit Inc..........C.......650 944-2840
141 Corona Way Portola Valley (94028) ***(P-15367)***
Intuit Inc..........C.......650 944-6000
180 Jefferson Dr Menlo Park (94025) ***(P-15368)***

Intuit Inc...B.......858 215-8000
7545 Torrey Santa Fe Rd San Diego (92129) ***(P-15369)***
Invarian, Santa Clara *Also called Silvaco Inc* ***(P-15692)***
Inveserve Corporation...D.......626 458-3435
123 S Chapel Ave Alhambra (91801) ***(P-11211)***
Invesmart Inc...D.......408 961-2800
55 Almaden Blvd Ste 800 San Jose (95113) ***(P-10393)***
Investlinc Group LLC (PA)...D.......310 997-0580
1230 Rosecrans Ave # 600 Manhattan Beach (90266) ***(P-16854)***
Investlinc Group, The, Manhattan Beach *Also called Investlinc Group LLC* ***(P-16854)***
Investment Banking, Los Angeles *Also called J Alexander Investments Inc* ***(P-11755)***
Investment Real Estate, San Jose *Also called Zell Associates Inc* ***(P-9776)***
Investment Tech Group Inc...C.......310 216-6777
400 Crprate Pinte Ste 855 Culver City (90230) ***(P-9701)***
Investor's Property Services, Irvine *Also called R & K Interests Inc* ***(P-12781)***
Investors Capital MGT Group...B.......310 553-5175
10390 Santa Monica Blvd Los Angeles (90025) ***(P-26269)***
Investors MGT Tr RE Group Inc (PA)...E.......818 784-4700
15303 Ventura Blvd # 200 Sherman Oaks (91403) ***(P-10740)***
Invitae Corporation (PA)...C.......415 374-7782
1400 16th St San Francisco (94103) ***(P-26084)***
Invitation Homes Inc...D.......805 372-2900
465 N Halstead St Ste 150 Pasadena (91107) ***(P-10612)***
Inyo Mono Advcts Fr Cmmnty Act (PA)...D.......760 873-8557
137 E South St Bishop (93514) ***(P-24183)***
Inyo Sheriff Office, Independence *Also called Sheriffs Offices* ***(P-22819)***
Inzunza Real Estate Inc...D.......951 544-8801
25310 Madison Ave Ste 101 Murrieta (92562) ***(P-11212)***
Iogear, Irvine *Also called Aten Technology Inc* ***(P-6800)***
Ion Media Networks Inc...E.......818 953-7193
2531 Nina St Pasadena (91107) ***(P-5614)***
Ionics Altrpure Wtr Crparation...D.......562 948-2188
7777 Industry Ave Pico Rivera (90660) ***(P-8589)***
Iotec, Santa Fe Springs *Also called Integrated Office Tech LLC* ***(P-6750)***
Ip Access International...E.......949 655-1000
31831 Cmno Capistrno 300a San Juan Capistrano (92675) ***(P-16039)***
Ip Infusion Inc (HQ)...D.......408 400-1900
3965 Freedom Cir Ste 200 Santa Clara (95054) ***(P-15621)***
Ip International Inc...E.......650 403-7800
1510 Fashion Island Blvd # 104 San Mateo (94404) ***(P-16040)***
Ipass Inc...D.......650 232-4100
15241 Laguna Canyon Rd # 100 Irvine (92618) ***(P-15622)***
Ipass Inc (HQ)...D.......650 232-4100
3800 Bridge Pkwy Redwood City (94065) ***(P-5428)***
Ipayables Inc (PA)...D.......949 215-9122
95 Argonaut Ste 270 Aliso Viejo (92656) ***(P-15370)***
Ipayment Inc (HQ)...D.......212 802-7200
30721 Russell Ranch Rd # 200 Westlake Village (91362) ***(P-16855)***
IPC (usa) Inc (HQ)...D.......949 648-5600
4 Hutton Cntre Dr Ste 700 Santa Ana (92707) ***(P-8733)***
IPC Healthcare Inc (HQ)...C.......888 447-2362
4605 Lankershim Blvd North Hollywood (91602) ***(P-19028)***
Ipd, Torrance *Also called Industrial Parts Depot LLC* ***(P-7550)***
Ipitek Inc...C.......760 438-1010
2461 Impala Dr Carlsbad (92010) ***(P-2522)***
Ipolipo Inc...D.......408 916-5290
440 N Wolfe Rd Sunnyvale (94085) ***(P-15371)***
Ips, Woodland Hills *Also called Interstate Protective Services* ***(P-16326)***
Ips Group Inc (PA)...D.......858 404-0607
7737 Kenamar Ct San Diego (92121) ***(P-5790)***
Ipsos Otx Corporation (HQ)...C.......310 736-3400
300 Crprate Pinte Ste 500 Culver City (90230) ***(P-25912)***
Ipsos Public Affairs Inc...C.......559 451-2820
3402 N Blackstone Ave Fresno (93726) ***(P-25913)***
Iptor Supply Chain Systems USA (HQ)...C.......916 542-2820
915 Highland Pointe Dr # 250 Roseville (95678) ***(P-14887)***
Iqa Solutions Inc...D.......562 420-1000
4089 E Conant St Long Beach (90808) ***(P-25144)***
Iqms (HQ)...C.......805 227-1122
2231 Wisteria Ln Paso Robles (93446) ***(P-15372)***
Iqtalent Partners LLC...D.......888 501-4787
171 Main St Ste 284 Los Altos (94022) ***(P-14313)***
Irby Construction Company...D.......760 344-4478
100 W Keystone Rd Brawley (92227) ***(P-1868)***
IRC Technologies Inc (PA)...D.......949 476-8626
2901 Pullman St Santa Ana (92705) ***(P-3064)***
Irell & Manella LLP (PA)...B.......310 277-1010
1800 Avenue Of The Stars # 900 Los Angeles (90067) ***(P-22581)***
Irell & Manella LLP...D.......949 760-0991
840 Nwport Ctr Dr Ste 400 Newport Beach (92660) ***(P-22582)***
Irene Swindell's Adult Day Car, San Francisco *Also called Institute On Aging* ***(P-23278)***
Irise (PA)...D.......800 556-0399
2381 Rosecrans Ave # 100 El Segundo (90245) ***(P-14888)***
Irish Communication Company (HQ)...D.......626 288-6170
2649 Stingle Ave Rosemead (91770) ***(P-1869)***
Irish Construction (HQ)...C.......626 288-8530
2641 River Ave Rosemead (91770) ***(P-1870)***
Irish Construction...D.......408 612-8440
19490 Monterey St Morgan Hill (95037) ***(P-1871)***
Irish Construction...D.......619 713-1991
1329 Sweetwater Ln Spring Valley (91977) ***(P-1872)***
Irish Construction...D.......209 576-8766
1028 Marchy Ln Ceres (95307) ***(P-1873)***
Iron Law Inc (PA)...D.......844 476-6529
663 S Rancho Santa Fe Rd San Marcos (92078) ***(P-22583)***
Iron Mountain Assurance Corp, Milpitas *Also called Iron Mountain Fulfillment* ***(P-13725)***
Iron Mountain Fulfillment (HQ)...E.......408 945-1600
565 Sinclair Frontage Rd Milpitas (95035) ***(P-13725)***
Iron Mountain Incorporated...D.......510 798-6387
30481 Whipple Rd Union City (94587) ***(P-16528)***
Iron Mountain Incorporated...D.......661 775-9008
28751 Witherspoon Pkwy Valencia (91355) ***(P-4567)***
Iron Mountain Incorporated...D.......562 345-6900
P.O. Box 7877 Newport Beach (92658) ***(P-4568)***
Iron Mountain Info MGT LLC...D.......714 526-0916
12958 Midway Pl Cerritos (90703) ***(P-4569)***
Iron Systems Inc...D.......408 943-8000
980 Mission Ct Fremont (94539) ***(P-6854)***
Iron Workers Local 433...E.......909 884-5500
252 Hillcrest Ave San Bernardino (92408) ***(P-11788)***
Ironclad Inc...D.......818 404-2777
325 5th St San Francisco (94107) ***(P-14889)***
Ironclad Security Services Inc...D.......408 773-2800
3561 Homestead Rd Ste 600 Santa Clara (95051) ***(P-16327)***
Ironworkers Union, Pasadena *Also called Ironwrker Emplyees Beneft Corp* ***(P-11789)***
Ironwrker Emplyees Beneft Corp...D.......626 792-7337
131 N El Molino Ave # 330 Pasadena (91101) ***(P-11789)***
Irp Lax Hotel LLC...C.......310 645-4600
9750 Airport Blvd Los Angeles (90045) ***(P-12478)***
Irri-Scape Construction Inc...D.......951 694-6936
20182 Carancho Rd Temecula (92590) ***(P-831)***
Irvine APT Communities LP (HQ)...C.......949 720-5600
110 Innovation Dr Irvine (92617) ***(P-10741)***
Irvine Company LLC...D.......949 653-5300
1 Golf Club Dr Irvine (92618) ***(P-24842)***
Irvine Company Office Property, Newport Beach *Also called Irvine Eastgate Office II LLC* ***(P-11858)***
Irvine Eastgate Office II LLC...A.......949 720-2000
550 Newport Center Dr Newport Beach (92660) ***(P-11858)***
Irvine Medical Center, Orange *Also called University California Irvine* ***(P-21343)***
Irvine Pharmaceutical Svcs Inc...D.......949 439-6677
30262 Crown Valley Pkwy Laguna Niguel (92677) ***(P-26085)***
Irvine Police Department, Irvine *Also called City of Irvine* ***(P-24394)***
Irvine Ranch Water District (PA)...C.......949 453-5300
15600 Sand Canyon Ave Irvine (92618) ***(P-6071)***
Irvine Ranch Water District...C.......949 453-5300
3512 Michelson Dr Irvine (92612) ***(P-6072)***
Irvine Regional Hospital, Anaheim *Also called Tenet Healthsystem Medical* ***(P-21306)***
Irvine Technology Corporation...C.......714 445-2624
17900 Von Karman Ave # 100 Irvine (92614) ***(P-14314)***
Irvine Unified School Distict...D.......949 936-5300
100 Nightmist Irvine (92618) ***(P-3816)***
Irvine Valencia Growers...D.......949 936-8000
11501 Jeffrey Rd Irvine (92602) ***(P-223)***
Irwin Naturals...D.......310 306-3636
5310 Beethoven St Los Angeles (90066) ***(P-7952)***
Irwindale 6000, Irwindale *Also called Southern California Edison Co* ***(P-5939)***
ISA, Van Nuys *Also called Interviewing Service Amer LLC* ***(P-25911)***
Isaac Fair Corporation...D.......858 369-8000
3661 Valley Centre Dr San Diego (92130) ***(P-14890)***
Isabel Garreton Inc (PA)...C.......310 833-7768
770 Miraflores San Pedro (90731) ***(P-8079)***
Iscs Inc...C.......408 362-3000
100 Great Oaks Blvd # 100 San Jose (95119) ***(P-14891)***
ISE Labs Inc (HQ)...C.......510 687-2500
46800 Bayside Pkwy Fremont (94538) ***(P-26086)***
Isearch Media LLC...D.......415 358-0882
1710 S Amphlett Blvd # 320 San Mateo (94402) ***(P-13528)***
Iserve Residential Lending LLC...D.......858 486-4169
16745 W Bernardo Dr # 100 San Diego (92127) ***(P-9565)***
Ishares, San Francisco *Also called Blackrock Instnl Tr Nat Assn* ***(P-11718)***
Isheriff Inc...C.......650 412-4300
555 Twin Dolphin Dr # 135 Redwood City (94065) ***(P-14892)***
ISI Inspection Services Inc (PA)...D.......510 900-2101
1798 University Ave Berkeley (94703) ***(P-16856)***
Islamic Relief USA...D.......714 676-1300
6131 Orangethorpe Ave # 280 Buena Park (90620) ***(P-23287)***
Island Hospitality MGT LLC...E.......408 720-1000
750 Lakeway Dr Sunnyvale (94085) ***(P-12479)***
Island Hospitality MGT LLC...D.......650 574-4700
2000 Winward Way San Mateo (94404) ***(P-12480)***
Island Hospitality MGT LLC...D.......408 720-8893
1080 Stewart Dr Sunnyvale (94085) ***(P-12481)***
Island Hospitality MGT LLC...E.......909 937-6788
2025 Convention Ctr Way Ontario (91764) ***(P-12482)***
Island Hospitality MGT LLC...D.......650 591-8600
400 Concourse Dr Belmont (94002) ***(P-12483)***
Island Pacific Supermarket, City of Industry *Also called Abacus Business Capital Inc* ***(P-8144)***
Islands Restaurant & Lounge, San Diego *Also called Crown Plaza SD* ***(P-12190)***
Isolutecom Inc (PA)...E.......805 498-6259
9 Northam Ave Newbury Park (91320) ***(P-15373)***
Isotis Orthobiologics Inc...C.......949 595-8710
2 Goodyear Ste A Irvine (92618) ***(P-25770)***
Ispace Inc...C.......310 563-3800
2381 Rosecrans Ave # 110 El Segundo (90245) ***(P-16041)***
Isr Holdings, Roseville *Also called Intercare Specialty Risk Ins* ***(P-10388)***
Israel Discount Bank New York...C.......213 861-6440
888 S Figueroa St Ste 550 Los Angeles (90017) ***(P-9212)***
Israel Pops Orchestra...E.......818 343-6450
4841 Alonzo Ave Encino (91316) ***(P-17984)***
ISS Facility Services Inc...B.......650 593-9774
40563 Encyclopedia Cir Fremont (94538) ***(P-13954)***
Ists Worldwide Inc...C.......510 794-1400
2201 Walnut Ave Ste 210 Fremont (94538) ***(P-16042)***

ALPHABETIC

Employee Codes: A=Over 500 employees, B=251-500
C=101-250, D=51-100, E=50
2020 Directory of California
Wholesalers and Services Companies
© Mergent Inc. 1-800-342-5647
1309

Isys Solutions Inc ....D....714 521-7656
2601 Saturn St Ste 302 Brea (92821) ***(P-26653)***
It Is Written, Riverside *Also called Adventist Media Center Inc* ***(P-17883)***
Ita Group Inc ....C....415 277-3200
455 Market St Ste 1450 San Francisco (94105) ***(P-26654)***
Italent Corporation (PA) ....C....408 496-6200
27 Devine St Ste 20 San Jose (95110) ***(P-16043)***
Italent Digital, San Jose *Also called Italent Corporation* ***(P-16043)***
Italfoods Inc ....D....650 877-0724
205 Shaw Rd South San Francisco (94080) ***(P-8590)***
Itc Srvice Group Acqsition LLC (HQ) ....E....877 370-4482
7777 Greenback Ln Ste 201 Citrus Heights (95610) ***(P-27098)***
Itco Solutions Inc ....B....650 367-0514
1003 Whitehall Ln Redwood City (94061) ***(P-16044)***
Itd Print Solutions, Los Angeles *Also called Imaging Technologies Group LLC* ***(P-7858)***
Itek Services Inc ....D....949 770-4835
25501 Arctic Ocean Dr Lake Forest (92630) ***(P-16045)***
Itera Software, Irvine *Also called Vision Solutions Inc* ***(P-16154)***
Ito Farms, Westminster *Also called B & E Farms Inc* ***(P-87)***
Itrenew Inc (HQ) ....E....408 744-9600
8356 Central Ave Newark (94560) ***(P-16046)***
Itron Inc ....A....510 844-2800
1111 Broadway Ste 1800 Oakland (94607) ***(P-2523)***
Itron Networked Solutions Inc (HQ) ....B....669 770-4000
230 W Tasman Dr San Jose (95134) ***(P-5791)***
Its Technologies Logistics LLC ....D....209 460-6023
6540 Austin Rd Stockton (95215) ***(P-5121)***
Iunlimited Incorporated ....C....916 218-6198
7801 Folsom Blvd Ste 203 Sacramento (95826) ***(P-16328)***
Iuoe Local 39, Sacramento *Also called Iuoe Sttonary Engineers Lcl 39* ***(P-24449)***
Iuoe Sttonary Engineers Lcl 39 ....E....916 928-0399
1620 N Market Blvd Sacramento (95834) ***(P-24449)***
IVBCF, Temecula *Also called Inland Valley Business and Com* ***(P-24841)***
Ivie McNeill Wyatt A Prof Law ....E....213 489-0028
444 S Flower St Ste 1800 Los Angeles (90071) ***(P-22584)***
Ivo Wall Experts Inc ....D....323 246-4026
5359 Sheila St Commerce (90040) ***(P-2802)***
Ivy Realty ....E....213 386-8888
611 S Wilton Pl Los Angeles (90005) ***(P-11213)***
Iw Golf Club, Inc, Indian Wells *Also called Indian Wells Country Club Inc* ***(P-18468)***
Iw Group (PA) ....D....310 289-5500
6300 Wilshire Blvd # 2150 Los Angeles (90048) ***(P-13529)***
Iworks Us Inc ....D....323 278-8363
2501 S Malt Ave Commerce (90040) ***(P-3265)***
Ixia, Santa Clara *Also called Net Optics Inc* ***(P-15419)***
Ixos Software Inc (PA) ....D....949 784-8000
8717 Research Dr Irvine (92618) ***(P-6855)***
Ixsystems Inc (PA) ....D....408 943-4100
2490 Kruse Dr San Jose (95131) ***(P-15374)***
Izmocars, San Francisco *Also called Homestar Systems Inc* ***(P-16022)***
Izt Mortgage Inc (PA) ....E....925 946-1858
3011 Citrus Cir Ste 202 Walnut Creek (94598) ***(P-9629)***
J & D Meat Company ....C....559 445-1123
4671 E Edgar Ave Fresno (93725) ***(P-8591)***
J & E Private Security Corp ....D....909 594-1111
3227 Producer Way Ste 110 Pomona (91768) ***(P-16329)***
J & J Acoustics Inc ....C....408 275-9255
2260 De La Cruz Blvd Santa Clara (95050) ***(P-2803)***
J & J Air Conditioning Inc ....D....408 920-0662
1086 N 11th St San Jose (95112) ***(P-2159)***
J & J Farms ....E....559 659-1457
36245 W Ashlan Ave Firebaugh (93622) ***(P-334)***
J & J Productions Incorporated ....E....714 535-0951
1775 E Lincoln Ave # 205 Anaheim (92805) ***(P-16857)***
J & L Collections Services Inc ....D....800 481-6006
8220 Longleaf Dr 400 Elk Grove (95758) ***(P-13687)***
J & L Vineyards ....D....559 268-1627
16492 Summit Crest Ln Clovis (93619) ***(P-134)***
J & M Inc ....E....925 724-0300
6700 National Dr Livermore (94550) ***(P-1874)***
J & O'S Commercial Tire Center, Richmond *Also called Rubber Dust Inc* ***(P-17318)***
J & P Financial Inc (PA) ....E....760 738-9000
330 W Felicita Ave Ste E1 Escondido (92025) ***(P-11214)***
J & P Solari ....D....209 931-1765
6302 Foppiano Ln Stockton (95212) ***(P-205)***
J & R Debenedetto Orchards Inc ....D....559 665-1712
26393 Road 22 1/2 Chowchilla (93610) ***(P-667)***
J & S Farm ....D....559 308-0294
803 W Kimball Ave Visalia (93277) ***(P-335)***
J A Contracting Inc ....B....559 733-4865
2209 W Tulare Ave Visalia (93277) ***(P-626)***
J Alexander Investments Inc (PA) ....D....213 687-8400
922 S Barrington Ave A Los Angeles (90049) ***(P-11755)***
J and J Wall Baking Co Inc ....D....916 381-1410
8806 Fruitridge Rd Sacramento (95826) ***(P-8288)***
J B A, Pasadena *Also called B Jacqueline and Assoc Inc* ***(P-14667)***
J B Bostick Company Inc (PA) ....D....714 238-2121
2870 E La Cresta Ave Anaheim (92806) ***(P-1734)***
J B Company ....D....916 929-3003
1825 Bell St Ste 100 Sacramento (95825) ***(P-1506)***
J B Hunt Transport Inc ....C....909 466-5361
11559 Jersey Blvd Rancho Cucamonga (91730) ***(P-4064)***
J B Hunt Transport Svcs Inc ....A....559 834-3852
3124 E Manning Ave Fowler (93625) ***(P-4065)***
J B Hunt Transport Svcs Inc ....A....619 230-0054
1620 5th Ave San Diego (92101) ***(P-5122)***
J B J Distributing, Fullerton *Also called Veg-Land Inc* ***(P-4335)***
J B Laquindanum & Associates ....E....707 648-0501
2608 Springs Rd Vallejo (94591) ***(P-13391)***
J Baron Inc ....D....949 451-1200
5299 Alton Pkwy Irvine (92604) ***(P-11215)***
J Brand Holdings LLC ....D....212 228-8181
1318 E 7th St Ste 260 Los Angeles (90021) ***(P-11675)***
J C C, San Rafael *Also called Bernard Osher Marin Jewish Com* ***(P-22943)***
J C Entertainment Ltg Svcs Inc ....D....818 252-7481
5435 W San Fernando Rd Los Angeles (90039) ***(P-17918)***
J C French & Company ....D....909 596-1423
2984 1st St Ste L La Verne (91750) ***(P-2359)***
J C Penney Purchasing Corp ....C....209 858-9463
700 Darcy Pkwy Lathrop (95330) ***(P-4434)***
J C Sales, Vernon *Also called Shims Bargain Inc* ***(P-9011)***
J C Towing Inc ....D....619 429-1492
2501 Faivre St Chula Vista (91911) ***(P-17420)***
J Craig Venter Institute Inc (PA) ....B....301 795-7000
4120 Capricorn Ln La Jolla (92037) ***(P-25998)***
J Crecelius Inc ....D....209 883-4826
5043 N Montpelier Rd Denair (95316) ***(P-336)***
J D L Motor Express ....D....619 232-6136
1250 Delevan Dr San Diego (92102) ***(P-3897)***
J D Rush Company Inc (HQ) ....C....661 392-1900
5900 E Lerdo Hwy Shafter (93263) ***(P-11790)***
J G Boswell Company ....D....559 992-2141
710 Bainum Ave Corcoran (93212) ***(P-506)***
J G Boswell Company ....C....661 327-7721
21101 Bear Mountain Blvd Bakersfield (93311) ***(P-13)***
J G Boswell Company ....B....559 992-5141
28001 S Dairy Ave Corcoran (93212) ***(P-14)***
J G Construction, Chino *Also called June A Grothe Construction Inc* ***(P-1517)***
J G Golfing Enterprises Inc ....E....909 885-2414
1494 S Waterman Ave San Bernardino (92408) ***(P-18257)***
J G Haddy Sales Co Inc (PA) ....C....951 685-4100
3401 Etiwanda Ave Jurupa Valley (91752) ***(P-4435)***
J Gelt Corporation ....E....619 424-8181
1424 30th St Ste C San Diego (92154) ***(P-23288)***
J Ginger Masonry LP (PA) ....B....951 688-5050
8188 Lincoln Ave Ste 100 Riverside (92504) ***(P-2717)***
J H Maddocks Photography ....D....818 842-7150
40 E Verdugo Ave Burbank (91502) ***(P-16579)***
J H Meek & Sons Inc ....E....530 662-1106
22075 County Road 99 Woodland (95695) ***(P-337)***
J H Synder Co LLC ....D....323 857-5546
5757 Wilshire Blvd Ph 30 Los Angeles (90036) ***(P-11216)***
J Harris Sim Inc (PA) ....D....858 437-0190
9685 Via Excelencia # 200 San Diego (92126) ***(P-1735)***
J I Miller, Granada Hills *Also called James I Miller* ***(P-579)***
J I T Supply, Norco *Also called JIT Corporation* ***(P-7285)***
J I T Transportation, Milpitas *Also called Dga Services Inc* ***(P-4204)***
J L S Concrete Pumping Inc ....D....805 643-0766
2055 N Ventura Ave Ventura (93001) ***(P-3165)***
J M A, San Mateo *Also called Judy Madrigal & Associates Inc* ***(P-19035)***
J M C International LLC ....E....559 256-1300
1470 W Herndon Ave # 100 Fresno (93711) ***(P-1507)***
J M Carden Sprinkler Co Inc ....D....323 258-8300
2909 Fletcher Dr Los Angeles (90065) ***(P-2160)***
J M Electric, Salinas *Also called Jensco Inc* ***(P-2526)***
J M Equipment Company Inc (PA) ....D....209 522-3271
321 Spreckels Ave Manteca (95336) ***(P-14171)***
J M Equipment Company Inc ....E....559 233-0187
3751 E Calwa Ave Fresno (93725) ***(P-7480)***
J M V B Inc ....D....714 288-9797
12118 Severn Way Riverside (92503) ***(P-2360)***
J Marchini & Son Inc ....D....559 665-2944
12000 Le Grand Rd Le Grand (95333) ***(P-338)***
J P Carroll Co Inc ....D....323 660-9230
5707 Milton Ave Whittier (90601) ***(P-2361)***
J P Consulting ....E....707 747-4800
4690 E 2nd St Ste 3 Benicia (94510) ***(P-26655)***
J P H Consulting Inc (PA) ....E....323 934-5660
1101 Crenshaw Blvd Los Angeles (90019) ***(P-20034)***
J P H Consulting Inc ....C....323 934-5660
4515 Huntington Dr S Los Angeles (90032) ***(P-20035)***
J P Original Corp (PA) ....D....626 839-4300
19101 E Walnut Dr N City of Industry (91748) ***(P-8135)***
J P Witherow Roofing Company ....D....619 297-4701
1083 N Cuyamaca St El Cajon (92020) ***(P-3065)***
J Paul Getty Trust ....D....310 440-7325
1200 Getty Center Dr # 400 Los Angeles (90049) ***(P-25914)***
J Perez Associates Inc (PA) ....D....562 801-5397
10833 Valley View St # 200 Cypress (90630) ***(P-3421)***
J R Industries, Westlake Village *Also called Jri Inc* ***(P-7287)***
J R Pierce Plumbing Company ....D....510 483-5473
14481 Wicks Blvd San Leandro (94577) ***(P-2161)***
J R Roberts Corp (HQ) ....D....916 729-5600
7745 Greenback Ln Ste 300 Citrus Heights (95610) ***(P-1508)***
J R Roberts Enterprises Inc ....C....916 729-5600
7745 Greenback Ln Ste 300 Citrus Heights (95610) ***(P-1509)***
J Redfern Inc ....C....925 371-3300
164 N L St Livermore (94550) ***(P-832)***
J Rivera Associates Inc ....D....415 617-5660
139 S Guild Ave Lodi (95240) ***(P-27283)***
J Robert Echter ....E....760 436-0188
1150 Quail Gardens Dr Encinitas (92024) ***(P-250)***
J T R Company Inc (PA) ....D....408 975-7733
1102 S 3rd St San Jose (95112) ***(P-7953)***
J T R Company Inc ....E....408 293-3272
1102 S 3rd St San Jose (95112) ***(P-4436)***

Mergent e-mail: customerrelations@mergent.com
1310
2020 Directory of California
Wholesalers and Services Companies
(P-0000) Products & Services Section entry number
(PA)=Parent Co (HQ)=Headquarters (DH)=Div Headquarters

J Vineyards & Winery, Healdsburg *Also called E & J Gallo Winery (P-129)*
J Vitale Landscape & Maint ....D....619 938-2435
8801 Cottonwood Ave Santee (92071) **(P-833)**
J W Floor Covering Inc (PA) ....C....858 536-8565
9881 Carroll Centre Rd San Diego (92126) **(P-3010)**
J Walter Thompson USA LLC ....D....415 268-5555
303 2nd St San Francisco (94107) **(P-13530)**
J Waters Inc ....D....866 424-1946
75 San Miguel Ave Ste 5 Salinas (93901) **(P-16330)**
J&G Berry Farms LLC ....C....831 750-9408
720 Rosemary Rd Santa Maria (93454) **(P-98)**
J&L Teamworks, Elk Grove *Also called J & L Collections Services Inc (P-13687)*
J&M Keystone Inc ....D....619 466-9876
2709 Via Orange Way Ste A Spring Valley (91978) **(P-13269)**
J&R Fleet Services LLC ....D....909 820-7000
210 Saint Katherine Dr La Canada Flintridge (91011) **(P-17335)**
J. Perez & Associates, Cypress *Also called J Perez Associates Inc (P-3421)*
J.B. Hunt Transport Services, Fowler *Also called J B Hunt Transport Svcs Inc (P-4065)*
J2 Cloud Services LLC (HQ) ....D....323 860-9200
6922 Hollywood Blvd # 500 Los Angeles (90028) **(P-5503)**
J2 Cloud Services, Inc., Los Angeles *Also called J2 Cloud Services LLC (P-5503)*
J2 Global Inc (PA) ....C....323 860-9200
6922 Hollywood Blvd # 500 Los Angeles (90028) **(P-5504)**
J5 Infrastructure Partners LLC ....D....949 299-5258
2030 Main St Ste 200 Irvine (92614) **(P-5262)**
J5th LLC ....D....619 487-1200
356 6th Ave San Diego (92101) **(P-12484)**
Ja Automation & Control LLC ....E....619 661-2591
6965 Cmino Mqladora Ste H San Diego (92154) **(P-7553)**
Jabez Building Services Inc ....D....714 776-7705
2094 Orange Ave Costa Mesa (92627) **(P-13955)**
Jabil Silver Creek Inc (HQ) ....C....669 255-2900
5981 Optical Ct San Jose (95138) **(P-17474)**
Jack Engle & Co (PA) ....D....323 589-8111
8440 S Alameda St Los Angeles (90001) **(P-7762)**
Jack H Caldwell & Sons Inc ....D....323 589-4008
4035 E 52nd St Maywood (90270) **(P-8490)**
Jack Jones Trucking Inc ....D....909 456-2500
1090 E Belmont St Ontario (91761) **(P-4066)**
Jack Kramer Club ....E....310 326-4404
11 Montecillo Dr Rllng HLS Est (90274) **(P-18471)**
Jack Morton Worldwide Inc ....D....310 967-2400
1840 Century Park E # 1800 Los Angeles (90067) **(P-13531)**
Jack Nadel Inc (PA) ....D....310 815-2600
8701 Bellanca Ave Los Angeles (90045) **(P-26656)**
Jack Nadel International, Los Angeles *Also called Jack Nadel Inc (P-26656)*
Jack Neal & Son Inc ....C....707 963-7303
360 Lafata St Saint Helena (94574) **(P-135)**
Jack P Selman ....D....714 639-9860
144 N Orange St Orange (92866) **(P-25461)**
Jack Parker Corp ....C....760 770-5000
4200 E Palm Canyon Dr Palm Springs (92264) **(P-12485)**
Jackie Hoofring ....E....818 961-7272
3390 Auto Mall Dr Westlake Village (91362) **(P-14315)**
Jackoway Tyreman Wertheimer Au ....D....310 553-0305
1925 Century Park E Fl 2 Los Angeles (90067) **(P-22585)**
Jacks Car Wash 3 ....D....559 438-8201
6745 N West Ave Fresno (93711) **(P-17377)**
Jackson Demarco Tidus Peter (PA) ....D....949 752-8585
2030 Main St Ste 1200 Irvine (92614) **(P-22586)**
Jackson & Blanc ....C....858 831-7900
7929 Arjons Dr San Diego (92126) **(P-2162)**
Jackson Construction (PA) ....E....916 381-8113
155 Cadillac Dr Sacramento (95825) **(P-1356)**
Jackson Family Wines Inc ....C....415 819-0301
1190 Kittyhawk Blvd Ste A Santa Rosa (95403) **(P-8813)**
Jackson Lewis PC ....E....415 394-9400
50 California St Ste 900 San Francisco (94111) **(P-22587)**
Jackson Lewis PC ....D....213 689-0404
725 S Figueroa St # 2500 Los Angeles (90017) **(P-22588)**
Jackson Shrub Supply Inc ....D....818 982-0100
11505 Vanowen St North Hollywood (91605) **(P-17746)**
Jackson Tull Chrtred Engineers ....E....310 658-2132
550 Continental Blvd # 195 El Segundo (90245) **(P-15623)**
Jacksons Hardware Inc ....D....415 870-4083
435 Du Bois St San Rafael (94901) **(P-7395)**
Jacmar Companies, The, Alhambra *Also called Pacific Ventures Ltd (P-26342)*
Jacmar Ddc LLC ....D....916 372-9795
3057 Promenade St West Sacramento (95691) **(P-8592)**
Jacmar Food Service Dist, West Sacramento *Also called Jacmar Ddc LLC (P-8592)*
Jacob Health Care Center, San Diego *Also called Premier Management Company (P-21844)*
Jacobs Atcs Fema A Joint Ventr ....D....571 218-1115
155 N Lake Ave Fl 5 Pasadena (91101) **(P-25145)**
Jacobs Civil Inc ....D....310 847-2500
1500 Hughes Way Ste B400 Long Beach (90810) **(P-25146)**
Jacobs Consultancy Inc ....D....650 579-7722
555 Airport Blvd Ste 300 Burlingame (94010) **(P-27099)**
Jacobs Cshman San Diego Fd Bnk ....E....858 527-1419
9850 Distribution Ave San Diego (92121) **(P-23289)**
Jacobs Engineering Company ....A....626 449-2171
1111 S Arroyo Pkwy Pasadena (91105) **(P-25147)**
Jacobs Engineering Group Inc ....D....925 423-7564
4435 First St Livermore (94551) **(P-1510)**
Jacobs Engineering Group Inc ....D....949 224-7585
2600 Michelson Dr Ste 500 Irvine (92612) **(P-25148)**
Jacobs Engineering Group Inc ....D....661 275-5685
37528 Morning Cir Palmdale (93550) **(P-25149)**
Jacobs Engineering Group Inc ....D....925 356-3900
2300 Clayton Rd Concord (94520) **(P-25150)**
Jacobs Engineering Group Inc ....D....310 847-2500
1500 Hughes Way Ste B400 Long Beach (90810) **(P-25151)**
Jacobs Engineering Group Inc ....D....909 974-2700
3257 E Guasti Rd Ste 130 Ontario (91761) **(P-25152)**
Jacobs Engineering Group Inc ....D....408 436-4936
1737 N 1st St Ste 300 San Jose (95112) **(P-25153)**
Jacobs Engineering Group Inc ....C....213 362-4336
1000 Wilshire Blvd # 2100 Los Angeles (90017) **(P-25154)**
Jacobs Engineering Group Inc ....D....626 578-3500
1111 S Arroyo Pkwy Pasadena (91105) **(P-25155)**
Jacobs Engineering Inc (HQ) ....C....626 578-3500
155 N Lake Ave Pasadena (91101) **(P-25156)**
Jacobs Farm/Del Cabo Inc ....D....650 827-1133
390 Swift Ave Ste 8 South San Francisco (94080) **(P-339)**
Jacobs Farm/Del Cabo Inc ....C....831 460-3500
144 Holm Rd Spc 42 Watsonville (95076) **(P-3898)**
Jacobs International Ltd Inc ....B....626 578-3500
155 N Lake Ave Pasadena (91101) **(P-25157)**
Jacobs Project Management Co ....D....949 224-7695
2600 Michelson Dr Ste 500 Irvine (92612) **(P-25158)**
Jacobs Project Management Co ....D....619 687-0110
402 W Broadway Ste 1450 San Diego (92101) **(P-25159)**
Jacobs Project Management Co ....D....510 457-2436
300 Frank H Ogawa Plz Oakland (94612) **(P-26657)**
Jacobs Technology Inc ....C....760 446-1549
1550 N Norma St Ridgecrest (93555) **(P-25160)**
Jacobs Tree Specialist Inc ....E....559 639-7138
2209 W Tulare Ave Visalia (93277) **(P-627)**
Jacobsson Engrg Cnstr Inc ....D....760 345-8700
72310 Varner Rd Thousand Palms (92276) **(P-1736)**
Jacobus Consulting Inc ....E....949 727-0720
15375 Barranca Pkwy B202 Irvine (92618) **(P-26658)**
Jade Global Inc (PA) ....D....408 899-7200
1731 Tech Dr Ste 350 San Jose (95110) **(P-15624)**
Jade Inc ....D....818 365-7137
11126 Sepulveda Blvd B Mission Hills (91345) **(P-2804)**
Jag Framing Inc ....E....818 822-7110
16741 Los Alimos St Granada Hills (91344) **(P-2942)**
Jag Professional Services Inc ....C....310 945-5648
2008 Walnut Ave Manhattan Beach (90266) **(P-27100)**
Jag Software Inc ....D....408 262-0572
2235 Skyline Dr Milpitas (95035) **(P-6856)**
Jagpreet Enterprises LLC ....C....510 336-8376
25823 Clawiter Rd Hayward (94545) **(P-8593)**
Jaguar Computer Systems Inc ....E....951 273-7950
4135 Indus Way Riverside (92503) **(P-6857)**
Jake Hey Incorporated ....C....323 856-5280
257 S Lake St Burbank (91502) **(P-16580)**
Jakes Crawfish & Seafood, Sacramento *Also called Pacific Sea Food Co Inc (P-8381)*
Jakks Sales Corporation ....E....424 268-9444
2951 28th St Ste 51 Santa Monica (90405) **(P-7735)**
Jakov P Dulcich & Sons ....C....661 792-6360
31956 Peterson Rd Mc Farland (93250) **(P-136)**
Jal Berry Farms LLC ....D....831 763-7200
1767 San Juan Rd Aromas (95004) **(P-99)**
Jalmar Properties Inc (PA) ....E....310 207-8481
12121 Wilshire Blvd # 1120 Los Angeles (90025) **(P-11217)**
Jalux Americas Inc (HQ) ....E....310 524-1000
390 N Pcf Csthwy Ste 2000 El Segundo (90245) **(P-14172)**
JAM Industries Inc ....D....310 254-0300
2101 E Via Arado Compton (90220) **(P-4437)**
Jam Warehouse, Compton *Also called JAM Industries Inc (P-4437)*
Jamboor Medical Corporation ....D....760 241-8063
12675 Hesperia Rd Victorville (92395) **(P-21927)**
Jamboree Management, Laguna Hills *Also called Jamboree Realty Corp (P-11218)*
Jamboree Realty Corp (PA) ....C....949 380-0300
22982 Mill Creek Dr Laguna Hills (92653) **(P-11218)**
Jamcracker Inc ....E....408 496-5500
4677 Old Ironsides Dr # 450 Santa Clara (95054) **(P-5429)**
James A Kiley MD, Folsom *Also called Dignity Health (P-18956)*
James B Branch Inc (PA) ....E....818 765-3521
4367 Clybourn Ave Toluca Lake (91602) **(P-4067)**
James C Jenkins Insur Svc Inc ....C....925 798-3334
1390 Willow Pass Rd Concord (94520) **(P-10394)**
James D Tate MD ....D....530 225-8710
2888 Eureka Way Ste 200 Redding (96001) **(P-19029)**
James E Roberts-Obayashi Corp ....C....925 820-0600
20 Oak Ct Danville (94526) **(P-1249)**
James Fedor Masonry Inc ....D....760 772-3036
54859 Bodine Dr Thermal (92274) **(P-2718)**
James G Parker Insurance Assoc (PA) ....D....559 222-7722
1753 E Fir Ave Fresno (93720) **(P-10395)**
James H Cowan & Associates Inc ....D....310 457-2574
5126 Clareton Dr Ste 200 Agoura Hills (91301) **(P-834)**
James Hardie Building Pdts Inc ....C....909 355-6500
10901 Elm Ave Fontana (92337) **(P-6630)**
James I Miller ....E....818 363-7444
17659 Chatsworth St Granada Hills (91344) **(P-579)**
James J Stevinson A Corp (PA) ....E....209 632-1681
25079 River Rd Stevinson (95374) **(P-396)**
James McCutcheon ....E....661 867-1810
17521 Walker Basin Rd Caliente (93518) **(P-1250)**
James McMinn Inc ....E....909 514-1231
21834 Cactus Ave Riverside (92518) **(P-1737)**
James Metals, Riverside *Also called Harbor Pipe and Steel Inc (P-7069)*
James Monroe School Pto ....E....760 772-4130
42100 Yucca Ln Bermuda Dunes (92203) **(P-24566)**
James R Glidewell Dental ....A....800 411-9723
2181 Dupont Dr Irvine (92612) **(P-21611)**

ALPHABETIC

Employee Codes: A=Over 500 employees, B=251-500
C=101-250, D=51-100, E=50
2020 Directory of California
Wholesalers and Services Companies
© Mergent Inc. 1-800-342-5647
1311

James R Glidewell Dental (PA)..........A.......949 440-2600
4141 Macarthur Blvd Newport Beach (92660) ***(P-21612)***
James-Timec International..........E.......707 642-2222
155 Corporate Pl Vallejo (94590) ***(P-1970)***
Jameson Properties Co Inc..........E.......213 487-3770
3530 Wilshire Blvd # 600 Los Angeles (90010) ***(P-10613)***
Jamison Childrens Home..........D.......661 334-3500
1010 Shalimar Dr Bakersfield (93306) ***(P-23290)***
Jamm Management LLC..........E.......510 437-5200
2447 Stanford Way Antioch (94531) ***(P-6448)***
Jan, North Hollywood *Also called Japanese Assistance Netwrk Inc* ***(P-16858)***
Jan Pro Clg Systems Sthern Cal..........E.......714 220-0500
2401 E Katella Ave # 525 Anaheim (92806) ***(P-13956)***
Jane McClurg..........D.......559 834-3080
4584 E Floral Ave Selma (93662) ***(P-137)***
Janet Hilton..........D.......310 851-7200
990 W 190th St Ste 300 Torrance (90502) ***(P-10396)***
Janet K Hartzler MD..........D.......760 340-3937
72057 Dinah Shore Dr D Rancho Mirage (92270) ***(P-19030)***
Janitorial, Santa Barbara *Also called Master Clean USA Inc* ***(P-13974)***
Janitorial Equipment Svcs Inc..........D.......951 205-8937
11752 Garden Grove Blvd # 100 Garden Grove (92843) ***(P-13957)***
Janssen Alzheimer Immunothera..........D.......650 794-2500
700 Gateway Blvd South San Francisco (94080) ***(P-25771)***
Janus Corporation (PA)..........D.......925 969-9200
1081 Shary Cir Concord (94518) ***(P-3422)***
Janus Corporation..........E.......951 479-0700
2025 Tandem Norco (92860) ***(P-3423)***
Janus Et Cie (PA)..........C.......310 601-2908
12310 Greenstone Ave Santa Fe Springs (90670) ***(P-6521)***
Janus of Santa Cruz..........D.......831 462-1060
200 7th Ave Ste 150 Santa Cruz (95062) ***(P-23291)***
Japan Airlines Co Ltd..........D.......310 607-2305
300 Continental Blvd # 620 El Segundo (90245) ***(P-4826)***
Japanese Assistance Netwrk Inc..........B.......818 505-6080
11135 Magnolia Blvd # 140 North Hollywood (91601) ***(P-16858)***
Japanese Cmnty Youth Council (PA)..........D.......415 202-7905
2012 Pine St San Francisco (94115) ***(P-24184)***
Japanese Retirement Home, Los Angeles *Also called Senior Keiro Health Care* ***(P-24070)***
Jaqui Foundation Inc..........E.......510 562-4721
675 Hegenberger Rd # 209 Oakland (94621) ***(P-27284)***
Jarka Enterprises Inc..........D.......916 491-6180
1059 Vine St Ste 108 Sacramento (95811) ***(P-3424)***
Jaroth Inc..........C.......925 553-3650
2001 Crow Canyon Rd # 200 San Ramon (94583) ***(P-2524)***
Jarrow Formulas Inc (PA)..........D.......310 204-6936
1824 S Robertson Blvd Los Angeles (90035) ***(P-7954)***
JAS Pacific..........C.......909 605-7777
201 N Euclid Ave Ste A Upland (91786) ***(P-25161)***
Jason Mechanical Inc..........E.......916 638-8763
1379 Fitzgerald Rd Rancho Cordova (95742) ***(P-2163)***
Jason Proctor Trnsp Co..........E.......559 992-1767
2375 Dairy Ave Corcoran (93212) ***(P-3688)***
Javelin Logistics Company Inc..........C.......800 577-1060
7025 Central Ave Newark (94560) ***(P-4438)***
Javelin Logistics Corporation (PA)..........E.......510 795-7287
7025 Central Ave Newark (94560) ***(P-4214)***
Jay Fisher Farms Inc..........E.......805 735-1598
2251 W Central Ave Lompoc (93436) ***(P-59)***
Jay's Catering, Garden Grove *Also called Mastroianni Family Entps Ltd* ***(P-13438)***
Jayasinghe Medical Group Inc (PA)..........D.......562 267-7000
200 S Beach Blvd Ste A2 La Habra (90631) ***(P-19031)***
Jaylaneentertainment Corp..........D.......707 820-2773
585 Fernando Dr Novato (94945) ***(P-13626)***
Jaynes Corporation California..........C.......619 233-4080
111 Elm St Fl 4 San Diego (92101) ***(P-1511)***
Jazzercise Inc (PA)..........D.......760 476-1750
2460 Impala Dr Carlsbad (92010) ***(P-18159)***
JB Dental Supply Co Inc (PA)..........C.......310 202-8855
17000 Kingsview Ave Carson (90746) ***(P-6972)***
JB Finish Inc..........D.......760 342-6300
82750 Atlantic St Indio (92203) ***(P-2943)***
JB Partners Group Inc..........C.......818 668-8201
18375 Ventura Blvd Tarzana (91356) ***(P-11219)***
JB Upland Ltd Liability Co..........E.......909 944-5456
9087 Arrow Rte Ste 140 Rancho Cucamonga (91730) ***(P-26659)***
Jbhunt Transport, San Diego *Also called J B Hunt Transport Svcs Inc* ***(P-5122)***
Jbs International Inc..........D.......650 373-4900
555 Airport Blvd Ste 400 Burlingame (94010) ***(P-25999)***
Jbsprotection, Fontana *Also called Jones Bold Security Inc* ***(P-16331)***
JC Foodservice Inc (PA)..........D.......626 299-3800
415 S Atlantic Blvd Monterey Park (91754) ***(P-6926)***
JC Party Rentals Inc..........D.......818 765-4819
11562 Vanowen St North Hollywood (91605) ***(P-14173)***
JC Resorts Inn..........D.......858 487-0700
17550 Bernardo Oaks Dr San Diego (92128) ***(P-12486)***
JC Resorts LLC..........B.......949 376-2779
1555 S Coast Hwy Laguna Beach (92651) ***(P-26270)***
JC Resorts LLC..........D.......760 944-1936
1275 Quail Gardens Dr Encinitas (92024) ***(P-26271)***
JC Sales, Commerce *Also called Shims Bargain Inc* ***(P-1377)***
Jck Hotels LLC..........D.......858 635-5566
9888 Mira Mesa Blvd San Diego (92131) ***(P-12487)***
Jcm Engineering Corp..........D.......909 923-3730
2690 E Cedar St Ontario (91761) ***(P-7692)***
Jct Company LLC..........E.......949 589-2021
29736 Avenida&Bandera Rancho Santa Margari (92688) ***(P-2164)***
Jcv Inc..........E.......714 871-2007
1118 W Orangethorpe Ave Fullerton (92833) ***(P-2805)***

JD Food, Fresno *Also called J & D Meat Company* ***(P-8591)***
JD Group, San Diego *Also called Brokerage Lgstics Slutions Inc* ***(P-4902)***
JD Miller Construction Inc..........E.......951 471-3513
506 W Graham Ave Ste 202 Lake Elsinore (92530) ***(P-2362)***
JD Power (HQ)..........D.......714 621-6200
3200 Park Center Dr Fl 13 Costa Mesa (92626) ***(P-25915)***
JD Power..........B.......805 418-8000
30870 Russell Ranch Rd Westlake Village (91362) ***(P-25916)***
Jdf Construction Inc..........E.......714 526-1120
201 Gemini Ave Brea (92821) ***(P-1140)***
Jdr Engineering Cons Inc..........C.......949 495-2063
30422 Via Lindosa Laguna Niguel (92677) ***(P-27101)***
JE Williams Trucking Inc..........E.......406 248-7397
1875 Century Park E # 600 Los Angeles (90067) ***(P-4068)***
Jean Mart Inc..........D.......323 752-7775
6700 Avalon Blvd Los Angeles (90003) ***(P-8080)***
JEANNE JUGAN, A RESIDENCE, San Pedro *Also called Little Sisters The Poor of La* ***(P-20085)***
Jeep Gear, Irvine *Also called Alcone Marketing Group Inc* ***(P-13470)***
Jeeva Corp..........D.......909 238-4073
750 E E St Unit B Ontario (91764) ***(P-2525)***
Jeff Boldt Farms, Kingsburg *Also called Jeff W Boldt Farms* ***(P-206)***
Jeff Carpenter Inc..........D.......951 657-5115
1380 W Oleander Ave Perris (92571) ***(P-3320)***
Jeff Kerber Pool Plst Inc..........B.......909 465-0677
166 San Lorenzo St Pomona (91766) ***(P-3425)***
Jeff Stover Inc..........D.......530 345-9427
260 Cohasset Rd Ste 190 Chico (95926) ***(P-18160)***
Jeff Tracy Inc..........E.......949 582-0877
15375 Barranca Pkwy A110 Irvine (92618) ***(P-2165)***
Jeff W Boldt Farms..........D.......559 318-6690
12725 S Smith Ave Kingsburg (93631) ***(P-206)***
Jeffco Painting & Coating Inc..........D.......707 562-1900
1260 Railroad Ave Vallejo (94592) ***(P-2363)***
Jeffer Mngels Btlr Mtchell LLP (PA)..........C.......310 203-8080
1900 Avenue Of The Stars Los Angeles (90067) ***(P-22589)***
Jeffer Mngels Btlr Mtchell LLP..........D.......415 398-8080
2 Embarcadero Ctr Fl 5 San Francisco (94111) ***(P-22590)***
Jefferies LLC..........D.......310 445-1199
11100 Santa Monica Blvd # 12 Los Angeles (90025) ***(P-9702)***
Jefferson California Congress..........D.......760 331-5500
6225 El Camino Real Carlsbad (92009) ***(P-24567)***
Jeffrey Pine Holdings LLC..........D.......619 442-0544
622 S Anza St El Cajon (92020) ***(P-20036)***
Jeffrey Rome & Associates..........D.......949 760-3929
1715 Port Charles Pl Newport Beach (92660) ***(P-25462)***
Jeld-Wen Inc..........B.......760 597-4201
2760 Progress St Ste B Vista (92081) ***(P-6631)***
Jeld-Wen Windows, Vista *Also called Jeld-Wen Inc* ***(P-6631)***
Jelem LLC..........E.......858 457-2202
1455 Frazee Rd Ste 500 San Diego (92108) ***(P-16859)***
Jelight Company Inc..........D.......949 380-8774
2 Mason Irvine (92618) ***(P-7157)***
Jemtown Inc..........E.......916 315-0555
6818 Five Star Blvd Rocklin (95677) ***(P-17378)***
Jenco Productions Inc (PA)..........C.......909 381-9453
401 S J St San Bernardino (92410) ***(P-16860)***
Jencor Door and Trim Inc..........E.......661 251-8161
26845 Oak Ave Ste 12 Canyon Country (91351) ***(P-2944)***
Jenkins Gales & Martinez Inc..........D.......310 645-0561
6033 W Century Blvd # 601 Los Angeles (90045) ***(P-26272)***
Jenny Craig Inc (PA)..........C.......760 696-4000
5770 Fleet St Carlsbad (92008) ***(P-13433)***
Jenny Craig Wght Loss Ctrs Inc (HQ)..........C.......760 696-4000
5770 Fleet St Carlsbad (92008) ***(P-13434)***
Jensco Inc..........E.......831 422-7819
400 Griffin St Salinas (93901) ***(P-2526)***
Jensen Corp Landscape Contr..........C.......408 446-4881
1983 Concourse Dr San Jose (95131) ***(P-835)***
Jensen Corp Landscape Contrs, San Jose *Also called Jensen Landscape Services Inc* ***(P-837)***
Jensen Corporate Holdings Inc (PA)..........C.......408 446-1118
1983 Concourse Dr San Jose (95131) ***(P-836)***
Jensen Enterprises Inc..........D.......916 992-8301
5400 Raley Blvd Sacramento (95838) ***(P-6723)***
Jensen Landscape Services Inc..........C.......408 446-1118
1983 Concourse Dr San Jose (95131) ***(P-837)***
Jensen Precast, Sacramento *Also called Jensen Enterprises Inc* ***(P-6723)***
Jeopardy Productions Inc..........C.......310 244-8855
10202 Washington Blvd Culver City (90232) ***(P-17619)***
Jeppesen Dataplan Inc..........C.......408 961-2825
225 W Santa Clara St # 1 San Jose (95113) ***(P-15871)***
Jeremiah Phillips LLC..........C.......650 697-7733
863 Malcolm Rd Burlingame (94010) ***(P-3899)***
Jerry Melton & Sons Cnstr, Taft *Also called Jerry Melton & Sons Cnstr* ***(P-1029)***
Jerry Melton & Sons Cnstr..........D.......661 765-5546
100 Jamison Ln Taft (93268) ***(P-1029)***
Jerry S Powell MD..........D.......916 734-5959
4501 X St Sacramento (95817) ***(P-19032)***
Jerry Thompson & Sons Pntg Inc..........C.......415 454-1500
3 Simms St San Rafael (94901) ***(P-2364)***
Jesse Alexander Transport..........D.......760 669-0379
9338 Azurite Ave Hesperia (92344) ***(P-5123)***
Jesse Lee Group Inc..........D.......510 351-3700
300 Crprate Pinte Ste 550 Culver City (90230) ***(P-26273)***
Jesse Lee Group Inc..........C.......209 832-2273
2586 Buthmann Ave Tracy (95376) ***(P-26274)***
Jessica Cosmetics Intl Inc..........D.......818 759-1050
13209 Saticoy St North Hollywood (91605) ***(P-7955)***

Jessica's Cosmetics, North Hollywood *Also called Jessica Cosmetics Intl Inc* ***(P-7955)***
Jet Delivery Inc (PA) ....D....800 716-7177
2169 Wright Ave La Verne (91750) ***(P-4273)***
Jet Edge International LLC ....D....818 442-0096
16700 Roscoe Blvd Hngr C Van Nuys (91406) ***(P-4741)***
Jet Health Inc (PA) ....A....949 356-6525
20 Fairbanks Ste 175 Irvine (92618) ***(P-22263)***
Jet Propulsion Laboratory, Pasadena *Also called California Institute Tech* ***(P-25974)***
Jet Sets, North Hollywood *Also called M Gaw Inc* ***(P-3431)***
Jet Source Inc ....D....760 438-0877
2056 Palomar Airport Rd Carlsbad (92011) ***(P-4776)***
Jetblue Airways Corporation ....D....718 286-7900
2627 N Hollywood Way Burbank (91505) ***(P-4669)***
Jetblue Airways Corporation ....D....510 381-1369
130 Alan Shepard Way M Oakland (94621) ***(P-4670)***
Jetblue Airways Corporation ....D....619 725-0807
3707 N Harbor Dr 1 San Diego (92101) ***(P-4671)***
Jetmore International, South El Monte *Also called Jetworld Inc* ***(P-6403)***
Jetmore Wind LLC ....A....888 903-6926
15445 Innovation Dr San Diego (92128) ***(P-5849)***
Jetro Cash and Carry Entps LLC ....D....916 492-2305
1275 Vine St Sacramento (95811) ***(P-8183)***
Jetro Cash and Carry Entps LLC ....C....714 666-8211
1265 N Kraemer Blvd Anaheim (92806) ***(P-8289)***
Jetro Cash and Carry Entps LLC ....D....415 920-2888
2045 Evans Ave San Francisco (94124) ***(P-8409)***
Jetro Cash and Carry Entps LLC ....D....323 964-1200
5333 W Jefferson Blvd Los Angeles (90016) ***(P-8771)***
Jetsuite Inc (PA) ....D....949 892-4300
18952 Macarthur Blvd # 200 Irvine (92612) ***(P-4742)***
Jett Pro Line Maintenance Inc (PA) ....D....909 980-0552
8225 White Oak Ave Rancho Cucamonga (91730) ***(P-4777)***
Jetworld Inc ....C....626 448-0150
2656 Chico Ave South El Monte (91733) ***(P-6403)***
Jewis Vocational & Counseling ....D....415 391-3600
225 Bush St Ste 400 San Francisco (94104) ***(P-23606)***
Jewish Cmnty Fndn of (PA) ....C....323 761-8700
6505 Wilshire Blvd Los Angeles (90048) ***(P-24568)***
Jewish Community Ctr Long Bch ....C....562 426-7601
3801 E Willow St Long Beach (90815) ***(P-23292)***
Jewish Community Fedrtn San Fr (PA) ....D....415 777-0411
121 Steuart St Fl 7 San Francisco (94105) ***(P-24185)***
Jewish Family and Chld Svcs ....D....650 931-1860
200 Channing Ave Palo Alto (94301) ***(P-23293)***
Jewish Family and Chld Svcs (PA) ....D....415 449-1200
2150 Post St San Francisco (94115) ***(P-23294)***
Jewish Family and Chld Svcs ....B....650 688-3030
200 Channing Ave Palo Alto (94301) ***(P-23295)***
Jewish Family Svc Los Angeles (PA) ....E....323 761-8800
3580 Wilshire Blvd Los Angeles (90010) ***(P-24406)***
Jewish Family Svc Los Angeles ....D....818 984-0276
12821 Victory Blvd North Hollywood (91606) ***(P-23296)***
Jewish Family Svc Los Angeles ....E....323 937-5900
330 N Fairfax Ave Los Angeles (90036) ***(P-23297)***
Jewish Family Svc San Diego (PA) ....D....858 637-3000
8804 Balboa Ave San Diego (92123) ***(P-23298)***
Jewish Fmly & Cmnty Svcs E Bay (PA) ....D....510 704-7475
2484 Shattuck Ave Ste 210 Berkeley (94704) ***(P-23299)***
JEWISH FREE LOAN ASSOCIATION, Los Angeles *Also called Jewish Family Svc Los Angeles* ***(P-24406)***
JEWISH HOME FOR THE AGED, San Francisco *Also called Hebrew Home For Aged Disabled* ***(P-20009)***
Jewish Home For The Aging of O ....C....949 364-0010
27356 Bellogente Mission Viejo (92691) ***(P-20037)***
Jewish Senior Living Group ....D....415 562-2600
302 Silver Ave San Francisco (94112) ***(P-10742)***
Jewish Vocational Services (PA) ....E....323 761-8888
6505 Wilshire Blvd # 200 Los Angeles (90048) ***(P-23607)***
Jezowski & Markel Contrs Inc ....C....714 978-2222
749 N Poplar St Orange (92868) ***(P-3166)***
JF Shea Construction Inc ....D....530 246-4292
17400 Clear Creek Rd Redding (96001) ***(P-1141)***
JF Shea Construction Inc ....D....949 526-8792
2 Ada Ste 200 Irvine (92618) ***(P-1142)***
JF Shea Construction Inc ....E....909 594-0998
675 Brea Canyon Rd Ste 8 Walnut (91789) ***(P-1143)***
JF Shea Construction Inc ....B....408 225-1475
6130 Monterey Hwy Ofc San Jose (95138) ***(P-1144)***
JF Shea Construction Inc ....C....925 245-3660
2580 Shea Center Dr Livermore (94551) ***(P-1145)***
Jfc International Inc (HQ) ....C....323 721-6100
7101 E Slauson Ave Commerce (90040) ***(P-8594)***
Jfc International Inc ....C....323 721-6900
7101 E Slauson Ave Commerce (90040) ***(P-8595)***
JFCS/EAST BAY, Berkeley *Also called Jewish Fmly & Cmnty Svcs E Bay* ***(P-23299)***
Jfe Shoji Trade America Inc (HQ) ....D....562 637-3500
301 E Ocean Blvd Ste 1750 Long Beach (90802) ***(P-7073)***
Jfp Company, Norco *Also called Anna Corporation* ***(P-2331)***
JH Bryant Jr Inc (PA) ....E....310 532-1840
17217 S Broadway Gardena (90248) ***(P-1357)***
Jh Capital Partners LP ....E....415 364-0300
451 Jackson St San Francisco (94111) ***(P-11924)***
Jhc Investment Inc ....D....714 751-2400
7 Hutton Centre Dr Santa Ana (92707) ***(P-12488)***
Jhp Produce Inc ....D....213 627-1093
1601 E Olympic Blvd # 200 Los Angeles (90021) ***(P-8491)***
Jiangsu Juwang Info Tech Co (PA) ....D....510 967-3729
195 Recino St Fremont (94539) ***(P-14893)***
Jiff Inc (HQ) ....B....415 829-1400
150 Spear St Ste 400 San Francisco (94105) ***(P-14894)***
Jifflenow, Sunnyvale *Also called Ipolipo Inc* ***(P-15371)***
Jiffy Lube, Los Alamitos *Also called Alamitos Enterprises LLC* ***(P-17406)***
Jilk Heavy Construction Inc ....D....310 830-6323
14732 S Maple Ave Gardena (90248) ***(P-1971)***
Jillians San Francisco CA ....D....415 369-6100
101 4th St Ste 170 San Francisco (94103) ***(P-16861)***
Jim & Doug Carters Automotive ....E....818 842-5702
2612 N Hollywood Way Burbank (91505) ***(P-17259)***
Jim Henson Company Inc (PA) ....D....323 856-6680
1416 N La Brea Ave Los Angeles (90028) ***(P-17620)***
Jim Murphy & Associates, Santa Rosa *Also called Murphy-True Inc* ***(P-1547)***
Jimenez Nursery Inc ....D....805 684-7955
3800 Via Real Carpinteria (93013) ***(P-251)***
Jimenez Nursery and Landscapes, Carpinteria *Also called Jimenez Nursery Inc* ***(P-251)***
Jimmy Kimmel Live, Los Angeles *Also called ABC Cable Networks Group* ***(P-5506)***
Jimmys Fashions ....E....818 790-8932
3135 Chadney Dr Glendale (91206) ***(P-16862)***
Jims Steel Supply LLC ....E....661 324-6514
3530 Buck Owens Blvd Bakersfield (93308) ***(P-26660)***
Jims Supply Co Inc (PA) ....D....661 616-6977
3500 Buck Owens Blvd Bakersfield (93308) ***(P-7074)***
Jinx Inc (PA) ....D....888 546-9266
13465 Gregg St Poway (92064) ***(P-7736)***
Jinx Hackwear/Jinx.com, Poway *Also called Jinx Inc* ***(P-7736)***
Jipc Management Inc ....A....949 916-2000
22342 Avenida Empresa # 220 Rcho STA Marg (92688) ***(P-26275)***
JIT Corporation ....D....805 238-5000
2790 Valley View Ave Norco (92860) ***(P-7285)***
Jj Fisher Construction Inc ....D....805 723-5220
261 W Dana St Ste 100 Nipomo (93444) ***(P-1738)***
Jj Grand Hotel ....D....213 383-3000
620 S Harvard Blvd Los Angeles (90005) ***(P-12489)***
JJ Mac Intyre Co Inc (PA) ....C....951 898-4300
4160 Temescal Canyon Rd Corona (92883) ***(P-13688)***
JJ Rios Farm Services Inc ....D....209 333-7467
4890 E Acampo Rd Acampo (95220) ***(P-628)***
Jjj Floor Covering Inc (PA) ....D....562 692-9008
4831 Passons Blvd Ste A Pico Rivera (90660) ***(P-3011)***
JJR Enterprises Inc (PA) ....D....916 363-2666
10491 Old Placerville Rd # 150 Sacramento (95827) ***(P-17457)***
Jk Consultants ....E....209 532-7772
160 Station Way Unit 102 Arroyo Grande (93421) ***(P-27102)***
Jk Imaging Ltd ....D....310 755-6848
17239 S Main St Gardena (90248) ***(P-6733)***
JKB Corporation ....E....562 905-3477
561 S Walnut St La Habra (90631) ***(P-3167)***
Jkf Auto Service Inc ....D....916 315-0555
6818 Five Star Blvd Rocklin (95677) ***(P-17379)***
Jla Home, Woodland *Also called E & E Co Ltd* ***(P-1118)***
Jla Home, Fremont *Also called E & E Co Ltd* ***(P-6553)***
Jlg Harvesting Inc ....B....831 422-7871
27 Zabala Rd Salinas (93908) ***(P-507)***
Jlp Landscape Contracting ....E....707 526-6285
901 7th St Santa Rosa (95404) ***(P-838)***
Jls Environmental Services Inc ....D....916 660-1525
3460 Swetzer Rd Loomis (95650) ***(P-26951)***
JM Roofing Company Inc ....D....805 966-3696
534 E Ortega St Santa Barbara (93103) ***(P-3066)***
JM Streamline Inc ....D....530 272-6806
154 Scandling Ave Grass Valley (95945) ***(P-1512)***
Jma Investments Ltd ....D....916 685-1355
9265 Beatty Dr Sacramento (95826) ***(P-839)***
Jmac Lending Inc ....D....949 390-2688
2510 Redhill Ave Santa Ana (92705) ***(P-9464)***
JMB Construction Inc ....D....650 267-5300
132 S Maple Ave South San Francisco (94080) ***(P-1875)***
Jmbm, Los Angeles *Also called Jeffer Mngels Btlr Mtchell LLP* ***(P-22589)***
Jme Inc (PA) ....C....201 896-8600
527 Prk Ave San Fernando San Fernando (91340) ***(P-7158)***
Jmg Security Systems Inc ....D....714 545-8882
17150 Newhope St Ste 109 Fountain Valley (92708) ***(P-2527)***
JMJ Financial Group (PA) ....E....949 340-6336
26800 Aliso Viejo Pkwy # 200 Aliso Viejo (92656) ***(P-9566)***
Jmp Securities LLC (HQ) ....D....415 835-8900
600 Montgomery St # 1100 San Francisco (94111) ***(P-9703)***
JMS Realtors Ltd (PA) ....C....559 490-1500
575 E Alluvial Ave # 101 Fresno (93720) ***(P-11220)***
Jmt Charitable Foundation ....D....415 974-6000
1 Market Ste 620 San Francisco (94105) ***(P-25620)***
Jn Projects Inc ....D....415 766-0273
333 Brannan St San Francisco (94107) ***(P-13435)***
Jnr Inc ....D....949 476-2788
19900 Macarthur Blvd # 700 Irvine (92612) ***(P-26661)***
Joan Kroc Center, Mission Viejo *Also called St Vincent De Paul Vlg Inc* ***(P-24875)***
Joan Young Co Realtors, Westlake Village *Also called Young Realtors* ***(P-11526)***
Job Options Incorporated ....A....909 890-4612
1110 S Washington Ave San Bernardino (92408) ***(P-13322)***
Jobs Plus, Chico *Also called Caminar* ***(P-21963)***
Jobs Plus, San Ramon *Also called Plus Group Inc* ***(P-14357)***
Jobvite Inc (PA) ....D....650 376-7200
1300 S El Camino Real # 400 San Mateo (94402) ***(P-26662)***
Joe & Mary Mottino YMCA, Oceanside *Also called YMCA of San Diego County* ***(P-24717)***
Joe Campagna ....D....619 222-0555
2830 Shelter Island Dr San Diego (92106) ***(P-11221)***
Joe Heidrick Enterprises Inc ....E....530 662-2339
36826 County Road 24 Woodland (95695) ***(P-8)***

ALPHABETIC

Employee Codes: A=Over 500 employees, B=251-500
C=101-250, D=51-100, E=50
2020 Directory of California
Wholesalers and Services Companies
© Mergent Inc. 1-800-342-5647
1313

Joe L Coelho Inc ....E.......209 667-2676
18637 E Bradbury Rd Turlock (95380) ***(P-4069)***
Joe Lunardi Electric Inc ....D.......707 545-4755
5334 Sebastopol Rd Santa Rosa (95407) ***(P-2528)***
Joe Pucci & Sons Seafoods, Hayward *Also called Blue River Seafood Inc* ***(P-8364)***
Joe's Auto Parks, Los Angeles *Also called L and R Auto Parks Inc* ***(P-17260)***
Joerns LLC (HQ) ....C.......800 966-6662
19748 Dearborn St Chatsworth (91311) ***(P-6973)***
Joes Sweeping Inc ....D.......562 929-4344
11914 Front St Norwalk (90650) ***(P-6215)***
Joguru Inc ....D.......855 526-4332
2600 El Camino Real Ste 4 Palo Alto (94306) ***(P-4854)***
Johannes Flowers Inc ....D.......805 684-5686
4990 Foothill Rd Carpinteria (93013) ***(P-252)***
John A Maida Enterprises ....E.......408 254-3100
P.O. Box 6144 San Jose (95150) ***(P-7859)***
John Aguilar & Company Inc ....D.......209 546-0171
1505 Navy Dr Stockton (95206) ***(P-3900)***
John Alden Life Insurance Co ....D.......818 595-7600
20950 Warner Center Ln A Woodland Hills (91367) ***(P-9869)***
John Brink General Contractor ....E.......530 583-2005
1760 W Lake Blvd Ste 3 Tahoe City (96145) ***(P-1739)***
John C Fremont Healthcare Dst ....C.......209 966-3631
5189 Hospital Rd Mariposa (95338) ***(P-20918)***
John Collins Co Inc ....D.......818 227-2190
5155 Cedarwood Rd Mgr Bonita (91902) ***(P-10743)***
John Deere Authorized Dealer, Fresno *Also called Vucovich Inc* ***(P-7512)***
John Deere Authorized Dealer, Manteca *Also called J M Equipment Company Inc* ***(P-14171)***
John Deere Authorized Dealer, Poway *Also called Bay City Equipment Inds Inc* ***(P-7128)***
John Deere Authorized Dealer, Firebaugh *Also called Thomason Tractor Co California* ***(P-7509)***
John Deere Authorized Dealer, Visalia *Also called Lawrence Tractor Coinc* ***(P-7502)***
John Deere Authorized Dealer, Colton *Also called A-Z Bus Sales Inc* ***(P-6376)***
John Deere Authorized Dealer, Lakeside *Also called Rdo Construction Equipment Co* ***(P-14111)***
John Deere Authorized Dealer, Sacramento *Also called Pape Machinery Inc* ***(P-7482)***
John Deere Authorized Dealer, Riverside *Also called Complete Coach Works* ***(P-17415)***
John Deere Authorized Dealer, Riverside *Also called Rdo Construction Equipment Co* ***(P-7506)***
John F Dmingue Attorney At Law ....C.......408 591-5180
10 Almaden Blvd Ste 1100 San Jose (95113) ***(P-22591)***
John F Kennedy Memorial Hosp ....A.......760 347-6191
47111 Monroe St Indio (92201) ***(P-20919)***
John F Knnedy Mem Hosp Emrgncy, Indio *Also called John F Kennedy Memorial Hosp* ***(P-20919)***
John F Otto Inc ....C.......916 441-6870
1717 2nd St Sacramento (95811) ***(P-1513)***
John G Shipley ....D.......714 626-2000
100 W Valencia Mesa Dr # 201 Fullerton (92835) ***(P-11222)***
John Gore Organization Inc ....D.......650 340-0469
255 S B St San Mateo (94401) ***(P-17919)***
John Grizzle Farming ....E.......760 356-4381
1395 Bonds Corner Rd Holtville (92250) ***(P-340)***
John H Kautz Farms ....E.......209 334-4786
5490 Bear Creek Rd Lodi (95240) ***(P-437)***
John Hancock, Irvine *Also called Signature Resources Insurance* ***(P-10494)***
John Hancock Life Insur Co USA (HQ) ....A.......213 689-0813
865 S Figueroa St # 3320 Los Angeles (90017) ***(P-10397)***
John Jackson Masonry ....D.......916 381-8021
5691 Power Inn Rd Ste B Sacramento (95824) ***(P-2719)***
John Jory Corporation (PA) ....B.......714 279-7901
2180 N Glassell St Orange (92865) ***(P-2806)***
John Kenney Construction Inc ....D.......805 884-1579
619 E Montecito St Santa Barbara (93103) ***(P-3168)***
John L Ginger Masonry Inc ....D.......951 688-5050
8188 Lincoln Ave Ste 100 Riverside (92504) ***(P-2720)***
John M Adams Jr MD ....D.......310 829-2663
1301 20th St Ste 150 Santa Monica (90404) ***(P-19033)***
John M Frank Construction Inc ....D.......714 210-3600
913 E 4th St Santa Ana (92701) ***(P-1514)***
John M Frank Service Group, Santa Ana *Also called John M Frank Construction Inc* ***(P-1514)***
John M Phillips LLC (PA) ....D.......562 595-7363
2755 Dawson Ave Signal Hill (90755) ***(P-14100)***
John M Phillips Oil Field Eqp, Signal Hill *Also called John M Phillips LLC* ***(P-14100)***
John Muir Behavioral Hlth Ctr ....C.......925 674-4100
2740 Grant St Concord (94520) ***(P-21413)***
John Muir Health ....A.......925 692-5600
5003 Commercial Cir Concord (94520) ***(P-20920)***
John Muir Health ....A.......925 952-2887
380 Civic Dr Ste 100 Pleasant Hill (94523) ***(P-20921)***
John Muir Health (HQ) ....A.......925 947-4449
1601 Ygnacio Valley Rd Walnut Creek (94598) ***(P-20922)***
John Muir Health ....E.......925 947-5300
1981 N Broadway Ste 180 Walnut Creek (94596) ***(P-20923)***
John Muir Health ....A.......925 939-3000
1601 Ygnacio Valley Rd Walnut Creek (94598) ***(P-20924)***
John Muir Health ....A.......925 682-8200
2540 East St Concord (94520) ***(P-20925)***
John Muir Med Ctr Cncord Cmpus, Concord *Also called John Muir Health* ***(P-20925)***
John Muir Medical Center, Walnut Creek *Also called John Muir Physician Network* ***(P-20929)***
John Muir Medical Center, Walnut Creek *Also called John Muir Health* ***(P-20924)***
John Muir Physician Network ....A.......925 952-2701
112 La Casa Via Ste 300 Walnut Creek (94598) ***(P-20926)***
John Muir Physician Network ....A.......925 685-0843
91 Gregory Ln Ste 15 Pleasant Hill (94523) ***(P-20927)***
John Muir Physician Network ....A.......925 682-8200
2540 East St Concord (94520) ***(P-20928)***
John Muir Physician Network (PA) ....A.......925 296-9700
1450 Treat Blvd Walnut Creek (94597) ***(P-20929)***
John Muir Physician Network ....B.......925 939-3000
1601 Ygnacio Valley Rd Walnut Creek (94598) ***(P-20930)***
John Muir Physician Network ....E.......925 838-4633
1505 Saint Alphonsus Way Alamo (94507) ***(P-19034)***
John Muir Physician Network ....A.......925 674-2200
2720 Grant St Concord (94520) ***(P-20931)***
John Paul USA (PA) ....C.......415 905-6088
575 Market St Ste 3050 San Francisco (94105) ***(P-14518)***
John Plane Construction Inc ....C.......415 468-0555
661 Hayne Rd Hillsborough (94010) ***(P-1515)***
John Shannon Mc Gee Co Inc ....E.......562 789-1777
8190 Byron Rd Whittier (90606) ***(P-7159)***
John Stewart Company ....D.......707 676-5660
191 Heritage Ln Dixon (95620) ***(P-11223)***
John Stewart Company ....E.......213 787-2700
888 S Figueroa St Ste 700 Los Angeles (90017) ***(P-11224)***
John Stewart Company ....C.......415 345-4400
2451 Meadowview Rd Sacramento (95832) ***(P-10744)***
John Stewart Company (PA) ....D.......415 345-4400
1388 Sutter St Ste 1100 San Francisco (94109) ***(P-11225)***
John Tillman Company, Compton *Also called Blake H Brown Inc* ***(P-7530)***
John Wayne Airport, Costa Mesa *Also called County of Orange* ***(P-4765)***
John Wayne Institute For Ctr ....C.......310 449-5253
2200 Santa Monica Blvd Santa Monica (90404) ***(P-26000)***
John's Incredible Pizza Co, Rcho STA Marg *Also called Jipc Management Inc* ***(P-26275)***
John's Pet Products, San Jose *Also called Johns Dog Food Distributing* ***(P-8596)***
Johnre Care LLC ....D.......951 658-6374
461 E Johnston Ave Hemet (92543) ***(P-20038)***
Johns Dog Food Distributing ....D.......408 275-1943
1633 Monterey Hwy San Jose (95112) ***(P-8596)***
Johnsen Construction Inc ....D.......530 642-2123
6448 Capitol Ave Diamond Springs (95619) ***(P-3169)***
Johnson & Johnson Pistaccios ....E.......818 242-7853
1720 Ben Lomond Dr Glendale (91202) ***(P-27)***
Johnson & Turner Painting Co ....E.......714 828-8282
8241 Electric Ave Stanton (90680) ***(P-2365)***
Johnson Air, Clovis *Also called Ladell Inc* ***(P-2179)***
Johnson Cntrls SEC Sltions LLC ....C.......818 428-6669
104 E Graham Pl Burbank (91502) ***(P-16529)***
Johnson Cntrls SEC Sltions LLC ....D.......951 787-0420
1120 Palmyrita Ave # 280 Riverside (92507) ***(P-16530)***
Johnson Cntrls SEC Sltions LLC ....C.......561 988-3600
3870 Murphy Canyon Rd # 140 San Diego (92123) ***(P-16531)***
Johnson Cntrls SEC Sltions LLC ....D.......650 634-9000
150 N Hill Dr Ste 3 Brisbane (94005) ***(P-16532)***
Johnson Cntrls SEC Sltions LLC ....D.......510 246-2862
3825 Bay Center Pl B Hayward (94545) ***(P-16533)***
Johnson Cntrls SEC Sltions LLC ....C.......714 223-2300
7565 Irvine Center Dr # 100 Irvine (92618) ***(P-16534)***
Johnson Contrls Authorized Dlr, Pleasant Hill *Also called Buildings Iot Inc* ***(P-7415)***
Johnson Controls ....D.......805 642-0366
1868 Palma Dr Ventura (93003) ***(P-2166)***
Johnson Controls ....C.......562 405-3817
12728 Shoemaker Ave Santa Fe Springs (90670) ***(P-16535)***
Johnson Controls ....D.......707 578-3212
3077 Wiljan Ct Ste B Santa Rosa (95407) ***(P-2167)***
Johnson Controls Inc ....D.......805 522-5555
1757 Tapo Canyon Rd # 120 Simi Valley (93063) ***(P-7286)***
Johnson Controls Inc ....D.......707 546-3042
2226 Northpoint Pkwy Santa Rosa (95407) ***(P-25162)***
Johnson Fain Inc ....D.......323 224-6000
1201 N Broadway Los Angeles (90012) ***(P-25463)***
Johnson La Follette ....D.......714 558-7008
2677 N Main St Ste 901 Santa Ana (92705) ***(P-22592)***
Johnson Machinery Co (PA) ....C.......951 686-4560
800 E La Cadena Dr Riverside (92507) ***(P-7481)***
Johnson Ranch Racquet Club, Roseville *Also called Spare-Time Inc* ***(P-18581)***
Johnson Service Group Inc ....A.......408 728-9510
950 S Bascom Ave San Jose (95128) ***(P-10614)***
Johnson/Johnson, Glendale *Also called Johnson & Johnson Pistaccios* ***(P-27)***
Johnston Farms Fmly Ltd Partnr ....D.......661 366-3201
13031 E Packinghouse Rd Edison (93220) ***(P-191)***
Johnston Vacuum Tank Service, Taft *Also called Watkins Construction Co Inc* ***(P-1931)***
Joie, Vernon *Also called Collected Group Company LLC* ***(P-8066)***
Joie De Vivre Hospitality LLC ....A.......408 335-1700
210 E Main St Los Gatos (95030) ***(P-2529)***
Joie De Vivre Hospitality LLC (PA) ....E.......415 835-0300
1750 Geary Blvd San Francisco (94115) ***(P-12490)***
Joie De Vivre Hospitality LLC ....D.......415 986-2000
386 Geary St San Francisco (94102) ***(P-26276)***
Joie De Vivre Hospitality LLC ....D.......650 879-1100
2001 Rossi Rd Pescadero (94060) ***(P-26277)***
Joie De Vivre Hospitality Inc ....D.......408 738-0500
910 E Fremont Ave Sunnyvale (94087) ***(P-12491)***
Jolly Roger Inn, Anaheim *Also called Edward Thomas Companies* ***(P-12239)***
Jomar Industries Inc ....E.......323 770-0505
1500 W 139th St Gardena (90249) ***(P-16863)***
Jon K Takata Corporation (PA) ....D.......510 315-5400
4142 Point Eden Way Hayward (94545) ***(P-23300)***
Jon Wayne Construction, Vista *Also called Jwc Construction Inc* ***(P-1252)***
Jonathan Beach Club, Santa Monica *Also called Jonathan Club* ***(P-18472)***
Jonathan Club (PA) ....B.......213 624-0881
545 S Figueroa St Los Angeles (90071) ***(P-24569)***
Jonathan Club ....C.......310 393-9245
850 Palisades Beach Rd Santa Monica (90403) ***(P-18472)***

Jonbec Care Incorporated (PA)....D....909 798-4003
1711 Plum Ln Redlands (92374) ***(P-20434)***
Jonce Thomas Construction Co....E....510 657-7171
3390 Seldon Ct Fremont (94539) ***(P-2945)***
Jones & Jones MGT Group Inc....C....818 594-0019
8220 Topanga Canyon Blvd Canoga Park (91304) ***(P-10745)***
Jones Bold Security Inc....D....562 316-6552
7520 Sleepy Creek Ave Fontana (92336) ***(P-16331)***
Jones Covey Group, Rancho Cucamonga *Also called Jones/Covey Group Incorporated* ***(P-3426)***
Jones Day Limited Partnership....D....858 314-1200
4655 Executive Dr # 1500 San Diego (92121) ***(P-22593)***
Jones Day Limited Partnership....D....415 626-3939
555 California St # 2600 San Francisco (94104) ***(P-22594)***
Jones Day Limited Partnership....D....949 851-3939
3161 Michelson Dr Ste 800 Irvine (92612) ***(P-22595)***
Jones Day Limited Partnership....D....650 739-3939
1755 Embarcadero Rd Palo Alto (94303) ***(P-22596)***
Jones Lang La Salle....D....213 239-6000
515 S Flower St Fl 13 Los Angeles (90071) ***(P-11859)***
Jones Lang Lasalle Inc....C....415 395-4900
4444 Mkt St Ste 1100 San Francisco (94111) ***(P-11226)***
Jones Lang Lsalle Americas Inc....C....949 296-3600
2211 Michelson Dr Irvine (92612) ***(P-9827)***
Jones Sign Co Inc....C....858 569-1400
9025 Balboa Ave Ste 150 San Diego (92123) ***(P-6927)***
Jones Valley Resorts, Redding *Also called Shasta Lake Resorts LP* ***(P-18757)***
Jones/Covey Group Incorporated....D....888 972-7581
9595 Lucas Ranch Rd # 100 Rancho Cucamonga (91730) ***(P-3426)***
Joni and Friends (PA)....D....818 707-5664
30009 Ladyface Ct Agoura (91301) ***(P-23301)***
Jonset Corporation....D....949 551-5151
16251 Construction Cir W Irvine (92606) ***(P-6350)***
Jopari Solutions Inc....D....925 459-5200
1855 Gateway Blvd Ste 500 Concord (94520) ***(P-16864)***
Jordana Cosmetics LLC....D....310 730-4400
2035 E 49th St Vernon (90058) ***(P-7956)***
Jordano's Food Service, Santa Barbara *Also called Jordanos Inc* ***(P-8772)***
Jordanos Inc (PA)....C....805 964-0611
550 S Patterson Ave Santa Barbara (93111) ***(P-8772)***
Jorge Pimental Diaz....C....661 344-5139
348 Manzanita Dr Delano (93215) ***(P-629)***
Jorgensen & Co, Fresno *Also called Jorgensen & Sons Inc* ***(P-7819)***
Jorgensen & Sons Inc (PA)....D....559 268-6241
2467 Foundry Park Ave Fresno (93706) ***(P-7819)***
Jose Vramontes....E....209 810-5384
14345 N Highway 88 Lodi (95240) ***(P-341)***
Joseph A Foroosh Dental Corp (PA)....D....760 241-3336
12640 Hesperia Rd Ste A Victorville (92395) ***(P-19613)***
Joseph C Sansone Company (PA)....D....818 226-3400
21300 Victory Blvd # 300 Woodland Hills (91367) ***(P-22597)***
Joseph Cozza Salon Inc (PA)....D....415 433-3030
77 Maiden Ln Fl 2 San Francisco (94108) ***(P-13351)***
Joseph Dipuzo....E....760 325-1200
601 E Tahquitz Canyon Way # 120 Palm Springs (92262) ***(P-13185)***
Joseph Farms Cheese, Atwater *Also called Gallo Cattle Co A Ltd Partnr* ***(P-392)***
Joseph J Albanese Inc....A....408 727-5700
851 Martin Ave Santa Clara (95050) ***(P-3170)***
Joseph Jensen Filtration Plant, Granada Hills *Also called Metropolitan Water District* ***(P-6088)***
Joseph T Ryerson & Son Inc....D....323 267-6000
4310 Bandini Blvd Vernon (90058) ***(P-7075)***
Josephine's Personnel Services, San Jose *Also called Josephines Prof Staffing* ***(P-14316)***
Josephines Prof Staffing (PA)....C....408 943-0111
2158 Ringwood Ave San Jose (95131) ***(P-14316)***
Joshua J Bodenstadt CPA A Prof....E....858 642-5050
4225 Executive Sq Ste 900 La Jolla (92037) ***(P-25621)***
Joy Senior Inc....C....805 577-0926
6593 Collins Dr Ste D10 Moorpark (93021) ***(P-21792)***
Joyent Inc....C....415 400-0600
655 Montgomery St # 1600 San Francisco (94111) ***(P-16047)***
Joyride Coffee Distrs LLC....D....718 841-7206
1485 Yosemite Ave San Francisco (94124) ***(P-8597)***
JP Allen Inc....B....818 841-4770
150 E Angeleno Ave Burbank (91502) ***(P-10746)***
JP Allen Extended Stay....E....818 841-4770
150 E Angeleno Ave Burbank (91502) ***(P-12492)***
JP Allen Extended Stay (PA)....C....818 956-0202
450 Pioneer Dr Glendale (91203) ***(P-12493)***
JP Morgan Securities LLC....D....310 201-2693
14061 Mercado Dr Del Mar (92014) ***(P-9704)***
JP Motorsports Inc....D....818 381-8313
11582 Sheldon St Sun Valley (91352) ***(P-3689)***
Jpa Landscape & Cnstr Inc....D....925 960-9602
256 Boeing Ct Livermore (94551) ***(P-840)***
Jpi Development Group Inc....D....951 973-7680
41205 Golden Gate Cir Murrieta (92562) ***(P-2168)***
Jpmorgan Chase Bank Nat Assn....C....707 864-4700
5095 Business Center Dr Fairfield (94534) ***(P-9097)***
Jpmorgan Chase Bank Nat Assn....C....949 429-6071
1995 Santa Ana Ave Costa Mesa (92627) ***(P-16865)***
Jpmorgan Chase Bank Nat Assn....D....626 795-5177
860 E Colorado Blvd Pasadena (91101) ***(P-9264)***
Jpmorgan Chase Bank Nat Assn....C....805 482-2902
502 Las Posas Rd Camarillo (93010) ***(P-16866)***
Jpmorgan Chase Bank Nat Assn....E....818 763-7343
12051 Ventura Blvd Studio City (91604) ***(P-9265)***
Jpmorgan Chase Bank Nat Assn....D....626 919-3129
100 S Vincent Ave Fl 1 West Covina (91790) ***(P-9098)***
Jpmorgan Chase Bank Nat Assn....E....619 424-8197
1100 Palm Ave Imperial Beach (91932) ***(P-9099)***
Jpmorgan Chase Bank Nat Assn....A....209 460-2888
400 E Main St Fl 2 Stockton (95202) ***(P-9280)***
Jpmorgan Xign Corporation....D....925 469-9446
7077 Koll Center Pkwy Pleasanton (94566) ***(P-25622)***
Jr Construction Inc....D....858 505-4760
8123 Engineer Rd San Diego (92111) ***(P-1516)***
JR Filanc Cnstr Co Inc (PA)....D....760 941-7130
740 N Andreasen Dr Escondido (92029) ***(P-1876)***
JR Perce Plbg Inc Sacramento....C....916 434-9554
3610 Cincinnati Ave Rocklin (95765) ***(P-2169)***
JR Simplot Company....C....559 439-3900
3265 W Figarden Dr Fresno (93711) ***(P-8841)***
JR Simplot Company....E....559 659-2033
35836 W Bullard Ave Firebaugh (93622) ***(P-8842)***
Jri Inc....E....818 706-2424
31280 La Baya Dr Westlake Village (91362) ***(P-7287)***
JS Homen Trucking Inc....D....209 723-9559
4224 Turlock Rd Snelling (95369) ***(P-3901)***
Js Hospitality Group LLC....D....805 988-3600
600 E Esplanade Dr Oxnard (93036) ***(P-12494)***
JS International Shipg Corp (PA)....D....650 697-3963
33215 Dowe Ave Union City (94587) ***(P-4974)***
JS Real Estate Prpts Inc....D....310 856-6868
134 W 168th St Gardena (90248) ***(P-3266)***
Jsi Shipping, Union City *Also called JS International Shipg Corp* ***(P-4974)***
Jsl Technologies Inc....B....805 985-7700
1451 N Rice Ave Ste A Oxnard (93030) ***(P-25163)***
JT Wimsatt Contg Co Inc (PA)....D....661 775-8090
28064 Avenue Stanford B Valencia (91355) ***(P-3171)***
Jt3 LLC....A....661 277-4900
190 S Wolfe Ave Bldg 1260 Edwards (93524) ***(P-25164)***
Jtb Americas Ltd (HQ)....D....310 303-3750
19700 Mariner Ave Torrance (90503) ***(P-4827)***
Juan Lopez....D....619 428-3138
3065 Beyer Blvd Ste B106 San Diego (92154) ***(P-1146)***
Judson Enterprises Inc (PA)....B....916 596-6721
2440 Gold River Rd # 100 Rancho Cordova (95670) ***(P-1251)***
Judy Madrigal & Associates Inc....A....650 873-3444
2000 Alameda De Las Pulga San Mateo (94403) ***(P-19035)***
Jules and Associates Inc....D....213 362-5600
515 S Figueroa St # 1900 Los Angeles (90071) ***(P-14174)***
Julio Gonzalez....D....310 310-4055
1417 S Fairfax Ave Apt 4 Los Angeles (90019) ***(P-27103)***
Julius Steve Construction Inc....E....949 369-7820
230 Calle Pintoresco San Clemente (92672) ***(P-1358)***
Jump Dance Convention, North Hollywood *Also called Break Floor Productions LLC* ***(P-17889)***
Jumpshot Inc....D....415 212-9250
333 Bryant St Ste 240 San Francisco (94107) ***(P-14895)***
Jumpstart Automotive Media, San Francisco *Also called Jumpstart Digital Mktg Inc* ***(P-26663)***
Jumpstart Digital Mktg Inc (HQ)....D....415 844-6336
550 Kearny St Ste 500 San Francisco (94108) ***(P-26663)***
Jumpstart Games Inc....D....424 645-4311
500 W 190th St Ste 300 Gardena (90248) ***(P-14896)***
June A Grothe Construction Inc....D....909 993-9393
15632 El Prado Rd Chino (91710) ***(P-1517)***
June Group LLC....D....858 450-4290
9444 Waples St Ste 100 San Diego (92121) ***(P-14519)***
Jungle Fun & Adventure, Concord *Also called Leisure Planet* ***(P-18717)***
Juniper Hotel, Cupertino *Also called Cupertino Lessee LLC* ***(P-12193)***
Juniper Networks Inc....A....408 745-2000
1137 Innovation Way B Sunnyvale (94089) ***(P-15625)***
Juniper Networks Inc....D....805 880-2000
6868 Cortona Dr Ste C Goleta (93117) ***(P-15626)***
Juniper Networks Inc....D....916 503-1593
1215 K St Fl 17 Sacramento (95814) ***(P-15627)***
Juniper Networks Inc....A....888 586-4737
1133 Innovation Way A Sunnyvale (94089) ***(P-15628)***
Jupiter Holding I Corp (HQ)....A....909 606-1416
13925 City Center Dr # 200 Chino Hills (91709) ***(P-7714)***
Jurlique Hlistic Skin Care Inc (PA)....E....914 998-8800
234 E Colo Blvd Ste 450 Pasadena (91101) ***(P-18161)***
Jurupa Stadium Cinema 14, Riverside *Also called Edwards Theatres Circuit Inc* ***(P-17832)***
Jury Insight, Playa Vista *Also called Kelton Research LLC* ***(P-25917)***
Just Desserts, Fairfield *Also called New Desserts Inc* ***(P-8617)***
Just Mortgage Inc....C....562 908-5000
8577 Haven Ave Ste 306 Rancho Cucamonga (91730) ***(P-9567)***
Justice California Department....A....916 324-5039
1300 I St Ste 720 Sacramento (95814) ***(P-27104)***
Justman Packaging & Display....D....323 728-8888
5819 Telegraph Rd Commerce (90040) ***(P-6928)***
Juvenile Hall, Indio *Also called County of Riverside* ***(P-23879)***
Juvenile Justice Division Cal....B....805 485-7951
3100 Wright Rd Camarillo (93010) ***(P-26278)***
Jvc Americas Corp....D....562 463-8110
11925 Pike St Santa Fe Springs (90670) ***(P-17435)***
Jvc Service & Engineering, Santa Fe Springs *Also called Jvc Americas Corp* ***(P-17435)***
Jvckenwood USA Corporation (HQ)....C....310 639-9000
2201 E Dominguez St Long Beach (90810) ***(P-7207)***
JVSLA, Los Angeles *Also called Jewish Vocational Services* ***(P-23607)***
JW Marriott Desert, Palm Desert *Also called Host Hotels & Resorts LP* ***(P-12389)***
JW Marriott Le Merigot, Santa Monica *Also called C W Hotels Ltd* ***(P-12102)***
Jwc Construction Inc (PA)....E....760 727-2494
2580 Fortune Way Vista (92081) ***(P-1252)***

A L P H A B E T I C

Employee Codes: A=Over 500 employees, B=251-500
C=101-250, D=51-100, E=50
2020 Directory of California
Wholesalers and Services Companies
© Mergent Inc. 1-800-342-5647
1315

Jwc Construction Inc...E...949 252-2107
4570 Campus Dr Newport Beach (92660) ***(P-1253)***
Jwch Institute Inc...D...562 867-7999
14371 Clark Ave Bellflower (90706) ***(P-22264)***
Jwch Institute Inc...D...323 562-5813
6912 Ajax Ave Bell (90201) ***(P-26001)***
Jwch Institute Inc...D...562 281-0306
12360 Firestone Blvd Norwalk (90650) ***(P-26002)***
JWdangelo Company Inc...E...562 690-1000
601 S Harbor Blvd La Habra (90631) ***(P-7673)***
Jwmcc Limited Partnership...B...310 277-1234
2151 Avenue Of The Stars Los Angeles (90067) ***(P-12495)***
Jyg Concrete Construction Inc...C...661 607-0337
24841 Avenue Tibbitts Valencia (91355) ***(P-3172)***
K & P Janitorial Services...D...310 540-8878
412 S Pacific Coast Hwy # 200 Redondo Beach (90277) ***(P-13958)***
K & S Air Conditioning Inc...C...714 685-0077
143 E Meats Ave Orange (92865) ***(P-2170)***
K & S Auto, Truck & Tractor, Bay Point *Also called K & S Towing & Transport* ***(P-26664)***
K & S Towing & Transport...D...925 709-0759
2780 Willow Pass Rd Bay Point (94565) ***(P-26664)***
K A Associates Inc...C...310 556-2721
1800 Avenue Of The Stars # 200 Los Angeles (90067) ***(P-9705)***
K B I, Anaheim *Also called Kinsbursky Bros Supply Inc* ***(P-7763)***
K C C, El Segundo *Also called Carson Kurtzman Consultants* ***(P-22413)***
K E, Irvine *Also called Kite Electric Inc* ***(P-2533)***
K E M A, Oakland *Also called Dnv GL Energy Insights USA Inc* ***(P-27051)***
K E S, San Diego *Also called Koam Engineering Systems Inc* ***(P-15630)***
K G O T V News Bureau...D...510 451-4772
520 3rd St Ste 200 Oakland (94607) ***(P-5544)***
K G S Electronics, Arcadia *Also called Gar Enterprises* ***(P-6840)***
K G Walters Cnstr Co Inc...D...707 527-9968
195 Concourse Blvd Ste A Santa Rosa (95403) ***(P-1972)***
K Hovnanian, Irvine *Also called K Hovnanian Companies Cal Inc* ***(P-1147)***
K Hovnanian Companies Cal Inc (HQ)...D...714 368-4500
400 Exchange Ste 200 Irvine (92602) ***(P-1147)***
K K R, Menlo Park *Also called Kohlberg Kravis Roberts Co LP* ***(P-11928)***
K K W Trucking Inc (PA)...B...909 869-1200
3100 Pomona Blvd Pomona (91768) ***(P-4439)***
K Line America Inc...E...714 861-5000
950 S Coast Dr Ste 178 Costa Mesa (92626) ***(P-4585)***
K O X R, Oxnard *Also called Koxr Spanish Radio* ***(P-5548)***
K P F F Consulting Engineers, Los Angeles *Also called Kpff Inc* ***(P-25179)***
K R Anderson Inc (PA)...D...408 825-1800
18330 Sutter Blvd Morgan Hill (95037) ***(P-8701)***
K R G, Valencia *Also called Krg Technologies Inc* ***(P-14904)***
K S B W- T V, Salinas *Also called Hearst Stations Inc* ***(P-5610)***
K S Fabrication & Machine Inc...C...661 617-1700
6205 District Blvd Bakersfield (93313) ***(P-1877)***
K S I, Bakersfield *Also called KS Industries LP* ***(P-1881)***
K S S C - F M, Los Angeles *Also called Entravsion Communications Corp* ***(P-5597)***
K S S J Radio-101.9 FM City, Sacramento *Also called Entercom Communications Corp* ***(P-5527)***
K T A Construction Inc...D...619 562-9464
1920 Cordell Ct Ste 105 El Cajon (92020) ***(P-1878)***
K T Lucky Co Inc...D...626 579-7272
10925 Schmidt Rd El Monte (91733) ***(P-8598)***
K T W Productions Inc...A...714 685-0428
6303 E Cedarbrooks Rd Orange (92867) ***(P-6565)***
K Tech Security & Protect Svc...C...619 858-5832
665 Alvin St San Diego (92114) ***(P-16332)***
K W K Trucking Inc...C...714 791-7928
6131 Manorfield Dr Huntington Beach (92648) ***(P-3902)***
K W P H Enterprises...A...559 443-5900
2911 E Tulare St Fresno (93721) ***(P-3690)***
K X T V Channel 10, Sacramento *Also called Kxtv Inc* ***(P-5630)***
K Y L D, San Francisco *Also called Iheartcommunications Inc* ***(P-5534)***
K&B Electric LLC...C...951 808-9501
290 Corporate Terrace Cir # 200 Corona (92879) ***(P-25165)***
K&B Engineering, Corona *Also called K&B Electric LLC* ***(P-25165)***
K&B Engineering...C...951 808-9501
290 Corporate Terrace Cir Corona (92879) ***(P-25166)***
K&I International Trade Inc...E...312 766-1848
3592 Rosemead Blvd # 220 Rosemead (91770) ***(P-6522)***
K&L Gates LLP...D...415 882-8200
55 2nd St Ste 1700 San Francisco (94105) ***(P-22598)***
K&L Gates LLP...E...310 552-5000
10100 Santa Monica Blvd # 700 Los Angeles (90067) ***(P-22599)***
K&M Construction...D...831 643-2819
642 Pine Ave Pacific Grove (93950) ***(P-1254)***
K&S, Orange *Also called K & S Air Conditioning Inc* ***(P-2170)***
K-Designers, Rancho Cordova *Also called Judson Enterprises Inc* ***(P-1251)***
K-LOVE RADIO NETWORK, Rocklin *Also called Educational Media Foundation* ***(P-5522)***
K-Micro Inc...D...310 442-3200
1618 Stanford St Santa Monica (90404) ***(P-6858)***
K/P LLC...E...510 614-7800
13947 Washington Ave San Leandro (94578) ***(P-13726)***
K3 Dev LLC...D...408 733-7950
725 S Fair Oaks Ave Sunnyvale (94086) ***(P-12496)***
Ka Management Inc...D...858 404-6080
5820 Oberlin Dr Ste 201 San Diego (92121) ***(P-26279)***
Kaa Design Group Inc...D...310 821-1400
4201 Redwood Ave Los Angeles (90066) ***(P-25464)***
Kabam Inc (HQ)...D...604 256-0054
575 Market St Ste 2450 San Francisco (94105) ***(P-14897)***
Kabc 790 Talk Radio, Los Angeles *Also called Cumulus Intrmdate Holdings Inc* ***(P-5519)***
Kabler Construction Svcs Inc...E...415 888-8812
467 Miller Ave Mill Valley (94941) ***(P-26665)***
Kaden Cash LLC...E...818 714-4665
15845 Jackson Dr Fontana (92336) ***(P-17985)***
Kadena Pacific Inc...E...951 990-7865
3421 Gato Ct Ste A Riverside (92507) ***(P-1518)***
Kagan Capital Management Inc...D...831 624-1536
126 Clock Tower Pl Carmel (93923) ***(P-9828)***
Kaidan Hospitality LP...D...530 221-8700
1830 Hilltop Dr Redding (96002) ***(P-12497)***
Kaimanu Outrigger Canoe Club...D...510 895-0435
13424 Doolittle Dr San Leandro (94577) ***(P-18711)***
Kainos Home & Training Ctr...E...650 361-1355
2761 Fair Oaks Ave Ste A Redwood City (94063) ***(P-23302)***
Kainos Work Activity Ctr, Redwood City *Also called Kainos Home & Training Ctr* ***(P-23302)***
Kaiser Foundation Health Plan, San Diego *Also called Southern Cal Prmnnte Med Group* ***(P-10049)***
Kaiser Foundation Health Plan, Union City *Also called Kaiser Foundation Hospitals* ***(P-9956)***
Kaiser Foundation Health Plan, San Francisco *Also called Kaiser Foundation Hospitals* ***(P-9957)***
Kaiser Foundation Health Plan, Pasadena *Also called Kaiser Foundation Hospitals* ***(P-9958)***
Kaiser Foundation Health Plan, Vallejo *Also called Kaiser Foundation Hospitals* ***(P-9959)***
Kaiser Foundation Health Plan, San Rafael *Also called Kaiser Foundation Hospitals* ***(P-9960)***
Kaiser Foundation Health Plan, Los Angeles *Also called Kaiser Foundation Hospitals* ***(P-9961)***
Kaiser Foundation Health Plan, Oakland *Also called Kaiser Foundation Hospitals* ***(P-9962)***
Kaiser Foundation Health Plan, Fresno *Also called Kaiser Foundation Hospitals* ***(P-9963)***
Kaiser Foundation Health Plan, Elk Grove *Also called Kaiser Foundation Hospitals* ***(P-9964)***
Kaiser Foundation Health Plan, Victorville *Also called Kaiser Foundation Hospitals* ***(P-9965)***
Kaiser Foundation Health Plan, San Diego *Also called Kaiser Foundation Hospitals* ***(P-9966)***
Kaiser Foundation Health Plan, San Diego *Also called Kaiser Foundation Hospitals* ***(P-9967)***
Kaiser Foundation Health Plan, Temecula *Also called Kaiser Foundation Hospitals* ***(P-9968)***
Kaiser Foundation Health Plan, Mission Hills *Also called Kaiser Foundation Hospitals* ***(P-9969)***
Kaiser Foundation Health Plan, Panorama City *Also called Kaiser Foundation Hospitals* ***(P-9970)***
Kaiser Foundation Health Plan, Hayward *Also called Kaiser Foundation Hospitals* ***(P-9971)***
Kaiser Foundation Health Plan, Los Angeles *Also called Kaiser Foundation Hospitals* ***(P-9972)***
Kaiser Foundation Health Plan, Anaheim *Also called Kaiser Foundation Hospitals* ***(P-9974)***
Kaiser Foundation Health Plan, Campbell *Also called Kaiser Foundation Hospitals* ***(P-9975)***
Kaiser Foundation Health Plan, Walnut Creek *Also called Kaiser Foundation Hospitals* ***(P-9976)***
Kaiser Foundation Health Plan, Clovis *Also called Kaiser Foundation Hospitals* ***(P-9977)***
Kaiser Foundation Health Plan, Woodland Hills *Also called Kaiser Foundation Hospitals* ***(P-9978)***
Kaiser Foundation Health Plan, Roseville *Also called Kaiser Foundation Hospitals* ***(P-9979)***
Kaiser Foundation Health Plan, Oakhurst *Also called Kaiser Foundation Hospitals* ***(P-9980)***
Kaiser Foundation Health Plan, Ontario *Also called Kaiser Foundation Hospitals* ***(P-9981)***
Kaiser Foundation Health Plan, Palm Desert *Also called Kaiser Foundation Hospitals* ***(P-9982)***
Kaiser Foundation Health Plan, Ventura *Also called Kaiser Foundation Hospitals* ***(P-9983)***
Kaiser Foundation Health Plan, Santa Ana *Also called Kaiser Foundation Hospitals* ***(P-9984)***
Kaiser Foundation Health Plan, San Bernardino *Also called Kaiser Foundation Hospitals* ***(P-9985)***
Kaiser Foundation Health Plan, Corona *Also called Kaiser Foundation Hospitals* ***(P-22265)***
Kaiser Foundation Health Plan, Chino *Also called Kaiser Foundation Hospitals* ***(P-9986)***
Kaiser Foundation Health Plan, Daly City *Also called Kaiser Foundation Hospitals* ***(P-9987)***
Kaiser Foundation Health Plan, Union City *Also called Kaiser Foundation Hospitals* ***(P-9988)***
Kaiser Foundation Health Plan, Tracy *Also called Kaiser Foundation Hospitals* ***(P-9989)***
Kaiser Foundation Health Plan, San Bruno *Also called Kaiser Foundation Hospitals* ***(P-9990)***
Kaiser Foundation Health Plan, Santa Rosa *Also called Kaiser Foundation Hospitals* ***(P-9991)***
Kaiser Foundation Health Plan, Santa Rosa *Also called Kaiser Foundation Hospitals* ***(P-9992)***
Kaiser Foundation Health Plan, Modesto *Also called Kaiser Foundation Hospitals* ***(P-9993)***
Kaiser Foundation Health Plan, Rohnert Park *Also called Kaiser Foundation Hospitals* ***(P-9994)***
Kaiser Foundation Health Plan, Alameda *Also called Kaiser Foundation Hospitals* ***(P-9995)***
Kaiser Foundation Health Plan, Oakland *Also called Kaiser Foundation Hospitals* ***(P-9996)***
Kaiser Foundation Health Plan, Bellflower *Also called Kaiser Foundation Hospitals* ***(P-9997)***
Kaiser Foundation Health Plan, Selma *Also called Kaiser Foundation Hospitals* ***(P-9998)***
Kaiser Foundation Health Plan, Orange *Also called Kaiser Foundation Hospitals* ***(P-9999)***
Kaiser Foundation Health Plan, Palm Springs *Also called Kaiser Foundation Hospitals* ***(P-10000)***
Kaiser Foundation Health Plan, Torrance *Also called Kaiser Foundation Hospitals* ***(P-10001)***
Kaiser Foundation Health Plan, Thousand Oaks *Also called Kaiser Foundation Hospitals* ***(P-10002)***
Kaiser Foundation Health Plan, Simi Valley *Also called Kaiser Foundation Hospitals* ***(P-10003)***
Kaiser Foundation Health Plan, San Juan Capistrano *Also called Kaiser Foundation Hospitals* ***(P-10004)***
Kaiser Foundation Health Plan, Fontana *Also called Kaiser Foundation Hospitals* ***(P-10005)***
Kaiser Foundation Health Plan, Downey *Also called Kaiser Foundation Hospitals* ***(P-10006)***
Kaiser Foundation Health Plan, San Jose *Also called Kaiser Foundation Hospitals* ***(P-10007)***
Kaiser Foundation Health Plan, North Hollywood *Also called Kaiser Foundation Hospitals* ***(P-10008)***

Mergent e-mail: customerrelations@mergent.com
1316
2020 Directory of California
Wholesalers and Services Companies
(P-0000) Products & Services Section entry number
(PA)=Parent Co (HQ)=Headquarters (DH)=Div Headquarters

Kaiser Foundation Health Plan, Fresno *Also called Kaiser Foundation Hospitals* ***(P-20977)***
Kaiser Foundation Health Plan, Modesto *Also called Kaiser Foundation Hospitals* ***(P-10009)***
Kaiser Foundation Health Plan, Orange *Also called Kaiser Foundation Hospitals* ***(P-10010)***
Kaiser Foundation Hospital.......E.......510 752-6295
4501 Broadway Oakland (94611) ***(P-21793)***
Kaiser Foundation Hospitals.......C.......714 279-4675
411 N Lakeview Ave Anaheim (92807) ***(P-19036)***
Kaiser Foundation Hospitals.......C.......949 262-5780
6 Willard Irvine (92604) ***(P-20932)***
Kaiser Foundation Hospitals.......B.......619 662-5107
4650 Palm Ave San Diego (92154) ***(P-11791)***
Kaiser Foundation Hospitals.......D.......510 675-5777
30116 Eigenbrodt Way Union City (94587) ***(P-9956)***
Kaiser Foundation Hospitals.......A.......408 361-2100
50 Great Oaks Blvd San Jose (95119) ***(P-21794)***
Kaiser Foundation Hospitals.......C.......949 425-3150
24502 Pacific Park Dr Aliso Viejo (92656) ***(P-19037)***
Kaiser Foundation Hospitals.......D.......619 542-7210
8889 Rio San Diego Dr San Diego (92108) ***(P-19038)***
Kaiser Foundation Hospitals.......C.......916 746-3937
1680 E Roseville Pkwy Roseville (95661) ***(P-20933)***
Kaiser Foundation Hospitals.......A.......707 393-4000
401 Bicentennial Way Santa Rosa (95403) ***(P-19039)***
Kaiser Foundation Hospitals.......A.......619 528-5888
4647 Zion Ave San Diego (92120) ***(P-11792)***
Kaiser Foundation Hospitals.......A.......818 719-2000
5601 De Soto Ave Woodland Hills (91367) ***(P-20934)***
Kaiser Foundation Hospitals.......A.......951 353-4000
12620 Prescott Ave Tustin (92782) ***(P-20935)***
Kaiser Foundation Hospitals.......C.......925 813-6500
4501 Sand Creek Rd Antioch (94531) ***(P-19040)***
Kaiser Foundation Hospitals.......C.......661 726-2500
43112 15th St W Lancaster (93534) ***(P-20936)***
Kaiser Foundation Hospitals.......D.......714 741-3448
12100 Euclid St Garden Grove (92840) ***(P-19041)***
Kaiser Foundation Hospitals.......D.......323 783-4011
4867 W Sunset Blvd Los Angeles (90027) ***(P-20937)***
Kaiser Foundation Hospitals.......D.......925 906-2380
320 Lennon Ln Walnut Creek (94598) ***(P-20938)***
Kaiser Foundation Hospitals.......D.......415 833-2616
2350 Geary Blvd Fl 2 San Francisco (94115) ***(P-9957)***
Kaiser Foundation Hospitals.......A.......925 295-4145
710 S Broadway Walnut Creek (94596) ***(P-22047)***
Kaiser Foundation Hospitals.......A.......626 851-1011
1011 Baldwin Park Blvd Baldwin Park (91706) ***(P-20939)***
Kaiser Foundation Hospitals.......C.......925 372-1000
200 Muir Rd Martinez (94553) ***(P-11793)***
Kaiser Foundation Hospitals.......A.......510 752-1000
3600 Broadway Oakland (94611) ***(P-19042)***
Kaiser Foundation Hospitals.......B.......562 657-9000
9333 Imperial Hwy Downey (90242) ***(P-20940)***
Kaiser Foundation Hospitals.......A.......415 833-2000
2425 Geary Blvd San Francisco (94115) ***(P-19043)***
Kaiser Foundation Hospitals (HQ).......C.......510 271-6611
1 Kaiser Plz Oakland (94612) ***(P-20941)***
Kaiser Foundation Hospitals.......E.......626 405-5000
393 E Walnut St Pasadena (91188) ***(P-9958)***
Kaiser Foundation Hospitals.......A.......510 752-1000
280 W Macarthur Blvd Oakland (94611) ***(P-20942)***
Kaiser Foundation Hospitals.......D.......707 645-2720
1761 Broadway St Ste 210 Vallejo (94589) ***(P-9959)***
Kaiser Foundation Hospitals.......D.......909 394-2530
1255 W Arrow Hwy San Dimas (91773) ***(P-20943)***
Kaiser Foundation Hospitals.......D.......888 750-0036
1301 California St Redlands (92374) ***(P-19044)***
Kaiser Foundation Hospitals.......D.......714 672-5100
1900 E Lambert Rd Brea (92821) ***(P-19045)***
Kaiser Foundation Hospitals.......A.......415 444-2000
99 Montecillo Rd San Rafael (94903) ***(P-19046)***
Kaiser Foundation Hospitals.......D.......619 528-2583
4405 Vandever Ave Fl 5 San Diego (92120) ***(P-20944)***
Kaiser Foundation Hospitals.......B.......510 307-1500
901 Nevin Ave Richmond (94801) ***(P-19047)***
Kaiser Foundation Hospitals.......A.......323 857-2000
6041 Cadillac Ave Los Angeles (90034) ***(P-19048)***
Kaiser Foundation Hospital.......A.......818 375-2000
13651 Willard St Panorama City (91402) ***(P-20945)***
Kaiser Foundation Hospitals.......B.......408 972-6010
280 Hospital Pkwy San Jose (95119) ***(P-20946)***
Kaiser Foundation Hospitals.......C.......909 609-3800
17284 Slover Ave Fontana (92337) ***(P-19049)***
Kaiser Foundation Hospitals.......D.......415 444-3522
820 Las Gallinas Ave San Rafael (94903) ***(P-9960)***
Kaiser Foundation Hospitals.......D.......800 954-8000
1550 W Manchester Ave Los Angeles (90047) ***(P-9961)***
Kaiser Foundation Hospitals.......D.......510 752-7864
255 W Macarthur Blvd Oakland (94611) ***(P-9962)***
Kaiser Foundation Hospitals.......D.......559 448-4555
4785 N 1st St Fresno (93726) ***(P-9963)***
Kaiser Foundation Hospitals.......D.......916 544-6000
10305 Promenade Pkwy Elk Grove (95757) ***(P-9964)***
Kaiser Foundation Hospitals.......D.......888 750-0036
14011 Park Ave Victorville (92392) ***(P-9965)***
Kaiser Foundation Hospitals.......D.......619 528-5000
17140 Bernardo Center Dr San Diego (92128) ***(P-9966)***
Kaiser Foundation Hospitals.......D.......619 528-5000
5893 Copley Dr San Diego (92111) ***(P-9967)***
Kaiser Foundation Hospitals.......D.......866 984-7483
27309 Madison Ave Temecula (92590) ***(P-9968)***
Kaiser Foundation Hospitals.......D.......888 778-5000
11001 Sepulveda Blvd Mission Hills (91345) ***(P-9969)***
Kaiser Foundation Hospitals.......D.......818 375-2028
8001 Ventura Canyon Ave Panorama City (91402) ***(P-9970)***
Kaiser Foundation Hospitals.......D.......510 454-1000
27303 Sleepy Hollow Ave S Hayward (94545) ***(P-9971)***
Kaiser Foundation Hospitals.......D.......800 954-8000
5620 Mesmer Ave Los Angeles (90230) ***(P-9972)***
Kaiser Foundation Hospitals.......A.......707 624-4000
1 Quality Dr Vacaville (95688) ***(P-19050)***
Kaiser Foundation Hospitals.......A.......209 839-3200
2185 W Grant Line Rd Tracy (95377) ***(P-19051)***
Kaiser Foundation Hospitals.......A.......510 675-4010
3555 Whipple Rd Union City (94587) ***(P-19052)***
Kaiser Foundation Hospitals.......A.......888 750-0036
10850 Arrow Rte Rancho Cucamonga (91730) ***(P-19053)***
Kaiser Foundation Hospitals.......A.......888 988-2800
5475 E La Palma Ave Anaheim (92807) ***(P-19054)***
Kaiser Foundation Hospitals.......A.......877 524-7373
3733 San Dimas St Bakersfield (93301) ***(P-19055)***
Kaiser Foundation Hospitals.......A.......888 988-2800
3460 E La Palma Ave Anaheim (92806) ***(P-19056)***
Kaiser Foundation Hospitals.......B.......661 395-3000
2615 Chester Ave Bakersfield (93301) ***(P-20947)***
Kaiser Foundation Hospitals.......A.......877 524-7373
2531 Chester Ave Bakersfield (93301) ***(P-19057)***
Kaiser Foundation Hospitals.......A.......661 337-7160
2620 Chester Ave Bakersfield (93301) ***(P-19058)***
Kaiser Foundation Hospitals.......A.......877 524-7373
1200 Discovery Dr Bakersfield (93309) ***(P-19059)***
Kaiser Foundation Hospitals.......A.......800 823-4040
10820 183rd St Cerritos (90703) ***(P-19060)***
Kaiser Foundation Hospitals.......A.......888 515-3500
2620 Las Posas Rd Camarillo (93010) ***(P-19061)***
Kaiser Foundation Hospitals.......A.......877 524-7373
8800 Ming Ave Bakersfield (93311) ***(P-19062)***
Kaiser Foundation Hospitals.......A.......562 463-4377
12801 Crossroads Pkwy S City of Industry (91746) ***(P-19063)***
Kaiser Foundation Hospitals.......A.......800 823-4040
9449 Imperial Hwy Downey (90242) ***(P-19064)***
Kaiser Foundation Hospitals.......A.......442 281-5000
2185 Citracado Pkwy Escondido (92029) ***(P-20948)***
Kaiser Foundation Hospitals.......A.......800 780-1277
1336 Bridgegate Dr Diamond Bar (91765) ***(P-19065)***
Kaiser Foundation Hospitals.......A.......760 739-3000
555 E Valley Pkwy Escondido (92025) ***(P-19066)***
Kaiser Foundation Hospitals.......A.......800 823-4040
9353 Imperial Hwy Downey (90242) ***(P-19067)***
Kaiser Foundation Hospitals.......A.......707 427-4000
1550 Gateway Blvd Fairfield (94533) ***(P-19068)***
Kaiser Foundation Hospitals.......A.......800 922-2000
26882 Towne Centre Dr # 1 Foothill Ranch (92610) ***(P-19069)***
Kaiser Foundation Hospitals.......A.......866 205-3595
9310 Sierra Ave Fontana (92335) ***(P-19070)***
Kaiser Foundation Hospitals.......A.......916 986-4178
285 Palladio Pkwy Folsom (95630) ***(P-19071)***
Kaiser Foundation Hospitals.......A.......800 780-1230
18600 S Figueroa St Gardena (90248) ***(P-19072)***
Kaiser Foundation Hospitals.......A.......818 832-7200
10605 Balboa Blvd Ste 330 Granada Hills (91344) ***(P-19073)***
Kaiser Foundation Hospitals.......A.......800 954-8000
501 N Orange St Glendale (91203) ***(P-19074)***
Kaiser Foundation Hospitals.......A.......866 984-7483
46900 Monroe St Indio (92201) ***(P-19075)***
Kaiser Foundation Hospitals.......B.......661 949-5000
1600 W Avenue J Lancaster (93534) ***(P-20949)***
Kaiser Foundation Hospitals.......A.......619 528-5000
3875 Avocado Blvd La Mesa (91941) ***(P-19076)***
Kaiser Foundation Hospitals.......A.......916 543-5153
1900 Dresden Dr Lincoln (95648) ***(P-19077)***
Kaiser Foundation Hospitals.......A.......661 951-0070
44444 20th St W Lancaster (93534) ***(P-19078)***
Kaiser Foundation Hospitals.......A.......310 325-6542
2081 Palos Verdes Dr N Lomita (90717) ***(P-19079)***
Kaiser Foundation Hospitals.......C.......424 251-7000
2040 Pacific Coast Hwy Lomita (90717) ***(P-22048)***
Kaiser Foundation Hospitals.......A.......310 604-5700
3830 Martin Luther King Lynwood (90262) ***(P-19080)***
Kaiser Foundation Hospitals.......A.......209 735-5000
4601 Dale Rd Modesto (95356) ***(P-19081)***
Kaiser Foundation Hospitals.......A.......888 778-5000
5250 Lankershim Blvd North Hollywood (91601) ***(P-19082)***
Kaiser Foundation Hospitals.......A.......209 735-5000
4125 Bangs Ave Modesto (95356) ***(P-19083)***
Kaiser Foundation Hospitals.......A.......562 807-6100
12501 Imperial Hwy Norwalk (90650) ***(P-19084)***
Kaiser Foundation Hospitals.......A.......909 724-5000
2295 S Vineyard Ave Ontario (91761) ***(P-19085)***
Kaiser Foundation Hospitals.......A.......888 515-3500
2200 E Gonzales Rd Oxnard (93036) ***(P-19086)***
Kaiser Foundation Hospitals.......A.......800 777-1256
73733 Fred Waring Dr Palm Desert (92260) ***(P-19087)***
Kaiser Foundation Hospitals.......A.......805 988-6300
2103 E Gonzales Rd Oxnard (93036) ***(P-19088)***
Kaiser Foundation Hospitals.......A.......510 243-4000
1301 Pinole Valley Rd Pinole (94564) ***(P-19089)***
Kaiser Foundation Hospitals.......A.......866 984-7483
University Park Ctr Palm Desert (92211) ***(P-19090)***
Kaiser Foundation Hospitals.......A.......951 248-4000
5225 Canyon Crest Dr Riverside (92507) ***(P-19091)***

Kaiser Foundation Hospitals ....A.......866 984-7483
14305 Meridian Pkwy Riverside (92518) *(P-19092)*
Kaiser Foundation Hospitals ....A.......858 847-3500
3851 Shaw Ridge Rd San Diego (92130) *(P-19093)*
Kaiser Foundation Hospitals ....A.......858 502-1350
4510 Viewridge Ave San Diego (92123) *(P-19094)*
Kaiser Foundation Hospitals ....A.......650 358-7000
1000 Franklin Pkwy San Mateo (94403) *(P-19095)*
Kaiser Foundation Hospitals ....C.......858 573-0090
7035 Convoy Ct San Diego (92111) *(P-22049)*
Kaiser Foundation Hospitals ....A.......510 454-1000
2500 Merced St San Leandro (94577) *(P-19096)*
Kaiser Foundation Hospitals ....A.......925 244-7600
2300 Camino Ramon San Ramon (94583) *(P-19097)*
Kaiser Foundation Hospitals ....A.......714 223-2606
3601 S Harbor Blvd Santa Ana (92704) *(P-19098)*
Kaiser Foundation Hospitals ....A.......888 778-5000
26415 Carl Boyer Dr Santa Clarita (91350) *(P-19099)*
Kaiser Foundation Hospitals ....A.......888 515-3500
145 Hodencamp Rd Thousand Oaks (91360) *(P-19100)*
Kaiser Foundation Hospitals ....A.......408 851-1000
1263 E Arques Ave Sunnyvale (94085) *(P-19101)*
Kaiser Foundation Hospitals ....A.......888 515-3500
322 E Thousand Oaks Blvd Thousand Oaks (91360) *(P-19102)*
Kaiser Foundation Hospitals ....A.......888 988-2800
2521 Michelle Dr Tustin (92780) *(P-19103)*
Kaiser Foundation Hospitals ....B.......925 598-2799
5820 Owens Dr Bldg E-2 Pleasanton (94588) *(P-20950)*
Kaiser Foundation Hospitals ....A.......408 972-7000
250 Hospital Pkwy San Jose (95119) *(P-19104)*
Kaiser Foundation Hospitals ....A.......650 299-2000
1100 Veterans Blvd Redwood City (94063) *(P-19105)*
Kaiser Foundation Hospitals ....A.......925 295-4000
1425 S Main St Walnut Creek (94596) *(P-19106)*
Kaiser Foundation Hospitals ....E.......323 881-5516
5119 Pomona Blvd Los Angeles (90022) *(P-11794)*
Kaiser Foundation Hospitals ....A.......310 325-5111
25825 Vermont Ave Harbor City (90710) *(P-19107)*
Kaiser Foundation Hospitals ....C.......415 833-9688
601 Van Ness Ave Ste 2008 San Francisco (94102) *(P-19108)*
Kaiser Foundation Hospitals ....D.......916 973-5000
1650 Response Rd Sacramento (95815) *(P-20951)*
Kaiser Foundation Hospitals ....A.......909 427-5000
9961 Sierra Ave Fontana (92335) *(P-19109)*
Kaiser Foundation Hospitals ....B.......619 641-4663
10990 San Dego Mission Rd San Diego (92108) *(P-20952)*
Kaiser Foundation Hospitals ....E.......619 528-5000
8080 Parkway Dr La Mesa (91942) *(P-20953)*
Kaiser Foundation Hospitals ....E.......661 398-5011
3501 Stockdale Hwy Bakersfield (93309) *(P-20954)*
Kaiser Foundation Hospitals ....E.......408 945-2900
770 E Calaveras Blvd Milpitas (95035) *(P-19110)*
Kaiser Foundation Hospitals ....A.......510 987-1000
1950 Franklin St Oakland (94612) *(P-19111)*
Kaiser Foundation Hospitals ....E.......951 601-6174
12815 Heacock St Moreno Valley (92553) *(P-11795)*
Kaiser Foundation Hospitals ....E.......951 353-2000
36450 Inland Valley Dr # 204 Wildomar (92595) *(P-20955)*
Kaiser Foundation Hospitals ....E.......714 562-3420
5 Centerpointe Dr La Palma (90623) *(P-19112)*
Kaiser Foundation Hospitals ....E.......818 552-3000
444 W Glenoaks Blvd Glendale (91202) *(P-19113)*
Kaiser Foundation Hospitals ....E.......626 440-5639
3280 E Foothill Blvd Pasadena (91107) *(P-19114)*
Kaiser Foundation Hospitals ....E.......714 685-3520
22550 Savi Ranch Pkwy Yorba Linda (92887) *(P-19115)*
Kaiser Foundation Hospitals ....E.......619 528-5000
1630 E Main St El Cajon (92021) *(P-20956)*
Kaiser Foundation Hospitals ....D.......323 562-6400
7825 Atlantic Ave Cudahy (90201) *(P-20957)*
Kaiser Foundation Hospitals ....E.......619 528-5000
250 Travelodge Dr El Cajon (92020) *(P-20958)*
Kaiser Foundation Hospitals ....E.......619 528-5000
732 N Broadway Escondido (92025) *(P-19116)*
Kaiser Foundation Hospitals ....E.......866 319-4269
1249 S Sunset Ave West Covina (91790) *(P-20959)*
Kaiser Foundation Hospitals ....E.......530 757-7100
1955 Cowell Blvd Davis (95618) *(P-19117)*
Kaiser Foundation Hospitals ....E.......310 517-2956
15446 S Western Ave Gardena (90249) *(P-20960)*
Kaiser Foundation Hospitals ....E.......818 592-3100
21263 Erwin St Woodland Hills (91367) *(P-20961)*
Kaiser Foundation Hospitals ....E.......916 631-3088
10725 International Dr Rancho Cordova (95670) *(P-20962)*
Kaiser Foundation Hospitals ....E.......707 765-3900
3900 Lakeville Hwy Petaluma (94954) *(P-20963)*
Kaiser Foundation Hospitals ....E.......415 899-7400
97 San Marin Dr Novato (94945) *(P-20964)*
Kaiser Foundation Hospitals ....E.......707 624-4000
1 Quality Dr Vacaville (95688) *(P-9973)*
Kaiser Foundation Hospitals ....A.......510 678-4000
27400 Hesperian Blvd Hayward (94545) *(P-19118)*
Kaiser Foundation Hospitals ....C.......650 903-3000
555 Castro St Fl 3 Mountain View (94041) *(P-20965)*
Kaiser Foundation Hospitals ....C.......916 784-4000
1001 Riverside Ave Roseville (95678) *(P-19119)*
Kaiser Foundation Hospitals ....D.......714 284-6634
1011 S East St Fl 1 Anaheim (92805) *(P-9974)*
Kaiser Foundation Hospitals ....A.......925 906-2000
501 Lennon Ln Walnut Creek (94598) *(P-20966)*

Kaiser Foundation Hospitals ....B.......925 847-5000
7601 Stoneridge Dr Pleasanton (94588) *(P-20967)*
Kaiser Foundation Hospitals ....C.......916 817-5200
2155 Iron Point Rd Folsom (95630) *(P-19120)*
Kaiser Foundation Hospitals ....D.......408 871-6500
220 E Hacienda Ave Campbell (95008) *(P-9975)*
Kaiser Foundation Hospitals ....B.......510 891-3400
2000 Brdwy Oakland (94612) *(P-20968)*
Kaiser Foundation Hospitals ....C.......661 334-2020
5055 California Ave # 110 Bakersfield (93309) *(P-20969)*
Kaiser Foundation Hospitals ....D.......925 926-3000
25 N Via Monte Walnut Creek (94598) *(P-9976)*
Kaiser Foundation Hospitals ....A.......650 742-2000
1200 El Camino Real South San Francisco (94080) *(P-19121)*
Kaiser Foundation Hospitals ....C.......323 298-3300
5105 W Goldleaf Cir Los Angeles (90056) *(P-22050)*
Kaiser Foundation Hospitals ....A.......916 688-2000
6600 Bruceville Rd Sacramento (95823) *(P-19122)*
Kaiser Foundation Hospitals ....C.......925 779-5000
3400 Delta Fair Blvd Antioch (94509) *(P-22051)*
Kaiser Foundation Hospitals ....B.......510 248-3000
39400 Paseo Padre Pkwy Fremont (94538) *(P-19123)*
Kaiser Foundation Hospitals ....C.......707 258-2500
3285 Claremont Way NAPA (94558) *(P-11796)*
Kaiser Foundation Hospitals ....A.......707 651-1000
975 Sereno Dr Vallejo (94589) *(P-20970)*
Kaiser Foundation Hospitals ....C.......213 580-7200
765 W College St Los Angeles (90012) *(P-21414)*
Kaiser Foundation Hospitals ....E.......866 340-5974
12470 Whittier Blvd Whittier (90602) *(P-20971)*
Kaiser Foundation Hospitals ....D.......661 222-2323
27107 Tourney Rd Santa Clarita (91355) *(P-19124)*
Kaiser Foundation Hospitals ....D.......559 324-5100
2071 Herndon Ave Clovis (93611) *(P-9977)*
Kaiser Foundation Hospitals ....D.......888 515-3500
21263 Erwin St Woodland Hills (91367) *(P-9978)*
Kaiser Foundation Hospitals ....D.......916 784-4050
1840 Sierra Gardens Dr Roseville (95661) *(P-9979)*
Kaiser Foundation Hospitals ....D.......559 658-8388
40595 Westlake Dr Oakhurst (93644) *(P-9980)*
Kaiser Foundation Hospitals ....D.......888 750-0036
2295 S Vineyard Ave Ontario (91761) *(P-9981)*
Kaiser Foundation Hospitals ....D.......760 360-1475
42575 Washington St Palm Desert (92211) *(P-9982)*
Kaiser Foundation Hospitals ....D.......888 515-3500
888 S Hill Rd Ventura (93003) *(P-9983)*
Kaiser Foundation Hospitals ....D.......888 988-2800
3401 S Harbor Blvd Santa Ana (92704) *(P-9984)*
Kaiser Foundation Hospitals ....D.......888 750-0036
1717 Date Pike San Bernardino (92404) *(P-9985)*
Kaiser Foundation Hospitals ....D.......866 984-7483
2055 Kellogg Ave Corona (92879) *(P-22265)*
Kaiser Foundation Hospitals ....D.......888 750-0036
11911 Central Ave Chino (91710) *(P-9986)*
Kaiser Foundation Hospitals ....D.......650 301-5860
395 Hickey Blvd Daly City (94015) *(P-9987)*
Kaiser Foundation Hospitals ....D.......510 675-2170
3553 Whipple Rd Union City (94587) *(P-9988)*
Kaiser Foundation Hospitals ....D.......209 832-6339
2417 Naglee Rd Tracy (95304) *(P-9989)*
Kaiser Foundation Hospitals ....D.......650 742-2100
901 El Camino Real San Bruno (94066) *(P-9990)*
Kaiser Foundation Hospitals ....D.......707 571-3835
3554 Round Barn Blvd Santa Rosa (95403) *(P-9991)*
Kaiser Foundation Hospitals ....D.......707 393-4033
3925 Old Redwood Hwy Santa Rosa (95403) *(P-9992)*
Kaiser Foundation Hospitals ....D.......855 268-4096
1320 Standiford Ave Modesto (95350) *(P-9993)*
Kaiser Foundation Hospitals ....D.......707 206-3000
5900 State Farm Dr # 100 Rohnert Park (94928) *(P-9994)*
Kaiser Foundation Hospitals ....D.......510 752-1190
2417 Central Ave Alameda (94501) *(P-9995)*
Kaiser Foundation Hospitals ....D.......510 251-0121
969 Broadway Oakland (94607) *(P-9996)*
Kaiser Foundation Hospitals ....D.......562 461-3084
9333 Rosecrans Ave Bellflower (90706) *(P-9997)*
Kaiser Foundation Hospitals ....D.......559 898-6000
2651 Highland Ave Selma (93662) *(P-9998)*
Kaiser Foundation Hospitals ....D.......714 748-7622
4201 W Chapman Ave Orange (92868) *(P-9999)*
Kaiser Foundation Hospitals ....D.......866 370-1942
1717 E Vista Chino Ste B2 Palm Springs (92262) *(P-10000)*
Kaiser Foundation Hospitals ....D.......800 780-1230
20790 Madrona Ave Torrance (90503) *(P-10001)*
Kaiser Foundation Hospitals ....D.......888 515-3500
365 E Hillcrest Dr Thousand Oaks (91360) *(P-10002)*
Kaiser Foundation Hospitals ....D.......888 515-3500
3900 Alamo St Simi Valley (93063) *(P-10003)*
Kaiser Foundation Hospitals ....D.......888 988-2800
30400 Camino Capistrano San Juan Capistrano (92675) *(P-10004)*
Kaiser Foundation Hospitals ....D.......909 427-3910
9961 Sierra Ave Fontana (92335) *(P-10005)*
Kaiser Foundation Hospitals ....D.......562 622-4190
12200 Bellflower Blvd Downey (90242) *(P-10006)*
Kaiser Foundation Hospitals ....D.......619 409-6405
3955 Bonita Rd Bonita (91902) *(P-20972)*
Kaiser Foundation Hospitals ....A.......951 353-2000
10800 Magnolia Ave Riverside (92505) *(P-19125)*
Kaiser Foundation Hospitals ....A.......909 427-5521
789 E Cooley Dr Colton (92324) *(P-11797)*

Mergent e-mail: customerrelations@mergent.com
1318

2020 Directory of California
Wholesalers and Services Companies

(P-0000) Products & Services Section entry number
(PA)=Parent Co (HQ)=Headquarters (DH)=Div Headquarters

ALPHABETIC SECTION
Kang Family Partners LLC

Kaiser Foundation Hospitals A 209 825-3700
1777 W Yosemite Ave Manteca (95337) ***(P-20973)***

Kaiser Foundation Hospitals C 408 972-3000
250 Hospital Pkwy Bldg D San Jose (95119) ***(P-19126)***

Kaiser Foundation Hospitals A 415 833-2000
2425 Geary Blvd San Francisco (94115) ***(P-19127)***

Kaiser Foundation Hospitals B 951 243-0811
27300 Iris Ave Moreno Valley (92555) ***(P-19128)***

Kaiser Foundation Hospitals D 408 972-3376
5755 Cottle Rd San Jose (95123) ***(P-10007)***

Kaiser Foundation Hospitals D 818 503-7082
11666 Sherman Way North Hollywood (91605) ***(P-10008)***

Kaiser Foundation Hospitals C 408 972-6700
275 Hospital Pkwy 765a San Jose (95119) ***(P-20974)***

Kaiser Foundation Hospitals B 310 419-3303
110 N La Brea Ave Inglewood (90301) ***(P-19129)***

Kaiser Foundation Hospitals B 626 440-5659
1055 E Colo Blvd Ste 100 Pasadena (91106) ***(P-20975)***

Kaiser Foundation Hospitals A 916 784-4000
1600 Eureka Rd Roseville (95661) ***(P-20976)***

Kaiser Foundation Hospitals A 559 448-4500
7300 N Fresno St Fresno (93720) ***(P-20977)***

Kaiser Foundation Hospitals A 559 448-4500
7300 N Fresno St Fresno (93720) ***(P-19130)***

Kaiser Foundation Hospitals B 888 750-0036
250 W San Jose Ave Claremont (91711) ***(P-20978)***

Kaiser Foundation Hospitals C 760 931-4228
6860 Avenida Encinas Carlsbad (92011) ***(P-19131)***

Kaiser Foundation Hospitals C 916 525-6300
7300 Wyndham Dr Sacramento (95823) ***(P-20979)***

Kaiser Foundation Hospitals D 310 513-6707
23621 Main St Carson (90745) ***(P-22052)***

Kaiser Foundation Hospitals C 209 476-3101
7373 West Ln Stockton (95210) ***(P-20980)***

Kaiser Foundation Hospitals D 209 557-1000
1625 I St Modesto (95354) ***(P-10009)***

Kaiser Foundation Hospitals D 888 988-2800
200 N Lewis St Fl 1 Orange (92868) ***(P-10010)***

Kaiser Foundation Hospitals A 408 851-1000
710 Lawrence Expy Santa Clara (95051) ***(P-20981)***

Kaiser Foundation Hospitals A 866 984-7483
182 Granite St Corona (92879) ***(P-11798)***

Kaiser Foundation Hospitals B 949 932-5000
6640 Alton Pkwy Irvine (92618) ***(P-11799)***

Kaiser Foundation Hospitals E 714 967-4700
1900 E 4th St Santa Ana (92705) ***(P-20982)***

Kaiser Fundation Hlth Plan Inc (PA) B 510 271-5800
1 Kaiser Plz Oakland (94612) ***(P-9908)***

Kaiser Fundation Hlth Plan Inc D 510 752-7644
3801 Howe St Oakland (94611) ***(P-10011)***

Kaiser Fundation Hlth Plan Inc D 510 271-5800
4460 Hacienda Dr Pleasanton (94588) ***(P-10012)***

Kaiser Fundation Hlth Plan Inc D 510 987-2255
1950 Franklin St Fl 3 Oakland (94612) ***(P-10013)***

Kaiser Group Holdings Inc D 510 419-6000
2101 Webster St Ste 1000 Oakland (94612) ***(P-25167)***

Kaiser Hlth Plan Asset MGT Inc E 510 271-5910
1 Kaiser Plz Ste 1333 Oakland (94612) ***(P-26280)***

Kaiser Manteca Medical Office C 209 825-3700
1721 W Yosemite Ave Manteca (95337) ***(P-21543)***

Kaiser Med Clinic C 650 903-2103
555 Castro St Mountain View (94041) ***(P-19132)***

Kaiser Med Security Services D 415 833-3683
2241 Geary Blvd San Francisco (94115) ***(P-16333)***

Kaiser Mental Health Center, Los Angeles *Also called Kaiser Foundation Hospitals* ***(P-21414)***
Kaiser Permanente, San Jose *Also called Kaiser Foundation Hospitals* ***(P-21794)***
Kaiser Permanente, San Diego *Also called Southern Cal Prmnnte Med Group* ***(P-19416)***
Kaiser Permanente, San Diego *Also called Kaiser Foundation Hospitals* ***(P-11792)***
Kaiser Permanente, Woodland Hills *Also called Kaiser Foundation Hospitals* ***(P-20934)***
Kaiser Permanente, Tustin *Also called Kaiser Foundation Hospitals* ***(P-20935)***
Kaiser Permanente, Lancaster *Also called Kaiser Foundation Hospitals* ***(P-20936)***
Kaiser Permanente, Garden Grove *Also called Kaiser Foundation Hospitals* ***(P-19041)***
Kaiser Permanente, Los Angeles *Also called Kaiser Foundation Hospitals* ***(P-20937)***
Kaiser Permanente, Walnut Creek *Also called Kaiser Foundation Hospitals* ***(P-22047)***
Kaiser Permanente, Baldwin Park *Also called Kaiser Foundation Hospitals* ***(P-20939)***
Kaiser Permanente, Oakland *Also called Kaiser Foundation Hospitals* ***(P-20941)***
Kaiser Permanente, Oakland *Also called Kaiser Foundation Hospitals* ***(P-20942)***
Kaiser Permanente, San Dimas *Also called Kaiser Foundation Hospitals* ***(P-20943)***
Kaiser Permanente, Redlands *Also called Kaiser Foundation Hospitals* ***(P-19044)***
Kaiser Permanente, Brea *Also called Kaiser Foundation Hospitals* ***(P-19045)***
Kaiser Permanente, San Rafael *Also called Kaiser Foundation Hospitals* ***(P-19046)***
Kaiser Permanente, Pasadena *Also called Southern Cal Prmnnte Med Group* ***(P-10053)***
Kaiser Permanente, San Diego *Also called Kaiser Foundation Hospitals* ***(P-20944)***
Kaiser Permanente, Richmond *Also called Kaiser Foundation Hospitals* ***(P-19047)***
Kaiser Permanente, Panorama City *Also called Kaiser Foundation Hospitals* ***(P-20945)***
Kaiser Permanente, San Jose *Also called Kaiser Foundation Hospitals* ***(P-19104)***
Kaiser Permanente, Redwood City *Also called Kaiser Foundation Hospitals* ***(P-19105)***
Kaiser Permanente, Walnut Creek *Also called Kaiser Foundation Hospitals* ***(P-19106)***
Kaiser Permanente, Los Angeles *Also called Kaiser Foundation Hospitals* ***(P-11794)***
Kaiser Permanente, Harbor City *Also called Kaiser Foundation Hospitals* ***(P-19107)***
Kaiser Permanente, Sacramento *Also called Kaiser Foundation Hospitals* ***(P-20951)***
Kaiser Permanente, Fontana *Also called Kaiser Foundation Hospitals* ***(P-19109)***
Kaiser Permanente, West Covina *Also called Kaiser Foundation Hospitals* ***(P-20959)***
Kaiser Permanente, Walnut Creek *Also called Kaiser Foundation Hospitals* ***(P-20966)***
Kaiser Permanente, Pleasanton *Also called Kaiser Foundation Hospitals* ***(P-20967)***
KAISER PERMANENTE, Oakland *Also called Kaiser Hlth Plan Asset MGT Inc* ***(P-26280)***
Kaiser Permanente, Bakersfield *Also called Kaiser Foundation Hospitals* ***(P-20969)***
Kaiser Permanente, South San Francisco *Also called Kaiser Foundation Hospitals* ***(P-19121)***
Kaiser Permanente, Antioch *Also called Kaiser Foundation Hospitals* ***(P-22051)***
Kaiser Permanente, Fremont *Also called Kaiser Foundation Hospitals* ***(P-19123)***
Kaiser Permanente, NAPA *Also called Kaiser Foundation Hospitals* ***(P-11796)***
Kaiser Permanente, Whittier *Also called Kaiser Foundation Hospitals* ***(P-20971)***
Kaiser Permanente, Santa Clarita *Also called Kaiser Foundation Hospitals* ***(P-19124)***
Kaiser Permanente, Colton *Also called Kaiser Foundation Hospitals* ***(P-11797)***
Kaiser Permanente, San Francisco *Also called Kaiser Foundation Hospitals* ***(P-19127)***
Kaiser Permanente, Inglewood *Also called Kaiser Foundation Hospitals* ***(P-19129)***
Kaiser Permanente, Pasadena *Also called Kaiser Foundation Hospitals* ***(P-20975)***
Kaiser Permanente, Downey *Also called Southern Cal Prmnnte Med Group* ***(P-10056)***
Kaiser Permanente, Roseville *Also called Kaiser Foundation Hospitals* ***(P-20976)***
Kaiser Permanente, Fresno *Also called Kaiser Foundation Hospitals* ***(P-19130)***
Kaiser Permanente, Claremont *Also called Kaiser Foundation Hospitals* ***(P-20978)***
Kaiser Permanente, Carson *Also called Kaiser Foundation Hospitals* ***(P-22052)***
Kaiser Permanente, Stockton *Also called Kaiser Foundation Hospitals* ***(P-20980)***
Kaiser Permanente, Santa Ana *Also called Kaiser Foundation Hospitals* ***(P-20982)***

Kaiser Permanente D 510 450-2109
3505 Broadway Oakland (94611) ***(P-20983)***

Kaiser Permanente Advice, Sacramento *Also called Kaiser Foundation Hospitals* ***(P-20979)***
Kaiser Permanente Division RES, Oakland *Also called Kaiser Foundation Hospitals* ***(P-20968)***
Kaiser Permanente Eye, Roseville *Also called Kaiser Foundation Hospitals* ***(P-20933)***
Kaiser Permanente Kearny, San Diego *Also called Kaiser Foundation Hospitals* ***(P-19094)***
Kaiser Permanente Member Svcs, Palm Desert *Also called Kaiser Foundation Hospitals* ***(P-19087)***
Kaiser Permanente Moreno, Moreno Valley *Also called Kaiser Foundation Hospitals* ***(P-19128)***
Kaiser Permanente San, San Francisco *Also called Kaiser Foundation Hospitals* ***(P-19043)***
Kaiser Permanente San, San Mateo *Also called Kaiser Foundation Hospitals* ***(P-19095)***
Kaiser Permanente San, San Leandro *Also called Kaiser Foundation Hospitals* ***(P-19096)***
Kaiser Permanente San, San Jose *Also called Kaiser Foundation Hospitals* ***(P-20974)***
Kaiser Permanente San Fran, San Francisco *Also called Kaiser Foundation Hospitals* ***(P-19108)***
Kaiser Permanente San Jose, San Jose *Also called Kaiser Foundation Hospitals* ***(P-19126)***
Kaiser Permanente Santa, Santa Rosa *Also called Kaiser Foundation Hospitals* ***(P-19039)***
Kaiser Permanente Santa, Santa Clara *Also called Kaiser Foundation Hospitals* ***(P-20981)***
Kaiser Permanente South, Sacramento *Also called Kaiser Foundation Hospitals* ***(P-19122)***
Kaiser Permanente West, Los Angeles *Also called Kaiser Foundation Hospitals* ***(P-19048)***
Kaiser Perminente, Folsom *Also called Kaiser Foundation Hospitals* ***(P-19120)***
Kaiser Prmanente Internet Svcs, Pleasanton *Also called Kaiser Foundation Hospitals* ***(P-20950)***
Kaiser Prmnente Downey Med Ctr, Downey *Also called Kaiser Foundation Hospitals* ***(P-20940)***
Kaiser Prmnnte Antioch Med Ctr, Antioch *Also called Kaiser Foundation Hospitals* ***(P-19040)***
Kaiser Prmnnte Hayward Med Ctr, Hayward *Also called Kaiser Foundation Hospitals* ***(P-19118)***
Kaiser Prmnnte Manteca Med Ctr, Manteca *Also called Kaiser Foundation Hospitals* ***(P-20973)***
Kaiser Prmnnte Modesto Med Ctr, Modesto *Also called Permanente Medical Group Inc* ***(P-10035)***
Kaiser Prmnnte Psadena Med Off, Pasadena *Also called Kaiser Foundation Hospitals* ***(P-19114)***
Kaiser Prmnnte Vallejo Med Ctr, Vallejo *Also called Kaiser Foundation Hospitals* ***(P-20970)***

Kaiser Radiology D 559 448-5541
7300 N Fresno St Fresno (93720) ***(P-21544)***

Kaiserair Inc (PA) C 510 569-9622
8735 Earhart Rd Oakland (94621) ***(P-4743)***

Kajima Construction Svcs Inc E 323 269-0020
250 E 1st St Ste 400 Los Angeles (90012) ***(P-1359)***

Kajima International, Los Angeles *Also called Kajima Construction Svcs Inc* ***(P-1359)***

Kal Krishnan Consulting Svcs (PA) D 510 893-3500
800 S Figueroa St # 1210 Los Angeles (90017) ***(P-26281)***

Kal Tool Co, Baldwin Park *Also called G K Tool Corp* ***(P-7392)***
Kaleidioscope Stadium Cinema, Mission Viejo *Also called Edwards Theatres Circuit Inc* ***(P-17835)***

Kallidus Inc D 877 554-2176
425 Market St Ste 2200 San Francisco (94105) ***(P-14898)***

Kalpana LLC (PA) B 949 610-8200
620 Newport Center Dr # 1600 Newport Beach (92660) ***(P-12498)***

Kalpana LLC C 619 543-9000
901 Camino Del Rio S San Diego (92108) ***(P-12499)***

Kamiya, Kenneth M Insurance, Torrance *Also called Charles M Kamiya and Sons Inc* ***(P-10315)***

Kamps Company C 209 823-8924
1262 Dupont Ct Manteca (95336) ***(P-14520)***

Kan-Di-Ki LLC (HQ) C 818 549-1880
2820 N Ontario St Burbank (91504) ***(P-21545)***

Kana Pipeline Inc D 714 986-1400
12620 Magnolia Ave Riverside (92503) ***(P-1879)***

Kana Software Inc (HQ) D 650 614-8300
2550 Walsh Ave Ste 120 Santa Clara (95051) ***(P-15375)***

Kandarian Agri Enterprises C 559 834-1501
116 W Adams Ave Fowler (93625) ***(P-138)***

Kaney Foods, San Luis Obispo *Also called Amk Foodservices Inc* ***(P-8155)***

Kang Family Partners LLC C 805 688-1000
555 Mcmurray Rd Buellton (93427) ***(P-12500)***

ALPHABETIC

Employee Codes: A=Over 500 employees, B=251-500
C=101-250, D=51-100, E=50
2020 Directory of California
Wholesalers and Services Companies
© Mergent Inc. 1-800-342-5647
1319

Kanopy Insurance Center LLC ....C......877 513-2434
545 N Mountain Ave # 205 Upland (91786) *(P-10233)*
Kapl Inc ....B......714 991-9543
1126 N Brookhurst St Anaheim (92801) *(P-25772)*
Karam Bath ....E......559 864-3868
1673 W Kamm Ave Caruthers (93609) *(P-139)*
Karcher Environmental Inc (PA) ....C......714 385-1490
2300 E Orangewood Ave Anaheim (92806) *(P-3427)*
Karen Kane Inc (PA) ....C......323 588-0000
2275 E 37th St Vernon (90058) *(P-8081)*
Karma Inc ....C......209 239-1222
410 Eastwood Ave Manteca (95336) *(P-20039)*
Karsyn Construction Inc ....D......559 271-2900
4697 W Jacquelyn Ave Fresno (93722) *(P-1519)*
Kasdan Smnds Riley Vaughan LLP (PA) ....D......949 851-9000
19900 Macarthur Blvd # 850 Irvine (92612) *(P-22600)*
Kash Apparel LLC ....D......213 747-8885
1437 E 20th St Los Angeles (90011) *(P-8082)*
Kaspick & Co LLC (HQ) ....D......650 585-4100
203 Redwood Shores Pkwy # 300 Redwood City (94065) *(P-10398)*
Kate Somerville Holdings LLC ....D......323 655-4170
144 S Beverly Dr Ste 500 Beverly Hills (90212) *(P-7957)*
Kate Summerville, Beverly Hills Also called Skin Health Experts Medic *(P-22124)*
Katella Properties ....C......562 596-5561
3902 Katella Ave Los Alamitos (90720) *(P-20040)*
Katerra Inc (PA) ....D......650 422-3572
2494 Sand Hill Rd Ste 100 Menlo Park (94025) *(P-1030)*
Katherine Bousson ....D......510 582-1166
1015 Palisade St Hayward (94542) *(P-18712)*
Katten Muchin Rosenman LLP ....C......310 788-4498
515 S Flower St Los Angeles (90071) *(P-22601)*
Katten Muchin Rosenman LLP ....C......415 360-5444
1999 Harrison St Ste 700 Oakland (94612) *(P-22602)*
Katten Muchin Rosenman LLP ....C......310 788-4400
2029 Century Park E # 2600 Los Angeles (90067) *(P-22603)*
Katz Media Group Inc ....D......323 966-5000
5700 Wilshire Blvd # 200 Los Angeles (90036) *(P-27105)*
Katzkin Leather Inc (PA) ....C......323 725-1243
6868 W Acco St Montebello (90640) *(P-8981)*
Kaufman & Broad, Los Angeles Also called Kaufman and Broad Limited *(P-1302)*
Kaufman & Broad, Los Angeles Also called Kbsa Inc *(P-1305)*
Kaufman and Broad Limited ....C......310 231-4000
10990 Wilshire Blvd Fl 7 Los Angeles (90024) *(P-1302)*
Kaufman Properties, Woodland Hills Also called 7410 Woodman Avenue LLC *(P-10679)*
Kautz Ironstone Vineyards, Murphys Also called Kautz Vineyards Inc *(P-140)*
Kautz Vineyards Inc (PA) ....D......209 728-1251
1894 6 Mile Rd Murphys (95247) *(P-140)*
Kava Holdings Inc (HQ) ....C......310 472-1211
701 Stone Canyon Rd Los Angeles (90077) *(P-12501)*
Kavaliro, Petaluma Also called AB Closing Corporation *(P-14216)*
Kawahara Nursery Inc ....C......408 779-2400
698 Burnett Ave Morgan Hill (95037) *(P-253)*
Kawai America Corporation (HQ) ....E......310 631-1771
2055 E University Dr Compton (90220) *(P-7820)*
KAWEAH DELTA DISTRICT HOSPITAL, Visalia Also called Kaweah Delta Health Care Dst *(P-20985)*
Kaweah Delta Health Care Dst ....C......559 591-5513
355 Monte Vista Dr Dinuba (93618) *(P-20984)*
Kaweah Delta Health Care Dst ....C......559 592-7128
1014 San Juan Ave Exeter (93221) *(P-19133)*
Kaweah Delta Health Care Dst (PA) ....A......559 624-2000
400 W Mineral King Ave Visalia (93291) *(P-20985)*
Kaweah Dlta Hlth Care Dst Gild ....C......559 624-3100
4945 W Cypress Ave Visalia (93277) *(P-22266)*
Kaweah Dlta Hlth Care Dst Gild ....C......559 592-7300
1014 San Juan Ave Ste A Exeter (93221) *(P-22267)*
Kaweah Dlta Hlth Care Dst Gild ....C......559 624-4800
1110 S Ben Maddox Way Visalia (93292) *(P-19134)*
Kawela One LLC ....D......650 843-5000
3000 El Camino Real Palo Alto (94306) *(P-22604)*
Kay Dix Inc ....E......916 776-1701
14400 Andrus Island Rd Isleton (95641) *(P-207)*
Kayne Anderson Rudni ....D......310 229-9260
1800 Avenue Of The Stars # 200 Los Angeles (90067) *(P-11729)*
Kaza Azteca America Inc ....C......818 241-5400
3900 W Alameda Ave # 1200 Burbank (91505) *(P-5615)*
Kazan McClain Satterley & ....C......877 995-6372
55 Harrison St Ste 400 Oakland (94607) *(P-22605)*
Kazarian/Jewett Inc ....E......562 594-5927
6621 Pcf Cast Hwy Ste 120 Long Beach (90803) *(P-1360)*
Kazeon Systems Inc ....D......650 641-8100
2841 Mission College Blvd Santa Clara (95054) *(P-14899)*
KB Home (PA) ....D......310 231-4000
10990 Wilshire Blvd Fl 5 Los Angeles (90024) *(P-1303)*
KB Home Coastal Inc ....D......310 231-4000
10990 Wilshire Blvd Fl 7 Los Angeles (90024) *(P-1304)*
KB Home Grater Los Angeles Inc (HQ) ....D......310 231-4000
10990 Wilshire Blvd # 700 Los Angeles (90024) *(P-1148)*
KB Home South Bay Inc ....C......925 983-2500
5000 Executive Pkwy # 125 San Ramon (94583) *(P-1255)*
Kbak TV Channel 29 CBS ....D......661 327-7955
1901 Westwind Dr Bakersfield (93301) *(P-5616)*
Kbaktv, Bakersfield Also called Fisher Communications Inc *(P-5603)*
Kbl Group International Ltd ....E......562 699-9995
9142 9150 Norwalk Blvd Santa Fe Springs (90670) *(P-8083)*
Kbl International, Santa Fe Springs Also called Kbl Group International Ltd *(P-8083)*
Kbm Building Services, San Diego Also called Kbm Fclity Sltons Holdings LLC *(P-13959)*
Kbm Fclity Sltons Holdings LLC ....B......858 467-0202
7976 Engineer Rd Ste 200 San Diego (92111) *(P-13959)*

Kbrwyle Tech Solutions LLC ....C......760 255-8322
850 E Main St Barstow (92311) *(P-25168)*
Kbrwyle Tech Solutions LLC ....B......805 734-2982
Vanonbrg Air Frc Bldg 660 Lompoc (93438) *(P-5792)*
Kbsa Inc ....D......310 231-4000
10990 Wilshire Blvd 7th Los Angeles (90024) *(P-1305)*
KC SERVICES, Buena Park Also called Korean Community Services Inc *(P-23307)*
Kcao, Hanford Also called Kings Community Action O *(P-23304)*
Kcb Builders, Long Beach Also called Kazarian/Jewett Inc *(P-1360)*
Kcb Towers Inc ....D......909 862-0322
27260 Meines St Highland (92346) *(P-3267)*
Kcbs News Radio 74 ....D......415 765-4112
865 Battery St San Francisco (94111) *(P-5545)*
Kcetlink (PA) ....C......714 241-4100
2900 W Alameda Ave # 600 Burbank (91505) *(P-5617)*
Kci Environmental Inc ....E......805 543-3311
207 Suburban Rd Ste 6 San Luis Obispo (93401) *(P-27285)*
KCRW FM RADIO, Santa Monica Also called Kcrw Foundation Inc *(P-24186)*
Kcrw Foundation Inc ....D......310 450-5183
1900 Pico Blvd Santa Monica (90405) *(P-24186)*
KCS Electric Inc ....D......623 551-1500
1585 N Harmony Cir Anaheim (92807) *(P-2530)*
Kcsm TV & Radio, San Mateo Also called San Mateo County Community *(P-5646)*
Kdc Construction, West Sacramento Also called Cirks Construction Inc *(P-1446)*
Kdc Inc (HQ) ....C......714 828-7000
4462 Corporate Center Dr Los Alamitos (90720) *(P-2531)*
Kdc Systems, Los Alamitos Also called Kdc Inc *(P-2531)*
Kdg Construction Consulting, Glendale Also called Kennard Development Group *(P-1256)*
KDI Elements ....C......760 345-9933
79431 Country Club Dr Bermuda Dunes (92203) *(P-2898)*
Kds Printing and Packaging Inc ....E......909 770-5400
13397 Marlay Ave Ste A Fontana (92337) *(P-16867)*
Kdtv, San Jose Also called Univision Television Group Inc *(P-5661)*
Kearn Alternative Care Inc (PA) ....B......661 631-2036
2029 21st St Bakersfield (93301) *(P-21795)*
Kearny Mesa Convalescent Hosp, San Diego Also called Linda Vista Manor Inc *(P-20084)*
Keating Dental Arts Inc ....C......949 955-2100
16881 Hale Ave Ste A Irvine (92606) *(P-21613)*
Keb Keb Magic Clown ....D......916 369-6054
637 Germaine Dr Galt (95632) *(P-18713)*
Kec Engineering ....C......951 734-3010
200 N Sherman Ave Corona (92882) *(P-1740)*
Keck Hospital of Usc ....D......800 872-2273
1500 San Pablo St Los Angeles (90033) *(P-20986)*
Kedren Acute Psychia Hospit An, Los Angeles Also called Kedren Community Hlth Ctr Inc *(P-21415)*
Kedren Community Hlth Ctr Inc ....C......323 524-0634
3800 S Figueroa St Los Angeles (90037) *(P-23303)*
Kedren Community Hlth Ctr Inc (PA) ....B......323 233-0425
4211 Avalon Blvd Los Angeles (90011) *(P-21415)*
Keeco LLC (PA) ....D......510 324-8800
30736 Wiegman Rd Hayward (94544) *(P-6566)*
Keefe Plumbing Services, Glendale Also called H L Moe Co Inc *(P-2149)*
Keen Account, Union City Also called Buffalo Distribution *(P-8123)*
Keenan & Associates ....D......650 306-0616
1791 Broadway St Ste 200 Redwood City (94063) *(P-10399)*
Keenan & Associates (HQ) ....B......310 212-3344
2355 Crenshaw Blvd # 200 Torrance (90501) *(P-10400)*
Keenan & Associates ....D......707 268-1616
626 H St Eureka (95501) *(P-10401)*
Keenan & Associates ....D......951 788-0330
3550 Vine St Ste 200 Riverside (92507) *(P-10402)*
Keenan & Associates ....D......916 858-2981
2868 Prospect Park Dr # 600 Rancho Cordova (95670) *(P-10403)*
Keenan & Associates ....E......408 441-0754
1740 Tech Dr Ste 300 San Jose (95110) *(P-10404)*
Keenan & Associates ....D......949 940-1760
901 Calle Amanecer # 200 San Clemente (92673) *(P-10405)*
Keenan Farms Inc ....D......559 945-1400
31510 Plymouth Ave Kettleman City (93239) *(P-177)*
Keenan Hopkins Suder & Stowell (PA) ....D......714 695-3670
5109 E La Palma Ave Ste A Anaheim (92807) *(P-2807)*
Keenan Hopkins Suder & Stowell ....D......714 695-3670
5109 E La Palma Ave Ste A Anaheim (92807) *(P-1520)*
Keeney Truck Lines Inc ....E......323 589-3231
3500 Fruitland Ave Maywood (90270) *(P-3903)*
Keep Truckin Inc (PA) ....E......855 434-3564
55 Hawthorne St Ste 400 San Francisco (94105) *(P-14900)*
Keesal Young Logan A Prof Corp (PA) ....D......562 436-2000
400 Oceangate Ste 1400 Long Beach (90802) *(P-22606)*
Keiro Nursing Home ....C......323 276-5700
2221 Lincoln Park Ave Los Angeles (90031) *(P-20987)*
KEIRO SENIOR HEALTH CARE, Los Angeles Also called Keiro Services *(P-26282)*
Keiro Services ....B......213 873-5700
420 E 3rd St Ste 1000 Los Angeles (90013) *(P-26282)*
Keisers Holdings LLC ....D......559 265-4700
411 S West Ave Fresno (93706) *(P-18162)*
Keith Development Corporation ....E......707 528-8703
2777 Cleveland Ave # 109 Santa Rosa (95403) *(P-11568)*
Keith T Kusunis MD ....D......909 469-9494
91767 N Orange Grv Ave Pomona (91767) *(P-22053)*
Keiwit Infrastructure West Co, Fairfield Also called Kiewit Corporation *(P-1522)*
Keker Van Nest & Peters LLP ....D......415 391-5400
633 Battery St Bsmt 91 San Francisco (94111) *(P-22607)*
Keller William Realty, Visalia Also called Beethoven Holdings Inc *(P-10934)*
Keller Williams Realtors, Visalia Also called Keller Williams Realty Inc *(P-11232)*
Keller Williams Realtors, Auburn Also called East Hall Investors Inc *(P-11109)*

Mergent e-mail: customerrelations@mergent.com
1320

2020 Directory of California
Wholesalers and Services Companies

(P-0000) Products & Services Section entry number
(PA)=Parent Co (HQ)=Headquarters (DH)=Div Headquarters

Keller Williams Realtors, Carmel Valley *Also called Keller Williams Realty* ***(P-11227)***
Keller Williams Realtors, Covina *Also called Keller Williams Realty* ***(P-11228)***
Keller Williams Realtors, Torrance *Also called Keller Williams Realty* ***(P-11229)***
Keller Williams Realtors, Victorville *Also called Keller Williams Realty* ***(P-11230)***
Keller Williams Realtors, Granite Bay *Also called Williams Keller Realty* ***(P-11519)***
Keller Williams Realtors, Corona *Also called Pro Group Inc* ***(P-11369)***
Keller Williams Realtors, Chino Hills *Also called Ch Market Center Inc* ***(P-11009)***
Keller Williams Realtors, Riverside *Also called Keller Williams Realty* ***(P-11231)***
Keller Williams Realty.....D.....831 622-6200
39 Calle De Los Ositos Carmel Valley (93924) ***(P-11227)***
Keller Williams Realty.....D.....626 384-2803
100 N Citrus Ave Covina (91723) ***(P-11228)***
Keller Williams Realty.....B.....310 375-3511
23670 Hawthorne Blvd # 100 Torrance (90505) ***(P-11229)***
Keller Williams Realty.....D.....760 951-5242
12530 Hesperia Rd Ste 110 Victorville (92395) ***(P-11230)***
Keller Williams Realty.....E.....951 215-0787
7898 Mission Grove Pkwy S # 102 Riverside (92508) ***(P-11231)***
Keller Williams Realty Inc.....D.....559 733-4100
400 E Main St Visalia (93291) ***(P-11232)***
Keller Wllams Rlty Bvrly Hills.....D.....310 432-6400
439 N Canon Dr Ste 300 Beverly Hills (90210) ***(P-11233)***
Kelley Drye & Warren LLP.....C.....310 712-6100
10100 Santa Monica Blvd Los Angeles (90067) ***(P-22608)***
Kelleyamerit Fleet Services, Walnut Creek *Also called Kelleyamerit Holdings Inc* ***(P-26283)***
Kelleyamerit Holdings Inc (PA).....D.....877 512-6374
1331 N Calif Blvd Ste 150 Walnut Creek (94596) ***(P-26283)***
Kellogg Andlson Accntancy Corp (PA).....D.....818 971-5100
21700 Oxnard St Ste 800 Woodland Hills (91367) ***(P-25623)***
Kellstrom Holding Corporation (PA).....D.....561 222-7455
100 N Pcf Cast Hwy Ste 19 El Segundo (90245) ***(P-7693)***
Kellwood Company LLC.....C.....626 934-4155
13085 Temple Ave City of Industry (91746) ***(P-8084)***
Kelly Moses Floors.....E.....951 296-5147
27430 Bostik Ct Ste 101 Temecula (92590) ***(P-2899)***
Kelly Paper Company (HQ).....E.....909 859-8200
288 Brea Canyon Rd Walnut (91789) ***(P-7847)***
Kellytoy Worldwide Inc.....D.....323 923-1300
4811 S Alameda St Vernon (90058) ***(P-7737)***
Kelomar Inc.....C.....760 344-5253
3949 Austin Rd Brawley (92227) ***(P-60)***
Kelpien Health Care, Montebello *Also called Beverly Community Hosp Assn* ***(P-20765)***
Kelton Research LLC (PA).....D.....310 479-4040
12121 Bluff Creek Dr Playa Vista (90094) ***(P-25917)***
Kelvin Hildebrand Inc.....E.....831 768-9104
6 Lewis Rd Royal Oaks (95076) ***(P-3904)***
Kemp Bros Construction Inc.....E.....562 236-5000
10135 Geary Ave Santa Fe Springs (90670) ***(P-1361)***
Kemper Insurance, Glendale *Also called Arthur J Gallagher & Co* ***(P-10274)***
Kemper Insurance, Visalia *Also called Mitchell Buckman Inc* ***(P-10428)***
Kemper Insurance, Kingsburg *Also called Van Beurden Insurance Svcs Inc* ***(P-10540)***
Kemper Insurance, Irvine *Also called USI South Coast* ***(P-10538)***
Kemper Insurance, Sacramento *Also called Interwest Insurance Svcs LLC* ***(P-10390)***
Kemper Insurance, Lafayette *Also called Arthur J Gallagher & Co* ***(P-10279)***
Ken Blanchard Companies, The, Escondido *Also called Blanchard Training and Dev Inc* ***(P-26530)***
Ken Grody Ford, Buena Park *Also called Ted Ford Jones Inc* ***(P-17350)***
Ken Real Estate Lease Ltd.....D.....714 778-1700
900 S Disneyland Dr Anaheim (92802) ***(P-12502)***
Ken Starr Inc.....D.....714 632-8789
1120 N Tustin Ave Anaheim (92807) ***(P-2171)***
Kenan Advantage Group Inc.....D.....323 582-3778
2709 E 37th St Vernon (90058) ***(P-4070)***
Kendal Floral Supply LLC (PA).....D.....760 431-4910
1960 Kellogg Ave Carlsbad (92008) ***(P-8900)***
Kendal North Bouquet Co, Carlsbad *Also called Kendal Floral Supply LLC* ***(P-8900)***
Kendall Farms LP.....E.....760 731-0681
4230 White Lilac Rd Fallbrook (92028) ***(P-254)***
Kendrick Co The, Seal Beach *Also called Kendrick Construction Services* ***(P-1362)***
Kendrick Construction Services.....D.....562 546-0200
3010 Old Ranch Pkwy # 470 Seal Beach (90740) ***(P-1362)***
Kenmore Residence Club, San Francisco *Also called Monroe Residence Club* ***(P-10781)***
Kennard Development Group.....D.....818 241-0800
1025 N Brand Blvd Ste 300 Glendale (91202) ***(P-1256)***
Kennedy Athletic Club (PA).....D.....805 466-6775
3534 El Camino Real Atascadero (93422) ***(P-18163)***
Kennedy Care Center, Los Angeles *Also called BV General Inc* ***(P-20520)***
Kennedy Care Center.....D.....323 651-0043
619 N Fairfax Ave Los Angeles (90036) ***(P-20604)***
Kennedy Care Ctr Kosher Certif, Los Angeles *Also called Kennedy Care Center* ***(P-20604)***
Kennedy Club Fitness.....D.....805 781-3488
188 Tank Farm Rd San Luis Obispo (93401) ***(P-18164)***
Kennedy Elementary School, San Diego *Also called San Diego Unified School Dst* ***(P-23782)***
Kennedy Jenks, San Francisco *Also called Kennedy/Jenks Consultants Inc* ***(P-25169)***
Kennedy Pipeline Company.....D.....949 380-8363
61 Argonaut Laguna Hills (92656) ***(P-1880)***
Kennedy-Wilson Inc (PA).....C.....310 887-6400
151 El Camino Dr Beverly Hills (90212) ***(P-11234)***
Kennedy/Jenks Consultants Inc (PA).....D.....415 243-2150
303 2nd St Ste 300s San Francisco (94107) ***(P-25169)***
Kenneth Brdwick Intr Dsgns Inc.....D.....310 274-9999
1615 Westwood Blvd # 201 Los Angeles (90024) ***(P-16868)***
Kenneth Corp.....A.....714 537-5160
12601 Garden Grove Blvd Garden Grove (92843) ***(P-20988)***
Kenneth Norris Cancer Hospital, Los Angeles *Also called Tenet Health Systems Norris* ***(P-21302)***
Kenneth P Slaught Inc.....E.....805 962-8989
200 E Carrillo St Ste 200 # 200 Santa Barbara (93101) ***(P-11235)***
Kenny Pabst.....E.....562 439-2147
248 Redondo Ave Long Beach (90803) ***(P-11236)***
Kenshoo Inc (HQ).....C.....877 536-7462
22 4th St Fl 7 San Francisco (94103) ***(P-26666)***
Kensington Agency Inc.....E.....619 280-6993
8469 La Mesa Blvd La Mesa (91942) ***(P-14521)***
Kensington Nursing Agency, La Mesa *Also called Kensington Agency Inc* ***(P-14521)***
Kensington Place, Walnut Creek *Also called Argonaut Kensington Associates* ***(P-22922)***
Kentfield Rehabilitation Hosp, Kentfield *Also called 1125 Sir Francis Drake Bouleva* ***(P-20728)***
Kentina, Temecula *Also called Sft Realty Galway Downs LLC* ***(P-11445)***
Kentmaster Mfg Co Inc (PA).....E.....626 359-8888
1801 S Mountain Ave Monrovia (91016) ***(P-7554)***
Kenwood Service Center West, Cerritos *Also called Usaco Service Corp* ***(P-17468)***
Kenyon Construction Inc.....B.....925 371-8102
63 Trevarno Rd D Livermore (94551) ***(P-3173)***
Kenyon Construction Inc.....D.....559 277-5645
4667 N Blythe Ave Fresno (93722) ***(P-2808)***
Kenyon Construction Inc.....C.....916 514-9502
3223 E St North Highlands (95660) ***(P-2809)***
Kenyon Construction Inc.....C.....209 462-4060
1286 N Broadway Ave Stockton (95205) ***(P-2810)***
Kenyon Plastering, North Highlands *Also called Kenyon Construction Inc* ***(P-2809)***
Kenyon Plastering, Stockton *Also called Kenyon Construction Inc* ***(P-2810)***
Kenyon Plastream, Livermore *Also called Kenyon Construction Inc* ***(P-3173)***
Keolis Transit America Inc.....C.....818 616-5254
14663 Keswick St Van Nuys (91405) ***(P-3542)***
Keolis Transit America Inc.....D.....559 621-5783
4488 N Blackstone Ave Fresno (93726) ***(P-3543)***
Keolis Transit America Inc.....D.....661 341-3910
660 W Avenue L Lancaster (93534) ***(P-3544)***
Keolis Transit America Inc (HQ).....E.....310 981-9500
6053 W Century Blvd # 900 Los Angeles (90045) ***(P-3691)***
Kerdus Plastering Inc.....C.....951 272-6720
575 6th St Norco (92860) ***(P-2811)***
Kerlan-Jobe Orthopedic Clinic (PA).....D.....310 665-7200
6801 Park Ter Ste 500 Los Angeles (90045) ***(P-19135)***
Kerman Telephone Co.....D.....559 846-4954
811 S Madera Ave Kerman (93630) ***(P-5430)***
Kermantelnet Internet Service.....D.....559 842-2223
811 S Madera Ave Kerman (93630) ***(P-5431)***
Kern 2008 Cmnty Partners LP.....D.....559 651-3559
1219 N Plaza Dr Visalia (93291) ***(P-1257)***
Kern Alternative Care Inc.....C.....661 631-2036
2029 21st St Bakersfield (93301) ***(P-21796)***
Kern Around Clock Foundation.....E.....661 324-3221
5251 Office Park Dr # 400 Bakersfield (93309) ***(P-26284)***
Kern Cnty Mntal Hlth Child Sys.....D.....661 868-8300
1111 Columbus St Ste 3000 Bakersfield (93305) ***(P-20435)***
Kern County Hospital Authority.....A.....661 326-2102
1700 Mount Vernon Ave Bakersfield (93306) ***(P-20989)***
Kern County Water Agency.....D.....661 634-1512
811 Nadine Ln Bakersfield (93308) ***(P-6073)***
Kern Direct Marketing, Woodland Hills *Also called Kern Organization Inc* ***(P-13532)***
Kern Family Helathcare, Bakersfield *Also called Kern Health Systems Inc* ***(P-19136)***
Kern Federal Credit Union, Bakersfield *Also called Kern Member Insurance Services* ***(P-9319)***
Kern Federal Credit Union.....D.....661 327-9461
1717 Truxtun Ave Bakersfield (93301) ***(P-9318)***
Kern Health Systems Inc.....D.....661 664-5000
9700 Stockdale Hwy Bakersfield (93311) ***(P-19136)***
Kern Member Insurance Services.....E.....661 327-9461
1717 Truxtun Ave Bakersfield (93301) ***(P-9319)***
Kern Organization Inc.....D.....818 703-8775
20955 Warner Center Ln Woodland Hills (91367) ***(P-13532)***
Kern Rdlgy Imaging Systems Inc (PA).....C.....661 326-9600
2301 Bahamas Dr Bakersfield (93309) ***(P-19137)***
Kern Regional Center (PA).....C.....661 327-8531
3200 N Sillect Ave Bakersfield (93308) ***(P-24187)***
Kern Ridge Growers LLC.....B.....661 854-3141
25429 Barbara St Arvin (93203) ***(P-508)***
Kern River Co Generation Co.....D.....661 392-2663
Sw China Grade Loop Bakersfield (93308) ***(P-5850)***
Kern River Outfitters, Bayside *Also called O A Outfitting Inc* ***(P-18730)***
Kern River Tours Inc.....D.....760 379-4616
2712 Mayfair Rd Lake Isabella (93240) ***(P-18714)***
Kern Schools Federal Credit Un (PA).....D.....661 833-7900
11500 Bolthouse Dr Bakersfield (93311) ***(P-9320)***
Kern Security Corporation.....D.....661 363-6874
2701 Fruitvale Ave Bakersfield (93308) ***(P-16536)***
Kern Security Systems, Bakersfield *Also called Kern Security Corporation* ***(P-16536)***
Kern Steel Fabrication Inc (PA).....D.....661 327-9588
627 Williams St Bakersfield (93305) ***(P-17515)***
Kernen Construction.....D.....707 826-8686
2350 Glendale Dr McKinleyville (95519) ***(P-1363)***
Kerria, Auburn *Also called Westview Healh Care Center* ***(P-20382)***
Kertel Communications Inc (HQ).....D.....559 432-5800
7600 N Palm Ave Ste 101 Fresno (93711) ***(P-2532)***
Kesari Hospitality LLC.....D.....619 298-1291
445 Hotel Cir S San Diego (92108) ***(P-12503)***
Kesq TV, Thousand Palms *Also called Gulf- California Broadcast Co* ***(P-5609)***
Ketchum Incorporated.....D.....310 437-2600
12777 W Jefferson Blvd # 120 Los Angeles (90066) ***(P-26913)***
Ketchum Incorporated.....D.....415 984-6100
1050 Battery St San Francisco (94111) ***(P-26914)***
Ketchum YMCA, Los Angeles *Also called Young Mens Chrstn Assn of La* ***(P-24755)***

A L P H A B E T I C

Employee Codes: A=Over 500 employees, B=251-500
C=101-250, D=51-100, E=50
2020 Directory of California
Wholesalers and Services Companies
© Mergent Inc. 1-800-342-5647
1321

Kevcomp Inc ......D......562 423-3028
4300 Long Beach Blvd # 720 Long Beach (90807) ***(P-25170)***
Kevcomp Engineering, Long Beach *Also called Kevcomp Inc* ***(P-25170)***
Kevin Persons Inc ......E......805 371-8746
2977 Los Feliz Dr Thousand Oaks (91362) ***(P-736)***
Key Air Cnditioning Contrs Inc ......D......562 941-2233
10905 Laurel Ave Santa Fe Springs (90670) ***(P-2172)***
Key Environmental Services, Los Angeles *Also called The Teecor Group Inc* ***(P-3477)***
Key Inn & Suites, Tustin *Also called Key Inn Ltd A Cal Ltd Partnr* ***(P-12504)***
Key Inn Ltd A Cal Ltd Partnr ......E......714 832-3220
1611 El Camino Real Tustin (92780) ***(P-12504)***
Key Largo Casino, Newport Beach *Also called Ambassador Gaming Inc* ***(P-18619)***
Keypoint Credit Union (PA) ......C......408 731-4100
2805 Bowers Ave Ste 105 Santa Clara (95051) ***(P-9397)***
Keystone Automotive Inds Inc ......D......909 986-4586
2530 Lindsey Privado Dr C Ontario (91761) ***(P-6449)***
Keystone NPS LLC (HQ) ......D......909 633-6354
11980 Mount Vernon Ave Grand Terrace (92313) ***(P-24188)***
Keystone PCF Property MGT Inc (PA) ......D......949 833-2600
16775 Von Karman Ave # 100 Irvine (92606) ***(P-11237)***
Keystone Schools-Ramona, Grand Terrace *Also called Keystone NPS LLC* ***(P-24188)***
Keystone Strategy LLC ......D......877 419-2623
150 Spear St Ste 1750 San Francisco (94105) ***(P-27106)***
Keyt Television, Santa Barbara *Also called Smith Broadcasting Group Inc* ***(P-5647)***
Kf Bella Vista Health Care, Ontario *Also called Bella Vista Healthcare Center* ***(P-19750)***
Kf Community Care LLC ......C......626 357-3207
2335 Mountain Ave Duarte (91010) ***(P-20605)***
Kf Ontario Healthcare LLC ......E......909 984-6713
1661 S Euclid Ave Ontario (91762) ***(P-20606)***
Kf Sunray LLC ......D......323 734-2171
3210 W Pico Blvd Los Angeles (90019) ***(P-20607)***
Kfa LLP ......D......310 399-7975
1625 Olympic Blvd Santa Monica (90404) ***(P-25465)***
Kfco Inc ......C......310 441-2483
12100 W Washington Blvd Los Angeles (90066) ***(P-3905)***
Kfi ......E......415 956-9812
1 Sansome St Fl 32 San Francisco (94104) ***(P-26285)***
Kfjc FM, Los Altos Hills *Also called Footh-De Anza Commun Colleg Di* ***(P-5531)***
Kforce Inc ......D......858 550-1645
4510 Executive Dr Ste 325 San Diego (92121) ***(P-14317)***
Kfsn Television LLC ......C......559 442-1170
1777 G St Fresno (93706) ***(P-5618)***
Kftv ......D......559 222-2121
601 W Univision Plz Fresno (93704) ***(P-5619)***
KG Berry Farms LLC ......C......805 680-6751
1660 Philbric Rd Santa Maria (93454) ***(P-342)***
KG Oldco Inc (HQ) ......E......408 980-8550
2270 Martin Ave Santa Clara (95050) ***(P-15629)***
Kgo 810am, San Francisco *Also called San Francisco Radio Assets LLC* ***(P-5565)***
Kgo Television Inc ......C......415 954-7777
900 Front St San Francisco (94111) ***(P-5620)***
Kgtv, San Diego *Also called EW Scripps Company* ***(P-5602)***
Kh Construction, Fresno *Also called Nevocal Enterprises Inc* ***(P-1058)***
Khan Academy Inc ......D......650 336-5426
1200 Villa St Ste 200 Mountain View (94041) ***(P-15376)***
Khanna Entps - II Ltd Partnr ......C......916 338-5800
5321 Date Ave Sacramento (95841) ***(P-12505)***
Khatri Inc ......E......209 576-1481
1608 Sunrise Ave Ste 6 Modesto (95350) ***(P-12506)***
Khatri Properties, Modesto *Also called Khatri Inc* ***(P-12506)***
Kheir, Los Angeles *Also called Korean Health Education* ***(P-23308)***
Khop, Stockton *Also called Cumulus Intrmdate Holdings Inc* ***(P-5520)***
Khoros LLC (PA) ......E......415 757-3100
1 Pier Ste 1a San Francisco (94111) ***(P-15377)***
Khp II San Diego Hotel LLC (PA) ......D......619 515-3000
1047 5th Ave San Diego (92101) ***(P-12507)***
Khp III Goleta LLC ......D......805 964-6241
5650 Calle Real Goleta (93117) ***(P-12508)***
Khs & S Contractors, Anaheim *Also called Keenan Hopkins Suder & Stowell* ***(P-2807)***
Khsl TV, Chico *Also called Catamount Broadcasting of Chic* ***(P-5584)***
Khss Contractors, Anaheim *Also called Keenan Hopkins Suder & Stowell* ***(P-1520)***
Kid Helping Kids, Santa Barbara *Also called San Marcos Kids Helpng Kids FN* ***(P-24642)***
Kid Stock Inc ......D......415 753-3737
1539 Funston Ave San Francisco (94122) ***(P-17920)***
Kidango Inc (PA) ......D......510 897-6900
44000 Old Warm Sprng Blvd Fremont (94538) ***(P-23733)***
Kidango Inc ......C......510 494-9601
4700 Calaveras Ave Fremont (94538) ***(P-23734)***
Kidder Mathews LLC ......C......858 509-1200
12230 El Camino Real # 400 San Diego (92130) ***(P-11238)***
Kidney Center Inc ......C......805 433-7777
50 Moreland Rd Simi Valley (93065) ***(P-21928)***
Kidney Dialysis Center Verdugo, Simi Valley *Also called Kidney Center Inc* ***(P-21928)***
Kids First Foundation ......C......760 631-7550
1025 Service Pl Ste 103 Vista (92084) ***(P-23964)***
Kids First Foundation ......D......760 631-7550
993 S Santa Fe Ave Ste C Vista (92083) ***(P-23965)***
Kids Klub Care Centers Inc (PA) ......D......626 795-2501
380 S Raymond Ave Pasadena (91105) ***(P-23735)***
Kids Klub Pasadena, Pasadena *Also called Kids Klub Care Centers Inc* ***(P-23735)***
Kids N Things Inc (PA) ......D......805 522-1011
4221 Cochran St Simi Valley (93063) ***(P-23736)***
Kids Overcoming LLC ......D......415 748-8052
40029 St Ste 204 Oakland (94609) ***(P-21797)***
Kids World Preschool, Temecula *Also called McCusker Enterprises Inc* ***(P-23750)***
Kids' Club YMCA Oxford School, Berkeley *Also called Young MNS Chrstn Assn of E Bay* ***(P-24771)***
Kidspace A Prticipatory Museum ......D......626 449-9144
480 N Arroyo Blvd Pasadena (91103) ***(P-24267)***
Kie Con, Antioch *Also called Kiewit Infrastructure West Co* ***(P-1745)***
Kie-Con Inc ......D......925 754-9494
3551 Wilbur Ave Antioch (94509) ***(P-1521)***
Kieckhafer Schiffer & Co LLP (PA) ......E......949 250-3900
6201 Oak Cyn Ste 200 Irvine (92618) ***(P-25624)***
Kier & Wright Civil ENGrs&srvy ......E......925 245-8788
2850 Collier Canyon Rd Livermore (94551) ***(P-25522)***
Kiewit Corporation ......D......707 439-7300
4650 Business Center Dr Fairfield (94534) ***(P-1522)***
Kiewit Corporation ......D......907 222-9350
10704 Shoemaker Ave Santa Fe Springs (90670) ***(P-1523)***
Kiewit Infrastructure West Co ......D......360 693-1478
12700 Stowe Dr Ste 180 Poway (92064) ***(P-1741)***
Kiewit Infrastructure West Co ......D......510 452-1400
1111 Broadway Oakland (94607) ***(P-1742)***
Kiewit Infrastructure West Co ......D......925 462-1088
3200 Busch Rd Pleasanton (94566) ***(P-1743)***
Kiewit Infrastructure West Co ......C......562 946-1816
10704 Shoemaker Ave Santa Fe Springs (90670) ***(P-1744)***
Kiewit Infrastructure West Co ......E......925 754-9494
3551 Wilbur Ave Antioch (94509) ***(P-1745)***
Kifm Smooth Jazz 981 Inc ......C......619 297-3698
1615 Murray Canyon Rd San Diego (92108) ***(P-5546)***
Kiid, Roseville *Also called Walt Disney Company* ***(P-5574)***
Kilcrew Productions ......D......619 564-2080
32811 Wesley St Wildomar (92595) ***(P-16869)***
Kilpatrick Twnsend Stckton LLP ......C......925 472-5000
2175 N California Blvd Walnut Creek (94596) ***(P-22609)***
Kilroy Realty Corporation (PA) ......D......310 481-8400
12200 W Olympic Blvd # 200 Los Angeles (90064) ***(P-11860)***
Kim Chong ......D......323 581-4700
2105 E 25th St Los Angeles (90058) ***(P-16870)***
Klma W Medical Center ......D......530 625-4114
535 Airport Rd Hoopa (95546) ***(P-22054)***
Kimball Tirey & St John LLP (PA) ......D......619 234-1690
7676 Hazard Center Dr # 900 San Diego (92108) ***(P-22610)***
Kimberlite Corporation ......D......209 948-2551
3728 Imperial Way Stockton (95215) ***(P-16537)***
Kimberlite Corporation (PA) ......D......559 264-9730
3621 W Beechwood Ave Fresno (93711) ***(P-16538)***
Kimberly Care Center Inc ......D......805 925-8877
820 W Cook St Santa Maria (93458) ***(P-20041)***
Kimco Staffing Services Inc ......A......310 622-1616
3415 S Sepulveda Blvd # 1100 Los Angeles (90034) ***(P-14318)***
Kimco Staffing Services Inc ......A......925 945-1444
1801 Oakland Blvd Ste 220 Walnut Creek (94596) ***(P-22268)***
Kimley-Horn and Associates Inc ......D......619 234-9411
401 B St Ste 600 San Diego (92101) ***(P-25171)***
Kimpton Hotel & Rest Group LLC ......D......415 885-2500
405 Taylor St San Francisco (94102) ***(P-12509)***
Kimpton Hotel & Rest Group LLC (HQ) ......D......415 397-5572
222 Kearny St Ste 200 San Francisco (94108) ***(P-12510)***
Kimpton Hotel & Rest Group LLC ......D......415 561-1100
425 N Point St San Francisco (94133) ***(P-12511)***
Kimpton Hotel & Rest Group LLC ......D......415 561-1111
2455 Mason St San Francisco (94133) ***(P-12512)***
Kimpton Hotel & Rest Group LLC ......D......415 292-0100
501 Geary St San Francisco (94102) ***(P-12513)***
Kincaid Industries Inc ......C......760 343-5457
31065 Plantation Dr Thousand Palms (92276) ***(P-2173)***
Kind Homecare Inc ......D......888 885-5463
3705 Haven Ave Ste 104 Menlo Park (94025) ***(P-21798)***
Kinder Mrgan Enrgy Partners LP ......E......310 518-7700
2000 E Sepulveda Blvd Carson (90810) ***(P-4570)***
Kinder Mrgan Enrgy Partners LP ......E......909 873-5100
2319 S Riverside Ave Bloomington (92316) ***(P-4810)***
Kinder Mrgan Lqds Trminals LLC ......D......415 467-8107
950 Tunnel Ave Brisbane (94005) ***(P-4571)***
Kinder Mrgan Lqds Trminals LLC ......D......619 283-6511
9950 San Diego Mission Rd San Diego (92108) ***(P-5964)***
Kinder Mrgan Lqds Trminals LLC ......D......408 435-7399
2150 Kruse Dr San Jose (95131) ***(P-4572)***
Kindercare Education LLC ......D......925 824-0267
3280 Crow Canyon Rd San Ramon (94583) ***(P-23737)***
Kindercare Learning Ctrs LLC ......D......562 961-8882
5251 E Las Lomas St Long Beach (90815) ***(P-23738)***
Kindred Healthcare Oper Inc ......C......925 692-5886
1800 Adobe St Concord (94520) ***(P-20042)***
Kindred Healthcare Oper Inc ......D......916 454-5752
4700 Elvas Ave Sacramento (95819) ***(P-20043)***
Kindred Healthcare Oper Inc ......D......805 487-7840
2641 S C St Oxnard (93033) ***(P-20608)***
Kindred Healthcare Oper Inc ......D......714 529-6842
875 N Brea Blvd Brea (92821) ***(P-20044)***
Kindred Healthcare Oper Inc ......C......909 862-0611
7534 Palm Ave Highland (92346) ***(P-20045)***
Kindred Healthcare Oper Inc ......D......925 443-1800
76 Fenton St Livermore (94550) ***(P-20046)***
Kindred Healthcare Oper Inc ......B......510 357-8300
2800 Benedict Dr San Leandro (94577) ***(P-20990)***
Kindred Healthcare Oper Inc ......B......909 391-0333
550 N Monterey Ave Ontario (91764) ***(P-20991)***
Kindred Healthcare Oper LLC ......C......916 457-6521
3500 Folsom Blvd Sacramento (95816) ***(P-20047)***
Kindred Healthcare Oper LLC ......C......502 596-7300
1940 El Cajon Blvd San Diego (92104) ***(P-20992)***
Kindred Healthcare Oper LLC ......C......760 471-2986
1586 W San Marcos Blvd San Marcos (92078) ***(P-20048)***

Kindred Healthcare Oper LLC ....C.......831 424-8072
720 E Romie Ln Salinas (93901) ***(P-20049)***
Kindred Healthcare Oper LLC ....D.......415 922-5085
2121 Pine St San Francisco (94115) ***(P-20050)***
Kindred Healthcare Oper LLC ....C.......415 566-1200
1575 7th Ave San Francisco (94122) ***(P-20051)***
Kindred Healthcare Operating........B.......650 697-1865
1609 Trousdale Dr Burlingame (94010) ***(P-21479)***
Kindred Healthcare Operating........C.......661 872-2121
2211 Mount Vernon Ave Bakersfield (93306) ***(P-20052)***
Kindred Healthcare Operating........C.......916 351-9151
223 Fargo Way Folsom (95630) ***(P-20053)***
Kindred Healthcare Operating........B.......310 642-0325
5525 W Slauson Ave Los Angeles (90056) ***(P-20993)***
Kindred Healthcare Operating........D.......951 688-8200
9020 Garfield St Riverside (92503) ***(P-20609)***
Kindred Hospital, San Leandro *Also called Kindred Healthcare Oper Inc* ***(P-20990)***
Kindred Hospital - Brea, Brea *Also called Kindred Healthcare Oper Inc* ***(P-20044)***
Kindred Hospital - Rancho, Rancho Cucamonga *Also called Knd Development 55 LLC* ***(P-20995)***
Kindred Hospital La Mirada, La Mirada *Also called Southern Cal Spcialty Care Inc* ***(P-21209)***
Kindred Hospital La Mirata, West Covina *Also called Southern Cal Spcialty Care Inc* ***(P-21207)***
Kindred Hospital San Diego, San Diego *Also called Kindred Healthcare Oper LLC* ***(P-20992)***
Kindred Nrsing Hlthcre- Bybrry, Concord *Also called Kindred Healthcare Oper Inc* ***(P-20042)***
Kindred Nursing, San Francisco *Also called Kindred Healthcare Oper LLC* ***(P-20050)***
Kindred Nursing and Reha, San Rafael *Also called Kindred Nursing Centers W LLC* ***(P-20994)***
Kindred Nursing Centers W LLC........D.......510 521-5600
516 Willow St Alameda (94501) ***(P-20054)***
Kindred Nursing Centers W LLC........D.......415 456-7170
1601 5th Ave San Rafael (94901) ***(P-20994)***
Kindred Nursing Centers W LLC........C.......530 243-6317
2120 Benton Dr Redding (96003) ***(P-20055)***
Kindred Nursing Centers W LLC........C.......209 957-4539
1517 Knickerbocker Dr Stockton (95210) ***(P-20056)***
Kindred Nursing Centers W LLC........C.......415 673-8405
1359 Pine St San Francisco (94109) ***(P-22055)***
Kindred Nursng & Healthcare, Livermore *Also called Kindred Healthcare Oper Inc* ***(P-20046)***
Kindred Transitional, Stockton *Also called Kindred Nursing Centers W LLC* ***(P-20056)***
Kindred Transitional Care, Alameda *Also called Kindred Nursing Centers W LLC* ***(P-20054)***
Kindred Transitional Care, Redding *Also called Kindred Nursing Centers W LLC* ***(P-20055)***
Kindred Transitional Care, San Francisco *Also called Kindred Nursing Centers W LLC* ***(P-22055)***
Kinecta Federal Credit Union (PA)........C.......310 643-5400
1440 Rosecrans Ave Manhattan Beach (90266) ***(P-9321)***
Kinemetrics Inc (HQ)........D.......626 795-2220
222 Vista Ave Pasadena (91107) ***(P-25172)***
Kinetic Systems Inc........E.......949 502-4856
1620 S Sunkist St Anaheim (92806) ***(P-2174)***
Kineticom Inc (PA)........D.......619 330-3100
8885 Rio San Diego Dr # 210 San Diego (92108) ***(P-14319)***
Kinetics Mechanical Svc Inc........D.......925 245-6200
6336 Patterson Pass Rd H Livermore (94550) ***(P-2175)***
King Hlmes Pterno Soriano LLP........E.......310 282-8989
1900 Avenue Of The Stars Los Angeles (90067) ***(P-22611)***
King & Spalding LLP........B.......415 318-1200
101 2nd St Ste 2300 San Francisco (94105) ***(P-22612)***
King Equipment LLC........D.......909 986-5300
1690 Ashley Way Colton (92324) ***(P-14175)***
King George Cabbage, Watsonville *Also called Guy George* ***(P-97)***
King Harbor Sports Center, Redondo Beach *Also called Sport Center Fitness Inc* ***(P-18202)***
King Janitorial Equipment Svcs, Garden Grove *Also called Janitorial Equipment Svcs Inc* ***(P-13957)***
King Monster Inc........D.......661 253-3000
27451 Tourney Rd Ste 140 Valencia (91355) ***(P-11239)***
King Relocation Services, Santa Fe Springs *Also called Van King & Storage Inc* ***(P-4162)***
King Security Services Inc........A.......415 556-5464
1159 7th St Novato (94945) ***(P-16334)***
King Ventures........C.......805 544-4444
285 Bridge St San Luis Obispo (93401) ***(P-11569)***
King-Reynolds Ventures LLC........D.......650 879-2136
2001 Rossi Rd Pescadero (94060) ***(P-16871)***
Kingcom(us) LLC (HQ)........C.......424 744-5697
3100 Ocean Park Blvd Santa Monica (90405) ***(P-15378)***
Kingdom Enterprise Films LLC........E.......818 963-2513
10812 Bothwell Rd Chatsworth (91311) ***(P-17621)***
Kingdom Express Inc........D.......310 258-0900
18640 Crenshaw Blvd Torrance (90504) ***(P-4071)***
Kingledon Inc........C.......805 643-6000
2055 Harbor Blvd Ventura (93001) ***(P-12514)***
Kings Arena Ltd Partnership........D.......916 928-0000
1 Sports Pkwy Sacramento (95834) ***(P-18066)***
Kings Casino Management Corp........B.......916 560-4405
6510 Antelope Rd Citrus Heights (95621) ***(P-18715)***
Kings Community Action O (PA)........D.......559 582-4386
1130 N 11th Ave Hanford (93230) ***(P-23304)***
Kings County Probation Dept., Hanford *Also called County of Kings* ***(P-23081)***
Kings County Truck Lines (HQ)........C.......559 686-2857
754 S Blackstone St Tulare (93274) ***(P-4072)***
Kings Credit Services........D.......559 322-2550
96 Shaw Ave Ste 221 Clovis (93612) ***(P-13689)***
Kings Garden LLC........C.......760 275-4969
3540 N Anza Rd Palm Springs (92262) ***(P-26667)***
Kings Garden Royal Deliveries, Palm Springs *Also called Kings Garden LLC* ***(P-26667)***
Kings Inn Hotel & Grille, San Diego *Also called Kings Inn Hotel San Diego* ***(P-12515)***
Kings Inn Hotel San Diego........D.......619 297-2231
1333 Hotel Cir S San Diego (92108) ***(P-12515)***
Kings Jewelry and Loan, Los Angeles *Also called Kings Pawnshop* ***(P-9630)***
Kings Nrsing Rhabilitaion Hosp, Hanford *Also called Wilshire Hlth & Cmnty Svcs Inc* ***(P-20726)***
Kings Nrsing Rhabilitation Ctr, Hanford *Also called Mission Medical Entps Inc* ***(P-20142)***
Kings Pawnshop........D.......213 383-5555
800 S Vermont Ave Los Angeles (90005) ***(P-9630)***
Kings Rehabilitation Center (PA)........D.......559 582-9234
490 E Hanford Armona Rd Hanford (93230) ***(P-23305)***
Kings River Conservation Dst........D.......559 237-5567
4886 E Jensen Ave Fresno (93725) ***(P-27286)***
Kings Seafood Company LLC........D.......714 793-1177
7691 Edinger Ave Huntington Beach (92647) ***(P-8371)***
Kings Seafood Company LLC........D.......714 771-6655
1521 W Katella Ave Orange (92867) ***(P-8372)***
Kings View........E.......209 357-0321
100 Airpark Rd Atwater (95301) ***(P-23608)***
Kings View........D.......559 582-9307
289 E 8th St Hanford (93230) ***(P-22056)***
Kings View Work Experience Ctr........E.......209 826-8118
703 I St Los Banos (93635) ***(P-9909)***
Kingsburg Apple Packers Inc........B.......559 897-5132
10363 Davis Ave Kingsburg (93631) ***(P-8492)***
Kingsburg Apple Partners LP........D.......559 897-5132
10363 Davis Ave Kingsburg (93631) ***(P-208)***
KINGSBURG CENTER, Kingsburg *Also called Sunbridge Care Entps W LLC* ***(P-20283)***
Kingsburg Center, Kingsburg *Also called Sunbridge Care Entps W Inc* ***(P-20282)***
Kingsburg Orchards, Kingsburg *Also called Kingsburg Apple Packers Inc* ***(P-8492)***
Kingsley Manor, Los Angeles *Also called Front Porch Communities* ***(P-19928)***
Kingspan Light & Air LLC........C.......714 540-8950
401 Goetz Ave Santa Ana (92707) ***(P-3067)***
Kingsview Corp........D.......209 533-6245
2 S Green St Sonora (95370) ***(P-22057)***
Kinsbursky Bros Supply Inc (PA)........D.......714 738-8516
125 E Commercial St Ste A Anaheim (92801) ***(P-7763)***
Kinship Center........D.......714 979-2365
18302 Irvine Blvd Ste 300 Tustin (92780) ***(P-23306)***
Kintera Inc (HQ)........D.......858 795-3000
9605 Scranton Rd Ste 200 San Diego (92121) ***(P-15379)***
Kintetsu Enterprises........D.......213 687-2000
328 E 1st St Los Angeles (90012) ***(P-26286)***
Kintetsu Enterprises Co Amer, Torrance *Also called Kintetsu Enterprises Co Amer* ***(P-12516)***
Kintetsu Enterprises Co Amer (HQ)........C.......310 782-9300
21241 S Wstn Ave Ste 100 Torrance (90501) ***(P-12516)***
Kintetsu Enterprises Co Amer........D.......213 617-2000
328 E 1st St Los Angeles (90012) ***(P-12517)***
Kioxia America Inc (HQ)........C.......408 526-2400
2610 Orchard Pkwy San Jose (95134) ***(P-7288)***
Kioxia America Inc........E.......916 986-4707
35 Iron Point Cir Ste 100 Folsom (95630) ***(P-25773)***
Kipp Foundation........C.......415 399-1556
135 Main St Ste 1700 San Francisco (94105) ***(P-24189)***
Kirkhill Aircraft Parts Co (PA)........C.......323 216-9136
3120 Enterprise St Brea (92821) ***(P-7694)***
Kirkhill Rubber Company........D.......562 803-1117
2500 E Thompson St Long Beach (90805) ***(P-7638)***
Kirkland & Ellis LLP........C.......415 439-1400
555 California St # 2700 San Francisco (94104) ***(P-22613)***
Kirkpatrick Ldscpg Svcs Inc........C.......760 347-6926
43752 Jackson St Indio (92201) ***(P-841)***
Kirschenman Enterprises Inc........D.......661 366-5736
10100 Digiorgio Rd Bakersfield (93307) ***(P-343)***
Kirschenman Enterprises Sls LP........B.......661 366-5736
12826 Edison Hwy Edison (93220) ***(P-16872)***
Kirschenman Packing Inc........C.......661 366-5736
12826 Edison Hwy Edison (93220) ***(P-509)***
Kisco Senior Living LLC........D.......415 664-6264
1601 19th Ave Ofc San Francisco (94122) ***(P-26287)***
Kisco Senior Living LLC........D.......415 491-1935
275 Los Ranchitos Rd San Rafael (94903) ***(P-10747)***
Kisco Senior Living LLC........D.......714 872-9785
1731 W Medical Center Dr Anaheim (92801) ***(P-10748)***
Kisco Senior Living LLC........D.......949 888-2250
21952 Buena Suerte Rcho STA Marg (92688) ***(P-10749)***
Kisco Senior Living LLC........D.......559 449-8070
1100 E Spruce Ave Ofc Fresno (93720) ***(P-10750)***
Kisco Senior Living LLC........D.......707 585-1800
1350 Oak View Cir Rohnert Park (94928) ***(P-10751)***
Kisco Senior Living LLC........E.......650 948-7337
1174 Los Altos Ave Ofc Los Altos (94022) ***(P-10752)***
Kissito Health Care Inc........D.......510 582-8311
442 Sunset Blvd Hayward (94541) ***(P-21799)***
Kissito Health Case Inc........D.......925 689-9222
3318 Willow Pass Rd Concord (94519) ***(P-21800)***
Kissito Health Case Inc........D.......510 357-4015
368 Juana Ave San Leandro (94577) ***(P-21801)***
Kissito Health Case Inc........C.......209 524-4817
1310 W Granger Ave Modesto (95350) ***(P-20057)***
Kit Carson Nursing & Rehab, Jackson *Also called Tutera Group Inc* ***(P-20338)***
Kitayama Brothers Inc........D.......831 722-8118
481 San Andreas Rd Watsonville (95076) ***(P-255)***
Kitayama Flowers, Watsonville *Also called Kitayama Brothers Inc* ***(P-255)***
Kitchen Mart Inc........D.......916 315-3535
4381 Granite Dr Ste C Rocklin (95677) ***(P-1149)***
Kite Electric Inc........C.......949 380-7471
2 Thomas Irvine (92618) ***(P-2533)***
Kite Pharma Inc (HQ)........C.......310 824-9999
2400 Broadway Ste 100 Santa Monica (90404) ***(P-25774)***

A L P H A B E T I C

Employee Codes: A=Over 500 employees, B=251-500
C=101-250, D=51-100, E=50
2020 Directory of California
Wholesalers and Services Companies
© Mergent Inc. 1-800-342-5647
1323

Kitson Landscape MGT Inc..........D.......805 681-9460
5787 Thornwood Dr Goleta (93117) ***(P-842)***
Kittridge Gardens, Reseda *Also called GK Management Co Inc* ***(P-11169)***
Kittridge Hotels & Resorts LLC..........D.......760 325-9676
150 S Indian Canyon Dr Palm Springs (92262) ***(P-12518)***
Kiwanis International Inc..........D.......209 578-1448
3201 Canterbury Ct Modesto (95350) ***(P-24570)***
Kjc Operating Company..........C.......760 762-5562
41100 Us Highway 395 Boron (93516) ***(P-5851)***
Kkhj 930 AM, Burbank *Also called Liberman Broadcasting Inc* ***(P-5556)***
Kkzz 1590..........E.......805 289-1400
2284 S Victoria Ave 2g Ventura (93003) ***(P-5547)***
Kl Cutting Service Inc..........C.......213 742-9001
2250 Maple Ave Los Angeles (90011) ***(P-13323)***
Klassen Corporation (PA)..........D.......661 327-0875
2021 Westwind Dr Bakersfield (93301) ***(P-1524)***
Klein Denatale Goldner Et Al (PA)..........D.......661 401-7755
4550 California Ave Fl 2 Bakersfield (93309) ***(P-22614)***
Klein Denatale Goldner Cooper, Bakersfield *Also called Klein Denatale Goldner Et Al* ***(P-22614)***
Klein Foods Inc..........D.......707 431-1533
11455 Old Redwood Hwy Healdsburg (95448) ***(P-141)***
Klein-Testan-Brundo..........E.......714 245-8888
1851 E 1st St Ste 100 Santa Ana (92705) ***(P-22615)***
Kleiner Prkins Cfeld Byers LLC (PA)..........C.......650 233-2750
2750 Sand Hill Rd Menlo Park (94025) ***(P-11925)***
Kleinfelder Inc (HQ)..........C.......619 831-4600
550 W C St Ste 1200 San Diego (92101) ***(P-25173)***
Kleinfelder Inc..........D.......559 486-0750
5125 N Gates Ave Ste 102 Fresno (93722) ***(P-25174)***
Kleinfelder Inc..........D.......925 484-1700
6700 Koll Center Pkwy # 120 Pleasanton (94566) ***(P-25175)***
Kleinfelder Inc..........D.......951 801-3681
3880 Lemon St Ste 300 Riverside (92501) ***(P-27107)***
Kleinfelder Inc..........D.......916 366-1701
2882 Prospect Park Dr # 200 Rancho Cordova (95670) ***(P-25176)***
Kleinfelder Associates..........A.......619 831-4600
550 W C St Ste 1200 San Diego (92101) ***(P-25177)***
Kleinpartners Capital Corp..........B.......310 426-2055
400 Continental Blvd # 600 El Segundo (90245) ***(P-11926)***
Klh Consulting Inc..........D.......707 575-9986
2324 Bethards Dr Santa Rosa (95405) ***(P-27108)***
Klink Citrus Association..........C.......559 798-1881
32921 Road 159 Ivanhoe (93235) ***(P-510)***
Klink Citrus Exchange, Ivanhoe *Also called Klink Citrus Association* ***(P-510)***
Klm Management Company..........D.......626 330-3479
14120 Valley Blvd City of Industry (91746) ***(P-8318)***
Klm Orthotic Laboratories Inc..........D.......661 295-2600
28280 Alta Vista Ave Valencia (91355) ***(P-6974)***
Kloeckner Metals Corporation..........D.......562 906-2020
9804 Norwalk Blvd Ste A Santa Fe Springs (90670) ***(P-7076)***
Kloeckner Metals Corporation..........E.......562 906-2020
9804 Norwalk Blvd Ste A Santa Fe Springs (90670) ***(P-7077)***
Kloeckner Metals Corporation..........D.......559 688-7980
2000 S O St Tulare (93274) ***(P-7078)***
Kloudgin, Sunnyvale *Also called Enterprise Signal Inc* ***(P-15321)***
Klx Inc..........D.......559 684-1037
3645 S K St Tulare (93274) ***(P-4073)***
Km Fresno Investors LLC..........E.......323 556-6600
6222 Wilshire Blvd # 650 Los Angeles (90048) ***(P-11927)***
Km Industrial Inc..........C.......562 786-6200
2375 W Esther St Long Beach (90813) ***(P-13960)***
KMA Emergency Services Inc..........D.......510 614-1420
14275 Wicks Blvd San Leandro (94577) ***(P-3692)***
Kmax TV, West Sacramento *Also called Sacramento Television Stns Inc* ***(P-5645)***
KMD Architects (PA)..........D.......415 398-5191
417 Montgomery St Ste 200 San Francisco (94104) ***(P-25466)***
Kmea (PA)..........D.......619 399-5900
2423 Hoover Ave National City (91950) ***(P-22616)***
Kmir-Tv6, Palm Desert *Also called Entravsion Communications Corp* ***(P-5598)***
Kml Enterprises Career Dev LLC..........C.......714 221-3100
1900 S State College Blvd Anaheim (92806) ***(P-16048)***
Kmph Fox 26..........C.......559 255-2600
5111 E Mckinley Ave Fresno (93727) ***(P-5621)***
Kms Fishermans Wharf LP..........C.......415 561-1100
425 N Point St San Francisco (94133) ***(P-12519)***
Knd Development 55 LLC..........D.......909 581-6400
10841 White Oak Ave Rancho Cucamonga (91730) ***(P-20995)***
Knet TV..........E.......323 469-5638
5757 Wilshire Blvd # 470 Los Angeles (90036) ***(P-5622)***
Kniesels Auto Collision Center..........E.......916 315-8888
4680 Pacific St Rocklin (95677) ***(P-17296)***
Knight Port Services, Compton *Also called Knight Transportation Inc* ***(P-4074)***
Knight Transportation Inc..........C.......888 549-7802
2960 E Victoria St Compton (90221) ***(P-4074)***
Knight-Calabasas LLC (PA)..........D.......818 222-3200
4515 Park Entrada Calabasas (91302) ***(P-18473)***
Knight-Calabasas LLC..........D.......415 453-4940
333 Biscayne Dr San Rafael (94901) ***(P-18474)***
Knight-Swift Trnsp Hldings Inc..........D.......209 858-1630
901 Darcy Pkwy Lathrop (95330) ***(P-4075)***
Knight-Swift Trnsp Hldings Inc..........D.......559 441-0340
2797 S Orange Ave Fresno (93725) ***(P-4076)***
Knight-Swift Trnsp Hldings Inc..........D.......951 360-0130
11888 Mission Blvd Jurupa Valley (91752) ***(P-4077)***
Knight-Swift Trnsp Hldings Inc..........D.......619 671-0588
6933 Calle De Linea Chula Vista (91911) ***(P-4078)***
Knights of Columbus..........D.......408 262-6609
871 Founders Ln Milpitas (95035) ***(P-24571)***
Knights of Columbus..........C.......805 525-7810
1344 Magnolia Dr Santa Paula (93060) ***(P-24572)***
Knit Generation Group Inc..........D.......213 221-5081
3818 S Broadway Los Angeles (90037) ***(P-26288)***
Kno Inc..........D.......408 844-8120
2200 Mission College Blvd Santa Clara (95054) ***(P-15380)***
Knobbe Martens Olson Bear LLP (PA)..........B.......949 760-0404
2040 Main St Fl 14 Irvine (92614) ***(P-22617)***
Knobbe Martens Olson Bear LLP..........D.......858 707-4000
12790 El Camino Real # 100 San Diego (92130) ***(P-22618)***
Knolls Convalescent Hospital (PA)..........C.......760 245-5361
16890 Green Tree Blvd Victorville (92395) ***(P-20058)***
Knolls Convalescent Hospital..........D.......760 245-6477
14973 Hesperia Rd Victorville (92395) ***(P-20059)***
Knolls West Enterprise..........D.......760 245-0107
16890 Green Tree Blvd Victorville (92395) ***(P-23966)***
Knolls West Post Acute LLC..........D.......760 245-5361
16890 Green Tree Blvd Victorville (92395) ***(P-20610)***
Knolls West Residential Care, Victorville *Also called Knolls West Enterprise* ***(P-23966)***
Knollwood Center, Riverside *Also called Knollwood Psychiatric and Chem* ***(P-21416)***
Knollwood Psychiatric and Chem..........D.......951 275-8400
5900 Brockton Ave Riverside (92506) ***(P-21416)***
KNOLLWOOD PSYCHIATRIC CENTER, Riverside *Also called Behavioral Health Resources* ***(P-21386)***
Knot Wedding Wire..........E.......530 242-1621
1679 Insight Pl Redding (96003) ***(P-5432)***
Knott's Berry Farm Hotel, Buena Park *Also called Knotts Berry Farm LLC* ***(P-12520)***
Knotts Berry Farm LLC..........C.......714 995-1111
7675 Crescent Ave Buena Park (90620) ***(P-12520)***
Knowledge Adventure, Torrance *Also called Knowledge Holdings Inc* ***(P-14901)***
Knowledge Holdings Inc (PA)..........D.......310 533-3400
2377 Crenshaw Blvd # 302 Torrance (90501) ***(P-14901)***
Knox Attorney Service Inc (PA)..........C.......619 233-9700
2250 4th Ave Ste 200 San Diego (92101) ***(P-22619)***
Knox Services, San Diego *Also called Knox Attorney Service Inc* ***(P-22619)***
Knox Services LLC (PA)..........D.......714 479-1650
1522 Brookhollow Dr Ste 3 Santa Ana (92705) ***(P-13763)***
Knudtson Building Maint Svc, Sherman Oaks *Also called Adhei Enterprises Inc* ***(P-13850)***
Ko Holdings LLC..........D.......949 629-3044
220 Newport Center Dr Newport Beach (92660) ***(P-22620)***
Koam Engineering Systems Inc..........C.......858 292-0922
7807 Convoy Ct Ste 200 San Diego (92111) ***(P-15630)***
Kobata Growers Inc (PA)..........D.......310 323-0662
17622 Van Ness Ave Torrance (90504) ***(P-256)***
Kobey Corporation Inc (PA)..........D.......619 523-2700
3740 Sports Arena Blvd # 2 San Diego (92110) ***(P-16873)***
Kobey Swap Meet At Spt Arena, San Diego *Also called Kobey Corporation Inc* ***(P-16873)***
Koce-TV Foundation..........D.......714 241-4100
3080 Bristol St Ste 400 Costa Mesa (92626) ***(P-5623)***
Koch-Armstrong General Engrg..........D.......619 561-2005
15315 Olde Highway 80 El Cajon (92021) ***(P-25178)***
Kodiak Roofing & Waterproofing, Roseville *Also called Dwayne Nash Industries Inc* ***(P-3049)***
Koeller Nbker Crlson Hluck LLP (PA)..........C.......949 864-3400
3 Park Plz Ste 1500 Irvine (92614) ***(P-22621)***
Kofax Inc (PA)..........B.......949 783-1000
15211 Laguna Canyon Rd Irvine (92618) ***(P-14902)***
Koffler Elec Mech Apprts Repai..........D.......510 567-0630
527 Whitney St San Leandro (94577) ***(P-7160)***
Kogoam, San Diego *Also called Iheartcommunications Inc* ***(P-5537)***
Kohlberg Kravis Roberts Co LP..........D.......650 233-6560
2800 Sand Hill Rd Ste 200 Menlo Park (94025) ***(P-11928)***
Kohls Corporation..........B.......909 382-4300
890 E Mill St San Bernardino (92408) ***(P-4440)***
Koit, San Francisco *Also called Bonneville International Corp* ***(P-5509)***
Kojenov Arkadi Nilovich..........E.......916 718-1790
5335 Hackberry Ln Sacramento (95841) ***(P-4975)***
Kolb Elementary School, Dublin *Also called Dublin Unified School District* ***(P-24400)***
Kole Imports..........D.......310 834-0004
24600 Main St Carson (90745) ***(P-8982)***
Koll Management Services Inc..........A.......949 833-3030
4343 Von Karman Ave Newport Beach (92660) ***(P-11240)***
Kollstar Golf Company, Newport Beach *Also called Kollwood Golf Operating LP* ***(P-18258)***
Kollwood Golf Operating LP..........B.......949 833-3025
4343 Von Karman Ave Newport Beach (92660) ***(P-18258)***
Komar Distribution Services, Jurupa Valley *Also called Charles Komar & Sons Inc* ***(P-4384)***
Kommonwealth Inc..........E.......310 278-7328
6420 Wilshire Blvd Los Angeles (90048) ***(P-8136)***
Kona Kai Resort Hotel, San Diego *Also called Westgroup Kona Kai LLC* ***(P-18610)***
Konami Digital Entrmt Inc (HQ)..........D.......310 220-8100
2381 Rosecrans Ave # 200 El Segundo (90245) ***(P-15381)***
Kondaur Capital Corporation (PA)..........C.......714 352-2038
333 S Anita Dr Ste 400 Orange (92868) ***(P-9568)***
Kong Inc..........E.......415 754-9283
251 Post St Ste 200 San Francisco (94108) ***(P-14903)***
Konica Minolta Business Soluti..........D.......909 824-2000
1831 Commercenter W San Bernardino (92408) ***(P-6755)***
Konica Minolta Business Soluti..........E.......310 214-6696
879 W 190th St Ste 200 Gardena (90248) ***(P-6756)***
Konica Minolta Hlthcare, Aliso Viejo *Also called Ambry Genetics Corporation* ***(P-21505)***
Koning & Associates Inc (PA)..........E.......408 265-3800
1631 Willow St Ste 220 San Jose (95125) ***(P-10406)***
Kono Farms Incorporated..........C.......760 397-7110
87481 Avenue 74 Thermal (92274) ***(P-61)***
KONOCTI TRANSPORTATION SERVICE, Lakeport *Also called People Services Inc* ***(P-24024)***

Konocti Vista Casino (PA)..........C.......707 262-1900
2755 Mission Rancheria Rd Lakeport (95453) ***(P-18716)***
Konoike-Pacific California Inc (HQ)..........D.......310 518-1000
1420 Coil Ave Wilmington (90744) ***(P-4441)***
Koos Manufacturing Inc..........A.......323 249-1000
2741 Seminole Ave South Gate (90280) ***(P-16874)***
Kopy Kat Attorney Service, Brea *Also called V A Anderson Enterprises Inc* ***(P-17141)***
Kor Hotel Groups Inc..........D.......310 309-8066
530 Pico Blvd Santa Monica (90405) ***(P-26289)***
Koram Insurance Center Inc..........D.......323 660-1000
3807 Wilshire Blvd # 400 Los Angeles (90010) ***(P-10407)***
Kore1 Inc..........D.......949 706-6990
530 Technology Dr Ste 150 Irvine (92618) ***(P-16049)***
Korea Tchnlgy Cmmnications USA, Burbank *Also called Eon Innovative Technology Inc* ***(P-16512)***
Korean Air Lines Co Ltd..........C.......310 646-4866
380 World Way Ste S4 Los Angeles (90045) ***(P-4672)***
Korean Airlines..........C.......310 417-5294
380 World Way Los Angeles (90045) ***(P-4673)***
Korean Airlines Co Ltd..........C.......310 410-2000
6101 W Imperial Hwy Los Angeles (90045) ***(P-4674)***
Korean Airlines Co Ltd..........D.......213 484-1900
1813 Wilshire Blvd # 400 Los Angeles (90057) ***(P-4675)***
Korean Arln Crgo Reservations, Los Angeles *Also called Korean Airlines Co Ltd* ***(P-4674)***
Korean Community Services Inc..........E.......714 527-6561
8633 Knott Ave Buena Park (90620) ***(P-23307)***
Korean Health Education (PA)..........D.......213 427-4000
3727 W 6th St Ste 210 Los Angeles (90020) ***(P-23308)***
Koreatown Youth and Cmnty Ctr (PA)..........D.......213 365-7400
3727 W 6th St Ste 300 Los Angeles (90020) ***(P-23309)***
Korn Ferry (PA)..........C.......310 552-1834
1900 Avenue Of The Stars # 2600 Los Angeles (90067) ***(P-26668)***
Kos-USA..........D.......213 747-2591
3434 S Broadway Los Angeles (90007) ***(P-8085)***
Kositch Enterprises Inc..........D.......510 657-4460
5700 Boscell Cmn Fremont (94538) ***(P-2534)***
Kotobuki-Ya Inc..........D.......650 344-7955
314 Lang Rd Burlingame (94010) ***(P-3545)***
Kountable Inc..........D.......310 613-5481
321 Pacific Ave Fl 3 San Francisco (94111) ***(P-16875)***
Koury Engrg Tstg & Insptn..........D.......310 851-8685
14280 Euclid Ave Chino (91710) ***(P-16876)***
Kovel/Fuller LLC..........D.......310 841-4444
9925 Jefferson Blvd Culver City (90232) ***(P-13533)***
Koxr Spanish Radio..........E.......805 487-0444
200 S A St Ste 400 Oxnard (93030) ***(P-5548)***
Kozuki Farming Inc..........D.......559 646-2652
16518 E Adams Ave Parlier (93648) ***(P-209)***
Kp International, Oakland *Also called Permanente Kaiser Intl* ***(P-10029)***
Kp LLC..........C.......510 346-0729
13951 Washington Ave San Leandro (94578) ***(P-13727)***
Kpac, Wilmington *Also called Konoike-Pacific California Inc* ***(P-4441)***
Kpcb, Menlo Park *Also called Kleiner Prkins Cfeld Byers LLC* ***(P-11925)***
Kpff Inc..........C.......310 665-1536
700 S Flower St Ste 2100 Los Angeles (90017) ***(P-25179)***
Kpff Inc..........D.......562 437-9100
400 Oceangate Ste 500 Long Beach (90802) ***(P-25180)***
Kpff Inc..........D.......415 989-1004
45 Fremont St Fl 28 San Francisco (94105) ***(P-25181)***
Kpff Consulting Engineers, San Francisco *Also called Kpff Inc* ***(P-25181)***
Kpisoft Inc..........D.......415 439-5228
50 California St Ste 1500 San Francisco (94111) ***(P-15382)***
Kpmg LLP..........E.......310 273-2770
9171 Wilshire Blvd # 500 Beverly Hills (90210) ***(P-25625)***
Kpmg LLP..........C.......858 750-7100
4655 Executive Dr # 1100 San Diego (92121) ***(P-25626)***
Kpmg LLP..........E.......415 963-5100
55 2nd St Ste 1400 San Francisco (94105) ***(P-25627)***
Kpmg LLP..........D.......703 286-8175
550 S Hope St Ste 1500 Los Angeles (90071) ***(P-25628)***
Kpmg LLP..........A.......212 758-9700
4464 Jasmine Ave Culver City (90232) ***(P-25629)***
Kpmg LLP..........E.......925 946-1300
2175 N Calif Blvd # 1000 Walnut Creek (94596) ***(P-25630)***
Kpmg LLP..........C.......916 448-4700
500 Capitol Mall Ste 2100 Sacramento (95814) ***(P-25631)***
Kpmg LLP..........E.......818 227-6900
21700 Oxnard St Ste 1800 Woodland Hills (91367) ***(P-25632)***
Kpower Sup McRswitch Inverters, Irvine *Also called Zippy Usa Inc* ***(P-7195)***
Kprs Construction Services Inc (PA)..........D.......714 672-0800
2850 Saturn St Ste 110 Brea (92821) ***(P-1525)***
Kpu Roofing..........E.......909 586-2531
1497 Freesia Way Beaumont (92223) ***(P-3068)***
Kpwr Inc..........D.......818 953-4200
2600 W Olive Ave Ste 850 Burbank (91505) ***(P-5549)***
Kpwr Power 106, Burbank *Also called Kpwr Inc* ***(P-5549)***
Kpwr Radio LLC..........C.......562 745-2300
9550 Firestone Blvd # 105 Downey (90241) ***(P-16877)***
Kpxn-TV, Pasadena *Also called Ion Media Networks Inc* ***(P-5614)***
Kqed Inc (PA)..........B.......415 864-2000
2601 Mariposa St San Francisco (94110) ***(P-5624)***
KQED PUBLIC MEDIA, San Francisco *Also called Kqed Inc* ***(P-5624)***
Kradjian Importing Company Inc (PA)..........D.......818 502-1313
5018 San Fernando Rd Glendale (91204) ***(P-8599)***
Kraft & Kennedy Inc..........D.......415 956-4000
1 Post St Ste 2600 San Francisco (94104) ***(P-15631)***
Kraft Foods, Fresno *Also called Kraft Heinz Foods Company* ***(P-8601)***
Kraft Heinz Foods Company..........B.......925 469-0057
5000 Hopyard Rd Ste 235 Pleasanton (94588) ***(P-8600)***
Kraft Heinz Foods Company..........E.......559 499-5300
1055 E North Ave Fresno (93725) ***(P-8601)***
Kramer-Wilson Company Inc (PA)..........C.......818 760-0880
6345 Balboa Blvd Ste 190 Encino (91316) ***(P-10099)***
Kranem Corporation..........C.......650 319-6743
560 S Winchester Blvd San Jose (95128) ***(P-15383)***
Kranz & Assoc Holdings LLC..........D.......650 854-4400
830 Menlo Ave Ste 100 Menlo Park (94025) ***(P-25633)***
Kratos Rt Logic Inc..........D.......858 812-7300
10680 Treena St Ste 600 San Diego (92131) ***(P-15632)***
Kratos Tech Trning Sltions Inc (HQ)..........C.......858 812-7300
10680 Treena St Fl 6 San Diego (92131) ***(P-15384)***
Kravitz Investment Svcs Inc..........D.......818 995-6100
16030 Ventura Blvd # 200 Encino (91436) ***(P-9829)***
Krayden, Morgan Hill *Also called K R Anderson Inc* ***(P-8701)***
Krazan & Associates (PA)..........D.......559 348-2200
215 W Dakota Ave Clovis (93612) ***(P-27109)***
KRC Builders Incorporated..........D.......916 417-1200
6141 W 4th St Rio Linda (95673) ***(P-2946)***
KRC Equipment LLC..........D.......760 744-1036
700 N Twin Oaks Valley Rd San Marcos (92069) ***(P-7501)***
KRC Los Altos, Los Altos *Also called Kisco Senior Living LLC* ***(P-10752)***
KRC Santa Margarita, Rcho STA Marg *Also called Kisco Senior Living LLC* ***(P-10749)***
Krcr TV, Redding *Also called California Oregon Broadcasting* ***(P-5583)***
Krcx 99 9 FM Tricolor, Sacramento *Also called Entravsion Communications Corp* ***(P-5528)***
Kretek International Inc (HQ)..........D.......805 531-8888
5449 Endeavour Ct Moorpark (93021) ***(P-8940)***
Krg Technologies Inc..........A.......661 257-9967
25000 Ave Stnford Ste 243 Valencia (91355) ***(P-14904)***
Krikorian Premiere Theatre LLC..........C.......626 305-7469
8290 La Palma Ave Buena Park (90620) ***(P-17847)***
Krikorian Premiere Theatre LLC..........C.......760 945-7469
25 Main St Vista (92083) ***(P-17848)***
Krikorian Premiere Theatre LLC..........D.......562 205-3456
8540 Whittier Blvd Pico Rivera (90660) ***(P-17849)***
Krishnamurti Foundation Amer (PA)..........D.......805 646-2726
134 Besant Rd Ojai (93023) ***(P-11769)***
Krlh-AM 590-AM, Glendale *Also called Salem Media Group Inc* ***(P-5564)***
Krm Risk Management Svcs Inc..........D.......559 277-4800
4270 W Richert Ave # 101 Fresno (93722) ***(P-26290)***
Kroeker Inc..........C.......559 237-3764
4627 S Chestnut Ave Fresno (93725) ***(P-3345)***
Kron, San Francisco *Also called Nexstar Broadcasting Inc* ***(P-5640)***
Kron-TV, San Francisco *Also called Chronicle Broadcasting Co* ***(P-5590)***
Kron-TV, San Francisco *Also called Young Brdcstg of San Francisco* ***(P-5663)***
Kronick Moskovitz Tiedemann (PA)..........D.......916 321-4500
400 Capitol Mall Fl 27 Sacramento (95814) ***(P-22622)***
Kronos Foods Corp..........D.......559 674-4445
2401 W Almond Ave Madera (93637) ***(P-8602)***
Kronos Incorporated..........D.......800 580-7374
240 Commerce Irvine (92602) ***(P-15385)***
Kros-Wise..........C.......619 607-2899
435 E Carmel St San Marcos (92078) ***(P-27110)***
Krth Radio 101 FM, Los Angeles *Also called Infinity Broadcasting Corp Cal* ***(P-5543)***
Krty Ltd A Cal Ltd Partnr..........E.......408 293-8030
1887 Monterey Hwy Ste 250 San Jose (95112) ***(P-5550)***
Krzr 103 7 FM, Fresno *Also called Iheartcommunications Inc* ***(P-5536)***
KS Fabrication & Machine, Bakersfield *Also called K S Fabrication & Machine Inc* ***(P-1877)***
KS Industries LP (PA)..........A.......661 617-1700
6205 District Blvd Bakersfield (93313) ***(P-1881)***
Ksby Communications LLC..........D.......805 541-6666
1772 Calle Joaquin San Luis Obispo (93405) ***(P-5625)***
Ksee, Fresno *Also called Nexstar Broadcasting Inc* ***(P-5639)***
Kseg-FM, Sacramento *Also called Entercom Communications Corp* ***(P-5525)***
KSFCU, Bakersfield *Also called Kern Schools Federal Credit Un* ***(P-9320)***
Ksi Corp (PA)..........D.......650 952-0815
839 Mitten Rd San Bruno (94066) ***(P-4976)***
Ksi Corp..........D.......650 952-0815
839 Mitten Rd Ste 200 Burlingame (94010) ***(P-4977)***
Ksi Engineering Inc..........E.......661 617-1700
6205 District Blvd Bakersfield (93313) ***(P-25182)***
Ksl II Mngement Operations LLC..........D.......760 564-8000
50905 Avenida Bermudas La Quinta (92253) ***(P-26291)***
KSL Media Inc..........C.......212 468-3395
15910 Ventura Blvd # 900 Encino (91436) ***(P-13653)***
Ksl Resorts Hotel Del Coronado..........C.......619 435-6611
1500 Orange Ave Coronado (92118) ***(P-12521)***
Ksm Healthcare Inc..........D.......818 242-1183
1400 W Glenoaks Blvd Glendale (91201) ***(P-20060)***
Kswb, Los Angeles *Also called Bonneville International Corp* ***(P-5508)***
Kswb Inc..........D.......858 492-9269
7191 Engineer Rd San Diego (92111) ***(P-5626)***
Ktff, Brisbane *Also called Lincoln Television Inc* ***(P-5632)***
Ktgy Group Inc..........E.......510 463-2097
1814 Franklin St Ste 400 Oakland (94612) ***(P-25467)***
Ktgy Group Inc (PA)..........D.......949 851-2133
17911 Von Karman Ave # 250 Irvine (92614) ***(P-25468)***
Ktgy Group Inc..........E.......310 394-2625
12555 W Jefferson Blvd # 100 Los Angeles (90066) ***(P-25469)***
Ktsf Channel 26..........E.......415 467-6397
100 Valley Dr Brisbane (94005) ***(P-5627)***
Ktvu Partnership Inc..........C.......510 834-1212
2 Jack London Sq Oakland (94607) ***(P-5628)***
Ktvu Television Fox 2, Oakland *Also called Ktvu Partnership Inc* ***(P-5628)***
Ktxl-Fox 40, Sacramento *Also called Channel 40 Inc* ***(P-5589)***

A
L
P
H
A
B
E
T
I
C

Employee Codes: A=Over 500 employees, B=251-500
C=101-250, D=51-100, E=50
2020 Directory of California
Wholesalers and Services Companies
© Mergent Inc. 1-800-342-5647
1325

Ku Kyoung........C.......510 582-2765
Unknown Redding (96003) ***(P-20061)***
Kuehne + Nagel Inc........E.......415 656-4100
150 W Hill Pl Brisbane (94005) ***(P-4978)***
Kuehne + Nagel Inc........D.......510 785-0555
2660 W Winton Ave Hayward (94545) ***(P-4979)***
Kuehne + Nagel Inc........D.......909 574-2300
9425 Nevada St Redlands (92374) ***(P-4980)***
Kugga Inc........D.......925 639-0721
1841 Sunnyvale Ave Walnut Creek (94597) ***(P-14905)***
Kuic Inc........D.......707 446-0200
555 Mason St Ste 245 Vacaville (95688) ***(P-5551)***
Kuic-FM, Vacaville *Also called Kuic Inc* ***(P-5551)***
Kumar Hotels Inc........C.......530 934-8900
545 N Humboldt Ave Willows (95988) ***(P-12522)***
Kunde Estate Winery, Kenwood *Also called Arthur Kunde & Sons Inc* ***(P-653)***
Kurt Meiswinkel Inc........E.......650 344-7200
1407 E 3rd Ave San Mateo (94401) ***(P-2812)***
Kusc Radio........E.......213 225-7400
1149 S Hill St Ste H100 Los Angeles (90015) ***(P-5552)***
Kushner & Associates, Calabasas *Also called Custom Tours Inc* ***(P-4872)***
Kusi TV Channel 51, San Diego *Also called McKinnon Broadcasting Company* ***(P-5634)***
Kut From The Kloth, City of Industry *Also called Swatfame Inc* ***(P-8113)***
Kutir Corporation........E.......510 402-4526
3237 Nathan Ct Fremont (94539) ***(P-14906)***
Kvea-Tv-Channel 52, Burbank *Also called Estrella Communications Inc* ***(P-5601)***
Kvie Inc (PA)........D.......916 929-5843
2030 W El Camino Ave # 100 Sacramento (95833) ***(P-5629)***
Kvie Channel 6, Sacramento *Also called Kvie Inc* ***(P-5629)***
Kvl Holdings Inc (PA)........E.......831 678-2132
37700 Foothill Rd Soledad (93960) ***(P-142)***
Kw International Inc........D.......310 747-1380
18511 S Broadwick St Rancho Dominguez (90220) ***(P-4981)***
Kw International Inc........B.......213 703-6914
18724 S Broadwick St Rancho Dominguez (90220) ***(P-4573)***
Kwan Wo Ironworks Inc........C.......415 822-9628
31628 Hayman St Hayward (94544) ***(P-3268)***
Kwik Wash Laundries, Union City *Also called CSC Serviceworks Holdings Inc* ***(P-13248)***
Kxp Advantage Services LLC (PA)........C.......424 320-5300
11777 San Vicente Blvd # 747 Los Angeles (90049) ***(P-4982)***
Kxtv Inc........C.......916 441-2345
400 Broadway Sacramento (95818) ***(P-5630)***
Kya Services LLC........E.......714 659-6476
1800 E Mcfadden Ave Santa Ana (92705) ***(P-3012)***
Kyakamena Sklled Nrsing Fcilty, Berkeley *Also called Sanhyd Inc* ***(P-20240)***
KYCC, Los Angeles *Also called Koreatown Youth and Cmnty Ctr* ***(P-23309)***
Kyocera Dcment Sltons Amer Inc........D.......925 849-3300
1855 Gateway Blvd Ste 400 Concord (94520) ***(P-6757)***
Kyocera International Inc........E.......714 428-3600
3565 Cadillac Ave Costa Mesa (92626) ***(P-7289)***
Kyocera International Inc........D.......310 647-2805
222 N Pacific Coast Hwy El Segundo (90245) ***(P-6734)***
Kyocera Technology Development, Concord *Also called Kyocera Dcment Sltons Amer Inc* ***(P-6757)***
Kyoto Grand Hotel, Los Angeles *Also called 120 South Los Angeles Street H* ***(P-11973)***
Kyoto Grand Hotel and Gardens, Los Angeles *Also called Crestline Hotels & Resorts Inc* ***(P-12188)***
Kyriba Corp (PA)........E.......858 210-3560
9620 Towne Cntre Dr 200 San Diego (92121) ***(P-15386)***
Kysmet Security & Patrol Inc........E.......831 710-2425
21 W Laurel Dr Ste 49 Salinas (93906) ***(P-16335)***
Kzsu 90.1 FM, Stanford *Also called Leland Stanford Junior Univ* ***(P-5554)***
L & J Farms Caraccioli LLC........E.......831 675-7901
27905 Corda Rd Gonzales (93926) ***(P-344)***
L & L Logic and Logistics LP........E.......707 795-2475
6 Hamilton Landing # 250 Novato (94949) ***(P-8137)***
L & L Nursery Supply Inc (PA)........C.......909 591-0461
2552 Shenandoah Way San Bernardino (92407) ***(P-8843)***
L & O Aliso Viejo LLC........D.......949 643-6700
50 Enterprise Aliso Viejo (92656) ***(P-12523)***
L & R Distributors Inc........B.......909 980-3807
9292 9th St Rancho Cucamonga (91730) ***(P-7999)***
L & S Investment Co Inc........D.......760 245-3461
14173 Green Tree Blvd Victorville (92395) ***(P-12524)***
L & T Meat Co........D.......323 262-2815
3050 E 11th St Los Angeles (90023) ***(P-8290)***
L & W Supply Corporation........E.......858 627-0811
7750 Convoy Ct San Diego (92111) ***(P-6690)***
L A County Hospital, Torrance *Also called County of Los Angeles* ***(P-18925)***
L A Cstm AP & Promotions Inc (PA)........D.......562 595-1770
2680 Temple Ave Long Beach (90806) ***(P-8035)***
L A Fitness Intl LLC........D.......805 289-9907
1760 S Victoria Ave Ventura (93003) ***(P-18165)***
L A Fitness Sports Clubs, Ventura *Also called L A Fitness Intl LLC* ***(P-18165)***
L A Fitness Sports Clubs, San Diego *Also called Fitness International LLC* ***(P-18147)***
L A Girl, Ontario *Also called Beauty 21 Cosmetics Inc* ***(P-7921)***
L A Hearne Company (PA)........D.......831 385-5441
512 Metz Rd King City (93930) ***(P-8844)***
L A Inflight Service Company, Gardena *Also called World Service West* ***(P-4805)***
L A Kings, Los Angeles *Also called Los Angles Kings Hockey CLB LP* ***(P-18072)***
L A P F C U, Van Nuys *Also called Los Angeles Police Credit Un* ***(P-9398)***
L A Party Rents Inc........D.......818 989-4300
13520 Saticoy St Van Nuys (91402) ***(P-14176)***
L A Philharmonic, Los Angeles *Also called Los Angeles Philharmonic Assn* ***(P-17990)***
L A Rubber Co, Los Angeles *Also called Mechanical Drives Co* ***(P-7643)***
L A S Transportation Inc........B.......559 264-6583
250 E Belmont Ave Fresno (93701) ***(P-4079)***
L A Services Inc........E.......310 838-0408
9405 Jefferson Blvd Culver City (90232) ***(P-2176)***
L A Swikard Inc........C.......858 408-3700
9520 Candida St San Diego (92126) ***(P-843)***
L A U S D, Pico Rivera *Also called Los Angeles Unified School Dst* ***(P-16898)***
L and R Auto Parks Inc........C.......213 784-3018
707 Wilshire Blvd # 4700 Los Angeles (90017) ***(P-17260)***
L B C Holdings U S A Corp (PA)........C.......650 873-0750
362 E Grand Ave South San Francisco (94080) ***(P-4828)***
L B Construction, Roseville *Also called Lancaster Burns Cnstr Inc* ***(P-2813)***
L Barrios and Associates Inc........E.......909 592-5893
302 E Fthill Blvd Ste 101 San Dimas (91773) ***(P-844)***
L C C H Associates Inc........E.......858 565-4424
4311 3rd Ave B San Diego (92103) ***(P-20611)***
L E Cooke Co........C.......559 732-9146
26333 Road 140 Visalia (93292) ***(P-257)***
L E Coppersmith Inc (PA)........D.......310 607-8000
525 S Douglas St Ste 100 El Segundo (90245) ***(P-4983)***
L E Coppersmith Inc........D.......310 607-8000
525 S Douglas St El Segundo (90245) ***(P-4984)***
L I Metal Systems........E.......562 948-5950
9041 Bermudez St Pico Rivera (90660) ***(P-3069)***
L J B, San Diego *Also called Tanvex Biopharma Usa Inc* ***(P-25848)***
L J Kruse Co........D.......510 644-0260
920 Pardee St Berkeley (94710) ***(P-2177)***
L J T Flowers Inc........D.......805 310-6036
2425 Bonita School Rd Nipomo (93444) ***(P-258)***
L J Trucking USA........D.......323 469-9663
120 S Anderson St Los Angeles (90033) ***(P-4080)***
L L V A R E, Redlands *Also called Loma Linda Vet Association For* ***(P-24584)***
L Lyon Distributing Inc........E.......909 798-7129
254 W Stuart Ave Redlands (92374) ***(P-16878)***
L R Investment Company........D.......213 627-8211
515 S Flower St Ste 3200 Los Angeles (90071) ***(P-17261)***
L S A Associates Inc (PA)........C.......949 553-0666
20 Executive Park Ste 200 Irvine (92614) ***(P-27111)***
L S P Ix, Hinkley *Also called Luz Solar Partners Ix* ***(P-5855)***
L Tech Network Services Inc........D.......562 222-1121
9926 Pioneer Blvd Ste 101 Santa Fe Springs (90670) ***(P-2535)***
L W Roth Insurance Agency........D.......916 721-6273
6060 Sunrise Vista Dr Citrus Heights (95610) ***(P-24345)***
L&D Farm Labor........E.......760 408-6311
53762 Sapphire Ln Coachella (92236) ***(P-630)***
L&G Cable Construction........D.......714 630-6174
2776 E Miraloma Ave Anaheim (92806) ***(P-3428)***
L&H Airco LLC........D.......916 677-1000
2530 Warren Dr Rocklin (95677) ***(P-2178)***
L&T Staffing Inc (PA)........B.......714 558-1821
950 W 17th St Ste E Santa Ana (92706) ***(P-14320)***
L'Auberge Del Mar, Del Mar *Also called Lhoberge Lessee Inc* ***(P-12552)***
L'Ermitage Hotel, Beverly Hills *Also called Raffles Lrmitage Beverly Hills* ***(P-12788)***
L-3 Communications Maripro Inc, Goleta *Also called L3 Maripro Inc* ***(P-25183)***
L-O Coronado Hotel Inc........A.......619 435-6611
1500 Orange Ave Coronado (92118) ***(P-12525)***
L-O Soma Hotel Inc........B.......415 974-6400
50 3rd St San Francisco (94103) ***(P-12526)***
L.A. Care Health Plan, Los Angeles *Also called Local Initiative Health Author* ***(P-10016)***
L.A. Cold Storage, Los Angeles *Also called Standard-Southern Corporation* ***(P-4353)***
L.A. Gay & Lesbian Center, Los Angeles *Also called Los Angeles Lgbt Center* ***(P-24194)***
L.A.cO., Whittier *Also called County Santtn Dist 2 of La Co* ***(P-6343)***
L3 Applied Technologies Inc........C.......510 577-7100
2700 Merced St San Leandro (94577) ***(P-25775)***
L3 Maripro Inc........D.......805 683-3881
1522 Cook Pl Goleta (93117) ***(P-25183)***
L3 Technologies Inc........D.......760 375-0390
117 S Gold Canyon St Ridgecrest (93555) ***(P-15633)***
La 1000 Santa Fe LLC........C.......213 205-1000
1000 S Santa Fe Ave Los Angeles (90021) ***(P-26292)***
La Asociacion Nacional Pro Per........B.......213 202-5900
1452 W Temple St Ste 100 Los Angeles (90026) ***(P-23310)***
La Asociacion Nacional Pro Per (PA)........A.......626 564-1988
234 E Colo Blvd Ste 300 Pasadena (91101) ***(P-23311)***
La Belle Days Spas and Salons, Palo Alto *Also called Beauty Bazar Inc* ***(P-13334)***
La Bonne Vie Inc........D.......805 773-5003
2723 Shell Beach Rd Shell Beach (93449) ***(P-18166)***
La Boulange, San Francisco *Also called Bay Bread LLC* ***(P-8550)***
La Boxing Franchise Corp........C.......714 668-0911
1241 E Dyer Rd Ste 100 Santa Ana (92705) ***(P-18167)***
LA Brands LLC........E.......323 234-5070
4726 Loma Vista Ave Vernon (90058) ***(P-8036)***
La Canada Flintridge Cntry CLB........D.......818 790-0611
5500 Godbey Dr La Canada (91011) ***(P-18475)***
La Cantina Doors Inc........E.......888 221-0141
1875 Ord Way Oceanside (92056) ***(P-6724)***
La Casa Mental Health Center, Long Beach *Also called Telecare Corporation* ***(P-21434)***
La Casa Mhrc, Long Beach *Also called Telecare Corporation* ***(P-21433)***
La Checker Cab Co, Van Nuys *Also called Checker Cab Co* ***(P-3745)***
La Cienega Associates........D.......310 854-0071
8500 Beverly Blvd Ste 501 Los Angeles (90048) ***(P-11241)***
La City Tours.com, Malibu *Also called Las Vegas Intrntnl Tours* ***(P-4855)***
La Clinica De La Raza Inc........C.......510 535-6300
1515 Fruitvale Ave Oakland (94601) ***(P-19138)***
La Clinica De La Raza Inc........B.......707 556-8100
243 Georgia St Vallejo (94590) ***(P-19139)***
La Clinica De La Raza Inc........B.......510 535-4700
3050 E 16th St Oakland (94601) ***(P-19614)***

Mergent e-mail: customerrelations@mergent.com
1326
2020 Directory of California
Wholesalers and Services Companies
(P-0000) Products & Services Section entry number
(PA)=Parent Co (HQ)=Headquarters (DH)=Div Headquarters

La Clinica De La Raza Inc.....B.....510 535-6200
1601 Fruitvale Ave Oakland (94601) ***(P-19140)***
La Clinica De La Raza Inc.....B.....925 431-1250
337 E Leland Rd Pittsburg (94565) ***(P-19615)***
La Costa Glen, Carlsbad *Also called Continuing Lf Communities LLC* ***(P-14251)***
La Costa Limousine (PA).....D.....760 438-4455
2770 Loker Ave W Carlsbad (92010) ***(P-3693)***
La Costa Resort & Spa, Carlsbad *Also called Lc Trs Inc* ***(P-12544)***
La County High Desert Hlth Sys.....B.....661 945-8461
44900 60th St W Lancaster (93536) ***(P-19141)***
LA COUNTY MUSEUM OF ART, Los Angeles *Also called Museum Associates* ***(P-24272)***
La County Probation, Whittier *Also called County of Los Angeles* ***(P-23091)***
La Cumbre Country Club.....D.....805 687-2421
4015 Via Laguna Santa Barbara (93110) ***(P-18476)***
La Curacao, Vernon *Also called Adir International LLC* ***(P-1327)***
La Department Water and Power.....D.....661 824-7900
17031 State Highway 14 Mojave (93501) ***(P-6009)***
La Familia Counseling Center.....D.....916 452-3601
5523 34th St Sacramento (95820) ***(P-23312)***
La Fitness, Mission Viejo *Also called Fitness International LLC* ***(P-18146)***
La Follette Johnson De Haas (PA).....C.....213 426-3600
865 S Figueroa St # 3200 Los Angeles (90017) ***(P-22623)***
La Grande Farm.....D.....530 473-5923
P.O. Box 370 Williams (95987) ***(P-62)***
La Habra Villa.....D.....714 529-1697
220 Newport Center Dr # 11 Newport Beach (92660) ***(P-23967)***
La Hotel Venture LLC.....B.....213 617-1133
333 S Figueroa St Los Angeles (90071) ***(P-12527)***
LA Hydro-Jet Rooter Svc Inc.....D.....818 768-4225
10639 Wixom St Sun Valley (91352) ***(P-17516)***
La Hydrojet, Sun Valley *Also called LA Hydro-Jet Rooter Svc Inc* ***(P-17516)***
La Inc Convention Vistors Bur.....D.....213 236-2301
333 S Hope St Ste 1800 Los Angeles (90071) ***(P-16879)***
La Joie Construction, San Mateo *Also called La Joie Jerry* ***(P-26293)***
La Joie Jerry.....E.....650 375-1808
418 Sonora Dr San Mateo (94402) ***(P-26293)***
La Jolla Bch & Tennis CLB Inc (PA).....C.....858 454-7126
2000 Spindrift Dr La Jolla (92037) ***(P-18477)***
La Jolla Bch & Tennis CLB Inc.....C.....858 459-8271
8110 Camino Del Oro La Jolla (92037) ***(P-12528)***
La Jolla Country Club Inc.....C.....858 454-9601
7301 High Ave La Jolla (92037) ***(P-18478)***
La Jolla Cove Hotel & Motel.....D.....858 459-2621
1155 Coast Blvd La Jolla (92037) ***(P-12529)***
La Jolla Cove Motel, La Jolla *Also called La Jolla Cove Hotel & Motel* ***(P-12529)***
La Jolla Group Inc (PA).....D.....949 428-2800
14350 Myford Rd Irvine (92606) ***(P-16880)***
La Jolla Inst For Allergy & Im, La Jolla *Also called La Jolla Inst For Immunology* ***(P-26003)***
La Jolla Inst For Immunology.....B.....858 752-6500
9420 Athena Cir La Jolla (92037) ***(P-26003)***
La Jolla Nrsing Rhbltation Ctr, La Jolla *Also called Covenant Care La Jolla LLC* ***(P-19845)***
La Jolla Nurses Home Care.....C.....858 454-9339
2223 Avenida De La Playa La Jolla (92037) ***(P-14321)***
La Jolla Orthopaedic.....D.....858 657-0055
4120 La Jolla Village Dr La Jolla (92037) ***(P-19142)***
La Jolla Pharmaceutical Co (PA).....C.....858 207-4264
4550 Towne Centre Ct San Diego (92121) ***(P-25776)***
LA JOLLA PLAYHOUSE, La Jolla *Also called Theat and Arts Found of San Di* ***(P-24680)***
La Jolla Village Towers 500.....D.....858 646-7700
8515 Costa Verde Blvd Ofc San Diego (92122) ***(P-20062)***
La Jolla YMCA, La Jolla *Also called YMCA of San Diego County* ***(P-24706)***
La Lakers, El Segundo *Also called Los Angeles Lakers Inc* ***(P-18069)***
La Laser Center Pc Cpmc.....D.....310 446-4400
10884 Santa Monica Blvd # 300 Los Angeles (90025) ***(P-19143)***
La Live Properties LLC.....E.....213 763-7700
800 W Olympic Blvd # 305 Los Angeles (90015) ***(P-17921)***
La Maestra Community Clinic, San Diego *Also called La Maestra Family Clinic Inc* ***(P-19144)***
La Maestra Community Hlth Ctrs, San Diego *Also called La Maestra Family Clinic Inc* ***(P-19146)***
La Maestra Family Clinic Inc.....D.....619 280-4213
4060 Fairmount Ave San Diego (92105) ***(P-19144)***
La Maestra Family Clinic Inc.....D.....619 501-1235
4305 University Ave # 120 San Diego (92105) ***(P-19145)***
La Maestra Family Clinic Inc (PA).....C.....619 584-1612
4060 Fairmount Ave San Diego (92105) ***(P-19146)***
La Mancha Development, Los Angeles *Also called A M S Partnership* ***(P-11537)***
La Mesa Disposal, Signal Hill *Also called Edco Disposal Corporation Inc* ***(P-3881)***
La Mesa Internal Medical Group, La Mesa *Also called La Mesa Intrnl Mdc Mdcl Gr* ***(P-19147)***
La Mesa Intrnl Mdc Mdcl Gr.....E.....619 460-4050
5111 Garfield St La Mesa (91941) ***(P-19147)***
La Mesa Lions Club.....D.....619 469-9988
4387 Summit Dr La Mesa (91941) ***(P-24573)***
La Mesa Medical Offices, La Mesa *Also called Kaiser Foundation Hospitals* ***(P-20953)***
La Metro Hauling, Long Beach *Also called USA Waste of California Inc* ***(P-6307)***
La Mirada Country Club, La Mirada *Also called American Golf Corporation* ***(P-18375)***
La Mirage, San Diego *Also called Regency Hill Associates* ***(P-10808)***
La Palma Care Center.....D.....714 772-7480
1130 W La Palma Ave Anaheim (92801) ***(P-20063)***
La Palma Hospital Medical Ctr.....B.....714 670-7400
7901 Walker St La Palma (90623) ***(P-20996)***
LA PALMA INTERCOMMUNITY HOSPITAL, La Palma *Also called La Palma Hospital Medical Ctr* ***(P-20996)***
La Palma Medical Offices, La Palma *Also called Kaiser Foundation Hospitals* ***(P-19112)***
La Palma Nursing Center, Long Beach *Also called 1130 W La Palma Ave Inc* ***(P-19704)***
La Palma Nursing Center, Anaheim *Also called La Palma Care Center* ***(P-20063)***
La Paz Geropsychiatric Center, Paramount *Also called Telecare Corporation* ***(P-21442)***
La Peer Health Systems, Beverly Hills *Also called La Peer Surgery Center LLC* ***(P-19148)***
La Peer Surgery Center LLC.....D.....310 360-9119
8920 Wilshire Blvd # 101 Beverly Hills (90211) ***(P-19148)***
La Petite Baleen Inc.....D.....650 588-7665
434 San Mateo Ave San Bruno (94066) ***(P-18168)***
La Petite Baleen Swim School, San Bruno *Also called La Petite Baleen Inc* ***(P-18168)***
La Posta Band Mission Indians, Boulevard *Also called La Posta Casino* ***(P-12530)***
La Posta Casino.....C.....619 824-4100
777 Crestwood Rd Boulevard (91905) ***(P-12530)***
La Provence Inc.....D.....760 736-3299
1370 W San Marcos Blvd # 130 San Marcos (92078) ***(P-8603)***
La Provence Bakery, San Marcos *Also called La Provence Inc* ***(P-8603)***
La Puerta.....E.....619 696-3466
560 4th Ave San Diego (92101) ***(P-24574)***
La Quinta Country Club.....D.....760 564-4151
77750 Avenue 50 La Quinta (92253) ***(P-18479)***
La Quinta Inn, Los Angeles *Also called Lq Management LLC* ***(P-12565)***
La Quinta Inn, San Francisco *Also called Mile Post Properties LLC* ***(P-12617)***
La Quinta Resort & Club, La Quinta *Also called Lqr Property LLC* ***(P-12566)***
La Rinconada Country Club Inc (PA).....D.....408 395-4181
14595 Clearview Dr Los Gatos (95032) ***(P-18480)***
LA RINCONADA GOLF AND COUNTRY, Los Gatos *Also called La Rinconada Country Club Inc* ***(P-18480)***
La Salette Rehab Convlesc Hos, Stockton *Also called Mariner Health Care Inc* ***(P-20121)***
La Salle Apartments.....D.....415 647-0607
30 Whitfield Ct Ste 1 San Francisco (94124) ***(P-10753)***
La Salle Preservation, San Francisco *Also called La Salle Apartments* ***(P-10753)***
La Sierra Care Center, Merced *Also called CF Merced La Sierra LLC* ***(P-19791)***
LA Specialty Produce Co (PA).....B.....562 741-2200
13527 Orden Dr Santa Fe Springs (90670) ***(P-8493)***
La Sports Arena, Los Angeles *Also called Los Angeles Mem Coliseum Comm* ***(P-24845)***
LA Sports Properties Inc.....C.....213 742-7500
1212 S Flower St Fl 5 Los Angeles (90015) ***(P-18067)***
La Steel Services Inc.....E.....951 393-2013
1760 California Ave # 201 Corona (92881) ***(P-3269)***
La Tavola LLC (PA).....D.....707 257-3358
2655 Napa Valley Corp Dr NAPA (94558) ***(P-13223)***
La Tortilla Factory Inc (PA).....B.....707 586-4000
3300 Westwind Blvd Santa Rosa (95403) ***(P-8604)***
La Verne Nursery Inc.....D.....805 521-0111
3653 Center St Piru (93040) ***(P-259)***
La Vida Del Mar Associates, Solana Beach *Also called Senior Resource Group LLC* ***(P-24071)***
La Vida Mltispecialty Med Ctrs.....D.....213 765-7500
1400 S Grand Ave Los Angeles (90015) ***(P-19149)***
La Voie & Sons Construction.....E.....916 408-6900
1061 Nichols Ct Rocklin (95765) ***(P-26294)***
La Works, Irwindale *Also called East San Gbriel Vly Consortium* ***(P-3665)***
Laaco Ltd (PA).....C.....213 622-1254
431 W 7th St Los Angeles (90014) ***(P-10876)***
Laaco Ltd.....D.....310 823-4567
4469 Admiralty Way Marina Del Rey (90292) ***(P-18481)***
LAAPOA, Los Angeles *Also called Los Angeles Airport Peace Offc* ***(P-24586)***
Lab-Gistics LLC.....C.....650 309-2627
885 Pacific Ave San Jose (95126) ***(P-25777)***
Labaya Beachcomber LP.....E.....805 278-6688
3101 Sturgis Rd Oxnard (93030) ***(P-17297)***
Labcyte Inc (HQ).....D.....408 747-2000
170 Rose Orchard Way # 200 San Jose (95134) ***(P-25778)***
Labite, Los Angeles *Also called Kfco Inc* ***(P-3905)***
Labmed Partners.....E.....949 242-9925
5000 Birch St Newport Beach (92660) ***(P-26669)***
LABOR EMPLOYMENT & TRAINING, Cerritos *Also called Uaw-Lbor Emplyment Trning Corp* ***(P-14445)***
Labor Finders Staffing, Fresno *Also called Labor Fnders of The Palm Bches* ***(P-14322)***
Labor Fnders of The Palm Bches.....D.....559 221-2023
4325 N Blackstone Ave Fresno (93726) ***(P-14322)***
Labor One Inc.....D.....559 430-4202
575 Minnewawa Ave Ste 3 Clovis (93612) ***(P-631)***
Labor Ready, Yuba City *Also called Trueblue Inc* ***(P-14575)***
Labor Ready, Santa Barbara *Also called Trueblue Inc* ***(P-14576)***
Laboratory Corporation America.....D.....818 361-7089
14901 Rinaldi St Ste 203 Mission Hills (91345) ***(P-21546)***
Laboratory Corporation America.....D.....510 635-4555
10930 Bigge St San Leandro (94577) ***(P-21547)***
Laboratory Specialty Gases.....C.....619 234-6060
2506 Market St San Diego (92102) ***(P-7555)***
Laborers Funds Administrative (PA).....D.....707 864-2800
220 Campus Ln Fairfield (94534) ***(P-24450)***
Laborers Trust Funds Nthrn Cal, Fairfield *Also called Laborers Funds Administrative* ***(P-24450)***
Labratory, San Francisco *Also called Permanente Medical Group Inc* ***(P-21088)***
Lac Club, Los Angeles *Also called Los Angles Clippers Foundation* ***(P-26677)***
Lac Group, Burbank *Also called Library Associates LLC* ***(P-14325)***
LACERA, Pasadena *Also called Los Angeles Cnty Emp Retiremnt* ***(P-10218)***
Laclinica, Pittsburg *Also called La Clinica De La Raza Inc* ***(P-19615)***
Lacma, Los Angeles *Also called Los Angeles Cnty Mseum of Art* ***(P-24270)***
Lacmta, Los Angeles *Also called Los Angeles County MTA* ***(P-3557)***
Laco Associates (PA).....E.....707 443-5054
21 W 4th St Eureka (95501) ***(P-25184)***
Lacolina Jr High CA Congress O.....D.....805 967-4506
4025 Foothill Rd Santa Barbara (93110) ***(P-24575)***
Laconstructora Co Inc.....E.....760 439-7686
2030 Broadway Oceanside (92054) ***(P-1150)***

A
L
P
H
A
B
E
T
I
C

Ladas & Parry LLP..........E.......323 934-2300
4525 Wilshire Blvd # 240 Los Angeles (90010) ***(P-22624)***

Ladd Construction Co, Redding *Also called Roy E Ladd Inc* ***(P-1783)***

Ladell Inc..........E.......559 650-2000
605 N Halifax Ave Clovis (93611) ***(P-2179)***

Ladera Ranch, San Juan Capistrano *Also called Rancho Mission Viejo LLC* ***(P-11391)***

Ladwp, Independence *Also called Los Angeles Dept Wtr & Pwr* ***(P-6080)***

Ladwp, Los Angeles *Also called Los Angeles Dept Wtr & Pwr* ***(P-6081)***

Ladwp, Los Angeles *Also called Los Angeles Dept Wtr & Pwr* ***(P-5854)***

Laedc, Los Angeles *Also called Economic Dev Corp of La County* ***(P-27055)***

Lafaltte Rhbilitation Care Ctr..........D.......209 466-2066
537 E Fulton St Stockton (95204) ***(P-20064)***

Lafayette Car Wash, Lafayette *Also called Prestige Car Wash Lafayette LP* ***(P-17394)***

Lafayette Park Hotel Corp (PA)..........B.......650 330-8888
1100 Alma St Ste 106 Menlo Park (94025) ***(P-12531)***

Lafayette Textile Inds LLC..........D.......323 264-2212
2051 E 55th St Vernon (90058) ***(P-8000)***

Laguna Bch Golf Bnglow Vlg LLC..........E.......949 499-2271
31106 Coast Hwy Laguna Beach (92651) ***(P-427)***

Laguna Bch Golf Bnglow Vlg LLC..........D.......949 499-2271
31106 Coast Hwy Laguna Beach (92651) ***(P-18259)***

Laguna Country Mart Ltd Inc..........E.......310 826-5635
12410 Santa Monica Blvd Los Angeles (90025) ***(P-10615)***

Laguna Creek Racquet Club, Elk Grove *Also called Spare-Time Inc* ***(P-18583)***

Laguna Hills Hotel Dev Ventr..........D.......949 586-5000
25205 La Paz Rd Laguna Hills (92653) ***(P-12532)***

Laguna Hills Surgery Center, Laguna Hills *Also called Cirrus Health II LP* ***(P-18898)***

Laguna Niguel Racquet Club, Laguna Niguel *Also called Spearman Clubs Inc* ***(P-18762)***

Laguna Playhouse (PA)..........C.......949 497-2787
606 Laguna Canyon Rd Laguna Beach (92651) ***(P-17922)***

Laguna Woods Golf Club..........E.......949 597-4336
24122 Moulton Pkwy Laguna Hills (92637) ***(P-18482)***

Laguna Woods Village..........A.......949 597-4267
24351 El Toro Rd Laguna Woods (92637) ***(P-11242)***

Laguna Woods Village Golf Club, Laguna Hills *Also called Laguna Woods Golf Club* ***(P-18482)***

Lahontan Golf Club..........C.......530 550-2400
12700 Lodgetrail Dr Truckee (96161) ***(P-18483)***

Laidlaw Education Services, San Bernardino *Also called First Student Inc* ***(P-3807)***

Laidlaw Education Services, Santa Ana *Also called First Student Inc* ***(P-3810)***

Laidlaw Educational Services, Palm Springs *Also called First Student Inc* ***(P-3805)***

Laidlaw Transit Services, Madera *Also called First Student Inc* ***(P-3813)***

Lake Arrowhead Cmnty Svcs Dst..........E.......909 337-6395
6727 Arrowhead Lake Rd Hesperia (92345) ***(P-24190)***

Lake Arrwhead Rsort Oprtor Inc (HQ)..........C.......909 336-1511
27984 Hwy 189 Lake Arrowhead (92352) ***(P-12533)***

Lake Balboa Care Center, Van Nuys *Also called Van Nuys Care Center Inc* ***(P-20714)***

Lake Bowl, Folsom *Also called Folsom Recreation Corp* ***(P-18032)***

Lake Cnty Trbal Hlth Cnsortium..........D.......707 263-8382
925 Bevins Ct Lakeport (95453) ***(P-19616)***

Lake County Home Loans..........E.......707 462-4000
350 E Gobbi St Ukiah (95482) ***(P-9569)***

Lake Elsinore Unified Schl Dst..........D.......951 253-7830
21641 Bundy Canyon Rd Wildomar (92595) ***(P-3817)***

Lake Elsinore Unified Schl Dst..........D.......951 253-7091
565 Chaney St Lake Elsinore (92530) ***(P-23739)***

Lake Elsn SC Trans, Wildomar *Also called Lake Elsinore Unified Schl Dst* ***(P-3817)***

Lake Forest Ll Master Homeown..........D.......949 586-0860
24752 Toledo Ln Lake Forest (92630) ***(P-24576)***

Lake Forest Nursing Center, Lake Forest *Also called Life Care Centers America Inc* ***(P-20075)***

Lake Hemet Municipal Wtr Dst (PA)..........D.......951 927-1816
26385 Fairview Ave Hemet (92544) ***(P-6074)***

Lake Merced Golf & Country CLB..........D.......650 755-2233
2300 Junipero Serra Blvd Daly City (94015) ***(P-18484)***

Lake Merritt Hotel Associates..........E.......510 832-2300
1800 Madison St Oakland (94612) ***(P-1258)***

Lake Mission Viejo Association..........D.......949 770-1313
22555 Olympiad Rd Mission Viejo (92692) ***(P-24577)***

Lake Mrritt Healthcare Ctr LLC..........D.......510 227-1806
309 Macarthur Blvd Oakland (94610) ***(P-26295)***

Lake Natoma Inn, Folsom *Also called Lake Natoma Lodging LP* ***(P-12534)***

Lake Natoma Lodging LP..........D.......916 351-1500
702 Gold Lake Dr Folsom (95630) ***(P-12534)***

Lake of The Pines Association..........E.......530 268-1141
11665 Lakeshore N Auburn (95602) ***(P-24578)***

LAKE OF THE PINES HOMEOWNERS, Auburn *Also called Lake of The Pines Association* ***(P-24578)***

Lake Park Retirement Residence, Oakland *Also called Califrnia-Nevada Methdst Homes* ***(P-20524)***

Lake Piru Marina, Valencia *Also called Pyramid Enterprises Inc* ***(P-18740)***

Lake San Marcos Resort, San Marcos *Also called Citizens Development Corp* ***(P-18421)***

Lake Tahoe Resort Hotel, South Lake Tahoe *Also called Roppongi-Tahoe Lp A Californi* ***(P-12838)***

Lake Tahoe Secret Witness..........D.......530 541-6800
1051 Al Tahoe Blvd South Lake Tahoe (96150) ***(P-16336)***

Lake Wildwood Association..........C.......530 432-1152
11255 Cottontail Way Penn Valley (95946) ***(P-24579)***

Lake Wildwood Golf Course., Penn Valley *Also called Lake Wildwood Association* ***(P-24579)***

Lakenor Auto Salvage, Santa Fe Springs *Also called Cadnchev Inc* ***(P-6495)***

Lakes Country Club Assn Inc (PA)..........B.......760 568-4321
161 Old Ranch Rd Palm Desert (92211) ***(P-18485)***

Lakes Country Club, The, Palm Desert *Also called Lakes Country Club Assn Inc* ***(P-18485)***

Lakeside Clubhouse, Daly City *Also called Olympic Club* ***(P-24605)***

Lakeside Fire Protection Dst..........D.......619 390-2350
12216 Lakeside Ave Lakeside (92040) ***(P-16881)***

Lakeside Golf Club..........D.......818 984-0601
4500 W Lakeside Dr Burbank (91505) ***(P-18260)***

Lakeside Grill, The, Yountville *Also called Vintners Golf Club* ***(P-18312)***

Lakeside Medical Systems, Northridge *Also called Lakeside Systems Inc* ***(P-26296)***

Lakeside Systems Inc..........A.......866 654-3471
8510 Balboa Blvd Ste 150 Northridge (91325) ***(P-26296)***

Lakeside Tax & Financial Svcs..........D.......619 561-2681
9748 Los Coches Rd Ste 3 Lakeside (92040) ***(P-16882)***

Lakeview Medical Offices, Anaheim *Also called Kaiser Foundation Hospitals* ***(P-19036)***

Lakeview Senior Center, Irvine *Also called City of Irvine* ***(P-23009)***

Lakewood Cerritos Dental Ctr..........D.......562 860-0388
5819 Adenmoor Ave Lakewood (90713) ***(P-19617)***

Lakewood Country Club, Lakewood *Also called American Golf Corporation* ***(P-18216)***

Lakewood Healthcare Center, Downey *Also called Healthcare Ctr of Downey LLC* ***(P-20006)***

Lakewood Manor North Inc..........D.......213 380-9175
831 S Lake St Los Angeles (90057) ***(P-20065)***

Lakewood Mem Pk Fnrl Svcs Inc..........E.......209 883-4465
900 Santa Fe Ave Hughson (95326) ***(P-11630)***

Lakewood Memorial Pk & Fnrl HM, Hughson *Also called Alderwoods (delaware) Inc* ***(P-11623)***

Lakewood Memorial Pk & Fnrl HM, Hughson *Also called Lakewood Mem Pk Fnrl Svcs Inc* ***(P-11630)***

Lakewood Park Health Center, Downey *Also called Mental Hlth Cnvlscent Svcs Inc* ***(P-20136)***

Lakewood Park Health Center (PA)..........B.......562 869-0978
12023 Lakewood Blvd Downey (90242) ***(P-16883)***

Lakewood Regional Medical Ctr, Lakewood *Also called Tenet Healthsystem Medical* ***(P-19501)***

Lakewood South Car Wash LLC..........E.......562 430-4975
11031 Alamitos Ave Los Alamitos (90720) ***(P-17380)***

Lakewood Y M C A Gymnastics, Lakewood *Also called Young Mens Chrstn Assc Gr L B* ***(P-24742)***

Lakin Tire of Calif, Santa Fe Springs *Also called Lakin Tire West Incorporated* ***(P-6488)***

Lakin Tire West Incorporated (PA)..........D.......562 802-2752
15305 Spring Ave Santa Fe Springs (90670) ***(P-6488)***

Lakos, Fresno *Also called Claude Laval Corporation* ***(P-7538)***

Lamanuzzi & Pantaleo LLC (PA)..........D.......559 432-3170
11767 Road 27 1/2 Madera (93637) ***(P-143)***

Lamesa City Public Works, La Mesa *Also called City of La Mesa* ***(P-1682)***

Lamon Construction Company Inc..........E.......530 671-1370
871 Von Geldern Way Yuba City (95991) ***(P-1526)***

Lamont Community Health Center, Bakersfield *Also called Clinica Sierra Vista* ***(P-18904)***

Lamp Inc..........C.......213 488-9559
2116 Arlington Ave Lbby Los Angeles (90018) ***(P-23968)***

Lamp Community, Los Angeles *Also called Lamp Inc* ***(P-23968)***

Lamp Liter Associates..........D.......559 733-4328
3130 W Main St Ste A Visalia (93291) ***(P-12535)***

Lamp Liter Inn, Visalia *Also called Lamp Liter Associates* ***(P-12535)***

Lancashire Group Incorporated..........B.......510 792-9384
37053 Cherry St Ste 210 Newark (94560) ***(P-26670)***

Lancaster Burns Cnstr Inc..........C.......916 624-8404
8655 Washington Blvd Roseville (95678) ***(P-2813)***

Lancaster Comm Srvcs Fndtn..........D.......661 723-6230
46008 7th St W Lancaster (93534) ***(P-17336)***

Lancaster Crdlgy Med Group Inc (PA)..........D.......661 726-3058
43847 Heaton Ave Ste B Lancaster (93534) ***(P-19150)***

Lancaster Jethawks..........D.......661 726-5400
45116 Valley Central Way Lancaster (93536) ***(P-18486)***

Land & Personnel Management, Kerman *Also called Hall Management Corp* ***(P-26253)***

Land Design Consultants Inc..........D.......626 578-7000
2700 E Foothill Blvd # 200 Pasadena (91107) ***(P-27112)***

Land Disposition Company, Irvine *Also called NRLL LLC* ***(P-11940)***

Land Forms Landscape Cnstr, Irvine *Also called Jeff Tracy Inc* ***(P-2165)***

Land Home Financial Svcs Inc (PA)..........E.......925 676-7038
1355 Willow Way Ste 250 Concord (94520) ***(P-9570)***

Land Scapes, Costa Mesa *Also called Dwiw Inc* ***(P-804)***

Land Services Landscape Contrs..........D.......510 656-8101
901 Brown Rd Fremont (94539) ***(P-11570)***

Landcare Logic, San Diego *Also called Shoreline Land Care Inc* ***(P-762)***

Landcare USA LLC..........D.......949 559-7771
216 N Clara St Santa Ana (92703) ***(P-845)***

Landcare USA LLC..........D.......760 747-1174
770 Metcalf St Escondido (92025) ***(P-846)***

Landcare USA LLC..........C.......805 520-9394
1196 Patricia Ave Simi Valley (93065) ***(P-847)***

Landcare USA LLC..........D.......707 836-1460
930 Shiloh Rd Bldg 44-B Windsor (95492) ***(P-848)***

Landcare USA LLC..........D.......714 936-9512
15606 Cornet St Santa Fe Springs (90670) ***(P-849)***

Landcare USA LLC..........D.......310 719-1008
1315 W 130th St Gardena (90247) ***(P-850)***

Landcare USA LLC..........D.......310 354-1520
4134 Temple City Blvd Rosemead (91770) ***(P-851)***

Landcare USA LLC..........C.......310 354-1520
1323 W 130th St Gardena (90247) ***(P-852)***

Landcare USA LLC..........D.......916 635-0936
3213 Fitzgerald Rd Rancho Cordova (95742) ***(P-853)***

Landcare USA LLC..........C.......858 453-1755
5248 Governor Dr San Diego (92122) ***(P-854)***

Landcare USA LLC..........C.......818 346-7552
7755 Deering Ave Canoga Park (91304) ***(P-855)***

Landcare USA LLC..........D.......408 727-4099
85 Old Tully Rd San Jose (95111) ***(P-856)***

Landco..........D.......818 612-0118
7333 Clybourn Ave Sun Valley (91352) ***(P-857)***

Mergent e-mail: customerrelations@mergent.com
1328

2020 Directory of California
Wholesalers and Services Companies

(P-0000) Products & Services Section entry number
(PA)=Parent Co (HQ)=Headquarters (DH)=Div Headquarters

Landesign Cnstr & Maint Inc....D....707 578-2657
1328 Airport Blvd Santa Rosa (95403) ***(P-858)***
Landforce Express Corporation....C....760 843-7839
17201 N D St Victorville (92394) ***(P-4081)***
Landmark Event Staffing....A....714 293-4248
4790 Irvine Blvd Ste 105 Irvine (92620) ***(P-16337)***
Landmark Event Staffing....A....510 632-9000
1965 Adams Ave San Leandro (94577) ***(P-14522)***
Landmark Health LLC (PA)....D....253 394-2566
7755 Center Ave Ste 630 Huntington Beach (92647) ***(P-21802)***
Landmark Healthcare Svcs Inc (HQ)....C....800 638-4557
1610 Arden Way Ste 280 Sacramento (95815) ***(P-19647)***
Landmark Hotels LLC....C....949 640-5040
312 Broadway St Ste 204 Laguna Beach (92651) ***(P-12536)***
Landmark Medical Center, Pomona *Also called Landmark Medical Services Inc* ***(P-21417)***
Landmark Medical Services Inc....D....909 593-2585
2030 N Garey Ave Pomona (91767) ***(P-21417)***
Landmark Princess, Laguna Beach *Also called Landmark Hotels LLC* ***(P-12536)***
Landmark Protection Inc....B....408 293-6300
675 N 1st St Ste 620 San Jose (95112) ***(P-8037)***
Landmark Realty Center, Rancho Palos Verdes *Also called Inman Spinosa & Buchan Inc* ***(P-11203)***
Landmark Services Inc....D....714 547-6308
410 N Fairview St Santa Ana (92703) ***(P-13961)***
Landmark Theatres, Los Angeles *Also called Silver Cinemas Acquisition Co* ***(P-17866)***
Landor Associates Intl Ltd (HQ)....C....415 365-1700
1001 Front St San Francisco (94111) ***(P-13788)***
Landsberg Los Angeles Div 1001, Montebello *Also called Orora Packaging Solutions* ***(P-7896)***
Landsberg Orora, Buena Park *Also called Orora Packaging Solutions* ***(P-7893)***
Landsberg San Diego Div 1007, San Marcos *Also called Orora North America* ***(P-7891)***
Landscape Center, Riverside *Also called B & B Nurseries Inc* ***(P-8881)***
Landscape Development Inc (PA)....B....661 295-1970
28447 Witherspoon Pkwy Valencia (91355) ***(P-859)***
Landscape Support Services....D....818 475-0680
12610 Saticoy St S North Hollywood (91605) ***(P-860)***
Lang Richert & Patch....E....559 228-6700
5200 N Palm Ave Ste 401 Fresno (93704) ***(P-22625)***
Langetwins Inc....D....209 339-4055
1298 E Jahant Rd Acampo (95220) ***(P-144)***
Langham Hotels International, Pasadena *Also called Langham Hotels Pacific Corp* ***(P-12537)***
Langham Hotels Pacific Corp....D....617 451-1900
1401 S Oak Knoll Ave Pasadena (91106) ***(P-12537)***
Langham Huntington Hotel & Spa, Pasadena *Also called Pacific Huntington Hotel Corp* ***(P-12695)***
Language Line Services Inc (HQ)....D....800 752-6096
1 Lower Ragsdale Dr # 2 Monterey (93940) ***(P-16884)***
Language Weaver Inc....D....310 437-7300
6060 Center Dr Ste 150 Los Angeles (90045) ***(P-14907)***
Lani, Irvine *Also called Loan Administration Netwrk Inc* ***(P-14326)***
Lanlogic Inc (HQ)....E....925 273-2300
248 Rickenbacker Cir Livermore (94551) ***(P-15634)***
Lansing Farming Co, Fresno *Also called Woolf Farming Co Cal Inc* ***(P-374)***
Lantern of Crescent City LLC....D....949 445-1000
1280 Marshall St Crescent City (95531) ***(P-20066)***
Lanting Hay Dealer Inc....D....909 563-5601
9032 Merrill Ave Ontario (91762) ***(P-8845)***
Lantz Security Systems Inc....B....805 496-5775
101 N Westlake Blvd # 200 Westlake Village (91362) ***(P-16338)***
Lantz Security Systems Inc....C....818 871-0193
4111 Las Virgenes Rd # 202 Calabasas (91302) ***(P-16539)***
Lantz Security Systems Inc (PA)....D....661 949-3565
43440 Sahuayo St Lancaster (93535) ***(P-16339)***
Lanwave Technology Inc....D....408 253-3883
20111 Stevens Creek Blvd # 260 Cupertino (95014) ***(P-25185)***
Lanza Vineyards Inc....E....707 864-0730
4756 Suisun Valley Rd Fairfield (94534) ***(P-145)***
Lapham Company Inc....D....510 531-6000
4844 Telegraph Ave Oakland (94609) ***(P-11243)***
Lapham Company Management, Oakland *Also called Lapham Company Inc* ***(P-11243)***
Larchmont Radiology Med Group....D....213 483-5953
2010 Wilshire Blvd # 409 Los Angeles (90057) ***(P-19151)***
Laren D Tan MD....D....909 558-4444
11234 Anderson St Loma Linda (92354) ***(P-19152)***
Largo Concrete Inc....A....909 981-7844
1690 W Foothill Blvd B Upland (91786) ***(P-3174)***
Largo Concrete Inc....A....408 874-2500
891 W Hamilton Ave Campbell (95008) ***(P-3175)***
Largo Concrete Inc....C....619 356-2142
1650 Hotel Cir N San Diego (92108) ***(P-1151)***
Lark Avenue Car Wash....D....408 371-2565
5005 Almaden Expy San Jose (95118) ***(P-17381)***
LARK Industries Inc (HQ)....C....714 701-4200
4900 E Hunter Ave Anaheim (92807) ***(P-16885)***
Larkin Leasing Inc....D....714 528-3232
674 N Batavia St Orange (92868) ***(P-1882)***
Larkspur Hsptality Dev MGT LLC....D....650 872-1515
670 Gateway Blvd South San Francisco (94080) ***(P-12538)***
Larrabee Brothrs Distribtng Co....D....805 922-2108
815 S Blosser Rd Santa Maria (93458) ***(P-8773)***
Larry Blair Realtor....E....650 991-5267
2488 Junipero Serra Blvd Daly City (94015) ***(P-11244)***
Larry Jacinto Construction Inc....D....909 794-2151
9555 N Wabash Ave Redlands (92374) ***(P-1746)***
Larry Jacinto Farming Inc....D....909 794-2276
9555 N Wabash Ave Redlands (92374) ***(P-668)***
Larsen Supply Co (PA)....D....562 698-0731
12055 Slauson Ave Santa Fe Springs (90670) ***(P-7430)***
Larson, Drake Sales, Thermal *Also called Drake Larson Ranchs* ***(P-128)***
Las Brisas, San Luis Obispo *Also called Harvest Management Sub LLC* ***(P-23948)***
Las Cumbres Observatory Global....E....805 880-1600
6740 Cortona Dr Ste 102 Goleta (93117) ***(P-26004)***
Las Flores Convalescent Hosp, Gardena *Also called Gardena Flores Inc* ***(P-19933)***
Las Posas Club Inc....D....805 482-1811
230 Ramona Pl Camarillo (93010) ***(P-18487)***
Las Posas Country Club....D....805 482-4518
955 Fairway Dr Camarillo (93010) ***(P-18488)***
Las Posas Road Medical Offices, Camarillo *Also called Kaiser Foundation Hospitals* ***(P-19061)***
Las Vegas / LA Express Inc (PA)....C....909 972-3100
1000 S Cucamonga Ave Ontario (91761) ***(P-4082)***
Las Vegas Intrntnl Tours....D....323 960-0300
18147 Coastline Dr Apt 1 Malibu (90265) ***(P-4855)***
Las Villas De Carlsbad, San Diego *Also called Villas De Carlsbad Ltd A Cali* ***(P-24108)***
Las Villas De Carlsbad, Oceanside *Also called Villas De Carlsbad Ltd A Cali* ***(P-24109)***
Las Villas Del Norte....D....760 741-1047
1325 Las Villas Way Escondido (92026) ***(P-20067)***
Las Virgenes Municipal Wtr Dst....C....818 251-2100
4232 Las Virgenes Rd Lbby Calabasas (91302) ***(P-6075)***
Lasaltte Hlth Rhbilitation Ctr, Stockton *Also called Five Star Qulty Care-CA II LLC* ***(P-19917)***
Lasco, Santa Fe Springs *Also called Larsen Supply Co* ***(P-7430)***
Laser Electric Inc (PA)....E....760 658-6626
2250 Micro Pl Ste 200 Escondido (92029) ***(P-2536)***
Laserfiche Document Imaging, Long Beach *Also called Compulink Management Ctr Inc* ***(P-15289)***
Lasertech Computer Distr Inc....D....626 435-2800
139 N Sunset Ave City of Industry (91744) ***(P-6859)***
Lasr Inc....C....877 591-9979
1517 Beverly Blvd Los Angeles (90026) ***(P-13764)***
Lassen Canyon Nursery Inc....D....530 938-4720
14735 Big Springs Rd Weed (96094) ***(P-100)***
Lassen Canyon Nursery Inc....D....209 599-7777
11651 Palm Ln Ripon (95366) ***(P-101)***
Lassen Canyon Nursery Inc (PA)....C....530 223-1075
1300 Salmon Creek Rd Redding (96003) ***(P-8184)***
Lassen Hse Assisted Living LLC....E....530 529-2900
705 Luther Rd Red Bluff (96080) ***(P-23969)***
Lassen Land Co....E....530 865-7676
320 E South St Orland (95963) ***(P-669)***
Lassen Medical Group Inc (PA)....D....530 527-0414
2450 Sster Mary Clumba Dr Red Bluff (96080) ***(P-19153)***
Lassen's, Ali Success System, Carlsbad *Also called Lassens Ali Leads Club* ***(P-24346)***
Lassens Ali Leads Club (PA)....D....760 434-3761
2644 Madison St Carlsbad (92008) ***(P-24346)***
Lassley Enterprises Inc....E....559 226-4300
1289 E Shaw Ave Fresno (93710) ***(P-10754)***
Last Frontier Healthcare Dst....C....530 233-5131
228 W Mcdowell Ave Alturas (96101) ***(P-20997)***
Lastline Inc....C....805 456-7075
6950 Hollister Ave # 101 Goleta (93117) ***(P-15387)***
Lastline Inc (PA)....D....805 456-7075
203 Redwood Shores Pkwy Redwood City (94065) ***(P-15388)***
Latara Enterprise Inc (PA)....C....909 623-9301
1716 W Holt Ave Pomona (91768) ***(P-21548)***
Latara Enterprise Inc....D....661 665-9780
9610 Stockdale Hwy Bakersfield (93311) ***(P-21549)***
Latara Enterprise Inc....D....760 256-3450
705 E Virginia Way Ste D Barstow (92311) ***(P-21550)***
Lateral Designs Inc....D....415 847-6618
639 Front St Fl 3 San Francisco (94111) ***(P-13789)***
Latham & Watkins LLP....C....650 328-4600
140 Scott Dr Menlo Park (94025) ***(P-22626)***
Latham & Watkins LLP....B....714 755-8288
1722 Skyhill Way Santa Ana (92705) ***(P-22627)***
Latham & Watkins LLP....C....858 523-5400
12670 High Bluff Dr # 100 San Diego (92130) ***(P-22628)***
Latham & Watkins LLP....B....818 753-5000
111 Univrsal Hllywd 257 Universal City (91608) ***(P-22629)***
Latham & Watkins LLP (PA)....A....213 485-1234
355 S Grand Ave Ste 1000 Los Angeles (90071) ***(P-22630)***
Latham & Watkins LLP....D....213 891-7108
555 W 5th St Ste 800 Los Angeles (90013) ***(P-22631)***
Latham & Watkins LLP....C....714 540-1235
650 Town Center Dr # 2000 Costa Mesa (92626) ***(P-22632)***
Latham & Watkins LLP....C....213 891-1200
520 S Grand Ave Ste 200 Los Angeles (90071) ***(P-22633)***
Latham & Watkins LLP....C....415 391-0600
505 Montgomery St # 1900 San Francisco (94111) ***(P-22634)***
Latham Pool Products Inc....E....530 473-5319
121 Crawford Rd Williams (95987) ***(P-3429)***
Lathrop & Gage LLP....D....310 789-4600
1888 Century Park E # 1000 Los Angeles (90067) ***(P-22635)***
Lattice Engines Inc (HQ)....D....877 460-0010
1820 Gateway Dr Ste 200 San Mateo (94404) ***(P-15635)***
Laugh Factory Inc....C....562 495-2844
151 S Pine Ave Long Beach (90802) ***(P-24843)***
Laughlin Falbo Levy Moresi LLP (PA)....D....510 628-0496
1001 Galaxy Way Ste 200 Concord (94520) ***(P-22636)***
Lauras House....D....949 361-3775
999 Corporate Dr Ste 225 Mission Viejo (92694) ***(P-23313)***
Laurel Convelescent Center, Fontana *Also called Sun Mar Management Services* ***(P-26412)***
Laurel Labor Services Inc....D....805 928-0113
727 Richmind Ct Santa Maria (93455) ***(P-14323)***
Laurel Park, Pomona *Also called Genesis Healthcare Corporation* ***(P-19937)***
Laurence-Hovenier Inc....C....951 736-2990
179 N Maple St Corona (92880) ***(P-2947)***

ALPHABETIC

Lav Hotel Corp ....C....858 454-0771
1132 Prospect St La Jolla (92037) ***(P-12539)***
Lava Beds National Monuments ....E....530 667-2282
1 Indian Wells Hqtrs Tulelake (96134) ***(P-24844)***
Lavine Lofgren Morris Engelb ....E....858 455-1200
4180 La Jolla Village Dr # 300 La Jolla (92037) ***(P-25634)***
Law Crossing (PA) ....D....626 243-1801
175 S Lake Ave Unit 200 Pasadena (91101) ***(P-23609)***
Law Enforcement Officers Inc ....C....855 477-3536
24000 Alicia Pkwy 17-229 Mission Viejo (92691) ***(P-16540)***
Law Offices Berglund & Johnson (PA) ....D....951 276-4783
21550 Oxnard St Ste 900 Woodland Hills (91367) ***(P-22637)***
Law Offices Juan J. Dominguez, Los Angeles *Also called Dominguez Firm Inc* ***(P-22486)***
Law Offices of James F. Holtz, San Diego *Also called Artiano Shinoff Abed* ***(P-22364)***
Law Offices of Thomas W ....C....858 883-2000
14286 Danielson St # 103 Poway (92064) ***(P-22638)***
Law School Financial Inc ....C....626 243-1800
175 S Lake Ave Unit 200 Pasadena (91101) ***(P-9448)***
Law School Loans, Pasadena *Also called Law School Financial Inc* ***(P-9448)***
Lawinfocom Inc ....D....800 397-3743
5901 Priestly Dr Ste 200 Carlsbad (92008) ***(P-15389)***
Lawndale Hlthcare Wllness Ctr ....D....310 679-3344
1700 Santa Fe Ave Ste 100 Long Beach (90813) ***(P-20068)***
Lawnman II Inc ....D....916 739-1420
4300 82nd St Ste C Sacramento (95826) ***(P-861)***
Lawrence B Bonas Company ....D....714 668-5250
3197 Arprt Loop Dr Ste C Costa Mesa (92626) ***(P-2366)***
Lawrence Berkeley National Lab, Emeryville *Also called University California Berkeley* ***(P-26042)***
Lawrence Berkeley National Lab, Berkeley *Also called United States Dept of Energy* ***(P-26039)***
Lawrence Family Jewish Commu (PA) ....C....858 362-1144
4126 Executive Dr La Jolla (92037) ***(P-24191)***
Lawrence Livermore Nat Lab, Livermore *Also called United States Dept of Energy* ***(P-25858)***
Lawrence Tractor Coinc (PA) ....D....559 734-7406
2436 E Valley Oaks Dr Visalia (93292) ***(P-7502)***
Lawson Mechanical Contractors (PA) ....D....916 381-5000
6090 S Watt Ave Sacramento (95829) ***(P-2180)***
Lawson Roofing Co Inc ....D....415 285-1661
1495 Tennessee St San Francisco (94107) ***(P-3070)***
Lawyers Title Company ....D....858 650-3900
4542 Ruffner St Ste 200 San Diego (92111) ***(P-10195)***
Lawyers Title Company (HQ) ....E....818 767-0425
7530 N Glenoaks Blvd Burbank (91504) ***(P-10196)***
Lawyers Title Insurance Corp ....D....949 223-5575
18551 Von Karman Ave # 100 Irvine (92612) ***(P-10197)***
Lax Hospitality LP ....C....310 670-9000
6225 W Century Blvd Los Angeles (90045) ***(P-12540)***
Lax Hotel Ventures LLC ....E....310 645-4600
9750 Airport Blvd Los Angeles (90045) ***(P-12541)***
Lax International Service Ctr ....D....310 337-8764
5800 W Century Blvd Los Angeles (90009) ***(P-16886)***
Lax Plaza Hotel ....C....310 902-2202
6333 Bristol Pkwy Culver City (90230) ***(P-12542)***
LAX Wheel Refinishing Inc ....D....323 269-1484
1520 Spence St Los Angeles (90023) ***(P-6450)***
Lax-C Inc ....E....323 343-9000
1100 N Main St Los Angeles (90012) ***(P-8185)***
Laxmi Group Inc ....D....408 329-7733
4699 Old Ironsides Dr # 100 Santa Clara (95054) ***(P-14908)***
Layfield USA Corporation (HQ) ....D....619 562-1200
2500 Sweetwater Springs B Spring Valley (91978) ***(P-3430)***
Layne Christensen Company ....C....909 390-2833
1717 W Park Ave Redlands (92373) ***(P-27113)***
Layton-Belling & Associates, Irvine *Also called Lba Inc* ***(P-26671)***
Lazar Landscape Design & Cnstr ....D....510 444-5195
2884 Ettie St Oakland (94608) ***(P-737)***
Laztrans Inc ....E....661 833-3783
5200 District Blvd Bakersfield (93313) ***(P-3906)***
Lb Funding LLC ....D....562 983-3400
701 W Ocean Blvd Long Beach (90831) ***(P-12543)***
Lb Hills Golf Club LLC ....D....760 775-2000
84000 Terra Lago Pkwy Indio (92203) ***(P-18261)***
Lba Inc (PA) ....C....949 833-0400
3347 Michelson Dr Ste 200 Irvine (92612) ***(P-26671)***
Lba Realty Fund III - III LLC ....D....949 833-0400
3347 Michelson Dr Ste 200 Irvine (92612) ***(P-11861)***
Lba Realty LLC (PA) ....E....949 833-0400
3347 Michelson Dr Ste 200 Irvine (92612) ***(P-11245)***
Lba Rlty Fund I-Company IV LLC ....D....949 955-9321
3347 Michelson Dr Ste 950 Irvine (92612) ***(P-11862)***
LBC Inc ....D....805 581-1068
1881 Duncan St Simi Valley (93065) ***(P-3071)***
LBC Mundial Corporation (HQ) ....D....650 873-0750
3563 Inv Blvd Ste 3 Hayward (94545) ***(P-4722)***
LBC North America, Hayward *Also called LBC Mundial Corporation* ***(P-4722)***
Lbf Enterprises (PA) ....D....925 461-7171
1264 Stealth St Livermore (94551) ***(P-7290)***
Lbi Media Inc ....A....818 729-5316
1845 W Empire Ave Burbank (91504) ***(P-5553)***
Lbs Financial Credit Union ....D....714 893-5111
1401 Quail St Ste 130 Newport Beach (92660) ***(P-9449)***
Lbs Financial Credit Union (PA) ....C....562 598-9007
5505 Garden Grove Blvd # 500 Westminster (92683) ***(P-9450)***
Lc Trs Inc ....A....760 438-9111
2100 Costa Del Mar Rd Carlsbad (92009) ***(P-12544)***
Ld Products Inc ....C....562 986-6940
3700 Cover St Long Beach (90808) ***(P-6860)***
LDI Mechanical Inc ....E....916 361-3925
3760 Happy Ln Sacramento (95827) ***(P-2181)***
LDI Mechanical Inc (PA) ....C....951 340-9685
1587 E Bentley Dr Corona (92879) ***(P-2182)***
LDI Transportation Inc ....D....909 620-7001
200 Erie St Pomona (91768) ***(P-4215)***
Ldla Clothing LLC ....D....323 312-2805
13071 Temple Ave La Puente (91746) ***(P-8086)***
Le Bleu Chateau Inc ....E....818 843-3141
1900 Grismer Ave Burbank (91504) ***(P-23970)***
Le Courier, Burbank *Also called Tidavater Inc* ***(P-17096)***
Le Crochet By Saro Inc (PA) ....E....818 846-3314
3333 W Pacific Ave Burbank (91505) ***(P-6567)***
Le Merdien Dlfina Santa Monica, Santa Monica *Also called Blue Devils Lessee LLC* ***(P-12075)***
Le Meridian Hotel, San Francisco *Also called Chesapeake Lodging Trust* ***(P-12138)***
Le Montrose Hotel ....D....310 855-1115
900 Hammond St Apt 434 West Hollywood (90069) ***(P-12545)***
Le Montrose Suite Hotel, West Hollywood *Also called Le Montrose Hotel* ***(P-12545)***
Le Parc Suite Hotel, West Hollywood *Also called Ols Hotels & Resorts LP* ***(P-12670)***
Le Parker Meridien Palm Sprng, Palm Springs *Also called Jack Parker Corp* ***(P-12485)***
Le Vecke Corporation (PA) ....D....951 681-8600
10810 Inland Ave Jurupa Valley (91752) ***(P-8774)***
Le Vecke Group, Jurupa Valley *Also called Le Vecke Corporation* ***(P-8774)***
Lead Staffing Corporation ....C....800 928-5561
216 S Citrus St Ste 397 West Covina (91791) ***(P-19678)***
Leader Drug Store, Torrance *Also called Little Company Mary Hospital* ***(P-21007)***
Leader Emergency Vehicles, South El Monte *Also called Leader Industries Inc* ***(P-3694)***
Leader Industries Inc ....C....626 575-0880
10941 Weaver Ave South El Monte (91733) ***(P-3694)***
Leadhealthstaff, Tarzana *Also called Advanced Medical Placement* ***(P-24123)***
Leadstack Inc ....D....628 200-3063
1390 Market St Ste 200 San Francisco (94102) ***(P-14324)***
Leaf Commercial Capital Inc ....E....866 219-7924
1100 Town & Country Rd Orange (92868) ***(P-26672)***
Leaf Communications Inc ....D....949 388-0192
1000 Calle Cordillera San Clemente (92673) ***(P-27114)***
League of California Cities (PA) ....D....916 658-8200
1400 K St Fl 4 Sacramento (95814) ***(P-26915)***
League of Wmen Voters Whittier ....E....562 947-5818
10011 Melgar Dr Whittier (90603) ***(P-24779)***
Leantaas Inc ....D....650 409-3501
471 El Cmino Real Ste 230 Santa Clara (95050) ***(P-14909)***
Lear Capital Inc ....D....310 571-0190
1990 S Bundy Dr Ste 600 Los Angeles (90025) ***(P-9706)***
LEARN, Whittier *Also called Rio Hondo Education Consortium* ***(P-23416)***
Learning Services Corporation ....E....760 746-3223
2335 Bear Valley Pkwy Escondido (92027) ***(P-22058)***
Learning Services Corporation ....E....408 848-4379
10855 De Bruin Way Gilroy (95020) ***(P-22059)***
Learning Services Northern Cal, Gilroy *Also called Learning Services Corporation* ***(P-22059)***
Learning Tree Pre-School, Tujunga *Also called Crescenta-Canada YMCA* ***(P-24531)***
Leasing Equipment, San Francisco *Also called Atel Capital Group* ***(P-9498)***
Leavitt Group Enterprises Inc ....C....707 465-6508
785 E Washington Blvd # 4 Crescent City (95531) ***(P-10408)***
Leavy Brothers Incorporated ....D....916 773-5636
4117 Elverta Rd Ste 102 Antelope (95843) ***(P-2814)***
Led Global LLC ....D....917 921-4315
1010 Wilshire Blvd Los Angeles (90017) ***(P-2183)***
Ledcor CMI Inc ....D....602 595-3017
6405 Mira Mesa Blvd # 100 San Diego (92121) ***(P-1364)***
Ledcor Management Services Inc ....E....858 527-6400
6405 Mira Mesa Blvd Ste 1 San Diego (92121) ***(P-26297)***
Ledesma & Meyer Cnstr Co Inc ....D....909 297-1100
9441 Haven Ave Rancho Cucamonga (91730) ***(P-1527)***
Ledesma & Meyer Dev Inc ....D....909 476-0590
9441 Haven Ave Rancho Cucamonga (91730) ***(P-26298)***
Ledra Brands Inc ....D....714 259-9959
15774 Gateway Cir Tustin (92780) ***(P-6568)***
Ledson Winery & Vineyards, Santa Rosa *Also called Steven N Ledson* ***(P-1200)***
Lee Burkhart Liu Inc ....D....415 580-6740
100 California St Ste 725 San Francisco (94111) ***(P-25470)***
Lee Hong Degerman Kang ....D....949 250-9954
3501 Jamboree Rd Ste 6000 Newport Beach (92660) ***(P-22639)***
Lee & Assoc Comm Real Est Svcs ....E....909 989-7771
3535 Inland Empire Blvd Ontario (91764) ***(P-11246)***
Lee & Associates Coml RE Svcs, Ontario *Also called Lee & Assoc Comm Real Est Svcs* ***(P-11246)***
Lee & Associates Coml RE Svcs (PA) ....E....949 727-1200
7700 Irvine Center Dr # 600 Irvine (92618) ***(P-11247)***
Lee & Associates Realty Group ....E....949 724-1000
100 Bayview Cir Ste 600 Newport Beach (92660) ***(P-11248)***
Lee & Ro Inc (PA) ....E....626 912-3391
1199 Fullerton Rd City of Industry (91748) ***(P-25186)***
Lee Bros Foodservices Inc (PA) ....C....408 275-0700
660 E Gish Rd San Jose (95112) ***(P-8186)***
Lee Industrial Catering, San Jose *Also called Lee Bros Foodservices Inc* ***(P-8186)***
Lee Jennings Target Ex Inc (PA) ....C....909 868-1040
1465 E Franklin Ave Pomona (91766) ***(P-3907)***
Lee Johnson ....C....858 481-4411
14750 El Camino Real Del Mar (92014) ***(P-20612)***
Lee Mar Aquarium & Pet Sups, Vista *Also called Lee-Mar Aquarium & Pet Sups* ***(P-8983)***
LEE& Associates, Newport Beach *Also called Lee & Associates Realty Group* ***(P-11248)***
Lee-Mar Aquarium & Pet Sups ....D....760 727-1300
2459 Dogwood Way Vista (92081) ***(P-8983)***
Lee-Victorville Hotel Corp ....C....760 245-3461
14173 Green Tree Blvd Victorville (92395) ***(P-12546)***

Leed Electric Inc ....D....562 270-9500
13138 Arctic Cir Santa Fe Springs (90670) ***(P-2537)***
Leed International LLC ....E....650 861-7883
1583 Shanghai Cir San Jose (95131) ***(P-27115)***
Leekilpatrick Management Inc ....D....818 500-9631
324 S Myrtle Ave Monrovia (91016) ***(P-26673)***
Leemah Electronics Inc ....C....415 394-1288
1080 Sansome St San Francisco (94111) ***(P-5852)***
Leerink Partners LLC ....D....800 778-1164
255 California St Fl 12 San Francisco (94111) ***(P-9707)***
Lees Maintenance Service Inc ....B....818 988-6644
14740 Keswick St Van Nuys (91405) ***(P-13962)***
Legacy and Nursing Rehab ....D....925 228-8383
1790 Muir Rd Martinez (94553) ***(P-20069)***
Legacy Farms LLC ....C....714 736-1800
1765 W Penhall Way Anaheim (92801) ***(P-8494)***
Legacy Frames ....D....310 537-4210
11220 Wright Rd Lynwood (90262) ***(P-7291)***
Legacy Global Logistics Svcs, San Jose *Also called Legacy Transportation Svcs Inc* ***(P-4216)***
Legacy Healthcare Center LLC ....D....626 798-0558
1570 N Fair Oaks Ave Pasadena (91103) ***(P-22269)***
Legacy Lifepoint Health Inc ....C....760 326-7100
1401 Bailey Ave Needles (92363) ***(P-20998)***
Legacy Marketing Group (PA) ....C....707 778-8638
2090 Marina Ave Petaluma (94954) ***(P-26674)***
Legacy Mech & Enrgy Svcs Inc ....D....925 820-6938
3130 Crow Canyon Pl # 410 San Ramon (94583) ***(P-2184)***
Legacy Partners Hollywood ....D....949 930-7706
1600 Vine St Los Angeles (90028) ***(P-10755)***
Legacy Partners Limited Inc ....D....760 747-2711
738 W Washington Ave A Escondido (92025) ***(P-1747)***
Legacy Paving, Escondido *Also called Legacy Partners Limited Inc* ***(P-1747)***
Legacy Prtners Residential Inc ....B....949 930-6600
5141 California Ave # 100 Irvine (92617) ***(P-26299)***
Legacy Prtners Residential Inc (PA) ....C....650 571-2250
950 Tower Ln Ste 900 Foster City (94404) ***(P-26300)***
Legacy Tile and Stone Inc ....E....951 296-1096
26825 Jefferson Ave Ste D Murrieta (92562) ***(P-2900)***
Legacy Transportation Svcs Inc (PA) ....C....408 294-9800
935 Mclaughlin Ave San Jose (95122) ***(P-4216)***
Legacy Vulcan LLC ....E....909 875-1150
2400 W Highland Ave San Bernardino (92407) ***(P-1057)***
Legal Enterprise, Calabasas *Also called Litigtion Rsrces of America-CA* ***(P-16894)***
Legal Recovery Law Offices Inc ....D....619 275-4001
5030 Camino De La Siesta # 340 San Diego (92108) ***(P-22640)***
Legal Solutions Holdings Inc ....C....800 244-3495
955 Overland Ct Ste 200 San Dimas (91773) ***(P-22641)***
Legalmatchcom (PA) ....E....415 946-0800
395 Oyster Point Blvd South San Francisco (94080) ***(P-22642)***
Legalzoomcom Inc (HQ) ....B....323 962-8600
101 N Brand Blvd Fl 11 Glendale (91203) ***(P-22643)***
Legend Films ....B....858 793-4420
2200 Faraday Ave Ste 100 Carlsbad (92008) ***(P-17747)***
Legend Merchant Group Inc ....E....415 957-9555
201 Mission St Ste 230 San Francisco (94105) ***(P-16887)***
Legend Transpotation, Yuba City *Also called New Legend Inc* ***(P-4101)***
Legend3d Inc ....D....858 793-4420
1500 N El Centro Ave # 100 Los Angeles (90028) ***(P-17622)***
Leggett & Platt Incorporated ....D....510 487-8063
31023 Huntwood Ave Hayward (94544) ***(P-13654)***
Legion Corporation ....D....415 829-7307
106 Sanchez St San Francisco (94114) ***(P-24580)***
Legion Industries ....E....650 743-6358
748 Lakemead Way Emerald Hills (94062) ***(P-16888)***
Legions Protective Svcs LLC ....E....310 819-8881
17201 S Figueroa St Gardena (90248) ***(P-16340)***
Legislative Counsel Tstg Off, Sacramento *Also called Office of The Legislative Coun* ***(P-27154)***
Legislative Data Center, Sacramento *Also called Office of The Legislative Coun* ***(P-5267)***
Legoland California LLC ....B....760 918-5346
1 Legoland Dr Carlsbad (92008) ***(P-18334)***
Legrande Affaire, Santa Clara *Also called Restivo Enterprises* ***(P-3714)***
Legrande Affaire Inc ....C....408 988-4884
651 Aldo Ave Santa Clara (95054) ***(P-3695)***
Lehar Sales Co ....D....510 465-3255
477 Forbes Blvd South San Francisco (94080) ***(P-8328)***
Lehman Brothers, Los Angeles *Also called Barclays Capital Inc* ***(P-9652)***
Lehr, Sacramento *Also called Stommel Inc* ***(P-2656)***
Lei AG Seattle, Los Angeles *Also called Lowe Enterprises Inc* ***(P-12564)***
Leichtag Assisted Living, Encinitas *Also called San Diego Hebrew Homes* ***(P-20232)***
Leidos Inc ....C....858 826-9090
2985 Scott St Vista (92081) ***(P-25779)***
Leidos Inc ....B....858 826-5552
4035 Hancock St San Diego (92110) ***(P-25780)***
Leidos Inc ....D....310 791-9671
1874 S Pacific Coast Hwy Redondo Beach (90277) ***(P-25781)***
Leidos Inc ....C....858 535-4499
9455 Towne Centre Dr # 200 San Diego (92121) ***(P-25782)***
Leidos Inc ....C....703 676-4300
10260 Campus Point Dr C San Diego (92121) ***(P-25783)***
Leidos Inc ....B....858 826-7670
1550 N Norma St Ridgecrest (93555) ***(P-15783)***
Leidos Inc ....C....858 826-9416
4161 Campus Point Ct San Diego (92121) ***(P-25784)***
Leidos Inc ....D....714 257-6400
590 W Central Ave Ste I Brea (92821) ***(P-25785)***
Leidos Inc ....C....310 524-3134
300 N Pacific Coast Hwy El Segundo (90245) ***(P-25786)***
Leidos Inc ....D....858 826-6616
10740 Thornmint Rd San Diego (92127) ***(P-25787)***
Leidos Inc ....D....510 428-2550
2000 Powell St Ste 1090 Emeryville (94608) ***(P-25788)***
Leidos Inc ....B....858 826-6000
1299 Prospect St La Jolla (92037) ***(P-25789)***
Leidos Inc ....D....858 826-6000
4065 Hancock St San Diego (92110) ***(P-25790)***
Leidos Inc ....C....858 826-7129
10010 Campus Point Dr San Diego (92121) ***(P-25791)***
Leidos Inc ....D....510 466-7138
505 14th St Ste 900 Oakland (94612) ***(P-25792)***
Leidos Inc ....B....916 974-8800
3800 Watt Ave Ste 210 Sacramento (95821) ***(P-15636)***
Leidos Inc ....D....910 574-4597
N Depo Rd Bldg 4530 Fort Irwin (92310) ***(P-25793)***
Leidos Engineering LLC ....D....714 257-6400
590 W Central Ave Ste I Brea (92821) ***(P-25187)***
Leidos Engineering LLC ....D....858 826-6000
4161 Campus Point Ct E San Diego (92121) ***(P-25188)***
Leidos Engrg & Sciences LLC ....D....619 542-3130
1330 30th St Ste A San Diego (92154) ***(P-25794)***
Leight Sales Co Inc ....D....310 223-1000
1611 S Catalina Ave L45 Redondo Beach (90277) ***(P-7396)***
Leighton & Associates, Irvine *Also called Gradient Engineers Inc* ***(P-25110)***
Leighton and Associates Inc (PA) ....D....949 250-1421
17781 Cowan Irvine (92614) ***(P-27116)***
Leighton Group Inc ....C....760 776-4192
75450 Gerald Ford Dr Palm Desert (92211) ***(P-24407)***
Leisure Care, Livermore *Also called Livermore Snior Lving Assoc LP* ***(P-10758)***
Leisure Care Inc ....D....949 645-6833
1455 Superior Ave Newport Beach (92663) ***(P-10756)***
Leisure Care LLC ....D....818 713-0900
8138 Woodlake Ave West Hills (91304) ***(P-20436)***
Leisure Care LLC ....E....714 974-1616
380 S Anaheim Hills Rd Anaheim (92807) ***(P-23971)***
Leisure Care LLC ....D....559 434-1237
9525 N Fort Washington Rd Fresno (93730) ***(P-23972)***
Leisure Court Nursing Center, Anaheim *Also called 1135 N Leisure Ct Inc* ***(P-19705)***
Leisure Glen Convalescent Ctr, Glendale *Also called Buena Ventura Care Center Inc* ***(P-20519)***
Leisure Planet ....C....925 687-4386
1975 Diamond Blvd Concord (94520) ***(P-18717)***
Leisure Sports Inc ....C....510 226-8500
46650 Landing Pkwy Fremont (94538) ***(P-18169)***
Leisure Sports Inc ....B....925 938-3058
2805 Jones Rd Walnut Creek (94597) ***(P-12547)***
Leisure Village Association ....D....805 484-2861
200 Leisure Village Dr Camarillo (93012) ***(P-24581)***
Leisure World Pharmacy, Seal Beach *Also called Tenet Healthsystem Medical* ***(P-19503)***
Leisure World Resales, Laguna Hills *Also called Professional Community MGT Cal* ***(P-11373)***
LEK Consulting LLC ....D....310 209-9800
1100 Glendon Ave Ste 2100 Los Angeles (90024) ***(P-26675)***
Leland Health Care Services, Hemet *Also called Physicians For Healthy Hospita* ***(P-21094)***
Leland House, San Francisco *Also called Catholic Chrts Cyo Archdiocs* ***(P-22972)***
Leland Stanford Junior Univ ....C....650 723-6254
1070 Arastradero Rd # 100 Palo Alto (94304) ***(P-25918)***
Leland Stanford Junior Univ ....D....650 725-4868
551 Srra Mall Mem Adtrium Memorial Auditorium Stanford (94305) ***(P-5554)***
Leland Stanford Junior Univ ....D....650 723-7863
1201 Welch Rd Stanford (94305) ***(P-19154)***
Leland Stanford Junior Univ ....E....650 723-2997
328 Lomita Dr Palo Alto (94305) ***(P-20999)***
Leland Stanford Junior Univ ....D....650 723-4150
Melcode 4020 Bldg 540 Stanford (94305) ***(P-26005)***
Leland Stanford Junior Univ ....C....650 723-2021
326 Galvez St Stanford (94305) ***(P-24582)***
Leland Stanford Junior Univ ....B....650 723-7546
476 Lomita Mall Palo Alto (94305) ***(P-25919)***
Leland Stanford Junior Univ ....D....650 723-9633
711 Serra St Stanford (94305) ***(P-2538)***
Leland Stanford Junior Univ ....A....650 725-2377
820 Quarry Rd Palo Alto (94304) ***(P-21000)***
Leland Stanford Junior Univ ....A....650 723-4000
2680 Hanover St Palo Alto (94304) ***(P-21001)***
Leland Stanford Junior Univ ....C....650 723-0107
450 Via Palou Mall Stanford (94305) ***(P-26006)***
Leland Stanford Junior Univ ....C....650 724-8899
397 Panama Mall Ste 360 Stanford (94305) ***(P-26007)***
Leland Stanford Junior Univ ....D....650 725-4416
211 Quarry Rd N229 Palo Alto (94304) ***(P-19155)***
Leland Stanford Junior Univ ....A....650 725-4617
1000 Welch Rd Palo Alto (94304) ***(P-21002)***
Leland Stanford Junior Univ ....A....650 725-2386
473 Via Ortega Stanford (94305) ***(P-21003)***
Leland Stanford Junior Univ ....A....650 725-6127
243 Panama St Stanford (94305) ***(P-21004)***
Leland Stanford Junior Univ ....D....650 723-0821
870 Campus Dr Stanford (94305) ***(P-19156)***
Leland Stanford Junior Univ ....A....650 723-4000
300 Pasteur Dr Stanford (94305) ***(P-21005)***
Leland Stanford Junior Univ ....D....650 723-4733
1201 Welch Rd Palo Alto (94305) ***(P-26008)***
Lemo USA Inc ....D....707 206-3700
635 Park Ct Rohnert Park (94928) ***(P-7292)***
Lemonlight Media Inc ....D....310 402-0275
226 S Glasgow Ave Inglewood (90301) ***(P-17623)***

Employee Codes: A=Over 500 employees, B=251-500
C=101-250, D=51-100, E=50
2020 Directory of California
Wholesalers and Services Companies
© Mergent Inc. 1-800-342-5647
1331

Lemore Transportation Inc (PA) ....D....925 689-6444
1420 Royal Industrial Way Concord (94520) ***(P-4083)***
Lender Processing Services Inc ....D....626 808-9000
3100 New York Dr Ste 200 Pasadena (91107) ***(P-15784)***
Lendingclub Asset MGT LLC ....B....415 632-5600
71 Stevenson St Ste 300 San Francisco (94105) ***(P-9631)***
Lendingclub Corporation (PA) ....C....415 632-5600
595 Market St Fl 4 San Francisco (94105) ***(P-16889)***
Lendlease US Construction Inc ....D....213 430-4660
800 W 6th St Ste 1600 Los Angeles (90017) ***(P-26301)***
Lendup, Oakland *Also called Flurish Inc* ***(P-9459)***
Lendus LLC ....A....925 295-9300
3240 Stone Valley Rd W Alamo (94507) ***(P-9571)***
Lendusa LLC (PA) ....D....925 295-9300
3240 Stone Valley Rd W Alamo (94507) ***(P-9572)***
Lenlyn Limited Which Will Do B (HQ) ....D....310 417-3432
6151 W Century Blvd Los Angeles (90045) ***(P-9439)***
Lennar, Rancho Santa Fe *Also called HCC Investors LLC* ***(P-18465)***
Lennar Builders, Irvine *Also called Lennar Homes California Inc* ***(P-1152)***
Lennar Corporation ....D....949 349-8000
15131 Alton Pkwy Ste 190 Irvine (92618) ***(P-1306)***
Lennar Homes Inc ....C....916 517-4950
3788 Edington Dr Rancho Cordova (95742) ***(P-1307)***
Lennar Homes Inc ....C....951 739-0267
980 Montecito Dr Ste 300 Corona (92879) ***(P-1308)***
Lennar Homes California Inc ....D....858 759-7200
18495 Seven Bridges Rd Santa Clara (95050) ***(P-1309)***
Lennar Homes California Inc (HQ) ....C....949 349-8000
15131 Alton Pkwy Ste 190 Irvine (92618) ***(P-1152)***
Lennar Multi Family Community, Aliso Viejo *Also called LMC Hollywood Highland* ***(P-1530)***
Lennar Partners of Los Angeles (PA) ....E....949 885-8500
4350 Von Karman Ave # 200 Newport Beach (92660) ***(P-16890)***
Lennox Industries Inc ....C....818 739-1616
19801 Nordhoff Pl Ste 109 Chatsworth (91311) ***(P-7453)***
Lenore John & Co (PA) ....C....619 232-6136
1250 Delevan Dr San Diego (92102) ***(P-8605)***
Lenox Financial Mortgage Corp ....C....949 428-5100
200 Sandpointe Ave # 800 Santa Ana (92707) ***(P-9573)***
Leo A Daly Company, Sacramento *Also called Leo A Daly Company* ***(P-25472)***
Leo A Daly Company ....D....213 627-9300
550 S Hope St Ste 2700 Los Angeles (90071) ***(P-25471)***
Leo A Daly Company ....D....916 564-3259
2150 River Plaza Dr Sacramento (95833) ***(P-25472)***
Leo Daly Company, Los Angeles *Also called Leo A Daly Company* ***(P-25471)***
Leo J Ryan Child Care Ctr, South San Francisco *Also called Peninsula Family Service* ***(P-23380)***
Leon Chien Corp ....D....626 964-8302
17843 Colima Rd City of Industry (91748) ***(P-9574)***
Leonard Anthony Valenti Inc ....D....408 848-9688
9110 Marcella Ave Gilroy (95020) ***(P-862)***
Leonard Chaidez Inc ....D....714 279-8173
2298 N Batavia St Orange (92865) ***(P-941)***
Leonard Chaidez Tree Service, Orange *Also called Leonard Chaidez Inc* ***(P-941)***
Leonards Carpet Service Inc ....E....858 453-9525
6767 Nancy Ridge Dr San Diego (92121) ***(P-3176)***
Leonid M Glosman DDS A D ....C....323 560-4514
5021 Florence Ave Bell (90201) ***(P-19618)***
Lereta LLC (PA) ....B....626 543-1765
1123 Park View Dr Covina (91724) ***(P-9708)***
Leroy Durbin ....D....562 531-2001
14620 Lakewood Blvd Bellflower (90706) ***(P-11249)***
Leroy Haynes Center, La Verne *Also called Haynes Family Programs Inc* ***(P-23952)***
Les Kelley Family Health Ctr ....D....310 319-4700
1920 Colorado Ave Santa Monica (90404) ***(P-19157)***
Lescure Company Inc ....D....925 283-2528
2301 Arnold Industrial Wa Concord (94520) ***(P-2185)***
Lesley Foundation ....D....650 726-4888
701 Arnold Way Bldg A Half Moon Bay (94019) ***(P-27117)***
Leslie Thompson, Newport Beach *Also called Compass Real Estate LLC* ***(P-10327)***
Level 10 Construction LP ....C....408 747-5000
1050 Entp Way Ste 250 Sunnyvale (94089) ***(P-1528)***
Level 9 Security Services ....E....562 949-7180
9020 Slauson Ave Ste 206 Pico Rivera (90660) ***(P-16341)***
Level 99, Gardena *Also called Phoenix Textile Inc* ***(P-8005)***
Level Four Business MGT LLC ....E....310 914-1600
11812 San Vicente Blvd # 400 Los Angeles (90049) ***(P-27118)***
Level-It Installations Ltd ....E....604 942-2022
2443 Fillmore St San Francisco (94115) ***(P-1529)***
Lever Inc ....D....415 458-2731
155 5th St 6 San Francisco (94103) ***(P-14910)***
Levin and Simes ....E....415 426-3000
353 Sacramento St # 2000 San Francisco (94111) ***(P-22644)***
Levin-Richmond Terminal Corp ....D....510 232-4422
402 Wright Ave Richmond (94804) ***(P-4613)***
Levy Cncessions At Staples Ctr, Los Angeles *Also called Levy Prmium Fdsrvice Ltd Prtnr* ***(P-1365)***
Levy Prmium Fdsrvice Ltd Prtnr ....D....213 742-7867
1111 S Figueroa St Los Angeles (90015) ***(P-1365)***
Lewis & Taylor LLC ....C....415 781-3496
440 Bryant St San Francisco (94107) ***(P-13963)***
Lewis & Taylor Bldg Svc Contrs, San Francisco *Also called Lewis & Taylor LLC* ***(P-13963)***
Lewis Brsbois Bsgard Smith LLP ....D....951 252-6150
28765 Single Oak Dr Ste 1 Temecula (92590) ***(P-22645)***
Lewis Brsbois Bsgard Smith LLP (PA) ....A....213 250-1800
633 W 5th St Ste 4000 Los Angeles (90071) ***(P-22646)***
Lewis Brsbois Bsgard Smith LLP ....D....619 233-1006
701 B St Ste 1900 San Diego (92101) ***(P-22647)***
Lewis Brsbois Bsgard Smith LLP ....C....415 362-2580
333 Bush St San Francisco (94104) ***(P-22648)***
Lewis Brsbois Bsgard Smith LLP ....E....909 387-1130
650 E Hospitality Ln # 600 San Bernardino (92408) ***(P-22649)***
Lewis Companies (PA) ....B....909 985-0971
1156 N Mountain Ave Upland (91786) ***(P-1310)***
Lewis Lifetime Tools, Poway *Also called Richmond Engineering Co Inc* ***(P-900)***
Lewis Marenstein Wicke Sherwin ....E....818 703-6000
20750 Ventura Blvd # 400 Woodland Hills (91364) ***(P-22650)***
Lewis PR Inc (HQ) ....D....415 432-2400
111 Sutter St Ste 850 San Francisco (94104) ***(P-26916)***
Lewis-Goetz and Company Inc ....D....916 366-9340
10182 Croydon Way Sacramento (95827) ***(P-7639)***
Lexani Wheel Corporation ....D....951 808-4220
2380 Railroad St Ste 101 Corona (92880) ***(P-6451)***
Lexicon Consulting Inc (PA) ....D....619 792-1530
420 S Magnolia Ave El Cajon (92020) ***(P-26952)***
Lexington Scenery & Props Inc ....C....818 768-5768
12800 Rangoon St Arleta (91331) ***(P-2948)***
Lexisnexis, Los Angeles *Also called Relx Inc* ***(P-15881)***
Lexisnexis Courtlink Inc ....C....425 974-5000
2101 K St Sacramento (95816) ***(P-24408)***
Lexmar Distribution Inc ....C....909 620-7001
200 Erie St Pomona (91768) ***(P-4084)***
Lexxiom Inc ....B....909 581-7313
7945 Cartilla Ave Ste A Rancho Cucamonga (91730) ***(P-26302)***
Lfk Law ....D....310 300-8464
9595 Wilshire Blvd # 900 Beverly Hills (90212) ***(P-22651)***
Lfp Ecommerce LLC ....D....314 428-5069
210 N Sunset Ave West Covina (91790) ***(P-16891)***
Lg Display America Inc ....E....760 692-0900
2791 Loker Ave W Carlsbad (92010) ***(P-7293)***
Lg Display America Inc (HQ) ....D....408 350-0190
2540 N 1st St Ste 400 San Jose (95131) ***(P-7294)***
Lh Indian Wells Operating LLC ....C....760 341-2200
4500 Indian Wells Ln Indian Wells (92210) ***(P-12548)***
Lh Universal Operating LLC ....B....818 980-1212
333 Unversal Hollywood Dr Universal City (91608) ***(P-12549)***
Lho Mssion Bay Rsie Lessee Inc ....B....619 276-4010
1775 E Mission Bay Dr San Diego (92109) ***(P-12550)***
Lho Santa Cruz One Lesse Inc ....C....831 475-5600
1 Chaminade Ln Santa Cruz (95065) ***(P-12551)***
Lhoberge Lessee Inc ....C....858 259-1515
1540 Camino Del Mar Del Mar (92014) ***(P-12552)***
Liberman Broadcasting Inc (PA) ....D....818 729-5300
1845 W Empire Ave Burbank (91504) ***(P-5555)***
Liberman Broadcasting Inc ....E....323 461-9300
1845 W Empire Ave Burbank (91504) ***(P-5556)***
Liberty Ambulance, Ridgecrest *Also called Poulin Corporation* ***(P-11949)***
Liberty Ambulance LLC ....D....562 741-6230
9441 Washburn Rd Downey (90242) ***(P-3696)***
Liberty American Mortgage Corp (PA) ....D....916 780-3000
193 Blue Ravine Rd # 240 Folsom (95630) ***(P-9632)***
Liberty Debt Relief LLC ....D....800 756-8447
333 City Blvd W Fl 17 Orange (92868) ***(P-13436)***
Liberty Dental Plan Cal Inc ....B....949 223-0007
340 Commerce Ste 100 Irvine (92602) ***(P-10014)***
Liberty Dental Plan Nevada Inc ....D....888 703-6999
340 Commerce Irvine (92602) ***(P-10015)***
Liberty Energy, South Lake Tahoe *Also called Liberty Utltles Clpeco Elc LLC* ***(P-5853)***
Liberty Engineering, Chatsworth *Also called Delaware Electro Inds Inc* ***(P-7142)***
Liberty Hardware Mfg Corp ....D....909 605-2300
5555 Jurupa St Ontario (91761) ***(P-7397)***
Liberty Healthcare of Oklahoma ....D....408 532-7677
4463 San Felipe Rd Ofc San Jose (95135) ***(P-20070)***
Liberty Landscaping Inc (PA) ....C....951 683-2999
5212 El Rivino Rd Riverside (92509) ***(P-863)***
Liberty Mutual Insurance Co ....C....310 316-9428
21515 Hawthorne Blvd # 550 Torrance (90503) ***(P-10100)***
Liberty Mutual Insurance Co ....C....415 957-1175
101 Mission St Ste 740 San Francisco (94105) ***(P-10101)***
Liberty Mutual Insurance Co ....C....916 294-9518
13405 Folsom Blvd Ste 200 Folsom (95630) ***(P-10102)***
Liberty Mutual Insurance Co ....D....909 476-6688
3633 Inland Empire Blvd # 280 Ontario (91764) ***(P-10103)***
Liberty Mutual Insurance Co ....C....714 937-1400
790 The City Dr S Ste 200 Orange (92868) ***(P-10104)***
Liberty Mutual Insurance Co ....C....781 740-1920
20500 Belshaw Ave Carson (90746) ***(P-10105)***
Liberty Mutual Insurance Co ....B....916 564-1792
1750 Howe Ave Ste 450 Sacramento (95825) ***(P-10106)***
Liberty Packing Company LLC (PA) ....C....209 826-7100
724 Main St Woodland (95695) ***(P-8495)***
Liberty Station Hhg Hotel LP ....D....619 221-1900
2592 Laning Rd San Diego (92106) ***(P-12553)***
Liberty Station Hhg Hotel LP ....E....619 222-0500
2576 Laning Rd San Diego (92106) ***(P-12554)***
Liberty Utilities Pk Wtr Corp (HQ) ....D....562 923-0711
9750 Washburn Rd Downey (90241) ***(P-6076)***
Liberty Utlties Clpeco Elc LLC ....D....800 782-2506
933 Eloise Ave South Lake Tahoe (96150) ***(P-5853)***
Library Associates LLC ....B....626 529-6786
3110 N San Fernando Blvd Burbank (91504) ***(P-14325)***
Libsource LLC ....C....323 852-1083
10390 Santa Monica Blvd Los Angeles (90025) ***(P-26303)***
Licensale Inc ....D....604 681-6888
900 Bush St Apt 205 San Francisco (94109) ***(P-11828)***
Lieberman RES Worldwide LLC (PA) ....C....310 553-0550
1900 Avenue Of The Stars Los Angeles (90067) ***(P-25920)***

Lieff Cabraser Heimann & (PA)............................C......415 788-0245
275 Battery St Ste 2800 San Francisco (94111) ***(P-22652)***

Life Alert Emergency Response (PA)............................C......800 247-0000
16027 Ventura Blvd # 400 Encino (91436) ***(P-16541)***

Life Care Center of Bellflower, Bellflower *Also called Life Care Centers America Inc* ***(P-20077)***

Life Care Center of La Habra, La Habra *Also called Life Care Centers America Inc* ***(P-20071)***

Life Care Center of Norwalk, Norwalk *Also called Life Care Centers America Inc* ***(P-20078)***

Life Care Center San Gabriel, San Gabriel *Also called Life Care Centers America Inc* ***(P-20073)***

Life Care Centers America Inc............................D......562 690-0852
1233 W La Habra Blvd La Habra (90631) ***(P-20071)***

Life Care Centers America Inc............................C......760 724-8222
304 N Melrose Dr Vista (92083) ***(P-20613)***

Life Care Centers America Inc............................C......562 947-8691
12200 La Mirada Blvd La Mirada (90638) ***(P-20072)***

Life Care Centers America Inc............................D......626 289-5365
909 W Santa Anita Ave San Gabriel (91776) ***(P-20073)***

Life Care Centers America Inc............................C......760 741-6109
1980 Felicita Rd Escondido (92025) ***(P-20074)***

Life Care Centers America Inc............................C......949 380-9380
25652 Old Trabuco Rd Lake Forest (92630) ***(P-20075)***

Life Care Centers America Inc............................C......562 943-7156
11926 La Mirada Blvd La Mirada (90638) ***(P-20076)***

Life Care Centers America Inc............................D......562 867-1761
16910 Woodruff Ave Bellflower (90706) ***(P-20077)***

Life Care Centers America Inc............................D......562 921-6624
12350 Rosecrans Ave Norwalk (90650) ***(P-20078)***

Life Care Centers America Inc............................B......760 252-2515
27555 Rimrock Rd Barstow (92311) ***(P-20079)***

Life Care Centers of Escondido, Escondido *Also called Life Care Centers America Inc* ***(P-20074)***

Life Cycle Engineering Inc............................D......619 785-5990
2535 Camino Del Rio S # 250 San Diego (92108) ***(P-13964)***

Life Enchancing Therapies, Upland *Also called Inland Empire Therapy Provider* ***(P-19670)***

Life Gnerations Healthcare LLC............................D......619 449-5555
8778 Cuyamaca St Santee (92071) ***(P-20614)***

Life Gnerations Healthcare LLC............................C......619 460-2330
7800 Parkway Dr La Mesa (91942) ***(P-20080)***

Life Ivf Center, Irvine *Also called Frank D Yelian MD PC* ***(P-18989)***

Life Line Screening Amer Ltd............................B......626 797-9774
2854 Casitas Ave Altadena (91001) ***(P-22270)***

Life Optons Vctnal Rsource Ctr (PA)............................C......805 735-3428
116 N I St Lompoc (93436) ***(P-23314)***

Life Steps Foundation Inc............................C......805 474-8431
1431 Pomeroy Rd Arroyo Grande (93420) ***(P-23315)***

Life Steps Foundation Inc............................D......562 436-0751
500 E 4th St Long Beach (90802) ***(P-23316)***

Life Steps Foundation Inc............................D......805 549-0150
1107 Johnson Ave San Luis Obispo (93401) ***(P-23317)***

Lifecare Assurance Company, Woodland Hills *Also called 21st Century Lf & Hlth Co Inc* ***(P-9894)***

Lifecare Assurance Company............................C......818 887-4436
21600 Oxnard St Fl 16 Woodland Hills (91367) ***(P-9910)***

Lifecare Health, Cerritos *Also called Healthview Inc* ***(P-23955)***

Lifecare Solutions, Pasadena *Also called Founders Healthcare LLC* ***(P-21744)***

Lifecare Systems Inc............................C......310 540-7676
4101 Torrance Blvd Torrance (90503) ***(P-20081)***

Lifehouse Inc (PA)............................B......415 472-2373
899 Northgate Dr Ste 500 San Rafael (94903) ***(P-23318)***

Lifeline Ambulance, Montebello *Also called Eastwestproto Inc* ***(P-3666)***

Lifeline Medical Transport, Ventura *Also called Ojai Ambulance Inc* ***(P-3704)***

Lifelong Medical Care (PA)............................E......510 704-6010
2344 6th St Berkeley (94710) ***(P-19158)***

Lifemoves (PA)............................E......650 685-5880
181 Constitution Dr Menlo Park (94025) ***(P-23319)***

Lifeproof, San Diego *Also called Treefrog Developments Inc* ***(P-7840)***

Liferay Inc (PA)............................D......877 543-3729
1400 Montefino Ave # 100 Diamond Bar (91765) ***(P-15637)***

Lifesigns Now Inc (PA)............................B......323 550-4210
2222 Laverna Ave Fl 1 Los Angeles (90041) ***(P-16892)***

Lifespan Care Management Agcy, Santa Cruz *Also called Lifespan Inc* ***(P-24192)***

Lifespan Inc............................D......831 469-4900
600 Frederick St Santa Cruz (95062) ***(P-24192)***

Lifestream, San Bernardino *Also called Blood Bank of San Bernardino A* ***(P-22189)***

Lifestreet Corporation............................D......650 508-2220
98 Battery St St 504 San Carlos (94070) ***(P-8984)***

Lifestreet Media, San Carlos *Also called Lifestreet Corporation* ***(P-8984)***

Lifestyles Senior Housing Man............................D......916 714-3755
9325 E Stockton Blvd Elk Grove (95624) ***(P-23320)***

Lifetime Entrmt Svcs LLC............................D......310 556-7500
2049 Century Park E # 840 Los Angeles (90067) ***(P-5631)***

Lifetime TV Network, Los Angeles *Also called Lifetime Entrmt Svcs LLC* ***(P-5631)***

Lifetouch Inc............................D......916 535-7733
7916 Alta Sunrise Ln Citrus Heights (95610) ***(P-13328)***

Lifetouch Nat Schl Studios Inc............................E......510 293-1818
30351 Huntwood Ave Hayward (94544) ***(P-13329)***

Lifetouch Portrait Studios Inc............................E......858 693-9197
9770 Carroll Centre Rd C San Diego (92126) ***(P-13330)***

Lifted Research Group, Irvine *Also called Hwmm* ***(P-8033)***

Light House Group, The, Pacific Palisades *Also called Lighthouse Capital Funding* ***(P-11929)***

Light Hse Memorials Receptions (PA)............................D......310 792-7599
5310 Torrance Blvd Torrance (90503) ***(P-13371)***

Light Rail, Sacramento *Also called Sacramento Regional Trnst Dist* ***(P-3832)***

Lightbeam Power Company Gridle............................D......800 696-7114
100 Century Center Ct # 100 San Jose (95112) ***(P-1883)***

Lightbeam Pwr Gridley Main LLC............................D......800 696-7114
100 Century Center Ct # 100 San Jose (95112) ***(P-1884)***

Lightbend Inc............................D......877 989-7372
625 Market St Ste 1000 San Francisco (94105) ***(P-14911)***

Lightbrdge Hspice Plltive Care, San Diego *Also called Lightbridge Hospice LLC* ***(P-21480)***

Lightbridge Hospice LLC (PA)............................D......858 458-2992
6155 Cornerstone Ct E San Diego (92121) ***(P-21480)***

Lightcrest LLC............................E......888 320-8495
1112 Montana Ave Ste 705 Santa Monica (90403) ***(P-15638)***

Lighthouse Capital Funding............................E......310 230-8335
15332 Antioch St Ste 540 Pacific Palisades (90272) ***(P-11929)***

Lighthouse Healthcare Ctr LLC............................D......323 564-4461
2222 Santa Ana S Los Angeles (90059) ***(P-20082)***

Lighthouse Living Services (PA)............................D......916 454-4381
3600 Power Inn Rd Ste H Sacramento (95826) ***(P-23321)***

Lighting Department, Burbank *Also called Twdc Enterprises 18 Corp* ***(P-5654)***

Lighting Technologies Intl LLC............................C......626 480-0755
13700 Live Oak Ave Baldwin Park (91706) ***(P-7161)***

Lightwaves 2020 Inc............................E......408 503-8888
1323 Great Mall Dr Milpitas (95035) ***(P-25795)***

Lilien LLC (HQ)............................E......415 389-7500
17 E Sir Francis Dr # 110 Larkspur (94939) ***(P-15639)***

Lily Holdings LLC............................D......559 222-4807
3510 E Shields Ave Fresno (93726) ***(P-20083)***

Limbach Company LP............................C......714 653-7000
1709 Apollo Ct Seal Beach (90740) ***(P-2186)***

Liminex Inc............................C......424 529-6960
200 N Supulveda Blvd Ste Hermosa Beach (90254) ***(P-14912)***

Limoneira Company (PA)............................C......805 525-5541
1141 Cummings Rd Ofc Santa Paula (93060) ***(P-511)***

Lims Inc............................D......925 803-7795
2880 Zanker Rd San Jose (95134) ***(P-8087)***

Linardos Enterprises Inc............................D......415 644-0827
75 Broadway San Francisco (94111) ***(P-26676)***

Lincoln (PA)............................D......510 273-4700
1266 14th St Oakland (94607) ***(P-22060)***

Lincoln Child Center Inc............................C......925 521-1270
51 Marina Blvd Pittsburg (94565) ***(P-23973)***

Lincoln Glen Manor............................C......408 267-1492
2671 Plummer Ave Ste A San Jose (95125) ***(P-20615)***

LINCOLN GLEN SKILLED NURSING, San Jose *Also called Lincoln Glen Manor* ***(P-20615)***

Lincoln Hills Golf Club............................E......916 543-9200
1005 Sun City Ln Lincoln (95648) ***(P-18262)***

Lincoln Mariners Assoc Ltd............................D......619 225-1473
4392 W Point Loma Blvd San Diego (92107) ***(P-10757)***

Lincoln Medical Offices, Lincoln *Also called Kaiser Foundation Hospitals* ***(P-19077)***

Lincoln Plaza Hotel Inc............................D......626 571-8818
123 S Lincoln Ave Monterey Park (91755) ***(P-12555)***

Lincoln Products, City of Industry *Also called Ferguson Enterprises Inc* ***(P-7420)***

Lincoln School Bus Trnsp............................D......209 953-8596
6749 Harrisburg Pl Stockton (95207) ***(P-3760)***

Lincoln Television Inc............................D......415 468-2626
100 Valley Dr Brisbane (94005) ***(P-5632)***

Lincoln Training Center and RE............................D......626 442-0621
2643 Loma Ave South El Monte (91733) ***(P-23610)***

Linda Beach Coop Pre-School............................E......510 547-4432
400 Highland Ave Piedmont (94611) ***(P-23740)***

Linda Loma Univ Hlth Care (HQ)............................D......909 558-2806
11370 Anderson St # 3900 Loma Linda (92350) ***(P-21006)***

Linda Loma Univ Hlth Care............................C......909 558-2851
11370 Anderson St # 2100 Loma Linda (92354) ***(P-19159)***

Linda Loma Univ Hlth Care (PA)............................A......909 558-4729
11175 Campus St Loma Linda (92350) ***(P-19160)***

Linda Loma Univ Hlth Care............................C......909 558-2840
11370 Anderson St # 3950 Loma Linda (92354) ***(P-19161)***

Linda Mar Care Center, Pacifica *Also called Pacifica Linda Mar Inc* ***(P-20183)***

Linda Placentia-Yorba............................D......714 985-8775
1301 E Orangethorpe Ave Placentia (92870) ***(P-4442)***

Linda Terra Farms (PA)............................C......559 867-3473
5494 W Mount Whitney Ave Riverdale (93656) ***(P-382)***

Linda Valley Care Center, Loma Linda *Also called Chancellor Hlth Care Cal I Inc* ***(P-20526)***

Linda Verde School............................E......661 942-0431
44924 5th St E Lancaster (93535) ***(P-24583)***

Linda Vista Health Care Center, San Diego *Also called San Diego Family Care* ***(P-19355)***

Linda Vista Manor Inc............................C......858 278-8121
7675 Family Cir San Diego (92111) ***(P-20084)***

Linda Yorba Water District (PA)............................D......714 701-3000
1717 E Miraloma Ave Placentia (92870) ***(P-6077)***

Lindamood-Bell Lrng Processes (PA)............................C......805 541-3836
406 Higuera St Ste 120 San Luis Obispo (93401) ***(P-23741)***

Lindbergh Parking Inc............................C......619 291-1508
3705 N Harbor Dr San Diego (92101) ***(P-17262)***

Lindburgh Child Development, Costa Mesa *Also called Orange Cnty Sprntndent Schools* ***(P-23764)***

Linden Crest Surgery Center............................D......310 601-3900
9735 Wilshire Blvd # 100 Beverly Hills (90212) ***(P-19162)***

Linden Lab, San Francisco *Also called Linden Research Inc* ***(P-14913)***

Linden Nut, Stockton *Also called Pearl Crop Inc* ***(P-527)***

Linden Optometry A Prof Corp............................D......323 681-5678
477 E Colorado Blvd Pasadena (91101) ***(P-19649)***

Linden Research Inc............................B......415 243-9000
945 Battery St San Francisco (94111) ***(P-14913)***

Lindhurst Dental Clinic............................E......530 743-4614
4941 Olivehurst Ave Olivehurst (95961) ***(P-19619)***

Lindhurst Family Health Center, Olivehurst *Also called Ampla Health* ***(P-18810)***

Lindley Fire Protection Co............................E......714 535-5761
2220 E Via Burton Anaheim (92806) ***(P-2187)***

Lindo Hanna & Abbott, Chico *Also called Interwest Insurance Svcs LLC* ***(P-10392)***

Employee Codes: A=Over 500 employees, B=251-500
C=101-250, D=51-100, E=50
2020 Directory of California
Wholesalers and Services Companies
© Mergent Inc. 1-800-342-5647
1333

Lindsay Fruit Company LLC D 559 562-1327
247 N Mount Vernon Ave Lindsay (93247) ***(P-16893)***
Lindsay Transportation C 707 374-6800
180 River Rd Rio Vista (94571) ***(P-7556)***
Lindsay Trnsp Solutions, Rio Vista *Also called Lindsay Transportation* ***(P-7556)***
Lindsay Wildlife Museum D 925 935-1978
1931 1st Ave Walnut Creek (94597) ***(P-24268)***
Line Hotel, The, Los Angeles *Also called Sydell Hotels LLC* ***(P-13011)***
Lineage Logistics LLC C 323 583-3163
3141 E 44th St Vernon (90058) ***(P-4347)***
Lineage Logistics LLC E 951 360-7970
3251 De Forest Cir Ste C Jurupa Valley (91752) ***(P-4348)***
Lineage Logistics Holdings LLC (PA) C 800 678-7271
1 Park Plz Ste 550 Irvine (92614) ***(P-4349)***
Lineage Logistics Holdings LLC A 909 874-1200
2551 S Lilac Ave Bloomington (92316) ***(P-4217)***
Linear Industries Ltd (PA) D 626 303-1130
1850 Enterprise Way Monrovia (91016) ***(P-7640)***
Liner Law, Los Angeles *Also called Liner LLP* ***(P-22653)***
Liner LLP C 310 500-3500
1100 Glendon Ave 14th Los Angeles (90024) ***(P-22653)***
Ling's, South El Monte *Also called Out of Shell LLC* ***(P-1373)***
Linkedin Corporation (HQ) C 650 687-3600
1000 W Maude Ave Sunnyvale (94085) ***(P-15872)***
Links Sgn Lngg Intrprtng, Shrd, Long Beach *Also called Goodwill Srvng The Ppl of Sthr* ***(P-16807)***
Linksys LLC C 310 751-5100
12045 Waterfront Dr Playa Vista (90094) ***(P-7295)***
Linksys LLC (HQ) B 949 270-8500
121 Theory Irvine (92617) ***(P-7296)***
Linkus Enterprises LLC B 559 256-6600
5595 W San Madele Ave Fresno (93722) ***(P-1885)***
Linkus Enterprises LLC (PA) C 530 229-9197
18631 Lloyd Ln Anderson (96007) ***(P-1886)***
Linnco LLC A 661 616-3900
5201 Truxtun Ave Bakersfield (93309) ***(P-987)***
Linne Entertainment LLC E 213 425-1146
1250 N June St Apt 305 Los Angeles (90038) ***(P-17624)***
Linquest Corporation (PA) C 323 924-1600
5140 W Goldleaf Cir # 40 Los Angeles (90056) ***(P-25189)***
Linwood Grdns Convalescent Ctr, Visalia *Also called Far West Inc* ***(P-19909)***
Linwood Nursery, La Grange *Also called Green Tree Nursery* ***(P-8895)***
Lion Brothers Farms-Newstone, Madera *Also called Lion Raisins Inc* ***(P-345)***
Lion Creek Crossing V, Oakland *Also called Lion Creek Senior Housing Part* ***(P-11250)***
Lion Creek Senior Housing Part D 510 878-9120
6710 Lion Way Oakland (94621) ***(P-11250)***
Lion Raisins Inc C 559 662-8686
12555 Road 9 Madera (93637) ***(P-345)***
Lion-Vallen Ltd Partnership E 760 385-4885
22 Area Aven A Bldg 2234 Camp Pendleton (92055) ***(P-26304)***
Lionakis C 949 955-1919
20371 Irvine Ave Ste 120 Newport Beach (92660) ***(P-25190)***
Lionakis (PA) C 916 558-1901
1919 19th St Sacramento (95811) ***(P-25191)***
Lions Gate Entertainment Inc (HQ) D 310 449-9200
2700 Colorado Ave Ste 200 Santa Monica (90404) ***(P-17625)***
Lions Gate Films Inc C 310 449-9200
2700 Colorado Ave Ste 200 Santa Monica (90404) ***(P-17626)***
Lionsgate Ht & Conference Ctr D 916 643-6222
3410 Westover St McClellan (95652) ***(P-12556)***
Lipman Insur Admnistrators Inc (PA) D 510 796-4676
39420 Liberty St Ste 260 Fremont (94538) ***(P-10217)***
Lippin Group Inc (PA) E 323 965-1990
6100 Wilshire Blvd # 400 Los Angeles (90048) ***(P-26917)***
Liquid Investments Inc (PA) C 858 509-8510
3840 Via De La Valle # 300 Del Mar (92014) ***(P-8775)***
Liquidate Direct LLC E 800 750-7617
2929 Washington Blvd Fl 2 Marina Del Rey (90292) ***(P-15640)***
Liquidity Services Inc D 714 738-6446
741 E Ball Rd Ste 200 Anaheim (92805) ***(P-8038)***
Lisi Inc (PA) D 650 348-4131
1600 W Hillsdale Blvd # 202 San Mateo (94402) ***(P-10409)***
Lisi Inc D 714 460-5153
2677 N Main St Ste 350 Santa Ana (92705) ***(P-10234)***
Lite Solar Corp C 562 256-1249
3553 Atlantic Ave Long Beach (90807) ***(P-2188)***
Lite-On Inc (HQ) E 408 946-4873
720 S Hillview Dr Milpitas (95035) ***(P-7297)***
Lite-On Sales and Dist Inc D 510 687-1800
726 S Hillview Dr Milpitas (95035) ***(P-6861)***
Lite-On U S A, Milpitas *Also called Lite-On Inc* ***(P-7297)***
Lithchem, Anaheim *Also called Retriev Technologies Inc* ***(P-6259)***
Lithia Motors Inc E 209 956-1930
3077 E Hammer Ln Stockton (95212) ***(P-17337)***
Litigtion Rsrces of America-CA (PA) D 818 878-9227
4232-1 Las Virgenes Rd Calabasas (91302) ***(P-16894)***
Little Citizens Schools Inc D 323 732-1212
4256 S Western Ave Los Angeles (90062) ***(P-23742)***
Little Co Mary Hosp Pavilion, Torrance *Also called Providence Health System* ***(P-11811)***
Little Company Mary Hospital A 310 540-7676
4101 Torrance Blvd Torrance (90503) ***(P-21007)***
Little Giant Bldg Maint Inc C 415 508-0282
15 Brooks Pl Pacifica (94044) ***(P-13965)***
Little Mary Amblatory Care Ctr, Torrance *Also called Del AMO Diagnostic Center* ***(P-22016)***
Little Peoples D 951 849-1959
39514 Brookside Ave Cherry Valley (92223) ***(P-23974)***
Little River Inn Inc D 707 937-5942
7901 N Highway 1 Little River (95456) ***(P-12557)***
Little River Inn and Golf Crse, Little River *Also called Little River Inn Inc* ***(P-12557)***
Little Sister's Truck Wash, Fallbrook *Also called Little Sisters Truck Wash Inc* ***(P-17386)***
Little Sisters of Poor C 415 751-6510
300 Lake St San Francisco (94118) ***(P-23975)***
Little Sisters The Poor of La D 310 548-0625
2100 S Western Ave San Pedro (90732) ***(P-20085)***
Little Sisters Truck Wash Inc D 760 343-3448
72189 Varner Rd Thousand Palms (92276) ***(P-17382)***
Little Sisters Truck Wash Inc D 760 947-4448
8899 Three Flags Ave Oak Hills (92344) ***(P-17383)***
Little Sisters Truck Wash Inc D 909 549-1862
14264 Valley Blvd Fontana (92335) ***(P-17384)***
Little Sisters Truck Wash Inc D 760 253-2277
2960 Lenwood Rd Barstow (92311) ***(P-17385)***
Little Sisters Truck Wash Inc (PA) D 760 731-3170
25 Rolling View Ln Fallbrook (92028) ***(P-17386)***
Littler Mendelson PC (PA) B 415 433-1940
333 Bush St Fl 34 San Francisco (94104) ***(P-22654)***
Littlethings Inc D 917 364-9277
642 Harrison St Fl 3 San Francisco (94107) ***(P-16050)***
Live International, Santa Monica *Also called Artisan Pictures Inc* ***(P-7798)***
Live Media LLC E 951 279-8877
1580 Magnolia Ave Corona (92879) ***(P-17986)***
Live Nation Entertainment Inc D 213 639-6178
7060 Hollywood Blvd Ste 2 Los Angeles (90028) ***(P-17987)***
Live Nation Entertainment Inc D 323 462-4785
151 El Camino Dr Fl 3 Beverly Hills (90212) ***(P-17988)***
Live Nation Entertainment Inc (PA) C 800 653-8000
9348 Civic Center Dr Lbby Beverly Hills (90210) ***(P-16895)***
Live Nation Merchandise Inc (HQ) E 415 247-7400
450 Mission St Ste 300 San Francisco (94105) ***(P-8985)***
Live Nation Worldwide Inc C 323 966-5066
6500 Wilshire Blvd # 200 Los Angeles (90048) ***(P-17923)***
Live Nation Worldwide Inc A 310 867-7000
9348 Civic Center Dr Lbby Beverly Hills (90210) ***(P-17924)***
Live Oak Rehab, San Gabriel *Also called Longwood Management Corp* ***(P-20622)***
Live Pos, La Jolla *Also called CSS Holdings Inc* ***(P-14745)***
Liveoffice LLC D 877 253-2793
900 Corporate Pointe Culver City (90230) ***(P-15390)***
Livermore Area Rcration Pk Dst C 925 373-5700
71 Trevarno Rd Livermore (94551) ***(P-18718)***
Livermore Area Rcration Pk Dst (PA) B 925 373-5700
4444 East Ave Livermore (94550) ***(P-18719)***
Livermore Casino, Livermore *Also called Sidjon Corporation* ***(P-12924)***
Livermore Snior Lving Assoc LP E 925 371-2300
900 E Stanley Blvd # 383 Livermore (94550) ***(P-10758)***
Livermore VA Medical Center, Livermore *Also called Veterans Health Administration* ***(P-19572)***
Livermore Valley Tennis Club D 925 443-7700
2000 Arroyo Rd Livermore (94550) ***(P-18170)***
Livescribe Inc E 503 290-4029
930 Roosevelt Irvine (92620) ***(P-6862)***
Livetime Software Inc E 415 905-4009
276 Avocado St Apt C102 Costa Mesa (92627) ***(P-15391)***
Liveuniverse Inc D 310 492-2200
9255 W Sunset Blvd # 1010 West Hollywood (90069) ***(P-13627)***
Livevox Inc (PA) D 415 671-6000
655 Montgomery St # 1190 San Francisco (94111) ***(P-27119)***
Liveworld Inc (PA) D 800 301-9507
4340 Stevens Creek Blvd # 101 San Jose (95129) ***(P-5433)***
Livhome Inc (PA) A 800 807-5854
5670 Wilshire Blvd # 500 Los Angeles (90036) ***(P-21803)***
Living Centers, Vallejo *Also called Empres Financial Services LLC* ***(P-19879)***
Living Colors Inc D 818 893-5068
16026 Rayen St North Hills (91343) ***(P-2367)***
Living Desert C 760 346-5694
47900 Portola Ave Palm Desert (92260) ***(P-24309)***
Living Doll, La Puente *Also called Ldla Clothing LLC* ***(P-8086)***
Living Opportunities MGT Co C 323 589-5956
6900 Seville Ave Huntington Park (90255) ***(P-10759)***
Livingston Community Health C 209 394-7913
600 B St Bldg A Livingston (95334) ***(P-19163)***
Livingston Health Center, Livingston *Also called Livingston Community Health* ***(P-19163)***
Livingston Mem Vna Hlth Corp B 805 642-0239
1996 Eastman Ave Ste 101 Ventura (93003) ***(P-26305)***
LIVINGSTON MEMORIAL VISITING N, Ventura *Also called Livingston Mem Vna Hlth Corp* ***(P-26305)***
Livingston Ranch, Livingston *Also called E & J Gallo Winery* ***(P-658)***
Livongo Health Inc (PA) E 866 435-5643
150 W Evelyn Ave Ste 150 # 150 Mountain View (94041) ***(P-21481)***
Lj Distributors Inc D 562 229-7660
12840 Leyva St Norwalk (90650) ***(P-8496)***
LJ Walch Co Inc D 925 449-9252
6600 Preston Ave Livermore (94551) ***(P-7695)***
LJC Construction Inc D 209 668-2700
712 W Harding Rd Turlock (95380) ***(P-3072)***
Ljg, Irvine *Also called La Jolla Group Inc* ***(P-16880)***
LL Frank Work Center, Los Angeles *Also called Abilityfirst* ***(P-22892)***
LLC Brewer Crane D 619 390-8252
12570 Highway 67 Bldg 10 Lakeside (92040) ***(P-14101)***
LLC Woodward West C 661 822-7900
28400 Stallion Springs Dr Tehachapi (93561) ***(P-12558)***
Lloyd Pest Control Co D 951 232-9687
19161 Newhall St North Palm Springs (92258) ***(P-13823)***
Lloyd Pest Control Co E 714 979-6021
566 E Dyer Rd Santa Ana (92707) ***(P-13824)***
LLP Downey Brand D 775 329-5900
621 Capitol Mall Fl 18 Sacramento (95814) ***(P-22655)***

Mergent e-mail: customerrelations@mergent.com 2020 Directory of California (P-0000) Products & Services Section entry number
1334 Wholesalers and Services Companies (PA)=Parent Co (HQ)=Headquarters (DH)=Div Headquarters

LLP Downey Brand.....D.....415 848-4800
455 Market St Ste 1500 San Francisco (94105) ***(P-22656)***
LLP Locke Lord.....C.....415 318-8800
101 Montgomery St # 1950 San Francisco (94104) ***(P-22657)***
LLP Locke Lord.....D.....949 423-2100
660 Nwport Ctr Dr Ste 900 Newport Beach (92660) ***(P-22658)***
LLP Mayer Brown.....A.....650 331-2000
2 Palo Alto Sq Ste 300 Palo Alto (94306) ***(P-22659)***
LLP Mayer Brown.....C.....213 229-9500
350 S Grand Ave Ste 2500 Los Angeles (90071) ***(P-22660)***
LLP Moss Adams.....D.....916 503-8100
2882 Prospect Park Dr # 300 Rancho Cordova (95670) ***(P-25635)***
LLP Moss Adams.....D.....818 577-1822
21700 Oxnard St Ste 300 Woodland Hills (91367) ***(P-25636)***
LLP Moss Adams.....E.....209 955-6100
3121 W March Ln Ste 100 Stockton (95219) ***(P-25637)***
LLP Moss Adams.....C.....415 956-1500
101 2nd St Ste 900 San Francisco (94105) ***(P-25638)***
LLP Moss Adams.....C.....408 369-2400
635 Campbell Tech Pkwy # 100 Campbell (95008) ***(P-25639)***
LLP Moss Adams.....C.....310 477-0450
10960 Wilshire Blvd # 1100 Los Angeles (90024) ***(P-25640)***
LLP Moss Adams.....D.....707 224-4001
1000 Main St NAPA (94559) ***(P-25641)***
LLP Moss Adams.....E.....949 221-4000
2040 Main St Ste 900 Irvine (92614) ***(P-25642)***
LLP Moss Adams.....D.....858 627-1400
4747 Executive Dr # 1300 San Diego (92121) ***(P-25643)***
LLP Robins Kaplan.....D.....310 552-0130
2049 Century Park E # 3400 Los Angeles (90067) ***(P-22661)***
Llu Advntist Hlth Sciences Ctr.....D.....909 558-4386
101 E Redlands Blvd San Bernardino (92408) ***(P-19164)***
Llu Center For Fertility, Loma Linda *Also called Linda Loma Univ Hlth Care* ***(P-19161)***
LLUMC, Loma Linda *Also called Loma Linda University Med Ctr* ***(P-21011)***
Lmb Mortgage Services Inc (HQ).....C.....310 348-6800
4859 W Slauson Ave # 405 Los Angeles (90056) ***(P-9575)***
Lmb Opco LLC.....B.....310 348-6800
12181 Bluff Creek Dr Playa Vista (90094) ***(P-9633)***
LMC Hollywood Highland.....B.....949 448-1600
95 Enterprise Ste 200 Aliso Viejo (92656) ***(P-1530)***
LMC West Inc.....E.....209 869-0144
5300 Claus Rd Riverbank (95367) ***(P-7557)***
Lmno Cable Group, Encino *Also called Lmno Productions Inc* ***(P-17627)***
Lmno Productions Inc.....C.....818 995-5555
15821 Ventura Blvd # 320 Encino (91436) ***(P-17627)***
LMS Corporation.....E.....310 641-4222
300 Crprate Pinte Ste 301 Culver City (90230) ***(P-16896)***
LN Curtis and Sons (PA).....D.....510 839-5111
1800 Peralta St Oakland (94607) ***(P-7674)***
Lo Bue Bros Inc.....C.....559 562-6367
713 E Hermosa St Lindsay (93247) ***(P-512)***
Lo Bue Bros East, Lindsay *Also called Lo Bue Bros Inc* ***(P-512)***
Loan Administration Netwrk Inc.....D.....949 752-5246
18952 Macarthur Blvd # 315 Irvine (92612) ***(P-14326)***
Loan Now.....D.....714 352-2250
3100 S Harbor Blvd # 180 Santa Ana (92704) ***(P-9465)***
Loandepotcom LLC.....A.....760 797-6000
901 N Palm Canyon Dr Palm Springs (92262) ***(P-9576)***
Loandepotcom LLC (PA).....A.....888 337-6888
26642 Towne Centre Dr Foothill Ranch (92610) ***(P-9577)***
Lobel Financial Corporation (PA).....D.....714 995-3333
1150 N Magnolia Ave Anaheim (92801) ***(P-9466)***
Local 250 Health Care Wkrs Un, Oakland *Also called Health Care Workers Union* ***(P-10607)***
Local 442, Santa Barbara *Also called International Alliance Thea* ***(P-24442)***
Local Corporation (PA).....D.....949 784-0800
7555 Irvine Center Dr Irvine (92618) ***(P-13534)***
Local Initiative Health Author.....A.....213 694-1250
1055 W 7th St Fl 10 Los Angeles (90017) ***(P-10016)***
Local Media San Diego LLC.....D.....858 888-7000
6160 Cornerstone Ct E # 150 San Diego (92121) ***(P-5557)***
Local.com, Irvine *Also called Local Corporation* ***(P-13534)***
Location Labs Inc.....D.....510 601-7012
2100 Powell St Fl 14 Emeryville (94608) ***(P-14914)***
Location Services LLC (PA).....D.....800 588-0097
2365 Iron Point Rd # 160 Folsom (95630) ***(P-5124)***
Locator Services Inc.....C.....619 229-6100
4616 Mission Gorge Pl San Diego (92120) ***(P-16342)***
Lockeford Spring Golf Course (PA).....C.....209 333-6275
16360 N Highway 88 Lodi (95240) ***(P-18489)***
Lockheed Martin Corporation.....C.....415 402-0406
255 California St Ste 400 San Francisco (94111) ***(P-25192)***
Lockheed Martin Corporation.....C.....760 386-2572
South Loop Bldg 821 Fort Irwin (92310) ***(P-4443)***
Lockheed Martin Government Ser.....E.....323 721-6979
500 N Via Val Verde Montebello (90640) ***(P-16051)***
Lockheed Martin Orincon Corp (HQ).....C.....858 455-5530
10325 Meanley Dr San Diego (92131) ***(P-14915)***
Lockton Companies LLC- Pacifi (HQ).....B.....213 689-0500
777 S Figueroa St # 5200 Los Angeles (90017) ***(P-10410)***
Lockton Insurance Brokers, Los Angeles *Also called Lockton Companies LLC-Pacifi* ***(P-10410)***
Locums Unlimited LLC.....B.....619 550-3763
4141 Jutland Dr Ste 305 San Diego (92117) ***(P-19679)***
Lodge At Tiburon, Belvedere Tiburon *Also called 1651 Tiburon Hotel LLC* ***(P-11976)***
Lodge At Tiburon, The, Belvedere Tiburon *Also called Tiburon Hotel LLC* ***(P-13024)***
Lodge Inn and Health Center, Chico *Also called Terraces Retirement Community* ***(P-24094)***
Lodgen Lacher Golditch Sard.....E.....818 783-0570
16530 Ventura Blvd # 305 Encino (91436) ***(P-25644)***
Lodgeworks LP.....D.....707 690-9800
1230 1st St NAPA (94559) ***(P-12559)***
Lodi Development Inc.....E.....209 367-7600
1420 S Mills Ave Ste E Lodi (95242) ***(P-11571)***
Lodi Memorial Hosp Assn Inc (HQ).....A.....209 334-3411
975 S Fairmont Ave Lodi (95240) ***(P-21008)***
Lodi Memorial Hosp Assn Inc.....E.....209 339-7583
1200 W Vine St Lodi (95240) ***(P-21009)***
Lodi Memorial Hosp Assn Inc.....C.....209 333-3100
800 S Lower Sacramento Rd Lodi (95242) ***(P-19165)***
Lodi Unified School District.....D.....209 331-7181
1305 E Vine St Lodi (95240) ***(P-13966)***
Lodi Unified School District.....C.....209 331-7169
820 S Cuff Ave Lodi (95240) ***(P-3818)***
Loeb & Loeb LLP (PA).....C.....310 282-2000
10100 Santa Monica Blvd # 2200 Los Angeles (90067) ***(P-22662)***
Loews Coronado Bay Resort, Coronado *Also called 51st St & 8th Ave Corp* ***(P-11984)***
Loews Corporation.....B.....619 424-4000
4000 Coronado Bay Rd Coronado (92118) ***(P-10411)***
Loews Hollywood Hotel LLC.....B.....323 450-2235
1755 N Highland Ave Hollywood (90028) ***(P-12560)***
Loews Regency San Francisco, San Francisco *Also called San Francisco Hotel Group LLC* ***(P-12874)***
Loews Santa Monica Beach Hotel, Santa Monica *Also called Dtrs Santa Monica LLC* ***(P-12232)***
Loewy Enterprises.....D.....323 726-3838
500 Burning Tree Rd Fullerton (92833) ***(P-8497)***
Logcap IV - Task Order 7, Fort Irwin *Also called Dyncorp International LLC* ***(P-4769)***
Logicmonitor Inc (PA).....C.....805 617-3884
820 State St Fl 5 Santa Barbara (93101) ***(P-15873)***
Logictier Inc.....C.....650 235-6600
7 41st Ave 76 San Mateo (94403) ***(P-16052)***
Logility Inc.....D.....858 565-4238
4885 Greencraig Ln 200 San Diego (92123) ***(P-14916)***
Login Consulting Services Inc.....D.....310 607-9091
300 Continental Blvd # 530 El Segundo (90245) ***(P-16053)***
Loginext Solutions Inc.....D.....339 244-0380
5002 Spring Crest Ter Fremont (94536) ***(P-15392)***
Logistical Support LLC.....C.....818 341-3344
20409 Prairie St Chatsworth (91311) ***(P-7696)***
Logistics Team, Walnut *Also called Amerifreight Inc* ***(P-4372)***
Logix Development Corporation.....D.....888 505-6449
473 Post St Camarillo (93010) ***(P-14917)***
Logix Federal Credit Union (PA).....C.....888 718-5328
2340 N Hollywood Way Burbank (91505) ***(P-9322)***
Loglogic Inc.....C.....408 215-5900
110 Rose Orchard Way San Jose (95134) ***(P-14918)***
Logo Design Pros, San Francisco *Also called Lateral Designs Inc* ***(P-13789)***
Logomark Inc.....C.....714 675-6100
1201 Bell Ave Tustin (92780) ***(P-8986)***
Lois Lauer Realty.....C.....909 748-7000
1998 Orange Tree Ln Redlands (92374) ***(P-11251)***
Loma Cleaning Service, Fremont *Also called ISS Facility Services Inc* ***(P-13954)***
Loma Linda Catering Center, Loma Linda *Also called Loma Linda University Med Ctr* ***(P-21012)***
Loma Linda Community Hospital, Loma Linda *Also called Loma Linda University Med Ctr* ***(P-21015)***
Loma Linda Faculty Med Group, Loma Linda *Also called Linda Loma Univ Hlth Care* ***(P-19159)***
Loma Linda Healthcare Sys 605, Loma Linda *Also called Veterans Health Administration* ***(P-19573)***
Loma Linda Pharmacy, Loma Linda *Also called Loma Linda University Med Ctr* ***(P-21014)***
Loma Linda University.....D.....909 558-6422
1911 W Park Ave Redlands (92373) ***(P-19166)***
Loma Linda University Med Ctr.....C.....909 558-2100
11370 Anderson St 2100 Loma Linda (92350) ***(P-21010)***
Loma Linda University Med Ctr (HQ).....A.....909 558-4000
11234 Anderson St Loma Linda (92354) ***(P-21011)***
Loma Linda University Med Ctr.....D.....909 558-8244
11175 Campus St Loma Linda (92350) ***(P-21012)***
Loma Linda University Med Ctr.....B.....909 558-9275
1710 Barton Rd Redlands (92373) ***(P-21013)***
Loma Linda University Med Ctr.....C.....909 558-4216
11223 Campus St Loma Linda (92354) ***(P-21014)***
Loma Linda University Med Ctr.....C.....909 558-3096
11265 Mountain View Ave E Loma Linda (92354) ***(P-21804)***
Loma Linda University Med Ctr.....C.....909 796-0167
25333 Barton Rd Loma Linda (92350) ***(P-21015)***
Loma Linda Vet Association For.....D.....909 583-6250
710 Brookside Ave Ste 2 Redlands (92373) ***(P-24584)***
Loma Riviera Community Assn.....D.....619 224-1313
9610 Waples St San Diego (92121) ***(P-24585)***
Loma Vista Nursery.....D.....714 779-5583
18272 Bastanchury Rd Yorba Linda (92886) ***(P-8901)***
Loma Vista Nursery 2, Yorba Linda *Also called Loma Vista Nursery* ***(P-8901)***
Lomas Santa Fe Country Club, Solana Beach *Also called American Golf Corporation* ***(P-18357)***
Lombardo Diamnd Core Drlg Inc.....D.....408 727-7922
2225 De La Cruz Blvd Santa Clara (95050) ***(P-3177)***
Lombardy Holdings Inc (PA).....C.....951 808-4550
151 Kalmus Dr Ste F6 Costa Mesa (92626) ***(P-1887)***
Lomita Care Center, Lomita *Also called Lomita Verde Inc* ***(P-20616)***
Lomita Medical Offices, Lomita *Also called Kaiser Foundation Hospitals* ***(P-19079)***
Lomita Verde Inc.....D.....310 325-1970
1955 Lomita Blvd Lomita (90717) ***(P-20616)***
Lompoc Convlsnt Care Ctr, Lompoc *Also called Lompoc Valley Medical Center* ***(P-21018)***

ALPHABETIC

Employee Codes: A=Over 500 employees, B=251-500
C=101-250, D=51-100, E=50
2020 Directory of California
Wholesalers and Services Companies
© Mergent Inc. 1-800-342-5647
1335

Lompoc Family YMCA, Lompoc *Also called Channel Islands Young Mens Ch (P-24514)*

Lompoc Honda Body Shop, Lompoc *Also called Zikakis Auto Holdings LLC (P-17315)*

Lompoc Skilled Care Center, Lompoc *Also called Lompoc Valley Medical Center (P-21017)*

Lompoc Skilled Nursing & Rehab, Lompoc *Also called Ghc of Lompoc LLC (P-22031)*

Lompoc Valley Medical Center....C....805 735-9229
1111 E Ocean Ave Ste 2 Lompoc (93436) *(P-21016)*

Lompoc Valley Medical Center (PA)....B....805 737-3300
1515 E Ocean Ave Lompoc (93436) *(P-21017)*

Lompoc Valley Medical Center....C....805 736-3466
216 N 3rd St Lompoc (93436) *(P-21018)*

Lone Cypress Company LLC....A....831 624-3811
17 Mile Dr Pebble Beach (93953) *(P-12561)*

Lone Cypress Company LLC....D....831 625-8507
1567 Cypress Dr Pebble Beach (93953) *(P-18490)*

Lone Tree Convalescent Hosp....C....925 754-0470
4001 Lone Tree Way Antioch (94509) *(P-20086)*

LONE TREE GOLF COURSE, Antioch *Also called Antioch Public Golf Corp (P-18220)*

Lonestar Sierra LLC....C....866 575-5680
1820 W Orangewood Ave Orange (92868) *(P-7641)*

Long & Levit LLP....E....415 397-2222
465 California St Ste 500 San Francisco (94104) *(P-22663)*

Long Bch Convention Entrmt Ctr, Long Beach *Also called City of Long Beach (P-16697)*

Long Bch Museum Art Foundation....D....562 439-2119
2300 E Ocean Blvd Long Beach (90803) *(P-24269)*

Long Bch Unfied Schl Dst Lbusd, Long Beach *Also called Long Beach Unified School Dst (P-14327)*

Long Beach Airport, Long Beach *Also called City of Long Beach (P-4758)*

Long Beach Behavioral Health U....D....310 221-6336
3200 Long Beach Blvd Long Beach (90807) *(P-22271)*

Long Beach Cap, Long Beach *Also called Long Beach Cmnty Action Partnr (P-24193)*

Long Beach Care Center Inc....C....562 426-6141
2615 Grand Ave Long Beach (90815) *(P-20087)*

Long Beach City College Whse, Long Beach *Also called Long Beach Cmnty College Dst (P-4444)*

Long Beach City Fleet Services, Long Beach *Also called City of Long Beach (P-17325)*

Long Beach Cmnty Action Partnr....C....562 216-4600
117 W Victoria St Long Beach (90805) *(P-24193)*

Long Beach Cmnty College Dst....A....562 938-4291
1855 Walnut Ave Long Beach (90806) *(P-4444)*

Long Beach Convention Center, Long Beach *Also called Smg Holdings LLC (P-10652)*

Long Beach Cty Flt Svc Ofc, Long Beach *Also called City of Long Beach (P-22418)*

Long Beach Day Nursery (PA)....D....562 421-1488
1548 Chestnut Ave Long Beach (90813) *(P-23743)*

Long Beach Day Nursery....E....562 421-1488
3965 N Bellflower Blvd Long Beach (90808) *(P-23744)*

Long Beach Golden Sails Inc....D....562 596-1631
23545 Crenshaw Blvd # 100 Torrance (90505) *(P-12562)*

Long Beach Hilton, The, Long Beach *Also called World Trade Ctr Ht Assoc Ltd (P-13115)*

Long Beach Investment Group....E....562 595-7277
2041 Pacific Coast Hwy Lomita (90717) *(P-9578)*

Long Beach Marriott, Long Beach *Also called Ruffin Hotel Corp of Cal (P-12854)*

Long Beach Memorial Med Ctr (HQ)....A....562 933-2000
2801 Atlantic Ave Fl 2 Long Beach (90806) *(P-21019)*

Long Beach Pain Center, Long Beach *Also called Healthsmart Pacific Inc (P-20906)*

Long Beach Public Transit, Long Beach *Also called Long Beach Public Trnsp Co (P-3761)*

Long Beach Public Trnsp Co....B....562 591-2301
1300 Gardenia Ave Long Beach (90813) *(P-3546)*

Long Beach Public Trnsp Co (PA)....A....562 591-8753
1963 E Anaheim St Long Beach (90813) *(P-3761)*

Long Beach Public Trnsp Co....D....562 591-8753
1963 E Anaheim St Long Beach (90813) *(P-3547)*

Long Beach Unified School Dst....A....562 491-1281
999 Atlantic Ave Fl 3 Long Beach (90813) *(P-14327)*

Long Beach Unified School Dst....D....562 426-6176
2700 Pine Ave Long Beach (90806) *(P-3819)*

Long Beach Unified School Dst....C....562 997-7550
2425 Webster Ave Long Beach (90810) *(P-13967)*

Long Beach Unified School Dst....A....562 493-3596
3351 Val Verde Ave Long Beach (90808) *(P-16897)*

Long Beach Yacht Club....D....562 598-9401
6201 E Appian Way Long Beach (90803) *(P-18491)*

Long Dragon Financial Service, Arcadia *Also called Long Dragon Realty Co Inc (P-11252)*

Long Dragon Realty Co Inc....C....626 309-7999
2633 S Baldwin Ave Arcadia (91007) *(P-11252)*

Long Point Development LLC....A....310 265-2800
100 Terranea Way Rancho Palos Verdes (90275) *(P-12563)*

Long Swimming Pool Steel Inc....E....714 524-8172
3920 E Coronado St # 205 Anaheim (92807) *(P-3270)*

Long-Lok Fasteners Corporation....E....310 667-4200
20501 Belshaw Ave Carson (90746) *(P-7398)*

LONGSHOREMEN'S & WAREHOUSEMENS, Stockton *Also called International Longshoremens (P-24445)*

Longust Distributing LLC....E....480 820-6244
1206 N Miller St Unit A Anaheim (92806) *(P-6569)*

Longwood Management, San Dimas *Also called San Dimas Retirement Center (P-10810)*

Longwood Management Corp....C....310 679-1461
11834 Inglewood Ave Hawthorne (90250) *(P-20088)*

Longwood Management Corp....D....323 735-5146
2000 W Washington Blvd Los Angeles (90018) *(P-20617)*

Longwood Management Corp....E....818 781-6348
6728 Sepulveda Blvd Van Nuys (91411) *(P-10760)*

Longwood Management Corp....D....562 693-5240
7716 Pickering Ave Whittier (90602) *(P-21020)*

Longwood Management Corp....D....818 246-7174
605 W Broadway Glendale (91204) *(P-20618)*

Longwood Management Corp....D....818 881-7414
7836 Reseda Blvd Reseda (91335) *(P-21021)*

Longwood Management Corp....D....818 360-1864
17922 San Frnando Msn Granada Hills (91344) *(P-20089)*

Longwood Management Corp....D....626 280-2293
8101 Hill Dr Rosemead (91770) *(P-20090)*

Longwood Management Corp....C....626 280-4820
8035 Hill Dr Rosemead (91770) *(P-20091)*

Longwood Management Corp....D....323 737-7778
2190 W Adams Blvd Los Angeles (90018) *(P-20619)*

Longwood Management Corp....C....213 382-8461
1240 S Hoover St Los Angeles (90006) *(P-20620)*

Longwood Management Corp....C....818 980-8200
11429 Ventura Blvd Studio City (91604) *(P-20621)*

Longwood Management Corp....D....818 884-7100
895 E Pasadena St Pomona (91767) *(P-10761)*

Longwood Management Corp....E....323 933-1560
1900 S Longwood Ave Los Angeles (90016) *(P-20092)*

Longwood Management Corp....D....626 289-3763
537 W Live Oak St San Gabriel (91776) *(P-20622)*

Longwood Management Corp....D....714 962-5531
9925 La Alameda Ave Fountain Valley (92708) *(P-23976)*

Longwood Management Corp....C....562 432-5751
1913 E 5th St Long Beach (90802) *(P-20623)*

Longwood Management Inc....D....310 370-5828
20920 Earl St Ofc Torrance (90503) *(P-10762)*

Longwood Manor....C....323 935-1157
4853 W Washington Blvd Los Angeles (90016) *(P-20093)*

Longwood Manor Convalescent HM, Los Angeles *Also called Longwood Manor (P-20093)*

Loofs Lite A Line....E....562 436-2978
2500 Long Beach Blvd Long Beach (90806) *(P-18319)*

Lookout Inc (PA)....C....650 241-2358
1 Front St Ste 3100 San Francisco (94111) *(P-16542)*

Lookout Productions LLC....E....310 408-5687
3748 W 9th St Apt 403 Los Angeles (90019) *(P-17628)*

Loomis Armored Us LLC....D....619 232-5106
3555 Aero Ct San Diego (92123) *(P-16343)*

Loomis Armored Us LLC....D....916 441-1091
315 12th St Sacramento (95814) *(P-16344)*

Loomworks Apparel, Irvine *Also called Delta Galil USA Inc (P-8068)*

Looney Bins Inc (PA)....D....818 485-8200
12153 Montague St Pacoima (91331) *(P-6216)*

Loop Media Inc....D....650 704-7409
3900 W Alameda Ave # 1200 Burbank (91505) *(P-14919)*

Lopez Canyon Landfill....C....818 834-5122
11950 Lopez Canyon Rd Sylmar (91342) *(P-6217)*

Lopez Harvesting....D....559 568-2553
24079 Avenue 196 Strathmore (93267) *(P-453)*

Lorber Greenfield & Polito LLP (PA)....D....858 486-6757
13985 Stowe Dr Poway (92064) *(P-22664)*

Loring Smart Roast Inc....D....707 526-7215
3200 Dutton Ave Ste 413 Santa Rosa (95407) *(P-7558)*

Loring Ward, San Jose *Also called Bam Advisor Services LLC (P-9795)*

Los Adobes De Maria, Santa Maria *Also called Peoples Self-Help Housing Corp (P-27167)*

Los Alamitos Hemo Dialysis Ctr, Los Alamitos *Also called Los Almtos Hmodialysis Ctr Inc (P-21929)*

Los Alamitos Medical Ctr Inc (HQ)....A....714 826-6400
3751 Katella Ave Los Alamitos (90720) *(P-21022)*

Los Almtos Hmodialysis Ctr Inc....D....562 426-8881
3810 Katella Ave Los Alamitos (90720) *(P-21929)*

Los Altos Center, Los Altos *Also called Palo Alto Medical Foundation (P-19262)*

Los Altos Food Products Inc....C....626 330-6555
450 Baldwin Park Blvd City of Industry (91746) *(P-8319)*

Los Altos Golf and Country CLB....D....650 947-3100
1560 Country Club Dr Los Altos (94024) *(P-18492)*

Los Altos YMCA, Long Beach *Also called Young Mens Chrstn Assc Gr L B (P-24743)*

Los Alts Sub-Acute Rhbltn, Los Altos *Also called Covenant Care California LLC (P-19842)*

Los Amigos Country Club Inc....D....562 923-9696
7295 Quill Dr Downey (90242) *(P-18493)*

Los Amigos Golf Course, Downey *Also called Los Amigos Country Club Inc (P-18493)*

Los Angeles Airport Peace Offc....B....310 242-5218
6080 Center Dr Fl 6 Los Angeles (90045) *(P-24586)*

Los Angeles Angels of Anaheim, Anaheim *Also called Angels Baseball LP (P-18049)*

Los Angeles Athletic Club Inc....C....213 625-2211
431 W 7th St Los Angeles (90014) *(P-18171)*

Los Angeles Branch, Los Angeles *Also called Federal Rsrve Bnk San Frncisco (P-9026)*

Los Angeles Branch, Commerce *Also called Jfc International Inc (P-8595)*

Los Angeles Cardiology Assoc (PA)....D....213 977-0419
1245 Wilshire Blvd # 703 Los Angeles (90017) *(P-19167)*

Los Angeles Chargers, Costa Mesa *Also called Chargers Football Company LLC (P-18058)*

Los Angeles Chmber Orchstra....D....213 622-7001
350 S Figueroa St Ste 183 Los Angeles (90071) *(P-17989)*

Los Angeles City Hauling, Sun Valley *Also called USA Waste of California Inc (P-6298)*

Los Angeles Clippers, Los Angeles *Also called LA Sports Properties Inc (P-18067)*

Los Angeles Cnty Dev Svc Fndtn....C....213 383-1300
3303 Wilshire Blvd # 700 Los Angeles (90010) *(P-22272)*

Los Angeles Cnty Emp Retiremnt (PA)....B....626 564-6000
300 N Lake Ave Ste 720 Pasadena (91101) *(P-10218)*

Los Angeles Cnty Mseum of Art....D....323 857-6000
5905 Wilshire Blvd Los Angeles (90036) *(P-24270)*

Los Angeles Cnty Mtro Trnspt, Los Angeles *Also called Los Angeles County MTA (P-3552)*

Los Angeles Cold Storage, Los Angeles *Also called Standard-Southern Corporation (P-4354)*

Los Angeles Cold Storage Co, Los Angeles *Also called Standard-Southern Corporation (P-4352)*

Los Angeles Community Hospital, Los Angeles *Also called Alta Hospitals System LLC (P-20742)*

Los Angeles Conven and Exh....B....213 741-1151
1201 S Figueroa St Los Angeles (90015) *(P-10616)*

Mergent e-mail: customerrelations@mergent.com
1336
2020 Directory of California
Wholesalers and Services Companies
(P-0000) Products & Services Section entry number
(PA)=Parent Co (HQ)=Headquarters (DH)=Div Headquarters

Los Angeles Convention Center, Los Angeles *Also called AEG Management Lacc LLC* ***(P-26124)***

Los Angeles Country Club ... C ... 310 276-6104
10101 Wilshire Blvd Los Angeles (90024) ***(P-18494)***

Los Angeles County, Pacoima *Also called County of Los Angeles* ***(P-18928)***

Los Angeles County Bar Assn (PA) ... D ... 213 627-2727
1055 W 7th St Ste 2700 Los Angeles (90017) ***(P-24409)***

Los Angeles County Fair Assn (PA) ... D ... 909 623-3111
1101 W Mckinley Ave Pomona (91768) ***(P-18720)***

Los Angeles County MTA ... C ... 213 922-6308
9201 Canoga Ave Chatsworth (91311) ***(P-3548)***

Los Angeles County MTA ... C ... 213 922-5887
900 Lyon St Los Angeles (90012) ***(P-3549)***

Los Angeles County MTA ... C ... 213 922-6301
1130 E 6th St Los Angeles (90021) ***(P-3550)***

Los Angeles County MTA ... B ... 213 922-6203
630 W Avenue 28 Los Angeles (90065) ***(P-3551)***

Los Angeles County MTA ... C ... 213 922-6202
1 Gateway Plz Los Angeles (90012) ***(P-3552)***

Los Angeles County MTA (PA) ... A ... 323 466-3876
1 Gateway Plz Fl 25 Los Angeles (90012) ***(P-3553)***

Los Angeles County MTA ... A ... 213 922-6207
8800 Santa Monica Blvd Los Angeles (90069) ***(P-3554)***

Los Angeles County MTA ... B ... 213 922-6215
11900 Branford St Sun Valley (91352) ***(P-3555)***

Los Angeles County MTA ... B ... 213 533-1506
720 E 15th St Los Angeles (90021) ***(P-3556)***

Los Angeles County MTA ... C ... 213 922-5012
470 Bauchet St Los Angeles (90012) ***(P-3557)***

Los Angeles County MTA ... C ... 310 392-8636
100 Sunset Ave Venice (90291) ***(P-3558)***

Los Angeles County MTA ... C ... 213 244-6783
818 W 7th St Ste 500 Los Angeles (90017) ***(P-3559)***

Los Angeles County MTA ... C ... 213 626-4455
320 S Santa Fe Ave Los Angeles (90013) ***(P-3560)***

Los Angeles County Pub Works, South Gate *Also called County of Los Angeles* ***(P-22217)***

Los Angeles Cty Rnch Los Amgos ... A ... 562 385-7111
7601 Imperial Hwy Downey (90242) ***(P-20437)***

Los Angeles Dept Convetion Tou, Los Angeles *Also called Los Angeles Conven and Exh* ***(P-10616)***

Los Angeles Dept Wtr & Pwr ... A ... 323 256-8079
4030 Crenshaw Blvd Los Angeles (90008) ***(P-6078)***

Los Angeles Dept Wtr & Pwr ... A ... 213 367-1342
11801 Sheldon St Sun Valley (91352) ***(P-6079)***

Los Angeles Dept Wtr & Pwr ... A ... 760 878-2156
201 S Webster St Independence (93526) ***(P-6080)***

Los Angeles Dept Wtr & Pwr (PA) ... C ... 213 367-4211
111 N Hope St Los Angeles (90012) ***(P-6081)***

Los Angeles Dept Wtr & Pwr ... D ... 213 367-4211
111 N Hope St Los Angeles (90012) ***(P-5854)***

Los Angeles Dept Wtr & Pwr ... A ... 213 367-5706
1141 W 2nd St Bldg D Los Angeles (90012) ***(P-6082)***

Los Angeles Dept Wtr & Pwr ... D ... 310 524-8500
12700 Vista Del Mar Playa Del Rey (90293) ***(P-6010)***

Los Angeles Deseret Industries, Los Angeles *Also called Church of Jsus Chrst of Ld STS* ***(P-17471)***

Los Angeles District Office, Glendale *Also called State Compensation Insur Fund* ***(P-10140)***

Los Angeles Dodgers LLC ... A ... 323 224-1507
1000 Vin Scully Ave Los Angeles (90090) ***(P-18068)***

Los Angeles Dr-In Theatre Co, Montclair *Also called Mission Drive-In Theatre Co* ***(P-17874)***

Los Angeles Engineering Inc ... C ... 626 869-1400
633 N Barranca Ave Covina (91723) ***(P-25193)***

Los Angeles Equestrian Center ... D ... 818 840-9063
480 W Riverside Dr Burbank (91506) ***(P-606)***

Los Angeles Federal Credit Un (PA) ... D ... 818 242-8640
300 S Glendale Ave # 100 Glendale (91205) ***(P-9323)***

Los Angeles Free Clinic (PA) ... B ... 323 653-8622
8405 Beverly Blvd Los Angeles (90048) ***(P-19168)***

Los Angeles Free Clinic ... D ... 323 653-8622
8405 Beverly Blvd Los Angeles (90048) ***(P-19169)***

Los Angeles Freightliner, Fontana *Also called Los Angeles Truck Centers LLC* ***(P-6404)***

Los Angeles Job Corps ... C ... 213 748-0135
4867 E 61st St Apt C Maywood (90270) ***(P-23611)***

Los Angeles Lakers Inc ... C ... 310 426-6000
2275 E Mariposa Ave El Segundo (90245) ***(P-18069)***

Los Angeles Lawyer Magazine, Los Angeles *Also called Los Angeles County Bar Assn* ***(P-24409)***

Los Angeles Lgbt Center (PA) ... C ... 323 993-7618
1625 Schrader Blvd Los Angeles (90028) ***(P-24194)***

Los Angeles Magazine, Los Angeles *Also called Emmis Publishing Corporation* ***(P-8871)***

Los Angeles Marriott Downtown, Los Angeles *Also called La Hotel Venture LLC* ***(P-12527)***

Los Angeles Mem Coliseum Comm ... B ... 213 747-7111
3911 S Figueroa St Los Angeles (90037) ***(P-24845)***

Los Angeles Mission Inc (PA) ... D ... 213 629-1227
303 E 5th St Los Angeles (90013) ***(P-23977)***

Los Angeles Organizing ... E ... 310 407-0539
10900 Wilshire Blvd # 710 Los Angeles (90024) ***(P-18495)***

Los Angeles Orphan Asylum Inc ... C ... 323 283-9311
7600 Graves Ave Rosemead (91770) ***(P-23978)***

Los Angeles Orphans Home Soc (HQ) ... C ... 323 463-2119
815 N El Centro Ave Los Angeles (90038) ***(P-23979)***

Los Angeles Philharmonic Assn (PA) ... A ... 213 972-7300
151 S Grand Ave Los Angeles (90012) ***(P-17990)***

Los Angeles Police Command ... B ... 877 275-5273
100 W 1st St Los Angeles (90012) ***(P-24846)***

Los Angeles Police Credit Un (PA) ... D ... 818 787-6520
16150 Sherman Way Van Nuys (91406) ***(P-9398)***

Los Angeles Rams LLC (PA) ... D ... 314 982-7267
29899 Agoura Rd Agoura Hills (91301) ***(P-18070)***

Los Angeles Regional Food Bank ... C ... 323 234-3030
1734 E 41st St Vernon (90058) ***(P-23322)***

Los Angeles Regional Office, Brea *Also called International Code Council Inc* ***(P-24405)***

Los Angeles Regional Office, Pasadena *Also called Employee Benefits Security ADM* ***(P-10216)***

Los Angeles Residential Comm F ... D ... 661 296-8636
29890 Bouquet Canyon Rd Santa Clarita (91390) ***(P-23980)***

Los Angeles Rubber Company (PA) ... D ... 323 263-4131
2915 E Washington Blvd Los Angeles (90023) ***(P-7642)***

Los Angeles SEC National (PA) ... E ... 323 651-2930
543 N Fairfax Ave Los Angeles (90036) ***(P-23323)***

Los Angeles Senior Citizen ... D ... 310 271-9670
1425 S Wooster St Los Angeles (90035) ***(P-10763)***

Los Angeles South Bay Dst Off, Long Beach *Also called Rehabilitation California Dept* ***(P-23408)***

Los Angeles Terminal, Los Angeles *Also called El Pas-Los Angles Lmsne Ex Inc* ***(P-3774)***

Los Angeles Truck Centers LLC ... C ... 909 510-4000
13800 Valley Blvd Fontana (92335) ***(P-6404)***

Los Angeles Turf Club Inc (HQ) ... C ... 626 574-6330
285 W Huntington Dr Arcadia (91007) ***(P-18085)***

Los Angeles Unified School Dst ... B ... 818 997-2640
6651 Balboa Blvd Van Nuys (91406) ***(P-22061)***

Los Angeles Unified School Dst ... C ... 213 485-3691
200 N Main St Ste 1400 Los Angeles (90012) ***(P-15922)***

Los Angeles Unified School Dst ... C ... 323 753-3175
816 W 51st St Los Angeles (90037) ***(P-24587)***

Los Angeles Unified School Dst ... D ... 323 939-7322
1212 Queen Anne Pl Los Angeles (90019) ***(P-23745)***

Los Angeles Unified School Dst ... A ... 213 847-6911
200 N Main St Ste 1400 Los Angeles (90012) ***(P-15785)***

Los Angeles Unified School Dst ... C ... 310 258-2000
8810 Emerson Ave Los Angeles (90045) ***(P-23324)***

Los Angeles Unified School Dst ... D ... 562 654-9007
8525 Rex Rd Pico Rivera (90660) ***(P-16898)***

Los Angeles Unified School Dst ... E ... 310 808-1500
17729 S Figueroa St Gardena (90248) ***(P-13968)***

Los Angeles Unified School Dst ... C ... 310 518-1128
1468 N Marine Ave Wilmington (90744) ***(P-23325)***

Los Angeles Unified School Dst ... C ... 818 363-5061
10900 Hayvenhurst Ave Granada Hills (91344) ***(P-24588)***

Los Angeles World Airports (PA) ... C ... 310 646-7911
6320 W 96th St Los Angeles (90045) ***(P-4778)***

Los Angeles World Airports ... D ... 909 544-5490
1230 Tower St Ontario (91761) ***(P-4779)***

Los Angles Ambulatory Care Ctr, Los Angeles *Also called Veterans Health Administration* ***(P-19578)***

Los Angles Arbretum Foundation ... D ... 626 821-3222
301 N Baldwin Ave Arcadia (91007) ***(P-24310)***

Los Angles Area Chmber Cmmerce ... D ... 213 580-7500
350 S Bixel St Los Angeles (90017) ***(P-24347)***

Los Angles Child Gdance Clinic (PA) ... C ... 323 373-2400
3031 S Vermont Ave Los Angeles (90007) ***(P-23326)***

Los Angles Clippers Foundation ... D ... 213 742-7555
1111 S Figueroa St # 1100 Los Angeles (90015) ***(P-26677)***

Los Angles Cnty Cntl Jail Hosp, Los Angeles *Also called County of Los Angeles* ***(P-20817)***

Los Angles Cnty Employees Assn ... D ... 213 368-8660
1545 Wilshire Blvd Los Angeles (90017) ***(P-24451)***

Los Angles Dst Off Policy Svcs, Monterey Park *Also called State Compensation Insur Fund* ***(P-10146)***

Los Angles Homecare Pediatrics, Los Angeles *Also called Maxim Healthcare Services Inc* ***(P-21810)***

Los Angles Jewish HM For Aging (PA) ... A ... 818 774-3000
7150 Tampa Ave Reseda (91335) ***(P-20094)***

Los Angles Jewish HM For Aging ... B ... 818 774-3000
18855 Victory Blvd Reseda (91335) ***(P-20095)***

Los Angles Kings Hockey CLB LP ... C ... 310 535-4502
555 N Nash St El Segundo (90245) ***(P-18071)***

Los Angles Kings Hockey CLB LP (PA) ... C ... 888 546-4752
800 W Olympic Blvd Los Angeles (90015) ***(P-18072)***

Los Angles Trism Convention Bd (PA) ... D ... 213 624-7300
633 W 5th St Ste 1800 Los Angeles (90071) ***(P-16899)***

Los Angles Universal Preschool ... C ... 213 416-1200
515 S Figueroa St Ste 900 Los Angeles (90071) ***(P-23746)***

LOS BANOS NURSING AND REHAB, Los Banos *Also called Para & Palli Inc* ***(P-20186)***

Los Banos School District, Los Banos *Also called Facilities Operation and Trnsp* ***(P-3800)***

Los Defensores Inc ... E ... 310 519-4050
20101 Hamilton Ave # 300 Torrance (90502) ***(P-13535)***

Los Dos Valles Harvstg & Pkg ... C ... 805 739-1688
2365 Westgate Rd Santa Maria (93455) ***(P-454)***

Los Gatos Meadows, Los Gatos *Also called Episcopal Senior Communities* ***(P-23917)***

Los Gatos Senior Living LLC ... E ... 408 356-9146
16605 Lark Ave Los Gatos (95032) ***(P-20624)***

Los Gtos Oaks Cnvalescent Hosp, Los Gatos *Also called Los Gatos Senior Living LLC* ***(P-20624)***

Los Osos Management Co Inc (PA) ... D ... 559 733-4328
3130 W Main St Ste A Visalia (93291) ***(P-11253)***

Los Padres Bank, Solvang *Also called Pacific Western Bank* ***(P-9231)***

Los Palos Convalescent Hosp, San Pedro *Also called San Pedro Convalescent HM Inc* ***(P-20238)***

Los Posadas Service Center, Camarillo *Also called Telecare Corporation* ***(P-21439)***

Los Prietos Boys Camp ... D ... 805 692-1750
3900 Paradise Rd Santa Barbara (93105) ***(P-23981)***

Los Robles Bank ... D ... 805 373-6763
33 W Thousand Oaks Blvd Thousand Oaks (91360) ***(P-9213)***

ALPHABETIC

Employee Codes: A=Over 500 employees, B=251-500
C=101-250, D=51-100, E=50
2020 Directory of California
Wholesalers and Services Companies
© Mergent Inc. 1-800-342-5647
1337

Los Robles Hospital & Med Ctr (HQ) ....D....805 497-2727
215 W Janss Rd Thousand Oaks (91360) ***(P-21023)***
Los Serranos Golf & Cntry CLB, Chino Hills *Also called Los Serranos Golf Club* ***(P-18263)***
Los Serranos Golf Club ....C....909 597-1769
15656 Yorba Ave Chino Hills (91709) ***(P-18263)***
Los Verdes Golf Course, Rancho Palos Verdes *Also called American Golf Corporation* ***(P-18371)***
Los Verdes Golf Curse, Rancho Palos Verdes *Also called Los Verdes MNS Golf Cntry CLB* ***(P-18264)***
Los Verdes MNS Golf Cntry CLB ....E....310 377-7370
7000 Los Verdes Dr Ste 1 Rancho Palos Verdes (90275) ***(P-18264)***
Lost Canyons Golf Course, Simi Valley *Also called Big Sky Country Club LLC* ***(P-18222)***
Lotus Communications Corp (PA) ....D....323 512-2225
3301 Barham Blvd Ste 200 Los Angeles (90068) ***(P-5558)***
Lotus Interworks Inc ....C....310 442-3330
10801 National Blvd # 500 Los Angeles (90064) ***(P-26678)***
Lou Bozigian ....D....661 948-4737
5900 Alleppo Ln Palmdale (93551) ***(P-11254)***
Louie Almeida & Settler (PA) ....D....818 461-9559
303 N Glenoaks Blvd # 400 Burbank (91502) ***(P-22665)***
Louis Luskin & Sons Inc ....D....323 938-5142
6004 Venice Blvd Los Angeles (90034) ***(P-2189)***
Louis Wurth and Company (HQ) ....D....714 529-1771
895 Columbia St Brea (92821) ***(P-7399)***
Lounge 22 LLC (PA) ....D....818 502-0700
211 N Brand Blvd Glendale (91203) ***(P-14177)***
Loup Logistics Company ....C....661 370-4341
2121 S Browning Rd Delano (93215) ***(P-4985)***
Loupe, San Francisco *Also called Plangrid Inc* ***(P-15476)***
LOVARC, Lompoc *Also called Life Optons Vctnal Rsource Ctr* ***(P-23314)***
Lovazzano Mechanical Inc ....D....650 367-6216
189 Constitution Dr Menlo Park (94025) ***(P-2190)***
Lovco Construction Inc ....C....562 595-1601
1300 E Burnett St Signal Hill (90755) ***(P-3321)***
Love Lifted US Youth Services ....E....818 471-0594
6356 Van Nuys Blvd # 229 Van Nuys (91401) ***(P-18172)***
Lovely Living Homecare ....D....909 625-7999
112 Harvard Ave Claremont (91711) ***(P-21805)***
Low Ball & Lynch A Prof Corp (PA) ....D....415 981-6630
505 Montgomery St Fl 7 San Francisco (94111) ***(P-22666)***
Lowcom LLC ....C....213 408-0080
818 W 7th St Ste 700 Los Angeles (90017) ***(P-13536)***
Lowe Enterprises Inc ....C....310 820-6661
11777 San Vicente Blvd # 900 Los Angeles (90049) ***(P-11255)***
Lowe Enterprises Inc (PA) ....C....310 820-6661
11777 San Vicente Blvd # 900 Los Angeles (90049) ***(P-12564)***
Lowe Enterprises Coml Group, Los Angeles *Also called Lowe Enterprises RE Group* ***(P-11573)***
Lowe Enterprises Inc ....D....310 820-6661
11777 San Vincente Blvd S Los Angeles (90049) ***(P-11572)***
Lowe Enterprises RE Group ....D....310 820-6661
11777 San Vicente Blvd # 900 Los Angeles (90049) ***(P-11573)***
Lowenstein Sandler LLP ....E....650 433-5800
390 Lytton Ave Palo Alto (94301) ***(P-22667)***
Lowermybills, Los Angeles *Also called Lmb Mortgage Services Inc* ***(P-9575)***
Lowermybills, Playa Vista *Also called Lmb Opco LLC* ***(P-9633)***
Lowrates.com, 1st Liberty, Buena Park *Also called Sun West Mortgage Company Inc* ***(P-9605)***
Loyal Svc Unt Spec Team, Long Beach *Also called Michael McCarthy* ***(P-16352)***
Loyal3 Holdings Inc ....D....415 981-0700
150 California St Ste 400 San Francisco (94111) ***(P-16900)***
Loyalton At Rancho Solano ....D....707 425-3588
3350 Cherry Hills Ct Ofc Fairfield (94534) ***(P-23982)***
Loyda Yu Real Estate Inc ....D....619 475-7777
860 Kuhn Dr Ste 200 Chula Vista (91914) ***(P-11256)***
Loyola Marymount University ....C....310 338-2866
1 Lmu Dr Ste 100 Los Angeles (90045) ***(P-5559)***
Lozano Car Wash, Mountain View *Also called Lozano Inc* ***(P-17387)***
Lozano Inc ....C....650 941-0590
2690 W El Camino Real Mountain View (94040) ***(P-17387)***
Lozano Plumbing Services Inc ....C....951 683-4840
3615 Presley Ave Riverside (92507) ***(P-2191)***
Lozano Smith LLP ....C....559 431-5600
7404 N Spalding Ave Fresno (93720) ***(P-22668)***
Lozano Smith A Prof Corp (PA) ....D....559 431-5600
7404 N Spalding Ave Fresno (93720) ***(P-22669)***
LPA Inc (PA) ....C....949 261-1001
5301 California Ave # 100 Irvine (92617) ***(P-25473)***
LPA Inc ....C....408 780-7200
60 S Market St Ste 150 San Jose (95113) ***(P-25474)***
Lpa Insurance Agency Inc ....D....916 286-7850
3800 Watt Ave Ste 147 Sacramento (95821) ***(P-15393)***
Lpas Inc ....D....916 443-0335
2484 Natomas Park Dr # 100 Sacramento (95833) ***(P-25475)***
Lpcc, Camarillo *Also called Las Posas Country Club* ***(P-18488)***
Lpl Holdings Inc (HQ) ....C....858 450-9606
4707 Executive Dr San Diego (92121) ***(P-26679)***
Lpsh Holdings Inc ....A....951 926-1176
3570 W Florida Ave # 168 Hemet (92545) ***(P-2192)***
Lq Management LLC ....D....310 645-2200
5249 W Century Blvd Los Angeles (90045) ***(P-12565)***
Lqr Property LLC ....D....760 564-4111
49499 Eisenhower Dr La Quinta (92253) ***(P-12566)***
Lres Corporation (PA) ....D....714 520-5737
765 The City Dr S Ste 300 Orange (92868) ***(P-11257)***
Lrw Group, Los Angeles *Also called Lieberman RES Worldwide LLC* ***(P-25920)***
Lrw Investments LLC ....D....310 337-1944
9700 Bellanca Ave Los Angeles (90045) ***(P-17263)***

LS Farms LLC ....B....661 792-3192
6111 De La Guerra Ter Bakersfield (93306) ***(P-346)***
Lsf Central Cal Adult Svcs, Arroyo Grande *Also called Life Steps Foundation Inc* ***(P-23315)***
Lsf9 Cypress Holdings LLC ....A....714 380-3127
2741 Walnut Ave Ste 200 Tustin (92780) ***(P-6725)***
LSI - Silvercreek LLC ....C....408 226-8080
800 Embedded Way Ste 80 San Jose (95138) ***(P-18173)***
Ltc Pharmacy, Riverside *Also called Pharmerica Long-Term Care LLC* ***(P-7975)***
Ltd Eyewear, Chatsworth *Also called Atlantic Optical Co Inc* ***(P-7021)***
LTS Associate Inc (PA) ....E....626 435-2838
18738 San Jose Ave City of Industry (91748) ***(P-7298)***
Luberski Inc ....D....951 271-3866
1811 Mountain Ave Norco (92860) ***(P-8329)***
Lucasfilm Coml Productions, San Francisco *Also called Lucasfilm Ltd LLC* ***(P-17629)***
Lucasfilm Ltd LLC (HQ) ....C....415 623-1000
1110 Gorgas Ave Bldg C-Hr San Francisco (94129) ***(P-17629)***
Lucich Santos Farms ....C....209 892-6500
12631 Rogers Rd Patterson (95363) ***(P-347)***
Lucid Design Group Inc ....D....510 907-0400
55 Harrison St 200 Oakland (94607) ***(P-15641)***
Lucid Vr Inc ....D....408 391-0506
4500 Great America Pkwy Santa Clara (95054) ***(P-14920)***
Lucideus Inc ....C....650 843-0988
3260 Hillview Ave Palo Alto (94304) ***(P-14921)***
Lucile Packard Childrens Hosp ....D....650 321-2545
730 Welch Rd Ste B Palo Alto (94304) ***(P-21024)***
Lucile Salter Packard Chil ....C....925 277-7550
5601 Norris Canyon Rd # 230 San Ramon (94583) ***(P-19170)***
Lucile Salter Packard Chil ....C....650 736-2142
4100 Bohannon Dr Menlo Park (94025) ***(P-21482)***
Lucile Salter Packard Chil (PA) ....D....650 497-8000
725 Welch Rd Palo Alto (94304) ***(P-21483)***
Lucile Salter Packard Chil ....C....650 723-5791
300 Pasteur Dr Stanford (94305) ***(P-21484)***
Lucky Chances Inc ....A....650 758-2237
1700 Hillside Blvd Colma (94014) ***(P-12567)***
Lucky Chances Casino, Colma *Also called Lucky Chances Inc* ***(P-12567)***
Lucky Farms Inc ....D....909 799-6688
1194 E Brier Dr San Bernardino (92408) ***(P-63)***
Lucky Installations ....E....562 948-5950
9041 Bermudez St Pico Rivera (90660) ***(P-3073)***
Lucky Lady Card Room, San Diego *Also called California Club Lucky Lady* ***(P-12106)***
Lucky Strike Entertainment LLC ....D....818 933-3752
6801 Hollywood Blvd # 143 Los Angeles (90028) ***(P-18036)***
Lucky Strike Entertainment LLC ....C....818 933-0872
15260 Ventura Blvd # 1110 Sherman Oaks (91403) ***(P-18037)***
Lucky Strike Entertainment LLC ....D....248 374-3420
20 City Blvd W Ste G2 Orange (92868) ***(P-18038)***
LUCKY STRIKE ENTERTAINMENT, L.L.C., Los Angeles *Also called Lucky Strike Entertainment LLC* ***(P-18036)***
LUCKY STRIKE ENTERTAINMENT, L.L.C., Sherman Oaks *Also called Lucky Strike Entertainment LLC* ***(P-18037)***
LUCKY STRIKE ENTERTAINMENT, L.L.C., Orange *Also called Lucky Strike Entertainment LLC* ***(P-18038)***
Lufthnsa Crgo Aktngesellschaft ....C....310 242-2590
5721 W Imperial Hwy Los Angeles (90045) ***(P-4986)***
Luis Esparza Services Inc ....B....661 766-2344
183 Hwy 33 Maricopa (93252) ***(P-14328)***
Lukenbill Enterprises ....D....916 454-2400
3600 Power Inn Rd Ste H Sacramento (95826) ***(P-4676)***
Luma Pictures Inc ....C....310 888-8738
1424 2nd St Santa Monica (90401) ***(P-17748)***
Lumberyard Plaza Mall, Los Angeles *Also called Laguna Country Mart Ltd Inc* ***(P-10615)***
Lumens LLC (HQ) ....D....916 444-5585
2020 L St Ste Ll10 Sacramento (95811) ***(P-7162)***
Lumetra Healthcare Solutions ....E....415 677-2000
44 Montgomery St Ste 810 San Francisco (94104) ***(P-27120)***
Lumina At Home, Los Angeles *Also called Lumina Healthcare LLC* ***(P-21806)***
Lumina Healthcare LLC (PA) ....D....888 958-6462
5220 Pacific Concourse Dr Los Angeles (90045) ***(P-21806)***
Luminance, Commerce *Also called American De Rosa Lamparts LLC* ***(P-7121)***
Luminar Technologies Inc ....D....650 849-8797
1891 Page Mill Rd 200 Palo Alto (94304) ***(P-26009)***
Lunares, San Francisco *Also called Sunday Bazaar Inc* ***(P-6585)***
Lunarpages, La Habra *Also called Add2net Inc* ***(P-15936)***
Lund Construction Co ....C....916 344-5800
5302 Roseville Rd North Highlands (95660) ***(P-25194)***
Lund Equipment LP ....E....916 344-5800
5302 Roseville Rd North Highlands (95660) ***(P-1748)***
Lundblade Builders, Eureka *Also called Fred H Lundblade Jr* ***(P-10592)***
Lundstrom & Associates Inc ....E....619 641-5900
4804 Sunrise Hills Dr El Cajon (92020) ***(P-25195)***
Luppen and Hawley Inc ....C....916 456-7831
6330 N Point Way Sacramento (95831) ***(P-2193)***
Lupton Excavation Inc ....D....916 387-1104
8467 Florin Rd Sacramento (95828) ***(P-3322)***
Lusardi Construction Co ....C....925 829-1114
6376 Clark Ave Dublin (94568) ***(P-1531)***
Lusive Decor ....E....323 227-9207
3400 Medford St Los Angeles (90063) ***(P-27121)***
Luth Research Inc (PA) ....B....619 234-5884
1365 4th Ave San Diego (92101) ***(P-25921)***
Luther Burbank Corporation ....D....949 428-8043
20 Pacifica Ste 600 Irvine (92618) ***(P-9266)***
Luther Burbank Mem Foundation ....D....707 546-3600
50 Mark West Springs Rd Santa Rosa (95403) ***(P-17925)***
Luther Burbank Savings (HQ) ....E....707 578-9216
500 3rd St Santa Rosa (95401) ***(P-9289)***

Lutheran Health Facility, Burbank *Also called Front Porch Communities & Svcs* ***(P-20560)***
Lutrel Trucking Inc..........D......661 397-9756
12856 Old River Rd Bakersfield (93311) ***(P-4987)***
Luxar Tech Inc..........C......408 835-2551
42840 Christy St Ste 231 Fremont (94538) ***(P-5434)***
Luxe City Center, Los Angeles *Also called Emerik Hotel Corp* ***(P-12249)***
Luxe Light and Home, Los Angeles *Also called Lusive Decor* ***(P-27121)***
Luxe Sunset Boulevard Hotel, Los Angeles *Also called E H Summit Inc* ***(P-12234)***
Luxera Inc..........E......510 456-7690
39300 Civic Center Dr # 145 Fremont (94538) ***(P-13969)***
Luxn Inc..........D......408 213-7437
580 Maude Ct Sunnyvale (94085) ***(P-5793)***
Luxor Cabs Inc..........D......415 282-4141
531 Bay Shore Blvd San Francisco (94124) ***(P-3746)***
Luxottica, Ontario *Also called Oakley Inc* ***(P-4464)***
Luz Solar Partners Ix..........D......760 762-3113
43880 Harper Lake Rd Hinkley (92347) ***(P-5855)***
Lydia C Gonzalez..........E......650 299-4707
1400 Veterans Blvd Redwood City (94063) ***(P-23327)***
Lyell Immunopharma Inc..........C......650 383-5381
401 E Jamie Ct South San Francisco (94080) ***(P-16901)***
Lyft Inc (PA)..........B......844 250-2773
185 Berry St Ste 5000 San Francisco (94107) ***(P-3697)***
Lyle Company..........D......916 266-7000
3140 Gold Camp Dr Ste 30 Rancho Cordova (95670) ***(P-27122)***
Lymi Inc (PA)..........D......213 434-2772
2263 E Vernon Ave Vernon (90058) ***(P-8088)***
Lynberg & Watkins A Prof Corp (PA)..........E......213 624-8700
1150 S Olive St Fl 18 Los Angeles (90015) ***(P-22670)***
Lynberg & Watkins Attys At Law, Los Angeles *Also called Lynberg & Watkins A Prof Corp* ***(P-22670)***
Lynch Ambulance Service, Anaheim *Also called Filyn Corporation* ***(P-3671)***
Lynch Creek Medical Management, Petaluma *Also called Crocodile Bay Lodge* ***(P-13137)***
Lynch Gilardi & Grummer LLP..........E......415 397-2800
170 Columbus Ave Fl 5 San Francisco (94133) ***(P-22671)***
Lyngso Garden Materials Inc..........E......650 364-1730
345 Shoreway Rd San Carlos (94070) ***(P-6691)***
Lynup Corporation..........D......858 207-4610
16875 W Bernardo Dr # 110 San Diego (92127) ***(P-26680)***
Lynwood Medical Offices, Lynwood *Also called Kaiser Foundation Hospitals* ***(P-19080)***
Lynx Software Technologies Inc (PA)..........D......408 979-3900
855 Embedded Way San Jose (95138) ***(P-15394)***
Lyon & Associates Realtors, Sacramento *Also called William L Lyon & Assoc Inc* ***(P-11517)***
Lyon Promenade LLC..........E......949 252-9101
4901 Birch St Newport Beach (92660) ***(P-1311)***
Lyon Real Estate, Sacramento *Also called William L Lyon & Assoc Inc* ***(P-26462)***
Lyon Real Estate..........D......916 355-7000
150 Natoma Station Dr # 300 Folsom (95630) ***(P-11258)***
Lyon Realtors, Fair Oaks *Also called William L Lyon & Assoc Inc* ***(P-11518)***
Lyon Realty..........C......916 962-0111
8814 Madison Ave Fair Oaks (95628) ***(P-11259)***
Lyon Realty..........C......530 295-4444
4340 Golden Center Dr A Placerville (95667) ***(P-10877)***
Lyon Realty (PA)..........A......916 574-8800
2280 Del Paso Rd Ste 100 Sacramento (95834) ***(P-11260)***
Lyons Security Service Inc..........D......714 401-4850
P.O. Box 18955 Anaheim (92817) ***(P-16543)***
Lyons Security Service Inc..........D......916 925-9667
655 University Ave # 240 Sacramento (95825) ***(P-16345)***
Lytton Garden II, Palo Alto *Also called Community Housing Inc* ***(P-23870)***
Lytton Rancheria..........A......510 215-7888
13255 San Pablo Ave San Pablo (94806) ***(P-18721)***
Lz Management Group LLC..........D......714 957-4061
720 Paularino Ave Costa Mesa (92626) ***(P-26306)***
M & A Mortgage Inc..........D......714 560-1970
1600 N Broadway Ste 1020 Santa Ana (92706) ***(P-9634)***
M & C, Los Angeles *Also called Murchison & Cumming LLP* ***(P-22714)***
M & G Jewelers Inc..........D......909 989-2929
10823 Edison Ct Rancho Cucamonga (91730) ***(P-17470)***
M & H Realty Partners LP..........D......415 693-9000
353 Sacramento St Fl 21 San Francisco (94111) ***(P-11930)***
M & J Seafood Company Inc..........D......562 529-2786
6859 Walthall Way Paramount (90723) ***(P-8373)***
M & L Plumbing Co Inc..........E......559 291-5525
3540 N Duke Ave Fresno (93727) ***(P-2194)***
M & M Distributors, Los Angeles *Also called Wiemar Distributors Inc* ***(P-8539)***
M & M Electric, Sacramento *Also called May-Han Electric Inc* ***(P-2545)***
M & M Plumbing Inc..........D......951 354-5388
6782 Columbus St Riverside (92504) ***(P-2195)***
M & R Joint Venture Electrical..........D......909 598-7700
231 Benton Ct Walnut (91789) ***(P-2539)***
M & S Acquisition Corporation (PA)..........C......213 385-1515
707 Wilshire Blvd # 5200 Los Angeles (90017) ***(P-11261)***
M & S Security Services Inc..........D......661 397-9616
2900 L St Bakersfield (93301) ***(P-16346)***
M & S SUPPLY CO, Eureka *Also called McMurray & Sons Inc* ***(P-3076)***
M & S Trading Inc..........D......714 241-7190
15778 Gateway Cir Tustin (92780) ***(P-8039)***
M & T Calf Ranch..........D......559 686-7663
14998 Avenue 192 Tulare (93274) ***(P-379)***
M A A C Project, Chula Vista *Also called Metropolitan Area Advisory Com* ***(P-23613)***
M A C, Northridge *Also called Mikuni American Corporation* ***(P-6454)***
M Arthur Gensler Jr Assoc Inc..........E......408 885-8100
225 W Santa Clara St San Jose (95113) ***(P-25476)***
M Arthur Gensler Jr Assoc Inc (PA)..........B......415 433-3700
45 Fremont St Ste 1500 San Francisco (94105) ***(P-25477)***
M Arthur Gensler Jr Assoc Inc..........C......510 625-7400
2101 Webster St Ste 2000 Oakland (94612) ***(P-25478)***
M Arthur Gensler Jr Assoc Inc..........C......213 927-3600
500 S Figueroa St Los Angeles (90071) ***(P-25479)***
M Arthur Gensler Jr Assoc Inc..........D......949 863-9434
4675 Macarthur Ct Ste 100 Newport Beach (92660) ***(P-25480)***
M B, San Jose *Also called Marquez Brothers Intl Inc* ***(P-8188)***
M B M, Pleasanton *Also called McLane Foodservice Dist Inc* ***(P-8292)***
M Bar C Construction Inc..........D......760 744-4131
1770 La Costa Meadows Dr San Marcos (92078) ***(P-3271)***
M Block & Sons Inc..........C......909 335-6684
26875 Pioneer Ave Redlands (92374) ***(P-4445)***
M C, Los Angeles *Also called Muir-Chase Plumbing Co Inc* ***(P-2205)***
M C Builder Corp..........E......760 323-8010
3500 E Tachevah Dr Ste C Palm Springs (92262) ***(P-2368)***
M C C, Brea *Also called Mercury Casualty Company* ***(P-10107)***
M Caratan Inc..........C......661 725-2566
33787 Cecil Ave Delano (93215) ***(P-146)***
M E Nollkamper Inc (PA)..........E......951 737-9300
940 Manor Way Corona (92882) ***(P-26681)***
M F Maher Inc..........D......707 552-2774
490 Ryder St Vallejo (94590) ***(P-1749)***
M F Salta Co Inc (PA)..........D......562 421-2512
20 Executive Park Ste 150 Irvine (92614) ***(P-26682)***
M Gaw Inc..........D......818 503-7997
6910 Farmdale Ave North Hollywood (91605) ***(P-3431)***
M H Deyoung Memorial, San Francisco *Also called Corportion of Fine Arts Mseums* ***(P-24258)***
M H Podell Company (PA)..........D......415 296-8800
22 Battery St Ste 404 Burlingame (94010) ***(P-11574)***
M I G, Berkeley *Also called Moore Iacofano Goltsman Inc* ***(P-27139)***
M I I, Bakersfield *Also called Mechanical Industries Inc* ***(P-3273)***
M J D Concrete Works, Agoura Hills *Also called Mjd Construction Corp* ***(P-1165)***
M K H Inc..........D......818 882-9274
8870 Tampa Ave Northridge (91324) ***(P-17388)***
M K S Construction Inc..........C......916 446-2521
471 Bannon St Sacramento (95811) ***(P-1153)***
M K Technical Services Inc..........E......408 528-0401
4349 San Felipe Rd San Jose (95135) ***(P-14523)***
M L Stern & Co LLC (HQ)..........C......323 658-4400
8350 Wilshire Blvd Fl 1 Beverly Hills (90211) ***(P-9709)***
M M C, Covina *Also called Davita Magan Management Inc* ***(P-18943)***
M M Direct Marketing Inc..........B......714 265-4100
14271 Corporate Dr Garden Grove (92843) ***(P-13728)***
M M Fab Inc..........D......310 763-3800
2300 E Gladwick St Compton (90220) ***(P-8001)***
M Network Television Inc..........E......818 756-5150
6007 Sepulveda Blvd Van Nuys (91411) ***(P-5633)***
M O C Insurance Services, San Francisco *Also called Maroevich OShea & Coghlan* ***(P-10415)***
M O Dion & Sons Inc (PA)..........D......562 432-3946
1543 W 16th St Long Beach (90813) ***(P-8734)***
M P M & Associates Inc..........D......818 708-9676
7011 Hayvenhurst Ave F Van Nuys (91406) ***(P-1532)***
M P O Inc (HQ)..........D......562 628-1007
3760 Kilroy Airport Way # 5 Long Beach (90806) ***(P-7958)***
M P Vacuum Truck Service, Bakersfield *Also called Mp Environmental Services Inc* ***(P-6226)***
M R S, American Canyon *Also called Medical Receivables Solutions* ***(P-26705)***
M S, Pleasant Hill *Also called Mark Scott Construction Inc* ***(P-1535)***
M S E Enterprises Inc (PA)..........D......818 223-3500
23622 Calabasas Rd # 200 Calabasas (91302) ***(P-11262)***
M S International Inc (PA)..........B......714 685-7500
2095 N Batavia St Orange (92865) ***(P-6692)***
M Squared Consulting, San Francisco *Also called Collabrus Inc* ***(P-25561)***
M T C, Los Angeles *Also called Mutual Trading Co Inc* ***(P-8612)***
M T C, San Francisco *Also called Metropolitan Trnsp Comm* ***(P-3563)***
M T C, City of Industry *Also called Micro-Technology Concepts Inc* ***(P-6872)***
M T C Holdings (HQ)..........E......912 651-4000
3 Embarcadero Ctr Ste 550 San Francisco (94111) ***(P-4614)***
M T D, Santa Barbara *Also called Santa Barbara Metro Trnst Dst* ***(P-3599)***
M T M & M Inc..........D......626 445-2922
3333 Peck Rd Monrovia (91016) ***(P-14102)***
M T R, Newark *Also called Membrane Technology & RES Inc* ***(P-25796)***
M Timm Development Inc (PA)..........C......805 963-0358
233 E Carrillo St Ste D Santa Barbara (93101) ***(P-11575)***
M V E, Modesto *Also called Mve Inc* ***(P-25227)***
M X R, San Diego *Also called Merry X-Ray Chemical Corp* ***(P-6977)***
M Z T, Santa Ana *Also called Macro-Z-Technology Company* ***(P-1750)***
M&C Hotel Interests Inc..........D......310 399-9344
530 Pico Blvd Santa Monica (90405) ***(P-12568)***
M&M Asseet Management Gnl..........D......310 769-6669
2936 W El Segundo Blvd Gardena (90249) ***(P-10764)***
M-E Engineers Inc..........D......310 842-8700
600 Wilshire Blvd # 1200 Los Angeles (90017) ***(P-25196)***
M-N-Z Janitorial Services Inc..........C......323 851-4115
2109 W Burbank Blvd Burbank (91506) ***(P-13970)***
M-S Cash Drawer Corporation (PA)..........D......626 792-2111
2085 E Foothill Blvd B Pasadena (91107) ***(P-6758)***
M4 Wind Services Inc..........D......562 981-7797
4020 Long Beach Blvd Fl 2 Long Beach (90807) ***(P-27287)***
M4dev LLC..........D......619 696-6300
2137 Pacific Hwy Ste A San Diego (92101) ***(P-12569)***
M6 Dev LLC..........E......714 533-2101
1801 S Harbor Blvd Anaheim (92802) ***(P-12570)***
MA Laboratories Inc..........D......626 820-8988
18725 San Jose Ave City of Industry (91748) ***(P-6863)***

ALPHABETIC

Employee Codes: A=Over 500 employees, B=251-500
C=101-250, D=51-100, E=50
2020 Directory of California
Wholesalers and Services Companies
© Mergent Inc. 1-800-342-5647
1339

MA Labs, City of Industry *Also called MA Laboratories Inc* ***(P-6863)***
MA Steiner Construction Inc ....D....916 988-6300
8854 Greenback Ln Ste 1 Orangevale (95662) ***(P-1366)***
Maac Project, Chula Vista *Also called Metropolitan Area Advisory Com* ***(P-23615)***
Maac Project Cwbh, San Diego *Also called Metropolitan Area Advisory Com* ***(P-23614)***
Mabie Marketing Group Inc....C....858 279-5585
8352 Clairemont Mesa Blvd San Diego (92111) ***(P-16902)***
Mac Arthur Co....C....916 226-5706
1420b Enterprise Blvd West Sacramento (95691) ***(P-6715)***
Mac Kenzie Warehouse, San Francisco *Also called S F Auto Parts Whse Inc* ***(P-6466)***
Macarthur Transit Community....C....415 989-1111
345 Spear St Ste 700 San Francisco (94105) ***(P-1154)***
Maccarthy House, San Jose *Also called Momentum For Mental Health* ***(P-24197)***
Macdonald Housing Partners LP....E....510 620-0865
350 Macdonald Ave Ste 100 Richmond (94801) ***(P-11263)***
Macdonald Mott Group Inc....D....323 903-4100
3699 Crenshaw Blvd Los Angeles (90016) ***(P-25197)***
Macdonald Mott Group Inc....D....925 469-8010
12647 Alcosta Blvd San Ramon (94583) ***(P-25198)***
Macdonald Mott LLC....D....408 321-5900
3103 N 1st St Bldg B San Jose (95134) ***(P-25199)***
Macdonald Mott LLC....D....916 399-0580
180 Promenade Cir Ste 300 Sacramento (95834) ***(P-25200)***
Macerich Company (PA)....D....310 394-6000
401 Wilshire Blvd Ste 700 Santa Monica (90401) ***(P-11863)***
Macerich Company....E....562 861-9233
251 Stonewood St Downey (90241) ***(P-10617)***
Macerich Company....D....310 474-5940
10800 W Pico Blvd Ste 312 Los Angeles (90064) ***(P-11264)***
Macfarlane Partners LLC (PA)....D....415 356-2500
201 Spear St Ste 1000 San Francisco (94105) ***(P-11730)***
Machado & Sons Cnstr Inc....E....209 632-5260
1000 S Kilroy Rd Turlock (95380) ***(P-1155)***
Machine Tools Supply, Costa Mesa *Also called Mt Supply Inc* ***(P-7645)***
Machine Zone Inc (PA)....D....650 320-1678
1050 Page Mill Rd Palo Alto (94304) ***(P-14922)***
Machining Time Savers Inc....D....714 635-7373
1338 S State College Pkwy Anaheim (92806) ***(P-7559)***
Machintel Corporation....D....617 517-3090
4225 Executive Sq Ste 955 La Jolla (92037) ***(P-13537)***
Macias Gini & OConnell LLP (PA)....D....916 928-4600
3000 S St Ste 300 Sacramento (95816) ***(P-25645)***
Mackay Smps Cvil Engineers Inc (PA)....D....925 416-1790
5142 Franklin Dr Ste C Pleasanton (94588) ***(P-25201)***
Mackenzie Landscape A Cal Corp....D....951 679-5477
33380 Bailey Park Blvd Menifee (92584) ***(P-864)***
Mackevision Corporation....C....248 656-6566
1255 Treat Blvd Ste 250 Walnut Creek (94597) ***(P-15642)***
Macmurray Pacific, San Francisco *Also called Wildenradt-Mcmurray Inc* ***(P-7412)***
Macpherson's, Emeryville *Also called Art Supply Enterprises Inc* ***(P-8951)***
Macqurie Arcft Lsg Svcs US Inc....D....415 829-6600
2 Embarcadero Ctr Ste 200 San Francisco (94111) ***(P-14178)***
Macro-Pro Inc (PA)....C....562 595-0900
2400 Grand Ave Long Beach (90815) ***(P-16903)***
Macro-Z-Technology Company (PA)....D....714 564-1130
841 E Washington Ave Santa Ana (92701) ***(P-1750)***
Macronix America Inc (HQ)....D....408 262-8887
680 N Mccarthy Blvd # 200 Milpitas (95035) ***(P-7299)***
Macsei Industries Corporation....D....323 233-7864
1784 E Vernon Ave Vernon (90058) ***(P-8410)***
Macys Inc....D....916 373-0333
6200 Franklin Blvd Sacramento (95824) ***(P-4574)***
Mad Dog Express Inc (PA)....D....650 588-1900
299 Lawrence Ave South San Francisco (94080) ***(P-3908)***
Mad Dogg Athletics Inc (PA)....D....310 823-7008
2111 Narcissus Ct Venice (90291) ***(P-8089)***
MAD RIVER COMMUNITY HOSPITAL, Arcata *Also called American Hospital Mgt Corp* ***(P-20746)***
Madaluxe Group LLC (PA)....E....562 296-1055
1760 Apollo Ct Seal Beach (90740) ***(P-8090)***
Madden Corporation....D....714 922-1670
733 W Taft Ave Orange (92865) ***(P-16904)***
Maddox Dairy LLC....D....559 866-5308
12863 W Kamm Ave Spc 2 Riverdale (93656) ***(P-397)***
Maddox Dairy A Ltd Partnership (PA)....D....559 867-3545
12863 W Kamm Ave Spc 2 Riverdale (93656) ***(P-398)***
Maddox Dairy A Ltd Partnership....E....559 867-4457
7285 W Davis Ave Riverdale (93656) ***(P-399)***
Maddox Farms....D....559 866-5308
12840 W Kamm Ave Riverdale (93656) ***(P-348)***
Made In USA Foundation Inc....E....310 623-3872
11950 San Vicente Blvd # 220 Los Angeles (90049) ***(P-24589)***
Mader News Inc....D....818 551-5000
913 Ruberta Ave Glendale (91201) ***(P-8874)***
Madera Cnty Bhvioral Hlth Svcs....C....559 673-3508
209 E 7th St Madera (93638) ***(P-22062)***
Madera Community Hospital....C....559 675-5530
1210 E Almond Ave Ste A Madera (93637) ***(P-21025)***
Madera Community Hospital....C....559 665-3768
285 Hospital Dr Chowchilla (93610) ***(P-21026)***
Madera Community Hospital (PA)....B....559 675-5555
1250 E Almond Ave Madera (93637) ***(P-21027)***
Madera Convalescent Hospital (PA)....C....559 673-9228
517 S A St Madera (93638) ***(P-20096)***
Madera Convalescent Hospital....D....209 723-8814
1255 B St Merced (95341) ***(P-21418)***
Madera Convalescent Hospital....C....209 723-2911
510 W 26th St Merced (95340) ***(P-20625)***
Madera Convalescent Hospital....D....530 885-7051
260 Racetrack St Auburn (95603) ***(P-20097)***
Madera County Probation Dept, Madera *Also called County of Los Angeles* ***(P-23111)***
Madera County Road Department, Madera *Also called County of Madera* ***(P-17416)***
Madera Private Security Patrol....D....559 662-1546
910 W Yosemite Ave Madera (93637) ***(P-16347)***
Madera Quality Nut, Madera *Also called Ready Roast Nut Company LLC* ***(P-531)***
Maderas Golf Club....D....858 451-8100
17750 Old Coach Rd Poway (92064) ***(P-18265)***
Madison Care Center LLC....D....619 444-1107
1391 E Madison Ave El Cajon (92021) ***(P-20098)***
Madison Club Owners Assn....C....760 777-9320
53035 Meriwether Way La Quinta (92253) ***(P-18266)***
Madison Club, The, La Quinta *Also called Madison Club Owners Assn* ***(P-18266)***
Madison Materials....D....714 664-0159
1035 E 4th St Santa Ana (92701) ***(P-6218)***
Madison Radiology Med Group....D....626 793-8189
65 N Madison Ave Ste M250 Pasadena (91101) ***(P-19171)***
Madison Square Building, Oakland *Also called San Francisco Bay Area Rapid* ***(P-3592)***
Madrona Mnr Wine Cntry Inn....D....707 433-4231
1001 Westside Rd Healdsburg (95448) ***(P-12571)***
Madrone Vineyard Management, Sonoma *Also called Clarbec Inc* ***(P-123)***
Maersk Inc....D....714 428-5500
555 Anton Blvd Ste 300 Costa Mesa (92626) ***(P-4988)***
Maersk Line, Costa Mesa *Also called Maersk Inc* ***(P-4988)***
Mafab Inc (PA)....D....714 893-0551
1925 Century Park E # 650 Los Angeles (90067) ***(P-11676)***
Magagnini, Newark *Also called Intelliswift Software Inc* ***(P-14880)***
Magana Labor Services Inc....C....805 524-0446
2896 W Telegraph Rd Fillmore (93015) ***(P-14329)***
Magarro Farms....D....949 859-6506
23322 Peralta Dr Ste 3 Laguna Hills (92653) ***(P-513)***
Magave Tequila Inc....E....415 515-3536
6 Park Pl Belvedere Tiburon (94920) ***(P-8814)***
Magdalena Ecke Family YMCA, Encinitas *Also called YMCA of San Diego County* ***(P-24710)***
MAGELLAN HEALTH, San Diego *Also called Aurora Behavioral Health Care* ***(P-21381)***
Magento, Los Angeles *Also called Xcommerce Inc* ***(P-16163)***
Maggiora Bros Drilling Inc (PA)....D....831 724-1338
595 Airport Blvd Watsonville (95076) ***(P-3245)***
Magic 92.5, San Diego *Also called Local Media San Diego LLC* ***(P-5557)***
Magic Bullet, Los Angeles *Also called Homeland Housewares LLC* ***(P-7206)***
Magic International, Santa Monica *Also called Mens Apparel Guild In Cal Inc* ***(P-24348)***
Magic Mountain LLC....B....661 255-4100
26101 Magic Mountain Pkwy Valencia (91355) ***(P-17926)***
Magic Workforce Solutions LLC....A....310 246-6153
9100 Wilsh Blvd Ste 700e Beverly Hills (90212) ***(P-26918)***
Magma Design Automation Inc (HQ)....B....408 565-7500
1650 Tech Dr Ste 100 San Jose (95110) ***(P-14923)***
Magnell Associate Inc....C....626 271-1420
9997 Rose Hills Rd Whittier (90601) ***(P-4446)***
Magnell Associate Inc (HQ)....C....626 271-9700
17560 Rowland St City of Industry (91748) ***(P-6864)***
Magnell Associate Inc....D....626 271-1580
18045 Rowland St City of Industry (91748) ***(P-6865)***
Magnesite Specialties Inc....E....858 578-4186
8686 Production Ave Ste A San Diego (92121) ***(P-3013)***
Magnetic Imaging Affilates....D....510 204-1820
5730 Telegraph Ave Oakland (94609) ***(P-21551)***
Magnetika Inc (PA)....D....310 527-8100
2041 W 139th St Gardena (90249) ***(P-7163)***
Magnolia Convalescent Hospital, Riverside *Also called Magnolia Rhbltion Nursing Ctr* ***(P-20626)***
Magnolia Grdns Convalescent HM, Granada Hills *Also called Longwood Management Corp* ***(P-20089)***
Magnolia of Millbrae Inc....D....650 697-7700
201 Chadbourne Ave Millbrae (94030) ***(P-23983)***
Magnolia Post Acute Care, El Cajon *Also called Magnolia Special Care Center* ***(P-20438)***
Magnolia Rhbltion Nursing Ctr....C....951 688-4321
8133 Magnolia Ave Riverside (92504) ***(P-20626)***
Magnolia Special Care Center....D....619 442-8826
635 S Magnolia Ave El Cajon (92020) ***(P-20438)***
Magnolia Ventures Ltd....D....213 389-6900
4032 Wilshire Blvd Fl 6 Los Angeles (90010) ***(P-16905)***
Magnum Drywall Inc....D....510 979-0420
42027 Boscell Rd Fremont (94538) ***(P-2815)***
Magnum USA, Van Nuys *Also called Hi-TEC Sports Usa Inc* ***(P-8134)***
Magnus Security....E....619 546-7789
2667 Camino Del Rio S San Diego (92108) ***(P-16348)***
Magnus Tech Solutions Inc....D....408 963-0808
5205 Prospect Rd Ste 135 San Jose (95129) ***(P-14924)***
Maguire Aviation, Van Nuys *Also called 16700 Roscoe Associates LLC* ***(P-18345)***
Maguire Aviation Group LLC....E....818 989-2300
7155 Valjean Ave Van Nuys (91406) ***(P-4744)***
Maguire Properties Twr 17 LLC....D....310 857-1100
1733 Ocean Ave Fl 4 Santa Monica (90401) ***(P-11864)***
Maher M F Concrete Cnstr, Vallejo *Also called M F Maher Inc* ***(P-1749)***
Mahony, John MD, San Pablo *Also called Brookside Community Health Ctr* ***(P-22193)***
MAI Systems, Lake Forest *Also called Infor (us) Inc* ***(P-15357)***
Maida Specialties Co, San Jose *Also called John A Maida Enterprises* ***(P-7859)***
Mail Boxes Etc, San Diego *Also called UPS Store Inc* ***(P-17139)***
Mailmark Enterprises LLC....E....818 407-0660
8587 Canoga Ave Canoga Park (91304) ***(P-13729)***
Main Electric Supply Co LLC (PA)....D....949 833-3052
3600 W Segerstrom Ave Santa Ana (92704) ***(P-7164)***
Main Electric Supply Co LLC....D....951 784-2900
461 Main St Riverside (92501) ***(P-7165)***

Main Frame Construction, Santa Clarita *Also called Santa Clarita Valley Bldrs Inc* ***(P-2975)***
Main Freight Sfo, South San Francisco *Also called Watchpoint Logistics Inc* ***(P-5082)***
Main Hospital, San Jose *Also called HCA Inc* ***(P-20901)***
Main Street Fibers Inc.......D.......909 986-6310
608 E Main St Ontario (91761) ***(P-6219)***
Main Street Specialty Surgery.......D.......714 704-1900
280 S Mn St Ste 100 Orange (92868) ***(P-21028)***
Mainfreight Inc (HQ).......D.......310 900-1974
1400 Glenn Curtiss St Carson (90746) ***(P-4989)***
Maintech Incorporated.......C.......714 921-8000
2401 N Glassell St Orange (92865) ***(P-14925)***
Maintenance, Long Beach *Also called Long Beach Unified School Dst* ***(P-13967)***
Maintenance & Operation Dept, Montebello *Also called Montebello Unified School* ***(P-13986)***
Maintenance & Operations, Lodi *Also called Lodi Unified School District* ***(P-13966)***
Maintenance & Trnsp Fcilty, Irvine *Also called Irvine Unified School Distict* ***(P-3816)***
Maintenance Department, Petaluma *Also called Transportation California Dept* ***(P-1802)***
Maintenance Department, Fresno *Also called Fresno Unified School District* ***(P-13931)***
Maintenance Dept, Gardena *Also called Los Angeles Unified School Dst* ***(P-13968)***
Maintenance Dept, Brea *Also called City of Brea* ***(P-26934)***
Maintenance Service For The Cy.......D.......510 865-3778
1616 Fortmann Way Alameda (94501) ***(P-13971)***
Maintenance Staff Inc.......A.......562 493-3982
122 W 8th St Long Beach (90813) ***(P-13972)***
Majestic Industry Hills LLC.......B.......626 810-4455
1 Industry Hills Pkwy City of Industry (91744) ***(P-12572)***
Majestic Terminal Services Inc.......D.......909 390-1210
9568 Archibald Ave # 100 Rancho Cucamonga (91730) ***(P-26683)***
Majesty One Properties Inc.......C.......909 980-8000
6249 Quartz St Rancho Cucamonga (91701) ***(P-11265)***
Major Transportation Svcs Inc.......E.......559 485-5949
3342 N Weber Ave Fresno (93722) ***(P-4085)***
Makallon La Jolla Properties, Newport Beach *Also called Makar Properties LLC* ***(P-11576)***
Makar Anaheim LLC.......A.......714 740-4431
777 W Convention Way Anaheim (92802) ***(P-12573)***
Makar Properties LLC (PA).......A.......949 255-1100
4100 Macarthur Blvd # 150 Newport Beach (92660) ***(P-11576)***
Maker Studios Inc (HQ).......C.......310 606-2182
3515 Eastham Dr Culver City (90232) ***(P-17991)***
Makita USA Inc (HQ).......C.......714 522-8088
14930 Northam St La Mirada (90638) ***(P-7400)***
Malaga Financial Corporation (PA).......D.......310 375-9000
2514 Via Tejon Palos Verdes Estates (90274) ***(P-9290)***
Malco Maintenance Inc.......D.......714 630-0194
3703 E Melville Way Anaheim (92806) ***(P-3432)***
Malco Services, Anaheim *Also called Malco Maintenance Inc* ***(P-3432)***
Malco Services Inc.......D.......714 630-0194
3703 E Melville Way Anaheim (92806) ***(P-26684)***
Malcolm & Cisneros A Law Corp.......C.......949 252-1039
2112 Business Center Dr # 100 Irvine (92612) ***(P-22672)***
Malcolm Cisneros, Irvine *Also called Malcolm & Cisneros A Law Corp* ***(P-22672)***
Malcolm Drilling Company Inc (PA).......C.......415 901-4400
92 Natoma St Ste 400 San Francisco (94105) ***(P-3433)***
Malibu Beach Inn, Malibu *Also called Mbipch LLC* ***(P-12604)***
Malibu Canyon Ldscp & Maint.......D.......805 523-2676
2046 Tierra Rejada Rd Moorpark (93021) ***(P-738)***
Malibu Castle, Aliso Viejo *Also called Apex Parks Group LLC* ***(P-18623)***
Malibu Castle.......E.......210 341-6663
27061 Aliso Creek Rd # 100 Aliso Viejo (92656) ***(P-18335)***
Malibu Conference Center Inc.......B.......818 889-6440
327 Latigo Canyon Rd Malibu (90265) ***(P-10618)***
Malibu Country Club, Malibu *Also called California Fuji International* ***(P-18226)***
Malibu Design Group.......E.......323 271-1700
5445 Jillson St Commerce (90040) ***(P-8091)***
Malibu Grand Prix 51, Redwood City *Also called Festival Fun Parks LLC* ***(P-18331)***
Malibu It Labs LLC.......D.......408 650-6100
1250 Borregas Ave Sunnyvale (94089) ***(P-26087)***
Malibu Lagoon Museum, Malibu *Also called Parks and Recreation Cal Dept* ***(P-24281)***
Malibu Limousine Service, Marina Del Rey *Also called Executive Network Entps Inc* ***(P-3670)***
Malibu Realty Inc.......E.......310 457-5124
22809 Pacific Coast Hwy Malibu (90265) ***(P-11266)***
Malibu Realty Property MGT, Malibu *Also called Malibu Realty Inc* ***(P-11266)***
Malikco LLC.......E.......925 974-3555
2121 N Calif Blvd Ste 290 Walnut Creek (94596) ***(P-15395)***
Malka Communications Group Inc.......E.......818 239-4431
15260 Ventura Blvd # 1200 Sherman Oaks (91403) ***(P-27288)***
Mallcraft Inc.......E.......626 765-9100
2225 Windsor Ave Altadena (91001) ***(P-1533)***
Malloy Orchards Inc.......C.......530 695-1861
925 Koch Ln Live Oak (95953) ***(P-210)***
Maloof Sport Entertainment, Sacramento *Also called Kings Arena Ltd Partnership* ***(P-18066)***
Malwarebytes Corporation.......A.......408 852-4336
3979 Freedom Cir Fl 12 Santa Clara (95054) ***(P-14926)***
Mamco Inc (PA).......C.......951 776-9300
764 Ramona Expy Ste C Perris (92571) ***(P-1751)***
Mammography Center, Lompoc *Also called Lompoc Valley Medical Center* ***(P-21016)***
MAMMOTH HOSPITAL, Mammoth Lakes *Also called Southern Mono Healthcare Dst* ***(P-21215)***
Mammoth Mountain Inn, Mammoth Lakes *Also called Mammoth Mountain Ski Area LLC* ***(P-12574)***
Mammoth Mountain Lake Corp.......B.......760 934-2571
10001 Minaret Rd Mammoth Lakes (93546) ***(P-13150)***
Mammoth Mountain Ski Area LLC (HQ).......B.......760 934-2571
10001 Minaret Rd Mammoth Lakes (93546) ***(P-12574)***
Mamone James M, Roseville *Also called Sutter Health* ***(P-21251)***
Managed Care Systems Kern Cnty.......D.......661 716-7100
5251 Office Park Dr # 405 Bakersfield (93309) ***(P-10412)***
Managed Health Network.......A.......714 934-5519
7755 Center Ave Ste 700 Huntington Beach (92647) ***(P-10017)***
Managed Health Network (HQ).......B.......415 460-8168
2370 Kerner Blvd San Rafael (94901) ***(P-10018)***
Managed Homecare Inc.......E.......951 341-0782
17682 Mitchell N Ste 100 Irvine (92614) ***(P-21807)***
Management Associates, Saint Helena *Also called Silverado Orchards* ***(P-10814)***
Management Success, Monrovia *Also called Leekilpatrick Management Inc* ***(P-26673)***
Management Tech Consulting LLC.......D.......323 851-5008
7738 Skyhill Dr Los Angeles (90068) ***(P-27123)***
Management Trust Assn Inc.......C.......805 496-5514
100 E Thousand Oaks Blvd Thousand Oaks (91360) ***(P-11800)***
Management Trust Assn Inc.......C.......858 547-4373
9815 Carroll Canyon Rd San Diego (92131) ***(P-11801)***
Management Trust Assn Inc.......C.......951 694-1758
4160 Temescal Canyon Rd # 202 Corona (92883) ***(P-11802)***
Management Trust Assn Inc (PA).......D.......714 285-2626
15661 Red Hill Ave # 201 Tustin (92780) ***(P-11803)***
Management Trust Assn Inc.......C.......562 926-3372
12607 Hiddencreek Way R Cerritos (90703) ***(P-26685)***
Management Trust, The, Tustin *Also called Management Trust Assn Inc* ***(P-11803)***
Manas Hospitality LLC.......E.......619 298-1291
445 Hotel Cir S San Diego (92108) ***(P-12575)***
Manatt Phelps & Phillips LLP.......E.......714 371-2500
695 Town Center Dr # 1400 Costa Mesa (92626) ***(P-22673)***
Manchester Band Pomo Indians.......D.......707 882-2788
24 Mamie Laiwa Dr Point Arena (95468) ***(P-23328)***
Manchester Center, Fresno *Also called US Property Group Inc* ***(P-10667)***
Manchester Grand Resorts LP.......A.......619 232-1234
1 Market Pl Fl 33 San Diego (92101) ***(P-12576)***
Manchester Point Arena, Point Arena *Also called Manchester Band Pomo Indians* ***(P-23328)***
Manchster Grnd Hyatt San Diego, San Diego *Also called Manchester Grand Resorts LP* ***(P-12576)***
Manchster Mnor Cnvlescent Hosp.......D.......323 753-1789
837 W Manchester Ave Los Angeles (90044) ***(P-20099)***
Mandalay Baseball Properties, Los Angeles *Also called Mandalay Sports Entrmt LLC* ***(P-18073)***
Mandalay Sports Entrmt LLC (PA).......D.......323 549-4300
4751 Wilshire Blvd Fl 3 Los Angeles (90010) ***(P-18073)***
Manduka LLC (HQ).......E.......310 426-1495
2121 Park Pl Ste 250 El Segundo (90245) ***(P-7715)***
Mangan Inc (PA).......D.......310 835-8080
3901 Via Oro Ave Long Beach (90810) ***(P-25202)***
Mangold Property Management.......D.......831 372-1338
575 Calle Principal Monterey (93940) ***(P-11267)***
Mangrove Lab & X-Ray, Chico *Also called Mangrove Medical Group* ***(P-19172)***
Mangrove Medical Group.......E.......530 345-0064
1040 Mangrove Ave Chico (95926) ***(P-19172)***
Manhattan Country Club, Manhattan Beach *Also called 1334 Partners LP* ***(P-18344)***
Manheim Riverside Auto Auction, Riverside *Also called Cox Automotive Inc* ***(P-6391)***
Manheim San Diego, Oceanside *Also called Cox Automotive Inc* ***(P-6392)***
Manhole Adjusting Contrs Inc.......E.......323 725-1387
9500 Beverly Rd Pico Rivera (90660) ***(P-1752)***
Maniflo Money Exchange Inc.......D.......619 434-7200
1442 Highland Ave National City (91950) ***(P-9440)***
Mann Lake Ltd.......E.......530 662-4061
500 Santa Anita Dr Woodland (95776) ***(P-8846)***
Mann Packing Co Inc (HQ).......B.......831 422-7405
1333 Schilling Pl Salinas (93901) ***(P-514)***
Mann Packing Co Inc.......D.......831 796-2670
1347 Harkins Rd Salinas (93901) ***(P-5095)***
Mann Packing Co Inc.......D.......831 245-0814
49 Katherine St Gonzales (93926) ***(P-5096)***
Mann Packing Pea Plant, Salinas *Also called Mann Packing Co Inc* ***(P-5095)***
Mann Theaters, Burbank *Also called WF Cinema Holdings LP* ***(P-17870)***
Mann's Theatres, Los Angeles *Also called Weststar Cinemas Inc* ***(P-17868)***
Manning Gardens Inc.......E.......559 834-2586
2113 E Manning Ave Fresno (93725) ***(P-20100)***
Manning Gardens Care Ctr Inc.......D.......559 834-2586
2113 E Manning Ave Fresno (93725) ***(P-20101)***
Manning Grdns Cnvalescent Hosp, Fresno *Also called Manning Gardens Inc* ***(P-20100)***
Manning Kass Ellrod Ram Trestr (PA).......C.......213 624-6900
801 S Figueroa St Fl 15 Los Angeles (90017) ***(P-22674)***
Manor At Santa Teresita Hosp, Duarte *Also called Santa Teresita Inc* ***(P-21168)***
Manor Bell L P.......D.......707 526-9782
790 Sonoma Ave Santa Rosa (95404) ***(P-1312)***
Manor Care, Fountain Valley *Also called Hcr Manorcare Med Svcs Fla LLC* ***(P-19998)***
Manor Care, Citrus Heights *Also called Hcr Manorcare Med Svcs Fla LLC* ***(P-19999)***
Manor Care, Sunnyvale *Also called Hcr Manorcare Med Svcs Fla LLC* ***(P-20001)***
Manor Care Sunnyvale Ca LLC.......D.......408 735-7200
1150 Tilton Dr Sunnyvale (94087) ***(P-20102)***
Manorcare Health Services, Walnut Creek *Also called Hcr Manorcare Med Svcs Fla LLC* ***(P-19997)***
Manorcare Health Svcs Hemet, Hemet *Also called Hcr Manorcare Med Svcs Fla LLC* ***(P-20000)***
Manorcare Health Svcs Rossmoor, Walnut Creek *Also called Hcr Manorcare Med Svcs Fla LLC* ***(P-20002)***
Manorcare Hlth Svcs Encinitas, Encinitas *Also called Hcr Manorcare Med Svcs Fla LLC* ***(P-20003)***
Manorcare Hlth Svcs Sunnyvale, Sunnyvale *Also called Manor Care Sunnyvale Ca LLC* ***(P-20102)***
Manpower, San Diego *Also called United States Dept of Navy* ***(P-14578)***
Manpower, San Diego *Also called CPM Ltd Inc* ***(P-14498)***
Mansion Hospitality Services.......D.......916 643-6222
3410 Westover St McClellan (95652) ***(P-26686)***

ALPHABETIC

Employee Codes: A=Over 500 employees, B=251-500
C=101-250, D=51-100, E=50
2020 Directory of California
Wholesalers and Services Companies
© Mergent Inc. 1-800-342-5647
1341

Manteca Care Rhabilitation Ctr, Manteca *Also called Karma Inc* ***(P-20039)***
Mantech International Corp ....C....858 492-9938
8328 Clairemont Mesa Blvd San Diego (92111) ***(P-15643)***
Mantech International Corp ....C....310 765-9324
615 N Nash St Ste 200 El Segundo (90245) ***(P-15644)***
Mantech Systems Engrg Corp ....D....858 292-9000
8328 Clairemont Mesa Blvd # 100 San Diego (92111) ***(P-27124)***
Manufacturers Bank (HQ) ....C....213 489-6200
515 S Figueroa St Fl 4 Los Angeles (90071) ***(P-9214)***
Manufacturing Facility, Davis *Also called Schilling Robotics LLC* ***(P-25299)***
MAOF, Montebello *Also called Mexican Amrcn Oprtnty Fndation* ***(P-23339)***
Maof Commerce, Commerce *Also called Mexican Amrcn Oprtnty Fndation* ***(P-23340)***
Map Cargo Global Logistics (PA) ....D....310 297-8300
2501 Santa Fe Ave Redondo Beach (90278) ***(P-4990)***
Map Energy LLC ....D....650 324-9095
3000 El Camino Real Palo Alto (94306) ***(P-9710)***
Maple Dairy LP ....D....661 396-9600
15857 Bear Mountain Blvd Bakersfield (93311) ***(P-400)***
Maplebear Inc (PA) ....D....888 246-7822
50 Beale St Ste 600 San Francisco (94105) ***(P-3909)***
Mapp Digital Us LLC ....C....619 295-1856
3655 Nobel Dr Ste 500 San Diego (92122) ***(P-26687)***
Mapr Data Technologies, Santa Clara *Also called Mapr Technologies Inc* ***(P-14927)***
Mapr Technologies Inc (PA) ....B....408 914-2390
4555 Great America Pkwy # 201 Santa Clara (95054) ***(P-14927)***
Mar-Kell Seal, Irvine *Also called Quadion LLC* ***(P-9842)***
Marathon Construction Corp ....D....619 276-4401
10108 Riverford Rd Lakeside (92040) ***(P-1973)***
Marathon General Inc ....D....760 738-9714
1728 Mission Rd Escondido (92029) ***(P-1753)***
Marathon Industries Inc ....C....661 286-1520
25597 Springbrook Ave Santa Clarita (91350) ***(P-6405)***
Marathon Land Inc (PA) ....C....805 488-3585
2599 E Hueneme Rd Oxnard (93033) ***(P-260)***
Marathon Staffing Solutions ....D....978 649-6230
2950 Beacon Blvd Ste 45 West Sacramento (95691) ***(P-14524)***
Marathon Truck Bodies, Santa Clarita *Also called Marathon Industries Inc* ***(P-6405)***
Maravilla Foundation (PA) ....D....323 721-4162
5729 Union Pacific Ave Commerce (90022) ***(P-24590)***
Marbella Country Club ....C....949 248-3700
30800 Golf Club Dr San Juan Capistrano (92675) ***(P-18496)***
Marbella Golf & Country Club ....C....949 248-3700
30800 Golf Club Dr San Juan Capistrano (92675) ***(P-18497)***
Marblewest Inc ....E....714 847-6472
7421 Vincent Cir Huntington Beach (92648) ***(P-2901)***
Marbleworks, Huntington Beach *Also called Marblewest Inc* ***(P-2901)***
Marborg Industries (PA) ....B....805 963-1852
728 E Yanonali St Santa Barbara (93103) ***(P-6220)***
March International Inc ....E....909 821-5128
1249 S Dmnd Bar Blvd 20 Diamond Bar (91765) ***(P-1974)***
Marchini Inc ....E....209 389-4566
12006 Le Grand Rd Le Grand (95333) ***(P-349)***
Marco Crane & Rigging Co ....D....619 938-8080
10168 Channel Rd Lakeside (92040) ***(P-14103)***
Marco Roofing, Fremont *Also called Milan Corporation* ***(P-3078)***
Marcolin USA Inc ....D....415 383-6348
6 Janet Way Apt 116 Belvedere Tiburon (94920) ***(P-7023)***
Marcos Auto Body Inc (PA) ....D....626 286-5691
1390 E Palm St Altadena (91001) ***(P-17298)***
Marcum LLP ....D....415 543-6900
303 2nd St Ste 950 San Francisco (94107) ***(P-25646)***
Marcum LLP ....D....310 432-7400
2049 Century Park E # 300 Los Angeles (90067) ***(P-25647)***
Marcus & Millichap Inc (PA) ....D....818 212-2250
23975 Park Sorrento # 400 Calabasas (91302) ***(P-11268)***
Marcus & Millichap Capitl Corp ....E....818 212-2250
23975 Park Sorrento # 400 Calabasas (91302) ***(P-11269)***
Marcus & Millichap Real Estate ....E....415 391-9220
750 Battery St Fl 5 San Francisco (94111) ***(P-11270)***
Marcus Buckingham Company ....D....323 302-9810
8350 Wilshire Blvd # 200 Beverly Hills (90211) ***(P-26688)***
Marcus Millichap Corp RE Svcs (HQ) ....D....650 391-1700
2626 Hanover St Palo Alto (94304) ***(P-11271)***
Marcus Millichap Reis Nev Inc ....D....650 494-1400
23975 Park Sorrento # 400 Calabasas (91302) ***(P-11272)***
Marcus Mllchap RE Inv Svcs Inc (HQ) ....E....818 212-2250
23975 Park Sorrento # 400 Calabasas (91302) ***(P-11273)***
Mardx Diagnostics Inc ....D....760 929-0500
5919 Farnsworth Ct Carlsbad (92008) ***(P-6975)***
Mare Island Outpatient Clinic, Vallejo *Also called Veterans Health Administration* ***(P-19555)***
Marelich Mechanical Co Inc (HQ) ....D....510 785-5500
24041 Amador St Hayward (94544) ***(P-2196)***
Margate Construction Inc ....C....310 830-8610
25007 Figueroa St Carson (90745) ***(P-1888)***
MARGUERITE GARDENS, La Canada Flintridge *Also called California Peo Home* ***(P-23847)***
Mariadb Usa Inc ....D....847 562-9000
350 Bay St Ste 100-319 San Francisco (94133) ***(P-6866)***
Mariak Industries Inc ....B....310 661-4400
575 W Manville St Rancho Dominguez (90220) ***(P-6570)***
Mariak Window Fashion, Rancho Dominguez *Also called Mariak Industries Inc* ***(P-6570)***
Marian Extended Care Cntr, Santa Maria *Also called Dignity Health* ***(P-19865)***
Marian Home Care and Hospice, Santa Maria *Also called Dignity Health* ***(P-21730)***
Marian Hospital Homecare, Arroyo Grande *Also called Dignity Health* ***(P-21729)***
Marian Regional Medical Center, Santa Maria *Also called Dignity Health* ***(P-20831)***
Marian West, Santa Maria *Also called Dignity Health* ***(P-20851)***
Mariani Nut Company Inc ....D....530 795-2225
12 Baker St Winters (95694) ***(P-178)***
Mariani Packing Co Inc (PA) ....B....707 452-2800
500 Crocker Dr Vacaville (95688) ***(P-515)***
Marianne Frostig Center (PA) ....E....626 791-1255
971 N Altadena Dr Pasadena (91107) ***(P-24410)***
Maricopa Packers, Bakersfield *Also called Sun Pacific Maricopa* ***(P-544)***
Marie Cllender Wholesalers Inc ....D....951 737-6760
170 E Rincon St Corona (92879) ***(P-8291)***
Marika Group Inc ....D....858 537-5300
8960 Carroll Way San Diego (92121) ***(P-8092)***
Marin Abused Women's Services, San Rafael *Also called Center For Domestic Peace* ***(P-22978)***
Marin Airporter Chrtr & Tours, San Rafael *Also called Marin Airporter Inc* ***(P-3561)***
Marin Airporter Inc (PA) ....D....415 256-8833
8 Lovell Ave San Rafael (94901) ***(P-3561)***
Marin City Library, Sausalito *Also called County of Marin* ***(P-23112)***
Marin Clean Energy ....D....415 464-6028
1125 Tamalpais Ave San Rafael (94901) ***(P-5856)***
Marin Cnvlscent Rhblttion Hosp ....D....415 435-4554
30 Hacienda Dr Belvedere Tiburon (94920) ***(P-20103)***
Marin Community Clinic ....D....415 448-1500
9 Commercial Blvd Ste 100 Novato (94949) ***(P-19173)***
Marin Community Clinics, Novato *Also called Marin Community Clinic* ***(P-19173)***
Marin Country Club Inc ....D....415 382-6700
500 Country Club Dr Novato (94949) ***(P-18498)***
Marin County Sart Program ....D....415 892-1628
655 Canyon Rd Novato (94947) ***(P-21419)***
Marin County Welfare Dept, San Rafael *Also called County of Marin* ***(P-23113)***
Marin General Hospital ....A....415 925-7000
250 Bon Air Rd Kentfield (94904) ***(P-21029)***
Marin Horizon School Inc ....E....415 388-8408
305 Montford Ave Mill Valley (94941) ***(P-23747)***
Marin Humane Society ....D....415 883-4621
171 Bel Marin Keys Blvd Novato (94949) ***(P-24847)***
Marin Industrial Distributors, San Rafael *Also called Jacksons Hardware Inc* ***(P-7395)***
Marin Labor Services ....C....805 525-7730
277 Country View Ct Santa Paula (93060) ***(P-632)***
Marin Municipal Water District (PA) ....C....415 945-1455
220 Nellen Ave Corte Madera (94925) ***(P-6083)***
Marin Resource Recovery Center, San Rafael *Also called Marin Sanitary Service* ***(P-6221)***
Marin Sanitary Service (PA) ....D....415 456-2601
1050 Andersen Dr San Rafael (94901) ***(P-6221)***
Marin Snior Crdnting Cncil Inc ....D....415 454-0964
930 Tamalpais Ave San Rafael (94901) ***(P-23329)***
Marin Software Incorporated (PA) ....C....415 399-2580
123 Mission St Fl 27 San Francisco (94105) ***(P-15786)***
Marina Auto Body Shop Inc ....E....310 822-6615
721 Washington Blvd Marina Del Rey (90292) ***(P-17299)***
Marina Autobody, Marina Del Rey *Also called Williamson Enterprises Inc* ***(P-17313)***
Marina Breeze, San Leandro *Also called Vasona Management Inc* ***(P-10833)***
Marina Care Center, Culver City *Also called D K Fortune & Associates Inc* ***(P-20544)***
Marina City Club LP A Cali ....C....310 822-0611
4333 Admiralty Way Marina Del Rey (90292) ***(P-10765)***
Marina Convalescent Center, Fremont *Also called C J Health Services Inc* ***(P-19768)***
Marina Inn, San Leandro *Also called Apple Inns Inc* ***(P-12014)***
Marina International Hotel, Venice *Also called Outrigger Hotels Hawaii* ***(P-12680)***
Marina International Hotel, Marina Del Rey *Also called Al Anwa USA Incorporated* ***(P-11997)***
Marina Landscape Maint Inc ....B....714 939-6600
1900 S Lewis St Anaheim (92805) ***(P-739)***
Marine Avenue Adult Center, Wilmington *Also called Los Angeles Unified School Dst* ***(P-23325)***
Marine Band San Diego ....E....619 524-1754
1400 Russell Ave San Diego (92140) ***(P-17992)***
Marine Corps United States ....A....760 725-1304
Camp Pendleton Oceanside (92055) ***(P-21485)***
Marine Corps United States ....E....760 430-4709
A St Bldg 1341 Camp Pendleton (92055) ***(P-12577)***
Marine Corps Community Svcs, San Diego *Also called Business and Support Services* ***(P-18637)***
MARINE FIREMENS UNION, San Francisco *Also called Pacific CST Mar Fireman Oilers* ***(P-24455)***
Marine Holding US Corp ....A....805 529-2000
6000 Condor Dr Moorpark (93021) ***(P-11931)***
Marine Mammal Center (PA) ....E....415 339-0430
2000 Bunker Rd Sausalito (94965) ***(P-580)***
Marine Room Restaurant, La Jolla *Also called La Jolla Bch & Tennis CLB Inc* ***(P-18477)***
Marine Technical Services Inc ....D....310 549-8030
211 N Marine Ave Wilmington (90744) ***(P-16906)***
Marine World/Africa USA, Vallejo *Also called City of Vallejo* ***(P-18326)***
Mariner, San Jose *Also called Health & Rehabilitation Center* ***(P-20004)***
Mariner LLC ....C....858 795-2100
11512 El Camino Real # 370 San Diego (92130) ***(P-26689)***
Mariner Health Care Inc ....D....310 371-4628
4109 Emerald St Torrance (90503) ***(P-20104)***
Mariner Health Care Inc ....C....510 792-3743
39022 Presidio Way Fremont (94538) ***(P-20105)***
Mariner Health Care Inc ....C....408 842-9311
8170 Murray Ave Gilroy (95020) ***(P-20106)***
Mariner Health Care Inc ....C....408 298-3950
2065 Forest Ave San Jose (95128) ***(P-20107)***
Mariner Health Care Inc ....C....916 422-4825
7400 24th St Sacramento (95822) ***(P-20108)***
Mariner Health Care Inc ....C....510 232-5945
13484 San Pablo Ave San Pablo (94806) ***(P-20109)***
Mariner Health Care Inc ....C....310 677-9114
100 S Hillcrest Blvd Inglewood (90301) ***(P-20110)***

Mariner Health Care Inc...D...323 665-1185
3032 Rowena Ave Los Angeles (90039) ***(P-20111)***
Mariner Health Care Inc...C...530 756-1800
1850 E 8th St Davis (95616) ***(P-20112)***
Mariner Health Care Inc...C...818 246-5677
430 N Glendale Ave Glendale (91206) ***(P-20113)***
Mariner Health Care Inc...D...831 475-6323
675 24th Ave Santa Cruz (95062) ***(P-20114)***
Mariner Health Care Inc...D...510 538-4424
1768 B St Hayward (94541) ***(P-20115)***
Mariner Health Care Inc...C...510 785-2880
19700 Hesperian Blvd Hayward (94541) ***(P-20116)***
Mariner Health Care Inc...D...562 942-7019
8925 Mines Ave Pico Rivera (90660) ***(P-20117)***
Mariner Health Care Inc...D...415 479-3610
45 Professional Ctr Pkwy San Rafael (94903) ***(P-20118)***
Mariner Health Care Inc...D...408 377-9275
2065 Los Gatos Almaden Rd San Jose (95124) ***(P-20119)***
Mariner Health Care Inc...D...510 261-5200
3025 High St Oakland (94619) ***(P-20120)***
Mariner Health Care Inc...C...209 466-2066
537 E Fulton St Stockton (95204) ***(P-20121)***
Mariner Health Care Inc...D...818 985-5990
13000 Victory Blvd North Hollywood (91606) ***(P-20122)***
Mariner Health Care Inc...D...818 957-0850
3050 Montrose Ave La Crescenta (91214) ***(P-20123)***
Mariner Health Care Inc...C...916 481-5500
3400 Alta Arden Expy Sacramento (95825) ***(P-20124)***
Mariner Square Athletic Inc...D...510 523-8011
2227 Mariner Square Loop Alameda (94501) ***(P-18174)***
Mariner Systems Inc (PA)...D...305 266-7255
114 C Ave Coronado (92118) ***(P-16907)***
Mariner Wealth Advisors, San Diego *Also called Mariner LLC* ***(P-26689)***
Mariner's Point Golf Course, Foster City *Also called Vb Golf LLC* ***(P-18310)***
Mariners Cove Apartments, San Diego *Also called Lincoln Mariners Assoc Ltd* ***(P-10757)***
Marines Memorial Association...C...415 673-6672
609 Sutter St San Francisco (94102) ***(P-24591)***
MARINES' MEMORIAL CLUB & HOTEL, San Francisco *Also called Marines Memorial Association* ***(P-24591)***
Marinow Harry MD Facs Inc...E...562 430-3561
3742 Katella Ave Ste 401 Los Alamitos (90720) ***(P-19174)***
Mariposa Horticultural Entps, Irwindale *Also called Mariposa Landscapes Inc* ***(P-865)***
Mariposa Landscapes Inc (PA)...D...626 960-0196
6232 Santos Diaz St Irwindale (91702) ***(P-865)***
Maritime Management...B...916 392-3000
2368 Maritime Dr Ste 100 Elk Grove (95758) ***(P-26307)***
Maritzcx Research LLC...D...310 783-4300
20285 S Wstn Ave Ste 101 Torrance (90501) ***(P-4856)***
Maritzcx Research LLC...A...310 525-1300
3901 Via Oro Ave Ste 200 Long Beach (90810) ***(P-25922)***
Mariz Berry Farms...C...805 981-9908
1650 E Gonzales Rd Oxnard (93036) ***(P-102)***
Mark & Fred Enterprises...C...714 821-1993
645 S Beach Blvd Anaheim (92804) ***(P-20125)***
Mark 1 Mortgage Corporation (PA)...E...714 752-5700
1342 E Chapman Ave Orange (92866) ***(P-9635)***
Mark Clemons...C...760 361-1531
4584 Adobe Rd Twentynine Palms (92277) ***(P-4086)***
Mark Diversified Inc...E...916 923-6275
650 Howe Ave Ste 1045 Sacramento (95825) ***(P-1534)***
Mark E Jacobson M D...D...707 571-4022
1260 N Dutton Ave Ste 230 Santa Rosa (95401) ***(P-19175)***
Mark Garcia...D...707 446-4529
5131 Ellsworth Rd Ste B Vacaville (95688) ***(P-13973)***
Mark H Leibenhaut MD...E...916 454-6600
2800 L St Ste 110 Sacramento (95816) ***(P-19176)***
Mark Herzog & Company Inc...D...818 762-4640
4640 Lankershim Blvd North Hollywood (91602) ***(P-17630)***
Mark III Construction Inc (PA)...D...916 381-8080
5101 Florin Perkins Rd Sacramento (95826) ***(P-2540)***
Mark III Dvlpers Dsgn/Builders, Sacramento *Also called Mark III Construction Inc* ***(P-2540)***
Mark Land Electric Inc...D...818 883-5110
7876 Deering Ave Canoga Park (91304) ***(P-2541)***
Mark One Corporation...E...209 537-4581
1711 Richland Ave Ceres (95307) ***(P-20627)***
Mark R Eggen Construction Inc...E...949 661-2674
34145 Pacific Coast Hwy # 325 Dana Point (92629) ***(P-1156)***
Mark Roberts, Santa Ana *Also called Celmol Inc* ***(P-8956)***
Mark Scott Construction Inc...D...209 982-0502
241 Frank West Cir # 200 Stockton (95206) ***(P-1259)***
Mark Scott Construction Inc (PA)...E...925 944-0502
2835 Contra Costa Blvd Pleasant Hill (94523) ***(P-1535)***
Mark Twain Conv. Hospital, San Andreas *Also called Avalon Care Center* ***(P-19733)***
Mark Twain Medical Center (HQ)...C...209 754-3521
768 Mountain Ranch Rd San Andreas (95249) ***(P-21030)***
Mark Twain Medical Center...B...209 754-1487
768 Mountain Ranch Rd San Andreas (95249) ***(P-21031)***
Mark Twain St Josephs Hospital, San Andreas *Also called Dignity Health* ***(P-20846)***
Mark Twain St Josephs Hospital, San Andreas *Also called Mark Twain Medical Center* ***(P-21030)***
Markel Corp...B...818 595-0600
21600 Oxnard St Ste 900 Woodland Hills (91367) ***(P-10413)***
Markel West Inc...E...818 595-0600
21600 Oxnard St Ste 400 Woodland Hills (91367) ***(P-10414)***
Marker Hotel, The, San Francisco *Also called Geary Darling Lessee Inc* ***(P-12291)***
Market Centre, Livermore *Also called Unified Grocers Inc* ***(P-8274)***
Market Hall Foods, Oakland *Also called Pasta Shop* ***(P-8626)***

Market Scan Info Systems Inc (PA)...C...805 823-4258
815b Camarillo Springs Rd Camarillo (93012) ***(P-14928)***
Market Tech Media Corporation...D...661 257-4745
27220 Turnberry Ln # 190 Valencia (91355) ***(P-13790)***
Marketbridge Corp...D...240 752-1800
601 Montgomery St Ste 650 San Francisco (94111) ***(P-26690)***
Marketing Department, San Francisco *Also called Morrison & Foerster LLP* ***(P-22708)***
Marketing Professionals Inc...B...714 578-0500
5100 E La Palma Ave # 116 Anaheim (92807) ***(P-26691)***
Marketing Sales & Dist Div, Fontana *Also called Weyerhaeuser Company* ***(P-6667)***
Marketo Inc (HQ)...C...650 376-2300
901 Mariners Island Blvd # 200 San Mateo (94404) ***(P-14929)***
Marketwatch Inc (HQ)...D...415 439-6400
201 California St Fl 13 San Francisco (94111) ***(P-16574)***
Marketwire Inc (HQ)...D...310 765-3200
100 N Pacific Coast Hwy El Segundo (90245) ***(P-16575)***
Marklogic Corporation (PA)...C...650 655-2300
999 Skyway Rd Ste 200 San Carlos (94070) ***(P-14930)***
Markmonitor Holdings Inc...B...415 278-8400
425 Market St Ste 500 San Francisco (94105) ***(P-14931)***
Markmonitor Inc (HQ)...D...415 278-8400
50 California St Ste 200 San Francisco (94111) ***(P-16054)***
Markstein Bev Co Sacramento...C...916 920-3911
60 Main Ave Sacramento (95838) ***(P-8776)***
Markstein Beverage Co...C...760 744-9100
505 S Pacific St San Marcos (92078) ***(P-8777)***
Markstein Beverage Company, Sacramento *Also called Markstein Bev Co Sacramento* ***(P-8776)***
Marksys LLC...D...916 745-4883
3725 Cincinnati Ave # 200 Rocklin (95765) ***(P-26692)***
Marksys Holdings LLC...D...916 745-4883
3725 Cincinnati Ave # 200 Rocklin (95765) ***(P-26693)***
Markwins Beauty Products Inc...D...909 595-8898
22067 Ferrero City of Industry (91789) ***(P-7959)***
Markwins International Corp (PA)...C...909 595-8898
22067 Ferrero Walnut (91789) ***(P-7960)***
Marland Co LP...E...213 614-6171
444 S Flower St Ste 1200 Los Angeles (90071) ***(P-192)***
Marlin Alliance Inc...D...619 450-1717
3990 Old Town Ave Ste A San Diego (92110) ***(P-27125)***
Marlin Equity Partners LLC (PA)...D...310 364-0100
338 Pier Ave Hermosa Beach (90254) ***(P-9830)***
Marlin Equity Partners III LP (PA)...C...310 364-0100
338 Pier Ave Hermosa Beach (90254) ***(P-11932)***
Marlinda Imperial Hospital, Pasadena *Also called Two Palms Nursing Center Inc* ***(P-20704)***
Marlinda Management Inc (PA)...C...310 631-6122
3351 E Imperial Hwy Lynwood (90262) ***(P-20628)***
Marlora Investments LLC...D...562 494-3311
3801 E Anaheim St Long Beach (90804) ***(P-20126)***
MARLORA POST ACCUTE REHABILITAT, Long Beach *Also called Marlora Investments LLC* ***(P-20126)***
Marmalade LLC...E...310 317-4242
3894 Cross Creek Rd Malibu (90265) ***(P-16908)***
Marmalade Cafes, Malibu *Also called Marmalade LLC* ***(P-16908)***
Marmol Radziner...D...310 826-6222
12210 Nebraska Ave Los Angeles (90025) ***(P-25481)***
Marna Health Services Inc...D...909 882-2965
4280 Cypress Dr San Bernardino (92407) ***(P-20629)***
Marne Construction Inc...D...714 935-0995
749 N Poplar St Orange (92868) ***(P-3178)***
Maroevich OShea & Coghlan...D...415 957-0600
44 Montgomery St Ste 1700 San Francisco (94104) ***(P-10415)***
Marquee Fire Protection (PA)...D...916 641-7997
710 W Stadium Ln Sacramento (95834) ***(P-2197)***
Marques Pipeline Inc...E...916 923-3434
7225 26th St Sacramento (95834) ***(P-25203)***
Marquez Brothers Advg Agcy...D...408 960-2700
5801 Rue Ferrari San Jose (95138) ***(P-16909)***
Marquez Brothers Entps Inc...C...626 330-3310
15480 Valley Blvd City of Industry (91746) ***(P-8187)***
Marquez Brothers Intl Inc (PA)...C...408 960-2700
5801 Rue Ferrari San Jose (95138) ***(P-8188)***
Marquez Brothers Intl Inc...D...323 722-8103
1329 W Olympic Blvd Montebello (90640) ***(P-8189)***
Marquez Brothers Intl Inc...C...559 584-8000
179 S 11th Ave Hanford (93230) ***(P-8190)***
Marrakesh Management Corp...E...760 568-2688
47000 Marrakesh Dr Palm Desert (92260) ***(P-11274)***
Marriot Courtyard...E...415 775-1103
580 Beach St San Francisco (94133) ***(P-12578)***
Marriott, Riverside *Also called Sunstone Hotel Management Inc* ***(P-12999)***
Marriott, Los Angeles *Also called Renaissance Hotel MGT Co LLC* ***(P-12803)***
Marriott, San Diego *Also called Host Hotels & Resorts LP* ***(P-12387)***
Marriott, Santa Monica *Also called Cwgp Limited Partnership* ***(P-12196)***
Marriott, San Jose *Also called Host International Inc* ***(P-12399)***
Marriott, San Diego *Also called Hhlp San Diego Lessee LLC* ***(P-12349)***
Marriott, Visalia *Also called Welcome Group Management LLC* ***(P-13081)***
Marriott, Pleasanton *Also called Pleasanton Project Owner LLC* ***(P-12762)***
Marriott, Newport Beach *Also called Wj Newport LLC* ***(P-13110)***
Marriott, NAPA *Also called Sunstone Hotel Investors LLC* ***(P-12995)***
Marriott, Oakland *Also called Oakland Renaissance Associates* ***(P-12657)***
Marriott, Burbank *Also called Shc Burbank II LLC* ***(P-12910)***
Marriott, Newport Beach *Also called Host Hotels & Resorts LP* ***(P-12395)***
Marriott, Lake Arrowhead *Also called Lake Arrwhead Rsort Oprtor Inc* ***(P-12533)***
Marriott, Santa Monica *Also called Windsor Capital Group Inc* ***(P-13103)***
Marriott, Fullerton *Also called Merritt Hospitality LLC* ***(P-12612)***

A L P H A B E T I C

Marriott, Walnut Creek *Also called Zks Real Estate Partners LLC (P-13134)*
Marriott, Woodland Hills *Also called HEI Hospitality LLC (P-12345)*
Marriott, San Francisco *Also called Renaissance Hotel MGT Co LLC (P-12805)*
Marriott, Baldwin Park *Also called Ols Hotels & Resorts LLC (P-12669)*
Marriott, Pleasanton *Also called Pyramid Advisors Ltd Partnr (P-12775)*
Marriott, Manhattan Beach *Also called Host Hotels & Resorts LP (P-12397)*
Marriott, Marina Del Rey *Also called Host Hotels & Resorts LP (P-12398)*
Marriott, Riverside *Also called Windsor Capital Group Inc (P-13109)*
Marriott Burbank, Burbank *Also called AWH Burbank Hotel LLC (P-12028)*
Marriott Burbank, Burbank *Also called Spire Concessions LLC (P-12953)*
Marriott Fisherman's Wharf, San Francisco *Also called Host Hotels & Resorts Inc (P-12384)*
Marriott Foundation For People ....D......510 834-4700
  344 Thomas L Berkley Way Oakland (94612) *(P-23612)*
Marriott Grand Residence ....B......530 542-8400
  1001 Heavenly Village Way South Lake Tahoe (96150) *(P-12579)*
Marriott International Inc ....C......760 431-9399
  5835 Owens Ave Carlsbad (92008) *(P-12580)*
Marriott International Inc ....C......714 209-6586
  4381 Myra Ave Cypress (90630) *(P-12581)*
Marriott International Inc ....C......858 523-1700
  11966 El Camino Real San Diego (92130) *(P-12582)*
Marriott International Inc ....A......310 641-5700
  5855 W Century Blvd Los Angeles (90045) *(P-12583)*
Marriott International Inc ....D......415 947-0700
  299 2nd St San Francisco (94105) *(P-12584)*
Marriott International Inc ....D......619 831-0225
  900 Bayfront Ct San Diego (92101) *(P-12585)*
Marriott International Inc ....C......510 413-3700
  46100 Landing Pkwy Fremont (94538) *(P-12586)*
Marriott International Inc ....B......949 724-3606
  18000 Von Karman Ave Irvine (92612) *(P-12587)*
Marriott International Inc ....B......858 587-1414
  4240 La Jolla Village Dr La Jolla (92037) *(P-12588)*
Marriott International Inc ....C......831 649-4234
  350 Calle Principal Monterey (93940) *(P-12589)*
Marriott International Inc ....C......562 425-5210
  4700 Airport Plaza Dr Long Beach (90815) *(P-12590)*
Marriott International Inc ....C......310 725-9696
  14400 Aviation Blvd Hawthorne (90250) *(P-12591)*
Marriott International Inc ....C......510 657-4600
  39802 Cedar Blvd Newark (94560) *(P-12592)*
Marriott International Inc ....C......707 935-6600
  1325 Broadway Sonoma (95476) *(P-12593)*
Marriott International Inc ....C......714 545-5261
  3130 S Harbor Blvd # 500 Santa Ana (92704) *(P-12594)*
Marriott International Inc ....C......213 284-3862
  900 W Olympic Blvd Los Angeles (90015) *(P-12595)*
Marriott International Inc ....C......650 692-9100
  1800 Old Bayshore Hwy Burlingame (94010) *(P-12596)*
Marriott International Inc ....D......619 831-0224
  900 Bayfront Ct San Diego (92101) *(P-12597)*
Marriott Los Angeles Downtown, Los Angeles *Also called Interstate Hotels Resorts Inc (P-12472)*
Marriott Rsrts Hspitality Corp 760 779-1200
  1091 Pinehurst Ln Palm Desert (92260) *(P-12598)*
Marriott San Dego Gslamp Qrter, San Diego *Also called San Diego Hotel Company LLC (P-12870)*
Marriott Vacation Club Pulse, San Francisco *Also called PHF Ruby LLC (P-12751)*
Marriotts Newport Coast Villa ....D......949 464-6000
  23000 Newport Coast Dr Newport Beach (92657) *(P-12599)*
Marriotts Shadow Ridge ....D......760 674-2600
  9003 Shadow Ridge Rd Palm Desert (92211) *(P-12600)*
Marrow Meadows, Walnut *Also called M & R Joint Venture Electrical (P-2539)*
Marsh & McLennan Agency LLC ....D......949 544-8460
  1 Polaris Way Ste 300 Aliso Viejo (92656) *(P-10416)*
Marsh & McLennan Agency LLC ....D......415 243-4160
  201 California St Ste 900 San Francisco (94111) *(P-10417)*
Marsh & McLennan Agency LLC ....D......858 457-3414
  9171 Towne Centre Dr # 500 San Diego (92122) *(P-10418)*
Marsh & McLennan Companies Inc ....D......213 346-5555
  777 S Figueroa St # 2200 Los Angeles (90017) *(P-10419)*
Marsh Consulting Group ....D......239 433-5500
  2626 Summer Ranch Rd Paso Robles (93446) *(P-16910)*
Marsh USA Inc ....D......415 743-8000
  345 California St # 1300 San Francisco (94104) *(P-10420)*
Marsh USA Inc ....D......408 467-5600
  1735 Tech Dr Ste 790 San Jose (95110) *(P-10421)*
Marshall Hospital, Placerville *Also called Marshall Medical Center (P-21033)*
Marshall Medical Center ....C......916 933-2273
  1100 Marshall Way El Dorado Hills (95762) *(P-21032)*
Marshall Medical Center (PA) ....A......530 622-1441
  1100 Marshall Way Placerville (95667) *(P-21033)*
Marshall S Ezralow & Assoc, Calabasas *Also called M S E Enterprises Inc (P-11262)*
Marshall, Spector MD, San Gabriel *Also called Facey Medical Foundation (P-22245)*
Martech Medical Products Inc ....D......215 256-8833
  565 Clara Nofal Rd Calexico (92231) *(P-19177)*
Marthas Village & Kitchen ....D......760 347-4741
  83791 Date Ave Indio (92201) *(P-23330)*
Marticus Electric Inc ....D......916 368-2186
  9266 Beatty Dr Ste D Sacramento (95826) *(P-2542)*
Martin AC Partners Inc ....C......213 683-1900
  444 S Flower St Ste 1200 Los Angeles (90071) *(P-25482)*
Martin Associates Group Inc (PA) ....D......213 483-6490
  950 S Grand Ave Fl 4 Los Angeles (90015) *(P-25204)*
Martin ATI-AC Inc (PA) ....D......925 648-8800
  4750 Willow Rd Ste 250 Pleasanton (94588) *(P-25483)*

Martin Bros/Marcowall Inc (PA) ....C......310 532-5335
  17104 S Figueroa St Gardena (90248) *(P-2816)*
Martin Brothers Construction (PA) ....D......916 386-1600
  8801 Folsom Blvd Ste 260 Sacramento (95826) *(P-1754)*
MARTIN DE PORRES HOUSE, San Francisco *Also called MD P Foundation Inc (P-23332)*
Martin Integrated Systems ....D......714 998-9100
  2330 N Pacific St Orange (92865) *(P-2817)*
Martin Lther King/Drew Med Ctr ....D......310 773-4926
  1670 E 120th St Los Angeles (90059) *(P-19178)*
Martin Lthr Kng Chldr Ctr, Pittsburg *Also called State Preschool (P-23791)*
Martin Resorts Inc (PA) ....B......805 545-7900
  1201 Palm St San Luis Obispo (93408) *(P-12601)*
Martin, John A & Associates, Los Angeles *Also called Martin Associates Group Inc (P-25204)*
Martin-Brower Company LLC ....C......209 466-2980
  4704 Fite Ct Stockton (95215) *(P-8191)*
Martina Landscape Inc ....D......408 871-8800
  811 Camden Ave Campbell (95008) *(P-866)*
Martinez Farms Inc ....B......619 661-6571
  2433 Cactus Rd San Diego (92154) *(P-261)*
Martinez Medical Offices, Martinez *Also called Kaiser Foundation Hospitals (P-11793)*
Martis Camp Club ....B......530 550-6000
  7951 Fleur Du Lac Ct Truckee (96161) *(P-23331)*
Martrac, Fresno *Also called UPS Ground Freight Inc (P-4151)*
Marty Franich Leasing Co ....E......831 724-2463
  555 Auto Center Dr Watsonville (95076) *(P-17229)*
Marty's Cutting Service, Vernon *Also called Martys Cutting Inc (P-16911)*
Martys Cutting Inc ....D......323 582-5758
  2615 Fruitland Ave Vernon (90058) *(P-16911)*
Maruchan Inc ....D......949 789-2300
  15800 Laguna Canyon Rd Irvine (92618) *(P-4447)*
Marwit Capital Partners II LP (PA) ....B......949 861-3636
  24 Corporate Plaza Dr # 100 Newport Beach (92660) *(P-9506)*
Mary and Friends ....C......562 691-1575
  1101 Farrington Dr La Habra (90631) *(P-23984)*
Mary Grahams Childrens Shelter, French Camp *Also called County of San Joaquin (P-23154)*
Mary Hlth SCK Cnvlscnt &NRsng ....D......805 498-3644
  2929 Theresa Dr Newbury Park (91320) *(P-20127)*
Marycrest Manor ....D......310 838-2778
  10664 Saint James Dr Culver City (90230) *(P-20630)*
Marymount Villa LLC ....D......510 895-5007
  345 Davis St Ofc San Leandro (94577) *(P-20439)*
MARYSVILLE CARE CENTER, Marysville *Also called Marysvlle Nrsing Rehab Ctr LLC (P-20128)*
Marysville Post-Acute, Marysville *Also called Melon Holdings LLC (P-20135)*
Marysvlle Nrsing Rehab Ctr LLC ....D......530 742-7311
  1617 Ramirez St Marysville (95901) *(P-20128)*
Maryvale ....D......626 280-6510
  7600 Graves Ave Rosemead (91770) *(P-23985)*
Maryvale Day Care Center ....C......626 357-1514
  2502 Huntington Dr Duarte (91010) *(P-23748)*
Maryvale Day Care Center (PA) ....D......626 280-6511
  7600 Graves Ave Rosemead (91770) *(P-23749)*
Maryvale Edcatn Fmly Rsrce Ctr, Duarte *Also called Maryvale Day Care Center (P-23748)*
MARYVALE EDUCATIONAL DAY CARE, Rosemead *Also called Maryvale Day Care Center (P-23749)*
Masa's, San Francisco *Also called San Francisco Hotel Associates (P-12873)*
MASADA HOMES, Gardena *Also called Counseling and Research Assoc (P-23874)*
Masada Homes Foster Fmly Agcy, Lancaster *Also called Counseling and Research Assoc (P-23875)*
Masco, San Jose *Also called Topbuild Services Group Corp (P-3479)*
Mashburn Trnsp Svcs Inc ....C......661 763-5724
  1423 Kern St Taft (93268) *(P-4087)*
Masker Painting, Oakland *Also called George E Masker Inc (P-2352)*
Mason McDuffie Mortgage Corp (PA) ....D......925 242-4400
  2010 Crow Canyon Pl # 400 San Ramon (94583) *(P-9579)*
Mason Street Opco LLC ....A......415 772-5000
  950 Mason St San Francisco (94108) *(P-12602)*
Mason-Mcduffie Real Estate Inc ....D......510 705-8611
  2095 Rose St Ste 100 Berkeley (94709) *(P-11275)*
Mason-Mcduffie Real Estate Inc ....D......925 932-1000
  2051 Mt Diablo Blvd Walnut Creek (94596) *(P-11276)*
Mason-Mcduffie Real Estate Inc ....D......925 776-2740
  5887 Lone Tree Way Ste A Antioch (94531) *(P-11277)*
Mason-Mcduffie Real Estate Inc ....E......510 886-7511
  21060 Redwood Rd Ste 100 Castro Valley (94546) *(P-11278)*
Mason-Mcduffie Real Estate Inc ....D......510 834-2010
  3320 Grand Ave Oakland (94610) *(P-11279)*
Mason-Mcduffie Real Estate Inc ....D......925 734-5000
  5950 Stoneridge Dr Pleasanton (94588) *(P-11280)*
Mason-West Inc ....E......619 226-8253
  3910 Chapman St Ste D San Diego (92110) *(P-7560)*
Masonic Home For Adults, Union City *Also called Masonic Homes of California (P-23987)*
Masonic Homes of California (PA) ....B......415 776-7000
  1111 California St San Francisco (94108) *(P-23986)*
Masonic Homes of California ....B......510 441-3700
  34400 Mission Blvd Union City (94587) *(P-23987)*
Masonic Homes of California ....D......626 251-2200
  3823 N Reeder Ave Covina (91724) *(P-23988)*
Masonry Concepts Inc ....D......562 802-3700
  15408 Cornet St Santa Fe Springs (90670) *(P-2721)*
Mass Electric Construction Co ....D......800 933-6322
  1925 Wright Ave Ste D La Verne (91750) *(P-2543)*
Massachusetts Mutl Lf Insur Co ....D......323 965-6339
  8383 Wilshire Blvd # 600 Beverly Hills (90211) *(P-9870)*

Massage Place .... C 310 204-3004
2516 Overland Ave Los Angeles (90064) *(P-13437)*
Massdrop Inc (PA) .... D 415 340-2999
710 Sansome St San Francisco (94111) *(P-16912)*
Massmutual, Beverly Hills *Also called Massachusetts Mutl Lf Insur Co (P-9870)*
Massnexus, Studio City *Also called Dpr Holdings LLC (P-11657)*
Massolo Trucking LLC (PA) .... E 831 424-7205
18765 Gould Rd Salinas (93908) *(P-3910)*
Master Clean USA Inc .... E 805 681-0950
5511 Ekwill St Ste D Santa Barbara (93111) *(P-13974)*
Master Design Drywall Inc .... C 760 480-9001
360 S Spruce St Escondido (92025) *(P-2818)*
Master Disposal Co .... E 626 444-6789
1980 S Reservoir St Pomona (91766) *(P-6222)*
Master Drywall Inc .... C 707 448-8659
6727 Bucktown Ln Vacaville (95688) *(P-2819)*
Master Rent, Fresno *Also called Automatic Leasing Inc (P-13245)*
Master Roofing Systems Inc .... D 415 407-4450
52 S Linden Ave Ste 5 South San Francisco (94080) *(P-3074)*
Master-Chef's Linen Rental, Los Angeles *Also called American Textile Maint Co (P-13198)*
Mastroianni Family Entps Ltd. .... D 310 952-1700
10581 Garden Grove Blvd Garden Grove (92843) *(P-13438)*
Masudas Landscape Services .... D 408 379-7100
423 Salmar Ave Campbell (95008) *(P-740)*
Mat Express, San Diego *Also called MAT Parcel Express Inc (P-3911)*
MAT Parcel Express Inc (PA) .... D 619 849-9600
2719 Kurtz St Ste C San Diego (92110) *(P-3911)*
Matagrano Inc .... D 650 829-4829
440 Forbes Blvd South San Francisco (94080) *(P-8778)*
Matched Care Gvrs Cntns Care, Atherton *Also called Matched Caregivers Inc (P-21808)*
Matched Caregivers Inc .... C 408 560-2382
95 Wilburn Ave Atherton (94027) *(P-21808)*
Mater Misericordiae Hospital (PA) .... A 209 564-5000
333 Mercy Ave Merced (95340) *(P-21034)*
Material Handling Supply Inc (HQ) .... D 562 921-7715
12900 Firestone Blvd Santa Fe Springs (90670) *(P-7561)*
Material Transport, Sacramento *Also called Pacific Coast Trnsp Svcs Inc (P-5132)*
Materials Marketing .... D 949 729-9881
250 Baker St Ste 100 Costa Mesa (92626) *(P-26694)*
Matesta Corporation .... C 949 874-6052
5620 Knott Ave Buena Park (90621) *(P-8093)*
Matheny Sars Linkert Jaime LLP .... D 916 978-3434
3638 American River Dr Sacramento (95864) *(P-22675)*
Mather Aviation LLC (PA) .... D 916 364-4711
10360 Macready Ave Mather (95655) *(P-4780)*
Matheson Fast Freight Inc .... D 209 342-0184
9785 Goethe Rd Sacramento (95827) *(P-4088)*
Matheson Fast Freight Inc (HQ) .... D 916 686-4600
9780 Dino Dr Elk Grove (95624) *(P-4089)*
Matheson Trucking Inc (HQ) .... E 916 685-2330
9785 Goethe Rd Sacramento (95827) *(P-4090)*
Matich Corporation (PA) .... D 909 382-7400
1596 E Harry Shepard Blvd San Bernardino (92408) *(P-1755)*
Matich Corporation .... E 951 849-8280
13984 Apache Trl Cabazon (92230) *(P-1756)*
Matrix Aviation Services Inc .... C 310 337-3037
6171 W Century Blvd Ste 1 Los Angeles (90045) *(P-4877)*
Matrix Environmental Inc .... D 562 236-2704
2330 Cherry Indus Cir Long Beach (90805) *(P-3434)*
Matrix Group International Inc. .... D 626 960-6205
1520 W Cameron Ave West Covina (91790) *(P-1157)*
Matrix Industries Inc .... B 562 236-2700
2330 E Cherry Indus Cir Long Beach (90805) *(P-3435)*
Matrix Resources Inc. .... D 415 644-0642
1 Embarcadero Ctr Ste 500 San Francisco (94111) *(P-14330)*
Matrix Surfaces Inc .... D 714 696-5449
5449 E La Palma Ave Anaheim (92807) *(P-2902)*
Matson Alarm Co Inc (PA) .... E 559 438-8000
581 W Fallbrook Ave # 100 Fresno (93711) *(P-2544)*
Matson Navigation Company Inc (HQ) .... C 510 628-4000
555 12th St Fl 7 Oakland (94607) *(P-4587)*
Matsui Nursery Inc (PA) .... D 831 422-6433
1645 Old Stage Rd Salinas (93908) *(P-262)*
Matsushita International Corp (PA) .... D 949 498-1000
1141 Via Callejon San Clemente (92673) *(P-11933)*
Matt Construction Corporation (PA) .... C 562 903-2277
9814 Norwalk Blvd Ste 100 Santa Fe Springs (90670) *(P-26695)*
Matt-Colombo A Joint Venture .... D 562 903-2277
9814 Norwalk Blvd Ste 100 Santa Fe Springs (90670) *(P-1536)*
Matterport Inc (PA) .... C 888 993-8990
352 E Java Dr Sunnyvale (94089) *(P-6867)*
Matthew Burns .... D 209 676-4940
617 Flower St Folsom (95630) *(P-1537)*
Matthews International Corp .... E 951 654-9123
580 S State St Ste 8 San Jacinto (92583) *(P-17517)*
Matthews Real Estate Inv Svcs, El Segundo *Also called Matthews Retail Group Inc (P-11231)*
Matthews Retail Group Inc .... D 866 889-0550
841 Apollo St Ste 150 El Segundo (90245) *(P-11281)*
Mattress Liqidation, Rancho Cucamonga *Also called Hibshman Trading Corporation (P-8076)*
Matus International Inc .... C 562 435-5200
1120 De Forest Ave Long Beach (90813) *(P-4991)*
Maud Booth Family Center, North Hollywood *Also called Volunteers of Amer Los Angeles (P-23537)*
Maverick Hotel Partners LLC .... B 415 655-9526
50 California St San Francisco (94111) *(P-26308)*

Max Group Corporation (PA) .... D 626 935-0050
17011 Green Dr City of Industry (91745) *(P-6868)*
Max Leather .... E 310 841-6990
8533 Washington Blvd Culver City (90232) *(P-8987)*
Max Mri Imaging Inc (PA) .... E 818 382-2220
17530 Ventura Blvd # 105 Encino (91316) *(P-21552)*
Max Sommers Real Estate .... D 310 560-1499
615 Esplanade Unit 312 Redondo Beach (90277) *(P-11282)*
Max Sportsters Inc .... E 408 446-8330
10050 N Foothill Blvd # 200 Cupertino (95014) *(P-26309)*
Max/Mr Imaging Inc .... D 818 382-2220
17530 Ventura Blvd # 105 Encino (91316) *(P-21553)*
Maxco Supply Inc (PA) .... C 559 646-8449
605 S Zediker Ave Parlier (93648) *(P-7883)*
Maxco Supply Inc .... D 559 646-6700
8419 Di Giorgio Rd Lamont (93241) *(P-7884)*
Maxgen Energy Services Corp (HQ) .... D 714 908-5266
1690 Scenic Ave Costa Mesa (92626) *(P-6003)*
Maxim Crane Works LP .... C 209 464-7635
2373 S Mariposa Rd Stockton (95205) *(P-14104)*
Maxim Healthcare Services Inc .... C 408 914-7478
631 River Oaks Pkwy San Jose (95134) *(P-14525)*
Maxim Healthcare Services Inc .... A 805 278-4593
500 E Esplanade Dr Oxnard (93036) *(P-21809)*
Maxim Healthcare Services Inc .... E 866 465-5678
3580 Wilshire Blvd # 1000 Los Angeles (90010) *(P-14526)*
Maxim Healthcare Services Inc .... C 323 937-9410
4221 Wilshire Blvd # 130 Los Angeles (90010) *(P-21810)*
Maxim Healthcare Services Inc .... B 951 684-4148
1845 Bus Ctr Dr Ste 112 San Bernardino (92408) *(P-14527)*
Maxim Lighting .... C 626 956-4200
253 Vineland Ave City of Industry (91746) *(P-7166)*
Maxim Planning Group .... D 818 425-4343
1214 E Colorado Blvd Pasadena (91106) *(P-27126)*
Maxim Services Ltd Inc .... D 925 969-1907
2470 Estand Way Pleasant Hill (94523) *(P-13975)*
Maximum Fitness LLC .... E 707 447-0606
135 Dobbins St Vacaville (95688) *(P-18175)*
Maximus Inc .... D 916 673-2175
625 Coolidge Dr Ste 100 Folsom (95630) *(P-26696)*
Maximus Inc .... D 916 364-6610
11050 Olson Dr Ste 100 Rancho Cordova (95670) *(P-21811)*
Maximus CA Healthy Family, Folsom *Also called Maximus Inc (P-26696)*
Maximus Holdings Inc .... A 650 935-9500
2475 Hanover St Palo Alto (94304) *(P-15396)*
Maximus Real Estate Partners .... D 415 584-4832
1 Maritime Plz Ste 1900 San Francisco (94111) *(P-10878)*
Maxon Lift Corporation .... C 562 464-0099
11921 Slauson Ave Santa Fe Springs (90670) *(P-7562)*
Maxonic Inc .... D 408 739-4900
2542 S Bascom Ave Ste 190 Campbell (95008) *(P-16055)*
Maxplore Technologies Inc .... D 925 621-1400
4450 Rosewood Dr Ste 200 Pleasanton (94588) *(P-14932)*
Maxson Young Assoc Inc .... C 415 228-6400
180 Montgomery St # 2100 San Francisco (94104) *(P-10422)*
Maxus USA, Los Angeles *Also called Essense (P-27273)*
Maxwell Hotel, The, San Francisco *Also called Joie De Vivre Hospitality LLC (P-26276)*
Maxwell Petersen Associates .... E 714 230-3150
13950 Milton Ave Ste 200 Westminster (92683) *(P-26697)*
Maxx Metals Inc .... D 650 654-1500
355 Quarry Rd San Carlos (94070) *(P-7079)*
Maxzone Vehicle Lighting Corp (HQ) .... E 909 822-3288
15889 Slover Ave Unit A Fontana (92337) *(P-6452)*
May-Han Electric Inc. .... D 916 929-0150
1600 Auburn Blvd Sacramento (95815) *(P-2545)*
Mayacama Golf Club LLC .... C 707 569-2900
1240 Mayacama Club Dr Santa Rosa (95403) *(P-18499)*
MAYACAMA INDUSTRIES, Ukiah *Also called Ukiah Vly Assn For Hbilitation (P-23649)*
Mayer Associates .... D 310 274-5553
9090 Wilshire Blvd Fl 3 Beverly Hills (90211) *(P-10766)*
Mayer Brown & Platt, Los Angeles *Also called LLP Mayer Brown (P-22660)*
Mayesh Wholesale Florist Inc (PA). .... E 310 342-0980
5401 W 104th St Los Angeles (90045) *(P-8902)*
Mayfair Hotel .... D 213 484-9789
1430 Amherst Ave Apt 5 Los Angeles (90025) *(P-12603)*
Maynard Cooper & Gale PC .... C 415 704-7433
600 Montgomery St # 2600 San Francisco (94111) *(P-22676)*
Mayor Office, Pasadena *Also called City of Pasadena (P-13879)*
Mayoral Bros .... B 707 693-9111
420 Hillcrest Cir Dixon (95620) *(P-633)*
Maywood Acres Health Care Ctr, Oxnard *Also called Kindred Healthcare Oper Inc (P-20608)*
MAYWOOD ACRES HEALTHCARE, Oxnard *Also called Milwood Healthcare Inc (P-10622)*
Maywood Halthcare Wellness Ctr .... E 323 560-0720
6025 Pine Ave Maywood (90270) *(P-20129)*
Mazar Corp .... D 909 292-8269
3200 E Guasti Rd Ste 100 Ontario (91761) *(P-16349)*
Mazda Research & Dev of N Amer .... D 949 852-8898
1421 Reynolds Ave Irvine (92614) *(P-25205)*
Mazzetti Inc (PA) .... E 415 362-3266
220 Montgomery St Ste 650 San Francisco (94104) *(P-25206)*
Mazzetti GBA, San Francisco *Also called Mazzetti Inc (P-25206)*
MB Coatings Inc. .... D 714 625-2118
571 N Poplar St Ste G Orange (92868) *(P-16913)*
MB Herzog Electric Inc .... C 562 531-2002
15709 Illinois Ave Paramount (90723) *(P-2546)*
Mbari, Moss Landing *Also called Monterey Bay Aquarium RES Inst (P-26012)*
MBC Systems, Santa Ana *Also called Medical Network Inc (P-26312)*
Mbe, Pasadena *Also called Ttg Engineers (P-25356)*

A
L
P
H
A
B
E
T
I
C

Mbh Architects Inc......C......510 865-8663
960 Atlantic Ave Alameda (94501) ***(P-25484)***
Mbh Enterprises Inc......D......510 302-6680
1430 Franklin St Ste 201 Oakland (94612) ***(P-6869)***
MBI, Stockton *Also called Midstate Barrier Inc* ***(P-1760)***
Mbipch LLC......D......310 456-6444
22211 Pacific Coast Hwy Malibu (90265) ***(P-12604)***
MBK Laguna, Irvine *Also called MBK Real Estate Companies* ***(P-11283)***
MBK Real Estate Companies......E......949 789-8300
4 Park Plz Ste 1700 Irvine (92614) ***(P-11283)***
MBK Real Estate Ltd A Calfor......D......831 438-7533
100 Lockewood Ln Scotts Valley (95066) ***(P-10767)***
MBK Real Estate Ltd A Calfor (HQ)......D......949 789-8300
4 Park Plz Ste 1700 Irvine (92614) ***(P-11284)***
MBK Real Estate Ltd A Califor......E......310 399-3227
2107 Ocean Ave Ofc Santa Monica (90405) ***(P-10768)***
MBK Senior Living LLC......D......951 506-5555
41780 Btterfield Stage Rd Temecula (92592) ***(P-20631)***
Mbm, Irvine *Also called McLane Foodservice Dist Inc* ***(P-8193)***
Mbp Land LLC......D......619 291-5720
595 Hotel Cir S San Diego (92108) ***(P-12605)***
Mbs Equipment Company (PA)......D......310 558-3100
12800 Foothill Blvd Sylmar (91342) ***(P-17749)***
Mc Graw Commercial Insur Svc......D......714 939-9875
8185 E Kaiser Blvd Anaheim (92808) ***(P-10423)***
Mc Laughlin Mine, Lower Lake *Also called Barrick Gold Corporation* ***(P-968)***
Mc Namara Dodge Ney Beatt (PA)......D......925 939-5330
3480 Buskirk Ave Ste 250 Pleasant Hill (94523) ***(P-22677)***
MCA Music, Universal City *Also called Universal Studios Company LLC* ***(P-17695)***
McAfee Inc......D......858 967-2342
6707 Barnhurst Dr San Diego (92117) ***(P-15397)***
McAfee LLC (HQ)......C......888 847-8766
2821 Mission College Blvd Santa Clara (95054) ***(P-15398)***
McAfee Finance 2 LLC......A......888 847-8766
2821 Mission College Blvd Santa Clara (95054) ***(P-15399)***
McAfee Security LLC......A......866 622-3911
2821 Mission College Blvd Santa Clara (95054) ***(P-15400)***
McAlister Inst For Trtmnt Edca (PA)......C......619 442-0277
1400 N Johnson Ave # 101 El Cajon (92020) ***(P-22063)***
McAlister Institute For Treat......D......760 726-4451
3923 Waring Rd Oceanside (92056) ***(P-22064)***
MCASD, San Diego *Also called Museum Cntmprary Art San Diego* ***(P-24273)***
MCB-Cjs LLC......D......714 230-3600
5312 Bolsa Ave Huntington Beach (92649) ***(P-26698)***
McCain Inc (HQ)......C......760 727-8100
2365 Oak Ridge Way Vista (92081) ***(P-7563)***
McCallum Theatre, Palm Desert *Also called Friends of Cultural Center Inc* ***(P-17910)***
McCampbell Analytical Inc......D......925 252-9262
1534 Willow Pass Rd Pittsburg (94565) ***(P-26088)***
McCann World Group Inc (PA)......D......415 262-5500
653 Front St San Francisco (94111) ***(P-13538)***
McCann-Erickson Corporation (HQ)......D......415 348-5600
135 Main St Fl 21 San Francisco (94105) ***(P-13539)***
McCann-Erickson Usa Inc......C......415 262-5600
600 Battery St Fl 1 San Francisco (94111) ***(P-25923)***
McCarthy Bldg Companies Inc......B......949 851-8383
20401 Sw Birch St Ste 200 Newport Beach (92660) ***(P-1538)***
McCarthy Bldg Companies Inc......D......949 851-8383
20401 Sw Birch St Ste 300 Newport Beach (92660) ***(P-1539)***
McCarthy Construction, Lawndale *Also called McCarthy Framing Construction* ***(P-2949)***
McCarthy Framing Construction......D......310 219-3038
15133 Grevillea Ave Lawndale (90260) ***(P-2949)***
McClatchy Company......A......916 321-1941
2100 Q St Sacramento (95816) ***(P-27289)***
McClellan Business Park LLC......D......916 965-7100
3140 Peacekeeper Way McClellan (95652) ***(P-26699)***
McClellan Facilities Svcs LLC......D......916 965-7100
3140 Peacekeeper Way McClellan (95652) ***(P-10619)***
McClellan Hospitality Svcs LLC......D......916 965-7100
3140 Peacekeeper Way McClellan (95652) ***(P-12606)***
McClenahan Pest Control Inc......E......650 326-8781
1 Arastradero Rd Portola Valley (94028) ***(P-13825)***
McClenahan S P Co Tree Service, Portola Valley *Also called SP McClenahan Co* ***(P-945)***
McClintock Enterprises Inc......D......619 579-5300
777 Gable Way El Cajon (92020) ***(P-3778)***
McClone Construction Company......C......559 431-9411
4340 Product Dr Cameron Park (95682) ***(P-1158)***
McClure Convalescent Hospital, Oakland *Also called Independent Quality Care Inc* ***(P-20601)***
McCollisters Trnsp Group Inc......D......909 428-5700
10672 Jasmine St Fontana (92337) ***(P-4091)***
McCormack Roofng Constrctn & E......D......714 777-4040
1260 N Hancock St Ste 108 Anaheim (92807) ***(P-3075)***
McCormick Barstow, Fresno *Also called McCormick Barstow Shepprd Wayt* ***(P-22678)***
McCormick Barstow Shepprd Wayt (PA)......D......559 433-1300
7647 N Fresno St Fresno (93720) ***(P-22678)***
McCoy's Patrol Service, Suisun City *Also called Hal-Mar-Jac Enterprises* ***(P-16317)***
McCuen Construction Inc (PA)......E......916 652-7824
3269 Swetzer Rd Loomis (95650) ***(P-1540)***
McCullough Construction Inc......D......707 825-1014
57 Aldergrove Rd Arcata (95521) ***(P-1757)***
McCusker Enterprises Inc......D......951 699-9777
29879 Santiago Rd Temecula (92592) ***(P-23750)***
McCutcheon Enterprises Inc......D......559 864-3200
604 W Nebraska Ave Fresno (93706) ***(P-147)***
McDermott Will & Emery LLP......C......310 277-4110
2049 Century Park E # 3200 Los Angeles (90067) ***(P-22679)***
McDermott Will & Emery LLP......D......949 757-7165
18565 Jamboree Rd Ste 250 Irvine (92612) ***(P-22680)***
McE, San Rafael *Also called Marin Clean Energy* ***(P-5856)***
McE Corporation (PA)......D......925 803-4111
4000 Industrial Way Concord (94520) ***(P-1758)***
McElvany Inc......D......209 826-1102
13343 Johnson Rd Los Banos (93635) ***(P-1889)***
McFadden Farm......E......707 743-1122
16000 Powerhouse Rd Potter Valley (95469) ***(P-6)***
McGee Company, Whittier *Also called John Shannon Mc Gee Co Inc* ***(P-7159)***
McGrath Rentcorp......D......925 606-9200
5700 Las Positas Rd Livermore (94551) ***(P-14179)***
McGrath Rentcorp......C......877 221-2813
5700 Las Positas Rd Livermore (94551) ***(P-7564)***
McGrath Rentcorp (PA)......C......925 606-9200
5700 Las Positas Rd Livermore (94551) ***(P-7565)***
McGraw Insurance Services, Anaheim *Also called Mc Graw Commercial Insur Svc* ***(P-10423)***
McGreever and Danlee Very, Azusa *Also called Morris National Inc* ***(P-8611)***
McGuire and Hester (PA)......B......510 632-7676
2810 Harbor Bay Pkwy Alameda (94502) ***(P-1890)***
McGuire Contracting Inc......D......909 357-1200
16579 Slover Ave Fontana (92337) ***(P-3179)***
McGuire Talent Inc......D......909 527-7006
8608 Utica Ave Ste 220 Rancho Cucamonga (91730) ***(P-17927)***
McGuirewoods LLP......D......310 315-8200
1800 Century Park E Fl 8 Los Angeles (90067) ***(P-22681)***
Mch, Madera *Also called Madera Community Hospital* ***(P-21027)***
McHc, Ukiah *Also called Mendocino Cmnty Hlth Clnic Inc* ***(P-19193)***
McHenry Bowl Inc......E......209 571-2695
3700 Mchenry Ave Modesto (95356) ***(P-18039)***
McHenry Medical Group Inc......D......209 577-3388
1541 Florida Ave Ste 200 Modesto (95350) ***(P-19179)***
MCI Communications Svcs Inc......C......213 625-1005
700 S Flower St Ste 1600 Los Angeles (90017) ***(P-5435)***
McIntyre......D......510 614-5890
14680 Wicks Blvd San Leandro (94577) ***(P-26700)***
McIntyre Company (PA)......D......909 962-6322
2817 E Cedar St Ste 200 Ontario (91761) ***(P-3272)***
McIntyre Vineyards, Carmel *Also called Monterey Pacific Inc* ***(P-673)***
McKann World Group, San Francisco *Also called McCann-Erickson Usa Inc* ***(P-25923)***
McKee Electric, Bakersfield *Also called Surgener Electric Inc* ***(P-2662)***
McKesson Corporation......D......951 686-3575
6969 Brockton Ave Ste B Riverside (92506) ***(P-7961)***
McKesson Corporation......D......510 666-0854
3000 Colby St Berkeley (94705) ***(P-7962)***
McKesson Corporation......C......562 463-2100
9501 Norwalk Blvd Santa Fe Springs (90670) ***(P-7963)***
McKesson Corporation......D......916 636-8700
11000 Trade Center Dr Rancho Cordova (95670) ***(P-7964)***
McKesson Drug, Santa Fe Springs *Also called McKesson Corporation* ***(P-7963)***
McKesson Medical-Surgical Inc......D......800 767-6339
16043 El Prado Rd Chino (91708) ***(P-7965)***
McKesson Medical-Surgical Inc......D......805 375-8800
1525 Rnch Conejo Blvd # 104 Newbury Park (91320) ***(P-7966)***
McKesson Ptent Care Sltons Inc (HQ)......D......412 507-0077
9235 Activity Rd Ste 105 San Diego (92126) ***(P-22273)***
McKinley Childrens Center Inc (PA)......C......909 599-1227
762 Cypress St San Dimas (91773) ***(P-23989)***
McKinley Equipment Corporation (PA)......D......800 770-6094
17611 Armstrong Ave Irvine (92614) ***(P-7566)***
McKinley Home Foundation......D......909 599-1227
762 Cypress St San Dimas (91773) ***(P-24195)***
MCKINLEY PARK CARE CENTER, Sacramento *Also called Azalea Holdings LLC* ***(P-20757)***
McKinley Plaza LLC......D......619 405-6307
2401 E Division St National City (91950) ***(P-26310)***
McKinnon Broadcasting Company (HQ)......C......858 571-5151
4575 Viewridge Ave San Diego (92123) ***(P-5634)***
McKinnon Publishing Company......A......858 571-5151
4575 Viewridge Ave San Diego (92123) ***(P-5635)***
McKinsey & Company Inc......E......424 249-1000
2000 Avenue Of The Stars # 800 Los Angeles (90067) ***(P-26701)***
McKinsey & Company Inc......B......415 981-0250
555 California St # 4800 San Francisco (94104) ***(P-26702)***
McKinsey & Company Inc......D......650 494-6262
3075 Hansen Way Bldg A Palo Alto (94304) ***(P-26703)***
McKool Smith Hennigan......D......213 694-1200
300 S Grand Ave Ste 2900 Los Angeles (90071) ***(P-22682)***
McKowskis Maint Systems Inc......D......619 269-4600
10979 San Dego Mission Rd San Diego (92108) ***(P-13976)***
McLane Company Inc......C......209 221-7500
800 E Pescadero Ave Tracy (95304) ***(P-8192)***
McLane Foodservice Dist Inc......C......909 484-6100
3051 N Church St Rancho Cucamonga (91730) ***(P-8411)***
McLane Foodservice Dist Inc......D......252 985-7200
5675 Sunol Blvd Pleasanton (94566) ***(P-8292)***
McLane Foodservice Dist Inc......D......714 863-0163
17872 Cartwright Rd Irvine (92614) ***(P-8193)***
McLane/Pacific Inc......B......209 725-2500
3876 E Childs Ave Merced (95341) ***(P-8194)***
MCM Construction Inc (PA)......D......916 334-1221
6413 32nd St North Highlands (95660) ***(P-1822)***
MCM Construction Inc......D......310 549-9207
708 Pier A St Wilmington (90744) ***(P-3180)***
MCM Construction Inc......C......909 875-0533
19010 Slover Ave Bloomington (92316) ***(P-1823)***
McM Partners Inc......D......925 463-9500
6111 Johnson Ct Ste 110 Pleasanton (94588) ***(P-11285)***
McManis Faulkner A Prof Corp......E......408 279-8700
50 W San Fernando St # 1000 San Jose (95113) ***(P-22683)***

McMillan Data Cmmnications Inc.....D.....415 826-5100
1950 Cesar Chavez San Francisco (94124) ***(P-2547)***
McMillan Electric.....B.....415 826-5100
1950 Cesar Chavez San Francisco (94124) ***(P-2548)***
McMillan Farm Management.....C.....951 676-2045
29379 Rancho California R Temecula (92591) ***(P-26311)***
McMillen Jacobs Associates Inc.....D.....530 497-5407
3954 Carson Rd Camino (95709) ***(P-25207)***
McMillin Communities Inc.....A.....951 506-3303
41687 Temeku Dr Temecula (92591) ***(P-18267)***
McMillin Companies LLC (PA).....D.....619 477-4117
2750 Womble Rd Ste 102 San Diego (92106) ***(P-11934)***
McMillin Construction Svcs LP.....E.....619 477-4170
2750 Womble Rd San Diego (92106) ***(P-1159)***
McMillin Homes, San Diego *Also called McMillin Companies LLC* ***(P-11934)***
McMillin Homes, San Diego *Also called McMillin Management Svcs LP* ***(P-11731)***
McMillin Management Svcs LP (HQ).....C.....619 477-4117
2750 Womble Rd Ste 102 San Diego (92106) ***(P-11731)***
McMillin RE & Mrtg Co Inc.....D.....619 422-4500
320 E H St Chula Vista (91910) ***(P-11286)***
McMurray & Sons Inc (PA).....D.....707 443-3088
1818 Allard Ave Eureka (95503) ***(P-3076)***
McMurray Stern, Santa Fe Springs *Also called Gatehouse Msi LLC* ***(P-2935)***
MCP Industries Inc.....D.....562 944-5511
10039 Norwalk Blvd Santa Fe Springs (90670) ***(P-8702)***
MCR Printing and Packg Corp.....C.....619 488-3012
8830 Siempre Viva Rd San Diego (92154) ***(P-4448)***
MCS, Bakersfield *Also called Managed Care Systems Kern Cnty* ***(P-10412)***
McWong Envmtl & Enrgy Group.....E.....916 371-8080
1921 Arena Blvd Sacramento (95834) ***(P-27127)***
MD Imaging Inc A Prof Med Corp.....D.....530 243-1249
2020 Court St Redding (96001) ***(P-19180)***
MD P Foundation Inc.....C.....415 552-0240
225 Potrero Ave San Francisco (94103) ***(P-23332)***
Mda US Systems LLC, Pasadena *Also called Ssl Robotics LLC* ***(P-25316)***
Mdcc, Covina *Also called Mohan Dialysis Ctr of Covina* ***(P-21931)***
Mddr Inc.....C.....714 792-1993
555 Vanguard Way Brea (92821) ***(P-2198)***
MDE Electric, Sunnyvale *Also called MDE Electric Company Inc* ***(P-2549)***
MDE Electric Company Inc.....E.....408 738-8600
152 Commercial St Sunnyvale (94086) ***(P-2549)***
MDE Semiconductor Inc.....D.....760 564-8656
201 Shipyard Way Ste C Newport Beach (92663) ***(P-7300)***
Mds Consulting (PA).....D.....949 251-8821
17320 Red Hill Ave # 350 Irvine (92614) ***(P-25208)***
ME and ME Inc.....D.....818 891-0197
14536 Roscoe Blvd Ste 112 Van Nuys (91402) ***(P-14528)***
ME Fox & Company Inc.....D.....408 435-8510
128 Component Dr San Jose (95131) ***(P-8779)***
Mea Digital Worx LLC.....E.....619 238-8923
530 B St Ste 1900 San Diego (92101) ***(P-13540)***
Meadow Club.....D.....415 453-3274
1001 Bolinas Rd Fairfax (94930) ***(P-18500)***
Meadow Glen Apartments, Sacramento *Also called John Stewart Company* ***(P-10744)***
Meadow View Manor Inc.....D.....530 272-2273
396 Dorsey Dr Grass Valley (95945) ***(P-20130)***
Meadowbrook Bhavioral Hlth Ctr, Los Angeles *Also called Genesis Healthcare Corporation* ***(P-19936)***
Meadowbrook Convalescent Hosp.....D.....951 658-2293
461 E Johnston Ave Hemet (92543) ***(P-23990)***
Meadowbrook Senior Living.....D.....818 991-3544
5217 Chesebro Rd Agoura Hills (91301) ***(P-23333)***
Meadowbrook Village Christian.....C.....760 746-2500
100 Holland Gln Escondido (92026) ***(P-23991)***
Meadowood Care Center, Stockton *Also called Meadowood Hlth Rehabilitation* ***(P-20131)***
Meadowood Hlth Rehabilitation.....B.....209 956-3444
3110 Wagner Heights Rd Stockton (95209) ***(P-20131)***
Meadowood Nursing Center, Clearlake *Also called Vindra Inc* ***(P-20361)***
Meadows Nappa Valley Care Ctr, NAPA *Also called California Odd Fellows* ***(P-10708)***
Meadows of NAPA Valley, NAPA *Also called California Odd Fellows* ***(P-10707)***
Meadows Senior Living, The, Elk Grove *Also called Lifestyles Senior Housing Man* ***(P-23320)***
MEALS ON WHEELS, San Diego *Also called Meals-On-Wheels Grtr Sn Diego* ***(P-23337)***
Meals On Wheels Diablo Region (PA).....D.....925 937-8311
1300 Civic Dr Fl 1 Walnut Creek (94596) ***(P-23334)***
Meals On Wheels-The Health Tr.....E.....408 961-9870
1400 Parkmoor Ave Ste 230 San Jose (95126) ***(P-23335)***
Meals On Whels San Frncsco Inc.....E.....415 920-1111
1375 Fairfax Ave San Francisco (94124) ***(P-23336)***
Meals-On-Wheels Grtr Sn Diego (PA).....D.....619 260-6110
2254 San Diego Ave # 200 San Diego (92110) ***(P-23337)***
Meany Wilson L P.....E.....415 905-5300
4 Embarcadero Ctr # 3330 San Francisco (94111) ***(P-11577)***
Mearsk, San Pedro *Also called APM Terminals Pacific LLC* ***(P-4894)***
Meathead Movers.....D.....805 349-8000
101 W Canon Perdido St Santa Maria (93454) ***(P-4092)***
Meathead Movers Inc.....D.....805 496-1416
300 Rolling Oaks Dr Thousand Oaks (91361) ***(P-4093)***
Meathead Movers Inc (PA).....D.....805 544-6328
3600 S Higuera St San Luis Obispo (93401) ***(P-4094)***
Meathead Movers Inc.....D.....805 437-5100
412 Calle San Pablo Camarillo (93012) ***(P-4095)***
Meathead Movers Inc.....D.....805 966-6328
1524 State St Santa Barbara (93101) ***(P-4096)***
Mechanical Drives and Belting, Los Angeles *Also called Los Angeles Rubber Company* ***(P-7642)***
Mechanical Drives Co (PA).....D.....323 263-4131
2915 E Washington Blvd Los Angeles (90023) ***(P-7643)***
Mechanical Industries Inc.....E.....661 634-9477
314 Yampa St Bakersfield (93307) ***(P-3273)***
Mechanics Bank (HQ).....C.....800 797-6324
1111 Civic Dr Walnut Creek (94596) ***(P-9267)***
Mechanics Bank.....B.....855 272-2886
18400 Von Karman Ave Irvine (92612) ***(P-9215)***
Mechanics Bank.....D.....510 741-7545
725 Alfred Nobel Dr Hercules (94547) ***(P-9216)***
Mechanics Bank.....C.....831 422-6642
301 Main St Salinas (93901) ***(P-9217)***
Med Focus/California Radiology, Santa Monica *Also called Stephen B Meisel MD A Med Corp* ***(P-19453)***
Med Staffing LLC.....E.....510 795-0114
1860 Mowry Ave Ste 302 Fremont (94538) ***(P-14529)***
Med-Data Incorporated.....D.....916 771-1362
3741 Douglas Blvd Ste 170 Roseville (95661) ***(P-25648)***
Med-Legal LLC.....C.....626 653-5160
4401 Atlantic Ave Long Beach (90807) ***(P-22684)***
Med-Life Ambulance Services.....D.....818 242-1785
4304 Alger St Los Angeles (90039) ***(P-3698)***
Medallia Inc (PA).....C.....650 321-3000
575 Market St Ste 1850 San Francisco (94105) ***(P-15401)***
Medallion Cnstr Clean-Up, Mountain View *Also called Service By Medallion* ***(P-14044)***
Medallion Landscape MGT Inc (PA).....D.....408 782-7500
10 San Bruno Ave Morgan Hill (95037) ***(P-741)***
Medamerica Billing Svcs Inc (HQ).....D.....209 491-7710
1601 Cummins Dr Ste D Modesto (95358) ***(P-25649)***
Medasend Biomedical Inc (PA).....C.....800 200-3581
1402 Daisy Ave Long Beach (90813) ***(P-22274)***
Medata Inc (PA).....D.....714 918-1310
5 Peters Canyon Rd # 250 Irvine (92606) ***(P-15402)***
Medex Pratice Solutions Inc.....D.....209 845-1346
4725 Enterprise Way Ste 1 Modesto (95356) ***(P-25650)***
Medfocus Radiology Network, Santa Monica *Also called Stephen B Meisel MD PC* ***(P-19452)***
Medi-Flight Northern Cal, Modesto *Also called Sutter Central Vly Hospitals* ***(P-4747)***
Medi-Van Ambulette, Los Angeles *Also called Health Link Medi Van* ***(P-5117)***
Media All Stars Inc.....D.....858 300-9600
8525 Gibbs Dr Ste 206 San Diego (92123) ***(P-16914)***
Media Arts Lab, Santa Monica *Also called Tbwa Worldwide Inc* ***(P-13585)***
Media Design Group, Los Angeles *Also called Revenue Frontier LLC* ***(P-13661)***
Media Services, Los Angeles *Also called Oberman Tivoli & Pickert Inc* ***(P-15669)***
Media Temple Inc.....C.....877 578-4000
12130 Millennium Ste 300 Playa Vista (90094) ***(P-5436)***
Media Vntures Entrmt Group LLC.....E.....310 260-3171
1547 14th St Santa Monica (90404) ***(P-17631)***
Mediabrands Worldwide Inc (HQ).....A.....212 605-7000
653 Front St San Francisco (94111) ***(P-13655)***
Mediabrands Worldwide Inc.....B.....323 370-8000
5700 Wilshire Blvd # 400 Los Angeles (90036) ***(P-13541)***
Mediaplatform Inc.....D.....310 909-8410
8383 Wilshire Blvd # 460 Beverly Hills (90211) ***(P-17632)***
Mediaplex Inc (HQ).....D.....818 575-4500
30699 Russell Ranch Rd # 250 Westlake Village (91362) ***(P-13542)***
Medic Ambulance Service Inc (PA).....C.....707 644-1761
506 Couch St Vallejo (94590) ***(P-3699)***
Medical Billing Services, Monrovia *Also called California Business Bureau Inc* ***(P-13672)***
Medical Care Professionals.....D.....650 583-9898
363 El Cmino Real Ste 215 South San Francisco (94080) ***(P-20132)***
Medical Care Services Division, San Diego *Also called County of San Diego* ***(P-22219)***
Medical Center, San Diego *Also called University Cal San Diego* ***(P-21334)***
Medical Center, San Bernardino *Also called Far West Inc* ***(P-19911)***
Medical Center, Ventura *Also called County of Ventura* ***(P-23181)***
Medical Centre, Sacramento *Also called University California Davis* ***(P-21339)***
Medical Couriers Inc.....D.....916 452-5700
176 Otto Cir Sacramento (95822) ***(P-3912)***
Medical Couriers Inc.....D.....650 872-1144
1611 Neptune Dr San Leandro (94577) ***(P-4274)***
Medical Ex Courier Systems, Orange *Also called Mx Courier Systems Inc* ***(P-16937)***
Medical Examiner, San Diego *Also called County of San Diego* ***(P-20819)***
Medical Examiner Forensic Ctr, San Diego *Also called County of San Diego* ***(P-22221)***
Medical Eye Services Inc.....D.....714 619-4660
345 Baker St Costa Mesa (92626) ***(P-10424)***
Medical Group Bverly Hills Inc (PA).....E.....310 385-3200
200 N Robertson Blvd Beverly Hills (90211) ***(P-19181)***
Medical Group Bverly Hills Inc.....E.....310 247-4646
250 N Robertson Blvd # 603 Beverly Hills (90211) ***(P-19182)***
Medical Hill Rehabilitation, Oakland *Also called Ocadian Care Centers LLC* ***(P-20169)***
Medical HM Care Professionals, Redding *Also called Medical Home Specialists Inc* ***(P-14530)***
Medical Home Specialists Inc.....C.....530 226-5577
2115 Churn Creek Rd Redding (96002) ***(P-14530)***
Medical Inst of Little Co Mary, Torrance *Also called Lifecare Systems Inc* ***(P-20081)***
Medical Insurance Exchange Cal.....D.....510 596-4935
6250 Claremont Ave Oakland (94618) ***(P-10425)***
Medical Investment Co.....C.....818 360-1003
16553 Rinaldi St Granada Hills (91344) ***(P-20632)***
Medical Management Cons Inc.....A.....858 587-0609
6046 Cornerstone Ct W San Diego (92121) ***(P-26704)***
Medical Management Cons Inc (PA).....E.....310 659-3835
8150 Beverly Blvd Los Angeles (90048) ***(P-14531)***
Medical Network Inc.....D.....949 863-0022
1809 E Dyer Rd Ste 311 Santa Ana (92705) ***(P-26312)***
Medical Receivables Solutions.....E.....707 980-6733
101 W American Canyon Rd American Canyon (94503) ***(P-26705)***
Medical Specialties Managers.....C.....714 571-5000
1 City Blvd W Ste 1100 Orange (92868) ***(P-26706)***

ALPHABETIC

Employee Codes: A=Over 500 employees, B=251-500
C=101-250, D=51-100, E=50
2020 Directory of California
Wholesalers and Services Companies
© Mergent Inc. 1-800-342-5647
1347

Medical Specialty Billing, Orange *Also called Medical Specialties Managers* ***(P-26706)***
Medical Support Services, Los Angeles *Also called MSS Nurses Registry Inc* ***(P-14536)***
Medical Support Services..........D.......323 860-7994
6660 W Sunset Blvd Ste J Los Angeles (90028) ***(P-14532)***
Medical Transcription Billing..........A.......800 869-3700
405 Kenyon St Ste 300 San Diego (92110) ***(P-15403)***
Medicl Imgng Ctr of Southrn CA..........D.......310 829-9788
2811 Wilshire Blvd # 100 Santa Monica (90403) ***(P-19183)***
Medico Professional Linen Svc, Los Angeles *Also called American Textile Maint Co* ***(P-13195)***
Medicrest of California 1..........D.......909 626-1294
5119 Bandera St Montclair (91763) ***(P-20133)***
Medimpact Hlthcare Systems Inc (HQ)..........A.......858 566-2727
10181 Scripps Gateway Ct San Diego (92131) ***(P-24411)***
Medina Concrete Construction..........E.......909 474-9640
2368 W 1st Ave San Bernardino (92407) ***(P-3181)***
Medina Construction, Riverside *Also called Bens Asphalt & Maint Co Inc* ***(P-1672)***
Mediscan Diagnostic Svcs LLC..........D.......818 758-4224
21050 Califa St Ste 100 Woodland Hills (91367) ***(P-14533)***
Mediscan Staffing Services, Woodland Hills *Also called Mediscan Diagnostic Svcs LLC* ***(P-14533)***
Mediscan Staffing Services, Woodland Hills *Also called New Mediscan II LLC* ***(P-14539)***
Meditab Software Inc..........C.......510 632-2021
333 Hegenberger Rd # 800 Oakland (94621) ***(P-15404)***
Medley Communications Inc..........D.......760 294-4579
255 N Ash St Escondido (92027) ***(P-2550)***
Medley Communications Inc (PA)..........C.......951 245-5200
43015 Black Deer Loop # 203 Temecula (92590) ***(P-2551)***
Medlin Development..........E.......909 825-5296
320 Tropicana Ranch Rd Colton (92324) ***(P-867)***
Mednax Inc..........C.......408 254-8257
225 N Jackson Ave San Jose (95116) ***(P-19184)***
Mednax Inc..........C.......626 574-3050
300 W Huntington Dr Arcadia (91007) ***(P-19185)***
Mednax Inc..........C.......949 587-9037
24411 Health Center Dr Laguna Hills (92653) ***(P-19186)***
Mednax Inc..........C.......310 375-7172
23441 Madison St Ste 215 Torrance (90505) ***(P-19187)***
Mednax Inc..........C.......650 625-0127
2204 Grant Rd Mountain View (94040) ***(P-19188)***
Medpoint Management..........E.......818 702-0100
6400 Canoga Ave Ste 163 Woodland Hills (91367) ***(P-19189)***
Medric, Burlingame *Also called Acumen LLC* ***(P-15553)***
Medsphere Systems Corporation (PA)..........D.......760 692-3700
1903 Wright Pl Ste 120 Carlsbad (92008) ***(P-26707)***
Medstar LLC..........D.......916 669-0550
20 Busneca Pk Way Ste 100 Sacramento (95828) ***(P-3700)***
Medstop Medical, North Hollywood *Also called Morigon Technologies LLC* ***(P-6979)***
Medterra Cbd LLC..........D.......800 971-1288
9801 Research Dr Irvine (92618) ***(P-28)***
Medusind Solutions Inc (HQ)..........A.......949 240-8895
31103 Rancho Viejo Rd San Juan Capistrano (92675) ***(P-16915)***
Meeting Services Inc..........D.......858 348-0100
1125 Joshua Way Vista (92081) ***(P-14180)***
Mega Appraisers Inc..........A.......818 246-7370
14724 Ventura Blvd # 800 Sherman Oaks (91403) ***(P-16916)***
Mega Builders, Chatsworth *Also called A I T Development Corp* ***(P-1070)***
Mega Farm Labor Services Inc..........C.......661 229-8077
110 S Montclair St # 103 Bakersfield (93309) ***(P-14331)***
Mega Professional Intl..........D.......408 946-1500
995 Montague Expy Ste 121 Milpitas (95035) ***(P-14933)***
Megapath, Pleasanton *Also called Covad Communications Group Inc* ***(P-5382)***
Megapath, Pleasanton *Also called Gtt Communications (mp) Inc* ***(P-5415)***
Megapath Inc (PA)..........D.......877 611-6342
6800 Koll Center Pkwy # 200 Pleasanton (94566) ***(P-5437)***
Meiko America Inc..........D.......951 360-0281
12300 Riverside Dr Eastvale (91752) ***(P-4449)***
Mejico Express Inc (PA)..........C.......714 690-8300
14849 Firestone Blvd Fl 1 La Mirada (90638) ***(P-4723)***
Mek Norwood Pines LLC..........D.......916 922-7177
500 Jessie Ave Sacramento (95838) ***(P-20134)***
Mekanism Inc (PA)..........E.......415 908-4000
640 2nd St Fl 3 San Francisco (94107) ***(P-13543)***
Meks's Auto Body, Concord *Also called Mike Roses Auto Body Inc* ***(P-17300)***
Mekwus Solar Energy..........D.......510 731-4134
20283 Santa Maria Ave # 2103 Castro Valley (94546) ***(P-5996)***
Mel Bernie and Company Inc (PA)..........C.......818 841-1928
3000 W Empire Ave Burbank (91504) ***(P-7790)***
Mel Bernie and Company Inc..........C.......818 841-1928
3000 W Empire Ave Burbank (91504) ***(P-8094)***
Melano Enterprises, Oceanside *Also called Mellano & Co* ***(P-8904)***
Melissa Bradley RE Inc..........D.......707 258-3900
3249 Browns Valley Rd NAPA (94558) ***(P-11287)***
Melissa Bradley RE Inc..........D.......707 536-0888
1401 4th St Santa Rosa (95404) ***(P-11288)***
Melissa Bradley RE Inc..........D.......415 435-2705
1690 Tiburon Blvd Belvedere Tiburon (94920) ***(P-11289)***
Melissa Bradley RE Inc..........D.......415 209-1000
1701 Novato Blvd Ste 100 Novato (94947) ***(P-11290)***
Melissas World Variety Produce, Vernon *Also called World Variety Produce Inc* ***(P-8541)***
Mellano & Co (PA)..........B.......213 622-0796
766 Wall St Los Angeles (90014) ***(P-8903)***
Mellano & Co..........C.......760 433-9550
734 Wilshire Rd Oceanside (92057) ***(P-8904)***
Mellano Enterprises, Los Angeles *Also called Mellano & Co* ***(P-8903)***
Mellennia Holdings, Los Angeles *Also called Millennia Holdings Inc* ***(P-26719)***
Mellor, Anna B MD, Torrance *Also called South Bay Family Medical Group* ***(P-19407)***
Melmet Steven J Law Ofc..........D.......949 263-1000
2912 Daimler St Santa Ana (92705) ***(P-22685)***
Melo Concrete Construction..........D.......408 842-3484
5820 Obata Way Gilroy (95020) ***(P-3182)***
Melon Holdings LLC..........D.......530 742-7311
1617 Ramirez St Marysville (95901) ***(P-20135)***
Melos Plst Lthg & Drywall..........D.......559 237-0028
2038 E Jensen Ave Fresno (93706) ***(P-2820)***
Meltwater News US Inc (HQ)..........D.......415 829-5900
225 Bush St Ste 1000 San Francisco (94104) ***(P-16576)***
Membrane Technology & RES Inc..........D.......650 328-2228
39630 Eureka Dr Newark (94560) ***(P-25796)***
Memco Holdings Inc..........C.......310 277-0057
10390 Santa Monica Blvd # 210 Los Angeles (90025) ***(P-11291)***
Memeged Tevuot Shemesh (PA)..........C.......866 575-1211
5550 Topanga Canyon Blvd # 280 Woodland Hills (91367) ***(P-2199)***
Memo Scaffolding Inc..........D.......562 404-8600
12722 Carmenita Rd Santa Fe Springs (90670) ***(P-3436)***
Memon Aamir..........E.......818 339-8810
20832 Roscoe Blvd Ste 207 Winnetka (91306) ***(P-16350)***
Memor Ortho Surgic Group A M..........D.......562 424-6666
2760 Atlantic Ave Long Beach (90806) ***(P-19190)***
Memorex Products Inc..........C.......562 653-2800
17777 Center Court Dr N S Cerritos (90703) ***(P-7208)***
Memorial Center, Bakersfield *Also called Bakersfield Memorial Hospital* ***(P-20758)***
Memorial Counseling Assoc Inc..........D.......562 961-0155
4525 E Atherton St Long Beach (90815) ***(P-19191)***
Memorial Healthtec Labratories..........A.......714 962-4677
9920 Talbert Ave Fountain Valley (92708) ***(P-25797)***
MEMORIAL HOSPITAL OF GARDENA, Gardena *Also called Gardena Hospital LP* ***(P-20885)***
Memorial Medical Center, Modesto *Also called Sutter Central Vly Hospitals* ***(P-21247)***
Memorial Psychiatric Hlth Svcs..........E.......562 494-9243
4525 E Atherton St Long Beach (90815) ***(P-19192)***
Memorialcare Surgical Center A..........D.......714 369-1100
18111 Brookhurst St # 3200 Fountain Valley (92708) ***(P-21035)***
Memory To Go..........D.......310 446-0111
10801 National Blvd # 101 Los Angeles (90064) ***(P-6870)***
Memoryten Inc (PA)..........D.......408 516-4141
2995 Mead Ave Santa Clara (95051) ***(P-6871)***
Memoryx, Santa Clara *Also called Memoryten Inc* ***(P-6871)***
Mendelsohn/Zien Advg LLC..........D.......310 444-1990
11901 Santa Monica Blvd # 618 Los Angeles (90025) ***(P-13544)***
Mendes Calf Ranch..........D.......559 688-4708
13356 Avenue 168 Tipton (93272) ***(P-377)***
Mendicino Cast Otptent Surgery, Fort Bragg *Also called Mendocino Coast District Hosp* ***(P-21037)***
Mendocino Cmnty Hlth Clnic Inc (PA)..........C.......707 468-1010
333 Laws Ave Ukiah (95482) ***(P-19193)***
Mendocino Coast Clinics Inc..........D.......707 964-1251
205 South St Fort Bragg (95437) ***(P-22065)***
Mendocino Coast District Hosp (PA)..........B.......707 961-1234
700 River Dr Fort Bragg (95437) ***(P-21036)***
Mendocino Coast District Hosp..........C.......707 961-4736
700 River Dr Fort Bragg (95437) ***(P-21037)***
Mendocino Forest Pdts Co LLC..........C.......707 468-1431
850 Kunzler Ranch Rd Ukiah (95482) ***(P-6632)***
Mendocino Forest Pdts Co LLC (PA)..........B.......707 620-2961
3700 Old Redwood Hwy # 200 Santa Rosa (95403) ***(P-6633)***
Mendocino Forest Pdts Co LLC..........D.......707 485-6800
6375 N State St Calpella (95418) ***(P-6634)***
Mendocino Forest Pdts Co LLC..........D.......707 620-2961
6500 Durable Mill Rd Calpella (95418) ***(P-7821)***
Mendocino Hotel & Grdn Suites, Mendocino *Also called Mendocino Hotel & Resort Corp* ***(P-12607)***
Mendocino Hotel & Resort Corp..........D.......707 937-0511
45080 Main St Mendocino (95460) ***(P-12607)***
Mendocino Transit Authority..........D.......707 462-1422
111 Boatyard Dr Fort Bragg (95437) ***(P-3562)***
Menemsha Development Group Inc (PA)..........C.......310 343-3430
20521 Earl St Torrance (90503) ***(P-1541)***
Menemsha Solutions, Torrance *Also called Menemsha Development Group Inc* ***(P-1541)***
Menifee Lakes Country Club, Ontario *Also called Menifee Management Corp* ***(P-18501)***
Menifee Management Corp..........D.......951 672-4824
3200 E Guasti Rd Ste 100 Ontario (91761) ***(P-18501)***
Menifee Valley Hospital Center, Sun City *Also called Physicians For Healthy Hospita* ***(P-21093)***
Menke & Associates Inc (PA)..........D.......415 362-5200
1 Kaiser Plz Ste 505 Oakland (94612) ***(P-27128)***
Menlo Circus Club..........D.......650 322-4616
190 Park Ln Atherton (94027) ***(P-18502)***
Menlo Country Club..........E.......650 369-2342
2300 Woodside Rd Woodside (94062) ***(P-18503)***
Menlo Gateway Inc..........D.......650 356-2900
303 Vintage Park Dr # 250 Foster City (94404) ***(P-10854)***
Menlo Park VA Medical Center, Menlo Park *Also called Veterans Health Administration* ***(P-19574)***
Menlo Park-Atherton Education (PA)..........D.......650 325-0100
181 Encinal Ave Atherton (94027) ***(P-24848)***
Menlo Security Inc (PA)..........D.......650 614-1705
2300 Geng Rd Ste 200 Palo Alto (94303) ***(P-14934)***
Mens Apparel Guild In Cal Inc..........D.......310 857-7500
2901 28th St Ste 100 Santa Monica (90405) ***(P-24348)***
Mental Health Amer Los Angeles..........D.......562 437-6717
456 Elm Ave Long Beach (90802) ***(P-23338)***
Mental Health Assn Orange Cnty, Santa Ana *Also called Orange Cnty Assn For Mntal HLT* ***(P-24415)***
Mental Health California Dept..........B.......707 449-6504
1600 California Dr Vacaville (95696) ***(P-21420)***

Mental Health Department, Oakland *Also called La Clinica De La Raza Inc* ***(P-19140)***
Mental Health Dept, Van Nuys *Also called Los Angeles Unified School Dst* ***(P-22061)***
Mental Health Dept of, Arcadia *Also called County of Los Angeles* ***(P-23102)***
Mental Health Dept of, Artesia *Also called County of Los Angeles* ***(P-21999)***
Mental Health Dept of, Long Beach *Also called County of Los Angeles* ***(P-18929)***
Mental Health Services, Stockton *Also called County of San Joaquin* ***(P-22005)***
Mental Health Services, Red Bluff *Also called County of Tehama* ***(P-23175)***
Mental Health Systems Inc (PA).......D.......858 573-2600
9465 Farnham St San Diego (92123) ***(P-22066)***
Mental Hlth Cnvlscent Svcs Inc.......B.......562 869-0978
12023 Lakewood Blvd Downey (90242) ***(P-20136)***
Mental Hlth Sbstnce Abuse Svcs, Auburn *Also called County of Placer* ***(P-23127)***
Mental Hlth Svcs For Kngs Cnty, Hanford *Also called Kings View* ***(P-22056)***
Mentor Media (usa) Sup.......D.......909 930-0800
3768 Milliken Ave Ste A Eastvale (91752) ***(P-26313)***
Mentor Worldwide LLC.......B.......805 681-6000
5425 Hollister Ave Santa Barbara (93111) ***(P-6976)***
Menzies Aviation (texas) Inc.......D.......909 937-3998
1049 S Vineyard Ave Ontario (91761) ***(P-4781)***
Merabi & Sons LLC.......C.......818 817-0006
14545 Friar St Ste 101 Van Nuys (91411) ***(P-11865)***
Mercado Latino Inc (PA).......D.......626 333-6862
245 Baldwin Park Blvd City of Industry (91746) ***(P-8195)***
Mercado Latino Inc.......E.......510 475-5500
33430 Western Ave Union City (94587) ***(P-8196)***
Merced Convalescent Hospital, Merced *Also called Madera Convalescent Hospital* ***(P-20625)***
Merced Irrigation District (PA).......E.......209 722-5761
744 W 20th St Merced (95340) ***(P-5857)***
Merced Irrigation District.......C.......209 722-2719
3321 Franklin Rd Merced (95348) ***(P-6365)***
Merced School Employees F C U (PA).......D.......209 383-5550
1021 Olivewood Dr Merced (95348) ***(P-9324)***
Merced Transportation Company.......D.......209 384-2575
300 Grogan Ave Merced (95341) ***(P-3820)***
Mercedes Diaz Homes Inc.......D.......562 945-4576
7239 Washington Ave # 100 Whittier (90602) ***(P-23992)***
Mercedes-Benz RE.......E.......310 547-6086
4031 Via Oro Ave Long Beach (90810) ***(P-25798)***
Mercer (us) Inc.......C.......213 346-2200
777 S Figueroa St # 2400 Los Angeles (90017) ***(P-26708)***
Mercer (us) Inc.......C.......415 743-8700
4 Embarcadero Ctr Lbby 4 # 4 San Francisco (94111) ***(P-26709)***
Mercer (us) Inc.......D.......949 222-1300
17901 Von Karman Ave # 1100 Irvine (92614) ***(P-26710)***
Mercer Global Securities LLC.......D.......805 565-1681
1801 E Cabrillo Blvd A Santa Barbara (93108) ***(P-9831)***
Mercer Health & Benefits, San Francisco *Also called Mercer (us) Inc* ***(P-26709)***
Merchant Services, Irvine *Also called Universal Card Inc* ***(P-17134)***
Merchant Services Inc (PA).......B.......817 725-0900
1 S Van Ness Ave Fl 5 San Francisco (94103) ***(P-15787)***
Merchant Valley Corp.......E.......916 410-2021
1786 Jayne Ave Coalinga (93210) ***(P-12608)***
Merchant Valley Corporation.......C.......916 786-7227
1808 Avondale Dr Roseville (95747) ***(P-24349)***
Merchants Bank California N A.......D.......310 549-4350
1 Civic Plaza Dr Ste 100 Carson (90745) ***(P-9100)***
Merchants Bank of Commerce (HQ).......D.......530 224-7355
1951 Churn Creek Rd Redding (96002) ***(P-9101)***
Merchants Building Maint Co.......B.......714 973-9272
1639 E Edinger Ave Ste C Santa Ana (92705) ***(P-13977)***
Merchants Building Maint Co (PA).......D.......323 881-6701
1190 Monterey Pass Rd Monterey Park (91754) ***(P-13978)***
Merchants Building Maint Co.......B.......858 455-0163
9555 Dist Ave 102 San Diego (92121) ***(P-13979)***
Merchants Building Maint Co.......C.......909 622-8260
1995 W Holt Ave Pomona (91768) ***(P-13980)***
Merchants Building Maint Co.......C.......323 881-8902
606 Monterey Paca Rd 20 Ste 202 Monterey Park (91754) ***(P-13981)***
Merchsource LLC (PA).......D.......800 374-2744
7755 Irvine Center Dr Irvine (92618) ***(P-7738)***
Mercies Home (PA).......E.......661 832-3424
910 S Real Rd Bakersfield (93309) ***(P-23751)***
Mercury Air Cargo Inc (HQ).......C.......310 258-6100
6040 Avion Dr Ste 200 Los Angeles (90045) ***(P-4782)***
Mercury Casualty Company (HQ).......A.......323 937-1060
555 W Imperial Hwy Brea (92821) ***(P-10107)***
Mercury Defense Systems Inc (HQ).......D.......714 898-8200
10855 Bus Ctr Dr Bldg A Cypress (90630) ***(P-15788)***
Mercury General Corporation (PA).......D.......323 937-1060
4484 Wilshire Blvd Los Angeles (90010) ***(P-10108)***
Mercury Insurance Broker, Santa Monica *Also called Mercury Insurance Company* ***(P-10111)***
Mercury Insurance Company.......D.......714 671-6700
555 W Imperial Hwy Brea (92821) ***(P-10109)***
Mercury Insurance Company.......D.......916 353-4859
104 Woodmere Rd Folsom (95630) ***(P-10110)***
Mercury Insurance Company.......D.......310 451-4943
1433 Santa Monica Blvd Santa Monica (90404) ***(P-10111)***
Mercury Insurance Company.......D.......714 255-5000
1700 Greenbriar Ln Brea (92821) ***(P-10112)***
Mercury Insurance Company (HQ).......C.......323 937-1060
4484 Wilshire Blvd Los Angeles (90010) ***(P-10113)***
Mercury Insurance Company.......D.......858 694-4100
9635 Gran Rdge Dr Ste 200 San Diego (92123) ***(P-10114)***
Mercury Insurance Company.......D.......661 291-6470
27200 Tourney Rd Ste 400 Valencia (91355) ***(P-10115)***
Mercury Insurance Group, Folsom *Also called Mercury Insurance Company* ***(P-10110)***
Mercury Insurance Services LLC.......A.......323 937-1060
4484 Wilshire Blvd Los Angeles (90010) ***(P-10116)***
Mercury Mailing Systems Inc.......D.......323 730-0307
2727 Exposition Blvd Los Angeles (90018) ***(P-13730)***
Mercury Messenger Service Inc.......E.......818 989-3115
16735 Saticoy St Ste 104 Van Nuys (91406) ***(P-16917)***
Mercury Systems, Cypress *Also called Mercury Defense Systems Inc* ***(P-15788)***
Mercury World Cargo, Los Angeles *Also called Mercury Air Cargo Inc* ***(P-4782)***
Mercy Air Tri-County LLC.......C.......909 829-1051
1670 Miro Way Rialto (92376) ***(P-4745)***
Mercy Foundation North.......D.......530 247-3424
2625 Edith Ave Ste E Redding (96001) ***(P-22275)***
Mercy General Hospital, Sacramento *Also called Mercy HM Svcs A Cal Ltd Partnr* ***(P-21042)***
Mercy General Hospital, Sacramento *Also called Dignity Health* ***(P-21524)***
Mercy General Hospital Bus Off, Sacramento *Also called Dignity Health* ***(P-20848)***
Mercy HM Svcs A Cal Ltd Partnr.......C.......661 632-5234
2215 Truxtun Ave Bakersfield (93301) ***(P-21038)***
Mercy HM Svcs A Cal Ltd Partnr (HQ).......A.......530 225-6000
2175 Rosaline Ave Ste A Redding (96001) ***(P-21039)***
Mercy HM Svcs A Cal Ltd Partnr.......B.......530 225-6000
2175 Rosaline Ave Ste A Redding (96001) ***(P-21040)***
Mercy HM Svcs A Cal Ltd Partnr.......B.......530 926-6111
914 Pine St Mount Shasta (96067) ***(P-21041)***
Mercy HM Svcs A Cal Ltd Partnr.......A.......916 453-4545
4001 J St Sacramento (95819) ***(P-21042)***
Mercy HM Svcs A Cal Ltd Partnr.......B.......209 564-4200
2740 M St Merced (95340) ***(P-21043)***
Mercy HM Svcs A Cal Ltd Partnr.......A.......916 983-7400
1650 Creekside Dr Folsom (95630) ***(P-19194)***
Mercy HM Svcs A Cal Ltd Partnr.......D.......530 245-4070
1544 Market St Redding (96001) ***(P-21812)***
Mercy Hospital, Bakersfield *Also called Dignity Health* ***(P-20855)***
Mercy Hospital of Folsom, Folsom *Also called Mercy HM Svcs A Cal Ltd Partnr* ***(P-19194)***
Mercy House Living Centers.......C.......714 836-7188
807 N Garfield St Santa Ana (92701) ***(P-24350)***
Mercy Housing Calif Xxv, Sacramento *Also called Mercy Housing California Xxvi* ***(P-11292)***
Mercy Housing California Xxvi.......D.......916 414-4400
2512 River Plaza Dr Sacramento (95833) ***(P-11292)***
Mercy Hse Trnstnal Living Ctrs, Santa Ana *Also called Mercy House Living Centers* ***(P-24350)***
Mercy Hsing California Xxxiv.......D.......415 503-0816
66 9th St San Francisco (94103) ***(P-10769)***
Mercy Medical, Red Bluff *Also called Lassen Medical Group Inc* ***(P-19153)***
Mercy Medical Center, Merced *Also called Mercy HM Svcs A Cal Ltd Partnr* ***(P-21043)***
Mercy Medical Center - Redding, Redding *Also called Mercy HM Svcs A Cal Ltd Partnr* ***(P-21039)***
MERCY MEDICAL CENTER MERCED, Merced *Also called Mater Misericordiae Hospital* ***(P-21034)***
Mercy Medical Center Redding, Redding *Also called Dignity Health* ***(P-20843)***
Mercy Retirement and Care Ctr.......C.......510 534-8540
3431 Foothill Blvd Oakland (94601) ***(P-23993)***
Mercy San Juan Med Trauma Ctr, Carmichael *Also called Dignity Health* ***(P-20833)***
Mercy San Juan Medical Center, Carmichael *Also called Dignity Health* ***(P-20841)***
Meredith Baer & Associates, South Gate *Also called Meribear Productions Inc* ***(P-16918)***
Merex Group, El Segundo *Also called Kellstrom Holding Corporation* ***(P-7693)***
Meribear Productions Inc.......D.......310 204-5353
4100 Ardmore Ave South Gate (90280) ***(P-16918)***
Merical LLC (PA).......D.......714 238-7225
2995 E Miraloma Ave Anaheim (92806) ***(P-16919)***
Merical LLC.......D.......714 685-0977
447 W Freedom Ave Orange (92865) ***(P-16920)***
Merical LLC.......C.......714 283-9551
233 E Bristol Ln Orange (92865) ***(P-16921)***
Merical/Vita-Pak, Orange *Also called Merical LLC* ***(P-16921)***
Meridian Gold Inc.......C.......209 785-3222
4461 Rock Creek Rd Copperopolis (95228) ***(P-970)***
Meridian Holdings.......D.......805 539-2752
2580 El Camino Real Atascadero (93422) ***(P-7431)***
Meridian Industrial Trust.......D.......415 281-3900
455 Market St Ste 1700 San Francisco (94105) ***(P-11866)***
Meridian Knwldge Solutions LLC (HQ).......D.......913 985-9625
80 Iron Pont Cir Ste 100 Folsom (95630) ***(P-26711)***
Meridian Management Group.......C.......415 434-9700
1145 Bush St San Francisco (94109) ***(P-11293)***
Meridian Medical Offices, Riverside *Also called Kaiser Foundation Hospitals* ***(P-19092)***
Meridian Rack & Pinion Inc.......C.......858 587-8777
6740 Cobra Way Ste 200 San Diego (92121) ***(P-6453)***
Meridian Textiles Inc (PA).......D.......323 869-5700
6415 Canning St Commerce (90040) ***(P-8002)***
Meridian Vineyards, Paso Robles *Also called Treasury Wine Estates Americas* ***(P-166)***
Meridian World Travel, Menlo Park *Also called Peninsula World Travel LLC* ***(P-4831)***
Meringcarson Holdings (PA).......D.......916 441-0571
1700 I St Ste 210 Sacramento (95811) ***(P-13545)***
Meristar San Pedro Hilton LLC.......C.......310 514-3344
2800 Via Cabrillo Marina San Pedro (90731) ***(P-12609)***
Merit Logistics LLC.......A.......949 481-0685
33332 Valle Rd Ste 100 San Juan Capistrano (92675) ***(P-5125)***
Merit Property Management Inc, Irvine *Also called Firstservice Residential* ***(P-11154)***
Merit Technologies LLC.......D.......858 623-9800
10509 Vista Sorrento Pkwy # 420 San Diego (92121) ***(P-26712)***
Meritage Resort LLC.......B.......707 251-1900
875 Bordeaux Way NAPA (94558) ***(P-12610)***
Meritage Resort and Spa, The, NAPA *Also called Meritage Resort LLC* ***(P-12610)***
Meriwest Credit Union (PA).......C.......408 363-3200
5615 Chesbro Ave Ste 100 San Jose (95123) ***(P-9325)***
Merli Concrete Pumping, Gardena *Also called Stefan Merli Plastering Co Inc* ***(P-3222)***
Merlin Global Services LLC.......C.......904 305-9559
440 Stevens Ave Ste 150 Solana Beach (92075) ***(P-4746)***

Employee Codes: A=Over 500 employees, B=251-500
C=101-250, D=51-100, E=50
2020 Directory of California
Wholesalers and Services Companies
© Mergent Inc. 1-800-342-5647
1349

Merlin Securities LLC......D......415 848-0269
45 Fremont St Ste 3000 San Francisco (94105) ***(P-9711)***
Merlot Film Productions Inc......C......323 575-2906
7800 Beverly Blvd Los Angeles (90036) ***(P-17633)***
Meroform Systems USA, Tustin *Also called Absolute Exhibits Inc* ***(P-16595)***
Merrill Gardens......D......510 790-1645
2860 Country Dr Ofc Fremont (94536) ***(P-10855)***
Merrill Gardens At Bankers Hl, San Diego *Also called Merrill Gardens LLC* ***(P-10772)***
Merrill Gardens LLC......D......707 447-7496
799 Yellowstone Dr Vacaville (95687) ***(P-11294)***
Merrill Gardens LLC......D......707 553-2698
350 Locust Dr Apt L215 Vallejo (94591) ***(P-10770)***
Merrill Gardens LLC......D......707 585-7878
4855 Snyder Ln Apt 152 Rohnert Park (94928) ***(P-10771)***
Merrill Gardens LLC......D......619 961-4990
2567 2nd Ave San Diego (92103) ***(P-10772)***
Merrill Gardens LLC......D......714 842-6569
17200 Goldenwest St # 101 Huntington Beach (92647) ***(P-10773)***
Merrill Gardens LLC......D......408 370-6431
2115 Winchester Blvd Campbell (95008) ***(P-10774)***
Merrill Gardens LLC......D......805 310-4102
1220 Suey Rd Bldg A Santa Maria (93454) ***(P-10775)***
Merrill Gardens LLC......D......707 996-7101
800 Oregon St Sonoma (95476) ***(P-10776)***
Merrill Gardens LLC......D......209 823-0164
430 N Union Rd Manteca (95337) ***(P-10777)***
Merrill Gardens LLC......D......562 693-0505
13250 Philadelphia St Ofc Whittier (90601) ***(P-10778)***
Merrill Gardns At Chateau Whit, Whittier *Also called Merrill Gardens LLC* ***(P-10778)***
Merrill Lynch Pierce Fenner......D......650 473-7888
333 Middlefield Rd Menlo Park (94025) ***(P-9712)***
Merrill Lynch Pierce Fenner......D......818 528-7809
16830 Ventura Blvd # 601 Encino (91436) ***(P-9713)***
Merrill Lynch Pierce Fenner......D......650 842-2440
3075b Hansen Way Palo Alto (94304) ***(P-9714)***
Merrill Lynch Pierce Fenner......E......661 802-0764
730 Patricia Dr San Luis Obispo (93405) ***(P-9715)***
Merrill Lynch Pierce Fenner......C......949 467-3760
520 Newport Center Dr # 1900 Newport Beach (92660) ***(P-9716)***
Merrill Lynch Pierce Fenner......D......626 304-1596
800 E Colo Blvd Ste 400 Pasadena (91101) ***(P-9636)***
Merrill Lynch Pierce Fenner......C......800 964-5182
300 E Esplanade Dr Oxnard (93036) ***(P-9717)***
Merrill Lynch Pierce Fenner......C......650 473-7888
333 Middlefield Rd # 202 Menlo Park (94025) ***(P-9718)***
Merrill Lynch Pierce Fenner......C......619 699-3700
701 B St Ste 2350 San Diego (92101) ***(P-9719)***
Merrill Lynch Pierce Fenner......E......408 283-3000
50 W San Fernando St # 16 San Jose (95113) ***(P-9720)***
Merrill Lynch Pierce Fenner......D......714 257-4400
145 S State College Blvd # 300 Brea (92821) ***(P-9779)***
Merrill Lynch Pierce Fenner......C......310 407-3900
2049 Century Park E # 1100 Los Angeles (90067) ***(P-9721)***
Merrill Lynch Pierce Fenner......D......925 945-4800
1331 N Calif Blvd Ste 400 Walnut Creek (94596) ***(P-9722)***
Merrill Lynch Pierce Fenner......E......415 274-7000
101 California St Fl 24 San Francisco (94111) ***(P-9723)***
Merrill Lynch Pierce Fenner......D......626 844-8500
800 E Colo Blvd Ste 400 Pasadena (91101) ***(P-9780)***
Merrill Lynch Pierce Fenner......D......949 859-2900
100 Spectrum Center Dr # 1100 Irvine (92618) ***(P-9724)***
Merrill Lynch Pierce Fenner......D......858 456-3600
7825 Fay Ave Ste 300 La Jolla (92037) ***(P-9725)***
Merrill Lynch Wealth MGT, Pasadena *Also called Merrill Lynch Pierce Fenner* ***(P-9636)***
Merritt Hawkins & Assoc LLC (HQ)......C......858 792-0711
12400 High Bluff Dr San Diego (92130) ***(P-14534)***
Merritt Hospitality LLC......C......562 983-3400
701 W Ocean Blvd Long Beach (90831) ***(P-12611)***
Merritt Hospitality LLC......C......714 738-7800
2701 Nutwood Ave Fullerton (92831) ***(P-12612)***
Merry X-Ray Chemical Corp (PA)......C......858 565-4472
4909 Murphy Canyon Rd # 120 San Diego (92123) ***(P-6977)***
Meruelo Enterprises, Downey *Also called Cantamar Property MGT Inc* ***(P-10961)***
Meruelo Enterprises Inc (PA)......A......562 745-2300
9550 Firestone Blvd # 105 Downey (90241) ***(P-1542)***
Mesa Cnsld Wtr Dst Imprv Corp (PA)......D......949 631-1200
1965 Placentia Ave Costa Mesa (92627) ***(P-6084)***
Mesa Cold Strg 4145, Fullerton *Also called US Foods Inc* ***(P-8666)***
Mesa Counselling......E......909 421-9301
850 E Foothill Blvd Rialto (92376) ***(P-26713)***
Mesa Distributing Coinc (HQ)......C......858 452-2300
3840 Via De La Valle # 300 Del Mar (92014) ***(P-8780)***
Mesa Energy Systems Inc (HQ)......C......949 460-0460
2 Cromwell Irvine (92618) ***(P-2200)***
Mesa Energy Systems Inc......D......559 277-7900
3980 N Chestnut Ave Fresno (93726) ***(P-2201)***
Mesa Energy Systems Inc......C......818 756-0500
16130 Sherman Way Van Nuys (91406) ***(P-2202)***
Mesa Management Inc......D......949 851-0995
1451 Quail St Ste 201 Newport Beach (92660) ***(P-11295)***
Mesa Pointe Stadium 12, Costa Mesa *Also called Edwards Theatres Circuit Inc* ***(P-17833)***
Mesa Properties GP......D......949 857-1905
25 Mauchly Ste 305 Irvine (92618) ***(P-12613)***
Mesa Verde Convalescent Hosp......C......949 548-5584
661 Center St Costa Mesa (92627) ***(P-20137)***
Mesa Verde Country Club......C......714 549-0377
3000 Club House Rd Costa Mesa (92626) ***(P-18504)***
Mesa Verde Partners......D......714 540-7500
1701 Golf Course Dr Costa Mesa (92626) ***(P-18268)***
Mesa Verde Prosecute Care, Costa Mesa *Also called Mesa Verde Convalescent Hosp* ***(P-20137)***
Mesa Vineyard Management Inc......D......805 925-7200
2570 Prell Rd Santa Maria (93454) ***(P-670)***
Mesa Vineyard Management Inc (PA)......D......805 434-4100
110 Gibson Rd Templeton (93465) ***(P-671)***
MESA WATER DISTRICT, Costa Mesa *Also called Mesa Cnsld Wtr Dst Imprv Corp* ***(P-6084)***
Message Broadcast LLC......E......949 428-3111
4685 Macarthur Ct Ste 250 Newport Beach (92660) ***(P-16922)***
Message Center Communication......E......858 974-7419
6779 Mesa Ridge Rd # 100 San Diego (92121) ***(P-16923)***
Messenger Express (PA)......C......213 614-0475
5435 Cahuenga Blvd Ste C North Hollywood (91601) ***(P-4275)***
Messenger Express......D......858 550-1400
10671 Roselle St Ste 200 San Diego (92121) ***(P-4276)***
Metabyte Inc......D......510 405-1117
39300 Civic Center Dr # 260 Fremont (94538) ***(P-16056)***
Metagenics Inc (HQ)......C......949 366-0818
25 Enterprise Ste 200 Aliso Viejo (92656) ***(P-7967)***
Metagenics Inc......D......800 692-9400
100 Avenida La Pata San Clemente (92673) ***(P-7968)***
Metaswitch Networks......E......415 513-1500
1751 Harbor Bay Pkwy # 125 Alameda (94502) ***(P-14935)***
Method Studios LLC......D......310 434-6500
3401 Exposition Blvd Santa Monica (90404) ***(P-17634)***
Methodist Hosp Southern Cal (PA)......A......626 898-8000
300 W Huntington Dr Arcadia (91007) ***(P-21044)***
Methodist Hospital of S CA......D......626 574-3755
300 W Huntington Dr Arcadia (91007) ***(P-21045)***
Methodist Hospital Sacramento, Sacramento *Also called Dignity Health* ***(P-20847)***
MetLife, San Francisco *Also called Metropolitan Life Insur Co* ***(P-10426)***
Metric Equipment Sales Inc......D......510 264-0887
25841 Industrial Blvd # 200 Hayward (94545) ***(P-7301)***
Metrick Property Management, San Francisco *Also called Blackrock Holdco 2 Inc* ***(P-10943)***
Metricstream Inc (PA)......C......650 620-2900
2479 E Byshore Rd Ste 260 Palo Alto (94303) ***(P-15405)***
Metricus Inc......C......650 328-2500
P.O. Box 458 Palo Alto (94302) ***(P-16924)***
Metro Bldrs & Engineers Group, Newport Beach *Also called Houalla Enterprises Ltd* ***(P-1502)***
Metro Building Maintenance, Los Angeles *Also called US Metro Group Inc* ***(P-14079)***
Metro City, Sherman Oaks *Also called Metro Home Loan Inc* ***(P-9580)***
Metro Home Loan Inc......D......818 461-9840
15301 Ventura Blvd # 400 Sherman Oaks (91403) ***(P-9580)***
Metro One Telecom Inc......C......626 337-8100
4900 Rivergrade Rd B210 Irwindale (91706) ***(P-13546)***
Metro Pcs, Los Angeles *Also called Richards Group Inc* ***(P-13569)***
Metro Rf, Ontario *Also called R F Metro Services Inc* ***(P-5798)***
Metro-Goldwyn-Mayer Inc (HQ)......B......310 449-3000
245 N Beverly Dr Beverly Hills (90210) ***(P-17635)***
Metrolux 14 Theatres, Los Angeles *Also called Metrolux Theatres* ***(P-17788)***
Metrolux Theatres......D......310 858-2800
8727 W 3rd St Los Angeles (90048) ***(P-17788)***
Metromile Inc (PA)......D......888 244-1702
690 Folsom St Ste 200 San Francisco (94107) ***(P-10117)***
Metron Incorporated......E......858 792-8904
12250 El Camino Real # 260 San Diego (92130) ***(P-26714)***
Metron-Athene Inc (PA)......D......949 588-5757
23046 Avnida De La Crlota Carlota Laguna Hills (92653) ***(P-14936)***
Metropcs-Fremont, Fremont *Also called T-Mobile Usa Inc* ***(P-5273)***
Metropcs-Modesto, Modesto *Also called T-Mobile Usa Inc* ***(P-5274)***
Metropcs-Van Ness, San Francisco *Also called T-Mobile Usa Inc* ***(P-5275)***
Metroplex Theatres LLC......A......310 856-1270
2275 W 190th St Ste 201 Torrance (90504) ***(P-17850)***
Metroplitan Oakland Intl Arprt, Oakland *Also called Port Dept City of Oakland* ***(P-4787)***
Metropolis Hotel MGT LLC......C......213 683-4855
899 Francisco St Los Angeles (90017) ***(P-12614)***
Metropolitan Area Advisory Com (PA)......D......619 426-3595
1355 Third Ave Chula Vista (91911) ***(P-23613)***
Metropolitan Area Advisory Com......B......619 255-7284
1102 Cesar E Chavez Pkwy San Diego (92113) ***(P-23614)***
Metropolitan Area Advisory Com......C......619 420-8981
1355 Third Ave Chula Vista (91911) ***(P-23615)***
Metropolitan Club......D......415 673-0600
640 Sutter St San Francisco (94102) ***(P-18505)***
Metropolitan Dst Private SEC......D......661 942-3999
44262 Division St Ste A Lancaster (93535) ***(P-16351)***
Metropolitan Elec Cnstr Inc......C......415 642-3000
2400 3rd St San Francisco (94107) ***(P-2552)***
Metropolitan Life Insur Co......B......415 536-1065
425 Market St Ste 960 San Francisco (94105) ***(P-10426)***
Metropolitan Trnsp Comm (PA)......C......415 778-6700
375 Beale St Ste 800 San Francisco (94105) ***(P-3563)***
Metropolitan Waste Disposal, Paramount *Also called Calmet Inc* ***(P-6175)***
Metropolitan Water District......E......909 890-3776
1820 Commercenter Cir San Bernardino (92408) ***(P-6085)***
Metropolitan Water District......E......951 688-5672
18250 La Sierra Ave Riverside (92503) ***(P-6086)***
Metropolitan Water District......D......714 577-5031
3972 Valley View Ave Yorba Linda (92886) ***(P-6087)***
Metropolitan Water District......D......818 368-3731
13100 Balboa Blvd Granada Hills (91344) ***(P-6088)***
Metropolitan Water District......B......909 593-7474
700 Moreno Ave La Verne (91750) ***(P-6089)***
Metropolitan Water District......D......951 926-7095
33752 Newport Rd Winchester (92596) ***(P-6090)***
Metropolitan Water District......D......951 780-1511
550 E Alessandro Blvd Riverside (92508) ***(P-6091)***

Mergent e-mail: customerrelations@mergent.com
1350
2020 Directory of California
Wholesalers and Services Companies
(P-0000) Products & Services Section entry number
(PA)=Parent Co (HQ)=Headquarters (DH)=Div Headquarters

Metropolitan Water District.....A.....310 832-6106
2300 Palos Verdes Dr N Rllng HLS Est (90274) *(P-6092)*
Metropolitan Water District.....D.....951 926-1501
33740 Borel Rd Winchester (92596) *(P-6093)*
Metropolitan Water Lavern, La Verne *Also called Metropolitan Water District (P-6089)*
Metropower Inc.....D.....562 305-9617
941 Grand Ave Long Beach (90804) *(P-2553)*
Metropro Road Services Inc (PA).....D.....714 556-7600
2550 S Garnsey St Santa Ana (92707) *(P-17421)*
Meus, Cypress *Also called Mitsubishi Electric Us Inc (P-3361)*
Mexican Amrcn Oprtnty Fndation (PA).....D.....323 890-9600
401 N Garfield Ave Montebello (90640) *(P-23339)*
Mexican Amrcn Oprtnty Fndation.....E.....323 588-7320
2650 Zoe Ave Fl 3 Huntington Park (90255) *(P-23752)*
Mexican Amrcn Oprtnty Fndation.....D.....323 890-1555
5657 E Washington Blvd Commerce (90040) *(P-23340)*
Mexican Heritg Ctr Gallery Inc.....D.....209 969-9306
111 S Sutter St Stockton (95202) *(P-24271)*
Meyer Coatings Inc.....E.....714 467-4600
1927 N Glassell St Orange (92865) *(P-2369)*
Meyer Corporation US.....D.....707 399-2100
2001 Meyer Way Fairfield (94533) *(P-6571)*
Meyer Properties Corp (PA).....D.....949 862-0500
4320 Von Karman Ave Newport Beach (92660) *(P-11578)*
Meyers Nave Riback Silver & (PA).....C.....510 351-4300
555 12th St Ste 1500 Oakland (94607) *(P-22686)*
Meyers Earthwork Inc.....D.....530 365-8858
4150 Fig Tree Ln Redding (96002) *(P-3323)*
Meyers Farming, Firebaugh *Also called Oxford Farms Inc (P-675)*
Meyers Group, Costa Mesa *Also called Hanley Wood Mkt Intelligence (P-25905)*
Meyers Research LLC.....D.....925 362-1028
675 Hartz Ave Danville (94526) *(P-26715)*
Mf Daily Oxnard Ranch Partnr.....E.....805 646-5633
1033 E Ojai Ave Ojai (93023) *(P-18269)*
Mf Services Company LLC (HQ).....D.....949 474-5800
4350 Von Karman Ave # 400 Newport Beach (92660) *(P-26716)*
Mfi Recovery Center (PA).....C.....951 683-6596
5870 Arlington Ave # 103 Riverside (92504) *(P-22067)*
Mfw Partners.....E.....858 454-8857
1120 Silverado St La Jolla (92037) *(P-10620)*
MGA Entertainment Inc (PA).....B.....818 894-2525
9220 Winnetka Ave Chatsworth (91311) *(P-7739)*
MGA Healthcare California Inc.....E.....310 324-5591
879 W 190th St Ste 700 Gardena (90248) *(P-14535)*
Mgb Construction Inc.....C.....951 342-0303
91 Commercial Ave Riverside (92507) *(P-1759)*
Mge Underground Inc.....D.....805 238-3510
816 26th St Paso Robles (93446) *(P-1891)*
Mggb Inc.....C.....714 226-0520
10841 Noel St Ste 110 Los Alamitos (90720) *(P-25209)*
Mgh Corporation.....E.....323 754-1408
1202 W 101st St Los Angeles (90044) *(P-23994)*
Mgi, Newark *Also called Mickwee Group Inc (P-16925)*
MGM, Beverly Hills *Also called Metro-Goldwyn-Mayer Inc (P-17635)*
MGM and Ua Services Company.....A.....310 449-3000
245 N Beverly Dr Beverly Hills (90210) *(P-27290)*
MGM Drywall Inc.....D.....408 292-4085
1050 Coml St Ste 102 San Jose (95112) *(P-2821)*
Mgr Services Inc.....D.....909 981-4466
1425 W Foothill Blvd # 300 Upland (91786) *(P-11296)*
MGT Industries Inc.....D.....310 324-3152
19034 S Vermont Ave Gardena (90248) *(P-26314)*
Mhh Holdings Inc.....C.....949 651-9903
5653 Alton Pkwy Irvine (92618) *(P-8606)*
Mhh Holdings Inc.....C.....626 744-9370
415 S Lake Ave Ste 108 Pasadena (91101) *(P-8607)*
Mhn Government Services LLC.....C.....916 294-4941
2370 Kerner Blvd San Rafael (94901) *(P-23341)*
MHRP Resort Inc.....D.....760 249-5808
24510 Highway 2 Wrightwood (92397) *(P-12615)*
MHS, San Diego *Also called Mental Health Systems Inc (P-22066)*
MHS, Fresno *Also called Turn Behavioral Hlth Svcs Inc (P-22146)*
MHS Customer Service Inc.....D.....858 695-2151
7586 Trade St Ste C San Diego (92121) *(P-14332)*
Mhx LLC.....D.....800 234-2098
22707 Wilmington Ave Carson (90745) *(P-4992)*
Mias Fashion Mfg Co Inc.....B.....562 906-1060
12623 Cisneros Ln Santa Fe Springs (90670) *(P-8095)*
Michaael S Hensley.....C.....650 692-7007
180 W Hill Pl Brisbane (94005) *(P-13439)*
Michael A Meczka.....E.....310 670-4824
5757 W Century Blvd # 120 Los Angeles (90045) *(P-25924)*
Michael B Mayock Inc.....D.....415 456-9306
1945 Francisco Blvd E # 31 San Rafael (94901) *(P-2822)*
Michael Baker Jr Inc.....D.....805 383-3373
5051 Verdugo Way Ste 300 Camarillo (93012) *(P-25210)*
Michael Baker Intl Inc.....C.....510 879-0950
1 Kaiser Plz Ste 1150 Oakland (94612) *(P-25211)*
Michael Baker Intl Inc.....D.....916 361-8384
2729 Prospect Park Dr # 220 Rancho Cordova (95670) *(P-27129)*
Michael Baker Intl Inc.....D.....858 453-3602
9755 Clairemont Mesa Blvd San Diego (92124) *(P-27130)*
Michael Baker Intl Inc.....E.....909 974-4900
3300 E Guasti Rd Ste 100 Ontario (91761) *(P-27131)*
Michael Baker Intl Inc.....D.....951 676-8042
40810 County Center Dr # 100 Temecula (92591) *(P-25212)*
Michael Bruington.....E.....831 663-1772
9 Soledad Dr Ste E Monterey (93940) *(P-1160)*
Michael Dusi Trucking Inc.....D.....805 237-9499
4305 Second Wind Way Paso Robles (93446) *(P-4097)*
Michael Jon Designs, Vernon *Also called Morgan Fabrics Corporation (P-8004)*
Michael Madden Co Inc.....D.....800 834-6248
2825 Warner Ave Irvine (92606) *(P-7885)*
Michael Maguire & Associates.....E.....714 435-7500
611 Anton Blvd Ste 900 Costa Mesa (92626) *(P-10427)*
Michael McCarthy.....E.....310 800-5367
3233 E Broadway Long Beach (90803) *(P-16352)*
Michael P Byko DDS A Prof Corp (PA).....D.....909 888-7817
164 W Hospitality Ln # 14 San Bernardino (92408) *(P-19620)*
Michael Reyes.....C.....909 444-0120
577 N D St Ste 111a14 San Bernardino (92401) *(P-1543)*
Michael S Duffy Sr Do Inc.....D.....619 461-3717
1501 5th Ave Ste 100 San Diego (92101) *(P-19195)*
Michael SD Nagatini.....D.....559 738-7502
5400 W Hillsdale Ave Visalia (93291) *(P-19196)*
Michael Sullivan & Assoc LLP.....C.....310 337-4480
400 Continental Blvd # 250 El Segundo (90245) *(P-22687)*
Michael W Morgan.....E.....760 344-5253
3949 Austin Rd Brawley (92227) *(P-64)*
Michael-Antonio Studio, Montclair *Also called E M S Trading Inc (P-8130)*
Michaels Stores Inc.....C.....661 951-3500
3501 W Avenue H Lancaster (93536) *(P-4450)*
Michaels Trnsp Svc Inc.....D.....707 674-6013
140 Yolano Dr Vallejo (94589) *(P-3770)*
Michaelson Connor & Boul (PA).....D.....714 230-3600
5312 Bolsa Ave Huntington Beach (92649) *(P-26717)*
Micheli Farms Inc.....E.....530 695-9022
6005 Highway 99 Live Oak (95953) *(P-211)*
Michelle Pasternak, Los Angeles *Also called SM 10000 Property LLC (P-11604)*
Michelson Laboratories Inc (PA).....D.....562 928-0553
6280 Chalet Dr Commerce (90040) *(P-26089)*
Mickey Wall Painting Inc.....E.....209 669-0557
250 East Ave Turlock (95380) *(P-2370)*
Mickwee Group Inc.....D.....510 651-5527
5600 Mowry School Rd # 230 Newark (94560) *(P-16925)*
Micon Construction Cal Inc.....D.....714 666-0203
1616 Sierra Madre Cir Placentia (92870) *(P-1544)*
Micro Holding Corp.....A.....415 788-5111
1 Maritime Plz Fl 12 San Francisco (94111) *(P-15789)*
Micro P Technologies, El Segundo *Also called Pcm Sales Inc (P-6882)*
Micro-Mechanics Inc.....E.....408 779-2927
465 Woodview Ave Morgan Hill (95037) *(P-7302)*
Micro-Pro Microfilming Svcs, Long Beach *Also called Macro-Pro Inc (P-16903)*
Micro-Technology Concepts Inc.....D.....626 839-6800
17837 Rowland St City of Industry (91748) *(P-6872)*
Microbial Diseases Laboratory, Richmond *Also called Department Health Care Svcs (P-21521)*
Microconstants Inc.....E.....858 652-4600
9050 Camino Santa Fe San Diego (92121) *(P-25799)*
Microfinancial Incorporated.....C.....805 367-8900
2801 Townsgate Rd Westlake Village (91361) *(P-14181)*
Microlease, Hayward *Also called Metric Equipment Sales Inc (P-7301)*
Microlease Inc (HQ).....D.....866 520-0200
6060 Sepulveda Blvd Van Nuys (91411) *(P-14182)*
Micromenders Inc (PA).....D.....415 344-0917
1388 Sutter St Ste 650 San Francisco (94109) *(P-6873)*
Microsoft Corporation.....D.....650 964-7200
1085 La Avenida St Mountain View (94043) *(P-15406)*
Microsoft Corporation.....D.....619 849-5872
7007 Friars Rd San Diego (92108) *(P-15407)*
Microsoft Corporation.....C.....650 693-1009
1020 Entp Way Bldg B Sunnyvale (94089) *(P-15408)*
Microsoft Corporation.....C.....949 263-3000
3 Park Plz Ste 1800 Irvine (92614) *(P-15409)*
Microsoft Corporation.....D.....213 806-7300
13031 W Jefferson Blvd # 200 Playa Vista (90094) *(P-15410)*
Microsoft Corporation.....C.....415 972-6400
555 California St Ste 200 San Francisco (94104) *(P-15411)*
Microsoft Corporation.....D.....408 987-9608
2045 Lafayette St Santa Clara (95050) *(P-15412)*
Microtek Lab Inc (HQ).....C.....310 687-5823
13337 South St Cerritos (90703) *(P-6759)*
Mid Century Insurance Company.....C.....323 932-7116
6303 Owensmouth Ave Woodland Hills (91367) *(P-10118)*
MID PENN HOUSING, Saratoga *Also called Saratoga Court Inc (P-10859)*
Mid Rckland Imging Prtners Inc (HQ).....E.....310 445-2800
1510 Cotner Ave Los Angeles (90025) *(P-21554)*
Mid State Steel Erection (PA).....D.....209 464-9497
1916 Cherokee Rd Stockton (95205) *(P-3274)*
Mid Valley Labor Services Inc.....B.....559 661-6390
19358 Avenue 18 1/2 Madera (93637) *(P-14333)*
Mid Valley Packaging & Sup Co, Fowler *Also called Gahvejian Enterprises Inc (P-7879)*
Mid Valley Plastering Inc.....B.....209 858-9766
15300 Mckinley Ave Lathrop (95330) *(P-2823)*
Mid Vlley Racquetball Athc CLB.....C.....818 705-6500
18420 Hart St Reseda (91335) *(P-18506)*
Mid Wilshire Health Care Ctr.....D.....213 483-9921
676 S Bonnie Brae St Los Angeles (90057) *(P-20138)*
Mid-Cities Association Inc (PA).....D.....310 537-4510
14208 Towne Ave Los Angeles (90061) *(P-23616)*
Mid-Peninsula Roofing Inc.....D.....650 375-7850
1326 Marsten Rd Burlingame (94010) *(P-3077)*
Mid-Peninsula Tyrella Corp (PA).....D.....650 299-8000
658 Bair Island Rd # 300 Redwood City (94063) *(P-10779)*
Mid-Valley Athletic Club, Reseda *Also called Mid Vlley Racquetball Athc CLB (P-18506)*
Mid-Valley Y M C A, Van Nuys *Also called Young Mens Chrstn Assn of La (P-24749)*

Employee Codes: A=Over 500 employees, B=251-500
C=101-250, D=51-100, E=50
2020 Directory of California
Wholesalers and Services Companies
© Mergent Inc. 1-800-342-5647
1351

Mida Industries Inc...C...562 616-1020
6101 Obispo Ave Long Beach (90805) ***(P-13982)***
Midas Express Los Angeles Inc...C...310 609-0366
11854 Alameda St Lynwood (90262) ***(P-4451)***
Midland Credit Management Inc (HQ)...A...877 240-2377
3111 Camino Del Rio N # 103 San Diego (92108) ***(P-9487)***
Midland Express Credit LLC...D...800 961-3904
2037 W Bullard Ave # 316 Fresno (93711) ***(P-26718)***
Midmark Diagnostics Group, Gardena *Also called Brentwood Medical Tech Corp* ***(P-6955)***
Midnight Auto Recycling LLC...E...909 884-5308
434 E 6th St San Bernardino (92410) ***(P-7764)***
Midnight Mission (PA)...D...213 624-9258
601 S San Pedro St Los Angeles (90014) ***(P-24592)***
Midnite Air Corp...E...310 330-2300
8801 Bellanca Ave Los Angeles (90045) ***(P-4724)***
Midnite Air Corp (HQ)...D...310 910-9199
5001 Arprt Plz Dr Ste 250 Long Beach (90815) ***(P-4725)***
Midori Landscape Inc...D...714 751-8792
3231 S Main St Santa Ana (92707) ***(P-868)***
Midori Landscaping, Santa Ana *Also called Midori Landscape Inc* ***(P-868)***
MIDPEN HOUSING, Foster City *Also called Menlo Gateway Inc* ***(P-10854)***
MIDPEN HOUSING, San Jose *Also called Vivente 1 Inc* ***(P-10860)***
Midpen Housing Corporation...B...650 356-2900
303 Vintage Park Dr # 250 Foster City (94404) ***(P-11579)***
Midpen Resident Services Corp...B...650 356-2965
303 Vintage Park Dr # 250 Foster City (94404) ***(P-10856)***
Midpeninsul Rgnl Opn Sp...D...650 691-1200
330 Distel Cir Los Altos (94022) ***(P-27291)***
Midstate Barrier Inc...D...209 944-9565
3291 S Highway 99 Stockton (95215) ***(P-1760)***
Midstate Construction Corp...D...707 762-3200
1180 Holm Rd Ste A Petaluma (94954) ***(P-1161)***
Midway Car Rental, North Hollywood *Also called Midway Rent A Car Inc* ***(P-17230)***
Midway Clinic Cars, Los Angeles *Also called Midway Rent A Car Inc* ***(P-17220)***
Midway International Inc...E...562 921-2255
13131 166th St Cerritos (90703) ***(P-8988)***
Midway Motors...D...310 649-5549
6151 W Century Blvd # 100 Los Angeles (90045) ***(P-17219)***
Midway Rent A Car Inc...C...818 985-9770
4201 Lankershim Blvd North Hollywood (91602) ***(P-17230)***
Midway Rent A Car Inc...D...310 445-4355
1800 S Sepulveda Blvd Los Angeles (90025) ***(P-17220)***
Midwest Enviromental Control...E...661 255-0722
22430 13th St Santa Clarita (91321) ***(P-25800)***
Mig Management Services LLC...D...949 474-5800
660 Newport Center Dr Newport Beach (92660) ***(P-26315)***
Mighty Enterprises Inc...D...310 516-7478
19706 Normandie Ave Torrance (90502) ***(P-7567)***
Mighty Leaf Tea...D...415 491-2650
100 Smith Ranch Rd # 120 San Rafael (94903) ***(P-8608)***
Mighty USA, Torrance *Also called Mighty Enterprises Inc* ***(P-7567)***
Mikado Best Western Hotel, North Hollywood *Also called Mikado Hotels Inc* ***(P-12616)***
Mikado Hotels Inc...E...818 763-9141
12600 Riverside Dr North Hollywood (91607) ***(P-12616)***
Mikaelian & Sons Inc...C...559 591-6324
10368 Avenue 400 Dinuba (93618) ***(P-65)***
Mike Brown Electric Co...D...707 792-8100
561a Mercantile Dr Cotati (94931) ***(P-2554)***
Mike Campbell & Associates Ltd...A...626 369-3981
10907 Downey Ave Ste 203 Downey (90241) ***(P-4350)***
Mike Campbell Assoc Logictics, Downey *Also called Mike Campbell & Associates Ltd* ***(P-4350)***
Mike Champlin...D...925 961-1004
4374 Contractors Cmn Livermore (94551) ***(P-2371)***
Mike Champlin Painting, Livermore *Also called Mike Champlin* ***(P-2371)***
Mike Jensen Farms...C...559 897-4192
13138 S Bethel Ave Kingsburg (93631) ***(P-212)***
Mike McCall Landscape Inc...C...925 363-8100
4749 Clayton Rd Concord (94521) ***(P-869)***
Mike Parker Landscape, Santa Ana *Also called Mpl Enterprises Inc* ***(P-873)***
Mike Roses Auto Body Inc...E...925 686-1739
2001 Fremont St Concord (94520) ***(P-17300)***
Mike Rovner Construction Inc...C...949 458-1562
22600 Lambert St Lake Forest (92630) ***(P-26316)***
Mike Rovner Construction Inc...C...408 453-6070
1758 Junction Ave Ste C San Jose (95112) ***(P-1162)***
Miken Clothing, Commerce *Also called Miken Sales Inc* ***(P-8096)***
Miken Sales Inc (PA)...D...323 266-2560
7230 Oxford Way Commerce (90040) ***(P-8096)***
Mikuni American Corporation (HQ)...D...310 676-0522
8910 Mikuni Ave Northridge (91324) ***(P-6454)***
Milan Corporation...E...510 656-6400
43230 Osgood Rd Fremont (94539) ***(P-3078)***
Milauskas Eye Institute, Rancho Mirage *Also called Outpatnt Eye Srgry Ctr of Dsrt* ***(P-19252)***
Milbank Global Securities, Los Angeles *Also called Milbank Tweed Hdley McCloy LLP* ***(P-22688)***
Milbank Tweed Hdley McCloy LLP...C...424 386-4000
2029 Century Park E # 3300 Los Angeles (90067) ***(P-22688)***
Milco Constructors Inc...E...562 595-1977
3930b Cherry Ave Long Beach (90807) ***(P-1975)***
Mile Post Properties LLC...D...415 673-4711
1050 Van Ness Ave San Francisco (94109) ***(P-12617)***
Mile Square Golf Course...C...714 962-5541
10401 Warner Ave Fountain Valley (92708) ***(P-18270)***
Miles Construction Group Inc...E...951 260-2504
42020 Winchester Rd Temecula (92590) ***(P-1163)***
Milestone Hospice...C...310 782-1177
1025 W 190th St Ste 450 Gardena (90248) ***(P-21813)***
Milestone Technologies Inc (PA)...C...510 651-2454
3101 Skyway Ct Fremont (94539) ***(P-15645)***
Milestone Topco Inc (HQ)...A...650 376-2300
901 Mariners Island Blvd San Mateo (94404) ***(P-11677)***
Milestones Adult Dev Ctr...D...707 644-0464
1 Florida St Vallejo (94590) ***(P-23342)***
Milestones of Development Inc...D...707 644-0496
1 Florida St Vallejo (94590) ***(P-20440)***
Milhous Feed...C...530 292-3242
24077 State Highway 49 Nevada City (95959) ***(P-8847)***
Milken Family Foundation...C...310 570-4800
1250 4th St Fl 1 Santa Monica (90401) ***(P-24593)***
Milken Institute...E...310 570-4600
1250 4th St Santa Monica (90401) ***(P-26010)***
Mill Creek Manor, Mentone *Also called Nice Avenue LLC* ***(P-20156)***
Mill Valley Parks & Recreation, Mill Valley *Also called City of Mill Valley* ***(P-18659)***
Mill Valley Refuse Service Inc...D...415 457-2287
112 Front St San Rafael (94901) ***(P-6223)***
Millbrae Serra Sanitarium...C...650 697-8386
150 Serra Ave Millbrae (94030) ***(P-20633)***
Millbrae Srra Cnvalescent Hosp, Millbrae *Also called Millbrae Serra Sanitarium* ***(P-20633)***
Millbrae Wcp Hotel II LLC...E...650 443-5500
401 E Millbrae Ave Millbrae (94030) ***(P-12618)***
Millenia Development...E...951 660-5691
929 Bettina Way San Jacinto (92582) ***(P-1164)***
Millenium Athletic Club LLc...D...805 562-3845
170 Los Carneros Way Goleta (93117) ***(P-18176)***
Millennia Holdings Inc...D...213 252-1230
3731 Wilshire Blvd # 618 Los Angeles (90010) ***(P-26719)***
Millennia Stainless Inc...D...562 946-3545
10016 Romandel Ave Santa Fe Springs (90670) ***(P-7644)***
Millennial Brands LLC (PA)...D...866 938-4806
2000 Crow Canyon Pl # 300 San Ramon (94583) ***(P-8138)***
Millennium Biltmore Hotel, Los Angeles *Also called Whb Corporation* ***(P-13094)***
Millennium Engrg Integration...D...703 413-7750
350 N Akron Rd Moffett Field (94035) ***(P-25213)***
Millennium Health LLC...B...877 451-3534
16981 Via Tazon Ste F San Diego (92127) ***(P-26090)***
Millennium Transportation Inc...D...714 956-7882
3164 E La Palma Ave Ste D Anaheim (92806) ***(P-4993)***
Miller Starr & Regalia A Pro (PA)...D...925 935-9400
1331 N Calif Blvd Ste 500 Walnut Creek (94596) ***(P-22689)***
Miller & Associates LLP...D...310 315-1100
2530 Wilshire Blvd Fl 1 Santa Monica (90403) ***(P-22690)***
Miller Children's Hospital, Long Beach *Also called Long Beach Memorial Med Ctr* ***(P-21019)***
Miller Environmental Inc...C...714 385-0099
1130 W Trenton Ave Orange (92867) ***(P-3346)***
Millers Progressive Care, Riverside *Also called Wilmon Corporation* ***(P-20388)***
Millie and Severson Inc...D...562 493-3611
3601 Serpentine Dr Los Alamitos (90720) ***(P-1367)***
Milliman Inc...E...415 403-1333
650 California St Fl 21 San Francisco (94108) ***(P-27292)***
Millmens Local 1496...E...559 275-8676
6190 N Cecelia Ave Fresno (93722) ***(P-24452)***
Mills Corporation...D...909 484-8300
1 Mills Cir Ste 1 # 1 Ontario (91764) ***(P-10621)***
Mills-Peninsula Health HM Care, San Mateo *Also called Alliance Hospital Services* ***(P-21654)***
Millsap Degnan & Assoc Inc...D...415 472-4244
4280 Redwood Hwy Ste 10 San Rafael (94903) ***(P-25214)***
Millward Brown LLC...E...310 309-3352
2425 Olympic Blvd 240e Santa Monica (90404) ***(P-25925)***
Millwork Holdings, Irvine *Also called Alton Irvine Inc* ***(P-6502)***
Milo Wind Project LLC...D...888 903-6926
15445 Innovation Dr San Diego (92128) ***(P-5858)***
Milpitas Medical Offices, Milpitas *Also called Kaiser Foundation Hospitals* ***(P-19110)***
Milspec Industries Inc (HQ)...D...213 680-9690
5825 Greenwood Ave Commerce (90040) ***(P-7401)***
Milt & Michael Master Dry Clrs, Burbank *Also called Shadkor Inc* ***(P-13259)***
Miltenyi Biotec Inc (HQ)...D...530 745-2800
2303 Lindbergh St Auburn (95602) ***(P-6978)***
Milwood Healthcare Inc...D...626 274-4345
2641 S C St Oxnard (93033) ***(P-10622)***
Mimg Medical Management LLC...D...949 282-1600
26522 La Alameda Ste 120 Mission Viejo (92691) ***(P-26317)***
Minami Tamaki LLP...E...415 788-9000
360 Post St Fl 8 San Francisco (94108) ***(P-22691)***
Mind Dragon Inc...E...877 367-6060
36002 Pansy St Winchester (92596) ***(P-27132)***
Mind Research Institute...C...949 345-8700
111 Academy Ste 100 Irvine (92617) ***(P-26011)***
Mindbody Inc (PA)...C...877 755-4279
4051 Broad St Ste 220 San Luis Obispo (93401) ***(P-15790)***
Mindfull Body...D...415 931-2639
2876 California St San Francisco (94115) ***(P-18722)***
Mindlance Inc...C...858 433-9298
10679 Westview Pkwy Fl 2 San Diego (92126) ***(P-26720)***
Mindless Entertainment, North Hollywood *Also called 51 Minds Entertainment LLC* ***(P-17958)***
Mindsource Inc...D...650 314-6400
555 Clyde Ave Ste 100 Mountain View (94043) ***(P-14937)***
Mindwave Software, San Diego *Also called Isaac Fair Corporation* ***(P-14890)***
Mine Fashion, Los Angeles *Also called Edgemine Inc* ***(P-8070)***
Minegar Contracting Inc...E...760 598-5001
925 Poinsettia Ave Ste 10 Vista (92081) ***(P-3183)***
Minerva Networks Inc (PA)...D...800 806-9594
1600 Technology Dr Fl 8 San Jose (95110) ***(P-14938)***
Mineta San Jose Intl Arprt, San Jose *Also called City of San Jose* ***(P-4761)***
Ming Medical Offices, Bakersfield *Also called Kaiser Foundation Hospitals* ***(P-19062)***

Minilec Service Inc......E......818 341-1125
9207 Deering Ave Ste A Chatsworth (91311) ***(P-17436)***
Minilec Service-Los Angeles BR, Chatsworth *Also called Minilec Service Inc* ***(P-17436)***
Miniluxe Inc......D......424 442-1630
11965 San Vicente Blvd Los Angeles (90049) ***(P-13352)***
Minimalisms Inc......D......415 309-3108
49 Missouri St Apt 10 San Francisco (94107) ***(P-16926)***
Minimatics Inc (PA)......D......650 969-5630
3445 De La Cruz Blvd Santa Clara (95054) ***(P-7303)***
Minka Group, Corona *Also called Minka Lighting Inc* ***(P-7167)***
Minka Lighting Inc (PA)......D......951 735-9220
1151 Bradford Cir Corona (92882) ***(P-7167)***
Minolta Business Systems, Gardena *Also called Konica Minolta Business Soluti* ***(P-6756)***
Minority Aids Project Inc......D......323 936-4949
5147 W Jefferson Blvd Los Angeles (90016) ***(P-23343)***
Minshew Brothers Stl Cnstr Inc......C......619 561-5700
12578 Vigilante Rd Lakeside (92040) ***(P-1368)***
Mintie Corporation (PA)......D......323 225-4111
1114 N San Fernando Rd Los Angeles (90065) ***(P-13983)***
Mintie Technologies, Los Angeles *Also called Mintie Corporation* ***(P-13983)***
Mintz Levin Cohn Ferris GL......D......858 314-1500
3580 Carmel Mountain Rd # 300 San Diego (92130) ***(P-22692)***
Mira Mesa Stadium 18, San Diego *Also called Edwards Theatres Circuit Inc* ***(P-17836)***
Mirabella Farms Inc......D......559 237-4495
5551 S Orange Ave Fresno (93725) ***(P-148)***
Miracle Home Health Agency......E......562 653-0668
13146 Mungo Ct Rancho Cucamonga (91739) ***(P-21814)***
Mirada, Long Beach *Also called Motion Theory Inc* ***(P-13792)***
Mirada Hills Rehb & Conva, La Mirada *Also called Life Care Centers America Inc* ***(P-20072)***
Miramar Ford Truck Sales Inc......D......619 272-5340
6066 Miramar Rd San Diego (92121) ***(P-6406)***
Miramar Hotel, Santa Barbara *Also called Morgans Hotel Group MGT LLC* ***(P-12631)***
Miramar Transportation Inc......D......858 693-0071
9340 Cabot Dr Ste I San Diego (92126) ***(P-4994)***
Miramar Truck Center, San Diego *Also called Transwest San Diego LLC* ***(P-4237)***
Miramax Film Ny LLC (HQ)......D......310 409-4321
1901 Avenue Of The Stars # 2000 Los Angeles (90067) ***(P-17636)***
Miramed Global Services Inc......A......805 277-1017
199 E Thsand Oaks Blvd Thousand Oaks (91360) ***(P-27133)***
Miramnte High Schl Parents CLB......C......925 280-3965
750 Moraga Way Orinda (94563) ***(P-24196)***
Miramonte Enterprises LLC......C......951 658-9441
275 N San Jacinto St Hemet (92543) ***(P-20139)***
Mirion Technologies Gds Inc (HQ)......C......949 419-1000
2652 Mcgaw Ave Irvine (92614) ***(P-26091)***
Mirnavseh Inc......D......858 335-2470
8436 Florissant Ct San Diego (92129) ***(P-14939)***
Mirum Inc......C......619 237-5552
350 10th Ave Ste 1200 San Diego (92101) ***(P-13791)***
Mis Sciences Corp......C......818 847-0213
2550 N Hollywood Way Burbank (91505) ***(P-5438)***
Mishima Foods USA Inc (PA)......D......310 787-1533
2340 Plaza Del Amo # 105 Torrance (90501) ***(P-8197)***
Mission Ambulance Inc......D......951 272-2300
1055 E 3rd St Corona (92879) ***(P-3701)***
MISSION BARGAIN CENTER, Oxnard *Also called Rescue Mission Alliance* ***(P-24859)***
MISSION BAY AQUATIC CENTER, San Diego *Also called Associated Students San Diego* ***(P-24791)***
Mission Beverage Co (HQ)......C......323 266-6238
550 S Mission Rd Los Angeles (90033) ***(P-8781)***
Mission Car Wash......E......707 537-2040
59 Mission Cir Santa Rosa (95409) ***(P-17389)***
Mission Car Wash & Quik Lube, Santa Rosa *Also called Mission Car Wash* ***(P-17389)***
MISSION CARE CENTER, Riverside *Also called Riverside Equities LLC* ***(P-20218)***
Mission Care Center, Rosemead *Also called Ensign Group Inc* ***(P-19887)***
Mission Cmmons Rtrment Rsdence, Redlands *Also called Harvest Facility Holdings LP* ***(P-10735)***
Mission Community Hospital, Panorama City *Also called Deanco Healthcare LLC* ***(P-20825)***
Mission Courier Inc......D......916 484-1992
3204 Orange Grove Ave North Highlands (95660) ***(P-16927)***
Mission De La Casa, San Jose *Also called Careage Inc* ***(P-19779)***
Mission Drive-In Theatre Co......D......909 465-9219
4407 State St Montclair (91763) ***(P-17874)***
MISSION ELECTRIC COMPANY, Fremont *Also called Kositch Enterprises Inc* ***(P-2534)***
Mission Energy Holding Company......A......949 752-5588
2600 Michelson Dr # 1700 Irvine (92612) ***(P-11678)***
Mission Federal Credit Union (PA)......A......858 546-2184
5785 Oberlin Dr Ste 312 San Diego (92121) ***(P-9326)***
Mission Federal Services LLC (PA)......C......858 524-2850
10325 Meanley Dr San Diego (92131) ***(P-9327)***
Mission Hills Country Club Inc......C......760 324-9400
34600 Mission Hills Dr Rancho Mirage (92270) ***(P-18507)***
Mission Hills Healthcare Ctr, San Diego *Also called Mission Hills Healthcare Inc* ***(P-20140)***
Mission Hills Healthcare Inc......D......619 297-4086
726 Torrance St San Diego (92103) ***(P-20140)***
Mission Hills Mortgage Bankers, Irvine *Also called Mission Hills Mortgage Corp* ***(P-9581)***
Mission Hills Mortgage Corp (HQ)......C......714 972-3832
18500 Von Karman Ave # 1100 Irvine (92612) ***(P-9581)***
Mission Hills Post Acute Care......D......619 297-4484
3680 Reynard Way San Diego (92103) ***(P-23995)***
Mission Hills Senior Living......D......760 770-7737
34560 Bob Hope Dr Rancho Mirage (92270) ***(P-23996)***
Mission Hosp Regional Med Ctr (PA)......A......949 364-1400
27700 Medical Center Rd Mission Viejo (92691) ***(P-21046)***
Mission Hospice & HM Care Inc (PA)......C......650 554-1000
1670 S Amphlett Blvd # 300 San Mateo (94402) ***(P-24849)***
Mission Inn Hotel and Spa, The, Riverside *Also called Historic Mission Inn Corp* ***(P-12365)***
Mission Internal Med Group Inc......C......949 364-3570
26800 Crown Valley Pkwy # 103 Mission Viejo (92691) ***(P-19197)***
Mission Internal Med Group Inc......C......949 364-3605
27882 Forbes Rd Ste 110 Laguna Niguel (92677) ***(P-19198)***
Mission Landscape Service......D......909 947-7290
952 E Francis St Ontario (91761) ***(P-870)***
Mission Lane LLC......D......408 505-3081
101 2nd St Ste 350 San Francisco (94105) ***(P-16928)***
Mission Ldscp Companies Inc......C......714 545-9962
536 E Dyer Rd Santa Ana (92707) ***(P-742)***
Mission Linen & Uniform Svc, Oceanside *Also called Mission Linen Supply* ***(P-13224)***
Mission Linen & Uniform Svc, Sacramento *Also called Mission Linen Supply* ***(P-13226)***
Mission Linen & Uniform Svc, Salinas *Also called Mission Linen Supply* ***(P-13227)***
Mission Linen & Uniform Svc, Fresno *Also called Mission Linen Supply* ***(P-13229)***
Mission Linen & Uniform Svc, Oxnard *Also called Mission Linen Supply* ***(P-13230)***
Mission Linen & Uniform Svc, San Francisco *Also called Mission Linen Supply* ***(P-13231)***
Mission Linen & Uniform Svc, Salinas *Also called Mission Linen Supply* ***(P-13300)***
Mission Linen & Uniform Svc, Santa Barbara *Also called Mission Linen Supply* ***(P-13232)***
Mission Linen & Uniform Svc, Chico *Also called Mission Linen Supply* ***(P-13233)***
Mission Linen & Uniform Svc, Sacramento *Also called Mission Linen Supply* ***(P-13301)***
Mission Linen & Uniform Svc, Santa Maria *Also called Mission Linen Supply* ***(P-13234)***
Mission Linen & Uniform Svc, Chino *Also called Mission Linen Supply* ***(P-13235)***
Mission Linen Supply......C......760 757-9099
2727 Industry St Oceanside (92054) ***(P-13224)***
Mission Linen Supply......E......805 772-4451
399 Errol St Morro Bay (93442) ***(P-13225)***
Mission Linen Supply......C......916 423-3179
7520 Reese Rd Sacramento (95828) ***(P-13226)***
Mission Linen Supply......D......831 424-1707
315 Kern St Salinas (93905) ***(P-13227)***
Mission Linen Supply......D......510 996-3416
6590 Central Ave Newark (94560) ***(P-13984)***
Mission Linen Supply......D......707 443-8681
1401 Summer St Eureka (95501) ***(P-13228)***
Mission Linen Supply......D......559 268-0647
2555 S Orange Ave Fresno (93725) ***(P-13229)***
Mission Linen Supply......D......805 485-6794
505 Maulhardt Ave Oxnard (93030) ***(P-13230)***
Mission Linen Supply......C......510 429-7305
550 Florida St San Francisco (94110) ***(P-13231)***
Mission Linen Supply......C......831 424-1753
435 W Market St Salinas (93901) ***(P-13300)***
Mission Linen Supply......E......805 962-7687
712 E Montecito St Santa Barbara (93103) ***(P-13232)***
Mission Linen Supply......E......530 342-4110
1340 W 7th St Chico (95928) ***(P-13233)***
Mission Linen Supply......C......916 423-3135
7524 Reese Rd Sacramento (95828) ***(P-13301)***
Mission Linen Supply......D......805 922-3579
602 S Western Ave Santa Maria (93458) ***(P-13234)***
Mission Linen Supply......B......909 393-5589
5400 Alton Way Chino (91710) ***(P-13235)***
Mission Linen Supply & Svcs, Eureka *Also called Mission Linen Supply* ***(P-13228)***
Mission Medical Entps Inc......C......559 582-2871
1007 W Lacey Blvd Hanford (93230) ***(P-20141)***
Mission Medical Entps Inc......D......559 582-4414
851 Leslie Ln Hanford (93230) ***(P-20142)***
Mission Neighborhood Hlth Ctr (PA)......C......415 552-3870
240 Shotwell St San Francisco (94110) ***(P-19199)***
Mission Oaks Hospital, Los Gatos *Also called Good Samaritan Hospital LP* ***(P-20894)***
Mission Oaks Recreation Pk Dst......D......916 488-2810
3344 Mission Ave Carmichael (95608) ***(P-18723)***
Mission Peak Orthopedics......D......510 797-3933
5924 Stoneridge Dr # 200 Pleasanton (94588) ***(P-19200)***
Mission Pets Inc......E......415 904-9914
986 Mission St Fl 5 San Francisco (94103) ***(P-8989)***
Mission Pines Apts, Martinez *Also called Braddock & Logan Inc* ***(P-10698)***
Mission Produce Inc......D......805 981-3650
3803 Dufau Rd Oxnard (93033) ***(P-8498)***
Mission Ranch Inc......E......831 624-6436
26270 Dolores St Carmel (93923) ***(P-12619)***
Mission Security and Patrol......D......805 899-3039
27 W Anapamu St Ste 141 Santa Barbara (93101) ***(P-16353)***
Mission Series Inc......E......714 736-1000
1585 W Mission Blvd Pomona (91766) ***(P-7969)***
Mission Skilled Nursing Home, Santa Clara *Also called Covenant Care California LLC* ***(P-19829)***
Mission Stuart Ht Partners LLC......C......415 278-3700
8 Mission St San Francisco (94105) ***(P-12620)***
Mission Terrace, Santa Barbara *Also called Cliff View Terrace Inc* ***(P-23868)***
Mission Trail Wste Systems Inc......D......408 727-5365
1060 Richard Ave Santa Clara (95050) ***(P-3913)***
Mission Truck Sales......D......408 436-2920
780 E Brokaw Rd San Jose (95112) ***(P-17231)***
Mission Valley Bancorp......D......818 394-2300
9116 Sunland Blvd Sun Valley (91352) ***(P-11639)***
Mission Valley Ht Operator Inc......D......619 291-5720
595 Hotel Cir S San Diego (92108) ***(P-12621)***
Mission Valley Hts Surgery Ctr......D......619 291-3737
7485 Mission Valley Rd # 106 San Diego (92108) ***(P-19201)***
Mission Valley Truck Center, San Jose *Also called Mission Truck Sales* ***(P-17231)***
Mission Valley V A, San Diego *Also called Veterans Health Administration* ***(P-19569)***
Mission Valley YMCA, San Diego *Also called YMCA of San Diego County* ***(P-24715)***
Mission Viejo Country Club......C......949 582-1550
26200 Country Club Dr Mission Viejo (92691) ***(P-18508)***
Mission View Health Center, San Luis Obispo *Also called Compass Health Inc* ***(P-20530)***

ALPHABETIC

Employee Codes: A=Over 500 employees, B=251-500
C=101-250, D=51-100, E=50
2020 Directory of California
Wholesalers and Services Companies
© Mergent Inc. 1-800-342-5647
1353

Mission Villa LLC.....E.....650 756-1995
995 E Market St Daly City (94014) ***(P-23997)***
Mission Vlla Alzhmers Rsidence.....E.....408 559-8301
3333 S Bascom Ave Campbell (95008) ***(P-23998)***
Mist Systems Inc.....C.....408 326-0346
1601 S De Anza Blvd # 248 Cupertino (95014) ***(P-15646)***
Mistras Group Inc.....D.....661 829-1192
21215 Kratzmeyer Rd A Bakersfield (93314) ***(P-25215)***
Mistras Group Inc.....D.....562 597-3932
2230 E Artesia Blvd Long Beach (90805) ***(P-25216)***
Mistras Group Inc.....D.....323 583-1653
8427 Atlantic Ave Cudahy (90201) ***(P-25217)***
Mistras Group Inc.....E.....707 746-5870
6170 Egret Ct Benicia (94510) ***(P-26092)***
Mistras Impro, Bakersfield *Also called Mistras Group Inc* ***(P-25215)***
Mitch Brown Construction Inc.....D.....559 781-6389
14200 Road 284 Porterville (93257) ***(P-1976)***
Mitchell Buckman Inc (PA).....D.....559 733-1181
500 N Santa Fe St Visalia (93292) ***(P-10428)***
Mitchell Concrete, Rancho Cordova *Also called Mitchell Jones Concrete Inc* ***(P-3184)***
Mitchell Engineering.....E.....415 227-1040
1395 Evans Ave San Francisco (94124) ***(P-3324)***
Mitchell International Inc (HQ).....C.....858 368-7000
6220 Greenwich Dr San Diego (92122) ***(P-14940)***
Mitchell Jones Concrete Inc.....C.....916 638-6870
3185 Fitzgerald Rd Rancho Cordova (95742) ***(P-3184)***
Mitchell Silberberg Knupp LLP (PA).....C.....310 312-2000
2049 Century Park E Fl 18 Los Angeles (90067) ***(P-22693)***
Mitchell Vineyard Management, Saint Helena *Also called Mitchell Vineyards LLC* ***(P-672)***
Mitchell Vineyards LLC.....D.....707 963-7050
1831 Sarahs Way Saint Helena (94574) ***(P-672)***
Mitchells Group Home, Los Angeles *Also called Mgh Corporation* ***(P-23994)***
Mitsuba Corporation.....D.....909 374-2631
2509 Reata Pl Diamond Bar (91765) ***(P-6874)***
Mitsubishi Electric Us Inc (HQ).....C.....714 220-2500
5900 Katella Ave Ste A Cypress (90630) ***(P-3361)***
Mitsubishi Electric Us Inc.....D.....714 934-5300
7345 Orangewood Ave Garden Grove (92841) ***(P-7304)***
Mitsubishi Motors Cr Amer Inc (HQ).....B.....714 799-4730
6400 Katella Ave Cypress (90630) ***(P-9467)***
Mitsubishi Warehouse Cal Corp.....D.....310 886-5500
3040 E Victoria St Compton (90221) ***(P-4452)***
Mitsui & Co (usa) Inc.....D.....213 896-1100
601 S Figueroa St # 1900 Los Angeles (90017) ***(P-7080)***
Mitsui USA, Los Angeles *Also called Mitsui & Co (usa) Inc* ***(P-7080)***
Mitzel Company, Santa Ana *Also called Ralph D Mitzel Inc* ***(P-14110)***
Mixpanel Inc (PA).....D.....415 688-4001
1 Front St Ste 2800 San Francisco (94111) ***(P-14941)***
Miyako Hotels.....D.....213 617-2000
328 E 1st St Ste 510 Los Angeles (90012) ***(P-12622)***
Mizuho Securities USA Inc.....D.....415 268-5500
3 Embarcadero Ctr # 1620 San Francisco (94111) ***(P-9726)***
Mj Star-Lite Inc.....E.....818 717-0834
9232 Independence Ave Chatsworth (91311) ***(P-2555)***
MJB Partners LLC.....D.....909 623-2481
651 N Main St Pomona (91768) ***(P-20143)***
Mjd Construction Corp.....D.....818 575-9864
28244 Dorothy Dr Agoura Hills (91301) ***(P-1165)***
Mjp Empire Inc (PA).....B.....714 564-7900
1682 Langley Ave Fl 2 Irvine (92614) ***(P-2372)***
Mkni, Visalia *Also called Morgan Kleppe & Nash* ***(P-10430)***
ML Electricworks Inc.....D.....951 687-5078
11325 Magnolia Ave Riverside (92505) ***(P-2556)***
ML Prior Inc.....C.....626 653-5160
955 Berrand Ct Ste 200 San Dimas (91773) ***(P-22694)***
Mladen Buntich Cnstr Co Inc.....D.....909 920-9977
1500 W 9th St Upland (91786) ***(P-1892)***
Mlim Holdings LLC.....A.....619 299-3131
350 Camino De La Reina San Diego (92108) ***(P-11679)***
Mlslistings Inc.....D.....408 874-0200
740 Kifer Rd Sunnyvale (94086) ***(P-26721)***
Mm Advertising, Cypress *Also called Money Mailer LLC* ***(P-13731)***
MMC, San Diego *Also called Medical Management Cons Inc* ***(P-26704)***
MMC, Los Angeles *Also called Medical Management Cons Inc* ***(P-14531)***
Mmi Services Inc.....C.....661 589-9366
4042 Patton Way Bakersfield (93308) ***(P-1031)***
MNS Engineers Inc (PA).....D.....805 692-6921
201 N Calle Cesar Santa Barbara (93103) ***(P-25218)***
MNX, Long Beach *Also called Midnite Air Corp* ***(P-4725)***
Moaddel Law Firm APC.....E.....323 999-5099
3435 Wilshire Blvd # 2430 Los Angeles (90010) ***(P-22695)***
Mobica US Inc.....A.....650 450-6654
2570 N 1st St Fl 2 San Jose (95131) ***(P-15647)***
Mobile Application, Santa Clara *Also called Soundhound Inc* ***(P-15119)***
Mobile Hm Communities of Amer (PA).....C.....408 279-5200
1122 Willow St Ste 200 San Jose (95125) ***(P-10863)***
Mobile Modular, Livermore *Also called McGrath Rentcorp* ***(P-7564)***
Mobileiron Inc (PA).....C.....650 919-8100
401 E Middlefield Rd Mountain View (94043) ***(P-15413)***
Mobilenet Services Inc (PA).....C.....949 951-4444
18 Morgan Ste 200 Irvine (92618) ***(P-25219)***
Mobilitie Investments III LLC.....C.....877 999-7070
2955 Red Hill Ave Ste 200 Costa Mesa (92626) ***(P-5263)***
Mobilitie Services LLC.....B.....877 999-7070
660 Newport Center Dr Newport Beach (92660) ***(P-5439)***
Mobilityware, Irvine *Also called Upstanding LLC* ***(P-15528)***
Mobilityware LLC (PA).....D.....949 788-9900
440 Exchange Ste 100 Irvine (92602) ***(P-14942)***
Mobilygen Corporation.....D.....408 601-1000
160 Rio Robles San Jose (95134) ***(P-7305)***
Mobis Parts America LLC (HQ).....D.....786 515-1101
10550 Talbert Ave Fl 4 Fountain Valley (92708) ***(P-6455)***
Mobis Wholesale, Carpinteria *Also called Ocean Breeze International* ***(P-266)***
Mobitv Inc.....D.....510 981-1303
1900 Powell St Ste 900 Emeryville (94608) ***(P-5440)***
Mobpartner Inc.....D.....650 300-6388
4151 Mddlfield Rd Ste 100 San Francisco (94103) ***(P-13607)***
Moc Products Company Inc.....D.....510 635-1230
9840 Kitty Ln Oakland (94603) ***(P-17422)***
Mocana Corporation.....D.....415 617-0055
111 W Evelyn Ave Ste 210 Sunnyvale (94086) ***(P-15791)***
Mocean, Burbank *Also called Cmp Film & Design Burbank LLC* ***(P-26904)***
Mocean LLC.....C.....310 481-0808
2440 S Sepulveda Blvd # 150 Los Angeles (90064) ***(P-15792)***
Mocha, Oakland *Also called Museum of Childrens Art* ***(P-18726)***
Mochahost.com, San Jose *Also called Mochanin LLC* ***(P-15793)***
Mochanin LLC.....D.....408 432-7259
2880 Zanker Rd Ste 203 San Jose (95134) ***(P-15793)***
Mocse Federal Credit Union.....D.....209 572-3600
3600 Coffee Rd Modesto (95355) ***(P-9328)***
Mod Vid Film, Glendale *Also called Modern Videofilm Inc* ***(P-17750)***
Modern Building Inc.....E.....530 891-4533
3083 Southgate Ln Chico (95928) ***(P-1369)***
Modern Button Company of Cal.....E.....213 747-7431
3957 S Hill St Los Angeles (90037) ***(P-8003)***
Modern Dev Co A Ltd Partnr.....D.....949 646-6400
7900 All America City Way Paramount (90723) ***(P-16929)***
Modern Hr Inc.....B.....310 270-9800
9000 W Sunset Blvd # 900 West Hollywood (90069) ***(P-26722)***
Modern Parking Inc.....D.....310 821-1081
14110 Palawan Way Marina Del Rey (90292) ***(P-17264)***
Modern Videofilm Inc.....C.....818 637-6800
1733 Flower St Glendale (91201) ***(P-17750)***
Modern Videofilm Inc (PA).....C.....818 840-1700
2300 W Empire Ave Burbank (91504) ***(P-17751)***
Modesto & Empire Traction Co (HQ).....D.....209 524-4631
530 11th St Modesto (95354) ***(P-3502)***
Modesto Court Room Inc.....D.....209 577-1060
2012 Mchenry Ave Modesto (95350) ***(P-18509)***
Modesto Hospitality LLC.....C.....209 526-6000
1150 9th St Modesto (95354) ***(P-12623)***
Modesto Hospitality Lessee LLC.....D.....209 526-6000
1150 9th St Ste C Modesto (95354) ***(P-12624)***
Modesto Imaging Center, Modesto *Also called Radnet Management Inc* ***(P-26372)***
Modesto Industrial Elec Co Inc (PA).....C.....209 527-2800
1417 Coldwell Ave Modesto (95350) ***(P-2557)***
Modesto Irrigation District.....B.....209 526-7563
1231 11th St Modesto (95354) ***(P-5859)***
Modesto Irrigation District (PA).....C.....209 526-7337
1231 11th St Modesto (95354) ***(P-5860)***
Modesto Irrigation District.....B.....209 526-7373
929 Woodland Ave Modesto (95351) ***(P-5861)***
Modesto Medical Offices, Modesto *Also called Kaiser Foundation Hospitals* ***(P-19081)***
Modesto Wstewater Trtmnt Plant.....D.....209 577-5300
1221 Sutter Ave Modesto (95351) ***(P-6224)***
Modoc County ADM Svcs, Alturas *Also called County of Modoc* ***(P-23116)***
MODOC MEDICAL CENTER, Alturas *Also called Last Frontier Healthcare Dst* ***(P-20997)***
Modrine Limited.....D.....213 269-5466
750 N Diamond Bar Blvd Diamond Bar (91765) ***(P-14943)***
Modular Systems Inc.....D.....805 963-9350
800 Garden St Ste K Santa Barbara (93101) ***(P-11297)***
Moffatt & Nichol.....E.....925 944-5411
2001 N Main St Ste 360 Walnut Creek (94596) ***(P-25220)***
Moffatt & Nichol.....D.....657 261-2699
555 Anton Blvd Ste 400 Costa Mesa (92626) ***(P-25221)***
Moffatt & Nichol.....E.....510 645-1238
1300 Clay St Oakland (94612) ***(P-25222)***
Moffatt & Nichol.....D.....562 426-9551
4225 E Conant St Ste 201 Long Beach (90808) ***(P-25223)***
Moffitt H C Hospital.....C.....415 476-1000
505 Parnassus Ave San Francisco (94143) ***(P-21047)***
Mofo, San Francisco *Also called Morrison & Foerster LLP* ***(P-22706)***
Mogannam and Whalen Med Corp, Los Angeles *Also called Whalen Medical Corporation* ***(P-23545)***
Mohan Dialysis Center Industry.....D.....626 333-3801
15757 E Valley Blvd City of Industry (91744) ***(P-21930)***
Mohan Dialysis Ctr of Covina.....D.....626 859-2522
158 W College St Covina (91723) ***(P-21931)***
Mojo Networks Inc (PA).....C.....650 961-1111
5453 Great America Pkwy Santa Clara (95054) ***(P-14944)***
Mola Inc.....C.....323 582-0088
2957 E 46th St Vernon (90058) ***(P-8097)***
Mold Testing and Inspection.....D.....760 643-1834
4785 Sequoia Pl Oceanside (92057) ***(P-16930)***
Molina Healthcare Inc.....B.....858 614-1580
9275 Sky Park Ct Ste 400 San Diego (92123) ***(P-22276)***
Molina Healthcare Inc.....C.....909 546-7116
790 E Foothill Blvd Rialto (92376) ***(P-19202)***
Molina Healthcare Inc.....B.....888 562-5442
604 Pine Ave Long Beach (90802) ***(P-19203)***
Molina Healthcare Inc.....B.....310 221-3031
1500 Hughes Way Long Beach (90810) ***(P-10019)***
Molina Healthcare Inc (PA).....A.....562 435-3666
200 Oceangate Ste 100 Long Beach (90802) ***(P-19204)***
Molina Healthcare Inc.....B.....562 435-3666
1 Golden Shore Long Beach (90802) ***(P-22277)***

Molina Healthcare California ....C....800 526-8196
200 Oceangate Ste 100 Long Beach (90802) ***(P-19205)***
Molina Healthcare of Californi ....A....562 435-3666
200 Oceangate Ste 100 Long Beach (90802) ***(P-9911)***
Molinas Pntg Wallcovering Inc ....D....925 228-7487
4285 Pacheco Blvd Martinez (94553) ***(P-2373)***
Molly Maid, La Verne *Also called Steve and Beth Chaput* ***(P-14058)***
Molly Maid ....E....949 367-8000
24412 Muirlands Blvd A Lake Forest (92630) ***(P-13985)***
Momentous Insurance Brkg Inc ....D....818 933-2700
5990 Sepulvda Blvd # 550 Van Nuys (91411) ***(P-10429)***
Momentum For Mental Health ....D....408 261-7777
2001 The Alameda San Jose (95126) ***(P-24197)***
Moms Orange County ....E....714 972-2610
1128 W Santa Ana Blvd Santa Ana (92703) ***(P-21815)***
Monarch Bay Golf Resort ....D....510 895-2162
13800 Monarch Bay Dr San Leandro (94577) ***(P-18271)***
Monarch Beach Golf Links (HQ) ....D....949 240-8247
50 Monarch Beach Resort N Dana Point (92629) ***(P-18272)***
Monarch Healthcare A Medical (HQ) ....D....949 923-3200
11 Technology Dr Irvine (92618) ***(P-19206)***
Monarch Landscape Holdings LLC (PA) ....C....213 816-1750
550 S Hope St Ste 1675 Los Angeles (90071) ***(P-871)***
Monarch Nut Company LLC ....C....661 725-6458
786 Road 188 Delano (93215) ***(P-516)***
Monarch Place Piedmont LLC ....C....510 658-9266
4500 Gilbert St Oakland (94611) ***(P-23999)***
Monarchy Diamond Inc ....B....213 924-1161
550 S Hill St Ste 1088 Los Angeles (90013) ***(P-1068)***
Monark LP ....D....310 769-6669
2804 W El Segundo Blvd Gardena (90249) ***(P-10780)***
Mondelez Global LLC ....D....909 605-0140
5815 Clark St Ontario (91761) ***(P-8609)***
Mondrian Hotel, Los Angeles *Also called Morgans Hotel Group MGT LLC* ***(P-12632)***
Money Mailer LLC (PA) ....C....714 889-3800
6261 Katella Ave Ste 200 Cypress (90630) ***(P-13731)***
Monico Alloys Inc (PA) ....D....310 928-0168
3039 E Ana St Compton (90221) ***(P-7081)***
Monique Suraci ....D....951 677-8111
41885 Ivy St Murrieta (92562) ***(P-18177)***
Mono Nation ....D....559 877-2450
58288 Road 225 North Fork (93643) ***(P-23344)***
Mono Wind Casino ....D....559 855-4350
37302 Rancheria Ln Auberry (93602) ***(P-12625)***
Monoprice Inc (HQ) ....C....909 989-6887
1 Pointe Dr Ste 400 Brea (92821) ***(P-7822)***
Monoprice.com, Brea *Also called Monoprice Inc* ***(P-7822)***
Monroe Residence Club ....D....415 771-9119
1570 Sutter St San Francisco (94109) ***(P-10781)***
Monrovia Convalescent Hospital ....D....626 359-6618
1220 Huntington Dr Duarte (91010) ***(P-20144)***
Monrovia Growes, Azusa *Also called Monrovia Nursery Company* ***(P-263)***
Monrovia Health Center ....D....626 256-1600
330 W Maple Ave Monrovia (91016) ***(P-19207)***
Monrovia Memorial Hospital, Monrovia *Also called Alakor Healthcare LLC* ***(P-20739)***
Monrovia Nursery Company (PA) ....A....626 334-9321
817 E Monrovia Pl Azusa (91702) ***(P-263)***
Monrovia Ranch Market, Victorville *Also called E & T Foods Inc* ***(P-426)***
Monrovia Service Center, Monrovia *Also called Southern California Edison Co* ***(P-5928)***
Monsanto Company ....B....530 669-6224
37437 State Highway 16 Woodland (95695) ***(P-8499)***
Monster Inc (PA) ....B....415 840-2000
601 Gateway Blvd Ste 900 South San Francisco (94080) ***(P-7823)***
Monster Energy Company (HQ) ....C....951 739-6200
1 Monster Way Corona (92879) ***(P-8610)***
Monster Mechanical Inc ....D....408 727-8362
1521 Terminal Ave San Jose (95112) ***(P-2203)***
Monster Products, South San Francisco *Also called Monster Inc* ***(P-7823)***
Montage Beverly Hills, Beverly Hills *Also called Montage Hotels & Resorts LLC* ***(P-12626)***
Montage Health ....A....831 625-4821
P.O. Box Hh Monterey (93942) ***(P-19208)***
Montage Health (PA) ....A....831 625-4830
23625 Holman Hwy Monterey (93940) ***(P-26318)***
Montage Hotels & Resorts LLC ....B....310 499-4199
225 N Canon Dr Beverly Hills (90210) ***(P-12626)***
Montage Hotels & Resorts LLC (PA) ....A....949 715-5002
3 Ada Ste 100 Irvine (92618) ***(P-12627)***
Montage Laguna Beach, Irvine *Also called Montage Hotels & Resorts LLC* ***(P-12627)***
Montalvo Arts Center, Saratoga *Also called Montalvo Association* ***(P-24311)***
Montalvo Association ....D....408 961-5800
15400 Montalvo Rd Saratoga (95070) ***(P-24311)***
Montana Investigation, San Francisco *Also called Black Bear Security Services* ***(P-16209)***
MONTCLAIR HOSPITAL MEDICAL CENTER, Montclair *Also called Prime Healthcare Svcs III LLC* ***(P-21112)***
Montclair Hotels Mb LLC ....D....925 687-5500
1050 Burnett Ave Concord (94520) ***(P-12628)***
Montclair Mnor Cnvlescent Hosp, Montclair *Also called Medicrest of California 1* ***(P-20133)***
Montclair Physical Therapy, Claremont *Also called Pomona Valley Hospital Med Ctr* ***(P-21104)***
Monte Nido & Affiliates, Calabasas *Also called Monte Nido Holdings LLC* ***(P-24000)***
Monte Nido Holdings LLC ....C....818 457-9958
514 Live Oak Circle Dr Calabasas (91302) ***(P-24000)***
Monte Vista Grove Homes ....D....626 796-6135
2889 San Pasqual St Pasadena (91107) ***(P-24001)***
Monte Vista Retirement Lodge ....D....619 465-1331
2211 Massachusetts Ave Lemon Grove (91945) ***(P-10782)***
Monte Vista School, Redding *Also called County of Shasta* ***(P-23715)***
Monte Vista Village, Lemon Grove *Also called Monte Vista Retirement Lodge* ***(P-10782)***
Monte Vsta Mem Schlrship Assoc ....E....831 722-8178
2 School Way Watsonville (95076) ***(P-27134)***
Montebello School Transportion ....D....323 887-7900
505 S Greenwood Ave Montebello (90640) ***(P-3821)***
Montebello Transit ....C....323 887-4600
400 S Taylor Ave Montebello (90640) ***(P-3564)***
Montebello Unified School ....D....323 887-2140
500 Hendricks St Fl 2 Montebello (90640) ***(P-13986)***
Montecito Family YMCA, Santa Barbara *Also called Channel Islands Young Mens Ch* ***(P-24517)***
Montecito Fire Protection Dst ....E....805 969-7762
595 San Ysidro Rd Santa Barbara (93108) ***(P-24594)***
Montecito Retirement Assn ....B....805 969-8011
300 Hot Springs Rd Santa Barbara (93108) ***(P-20145)***
Montecito Sequoia Inc ....D....559 565-3388
8000 Generals Hwy Kings Canyon Nationa (93633) ***(P-12629)***
Montecito Sequoia Lodge, Kings Canyon Nationa *Also called Montecito Sequoia Inc* ***(P-12629)***
Montego Heights Lodge, Walnut Creek *Also called Atria Senior Living Inc* ***(P-10689)***
Monterey Bay Acadamy Laundry ....D....831 728-1481
675 Beach Dr Watsonville (95076) ***(P-13181)***
Monterey Bay Aqar Foundation (PA) ....B....831 648-4800
886 Cannery Row Monterey (93940) ***(P-24312)***
Monterey Bay Aquarium RES Inst ....C....831 775-1700
7700 Sandholdt Rd Moss Landing (95039) ***(P-26012)***
Monterey Bay Bouquet Acquisit ....C....831 786-2700
481 San Andreas Rd Watsonville (95076) ***(P-8905)***
Monterey Bay Masonry Inc ....E....408 289-8295
333 Phelan Ave San Jose (95112) ***(P-2722)***
Monterey Beach Hotel, Monterey *Also called Zhg Inc* ***(P-13133)***
Monterey Construction Company, Salinas *Also called Reegs Inc* ***(P-1268)***
Monterey Country Club, Palm Desert *Also called American Golf Corporation* ***(P-18374)***
Monterey County Office Educatn ....D....831 755-0324
901 Blanco Cir Salinas (93901) ***(P-25926)***
Monterey County Public Works, Salinas *Also called County of Monterey* ***(P-1694)***
Monterey County Sheriffs Dept, Salinas *Also called County of Monterey* ***(P-24821)***
Monterey Credit Union (PA) ....D....831 647-1000
501 E Franklin St Monterey (93940) ***(P-9329)***
Monterey Dental Group ....D....831 373-3068
333 El Dorado St Monterey (93940) ***(P-19621)***
Monterey Financial Svcs Inc (PA) ....C....760 639-3500
4095 Avenida De La Plata Oceanside (92056) ***(P-9468)***
Monterey Healthcare & Wellness ....D....626 280-3220
1267 San Gabriel Blvd Rosemead (91770) ***(P-20146)***
Monterey Mechanical Co (PA) ....E....510 632-3173
8275 San Leandro St Oakland (94621) ***(P-1977)***
Monterey Mushrooms Inc (PA) ....E....831 763-5300
260 Westgate Dr Watsonville (95076) ***(P-293)***
Monterey Mushrooms Inc ....B....408 779-4191
642 Hale Ave Morgan Hill (95037) ***(P-294)***
Monterey Mushrooms Inc ....A....831 728-8300
777 Maher Ct Royal Oaks (95076) ***(P-295)***
Monterey Mushrooms-Morgan Hill, Morgan Hill *Also called Monterey Mushrooms Inc* ***(P-294)***
Monterey One Water (PA) ....D....831 372-3367
5 Harris Ct Bldg D Monterey (93940) ***(P-6131)***
Monterey Pacific Inc (PA) ....E....831 678-4845
169 The Crossroads Blvd Carmel (93923) ***(P-673)***
Monterey Park Branch, Monterey Park *Also called Cathay Bank* ***(P-9178)***
Monterey Park Hospital, Monterey Park *Also called Monterey Park Hospital* ***(P-21048)***
Monterey Park Hospital ....C....626 570-9000
900 S Atlantic Blvd Monterey Park (91754) ***(P-21048)***
Monterey Peninsula Country CLB ....C....831 373-1556
3000 Club Rd Pebble Beach (93953) ***(P-18510)***
Monterey Peninsula Dntl Group ....D....831 373-3068
333 El Dorado St Monterey (93940) ***(P-19622)***
Monterey Peninsula Hospital ....E....831 373-0924
576 Hartnell St Ste 260 Monterey (93940) ***(P-21049)***
Monterey Pines Sklld Nursg Fac ....D....831 373-3716
1501 Skyline Dr Monterey (93940) ***(P-20147)***
Monterey Pk Convalescent Hosp ....D....626 280-0280
416 N Garfield Ave Monterey Park (91754) ***(P-20634)***
Monterey Plaza Hotel & Spa, Monterey *Also called Monterey Plaza Ht Ltd Partnr* ***(P-12630)***
Monterey Plaza Ht Ltd Partnr ....B....800 334-3999
400 Cannery Row Monterey (93940) ***(P-12630)***
Monterey Rgional Waste MGT Dst ....C....831 384-5313
14201 Del Monte Blvd Marina (93933) ***(P-6225)***
Monterey-Salinas Transit Corp ....C....831 754-2804
1375 Burton Ave Salinas (93901) ***(P-3762)***
Montesquieu Corp ....D....877 705-5669
8929 Aero Dr Ste C San Diego (92123) ***(P-8815)***
Montesquieu Vins & Domaines, San Diego *Also called Montesquieu Corp* ***(P-8815)***
Montessori Learning Commons (PA) ....D....916 444-7786
1123 D St Sacramento (95814) ***(P-23753)***
Montessori On The Lake, Lake Forest *Also called Environments For Learning Inc* ***(P-23723)***
Montetisea Framing, Denair *Also called J Crecelius Inc* ***(P-336)***
Montgomery Tank Lines, South Gate *Also called Quality Carriers Inc* ***(P-4115)***
Montpelier Nut Company Inc (PA) ....D....209 566-9084
1518 K St Modesto (95354) ***(P-8358)***
Montpelier Orchards MGT Co Inc ....E....209 883-4079
4931 S Montpelier Rd Denair (95316) ***(P-517)***
Montrenes Financial Svcs Inc ....D....562 795-0450
27 Montpellier Newport Beach (92660) ***(P-16931)***
Montrose Environmental Corp ....B....925 680-4300
2825 Verne Roberts Cir Antioch (94509) ***(P-27135)***

ALPHABETIC

Employee Codes: A=Over 500 employees, B=251-500
C=101-250, D=51-100, E=50
2020 Directory of California
Wholesalers and Services Companies
© Mergent Inc. 1-800-342-5647
1355

Montrose Envmtl Group Inc (PA) ... D ... 949 988-3500
1 Park Plz Ste 1000 Irvine (92614) ***(P-27136)***
Montrose Envmtl Group Inc ... A ... 714 332-8646
1631 E Saint Andrew Pl Santa Ana (92705) ***(P-27137)***
Montrose Water and Sustainabil ... D ... 949 988-3500
1 Park Plz Ste 1000 Irvine (92614) ***(P-27138)***
Monument Construction Inc ... D ... 408 778-1350
16200 Vineyard Blvd # 100 Morgan Hill (95037) ***(P-872)***
Monument Security Inc ... C ... 510 430-3540
24301 Suthland Dr Ste 312 Hayward (94545) ***(P-16354)***
Monument Security Inc (PA) ... C ... 916 564-4234
4926 43rd St Ste 10 McClellan (95652) ***(P-16355)***
Moog Inc ... D ... 650 210-9000
2581 Leghorn St Mountain View (94043) ***(P-25224)***
Moon Mountain Farms LLC ... E ... 805 521-1742
3846 E Telegraph Rd Fillmore (93015) ***(P-350)***
Mooney Farms ... E ... 530 899-2661
1220 Fortress St Chico (95973) ***(P-518)***
Moonlight Companies, Reedley *Also called Moonlight Packing Corporation* ***(P-8500)***
Moonlight Packing Corporation ... A ... 559 638-7799
17770 E Huntsman Ave Reedley (93654) ***(P-5097)***
Moonlight Packing Corporation (PA) ... C ... 559 638-7799
17719 E Huntsman Ave Reedley (93654) ***(P-8500)***
Moonstone Hotel Properties, Cambria *Also called Moonstone Management Corp* ***(P-11298)***
Moonstone Management Corp (PA) ... C ... 805 927-4200
2905 Burton Dr Cambria (93428) ***(P-11298)***
Moor Products, Mission Viejo *Also called Greenleaf Paper Products* ***(P-7882)***
Moore Business Forms, Walnut Creek *Also called R R Donnelley & Sons Company* ***(P-3505)***
Moore Business Forms, Temecula *Also called RR Donnelley & Sons Company* ***(P-7864)***
Moore Foundations Inc ... E ... 818 698-4737
7046 Darby Ave Reseda (91335) ***(P-24595)***
Moore Iacofano Goltsman Inc (PA) ... D ... 510 845-7549
800 Hearst Ave Berkeley (94710) ***(P-27139)***
Moore Law Group A Prof Corp ... D ... 714 431-2000
3710 S Susan St Ste 210 Santa Ana (92704) ***(P-22696)***
Moore Twining Associates Inc (PA) ... D ... 559 268-7021
2527 Fresno St Fresno (93721) ***(P-26093)***
Moorefield Construction Inc (PA) ... D ... 714 972-0700
600 N Tustin Ave Ste 210 Santa Ana (92705) ***(P-1545)***
Mooretown Rancheria ... B ... 530 533-3885
3 Alverda Dr Oroville (95966) ***(P-18320)***
Mooretown Rancheria (PA) ... E ... 530 533-3625
1 Alverda Dr Oroville (95966) ***(P-18724)***
Moorpark Active Adult Center, Moorpark *Also called City of Moorpark* ***(P-23011)***
Moose Family Center 545, Santa Cruz *Also called Moose International Inc* ***(P-24596)***
Moose International Inc ... C ... 831 438-1817
2470 El Rancho Dr Santa Cruz (95060) ***(P-24596)***
Moov Corporation ... C ... 877 666-8932
123 Mission St Ste 1000 San Francisco (94105) ***(P-14945)***
Moovweb, San Francisco *Also called Moov Corporation* ***(P-14945)***
Mopar Enterprises ... D ... 858 492-1123
1710 Dornoch Ct Ste A San Diego (92154) ***(P-13732)***
Morada Produce Company LP ... A ... 209 546-0426
500 N Jack Tone Rd Stockton (95215) ***(P-519)***
Moraga Cntry CLB Hmowners Assn ... D ... 925 376-2200
1600 Saint Andrews Dr Moraga (94556) ***(P-18511)***
Morale Welfare Recreation Fund ... C ... 831 242-6631
4260 Gigling Rd Seaside (93955) ***(P-24198)***
More Truck Lines Inc ... D ... 951 371-6673
1776 All American Way Corona (92879) ***(P-3914)***
MORE WORKSHOP, Placerville *Also called Mother Lode Rehabilit* ***(P-24002)***
Moreland PCF Snoqualmie LLC ... C ... 661 322-1081
5060 California Ave # 1150 Bakersfield (93309) ***(P-11580)***
Moreno & Associates Inc ... D ... 408 924-0353
1260 Birchwood Dr Sunnyvale (94089) ***(P-13987)***
Moreno Valley Family Hlth Ctr, Moreno Valley *Also called Community Health Systems Inc* ***(P-18914)***
Moreno Valley Heacock Med Offs, Moreno Valley *Also called Kaiser Foundation Hospitals* ***(P-11795)***
Morgan Lewis & Bockius LLP ... A ... 415 393-2000
1 Market St Ste 500 San Francisco (94105) ***(P-22697)***
Morgan Lewis & Bockius LLP ... D ... 650 843-4000
1400 Page Mill Rd Palo Alto (94304) ***(P-22698)***
Morgan Lewis & Bockius LLP ... C ... 949 399-7000
600 Anton Blvd Ste 1800 Costa Mesa (92626) ***(P-22699)***
Morgan Lewis & Bockius LLP ... C ... 213 612-2500
300 S Grand Ave Ste 2200 Los Angeles (90071) ***(P-22700)***
Morgan Lewis & Bockius LLP ... B ... 415 442-1000
1 Market Plz Lbby 1 # 1 San Francisco (94105) ***(P-22701)***
Morgan Lewis & Bockius LLP ... C ... 213 612-2500
300 S Grand Ave Ste 2200 Los Angeles (90071) ***(P-22702)***
Morgan Creek Productions (PA) ... D ... 310 432-4848
10351 Santa Monica Blvd # 200 Los Angeles (90025) ***(P-17789)***
Morgan Fabrics Corporation (PA) ... D ... 323 583-9981
4265 Exchange Ave Vernon (90058) ***(P-8004)***
Morgan Farm LLC ... D ... 831 726-5120
201 Vista Dr Watsonville (95076) ***(P-103)***
Morgan Kleppe & Nash ... D ... 559 732-3436
501 N Church St Visalia (93291) ***(P-10430)***
Morgan Linen Service, Los Angeles *Also called Morgan Services Inc* ***(P-13236)***
Morgan Services Inc ... D ... 213 485-9666
905 Yale St Los Angeles (90012) ***(P-13236)***
Morgan Stanley, San Francisco *Also called TransMontaigne PDT Svcs LLC* ***(P-5142)***
Morgan Stanley ... D ... 949 760-2440
800 Nwport Ctr Dr Ste 500 Newport Beach (92660) ***(P-9832)***
Morgan Stanley ... D ... 626 405-9313
55 S Lake Ave Ste 800 Pasadena (91101) ***(P-9727)***
Morgan Stanley ... E ... 858 597-7777
4350 La Jolla Village Dr # 1000 San Diego (92122) ***(P-9728)***
Morgan Stanley ... C ... 949 809-1200
1901 Main St Ste 700 Irvine (92614) ***(P-9729)***
Morgan Stanley & Co LLC ... E ... 916 444-8041
407 Capitol Mall Ste 1900 Sacramento (95814) ***(P-9730)***
Morgan Stanley & Co LLC ... E ... 559 431-5900
5250 N Palm Ave Ste 321 Fresno (93704) ***(P-9731)***
Morgan Stanley & Co LLC ... D ... 714 836-5181
2677 N Main St Fl 10 Santa Ana (92705) ***(P-9732)***
Morgan Stanley & Co LLC ... D ... 619 236-1331
101 W Broadway Ste 1800 San Diego (92101) ***(P-9733)***
Morgan Stanley & Co LLC ... D ... 661 663-8100
9100 Ming Ave Ste 205 Bakersfield (93311) ***(P-9734)***
Morgan Stanley & Co LLC ... D ... 510 839-8080
1999 Harrison St Ste 2200 Oakland (94612) ***(P-9735)***
Morgan Stanley & Co LLC ... D ... 650 340-6550
216 Lorton Ave Burlingame (94010) ***(P-9736)***
Morgan Stanley & Co LLC ... D ... 310 319-5200
1453 3rd St Ste 200 Santa Monica (90401) ***(P-9737)***
Morgan Stanley & Co LLC ... D ... 408 947-2200
225 W Santa Clara St # 900 San Jose (95113) ***(P-9738)***
Morgan Stanley & Co LLC ... C ... 310 285-4800
9665 Wilshire Blvd # 600 Beverly Hills (90212) ***(P-9739)***
Morgan Stanley & Co LLC ... B ... 415 693-6000
101 California St Fl 3 San Francisco (94111) ***(P-9740)***
Morgan Truck Body LLC ... D ... 951 689-0800
7888 Lincoln Ave Riverside (92504) ***(P-3915)***
Morgans Hotel Group MGT LLC ... C ... 805 969-2203
1555 S Jameson Ln Santa Barbara (93108) ***(P-12631)***
Morgans Hotel Group MGT LLC ... C ... 323 650-8999
8440 W Sunset Blvd Los Angeles (90069) ***(P-12632)***
Morgans Hotel Group MGT LLC ... C ... 415 775-4700
495 Geary St San Francisco (94102) ***(P-12633)***
Morigon Technologies LLC ... E ... 818 764-8880
7615 Fulton Ave North Hollywood (91605) ***(P-6979)***
Morley Construction, Santa Monica *Also called MSC Service Co* ***(P-25651)***
Morley Construction Company (HQ) ... D ... 310 399-1600
3330 Ocean Park Blvd # 101 Santa Monica (90405) ***(P-3185)***
Morning Star Company The, Woodland *Also called Liberty Packing Company LLC* ***(P-8495)***
Morningside Community Assn ... D ... 760 328-3323
82 Mayfair Dr Rancho Mirage (92270) ***(P-24597)***
Morningside Corecare Assoc LP ... C ... 650 854-5600
2180 Sand Hill Rd Ste 200 Menlo Park (94025) ***(P-20148)***
Morningside of Fullerton, Fullerton *Also called Corecare I I I* ***(P-23873)***
Morphosis Architects ... D ... 310 453-2247
3440 Wesley St Culver City (90232) ***(P-25485)***
Morphotrak LLC (HQ) ... C ... 714 238-2000
5515 E La Palma Ave # 100 Anaheim (92807) ***(P-15648)***
Morris & Willner Partners ... D ... 949 705-0682
201 Sandpointe Ave # 200 Santa Ana (92707) ***(P-26723)***
Morris Distributing Inc ... D ... 707 769-7294
3800a Lakeville Hwy Petaluma (94954) ***(P-8782)***
Morris Grritano Insur Agcy Inc ... D ... 805 543-6887
1122 Laurel Ln San Luis Obispo (93401) ***(P-10431)***
Morris National Inc (HQ) ... D ... 626 385-2000
760 N Mckeever Ave Azusa (91702) ***(P-8611)***
Morris Polich & Purdy LLP (PA) ... D ... 213 891-9100
1055 W 7th St Ste 2400 Los Angeles (90017) ***(P-22703)***
Morrison & Foerster LLP ... B ... 650 813-5600
755 Page Mill Rd Ste A100 Palo Alto (94304) ***(P-22704)***
Morrison & Foerster - Library, Palo Alto *Also called Morrison & Foerster LLP* ***(P-22704)***
Morrison & Foerster LLP ... C ... 213 892-5200
707 Wilshire Blvd # 6000 Los Angeles (90017) ***(P-22705)***
Morrison & Foerster LLP (PA) ... B ... 415 268-7000
425 Market St Fl 30 San Francisco (94105) ***(P-22706)***
Morrison & Foerster LLP ... C ... 858 720-5100
12531 High Bluff Dr # 100 San Diego (92130) ***(P-22707)***
Morrison & Foerster LLP ... C ... 415 268-7178
425 Market St Fl 32 San Francisco (94105) ***(P-22708)***
Morrison & Foerster LLP ... E ... 925 295-3300
425 Market St Fl 32 San Francisco (94105) ***(P-22709)***
Morrison Concrete Inc ... E ... 562 802-1450
14114 Rosecrans Ave Ste C Santa Fe Springs (90670) ***(P-3186)***
Morrison Health Care, Palm Springs *Also called Morrison MGT Specialists Inc* ***(P-26319)***
Morrison Landscape ... E ... 714 571-0455
1225 E Wakeham Ave Santa Ana (92705) ***(P-7114)***
Morrison MGT Specialists, Fresno *Also called Morrison MGT Specialists Inc* ***(P-22278)***
Morrison MGT Specialists Inc ... C ... 559 459-6449
2823 Fresno St Fresno (93721) ***(P-22278)***
Morrison MGT Specialists Inc ... D ... 760 323-6296
1150 N Indian Canyon Dr Palm Springs (92262) ***(P-26319)***
Morrison MGT Specialists Inc ... D ... 530 332-7557
1531 Esplanade Chico (95926) ***(P-26320)***
Morrison MGT Specialists Inc ... D ... 818 364-4219
14445 Olive View Dr Sylmar (91342) ***(P-26321)***
Morro Bay Public Works ... D ... 805 772-6261
955 Shasta Ave Morro Bay (93442) ***(P-1761)***
Morrow-Meadows Corporation (PA) ... A ... 858 974-3650
231 Benton Ct City of Industry (91789) ***(P-2558)***
Morse Court Apartments, Sunnyvale *Also called Mp Morse Court Associates* ***(P-10857)***
Mortgage Capital Assoc Inc ... D ... 310 477-6877
11150 W Olympic Blvd # 1160 Los Angeles (90064) ***(P-9582)***
Mortgage Capital Partners Inc ... D ... 310 295-2900
12400 Wilshire Blvd # 900 Los Angeles (90025) ***(P-9583)***
Mortgage Corp America Inc ... D ... 805 582-2220
2315 Kuehner Dr Ste 115 Simi Valley (93063) ***(P-9637)***
Mortgage Corp of America, Simi Valley *Also called Mortgage Corp America Inc* ***(P-9637)***

Mortgage Fax Inc ....D....714 899-2656
18685 Main St Ste 101 Huntington Beach (92648) ***(P-13716)***
Mortgage Works Financial, Redlands *Also called Mountain West Financial Inc* ***(P-9584)***
Morton & Pitalo Inc (PA) ....D....916 984-7621
75 Iron Point Cir Ste 120 Folsom (95630) ***(P-25225)***
Morton Bakar Center, Alameda *Also called Garfield Nursing Home Inc* ***(P-19934)***
Morton Bakar Center, Hayward *Also called Telecare Corporation* ***(P-21436)***
Morton Golf LLC ....D....916 481-4653
3645 Fulton Ave Sacramento (95821) ***(P-18273)***
Mosaic ....D....858 397-2261
10991 Via Banco San Diego (92126) ***(P-26322)***
Mosaic Quest, San Diego *Also called Mosaic* ***(P-26322)***
Moschip Semiconductor Tech USA ....C....408 737-7141
3335 Kifer Rd Santa Clara (95051) ***(P-7306)***
Moshun Group LLC ....D....855 258-2220
1968 S Coast Hwy Laguna Beach (92651) ***(P-26323)***
Moskow, Lonnie J MD, Laguna Hills *Also called South County Orthopedic Specia* ***(P-19409)***
Moss & Company Inc (PA) ....D....310 453-0911
15300 Ventura Blvd # 418 Sherman Oaks (91403) ***(P-11299)***
Moss Landing Marine Labs ....C....831 771-4400
8272 Moss Landing Rd Moss Landing (95039) ***(P-21555)***
Moss Landing Power Plant, Moss Landing *Also called Dynegy Moss Landing LLC* ***(P-5832)***
Motech Americas LLC ....B....302 451-7500
1300 Valley Vista Dr # 207 Diamond Bar (91765) ***(P-25801)***
Motel 6 Operating LP ....D....310 419-1234
5101 W Century Blvd Inglewood (90304) ***(P-12634)***
Mother Lode Rehabilit ....C....530 622-4848
415 Placerville Dr Ste J Placerville (95667) ***(P-24002)***
Motherlode Investors LLC ....D....209 736-8112
711 Mccauley Ranch Rd Angels Camp (95222) ***(P-18274)***
Motiga Inc ....D....425 748-8509
100 Rdwood Shres Pkwy 4 Redwood City (94065) ***(P-14946)***
Motion Math Inc ....C....415 590-2961
582 Market St Ste 511 San Francisco (94104) ***(P-14947)***
Motion Pcture Hlth Wlfare Fund ....C....818 769-0007
11365 Ventura Blvd # 300 Studio City (91604) ***(P-10219)***
Motion Picture and TV Fund (PA) ....A....818 876-1777
23388 Mulholland Dr # 200 Woodland Hills (91364) ***(P-21050)***
Motion Picture Assn Amer Inc (PA) ....C....818 995-6600
15301 Ventura Blvd Bldg E Sherman Oaks (91403) ***(P-24351)***
Motion Picture Industry Plans ....C....818 769-0007
11365 Ventura Blvd # 300 Studio City (91604) ***(P-10220)***
Motion Solutions, Aliso Viejo *Also called Bearing Engineers Inc* ***(P-7627)***
Motion Theory Inc ....C....310 396-9433
444 W Ocean Blvd Ste 1400 Long Beach (90802) ***(P-13792)***
Motivational Fulfillmen, Chino *Also called Motivational Marketing Inc* ***(P-4453)***
Motivational Fulfillment, Chino *Also called Motivational Marketing Inc* ***(P-4995)***
Motivational Marketing Inc ....C....909 517-2200
15785 Mountain Ave Chino (91708) ***(P-4453)***
Motivational Marketing Inc ....D....909 517-2200
16133 Fern Ave Chino (91708) ***(P-4995)***
Motivational Marketing Inc (PA) ....D....909 517-2200
15820 Euclid Ave Chino (91708) ***(P-16932)***
Motivational Systems Inc (PA) ....D....619 474-8246
2200 Cleveland Ave National City (91950) ***(P-13793)***
Motive Energy Inc (PA) ....D....714 888-2525
125 E Coml St Bldg B Anaheim (92801) ***(P-7168)***
Motive Nation, Downey *Also called Rockview Dairies Inc* ***(P-8640)***
Motivtnal Flfllment Lgstics Sv, Chino *Also called Motivational Marketing Inc* ***(P-16932)***
Motor Vehicle Software Corp (PA) ....D....818 706-1949
29901 Agoura Rd Agoura Hills (91301) ***(P-26724)***
Motorola Mobility LLC ....D....858 455-1500
6450 Sequence Dr San Diego (92121) ***(P-7307)***
Moulton Logistics Management (PA) ....D....818 997-1800
7855 Hayvenhurst Ave Van Nuys (91406) ***(P-4454)***
Moulton Niguel Water (PA) ....D....949 831-2500
27500 La Paz Rd Laguna Niguel (92677) ***(P-6094)***
Mount Diablo Medical Center, Concord *Also called John Muir Physician Network* ***(P-20928)***
Mount Hermon Association Inc (PA) ....D....831 335-4466
37 Conference Dr Mount Hermon (95041) ***(P-13151)***
Mount Miguel Covenant Village, Spring Valley *Also called Evangelical Covenant Church* ***(P-23922)***
Mount Rbdoux Convalescent Hosp ....C....951 681-2200
6401 33rd St Riverside (92509) ***(P-20149)***
Mount San Jacinto Win Pk Auth ....D....760 325-1449
1 Tramway Rd Palm Springs (92262) ***(P-18725)***
Mount Shasta Resort, Mount Shasta *Also called Siskiyou Lake Golf Resort Inc* ***(P-18299)***
Mount View Hotel, Calistoga *Also called Mv Hospitality Inc* ***(P-18180)***
Mount View Spa, Calistoga *Also called Spa Partners Inc* ***(P-18200)***
Mount Woodson Country Club, Ramona *Also called Spe Go Holdings Inc* ***(P-18300)***
Mountain Comm Hlth Cre Dist ....C....530 623-5541
410 N Taylor St Weaverville (96093) ***(P-21051)***
Mountain Comm Hlth Cre Dist (PA) ....C....530 623-5541
60 Easter Ave Weaverville (96093) ***(P-21052)***
Mountain Gear Corporation ....C....626 851-2488
4889 4th St Irwindale (91706) ***(P-8040)***
Mountain High Resort Assoc LLC ....A....760 249-5808
24512 Highway 2 Wrightwood (92397) ***(P-11300)***
Mountain High Ski Resort, Wrightwood *Also called MHRP Resort Inc* ***(P-12615)***
Mountain Meadow Mushrooms Inc ....D....760 749-1201
26948 N Broadway Escondido (92026) ***(P-296)***
Mountain Play Association ....E....415 383-1100
1556 4th St B San Rafael (94901) ***(P-17928)***
Mountain Retreat Incorporated ....D....925 838-7780
111 Deerwood Rd Ste 100 San Ramon (94583) ***(P-11581)***
MOUNTAIN SHADOWS COMMUNITY HOM, Escondido *Also called Mountain Shadows Support Group* ***(P-20441)***
Mountain Shadows Support Group (PA) ....D....760 743-3714
2067 W El Norte Pkwy Escondido (92026) ***(P-20441)***
Mountain Springs Kirkwood LLC ....C....209 258-6000
1501 Kirkwood Meadows Dr Kirkwood (95646) ***(P-12635)***
Mountain Top Comm Svcs LLC ....E....909 798-4400
1902 Orange Tree Ln Redlands (92374) ***(P-27140)***
Mountain Valley Child and Fami ....C....530 265-9057
24077 State Highway 49 Nevada City (95959) ***(P-20442)***
Mountain Valley Express Co Inc (PA) ....D....209 823-2168
6750 Longe St Ste 100 Stockton (95206) ***(P-4098)***
Mountain Valley Express Co Inc ....C....562 630-5500
7701 Rosecrans Ave Paramount (90723) ***(P-4996)***
Mountain View AG Services Inc ....A....559 528-6004
13281 Avenue 416 Orosi (93647) ***(P-634)***
Mountain View Child Care Inc ....C....818 252-5863
10716 La Tuna Canyon Rd Sun Valley (91352) ***(P-23754)***
Mountain View Child Care Inc (PA) ....B....909 796-6915
1720 Mountain View Ave Loma Linda (92354) ***(P-21053)***
Mountain View Cnvalescent Hosp ....E....818 367-1033
13333 Fenton Ave Sylmar (91342) ***(P-20150)***
Mountain View Healthcare Ctr, Mountain View *Also called Balboa Enterprises Inc* ***(P-19744)***
Mountain View Physical Therapy ....D....909 949-6235
299 W Fthill Blvd Ste 200 Upland (91786) ***(P-19680)***
Mountain View Sport Club, Mountain View *Also called 24 Hour Fitness Usa Inc* ***(P-18112)***
Mountain West Financial Inc (PA) ....B....909 793-1500
1209 Nevada St Ste 200 Redlands (92374) ***(P-9584)***
Mountain-Pacific Financial (PA) ....D....858 456-8420
1010 Prospect St Ste 300 La Jolla (92037) ***(P-11301)***
Mountains Community Hosp Fndtn ....C....909 336-3651
29101 Hospital Rd Lake Arrowhead (92352) ***(P-21054)***
Mountasia Family Fun Center, Santa Clarita *Also called Mountasia of Santa Clarita* ***(P-13440)***
Mountasia Family Fun Center ....D....661 253-4386
21516 Golden Triangle Rd Santa Clarita (91350) ***(P-18336)***
Mountasia of Santa Clarita ....D....661 253-4386
21516 Golden Triangle Rd Santa Clarita (91350) ***(P-13440)***
Mounting Systems Inc ....D....916 374-8872
180 Promenade Cir Ste 300 Sacramento (95834) ***(P-2204)***
Move Inc ....C....818 701-0012
8428 Calvin Ave Northridge (91324) ***(P-11302)***
Move Inc (HQ) ....B....408 558-7100
3315 Scott Blvd Ste 250 Santa Clara (95054) ***(P-11303)***
Move Co ....C....805 557-2300
30700 Russell Ranch Rd # 100 Westlake Village (91362) ***(P-11304)***
Move Sales Inc (HQ) ....D....805 557-2300
3315 Scott Blvd Ste 250 Santa Clara (95054) ***(P-13441)***
Mover Services Inc ....E....310 868-5143
721 E Compton Blvd Rancho Dominguez (90220) ***(P-3437)***
Movie Movers, West Hollywood *Also called Quixote Mm LLC* ***(P-17761)***
Movieclips.com, Los Angeles *Also called Zefr Inc* ***(P-17720)***
Moving Solutions Inc ....C....408 920-0110
7093 Central Ave Newark (94560) ***(P-4218)***
Movocash Inc ....E....650 722-3990
530 Lytton Ave Fl 2 Palo Alto (94301) ***(P-14948)***
Movoto LLC ....D....888 766-8686
1900 S Norfolk St Ste 222 San Mateo (94403) ***(P-11305)***
Mowery Thomason Inc ....C....714 666-1717
1225 N Red Gum St Anaheim (92806) ***(P-2824)***
Moya Farm Labor Services, Reedley *Also called Moya Juan Farm Labor Services* ***(P-635)***
Moya Juan Farm Labor Services ....C....559 638-9498
7919 S Alta Ave Reedley (93654) ***(P-635)***
Moyes Custom Furniture Inc ....E....714 729-0234
3431 E La Palma Ave Ste 3 Anaheim (92806) ***(P-17472)***
Moyles Central Vly Hlth Care (PA) ....B....559 688-0288
999 N M St Tulare (93274) ***(P-20151)***
Moyles Central Vly Hlth Care ....C....559 782-1509
1100 W Morton Ave Porterville (93257) ***(P-20152)***
Moyles Health Care Inc ....A....559 686-1601
604 E Merritt Ave Tulare (93274) ***(P-20635)***
Mozilla Corporation (HQ) ....A....650 903-0800
331 E Evelyn Ave Mountain View (94041) ***(P-15649)***
Mozilla Foundation (PA) ....A....650 903-0800
331 E Evelyn Ave Mountain View (94041) ***(P-14949)***
Mozingo Construction Inc ....E....209 848-0160
751 Wakefield Ct Oakdale (95361) ***(P-3325)***
Mp Aero LLC ....D....818 901-9828
7701 Woodley Ave Van Nuys (91406) ***(P-3438)***
Mp Environmental Services Inc (PA) ....C....800 458-3036
3400 Manor St Bakersfield (93308) ***(P-6226)***
Mp Holdings, McClellan *Also called McClellan Business Park LLC* ***(P-26699)***
Mp Mine Operations LLC ....C....702 277-0848
67750 Bailey Rd Mountain Pass (92366) ***(P-1064)***
Mp Morse Court Associates ....D....408 734-9442
825 Morse Ave Sunnyvale (94085) ***(P-10857)***
Mp Shoreline Assoc Ltd Partnr ....E....650 966-1327
460 N Shoreline Blvd Mountain View (94043) ***(P-10783)***
Mp Tice Oaks Associates A CA ....D....650 356-2976
2150 Valley Blvd Walnut Creek (94595) ***(P-11306)***
Mpc Productions LLC ....D....310 418-8115
12035 Killion St Sherman Oaks (91401) ***(P-17993)***
Mpcc, Pebble Beach *Also called Monterey Peninsula Country CLB* ***(P-18510)***
Mpic, Milpitas *Also called Mega Professional Intl* ***(P-14933)***
Mpl Enterprises Inc ....D....714 545-1717
2302 S Susan St Santa Ana (92704) ***(P-873)***
Mpower Communications Corp (HQ) ....D....866 699-8242
515 S Flower St Los Angeles (90071) ***(P-5441)***
Mpp Brea Div 6079, Brea *Also called Orora Packaging Solutions* ***(P-7894)***
Mpp Fullerton Div 6061, Fullerton *Also called Orora Packaging Solutions* ***(P-7897)***

ALPHABETIC

Employee Codes: A=Over 500 employees, B=251-500
C=101-250, D=51-100, E=50
2020 Directory of California
Wholesalers and Services Companies
© Mergent Inc. 1-800-342-5647
1357

Mpp San Diego Div 6064, San Marcos *Also called Orora North America* ***(P-7889)***
MPS Security, Murrieta *Also called National Bus Investigations* ***(P-16939)***
Mq Power, Cypress *Also called Multiquip Inc* ***(P-7169)***
Mr Clean Maintenance Systems, Bloomington *Also called Chiro Inc* ***(P-7668)***
Mr Cool, Fresno *Also called Donald P Dick AC Inc* ***(P-2117)***
Mr Copy Inc (HQ)..........D.......858 573-6300
5657 Copley Dr San Diego (92111) ***(P-6760)***
Mr Mailer, Baldwin Park *Also called All Direct Mail Services Inc* ***(P-13718)***
Mr Rooter, Fremont *Also called Growith Inc* ***(P-17502)***
Mr Rooter, Ventura *Also called D S R Inc* ***(P-17495)***
Mrc, Smart Tech Solutions, San Diego *Also called Mr Copy Inc* ***(P-6760)***
Mrca Fire Division..........E.......818 880-4752
1670 Las Virgenes Cyn Rd Calabasas (91302) ***(P-24598)***
Mrs Gochs Natural Fd Mkts Inc..........C.......619 294-2800
711 University Ave San Diego (92103) ***(P-4455)***
Mrt Inc..........E.......949 348-2292
19781 Pauling Foothill Ranch (92610) ***(P-13733)***
MRWPCA, Monterey *Also called Monterey One Water* ***(P-6131)***
Ms Bubbles Inc (PA)..........D.......323 544-0300
2731 S Alameda St Los Angeles (90058) ***(P-8098)***
MS Industrial Shtmtl Inc..........C.......951 272-6610
1731 Pomona Rd Corona (92880) ***(P-3079)***
Msas Cargo International, Brisbane *Also called Dhl Supply Chain (usa)* ***(P-4925)***
Msblous LLC..........D.......909 929-9689
11671 Dayton Dr Rancho Cucamonga (91730) ***(P-4456)***
MSC Chatsworth..........D.......818 718-7696
9324 Corbin Ave Northridge (91324) ***(P-7824)***
MSC Metalworking, City of Industry *Also called Rutland Tool & Supply Co* ***(P-7654)***
MSC Service Co..........D.......310 399-1600
3330 Ocean Park Blvd # 101 Santa Monica (90405) ***(P-25651)***
Msci Barra, Berkeley *Also called Barra LLC* ***(P-15254)***
Mscsoftware Corporation (HQ)..........C.......714 540-8900
4675 Macarthur Ct Ste 900 Newport Beach (92660) ***(P-15414)***
Mscsoftware Corporation..........B.......714 540-8900
4675 Macarthur Ct Ste 900 Newport Beach (92660) ***(P-15650)***
Msd Capital LP..........D.......310 458-3600
100 Wilshire Blvd # 1450 Santa Monica (90401) ***(P-11935)***
MSEFCU, Merced *Also called Merced School Employees F C U* ***(P-9324)***
Mshift Inc..........E.......408 437-2740
39899 Balentine Dr # 235 Newark (94560) ***(P-14950)***
MSI, Santa Barbara *Also called Modular Systems Inc* ***(P-11297)***
MSI, Orange *Also called M S International Inc* ***(P-6692)***
MSI Computer Corp (HQ)..........D.......626 913-0828
901 Canada Ct City of Industry (91748) ***(P-6875)***
MSI Invntory Srvce-Los Angeles, Covina *Also called Accu-Count Inventory Svcs Inc* ***(P-16600)***
MSI Production Services, Vista *Also called Meeting Services Inc* ***(P-14180)***
Msj Healthcare LLC..........E.......818 244-8446
3452 E Fthill Blvd Ste 70 Pasadena (91107) ***(P-21816)***
Msl Electric Inc..........D.......714 693-4837
2918 E La Jolla St Anaheim (92806) ***(P-2559)***
Msla Management LLC..........C.......626 824-6020
1294 E Colorado Blvd Pasadena (91106) ***(P-27141)***
Msr Hotels & Resorts Inc..........D.......408 496-6400
2885 Lakeside Dr Santa Clara (95054) ***(P-12636)***
MSS Nurses Registry Inc..........D.......323 467-5717
6660 W Sunset Blvd Ste J Los Angeles (90028) ***(P-14536)***
Mt Dblo Resource Recovery LLC..........B.......925 682-9113
4080 Mallard Dr Concord (94520) ***(P-3916)***
MT DIABLO CENTER ADULT DAY HEA, Pleasant Hill *Also called Choice In Aging* ***(P-21980)***
Mt Diablo Heart Health Center, Concord *Also called John Muir Physician Network* ***(P-20931)***
Mt Diablo Medical Center, Walnut Creek *Also called John Muir Physician Network* ***(P-20930)***
Mt Eden Nursery Co Inc (PA)..........E.......408 213-5777
2124 Bering Dr San Jose (95131) ***(P-10879)***
Mt Hamilton Grange..........D.......408 513-5528
2840 Aborn Rd San Jose (95135) ***(P-24199)***
Mt Miquel Covenant Village..........C.......619 479-4790
325 Kempton St Spring Valley (91977) ***(P-20636)***
Mt Rubidoux Convalescent Hosp, San Bernardino *Also called Waterman Convalescent Hospital* ***(P-20371)***
Mt Sinai Mem Pk & Mortuary, Los Angeles *Also called Sinai Temple* ***(P-13379)***
Mt Supply Inc (HQ)..........C.......800 938-6658
3505 Cadillac Ave Ste K2 Costa Mesa (92626) ***(P-7645)***
Mt View Apartments LLC..........D.......925 866-8429
3170 Crow Canyon Pl # 165 San Ramon (94583) ***(P-10784)***
MT&i, Oceanside *Also called Mold Testing and Inspection* ***(P-16930)***
Mtc Distributing (PA)..........C.......209 523-6449
4900 Stoddard Rd Modesto (95356) ***(P-8941)***
Mtc Financial Inc..........E.......949 252-8300
17100 Gillette Ave Irvine (92614) ***(P-11804)***
Mtc Transportation, Twentynine Palms *Also called Mark Clemons* ***(P-4086)***
Mtc Worldwide Corp..........D.......626 839-6800
17837 Rowland St City of Industry (91748) ***(P-6876)***
Mthuron Inc..........C.......925 932-4101
1903 Rutan Dr Livermore (94551) ***(P-2903)***
MTI, San Diego *Also called Merit Technologies LLC* ***(P-26712)***
Mtm & Thomasville Co..........D.......626 934-1112
16035 Phoenix Dr City of Industry (91745) ***(P-1546)***
Mtv Networks, Los Angeles *Also called Viacom Networks* ***(P-17701)***
Muehlhan Certifed Coatings Inc..........C.......707 639-4414
2320 Cordelia Rd Fairfield (94534) ***(P-3439)***
Mueller Grooming & Pet Sups, Sacramento *Also called Mueller Pet Medical Center* ***(P-581)***
Mueller Pet Medical Center..........E.......916 428-9202
7625 Freeport Blvd Sacramento (95832) ***(P-581)***
Mufg Bank Ltd..........D.......213 488-3700
777 S Figueroa St Ste 600 Los Angeles (90017) ***(P-9268)***
Mufg Union Bank Foundation..........A.......213 236-5000
445 S Figueroa St Ste 710 Los Angeles (90071) ***(P-9102)***
Mufg Union Bank National Assn (HQ)..........A.......415 705-7000
400 California St Fl 14 San Francisco (94104) ***(P-9103)***
Mufg Union Bank National Assn..........E.......213 972-5500
120 S San Pedro St Los Angeles (90012) ***(P-9104)***
Mufg Union Bank National Assn..........D.......805 564-6410
20 E Carrillo St Santa Barbara (93101) ***(P-9105)***
Mufg Union Bank National Assn..........D.......310 550-6522
9460 Wilshire Blvd # 200 Beverly Hills (90212) ***(P-9106)***
Mufg Union Bank National Assn..........D.......619 230-4666
1201 5th Ave San Diego (92101) ***(P-9218)***
Mufg Union Bank National Assn..........D.......213 312-4500
900 S Main St Los Angeles (90015) ***(P-9107)***
Mufg Union Bank National Assn..........E.......310 354-4700
15800 S Western Ave Gardena (90247) ***(P-9108)***
Mufg Union Bank National Assn..........D.......510 891-2495
460 Hegenberger Rd Fl 3 Oakland (94621) ***(P-9109)***
Muir Labs..........B.......925 947-3335
1601 Ygnacio Valley Rd Walnut Creek (94598) ***(P-21055)***
Muir Orthopedic Specialists..........C.......925 939-8585
2405 Shadelands Dr # 210 Walnut Creek (94598) ***(P-19209)***
Muir-Chase Plumbing Co Inc..........D.......818 500-1940
4530 Brazil St Ste 1 Los Angeles (90039) ***(P-2205)***
Muirlab, Walnut Creek *Also called Muir Labs* ***(P-21055)***
Mulechain Inc..........D.......888 456-8881
2901 W Coast Hwy Ste 200 Newport Beach (92663) ***(P-3917)***
Mulesoft Inc..........A.......415 229-2009
50 Fremont St Ste 300 San Francisco (94105) ***(P-15415)***
Mulhearn Group, Hacienda Heights *Also called Berkshire Hattaway Home Servcs* ***(P-10937)***
Mulhearn Realtors Inc..........D.......562 860-2443
11306 183rd St Ste 101 Cerritos (90703) ***(P-11307)***
Mulholland SEC & Patrol Inc..........B.......818 755-0202
11454 San Vicente Blvd Fl Los Angeles (90049) ***(P-16356)***
Mullen & Henzell LLP..........E.......805 966-1501
112 E Victoria St Santa Barbara (93101) ***(P-22710)***
Muller Ranch LLC..........D.......530 662-0105
15810 County Road 95 Woodland (95695) ***(P-2)***
Muller-Ing-Gateway LLC..........D.......951 687-2900
23521 Paseo De Valencia # 200 Laguna Hills (92653) ***(P-10623)***
Mulligan Family Fun Center, Murrieta *Also called Mulligan Ltd A Cal Ltd Partnr* ***(P-18338)***
Mulligan Family Fun Center, Los Alamitos *Also called Mulligan Limited* ***(P-18337)***
Mulligan Limited (PA)..........D.......714 484-6799
4281 Katella Ave Ste 228 Los Alamitos (90720) ***(P-18337)***
Mulligan Ltd A Cal Ltd Partnr..........D.......951 696-9696
24950 Madison Ave Murrieta (92562) ***(P-18338)***
Mullikin Medical Center, Stockton *Also called Caremark Rx LLC* ***(P-18871)***
Mulroses Usa Inc..........D.......213 489-1761
741 S San Pedro St Los Angeles (90014) ***(P-264)***
Multi Mechanical Inc..........D.......714 632-7404
469 Blaine St Corona (92879) ***(P-2206)***
Multi Specialty Group Practice, Yuba City *Also called Sutter North Med Foundation* ***(P-19491)***
Multi Specialty Medical Svc, Visalia *Also called Visalia Medical Clinic Inc* ***(P-19583)***
Multi-Pak Corporation..........D.......818 709-0508
20131 Bahama St Chatsworth (91311) ***(P-16933)***
Multimodal Esquer Inc..........D.......619 710-0477
8856 Siempre Viva Rd San Diego (92154) ***(P-4099)***
Multipak, Chatsworth *Also called Multi-Pak Corporation* ***(P-16933)***
MULTIPLIER, Oakland *Also called Trust For Cnsrvtion Innovation* ***(P-27240)***
Multipoint Wireless LLC..........E.......714 262-4172
2549 Eastbluff Dr Ste 474 Newport Beach (92660) ***(P-25226)***
Multiquip Inc (HQ)..........B.......310 537-3700
6141 Katella Ave Ste 200 Cypress (90630) ***(P-7169)***
Multiven Inc..........E.......408 828-2715
303 Twin Dolphin Dr # 600 Redwood City (94065) ***(P-16057)***
Multivision Inc (HQ)..........D.......510 740-5600
66 Franklin St Fl 3 Oakland (94607) ***(P-16934)***
Munger Tolles & Olson LLP..........C.......213 683-9100
350 S Grand Ave Fl 50 Los Angeles (90071) ***(P-22711)***
Munger Bros LLC..........A.......661 721-0390
786 Road 188 Delano (93215) ***(P-224)***
Munger Farm, Delano *Also called Munger Bros LLC* ***(P-224)***
Munger Farms, Delano *Also called Monarch Nut Company LLC* ***(P-516)***
Munger Tolles Olson Foundation (PA)..........B.......213 683-9100
350 S Grand Ave Fl 50 Los Angeles (90071) ***(P-22712)***
Munger Tolles Olson Foundation..........E.......415 512-4000
560 Mission St Fl 27 San Francisco (94105) ***(P-22713)***
Muni-Fed Energy Inc..........E.......714 321-3346
192 N Marina Dr Long Beach (90803) ***(P-2207)***
Municipal Svcs Agency, Sacramento *Also called County of Sacramento* ***(P-1816)***
Muniservices LLC (HQ)..........C.......800 800-8181
7625 N Palm Ave Ste 108 Fresno (93711) ***(P-26725)***
Mural, San Francisco *Also called Tactivos Inc* ***(P-5478)***
Muranaka Farm..........C.......805 529-0201
11018 W Los Angeles Ave Moorpark (93021) ***(P-351)***
Murano Group..........D.......949 409-1079
30211 Ave De Las Bndra Rcho STA Marg (92688) ***(P-16357)***
Murchison & Cumming LLP (PA)..........D.......213 623-7400
801 S Grand Ave Ste 900 Los Angeles (90017) ***(P-22714)***
Murcor Inc..........C.......909 623-4001
740 Corp Ctr Dr Pomona (91768) ***(P-11308)***
Murphy (PA)..........D.......415 788-1900
88 Kearny St Fl 10 San Francisco (94108) ***(P-22715)***
Murphy McKay & Associates Inc..........E.......925 283-9555
3468 Mt Diablo Blvd B108 Lafayette (94549) ***(P-16058)***

Murphy OBrien Inc.......D.......310 453-2539
11444 W Olympic Blvd # 600 Los Angeles (90064) ***(P-26919)***
Murphy-True Inc.......D.......707 576-7337
464 Kenwood Ct Ste B Santa Rosa (95407) ***(P-1547)***
Murray Company, E Rncho Dmngz *Also called Murray Plumbing and Htg Corp* ***(P-2208)***
Murray Plumbing and Htg Corp (PA).......A.......310 637-1500
18414 S Santa Fe Ave E Rncho Dmngz (90221) ***(P-2208)***
Murrieta Day Spa, Murrieta *Also called Monique Suraci* ***(P-18177)***
Murrieta Gardens Senior Living.......D.......951 600-7676
18878 E Armstead St Azusa (91702) ***(P-20443)***
Murrietta Circuits.......D.......714 970-2430
5000 E Landon Dr Anaheim (92807) ***(P-2560)***
Mursion Inc (PA).......D.......415 746-9631
303 2nd St Ste 460 San Francisco (94107) ***(P-15416)***
Murtaugh Myer Nlson Trglia LLP.......D.......949 794-4000
2603 Main St Ste 900 Irvine (92614) ***(P-22716)***
Muscle Improvement Inc.......D.......310 374-5522
200 N Harbor Dr Redondo Beach (90277) ***(P-18178)***
Musclebound Inc (PA).......B.......818 349-0123
19835 Nordhoff St Northridge (91324) ***(P-18179)***
Muscolino Inventory Svc Inc.......E.......209 576-8469
1620 N Carptr Rd Ste D50 Modesto (95351) ***(P-16935)***
Muse Concrete Contractors Inc.......D.......530 226-5151
8599 Commercial Way Redding (96002) ***(P-1762)***
Museum Associates.......B.......323 857-6172
5905 Wilshire Blvd Los Angeles (90036) ***(P-24272)***
Museum Cntmprary Art San Diego.......D.......858 454-3541
1100 Kettner Blvd San Diego (92101) ***(P-24273)***
Museum of Childrens Art.......E.......510 465-8770
1221 Broadway Oakland (94612) ***(P-18726)***
Museum of Contemporary Art (PA).......C.......213 626-6222
250 S Grand Ave Los Angeles (90012) ***(P-24274)***
Museum of Latin American Art.......E.......562 437-1689
628 Alamitos Ave Long Beach (90802) ***(P-24275)***
MUSIC CENTER UNIFIED FUND, Los Angeles *Also called Performing Arts Center of La C* ***(P-17935)***
Music Circus, Sacramento *Also called Broadway Sacramento* ***(P-17891)***
Music Collective LLC.......E.......818 508-3303
12711 Ventura Blvd # 110 Studio City (91604) ***(P-17752)***
Music Intllgnce Neuro Dev Inst, Irvine *Also called Mind Research Institute* ***(P-26011)***
Musick Peeler & Garrett LLP (PA).......C.......213 629-7600
624 S Grand Ave Ste 2000 Los Angeles (90017) ***(P-22717)***
Musicmatch Inc.......C.......858 485-4300
16935 W Bernardo Dr # 270 San Diego (92127) ***(P-15417)***
Mutesix Group Inc.......C.......310 215-3467
6080 Center Dr Ste 900 Los Angeles (90045) ***(P-13547)***
Mutesix, An Iprospect Company, Los Angeles *Also called Mutesix Group Inc* ***(P-13547)***
Muth Development Co Inc.......D.......714 527-2239
11100 Beach Blvd Stanton (90680) ***(P-10624)***
Mutual Assist Network Del Paso (PA).......E.......916 927-7694
811 Grand Ave Ste A Sacramento (95838) ***(P-23345)***
Mutual Trading Co Inc (HQ).......C.......213 626-9458
431 Crocker St Los Angeles (90013) ***(P-8612)***
Mutual Trading Co Inc.......E.......858 748-9458
13790 Stowe Dr Ste A Poway (92064) ***(P-8613)***
Mv Hospitality Inc.......E.......707 942-6877
1457 Lincoln Ave Calistoga (94515) ***(P-18180)***
Mv Medical Management.......D.......323 257-7637
1860 Colo Blvd Ste 200 Los Angeles (90041) ***(P-26726)***
Mv Transportation Inc.......D.......323 666-0856
13690 Vaughn St San Fernando (91340) ***(P-3565)***
Mv Transportation Inc.......C.......510 351-1603
1944 Williams St San Leandro (94577) ***(P-5126)***
Mv Transportation Inc.......D.......818 409-3387
1242 Los Angeles St Glendale (91204) ***(P-3566)***
Mv Transportation Inc.......C.......831 373-1395
1375 Burton Ave Salinas (93901) ***(P-5127)***
Mv Transportation Inc.......D.......209 547-7879
1250 S Wilson Way Ste A1 Stockton (95205) ***(P-3567)***
Mv Transportation Inc.......D.......209 339-1972
24 S Sacramento St Lodi (95240) ***(P-3568)***
Mv Transportation Inc.......D.......805 557-7372
265 S Rancho Rd Thousand Oaks (91361) ***(P-5128)***
Mv Transportation Inc.......D.......707 446-5573
479 Mason St Ste 221 Vacaville (95688) ***(P-3569)***
Mv Transportation Inc.......C.......415 206-7386
3550 3rd St San Francisco (94124) ***(P-3570)***
Mv Transportation Inc.......D.......562 790-8642
7231 Rosecrans Ave Paramount (90723) ***(P-5129)***
Mve Inc (PA).......D.......209 526-4214
1117 L St Modesto (95354) ***(P-25227)***
Mve + Partners Inc (PA).......D.......949 809-3388
1900 Main St Ste 800 Irvine (92614) ***(P-25486)***
Mventix Inc (PA).......B.......818 337-3747
21600 Oxnard St Ste 1700 Woodland Hills (91367) ***(P-16936)***
Mvf World Wide Services, Burbank *Also called Modern Videofilm Inc* ***(P-17751)***
Mvp Partners, Santa Ana *Also called Colton Real Estate Group* ***(P-10870)***
Mw Partners, Santa Ana *Also called Morris & Willner Partners* ***(P-26723)***
Mw2 Consulting LLC.......D.......408 573-6310
981 Manor Way Los Altos (94024) ***(P-26727)***
MWH Americas Inc.......D.......805 683-2409
437 2nd St Solvang (93463) ***(P-25228)***
MWH Americas Inc.......C.......626 386-1100
750 Royal Oaks Dr Ste 100 Monrovia (91016) ***(P-25229)***
MWH Americas Inc.......D.......415 430-1800
44 Montgomery St Ste 1400 San Francisco (94104) ***(P-25230)***
MWH Americas Inc.......D.......626 796-9141
618 Michillinda Ave # 200 Arcadia (91007) ***(P-25231)***
Mws Precision Wire Inds Inc.......D.......818 991-8553
31200 Cedar Valley Dr Westlake Village (91362) ***(P-7082)***
Mws Wire Industries, Westlake Village *Also called Mws Precision Wire Inds Inc* ***(P-7082)***
Mwss, Irvine *Also called Montrose Water and Sustainabil* ***(P-27138)***
Mx Courier Systems Inc.......E.......714 288-8622
990 N Tustin St Orange (92867) ***(P-16937)***
Mxb Battery Operations LP.......D.......415 230-8000
717 Battery St San Francisco (94111) ***(P-24599)***
Mxic, Milpitas *Also called Macronix America Inc* ***(P-7299)***
My Ally Inc.......D.......650 387-9118
1000 Elwell Ct Ste 105 Palo Alto (94303) ***(P-15651)***
My Choice Inhome Care LLC.......D.......951 244-8770
31610 Rr Cyn Rd Ste 4 Canyon Lake (92587) ***(P-21817)***
MY DAY COUNTS, Anaheim *Also called Orange Cnty Adult Achvment Ctr* ***(P-16968)***
My Express Freight, Beverly Hills *Also called G Katen Partners Ltd Lblty Co* ***(P-4950)***
My Kids Dentist.......B.......951 600-1062
24635 Madison Ave Ste E Murrieta (92562) ***(P-19623)***
My Office Inc.......D.......858 549-6700
6060 Nncy Rdge Dr Ste 100 San Diego (92121) ***(P-3440)***
My Points.com, San Francisco *Also called Mypointscom LLC* ***(P-13548)***
My Wireless, Santa Ana *Also called B-Per Electronic Inc* ***(P-5197)***
Mya Systems Inc.......E.......877 679-0952
27 Maiden Ln Ste 300 San Francisco (94108) ***(P-14334)***
Mycase, San Diego *Also called Appfolio Inc* ***(P-15240)***
Mycleanpc, Santa Monica *Also called Realdefense LLC* ***(P-16552)***
Myers & Sons Construction LP.......D.......424 227-3285
5200 W Century Blvd Los Angeles (90045) ***(P-1763)***
Myers & Sons Construction LP (PA).......C.......916 283-9950
4600 Northgate Blvd # 100 Sacramento (95834) ***(P-1764)***
Myers Capital Partners LLC.......E.......626 568-1398
790 S Oak Knoll Ave Pasadena (91106) ***(P-9741)***
Myers FSI, Ontario *Also called Myers Power Products Inc* ***(P-7170)***
Myers Power Products Inc (PA).......C.......909 923-1800
2950 E Philadelphia St Ontario (91761) ***(P-7170)***
Myers Tire Supply Dist Inc.......D.......602 233-1037
107 Exchange Pl Pomona (91768) ***(P-6456)***
Myers Tire Supply Division, Pomona *Also called Myers Tire Supply Dist Inc* ***(P-6456)***
Mygrant Glass Company Inc (PA).......E.......510 785-4360
3271 Arden Rd Hayward (94545) ***(P-6457)***
Myinternetservicescom LLC.......D.......213 256-0575
1010 E Union St Ste 125 Pasadena (91106) ***(P-5442)***
Myoscience, Inc., Fremont *Also called Pacira Cryotech Inc* ***(P-27163)***
Mypointscom LLC (HQ).......D.......415 615-1100
44 Montgomery St Ste 1050 San Francisco (94104) ***(P-13548)***
Myra Investment and Dev Corp.......D.......209 834-2343
47 W 6th St Tracy (95376) ***(P-11867)***
Myriad Flowers International.......D.......805 684-8079
4601 Foothill Rd Carpinteria (93013) ***(P-8906)***
Myriad Womens Health Inc.......B.......888 268-6795
180 Kimball Way South San Francisco (94080) ***(P-21556)***
Mystic Inc (PA).......D.......213 746-8538
2444 Porter St Los Angeles (90021) ***(P-8099)***
MYYOGAWORKS, Culver City *Also called Yogaworks Inc* ***(P-18785)***
Mza Events Inc (PA).......E.......213 201-1348
3550 Wilshire Blvd # 1012 Los Angeles (90010) ***(P-16938)***
N & S Tractor Co (PA).......D.......209 383-5888
600 S St 59 Merced (95341) ***(P-17518)***
N A C O, Groveland *Also called Thousand Trails Inc* ***(P-13165)***
N A T C, Pleasanton *Also called North American Title Co Inc* ***(P-10198)***
N A Tomatobank.......D.......626 759-9200
901 S Baldwin Ave Arcadia (91007) ***(P-9269)***
N Compass International Inc.......C.......323 785-1700
8223 Santa Monica Blvd West Hollywood (90046) ***(P-26728)***
N G A Associates.......E.......760 726-4015
205 W Alvarado St Fallbrook (92028) ***(P-10625)***
N G I, Brea *Also called Nevell Group Inc* ***(P-1550)***
N H A, San Diego *Also called Neighborhood House Association* ***(P-23347)***
N I D, Grass Valley *Also called Nevada Irrigation District* ***(P-6366)***
N Model Inc (PA).......C.......650 610-4600
777 Mariners Island Blvd San Mateo (94404) ***(P-14951)***
N N R, Carson *Also called Nnr Global Logistics USA Inc* ***(P-5005)***
N Qiagen Amercn Holdings Inc (HQ).......C.......800 426-8157
27220 Turnberry Ln # 200 Valencia (91355) ***(P-7970)***
N S B N Investments Llc.......D.......310 273-2501
9454 Wilshire Blvd Fl 4 Beverly Hills (90212) ***(P-11936)***
N T S, Woodland Hills *Also called Network Telephone Services Inc* ***(P-16945)***
N Th Degree, Foothill Ranch *Also called Nth Degree Inc* ***(P-16955)***
N V H, San Leandro *Also called N V Heathorn Inc* ***(P-2209)***
N V Heathorn Inc.......D.......510 569-9100
1155 Beecher St San Leandro (94577) ***(P-2209)***
N V Landscape Inc.......D.......661 286-8888
24400 Walnut St Ste D Newhall (91321) ***(P-874)***
N-U Enterprise, Irvine *Also called Ancca Corporation* ***(P-2747)***
N2 Acquisition Company Inc.......D.......714 942-3563
14440 Myford Rd Irvine (92606) ***(P-11680)***
N2 Imaging Systems, Irvine *Also called N2 Acquisition Company Inc* ***(P-11680)***
Nabisco, Ontario *Also called Mondelez Global LLC* ***(P-8609)***
Nabors Well Services Co.......D.......805 648-2731
2567 N Ventura Ave C Ventura (93001) ***(P-1032)***
Nabors Well Services Co.......C.......661 588-6140
1025 Earthmover Ct Bakersfield (93314) ***(P-1033)***
Nabors Well Services Co.......B.......661 589-3970
7515 Rosedale Hwy Bakersfield (93308) ***(P-1034)***
Nabors Well Services Co.......C.......310 639-7074
19431 S Santa Fe Ave Compton (90221) ***(P-1035)***

Nabors Well Services Co ...D.......661 392-7668
1954 James Rd Bakersfield (93308) ***(P-1036)***
Nadel Inc (PA)...D.......310 826-2100
1990 S Bundy Dr Ste 400 Los Angeles (90025) ***(P-25487)***
Nader Mehr DDS Inc ...D.......562 634-2477
555 Anton Blvd Ca Costa Mesa (92626) ***(P-19624)***
Nafithat Alsharq, La Mesa *Also called Abbood Zeyad* ***(P-24897)***
NAFTA Distributors...E.......909 605-7515
5120 Santa Ana St Ontario (91761) ***(P-8198)***
Nafta Shoes Inc...D.......626 369-9681
14632 Nelson Ave City of Industry (91744) ***(P-13367)***
Nagarro Inc (HQ)...D.......408 436-6170
2001 Gateway Pl Ste 100w San Jose (95110) ***(P-15652)***
Nagra, San Francisco *Also called Opentv Inc* ***(P-15435)***
Nagra Usa Inc (HQ)...D.......310 335-5225
841 Apollo St Ste 300 El Segundo (90245) ***(P-7568)***
Naht Care At, San Diego *Also called Neighborhood House Association* ***(P-23348)***
Nail Emporium...E.......714 779-9889
1517 N Harmony Cir Anaheim (92807) ***(P-7675)***
Nail Emporium Beauty Supply, Anaheim *Also called Nail Emporium* ***(P-7675)***
Naimies Beauty Center Inc (PA)...D.......818 655-9933
12640 Riverside Dr Valley Village (91607) ***(P-7676)***
Naimies Film & TV Beauty Sup, Valley Village *Also called Naimies Beauty Center Inc* ***(P-7676)***
Nakase Brothers Wholesale Nurs (PA)...D.......949 855-4388
9441 Krepp Dr Huntington Beach (92646) ***(P-8907)***
Nakase Brothers Wholesale Nurs...C.......949 855-4388
20621 Lake Forest Dr Lake Forest (92630) ***(P-8908)***
Nalco Company LLC...D.......925 957-9720
1320 Arnold Dr Ste 246 Martinez (94553) ***(P-8703)***
Nallatech Inc...D.......805 383-8997
741 Flynn Rd Camarillo (93012) ***(P-7308)***
Namm, Carlsbad *Also called National Assn Mus Mrchants Inc* ***(P-24352)***
Nan Fang Dist Group Inc...D.......510 297-5382
2100 Williams St San Leandro (94577) ***(P-7569)***
Nan McKay and Associates Inc...D.......619 258-1855
1810 Gillespie Way # 202 El Cajon (92020) ***(P-26729)***
Nancy Smith Construction Inc...E.......510 923-1671
47 Yorkshire Dr Oakland (94618) ***(P-1260)***
Nanolab Technologies Inc (PA)...D.......408 433-3320
1708 Mccarthy Blvd Milpitas (95035) ***(P-26094)***
Nantbioscience Inc...D.......310 883-1300
9920 Jefferson Blvd Culver City (90232) ***(P-6980)***
Nanthealth Inc (HQ)...D.......310 883-1300
9920 Jefferson Blvd Culver City (90232) ***(P-15653)***
Nantmobile LLC...C.......310 883-7888
9920 Jefferson Blvd Culver City (90232) ***(P-14952)***
Nantworks LLC (PA)...D.......310 883-1300
9920 Jefferson Blvd Culver City (90232) ***(P-15654)***
NAPA Auto Parts, NAPA *Also called County of NAPA* ***(P-23118)***
NAPA County Juvenile Probation, NAPA *Also called County of NAPA* ***(P-23119)***
NAPA Es Leasing LLC...C.......707 253-9540
1075 California Blvd NAPA (94559) ***(P-12637)***
NAPA Golf Associates LLC...D.......707 257-1900
2555 Jameson Canyon Rd NAPA (94558) ***(P-18512)***
NAPA Nursing Center Inc...C.......707 257-0931
3275 Villa Ln NAPA (94558) ***(P-20153)***
NAPA Sanitation District...E.......707 254-9231
1515 Soscol Ferry Rd NAPA (94558) ***(P-6132)***
NAPA Solano Cmnty Blood Ctr, Fairfield *Also called Vitalant Research Institute* ***(P-22342)***
NAPA State Hospital, NAPA *Also called Califrnia Dept State Hospitals* ***(P-21389)***
NAPA Sunrise Rotary Club Inc...D.......707 257-9564
P.O. Box 5324 NAPA (94581) ***(P-24600)***
NAPA Valley Country Club...D.......707 252-1111
3385 Hagen Rd NAPA (94558) ***(P-18513)***
NAPA Valley Lodge LP...D.......707 875-3525
103 Coast Highway 1 Bodega Bay (94923) ***(P-12638)***
NAPA Valley Marriott, NAPA *Also called IA Lodging NAPA Solano Trs LLC* ***(P-12453)***
NAPA Valley PSI Inc...D.......707 255-0177
651 Trabajo Ln NAPA (94559) ***(P-23617)***
NAPA Valley Railroad Co, NAPA *Also called NAPA Valley Wine Train LLC* ***(P-18727)***
NAPA Valley Wine Train LLC (HQ)...C.......707 253-2160
1275 Mckinstry St NAPA (94559) ***(P-18727)***
NAPA West, Five Points *Also called ATI Machinery Inc* ***(P-7498)***
Napastyle Inc (PA)...E.......707 251-5100
360 Industrial Ct Ste A NAPA (94558) ***(P-13628)***
Narven Enterprises Inc...D.......619 239-2261
1430 7th Ave Ste B San Diego (92101) ***(P-12639)***
Nasser Company Inc (PA)...D.......714 279-2100
22720 Savi Ranch Pkwy Yorba Linda (92887) ***(P-8199)***
Nasser Company of Arizona, Yorba Linda *Also called Nasser Company Inc* ***(P-8199)***
Nat Geo TV, Los Angeles *Also called Fox Networks Group Inc* ***(P-5722)***
Nat L Eggert Operations Center, El Cajon *Also called Helix Water District* ***(P-6067)***
Nat Sim Corp...D.......818 705-3131
7405 Woodley Ave Van Nuys (91406) ***(P-7860)***
NAT'L ASSN FOR HISPANIC ELDERL, Pasadena *Also called La Asociacion Nacional Pro Per* ***(P-23311)***
Natera Inc (PA)...C.......650 249-9090
201 Industrial Rd Ste 410 San Carlos (94070) ***(P-21557)***
National Air Inc...C.......619 299-2500
2053 Kurtz St San Diego (92110) ***(P-2210)***
National Air and Energy, San Diego *Also called National Air Inc* ***(P-2210)***
National Air Cargo Inc...D.......310 662-4766
222 N Sepulveda Blvd # 2000 El Segundo (90245) ***(P-4997)***
National Apartment Flrg LLC...D.......800 773-6904
3205 Ocean Park Blvd # 180 Santa Monica (90405) ***(P-3014)***
National Assn For Hispanic, Los Angeles *Also called La Asociacion Nacional Pro Per* ***(P-23310)***
National Assn Ltr Carriers...B.......805 543-7329
4251 S Higuera St San Luis Obispo (93401) ***(P-24453)***
National Assn Ltr Carriers...B.......415 362-0214
2310 Mason St Fl 4 San Francisco (94133) ***(P-24454)***
National Assn Ltr Crrers BR 52, San Luis Obispo *Also called National Assn Ltr Carriers* ***(P-24453)***
National Assn Mus Mrchants Inc...D.......760 438-8001
5790 Armada Dr Carlsbad (92008) ***(P-24352)***
National Association For Self, Citrus Heights *Also called L W Roth Insurance Agency* ***(P-24345)***
National Builder Services Inc...D.......714 634-7800
3835 E Thousand Oaks Blvd R Westlake Village (91362) ***(P-14537)***
National Bus Investigations...D.......951 677-3500
25020 Las Brisas Rd Ste A Murrieta (92562) ***(P-16939)***
National Business Group Inc (PA)...D.......818 221-6000
15319 Chatsworth St Mission Hills (91345) ***(P-14105)***
National Cble Cmmnications LLC...D.......310 231-0745
11150 Santa Monica Blvd # 900 Los Angeles (90025) ***(P-13656)***
National Cement, Duarte *Also called United Hauling Corp* ***(P-17191)***
National Center On Deafness...D.......818 677-2054
18111 Nordhoff St Northridge (91330) ***(P-23346)***
National City Family Clinic, National City *Also called Centro De Salud De La Comuni* ***(P-21976)***
National Cmnty Renaissance Cal (PA)...D.......909 483-2444
9421 Haven Ave Rancho Cucamonga (91730) ***(P-11582)***
National Cnstr Rentals Inc (HQ)...D.......818 221-6000
15319 Chatsworth St Mission Hills (91345) ***(P-14183)***
National Commercial Services...D.......818 701-4400
6644 Valjean Ave Ste 100 Van Nuys (91406) ***(P-13690)***
National Community Renaissance (PA)...D.......909 483-2444
9421 Haven Ave Rancho Cucamonga (91730) ***(P-13173)***
National Construction & Maint...E.......909 888-7042
23846 Sunnymead Blvd # 10 Moreno Valley (92553) ***(P-1548)***
National Council Negro Women...D.......415 564-4153
784 Cole St San Francisco (94117) ***(P-24850)***
National Credit Industries Inc...D.......626 967-4355
1100 Via Verde San Dimas (91773) ***(P-9638)***
National Custom Packing Inc...E.......831 724-2026
13526 Blackie Rd Castroville (95012) ***(P-520)***
National Ecnomic RES Assoc Inc...D.......213 346-3000
777 S Figueroa St # 1950 Los Angeles (90017) ***(P-25927)***
National Everclean Svcs Inc...D.......877 532-5326
28632 Roadside Dr Ste 275 Agoura Hills (91301) ***(P-26095)***
National Fail Safe Inc...E.......562 493-5447
6442 Industry Way Westminster (92683) ***(P-2561)***
National Fail-Safe SEC Systems, Westminster *Also called National Fail Safe Inc* ***(P-2561)***
National Film Laboratories...C.......323 466-0281
900 Glenneyre St Laguna Beach (92651) ***(P-17753)***
National Fitness Testing, Los Angeles *Also called Young Mens Chrstn Assn of La* ***(P-24753)***
National Fncl Srvcs Cnsrtm LLC...D.......650 572-2872
3161 Los Prados St San Mateo (94403) ***(P-26730)***
National General Insurance Co...D.......909 944-8085
3633 Inland Empire Blvd # 700 Ontario (91764) ***(P-10432)***
National Golf Properties LLC...D.......415 488-4030
5800 Sir Francis Drake San Geronimo (94963) ***(P-18275)***
National Hospitality LLC...D.......805 688-8000
400 Alisal Rd Solvang (93463) ***(P-12640)***
National Hot Rod Association (PA)...C.......626 914-4761
2035 E Financial Way Glendora (91741) ***(P-18086)***
National Insurance Associates, Solana Beach *Also called National Insurance Housing* ***(P-27142)***
National Insurance Housing...D.......800 550-1911
265 Santa Helena Ste 210 Solana Beach (92075) ***(P-27142)***
National Lgal Studies Inst Inc...E.......951 653-4240
23962 Alssndro Blvd Ste P Moreno Valley (92553) ***(P-16940)***
National Link Incorporated...D.......909 670-1900
2235 Auto Centre Dr Glendora (91740) ***(P-6761)***
National Liquidators...E.......949 631-6715
2715 W Coast Hwy Newport Beach (92663) ***(P-7716)***
National Marine Fisheries Svc...C.......858 546-7081
8604 La Jolla Shores Dr La Jolla (92037) ***(P-25802)***
National Mentor Inc...D.......909 483-2505
9166 Anaheim Pl Ste 200 Rancho Cucamonga (91730) ***(P-23618)***
National Mentor Inc...E.......661 387-1000
2131 Mars Ct Bakersfield (93308) ***(P-24200)***
National Notary Association...C.......818 739-4071
9350 De Soto Ave Chatsworth (91311) ***(P-24412)***
NATIONAL NURSES UNITED, Oakland *Also called California Nurses Association* ***(P-24386)***
National Opinion Research Ctr...C.......415 315-2000
50 California St Ste 1500 San Francisco (94111) ***(P-25928)***
National Opinion Research Ctr...D.......415 315-3800
1250 Borregas Ave Sunnyvale (94089) ***(P-25929)***
National Organization of...C.......800 489-0210
18663 Ventura Blvd Tarzana (91356) ***(P-22279)***
National Parking & Valet, Monterey *Also called Pacific Parking & Valet LLC* ***(P-6352)***
National Paving Company Inc...D.......951 369-1332
4361 Fort Dr Riverside (92509) ***(P-1765)***
National Planning Corporation...C.......800 881-7174
100 N Pacific Coast Hwy # 1800 El Segundo (90245) ***(P-9469)***
National Pub Sfety SEC Svcs In...D.......619 579-1660
490 N Magnolia Ave El Cajon (92020) ***(P-16358)***
National Railroad Pass Corp...C.......619 239-9989
1050 Kettner Blvd Ste 1 San Diego (92101) ***(P-3503)***
National Rehab, San Diego *Also called McKesson Ptent Care Sltons Inc* ***(P-22273)***
National Rent A Car, Oakland *Also called National Rental (us) Inc* ***(P-17221)***
National Rent A Car, Santa Clara *Also called National Rental (us) Inc* ***(P-17222)***

National Rental (us) Inc .... D 510 877-4507
7600 Earhart Rd Ste 4 Oakland (94621) ***(P-17221)***

National Rental (us) Inc .... D 408 492-0501
2752 De La Cruz Blvd Santa Clara (95050) ***(P-17222)***

National Research Group Inc .... B 323 817-2000
6255 W Sunset Blvd Fl 19 Los Angeles (90028) ***(P-25930)***

National Retail Trnsp Inc .... D 310 605-3777
355 W Carob St Compton (90220) ***(P-4100)***

National Rtrement Partners Inc (PA) .... D 949 488-8726
34700 Pacific Coast Hwy Capistrano Beach (92624) ***(P-10433)***

National Safe, Fullerton *Also called Henry Bros Electronics Inc* ***(P-15608)***

National Safety Services .... E 714 679-9118
3400 Avenue Of The Arts Costa Mesa (92626) ***(P-27143)***

National Sales Corp .... D 323 586-0200
7250 Oxford Way Commerce (90040) ***(P-8990)***

National Security, San Diego *Also called Leidos Inc* ***(P-25790)***

National Security Industries .... B 916 779-0640
1217 Del Paso Blvd Ste A Sacramento (95815) ***(P-16544)***

National Security Industries .... B 831 425-2052
501 Mission St Ste 1a Santa Cruz (95060) ***(P-16359)***

National Security Santa Cruz, Santa Cruz *Also called National Security Industries* ***(P-16359)***

National Security Tech LLC .... D 925 960-2500
161 S Vasco Rd Ste A Livermore (94551) ***(P-25232)***

National Surety Corporation .... A 415 899-2000
1465 N Mcdowell Blvd # 100 Petaluma (94954) ***(P-10165)***

National Therapeutic Svcs Inc (PA) .... D 866 311-0003
3822 Campus Dr Ste 100 Newport Beach (92660) ***(P-22068)***

National Tire Wholesale, Fresno *Also called Carrolls LLC* ***(P-6484)***

National Tube & Steel, Mission Hills *Also called National Business Group Inc* ***(P-14105)***

National Veterinary Assoc Inc .... D 707 462-8625
2300 N State St Ukiah (95482) ***(P-582)***

National Veterinary Assoc Inc (PA) .... C 805 777-7722
29229 Canwood St Ste 100 Agoura Hills (91301) ***(P-583)***

NationaLease, San Diego *Also called Miramar Ford Truck Sales Inc* ***(P-6406)***

Nationbuilder, Los Angeles *Also called 3dna Corp* ***(P-14602)***

Nationl Medcl Assn Comp Health .... D 619 231-9300
3177 Ocean View Blvd San Diego (92113) ***(P-22069)***

Nations Capital Group LLC .... E 818 793-2050
5353 Balboa Blvd Ste 300 Encino (91316) ***(P-9488)***

Nations Direct Lender & In .... C 800 969-7779
160 S Old Springs Rd # 260 Anaheim (92808) ***(P-16941)***

Nations First Capital LLC .... D 855 396-3600
516 Gibson Dr Ste 160 Roseville (95678) ***(P-9507)***

Nations Petroleum Cal LLC .... D 661 387-6402
9600 Ming Ave Ste 300 Bakersfield (93311) ***(P-1005)***

Nations Surgery Center, Encino *Also called Nations Capital Group LLC* ***(P-9488)***

Nationwide Environmental Svcs, Norwalk *Also called Joes Sweeping Inc* ***(P-6215)***

Nationwide Funding LLC .... E 949 679-3600
5520 Trabuco Rd Ste 100 Irvine (92620) ***(P-9508)***

Nationwide Guard Services Inc .... D 909 608-1112
9327 Fairway View Pl # 200 Rancho Cucamonga (91730) ***(P-16360)***

Nationwide Legal LLC (PA) .... D 213 249-9999
1609 James M Wood Blvd Los Angeles (90015) ***(P-22718)***

Nationwide Theatres Corp (HQ) .... D 310 657-8420
120 N Robertson Blvd Fl 3 Los Angeles (90048) ***(P-17875)***

Nationwide Theatres Corp .... D 562 421-8448
2500 Carson St Lakewood (90712) ***(P-18040)***

Nationwide Trans Inc (PA) .... D 909 355-3211
1633 S Campus Ave Ontario (91761) ***(P-4998)***

Native American Health Ctr Inc (PA) .... D 510 535-4400
2950 International Blvd Oakland (94601) ***(P-19210)***

Native Sons Landscaping Inc .... E 925 837-8175
25 Beta Ct Ste L San Ramon (94583) ***(P-875)***

Natividad Medical Center .... A 831 755-4111
1441 Constitution Blvd Salinas (93906) ***(P-21056)***

Natomas Marketplace 16, Sacramento *Also called Regal Cinemas Inc* ***(P-17862)***

Natomas Racquet Club, Sacramento *Also called Spare-Time Inc* ***(P-18201)***

Natural Health Trends Corp .... D 310 541-0888
609 Deep Valley Dr # 390 Rllng HLS Est (90274) ***(P-22280)***

Natural History Museum of Los .... B 213 763-3442
900 Exposition Blvd Los Angeles (90007) ***(P-24276)***

Natural Rsrces Def Council Inc .... D 310 434-2300
1314 2nd St Santa Monica (90401) ***(P-24601)***

Naturally Aged Flooring, Moorpark *Also called Ace Floor Co Inc* ***(P-2993)***

Naturebridge .... D 415 332-5771
1033 Fort Cronkhite Sausalito (94965) ***(P-24851)***

Natures Image Inc .... D 949 680-4400
20361 Hermana Cir Lake Forest (92630) ***(P-743)***

Natures Produce Company .... D 323 235-4343
3305 Bandini Blvd Vernon (90058) ***(P-8501)***

Naumann/Hobbs Material .... C 909 427-0125
8575 Cherry Ave Fontana (92335) ***(P-7570)***

Naumann/Hobbs Material .... C 858 207-6274
1600 E Mission Rd San Marcos (92069) ***(P-7571)***

Naumes Inc .... E 530 743-2055
3792 Feather River Blvd Olivehurst (95961) ***(P-265)***

Naval Coating Inc .... C 619 234-8366
3475 E St San Diego (92102) ***(P-3441)***

Naval Dental Center, San Diego *Also called United States Dept of Navy* ***(P-19520)***

Naval Fac Eng Cmmd SW Wrkng CA .... D 619 532-1158
1220 Pacific Hwy San Diego (92132) ***(P-25233)***

Naval Hospital Lemoore, Lemoore *Also called United States Dept of Navy* ***(P-21325)***

Naval Medical Center, San Diego *Also called United States Dept of Navy* ***(P-21326)***

Naval Medical Clinic, Port Hueneme *Also called United States Dept of Navy* ***(P-19523)***

Naval Research, San Diego *Also called United States Dept of Navy* ***(P-25859)***

Naval Research Lab, Monterey *Also called United States Dept of Navy* ***(P-25860)***

Navigant Consulting Inc .... D 213 452-4516
300 S Grand Ave Ste 3850 Los Angeles (90071) ***(P-26731)***

Navigant Cymetrix Corporation .... C 424 201-6300
1515 W 190th St Ste 350 Gardena (90248) ***(P-26324)***

Navigate Biopharma Svcs Inc .... C 866 992-4939
1890 Rutherford Rd Carlsbad (92008) ***(P-26013)***

Navis Holdings LLC .... C 510 267-5000
55 Harrison St Ste 600 Oakland (94607) ***(P-14953)***

Navisite LLC .... E 408 965-9000
2805 Lafayette St Santa Clara (95050) ***(P-5443)***

Navitas LLC .... E 415 883-8116
15 Pamaron Way Novato (94949) ***(P-8614)***

Navitas Naturals, Novato *Also called Navitas LLC* ***(P-8614)***

Navmedwest, San Diego *Also called United States Dept of Navy* ***(P-19524)***

Navy Bachelor Quarters, Ridgecrest *Also called Navy Exchange Service Command* ***(P-13174)***

Navy Exchange Service Command .... D 760 939-8681
1395 Hussey Rd Ridgecrest (93555) ***(P-13174)***

Navy Exchange Service Command .... C 909 517-2640
4250 Eucalyptus Ave Chino (91710) ***(P-4457)***

Navy Federal Credit Union .... C 888 842-6328
2040 Harbison Dr Vacaville (95687) ***(P-9330)***

Navy Hospital, Lemoore *Also called United States Dept of Navy* ***(P-21324)***

Nazareth House, Fresno *Also called Congregation of Poor Sisters* ***(P-23871)***

Nazareth House, San Rafael *Also called Sisters of Nazareth* ***(P-20689)***

Nazareth House, San Diego *Also called Poor Sisters of Nazareth of SA* ***(P-24028)***

Nazzareno Electric Co Inc .... D 714 712-4744
1250 E Gene Autry Way Anaheim (92805) ***(P-2562)***

NBBJ LP .... E 213 243-3333
523 W 6th St Ste 300 Los Angeles (90014) ***(P-25488)***

NBC 7/Channel 39, San Diego *Also called Station Venture Operations LP* ***(P-5648)***

NBC Consulting Inc .... D 310 798-5000
2110 Artesia Blvd Ste 323 Redondo Beach (90278) ***(P-26732)***

NBC Subsidiary (knbc-Tv) LLC .... C 818 684-5746
100 Unvrsal Cy Plz Bldg 2 Universal City (91608) ***(P-5636)***

NBC Universal Inc .... C 818 260-5746
3000 W Alameda Ave Burbank (91523) ***(P-5637)***

NC Fit Inc .... D 408 910-6748
647 N Santa Cruz Ave C Los Gatos (95030) ***(P-18181)***

NC Interactive LLC .... D 650 393-2200
1900 S Norfolk St Ste 125 San Mateo (94403) ***(P-15418)***

NC Interactive LLC .... D 512 623-8700
1 Polaris Way Ste 110 Aliso Viejo (92656) ***(P-16059)***

Nca,, Los Angeles *Also called National Cble Cmmnications LLC* ***(P-13656)***

NCALC, Chico *Also called Northern Cal Adptive Lving Ctr* ***(P-24007)***

Ncc Group Inc (HQ) .... D 415 268-9300
123 Mission St Ste 1020 San Francisco (94105) ***(P-16060)***

Ncire, San Francisco *Also called Northern California Institute* ***(P-24203)***

Ncjw La, Los Angeles *Also called Los Angeles SEC National* ***(P-23323)***

NCM, Moreno Valley *Also called National Construction & Maint* ***(P-1548)***

Ncompass International, West Hollywood *Also called N Compass International Inc* ***(P-26728)***

Ncpa, Roseville *Also called Northern California Power Agcy* ***(P-5862)***

Ncpa- Plant 1, Middletown *Also called Northern California Power Agcy* ***(P-5863)***

Ncsoft, Aliso Viejo *Also called NC Interactive LLC* ***(P-16059)***

NCTD, Oceanside *Also called North County Transit District* ***(P-3571)***

ND Systems Inc .... D 408 776-0085
5750 Hellyer Ave San Jose (95138) ***(P-13657)***

Ndga, Santa Clara *Also called Bandai Namco Entrmt Amer Inc* ***(P-7727)***

Nds Americas Inc (HQ) .... D 714 434-2100
3500 Hyland Ave Costa Mesa (92626) ***(P-5731)***

Nds Surgical Imaging LLC .... C 408 776-0085
5750 Hellyer Ave San Jose (95138) ***(P-6981)***

Ndti, Ridgecrest *Also called New Directions Tech Inc* ***(P-15662)***

Neal Electric Corp (HQ) .... D 858 513-2525
2790 Business Park Dr Vista (92081) ***(P-2563)***

Neal Trucking Inc .... D 951 685-5048
9749 Bellegrave Ave Riverside (92509) ***(P-3918)***

Neals Janitorial Service .... E 408 271-9944
1588 Calco Creek Dr San Jose (95127) ***(P-13988)***

Near-Cal Corp .... E 951 245-5400
512 Chaney St Lake Elsinore (92530) ***(P-1549)***

Neardata Inc .... D 818 249-2469
4502 Dyer St Ste 103 La Crescenta (91214) ***(P-26733)***

Neardata Systems, La Crescenta *Also called Neardata Inc* ***(P-26733)***

Ned E Dunphy .... D 661 395-1000
4550 California Ave Fl 2 Bakersfield (93309) ***(P-22719)***

Ned L Webster Concrete Cnstr .... D 805 529-4900
8800 Grimes Canyon Rd Moorpark (93021) ***(P-3187)***

Nederlander of California Inc .... E 323 468-1700
6233 Hollywood Blvd Fl 2 Los Angeles (90028) ***(P-10626)***

Neese Inc .... E 707 544-4444
588 Roseland Ave Santa Rosa (95407) ***(P-3747)***

Nefab Packaging West LLC .... D 408 678-2516
8477 Central Ave Newark (94560) ***(P-16942)***

Neff Construction, Ontario *Also called Southtown Industrial Park* ***(P-10657)***

Nehemiah Construction Inc .... E 707 746-6815
12150 Tributary Ln P Rancho Cordova (95670) ***(P-1766)***

Nehemiah Progressive Housing D .... D 916 231-1999
424 N 7th St Ste 250 Sacramento (95811) ***(P-11583)***

Neighborhood Healthcare .... D 951 225-6400
41840 Enterprise Cir N Temecula (92590) ***(P-22281)***

Neighborhood Healthcare .... D 619 390-9975
10039 Vine St Ste A Lakeside (92040) ***(P-22282)***

Neighborhood Healthcare .... C 760 737-6903
401 E Valley Pkwy Escondido (92025) ***(P-22283)***

Neighborhood Healthcare (PA) .... E 760 520-8372
425 N Date St Ste 203 Escondido (92025) ***(P-19211)***

Employee Codes: A=Over 500 employees, B=251-500
C=101-250, D=51-100, E=50
2020 Directory of California
Wholesalers and Services Companies
© Mergent Inc. 1-800-342-5647
1361

Neighborhood Healthcare..........D.......619 440-2751
855 E Madison Ave El Cajon (92020) ***(P-19212)***
Neighborhood Healthcare..........D.......760 737-2000
460 N Elm St Escondido (92025) ***(P-19213)***
Neighborhood House Association..........D.......619 262-8199
4111 Home Ave Ste F San Diego (92105) ***(P-23755)***
Neighborhood House Association (PA)..........B.......858 715-2642
5660 Copley Dr San Diego (92111) ***(P-23347)***
Neighborhood House Association..........E.......619 527-1287
4425 Federal Blvd Ste 24 San Diego (92102) ***(P-23348)***
Neighborhood House Association..........D.......619 263-7761
841 S 41st St San Diego (92113) ***(P-23349)***
Neighborhood Hse Assoc Fmily, San Diego *Also called Neighborhood House Association* ***(P-23349)***
Neighborhood Preservation Div, Stockton *Also called County of San Joaquin* ***(P-24165)***
Neil Dymott Frank McFall..........C.......619 238-1712
110 W A St San Diego (92101) ***(P-22720)***
Neil Bassetti Farms..........E.......831 674-2040
41715 Espinosa Rd Greenfield (93927) ***(P-66)***
Neil Dymott Perkins Brown, San Diego *Also called Neil Dymott Frank McFall* ***(P-22720)***
Neilson Marketing Services, Laguna Hills *Also called Nms Data Inc* ***(P-27148)***
Nelson Shelton & Associates..........C.......310 271-2229
355 N Canon Dr Beverly Hills (90210) ***(P-11309)***
Nelson & Associates Inc..........D.......562 921-4423
12816 Leffingwell Ave Santa Fe Springs (90670) ***(P-7171)***
Nelson & Sons Electric Inc..........E.......209 667-4343
401 N Walnut Rd Turlock (95380) ***(P-2564)***
Nelson Bros Property MGT Inc..........C.......949 916-7300
16b Journey Ste 200 Aliso Viejo (92656) ***(P-26325)***
Nelson Brothers Property MGT, Aliso Viejo *Also called Nelson Bros Property MGT Inc* ***(P-26325)***
Nelson Moving & Storage Inc..........E.......949 582-0380
25742 Atlantic Ocean Dr Lake Forest (92630) ***(P-4219)***
Nelson North American, Lake Forest *Also called Nelson Moving & Storage Inc* ***(P-4219)***
Nelson, Shelton, & Associates, Beverly Hills *Also called Nelson Shelton & Associates* ***(P-11309)***
Neo Tech, Chatsworth *Also called Oncore Manufacturing LLC* ***(P-25242)***
Neogov, El Segundo *Also called Governmentjobscom Inc* ***(P-15339)***
Neonatal Medical Assoc Inc..........B.......562 933-8100
1022 E Tehachapi Dr Long Beach (90807) ***(P-19214)***
Neonroots LLC..........C.......310 907-9210
8560 W Sunset Blvd # 500 West Hollywood (90069) ***(P-14954)***
Neopets Inc..........E.......818 551-4338
412 W Broadway Ste 303 Glendale (91204) ***(P-5444)***
Neostyle Eyewear Corporation..........D.......760 305-4004
2651 La Mirada Dr Ste 150 Vista (92081) ***(P-7024)***
Neovia Logistics Dist LP..........C.......626 359-4500
600 Live Oak Ave Irwindale (91706) ***(P-4999)***
Nep Group Inc..........E.......951 279-8877
1580 Magnolia Ave Corona (92879) ***(P-17637)***
Nep Group Inc..........D.......412 423-1354
7635 Airport Bus Pkwy Van Nuys (91406) ***(P-17638)***
Nephrology, Los Angeles *Also called Cedars-Sinai Medical Center* ***(P-18877)***
Neps Worldwide, La Mirada *Also called Northeast Protective Svcs Inc* ***(P-16364)***
Neptune Management Corporation..........D.......510 797-2269
4065 Mowry Ave Fremont (94538) ***(P-13372)***
Neptune Management Corporation..........D.......916 771-5300
9650 Fairway Dr 120 Roseville (95678) ***(P-13373)***
Ner Precious Metals Inc..........D.......310 367-3179
640 St Hill St Ste 450 Los Angeles (90014) ***(P-7791)***
Nerys Logistics Inc..........C.......619 616-2124
9925 Airway Rd San Diego (92154) ***(P-5130)***
Nest Labs Inc..........D.......855 469-6378
3400 Hillview Ave Palo Alto (94304) ***(P-7309)***
Nestle Dreyers Ice Cream Co..........C.......909 595-0677
351 Cheryl Ln Walnut (91789) ***(P-8320)***
Nestle Ice Cream Company..........A.......661 398-3500
7301 District Blvd Bakersfield (93313) ***(P-8321)***
Nestle Usa Inc..........C.......408 846-6892
6205 Engel Way Gilroy (95020) ***(P-8322)***
Nestle Waters North Amer Inc..........C.......714 532-6220
619 N Main St Orange (92868) ***(P-8615)***
Nestor Enterprises LLC..........E.......209 727-5711
13852 E Peltier Rd Acampo (95220) ***(P-149)***
Nestwise LLC..........B.......855 444-6378
9785 Towne Centre Dr San Diego (92121) ***(P-16943)***
Net Eternity, Redding *Also called Alexandria Clayton* ***(P-15555)***
Net Express..........D.......510 887-4395
32 Snyder Way Fremont (94536) ***(P-15655)***
Net Optics Inc..........D.......408 737-7777
5301 Stevens Creek Blvd Santa Clara (95051) ***(P-15419)***
Net4site LLC..........D.......408 427-3004
3350 Scott Blvd Bldg 34b Santa Clara (95054) ***(P-26734)***
Netafim Irrigation Inc (HQ)..........C.......559 453-6800
5470 E Home Ave Fresno (93727) ***(P-7503)***
Netapp Inc..........C.......949 754-6600
300 Spectrum Center Dr # 900 Irvine (92618) ***(P-15656)***
Netapp Inc..........C.......408 822-3402
1299 Orleans Dr Sunnyvale (94089) ***(P-15657)***
Netapp Inc..........C.......818 227-5025
6320 Canoga Ave Ste 1500 Woodland Hills (91367) ***(P-15658)***
Netapp Inc..........C.......408 419-5301
1345 Crossman Ave Sunnyvale (94089) ***(P-15659)***
Netapp Inc..........C.......408 822-3803
3334 Meadowlands Ln San Jose (95135) ***(P-15660)***
Netball America Inc..........E.......888 221-3650
5101 Audrey Dr Huntington Beach (92649) ***(P-16944)***
Netbase Solutions Inc (PA)..........D.......650 810-2100
3960 Freedom Cir 201 Santa Clara (95054) ***(P-15794)***
Netcontinuum Inc..........D.......408 961-5600
1454 Almaden Valley Dr San Jose (95120) ***(P-16545)***
Netcube Systems Inc..........D.......650 862-7858
1275 Arbor Ave Los Altos (94024) ***(P-15420)***
Netease Information Tech Corp..........D.......415 612-7866
2000 Sierra Point Pkwy # 800 Brisbane (94005) ***(P-14955)***
Netenrich Inc (PA)..........D.......408 436-5900
2590 N 1st St Ste 300 San Jose (95131) ***(P-16061)***
Netflix Inc..........A.......408 540-3700
121 Albright Way Los Gatos (95032) ***(P-17876)***
Netflix Productions LLC..........C.......323 960-3457
5555 Melrose Ave Los Angeles (90038) ***(P-17639)***
Netline Corporation (PA)..........D.......408 374-4200
750 University Ave # 200 Los Gatos (95032) ***(P-26735)***
Netlinx Publishing Solutions, Sacramento *Also called System Integrators Inc* ***(P-15700)***
Netnow..........B.......408 370-0425
41 Heritage Village Ln Campbell (95008) ***(P-5445)***
Netpace Inc..........D.......925 543-7760
5000 Executive Pkwy # 530 San Ramon (94583) ***(P-16062)***
Netpolarity Inc..........B.......408 971-1100
900 E Campbell Ave Campbell (95008) ***(P-14335)***
Netronix Integration Inc (PA)..........D.......408 573-1444
2170 Paragon Dr San Jose (95131) ***(P-2565)***
Netskope Inc (PA)..........D.......800 979-6988
2445 Augustine Dr Fl 3 Santa Clara (95054) ***(P-14956)***
Netsource Inc..........D.......415 831-3681
5955 Geary Blvd San Francisco (94121) ***(P-14336)***
Netsuite Inc (HQ)..........C.......650 627-1000
2955 Campus Dr Ste 100 San Mateo (94403) ***(P-15421)***
Netversant - Silicon Vly Inc (PA)..........C.......510 771-1200
47811 Warm Springs Blvd Fremont (94539) ***(P-2566)***
Network Automation Inc..........E.......213 738-1700
3530 Wilshire Blvd # 1800 Los Angeles (90010) ***(P-15422)***
Network Global Logistics LLC..........C.......888 285-7447
13479 Valley Blvd Fontana (92335) ***(P-4458)***
Network Intgrtion Partners Inc..........D.......909 919-2800
11981 Jack Benny Dr # 103 Rancho Cucamonga (91739) ***(P-15661)***
Network Management Group Inc (PA)..........C.......323 263-2632
1100 S Flower St Ste 3110 Los Angeles (90015) ***(P-26326)***
Network Medical Management Inc..........C.......626 282-0288
1668 S Grfeld Ave Ste 100 Alhambra (91801) ***(P-26327)***
Network Telephone Services Inc (PA)..........B.......800 742-5687
21135 Erwin St Woodland Hills (91367) ***(P-16945)***
Networked Insurance Agents LLC..........C.......800 682-8476
443 Crown Point Cir Ste A Grass Valley (95945) ***(P-10434)***
Netzero Inc (HQ)..........C.......805 418-2000
21301 Burbank Blvd Fl 3 Woodland Hills (91367) ***(P-14957)***
Neuberg Nuberg Importers Group..........E.......800 832-2742
6001 Santa Monica Blvd Los Angeles (90038) ***(P-6572)***
Neudesic LLC (PA)..........C.......949 754-4500
200 Spectrum Center Dr # 2000 Irvine (92618) ***(P-16063)***
Neuintel LLC (PA)..........D.......949 625-6117
20 Pacifica Ste 1000 Irvine (92618) ***(P-14958)***
Neuro Drinks, Sherman Oaks *Also called Neurobrands LLC* ***(P-8616)***
Neurobrands LLC..........C.......310 393-6444
15303 Ventura Blvd # 675 Sherman Oaks (91403) ***(P-8616)***
Neuron Esb, Irvine *Also called Neudesic LLC* ***(P-16063)***
Neuropace Inc..........D.......650 237-2700
455 Bernardo Ave Mountain View (94043) ***(P-25803)***
Neurosurgery, Eureka *Also called St Joseph Hospital* ***(P-21226)***
Nevada County Behavioral Hlth..........E.......530 265-1450
500 Crown Point Cir # 120 Grass Valley (95945) ***(P-22070)***
Nevada Irrigation District (PA)..........C.......530 273-6185
1036 W Main St Grass Valley (95945) ***(P-6366)***
Nevada Republic Electric N Inc..........C.......916 294-0140
11855 White Rock Rd Rancho Cordova (95742) ***(P-2567)***
Nevada Truck & Trailer Repair, West Sacramento *Also called Fredericksen Tank Lines Inc* ***(P-4049)***
Nevell Group Inc (PA)..........C.......714 579-7501
3001 Enterprise St # 200 Brea (92821) ***(P-1550)***
Neversoft Entertainment Inc..........C.......818 610-4100
21255 Burbank Blvd # 600 Woodland Hills (91367) ***(P-14959)***
Neville Alleyne MD, Oceanside *Also called Tri City Orthopedic Sgy & Mdcl* ***(P-19510)***
Nevin Levy LLP A Partnership..........D.......415 800-5770
50 California St Ste 1500 San Francisco (94111) ***(P-11310)***
Nevins Adams Properties, Santa Barbara *Also called Nevins-Adams Properties Inc* ***(P-10627)***
Nevins-Adams Properties Inc (PA)..........C.......805 963-2884
920 Garden St Ste A Santa Barbara (93101) ***(P-10627)***
Nevocal Enterprises Inc..........D.......559 277-0700
5320 N Barcus Ave Fresno (93722) ***(P-1058)***
New Advances For People Disabi..........D.......661 327-0188
1120 21st St Bakersfield (93301) ***(P-24201)***
New Age Electric Inc..........D.......408 279-8787
1085 N 11th St San Jose (95112) ***(P-2568)***
New Air LLC..........E.......657 257-4349
6600 Katella Ave Cypress (90630) ***(P-7209)***
New Alliance Insurance Brokers..........E.......424 205-6700
3700 Santa Fe Ave Ste 300 Long Beach (90810) ***(P-10435)***
New American Funding, Tustin *Also called Broker Solutions Inc* ***(P-26540)***
New Bi US Gaming LLC..........D.......858 592-2472
10920 Via Frontera # 420 San Diego (92127) ***(P-15423)***
New Bridge Foundation Inc..........D.......510 548-7270
2323 Hearst Ave Berkeley (94709) ***(P-23350)***
New Bridge Foundation Inc..........D.......510 548-7270
1820 Scenic Ave Berkeley (94709) ***(P-21486)***

Mergent e-mail: customerrelations@mergent.com
1362
2020 Directory of California
Wholesalers and Services Companies
(P-0000) Products & Services Section entry number
(PA)=Parent Co (HQ)=Headquarters (DH)=Div Headquarters

New Bthny Rsdntl CRE&sklld..........D.......209 827-8933
1441 Berkeley Dr Los Banos (93635) ***(P-20154)***
New CAM Commerce Solutions LLC..........D.......714 338-0200
5555 Garden Grove Blvd # 100 Westminster (92683) ***(P-15424)***
New Century Media Corp..........E.......562 695-1000
2727 Pellissier Pl City of Industry (90601) ***(P-7825)***
New Century Science & Tech..........D.......626 581-5500
18031 Cortney Ct City of Industry (91748) ***(P-7717)***
New Childrens Museum..........D.......619 233-8792
200 W Island Ave San Diego (92101) ***(P-24277)***
New Cingular Wireless Svcs Inc..........D.......562 924-0000
P.O. Box 68055 Artesia (90702) ***(P-5264)***
New Civic Company Ltd..........C.......415 986-1668
870 Market St Ste 1168 San Francisco (94102) ***(P-11937)***
New Colusa Indian Bingo..........B.......530 458-8844
3770 State Highway 45 Colusa (95932) ***(P-18728)***
NEW COVENANT CARE CENTER OF DI, Dinuba *Also called New Covenant Care of Dinuba* ***(P-20155)***
New Covenant Care of Dinuba..........D.......559 591-3300
1730 S College Ave Dinuba (93618) ***(P-20155)***
New Crew Production Corp..........C.......323 234-8880
1100 W 135th St Gardena (90247) ***(P-16946)***
New Day Staffing Inc..........C.......619 481-5400
5920 Friars Rd Ste 104 San Diego (92108) ***(P-14538)***
New Deal Studios Inc..........D.......310 578-9929
1812 W Burbank Blvd Burbank (91506) ***(P-17754)***
New Desserts Inc..........D.......415 780-6860
5000 Fulton Dr Fairfield (94534) ***(P-8617)***
New Directions Inc (PA)..........D.......310 914-4045
11303 Wilshire Blvd Los Angeles (90025) ***(P-23351)***
New Directions For Veterans, Los Angeles *Also called New Directions Inc* ***(P-23351)***
New Directions Tech Inc (PA)..........D.......760 384-2444
137 W Drummond Ave Ste A Ridgecrest (93555) ***(P-15662)***
New Discovery Inc..........D.......925 783-6613
1475 Clubhouse Dr Byron (94505) ***(P-18514)***
New Discovery Inc..........D.......925 634-0505
2600 Cherry Hills Dr Byron (94505) ***(P-18276)***
New Dream Network LLC (PA)..........D.......626 644-9466
135 S State College Blvd Brea (92821) ***(P-5446)***
New Dream Network LLC..........D.......323 375-3842
707 Wilshire Blvd # 5050 Los Angeles (90017) ***(P-5447)***
New Earth Enterprises Inc..........D.......760 942-1298
3790 Manchester Ave Encinitas (92024) ***(P-744)***
New Economics For Women (PA)..........D.......213 483-2060
303 Loma Dr Los Angeles (90017) ***(P-23352)***
New England Financial, Woodland Hills *Also called Russon Financial Services Inc* ***(P-26801)***
New England Shtmtl Works Inc..........C.......559 268-7375
2731 S Cherry Ave Fresno (93706) ***(P-25234)***
New Figueroa Hotel Inc..........D.......213 627-8971
1000 S Hope St Apt 201 Los Angeles (90015) ***(P-12641)***
New First Fincl Resources LLC..........C.......949 223-2160
100 Spectrum Center Dr # 400 Irvine (92618) ***(P-9871)***
New Haven Youth Fmly Svcs Inc..........C.......760 630-4060
P.O. Box 1199 Vista (92085) ***(P-23353)***
New Home Company Inc (PA)..........D.......949 382-7800
85 Enterprise Ste 450 Aliso Viejo (92656) ***(P-1313)***
New Home Feed, Oakland *Also called Zillow Group Inc* ***(P-15838)***
New Home Professionals..........C.......925 556-1555
6500 Dublin Blvd Ste 201 Dublin (94568) ***(P-11311)***
New Hope Care Center, Tracy *Also called Jesse Lee Group Inc* ***(P-26274)***
New Hope Harvesting LLC..........D.......805 478-4469
918 Nita Ct Santa Maria (93454) ***(P-455)***
New Image Landscape Company..........D.......510 226-9191
3250 Darby Cmn Fremont (94539) ***(P-876)***
New Legend Inc..........B.......530 674-3100
1235 Oswald Rd Yuba City (95991) ***(P-4101)***
New Legend Inc..........C.......855 210-2300
8613 Etiwanda Ave Rancho Cucamonga (91739) ***(P-4102)***
New Mediscan II LLC..........D.......866 758-4224
21050 Califa St 100 Woodland Hills (91367) ***(P-14539)***
New Ngc Inc..........E.......510 234-6745
1040 Canal Blvd Richmond (94804) ***(P-7765)***
New Paradigm Productions Inc (PA)..........D.......415 924-8000
39 Mesa St Ste 212 San Francisco (94129) ***(P-17640)***
New Port Orthopedic Institute..........D.......949 722-5071
19582 Beach Blvd Ste 118 Huntington Beach (92648) ***(P-19215)***
New Pride Corporation..........D.......323 584-6608
5101 Pacific Blvd Vernon (90058) ***(P-8100)***
New Pride Tire Inc..........E.......310 631-7000
1511 E Orangethorpe Ave D Fullerton (92831) ***(P-17317)***
New Regency Productions Inc (PA)..........D.......310 369-8300
10201 W Pico Blvd Bldg 12 Los Angeles (90064) ***(P-17641)***
New Relic Inc (PA)..........C.......650 777-7600
188 Spear St Ste 1200 San Francisco (94105) ***(P-15425)***
New Solar Incorporated..........E.......888 886-0103
1525 Mccarthy Blvd Milpitas (95035) ***(P-26328)***
New Start Home Health Care Inc..........C.......818 665-7898
21515 Vanowen St Ste 205 Canoga Park (91303) ***(P-23354)***
New Stockton Poultry Inc..........E.......209 466-1952
302 S San Joaquin St Stockton (95203) ***(P-8330)***
New View Landscape Inc..........D.......818 222-8972
24860 Calabasas Rd Calabasas (91302) ***(P-877)***
New Visa Health Services Inc..........B.......760 723-0053
3414 Preakness Ct Fallbrook (92028) ***(P-20637)***
New Vista Behavioral Hlth LLC..........D.......949 284-0095
3 Park Plz Ste 550 Irvine (92614) ***(P-20444)***
New Vista Health Services..........C.......310 477-5501
1516 Sawtelle Blvd Los Angeles (90025) ***(P-20638)***
New Vista Health Services..........C.......818 352-1421
8647 Fenwick St Sunland (91040) ***(P-20639)***
New Vista Health Services (PA)..........B.......559 298-3236
1987 Vartikian Ave Clovis (93611) ***(P-20640)***
New Vista Pst Act Care Cntr, Los Angeles *Also called New Vista Health Services* ***(P-20638)***
New Vsta Nrsing Rhbltation Ctr, Sunland *Also called New Vista Health Services* ***(P-20639)***
New Wave Entertainment, Burbank *Also called NW Entertainment Inc* ***(P-17643)***
New Way Landscape & Tree Svcs..........C.......858 505-8300
7485 Ronson Rd San Diego (92111) ***(P-878)***
New Way LLC..........E.......925 688-1520
1130 Burnett Ave Ste G Concord (94520) ***(P-24003)***
New West Partitions..........C.......916 456-8365
2550 Sutterville Rd Sacramento (95820) ***(P-2825)***
New York Life Insurance Co..........B.......650 571-1220
1300 S El Cmno Real 400 San Mateo (94402) ***(P-10436)***
New York Life Insurance Co..........D.......925 809-7020
191 Sand Creek Rd Ste 200 Brentwood (94513) ***(P-9872)***
New York Life Insurance Co..........D.......714 255-5100
675 Placentia Ave Ste 250 Brea (92821) ***(P-9873)***
New York Life Insurance Co..........D.......805 898-7625
3757 State St Ste 310 Santa Barbara (93105) ***(P-9874)***
New York Life Insurance Co..........D.......818 662-7500
801 N Brand Blvd Glendale (91203) ***(P-9875)***
New York Life Insurance Co..........D.......408 392-9782
1731 Tech Dr Ste 400 San Jose (95110) ***(P-9876)***
New York Life Insurance Co..........D.......559 447-3900
205 E Rver Pk Cir Ste 250 Fresno (93720) ***(P-10437)***
New York Life Insurance Co..........D.......951 354-2094
4204 Riverwalk Pkwy # 200 Riverside (92505) ***(P-9877)***
New York Life Insurance Co..........D.......949 797-2400
2020 Main St Ste 1200 Irvine (92614) ***(P-9878)***
New York Life Insurance Co..........E.......415 393-6060
425 Market St Fl 16 San Francisco (94105) ***(P-10438)***
New York Life Insurance Co..........D.......916 774-6200
2999 Douglas Blvd Ste 350 Roseville (95661) ***(P-9879)***
New York Life Insurance Co..........C.......858 623-8600
4365 Executive Dr Ste 800 San Diego (92121) ***(P-9880)***
New York Life Insurance Co..........D.......415 999-9576
2633 Camino Ramon Ste 525 San Ramon (94583) ***(P-9881)***
New York Life Insurance Co..........E.......805 656-4598
300 E Esplanade Dr # 2050 Oxnard (93036) ***(P-9882)***
New York Life Insurance Co..........E.......323 782-3000
6300 Wilshire Blvd # 1900 Los Angeles (90048) ***(P-9883)***
New York Life Insurance Co..........D.......559 447-3900
7112 N Fresno St Ste 100 Fresno (93720) ***(P-10439)***
New York Life Insurance Co..........D.......909 305-6500
140 Via Verde Ste 200 San Dimas (91773) ***(P-9884)***
Newark Courtyard By Marriott..........D.......510 792-5200
34905 Newark Blvd Newark (94560) ***(P-12642)***
NEWARK CRISIS CENTER, Newark *Also called Second Chance Inc* ***(P-23455)***
Neway Packaging Corp (PA)..........D.......602 454-9000
1973 E Via Arado Rancho Dominguez (90220) ***(P-7886)***
Newco Distributors Inc..........D.......909 291-2240
9060 Rochester Ave Rancho Cucamonga (91730) ***(P-8848)***
Newcomb Academy, Long Beach *Also called Long Beach Unified School Dst* ***(P-16897)***
Newland Group Inc (PA)..........E.......858 455-7503
4790 Eastgate Mall # 150 San Diego (92121) ***(P-11584)***
Newland Northwest, San Diego *Also called Newland Group Inc* ***(P-11584)***
Newland Real Estate Group LLC (HQ)..........D.......858 455-7503
4790 Eastgate Mall # 150 San Diego (92121) ***(P-9833)***
Newma Garris Gilmo + Partne I..........D.......949 756-0818
3100 Bristol St Ste 400 Costa Mesa (92626) ***(P-25489)***
Newmark & Company RE Inc..........D.......714 667-8252
1551 N Tustin Ave Ste 300 Santa Ana (92705) ***(P-26736)***
Newmark & Company RE Inc..........D.......949 608-2000
4675 Macarthur Ct # 1600 Newport Beach (92660) ***(P-11312)***
Newmark Grubb Knight Frank, Santa Ana *Also called Newmark & Company RE Inc* ***(P-26736)***
Newmark Grubb Knight Frank, Newport Beach *Also called Newmark & Company RE Inc* ***(P-11312)***
Newmeyer & Dillion LLP (PA)..........C.......949 854-7000
895 Dove St Fl 5 Newport Beach (92660) ***(P-22721)***
Newport Apparel Corporation (PA)..........D.......310 605-1900
1215 W Walnut St Compton (90220) ***(P-8101)***
Newport Bay Hospital, Newport Beach *Also called Beacon Healthcare Services* ***(P-21384)***
Newport Bch Marriott Ht & Spa, Newport Beach *Also called Host Hotels & Resorts LP* ***(P-12386)***
Newport Beach Country Club Inc..........D.......949 644-9550
1 Clubhouse Dr Newport Beach (92660) ***(P-18515)***
Newport Beach Orthopedic Inst..........D.......949 722-7038
22 Corporate Plaza Dr Newport Beach (92660) ***(P-19216)***
Newport Beach Surgery Ctr LLC..........C.......949 631-0988
361 Hospital Rd Ste 124 Newport Beach (92663) ***(P-19217)***
Newport Ch International LLC (PA)..........D.......714 572-8881
1100 W Town And Country R Orange (92868) ***(P-7766)***
Newport Diagnostic Center Inc (PA)..........D.......949 760-3025
1605 Avocado Ave Newport Beach (92660) ***(P-21558)***
Newport Diversified Inc..........C.......562 921-4359
13963 Alondra Blvd Santa Fe Springs (90670) ***(P-16947)***
Newport Diversified Inc..........D.......619 449-7800
1286 Fletcher Pkwy El Cajon (92020) ***(P-16948)***
Newport Fmly Mdcne/A Med Group..........D.......949 644-1025
520 Superior Ave Newport Beach (92663) ***(P-19218)***
Newport Group Inc (PA)..........C.......925 328-4540
1350 Treat Blvd Ste 300 Walnut Creek (94597) ***(P-26329)***
Newport Harbor Radiology Assoc..........D.......949 721-8191
360 San Miguel Dr # 105106 Newport Beach (92660) ***(P-19219)***
Newport Hospitality Group Inc..........C.......661 323-1900
801 Truxtun Ave Bakersfield (93301) ***(P-12643)***

ALPHABETIC

Newport Hotel Capital LLC ......C......714 758-0900
1221 S Harbor Blvd Anaheim (92805) ***(P-12644)***
Newport Imaging Center, Newport Beach *Also called Newport Harbor Radiology Assoc* ***(P-19219)***
Newport Meat Company, Irvine *Also called Newport Meat Southern Cal Inc* ***(P-8412)***
Newport Meat Southern Cal Inc ......C......949 399-4200
16691 Hale Ave Irvine (92606) ***(P-8412)***
Newport Mesa Memory Care Cmnty, Costa Mesa *Also called Silverado Senior Living Inc* ***(P-20455)***
Newport Pacific Capital Co Inc (PA) ......C......949 852-5575
17300 Red Hill Ave # 280 Irvine (92614) ***(P-11313)***
Newport Radio Surgery Center, Newport Beach *Also called Newport Diagnostic Center Inc* ***(P-21558)***
Newport Television LLC ......C......559 761-0243
4880 N 1st St Fresno (93726) ***(P-17929)***
Newport Television LLC ......D......661 283-1700
2120 L St Bakersfield (93301) ***(P-5638)***
Newshire Investment, Los Angeles *Also called Otts Asia* ***(P-11944)***
Newstar Fresh Foods LLC ......D......831 758-7800
126 Sun St Salinas (93901) ***(P-521)***
Newstar Fresh Foods LLC (PA) ......C......888 782-7220
850 Work St Ste 101 Salinas (93901) ***(P-8502)***
Newsways Distributors, Los Angeles *Also called Newsways Services Inc* ***(P-8875)***
Newsways Services Inc ......C......323 258-6000
1324 Cypress Ave Los Angeles (90065) ***(P-8875)***
Newton Softed Inc ......E......949 396-6192
2807 Mcgaw Ave Irvine (92614) ***(P-27144)***
Newval Chemical, Orange *Also called Marne Construction Inc* ***(P-3178)***
Newwest Funding, Downey *Also called Newwest Mortgage Company* ***(P-9639)***
Newwest Mortgage Company ......D......562 861-8393
8255 Firestone Blvd # 101 Downey (90241) ***(P-9639)***
Nex Systems, Stockton *Also called Designers LLC* ***(P-13267)***
Nexant Inc (PA) ......D......415 369-1000
101 2nd St Ste 1000 San Francisco (94105) ***(P-27145)***
Nexcare Collaborative (PA) ......E......818 907-0322
15477 Ventura Blvd Sherman Oaks (91403) ***(P-23355)***
Nexgenix Inc (PA) ......B......714 665-6240
2 Peters Canyon Rd # 200 Irvine (92606) ***(P-14960)***
Nexgrill Industries Inc (PA) ......D......909 598-8799
14050 Laurelwood Pl Chino (91710) ***(P-6573)***
Nexinfo Solutions Inc ......E......714 368-1452
8502 E Chapman Ave # 364 Orange (92869) ***(P-6877)***
Nexsentio Inc ......D......408 392-9249
1346 Ridder Park Dr San Jose (95131) ***(P-13989)***
Nexstar Broadcasting Inc ......C......559 222-2411
5035 E Mckinley Ave Fresno (93727) ***(P-5639)***
Nexstar Broadcasting Inc ......B......415 441-4444
900 Front St Ste 300 San Francisco (94111) ***(P-5640)***
Nexstar Digital LLC ......D......310 971-9300
12777 W Jefferson Blvd Los Angeles (90066) ***(P-13549)***
Next Door Sltons To Dom Vlence ......D......408 279-2962
234 E Gish Rd Ste 200 San Jose (95112) ***(P-24202)***
Next Image Medical Inc (PA) ......D......858 847-9185
3390 Carmel Mountain Rd # 150 San Diego (92121) ***(P-26737)***
Next Management LLC ......E......323 782-0038
8447 Wilshire Blvd # 301 Beverly Hills (90211) ***(P-26738)***
Next Management Co, Beverly Hills *Also called Next Management LLC* ***(P-26738)***
Next Trucking Inc ......C......855 688-6398
2383 Utah Ave Ste 108 El Segundo (90245) ***(P-5000)***
Next Venture Inc ......D......818 637-2888
560 Rverdale Drv Glendale Glendale (91204) ***(P-1551)***
Nextdoorcom Inc ......D......415 236-0000
875 Stevenson St Ste 100 San Francisco (94103) ***(P-15874)***
Nextel Communications Inc ......D......323 290-2400
1810 W Slauson Ave Ste G Los Angeles (90047) ***(P-5265)***
Nextel Communications Inc ......D......925 682-2355
272 Sun Valley Mall Concord (94520) ***(P-5266)***
Nextgen Healthcare Inc (PA) ......C......949 255-2600
18111 Von Karman Ave # 8 Irvine (92612) ***(P-15426)***
Nextgen Healthcare Info System (HQ) ......D......949 255-2600
18111 Von Karman Ave Irvine (92612) ***(P-14961)***
Nextpoint Inc (PA) ......D......310 360-5904
8750 Wilshire Blvd 300e Beverly Hills (90211) ***(P-5448)***
Nextracker Inc (HQ) ......D......510 270-2500
6200 Paseo Padre Pkwy Fremont (94555) ***(P-7432)***
Nextroll Inc (PA) ......C......877 723-7655
2300 Harrison St Fl 2 San Francisco (94110) ***(P-13550)***
Nexus Healthcare Solutions Inc ......E......310 448-2693
648 N St Andrews Pl Los Angeles (90004) ***(P-22284)***
NFFE-IAM 2152, Needles *Also called International Assoc of Machini* ***(P-24443)***
Nfl Network, Culver City *Also called Nfl Properties LLC* ***(P-17930)***
Nfl Properties LLC ......B......310 840-4635
10950 Wash Blvd Ste 100 Culver City (90232) ***(P-17930)***
Nfp Advisors, Simi Valley *Also called Nfp Property & Casualty Svcs* ***(P-26739)***
Nfp Property & Casualty Svcs ......E......805 579-1900
2450 Tapo St Simi Valley (93063) ***(P-26739)***
NGL, Fontana *Also called Network Global Logistics LLC* ***(P-4458)***
Ngs Group Inc ......D......323 735-1700
4152 W Washington Blvd Los Angeles (90018) ***(P-8618)***
Nguyen, Myhanh MD, Sunnyvale *Also called Sutter Health* ***(P-19478)***
Nhca Inc ......C......310 519-8200
2330 Grand Ave Long Beach (90815) ***(P-12645)***
Nhn Global Inc (PA) ......C......424 672-1177
3530 Wilshire Blvd Ste 16 Los Angeles (90010) ***(P-8102)***
Nhr Newco Holdings LLC (HQ) ......D......805 964-9975
6500 Hollister Ave # 210 Santa Barbara (93117) ***(P-6878)***
Nhra, Glendora *Also called National Hot Rod Association* ***(P-18086)***

Ni Ki Cruz LLC ......D......408 332-7616
5255 Stevens Creek Blvd Santa Clara (95051) ***(P-26740)***
Ni Microwave Components, Santa Clara *Also called Phase Matrix Inc* ***(P-7320)***
Niacc-Avitech Technologies Inc (PA) ......D......559 291-2500
245 W Dakota Ave Clovis (93612) ***(P-17519)***
Nibbelink Masonry Cnstr Corp ......D......661 948-7859
2010 W Avenue K Lancaster (93536) ***(P-2723)***
Nibbi Bros Associates Inc ......C......415 863-1820
1000 Brannan St Ste 102 San Francisco (94103) ***(P-1261)***
Nibbi Bros Concrete, San Francisco *Also called Nibbi Bros Associates Inc* ***(P-1261)***
Nic Partners, Rancho Cucamonga *Also called Network Intgrtion Partners Inc* ***(P-15661)***
Nice Avenue LLC ......D......909 794-1189
2278 Nice Ave Mentone (92359) ***(P-20156)***
Nicholas A Stevens, Burlingame *Also called M H Podell Company* ***(P-11574)***
Nicholas B Macy Dvm ......D......831 475-5400
2585 Soquel Dr Santa Cruz (95065) ***(P-584)***
Nicholas Grant Corporation ......D......619 390-3900
12570 Highway 67 Lakeside (92040) ***(P-1767)***
Nicholas Lane Contractors Inc ......B......714 630-7630
1157 N Red Gum St Anaheim (92806) ***(P-1166)***
Nichols Inst Reference Labs (HQ) ......A......949 728-4000
33608 Ortega Hwy San Juan Capistrano (92675) ***(P-21559)***
Nichols Lumber & Hardware Co ......D......626 960-4802
13470 Dalewood St Baldwin Park (91706) ***(P-6635)***
Nichols Melburg Rossetto Assoc (PA) ......E......530 222-3300
300 Knollcrest Dr Redding (96002) ***(P-25490)***
Nick and MO, Irwindale *Also called Wor International Inc* ***(P-8051)***
Nicks Cove Inc ......D......415 663-1033
23240 Ca 1 Marshall (94940) ***(P-12646)***
Nicola International Inc ......C......818 767-1133
11119 Dora St Sun Valley (91352) ***(P-8619)***
Nicole Pttrson Crt Rprting LLC ......E......559 400-2407
545 E Alluvial Ave # 109 Fresno (93720) ***(P-22722)***
Nidek Incorporated ......E......510 226-5700
2040 Corporate Ct San Jose (95131) ***(P-7025)***
Nielsen Company (us) LLC ......B......323 817-2000
6255 W Sunset Blvd Fl 20 Los Angeles (90028) ***(P-25931)***
Nielsen Company (us) LLC ......C......858 677-9542
5375 Mira Sorrento Pl # 400 San Diego (92121) ***(P-25932)***
Nielsen Company (us) LLC ......D......323 462-0050
6255 W Sunset Blvd Fl 19 Los Angeles (90028) ***(P-25933)***
Nielsen Media Research, Los Angeles *Also called Nielsen Company (us) LLC* ***(P-25931)***
Nielsen Mobile LLC (HQ) ......C......917 435-9301
1010 Battery St San Francisco (94111) ***(P-16949)***
Nielsens Creamery (PA) ......D......559 686-4744
21346 Road 140 Tulare (93274) ***(P-401)***
Nieves Landscape Inc ......C......714 835-7332
1629 E Edinger Ave Santa Ana (92705) ***(P-879)***
Nifty Thrift, Concord *Also called Futures Explored* ***(P-23240)***
Nightingale Vantagemed Corp (HQ) ......D......916 638-4744
10670 White Rock Rd Rancho Cordova (95670) ***(P-15427)***
Nightrider Overnite Copy Svc, San Francisco *Also called Ricoh Usa Inc* ***(P-6768)***
Nightrider Overnite Copy Svc, Oakland *Also called Ricoh Usa Inc* ***(P-6770)***
Nihon Kohden America Inc (HQ) ......D......949 580-1555
15353 Barranca Pkwy Irvine (92618) ***(P-6982)***
Nijjar Realty Inc (PA) ......D......626 575-0062
4900 Santa Anita Ave 2b El Monte (91731) ***(P-11314)***
Nikewoman ......E......408 942-6457
447 Great Mall Dr Milpitas (95035) ***(P-8139)***
Nikken Global Inc (HQ) ......C......949 789-2000
18301 Von Karman Ave # 120 Irvine (92612) ***(P-7677)***
Nikon Precision Inc (HQ) ......C......650 508-4674
1399 Shoreway Rd Belmont (94002) ***(P-7572)***
Nines Restaurant ......D......925 516-3413
100 Summerset Dr Brentwood (94513) ***(P-26741)***
Ning Trucking Inc ......D......415 544-2531
1160 Battery St San Francisco (94111) ***(P-3919)***
Ninos Latino Unidos FSA ......D......562 801-5454
10016 Pioneer Blvd # 123 Santa Fe Springs (90670) ***(P-24004)***
Ninyo & Moore Geotechnical (PA) ......D......858 576-1000
5710 Ruffin Rd San Diego (92123) ***(P-27146)***
Ninyo & Moore Geotechnical ......D......949 753-7070
475 Goddard Ste 200 Irvine (92618) ***(P-27147)***
Nipomo Dial A Ride ......D......805 929-2881
179 Cross St San Luis Obispo (93401) ***(P-3702)***
Nippon Ex Nec Lgstics Amer Inc ......D......310 604-6100
18615 S Ferris Pl Rancho Dominguez (90220) ***(P-3920)***
Nippon Express USA Inc ......E......310 532-6300
970 Francisco St Torrance (90502) ***(P-5001)***
Nippon Express USA Inc ......D......310 532-6300
300 Westmont Dr San Pedro (90731) ***(P-5002)***
Nippon Express USA Inc ......D......310 535-7200
2233 E Grand Ave El Segundo (90245) ***(P-5003)***
Nippon Travel Agency Amer Inc ......D......310 768-1817
1411 W 190th St Ste 650 Gardena (90248) ***(P-4829)***
Nippon Travel Agency PCF Inc (HQ) ......D......310 768-0017
1025 W 190th St Ste 300 Gardena (90248) ***(P-4830)***
Nissan North America Inc ......D......916 920-4712
3939 N Freeway Blvd Sacramento (95834) ***(P-4459)***
Nissan of Stockton, Stockton *Also called Lithia Motors Inc* ***(P-17337)***
Nissen Vineyard Services Inc ......D......707 963-3480
1226 Spring St Saint Helena (94574) ***(P-674)***
Nissin Intl Trnspt USA Inc (HQ) ......E......310 222-8500
1540 W 190th St Torrance (90501) ***(P-5004)***
Nisum Technologies Inc ......A......714 619-7989
71 Stevenson St Ste 446 San Francisco (94105) ***(P-14962)***
Nisum Technologies Inc ......A......714 579-7979
46231 Landing Pkwy Fremont (94538) ***(P-14963)***

Nitai Partners Inc ....D....855 879-2847
1761 Reichert Way Chula Vista (91913) ***(P-14964)***
Nitro Software Inc ....C....415 632-4894
150 Spear St Ste 1500 San Francisco (94105) ***(P-14965)***
Nittany Lion Landscaping Inc ....D....714 635-1788
14770 Firestone Blvd # 203 La Mirada (90638) ***(P-880)***
Nitto Avecia Pharma Svcs Inc (HQ) ....C....949 951-4425
10 Vanderbilt Irvine (92618) ***(P-26096)***
Nitto Denko Technical Corp ....D....760 435-7011
501 Via Del Monte Oceanside (92058) ***(P-25934)***
Nixon Inc (PA) ....C....760 944-0900
701 S Coast Highway 101 Encinitas (92024) ***(P-7792)***
Nixon Peabody LLP ....C....415 984-8200
1 Embarcadero Ctr # 3200 San Francisco (94111) ***(P-22723)***
Nixon Peabody LLP ....D....213 629-6000
555 W 5th St Fl 30 Los Angeles (90013) ***(P-22724)***
Nixon Watches, Encinitas *Also called Nixon Inc* ***(P-7792)***
Nl Services, La Mirada *Also called Nittany Lion Landscaping Inc* ***(P-880)***
NLc Enterprises Incorporated ....E....562 693-3590
15710 Leffingwell Rd Whittier (90604) ***(P-16950)***
Nlsi, Moreno Valley *Also called National Lgal Studies Inst Inc* ***(P-16940)***
Nmi Holdings Inc ....B....855 530-6642
2100 Powell St Fl 12th Emeryville (94608) ***(P-10166)***
Nmi Industrial Holdings Inc ....D....916 635-7030
8503 Weyand Ave Sacramento (95828) ***(P-25235)***
Nmms Twin Peaks LLC ....D....818 710-6100
5850 Canoga Ave Ste 650 Woodland Hills (91367) ***(P-11315)***
NMN Construction Inc ....D....707 763-6981
1077 Lakeville St Petaluma (94952) ***(P-3188)***
Nmr Design, Redding *Also called Nichols Melburg Rossetto Assoc* ***(P-25490)***
Nms Data Inc ....E....949 472-2700
23172 Plaza Pointe Dr # 205 Laguna Hills (92653) ***(P-27148)***
Nms Management Inc ....D....619 425-0440
155 W 35th St Ste A National City (91950) ***(P-13990)***
Nms Properties Inc ....D....310 475-7600
1430 5th St Ste 101 Santa Monica (90401) ***(P-11316)***
NMWD, Novato *Also called North Marin Water District* ***(P-6095)***
Nna Insurance Services, Chatsworth *Also called Nna Services LLC* ***(P-16951)***
NNA Insurance Services ....C....818 739-4071
9350 De Soto Ave Chatsworth (91311) ***(P-10440)***
Nna Services, Chatsworth *Also called National Notary Association* ***(P-24412)***
NNA Services ....C....818 739-4071
9350 De Soto Ave Chatsworth (91311) ***(P-24413)***
Nna Services LLC ....C....818 739-4071
9350 De Soto Ave Chatsworth (91311) ***(P-16951)***
Nnj Services Inc ....C....858 550-7900
9610 Waples St San Diego (92121) ***(P-11317)***
Nnn Realty Investors LLC ....B....714 667-8252
19700 Fairchild Ste 300 Irvine (92612) ***(P-11938)***
Nnncc Ranch ....D....559 626-4890
7602 Monson Ave Orange Cove (93646) ***(P-16952)***
Nnr Global Logistics USA Inc ....C....310 357-2100
21023 Main St Ste D Carson (90745) ***(P-5005)***
No Barriers ....D....707 451-1947
479 Mason St Ste 325 Vacaville (95688) ***(P-23356)***
No More Dirt Inc ....C....415 821-6757
1699 Valencia St San Francisco (94110) ***(P-13991)***
No Ordinary Moments Inc ....C....714 848-3800
16742 Gothard St Ste 115 Huntington Beach (92647) ***(P-21818)***
No Shnacks Inc ....E....909 293-8747
7480 Harvard Ct Fontana (92336) ***(P-26330)***
Noah Concrete Corporation ....D....408 842-7211
5900 Rossi Ln Gilroy (95020) ***(P-3189)***
Nob Hill Properties Inc ....B....415 474-5400
1075 California St San Francisco (94108) ***(P-12647)***
Nobelbiz Inc ....E....760 405-0105
5759 Fleet St Ste 210 Carlsbad (92008) ***(P-27293)***
Noble Aew Vineyard Creek LLC ....D....707 284-1234
170 Railroad St Santa Rosa (95401) ***(P-12648)***
Noble Credit Union (PA) ....E....559 252-5000
2580 W Shaw Ln Frnt Fresno (93711) ***(P-9331)***
Noble Energy, Seal Beach *Also called Samedan Oil Corporation* ***(P-991)***
Noble House Home Furn LLC (PA) ....D....818 884-7059
21325 Superior St Chatsworth (91311) ***(P-6523)***
Noble Rents Inc ....D....855 767-4424
8314 Slauson Ave Pico Rivera (90660) ***(P-14106)***
Noble Tower Preservation LP ....D....510 444-5228
1515 Lakeside Dr Oakland (94612) ***(P-11318)***
Noble/Utah Long Beach LLC ....C....562 436-3000
333 E Ocean Blvd Long Beach (90802) ***(P-12649)***
Noblesse Oblige Inc ....C....760 353-3336
2015 Silsbee Rd El Centro (92243) ***(P-456)***
Nohl Ranch Inn, Anaheim *Also called Leisure Care LLC* ***(P-23971)***
Noia Residential Services Inc 559 485-5555
606 E Belmont Ave Ste 101 Fresno (93701) ***(P-24005)***
Noiro West LLC ....C....619 819-6620
701 A St San Diego (92101) ***(P-12650)***
Noland Hamerly Etienne (PA) ....E....831 372-7525
333 Salinas St Salinas (93901) ***(P-22725)***
Nolte Associates, Sacramento *Also called Nv5 Inc* ***(P-25238)***
Nolte, George S & Associates, San Diego *Also called Nv5 Inc* ***(P-25239)***
Nominum Inc ....E....650 381-6000
3355 Scott Blvd Fl 3 Santa Clara (95054) ***(P-15428)***
Nomura Securities Intl Inc ....B....415 445-3831
425 California St # 2600 San Francisco (94104) ***(P-9742)***
Nongshim America Inc (HQ) ....C....909 481-3698
12155 6th St Rancho Cucamonga (91730) ***(P-8200)***
Noodle Analytics Inc ....D....415 412-2139
115 Sansome St Fl 8 San Francisco (94104) ***(P-14966)***
Noodle.ai, San Francisco *Also called Noodle Analytics Inc* ***(P-14966)***
Nor-Cal Beverage Co Inc (PA) ....B....916 372-0600
2150 Stone Blvd West Sacramento (95691) ***(P-8783)***
Nor-Cal Beverage Co Inc ....C....714 526-8600
1226 N Olive St Anaheim (92801) ***(P-16953)***
Nor-Cal Medical Temps, Belvedere Tiburon *Also called Pharmacy Temps Inc* ***(P-14543)***
Nor-Cal Moving Services (PA) ....C....510 371-4942
3129 Corporate Pl Hayward (94545) ***(P-4220)***
Nor-Cal Moving Services ....D....408 954-1175
560 E Trimble Rd San Jose (95131) ***(P-4221)***
Nor-Cal Pipeline Services ....D....530 673-3886
1875 S River Rd West Sacramento (95691) ***(P-1893)***
Nor-Cal Produce Inc ....C....916 373-0830
2995 Oates St West Sacramento (95691) ***(P-4460)***
Nor-Wall Inc (PA) ....E....707 445-5445
518 W Clark St Eureka (95501) ***(P-18516)***
Nora Lighting Inc ....D....800 686-6672
6505 Gayhart St Commerce (90040) ***(P-7172)***
Norac Additives LLC ....D....909 321-5952
813 Towne Center Dr Pomona (91767) ***(P-8704)***
Noralco Inc ....C....209 551-4545
20001 Mchenry Ave Escalon (95320) ***(P-522)***
Norcal Inc ....C....714 224-3949
1400 Moonstone Brea (92821) ***(P-2950)***
Norcal Ambulance Services, Oakland *Also called North Star Emergency Svcs Inc* ***(P-3703)***
Norcal Beverage Co, Anaheim *Also called Nor-Cal Beverage Co Inc* ***(P-16953)***
Norcal Care Centers Inc ....D....925 757-8787
1210 A St Antioch (94509) ***(P-20641)***
Norcal Gold Inc ....E....916 984-8778
2340 E Bidwell St Folsom (95630) ***(P-11319)***
Norcal Inc ....C....714 224-3949
1400 Moonstone Brea (92821) ***(P-2951)***
Norcal Mutual Insurance Co (PA) ....B....415 397-9703
575 Market St Fl 10 San Francisco (94105) ***(P-10441)***
Norcal Painters Inc ....D....415 566-6800
60 29th St 241 San Francisco (94110) ***(P-2374)***
Norco Auto Wash, Fountain Valley *Also called Norco Hills Car Wash* ***(P-17390)***
Norco Fire Department ....A....951 737-8097
3902 Hillside Ave Norco (92860) ***(P-10221)***
Norco Hills Car Wash ....E....951 279-4398
18020 Magnolia St Fountain Valley (92708) ***(P-17390)***
Norco Ranch Inc (HQ) ....B....951 737-6735
12005 Cabernet Dr Fontana (92337) ***(P-428)***
Nordby Construction Co ....E....707 526-4500
1550 Airport Blvd Ste 101 Santa Rosa (95403) ***(P-1552)***
Nordby Wine Caves, Santa Rosa *Also called Nordby Construction Co* ***(P-1552)***
Nordic Industries Inc ....D....530 742-7124
1437 Furneaux Rd Olivehurst (95961) ***(P-1978)***
Nordic Security Services, Newport Beach *Also called Dansk Enterprises Inc* ***(P-16253)***
Nordic/Great Lakes E&I JV ....D....530 742-7124
1437 Furneaux Rd Olivehurst (95961) ***(P-1979)***
Nordman Cormany Hair & Compton ....C....805 485-1000
1000 Town Center Dr Fl 6 Oxnard (93036) ***(P-22726)***
Nordstrom, South Gate *Also called Rick Studer* ***(P-4119)***
Nordstrom Inc ....B....909 390-1040
1600 S Milliken Ave Ontario (91761) ***(P-4461)***
Noritsu America Corporation (HQ) ....C....714 521-9040
6900 Noritsu Ave Buena Park (90620) ***(P-6735)***
Noritz America Corporation (HQ) ....D....714 433-2905
11160 Grace Ave Fountain Valley (92708) ***(P-7454)***
Norland Group ....C....408 855-8255
3350 Scott Blvd Ste 6501 Santa Clara (95054) ***(P-16064)***
Norlyn Builders Newport Beach, Newport Beach *Also called Leisure Care Inc* ***(P-10756)***
Norman Charter, Santa Fe Springs *Also called Norman International Inc* ***(P-6574)***
Norman Industrial Mtls Inc (PA) ....C....818 729-3333
8300 San Fernando Rd Sun Valley (91352) ***(P-7083)***
Norman Industrial Mtls Inc ....E....858 277-8200
7550 Ronson Rd San Diego (92111) ***(P-7084)***
Norman International Inc ....D....562 946-0420
12301 Hawkins St Santa Fe Springs (90670) ***(P-6574)***
Norman S Wright Mech Eqp Corp (PA) ....D....415 467-7600
99 S Hill Dr Ste A Brisbane (94005) ***(P-7455)***
Normand/Wlshire Rtrment Ht Inc ....D....818 373-5429
6700 Sepulveda Blvd Van Nuys (91411) ***(P-10785)***
Normandie Casino & Showroom, Rancho Palos Verdes *Also called Normandie Club LP* ***(P-18729)***
Normandie Club LP ....A....310 352-3486
57 Via Malona Rancho Palos Verdes (90275) ***(P-18729)***
Normandin Auto Brokers ....D....408 266-2824
900 Cptl Expy Aut Mall San Jose (95136) ***(P-6407)***
Normans Nursery Inc (PA) ....E....626 285-9795
8665 Duarte Rd San Gabriel (91775) ***(P-8909)***
Normans Nursery Inc ....B....805 684-5442
5800 Via Real Carpinteria (93013) ***(P-8910)***
Normans Nursery Inc ....C....209 887-2033
6250 N Escalon Bellota Rd Linden (95236) ***(P-8911)***
Norogachi Construction Inc/CA ....D....916 236-4201
600 Industrial Dr Ste 100 Galt (95632) ***(P-2826)***
Norse Dairy Systems, Los Angeles *Also called Interbake Foods LLC* ***(P-8588)***
Nortech Waste LLC ....C....916 645-5230
3033 Fiddyment Rd Roseville (95747) ***(P-6227)***
North Amercn Science Assoc Inc ....D....949 951-3110
9 Morgan Irvine (92618) ***(P-26097)***
North American Acceptance Corp ....C....714 868-3195
3191 Red Hill Ave Ste 100 Costa Mesa (92626) ***(P-9470)***
North American Cinemas Inc ....B....707 571-1412
409 Aviation Blvd Santa Rosa (95403) ***(P-17851)***
North American Client Svcs Inc (PA) ....C....949 240-2423
5150 E A Palma Ave 206 Anaheim (92807) ***(P-26331)***

ALPHABETIC

Employee Codes: A=Over 500 employees, B=251-500
C=101-250, D=51-100, E=50
2020 Directory of California
Wholesalers and Services Companies
© Mergent Inc. 1-800-342-5647
1365

North American Health Care ....D......530 662-9193
  625 Cottonwood St Woodland (95695) *(P-26332)*
North American Med MGT Cal Inc (HQ) ....D......909 605-8000
  3281 E Guasti Rd Fl 7 Ontario (91761) *(P-26333)*
North American Security Inc ....B......310 630-4840
  550 E Carson Plaza Dr # 222 Carson (90746) *(P-16361)*
North American Title Co Inc ....D......925 399-3000
  6612 Owens Dr 100 Pleasanton (94588) *(P-10198)*
North American Van Lines, Corona *Also called South Coast Logistics (P-4232)*
North American Van Lines, Newark *Also called Moving Solutions Inc (P-4218)*
North Amrcn SEC Investigations ....D......323 634-1911
  550 E Carson Plaza Dr Carson (90746) *(P-16362)*
NORTH AREA COMMUNITY MENTAL HE, Sacramento *Also called Terkensha Associates
Inc (P-23499)*
North Bay Auto Auction, Fairfield *Also called Wind River Enterprises Inc (P-6415)*
North Bay Childrens Center (PA) ....D......415 883-6222
  932 C St Novato (94949) *(P-23756)*
North Bay Construction Inc ....D......707 283-0093
  431 Payran St Petaluma (94952) *(P-1768)*
North Bay Construction Inc ....E......707 836-8500
  930 Shiloh Rd Bldg 46 Windsor (95492) *(P-3190)*
North Bay Developmental (PA) ....D......707 256-1224
  10 Executive Ct Ste A NAPA (94558) *(P-23619)*
North Bay Distribution Inc ....D......707 450-1219
  2029 E Monte Vista Ave Vacaville (95688) *(P-8041)*
North Bay Distribution Inc (PA) ....D......707 452-9984
  2050 Cessna Dr Vacaville (95688) *(P-4462)*
North Bay Eye Assoc A Med Corp. ....D......707 206-0849
  50 Professional Center Dr # 210 Rohnert Park (94928) *(P-19220)*
North Bay Eye Assoc Med Group, Rohnert Park *Also called North Bay Eye Assoc A Med
Corp (P-19220)*
North Bay Pool and Spa, Monrovia *Also called Vivopools LLC (P-17154)*
North Bay Regional Center, NAPA *Also called North Bay Developmental (P-23619)*
North Coast Cleaning Services ....E......707 269-0838
  211 7th St Eureka (95501) *(P-13992)*
North Coast Fabricators Inc ....E......707 822-4629
  4801 West End Rd Arcata (95521) *(P-1370)*
North Coast Fisheries LLC ....D......707 579-0679
  2255 Challenger Way # 101 Santa Rosa (95407) *(P-8374)*
North Coast Home Care Inc ....D......760 260-8700
  5731 Palmer Way Ste F Carlsbad (92010) *(P-21819)*
North Coast Presbyterian Ch ....D......760 753-2535
  1831 S El Camino Real Encinitas (92024) *(P-23757)*
North Coast Surgery Center ....D......760 940-0997
  3903 Waring Rd Oceanside (92056) *(P-19221)*
North Counties Drywall Inc ....E......707 996-0198
  20563 Broadway Sonoma (95476) *(P-2827)*
North County Health Prj Inc (PA) ....C......760 736-6755
  150 Valpreda Rd Frnt San Marcos (92069) *(P-19222)*
North County Ob-Gyn Med Group ....E......858 453-0753
  9850 Genesee Ave Ste 600 La Jolla (92037) *(P-19223)*
NORTH COUNTY SERVICES, San Marcos *Also called North County Health Prj Inc (P-19222)*
North County Transit District (PA) ....C......760 966-6500
  810 Mission Ave Oceanside (92054) *(P-3571)*
North Hollywood Medical Offs, North Hollywood *Also called Kaiser Foundation
Hospitals (P-19082)*
North La County Regional Ctr (PA) ....B......818 778-1900
  15400 Sherman Way Ste 170 Van Nuys (91406) *(P-27149)*
North La County Regional Ctr ....D......661 945-6761
  43210 Gingham Ave Ste 6 Lancaster (93535) *(P-27150)*
North Marin Water District (PA) ....E......415 897-4133
  999 Rush Creek Pl Novato (94945) *(P-6095)*
North Modesto Kiwanis Club, Modesto *Also called Kiwanis International Inc (P-24570)*
North Orange Cnty Fmly Y M C A, Fullerton *Also called YMCA of North Orange
County (P-24704)*
North Orange Coast Pntg Inc ....D......951 279-2694
  3969 Sierra Ave Norco (92860) *(P-2375)*
North Orange County Svc Ctr, Fullerton *Also called Southern California Edison Co (P-5934)*
North Pt Hlth Wellness Ctr LLC ....D......559 320-2200
  668 E Bullard Ave Fresno (93710) *(P-20157)*
North Ranch Country Club ....C......818 889-3531
  4761 Valley Spring Dr Westlake Village (91362) *(P-18517)*
North Ridge Country Club ....D......916 967-5717
  7600 Madison Ave Fair Oaks (95628) *(P-18518)*
North River Ranch LLC ....E......714 556-6244
  3601 W Pendleton Ave Santa Ana (92704) *(P-104)*
North San Jose Job Center, San Jose *Also called Work2future Foundation (P-23659)*
North Shore Greenhouses Inc ....C......760 397-0400
  82900 Johnson St Thermal (92274) *(P-297)*
North Shore Investment Inc ....D......707 464-6151
  1280 Marshall St Crescent City (95531) *(P-20158)*
North Shore Living Herbs, Thermal *Also called North Shore Greenhouses Inc (P-297)*
North Sonoma County Hosp Dst ....C......707 431-6500
  1375 University St Healdsburg (95448) *(P-21057)*
North Star Building Maint Inc ....D......805 518-0417
  2828 Cochran St Ste 214 Simi Valley (93065) *(P-13993)*
North Star Emergency Svcs Inc ....D......510 452-3400
  2537 Willow St Oakland (94607) *(P-3703)*
North State Elec Contrs Inc ....D......916 572-0571
  11101 White Rock Rd Rancho Cordova (95670) *(P-2569)*
North State Imaging, Chico *Also called North State Radiology (P-19224)*
North State Radiology ....E......530 898-0504
  1702 Esplanade Chico (95926) *(P-19224)*
North State Security Inc ....D......530 243-0295
  1970 Hartnell Ave Redding (96002) *(P-16363)*
North Valley Construction Inc ....D......925 373-1246
  4010 Raymond Rd Livermore (94551) *(P-3442)*

North Valley Nursing Center, Tujunga *Also called Sun Mar Management Services (P-26414)*
North West Learning Center ....E......559 228-3057
  3485 W Ashcroft Ave Fresno (93722) *(P-23758)*
North Wind Cnstr Svcs LLC ....D......916 333-3015
  730 Howe Ave Ste 700 Sacramento (95825) *(P-1167)*
Northbay Healthcare Corp (PA) ....C......707 646-5000
  1200 B Gale Wilson Blvd Fairfield (94533) *(P-21058)*
Northbay Healthcare Group (PA) ....A......707 646-5000
  1200 B Gale Wilson Blvd Fairfield (94533) *(P-21059)*
Northbay Healthcare Group ....A......707 446-4000
  1000 Nut Tree Rd Vacaville (95687) *(P-21060)*
Northbay Healthcare System, Fairfield *Also called Northbay Healthcare Corp (P-21058)*
Northbay Medical Center, Fairfield *Also called Northbay Healthcare Group (P-21059)*
Northbound Treatment Services, Newport Beach *Also called National Therapeutic Svcs
Inc (P-22068)*
Northcoast Childrens Services ....D......530 629-2283
  730 Hwy 96 Willow Creek (95573) *(P-23357)*
Northcountry Clinic ....D......707 822-2481
  785 18th St Arcata (95521) *(P-19225)*
Northeast Community Clinic ....D......323 373-9400
  1414 S Grand Ave Ste 380 Los Angeles (90015) *(P-19226)*
Northeast Community Clinics, Los Angeles *Also called La Vida Mltispecialty Med
Ctrs (P-19149)*
Northeast Protective Svcs Inc ....D......800 577-0899
  16040 Peppertree Ln La Mirada (90638) *(P-16364)*
Northeast Valley Health Corp ....D......818 340-3570
  7107 Remmet Ave Canoga Park (91303) *(P-22285)*
Northeast Valley Health Corp ....D......818 432-4400
  7223 Fair Ave Sun Valley (91352) *(P-22286)*
Northeast Valley Health Corp (PA) ....D......818 898-1388
  1172 N Maclay Ave San Fernando (91340) *(P-23358)*
Northeast Valley Health Corp ....D......818 365-8086
  1600 San Fernando Rd San Fernando (91340) *(P-19227)*
Northeast Valley Health Corp ....D......818 896-0531
  12756 Van Nuys Blvd Pacoima (91331) *(P-19228)*
Northeastern Rur Hlth Clinics (PA) ....D......530 251-5000
  1850 Spring Ridge Dr Susanville (96130) *(P-19229)*
Northern CA Cngrgtnl Rtmt ....C......831 624-1281
  8545 Carmel Valley Rd Carmel (93923) *(P-20642)*
Northern CA Retiredd Ofcrs ....C......707 432-1200
  2600 Estates Dr Fairfield (94533) *(P-24006)*
Northern Cal Adptive Lving Ctr (PA) ....C......530 894-2726
  2725 Esplanade Chico (95973) *(P-24007)*
Northern Cal Rehabilitation, Redding *Also called Ocadian Care Centers LLC (P-20168)*
Northern Cal Ret Clks-Emp Fund ....C......925 746-7530
  190 N Wiget Ln Ste 110 Walnut Creek (94598) *(P-11805)*
Northern Cal Yuth Fmly Prgrams (PA) ....D......530 893-2316
  2577 California Park Dr Chico (95928) *(P-24008)*
Northern California Hlth Care ....D......530 223-2332
  16201 Plateau Cir Redding (96001) *(P-21820)*
Northern California Inalliance ....C......530 633-9695
  411 4th St Wheatland (95692) *(P-23359)*
Northern California Inalliance (PA) ....C......916 381-1300
  6950 21st Ave Sacramento (95820) *(P-23360)*
Northern California Institute ....B......415 750-6954
  4150 Clement St San Francisco (94121) *(P-24203)*
Northern California Mkt Area, Sacramento *Also called Veritiv Operating Company (P-7907)*
Northern California Power Agcy (PA) ....D......916 781-3636
  651 Commerce Dr Roseville (95678) *(P-5862)*
Northern California Power Agcy ....D......707 987-2381
  12000 Ridge Rd Middletown (95461) *(P-5863)*
Northern California Presbyteri ....D......415 464-1767
  501 Via Casitas Ofc Greenbrae (94904) *(P-20643)*
Northern California Presbyteri ....B......415 922-9700
  1400 Geary Blvd San Francisco (94109) *(P-20159)*
Northern California Region, San Mateo *Also called Securitas SEC Svcs USA Inc (P-16407)*
Northern California Region, Stockton *Also called Securitas SEC Svcs USA Inc (P-16409)*
Northern California Region, Fresno *Also called Securitas SEC Svcs USA Inc (P-16410)*
Northern California Region, Redding *Also called Securitas SEC Svcs USA Inc (P-16415)*
Northern California Region, Petaluma *Also called Securitas SEC Svcs USA Inc (P-16418)*
Northern California Region, Eureka *Also called Securitas SEC Svcs USA Inc (P-16420)*
Northern California Region, Palm Desert *Also called Securitas SEC Svcs USA Inc (P-16423)*
Northern California Region, Salinas *Also called Securitas SEC Svcs USA Inc (P-16424)*
Northern California Regional, Sacramento *Also called Granite Construction
Company (P-1966)*
Northern California Rehab ....C......530 246-9000
  2801 Eureka Way Redding (96001) *(P-21061)*
Northern Division, Pittsburg *Also called Arb Inc (P-4373)*
Northern Hydro, Big Creek *Also called Southern California Edison Co (P-5927)*
Northern Inyo Healthcare Dst ....B......760 873-5811
  150 Pioneer Ln Bishop (93514) *(P-21062)*
NORTHERN INYO HOSPITAL, Bishop *Also called Northern Inyo Healthcare Dst (P-21062)*
Northern Mono Chamber Commerce ....E......530 208-6078
  115281 Us Highway 395 Topaz (96133) *(P-24353)*
Northern Queen Inc ....D......530 265-4492
  400 Railroad Ave Nevada City (95959) *(P-12651)*
Northern Queen Inn, Nevada City *Also called Northern Queen Inc (P-12651)*
Northern Reg. Sub Base, Bakersfield *Also called Southern California Gas Co (P-5976)*
Northern Rfrigerated Trnsp Inc (PA) ....C......209 664-3800
  2700 W Main St Turlock (95380) *(P-4103)*
Northern Trust Company ....E......310 282-3800
  2049 Century Park E # 3600 Los Angeles (90067) *(P-9110)*
Northern Valley Catholic Socia ....C......530 241-0552
  2400 Washington Ave Redding (96001) *(P-23361)*
Northern Vly Indian Hlth Inc ....D......530 896-9400
  845 W East Ave Chico (95926) *(P-19625)*

Mergent e-mail: customerrelations@mergent.com
1366

2020 Directory of California
Wholesalers and Services Companies

(P-0000) Products & Services Section entry number
(PA)=Parent Co (HQ)=Headquarters (DH)=Div Headquarters

Northern Vly Indian Hlth Inc ....D....530 661-4400
175 W Court St Woodland (95695) ***(P-21421)***
Northfield Medical Inc ....C....248 268-2500
13631 Pawnee Rd Apple Valley (92308) ***(P-17520)***
Northgate Branch, San Rafael *Also called Bank of Marin* ***(P-9164)***
Northgate Care Center ....D....415 479-1230
40 Professional Ctr Pkwy San Rafael (94903) ***(P-20644)***
Northgate Convalescent Hosp, San Rafael *Also called Independent Quality Care Inc* ***(P-20599)***
Northgate Ter Cmnty Partner LP ....E....510 465-9346
550 24th St Oakland (94612) ***(P-11320)***
Northgate Terrace Apts ....D....530 671-2026
1290 Northgate Dr Apt 48 Yuba City (95991) ***(P-10786)***
Northland Control Systems Inc (PA) ....C....510 226-1015
1533 California Cir Milpitas (95035) ***(P-2570)***
Northpoint Day Treatment Sch, Northridge *Also called Child and Family Guidance Ctr* ***(P-21978)***
Northpointe Apartment Homes, Long Beach *Also called Parwood Preservation LP* ***(P-11351)***
Northpointe Healthcare Centre, Fresno *Also called North Pt Hlth Wellness Ctr LLC* ***(P-20157)***
Northridge 07 A LLC ....D....818 505-6777
12411 Ventura Blvd Studio City (91604) ***(P-10628)***
Northridge Fashion Center 10, Northridge *Also called Pacific Theaters* ***(P-17799)***
Northridge Nursing Center, Reseda *Also called Longwood Management Corp* ***(P-21021)***
Northrop Grumman Federal Cr Un (PA) ....D....310 808-4000
879 W 190th St Ste 800 Gardena (90248) ***(P-9399)***
Northrop Grumman Innovation ....D....818 887-8100
9401 Corbin Ave Northridge (91324) ***(P-25804)***
Northrop Grumman Systems Corp ....B....858 514-0400
9326 Spectrum Center Blvd San Diego (92123) ***(P-14967)***
Northrop Grumman Systems Corp ....A....858 592-3000
1 Rancho Carmel Dr San Diego (92128) ***(P-25805)***
Northrop Grumman Systems Corp ....C....650 604-6056
P.O. Box 81 Moffett Field (94035) ***(P-15663)***
Northrop Grumman Systems Corp ....D....805 987-9739
5161 Verdugo Way Camarillo (93012) ***(P-15664)***
Northstar, Irvine *Also called Custom Business Solutions Inc* ***(P-6747)***
Northstar Contg Group Inc ....D....714 639-7600
13320 Cambridge St Santa Fe Springs (90670) ***(P-3347)***
Northstar Contg Group Inc (HQ) ....D....510 491-1330
2614-20 Barrington Ct Hayward (94545) ***(P-3443)***
Northstar Dem & Remediation LP (HQ) ....C....714 672-3500
404 N Berry St Brea (92821) ***(P-3348)***
Northstar Senior Living Inc ....A....530 242-8300
2334 Washington Ave Ste A Redding (96001) ***(P-26334)***
Northstar Technology Corp (PA) ....C....949 788-0738
32 Mauchly Ste C Irvine (92618) ***(P-14968)***
Northstar-At-Tahoe, Truckee *Also called Trimont Land Company* ***(P-11489)***
Northstate Plastering Inc ....D....707 207-0950
2210 Cordelia Rd Fairfield (94534) ***(P-3191)***
Northwest Excavating Inc ....D....818 349-5861
18201 Napa St Northridge (91325) ***(P-14107)***
Northwest Hotel Corporation (PA) ....D....714 776-6120
1380 S Harbor Blvd Anaheim (92802) ***(P-12652)***
Northwest Insurance Agency ....D....707 573-1300
418 B St Ste 100 Santa Rosa (95401) ***(P-10442)***
Northwest Landscape Maint Co ....E....408 298-6489
283 Kinney Dr San Jose (95112) ***(P-881)***
Northwest Landscape Services, Los Angeles *Also called Vaughn Weedman Inc* ***(P-922)***
Northwest Medical Group Inc ....D....559 271-6302
7355 N Palm Ave Ste 100 Fresno (93711) ***(P-19230)***
Northwest Medical Pharmacy, Fresno *Also called Northwest Physicians Med Group* ***(P-19231)***
Northwest Physicians Med Group ....D....559 271-6370
7355 N Palm Ave Ste 100 Fresno (93711) ***(P-19231)***
Northwest Recycler Core, Riverside *Also called Recycler Core Company Inc* ***(P-6464)***
Northwest Staffing Resources ....A....916 960-2668
701 University Ave # 120 Sacramento (95825) ***(P-14337)***
Northwestern Bell Telephones, City of Industry *Also called Unical Enterprises Inc* ***(P-6915)***
Northwestern Mutl Fincl Netwrk (PA) ....C....619 234-3111
4225 Executive Sq # 1250 La Jolla (92037) ***(P-10443)***
NORTON SCIENCE AND LANGUAGE AC, Apple Valley *Also called High Desert Partnership* ***(P-25906)***
Norton Simon Museum ....D....626 449-6840
411 W Colorado Blvd Pasadena (91105) ***(P-24278)***
Norwalk Community Hospital ....D....562 863-4763
13222 Bloomfield Ave Norwalk (90650) ***(P-21063)***
Norwalk La Mirada Unif ....D....714 521-0970
15135 Escalona Rd La Mirada (90638) ***(P-24414)***
Norwalk Marriott Hotel, Paramount *Also called Goldenpark LLC* ***(P-12301)***
Norwalk Meadows Nursing Ctr LP ....C....562 864-2541
10625 Leffingwell Rd Norwalk (90650) ***(P-20160)***
Norwalk Medical Offices, Norwalk *Also called Kaiser Foundation Hospitals* ***(P-19084)***
Norwalk Transit System ....D....562 929-5550
12650 Imperial Hwy Norwalk (90650) ***(P-3572)***
Norwest Venture Partners VI LP ....D....650 289-2243
525 University Ave # 800 Palo Alto (94301) ***(P-11939)***
Nossaman LLP (PA) ....D....213 612-7800
777 S Figueroa St # 3400 Los Angeles (90017) ***(P-22727)***
Nossaman LLP ....D....760 918-0500
1925 Palomar Oaks Way # 220 Carlsbad (92008) ***(P-22728)***
Nossaman LLP ....E....415 398-3600
50 California St Ste 3400 San Francisco (94111) ***(P-22729)***
Nossaman LLP ....E....949 833-7800
18101 Von Karman Ave # 1800 Irvine (92612) ***(P-22730)***
Not Your Daughters Jeans, Vernon *Also called Nydj Apparel LLC* ***(P-8103)***
Notellage Corporation ....E....323 257-8151
4681 Eagle Rock Blvd Los Angeles (90041) ***(P-20645)***
Notthoff Engineering, Huntington Beach *Also called AMG Huntington Beach LLC* ***(P-24934)***
Nourmand & Associates ....E....310 274-4000
421 N Beverly Dr Ste 200 Beverly Hills (90210) ***(P-11321)***
Nova ATL Elc A Joint Ventr ....D....707 265-1100
185 Devlin Rd NAPA (94558) ***(P-1980)***
Nova Brink A Joint Venture ....D....707 265-1100
185 Devlin Rd NAPA (94558) ***(P-1981)***
Nova Container Freight Station, Carson *Also called H Rauvel Inc* ***(P-4426)***
Nova Development, Calabasas *Also called Avanquest North America LLC* ***(P-6802)***
Nova Group Inc (HQ) ....C....707 265-1100
185 Devlin Rd NAPA (94558) ***(P-1894)***
Nova Lane Constructors A JV ....D....707 265-1100
185 Devlin Rd NAPA (94558) ***(P-1982)***
Nova Ortho-Med Inc (PA) ....E....310 352-3600
1470 Beachey Pl Carson (90746) ***(P-6983)***
Nova Skilled Home Health Inc ....C....323 658-6232
3300 N San Fernando Blvd Burbank (91504) ***(P-22287)***
Nova-Cpf Inc ....C....707 257-3200
7411 Napa Vallejo Hwy NAPA (94558) ***(P-1895)***
Nova/Tic Gov Proj JV ....C....707 257-3200
185 Devlin Rd NAPA (94558) ***(P-1896)***
Novacap LLC ....B....661 295-5920
25111 Anza Dr Valencia (91355) ***(P-7310)***
Novalogic Inc (PA) ....D....818 880-1997
27489 Agoura Rd Ste 300 Agoura Hills (91301) ***(P-14969)***
Novare Nat Settlement Svc LLC ....E....714 352-4088
320 Commerce Ste 150 Irvine (92602) ***(P-9111)***
Novariant Inc (PA) ....D....510 933-4800
46610 Landing Pkwy Fremont (94538) ***(P-25236)***
Novastar Post Inc ....D....323 467-5020
23466 Hatteras St Woodland Hills (91367) ***(P-17642)***
Novatime Technology Inc (HQ) ....D....909 895-8100
9680 Haven Ave Ste 200 Rancho Cucamonga (91730) ***(P-14338)***
Novato Disposal Service Inc (PA) ....D....707 765-9995
3417 Standish Ave Santa Rosa (95407) ***(P-6228)***
Novato Fire Protection Dist ....D....415 878-2690
95 Rowland Way Novato (94945) ***(P-16954)***
Novato Healthcare Center LLC ....C....415 897-6161
1565 Hill Rd Novato (94947) ***(P-20161)***
Novato Medical Offices, Novato *Also called Kaiser Foundation Hospitals* ***(P-20964)***
Novo Construction Inc (PA) ....C....650 701-1500
1460 Obrien Dr Menlo Park (94025) ***(P-1553)***
Novo Engineering Inc (PA) ....D....760 598-6686
1350 Specialty Dr Ste A Vista (92081) ***(P-25237)***
Novo Nordisk Biotech, Davis *Also called Novozymes Inc* ***(P-25935)***
Novogradac & Company LLP ....E....415 356-8000
246 1st St Ste 500 San Francisco (94105) ***(P-25652)***
Novozymes Inc (HQ) ....D....530 757-8100
1445 Drew Ave Davis (95618) ***(P-25935)***
Novozymes Us Inc ....A....530 757-8100
1445 Drew Ave Davis (95618) ***(P-11681)***
Nowcom Corporation ....D....323 938-6449
4751 Wilshire Blvd # 205 Los Angeles (90010) ***(P-16065)***
Nowher Partners LLC ....D....818 857-3366
26767 Agoura Rd Ste A Calabasas (91302) ***(P-8620)***
Nozomi Networks Inc (HQ) ....D....800 314-6114
575 Market St Ste 3650 San Francisco (94105) ***(P-16546)***
NP Mechanical Inc ....B....951 667-4220
9225 Stellar Ct Ste A Corona (92883) ***(P-2211)***
Npario Inc ....D....650 461-9696
350 Cambridge Ave Ste 330 Palo Alto (94306) ***(P-14970)***
Nph Medical Services ....D....530 899-2255
555 Flying V St Ste 5 Chico (95928) ***(P-14339)***
Nphase LLC ....D....312 577-1650
6195 Lusk Blvd Ste 200 San Diego (92121) ***(P-5794)***
Npl Anaheim Investments LLC ....D....714 750-2010
2010 S Harbor Blvd Anaheim (92802) ***(P-12653)***
NPS Marketing ....B....916 941-5510
3381 Sage Rose Ln Placerville (95667) ***(P-26742)***
Nr 2 Group Inc ....E....626 251-6681
1561 Chapin Unit C Baldwin Park (91706) ***(P-3921)***
NRC Environmental Services Inc ....D....562 432-1304
3777 Long Beach Blvd Long Beach (90807) ***(P-6229)***
NRC Environmental Services Inc (HQ) ....D....510 749-1390
1605 Ferry Pt Alameda (94501) ***(P-6351)***
Nrea-TRC 711 LLC ....C....213 488-3500
711 S Hope St Los Angeles (90017) ***(P-12654)***
NRG California South LP ....D....909 899-7241
8996 Etiwanda Ave Rancho Cucamonga (91739) ***(P-5864)***
NRG Clean Power Inc ....E....818 444-2020
7012 Owensmouth Ave Canoga Park (91303) ***(P-5865)***
NRG El Segundo Operations Inc ....D....310 615-6344
301 Vista Del Mar El Segundo (90245) ***(P-5866)***
NRG Energy Inc ....D....913 689-3904
3201 Wilbur Ave Antioch (94509) ***(P-5867)***
NRG Power Inc ....D....714 424-6484
3011 S Shannon St Santa Ana (92704) ***(P-2571)***
Nrhc, Susanville *Also called Northeastern Rur Hlth Clinics* ***(P-19229)***
Nri Distribution, Los Angeles *Also called Nri Usa LLC* ***(P-5006)***
Nri Usa LLC (PA) ....D....323 345-6456
13200 S Broadway Los Angeles (90061) ***(P-5006)***
Nri Usa LLC ....D....323 345-6456
227 E Compton Blvd Gardena (90248) ***(P-5007)***
NRLL LLC ....E....949 768-7777
1 Mauchly Irvine (92618) ***(P-11940)***
Nrp Holding Co Inc (PA) ....C....949 583-1000
1 Mauchly Irvine (92618) ***(P-11682)***
Nrt, Concord *Also called Goldman Avram* ***(P-26244)***
Nrt Commercial Utah LLC ....D....626 449-5222
42 S Pasadena Ave Pasadena (91105) ***(P-11322)***

A L P H A B E T I C

Employee Codes: A=Over 500 employees, B=251-500
C=101-250, D=51-100, E=50
2020 Directory of California
Wholesalers and Services Companies
© Mergent Inc. 1-800-342-5647
1367

Nsbn, Los Angeles *Also called Cliftonlarsonallen LLP* ***(P-25558)***
Nsg Technology Inc.....B.....408 547-8770
1705 Junction Ct Ste 200 San Jose (95112) ***(P-17458)***
Nsv International Corp.....D.....562 438-3836
1250 E 29th St Signal Hill (90755) ***(P-6458)***
Nsw Real Estate Holdings LLC.....D.....415 467-7600
99 S Hill Dr Ste A Brisbane (94005) ***(P-11323)***
Nt Sunset Inc.....E.....510 420-3772
2220 Livingston St # 201 Oakland (94606) ***(P-26014)***
Nta America, Gardena *Also called Nippon Travel Agency Amer Inc* ***(P-4829)***
Nta Pacific, Gardena *Also called Nippon Travel Agency PCF Inc* ***(P-4830)***
Ntent Inc.....D.....760 930-7600
1808 Aston Ave Ste 170 Carlsbad (92008) ***(P-14971)***
Nth Degree Inc.....E.....714 734-4155
27092 Burbank Foothill Ranch (92610) ***(P-16955)***
NTN Buzztime Inc (PA).....C.....760 438-7400
1800 Aston Ave Ste 100 Carlsbad (92008) ***(P-15429)***
Ntrust Infotech Inc.....D.....562 207-1600
230 Commerce Ste 180 Irvine (92602) ***(P-15430)***
NTS It Care Inc.....C.....408 480-4083
1605 S Main St Ste 125 Milpitas (95035) ***(P-14972)***
NTS Technical Systems.....D.....909 863-5150
3505 E 3rd St San Bernardino (92408) ***(P-26098)***
NTS Technical Systems.....C.....714 879-6110
1536 E Valencia Dr Fullerton (92831) ***(P-26099)***
NTS Technical Systems.....D.....661 259-8184
20970 Centre Pointe Pkwy Santa Clarita (91350) ***(P-26100)***
NTS Technical Systems.....E.....510 578-3500
41039 Boyce Rd Fremont (94538) ***(P-26101)***
Ntt Data Inc.....D.....213 228-2500
1000 Corporate Center Dr # 140 Monterey Park (91754) ***(P-15665)***
Ntt Data Services Corporation.....D.....310 342-3200
6701 Center Dr W Ste 1000 Los Angeles (90045) ***(P-15904)***
Nu Flow America Inc (PA).....D.....619 275-9130
7710 Kenamar Ct San Diego (92121) ***(P-2212)***
Nu Horizons Electronics Corp.....E.....408 946-4154
890 N Mccarthy Blvd San Jose (95131) ***(P-7311)***
Nuance Communications Inc.....C.....650 847-0000
1005 Hamilton Ct Menlo Park (94025) ***(P-14973)***
Nucompass Mobility Svcs Inc (PA).....D.....925 734-3434
6800 Koll Center Pkwy Pleasanton (94566) ***(P-16956)***
Nucourse Distribution Inc.....D.....866 655-4366
22342 Avenida Empresa # 200 Rcho STA Marg (92688) ***(P-7312)***
Nuevacare LLC.....D.....650 396-3596
2100 Geng Rd Ste 210 Palo Alto (94303) ***(P-20162)***
Nuevo Amnecer Latino Chld Svcs (PA).....D.....323 720-9951
5400 Pomona Blvd Los Angeles (90022) ***(P-23362)***
Nugget Market Inc.....D.....916 226-2626
7101 Elk Grove Blvd Elk Grove (95758) ***(P-27151)***
Nugget Market Inc.....C.....530 662-5479
157 Main St Woodland (95695) ***(P-4463)***
Nugget Mkts Pharmacy, Woodland *Also called Nugget Market Inc* ***(P-4463)***
Nulaid Foods Inc (PA).....D.....209 599-2121
200 W 5th St Ripon (95366) ***(P-8331)***
Numero Uno Market.....D.....323 231-9403
4373 S Vermont Ave Los Angeles (90037) ***(P-11941)***
Numero Uno Market.....D.....213 381-1734
9127 S Figueroa St Los Angeles (90003) ***(P-11942)***
Nuna Health, San Francisco *Also called Nuna Incorporated* ***(P-14974)***
Nuna Incorporated.....D.....415 942-5200
370 Townsend St San Francisco (94107) ***(P-14974)***
Nunes Company Inc (PA).....E.....831 751-7510
925 Johnson Ave Salinas (93901) ***(P-8503)***
Nunes Cooling Inc.....E.....831 751-7510
925 Johnson Ave Salinas (93901) ***(P-523)***
Nurlogic Design Inc (HQ).....D.....858 455-7570
5580 Morehouse Dr San Diego (92121) ***(P-15666)***
Nurse Providers Inc.....A.....650 992-8559
355 Gellert Blvd Ste 110 Daly City (94015) ***(P-14340)***
Nursecore Management Svcs LLC.....A.....805 938-7660
1010 S Broadway Santa Maria (93454) ***(P-24009)***
Nursefinders LLC (HQ).....C.....858 314-7427
12400 High Bluff Dr San Diego (92130) ***(P-14341)***
Nurses & Prof Hlth Care, Chico *Also called Nph Medical Services* ***(P-14339)***
Nurses Internet Staffing Svcs (PA).....C.....323 720-9900
6055 E Wash Blvd Ste 409 Commerce (90040) ***(P-14342)***
Nurses Tuch HM Hlth Prvder Inc.....E.....818 500-4877
135 S Jackson St Ste 100 Glendale (91205) ***(P-21821)***
Nursing & Rehab At Home.....D.....650 286-4272
1660 S Amphlett Blvd # 112 San Mateo (94402) ***(P-21822)***
Nursing Registry, Daly City *Also called Nurse Providers Inc* ***(P-14340)***
Nurturing Tots Inc.....D.....818 996-1602
3784 Winford Dr Tarzana (91356) ***(P-23759)***
Nushake Inc.....D.....209 239-8616
319 S Parallel Ave Ripon (95366) ***(P-3080)***
Nushake Roofing, Ripon *Also called Nushake Inc* ***(P-3080)***
Nussbaum, Barry Company, Solana Beach *Also called BNC Real Estate* ***(P-10946)***
Nutanix Inc (PA).....A.....408 216-8360
1740 Tech Dr Ste 150 San Jose (95110) ***(P-14975)***
Nutec Enterprises Inc.....D.....661 287-3200
24200 Magic Mountain Pkwy # 105 Valencia (91355) ***(P-11324)***
Nutra-Figs, Fresno *Also called San Joaquin Figs Inc* ***(P-538)***
Nutrien AG Solutions Inc.....D.....760 355-1133
305 Larsen Rd Imperial (92251) ***(P-8849)***
Nutrien AG Solutions Inc.....D.....805 922-5848
1335 W Main St Santa Maria (93458) ***(P-8850)***
Nutrien AG Solutions Inc.....E.....559 884-6010
21929 S Lassen Five Points (93624) ***(P-8851)***
Nutrien AG Solutions Inc.....D.....831 757-5391
1143 Terven Ave Salinas (93901) ***(P-8852)***
Nutririon Services, Santa Ana *Also called Santa Ana Unified School Dst* ***(P-22318)***
Nutrition Parent LLC.....A.....650 321-4910
1950 University Ave # 350 East Palo Alto (94303) ***(P-11943)***
Nutrition Services, San Bernardino *Also called San Bernardino City Unf School* ***(P-22313)***
Nuvi Global.....A.....559 306-2646
518 W Henderson Ave Apt 9 Porterville (93257) ***(P-6984)***
Nuvision Fincl Federal Cr Un (PA).....C.....714 375-8000
7812 Edinger Ave Ste 100 Huntington Beach (92647) ***(P-9400)***
Nuvoton Technology Corp Amer.....D.....408 544-1718
2727 N 1st St San Jose (95134) ***(P-7313)***
Nuworld Business Systems, Cerritos *Also called Young Systems Corporation* ***(P-6783)***
Nv5 Inc (HQ).....D.....916 641-9100
2525 Natomas Park Dr # 300 Sacramento (95833) ***(P-25238)***
Nv5 Inc.....C.....858 385-0500
15092 Avenue Of Science # 200 San Diego (92128) ***(P-25239)***
Nv5 Inc.....D.....916 641-9100
2495 Natomas Park Dr # 300 Sacramento (95833) ***(P-25240)***
Nvision Laser Eye Centers Inc (PA).....D.....909 605-1975
3155d Sedona Ct 100 Ontario (91764) ***(P-19232)***
Nvision Laser Eye Centers Inc.....D.....949 951-1457
24022 Calle De La Plata Laguna Hills (92653) ***(P-19681)***
Nvision Laser Eye Centers Inc.....D.....415 421-8667
711 Van Ness Ave Ste 320 San Francisco (94102) ***(P-19233)***
NW Entertainment Inc (PA).....C.....818 295-5000
2660 W Olive Ave Burbank (91505) ***(P-17643)***
NW Manor Community Partners LP.....D.....714 662-5565
17782 Sky Park Cir Irvine (92614) ***(P-11585)***
NW Packaging LLC (PA).....D.....909 706-3627
1201 E Lexington Ave Pomona (91766) ***(P-8991)***
Nwp Services Corporation (HQ).....C.....949 253-2500
535 Anton Blvd Ste 1100 Costa Mesa (92626) ***(P-15431)***
NY Transport Inc.....D.....909 355-9832
10191 Redwood Ave Fontana (92335) ***(P-4104)***
Nydj Apparel LLC.....C.....323 581-9040
5401 S Soto St Vernon (90058) ***(P-8103)***
Nygard Inc.....D.....310 776-8900
14401 S San Pedro St Gardena (90248) ***(P-8104)***
Nyse Arca Inc.....B.....415 393-4000
115 Sansome St San Francisco (94104) ***(P-9781)***
Nzg Specialties Inc (PA).....D.....310 216-7575
2580 Santa Fe Ave Redondo Beach (90278) ***(P-8201)***
O & R, Glendale *Also called Rev Enterprises* ***(P-16393)***
O & S Holdings LLC.....E.....310 207-8600
11611 San Vicente Blvd Los Angeles (90049) ***(P-11586)***
O A Outfitting Inc.....D.....707 498-2917
6602 Wofford Heights Blvd Bayside (95524) ***(P-18730)***
O C Jones & Sons Inc (PA).....C.....510 526-3424
1520 4th St Berkeley (94710) ***(P-1769)***
O C Jones & Sons Inc.....D.....510 663-6911
155 Filbert St Ste 209 Oakland (94607) ***(P-27152)***
O C McDonald Co Inc.....C.....408 295-2182
1150 W San Carlos St San Jose (95126) ***(P-2213)***
O C Sailing Club Inc.....D.....510 843-4200
1 Spinnaker Way Berkeley (94710) ***(P-18731)***
O E C Shipg Los Angeles Inc.....E.....562 926-7186
13100 Alondra Blvd # 100 Cerritos (90703) ***(P-5008)***
O H I, Irvine *Also called European Hotl Invstrs of CA* ***(P-12258)***
O P I Products Inc (HQ).....B.....818 759-8688
13034 Saticoy St North Hollywood (91605) ***(P-7678)***
O'Connor Hospital, San Jose *Also called Verity Health System Cal Inc* ***(P-21357)***
O'Connor Hospital Pedia Center, San Jose *Also called OConnor Hospital* ***(P-21065)***
O'Connor Wound Care Clinic, San Jose *Also called OConnor Hospital* ***(P-21066)***
O'Neill Vintners & Distillers, Parlier *Also called ONeill Beverages Co LLC* ***(P-150)***
O'Neill Vintners & Distillers, Larkspur *Also called ONeill Beverages Co LLC* ***(P-151)***
O.H. Kruse Grain and Milling, Goshen *Also called Western Milling LLC* ***(P-8862)***
O1 Communications Inc.....D.....888 444-1111
4359 Town Center Blvd # 217 El Dorado Hills (95762) ***(P-5449)***
O2 Micro Inc.....D.....408 987-5920
3118 Patrick Henry Dr Santa Clara (95054) ***(P-15667)***
O2a, Paso Robles *Also called Omega 2 Alpha Services LLC* ***(P-26745)***
Oak Creek LP.....D.....909 860-5440
21725 Gateway Center Dr Diamond Bar (91765) ***(P-12655)***
Oak Creek Apartments.....E.....650 327-1600
1600 Sand Hill Rd Palo Alto (94304) ***(P-10787)***
Oak Creek Golf Club, Irvine *Also called Irvine Company LLC* ***(P-24842)***
Oak Distribution, Los Angeles *Also called Oak Paper Products Co Inc* ***(P-7887)***
Oak Grove Center, Murrieta *Also called Oak Grove Inst Foundation Inc* ***(P-19234)***
Oak Grove Inst Foundation Inc (PA).....B.....951 677-5599
24275 Jefferson Ave Murrieta (92562) ***(P-19234)***
Oak Harbor Freight Lines Inc.....D.....510 608-8841
6700 Smith Ave Newark (94560) ***(P-4105)***
Oak Harbor Freight Lines Inc.....D.....916 371-3960
832 F St West Sacramento (95605) ***(P-4106)***
Oak Hill Capital Partners LP.....A.....650 234-0500
2775 Sand Hill Rd Ste 220 Menlo Park (94025) ***(P-21823)***
Oak Knoll Convalescent Center.....D.....707 778-8686
450 Hayes Ln Petaluma (94952) ***(P-20163)***
Oak Paper Products Co Inc (PA).....C.....323 268-0507
3686 E Olympic Blvd Los Angeles (90023) ***(P-7887)***
Oak River Rehabilitation.....C.....530 365-0025
3300 Franklin St Anderson (96007) ***(P-20164)***
Oak Springs Nursery Inc.....D.....818 367-5832
13761 Eldridge Ave Sylmar (91342) ***(P-6367)***
Oak Street Physical Therapy, Lomita *Also called Kaiser Foundation Hospitals* ***(P-22048)***
Oak Valley Golf Club, Beaumont *Also called California Oak Valley Golf* ***(P-18227)***

Oak Valley Hospital District (HQ)....B....209 847-3011
350 S Oak Ave Oakdale (95361) ***(P-21064)***
Oak Valley Hotel LLC....D....619 297-1101
2270 Hotel Cir N San Diego (92108) ***(P-12656)***
Oak View Snoma Hlls Apartments, Rohnert Park *Also called Kisco Senior Living LLC* ***(P-10751)***
Oakdale Golf and Country Club....D....209 847-2984
243 N Stearns Rd Oakdale (95361) ***(P-18519)***
Oakdale Heights Senior Living....E....661 663-9671
3209 Brookside Dr Bakersfield (93311) ***(P-20165)***
Oakdale Irrgtion Dst Fing Corp....D....209 847-0341
1205 E F St Oakdale (95361) ***(P-6096)***
Oakdale Memorial Park (PA)....D....626 335-0281
1401 S Grand Ave Glendora (91740) ***(P-11631)***
Oakhurst Country Club, Clayton *Also called American Golf Corporation* ***(P-18368)***
OAKHURST HEALTHCARE & WELLNESS, Oakhurst *Also called Oakhurst Skilled Nursing Welln* ***(P-20166)***
Oakhurst Industries Inc....D....510 265-2400
3265 Investment Blvd Hayward (94545) ***(P-8202)***
Oakhurst Skilled Nursing Welln....D....559 683-2244
40131 Highway 49 Oakhurst (93644) ***(P-20166)***
Oakland Athletics, Oakland *Also called Athletics Investment Group LLC* ***(P-18051)***
Oakland District Office, Oakland *Also called State Compensation Insur Fund* ***(P-10132)***
Oakland Healthcare & Wellness....C....323 330-6572
3030 Webster St Oakland (94609) ***(P-20167)***
Oakland Ice Center, Oakland *Also called City of Oakland* ***(P-18662)***
Oakland Medical Center, Oakland *Also called Kaiser Foundation Hospitals* ***(P-19042)***
Oakland Mrriott Hotels Resorts, Oakland *Also called Oakland Renaissance Associates* ***(P-12658)***
Oakland Mrtime Spport Svcs Inc....E....510 868-1005
11 Burma Rd Oakland (94607) ***(P-4635)***
Oakland Museum of California....D....510 318-8400
1000 Oak St Oakland (94607) ***(P-24279)***
Oakland Pallet Company Inc (PA)....C....510 278-1291
2500 Grant Ave San Lorenzo (94580) ***(P-6636)***
Oakland Private Industry Counc....D....510 768-4400
268 Grand Ave Oakland (94610) ***(P-23620)***
Oakland Public Education Fund....D....510 221-6968
520 3rd St Ste 109 Oakland (94607) ***(P-11770)***
Oakland Renaissance Associates....D....510 451-4000
1001 Broadway Oakland (94607) ***(P-12657)***
Oakland Renaissance Associates....B....510 451-4000
1001 Broadway Oakland (94607) ***(P-12658)***
Oakland Shops/Annex, Oakland *Also called San Francisco Bay Area Rapid* ***(P-3590)***
Oakland Unified School Dst....D....510 729-7775
9860 Sunnyside St Oakland (94603) ***(P-24602)***
Oakland Unified School Dst....C....510 535-2717
955 High St Oakland (94601) ***(P-13994)***
Oakland V A Outpatient Clinic, Oakland *Also called Veterans Health Administration* ***(P-19562)***
Oakland Zoo In Knowland Park, Oakland *Also called Conservation Society Cal* ***(P-24306)***
Oakley Inc....D....951 685-0038
11296 Harrell Ontario (91761) ***(P-4464)***
Oakley Union School District....D....925 625-5060
1100 Ohara Ave Oakley (94561) ***(P-24603)***
Oakmont Country Club....C....818 542-4260
3100 Country Club Dr Glendale (91208) ***(P-18520)***
Oakmont Golf Club Inc....D....707 538-2454
7025 Oakmont Dr Santa Rosa (95409) ***(P-18277)***
Oakridge Care Center, Oakland *Also called A T Associates Inc* ***(P-20476)***
Oakridge Landscape Inc (PA)....D....661 295-7228
28064 Avenue Stanford K Valencia (91355) ***(P-438)***
Oaks Diagnostics Inc (PA)....D....310 855-0035
6310 San Vicente Blvd Los Angeles (90048) ***(P-19235)***
Oaks Post Acute, The, Petaluma *Also called Trestles Holdings LLC* ***(P-11700)***
Oaks, The, Petaluma *Also called Oak Knoll Convalescent Center* ***(P-20163)***
Oaktree Capital Management LP (HQ)....C....213 830-6300
333 S Grand Ave Ste 2800 Los Angeles (90071) ***(P-9834)***
Oaktree Holdings Inc....A....213 830-6300
333 S Grand Ave Ste 2800 Los Angeles (90071) ***(P-11732)***
Oaktree Real Estate Opportunit....A....213 830-6300
333 S Grand Ave Fl 28 Los Angeles (90071) ***(P-11733)***
Oaktree Strategic Income LLC....A....213 830-6300
333 S Grand Ave Fl 28 Los Angeles (90071) ***(P-11734)***
Oakview Convalescent Hospital....E....818 352-4426
9166 Tujunga Canyon Blvd Tujunga (91042) ***(P-20646)***
Oakville Produce Partners LLC....C....415 647-2991
453 Valley Dr Brisbane (94005) ***(P-8504)***
Oakwood Apartments, Woodland Hills *Also called R & B Realty Group* ***(P-10803)***
Oakwood Apts, Marina Del Rey *Also called R & B Realty Group* ***(P-10804)***
Oakwood Athletic Club, Lafayette *Also called Clubsport San Ramon LLC* ***(P-18132)***
Oakwood Garden Apts, Los Angeles *Also called R & B Realty Group* ***(P-10802)***
Oakwood Gardens Care Center, Fresno *Also called Lily Holdings LLC* ***(P-20083)***
Oakwood Village, Auburn *Also called Horizon West Inc* ***(P-26077)***
Oakwood Worldwide, Long Beach *Also called R & B Realty Group LP* ***(P-11386)***
Oasis Brands Inc....D....540 658-2830
100 S Anaheim Blvd # 280 Anaheim (92805) ***(P-7888)***
Oasis Country Club, Palm Desert *Also called Oasis Palm Dsert Hmowners Assn* ***(P-18521)***
Oasis Date Gardens, Thermal *Also called Woodspur Farming LLC* ***(P-373)***
Oasis IPA, Palm Springs *Also called Desert Medical Group Inc* ***(P-18951)***
Oasis Mental Health Trtmnt Ctr....C....760 863-8609
47915 Oasis St Indio (92201) ***(P-21422)***
Oasis Palm Dsert Hmowners Assn....D....760 345-5661
42330 Casbah Way Palm Desert (92211) ***(P-18521)***
Oasis Repower LLC....A....888 903-6926
15445 Innovation Dr San Diego (92128) ***(P-5868)***
Oasis Technology Inc....D....805 445-4833
601 E Daily Dr Ste 226 Camarillo (93010) ***(P-15668)***
Oates Buzz Enterprises....D....916 381-3600
555 Capitol Mall Ste 900 Sacramento (95814) ***(P-10629)***
Oatey Supply Chain Svcs Inc....E....510 797-4677
6600 Smith Ave Newark (94560) ***(P-7433)***
Ob Usa Inc....C....213 465-4876
931 S Cypress St La Habra (90631) ***(P-8784)***
Oberman Tivoli & Pickert Inc....C....310 440-9600
500 S Sepulveda Blvd # 500 Los Angeles (90049) ***(P-15669)***
Obey Clothing, Irvine *Also called One 3 Two Inc* ***(P-8105)***
Objective Systems Integrators (HQ)....E....916 467-1500
2365 Iron Point Rd # 170 Folsom (95630) ***(P-14976)***
Oblong Industries Inc (HQ)....C....213 683-8863
923 E 3rd St Ste 111 Los Angeles (90013) ***(P-14977)***
OBryant Electric Inc....C....818 407-1986
9314 Eton Ave Chatsworth (91311) ***(P-2572)***
Obscura Digital Incorporated....E....415 227-9979
14 Louisiana St San Francisco (94107) ***(P-13629)***
Observatories of The Carnegie, Pasadena *Also called Carnegie Institution Wash* ***(P-25980)***
Oc 405 Partners Joint Venture....D....858 251-2200
3100 W Lake Center Dr # 200 Santa Ana (92704) ***(P-1824)***
Oc Accessories LLC....D....949 229-2410
4533 Macarthur Blvd A-2032 Newport Beach (92660) ***(P-16957)***
OC Communications Inc (PA)....C....916 686-3700
2204 Kausen Dr Ste 100 Elk Grove (95758) ***(P-5732)***
Oc Engineering....D....714 667-3212
300 N Flower St Santa Ana (92703) ***(P-25241)***
OC FOOD BANK, Garden Grove *Also called Community Action Partnershi* ***(P-23026)***
Oc IV A California LP....E....925 734-5800
4511 Willow Rd Ste 1 Pleasanton (94588) ***(P-17338)***
Oc Public Works, Santa Ana *Also called Ocpw* ***(P-24204)***
OC Special Events SEC Inc....C....714 541-4111
1232 Village Way Ste K Santa Ana (92705) ***(P-16365)***
Oc Waste & Recycling, Santa Ana *Also called County of Orange* ***(P-6190)***
Ocadian Care Centers LLC....C....530 246-9000
2801 Eureka Way Redding (96001) ***(P-20168)***
Ocadian Care Centers LLC....D....510 832-3222
475 29th St Oakland (94609) ***(P-20169)***
Ocadian Care Centers LLC....D....415 461-9700
1220 S Eliseo Dr Greenbrae (94904) ***(P-20170)***
Ocadian Care Centers LLC....D....415 499-1000
1550 Silveira Pkwy San Rafael (94903) ***(P-20171)***
Ocadian Care Centers LLC....E....408 295-2665
75 N 13th St San Jose (95112) ***(P-20172)***
Ocb Riverside, Riverside *Also called American Reprographics Co LLC* ***(P-13752)***
Occidental Cnty Sanitation Dst....D....707 547-1900
404 Aviation Blvd Santa Rosa (95403) ***(P-6133)***
Occupational Health Services, San Jose *Also called El Camino Hospital* ***(P-21471)***
Occupational Medicine, Salinas *Also called Natividad Medical Center* ***(P-21056)***
Occupational Therapy Training, Torrance *Also called Special Service For Groups Inc* ***(P-24229)***
Occupnl Urgnt Care Hlth Syst....B....916 374-4600
750 Riverpoint Dr West Sacramento (95605) ***(P-22288)***
Ocean Avenue LLC....B....310 576-7777
101 Wilshire Blvd Santa Monica (90401) ***(P-12659)***
Ocean Blue Envmtl Svcs Inc (PA)....D....562 624-4120
925 W Esther St Long Beach (90813) ***(P-3922)***
Ocean Breeze International....D....805 684-1747
3910 Via Real Carpinteria (93013) ***(P-266)***
Ocean Breeze Manufacturing....D....323 586-8760
1961 Hawkins Cir Los Angeles (90001) ***(P-16958)***
Ocean Colony Partners LLC....C....650 726-5764
2450 Cabrillo Hwy S # 200 Half Moon Bay (94019) ***(P-11587)***
Ocean Dream, Commerce *Also called Malibu Design Group* ***(P-8091)***
Ocean Fresh Fish Seafood Mktg, Los Angeles *Also called Ocean Group Inc* ***(P-8375)***
Ocean Group Inc (PA)....D....213 622-3677
1100 S Santa Fe Ave Los Angeles (90021) ***(P-8375)***
Ocean Holiday LP....D....760 231-7000
1401 Carmelo Dr Oceanside (92054) ***(P-12660)***
Ocean House Retirement Inn, Santa Monica *Also called MBK Real Estate Ltd A Califor* ***(P-10768)***
Ocean Knight Shipping Inc....C....310 885-3388
19516 S Susana Rd # 101 Compton (90221) ***(P-5009)***
Ocean Links Corporation....D....650 726-1800
2 Miramontes Point Rd Half Moon Bay (94019) ***(P-18278)***
Ocean Mist Farming Company (PA)....C....831 633-2144
10855 Ocean Mist Pkwy A Castroville (95012) ***(P-67)***
Ocean Mist Farms, Castroville *Also called California Artichoke & Vegetab* ***(P-474)***
Ocean Mist Farms, Castroville *Also called Ocean Mist Farming Company* ***(P-67)***
Ocean Park Community Center....C....310 828-6717
1447 16th St Santa Monica (90404) ***(P-27153)***
Ocean Park Health Center....E....415 753-8100
1351 24th Ave San Francisco (94122) ***(P-19236)***
Ocean Park Hotels Inc....C....831 373-6141
1000 Aguajito Rd Monterey (93940) ***(P-12661)***
Ocean Park Hotels Inc....D....661 284-3200
27710 The Old Rd Valencia (91355) ***(P-12662)***
Ocean Park Hotels Mmex LLC....E....661 284-2101
27513 Wayne Mills Pl Valencia (91355) ***(P-12663)***
Ocean Queen 87 Inc....E....323 585-1200
4511 Everett Ave Vernon (90058) ***(P-8376)***
Ocean Service, San Diego *Also called Overseas Service Corporation* ***(P-27297)***
Ocean View Flowers LLC....C....800 736-5608
1105 Union Sugar Ave Lompoc (93436) ***(P-267)***
Ocean View Manor LP....D....805 781-3088
3533 Empleo St San Luis Obispo (93401) ***(P-10880)***

ALPHABETIC

Employee Codes: A=Over 500 employees, B=251-500
C=101-250, D=51-100, E=50
2020 Directory of California
Wholesalers and Services Companies
© Mergent Inc. 1-800-342-5647
1369

Ocean View Manor Apartments, San Luis Obispo *Also called Ocean View Manor LP* ***(P-10880)***
Oceanland Customhouse Broker, City of Industry *Also called Oceanland Service Inc* ***(P-5010)***
Oceanland Service Inc (PA).....D.....626 573-8429
15241 Don Julian Rd City of Industry (91745) ***(P-5010)***
Oceans Eleven Casino.....B.....760 439-6988
121 Brooks St Oceanside (92054) ***(P-12664)***
Oceanside Hlthcare Stffing Inc.....C.....213 503-5649
2216 El Camino Rela 211 Santa Clarita (91350) ***(P-22289)***
Oceanside Laundry LLC.....D.....831 722-4358
675 Beach Dr Watsonville (95076) ***(P-13249)***
Oceanside Lifeguards.....D.....760 435-4500
300 N Coast Hwy Oceanside (92054) ***(P-18732)***
Oceanview Produce Company.....D.....805 488-6401
5713 W Gonzales Rd Oxnard (93036) ***(P-68)***
Oceanx LLC (HQ).....D.....310 774-4088
100 N Pacific Coast Hwy El Segundo (90245) ***(P-16959)***
Ocm Real Estate Opportunities.....A.....213 830-6300
333 S Grand Ave Fl 28 Los Angeles (90071) ***(P-11735)***
Ocmban, Irvine *Also called Ocmbc Inc* ***(P-9585)***
Ocmbc Inc.....D.....714 479-0999
19000 Macarthur Blvd # 200 Irvine (92612) ***(P-9585)***
OConnell Landscape Maint Inc.....E.....760 630-4963
4600 Leisure Village Way Oceanside (92056) ***(P-882)***
OConner Woods A California.....D.....209 956-3400
3400 Wagner Heights Rd Stockton (95209) ***(P-10788)***
Oconnor Hospital, San Jose *Also called OConnor Imaging Med Group Inc* ***(P-19237)***
OConnor Hospital.....D.....408 947-2929
2039 Forest Ave San Jose (95128) ***(P-21065)***
OConnor Hospital (HQ).....A.....408 947-2500
2105 Forest Ave San Jose (95128) ***(P-21066)***
OConnor Imaging Med Group Inc.....D.....408 947-2992
2105 Forest Ave San Jose (95128) ***(P-19237)***
OConnor Pest Control Visalia.....D.....559 366-4853
1728 W Prospect Ave Visalia (93291) ***(P-13826)***
OConnor Woods Housing Corp.....D.....209 956-3400
3400 Wagner Heights Rd Stockton (95209) ***(P-10789)***
Ocpw.....A.....714 955-0255
601 N Ross St Santa Ana (92701) ***(P-24204)***
Octa, Orange *Also called Orange County Trnsp Auth* ***(P-3576)***
Odc (PA).....D.....415 863-6606
351 Shotwell St San Francisco (94110) ***(P-17881)***
Odc Theater.....D.....415 863-6606
351 Shotwell St San Francisco (94110) ***(P-17931)***
Odd Fellow-Rebekah Chld HM Cal (PA).....C.....408 846-2100
290 I O O F Ave Gilroy (95020) ***(P-24010)***
Odd Fellow-Rebekah Chld HM Cal.....D.....831 775-0348
1260 S Main St Ste 101 Salinas (93901) ***(P-24011)***
Odd Fellows Home California.....B.....408 741-7100
14500 Fruitvale Ave # 3000 Saratoga (95070) ***(P-24012)***
Oddworld Inhabitants Inc.....D.....805 503-3000
869 Monterey St San Luis Obispo (93401) ***(P-15432)***
Odesus Inc (PA).....D.....310 473-4600
11766 Wilshire Blvd # 400 Los Angeles (90025) ***(P-16066)***
Odona Central Security Inc.....C.....323 728-8818
71 N San Gabriel Blvd Pasadena (91107) ***(P-16366)***
Ods Technologies LP.....C.....310 242-9400
6701 Center Dr W Ste 160 Los Angeles (90045) ***(P-5641)***
Odu-Usa Inc (HQ).....D.....805 484-0540
300 Camarillo Ranch Rd A Camarillo (93012) ***(P-7314)***
Odyssey Environmental Services, Lodi *Also called Odyssey Landscaping Co Inc* ***(P-3192)***
Odyssey Healthcare Inc.....D.....714 245-7420
525 Cabrillo Park Dr # 150 Santa Ana (92701) ***(P-20173)***
Odyssey Healthcare Inc.....D.....408 626-4868
1500 E Hamilton Ave # 212 Campbell (95008) ***(P-20174)***
Odyssey Healthcare Inc.....D.....858 565-2499
9444 Balboa Ave Ste 290 San Diego (92123) ***(P-21824)***
Odyssey Healthcare Inc.....E.....760 674-0066
74350 Country Club Dr Palm Desert (92260) ***(P-20647)***
Odyssey Healthcare Inc.....D.....760 241-7044
17290 Jasmine St Ste 104 Victorville (92395) ***(P-21825)***
Odyssey Landscaping Co Inc.....D.....209 369-6197
5400 W Highway 12 Lodi (95242) ***(P-3192)***
Odyssey Telecorp Inc.....C.....650 470-7550
550 Lytton Ave Fl 2 Palo Alto (94301) ***(P-5450)***
Oec Group, Cerritos *Also called O E C Shipg Los Angeles Inc* ***(P-5008)***
Oel/Hhh Inc.....D.....818 246-6050
1833 Victory Blvd Glendale (91201) ***(P-25491)***
OES Equipment LLC (PA).....D.....510 284-1900
37421 Centralmont Pl Fremont (94536) ***(P-14184)***
Off Duty Officers Inc.....A.....888 408-5900
2365 La Mirada Dr Vista (92081) ***(P-16367)***
Office Cmnty Inv Infrstructure, San Francisco *Also called Successor To San Francisco* ***(P-27220)***
Office Depot Inc.....D.....916 927-0171
7531 Quail Vista Ln Citrus Heights (95610) ***(P-6762)***
Office Furniture Outlet, Modesto *Also called Wardens Office Inc* ***(P-7869)***
Office Movers Inc.....E.....408 254-5010
4020 Nelson Ave Ste 200 Concord (94520) ***(P-4222)***
Office of Child Development.....D.....310 842-4230
10800 Farragut Dr Culver City (90230) ***(P-23760)***
Office of Inspector General, Los Angeles *Also called Los Angeles County MTA* ***(P-3559)***
Office of Nutritional Services, Visalia *Also called Visalia Unified School Dst* ***(P-23526)***
Office of Technology, Rancho Cordova *Also called Technology Services Cal Dept* ***(P-16132)***
Office of The Legislative Coun.....B.....916 341-8708
1100 J St Fl 7 Sacramento (95814) ***(P-5267)***
Office of The Legislative Coun.....A.....916 445-3796
925 L St Ste 900 Sacramento (95814) ***(P-27154)***
Office On Aging, ADRC Of River, Riverside *Also called County of Riverside* ***(P-23135)***
Office Star Products, Ontario *Also called Blumenthal Distributing Inc* ***(P-6507)***
Office Team, Menlo Park *Also called Robert Half International Inc* ***(P-14400)***
Office Team, San Ramon *Also called Robert Half International Inc* ***(P-14404)***
OfficeMax Incorporated.....D.....951 485-9353
7300 Chapman Ave Garden Grove (92841) ***(P-4465)***
Officer Off Duty, Rcho STA Marg *Also called Murano Group* ***(P-16357)***
Officeteam, San Jose *Also called Robert Half International Inc* ***(P-14389)***
Officeteam, Irvine *Also called Robert Half International Inc* ***(P-14401)***
Officeworks Inc.....D.....510 444-2161
300 Frank H Ste 269 Oakland (94612) ***(P-14343)***
Officeworks Inc.....D.....951 784-2534
11801 Pierce St Fl 2 Riverside (92505) ***(P-14344)***
Official Police Garage Assn of.....A.....805 624-0572
67 W Boulder Creek Rd Simi Valley (93065) ***(P-4631)***
Offshore Crane & Service Co (PA).....D.....805 648-3348
1375 N Olive St Ste A Ventura (93001) ***(P-14108)***
Ofi Markesa International, Vernon *Also called Orient Fisheries Inc* ***(P-8378)***
Ogilvy & Mather Worldwide Inc.....D.....310 280-2200
2425 Olympic Blvd 2200w Santa Monica (90404) ***(P-13551)***
Ogilvy Pub Rltons Wrldwide Inc.....D.....916 231-7700
1530 J St Sacramento (95814) ***(P-26920)***
Ogletree Deakins Nash Smoak.....D.....415 442-4810
1 Market St Ste 1300 San Francisco (94105) ***(P-22731)***
OGrady Paving Inc.....C.....650 966-1926
2513 Wyandotte St Mountain View (94043) ***(P-1770)***
OH My Green Inc.....D.....650 989-8181
1845 Rollins Rd Burlingame (94010) ***(P-8621)***
OHagin Manufacturing LLC.....E.....707 872-3620
210 Classic Ct Ste 100 Rohnert Park (94928) ***(P-2214)***
OHagins Inc.....D.....707 303-3660
210 Classic Ct Ste 100 Rohnert Park (94928) ***(P-2215)***
Ohana Partners Inc (PA).....D.....408 856-3232
454 S Abbott Ave Milpitas (95035) ***(P-14185)***
Ohi Resort Hotels LLC.....D.....714 867-5555
12021 Harbor Blvd Garden Grove (92840) ***(P-12665)***
Ohl, Redlands *Also called Geodis Logistics LLC* ***(P-4418)***
Ohl LLC.....C.....650 872-3399
1162 Cherry Ave San Bruno (94066) ***(P-26743)***
Oil Changers, Pleasanton *Also called Oc IV A California LP* ***(P-17338)***
Oil Well Service Company (PA).....C.....562 612-0600
10840 Norwalk Blvd Santa Fe Springs (90670) ***(P-1037)***
Oilfield Electric & Motor, Ventura *Also called Oilfield Electric Company* ***(P-2573)***
Oilfield Electric Company.....D.....805 648-3131
1801 N Ventura Ave Ventura (93001) ***(P-2573)***
Oj Insulation LP.....D.....408 842-6315
5820 Obata Way Ste B Gilroy (95020) ***(P-2828)***
Oj Insulation LP.....E.....760 839-3200
2061 Albergrov Ave Escondido (92029) ***(P-2829)***
Oj Insulation LP.....D.....760 200-4343
78 015 Wildcat Dr Palm Desert (92211) ***(P-2830)***
Oj Insulation LP (PA).....C.....626 812-6070
600 S Vincent Ave Azusa (91702) ***(P-2831)***
Oj Insulation & Fireplaces, Escondido *Also called Oj Insulation LP* ***(P-2829)***
Ojai Ambulance Inc.....E.....805 653-9111
632 E Thompson Blvd Ventura (93001) ***(P-3704)***
Ojai Valley Community Hospital, Ojai *Also called Community Memorial Health Sys* ***(P-20804)***
Ojai Valley Inn & Spa, Ojai *Also called Ovis Llc* ***(P-12682)***
Ojai Valley Inn Golf Course.....A.....805 646-2420
905 Country Club Rd Ojai (93023) ***(P-12666)***
Ojai Valley Spa, Ojai *Also called Ojai Valley Inn Golf Course* ***(P-12666)***
OK Produce, Fresno *Also called Charlies Enterprises* ***(P-4385)***
Okabe International Inc (PA).....E.....415 921-0808
1739 Buchanan St Ste B San Francisco (94115) ***(P-4857)***
Okta Inc (PA).....C.....888 722-7871
100 1st St Ste 600 San Francisco (94105) ***(P-15433)***
Olam Americas Inc (HQ).....A.....559 447-1390
25 Union Pl Ste 3 Fresno (93720) ***(P-524)***
Olam LLC.....E.....559 446-6420
205 E Rver Pk Cir Ste 310 Fresno (93720) ***(P-15)***
Olam Spces Vgtable Ingredients, Fresno *Also called Olam West Coast Inc* ***(P-525)***
Olam West Coast Inc (HQ).....C.....559 447-1390
205 E Rver Pk Pl Ste 3 Fresno (93720) ***(P-525)***
Old Dominion Freight Line Inc.....C.....323 725-3400
1225 Washington Blvd Montebello (90640) ***(P-4107)***
Old Globe Theatre.....B.....619 234-5623
1363 Old Globe Way San Diego (92101) ***(P-17932)***
Old Republic Contractors Ins.....D.....626 683-5200
225 S Lake Ave Ste 900 Pasadena (91101) ***(P-10444)***
Old Republic HM Protection Inc.....B.....925 866-1500
2 Annabel Ln Ste 112 San Ramon (94583) ***(P-10445)***
Old Republic Title Company.....A.....818 240-1936
101 N Brand Blvd Ste 1400 Glendale (91203) ***(P-10199)***
Old Republic Title Company.....E.....831 757-8051
584 S Main St Salinas (93901) ***(P-10200)***
Old Town Fmly Hospitality Corp.....C.....619 246-8010
4962 Concannon Ct San Diego (92130) ***(P-12667)***
Old Town Gallery of Fine Art, Auburn *Also called Auburn Old Town Gallery* ***(P-18629)***
Old Town Trlley Turs San Diego.....D.....619 298-8687
2115 Kurtz St San Diego (92110) ***(P-4858)***
Olde Thompson LLC.....C.....805 983-0388
3250 Camino Del Sol Oxnard (93030) ***(P-6575)***
Oldenkamp Trucking Inc (PA).....D.....661 833-3400
13535 S Union Ave Bakersfield (93307) ***(P-3923)***
Older Adults Care Management (PA).....C.....650 329-1411
881 Fremont Ave Ste A2 Los Altos (94024) ***(P-23363)***

Mergent e-mail: customerrelations@mergent.com
1370
2020 Directory of California
Wholesalers and Services Companies
(P-0000) Products & Services Section entry number
(PA)=Parent Co (HQ)=Headquarters (DH)=Div Headquarters

Ole Health...E.......707 254-1770
1100 Trancas St Ste 300 NAPA (94558) ***(P-19238)***
Oleander Holdings LLC...D.......916 331-4590
5255 Hemlock St Sacramento (95841) ***(P-20175)***
Olen Commercial Realty Corp...B.......949 644-6536
7 Corporate Plaza Dr Newport Beach (92660) ***(P-10630)***
Olen Companies, The, Newport Beach *Also called Olen Residential Realty Corp* ***(P-1262)***
Olen Residential Realty, Newport Beach *Also called Olen Commercial Realty Corp* ***(P-10630)***
Olen Residential Realty Corp (HQ)...D.......949 644-6536
7 Corporate Plaza Dr Newport Beach (92660) ***(P-1262)***
Olive Crest...D.......760 341-8507
73700 Dinah Shore Dr # 101 Palm Desert (92211) ***(P-24013)***
Olive Crest...D.......562 216-8841
917 Pine Ave Long Beach (90813) ***(P-24014)***
Olive Crest (PA)...B.......714 543-5437
2130 E 4th St Ste 200 Santa Ana (92705) ***(P-24015)***
Olive Crest Op, Long Beach *Also called Olive Crest* ***(P-24014)***
Olive Grove Retirement Resort...D.......951 687-2241
7858 California Ave Riverside (92504) ***(P-10790)***
Olive Hill Greenhouses...D.......760 728-4596
3508 Olive Hill Rd Fallbrook (92028) ***(P-268)***
Olive Knolls Christian School...D.......661 393-3566
6201 Fruitvale Ave Bakersfield (93308) ***(P-23761)***
Olive Ridge Post Acute Care, Oroville *Also called Evergreen At Oroville LLC* ***(P-19902)***
Olive US Bidco Inc (HQ)...E.......800 662-1711
25341 Commercentre Dr Lake Forest (92630) ***(P-16547)***
Olive View-Ucla Medical Center (PA)...D.......818 364-1555
14445 Olive View Dr Sylmar (91342) ***(P-19239)***
Olive View/Ucla Education &...D.......818 364-3434
14445 Olive View Dr Sylmar (91342) ***(P-26015)***
Olive Vista, Center, Pomona *Also called Genesis Healthcare Corporation* ***(P-19938)***
Olivenhain Municipal Water Dst...D.......760 753-6466
1966 Olivenhain Rd Encinitas (92024) ***(P-6097)***
Oliver & Company Inc...D.......510 412-9090
1300 S 51st St Richmond (94804) ***(P-1554)***
Olivermcmillan LLC (HQ)...D.......619 321-1111
733 8th Ave San Diego (92101) ***(P-11588)***
Olivet International Inc (PA)...D.......951 681-8888
11015 Hopkins St Jurupa Valley (91752) ***(P-7826)***
Olivieri Enterprises LP...C.......916 791-7857
210 Estates Dr Ste 200 Roseville (95678) ***(P-2952)***
Ols Hotels & Resorts LLC (PA)...A.......818 905-8280
16000 Ventura Blvd # 1010 Encino (91436) ***(P-12668)***
Ols Hotels & Resorts LLC...A.......626 962-6000
14635 Bldwin Pk Towne Ctr Baldwin Park (91706) ***(P-12669)***
Ols Hotels & Resorts LP...C.......310 855-1115
733 W Knoll Dr West Hollywood (90069) ***(P-12670)***
Olson & Assoc...D.......714 878-6649
3448 Lupine Cir Ste 102 Costa Mesa (92626) ***(P-16067)***
Olson Company LLC (PA)...D.......562 596-4770
3010 Old Ranch Pkwy # 100 Seal Beach (90740) ***(P-1168)***
Olson Company, The, Seal Beach *Also called Olson Urban Housing LLC* ***(P-11589)***
Olson Homes, Seal Beach *Also called Olson Company LLC* ***(P-1168)***
Olson Urban Housing LLC...D.......562 596-4770
3010 Old Ranch Pkwy # 100 Seal Beach (90740) ***(P-11589)***
Oltmans Construction Co (PA)...D.......562 948-4242
10005 Mission Mill Rd Whittier (90601) ***(P-1371)***
Oltmans Investment Company...E.......562 948-4242
10005 Mission Mill Rd Whittier (90601) ***(P-10631)***
Oltmans Property Management, Whittier *Also called Oltmans Investment Company* ***(P-10631)***
Olympia Convalescent Hospital...C.......213 487-3000
1100 S Alvarado St Los Angeles (90006) ***(P-20648)***
Olympia Health Care LLC...A.......323 938-3161
5900 W Olympic Blvd Los Angeles (90036) ***(P-21067)***
Olympia Medical Center, Los Angeles *Also called Olympia Health Care LLC* ***(P-21067)***
Olympic Circle Sailing Club, Berkeley *Also called O C Sailing Club Inc* ***(P-18731)***
Olympic Club...D.......415 676-1412
665 Sutter St San Francisco (94102) ***(P-18522)***
Olympic Club (PA)...C.......415 345-5100
524 Post St San Francisco (94102) ***(P-24604)***
Olympic Club...C.......415 404-4300
599 Skyline Dr Daly City (94015) ***(P-24605)***
Olympic Construction, Roseville *Also called Olivieri Enterprises LP* ***(P-2952)***
Olympic Frt & Vegatable Distr, Los Angeles *Also called Coast Citrus Distributors* ***(P-8447)***
Olympic Investors Ltd...D.......925 322-8996
1908 Olympic Blvd Walnut Creek (94596) ***(P-18523)***
Olympic Security, Bellflower *Also called Advent Securities Investments* ***(P-9649)***
Olympix Fitness LLC...D.......562 366-4600
4101 E Olympic Plz Long Beach (90803) ***(P-18182)***
Olympus Adhc Inc...E.......310 572-7272
11613 Washington Pl Los Angeles (90066) ***(P-23762)***
Olympus Adult Day Hlthcare Ctr, Los Angeles *Also called Olympus Adhc Inc* ***(P-23762)***
Olympus America Inc...C.......949 466-3548
23342 Madero Mission Viejo (92691) ***(P-6985)***
OLYMPUS AMERICA INC., Mission Viejo *Also called Olympus America Inc* ***(P-6985)***
Olympus Building Services Inc...A.......760 750-4629
441 La Moree Rd San Marcos (92078) ***(P-26953)***
Olympus Power LLC...C.......661 393-6885
34759 Lencioni Ave Bakersfield (93308) ***(P-5869)***
Om Food Sejal Enterprises Inc...D.......626 712-3138
449 W Allen Ave Ste 111 San Dimas (91773) ***(P-26744)***
Omar Orozco...D.......530 723-0849
816 Gibson Rd Woodland (95695) ***(P-636)***
Omar Orozco's Contracting, Woodland *Also called Omar Orozco* ***(P-636)***
Omega 2 Alpha Services LLC...D.......805 610-2249
935 Riverside Ave Ste 23 Paso Robles (93446) ***(P-26745)***
Omega Insurance Services...E.......714 973-0311
721 S Parker St Ste 300 Orange (92868) ***(P-10446)***
Omega Management Services, Corning *Also called Omega Waste Management Inc* ***(P-26746)***
Omega Moulding West LLC...C.......323 261-3510
5500 Lindbergh Ln Bell (90201) ***(P-6576)***
Omega Security Services & Cons...D.......818 831-1100
10611 Garden Grove Ave # 2 Northridge (91326) ***(P-16368)***
Omega Walnut Inc...E.......530 865-0136
7233 County Road 24 Orland (95963) ***(P-526)***
Omega Waste Management Inc...D.......530 824-1890
957 Colusa St Corning (96021) ***(P-26746)***
Omega/Cinema Props Inc...D.......323 466-8201
5857 Santa Monica Blvd Los Angeles (90038) ***(P-17755)***
Omelet LLC (PA)...D.......213 427-6400
3540 Hayden Ave Culver City (90232) ***(P-13552)***
OMelveny & Myers LLP (PA)...A.......213 430-6000
400 S Hope St Fl 19 Los Angeles (90071) ***(P-22732)***
OMelveny & Myers LLP...C.......949 760-9600
610 Nwport Ctr Dr Fl 17 Flr 17 Newport Beach (92660) ***(P-22733)***
OMelveny & Myers LLP...C.......310 553-6700
1999 Avenue Of The Stars # 600 Los Angeles (90067) ***(P-22734)***
OMelveny & Myers LLP...C.......650 473-2600
2765 Sand Hill Rd Menlo Park (94025) ***(P-22735)***
OMelveny & Myers LLP...C.......415 984-8700
2 Embarcadero Ctr Fl 28 San Francisco (94111) ***(P-22736)***
Omni Family Health (PA)...D.......661 459-1900
4900 California Ave 400b Bakersfield (93309) ***(P-19240)***
Omni Hotels Corporation...B.......760 568-2727
41000 Bob Hope Dr Rancho Mirage (92270) ***(P-12671)***
Omni Hotels Corporation...B.......619 231-6664
675 L St San Diego (92101) ***(P-12672)***
Omni Hotels Corporation...B.......415 677-9494
500 California St San Francisco (94104) ***(P-12673)***
Omni Hotels Corporation...C.......213 617-3300
251 S Olive St Fl 1 Los Angeles (90012) ***(P-12674)***
Omni La Costa Resort & Spa LLC...E.......760 438-9111
2100 Costa Del Mar Rd Carlsbad (92009) ***(P-12675)***
Omni Seals, Inc., Rancho Cucamonga *Also called Smith International Inc* ***(P-1044)***
Omni Womens Hlth Med Group Inc...D.......559 441-4271
2550 Merced St Fresno (93721) ***(P-19241)***
Omnia Italian Design LLC...C.......909 393-4400
4900 Edison Ave Chino (91710) ***(P-6524)***
Omnicare Inc...D.......510 293-9663
20967 Cabot Blvd Hayward (94545) ***(P-7971)***
Omniduct, Buena Park *Also called ECB Corp* ***(P-2122)***
Omnify Software, Foster City *Also called Arena Solutions Inc* ***(P-15243)***
Omnikron Systems Inc...D.......818 591-7890
20920 Warner Center Ln A Woodland Hills (91367) ***(P-16068)***
Omninet Twin Towers Gp LLC...E.......310 300-4100
9420 Wilshire Blvd # 400 Beverly Hills (90212) ***(P-11325)***
Omninet Twin Towers LP...E.......310 300-4110
9420 Wilshire Blvd # 400 Beverly Hills (90212) ***(P-11326)***
Omniteam Inc...C.......562 923-9660
9300 Hall Rd Downey (90241) ***(P-7462)***
Omnitrans Inc...B.......909 383-1680
234 S I St San Bernardino (92410) ***(P-24016)***
Omnitrans Inc...C.......909 379-7100
4748 Arrow Hwy Montclair (91763) ***(P-3573)***
Omnitrans Access, San Bernardino *Also called Omnitrans Inc* ***(P-24016)***
Omniupdate Inc...D.......805 484-9400
1320 Flynn Rd Ste 100 Camarillo (93012) ***(P-14978)***
On Call Consulting, Thousand Oaks *Also called Miramed Global Services Inc* ***(P-27133)***
On Central Realty Inc...B.......323 543-8500
1648 Colorado Blvd Los Angeles (90041) ***(P-11327)***
On Lok Inc...D.......415 292-8888
1333 Bush St San Francisco (94109) ***(P-19242)***
On Lok Life Ways, Fremont *Also called On Lok Senior Health Services* ***(P-10021)***
On Lok Lifeways, San Francisco *Also called On Lok Senior Health Services* ***(P-10020)***
On Lok Senior Health Services (PA)...A.......415 292-8888
1333 Bush St San Francisco (94109) ***(P-10020)***
On Lok Senior Health Services...E.......510 249-2700
3683 Peralta Blvd Fremont (94536) ***(P-10021)***
On My Own Indepedent Living...D.......707 938-9156
920 1st St W Sonoma (95476) ***(P-20649)***
On The Move...E.......707 251-9432
780 Lincoln Ave NAPA (94558) ***(P-24205)***
On Trac Overhead Door Co Inc...E.......909 799-8555
1430 Richardson St San Bernardino (92408) ***(P-2953)***
On-Scene Security Services Inc...E.......661 263-2343
P.O. Box 800147 Santa Clarita (91380) ***(P-16369)***
On-Site Lasermedic Corporation (PA)...D.......818 775-9111
21540 Prairie St Ste D Chatsworth (91311) ***(P-15923)***
On-Site Manager Inc (HQ)...E.......866 266-7483
307 Orchard Cy Dr Ste 110 Campbell (95008) ***(P-16960)***
On-Time AC & Htg Inc (PA)...C.......925 598-1911
7020 Commerce Dr Pleasanton (94588) ***(P-2216)***
On24 Inc (PA)...B.......877 202-9599
50 Beale St Ste 800 San Francisco (94105) ***(P-15434)***
Onboardiq Inc...E.......480 433-1197
275 Sacramento St Ste 300 San Francisco (94111) ***(P-15875)***
Oncore Manufacturing LLC (HQ)...A.......818 734-6500
9340 Owensmouth Ave Chatsworth (91311) ***(P-25242)***
One Inc (PA)...D.......866 343-6940
620 Coolidge Dr Ste 200 Folsom (95630) ***(P-26335)***
One 3 Two Inc...C.......949 596-8400
17353 Derian Ave Irvine (92614) ***(P-8105)***
One California Plaza, Los Angeles *Also called Hill Farrer & Burrill* ***(P-22569)***

Employee Codes: A=Over 500 employees, B=251-500
C=101-250, D=51-100, E=50
2020 Directory of California
Wholesalers and Services Companies
© Mergent Inc. 1-800-342-5647
1371

One Call Medical Inc...D...818 346-8700
8501 Fllbrook Ave Ste 100 Canoga Park (91304) *(P-26747)*
One Call Plumber Goleta...D...805 284-0441
140 Nectarine Ave Apt 4 Goleta (93117) *(P-13442)*
One Call Plumber Santa Barbara...D...805 364-6337
1016 Cliff Dr Apt 309 Santa Barbara (93109) *(P-2217)*
One Diversified LLC...D...408 969-1972
3275 Edward Ave Santa Clara (95054) *(P-27155)*
One Embarcadero Center Venture...D...415 772-0700
4 Embarcadero Ctr Ste 1 San Francisco (94111) *(P-11868)*
One Heart World Which Will Do...D...415 379-4762
1818 Pacheco St San Francisco (94116) *(P-16961)*
One K Studios LLC...E...818 531-3800
3400 W Olive Ave Ste 300 Burbank (91505) *(P-13794)*
One Legal Inc...D...213 617-1212
350 S Figueroa St Ste 385 Los Angeles (90071) *(P-16962)*
One Medical Group, San Francisco *Also called 1life Healthcare Inc (P-22165)*
One Medical Group Inc (PA)...D...415 578-3100
1 Embarcadero Ctr Ste 500 San Francisco (94111) *(P-19243)*
One Medical Group Inc...D...415 529-4522
3885 24th St San Francisco (94114) *(P-19244)*
One Medical Group Inc...D...212 530-2288
1 Embarcadero Ctr Ste 500 San Francisco (94111) *(P-19245)*
One Nob Hill Associates LLC...D...415 392-3434
999 California St San Francisco (94108) *(P-12676)*
One Planet Ops Inc (PA)...C...925 983-2800
1820 Bonanza St Ste 200 Walnut Creek (94596) *(P-13553)*
One Rock Capital Partners LLC...D...213 292-5870
11601 Wilshire Blvd # 1960 Los Angeles (90025) *(P-9835)*
One Silver Serve Inc...E...818 995-6444
17835 Ventura Blvd # 108 Encino (91316) *(P-13995)*
One Source Supply Solutions, Buena Park *Also called Onesource Distributors LLC (P-7173)*
One Stop Program, Los Angeles *Also called Uaw-Lbor Emplyment Trning Corp (P-14444)*
One Town Center Associates LLC...E...714 435-2100
3315 Fairview Rd Costa Mesa (92626) *(P-10632)*
One Workplace L Ferrari, San Francisco *Also called One Workplace L Ferrari LLC (P-6525)*
One Workplace L Ferrari LLC...E...415 357-2200
475 Brannan St San Francisco (94107) *(P-6525)*
One10 LLC...D...415 398-3534
180 Montgomery St San Francisco (94104) *(P-26748)*
One10 LLC...D...415 844-2200
735 Battery St Fl 1 San Francisco (94111) *(P-26749)*
Onebill Software Inc...D...844 462-7638
3080 Olcott St Ste D230 Santa Clara (95054) *(P-14979)*
Onebody Inc...D...510 285-2000
2000 Powell St Ste 555 Emeryville (94608) *(P-21826)*
Onecalifornia Bank, Oakland *Also called Beneficial State Bank (P-9175)*
Onegeneration (PA)...D...818 708-6625
17400 Victory Blvd Van Nuys (91406) *(P-23364)*
Onegeneration Adult Day Health, Van Nuys *Also called Onegeneration (P-23364)*
Onehealth Solutions Inc...D...858 947-6333
420 Stevens Ave Ste 200 Solana Beach (92075) *(P-16069)*
ONeill Beverages Co LLC...C...559 638-3544
8418 S Lac Jac Ave Parlier (93648) *(P-150)*
ONeill Beverages Co LLC (PA)...D...844 825-6600
101 Larkspur Landing Cir Larkspur (94939) *(P-151)*
Onelegacy (PA)...D...213 625-0665
221 S Figueroa St Ste 500 Los Angeles (90012) *(P-22290)*
Onemain Holdings Inc...D...209 869-8030
2401 Claribel Rd Ste C Riverbank (95367) *(P-9586)*
Onemain Holdings Inc...D...909 392-5578
2278 Foothill Blvd La Verne (91750) *(P-9836)*
Onemain Holdings Inc...D...951 245-5029
31712 Casino Dr Ste 6a Lake Elsinore (92530) *(P-9587)*
Oneoc (PA)...D...714 953-5757
1901 E 4th St Ste 100 Santa Ana (92705) *(P-24852)*
Onesource Distributors LLC...D...714 685-5378
6530 Altura Blvd Buena Park (90620) *(P-7173)*
Oneunited Bank...D...323 295-3381
3683 Crenshaw Blvd Los Angeles (90016) *(P-9219)*
Onewest Bank, Culver City *Also called CIT Bank NA (P-9065)*
Onewest Bank NA...D...562 433-0971
3500 E 7th St Long Beach (90804) *(P-9281)*
Online Communications Inc...C...916 652-7253
3291 Swetzer Rd Loomis (95650) *(P-2574)*
Online Technical Services Inc (PA)...E...408 378-1100
1901 S Bascom Ave Ste 840 Campbell (95008) *(P-14345)*
Onmycare Home Health, Fremont *Also called Onmycare LLC (P-21827)*
Onmycare LLC...D...510 858-2273
39159 Paseo Padre Pkwy # 304 Fremont (94538) *(P-21827)*
Onrad Inc...D...800 848-5876
1770 Iowa Ave Ste 280 Riverside (92507) *(P-19246)*
Onrad Medical Group, Riverside *Also called Onrad Inc (P-19246)*
Onsite Consulting LLC...D...323 401-3190
5042 Wilshire Blvd # 135 Los Angeles (90036) *(P-27156)*
Onsite Health Inc (PA)...D...949 305-2253
85 Argonaut Ste 220 Aliso Viejo (92656) *(P-22291)*
Onsolve LLC...D...858 724-1200
3398 Carmel Mountain Rd # 100 San Diego (92121) *(P-14980)*
Ontario Airport Hotel Corp...C...408 562-6709
4949 Great America Pkwy Santa Clara (95054) *(P-12677)*
Ontario Community Hospital, Ontario *Also called Kindred Healthcare Oper Inc (P-20991)*
Ontario Convention Center, Ontario *Also called Smg Food and Beverage LLC (P-17059)*
Ontario Convention Center Corp...C...909 937-3000
2000 E Convention Ctr Way Ontario (91764) *(P-16963)*
Ontario Health Educatn Co Inc...E...951 817-8553
3130 Sedona Ct Ontario (91764) *(P-21828)*
Ontario Healthcare Center, Ontario *Also called Kf Ontario Healthcare LLC (P-20606)*
Ontario Mills Shopping Center, Ontario *Also called Mills Corporation (P-10621)*
Ontario Montclar Sch Dist Food...C...909 930-6360
1525 S Bon View Ave Ontario (91761) *(P-22292)*
Ontario Refrigeration Svc Inc (PA)...D...909 984-2771
635 S Mountain Ave Ontario (91762) *(P-2218)*
Ontario Vineyard Medical Offs, Ontario *Also called Kaiser Foundation Hospitals (P-19085)*
Ontario-Don, Ontario *Also called Synnex Corporation (P-4510)*
Ontario/Montclair YMCA, Ontario *Also called West End Yung MNS Christn Assn (P-24696)*
Ontel Security Services Inc...D...209 521-0200
2125 Wylie Dr Ste 11 Modesto (95355) *(P-16370)*
Ontic Engineering and Mfg Inc (HQ)...B...818 678-6555
20400 Plummer St Chatsworth (91311) *(P-7697)*
Ontrac, Santa Maria *Also called Express Messenger Systems Inc (P-4256)*
Ontrac, Compton *Also called Express Messenger Systems Inc (P-4258)*
Ontrac, Fresno *Also called Express Messenger Systems Inc (P-4261)*
Oocl (usa) Inc...D...408 576-6543
2700 Zanker Rd Ste 200 San Jose (95134) *(P-5011)*
Oocl (usa) Inc...D...562 499-2600
111 W Ocean Blvd Ste 1800 Long Beach (90802) *(P-5012)*
Oocl (usa) Inc...D...562 499-2600
17777 Center Court Dr N # 500 Cerritos (90703) *(P-5013)*
Ooma Inc (PA)...C...650 566-6600
525 Almanor Ave Ste 200 Sunnyvale (94085) *(P-15795)*
Ooyala Inc (HQ)...D...650 961-3400
2099 Gateway Pl Ste 600 San Jose (95110) *(P-14981)*
Op Bancorp...C...213 892-9999
1000 Wilshire Blvd # 500 Los Angeles (90017) *(P-9220)*
Opal Fry and Son...E...661 858-2523
Maricopa Hwy Bakersfield (93307) *(P-69)*
Opal Soft Inc...D...408 267-2211
1288 Kifer Rd Ste 201 Sunnyvale (94086) *(P-16070)*
Opallios Inc...E...408 769-4594
4633 Old Ironsides Dr # 315 Santa Clara (95054) *(P-27157)*
Opalsoft, Sunnyvale *Also called Opal Soft Inc (P-16070)*
Oparc...D...909 598-8055
355 S Lemon Ave Ste J Walnut (91789) *(P-23365)*
Oparc (PA)...E...909 982-4090
9029 Vernon Ave Montclair (91763) *(P-23621)*
Open Door Community Hlth Ctrs...D...707 826-8610
770 10th St Arcata (95521) *(P-22071)*
Open Door Community Hlth Ctrs (PA)...D...707 826-8642
670 9th St Ste 203cfo Arcata (95521) *(P-22072)*
Open Text Inc (HQ)...C...650 645-3000
2950 S Delaware St San Mateo (94403) *(P-14982)*
Opendoor Labs Inc (PA)...D...415 510-7213
1 Post St Fl 11 San Francisco (94104) *(P-11328)*
Opendoor Labs Inc...D...888 352-7075
8880 Cal Center Dr # 400 Sacramento (95826) *(P-11329)*
Opendoor Labs Inc...D...888 352-7075
11801 Pierce St Ste 200 Riverside (92505) *(P-11330)*
Opendoor Property, Sacramento *Also called Opendoor Labs Inc (P-11329)*
Opendoor Property, Riverside *Also called Opendoor Labs Inc (P-11330)*
Openpopcom Inc (PA)...D...714 249-7044
5422 Beach Blvd Buena Park (90621) *(P-27158)*
Opentable Inc (HQ)...C...415 344-4200
1 Montgomery St Ste 700 San Francisco (94104) *(P-16964)*
Opentv Inc (HQ)...C...415 962-5000
275 Sacramento St Ste Sl1 San Francisco (94111) *(P-15435)*
Openx Technologies Inc (HQ)...C...855 673-6948
888 E Walnut St Fl 2 Pasadena (91101) *(P-13554)*
Opera San Jose Inc...D...408 437-4450
2149 Paragon Dr San Jose (95131) *(P-17933)*
Operam Inc...D...855 673-7261
1041 N Formosa Ave 500 West Hollywood (90046) *(P-26750)*
Operating Engineers Funds Inc (PA)...C...866 400-5200
100 Corson St Ste 222 Pasadena (91103) *(P-11806)*
Operating Engineers Loca...C...408 782-9803
325 Digital Dr Morgan Hill (95037) *(P-25243)*
Operation Samahan Inc...C...619 477-4451
10737 Camino Ruiz Ste 235 San Diego (92126) *(P-19247)*
Operation Technology Inc (PA)...D...949 462-0100
17 Goodyear Ste 100 Irvine (92618) *(P-14983)*
Operations, Los Angeles *Also called Wells Fargo Bank NA (P-9126)*
Operations Control Center, Oakland *Also called San Francisco Bay Area Rapid (P-3586)*
Operations/Risk Group, Pasadena *Also called Parsons Constructors Inc (P-26347)*
Operatix Inc...D...408 332-5796
111 N Market St Ste 300 San Jose (95113) *(P-26751)*
Opex Communications Inc...E...562 968-5420
3777 Long Beach Blvd # 400 Long Beach (90807) *(P-5451)*
Oplink Communications LLC (HQ)...D...510 933-7200
46360 Fremont Blvd Fremont (94538) *(P-5795)*
Oplink Communications, Inc., Fremont *Also called Oplink Communications LLC (P-5795)*
Oportun Financial Corporation (PA)...A...650 810-8823
2 Circle Star Way San Carlos (94070) *(P-16965)*
Oprah Winfrey Network, West Hollywood *Also called Own LLC (P-5733)*
Opsec Specialized Protection...D...661 942-3999
44262 Division St Ste A Lancaster (93535) *(P-16371)*
Opswat Inc (PA)...D...415 590-7300
398 Kansas St San Francisco (94103) *(P-14984)*
Optics Laboratory Inc...D...626 350-1926
9480 Telstar Ave Ste 3 El Monte (91731) *(P-21560)*
Optim, Pleasanton *Also called Unchained Labs (P-21595)*
Optima Building Services Maint...D...707 586-6640
210 Mountain View Ave Santa Rosa (95407) *(P-13996)*
Optima Mortgage Corporation...D...714 389-4650
2081 Bus Ctr Dr Ste 230 Irvine (92612) *(P-9588)*
Optima Network Services Inc (HQ)...D...305 599-1800
15345 Fairfield Ranch Rd # 225 Chino Hills (91709) *(P-27294)*

Optima Tax Relief LLC	C	714 361-4636
3100 S Harbor Blvd # 250 Santa Ana (92704) *(P-13392)*		
Optimal Health Services Inc	D	661 393-4483
1227 Chester Ave Bakersfield (93301) *(P-21829)*		
Optimal Hospice Care, Bakersfield *Also called Optimal Hospice Foundation (P-21830)*		
Optimal Hospice Foundation	C	661 716-4000
1675 Chester Ave Ste 401 Bakersfield (93301) *(P-21830)*		
Optimizely Inc (PA)	B	415 376-4598
631 Howard St Ste 100 San Francisco (94105) *(P-14985)*		
Optimum Inc (PA)	E	909 990-0767
17890 Valley Blvd Ste A Bloomington (92316) *(P-25244)*		
Optimum Con Fundations USA Inc		877 212-7994
6258 Rustic Ln Jurupa Valley (92509) *(P-3193)*		
Optimum Solutions Group LLC	C	415 954-7100
419 Ponderosa Ct Lafayette (94549) *(P-15436)*		
Optio Solutions LLC	C	800 360-2827
1444 N Mcdowell Blvd Petaluma (94954) *(P-13691)*		
Option Care Home Care Inc		818 351-3000
9401 Chivers Ave Sun Valley (91352) *(P-21831)*		
Option One Home Med Eqp Inc	C	909 478-5413
1220 Research Dr Ste A Redlands (92374) *(P-14089)*		
Options Family of Services	E	805 462-8544
5755 Valentina Ave Atascadero (93422) *(P-22073)*		
Options For Learning	D	626 308-2411
2001 Elm St Alhambra (91803) *(P-23763)*		
Optisource Technologies Inc	E	714 288-0825
1855 W Katella Ave # 170 Orange (92867) *(P-13765)*		
Optumrx Inc	B	760 804-2399
2858 Loker Ave E Ste 100 Carlsbad (92010) *(P-10022)*		
Optumrx Inc (HQ)	B	714 825-3600
2300 Main St Irvine (92614) *(P-10023)*		
Opus 2 International Inc	E	888 960-3117
100 Pine St Ste 775 San Francisco (94111) *(P-16966)*		
Opus Bank	C	714 578-7500
200 W Commonwealth Ave Fullerton (92832) *(P-9270)*		
Opus Inspection Inc	D	714 999-6727
1410 S Acacia Ave Ste A Fullerton (92831) *(P-14986)*		
Opya Inc	D	650 931-6300
1720 S Amphlett Blvd # 110 San Mateo (94402) *(P-22074)*		
Ora Pacific Regional Field Off	D	949 608-2907
19701 Fairchild Irvine (92612) *(P-16967)*		
Oracle, San Mateo *Also called Netsuite Inc (P-15421)*		
Oracle America Inc	C	408 276-4300
4220 Network Cir Santa Clara (95054) *(P-15437)*		
Oracle America Inc	D	415 908-3609
475 Sansome St Fl 15 San Francisco (94111) *(P-15438)*		
Oracle America Inc	C	408 276-3331
4120 Network Cir Santa Clara (95054) *(P-15439)*		
Oracle America Inc	D	925 694-3314
5815 Owens Dr Pleasanton (94588) *(P-15440)*		
Oracle America Inc	D	858 625-5044
9540 Towne Centre Dr San Diego (92121) *(P-15441)*		
Oracle America Inc	C	408 276-7534
4230 Leonard Stocking Dr Santa Clara (95054) *(P-15442)*		
Oracle America Inc	D	800 633-0584
500 Oracle Pkwy Redwood City (94065) *(P-6879)*		
Oracle Corp	A	650 506-7000
17901 Von Karman Ave # 800 Irvine (92614) *(P-27295)*		
Oracle Corporation	C	713 654-0919
279 Barnes Rd Tustin (92782) *(P-15443)*		
Oracle Corporation	B	650 607-5402
214 Clarence Ave Sunnyvale (94086) *(P-15444)*		
Oracle Corporation	B	650 678-3612
1408 Antigua Ln Foster City (94404) *(P-15445)*		
Oracle Corporation	B	408 421-2890
1490 Newhall St Santa Clara (95050) *(P-15446)*		
Oracle Corporation	B	408 276-5552
231 Kerry Dr Santa Clara (95050) *(P-15447)*		
Oracle Corporation	B	408 276-3822
3084 Thurman Dr San Jose (95148) *(P-15448)*		
Oracle Corporation	B	858 202-0648
9890 Towne Centre Dr # 150 San Diego (92121) *(P-15449)*		
Oracle Corporation	B	650 506-9864
3532 Eastin Pl Santa Clara (95051) *(P-15450)*		
Oracle Corporation	B	408 390-8623
372 Calero Ave San Jose (95123) *(P-15451)*		
Oracle Corporation	C	415 402-7200
525 Market St San Francisco (94105) *(P-15452)*		
Oracle Corporation	B	916 435-8342
6224 Hummingbird Ln Rocklin (95765) *(P-15453)*		
Oracle Corporation	B	877 767-2253
5805 Owens Dr Pleasanton (94588) *(P-15454)*		
Oracle Corporation	B	925 694-6258
3925 Emerald Isle Ln San Jose (95135) *(P-15455)*		
Oracle Corporation	B	510 471-6971
5863 Carmel Way Union City (94587) *(P-15456)*		
Oracle Corporation	B	310 258-7500
200 Crprate Pinte Ste 200 Culver City (90230) *(P-15457)*		
Oracle Corporation	B	310 343-7405
200 N Pacific Coast Hwy # 400 El Segundo (90245) *(P-15458)*		
Oracle Corporation	B	916 315-3500
1001 Sunset Blvd Rocklin (95765) *(P-15459)*		
Oracle Corporation (PA)	A	650 506-7000
500 Oracle Pkwy Redwood City (94065) *(P-16071)*		
Oracle Systems Corporation	D	818 817-2900
200 Crprate Pinte Ste 200 Culver City (90230) *(P-15460)*		
Oracle Systems Corporation	D	650 506-8648
102 Santa Barbara Ave Daly City (94014) *(P-15461)*		
Oracle Systems Corporation	B	650 654-7606
301 Island Pkwy Belmont (94002) *(P-15462)*		

Oracle Systems Corporation	C	650 506-6780
500 Oracle Pkwy San Mateo (94403) *(P-15463)*		
Oracle Systems Corporation	B	650 506-0300
10 Twin Dolphin Dr Redwood City (94065) *(P-15464)*		
Oracle Systems Corporation (HQ)	A	650 506-7000
500 Oracle Pkwy Redwood City (94065) *(P-16072)*		
Oracle Systems Corporation	B	925 694-3000
5840 Owens Dr Pleasanton (94588) *(P-15465)*		
Oracle Systems Corporation	D	949 224-1000
2010 Main St Ste 450 Irvine (92614) *(P-15466)*		
Oracle Systems Corporation	B	949 623-9460
17901 Von Karman Ave # 800 Irvine (92614) *(P-15467)*		
Oracle Taleo LLC	A	925 452-3000
4140 Dublin Blvd Ste 400 Dublin (94568) *(P-15468)*		
Orange Belt Adventures, Visalia *Also called Orange Belt Stages (P-3779)*		
Orange Belt Stages (PA)	D	559 733-4408
2134 E Mineral King Ave Visalia (93292) *(P-3779)*		
Orange Cast Title Southern Cal	D	714 822-3211
2461 W La Palma Ave Fl 1 Anaheim (92801) *(P-11534)*		
Orange Cnty Adult Achvment Ctr	C	714 744-5301
225 W Carl Karcher Way Anaheim (92801) *(P-16968)*		
Orange Cnty Assn For Mntal HLT (PA)	D	714 547-7559
1971 E 4th St Ste 130 Santa Ana (92705) *(P-24415)*		
Orange Cnty Conservation Corps	D	714 451-1301
1853 N Raymond Ave Anaheim (92801) *(P-23622)*		
Orange Cnty George M Raymond N, Orange *Also called Raymond Group (P-26374)*		
Orange Cnty Sprntndent Schools	D	949 650-2506
220 23rd St Costa Mesa (92627) *(P-23764)*		
Orange Coast Building Services	C	714 453-6300
2191 S Dupont Dr Anaheim (92806) *(P-1372)*		
Orange Coast Ctr For Surgl Cr, Fountain Valley *Also called Memorialcare Surgical Center A (P-21035)*		
Orange Coast Masonry Acquisit	D	714 538-4386
601 N Batavia St Orange (92868) *(P-2724)*		
Orange Coast Memorial Med Ctr (HQ)	D	714 378-7000
9920 Talbert Ave Fountain Valley (92708) *(P-21068)*		
Orange Coast Service Center, Westminster *Also called Southern California Edison Co (P-5947)*		
Orange Coast Title Company (PA)	D	714 558-2836
1551 N Tustin Ave Ste 300 Santa Ana (92705) *(P-16969)*		
Orange Coast Wns Med Group Inc (PA)	D	949 829-5500
24411 Health Center Dr # 200 Laguna Hills (92653) *(P-19248)*		
Orange County Child Abuse	D	714 543-4333
2390 E Orangewood Ave # 300 Anaheim (92806) *(P-23366)*		
Orange County Cncl Bsa (PA)	D	714 546-4990
1211 E Dyer Rd Ste 100 Santa Ana (92705) *(P-24606)*		
Orange County Dept Education	A	714 730-7301
300 S C St Tustin (92780) *(P-26336)*		
Orange County Employees Retir	D	714 558-6200
2223 S Wellington Ave Santa Ana (92701) *(P-11736)*		
Orange County Head Start (PA)	D	714 241-8920
2501 Pullman St Santa Ana (92705) *(P-23765)*		
Orange County Head Start	D	714 761-4967
9200 W Pacific Pl Anaheim (92804) *(P-23766)*		
Orange County Head Start	E	714 241-8920
14422 Hammon Ln Huntington Beach (92647) *(P-23767)*		
Orange County Health Auth	B	714 246-8500
505 City Pkwy W Orange (92868) *(P-24416)*		
Orange County Health Care Agcy	D	714 568-5683
405 W 5th St Ste 700 Santa Ana (92701) *(P-24417)*		
Orange County One Stop Center	D	714 241-4900
5405 Grdn Rd Blvd Ste 100 Westminster (92683) *(P-14346)*		
Orange County Plst Co Inc	C	714 957-1971
3191 Arprt Loop Dr Ste B1 Costa Mesa (92626) *(P-2832)*		
Orange County Produce LLC	D	949 451-0880
11405 Jeffrey Rd Irvine (92602) *(P-105)*		
Orange County Royale Convlscnt	D	949 458-6346
23228 Madero Mission Viejo (92691) *(P-21069)*		
Orange County Royale Convlscnt (PA)	B	714 546-6450
1030 W Warner Ave Santa Ana (92707) *(P-20650)*		
Orange County Sanitation (PA)	B	714 962-2411
10844 Ellis Ave Fountain Valley (92708) *(P-6230)*		
Orange County Sanitation	C	714 962-2411
22212 Brookhurst St Huntington Beach (92646) *(P-6134)*		
Orange County Service Center, San Clemente *Also called San Diego Gas & Electric Co (P-5998)*		
Orange County Services Inc	E	714 541-9753
3022 N Hesperian St Santa Ana (92706) *(P-2219)*		
Orange County Trnsp Auth, Orange *Also called Orange County Trnsp Auth (P-3575)*		
Orange County Trnsp Auth	A	714 560-6282
11790 Cardinal Cir Garden Grove (92843) *(P-3574)*		
Orange County Trnsp Auth (PA)	B	714 636-7433
550 S Main St Orange (92868) *(P-3575)*		
Orange County Trnsp Auth	A	714 999-1726
600 S Main St Ste 910 Orange (92868) *(P-3576)*		
Orange County Water District	C	714 378-3200
18700 Ward St Fountain Valley (92708) *(P-6098)*		
Orange County-Irvine Med Ctr, Irvine *Also called Kaiser Foundation Hospitals (P-11799)*		
Orange Countys Credit Union (PA)	C	714 755-5900
1721 E Saint Andrew Pl Santa Ana (92705) *(P-9332)*		
Orange Courier Inc	B	714 384-3600
3731 W Warner Ave Santa Ana (92704) *(P-16970)*		
Orange Cove Health Center, Orange Cove *Also called United Health Ctrs San Joaquin (P-22151)*		
Orange Health Solutions Inc	D	661 310-9333
28480 Ave Stnford Ste 300 Valencia (91355) *(P-14987)*		
Orange Healthcare & Wellness	C	714 633-3568
920 W La Veta Ave Orange (92868) *(P-20176)*		

Employee Codes: A=Over 500 employees, B=251-500
C=101-250, D=51-100, E=50

2020 Directory of California
Wholesalers and Services Companies

© Mergent Inc. 1-800-342-5647

1373

A
L
P
H
A
B
E
T
I
C

Orange Labs, San Francisco *Also called France Telecom RES & Dev LLC* ***(P-25896)***
Orange Pacific Plumbing Inc..........D.......714 992-4547
801 Panorama Rd Fullerton (92831) ***(P-2220)***
Orange Silicon Valley..........D.......415 243-1500
60 Spear St Ste 1100 San Francisco (94105) ***(P-27159)***
Orangepeople LLC..........D.......949 535-1308
300 Spectrum Center Dr Irvine (92618) ***(P-27296)***
Orangewood Foundation..........D.......714 619-0200
1575 E 17th St Santa Ana (92705) ***(P-23367)***
Orbital Sciences Corporation..........B.......703 406-5000
2401 E El Segundo Blvd # 200 El Segundo (90245) ***(P-25806)***
Orchard - Post Acute Care Ctr..........A.......562 693-7701
12385 Washington Blvd Whittier (90606) ***(P-20177)***
Orchard Holdings Group Inc..........C.......949 502-8300
1 Venture Ste 300 Irvine (92618) ***(P-11331)***
Orchard Horror Film LLC..........E.......212 203-6147
15715 Woodvale Rd Encino (91436) ***(P-17994)***
Orchard Hospital..........C.......530 846-9000
240 Spruce St Gridley (95948) ***(P-21070)***
Orchard Hotel, San Francisco *Also called Orchard International Group* ***(P-12678)***
Orchard International Group (PA)..........D.......415 362-8878
665 Bush St San Francisco (94108) ***(P-12678)***
Orchard Medical Offices, Downey *Also called Kaiser Foundation Hospitals* ***(P-19064)***
Orchard Park, Clovis *Also called Regent Assisted Living Inc* ***(P-24047)***
Orchid MPS..........D.......714 549-9203
3233 W Harvard St Santa Ana (92704) ***(P-6986)***
Orco Block, Stanton *Also called Muth Development Co Inc* ***(P-10624)***
Orcutt Lions Club..........D.......805 937-0158
126 S Broadway St Orcutt (93455) ***(P-24853)***
Ore-Cal Corp (PA)..........D.......213 623-8493
634 Crocker St Los Angeles (90021) ***(P-8377)***
Oregon PCF Bldg Pdts Calif Inc..........D.......916 381-8051
8185 Signal Ct Ste A Sacramento (95824) ***(P-6637)***
Oregon PCF Bldg Pdts Maple Inc..........C.......909 627-4043
2401 E Philadelphia St Ontario (91761) ***(P-6638)***
Oren's Replay, Van Nuys *Also called Factory 2-U Import Export Inc* ***(P-8073)***
Orenda Center..........D.......707 565-7450
1430 Neotomas Ave Santa Rosa (95405) ***(P-22075)***
Orepac Building Products, Sacramento *Also called Oregon PCF Bldg Pdts Calif Inc* ***(P-6637)***
Orepac Millwork Products, Ontario *Also called Oregon PCF Bldg Pdts Maple Inc* ***(P-6638)***
Oreq Corporation..........E.......951 296-5076
42306 Remington Ave Temecula (92590) ***(P-26337)***
Organic Inc..........D.......310 543-4600
390 Amapola Ave Ste 8 Torrance (90501) ***(P-16073)***
Organic Inc (HQ)..........C.......415 581-5300
600 California St Fl 8 San Francisco (94108) ***(P-16074)***
Organic & Sustainable Buty Inc..........E.......310 815-8201
5933 Bowcroft St Los Angeles (90016) ***(P-13353)***
Organic Affinity LLC..........D.......801 870-7433
3980 Hopevale Dr Sherman Oaks (91403) ***(P-7315)***
Organic Holdings Inc..........B.......415 581-5300
600 California St Fl 8 San Francisco (94108) ***(P-13555)***
Organic On, San Francisco *Also called Organic Holdings Inc* ***(P-13555)***
Organic Pastures Dairy Co LLC..........E.......559 846-9732
7221 S Jameson Ave Fresno (93706) ***(P-402)***
Organztion Amrcn Kdaly Edctors..........E.......310 441-3555
10801 National Blvd # 590 Los Angeles (90064) ***(P-24854)***
Orient Fisheries Inc..........D.......323 588-4185
1912 E Vernon Ave Ste 110 Vernon (90058) ***(P-8378)***
Oriental Motor USA Corporation (HQ)..........D.......310 715-3300
570 Alaska Ave Torrance (90503) ***(P-7174)***
Oriental Trading Co, Richmond *Also called Ctc Food International Inc* ***(P-8571)***
Origaudio, Fountain Valley *Also called Forty Four Group LLC* ***(P-13508)***
Origin Systems Inc..........B.......650 628-1500
209 Redwood Shores Pkwy Redwood City (94065) ***(P-14988)***
Original Mowbrays Tree Svc Inc (PA)..........C.......909 383-7009
1845 Bus Ctr Dr Ste 215 San Bernardino (92408) ***(P-942)***
Original Petes Pizza Inc..........E.......916 442-6770
2001 J St Sacramento (95811) ***(P-11829)***
Original Seatbeltbag , The, Santa Ana *Also called Harveys Industries Inc* ***(P-8075)***
Original Sid Blackman Plbg Inc..........D.......760 352-3632
1160 S 2nd St El Centro (92243) ***(P-2221)***
Orinda Convalescent Hospital..........D.......925 254-6500
11 Altarinda Rd Orinda (94563) ***(P-20651)***
Orinda Country Club..........D.......925 254-4313
315 Camino Sobrante Orinda (94563) ***(P-18524)***
Orion - Rand, Simi Valley *Also called Rand Medical Billing Inc* ***(P-25668)***
Orion Construction Corporation..........D.......760 597-9660
2185 La Mirada Dr Vista (92081) ***(P-1897)***
Orion Pictures Corporation..........A.......310 449-3000
245 N Beverly Dr Beverly Hills (90210) ***(P-17644)***
Orion Security, San Jose *Also called Yosh Enterprises Inc* ***(P-16484)***
Oritz Corporation (PA)..........C.......650 692-8000
1555 Old Bayshore Hwy # 400 Burlingame (94010) ***(P-8413)***
Ormat Nevada Inc..........E.......760 353-8200
947 Dogwood Rd Heber (92249) ***(P-6011)***
Ormesa LLC..........D.......760 356-3020
3300 E Evan Hewes Hwy Holtville (92250) ***(P-5870)***
Orohealth Corporation..........A.......530 534-9183
900 Oro Dam Blvd E Oroville (95965) ***(P-19249)***
Orora North America..........D.......760 510-7170
664 N Twin Oaks Valley Rd San Marcos (92069) ***(P-7889)***
Orora North America..........C.......626 284-9524
3201 W Mission Rd Alhambra (91803) ***(P-7890)***
Orora North America..........D.......760 510-7000
664 N Twin Oaks Valley Rd San Marcos (92069) ***(P-7891)***
Orora North America..........C.......714 562-6002
6200 Caballero Blvd Buena Park (90620) ***(P-7892)***
Orora Packaging Solutions (HQ)..........D.......714 562-6000
6600 Valley View St Buena Park (90620) ***(P-7893)***
Orora Packaging Solutions..........D.......714 984-2300
3200 Enterprise St Brea (92821) ***(P-7894)***
Orora Packaging Solutions..........D.......510 487-1211
33463 Western Ave Union City (94587) ***(P-7895)***
Orora Packaging Solutions..........C.......323 832-2000
1640 S Greenwood Ave Montebello (90640) ***(P-7896)***
Orora Packaging Solutions..........C.......714 278-6000
1901 E Rosslynn Ave Fullerton (92831) ***(P-7897)***
Orora Packaging Solutions..........D.......714 773-0124
1911 E Rosslynn Ave Fullerton (92831) ***(P-7898)***
Oroville Hosp Post Acute Ctr, Oroville *Also called 1000 Executive Parkway LLC* ***(P-19703)***
Oroville Hospital, Oroville *Also called Orohealth Corporation* ***(P-19249)***
Oroville Hospital..........D.......530 538-8700
2353 Myers St Ste B Oroville (95966) ***(P-19682)***
Oroville Internal Meds Group..........E.......530 538-3171
2721 Olive Hwy Ste 12 Oroville (95966) ***(P-19250)***
Orrick Hrrington Sutcliffe LLP (PA)..........C.......415 773-5700
405 Howard St San Francisco (94105) ***(P-22737)***
Orrick Hrrington Sutcliffe LLP..........C.......650 614-7400
1000 Marsh Rd Menlo Park (94025) ***(P-22738)***
Orrick Hrrington Sutcliffe LLP..........C.......650 614-7454
1020 Marsh Rd Menlo Park (94025) ***(P-22739)***
Orrick Hrrington Sutcliffe LLP..........C.......213 629-2020
777 S Figueroa St # 3200 Los Angeles (90017) ***(P-22740)***
Orrick Hrrington Sutcliffe LLP..........D.......916 447-9200
400 Capitol Mall Ste 3000 Sacramento (95814) ***(P-22741)***
Ortega Elementary Pto..........D.......650 738-6670
1283 Terra Nova Blvd Pacifica (94044) ***(P-24607)***
Ortega High School, Lake Elsinore *Also called Lake Elsinore Unified Schl Dst* ***(P-23739)***
Orthocad, San Jose *Also called Cadent Inc* ***(P-15564)***
Orthopaedic Hospital (PA)..........C.......213 742-1000
403 W Adams Blvd Los Angeles (90007) ***(P-21071)***
Orthopaedic Inst For Children, Los Angeles *Also called Orthopaedic Hospital* ***(P-21071)***
Orthopedic Consultants (PA)..........E.......818 788-7343
16311 Ventura Blvd # 800 Encino (91436) ***(P-19251)***
Orthopedics Department, Los Angeles *Also called Southern Cal Prmnnte Med Group* ***(P-19421)***
Ortiz Asphalt Paving Inc..........E.......951 966-7060
16588 Farmington St Hesperia (92345) ***(P-1771)***
Ortiz Enterprises Incorporated (PA)..........D.......949 753-1414
6 Cushing Ste 200 Irvine (92618) ***(P-1772)***
Orwick Fresh Foods Inc..........E.......909 985-5604
7940 Cherry Ave Ste 203 Fontana (92336) ***(P-8622)***
Osage Hlthcare Wellness Centre, Inglewood *Also called Centinela Sklld Nrsng & Wllnss* ***(P-19788)***
Osata Enterprises Inc..........D.......888 445-6237
225 S Aviation Blvd El Segundo (90245) ***(P-8140)***
Oscar Valero..........E.......530 668-4342
1685 Jones St Woodland (95776) ***(P-352)***
Oshman Family Jewish Cmnty Ctr..........C.......650 223-8700
3921 Fabian Way Palo Alto (94303) ***(P-23368)***
Oshyn Inc..........D.......213 483-1770
100 W Broadway Ste 330 Long Beach (90802) ***(P-14989)***
OSI, Folsom *Also called Objective Systems Integrators* ***(P-14976)***
OSI Digital Inc..........E.......949 724-8300
2525 Main St Ste 350 Irvine (92614) ***(P-16075)***
OSI Engineering Inc..........C.......408 550-2800
901 Campisi Way Ste 160 Campbell (95008) ***(P-25245)***
OSI Software, San Leandro *Also called Osisoft LLC* ***(P-14990)***
Osisoft LLC (PA)..........B.......510 297-5800
1600 Alvarado St San Leandro (94577) ***(P-14990)***
Osram Opto Semiconductors Inc..........D.......408 588-3800
1150 Kifer Rd Ste 100 Sunnyvale (94086) ***(P-7316)***
Osram Opto Semiconductors Inc (HQ)..........E.......408 962-3736
1150 Kifer Rd Ste 100 Sunnyvale (94086) ***(P-7317)***
Osscim Inc..........E.......714 680-0015
172 E Orangethorpe Ave Placentia (92870) ***(P-3081)***
Ost Crane Service, Ventura *Also called Ost Trucks and Cranes Inc* ***(P-16971)***
Ost Trucks and Cranes Inc..........D.......805 643-9963
2951 N Ventura Ave Ventura (93001) ***(P-16971)***
Ostcs, Covina *Also called Outsource Testing Inc* ***(P-27160)***
Ostendo Technologies Inc (PA)..........D.......760 710-3003
6185 Paseo Del Norte # 200 Carlsbad (92011) ***(P-25807)***
Osterhout Design Group, San Francisco *Also called Osterhout Group Inc* ***(P-16972)***
Osterhout Group Inc..........E.......415 644-4000
200 Brannan St Apt 326 San Francisco (94107) ***(P-16972)***
OTasty Foods Inc..........D.......626 330-1229
160 S Hacienda Blvd City of Industry (91745) ***(P-8293)***
Otay Lakes Road Branch, Chula Vista *Also called Citibank National Association* ***(P-9082)***
Otay Mesa Medical Offices, San Diego *Also called Kaiser Foundation Hospitals* ***(P-11791)***
Otay Water District..........C.......619 670-2222
2554 Swetwater Sprng Blvd Spring Valley (91978) ***(P-6099)***
Otb Acquisition LLC..........C.......520 458-0540
770 S Brea Blvd Ste 227 Brea (92821) ***(P-12679)***
Otis Elevator Company..........E.......323 342-4500
2701 Media Center Dr # 2 Los Angeles (90065) ***(P-7573)***
Otis Elevator Company..........E.......714 758-9593
711 E Ball Rd Ste 200 Anaheim (92805) ***(P-17521)***
Otis Elevator Company..........C.......415 546-0880
444 Spear St Ste 100 San Francisco (94105) ***(P-17522)***
Otis Elevator Intl Inc..........D.......510 874-5129
1358 14th St Oakland (94607) ***(P-3362)***
Otr Global LLC..........E.......415 675-7660
155 Montgomery St Ste 501 San Francisco (94104) ***(P-25936)***
Otto Cap, Ontario *Also called Otto International Inc* ***(P-8042)***
OTTO CONSTRUCTION, Sacramento *Also called John F Otto Inc* ***(P-1513)***

Mergent e-mail: customerrelations@mergent.com 2020 Directory of California (P-0000) Products & Services Section entry number
1374 Wholesalers and Services Companies (PA)=Parent Co (HQ)=Headquarters (DH)=Div Headquarters

Otto International Inc (PA) ....D....909 937-1998
3550 Jurupa St Ste A Ontario (91761) ***(P-8042)***
Otts Asia ....D....562 259-3447
10015 Baring Cross St Los Angeles (90044) ***(P-11944)***
Ouch Systems, West Sacramento *Also called Occupnl Urgnt Care Hlth Syst* ***(P-22288)***
Oum & Co LLP (PA) ....D....415 434-3744
601 California St # 1800 San Francisco (94108) ***(P-25653)***
Our House, Vallejo *Also called Crestwood Behavioral Hlth Inc* ***(P-21405)***
Our Huse Rsdntial Care Ctr Inc ....D....559 674-8670
109 E Central Ave Madera (93638) ***(P-20652)***
Our Lady of Fatima Villa Inc ....D....408 741-2950
20400 Srtoga Los Gatos Rd Saratoga (95070) ***(P-20178)***
Our Lady of Grace P T G ....E....619 466-0055
2766 Navajo Rd El Cajon (92020) ***(P-16973)***
Our Watch ....D....714 622-5852
12832 Valley View St # 211 Garden Grove (92845) ***(P-21832)***
Our Way, Oceanside *Also called E R I T Inc* ***(P-23912)***
Out of Shell LLC ....C....626 401-1923
9658 Remer St South El Monte (91733) ***(P-1373)***
Outcast Agency LLC ....C....415 392-8282
100 Montgomery St # 1202 San Francisco (94104) ***(P-26921)***
Outfront Media Inc ....C....408 457-0111
2635 N 1st St Ste 236 San Jose (95134) ***(P-13608)***
Outfront Media LLC ....D....510 527-3350
1695 Eastshore Hwy Berkeley (94710) ***(P-13609)***
Outlook Amusements Inc ....C....818 433-3800
2900 W Alameda Ave # 400 Burbank (91505) ***(P-16076)***
Outpatient Rehabilitation Svcs, Walnut Creek *Also called John Muir Health* ***(P-20923)***
Outpatnt Eye Srgry Ctr of Dsrt ....E....760 340-3937
72057 Dinah Shore Dr D1 Rancho Mirage (92270) ***(P-19252)***
Outreach & Escort Inc (PA) ....D....408 678-8585
2221 Oakland Rd Ste 200 San Jose (95131) ***(P-23369)***
Outrigger Hotels Hawaii ....D....310 301-2000
4200 Admiralty Way Venice (90292) ***(P-12680)***
Outrigger Hotels Hawaii ....D....323 491-9015
8462 W Sunset Blvd West Hollywood (90069) ***(P-12681)***
Outside Lines Inc ....E....714 637-4747
2150 S Towne Cntre Pl 1 Anaheim (92806) ***(P-745)***
Outsource Testing Inc ....D....909 592-8898
1278 Center Court Dr Covina (91724) ***(P-27160)***
Ovations Fanfare ....D....714 708-1880
88 Fair Dr Costa Mesa (92626) ***(P-26338)***
Over 60 Health Center, Berkeley *Also called Lifelong Medical Care* ***(P-19158)***
Overaa Construction, Richmond *Also called C Overaa & Co* ***(P-1336)***
Overaa Construction, San Pablo *Also called C Overaa & Co* ***(P-1337)***
Overhead Door Corporation ....D....714 680-0600
1617 N Orangethorpe Way Anaheim (92801) ***(P-2954)***
Overland Pacific & Cutler LLC (PA) ....D....800 400-7356
3750 Schaufele Ave # 150 Long Beach (90808) ***(P-16974)***
Overmiller Inc ....D....925 798-2122
195 Mason Cir Concord (94520) ***(P-17523)***
Overseas Service Corporation ....C....858 408-0751
8221 Arjons Dr Ste B2 San Diego (92126) ***(P-27297)***
Overseenet (PA) ....C....213 408-0080
550 S Hope St Ste 200 Los Angeles (90071) ***(P-13556)***
Overton Security Services Inc ....C....510 791-7380
39300 Civic Center Dr # 370 Fremont (94538) ***(P-16372)***
Ovis Llc ....A....805 646-5511
905 Country Club Rd Ojai (93023) ***(P-12682)***
Owen & Company ....D....916 993-2700
1455 Response Rd Ste 260 Sacramento (95815) ***(P-10447)***
Owens & Minor Inc ....D....909 944-2100
5125 Ontario Mills Pkwy Ontario (91764) ***(P-6987)***
Owens & Minor Inc ....D....209 833-4600
18520 Stanford Rd Tracy (95377) ***(P-6988)***
Owens Corning Sales LLC ....B....408 235-1351
960 Central Expy Santa Clara (95050) ***(P-6716)***
Owl Companies (PA) ....A....949 797-2000
2465 Campus Dr Irvine (92612) ***(P-23623)***
Owl Education and Training ....A....949 797-2000
2465 Campus Dr Irvine (92612) ***(P-23624)***
Own LLC ....C....323 602-5500
1041 N Formosa Ave West Hollywood (90046) ***(P-5733)***
Ownit Mortgage Solutions Inc ....B....513 872-6922
4360 Park Terrace Dr # 100 Westlake Village (91361) ***(P-9589)***
Oxford Farms Inc ....E....559 659-3033
901 N St Ste 103 Firebaugh (93622) ***(P-675)***
Oxford Palace Hotel ....D....213 382-7756
745 S Oxford Ave Los Angeles (90005) ***(P-12683)***
Oxford Suites Chico, Chico *Also called Baney Corporation* ***(P-12035)***
Oxgord Incorporated ....C....800 221-0718
16325 S Avalon Blvd Gardena (90248) ***(P-8992)***
Oxnard 2103 East Gonzales Road, Oxnard *Also called Kaiser Foundation Hospitals* ***(P-19088)***
Oxnard 2200 East Gonzales, Oxnard *Also called Kaiser Foundation Hospitals* ***(P-19086)***
Oxnard Beach Hotel LP ....E....805 488-6560
350 E Port Hueneme Rd Port Hueneme (93041) ***(P-12684)***
Oxnard Family Circle Adhc, Oxnard *Also called Family Circle Inc* ***(P-23217)***
Oxnard Manor Healthcare Ctr LP ....D....805 983-0324
1400 W Gonzales Rd Oxnard (93036) ***(P-20179)***
Oxnard Perfrmn Arts & Convtn ....E....805 486-2424
800 Hobson Way Oxnard (93030) ***(P-16975)***
Oxnard Veterans Center, Oxnard *Also called Veterans Health Administration* ***(P-19568)***
OXY USA Inc ....C....661 869-8000
9600 Ming Ave Ste 300 Bakersfield (93311) ***(P-988)***
P & D Consultants Inc (HQ) ....E....714 835-4447
999 W Town And Country Rd Orange (92868) ***(P-25246)***
P & P Agrilabor ....D....831 679-2307
Highway 101 Floretta Rd Chualar (93925) ***(P-14347)***
P & R Paper Supply Co Inc (PA) ....C....909 389-1811
1898 E Colton Ave Redlands (92374) ***(P-7899)***
P A C E, Los Angeles *Also called Pacific Asian Consortm Emplymn* ***(P-23625)***
P A T H, Los Angeles *Also called People Assisting Homeless* ***(P-23383)***
P B C Pavers Inc ....D....714 278-0488
1560 W Lambert Rd Brea (92821) ***(P-2376)***
P B I, Long Beach *Also called Pbi-Birkenwald Market Eqp Inc* ***(P-6929)***
P C A, Livermore *Also called Pen-Cal Administrators Inc* ***(P-26350)***
P C A Farm Management LLC ....A....661 720-2400
1901 S Lexington St Delano (93215) ***(P-676)***
P C I & Associates, San Diego *Also called PCI Collections Inc* ***(P-13692)***
P C M, Foothill Ranch *Also called Professional Community MGT Cal* ***(P-11370)***
P C S, Concord *Also called Patriot Contract Services LLC* ***(P-4586)***
P H B Contracting Inc ....C....760 347-7290
43180 Sunburst St Indio (92201) ***(P-2833)***
P H I, South San Francisco *Also called Peking Handicraft Inc* ***(P-6578)***
P H Ranch Inc ....E....209 358-5111
6335 Oakdale Rd Winton (95388) ***(P-403)***
P H S Management Group (PA) ....E....714 547-7551
721 N Eckhoff St Orange (92868) ***(P-26752)***
P J J Enterprises Inc ....D....619 232-6136
1250 Delevan Dr San Diego (92102) ***(P-14186)***
P J'S Construction Supplies, Fremont *Also called PJs Lumber Inc* ***(P-6645)***
P K B Investments Inc ....C....559 243-1224
745 E Locust Ave Ste 105 Fresno (93720) ***(P-26753)***
P M B, San Diego *Also called Pacific Medical Buildings LP* ***(P-11334)***
P M C A, Burlingame *Also called Provident Mrtg Cpitl Assoc Inc* ***(P-9596)***
P Monterey LP ....D....831 250-6159
47 Via Cimarron Monterey (93940) ***(P-24017)***
P Murphy & Associates Inc ....C....818 841-2002
359 E Magnolia Blvd Ste G Burbank (91502) ***(P-14991)***
P R N Convalescent Hospital ....D....818 352-3158
7912 Topley Ln Sunland (91040) ***(P-20180)***
P R P, Costa Mesa *Also called Profit Recovery Partners LLC* ***(P-27172)***
P U I, Irvine *Also called Projections Unlimited Inc* ***(P-7323)***
P W C, San Dimas *Also called Pacific W Space Cmmnctions Inc* ***(P-1900)***
P& JP Brokerage LLC ....E....310 801-9707
15301 Ventura Blvd Ste P2 Sherman Oaks (91403) ***(P-5014)***
P-Wave Holdings LLC ....A....310 209-3010
10877 Wilshire Blvd Los Angeles (90024) ***(P-11945)***
P.J.'s Rebar, Turlock *Also called PJs Lumber Inc* ***(P-3278)***
P2s Engineering, Long Beach *Also called P2s Inc* ***(P-25247)***
P2s Inc ....C....562 497-2999
5000 E Spring St Ste 800 Long Beach (90815) ***(P-25247)***
P8ge Consulting Inc ....E....310 666-2301
8406 Beverly Blvd Los Angeles (90048) ***(P-27161)***
Paat & Kimmel Development Inc ....D....909 315-8074
600 N Mountain Ave Upland (91786) ***(P-1555)***
Pac West Land Care Inc ....C....760 630-0231
408 Olive Ave Vista (92083) ***(P-883)***
Pac-12 Enteprises LLC ....C....415 580-4200
360 3rd St Ste 300 San Francisco (94107) ***(P-13630)***
Pacbell, San Francisco *Also called Pacific Bell Telephone Company* ***(P-5452)***
Paccar Leasing Corporation ....C....559 268-4344
2892 E Jensen Ave Fresno (93706) ***(P-17178)***
Pace Inc ....D....925 602-0900
2301 Arnold Industrial Wa Concord (94520) ***(P-2834)***
Pace Administrator To Work, Los Angeles *Also called Pacific Asian Consortm Emplymn* ***(P-23370)***
Pace Drywall, Concord *Also called Pace Inc* ***(P-2834)***
Pace Supply Corp (PA) ....D....707 755-2499
6000 State Farm Dr # 200 Rohnert Park (94928) ***(P-7434)***
Pacheco Brothers Gardening Inc (PA) ....D....510 732-6330
20973 Cabot Blvd Hayward (94545) ***(P-746)***
Pachinko World Inc ....C....714 895-7772
5912 Bolsa Ave Ste 108 Huntington Beach (92649) ***(P-18321)***
Pachulski Stang Zehl Jones LLP (PA) ....D....310 277-6910
10100 Santa Monica Blvd # 1100 Los Angeles (90067) ***(P-22742)***
Pacific Airworks Group LLC ....D....909 815-7012
255 S Leland Norton Way San Bernardino (92408) ***(P-25248)***
Pacific American Fish Co Inc (PA) ....B....323 319-1551
5525 S Santa Fe Ave Vernon (90058) ***(P-8379)***
Pacific Aquascape Inc ....D....714 843-5734
17520 Newhope St Ste 120 Fountain Valley (92708) ***(P-3444)***
Pacific Asian Consortm Emplymn ....D....213 989-3228
1055 Wilshire Blvd # 1475 Los Angeles (90017) ***(P-23370)***
Pacific Asian Consortm Emplymn (PA) ....C....213 353-3982
1055 Wilshire Blvd Ste 14 Los Angeles (90017) ***(P-23625)***
Pacific Aviation Corporation ....C....650 821-1190
P.O. Box 250758 San Francisco (94125) ***(P-4783)***
Pacific Aviation Corporation (PA) ....C....310 646-4015
201 Continental Blvd # 220 El Segundo (90245) ***(P-4784)***
Pacific Bay Properties (PA) ....E....949 440-7200
4041 Macarthur Blvd # 500 Newport Beach (92660) ***(P-1169)***
Pacific Beach House LLC (PA) ....D....650 712-0220
4100 Cabrillo Hwy N Half Moon Bay (94019) ***(P-12685)***
Pacific Bell Telephone Company (HQ) ....A....415 542-9000
430 Bush St Fl 3 San Francisco (94108) ***(P-5452)***
Pacific Boring Incorporated ....E....559 864-9444
1985 W Mountain View Ave Caruthers (93609) ***(P-1898)***
Pacific Building Group ....D....858 552-0600
13541 Stoney Creek Rd San Diego (92129) ***(P-2835)***
Pacific Building Group (PA) ....C....858 552-0600
9752 Aspen Creek Ct # 100 San Diego (92126) ***(P-1556)***

ALPHABETIC

Employee Codes: A=Over 500 employees, B=251-500
C=101-250, D=51-100, E=50
2020 Directory of California
Wholesalers and Services Companies
© Mergent Inc. 1-800-342-5647
1375

Pacific Building Maint Inc ...D 805 969-5221
130 Garden St Bldg 2b1 Santa Barbara (93101) ***(P-13997)***
Pacific Cambria Inc ...D 805 927-6114
2905 Burton Dr Cambria (93428) ***(P-12686)***
Pacific Capital Companies LLC ...C 800 583-3015
11620 Wilshire Blvd Los Angeles (90025) ***(P-9509)***
Pacific Care Inc ...D 562 494-6500
1903 Redondo Ave Long Beach (90755) ***(P-21833)***
Pacific Cast Bnkers Bancshares (PA) ...D 415 399-1900
1676 N Calif Blvd Ste 300 Walnut Creek (94596) ***(P-9221)***
Pacific Cast Sightseeing Tours, Anaheim *Also called Coach Usa Inc* ***(P-3772)***
Pacific Centrex Services Inc ...D 818 623-2300
114 E Haley St Ste A Santa Barbara (93101) ***(P-5453)***
Pacific Cheese Co Inc (PA) ...C 510 784-8800
21090 Cabot Blvd Hayward (94545) ***(P-8323)***
Pacific Chemical Dist Corp (HQ) ...D 714 521-7161
6250 Caballero Blvd Buena Park (90620) ***(P-4575)***
Pacific Choice Seafood Company ...B 707 442-2981
1 Commercial St Eureka (95501) ***(P-8380)***
Pacific Cities Management Inc (PA) ...D 916 348-1188
6056 Rutland Dr Ste 1 Carmichael (95608) ***(P-11332)***
Pacific City Hotel LLC ...B 714 698-6100
21080 Pacific Coast Hwy Huntington Beach (92648) ***(P-12687)***
Pacific Civil & Strl Cons LLC ...E 916 421-1000
7415 Greenhaven Dr # 100 Sacramento (95831) ***(P-25249)***
Pacific Clay Products Inc ...C 661 857-1401
14741 Lake St Lake Elsinore (92530) ***(P-6693)***
Pacific Cleaning Service Inc ...E 949 829-8790
3334 Pacific Coast Hwy # 205 Corona Del Mar (92625) ***(P-13998)***
Pacific Clinics ...D 562 949-8455
11721 Telegraph Rd Ste A Santa Fe Springs (90670) ***(P-22076)***
Pacific Clinics Foundation ...D 626 796-3453
855 N Orange Grove Blvd Pasadena (91103) ***(P-23371)***
Pacific Club (PA) ...D 949 955-1123
4110 Macarthur Blvd Newport Beach (92660) ***(P-18525)***
Pacific Coast Bankers Bank ...D 415 399-1900
1676 N Calif Blvd Ste 300 Walnut Creek (94596) ***(P-9222)***
Pacific Coast Care Center, Salinas *Also called Kindred Healthcare Oper LLC* ***(P-20049)***
Pacific Coast Companies Inc ...C 916 631-6500
10600 White Rock Rd # 100 Rancho Cordova (95670) ***(P-16976)***
Pacific Coast Container Inc (PA) ...C 510 346-6100
432 Estudillo Ave Ste 1 San Leandro (94577) ***(P-5131)***
Pacific Coast Drum Company ...D 626 443-3096
2200 Rosemead Blvd 2204 El Monte (91733) ***(P-7646)***
Pacific Coast Equipment Co Inc (PA) ...E 714 630-5957
3839 E Coronado St Anaheim (92807) ***(P-3363)***
Pacific Coast Lacquer, Los Angeles *Also called Berg Lacquer Co* ***(P-8944)***
Pacific Coast Ldscp MGT Inc ...D 925 513-2310
3960 Holway Dr Byron (94514) ***(P-747)***
Pacific Coast Manor, Capitola *Also called Covenant Care LLC* ***(P-19826)***
Pacific Coast Nursery Inc ...D 714 630-4868
2885 E La Cresta Ave Anaheim (92806) ***(P-8912)***
Pacific Coast Produce Inc ...E 805 240-3385
950 Mountain View Ave # 1 Oxnard (93030) ***(P-8505)***
Pacific Coast Producers ...B 209 365-9982
650 S Guild Ave Lodi (95240) ***(P-16977)***
Pacific Coast Services Inc ...A 209 956-2532
3202 W March Ln Ste D Stockton (95219) ***(P-21834)***
Pacific Coast Sightseeing Tour ...C 714 507-1157
2001 S Manchester Ave Anaheim (92802) ***(P-4859)***
Pacific Coast Supply LLC ...D 805 434-4800
626 N Main St Templeton (93465) ***(P-6639)***
Pacific Coast Supply LLC ...C 916 481-2220
4290 Roseville Rd North Highlands (95660) ***(P-6640)***
Pacific Coast Supply LLC (HQ) ...C 916 971-2301
4290 Roseville Rd North Highlands (95660) ***(P-6641)***
Pacific Coast Sweeping, Rancho Santa Margari *Also called Wendt Landscape Services Inc* ***(P-927)***
Pacific Coast Title Company ...D 818 244-5273
200 W Glenoaks Blvd # 100 Glendale (91202) ***(P-11535)***
Pacific Coast Trnsp Svcs Inc ...E 916 266-5300
7500 San Joaquin St Sacramento (95820) ***(P-5132)***
Pacific Coast Truck and Whse (PA) ...E 619 661-5451
692 Anita St Chula Vista (91911) ***(P-6459)***
Pacific Communications Assoc ...E 925 634-1203
761 2nd St Brentwood (94513) ***(P-27162)***
Pacific Compensation Insur Co ...C 818 575-8500
1 Baxter Way Ste 170 Westlake Village (91362) ***(P-10448)***
Pacific Composite Mtls Inc ...E 310 956-5357
9655 Gran Rdge Dr Ste 200 San Diego (92123) ***(P-26754)***
Pacific Concept Laundry, Los Angeles *Also called E & C Fashion Inc* ***(P-16757)***
Pacific Contours Corporation (PA) ...D 714 693-1260
5340 E Hunter Ave Anaheim (92807) ***(P-7698)***
Pacific Couriers, El Monte *Also called Integrated Parcel Network* ***(P-4272)***
Pacific Crossing LLC ...C 949 679-2588
95 Argonaut Ste 100 Aliso Viejo (92656) ***(P-15670)***
Pacific CST Mar Fireman Oilers (PA) ...D 415 362-4592
240 2nd St Fl 2 San Francisco (94105) ***(P-24455)***
Pacific Cycle Inc ...E 909 481-5613
9282 Pittsburgh Ave Rancho Cucamonga (91730) ***(P-4466)***
Pacific Cycle P Finished Goods, Rancho Cucamonga *Also called Pacific Cycle Inc* ***(P-4466)***
Pacific Dental Services LLC (PA) ...B 714 845-8500
17000 Red Hill Ave Irvine (92614) ***(P-19626)***
Pacific Design Directions Inc ...E 714 685-7766
8171 E Kaiser Blvd Anaheim (92808) ***(P-1170)***
Pacific Dining Food Svc MGT, Fremont *Also called Page Front Catering* ***(P-7679)***
Pacific Eagle Holdings Corp ...D 415 398-2473
353 Sacramento St Ste 360 San Francisco (94111) ***(P-10633)***
Pacific Earth Resources (PA) ...D 805 986-8277
305 Hueneme Rd Camarillo (93012) ***(P-269)***
Pacific Eastern Intl Pdts ...D 714 538-3434
12551 Barrett Ln Santa Ana (92705) ***(P-8993)***
Pacific Eastern Intl Pdts I, Santa Ana *Also called Pacific Eastern Intl Pdts* ***(P-8993)***
Pacific Echo Inc ...D 310 539-1822
23540 Telo Ave Torrance (90505) ***(P-7647)***
Pacific Energy Fuels Company ...A 415 973-8200
77 Beale St Ste 100 San Francisco (94105) ***(P-5970)***
Pacific Engineering Builders ...D 650 557-1238
1009 Terra Nova Blvd Pacifica (94044) ***(P-1557)***
Pacific Equities Captl ...D 310 477-5300
1640 S Sepulveda Blvd # 308 Los Angeles (90025) ***(P-10881)***
Pacific Event Productions Inc (PA) ...C 858 458-9908
6989 Corte Santa Fe San Diego (92121) ***(P-13443)***
Pacific Excavation Inc ...D 916 686-2800
9796 Kent St Elk Grove (95624) ***(P-3326)***
Pacific Exteriors, La Habra *Also called Quail Engineering Inc* ***(P-1778)***
Pacific Exteriors Inc ...D 714 265-1998
13911 Enterprise Dr Ste B Garden Grove (92843) ***(P-2836)***
Pacific Eye Associated Inc ...D 415 923-3007
2100 Webster St Ste 214 San Francisco (94115) ***(P-19253)***
Pacific Fire Safety, Pomona *Also called Ferguson Fire Fabrication Inc* ***(P-7426)***
Pacific Foods & Dist Inc ...D 714 547-0787
3431 W Carriage Dr Santa Ana (92704) ***(P-8623)***
Pacific Fresh Sea Food Company (HQ) ...C 916 419-5500
1420 National Dr Sacramento (95834) ***(P-8294)***
Pacific Fresh Seafood Company, Wilmington *Also called Pacific Sea Food Co Inc* ***(P-8382)***
Pacific Frnsic Psychlogy Assoc ...D 925 253-3111
9261 Folsom Blvd Ste 300 Sacramento (95826) ***(P-22077)***
Pacific Gardens, Santa Clara *Also called Community Home Partners LLC* ***(P-20418)***
Pacific Gardens Hlth Care Ctr, Fresno *Also called Covenant Care California LLC* ***(P-19834)***
Pacific Gas and Electric Co ...D 415 973-7000
425 Beck Ave Fairfield (94533) ***(P-5871)***
Pacific Gas and Electric Co ...D 415 972-5654
150 Spear St Ste 1770 San Francisco (94105) ***(P-5872)***
Pacific Gas and Electric Co (HQ) ...A 415 973-7000
77 Beale St San Francisco (94105) ***(P-5873)***
Pacific Gas and Electric Co ...C 916 375-5005
885 Embarcadero Dr West Sacramento (95605) ***(P-5874)***
Pacific Gas and Electric Co ...C 916 923-7007
2730 Gateway Oaks Dr # 220 Sacramento (95833) ***(P-5875)***
Pacific Gas and Electric Co ...D 510 450-5744
4525 Hollis St Oakland (94608) ***(P-5876)***
Pacific Gas and Electric Co ...B 510 784-3253
24300 Clawiter Rd Hayward (94545) ***(P-5971)***
Pacific Gas and Electric Co ...B 650 592-9411
1970 Industrial Way Belmont (94002) ***(P-5877)***
Pacific Gas and Electric Co ...B 925 757-2000
777 Railroad Ave Pittsburg (94565) ***(P-5878)***
Pacific Gas and Electric Co ...B 559 263-7361
650 O St Fresno (93721) ***(P-5879)***
Pacific Gas and Electric Co ...E 707 765-5118
210 Corona Rd Petaluma (94954) ***(P-5880)***
Pacific Gas and Electric Co ...C 530 477-3245
788 Taylorville Rd Grass Valley (95949) ***(P-5881)***
Pacific Gas and Electric Co ...C 800 756-7243
111 Stony Cir Santa Rosa (95401) ***(P-5882)***
Pacific Gas and Electric Co ...C 530 894-4739
460 Rio Lindo Ave Chico (95926) ***(P-5972)***
Pacific Gas and Electric Co ...D 925 676-0948
4690 Evora Rd Concord (94520) ***(P-5883)***
Pacific Gas and Electric Co ...E 530 621-7237
4636 Missouri Flat Rd Placerville (95667) ***(P-5884)***
Pacific Gas and Electric Co ...C 530 532-4093
1567 Huntoon St Oroville (95965) ***(P-5885)***
Pacific Gas and Electric Co ...A 805 506-5280
9 Mi Nw Of Avila Bch Avila Beach (93424) ***(P-5886)***
Pacific Gas and Electric Co ...D 530 389-2202
33995 Alta Bonny Nook Rd Alta (95701) ***(P-5887)***
Pacific Gas and Electric Co ...C 530 365-7672
3600 Meadow View Dr Redding (96002) ***(P-5888)***
Pacific Gas and Electric Co ...E 530 889-3102
12840 Bill Clark Way Auburn (95602) ***(P-5889)***
Pacific Gas and Electric Co ...D 925 674-6305
1850 Gateway Blvd Ste 800 Concord (94520) ***(P-5890)***
Pacific Gas and Electric Co ...C 530 865-4461
810 4th St Orland (95963) ***(P-5891)***
Pacific Gas and Electric Co ...C 209 942-1523
4040 West Ln Stockton (95204) ***(P-5892)***
Pacific Gas and Electric Co ...E 831 648-3231
2311 Garden Rd Monterey (93940) ***(P-5893)***
Pacific Gas and Electric Co ...C 510 770-2025
42105 Boyce Rd Fremont (94538) ***(P-5894)***
Pacific Gas and Electric Co ...D 707 444-0700
1000 King Salmon Ave Eureka (95503) ***(P-5895)***
Pacific Gas and Electric Co ...E 559 855-6112
33755 Old Mill Rd Auberry (93602) ***(P-5896)***
Pacific Gas and Electric Co ...C 650 755-1236
450 Eastmoor Ave Daly City (94015) ***(P-5897)***
Pacific Gas and Electric Co ...E 209 576-6636
1524 N Carpenter Rd Modesto (95351) ***(P-5898)***
Pacific Gas and Electric Co ...D 209 942-1787
3136 Boeing Way 2nd Stockton (95206) ***(P-5899)***
Pacific Gas and Electric Co ...C 916 275-2763
5555 Florin Perkins Rd Sacramento (95826) ***(P-5900)***
Pacific Gas and Electric Co ...C 925 373-2623
3797 1st St Livermore (94551) ***(P-5901)***
Pacific Gas and Electric Co ...B 530 757-5803
316 L St Davis (95616) ***(P-5902)***

Mergent e-mail: customerrelations@mergent.com
1376
2020 Directory of California
Wholesalers and Services Companies
(P-0000) Products & Services Section entry number
(PA)=Parent Co (HQ)=Headquarters (DH)=Div Headquarters

Pacific Gas and Electric Co ....B....415 695-3513
2180 Harrison St San Francisco (94110) ***(P-5903)***
Pacific Gas and Electric Co ....D....408 945-6215
66 Ranch Dr Milpitas (95035) ***(P-5904)***
Pacific Gas and Electric Co ....D....209 295-2651
28570 Tiger Creek Rd Pioneer (95666) ***(P-5905)***
Pacific Gas and Electric Co ....D....661 398-5918
4201 Arrow St Bakersfield (93308) ***(P-5906)***
Pacific Gas and Electric Co ....D....805 434-4418
160 Cow Meadow Pl Templeton (93465) ***(P-5907)***
Pacific Gas Turbine Center LLC ....C....858 877-2910
7007 Consolidated Way San Diego (92121) ***(P-17524)***
Pacific Golf & Country Club ....D....949 498-6604
200 Avenida La Pata San Clemente (92673) ***(P-18526)***
Pacific Grain & Foods LLC (PA) ....C....559 276-2580
4067 W Shaw Ave Ste 116 Fresno (93722) ***(P-8679)***
Pacific Grain and Foods, Fresno *Also called Pacific Grain & Foods LLC* ***(P-8679)***
Pacific Green Landscape Inc (PA) ....C....619 390-1546
8834 Winter Gardens Blvd Lakeside (92040) ***(P-884)***
Pacific Groservice Inc ....B....408 727-4826
567 Cinnabar St San Jose (95110) ***(P-8942)***
Pacific Grove Aslmar Oper Corp ....C....831 372-8016
800 Asilomar Blvd Pacific Grove (93950) ***(P-12688)***
Pacific Grove Cnvalescent Hosp ....D....831 375-2695
200 Lighthouse Ave Pacific Grove (93950) ***(P-20653)***
Pacific Grove Hospital, Riverside *Also called Vista Behavioral Health Inc* ***(P-21446)***
Pacific Growth Equities LLC ....D....415 274-6800
1 Bush St Fl 17 San Francisco (94104) ***(P-9743)***
Pacific Gtwy Wrkfrce Prtnr Inc ....E....562 570-3700
4811 Arprt Plz Dr Ste 200 Long Beach (90815) ***(P-14348)***
Pacific Harbor Line Inc (HQ) ....C....310 834-4594
705 N Henry Ford Ave Wilmington (90744) ***(P-3504)***
Pacific Haven Convalescent HM, Garden Grove *Also called Pacific Haven Convalescent HM* ***(P-20654)***
Pacific Haven Convalescent HM ....D....714 534-1942
12072 Trask Ave Garden Grove (92843) ***(P-20654)***
Pacific Health and Welness, Redondo Beach *Also called NBC Consulting Inc* ***(P-26732)***
Pacific Health Corporation ....B....714 619-7797
3699 Wilshire Blvd # 540 Los Angeles (90010) ***(P-21072)***
Pacific Home Works Inc ....C....310 781-3012
20725 S Wstn Ave Ste 100 Torrance (90501) ***(P-3445)***
Pacific Homecare Services, Stockton *Also called Pacific Coast Services Inc* ***(P-21834)***
Pacific Homes Foundation ....D....818 729-8106
303 N Lennox Glenoaks1000 # 1000 Burbank (91502) ***(P-20655)***
Pacific Hotel Dev Ventr LP ....C....650 347-8260
625 El Camino Real Palo Alto (94301) ***(P-12689)***
Pacific Hotel Management LLC (PA) ....A....650 347-8260
400 S El Camino Real # 200 San Mateo (94402) ***(P-12690)***
Pacific Hotel Management LLC ....C....510 547-7888
1603 Powell St Emeryville (94608) ***(P-12691)***
Pacific Hotel Management LLC ....C....510 262-0700
3150 Garrity Way Richmond (94806) ***(P-12692)***
Pacific Hotel Management LLC ....B....650 328-2800
625 El Camino Real Palo Alto (94301) ***(P-12693)***
Pacific Hotel Management Inc ....C....949 608-1091
4545 Macarthur Blvd Newport Beach (92660) ***(P-12694)***
Pacific Housing Management (PA) ....D....714 508-1777
945 Katella St Laguna Beach (92651) ***(P-11333)***
Pacific Huntington Hotel Corp ....A....626 568-3900
1401 S Oak Knoll Ave Pasadena (91106) ***(P-12695)***
Pacific Hydrotech Corporation ....C....951 943-8803
314 E 3rd St Perris (92570) ***(P-25250)***
Pacific Indemnity Company ....B....213 622-2334
555 S Flower St Ste 300 Los Angeles (90071) ***(P-10449)***
Pacific Inn, The, Seal Beach *Also called Saga Seal Co Ltd* ***(P-12862)***
Pacific Inptient Med Group Inc ....D....415 485-8824
9 Jeffrey Ct Novato (94945) ***(P-19254)***
Pacific Insulation, Commerce *Also called Farwest Insulation Contracting* ***(P-2787)***
Pacific Interior Design, Anaheim *Also called Pacific Design Directions Inc* ***(P-1170)***
Pacific Interior Medicine, San Francisco *Also called Arlene Keller MD* ***(P-18823)***
Pacific International Mktg, Salinas *Also called Pacific Intl Vgetable Mktg Inc* ***(P-8506)***
Pacific Intl Vgetable Mktg Inc (PA) ....D....831 422-3745
740 Airport Blvd Salinas (93901) ***(P-8506)***
Pacific Investment MGT Co LLC (HQ) ....C....949 720-6000
650 Newport Center Dr Newport Beach (92660) ***(P-11737)***
Pacific Labor Services Inc ....E....805 488-4625
5690 Cypress Rd Oxnard (93033) ***(P-13139)***
Pacific Lath & Plaster, Escondido *Also called Master Design Drywall Inc* ***(P-2818)***
Pacific Legal Foundation (PA) ....E....916 419-7111
930 G St Sacramento (95814) ***(P-22743)***
Pacific Leisure Management, San Francisco *Also called Okabe International Inc* ***(P-4857)***
Pacific Life & Annuity Company ....A....949 219-3011
700 Newport Center Dr Newport Beach (92660) ***(P-9885)***
Pacific Lighting Mfr Inc ....D....310 327-7711
2329 E Pacifica Pl Compton (90220) ***(P-7175)***
Pacific Lighting Mfr Inc ....D....310 327-7711
2329 E Pacifica Pl Rancho Dominguez (90220) ***(P-7176)***
Pacific Line Clean-Up Inc ....C....949 348-0245
27601 Forbes Rd Ste 29 Laguna Niguel (92677) ***(P-3446)***
Pacific Lodge Boy's Home, Woodland Hills *Also called Pacific Lodge Youth Services* ***(P-24018)***
Pacific Lodge Youth Services ....C....818 347-1577
4900 Serrania Ave Woodland Hills (91364) ***(P-24018)***
Pacific Logistics Corp (PA) ....C....562 478-4700
7255 Rosemead Blvd Pico Rivera (90660) ***(P-5015)***
Pacific Maritime Group Inc (PA) ....C....619 533-7932
1444 Cesar E Chavez Pkwy San Diego (92113) ***(P-4632)***
Pacific Medical Inc (PA) ....C....800 726-9180
1700 N Chrisman Rd Tracy (95304) ***(P-16978)***
Pacific Medical Buildings LP ....D....858 794-1900
3394 Carmel Mountain Rd # 200 San Diego (92121) ***(P-11334)***
Pacific Mercantile Bank (HQ) ....E....714 438-2500
949 S Coast Dr Ste 300 Costa Mesa (92626) ***(P-9223)***
Pacific Metals Group LLC ....E....909 218-8889
787 S Wanamaker Ave Ontario (91761) ***(P-7085)***
Pacific Metro Electric Inc ....D....209 939-3222
3150 E Fremont St Stockton (95205) ***(P-2575)***
Pacific Metro LLC (PA) ....B....408 201-5000
18715 Madrone Pkwy Morgan Hill (95037) ***(P-8994)***
Pacific Monarch Resorts Inc ....D....949 228-1396
7 Grenada St Laguna Niguel (92677) ***(P-11335)***
Pacific Monarch Resorts Inc (PA) ....D....949 609-2400
4000 Macarthur Blvd # 600 Newport Beach (92660) ***(P-11336)***
Pacific Mortgage Resources, Walnut Creek *Also called Diablo Realty Inc* ***(P-11091)***
Pacific Mutual Distributors, Newport Beach *Also called Pacific Select Distributors* ***(P-9744)***
Pacific Occptnal Medicine Svcs ....E....562 997-2290
2776 Pacific Ave Long Beach (90806) ***(P-21073)***
Pacific Outdoor Living, Sun Valley *Also called Pro Ponds West Inc* ***(P-752)***
Pacific Outdoor Living, Sun Valley *Also called Pacific Pavingstone Inc* ***(P-3194)***
Pacific Palms Healthcare LLC ....D....562 433-6791
1020 Termino Ave Long Beach (90804) ***(P-21835)***
Pacific Paper Converting Inc (PA) ....D....323 888-1330
6023 Bandini Blvd Los Angeles (90040) ***(P-7900)***
Pacific Park, Santa Monica *Also called Santa Monica Amusements LLC* ***(P-18340)***
Pacific Park Management ....C....415 440-4840
1300 Fillmore St San Francisco (94115) ***(P-26339)***
Pacific Parking & Valet LLC ....C....831 646-0426
2555 Garden Rd Monterey (93940) ***(P-6352)***
Pacific Partners MGT Svcs Inc ....D....650 358-5804
1051 E Hillsdale Blvd Foster City (94404) ***(P-26340)***
Pacific Partners MSI, Foster City *Also called Pacific Partners MGT Svcs Inc* ***(P-26340)***
Pacific Parts International, Canoga Park *Also called Richard Huetter Inc* ***(P-6465)***
Pacific Pavingstone Inc ....C....818 244-4000
8309 Tujunga Ave Unit 201 Sun Valley (91352) ***(P-3194)***
Pacific Pharma Inc ....A....714 246-4600
18600 Von Karman Ave Irvine (92612) ***(P-7972)***
Pacific Pioneer Insur Group, Cypress *Also called Pacific Pioneer Insur Group* ***(P-10450)***
Pacific Pioneer Insur Group (PA) ....C....714 228-7888
6363 Katella Ave Cypress (90630) ***(P-10450)***
Pacific Plms Conference Resort, City of Industry *Also called Majestic Industry Hills LLC* ***(P-12572)***
Pacific Plug and Liner, Watsonville *Also called Smith Gardens Inc* ***(P-282)***
Pacific Premier Bank (HQ) ....C....714 431-4000
17901 Von Karman Ave Irvine (92614) ***(P-9224)***
Pacific Premier Bank ....D....213 626-0085
333 S Grand Ave Ste 3560 Los Angeles (90071) ***(P-9225)***
Pacific Process Systems Inc (PA) ....D....661 321-9681
7401 Rosedale Hwy Bakersfield (93308) ***(P-1038)***
Pacific Production Plumbing (PA) ....E....951 509-3100
1584 Pioneer Way El Cajon (92020) ***(P-2222)***
Pacific Program/Design Managem ....D....626 440-2000
100 W Walnut St Pasadena (91124) ***(P-26341)***
Pacific Properties Realty, Hawthorne *Also called Argon Enterprises Inc* ***(P-10919)***
Pacific Protection Services ....D....818 313-9369
22144 Clarendon St # 110 Woodland Hills (91367) ***(P-16373)***
Pacific Pulmonary Services Co, Petaluma *Also called Braden Partners LP A Calif* ***(P-21684)***
Pacific Racing Association ....C....510 559-7300
1100 Eastshore Hwy Albany (94710) ***(P-18087)***
Pacific Rebar Inc ....D....909 984-7199
501 S Oaks Ave Ontario (91762) ***(P-3275)***
Pacific Regional Laboratory SW, Irvine *Also called Ora Pacific Regional Field Off* ***(P-16967)***
Pacific Rehabilitation & Wel ....D....707 443-9767
2211 Harrison Ave Eureka (95501) ***(P-20181)***
Pacific Relocation Consultants, Long Beach *Also called Overland Pacific & Cutler LLC* ***(P-16974)***
Pacific Restoration Group Inc ....E....951 940-6069
325 E Ellis Ave Perris (92570) ***(P-748)***
Pacific Retirement Svcs Inc ....C....530 753-1450
1515 Shasta Dr Ofc Davis (95616) ***(P-24019)***
Pacific Rim Contractors Inc ....D....714 641-7380
1315 E Saint Andrew Pl B Santa Ana (92705) ***(P-2837)***
Pacific Rim Mech Contrs Inc ....D....714 285-2600
1701 E Edinger Ave Ste F2 Santa Ana (92705) ***(P-2223)***
Pacific Rim Mech Contrs Inc (PA) ....B....858 974-6500
7655 Convoy Ct San Diego (92111) ***(P-2224)***
Pacific Rim Realty Group ....E....805 553-9562
740 Lucille Ct Moorpark (93021) ***(P-11337)***
Pacific Rim Resources Srch ....C....714 638-0307
14148 Brookhurst St Garden Grove (92843) ***(P-14349)***
Pacific Sd/Pcfic Arbor Nrsries, Camarillo *Also called Pacific Earth Resources* ***(P-269)***
Pacific Sea Food Co Inc ....D....916 419-5500
1420 National Dr Sacramento (95834) ***(P-8381)***
Pacific Sea Food Co Inc ....E....310 835-4343
605 Flint Ave Wilmington (90744) ***(P-8382)***
Pacific Seafood Sacramento, Sacramento *Also called Pacific Fresh Sea Food Company* ***(P-8294)***
Pacific Secured Equities Inc ....B....916 677-2500
6020 West Oaks Blvd # 100 Rocklin (95765) ***(P-26755)***
Pacific Select Distributors ....D....949 219-3011
700 Newport Center Dr # 4 Newport Beach (92660) ***(P-9744)***
Pacific Service Credit Union (PA) ....D....888 858-6878
3000 Clayton Rd Concord (94519) ***(P-9333)***
Pacific Shores Masonry ....E....951 371-8550
1369 Walker Ln Corona (92879) ***(P-2725)***

Employee Codes: A=Over 500 employees, B=251-500
C=101-250, D=51-100, E=50
2020 Directory of California
Wholesalers and Services Companies
© Mergent Inc. 1-800-342-5647
1377

Pacific Shores Med Group Inc (PA)............D.......562 590-0345
1043 Elm Ave Ste 104 Long Beach (90813) ***(P-19255)***
Pacific Slope Tree Coop Inc............E.......415 663-1300
11201 State Rte One 201 Point Reyes Station (94956) ***(P-943)***
Pacific Snow Valley Resort LLC............D.......909 866-3121
40650 Village Dr Big Bear Lake (92315) ***(P-12696)***
Pacific Southwest, Long Beach *Also called Foss Maritime Company Llc* ***(P-4584)***
Pacific Southwest Cnstr & Eqp............D.......619 445-5190
2308 Shaylene Way Alpine (91901) ***(P-1899)***
Pacific Southwest Instruments, Corona *Also called Pacwest Instrument Labs Inc* ***(P-17525)***
Pacific Spanish Network Inc............D.......619 427-6323
296 H St Ste 300 Chula Vista (91910) ***(P-5560)***
Pacific Specialty Insurance Co............E.......800 303-5000
2200 Geng Rd Ste 200 Palo Alto (94303) ***(P-10451)***
Pacific State Bancorp............D.......209 870-3214
1899 W March Ln Stockton (95207) ***(P-9282)***
Pacific States Industries Inc............C.......707 894-4242
31401 Mccray Rd Cloverdale (95425) ***(P-6642)***
Pacific Steel Group............C.......858 449-7219
2755 S Willow Ave Bloomington (92316) ***(P-7086)***
Pacific Steel Group............D.......707 297-8922
Gilmore Ave Bldg 411 Stockton (95203) ***(P-7087)***
Pacific Sthwest Structures Inc............C.......619 469-2323
7845 Lemon Grove Way A Lemon Grove (91945) ***(P-3195)***
Pacific Strucframe LLC............D.......951 405-8536
1600 Chicago Ave Ste R11 Riverside (92507) ***(P-3082)***
Pacific Structures Inc (PA)............C.......415 970-5434
457 Minna St San Francisco (94103) ***(P-3196)***
Pacific Structures Cnstr Inc............E.......740 480-4133
101 State Pl Ste E Escondido (92029) ***(P-3197)***
Pacific Sttes Envmtl Cntrs Inc............E.......925 803-4333
11555 Dublin Blvd Dublin (94568) ***(P-1558)***
Pacific Suites Hotel, Santa Monica *Also called Windsor Capital Group Inc* ***(P-13100)***
Pacific Sun Labor............D.......760 556-5085
350 G St Brawley (92227) ***(P-637)***
Pacific Supply, Santa Ana *Also called Beacon Sales Acquisition Inc* ***(P-6710)***
Pacific Symphony............D.......714 755-5788
17620 Fitch Ste 100 Irvine (92614) ***(P-17995)***
Pacific Systems Interiors Inc............C.......310 436-6820
190 E Arrow Hwy Ste D San Dimas (91773) ***(P-2838)***
Pacific Tank Lines Inc............D.......951 680-1900
5230 Wilson St Ste A Riverside (92509) ***(P-5968)***
Pacific Telemanagement Svcs, San Ramon *Also called Jaroth Inc* ***(P-2524)***
Pacific Terrace, San Diego *Also called Bartell Hotels* ***(P-12040)***
Pacific Terrace Inn, Coronado *Also called El Cordova Hotel* ***(P-12242)***
Pacific Theaters............D.......818 501-5121
9400 Shirley Ave Northridge (91324) ***(P-17799)***
Pacific Theaters Inc (PA)............C.......310 657-8420
120 N Robertson Blvd Fl 3 Los Angeles (90048) ***(P-17852)***
Pacific Theaters Inc............D.......310 607-0007
831 S Nash St El Segundo (90245) ***(P-17853)***
Pacific Theaters Inc............D.......562 634-1183
4821 Del Amo Blvd Lakewood (90712) ***(P-17854)***
Pacific Theatres Entrmt Corp (HQ)............D.......310 659-9432
120 N Robertson Blvd Fl 3 Los Angeles (90048) ***(P-17855)***
Pacific Thtres Cmmerce Theatre, Commerce *Also called Commerce Center Theatres* ***(P-17829)***
Pacific Towboat & Salvage Co, Long Beach *Also called Foss Maritime Co Inc* ***(P-4630)***
Pacific Towing, Stockton *Also called Covey Auto Express Inc* ***(P-17417)***
Pacific Toxicology Labs............D.......818 598-3110
9348 De Soto Ave Chatsworth (91311) ***(P-26102)***
Pacific Trellis Fruit LLC (PA)............C.......323 859-9600
2301 E 7th St Ste C200 Los Angeles (90023) ***(P-8507)***
Pacific Tugboat Service, San Diego *Also called Pacific Maritime Group Inc* ***(P-4632)***
Pacific Union Club............D.......415 775-1234
1000 California St San Francisco (94108) ***(P-24608)***
Pacific Union Co............D.......415 789-8686
1550 Tiburon Blvd Ste U Belvedere (94920) ***(P-11338)***
Pacific Union Co............D.......415 474-6600
1699 Van Ness Ave San Francisco (94109) ***(P-11339)***
Pacific Union Homes Inc (PA)............D.......925 314-3800
675 Hartz Ave Ste 300 Danville (94526) ***(P-11590)***
Pacific Union Intl Inc............B.......415 461-8686
23 Ross Cmn Ross (94957) ***(P-11340)***
Pacific Union Intl Inc............A.......707 934-2300
135 W Napa St Ste 200 Sonoma (95476) ***(P-9640)***
Pacific Union Intl Inc............B.......510 338-1379
1900 Mountain Blvd # 102 Oakland (94611) ***(P-11341)***
Pacific Union RE Group (HQ)............D.......415 929-7100
1699 Van Ness Ave 2 San Francisco (94109) ***(P-11342)***
Pacific Union Residental Brkg............D.......510 339-6460
1900 Mountain Blvd # 102 Oakland (94611) ***(P-11343)***
Pacific Utlity Instllation Inc............D.......714 970-6430
1585 N Harmony Cir Anaheim (92807) ***(P-2576)***
Pacific Ventures Ltd............C.......626 576-0737
2200 W Valley Blvd Alhambra (91803) ***(P-26342)***
Pacific View Companies, La Mesa *Also called Pvcc Inc* ***(P-10636)***
Pacific Vision Services Inc............D.......909 824-6090
1900 E Washington St Colton (92324) ***(P-19650)***
Pacific W Space Cmmnctions Inc............D.......909 592-4321
900 W Gladstone St San Dimas (91773) ***(P-1900)***
Pacific West Lath & Plaster............E.......916 387-5773
6853 Mccomber St Sacramento (95828) ***(P-2839)***
Pacific West Security Inc............D.......801 748-1034
1587 Schallenberger Rd San Jose (95131) ***(P-16548)***
Pacific West Tree Service, Vista *Also called Pac West Land Care Inc* ***(P-883)***
Pacific Western Bank............B.......858 756-3023
6110 El Tordo Rancho Santa Fe (92067) ***(P-9112)***
Pacific Western Bank............C.......213 430-7000
818 W 7th St Ste 220 Los Angeles (90017) ***(P-9226)***
Pacific Western Bank............E.......310 996-9100
11150 W Olympic Blvd # 100 Los Angeles (90064) ***(P-9227)***
Pacific Western Bank............C.......760 432-1350
900 Canterbury Pl Ste 300 Escondido (92025) ***(P-9228)***
Pacific Western Bank............D.......760 918-2469
5900 La Place Ct Ste 200 Carlsbad (92008) ***(P-9113)***
Pacific Western Bank............D.......619 562-6400
9955 Mission Gorge Rd Santee (92071) ***(P-9229)***
Pacific Western Bank............D.......858 436-3500
12481 High Bluff Dr # 350 San Diego (92130) ***(P-9230)***
Pacific Western Bank............D.......760 432-1100
900 Cantebury Pl Ste 300 Escondido (92025) ***(P-9114)***
Pacific Western Bank............C.......805 688-6644
610 Alamo Pintado Rd Solvang (93463) ***(P-9231)***
Pacific Western Sales (PA)............D.......714 572-6730
2980 Enterprise St Ste A Brea (92821) ***(P-8995)***
Pacific Wine Distributors Inc............D.......626 471-9997
15751 Tapia St Irwindale (91706) ***(P-3924)***
Pacific Ygnacio Corporation............D.......925 939-3275
201 California St Ste 500 San Francisco (94111) ***(P-10882)***
Pacifica Care Center............C.......650 355-5622
385 Esplanade Ave Pacifica (94044) ***(P-20182)***
Pacifica Companies LLC (PA)............D.......619 296-9000
1775 Hancock St Ste 200 San Diego (92110) ***(P-11869)***
Pacifica Consulting Services, Culver City *Also called Servicon Systems Inc* ***(P-26954)***
Pacifica Crossroads, San Ramon *Also called Pacifica Reflections* ***(P-1314)***
Pacifica Hiorange LP............D.......714 556-3838
2720 Hotel Ter Santa Ana (92705) ***(P-12697)***
Pacifica Hospital of Valley, Sun Valley *Also called Pacifica of Valley Corporation* ***(P-21074)***
Pacifica Hosts Inc............C.......310 670-9000
6225 W Century Blvd Los Angeles (90045) ***(P-12698)***
Pacifica Hosts Inc............C.......619 296-9000
700 16th St Sacramento (95814) ***(P-12699)***
Pacifica Hotel & Conference Ce............C.......310 649-1776
6161 W Centinela Ave Culver City (90230) ***(P-12700)***
Pacifica Hotel Company............C.......619 221-8000
1551 Shelter Island Dr San Diego (92106) ***(P-12701)***
Pacifica Hotel Company (HQ)............E.......805 957-0095
39 Argonaut Aliso Viejo (92656) ***(P-11344)***
Pacifica Hotel Company............E.......650 726-9000
2400 Cabrillo Hwy S Half Moon Bay (94019) ***(P-12702)***
Pacifica Katie Avenue LLC............D.......619 296-9000
1775 Hancock St Ste 100 San Diego (92110) ***(P-25937)***
Pacifica Linda Mar Inc............D.......650 359-4800
751 San Pedro Terrace Rd Pacifica (94044) ***(P-20183)***
Pacifica Nursing & Rehab Ctr, Pacifica *Also called Pacifica Care Center* ***(P-20182)***
Pacifica of Valley Corporation............A.......818 767-3310
9449 San Fernando Rd Sun Valley (91352) ***(P-21074)***
Pacifica Reflections............E.......925 275-9800
405 Reflections Cir San Ramon (94583) ***(P-1314)***
Pacifica San Jose LP............C.......619 296-9000
1775 Hancock St Ste 100 San Diego (92110) ***(P-12703)***
Pacifica Services Inc............D.......626 405-0131
106 S Mentor Ave Ste 200 Pasadena (91106) ***(P-25251)***
Pacifica Trucks LLC............D.......310 549-1351
1450 Dominguez St Carson (90810) ***(P-5016)***
Pacificare, Concord *Also called United Behavioral Health* ***(P-10059)***
Pacificare Dental............C.......661 631-8613
3110 W Lake Center Dr Santa Ana (92704) ***(P-10024)***
Pacificare Health Plan Admin (HQ)............B.......714 825-5200
3120 W Lake Center Dr Santa Ana (92704) ***(P-10025)***
Pacificare Health Systems, Huntington Beach *Also called Unitedhealth Group Inc* ***(P-10060)***
Pacificare Health Systems, Cypress *Also called Unitedhealth Group Inc* ***(P-10061)***
Pacificare Health Systems LLC (HQ)............A.......714 952-1121
5995 Plaza Dr Cypress (90630) ***(P-10026)***
Pacificare of California, Cypress *Also called Uhc of California* ***(P-10058)***
Pacificdental Benefits Inc (PA)............C.......925 363-6000
2300 Clayton Rd Ste 1000 Concord (94520) ***(P-10027)***
Paciolan LLC (HQ)............D.......866 722-4652
5291 California Ave # 100 Irvine (92617) ***(P-15469)***
Pacira Cryotech Inc............E.......800 442-0989
46400 Fremont Blvd Fremont (94538) ***(P-27163)***
Pacira Pharmaceuticals Inc............C.......858 625-2424
10578 Science Center Dr San Diego (92121) ***(P-7973)***
Pack & Crate Services Inc............E.......760 737-6893
238 N Quince St Escondido (92025) ***(P-4223)***
Packaging Innovators LLC............D.......925 371-2000
6650 National Dr Livermore (94550) ***(P-7901)***
Packaging Manufacturing Inc............C.......619 498-9199
2475 Pseo De Las Americas San Diego (92154) ***(P-8996)***
Packard Childrens Hlth Aliance............D.......650 497-8000
725 Welch Rd Palo Alto (94304) ***(P-19256)***
Packard Hospitality Group LLC............C.......858 277-4305
9555 Chesapeake Dr # 202 San Diego (92123) ***(P-26343)***
Packard Medical Group Inc............D.......650 724-3637
770 Welch Rd Palo Alto (94304) ***(P-19257)***
Packard Realty Inc............D.......310 649-5151
9901 S La Cienega Blvd Los Angeles (90045) ***(P-12704)***
Packet Design Inc............D.......408 490-1000
1 Almaden Blvd Ste 1150 San Jose (95113) ***(P-14992)***
Packetvideo Corporation (HQ)............D.......858 731-5300
10350 Science Center Dr San Diego (92121) ***(P-14993)***
PacLease, Fresno *Also called Paccar Leasing Corporation* ***(P-17178)***
Paclo, Pico Rivera *Also called Pacific Logistics Corp* ***(P-5015)***
Pacmet Aerospace, Ontario *Also called Pacific Metals Group LLC* ***(P-7085)***
Pactiv LLC............C.......559 251-7351
5370 E Home Ave Fresno (93727) ***(P-8997)***

Pactiv LLC ....D....530 529-3340
1 Diamond Ave Red Bluff (96080) ***(P-8998)***
Pactiv Packaging Inc (HQ) ....D....323 513-9000
3751 Seville Ave Vernon (90058) ***(P-8999)***
Pacwend III Inc ....D....209 577-6690
1308 Kansas Ave Ste 6 Modesto (95351) ***(P-26344)***
Pacwest Instrument Labs Inc ....D....951 737-0790
1721 Railroad St Corona (92880) ***(P-17525)***
Padi Americas Inc ....C....949 858-7234
30151 Tomas Rcho STA Marg (92688) ***(P-24418)***
Padilla Construction Company ....C....714 685-8500
205 W Bristol Ln Orange (92865) ***(P-2840)***
Padilla Farm Labor Inc ....C....559 562-1166
20486 Road 196 Lindsay (93247) ***(P-193)***
Padre Dam Municipal Water Dst (PA) ....D....619 258-4617
9300 Fanita Pkwy Santee (92071) ***(P-6100)***
Padres LP ....A....619 795-5000
100 Park Blvd Petco Park San Diego (92101) ***(P-18074)***
Pae Consulting Engineers Inc ....D....503 226-2921
48 Golden Gate Ave San Francisco (94102) ***(P-25252)***
Pafco, Vernon *Also called Pacific American Fish Co Inc* ***(P-8379)***
Paganini Companies, San Francisco *Also called Paganini Electric Corporation* ***(P-2577)***
Paganini Electric Corporation ....C....415 575-3900
190 Hubbell St Ste 200 San Francisco (94107) ***(P-2577)***
Page Front Catering ....D....408 406-8487
34793 Ardentech Ct Fremont (94555) ***(P-7679)***
Pagerduty Inc (PA) ....C....844 800-3889
600 Townsend St Ste 200e San Francisco (94103) ***(P-15470)***
Paglia & Associates Cnstr ....D....714 982-5151
2790 E Regal Park Dr Anaheim (92806) ***(P-1171)***
Pahc Apartments Inc ....E....650 321-9709
2595 E Byshore Rd Ste 200 Palo Alto (94303) ***(P-10791)***
Pain Management Specialists PC ....E....805 544-7246
1551 Bishop St Ste 230 San Luis Obispo (93401) ***(P-19258)***
Paiute Palace Casino, Bishop *Also called Bishop Paiute Gaming Corp* ***(P-12073)***
Pajaro Valley Prevntn & Studen ....D....831 728-6445
335 E Lake Ave Watsonville (95076) ***(P-23372)***
Pak West Paper & Packaging, Santa Ana *Also called Blower-Dempsay Corporation* ***(P-8952)***
Paklab, Chino *Also called Universal Packg Systems Inc* ***(P-4526)***
Pala Band of Mission Indians ....C....760 207-2603
3478 Sunset Dr Fallbrook (92028) ***(P-17996)***
Pala Casino Spa & Resort ....A....760 510-5100
11154 Highway 76 Pala (92059) ***(P-12705)***
Pala Mesa Limited Partnership ....C....760 728-5881
2001 Old Highway 395 Fallbrook (92028) ***(P-12706)***
Pala Mesa Resort, Fallbrook *Also called Pala Mesa Limited Partnership* ***(P-12706)***
Palace Business Solutions, Santa Cruz *Also called Trowbridge Enterprises* ***(P-7867)***
Palace Entertainment Inc (HQ) ....E....949 261-0404
4590 Macarthur Blvd # 400 Newport Beach (92660) ***(P-18733)***
Palace of The Legion Honor, San Francisco *Also called Corportion of Fine Arts Mseums* ***(P-24257)***
Palace Park, Irvine *Also called Festival Fun Parks LLC* ***(P-18695)***
Palace Sports & Entrmt LLC, Beverly Hills *Also called Pse Holding LLC* ***(P-18075)***
Paladin Eastside Services Inc ....D....323 890-0180
111 S Grfield Ave Ste 101 Montebello (90640) ***(P-24020)***
Paladin Home Care ....E....510 526-2273
555 Pierce St Ste Cml 4 Albany (94706) ***(P-20656)***
Paladin Private Security, Sacramento *Also called Paladin Prtction Spcalists Inc* ***(P-16374)***
Paladin Prtction Spcalists Inc ....C....916 331-3175
320 Commerce Cir Sacramento (95815) ***(P-16374)***
Paladin Realty Partners LLC (PA) ....E....310 914-2410
10880 Wilshire Blvd # 1400 Los Angeles (90024) ***(P-11345)***
Paladin Technologies Inc ....C....858 668-1705
13000 Gregg St Ste B Poway (92064) ***(P-16979)***
Palantir Technologies Inc (PA) ....C....650 815-0200
100 Hamilton Ave Ste 300 Palo Alto (94301) ***(P-14994)***
Palantir Usg Inc (HQ) ....C....650 815-0200
635 Waverley St Palo Alto (94301) ***(P-14995)***
Palcare Inc ....E....650 340-1289
945 California Dr Burlingame (94010) ***(P-23768)***
Palecek Imports Inc (PA) ....D....510 236-7730
601 Parr Blvd Richmond (94801) ***(P-6526)***
Palisades Interactive, Santa Monica *Also called Palisades Media Group Inc* ***(P-13658)***
Palisades Media Group Inc (PA) ....D....310 564-5400
1601 Cloverf Blvd 6000n Santa Monica (90404) ***(P-13658)***
Palisades Optimist Foundation ....D....310 454-4111
15312 Whitfield Ave Pacific Palisades (90272) ***(P-24609)***
Palisades Ranch Inc ....B....323 581-6161
5925 Alcoa Ave Vernon (90058) ***(P-8203)***
Pall Fortebio LLC ....D....650 322-1360
47661 Fremont Blvd Fremont (94538) ***(P-25808)***
Palm Canyon Resort & Spa, Palm Springs *Also called Diamond Resorts LLC* ***(P-12208)***
Palm Desert Community Assn, Palm Desert *Also called Sun City Palm Dsert Cmnty Assn* ***(P-24665)***
Palm Desert Greens Association ....D....760 346-8005
73750 Country Club Dr Palm Desert (92260) ***(P-24610)***
Palm Desert Medical Offices, Palm Desert *Also called Kaiser Foundation Hospitals* ***(P-19090)***
Palm Desert Town Center, Palm Desert *Also called West Ville Palm Desert* ***(P-10671)***
Palm Drive Healthcare District, Sebastopol *Also called County of Sonoma* ***(P-20820)***
Palm Dsert Rcrtl Fclities Corp ....D....760 346-0015
38995 Desert Willow Dr Palm Desert (92260) ***(P-18279)***
Palm Garden Hotel, Thousand Oaks *Also called Ventu Park LLC* ***(P-13061)***
Palm Grdns Rsdntial Care Fclty ....E....530 661-0574
240 Palm Ave Woodland (95695) ***(P-24021)***
Palm Grove Health Care, Torrance *Also called Unified Inv Programs Inc* ***(P-22335)***
Palm Grove Healthcare, Beaumont *Also called David-Kleis II LLC* ***(P-22223)***
Palm Harbor Residency LP ....C....562 595-4551
3501 Cedar Ave Long Beach (90807) ***(P-20657)***
PALM SPRINGS AERIAL TRAMWAY, Palm Springs *Also called Mount San Jacinto Win Pk Auth* ***(P-18725)***
Palm Springs Art Museum Inc ....D....760 322-4800
101 N Museum Dr Palm Springs (92262) ***(P-24280)***
Palm Springs Convention Center, Palm Springs *Also called Smg Holdings Inc* ***(P-26822)***
Palm Springs Disposal Services ....D....760 327-1351
4690 E Mesquite Ave Palm Springs (92264) ***(P-6231)***
Palm Springs Health Care Ctr, Palm Springs *Also called Five Star Quality Care Inc* ***(P-26230)***
Palm Springs Renaissance, Palm Springs *Also called Remington Hotel Corporation* ***(P-12800)***
Palm Sprng Riviera Resorts Spa, Palm Springs *Also called Riviera Reincarnate LLC* ***(P-12833)***
Palm Ter Hlth Care Rhblitation, Laguna Hills *Also called Gate Three Healthcare LLC* ***(P-23936)***
Palm Terrace Care Center, Riverside *Also called T C H P Inc* ***(P-20331)***
Palmcrest Grand Care Ctr Inc ....D....562 595-4551
3501 Cedar Ave Long Beach (90807) ***(P-20184)***
Palmcrest North Convalescent, Long Beach *Also called Palm Harbor Residency LP* ***(P-20657)***
Palmdale Area, Lancaster *Also called Granite Construction Company* ***(P-1718)***
Palmdale Center For Pain MGT ....E....661 267-6876
819 Auto Center Dr Palmdale (93551) ***(P-19259)***
Palmdale Med Mental Hlth Svcs, Santa Clarita *Also called American Health Services LLC* ***(P-18806)***
Palmdale Resort Inc ....E....661 947-8055
38630 5th St W Palmdale (93551) ***(P-12707)***
Palmdale Water District ....D....661 947-4111
2029 E Avenue Q Palmdale (93550) ***(P-6101)***
Palmdale Womans Club ....D....661 266-3008
2141 E Avenue Q Palmdale (93550) ***(P-13444)***
Palmetto Hospitality ....E....650 843-0795
4216 El Camino Real Palo Alto (94306) ***(P-12708)***
Palo Alpo Medical Foudation, Palo Alto *Also called Sutter Health* ***(P-19480)***
Palo Alto Clinic, Palo Alto *Also called Palo Alto Medical Foundation* ***(P-19261)***
Palo Alto Commons ....D....650 320-8626
4075 El Camino Way Palo Alto (94306) ***(P-24022)***
Palo Alto Community Child Care ....D....650 855-9828
890 Escondido Rd Stanford (94305) ***(P-23769)***
Palo Alto Egg and Food Svc Co ....E....510 456-2420
6691 Clark Ave Newark (94560) ***(P-8204)***
Palo Alto Family Y M C A ....E....650 856-9622
3412 Ross Rd Palo Alto (94303) ***(P-24611)***
Palo Alto Food Company, Newark *Also called Palo Alto Egg and Food Svc Co* ***(P-8204)***
Palo Alto Hills Golf An ....D....650 948-1800
3000 Alexis Dr Palo Alto (94304) ***(P-13445)***
Palo Alto Med Fndtion STA Cruz ....A....831 458-5670
2025 Soquel Ave Santa Cruz (95062) ***(P-21075)***
Palo Alto Medical Clinic ....E....650 321-4121
795 El Camino Real Palo Alto (94301) ***(P-19260)***
Palo Alto Medical Foundation (HQ) ....A....650 321-4121
795 El Camino Real Palo Alto (94301) ***(P-19261)***
Palo Alto Medical Foundation ....D....650 254-5200
370 Distel Cir Los Altos (94022) ***(P-19262)***
Palo Alto Medical Foundation ....D....408 730-4390
201 Old San Francisco Rd Sunnyvale (94086) ***(P-19263)***
Palo Alto Medical Foundation ....D....408 524-5900
1085 W El Camino Real Sunnyvale (94087) ***(P-19264)***
Palo Alto Medical Foundation ....E....650 326-8120
795 El Camino Real Palo Alto (94301) ***(P-25809)***
Palo Alto Nursing Center, Palo Alto *Also called Covenant Care California LLC* ***(P-19828)***
Palo Alto Research Center Inc ....C....650 812-4000
3333 Coyote Hill Rd Palo Alto (94304) ***(P-25810)***
Palo Alto VA Medical Center, Palo Alto *Also called Veterans Health Administration* ***(P-19561)***
Palo Alto Vineyard MGT LLC ....D....707 996-7725
50 Adobe Canyon Rd Kenwood (95452) ***(P-638)***
Palo Alto Vterans Inst For RES ....C....650 858-3970
3801 Miran Ave Bldg 101a Palo Alto (94304) ***(P-26016)***
Palo Verde Health Care Dst ....C....760 922-4115
250 N 1st St Blythe (92225) ***(P-21076)***
Palo Verde Hospital, Blythe *Also called Palo Verde Health Care Dst* ***(P-21076)***
Palo Verde Hospital Assn ....C....760 922-4115
250 N 1st St Blythe (92225) ***(P-21077)***
Palo Verde Irrigation District ....D....760 922-3144
180 W 14th Ave Blythe (92225) ***(P-6368)***
Palomar Fmly Cunseling Svc Inc (PA) ....D....760 741-2660
1002 E Grand Ave Escondido (92025) ***(P-23373)***
Palomar Gem & Mineral Club ....D....760 743-0809
2120 Mission Rd Ste 260 Escondido (92029) ***(P-18527)***
Palomar Health ....B....858 675-5360
555 E Valley Pkwy 6 Escondido (92025) ***(P-21078)***
Palomar Health (PA) ....C....442 281-5000
456 E Grand Ave Escondido (92025) ***(P-21079)***
Palomar Health ....A....760 739-3000
2185 Citracado Pkwy Escondido (92029) ***(P-21080)***
Palomar Health ....B....858 613-4000
15615 Pomerado Rd Poway (92064) ***(P-21081)***
Palomar Health Downtown Campus, Escondido *Also called Kaiser Foundation Hospitals* ***(P-19066)***
Palomar Holdings Inc ....D....619 567-5290
7979 Ivanhoe Ave Ste 500 La Jolla (92037) ***(P-10119)***
Palomar Medical Center, Escondido *Also called Palomar Health* ***(P-21079)***
Palomar Medical Center, Escondido *Also called Kaiser Foundation Hospitals* ***(P-20948)***
Palomar Medical Center, Escondido *Also called Palomar Health* ***(P-21080)***

ALPHABETIC

Palomar San Diego, San Diego *Also called Khp II San Diego Hotel LLC* ***(P-12507)***

Palomar Vista Healthcare Ctr, Escondido *Also called Ensign Group Inc* ***(P-19886)***

Palomar Vista Healthcare Ctr, Escondido *Also called West Escondido Healthcare LLC* ***(P-20377)***

Palos Verdes Beach & Athc CLB ... D ... 310 375-8777
389 Paseo Del Mar Palos Verdes Estates (90274) ***(P-18528)***

Palos Verdes Bowl, Torrance *Also called Crenshaw Bowling* ***(P-18031)***

Palp Inc ... C ... 562 599-5841
2230 Lemon Ave Long Beach (90806) ***(P-1773)***

Palumbo Lawyers LLP (PA) ... D ... 949 442-0300
15635 Alton Pkwy Ste 300 Irvine (92618) ***(P-22744)***

Pam's Delivery Svc & Nat Msgnr, Orange *Also called Madden Corporation* ***(P-16904)***

Pama Management Co ... E ... 951 929-0340
123 N Inez St Ste 16 Hemet (92543) ***(P-26345)***

Pamc Ltd (PA) ... A ... 213 624-8411
531 W College St Los Angeles (90012) ***(P-21082)***

Pamc Health Foundation, Los Angeles *Also called Pamc Ltd* ***(P-21082)***

Pamona Valley Physical Therapy, Claremont *Also called Pomona Valley Hospital Med Ctr* ***(P-19686)***

Pamona Vallley Hospital, Pomona *Also called Pomona Valley Hospital Med Ctr* ***(P-21487)***

Pan American Bank Fsb ... B ... 949 224-1917
18191 Von Karman Ave # 300 Irvine (92612) ***(P-9283)***

Pan Pacific Petroleum Co Inc (PA) ... B ... 562 928-0100
9302 Garfield Ave South Gate (90280) ***(P-4108)***

Pan Pacific Petroleum Co Inc ... D ... 661 589-3200
1850 Coffee Rd Bakersfield (93308) ***(P-4109)***

Pan Pacific San Diego, San Diego *Also called Pan Pcfic Htels Rsrts Amer Inc* ***(P-12709)***

Pan Pcfic Htels Rsrts Amer Inc ... B ... 619 239-4500
400 W Broadway San Diego (92101) ***(P-12709)***

Pan-Pacific Mechanical LLC (PA) ... C ... 949 474-9170
18250 Euclid St Fountain Valley (92708) ***(P-2225)***

Pan-Pacific Mechanical LLC ... A ... 650 561-8810
1205 Chrysler Dr Menlo Park (94025) ***(P-2226)***

Pan-Pacific Mechanical LLC ... C ... 858 764-2464
11622 El Camino Real San Diego (92130) ***(P-2227)***

Pan-Pacific Plumbing & Mech, San Diego *Also called Pan-Pacific Mechanical LLC* ***(P-2227)***

Pana-Pacific, Fresno *Also called Brix Group Inc* ***(P-7241)***

Panalpina Inc ... E ... 650 825-3036
400 Oyster Point Blvd # 30 South San Francisco (94080) ***(P-5017)***

Panalpina Inc ... D ... 310 819-4060
19900 S Vermont Ave Ste A Torrance (90502) ***(P-5018)***

Panama-Buena Vista Un Schl Dst ... C ... 661 397-2205
5901 Schirra Ct Bakersfield (93313) ***(P-13999)***

Panama-Buena Vista Un Schl Dst ... D ... 661 831-7879
4200 Ashe Rd Bakersfield (93313) ***(P-4467)***

Panaroma Gardens, Panorama City *Also called Ensign Group Inc* ***(P-19883)***

Panasas Inc (PA) ... D ... 408 215-6800
969 W Maude Ave Sunnyvale (94085) ***(P-14996)***

Panasonic ... C ... 949 581-0661
26160 Enterprise Way Lake Forest (92630) ***(P-7210)***

Panasonic Avionics Corporation ... D ... 949 472-2376
26211 Enterprise Way Lake Forest (92630) ***(P-25253)***

Panasonic Avionics Corporation (HQ) ... B ... 949 672-2000
26200 Enterprise Way Lake Forest (92630) ***(P-25254)***

Panasonic Broadcast TV Systems, Los Angeles *Also called Panasonic Corp North America* ***(P-7211)***

Panasonic Corp North America ... C ... 323 436-3500
3330 Chnga Blvd W Ste 505 Los Angeles (90068) ***(P-7211)***

Panasonic Corp North America ... E ... 619 661-1134
2001 Sanyo Ave San Diego (92154) ***(P-7212)***

Panasonic Corp North America ... D ... 201 348-7000
2033 Gateway Pl Ste 200 San Jose (95110) ***(P-7213)***

Panasonic Corp North America ... C ... 408 861-3900
10900 N Tantau Ave 200 Cupertino (95014) ***(P-25811)***

Panasonic Corp North America ... D ... 619 661-1134
7625 Panasonic Way San Diego (92154) ***(P-7214)***

Panattoni Development Co Inc (PA) ... D ... 916 381-1561
2442 Dupont Dr Irvine (92612) ***(P-11346)***

Panavision Group, Woodland Hills *Also called Panavision Inc* ***(P-14187)***

Panavision Inc (PA) ... B ... 818 316-1000
6101 Variel Ave Woodland Hills (91367) ***(P-14187)***

Pancan, Manhattan Beach *Also called Pancreatic Cancr Actn Netwrk I* ***(P-22293)***

Pancreatic Cancr Actn Netwrk I (PA) ... C ... 310 725-0025
1500 Rosecrans Ave # 200 Manhattan Beach (90266) ***(P-22293)***

Pandol & Sons ... E ... 661 725-3755
401 Road 192 Delano (93215) ***(P-152)***

Pandora Marketing LLC ... D ... 800 705-6856
26970 Aliso Viejo Pkwy # 150 Aliso Viejo (92656) ***(P-26756)***

Pandora Media LLC (HQ) ... C ... 510 451-4100
2100 Franklin St Ste 700 Oakland (94612) ***(P-5561)***

Pangea Corporation ... E ... 949 443-0666
34145 Pacific Coast Hwy Dana Point (92629) ***(P-27298)***

Panoche Water District ... E ... 209 364-6136
52027 W Althea Ave Firebaugh (93622) ***(P-6369)***

Panorama Madows Nursing Ctr LP ... D ... 818 894-5707
14857 Roscoe Blvd Panorama City (91402) ***(P-20185)***

Panorama Park Apts ... D ... 661 325-4047
401 W Columbus St Apt 64 Bakersfield (93301) ***(P-10792)***

Panoramic Doors LLC ... D ... 760 722-1300
3265 Production Ave Ste A Oceanside (92058) ***(P-2955)***

Pantheon Systems Inc (PA) ... D ... 855 927-9387
717 California St San Francisco (94108) ***(P-15796)***

Panzura Inc ... D ... 408 457-8504
695 Campbell Tech Pkwy # 225 Campbell (95008) ***(P-15671)***

Pape Machinery Inc ... D ... 916 922-7181
2850 El Centro Rd Sacramento (95833) ***(P-7482)***

Pape Material Handling Inc ... D ... 510 659-4100
47132 Kato Rd Fremont (94538) ***(P-7574)***

Pape Trucks Inc ... D ... 559 268-4344
2892 E Jensen Ave Fresno (93706) ***(P-17339)***

Pape' Kenworth, Fresno *Also called Pape Trucks Inc* ***(P-17339)***

Paper Company, The, Irvine *Also called Michael Madden Co Inc* ***(P-7885)***

Paper Cutters, Los Angeles *Also called Pacific Paper Converting Inc* ***(P-7900)***

Paper Mart Indus & Ret Packg, Orange *Also called Frick Paper Company* ***(P-7878)***

Papercraft Los Angeles, Cerritos *Also called Bunzl Usa Inc* ***(P-7874)***

Papich Construction Co Inc (PA) ... C ... 805 473-3016
398 Sunrise Ter Arroyo Grande (93420) ***(P-3327)***

Pappas Telecasting Company, Fresno *Also called Kmph Fox 26* ***(P-5621)***

Par Electrical Contractors Inc ... D ... 760 291-1192
525 Corporate Dr Escondido (92029) ***(P-2578)***

Par Electrical Contractors Inc ... D ... 909 854-2880
11276 5th St Ste 100 Rancho Cucamonga (91730) ***(P-2579)***

Par Electrical Contractors Inc ... D ... 707 693-1237
1416 Midway Rd Vacaville (95688) ***(P-2580)***

Par Engineering Inc ... E ... 626 964-8700
17855 Arenth Ave City of Industry (91748) ***(P-2228)***

PAR SERVICES, Culver City *Also called Exceptional Chld Foundation* ***(P-23594)***

Par Services, Los Angeles *Also called Exceptional Chld Foundation* ***(P-23595)***

Para & Palli Inc ... D ... 209 826-0790
931 Idaho Ave Los Banos (93635) ***(P-20186)***

Para Los Ninos ... C ... 213 623-3942
845 E 6th St Los Angeles (90021) ***(P-23770)***

Paracelsus Los Angeles Comm ... C ... 323 267-0477
4081 E Olympic Blvd Los Angeles (90023) ***(P-21083)***

Paradigm Industries Inc ... D ... 310 965-1900
2522 E 37th St Vernon (90058) ***(P-16980)***

Paradigm Information Services ... D ... 858 693-6115
10755 F Scrps Pwy Pkwy424 San Diego (92131) ***(P-27299)***

Paradigm Music LLC (PA) ... D ... 310 288-8000
360 N Crescent Dr Beverly Hills (90210) ***(P-17934)***

Paradigm Staffing Solutions ... E ... 510 663-7860
1970 Broadway Ste 615 Oakland (94612) ***(P-14350)***

Paradise Ambulance Service, Chico *Also called First Responder Ems Inc* ***(P-3673)***

Paradise Building Services ... C ... 909 399-0707
9664 Hermosa Ave Rancho Cucamonga (91730) ***(P-14000)***

Paradise Electric Inc ... D ... 619 449-4141
697 Greenfield Dr El Cajon (92021) ***(P-2581)***

Paradise Lessee Inc ... B ... 858 274-4630
1404 Vacation Rd San Diego (92109) ***(P-12710)***

Paradise Point Resort, San Diego *Also called Westgroup San Diego Associates* ***(P-13087)***

Paradise Point Resort & Spa, San Diego *Also called Paradise Lessee Inc* ***(P-12710)***

Paradise Ridge Fmly Resources, Paradise *Also called Youth For Change* ***(P-23551)***

Paradise Solid Waste, Paradise *Also called USA Waste of California Inc* ***(P-6309)***

PARADISE VALLEY ESTATES, Fairfield *Also called Northern CA Retiredd Ofcrs* ***(P-24006)***

Paradise Valley Hospital ... D ... 619 472-7474
180 Otay Lakes Rd Ste 100 Bonita (91902) ***(P-21084)***

Paradise Vly Hlth Care Ctr Inc ... D ... 619 470-6700
2575 E 8th St National City (91950) ***(P-20187)***

Paragon Coml Bldg Maint Inc ... D ... 916 334-8801
6731 32nd St Ste J North Highlands (95660) ***(P-14001)***

Paragon Health & Rehab CT ... E ... 559 638-3578
1090 E Dinuba Ave Reedley (93654) ***(P-22078)***

Paragon Industries Inc ... D ... 714 778-8453
1235 S State College Blvd Anaheim (92806) ***(P-6694)***

Paragon Partners Ltd (PA) ... D ... 714 379-3376
5660 Katella Ave Ste 100 Cypress (90630) ***(P-27164)***

Paragon Plastics Co Div, Chino *Also called Consolidated Plastics Corp* ***(P-8684)***

Paragon Real Estate Group ... D ... 415 323-4066
350 Rhode Island St San Francisco (94103) ***(P-11347)***

Paragon Services Engineering, San Diego *Also called San Diego Services LLC* ***(P-25296)***

Paragon Textiles Inc ... D ... 310 323-7500
13003 S Figueroa St Los Angeles (90061) ***(P-8106)***

Parallax Capital Partners LLC (PA) ... C ... 949 296-4800
23332 Mill Creek Dr # 155 Laguna Hills (92653) ***(P-11756)***

Parallel Advisors LLC ... D ... 866 627-6984
150 Spear St Ste 950 San Francisco (94105) ***(P-16981)***

Paramount, San Francisco *Also called Third & Mission Associates LLC* ***(P-11481)***

Paramount Citrus, Delano *Also called Wonderful Company LLC* ***(P-196)***

Paramount Citrus Packing Co, Delano *Also called Wonderful Citrus Packing LLC* ***(P-563)***

Paramount Convalescent Hosp, Paramount *Also called Paramunt Cnvalescent Group Inc* ***(P-20658)***

Paramount Equity Mortgage LLC ... C ... 916 290-9999
22 Executive Park Ste 100 Irvine (92614) ***(P-9590)***

Paramount Export Company ... D ... 858 452-8101
5875 Lamas St San Diego (92122) ***(P-8508)***

Paramount Farming, Shafter *Also called Wonderful Orchards LLC* ***(P-181)***

Paramount Pictures, Los Angeles *Also called Paramount Television Service* ***(P-17646)***

Paramount Pictures Corporation (HQ) ... A ... 323 956-5000
5555 Melrose Ave Los Angeles (90038) ***(P-17645)***

Paramount Properties, Beverly Hills *Also called Rodeo Realty Inc* ***(P-11425)***

Paramount Properties, Woodland Hills *Also called Rodeo Realty Inc* ***(P-11428)***

Paramount Properties Encino BR, Encino *Also called Rodeo Realty Inc* ***(P-11423)***

Paramount Studios, Los Angeles *Also called Paramount Pictures Corporation* ***(P-17645)***

Paramount Swap Meet, Paramount *Also called Modern Dev Co A Ltd Partnr* ***(P-16929)***

Paramount Television Service ... A ... 323 956-5000
5555 Melrose Ave Rm 204 Los Angeles (90038) ***(P-17646)***

Paramount Theatre of Arts Inc ... D ... 510 893-2300
2025 Broadway Oakland (94612) ***(P-17856)***

Paramount Trnsp Systems Inc (PA) ... E ... 760 510-7979
1350 Grand Ave San Marcos (92078) ***(P-5019)***

Paramount Farms, Lost Hills *Also called Roll Properties Intl Inc* ***(P-11953)***

Paramunt Cnvalescent Group Inc ... D ... 562 634-6895
8558 Rosecrans Ave Paramount (90723) ***(P-20658)***

Mergent e-mail: customerrelations@mergent.com
1380
2020 Directory of California
Wholesalers and Services Companies
(P-0000) Products & Services Section entry number
(PA)=Parent Co (HQ)=Headquarters (DH)=Div Headquarters

Paramunt Contrs Developers Inc............E.......323 464-7050
6464 W Sunset Blvd # 700 Los Angeles (90028) ***(P-11348)***
Paramunt Madows Nursing Ctr LP............D.......562 531-0990
7039 Alondra Blvd Paramount (90723) ***(P-26346)***
Parasec Incorporated (PA)............D.......916 576-7000
2804 Gateway Oaks Dr # 100 Sacramento (95833) ***(P-22745)***
Parasoft Corporation (PA)............E.......626 256-3680
101 E Huntington Dr Fl 2 Monrovia (91016) ***(P-6880)***
Paratransit Incorporated (PA)............C.......916 429-2009
2501 Florin Rd Sacramento (95822) ***(P-3705)***
Paratransit Incorporated............C.......209 522-2300
3300 Tully Rd Modesto (95350) ***(P-3706)***
Parc, Palo Alto *Also called Palo Alto Research Center Inc* ***(P-25810)***
Parc 55 Hotel, San Francisco *Also called Rp/Kinetic Parc 55 Owner LLC* ***(P-12845)***
Parc Management LLC............A.......925 609-1364
1950 Waterworld Pkwy Concord (94520) ***(P-18734)***
Parc Specialty Contractors............D.......916 992-5405
1400 Vinci Ave Sacramento (95838) ***(P-3447)***
PARCA, Burlingame *Also called Partners Advctes For Rmrkble C* ***(P-23374)***
Parcell Steel Corp (PA)............C.......951 471-3200
26365 Earthmover Cir Corona (92883) ***(P-3276)***
Pardee Homes (HQ)............D.......310 955-3100
177 E Colo Blvd Ste 550 Pasadena (91105) ***(P-11591)***
Pardee Tree Nursery............D.......760 630-5400
30970 Via Puerta Del Sol Oceanside (92057) ***(P-8913)***
Parenthood of Planned............D.......415 821-1282
1650 Valencia St San Francisco (94110) ***(P-24612)***
Parenthood of Planned............D.......707 527-7656
1140 Sonoma Ave Ste 3 Santa Rosa (95405) ***(P-22079)***
Parenthood of Planned (PA)............D.......619 881-4500
1075 Camino Del Rio S # 100 San Diego (92108) ***(P-22080)***
Parenthood of Planned............D.......951 222-3101
12900 Frederick St Ste C Moreno Valley (92553) ***(P-22081)***
Parenthood of Planned............D.......530 351-7100
2935 Bechelli Ln Redding (96002) ***(P-22082)***
Parents Place, Palo Alto *Also called Jewish Family and Chld Svcs* ***(P-23295)***
Parents United, San Jose *Also called Giarretto Institute* ***(P-23242)***
Pareto Networks Inc............C.......877 727-8020
1183 Bordeaux Dr Ste 22 Sunnyvale (94089) ***(P-5454)***
Parexel International Corp............C.......818 254-7076
1560 E Chevy Chase Dr # 140 Glendale (91206) ***(P-25812)***
Paribas Asset Management Inc............D.......415 772-1300
1 Front St Fl 23 San Francisco (94111) ***(P-9415)***
Paris Blues Inc (PA)............D.......310 605-2000
2397 Miguel Miranda Ave Duarte (91010) ***(P-11683)***
Park and Recreation, San Diego *Also called City of San Diego* ***(P-21461)***
Park and Recreation, Folsom *Also called City of Folsom* ***(P-18654)***
Park Central Hotel Fresno, Fresno *Also called Park Inn By Readisson Fresno* ***(P-12738)***
Park Central Ht San Francisco, San Francisco *Also called Viva Soma Lessee Inc* ***(P-26451)***
Park Cleaners Inc (PA)............D.......626 281-5942
419 Mcgroarty St San Gabriel (91776) ***(P-13237)***
Park Cntl Care Rhblitation Ctr............D.......510 797-5300
2100 Parkside Dr Fremont (94536) ***(P-20188)***
Park Disposal Service, Buena Park *Also called Edco Disposal Corporation Inc* ***(P-6199)***
Park Hotels & Resorts Inc............B.......805 564-4333
633 E Cabrillo Blvd Santa Barbara (93103) ***(P-12711)***
Park Hotels & Resorts Inc............D.......408 942-0400
901 E Calaveras Blvd Milpitas (95035) ***(P-12712)***
Park Hotels & Resorts Inc............D.......714 990-6000
900 E Birch St Brea (92821) ***(P-12713)***
Park Hotels & Resorts Inc............B.......619 276-4010
1775 E Mission Bay Dr San Diego (92109) ***(P-12714)***
Park Hotels & Resorts Inc............B.......415 771-1400
333 Ofarrell St San Francisco (94102) ***(P-12715)***
Park Hotels & Resorts Inc............C.......510 635-5000
1 Hegenberger Rd Oakland (94621) ***(P-12716)***
Park Hotels & Resorts Inc............E.......858 450-4569
10950 N Torrey Pines Rd La Jolla (92037) ***(P-12717)***
Park Hotels & Resorts Inc............D.......707 253-9540
1075 California Blvd NAPA (94559) ***(P-12718)***
Park Hotels & Resorts Inc............C.......909 980-3420
700 N Haven Ave Ontario (91764) ***(P-12719)***
Park Hotels & Resorts Inc............C.......626 577-1000
168 S Los Robles Ave Pasadena (91101) ***(P-12720)***
Park Hotels & Resorts Inc............B.......415 392-8000
55 Cyril Magnin St San Francisco (94102) ***(P-12721)***
Park Hotels & Resorts Inc............D.......626 915-3441
1211 E Garvey St Covina (91724) ***(P-12722)***
Park Hotels & Resorts Inc............C.......310 415-3340
9876 Wilshire Blvd Beverly Hills (90210) ***(P-12723)***
Park Hotels & Resorts Inc............C.......530 543-2126
4130 Lake Tahoe Blvd South Lake Tahoe (96150) ***(P-12724)***
Park Hotels & Resorts Inc............C.......650 342-4600
150 Anza Blvd Burlingame (94010) ***(P-12725)***
Park Hotels & Resorts Inc............C.......626 445-8525
211 E Huntington Dr Arcadia (91006) ***(P-12726)***
Park Hotels & Resorts Inc............D.......562 861-1900
8425 Firestone Blvd Downey (90241) ***(P-12727)***
Park Hotels & Resorts Inc............D.......714 739-5600
7762 Beach Blvd Buena Park (90620) ***(P-12728)***
Park Hotels & Resorts Inc............C.......909 980-0400
700 N Haven Ave Ontario (91764) ***(P-12729)***
Park Hotels & Resorts Inc............C.......626 270-2700
225 W Valley Blvd San Gabriel (91776) ***(P-12730)***
Park Hotels & Resorts Inc............C.......949 553-8332
2120 Main St Irvine (92614) ***(P-12731)***
Park Hotels & Resorts Inc............B.......714 540-7000
3050 Bristol St Costa Mesa (92626) ***(P-12732)***
Park Hotels & Resorts Inc............C.......310 410-4000
5711 W Century Blvd Los Angeles (90045) ***(P-12733)***
Park Hotels & Resorts Inc............D.......714 632-1221
3100 E Frontera St Anaheim (92806) ***(P-12734)***
Park Hotels & Resorts Inc............D.......650 589-3400
250 Gateway Blvd South San Francisco (94080) ***(P-12735)***
Park Hotels & Resorts Inc............E.......530 541-6122
901 Ski Run Blvd South Lake Tahoe (96150) ***(P-12736)***
Park Hyatt Aviara, Carlsbad *Also called Aviara Resort Associates* ***(P-12027)***
Park Inn, Anaheim *Also called Badalian Enterprises Inc* ***(P-12033)***
Park Inn By Radisson............D.......559 226-2200
3737 N Blackstone Ave Fresno (93726) ***(P-12737)***
Park Inn By Readisson Fresno............D.......559 226-2200
3737 N Blackstone Ave Fresno (93726) ***(P-12738)***
Park Labrea Management, Los Angeles *Also called Plb Management LLC* ***(P-10799)***
Park Landscape Maint 1-2-3-4, Rcho STA Marg *Also called Park Landscape Maintenance* ***(P-885)***
Park Landscape Maintenance (PA)............B.......949 546-8300
22421 Gilberto Ste A Rcho STA Marg (92688) ***(P-885)***
Park Lane A Classic Residenc, Monterey *Also called Classic Park Lane Partnership* ***(P-10711)***
Park Lane, The, Monterey *Also called P Monterey LP* ***(P-24017)***
Park Maintenance, Torrance *Also called City of Torrance* ***(P-18666)***
Park Manor Suites, San Diego *Also called Gentry Associates LLC* ***(P-12292)***
Park Marino Convalescent Ctr............E.......626 463-4105
2585 E Washington Blvd Pasadena (91107) ***(P-20659)***
Park n Fly Inc............D.......310 417-3566
6351 W Century Blvd Los Angeles (90045) ***(P-17265)***
Park Newport Apartments, Newport Beach *Also called Park Newport Ltd* ***(P-10793)***
Park Newport Ltd (PA)............D.......949 644-1900
1 Park Newport Newport Beach (92660) ***(P-10793)***
Park One Lax, Los Angeles *Also called Park n Fly Inc* ***(P-17265)***
PARK PASEO, Glendale *Also called Cal Southern Presbt Homes* ***(P-10705)***
Park Plaza Hotel............E.......510 635-5300
150 Hegenberger Rd Oakland (94621) ***(P-12739)***
Park Regency Inc............D.......818 363-6116
10146 Balboa Blvd Granada Hills (91344) ***(P-11349)***
Park Shadelands Medical Offs, Walnut Creek *Also called Kaiser Foundation Hospitals* ***(P-20938)***
Park Uniform Rentals, San Gabriel *Also called Park Cleaners Inc* ***(P-13237)***
Park View Gardens, Santa Rosa *Also called Ensign Group Inc* ***(P-19885)***
PARK VISTA AT MORNINGSIDE, Fullerton *Also called Corecare V A Cal Ltd Partnr* ***(P-19815)***
Park West Rescom Inc............C.......949 546-8300
22421 Gilberto Rcho STA Marg (92688) ***(P-886)***
Parkco Building Company............D.......714 444-1441
3190 Airport Loop Dr F Costa Mesa (92626) ***(P-1559)***
Parker Landscape Dev Inc............E.......916 383-4071
6011 Franklin Blvd Sacramento (95824) ***(P-749)***
Parker Milliken Clark OHar............D.......818 784-8087
555 S Flower St Fl 30 Los Angeles (90071) ***(P-22746)***
Parker Stanbury LLP (PA)............D.......619 528-1259
444 S Flower St Ste 1900 Los Angeles (90071) ***(P-22747)***
Parker Station, Woodland Hills *Also called Guarachi Wine Partners Inc* ***(P-8811)***
Parkers Retirement Residence, Fountain Valley *Also called Longwood Management Corp* ***(P-23976)***
Parkhurst Terrace............D.......831 685-0800
100 Parkhurst Cir Aptos (95003) ***(P-1263)***
Parking Company of America............D.......562 862-2118
523 W 6th St Ste 528 Los Angeles (90014) ***(P-17266)***
Parking Concepts Inc............E.......310 208-1611
1036 Broxton Ave Los Angeles (90024) ***(P-17267)***
Parking Concepts Inc............E.......213 746-5764
1801 Georgia St Los Angeles (90015) ***(P-17268)***
Parking Concepts Inc............C.......310 821-1081
14110 Palawan Way Venice (90292) ***(P-17269)***
Parking Concepts Inc............E.......213 623-2661
800 Wilshire Blvd Los Angeles (90017) ***(P-17270)***
Parking Concepts Inc............D.......310 322-5008
12001 Vista Del Mar Playa Del Rey (90293) ***(P-17271)***
Parking Network Inc............C.......213 613-1500
255 S Grand Ave Apt 314 Los Angeles (90012) ***(P-3448)***
Parking Spot, The, Los Angeles *Also called Prg Parking Century LLC* ***(P-17273)***
Parking Spot, The, Los Angeles *Also called Tps Parking Management LLC* ***(P-17277)***
Parkinsons Institute............D.......800 786-2958
2500 Hospital Dr Bldg 10 Mountain View (94040) ***(P-26017)***
Parkmerced Investors LLC............E.......877 243-5544
3711 19th Ave San Francisco (94132) ***(P-14188)***
Parks & Recreation, Commerce *Also called City of Commerce* ***(P-18651)***
Parks & Recreation Dept, Los Angeles *Also called City of Los Angeles* ***(P-24255)***
Parks & Recreation Dept, Spring Valley *Also called County of San Diego* ***(P-23149)***
Parks & Recreation Dept, Los Angeles *Also called City of Los Angeles* ***(P-13146)***
Parks and Recreation Cal Dept............E.......209 763-5121
2000 Camanche Rd Ofc Ione (95640) ***(P-18735)***
Parks and Recreation Cal Dept............D.......310 456-8432
23200 Pacific Coast Hwy Malibu (90265) ***(P-24281)***
Parks Department, Redwood City *Also called County of San Mateo* ***(P-13160)***
Parks Recreation Libraries, Orange *Also called City of Orange* ***(P-18663)***
Parks-Rcreation-Community Svcs, Irvine *Also called City of Irvine* ***(P-18658)***
Parkside Lending LLC............D.......415 771-3700
180 Redwood St Ste 250 San Francisco (94102) ***(P-9745)***
Parkside Special Care Center............D.......619 442-7744
444 W Lexington Ave El Cajon (92020) ***(P-20189)***
PARKTREE COMMUNITY HEALTH CENT, Pomona *Also called Pomona Community Health Center* ***(P-24420)***

Employee Codes: A=Over 500 employees, B=251-500
C=101-250, D=51-100, E=50
2020 Directory of California
Wholesalers and Services Companies
© Mergent Inc. 1-800-342-5647
1381

Parkview Cmnty Hosp Med Ctr.......A.......951 354-7404
3865 Jackson St Riverside (92503) ***(P-21085)***
Parkview Jlian Cnvlescent Hosp.......C.......661 831-9150
1801 Julian Ave Bakersfield (93304) ***(P-20190)***
Parkway Apartments LLC.......E.......925 866-8429
3170 Crow Canyon Pl # 165 San Ramon (94583) ***(P-10794)***
Parkwood Landscape Maint Inc.......D.......818 988-9677
16443 Hart St Van Nuys (91406) ***(P-887)***
Parma Management Co Inc.......E.......858 457-4999
6390 Greenwich Dr Ste 150 San Diego (92122) ***(P-11350)***
Parole Unit Office, Eureka *Also called Correctons Rhbltation Cal Dept* ***(P-23051)***
Parpro Holdings Co Ltd.......C.......619 498-9004
9355 Airway Rd Ste 4 San Diego (92154) ***(P-11684)***
Parron Hall Office Interiors, San Diego *Also called Parron-Hall Corporation* ***(P-6527)***
Parron-Hall Corporation.......D.......858 268-1212
9655 Gran Ridge Dr Ste 10 San Diego (92123) ***(P-6527)***
Parsec Inc.......A.......323 268-5011
4940 Sheila St Commerce (90040) ***(P-5133)***
Parsec Inc.......D.......323 276-3116
750 Lamar St Los Angeles (90031) ***(P-5134)***
Parsons Brnckrhoff Hldings Inc.......D.......916 567-2500
2329 Oakes Dr Ste 200 Sacramento (95833) ***(P-26757)***
Parsons Constructors Inc.......A.......626 440-2000
100 W Walnut St Pasadena (91124) ***(P-26347)***
Parsons Corporation.......C.......714 562-5725
1 Centerpointe Dr Ste 210 La Palma (90623) ***(P-1983)***
Parsons Corporation.......D.......415 490-2400
44 Montgomery St Ste 880 San Francisco (94104) ***(P-1774)***
Parsons Engrg Science Inc (HQ).......B.......626 440-2000
100 W Walnut St Pasadena (91124) ***(P-25255)***
Parsons Government Svcs Inc (HQ).......B.......626 440-2000
100 W Walnut St Pasadena (91124) ***(P-25256)***
Parsons Government Svcs Inc.......D.......925 313-3217
2000 Marina Vista Ave Martinez (94553) ***(P-25257)***
Parsons Government Svcs Inc (HQ).......D.......949 768-8161
25531 Commercentre Dr Lake Forest (92630) ***(P-25258)***
Parsons Government Svcs Inc.......B.......619 685-0085
525 B St Ste 1600 San Diego (92101) ***(P-25259)***
Parsons Group Inc (PA).......D.......805 564-3341
1 N Calle Chavez Ste 200 Santa Barbara (93101) ***(P-10795)***
Parsons Gvrnment Svcs Intl Inc.......B.......626 440-6000
100 W Walnut St Pasadena (91124) ***(P-1560)***
Parsons Project Services Inc.......C.......626 440-4000
100 W Walnut St Pasadena (91124) ***(P-1374)***
Parsons Services Company.......A.......626 440-2000
100 W Walnut St Pasadena (91124) ***(P-25260)***
Parsons Technical Services Inc.......D.......626 440-3998
100 W Walnut St Pasadena (91124) ***(P-25261)***
Parsons Wtr Infrastructure Inc.......A.......626 440-7000
100 W Walnut St Pasadena (91124) ***(P-25262)***
Parthenon Capital LLC.......A.......415 913-3900
4 Embarcadero Ctr # 2500 San Francisco (94111) ***(P-11946)***
Parthenon DCS Holdings LLC.......A.......925 960-4800
4 Embarcadero Ctr San Francisco (94111) ***(P-26348)***
Participant Channel Inc.......D.......310 550-7715
331 Foothill Rd Fl 3 Beverly Hills (90210) ***(P-5642)***
Participant Media LLC (PA).......D.......310 550-5100
331 Foothill Rd Fl 3 Beverly Hills (90210) ***(P-17647)***
Partitions Installation Inc.......D.......562 207-9868
13021 Leffingwell Ave Santa Fe Springs (90670) ***(P-3449)***
Partner Assessment Corporation (PA).......C.......800 419-4923
2154 Torrance Blvd # 200 Torrance (90501) ***(P-25263)***
Partner Engineering & Science, Torrance *Also called Partner Assessment Corporation* ***(P-25263)***
Partner Hero Inc.......E.......888 968-2767
1001 Avenida Pico C260 San Clemente (92673) ***(P-16982)***
Partners Advctes For Rmrkble C.......D.......650 312-0730
800 Airport Blvd Ste 320 Burlingame (94010) ***(P-23374)***
Partners Capital Group Inc (PA).......D.......949 916-3900
201 Sandpointe Ave # 500 Santa Ana (92707) ***(P-16983)***
Partners For Community Access.......D.......510 558-6700
708 Gilman St Berkeley (94710) ***(P-23375)***
Partners In Leadership LLC (HQ).......D.......951 694-5596
27555 Ynez Rd Ste 300 Temecula (92591) ***(P-26758)***
Partners In Leadership Interme (PA).......D.......951 506-6878
27555 Ynez Rd Temecula (92591) ***(P-26759)***
Partners Information Tech Inc (HQ).......D.......714 736-4487
7101 Village Dr Buena Park (90621) ***(P-16077)***
Partners Risk Specialists.......E.......619 326-0840
6136 Mission Gorge Rd # 125 San Diego (92120) ***(P-27165)***
Partnership Health Plan Cal.......B.......707 863-4100
4665 Business Center Dr Fairfield (94534) ***(P-10028)***
Partos Agency LLC.......D.......310 458-7800
247 Windward Ave Venice (90291) ***(P-16984)***
Partos Company, The, Venice *Also called Partos Agency LLC* ***(P-16984)***
Parts.......D.......916 371-3115
2445 Evergreen Ave West Sacramento (95691) ***(P-17179)***
Partschannel Inc.......E.......562 654-3400
8905 Rex Rd Pico Rivera (90660) ***(P-6460)***
Partsearch Technologies Inc.......E.......661 257-7700
25158 Avenue Stanford Santa Clarita (91355) ***(P-7318)***
Party Pantry Garden Room.......E.......714 899-0626
12777 Knott St Garden Grove (92841) ***(P-13446)***
Parwood Preservation LP.......D.......562 531-7880
5441 N Paramount Blvd Long Beach (90805) ***(P-11351)***
Paryroll Department, Redwood City *Also called Verity Health System Cal Inc* ***(P-21358)***
Pasadena Baking Co.......E.......626 796-5093
70 W Pal Meto Ave Pasadena (91105) ***(P-8624)***
Pasadena Billing Associates.......D.......626 795-6596
225 S Lake Ave Ste 535 Pasadena (91101) ***(P-25654)***
Pasadena Center Operating Co.......C.......626 795-9311
300 E Green St Pasadena (91101) ***(P-16985)***
Pasadena Child Dev Assoc Inc.......D.......626 793-7350
620 N Lake Ave Pasadena (91101) ***(P-22083)***
Pasadena Child Development Ass.......D.......626 793-7350
620 N Lake Ave Pasadena (91101) ***(P-23376)***
Pasadena Chld Training Soc.......C.......626 798-0853
2933 El Nido Dr Altadena (91001) ***(P-24023)***
Pasadena Convention Center, Pasadena *Also called Pasadena Center Operating Co* ***(P-16985)***
Pasadena Cyto Pathology Lab.......B.......626 397-8616
100 W Calif Blvd Fl 3 Pasadena (91105) ***(P-21086)***
Pasadena Hospital Assn Ltd.......D.......626 397-3322
716 S Fair Oaks Ave Pasadena (91105) ***(P-20191)***
Pasadena Hotel Dev Ventr LP.......D.......626 449-4000
303 Cordova St Pasadena (91101) ***(P-12740)***
Pasadena Humane Society.......D.......626 792-7151
361 S Raymond Ave Pasadena (91105) ***(P-24855)***
Pasadena Madows Nursing Ctr LP.......D.......626 796-1103
150 Bellefontaine St Pasadena (91105) ***(P-20192)***
Pasadena Model Railroad Club.......D.......323 222-1718
5458 Alhambra Ave Los Angeles (90032) ***(P-18529)***
Pasadena Rbles Acquisition LLC.......D.......626 577-1000
168 S Los Robles Ave Pasadena (91101) ***(P-12741)***
Pasadena Rehabilitation Inst, Pasadena *Also called Algos Inc A Medical Corp* ***(P-21947)***
Pasadena Sport Club, Pasadena *Also called 24 Hour Fitness Usa Inc* ***(P-18096)***
Pasadena Vision, Pasadena *Also called Linden Optometry A Prof Corp* ***(P-19649)***
Pasea Hotel & Spa, Huntington Beach *Also called Pacific City Hotel LLC* ***(P-12687)***
Paseo Vlg Hsing Partners LP.......E.......714 991-9172
1115 N Citron St Anaheim (92801) ***(P-10796)***
Pasha Distribution Svcs LLC.......D.......714 889-2460
3010 Old Ranch Pkwy # 220 Seal Beach (90740) ***(P-5020)***
Pasha Freight, San Rafael *Also called Pasha Group* ***(P-5021)***
Pasha Group (PA).......B.......415 927-6400
4040 Civic Center Dr # 350 San Rafael (94903) ***(P-5021)***
Pasha Group.......C.......310 735-0952
19020 S Dminguez Hills Dr Compton (90220) ***(P-5022)***
Pasha Hawaii Trnspt Lines LLC.......D.......510 271-1400
1425 Maritime St Oakland (94607) ***(P-4588)***
Pasha Hawaii Trnspt Lines LLC (PA).......C.......415 927-6400
4040 Civic Center Dr # 350 San Rafael (94903) ***(P-4594)***
Pasha Stevedoring Terminals LP.......E.......310 233-2006
802 S Fries Ave Wilmington (90744) ***(P-4615)***
Pasha Stevedoring Terminals LP.......E.......415 927-6353
802 S Fries Ave Wilmington (90744) ***(P-4589)***
Paskenta Band Nomlaki Indians.......B.......530 528-3500
2655 Everett Freeman Way Corning (96021) ***(P-12742)***
Paso Robles Hotel, Paso Robles *Also called Paso Robles Inn LLC* ***(P-12743)***
Paso Robles Inn LLC.......D.......805 238-2660
1103 Spring St Paso Robles (93446) ***(P-12743)***
Paso Robles Tank Inc (PA).......D.......805 227-1641
825 26th St Paso Robles (93446) ***(P-3277)***
Passages, Malibu *Also called Grasshopper House LLC* ***(P-23247)***
Passco Companies LLC (PA).......D.......949 442-1000
2050 Main St Ste 650 Irvine (92614) ***(P-11352)***
Passprt Accept Fclty Los Angel.......D.......323 460-4811
1425 N Cherokee Ave Los Angeles (90093) ***(P-16986)***
Pasta Piccinini Inc.......D.......626 798-0841
950 N Fair Oaks Ave Pasadena (91103) ***(P-8625)***
Pasta Shop (PA).......D.......510 250-6005
5655 College Ave Ste 201 Oakland (94618) ***(P-8626)***
Patelco Credit Union.......D.......925 785-9487
310 Hartz Ave Danville (94526) ***(P-9334)***
Patelco Credit Union (PA).......C.......800 358-8228
5050 Hopyard Rd Pleasanton (94588) ***(P-9335)***
Patenaude & Felix A Prof Corp (PA).......D.......858 244-7600
4545 Murphy Canyon Rd # 3 San Diego (92123) ***(P-22748)***
Pater Digintas Inc.......D.......831 624-1875
23795 Holman Hwy Monterey (93940) ***(P-20193)***
Pathfinder Health Inc.......C.......714 636-5649
10051 Lampson Ave Garden Grove (92840) ***(P-21836)***
Pathfinder Services, Folsom *Also called Location Services LLC* ***(P-5124)***
Pathnostics, Irvine *Also called Cap Diagnostics LLC* ***(P-21510)***
Pathpoint.......D.......805 782-8890
11491 Los Osos Valley Rd San Luis Obispo (93405) ***(P-23626)***
Pathstone Family Office LLC.......C.......888 750-7284
1900 Avenue Of The Los Angeles (90067) ***(P-11353)***
Pathstone Federal Street, Los Angeles *Also called Pathstone Family Office LLC* ***(P-11353)***
Pathway Capital Management LP (PA).......D.......949 622-1000
18575 Jamboree Rd Ste 700 Irvine (92612) ***(P-26349)***
Pathway Inc.......D.......909 890-1070
287 W Orange Show Ln San Bernardino (92408) ***(P-23377)***
Pathway Society.......E.......408 244-1834
102 S 11th St San Jose (95112) ***(P-22084)***
Pathway To Choices Inc.......D.......510 724-9044
751 Belmont Way Pinole (94564) ***(P-23378)***
Pathways, Oakland *Also called Hospice & Home Health of E Bay* ***(P-21776)***
Pathways Home Health.......E.......650 634-0133
395 Oyster Point Blvd # 128 South San Francisco (94080) ***(P-22294)***
Pathways La (PA).......E.......213 427-2700
3325 Wilshire Blvd # 1100 Los Angeles (90010) ***(P-23379)***
Patient Business Services, Escondido *Also called Palomar Health* ***(P-21078)***
Patientpop Inc.......D.......844 487-8399
214 Wilshire Blvd Santa Monica (90401) ***(P-15471)***
Patients Hospital.......D.......530 225-8700
2900 Eureka Way Redding (96001) ***(P-21087)***
Patientsafe Solutions Inc (PA).......D.......858 746-3100
9330 Scranton Rd Ste 325 San Diego (92121) ***(P-14997)***

Patina Freight Inc...C...909 444-1025
525 S Lemon Ave Walnut (91789) ***(P-4468)***
Patina Freight Inc...D...310 764-4395
1650 S Central Ave Compton (90220) ***(P-5023)***
Patra Corporation (PA)...C...415 595-9987
1107 Inv Blvd Ste 100 El Dorado Hills (95762) ***(P-9886)***
Patric Communications Inc (PA)...C...619 579-2898
15215 Alton Pkwy Ste 200 Irvine (92618) ***(P-2582)***
Patrick Dean Bryan...D...530 273-5484
12481 Lttle Deer Creek Ln Nevada City (95959) ***(P-3450)***
Patrick Industries Inc...C...909 350-4440
13414 Slover Ave Fontana (92337) ***(P-6695)***
Patrick K Willis Company Inc...B...800 398-6480
5118 Rbert J Mathews Pkwy El Dorado Hills (95762) ***(P-16987)***
Patricks Construction Clean-Up...D...916 452-5495
7851 14th Ave Sacramento (95826) ***(P-1984)***
Patriot Brokerage Inc...D...910 227-4142
7840 Foothill Blvd Ste H Sunland (91040) ***(P-5024)***
Patriot Communications LLC (PA)...D...888 833-4711
3415 S Sepulveda Blvd # 800 Los Angeles (90034) ***(P-27166)***
Patriot Contract Services LLC...B...925 296-2000
1320 Willow Pass Rd # 485 Concord (94520) ***(P-4586)***
Patrol Masters Inc...C...714 426-2526
1651 E 4th St Ste 150 Santa Ana (92701) ***(P-16375)***
Patron Solutions LLC...C...949 823-1700
5171 California Ave # 200 Irvine (92617) ***(P-15472)***
Pattern Energy Group LP (PA)...D...415 283-4000
1088 Sansome St San Francisco (94111) ***(P-5908)***
Pattern Renewables 2 LP (HQ)...C...415 283-4000
1088 Sansome St San Francisco (94111) ***(P-2229)***
Patterson Dental 426, El Segundo *Also called Patterson Dental Supply Inc* ***(P-6989)***
Patterson Dental 454, Roseville *Also called Patterson Dental Supply Inc* ***(P-6990)***
Patterson Dental 590, Dinuba *Also called Patterson Dental Supply Inc* ***(P-6991)***
Patterson Dental Supply Inc...D...310 426-3100
185 S Douglas St Ste 100 El Segundo (90245) ***(P-6989)***
Patterson Dental Supply Inc...D...916 780-5100
1030 Winding Creek Rd # 150 Roseville (95678) ***(P-6990)***
Patterson Dental Supply Inc...D...559 595-1450
800 Monte Vista Dr Dinuba (93618) ***(P-6991)***
Patterson Dental Supply Inc...E...818 435-1368
9200 Oakdale Ave Ste 500 Chatsworth (91311) ***(P-14998)***
Patterson Ritner Lockwood (PA)...D...818 241-8001
620 N Brand Blvd Fl 3 Glendale (91203) ***(P-22749)***
Patton Air Conditioning, Fresno *Also called Patton Sheet Metal Works Inc* ***(P-3083)***
Patton Sales Corp (PA)...C...909 988-0661
1095 E California St Ontario (91761) ***(P-7088)***
Patton Sheet Metal Works Inc...E...559 486-5222
272 N Palm Ave Fresno (93701) ***(P-3083)***
Patton State Hospital, Patton *Also called Califrnia Dept State Hospitals* ***(P-21390)***
Patton's Steel, Ontario *Also called Patton Sales Corp* ***(P-7088)***
Paul Calvo and Company...E...626 814-8000
1619 W Garvey Ave N # 201 West Covina (91790) ***(P-11354)***
Paul Graham Drilling & Svc Co...C...707 374-5123
2500 Airport Rd Rio Vista (94571) ***(P-999)***
Paul Hastings LLP...D...714 668-6200
695 Town Ctr Santa Ana (92704) ***(P-22750)***
Paul Hastings LLP...C...714 668-6200
695 Town Center Dr # 120 Costa Mesa (92626) ***(P-22751)***
Paul Hastings LLP (PA)...C...213 683-6000
515 S Flower St Fl 25 Los Angeles (90071) ***(P-22752)***
Paul Hastings LLP...D...858 458-3000
4747 Executive Dr # 1200 San Diego (92121) ***(P-22753)***
Paul Hastings LLP...C...415 856-7000
101 California St Fl 48 San Francisco (94111) ***(P-22754)***
Paul Hastings LLP...C...650 320-1800
1117 California Ave Palo Alto (94304) ***(P-22755)***
Paul Kagan Associates, Carmel *Also called Kagan Capital Management Inc* ***(P-9828)***
Paul Maurer Company...D...714 231-8241
16081 Warren Ln Huntington Beach (92649) ***(P-18736)***
Paul Maurer Shows, Huntington Beach *Also called Paul Maurer Company* ***(P-18736)***
Paul Mitchell John Systems (PA)...D...310 248-3888
20705 Centre Pointe Pkwy Santa Clarita (91350) ***(P-7974)***
Paul Pietrzyk...E...209 726-5034
1142 Acapulco Ct Merced (95348) ***(P-2841)***
Paul Trucking, Watsonville *Also called Amar Transportation Inc* ***(P-3963)***
Paul Williams Tile Co Inc...D...760 772-7440
77570 Springfield Ln K Palm Desert (92211) ***(P-2904)***
Pauls Drywall, Merced *Also called Paul Pietrzyk* ***(P-2841)***
Paulus Engineering Inc...D...714 632-3322
2871 E Coronado St Anaheim (92806) ***(P-1901)***
Pauma Band of Mission Indians...B...760 742-2177
777 Pauma Reservation Rd Pauma Valley (92061) ***(P-12744)***
Pauma Valley Country Club...D...760 742-1230
15835 Pauma Valley Dr Pauma Valley (92061) ***(P-18530)***
Pave-Tech Inc...E...760 727-8700
2231 La Mirada Dr Vista (92081) ***(P-1775)***
Pavement Recycling Systems Inc (PA)...C...951 682-1091
10240 San Sevaine Way Jurupa Valley (91752) ***(P-7767)***
Pavex Construction Company, Redwood City *Also called Granite Rock Co* ***(P-1728)***
Pavigym America Corp...D...858 414-8624
1902 Wright Pl Fl 2 Carlsbad (92008) ***(P-6577)***
Pavilion Surgery Center LLC...D...714 744-8850
1140 W La Veta Ave Orange (92868) ***(P-19265)***
Pavir, Palo Alto *Also called Palo Alto Vterans Inst For RES* ***(P-26016)***
Pavletich Elc Cmmnications Inc (PA)...D...661 589-9473
6308 Seven Seas Ave Bakersfield (93308) ***(P-2583)***
Paxata Inc...D...650 542-7897
1800 Seaport Blvd 1 Redwood City (94063) ***(P-15473)***
Paychex Inc...D...559 432-1100
9 E River Park Pl E # 210 Fresno (93720) ***(P-25655)***
Paychex Inc...D...858 547-2920
2385 Northside Dr Ste 100 San Diego (92108) ***(P-25656)***
Paychex Inc...E...951 682-6100
1420 Iowa Ave Ste 100 Riverside (92507) ***(P-25657)***
Paychex Inc...D...310 338-7900
300 Crprate Pinte Ste 150 Culver City (90230) ***(P-25658)***
Paychex Benefit Tech Inc...C...800 322-7292
2385 Northside Dr Ste 100 San Diego (92108) ***(P-5455)***
Paycycle Inc...D...866 729-2925
210 Portage Ave Palo Alto (94306) ***(P-5456)***
Paydarfar Industries Inc...D...949 481-3267
26054 Acero Mission Viejo (92691) ***(P-6881)***
Payden and Rygel (PA)...C...213 625-1900
333 S Grand Ave Ste 3200 Los Angeles (90071) ***(P-9837)***
Payless Patio & Rockery, San Jose *Also called County Building Materials Inc* ***(P-6614)***
Paylocity Holding Corporation...B...847 956-4850
2107 Livingston St Oakland (94606) ***(P-15474)***
Payment Processing Inc...C...510 795-2290
8200 Central Ave Newark (94560) ***(P-14999)***
Payne & Fears LLP (PA)...D...949 851-1101
4 Park Plz Ste 1100 Irvine (92614) ***(P-22756)***
Payne Brothers Ranches...D...530 662-2354
13330 County Road 102 Woodland (95776) ***(P-70)***
Payne, E L Company, Los Angeles *Also called E L Payne Heating Company* ***(P-2120)***
Payoff Inc...D...949 430-0630
3200 Park Center Dr # 800 Costa Mesa (92626) ***(P-9471)***
Paypal Inc (HQ)...C...877 981-2163
2211 N 1st St San Jose (95131) ***(P-5457)***
Paypal Holdings Inc (PA)...D...408 967-1000
2211 N 1st St San Jose (95131) ***(P-16988)***
Paypros, Newark *Also called Payment Processing Inc* ***(P-14999)***
Payroll Dept., Chico *Also called Enloe Medical Center* ***(P-18973)***
Paystack Inc...D...415 941-8102
201 Spear St Ste 1100 San Francisco (94105) ***(P-15000)***
Pb Car Movers...D...310 283-2741
5510 W 120th St Hawthorne (90250) ***(P-16989)***
Pbc Companies, Brea *Also called Peterson Bros Contruction Inc* ***(P-3201)***
Pbfy Flexible Packaging, Brea *Also called Pacific Western Sales* ***(P-8995)***
Pbi-Birkenwald Market Eqp Inc (PA)...E...562 595-4785
2667 Gundry Ave Long Beach (90755) ***(P-6929)***
PBM Maintenance Corp...B...818 771-1100
8523 Lankershim Blvd Sun Valley (91352) ***(P-14002)***
Pbms Inc...D...213 386-2552
1909 Wilshire Blvd Los Angeles (90057) ***(P-14003)***
Pbp Hotel LLC...D...619 881-6900
1515 Hotel Cir S San Diego (92108) ***(P-11592)***
PBR Twin Peaks, Woodland Hills *Also called Nmms Twin Peaks LLC* ***(P-11315)***
Pbs Paymaster Sales & Service, Santa Rosa *Also called Protective Business & Health* ***(P-15802)***
Pbs Socal, Costa Mesa *Also called Koce-TV Foundation* ***(P-5623)***
PC Mechanical Inc...E...805 925-2888
2803 Industrial Pkwy Santa Maria (93455) ***(P-1039)***
PCA, Los Angeles *Also called Beres Consulting* ***(P-24324)***
Pcamp, Los Angeles *Also called Parking Company of America* ***(P-17266)***
PCC Northwest, San Leandro *Also called Pacific Coast Container Inc* ***(P-5131)***
Pcg Technology Consulting, Sacramento *Also called Public Consulting Group Inc* ***(P-26777)***
Pcha, Palo Alto *Also called Packard Childrens Hlth Aliance* ***(P-19256)***
PCI, San Diego *Also called Project Concern International* ***(P-24356)***
PCI Collections Inc...B...619 595-3114
402 W Broadway Fl 4 San Diego (92101) ***(P-13692)***
PCL Construction Services Inc...C...818 246-3481
500 N Brand Blvd Ste 1500 Glendale (91203) ***(P-1561)***
PCL Construction Services Inc...C...818 509-7816
100 Universal City Plz North Hollywood (91608) ***(P-1562)***
PCL Industrial Services Inc...B...661 832-3995
1500 S Union Ave Bakersfield (93307) ***(P-1563)***
Pcm, Laguna Woods *Also called Professional Community MGT Cal* ***(P-11372)***
Pcm, Foothill Ranch *Also called Professional Community MGT Cal* ***(P-10858)***
Pcm Sales Inc (HQ)...C...310 354-5600
1940 E Mariposa Ave El Segundo (90245) ***(P-6882)***
Pcs Mobile Solutions LLC...D...323 567-2490
3534 Tweedy Blvd South Gate (90280) ***(P-5458)***
Pcs Property Managment LLC...C...310 231-1000
11859 Wilshire Blvd # 600 Los Angeles (90025) ***(P-11355)***
Pcs1, Santa Barbara *Also called Pacific Centrex Services Inc* ***(P-5453)***
Pcv Murcor Real Estate Svcs, Pomona *Also called Murcor Inc* ***(P-11308)***
Pcwc, Ontario *Also called Chino-Pacific Warehouse Corp* ***(P-4386)***
Pd Liquidation Inc...C...818 772-0100
21350 Lassen St Chatsworth (91311) ***(P-9000)***
PDC Capital Group LLC...D...866 500-8550
250 Fischer Ave Costa Mesa (92626) ***(P-11593)***
Pdf Solutions Inc (PA)...D...408 280-7900
2858 De La Cruz Blvd Santa Clara (95050) ***(P-15001)***
PDM Steel Service Centers...D...408 988-3000
3500 Bassett St Santa Clara (95054) ***(P-7089)***
PDM Steel Service Centers...E...559 442-1410
4005 E Church Ave Fresno (93725) ***(P-7090)***
PDM Steel Service Centers...D...209 234-0548
936 Performance Dr Stockton (95206) ***(P-7091)***
PDQ Automatic Transm Parts Inc...D...916 681-7701
8380 Tiogawoods Dr Sacramento (95828) ***(P-17321)***
PDQ Enterprises Inc...D...818 504-4900
11037 Penrose Ave Los Angeles (91331) ***(P-14189)***
Pdrfc, Palm Desert *Also called Palm Dsert Rcrtl Fclities Corp* ***(P-18279)***
Pds, Irvine *Also called Pacific Dental Services LLC* ***(P-19626)***

ALPHABETIC

Employee Codes: A=Over 500 employees, B=251-500
C=101-250, D=51-100, E=50
2020 Directory of California
Wholesalers and Services Companies
© Mergent Inc. 1-800-342-5647
1383

Pds Tech Inc......A......408 916-4848
1798 Tech Dr Ste 130 San Jose (95110) ***(P-14351)***
Pds Tech Inc......D......214 647-9600
3100 S Harbor Blvd # 135 Santa Ana (92704) ***(P-14352)***
Peace Action West (PA)......E......510 830-3600
2201 Broadway Ste 321 Oakland (94612) ***(P-24780)***
Peace Keepers Private Security......D......925 978-4140
2734b Delta Fair Blvd Antioch (94509) ***(P-16376)***
Peaceful Hearts Home Care Inc......D......951 541-9343
387 Magnolia Ave Ste 103 Corona (92879) ***(P-21837)***
Peach Inc......C......323 654-2333
1311 N Highland Ave Los Angeles (90028) ***(P-4277)***
Peach Love California, Vernon *Also called Incremento Inc* ***(P-8078)***
Peach Tree Healthcare......D......530 749-3242
5730 Packard Ave Ste 500 Marysville (95901) ***(P-19266)***
Peachwood Medical Group Clovis......D......559 324-6200
275 W Herndon Ave Clovis (93612) ***(P-19267)***
Peacock Gap Golf & Country CLB, San Rafael *Also called Knight-Calabasas LLC* ***(P-18474)***
Peacock Stes Resort Ltd Partnr......D......714 535-8255
1745 S Anaheim Blvd Anaheim (92805) ***(P-12745)***
Pearce Industries Inc......D......661 695-3420
6558 Meany Ave Bakersfield (93308) ***(P-7483)***
Pearce Services LLC (HQ)......E......805 237-7480
3720 La Cruz Way Paso Robles (93446) ***(P-1902)***
Pearl Crop Inc (PA)......D......209 808-7575
1550 Industrial Dr Stockton (95206) ***(P-527)***
Pearlman Borska & Wax LLP (PA)......D......818 501-4343
15910 Ventura Blvd Fl 18 Encino (91436) ***(P-22757)***
Pearson Realty (PA)......D......559 432-6200
7480 N Palm Ave Ste 101 Fresno (93711) ***(P-11356)***
Pebble Beach Company, Pebble Beach *Also called I Cypress Company* ***(P-12452)***
Pechanga Development Corp......A......951 695-4655
45000 Pechanga Pkwy Temecula (92592) ***(P-12746)***
Pechanga Resort & Casino, Temecula *Also called Pechanga Development Corp* ***(P-12746)***
Peci, San Francisco *Also called Clearesult Consulting Inc* ***(P-27033)***
Peck & Hiller Company......D......707 258-8800
870 Napa Vally Corp Way NAPA (94558) ***(P-3198)***
Pecs, Rancho Cucamonga *Also called Professnal Elec Cnstr Svcs Inc* ***(P-2593)***
Pedestal Capital II LLC......D......562 863-5555
13111 Sycamore Dr Norwalk (90650) ***(P-11947)***
Pedi Center, Bakersfield *Also called Dignity Health* ***(P-20854)***
Pediatric & Family Medical Ctr......C......213 342-3325
1530 S Olive St Los Angeles (90015) ***(P-22085)***
Pediatric Cancer Research, Orange *Also called Childrens Healthcare Cal* ***(P-18894)***
Pediatric Physical Rehab Clnc......E......559 353-6130
9300 Valley Childrens Pl Madera (93636) ***(P-22086)***
Pediatric Therapy Network......D......310 328-0276
1815 W 213th St Ste 100 Torrance (90501) ***(P-22087)***
Peed Equipment Company......E......951 657-0900
43466 Business Park Dr Temecula (92590) ***(P-14109)***
Peekay Investments Prpts LLC......E......714 403-1923
901 N China Lake Blvd Ridgecrest (93555) ***(P-12747)***
Peerless Building Maint Co, Chatsworth *Also called Tuttle Family Enterprises Inc* ***(P-14068)***
Peerless Building Maint Inc......D......530 222-6369
4665 Mountain Lakes Blvd Redding (96003) ***(P-14004)***
Peerless Maintenance Service......B......714 871-3380
1100 S Euclid St La Habra (90631) ***(P-14005)***
Peeters Transportation Co......E......800 356-5877
451 Eccles Ave South San Francisco (94080) ***(P-4110)***
Peeters/Mayflower, South San Francisco *Also called Peeters Transportation Co* ***(P-4110)***
Pegasus Building Svcs Co Inc......C......858 444-2290
7966 Arjons Dr Ste A San Diego (92126) ***(P-14006)***
Pegasus Building Svcs Co Inc (PA)......C......858 444-2290
7966 Arjons Dr Ste A San Diego (92126) ***(P-14007)***
Pegasus Home Health Care A CA......D......818 551-1932
132 N Artsakh St Glendale (91206) ***(P-21838)***
Pegasus Home Health Services, Glendale *Also called Pegasus Home Health Care A CA* ***(P-21838)***
Pegasus Maritime Inc......D......714 728-8565
535 N Brand Blvd Ste 400 Glendale (91203) ***(P-5025)***
Pegasus Risk Management Inc (PA)......D......209 574-2800
642 Galaxy Way Modesto (95356) ***(P-10452)***
Pegasus Squire Inc......D......866 208-6837
12021 Wilshire Blvd Ste 7 Los Angeles (90025) ***(P-16078)***
Peggs Company Inc (PA)......D......253 584-9548
4851 Felspar St Riverside (92509) ***(P-17526)***
Peking Handicraft Inc (PA)......C......650 871-3788
1388 San Mateo Ave South San Francisco (94080) ***(P-6578)***
Pelco By Schneider Electric, Chino *Also called Schneider Electric Usa Inc* ***(P-4500)***
Pelomar Family YMCA, Escondido *Also called YMCA of San Diego County* ***(P-24708)***
Peltzer Groves......E......559 804-0661
34286 Road 188 Woodlake (93286) ***(P-194)***
Pemer Packing Co Inc......A......831 758-8586
20260 Spence Rd Salinas (93908) ***(P-14353)***
Pen-Cal Administrators Inc......D......925 251-3400
7633 Suthfront Rd Ste 120 Livermore (94551) ***(P-26350)***
Pena Grading & Demolition Inc......E......818 768-5202
11253 Vinedale St Sun Valley (91352) ***(P-1776)***
Pena Trucking, Sun Valley *Also called Pena Grading & Demolition Inc* ***(P-1776)***
Pena's Recycling Center, Cutler *Also called Penas Disposal Inc* ***(P-6232)***
Penas Disposal Inc......D......559 528-3909
12094 Avenue 408 Cutler (93615) ***(P-6232)***
Penguin Computing Inc (HQ)......D......415 954-2800
45800 Northport Loop W Fremont (94538) ***(P-6883)***
Penhall Company......D......510 357-8810
13750 Catalina St San Leandro (94577) ***(P-3199)***
Penhall San Leandro 153, San Leandro *Also called Penhall Company* ***(P-3199)***
Peninou French Ldry & Clrs Inc (PA)......D......800 392-2532
101 S Maple Ave South San Francisco (94080) ***(P-13324)***
Peninsula Beverly Hill's, Beverly Hills *Also called Belvedere Hotel Partnership* ***(P-12053)***
Peninsula Beverly Hills, The, Beverly Hills *Also called Belvedere Partnership* ***(P-12054)***
Peninsula Community Foundation......D......650 358-9369
1700 S El Camino Real # 300 San Mateo (94402) ***(P-24613)***
Peninsula Crrdor Jint Pwers Bd......C......650 508-6200
1250 San Carlos Ave San Carlos (94070) ***(P-3577)***
Peninsula Custom Homes Inc......D......650 574-0241
1401 Old County Rd San Carlos (94070) ***(P-1172)***
Peninsula Family Service (PA)......D......650 403-4300
24 2nd Ave San Mateo (94401) ***(P-23771)***
Peninsula Family Service......D......650 403-4300
2635 N 1st St San Jose (95134) ***(P-23772)***
Peninsula Family Service......D......650 952-6848
1200 Miller Ave South San Francisco (94080) ***(P-23380)***
Peninsula Family YMCA Sunshine, San Diego *Also called YMCA of San Diego County* ***(P-24712)***
Peninsula Jewish Community Ctr......C......650 212-7522
800 Foster City Blvd Foster City (94404) ***(P-23381)***
Peninsula Pathology Associates, South San Francisco *Also called Pennisula Pthlogists Med Group* ***(P-21561)***
Peninsula Regent, The, San Mateo *Also called Bay Area Senior Services Inc* ***(P-22936)***
Peninsula South Bay, Millbrae *Also called Vitalant Research Institute* ***(P-22339)***
Peninsula Volunteers Inc (PA)......E......650 326-0665
800 Middle Ave Menlo Park (94025) ***(P-23382)***
Peninsula Womens Health (PA)......E......650 692-3818
1828 El Camino Real Ste 8 Burlingame (94010) ***(P-19268)***
Peninsula World Travel LLC (PA)......E......650 328-2030
825 Santa Cruz Ave Menlo Park (94025) ***(P-4831)***
Peninsula YMCA, San Mateo *Also called Young Mens Christian Assoc SF* ***(P-24734)***
Pennacchio Tile Inc......D......707 586-8858
655 Carlson Ct Rohnert Park (94928) ***(P-2905)***
Penney Lawn Service Inc......D......661 587-4788
4000 Allen Rd Bakersfield (93314) ***(P-888)***
Pennisula Pthlogists Med Group......D......650 616-2940
393 E Grand Ave Ste I South San Francisco (94080) ***(P-21561)***
Pennmar, El Monte *Also called San Gbriel Vly Cnvlescent Hosp* ***(P-21425)***
Penny Lane Centers (PA)......B......818 892-3423
15305 Rayen St North Hills (91343) ***(P-24206)***
Penny Lane Centers......C......818 892-3423
15317 Rayen St North Hills (91343) ***(P-24207)***
Penny Lane Centers......C......562 903-4135
10330 Pioneer Blvd # 290 Santa Fe Springs (90670) ***(P-24208)***
Penny Lane Centers......C......818 892-3423
15331 Rayen St North Hills (91343) ***(P-24209)***
Penny Lane Centers......C......818 892-1112
15302 Rayen St North Hills (91343) ***(P-24210)***
Penny Lane Centers......C......818 892-3423
15256 Acre St North Hills (91343) ***(P-24211)***
Penny Lane Centers......C......818 892-3423
1020 E Palmdale Blvd Palmdale (93550) ***(P-24212)***
Penny Lane Centers......C......323 318-9960
2450 S Atl Blvd Ste 101 Commerce (90040) ***(P-24213)***
Penny Lane Centers......C......661 274-0770
43520 Division St Lancaster (93535) ***(P-24214)***
Penny Lawn Service, Bakersfield *Also called Penney Lawn Service Inc* ***(P-888)***
Penny Roofing Company......E......323 731-5424
2501 Exposition Blvd Los Angeles (90018) ***(P-3084)***
Pennymac, Agoura Hills *Also called Private Nat Mrtg Acceptance LLC* ***(P-9593)***
Pennymac Corp......C......818 878-8416
27001 Agoura Rd Agoura Hills (91301) ***(P-9641)***
Pennymac Financial Svcs Inc......A......949 341-0020
36 Discovery Irvine (92618) ***(P-26760)***
Pension Administrators Inc (PA)......C......949 253-4080
17701 Mitchell N Irvine (92614) ***(P-13734)***
Penske Automotive Group Inc......C......858 430-2320
4750 Kearny Mesa Rd San Diego (92111) ***(P-17180)***
Penske Automotive Group Inc......E......415 492-1922
17 Woodland Ave San Rafael (94901) ***(P-17181)***
Penske Automotive Group Inc......E......408 293-7688
803 S 1st St San Jose (95110) ***(P-17182)***
Penske Logistics LLC......D......800 529-6531
2090 Etiwanda Ave Ontario (91761) ***(P-4111)***
Penske Media Corporation (PA)......D......310 321-5000
11175 Santa Monica Blvd Los Angeles (90025) ***(P-13631)***
Penske Truck Leasing Co LP......E......213 628-1255
2300 E Olympic Blvd Los Angeles (90021) ***(P-17183)***
Penske Truck Leasing Co LP......D......310 327-3116
19646 Figueroa St Long Beach (90745) ***(P-17184)***
Penske Truck Leasing Co LP......E......559 268-7000
3080 E Malaga Ave Fresno (93725) ***(P-17185)***
Pentair Equipment Protection, San Diego *Also called Schroff Inc* ***(P-17460)***
Pentel of America Ltd (HQ)......C......310 320-3831
2715 Columbia St Torrance (90503) ***(P-7861)***
Pentel of America Ltd......E......909 975-2200
4000 E Airport Dr Ste C Ontario (91761) ***(P-7862)***
Pentron Clinical Tech LLC......D......203 265-7397
1717 W Collins Ave Orange (92867) ***(P-21562)***
Penwal Industries Inc......D......909 466-1555
10611 Acacia St Rancho Cucamonga (91730) ***(P-1564)***
People Assisting Homeless......C......323 644-2216
340 N Madison Ave Los Angeles (90004) ***(P-23383)***
People Center Inc......E......781 864-1232
2443 Fillmore St 380-7 San Francisco (94115) ***(P-15475)***
People Concern......C......310 883-1222
1751 Cloverfield Blvd Santa Monica (90404) ***(P-23384)***

Mergent e-mail: customerrelations@mergent.com
1384
2020 Directory of California
Wholesalers and Services Companies
(P-0000) Products & Services Section entry number
(PA)=Parent Co (HQ)=Headquarters (DH)=Div Headquarters

People Concern ....C....310 450-0650
1751 Cloverfield Blvd Santa Monica (90404) ***(P-23385)***
People Creating Success Inc....D....661 225-9700
1607 E Palmdale Blvd H Palmdale (93550) ***(P-23386)***
People Creating Success Inc....C....805 644-9480
380 Arneill Rd Camarillo (93010) ***(P-19269)***
People Creating Success Inc....C....805 692-5290
5350 Hollister Ave Ste I Santa Barbara (93111) ***(P-23387)***
People Onesource, Long Beach *Also called Covenant Industries Inc* ***(P-14252)***
People Science Inc....E....888 924-1004
951 Mariners Island Blvd San Mateo (94404) ***(P-14354)***
People Services Inc (PA)....D....707 263-3810
4195 Lakeshore Blvd Lakeport (95453) ***(P-24024)***
People's Place, Torrance *Also called Topwin Corporation* ***(P-8048)***
Peopleai Inc....D....888 997-3675
475 Brannan St Ste 320 San Francisco (94107) ***(P-15002)***
Peopleready Inc....E....760 433-4980
1405 Carmelo Dr 5112 Oceanside (92054) ***(P-14540)***
Peoples Care Inc....C....760 962-1900
13901 Amargosa Rd Ste 101 Victorville (92392) ***(P-21839)***
Peoples Care Inc....C....562 320-0174
12215 Telg Rd Ste 208 Santa Fe Springs (90670) ***(P-23773)***
Peoples Choice Home (PA)....D....949 494-6167
7515 Irvine Center Dr Irvine (92618) ***(P-9591)***
Peoples Choice Staffing Inc....D....951 735-0550
4218 Green River Rd # 101 Corona (92880) ***(P-14355)***
Peoples Self-Help Housing Corp....D....805 349-9341
1026 W Boone St Santa Maria (93458) ***(P-27167)***
Peoplespace, Irvine *Also called Interior Office Solutions Inc* ***(P-16847)***
Peopleware Technical Resources....D....310 640-2406
302 W Grand Ave Ste 4 El Segundo (90245) ***(P-14356)***
Pep Boys Manny Moe Jack of Cal....E....562 908-4400
11456 Washington Blvd Whittier (90606) ***(P-17340)***
Pep Creations, San Diego *Also called Pacific Event Productions Inc* ***(P-13443)***
Pepper Tree Inn....D....530 583-3711
645 N Lake Blvd Tahoe City (96145) ***(P-12748)***
Peppermill Casinos Inc....C....925 671-7711
4021 Port Chicago Hwy Concord (94520) ***(P-12749)***
Peppermint Ridge (PA)....D....951 273-7320
825 Magnolia Ave Corona (92879) ***(P-24025)***
Pepsi-Cola Metro Btlg Co Inc....D....707 535-4560
3029 Coffey Ln Santa Rosa (95403) ***(P-8627)***
Pepsi-Cola Metro Btlg Co Inc....C....209 557-5100
200 River Rd Modesto (95351) ***(P-8628)***
Pepsi-Cola Metro Btlg Co Inc....B....951 697-3200
6659 Sycamore Canyon Blvd Riverside (92507) ***(P-7463)***
Pereira & ODell LLC (PA)....D....415 284-9916
215 2nd St Ste 100 San Francisco (94105) ***(P-13557)***
Perez Contracting LLC....C....661 399-2700
12620 Snow Rd Bakersfield (93314) ***(P-677)***
Perfect Bar LLC....D....866 628-8548
3931 Sorrento Valley Blvd San Diego (92121) ***(P-8629)***
Perfect Snacks, San Diego *Also called Perfect Bar LLC* ***(P-8629)***
Perfect Workout Inc (PA)....D....949 943-7281
150 N El Camino Real Encinitas (92024) ***(P-18183)***
Perfect World Entrmt Inc....C....650 590-7700
101 Redwood Shr Pkwy # 400 Redwood City (94065) ***(P-15003)***
Perfection Glass Inc....E....951 674-0240
554 3rd St Lake Elsinore (92530) ***(P-3295)***
Performance Building Services....C....949 364-4364
22642 Lambert St Ste 409 Lake Forest (92630) ***(P-14008)***
Performance Cleanroom Services, Lake Forest *Also called Performance Building Services* ***(P-14008)***
Performance Contracting Inc....E....925 273-3800
1943 Rutan Dr Livermore (94551) ***(P-1375)***
Performance Contracting Inc....D....913 310-7120
4955 E Landon Dr Anaheim (92807) ***(P-3364)***
Performance Designed Pdts LLC (HQ)....D....323 234-9911
9179 Aero Dr San Diego (92123) ***(P-7740)***
Performance Food Group Inc....D....800 697-7662
16639 Gale Ave City of Industry (91745) ***(P-8205)***
Performance Food Group Inc....D....925 456-8664
6211 Las Positas Rd Livermore (94551) ***(P-8630)***
Performance Food Group Inc....C....831 462-4400
1047 17th Ave Santa Cruz (95062) ***(P-8206)***
Performance Foodservice, Livermore *Also called Performance Food Group Inc* ***(P-8630)***
Performance Roma Southern Cal, City of Industry *Also called Performance Food Group Inc* ***(P-8205)***
Performance Sheets LLC....C....626 333-0195
440 Baldwin Park Blvd City of Industry (91746) ***(P-3085)***
PERFORMANCE TEAM FREIGHT SYSTEM, INC., Santa Fe Springs *Also called Performance Team Frt Sys Inc* ***(P-4469)***
Performance Team Frt Sys Inc....D....562 741-1300
12816 Shoemaker Ave Santa Fe Springs (90670) ***(P-4469)***
Performance Team Frt Sys Inc....C....310 241-4100
401 Westmont Dr San Pedro (90731) ***(P-4470)***
Performance Team Frt Sys Inc....D....562 345-2200
1331 Torrance Blvd Torrance (90501) ***(P-5026)***
Performance Team Frt Sys Inc....C....424 358-6943
1651 California St Redlands (92374) ***(P-5027)***
Performance Team LLC....B....801 301-1732
1651 California St Ste A Redlands (92374) ***(P-5028)***
Performance Team LLC (PA)....C....562 345-2200
2240 E Maple Ave El Segundo (90245) ***(P-5029)***
Performance Tech Partners LLC....C....800 787-4143
500 Capitol Mall Ste 2350 Sacramento (95814) ***(P-16079)***
Performance Warehouse Co....D....916 920-2221
901 Arden Way Sacramento (95815) ***(P-6461)***
Performant Financial Corp (PA)....D....925 960-4800
333 N Canyons Pkwy # 100 Livermore (94551) ***(P-15876)***
Performant Recovery Inc....C....209 858-3500
17080 S Harlan Rd Lathrop (95330) ***(P-13693)***
Performant Recovery Inc (HQ)....C....209 858-3994
333 N Canyons Pkwy # 100 Livermore (94551) ***(P-13694)***
Performant Technologies Inc....B....925 960-4800
333 N Canyons Pkwy # 100 Livermore (94551) ***(P-9838)***
Performing Arts Center of La C....C....213 972-7211
135 N Grand Ave Los Angeles (90012) ***(P-17935)***
Performnce Foodservice-Ledyard, Santa Cruz *Also called Performance Food Group Inc* ***(P-8206)***
Perillo Industries Inc....E....805 498-9838
2150 Anchor Ct Ste A Newbury Park (91320) ***(P-7319)***
Perkins Coie LLP....D....415 725-1313
3150 Porter Dr Palo Alto (94304) ***(P-22758)***
Perkins Coie LLP....D....310 788-9900
1620 26th St Ste 600s Santa Monica (90404) ***(P-22759)***
Perkins Coie LLP....E....415 344-7000
505 Howard St Ste 1000 San Francisco (94105) ***(P-22760)***
Perkowitz & Ruth Architects, Long Beach *Also called Rdc-S111 Inc* ***(P-25494)***
Perkstreet Financial Inc....E....978 801-1177
1100 La Avenida St Ste A Mountain View (94043) ***(P-26761)***
Perlegen Sciences Inc....C....650 625-4500
35473 Dumbarton Ct Newark (94560) ***(P-25813)***
Permanente Federation LLC....D....510 625-6920
1 Kaiser Plz Fl 27 Oakland (94612) ***(P-26762)***
Permanente Kaiser Intl (HQ)....C....510 271-5910
1 Kaiser Plz Oakland (94612) ***(P-10029)***
Permanente Medical Group, Mountain View *Also called Kaiser Foundation Hospitals* ***(P-20965)***
Permanente Medical Group Inc....D....559 448-4500
7300 N Fresno St Fresno (93720) ***(P-19270)***
Permanente Medical Group Inc....D....916 688-2055
6600 Bruceville Rd Sacramento (95823) ***(P-19271)***
Permanente Medical Group Inc....D....650 742-2100
901 El Camino Real San Bruno (94066) ***(P-19272)***
Permanente Medical Group Inc....D....707 393-4000
3558 Round Barn Blvd Santa Rosa (95403) ***(P-19273)***
Permanente Medical Group Inc....D....415 833-2000
2425 Geary Blvd San Francisco (94115) ***(P-21088)***
Permanente Medical Group Inc....D....408 972-6883
275 Hospital Pkwy Ste 470 San Jose (95119) ***(P-19274)***
Permanente Medical Group Inc....D....925 372-1000
200 Muir Rd Martinez (94553) ***(P-19275)***
Permanente Medical Group Inc....D....510 752-1000
3779 Piedmont Ave Oakland (94611) ***(P-19276)***
Permanente Medical Group Inc....D....510 248-3000
39400 Paseo Padre Pkwy Fremont (94538) ***(P-19277)***
Permanente Medical Group Inc....D....408 945-2900
770 E Calaveras Blvd Milpitas (95035) ***(P-19278)***
Permanente Medical Group Inc....D....925 813-6149
4501 Sand Creek Rd Antioch (94531) ***(P-19279)***
Permanente Medical Group Inc....D....650 827-6500
220 Oyster Point Blvd South San Francisco (94080) ***(P-10030)***
Permanente Medical Group Inc....D....650 299-2000
1150 Veterans Blvd Redwood City (94063) ***(P-19280)***
Permanente Medical Group Inc....D....650 299-2015
910 Marshall St Redwood City (94063) ***(P-19281)***
Permanente Medical Group Inc....D....510 231-5406
914 Marina Way S Richmond (94804) ***(P-19282)***
Permanente Medical Group Inc....D....510 454-1000
2500 Merced St San Leandro (94577) ***(P-19283)***
Permanente Medical Group Inc....D....650 598-2852
900 Veterans Blvd Ste 400 Redwood City (94063) ***(P-10031)***
Permanente Medical Group Inc (HQ)....B....866 858-2226
1950 Franklin St Fl 18th Oakland (94612) ***(P-22295)***
Permanente Medical Group Inc....D....415 444-2000
99 Montecillo Rd San Rafael (94903) ***(P-19284)***
Permanente Medical Group Inc....D....925 906-2000
320 Lennon Ln Walnut Creek (94598) ***(P-19285)***
Permanente Medical Group Inc....D....415 209-2444
100 Rowland Way Ste 125 Novato (94945) ***(P-19286)***
Permanente Medical Group Inc....D....415 899-7400
97 San Marin Dr Novato (94945) ***(P-19287)***
Permanente Medical Group Inc....D....510 559-5119
1725 Eastshore Hwy Berkeley (94710) ***(P-10032)***
Permanente Medical Group Inc....D....916 784-4000
1600 Eureka Rd Roseville (95661) ***(P-19288)***
Permanente Medical Group Inc....C....415 833-2000
2238 Geary Blvd San Francisco (94115) ***(P-10033)***
Permanente Medical Group Inc....D....510 559-5338
1750 2nd St Berkeley (94710) ***(P-19289)***
Permanente Medical Group Inc....D....707 765-3900
3900 Lakeville Hwy Petaluma (94954) ***(P-19290)***
Permanente Medical Group Inc....E....707 427-4000
1550 Gateway Blvd Fairfield (94533) ***(P-21089)***
Permanente Medical Group Inc....E....209 476-2000
1305 Tommydon St Stockton (95210) ***(P-19291)***
Permanente Medical Group Inc....D....510 675-4010
3555 Whipple Rd Union City (94587) ***(P-10034)***
Permanente Medical Group Inc....D....925 243-2600
3000 Las Positas Rd Livermore (94551) ***(P-19292)***
Permanente Medical Group Inc....C....916 631-3000
10725 International Dr Rancho Cordova (95670) ***(P-19293)***
Permanente Medical Group Inc....D....650 358-7000
1000 Franklin Pkwy San Mateo (94403) ***(P-19294)***
Permanente Medical Group Inc....D....209 735-5000
4601 Dale Rd Modesto (95356) ***(P-10035)***

Employee Codes: A=Over 500 employees, B=251-500
C=101-250, D=51-100, E=50
2020 Directory of California
Wholesalers and Services Companies
© Mergent Inc. 1-800-342-5647
1385

Permanente Medical Group Inc........D.......707 765-3930
1617 Broadway St Vallejo (94590) ***(P-19295)***
Permanente Medical Group Inc........D.......510 625-6262
1800 Harrison St Fl 7th Oakland (94612) ***(P-19296)***
Permanente Medical Group Inc........D.......510 752-1190
235 W Macarthur Blvd Oakland (94611) ***(P-19297)***
Permanente Medical Group Inc........D.......209 476-3737
7373 West Ln Stockton (95210) ***(P-19298)***
Permanente Medical Group Inc........D.......650 301-5860
395 Hickey Blvd Fl 1 Daly City (94015) ***(P-19299)***
Permanentee Medical Group, Roseville *Also called Kaiser Foundation Hospitals* ***(P-19119)***
Permits Today LLC........D.......626 585-2931
140 S Lake Ave Ste 323 Pasadena (91101) ***(P-16990)***
Pernixdata Inc........D.......408 724-8413
1740 Tech Dr Ste 150 San Jose (95110) ***(P-15004)***
Perona Langer Beck A Prof Corp........D.......562 426-6155
300 E San Antonio Dr Long Beach (90807) ***(P-22761)***
Perquest Inc........D.......510 740-6300
268 Bush St San Francisco (94104) ***(P-25659)***
Perr & Knight Inc (PA)........D.......310 230-9339
401 Wilshire Blvd Ste 300 Santa Monica (90401) ***(P-10453)***
Perrin Bernard Supowitz LLC (PA)........D.......323 981-2800
5496 Lindbergh Ln Bell (90201) ***(P-8207)***
Perris Valley Cmnty Hosp LLC (PA)........B.......951 436-5000
2224 Medical Center Dr Perris (92571) ***(P-21090)***
Perris Valley Cmnty Hosp LLC........C.......909 581-6400
10841 White Oak Ave Rancho Cucamonga (91730) ***(P-21091)***
Perris Vly Skydiving Schl Inc........E.......951 657-1664
2091 Goetz Rd Perris (92570) ***(P-18737)***
Perry & Shaw Inc........D.......619 390-6500
9029 Park Plaza Dr # 104 La Mesa (91942) ***(P-25264)***
Perry Coast Construction Inc........C.......951 774-0677
14130 Meridian Pkwy Riverside (92518) ***(P-1565)***
Perry Floor Systems Inc........D.......909 949-1211
963 Seaboard Ct Upland (91786) ***(P-3200)***
Perry-Smith LLP........D.......916 441-1000
400 Capitol Mall Ste 1400 Sacramento (95814) ***(P-25660)***
Persistant Systems, Santa Clara *Also called Persistent Tlcom Solutions Inc* ***(P-15006)***
Persistent Systems Inc (HQ)........D.......408 216-7010
2055 Laurelwood Rd # 210 Santa Clara (95054) ***(P-15005)***
Persistent Tlcom Solutions Inc........E.......408 216-7010
2055 Laurelwood Rd # 210 Santa Clara (95054) ***(P-15006)***
Personagraph Corporation........D.......408 616-1600
920 Stewart Dr Ste 100 Sunnyvale (94085) ***(P-15007)***
PERSONAL CARE SERVICES, Santa Barbara *Also called Visiting Care & Companions Inc* ***(P-21893)***
Personal Protective Svcs Inc (PA)........D.......650 344-3302
398 Beach Rd Fl 2 Burlingame (94010) ***(P-16377)***
Personalis Inc........C.......650 752-1300
1330 Obrien Dr Menlo Park (94025) ***(P-21563)***
Personlzed Hmcare Hmmaker Agcy........D.......916 979-4975
4700 Northgate Blvd Sacramento (95834) ***(P-21840)***
Personnel Plus Inc (PA)........C.......562 712-5490
12052 Imperial Hwy # 200 Norwalk (90650) ***(P-14541)***
Personnel Preference Inc........C.......530 938-3909
150 Boles St Ste A Weed (96094) ***(P-14542)***
Perspecta Engineering Inc........D.......408 961-3250
1315 Dell Ave Campbell (95008) ***(P-15672)***
Perterman, San Jose *Also called Durham School Services* ***(P-3791)***
Perverted Jstice Fundation Inc........C.......310 910-9380
703 Pier Ave Ste B154 Hermosa Beach (90254) ***(P-11771)***
Pescadero Conservation Aliance........E.......650 879-1441
4100 Cabrillo Hwy Pescadero (94060) ***(P-24614)***
Pescatore, San Francisco *Also called Kimpton Hotel & Rest Group LLC* ***(P-12512)***
PET POURRI, Milpitas *Also called Humane Society Silicon Valley* ***(P-24839)***
Petalon Landscape MGT Inc........D.......408 453-3998
1766 Rogers Ave San Jose (95112) ***(P-889)***
Petaluma Health Center Inc........B.......707 559-7500
1179 N Mcdowell Blvd A Petaluma (94954) ***(P-19300)***
Petaluma Medical Offices, Petaluma *Also called Kaiser Foundation Hospitals* ***(P-20963)***
Petaluma Valley Hospital, Petaluma *Also called Srm Alliance Hospital Services* ***(P-21218)***
Petaluma Valley Hospital, Petaluma *Also called St Joseph Health System* ***(P-21222)***
Petco, San Diego *Also called Interntional Pet Sups Dist Inc* ***(P-8980)***
Petco Animal Supplies Inc (HQ)........B.......858 453-7845
10850 Via Frontera San Diego (92127) ***(P-5098)***
Pete Santellan........C.......559 564-3748
176 S Valencia Blvd Ste C Woodlake (93286) ***(P-639)***
Peter H Mattson & Co Inc........D.......650 356-2500
343 Hatch Dr Foster City (94404) ***(P-25814)***
Peter J Wolk MD........E.......530 534-6517
2721 Olive Hwy Oroville (95966) ***(P-19301)***
Peter Kiewit Sons Inc........C.......909 962-6001
1925 Wright Ave Ste C La Verne (91750) ***(P-1777)***
Petersen Builders Inc........E.......707 838-3035
7706 Bell Rd Ste A Windsor (95492) ***(P-1173)***
Petersen-Dean Inc........D.......661 254-3322
21616 Golden Triangle Rd # 101 Santa Clarita (91350) ***(P-3086)***
Petersen-Dean Inc........E.......707 469-7470
1705 Enterprise Dr Fairfield (94533) ***(P-3087)***
Petersen-Dean Inc........C.......714 629-9670
2210 S Dupont Dr Anaheim (92806) ***(P-3088)***
Petersen-Dean Commercial Inc........C.......707 469-7470
1705 Enterprise Dr Fairfield (94533) ***(P-3089)***
Petersendean, Fairfield *Also called Petersen-Dean Commercial Inc* ***(P-3089)***
Petersendean, Santa Clarita *Also called Petersen-Dean Inc* ***(P-3086)***
Petersendean, Anaheim *Also called Petersen-Dean Inc* ***(P-3088)***
Peterson Bros Construction, Brea *Also called P B C Pavers Inc* ***(P-2376)***
Peterson Bros Contruction Inc........A.......714 278-0488
1560 W Lambert Rd Brea (92821) ***(P-3201)***
Peterson Cat, San Leandro *Also called Peterson Machinery Co* ***(P-6930)***
Peterson Family Inc........D.......559 897-5064
38694 Road 16 Kingsburg (93631) ***(P-213)***
Peterson Hydraulics Inc (PA)........D.......310 323-3155
1653 W El Segundo Blvd Gardena (90249) ***(P-17527)***
Peterson Machinery Co (PA)........D.......541 302-9199
955 Marina Blvd San Leandro (94577) ***(P-6930)***
Peterson Painting Inc........B.......925 455-5864
5750 La Ribera St Livermore (94550) ***(P-2377)***
Petes Connection Inc........E.......760 723-1972
407 Ranger Rd Fallbrook (92028) ***(P-5734)***
Petit Ermitage, West Hollywood *Also called Valadon Hotel LLC* ***(P-13059)***
Petrelli Electric Inc........D.......661 268-7312
11615 Davenport Rd Agua Dulce (91390) ***(P-2584)***
Petrochem Insulation Inc........C.......310 638-6663
19010 S Alameda St Compton (90221) ***(P-2842)***
Petrol Advertising, Burbank *Also called Todda Merger Sub Inc* ***(P-13587)***
Petroleum Sales Inc........D.......415 256-1600
2066 Redwood Hwy Greenbrae (94904) ***(P-989)***
Petroleum Sales Inc (PA)........C.......415 256-1600
1475 2nd St San Rafael (94901) ***(P-17391)***
Petroquip, Santa Ana *Also called G W Maintenance Inc* ***(P-7634)***
Pets Unlimited........C.......415 563-6700
2343 Fillmore St San Francisco (94115) ***(P-24856)***
Petti Kohn Ingrassia & L PR Co........D.......310 649-5772
11622 El Camino Real San Diego (92130) ***(P-22762)***
Pexs International Inc........C.......626 365-6706
1400 Midvale Ave Apt 408 Los Angeles (90024) ***(P-16080)***
Pf West LLC........C.......415 479-9600
101 Lucas Valley Rd # 150 San Rafael (94903) ***(P-18184)***
Pfitech, Huntington Beach *Also called Precise Fit Limited One LLC* ***(P-14358)***
Pfizer Inc........A.......858 622-3000
10777 Science Center Dr San Diego (92121) ***(P-26018)***
Pfl Security, Rancho Mirage *Also called Protect-For-Less Security Svcs* ***(P-16551)***
Pfyffer Associates Inc........E.......831 423-8572
2611 Mission St Santa Cruz (95060) ***(P-71)***
PG&e, Fairfield *Also called Pacific Gas and Electric Co* ***(P-5871)***
PG&e, San Francisco *Also called Pacific Gas and Electric Co* ***(P-5872)***
PG&e, San Francisco *Also called Pacific Gas and Electric Co* ***(P-5873)***
PG&e, West Sacramento *Also called Pacific Gas and Electric Co* ***(P-5874)***
PG&e, Sacramento *Also called Pacific Gas and Electric Co* ***(P-5875)***
PG&e, Hayward *Also called Pacific Gas and Electric Co* ***(P-5971)***
PG&e, Pittsburg *Also called Pacific Gas and Electric Co* ***(P-5878)***
PG&e, Fresno *Also called Pacific Gas and Electric Co* ***(P-5879)***
PG&e, Petaluma *Also called Pacific Gas and Electric Co* ***(P-5880)***
PG&e, Grass Valley *Also called Pacific Gas and Electric Co* ***(P-5881)***
PG&e, Chico *Also called Pacific Gas and Electric Co* ***(P-5972)***
PG&e, Concord *Also called Pacific Gas and Electric Co* ***(P-5883)***
PG&e, Placerville *Also called Pacific Gas and Electric Co* ***(P-5884)***
PG&e, Oroville *Also called Pacific Gas and Electric Co* ***(P-5885)***
PG&e, Avila Beach *Also called Pacific Gas and Electric Co* ***(P-5886)***
PG&e, Alta *Also called Pacific Gas and Electric Co* ***(P-5887)***
PG&e, Redding *Also called Pacific Gas and Electric Co* ***(P-5888)***
PG&e, Auburn *Also called Pacific Gas and Electric Co* ***(P-5889)***
PG&e, Concord *Also called Pacific Gas and Electric Co* ***(P-5890)***
PG&e, Stockton *Also called Pacific Gas and Electric Co* ***(P-5892)***
PG&e, San Francisco *Also called Pacific Energy Fuels Company* ***(P-5970)***
PG&e, Monterey *Also called Pacific Gas and Electric Co* ***(P-5893)***
PG&e, Fremont *Also called Pacific Gas and Electric Co* ***(P-5894)***
PG&e, Eureka *Also called Pacific Gas and Electric Co* ***(P-5895)***
PG&e, Auberry *Also called Pacific Gas and Electric Co* ***(P-5896)***
PG&e, Daly City *Also called Pacific Gas and Electric Co* ***(P-5897)***
PG&e, Modesto *Also called Pacific Gas and Electric Co* ***(P-5898)***
PG&e, Stockton *Also called Pacific Gas and Electric Co* ***(P-5899)***
PG&e, Sacramento *Also called Pacific Gas and Electric Co* ***(P-5900)***
PG&e, Livermore *Also called Pacific Gas and Electric Co* ***(P-5901)***
PG&e, Davis *Also called Pacific Gas and Electric Co* ***(P-5902)***
PG&e, San Francisco *Also called Pacific Gas and Electric Co* ***(P-5903)***
PG&e, Milpitas *Also called Pacific Gas and Electric Co* ***(P-5904)***
PG&e, Pioneer *Also called Pacific Gas and Electric Co* ***(P-5905)***
PG&e, Bakersfield *Also called Pacific Gas and Electric Co* ***(P-5906)***
PG&e, Templeton *Also called Pacific Gas and Electric Co* ***(P-5907)***
Pgande........E.......209 942-1745
10901 E Highway 120 Manteca (95336) ***(P-24354)***
PGS 360, City of Industry *Also called Prime Global Solutions Inc* ***(P-5033)***
Phamatech Incorporated........C.......858 643-5555
15175 Innovation Dr San Diego (92128) ***(P-26103)***
Pharmaco Inc........D.......310 328-3897
19500 Normandie Ave Torrance (90502) ***(P-21841)***
Pharmacy At Cares, The, Sacramento *Also called Cares Community Health* ***(P-18875)***
Pharmacy Temps Inc........E.......415 459-5211
2125 Paradise Dr Belvedere Tiburon (94920) ***(P-14543)***
Pharmerica Long-Term Care LLC........D.......951 784-1616
1130 Palmyrita Ave # 350 Riverside (92507) ***(P-7975)***
Phase 3 Communications Inc........D.......408 946-9011
3091 Monterey Hwy San Jose (95111) ***(P-2585)***
Phase Matrix Inc........E.......954 490-9429
4600 Patrick Henry Dr Santa Clara (95054) ***(P-7320)***
PHD Marketing Inc........D.......909 620-1000
1373 Ridgeway St Pomona (91768) ***(P-9001)***

Mergent e-mail: customerrelations@mergent.com
1386
2020 Directory of California
Wholesalers and Services Companies
(P-0000) Products & Services Section entry number
(PA)=Parent Co (HQ)=Headquarters (DH)=Div Headquarters

Phelan & Taylor Produce Co..............C......805 489-2413
1860 Pacific Coast Hwy Oceano (93445) ***(P-528)***
Phelps Group..............E......310 752-4400
12121 W Bluff Dr Ste 200 Playa Vista (90094) ***(P-13558)***
Phelps United LLC..............D......657 212-8050
3183 Red Hill Ave Costa Mesa (92626) ***(P-6884)***
Phenomenon Mktg & Entrmt LLC (PA)..............D......323 648-4000
5900 Wilshire Blvd Fl 28 Los Angeles (90036) ***(P-26763)***
PHF II Burbank LLC..............C......818 843-6000
2500 N Hollywood Way Burbank (91505) ***(P-12750)***
PHF Ruby LLC..............C......415 885-4700
2620 Jones St San Francisco (94133) ***(P-12751)***
Phfe Wic Program..............C......626 856-6650
12871 Schabarum Ave Irwindale (91706) ***(P-23388)***
Phg Engineering Services LLC..............D......714 283-8288
180 N Rverview Dr Ste 165 Anaheim (92808) ***(P-25265)***
PHH, Hemet *Also called Physicians For Healthy Hospita* ***(P-21092)***
PHI Delta Theta Inc..............E......818 885-9940
17740 Halsted St Northridge (91325) ***(P-13175)***
Phifactor Technologies LLC..............D......424 234-9494
6415 Surfside Way Malibu (90265) ***(P-21564)***
Phihong USA Corp (HQ)..............D......510 445-0100
47800 Fremont Blvd Fremont (94538) ***(P-6885)***
Philip DAmato Racing LLC..............D......949 830-7027
28202 Palmada Mission Viejo (92692) ***(P-18088)***
Philip West Industrial Service, Long Beach *Also called PSC Industrial Outsourcing LP* ***(P-6236)***
Philippine Airlines..............D......310 646-1981
11001 Aviation Blvd Los Angeles (90045) ***(P-4677)***
Philippine Airlines Inc..............C......415 217-3100
447 Sutter St Ste 200 San Francisco (94108) ***(P-4678)***
Philips Hlthcare Infrmtics Inc (HQ)..............C......650 293-2300
4430 Rosewood Dr Ste 200 Pleasanton (94588) ***(P-15008)***
Philips Medical Systems Clevel..............D......949 699-2300
1 Marconi Irvine (92618) ***(P-6992)***
Phillips & Assoc Law Offs PC..............D......510 464-8040
1300 Clay St Ste 600 Oakland (94612) ***(P-22763)***
Phillips Farms..............E......559 798-1871
33771 Road 156 Visalia (93292) ***(P-214)***
Phillips Plywood Co Inc..............D......818 897-7736
13599 Desmond St Pacoima (91331) ***(P-6643)***
Philmont Management Inc..............D......213 380-0159
3450 Wilshire Blvd # 850 Los Angeles (90010) ***(P-1566)***
Philotic Inc..............D......510 730-1740
524 3rd St San Francisco (94107) ***(P-15009)***
Phoenix American Incorporated (PA)..............D......415 485-4500
2401 Kerner Blvd San Rafael (94901) ***(P-5735)***
Phoenix Engineering Co Inc..............D......310 532-1134
550 E Carson Plaza Dr # 112 Carson (90746) ***(P-14544)***
Phoenix Home Lf Mutl Insur Co, Hemet *Also called Anka Behavioral Health Inc* ***(P-10257)***
Phoenix House Orange County..............D......714 953-9373
1207 E Fruit St Santa Ana (92701) ***(P-24026)***
Phoenix Houses Los Angeles Inc..............D......818 686-3000
11600 Eldridge Ave Lake View Terrace (91342) ***(P-24027)***
PHOENIX HSE FNDTN, INC. & AF, Lake View Terrace *Also called Phoenix Houses Los Angeles Inc* ***(P-24027)***
Phoenix International, Torrance *Also called CH Robinson Freight Svcs Ltd* ***(P-4912)***
Phoenix Intl Holdings Inc..............C......619 207-0871
127 Press Ln Chula Vista (91910) ***(P-16991)***
Phoenix Personnel, Carson *Also called Phoenix Engineering Co Inc* ***(P-14544)***
Phoenix Satellite TV US Inc..............E......626 388-1188
3810 Durbin St Baldwin Park (91706) ***(P-5736)***
Phoenix Textile Inc..............D......213 239-9640
910 S Los Angeles St Los Angeles (90015) ***(P-16992)***
Phoenix Textile Inc (PA)..............D......310 715-7090
14600 S Broadway Gardena (90248) ***(P-8005)***
Phone App Company, The, Hermosa Beach *Also called Southbay Website Design LLC* ***(P-15816)***
Phone Ware Inc..............B......858 530-8550
8902 Activity Rd Ste A San Diego (92126) ***(P-16993)***
Photo Holdings LLC..............A......650 610-5200
2800 Bridge Pkwy Redwood City (94065) ***(P-11685)***
Photo TLC Inc..............C......415 462-0010
3925 Cypress Dr Petaluma (94954) ***(P-16581)***
Photocenter Imaging, Burbank *Also called J H Maddocks Photography* ***(P-16579)***
Phs / Mwa (HQ)..............E......950 695-1008
42355 Rio Nedo Temecula (92590) ***(P-4785)***
Phs Staffing, Seal Beach *Also called Premier Healthcare Svcs LLC* ***(P-14360)***
Phs/Mwa Aviation Services, Temecula *Also called Phs / Mwa* ***(P-4785)***
Phtl, San Rafael *Also called Pasha Hawaii Trnspt Lines LLC* ***(P-4594)***
Physical Distribution Svc Inc (PA)..............D......323 881-0886
16000 Heron Ave La Mirada (90638) ***(P-4471)***
Physical Optics Corporation (PA)..............D......310 320-3088
1845 W 205th St Torrance (90501) ***(P-25815)***
Physical Rehabilitation Netwrk..............E......408 570-0510
2833 Junction Ave Ste 206 San Jose (95134) ***(P-19683)***
Physical Rhbltation Netwrk LLC..............C......646 430-2300
1632 Puente Ave Baldwin Park (91706) ***(P-22088)***
Physical Rhbltation Netwrk LLC (PA)..............D......760 931-8310
3025 Crte Del Ngal Ste 20 Carlsbad (92011) ***(P-19684)***
Physical Therapy Hand Ctrs Inc..............E......760 233-9655
1815 E Valley Pkwy Ste 5 Escondido (92027) ***(P-19685)***
Physical Therapy Unit, Burbank *Also called Therapeutic Associates Inc* ***(P-19697)***
Physical/Occupational Therapy, Madera *Also called Pediatric Physical Rehab Clnc* ***(P-22086)***
Physician Assoc San Gabriel..............C......626 817-8300
199 S Los Robles Ave Pasadena (91101) ***(P-10036)***
Physician Management Group Inc..............C......858 309-6300
3860 Calle Fortunada # 210 San Diego (92123) ***(P-26351)***

PHYSICIAN OFFICE SUPPORT SERVI, Torrance *Also called Torrance Memorial Medical Ctr* ***(P-21311)***
PHYSICIAN OFFICE SUPPORT SERVI, Torrance *Also called Torrance Health Assn Inc* ***(P-21310)***
Physician Weblink MGT Svcs, Irvine *Also called Syntiro Healthcare Services* ***(P-26419)***
Physician Weblink of Cal (HQ)..............C......949 923-3201
7 Technology Dr Irvine (92618) ***(P-26352)***
Physicians Automated Lab Inc (HQ)..............D......661 325-0744
820 34th St Ste 102 Bakersfield (93301) ***(P-21565)***
Physicians Choice LLC..............D......818 340-9988
21860 Burbank Blvd # 120 Woodland Hills (91367) ***(P-25661)***
Physicians Choice HM Hlth Inc..............E......310 793-1616
3220 Sepulveda Blvd # 100 Torrance (90505) ***(P-21842)***
Physicians For Healthy Hospita (HQ)..............D......951 652-2811
1117 E Devonshire Ave Hemet (92543) ***(P-21092)***
Physicians For Healthy Hospita..............B......951 679-8888
28400 Mccall Blvd Sun City (92585) ***(P-21093)***
Physicians For Healthy Hospita..............C......951 652-2811
371 N Weston Pl Hemet (92543) ***(P-21094)***
Physicians For Healthy Hospita..............C......951 652-2811
1280 S Buena Vista St San Jacinto (92583) ***(P-21095)***
Physicians Referral Service, Lancaster *Also called Lancaster Crdlgy Med Group Inc* ***(P-19150)***
Piazza Trucking, South Gate *Also called Samuel J Piazza & Son Inc* ***(P-4229)***
Piccadilly Hospitality LLC..............E......559 348-5520
2305 W Shaw Ave Fresno (93711) ***(P-12752)***
Piccadilly Inn Airport, Fresno *Also called Art Piccadilly Shaw LLC* ***(P-12019)***
Piccadilly Inn Shaw, Fresno *Also called Piccadilly Hospitality LLC* ***(P-12752)***
Pick Pull Auto Dismantling Inc (HQ)..............E......916 689-2000
10850 Gold Center Dr # 325 Rancho Cordova (95670) ***(P-6496)***
Pick-A-Part, Monrovia *Also called M T M & M Inc* ***(P-14102)***
Pick-A-Part Auto Wrecking..............D......559 485-3071
9445 Cambridge St Cypress (90630) ***(P-7768)***
Pickford Realty Inc..............D......805 782-6000
1015 Nipomo St Ste 100 San Luis Obispo (93401) ***(P-11357)***
Pickleback Nola LLC..............E......504 605-0911
1102 7th Pl Hermosa Beach (90254) ***(P-17648)***
Pickwick Hotel The, San Francisco *Also called Yhb San Francisco LLC* ***(P-13131)***
Pico Cleaner Inc (PA)..............D......310 274-2431
9150 W Pico Blvd Los Angeles (90035) ***(P-13257)***
Pico Party Rents, Los Angeles *Also called Pico Rents Inc* ***(P-14190)***
Pico Rents Inc..............D......310 275-9431
13414 S Figueroa St Los Angeles (90061) ***(P-14190)***
PICO WOOSTER SENIOR HOUSING, Los Angeles *Also called Los Angeles Senior Citizen* ***(P-10763)***
Picsart Inc..............D......415 757-6800
1 Market St Fl 32 San Francisco (94105) ***(P-15010)***
Picture It On Canvas Inc..............D......858 679-1200
1800 Seaport Blvd Redwood City (94063) ***(P-16582)***
Pie Town Productions Inc..............C......818 255-9300
5433 Laurel Canyon Blvd North Hollywood (91607) ***(P-17649)***
Piedmont Gardens, Oakland *Also called American Baptist Homes of West* ***(P-23818)***
Piedmont Transfer & Storage..............E......408 288-5600
1555 S 7th St Ste A San Jose (95112) ***(P-4112)***
Piege Co (PA)..............C......818 727-9100
20120 Plummer St Chatsworth (91311) ***(P-8043)***
Piehl, Joel J DDS, Hawthorne *Also called Schnierow Dental Care* ***(P-19630)***
Pier 39 Limited Partnership (PA)..............C......415 705-5500
Beach Embarcadero Level 3 San Francisco (94133) ***(P-10634)***
Pier Pont Hotel LP..............E......805 643-6144
550 San Jon Rd Ventura (93001) ***(P-12753)***
Pier Restaurant, San Francisco *Also called Blue and Gold Fleet* ***(P-4598)***
Pierce Brothers (HQ)..............D......818 763-9121
10621 Victory Blvd North Hollywood (91606) ***(P-13374)***
Pierce Enterprises, El Monte *Also called Wgg Enterprises Inc* ***(P-2878)***
Pierpont Inn Inc..............E......805 643-0245
550 San Jon Rd Ventura (93001) ***(P-12754)***
Pierre Landscape Inc..............C......626 587-2121
5455 2nd St Irwindale (91706) ***(P-750)***
Pigeon and Poodle, City of Industry *Also called Ardmore Home Design Inc* ***(P-6542)***
Pih Health, Whittier *Also called Interhealth Corp* ***(P-20917)***
Pih Health Hospital - Downey..............A......562 698-0811
11500 Brookshire Ave Downey (90241) ***(P-21096)***
Pih Health Hospital - Whitti..............B......626 357-6876
122 N Primrose Ave Apt A Monrovia (91016) ***(P-21097)***
Pih Health Hospital - Whitti..............A......562 904-5482
11500 Brookshire Ave Downey (90241) ***(P-21098)***
Pih Health Hospital - Whittier (PA)..............A......562 698-0811
12401 Washington Blvd Whittier (90602) ***(P-21099)***
Pilgrim Haven Retirement Home, Los Altos *Also called American Baptist Homes of West* ***(P-20488)***
Pilgrim Operations LLC..............B......818 478-4500
12020 Chanl Blvd Ste 200 North Hollywood (91607) ***(P-6736)***
Pilgrim Place Beauty Salon, Claremont *Also called Pilgrim Place In Claremont* ***(P-13354)***
Pilgrim Place In Claremont (PA)..............C......909 399-5500
625 Mayflower Rd Claremont (91711) ***(P-20660)***
Pilgrim Place In Claremont..............C......909 621-9581
721 Harrison Ave Claremont (91711) ***(P-13354)***
Pillar Data Systems Inc..............B......408 503-4000
2840 Junction Ave San Jose (95134) ***(P-15011)***
Pillsbury Winthrop Shaw..............C......415 983-1000
4 Embarcadero Ctr Fl 22 San Francisco (94111) ***(P-22764)***
Pillsbury Winthrop Shaw..............C......213 488-7100
725 S Figueroa St # 2900 Los Angeles (90017) ***(P-22765)***
Pillsbury Winthrop Shaw..............C......415 983-1865
29 Eucalyptus Rd Berkeley (94705) ***(P-22766)***

ALPHABETIC

Employee Codes: A=Over 500 employees, B=251-500
C=101-250, D=51-100, E=50
2020 Directory of California
Wholesalers and Services Companies
© Mergent Inc. 1-800-342-5647
1387

Pillsbury Winthrop Shaw ....D....858 509-4000
12255 El Camino Real # 300 San Diego (92130) ***(P-22767)***
Pillsbury Winthrop Shaw ....B....415 983-1075
50 Fremont St Ste 522 San Francisco (94105) ***(P-22768)***
Pillsbury Winthrop Shaw ....C....650 233-4500
2550 Hanover St Palo Alto (94304) ***(P-22769)***
Pilot Automotive, City of Industry *Also called Pilot Inc* ***(P-4472)***
Pilot Freight Services, San Diego *Also called Miramar Transportation Inc* ***(P-4994)***
Pilot Inc (PA) ....D....626 937-6988
13000 Temple Ave City of Industry (91746) ***(P-4472)***
Pilot Painting & Construction, Cypress *Also called Power Maintenance Services Inc* ***(P-2378)***
Pimco, Newport Beach *Also called Pacific Investment MGT Co LLC* ***(P-11737)***
Pimco Funds Distribution Co ....B....949 720-4761
840 Nwport Ctr Dr Ste 100 Newport Beach (92660) ***(P-11738)***
Pimco Mortgage Income Tr Inc ....B....949 720-6000
650 Newport Center Dr Newport Beach (92660) ***(P-11807)***
Pina Vineyard Management LLC ....E....707 944-2229
7960 Silverado Trl NAPA (94558) ***(P-678)***
Pinamar LLC ....D....925 243-8979
6909 Las Positas Rd Ste D Livermore (94551) ***(P-14191)***
Pinasco Mechinical, Stockton *Also called Pinasco Plumbing & Heating Inc* ***(P-2230)***
Pinasco Plumbing & Heating Inc ....E....209 463-7793
2145 E Taylor St Stockton (95205) ***(P-2230)***
Pindler & Pindler Inc (PA) ....D....805 531-9090
11910 Poindexter Ave Moorpark (93021) ***(P-8006)***
Pine & Powell Partners LLC ....D....415 989-3500
905 California St San Francisco (94108) ***(P-12755)***
Pine Company, Culver City *Also called Pine Data Processing Inc* ***(P-15797)***
Pine Crest, Maywood *Also called Maywood Halthcare Wellness Ctr* ***(P-20129)***
Pine Data Processing Inc ....D....310 815-5700
10559 Jefferson Blvd Culver City (90232) ***(P-15797)***
Pine Grove Healthcare ....D....626 285-3131
126 N San Gabriel Blvd San Gabriel (91775) ***(P-20194)***
PINE KNOLL PUBLICATIONS, Redlands *Also called Study Tapes* ***(P-17679)***
Pine Mountain Lake Association (PA) ....C....209 962-4080
19228 Pine Mountain Dr Groveland (95321) ***(P-24615)***
Pine Tree Lumber Company LP (PA) ....D....760 745-0411
707 N Andreasen Dr Escondido (92029) ***(P-6644)***
Pinedridge Care Ctr, San Rafael *Also called Mariner Health Care Inc* ***(P-20118)***
Pinegrove Hlthcare Wllness Ctr, San Gabriel *Also called Fernview Convalescent Hospital* ***(P-19912)***
Pinelands Preservation Inc ....D....609 703-0359
4501 Auburn Blvd Ste 201 Sacramento (95841) ***(P-890)***
Piner's Medical Supply, NAPA *Also called Piners Nursing Home Inc* ***(P-20195)***
Piners Nursing Home Inc ....D....707 224-7925
1800 Pueblo Ave NAPA (94558) ***(P-20195)***
Pinery LLC ....D....858 675-3575
13701 Highland Valley Rd Escondido (92025) ***(P-959)***
Pines At Plcrvlle Hlthcare Ctr, Placerville *Also called Gladiolus Holdings LLC* ***(P-19941)***
Pink Diamonds, Vernon *Also called Stone Blue Inc* ***(P-13312)***
Pinnacle 1617 LLC ....E....619 239-9600
1617 1st Ave San Diego (92101) ***(P-12756)***
Pinnacle Builders Inc ....B....916 372-5000
1911 Douglas Blvd Ste 85 Roseville (95661) ***(P-1174)***
Pinnacle Communication Svcs, Glendale *Also called Pinnacle Networking Svcs Inc* ***(P-2586)***
Pinnacle Contracting Corp ....E....818 888-6548
21800 Burbank Blvd # 210 Woodland Hills (91367) ***(P-1567)***
Pinnacle Electrical Svcs Inc ....D....818 241-6009
730 Fairmont Ave Ste 100 Glendale (91203) ***(P-27168)***
Pinnacle Escrow Company, Northridge *Also called Pinnacle Estate Properties* ***(P-11358)***
Pinnacle Estate Properties (PA) ....C....818 993-4707
9137 Reseda Blvd Northridge (91324) ***(P-11358)***
Pinnacle Funding Group Inc ....E....925 552-5302
2092 Omega Rd Ste H San Ramon (94583) ***(P-9642)***
Pinnacle Networking Services, Glendale *Also called Pinnacle Electrical Svcs Inc* ***(P-27168)***
Pinnacle Networking Svcs Inc ....D....818 241-6009
730 Fairmont Ave Glendale (91203) ***(P-2586)***
Pinnacle Rvrside Hspitality LP ....C....951 784-8000
3400 Market St Riverside (92501) ***(P-12757)***
Pinnacle Telecom Inc (PA) ....E....916 426-1000
8100 Sierra College Blvd Roseville (95661) ***(P-15673)***
Pinnacle Travel Services LLC ....C....310 414-1787
390 N Pacific Coast Hwy El Segundo (90245) ***(P-4832)***
Pinner Construction Co Inc (PA) ....D....714 490-4000
1255 S Lewis St Anaheim (92805) ***(P-1568)***
Pinole Assisted Living Cmnty ....D....510 758-1122
2850 Estates Ave Pinole (94564) ***(P-10797)***
Pinole Medical Offices, Pinole *Also called Kaiser Foundation Hospitals* ***(P-19089)***
Pinole Senior Center ....D....510 724-9800
2500 Charles St Pinole (94564) ***(P-23389)***
PINOLE SENIOR VILLAGE, Pinole *Also called Pinole Assisted Living Cmnty* ***(P-10797)***
Pinsetters Inc ....D....916 488-7545
2600 Watt Ave Sacramento (95821) ***(P-18041)***
Pinterest Inc ....C....415 400-4645
808 Brannan St San Francisco (94103) ***(P-13659)***
Pinterest Inc (PA) ....C....415 617-5585
808 Brannan St San Francisco (94103) ***(P-15877)***
Pioneer Health Care Services ....C....925 631-9100
1640 School St Ste 100 Moraga (94556) ***(P-26353)***
Pioneer House, Sacramento *Also called Cathedral Pioneer Church Homes* ***(P-19783)***
Pioneer Medical Group Inc ....D....562 862-2775
11411 Brookshire Ave # 108 Downey (90241) ***(P-19302)***
Pioneer Medical Group Inc ....D....562 229-0902
16510 Bloomfield Ave Cerritos (90703) ***(P-19303)***
Pioneer Sands LLC ....D....949 728-0171
31302 Ortega Hwy San Juan Capistrano (92675) ***(P-1060)***
Pioneer Square Hotel Company ....E....415 346-2323
1940 Fillmore St San Francisco (94115) ***(P-12758)***
Pioneer Theatres Inc ....C....310 532-8183
2500 Redondo Beach Blvd Torrance (90504) ***(P-16994)***
Pioneer Towers Rhf Partners LP ....E....916 443-6548
515 P St Ofc Sacramento (95814) ***(P-10798)***
Pioneers Mem Healthcare Dst (PA) ....A....760 351-3333
207 W Legion Rd Brawley (92227) ***(P-21100)***
PIONEERS MEMORIAL HOSPITAL, Brawley *Also called Pioneers Mem Healthcare Dst* ***(P-21100)***
Pipe Dream Products, Chatsworth *Also called Pd Liquidation Inc* ***(P-9000)***
Pipe Restoration Inc ....E....714 564-7600
3122 W Alpine St Santa Ana (92704) ***(P-2231)***
Pipeline Plumbing, Norco *Also called F J Hoover Plumbing Inc* ***(P-2132)***
Pipeline Restoration Plumbing ....E....714 957-5836
2700 S Main St Ste E Santa Ana (92707) ***(P-2232)***
Pircher Nichols & Meeks (PA) ....D....310 201-0132
1925 Century Park E # 1700 Los Angeles (90067) ***(P-22770)***
Pismo Beach Athletic Club ....E....805 773-3011
1751 Price St Pismo Beach (93449) ***(P-18185)***
Pismo Coast Village Inc ....D....805 773-1811
165 S Dolliver St Pismo Beach (93449) ***(P-12759)***
Piston Agency, San Diego *Also called Mea Digital Worx LLC* ***(P-13540)***
Pit River Casino, Burney *Also called Pit River Tribal Council* ***(P-18738)***
Pit River Health Service Inc (PA) ....D....530 335-3651
36977 Park Ave Burney (96013) ***(P-22296)***
Pit River Health Services, Burney *Also called Pit River Tribal Council* ***(P-19304)***
Pit River Tribal Council ....D....530 335-3651
36977 Park Ave Burney (96013) ***(P-19304)***
Pit River Tribal Council ....D....530 335-2334
20265 Tamarack Ave Burney (96013) ***(P-18738)***
Pitco Foods, San Jose *Also called Pacific Groservice Inc* ***(P-8942)***
Pitco Foods, San Jose *Also called Pittsburg Wholesale Groc Inc* ***(P-8209)***
Pitney Bowes Presort Svcs Inc ....C....310 763-4615
18550 S Broadwick St Compton (90220) ***(P-16995)***
Pitney Bowes Presort Svcs Inc ....D....415 468-1660
125 Valley Dr Brisbane (94005) ***(P-16996)***
Pitts & Bachmann Realtors Inc ....D....805 963-1391
1436 State St Santa Barbara (93101) ***(P-11359)***
Pittsburg Care Center Ltd ....E....925 432-3831
535 School St Pittsburg (94565) ***(P-20196)***
Pittsburg Skilled Nursing ....D....925 808-6540
535 School St Pittsburg (94565) ***(P-20197)***
Pittsburg Wholesale Groc Inc ....D....916 372-7772
1670 Overland Ct West Sacramento (95691) ***(P-8208)***
Pittsburg Wholesale Groc Inc (PA) ....C....916 372-7772
567 Cinnabar St San Jose (95110) ***(P-8209)***
Pivot Interiors Inc ....D....949 988-5400
3200 Park Center Dr # 100 Costa Mesa (92626) ***(P-2587)***
Pivot Systems Inc ....C....408 435-1000
4320 Stevens Creek Blvd San Jose (95129) ***(P-15012)***
Pivotal Software Inc (HQ) ....C....415 777-4868
875 Howard St Fl 5 San Francisco (94103) ***(P-15013)***
Pivotcloud Inc ....E....408 475-6090
1230 Midas Way Ste 210 Sunnyvale (94085) ***(P-15014)***
Pixar (HQ) ....A....510 922-3000
1200 Park Ave Emeryville (94608) ***(P-17650)***
Pixar Animation Studios, Emeryville *Also called Pixar* ***(P-17650)***
Pixelmags Inc ....D....310 598-7303
1800 Century Park E # 600 Los Angeles (90067) ***(P-15015)***
Pixelogic Media Partners LLC ....C....818 861-2001
4000 W Alameda Ave # 110 Burbank (91505) ***(P-17756)***
Pixi Inc ....D....310 670-7767
10351 Santa Monica Blvd # 410 Los Angeles (90025) ***(P-7976)***
Pixi Beauty, Los Angeles *Also called Pixi Inc* ***(P-7976)***
Pixim Inc ....D....650 934-0550
1730 N 1st St San Jose (95112) ***(P-15674)***
Pixior LLC (PA) ....D....323 721-2221
5901 S Eastern Ave Commerce (90040) ***(P-16997)***
Pjbs Holdings Inc (PA) ....D....661 822-5273
1401 Goodrick Dr Tehachapi (93561) ***(P-6233)***
PJs Lumber Inc ....D....209 850-9444
250 D St Turlock (95380) ***(P-3278)***
PJs Lumber Inc ....C....510 743-5300
45055 Fremont Blvd Fremont (94538) ***(P-6645)***
Pk Autobody Inc ....E....559 298-9691
361 N Minnewawa Ave Clovis (93612) ***(P-17301)***
Pk Management LLC ....B....818 808-0600
15301 Ventura Blvd # 570 Sherman Oaks (91403) ***(P-26354)***
Pk Nevada LLC ....E....310 255-0025
1317 5th St Fl 2 Santa Monica (90401) ***(P-11360)***
Pkl Services Inc ....C....858 679-1755
14265 Danielson St C1 Poway (92064) ***(P-17528)***
Place Asian Amrcn Rcovery Svcs, San Jose *Also called Asian Amercn Recovery Svcs Inc* ***(P-21448)***
Placentia Linda Hospital, Placentia *Also called Tenet Healthsystem Medical* ***(P-21499)***
Placer Co Bar Association (PA) ....B....916 557-9181
P.O. Box 4598 Auburn (95604) ***(P-24419)***
Placer County ADM Svcs ....C....530 886-5401
2962 Richardson Dr Auburn (95603) ***(P-27300)***
Placer County Water Agency (PA) ....D....530 823-4850
144 Ferguson Rd Auburn (95603) ***(P-5909)***
Placer County- Adult Sys Care ....D....530 886-2974
11533 C Ave Auburn (95603) ***(P-22089)***
Placervlle Pnes Cnvlscent Hosp ....C....530 622-3400
1040 Marshall Way Placerville (95667) ***(P-20661)***
Plaid Inc (PA) ....D....415 799-1354
1098 Harrison St San Francisco (94103) ***(P-15878)***

Plan Member Financial Corp ......D......800 874-6910
6187 Carpinteria Ave Carpinteria (93013) ***(P-9839)***
Plan-It Interactive Inc (PA) ......E......707 752-6010
150 W Industrial Way Benicia (94510) ***(P-13447)***
Plan-It Life Inc ......D......951 742-7561
5729 Vista Del Caballero Riverside (92509) ***(P-23390)***
Planet Fitness, San Rafael *Also called Pf West LLC* ***(P-18184)***
Planet Group Inc ......D......402 491-3560
5796 Armada Dr Ste 300 Carlsbad (92008) ***(P-15675)***
Planet Labs Inc (PA) ......D......415 829-3313
645 Harrison St Fl 4 San Francisco (94107) ***(P-15798)***
Plangrid Inc (HQ) ......D......800 646-0796
2111 Mission St Ste 400 San Francisco (94110) ***(P-15476)***
Planmember Services, Carpinteria *Also called Plan Member Financial Corp* ***(P-9839)***
Planned Parenthood Federation ......D......949 548-8830
601 W 19th St Ste B Costa Mesa (92627) ***(P-22090)***
Planned Parenthood Federation ......D......916 446-5247
555 Capitol Mall Ste 510 Sacramento (95814) ***(P-22091)***
Planned Parenthood Los Angeles (PA) ......D......213 284-3200
400 W 30th St Los Angeles (90007) ***(P-22092)***
Planned Parenthood Mar Monte (PA) ......D......831 373-1709
316 N Main St Ste 100 Salinas (93901) ***(P-22093)***
Planned Parenthood Nthrn Cal, Concord *Also called Planned Prnthod Shst-Dblo Inc* ***(P-22095)***
Planned Parenthood/Orange and (PA) ......C......714 633-6373
700 S Tustin St Fl 1 Orange (92866) ***(P-22094)***
Planned Prnthod Shst-Dblo Inc (PA) ......E......925 676-0300
2185 Pacheco St Concord (94520) ***(P-22095)***
Planned Prnthood Cal Cntl Cast, Santa Barbara *Also called Planned Prnthood Cal Cntl Cast* ***(P-22096)***
Planned Prnthood Cal Cntl Cast (PA) ......D......805 963-2445
518 Garden St Santa Barbara (93101) ***(P-22096)***
Planned Prnthood Mar Monte Inc ......C......408 287-7529
1691 The Alameda San Jose (95126) ***(P-22097)***
Planned Prnthood Mar Monte Inc (PA) ......D......408 287-7532
1691 The Alameda San Jose (95126) ***(P-22098)***
Planned Prnthood Mar Monte Inc ......D......949 768-3643
26302 La Paz Rd 200 Mission Viejo (92691) ***(P-22099)***
Plannet Consulting LLC ......D......714 982-5800
2951 Saturn St Ste E Brea (92821) ***(P-16081)***
Planning and Public Works Agcy, Willows *Also called County of Glenn* ***(P-1689)***
Planprescriber Inc ......B......650 584-2700
440 E Middlefield Rd Mountain View (94043) ***(P-10454)***
Plant 04, Reedley *Also called Moonlight Packing Corporation* ***(P-5097)***
Plant Holdings Inc (HQ) ......B......951 719-2100
42555 Rio Nedo Temecula (92590) ***(P-11686)***
Plant Maintenance Inc ......C......925 228-3285
1330 Arnold Dr Ste 147 Martinez (94553) ***(P-14545)***
Plant Sciences Inc ......E......530 398-4042
234 Juniper Knoll Rd Macdoel (96058) ***(P-8914)***
Plant Source Inc ......E......760 743-7743
2029 Sycamore Dr San Marcos (92069) ***(P-270)***
Plant Tape Usa Inc (HQ) ......E......831 455-2255
1 Harris Rd Fl 1 # 1 Salinas (93908) ***(P-439)***
Plantasia Inc ......D......310 375-0387
2550 Via Tejon Ste 3f Palos Verdes Estates (90274) ***(P-891)***
Plantasia Landscaping, Palos Verdes Estates *Also called Plantasia Inc* ***(P-891)***
Plantation Golf Club Inc ......D......760 775-3688
50994 Monroe St Indio (92201) ***(P-18531)***
Plantel Nurseries Inc ......B......805 349-8952
2775 E Clark Ave Santa Maria (93455) ***(P-8915)***
Planters Hay Inc ......D......760 344-0620
1295 E St 78 Brawley (92227) ***(P-8853)***
Plasma Collection Centers Inc ......C......323 441-7720
2410 Lillyvale Ave Los Angeles (90032) ***(P-22297)***
Plastiflex Company Inc (HQ) ......C......619 662-8792
601 E Palomar St Ste 424 Chula Vista (91911) ***(P-16998)***
Platinum Clg Indianapolis LLC ......B......310 584-8000
1522 2nd St Santa Monica (90401) ***(P-14009)***
Platinum Empire Group Inc ......C......310 821-5888
3521 Lomita Blvd Ste 202b Torrance (90505) ***(P-14546)***
Platinum Equity, Beverly Hills *Also called Finn Holding Corporation* ***(P-4593)***
Platinum Equity Partners Inc ......C......714 444-3100
3131 S Standard Ave Santa Ana (92705) ***(P-17302)***
Platinum Facilities Services ......C......408 998-9004
1530 Oakland Rd Ste 120 San Jose (95112) ***(P-14010)***
Platinum Group Companies Inc (PA) ......C......818 721-3800
22560 La Quilla Dr Chatsworth (91311) ***(P-11687)***
Platinum Healthcare Staffing, Torrance *Also called Platinum Empire Group Inc* ***(P-14546)***
Platinum Landscape Inc ......C......760 200-3673
42575 Melanie Pl Ste C Palm Desert (92211) ***(P-751)***
Platinum Protection Group Inc ......D......800 824-1097
8018 E Santa Ana Cyn Rd Anaheim (92808) ***(P-16378)***
Platinum Roofing Inc ......D......408 280-5028
800 Charcot Ave Ste 107 San Jose (95131) ***(P-3090)***
Platinum Strands Salon ......D......714 532-2633
3443 E Chapman Ave Orange (92869) ***(P-13355)***
Platinum Visual Systems, Corona *Also called ABC School Equipment Inc* ***(P-7026)***
Platt Security Services, Long Beach *Also called Platt Security Systems Inc* ***(P-16379)***
Platt Security Systems Inc ......C......562 986-4484
3275 E Grant St Ste D Long Beach (90755) ***(P-16379)***
Playa Proper Jv LLC ......D......310 645-0400
8639 Lincoln Blvd Los Angeles (90045) ***(P-12760)***
Playboy Enterprises Inc (PA) ......D......310 424-1800
9346 Civic Center Dr # 200 Beverly Hills (90210) ***(P-17651)***
Playboy Entrmt Group Inc (HQ) ......C......323 276-4000
2300 W Empire Ave Burbank (91504) ***(P-17652)***
Playboy Magazine, Beverly Hills *Also called Playboy Enterprises Inc* ***(P-17651)***
Playmar Inc ......D......408 324-1930
2502 Channing Ave San Jose (95131) ***(P-6696)***
Playphone Inc ......D......408 261-6200
3031 Tisch Way Ste 110pw San Jose (95128) ***(P-15016)***
Playspan LLC ......E......408 617-9155
2900 Gordon Ave Ste 201 Santa Clara (95051) ***(P-9489)***
Playworks Education Energized (PA) ......E......510 893-4180
638 3rd St Oakland (94607) ***(P-18739)***
Playwrights Foundation Inc ......D......415 626-2176
1616 16th St Ste 350 San Francisco (94103) ***(P-17936)***
Plaza De La Raza Child Develop ......D......323 224-1788
225 N Avenue 25 Los Angeles (90031) ***(P-23774)***
Plaza De La Raza Child Develop ......D......562 695-1070
6411 Norwalk Blvd Whittier (90606) ***(P-23775)***
Plaza De La Raza Child Develop (PA) ......D......562 776-1301
13300 Crssrds Pkwy N 44 La Puente (91746) ***(P-23776)***
Plaza Hand Carwash Inc ......E......951 697-4420
23100 Alssndro Blvd Ste B Moreno Valley (92553) ***(P-17392)***
Plaza Home Mortgage Inc (PA) ......E......858 346-1200
4820 Eastgate Mall # 100 San Diego (92121) ***(P-9592)***
Plaza Home Mortgage Inc ......C......714 508-6406
6420 Sequence Dr Ste 200 San Diego (92121) ***(P-9746)***
Plaza Manor Preservation LP ......A......619 475-2125
2615 E Plaza Blvd National City (91950) ***(P-11361)***
Plb Management LLC ......E......323 549-5400
6200 W 3rd St Los Angeles (90036) ***(P-10799)***
PLD Enterprises Inc ......D......213 626-4444
440 Stanford Ave Los Angeles (90013) ***(P-8383)***
PLD Enterprises Inc (PA) ......D......310 547-3366
1621 W 25th St Ste 228 San Pedro (90732) ***(P-8384)***
Plda Inc ......D......408 273-4528
2570 N 1st St 218 San Jose (95131) ***(P-10883)***
Pleasant Canyon Hotel Inc ......E......925 847-0535
11920 Dublin Canyon Rd Pleasanton (94588) ***(P-12761)***
Pleasant Care of Vista ......C......760 945-3033
247 E Bobier Dr Vista (92084) ***(P-20198)***
Pleasant Hawaiian Holiday, Westlake Village *Also called Pleasant Holidays LLC* ***(P-4860)***
Pleasant Hl Byshore Dspsal Inc ......C......925 685-4711
441 N Buchanan Cir Pacheco (94553) ***(P-6234)***
Pleasant Holidays LLC (HQ) ......B......818 991-3390
2404 Townsgate Rd Westlake Village (91361) ***(P-4860)***
Pleasant Valley Flowers Inc ......B......805 986-2776
3132 E Pleasant Valley Rd Oxnard (93033) ***(P-298)***
Pleasant View Convalescent Hos ......C......408 253-9034
22590 Voss Ave Cupertino (95014) ***(P-20662)***
Pleasanton Hilton Hotel, Pleasanton *Also called American Property Management* ***(P-12003)***
Pleasanton Project Owner LLC ......D......925 847-7592
11950 Dublin Canyon Rd Pleasanton (94588) ***(P-12762)***
Pleasantview Industries Inc ......D......661 296-6700
27921 Urbandale Ave Saugus (91350) ***(P-22100)***
Plex Systems Inc ......C......248 391-8001
4305 Hacienda Dr Ste 500 Pleasanton (94588) ***(P-15799)***
Plexicor Inc (PA) ......E......714 918-8700
3598 Cadillac Ave Costa Mesa (92626) ***(P-16549)***
Plh Aviation Services Inc ......E......310 417-0124
7251 World Way W Los Angeles (90045) ***(P-4786)***
Plott Family Care Center, Riverside *Also called Mount Rbdoux Convalescent Hosp* ***(P-20149)***
Plott Family Home Care, San Bernardino *Also called Plott Management Co* ***(P-20199)***
Plott Management Co ......D......909 883-0288
264 E 18th St San Bernardino (92404) ***(P-20199)***
Plowboy Landscapes Inc ......D......805 643-4966
2190 N Ventura Ave Ventura (93001) ***(P-892)***
Plpc, City of Industry *Also called Private Label Pc LLC* ***(P-6886)***
Plug & Play LLC ......D......650 722-2195
370 Convention Way Redwood City (94063) ***(P-11948)***
Plug Connection Inc ......D......760 631-0992
2627 Ramona Dr Vista (92084) ***(P-271)***
Plum Healthcare Group LLC ......D......909 793-2609
1620 W Fern Ave Redlands (92373) ***(P-16999)***
Plum Healthcare Group LLC (PA) ......D......760 471-0388
100 E San Marcos Blvd # 200 San Marcos (92069) ***(P-20200)***
Plum Healthcare Group LLC ......D......408 998-8447
1990 Fruitdale Ave San Jose (95128) ***(P-20201)***
Plum Healthcare Group LLC ......C......619 873-2500
1391 E Madison Ave El Cajon (92021) ***(P-20202)***
Plumas District Hospital (PA) ......C......530 283-2121
1065 Bucks Lake Rd Quincy (95971) ***(P-21101)***
Plumas District Hospital ......C......530 283-0650
1045 Bucks Lake Rd Quincy (95971) ***(P-19305)***
Plumas Rural Services ......D......530 283-2725
711 E Main St Quincy (95971) ***(P-23391)***
Plumb Tech Inc ......D......310 322-4925
1242 E Maple Ave El Segundo (90245) ***(P-2233)***
Plumbing Master, Riverside *Also called Lozano Plumbing Services Inc* ***(P-2191)***
Plumbing Piping & Cnstr Inc ......D......714 821-0490
5950 Lakeshore Dr Cypress (90630) ***(P-2234)***
Plumbing Systems West Inc ......D......909 794-3823
31491 Outer Highway 10 Redlands (92373) ***(P-2235)***
Plume Design Inc ......D......408 498-5512
290 California Ave # 200 Palo Alto (94306) ***(P-15676)***
Plume Wifi, Palo Alto *Also called Plume Design Inc* ***(P-15676)***
Plummer Vlg Preservation LP ......D......818 891-0646
15450 Plummer St North Hills (91343) ***(P-10800)***
Plumpjack The, Olympic Valley *Also called Cncml A California Ltd Partnr* ***(P-12158)***
Plus Group Inc ......D......925 831-8551
2551 Sn Rmn Vlly Blvd 2 San Ramon (94583) ***(P-14357)***
Plx Technology Inc ......C......408 435-7400
1320 Ridder Park Dr San Jose (95131) ***(P-15477)***

ALPHABETIC

Employee Codes: A=Over 500 employees, B=251-500
C=101-250, D=51-100, E=50
2020 Directory of California
Wholesalers and Services Companies
© Mergent Inc. 1-800-342-5647
1389

Ply Gem Pacific Windows Corp..........D.......951 272-1300
235 Radio Rd Corona (92879) ***(P-6646)***
PLYMOUTH SQUARE, Stockton *Also called Stockton Congregational Home* ***(P-24087)***
Plymouth Square, Stockton *Also called Retirement Housing Foundation* ***(P-11418)***
Plymouth Village, Redlands *Also called American Baptist Homes of West* ***(P-20487)***
Pm2net, Irvine *Also called Newton Softed Inc* ***(P-27144)***
Pmbc, Costa Mesa *Also called Pacific Mercantile Bank* ***(P-9223)***
PMC Leaders In Chemicals Inc (HQ)..........C.......818 896-1101
12243 Branford St Sun Valley (91352) ***(P-8705)***
Pmd Industries Inc..........E.......949 222-0999
703 Randolph Ave Costa Mesa (92626) ***(P-2588)***
Pmk-Bnc Inc (PA)..........C.......310 854-0455
1840 Century Park E # 1400 Los Angeles (90067) ***(P-26922)***
Pmk-Bnc Inc..........E.......310 854-4800
8687 Melrose Ave Fl 8th Los Angeles (90069) ***(P-26923)***
Pmt Crdit Risk Trnsf Tr 2015-1..........D.......818 224-7028
3043 Townsgate Rd Westlake Village (91361) ***(P-11808)***
Pmt Crdit Risk Trnsf Tr 2015-2..........C.......818 224-7442
3043 Townsgate Rd Westlake Village (91361) ***(P-11809)***
Pmt Issuer Trust - Fmsr..........C.......818 224-7028
3043 Townsgate Rd Westlake Village (91361) ***(P-11870)***
PNC, San Francisco *Also called Esurance Insurance Svcs Inc* ***(P-10349)***
Pnc Inc..........D.......619 713-2278
2533 Folex Way Spring Valley (91978) ***(P-8414)***
PNC Bank National Association..........D.......626 432-4500
2 N Lake Ave Ste 440 Pasadena (91101) ***(P-9115)***
PNC Bank National Association..........D.......626 351-2211
465 N Halstead St Ste 160 Pasadena (91107) ***(P-9116)***
Pnmac Gmsr Issuer Trust..........A.......818 746-2271
3043 Townsgate Rd Westlake Village (91361) ***(P-11810)***
Point Blue Cnservation Science, Petaluma *Also called Point Reyes Bird Observator* ***(P-24857)***
Point Blue Cnservation Science, Petaluma *Also called Point Reyes Bird Observatory* ***(P-26019)***
Point Loma Convalescent Hosp..........C.......619 224-4141
3202 Duke St San Diego (92110) ***(P-20203)***
Point Loma Post Acute Care Ctr, San Diego *Also called Point Loma Rhblitation Ctr LLC* ***(P-20204)***
Point Loma Rhblitation Ctr LLC..........C.......619 224-4141
3202 Duke St San Diego (92110) ***(P-20204)***
Point of View Inc..........D.......909 860-0705
947 N Del Sol Ln Diamond Bar (91765) ***(P-15017)***
Point One Elec Systems Inc..........D.......925 667-2935
6751 Southfront Rd Livermore (94551) ***(P-2589)***
Point Reyes Bird Observator..........D.......415 868-0371
3820 Cypress Dr Ste 11 Petaluma (94954) ***(P-24857)***
Point Reyes Bird Observatory..........D.......707 781-2555
3820 Cypress Dr Ste 11 Petaluma (94954) ***(P-26019)***
Point360..........D.......818 556-5700
1133 N Hollywood Way Burbank (91505) ***(P-17757)***
Point360 (PA)..........C.......818 565-1400
2701 Media Center Dr Los Angeles (90065) ***(P-17758)***
Pointdirect Transport Inc..........D.......909 371-0837
10858 Almond Ave Fontana (92337) ***(P-5030)***
Pointe At Lantern Crest, The, Santee *Also called Santee Senior Retirement Com* ***(P-23453)***
Pointspeed Inc..........D.......650 638-3720
135 Wyndham Dr Portola Valley (94028) ***(P-16082)***
Poison Spyder Customs Inc..........A.......951 849-5911
2360 Boswell Rd Chula Vista (91914) ***(P-17423)***
Polar Tankers Inc (HQ)..........D.......562 388-1400
300 Oceangate Long Beach (90802) ***(P-4590)***
Polarion Software Inc..........D.......877 572-4005
1001 Marina Village Pkwy # 403 Alameda (94501) ***(P-15478)***
Polaris Building Maintenance..........D.......650 964-9400
2580 Wyandotte St Ste E Mountain View (94043) ***(P-14011)***
Polaris Home Care LLC..........D.......408 400-7020
830 Stewart Dr Ste 211 Sunnyvale (94085) ***(P-21843)***
Polaris Networks Incorporated..........D.......408 625-7273
14856 Holden Way San Jose (95124) ***(P-15018)***
Polaris Research & Development..........D.......415 777-3229
390 4th St Fl 1 San Francisco (94107) ***(P-27169)***
Polaris Wireless Inc..........E.......408 492-8900
301 N Whisman Rd Mountain View (94043) ***(P-15019)***
Polestar Labs Inc..........D.......760 480-2600
1223 Pacific Oaks Pl # 102 Escondido (92029) ***(P-6993)***
Polexis Inc..........D.......858 812-7300
10680 Treena St Fl 6 San Diego (92131) ***(P-15020)***
Police Department, Oakland *Also called San Francisco Bay Area Rapid* ***(P-3591)***
Police Department, Berkeley *Also called City of Berkeley* ***(P-25555)***
Policeone Academy, San Francisco *Also called Praetorian Group* ***(P-16083)***
Poliseek Ais Insur Sltions Inc..........D.......866 480-7335
17785 Center Court Dr N # 250 Cerritos (90703) ***(P-10455)***
Pollard Crnert Crwford Stevens..........E.......626 793-4440
35 N Lake Ave Ste 500 Pasadena (91101) ***(P-22771)***
Polsinelli LLP, Los Angeles *Also called Polsinelli PC* ***(P-22772)***
Polsinelli PC..........D.......310 556-1801
2049 Century Park E Los Angeles (90067) ***(P-22772)***
Poltex Company Inc..........D.......619 669-1846
14748 Wild Colt Pl Jamul (91935) ***(P-15021)***
Polycomp Administrative Svcs..........E.......916 773-3480
3000 Lava Ridge Ct # 130 Roseville (95661) ***(P-10456)***
Polymer Technology Group, The, Berkeley *Also called DSM Biomedical Inc* ***(P-25739)***
Polypeptide Laboratories Inc (HQ)..........D.......310 782-3569
365 Maple Ave Torrance (90503) ***(P-21566)***
Polypeptide Labs San Diego LLC..........D.......858 408-0808
9395 Cabot Dr San Diego (92126) ***(P-25816)***
Polyvore Inc..........D.......650 968-1195
701 First Ave Sunnyvale (94089) ***(P-9002)***

Pom Medical LLC..........D.......805 306-2105
11959 Discovery Ct Moorpark (93021) ***(P-6994)***
Pomerado Hospital, Poway *Also called Palomar Health* ***(P-21081)***
Pomerado Operations LLC..........D.......858 487-6242
12696 Monte Vista Rd Poway (92064) ***(P-20205)***
Pomeroy Rcrtion Rhbltation Ctr (PA)..........C.......415 665-4100
207 Skyline Blvd San Francisco (94132) ***(P-23392)***
Pomona City Refuse Collection, Pomona *Also called City of Pomona* ***(P-6182)***
Pomona College..........C.......909 621-8000
333 N College Way Claremont (91711) ***(P-13735)***
Pomona Community Health Center..........D.......909 630-7927
1450 E Holt Ave Pomona (91767) ***(P-24420)***
Pomona Housing Partners LP..........E.......909 622-1010
1731 W Holt Ave Pomona (91768) ***(P-11362)***
Pomona Intergenerational, Pomona *Also called Pomona Housing Partners LP* ***(P-11362)***
Pomona Valley Harley-Davidson, Montclair *Also called Pomona Valley Motorcycles Inc* ***(P-17529)***
Pomona Valley Hospital Med Ctr (PA)..........A.......909 865-9500
1798 N Garey Ave Pomona (91767) ***(P-21102)***
Pomona Valley Hospital Med Ctr..........A.......909 865-9104
1601 Monte Vista Ave Claremont (91711) ***(P-21103)***
Pomona Valley Hospital Med Ctr..........C.......909 865-9700
1798 N Garey Ave Pomona (91767) ***(P-21487)***
Pomona Valley Hospital Med Ctr..........D.......909 621-7956
1775 Monte Vista Ave Claremont (91711) ***(P-19686)***
Pomona Valley Hospital Med Ctr..........A.......909 865-9977
1601 Monte Vista Ave # 270 Claremont (91711) ***(P-21104)***
Pomona Valley Motorcycles Inc..........D.......909 981-9500
8710 Central Ave Montclair (91763) ***(P-17529)***
Pomona Valley Workshop (PA)..........D.......909 624-3555
4650 Brooks St Montclair (91763) ***(P-23627)***
Pomona Vista Care Center, Pomona *Also called MJB Partners LLC* ***(P-20143)***
Pomwonderful LLC (HQ)..........C.......310 966-5800
11444 W Olympic Blvd Los Angeles (90064) ***(P-8631)***
Pomwonderful LLC..........D.......310 966-5800
900 Airport Blvd Mendota (93640) ***(P-8632)***
Ponder Environmental Svcs Inc (PA)..........D.......707 748-7775
4563 E 2nd St Benicia (94510) ***(P-27170)***
Ponderosa Builders Inc..........A.......714 434-9494
3300 W Macarthur Blvd Santa Ana (92704) ***(P-14012)***
Ponderosa Electric Inc..........D.......949 253-3100
3911 E La Palma Ave Ste D Anaheim (92807) ***(P-2590)***
Ponderosa Mobile Estates, San Francisco *Also called Marcus & Millichap Real Estate* ***(P-11270)***
Ponte Vineyard Inn..........D.......951 587-6688
35001 Rancho Cal Rd Temecula (92591) ***(P-12763)***
Ponto Nursery Inc..........D.......760 724-6003
2545 Ramona Dr Vista (92084) ***(P-8916)***
Ponyai Inc..........C.......650 281-4639
3501 Gateway Blvd Fremont (94538) ***(P-15022)***
Pool Pals Division, Temecula *Also called Oreq Corporation* ***(P-26337)***
Poor Sisters of Nazareth of SA..........D.......619 563-0480
6333 Rancho Mission Rd San Diego (92108) ***(P-24028)***
Pop Media Networks LLC (HQ)..........D.......323 856-4000
5510 Lincoln Blvd Ste 400 Playa Vista (90094) ***(P-17997)***
Poppy Hills Inc..........D.......831 625-1513
3200 Lopez Rd Pebble Beach (93953) ***(P-18280)***
Poppy Ridge Golf Course, Livermore *Also called Poppy Ridge Inc* ***(P-18281)***
Poppy Ridge Inc..........D.......925 456-8229
4280 Greenville Rd Livermore (94550) ***(P-18281)***
Poppy State Express Inc..........D.......209 664-3950
2700 W Main St Turlock (95380) ***(P-4113)***
Porchlight Inc..........D.......562 989-5100
3800 Kilroy Airport Way Long Beach (90806) ***(P-20663)***
Porrey Pines Bank Inc..........B.......510 899-7500
1951 Webster St Oakland (94612) ***(P-9117)***
Port Dept City of Oakland (PA)..........B.......510 627-1100
530 Water St Fl 3 Oakland (94607) ***(P-4616)***
Port Dept City of Oakland..........C.......510 563-3300
1 Airport Dr Ste 45 Oakland (94621) ***(P-4787)***
Port Logistics Group Inc..........D.......909 539-0478
14210 Telephone Ave Chino (91710) ***(P-4224)***
Port Logistics Group Inc..........D.......310 669-2551
19801 S Santa Fe Ave Compton (90221) ***(P-4225)***
Port Logistics Group Inc..........E.......909 539-9773
5026 Chino Hills Pkwy Chino (91710) ***(P-4226)***
Port of Long Bch Employees CLB..........B.......562 590-4102
4801 Airport Plaza Dr Long Beach (90815) ***(P-24456)***
Port of Los Angeles, Wilmington *Also called City of Los Angeles* ***(P-3827)***
Port of Los Angeles..........D.......310 732-3508
425 S Palos Verdes St San Pedro (90731) ***(P-4617)***
Port of Oakland, Oakland *Also called Port Dept City of Oakland* ***(P-4616)***
Port of Sacramento, West Sacramento *Also called Sacramento-Yolo Port District* ***(P-4619)***
PORT OF SAN DIEGO, San Diego *Also called San Diego Unified Port Dst* ***(P-4622)***
PORT OF STOCKTON, Stockton *Also called Stockton Port District* ***(P-4625)***
Port Royal Marina, Torrance *Also called California Yacht Marina Inc* ***(P-4633)***
Portellus Inc..........D.......949 250-9600
2522 Chambers Rd Ste 100 Tustin (92780) ***(P-15479)***
Porteous Enterprises Inc..........C.......310 549-9180
22795 Utility Way Carson (90745) ***(P-7402)***
Porter Construction Co Inc..........C.......831 455-3020
18931 Portola Dr Ste A Salinas (93908) ***(P-1175)***
Porter Crispin & LLC Bogusky..........C.......305 859-2070
2110 Colorado Ave Ste 200 Santa Monica (90404) ***(P-13559)***
Porter Ranch Development Co..........D.......323 655-7330
8383 Wilshire Blvd # 700 Beverly Hills (90211) ***(P-1315)***
Porter Valley Catering, Northridge *Also called Porter Valley Country Club* ***(P-18532)***

Porter Valley Country Club ....C....818 360-1071
19216 Singing Hills Dr Northridge (91326) ***(P-18532)***
Portermatt Electric Inc ....D....714 596-8788
5431 Production Dr Huntington Beach (92649) ***(P-2591)***
Porterville Annex, Porterville *Also called Family Healthcare Network* ***(P-18982)***
Porterville Convalescent Hosp, Porterville *Also called Moyles Central Vly Hlth Care* ***(P-20152)***
Porterville Developmental Ctr, Porterville *Also called Developmental Svcs Cal Dept* ***(P-19864)***
Porterville Sheltered Workshop ....D....559 684-9168
1853 E Cross Ave Tulare (93274) ***(P-6995)***
Portfolio Hotels & Resorts LLC ....E....831 375-2411
700 Munras Ave Monterey (93940) ***(P-12764)***
Porto Vista Hotel, San Diego *Also called 1835 Columbia Street LP* ***(P-11977)***
Portofino Hotel Partners LP ....C....310 379-8481
260 Portofino Way Redondo Beach (90277) ***(P-12765)***
Portofino Inn & Suites Anaheim ....A....714 782-7600
1831 S Harbor Blvd Anaheim (92802) ***(P-12766)***
Portola Hotel & Spa, Monterey *Also called Custom House Hotel LP* ***(P-12195)***
Ports America Inc ....D....510 749-7400
1601 Harbor Bay Pkwy # 150 Alameda (94502) ***(P-4618)***
Portworx Inc ....D....650 386-0766
4940 El Camino Real # 200 Los Altos (94022) ***(P-15023)***
Posada Royale Hotel & Suites ....E....805 584-6300
1775 Madera Rd Simi Valley (93065) ***(P-12767)***
Posca Brothers Dental Lab ....D....562 427-1811
641 W Willow St Long Beach (90806) ***(P-21614)***
Posh Bagel Inc (PA) ....D....408 980-8451
445 Nelo St Santa Clara (95054) ***(P-8633)***
Positive Choice Wellness Ctr, San Diego *Also called Kaiser Foundation Hospitals* ***(P-22049)***
Post Alarm Systems (PA) ....D....626 446-7159
47 E Saint Joseph St Arcadia (91006) ***(P-16550)***
Post Alarm Systems Patrol Svcs, Arcadia *Also called Post Alarm Systems* ***(P-16550)***
Post Group Inc (PA) ....C....323 462-2300
1415 N Cahuenga Blvd Los Angeles (90028) ***(P-17759)***
Post Modern Edit LLC ....D....310 396-7375
4551 Glencoe Ave Ste 210 Marina Del Rey (90292) ***(P-17653)***
Post Modern Edit LLC (PA) ....D....949 608-8700
2941 Alton Pkwy Irvine (92606) ***(P-17654)***
Post Street Renaissance ....B....415 563-0303
545 Post St San Francisco (94102) ***(P-12768)***
Post Surgical Recovery Center, Huntington Beach *Also called Friedman Professional Mgt Co* ***(P-18991)***
Postaer Rubin and Associates (PA) ....C....310 394-4000
2525 Colorado Ave Ste 100 Santa Monica (90404) ***(P-13560)***
Postman Inc ....D....415 796-6470
595 Market St Ste 1130 San Francisco (94105) ***(P-15024)***
Postmates Inc (PA) ....C....800 882-6106
201 3rd St Fl 2 San Francisco (94103) ***(P-5135)***
Potawot Health Clinic, Arcata *Also called United Indian Health Svcs Inc* ***(P-19516)***
Potential Industries Inc (PA) ....C....310 807-4466
922 E E St Wilmington (90744) ***(P-6235)***
Potter Roemer LLC (HQ) ....D....626 855-4890
17451 Hurley St City of Industry (91744) ***(P-6647)***
Poulin Corporation (PA) ....D....760 375-6531
111 S Mahan St Ridgecrest (93555) ***(P-11949)***
Poumtjack Hotels, NAPA *Also called Carneros Inn LLC* ***(P-12117)***
Poundex Associates Corporation ....D....909 444-5878
21490 Baker Pkwy City of Industry (91789) ***(P-6528)***
Powell Works Inc ....B....909 861-6699
17807 Maclaren St Ste B La Puente (91744) ***(P-7575)***
Power 106 Radio ....D....818 953-4200
2600 W Olive Ave Fl 8 Burbank (91505) ***(P-5562)***
Power Engineers Incorporated ....D....714 507-2700
731 E Ball Rd Ste 100 Anaheim (92805) ***(P-25266)***
Power Engineers Incorporated ....D....925 372-9284
218 Loreto Ct Martinez (94553) ***(P-25267)***
Power Generation Entps Inc ....C....818 484-8550
11411 Cumpston St Ste 104 North Hollywood (91601) ***(P-7576)***
Power Logistics, Stockton *Also called Exel N Amercn Logistics Inc* ***(P-4345)***
Power Maintenance Services Inc ....D....714 229-5900
5555 Corporate Ave Cypress (90630) ***(P-2378)***
Power Plant, Glendale *Also called City of Glendale* ***(P-5820)***
Power Plus, Perris *Also called SR Bray LLC* ***(P-14200)***
Power Plus, Anaheim *Also called SR Bray LLC* ***(P-2649)***
Power Plus LLC ....D....714 507-1881
1210 N Red Gum St Anaheim (92806) ***(P-7177)***
Power Plus Solutions Corp ....E....714 507-1881
1210 N Red Gum St Anaheim (92806) ***(P-2592)***
Powerhouse Building Inc ....D....415 446-0188
4320 Redwood Hwy Ste 200 San Rafael (94903) ***(P-3202)***
Powerhouse Realty Inc ....D....323 562-7777
3452 E Florence Ave Huntington Park (90255) ***(P-11363)***
Powerlight, Richmond *Also called Sunpower Corporation Systems* ***(P-2291)***
Powermatic Associates, Livermore *Also called Lbf Enterprises* ***(P-7290)***
Powerplant Mint Spcialists Inc ....C....714 427-6900
2900 Bristol St Ste H202 Costa Mesa (92626) ***(P-1985)***
Powerreviews Oc LLC ....D....415 315-9208
180 Montgomery St # 1800 San Francisco (94104) ***(P-15025)***
Powerschool Group LLC (HQ) ....C....916 288-1636
150 Parkshore Dr Folsom (95630) ***(P-15480)***
Ppc Enterprises Inc ....C....951 354-5402
5920 Rickenbacker Ave Riverside (92504) ***(P-2236)***
Pphm Inc ....D....714 508-6100
14282 Franklin Ave Tustin (92780) ***(P-7977)***
Ppic, San Francisco *Also called Public Policy Institute Cal* ***(P-24357)***
Ppm Real Estate Inc ....D....510 758-5636
3575 San Pablo Dam Rd El Sobrante (94803) ***(P-11364)***
Ppmc, Corona *Also called Primary Provider MGT Co Inc* ***(P-26358)***
Pponext Inc ....B....888 446-6098
1501 Hughes Way Ste 400 Long Beach (90810) ***(P-22298)***
Pps Parking Inc ....A....949 223-8707
1800 E Garry Ave Ste 107 Santa Ana (92705) ***(P-13448)***
PQL Inc (PA) ....E....805 579-8279
2285 Ward Ave Simi Valley (93065) ***(P-7178)***
PR Rancho Hotel LLC ....D....916 638-4141
11260 Point East Dr Rancho Cordova (95742) ***(P-12769)***
Practice Fusion Inc (HQ) ....C....415 346-7700
731 Market St Ste 400 San Francisco (94103) ***(P-15026)***
Practice Wares Inc ....E....916 526-2674
2377 Gold Meadow Way Gold River (95670) ***(P-6996)***
Practicewares Dental Supply, Gold River *Also called Practice Wares Inc* ***(P-6996)***
Praetorian Event Services, Petaluma *Also called Praetorian USA* ***(P-13449)***
Praetorian Group (PA) ....E....415 962-8310
200 Green St Ste 200 # 200 San Francisco (94111) ***(P-16083)***
Praetorian USA ....D....707 780-8020
925 Lakeville St 129 Petaluma (94952) ***(P-13449)***
Pragiti Inc ....D....408 689-7214
3312 Woodward Ave Santa Clara (95054) ***(P-16084)***
Prairie City Commons LLC ....D....916 458-0303
645 Willard Dr Folsom (95630) ***(P-20445)***
Prairie City Landing, Folsom *Also called Prairie City Commons LLC* ***(P-20445)***
Prajin 1 Stop Distributors Inc (PA) ....E....323 395-5302
5701 Pacific Blvd 5711 Huntington Park (90255) ***(P-7827)***
Prajin Discount Distributors, Huntington Park *Also called Prajin 1 Stop Distributors Inc* ***(P-7827)***
Pramira Inc ....C....800 678-1169
1422 Edinger Ave Ste 250 Tustin (92780) ***(P-16085)***
Prana Living LLC (HQ) ....D....866 915-6457
3209 Lionshead Ave Carlsbad (92010) ***(P-8044)***
Pratt Industries Inc ....E....805 483-5331
1051 S Rose Ave Oxnard (93030) ***(P-9003)***
Praxair Inc ....D....562 983-2100
2300 E Pacific Coast Hwy Wilmington (90744) ***(P-8706)***
Praxair Inc ....D....562 427-0099
2677 Signal Pkwy Long Beach (90755) ***(P-7577)***
PRC ....D....415 777-0333
170 9th St San Francisco (94103) ***(P-24215)***
PRC Builders Inc ....D....949 529-7011
1820 E Garry Ave Ste 211 Santa Ana (92705) ***(P-1264)***
Prdctions N Fremantle Amer Inc (HQ) ....D....818 748-1100
2900 W Alameda Ave # 800 Burbank (91505) ***(P-17937)***
Pre Con Industries Inc ....E....805 345-3147
514 Work St Salinas (93901) ***(P-26355)***
Pre Con Industries Inc ....E....805 481-7305
950 Riata Ln Nipomo (93444) ***(P-2956)***
Pre-Employcom ....D....800 300-1821
3655 Meadow View Dr Redding (96002) ***(P-16380)***
Pre-Employcom Inc ....D....800 300-1821
3655 Meadow View Dr Redding (96002) ***(P-17000)***
Precept Inc (HQ) ....D....949 955-1430
130 Theory Ste 200 Irvine (92617) ***(P-10457)***
Precept Group The, Irvine *Also called Precept Inc* ***(P-10457)***
Precious Enterprises Inc ....D....408 265-2226
14130 Douglass Ln Saratoga (95070) ***(P-23777)***
Precise Auto Protection, Azusa *Also called Precise Enterprises LLC* ***(P-26764)***
Precise Distribution Inc ....E....951 367-1037
12215 Holly St Riverside (92509) ***(P-4473)***
Precise Enterprises LLC ....E....818 599-6450
751 W 9th St Azusa (91702) ***(P-26764)***
Precise Fit Limited One LLC ....B....310 824-1800
17011 Beach Blvd Ste 900 Huntington Beach (92647) ***(P-14358)***
Preciseq Inc ....D....310 709-6094
11601 Wilshire Blvd Fl 5 Los Angeles (90025) ***(P-16086)***
Precision Auto Body, Reseda *Also called Auto Body Management Inc* ***(P-17281)***
Precision Auto Detailing LLC ....D....650 992-9775
700 Serramonte Blvd Colma (94014) ***(P-17393)***
Precision Framing Inc ....B....916 791-7464
1504 Eureka Rd Ste 160 Roseville (95661) ***(P-2957)***
Precision Home Care LLC ....D....916 749-4051
2365 Iron Point Rd # 270 Folsom (95630) ***(P-23393)***
Precision Ideo Inc ....B....650 688-3400
780 High St Palo Alto (94301) ***(P-17001)***
Precision Medical Products Inc ....D....573 474-9302
2217 Plaza Dr Rocklin (95765) ***(P-19306)***
Precision Relocation Inc ....C....714 690-9344
16055 Heron Ave Ste B La Mirada (90638) ***(P-4227)***
Precision Television Inc ....D....925 825-5296
2350 Stanwell Dr Concord (94520) ***(P-17437)***
Precision Toxicology LLC ....D....800 635-6901
4215 Sorrento Valley Blvd San Diego (92121) ***(P-21567)***
Precision TV, Concord *Also called Precision Television Inc* ***(P-17437)***
Predentials, Oakland *Also called Mason-Mcduffie Real Estate Inc* ***(P-11279)***
Predicate Logic Inc (PA) ....D....858 715-0100
6498 Weathers Pl Ste 200 San Diego (92121) ***(P-25268)***
Predicine Inc ....E....650 300-2188
3555 Arden Rd Hayward (94545) ***(P-19307)***
Preferred Brokers Inc (PA) ....D....661 836-2345
9100 Ming Ave Ste 100 Bakersfield (93311) ***(P-11365)***
Preferred Construction Co Inc ....D....714 630-3004
3926 E Broadway Long Beach (90803) ***(P-1569)***
Preferred Employers Insur Co ....D....619 688-3900
9797 Aero Dr Ste 200 San Diego (92123) ***(P-10458)***
Preferred Financial, San Ramon *Also called A D Bilich Inc* ***(P-9513)***

A L P H A B E T I C

Employee Codes: A=Over 500 employees, B=251-500
C=101-250, D=51-100, E=50
2020 Directory of California
Wholesalers and Services Companies
© Mergent Inc. 1-800-342-5647
1391

Preferred Frzr Svcs - Lbf LLC .... D 323 263-8811
4901 Bandini Blvd Vernon (90058) ***(P-4351)***

Preferred Hlthcare Rgistry Inc .... C 800 787-6787
4909 Murphy Canyon Rd # 310 San Diego (92123) ***(P-14359)***

Preferred Insulation Contrs (PA) .... D 951 735-3725
1691 Jenks Dr Corona (92880) ***(P-3451)***

Preferred Plumbing and Drain, North Highlands *Also called AAA Drain Patrol* ***(P-2012)***

Preferred Produce, Salinas *Also called Elioco Produce Inc* ***(P-618)***

Preferred Valet Parking LLC .... E 619 233-7275
2568 Violet St San Diego (92105) ***(P-17272)***

Pregis LLC .... D 510 404-1360
33340 Central Ave Union City (94587) ***(P-9004)***

Prellis Mortgage Company, Granada Hills *Also called C21 Peak* ***(P-10957)***

Prelude Systems Inc (PA) .... C 949 208-7126
5 Corporate Park Ste 140 Irvine (92606) ***(P-16087)***

PRELUDESYS, Irvine *Also called Prelude Systems Inc* ***(P-16087)***

Premier America Credit Union (PA) .... C 818 772-4000
19867 Prairie St Lbby Chatsworth (91311) ***(P-9401)***

Premier Auto W Covina LLC .... D 626 858-7202
777 W Orangethorpe Ave Placentia (92870) ***(P-17341)***

Premier Building Maint Svcs, Los Angeles *Also called Pbms Inc* ***(P-14003)***

Premier Business Centers, Irvine *Also called Premier Office Centers LLC* ***(P-17002)***

Premier Care Ctr For Palm Sprn, Palm Springs *Also called Ensign Palm I LLC* ***(P-19888)***

Premier Commercial Bancorp .... D 714 978-2400
2400 E Katella Ave # 125 Anaheim (92806) ***(P-9232)***

Premier Dealer Services Inc .... D 858 810-1700
9449 Balboa Ave Ste 300 San Diego (92123) ***(P-10459)***

Premier Drywall, Salinas *Also called Pre Con Industries Inc* ***(P-26355)***

Premier Drywall .... D 805 928-3397
725 Oak St Santa Maria (93454) ***(P-2843)***

Premier Exec Solutions Inc .... E 310 989-9925
269 S Beverly Dr Ste 981 Beverly Hills (90212) ***(P-27171)***

Premier Floor Care Inc (PA) .... C 925 679-4901
390 Carrol Ct Ste C Brentwood (94513) ***(P-14013)***

Premier Healthcare Svcs LLC (HQ) .... C 626 204-7930
3030 Old Ranch Pkwy # 100 Seal Beach (90740) ***(P-14360)***

Premier Hlthcare Solutions Inc .... B 858 569-8629
12225 El Camino Real San Diego (92130) ***(P-26356)***

Premier IMS Insurance Services, San Diego *Also called Premier Hlthcare Solutions Inc* ***(P-26356)***

Premier Infusion Care, Torrance *Also called Pharmaco Inc* ***(P-21841)***

Premier Insite Group Inc .... D 562 741-5018
111 W Ocean Blvd Ste 400 Long Beach (90802) ***(P-14361)***

Premier Mailing Inc .... E 562 408-2134
14522 Garfield Ave Paramount (90723) ***(P-13736)***

Premier Mailing Services, Paramount *Also called Premier Mailing Inc* ***(P-13736)***

Premier Management Company, Los Angeles *Also called B H Premier Inc* ***(P-21679)***

Premier Management Company .... E 619 582-5168
4075 54th St San Diego (92105) ***(P-21844)***

Premier Meat Company, Vernon *Also called Wayne Provision Co Inc* ***(P-8422)***

Premier Medical Transport Inc .... D 888 353-9556
260 N Palm St 200 Brea (92821) ***(P-5031)***

Premier Medical Trnsp Inc .... D 909 433-3939
575 Maple Ct Ste A Colton (92324) ***(P-3707)***

Premier Mushrooms LP (PA) .... C 530 458-2700
2880 Niagara Ave Colusa (95932) ***(P-8509)***

Premier Mushrooms LP .... C 530 458-2700
2847 Niagara Ave Colusa (95932) ***(P-299)***

Premier Nursing Services Inc (PA) .... A 562 437-4313
444 W Ocean Blvd Ste 1050 Long Beach (90802) ***(P-14362)***

Premier Office Centers LLC (PA) .... E 949 253-4616
2102 Business Center Dr Irvine (92612) ***(P-17002)***

Premier Packaging/Assembly, Santa Fe Springs *Also called Haringa Inc* ***(P-16816)***

Premier Plumbing Company, Riverside *Also called Ppc Enterprises Inc* ***(P-2236)***

Premier Pools and Spas Lp (PA) .... D 916 852-0223
11250 Pyrites Way Gold River (95670) ***(P-3452)***

Premier Residential Svcs LLC .... D 760 773-4081
43100 Cook St Ste 101 Palm Desert (92211) ***(P-13450)***

Premier Source LLC .... D 415 349-2010
999 Bayhill Dr Fl 3 San Bruno (94066) ***(P-26020)***

Premier Tile & Marble .... D 310 516-1712
15000 S Main St Gardena (90248) ***(P-2906)***

Premier Valley Inc A Cal Corp (PA) .... D 209 847-6111
1414 E F St Bldg A Oakdale (95361) ***(P-11366)***

Premiere Financial .... D 760 518-5034
6498 Willow Pl Carlsbad (92011) ***(P-9840)***

Premiere Packing, Shafter *Also called Grimmway Enterprises Inc* ***(P-325)***

Premiere Properties, Carlsbad *Also called Premiere Financial* ***(P-9840)***

Premiere Radio Network Inc (HQ) .... C 818 377-5300
15260 Ventura Blvd # 400 Sherman Oaks (91403) ***(P-17938)***

Premium Harvesting, Salinas *Also called Premium Packing Inc* ***(P-457)***

Premium Packing Inc .... C 831 443-6855
449 Harrison Rd Salinas (93907) ***(P-457)***

Premium Quality Lighting, Simi Valley *Also called PQL Inc* ***(P-7178)***

Premium Rock Drywall Inc .... D 818 676-3350
31348 Via Colinas Ste 103 Westlake Village (91362) ***(P-2844)***

Premium Trnsp Svcs Inc (PA) .... D 310 816-0260
18735 S Ferris Pl Rancho Dominguez (90220) ***(P-4474)***

Prentice Hall Legal Fincl Svcs, Sacramento *Also called Corporation Service Company* ***(P-13894)***

Presbyterian Health Physicians .... C 562 464-4717
6557 Greenleaf Ave Whittier (90601) ***(P-21105)***

Presbyterian Inter Cmnty Hosp, Whittier *Also called Interhealth Services Inc* ***(P-21790)***

Preschool Service, San Bernardino *Also called County of San Bernardino* ***(P-23712)***

Prescott Companies (PA) .... C 760 634-4700
5950 La Place Ct Ste 200 Carlsbad (92008) ***(P-11367)***

Prescott Hotel, The, San Francisco *Also called Post Street Renaissance* ***(P-12768)***

Prescription Solutions, Carlsbad *Also called Optumrx Inc* ***(P-10022)***

Prescription Solutions, Irvine *Also called Optumrx Inc* ***(P-10023)***

Prescription Solutions .... A 760 804-2370
2858 Loker Ave E Ste 100 Carlsbad (92010) ***(P-26765)***

Preserve Golf Club Inc .... E 831 620-6871
1 Rancho San Carlos Rd Carmel (93923) ***(P-18282)***

Presidian Hotel, Visalia *Also called Viscamar LLC* ***(P-13067)***

Presidio Community YMCA, San Francisco *Also called Young Mens Christian Assoc SF* ***(P-24733)***

Presidio Components Inc .... C 858 578-9390
7169 Construction Ct San Diego (92121) ***(P-7321)***

Presidio Hotel Group LLC (PA) .... C 707 429-6000
1011 10th St Sacramento (95814) ***(P-12770)***

Presidio Hotel Group LLC .... D 916 631-7500
10713 White Rock Rd Rancho Cordova (95670) ***(P-12771)***

Presidio Wealth Management LLC .... E 415 449-2500
101 California St # 2400 San Francisco (94111) ***(P-9841)***

Presido YMCA, San Francisco *Also called Young Mens Christian Assnsf* ***(P-24728)***

Pressed Juicery Inc .... E 559 777-8900
3530 E Church Ave Fresno (93725) ***(P-8634)***

Prestige Asstd Lvng in Chico, Chico *Also called Caldwell Ventures LLC* ***(P-19771)***

Prestige Auto Collision Inc .... D 949 470-6031
23726 Via Fabricante Mission Viejo (92691) ***(P-17303)***

Prestige Car Wash Lafayette LP .... E 925 283-1190
3319 Mt Diablo Blvd Lafayette (94549) ***(P-17394)***

Prestige Concrete .... D 858 679-2772
13507 Midland Rd Poway (92064) ***(P-3203)***

Prestige Preschools Inc (PA) .... D 818 957-1170
3795 La Crescenta Ave # 200 Glendale (91208) ***(P-23778)***

Prestige Protection, San Ramon *Also called Universal Protection Svc LP* ***(P-16467)***

Prestige Sales II LLC .... D 714 632-8020
1038 E Bastanchury Rd Fullerton (92835) ***(P-8635)***

Prestige Security Service Inc .... B 310 670-5999
5721 W Slauson Ave # 120 Culver City (90230) ***(P-16381)***

Prestige Too Auto Body Inc .... E 310 787-8852
11899 Woodruff Ave Downey (90241) ***(P-17304)***

Preston Pipelines Inc (PA) .... C 408 262-1418
133 Bothelo Ave Milpitas (95035) ***(P-1903)***

Preston Wynne Spa Inc .... D 408 741-1750
14567 Big Basin Way A2 Saratoga (95070) ***(P-18186)***

Prevent Life Safety Svcs Inc .... E 925 667-2088
1410 Stealth St Livermore (94551) ***(P-17003)***

Prevention Institute .... D 510 444-4133
221 Oak St Ste A Oakland (94607) ***(P-26766)***

Prg (california) Inc .... E 818 252-2600
1245 Aviation Pl San Fernando (91340) ***(P-17655)***

Prg Parking Century LLC .... D 310 642-0947
5701 W Century Blvd Los Angeles (90045) ***(P-17273)***

Prh Pro Inc .... C 714 510-7226
13089 Peyton Dr Ste C362 Chino Hills (91709) ***(P-7648)***

PRI Medical Technologies Inc (HQ) .... D 818 394-2800
10939 Pendleton St Sun Valley (91352) ***(P-6997)***

Pribuss Engineering Inc .... D 650 588-0447
523 Mayfair Ave South San Francisco (94080) ***(P-2237)***

Price Associates .... E 818 995-9216
15760 Ventura Blvd # 1100 Encino (91436) ***(P-22773)***

Price Law Group A Prof Corp (PA) .... C 818 995-4540
15760 Ventura Blvd # 1100 Encino (91436) ***(P-22774)***

Price Postel and Parma LLP .... D 805 962-0011
200 E Carrillo St Ste 400 Santa Barbara (93101) ***(P-22775)***

Price Spider, Irvine *Also called Neuintel LLC* ***(P-14958)***

Price, Stuart, Encino *Also called Price Associates* ***(P-22773)***

Pricemetrix Usa Inc .... E 714 357-6192
3 Bridgeport Rd Newport Coast (92657) ***(P-15800)***

Pricewaterhousecoopers LLP .... B 949 437-5200
2020 Main St Ste 400 Irvine (92614) ***(P-25662)***

Pricewaterhousecoopers LLP .... A 408 817-3700
488 Almaden Blvd Ste 1800 San Jose (95110) ***(P-25663)***

Pricewaterhousecoopers LLP .... B 858 677-2400
5375 Mira Sorrento Pl San Diego (92121) ***(P-25664)***

Pricewaterhousecoopers LLP .... D 916 930-8100
400 Capitol Mall Ste 600 Sacramento (95814) ***(P-25665)***

Pricewaterhousecoopers LLP .... B 415 498-5000
3 Embarcadero Ctr Fl 20 San Francisco (94111) ***(P-25666)***

Pride Auto Body, Van Nuys *Also called Pride Collision Centers Inc* ***(P-17305)***

Pride Collision Centers Inc (PA) .... D 818 909-0660
7950 Haskell Ave Van Nuys (91406) ***(P-17305)***

Pride Industries (PA) .... C 916 788-2100
10030 Foothills Blvd Roseville (95747) ***(P-4576)***

Pride Industries .... C 805 985-8481
Cbc Base Bldg 19 43rd St Port Hueneme (93041) ***(P-1265)***

Pride Industries .... C 530 888-0331
13080 Earhart Ave Auburn (95602) ***(P-23628)***

Pride Industries .... D 530 477-1832
12451 Loma Rica Dr Grass Valley (95945) ***(P-23629)***

Pride Industries .... D 916 334-5415
3608 Madison Ave Ste 43 North Highlands (95660) ***(P-23630)***

Pride Industries .... C 916 649-9499
1281 National Dr Sacramento (95834) ***(P-27301)***

Prima Royale, Pasadena *Also called Prima Royale Enterprises Ltd* ***(P-8141)***

Prima Royale Enterprises Ltd .... D 626 960-8388
150 S Los Robles Ave # 100 Pasadena (91101) ***(P-8141)***

Primal Blueprint, Oxnard *Also called Primal Nutrition LLC* ***(P-7979)***

Primal Elements Inc .... D 714 899-0757
18062 Redondo Cir Huntington Beach (92648) ***(P-7978)***

Primal Nutrition LLC .... E 310 317-4414
1631 S Rose Ave Oxnard (93033) ***(P-7979)***

Primary Care Assod Med Group (PA) ....D....760 471-7505
1635 Lake San Marcos Dr # 201 San Marcos (92078) ***(P-26357)***
Primary Color Systems Corp ....C....310 841-0250
401 Coral Cir El Segundo (90245) ***(P-13771)***
Primary Critical Care Medical ....C....818 847-9950
620 N Brand Blvd Ste 500 Glendale (91203) ***(P-19308)***
Primary Eyecare Network, Alameda *Also called Abb/Con-Cise Optical Group LLC* ***(P-7019)***
Primary Freight Services Inc (PA) ....D....310 635-3000
6545 Caballero Blvd Buena Park (90620) ***(P-5032)***
Primary Provider MGT Co Inc (PA) ....C....951 280-7700
2115 Compton Ave Ste 301 Corona (92881) ***(P-26358)***
Prime Administration LLC ....A....323 549-7155
357 S Curson Ave Los Angeles (90036) ***(P-11871)***
Prime Clinical Systems (PA) ....D....626 449-1705
3675 Huntington Dr Ste A Pasadena (91107) ***(P-15027)***
Prime Communications LP ....D....951 253-3304
29273 Central Ave Lake Elsinore (92532) ***(P-5268)***
Prime Focus North America Inc (PA) ....D....323 461-7887
5750 Hannum Ave Ste 100 Culver City (90230) ***(P-17760)***
Prime Focus World, Culver City *Also called Prime Focus North America Inc* ***(P-17760)***
Prime Global Solutions Inc (PA) ....D....800 424-7746
15801 E Valley Blvd City of Industry (91744) ***(P-5033)***
Prime Group, Los Angeles *Also called Prime Administration LLC* ***(P-11871)***
Prime Health Care Svcs Grdn Gr ....B....714 537-5160
12601 Garden Grove Blvd Garden Grove (92843) ***(P-21106)***
Prime Healthcare Anaheim LLC ....A....714 827-3000
3033 W Orange Ave Anaheim (92804) ***(P-21107)***
Prime Healthcare Centinela LLC ....A....310 673-4660
555 E Hardy St Inglewood (90301) ***(P-21108)***
Prime Healthcare Services, Ontario *Also called Bio-Med Services Inc* ***(P-22185)***
Prime Healthcare Services ....A....530 244-5400
1100 Butte St Redding (96001) ***(P-21109)***
Prime Healthcare Services - Sh ....A....818 981-7111
4929 Van Nuys Blvd Sherman Oaks (91403) ***(P-26767)***
Prime Healthcare Servs Sh ....A....530 244-5458
1450 Liberty St Redding (96001) ***(P-21110)***
Prime Healthcare Svcs II LLC ....B....818 981-7111
4929 Van Nuys Blvd Sherman Oaks (91403) ***(P-21111)***
Prime Healthcare Svcs III LLC (HQ) ....C....909 625-5411
5000 San Bernardino St Montclair (91763) ***(P-21112)***
Prime Healthcare-San Dimas LLC ....B....909 599-6811
1350 W Covina Blvd San Dimas (91773) ***(P-21113)***
Prime Hlthcare Hntngton Bch ....B....714 843-5000
17772 Beach Blvd Huntington Beach (92647) ***(P-21114)***
Prime International Security ....D....310 670-4565
1630 Centinela Ave # 209 Inglewood (90302) ***(P-16382)***
Prime Security, Inglewood *Also called Prime International Security* ***(P-16382)***
Prime Stop, Moreno Valley *Also called Plaza Hand Carwash Inc* ***(P-17392)***
Prime Tech Cabinets Inc ....C....949 757-4900
2215 S Standard Ave Santa Ana (92707) ***(P-2958)***
Prime Time Athletic Club Inc ....D....650 204-3662
1730 Rollins Rd Burlingame (94010) ***(P-18187)***
Prime Time International, Coachella *Also called Sun and Sands Enterprises LLC* ***(P-79)***
Prime-Line Products Company (HQ) ....B....909 887-8118
26950 San Bernardino Ave Redlands (92374) ***(P-7403)***
Primecare Quality HM Care Inc ....D....949 681-3515
2372 Morse Ave Irvine (92614) ***(P-1176)***
Primeco Painting & Cnstr ....D....760 967-8278
220 Oceanside Blvd Oceanside (92054) ***(P-2379)***
Primed MGT Consulting Svcs Inc ....B....925 327-6710
2409 Camino Ramon San Ramon (94583) ***(P-26359)***
Primerica Financial Svcs Inc ....D....951 695-4325
27470 Jefferson Ave 5a Temecula (92590) ***(P-10460)***
Primerica Life Insurance Co ....C....650 323-2554
260 Sheridan Ave Ste B42 Palo Alto (94306) ***(P-10461)***
Primerica Life Insurance Co ....C....661 947-9070
41307 12th St W Ste 200 Palmdale (93551) ***(P-10462)***
Primerica Life Insurance Co ....C....951 652-6190
175 N Cawston Ave Hemet (92545) ***(P-10463)***
Primero Systems Incorporated ....D....866 426-0779
14123 Rasmussen Way San Diego (92129) ***(P-15028)***
Primetime International Inc ....D....760 399-4166
86705 Avenue 54 Ste A Coachella (92236) ***(P-8510)***
Primex Clinical Labs Inc (PA) ....D....818 779-0496
16742 Stagg St Ste 120 Van Nuys (91406) ***(P-21568)***
Primitive Logic Inc ....D....415 391-8080
704 Sansome St San Francisco (94111) ***(P-16088)***
Primm Valley Golf Club ....D....702 679-5509
1 Yates Wells Rd Nipton (92364) ***(P-18283)***
Primrose Alzheimers Living (PA) ....E....707 568-4355
726 College Ave Santa Rosa (95404) ***(P-24029)***
Primrose Alzheimers Living ....E....707 578-8360
2080 Guerneville Rd Santa Rosa (95403) ***(P-24030)***
Primrose Alzheimers Living ....D....916 392-3510
7707 Rush River Dr Sacramento (95831) ***(P-24031)***
Primrose Sacramento, Sacramento *Also called Primrose Alzheimers Living* ***(P-24031)***
Primus Group Inc (PA) ....E....805 922-0055
2810 Industrial Pkwy Santa Maria (93455) ***(P-26768)***
Primus Labs, Santa Maria *Also called Primus Group Inc* ***(P-26768)***
Primx Entertainment LLC ....E....818 324-5229
9664 Andora Ave Chatsworth (91311) ***(P-17998)***
Princess Cruise Lines Ltd ....A....661 753-2197
24833 Anza Dr Santa Clarita (91355) ***(P-4833)***
Princess Cruise Lines Ltd (HQ) ....A....661 753-0000
24305 Town Center Dr Santa Clarita (91355) ***(P-4596)***
Princess Cruises, Santa Clarita *Also called Princess Cruise Lines Ltd* ***(P-4833)***
Princess Cruises, Santa Clarita *Also called Princess Cruise Lines Ltd* ***(P-4596)***
Princess Cruises and Tours Inc (HQ) ....A....206 336-6000
24305 Town Center Dr # 200 Valencia (91355) ***(P-4834)***
Principal Financial Group Inc ....D....818 243-7141
500 N Brand Blvd Ste 1800 Glendale (91203) ***(P-10464)***
Principal Financial Group Inc ....D....559 261-2000
1350 E Spruce Ave Ste 100 Fresno (93720) ***(P-9887)***
Principles Inc (PA) ....D....323 681-2575
1680 N Fair Oaks Ave Pasadena (91103) ***(P-22101)***
Prindle Decker & Amaro LLP (PA) ....D....562 436-3946
310 Golden Shore Fl 4 Long Beach (90802) ***(P-22776)***
Printing Inds Assn Suthern Cal ....D....323 728-9500
5800 S Eastrn Ave Ste 400 Commerce (90040) ***(P-24355)***
Printing Technology Inc ....C....818 576-9220
9831 Independence Ave Chatsworth (91311) ***(P-7649)***
Priority 1 Warehousing Inc (PA) ....D....209 824-8876
2577 W Yosemite Ave Manteca (95337) ***(P-4475)***
Priority Building Services LLC ....B....858 695-1326
7313 Carroll Rd Ste G San Diego (92121) ***(P-14014)***
Priority Building Services LLC (PA) ....D....714 255-2940
521 Mercury Ln Brea (92821) ***(P-14015)***
Priority Cooling, Firebaugh *Also called Tri-State AG Inc* ***(P-6360)***
Priority Dispatch Service Inc ....D....408 400-3860
309 Laurelwood Rd Ste 10 Santa Clara (95054) ***(P-4278)***
Priority Landscape Services, Brea *Also called Priority Building Services LLC* ***(P-14015)***
Priority One Credit Union (PA) ....D....323 682-1999
1631 Huntington Dr South Pasadena (91030) ***(P-9336)***
Priority One Med Trnspt Inc (PA) ....D....909 948-4400
9327 Fairway View Pl # 300 Rancho Cucamonga (91730) ***(P-3708)***
Priority One Support, Irvine *Also called Alorica Inc* ***(P-15720)***
Prism Electronics Corp (PA) ....E....408 778-7050
900 Lightpost Way 100 Morgan Hill (95037) ***(P-7322)***
Prison Industry Authority-Pia ....D....559 386-6060
1 Kings Way Avenal (93204) ***(P-22777)***
Pritchett Rapf and Associates ....D....310 456-6771
23732 Malibu Rd Malibu (90265) ***(P-11368)***
Private Industry Cncl Slno Cty (PA) ....E....707 864-3370
500 Chadbourne Rd Fairfield (94534) ***(P-14363)***
Private Label Pc LLC ....C....626 965-8686
748 Epperson Dr Ste B City of Industry (91748) ***(P-6886)***
Private Medical-Care Inc ....C....562 924-8311
12898 Towne Center Dr Cerritos (90703) ***(P-10037)***
Private Nat Mrtg Accptance LLC (HQ) ....A....818 224-7401
6101 Condor Dr Agoura Hills (91301) ***(P-9593)***
Privilege International Inc ....D....323 585-0777
2323 Firestone Blvd South Gate (90280) ***(P-6529)***
Priyo Inc ....E....408 248-2507
605 Tumbleweed Cmn Fremont (94539) ***(P-15029)***
Prize Proz ....E....909 509-8600
1500 S Hellman Ave Ontario (91761) ***(P-26769)***
Prn LLC (HQ) ....D....415 805-2525
600 Montgomery St # 1800 San Francisco (94111) ***(P-15030)***
Prn Ambulance LLC ....B....818 810-3600
8928 Sepulveda Blvd North Hills (91343) ***(P-3709)***
Prn Radio Networks, Sherman Oaks *Also called Premiere Radio Network Inc* ***(P-17938)***
Pro Act LLC ....D....831 655-4250
40 Ragsdale Dr Ste 200 Monterey (93940) ***(P-8511)***
Pro America Premium Tools, Baldwin Park *Also called American Kal Enterprises Inc* ***(P-7378)***
Pro Building Maintenance Inc ....C....951 279-3386
149 N Maple St Ste H Corona (92880) ***(P-14016)***
Pro Care 2000 Home Health Care, Long Beach *Also called Pacific Care Inc* ***(P-21833)***
Pro Group Inc ....C....951 271-3000
4160 Temescal Canyon Rd # 500 Corona (92883) ***(P-11369)***
Pro Loaders Inc (PA) ....C....909 355-5531
14032 Santa Ana Ave Fontana (92337) ***(P-5034)***
Pro Pacific Fresh, Durham *Also called Chico Produce Inc* ***(P-8442)***
Pro Ponds West Inc ....D....818 244-4000
8309 Tujunga Ave Unit 201 Sun Valley (91352) ***(P-752)***
Pro Specialties Group Inc ....D....858 541-1100
8221 Arjons Dr Ste F San Diego (92126) ***(P-9005)***
Pro Structural Inc ....D....951 526-2010
26105 Sherman Rd Menifee (92585) ***(P-2726)***
Pro Unlimited Inc ....E....650 344-1099
1350 Bayshore Hwy Ste 350 Burlingame (94010) ***(P-26360)***
Pro-Craft Construction Inc ....C....909 790-5222
500 Iowa St Ste 100 Redlands (92373) ***(P-2238)***
Pro-Med Hlth Care Admnistrator ....D....909 932-1045
4150 Concours Ste 100 Ontario (91764) ***(P-26361)***
Pro-Tech Design & Mfg Inc ....D....562 207-1680
14561 Marquardt Ave Santa Fe Springs (90670) ***(P-17004)***
Pro-Tek Consulting (PA) ....C....805 807-5571
21300 Victory Blvd # 240 Woodland Hills (91367) ***(P-16089)***
Pro-Wash Inc ....D....323 756-6000
9117 S Main St Los Angeles (90003) ***(P-13250)***
Proactiv, El Segundo *Also called Guthy-Renker LLC* ***(P-7814)***
Proactive Bus Solutions Inc ....C....510 302-0120
428 13th St Fl 5 Oakland (94612) ***(P-26362)***
Proactive Risk Management Inc ....D....213 840-8856
22617 Hawthorne Blvd Torrance (90505) ***(P-26363)***
Proactive Technical Svcs Inc ....E....408 531-6040
2350 Mission College Blvd # 246 Santa Clara (95054) ***(P-15031)***
Probation, Red Bluff *Also called County of Tehama* ***(P-23176)***
Probation Department, Fresno *Also called County of Fresno* ***(P-23068)***
Probation Department, Pasadena *Also called County of Los Angeles* ***(P-23082)***
Probation Department, Lancaster *Also called County of Los Angeles* ***(P-23084)***
Probation Department, Redwood City *Also called County of San Mateo* ***(P-23157)***
Probation Department, San Mateo *Also called County of San Mateo* ***(P-23158)***
Probation Department, San Mateo *Also called County of San Mateo* ***(P-23159)***
Probation Department, Clovis *Also called County of Fresno* ***(P-23069)***
Probation Department, Sacramento *Also called Sacramento County Off Educatn* ***(P-23421)***

A L P H A B E T I C

Employee Codes: A=Over 500 employees, B=251-500
C=101-250, D=51-100, E=50
2020 Directory of California
Wholesalers and Services Companies
© Mergent Inc. 1-800-342-5647
1393

Probation Department, Los Angeles *Also called County of Los Angeles* ***(P-23092)***

Probation Department, East Palo Alto *Also called County of San Mateo* ***(P-23160)***

Probation Department, San Mateo *Also called County of San Mateo* ***(P-23163)***

Probation Department, Redwood City *Also called County of San Mateo* ***(P-23164)***

Probation Dept, San Diego *Also called County of San Diego* ***(P-23146)***

Probation Dept, Anaheim *Also called County of Orange* ***(P-23121)***

Probation Dept, Westminster *Also called County of Orange* ***(P-23122)***

Probation Dept, Modesto *Also called County of Stanislaus* ***(P-23171)***

Probation Dept, Los Angeles *Also called County of Los Angeles* ***(P-23090)***

Probation Dept, Rancho Cucamonga *Also called County of San Bernardino* ***(P-23140)***

Probation Dept, Santa Barbara *Also called Santa Barbara County of* ***(P-23444)***

Probation Dept, Santa Maria *Also called Santa Barbara County of* ***(P-23445)***

Probation Dept, Santa Monica *Also called County of Los Angeles* ***(P-23100)***

Probation Dept, Van Nuys *Also called County of Los Angeles* ***(P-23101)***

Probation Dept, Los Angeles *Also called County of Los Angeles* ***(P-23103)***

Probation Dept, Los Angeles *Also called County of Los Angeles* ***(P-23106)***

Probation Dept, Compton *Also called County of Los Angeles* ***(P-23107)***

Probation Dept, Pasadena *Also called County of Los Angeles* ***(P-23108)***

Probation Dept, San Jose *Also called Santa Clara County of* ***(P-23450)***

Probation Dept, Auburn *Also called County of Placer* ***(P-23128)***

Probation Dept, Santa Barbara *Also called Santa Barbara County of* ***(P-23447)***

Probation Dept-Juvenile, Bakersfield *Also called County of Kern* ***(P-23075)***

Probation Dept-Juvenile Div, Morgan Hill *Also called Santa Clara County of* ***(P-24065)***

Probe Information Services Inc......C......916 676-1826
6375 Auburn Blvd Citrus Heights (95621) ***(P-16383)***

Prober & Raphael A Law Corp......D......818 227-0100
20750 Ventura Blvd # 100 Woodland Hills (91364) ***(P-22778)***

Prober & Raphael, ALC, Woodland Hills *Also called Prober & Raphael A Law Corp* ***(P-22778)***

Procel Temporary Services Inc......B......310 372-0560
222 W 6th St Ste 370 San Pedro (90731) ***(P-14547)***

Procera Networks Inc (HQ)......D......510 230-2777
2055 Junction Ave Ste 105 San Jose (95131) ***(P-15032)***

Processing Office, Corcoran *Also called J G Boswell Company* ***(P-506)***

Procida Landscape Inc......C......916 387-5296
8465 Specialty Cir Sacramento (95828) ***(P-893)***

Procore Technologies Inc (PA)......A......866 477-6267
6309 Carpinteria Ave Carpinteria (93013) ***(P-15033)***

Procter & Gamble Distrg LLC......B......209 538-3987
1992 Rockefeller Dr Ceres (95307) ***(P-8707)***

Procter & Gamble Distrg LLC......B......925 867-4900
2010 Crow Canyon Pl # 230 San Ramon (94583) ***(P-8708)***

Proctoru Inc......B......205 870-8122
3687 Old Sta Pleasanton (94588) ***(P-15879)***

Prodata Research, San Diego *Also called Soleil Communications LLC* ***(P-25944)***

Prodege LLC (PA)......D......310 294-9599
100 N Pacific Coast Hwy # 800 El Segundo (90245) ***(P-15034)***

Produce Company......C......310 508-7760
16809 Bellflower Blvd # 32 Bellflower (90706) ***(P-8512)***

Produce Exchange Incorporated (HQ)......D......925 454-8700
7407 Southfront Rd Livermore (94551) ***(P-8513)***

Producer -Writers Guild......D......818 846-1015
2900 W Alameda Ave # 1100 Burbank (91505) ***(P-10222)***

Producers Dairy Foods Inc (PA)......C......559 264-6583
250 E Belmont Ave Fresno (93701) ***(P-8295)***

Produces Dairy, Fresno *Also called L A S Transportation Inc* ***(P-4079)***

Product Development Corp (PA)......C......831 333-1100
30 Ragsdale Dr Ste 101 Monterey (93940) ***(P-17005)***

Product Partners, Santa Monica *Also called Beachbody LLC* ***(P-13614)***

Product Quality Partners Inc......D......925 484-6491
450 Main St Ste 207 Pleasanton (94566) ***(P-16090)***

Production Delivery Svcs Inc......D......562 777-0060
12133 Greenstone Ave Santa Fe Springs (90670) ***(P-4114)***

Production Fcilities Unlimited, La Puente *Also called San Gabriel Vly Training Ctr* ***(P-23634)***

Production Framing Inc......D......916 978-2843
2000 Opportunity Dr # 140 Roseville (95678) ***(P-2959)***

Production Framing Systems Inc (PA)......C......916 978-2888
2000 Opportunity Dr # 140 Roseville (95678) ***(P-2960)***

Production Plus Plumbing Inc......C......760 597-0235
2472 Grand Ave Vista (92081) ***(P-2239)***

Production Special Events Svcs......E......818 831-5326
17326 Devonshire St Northridge (91325) ***(P-17939)***

Production Transport, Santa Fe Springs *Also called Production Delivery Svcs Inc* ***(P-4114)***

Productos Chata, Chula Vista *Also called Culinary Hispanic Foods Inc* ***(P-8572)***

Professional Building Maint, Sun Valley *Also called PBM Maintenance Corp* ***(P-14002)***

Professional Bureau of Collect......C......916 685-3399
9675 Elk Grove Florin Rd Elk Grove (95624) ***(P-13695)***

Professional Cabinet Solutions......C......909 614-2900
11350 Riverside Dr Frnt Jurupa Valley (91752) ***(P-2961)***

Professional Community MGT Cal (PA)......E......800 369-7260
27051 Towne Centre Dr # 200 Foothill Ranch (92610) ***(P-11370)***

Professional Community MGT Cal......E......951 845-2191
850 Country Club Dr Banning (92220) ***(P-11371)***

Professional Community MGT Cal......C......949 206-0580
24351 El Toro Rd Laguna Woods (92637) ***(P-11372)***

Professional Community MGT Cal......D......949 768-7261
27051 Towne Centre Dr # 200 Foothill Ranch (92610) ***(P-10858)***

Professional Community MGT Cal......C......949 597-4200
23522 Paseo De Valencia Laguna Hills (92653) ***(P-11373)***

Professional Construction Svcs, Rancho Cucamonga *Also called Rwc Enterprises Inc* ***(P-25291)***

Professional Exchange Svc......E......559 229-6249
4747 N 1st St Ste 140 Fresno (93726) ***(P-17006)***

Professional Golf MGT LLC......D......760 564-0804
49155 Vista Estrella La Quinta (92253) ***(P-26364)***

Professional Health Tech......D......858 449-1599
8131 Calle Del Cielo La Jolla (92037) ***(P-19309)***

Professional Hospital Sup Inc (HQ)......A......951 699-5000
42500 Winchester Rd Temecula (92590) ***(P-6998)***

Professional Insur Assoc Inc (PA)......E......650 592-7333
1100 Industrial Rd Ste 3 San Carlos (94070) ***(P-10465)***

Professional Janitorial Svc......E......310 410-1452
234 Eucalyptus Dr B El Segundo (90245) ***(P-14017)***

Professional Maint Systems, San Diego *Also called Professional Maint Systems Inc* ***(P-14018)***

Professional Maint Systems Inc......A......619 276-1150
4912 Naples St San Diego (92110) ***(P-14018)***

Professional Medical MGT, Hemet *Also called Hemet Valley Imaging Med Group* ***(P-19009)***

Professional Produce......D......323 277-1550
2570 E 25th St Los Angeles (90058) ***(P-8514)***

Professional Security Cons (PA)......C......310 207-7729
11454 San Vicente Blvd # 2 Los Angeles (90049) ***(P-16384)***

Professional Services Company, San Francisco *Also called Shenyang Zhong Yi Tin-Plating* ***(P-10644)***

Professional Staffing, Granada Hills *Also called PS National Inc* ***(P-14369)***

Professional Staffing Associat, Downey *Also called Rancho Los Amigos Nationa* ***(P-23399)***

Professional Svcs Med Group, Huntington Park *Also called All Care Medical Group Inc* ***(P-18792)***

Professionals Choice Sport......D......619 873-1100
2025 Gillespie Way # 106 El Cajon (92020) ***(P-8854)***

Professnal Cmmnctons Netwrk LP (PA)......E......951 275-9149
6774 Magnolia Ave Riverside (92506) ***(P-17007)***

Professnal Creer Placementscom......E......415 615-0688
1990 N Calif Blvd Fl 8 Walnut Creek (94596) ***(P-14364)***

Professnal Elec Cnstr Svcs Inc......C......909 373-4100
9112 Santa Anita Ave Rancho Cucamonga (91730) ***(P-2593)***

Professnal Ldscp Solutions Inc......E......916 424-3815
6108 27th St Ste C Sacramento (95822) ***(P-753)***

Professnal Rgistry Netwrk Corp......C......714 394-4071
20132 Canyon Dr Yorba Linda (92886) ***(P-14365)***

Professonal Technical SEC Svcs......B......510 645-9200
1970 Broadway Ste 840 Oakland (94612) ***(P-16385)***

Professonal Tele Answering Svc, Chatsworth *Also called Seven One Inc* ***(P-17054)***

Professsional Insurance, San Carlos *Also called Professional Insur Assoc Inc* ***(P-10465)***

Proficient LLC......D......310 519-8200
601 S Palos Verdes St San Pedro (90731) ***(P-12772)***

Proficio Inc (PA)......E......800 779-5042
3264 Grey Hawk Ct Carlsbad (92010) ***(P-6887)***

Profile of Santa Cruz......D......831 479-0393
2045 40th Ave Ste B Capitola (95010) ***(P-14366)***

Profit Recovery Partners LLC......D......949 851-2777
2995 Red Hill Ave Ste 200 Costa Mesa (92626) ***(P-27172)***

Proform Interior Cnstr Inc......D......619 881-0041
663 33rd St Ste C San Diego (92102) ***(P-3453)***

Progauge Technologies Inc......E......661 392-9600
2331 Cepheus Ct Bakersfield (93308) ***(P-7578)***

Progenity Inc (PA)......C......760 494-1555
4330 La Jolla Village Dr # 200 San Diego (92122) ***(P-21569)***

Progress Foundation......D......415 553-3100
52 Dore St San Francisco (94103) ***(P-24616)***

Progress Glass Co Inc (PA)......C......415 824-7040
25 Patterson St San Francisco (94124) ***(P-3296)***

Progress House Inc (PA)......D......530 626-9240
2844 Coloma St Ste A&B Placerville (95667) ***(P-24032)***

PROGRESSIN DRYWALL, Lancaster *Also called Excel Contractors Inc* ***(P-1121)***

Progressive Computing LLC......D......858 707-0707
3615 Krny Vlla Rd Ste 105 San Diego (92123) ***(P-15035)***

Progressive Corporation......D......626 232-1540
2470 Via Mariposa San Dimas (91773) ***(P-10120)***

Progressive Corporation......D......440 461-5000
150 N Hill Dr Ste 9 Brisbane (94005) ***(P-10121)***

Progressive Floor Covering Inc......E......714 213-8805
924 S Highland Ave Fullerton (92832) ***(P-3015)***

Progressive Insurance, San Dimas *Also called Progressive Corporation* ***(P-10120)***

Progressive Insurance, Brisbane *Also called Progressive Corporation* ***(P-10121)***

Progressive Management Systems, West Covina *Also called RM Galicia Inc* ***(P-13698)***

Progressive Marketing Group, Commerce *Also called Progressive Produce LLC* ***(P-8515)***

Progressive Power Group Inc......E......714 899-2300
12552 Western Ave Garden Grove (92841) ***(P-2240)***

Progressive Produce LLC (HQ)......C......323 890-8100
5790 Peachtree St Commerce (90040) ***(P-8515)***

Progressive Roofing, Stockton *Also called Progressive Services Inc* ***(P-3091)***

Progressive Services Inc......D......209 824-2837
3832 S Highway 99 Ste A Stockton (95215) ***(P-3091)***

Progressive Solutions, San Jose *Also called Sarpa-Feldman Enterprises Inc* ***(P-17046)***

Progressive Sub-Acute Care......C......408 378-8875
13425 Sousa Ln Saratoga (95070) ***(P-21488)***

Progressive Trnsp Svcs Inc......D......510 268-3776
19500 S Alameda St Compton (90221) ***(P-7650)***

Progrssive Employment Concepts (PA)......D......916 723-3112
6060 Sunrise Vista Dr # 1875 Citrus Heights (95610) ***(P-23631)***

Project Air Force, Santa Monica *Also called Air Force US Dept of* ***(P-25959)***

Project Boat Holdings LLC......A......310 712-1850
360 N Crescent Dr Bldg S Beverly Hills (90210) ***(P-11688)***

Project Concern International (PA)......D......858 279-9690
5151 Murphy Canyon Rd # 320 San Diego (92123) ***(P-24356)***

Project Consulting Specialists......E......650 265-2400
425 N Whisman Rd Ste 600 Mountain View (94043) ***(P-27173)***

Project Design Consultants......D......619 235-6471
701 B St Ste 800 San Diego (92101) ***(P-27174)***

Project Go Incorporated......E......916 782-3443
801 Vernon St Roseville (95678) ***(P-3454)***

Project Management Institute......D......760 458-6198
8895 Towne Centre Dr San Diego (92122) ***(P-26365)***
Project Open Hand (PA)......D......415 292-3400
730 Polk St Fl 3 San Francisco (94109) ***(P-23394)***
Project Six......D......818 781-0360
13130 Burbank Blvd Sherman Oaks (91401) ***(P-17008)***
Project Skyline Intermediate H......A......310 712-1850
360 N Crescent Dr Bldg S Beverly Hills (90210) ***(P-11689)***
Projections Unlimited Inc (PA)......E......714 544-2700
15311 Barranca Pkwy Irvine (92618) ***(P-7323)***
Projistics, San Jose *Also called Nagarro Inc* ***(P-15652)***
Proland Property Managment LLC (PA)......D......213 738-8175
2510 W 7th St Fl 2 Los Angeles (90057) ***(P-11374)***
Prolifics Inc (HQ)......B......212 267-7722
24025 Park Sorrento # 405 Calabasas (91302) ***(P-16091)***
Prolifics Testing Inc......D......925 485-9535
24025 Park Sorrento # 405 Calabasas (91302) ***(P-15036)***
Prologic Rdmption Slutions Inc (PA)......A......310 322-7774
2121 Rosecrans Ave El Segundo (90245) ***(P-17009)***
Prologis Inc (PA)......B......415 394-9000
Bay 1 Pier 1 San Francisco (94111) ***(P-11872)***
Prologis LP (HQ)......B......415 394-9000
Bay 1 Pier 1 San Francisco (94111) ***(P-11873)***
Prologue Films (PA)......E......310 589-9090
534 Victoria Ave Venice (90291) ***(P-13795)***
Promab Biotechnologies Inc......D......510 860-4615
2600 Hilltop Dr San Pablo (94806) ***(P-25817)***
Promed Hlth Care Admnistrators......D......909 932-1045
9302 Pttsbrgh Ave Ste 220 Rancho Cucamonga (91730) ***(P-19310)***
Promesa Behavioral Health......D......209 725-3114
2815 G St Merced (95340) ***(P-24033)***
Promesa Behavioral Health (PA)......C......559 439-5437
7120 N Marks Ave Fresno (93711) ***(P-24034)***
Prometheus RE Group Inc (PA)......C......650 931-3400
1900 S Norfolk St Ste 150 San Mateo (94403) ***(P-11375)***
Promise Technology Inc......D......408 228-1400
580 Cottonwood Dr Milpitas (95035) ***(P-6888)***
Promo Shop Inc (PA)......D......310 821-1780
5420 Mcconnell Ave Los Angeles (90066) ***(P-26770)***
Promote Media LP......D......323 433-7950
8484 Wilshire Blvd # 630 Beverly Hills (90211) ***(P-26771)***
Proof of Concept Poc Lab, Sunnyvale *Also called Juniper Networks Inc* ***(P-15625)***
Proofpoint Inc (PA)......C......408 517-4710
892 Ross Dr Sunnyvale (94089) ***(P-15037)***
Proove Medical Labs Inc......C......949 427-5303
15326 Elton Pkwy Irvine (92618) ***(P-21570)***
Propak Logistics Inc......D......559 782-8696
1300 S F St Porterville (93257) ***(P-17530)***
Propane Transport Service Inc......C......209 823-8005
903 W Center St Ste 7 Manteca (95337) ***(P-3925)***
Propath Inc......E......949 341-8000
17891 Cartwright Rd # 100 Irvine (92614) ***(P-14367)***
Propel Software Corporation......C......408 571-6300
1010 Rincon Cir San Jose (95131) ***(P-16092)***
Property I D, Los Angeles *Also called I D Property Corporation* ***(P-11199)***
Property Insight......C......909 876-6505
202 E Airport Dr Ste 210 San Bernardino (92408) ***(P-10635)***
Property Maintenance Company (PA)......C......408 297-7849
255 W Julian St Ste 301 San Jose (95110) ***(P-14019)***
Property Management, Riverside *Also called Real Estate California Dept* ***(P-11401)***
Property Management Assoc Inc (PA)......C......323 295-2000
6011 Bristol Pkwy Culver City (90230) ***(P-11376)***
Property Management Cons (PA)......E......858 485-9811
11717 Bernardo Plaza Ct # 220 San Diego (92128) ***(P-11377)***
Propertyplus Insur Agcy Inc......A......818 432-2640
21820 Burbank Blvd # 130 Woodland Hills (91367) ***(P-10466)***
Prophet Brand Strategy (PA)......E......415 677-0909
1 Bush St Fl 7 San Francisco (94104) ***(P-26772)***
Proponent, Brea *Also called Kirkhill Aircraft Parts Co* ***(P-7694)***
Proprocess Corporation......D......800 624-6717
20281 Harvill Ave Perris (92570) ***(P-7579)***
Propulsion Controls Engrg (PA)......D......619 235-0961
1620 Rigel St San Diego (92113) ***(P-17531)***
Pros Incorporated......D......661 589-5400
3400 Patton Way Bakersfield (93308) ***(P-1040)***
Proscape Landscape, Signal Hill *Also called Fenderscape Inc* ***(P-811)***
Prosciento Inc......C......619 427-1300
855 Third Ave Ste 3340 Chula Vista (91911) ***(P-25818)***
Proskauer Rose LLP......D......310 557-2900
2049 Century Park E # 3200 Los Angeles (90067) ***(P-22779)***
Prosoft Technology Inc (HQ)......D......661 716-5100
9201 Camino Media Ste 200 Bakersfield (93311) ***(P-5796)***
Prospance Inc (PA)......D......925 415-2394
4221 Bus Ctr Dr Ste 1 Fremont (94538) ***(P-15038)***
Prospect Enterprises Inc (PA)......C......213 599-5700
625 Kohler St Los Angeles (90021) ***(P-8385)***
Prospect Medical Group Inc (HQ)......B......714 796-5900
1920 E 17th St Ste 200 Santa Ana (92705) ***(P-26366)***
Prospect Medical Holdings Inc (PA)......D......310 943-4500
3415 S Sepulveda Blvd # 9 Los Angeles (90034) ***(P-19311)***
Prosper Funding LLC......D......415 593-5400
101 2nd St Fl 15 San Francisco (94105) ***(P-9490)***
Prosper Marketplace Inc (PA)......D......415 593-5400
221 Main St Fl 3 San Francisco (94105) ***(P-9643)***
Prostavar Rx, Los Angeles *Also called Superbalife International LLC* ***(P-7986)***
Prosum Inc (PA)......D......310 426-0600
2201 Park Pl Ste 102 El Segundo (90245) ***(P-15801)***
Prosum Technology Services, El Segundo *Also called Prosum Inc* ***(P-15801)***

Protec Association Services (PA)......C......858 569-1080
10180 Willow Creek Rd San Diego (92131) ***(P-14020)***
Protec Building Services, San Diego *Also called Protec Association Services* ***(P-14020)***
Protech Construction, Anaheim *Also called Paglia & Associates Cnstr* ***(P-1171)***
Protect-For-Less Security Svcs......E......760 343-1192
72877 Dinah Shore Dr Rancho Mirage (92270) ***(P-16551)***
Protect-US......C......714 721-8127
12397 Lewis St Ste 202 Garden Grove (92840) ***(P-16386)***
Protected Outcomes Corporation......D......203 545-9565
9663 Santa Monica Blvd Beverly Hills (90210) ***(P-16387)***
Protection Specialists......B......818 503-1306
6841 Whitsett Ave Apt 104 North Hollywood (91605) ***(P-16388)***
Protective Business & Health......D......845 354-5372
3785 Brickway Blvd # 200 Santa Rosa (95403) ***(P-15802)***
Protege Builders Inc......E......916 825-8478
4306 Pinell St Sacramento (95838) ***(P-2962)***
Proteus Inc......C......661 721-5800
1816 Cecil Ave Delano (93215) ***(P-23395)***
Prothena Biosciences Inc......E......650 837-8550
331 Oyster Point Blvd South San Francisco (94080) ***(P-26021)***
Protiviti Inc......D......925 913-1000
2613 Camino Ramon San Ramon (94583) ***(P-26773)***
Protiviti Inc (HQ)......D......650 234-6000
2884 Sand Hill Rd Ste 200 Menlo Park (94025) ***(P-26774)***
Protiviti Inc......D......213 327-1400
400 S Hope St Ste 900 Los Angeles (90071) ***(P-26775)***
Protosource Corporation......D......559 490-8600
2511 W Shaw Ave Ste 102 Fresno (93711) ***(P-15803)***
Prototypes Centers For Innov......C......213 542-3838
1000 N Alameda St Ste 390 Los Angeles (90012) ***(P-23396)***
Prototypes Women's Center, Pomona *Also called Healthright 360* ***(P-23255)***
Protransport-1 LLC (HQ)......A......707 975-2386
720 Portal St Cotati (94931) ***(P-3710)***
Protravel International LLC......D......310 271-9566
9171 Wilshire Blvd # 428 Beverly Hills (90210) ***(P-4835)***
Proven Solutions Inc......D......310 933-4544
11150 Santa Monica Blvd # 1060 Los Angeles (90025) ***(P-14368)***
Providence Health & Services F......A......818 843-5111
501 S Buena Vista St Burbank (91505) ***(P-21115)***
Providence Health & Services S......D......310 832-3311
1300 W 7th St San Pedro (90732) ***(P-21116)***
Providence Health & Svcs - Ore......B......510 444-0839
540 23rd St Oakland (94612) ***(P-21117)***
Providence Health & Svcs - Ore......B......818 365-8051
15031 Rinaldi St Mission Hills (91345) ***(P-21118)***
Providence Health System......A......818 898-4530
15031 Rinaldi St Mission Hills (91345) ***(P-19312)***
Providence Health System......A......818 898-4561
15031 Rinaldi St Mission Hills (91345) ***(P-21119)***
Providence Health System......A......310 832-3311
1300 W 7th St San Pedro (90732) ***(P-21120)***
Providence Health System......A......818 843-5111
501 S Buena Vista St Burbank (91505) ***(P-21121)***
Providence Health System......D......310 514-5270
1322 W 6th St San Pedro (90732) ***(P-21122)***
Providence Health System......C......310 543-5900
4320 Maricopa St Torrance (90503) ***(P-11811)***
Providence Health System......C......310 370-5895
3551 Voyager St Ste 201 Torrance (90503) ***(P-11812)***
Providence Health System......C......818 846-8141
511 S Buena Vista St Burbank (91505) ***(P-11813)***
Providence Health System......C......310 370-5895
4101 Torrance Blvd Torrance (90503) ***(P-21845)***
Providence Health System......C......310 303-6970
4101 Torrance Blvd Torrance (90503) ***(P-26367)***
Providence Holy Cross (PA)......D......818 365-8051
15031 Rinaldi St Mission Hills (91345) ***(P-21123)***
Providence Holy Cross Med Ctr, Mission Hills *Also called Providence Health System* ***(P-21119)***
Providence Holy Cross Med Ctr, Mission Hills *Also called Providence Health & Svcs - Ore* ***(P-21118)***
Providence Little Company of M, San Pedro *Also called Providence Health & Services S* ***(P-21116)***
Providence Seminars Inc......D......760 827-2100
6349 Palomar Oaks Ct Carlsbad (92011) ***(P-26776)***
Providence Service Corporation......E......661 765-7025
1021 4th St Taft (93268) ***(P-22102)***
Providence Speech Hearing Ctr......E......714 639-4990
1301 W Providence Ave Orange (92868) ***(P-22103)***
Providence St Johns Hlth Ctr......B......310 829-6562
2121 Santa Monica Blvd Santa Monica (90404) ***(P-21124)***
Providence St Joseph Med Ctr, Burbank *Also called Therapeutic Associates Inc* ***(P-21500)***
Providence Tarzana Medical Ctr......A......818 881-0800
18321 Clark St Tarzana (91356) ***(P-21125)***
Provident Bank, Riverside *Also called Provident Savings Bank LLC* ***(P-9233)***
Provident Bank, Riverside *Also called Provident Savings Bank* ***(P-9285)***
Provident Care Inc......C......209 578-1210
1025 14th St Modesto (95354) ***(P-24035)***
Provident Credit Union (PA)......C......650 508-0300
303 Twin Dolphin Dr # 303 Redwood City (94065) ***(P-9402)***
Provident Financial Management......D......310 282-0477
3130 Wilshire Blvd # 600 Santa Monica (90403) ***(P-26368)***
Provident Fincl Holdings Inc......D......916 709-3257
9245 Laguna Springs Dr # 13 Elk Grove (95758) ***(P-9594)***
Provident Funding Assoc LP (PA)......E......650 652-1300
851 Traeger Ave Ste 100 San Bruno (94066) ***(P-9595)***
Provident Group Crown Pnte LLC......D......951 737-7482
737 Magnolia Ave Ofc Corona (92879) ***(P-10801)***

Employee Codes: A=Over 500 employees, B=251-500
C=101-250, D=51-100, E=50
2020 Directory of California
Wholesalers and Services Companies
© Mergent Inc. 1-800-342-5647
1395

Provident Mrtg Cpitl Assoc Inc....A....650 652-1300
1633 Bayshore Hwy Ste 155 Burlingame (94010) ***(P-9596)***
Provident Savings Bank (HQ)....D....951 782-6177
6570 Magnolia Ave Riverside (92506) ***(P-9284)***
Provident Savings Bank....D....951 686-6060
6674 Brockton Ave Riverside (92506) ***(P-9285)***
Provident Savings Bank LLC....D....951 686-6060
3756 Central Ave Riverside (92506) ***(P-9233)***
Providnce Holy Cross Fundation, Burbank *Also called Providence Health & Services F* ***(P-21115)***
Provoast Automation Controls (PA)....D....858 748-2237
12635 Danielson Ct # 205 Poway (92064) ***(P-7580)***
Prowall Lath and Plaster....D....760 480-9001
360 S Spruce St Escondido (92025) ***(P-2845)***
Proxim Wireless Corporation....C....408 383-7600
2114 Ringwood Ave San Jose (95131) ***(P-25938)***
Prs/Roebbelen JV....E....916 641-0324
4811 Tunis Rd Sacramento (95835) ***(P-1570)***
Prsi, Jurupa Valley *Also called Pavement Recycling Systems Inc* ***(P-7767)***
Prudential, Encino *Also called Burkshire Has A Way Home Servc* ***(P-10951)***
Prudential, Pleasanton *Also called McM Partners Inc* ***(P-11285)***
Prudential, San Diego *Also called Joe Canpagna* ***(P-11221)***
Prudential, San Luis Obispo *Also called Pickford Realty Inc* ***(P-11357)***
Prudential, Thousand Oaks *Also called Gemmm Corp* ***(P-11165)***
Prudential, Berkeley *Also called Mason-Mcduffie Real Estate Inc* ***(P-11275)***
Prudential, Walnut Creek *Also called Mason-Mcduffie Real Estate Inc* ***(P-11276)***
Prudential, Santa Maria *Also called Hunter Realty Inc* ***(P-11197)***
Prudential, Chula Vista *Also called Coronado Financial Corp* ***(P-11078)***
Prudential, Antioch *Also called Mason-Mcduffie Real Estate Inc* ***(P-11277)***
Prudential, Rancho Cucamonga *Also called Empire Estates Inc* ***(P-11113)***
Prudential, Valencia *Also called Nutec Enterprises Inc* ***(P-11324)***
Prudential 24 Hour Real Estate....D....562 861-7257
8635 Florence Ave Ste 101 Downey (90240) ***(P-11378)***
Prudential Amrcn Rlty A Cal LP....E....818 993-8900
9003 Reseda Blvd Ste 105 Northridge (91324) ***(P-11379)***
Prudential CA Realty....D....510 487-6088
39275 Mssion Blvd Ste 103 Fremont (94539) ***(P-11380)***
Prudential California Realty....D....415 664-9400
677 Portola Dr San Francisco (94127) ***(P-11381)***
Prudential California Realty....D....858 487-3520
976 Main St Ste A Ramona (92065) ***(P-11382)***
Prudential Cleanroom Services, Milpitas *Also called Prudential Overall Supply* ***(P-13306)***
Prudential Cleanroom Services, Commerce *Also called Prudential Overall Supply* ***(P-13307)***
Prudential Dust Control, Riverside *Also called Prudential Overall Supply* ***(P-13304)***
Prudential Insur Co of Amer....E....949 440-5300
3333 Michelson Dr Ste 820 Irvine (92612) ***(P-10467)***
Prudential Insur Co of Amer....D....415 398-7310
101 California St Fl 40 San Francisco (94111) ***(P-10468)***
Prudential Insur Co of Amer....E....818 990-2122
15303 Ventura Blvd # 1550 Sherman Oaks (91403) ***(P-10469)***
Prudential Insur Co of Amer....D....415 486-3050
180 Montgomery St # 1900 San Francisco (94104) ***(P-10038)***
Prudential Insur Co of Amer....D....818 901-0028
5990 Sepulvda Blvd # 300 Van Nuys (91411) ***(P-10470)***
Prudential Malibu Realty, Malibu *Also called Terra Coastal Properties Inc* ***(P-11478)***
Prudential Norcal Realty, Carmichael *Also called Diez & Leis RE Group Inc* ***(P-11093)***
Prudential Overall Supply....D....323 724-4888
6920 Bandini Blvd Commerce (90040) ***(P-13302)***
Prudential Overall Supply (PA)....D....949 250-4855
1661 Alton Pkwy Irvine (92606) ***(P-13303)***
Prudential Overall Supply....C....951 687-0440
6997 Jurupa Ave Riverside (92504) ***(P-13304)***
Prudential Overall Supply....D....760 727-7163
2485 Ash St Vista (92081) ***(P-13305)***
Prudential Overall Supply....D....408 719-0886
1437 N Milpitas Blvd Milpitas (95035) ***(P-13306)***
Prudential Overall Supply....D....323 722-0636
6948 Bandini Blvd Commerce (90040) ***(P-13307)***
Prudential Overall Supply....D....559 264-8231
1260 E North Ave Fresno (93725) ***(P-13308)***
Prudential Overall Supply....D....805 529-0833
5300 Gabbert Rd Moorpark (93021) ***(P-13238)***
Prudential RE Affiliates Inc, Irvine *Also called Brer Affiliates LLC* ***(P-11825)***
Prudential Realty Corp....D....415 566-9800
1430 Taraval St San Francisco (94116) ***(P-11383)***
Prudential Security Services, Los Angeles *Also called Eastside Group Corporation* ***(P-16264)***
Pruitthealth Inc....E....626 810-5567
1982 Camwood Ave City of Industry (91748) ***(P-20664)***
Prutel Joint Venture....A....949 240-2000
1 Ritz Carlton Dr Dana Point (92629) ***(P-12773)***
PS Arts....E....310 586-1017
6701 Center Dr W Ste 550 Los Angeles (90045) ***(P-27175)***
PS Business Parks Inc (PA)....D....818 244-8080
701 Western Ave Glendale (91201) ***(P-11874)***
PS Business Parks LP....D....818 244-8080
701 Western Ave Glendale (91201) ***(P-11384)***
PS Development Corporation....D....818 340-0965
21625 Prairie St Chatsworth (91311) ***(P-2594)***
PS Environmental Svcs Inc....D....310 373-6259
23775 Madison St Torrance (90505) ***(P-17010)***
PS National Inc....B....818 366-1300
17645 Chatsworth St Granada Hills (91344) ***(P-14369)***
PS Partners III Ltd....C....818 244-8080
701 Western Ave Ste 200 Glendale (91201) ***(P-4476)***
Ps2 (PA)....D....310 243-2980
17903 S Hobart Blvd Gardena (90248) ***(P-2380)***
Ps24 Inc....D....415 834-5105
65 Division St San Francisco (94103) ***(P-26369)***
PSC Industrial Outsourcing LP....C....310 325-1600
19340 Van Ness Ave Torrance (90501) ***(P-17532)***
PSC Industrial Outsourcing LP....D....562 997-6000
1661 E 32nd St Long Beach (90807) ***(P-6236)***
PSC Industrial Outsourcing LP....D....831 627-2595
62117 Railroad St San Ardo (93450) ***(P-3926)***
Pse Holding LLC (HQ)....B....248 377-0165
360 N Crescent Dr Beverly Hills (90210) ***(P-18075)***
PSI Fire....E....408 842-9308
820 Eschenburg Dr Gilroy (95020) ***(P-15039)***
Psi3g Inc....D....916 803-2879
2979 Promenade St Ste 100 West Sacramento (95691) ***(P-6579)***
Psinapse Technology Ltd....D....925 225-0400
1063 Serpentine Ln Ste A Pleasanton (94566) ***(P-14370)***
Pslq Inc....D....951 795-4260
28910 Rancho California R Temecula (92590) ***(P-1266)***
Psomas....C....714 751-7373
3 Hutton Cntre Dr Ste 200 Santa Ana (92707) ***(P-25523)***
Psomas....E....760 843-5700
14369 Park Ave Ste 101b Victorville (92392) ***(P-25524)***
Psomas (PA)....C....213 223-1400
555 S Flower St Ste 4300 Los Angeles (90071) ***(P-25525)***
Psomas....C....916 788-8122
1075 Crkside Rdg Dr # 200 Roseville (95678) ***(P-25269)***
Psychemedics Corporation....D....310 216-7776
5750 Hannum Ave Ste 100 Culver City (90230) ***(P-26104)***
Psychiatric Ctrs At San Diego (PA)....D....619 528-4600
4542 Ruffner St Ste 200 San Diego (92111) ***(P-19313)***
Psychiatric Health Facility, Placerville *Also called County of El Dorado* ***(P-21398)***
Psychiatric Solutions Inc....C....626 286-1191
4619 Rosemead Blvd Rosemead (91770) ***(P-22104)***
Psychiatric Solutions Inc....C....916 288-0300
8001 Bruceville Rd Sacramento (95823) ***(P-19314)***
Psychiatric Solutions Inc....C....916 489-3336
4250 Auburn Blvd Sacramento (95841) ***(P-21423)***
Psychiatric Solutions Inc....C....510 796-1100
39001 Sundale Dr Fremont (94538) ***(P-19315)***
Psychiatric Solutions Inc....C....951 789-4405
17241 Van Buren Blvd Riverside (92504) ***(P-19316)***
Psynergy Programs Inc....D....408 776-0422
18225 Hale Ave Morgan Hill (95037) ***(P-24036)***
Pszyjw, Los Angeles *Also called Pachulski Stang Zehl Jones LLP* ***(P-22742)***
Pt Gaming LLC....A....323 260-5060
235 Oregon St El Segundo (90245) ***(P-12774)***
Pt Logistics Inc....E....831 728-4535
144 W Lake Ave Ste B Watsonville (95076) ***(P-3927)***
Pta CA Cngress of Parnts Eagle, Chino Hills *Also called Chino Valley Unified Schl Dst* ***(P-24524)***
Pta CA Cngrss of Parnts Tchrs....D....714 836-2700
3030 N Hesperian St Santa Ana (92706) ***(P-24617)***
Pta CA Cngrss of Prnts, San Jose *Also called Berryessa Union School Dst* ***(P-24481)***
Pta CA Cong Prents Emperor Sch....D....626 548-5084
6415 N Muscatel Ave San Gabriel (91775) ***(P-24618)***
Pta CA Cong Prents Kelley Schl....E....760 331-5800
4885 Kelly Dr Carlsbad (92008) ***(P-24619)***
Pta CA Congress of Parents....E....818 340-6700
5014 Serrania Ave Woodland Hills (91364) ***(P-24620)***
Pta CA Congrss of Prnts, San Ysidro *Also called San Ysidro School District* ***(P-24644)***
Pta Calfrnia Congress of, Fresno *Also called Central Unified School Dst* ***(P-24512)***
Pta Calif Congress of Parents, Oakley *Also called Oakley Union School District* ***(P-24603)***
Pta California Cong P A S Elem....E....925 606-4700
5280 Irene Way Livermore (94550) ***(P-24621)***
Pta California Congress of, Hemet *Also called Hemet Unified School District* ***(P-24561)***
Pta California Congress of, Lancaster *Also called Linda Verde School* ***(P-24583)***
Pta California Congress of Par....E....559 622-3195
2121 E Laura Ave Visalia (93292) ***(P-24622)***
Pta California Congress of Par....D....310 328-3100
21514 Halldale Ave Torrance (90501) ***(P-24623)***
Ptac Carmel Valley Mid School....D....858 481-8221
3800 Mykonos Ln San Diego (92130) ***(P-24624)***
Ptac Don L Rhee Elem Sch R Pta....D....925 376-4441
90 Laird Dr Moraga (94556) ***(P-24625)***
Ptac Rail Ranch Elem School....D....951 696-1404
25030 Via Santee Murrieta (92563) ***(P-24626)***
Pti, Chatsworth *Also called Printing Technology Inc* ***(P-7649)***
Pti Solutions, Roseville *Also called Pinnacle Telecom Inc* ***(P-15673)***
Ptr Group Inc....E....951 965-1822
652 S Joyce Ave Rialto (92376) ***(P-26370)***
Pts Advance....C....949 268-4000
2860 Michelle Ste 150 Irvine (92606) ***(P-14371)***
Ptsi Managed Services Inc....D....626 440-3118
100 W Walnut St Pasadena (91124) ***(P-25270)***
Pub Works/Community Dev, Santa Barbara *Also called Santa Barbara City of* ***(P-17045)***
Public Communications Svcs Inc....C....310 231-1000
11859 Wilshire Blvd # 600 Los Angeles (90025) ***(P-5459)***
Public Consulting Group Inc....D....916 565-8090
2150 River Plaza Dr # 380 Sacramento (95833) ***(P-26777)***
Public Counsel....D....213 385-2977
610 S Ardmore Ave Los Angeles (90005) ***(P-22780)***
Public Defender, Fullerton *Also called County of Orange* ***(P-22444)***
Public Defender, Compton *Also called County of Los Angeles* ***(P-22441)***
Public Defender Administration, Los Angeles *Also called County of Los Angeles* ***(P-22440)***
Public Defender's Office, Fresno *Also called County of Fresno* ***(P-22435)***
Public Defender- Main Office, Riverside *Also called County of Riverside* ***(P-22445)***
Public Defenders Office, Los Angeles *Also called County of Los Angeles* ***(P-22437)***

Mergent e-mail: customerrelations@mergent.com
1396
2020 Directory of California
Wholesalers and Services Companies
(P-0000) Products & Services Section entry number
(PA)=Parent Co (HQ)=Headquarters (DH)=Div Headquarters

Public Employees Retirement ....B.......916 795-3400
400 Q St Sacramento (95811) ***(P-10223)***
Public Health California Dept ....C.......213 620-6160
320 W 4th St Ste 830 Los Angeles (90013) ***(P-19317)***
Public Health California Dept ....C.......661 835-4668
2400 Wible Rd Ste 14 Bakersfield (93304) ***(P-19318)***
Public Health California Dept ....C.......510 412-1502
850 Marina Bay Pkwy F175 Richmond (94804) ***(P-19319)***
Public Health Department, El Centro *Also called County of Imperial* ***(P-22211)***
Public Health Dept, Santa Barbara *Also called Santa Barbara County of* ***(P-22319)***
Public Health Di, Lakeport *Also called County Lake Health Services* ***(P-24397)***
Public Health Institute ....C.......916 285-1231
1825 Bell St Ste 203 Sacramento (95825) ***(P-22299)***
Public Health Institute (PA) ....D.......510 285-5500
555 12th St Ste 1050 Oakland (94607) ***(P-26022)***
Public Health Nursing Service, Sacramento *Also called County of Sacramento* ***(P-19823)***
Public Hlth Fndation Entps Inc ....C.......626 856-6600
12781 Schabarum Ave Irwindale (91706) ***(P-22300)***
Public Hlth Fndation Entps Inc ....C.......323 261-6388
3648 E Olympic Blvd Los Angeles (90023) ***(P-22301)***
Public Hlth Fndation Entps Inc ....C.......562 801-2323
8666 Whittier Blvd Pico Rivera (90660) ***(P-22302)***
Public Hlth Fndation Entps Inc ....C.......323 263-0262
277 S Atlantic Blvd Los Angeles (90022) ***(P-24627)***
Public Hlth Fndation Entps Inc ....C.......323 733-9381
1649 W Washington Blvd Los Angeles (90007) ***(P-22303)***
Public Hlth Fndation Entps Inc ....C.......310 320-5215
1640 W Carson St Ste G Torrance (90501) ***(P-24628)***
Public Hlth Fndation Entps Inc ....C.......310 518-2835
125 E Anaheim St Wilmington (90744) ***(P-22304)***
Public Hlth Fndation Entps Inc ....C.......626 856-6618
12781 Shama Rd El Monte (91732) ***(P-22305)***
Public Hlth Fndation Entps Inc (PA) ....C.......800 201-7320
13300 Crssrds Pkwy N City of Industry (91746) ***(P-24629)***
Public Investment Corporation ....C.......310 451-5227
4340 Eucalyptus Ave Chino (91710) ***(P-11594)***
Public Policy Institute Cal (PA) ....D.......415 291-4400
500 Washington St Ste 600 San Francisco (94111) ***(P-24357)***
Public Security Inc ....E.......323 293-9884
3860 Crenshaw Blvd # 223 Los Angeles (90008) ***(P-16389)***
Public Service Yard, Glendale *Also called City of Glendale* ***(P-6031)***
Public Services, Coronado *Also called City of Coronado* ***(P-5994)***
Public Social Service, Norco *Also called County of Riverside* ***(P-23129)***
Public Social Services, Moreno Valley *Also called County of Riverside* ***(P-18932)***
Public Social Services, Lake Elsinore *Also called County of Riverside* ***(P-23131)***
Public Social Services, Los Angeles *Also called County of Los Angeles* ***(P-23096)***
Public Social Services, Canyon Country *Also called County of Los Angeles* ***(P-10214)***
Public Social Services, Norwalk *Also called County of Los Angeles* ***(P-23104)***
Public Storage (PA) ....C.......818 244-8080
701 Western Ave Glendale (91201) ***(P-4477)***
Public Storage Prpts IV Ltd ....D.......818 244-8080
701 Western Ave Glendale (91201) ***(P-4478)***
Public Storage Prpts Xviii Inc ....D.......818 244-8080
701 Western Ave Ste 200 Glendale (91201) ***(P-4479)***
Public Work Dept, Burlingame *Also called Street and Sewer Yard Corp* ***(P-6139)***
Public Works, Imperial *Also called County of Imperial* ***(P-1690)***
Public Works, Corona *Also called City of Corona* ***(P-6007)***
Public Works and Highway Dept, Burlingame *Also called City of Burlingame* ***(P-1679)***
Public Works Department, Morgan Hill *Also called City of Morgan Hill* ***(P-27029)***
Public Works Department, Woodland *Also called City of Woodland* ***(P-26935)***
Public Works Department, Woodland *Also called City of Woodland* ***(P-25007)***
Public Works Dept, Los Angeles *Also called City of Los Angeles* ***(P-25004)***
Public Works Dept, Hayward *Also called County of Alameda* ***(P-1687)***
Public Works Dept, Auburn *Also called County of Placer* ***(P-25021)***
Public Works Dept, Palmdale *Also called City of Palmdale* ***(P-13878)***
Public Works Engineering Div, Daly City *Also called City of Daly City* ***(P-25002)***
Public Works Office, Vacaville *Also called City of Vacaville* ***(P-25006)***
Public Works Superintendent, Alameda *Also called Maintenance Service For The Cy* ***(P-13971)***
Public Works, Dept of, Palmdale *Also called County of Los Angeles* ***(P-1691)***
Public Works, Dept of, Los Angeles *Also called County of Los Angeles* ***(P-1692)***
Publis Works, Lomita *Also called City of Lomita* ***(P-6032)***
Pubmatic Inc (PA) ....D.......650 351-9162
305 Main St Fl 1 Redwood City (94063) ***(P-13561)***
Pubnub Inc (PA) ....D.......415 223-7552
460 Bryant St Fl 2 San Francisco (94107) ***(P-15040)***
Puente Hills Landfill, Whittier *Also called County Santtn Dist 2 of La Co* ***(P-6191)***
Pulmonary Medicine Assoc ....D.......916 733-5040
2801 K St Ste 500 Sacramento (95816) ***(P-19320)***
Pulp Studio Incorporated ....D.......310 815-4999
2100 W 139th St Gardena (90249) ***(P-13796)***
Pulse Biosciences Inc ....D.......510 906-4600
3957 Point Eden Way Hayward (94545) ***(P-25819)***
Pulse Secure LLC (HQ) ....D.......408 372-9600
2700 Zanker Rd Ste 200 San Jose (95134) ***(P-15041)***
Pulse-Link Inc ....D.......760 448-4690
2730 Loker Ave W Carlsbad (92010) ***(P-25820)***
Pulte Home Company LLC ....D.......925 249-3200
6210 Stoneridge Mall Rd Pleasanton (94588) ***(P-1177)***
Punch Studio LLC (PA) ....C.......310 390-9900
6025 W Slauson Ave Culver City (90230) ***(P-7863)***
Punctus Temporis Translations ....E.......510 309-0888
5201 Great America Pkwy Santa Clara (95054) ***(P-17011)***
Pupil Transportation, Whittier *Also called County of Los Angeles* ***(P-3790)***
Puratos Bakery Supply, Rancho Cucamonga *Also called Puratos Corporation* ***(P-4334)***
Puratos Corporation ....D.......909 484-1312
11167 White Birch Dr Rancho Cucamonga (91730) ***(P-4334)***
Purcell-Murray Company Inc (PA) ....D.......415 468-6620
1744 Rollins Rd Burlingame (94010) ***(P-7435)***
Purchasing & Warehouse, Bakersfield *Also called Panama-Buena Vista Un Schl Dst* ***(P-4467)***
Purchasing Department, Redlands *Also called City of Redlands* ***(P-6183)***
Purchasing Department, Ventura *Also called Community Mem HSP/Sn Benua* ***(P-20803)***
Pure Beauty-A Freeman Company, Union City *Also called Purebeauty Inc* ***(P-7680)***
Pure Luxury Limousine Service ....C.......800 626-5466
4246 Petaluma Blvd N Petaluma (94952) ***(P-3711)***
Pure Luxury Worldwide Trnsp, Petaluma *Also called Pure Luxury Limousine Service* ***(P-3711)***
Purebeauty Inc ....E.......510 477-7950
32920 Alvarado Niles Rd # 220 Union City (94587) ***(P-7680)***
Puregear, Irwindale *Also called Superior Communications Inc* ***(P-7349)***
Purism Spc ....E.......415 555-1212
5670 El Camino Real Ste E Carlsbad (92008) ***(P-7324)***
Purolator International Inc ....D.......888 511-4811
2310 E Gladwick St Compton (90220) ***(P-5035)***
Puronics Retail Services Inc ....D.......925 456-7000
5775 Las Positas Rd Livermore (94551) ***(P-2241)***
Purosil Division, Santa Fe Springs *Also called MCP Industries Inc* ***(P-8702)***
Purple Communications Inc ....C.......510 268-0120
1000 Broadway Ste 252 Oakland (94607) ***(P-5797)***
Pvcc Inc (PA) ....D.......619 463-4040
8100 La Mesa Blvd Ste 101 La Mesa (91942) ***(P-10636)***
PVHMC, Pomona *Also called Pomona Valley Hospital Med Ctr* ***(P-21102)***
Pw Fund B LP ....D.......916 379-3852
7585 Longe St Stockton (95206) ***(P-11739)***
PW Gillibrand Co Inc (PA) ....D.......805 526-2195
4537 Ish Dr Simi Valley (93063) ***(P-1061)***
Pw Jade LLC ....D.......707 843-5192
1825 4th St Santa Rosa (95404) ***(P-21846)***
PW Stephens Envmtl Inc (PA) ....D.......714 892-2028
15201 Pipeline Ln Ste B Huntington Beach (92649) ***(P-3455)***
PW Stephens Envmtl Inc ....D.......510 651-9506
4047 Clipper Ct Fremont (94538) ***(P-3456)***
PWC STRategy& (us) LLC ....C.......415 498-5000
3 Embarcadero Ctr Fl 20 San Francisco (94111) ***(P-26778)***
Pwp, Vernon *Also called Pactiv Packaging Inc* ***(P-8999)***
Pws Inc (PA) ....D.......323 721-8832
12020 Garfield Ave South Gate (90280) ***(P-7681)***
PWS Holdings LLC ....C.......323 721-8832
6500 Flotilla St Commerce (90040) ***(P-13251)***
Pyj V A California Ltd Partnr ....D.......805 495-8437
4812 Lakeview Canyon Rd Westlake Village (91361) ***(P-18284)***
Pyramid Advisors Ltd Partnr ....D.......925 847-6000
11950 Dublin Canyon Rd Pleasanton (94588) ***(P-12775)***
Pyramid Alternatives Inc (PA) ....E.......650 355-8787
480 Manor Pl Pacifica (94044) ***(P-22105)***
Pyramid Enterprises Inc (PA) ....D.......661 702-1420
28368 Constellation Rd # 380 Valencia (91355) ***(P-18740)***
Pyramid Flowers Inc ....C.......805 382-8070
3813 Doris Ave Oxnard (93030) ***(P-272)***
Pyramid Logistics Services Inc (PA) ....D.......714 903-2600
14650 Hoover St Westminster (92683) ***(P-4480)***
Pyramid Painting Inc ....E.......650 903-9791
2925 Bayview Dr Fremont (94538) ***(P-2381)***
Pyramid Peak Corporation ....D.......949 769-8600
450 Nwport Ctr Dr Ste 650 Newport Beach (92660) ***(P-11950)***
Pyramid Produce Inc ....C.......661 366-5736
12826 Edison Hwy Bakersfield (93307) ***(P-640)***
Pyro-Comm Systems Inc (PA) ....C.......714 902-8000
15531 Container Ln Huntington Beach (92649) ***(P-2595)***
Q Analysts LLC (PA) ....D.......408 907-8500
4320 Stevens Creek Blvd # 130 San Jose (95129) ***(P-26779)***
Q B C, Los Angeles *Also called Qualified Blling Cllctions LLC* ***(P-13697)***
Q S H Properties Inc ....D.......714 957-9200
2701 Hotel Ter Santa Ana (92705) ***(P-12776)***
Q S I, South San Francisco *Also called Quality Systems Installations* ***(P-3457)***
Q S San Luis Obispo LP ....E.......805 541-5001
1631 Monterey St San Luis Obispo (93401) ***(P-12777)***
Q-Free America Inc ....D.......855 737-3387
5962 La Place Ct 150 Carlsbad (92008) ***(P-27176)***
Q1media Inc ....D.......512 388-2300
300 Continental Blvd # 615 El Segundo (90245) ***(P-13562)***
Qad Inc (PA) ....C.......805 566-6000
100 Innovation Pl Santa Barbara (93108) ***(P-15481)***
Qal Affiliate Inc ....E.......408 238-5111
2680 S White Rd Ste 150 San Jose (95148) ***(P-11385)***
Qantas Vctons Nwmans Vacations, Los Angeles *Also called Helloworld Travel Svcs USA Inc* ***(P-4822)***
Qbi LLC (PA) ....D.......818 594-4900
21031 Ventura Blvd # 1200 Woodland Hills (91364) ***(P-25667)***
Qc Wall Systems, Rancho Murieta *Also called Energy Store of California Inc* ***(P-2128)***
Qcommission, San Mateo *Also called Cellarstone Inc* ***(P-15956)***
Qct LLC ....A.......510 270-6111
1010 Rincon Cir San Jose (95131) ***(P-15677)***
Qlm Consulting Inc ....E.......415 331-9292
2400 Bridgeway Ste 290 Sausalito (94965) ***(P-26780)***
Qmadix Inc ....D.......818 988-4300
14350 Arminta St Panorama City (91402) ***(P-7325)***
Qre Operating LLC ....C.......213 225-5900
707 Wilshire Blvd # 4600 Los Angeles (90017) ***(P-1006)***
Qsolv Inc ....C.......408 429-0918
440 N Wolfe Rd Ste 26 Sunnyvale (94085) ***(P-15678)***

Employee Codes: A=Over 500 employees, B=251-500
C=101-250, D=51-100, E=50
2020 Directory of California
Wholesalers and Services Companies
© Mergent Inc. 1-800-342-5647
1397

Qtc Management Inc (HQ)......C......800 260-1515
924 Overland Ct San Dimas (91773) ***(P-22306)***
Qtc Mdcal Group Inc A Med Corp......A......800 260-1515
924 Overland Ct San Dimas (91773) ***(P-22307)***
Quad Knopf Inc (PA)......E......559 733-0440
901 E Main St Visalia (93292) ***(P-25271)***
Quad/Graphics Inc......C......916 371-9500
1201 Shore St West Sacramento (95691) ***(P-13563)***
Quadion LLC......A......714 546-0994
17651 Armstrong Ave Irvine (92614) ***(P-9842)***
Quadra Productions Inc......C......310 244-1234
10202 Washington Blvd Culver City (90232) ***(P-17656)***
Quadramed Corporation......A......951 736-6290
800 S Main St Corona (92882) ***(P-13696)***
Quadrant Components Inc......D......510 656-9988
46567 Fremont Blvd Fremont (94538) ***(P-6889)***
Quadriga Inc......D......650 270-6326
555 Clfornia Ave Ste 4925 San Francisco (94104) ***(P-15042)***
Quadrix Information Tech Inc......E......424 603-2140
10736 Jefferson Blvd # 132 Culver City (90230) ***(P-27177)***
Quadrixit, Culver City *Also called Quadrix Information Tech Inc* ***(P-27177)***
Quail Engineering Inc......E......714 636-0612
2230 E Lambert Rd La Habra (90631) ***(P-1778)***
Quail H Farms LLC......A......209 394-8001
5301 Robin Ave Livingston (95334) ***(P-29)***
Quail Hill Investments Inc......C......408 978-9000
1124 Meridian Ave San Jose (95125) ***(P-11875)***
Quail Lodge Inc......C......831 624-1581
8205 Valley Greens Dr Carmel (93923) ***(P-12778)***
Quail Park Retirement Village......D......559 624-3500
4520 W Cypress Ave Visalia (93277) ***(P-20446)***
Quail Ridge Senior Living, Grass Valley *Also called Grass Valley LLC* ***(P-23941)***
Quails Inn Motel, San Marcos *Also called San Marcos Caterers Inc* ***(P-12878)***
Quailty Inn of Barstow, Barstow *Also called Darensburg Roghair & Renier* ***(P-12200)***
Quake City Caps, Los Angeles *Also called Quake City Casuals Inc* ***(P-8045)***
Quake City Casuals Inc......C......213 746-0540
1800 S Flower St Los Angeles (90015) ***(P-8045)***
Quakehold, Vista *Also called Ready America Inc* ***(P-7829)***
QUAKER GARDENS, Stanton *Also called California Friends Homes* ***(P-23846)***
Quaker Oats Company......E......714 526-8800
2501 E Orangethorpe Ave Fullerton (92831) ***(P-4481)***
Quaker Pet Group Inc......D......415 721-7400
160 Mitchell Blvd San Rafael (94903) ***(P-9006)***
Qualcomm International Inc (HQ)......A......858 587-1121
5775 Morehouse Dr San Diego (92121) ***(P-11830)***
Qualfax Inc......D......562 988-1272
3605 Long Beach Blvd # 428 Long Beach (90807) ***(P-17012)***
Qualia Collection Services, Petaluma *Also called Optio Solutions LLC* ***(P-13691)***
Qualified Benefits, Woodland Hills *Also called Qbi LLC* ***(P-25667)***
Qualified Benefits Inc......E......818 594-4900
21021 Ventura Blvd # 100 Woodland Hills (91364) ***(P-10471)***
Qualified Blling Cllctions LLC......C......323 556-3470
4601 Wilshire Blvd Fl 3 Los Angeles (90010) ***(P-13697)***
Quality Auto Craft Inc......A......925 426-0120
3295 Bernal Ave Ste B Pleasanton (94566) ***(P-17342)***
Quality Carriers Inc......D......800 282-2031
5042 Cecelia St South Gate (90280) ***(P-4115)***
Quality Childrens Services (PA)......C......760 942-3433
6108 Innovation Way Carlsbad (92009) ***(P-23779)***
Quality Claims Management Corp......D......619 450-8600
2763 Camino Del Rio S San Diego (92108) ***(P-10472)***
Quality Coast Incorporated......E......619 443-9192
2462 Main St Ste H Chula Vista (91911) ***(P-14021)***
Quality Construction, Tarzana *Also called Zohar Construction Inc* ***(P-1225)***
Quality Electrical Services, Costa Mesa *Also called Edward Straling* ***(P-2480)***
QUALITY FOSTER CARE, Fresno *Also called Quality Group Homes Inc* ***(P-24216)***
Quality Group Homes Inc......C......916 930-0066
250 Dos Rios St Ste A1 Sacramento (95811) ***(P-1178)***
Quality Group Homes Inc (PA)......C......559 255-8519
4928 E Clinton Way # 108 Fresno (93727) ***(P-24216)***
Quality Home Loans......C......818 206-6600
27001 Agoura Rd Ste 200 Agoura Hills (91301) ***(P-9597)***
Quality Hotel Airport, Arcadia *Also called Goodrich Lax A Cal Ltd Partnr* ***(P-12303)***
Quality In-Hmecare Specialists......D......530 303-3477
1166 Broadway Ste T Placerville (95667) ***(P-21847)***
Quality Inn, San Luis Obispo *Also called Q S San Luis Obispo LP* ***(P-12777)***
Quality Inn, Santa Ana *Also called Q S H Properties Inc* ***(P-12776)***
Quality Inv Prpts Scrmento LLC......D......916 679-2100
1100 N Market Blvd Sacramento (95834) ***(P-15804)***
Quality Laminating, Pacoima *Also called Phillips Plywood Co Inc* ***(P-6643)***
Quality Loan Service Corp......B......619 645-7711
2763 Camino Del Rio S San Diego (92108) ***(P-11814)***
Quality Long Term Care Nev Inc......D......818 361-0191
14122 Hubbard St Sylmar (91342) ***(P-20206)***
Quality Management, Stanford *Also called Stanford Health Care* ***(P-21238)***
Quality Marine, Los Angeles *Also called Allaquaria LLC* ***(P-8948)***
Quality Planning Corporation......D......415 369-0707
388 Market St Ste 750 San Francisco (94111) ***(P-26781)***
Quality Plus Auto Parts Inc......E......619 424-9991
1333 30th St Ste C San Diego (92154) ***(P-6462)***
Quality Production Svcs Inc......D......310 406-3350
18711 S Broadwick St Compton (90220) ***(P-2846)***
Quality Reinforcing Inc......D......858 748-8400
13275 Gregg St Poway (92064) ***(P-3279)***
Quality Systems Installations......D......650 875-9000
212 Shaw Rd Ste 3 South San Francisco (94080) ***(P-3457)***
Quality Tech Svcs Sacramento, Sacramento *Also called Quality Inv Prpts Scrmento LLC* ***(P-15804)***
Quality Techniques Engrg Cnstr, Rocklin *Also called Quality Telecom Consultants* ***(P-1904)***
Quality Telecom Consultants (PA)......D......916 315-0500
3740 Cincinnati Ave Rocklin (95765) ***(P-1904)***
Quality Temp Staffing, Granada Hills *Also called Siracusa Enterprises Inc* ***(P-14420)***
Quality Wall Systems Inc......D......951 739-4409
104 S Maple St Corona (92880) ***(P-2382)***
Qualitylogic Inc (PA)......C......805 531-9030
2245 1st St Ste 103 Simi Valley (93065) ***(P-27178)***
Qualstaff Resources, San Diego *Also called June Group LLC* ***(P-14519)***
Qualys Inc (PA)......C......650 801-6100
919 E Hillsdale Blvd Fl 4 Foster City (94404) ***(P-15043)***
Quantbiome Inc......E......408 421-0315
1475 Veterans Blvd Redwood City (94063) ***(P-19321)***
Quantcast Corporation (PA)......D......800 293-5706
795 Folsom St Fl 5 San Francisco (94107) ***(P-15044)***
Quantos Payroll, Los Angeles *Also called Film Payroll Services Inc* ***(P-25596)***
Quantum Bhvioral Solutions Inc (PA)......D......626 531-6999
445 S Figueroa St # 3100 Los Angeles (90071) ***(P-19687)***
Quantum Bhvioral Solutions Inc......D......626 531-6999
2400 E Katella Ave # 800 Anaheim (92806) ***(P-19688)***
Quantum Solutions Inc......E......818 577-4555
5146 Douglas Fir Rd # 205 Calabasas (91302) ***(P-16093)***
Quantum Technologies Inc......C......949 399-4500
25242 Arctic Ocean Dr Lake Forest (92630) ***(P-990)***
Quantum3d Government Systems, Milpitas *Also called Cg2 Inc* ***(P-25984)***
Quarry At La Quinta Inc (PA)......D......760 777-1100
41865 Boardwalk Ste 214 Palm Desert (92211) ***(P-18285)***
Quarry Collection, Huntington Beach *Also called GBI Tile & Stone Inc* ***(P-6686)***
Quartus Engineering Inc (PA)......D......858 875-6000
9689 Towne Centre Dr San Diego (92121) ***(P-25272)***
Quartz Hill Post Acute, Redding *Also called Honolua Bay Holdings LLC* ***(P-11671)***
Quartz Logistics Inc......D......626 606-2001
780 Nogales St Ste D City of Industry (91748) ***(P-5036)***
Qubera Solutions Inc......E......650 294-4460
676 Gail Ave Apt 26 Sunnyvale (94086) ***(P-16094)***
Quechan Gaming Commission, Winterhaven *Also called Quechan Indian Tribe* ***(P-18741)***
Quechan Indian Tribe......B......760 572-2413
450 Quechan Rd Winterhaven (92283) ***(P-18741)***
Queen Anne Early Education Ctr, Los Angeles *Also called Los Angeles Unified School Dst* ***(P-23745)***
Queen Mary Hotel, Long Beach *Also called RMS Foundation Inc* ***(P-12836)***
Queen Mary, The, Long Beach *Also called Urban Commons Queensway LLC* ***(P-13056)***
Queen of Angels Hollywood Pres......A......213 413-3000
1300 N Vermont Ave Los Angeles (90027) ***(P-21126)***
Queen of The Valley Campus, West Covina *Also called Citrus Vly Hlth Partners Inc* ***(P-20790)***
Queen of The Valley Hospital, West Covina *Also called Citrus Valley Medical Ctr Inc* ***(P-20788)***
Queen of Valley Hospital......A......626 962-4011
1115 S Sunset Ave West Covina (91790) ***(P-21127)***
Queen of Valley Medical Center (HQ)......A......707 252-4411
1000 Trancas St NAPA (94558) ***(P-21128)***
Queensbay Hotel LLC (PA)......C......562 628-0625
444 W Ocean Blvd Long Beach (90802) ***(P-12779)***
Queensbay Hotel LLC......D......562 481-3910
700 Queensway Dr Long Beach (90802) ***(P-12780)***
Queenscare Fmly Clinics-Eastsd, Los Angeles *Also called Queenscare Health Centers* ***(P-19322)***
Queenscare Health Centers......D......323 780-4510
4816 E 3rd St Los Angeles (90022) ***(P-19322)***
Queenscare Health Centers......D......323 644-6180
4618 Fountain Ave Los Angeles (90029) ***(P-19323)***
Quercus Ranch, Kelseyville *Also called BT Holdings Inc* ***(P-201)***
Quest Components Inc......E......626 333-5858
14711 Clark Ave City of Industry (91745) ***(P-7326)***
Quest Dgnstics Clncal Labs Inc......B......408 975-1015
2369 Bering Dr San Jose (95131) ***(P-21571)***
Quest Dgnstics Clncal Labs Inc......B......661 964-6582
26081 Avenue Hall 150 Valencia (91355) ***(P-21572)***
Quest Diagn Nichols Inst Valen, Valencia *Also called Specialty Laboratories Inc* ***(P-21593)***
Quest Diagnostics, West Hills *Also called Unilab Corporation* ***(P-21596)***
Quest Diagnostics Incorporated......B......925 687-2514
401 Gregory Ln Ste 146 Pleasant Hill (94523) ***(P-21573)***
Quest Diagnostics Incorporated......B......949 728-4235
33608 Ortega Hwy Mission Viejo (92675) ***(P-21574)***
Quest Diagnostics Incorporated......D......559 438-2893
1275 E Spruce Ave Ste 102 Fresno (93720) ***(P-21575)***
Quest Discovery Services Inc......D......310 769-5557
700 E Bonita Ave Pomona (91767) ***(P-14548)***
Quest Discovery Services Inc......D......916 483-7030
4600 Roseville Rd Ste 200 North Highlands (95660) ***(P-14549)***
Quest Group (PA)......D......949 585-0111
2621 White Rd Irvine (92614) ***(P-7828)***
Quest Intl Monitor Svc Inc (PA)......D......949 581-9900
60-65 Parker Irvine (92618) ***(P-15924)***
Quest Media & Supplies Inc (PA)......D......916 338-7070
9000 Fthills Blvd Ste 100 Roseville (95747) ***(P-15679)***
Quest Nutrition LLC (PA)......C......562 272-0180
777 S Avi Blvd Ste 100 El Segundo (90245) ***(P-8636)***
Quest Software Inc......D......415 373-2222
118 2nd St Fl 6 San Francisco (94105) ***(P-15482)***
Quest Software Inc (HQ)......A......949 754-8000
4 Polaris Way Aliso Viejo (92656) ***(P-15680)***
Quest Software Inc......D......949 754-8000
4 Polaris Way Aliso Viejo (92656) ***(P-15483)***
Questmark, Ontario *Also called Centimark Corporation* ***(P-3033)***

Mergent e-mail: customerrelations@mergent.com 2020 Directory of California (P-0000) Products & Services Section entry number
1398 Wholesalers and Services Companies (PA)=Parent Co (HQ)=Headquarters (DH)=Div Headquarters

Questus Inc (PA).....E.....415 677-5719
3350 E Birch St Ste 110 Brea (92821) ***(P-15805)***
Quetico LLC (PA).....D.....909 628-6200
5521 Schaefer Ave Chino (91710) ***(P-9007)***
Quick Systems Inc.....E.....702 335-3574
5042 Wilshire Blvd # 28533 Los Angeles (90036) ***(P-2242)***
Quick-N-Ezee Indian Foods, Hayward *Also called Jagpreet Enterprises LLC* ***(P-8593)***
Quicken Inc.....C.....650 564-3399
3760 Haven Ave Menlo Park (94025) ***(P-15045)***
Quicken Sub, LLC, Menlo Park *Also called Quicken Inc* ***(P-15045)***
Quicksilver Delivery Inc.....D.....415 431-1600
129 Kissling St San Francisco (94103) ***(P-3712)***
Quicksilver Delivery Service, San Francisco *Also called Quicksilver Delivery Inc* ***(P-3712)***
Quigley-Simpson La, Los Angeles *Also called Quigly-Simpson Heppelwhite Inc* ***(P-13564)***
Quigly-Simpson Heppelwhite Inc.....C.....310 996-5800
11601 Wilshire Blvd Fl 7 Los Angeles (90025) ***(P-13564)***
Quik Pick Express Delivery Svc, Carson *Also called Quik Pick Express LLC* ***(P-3928)***
Quik Pick Express LLC.....D.....310 763-3000
1021 E 233rd St Carson (90745) ***(P-3928)***
Quik Pick Express LLC.....C.....310 763-3000
1021 E 233rd St Carson (90745) ***(P-5037)***
Quik-Shor, Downey *Also called Westar Manufacturing Inc* ***(P-3492)***
Quincy Family Medicine, Quincy *Also called Plumas District Hospital* ***(P-19305)***
Quinn Company.....D.....818 767-7171
13275 Golden State Rd Sylmar (91342) ***(P-7484)***
Quinn Company.....D.....661 393-5800
2200 Pegasus Dr Bakersfield (93308) ***(P-7485)***
Quinn Company.....D.....805 485-2171
801 Del Norte Blvd Oxnard (93030) ***(P-7486)***
Quinn Company.....D.....805 925-8611
1655 Carlotti Dr Santa Maria (93454) ***(P-7487)***
Quinn Emanuel Urquhart.....E.....415 875-6600
50 California St Ste 2200 San Francisco (94111) ***(P-22781)***
Quinn Emanuel Urquhart.....D.....650 801-5000
555 Twin Dolphin Dr Fl 5 Redwood City (94065) ***(P-22782)***
Quinn Emanuel Urquhart (PA).....B.....213 443-3000
865 S Figueroa St Fl 10 Los Angeles (90017) ***(P-22783)***
Quinn Group Inc.....D.....805 485-2171
801 Del Norte Blvd Oxnard (93030) ***(P-7504)***
Quinn Group Inc.....C.....661 393-5800
2200 Pegasus Dr Bakersfield (93308) ***(P-7505)***
Quinn Group Inc.....A.....831 758-8461
1300 Abbott St Salinas (93901) ***(P-7488)***
Quinn Lift Inc.....D.....831 758-4086
1300 Abbott St Salinas (93901) ***(P-7581)***
Quinn Shepherd Machinery.....B.....562 463-6000
10006 Rose Hills Rd City of Industry (90601) ***(P-7489)***
Quinstar Technology Inc.....D.....310 320-1111
24085 Garnier St Torrance (90505) ***(P-7327)***
Quinstreet Inc (PA).....E.....650 578-7700
950 Tower Ln Ste 600 Foster City (94404) ***(P-17013)***
Quiring Corporation.....D.....559 432-2800
5118 E Clinton Way # 201 Fresno (93727) ***(P-1571)***
Quiring General LLC.....D.....559 432-2800
5118 E Clinton Way # 201 Fresno (93727) ***(P-1572)***
Quixote Mm LLC.....E.....323 851-5030
1011 N Fuller Ave Ste B West Hollywood (90046) ***(P-17761)***
Quixote Production Vehicles, West Hollywood *Also called Quixote Studios LLC* ***(P-14192)***
Quixote Studios LLC (PA).....E.....323 851-5030
1011 N Fuller Ave West Hollywood (90046) ***(P-14192)***
Quixote Studios LLC.....E.....818 252-7722
11473 Penrose St Sun Valley (91352) ***(P-17233)***
Qumu Inc (HQ).....D.....650 396-8530
1100 Grundy Ln Ste 110 San Bruno (94066) ***(P-15484)***
Quotient Technology Inc (PA).....C.....650 605-4600
400 Logue Ave Mountain View (94043) ***(P-13660)***
Quova Inc.....D.....650 965-2898
401 Castro St Fl 3 Mountain View (94041) ***(P-27179)***
Qupid Shoe, Walnut *Also called East Lion Corporation* ***(P-8131)***
Quri Inc.....E.....415 413-0100
655 Montgomery St Lbby 1 San Francisco (94111) ***(P-25939)***
Qw Media International LLC.....E.....949 200-4616
620 Newport Center Dr # 11 Newport Beach (92660) ***(P-13632)***
Qwest Corporation.....D.....925 974-4908
1350 Treat Blvd Ste 200 Walnut Creek (94597) ***(P-5460)***
Qy Research Inc.....D.....626 295-2442
17890 Castleton St City of Industry (91748) ***(P-26782)***
R T A, Riverside *Also called Riverside Transit Agency* ***(P-3579)***
R & A Painting Inc.....D.....916 688-3955
11730 Sheldon Lake Dr Elk Grove (95624) ***(P-2383)***
R & B Realty Group.....D.....323 851-3450
3600 Barham Blvd Los Angeles (90068) ***(P-10802)***
R & B Realty Group.....D.....818 710-5400
22122 Victory Blvd Woodland Hills (91367) ***(P-10803)***
R & B Realty Group.....D.....310 751-4545
4111 Via Marina Marina Del Rey (90292) ***(P-10804)***
R & B Realty Group LP.....A.....310 478-1021
1 World Trade Ctr # 2400 Long Beach (90831) ***(P-11386)***
R & B Reinforcing Steel Corp.....D.....909 591-1726
13581 5th St Chino (91710) ***(P-3280)***
R & B Wholesale Distrs Inc (PA).....C.....909 230-5400
2350 S Milliken Ave Ontario (91761) ***(P-7215)***
R & D Leasing Inc.....D.....559 924-1276
19101 Kent Ave Lemoore (93245) ***(P-14193)***
R & G Enterprises.....C.....559 781-1351
627 N Main St Porterville (93257) ***(P-458)***
R & K Interests Inc (PA).....C.....949 900-6160
15707 Rockfield Blvd # 225 Irvine (92618) ***(P-12781)***
R & N Packing Co.....C.....209 364-6101
47920 W Nees Ave Firebaugh (93622) ***(P-529)***
R & R Electric.....E.....310 785-0288
2029 Century Park E A4 Los Angeles (90067) ***(P-2596)***
R & R Maher Construction Co.....E.....707 552-0330
1324 Lemon St Vallejo (94590) ***(P-3204)***
R & R Profession.....C.....760 754-9020
2216 S El Camino Real # 211 Oceanside (92054) ***(P-19689)***
R & S Erection Incorporated (PA).....D.....510 483-3710
2057 W Avenue 140th San Leandro (94577) ***(P-2963)***
R & S Floor Covering, Riverside *Also called R&S Carpet Services Inc* ***(P-6580)***
R & S Investments LLC.....D.....415 591-2700
1 Bush St Fl 9 San Francisco (94104) ***(P-11740)***
R & V Management Corporation.....D.....619 429-3305
768 Hollister St San Diego (92154) ***(P-26371)***
R A Schreiber Plumbing.....E.....619 659-3101
2358 Tavern Rd Alpine (91901) ***(P-2243)***
R and R Labor Inc.....B.....831 638-0290
710 Kirkpatric Ct Ste A Hollister (95023) ***(P-641)***
R and R Prof Hlthcare Staffing, Santa Clarita *Also called Oceanside Hlthcare Stffing Inc* ***(P-22289)***
R and R Professional Medical, Oceanside *Also called R & R Profession* ***(P-19689)***
R B International Inc (PA).....E.....626 357-7652
109 N Ivy Ave Ste D Monrovia (91016) ***(P-7582)***
R B Spencer Inc.....D.....530 674-8307
1188 Hassett Ave Yuba City (95991) ***(P-2244)***
R C H, San Francisco *Also called Pomeroy Rcrtion Rhbltation Ctr* ***(P-23392)***
R C Hotels Inc.....D.....714 891-0123
7667 Center Ave Huntington Beach (92647) ***(P-12782)***
R C I Enterprises Inc.....E.....310 370-5900
3848 Del Amo Blvd Ste 301 Torrance (90503) ***(P-7031)***
R C I Image Systems, Torrance *Also called R C I Enterprises Inc* ***(P-7031)***
R C O Reforesting, Yreka *Also called RCO Reforesting Inc* ***(P-965)***
R C Roberts & Co (PA).....C.....415 456-8600
801 A St San Rafael (94901) ***(P-10864)***
R D S Unlimited Inc.....E.....619 443-0221
14372 Olde Highway 80 E El Cajon (92021) ***(P-2964)***
R DS For Healthcare.....E.....209 333-2115
1420 W Kettleman Ln N5 Lodi (95242) ***(P-19690)***
R E Cuddie Co.....E.....408 998-1250
1751 Junction Ave San Jose (95112) ***(P-3016)***
R E Maher Inc.....D.....707 642-3907
4545 Hess Rd American Canyon (94503) ***(P-3205)***
R F Macdonald Co (PA).....C.....510 784-0110
25920 Eden Landing Rd Hayward (94545) ***(P-7583)***
R F Metro Services Inc (PA).....D.....909 230-4920
2320 S Archibald Ave Ontario (91761) ***(P-5798)***
R F R Corporation.....D.....800 346-7663
3310 Verdugo Rd Los Angeles (90065) ***(P-11595)***
R Fellen Inc.....D.....559 233-6248
2939 S Peach Ave Fresno (93725) ***(P-20207)***
R G Canning Enterprises Inc.....C.....323 560-7469
4515 E 59th Pl Maywood (90270) ***(P-17014)***
R G Vanderweil Engineers LLP.....C.....562 256-8623
3760 Kilroy Airport Way # 230 Long Beach (90806) ***(P-25273)***
R H D, Corona *Also called Ranch House Doors Inc* ***(P-2966)***
R H O Capital Partners Inc.....E.....650 463-0300
525 University Ave # 1350 Palo Alto (94301) ***(P-11951)***
R H Phillips Inc (HQ).....C.....530 757-5557
26836 County Road 12a Esparto (95627) ***(P-153)***
R H Phillips Vineyard, Esparto *Also called R H Phillips Inc* ***(P-153)***
R Haupt Roofing Construction.....E.....310 515-9709
1305 W 132nd St Fl 2 Gardena (90247) ***(P-3092)***
R J Dailey Construction Co.....D.....650 948-5196
401 1st St Los Altos (94022) ***(P-1179)***
R J Daum Construction Co (PA).....C.....714 894-4300
11581 Monarch St Garden Grove (92841) ***(P-1573)***
R J M Construction Inc.....E.....909 794-8853
224 Donna Dr Redlands (92374) ***(P-1574)***
R Joy Inc.....D.....530 832-5760
1584 Wolf Meadows Ln Portola (96122) ***(P-25274)***
R K I, Union City *Also called Rki Instruments Inc* ***(P-7587)***
R K Properties, Long Beach *Also called Rance King Properties Inc* ***(P-10807)***
R L G, San Mateo *Also called Research Libraries Group Inc* ***(P-15884)***
R L Jones-San Diego Inc (PA).....D.....760 357-3177
1778 Zinetta Rd Ste A Calexico (92231) ***(P-5038)***
R L Jones-San Diego Inc.....D.....760 357-0140
1778 Zinetta Rd Ste A1 Calexico (92231) ***(P-5039)***
R L Klein & Associates.....D.....562 427-5577
3553 Atlantic Ave Ste A Long Beach (90807) ***(P-14550)***
R L Safety Inc.....E.....408 557-0887
2157 Cherrystone Dr San Jose (95128) ***(P-23397)***
R M A Group Inc (PA).....D.....909 980-6096
12130 Santa Margarita Ct Rancho Cucamonga (91730) ***(P-25275)***
R M B Packaging Co Inc.....E.....818 998-0658
9667 Canoga Ave Chatsworth (91311) ***(P-9008)***
R M B SEC Cnslting Invstgtions, Fountain Valley *Also called Bell Private Security Inc* ***(P-16208)***
R M Harris Company Inc.....D.....925 335-3000
1000 Howe Rd Ste 200 Martinez (94553) ***(P-1825)***
R M Matovu Memorial.....E.....412 337-5975
327 Consuelo Dr Santa Barbara (93110) ***(P-21129)***
R Mc Closkey Insurance Agency.....C.....949 223-8100
4001 Macarthur Blvd # 300 Newport Beach (92660) ***(P-10473)***
R Mora Farm Labor.....E.....661 746-2858
930 5th St Wasco (93280) ***(P-642)***
R N D Enterprises, Lancaster *Also called BDR Industries Inc* ***(P-5666)***

ALPHABETIC

Employee Codes: A=Over 500 employees, B=251-500
C=101-250, D=51-100, E=50
2020 Directory of California
Wholesalers and Services Companies
© Mergent Inc. 1-800-342-5647
1399

R N Priority Nursing Service.....D.....760 635-7776
P.O. Box 234216 Encinitas (92023) ***(P-14372)***
R Navarro Landscape Services.....D.....562 690-6414
359 West Rd La Habra Heights (90631) ***(P-894)***
R P Direct, Santa Monica *Also called Postaer Rubin and Associates* ***(P-13560)***
R P M C Travel, Calabasas *Also called Rpmc Inc* ***(P-26924)***
R P S Resort Corp.....C.....760 327-8311
1600 N Indian Canyon Dr Palm Springs (92262) ***(P-12783)***
R Q Construction Inc.....C.....760 631-7707
3194 Lionshead Ave Carlsbad (92010) ***(P-1575)***
R R Donnelley & Sons Company.....E.....310 784-8485
18915 S Laurel Park Rd Rancho Dominguez (90220) ***(P-13737)***
R R Donnelley & Sons Company.....E.....925 951-1320
1646 N Calif Blvd Ste 510 Walnut Creek (94596) ***(P-3505)***
R Ranch Market.....A.....714 573-1182
1112 Walnut Ave Tustin (92780) ***(P-429)***
R S P, Commerce *Also called Rolled Steel Products Corp* ***(P-7099)***
R S Software India Limited.....D.....408 382-1200
1900 Mccarthy Blvd # 103 Milpitas (95035) ***(P-16095)***
R Stanley Security Service.....D.....661 634-9283
403 18th St Bakersfield (93301) ***(P-16390)***
R Systems Inc (HQ).....D.....916 939-9696
5000 Windplay Dr Ste 5 El Dorado Hills (95762) ***(P-15681)***
R T Framing Corporation.....D.....805 496-3985
299 W Hillcrest Dr # 212 Thousand Oaks (91360) ***(P-2965)***
R T I, Sunnyvale *Also called Real-Time Innovations Inc* ***(P-15051)***
R W Garcia Co Inc (PA).....E.....408 287-4616
100 Enterprise Way C230 Scotts Valley (95066) ***(P-8359)***
R W Lyall & Company Inc (HQ).....C.....951 270-1500
2665 Research Dr Corona (92882) ***(P-1007)***
R W Zant Co (PA).....D.....323 980-5457
1470 E 4th St Los Angeles (90033) ***(P-8415)***
R&M USA Inc.....D.....408 945-6626
840 Yosemite Way Milpitas (95035) ***(P-7328)***
R&S Carpet Services Inc.....D.....909 740-6645
1485 Spruce St Ste C106 Riverside (92507) ***(P-6580)***
R-Bros Painting Inc.....E.....408 291-6820
707 W Hedding St San Jose (95110) ***(P-2384)***
R2c Group, San Francisco *Also called Respond 2 LLC* ***(P-17662)***
R2g Enterprises Inc.....D.....510 489-6218
31154 San Benito St Hayward (94544) ***(P-3093)***
R3 Strategic Support Group Inc.....D.....800 418-2040
1050 B Ave Ste A Coronado (92118) ***(P-26783)***
Ra Hughes Enterprises In.....E.....619 390-4880
9316 Abraham Way Santee (92071) ***(P-2245)***
RABBIT HAVEN THE, Scotts Valley *Also called Ava The Rabbit Haven Inc* ***(P-26997)***
RAC, Corcoran *Also called Recreational Assn Corcoran* ***(P-24631)***
RAC & Associates.....D.....858 694-5800
9541 Ridgehaven Ct San Diego (92123) ***(P-14090)***
Race Street Partners Inc (PA).....D.....408 294-6161
967 W Hedding St San Jose (95126) ***(P-8332)***
Racelegal Com.....E.....619 265-8159
315 Fourth Ave Chula Vista (91910) ***(P-24858)***
Racquet Club of Irvine.....D.....949 786-3000
5 Ethel Coplen Way Ste 5 # 5 Irvine (92612) ***(P-18533)***
Racquetball World, Canoga Park *Also called Bay Clubs Inc* ***(P-18389)***
Radar Medical Systems Inc.....D.....440 337-9521
1510 Cotner Ave Los Angeles (90025) ***(P-27302)***
Radford Alexander Corporation.....D.....310 523-2555
14700 S Avalon Blvd Gardena (90248) ***(P-3929)***
Radford Studio Center Inc.....B.....818 655-5000
4024 Radford Ave Studio City (91604) ***(P-17940)***
Radiant Logic Inc (PA).....D.....415 209-6800
75 Rowland Way Ste 300 Novato (94945) ***(P-15046)***
Radiant Services Corp (PA).....C.....310 327-6300
651 W Knox St Gardena (90248) ***(P-13182)***
Radiation Medical Group Inc (PA).....E.....619 220-4100
9333 Genesee Ave Ste 300 San Diego (92121) ***(P-19324)***
Radica Enterprises Ltd.....D.....310 252-2000
333 Continental Blvd El Segundo (90245) ***(P-7741)***
Radica USA, El Segundo *Also called Radica Enterprises Ltd* ***(P-7741)***
Radio Station, Los Angeles *Also called Loyola Marymount University* ***(P-5559)***
Radio Station Kfbs, La Mirada *Also called Far East Broadcasting Co Inc* ***(P-5530)***
Radio Time, San Francisco *Also called Tunein Inc* ***(P-5570)***
Radiology Department Cal Hosp.....E.....213 742-5840
1338 S Hope St Fl 4 Los Angeles (90015) ***(P-19325)***
Radiology Prtners Holdings LLC (PA).....D.....424 290-8004
2330 Utah Ave Ste 200 El Segundo (90245) ***(P-19326)***
Radiometer America Inc (HQ).....C.....800 736-0600
250 S Kraemer Blvd Ms Brea (92821) ***(P-6999)***
Radison Hotel Newport Beach, Newport Beach *Also called Pacific Hotel Management Inc* ***(P-12694)***
Radisson Hotel At Usc.....C.....213 748-4141
3540 S Figueroa St Los Angeles (90007) ***(P-12784)***
Radisson Hotel La Westside, Culver City *Also called Pacifica Hotel & Conference Ce* ***(P-12700)***
Radisson Hotel Phoenix Cy Ctr, Anaheim *Also called Sunshine Midtown LLC* ***(P-12988)***
Radisson Hotel Santa Maria.....D.....805 928-8000
3455 Skyway Dr Santa Maria (93455) ***(P-12785)***
Radisson Ht Fishermans Wharf.....D.....415 392-6700
250 Beach St San Francisco (94133) ***(P-12786)***
Radisson Ht Frsno Cnfrence Ctr, Fresno *Also called Hl Fresno Hospitality LLC* ***(P-12351)***
Radisson Inn, Los Angeles *Also called Pacifica Hosts Inc* ***(P-12698)***
Radisson Inn, Berkeley *Also called Boykin Mgt Co Ltd Lblty Co* ***(P-12080)***
Radisson Inn, Los Angeles *Also called Radisson Hotel At Usc* ***(P-12784)***
Radisson Inn, Westlake Village *Also called Amgreen-Karena Ht Partnr Ltd* ***(P-12005)***
Radisson Inn, Sunnyvale *Also called S R H H Inc* ***(P-12856)***
Radisson Inn, San Diego *Also called Rancho Bernardo Partners Ltd* ***(P-12791)***
Radisson Inn, Union City *Also called Interstate Hotels Resorts Inc* ***(P-12475)***
Radisson Inn, Agoura Hills *Also called Ww Lbv Inc* ***(P-13118)***
Radisson Inn, Los Angeles *Also called Lax Hospitality LP* ***(P-12540)***
Radisson Inn, Los Angeles *Also called Radlax Gateway Hotel LLC* ***(P-12787)***
Radisson Inn, San Bernardino *Also called First Hotels International Inc* ***(P-12266)***
Radisson Plaza Hotel Inn, San Jose *Also called Silicon Valley Hwang LLC* ***(P-12926)***
Radisson Suites Anaheim, Buena Park *Also called Golden Hotel LLC* ***(P-12298)***
Radius Product Development Inc.....A.....408 361-6000
6375 San Ignacio Ave San Jose (95119) ***(P-25276)***
Radix Textile Inc.....D.....323 234-1667
745 Kohler St Los Angeles (90021) ***(P-8007)***
Radlax Gateway Hotel LLC.....B.....310 670-9000
6225 W Century Blvd Los Angeles (90045) ***(P-12787)***
Radleys.....E.....310 765-2223
3780 Wilshire Blvd Los Angeles (90010) ***(P-17657)***
Radnet Inc (PA).....C.....310 445-2800
1510 Cotner Ave Los Angeles (90025) ***(P-21576)***
Radnet Management Inc.....D.....209 524-6800
157 E Coolidge Ave Modesto (95350) ***(P-26372)***
Radnet Management Inc.....D.....323 549-3000
8750 Wilshire Blvd # 100 Beverly Hills (90211) ***(P-19327)***
Radonich Corp.....E.....408 275-8888
886 Faulstich Ct San Jose (95112) ***(P-2597)***
Rady Childrens Hosp & Hlth Ctr (PA).....A.....858 576-1700
3020 Childrens Way San Diego (92123) ***(P-21489)***
Rady Chld Hospital-San Diego (HQ).....A.....858 576-1700
3020 Childrens Way San Diego (92123) ***(P-21130)***
Rady Chld Hospital-San Diego.....D.....858 966-5833
8022 Birmingham Dr # 22 San Diego (92123) ***(P-26373)***
Rafael Convalescent Hospital.....C.....415 479-3450
234 N San Pedro Rd San Rafael (94903) ***(P-20665)***
Raffles Lrmitage Beverly Hills.....C.....310 278-3344
9291 Burton Way Beverly Hills (90210) ***(P-12788)***
Raging Waters San Dimas 703, San Dimas *Also called Festival Fun Parks LLC* ***(P-7709)***
Raging Wire, Sacramento *Also called Ragingwire Data Centers Inc* ***(P-15905)***
Ragingwire Data Centers Inc (HQ).....B.....916 286-3000
1625 National Dr Sacramento (95834) ***(P-15905)***
Rahf IV Casa Panorama LP.....E.....216 621-6060
14555 Osborne St Panorama City (91402) ***(P-10805)***
Rahf IV Grove LP.....E.....216 621-6060
227 W H St Ontario (91762) ***(P-10806)***
Rahi Systems Inc (PA).....C.....510 651-2205
48303 Fremont Blvd Fremont (94538) ***(P-27180)***
Railpros Inc (PA).....D.....714 734-8765
15265 Alton Pkwy Ste 140 Irvine (92618) ***(P-25277)***
Railpros Field Services.....E.....877 315-0513
1 Ada Ste 200 Irvine (92618) ***(P-25278)***
Railroad Technology, Sacramento *Also called Macdonald Mott LLC* ***(P-25200)***
Rain Bird Corporation.....D.....619 661-4493
2475-A Paseo De Las Ameri San Diego (92154) ***(P-6370)***
Rain Bird Distribution Corp.....D.....626 963-9311
1000 W Sierra Madre Ave Azusa (91702) ***(P-1986)***
Rain Creek Baking, Madera *Also called Kronos Foods Corp* ***(P-8602)***
Rain For Rent, Bakersfield *Also called Western Oilfields Supply Co* ***(P-14209)***
Rainbow - Brite Indus Svcs LLC.....D.....559 925-2580
463 E Salmon River Dr Fresno (93730) ***(P-14022)***
Rainbow Camp Inc.....E.....310 456-3066
26619 Marigold Ct Calabasas (91302) ***(P-18742)***
Rainbow Disposal Co Inc (HQ).....C.....714 847-3581
17121 Nichols Ln Huntington Beach (92647) ***(P-6237)***
Rainbow Farms, Denair *Also called Valley Fresh Foods Inc* ***(P-414)***
Rainbow Home Care Services.....D.....714 544-8070
1560 Brookhollow Dr # 100 Santa Ana (92705) ***(P-21848)***
Rainbow Municipal Water Dst.....D.....760 728-1178
3707 Old Highway 395 Fallbrook (92028) ***(P-6102)***
Rainbow Ranches Inc.....C.....661 858-2266
13650 Copus Rd Bakersfield (93313) ***(P-353)***
Rainbow Realty Corporation.....D.....949 770-9626
24221 Paseo De Valencia Laguna Woods (92637) ***(P-11387)***
Rainbow Refuse Recycling, Huntington Beach *Also called Rainbow Disposal Co Inc* ***(P-6237)***
Rainbow Sandals Inc.....E.....949 276-4431
900 Calle Negocio San Clemente (92673) ***(P-8142)***
Rainbow Transfer Recycling.....C.....714 847-5818
17121 Nichols Ln Huntington Beach (92647) ***(P-6238)***
Rainbow Vending & Distributing, San Diego *Also called Canteen Vending - San Diego* ***(P-8339)***
Rainbow Wtrprofing Restoration.....C.....415 641-1578
600 Treat Ave San Francisco (94110) ***(P-3458)***
Raincross Hospitality Corp (PA).....D.....951 346-4700
3637 5th St Riverside (92501) ***(P-13451)***
Raines Law Group LLP.....E.....310 440-4100
9720 Wilshire Blvd Fl 5 Beverly Hills (90212) ***(P-22784)***
Rainforest Qa Inc.....C.....650 866-1407
600 Battery St Fl 2 San Francisco (94111) ***(P-15047)***
Rainier Financial Group LLC.....E.....310 335-9200
2321 Rosecrans Ave # 4270 El Segundo (90245) ***(P-26784)***
Raintree Systems Inc.....D.....951 252-9400
27307 Via Industria Temecula (92590) ***(P-15048)***
Raiser Senior Services LLC.....D.....650 342-4106
601 Laurel Ave Apt 903 San Mateo (94401) ***(P-24037)***
Raison D'Etre Bakery, South San Francisco *Also called Ashbury Market Inc* ***(P-8547)***
Rakon America LLC.....A.....847 930-5100
7600 Dublin Blvd Ste 220 Dublin (94568) ***(P-7329)***
Rakstar Production, Los Angeles *Also called Entertainment & Sports Today* ***(P-5595)***

Rakworx Inc....C....949 215-1362
23122 Alcalde Dr Ste C Laguna Hills (92653) ***(P-15925)***
Raleigh Enterprises Inc (PA)....C....310 899-8900
5300 Melrose Ave Fl 4 Los Angeles (90038) ***(P-12789)***
Raleigh Enterprises Inc....C....323 466-3111
5300 Melrose Ave Fl 3 Los Angeles (90038) ***(P-17762)***
Raleigh Holdings, Los Angeles *Also called Raleigh Enterprises Inc **(P-12789)***
Raleigh Studios, Los Angeles *Also called Raleigh Enterprises Inc **(P-17762)***
Raleys....B....916 928-0575
4061 Gateway Park Blvd Sacramento (95834) ***(P-4482)***
Raleys Distribution Ctr 836, Sacramento *Also called Raleys **(P-4482)***
Ralison International Inc....E....909 393-0008
15328 Central Ave Chino (91710) ***(P-7769)***
Ralph Collazo Packing Inc....D....760 353-0856
72 E Main St Ste A Heber (92249) ***(P-17015)***
Ralph D Mitzel Inc....D....714 554-4745
1520 N Fairview St Santa Ana (92706) ***(P-14110)***
Ralphs 00134, Glendale *Also called Ralphs Grocery Company **(P-4483)***
Ralphs 00173, Downey *Also called Ralphs Grocery Company **(P-4487)***
Ralphs 6, Encino *Also called Ralphs Grocery Company **(P-4486)***
Ralphs 96, Pasadena *Also called Ralphs Grocery Company **(P-4488)***
Ralphs Grocery Company....C....818 549-0035
211 N Glendale Ave Glendale (91206) ***(P-4483)***
Ralphs Grocery Company....A....310 637-1101
4841-45 San Fernando W Los Angeles (90039) ***(P-4484)***
Ralphs Grocery Company....D....562 633-0830
13525 Lakewood Blvd Downey (90242) ***(P-4485)***
Ralphs Grocery Company....C....818 345-6882
17840 Ventura Blvd Encino (91316) ***(P-4486)***
Ralphs Grocery Company....D....562 869-2042
9200 Lakewood Blvd Downey (90240) ***(P-4487)***
Ralphs Grocery Company....D....626 793-7480
160 N Lake Ave Pasadena (91101) ***(P-4488)***
Ram Commercial Enterprises Inc....E....916 429-1205
5896 S Land Park Dr Sacramento (95822) ***(P-11388)***
Ram Mechanical Inc....D....209 531-9155
3506 Moore Rd Ceres (95307) ***(P-2246)***
Ramada Clock Tower Inn, Ventura *Also called Clocktower Inn **(P-12155)***
Ramada Inn, Fresno *Also called Fresno Hotel Partners LP **(P-12285)***
Ramada Inn, Sunnyvale *Also called Executive Inn Inc **(P-12260)***
Ramada Inn, San Diego *Also called Royal Hospitality Incorporated **(P-12843)***
Ramada Inn, San Diego *Also called Trigild International Inc **(P-13043)***
Ramada Inn, Hawthorne *Also called Calhot Illinios LLC **(P-12104)***
Ramada Inn, Redondo Beach *Also called D & W LLC **(P-12199)***
Ramada Plaza Ht Anaheim Resort....C....714 991-6868
515 W Katella Ave Anaheim (92802) ***(P-12790)***
Ramada Plz Ht San Dego/ Ht Cir, San Diego *Also called G5 Global Partners Ix LLC **(P-12286)***
Ramboll Environ, Irvine *Also called Ramboll US Corporation **(P-27303)***
Ramboll Environ US Corporation....D....510 655-7400
2200 Powell St Ste 700 Emeryville (94608) ***(P-27181)***
Ramboll Environ US Corporation....D....949 261-5151
5 Park Plz Ste 500 Irvine (92614) ***(P-27182)***
Ramboll Environment & Health, Irvine *Also called Ramboll Environ US Corporation **(P-27182)***
Ramboll US Corporation....E....949 798-3604
5 Park Plz Ste 500 Irvine (92614) ***(P-27303)***
Ramcar Batteries Inc....E....323 726-1212
2700 Carrier Ave Commerce (90040) ***(P-6463)***
Ramcast Ornamental Sup Co Inc (PA)....C....323 585-1625
2201 Firestone Blvd Los Angeles (90002) ***(P-7092)***
Ramco Employment Services, Oxnard *Also called Ramco Enterprises LP **(P-530)***
Ramco Enterprises LP....A....805 922-9888
325 Plaza Dr Ste 1 Santa Maria (93454) ***(P-14373)***
Ramco Enterprises LP....A....831 722-3370
585 Auto Center Dr Watsonville (95076) ***(P-14374)***
Ramco Enterprises LP....A....805 486-9328
520 E 3rd St Ste B Oxnard (93030) ***(P-530)***
Ramkade Insurance Services....D....818 444-1340
21550 Oxnard St Ste 500 Woodland Hills (91367) ***(P-10474)***
Ramona Care Center Inc....C....626 442-5721
11900 Ramona Blvd El Monte (91732) ***(P-20208)***
Ramona Community Services Corp (HQ)....C....951 658-9288
890 W Stetson Ave Ste A Hemet (92543) ***(P-21849)***
Ramona Nrsing Rhbilitation Ctr, El Monte *Also called Ramona Care Center Inc **(P-20208)***
Ramona Rehabilitation and Post....C....951 652-0011
485 W Johnston Ave Hemet (92543) ***(P-21131)***
RAMONA VNA & HOSPICE, Hemet *Also called Ramona Community Services Corp **(P-21849)***
Rams Hill Country Club....D....760 767-4259
1881 Rams Hill Rd Borrego Springs (92004) ***(P-18534)***
Ramsell Public Health Rx LLC....D....510 587-2600
200 Webster St Ste 300 Oakland (94607) ***(P-10475)***
Ramsey Real Estate Group....E....800 685-7734
13714 Boquita Dr Del Mar (92014) ***(P-11389)***
Ramsey-Shilling Residential RE....D....323 851-5512
3360 Barham Blvd Los Angeles (90068) ***(P-11390)***
Ramsgate Engineering Inc....D....661 392-0050
2331 Cepheus Ct Bakersfield (93308) ***(P-25279)***
Rance King Properties Inc (PA)....C....562 240-1000
3737 E Broadway Long Beach (90803) ***(P-10807)***
Ranch At Laguna Beach, The, Laguna Beach *Also called Laguna Bch Golf Bnglow Vlg LLC **(P-427)***
Ranch At Little Hills, The, San Ramon *Also called Concessionaires Urban Park **(P-18674)***
Ranch Golf Club....D....408 270-0557
4601 Hill Top View Ln San Jose (95138) ***(P-18286)***
Ranch Hand Entertainment Inc....D....612 396-2632
11333 Moorpark St Pmb 441 Studio City (91602) ***(P-17658)***
Ranch House Doors Inc....D....951 278-2884
1527 Pomona Rd Corona (92880) ***(P-2966)***
Ranching Shop, Corcoran *Also called J G Boswell Company **(P-14)***
Rancho Bernardo Golf Club....D....858 487-1134
17550 Bernardo Oaks Dr San Diego (92128) ***(P-18743)***
Rancho Bernardo Partners Ltd....D....858 451-6600
11520 W Bernardo Ct San Diego (92127) ***(P-12791)***
Rancho California Landscaping....E....310 768-1680
13801 S Western Ave Gardena (90249) ***(P-895)***
Rancho California Water Dst (PA)....C....951 296-6900
42135 Winchester Rd Temecula (92590) ***(P-6103)***
Rancho Ccamonga Cmnty Hosp LLC....C....909 581-6400
10841 White Oak Ave Rancho Cucamonga (91730) ***(P-21132)***
Rancho Clinic Rancho San Diego, La Mesa *Also called Scripps Health **(P-19377)***
Rancho Cordova Medical Offices, Rancho Cordova *Also called Kaiser Foundation Hospitals **(P-20962)***
Rancho Cucamonga Medical Offs, Rancho Cucamonga *Also called Kaiser Foundation Hospitals **(P-19053)***
Rancho Cucamonga Sport Club, Rancho Cucamonga *Also called 24 Hour Fitness Usa Inc **(P-18097)***
Rancho De Sus Ninos Inc....D....619 661-9232
P.O. Box 360 Potrero (91963) ***(P-24038)***
Rancho Del Oro Ldscp Maint Inc....D....760 726-0215
4167 Avenida De La Plata Oceanside (92056) ***(P-754)***
Rancho Foods Inc....D....323 585-0503
2528 E 37th St Vernon (90058) ***(P-8416)***
Rancho Jurupa Park....E....951 684-7032
4800 Crestmore Rd Riverside (92509) ***(P-18744)***
Rancho La Quinta Country Club, La Quinta *Also called TD Desert Dev Ltd Partnr **(P-11613)***
Rancho Laguna Farms LLC....D....805 925-7805
2410 W Main St Santa Maria (93458) ***(P-354)***
Rancho Leonero Resort....E....760 438-2905
5671 Palmer Way Ste E Carlsbad (92010) ***(P-12792)***
Rancho Los Amigos Nationa....B....562 401-7111
7601 Imperial Hwy Downey (90242) ***(P-23398)***
Rancho Los Amigos Nationa....A....562 401-7111
7601 Imperial Hwy Downey (90242) ***(P-23399)***
Rancho Los Amigos Nationa....B....562 401-7266
12852 Erickson Ave Downey (90242) ***(P-23400)***
Rancho Los Amigos Nationa (PA)....D....562 401-7111
7601 Imperial Hwy Downey (90242) ***(P-23401)***
Rancho Mission Viejo LLC (PA)....D....949 240-3363
28811 Ortega Hwy San Juan Capistrano (92675) ***(P-11391)***
Rancho Murieta Country Club....D....916 354-2400
7000 Alameda Dr Rancho Murieta (95683) ***(P-18535)***
Rancho Niguel Dental Group....E....949 249-4180
30140 Town Center Dr Laguna Niguel (92677) ***(P-19627)***
Rancho Pacific Electric Inc....E....909 476-1022
9063 Santa Anita Ave Rancho Cucamonga (91730) ***(P-2598)***
Rancho Penasquitos Sport Club, San Diego *Also called 24 Hour Fitness Usa Inc **(P-18113)***
Rancho Physical Therapy Inc....C....760 752-1011
277 Rancheros Dr San Marcos (92069) ***(P-19691)***
Rancho Physical Therapy Inc (PA)....D....951 696-9353
24630 Washington Ave # 200 Murrieta (92562) ***(P-19692)***
Rancho Research Institute....C....562 401-8111
7601 Imperial Hwy Downey (90242) ***(P-26023)***
Rancho Salinas Packing Inc....C....831 758-3624
2376 Alisal Rd Salinas (93908) ***(P-643)***
Rancho San Antonio Boys HM Inc (PA)....C....818 882-6400
21000 Plummer St Chatsworth (91311) ***(P-24039)***
Rancho San Antonio Medical Ctr, Rancho Cucamonga *Also called San Antonio Community Hospital **(P-21150)***
Rancho San Antonio Retirement....B....650 265-2637
23500 Cristo Rey Dr Cupertino (95014) ***(P-24040)***
Rancho San Diego Cinema 16, El Cajon *Also called Edwards Theatres Circuit Inc **(P-17834)***
Rancho San Diego Medical Offs, La Mesa *Also called Kaiser Foundation Hospitals **(P-19076)***
Rancho San Joaquin Golf Course, Irvine *Also called American Golf Corporation **(P-18359)***
Rancho Santa Ana Botanic Grdn....D....909 625-8767
1500 N College Ave Claremont (91711) ***(P-24313)***
Rancho Santa Fe, Rancho Santa Fe *Also called Pacific Western Bank **(P-9112)***
Rancho Santa Fe Association A....D....858 756-1182
5827 Viadelacumere Rancho Santa Fe (92067) ***(P-18536)***
Rancho Santa Fe Protective Svc....E....760 433-8887
1991 Village Park Way # 100 Encinitas (92024) ***(P-16391)***
Rancho Sante Fe Golf Club, Rancho Santa Fe *Also called Rancho Santa Fe Association A **(P-18536)***
Rancho Simi Recreation Pk Dst (PA)....D....805 584-4400
4201 Guardian St Simi Valley (93063) ***(P-18745)***
Rancho Speciality Hospital, Rancho Cucamonga *Also called Rancho Ccamonga Cmnty Hosp LLC **(P-21132)***
Rancho Springs Medical Center, Murrieta *Also called Southwest Healthcare Sys Aux **(P-21217)***
Rancho Valencia Resort....B....858 756-1123
5921 Valencia Cir Rancho Santa Fe (92067) ***(P-12793)***
Rancho Vista Health Center....C....760 941-1480
200 Grapevine Rd Apt 15 Vista (92083) ***(P-20447)***
Rancho West Landscape....E....951 301-3979
39140 Pala Vista Dr Temecula (92591) ***(P-896)***
Rancho Wholesale, Chino *Also called Redwood Products Chino Inc **(P-6648)***
Ranchwood Contractors Inc....D....209 826-6200
923 E Pacheco Blvd Los Banos (93635) ***(P-1576)***
Rand Medical Billing Inc....D....805 578-8300
1633 Erringer Rd Fl 1 Simi Valley (93065) ***(P-25668)***
Rand Technology LLC (PA)....D....949 255-5700
15225 Alton Pkwy Unit 100 Irvine (92618) ***(P-7330)***

ALPHABETIC

Employee Codes: A=Over 500 employees, B=251-500
C=101-250, D=51-100, E=50
2020 Directory of California
Wholesalers and Services Companies
© Mergent Inc. 1-800-342-5647
1401

Randall Mc-Anany Company..........D......310 822-3344
1528 W 178th St Gardena (90248) ***(P-2385)***
Randall-Bold Wtr Trtmnt Plant, Oakley *Also called Contra Costa Water District* ***(P-6040)***
Randazzo Enterprises Inc..........D......831 633-4420
13550 Blackie Rd Castroville (95012) ***(P-3349)***
Rando AAA Hvac Inc..........E......408 293-4717
1712 Stone Ave Ste 1 San Jose (95125) ***(P-2247)***
Randstad Finance & Accounting, Burlingame *Also called Randstad Professionals Us LLC* ***(P-14377)***
Randstad North America Inc..........C......559 297-0054
7014 N Cedar Ave Fresno (93720) ***(P-14551)***
Randstad North America Inc..........C......559 582-2700
106 E 7th St Hanford (93230) ***(P-14375)***
Randstad North America Inc..........B......559 592-6700
1110 W Visalia Rd Ste 116 Exeter (93221) ***(P-14552)***
Randstad North America Inc..........C......415 397-3384
27 Maiden Ln Ste 202 San Francisco (94108) ***(P-14376)***
Randstad Professionals Us LLC..........C......650 343-5111
111 Anza Blvd Ste 202 Burlingame (94010) ***(P-14377)***
Randstad Technologies LLC..........D......619 798-7300
8880 Rio San Diego Dr # 107 San Diego (92108) ***(P-14378)***
Range Generation Next LLC..........D......310 647-9438
105 13th St Bldg 6525 Vandenberg Afb (93437) ***(P-25280)***
Range Generation Next LLC..........E......310 647-9438
Pillar Point Air Sta El Granada (94018) ***(P-27183)***
Ranger Pipelines Incorporated..........C......415 822-3700
1790 Yosemite Ave San Francisco (94124) ***(P-1905)***
Ranscapes Inc..........E......866 883-9297
30 Hughes Ste 209 Irvine (92618) ***(P-14023)***
Ransome Company..........E......510 686-9900
1933 Williams St San Leandro (94577) ***(P-1577)***
Rantec Power Systems Inc (HQ)..........D......805 596-6000
1173 Los Olivos Ave Los Osos (93402) ***(P-7331)***
Raphaels Party Rentals Inc (PA)..........C......858 444-1692
8606 Miramar Rd San Diego (92126) ***(P-14194)***
Rapid Product Dev Group Inc..........C......760 703-5770
300 W Grand Ave Escondido (92025) ***(P-27184)***
Rapid Solutions Consulting LLC..........E......415 226-1131
1900 S Norfolk St Ste 350 San Mateo (94403) ***(P-15049)***
Rapp Worldwide Inc..........D......310 563-7200
12777 W Jefferson Blvd Los Angeles (90066) ***(P-13565)***
Rapport Worldwide, San Francisco *Also called Mediabrands Worldwide Inc* ***(P-13655)***
Ras, Sacramento *Also called Mark H Leibenhaut MD* ***(P-19176)***
Ras Management Inc (PA)..........E......510 727-1800
4545 Crow Canyon Pl Castro Valley (94552) ***(P-4489)***
Rashman Corporation..........D......818 993-3030
8600 Wilbur Ave Northridge (91324) ***(P-7000)***
Ratcliff Architects..........D......510 899-6400
5856 Doyle St Emeryville (94608) ***(P-25492)***
Raul V Acevedo..........E......559 791-1304
1638 W Castle Ave Porterville (93257) ***(P-944)***
Rava Ranches Inc..........E......831 385-3285
700 Airport Rd King City (93930) ***(P-430)***
Raven Biotechnologies Inc..........D......650 624-2600
1 Corporate Dr South San Francisco (94080) ***(P-25821)***
Ravenswood Family Health Ctr, East Palo Alto *Also called South Cnty Cmnty Hlth Ctr Inc* ***(P-22325)***
Ravenswood Solutions Inc (HQ)..........D......650 241-3661
3065 Skyway Ct Fremont (94539) ***(P-15682)***
Ravig Inc..........D......925 526-1234
510 Garcia Ave Ste E Pittsburg (94565) ***(P-6890)***
Rawitser Golf Shop Mike..........E......408 441-4653
1560 Oakland Rd San Jose (95131) ***(P-18287)***
Rawlings Mechanical Corp (PA)..........D......323 875-2040
11615 Pendleton St Sun Valley (91352) ***(P-2248)***
Ray Stone, Sacramento *Also called Brunswick Corner Partnership* ***(P-10949)***
Ray W Choi..........D......714 783-1000
731 E Ball Rd Ste 100 Anaheim (92805) ***(P-26785)***
Rayco Electric, Rancho Cordova *Also called Rci Electric Inc* ***(P-2600)***
Raycon Construction Inc..........E......805 525-5256
1795 E Lemonwood Dr Santa Paula (93060) ***(P-2727)***
Raylee Electric..........E......916 408-7556
1202 Tarapin Ln Lincoln (95648) ***(P-2599)***
Raymak Automotive Inc..........E......310 329-8910
15600 S Main St Gardena (90248) ***(P-17343)***
Raymond Brown Company, San Francisco *Also called Walter E McGuire RE Inc* ***(P-11506)***
Raymond Group (PA)..........C......714 771-7670
520 W Walnut Ave Orange (92868) ***(P-26374)***
Raymond Handling Concepts Corp (HQ)..........D......510 745-7500
41400 Boyce Rd Fremont (94538) ***(P-17533)***
Raymond Handling Solutions Inc (HQ)..........C......562 944-8067
9939 Norwalk Blvd Santa Fe Springs (90670) ***(P-7584)***
Raymond Handling Solutions Inc..........D......909 930-9399
4602 E Brickell St Ontario (91761) ***(P-7585)***
RAYNER EQUIPMENT SYSTEMS, Sacramento *Also called California Pavement Maint Inc* ***(P-1676)***
Raytheon Command and Control..........E......714 446-3232
2000 E El Segundo Blvd El Segundo (90245) ***(P-7332)***
Raytheon Command and Control (HQ)..........A......714 446-3118
1801 Hughes Dr Fullerton (92833) ***(P-7333)***
Raytheon Company..........C......858 455-9741
9985 Pcf Hts Blvd Ste 200 San Diego (92121) ***(P-25281)***
Raytheon Company..........C......310 647-9438
2000 E El Segundo Blvd El Segundo (90245) ***(P-25282)***
Raytheon Company..........D......805 562-2941
75 Coromar Dr Goleta (93117) ***(P-17016)***
Raytheon Company..........B......760 386-2572
988 Inner Loop Rd Fort Irwin (92310) ***(P-17459)***
Rayv Inc..........E......310 600-2959
6380 Wilshire Blvd # 1006 Los Angeles (90048) ***(P-15683)***
Razavi Corporation..........D......619 465-8010
7979 La Mesa Blvd La Mesa (91942) ***(P-20209)***
Razor USA LLC (PA)..........D......562 345-6000
12723 166th St Cerritos (90703) ***(P-7718)***
RB Anglers Club..........D......858 487-6484
12578 Cresta Pl San Diego (92128) ***(P-18537)***
Rbb Architects Inc (PA)..........D......310 479-1473
10980 Wilshire Blvd Los Angeles (90024) ***(P-25493)***
Rbc Capital Markets LLC..........E......310 273-7600
9665 Wilshire Blvd Fl 4 Beverly Hills (90212) ***(P-9747)***
Rbc Transport Dynamics Corp..........C......203 267-7001
3131 W Segerstrom Ave Santa Ana (92704) ***(P-7651)***
Rbi Bearings, Monrovia *Also called R B International Inc* ***(P-7582)***
RC Construction Services, Rialto *Also called Robert Clapper Cnstr Svcs Inc* ***(P-1583)***
RC Packing LLC..........B......831 675-0308
26769 El Camino Real Gonzales (93926) ***(P-459)***
RC Wendt Painting Inc..........C......714 960-2700
21612 Surveyor Cir Huntington Beach (92646) ***(P-2386)***
RCA Properties, Paso Robles *Also called RE Max Parkside Real Estate* ***(P-11393)***
Rcac, West Sacramento *Also called Rural Cmnty Assistance Corp* ***(P-23417)***
Rcb Corporation (PA)..........D......916 567-2600
2485 Natomas Park Dr # 100 Sacramento (95833) ***(P-9234)***
Rcc Facility Incorporated..........D......510 658-2041
210 40th Street Way Oakland (94611) ***(P-20666)***
Rci, Irvine *Also called Racquet Club of Irvine* ***(P-18533)***
Rci Electric Inc..........D......916 858-8000
3144 Fitzgerald Rd Rancho Cordova (95742) ***(P-2600)***
RCO Reforesting Inc..........E......530 842-7647
1332 Fairlane Rd Ste A Yreka (96097) ***(P-965)***
Rcs World Travel, Ventura *Also called Registration Ctrl Systems Inc* ***(P-17018)***
Rcsn Inc..........C......714 965-0244
10221 Slater Ave Ste 214 Fountain Valley (92708) ***(P-14379)***
RCWD, Temecula *Also called Rancho California Water Dst* ***(P-6103)***
Rd Solutions, Encino *Also called Integrted Spport Solutions Inc* ***(P-27095)***
Rdc-S111 Inc (PA)..........D......562 628-8000
111 W Ocean Blvd Ste 21 Long Beach (90802) ***(P-25494)***
Rdi Engineering, Monterey Park *Also called Roque Development and Inv* ***(P-25289)***
Rdl Reference Laboratory, Los Angeles *Also called Rheumatology Diagnostics Lab* ***(P-21580)***
RDM Electric Co Inc (PA)..........D......909 591-0990
4260 E Brickell St Ontario (91761) ***(P-2601)***
Rdo Construction Equipment Co..........D......619 443-3758
10108 Riverford Rd Lakeside (92040) ***(P-14111)***
Rdo Construction Equipment Co..........E......951 778-3700
20 Iowa Ave Riverside (92507) ***(P-7506)***
Rdo Vermeer LLC..........D......916 643-0999
3980 Research Dr Sacramento (95838) ***(P-7490)***
Rdr Builders LP..........D......209 368-7561
1806 W Kettleman Ln Ste F Lodi (95242) ***(P-1267)***
Rdr Production Builders, Lodi *Also called Rdr Builders LP* ***(P-1267)***
RE Barren Ridge 1 LLC..........C......415 675-1500
300 California St Fl 7 San Francisco (94104) ***(P-5910)***
RE Infolink, Sunnyvale *Also called Mlslistings Inc* ***(P-26721)***
RE La Mesa LLC..........D......415 675-1500
300 California St Fl 8 San Francisco (94104) ***(P-1987)***
RE Max 2000 Realty, City of Industry *Also called Leon Chien Corp* ***(P-9574)***
RE Max All Cities Lk Arrowhead..........E......909 337-6111
28200 Highway 189 Lake Arrowhead (92352) ***(P-11392)***
RE Max Parkside Real Estate..........D......805 239-3310
711 12th St Paso Robles (93446) ***(P-11393)***
RE Max Westlake Investments, Daly City *Also called Casbn Investment Inc* ***(P-10967)***
RE Milano Plumbing Corp..........E......925 500-1372
4881 Sunrise Dr Ste B Martinez (94553) ***(P-2249)***
Re/Max, Westlake Village *Also called Remax Olson* ***(P-11416)***
Re/Max, Los Alamitos *Also called College Park Realty Inc* ***(P-11061)***
Re/Max, Sacramento *Also called Remax Gold* ***(P-11414)***
Re/Max, Upland *Also called Diamond Ridge Corporation* ***(P-11092)***
Re/Max, Yorba Linda *Also called Yorba Properties Corp* ***(P-11525)***
Re/Max, Irvine *Also called J Baron Inc* ***(P-11215)***
Re/Max, Ventura *Also called Evans/Sipes Inc* ***(P-11118)***
Re/Max, La Jolla *Also called Mountain-Pacific Financial* ***(P-11301)***
Re/Max, Cypress *Also called Riphagen & Bullerdick Inc* ***(P-11420)***
Re/Max, Folsom *Also called Norcal Gold Inc* ***(P-11319)***
Re/Max, Costa Mesa *Also called Remax Metro Inc* ***(P-11415)***
Re/Max..........E......661 616-4040
201 New Stine Rd Ste 300 Bakersfield (93309) ***(P-11394)***
Re/Max LLC..........E......303 770-5531
1071 E 16th St Upland (91784) ***(P-11395)***
Re/Max Beach Cities Realty Mar..........C......310 376-2225
400 S Sepulveda Blvd # 100 Manhattan Beach (90266) ***(P-11396)***
Re/Max Magic..........E......661 616-4040
11420 Ming Ave Ste 530 Bakersfield (93311) ***(P-11397)***
RE/Max of Valencia Inc (PA)..........C......661 255-2650
25101 The Old Rd Santa Clarita (91381) ***(P-11398)***
Re/Max Plos Vrdes Rlty / Exces..........E......310 541-5224
450 Silver Spur Rd Rancho Palos Verdes (90275) ***(P-11399)***
Re/Maxcc, Walnut Creek *Also called C C Connection Inc* ***(P-10955)***
Reach Out West End..........D......909 982-8641
1126 W Foothill Blvd # 250 Upland (91786) ***(P-24217)***
Reaching For Independence Inc..........D......707 725-9010
609 14th St Fortuna (95540) ***(P-24218)***
Reachlocal Inc (HQ)..........C......818 274-0260
21700 Oxnard St Ste 1600 Woodland Hills (91367) ***(P-13566)***

Mergent e-mail: customerrelations@mergent.com
1402
2020 Directory of California
Wholesalers and Services Companies
(P-0000) Products & Services Section entry number
(PA)=Parent Co (HQ)=Headquarters (DH)=Div Headquarters

Reading and Beyond ... D ... 559 840-1068
4670 E Butler Ave Fresno (93702) ***(P-24630)***
Reading Entertainment Inc (HQ) ... D ... 213 235-2226
500 Citadel Dr Ste 300 Commerce (90040) ***(P-17857)***
Reading International Inc ... E ... 951 696-7045
41090 California Oaks Rd Murrieta (92562) ***(P-17858)***
Reading International Inc ... D ... 858 207-2606
11620 Carmel Mountain Rd San Diego (92128) ***(P-17859)***
Reading International Inc ... C ... 916 442-0985
2508 Land Park Dr Sacramento (95818) ***(P-17860)***
Reading International Inc (PA) ... D ... 213 235-2240
5995 Sepulveda Blvd Fl 3 Culver City (90230) ***(P-17861)***
Reading Partners ... D ... 408 945-5720
600 Valley Way Milpitas (95035) ***(P-23402)***
Ready America Inc (PA) ... D ... 760 295-0234
1399 Specialty Dr Vista (92081) ***(P-7829)***
Ready Roast Nut Company LLC (PA) ... D ... 559 661-1696
2805 Falcon Dr Madera (93637) ***(P-531)***
Readylink Inc ... D ... 760 343-7000
72030 Metroplex Dr Thousand Palms (92276) ***(P-14380)***
Readylink Healthcare ... D ... 760 343-7000
72030 Metroplex Dr Thousand Palms (92276) ***(P-14381)***
Real Estate America Inc ... D ... 510 594-3100
2000 Powell St Ste 100 Emeryville (94608) ***(P-11400)***
Real Estate California Dept ... D ... 951 715-0130
3737 Main St Ofc Riverside (92501) ***(P-11401)***
Real Estate Digital LLC ... C ... 800 234-2139
27081 Aliso Creek Rd # 200 Aliso Viejo (92656) ***(P-15050)***
Real Estate Equity Exchange ... D ... 415 992-4200
650 California St Fl 18 San Francisco (94108) ***(P-9598)***
Real Estate Image Inc ... C ... 714 502-3900
1415 S Acacia Ave Fullerton (92831) ***(P-13738)***
Real Good Food Company LLC ... C ... 909 744-0073
111 N Artsakh St Ste 201 Glendale (91206) ***(P-8637)***
Real Goods Solar Inc ... C ... 951 304-3301
41567 Cherry St Murrieta (92562) ***(P-2250)***
Real Human Svcs & Workforce, Crescent City *Also called Del Norte Workforce Center* ***(P-23590)***
Real Property Systems Inc ... C ... 760 243-1143
1443 E Washington Blvd Pasadena (91104) ***(P-11402)***
Real Software Systems LLC (PA) ... D ... 818 313-8000
21255 Burbank Blvd # 220 Woodland Hills (91367) ***(P-15485)***
Real Time Information Svcs Inc ... E ... 559 222-6456
191 W Shaw Ave Ste 106 Fresno (93704) ***(P-14553)***
Real Time Staffing Services ... D ... 805 882-2200
301 Mentor Dr 210 Santa Barbara (93111) ***(P-14382)***
Real-Time Innovations Inc ... D ... 408 990-7400
232 E Java Dr Sunnyvale (94089) ***(P-15051)***
Real-Time Staffing Services, Fresno *Also called Real Time Information Svcs Inc* ***(P-14553)***
Realdefense LLC ... D ... 310 693-5935
1541 Ocean Ave Ste 200 Santa Monica (90401) ***(P-16552)***
Really Likeable People Inc ... E ... 760 431-5577
2251 Las Palmas Dr Carlsbad (92011) ***(P-8143)***
REALM, Milpitas *Also called R&M USA Inc* ***(P-7328)***
Realogy Holdings Corp ... B ... 707 284-1111
3554 Round Barn Blvd Santa Rosa (95403) ***(P-11403)***
Realsuite SM, Santa Clara *Also called Move Inc* ***(P-11303)***
Realtor Sfr Green ... E ... 858 488-4090
4090 Mission Blvd San Diego (92109) ***(P-11404)***
Realty Concepts, Fresno *Also called JMS Realtors Ltd* ***(P-11220)***
Realty Executives, Escondido *Also called J & P Financial Inc* ***(P-11214)***
Realty Executives ... C ... 661 286-8600
26650 The Old Rd Ste 300 Valencia (91381) ***(P-11405)***
Realty Group San Diego, Carlsbad *Also called Richard Realty Group Inc* ***(P-11419)***
Realty One Group Inc ... D ... 951 565-8105
19322 Jesse Ln Riverside (92508) ***(P-11406)***
Realty One Group Solution, Valencia *Also called King Monster Inc* ***(P-11239)***
Realty World, Wheatland *Also called Wheatland School District* ***(P-11516)***
Reaume and Associates Inc ... D ... 310 398-5768
11527 W Washington Blvd Los Angeles (90066) ***(P-25283)***
Reaume, E M & Associates, Los Angeles *Also called Reaume and Associates Inc* ***(P-25283)***
Rebar Engineering Inc ... C ... 562 946-2461
10706 Painter Ave Santa Fe Springs (90670) ***(P-3281)***
Rebas Inc ... C ... 562 941-4155
12907 Imperial Hwy Santa Fe Springs (90670) ***(P-7586)***
Rebecca Terley ... D ... 562 925-4252
9028 Rose St Bellflower (90706) ***(P-20210)***
Rebekah Children's Services, Gilroy *Also called Odd Fellow-Rebekah Chld HM Cal* ***(P-24010)***
Rebekah Children's Services, Salinas *Also called Odd Fellow-Rebekah Chld HM Cal* ***(P-24011)***
Rec Center ... C ... 415 831-6818
501 Stanyan St San Francisco (94117) ***(P-7719)***
Reche Cyn Regional Rehab Ctr, Colton *Also called Reche Cyn Rhblitation Hlth Ctr* ***(P-20211)***
Reche Cyn Rhblitation Hlth Ctr ... B ... 909 370-4411
1350 Reche Canyon Rd Colton (92324) ***(P-20211)***
Reciprocity Inc ... E ... 415 851-8667
3043 Mission St San Francisco (94110) ***(P-15052)***
Recology Inc (PA) ... D ... 415 875-1000
50 California St Ste 2400 San Francisco (94111) ***(P-6239)***
Recology Inc ... D ... 415 330-1300
Tunnel Ave And Beatty Rd San Francisco (94134) ***(P-6240)***
Recology Inc ... D ... 916 379-3300
245 N 1st St Dixon (95620) ***(P-6241)***
Recology Inc ... D ... 415 970-1582
100 Cargo Way San Francisco (94124) ***(P-6242)***
Recology Inc ... D ... 530 533-5868
2720 S 5th Ave Oroville (95965) ***(P-6243)***
Recology Inc ... C ... 415 330-1400
501 Tunnel Ave San Francisco (94134) ***(P-6244)***
Recology Los Altos ... D ... 650 961-8044
650 Martin Ave Santa Clara (95050) ***(P-6245)***
Recology San Francisco ... C ... 415 468-1752
501 Tunnel Ave San Francisco (94134) ***(P-6246)***
Recology San Mateo County ... D ... 650 595-3900
225 Shoreway Rd San Carlos (94070) ***(P-6247)***
Recology Sonoma Marin ... B ... 707 586-8261
3400 Standish Ave Santa Rosa (95407) ***(P-17017)***
Recology South Valley (HQ) ... D ... 408 842-3358
1351 Pacheco Pass Hwy Gilroy (95020) ***(P-6248)***
Recology Sunset Scavenger, San Francisco *Also called Sunset Scavenger Company* ***(P-6289)***
Recology Sustainable Crushing, San Francisco *Also called Recology Inc* ***(P-6242)***
Recology Vacaville Solano ... D ... 707 448-2945
1 Town Sq Ste 200 Vacaville (95688) ***(P-6249)***
Recology Vallejo (HQ) ... C ... 707 552-3110
2021 Broadway St Vallejo (94589) ***(P-6250)***
Recology Yuba-Sutter ... D ... 530 743-6933
3001 N Levee Rd Marysville (95901) ***(P-6251)***
Recon Environmental Inc (PA) ... D ... 619 308-9333
1927 5th Ave Ste 200 San Diego (92101) ***(P-27185)***
Recon Refractory & Cnstr Inc ... E ... 562 988-7981
3914 Cherry Ave Ste B Long Beach (90807) ***(P-25284)***
Records Center/Storage, Oakland *Also called San Francisco Bay Area Rapid* ***(P-3587)***
Recovery Place Inc ... D ... 954 200-8308
5000 E Spring St Ste 650 Long Beach (90815) ***(P-21490)***
Recovery Solutions Santa Ana, Santa Ana *Also called CRC Health Corporate* ***(P-22014)***
Recp Cy Oxnard LLC ... D ... 805 604-7527
600 E Esplanade Dr Oxnard (93036) ***(P-12794)***
Recp Rl Oxnard LLC ... C ... 805 278-2200
2101 W Vineyard Ave Oxnard (93036) ***(P-12795)***
Recp/Wndsor Scramento Ventr LP ... D ... 916 455-6800
4422 Y St Sacramento (95817) ***(P-12796)***
Recreation Complex, South Lake Tahoe *Also called City of South Lake Tahoe* ***(P-18665)***
Recreation Dept, Coronado *Also called City of Coronado* ***(P-18653)***
Recreation Park Golf Course 18, Long Beach *Also called American Golf Corporation* ***(P-18217)***
Recreational Assn Corcoran ... D ... 559 992-5171
900 Dairy Ave Corcoran (93212) ***(P-24631)***
Recurve Inc ... D ... 510 540-4860
220 Montgomery St Ste 820 San Francisco (94104) ***(P-17447)***
Recycle Waste, Santa Clara *Also called Mission Trail Wste Systems Inc* ***(P-3913)***
Recycled Wood Products, Pomona *Also called Rwp Transfer Inc* ***(P-7833)***
Recycler Core Company Inc ... D ... 951 276-1687
2727 Kansas Ave Riverside (92507) ***(P-6464)***
Recyclers I Electronic ... D ... 317 522-1414
7815 N Palm Ave Ste 140 Fresno (93711) ***(P-6252)***
Recycling Industries Inc ... D ... 916 452-3961
4741 Watt Ave North Highlands (95660) ***(P-6253)***
Red and White Fleet, San Francisco *Also called Golden Gate Scnic Stmship Corp* ***(P-4603)***
Red Blossom Farms, Salinas *Also called Red Blossom Sales Inc* ***(P-355)***
Red Blossom Sales Inc ... B ... 805 349-9404
865 Black Rd Santa Maria (93458) ***(P-106)***
Red Blossom Sales Inc ... A ... 831 751-9169
9 Harris Pl Salinas (93901) ***(P-355)***
Red Bull Distribution Co Inc (HQ) ... D ... 916 515-3501
1740 Stewart St Santa Monica (90404) ***(P-8638)***
Red Carpet Car Wash, Visalia *Also called Bowie Enterprises* ***(P-17363)***
Red Carpet Car Wash, Fresno *Also called Bowie Enterprises* ***(P-17364)***
Red Carpet Car Wash, Clovis *Also called Bowie Enterprises* ***(P-17365)***
Red Carpet Car Wash, Fresno *Also called Bowie Enterprises* ***(P-17412)***
Red Chamber Co (PA) ... B ... 323 234-9000
1912 E Vernon Ave Vernon (90058) ***(P-8386)***
Red Condor Inc ... D ... 707 569-7419
1300 Valley House Dr # 115 Rohnert Park (94928) ***(P-15053)***
Red Earth Casino, Thermal *Also called Torres-Martinez* ***(P-13030)***
Red Earth Casino ... C ... 760 395-1200
3089 Norm Niver Rd Thermal (92274) ***(P-12797)***
Red Hawk Casino, Placerville *Also called Shingle Sprng Trbal Gming Auth* ***(P-18758)***
Red Hawk Fire & SEC CA Inc ... D ... 510 438-1300
4384 Enterprise Pl Fremont (94538) ***(P-2602)***
Red Hawk Fire & SEC CA Inc ... C ... 714 685-8100
1640 N Batavia St Orange (92867) ***(P-2603)***
Red Hawk Fire & SEC CA Inc (HQ) ... D ... 818 683-1500
7605 N San Fernando Rd Los Angeles (90065) ***(P-2604)***
Red Hawk Fire & SEC CA Inc ... D ... 760 233-9787
920 S Andreasen Dr # 102 Escondido (92029) ***(P-2605)***
Red Hawk Fire & Security LLC ... D ... 323 276-3100
2705 Media Center Dr Los Angeles (90065) ***(P-16553)***
Red Hill Country Club ... D ... 909 982-1358
8358 Red Hl Cntry Clb Dr Rancho Cucamonga (91730) ***(P-18538)***
Red Interactive Agency LLC (PA) ... D ... 310 399-4242
3420 Ocean Park Blvd # 3080 Santa Monica (90405) ***(P-13567)***
Red Lion Hotel Redding, Redding *Also called Kaidan Hospitality LP* ***(P-12497)***
Red One - PSI Joint Ventr LLC ... E ... 559 772-8264
310 W Murray Ave Visalia (93291) ***(P-1578)***
Red Peak Group LLC ... D ... 818 222-7762
23975 Park Sorrento # 410 Calabasas (91302) ***(P-26786)***
Red Pocket Inc ... D ... 888 993-3888
2060d E Avenida De Los Thousand Oaks (91362) ***(P-5461)***
Red Pocket Mobile, Thousand Oaks *Also called Red Pocket Inc* ***(P-5461)***
Red Pointe Roofing LP (PA) ... D ... 714 685-0010
1814 N Neville St Orange (92865) ***(P-3094)***
Red Tail Golf Assoc, Rancho Santa Fe *Also called Farms Golf Club Inc* ***(P-18246)***

Employee Codes: A=Over 500 employees, B=251-500
C=101-250, D=51-100, E=50
2020 Directory of California
Wholesalers and Services Companies
© Mergent Inc. 1-800-342-5647
1403

Red Top Rice Growers..E......530 868-5975
  3200 8th St Biggs (95917) *(P-532)*
Redbarn Pet Products Inc (PA)...........................C......562 495-7315
  3229 E Spring St Ste 310 Long Beach (90806) *(P-9009)*
Redbarn Premium Pet Products, Long Beach Also called Redbarn Pet Products
Inc *(P-9009)*
Redbull Distribution Co Colo, Santa Monica Also called Red Bull Distribution Co
Inc *(P-8638)*
Redding Aero Enterprises Inc...............................D......530 224-2300
  3775 Flight Ave Ste 100 Redding (96002) *(P-3578)*
Redding Bank of Commerce, Redding Also called Merchants Bank of Commerce *(P-9101)*
Redding District Office, Redding Also called State Compensation Insur Fund *(P-10134)*
Redding Drywall Systems Inc................................E......530 222-8767
  3092 Crossroads Dr Redding (96003) *(P-2847)*
Redding Family Medicine Assoc.............................E......530 244-4907
  2510 Airpark Dr Ste 201 Redding (96001) *(P-19328)*
Redding Jet Center, Redding Also called Redding Aero Enterprises Inc *(P-3578)*
Redding Medical Group, Redding Also called David Civalier MD Inc *(P-18941)*
Redding Medical Home Care, Redding Also called Tenet Healthsystem Medical *(P-21882)*
Redding Pathologists Lab......................................D......530 225-8050
  2036 Railroad Ave Redding (96001) *(P-21577)*
Redding Ranch Indian Hlth CL, Redding Also called Redding Rancheria *(P-22308)*
Redding Rancheria (PA)..D......530 225-8979
  2000 Redding Rancheria Rd Redding (96001) *(P-12798)*
Redding Rancheria...D......530 224-2700
  1441 Liberty St Redding (96001) *(P-22308)*
Redding Tree Growers Corp....................................D......559 594-9299
  18985 Avenue 256 Apt A Exeter (93221) *(P-966)*
Redding V A Outpatient Clinic, Redding Also called Veterans Health
Administration *(P-19560)*
Redding Veterans Home, The, Redding Also called Veterans Affairs Cal Dept *(P-20351)*
Redevelopment Agency of The Ci............................D......707 421-7309
  701 Civic Center Blvd Suisun City (94585) *(P-27186)*
Redfin Corporation...B......206 340-8794
  655 Montgomery St # 1430 San Francisco (94111) *(P-11407)*
Redgate Memorial Hospital, Long Beach Also called Behavioral Health Services
Inc *(P-22939)*
Redhill Group Inc..D......949 752-5900
  18010 Sky Park Cir # 275 Irvine (92614) *(P-25940)*
Redhorse Constructors Inc......................................D......415 492-2020
  36 Professional Ctr Pkwy San Rafael (94903) *(P-1180)*
Redis Labs Inc..D......415 930-9666
  700 E El Camino Real # 250 Mountain View (94040) *(P-15054)*
Redlands Cmnty Hosp Foundation............................C......909 793-1382
  1875 Barton Rd Redlands (92373) *(P-20667)*
REDLANDS COMMUNITY HOSPITAL, Redlands Also called RHS Corp *(P-26380)*
Redlands Community Hospital (PA).........................D......909 335-5500
  350 Terracina Blvd Redlands (92373) *(P-21133)*
Redlands Country Club...D......909 793-2661
  1749 Garden St Redlands (92373) *(P-18539)*
Redlands Division, Redlands Also called American Med *(P-3622)*
Redlands Employment Services................................B......951 688-0083
  4295 Jurupa St Ste 110 Ontario (91761) *(P-14383)*
Redlands Foothill Groves...E......909 793-2164
  304 9th St Redlands (92374) *(P-533)*
Redlands Ford Inc...D......909 793-3211
  1121 W Colton Ave Redlands (92374) *(P-17306)*
Redlands Health Care Group, Redlands Also called Plum Healthcare Group LLC *(P-16999)*
REDLANDS HEALTHCARE CENTER, Redlands Also called Ash Holdings LLC *(P-19726)*
Redlands Recycling, Riverside Also called Riverside Scrap Ir & Met Corp *(P-7770)*
Redlands Staffing Services, Ontario Also called Redlands Employment Services *(P-14383)*
Redline Courier Service, Mission Hills Also called RLCS Inc *(P-4726)*
Redman Container, Carson Also called Calko Transport Company Inc *(P-4198)*
Redrocks Fumigation, San Jose Also called Homeguard Incorporated *(P-13822)*
Redseal Inc..D......408 641-2200
  1600 Technology Dr Fl 4 San Jose (95110) *(P-15486)*
Redstone Print & Mail Inc.......................................D......916 318-6450
  910 Riverside Pkwy Ste 40 West Sacramento (95605) *(P-26787)*
Redwood, Culver City Also called Wovexx Holdings Inc *(P-5809)*
Redwood Bridge Club...D......619 296-4274
  3111 6th Ave San Diego (92103) *(P-18540)*
Redwood Building Maint Co.....................................D......707 782-9100
  1364 N Mcdowell Blvd B Petaluma (94954) *(P-14024)*
Redwood Coast Medical Services (PA).....................E......707 884-1721
  46900 Ocean Dr Gualala (95445) *(P-19329)*
Redwood Coast Regional (PA).................................D......707 462-3832
  1116 Airport Park Blvd Ukiah (95482) *(P-23403)*
Redwood Coast Regional..E......707 445-0893
  525 2nd St Ste 300 Eureka (95501) *(P-23404)*
REDWOOD COAST REGIONAL CENTER, Ukiah Also called Redwood Coast
Regional *(P-23403)*
Redwood Coast Regional Center, Eureka Also called Redwood Coast Regional *(P-23404)*
Redwood Coast Seniors Inc.....................................D......707 964-0443
  490 N Harold St Fort Bragg (95437) *(P-23405)*
Redwood Community Services (PA)..........................C......707 467-2000
  631 S Orchard Ave Ukiah (95482) *(P-23406)*
Redwood Convalescent Hospital...............................D......510 537-8848
  22103 Redwood Rd Castro Valley (94546) *(P-20668)*
Redwood Credit Union..D......800 479-7928
  1129 S Cloverdale Blvd A Cloverdale (95425) *(P-9337)*
Redwood Credit Union (PA).....................................C......707 545-4000
  3033 Cleveland Ave # 100 Santa Rosa (95403) *(P-9338)*
Redwood Credit Union..D......800 479-7928
  1390 Market St San Francisco (94102) *(P-9339)*
Redwood Elderlink & Homelink, Escondido Also called Redwood Elderlink Scph *(P-24041)*

Redwood Elderlink Scph...B......760 480-1030
  710 W 13th Ave Escondido (92025) *(P-24041)*
Redwood Electric Group Inc (PA)............................A......707 451-7348
  2775 Northwestern Pkwy Santa Clara (95051) *(P-2606)*
Redwood Empir..D......707 586-5533
  3400 Standish Ave Santa Rosa (95407) *(P-6254)*
Redwood Empire Addctons Prgram, Santa Rosa Also called Drug Abuse Alternatives
Center *(P-22019)*
Redwood Empire Division, Cloverdale Also called Pacific States Industries Inc *(P-6642)*
Redwood Empire Ice Oprtons LLC (PA).....................D......707 546-7147
  1667 W Steele Ln Santa Rosa (95403) *(P-18746)*
Redwood Empire Packing Inc...................................C......707 462-5521
  8801 Old River Rd Ukiah (95482) *(P-534)*
Redwood Empire Vineyard Mgt..................................D......707 857-3401
  22000 Geyserville Ave Geyserville (95441) *(P-679)*
Redwood Health Club (PA).......................................D......707 468-0441
  3101 S State St Ukiah (95482) *(P-18188)*
Redwood Healthcare Staffing....................................D......619 238-4180
  600 B St Ste 1570 San Diego (92101) *(P-14554)*
Redwood Memorial Hosp Fortuna (PA).....................C......707 725-7327
  3300 Renner Dr Fortuna (95540) *(P-21134)*
Redwood Painting Co Inc...C......925 432-4500
  620 W 10th St Pittsburg (94565) *(P-2387)*
Redwood Products Chino Inc....................................D......909 923-5656
  9301 Remington Ave Chino (91710) *(P-6648)*
Redwood Regional Medical Group, Santa Rosa Also called Sotoyome Medical Building
LLC *(P-10654)*
Redwood Regional Medical Group.............................D......707 463-3636
  1165 S Dora St Bldg H Ukiah (95482) *(P-19330)*
Redwood Regional Medical Group (PA)......................D......707 525-4080
  990 Sonoma Ave Ste 15 Santa Rosa (95404) *(P-21578)*
Redwood Regional Oncology Ctr, Santa Rosa Also called Redwood Regional Medical
Group *(P-21578)*
Redwood Senior Homes & Svcs, Escondido Also called Cal Southern Presbt
Homes *(P-23844)*
Redwood Town Court, Escondido Also called Cal Southern Presbt Homes *(P-23845)*
Redwood Toxicology Lab Inc....................................C......707 577-7958
  3650 Westwind Blvd Santa Rosa (95403) *(P-21579)*
Redwood Valley Industrial Park................................D......707 485-8766
  8800 West Rd Redwood Valley (95470) *(P-4490)*
REDWOODS, THE, Mill Valley Also called The Redwoods A Cmnty Seniors *(P-24095)*
Reed Brothers Security, Oakland Also called Security Central Inc *(P-17544)*
Reed Smith LLP...D......415 659-5964
  2 Embarcadero Ctr Fl 20 San Francisco (94111) *(P-22785)*
Reed Smith LLP...C......213 457-8000
  355 S Grand Ave Ste 2900 Los Angeles (90071) *(P-22786)*
Reed Smith LLP...C......415 543-8700
  101 2nd St Ste 1800 San Francisco (94105) *(P-22787)*
Reed Smith LLP...C......415 543-8700
  2 Embarcadero Ctr Fl 21 San Francisco (94111) *(P-22788)*
Reed Thomas Company Inc......................................D......714 558-7691
  1025 N Santiago St Santa Ana (92701) *(P-3328)*
Reegs Inc...D......831 455-7931
  88 Monterey Salinas Hwy A Salinas (93908) *(P-1268)*
Reel Security California Inc.......................................D......818 928-4737
  15303 Ventura Blvd # 1080 Sherman Oaks (91403) *(P-16392)*
Reeve Trucking Company Inc (PA)............................D......209 948-4061
  5050 Carpenter Rd Stockton (95215) *(P-4116)*
Reeve-Knight Construction Inc..................................D......916 786-5112
  128 Ascot Dr Roseville (95661) *(P-1579)*
Reeves Tractor Service Inc.......................................D......714 692-4020
  5455 Blue Ridge Dr Yorba Linda (92887) *(P-1779)*
Refactored Materials, Emeryville Also called Bolt Threads Inc *(P-25726)*
Referral Realty Cupertino, Cupertino Also called Z & M Associates Inc *(P-11527)*
Referral Realty Inc..D......408 996-8100
  1601 S De Anza Blvd # 150 Cupertino (95014) *(P-11408)*
Refinery Av LLC...E......818 843-0004
  14455 Ventura Blvd Fl 3 Sherman Oaks (91423) *(P-13797)*
Refinery, The, Sherman Oaks Also called Waldberg Inc *(P-13640)*
Reflections and Enclave Hoa, Irvine Also called Keystone PCF Property MGT Inc *(P-11237)*
Reflektion Inc (PA)..E......650 293-0800
  1510 Fashion Island Blvd # 100 San Mateo (94404) *(P-15055)*
Reformation, The, Vernon Also called Lymi Inc *(P-8088)*
Refrigeration Hdwr Sup Corp....................................E......818 768-3636
  9021 Norris Ave Sun Valley (91352) *(P-7464)*
Refrigeration Solutions LLC....................................C......916 281-2000
  1166 National Dr Ste 10 Sacramento (95834) *(P-2251)*
Refugee Resettlement, San Diego Also called Catholic Charities Diocese San *(P-22965)*
Refuse Department, Lemoore Also called City of Lemoore *(P-6181)*
Regal Cinemas Inc...D......916 419-0205
  3561 Truxel Rd Sacramento (95834) *(P-17862)*
Regal Cinemas Inc...D......310 544-3042
  550 Deep Valley Dr # 339 Rllng HLS Est (90274) *(P-17863)*
Regal Medical Group Inc (PA)...................................D......818 654-3400
  8510 Balboa Blvd Ste 275 Northridge (91325) *(P-24421)*
Regatta Tropicals Ltd (PA).......................................D......805 473-1320
  1742 Manhattan Ave Ste C Grover Beach (93433) *(P-8516)*
Regency, San Jose Also called Liberty Healthcare of Oklahoma *(P-20070)*
Regency Caterers By Hyatt, San Diego Also called Hyatt Hotels Management Corp *(P-12447)*
Regency Centers LP..A......760 724-9795
  40 Main St Vista (92083) *(P-20212)*
Regency Enterprises, Los Angeles Also called New Regency Productions Inc *(P-17641)*
Regency Enterprises Inc (PA)....................................B......818 901-0255
  9261 Jordan Ave Chatsworth (91311) *(P-7179)*
Regency Fire Protection Inc......................................D......818 982-0126
  7651 Densmore Ave Van Nuys (91406) *(P-2252)*
REGENCY HEALTH SERVICES, Covina Also called Covina Rehabilitation Center *(P-19848)*

Regency Hill Associates ....D....619 281-5200
6560 Ambrosia Dr San Diego (92124) *(P-10808)*
Regency Inn, Bakersfield *Also called Days Inn Bakersfield (P-12203)*
Regency Inn, Costa Mesa *Also called US Hotel and Resort MGT Inc (P-13058)*
Regency Lighting, Chatsworth *Also called Regency Enterprises Inc (P-7179)*
Regency Oaks Care Center ....C....562 498-3368
3850 E Esther St Long Beach (90804) *(P-20213)*
Regency Park, Pasadena *Also called Zenith Health Care (P-11528)*
Regency Park El Molino, Pasadena *Also called Regency Park Senior Living Inc (P-11409)*
Regency Park Oak Knoll, Pasadena *Also called Regency Park Senior Living Inc (P-24042)*
Regency Park Senior Living Inc ....D....626 396-4911
255 S Oak Knoll Ave Pasadena (91101) *(P-24042)*
Regency Park Senior Living Inc ....D....626 578-0460
245 S El Molino Ave Pasadena (91101) *(P-11409)*
Regency Theatres Inc ....E....818 224-3825
26901 Agoura Rd Ste 150 Agoura Hills (91301) *(P-17864)*
Regenesis Bioremediation Pdts (PA) ....E....949 366-8000
1011 Calle Sombra San Clemente (92673) *(P-27187)*
Regent LP (PA) ....D....310 299-4100
9720 Wilshire Blvd Beverly Hills (90212) *(P-11952)*
Regent Aerospace Corporation (PA) ....C....661 257-3000
28110 Harrison Pkwy Valencia (91355) *(P-3459)*
Regent Assisted Living Inc ....D....626 332-3344
150 S Grand Ave Ofc West Covina (91791) *(P-24043)*
Regent Assisted Living Inc ....E....661 663-8400
8100 Westwold Dr Ofc Bakersfield (93311) *(P-24044)*
Regent Assisted Living Inc ....D....209 491-0800
2325 St Pauls Way Modesto (95355) *(P-24045)*
Regent Assisted Living Inc ....D....831 459-8400
80 Front St Santa Cruz (95060) *(P-24046)*
Regent Assisted Living Inc ....D....559 325-8400
675 W Alluvial Ave Ofc Clovis (93611) *(P-24047)*
Regent At Laurel Springs, Bakersfield *Also called Regent Assisted Living Inc (P-24044)*
Regent Court, Modesto *Also called Regent Assisted Living Inc (P-24045)*
Regent Senior Living W Covina, West Covina *Also called Regent Assisted Living Inc (P-24043)*
Regent Worldwide Sales LLC ....E....310 806-4288
10990 Wilshire Blvd Los Angeles (90024) *(P-17659)*
Regents Point, Irvine *Also called Cal Southern Presbt Homes (P-10702)*
Region Dev & Affairs Off, Salinas *Also called Planned Parenthood Mar Monte (P-22093)*
Regional Center, Chico *Also called Far Northern Coordinating Coun (P-23224)*
Regional Center For Devlpmtnly, Lancaster *Also called North La County Regional Ctr (P-27150)*
Regional Center of E Bay Inc ....C....510 618-6100
500 Davis St Ste 100 San Leandro (94577) *(P-23407)*
Regional Connector Constrs ....E....951 368-6400
1995 Agua Mansa Rd Riverside (92509) *(P-1181)*
Regional Investment & MGT LLC ....E....310 821-1945
4640 Admiralty Way # 1050 Marina Del Rey (90292) *(P-1269)*
Regional Medical Ctr San Jose, San Jose *Also called San Jose Medical Systems Lp (P-21158)*
Regional Office, Redlands *Also called Southern California Gas Co (P-5978)*
Regional Transportation Comm, San Diego *Also called San Diego Assn Governments (P-24360)*
Regis Corporation ....E....310 274-8791
9403 Santa Monica Blvd Beverly Hills (90210) *(P-13356)*
Registrar of Voters, Santa Ana *Also called County of Orange (P-24778)*
Registration Ctrl Systems Inc (PA) ....D....805 654-0171
1833 Portola Rd Unit B Ventura (93003) *(P-17018)*
Registry Monitoring Ins Srvcs ....C....800 400-4924
5388 Sterling Center Dr Westlake Village (91361) *(P-11410)*
Registry Network Inc (PA) ....C....760 966-3700
1207 Carlsbad Village Dr X Carlsbad (92008) *(P-14555)*
Regulus Therapeutics Inc ....D....858 202-6300
10628 Science Center Dr # 225 San Diego (92121) *(P-26024)*
Rehab Associates, Long Beach *Also called Eric D Feldman MD Inc (P-18975)*
Rehab West Inc ....E....619 518-3710
277 Rancheros Dr Ste 190 San Marcos (92069) *(P-10476)*
Rehabilitation California Dept ....E....562 422-8325
4300 Long Beach Blvd # 200 Long Beach (90807) *(P-23408)*
Rehabilitation Center, Lodi *Also called Lodi Memorial Hosp Assn Inc (P-19165)*
Rehabilitation Inst of Sthrn C, Orange *Also called Rio (P-22111)*
Rehablitation Inst Orange Cnty, Orange *Also called Rehabltation Inst Southern Cal (P-22106)*
Rehabltation Inst Southern Cal (PA) ....C....714 633-7400
1800 E La Veta Ave Orange (92866) *(P-22106)*
Rehabltion Cntre of Bvrly Hlls ....C....323 782-1500
580 S San Vicente Blvd Los Angeles (90048) *(P-20214)*
Rehablttion Cntre of Bkrsfield, Bakersfield *Also called Bakersfield Healthcare (P-19743)*
Rehabworks At Freedom Village, Lake Forest *Also called Freedom Village Healthcare Ctr (P-19924)*
Reichardt Duck Farm Inc ....D....707 762-6314
3770 Middle Two Rock Rd Petaluma (94952) *(P-420)*
Reichert Lengfeld Ltd Partnr ....D....510 845-1077
725 Folger Ave Albany (94710) *(P-12799)*
Reid & Helly ....D....951 682-1771
3880 Lemon St Fl 5 Riverside (92501) *(P-22789)*
Reign Accessories Inc ....E....310 297-6400
4000 Redondo Beach Ave Redondo Beach (90278) *(P-26375)*
Reilly Worldwide Inc ....E....310 449-4065
3000 Olympic Blvd Santa Monica (90404) *(P-17660)*
Reinhardt Roofing Inc ....D....510 713-7014
19258 Donna Ct Morgan Hill (95037) *(P-3095)*
Related Technologies Inc ....D....916 357-5900
81 Blue Ravine Rd Ste 230 Folsom (95630) *(P-15056)*
Relational Investors LLC ....D....858 704-3333
12400 High Bluff Dr Ste 6 San Diego (92130) *(P-9843)*
Relationedge LLC ....C....858 451-4665
10120 Pacific Heights Blv San Diego (92121) *(P-15880)*
Releasepoint, Claremont *Also called Western Feld Invstigations Inc (P-15894)*
Reliable Caregivers Inc ....C....415 436-0100
1700 California St # 400 San Francisco (94109) *(P-21850)*
Reliable Carriers Inc ....E....818 252-6400
9122 Glenoaks Blvd Sun Valley (91352) *(P-4117)*
Reliable Co, Glendale *Also called Coinmach Corporation (P-13247)*
Reliable Energy Management Inc ....D....562 984-5511
7201 Rosecrans Ave Paramount (90723) *(P-2253)*
Reliable Gardens Inc ....D....818 904-9801
7837 Burnet Ave Van Nuys (91405) *(P-897)*
Reliable Graphics, Van Nuys *Also called ARC Document Solutions Inc (P-13756)*
Reliable Health Care Svcs Inc ....E....310 397-2229
5705 Sepulveda Blvd Culver City (90230) *(P-14556)*
Reliable Interiors Inc ....C....951 371-3390
104 S Maple St Corona (92880) *(P-26376)*
Reliable Nursing Solutions ....D....760 946-9191
16057 Kamana Rd Ste B Apple Valley (92307) *(P-14384)*
Reliable Wholesale Lumber Inc (PA) ....D....714 848-8222
7600 Redondo Cir Huntington Beach (92648) *(P-6649)*
Reliance Company, Los Angeles *Also called Zastrow Construction Inc (P-1286)*
Reliance Intermodal Inc ....D....209 946-0200
1919 Martin Luther King Stockton (95210) *(P-8210)*
Reliance Steel & Aluminum Co (PA) ....D....213 687-7700
350 S Grand Ave Ste 5100 Los Angeles (90071) *(P-7093)*
Reliance Steel & Aluminum Co ....D....510 476-4400
33201 Western Ave Union City (94587) *(P-7094)*
Reliance Steel & Aluminum Co ....D....562 695-0467
9351 Norwalk Blvd Santa Fe Springs (90670) *(P-7095)*
Reliance Steel & Aluminum Co ....C....714 736-4800
15090 Northam St La Mirada (90638) *(P-7096)*
Reliance Steel & Aluminum Co ....C....323 583-6111
2537 E 27th St Vernon (90058) *(P-7097)*
Reliance Steel & Aluminum Co ....D....562 944-3322
12034 Greenstone Ave Santa Fe Springs (90670) *(P-7098)*
Reliance Steel Company, Vernon *Also called Reliance Steel & Aluminum Co (P-7097)*
Reliant Funding Group, San Diego *Also called Reliant Services Group LLC (P-9491)*
Reliant Services Group LLC ....C....877 850-0998
9540 Towne Centre Dr # 100 San Diego (92121) *(P-9491)*
Relibale Carries, Sun Valley *Also called Reliable Carriers Inc (P-4117)*
Religious Technology Center ....D....323 663-3258
1710 Ivar Ave Ste 1100 Los Angeles (90028) *(P-11831)*
Rels LLC ....A....949 214-1000
40 Pacifica Ste 900 Irvine (92618) *(P-11411)*
Rels Valuation, Irvine *Also called Rels LLC (P-11411)*
Relx Inc ....D....213 627-1130
555 W 5th St Ste 4500 Los Angeles (90013) *(P-15881)*
REM Eye Wear, Sun Valley *Also called REM Optical Company Inc (P-7032)*
REM Optical Company Inc ....D....818 504-3950
10941 La Tuna Canyon Rd Sun Valley (91352) *(P-7032)*
Remax Accord, Pleasanton *Also called S&J Stadtler Inc (P-11436)*
Remax Active Realty ....E....510 505-1660
4056 Decoto Rd Fremont (94555) *(P-11412)*
Remax Active Teal State, Fremont *Also called Remax Active Realty (P-11412)*
Remax All Stars Realty ....D....951 739-4000
765 N Main St Corona (92880) *(P-11413)*
Remax Champions Real Estate, Upland *Also called Re/Max LLC (P-11395)*
Remax College Park Realty, Long Beach *Also called College Park Realty Inc (P-11062)*
Remax Estate Properties, Rancho Palos Verdes *Also called Re/Max Plos Vrdes Rlty / Exces (P-11399)*
Remax Gold ....D....916 609-2800
3620 Fair Oaks Blvd # 300 Sacramento (95864) *(P-11414)*
Remax Legends, Alta Loma *Also called Inland Empire RE Solutions (P-11202)*
Remax Metro Inc ....D....714 557-2544
150 Paularino Ave Ste 125 Costa Mesa (92626) *(P-11415)*
Remax Olson ....D....805 267-4929
30699 Russell Ranch Rd Westlake Village (91362) *(P-11416)*
Remax Value Properties, San Jose *Also called Quail Hill Investments Inc (P-11875)*
Remax VIP, Bell Gardens *Also called Auchante Inc (P-10924)*
Remedy Intelligent Staffing, Aliso Viejo *Also called Remedytemp Inc (P-14557)*
Remedytemp Inc (HQ) ....C....949 425-7600
101 Enterprise Ste 100 Aliso Viejo (92656) *(P-14557)*
Remi Vista Inc (PA) ....C....530 245-5805
2701 Park Marina Dr Redding (96001) *(P-24048)*
Remington Club I & II, San Diego *Also called Five Star Quality Care Inc (P-19915)*
Remington Hotel Corporation ....D....760 322-6000
888 E Tahquitz Canyon Way Palm Springs (92262) *(P-12800)*
Remington Hotel Corporation ....D....310 553-6561
1150 S Beverly Dr Los Angeles (90035) *(P-12801)*
Remote Control Productions Inc (PA) ....E....310 260-0171
1547 14th St Santa Monica (90404) *(P-17661)*
Renaissance Clubsport, Walnut Creek *Also called Leisure Sports Inc (P-12547)*
Renaissance Hotel Clubsport, Aliso Viejo *Also called L & O Aliso Viejo LLC (P-12523)*
Renaissance Hotel Holdings Inc ....D....707 935-6600
1325 Broadway Sonoma (95476) *(P-12802)*
Renaissance Hotel MGT Co LLC ....B....310 337-2800
9620 Airport Blvd Los Angeles (90045) *(P-12803)*
Renaissance Hotel MGT Co LLC ....A....760 773-4444
44400 Indian Wells Ln Indian Wells (92210) *(P-12804)*
Renaissance Hotel MGT Co LLC ....C....415 989-3500
905 California St San Francisco (94108) *(P-12805)*
Renaissance Indian Wells, Indian Wells *Also called Renaissance Hotel MGT Co LLC (P-12804)*
Renaissance Palm Springs, Palm Springs *Also called HHC Trs Portsmouth LLC (P-12348)*

ALPHABETIC

Employee Codes: A=Over 500 employees, B=251-500
C=101-250, D=51-100, E=50
2020 Directory of California
Wholesalers and Services Companies
© Mergent Inc. 1-800-342-5647
1405

Renaissance Palm Springs Hotel, Palm Springs *Also called Crestline Hotels & Resorts LLC* ***(P-12189)***
Renaissnce Esmralda Resort Spa......D......760 773-4444
44400 Indian Wells Ln Indian Wells (92210) ***(P-12806)***
Renal Center, Orange *Also called St Joseph Hospital of Orange* ***(P-21229)***
Renal Treatment Ctrs - Cal Inc......D......714 990-0110
595 Tamarack Ave Ste A Brea (92821) ***(P-21932)***
Renal Treatment Ctrs - Cal Inc......D......949 930-6882
15271 Laguna Canyon Rd Irvine (92618) ***(P-21933)***
Renesas Electronics Amer Inc......A......408 588-6750
1541 Rollins Rd Burlingame (94010) ***(P-7334)***
Reneson Hotels Inc (PA)......D......650 449-5353
2700 Junipero Serra Blvd Daly City (94015) ***(P-12807)***
Reneson Hotels Inc......C......415 621-7001
112 7th St San Francisco (94103) ***(P-12808)***
Renew Health Group LLC......E......310 625-2838
107 W Lemon Ave Monrovia (91016) ***(P-26788)***
Renn Transportation Inc......D......408 842-3545
8845 Forest St Gilroy (95020) ***(P-4118)***
Reno Tenco, Boron *Also called Rio Tinto Minerals Inc* ***(P-974)***
Renova Energy Corp......E......760 568-3413
75181 Mediterranean Palm Desert (92211) ***(P-2254)***
Renovate America Inc......C......858 605-5333
15073 Ave Of Science # 200 San Diego (92128) ***(P-15057)***
Renovo Solutions LLC......B......714 599-7969
4 Executive Cir Ste 185 Irvine (92614) ***(P-26377)***
Rent.com, Los Angeles *Also called Viva Group Inc* ***(P-10841)***
Renteria Santiago J Farm Labo......C......661 792-0052
137 W Kern Ave Mc Farland (93250) ***(P-14385)***
Rentjuice Corporation......D......415 376-0369
225 Bush St Ste 1100 San Francisco (94104) ***(P-5462)***
Rentokil North America Inc......D......562 802-2238
15415 Marquardt Ave Santa Fe Springs (90670) ***(P-8855)***
Rentpayment.com, Walnut Creek *Also called Yapstone Inc* ***(P-17173)***
Renty LLC......E......858 560-0066
8025 Clairemont Mesa Blvd San Diego (92111) ***(P-3713)***
Renwood Realtytrac LLC (PA)......D......949 502-8300
1 Venture Ste 300 Irvine (92618) ***(P-15882)***
Replanet LLC......D......951 892-3079
9910 6th St Rancho Cucamonga (91730) ***(P-6255)***
Reprints Desk Inc......D......310 477-0354
15821 Ventura Blvd # 165 Encino (91436) ***(P-15883)***
Reproductive Science Center......D......925 867-1800
100 Park Pl Ste 200 San Ramon (94583) ***(P-19331)***
Reproductive Science Ctr Bay, San Ramon *Also called Reproductive Science Center* ***(P-19331)***
Republic Electric Inc......D......916 294-0140
3820 Happy Ln Sacramento (95827) ***(P-2607)***
Republic Electric West Inc......D......916 294-0140
3820 Happy Ln Sacramento (95827) ***(P-2608)***
Republic Indemnity Co Amer......D......415 981-3200
100 Pine St Fl 14 San Francisco (94111) ***(P-10122)***
Republic Indemnity Co Amer (HQ)......C......818 990-9860
15821 Ventura Blvd # 370 Encino (91436) ***(P-10123)***
Republic Indemnity Company Cal......C......818 990-9860
15821 Ventura Blvd # 370 Encino (91436) ***(P-10124)***
Republic Master Chefs Textile, Long Beach *Also called American Textile Maint Co* ***(P-13197)***
Republic Services, Salinas *Also called BFI Waste Systems N Amer Inc* ***(P-6163)***
Republic Services Inc......E......909 370-3377
2059 E Steel Rd Colton (92324) ***(P-6256)***
Republic Services Inc......D......310 527-6980
1449 W Rosecrans Ave Gardena (90249) ***(P-6257)***
Republic Services Inc......D......805 385-8060
111 S Del Norte Blvd Oxnard (93030) ***(P-6258)***
Republic Svcs Vsco Rd Landfill......E......925 447-0491
4001 N Vasco Rd Livermore (94551) ***(P-7216)***
Republic Uniform, Long Beach *Also called American Textile Maint Co* ***(P-13196)***
Reputation Impression LLC......D......858 633-4500
9245 Activity Rd Ste 106 San Diego (92126) ***(P-26789)***
Reputation Management Cons Inc......D......949 682-7906
1720 E Garry Ave Ste 103 Santa Ana (92705) ***(P-26790)***
Reputationcom Inc (PA)......C......650 381-3056
1400 A Sport Blvd Ste 401 Redwood City (94063) ***(P-16554)***
RES-Care Inc......D......800 707-8781
17291 Irvine Blvd Ste 150 Tustin (92780) ***(P-21851)***
RES-Care Inc......C......818 637-7727
611 S Central Ave Glendale (91204) ***(P-20448)***
RES-Care California Inc......E......626 334-7862
200 W Paramount St Azusa (91702) ***(P-20449)***
Res.net, Lake Forest *Also called US Real Estate Services Inc* ***(P-11495)***
Rescom Services Inc......D......760 930-3900
1637 Kings Way Vista (92084) ***(P-898)***
Rescue Agency Pub Beneft LLC (PA)......D......619 231-7555
2437 Morena Blvd San Diego (92110) ***(P-13568)***
Rescue Children Inc......E......559 268-1123
335 G St Fresno (93706) ***(P-23409)***
Rescue Concrete Inc......D......916 852-2400
9275 Beatty Dr Sacramento (95826) ***(P-3206)***
Rescue Mission Alliance (PA)......D......805 487-1234
315 N A St Oxnard (93030) ***(P-24859)***
Rescue Mission Alliance......E......805 201-4341
125 S Harrison Ave Oxnard (93030) ***(P-22309)***
Rescue Rooter, Hayward *Also called American Residential Svcs LLC* ***(P-2047)***
Rescue Rooter, Orange *Also called American Residential Svcs LLC* ***(P-2048)***
Rescue Rooter, Sylmar *Also called American Residential Svcs LLC* ***(P-2049)***
Rescue Rooter Bay Area North, San Leandro *Also called American Residential Svcs LLC* ***(P-2046)***
Rescue Rooter Bay Area South, San Jose *Also called American Residential Svcs LLC* ***(P-17483)***
Rescue Rotter, Riverside *Also called American Residential Svcs LLC* ***(P-2045)***
Research, San Diego *Also called Sun Pharmaceuticals Inc* ***(P-25840)***
Research & Dev & Mfg Site, San Diego *Also called Pacira Pharmaceuticals Inc* ***(P-7973)***
Research Affiliates Capital LP......D......949 325-8700
620 Nwport Ctr Dr Ste 900 Newport Beach (92660) ***(P-9844)***
Research Affiliates LLC......D......949 325-8700
620 Nwport Ctr Dr Ste 900 Newport Beach (92660) ***(P-9845)***
Research Libraries Group Inc......D......650 288-1288
777 Mariners Island Blvd # 550 San Mateo (94404) ***(P-15884)***
Research Management Cons Inc (PA)......D......805 987-5538
816 Camarillo Springs Rd J Camarillo (93012) ***(P-27188)***
Research of America......C......916 443-4722
1232 Q St Ste 100 Sacramento (95811) ***(P-15806)***
Research Solutions Inc (PA)......C......310 477-0354
15821 Ventura Blvd # 165 Encino (91436) ***(P-17019)***
Research Triangle Institute......D......510 849-4942
2150 Shattuck Ave Ste 800 Berkeley (94704) ***(P-26791)***
Reservation Ranch (PA)......C......707 487-3516
356 Sarina Rd N Smith River (95567) ***(P-12809)***
Reserve At Spanos Park, The, Stockton *Also called American Golf Corporation* ***(P-18361)***
Reserve Club......D......760 674-2222
49400 Desert Butte Trl Indian Wells (92210) ***(P-18541)***
Residence In Anaheim, Anaheim *Also called Holiday Garden SF Corp* ***(P-12371)***
Residence Inn By Mariott, San Diego *Also called J5th LLC* ***(P-12484)***
Residence Inn By Marriot Lax/C, Los Angeles *Also called Svi Lax LLC* ***(P-13006)***
Residence Inn By Marriott, Oxnard *Also called Windsor Capital Group Inc* ***(P-13099)***
Residence Inn By Marriott, Pleasanton *Also called Pleasant Canyon Hotel Inc* ***(P-12761)***
Residence Inn By Marriott, San Diego *Also called Marriott International Inc* ***(P-12597)***
Residence Inn By Marriott, San Mateo *Also called Island Hospitality MGT LLC* ***(P-12480)***
Residence Inn By Marriott, Ontario *Also called Island Hospitality MGT LLC* ***(P-12482)***
Residence Inn By Marriott, Los Angeles *Also called Sunstone Hotel Properties Inc* ***(P-13000)***
Residence Inn By Marriott, Manhattan Beach *Also called Sunstone Hotel Properties Inc* ***(P-13001)***
Residence Inn By Marriott, Los Angeles *Also called Beverly Sunstone Hills LLC* ***(P-12066)***
Residence Inn By Marriott, La Mirada *Also called B S A Partners* ***(P-12032)***
Residence Inn By Marriott......D......559 222-8900
5322 N Diana St Fresno (93710) ***(P-12810)***
Residence Inn By Marriott......D......714 533-3555
1700 S Clementine St Anaheim (92802) ***(P-12811)***
Residence Inn By Marriott......D......714 996-0555
700 W Kimberly Ave Placentia (92870) ***(P-12812)***
Residence Inn By Marriott......D......858 673-1900
11002 Rancho Carmel Dr San Diego (92128) ***(P-12813)***
Residence Inn By Marriott LLC......D......858 587-1770
5852 Stadium St San Diego (92122) ***(P-12814)***
Residence Inn By Marriott LLC......C......760 776-0050
38305 Cook St Palm Desert (92211) ***(P-12815)***
Residence Inn By Marriott LLC......C......310 333-0888
2135 E El Segundo Blvd El Segundo (90245) ***(P-12816)***
Residence Inn By Marriott LLC......C......858 278-2100
5400 Kearny Mesa Rd San Diego (92111) ***(P-12817)***
Residence Inn By Marriott LLC......C......909 937-6788
2025 Convention Ctr Way Ontario (91764) ***(P-12818)***
Residence Inn By Marriott LLC......C......951 371-0107
1015 Montecito Dr Corona (92879) ***(P-12819)***
Residence Inn By Marriott LLC......C......562 595-0909
4111 E Willow St Long Beach (90815) ***(P-12820)***
Residence Inn By Marriott LLC......C......925 689-1010
700 Ellinwood Way Pleasant Hill (94523) ***(P-12821)***
Residence Inn La Lax El Segndo, El Segundo *Also called Hit Portfolio I NTC Trs LP* ***(P-12367)***
Residence Inn San Diego, San Diego *Also called Rt San Diego LLC* ***(P-12850)***
Residence Mutual Insurance Co......D......949 724-9402
2172 Dupont Dr Ste 220 Irvine (92612) ***(P-10125)***
Resident Group Services Inc (PA)......C......714 630-5300
1156 N Grove St Anaheim (92806) ***(P-899)***
Residential Bancorp (PA)......D......330 499-8333
22632 Goln Spgs Dr Ste 20 Diamond Bar (91765) ***(P-9599)***
Residential Design Service, Anaheim *Also called LARK Industries Inc* ***(P-16885)***
Residential Fire Systems Inc......D......714 666-8450
8085 E Crystal Dr Anaheim (92807) ***(P-2255)***
Residential Mortgage Ctr 39, El Segundo *Also called City National Bank* ***(P-9091)***
Residential Plumbing, San Jose *Also called Aqualine Piping Inc* ***(P-2057)***
Residential Wall Systems, Corona *Also called Quality Wall Systems Inc* ***(P-2382)***
Residnce By Mria San Dego Cntl, San Diego *Also called Rt Sd-Denver LP* ***(P-12851)***
Residnce Inn By Mrriott Irvine......D......949 380-3000
10 Morgan Irvine (92618) ***(P-12822)***
Residnce Inn By Mrriott Oxnard, Oxnard *Also called Recp Rl Oxnard LLC* ***(P-12795)***
Residnce Inn By Mrrott Stckton, Stockton *Also called Castlehill Properties Inc* ***(P-12124)***
Residncy Prgram Natividad Hosp, Salinas *Also called County of Monterey* ***(P-20818)***
Residntial Alzheimers Care Inc......C......858 565-4424
9619 Chesapeake Dr # 103 San Diego (92123) ***(P-26378)***
Resmex Partners LLC......E......415 440-2737
438 Geary St San Francisco (94102) ***(P-17020)***
Resolution Economics Group LLC (PA)......D......310 275-9137
1925 Century Park E Fl 15 Los Angeles (90067) ***(P-27189)***
Resolve Systems LLC (PA)......D......949 325-0120
2302 Martin Ste 225 Irvine (92612) ***(P-15058)***
Resonate Inc (PA)......C......408 545-5500
90 Great Oaks Blvd # 205 San Jose (95119) ***(P-15059)***
Resort At Pelican Hill LLC......C......949 467-6800
22701 Pelican Hill Rd S Newport Coast (92657) ***(P-12823)***

Mergent e-mail: customerrelations@mergent.com
1406
2020 Directory of California
Wholesalers and Services Companies
(P-0000) Products & Services Section entry number
(PA)=Parent Co (HQ)=Headquarters (DH)=Div Headquarters

Resort At Squaw Creek, Alpine Meadows *Also called Squaw Creek Associates LLC* ***(P-12955)***
Resort Campground Intl, Lytle Creek *Also called Burlingame Industries Inc* ***(P-13157)***
Resort Parking Services Inc ....C......760 328-4041
39755 Berkey Dr B Palm Desert (92211) ***(P-17274)***
Resort Procomm Inc ....D......858 866-6280
9550 Waples St Ste 105 San Diego (92121) ***(P-26792)***
Resortime.com, Carlsbad *Also called Grand Pacific Resorts Inc* ***(P-16810)***
Resource Collection Inc ....A......310 219-3272
3771 W 242nd St Ste 205 Torrance (90505) ***(P-14025)***
Resource Connection of Amador (PA) ....D......209 754-3114
444 E Saint Charles St San Andreas (95249) ***(P-23410)***
Resource Connection of Amador ....D......209 223-7685
430 Sutter Hill Rd Sutter Creek (95685) ***(P-23411)***
RESOURCE CONNECTION, THE, San Andreas *Also called Resource Connection of Amador* ***(P-23410)***
Resource Environmental Inc ....D......562 468-7000
6634 Schilling Ave Long Beach (90805) ***(P-1580)***
Resource Management Group Inc (PA) ....D......858 677-0884
4686 Mercury St San Diego (92111) ***(P-5040)***
Resource Rfrral Child Care Dev ....E......559 673-9173
1225 Gill Ave Madera (93637) ***(P-23412)***
Resource Staffing Group, Sacramento *Also called Northwest Staffing Resources* ***(P-14337)***
Resources Connection Inc ....D......714 430-6550
695 Town Center Dr # 600 Costa Mesa (92626) ***(P-26793)***
Resources Connection Inc (PA) ....A......714 430-6400
17101 Armstrong Ave # 100 Irvine (92614) ***(P-26794)***
Resources Connection LLC (HQ) ....D......714 430-6400
17101 Armstrong Ave # 100 Irvine (92614) ***(P-14386)***
Resources Global Professionals, Irvine *Also called Resources Connection LLC* ***(P-14386)***
Resources Global Professionals, Costa Mesa *Also called Resources Connection Inc* ***(P-26793)***
Resources Global Professionals, Irvine *Also called Resources Connection Inc* ***(P-26794)***
RESPITE SERVICE, Yuba City *Also called Tri County Respite Care Svc* ***(P-23509)***
Respond 2 LLC ....D......415 398-4200
727 Ansome St San Francisco (94111) ***(P-17662)***
Response 1 Medical Staffing ....C......916 932-0430
1101 Inv Blvd Ste 140 El Dorado Hills (95762) ***(P-14387)***
Responselogix Inc ....C......408 220-6505
3031 Tisch Way Ste 115 San Jose (95128) ***(P-26379)***
Responsible Med Solutions Corp ....E......951 308-0024
41715 Winchester Rd # 101 Temecula (92590) ***(P-19332)***
Responsys Inc (HQ) ....D......650 745-1700
1100 Grundy Ln Ste 300 San Bruno (94066) ***(P-15060)***
Responsys.com, San Bruno *Also called Responsys Inc* ***(P-15060)***
Restaurant Depot, Sacramento *Also called Jetro Cash and Carry Entps LLC* ***(P-8183)***
Restaurant Depot, San Francisco *Also called Jetro Cash and Carry Entps LLC* ***(P-8409)***
Restaurant Depot ....E......714 378-3535
17332 Gothard St Huntington Beach (92647) ***(P-8211)***
Restaurant Depot LLC ....C......408 344-0107
520 Brennan St San Jose (95131) ***(P-8296)***
Restaurant Depot LLC ....C......714 666-9205
1265 N Kraemer Blvd Anaheim (92806) ***(P-8785)***
Restaurant Depot LLC ....C......626 744-0204
180 N San Gabriel Blvd Pasadena (91107) ***(P-8297)***
Restaurant Depot LLC ....D......310 516-7400
19901 Hamilton Ave Ste A Torrance (90502) ***(P-8786)***
Restaurant Depot LLC ....C......415 920-2888
2045 Evans Ave San Francisco (94124) ***(P-8787)***
Restaurant Depot LLC ....C......323 964-1220
5333 W Jefferson Blvd Los Angeles (90016) ***(P-8788)***
Restaurant Depot LLC ....C......510 628-0600
400 High St Oakland (94601) ***(P-8298)***
Restaurant Depot LLC ....C......714 378-3535
17332 Gothard St Huntington Beach (92647) ***(P-8299)***
Restaurant Depot LLC ....D......562 634-6771
2300 E 68th St Long Beach (90805) ***(P-8300)***
Restaurant Depot LLC ....C......818 376-7687
15853 Strathern St Van Nuys (91406) ***(P-8789)***
Restec Contractors Inc ....D......510 670-0100
22955 Kidder St Hayward (94545) ***(P-3460)***
Restivo Enterprises ....D......408 988-4884
2590 Lafayette St Santa Clara (95050) ***(P-3714)***
Restoration Management Company, Hayward *Also called Jon K Takata Corporation* ***(P-23300)***
Restoration Resources, Rocklin *Also called Sierra View Landscape Inc* ***(P-907)***
Restoration Resources Hrs, Rocklin *Also called Habitat Rstration Sciences Inc* ***(P-27086)***
Restore Motion, Foothill Ranch *Also called Team Makena LLC* ***(P-7009)***
Result Group Inc ....D......480 777-7130
2603 Main St Ste 710 Irvine (92614) ***(P-15684)***
Retail Pro International LLC (PA) ....D......916 605-7200
400 Plaza Dr Ste 200 Folsom (95630) ***(P-15061)***
Retail Pro Software, Folsom *Also called Retail Pro International LLC* ***(P-15061)***
Retail Services & Systems Inc ....D......916 984-6923
2765 E Bidwell St Folsom (95630) ***(P-27190)***
Retail Services & Systems Inc ....D......805 494-0108
394 N Moorpark Rd Thousand Oaks (91360) ***(P-27191)***
Retail Services Wis Corp ....D......951 653-1472
13800 Heacock St D135c Moreno Valley (92553) ***(P-17021)***
Retail Services Wis Corp ....C......916 485-3427
3800 Watt Ave Ste 101 Sacramento (95821) ***(P-17022)***
Retail Services Wis Corp ....D......714 637-3431
1838 N Tustin St Ste A Orange (92865) ***(P-17023)***
Retail Services Wis Corp ....E......818 772-4969
21354 Nordhoff St Ste 108 Chatsworth (91311) ***(P-17024)***
Retail Services Wis Corp ....D......818 407-2680
19420 Business Center Dr Northridge (91324) ***(P-17025)***
Retail Services Wis Corp ....D......805 644-5422
1932 Eastman Ave Ventura (93003) ***(P-17026)***
Retailnext Inc (PA) ....D......408 884-2162
60 S Market St Ste 1000 San Jose (95113) ***(P-15062)***
Retailnext Inc ....C......408 298-2585
845 Market St Ste 450 San Francisco (94103) ***(P-25941)***
Retinal Consultants Inc ....D......530 899-2251
19 Ilahee Ln Chico (95973) ***(P-19333)***
Retinal Consultants Inc (PA) ....E......916 454-4861
3939 J St Ste 106 Sacramento (95819) ***(P-19334)***
Retirement Housing Foundation (PA) ....D......562 257-5100
911 N Studebaker Rd # 100 Long Beach (90815) ***(P-11417)***
Retirement Housing Foundation ....C......530 823-6131
750 Auburn Ravine Rd Auburn (95603) ***(P-24049)***
Retirement Housing Foundation ....D......209 466-4341
1319 N Madison St Ofc Stockton (95202) ***(P-11418)***
Retirement Lf Care Communities ....D......510 505-0555
3800 Walnut Ave Apt 401 Fremont (94538) ***(P-24050)***
Retreat & Conference Center ....E......707 252-3810
4401 Redwood Rd NAPA (94558) ***(P-13452)***
Retriev Technologies Inc (PA) ....D......714 738-8516
125 E Commercial St Ste A Anaheim (92801) ***(P-6259)***
Retronix International Inc ....D......949 388-6930
65 Enterprise Aliso Viejo (92656) ***(P-17534)***
Retronix Semiconductors, Aliso Viejo *Also called Retronix International Inc* ***(P-17534)***
Rett Inc ....D......619 231-0403
402 W Broadway Ste 400 San Diego (92101) ***(P-13804)***
Reuben H Fleet Science Center ....C......619 238-1233
1875 El Prado San Diego (92101) ***(P-24282)***
Reutlinger Community ....C......925 964-2062
4000 Camino Tassajara Danville (94506) ***(P-23413)***
REUTLINGER COMMUNITY FOR JEWIS, Danville *Also called Reutlinger Community* ***(P-23413)***
Rev Enterprises ....E......818 551-7111
417 Arden Ave Ste 103 Glendale (91203) ***(P-16393)***
Revchem Composites Inc (PA) ....D......909 877-8477
2720 S Willow Ave B Bloomington (92316) ***(P-6717)***
Revchem Plastics, Bloomington *Also called Revchem Composites Inc* ***(P-6717)***
Reveal Imaging, Vista *Also called Leidos Inc* ***(P-25779)***
Revel Travel At Altour, Beverly Hills *Also called Revel Travel Service Inc* ***(P-4836)***
Revel Travel Service Inc ....D......310 553-5555
449 S Beverly Dr Ste 101 Beverly Hills (90212) ***(P-4836)***
Revenue Frontier LLC ....D......310 584-9200
6922 Hollywood Blvd 2 Los Angeles (90028) ***(P-13661)***
Revenue, Dept of, San Jose *Also called Santa Clara County of* ***(P-13699)***
Review Boost, Carlsbad *Also called Intravas Inc* ***(P-26652)***
Revinate Inc ....D......415 671-4703
1 Letterman Dr San Francisco (94129) ***(P-15063)***
Revjet ....C......650 508-2215
981 Industrial Rd Ste F San Carlos (94070) ***(P-15487)***
Revolt Media and Tv LLC ....C......323 645-3000
1800 N Highland Ave Fl 7 Los Angeles (90028) ***(P-5643)***
Revolution Medicines Inc (PA) ....D......650 481-6801
700 Saginaw Dr Redwood City (94063) ***(P-25822)***
Revolution Studios Dist Co LP (PA) ....D......310 255-7000
225 Santa Monica Blvd # 900 Santa Monica (90401) ***(P-17790)***
Rew Inc ....D......805 541-1308
973 Higuera St Ste A San Luis Obispo (93401) ***(P-10039)***
Rew Inc, Riverside *Also called Roy E Whitehead Inc* ***(P-2971)***
Rex Moore Group Inc ....B......916 372-1300
6001 Outfall Cir Sacramento (95828) ***(P-2609)***
Rex More Elec Contrs Engineers (PA) ....A......916 372-1300
6001 Outfall Cir Sacramento (95828) ***(P-2610)***
Rex More Elec Contrs Engineers ....D......559 294-1300
5803 E Harvard Ave Fresno (93727) ***(P-2611)***
Rex More Elec Contrs Engineers ....D......510 785-1300
6001 Outfall Cir Sacramento (95828) ***(P-2612)***
Rey Con Construction Inc ....C......805 525-8134
1795 E Lemonwood Dr Santa Paula (93060) ***(P-3207)***
Rey-Crest Roofg Waterproofing, Los Angeles *Also called Rey-Crest Roofg Waterproofing* ***(P-3461)***
Rey-Crest Roofg Waterproofing ....D......323 257-9329
3065 Verdugo Rd Los Angeles (90065) ***(P-3461)***
Reyes Coca-Cola Bottling LLC ....D......818 362-4307
12925 Bradley Ave Sylmar (91342) ***(P-8639)***
Reyes Holdings LLC ....B......858 452-2300
8870 Liquid Ct San Diego (92121) ***(P-9748)***
Reynen & Bardis Construction (PA) ....C......916 366-3665
10630 Mather Blvd Mather (95655) ***(P-1182)***
Reynolds Cleaning Services Inc ....C......650 599-0202
544 Lakemead Way Emerald Hills (94062) ***(P-14026)***
Reynolds Health Industries ....D......562 591-7621
1201 Walnut Ave Long Beach (90813) ***(P-20669)***
RFI Communications SEC Systems, San Jose *Also called RFI Enterprises Inc* ***(P-2613)***
RFI Enterprises Inc (PA) ....D......408 298-5400
360 Turtle Creek Ct San Jose (95125) ***(P-2613)***
Rfid Corporation ....C......925 473-9978
701 Willow Pass Rd Ste 10 Pittsburg (94565) ***(P-13239)***
Rfid Textile Services Inc ....C......714 998-6109
1575 N Case St Orange (92867) ***(P-13309)***
Rfid Textile Services Inc ....D......909 623-5135
300 E Commercial St Pomona (91767) ***(P-13240)***
Rfid Textile Services Inc ....D......408 840-7504
8190 Murray Ave Gilroy (95020) ***(P-13310)***
Rfj Corporation ....D......415 824-6890
930 Innes Ave San Francisco (94124) ***(P-2848)***
Rfj Meiswinkel, San Francisco *Also called Rfj Corporation* ***(P-2848)***
Rfmw, San Jose *Also called Tti Inc* ***(P-7357)***

ALPHABETIC

Employee Codes: A=Over 500 employees, B=251-500
C=101-250, D=51-100, E=50
2020 Directory of California
Wholesalers and Services Companies
© Mergent Inc. 1-800-342-5647
1407

Rggd Inc (PA)..........D.......323 581-6617
4950 S Santa Fe Ave Vernon (90058) ***(P-7830)***
Rgis LLC..........D.......661 827-9195
5500 Ming Ave Ste 185 Bakersfield (93309) ***(P-17027)***
Rgis LLC..........D.......805 644-0454
1787 Mesa Verde Ave Ventura (93003) ***(P-17028)***
Rgis LLC..........D.......916 387-9692
8801 Folsom Blvd Ste 173 Sacramento (95826) ***(P-17029)***
Rgis LLC..........C.......248 651-2511
500 E Olive Ave Ste 240 Burbank (91501) ***(P-17030)***
Rgis LLC..........D.......925 829-2875
7567 Amador Valley Blvd Dublin (94568) ***(P-17031)***
Rgis LLC..........D.......408 243-9141
4320 Stevens Creek Blvd San Jose (95129) ***(P-17032)***
Rgis LLC..........D.......661 702-8987
25115 Avenue Stanford Valencia (91355) ***(P-17033)***
Rgis LLC..........D.......530 898-1015
20 Landing Cir Ste 100 Chico (95973) ***(P-17034)***
Rgnext, Vandenberg Afb *Also called Range Generation Next LLC* ***(P-25280)***
Rgnext, El Granada *Also called Range Generation Next LLC* ***(P-27183)***
Rgs Services, Anaheim *Also called Resident Group Services Inc* ***(P-899)***
Rh, Alamo *Also called Round Hill Country Club* ***(P-18550)***
Rh Framing Inc..........C.......831 759-8860
815 Quail Ridge Ln Salinas (93908) ***(P-2967)***
Rhc Equipment LLC..........E.......530 892-1918
5237 Mallard Estates Rd Chico (95973) ***(P-1581)***
Rhcc, Fremont *Also called Raymond Handling Concepts Corp* ***(P-17533)***
Rheumatology Diagnostics Lab..........D.......310 253-5455
10755 Venice Blvd Los Angeles (90034) ***(P-21580)***
Rhf Plymouth Tower..........D.......951 248-0456
3401 Lemon St Ofc Riverside (92501) ***(P-24051)***
Rhi, Santa Rosa *Also called Richard Hancock Inc* ***(P-2968)***
Rhino Building Services Inc..........C.......858 455-1440
6650 Flanders Dr Ste K San Diego (92121) ***(P-14027)***
Rhino Ready Mix Trucking Inc (PA)..........E.......661 679-3643
3701 Pegasus Dr Ste 126 Bakersfield (93308) ***(P-3930)***
RHO Chem LLC (HQ)..........E.......323 776-6234
425 Isis Ave Inglewood (90301) ***(P-6353)***
RHODA GOLDMAN PLAZA, San Francisco *Also called Scott Street Senior Housing Co* ***(P-20451)***
Rhodes Retail Services Inc..........D.......916 714-9233
8603 Excelsior Rd Elk Grove (95624) ***(P-26795)***
RHS Corp..........A.......909 335-5500
350 Terracina Blvd Redlands (92373) ***(P-26380)***
Rhumbix Inc..........D.......435 764-3014
1169 Howard St San Francisco (94103) ***(P-17035)***
Rhythmone LLC..........D.......650 961-9024
800 W El Camino Real Mountain View (94040) ***(P-15064)***
Rhythmone LLC (HQ)..........D.......415 655-1450
601 Montgomery St Fl 16 San Francisco (94111) ***(P-5463)***
Ria Financial Service, Buena Park *Also called Continental Exch Solutions Inc* ***(P-9429)***
Ria Financial Services, Buena Park *Also called Continental Exch Solutions Inc* ***(P-16717)***
Riad Adoumie MD..........D.......310 373-6864
23560 Madison St Ste 110 Torrance (90505) ***(P-19335)***
Rialto Bioenergy Facility LLC..........C.......760 436-8870
5780 Fleet St Ste 310 Carlsbad (92008) ***(P-25285)***
RICA, Encino *Also called Republic Indemnity Company Cal* ***(P-10124)***
Rice Drywall Inc..........D.......714 543-5400
919 E 6th St Santa Ana (92701) ***(P-2849)***
Rich Meiers Landscaping Inc (PA)..........D.......661 723-2220
652 W Avenue L14 Lancaster (93534) ***(P-755)***
Richard Bagdasarian Inc..........D.......760 396-2168
65500 Lincoln St Mecca (92254) ***(P-154)***
Richard Burns MD..........D.......951 296-9300
41637 Margarita Rd # 100 Temecula (92591) ***(P-19336)***
Richard H Vila, Richmond *Also called Vila Construction Co* ***(P-1640)***
Richard Hancock Inc..........E.......707 528-4900
1029 3rd St Santa Rosa (95404) ***(P-2968)***
Richard Huetter Inc..........D.......818 700-8001
21050 Osborne St Canoga Park (91304) ***(P-6465)***
Richard Iest Dairy, Madera *Also called Iest Family Farms* ***(P-395)***
Richard Iest Dairy Inc..........D.......559 673-2635
13507 Road 17 Madera (93637) ***(P-30)***
Richard J Mendoza Inc..........D.......415 644-0180
501 2nd St Ste 330 San Francisco (94107) ***(P-10126)***
Richard J Metz MD Inc..........E.......310 553-3189
2080 Century Park E # 1609 Los Angeles (90067) ***(P-19337)***
Richard Joy Engineering, Portola *Also called R Joy Inc* ***(P-25274)***
Richard K Newman and Assoc Inc (PA)..........E.......661 634-1130
121 Monterey St Bakersfield (93305) ***(P-13241)***
Richard Realty Group Inc..........D.......760 603-8377
2792 Gateway Rd Ste 103 Carlsbad (92009) ***(P-11419)***
Richard Shames MD..........D.......415 388-0456
25 Mitchell Blvd Ste 8 San Rafael (94903) ***(P-19338)***
Richard Swanson Inc..........D.......209 632-3883
17659 Swanson Rd Delhi (95315) ***(P-179)***
Richard Wilson Wellington..........D.......626 812-7881
1025 N Todd Ave Azusa (91702) ***(P-273)***
Richards Watson & Gershon PC (PA)..........C.......213 626-8484
355 S Grand Ave Fl 40 Los Angeles (90071) ***(P-22790)***
Richards Group Inc..........C.......214 891-5700
888 S Figueroa St # 1400 Los Angeles (90017) ***(P-13569)***
Richards Grove Saralees Vinyrd..........D.......707 837-9200
1998 Jones Rd Windsor (95492) ***(P-155)***
Richmond American Homes..........E.......818 908-3267
16600 Sherman Way Ste 180 Van Nuys (91406) ***(P-1183)***
Richmond Area Mlt-Services Inc..........D.......415 392-4453
720 Sacramento St San Francisco (94108) ***(P-22107)***
Richmond Area Mlt-Services Inc..........D.......415 689-5662
1375 Mission St San Francisco (94103) ***(P-22108)***
Richmond Area Mlt-Services Inc..........D.......415 579-3021
1282 Market St San Francisco (94102) ***(P-22109)***
Richmond Area Mlt-Services Inc (PA)..........D.......415 800-0699
4355 Geary Blvd San Francisco (94118) ***(P-22110)***
Richmond Country Club..........D.......510 231-2241
1 Markovich Ln Richmond (94806) ***(P-18542)***
Richmond District YMCA, San Francisco *Also called Young Mens Christian Assoc SF* ***(P-24736)***
Richmond Dst Neighborhood Ctr (PA)..........D.......415 751-6600
741 30th Ave San Francisco (94121) ***(P-23414)***
Richmond Engineering Co Inc..........C.......800 589-7058
15472 Markar Rd Poway (92064) ***(P-900)***
Richmond Peak Quality, Richmond *Also called Richmond Wholesale Meat Co* ***(P-8417)***
Richmond Plastering Inc..........E.......562 924-4202
12102 Centralia Rd Ste B Hawaiian Gardens (90716) ***(P-2850)***
Richmond Repair Shop, Richmond *Also called San Francisco Bay Area Rapid* ***(P-3588)***
Richmond Rescue Mission (PA)..........D.......510 215-4555
2114 Macdonald Ave Richmond (94801) ***(P-23415)***
Richmond Sanitary Service Inc (HQ)..........C.......510 262-7100
3260 Blume Dr Ste 100 Richmond (94806) ***(P-6354)***
Richmond Wholesale Meat Co..........D.......510 233-5111
2920 Regatta Blvd Richmond (94804) ***(P-8417)***
Richmond Yard Tower, Richmond *Also called San Francisco Bay Area Rapid* ***(P-3589)***
Rick Engineering Company, San Diego *Also called Glenn A Rick Engrg & Dev Co* ***(P-25107)***
Rick H Hitch Plastering Inc..........C.......916 334-3591
3306 Orange Grove Ave North Highlands (95660) ***(P-2851)***
Rick Hamm Construction Inc..........D.......714 532-0815
201 W Carleton Ave Orange (92867) ***(P-1780)***
Rick Solomon Enterprises Inc (PA)..........D.......310 280-3700
8460 Higuera St Culver City (90232) ***(P-8046)***
Rick Studer..........E.......323 357-1720
2610 Wisconsin Ave South Gate (90280) ***(P-4119)***
Rick Weiss New Hope Apartments..........E.......310 395-1026
1637 Appian Way Santa Monica (90401) ***(P-10809)***
Ricoh Business Solutions, Huntington Beach *Also called Ricoh Usa Inc* ***(P-6766)***
Ricoh Usa Inc..........D.......916 638-3333
3046 Prospect Park Dr # 100 Rancho Cordova (95670) ***(P-6763)***
Ricoh Usa Inc..........D.......408 436-1000
460 E Brokaw Rd San Jose (95112) ***(P-6764)***
Ricoh Usa Inc..........E.......818 294-8601
9430 Topanga Canyon Blvd # 100 Chatsworth (91311) ***(P-6765)***
Ricoh Usa Inc..........E.......714 396-0568
17011 Beach Blvd Ste 1000 Huntington Beach (92647) ***(P-6766)***
Ricoh Usa Inc..........D.......213 629-1838
6330 Variel Ave Woodland Hills (91367) ***(P-6767)***
Ricoh Usa Inc..........D.......415 392-6850
333 Bush St Ste 2500 San Francisco (94104) ***(P-6768)***
Ricoh Usa Inc..........E.......818 703-0265
21820 Burbank Blvd # 229 Woodland Hills (91367) ***(P-6769)***
Ricoh Usa Inc..........E.......510 839-6399
1300 Clay St Ste 165 Oakland (94612) ***(P-6770)***
Ricoh Usa Inc..........C.......925 988-4000
1390 Willow Pass Rd # 480 Concord (94520) ***(P-6771)***
Ricoh Usa Inc..........D.......949 225-2300
16969 Von Karman Ave Irvine (92606) ***(P-6772)***
Ride At Home Care, Corona *Also called Bmb 1 LLC* ***(P-20509)***
Ride On Transportation, San Luis Obispo *Also called United Cerebral Palsy Assoc of* ***(P-3732)***
Rideout Memorial Hospital (HQ)..........A.......530 749-4416
726 4th St Marysville (95901) ***(P-21135)***
Ridgecrest Regional Hospital..........B.......760 499-7260
1011 N China Lake Blvd Ridgecrest (93555) ***(P-19339)***
Ridgecrest Regional Hospital (PA)..........D.......760 446-3551
1081 N China Lake Blvd Ridgecrest (93555) ***(P-21136)***
Ridgeside Construction Inc..........D.......909 218-7593
4345 E Lowell St Ste A Ontario (91761) ***(P-1184)***
Ridgeside Finishing, Ontario *Also called Ridgeside Construction Inc* ***(P-1184)***
Ridgetop Energy LLC..........E.......661 822-2400
7021 Oak Creek Rd Mojave (93501) ***(P-5911)***
Ridgway, Santa Rosa *Also called Finley Swim Center* ***(P-18697)***
Riebes Auto Parts, Yuba City *Also called Bi Warehousing Inc* ***(P-6426)***
Right At Home, Fountain Valley *Also called In Home Comfort and Care Inc* ***(P-21785)***
Right At Home, Santa Rosa *Also called Pw Jade LLC* ***(P-21846)***
Right At Home, Pasadena *Also called Good Works LLC* ***(P-21752)***
Right At Home..........D.......310 313-0600
3435 Ocean Park Blvd # 110 Santa Monica (90405) ***(P-21852)***
Right Choice In-Home Care Inc..........A.......818 836-6001
7104 Owensmouth Ave Canoga Park (91303) ***(P-21853)***
Right Stuff Health Club, The, San Jose *Also called SIM Investment Corporation* ***(P-18194)***
Rightpoint Consulting LLC..........C.......310 451-4619
1453 3rd Street Promenade Santa Monica (90401) ***(P-16096)***
Rightscale Inc (PA)..........D.......805 500-4164
402 E Gutierrez St Santa Barbara (93101) ***(P-15065)***
Riivos Inc..........D.......415 813-1840
101 California St # 1500 San Francisco (94111) ***(P-2614)***
Rika Corporation..........D.......949 830-9050
332 W Brenna Ln Orange (92867) ***(P-3282)***
Rimrock High Income Plus Fund..........E.......949 381-7800
100 Innovation Dr Ste 200 Irvine (92617) ***(P-11757)***
Rinaldi Convalescent Hospital, Granada Hills *Also called Medical Investment Co* ***(P-20632)***
Rinaldi Tile & Marble, Royal Oaks *Also called Gino Rinaldi Inc* ***(P-2897)***
Rincon Consultants Inc..........C.......559 228-9925
255 W Fallbrook Ave # 103 Fresno (93711) ***(P-27192)***
Rincon Pacific LLC..........D.......805 986-8806
1312 Del Norte Rd Camarillo (93010) ***(P-107)***

Rincon Technology Inc (PA) ....E....805 684-8100
810 E Montecito St Santa Barbara (93103) ***(P-7033)***
Ringadoc, San Francisco *Also called Practice Fusion Inc* ***(P-15026)***
Ringcentral Inc (PA) ....D....650 472-4100
20 Davis Dr Belmont (94002) ***(P-15807)***
Rinks Anaheim Ice, The, Anaheim *Also called Anaheim Ice* ***(P-18621)***
Rio ....C....714 633-7400
1800 E La Veta Ave Orange (92866) ***(P-22111)***
Rio Bravo Ranch Shop ....E....661 872-5050
15701 Highway 178 Bakersfield (93306) ***(P-431)***
Rio Bravo Rocklin, Lincoln *Also called Rocklin Power Investors LP* ***(P-5912)***
Rio Hondo Community Dev Corp ....D....626 401-2784
11706 Ramona Blvd Ste 107 El Monte (91732) ***(P-24219)***
Rio Hondo Education Consortium ....C....562 945-0150
7200 Greenleaf Ave # 300 Whittier (90602) ***(P-23416)***
Rio Mesa Farms LLC ....D....831 728-1965
75 Sakata Ln Watsonville (95076) ***(P-108)***
Rio Seo, San Diego *Also called Riosoft Holdings Inc* ***(P-15066)***
Rio Tinto Minerals Inc ....C....760 762-7121
14486 Borax Rd Boron (93516) ***(P-974)***
Rio Vista Development Company (PA) ....C....818 980-8000
4222 Vineland Ave North Hollywood (91602) ***(P-12824)***
Rio Vista Ventures LLC (PA) ....E....760 480-8502
15651 Old Milky Way Escondido (92027) ***(P-8212)***
Rio Vista Ventures LLC ....E....559 897-6730
3646 Avenue 416 Reedley (93654) ***(P-8213)***
Riolo Transportation Inc ....C....760 729-4405
2725 Jefferson St Ste 2d Carlsbad (92008) ***(P-5136)***
Rios Farming Company LLC ....C....707 965-2587
3851 Chiles Pope Vly Rd Saint Helena (94574) ***(P-156)***
Riosoft Holdings Inc ....E....858 529-5005
9255 Towne Centre Dr # 750 San Diego (92121) ***(P-15066)***
Riot Games Inc (HQ) ....C....310 207-1444
12333 W Olympic Blvd Los Angeles (90064) ***(P-15067)***
Ripcord Inc ....D....408 838-7446
30955 Huntwood Ave Hayward (94544) ***(P-25286)***
Riphagen & Bullerdick Inc ....E....714 763-2100
5925 Ball Rd Cypress (90630) ***(P-11420)***
Ripple Foods Pbc ....D....510 269-2563
901 Gilman St Ste A Berkeley (94710) ***(P-25823)***
Rippling, San Francisco *Also called People Center Inc* ***(P-15475)***
Rls Electrical Contrs Inc ....E....951 688-8049
7330 Sycamore Canyon Blvd # 1 Riverside (92508) ***(P-2615)***
Risk Management, San Bernardino *Also called Llu Advntist Hlth Sciences Ctr* ***(P-19164)***
Risk Management Solutions Inc (HQ) ....C....510 505-2500
7575 Gateway Blvd Ste 300 Newark (94560) ***(P-11832)***
Riskalyze Inc ....C....530 748-1660
373 Elm Ave Auburn (95603) ***(P-16097)***
Ritchie Plumbing Inc ....C....949 709-7575
11320 Lombardy Ln Moreno Valley (92557) ***(P-2256)***
Rite Aid Drug Palace Inc ....E....530 661-1800
1755 E Beamer St Woodland (95776) ***(P-4491)***
Rite of Pass Athl Trai Cent ....C....209 736-4500
10400 Fricot City Rd San Andreas (95249) ***(P-24052)***
Rite Way Enterprises ....E....818 376-6960
7131 Valjean Ave Van Nuys (91406) ***(P-5041)***
Rite-Way Meat Packers Inc ....D....323 826-2144
5151 Alcoa Ave Vernon (90058) ***(P-8418)***
Ritz Carlton, Rancho Mirage *Also called Ritz-Carlton Hotel Company LLC* ***(P-12826)***
Ritz Carlton Rancho Mirage, Rancho Mirage *Also called Ritz-Carlton Hotel Company LLC* ***(P-12830)***
Ritz Companies, Irvine *Also called Savoy Contractors Group Inc* ***(P-1189)***
Ritz-Carlton Halfmoon Bay, Half Moon Bay *Also called Bre Diamond Hotel LLC* ***(P-12082)***
Ritz-Carlton Hotel Company LLC ....B....415 781-9000
690 Market St San Francisco (94104) ***(P-12825)***
Ritz-Carlton Hotel Company LLC ....B....760 321-8282
68900 Frank Sinatra Dr Rancho Mirage (92270) ***(P-12826)***
Ritz-Carlton Hotel Company LLC ....B....949 240-5020
1 Ritz Carlton Dr Dana Point (92629) ***(P-12827)***
Ritz-Carlton Hotel Company LLC ....A....805 968-0100
8301 Hollister Ave Santa Barbara (93117) ***(P-12828)***
Ritz-Carlton Hotel Company LLC ....B....415 773-6168
600 Stockton St San Francisco (94108) ***(P-12829)***
Ritz-Carlton Hotel Company LLC ....B....760 321-8282
68900 Frank Sinatra Dr Rancho Mirage (92270) ***(P-12830)***
Ritz-Carlton Ht Marina Del Rey, Venice *Also called Host Hotels & Resorts LP* ***(P-12393)***
Ritz-Carlton Laguna Niguel, Dana Point *Also called Prutel Joint Venture* ***(P-12773)***
Ritz-Carlton Lake Tahoe, The, Truckee *Also called Bhr Trs Tahoe LLC* ***(P-12069)***
Ritz-Carlton Marina Del Rey ....D....310 823-1700
4375 Admiralty Way Marina Del Rey (90292) ***(P-12831)***
Ritz-Carlton San Francisco, San Francisco *Also called Ritz-Carlton Hotel Company LLC* ***(P-12829)***
River Bend Holdings LLC ....C....916 371-1890
2215 Oakmont Way West Sacramento (95691) ***(P-20215)***
River Bend Nursing Center, West Sacramento *Also called River Bend Holdings LLC* ***(P-20215)***
River City Auto Recovery Inc ....D....916 851-1100
3401 Fitzgerald Rd Rancho Cordova (95742) ***(P-17036)***
River City Bank, Sacramento *Also called Rcb Corporation* ***(P-9234)***
River City Bank (HQ) ....D....916 567-2600
2485 Natomas Park Dr # 100 Sacramento (95833) ***(P-9235)***
River Cy Basbal Inv Group LLC (PA) ....D....916 376-4700
400 Ball Park Dr West Sacramento (95691) ***(P-18076)***
River Cy Geoprofessionals Inc ....D....916 372-1434
3050 Industrial Blvd West Sacramento (95691) ***(P-25287)***
River Island Country Club Inc ....D....559 781-2917
31989 River Island Dr Porterville (93257) ***(P-18543)***
River Maid Land Co A Cal Ll (PA) ....B....209 369-3586
6011 E Pine St Lodi (95240) ***(P-535)***
River Oak Center For Children ....C....916 226-2800
9412 Big Horn Blvd Ste 6 Elk Grove (95758) ***(P-19693)***
River Oak Center For Children (PA) ....C....916 609-5100
5445 Laurel Hills Dr Sacramento (95841) ***(P-22112)***
River Oak Center For Children ....D....916 550-5600
5445 Laurel Hills Dr Sacramento (95841) ***(P-20670)***
River Ranch Fresh Foods LLC (HQ) ....B....831 758-1390
911 Blanco Cir Ste B Salinas (93901) ***(P-8517)***
River Ridge Farms Inc ....D....805 647-6880
3135 Los Angeles Ave Oxnard (93036) ***(P-274)***
River Ridge Golf Club, Oxnard *Also called High Tide and Green Grass Inc* ***(P-18254)***
River Ridge Golf Club ....D....805 981-8724
2401 W Vineyard Ave Oxnard (93036) ***(P-18544)***
River Ridge Gulf Course, Oxnard *Also called City of Oxnard* ***(P-18231)***
River Rock Casino, Geyserville *Also called River Rock Entertainment Auth* ***(P-12832)***
River Rock Entertainment Auth ....A....707 857-2777
3250 Highway 128 Geyserville (95441) ***(P-12832)***
River Rock Equipment LLC ....D....916 791-1609
216 Kenroy Ln Roseville (95678) ***(P-11690)***
Rivera Sanitarium Inc ....D....562 949-2591
7246 Rosemead Blvd Pico Rivera (90660) ***(P-20216)***
Riverbed Technology Inc (HQ) ....D....415 247-8800
680 Folsom St Ste 500 San Francisco (94107) ***(P-6891)***
Riverside Aditorium Events Ctr, Riverside *Also called Raincross Hospitality Corp* ***(P-13451)***
Riverside Auto Auction, Anaheim *Also called Califrnia Auto Dalers Exch LLC* ***(P-6386)***
Riverside Bhvral Heathcare Ctr, Riverside *Also called Riverside Sanitarium LLC* ***(P-20220)***
Riverside Care Inc ....C....951 683-7111
4301 Caroline Ct Riverside (92506) ***(P-20217)***
Riverside Cmnty Hlth Systems (HQ) ....D....951 788-3000
4445 Magnolia Ave Fl 6 Riverside (92501) ***(P-21137)***
Riverside Cnty Probation Dept, Riverside *Also called County of Riverside* ***(P-23136)***
Riverside Cnty Rgional Med Ctr, Riverside *Also called Riverside University Health* ***(P-21139)***
Riverside Cnvalescent Hosp Inc ....D....530 343-5595
375 Cohasset Rd Chico (95926) ***(P-20671)***
Riverside Community Hospital, Riverside *Also called Riverside Cmnty Hlth Systems* ***(P-21137)***
Riverside Community Hospital, Riverside *Also called Riverside Healthcare System LP* ***(P-21138)***
Riverside Companion Services, San Bernardino *Also called Maxim Healthcare Services Inc* ***(P-14527)***
Riverside Convention Center, Riverside *Also called Entrepreneurial Hospitality* ***(P-16766)***
Riverside Convention Center, Riverside *Also called City of Riverside* ***(P-16699)***
Riverside County Flood Control ....C....951 955-1200
1995 Market St Riverside (92501) ***(P-27304)***
Riverside Dialysis Center ....E....951 682-2700
4361 Latham St Ste 100 Riverside (92501) ***(P-21934)***
Riverside District Office, Riverside *Also called State Compensation Insur Fund* ***(P-10143)***
Riverside Equities LLC ....D....951 688-2222
8487 Magnolia Ave Riverside (92504) ***(P-20218)***
Riverside Health Care Corp ....D....209 523-5667
1611 Scenic Dr Modesto (95355) ***(P-20672)***
Riverside Health Care Corp (PA) ....D....530 897-5100
1469 Humboldt Rd Ste 175 Chico (95928) ***(P-20673)***
Riverside Health Care Corp ....D....916 446-2506
1090 Rio Ln Sacramento (95822) ***(P-20219)***
Riverside Healthcare System LP ....A....951 788-3000
4445 Magnolia Ave Riverside (92501) ***(P-21138)***
Riverside Marriott, Riverside *Also called Pinnacle Rvrside Hspitality LP* ***(P-12757)***
Riverside Med Clnic Ptient Ctr, Riverside *Also called Riverside Medical Clinic Inc* ***(P-19341)***
Riverside Medical Center, Riverside *Also called Kaiser Foundation Hospitals* ***(P-19125)***
Riverside Medical Clinic Inc ....B....951 683-6370
7117 Brockton Ave Riverside (92506) ***(P-19340)***
Riverside Medical Clinic Inc (PA) ....B....951 683-6370
3660 Arlington Ave Riverside (92506) ***(P-19341)***
Riverside Nursery & Ldscp Inc ....D....559 275-1891
4763 W Spruce Ave Ste 111 Fresno (93722) ***(P-8917)***
Riverside Research Institute ....E....949 631-0107
3333 W Coast Hwy Ste 101 Newport Beach (92663) ***(P-26025)***
Riverside Sanitarium LLC ....D....951 684-7701
4580 Palm Ave Riverside (92501) ***(P-20220)***
Riverside Scrap Ir & Met Corp (PA) ....E....951 686-2120
2993 6th St Riverside (92507) ***(P-7770)***
Riverside Transit Agency (PA) ....B....951 565-5000
1825 3rd St Riverside (92507) ***(P-3579)***
Riverside University Health (PA) ....D....951 358-5000
4065 County Circle Dr Riverside (92503) ***(P-21139)***
Riverside University Health ....A....951 486-4000
26520 Cactus Ave Moreno Valley (92555) ***(P-21140)***
Riverside-San Bernardino (PA) ....C....909 864-1097
11980 Mount Vernon Ave Grand Terrace (92313) ***(P-19342)***
Riverside-San Bernardino ....C....951 849-4761
11555 1/2 Potrero Rd Banning (92220) ***(P-22113)***
Riverside-San Bernardino ....D....951 654-0803
607 Donna Way San Jacinto (92583) ***(P-19343)***
Riverview Golf and Country CLB ....D....530 224-2254
4200 Bechelli Ln Redding (96002) ***(P-18545)***
Riverwalk PST-Cute Rhblitation, Mission Viejo *Also called Rock Canyon Healthcare Inc* ***(P-21855)***
Riviera Finance of Texas Inc (PA) ....C....310 540-3993
220 Avenue I Redondo Beach (90277) ***(P-9492)***
Riviera Health Care Center, Pico Rivera *Also called Riviera Nursing & Conva* ***(P-20221)***
Riviera Nursing & Conva ....C....562 806-2576
8203 Telegraph Rd Pico Rivera (90660) ***(P-20221)***
Riviera Partners LLC (PA) ....D....877 748-4372
141 10th St San Francisco (94103) ***(P-14388)***

Employee Codes: A=Over 500 employees, B=251-500
C=101-250, D=51-100, E=50
2020 Directory of California
Wholesalers and Services Companies
© Mergent Inc. 1-800-342-5647
1409

Riviera Reincarnate LLC .... D 760 327-8311
1600 N Indian Canyon Dr Palm Springs (92262) *(P-12833)*
Rivio Inc .... E 408 653-4400
2500 Augustine Dr Ste 100 Santa Clara (95054) *(P-5464)*
Rizal Community Center, Sacramento *Also called Southgate Recreation & Pk Dst (P-23477)*
RJ Allen Inc .... D 714 539-1022
10392 Stanford Ave Garden Grove (92840) *(P-14112)*
RJ Noble Company (PA) .... C 714 637-1550
15505 E Lincoln Ave Orange (92865) *(P-1781)*
Rjb Enterprises Inc .... E 714 484-3101
2579 W Woodland Dr Anaheim (92801) *(P-2616)*
RJN Investigations Inc .... D 951 686-7638
360 E 1st St Ste 696 Tustin (92780) *(P-16394)*
Rjp Framing Inc .... C 916 941-3934
1139 Sibley St Ste 100 Folsom (95630) *(P-2969)*
RJS & Associates Inc .... C 510 670-9111
1675 Sabre St Hayward (94545) *(P-3208)*
RK Electric Inc .... C 510 580-2850
42021 Osgood Rd Fremont (94539) *(P-2617)*
Rk Logistics Group Inc .... C 510 298-5128
44951 Industrial Dr Fremont (94538) *(P-5042)*
Rk Logistics Group Inc (PA) .... D 408 942-8107
41707 Christy St Fremont (94538) *(P-4492)*
Rki Instruments Inc (PA) .... D 510 441-5656
33248 Central Ave Union City (94587) *(P-7587)*
Rl Properties, Albany *Also called Reichert Lengfeld Ltd Partnr (P-12799)*
RLCS Inc (PA) .... D 818 898-1164
10550 Sepulveda Blvd # 203 Mission Hills (91345) *(P-4726)*
Rlh Fire Protection, Bakersfield *Also called CMA Fire Protection (P-2098)*
Rlj Hgn Emeryville Lessee LP .... D 510 658-9300
1800 Powell St Emeryville (94608) *(P-12834)*
Rljhgn Emeryville Lessee LP .... C 510 658-9300
1800 Powell St Emeryville (94608) *(P-12835)*
RM Galicia Inc .... C 626 813-6200
1521 W Cameron Ave # 100 West Covina (91790) *(P-13698)*
RMA Group, Rancho Cucamonga *Also called R M A Group Inc (P-25275)*
RMC Painting & Restoration, Burlingame *Also called Robert Meuschke Company Inc (P-2388)*
RMC Transport, Riverside *Also called Bledsoe Masonry Inc (P-2705)*
Rmci, Camarillo *Also called Research Management Cons Inc (P-27188)*
Rmd Group Inc .... B 562 866-9288
2311 E South St Long Beach (90805) *(P-26796)*
Rmg Recycling, San Diego *Also called Resource Management Group Inc (P-5040)*
Rmi International Inc .... D 310 781-6768
1919 Torrance Blvd Torrance (90501) *(P-16395)*
Rmis, Westlake Village *Also called Registry Monitoring Ins Srvcs (P-11410)*
RMR Construction Company .... C 415 647-0884
2424 Oakdale Ave San Francisco (94124) *(P-1582)*
RMS Foundation Inc .... A 562 435-3511
1126 Queens Hwy Long Beach (90802) *(P-12836)*
Rmt Landscape Contractors Inc .... E 510 568-3208
421 Pendleton Way Oakland (94621) *(P-901)*
RNA Ann Arbor Incorporated .... D 877 762-7511
508 S Smith Ave Ste A202 Corona (92882) *(P-14028)*
Rnc Capital Management LLC .... D 310 477-6543
11601 Wilshire Blvd Ph 25 Los Angeles (90025) *(P-9846)*
Rnc Genter Capital Management, Los Angeles *Also called Rnc Capital Management LLC (P-9846)*
Rncmba Inc .... C 661 395-1700
4801 Truxtun Ave Bakersfield (93309) *(P-14558)*
Road Dept, San Andreas *Also called County of Calaveras (P-23063)*
Road Safety Inc .... C 916 543-4600
4335 Pacific St Ste A Rocklin (95677) *(P-17037)*
Roadex America Inc .... D 310 878-9800
1515 W 178th St Gardena (90248) *(P-4493)*
Roadium Open Air Market, Torrance *Also called Pioneer Theatres Inc (P-16994)*
Roadrunner Shuttle, Camarillo *Also called Airport Connection Inc (P-3522)*
Robbins Geller Rudman Dowd LLP (PA) .... B 619 231-1058
655 W Broadway Ste 1900 San Diego (92101) *(P-22791)*
Robert A Bothman Inc (PA) .... C 408 279-2277
2690 Scott Blvd Santa Clara (95050) *(P-3209)*
Robert A Hall .... D 707 837-8564
9769 Dawn Way Windsor (95492) *(P-14559)*
Robert Alves Farms Inc .... D 559 896-3309
10642 E Dinuba Ave Selma (93662) *(P-157)*
Robert B Diemer Trtmnt Plant, Yorba Linda *Also called Metropolitan Water District (P-6087)*
Robert C Hamilton .... D 626 794-4103
1760 N Fair Oaks Ave Pasadena (91103) *(P-24053)*
Robert Cecchini Inc .... D 925 634-4400
5301 Orwood Rd Brentwood (94513) *(P-72)*
Robert Clapper Cnstr Svcs Inc .... D 909 829-3688
2223 N Locust Ave Rialto (92377) *(P-1583)*
Robert Consl Englekirk Strctrl (PA) .... D 323 733-6673
2116 Arlington Ave Lbby Los Angeles (90018) *(P-25288)*
Robert Cromeans Salon (PA) .... E 858 270-9975
410 A St San Diego (92101) *(P-13357)*
Robert Half International Inc .... D 408 961-2975
10 Almaden Blvd Ste 900 San Jose (95113) *(P-14389)*
Robert Half International Inc .... D 831 241-9042
4 Lower Ragsdale Dr # 101 Monterey (93940) *(P-14390)*
Robert Half International Inc (PA) .... D 650 234-6000
2884 Sand Hill Rd Ste 200 Menlo Park (94025) *(P-14560)*
Robert Half International Inc .... D 925 930-7766
3000 Oak Rd Walnut Creek (94597) *(P-14391)*
Robert Half International Inc .... D 951 779-9081
2280 Market St Ste 220 Riverside (92501) *(P-14392)*
Robert Half International Inc .... E 408 293-8611
10 Almaden Blvd Ste 900 San Jose (95113) *(P-14393)*
Robert Half International Inc .... D 800 356-1994
P.O. Box 743295 Los Angeles (90074) *(P-14394)*
Robert Half International Inc .... D 888 744-9202
4225 Executive Sq Ste 300 La Jolla (92037) *(P-14395)*
Robert Half International Inc .... C 415 434-1900
50 California St Ste 1000 San Francisco (94111) *(P-14396)*
Robert Half International Inc .... E 650 574-8200
1850 Gateway Dr Ste 200 San Mateo (94404) *(P-14397)*
Robert Half International Inc .... D 650 234-6000
2884 Sand Hill Rd Ste 200 Menlo Park (94025) *(P-14398)*
Robert Half International Inc .... D 650 234-6000
2884 Sand Hill Rd Ste 200 Menlo Park (94025) *(P-14399)*
Robert Half International Inc .... D 650 234-6000
2884 Sand Hill Rd Ste 200 Menlo Park (94025) *(P-14400)*
Robert Half International Inc .... D 949 476-3199
18200 Von Karman Ave # 800 Irvine (92612) *(P-14401)*
Robert Half International Inc .... D 626 463-2037
790 E Colo Blvd Ste 650 Pasadena (91101) *(P-14402)*
Robert Half International Inc .... D 650 812-9790
3600 W Byshore Rd Ste 103 Palo Alto (94303) *(P-14403)*
Robert Half International Inc .... E 925 913-1000
2613 Camino Ramon San Ramon (94583) *(P-14404)*
Robert Half MGT Resources .... E 510 271-0910
1999 Harrison St Ste 1100 Oakland (94612) *(P-14405)*
Robert Heely Construction, Bakersfield *Also called Robert Heely Construction LP (P-1041)*
Robert Heely Construction LP (PA) .... B 661 617-1400
5401 Woodmere Dr Bakersfield (93313) *(P-1041)*
Robert J Echter Foxpoint Farms, Encinitas *Also called J Robert Echter (P-250)*
Robert Kaufman Co Inc .... E 310 538-3482
135 W 132nd St Los Angeles (90061) *(P-8008)*
Robert Kinsella Inc .... D 949 453-9533
15375 Barranca Pkwy G107 Irvine (92618) *(P-8214)*
Robert Meuschke Company Inc .... E 650 342-3993
1039 Edwards Rd Burlingame (94010) *(P-2388)*
Robert Morken Construction .... E 530 386-1512
1300 Regency Way Ste 59 Kings Beach (96143) *(P-1185)*
Robert Quintero Labor Contg .... E 559 732-6954
1827 S Bardo St Visalia (93277) *(P-14406)*
Robert Sknner Filtration Plant, Winchester *Also called Metropolitan Water District (P-6093)*
Robert W Baird & Co Inc .... A 530 271-3000
360 Sierra College Dr # 200 Grass Valley (95945) *(P-10235)*
Robert Young Family Ltd Partnr .... D 707 433-3228
4950 Red Winery Rd Geyserville (95441) *(P-680)*
Robert Young Vineyards, Geyserville *Also called Robert Young Family Ltd Partnr (P-680)*
Robert's Lumber, Bloomington *Also called Roberts Lumber Sales Inc (P-6650)*
Robertas Labor Contracting .... B 831 678-8176
137 Main St Soledad (93960) *(P-14407)*
Roberts & Associates Inc .... D 951 727-4357
8175 Limonite Ave Ste A1 Riverside (92509) *(P-21854)*
Roberts Lumber Sales Inc .... D 909 350-9164
2661 S Lilac Ave Bloomington (92316) *(P-6650)*
Robertson Piper Management LLC .... C 650 625-8333
963 Fremont Ave Los Altos (94024) *(P-26797)*
Robinsn Clgne Rsn Shpr Dvs Inc .... D 619 338-4060
620 Nwport Ctr Dr Ste 700 San Diego (92101) *(P-22792)*
Robinson & Sons .... D 530 265-5844
293 Lower Grass Valley Rd # 201 Nevada City (95959) *(P-380)*
Robinson and Enterprises, Nevada City *Also called Robinson & Sons (P-380)*
Robinson and Wood Inc .... D 408 298-7120
160 W Santa Clara St # 1000 San Jose (95113) *(P-22793)*
Robinson Company Contrs Inc .... D 619 697-6040
8871 Troy St Spring Valley (91977) *(P-2257)*
Robinson Electric, Spring Valley *Also called Robinson Company Contrs Inc (P-2257)*
Robinson Fresh, Torrance *Also called C H Robinson Intl Inc (P-4903)*
Robinson Ranch Golf LLC .... C 818 885-0599
27734 Sand Canyon Rd Santa Clarita (91387) *(P-18288)*
Roblox Corporation .... B 888 858-2569
970 Park Pl San Mateo (94403) *(P-15488)*
Robotics Institute, Pleasanton *Also called Carnegie Mellon University (P-25879)*
Rocha Transportation, Modesto *Also called Ed Rocha Livestock Trnsp Inc (P-4008)*
Rocha, Jill B MD, Ventura *Also called West Ventura Family Care Ctr (P-19594)*
Rock Canyon Healthcare Inc .... C 719 404-1000
27101 Puerta Real Ste 450 Mission Viejo (92691) *(P-21855)*
Rock Paper Scissors LLC .... E 310 586-0600
2308 Broadway Santa Monica (90404) *(P-17663)*
Rock-It Cargo USA LLC .... D 310 455-1900
120 N Topanga Canyon Blvd # 215 Topanga (90290) *(P-5043)*
Rock-It Cargo USA LLC .... D 215 947-5400
5343 W Imperial Hwy # 900 Los Angeles (90045) *(P-5137)*
Rock-It Cargo USA LLC .... C 310 410-0935
5343 W Imperial Hwy # 900 Los Angeles (90045) *(P-5044)*
Rockefeller Group Dev Corp .... D 949 468-1800
4 Park Plz Ste 840 Irvine (92614) *(P-11596)*
Rocket Dog Brands, San Ramon *Also called Millennial Brands LLC (P-8138)*
Rocket Farms Inc (PA) .... C 800 227-5229
2651 Cabrillo Hwy N Half Moon Bay (94019) *(P-275)*
Rocket Farms Herbs Inc .... B 562 340-5108
370 Espinosa Rd Salinas (93907) *(P-356)*
Rocket Smog Inc .... D 310 390-7664
11413 W Washington Blvd Los Angeles (90066) *(P-17344)*
Rockey Murata Landscaping .... D 562 921-3210
15417 Cornet St Santa Fe Springs (90670) *(P-756)*
Rockland Builders Services Inc .... D 619 592-9582
3261 1/2 Main St Chula Vista (91911) *(P-1584)*
Rocklin Power Investors LP .... D 916 645-3383
3100 Thunder Valley Ct Lincoln (95648) *(P-5912)*
Rockport ADM Svcs LLC (PA) .... D 323 330-6500
5900 Wilshire Blvd # 1600 Los Angeles (90036) *(P-26798)*

Mergent e-mail: customerrelations@mergent.com
1410
2020 Directory of California
Wholesalers and Services Companies
(P-0000) Products & Services Section entry number
(PA)=Parent Co (HQ)=Headquarters (DH)=Div Headquarters

Rockport Healthcare Services, Los Angeles *Also called Rockport ADM Svcs LLC* ***(P-26798)***
Rockstar San Diego..........C.......760 929-0700
2200 Faraday Ave Ste 200 Carlsbad (92008) ***(P-15808)***
Rockview Dairies Inc (PA)..........C.......562 927-5511
7011 Stewart And Gray Rd Downey (90241) ***(P-8640)***
Rocky Coast Builders Inc..........D.......760 489-7770
135 Market Pl Escondido (92029) ***(P-2970)***
Rocky Point Care Center, Lakeport *Also called Windflower Holdings LLC* ***(P-20389)***
Rodbat Security Services, Torrance *Also called Rmi International Inc* ***(P-16395)***
Rodda Electric Inc (PA)..........D.......925 240-6024
380 Carrol Ct Ste L Brentwood (94513) ***(P-2258)***
Roddy Ranch Pbc LLC..........D.......925 978-4653
1 Tour Way Antioch (94531) ***(P-18546)***
Rodeo Realty Inc..........D.......818 986-7300
15300 Ventura Blvd # 500 Sherman Oaks (91403) ***(P-11421)***
Rodeo Realty Inc..........D.......310 873-0100
11940 San Vicente Blvd Los Angeles (90049) ***(P-11422)***
Rodeo Realty Inc..........D.......818 285-3700
17501 Ventura Blvd Encino (91316) ***(P-11423)***
Rodeo Realty Inc..........D.......818 308-8273
12345 Ventura Blvd Ste A Studio City (91604) ***(P-11424)***
Rodeo Realty Inc (PA)..........D.......818 349-9997
9171 Wilshire Blvd # 321 Beverly Hills (90210) ***(P-11425)***
Rodeo Realty Inc..........D.......818 349-9997
9338 Reseda Blvd Ste 102 Northridge (91324) ***(P-11426)***
Rodeo Realty Inc..........D.......818 657-4609
23901 Calabasas Rd # 1050 Calabasas (91302) ***(P-11427)***
Rodeo Realty Inc..........D.......818 999-2030
21031 Ventura Blvd # 100 Woodland Hills (91364) ***(P-11428)***
Rodeway Inn, Tahoe City *Also called Pepper Tree Inn* ***(P-12748)***
Rodgers Security Service Inc..........C.......310 684-3016
8726 S Sepulveda Blvd Los Angeles (90045) ***(P-16396)***
Rodgers Trucking Co, San Leandro *Also called Frank Ghiglione Inc* ***(P-3888)***
Rodgz Farm Labor Contg LLC..........D.......530 329-8403
4422 College Way Olivehurst (95961) ***(P-644)***
Rodin & Co Inc..........D.......818 358-3427
7411 Laurel Canyon Blvd # 10 North Hollywood (91605) ***(P-2389)***
Rodney Strong Vineyards, Healdsburg *Also called Klein Foods Inc* ***(P-141)***
Roebbelen Construction Inc..........D.......916 939-4000
1241 Hawks Flight Ct El Dorado Hills (95762) ***(P-1585)***
Roebbelen Contracting Inc..........B.......916 939-4000
1241 Hawks Flight Ct El Dorado Hills (95762) ***(P-1586)***
Rogan Building Services Inc..........E.......951 248-1261
1531 7th St Riverside (92507) ***(P-14029)***
Roger L Crumley MD Inc..........E.......714 456-5750
101 City Dr S Bldg 56 5 Orange (92868) ***(P-19344)***
Rogers Poultry Co (PA)..........D.......323 585-0802
5050 S Santa Fe Ave Vernon (90058) ***(P-8333)***
Rogers Poultry Co..........D.......800 585-0802
2020 E 67th St Los Angeles (90001) ***(P-8334)***
Rogers Trucking, San Leandro *Also called Frank Ghiglione Inc* ***(P-3889)***
Roi Communications Inc (PA)..........E.......831 430-0170
5274 Scotts Valley Dr # 107 Scotts Valley (95066) ***(P-26799)***
Roku Inc (PA)..........B.......408 556-9040
150 Winchester Cir Los Gatos (95032) ***(P-5737)***
Roland Corporation US (HQ)..........C.......323 890-3700
5100 S Eastern Ave Los Angeles (90040) ***(P-7831)***
Roland Dga Corporation (HQ)..........C.......949 727-2100
15363 Barranca Pkwy Irvine (92618) ***(P-6892)***
Roll Properties Intl Inc..........C.......661 797-6500
13646 Highway 33 Lost Hills (93249) ***(P-11953)***
Roll Technology West, Pittsburg *Also called Chrome Deposit Corp* ***(P-7053)***
Rolled Steel Products Corp (PA)..........D.......323 723-8836
2187 Garfield Ave Commerce (90040) ***(P-7099)***
Rolling Hills Casino, Corning *Also called Paskenta Band Nomlaki Indians* ***(P-12742)***
Rolling Hills Club, Novato *Also called Tennis Everyone Incorporated* ***(P-18593)***
Rolling Hills Estates City of, Rllng HLS Est *Also called Rolling Hlls Esttes Tennis CLB* ***(P-18747)***
Rolling Hlls Esttes Tennis CLB..........E.......310 541-4585
25851 Hawthorne Blvd Rllng HLS Est (90275) ***(P-18747)***
Rollins Inc..........D.......559 292-8222
5830 E Shields Ave Fresno (93727) ***(P-13827)***
Roman Cath Arch of Los Angels..........E.......310 836-5500
5835 W Slauson Ave Culver City (90230) ***(P-13375)***
Roman Cath Arch of Los Angels..........A.......805 687-8811
199 N Hope Ave Santa Barbara (93110) ***(P-13376)***
Roman Catholic Archdiocese of..........D.......650 756-2060
1500 Old Mission Rd Daly City (94014) ***(P-11632)***
Roman Cthlic Bishp of San Jose..........A.......833 304-0763
22555 Cristo Rey Dr Los Altos (94024) ***(P-11633)***
Roman Cthlic Bshp of Snta Rosa..........C.......707 528-8712
987 Airway Ct Santa Rosa (95403) ***(P-24220)***
Romark Logistics of California..........D.......909 356-5600
13521 Santa Ana Ave Ste A Fontana (92337) ***(P-4494)***
Romero Construction, Escondido *Also called Romero General Cnstr Corp* ***(P-1782)***
Romero General Cnstr Corp..........C.......760 489-8412
2150 N Centre City Pkwy Escondido (92026) ***(P-1782)***
Romex Textiles Inc (PA)..........E.......213 749-9090
785 E 14th Pl Los Angeles (90021) ***(P-8009)***
Ron D & Shelley N Horn..........E.......559 834-2118
30912 Moonflower Ln Murrieta (92563) ***(P-158)***
Ron Filice Enterprises Inc..........E.......408 294-0477
738 N 1st St Ste 202 San Jose (95112) ***(P-10477)***
Ron Nurss Inc..........D.......916 631-9761
11290 Sunrise Park Dr B Rancho Cordova (95742) ***(P-3210)***
Ron's Pharmacy Services, San Diego *Also called Belville Enterprises Inc* ***(P-18838)***
Ronald J Lemieux Assoc Law Off..........D.......562 375-0095
4195 N Viking Way Ste E Long Beach (90808) ***(P-22794)***
Ronald L Wolfe & Assoc Inc..........E.......805 964-6770
173 Chapel St Santa Barbara (93111) ***(P-11429)***
Ronald Reagan Building, Los Angeles *Also called Ucla Health System* ***(P-21319)***
Ronald Reagan Presdntl Library, Simi Valley *Also called Ronald Reagan Presidential* ***(P-24283)***
Ronald Reagan Presidential..........D.......805 522-2977
40 Presidential Dr # 200 Simi Valley (93065) ***(P-24283)***
Ronald Reagan Ucla Medical Ctr, Los Angeles *Also called University Cal Los Angeles* ***(P-21333)***
Rongcheng Trading LLC..........E.......626 338-1090
19319 Arenth Ave City of Industry (91748) ***(P-8419)***
Ronsin Photocopy Inc (PA)..........D.......909 594-5995
215 Lemon Creek Dr Walnut (91789) ***(P-17038)***
Roofing Constructors Inc..........C.......415 648-6472
15002 Wicks Blvd San Leandro (94577) ***(P-3096)***
Roofing Supply Group LLC..........D.......424 269-7330
14128 Kornblum Ave Hawthorne (90250) ***(P-6718)***
Roofing Wholesale Co Inc..........D.......909 825-8440
118 Commercial Rd San Bernardino (92408) ***(P-6719)***
Roosevelt Hotel LLC..........C.......323 466-7000
7000 Hollywood Blvd Los Angeles (90028) ***(P-12837)***
Roost, Sausalito *Also called Gate Five Group LLC* ***(P-6559)***
Rooster Run Golf Club Inc..........E.......707 778-1211
2301 E Washington St Petaluma (94954) ***(P-18289)***
Rope Partner Inc..........D.......831 460-9448
125 Mcpherson St Ste B Santa Cruz (95060) ***(P-7652)***
Ropers Majeski Kohn & Bentley, Redwood City *Also called Ropers Majeski Kohn Bentley* ***(P-22795)***
Ropers Majeski Kohn Bentley (PA)..........D.......650 364-8200
1001 Marshall St Fl 3 Redwood City (94063) ***(P-22795)***
Ropes & Gray LLP..........B.......415 315-6300
3 Embarcadero Ctr Ste 300 San Francisco (94111) ***(P-22796)***
Ropes & Gray LLP..........D.......650 617-4000
1900 University Ave # 600 East Palo Alto (94303) ***(P-22797)***
Roppongi-Tahoe Lp A Californi..........C.......530 544-5400
4130 Lake Tahoe Blvd South Lake Tahoe (96150) ***(P-12838)***
Roque Development and Inv..........D.......626 427-9077
227 E Pomona Blvd Ste B Monterey Park (91755) ***(P-25289)***
Rore Inc (PA)..........D.......858 404-7393
5151 Shoreham Pl Ste 260 San Diego (92122) ***(P-1587)***
Rosanna Inc..........C.......714 751-5100
3350 Avenue Of The Arts Costa Mesa (92626) ***(P-12839)***
Rosano Partners..........E.......213 802-0300
3530 Wilshire Blvd # 1750 Los Angeles (90010) ***(P-11430)***
Rosary Academy Parent Council..........D.......714 879-6302
1340 N Acacia Ave Fullerton (92831) ***(P-24632)***
Roscoe Real Estate Ltd Partnr..........D.......310 260-7500
1819 Ocean Ave Santa Monica (90401) ***(P-12840)***
Rose & Shore Inc..........B.......323 826-2144
5151 Alcoa Ave Vernon (90058) ***(P-17039)***
Rose Bowl Aquatics Center..........D.......626 564-0330
360 N Arroyo Blvd Pasadena (91103) ***(P-18547)***
Rose Brand Wipers Inc..........D.......818 505-6290
11440 Sheldon St Sun Valley (91352) ***(P-17941)***
ROSE GARDEN CONVALESCENT CENTE, Pasadena *Also called David Ross Inc* ***(P-19857)***
Rose Hills Co, Whittier *Also called Rose Hills Mortuary Inc* ***(P-13377)***
Rose Hills Company (HQ)..........A.......562 699-0921
3888 Workman Mill Rd Whittier (90601) ***(P-11634)***
Rose Hills Holdings Corp (PA)..........B.......562 699-0921
3888 Workman Mill Rd Whittier (90601) ***(P-11635)***
Rose Hills Mem Pk & Mortuary, Whittier *Also called Rose Hills Company* ***(P-11634)***
Rose Hills Mem Pk & Mortuary, Whittier *Also called Rose Hills Holdings Corp* ***(P-11635)***
Rose Hills Mortuary Inc..........A.......562 699-0921
3888 Workman Mill Rd Whittier (90601) ***(P-13377)***
Rose International Inc..........C.......636 812-4000
450 N Brand Blvd Fl 6 Glendale (91203) ***(P-15068)***
Rose International Inc..........C.......636 812-4000
4000 Executive Pkwy # 150 San Ramon (94583) ***(P-27193)***
Rose International Inc..........E.......636 812-4000
18952 Macarthur Blvd # 440 Irvine (92612) ***(P-27194)***
Rose Thompson Company..........D.......760 736-6020
949 Cassou Rd San Marcos (92069) ***(P-276)***
Roseburg Forest Products Co..........C.......530 938-2721
98 Mill St Weed (96094) ***(P-6651)***
Rosecrans Care Center, Gardena *Also called Health Care Investments Inc* ***(P-20005)***
Rosemary Childrens Services (PA)..........C.......626 844-3033
36 S Kinneloa Ave 200 Pasadena (91107) ***(P-24054)***
Rosemont Media LLC..........E.......858 200-0044
1010 Turquoise St Ste 201 San Diego (92109) ***(P-13570)***
Rosen Electronics LLC..........D.......951 898-9808
2500 E Francis St Ontario (91761) ***(P-7832)***
Rosendin Electric Inc (PA)..........A.......408 286-2800
880 Mabury Rd San Jose (95133) ***(P-2618)***
Rosendin Electric Inc..........A.......714 739-1334
1730 S Anaheim Way Anaheim (92805) ***(P-2619)***
Rosendin Electric Inc..........A.......408 321-2200
2698 Orchard Pkwy San Jose (95134) ***(P-2620)***
Rosendin Electric Inc..........C.......415 495-9300
2121 Oakdale Ave San Francisco (94124) ***(P-2621)***
Rosendin Electric Inc..........A.......415 495-9300
1001 Potrero Ave San Francisco (94110) ***(P-2622)***
ROSENER HOUSE, Menlo Park *Also called Peninsula Volunteers Inc* ***(P-23382)***
Rosenthal Group, The, Venice *Also called Trg Inc* ***(P-11487)***
Roseryan Inc..........D.......510 456-3056
35473 Dumbarton Ct Newark (94560) ***(P-25669)***
Roseville Care Center, Roseville *Also called Crocus Holdings LLC* ***(P-19853)***
Roseville Convalescent Hosp, Roseville *Also called Horizon West Healthcare Inc* ***(P-21477)***
Roseville Foothils and Jct, Roseville *Also called Wells Fargo Bank National Assn* ***(P-9137)***

ALPHABETIC

Employee Codes: A=Over 500 employees, B=251-500
C=101-250, D=51-100, E=50
2020 Directory of California
Wholesalers and Services Companies
© Mergent Inc. 1-800-342-5647
1411

Roseville Imaging, Roseville *Also called Sutter Health* ***(P-21594)***
Roseville Sportworld Inc..........D.......916 783-8550
1009 Orlando Ave Roseville (95661) ***(P-18748)***
Roseville Towne Place Suites..........D.......916 782-2232
10569 Fairway Dr Roseville (95678) ***(P-12841)***
Rosewood Convalescent Hospital, Pleasant Hill *Also called Dreamctchers Empwerment Netwrk* ***(P-23908)***
Rosewood Rehabilitation, Carmichael *Also called Carmichael Care Inc* ***(P-19780)***
Rosewood Retirement Community, Bakersfield *Also called American Baptist Homes of West* ***(P-20486)***
Ross F Carroll Inc..........E.......209 848-5959
8873 Warnerville Rd Oakdale (95361) ***(P-25290)***
Ross Valley Homes Inc..........D.......415 461-2300
501 Via Casitas Greenbrae (94904) ***(P-20450)***
Rossi Hamerslough Reishchl &..........D.......408 244-4570
1960 The Alameda Ste 200 San Jose (95126) ***(P-22798)***
Rossin Steel Inc..........C.......619 656-9200
2660 Cactus Rd San Diego (92154) ***(P-7100)***
Rossmoor, Walnut Creek *Also called Golden Rain Foundation* ***(P-11172)***
Rossmoor Carwash, Los Alamitos *Also called Lakewood South Car Wash LLC* ***(P-17380)***
Rotary and Miission Systems, Fort Irwin *Also called Lockheed Martin Corporation* ***(P-4443)***
Rotary CLB PCF Grove Char Fund..........D.......831 372-3877
706 Forest Ave Pacific Grove (93950) ***(P-18548)***
Rotary Club, Palo Cedro *Also called Rotary International* ***(P-24633)***
ROTARY CLUB OF NAPA SUNRISE OF, NAPA *Also called NAPA Sunrise Rotary Club Inc* ***(P-24600)***
Rotary International..........D.......530 547-5272
9839 Meadowlark Way Palo Cedro (96073) ***(P-24633)***
Roth Capital Partners LLC (PA)..........D.......800 678-9147
888 San Clemente Dr # 400 Newport Beach (92660) ***(P-9749)***
Roth Staffing Companies LP (PA)..........D.......714 939-8600
450 N State College Blvd Orange (92868) ***(P-14561)***
Rothfleisch Ranches Inc..........D.......760 344-1819
129 S El Cerrito Dr Brawley (92227) ***(P-681)***
Roto Rooter Plumbing & Drain S..........E.......951 658-8541
2141 Industrial Ct Ste B Vista (92081) ***(P-17535)***
Roto Rooter Plumbing & Svc Co, Mission Viejo *Also called Hoffman Southwest Corp* ***(P-17505)***
Roto-Rooter, Anaheim *Also called Hoffman Southwest Corp* ***(P-17504)***
Roto-Rooter, Concord *Also called Overmiller Inc* ***(P-17523)***
Roto-Rooter, Rancho Cucamonga *Also called Hoffman Southwest Corp* ***(P-17506)***
Roto-Rooter Services Company..........D.......650 322-2366
220 Demeter St East Palo Alto (94303) ***(P-17536)***
Rotorcraft Support Inc..........D.......818 997-7667
67 D St Fillmore (93015) ***(P-4788)***
Rouche O Edgar DDS, Riverside *Also called American Dntl Partners of Cal* ***(P-19602)***
Roughan Associates At Linc..........E.......626 351-0991
465 N Halstead St Ste 120 Pasadena (91107) ***(P-27195)***
Round Hill Country Club..........C.......925 934-8211
3169 Roundhill Rd Alamo (94507) ***(P-18549)***
Round Hill Country Club..........E.......925 934-8211
3169 Roundhill Rd Alamo (94507) ***(P-18550)***
Round Valley Indian Health Ctr..........D.......707 983-6182
Hwy 162 Biggar Ln Covelo (95428) ***(P-19345)***
Roundabout Entertainment Inc..........D.......818 842-9300
217 S Lake St Burbank (91502) ***(P-17664)***
Rounseville Rehabilitation Ctr, Oakland *Also called Rcc Facility Incorporated* ***(P-20666)***
Rountree Plumbing and Htg Inc..........D.......650 298-0300
1624 Santa Clara Dr 130 Roseville (95661) ***(P-2259)***
Roux Associates Inc..........D.......562 446-8600
5150 E Pacific Coast Hwy # 450 Long Beach (90804) ***(P-27196)***
Rowan Incorporated..........D.......760 692-0700
2778 Loker Ave W Carlsbad (92010) ***(P-2623)***
Rowan Electric, Carlsbad *Also called Rowan Incorporated* ***(P-2623)***
Rowland Convalescent Hosp Inc..........D.......626 967-2741
330 W Rowland St Covina (91723) ***(P-20222)***
ROWLAND, THE, Covina *Also called Rowland Convalescent Hosp Inc* ***(P-20222)***
Roy C Shannon MD, Oroville *Also called Oroville Internal Meds Group* ***(P-19250)***
Roy Carrington Inc..........D.......530 893-2100
2460 Ceres Ave Chico (95926) ***(P-14408)***
Roy E Ladd Inc..........E.......530 241-6102
3724 Sunlight Ct Redding (96001) ***(P-1783)***
Roy E Whitehead Inc..........D.......951 682-1490
2245 Via Cerro Riverside (92509) ***(P-2971)***
Roy Jorgensen Associates Inc..........D.......310 468-2478
19001 S Western Ave Torrance (90501) ***(P-14030)***
Roy Miller Freight Lines LLC (PA)..........D.......714 632-5511
3165 E Coronado St Anaheim (92806) ***(P-3931)***
Royal Airline Linen Inc..........D.......310 677-9885
125 N Ash Ave Inglewood (90301) ***(P-13183)***
Royal Ambulance Inc..........C.......510 568-6161
14472 Wicks Blvd San Leandro (94577) ***(P-3715)***
Royal Care Skilled Nursing Ctr, Long Beach *Also called Covenant Care California LLC* ***(P-19831)***
Royal Coach Tours (PA)..........C.......408 279-4801
630 Stockton Ave San Jose (95126) ***(P-3780)***
Royal Convalescent Hospital..........D.......760 344-5431
320 Cattle Call Dr Brawley (92227) ***(P-20223)***
Royal Crest Building Maint..........E.......714 562-5034
8601 Roland St Ste E Buena Park (90621) ***(P-14031)***
Royal Crest Healthcare, Covina *Also called Cruz Hoffstetter LLC* ***(P-16731)***
Royal Express Inc (PA)..........C.......559 272-3500
3545 E Date Ave Fresno (93725) ***(P-4228)***
Royal Glass Company Inc..........D.......408 969-0444
3200 De La Cruz Blvd Santa Clara (95054) ***(P-3297)***

Royal Gorge Crss Cntry Ski Rst, Soda Springs *Also called Royal Gorge Nordic Ski Resort* ***(P-12842)***
Royal Gorge Nordic Ski Resort (PA)..........C.......530 426-3871
9411 Hillside Rd Soda Springs (95728) ***(P-12842)***
Royal Hospitality Incorporated..........D.......858 278-0800
5550 Kearny Mesa Rd San Diego (92111) ***(P-12843)***
Royal Investigation Patrol Inc..........D.......510 352-6800
2950 Merced St Ste 108 San Leandro (94577) ***(P-16397)***
Royal Laundry, South San Francisco *Also called American Etc Inc* ***(P-13177)***
Royal Mountain King, Copperopolis *Also called Meridian Gold Inc* ***(P-970)***
Royal Oaks, Duarte *Also called Cal Southern Presbt Homes* ***(P-10706)***
Royal Oaks Enterprises Inc..........E.......408 779-2362
15480 Watsonville Rd Morgan Hill (95037) ***(P-300)***
Royal Oaks Manor, Duarte *Also called Begroup* ***(P-19749)***
Royal Oaks Mushroom, Morgan Hill *Also called Royal Oaks Enterprises Inc* ***(P-300)***
Royal Packing Dcf..........D.......559 945-2537
32839 S Lassen Ave Huron (93234) ***(P-73)***
Royal Paper Corp (PA)..........D.......562 903-9030
10232 Palm Dr Santa Fe Springs (90670) ***(P-7902)***
Royal Plywood Company LLC..........D.......916 426-3292
6003 88th St Ste 100 Sacramento (95828) ***(P-6652)***
Royal Plywood Company LLC (PA)..........D.......562 404-2989
14171 Park Pl Cerritos (90703) ***(P-6653)***
Royal Poultry, Vernon *Also called Golden West Trading Inc* ***(P-8405)***
Royal Roofing Construction Co, Placentia *Also called Osscim Inc* ***(P-3081)***
Royal Scandinavian Inn, Solvang *Also called National Hospitality LLC* ***(P-12640)***
Royal Specialty Undwrt Inc..........D.......818 922-6700
15303 Ventura Blvd # 500 Sherman Oaks (91403) ***(P-10127)***
Royal Supply Midwest, Santa Fe Springs *Also called Royal Paper Corp* ***(P-7902)***
Royal Terrace Healthcare..........D.......626 256-4654
1340 Highland Ave Duarte (91010) ***(P-20224)***
Royal Truck Body, Carson *Also called Fortress Resources LLC* ***(P-17328)***
Royal Trucking, Concord *Also called Lemore Transportation Inc* ***(P-4083)***
Royal West Drywall Inc..........D.......951 271-4600
2008 2nd St Norco (92860) ***(P-2852)***
Royale Hlth Care Mission Viejo, Mission Viejo *Also called Orange County Royale Convlscnt* ***(P-21069)***
Royalty Tours..........E.......408 279-4801
630 Stockton Ave San Jose (95126) ***(P-4861)***
Rp Realty Partners LLC..........E.......310 207-6990
990 W 8th St Ste 600 Los Angeles (90017) ***(P-10637)***
Rp Scs Wsd Hotel LLC..........D.......619 398-3020
421 W B St San Diego (92101) ***(P-12844)***
Rp/Kinetic Parc 55 Owner LLC..........B.......415 392-8000
55 Cyril Magnin St San Francisco (94102) ***(P-12845)***
RPC Old Town Avenue Owner LLC..........D.......619 299-7400
3900 Old Town Ave San Diego (92110) ***(P-12846)***
RPC Old Town Jefferson..........D.......619 725-4221
2435 Jefferson St San Diego (92110) ***(P-12847)***
Rpd Hotels 18 LLC (PA)..........A.......213 746-1531
2361 Rosecrans Ave # 150 El Segundo (90245) ***(P-12848)***
RPI Carlsbad LP..........C.......760 729-6183
2525 El Camino Real # 100 Carlsbad (92008) ***(P-10638)***
RPM Consolidated Services Inc (PA)..........D.......714 388-3500
1901 Raymer Ave Fullerton (92833) ***(P-4495)***
RPM Mechanical - A Joint Ventr..........D.......858 565-4131
2919 E Victoria St Compton (90221) ***(P-2260)***
RPM Mortgage, Alamo *Also called Lendusa LLC* ***(P-9572)***
RPM Transportation Inc (HQ)..........C.......714 388-3500
11660 Arroyo Ave Santa Ana (92705) ***(P-4120)***
Rpmc Inc (PA)..........D.......818 222-7762
23975 Park Sorrento # 410 Calabasas (91302) ***(P-26924)***
Rpx Corporation (HQ)..........D.......866 779-7641
1 Market Plz Towes San Francisco (94105) ***(P-11833)***
Rq Construction LLC..........C.......760 631-7707
3194 Lionshead Ave Carlsbad (92010) ***(P-1376)***
RR Donnelley, Rancho Dominguez *Also called R R Donnelley & Sons Company* ***(P-13737)***
RR Donnelley & Sons Company..........D.......951 296-2890
40610 County Center Dr # 100 Temecula (92591) ***(P-7864)***
Rri, Downey *Also called Rancho Research Institute* ***(P-26023)***
Rrm Construction Inc..........E.......562 440-3539
9135 Cord Ave Downey (90240) ***(P-1270)***
Rrm Design Group (PA)..........D.......805 439-0442
3765 S Higuera St Ste 102 San Luis Obispo (93401) ***(P-25495)***
Rromeo Corporation..........D.......714 640-3800
535 Anton Blvd Ste 200 Costa Mesa (92626) ***(P-26381)***
Rrt Enterprises LP..........B.......323 653-1521
855 N Fairfax Ave Los Angeles (90046) ***(P-20225)***
Rruff-Rocklin Residents Unite..........E.......415 806-2778
3031 St Rocklin (95765) ***(P-24634)***
Rs Calibration Services Inc..........E.......925 462-4217
1047 Serpentine Ln # 500 Pleasanton (94566) ***(P-17537)***
Rsa Films Inc (PA)..........D.......310 659-1577
634 N La Peer Dr West Hollywood (90069) ***(P-17665)***
RSC Associates Inc (PA)..........C.......530 893-8228
3120 Cohasset Rd Ste 5 Chico (95973) ***(P-11431)***
Rse, Sacramento *Also called Runyon Saltzman Inc* ***(P-13572)***
Rsf Protective Services, Encinitas *Also called Rancho Santa Fe Protective Svc* ***(P-16391)***
RSI Insurance Brokers Inc (HQ)..........E.......714 546-6616
4000 Westerly Pl Ste 110 Newport Beach (92660) ***(P-10478)***
RSI Professional Cab Solutions, Jurupa Valley *Also called Professional Cabinet Solutions* ***(P-2961)***
RSM US LLP..........D.......415 848-5300
44 Montgomery St Ste 3900 San Francisco (94104) ***(P-25670)***
RSM US LLP..........D.......949 255-6500
18401 Von Karman Ave # 500 Irvine (92612) ***(P-25671)***

Mergent e-mail: customerrelations@mergent.com
1412
2020 Directory of California
Wholesalers and Services Companies
(P-0000) Products & Services Section entry number
(PA)=Parent Co (HQ)=Headquarters (DH)=Div Headquarters

RSM US LLP...D.......408 572-4440
100 W San Fernando St San Jose (95113) *(P-25672)*
Rss, Los Angeles *Also called Rodgers Security Service Inc (P-16396)*
Rsui Group, Sherman Oaks *Also called Royal Specialty Undwrt Inc (P-10127)*
Rt Pasad Hotel Partners LP...C.......626 403-7600
180 N Fair Oaks Ave Pasadena (91103) *(P-12849)*
Rt San Diego LLC...E.......858 278-2100
5400 Kearny Mesa Rd San Diego (92111) *(P-12850)*
Rt Sd-Denver LP...E.......858 278-2100
5400 Kearny Mesa Rd San Diego (92111) *(P-12851)*
RTC, Los Angeles *Also called Religious Technology Center (P-11831)*
RTC Aerospace, Chatsworth *Also called Logistical Support LLC (P-7696)*
Rte Enterprises Inc...D.......818 999-5300
21530 Roscoe Blvd Canoga Park (91304) *(P-2390)*
Ruan...D.......209 634-4928
830 W Glenwood Ave Turlock (95380) *(P-3932)*
Ruann Dairy, Riverdale *Also called Maddox Dairy A Ltd Partnership (P-399)*
Rubber Dust Inc (PA)...D.......510 237-6344
533 S 13th St Richmond (94804) *(P-17318)*
Rubicon B Hacienda LLC...D.......424 290-5000
525 N Pacific Coast Hwy El Segundo (90245) *(P-12852)*
Rubicon B Hacienda LLC...D.......424 290-5555
475 N Pacific Coast Hwy El Segundo (90245) *(P-12853)*
Rubicon Enterprises Inc...C.......510 235-1516
2500 Bissell Ave Richmond (94804) *(P-14032)*
RUBICON PROGRAMS, Richmond *Also called Rubicon Enterprises Inc (P-14032)*
Rubicon Programs Incorporated (PA)...D.......510 235-1516
2500 Bissell Ave Richmond (94804) *(P-14033)*
Rubicon Project Inc (PA)...C.......310 207-0272
12181 Bluff Creek Dr Fl 4 Los Angeles (90094) *(P-13571)*
Rubidoux Family Care Center, Riverside *Also called County of Riverside (P-18931)*
Rubrik Inc (PA)...D.......650 300-5862
1001 Page Mill Rd Bldg 2 Palo Alto (94304) *(P-15809)*
Ruby Burma Investment LLC...D.......650 590-0545
612 El Camino Real San Carlos (94070) *(P-26382)*
Ruby Creek Resources Inc...E.......212 671-0404
11835 W Olympic Blvd Los Angeles (90064) *(P-26800)*
Ruby Hill Golf Club LLC...D.......925 417-5840
3400 W Ruby Hill Dr Pleasanton (94566) *(P-18290)*
Ruby Industrial Tech LLC...E.......909 390-7919
910 S Wanamaker Ave Ontario (91761) *(P-7653)*
Ruby Sky, Los Gatos *Also called Inner Circle Entertainment (P-8357)*
Ruckus Wireless Inc (HQ)...C.......650 265-4200
350 W Java Dr Sunnyvale (94089) *(P-5465)*
Ruder, Michael MD, Palo Alto *Also called Cardic Arithmias (P-18866)*
Rudolph and Sletten Inc (HQ)...D.......650 216-3600
2 Circle Star Way Fl 4 San Carlos (94070) *(P-1588)*
Rudy Carrillo Drywall Inc...D.......818 841-2011
1913 W Magnolia Blvd Burbank (91506) *(P-2853)*
Ruffin Hotel Corp of Cal...B.......562 425-5210
4700 Airport Plaza Dr Long Beach (90815) *(P-12854)*
Rugby Laboratories Inc (HQ)...D.......951 270-1400
311 Bonnie Cir Corona (92880) *(P-7980)*
Rugged Engineered Pdts Sector, San Diego *Also called Epsilon Systems Solutions Inc (P-25063)*
Ruhs-Emergency Department, Moreno Valley *Also called Riverside University Health (P-21140)*
Ruiz Janitorial Co Inc...E.......650 222-2078
446 Heller St Redwood City (94063) *(P-14034)*
Runa Hr Holdings Inc...D.......562 883-3546
3067 E 1st St Long Beach (90803) *(P-15069)*
Runway Liquidation LLC (HQ)...C.......323 589-2224
2761 Fruitland Ave Vernon (90058) *(P-8107)*
Runyon Saltzman Inc...D.......916 446-9900
2020 L St Ste 100 Sacramento (95811) *(P-13572)*
Rural Cmnty Assistance Corp (PA)...D.......916 447-2854
3120 Freeboard Dr Ste 201 West Sacramento (95691) *(P-23417)*
Rural/Metro Corporation...C.......510 266-0885
2364 W Winton Ave Hayward (94545) *(P-3716)*
Rural/Metro Corporation...C.......888 876-0740
1345 Vander Way San Jose (95112) *(P-3717)*
Rural/Metro San Diego Inc...D.......619 280-6060
10405 San Diego Mission R San Diego (92108) *(P-3718)*
Rush Computer Rentals, West Hills *Also called Electro Rent Corporation (P-14156)*
Rush Order Inc (PA)...E.......408 848-3525
6600 Silacci Way Gilroy (95020) *(P-4496)*
Rushmore Loan MGT Svcs LLC (PA)...A.......949 727-4798
15480 Laguna Canyon Rd Irvine (92618) *(P-9600)*
Russell Fisher Partnership...E.......714 842-4453
16061 Beach Blvd Huntington Beach (92647) *(P-17395)*
Russell Fisher Partnership (PA)...D.......909 930-5420
18971 Beach Blvd Huntington Beach (92648) *(P-17396)*
Russell Mechanical Inc...D.......916 635-2522
3251 Monier Cir Ste A Rancho Cordova (95742) *(P-2261)*
Russian River Health Center...E.......707 869-2849
16319 3rd St Guerneville (95446) *(P-19346)*
Russon Financial Services Inc...D.......818 999-2800
19935 Ventura Blvd # 100 Woodland Hills (91364) *(P-26801)*
Rustic Canyon Group LLC...D.......310 998-8000
201 Santa Monica Blvd # 500 Santa Monica (90401) *(P-11954)*
Rustic Canyon Partners, Santa Monica *Also called Rustic Canyon Group LLC (P-11954)*
Rutan & Tucker LLP (PA)...B.......714 641-5100
611 Anton Blvd Ste 1400 Costa Mesa (92626) *(P-22799)*
Ruth Barajas...E.......415 977-6949
965 Mission St Ste 520 San Francisco (94103) *(P-23418)*
Rutherford Co Inc (PA)...D.......323 666-5284
2107 Crystal St Los Angeles (90039) *(P-2854)*
Rutland Tool & Supply Co (HQ)...C.......562 566-5000
2225 Workman Mill Rd City of Industry (90601) *(P-7654)*
Rutledge Claims Management Inc...D.......858 883-2000
14286 Danielson St # 103 Poway (92064) *(P-10479)*
Ruuhwa Dann and Associates Inc...D.......909 467-4800
1541 Brooks St Ontario (91762) *(P-6260)*
Rvtlzation Anaheim II Partners...D.......714 520-4041
1515 S Calle Del Mar Anaheim (92802) *(P-11432)*
RW Lynch Co Inc (PA)...D.......925 837-3877
2333 San Ramon Valley Blv San Ramon (94583) *(P-13573)*
RW&g, Los Angeles *Also called Richards Watson & Gershon PC (P-22790)*
Rwc Enterprises Inc...E.......909 373-4100
9130 Santa Anita Ave Rancho Cucamonga (91730) *(P-25291)*
Rwp Transfer Inc...E.......909 868-6882
1313 E Phillips Blvd Pomona (91766) *(P-7833)*
Rwr Homes Inc (PA)...D.......805 413-1792
1014 S Westlake Blvd # 14 Westlake Village (91361) *(P-11597)*
Rx Pro Health LLC...A.......858 369-4050
12400 High Bluff Dr San Diego (92130) *(P-14562)*
Rxsight Inc...E.......949 521-7830
100 Columbia Ste 120 Aliso Viejo (92656) *(P-25824)*
Ryan Herco Flow Solutions, Burbank *Also called Ryan Herco Products Corp (P-7436)*
Ryan Herco Products Corp (HQ)...D.......818 841-1141
3010 N San Fernando Blvd Burbank (91504) *(P-7436)*
Ryan Shroads...E.......310 936-5966
5110 E Washington Blvd Commerce (90040) *(P-17040)*
Ryans Express Trnsp Svcs Inc (PA)...D.......310 219-2960
19500 Mariner Ave Torrance (90503) *(P-3781)*
Ryde Hotel LLC...E.......916 776-1318
14340 State Highway 160 Walnut Grove (95690) *(P-12855)*
Ryde Motel, Walnut Grove *Also called Ryde Hotel LLC (P-12855)*
Ryder Integrated Logistics Inc...E.......818 701-9332
19133 Parthenia St Northridge (91324) *(P-17186)*
Ryder Truck Rental Inc...C.......415 285-0756
2700 3rd St San Francisco (94107) *(P-17187)*
Ryder Truck Rental Inc...D.......562 921-0033
13630 Firestone Blvd Santa Fe Springs (90670) *(P-17188)*
Ryder Truck Rental Inc...D.......909 980-3137
9608 Santa Anita Ave Rancho Cucamonga (91730) *(P-17189)*
Rye Electric Inc...E.......949 441-0545
3940 Electric Ave Laguna Hills (92653) *(P-2624)*
Ryland Hmes Inlnd Empire Cstmr...D.......951 273-3473
1250 Corona Pointe Ct # 100 Corona (92879) *(P-1186)*
Ryland Homes, Carlsbad *Also called Calatlantic Group Inc (P-1290)*
Ryland Homes of Texas Inc...C.......805 367-3800
15360 Barranca Pkwy Irvine (92618) *(P-1316)*
Ryot Corp...D.......323 356-1787
11995 Bluff Creek Dr Playa Vista (90094) *(P-13798)*
S & J, Los Angeles *Also called Sam Jung USA Inc (P-8010)*
S & J Ranches LLC...D.......559 437-2600
39639 Avenue 10 Madera (93636) *(P-536)*
S & M Moving Systems, Santa Fe Springs *Also called Van Torrance & Storage Company (P-4241)*
S & M Moving Systems...D.......510 497-2300
48551 Warm Springs Blvd Fremont (94539) *(P-4121)*
S & P Company (PA)...D.......415 332-0550
100 Shoreline Hwy B395 Mill Valley (94941) *(P-11433)*
S & S Construction Co, Beverly Hills *Also called Shapell Industries LLC (P-11600)*
S & S Construction Services, El Monte *Also called S & S Rent-A-Fence Inc (P-14195)*
S & S Ranch Inc...D.......559 655-3491
904 S Lyon Ave Mendota (93640) *(P-440)*
S & S Rent-A-Fence Inc...D.......818 896-7710
4511 Rowland Ave El Monte (91731) *(P-14195)*
S & S Supplies and Solutions, Fairfield *Also called S & S Tool & Supply Inc (P-7655)*
S & S Tool & Supply Inc (HQ)...D.......925 313-0360
2700 Maxwell Way Fairfield (94534) *(P-7655)*
S A Cali-U Acoustics Inc...D.......805 376-9300
1111 Rnch Conejo Blvd # 501 Thousand Oaks (91320) *(P-2855)*
S A Camp Companies (PA)...E.......661 399-4451
17876 Zerker Rd Bakersfield (93308) *(P-7507)*
S A Camp Pump Company...D.......661 399-2976
17876 Zerker Rd Bakersfield (93308) *(P-17538)*
S A S, Concord *Also called Bay Alarm Company (P-2430)*
S A S, Millbrae *Also called Trans World Maintenance Inc (P-2401)*
S and R Towing Inc (PA)...E.......760 722-6686
1060 Airport Rd Oceanside (92058) *(P-17424)*
S B C, Fresno *Also called AT&T Services Inc (P-5195)*
S B C, Monterey *Also called AT&T Services Inc (P-5332)*
S B C Senior Care Inc...D.......805 560-6995
101 W Anapamu St Ste C Santa Barbara (93101) *(P-21856)*
S B Communications, Hawthorne *Also called South Bay Rgonal Pub Comm Auth (P-5800)*
S B M, McClellan *Also called Sbm Site Services LLC (P-14039)*
S C A, Victorville *Also called Comav Technical Services LLC (P-4763)*
S C A G, Los Angeles *Also called Cal Southern Assn Governments (P-27010)*
S C I R E, Long Beach *Also called Southern California Institute (P-26031)*
S C L, Gardena *Also called Schumacher Cargo Logistics Inc (P-5046)*
S C P M G, Fontana *Also called Southern Cal Prmnnte Med Group (P-21206)*
S C P M G, Colton *Also called Southern Cal Prmnnte Med Group (P-19422)*
S C P M G, El Cajon *Also called Southern Cal Prmnnte Med Group (P-19424)*
S C P M G, Anaheim *Also called Southern Cal Prmnnte Med Group (P-19425)*
S C P M G, San Juan Capistrano *Also called Southern Cal Prmnnte Med Group (P-19426)*
S C P M G, Yorba Linda *Also called Southern Cal Prmnnte Med Group (P-19427)*
S C P M G, Santa Ana *Also called Southern Cal Prmnnte Med Group (P-19428)*
S C P M G, San Diego *Also called Southern Cal Prmnnte Med Group (P-19429)*
S C P M G, Escondido *Also called Southern Cal Prmnnte Med Group (P-19430)*

ALPHABETIC

Employee Codes: A=Over 500 employees, B=251-500
C=101-250, D=51-100, E=50
2020 Directory of California
Wholesalers and Services Companies
© Mergent Inc. 1-800-342-5647
1413

S C P M G, San Dimas *Also called Southern Cal Prmnnte Med Group* **(P-10054)**
S C P M G, Cudahy *Also called Southern Cal Prmnnte Med Group* **(P-19431)**
S C P M G, Woodland Hills *Also called Southern Cal Prmnnte Med Group* **(P-19432)**
S C P M G, Santa Clarita *Also called Southern Cal Prmnnte Med Group* **(P-19433)**
S C S, North Highlands *Also called Security Contractor Svcs Inc* **(P-6726)**
S C Security Inc........E........661 251-6999
26752 Oak Ave Ste C Santa Clarita (91351) **(P-16398)**
S C Tile and Surfaces, El Cajon *Also called S C Tile Company Inc* **(P-2907)**
S C Tile Company Inc........E........619 669-1575
606 S Marshall Ave El Cajon (92020) **(P-2907)**
S C Yamamoto, La Habra *Also called Shinsuke Clifford Yamamoto* **(P-906)**
S D I, Lakeside *Also called Standard Drywall Inc* **(P-2862)**
S D O A, San Diego *Also called San Diego Orthopaedic Associat* **(P-19357)**
S D Property Management Inc........D........323 658-7990
14937 Delano St Van Nuys (91411) **(P-11434)**
S D Y S, San Diego *Also called San Diego Youth Services Inc* **(P-23432)**
S E C C Corporation........D........760 246-6218
16224 Koala Rd Adelanto (92301) **(P-1906)**
S E O P Inc........C........949 682-7906
1621 Alton Pkwy Ste 150 Irvine (92606) **(P-26802)**
S E Pipe Line Construction Co........D........562 868-9771
11832 Bloomfield Ave Santa Fe Springs (90670) **(P-1907)**
S F Auto Parts Whse Inc........D........415 255-0115
6000 3rd St San Francisco (94124) **(P-6466)**
S F Broadcasting of Wisconsin........C........310 586-2410
2425 Olympic Blvd Santa Monica (90404) **(P-5644)**
S G D Enterprises........E........323 658-1047
14937 Delano St Van Nuys (91411) **(P-902)**
S G S Produce, Los Angeles *Also called Shapiro-Gilman-Shandler Co* **(P-8522)**
S H E, Visalia *Also called Self Help Enterprises* **(P-24656)**
S I J Inc........E........951 304-9444
26035 Jefferson Ave Murrieta (92562) **(P-2972)**
S J Amoroso Cnstr Co Inc (PA)........B........650 654-1900
390 Bridge Pkwy Redwood City (94065) **(P-1589)**
S J General Building Maint........D........408 392-0800
919 Berryessa Rd Ste 10 San Jose (95133) **(P-14035)**
S J S Link International Inc (PA)........E........310 860-7666
468 N Camden Dr Ste 311 Beverly Hills (90210) **(P-8301)**
S J W, San Jose *Also called San Jose Water Company* **(P-6112)**
S K & A Information Svcs Inc (HQ)........D........949 476-2051
2601 Main St Ste 650 Irvine (92614) **(P-25942)**
S K S Enterprises Inc (PA)........D........209 599-4095
11830 French Camp Rd Manteca (95336) **(P-412)**
S L H C C Inc........E........916 457-6521
3500 Folsom Blvd Sacramento (95816) **(P-20226)**
S M G, San Francisco *Also called Smg Holdings Inc* **(P-10651)**
S M U D, Sacramento *Also called Sacramento Municpl Utility Dst* **(P-5913)**
S P R E Inc........D........510 222-8340
3223 Blume Dr Richmond (94806) **(P-11435)**
S P Richards Company........D........951 681-3114
10235 San Sevaine Way # 120 Jurupa Valley (91752) **(P-7865)**
S P Thomas Co of Northern Cal (PA)........D........916 786-2040
1201 Plumber Way Ste 112 Roseville (95678) **(P-11598)**
S R H H Inc........E........408 247-0800
1085 E El Camino Real Sunnyvale (94087) **(P-12856)**
S R I C B I........D........650 859-4865
333 Ravenswood Ave Menlo Park (94025) **(P-27197)**
S R J, San Clemente *Also called Julius Steve Construction Inc* **(P-1358)**
S R Mutual Funds, City of Industry *Also called California Country Club* **(P-18412)**
S S 8, Milpitas *Also called Ss8 Networks Inc* **(P-5802)**
S S F, South San Francisco *Also called Ssf Imported Auto Parts LLC* **(P-6472)**
S S I, Oxnard *Also called Synectic Solutions Inc* **(P-16123)**
S S W Mechanical Cnstr Inc........C........760 327-1481
670 S Oleander Rd Palm Springs (92264) **(P-2262)**
S Stamoules Inc........A........559 655-9777
904 S Lyon Ave Mendota (93640) **(P-537)**
S T L, Sacramento *Also called Sacramento Theatrical Ltg Ltd* **(P-17942)**
S Taylor Construction Inc........C........310 291-4505
23905 Clinton Keith Rd Wildomar (92595) **(P-1187)**
S W Construction Inc........C........714 978-7871
1145 E Stanford Ct Anaheim (92805) **(P-2973)**
S W K Properties LLC........D........714 481-6300
2726 S Grand Ave Lbby Santa Ana (92705) **(P-12857)**
S W K Properties LLC (PA)........C........213 383-9204
3807 Wilshire Blvd # 1226 Los Angeles (90010) **(P-12858)**
S W P T X Inc........C........714 564-7900
1682 Langley Ave Irvine (92614) **(P-2391)**
S&B Surgery Center II, Rllng HLS Est *Also called Spalding Srgcl Ctr of Bvrly Hl* **(P-19439)**
S&E Gourmet Cuts Inc........C........909 370-0155
379 Industrial Rd San Bernardino (92408) **(P-8360)**
S&F Management Company Inc........A........209 846-9744
2030 Evergreen Ave Modesto (95350) **(P-20227)**
S&F Management Company LLC........A........310 385-1088
25919 Gading Rd Hayward (94544) **(P-22310)**
S&F Management Company LLC........A........916 922-8855
501 Jessie Ave Sacramento (95838) **(P-23419)**
S&F Management Company LLC........A........209 466-0456
442 E Hampton St Stockton (95204) **(P-20228)**
S&F Management Company LLC (PA)........C........310 385-1090
9200 W Sunset Blvd # 700 West Hollywood (90069) **(P-20229)**
S&J Stadtler Inc........B........925 847-8900
5980 Stoneridge Dr # 122 Pleasanton (94588) **(P-11436)**
S&P Global Inc........C........831 393-6044
1566 Moffett St Salinas (93905) **(P-9847)**
S&W Seed Company (PA)........D........559 884-2535
106 K St Fl 3 Sacramento (95814) **(P-31)**
S.p Richards, Jurupa Valley *Also called S P Richards Company* **(P-7865)**
SA Camp Pump and Drilling Co, Bakersfield *Also called S A Camp Pump Company* **(P-17538)**
SA Photonics Inc........D........408 560-3500
120 Knowles Dr Los Gatos (95032) **(P-27198)**
SA Recycling LLC........D........619 238-6740
3055 Commercial St San Diego (92113) **(P-6261)**
SA Recycling LLC........D........323 564-5601
10313 S Alameda St Los Angeles (90002) **(P-6262)**
SA Recycling LLC........D........714 667-7898
2006 W 5th St Santa Ana (92703) **(P-6263)**
SA Recycling LLC........D........323 875-2520
9754 San Fernando Rd Sun Valley (91352) **(P-6264)**
SA Recycling LLC........D........559 688-0271
2525 S K St Tulare (93274) **(P-6265)**
SA Recycling LLC........D........805 486-7525
521 N Rice Ave Oxnard (93030) **(P-6266)**
SA Recycling LLC........D........626 359-5815
2495 Buena Vista St Duarte (91010) **(P-6267)**
SA Recycling LLC........D........323 723-8327
1540 S Greenwood Ave Montebello (90640) **(P-6268)**
SA Recycling LLC........D........559 237-6677
3489 S Chestnut Ave Fresno (93725) **(P-6269)**
SA Recycling LLC........D........760 391-5591
48100 Harrison St Coachella (92236) **(P-6270)**
SA Recycling LLC........D........626 444-9530
12301 Valley Blvd El Monte (91732) **(P-6271)**
SA Recycling LLC........D........661 327-3559
2000 E Brundage Ln Bakersfield (93307) **(P-6272)**
SA Recycling LLC........D........909 622-3337
11614 Eastend Ave Chino (91710) **(P-6273)**
SA Recycling LLC (PA)........C........714 632-2000
2411 N Glassell St Orange (92865) **(P-6274)**
SA Recycling LLC........D........661 723-1383
42353 8th St E Lancaster (93535) **(P-6275)**
SA Recycling LLC........D........909 825-1662
790 E M St Colton (92324) **(P-6276)**
SA Recycling LLC........D........714 632-2000
3202 Main St San Diego (92113) **(P-6277)**
Sa-Tech, Oxnard *Also called Systems Application & Tech Inc* **(P-25329)**
Saa Sierra Programs LLC........D........530 541-1244
130 Fallen Leaf Rd South Lake Tahoe (96150) **(P-24635)**
Saalex Corp (PA)........C........805 482-1070
811 Camarillo Springs Rd A Camarillo (93012) **(P-25292)**
Saalex Solutions, Camarillo *Also called Saalex Corp* **(P-25292)**
Saama Technologies Inc (PA)........C........408 371-1900
900 E Hamilton Ave # 200 Campbell (95008) **(P-15070)**
Saarman Construction Ltd........C........415 749-2700
683 Mcallister St San Francisco (94102) **(P-1271)**
Saatchi & Saatchi N Amer Inc........C........310 437-2500
13031 W Jefferson Blvd Los Angeles (90094) **(P-13574)**
Saba Software Inc (PA)........D........877 722-2101
4120 Dublin Blvd Ste 200 Dublin (94568) **(P-15489)**
Sabah International Inc (HQ)........D........925 463-0431
5925 Stoneridge Dr Pleasanton (94588) **(P-2625)**
Saban Brands LLC (HQ)........D........310 557-5230
10100 Santa Monica Blvd # 500 Los Angeles (90067) **(P-26803)**
Saban Community Clinic, Los Angeles *Also called Los Angeles Free Clinic* **(P-19168)**
Saban Films LLC........D........310 203-5850
10100 Santa Monica Blvd # 2525 Los Angeles (90067) **(P-17877)**
Saban Research Institute, The, Los Angeles *Also called Childrens Hospital Los Angeles* **(P-25986)**
Saber, Murrieta *Also called South Coast Piering Inc* **(P-1607)**
Saber Plumbing Inc........D........760 480-5716
325 Market Pl Escondido (92029) **(P-2263)**
Sabu Enterprises Inc........E........626 443-1351
5044 Buffington Rd El Monte (91732) **(P-20674)**
Sac Health System (PA)........D........909 382-7100
1455 3rd Ave San Bernardino (92408) **(P-19628)**
Sac International Steel Inc (PA)........D........323 232-2467
6130 Avalon Blvd Los Angeles (90003) **(P-7101)**
Sac River Outfitters........D........530 275-3500
1403 Edgewood Dr Redding (96003) **(P-18749)**
Sac Val Waste Disposal, Sacramento *Also called USA Waste of California Inc* **(P-3947)**
Saccani Distributing Company........D........916 441-0213
2600 5th St Sacramento (95818) **(P-8790)**
Sackett National Holdings Inc........C........866 834-6242
2605 Camino Del Rio S # 400 San Diego (92108) **(P-26804)**
Sacramento 49er, Sacramento *Also called Sacramnto Forty Niner Trvl Plz* **(P-12861)**
Sacramento Area Sewer District (PA)........B........916 876-6000
10060 Goethe Rd Sacramento (95827) **(P-6278)**
Sacramento Childrens Home........D........916 927-5059
1217 Del Paso Blvd Ste B Sacramento (95815) **(P-24055)**
Sacramento Childrens Home (PA)........C........916 452-3981
2750 Sutterville Rd Sacramento (95820) **(P-24056)**
Sacramento Chinese Community S........C........916 442-4228
420 I St Ste 5 Sacramento (95814) **(P-23420)**
Sacramento County Off Educatn........E........916 875-0300
9750 Bus Park Dr Ste 220 Sacramento (95827) **(P-23421)**
Sacramento County Water Agency........D........916 874-6851
827 7th St Ste 301 Sacramento (95814) **(P-6104)**
Sacramento Credit Union (PA)........D........916 444-6070
800 H St Ste 100 Sacramento (95814) **(P-9403)**
Sacramento Cy Unified Schl Dst (PA)........B........916 643-7400
5735 47th Ave Sacramento (95824) **(P-24636)**
Sacramento District Office, Sacramento *Also called State Compensation Insur Fund* **(P-10141)**
Sacramento Div, West Sacramento *Also called Quad/Graphics Inc* **(P-13563)**
Sacramento Ear Nose & Throat (PA)........D........916 736-3399
1111 Expo Blvd Bldg 700 Sacramento (95815) **(P-19347)**

Mergent e-mail: customerrelations@mergent.com
1414
2020 Directory of California
Wholesalers and Services Companies
(P-0000) Products & Services Section entry number
(PA)=Parent Co (HQ)=Headquarters (DH)=Div Headquarters

Sacramento Employement & Train ....C....916 263-3800
925 Del Paso Blvd Ste 100 Sacramento (95815) *(P-23632)*
Sacramento Employement & Train (PA) ....C....916 263-3800
925 Del Paso Blvd Ste 100 Sacramento (95815) *(P-23633)*
Sacramento Harness Association ....D....916 239-4040
1600 Exposition Blvd Sacramento (95815) *(P-24358)*
Sacramento Heart and Cardiovas (PA) ....D....916 830-2000
500 University Ave # 100 Sacramento (95825) *(P-19348)*
Sacramento Hotel Partners LLC ....D....916 326-5000
100 Capitol Mall Sacramento (95814) *(P-12859)*
Sacramento Hotel Partners LLC (PA) ....D....408 249-2500
100 Saratoga Ave Ste 300 Santa Clara (95051) *(P-12860)*
Sacramento Kenworth, Sacramento *Also called Ssmb Pacific Holding Co Inc (P-6411)*
Sacramento Loaves & Fishes (PA) ....D....916 446-0874
1351 N C St Ste 22 Sacramento (95811) *(P-23422)*
Sacramento Mental Hlth Clinic, Mather *Also called Veterans Health Administration (P-19558)*
Sacramento Municpl Utility Dst (PA) ....A....916 452-3211
6201 S St Sacramento (95817) *(P-5913)*
Sacramento Municpl Utility Dst ....A....916 452-3211
6201 S St Sacramento (95817) *(P-5914)*
Sacramento Municpl Utility Dst ....A....916 452-3211
6201 S St Sacramento (95817) *(P-17356)*
Sacramento Municpl Utility Dst ....D....916 732-5155
6301 S St Sacramento (95817) *(P-5915)*
Sacramento Municpl Utility Dst ....B....916 732-5616
6201 S St Sacramento (95817) *(P-5916)*
Sacramento Operating Co LP ....C....916 422-4825
7400 24th St Sacramento (95822) *(P-20230)*
Sacramento Packing Inc ....B....530 671-4488
833 Tudor Rd Yuba City (95991) *(P-215)*
Sacramento Post-Acute, Sacramento *Also called Oleander Holdings LLC (P-20175)*
Sacramento Prestige Gunite Inc ....E....916 723-0404
8634 Antelope North Rd Antelope (95843) *(P-3211)*
Sacramento Reg Co Sanit Dist (PA) ....A....916 876-6000
10060 Goethe Rd Sacramento (95827) *(P-6355)*
Sacramento Reg Co Sanit Dist ....B....916 875-9000
8521 Laguna Station Rd Elk Grove (95758) *(P-6135)*
Sacramento Regional Trnst Dist (PA) ....A....916 726-2877
1400 29th St Sacramento (95816) *(P-3580)*
Sacramento Regional Trnst Dist ....C....916 321-2800
1400 29th St Sacramento (95816) *(P-3581)*
Sacramento Regional Trnst Dist ....C....916 869-8611
2700 Academy Way Sacramento (95815) *(P-3832)*
Sacramento River Cats Baseball ....E....916 376-4700
400 Ball Park Dr West Sacramento (95691) *(P-18077)*
Sacramento Suburban Water Dst ....D....916 972-7171
3701 Marconi Ave Ste 100 Sacramento (95821) *(P-6105)*
Sacramento Suburban Water Dst ....D....916 972-7171
3701 Marconi Ave Ste 100 Sacramento (95821) *(P-6106)*
Sacramento Television Stns Inc (HQ) ....C....916 374-1452
2713 Kovr Dr West Sacramento (95605) *(P-5645)*
Sacramento Theatrical Ltg Ltd ....D....916 447-3258
950 Richards Blvd Sacramento (95811) *(P-17942)*
Sacramento V A Medical Center, Mather *Also called Veterans Health Administration (P-19571)*
Sacramento Valley Region 2, Gold River *Also called California Dept Fish Wildlife (P-13145)*
Sacramento Yolo Cnty Mosquito ....D....916 685-1022
8631 Bond Rd Elk Grove (95624) *(P-6356)*
Sacramento Zoological Society ....E....916 808-5888
3930 W Land Park Dr Sacramento (95822) *(P-24314)*
Sacramento-Yolo Port District ....C....916 371-8000
1110 W Capitol Ave West Sacramento (95691) *(P-4619)*
Sacramnto Forty Niner Trvl Plz ....C....916 927-4774
2828 El Centro Rd Sacramento (95833) *(P-12861)*
Sacramnto Mtro A Qulty MGT Dst ....D....916 874-4800
777 12th St Ste 300 Sacramento (95814) *(P-27199)*
Sacramnto Ntiv Amercn Hlth Ctr ....C....916 341-0575
2020 J St Sacramento (95811) *(P-19349)*
Sacromento Eductn Readng Lions ....E....916 228-2219
10461 Old Plza Vlle 130 Sacramento (95827) *(P-24637)*
Sada Systems Inc ....C....818 766-2400
5250 Lankershim Blvd # 620 North Hollywood (91601) *(P-16098)*
Sadaf Foods, Vernon *Also called Soofer Co Inc (P-8645)*
Saddle Back Valley YMCA, Mission Viejo *Also called Young Mens Chrstn Assn Orange (P-24759)*
Saddle Corp (PA) ....D....949 589-3422
23531 Ridge Route Dr C Laguna Hills (92653) *(P-3462)*
Saddleback Dialysis, Laguna Hills *Also called Dva Renal Healthcare Inc (P-21921)*
Saddleback Mem Med Lab Svcs, Laguna Hills *Also called Saddleback Memorial Med Ctr (P-21581)*
Saddleback Memorial Hospital, San Clemente *Also called San Clemente Medical Ctr LLC (P-21153)*
Saddleback Memorial Med Ctr (HQ) ....A....949 837-4500
24451 Health Center Dr # 1 Laguna Hills (92653) *(P-21141)*
Saddleback Memorial Med Ctr ....C....949 452-3405
24411 Health Center Dr Laguna Hills (92653) *(P-21581)*
Saddleback Valley Service Ctr, Irvine *Also called Southern California Edison Co (P-5945)*
Saddleback Vly ....D....949 586-1234
25631 Peter A Hartman Way Mission Viejo (92691) *(P-18551)*
Saddleback Waterproofing, Laguna Hills *Also called Saddle Corp (P-3462)*
Saddlemen, Compton *Also called Bst Enterprises Inc (P-6427)*
Sadie Rose Baking Co ....D....619 718-9532
2614 Temple Heights Dr Oceanside (92056) *(P-8641)*
Saehan Bank (PA) ....E....213 368-7700
3200 Wilshire Blvd # 700 Los Angeles (90010) *(P-9236)*
Safari Harvstg & Farming LLC ....B....805 925-2600
313 Plaza Dr Ste B12 Santa Maria (93454) *(P-357)*
Safe America Credit Union (PA) ....D....925 734-4111
6001 Gibraltar Dr Pleasanton (94588) *(P-9340)*
Safe Credit Union (PA) ....C....916 979-7233
2295 Iron Point Rd # 100 Folsom (95630) *(P-9404)*
Safe Credit Union ....E....916 979-7233
9055 Woodcreek Oaks Blvd # 150 Roseville (95747) *(P-9341)*
Safe Harbor Intl Relief ....E....949 858-6786
30615 Avnida De Las Flres Rancho Santa Margari (92688) *(P-24221)*
Safe Harbor Treatment Cen ....E....949 645-1026
1040 W 17th St Costa Mesa (92627) *(P-22114)*
Safe Refuge ....D....562 987-5722
1041 Redondo Ave Long Beach (90804) *(P-24057)*
Safe Security Inc ....B....925 830-4777
2440 Camino Ramon Ste 200 San Ramon (94583) *(P-16555)*
Safe-Guard Products Intl LLC ....D....800 742-7896
18100 Von Karman Ave # 150 Irvine (92612) *(P-10480)*
Safeco Door & Hardware Inc ....D....510 429-4768
31054 San Antonio St Hayward (94544) *(P-3298)*
Safeco Glass, Hayward *Also called Safeco Door & Hardware Inc (P-3298)*
Safeco Insurance Company Amer ....C....818 956-4250
330 N Brand Blvd Ste 680 Glendale (91203) *(P-10481)*
Safeguard Business Systems Inc ....C....805 486-9769
414 N A St Oxnard (93030) *(P-7866)*
Safeguard Health Entps Inc (HQ) ....B....800 880-1800
95 Enterprise Ste 100 Aliso Viejo (92656) *(P-10040)*
Safelite Autoglass, Sacramento *Also called Safelite Fulfillment Inc (P-17320)*
Safelite Fulfillment Inc ....D....916 442-4715
261 Richards Blvd Sacramento (95811) *(P-17320)*
Safely Home ....D....909 370-0343
461 Tennessee St Ste O Redlands (92373) *(P-21857)*
Safeop Surgical Inc ....D....760 494-6752
5818 El Camino Real Carlsbad (92008) *(P-21142)*
Safety Dynamics, Oakland *Also called Intelliguard Security Services (P-16323)*
Safety Security Patrol LLC ....D....909 888-7778
560 N Arrowhead Ave 3b San Bernardino (92401) *(P-16399)*
Safeway Stores Incorporated ....D....408 719-9460
750 Walsh Ave Santa Clara (95050) *(P-1590)*
Safeway Stores Incorporated ....B....209 833-4700
16900 W Schulte Rd Tracy (95377) *(P-4497)*
Safran, Anaheim *Also called Morphotrak LLC (P-15648)*
Safway Services LP ....E....650 652-9255
1660 Gilbreth Rd Burlingame (94010) *(P-7491)*
Safway Services LP ....E....707 745-2000
4072b Teal Ct Benicia (94510) *(P-7492)*
Sag- Aftra Federal ....D....818 562-3400
134 N Kenwood St Burbank (91505) *(P-9342)*
Sag-Aftra Foundation ....E....323 549-6708
5757 Wilshire Blvd Ph 1 Los Angeles (90036) *(P-24457)*
Saga Seal Co Ltd ....D....562 493-7501
600 Marina Dr Seal Beach (90740) *(P-12862)*
Sagan Systems Inc ....D....650 387-8485
201 California St # 1300 San Francisco (94111) *(P-15071)*
Sage Behavior Services Inc ....D....714 773-0077
505 E Commonwealth Ave Fullerton (92832) *(P-21424)*
Sage Electric Company ....D....818 718-9080
9144 Owensmouth Ave Chatsworth (91311) *(P-2626)*
Sage Group ....D....415 512-8200
33 Falmouth St San Francisco (94107) *(P-14409)*
Sage Hospitality Resources LLC ....D....626 357-5211
700 W Huntington Dr Monrovia (91016) *(P-12863)*
Sage Hospitality Resources LLC ....D....650 589-1600
2000 Shoreline Ct Brisbane (94005) *(P-12864)*
Sage Intacct Inc (HQ) ....E....408 878-0900
300 Park Ave Ste 1400 San Jose (95110) *(P-16099)*
Sage Software Inc ....D....949 753-1222
7595 Irvine Center Dr # 200 Irvine (92618) *(P-15885)*
Sage Software Inc ....C....650 579-3628
1380 Tatan Trail Rd Burlingame (94010) *(P-15490)*
Sage Software Holdings Inc (HQ) ....B....866 530-7243
6561 Irvine Center Dr Irvine (92618) *(P-15491)*
Sage Staffing Consultants Inc (PA) ....C....661 254-4026
27441 Tourney Rd Ste 150 Valencia (91355) *(P-14563)*
Sagepoint Financial Inc ....B....949 756-1462
3723 Birch St Ste 9 Newport Beach (92660) *(P-9848)*
Sahara, Artesia *Also called South Asian Help Referral Agcy (P-23471)*
Saia Inc ....C....916 483-8331
1508 Wyant Way Sacramento (95864) *(P-4122)*
Saia Motor Freight Line LLC ....E....916 690-8417
9119 Elkmont Dr Elk Grove (95624) *(P-4123)*
Saia Motor Freight Line LLC ....D....323 277-2880
2550 E 28th St Vernon (90058) *(P-4124)*
Saia Motor Freight Line LLC ....D....510 347-6890
1755 Aurora Dr San Leandro (94577) *(P-4125)*
Saia S Reno Barbara K, Sacramento *Also called Saia Inc (P-4122)*
Saic, San Diego *Also called Leidos Inc (P-25783)*
Saic, San Diego *Also called Science Applications Intl Corp (P-15687)*
Saic, Oakland *Also called Leidos Inc (P-25792)*
Saic Government Solutions, San Diego *Also called Science Applications Intl Corp (P-16102)*
Saiful/Bouquet Con Stru Eng (PA) ....D....626 304-2616
155 N Lake Ave Fl 6 Pasadena (91101) *(P-25293)*
Sailgp, San Francisco *Also called F50 League LLC (P-24829)*
Saint Agnes HM Hlth & Hospice, Fresno *Also called Trinity Home Health Svcs Inc (P-21887)*
Saint Agnes Med Providers Inc ....D....559 435-2630
1379 E Herndon Ave Fresno (93720) *(P-22311)*
Saint Agnes Medical Center (HQ) ....A....559 450-3000
1303 E Herndon Ave Fresno (93720) *(P-21143)*
Saint Baldricks Foundation, Simi Valley *Also called Vickie Lobello (P-24883)*

ALPHABETIC

Employee Codes: A=Over 500 employees, B=251-500
C=101-250, D=51-100, E=50
2020 Directory of California
Wholesalers and Services Companies
© Mergent Inc. 1-800-342-5647
1415

SAINT BARNABAS SENIOR SERVICES, Los Angeles *Also called St Barnbas Snior Ctr Los Angle* ***(P-23482)***
Saint Claires Nursing Ctr LLC ....C....916 392-4440
6248 66th Ave Sacramento (95823) ***(P-20231)***
Saint Helena Hosp Clearlake, Clearlake *Also called Adventist Health Clearlake* ***(P-20729)***
Saint Jhns Hlth Ctr Foundation ....C....310 315-6111
2200 Santa Monica Blvd Santa Monica (90404) ***(P-19350)***
Saint Jhns Hlth Ctr Foundation ....D....310 829-5511
2121 Santa Monica Blvd Santa Monica (90404) ***(P-23780)***
Saint Jhns Hlth Ctr Foundation ....B....310 829-8970
2020 Santa Monica Blvd 3rdfl3 Santa Monica (90404) ***(P-21144)***
SAINT JOHN'S WELL CHILD CENTER, Los Angeles *Also called St Johns Well Child* ***(P-19632)***
Saint Johns Child Fmly Dev Ctr, Santa Monica *Also called Saint Jhns Hlth Ctr Foundation* ***(P-23780)***
SAINT JOSEPH CENTER VOLUNTEER, Venice *Also called St Joseph Center* ***(P-23483)***
Saint Joseph Hlth Sys HM Hlth, Anaheim *Also called St Joseph Home Health Network* ***(P-21874)***
Saint Joseph Hlth Sys Hospice, Anaheim *Also called St Joseph Hospice* ***(P-23484)***
Saint Joseph Home Care Network ....D....707 206-9124
1165 Montgomery Dr Santa Rosa (95405) ***(P-24058)***
Saint Justin Education Fu ....D....323 221-3400
2415 Shoredale Ave Los Angeles (90031) ***(P-24222)***
Saint Louise Hospital ....B....408 848-2000
9400 N Name Uno Gilroy (95020) ***(P-21145)***
Saint Mary Medical Center, Long Beach *Also called Dignity Health* ***(P-20838)***
Saint Nicolas Vineyard, Soledad *Also called Kvl Holdings Inc* ***(P-142)***
Saint-Joseph Home Health ....E....408 244-5488
1525 Mccarthy Blvd # 208 Milpitas (95035) ***(P-22312)***
Sajahtera Inc ....A....310 276-2251
9641 Sunset Blvd Beverly Hills (90210) ***(P-12865)***
Sakata Seed America Inc (HQ) ....D....408 778-7758
18095 Serene Dr Morgan Hill (95037) ***(P-8856)***
Sakura Finetek USA Inc (HQ) ....C....310 972-7800
1750 W 214th St Torrance (90501) ***(P-7001)***
Salad Time Farms, Baldwin Park *Also called Tanimura & Antle Inc* ***(P-551)***
Saladinos Inc (PA) ....C....559 271-3700
3325 W Figarden Dr Fresno (93711) ***(P-8215)***
Salas OBrien Engineers Inc (PA) ....E....408 282-1500
305 S 11th St San Jose (95112) ***(P-25294)***
Salazar Labor Contracting ....D....760 746-0805
957 Sugarloaf Dr Escondido (92026) ***(P-645)***
Salem Christian Homes Inc (PA) ....C....909 614-0575
6921 Edison Ave Ste A Chino (91710) ***(P-24059)***
Salem Media Group Inc (PA) ....C....805 987-0400
4880 Santa Rosa Rd Camarillo (93012) ***(P-5563)***
Salem Media Group Inc ....D....818 956-5254
701 N Brand Blvd Ste 550 Glendale (91203) ***(P-5564)***
Salesforcecom Inc (PA) ....A....415 901-7000
415 Mission St Fl 3 San Francisco (94105) ***(P-15492)***
Salesforcecom/Foundation ....C....800 667-6389
The Landmark One St The Landma San Francisco (94105) ***(P-23423)***
Salesian Boys and Girls Club ....D....415 397-3068
680 Filbert St San Francisco (94133) ***(P-24638)***
Salient Global Technologies, Pittsburg *Also called Ravig Inc* ***(P-6890)***
Salinas Disposal Service, Hayward *Also called USA Waste of California Inc* ***(P-6301)***
Salinas Disposal Service, Salinas *Also called USA Waste of California Inc* ***(P-6310)***
Salinas Med Mngt Srvcs Org Inc ....D....831 751-7070
355 Abbott St Ste 100 Salinas (93901) ***(P-19351)***
Salinas Urgent Care, Salinas *Also called Salinas Valley Memorial Hlthca* ***(P-21149)***
Salinas Valley Medical Clinic ....B....831 424-7389
236 San Jose St Salinas (93901) ***(P-19352)***
Salinas Valley Memorial Hlthca ....B....831 759-3236
440 E Romie Ln Salinas (93901) ***(P-21146)***
Salinas Valley Memorial Hlthca ....B....831 884-5048
5 Lower Ragsdle Dr 102 Monterey (93940) ***(P-21147)***
Salinas Valley Memorial Hlthca (PA) ....D....831 757-4333
450 E Romie Ln Salinas (93901) ***(P-21148)***
Salinas Valley Memorial Hlthca ....B....831 757-3041
611 Abbott St Ste 101 Salinas (93901) ***(P-21491)***
Salinas Valley Memorial Hlthca ....B....831 755-7880
558 Abbott St Salinas (93901) ***(P-21149)***
Salinas Valley Memorial Hosp, Salinas *Also called Salinas Valley Memorial Hlthca* ***(P-21148)***
Salinas Valley Prime Care Med, Salinas *Also called Salinas Med Mngt Srvcs Org Inc* ***(P-19351)***
Salomon Smith Barney, El Segundo *Also called Citigroup Global Markets Inc* ***(P-9668)***
Salomon Smith Barney, Sacramento *Also called Citigroup Global Markets Inc* ***(P-9669)***
Salomon Smith Barney, Fresno *Also called Citigroup Global Markets Inc* ***(P-9674)***
Salon Lujon Inc ....D....714 738-1882
216 N Harbor Blvd Fullerton (92832) ***(P-13358)***
Salon Media Group Inc (PA) ....D....415 870-7566
870 Market St Ste 442 San Francisco (94102) ***(P-15886)***
Salon-Salon ....D....209 571-3500
1700 Mchenry Ave Ste 29 Modesto (95350) ***(P-13359)***
Salson Logistics Inc ....C....310 328-6800
1331 Torrance Blvd Torrance (90501) ***(P-5138)***
Salt Catering, Los Angeles *Also called Salt of Earth Productions Inc* ***(P-17041)***
Salt Lake Hotel Associates LP (PA) ....C....415 397-5572
222 Kearny St Ste 200 San Francisco (94108) ***(P-12866)***
Salt of Earth Productions Inc ....C....818 399-1860
1437 S Robertson Blvd Los Angeles (90035) ***(P-17041)***
Saltzburg Ray & Bergman LLP ....C....310 481-6700
12121 Wilshire Blvd # 600 Los Angeles (90025) ***(P-22800)***
Salu Beauty Inc ....D....916 475-1400
11344 Coloma Rd Ste 725 Gold River (95670) ***(P-24422)***
Salu.net, Gold River *Also called Salu Beauty Inc* ***(P-24422)***
Salud Para La Gente ....C....831 728-0222
195 Aviation Way Ste 200 Watsonville (95076) ***(P-19353)***
Salud Para La Gnte Hlth Clinic, Watsonville *Also called Salud Para La Gente* ***(P-19353)***
SALUS HOME HEALTH, Artesia *Also called Aspen Healthcare Corporation* ***(P-21673)***
Salutary Sports Clubs Inc ....E....530 677-5705
4242 Sports Club Dr Shingle Springs (95682) ***(P-18189)***
Salvador Martinez ....C....559 781-5150
2049 N Newcomb St Porterville (93257) ***(P-646)***
Salvation Army ....E....323 263-1206
8538 Bennett Ave Fontana (92335) ***(P-24860)***
Salvation Army ....D....213 553-3273
900 James M Wood Blvd Los Angeles (90015) ***(P-23424)***
Salvation Army ....D....916 441-5137
1615 D St Sacramento (95814) ***(P-23425)***
Salvation Army (HQ) ....C....562 491-8496
30840 Hawthorne Blvd Rancho Palos Verdes (90275) ***(P-23426)***
Salvation Army ....E....213 484-0772
2737 W Sunset Blvd Los Angeles (90026) ***(P-23427)***
Salvation Army ....D....209 466-3871
1247 S Wilson Way Stockton (95205) ***(P-22115)***
Salvation Army ....D....909 889-9605
363 S Doolittle Ave San Bernardino (92408) ***(P-22116)***
Salvation Army ....D....858 279-1100
2799 Health Center Dr San Diego (92123) ***(P-24060)***
Salvation Army ....D....415 643-8000
154 Oshaughnessy Blvd San Francisco (94127) ***(P-24061)***
Salvation Army Glden State Div (PA) ....D....415 553-3500
832 Folsom St Fl 6 San Francisco (94107) ***(P-23428)***
Salvation Army Ray & Joan ....B....619 287-5762
6845 University Ave San Diego (92115) ***(P-18190)***
Sam Hill & Sons Inc ....E....805 620-0828
2627 Beene Rd Ventura (93003) ***(P-1908)***
Sam Jung USA Inc ....D....323 231-0811
843 E 31st St Los Angeles (90011) ***(P-8010)***
Sam Trans, South San Francisco *Also called San Mateo County Transit Dst* ***(P-3598)***
Sam Trans, San Carlos *Also called San Mateo County Transit Dst* ***(P-3833)***
Samaritan Imaging Center ....A....213 977-2140
1245 Wilshire Blvd # 205 Los Angeles (90017) ***(P-21582)***
Samaritan Village Inc ....C....209 883-3212
7700 Fox Rd Hughson (95326) ***(P-23429)***
Samarkand Retirement Community, Santa Barbara *Also called Evangelical Covenant Church* ***(P-23923)***
Samba TV, San Francisco *Also called Free Stream Media Corp* ***(P-8973)***
Sambazon Inc (PA) ....D....877 726-2296
209 Avenida Fabricante # 200 San Clemente (92672) ***(P-8518)***
Sambreel Services LLC ....E....760 266-5090
5857 Owens Ave Ste 300 Carlsbad (92008) ***(P-15072)***
Same Swim LLC ....D....323 582-2588
2333 E 49th St Vernon (90058) ***(P-8108)***
Samedan Oil Corporation ....B....661 319-5038
1360 Landing Ave Seal Beach (90740) ***(P-991)***
Samiyatex, Los Angeles *Also called Paragon Textiles Inc* ***(P-8106)***
Sample Tile and Stone Inc ....D....951 776-8562
1410 Richardson St San Bernardino (92408) ***(P-2908)***
Samsung Electronics Amer Inc ....D....310 537-7000
18600 S Broadwick St Rancho Dominguez (90220) ***(P-7217)***
Samsung Electronics Amer Inc ....A....650 210-1000
665 Clyde Ave Mountain View (94043) ***(P-7335)***
Samsung International Inc (HQ) ....E....619 671-6859
333 H St Ste 6000 Chula Vista (91910) ***(P-7336)***
Samsung Research America Inc (HQ) ....E....408 544-5700
665 Clyde Ave Mountain View (94043) ***(P-25825)***
Samsung SDS America Inc ....D....408 638-8800
2665 N 1st St Ste 110 San Jose (95134) ***(P-15073)***
Samsung Semiconductor Inc (HQ) ....C....408 544-4000
3655 N 1st St San Jose (95134) ***(P-7337)***
Samuel Son & Co (usa) Inc ....E....323 722-0300
12389 Lower Azusa Rd Arcadia (91006) ***(P-7102)***
Samuel J Piazza & Son Inc (PA) ....D....323 357-1999
9001 Rayo Ave South Gate (90280) ***(P-4229)***
Samy Co, Cypress *Also called Hoyu America Co* ***(P-7951)***
San Andreas Regional Center (PA) ....C....408 374-9960
6203 San Ignacio Ave # 110 San Jose (95119) ***(P-23430)***
SAN ANTONIO COMMUNITY HOSPITAL, Rancho Cucamonga *Also called Assistnce Leag of Fthill Cmmnt* ***(P-24134)***
San Antonio Community Hospital ....E....909 948-8000
7777 Milliken Ave Ste A Rancho Cucamonga (91730) ***(P-21150)***
San Antonio Regional Hospital (PA) ....A....909 985-2811
999 San Bernardino Rd Upland (91786) ***(P-21151)***
San Benito Health Care Dst (PA) ....B....831 637-5711
911 Sunset Dr Ste A Hollister (95023) ***(P-21152)***
San Benito Htg & Shtmtl Inc ....D....831 637-1112
1771 San Felipe Rd Hollister (95023) ***(P-2264)***
San Bernabe Vineyards ....D....831 385-4897
53001 Oasis Rd King City (93930) ***(P-159)***
San Bernardino California City (PA) ....B....909 384-7272
290 N D St San Bernardino (92401) ***(P-22801)***
San Bernardino California City ....D....909 384-5111
300 N D St Fl 3 San Bernardino (92418) ***(P-24359)***
San Bernardino Care Company ....C....909 884-4781
467 E Gilbert St San Bernardino (92404) ***(P-20675)***
San Bernardino City Unf School ....D....909 388-6137
871 N J St San Bernardino (92411) ***(P-4498)***
San Bernardino City Unf School ....C....909 388-6100
956 W 9th St San Bernardino (92411) ***(P-14036)***
San Bernardino City Unf School ....D....909 388-6307
303 S K St San Bernardino (92410) ***(P-23781)***
San Bernardino City Unf School ....D....909 881-8000
1257 Northpark Blvd San Bernardino (92407) ***(P-22313)***

Mergent e-mail: customerrelations@mergent.com
1416
2020 Directory of California
Wholesalers and Services Companies
(P-0000) Products & Services Section entry number
(PA)=Parent Co (HQ)=Headquarters (DH)=Div Headquarters

San Bernardino Family YMCA, San Bernardino *Also called YMCA of East Valley (P-24702)*
San Bernardino Golf Club, San Bernardino *Also called J G Golfing Enterprises Inc (P-18257)*
San Bernardino Hilton (HQ)...C...909 889-0133
285 E Hospitality Ln San Bernardino (92408) ***(P-12867)***
San Bernardino Med Group Inc (PA)...C...909 883-8611
1700 N Waterman Ave San Bernardino (92404) ***(P-19354)***
San Bernardino Mtns Wildlife...E...909 226-6189
29450 Pine Ridge Dr Cedar Glen (92321) ***(P-423)***
San Bernardino Parole Unit 14, San Bernardino *Also called Correctons Rhbltation Cal Dept (P-23052)*
San Bernardino Symphony...D...909 381-5388
198 N Arrowhead Ave 2b San Bernardino (92408) ***(P-17999)***
San Brnrdino Pub Employees Assn...E...909 386-1260
433 N Sierra Way San Bernardino (92410) ***(P-24458)***
San Clemente Medical Ctr LLC...B...949 496-1122
654 Camino De Los Mares San Clemente (92673) ***(P-21153)***
San Clemente Villas By Sea...D...949 489-3400
660 Camino De Los Mares San Clemente (92673) ***(P-24062)***
San Dego Cnty Rgnal Arprt Auth (PA)...D...619 400-2400
3225 N Harbor Dr Fl 3 San Diego (92101) ***(P-4789)***
San Dego Cnty Rgnal Arprt Auth...C...619 400-2404
2320 Stillwater Rd San Diego (92101) ***(P-4790)***
San Dego Cnvntion Ctr Corp Inc (PA)...D...619 525-5000
111 W Harbor Dr San Diego (92101) ***(P-10639)***
San Dego Mission Vly Hilton Ht, San Diego *Also called Kalpana LLC (P-12499)*
San Dego Mrrott Marquis Marina...E...301 380-3000
333 W Harbor Dr San Diego (92101) ***(P-12868)***
San Dego Ntural History Museum, San Diego *Also called San Dego Soc of Ntural History (P-24284)*
San Dego Soc of Ntural History...D...619 232-3821
1788 El Prado San Diego (92101) ***(P-24284)***
San Diego Aerospace Museum...D...619 258-1221
335 Kenney St El Cajon (92020) ***(P-24285)***
San Diego Arcft Carier Museum...C...619 544-9600
910 N Harbor Dr San Diego (92101) ***(P-24286)***
San Diego Assn Governments (PA)...B...619 699-1900
401 B St Ste 800 San Diego (92101) ***(P-24360)***
San Diego Bay Area Elc Inc...D...858 748-2060
13100 Kirkham Way Ste 205 Poway (92064) ***(P-2627)***
San Diego Blood Bank (PA)...C...619 296-6393
3636 Gtwy Ctr Ave Ste 100 San Diego (92102) ***(P-22314)***
San Diego Blood Bnk Foundation, San Diego *Also called San Diego Blood Bank (P-22314)*
San Diego Car Accident Lawyers...E...858 201-4178
Maple St San Diego (92104) ***(P-22802)***
San Diego Cemetery Assn...D...858 453-2121
5600 Carroll Canyon Rd San Diego (92121) ***(P-13378)***
San Diego Center For Children (PA)...D...858 277-9550
3002 Armstrong St San Diego (92111) ***(P-20676)***
San Diego Choices, San Diego *Also called Telecare Corporation (P-21438)*
San Diego CLD Stg 4140, National City *Also called US Foods Inc (P-8670)*
San Diego Coastl Med Group Inc...C...760 901-5259
2201 Mission Ave Oceanside (92058) ***(P-22315)***
San Diego Community Hsing Corp...C...619 527-4633
230 Catania St San Diego (92113) ***(P-27200)***
San Diego Composites Inc...D...858 751-0450
9220 Activity Rd Ste 100 San Diego (92126) ***(P-25295)***
San Diego Correctional Fcilty, San Diego *Also called Corecivic Inc (P-26936)*
San Diego Country Club Inc...D...619 422-8895
88 L St Chula Vista (91911) ***(P-18552)***
San Diego Country Estates Assn...C...760 789-3788
24157 San Vicente Rd Ramona (92065) ***(P-24639)***
San Diego County Credit Union (PA)...C...877 732-2848
6545 Sequence Dr San Diego (92121) ***(P-9343)***
San Diego County Employees Ret...D...619 515-6800
2275 Rio Bonito Way # 100 San Diego (92108) ***(P-24459)***
San Diego County Water Auth (PA)...B...858 522-6600
4677 Overland Ave San Diego (92123) ***(P-6107)***
San Diego County Water Auth...D...760 480-1991
610 W 5th Ave Escondido (92025) ***(P-6108)***
San Diego District Office, San Diego *Also called State Compensation Insur Fund (P-10135)*
San Diego Family Care (PA)...D...858 279-0925
6973 Linda Vista Rd San Diego (92111) ***(P-19355)***
San Diego Family Care...C...619 563-0250
4290 Polk Ave San Diego (92105) ***(P-22316)***
San Diego Farah Partners...E...619 239-2261
1430 7th Ave Ste B San Diego (92101) ***(P-12869)***
San Diego Fish Market, San Diego *Also called Top of Market (P-26426)*
San Diego Gas & Electric Co (HQ)...C...619 696-2000
8326 Century Park Ct San Diego (92123) ***(P-5997)***
San Diego Gas & Electric Co...C...800 411-7343
990 Bay Blvd Chula Vista (91911) ***(P-5965)***
San Diego Gas & Electric Co...E...949 361-8090
662 Camino De Los Mares San Clemente (92673) ***(P-5998)***
San Diego Gas & Electric Co...C...760 438-6200
5016 Carlsbad Blvd Carlsbad (92008) ***(P-6012)***
San Diego Gas & Electric Co...C...619 699-1018
701 33rd St San Diego (92102) ***(P-5917)***
San Diego Gulls Hockey CLB LLC...D...619 359-4700
7676 Hazard Center Dr San Diego (92108) ***(P-18750)***
San Diego Harbor Excursion, Coronado *Also called Star & Crescent Boat Company (P-4608)*
San Diego Hbr Excursions Inc...D...619 234-4111
1050 N Harbor Dr San Diego (92101) ***(P-1988)***
San Diego Hebrew Homes (PA)...C...760 942-2695
211 Saxony Rd Encinitas (92024) ***(P-20232)***
San Diego Hospice...A...619 688-1600
2400 Historic Decatur Rd # 107 San Diego (92106) ***(P-21858)***
San Diego Hospice & Institute, San Diego *Also called San Diego Hospice (P-21858)*
San Diego Hotel Company LLC...C...619 696-0234
660 K St San Diego (92101) ***(P-12870)***
San Diego Hotel Lease LLC...C...619 446-3000
530 Broadway San Diego (92101) ***(P-12871)***
San Diego Humane Soc & Spca...D...619 299-7012
5500 Gaines St San Diego (92110) ***(P-24861)***
San Diego Imaging - Chula Vist (PA)...D...858 565-0950
8745 Aero Dr Ste 200 San Diego (92123) ***(P-19356)***
San Diego Land Systems...E...858 558-0542
8720 Miramar Pl San Diego (92121) ***(P-757)***
San Diego Lesbian Gay Bisexu...E...619 692-2077
3909 Centre St San Diego (92103) ***(P-23431)***
San Diego Lessee LLC...C...619 297-5466
7450 Hazard Center Dr San Diego (92108) ***(P-12872)***
San Diego Marriott Mission Vly, San Diego *Also called Ws Mmv Hotel LLC (P-13117)*
San Diego Med Svcs Entp LLC...B...619 280-6060
10405 Sn Diego Mn Rd 20 San Diego (92108) ***(P-3719)***
San Diego Messenger Inc...E...858 514-8866
4848 Ronson Ct Ste G San Diego (92111) ***(P-4279)***
San Diego Metro Trnst Sys...A...619 231-1466
1255 Imperial Ave # 1000 San Diego (92101) ***(P-3582)***
San Diego Mission Vly Hilton, San Diego *Also called HEI Mission Valley LP (P-12347)*
San Diego Mortgage & RE...E...619 334-7779
9461 Grsmnt Smt Dr Ste D La Mesa (91941) ***(P-11437)***
San Diego Mutal Trading, Poway *Also called Mutual Trading Co Inc (P-8613)*
San Diego Old Town, San Diego *Also called RPC Old Town Jefferson (P-12847)*
San Diego Opera Association (PA)...E...619 232-7636
233 A St Ste 500 San Diego (92101) ***(P-17943)***
San Diego Orthopaedic Associat...D...619 299-8500
4060 4th Ave Ste 700 San Diego (92103) ***(P-19357)***
San Diego Padres, San Diego *Also called Padres LP (P-18074)*
San Diego Pathologists Medical...C...619 297-4012
7592 Metro Dr Ste 406 San Diego (92108) ***(P-19358)***
San Diego Recyling Inc...B...619 287-7555
6670 Federal Blvd Lemon Grove (91945) ***(P-6279)***
San Diego Region, San Diego *Also called Water Resources Control Bd Cal (P-24371)*
San Diego Regional Ctr For Dev, National City *Also called San Diego-Imperial (P-23433)*
San Diego Rescue Mission Inc (PA)...D...619 819-1880
299 17th St San Diego (92101) ***(P-24223)***
San Diego Services LLC...C...858 654-0102
5415 Oberlin Dr San Diego (92121) ***(P-25296)***
San Diego Supercomputer Center, La Jolla *Also called University Cal San Diego (P-15831)*
San Diego Symphony Orchestra...C...619 235-0800
1245 7th Ave San Diego (92101) ***(P-18000)***
San Diego Testing Engineers...D...858 715-5800
7895 Convoy Ct Ste 18 San Diego (92111) ***(P-25297)***
San Diego Theatres Inc...C...619 615-4000
1100 3rd Ave San Diego (92101) ***(P-10640)***
San Diego Tourism Authority (PA)...D...619 232-3101
750 B St Ste 1500 San Diego (92101) ***(P-17042)***
San Diego Transit Corporation (PA)...A...619 238-0100
100 16th St San Diego (92101) ***(P-3583)***
San Diego Trolley Inc...B...619 595-4933
1341 Commercial St San Diego (92113) ***(P-3584)***
San Diego Unified Hbr Police, San Diego *Also called San Diego Unified Port Dst (P-4621)*
San Diego Unified Port Dst...C...619 686-6200
1400 Tidelands Ave National City (91950) ***(P-4620)***
San Diego Unified Port Dst...C...619 686-6585
3380 N Harbor Dr San Diego (92101) ***(P-4621)***
San Diego Unified Port Dst (PA)...C...619 686-6200
3165 Pacific Hwy San Diego (92101) ***(P-4622)***
San Diego Unified School Dst...D...619 266-4500
445 S 47th St San Diego (92113) ***(P-23782)***
San Diego Welders Supply, San Diego *Also called Westair Gases & Equipment Inc (P-7610)*
San Diego Wild Animal Park, Escondido *Also called Zoological Society San Diego (P-24317)*
San Diego Youth Services Inc (PA)...D...619 221-8600
3255 Wing St Ste 550 San Diego (92110) ***(P-23432)***
San Diego Zoo, San Diego *Also called Zoological Society San Diego (P-24318)*
San Diego-Imperial...D...619 336-6600
2727 Hoover Ave National City (91950) ***(P-23433)***
San Diego-Imperial Counties De (PA)...B...858 576-2996
4355 Ruffin Rd Ste 220 San Diego (92123) ***(P-23434)***
San Diego-Imperial Counties De...D...760 736-1200
1370 W Sn Mrcos Blvd # 100 San Marcos (92078) ***(P-23435)***
San Dimas Bushnell Building, Rosemead *Also called Southern California Edison Co (P-5941)*
SAN DIMAS COMMUNITY HOSPITAL, San Dimas *Also called Prime Healthcare-San Dimas LLC (P-21113)*
San Dimas Golf Inc...D...909 599-8486
1400 Avenida Entrada San Dimas (91773) ***(P-18553)***
San Dimas Luggage Company...D...909 510-8820
2095 S Archibald Ave Ontario (91761) ***(P-7834)***
San Dimas Medical Group Inc...D...661 663-4800
100 Old River Rd Bakersfield (93311) ***(P-19359)***
San Dimas Retirement Center (PA)...D...909 599-8441
834 W Arrow Hwy San Dimas (91773) ***(P-10810)***
San Fernando City of Inc...D...818 832-2400
10605 Balboa Blvd Ste 100 Granada Hills (91344) ***(P-22117)***
San Fernando Health Center, San Fernando *Also called Northeast Valley Health Corp (P-19227)*
San Fernando Juvenile Hall, Sylmar *Also called County of Los Angeles (P-23877)*
San Fernando Valley Community (PA)...B...818 901-4830
16360 Roscoe Blvd Fl 2 Van Nuys (91406) ***(P-22118)***
San Fernando Valley Interfaith, Van Nuys *Also called County of Los Angeles (P-23097)*
San Francisco City & County...D...415 695-5660
1520 Oakdale Ave San Francisco (94124) ***(P-23436)***
San Francisco 49ers, Santa Clara *Also called Forty Niners Football Co LLC (P-18061)*

San Francisco Aids Foundation (PA)..................................D......415 487-3000
  1035 Market St Ste 400 San Francisco (94103) *(P-23437)*
San Francisco Ballet Assn...C......415 865-2000
  455 Franklin St San Francisco (94102) *(P-17944)*
San Francisco Bay, San Francisco *Also called Charolais Care V Inc (P-21707)*
San Francisco Bay AR Tran Assn...................................C......510 501-5318
  915 San Antonio Ave Alameda (94501) *(P-24862)*
San Francisco Bay Area Councl.....................................D......510 577-9000
  1001 Davis St San Leandro (94577) *(P-24640)*
San Francisco Bay Area Rapid......................................E......510 464-6000
  1330 Broadway Oakland (94612) *(P-3585)*
San Francisco Bay Area Rapid......................................D......510 834-1297
  800 Madison St Oakland (94607) *(P-3586)*
San Francisco Bay Area Rapid......................................C......510 464-6126
  300 Lakeside Dr 23 Oakland (94612) *(P-3587)*
San Francisco Bay Area Rapid......................................C......510 233-6848
  1101 13th St Richmond (94801) *(P-3588)*
San Francisco Bay Area Rapid......................................D......510 233-7444
  1101 13th St Richmond (94801) *(P-3589)*
San Francisco Bay Area Rapid......................................A......510 286-2893
  601 E 8th St Oakland (94606) *(P-3590)*
San Francisco Bay Area Rapid......................................D......510 464-7000
  800 Madison St Oakland (94607) *(P-3591)*
San Francisco Bay Area Rapid......................................C......510 464-6000
  300 Lakeside Dr Fl 17 Oakland (94612) *(P-3592)*
San Francisco City & County..D......415 356-2700
  617 Mission St San Francisco (94105) *(P-23438)*
San Francisco City & County..D......415 356-2700
  617 Mission St San Francisco (94105) *(P-23439)*
San Francisco City & County..C......415 550-4600
  200 Paul Ave B San Francisco (94124) *(P-17357)*
San Francisco City Clinic...D......415 487-5500
  356 7th St San Francisco (94103) *(P-22119)*
San Francisco District Office, San Francisco *Also called California Dept
Rehabilitation (P-14239)*
San Francisco Federal Cr Un (PA).................................C......415 775-5377
  770 Golden Gate Ave Fl 1 San Francisco (94102) *(P-9344)*
San Francisco Fertility Ctrs..D......415 834-3000
  55 Francisco St Ste 300 San Francisco (94133) *(P-19360)*
San Francisco Food Bank..D......415 282-1900
  900 Pennsylvania Ave San Francisco (94107) *(P-23440)*
San Francisco Forty Niners..D......408 562-4949
  4949 Mrie P Debartolo Way Santa Clara (95054) *(P-11691)*
San Francisco Forty Niners (PA)...................................C......408 562-4949
  4949 Mrie P Debartolo Way Santa Clara (95054) *(P-18078)*
San Francisco Foundation...D......415 733-8500
  1 Embarcadero Ctr # 1400 San Francisco (94111) *(P-17043)*
San Francisco General Hospital, San Francisco *Also called Gastroenterology
Division (P-18994)*
San Francisco General Hospital, San Francisco *Also called City & County of San
Francisco (P-20791)*
San Francisco Health Authority (PA)...............................D......415 615-4407
  50 Beale St Fl 12 San Francisco (94105) *(P-24423)*
San Francisco Hilton & Towers, San Francisco *Also called Park Hotels & Resorts
Inc (P-12715)*
San Francisco Hotel Associates....................................D......415 392-4666
  650 Bush St San Francisco (94108) *(P-12873)*
San Francisco Hotel Group LLC...................................C......415 276-9888
  222 Sansome St San Francisco (94104) *(P-12874)*
San Francisco Ladies Protecti.......................................D......415 931-3136
  3400 Laguna St San Francisco (94123) *(P-24063)*
San Francisco Marriott Marquis, San Francisco *Also called Host Hotels & Resorts
LP (P-12391)*
San Francisco Marriott Un Sq, San Francisco *Also called Intercontinental Hotels
Group (P-12465)*
San Francisco Meritime N H P.......................................D......415 561-7000
  Fort Myson Ctr Bldg E265 San Francisco (94123) *(P-24287)*
San Francisco Opera Assn..A......415 861-4008
  301 Van Ness Ave San Francisco (94102) *(P-17945)*
San Francisco Partclr Cncl Sct.....................................D......415 255-3525
  525 5th St San Francisco (94107) *(P-23441)*
San Francisco Public Schools, San Francisco *Also called San Francisco City &
County (P-23436)*
San Francisco Radio Assets LLC (HQ)...........................C......415 216-1300
  750 Battery St Fl 2 San Francisco (94111) *(P-5565)*
San Francisco Reinsurance Co, Petaluma *Also called Allianz Reinsurance Amer Inc (P-9895)*
San Francisco Residential Care, San Francisco *Also called Self-Help For Elderly (P-23459)*
San Francisco Sightseeing, San Francisco *Also called Franciscan Lines Inc (P-3675)*
San Francisco Symphony Inc (PA)...............................B......415 552-8000
  201 Van Ness Ave San Francisco (94102) *(P-18001)*
San Francisco Tennis Club..D......415 777-9000
  645 5th St San Francisco (94107) *(P-18191)*
San Francisco Towers, San Francisco *Also called Covia Communities (P-23888)*
San Francisco Travel Assn..D......415 974-6900
  1 Front St Ste 2900 San Francisco (94111) *(P-17044)*
San Francisco Vamc, San Francisco *Also called Veterans Health Administration (P-19563)*
San Francisco Zoological Soc.......................................C......415 753-7080
  1 Zoo Rd San Francisco (94132) *(P-18751)*
San Fransisco Speciality Prod, Santa Fe Springs *Also called LA Specialty Produce
Co (P-8493)*
San Frncisco Incoming Svcs LLC (PA)..........................D......415 777-2288
  50 Quint St San Francisco (94124) *(P-4862)*
San Frncsco Bay Area Rpid Trns (PA).........................B......510 464-6000
  300 Lakeside Dr Oakland (94604) *(P-3593)*
San Frncsco Mrtime Nat Pk Assn (PA).........................E......415 561-6662
  Fort Mason Fl 2 Bldg E San Francisco (94123) *(P-24288)*

San Frncsco North/Petaluma KOA..............................E......707 763-1492
  20 Rainsville Rd Petaluma (94952) *(P-13164)*
San Frncsco Pub Utilities Comm, San Francisco *Also called City & County of San
Francisco (P-6029)*
San Frnndo Vly Intrfith Cuncil.......................................C......818 885-5220
  8956 Vanalden Ave Northridge (91324) *(P-24224)*
San Gabriel Ambulatory Sugery...................................A......626 300-5300
  207 S Santa Anita St G16 San Gabriel (91776) *(P-19361)*
San Gabriel Childrens Ctr Inc.......................................D......626 859-2089
  4740 N Grand Ave Covina (91724) *(P-24064)*
San Gabriel Convalescent Ctr, Rosemead *Also called Longwood Management
Corp (P-20091)*
San Gabriel Country Club..D......626 287-9671
  350 E Hermosa Dr San Gabriel (91775) *(P-18554)*
San Gabriel Nursery and Flor (PA)................................D......626 286-0787
  632 S San Gabriel Blvd San Gabriel (91776) *(P-277)*
San Gabriel Transit Inc..D......626 430-3650
  14913 Ramona Blvd Baldwin Park (91706) *(P-3748)*
San Gabriel Transit Inc (PA).......................................C......626 258-1310
  3650 Rockwell Ave El Monte (91731) *(P-3594)*
San Gabriel Transit Inc..D......818 771-0374
  7955 San Fernando Rd Sun Valley (91352) *(P-3749)*
San Gabriel Valley Cab Co, El Monte *Also called San Gabriel Transit Inc (P-3594)*
San Gabriel Valley Water Assn.....................................D......626 815-1305
  725 N Azusa Ave Azusa (91702) *(P-6109)*
San Gabriel Valley Water Co (PA).................................C......626 448-6183
  11142 Garvey Ave El Monte (91733) *(P-6110)*
San Gabriel Valley Water Co...D......909 822-2201
  8440 Nuevo Ave Fontana (92335) *(P-6111)*
San Gabriel Vly Training Ctr (PA)..................................D......626 330-3185
  400 S Covina Blvd La Puente (91746) *(P-23634)*
San Gabriel-Pomona Valley Hlg, Baldwin Park *Also called USA Waste of California
Inc (P-6302)*
SAN GABRIEL/POMONA REGIONAL CE, Pomona *Also called San Gabriel/Pomona
Valleys (P-23442)*
San Gabriel/Pomona Valleys.......................................B......909 620-7722
  75 Rancho Camino Dr Pomona (91766) *(P-23442)*
San Gbriel Vly Cnvlescent Hosp...................................D......626 401-1557
  3938 Cogswell Rd El Monte (91732) *(P-21425)*
San Gbriel Vly Med Ctr Fndtion.....................................A......626 289-5454
  438 W Las Tunas Dr San Gabriel (91776) *(P-21154)*
San Geronimo Golf Course, San Geronimo *Also called National Golf Properties
LLC (P-18275)*
San Gorgonio Memorial Hospital (PA)...........................C......951 845-1121
  600 N Highland Sprng Ave Banning (92220) *(P-21155)*
San Jacinto Healthcare, Hemet *Also called Miramonte Enterprises LLC (P-20139)*
San Joaquin Cnty Aging & Commu................................C......209 468-9455
  102 S San Joaquin St Stockton (95202) *(P-23443)*
San Joaquin Community Hospital, Bakersfield *Also called Kaiser Foundation
Hospitals (P-20947)*
San Joaquin Community Hospital (PA)...........................A......661 395-3000
  2615 Chester Ave Bakersfield (93301) *(P-21156)*
San Joaquin Country Club...D......559 439-3483
  3484 W Bluff Ave Fresno (93711) *(P-18555)*
San Joaquin County Adult Svcs, Stockton *Also called County of San Joaquin (P-23153)*
San Joaquin County Operations, Stockton *Also called American Medical Response
West (P-3645)*
San Joaquin Figs Inc...E......559 224-4492
  3564 N Hazel Ave Fresno (93722) *(P-538)*
San Joaquin Gardens, Fresno *Also called American Baptist Homes of West (P-23817)*
San Joaquin General Hospital.......................................A......209 468-6000
  500 W Hospital Rd French Camp (95231) *(P-21157)*
San Joaquin Hills Transporttn (PA)................................D......949 754-3400
  125 Pacifica Ste 100 Irvine (92618) *(P-1784)*
San Joaquin Regional Trnst Dst....................................C......209 948-5566
  421 E Weber Ave Stockton (95202) *(P-3595)*
San Joaquin Val UNI Air Pol (PA)..................................C......559 230-6000
  1990 E Gettysburg Ave Fresno (93726) *(P-27201)*
San Joaquin Val UNI Air Pol...D......209 497-1000
  2700 M St Ste 275 Bakersfield (93301) *(P-27202)*
San Joaquin Valley A P C D...D......559 230-6000
  1990 E Gettysburg Ave Fresno (93726) *(P-27203)*
San Joaquin Valley Intergrp...E......559 856-0559
  6048 E Cimarron Ave Fresno (93727) *(P-24863)*
San Joaquin Valley Railroad Co.....................................C......559 592-1857
  221 N F St Exeter (93221) *(P-3506)*
San Joaquin Valley Rehabili (HQ)..................................B......559 436-3600
  7173 N Sharon Ave Fresno (93720) *(P-22120)*
San Jose Airport Garden Hotel......................................D......408 793-3300
  1740 N 1st St San Jose (95112) *(P-12875)*
San Jose Airport Hotel LLC..C......408 793-3939
  1740 N 1st St San Jose (95112) *(P-12876)*
San Jose Arena Management LLC...............................C......510 623-7200
  44388 Old Warm Sprng Blvd Fremont (94538) *(P-26383)*
San Jose Chld Discovery Museum..................................D......408 298-5437
  180 Woz Way San Jose (95110) *(P-24289)*
San Jose Conservation Corps......................................C......408 283-7171
  2650 Senter Rd San Jose (95111) *(P-23635)*
San Jose Country Club...D......408 258-4901
  15571 Alum Rock Ave San Jose (95127) *(P-18556)*
San Jose District Office, San Jose *Also called State Compensation Insur Fund (P-10133)*
San Jose Earthquakes MGT LLC...................................C......408 556-7700
  451 El Cmino Real Ste 220 Santa Clara (95050) *(P-26384)*
San Jose Fairmont Lessee LLC...................................B......408 998-1900
  170 S Market St Lbby San Jose (95113) *(P-12877)*
SAN JOSE FOOTHILL FAMILY, San Jose *Also called Foothill Health Center Inc (P-18988)*

Mergent e-mail: customerrelations@mergent.com
1418

2020 Directory of California
Wholesalers and Services Companies

(P-0000) Products & Services Section entry number
(PA)=Parent Co (HQ)=Headquarters (DH)=Div Headquarters

San Jose Hlthcare Wellness Ctr, San Jose *Also called San Joses Healthcare & Well* ***(P-20233)***
San Jose Lessee LLC, San Jose *Also called Doubletree By Hilton San Jose* ***(P-12228)***
San Jose Medical Group / MGT, San Jose *Also called Verity Medical Foundation* ***(P-19554)***
San Jose Medical Systems Lp....A....408 259-5000
225 N Jackson Ave San Jose (95116) ***(P-21158)***
San Jose Municipal Golf Course, San Jose *Also called Rawitser Golf Shop Mike* ***(P-18287)***
San Jose Museum of Art Assn....D....408 271-6840
110 S Market St San Jose (95113) ***(P-24290)***
San Jose Redevelopment Agency....C....408 535-8500
200 E Santa Clara St 14th San Jose (95113) ***(P-27204)***
San Jose Sharks LLC....C....408 999-6810
525 W Santa Clara St San Jose (95113) ***(P-18079)***
San Jose Silicon Valley Cham....D....408 291-5250
101 W Santa Clara St San Jose (95113) ***(P-24361)***
San Jose State University....E....408 924-1000
1 Washington Sq San Jose (95112) ***(P-19362)***
San Jose Surgical Supply Inc (PA)....E....408 293-9033
902 S Bascom Ave San Jose (95128) ***(P-7002)***
San Jose Water Company (HQ)....C....408 288-5314
110 W Taylor St San Jose (95110) ***(P-6112)***
San Jose Water Company....C....408 298-0364
1221 S Bascom Ave San Jose (95128) ***(P-6113)***
San Joses Healthcare & Well....D....408 295-2665
75 N 13th St San Jose (95112) ***(P-20233)***
San Juan Golf Inc....E....949 493-1167
32120 San Juan Creek Rd San Juan Capistrano (92675) ***(P-18291)***
San Juan Hill Country Club, San Juan Capistrano *Also called San Juan Golf Inc* ***(P-18291)***
San Juan Oaks LLC....D....831 636-6113
3825 Union Rd Hollister (95023) ***(P-18292)***
San Juan Oaks Golf Club, Hollister *Also called San Juan Oaks LLC* ***(P-18292)***
San Leandro Healthcare Center, San Leandro *Also called Kissito Health Case Inc* ***(P-21801)***
San Leandro Healthcare Center....D....510 357-4015
368 Juana Ave San Leandro (94577) ***(P-20234)***
San Leandro Hospital LP....B....510 357-6500
13855 E 14th St San Leandro (94578) ***(P-21159)***
San Leandro Surgery Center Lt....D....510 276-2800
15035 E 14th St San Leandro (94578) ***(P-19363)***
San Lndro Care Rhblitation Ctr, San Leandro *Also called Sunbridge Healthcare LLC* ***(P-20464)***
San Lorenzo 0119, San Lorenzo *Also called Wells Fargo Bank National Assn* ***(P-9142)***
San Lorenzo Valley Water Dst (PA)....E....831 338-2153
13060 Highway 9 Boulder Creek (95006) ***(P-6114)***
San Lorenzo Village Shopg Ctr, San Mateo *Also called David D Bohannon Organization* ***(P-10580)***
San Luis Ambulance Service Inc....C....805 543-2626
3546 S Higuera St San Luis Obispo (93401) ***(P-3720)***
San Luis Care Center, Newman *Also called Avalon Care Ctr - Newman LLC* ***(P-19739)***
San Luis Dlta-Mendota Wtr Auth....D....209 835-2593
15990 Kelso Rd Byron (94514) ***(P-6371)***
San Luis Obispo County YMCA (PA)....D....805 543-8235
1020 Southwood Dr San Luis Obispo (93401) ***(P-24641)***
San Luis Obispo Golf....C....805 543-3400
255 Country Club Dr San Luis Obispo (93401) ***(P-18557)***
San Luis Obispo Regional....D....805 781-4465
179 Cross St Ste A San Luis Obispo (93401) ***(P-3596)***
San Luis Obispo VA Cboc, San Luis Obispo *Also called Veterans Health Administration* ***(P-19557)***
San Manuel Indian Bingo Casino (PA)....A....909 864-5050
777 San Manuel Blvd Highland (92346) ***(P-18752)***
San Marcos Caterers Inc....D....760 744-0120
1025 La Bonita Dr San Marcos (92078) ***(P-12878)***
San Marcos Kids Helpng Kids FN....C....800 659-6411
4750 Hollister Ave Santa Barbara (93110) ***(P-24642)***
SAN MARCOS MECHANICAL, Vista *Also called Industrial Coml Systems Inc* ***(P-2154)***
San Marcos Operating Co LP....D....760 471-2986
1586 W Square Marcos Blvd San Marcos (92078) ***(P-20235)***
San Marcos Stadium Cinema 18, San Marcos *Also called Edwards Theatres Circuit Inc* ***(P-17839)***
San Marino Manor....E....626 446-5263
6812 Oak Ave San Gabriel (91775) ***(P-20677)***
San Marino Plastering Inc....A....714 693-7840
4501 E La Palma Ave # 200 Anaheim (92807) ***(P-2856)***
San Mateo Cnty Expo Fair Assn....E....650 574-3247
2495 S Delaware St San Mateo (94403) ***(P-18753)***
San Mateo Cnty Pub Hlth Clinic....E....650 301-8600
380 90th St Daly City (94015) ***(P-22121)***
San Mateo County Community....D....650 574-6586
1700 W Hillsdale Blvd San Mateo (94402) ***(P-5646)***
SAN MATEO COUNTY EXPO CENTER, San Mateo *Also called San Mateo Cnty Expo Fair Assn* ***(P-18753)***
San Mateo County Transit Dst (PA)....C....650 508-6200
1250 San Carlos Ave San Carlos (94070) ***(P-3597)***
San Mateo County Transit Dst....B....650 588-4860
301 N Access Rd South San Francisco (94080) ***(P-3598)***
San Mateo County Transit Dst....C....650 508-6412
501 Pico Blvd San Carlos (94070) ***(P-3833)***
San Mateo Credit Union (PA)....D....650 363-1725
350 Convention Way # 300 Redwood City (94063) ***(P-9345)***
San Mateo Credit Union....C....650 363-1725
1515 S El Camino Real # 100 San Mateo (94402) ***(P-9346)***
SAN MATEO HEAD START PROGRAM, San Mateo *Also called Institute For Humn Social Dev* ***(P-23732)***
San Mateo Health Commission....C....650 616-0050
801 Gateway Blvd Ste 100 South San Francisco (94080) ***(P-22317)***
San Mateo Healthcare & Wellnes....D....650 692-3758
1100 Trousdale Dr Burlingame (94010) ***(P-20236)***
San Mateo Marriott, San Mateo *Also called Atrium Plaza LLC* ***(P-12025)***
San Mateo Sport Club, Burlingame *Also called 24 Hour Fitness Usa Inc* ***(P-18107)***
San Miguel Produce Inc....B....805 488-0981
4444 Navalair Rd Oxnard (93033) ***(P-74)***
SAN MIGUEL VILLA, Concord *Also called Tranquility Incorporated* ***(P-20701)***
San Onfre Nclear Gnerating Stn, San Clemente *Also called Southern California Edison Co* ***(P-5935)***
San Pablo Healthcare....C....510 235-3720
13328 San Pablo Ave San Pablo (94806) ***(P-20237)***
San Pablo Lodge 43....D....707 642-1391
342 Georgia St Vallejo (94590) ***(P-24643)***
San Pedro Convalescent HM Inc....D....310 832-6431
1430 W 6th St San Pedro (90732) ***(P-20238)***
San Pedro Hospital Pavilion, San Pedro *Also called Providence Health System* ***(P-21122)***
San Pedro Peninsula Hospital, San Pedro *Also called Providence Health System* ***(P-21120)***
San Psqual Band Mssion Indians....B....760 291-5500
16300 Nyemii Pass Rd Valley Center (92082) ***(P-12879)***
San Psqual Csino Dev Group Inc....E....760 291-5500
16300 Nyemii Pass Rd Valley Center (92082) ***(P-12880)***
San Rafael Hillcrest LLC....D....415 479-8800
1010 Northgate Dr San Rafael (94903) ***(P-12881)***
San Rafael Rock Quarry Inc (HQ)....D....415 459-7740
2350 Kerner Blvd Ste 200 San Rafael (94901) ***(P-1053)***
San Ramon Medical Offices, San Ramon *Also called Kaiser Foundation Hospitals* ***(P-19097)***
San Ramon Regional Med Ctr LLC....A....925 275-9200
6001 Norris Canyon Rd San Ramon (94583) ***(P-21160)***
San Salvador Pre-School, Colton *Also called Colton Joint Unified Schl Dst* ***(P-23704)***
San Tomas Convalescent Hosp, San Jose *Also called Aquinas Corporation* ***(P-19723)***
San Val Alarm System, Thousand Palms *Also called San Val Corp* ***(P-758)***
San Val Corp (PA)....B....760 346-3999
72203 Adelaid St Thousand Palms (92276) ***(P-758)***
San Vicente Inn & Golf Club, Ramona *Also called San Diego Country Estates Assn* ***(P-24639)***
San Ysidro Health, San Diego *Also called Centro De Salud De La Comuni* ***(P-21975)***
San Ysidro School District....D....619 428-4424
222 Avenida De La Madrid San Ysidro (92173) ***(P-24644)***
San-Mar Construction Co Inc....C....714 693-5400
4875 E La Palma Ave # 601 Anaheim (92807) ***(P-2974)***
Sanborn Theatres Inc....D....909 296-9728
41090 Calif Oaks Rd Murrieta (92562) ***(P-17865)***
Sanco Pipelines Incorporated....E....408 377-2793
727 University Ave Los Gatos (95032) ***(P-1909)***
Sanctuary, The, Redwood City *Also called Bay Clubs Inc* ***(P-18122)***
Sand Canyon Corporation (HQ)....D....949 727-9425
7595 Irvine Center Dr # 100 Irvine (92618) ***(P-9644)***
Sand Canyon LLC....D....949 551-2560
11 Strawberry Farm Rd Irvine (92612) ***(P-18293)***
Sand Dollar Holdings Inc (PA)....D....619 477-0185
1022 Bay Marina Dr # 106 National City (91950) ***(P-8420)***
Sandbar Solar and Electric, Santa Cruz *Also called Santa Cruz Westside Elc Inc* ***(P-2628)***
Sanderlings, Aptos *Also called Seascape Resort Ltd A Calif* ***(P-12898)***
Sanders & Wohrman Corporation....C....714 919-0446
709 N Poplar St Orange (92868) ***(P-2392)***
Sandhurst Convales Grp Ltd A....E....310 675-3304
13922 Cerise Ave Hawthorne (90250) ***(P-20239)***
Sandis Civil Engineers (PA)....D....408 636-0900
1700 Winchester Blvd Campbell (95008) ***(P-25526)***
Sandm San Dego Mrriott Del Mar....A....858 523-1700
11966 El Camino Real San Diego (92130) ***(P-12882)***
Sandoval Brothers Inc....D....831 678-1465
36503 Mile End Rd Soledad (93960) ***(P-14410)***
Sandoval Labor Contractor, Williams *Also called Elvira Sandoval* ***(P-14271)***
Sandrini Farms....D....661 792-3192
6111 De La Guerra Ter Bakersfield (93306) ***(P-160)***
Sands Rv Resort, San Rafael *Also called R C Roberts & Co* ***(P-10864)***
Sandwich Spot (PA)....D....916 492-2613
1630 18th St Sacramento (95811) ***(P-12883)***
Sanford Burnham Prebys Medical (PA)....A....858 795-5000
10901 N Torrey Pines Rd La Jolla (92037) ***(P-26026)***
Sangamo Therapeutics Inc (PA)....C....510 970-6000
501 Canal Blvd Richmond (94804) ***(P-25826)***
Sangiacomo Vineyards, Sonoma *Also called V Sangiacomo & Sons* ***(P-167)***
Sanhyd Inc....D....510 843-2131
2131 Carleton St Berkeley (94704) ***(P-20240)***
Sanitary Fill, San Francisco *Also called Recology Inc* ***(P-6244)***
Sanitation, Simi Valley *Also called Golden State Water Company* ***(P-6066)***
Sanitation Districts....A....562 908-4288
1955 Workman Mill Rd Whittier (90601) ***(P-6280)***
Sankara Eye Foundation USA....E....408 456-0555
1900 Mccarthy Blvd # 302 Milpitas (95035) ***(P-24864)***
Sansa Technology LLC....E....866 204-3710
6990 Village Pkwy Dublin (94568) ***(P-25827)***
Sansei Gardens Inc....C....510 226-9191
3250 Darby Cmn Fremont (94539) ***(P-903)***
Sansum Clinic (PA)....D....805 681-7700
470 S Patterson Ave Santa Barbara (93111) ***(P-19364)***
Sansum Clinic....E....805 682-6507
509 E Montecito St # 200 Santa Barbara (93103) ***(P-21859)***
Santa Ana City of....E....714 565-2600
1000 E Santa Ana Blvd # 108 Santa Ana (92701) ***(P-14411)***
Santa Ana Country Club....D....714 556-3000
20382 Newport Blvd Santa Ana (92707) ***(P-18558)***
Santa Ana District Office, Santa Ana *Also called State Compensation Insur Fund* ***(P-10130)***
Santa Ana Police Officers Assn....A....714 836-1211
1607 N Sycamore St Santa Ana (92701) ***(P-24645)***
Santa Ana Radiology Center....D....714 835-6055
1100 N Tustin Ave Ste A Santa Ana (92705) ***(P-19365)***

ALPHABETIC

Santa Ana Unified School Dst....D....714 431-1900
1749 Carnegie Ave Santa Ana (92705) ***(P-22318)***
Santa Anita Associates (PA)....D....626 447-2764
405 S Santa Anita Ave Arcadia (91006) ***(P-18294)***
Santa Anita Convalescent Hospi....C....626 579-0310
5522 Gracewood Ave Temple City (91780) ***(P-20241)***
Santa Anita Family Young....D....626 359-9244
501 S Mountain Ave Monrovia (91016) ***(P-23636)***
Santa Anita Golf Course, Arcadia *Also called Santa Anita Associates* ***(P-18294)***
Santa Anita Park, Arcadia *Also called Los Angeles Turf Club Inc* ***(P-18085)***
Santa Barbara City of....D....805 962-6464
1100 Anacapa St Dept 3 Santa Barbara (93101) ***(P-4863)***
Santa Barbara Airbus....D....805 964-7759
750 Technology Dr Goleta (93117) ***(P-3721)***
Santa Barbara City of....C....805 564-5485
630 Garden St Santa Barbara (93101) ***(P-17045)***
Santa Barbara Cnty Social Svcs, Santa Maria *Also called Santa Barbara Cottage Hospital* ***(P-21163)***
Santa Barbara Convalescent Ctr, Santa Barbara *Also called California Convalescent Hosp* ***(P-20521)***
Santa Barbara Cottage Care Ctr, Santa Barbara *Also called Cottage Care Center* ***(P-20807)***
Santa Barbara Cottage Hospital....A....805 569-7367
400 W Pueblo St Santa Barbara (93105) ***(P-21161)***
Santa Barbara Cottage Hospital (PA)....D....805 682-7111
400 W Pueblo St Santa Barbara (93105) ***(P-21162)***
Santa Barbara Cottage Hospital....C....805 346-7135
2125 Centerpointe Pkwy Santa Maria (93455) ***(P-21163)***
Santa Barbara County of....B....805 882-3700
117 E Carrillo St Santa Barbara (93101) ***(P-23444)***
Santa Barbara County of....C....805 614-1550
1410 S Broadway Ste L Santa Maria (93454) ***(P-23445)***
Santa Barbara County of....D....805 681-5100
345 Camino Del Remedio Santa Barbara (93110) ***(P-22319)***
Santa Barbara County of....C....805 737-7080
1100 W Laurel Ave Lompoc (93436) ***(P-23446)***
Santa Barbara County of....E....805 346-7540
312 E Cook St Ste D Santa Maria (93454) ***(P-22803)***
Santa Barbara County of....D....805 884-1600
429 N San Antonio Rd Santa Barbara (93110) ***(P-23447)***
Santa Barbara County of....C....866 901-3212
4 E Carrillo St Santa Barbara (93101) ***(P-23448)***
Santa Barbara Fabricare Inc....E....805 963-6677
14 W Gutierrez St Santa Barbara (93101) ***(P-13258)***
Santa Barbara Family YMCA, Santa Barbara *Also called Channel Islands Young Mens Ch* ***(P-24516)***
Santa Barbara Farms LLC (PA)....D....805 736-9776
1200 Union Sugar Ave Lompoc (93436) ***(P-75)***
Santa Barbara Metro Trnst Dst (PA)....D....805 963-3364
550 Olive St Santa Barbara (93101) ***(P-3599)***
Santa Barbara Museum....D....805 682-4711
2559 Puesta Del Sol Santa Barbara (93105) ***(P-24291)***
Santa Barbara Museum of Art (PA)....D....805 963-4364
1130 State St Santa Barbara (93101) ***(P-24292)***
Santa Barbara San Luis Obispo....C....800 421-2560
4050 Calle Real Santa Barbara (93110) ***(P-9912)***
Santa Barbara Service Center, Goleta *Also called Southern California Edison Co* ***(P-5943)***
Santa Barbara Trnsp Corp (HQ)....D....805 681-8355
6414 Hollister Ave Goleta (93117) ***(P-3822)***
Santa Barbara Trnsp Corp....D....805 928-0402
1331 Jason Way Santa Maria (93455) ***(P-3823)***
Santa Barbra Cttge Hsptl....B....805 569-7224
400 W Pueblo St Santa Barbara (93105) ***(P-21583)***
Santa Brbara Zlgcal Foundation....C....805 962-1673
500 Ninos Dr Santa Barbara (93103) ***(P-24315)***
Santa Catalina Island Company (PA)....D....310 510-2000
150 Metropole Ave Avalon (90704) ***(P-4864)***
Santa Clara County of....D....408 435-2000
2600 N 1st St San Jose (95134) ***(P-23449)***
Santa Clara Arques Med Offs, Sunnyvale *Also called Kaiser Foundation Hospitals* ***(P-19101)***
Santa Clara Cnty Fderal Cr Un (PA)....D....408 282-0700
1641 N 1st St Ste 245 San Jose (95112) ***(P-9347)***
Santa Clara County of....A....408 792-2704
3180 Newberry Dr Ste 150 San Jose (95118) ***(P-22804)***
Santa Clara County of....D....408 201-7600
19050 Malaguerra Ave Morgan Hill (95037) ***(P-24065)***
Santa Clara County of....C....408 885-7200
2325 Enborg Ln Fl 4 San Jose (95128) ***(P-25673)***
Santa Clara County of....E....408 885-6818
2325 Enborg Ln Ste 380 San Jose (95128) ***(P-21164)***
Santa Clara County of....C....408 355-2200
298 Garden Hill Dr Los Gatos (95032) ***(P-18754)***
Santa Clara County of....D....408 282-3200
1555 Berger Dr Fl 1 San Jose (95112) ***(P-13699)***
Santa Clara County of....C....408 435-2111
2314 N 1st St San Jose (95131) ***(P-23450)***
Santa Clara County of....C....408 885-7354
751 S Bascom Ave Fl 4 San Jose (95128) ***(P-25674)***
Santa Clara Hilton, The, Santa Clara *Also called Hostmark Investors Ltd Partnr* ***(P-26258)***
Santa Clara Tenant Corp....D....408 496-6400
2885 Lakeside Dr Santa Clara (95054) ***(P-12884)***
Santa Clara Valley Corporation....D....408 947-1100
715 N 1st St Ste 27 San Jose (95112) ***(P-14037)***
Santa Clara Valley Health & Ho, San Jose *Also called Santa Clara County of* ***(P-21164)***
Santa Clara Valley Medical Ctr....B....408 885-6300
2400 Moorpark Ave San Jose (95128) ***(P-19366)***
Santa Clara Valley Medical Ctr....A....408 885-5730
2220 Moorpark Ave San Jose (95128) ***(P-22320)***
Santa Clara Valley Trnsp Auth (PA)....A....408 321-2300
3331 N 1st St San Jose (95134) ***(P-3600)***
Santa Clara Valley Trnsp Auth....C....408 321-5559
3331 N 1st St Bldg B San Jose (95134) ***(P-3601)***
Santa Clara Valley Trnsp Auth....B....408 321-5555
3331 N 1st St San Jose (95134) ***(P-3763)***
Santa Clara Valley Water (PA)....A....408 265-2600
5750 Almaden Expy San Jose (95118) ***(P-6115)***
Santa Clara Valley Water....D....408 395-8121
400 More Ave Los Gatos (95032) ***(P-6116)***
Santa Clara Vlly Health/Hosptl, San Jose *Also called Santa Clara County of* ***(P-25674)***
Santa Clara Vly Job Career Ctr....D....805 933-8300
725 E Main St Ste 101 Santa Paula (93060) ***(P-14412)***
Santa Clara Vngard Booster CLB....E....408 727-5532
1795 Space Park Dr Santa Clara (95054) ***(P-24646)***
Santa Clara Woman's Club Adobe, Santa Clara *Also called Santa Clara Womens Club* ***(P-18559)***
Santa Clara Womens Club....D....408 246-8000
3260 The Alameda Santa Clara (95050) ***(P-18559)***
Santa Clarita City of....B....661 294-1287
28250 Constellation Rd Santa Clarita (91355) ***(P-3764)***
Santa Clarita City of....B....661 284-1423
23920 Valencia Blvd # 300 Santa Clarita (91355) ***(P-18755)***
Santa Clarita Athletic Club....D....661 255-3365
23942 Lyons Ave Ste 106 Newhall (91321) ***(P-18192)***
Santa Clarita Concrete....E....661 252-2012
16164 Sierra Hwy Santa Clarita (91390) ***(P-3212)***
Santa Clarita Convalescent HM, Newhall *Also called Valencia Health Care Inc* ***(P-20711)***
Santa Clarita Hauling/Blue, Santa Clarita *Also called USA Waste of California Inc* ***(P-6312)***
Santa Clarita Health Care Assn (PA)....D....661 253-8000
23845 Mcbean Pkwy Santa Clarita (91355) ***(P-26385)***
Santa Clarita Health Care Ctr, Santa Clarita *Also called Henry Mayo Newhall Mem Hosp* ***(P-22254)***
Santa Clarita Interiors Inc....D....661 253-0861
25682 Springbrook Ave # 130 Santa Clarita (91350) ***(P-3283)***
Santa Clarita Medical Group....E....661 255-6802
25775 Mcbean Pkwy Ste 209 Valencia (91355) ***(P-19367)***
Santa Clarita Swim Club, Valencia *Also called Academy Swim Club* ***(P-18347)***
Santa Clarita Valley Bldrs Inc....C....661 295-6722
24307 Magic Mountain Pkwy # 122 Santa Clarita (91355) ***(P-2975)***
SANTA CLARITA VALLEY SENIOR CE, Santa Clarita *Also called Santa Clarita Vlly Cmmtt Aging* ***(P-23451)***
Santa Clarita Valley Wtr Agcy....C....661 259-2737
26521 Summit Cir Santa Clarita (91350) ***(P-6117)***
Santa Clarita Vlly Cmmtt Aging....D....661 259-9444
22900 Market St Santa Clarita (91321) ***(P-23451)***
Santa Clarita Water Division, Santa Clarita *Also called Santa Clarita Valley Wtr Agcy* ***(P-6117)***
Santa Cruz County of....E....831 763-8400
1430 Freedom Blvd Ste D Watsonville (95076) ***(P-19368)***
Santa Cruz County of....D....831 454-2030
701 Ocean St Rm 530 Santa Cruz (95060) ***(P-15810)***
Santa Cruz County Symphony....E....831 462-0553
307 Church St Santa Cruz (95060) ***(P-18002)***
Santa Cruz Hotel Associates....C....831 426-4330
175 W Cliff Dr Santa Cruz (95060) ***(P-12885)***
Santa Cruz Medical Foundation (HQ)....D....831 458-5537
2025 Soquel Ave Santa Cruz (95062) ***(P-19369)***
Santa Cruz Metro Trnst Dst....D....831 469-1954
110 Vernon St Ste B Santa Cruz (95060) ***(P-3765)***
Santa Cruz Metro Trnst Dst....B....831 426-6080
135 Aviation Way Ste 2 Watsonville (95076) ***(P-3602)***
Santa Cruz Montessori School....E....831 476-1646
6230 Soquel Dr Aptos (95003) ***(P-23783)***
Santa Cruz Seaside Company (PA)....B....831 423-5590
400 Beach St Santa Cruz (95060) ***(P-18339)***
Santa Cruz Westside Elc Inc....D....831 469-8888
2656 Mission St Santa Cruz (95060) ***(P-2628)***
Santa Fe Pacific Pipeline, Bloomington *Also called Kinder Mrgan Enrgy Partners LP* ***(P-4810)***
Santa For Hire.com, Newport Beach *Also called Internet Booking Agencycom Inc* ***(P-14311)***
Santa Lucia Preserve Company....D....831 620-6760
1 Rancho San Carlos Rd Carmel (93923) ***(P-18560)***
Santa Margarita Water District (PA)....D....949 459-6400
26111 Antonio Pkwy Rcho STA Marg (92688) ***(P-6118)***
Santa Margarita YMCA Garrison, Oceanside *Also called YMCA of San Diego County* ***(P-24718)***
SANTA MARIA CARE CENTER, Santa Maria *Also called Kimberly Care Center Inc* ***(P-20041)***
Santa Maria Cinema 10, Santa Maria *Also called Edwards Theatres Circuit Inc* ***(P-17844)***
Santa Maria Hotel Corp....D....805 928-6000
2100 N Broadway Santa Maria (93454) ***(P-12886)***
Santa Maria Valley YMCA....C....805 937-8521
3400 Skyway Dr Santa Maria (93455) ***(P-24647)***
Santa Mnica Mntins Trils Cncil....D....818 222-4531
24735 Mulholland Hwy Woodland Hills (91302) ***(P-24648)***
Santa Mnica Wlshire Imging LLC....E....323 549-3055
5455 Wilshire Blvd Los Angeles (90036) ***(P-21584)***
Santa Monica City of....B....310 451-5444
1334 5th St Santa Monica (90401) ***(P-3766)***
Santa Monica Amusements LLC....B....310 451-9641
380 Santa Monica Pier Santa Monica (90401) ***(P-18340)***
Santa Monica Bay Physcians....C....310 459-2363
881 Alma Real Dr Ste 214 Pacific Palisades (90272) ***(P-19370)***
Santa Monica Bay Physicians He (PA)....D....310 417-5900
5767 W Century Blvd Los Angeles (90045) ***(P-19371)***
Santa Monica Bay Womens Club....E....310 395-1308
1210 4th St Santa Monica (90401) ***(P-24865)***
Santa Monica City of....D....310 399-5865
2802 4th St Santa Monica (90405) ***(P-23784)***

Mergent e-mail: customerrelations@mergent.com
1420
2020 Directory of California
Wholesalers and Services Companies
(P-0000) Products & Services Section entry number
(PA)=Parent Co (HQ)=Headquarters (DH)=Div Headquarters

ALPHABETIC SECTION SBC, Buena Park

Santa Monica City of......E......310 458-8551
1855 Main St Santa Monica (90401) ***(P-10641)***
Santa Monica Express Inc......D......310 458-6000
11150 W Olympic Blvd # 150 Los Angeles (90064) ***(P-3933)***
Santa Monica Family YMCA......D......310 451-7387
1332 6th St Santa Monica (90401) ***(P-24649)***
Santa Monica Hotel Owner LLC......C......310 395-3332
1707 4th St Santa Monica (90401) ***(P-12887)***
Santa Monica Hsr Ltd Partnr......C......310 395-3332
1707 4th St Santa Monica (90401) ***(P-12888)***
Santa Monica Orthopedic (PA)......D......310 315-2018
2020 Santa Monica Blvd # 230 Santa Monica (90404) ***(P-19372)***
Santa Monica Outpatient Center, Santa Monica *Also called Childrens Hospital Los Angeles* ***(P-20780)***
Santa Monica Proper Jv LLC......C......310 620-9990
700 Wilshire Blvd Santa Monica (90401) ***(P-12889)***
Santa Monica Seafood Company......C......310 393-5244
1000 Wilshire Blvd Santa Monica (90401) ***(P-8387)***
Santa Monica Sport Club, Santa Monica *Also called 24 Hour Fitness Usa Inc* ***(P-18105)***
Santa Monica Ucla Medical Ctr, Santa Monica *Also called University Cal Los Angeles* ***(P-21332)***
Santa Paula Hospital, Santa Paula *Also called Ventura County Medical Center* ***(P-19550)***
Santa Rosa & Sonoma Co Real Es......E......707 524-1124
1057 College Ave Santa Rosa (95404) ***(P-11438)***
Santa Rosa Berry Farms LLC......B......805 981-3060
3500 Camino Ave Ste 250 Oxnard (93030) ***(P-109)***
Santa Rosa Clinic, Santa Rosa *Also called Veterans Health Administration* ***(P-19565)***
Santa Rosa Community Hlth Ctrs (PA)......C......707 547-2222
3569 Round Barn Cir Santa Rosa (95403) ***(P-23452)***
Santa Rosa Convalescent Hosp, Santa Rosa *Also called Ashley Ltc Inc* ***(P-19727)***
Santa Rosa Dental Group......D......707 545-0944
1820 Sonoma Ave Ste 80 Santa Rosa (95405) ***(P-19629)***
Santa Rosa Golf & Country Club......D......707 546-3485
333 Country Club Dr Santa Rosa (95401) ***(P-18561)***
Santa Rosa Memorial Hospital (HQ)......A......707 546-3210
1165 Montgomery Dr Santa Rosa (95405) ***(P-21165)***
Santa Rosa Post Acute, Santa Rosa *Also called Santa Rosaidence Opco LLC* ***(P-20242)***
Santa Rosa Radiology Med Group (PA)......E......707 546-4062
121 Sotoyome St Santa Rosa (95405) ***(P-21585)***
Santa Rosa Rnchria Gaming Comm......D......559 924-6948
17225 Jersey Ave Lemoore (93245) ***(P-18003)***
Santa Rosa Surgery Center LP......D......707 575-5831
1111 Sonoma Ave Ste 214 Santa Rosa (95405) ***(P-21166)***
Santa Rosaidence Opco LLC......C......707 546-0471
4650 Hoen Ave Santa Rosa (95405) ***(P-20242)***
Santa Teresa Conv Hospital......D......562 948-1961
9140 Verner St Pico Rivera (90660) ***(P-21167)***
Santa Teresa Golf Center, San Jose *Also called Santa Teresa Golf Club* ***(P-18295)***
Santa Teresa Golf Club......D......408 225-2650
260 Bernal Rd San Jose (95119) ***(P-18295)***
Santa Teresita Inc (PA)......B......626 359-3243
819 Buena Vista St Duarte (91010) ***(P-21168)***
Santa Ynez Valley Cottage Hosp......D......805 688-6431
2050 Viborg Rd Solvang (93463) ***(P-21169)***
Santa Ynez Valley Marriott, Buellton *Also called Kang Family Partners LLC* ***(P-12500)***
Santaluz Club Inc......C......858 759-3120
8170 Caminito Santaluz E San Diego (92127) ***(P-18562)***
Santana Concrete......D......909 421-2218
4253 Fairgrounds St Riverside (92501) ***(P-3213)***
Santana Row Hotel Partners LP......C......408 551-0010
355 Santana Row Ste 1010 San Jose (95128) ***(P-12890)***
Sante Community Physicians, Fresno *Also called Sante Health System Inc* ***(P-9913)***
Sante Health System Inc (PA)......D......559 228-5400
7370 N Palm Ave Ste 101 Fresno (93711) ***(P-9913)***
Santee School District......D......619 956-5000
9665 Jeremy St Santee (92071) ***(P-24650)***
Santee Senior Retirement Com......C......619 955-0901
400 Lantern Crest Way Santee (92071) ***(P-23453)***
Santee Systems Services II......D......323 445-0044
229 E Gage Ave Los Angeles (90003) ***(P-23454)***
Santee Systems Services II LL......E......323 445-0044
229 E Gage Ave Los Angeles (90003) ***(P-18193)***
Santellan Farm Labor Contr, Woodlake *Also called Pete Santellan* ***(P-639)***
Santen Incorporated......D......415 268-9100
6401 Hollis St Ste 125 Emeryville (94608) ***(P-26027)***
Santos Legacy Builders LLC......D......916 439-2777
2829 Watt Ave 101 Sacramento (95821) ***(P-1188)***
Sants Clair Alcohol Meth Prog, San Jose *Also called Central Valley Clinic Inc* ***(P-21972)***
Sanyo Denki America Inc (HQ)......D......310 783-5400
468 Amapola Ave Torrance (90501) ***(P-6893)***
Sanyo Foods Corp America......C......714 730-1611
12442 Tustin Ranch Rd Tustin (92782) ***(P-18563)***
Sanzaru Games Inc......E......650 312-1000
1065 E Hillsdale Blvd Foster City (94404) ***(P-15074)***
Sap Labs LLC......D......650 849-4000
3475 Deer Creek Rd Palo Alto (94304) ***(P-15075)***
Sap Labs LLC (HQ)......B......650 849-4000
3410 Hillview Ave Palo Alto (94304) ***(P-15076)***
Sapho Inc......D......650 597-2746
1150 Bayhill Dr Ste 325 San Bruno (94066) ***(P-15077)***
Sapphire Softech Solutions LLC......D......888 357-5222
123 E 9th St Ste 323 Upland (91786) ***(P-16100)***
Sara, Cypress *Also called Scientific Applications & RES* ***(P-25828)***
Sarabian Farms, Sanger *Also called Virginia Sarabian* ***(P-217)***
Sarah Elizabeth Treusdell......E......661 949-0131
921 W Avenue J Ste C Lancaster (93534) ***(P-22122)***
Saratech, Mission Viejo *Also called Paydarfar Industries Inc* ***(P-6881)***
Saratoga Capital Inc......D......408 286-1000
233 W Santa Clara St San Jose (95113) ***(P-12891)***
Saratoga Court Inc......D......408 866-1392
18855 Cox Ave Saratoga (95070) ***(P-10859)***
Saratoga Retirement Community, Saratoga *Also called Odd Fellows Home California* ***(P-24012)***
Sarco Inc......E......949 888-5548
30412 Esperanza Rcho STA Marg (92688) ***(P-7338)***
Saro Lifestyle, Burbank *Also called Le Crochet By Saro Inc* ***(P-6567)***
Saroyan Lumber and Moulding Co, Huntington Park *Also called Saroyan Lumber Company Inc* ***(P-6654)***
Saroyan Lumber Company Inc (PA)......D......800 624-9309
6230 S Alameda St Huntington Park (90255) ***(P-6654)***
Sarpa-Feldman Enterprises Inc......D......408 982-1790
650 N King Rd San Jose (95133) ***(P-17046)***
Sas Entertainment Partners Inc......E......213 400-1901
6224 Greenleaf Ave Whittier (90601) ***(P-18004)***
Sas Institute Inc......D......949 250-9999
1148 N Lemon St Orange (92867) ***(P-15493)***
Sat, Sacramento *Also called Lpa Insurance Agency Inc* ***(P-15393)***
Satellite Dialysis, Modesto *Also called Satellite Healthcare Inc* ***(P-21935)***
Satellite Dialysis Centers, San Jose *Also called Satellite Healthcare Inc* ***(P-21936)***
Satellite First Communities LP (PA)......D......510 647-0700
1835 Alcatraz Ave Berkeley (94703) ***(P-10811)***
Satellite Healthcare Inc......D......209 578-0691
3500 Coffee Rd Ste 21 Modesto (95355) ***(P-21935)***
Satellite Healthcare Inc (PA)......D......650 404-3600
300 Santana Row Ste 300 # 300 San Jose (95128) ***(P-21936)***
Satellite Healthcare Inc......D......408 258-8720
2121 Alexian Dr Ste 118 San Jose (95116) ***(P-21937)***
Satellite Management Co (PA)......C......714 558-2411
1010 E Chestnut Ave Santa Ana (92701) ***(P-11439)***
Satellite Office, Van Nuys *Also called Southern Cal Orthpd Inst LP* ***(P-19412)***
Satellite Pros, Ontario *Also called Jeeva Corp* ***(P-2525)***
Sather Installation, Murrieta *Also called Sl Inc* ***(P-2977)***
Saticoy Country Club......D......805 647-1153
4450 Clubhouse Dr Somis (93066) ***(P-18564)***
Saticoy Fruit Exchange, Santa Paula *Also called Saticoy Lemon Association* ***(P-539)***
Saticoy Fruit Exchange, Ventura *Also called Saticoy Lemon Association* ***(P-195)***
Saticoy Lemon Association (PA)......D......805 654-6500
103 N Peck Rd Santa Paula (93060) ***(P-539)***
Saticoy Lemon Association......D......805 654-6500
7560 Bristol Rd Ventura (93003) ***(P-195)***
Saticoy Lemon Association......C......805 654-6543
600 E 3rd St Oxnard (93030) ***(P-24362)***
Satmetrix Systems Inc......C......650 227-8300
1820 Gateway Dr Ste 300 San Mateo (94404) ***(P-15078)***
Saturn Electric Inc......E......858 271-4100
7552 Trade St Ste A San Diego (92121) ***(P-2629)***
Sauce Labs Inc (PA)......D......855 677-0011
116 New Montgomery St # 3 San Francisco (94105) ***(P-15685)***
SAVA SENIOR CARE, Carmichael *Also called SSC Carmichael Operating Co LP* ***(P-20269)***
Savala Equipment Company Inc (PA)......D......949 552-1859
16402 Construction Cir E Irvine (92606) ***(P-14113)***
Savala Equipment Rentals, Irvine *Also called Savala Equipment Company Inc* ***(P-14113)***
Savant Construction Inc......D......909 614-4300
13830 Mountain Ave Chino (91710) ***(P-1591)***
Save Our Sunol......D......925 862-2263
2934 Kilkare Rd Sunol (94586) ***(P-24651)***
Save Queen LLC......B......562 435-3511
429 Shoreline Village Dr I Long Beach (90802) ***(P-12892)***
Savings Bank Mendocino County (PA)......C......707 462-6613
200 N School St Ukiah (95482) ***(P-9237)***
Saviynt Inc (PA)......C......310 641-1664
1301 E El Segundo Blvd El Segundo (90245) ***(P-26805)***
Savoy Contractors Group Inc......C......949 753-1919
8905 Research Dr Irvine (92618) ***(P-1189)***
Savvius Inc (HQ)......D......925 937-3200
1340 Treat Blvd Ste 500 Walnut Creek (94597) ***(P-15079)***
Sawmill, Ukiah *Also called Mendocino Forest Pdts Co LLC* ***(P-6632)***
Sawyers Heating & AC......D......209 416-7700
5272 Jerusalem Ct Ste D Modesto (95356) ***(P-2265)***
Saylor Lane Healthcare Center, Sacramento *Also called Kindred Healthcare Oper LLC* ***(P-20047)***
Saylor Lane Healthcare Center, Sacramento *Also called S L H C C Inc* ***(P-20226)***
Sb Product Group LLC......C......650 562-8221
1 Circle Star Way Fl 3 San Carlos (94070) ***(P-2630)***
Sbb Roofing Inc (PA)......C......323 254-2888
3310 Verdugo Rd Los Angeles (90065) ***(P-3097)***
SBC, San Diego *Also called AT&T Services Inc* ***(P-5322)***
SBC, San Ramon *Also called AT&T Services Inc* ***(P-5193)***
SBC, Monterey *Also called AT&T Services Inc* ***(P-5194)***
SBC, Jackson *Also called AT&T Services Inc* ***(P-5325)***
SBC, Anaheim *Also called AT&T Services Inc* ***(P-5327)***
SBC, San Diego *Also called AT&T Services Inc* ***(P-5328)***
SBC, Riverside *Also called AT&T Services Inc* ***(P-5330)***
SBC, Paso Robles *Also called AT&T Services Inc* ***(P-5331)***
SBC, Mountain View *Also called AT&T Services Inc* ***(P-5333)***
SBC, Los Angeles *Also called AT&T Services Inc* ***(P-5335)***
SBC, Santa Rosa *Also called AT&T Services Inc* ***(P-5339)***
SBC, Los Angeles *Also called AT&T Services Inc* ***(P-5342)***
SBC, San Jose *Also called AT&T Services Inc* ***(P-5343)***
SBC, San Francisco *Also called AT&T Services Inc* ***(P-5344)***
SBC, Buena Park *Also called AT&T Services Inc* ***(P-5346)***

ALPHABETIC

Employee Codes: A=Over 500 employees, B=251-500 C=101-250, D=51-100, E=50
2020 Directory of California Wholesalers and Services Companies
© Mergent Inc. 1-800-342-5647
1421

SBC, Concord *Also called AT&T Services Inc* ***(P-5347)***
SBC, Sacramento *Also called AT&T Services Inc* ***(P-5350)***
SBC, Oceanside *Also called AT&T Services Inc* ***(P-5351)***
SBC, Sacramento *Also called AT&T Services Inc* ***(P-5352)***
SBC, Concord *Also called AT&T Services Inc* ***(P-5353)***
SBC, San Diego *Also called AT&T Services Inc* ***(P-5354)***
SBC, Escondido *Also called AT&T Services Inc* ***(P-5355)***
SBC, Alhambra *Also called AT&T Services Inc* ***(P-5359)***
SBC, San Jose *Also called AT&T Services Inc* ***(P-5361)***
SBC Communications, Rancho Cordova *Also called AT&T Services Inc* ***(P-5338)***
SBE Contracting ....E....714 544-5066
17256 Red Hill Ave Irvine (92614) ***(P-2631)***
SBE Electrical Contracting Inc ....C....714 544-5066
2961 W Macarthur Blvd # 128 Santa Ana (92704) ***(P-2632)***
Sbm Management Services LP ....B....866 855-2211
5241 Arnold Ave McClellan (95652) ***(P-14038)***
Sbm Site Services LLC (PA) ....A....916 922-7600
5241 Arnold Ave McClellan (95652) ***(P-14039)***
SBMC, Ukiah *Also called Savings Bank Mendocino County* ***(P-9237)***
SBP, La Jolla *Also called Sanford Burnham Prebys Medical* ***(P-26026)***
SBPEA, San Bernardino *Also called San Brnrdino Pub Emplyees Assn* ***(P-24458)***
Sbrm Inc (PA) ....D....760 480-0208
2342 Meyers Ave Escondido (92029) ***(P-14040)***
Sbrpstc, San Jose *Also called South Bay Regl Public Safety T* ***(P-23639)***
SBSA, Redwood City *Also called Silicon Valley Clean Water* ***(P-6136)***
Sbsbtc, National City *Also called South Bay Sand Blasting and Ta* ***(P-17545)***
SC Builders Inc (PA) ....D....408 328-0688
910 Thompson Pl Sunnyvale (94085) ***(P-1592)***
SC Fuels, Orange *Also called Southern Counties Oil Co* ***(P-8716)***
SC Harp El Segundo LLC ....D....310 322-0999
1985 E Grand Ave El Segundo (90245) ***(P-12893)***
SC Wright Construction Inc ....B....619 698-6909
3838 Camino Del Rio Nth S San Diego (92108) ***(P-25298)***
Sca Enterprises Inc (PA) ....C....818 845-7621
3817 W Magnolia Blvd Burbank (91505) ***(P-17047)***
Scale Ai Inc ....D....617 803-5667
398 11th St San Francisco (94103) ***(P-15080)***
Scaleflux Inc ....D....408 628-2291
97 E Brokaw Rd Ste 260 San Jose (95112) ***(P-15686)***
Scalelab LLC (HQ) ....E....310 526-7524
6255 W Sunset Blvd # 850 Los Angeles (90028) ***(P-15081)***
Scalematrix Holdings Inc ....D....888 349-9994
5775 Kearny Villa Rd San Diego (92123) ***(P-16101)***
Scan, Long Beach *Also called Porchlight Inc* ***(P-20663)***
Scan California Management Co ....A....562 989-5100
3800 Kilroy Airport Way Long Beach (90806) ***(P-10041)***
Scan Group (PA) ....B....562 308-2733
3800 Kilroy Arprt Way # 100 Long Beach (90806) ***(P-10042)***
Scan Health Plan, Long Beach *Also called Senior Care* ***(P-10044)***
Scan-Vino LLC (PA) ....D....209 931-3570
5463 Cherokee Rd Stockton (95215) ***(P-4126)***
Scandia Family Fun Center, Sacramento *Also called Scandia Sports Inc* ***(P-18756)***
Scandia Sports Inc ....E....916 331-5757
5070 Hillsdale Blvd Sacramento (95842) ***(P-18756)***
Scantibodies Clinical Lab Inc ....E....866 249-1212
9236 Abraham Way Santee (92071) ***(P-21586)***
Scarborough Farms Inc ....C....805 483-9113
731 Pacific Ave Oxnard (93030) ***(P-76)***
Scat Enterprises Inc ....D....310 370-5501
1400 Kingsdale Ave Redondo Beach (90278) ***(P-6467)***
Scattergood Generation Plant, Playa Del Rey *Also called Los Angeles Dept Wtr & Pwr* ***(P-6010)***
SCC ESA Dept of Risk Mgmt ....D....408 441-4207
2310 N 1st St Ste 202 San Jose (95131) ***(P-10482)***
SCCH Inc ....D....562 494-5188
1880 Dawson Ave Signal Hill (90755) ***(P-26386)***
Scci, Orcutt *Also called Spiess Construction Co Inc* ***(P-1915)***
Scdrg Inc ....D....818 874-0830
473 S Carnegie Dr San Bernardino (92408) ***(P-13575)***
SCE, Rosemead *Also called Southern California Edison Co* ***(P-5925)***
SCE Eastern Hydro Division ....D....760 873-0767
4000 Bishop Creek Rd Bishop (93514) ***(P-5918)***
SCE FCU, Baldwin Park *Also called SCE Federal Credit Union* ***(P-9348)***
SCE Federal Credit Union (PA) ....D....626 960-6888
12701 Schabarum Ave Baldwin Park (91706) ***(P-9348)***
Scene7 Inc ....D....415 506-6000
6 Hamilton Landing # 150 Novato (94949) ***(P-15082)***
Scenic Circle Care Center, Modesto *Also called Riverside Health Care Corp* ***(P-20672)***
Scenic Route Inc ....E....818 896-6006
13516 Desmond St Pacoima (91331) ***(P-3463)***
Scga Golf Course MGT Inc ....D....951 677-7446
39500 Robrt Trnt Jnes Pkw Murrieta (92563) ***(P-18296)***
Schaefer Ambulance Service Inc ....B....323 468-1642
4627 Beverly Blvd Los Angeles (90004) ***(P-3722)***
Schaefer Mary-Judith ....D....562 634-3164
7202 Petterson Ln Paramount (90723) ***(P-3464)***
Schaefer Parking Lot Service, Paramount *Also called Schaefer Mary-Judith* ***(P-3464)***
Schafer Bros Trnsf Pano Movers (PA) ....D....310 835-7231
1981 E 213th St Carson (90810) ***(P-4499)***
Schafer Logistics, Carson *Also called Schafer Bros Trnsf Pano Movers* ***(P-4499)***
Schaper Construction Inc (PA) ....D....408 437-0337
1177 N 15th St San Jose (95112) ***(P-2393)***
Scharp's Oasis House, Los Angeles *Also called South Cntl Heatlh & Rehab Prog* ***(P-22128)***
Scheid Vineyards Inc (PA) ....D....831 455-9990
305 Hilltown Rd Salinas (93908) ***(P-161)***
Scheid Vineyards Inc ....C....707 433-1858
373 Healdsburg Ave Healdsburg (95448) ***(P-162)***
Schenker Inc ....D....650 745-3000
380 Littlefield Ave South San Francisco (94080) ***(P-5045)***
Scherzer International Corp (PA) ....D....818 227-2770
21650 Oxnard St Ste 300 Woodland Hills (91367) ***(P-17048)***
Schetter Electric, Sacramento *Also called M K S Construction Inc* ***(P-1153)***
Schetter Electric Inc (PA) ....D....916 446-2521
471 Bannon St Sacramento (95811) ***(P-2633)***
Schetter Electric Inc ....C....925 228-2424
737 Arnold Dr Ste D Martinez (94553) ***(P-2634)***
Schetter Electric LLC ....D....916 446-2521
471 Bannon St Sacramento (95811) ***(P-2635)***
Schick Moving & Storage Co (PA) ....D....714 731-5500
2721 Michelle Dr Tustin (92780) ***(P-4230)***
Schilling Paradise Corp ....C....619 449-4141
697 Greenfield Dr El Cajon (92021) ***(P-1910)***
Schilling Robotics LLC ....D....530 753-6718
201 Cousteau Pl Davis (95618) ***(P-25299)***
Schindler Elevator Corporation ....D....310 785-9775
2000 Avenue Of The Stars Los Angeles (90067) ***(P-17539)***
Schindler Elevator Corporation ....C....818 336-3000
16450 Fthill Blvd Ste 200 Sylmar (91342) ***(P-17540)***
Schirmer Fire Protection Eng ....D....213 630-2020
707 Wilshire Blvd # 2600 Los Angeles (90017) ***(P-10483)***
Schlumberger Technology Corp ....D....661 864-4750
2841 Pegasus Dr Bakersfield (93308) ***(P-1042)***
Schlumberger Technology Corp ....D....714 379-7332
12131 Industry St Garden Grove (92841) ***(P-1043)***
Schlumberger Well Services, Bakersfield *Also called Schlumberger Technology Corp* ***(P-1042)***
Schmidt Fire Protection Co Inc ....D....858 279-6122
4760 Murphy Canyon Rd # 100 San Diego (92123) ***(P-2266)***
Schmidt Phyllis MD Corporation ....A....213 613-1163
711 W College St Los Angeles (90012) ***(P-21170)***
SCHMITT HOUSE, El Monte *Also called Hope Hse For Mltple Hndicapped* ***(P-23961)***
Schneider Electric 600, Pleasanton *Also called Schneider Electric Usa Inc* ***(P-7180)***
Schneider Electric 650, Diamond Bar *Also called Schneider Electric Usa Inc* ***(P-7181)***
Schneider Electric Usa Inc ....D....925 462-0986
6160 Stoneridge Mall Rd # 200 Pleasanton (94588) ***(P-7180)***
Schneider Electric Usa Inc ....D....909 612-5400
21680 Gateway Center Dr # 300 Diamond Bar (91765) ***(P-7181)***
Schneider Electric Usa Inc ....D....909 438-2295
14725 Monte Vista Ave Chino (91710) ***(P-4500)***
Schneider National Inc ....C....661 858-1031
4193 Industrial Pkwy Dr Lebec (93243) ***(P-4127)***
Schneider National Inc ....C....909 574-2165
14392 Valley Blvd Fontana (92335) ***(P-4128)***
Schnierow Dental Care ....E....310 377-6453
13450 Hawthorne Blvd Hawthorne (90250) ***(P-19630)***
Schnitzer Steel Industries Inc ....D....510 444-3919
1101 Embarcadero W Oakland (94607) ***(P-7771)***
Scholastic Book Fairs Inc ....D....714 237-1100
2890 E White Star Ave Anaheim (92806) ***(P-8876)***
Scholastic Book Fairs Inc ....D....510 771-1700
42001 Christy St Fremont (94538) ***(P-8877)***
Scholls, Ontario *Also called Distribution Alternatives Inc* ***(P-4399)***
School Innovations Achievement (PA) ....D....916 933-2290
5200 Golden Foothill Pkwy El Dorado Hills (95762) ***(P-15494)***
Schools Financial Credit Union (PA) ....C....916 569-5400
1485 Response Rd Ste 126 Sacramento (95815) ***(P-9405)***
Schoolsfirst Federal Credit Un (PA) ....B....714 258-4000
2115 N Broadway Santa Ana (92706) ***(P-9349)***
Schoolwires Inc ....D....626 974-7600
645 S Barranca St West Covina (91791) ***(P-5799)***
Schramsberg Vineyards Company ....E....707 942-4558
1400 Schramsberg Rd Calistoga (94515) ***(P-163)***
Schricker, Oceanside *Also called Central Indiana Hdwr Co Inc* ***(P-7387)***
Schrimp, Roger Attorney, Oakdale *Also called Damrell Nelson Schrimp Pall* ***(P-22458)***
Schroff Inc ....C....858 740-2400
7328 Trade St San Diego (92121) ***(P-9010)***
Schroff Inc ....C....858 740-2400
7328 Trade St San Diego (92121) ***(P-17460)***
Schryver Med Sls & Mktg LLC ....C....303 371-0073
526 Mccormick St San Leandro (94577) ***(P-21587)***
Schryver Med Sls & Mktg LLC ....D....303 459-8160
8545 Arjons Dr San Diego (92126) ***(P-21588)***
Schryver Med Sls & Mktg LLC ....D....303 459-8160
1845 N Case St Orange (92865) ***(P-21589)***
Schryver Med Sls & Mktg LLC ....D....303 459-8150
310 N Cluff Ave Ste 212 Lodi (95240) ***(P-21590)***
Schubert Nursery (PA) ....D....831 753-0144
139 Zabala Rd Salinas (93908) ***(P-8918)***
Schuff Steel Company ....C....209 938-0869
10100 Trinity Pkwy # 400 Stockton (95219) ***(P-3284)***
Schulte Ranches ....D....805 563-0821
Rr 1 Box 228 Goleta (93117) ***(P-358)***
Schumacher Cargo Logistics Inc (PA) ....D....562 408-6677
550 W 135th St Gardena (90248) ***(P-5046)***
Schwager Davis Inc ....C....408 281-9300
198 Hillsdale Ave San Jose (95136) ***(P-1989)***
Schweizer Rena ....D....818 501-7100
15720 Ventura Blvd # 100 Encino (91436) ***(P-11440)***
SCI, North Hollywood *Also called Pierce Brothers* ***(P-13374)***
SCI, Corona Del Mar *Also called Service Corp International* ***(P-11444)***
SCI, Oceanside *Also called Service Corp International* ***(P-11636)***
Sci Inc ....D....951 245-7511
18501 Collier Ave B106 Lake Elsinore (92530) ***(P-3214)***

SCI Real Estate Invstments LLC ....D....310 361-8588
11620 Wilshire Blvd Fl 9 Los Angeles (90025) ***(P-11876)***
Scico, Avalon *Also called Santa Catalina Island Company* ***(P-4864)***
Scicon Technologies Corp (PA) ....D....661 295-8630
27525 Newhall Ranch Rd # 2 Valencia (91355) ***(P-25300)***
Scicon Technologies Corp ....D....949 252-1341
1300 Quail St Ste 208 Newport Beach (92660) ***(P-25301)***
Science Applications Intl Corp ....D....703 676-4300
4065 Hancock St Ste 110 San Diego (92110) ***(P-16102)***
Science Applications Intl Corp ....A....858 826-3061
4015 Hancock St San Diego (92110) ***(P-15687)***
Science Exchange Inc (PA) ....D....562 665-8978
435 Tasso St Ste 100 Palo Alto (94301) ***(P-16103)***
Science of Skincare LLC ....D....818 254-7961
3333 N San Fernando Blvd Burbank (91504) ***(P-7981)***
Scientific Applications & RES (PA) ....D....714 828-1465
6300 Gateway Dr Cypress (90630) ***(P-25828)***
Scientific Concepts Inc ....B....650 578-1142
303 Vintage Park Dr # 220 Foster City (94404) ***(P-17541)***
Scihp, Santa Rosa *Also called Sonoma County Indian Health PR* ***(P-19406)***
Scilex Holding Company (HQ) ....D....858 203-4100
4955 Directors Pl San Diego (92121) ***(P-7982)***
Scilex Pharmaceuticals Inc (HQ) ....D....949 441-2270
4955 Directors Pl Ste 100 San Diego (92121) ***(P-17049)***
Sciots Tract Association ....D....530 753-5219
937 Chestnut Ln Davis (95616) ***(P-24652)***
SCLARC, Los Angeles *Also called South Central Los* ***(P-24227)***
Scmg, San Diego *Also called Sharp Community Medical Group* ***(P-24424)***
Scmh, Whittier *Also called Southern California Mtl Hdlg* ***(P-7593)***
Scms, Aptos *Also called Santa Cruz Montessori School* ***(P-23783)***
Scope Seven LLC ....D....310 220-3939
2201 Park Pl Ste 100 El Segundo (90245) ***(P-7835)***
Scopely Inc (PA) ....C....323 400-6618
3530 Hayden Ave Ste A Culver City (90232) ***(P-15495)***
Scorpio Enterprises ....D....562 946-9464
12556 Mccann Dr Santa Fe Springs (90670) ***(P-2267)***
Scorpion Athc Booster CLB Inc ....E....805 482-2005
300 E Esplanade Dr # 250 Oxnard (93036) ***(P-24653)***
Scorpion Design LLC ....A....661 702-0100
27750 Entertainment Dr Valencia (91355) ***(P-13576)***
Scott A Porter Prof Corp ....D....916 929-1481
350 University Ave # 200 Sacramento (95825) ***(P-22805)***
Scott J Witlin Atty, Los Angeles *Also called Proskauer Rose LLP* ***(P-22779)***
Scott Jacks DDS Inc ....C....323 564-2444
4444 Tweedy Blvd South Gate (90280) ***(P-19631)***
Scott Place Associates ....D....650 345-8222
60 31st Ave San Mateo (94403) ***(P-11441)***
Scott Silva Concrete Inc ....D....916 859-0593
11374 Gold Dredge Way Rancho Cordova (95742) ***(P-3215)***
Scott Street Senior Housing Co ....C....415 345-5083
2180 Post St San Francisco (94115) ***(P-20451)***
Scott's Glass Service, Carson *Also called Scotts Labor Leasing Co Inc* ***(P-14413)***
Scottel Voice & Data Inc ....C....310 737-7300
6100 Center Dr Ste 720 Los Angeles (90045) ***(P-17461)***
Scottish American Insurance (PA) ....D....714 550-5050
2002 E Mcfadden Ave # 100 Santa Ana (92705) ***(P-10484)***
Scotts Labor Leasing Co Inc ....D....310 835-8388
22560 Lucerne St Carson (90745) ***(P-14413)***
Scotts Plant Service Co ....D....209 545-0903
6206 Carver Rd Modesto (95356) ***(P-904)***
SCR, Costa Mesa *Also called South Coast Repertory Inc* ***(P-17947)***
Screamline Investment Corp (PA) ....C....323 201-0114
2130 S Tubeway Ave Commerce (90040) ***(P-4865)***
Screen Actors Guild - American ....C....818 954-9400
3601 W Olive Ave Fl 2 Burbank (91505) ***(P-10224)***
Screen Actors Guild-Producers, Burbank *Also called Screen Actors Guild - American* ***(P-10224)***
Screen Spe Usa LLC (HQ) ....C....408 523-9140
820 Kifer Rd Ste B Sunnyvale (94086) ***(P-7339)***
Screenworks LLC ....D....951 279-8877
1900 Compton Ave Ste 101 Corona (92881) ***(P-13799)***
Screenworks Nep, Corona *Also called Screenworks LLC* ***(P-13799)***
Scribd Inc ....D....415 896-9890
460 Bryant St Fl 1 San Francisco (94107) ***(P-15887)***
Scrip Advantage Inc ....D....559 320-0052
4273 W Richert Ave # 110 Fresno (93722) ***(P-17050)***
Scripps Ambulatory Surgery Ctr, Encinitas *Also called Scripps Health* ***(P-21172)***
Scripps Aquarium, La Jolla *Also called Birch Aquarium At Scripps* ***(P-24303)***
Scripps Clinic ....C....858 794-1250
12395 El Camino Real San Diego (92130) ***(P-21171)***
Scripps Clinic - Encinitas, Encinitas *Also called Scripps Health* ***(P-19379)***
Scripps Clinic Carmel Valley ....B....858 554-8096
10666 N Torrey Pines Rd La Jolla (92037) ***(P-19373)***
Scripps Clinic Foundation ....A....858 554-9000
12395 El Camino Real San Diego (92130) ***(P-26387)***
Scripps Clinic Medical Group ....B....858 554-9606
10666 N Torrey Pines Rd La Jolla (92037) ***(P-19374)***
Scripps Clinic Ob-Gyn, San Diego *Also called Scripps Health* ***(P-19378)***
Scripps Del Mar, San Diego *Also called Scripps Health* ***(P-22123)***
Scripps Dialasys Inc (PA) ....E....619 453-9070
9870 Genesee Ave La Jolla (92037) ***(P-19375)***
Scripps Dialysis Center, La Jolla *Also called Scripps Dialasys Inc* ***(P-19375)***
Scripps Green Hospital, La Jolla *Also called Scripps Health* ***(P-21180)***
Scripps Health ....D....760 753-8413
320 Santa Fe Dr Ste 310 Encinitas (92024) ***(P-21172)***
Scripps Health ....B....760 806-9263
122 Civic Center Dr # 101 Vista (92084) ***(P-20243)***
Scripps Health ....D....858 622-9076
10140 Campus Point Dr San Diego (92121) ***(P-21173)***
Scripps Health ....D....619 294-8111
4077 5th Ave San Diego (92103) ***(P-21174)***
Scripps Health ....C....619 862-6600
237 Church Ave Chula Vista (91910) ***(P-19694)***
Scripps Health ....C....858 678-6966
10010 Campus Point Dr San Diego (92121) ***(P-24654)***
Scripps Health ....C....858 657-4218
10790 Rancho Bernardo Rd San Diego (92127) ***(P-20244)***
Scripps Health ....B....858 271-9770
15004 Innovation Dr San Diego (92128) ***(P-21175)***
Scripps Health ....B....619 245-2350
7565 Mission Valley Rd # 200 San Diego (92108) ***(P-21176)***
Scripps Health ....C....760 479-3900
477 N El Camino Real A208 Encinitas (92024) ***(P-19376)***
Scripps Health ....C....760 753-6501
354 Santa Fe Dr Encinitas (92024) ***(P-21177)***
Scripps Health ....D....619 670-5400
10862 Calle Verde La Mesa (91941) ***(P-19377)***
Scripps Health ....C....858 882-8350
9850 Genesee Ave Ste 600 San Diego (92121) ***(P-19378)***
Scripps Health ....A....619 691-7000
435 H St Chula Vista (91910) ***(P-21178)***
Scripps Health (PA) ....A....800 727-4777
10140 Campus Point Dr Ax415 San Diego (92121) ***(P-21179)***
Scripps Health ....B....858 455-9100
10666 N Torrey Pines Rd La Jolla (92037) ***(P-21180)***
Scripps Health ....B....619 294-8111
4077 Fifth Ave San Diego (92103) ***(P-21181)***
Scripps Health ....D....760 633-6915
310 Santa Fe Dr Ste 200 Encinitas (92024) ***(P-19379)***
Scripps Health ....B....858 764-3000
3811 Valley Centre Dr San Diego (92130) ***(P-21860)***
Scripps Health ....C....800 727-4777
10666 N Torrey Pines Rd La Jolla (92037) ***(P-21182)***
Scripps Health ....C....760 806-5700
488 E Valley Pkwy Ste 411 Escondido (92025) ***(P-19380)***
Scripps Health ....C....858 452-1279
9850 Genesee Ave Ste 900 La Jolla (92037) ***(P-24655)***
Scripps Health ....B....858 458-5100
9834 Genesee Ave Ste 311 La Jolla (92037) ***(P-19381)***
Scripps Health ....C....858 626-5200
9850 Genesee Ave Ste 620 La Jolla (92037) ***(P-19382)***
Scripps Health ....B....858 626-6150
9888 Genesee Ave La Jolla (92037) ***(P-21183)***
Scripps Health ....D....858 554-8892
10666 N Torrey Pines Rd La Jolla (92037) ***(P-19383)***
Scripps Health ....D....858 554-9489
10666 N Torrey Pines Rd La Jolla (92037) ***(P-19384)***
Scripps Health ....C....760 901-5200
3998 Vista Way Ste E Oceanside (92056) ***(P-19385)***
Scripps Health ....C....858 626-4123
9888 Genesee Ave La Jolla (92037) ***(P-21184)***
Scripps Health ....D....858 784-5888
10790 Rancho Bernardo Rd San Diego (92127) ***(P-19386)***
Scripps Health ....C....858 652-5504
10666 N Torrey Pines Rd La Jolla (92037) ***(P-25829)***
Scripps Health ....C....858 794-0160
3811 Valley Centre Dr San Diego (92130) ***(P-22123)***
Scripps Mem Hosp - Encinatas, Encinitas *Also called Scripps Health* ***(P-21177)***
Scripps Mem Hosp - La Jolla, La Jolla *Also called Scripps Health* ***(P-21184)***
Scripps Mem Hospital-La Jolla, La Jolla *Also called Scripps Health* ***(P-21183)***
Scripps Mercy Hospital, San Diego *Also called Scripps Health* ***(P-21174)***
Scripps Mercy Hospital, San Diego *Also called Scripps Health* ***(P-21181)***
Scripps Mercy Hospital ....D....619 294-8111
4077 5th Ave Mer35 San Diego (92103) ***(P-21185)***
Scripps Mercy Hospitals, Chula Vista *Also called Scripps Health* ***(P-21178)***
Scripps Ranch Recreation Club (PA) ....D....858 271-6222
9875 Aviary Dr San Diego (92131) ***(P-18565)***
Scripps Rancho Bernardo, San Diego *Also called Scripps Health* ***(P-21175)***
Scripps Research Institute ....D....858 242-1000
11119 N Torrey Pines Rd La Jolla (92037) ***(P-26028)***
Scripps Research Institute (PA) ....C....858 784-1000
10550 N Torrey Pines Rd La Jolla (92037) ***(P-26029)***
Scripps Shared Services, San Diego *Also called Scripps Health* ***(P-20244)***
Scripps Torrey Pines, La Jolla *Also called Scripps Health* ***(P-21182)***
Scripps Whttier Dbetes Program, San Diego *Also called Scripps Health* ***(P-21173)***
Script To Screen Inc ....D....714 558-3287
200 N Tustin Ave Ste 200 # 200 Santa Ana (92705) ***(P-17666)***
Scripto, Ontario *Also called Calico Brands Inc* ***(P-8955)***
Scst Inc (HQ) ....D....619 280-4321
6280 Riverdale St San Diego (92120) ***(P-26105)***
Scv Facilities Services ....D....310 803-4588
1907 W 75th St Los Angeles (90047) ***(P-14041)***
Scwa, Sacramento *Also called Sacramento County Water Agency* ***(P-6104)***
SCWD, Laguna Beach *Also called South Coast Water District* ***(P-6121)***
SD Deacon Corp California ....D....916 969-0900
7745 Greenback Ln Ste 250 Citrus Heights (95610) ***(P-1593)***
SD Hotel Circle LLC ....D....619 881-6800
2201 Hotel Cir S San Diego (92108) ***(P-12894)***
SD Sports MDCne&fmly Hlth Cntr ....D....619 229-3910
6699 Alvarado Rd Ste 2100 San Diego (92120) ***(P-19387)***
SD Stadium Hotel LLC ....D....858 278-9300
3805 Murphy Canyon Rd San Diego (92123) ***(P-12895)***
Sdcraa, San Diego *Also called San Dego Cnty Rgnal Arprt Auth* ***(P-4789)***
Sdg Enterprises ....D....805 777-7978
822 Hampshire Rd Ste H Westlake Village (91361) ***(P-2268)***

A L P H A B E T I C

Employee Codes: A=Over 500 employees, B=251-500
C=101-250, D=51-100, E=50
2020 Directory of California
Wholesalers and Services Companies
© Mergent Inc. 1-800-342-5647
1423

SDG&E, San Diego *Also called San Diego Gas & Electric Co* ***(P-5997)***

Sdi Media USA, Los Angeles *Also called SDI Media USA Inc* ***(P-17667)***

SDI Media USA Inc (HQ).....D.....323 602-5455
6060 Center Dr Ste 100 Los Angeles (90045) ***(P-17667)***

Sdl, Los Angeles *Also called Language Weaver Inc* ***(P-14907)***

SE San Diego Hotel LLC.....D.....619 515-3000
1047 5th Ave San Diego (92101) ***(P-12896)***

SE Scher Corporation.....A.....408 844-0772
1585 The Alameda San Jose (95126) ***(P-14564)***

SE Scher Corporation.....A.....858 546-8300
2525 Camino Del Rio S San Diego (92108) ***(P-14414)***

SE Scher Corporation.....B.....916 632-1363
6731 Five Star Blvd Ste C Rocklin (95677) ***(P-14415)***

Sea Breeze Collision, Tustin *Also called Sterling Collision Center LLC* ***(P-17312)***

Sea Breeze Financial Services (PA).....E.....949 223-9700
18191 Von Karman Ave # 150 Irvine (92612) ***(P-9601)***

Sea Breeze Health Care Inc.....C.....714 847-9671
7781 Garfield Ave Huntington Beach (92648) ***(P-20245)***

Sea Breeze Mortgage Services, Irvine *Also called Sea Breeze Financial Services* ***(P-9601)***

Sea Catch Seafoods, El Monte *Also called Atlanta Seafoods LLC* ***(P-8363)***

Sea Cliff Health Care, Huntington Beach *Also called Huntington Bch Cnvlescent Hosp* ***(P-20026)***

Sea Cliff Healthcare Center, Huntington Beach *Also called HB Healthcare Associates LLC* ***(P-19995)***

Sea View Medical Group Inc.....D.....805 373-5781
1901 Solar Dr Ste 265 Oxnard (93036) ***(P-22321)***

Sea West Cast Gard Fdral Cr Un (PA).....D.....510 568-4100
8750 Mountain Blvd Oakland (94605) ***(P-9350)***

Sea Win Inc.....E.....213 688-2899
526 Stanford Ave Los Angeles (90013) ***(P-8388)***

Sea-Air International Inc.....D.....310 338-0778
11222 S La Cienega Blvd # 100 Inglewood (90304) ***(P-5047)***

Sea-Logix LLC.....D.....510 271-1400
1425 Maritime St Oakland (94607) ***(P-4129)***

Seaboard Corporation.....B.....806 435-5935
10350 Hritg Pk Dr Ste 111 Santa Fe Springs (90670) ***(P-383)***

Seaboard Produce Distrs Inc.....D.....805 981-8001
710 Del Norte Blvd Oxnard (93030) ***(P-4501)***

Seabreeze Management Co Inc (PA).....D.....949 855-1800
26840 Aliso Viejo Pkwy # 100 Aliso Viejo (92656) ***(P-26388)***

Seabreeze Management Comp, Aliso Viejo *Also called Glenwood Village Cmnty Assn* ***(P-24553)***

Seacastle Inc.....D.....925 480-3000
4000 Executive Pkwy # 240 San Ramon (94583) ***(P-14196)***

Seacliff Country Club, Huntington Beach *Also called American Golf Corporation* ***(P-18366)***

Seacliff Inn Inc.....D.....831 661-4671
7500 Old Dominion Ct Aptos (95003) ***(P-12897)***

Seacoast Commerce Bank (HQ).....D.....858 432-7000
11939 Rncho Brnrdo Rd Ste San Diego (92128) ***(P-9271)***

Seacrest Convalescent Hosp Inc.....D.....310 833-3526
1416 W 6th St San Pedro (90732) ***(P-20246)***

Seafus Corporation.....E.....415 584-6100
1365 Lowrie Ave South San Francisco (94080) ***(P-14042)***

Seal Electric Inc.....C.....619 449-7323
1162 Greenfield Dr El Cajon (92021) ***(P-2636)***

Sealant Systems International.....D.....805 489-0490
125 Venture Dr Ste 210 San Luis Obispo (93401) ***(P-6489)***

Sealaska Envmtl Svcs LLC.....D.....619 564-8329
3838 Camino Del Rio N # 240 San Diego (92108) ***(P-27205)***

Seaman Nurseries Inc.....D.....559 665-1860
336 Robertson Blvd Ste A Chowchilla (93610) ***(P-441)***

Sean P OConnor.....D.....949 851-7323
1900 Main St Ste 700 Irvine (92614) ***(P-22806)***

Seaport Fish Company, Wilmington *Also called Star Fisheries* ***(P-8393)***

SEAPORT MEAT COMPANY, Spring Valley *Also called Pnc Inc* ***(P-8414)***

Search Agency Inc (PA).....D.....310 582-5700
801 N Brand Blvd Ste 1020 Glendale (91203) ***(P-13577)***

Search Engine Optimization Inc.....D.....760 929-0039
5841 Edison Pl Ste 140 Carlsbad (92008) ***(P-26806)***

Search Optics LLC (PA).....D.....858 678-0707
5770 Oberlin Dr San Diego (92121) ***(P-26807)***

Searles Valley Minerals Inc.....A.....760 372-2259
80201 Trona Rd Trona (93562) ***(P-1062)***

Sears, Benicia *Also called Innovel Solutions Inc* ***(P-4971)***

Sears, Delano *Also called Innovel Solutions Inc* ***(P-4972)***

Sears, Ontario *Also called Innovel Solutions Inc* ***(P-4973)***

Sears Roebuck and Co.....D.....925 246-1996
1001 Sunvalley Blvd Concord (94520) ***(P-17425)***

Sears Roebuck and Co.....D.....951 719-3528
40680 Winchester Rd Temecula (92591) ***(P-17426)***

Sears Roebuck and Co.....D.....530 751-4628
1235 Colusa Ave Yuba City (95991) ***(P-17427)***

Sears Roebuck and Co.....C.....714 256-7328
100 Brea Mall Brea (92821) ***(P-17542)***

Sears Roebuck and Co.....C.....909 390-4210
5691 E Philadelphia St Ontario (91761) ***(P-17543)***

Sears Roebuck and Co.....C.....619 590-3812
1406 N Johnson Ave El Cajon (92020) ***(P-17462)***

Sears Home Imprv Pdts Inc.....D.....858 790-7721
9586 Dist Ave Ste F San Diego (92121) ***(P-1190)***

Sears Service Center, El Cajon *Also called Sears Roebuck and Co* ***(P-17462)***

Seascape Golf Club, Aptos *Also called American Golf Corporation* ***(P-18373)***

Seascape Resort Ltd A Calif.....B.....831 662-7120
19 Seascape Vlg Aptos (95003) ***(P-12898)***

Seasholtz John.....C.....559 659-3805
1355 M St Firebaugh (93622) ***(P-77)***

Seaside Hotel Lessee Inc.....C.....310 260-7500
1819 Ocean Ave Santa Monica (90401) ***(P-17051)***

Seaside Laguna Inn & Suites.....D.....949 494-9717
1661 S Coast Hwy Laguna Beach (92651) ***(P-12899)***

Seaside Rfrigerated Trnspt Inc (PA).....E.....510 732-0472
7041 Las Positas Rd Ste H Livermore (94551) ***(P-4130)***

Season Produce Co Inc.....B.....213 689-0008
1601 E Olympic Blvd # 315 Los Angeles (90021) ***(P-8519)***

Seasons.....D.....562 691-1200
200 W Whittier Blvd La Habra (90631) ***(P-24066)***

Seatech Consulting Group Inc.....E.....310 356-6828
609 Deep Valley Dr # 200 Rllng HLS Est (90274) ***(P-16104)***

Seaver International.....D.....707 291-4929
4169 Green Valley Schl Rd Sebastopol (95472) ***(P-16105)***

Seaview Hlthcre & Rehab Ctr LL.....D.....707 443-5668
6400 Purdue Dr Eureka (95503) ***(P-24067)***

Seaview Industries.....E.....714 957-5073
2501 Harbor Blvd Costa Mesa (92626) ***(P-17052)***

Seaworld Global Logistics.....B.....310 208-9488
1421 Barry Ave Apt 5 Los Angeles (90025) ***(P-5048)***

Sebastian, Kerman *Also called Kerman Telephone Co* ***(P-5430)***

Sebastian, Fresno *Also called Kertel Communications Inc* ***(P-2532)***

Sebastian Enterprises Inc (PA).....D.....559 946-4954
811 S Madera Ave Kerman (93630) ***(P-5466)***

SEC Pac Inc.....D.....925 938-9200
1555 Riviera Ave Ste E Walnut Creek (94596) ***(P-11442)***

Seca Eqp Removal & Dismantle.....E.....209 543-1600
684 Bitritto Ct Modesto (95356) ***(P-3350)***

Seca Eqp Removal & Dismantling, Modesto *Also called Seca Eqp Removal & Dismantle* ***(P-3350)***

Secom International (PA).....D.....310 641-1290
15905 S Broadway Gardena (90248) ***(P-15688)***

Second Chance Inc (PA).....E.....510 792-4357
6330 Thornton Ave Ste B Newark (94560) ***(P-23455)***

Second Harvest Food.....D.....949 653-2900
8014 Marine Way Irvine (92618) ***(P-23456)***

Second Harvest Food Bank, San Jose *Also called Second Harvest Silicon Valley* ***(P-23457)***

Second Harvest Silicon Valley (PA).....C.....408 266-8866
750 Curtner Ave San Jose (95125) ***(P-23457)***

Second Image National LLC (PA).....C.....800 229-7477
170 E Arrow Hwy San Dimas (91773) ***(P-13766)***

Second Opinion Med Grp Inc.....D.....805 496-4315
2876 Sycamore Dr Ste 305 Simi Valley (93065) ***(P-10043)***

Second Street Corporation.....C.....310 394-5454
1111 2nd St Santa Monica (90403) ***(P-12900)***

Secova Inc.....C.....714 384-0530
3090 Bristol St Ste 200 Costa Mesa (92626) ***(P-26808)***

Secova Eservices Inc (HQ).....D.....714 384-0655
3090 Bristol St Ste 200 Costa Mesa (92626) ***(P-26809)***

Secret Charm LLC (PA).....C.....213 742-7744
1433 Walnut St Los Angeles (90011) ***(P-8109)***

Secrom Inc.....D.....310 830-4010
345 E Carson St Carson (90745) ***(P-20678)***

Sectek Inc.....D.....650 604-1785
Bldg 15 Mountain View (94035) ***(P-16556)***

Sectran Armored Truck Service, Pico Rivera *Also called Sectran Security Incorporated* ***(P-16400)***

Sectran Security Incorporated (PA).....C.....562 948-1446
7633 Industry Ave Pico Rivera (90660) ***(P-16400)***

Secure Net Alliance.....E.....818 848-4900
601 S Glenoaks Blvd # 409 Burbank (91502) ***(P-16401)***

Secure Nursing Service Inc.....B.....213 736-6771
3333 Wilshire Blvd # 625 Los Angeles (90010) ***(P-14416)***

Secure One Data Solutions LLC.....E.....562 924-7056
11090 Artesia Blvd Ste D Cerritos (90703) ***(P-15811)***

Secure Transportation Co Inc.....C.....858 790-3958
8304 Clairemont Mesa Blvd # 202 San Diego (92111) ***(P-5139)***

Secure Transportation Company.....D.....951 737-7300
12785 Magnolia Ave # 102 Riverside (92503) ***(P-3723)***

Secureauth Corporation (PA).....D.....949 777-6959
8845 Irvine Center Dr # 200 Irvine (92618) ***(P-15083)***

Securecom Inc.....E.....916 638-2855
4822 Golden Foothill Pkwy El Dorado Hills (95762) ***(P-2637)***

Securelion Security, Newark *Also called Courtesy Security Inc* ***(P-16244)***

Securitas Critical Infrastruct.....A.....858 560-0448
3914 Murphy Canyon Rd A120 San Diego (92123) ***(P-16402)***

Securitas Critical Infrastruct.....A.....310 817-2177
1835 W Orangewood Ave # 250 Orange (92868) ***(P-16403)***

Securitas Critical Infrastruct.....A.....805 685-1100
Rm 117 Bldg 7525 Vandenberg Afb (93437) ***(P-16404)***

Securitas Critical Infrastruct.....A.....310 426-3300
360 N Pacific Coast Hwy El Segundo (90245) ***(P-16405)***

Securitas Electronic SEC Inc.....D.....858 812-7349
7002 Convoy Ct San Diego (92111) ***(P-16557)***

Securitas SEC Svcs USA Inc.....C.....805 650-6285
5700 Ralston St Ventura (93003) ***(P-16406)***

Securitas SEC Svcs USA Inc.....C.....650 358-1556
1650 Borel Pl Ste 227 San Mateo (94402) ***(P-16407)***

Securitas SEC Svcs USA Inc.....C.....916 564-2009
2045 Hurley Way Sacramento (95825) ***(P-16408)***

Securitas SEC Svcs USA Inc.....C.....209 943-1401
3115 W March Ln Ste A Stockton (95219) ***(P-16409)***

Securitas SEC Svcs USA Inc.....C.....559 221-2302
10 E River Park Pl E # 220 Fresno (93720) ***(P-16410)***

Securitas SEC Svcs USA Inc.....C.....571 321-0913
750 Terrado Plz Ste 107 Covina (91723) ***(P-16411)***

Securitas SEC Svcs USA Inc.....C.....510 568-6818
505 Montgomery St San Francisco (94111) ***(P-16412)***

Mergent e-mail: customerrelations@mergent.com
1424
2020 Directory of California
Wholesalers and Services Companies
(P-0000) Products & Services Section entry number
(PA)=Parent Co (HQ)=Headquarters (DH)=Div Headquarters

Securitas SEC Svcs USA Inc......D......909 974-3160
430 N Vineyard Ave # 335 Ontario (91764) ***(P-16413)***
Securitas SEC Svcs USA Inc......C......760 353-8177
2344 S 2nd St Ste C El Centro (92243) ***(P-16414)***
Securitas SEC Svcs USA Inc......D......530 245-0256
2415 Larkspur Ln Ste B Redding (96002) ***(P-16415)***
Securitas SEC Svcs USA Inc......C......619 641-0049
1550 Hotel Cir N Ste 440 San Diego (92108) ***(P-16416)***
Securitas SEC Svcs USA Inc......B......818 706-6800
4330 Park Terrace Dr Westlake Village (91361) ***(P-16417)***
Securitas SEC Svcs USA Inc......C......707 586-1393
1304 Sthpint Blvd Ste 110 Petaluma (94954) ***(P-16418)***
Securitas SEC Svcs USA Inc......C......805 967-8987
5276 Hollister Ave # 204 Goleta (93111) ***(P-16419)***
Securitas SEC Svcs USA Inc......D......707 445-5463
1606 Koster St Ste A Eureka (95501) ***(P-16420)***
Securitas SEC Svcs USA Inc......C......916 569-4500
2045 Hurley Way Ste 175 Sacramento (95825) ***(P-16421)***
Securitas SEC Svcs USA Inc......C......951 676-3954
27450 Ynez Rd Ste 315 Temecula (92591) ***(P-16422)***
Securitas SEC Svcs USA Inc......C......559 221-2302
43-00 Cook St Ste 100 Palm Desert (92211) ***(P-16423)***
Securitas SEC Svcs USA Inc......C......831 444-9607
1611 Bunker Hill Way # 100 Salinas (93906) ***(P-16424)***
Securitas SEC Svcs USA Inc......C......909 865-4356
1101 W Mckinley Ave Pomona (91768) ***(P-16425)***
Securitas SEC Svcs USA Inc......C......323 832-9074
6055 E Wash Blvd Ste 155 Commerce (90040) ***(P-16426)***
Securitas SEC Svcs USA Inc......C......213 580-8825
1055 Wilshire Blvd Los Angeles (90017) ***(P-16427)***
Securitas SEC Svcs USA Inc......C......562 427-2737
1500 W Carson St Ste 109 Long Beach (90810) ***(P-16428)***
Securitas SEC Svcs USA Inc......C......310 787-0747
400 Crenshaw Blvd Ste 200 Torrance (90503) ***(P-16429)***
Securitas SEC Svcs USA Inc......C......714 385-9745
2870 Skypark Dr Ste 315 Torrance (90505) ***(P-16430)***
Securitas SEC Svcs USA Inc......C......760 245-1915
15428 Civic Dr Ste 305 Victorville (92392) ***(P-16431)***
Securitas SEC Svcs USA Inc......C......818 891-0458
16909 Parthenia St # 202 Northridge (91343) ***(P-16432)***
Securitas SEC Svcs USA Inc......C......818 706-6800
4330 Park Terrace Dr Westlake Village (91361) ***(P-16433)***
Securitech Security Services......C......213 387-5050
2733 N San Fernando Rd Los Angeles (90065) ***(P-16434)***
Security Alarm Fing Entps Inc......D......925 830-4786
2440 Camino Ramon Ste 200 San Ramon (94583) ***(P-16558)***
Security California Bancorp......D......951 368-2265
3403 10th St Ste 830 Riverside (92501) ***(P-9238)***
Security Central Inc......D......510 652-2477
4432 Telegraph Ave Oakland (94609) ***(P-17544)***
Security Company, Burbank *Also called Secure Net Alliance* ***(P-16401)***
Security Contractor Svcs Inc (PA)......D......916 338-4200
5339 Jackson St North Highlands (95660) ***(P-6726)***
Security Indust Spcialists Inc......C......323 924-9147
477 N Oak St Inglewood (90302) ***(P-16435)***
Security Indust Spcialists Inc (PA)......C......310 215-5100
6071 Bristol Pkwy Culver City (90230) ***(P-16436)***
Security Nat Mstr Holdg Co LLC (PA)......C......707 442-2818
323 5th St Eureka (95501) ***(P-9602)***
Security On-Demand Inc......E......858 563-5655
12121 Scripps Summit Dr # 320 San Diego (92131) ***(P-15689)***
Security On-Site Services Inc......D......916 988-6500
2210 Plaza Dr Ste 300 Rocklin (95765) ***(P-16559)***
Security One Inc......D......800 778-3017
1859 Streiff Ln Santa Rosa (95403) ***(P-16437)***
Security Pacific Home Loans, Westlake Village *Also called Ownit Mortgage Solutions Inc* ***(P-9589)***
Security Pacific RE Brkg, Richmond *Also called S P R E Inc* ***(P-11435)***
Security Pacific RE Brkg......D......510 245-9901
292 Violet Rd Hercules (94547) ***(P-11443)***
Security Pacific Real Estate, Walnut Creek *Also called SEC Pac Inc* ***(P-11442)***
Security Paving Company Inc (PA)......D......818 362-9200
3075 Townsgate Rd Ste 210 Westlake Village (91361) ***(P-1785)***
Security Signal Devices Inc (PA)......E......800 888-0444
1740 N Lemon St Anaheim (92801) ***(P-16560)***
Security Specialists, San Fernando *Also called Tyan Inc* ***(P-16463)***
Security Systems & Services, Riverside *Also called Ceed Security Corp* ***(P-16225)***
Secuto Music, Burbank *Also called Roundabout Entertainment Inc* ***(P-17664)***
Sedgwick Claims MGT Svcs Inc......B......916 771-2900
1410 Rocky Ridge Dr Ste 3 Roseville (95661) ***(P-10485)***
Sedgwick Claims MGT Svcs Inc......D......626 568-1415
3280 E Foothill Blvd # 350 Pasadena (91107) ***(P-10486)***
Sedgwick Claims MGT Svcs Inc......C......818 591-9444
24025 Park Sorrento # 200 Calabasas (91302) ***(P-10487)***
Sedgwick Claims MGT Svcs Inc......D......510 302-3000
2101 Webster St Oakland (94612) ***(P-10488)***
Sedgwick Claims MGT Svcs Inc......D......916 568-7394
1851 Heritage Ln Sacramento (95815) ***(P-10489)***
Sedgwick CMS Holdings Inc......A......909 477-5500
3633 Inland Empire Blvd Ontario (91764) ***(P-10490)***
Seecon Built Homes Inc......D......925 671-7711
4021 Port Chicago Hwy Concord (94520) ***(P-11599)***
Seed Dynamics Inc......D......831 424-1177
1081b Harkins Rd Salinas (93901) ***(P-540)***
Seedif Inc......E......408 930-3446
215 Hockney Ave Mountain View (94041) ***(P-14417)***
Seeds of Change Inc......C......310 764-7700
2555 S Dominguez Hills Dr Rancho Dominguez (90220) ***(P-8857)***
Seeley Brothers, Brea *Also called Norcal Inc* ***(P-2951)***
Seeley Brothers, Brea *Also called Norcal Inc* ***(P-2950)***
Seems Plumbing Co Inc......E......310 297-4969
5400 W Rosecrans Ave Lowr Hawthorne (90250) ***(P-2269)***
Seguin Mreau NAPA Coperage Inc......D......707 252-3408
151 Camino Dorado NAPA (94558) ***(P-7656)***
Segura Enterprises Inc......D......805 349-0550
1011 W Mccoy Ln Santa Maria (93455) ***(P-16438)***
Segura Security Services, Santa Maria *Also called Segura Enterprises Inc* ***(P-16438)***
Seidner-Miller Automotive Inc......E......909 394-3500
1253 S Lone Hill Ave Glendora (91740) ***(P-17345)***
Seiler LLP (PA)......C......650 365-4646
3 Lagoon Dr Ste 400 Redwood City (94065) ***(P-25675)***
Seiler LLP......D......415 392-2123
220 Montgomery St Ste 300 San Francisco (94104) ***(P-25676)***
Seirra Telephone, Oakhurst *Also called Sierra Tel Cmmunications Group* ***(P-5469)***
Seismic Software Inc (PA)......D......855 466-8748
12770 El Cmino Real Ste 3 San Diego (92130) ***(P-26389)***
SEIU Local 1021......C......510 350-9811
447 29th St Oakland (94609) ***(P-24460)***
Seiu Local 2015......C......213 985-0384
2910 Beverly Blvd Los Angeles (90057) ***(P-24461)***
Seiu Local 721......D......213 368-8660
1545 Wilshire Blvd # 100 Los Angeles (90017) ***(P-24462)***
Seiu Uhw-West, Commerce *Also called Seiu United Healthcare Workers* ***(P-24464)***
Seiu United Healthcare Workers (PA)......C......510 251-1250
560 Thomas L Berkley Way Oakland (94612) ***(P-24463)***
Seiu United Healthcare Workers......E......323 734-8399
5480 Ferguson Dr Commerce (90022) ***(P-24464)***
Sela Healthcare Inc (PA)......C......909 985-1981
867 E 11th St Upland (91786) ***(P-20247)***
Select Data Inc......C......714 577-1000
4155 E La Palma Ave # 250 Anaheim (92807) ***(P-15084)***
Select Harvest Usa LLC (PA)......D......209 668-2471
14827 W Harding Rd Turlock (95380) ***(P-8681)***
Select Home Care......D......805 777-3855
2393 Townsgate Rd Ste 100 Westlake Village (91361) ***(P-21861)***
Select Hotels Group LLC......E......510 623-6000
3101 W Warren Ave Fremont (94538) ***(P-12901)***
Select Hotels Group LLC......E......916 638-4141
11260 Point East Dr Rancho Cordova (95742) ***(P-12902)***
Select Personnel Services, Santa Barbara *Also called Select Temporaries LLC* ***(P-14418)***
Select Staffing, Santa Barbara *Also called Real Time Staffing Services* ***(P-14382)***
Select Staffing, Santa Barbara *Also called Employbridge LLC* ***(P-14272)***
Select Temporaries LLC (HQ)......D......805 882-2200
3820 State St Santa Barbara (93105) ***(P-14418)***
Selecta Products Inc (PA)......D......661 823-7050
1200 E Tehachapi Blvd Tehachapi (93561) ***(P-7182)***
Selecta Switch, Tehachapi *Also called Selecta Products Inc* ***(P-7182)***
Selectforce, Irvine *Also called Accurate Background LLC* ***(P-15843)***
Selectquote Insurance Services (PA)......C......415 543-7338
595 Market St Fl 10 San Francisco (94105) ***(P-10491)***
Selex Inc (PA)......D......707 836-8836
442 Longfellow St Livermore (94550) ***(P-3465)***
Selex Inc......D......707 836-8836
930 Shiloh Rd Windsor (95492) ***(P-3466)***
Self Help Enterprises (PA)......D......559 651-1000
8445 W Elowin Ct Visalia (93291) ***(P-24656)***
Self Serve Auto Dismantlers (PA)......C......714 630-8901
3200 E Frontera St Anaheim (92806) ***(P-6281)***
Self-Aid Workshop, Glendale *Also called Camble Center* ***(P-23574)***
Self-Help For Elderly......D......415 391-3843
777 Stockton St Ste 110 San Francisco (94108) ***(P-23458)***
Self-Help For Elderly (PA)......C......415 677-7600
731 Sansome St Ste 100 San Francisco (94111) ***(P-23459)***
Selig Construction Corp......E......530 893-5898
337 Huss Dr Chico (95928) ***(P-1191)***
Selligent Inc (HQ)......D......650 421-4255
1300 Island Dr Ste 200 Redwood City (94065) ***(P-15690)***
Selma Portuguese Azorian Assn......E......559 896-2508
1245 Nebraska Ave Selma (93662) ***(P-23460)***
Seltzer Caplan McMahon (PA)......C......619 685-3003
750 B St Ste 2100 San Diego (92101) ***(P-22807)***
Selu College, Inglewood *Also called Beckett Enterprise* ***(P-26526)***
Selvi-Vidovich LP......D......408 720-8500
865 W El Camino Real Sunnyvale (94087) ***(P-12903)***
Selzer Home Loans, Ukiah *Also called Lake County Home Loans* ***(P-9569)***
Sema, Diamond Bar *Also called Specialty Equipment Mkt Assn* ***(P-24367)***
Sema Inc (PA)......D......949 830-1400
4 Mason Ste A Irvine (92618) ***(P-25677)***
Sema Construction Inc......D......949 330-4300
6 Orchard Ste 150 Irvine (92618) ***(P-1826)***
Semans Communications (PA)......D......650 529-9984
112 Stonegate Rd Portola Vally (94028) ***(P-2638)***
Semantic Ai Inc (PA)......D......619 222-4050
4922 N Harbor Dr San Diego (92106) ***(P-15691)***
Semantic Research, San Diego *Also called Semantic Ai Inc* ***(P-15691)***
Semi (PA)......C......408 943-6900
673 S Milpitas Blvd Milpitas (95035) ***(P-24363)***
Semifreddi's Bakery, Alameda *Also called Semifreddis Inc* ***(P-8642)***
Semifreddis Inc (PA)......C......510 596-9930
1980 N Loop Rd Alameda (94502) ***(P-8642)***
Seminis Inc......D......831 623-4554
500 Lucy Brown Rd San Juan Bautista (95045) ***(P-25830)***
Seminis Inc (HQ)......B......805 485-7317
2700 Camino Del Sol Oxnard (93030) ***(P-25831)***
Seminis Vegetable Seeds Inc (HQ)......A......855 733-3834
2700 Camino Del Sol Oxnard (93030) ***(P-8858)***

Employee Codes: A=Over 500 employees, B=251-500
C=101-250, D=51-100, E=50
2020 Directory of California
Wholesalers and Services Companies
© Mergent Inc. 1-800-342-5647
1425

Sempra Energy (PA) ....A.......619 696-2000
488 8th Ave San Diego (92101) ***(P-6004)***
Sempra Energy ....A.......619 696-2000
9305 Lightwave Ave San Diego (92123) ***(P-5919)***
Sempra Energy Global Entps ....A.......619 696-2000
101 Ash St San Diego (92101) ***(P-5973)***
Sempra Energy International (HQ) ....A.......619 696-2000
101 Ash St San Diego (92101) ***(P-5920)***
Sempra Energy Utilities, San Diego *Also called Sempra Energy International* ***(P-5920)***
Sendmail Inc ....D.......510 594-5400
892 Ross Dr Sunnyvale (94089) ***(P-5467)***
Sendx Medical Inc (HQ) ....D.......760 930-6300
1945 Palomar Oaks Way # 100 Carlsbad (92011) ***(P-7003)***
Seneca Center, Fremont *Also called Seneca Family of Agencies* ***(P-23461)***
Seneca Family of Agencies ....D.......510 226-6180
40950 Chapel Way Fremont (94538) ***(P-23461)***
Seneca Family of Agency, Tustin *Also called Kinship Center* ***(P-23306)***
Seneca Healthcare District ....D.......530 258-1977
199 Reynolds Rd Chester (96020) ***(P-19388)***
Seneca Healthcare District (PA) ....C.......530 258-2151
130 Brentwood Dr Chester (96020) ***(P-21186)***
Seneca Hospital Almanor Clinic, Chester *Also called Seneca Healthcare District* ***(P-19388)***
Senegence International, Foothill Ranch *Also called Sgii Inc* ***(P-7983)***
Senior Assisted Living Comm Ch, Pleasant Hill *Also called Carlton Senior Living* ***(P-21700)***
Senior Care (PA) ....A.......562 989-5100
3800 Kilroy Airport Way Long Beach (90806) ***(P-10044)***
Senior Care ....D.......562 492-9878
2501 Cherry Ave Ste 380 Long Beach (90755) ***(P-10045)***
Senior Care Inc ....C.......619 928-5644
4960 Mills St La Mesa (91942) ***(P-24068)***
Senior Care Inc ....C.......619 817-8855
3423 Channel Way San Diego (92110) ***(P-24069)***
Senior Companions At Home ....E.......650 364-1265
650 El Camino Real Ste E Redwood City (94063) ***(P-21862)***
Senior Helpers South Coast, Fountain Valley *Also called His Passion Inc* ***(P-21765)***
Senior Keiro Health Care ....D.......323 263-9651
325 S Boyle Ave Los Angeles (90033) ***(P-24070)***
Senior Living Solutions LLC ....C.......408 385-1835
1725 S Bascom Ave Apt 105 Campbell (95008) ***(P-20452)***
SENIOR NUTRITION, Fort Bragg *Also called Redwood Coast Seniors Inc* ***(P-23405)***
Senior Resource Group LLC ....E.......858 519-0890
850 Del Mar Downs Rd # 338 Solana Beach (92075) ***(P-24071)***
Senior Services, Oxnard *Also called City of Oxnard* ***(P-23014)***
Seniors At Home, Palo Alto *Also called Jewish Family and Chld Svcs* ***(P-23293)***
Senomyx Inc ....D.......858 646-8300
4767 Nexus Center Dr San Diego (92121) ***(P-25832)***
Sensity Systems Inc (HQ) ....D.......408 841-4200
1237 E Arques Ave Sunnyvale (94085) ***(P-27206)***
Sentek Consulting Inc ....C.......619 543-9550
2811 Nimitz Blvd Ste G San Diego (92106) ***(P-16106)***
Sentek Global, San Diego *Also called Sentek Consulting Inc* ***(P-16106)***
Sentient Technologies USA LLC ....E.......415 422-9886
611 Mission St Fl 6 San Francisco (94105) ***(P-15085)***
Sentinel Acqstion Holdings Inc ....A.......310 201-4100
2000 Avenue Of The Stars Los Angeles (90067) ***(P-15086)***
Sentinel Monitoring Corp (HQ) ....C.......949 453-1550
220 Technology Dr Ste 200 Irvine (92618) ***(P-16561)***
Sentinel Offender Services LLC (PA) ....D.......949 453-1550
1290 N Hancock St Ste 103 Anaheim (92807) ***(P-16562)***
Sepulveda Ambulatory Care, North Hills *Also called Veterans Health Administration* ***(P-19570)***
Sequel Contractors Inc ....E.......562 802-7227
13546 Imperial Hwy Santa Fe Springs (90670) ***(P-1786)***
Sequenom Inc (HQ) ....D.......858 202-9000
3595 John Hopkins Ct San Diego (92121) ***(P-25833)***
Sequenom Center For Molecular ....B.......858 202-9051
3595 John Hopkins Ct San Diego (92121) ***(P-21591)***
Sequenom Laboratories, San Diego *Also called Sequenom Center For Molecular* ***(P-21591)***
Sequoia Adrc LP ....D.......650 364-5504
650 Main St Redwood City (94063) ***(P-23462)***
Sequoia Alchol DRG Rcovery Ctr, Redwood City *Also called Sequoia Adrc LP* ***(P-23462)***
Sequoia Beverage Company LP ....C.......559 651-2444
2122 N Plaza Dr Visalia (93291) ***(P-8791)***
Sequoia Bnefits Insur Svcs LLC ....D.......650 369-0200
1850 Gateway Dr Ste 600 San Mateo (94404) ***(P-26810)***
Sequoia Capital Operations LLC ....D.......650 854-3927
2800 Sand Hill Rd Ste 100 Menlo Park (94025) ***(P-11955)***
Sequoia Concepts Inc ....D.......818 409-6000
28632 Roadside Dr Ste 110 Agoura Hills (91301) ***(P-13700)***
Sequoia Consultants Inc ....D.......858 345-1544
11588 Sorrento Valley Rd San Diego (92121) ***(P-25302)***
Sequoia Enterprises Inc ....D.......559 592-9455
150 W Pine St Exeter (93221) ***(P-8520)***
Sequoia Environmental Svcs Inc ....D.......949 480-4742
1 University Dr Aliso Viejo (92656) ***(P-759)***
Sequoia Financial Services, Agoura Hills *Also called Sequoia Concepts Inc* ***(P-13700)***
Sequoia Health Services (HQ) ....D.......650 369-5811
170 Alameda De Las Pulgas Redwood City (94062) ***(P-21187)***
SEQUOIA HOSPITAL, Redwood City *Also called Sequoia Health Services* ***(P-21187)***
Sequoia Insurance Company (HQ) ....D.......831 655-9612
31 Upper Ragsdale Dr Monterey (93940) ***(P-10128)***
Sequoia Insurance Company ....D.......916 933-9524
P.O. Box 1510 Monterey (93942) ***(P-10492)***
Sequoia Orange, Exeter *Also called Sequoia Enterprises Inc* ***(P-8520)***
Sequoia Orange Co Inc (PA) ....D.......559 592-9455
150 W Pine St Exeter (93221) ***(P-541)***
Sequoia Residential Funding ....D.......415 389-7373
1 Belvedere Pl Ste 330 Mill Valley (94941) ***(P-9493)***
Sequoia Retail Systems Inc (HQ) ....D.......650 237-9000
2400 Wyandotte St B103 Mountain View (94043) ***(P-15087)***
Sequoia Senior Solutions Inc ....D.......707 263-3070
825 S Main St Lakeport (95453) ***(P-23463)***
Sequoia Senior Solutions Inc ....D.......707 621-9235
205 W Clay St Ukiah (95482) ***(P-23464)***
Sequoia Surgical Center LP ....E.......925 935-6700
2405 Shadelands Dr # 200 Walnut Creek (94598) ***(P-19389)***
Sequoia Surgical Pavilion, Walnut Creek *Also called Sequoia Surgical Center LP* ***(P-19389)***
Sequoia Wood Country Club ....D.......209 795-1000
1000 Cypress Point Dr Arnold (95223) ***(P-18566)***
Sequos-San Frncsco Residential, San Francisco *Also called Northern California Presbyteri* ***(P-20159)***
Seracada ....E.......626 486-0800
709 E Lavender Way Azusa (91702) ***(P-21863)***
Serco Inc ....C.......858 569-8979
9350 Waxie Way Ste 400 San Diego (92123) ***(P-25303)***
Serec Entertainment LLC ....E.......626 893-0600
1671 N Rocky Rd Upland (91784) ***(P-7404)***
Serene Ast LLC (HQ) ....D.......408 986-8544
3211 Scott Blvd Ste 201 Santa Clara (95054) ***(P-16107)***
Serfin Funds Transfer (PA) ....D.......626 457-3070
1000 S Fremont Ave A-O Alhambra (91803) ***(P-9441)***
Serimian M S D L Ranch ....E.......559 896-1517
10463 S Del Rey Ave Selma (93662) ***(P-359)***
Serpico Landscaping Inc ....E.......510 293-0341
1764 National Ave Hayward (94545) ***(P-760)***
Serra Community Med Clinic Inc ....C.......818 768-3000
9375 San Fernando Rd Sun Valley (91352) ***(P-19390)***
Serra Medical Clinic Inc ....D.......818 768-3000
9375 San Fernando Rd Sun Valley (91352) ***(P-19391)***
Serrania Charter Elementary, Woodland Hills *Also called Pta CA Congress of Parents* ***(P-24620)***
Serrano Associates LLC ....D.......916 939-3333
5005 Serrano Pkwy El Dorado Hills (95762) ***(P-18567)***
Serrano Country Club, El Dorado Hills *Also called Serrano Associates LLC* ***(P-18567)***
Serrano Country Club Inc ....C.......916 933-5005
5005 Serrano Pkwy P El Dorado Hills (95762) ***(P-18568)***
Serrano Covalescent Hospital ....D.......323 465-2106
5401 Fountain Ave Los Angeles (90029) ***(P-20248)***
Serrano Electric Inc ....E.......408 986-1570
1705 Russell Ave Santa Clara (95054) ***(P-2639)***
Serrano Hotel, San Francisco *Also called Kimpton Hotel & Rest Group LLC* ***(P-12509)***
Serrato-Mcdermott Inc ....D.......510 656-6233
43815 S Grimmer Blvd Fremont (94538) ***(P-6468)***
Servexo ....E.......323 527-9994
1515 W 190th St Ste 170 Gardena (90248) ***(P-16439)***
Servexo Protective Service, Gardena *Also called Servexo* ***(P-16439)***
Servi-Tech Controls Inc (PA) ....D.......559 264-6679
470 W Warwick Ave Clovis (93619) ***(P-2270)***
Servi-Tek Inc ....B.......858 638-7735
3970 Sorrento Valley Blvd San Diego (92121) ***(P-14043)***
Servi-Tek Janitorial Services, San Diego *Also called Servi-Tek Inc* ***(P-14043)***
Service 1st Electrical Svcs ....E.......714 630-9699
1092 N Armando St Anaheim (92806) ***(P-2640)***
Service By Medallion ....B.......650 625-1010
411 Clyde Ave Mountain View (94043) ***(P-14044)***
Service Champions, Pleasanton *Also called On-Time AC & Htg Inc* ***(P-2216)***
Service Cleaning and Maint, Los Angeles *Also called Service Parking Corporation* ***(P-17275)***
Service Corp International ....D.......949 644-2700
3500 Pacific View Dr Corona Del Mar (92625) ***(P-11444)***
Service Corp International ....D.......760 754-6600
1999 S El Camino Real Oceanside (92054) ***(P-11636)***
Service Employee Intl Un, Los Angeles *Also called Los Angles Cnty Employees Assn* ***(P-24451)***
Service Employees Intl Union, San Jose *Also called Service Workers Local 715* ***(P-24465)***
Service First Contractors ....E.......714 573-2200
2510 N Grand Ave Ste 110 Santa Ana (92705) ***(P-1594)***
Service Genius Los Angeles Inc ....D.......818 200-3379
9761 Variel Ave Chatsworth (91311) ***(P-2271)***
Service Hospitality LLC ....D.......925 566-8820
1050 Burnett Ave Concord (94520) ***(P-12904)***
Service King Cllision Repr Ctr, Oakland *Also called Service King Holdings LLC* ***(P-17307)***
Service King Cllision Repr Ctr, San Diego *Also called Service King Holdings LLC* ***(P-17308)***
Service King Cllision Repr Ctr, Fountain Valley *Also called Service King Holdings LLC* ***(P-17309)***
Service King Holdings LLC ....D.......510 562-9650
7801 Oakport St Oakland (94621) ***(P-17307)***
Service King Holdings LLC ....D.......619 219-3927
4660 Alvarado Canyon Rd San Diego (92120) ***(P-17308)***
Service King Holdings LLC ....D.......714 962-2600
18065 Euclid St Fountain Valley (92708) ***(P-17309)***
Service King Paint & Body LLC ....C.......925 301-8481
6080 Dublin Blvd Dublin (94568) ***(P-17310)***
Service Lathing Company ....E.......510 483-9732
1090 139th Ave San Leandro (94578) ***(P-2857)***
Service Master Industries Inc ....D.......760 480-0208
2342 Meyers Ave Escondido (92029) ***(P-17053)***
Service Parking Corporation ....D.......323 851-2416
3800 Barham Blvd Ste P1 Los Angeles (90068) ***(P-17275)***
Service Quality, Concord *Also called Customer Loyalty Builders Inc* ***(P-26577)***
Service Solutions Group LLC ....D.......626 960-9390
5367 2nd St Irwindale (91706) ***(P-17463)***
Service Transport Inc ....D.......951 403-3464
29991 Cyn Hls Rd Ste 137 Lake Elsinore (92532) ***(P-4231)***
Service Workers Local 715 (PA) ....D.......408 678-3300
2302 Zanker Rd San Jose (95131) ***(P-24465)***

ServiceMaster, South San Francisco *Also called Seafus Corporation* ***(P-14042)***
ServiceMaster, Merced *Also called Culver-Melin Enterprises* ***(P-13908)***
ServiceMaster, Santa Maria *Also called Skylstad-Schoelen Co Inc* ***(P-14053)***
ServiceMaster Company LLC ....D.......760 298-7001
1003 Hi Point St Los Angeles (90035) ***(P-14045)***
ServiceMaster Company LLC ....C.......714 245-1465
216 N Clara St Santa Ana (92703) ***(P-14046)***
Servicemax Inc (PA) ....D.......925 965-7859
4450 Rosewood Dr Ste 200 Pleasanton (94588) ***(P-15088)***
Servicetitan Inc (PA) ....D.......855 899-0970
801 N Brand Blvd Ste 700 Glendale (91203) ***(P-15089)***
Servicmster Clean By Integrity, Santa Barbara *Also called Pacific Building Maint Inc* ***(P-13997)***
Servicmster Cmplete Rstoration, Escondido *Also called Sbrm Inc* ***(P-14040)***
Servico Building Maint Co ....D.......707 935-1224
13732b Carmel Ave Glen Ellen (95442) ***(P-14047)***
Servicon Systems Inc ....A.......310 970-0700
3329 Jack Northrop Ave Hawthorne (90250) ***(P-3216)***
Servicon Systems Inc (PA) ....A.......310 204-5040
3965 Landmark St Culver City (90232) ***(P-26954)***
Serviz Inc ....D.......818 381-4826
15303 Ventura Blvd # 1600 Sherman Oaks (91403) ***(P-13453)***
SERVPRO Encino/Sherman Oaks, Encino *Also called One Silver Serve Inc* ***(P-13995)***
SERVPRO of Mendocino ....E.......707 462-3848
3001 S State St Ste 5 Ukiah (95482) ***(P-14048)***
SES, San Diego *Also called Superior Envmtl Svcs Inc* ***(P-14061)***
Ses LLC ....A.......949 727-3200
26561 Rancho Pkwy S Lake Forest (92630) ***(P-15090)***
Sesloc Federal Credit Union (PA) ....D.......805 543-1816
3855 Broad St San Luis Obispo (93401) ***(P-9351)***
Set A Head Start Westside, Sacramento *Also called Sacramento Employement & Train* ***(P-23632)***
Seta, Sacramento *Also called Sacramento Employement & Train* ***(P-23633)***
Sethi Management Inc ....C.......760 692-5288
6100 Innovation Way Carlsbad (92009) ***(P-26390)***
Sethi Management Inc ....D.......760 652-4010
183 Calle Magdalena # 101 Encinitas (92024) ***(P-12905)***
Seti Institute ....C.......650 961-6633
189 Bernardo Ave Ste 100 Mountain View (94043) ***(P-26030)***
Seti Institute, The, Mountain View *Also called Seti Institute* ***(P-26030)***
Seton Medical Center (HQ) ....A.......650 992-4000
1900 Sullivan Ave Daly City (94015) ***(P-21188)***
Seton Medical Center ....C.......650 563-7100
600 Marine Blvd Moss Beach (94038) ***(P-21189)***
Seton Medical Center ....D.......650 992-4000
1784 Sullivan Ave Ste 200 Daly City (94015) ***(P-21190)***
Seton Medical Center Coastside, Moss Beach *Also called Seton Medical Center* ***(P-21189)***
Setton Pstchio Terra Bella Inc (HQ) ....D.......559 535-6050
9370 Road 234 Terra Bella (93270) ***(P-8643)***
Seven Hospitality, Irvine *Also called State Group LLC* ***(P-26829)***
Seven Lakes Hm Assn Cntry CLB ....E.......760 328-2695
1 Desert Lakes Dr Palm Springs (92264) ***(P-18569)***
Seven Licensing Company LLC ....D.......323 881-0308
801 S Figueroa St # 2500 Los Angeles (90017) ***(P-8110)***
Seven Oaks Country Club ....C.......661 664-6404
2000 Grand Lakes Ave Bakersfield (93311) ***(P-18570)***
Seven One Inc (PA) ....D.......818 904-3435
21540 Prairie St Ste E Chatsworth (91311) ***(P-17054)***
Seven Resorts Inc (PA) ....B.......949 588-7100
9771 Irvine Center Dr Irvine (92618) ***(P-12906)***
Seven Seas Associates LLC ....C.......619 291-1300
411 Hotel Cir S San Diego (92108) ***(P-12907)***
Seven Seas Best Western, San Diego *Also called Seven Seas Associates LLC* ***(P-12907)***
Seven7 Brands, Los Angeles *Also called Seven Licensing Company LLC* ***(P-8110)***
Severson & Werson A Prof Corp ....D.......415 398-3344
1 Embarcadero Ctr Fl 26 San Francisco (94111) ***(P-22808)***
Severson Group Incorporated (PA) ....D.......562 493-3611
3601 Serpentine Dr Los Alamitos (90720) ***(P-1595)***
Seville Construction Svcs Inc ....D.......626 204-0800
199 S Hudson Ave Pasadena (91101) ***(P-26811)***
Sexy Hair Concepts ....D.......800 848-3383
9232 Eton Ave Chatsworth (91311) ***(P-8011)***
Seyfarth Shaw LLP ....C.......213 270-9600
601 S Figueroa St # 3300 Los Angeles (90017) ***(P-22809)***
Seyfarth Shaw LLP ....C.......310 277-7200
2029 Century Park E # 3400 Los Angeles (90067) ***(P-22810)***
Seyfarth Shaw LLP ....D.......415 397-2823
560 Mission St Fl 31 San Francisco (94105) ***(P-22811)***
Seymour Gale & Associates ....E.......213 622-5361
4501 Cedros Ave Unit 118 Sherman Oaks (91403) ***(P-8111)***
SF-MARIN FOOD BANK, San Francisco *Also called San Francisco Food Bank* ***(P-23440)***
Sf-Potrero Hill, San Francisco *Also called Citibank National Association* ***(P-9083)***
Sfadia Inc ....D.......323 622-1930
12505 Florence Ave Santa Fe Springs (90670) ***(P-2641)***
SFCU, Palo Alto *Also called Stanford Federal Credit Union* ***(P-9355)***
Sfd Partners LLC ....B.......415 392-7755
450 Powell St San Francisco (94102) ***(P-12908)***
SFF, Sacramento *Also called Sierra Forever Families* ***(P-23466)***
Sfi 2365 Iron Point LLC ....E.......415 395-9701
260 California St # 1100 San Francisco (94111) ***(P-10642)***
Sfi Carlsbad LLC ....E.......415 395-9701
260 California St # 1100 San Francisco (94111) ***(P-10643)***
Sfmc, Lynwood *Also called St Francis Medical Center* ***(P-19444)***
Sfn Group Inc ....D.......949 727-8500
114 Pacifica Ste 210 Irvine (92618) ***(P-14565)***
Sfn Group Inc ....C.......530 222-3434
3050 Bictor Ave Ste A Redding (96002) ***(P-14566)***
Sfo Airporter Inc (PA) ....D.......650 246-2734
160 S Linden Ave Ste 300 South San Francisco (94080) ***(P-3603)***
Sfo Airporter Inc ....D.......415 495-3909
325 5th St San Francisco (94107) ***(P-3604)***
Sfo Shuttle Bus Company, Stanford *Also called Imperial Parking (us) LLC* ***(P-17256)***
Sfo Shuttle Bus Company, Oakland *Also called Imperial Parking (us) LLC* ***(P-17257)***
Sfo Shuttle Bus Inc ....C.......650 877-0430
San Francisco Intl Arprt San Francisco (94128) ***(P-3605)***
Sfo-3 - San Francisco Full Svc, Brisbane *Also called Expeditors Intl Wash Inc* ***(P-4938)***
Sfpp LP (HQ) ....C.......714 560-4400
1100 W Town And Country R Orange (92868) ***(P-4809)***
Sft Realty Galway Downs LLC ....D.......951 232-1880
38801 Los Porralitos Temecula (92592) ***(P-11445)***
Sfusd Building Ground ....D.......415 695-5508
834 Toland St San Francisco (94124) ***(P-14049)***
Sfusd Jrotc Brigade ....D.......415 242-2546
2162 24th Ave San Francisco (94116) ***(P-15091)***
Sg Personnel LLC ....B.......831 444-0523
420 Espinosa Rd Salinas (93907) ***(P-278)***
Sg Personnel LLC ....D.......209 369-3018
5400 E Harney Ln Lodi (95240) ***(P-279)***
SGF Produce Holding Corp ....B.......714 630-6292
701 W Kimberly Ave # 210 Placentia (92870) ***(P-8521)***
Sgii Inc ....C.......949 521-6161
19651 Alter Foothill Ranch (92610) ***(P-7983)***
Sgokc, Beale Afb *Also called US Dept of the Air Force* ***(P-19535)***
SGS North America Inc ....D.......408 588-0200
1759 S Main St Ste 116 Milpitas (95035) ***(P-26106)***
Sgws of CA, Union City *Also called Southern Glazers Wine* ***(P-8816)***
Shadkor Inc ....D.......818 953-4627
4021 W Alameda Ave Burbank (91505) ***(P-13259)***
Shadow Animation LLC ....E.......323 466-7771
940 N Mansfield Ave Los Angeles (90038) ***(P-17668)***
Shadow Hlls Cnvlscent Hosp Inc ....D.......818 352-4438
10158 Sunland Blvd Sunland (91040) ***(P-20249)***
Shadow Mnt Rsort/Rcqut CL Tns, Palm Desert *Also called Destination Residences LLC* ***(P-12205)***
Shadowbrook Health Care Inc ....E.......530 534-1353
1 Gilmore Ln Oroville (95966) ***(P-20250)***
Shady Canyon Golf Club Inc ....C.......949 856-7000
100 Shady Canyon Dr Irvine (92603) ***(P-18571)***
Shaker Express, San Diego *Also called California Air Cartage Inc* ***(P-4660)***
Shalev Senior Living ....E.......818 780-4808
6245 Matilija Ave Van Nuys (91401) ***(P-24072)***
Shamrock Center, Burbank *Also called Shamrock Plus Inc* ***(P-9750)***
Shamrock Companies, The, Anaheim *Also called Shamrock Supply Company Inc* ***(P-7405)***
Shamrock Plus Inc ....E.......818 845-4444
4444 W Lakeside Dr Lbby Burbank (91505) ***(P-9750)***
Shamrock Supply Company Inc (PA) ....D.......714 575-1800
3366 E La Palma Ave Anaheim (92806) ***(P-7405)***
Shamrock-Hostmark Palm Desrt ....D.......760 340-6600
74700 Highway 111 Palm Desert (92260) ***(P-12909)***
Shandon Properties, Beverly Hills *Also called Gang Tyre Ramer & Brown Inc* ***(P-22525)***
Shapell Industries LLC (HQ) ....D.......323 655-7330
8383 Wilshire Blvd # 700 Beverly Hills (90211) ***(P-11600)***
Shapell Industries LLC ....E.......818 366-1132
11280 Corbin Ave Northridge (91326) ***(P-1192)***
Shapell's Home Center, Northridge *Also called Shapell Industries LLC* ***(P-1192)***
Shapiro Ben Basat Painting, Van Nuys *Also called C B B Z S Inc* ***(P-2337)***
Shapiro-Gilman-Shandler Co (PA) ....C.......213 593-1200
739 Decatur St Los Angeles (90021) ***(P-8522)***
Shapp International Trdg Inc ....C.......818 348-3000
6000 Reseda Blvd Tarzana (91356) ***(P-6655)***
Shapp Internatioonal, Tarzana *Also called Shapp International Trdg Inc* ***(P-6655)***
Share Our Selves Corporation ....D.......949 609-8199
1 Purpose Dr Lake Forest (92630) ***(P-22322)***
Shared Services, Torrance *Also called Securitas SEC Svcs USA Inc* ***(P-16429)***
Sharedata Inc ....D.......408 490-2500
2465 Augustine Dr Santa Clara (95054) ***(P-15496)***
Sharedta/E Trade Bus Solutions, Santa Clara *Also called Sharedata Inc* ***(P-15496)***
Sharespost Inc ....D.......800 279-7754
555 Montgomery St # 1400 San Francisco (94111) ***(P-11692)***
Sharethis Inc (PA) ....E.......650 641-0191
3000 El Camino Real 5-150 Palo Alto (94306) ***(P-13578)***
Sharf Woodward & Associates ....D.......818 989-2200
5900 Sepulvda Blvd # 104 Van Nuys (91411) ***(P-14419)***
Sharks Sports & Entrmt LLC ....A.......408 287-7070
525 W Santa Clara St San Jose (95113) ***(P-18080)***
Sharon Care Center LLC ....C.......323 655-2023
8167 W 3rd St Los Angeles (90048) ***(P-20251)***
Sharp Chula Vista Medical Ctr, Chula Vista *Also called Sharp Chula Vista Medical Ctr* ***(P-21191)***
Sharp Chula Vista Medical Ctr ....A.......619 502-5800
751 Medical Center Ct Chula Vista (91911) ***(P-21191)***
Sharp Chula Vista Medical Ctr ....D.......858 499-5150
8695 Spectrum Center Blvd San Diego (92123) ***(P-21192)***
Sharp Community Medical Group ....C.......858 499-4525
8695 Spectrum Center Blvd San Diego (92123) ***(P-24424)***
Sharp Fabric, Los Angeles *Also called Elijah Textiles Inc* ***(P-6555)***
Sharp Guard Services Inc ....A.......213 739-1900
3450 Wilshire Blvd # 1000 Los Angeles (90010) ***(P-16440)***
Sharp Health Care, San Diego *Also called Sharp Healthcare* ***(P-21194)***
Sharp Health Plan ....D.......858 499-8300
8520 Tech Way Ste 200 San Diego (92123) ***(P-10046)***
Sharp Healthcare ....C.......619 398-2988
7910 Frost St Ste 280 San Diego (92123) ***(P-19392)***

ALPHABETIC

Employee Codes: A=Over 500 employees, B=251-500
C=101-250, D=51-100, E=50
2020 Directory of California
Wholesalers and Services Companies

1427

Sharp Healthcare .... D 619 284-1400
3575 Euclid Ave San Diego (92105) ***(P-19393)***

Sharp Healthcare .... D 858 939-5434
8008 Frost St Ste 106 San Diego (92123) ***(P-21193)***

Sharp Healthcare .... D 619 297-0008
550 Washington St Ste 701 San Diego (92103) ***(P-19394)***

Sharp Healthcare .... D 619 442-0844
225 W Madison Ave Ste 1 El Cajon (92020) ***(P-19395)***

Sharp Healthcare .... C 619 446-1575
300 Fir St San Diego (92101) ***(P-19396)***

Sharp Healthcare .... D 858 653-6100
8901 Activity Rd San Diego (92126) ***(P-19397)***

Sharp Healthcare .... C 858 627-5152
3554 Ruffin Rd Ste Soca San Diego (92123) ***(P-21194)***

Sharp Healthcare .... D 760 806-5600
130 Cedar Rd Vista (92083) ***(P-21195)***

Sharp Healthcare .... D 858 541-4850
8080 Dagget St Ste 200 San Diego (92111) ***(P-21864)***

Sharp Healthcare .... C 858 499-2000
751 Medical Center Ct Chula Vista (91911) ***(P-20252)***

Sharp Healthcare .... D 858 616-8411
2020 Genesee Ave Fl 2 San Diego (92123) ***(P-19398)***

Sharp Healthcare .... D 800 827-4277
4510 Viewridge Ave San Diego (92123) ***(P-19399)***

Sharp Healthcare .... D 619 460-6200
8860 Center Dr Ste 450 La Mesa (91942) ***(P-19400)***

Sharp Healthcare .... D 858 616-8200
2020 Genesee Ave San Diego (92123) ***(P-19401)***

Sharp Home Care, San Diego *Also called Sharp Healthcare* ***(P-21864)***

Sharp Mary Birch H .... D 858 939-3400
3003 Health Center Dr San Diego (92123) ***(P-21196)***

Sharp McDonald Center .... A 858 637-6920
7989 Linda Vista Rd San Diego (92111) ***(P-21492)***

Sharp Memorial Hospital (HQ) .... A 858 939-3636
7901 Frost St San Diego (92123) ***(P-21197)***

Sharp Memorial Hospital .... C 858 278-4110
7850 Vista Hill Ave San Diego (92123) ***(P-21426)***

Sharp Mesa Vista Hospital, San Diego *Also called Sharp Memorial Hospital* ***(P-21426)***

Sharp Mission Park Medical Ctr, Vista *Also called Sharp Healthcare* ***(P-21195)***

Sharp Reece Stealy Med Group, San Diego *Also called Sharp Healthcare* ***(P-19399)***

Sharp Rees-Stealy, San Diego *Also called Sharp Healthcare* ***(P-21193)***

Sharp Rees-Stealy Div, San Diego *Also called Sharp Healthcare* ***(P-19396)***

SHARP REES-STEALY PHARMACY, San Diego *Also called Sharp Memorial Hospital* ***(P-21197)***

Shartsis Friese LLP .... C 415 421-6500
1 Maritime Plz Fl 18 San Francisco (94111) ***(P-22812)***

Shason Inc (PA) .... D 323 269-6666
5525 S Soto St Vernon (90058) ***(P-8012)***

Shasta Blood Center, San Francisco *Also called Vitalant Research Institute* ***(P-22340)***

Shasta Cattle Women, Cottonwood *Also called County of Shasta* ***(P-24527)***

Shasta Convalescent Center .... C 530 222-3630
3550 Churn Creek Rd Redding (96002) ***(P-20679)***

Shasta Convalescent Hospital, Redding *Also called Shasta Convalescent Center* ***(P-20679)***

Shasta County Calworks, Redding *Also called County of Shasta* ***(P-10215)***

Shasta County Head Start Child (PA) .... E 530 241-1036
375 Lake Blvd Ste 100 Redding (96003) ***(P-23785)***

Shasta Lake Resorts LP .... D 209 785-3300
22300 Jones Vly Marina Dr Redding (96003) ***(P-18757)***

Shasta Landscaping Inc .... D 760 744-6551
1340 Descanso Ave San Marcos (92069) ***(P-905)***

Shasta Livestock Auction Yard .... D 530 347-3793
3917 Main St Cottonwood (96022) ***(P-8680)***

Shasta Produce Co, South San Francisco *Also called Andrighetto Produce Inc* ***(P-3377)***

Shasta Regional Med Ctr Srmc, Redding *Also called Prime Healthcare Services* ***(P-21109)***

Shasta-Trinity Ranger Unit, Redding *Also called Forestry and Fire Protection* ***(P-964)***

Shattuck Health Care Inc .... D 510 665-2800
2829 Shattuck Ave Berkeley (94705) ***(P-20253)***

Shaw & Petersen Insurance Inc .... E 707 443-0845
1313 5th St Eureka (95501) ***(P-10493)***

Shaw Bakers LLC .... D 650 273-1440
320b Shaw Rd Ste B South San Francisco (94080) ***(P-8644)***

Shaw Industries Group Inc .... B 562 921-7209
15305 Valley View Ave Santa Fe Springs (90670) ***(P-6581)***

Shawmut Design and Cnstr, Los Angeles *Also called Shawmut Woodworking & Sup Inc* ***(P-1596)***

Shawmut Woodworking & Sup Inc .... C 323 602-1000
11390 W Olympic Blvd Fl 2 Los Angeles (90064) ***(P-1596)***

Shawnan, Downey *Also called Sialic Contractors Corporation* ***(P-1788)***

Shc Burbank II LLC .... C 818 843-6000
2500 N Hollywood Way Burbank (91505) ***(P-12910)***

Shc Reference Laboratory, Palo Alto *Also called Stanford Health Care* ***(P-21241)***

SHD, Chester *Also called Seneca Healthcare District* ***(P-21186)***

SHe Manages Properties Inc (PA) .... D 619 291-6300
9340 Hazard Way Ste B2 San Diego (92123) ***(P-11446)***

Shea Convalescent Hospital, Whittier *Also called Longwood Management Corp* ***(P-21020)***

Shea Family Care Somerset, El Cajon *Also called Somerset Special Care Center* ***(P-20458)***

Shea Homes, Irvine *Also called JF Shea Construction Inc* ***(P-1142)***

SHEA HOMES, Rio Vista *Also called Trilogy Rio Vista* ***(P-1389)***

Shea Homes, San Jose *Also called JF Shea Construction Inc* ***(P-1144)***

Shea Homes, Livermore *Also called JF Shea Construction Inc* ***(P-1145)***

Shea Homes Arizona Ltd Partnr .... D 909 594-9500
655 Brea Canyon Rd Walnut (91789) ***(P-11447)***

Shea Homes At Montage LLC .... D 909 594-9500
655 Brea Canyon Rd Walnut (91789) ***(P-1193)***

Shea Homes Lmtd Partnership A (HQ) .... E 909 594-9500
655 Brea Canyon Rd Walnut (91789) ***(P-1194)***

Shea Homes Ltd Prtnershp, Walnut *Also called Vistancia Marketing LLC* ***(P-26873)***

Shea Homes Vantis LLC .... D 909 594-9500
655 Brea Canyon Rd Walnut (91789) ***(P-1272)***

Shea Properties MGT Co Inc .... B 949 389-7000
130 Vantis Dr Ste 200 Aliso Viejo (92656) ***(P-11448)***

Shed Media US Inc .... D 323 904-4680
3800 Barham Blvd Ste 410 Los Angeles (90068) ***(P-13633)***

Sheedy Drayage Co (PA) .... D 415 648-7171
1215 Michigan St San Francisco (94107) ***(P-14114)***

Sheehan Construction Inc .... B 707 603-2610
477 Devlin Rd Ste 108 NAPA (94558) ***(P-1195)***

Shekinah Inc .... E 714 475-5460
7755 Center Ave Ste 1000 Huntington Beach (92647) ***(P-22813)***

Sheldon Mechanical Corporation .... D 661 286-1361
26015 Avenue Hall Santa Clarita (91355) ***(P-2272)***

Sheldon Ranches .... D 559 562-3978
25140 Burr Dr Lindsay (93247) ***(P-360)***

Shell Vacations LLC .... D 415 441-7100
501 Post St San Francisco (94102) ***(P-12911)***

Shelter Inc (PA) .... D 925 335-0698
1333 Willow Pass Rd # 206 Concord (94520) ***(P-23465)***

Shelter Point Hotel & Marina, San Diego *Also called Pacifica Hotel Company* ***(P-12701)***

Shelter Pointe Hotel & Marina, San Diego *Also called Shelter Pointe LLC* ***(P-4636)***

Shelter Pointe LLC .... C 619 221-8000
1551 Shelter Island Dr San Diego (92106) ***(P-4636)***

Shelton Construction Company .... D 714 903-7853
5628 Spinnaker Bay Dr Long Beach (90803) ***(P-1787)***

Shen Zhen New World II LLC .... D 818 980-1212
333 Unversal Hollywood Dr Universal City (91608) ***(P-12912)***

Shenyang Zhong Yi Tin-Plating .... C 415 788-2280
843 Clay St San Francisco (94108) ***(P-10644)***

Shepard Eye Center .... E 805 925-2637
1418 E Main St Ste 110 Santa Maria (93454) ***(P-19402)***

Sheplace Design Center, San Francisco *Also called Bay West Shwplace Invstors LLC* ***(P-10571)***

Sheppard Mullin Richter (PA) .... B 213 620-1780
333 S Hope St Fl 43 Los Angeles (90071) ***(P-22814)***

Sheppard Mullin Richter .... D 619 338-6500
12275 El Camino R Ste 200 San Diego (92130) ***(P-22815)***

Sheppard Mullin Richter .... D 415 434-9100
4 Embarcadero Ctr # 1700 San Francisco (94111) ***(P-22816)***

Sheppard Mullin Richter .... D 310 228-3700
1901 Avenue Of The Stars # 1600 Los Angeles (90067) ***(P-22817)***

Sheppard Mullin Richter .... D 714 513-5100
650 Town Center Dr Fl 10 Costa Mesa (92626) ***(P-22818)***

Sheppard Mullin, Los Angeles *Also called Sheppard Mullin Richter* ***(P-22814)***

Sheraton, San Francisco *Also called Interstate Hotels Resorts Inc* ***(P-12471)***

Sheraton, Santa Monica *Also called M&C Hotel Interests Inc* ***(P-12568)***

Sheraton, Los Angeles *Also called Hazens Investment LLC* ***(P-12343)***

Sheraton, Emeryville *Also called Pacific Hotel Management LLC* ***(P-12691)***

Sheraton, San Diego *Also called Dimension Development Two LLC* ***(P-12210)***

Sheraton, Pasadena *Also called Dallas Union Hotel Inc* ***(P-11850)***

Sheraton, San Diego *Also called Hst Lessee Boston LLC* ***(P-12422)***

Sheraton, San Diego *Also called 8110 Aero Holding LLC* ***(P-11988)***

Sheraton, La Jolla *Also called Bartell Hotels* ***(P-12042)***

Sheraton, Palo Alto *Also called Pacific Hotel Management LLC* ***(P-12693)***

Sheraton Carlsbad Resort & Spa, Carlsbad *Also called Grand Pacific Carlsbad Ht LP* ***(P-12305)***

Sheraton Downtown Los Angeles, Los Angeles *Also called Nrea-TRC 711 LLC* ***(P-12654)***

Sheraton Hotel San Jose, Milpitas *Also called Cni Thl Ops LLC* ***(P-12159)***

Sheraton Hotel Sunnyvale, Sunnyvale *Also called Sunnyvale Sof-X Owner L P* ***(P-12986)***

Sheraton Hotel Sunnyvale, Sunnyvale *Also called W2005 New Cntury Ht Prtflio LP* ***(P-13072)***

Sheraton Htl San Diego Msn Vly .... D 619 321-4602
1433 Camino Del Rio S San Diego (92108) ***(P-12913)***

Sheraton LLC .... B 415 362-5500
2500 Mason St San Francisco (94133) ***(P-12914)***

Sheraton LLC .... B 310 642-1111
6101 W Century Blvd Los Angeles (90045) ***(P-12915)***

Sheraton LLC .... B 916 447-1700
1230 J St 13th Sacramento (95814) ***(P-12916)***

Sheraton LLC .... B 909 204-6100
11960 Foothill Blvd Rancho Cucamonga (91739) ***(P-12917)***

Sheraton LLC .... B 925 463-3330
5990 Stoneridge Mall Rd Pleasanton (94588) ***(P-12918)***

Sheraton Ontario Airport Hotel, Los Angeles *Also called S W K Properties LLC* ***(P-12858)***

Sheraton Palo Alto, Palo Alto *Also called Pacific Hotel Dev Ventr LP* ***(P-12689)***

Sheraton Pasadena, Pasadena *Also called Pasadena Hotel Dev Ventr LP* ***(P-12740)***

Sheraton Pk Ht At Anheim Rsort, Anaheim *Also called Anaheim Hotel LLC* ***(P-12007)***

Sheraton Redding At The Sundia, Redding *Also called Sheraton Redding Hotel* ***(P-12919)***

Sheraton Redding Hotel .... D 530 364-2800
820 Sundial Bridge Dr Redding (96001) ***(P-12919)***

Sheraton San Diego Ht & Marina, San Diego *Also called Hst Lessee San Diego LP* ***(P-12423)***

Sheraton San Diego Ht & Marina, San Diego *Also called Host Hotels & Resorts LP* ***(P-12390)***

Sheraton San Diego Mission Vly, San Diego *Also called Sheraton Htl San Diego Msn Vly* ***(P-12913)***

Sheraton Sn Diego Htl Msn Vly, San Diego *Also called Ashford Trs Nickel LLC* ***(P-26141)***

Sheraton Sonoma Cnty Petaluma, Petaluma *Also called Sonoma Hotel Partners LP* ***(P-12945)***

Sheraton Suites San Diego, San Diego *Also called Noiro West LLC* ***(P-12650)***

Sheraton Universal Hotel, Universal City *Also called Shen Zhen New World II LLC* ***(P-12912)***

Sheraton Universal Hotel, North Hollywood *Also called SLC Operating Ltd Partnership* ***(P-13454)***

Mergent e-mail: customerrelations@mergent.com
1428

2020 Directory of California
Wholesalers and Services Companies

(P-0000) Products & Services Section entry number
(PA)=Parent Co (HQ)=Headquarters (DH)=Div Headquarters

Sheraton Universal Hotel, Universal City *Also called Lh Universal Operating LLC* ***(P-12549)***
Sheriff's Dept, Elk Grove *Also called County of Sacramento* ***(P-26941)***
Sheriff's Dept, San Francisco *Also called City & County of San Francisco* ***(P-23004)***
Sheriffs Offices ....D....760 878-0383
550 S Clay St Independence (93526) ***(P-22819)***
Sherman Oaks Health System ....D....818 981-7111
4929 Van Nuys Blvd Sherman Oaks (91403) ***(P-21198)***
Sherman Oaks Hospital, Sherman Oaks *Also called Prime Healthcare Svcs II LLC* ***(P-21111)***
Sherman Security ....C....909 941-4167
7218 Hermosa Ave Rancho Cucamonga (91701) ***(P-16441)***
Sherman Village Hlth Care Ctr, North Hollywood *Also called Hillsdale Group LP* ***(P-20594)***
Sherman Village Hlth Care Ctr, North Hollywood *Also called Coldwater Care Center LLC* ***(P-19808)***
Shermn-Lehr Cstm Tile Wrks Inc ....D....916 386-0417
5691 Power Inn Rd Ste A Sacramento (95824) ***(P-2909)***
Sherpaul Corporation ....D....760 639-6472
901 Hacienda Dr Ste B Vista (92081) ***(P-21865)***
Sherton Grdn Grove Anheim S Ht ....D....714 703-8400
12221 Harbor Blvd Garden Grove (92840) ***(P-12920)***
Sherwood Country Club ....C....805 496-3036
320 W Stafford Rd Thousand Oaks (91361) ***(P-18572)***
Sherwood Development Company (PA) ....E....805 496-1833
2300 Norfield Ct Thousand Oaks (91361) ***(P-11601)***
Sherwood Guest Home, Lynwood *Also called Marlinda Management Inc* ***(P-20628)***
Sherwood Healthcare Center, Sacramento *Also called H C C S Inc* ***(P-19989)***
Sherwood Mechanical Inc ....D....858 679-3000
6630 Top Gun St San Diego (92121) ***(P-2273)***
Sherwood Oaks Enterprises ....D....707 964-6333
130 Dana St Fort Bragg (95437) ***(P-20254)***
Sherwood Oaks Health Center, Fort Bragg *Also called Sherwood Oaks Enterprises* ***(P-20254)***
Sherwood Valley Rancheria ....D....707 459-7330
100 Kawi Pl Willits (95490) ***(P-12921)***
Sherwood Vllley Rnchria Casino, Willits *Also called Sherwood Valley Rancheria* ***(P-12921)***
Shibui Apartments, Torrance *Also called Hunt Enterprises Inc* ***(P-11196)***
Shield Healthcare, Valencia *Also called Shield-Denver Health Care Ctr* ***(P-7004)***
Shield Security Inc (HQ) ....B....714 210-1501
1551 N Tustin Ave Ste 650 Santa Ana (92705) ***(P-16442)***
Shield Security Inc ....C....818 239-5800
21110 Vanowen St Canoga Park (91303) ***(P-16443)***
Shield Security Inc ....B....562 283-1100
150 E Wardlow Rd Long Beach (90807) ***(P-16444)***
Shield Security Inc ....B....909 920-1173
265 N Euclid Ave Upland (91786) ***(P-16445)***
Shield-Denver Health Care Ctr (HQ) ....C....661 294-4200
27911 Franklin Pkwy Valencia (91355) ***(P-7004)***
Shields For Families (PA) ....D....323 242-5000
11601 S Western Ave Los Angeles (90047) ***(P-21493)***
Shields Nursing Centers Inc (PA) ....C....510 724-9911
606 Alfred Nobel Dr Hercules (94547) ***(P-20255)***
Shields Nursing Centers Inc ....D....510 525-3212
3230 Carlson Blvd El Cerrito (94530) ***(P-20256)***
Shieldx Networks Inc ....E....760 724-2700
4093 Oceanside Blvd Ste A Oceanside (92056) ***(P-15092)***
Shift Technologies Inc ....D....415 800-2038
2525 16th St Ste 310 San Francisco (94103) ***(P-6408)***
Shiftpixy Inc ....D....949 207-7184
1 Venture Ste 150 Irvine (92618) ***(P-27207)***
Shih Yu-Lang Central YMCA, San Francisco *Also called Young Mens Christian Assoc SF* ***(P-24738)***
Shii LLC ....E....909 354-8000
2151 E Cnvntn Ctr Way # 222 Ontario (91764) ***(P-11449)***
Shilpark Paint Automotive, Los Angeles *Also called Shilpark Paint Corporation* ***(P-8945)***
Shilpark Paint Corporation (PA) ....D....323 732-7093
1640 S Vermont Ave Los Angeles (90006) ***(P-8945)***
Shimadzu Medical Systems USA, Long Beach *Also called Shimadzu Precision Instrs Inc* ***(P-7699)***
Shimadzu Precision Instrs Inc (HQ) ....D....562 420-6226
3645 N Lakewood Blvd Long Beach (90808) ***(P-7699)***
Shimadzu Precision Instrs Inc ....D....310 217-8855
20101 S Vermont Ave Torrance (90502) ***(P-7005)***
Shimano North Amer Holdg Inc (HQ) ....C....949 951-5003
1 Holland Irvine (92618) ***(P-7720)***
Shimmick Construction Co Inc (HQ) ....C....510 777-5000
8201 Edgewater Dr Ste 202 Oakland (94621) ***(P-1990)***
Shims Bargain Inc (PA) ....D....323 881-0099
2600 S Soto St Vernon (90058) ***(P-9011)***
Shims Bargain Inc ....C....323 726-8800
7030 E Slauson Ave Commerce (90040) ***(P-1377)***
Shingle Sprng Trbal Gming Auth ....A....530 677-7000
1 Red Hawk Pkwy Placerville (95667) ***(P-18758)***
Shinsuke Clifford Yamamoto ....D....714 992-5783
2031 Emery Ave La Habra (90631) ***(P-906)***
Shinwoo P&C Usa Inc (PA) ....A....619 407-7164
2177 Britannia Blvd # 203 San Diego (92154) ***(P-17055)***
Shipbycom LLC ....D....626 271-9800
218 Machlin Ct Walnut (91789) ***(P-3934)***
Shipco Transport Inc ....D....562 295-2900
100 W Victoria St Long Beach (90805) ***(P-5049)***
Shiva-Shakthi, San Diego *Also called Marika Group Inc* ***(P-8092)***
Shn Cnslting Engnrs-Geologists, Eureka *Also called Shn Consulting Engin* ***(P-25304)***
Shn Consulting Engin (PA) ....D....707 441-8855
812 W Wabash Ave Eureka (95501) ***(P-25304)***
Sho-Air International Inc (PA) ....E....949 476-9111
5401 Argosy Ave Ste 102 Huntington Beach (92649) ***(P-5050)***
Shoei Foods USA Inc ....D....530 742-7866
1900 Feather River Blvd Olivehurst (95961) ***(P-8216)***
Shoffeitt Pipeline Inc ....D....949 581-1600
15801 Rockfield Blvd L Irvine (92618) ***(P-1911)***
Shook & Waller Cnstr Inc ....D....707 578-3933
7677 Bell Rd Ste 101 Windsor (95492) ***(P-2976)***
Shook Hardy & Bacon LLP ....D....415 544-1900
1 Montgomery St Ste 2700 San Francisco (94104) ***(P-22820)***
Shooter & Butts Inc ....E....925 460-5155
3768 Old Santa Rita Rd Pleasanton (94588) ***(P-761)***
Shopcore Properties LP (HQ) ....D....858 613-1800
10920 Via Frontera # 220 San Diego (92127) ***(P-11815)***
Shopkick Inc ....D....650 763-8727
2317 Broadway St Fl 3 Redwood City (94063) ***(P-15093)***
Shopper Inc ....B....805 527-6700
3987 Heritage Oak Ct Simi Valley (93063) ***(P-6931)***
Shoppes At Carlsbad, The, Carlsbad *Also called RPI Carlsbad LP* ***(P-10638)***
Shopping Center Mgt Corp ....D....650 617-8234
660 Stanford Shopping Ctr Palo Alto (94304) ***(P-10645)***
Shoppingcom Inc ....C....650 616-6500
199 Fremont St Fl 4 San Francisco (94105) ***(P-15812)***
Shopzilla.com, Santa Monica *Also called Connexity Inc* ***(P-5381)***
Shore Hotel ....D....310 458-1515
1515 Ocean Ave Santa Monica (90401) ***(P-12922)***
Shorebreeze Apartments, Mountain View *Also called Mp Shoreline Assoc Ltd Partnr* ***(P-10783)***
Shorecliff Properties, Pismo Beach *Also called T I C Hotels Inc* ***(P-13013)***
Shoreline Care Center, Oxnard *Also called Covenant Care California LLC* ***(P-19832)***
Shoreline Land Care Inc ....D....858 560-8555
7348 Trade St Ste B San Diego (92121) ***(P-762)***
Shoreline S Intermediate Care ....C....510 523-8857
430 Willow St Alameda (94501) ***(P-20453)***
Shorenstein Company LLC ....E....415 772-7000
235 Montgomery St Fl 15 San Francisco (94104) ***(P-10646)***
Shorenstein Properties LLC (PA) ....C....415 772-7000
235 Montgomery St Fl 16 San Francisco (94104) ***(P-10647)***
Shores Restaurant, La Jolla *Also called La Jolla Bch & Tennis CLB Inc* ***(P-12528)***
Shoreview Preservation LP ....D....415 647-6922
35 Lillian Ct San Francisco (94124) ***(P-10812)***
Shoring & Excavating, Santa Fe Springs *Also called Shoring Engineers* ***(P-3467)***
Shoring Engineers ....D....562 944-9331
12645 Clark St Santa Fe Springs (90670) ***(P-3467)***
Shotspotter Inc ....D....510 794-3100
7979 Gateway Blvd Ste 210 Newark (94560) ***(P-15497)***
Show Call Productions Inc ....B....619 602-0656
5212 Lenore Dr San Diego (92115) ***(P-17946)***
Showa Marine Inc (PA) ....D....213 627-4091
668 S Alameda St Ste A Los Angeles (90021) ***(P-8389)***
Showcase Installations, Santa Fe Springs *Also called Partitions Installation Inc* ***(P-3449)***
Showershapes, Ventura *Also called G W Surfaces* ***(P-3410)***
Showpad Inc (HQ) ....B....415 800-2033
301 Howard St Ste 500 San Francisco (94105) ***(P-16108)***
Showroom Interiors LLC ....C....323 348-1551
4900 E 50th St Vernon (90058) ***(P-14197)***
Shri Sidhi Vinayaka Hotel Inc ....C....855 922-5252
500 Leisure Ln Sacramento (95815) ***(P-12923)***
Shriner's Hospital, Pasadena *Also called Shriners Hspitals For Children* ***(P-21494)***
Shriners Hspitals For Children ....B....213 388-3151
909 S Fair Oaks Ave Pasadena (91105) ***(P-21494)***
Shriners Hspitals For Children ....B....916 453-2050
2425 Stockton Blvd Sacramento (95817) ***(P-21199)***
Shubin Services Inc ....E....714 259-0908
15031 Parkway Loop Ste A Tustin (92780) ***(P-6282)***
Shuler, Kurt MD, Davis *Also called Sutter Health* ***(P-21283)***
Shusters Transportation Inc ....D....707 459-4131
750 E Valley St Willits (95490) ***(P-3935)***
Shutterfly Inc (PA) ....C....650 610-5200
2800 Bridge Pkwy Ste 100 Redwood City (94065) ***(P-16583)***
Shutters On The Beach, Santa Monica *Also called By The Blue Sea LLC* ***(P-12100)***
Shutters On The Beach, Santa Monica *Also called Edward Thomas Hospitality Corp* ***(P-12240)***
SI Inc ....E....951 304-9444
26035 Jefferson Ave Murrieta (92562) ***(P-2977)***
Sia Engineering (usa) Inc ....D....310 693-7108
7001 W Imperial Hwy Los Angeles (90045) ***(P-25305)***
Sialic Contractors Corporation ....D....562 803-9977
12240 Woodruff Ave Downey (90241) ***(P-1788)***
Sick Child Care Center, The, San Jose *Also called Sjb Child Development Centers* ***(P-23787)***
Sideman & Bancroft LLP ....D....415 392-1960
1 Embarcadero Ctr Ste 860 San Francisco (94111) ***(P-22821)***
Sidjon Corporation ....D....925 606-6135
3571 1st St Livermore (94551) ***(P-12924)***
Sidley Austin LLP ....D....650 565-7000
1001 Page Mill Rd Bldg 1 Palo Alto (94304) ***(P-22822)***
Siemens AG ....C....650 969-9112
685 E Middlefield Rd Mountain View (94043) ***(P-25306)***
Siemens Healthineers, Mountain View *Also called Siemens AG* ***(P-25306)***
Siemens Industry Inc ....B....510 783-6000
2525 Barrington Ct Hayward (94545) ***(P-7183)***
Siemens Industry Inc ....C....510 783-6000
25821 Industrial Blvd # 300 Hayward (94545) ***(P-7588)***
Siemens Industry Inc ....D....909 627-6141
2420 S Reservoir St Pomona (91766) ***(P-7184)***
Siemens Industry Inc ....D....858 693-8711
9835 Carroll Ctre Rd 10 San Diego (92126) ***(P-7589)***
Siemens Industry Inc ....C....714 761-2200
6141 Katella Ave Cypress (90630) ***(P-7185)***
Siemens Med Solutions USA Inc ....B....650 694-5747
685 E Middlefield Rd Mountain View (94043) ***(P-7006)***

A L P H A B E T I C

Employee Codes: A=Over 500 employees, B=251-500
C=101-250, D=51-100, E=50
2020 Directory of California
Wholesalers and Services Companies
© Mergent Inc. 1-800-342-5647
1429

Siemens Mobility Inc ....D.......916 621-2700
5301 Price Ave McClellan (95652) ***(P-17346)***
Siemens PLM Software, Cypress *Also called Siemens Product Life Mgmt Sftw* ***(P-15094)***
Siemens Product Life Mgmt Sftw ....D.......714 952-6500
10824 Hope St Cypress (90630) ***(P-15094)***
Sierra At Taho Ski Resorts ....E.......530 659-7519
1111 Sierra At Tahoe Rd Twin Bridges (95735) ***(P-12925)***
Sierra Bancorp ....D.......559 449-8145
7029 N Ingram Ave Ste 101 Fresno (93650) ***(P-9239)***
Sierra Bay Contractors Inc ....E.......925 671-7711
4021 Port Chicago Hwy # 150 Concord (94520) ***(P-1378)***
Sierra Bookkeeping & Tax Svc ....D.......916 349-7610
5777 Madison Ave Ste 615 Sacramento (95841) ***(P-25678)***
Sierra Care Rehabilitation Ctr ....D.......916 782-3188
310 Oak Ridge Dr Roseville (95661) ***(P-20257)***
Sierra Cascade Blueberries ....E.......530 894-8728
12753 Doe Mill Rd Forest Ranch (95942) ***(P-110)***
Sierra Central Credit Union (PA) ....D.......530 671-3009
1351 Harter Pkwy Yuba City (95993) ***(P-9352)***
Sierra Club (PA) ....C.......415 977-5500
2101 Webster St Ste 1300 Oakland (94612) ***(P-24657)***
SIERRA CLUB BOOKS, Oakland *Also called Sierra Club* ***(P-24657)***
Sierra Cscade Fmly Opprtnities (PA) ....C.......530 283-1242
424 N Mill Creek Rd Quincy (95971) ***(P-23786)***
Sierra Disposal Service, South Lake Tahoe *Also called South Tahoe Refuse Co* ***(P-6286)***
Sierra Electric Co, San Francisco *Also called Stadtner Co Inc* ***(P-2653)***
Sierra Entertainment ....E.......530 666-9646
341 Industrial Way Woodland (95776) ***(P-3507)***
Sierra Equipment Leasing Inc ....E.......925 676-7300
1140 Suncast Ln El Dorado Hills (95762) ***(P-14198)***
Sierra Forest Products ....C.......559 535-4893
9000 Road 234 Terra Bella (93270) ***(P-6656)***
Sierra Forever Families ....D.......916 368-5114
8928 Volunteer Ln Ste 100 Sacramento (95826) ***(P-23466)***
Sierra Gold Nurseries Inc ....D.......530 674-1145
5320 Garden Hwy Yuba City (95991) ***(P-280)***
Sierra Group, Glendale *Also called Next Venture Inc* ***(P-1551)***
Sierra Health Services LLC ....E.......209 956-7725
2423 W March Ln Ste 100 Stockton (95207) ***(P-10047)***
Sierra Hills Care Center Inc ....D.......916 782-7007
1139 Cirby Way Roseville (95661) ***(P-20454)***
Sierra International McHy LLC ....D.......661 327-7073
1620 E Brundage Ln Frnt Bakersfield (93307) ***(P-7772)***
Sierra Lakes Golf Club ....D.......909 350-2500
16600 Clubhouse Dr Fontana (92336) ***(P-18297)***
Sierra Landscape & Maintenance ....D.......530 895-0263
546 Hickory St Chico (95928) ***(P-763)***
Sierra Lathing Company Inc ....C.......909 421-0211
1189 Leiske Dr Rialto (92376) ***(P-2858)***
Sierra Living Concepts Inc ....D.......510 402-4906
46560 Fremont Blvd # 414 Fremont (94538) ***(P-6582)***
Sierra Lobo Inc ....C.......626 510-6340
465 N Halstead St Ste 130 Pasadena (91107) ***(P-25307)***
Sierra Lodge 788, Oakhurst *Also called Sierra Masonic Association* ***(P-24658)***
Sierra Lumber & Decking, San Jose *Also called Sierra Lumber Co* ***(P-2978)***
Sierra Lumber Co ....C.......408 286-7071
1711 Senter Rd San Jose (95112) ***(P-2978)***
Sierra Manor Apts, Chico *Also called Hignell Incorporated* ***(P-10737)***
Sierra Masonic Association ....D.......559 683-7713
2166 Hwy 49 Oakhurst (93644) ***(P-24658)***
Sierra Mountain Express, El Dorado Hills *Also called Sierra Equipment Leasing Inc* ***(P-14198)***
Sierra Nevada Corporation ....C.......408 395-2004
985 University Ave Ste 4 Los Gatos (95032) ***(P-25308)***
Sierra Nevada Home Care, Grass Valley *Also called Sierra Nevada Memorial Hm Care* ***(P-21866)***
Sierra Nevada Memorial Hm Care ....D.......530 274-6350
1020 Mccourtney Rd Ste A Grass Valley (95949) ***(P-21866)***
Sierra Oaks Senior Living ....D.......530 241-5100
1520 Collyer Dr Redding (96003) ***(P-24073)***
Sierra Pacific 4117, Modesto *Also called US Foods Inc* ***(P-8667)***
Sierra Pacific Development ....D.......559 256-1300
1470 W Herndon Ave # 100 Fresno (93711) ***(P-11602)***
Sierra Pacific Dist Svcs Inc (PA) ....D.......209 572-2882
3731 Finch Rd Modesto (95357) ***(P-4502)***
Sierra Pacific Farms Inc (PA) ....D.......951 699-9980
43406 Business Park Dr Temecula (92590) ***(P-682)***
Sierra Pacific Htg & Air-Solar, Rancho Cordova *Also called Sierra PCF HM & Comfort Inc* ***(P-7456)***
Sierra Pacific Mortgage Co Inc ....D.......805 489-6060
104 Traffic Way Arroyo Grande (93420) ***(P-9603)***
Sierra Pacific Mortgage Co Inc (PA) ....A.......916 932-1700
1180 Iron Point Rd # 200 Folsom (95630) ***(P-9604)***
Sierra Pacific Ortho ....C.......559 256-5200
1630 E Herndon Ave Fresno (93720) ***(P-19403)***
Sierra Pacific Warehouse Group, Modesto *Also called Sierra Pacific Dist Svcs Inc* ***(P-4502)***
Sierra Pacific West Inc ....D.......760 599-0755
2125 La Mirada Dr Vista (92081) ***(P-1597)***
Sierra PCF HM & Comfort Inc ....D.......916 638-0543
2550 Mercantile Dr Ste D Rancho Cordova (95742) ***(P-7456)***
Sierra Railroad Company ....D.......530 554-2522
1222 Research Park Dr Davis (95618) ***(P-3508)***
Sierra Recycling & Dem Inc ....D.......661 327-7073
1620 E Brundage Ln Frnt Bakersfield (93307) ***(P-3351)***
Sierra Select Distributors Inc ....D.......916 483-9295
4320 Roseville Rd North Highlands (95660) ***(P-7218)***
Sierra Systems Inc (PA) ....C.......310 536-6288
222 N Pacific Coast Hwy # 1310 El Segundo (90245) ***(P-26812)***
Sierra Tel Business Systems, Oakhurst *Also called Sierra Tel Cmmunications Group* ***(P-5468)***
Sierra Tel Cmmunications Group ....D.......559 683-7777
40044 Highway 49 Ste C2 Oakhurst (93644) ***(P-5468)***
Sierra Tel Cmmunications Group (PA) ....D.......559 683-4611
49150 Road 426 Oakhurst (93644) ***(P-5469)***
Sierra Telephone Company Inc ....C.......559 683-4611
49150 Crane Valley Rd 426 Oakhurst (93644) ***(P-5470)***
Sierra Transport Inc ....D.......661 399-0246
12856 Old River Rd Bakersfield (93311) ***(P-3936)***
Sierra Valley Rehab Center ....C.......559 784-7375
301 W Putnam Ave Porterville (93257) ***(P-20680)***
Sierra View Care Center, Baldwin Park *Also called Sierra View Care Holdings LLC* ***(P-20258)***
Sierra View Care Holdings LLC ....D.......626 960-1971
14318 Ohio St Baldwin Park (91706) ***(P-20258)***
Sierra View Country Club ....D.......916 782-3741
105 Alta Vista Ave Roseville (95678) ***(P-18573)***
Sierra View District Hospital, Porterville *Also called Sierra View Local Hospital Dst* ***(P-21200)***
Sierra View Dst Hosp Leag Inc (PA) ....C.......559 784-1110
465 W Putnam Ave Porterville (93257) ***(P-19404)***
Sierra View Homes ....C.......559 637-2256
1155 E Springfield Ave Reedley (93654) ***(P-20259)***
SIERRA VIEW HOMES RESIDENTIAL, Reedley *Also called Sierra View Homes* ***(P-20259)***
Sierra View Landscape Inc ....E.......916 408-2990
3888 Cincinnati Ave Rocklin (95765) ***(P-907)***
Sierra View Local Hospital Dst ....B.......559 781-7877
283 Pearson Dr Porterville (93257) ***(P-21200)***
Sierra Vista 16 A LLC ....E.......818 505-6777
12411 Ventura Blvd Studio City (91604) ***(P-10648)***
Sierra Vista Extended Stay, Brea *Also called Otb Acquisition LLC* ***(P-12679)***
Sierra Vista Family Medical ....D.......805 582-4000
1227 E Los Angeles Ave Simi Valley (93065) ***(P-22323)***
Sierra Vista Hospital, Sacramento *Also called Psychiatric Solutions Inc* ***(P-19314)***
Sierra Vista Hospital Inc (HQ) ....A.......805 546-7600
1010 Murray Ave San Luis Obispo (93405) ***(P-21201)***
Sierra Vista Memory Care Cmnty, Azusa *Also called Silverado Senior Living Inc* ***(P-20683)***
Sierra Vista Regional Med Ctr, San Luis Obispo *Also called Sierra Vista Hospital Inc* ***(P-21201)***
Sierra Waste Transport Inc ....E.......916 386-9937
8191 Elder Creek Rd Sacramento (95824) ***(P-5140)***
Sierra Weatherization Co Inc ....D.......408 354-1900
43 E Main St Ste B Los Gatos (95030) ***(P-13579)***
Sierra West Construction Inc ....E.......530 268-7614
24744 Connie Ct Auburn (95602) ***(P-2979)***
Sierra West Home Care, Santa Monica *Also called Right At Home* ***(P-21852)***
Sierra Wireless America Inc (HQ) ....D.......760 444-5650
2738 Loker Ave W Ste A Carlsbad (92010) ***(P-5269)***
Sierra-Cascade Nursery Inc (PA) ....B.......530 254-6867
472-715 Johnson Rd Susanville (96130) ***(P-281)***
Sift Science Inc ....D.......415 882-7709
123 Mission St Fl 20 San Francisco (94105) ***(P-15095)***
Sight Machine Inc ....D.......888 461-5739
243 Vallejo St San Francisco (94111) ***(P-15498)***
Sigma Investment Holdings LLC ....E.......626 398-3098
2288 Villa Heights Rd Pasadena (91107) ***(P-1991)***
Sigma Kappa Sorority ....D.......510 540-9142
2409 Warring St Berkeley (94704) ***(P-13176)***
Sigma Networks Inc ....C.......408 876-4002
2191 Zanker Rd San Jose (95131) ***(P-5471)***
Sigma Services Inc (PA) ....D.......805 642-8377
2140 Eastman Ave Ste 110 Ventura (93003) ***(P-1598)***
Sigmanet Inc (HQ) ....C.......909 230-7500
4290 E Brickell St Ontario (91761) ***(P-6894)***
Sigmaways Inc ....D.......510 573-4208
39737 Paseo Padre Pkwy Fremont (94538) ***(P-26813)***
Sign of Dove ....D.......916 786-3277
707 Sunrise Ave Ofc Roseville (95661) ***(P-10813)***
Signal 88 LLC ....A.......714 713-5306
821 S Rockefeller Ave Ontario (91761) ***(P-16446)***
Signal Health Police Dept ....E.......562 989-7200
2745 Walnut Ave Signal Hill (90755) ***(P-24659)***
Signaldemand Inc ....E.......415 356-0800
101 Montgomery St Ste 400 San Francisco (94104) ***(P-15096)***
Signature Building Maint Inc ....D.......408 377-8066
4005 Clipper Ct Fremont (94538) ***(P-14050)***
Signature Consultants LLC ....D.......310 229-5731
8560 W Sunset Blvd Los Angeles (90069) ***(P-27208)***
Signature Consultants LLC ....C.......415 544-7510
44 Montgomery St Ste 1450 San Francisco (94104) ***(P-27305)***
Signature Flight Support Corp ....D.......559 981-2490
3050 N Winery Ave Fresno (93703) ***(P-4791)***
Signature Flight Support Corp ....D.......650 877-6800
1052 N Access Rd San Francisco (94128) ***(P-4792)***
Signature Flight Support Corp ....D.......818 464-9500
7240 Hayvenhurst Ave Van Nuys (91406) ***(P-4793)***
Signature Flight Support Corp ....D.......562 997-0700
3333 E Spring St Ste 205 Long Beach (90806) ***(P-4794)***
Signature Flooring Inc ....D.......714 558-9200
701 N Hariton St Orange (92868) ***(P-3017)***
SIGNATURE FLOORS, Orange *Also called Signature Flooring Inc* ***(P-3017)***
Signature Painting & Cnstr Inc ....E.......925 287-0444
1559 3rd Ave Walnut Creek (94597) ***(P-2394)***
Signature Properties Inc ....D.......925 463-1122
4670 Willow Rd Ste 200 Pleasanton (94588) ***(P-11603)***
Signature Resources Insurance ....D.......949 930-2400
19900 Macarthur Blvd # 920 Irvine (92612) ***(P-10494)***
Signature Services ....D.......949 851-9391
4425 Jamboree Rd Ste 250 Newport Beach (92660) ***(P-10649)***
Signatures Sni, San Francisco *Also called Live Nation Merchandise Inc* ***(P-8985)***

ALPHABETIC SECTION
Sinclair Concrete

Signet Testing Labs Inc (HQ)...E...510 887-8484
3526 Breakwater Ct Hayward (94545) ***(P-26107)***
Significant Cleaning Svcs LLC...C...408 559-5959
148 E Virginia St Ste 1 San Jose (95112) ***(P-14051)***
Sigue Corporation (PA)...D...818 837-5939
13190 Telfair Ave Sylmar (91342) ***(P-17056)***
Silicon Prime Technologies Inc...E...310 279-0222
4154 W 172nd St Torrance (90504) ***(P-15097)***
Silicon Valley Bank...D...818 382-2600
15260 Ventura Blvd # 1800 Sherman Oaks (91403) ***(P-9118)***
Silicon Valley Bank (HQ)...A...408 654-7400
3003 Tasman Dr Santa Clara (95054) ***(P-9272)***
Silicon Valley Clean Water...D...650 591-7121
1400 Radio Rd Redwood City (94065) ***(P-6136)***
Silicon Valley Exec Netwrk...A...408 746-5803
1336 Nelson Way Sunnyvale (94087) ***(P-27209)***
Silicon Valley Hwang LLC...C...408 452-0200
1471 N 4th St San Jose (95112) ***(P-12926)***
Silicon Valley Mechanical Inc...D...408 943-0380
2115 Ringwood Ave San Jose (95131) ***(P-2274)***
Silicon Valley Office, Menlo Park *Also called Winston & Strawn LLP* ***(P-22878)***
Silicon Valley Power, Santa Clara *Also called City of Santa Clara* ***(P-5821)***
Silicon Valley Sftwr Group LLC...E...844 946-7874
74 Tehama St San Francisco (94105) ***(P-15098)***
Silicon Vly Cmnty Foundation...C...650 450-5400
2440 W El Cmino Real Ste Mountain View (94040) ***(P-24660)***
Silicon Vly Educatn Foundation...A...408 790-9400
1400 Parkmoor Ave Ste 200 San Jose (95126) ***(P-24225)***
Silicon Vly Mntrey Bay Cncil I (PA)...D...408 279-2086
970 W Julian St San Jose (95126) ***(P-24661)***
Silicon Vly SEC & Patrol Inc (PA)...C...408 267-1539
1131 Luchessi Dr Ste 2 San Jose (95118) ***(P-16447)***
Siliconsage Construction Inc...C...408 916-3205
560 S Mathilda Ave Sunnyvale (94086) ***(P-1273)***
Siliconsystems Inc...D...949 900-9400
26840 Aliso Viejo Pkwy # 1 Aliso Viejo (92656) ***(P-7186)***
Siliconware Usa Inc (HQ)...E...408 573-5500
1735 Tech Dr Ste 300 Fl 3 San Jose (95110) ***(P-7340)***
Silla Automotive LLC...E...661 392-8880
1901 Mineral Ct Ste C Bakersfield (93308) ***(P-6469)***
SILLCREST NURSING HOME, San Bernardino *Also called Marna Health Services Inc* ***(P-20629)***
Silliker Labs Group Inc...E...714 226-0000
6360 Gateway Dr Cypress (90630) ***(P-26108)***
Silman Construction, San Leandro *Also called Silman Venture Corporation* ***(P-1379)***
Silman Venture Corporation (PA)...C...510 347-4800
1600 Factor Ave San Leandro (94577) ***(P-1379)***
Silv Communication Inc...D...213 381-7999
3460 Wilshire Blvd # 1100 Los Angeles (90010) ***(P-27210)***
Silva Artist Management,, Los Angeles *Also called Artist Silva Management LLC* ***(P-26140)***
Silva Farms LLC (PA)...B...831 675-2327
111 Alpine Dr Gonzales (93926) ***(P-78)***
Silva Trucking Inc...E...209 982-1114
36 W Mathews Rd French Camp (95231) ***(P-3937)***
Silvaco Inc (PA)...D...408 567-1000
2811 Mission College Blvd # 6 Santa Clara (95054) ***(P-15692)***
Silver Cinemas Acquisition Co (HQ)...D...310 473-6701
2222 S Barrington Ave Los Angeles (90064) ***(P-17866)***
Silver Creek Home Owners...E...408 559-1977
1935 Dry Creek Rd Ste 203 Campbell (95008) ***(P-26391)***
Silver Creek Industries Inc...C...951 943-5393
2830 Barrett Ave Perris (92571) ***(P-1599)***
Silver Creek Vly Cntry CLB Inc...C...408 239-5775
5460 Country Club Pkwy San Jose (95138) ***(P-18574)***
Silver Crk Vlly Ctry CLB HM Ow, Campbell *Also called Silver Creek Home Owners* ***(P-26391)***
Silver Fredman A Prof Law Corp...E...310 556-2356
2029 Century Park E # 1900 Los Angeles (90067) ***(P-22823)***
Silver Lake Financial, San Francisco *Also called Silver Lake Partners II LP* ***(P-11760)***
Silver Lake Partners LP (PA)...D...650 233-8120
2775 Sand Hill Rd Ste 100 Menlo Park (94025) ***(P-11758)***
Silver Lake Partners II LP...D...408 454-4732
10080 N Wolfe Rd Sw3190 Cupertino (95014) ***(P-11759)***
Silver Lake Partners II LP...C...415 293-4355
1 Market Plz San Francisco (94105) ***(P-11760)***
Silver Lakes Association...D...760 245-1606
15273 Orchard Hill Ln Helendale (92342) ***(P-24662)***
Silver Rock Resort Golf Club...D...760 777-8884
79179 Ahmanson Ln La Quinta (92253) ***(P-18298)***
Silver Service, San Andreas *Also called Mark Twain Medical Center* ***(P-21031)***
Silver Shield Security...C...408 435-1111
2107 N 1st St Ste 100 San Jose (95131) ***(P-16448)***
Silver Spur Christian Camp...D...209 928-4248
17301 Silver Spur Dr Tuolumne (95379) ***(P-13152)***
Silver Strand...E...818 701-9707
8945 Fullbright Ave Chatsworth (91311) ***(P-2980)***
Silverado Contractors Inc (PA)...D...510 658-9960
2855 Mandela Pkwy Fl 2 Oakland (94608) ***(P-3352)***
Silverado Energy Company...B...949 752-5588
18101 Von Karman Ave Irvine (92612) ***(P-5921)***
Silverado Framing & Cnstr...D...951 352-1100
3091 E La Cadena Dr Riverside (92507) ***(P-1196)***
Silverado Orchards (PA)...D...707 963-1461
601 Pope St Ofc Saint Helena (94574) ***(P-10814)***
Silverado Resort and Spa...A...707 257-0200
1600 Atlas Peak Rd NAPA (94558) ***(P-18575)***
Silverado Rsort Svcs Group LLC...B...707 257-0200
1600 Atlas Peak Rd NAPA (94558) ***(P-12927)***
Silverado Senior Living Inc...D...424 257-6418
514 N Prospect Ave # 120 Redondo Beach (90277) ***(P-20260)***
Silverado Senior Living Inc...D...650 226-8017
1301 Ralston Ave Ste A Belmont (94002) ***(P-20681)***
Silverado Senior Living Inc (PA)...D...949 240-7200
6400 Oak Cyn Ste 200 Irvine (92618) ***(P-20682)***
Silverado Senior Living Inc...D...626 650-9891
125 W Sierra Madre Ave Azusa (91702) ***(P-20683)***
Silverado Senior Living Inc...D...949 945-0189
350 W Bay St Costa Mesa (92627) ***(P-20455)***
Silverado Senior Living Inc...E...626 872-3941
1118 N Stoneman Ave Alhambra (91801) ***(P-20684)***
Silverado Senior Living Inc...D...760 456-5137
1500 Borden Rd Escondido (92026) ***(P-20685)***
Silverado Senior Living Inc...D...760 270-9917
335 Saxony Rd Encinitas (92024) ***(P-20686)***
Silverado Senior Living Inc...D...657 888-5752
240 E 3rd St Tustin (92780) ***(P-24074)***
Silverado Senior Living Inc...D...323 984-7313
330 N Hayworth Ave Los Angeles (90048) ***(P-20687)***
Silverado Senior Living Holdin...A...949 240-7200
6400 Oak Cyn Ste 200 Irvine (92618) ***(P-24075)***
Silvergate San Marcos, San Marcos *Also called Americare Hlth Retirement Inc* ***(P-10566)***
Silverline Construction Inc...C...408 437-8810
1752 Junction Ave Ste E San Jose (95112) ***(P-1197)***
Silverscreen Healthcare Inc...C...909 793-1382
1875 Barton Rd Redlands (92373) ***(P-20688)***
Silverscreen Healthcare Inc...D...818 763-8247
10830 Oxnard St North Hollywood (91606) ***(P-20261)***
Silverwood Landscape Cnstr Inc...E...714 427-6134
2209 S Lyon St Santa Ana (92705) ***(P-908)***
SIM Investment Corporation...D...408 445-3310
1329 Blossom Hill Rd San Jose (95118) ***(P-18194)***
Simas Floor Co Inc (PA)...C...916 452-4933
3550 Power Inn Rd Sacramento (95826) ***(P-3018)***
Simas Floor Co Design Center, Sacramento *Also called Simas Floor Co Inc* ***(P-3018)***
Simbol Inc...D...925 226-7400
6920 Koll Center Pkwy # 216 Pleasanton (94566) ***(P-25834)***
Simbol Materials, Pleasanton *Also called Simbol Inc* ***(P-25834)***
Simco Electronics (PA)...D...408 734-9750
3131 Jay St Ste 100 Santa Clara (95054) ***(P-17464)***
Simi Hills Golf Course, Simi Valley *Also called American Golf Corporation* ***(P-18376)***
Simi Radiology & Imaging...D...805 522-5978
4100 Guardian St Ste 205 Simi Valley (93063) ***(P-26814)***
Simi Valley Family YMCA, Simi Valley *Also called Young Mens Christian Asso* ***(P-18786)***
Simi Valley Plaza 10, Simi Valley *Also called Edwards Theatres Circuit Inc* ***(P-17843)***
Simi Vly Care & Rehabilitation, Simi Valley *Also called Chase Group Llc* ***(P-25880)***
Simi Vly Hosp & Hlth Care Svcs (HQ)...C...805 955-6000
2975 Sycamore Dr Simi Valley (93065) ***(P-19695)***
Simi West Inc...C...760 346-5502
999 Enchanted Way Simi Valley (93065) ***(P-12928)***
Simmons Construction Inc...E...661 636-1321
19252 Flypath Way Bakersfield (93308) ***(P-1600)***
Simon and Gladstone A Prof, Irvine *Also called Berger Kahn* ***(P-22380)***
Simon Mrtn-Vgue Wnklstein Mris, San Francisco *Also called A Smwm California Corporation* ***(P-25407)***
Simoni & Massoni Farms...E...925 634-2304
2510 Taylor Ln Byron (94514) ***(P-9)***
Simonian Brothers Inc (PA)...D...559 834-5921
511 N 7th St Fowler (93625) ***(P-542)***
Simonian Fruit, Fowler *Also called Simonian Brothers Inc* ***(P-542)***
Simple Luxuries LLC...E...310 627-6514
1560 N Sycamore Ave Rialto (92376) ***(P-3217)***
Simplehuman LLC (PA)...D...310 436-2250
19850 Magellan Dr Torrance (90502) ***(P-6583)***
Simpler Postage Inc (PA)...D...408 915-0063
1 Montgomery St Ste 400 San Francisco (94104) ***(P-5051)***
Simplex Time Recorder 480, San Diego *Also called Simplex Time Recorder LLC* ***(P-2642)***
Simplex Time Recorder LLC...D...858 740-0100
9855 Carroll Canyon Rd San Diego (92131) ***(P-2642)***
Simplot Growers Solutions, Firebaugh *Also called JR Simplot Company* ***(P-8842)***
Simply Fresh Fruit Inc...D...323 586-0000
4383 Exchange Ave Vernon (90058) ***(P-8523)***
Simpson & Simpson...D...213 736-6664
633 W 5th St Ste 3320 Los Angeles (90071) ***(P-26392)***
Simpson Delmore and Greene LLP (PA)...E...619 515-1194
600 W Broadway Ste 400 San Diego (92101) ***(P-22824)***
Simpson Gumpertz & Heger Inc...D...415 495-3700
100 Pine St Ste 1600 San Francisco (94111) ***(P-25309)***
Simpson Strong-Tie Intl Inc...D...925 560-9000
5956 W Las Positas Blvd Pleasanton (94588) ***(P-7103)***
Simpson Thacher & Bartlett LLP...C...650 251-5000
2475 Hanover St Palo Alto (94304) ***(P-22825)***
Sims Group USA Corporation...D...408 494-4242
1900 Monterey Hwy San Jose (95112) ***(P-7773)***
Sims Group USA Corporation (HQ)...D...510 412-5300
600 S 4th St Richmond (94804) ***(P-7774)***
Sims Group USA Corporation...D...510 236-0606
600 S 4th St Richmond (94804) ***(P-6283)***
Sims/LMC Recyclers, San Jose *Also called Sims Group USA Corporation* ***(P-7773)***
Simsmetal America, Richmond *Also called Sims Group USA Corporation* ***(P-7774)***
Sinai Temple...C...323 469-6000
5950 Forest Lawn Dr Los Angeles (90068) ***(P-13379)***
Sinanian Development Inc...D...818 996-9666
18980 Ventura Blvd # 200 Tarzana (91356) ***(P-1601)***
Sinclair Companies...C...619 238-1818
1055 2nd Ave San Diego (92101) ***(P-12929)***
Sinclair Concrete...D...916 663-0303
7205 Church St Penryn (95663) ***(P-3218)***

ALPHABETIC

Employee Codes: A=Over 500 employees, B=251-500
C=101-250, D=51-100, E=50
2020 Directory of California
Wholesalers and Services Companies
© Mergent Inc. 1-800-342-5647
1431

Sinecera Inc ... D ... 626 962-1087
5397 3rd St Irwindale (91706) ***(P-17057)***

Singapore Airlines Limited ... C ... 310 647-1922
222 N Pacific Coast Hwy # 1600 El Segundo (90245) ***(P-4679)***

Singerlewak LLP (PA) ... C ... 310 477-3924
10960 Wilshire Blvd Los Angeles (90024) ***(P-25679)***

Singerlewak LLP ... D ... 949 261-8600
2050 Main St Ste 700 Irvine (92614) ***(P-25680)***

Singerlewak LLP ... D ... 818 999-3924
21550 Oxnard St Ste 1000 Woodland Hills (91367) ***(P-25681)***

Singley Enterprises (PA) ... E ... 866 890-1776
121 Main Ave Sacramento (95838) ***(P-6657)***

Sintex Security Services Inc ... D ... 209 543-9044
501 Bangs Ave Ste D Modesto (95356) ***(P-16449)***

Sioux City Ht & Conference Ctr, Escondido *Also called Choa Hope LLC* ***(P-12141)***

Sippi Anne Riverside Ranch LLP ... E ... 661 871-9697
18200 Highway 178 Bakersfield (93306) ***(P-24076)***

Sir Francis Drake Hotel, San Francisco *Also called Huskies Lessee LLC* ***(P-12427)***

Sir Francis Drake Hotel, San Francisco *Also called Sfd Partners LLC* ***(P-12908)***

Siracusa Enterprises Inc ... D ... 818 831-1130
17737 Chtswrth St Ste 200 Granada Hills (91344) ***(P-14420)***

Sirva Inc ... C ... 925 824-3109
2010 Crow Canyon Pl San Ramon (94583) ***(P-4131)***

Sisa, Mountain View *Also called Samsung Research America Inc* ***(P-25825)***

Sisco Family Connection, Milpitas *Also called Bright Horizons Chld Ctrs LLC* ***(P-23679)***

Siskiyou Development Company ... D ... 530 938-2731
88 S Weed Blvd Edgewood (96094) ***(P-12930)***

Siskiyou Hospital Inc ... B ... 530 842-4121
444 Bruce St Yreka (96097) ***(P-21202)***

Siskiyou Lake Golf Resort Inc ... D ... 530 926-3030
1000 Siskiyou Lake Blvd Mount Shasta (96067) ***(P-18299)***

Siskiyou Opportunity Center (PA) ... C ... 530 926-4698
1516 S Mount Shasta Blvd Mount Shasta (96067) ***(P-23637)***

Sissc, Ridgecrest *Also called Leidos Inc* ***(P-15783)***

Sisters of Nazareth ... D ... 415 479-8282
245 Nova Albion Way San Rafael (94903) ***(P-20689)***

Sisters of Nzareth Los Angeles ... D ... 310 839-2361
3333 Manning Ave Los Angeles (90064) ***(P-24077)***

Sisters of Soul (sos) Youth ... D ... 909 533-4889
937 Via Lata Ste 400 Colton (92324) ***(P-24364)***

Sita Ram LLC ... D ... 209 223-0211
200 S State Highway 49 Jackson (95642) ***(P-12931)***

Site 210, Pacheco *Also called Pleasant Hl Byshore Dspsal Inc* ***(P-6234)***

Site 910, Santa Barbara *Also called BFI Waste Systems N Amer Inc* ***(P-6162)***

Site 916, Fremont *Also called BFI Waste Systems N Amer Inc* ***(P-6164)***

Site Crew Inc ... B ... 714 668-0100
3185 Airway Ave Ste G Costa Mesa (92626) ***(P-14052)***

Site L69, Milpitas *Also called Interntional Disposal Corp Cal* ***(P-6214)***

Site R45, Milpitas *Also called Browning-Ferris Industries LLC* ***(P-6168)***

Sitelite Holdings Inc ... C ... 949 265-6200
111 Theory Fl 2 Irvine (92617) ***(P-16109)***

Sitestuff Yardi Systems I (PA) ... D ... 805 966-3666
430 S Fairview Ave Goleta (93117) ***(P-26815)***

Sitetracker Inc ... D ... 408 838-9419
150 Grant Ave Ste A Palo Alto (94306) ***(P-26816)***

Siteworks Landscape Inc ... C ... 510 843-0409
5327 Jacuzzi St Ste 1b Richmond (94804) ***(P-764)***

Sitoa ... D ... 916 444-0008
6900 Airport Blvd Sacramento (95837) ***(P-3750)***

Sitonit Seating Inc ... C ... 714 995-4800
6415 Katella Ave Cypress (90630) ***(P-6530)***

Sitrick Brincko Group LLC ... D ... 310 788-2850
1840 Century Park E # 800 Los Angeles (90067) ***(P-26817)***

Six Continents Hotels Inc ... D ... 310 371-8525
19901 Prairie Ave Torrance (90503) ***(P-12932)***

Six Continents Hotels Inc ... D ... 818 989-5010
8244 Orion Ave Van Nuys (91406) ***(P-12933)***

Six Continents Hotels Inc ... D ... 213 748-1291
1020 S Figueroa St Los Angeles (90015) ***(P-12934)***

Six Continents Hotels Inc ... C ... 310 781-9100
19800 S Vermont Ave Torrance (90502) ***(P-12935)***

Six Continents Hotels Inc ... D ... 619 232-3861
1355 N Harbor Dr San Diego (92101) ***(P-12936)***

Six Continents Hotels Inc ... D ... 925 847-6000
11950 Dublin Canyon Rd # 609 Pleasanton (94588) ***(P-12937)***

Six Continents Hotels Inc ... D ... 619 795-4000
1110 A St San Diego (92101) ***(P-12938)***

Six Continents Hotels Inc ... D ... 619 474-2800
700 National City Blvd National City (91950) ***(P-12939)***

Six Flags Entertainment Corp ... B ... 916 924-3747
1600 Exposition Blvd Sacramento (95815) ***(P-18341)***

Six Flags Magic Mountain, Valencia *Also called Magic Mountain LLC* ***(P-17926)***

Six Point Harness ... E ... 323 462-3344
1759 Glendale Blvd Los Angeles (90026) ***(P-17763)***

Six Rivers National Bank (HQ) ... D ... 707 443-8400
402 F St Eureka (95501) ***(P-9119)***

Six Rivers Planned Parenthood ... D ... 707 442-5700
3225 Timber Fall Ct Eureka (95503) ***(P-24226)***

Sizmek Dsp Inc (HQ) ... C ... 650 595-1300
2000 Seaport Blvd Ste 400 Redwood City (94063) ***(P-16110)***

SJ Distributors Inc (PA) ... D ... 888 988-2328
625 Vista Way Milpitas (95035) ***(P-8302)***

Sjb Child Development Centers (PA) ... C ... 408 538-0200
1400 Parkmoor Ave Ste 220 San Jose (95126) ***(P-23787)***

Sjhs Sonoma County, Santa Rosa *Also called Santa Rosa Memorial Hospital* ***(P-21165)***

Sjrtd, Stockton *Also called San Joaquin Regional Trnst Dst* ***(P-3595)***

Sjsu Foundation ... A ... 408 924-1410
210 N 4th St Ste 300 San Jose (95112) ***(P-24866)***

Sjvi, Fresno *Also called San Joaquin Valley Intergrp* ***(P-24863)***

SJW Group (PA) ... B ... 408 279-7800
110 W Taylor St San Jose (95110) ***(P-6119)***

Sk Hynix America Inc (HQ) ... D ... 408 232-8000
3101 N 1st St San Jose (95134) ***(P-6895)***

Sk Sanctuary Day Spa Salon LLC ... E ... 858 459-2400
6919 La Jolla Blvd La Jolla (92037) ***(P-18195)***

SK&a, Irvine *Also called S K & A Information Svcs Inc* ***(P-25942)***

Skadden Arps Slate Meagher & F ... C ... 213 687-5000
300 S Grand Ave Ste 3400 Los Angeles (90071) ***(P-22826)***

Skanska Rocky Mountain Dst, Riverside *Also called Skanska USA Civil West Rocky M* ***(P-1992)***

Skanska USA Civil West Rocky M (HQ) ... D ... 970 565-8000
1995 Agua Mansa Rd Riverside (92509) ***(P-1992)***

Skanska USA Cvil W Cal Dst Inc (HQ) ... A ... 951 684-5360
1995 Agua Mansa Rd Riverside (92509) ***(P-1789)***

Skanska-Rados A Joint Venture ... D ... 213 978-0600
11390 W Olympic Blvd Los Angeles (90064) ***(P-1790)***

Skate Enterprises Inc ... D ... 562 924-0911
12356 Central Ave Chino (91710) ***(P-18759)***

Skatetown, Roseville *Also called Roseville Sportworld Inc* ***(P-18748)***

Skava, San Francisco *Also called Kallidus Inc* ***(P-14898)***

Skeffington Enterprises Inc ... D ... 714 540-1700
2200 S Yale St Santa Ana (92704) ***(P-11693)***

Skidmore Owings & Merrill LLP ... C ... 415 981-1555
1 Maritime Plz Fl 5 San Francisco (94111) ***(P-25496)***

Skidmore Owings & Merrill LLP ... C ... 310 651-9924
10100 Santa Monica Blvd Beverly Hills (90210) ***(P-25497)***

Skidmore Owings & Merrill LLP ... C ... 213 996-8366
555 W 5th St Fl 30 Los Angeles (90013) ***(P-25498)***

Skilled Healthcare LLC (HQ) ... D ... 949 282-5800
27442 Portola Pkwy # 200 Foothill Ranch (92610) ***(P-20262)***

Skilled Healthcare LLC ... D ... 323 663-3951
5154 W Sunset Blvd Los Angeles (90027) ***(P-20263)***

Skilled Nursing Facility, Taft *Also called West Side District Hospital* ***(P-21371)***

Skills Center Inc (PA) ... D ... 831 421-9900
220 Lincoln St Santa Cruz (95060) ***(P-23638)***

Skin Health Experts Medic ... D ... 310 623-6869
144 S Beverly Dr Ste 500 Beverly Hills (90212) ***(P-22124)***

Skirball Cultural Center ... C ... 310 440-4500
2701 N Sepulveda Blvd Los Angeles (90049) ***(P-24293)***

Skire Inc ... D ... 650 289-2600
500 Oracle Pkwy Redwood City (94065) ***(P-15099)***

Skitch, Redwood City *Also called Evernote Corporation* ***(P-14800)***

Skoll Foundation ... E ... 650 331-1031
250 University Ave Lbby Palo Alto (94301) ***(P-24867)***

Sky Chefs Inc ... C ... 650 652-7886
1845 Rollins Rd Burlingame (94010) ***(P-4503)***

Sky Court USA Inc ... C ... 805 497-9991
880 S Westlake Blvd Westlake Village (91361) ***(P-12940)***

Sky High Sports, Woodland Hills *Also called Skyhigh Woodland Hills LLC* ***(P-18760)***

Sky King, Sacramento *Also called Lukenbill Enterprises* ***(P-4676)***

Sky Park Gardens Assisted ... D ... 916 422-5650
5510 Sky Pkwy Ofc Sacramento (95823) ***(P-24078)***

Sky Scan Satelite Systems ... D ... 909 322-1393
9994 Willowbrook Rd Riverside (92509) ***(P-5738)***

Sky West Golf Course, Hayward *Also called Hayward Area Recreation Pkdist* ***(P-18251)***

Sky Zone LLC (HQ) ... D ... 310 734-0300
1201 W 5th St Ste T340 Los Angeles (90017) ***(P-18005)***

Skyblue Sewing Manufacturing ... E ... 415 777-9978
960 Mission St Fl 2 San Francisco (94103) ***(P-17058)***

Skybox Security Inc (PA) ... D ... 408 441-8060
2077 Gateway Pl Ste 200 San Jose (95110) ***(P-15100)***

Skyhigh Networks Inc (HQ) ... D ... 408 564-0278
900 E Hamilton Ave # 400 Campbell (95008) ***(P-16563)***

Skyhigh Woodland Hills LLC ... D ... 805 484-6300
6051 De Soto Ave Woodland Hills (91367) ***(P-18760)***

Skyhill Financial Inc ... D ... 714 657-3938
5772 Bolsa Ave Ste 100 Huntington Beach (92649) ***(P-11450)***

Skylar Film Studios LLC ... C ... 424 653-8902
13589 Mindanao Way # 11 Marina Del Rey (90292) ***(P-17764)***

Skylawn Memorial Park, Redwood City *Also called Chapel of Chimes* ***(P-11625)***

Skyles Insurance Agency ... E ... 916 361-9585
9840 Business Park Dr Sacramento (95827) ***(P-10495)***

SKYLIGHT CONVALESCENT CENTER, Long Beach *Also called Reynolds Health Industries* ***(P-20669)***

Skylight Hlthcare Systems Inc ... D ... 858 523-3700
10935 Vista Sorrento Pkwy # 350 San Diego (92130) ***(P-26818)***

Skyline Commercial Interiors (PA) ... D ... 415 908-1020
505 Sansome St Fl 7 San Francisco (94111) ***(P-1602)***

Skyline Construction, San Francisco *Also called Skyline Commercial Interiors* ***(P-1602)***

Skyline Consulting Group ... C ... 650 529-3455
13186 Skyline Blvd Woodside (94062) ***(P-26819)***

Skyline Health Care Center, San Jose *Also called Mariner Health Care Inc* ***(P-20107)***

Skyline Health Care Ctr, Los Angeles *Also called Mariner Health Care Inc* ***(P-20111)***

Skyline Healthcare & Wellness ... D ... 323 665-1185
3032 Rowena Ave Los Angeles (90039) ***(P-20264)***

Skyline Healthcare Center, Los Angeles *Also called Skyline Healthcare & Wellness* ***(P-20264)***

Skyline Place, Sonora *Also called Sonora Retirement Center Inc* ***(P-24081)***

Skylite Networks ... D ... 403 934-9349
761 Mabury Rd Ste 75 San Jose (95133) ***(P-15101)***

Skylstad-Schoelen Co Inc ... D ... 805 349-0503
3130 Skyway Dr Ste 701 Santa Maria (93455) ***(P-14053)***

Skynet USA Asset MGT Inc ... E ... 702 969-5599
17011 Beach Blvd Fl 9th Huntington Beach (92647) ***(P-26820)***

Mergent e-mail: customerrelations@mergent.com
1432
2020 Directory of California
Wholesalers and Services Companies
(P-0000) Products & Services Section entry number
(PA)=Parent Co (HQ)=Headquarters (DH)=Div Headquarters

Skyone Federal Credit Union (PA) ....D....310 491-7500
14600 Aviation Blvd Hawthorne (90250) ***(P-9353)***
Skypark, San Bruno *Also called Airport Parking Service Inc* ***(P-17244)***
Skypark At Santa's Village, Skyforest *Also called Spsv Entertainment LLC* ***(P-18010)***
Skype Inc ....D....650 493-7900
1 Microsoft Way Redmond Palo Alto (94304) ***(P-5472)***
Skypower Holdings LLC ....C....323 860-4900
4700 Wilshire Blvd Los Angeles (90010) ***(P-2275)***
Skyslope Inc ....D....916 833-2390
825 K St Fl 2 Sacramento (95814) ***(P-16111)***
Skyva Construction Inc ....E....916 726-4999
5781 Old Antelope N Rd Antelope (95843) ***(P-1198)***
Skywest Airlines Inc ....D....951 926-9511
32128 Chagall Ct Winchester (92596) ***(P-4680)***
Skywest Airlines Inc ....D....951 600-9181
26818 Bahama Way Murrieta (92563) ***(P-4681)***
SL Power Electronics Corp (PA) ....D....800 235-5929
6050 King Dr Ste A Ventura (93003) ***(P-7341)***
Slack Technologies Inc (PA) ....C....415 902-5526
500 Howard St Ste 100 San Francisco (94105) ***(P-15499)***
Slade Gorton & Co Inc ....D....714 676-4200
1 Centerpointe Dr Ste 311 La Palma (90623) ***(P-8390)***
Slade Industrial Landscape Inc ....D....818 885-1916
8838 Zelzah Ave Sherwood Forest (91325) ***(P-765)***
Slakey Brothers Inc ....E....408 494-0460
1480 Nicora Ave San Jose (95133) ***(P-7437)***
Slakey Brothers Inc ....E....209 556-1100
1001 Oates Ct Modesto (95358) ***(P-7104)***
Slate Creek Wind Project LLC ....A....888 903-6926
15445 Innovation Dr San Diego (92128) ***(P-5922)***
Slater Inc ....D....909 822-6800
11045 Rose Ave Fontana (92337) ***(P-1993)***
Slauson Plaza Med Group, Pico Rivera *Also called Altamed Health Services Corp* ***(P-22172)***
SLC Operating Ltd Partnership ....B....818 980-1212
333 Unversal Hollywood Dr North Hollywood (91608) ***(P-13454)***
Slch Inc (PA) ....E....626 798-0558
1920 N Fair Oaks Ave Pasadena (91103) ***(P-20265)***
Sleepio, San Francisco *Also called Big Health Inc* ***(P-20414)***
Sleepy Giant Entertainment Inc ....C....949 464-7986
4 San Joaquin Plz Ste 200 Newport Beach (92660) ***(P-15102)***
Sleepy Giant Entertainment Inc ....D....714 460-4113
3501 Jamboree Rd Ste 5000 Newport Beach (92660) ***(P-18006)***
Slide Go, Redlands *Also called Prime-Line Products Company* ***(P-7403)***
Sliding Door Co, The, Chatsworth *Also called Sliding Door Company* ***(P-6658)***
Sliding Door Company (PA) ....D....818 997-7855
20235 Bahama St Chatsworth (91311) ***(P-6658)***
SLM Services, Simi Valley *Also called Specialized Landscape MGT Svcs* ***(P-911)***
Slo Transitions, San Luis Obispo *Also called Transitions - Mental Hlth Assn* ***(P-22142)***
Slogcc, San Luis Obispo *Also called San Luis Obispo Golf* ***(P-18557)***
Slorta, San Luis Obispo *Also called San Luis Obispo Regional* ***(P-3596)***
SM 10000 Property LLC ....D....305 374-5700
10000 Santa Monica Blvd Los Angeles (90067) ***(P-11604)***
SM International, Fremont *Also called S & M Moving Systems* ***(P-4121)***
SMA America, Rocklin *Also called SMA Solar Technology Amer LLC* ***(P-7342)***
SMA Builders Inc ....E....818 994-8306
16134 Leadwell St Van Nuys (91406) ***(P-1199)***
SMA Solar Technology Amer LLC (HQ) ....D....916 625-0870
6020 West Oaks Blvd Rocklin (95765) ***(P-7342)***
Small Business Advertising Inc ....E....818 262-8923
24009 Ventura Blvd # 245 Calabasas (91302) ***(P-13662)***
Smart & Final Stores Inc ....A....858 748-0101
12339 Poway Rd Poway (92064) ***(P-8217)***
Smart & Final Stores Inc ....B....949 675-2396
3049 E Coast Hwy Corona Del Mar (92625) ***(P-8218)***
Smart & Final Stores Inc ....B....619 449-2396
9870 N Magnolia Ave Santee (92071) ***(P-8219)***
Smart & Final Stores Inc ....B....323 549-9586
4550 W Pico Blvd Los Angeles (90019) ***(P-8220)***
Smart & Final Stores Inc ....B....909 592-2190
1005 W Arrow Hwy San Dimas (91773) ***(P-8221)***
Smart & Final Stores Inc ....C....909 773-1813
13346 Limonite Ave Eastvale (92880) ***(P-8222)***
Smart & Final Stores Inc ....B....619 522-2014
150 B Ave Coronado (92118) ***(P-8223)***
Smart & Final Stores Inc ....B....916 486-6315
7223 Fair Oaks Blvd Carmichael (95608) ***(P-8224)***
Smart & Final Stores Inc ....B....805 574-1599
1464 E Grand Ave Arroyo Grande (93420) ***(P-8225)***
Smart & Final Stores Inc ....B....805 566-2174
850 Linden Ave Carpinteria (93013) ***(P-8226)***
Smart & Final Stores Inc ....B....714 549-2362
1308 W Edinger Ave Santa Ana (92704) ***(P-8227)***
Smart & Final Stores Inc ....B....619 390-1738
13439 Camino Canada El Cajon (92021) ***(P-8228)***
Smart & Final Stores Inc ....B....626 330-2495
15427 Amar Rd La Puente (91744) ***(P-8229)***
Smart & Final Stores Inc ....B....818 368-6409
18555 Devonshire St Northridge (91324) ***(P-8230)***
Smart & Final Stores Inc ....B....408 251-0109
1180 S King Rd San Jose (95122) ***(P-8231)***
Smart & Final Stores Inc ....B....562 438-0450
644 Redondo Ave Long Beach (90814) ***(P-8232)***
Smart & Final Stores Inc ....B....760 732-1480
1845 W Vista Way Vista (92083) ***(P-8233)***
Smart & Final Stores Inc ....B....805 237-0323
2121 Spring St Paso Robles (93446) ***(P-8234)***
Smart & Final Stores Inc ....B....760 434-2449
955 Carlsbad Village Dr Carlsbad (92008) ***(P-8235)***
Smart & Final Stores Inc ....C....619 668-9039
933 Sweetwater Rd Spring Valley (91977) ***(P-8236)***
Smart & Final Stores Inc ....B....949 581-1212
26911 Trabuco Rd Mission Viejo (92691) ***(P-8237)***
Smart & Final Stores Inc ....C....530 823-1205
2825 Grass Valley Hwy Auburn (95603) ***(P-8238)***
Smart & Final Stores Inc ....B....619 291-1842
2235 University Ave San Diego (92104) ***(P-8239)***
Smart & Final Stores Inc ....B....323 497-8528
615 N Pacific Coast Hwy Redondo Beach (90277) ***(P-8240)***
Smart & Final Stores Inc ....B....323 855-8434
240 S Diamond Bar Blvd Diamond Bar (91765) ***(P-8241)***
Smart & Final Stores Inc ....B....818 954-8631
3830 W Verdugo Ave Burbank (91505) ***(P-8242)***
Smart & Final Stores Inc ....B....661 722-6210
5038 W Avenue N Palmdale (93551) ***(P-8243)***
Smart & Final Stores Inc ....B....818 889-8253
5770 Lindero Canyon Rd Westlake Village (91362) ***(P-8244)***
Smart & Final Stores Inc ....B....805 647-4276
7800 Telegraph Rd Ventura (93004) ***(P-8245)***
Smart & Final Stores Inc ....C....619 589-7000
2800 Fletcher Pkwy El Cajon (92020) ***(P-8246)***
Smart & Final Stores Inc ....B....858 578-7343
10740 Westview Pkwy San Diego (92126) ***(P-8247)***
Smart & Final Stores Inc (PA) ....B....323 869-7500
600 Citadel Dr Commerce (90040) ***(P-8248)***
Smart & Final Stores Inc ....B....562 907-7037
13003 Whittier Blvd Whittier (90602) ***(P-8249)***
Smart & Final Stores Inc ....B....626 334-5189
303 E Foothill Blvd Azusa (91702) ***(P-8250)***
Smart & Final Stores Inc ....B....559 229-2944
2425 N Blackstone Ave Fresno (93703) ***(P-8251)***
Smart & Final Stores Inc ....B....408 941-9642
401 Jacklin Rd Milpitas (95035) ***(P-8252)***
Smart & Final Stores Inc ....B....559 297-9376
790 W Shaw Ave Clovis (93612) ***(P-8253)***
Smart & Final Stores LLC ....D....858 268-2400
4439 Genesee Ave San Diego (92117) ***(P-8254)***
Smart & Final Stores LLC ....D....858 270-8200
1260 Garnet Ave San Diego (92109) ***(P-8255)***
Smart & Final Stores LLC ....D....619 523-3640
3315 Rosecrans St Ste B San Diego (92110) ***(P-8256)***
Smart & Final Stores LLC (HQ) ....C....323 869-7500
600 Citadel Dr Commerce (90040) ***(P-8257)***
Smart & Final Stores LLC ....D....760 726-7274
471 College Blvd Oceanside (92057) ***(P-8258)***
Smart & Final Stores LLC ....D....619 291-8287
4175 Park Blvd San Diego (92103) ***(P-8259)***
Smart & Final Stores LLC ....D....858 350-7900
659 Lomas Santa Fe Dr Solana Beach (92075) ***(P-8260)***
Smart Energy Solar Inc ....C....800 405-1978
1641 Comm St Corona (92880) ***(P-2276)***
Smart Energy Systems LLC (PA) ....C....909 703-9609
19900 Macarthur Blvd Irvine (92612) ***(P-15103)***
Smart Energy Systems LLC ....C....909 703-9609
Michelson Dr Ste 3370 Irvine (92612) ***(P-15104)***
Smart Energy USA, Corona *Also called Smart Energy Solar Inc* ***(P-2276)***
Smart Living Company, Simi Valley *Also called Specialty Merchandise Corp* ***(P-9013)***
Smart Software Tstg Solutions ....D....833 778-7872
2450 Peralta Blvd Ste 202 Fremont (94536) ***(P-27211)***
Smart Systems Technologies (PA) ....D....949 367-9375
9 Goodyear Irvine (92618) ***(P-5923)***
Smartcues Inc, Mountain View *Also called Spotcues Inc* ***(P-6902)***
Smartdrive Systems Inc (PA) ....D....858 225-5550
4790 Estgate Mall Ste 200 San Diego (92121) ***(P-15105)***
Smartrevenuecom Inc ....B....203 733-9156
101 Cooper St Ste 205 Santa Cruz (95060) ***(P-25943)***
Smartway Express Inc ....C....559 272-3500
2660 S Railroad Ave Fresno (93725) ***(P-5052)***
Smartzip Analytics Inc ....D....855 661-1064
6200 Stoneridge Mall Rd Pleasanton (94588) ***(P-26821)***
Smashon Inc ....E....855 762-7466
1754 Tech Dr Ste 234 San Jose (95110) ***(P-16112)***
SMC Corporation of America ....E....408 943-9600
2841 Junction Ave Ste 110 San Jose (95134) ***(P-7590)***
SMC Networks Inc (HQ) ....D....949 679-8029
20 Mason Irvine (92618) ***(P-6896)***
Smci, Costa Mesa *Also called Software Management Cons Inc* ***(P-15112)***
Smci, Glendale *Also called Software Management Cons Inc* ***(P-16114)***
SMD Logistics Inc ....C....831 758-5300
26710 Encinal Rd Salinas (93908) ***(P-5053)***
Smg ....B....209 937-7433
3445 S El Dorado St Stockton (95206) ***(P-26955)***
Smg Food and Beverage LLC (PA) ....D....909 937-3000
2000 E Convention Ctr Way Ontario (91764) ***(P-17059)***
Smg Holdings Inc ....D....310 432-2893
225 E Broadway 312 Glendale (91205) ***(P-10650)***
Smg Holdings Inc ....C....650 738-8737
747 Howard St San Francisco (94103) ***(P-10651)***
Smg Holdings Inc ....B....559 445-8100
848 M St Fl 2nd Fresno (93721) ***(P-17060)***
Smg Holdings Inc ....D....760 325-6611
277 N Avenida Caballeros Palm Springs (92262) ***(P-26822)***
Smg Holdings LLC ....D....562 499-7611
300 E Ocean Blvd Long Beach (90802) ***(P-10652)***
Smg Management Facility, Ontario *Also called Ontario Convention Center Corp* ***(P-16963)***
Smg Stockton, Stockton *Also called Smg* ***(P-26955)***
Smg Stone Company Inc ....D....818 767-0000
8460 San Fernando Rd Sun Valley (91352) ***(P-2728)***

ALPHABETIC

Employee Codes: A=Over 500 employees, B=251-500
C=101-250, D=51-100, E=50
2020 Directory of California
Wholesalers and Services Companies
© Mergent Inc. 1-800-342-5647
1433

Smile Brands Group Inc (PA)......D......714 668-1300
100 Spectrum Center Dr # 1500 Irvine (92618) ***(P-26393)***
Smile Housing Corporation......D......805 772-6066
800 Quintana Rd Ste 2c Morro Bay (93442) ***(P-22125)***
Smile Keepers, Inglewood *Also called Interdent Inc* ***(P-19611)***
Smile Wide Dental, Irvine *Also called Universal Care Inc* ***(P-22152)***
Smisc Holdings LLC......E......707 938-8448
Hwy 121 Sonoma (95476) ***(P-18089)***
Smith & Sons Investment Co......E......949 646-9648
735 Ohms Way Costa Mesa (92627) ***(P-11451)***
Smith Barney, Los Angeles *Also called Citigroup Global Markets Inc* ***(P-9667)***
Smith Barney, Torrance *Also called Citigroup Global Markets Inc* ***(P-9671)***
Smith Barney, Irvine *Also called Citigroup Global Markets Inc* ***(P-9672)***
Smith Barney, La Jolla *Also called Citigroup Global Markets Inc* ***(P-9673)***
Smith Barney, Rllng HLS Est *Also called Citigroup Global Markets Inc* ***(P-9675)***
Smith Barneys, Menlo Park *Also called Citigroup Global Markets Inc* ***(P-9677)***
Smith Broadcasting Group Inc (PA)......C......805 965-0400
2315 Red Rose Way Santa Barbara (93109) ***(P-26394)***
Smith Broadcasting Group Inc......D......805 882-3933
730 Miramonte Dr Santa Barbara (93109) ***(P-5647)***
Smith Bros Inc (PA)......D......805 449-2841
2301 Townsgate Rd Ste A Westlake Village (91361) ***(P-2981)***
Smith Bros Finished Carpentry, Westlake Village *Also called Smith Bros Inc* ***(P-2981)***
Smith Brothers Restaurant Inc......D......626 577-2400
100 Corson St Lbby Pasadena (91103) ***(P-26395)***
Smith Coleman Inc......E......310 671-8271
707 N La Brea Ave Inglewood (90302) ***(P-11452)***
Smith Electric Service, Santa Maria *Also called Brannon Inc* ***(P-1335)***
Smith Gardens Inc......E......831 768-6300
750 Casserly Rd Watsonville (95076) ***(P-282)***
Smith International Inc......C......909 906-7900
11031 Jersey Blvd Ste A Rancho Cucamonga (91730) ***(P-1044)***
Smith Ranch......E......530 695-2521
1671 Campbell Rd Live Oak (95953) ***(P-216)***
Smith Residential Care Fcilty (PA)......D......559 584-8451
318 E 4th St Hanford (93230) ***(P-21867)***
Smith River Lucky 7 Casino......D......707 487-7777
350 N Indian Rd Smith River (95567) ***(P-12941)***
Smith-Emery Company (PA)......D......213 745-5312
781 E Washington Blvd Los Angeles (90021) ***(P-26823)***
Smith-Emery San Francisco Inc......C......415 642-7326
1940 Oakdale Ave San Francisco (94124) ***(P-17061)***
Smithgroup Inc......D......415 227-0100
301 Battery St Fl 7 San Francisco (94111) ***(P-25499)***
Smithgroup Inc......C......313 442-8351
301 Battery St Fl 7 San Francisco (94111) ***(P-25500)***
Smithgroupjjr, San Francisco *Also called Smithgroup Inc* ***(P-25500)***
Smoke Tree Inc......D......760 327-1221
1850 Smoke Tree Ln Palm Springs (92264) ***(P-12942)***
Smoke Tree Ranch, Palm Springs *Also called Smoke Tree Inc* ***(P-12942)***
Smp Construction & Maint Inc (PA)......D......925 961-9012
1813 Rutan Dr Ste A Livermore (94551) ***(P-1603)***
SMS Transportation......D......310 527-9200
18516 S Broadway Gardena (90248) ***(P-22827)***
SMS Transportation Svcs Inc......C......213 489-5367
865 S Figueroa St # 2750 Los Angeles (90017) ***(P-3606)***
Smss, Foster City *Also called Sony Interactive Entrmt LLC* ***(P-17063)***
Smud Energy Services, Sacramento *Also called Sacramento Municpl Utility Dst* ***(P-5915)***
Smuk Inc......C......323 904-4680
3800 Barham Blvd Ste 410 Los Angeles (90068) ***(P-17669)***
Snackademic, San Francisco *Also called Cesar Chavez Student Center* ***(P-10577)***
Snap Inc (PA)......C......310 399-3339
2772 Dnald Douglas Loop N Santa Monica (90405) ***(P-15106)***
Snap-On Incorporated......D......626 965-0668
19220 San Jose Ave City of Industry (91748) ***(P-7406)***
Snap-On Tools, City of Industry *Also called Snap-On Incorporated* ***(P-7406)***
Snapchat, Santa Monica *Also called Snap Inc* ***(P-15106)***
Snapdocs Inc......E......415 967-0136
100 Montgomery St # 2400 San Francisco (94104) ***(P-15107)***
Snapdragon Place 1 LP......D......805 659-3791
702 County Square Dr Ventura (93003) ***(P-10815)***
Snaplogic Inc (PA)......C......888 494-1570
1825 S Grant St Ste 550 San Mateo (94402) ***(P-15500)***
Sneary Construction Inc......E......909 982-1833
1182 Monte Vista Ave # 2 Upland (91786) ***(P-2859)***
Snell & Wilmer LLP......C......714 427-7000
600 Anton Blvd Ste 1400 Costa Mesa (92626) ***(P-22828)***
Snelling Employment LLC......D......510 769-4400
2203 Harvbor Bay Pkwy Alameda (94502) ***(P-14421)***
Snf Management......D......310 385-1090
9200 W Sunset Blvd # 700 West Hollywood (90069) ***(P-26396)***
Snoopy's Galary and Gift Shop, Santa Rosa *Also called Redwood Empire Ice Oprtons LLC* ***(P-18746)***
Snoozie Shavings Inc (PA)......D......707 464-6186
525 Elk Valley Rd Crescent City (95531) ***(P-4132)***
Snow Creek Resort, Mammoth Lakes *Also called Snowcreek Property Management* ***(P-11453)***
Snow Summit Mountain Resort, Big Bear City *Also called Snow Summit Ski Corporation* ***(P-18761)***
Snow Summit Ski Corporation (PA)......C......909 866-5766
880 Summit Blvd Big Bear Lake (92315) ***(P-12943)***
Snow Summit Ski Corporation......B......909 585-2517
43101 Goldmine Dr Big Bear City (92314) ***(P-18761)***
Snowbounders Ski Club......D......714 892-4897
5402 Tattershall Ave Westminster (92683) ***(P-18576)***
Snowcreek Property Management......E......760 934-3333
1254 Old Mammoth Rd Mammoth Lakes (93546) ***(P-11453)***
Snowflake Inc (PA)......C......844 766-9355
450 Concar Dr San Mateo (94402) ***(P-15108)***
Snowline Hspc Eldorado Cnty......C......916 817-2338
6520 Pleasant Valley Rd Diamond Springs (95619) ***(P-20456)***
Snowline Hspice El Dorado Cnty......C......530 621-7820
6520 Pleasant Valley Rd Diamond Springs (95619) ***(P-20457)***
Snyder Langston, Irvine *Also called Snyder Langston L P* ***(P-1604)***
Snyder Langston L P......D......949 863-9200
17962 Cowan Irvine (92614) ***(P-1604)***
So CA Edison, Rosemead *Also called Southern California Edison Co* ***(P-5953)***
So Cal Land Maintenance Inc......D......714 231-1454
2965 E Coronado St Anaheim (92806) ***(P-14054)***
So Cal Sandbags Inc......D......951 277-3404
12620 Bosley Ln Corona (92883) ***(P-7657)***
So Cal Ship Services......D......310 519-8411
971 S Seaside Ave San Pedro (90731) ***(P-4607)***
So Calif Stone Center, Encino *Also called Southern Cal Stone Ctr LLC* ***(P-19435)***
So California Ventures Ltd......D......714 524-0021
1101 Richfield Rd Placentia (92870) ***(P-1605)***
So-Cal Strl Stl Fbrication Inc......E......909 877-1299
130 S Spruce Ave Rialto (92376) ***(P-3285)***
Soaprojects Inc (PA)......D......650 960-9900
495 N Whisman Rd Ste 100 Mountain View (94043) ***(P-26824)***
Soapy Joes Inc (PA)......D......619 660-1113
11465 Woodside Ave Santee (92071) ***(P-17397)***
Sobaliving Llc......E......800 595-3803
22669 Pacific Coast Hwy Malibu (90265) ***(P-22324)***
Sobel Ross H Law Offices......E......310 788-8995
1875 Century Park E # 2000 Los Angeles (90067) ***(P-22829)***
Sobel, Ross Howell, Los Angeles *Also called Sobel Ross H Law Offices* ***(P-22829)***
Soboba Band Luiseno Indians......A......951 665-1000
22777 Soboba Rd San Jacinto (92583) ***(P-17062)***
Soboba Casino, San Jacinto *Also called Soboba Band Luiseno Indians* ***(P-17062)***
Soboba Indian Health Clinic, San Jacinto *Also called Riverside-San Bernardino* ***(P-19343)***
Sobol Philip A MD P C Inc......E......310 649-5894
8618 S Sepulveda Blvd # 130 Los Angeles (90045) ***(P-19405)***
SOBRIETY HOUSE, Long Beach *Also called Safe Refuge* ***(P-24057)***
Soc Pathology Med Group Inc......D......310 225-3244
2374 E Pacifica Pl Rancho Dominguez (90220) ***(P-21592)***
Soc/General Services/Bpm......D......415 703-5341
455 Golden Gate Ave # 2600 San Francisco (94102) ***(P-26397)***
Socal Coatings Inc......E......619 660-5395
2820 Via Orange Way Ste J Spring Valley (91978) ***(P-2395)***
Socal Home Care-Givers Svcs, Tustin *Also called RES-Care Inc* ***(P-21851)***
Socal Services Inc......C......858 453-1331
6336 Greenwich Dr Ste 100 San Diego (92122) ***(P-14422)***
Socal Sportsnet LLC......A......619 795-5000
100 Park Blvd San Diego (92101) ***(P-18007)***
Socal Uniform Rental, San Gabriel *Also called Cal Southern Services* ***(P-13212)***
Sociable Labs Inc......E......415 225-8740
25 Division St San Mateo (94402) ***(P-15813)***
Social Advocates For Y......C......619 283-9624
4275 El Cajon Blvd # 101 San Diego (92105) ***(P-23467)***
SOCIAL ADVOCATES FOR YOUTH, Santa Rosa *Also called Individuals Now* ***(P-23274)***
Social Advocates For Youth (PA)......E......805 928-1707
105 N Lincoln St Santa Maria (93458) ***(P-23468)***
Social Finance Inc (PA)......C......415 612-8229
234 1st St San Francisco (94105) ***(P-9645)***
Social Finance Inc......A......707 473-9889
375 Healdsburg Ave # 280 Healdsburg (95448) ***(P-9646)***
SOCIAL INTEREST SOLUTIONS, Oakland *Also called Center To Promote Healthcare A* ***(P-22200)***
SOCIAL REALITY, Los Angeles *Also called Srax Inc* ***(P-13580)***
Social Science Service Center......D......909 421-7120
18612 Santa Ana Ave Bloomington (92316) ***(P-21495)***
Social Service Dept- Admin, City of Industry *Also called County of Los Angeles* ***(P-26203)***
Social Services Agency, Santa Ana *Also called County of Orange* ***(P-23124)***
Social Services Agency, Orange *Also called County of Orange* ***(P-23125)***
Social Services Dept, Lompoc *Also called Santa Barbara County of* ***(P-23446)***
Social Services, Department of, Ukiah *Also called County of Mendocino* ***(P-23114)***
Social Studies School Service......D......310 839-2436
10200 Jefferson Blvd Culver City (90232) ***(P-7034)***
Social Vocational Services Inc......D......559 443-7119
1401 Fulton St Ste 510 Fresno (93721) ***(P-24079)***
Socialite Clothing, Los Angeles *Also called Kash Apparel LLC* ***(P-8082)***
Socialize Inc......E......415 529-4019
450 Townsend St 102 San Francisco (94107) ***(P-15501)***
Society For San Francisco......C......415 554-3000
201 Alabama St San Francisco (94103) ***(P-24868)***
Society For The Prevention of (PA)......D......888 772-2521
5026 W Jefferson Blvd Los Angeles (90016) ***(P-24869)***
Society of St Vincent (PA)......D......510 638-7600
2272 San Pablo Ave Oakland (94612) ***(P-24870)***
Society of St Vincent De (PA)......D......323 226-9645
210 N Avenue 21 Los Angeles (90031) ***(P-24871)***
Society6 LLC......E......310 394-6400
1655 26th St Santa Monica (90404) ***(P-15814)***
Sodexo Inc......D......818 952-2201
1812 Verdugo Blvd Fl 1 Glendale (91208) ***(P-26825)***
Sodexo Management Inc......D......925 325-9657
851 Howard St San Francisco (94103) ***(P-26398)***
Sodexo Management Inc......D......209 667-3634
1 University Cir Turlock (95382) ***(P-26399)***
Sodexo Operations LLC......D......831 582-3838
100 Campus Ctr Bldg 16 Seaside (93955) ***(P-26400)***
Sofa Holdco Dev LLC......D......847 713-0680
470 S Market St San Jose (95113) ***(P-15109)***

Soffietti Co.....D.....909 907-2277
236 W Orange Show San Bernardino (92408) *(P-7407)*
Sofi, San Francisco *Also called Social Finance Inc (P-9645)*
Sofitel Los Angeles, Los Angeles *Also called Accor Corp (P-11992)*
Sofitel Luxury Hotels, Los Angeles *Also called Beverly Blvd Leaseco LLC (P-12064)*
Soft Hq Holdings LLC.....E.....858 658-9200
6494 Weathers Pl Ste 200 San Diego (92121) *(P-16113)*
Softhq, San Diego *Also called Soft Hq Holdings LLC (P-16113)*
Softscript Inc.....A.....310 451-2110
2215 Campus Dr El Segundo (90245) *(P-13805)*
Softsol Resources Inc (HQ).....D.....510 824-2000
42808 Christy St Ste 100 Fremont (94538) *(P-15110)*
Software Ag Inc.....C.....408 490-5300
2901 Tasman Dr Ste 219 Santa Clara (95054) *(P-15502)*
Software AG of Virginia, Santa Clara *Also called Software Ag Inc (P-15502)*
Software AG Usa Inc.....C.....703 860-5050
1198 E Arques Ave Sunnyvale (94085) *(P-15111)*
Software Dev & Technical Svc, San Jose *Also called Sofa Holdco Dev LLC (P-15109)*
Software Dev Technical Support, San Diego *Also called Adler Dev LLC (P-14619)*
Software Dynamics Incorporated.....C.....818 992-3299
8501 Fllbrook Ave Ste 200 Canoga Park (91304) *(P-15693)*
Software Management Cons Inc.....D.....714 662-1841
959 S Coast Dr Ste 415 Costa Mesa (92626) *(P-15112)*
Software Management Cons Inc (PA).....B.....818 240-3177
500 Nth Brn Blvd Ste 1100 Glendale (91203) *(P-16114)*
Sohnen Barry As Co Trustee.....E.....562 946-3531
8945 Eice Rd Santa Fe Springs (90670) *(P-11816)*
Sohnen Enterprises Inc (PA).....E.....562 903-4957
13225 Marquardt Ave Santa Fe Springs (90670) *(P-17438)*
Soiree Valet Parking Service.....C.....415 284-9700
1470 Howard St San Francisco (94103) *(P-13455)*
Sol Transportation Inc.....E.....760 720-4327
2525 Ramona Dr Vista (92084) *(P-3724)*
Sola Impact Fund II LP.....E.....323 306-4648
9221 Kalmia St Los Angeles (90002) *(P-11454)*
Sola Impact Fund II LP.....E.....323 306-4648
1401 E 52nd St Los Angeles (90011) *(P-11455)*
Sola Impact Fund II LP.....E.....323 306-4648
1639 E 92nd St Los Angeles (90002) *(P-11456)*
Sola Impact Fund II LP.....E.....323 306-4648
629 E 48th St Los Angeles (90011) *(P-11457)*
Sola Impact Fund II LP.....E.....323 306-4648
11809 Robin St Los Angeles (90059) *(P-11458)*
Sola Rentals Inc.....E.....323 306-4648
8629 S Vermont Ave Los Angeles (90044) *(P-14199)*
Solag Disposal Co, San Juan Capistrano *Also called Solag Incorporated (P-6284)*
Solag Incorporated.....D.....949 728-1206
31641 Ortege Hwy San Juan Capistrano (92675) *(P-6284)*
Solairus Aviation, Petaluma *Also called Sunset Aviation LLC (P-4795)*
Solano County Mental Health.....E.....707 428-1131
9808 Venice Blvd Ste 700 Culver City (90232) *(P-23469)*
Solano County Probation Dept, Fairfield *Also called County of Solano (P-23168)*
SOLANO FAMILY & CHILDREN'S SER, Fairfield *Also called Solano Family & Chld Council (P-23788)*
Solano Family & Chld Council.....D.....707 863-3950
421 Executive Ct N Fairfield (94534) *(P-23788)*
Solano Garbage Company Inc.....D.....707 437-8900
2901 Industrial Ct Fairfield (94533) *(P-6285)*
Solano Gateway Realty Inc (PA).....D.....707 422-1725
2420 Martin Rd Ste 100 Fairfield (94534) *(P-11459)*
Solano Irrigation District.....D.....707 448-6847
810 Vaca Valley Pkwy # 201 Vacaville (95688) *(P-6372)*
Solano Pacific Corporation.....D.....707 745-6000
900 1st St Benicia (94510) *(P-11460)*
Solar Company Inc.....D.....510 888-9488
20861 Wilbeam Ave Ste 1 Castro Valley (94546) *(P-2277)*
Solar Energy LLC.....D.....818 449-5816
21600 Oxnard St Ste 1200 Woodland Hills (91367) *(P-2278)*
Solar Link International Inc.....C.....909 605-7789
4652 E Brickell St Ste A Ontario (91761) *(P-7658)*
Solar Spectrum LLC.....B.....844 777-6527
150 Linden St Oakland (94607) *(P-2279)*
Solari Enterprises Inc.....C.....714 282-2520
1507 W Yale Ave Orange (92867) *(P-10653)*
Solaris Paper Inc (PA).....D.....562 653-1680
100 S Anaheim Blvd # 280 Anaheim (92805) *(P-7903)*
Solarreserve Inc.....D.....310 315-2200
520 Broadway Fl 6 Santa Monica (90401) *(P-5924)*
Solartis LLC.....C.....310 251-4861
1601 N Sepulveda Blvd Manhattan Beach (90266) *(P-15113)*
Solcius LLC.....B.....951 772-0030
12155 Magnolia Ave 12b Riverside (92503) *(P-2280)*
Solcom Inc.....B.....510 940-2490
24801 Huntwood Ave Hayward (94544) *(P-1912)*
Solcom Communications Inc, Hayward *Also called Solcom Inc (P-1912)*
Solecon Industrial Contrs Inc.....D.....209 572-7390
1401 Mcwilliams Way Modesto (95351) *(P-2281)*
Soledad Cmnty Hlth Care Dst.....D.....831 678-2462
612 Main St Soledad (93960) *(P-20266)*
Soledad Medical Group, Soledad *Also called Soledad Cmnty Hlth Care Dst (P-20266)*
Soleeva Energy Inc.....D.....408 396-4954
1938 Junction Ave San Jose (95131) *(P-2282)*
Soleil Communications LLC.....D.....619 624-2888
2655 Camino Dl Rio N 11 San Diego (92108) *(P-25944)*
Solemnity Personnel.....E.....323 718-3979
2008 Camfiled Ave Commerce (90040) *(P-14423)*
Solestage Inc.....E.....909 576-1309
17651 Railroad St City of Industry (91748) *(P-15694)*
Solex Contracting Inc.....D.....951 308-1706
42146 Remington Ave Temecula (92590) *(P-1913)*
Solheim Lutheran Home.....C.....323 257-7518
2236 Merton Ave Los Angeles (90041) *(P-24080)*
Soli-Bond Inc.....E.....661 631-1633
4230 Foster Ave Bakersfield (93308) *(P-1045)*
Solid Commerce, Marina Del Rey *Also called Liquidate Direct LLC (P-15640)*
Solid Drywall, Antelope *Also called Leavy Brothers Incorporated (P-2814)*
Solid Oak Software Inc (PA).....D.....805 568-5415
1209 De La Vina St Ste B Santa Barbara (93101) *(P-6897)*
Solid Waste Services, San Marcos *Also called Edco Waste & Recycl Svcs Inc (P-6200)*
Solidcore Systems Inc (HQ).....D.....408 387-8400
3965 Freedom Cir Santa Clara (95054) *(P-15114)*
Soligent Distribution LLC (HQ).....D.....707 992-3100
1400 N Mcdowell Blvd # 201 Petaluma (94954) *(P-7343)*
Solimar Farms Inc.....D.....805 986-8806
1312 Del Norte Rd Camarillo (93010) *(P-111)*
Solimar Systems Inc (PA).....D.....619 849-2800
1515 2nd Ave San Diego (92101) *(P-15115)*
Solix Technologies Inc (PA).....D.....408 654-6446
4701 Patrick Henry Dr # 2001 Santa Clara (95054) *(P-15116)*
Solo W-2 Inc.....C.....925 680-0200
3478 Buskirk Ave Ste 1000 Pleasant Hill (94523) *(P-26826)*
Solo Workforce, Pleasant Hill *Also called Solo W-2 Inc (P-26826)*
Solomon Ward Sdnwurm Smith LLP.....D.....619 231-0303
401 B St Ste 1200 San Diego (92101) *(P-22830)*
Solopoint Solutions Inc.....D.....714 708-3639
150 Paularino Ave Ste 282 Costa Mesa (92626) *(P-25310)*
Solpac Inc.....C.....619 296-6247
2424 Congress St San Diego (92110) *(P-1606)*
Solpac Construction Inc.....C.....619 296-6247
2424 Congress St San Diego (92110) *(P-26401)*
Soltek Pacific, San Diego *Also called Solpac Inc (P-1606)*
SOLTEK PACIFIC CONSTRUCTION CO, San Diego *Also called Solpac Construction Inc (P-26401)*
Soltis Golf Incorporated.....D.....909 822-7000
869 W 9th St Upland (91786) *(P-1994)*
Solugenix Corporation (PA).....E.....866 749-7658
601 Valencia Ave Brea (92823) *(P-27212)*
Solugenix Corporation.....D.....866 749-7658
225 N Barranca St West Covina (91791) *(P-16115)*
Solute (PA).....D.....619 224-2810
1660 Hotel Cir N Ste 600 San Diego (92108) *(P-25311)*
Solute Consulting, San Diego *Also called Solute (P-25311)*
Solutions 2 Go LLC.....D.....949 825-7700
20091 Ellipse Lake Forest (92610) *(P-7742)*
Solv Inc.....C.....858 622-4040
16798 W Bernardo Dr San Diego (92127) *(P-15503)*
Solve All Facility Services, Oceanside *Also called Bergensons Property Svcs Inc (P-13869)*
Solve Healthcare Corporation (PA).....D.....949 891-0300
1300 Bristol St N Ste 285 Newport Beach (92660) *(P-27213)*
Solver Inc.....E.....310 691-5300
10780 Santa Monica Blvd # 370 Los Angeles (90025) *(P-6898)*
Soma Surgicenter.....E.....415 641-6889
1580 Valencia St San Francisco (94110) *(P-21203)*
Somansa Technologies Inc.....D.....408 297-1234
3003 N 1st St 301 San Jose (95134) *(P-6899)*
Somerford Place, Fresno *Also called Fresno Heritage Partners (P-19926)*
Somerford Place Encinitas, Encinitas *Also called Five Star Senior Living Inc (P-19919)*
Somerford Place Fresno, Fresno *Also called Five Star Quality Care Inc (P-19916)*
Somerford Place Stockton, Stockton *Also called Five Star Senior Living Inc (P-19920)*
Somerset Special Care Center.....D.....619 442-0245
151 Claydelle Ave El Cajon (92020) *(P-20458)*
Somis Pacific AG Management, Temecula *Also called Sierra Pacific Farms Inc (P-682)*
Sonata Software North Amer Inc (HQ).....D.....510 791-7220
2201 Walnut Ave Ste 180 Fremont (94538) *(P-15117)*
Sonic Industries Inc.....C.....310 532-8382
20030 Normandie Ave Torrance (90502) *(P-25312)*
Sonic Solutions Holdings Inc.....D.....408 562-8400
2830 De La Cruz Blvd Santa Clara (95050) *(P-15504)*
Sonicocom Inc.....D.....213 291-0475
2202 S Figueroa St Los Angeles (90007) *(P-16116)*
Sonicwall Inc (PA).....C.....888 557-6642
1033 Mccarthy Blvd Milpitas (95035) *(P-15695)*
Sonifi Solutions Inc.....C.....650 752-1980
1065 E Hillsdale Blvd # 228 Foster City (94404) *(P-5739)*
Sonim Technologies Inc (PA).....D.....650 378-8100
1875 S Grant St Ste 750 San Mateo (94402) *(P-5270)*
Sonitrol, San Jose *Also called Pacific West Security Inc (P-16548)*
Sonitrol Security Systems, Fresno *Also called Kimberlite Corporation (P-16538)*
Sonoma County Airport Ex Inc.....D.....707 837-8700
5807 Old Redwood Hwy Santa Rosa (95403) *(P-3607)*
Sonoma County Data Processing, Santa Rosa *Also called County of Sonoma (P-15744)*
Sonoma County Humane Society.....E.....707 542-0882
5345 Highway 12 Santa Rosa (95407) *(P-607)*
Sonoma County Indian Health PR (PA).....C.....707 521-4545
144 Stony Point Rd Santa Rosa (95401) *(P-19406)*
Sonoma County Water Agency.....C.....707 526-5370
404 Aviation Blvd Ste 0 Santa Rosa (95403) *(P-6120)*
Sonoma Hotel Operator Inc.....C.....707 938-9000
100 Boyes Blvd Sonoma (95476) *(P-12944)*
Sonoma Hotel Partners LP.....D.....707 283-2888
745 Baywood Dr Petaluma (94954) *(P-12945)*
Sonoma Life Support, Santa Rosa *Also called American Med Resp Amblnc Svc (P-3627)*
Sonoma Technology Inc.....D.....707 665-9900
1450 N Mcdowell Blvd Petaluma (94954) *(P-27214)*
Sonoma Valley Health Care Dst (PA).....B.....707 935-5000
347 Andrieux St Sonoma (95476) *(P-21204)*

ALPHABETIC

Employee Codes: A=Over 500 employees, B=251-500
C=101-250, D=51-100, E=50
2020 Directory of California
Wholesalers and Services Companies
© Mergent Inc. 1-800-342-5647
1435

SONOMA VALLEY HOSPITAL, Sonoma *Also called Sonoma Valley Health Care Dst* ***(P-21204)***
Sonoma Valley Womans Club D 707 938-8313
574 1st St E Sonoma (95476) ***(P-24663)***
Sonoma Vly Cnty Sanitation Dst C 707 547-1900
404 Aviation Blvd Santa Rosa (95403) ***(P-6137)***
Sonoma Vly Fire & Rescue Auth, Sonoma *Also called Valley Moon Fre Prtct Dist* ***(P-17144)***
Sonora Retirement Center Inc E 209 588-0373
12877 Sylva Ln Ofc Sonora (95370) ***(P-24081)***
Sonora Trade Company Inc D 619 878-5848
2127 Olympic Pkwy Chula Vista (91915) ***(P-9012)***
Sonoran Roofing Inc C 916 624-1080
4161 Citrus Ave Rocklin (95677) ***(P-3098)***
Sonshine Auto Body, Victorville *Also called Sonshine Collision Services* ***(P-17311)***
Sonshine Collision Services D 760 243-3185
17200 Jasmine St Victorville (92395) ***(P-17311)***
Sony Biotechnology Inc E 408 352-4257
1730 N 1st St Fl 2 San Jose (95112) ***(P-25835)***
Sony Corporation of America C 650 655-8000
2207 Bridgepointe Pkwy Foster City (94404) ***(P-15118)***
Sony Dadc New Mdia Sltions Inc C 310 760-8500
4499 Glencoe Ave Marina Del Rey (90292) ***(P-17791)***
Sony Electronics Inc C 714 508-7634
14450 Myford Rd Irvine (92606) ***(P-17670)***
Sony Electronics Inc B 415 833-4796
835 Howard St San Francisco (94103) ***(P-17671)***
Sony Electronics Inc C 310 835-6121
2201 E Carson St Carson (90810) ***(P-7219)***
Sony Interactive Entrmt LLC (HQ) C 310 981-1500
2207 Bridgepointe Pkwy Foster City (94404) ***(P-17063)***
Sony Logistics, Carson *Also called Sony Electronics Inc* ***(P-7219)***
Sony Music Entertainment Inc C 310 272-2555
9830 Wilshire Blvd Beverly Hills (90212) ***(P-7836)***
Sony Pictures Entrmt Inc B 310 840-8000
9050 Washington Blvd Culver City (90232) ***(P-17672)***
Sony Pictures Entrmt Inc B 310 202-1234
9336 Washington Blvd Culver City (90232) ***(P-18008)***
Sony Pictures Entrmt Inc B 310 244-3558
6527 W 82nd St Los Angeles (90045) ***(P-18009)***
Sony Pictures Entrmt Inc (HQ) A 310 244-4000
10202 Washington Blvd Culver City (90232) ***(P-17673)***
Sony Pictures Imageworks Inc A 310 840-8000
9050 Washington Blvd Culver City (90232) ***(P-15815)***
Sony Pictures Studios, Culver City *Also called Sony Pictures Entrmt Inc* ***(P-17673)***
Sony Pictures Studios Inc B 310 244-4000
1250 S Beverly Glen Blvd # 112 Los Angeles (90024) ***(P-17674)***
Sony Pictures Television Inc (HQ) B 310 244-7625
10202 Washington Blvd Culver City (90232) ***(P-17675)***
Sony Publishers, Beverly Hills *Also called Sony Music Entertainment Inc* ***(P-7836)***
Soofer Co Inc D 323 234-6666
2828 S Alameda St Vernon (90058) ***(P-8645)***
Sophia Lyn Convalescent Hosp, Pasadena *Also called Slch Inc* ***(P-20265)***
Soren McAdam Christianson LLP D 909 798-2222
2068 Orange Tree Ln # 100 Redlands (92374) ***(P-25682)***
Soroptmist Intl Huntington Bch E 714 271-9305
212 Utica Ave Huntington Beach (92648) ***(P-17064)***
Soroptomist Intl Tahoe Sierra E 530 573-1657
3050 Lake Tahoe Blvd South Lake Tahoe (96150) ***(P-24872)***
Sorrento Therapeutics Inc (PA) C 858 203-4100
4955 Directors Pl San Diego (92121) ***(P-25836)***
SOS Hosting, El Segundo *Also called Infrascale Inc* ***(P-6852)***
SOS Metals Inc (HQ) C 310 217-8848
201 E Gardena Blvd Gardena (90248) ***(P-7775)***
SOS Security Incorporated C 310 392-9600
2601 Ocean Park Blvd # 208 Santa Monica (90405) ***(P-16450)***
SOS Security Incorporated C 510 782-4900
26250 Industrial Blvd # 48 Hayward (94545) ***(P-16451)***
SOS Security LLC D 310 859-8248
331 N Beverly Dr Ste 3 Beverly Hills (90210) ***(P-16452)***
Sosa Granite & Marble Inc E 925 373-7675
7701 Marathon Dr Livermore (94550) ***(P-2910)***
Sosa Tile Co, Livermore *Also called Sosa Granite & Marble Inc* ***(P-2910)***
Sothebys Intl Rlty Inc E 310 456-6431
23405 Pacific Coast Hwy Malibu (90265) ***(P-11461)***
Soto Company Inc D 949 493-9403
34275 Camino Capistrano A Capistrano Beach (92624) ***(P-909)***
Soto Food Service, City of Industry *Also called Soto Provision Inc* ***(P-6584)***
Soto Provision Inc D 626 458-4600
488 Parriott Pl W City of Industry (91745) ***(P-6584)***
Sotoyome Medical Building LLC D 707 525-4000
990 Sonoma Ave Ste 15 Santa Rosa (95404) ***(P-10654)***
Souldriver Lessee Inc D 619 819-9500
435 6th Ave San Diego (92101) ***(P-12946)***
Soule Park Golf Course, Ojai *Also called Mf Daily Oxnard Ranch Partnr* ***(P-18269)***
Sound Mind and Body Inc D 206 547-2706
117 Via Yella Newport Beach (92663) ***(P-18196)***
Sound Technologies Inc D 760 918-9626
5810 Van Allen Way Carlsbad (92008) ***(P-7007)***
Sound-Crete Contractors Inc D 760 291-1240
530 Opper St Ste A Escondido (92029) ***(P-7493)***
Sound-Eklin, Carlsbad *Also called Sound Technologies Inc* ***(P-7007)***
Soundhound Inc (PA) D 408 441-3200
5400 Betsy Ross Dr Santa Clara (95054) ***(P-15119)***
Source 44 LLC C 877 916-6337
1921 Palomar Oaks Way # 205 Carlsbad (92008) ***(P-27215)***
Source Intelligence, Carlsbad *Also called Source 44 LLC* ***(P-27215)***
Source Logistics Center Corp D 323 887-3884
812 Union St Montebello (90640) ***(P-5054)***
Source Photonics Usa Inc (PA) C 818 773-9044
8521 Fllbrook Ave Ste 200 West Hills (91304) ***(P-7344)***
Source Rfrgn & Hvac Inc (HQ) C 714 578-2300
800 E Orangethorpe Ave Anaheim (92801) ***(P-2283)***
Sourcecorp Bps Nthrn Cal Inc D 530 893-7900
900 Fortress St Chico (95973) ***(P-6773)***
Sourcewise D 408 350-3200
2115 The Alameda San Jose (95126) ***(P-23470)***
Sourcing Solutions, Costa Mesa *Also called Phelps United LLC* ***(P-6884)***
South Asian Help Referral Agcy E 562 402-4132
17100 Pioneer Blvd # 260 Artesia (90701) ***(P-23471)***
South Bay Airport Shuttle D 408 225-4444
14420 Union Ave San Jose (95124) ***(P-3608)***
South Bay Bright Future Inc (PA) D 310 891-0096
24404 Vermont Ave Ste 206 Harbor City (90710) ***(P-24082)***
SOUTH BAY CENTER FOR COMMUNITY, Wilmington *Also called South Bay Ctr For Counseling* ***(P-23473)***
South Bay Community Services C 619 420-3620
430 F St Chula Vista (91910) ***(P-23472)***
South Bay Construction Company, Campbell *Also called B C C S Inc* ***(P-1412)***
South Bay Ctr For Counseling D 310 414-2090
540 N Marine Ave Wilmington (90744) ***(P-23473)***
South Bay Drive In Theatre, San Diego *Also called De Anza Land & Leisure Corp* ***(P-17830)***
South Bay Family Medical Group D 310 378-2234
3105 Lomita Blvd Torrance (90505) ***(P-19407)***
South Bay Freight System LLC (PA) D 626 271-9800
900 Turnbull Canyon Rd City of Industry (91745) ***(P-5055)***
South Bay Group, City of Industry *Also called South Bay Freight System LLC* ***(P-5055)***
South Bay Historical RR Soc E 408 243-3969
1005 Railroad Ave Santa Clara (95050) ***(P-24873)***
SOUTH BAY PACKAGING & ASSEMBLY, Carson *Also called South Bay Vocational Center* ***(P-23640)***
South Bay Power Plant, Chula Vista *Also called San Diego Gas & Electric Co* ***(P-5965)***
South Bay Regl Public Safety T E 408 270-6494
560 Bailey Ave San Jose (95141) ***(P-23639)***
South Bay Rgonal Pub Comm Auth E 310 973-1802
4440 W Broadway Hawthorne (90250) ***(P-5800)***
South Bay Sand Blasting and Ta D 619 238-8338
326 W 30th St National City (91950) ***(P-17545)***
South Bay Senior Services Inc D 310 338-8558
8929 S Sepulveda Blvd # 314 Los Angeles (90045) ***(P-21868)***
South Bay Senior Solutions Inc D 408 370-6360
1660 Hamilton Ave Ste 204 San Jose (95125) ***(P-21869)***
South Bay Vlla Preservation LP D 310 516-7325
13111 S San Pedro St Los Angeles (90061) ***(P-10816)***
South Bay Vocational Center E 424 215-4589
20706 Main St Carson (90745) ***(P-23640)***
South Baylo Acupuncture Clinic, Los Angeles *Also called South Baylo University* ***(P-22126)***
South Baylo University C 213 387-2414
2727 W 6th St Los Angeles (90057) ***(P-22126)***
South Capitol Cottage D 951 662-3026
15054 Daisy Rd Adelanto (92301) ***(P-27216)***
South Central Family Hlth Ctr D 323 908-4200
4425 S Central Ave Los Angeles (90011) ***(P-19408)***
South Central Los (PA) C 213 744-7000
2500 S Western Ave Los Angeles (90018) ***(P-24227)***
South China Sheet Metal Inc D 323 225-1522
1740 Albion St Los Angeles (90031) ***(P-2284)***
South Cntl Heatlh & Rehab Prog D 310 667-4070
2620 Industry Way Lynwood (90262) ***(P-22127)***
South Cntl Heatlh & Rehab Prog D 323 751-2677
5201 S Vermont Ave Los Angeles (90037) ***(P-22128)***
South Cnty Cmnty Hlth Ctr Inc (PA) D 650 330-7407
1885 Bay Rd East Palo Alto (94303) ***(P-22325)***
South Coast Air Qulty MGT Dst (PA) A 909 396-2000
21865 Copley Dr Diamond Bar (91765) ***(P-27217)***
South Coast Auto Insurance, Huntington Beach *Also called Freeway Insurance* ***(P-10366)***
South Coast Childrens Soc Inc C 909 478-3377
24950 Redlands Blvd Loma Linda (92354) ***(P-23474)***
South Coast Childrens Soc Inc C 909 364-9788
11780 Central Ave Chino (91710) ***(P-23475)***
South Coast Concrete Cnstr E 951 351-7777
6770 Central Ave Ste B Riverside (92504) ***(P-3219)***
South Coast Fencing Center D 714 549-2946
3518 W Lake Center Dr C Santa Ana (92704) ***(P-3468)***
South Coast Health Wellness E 951 686-9001
4768 Palm Ave Riverside (92501) ***(P-20267)***
South Coast Logistics E 714 894-4744
4160 Temescal Canyon Rd # 311 Corona (92883) ***(P-4232)***
South Coast Mechanical Inc D 714 738-6644
800 E Orangethorpe Ave Anaheim (92801) ***(P-2285)***
South Coast Piering Inc D 800 922-2488
41357 Date St Murrieta (92562) ***(P-1607)***
South Coast Plaza LLC (PA) D 714 546-0110
3333 Bristol St Ofc Costa Mesa (92626) ***(P-10655)***
South Coast Plaza LLC D 714 435-2000
3333 Bristol St Ofc Costa Mesa (92626) ***(P-10656)***
South Coast Plaza Mall, Costa Mesa *Also called South Coast Plaza LLC* ***(P-10656)***
South Coast Plaza Village, Costa Mesa *Also called South Coast Plaza LLC* ***(P-10655)***
South Coast Repertory Inc D 714 708-5500
655 Town Center Dr Costa Mesa (92626) ***(P-17947)***
South Coast Stone Paving D 714 835-0258
2618 N Baker St Santa Ana (92706) ***(P-1791)***
South Coast Trnsp & Dist Inc (PA) D 714 683-2300
1424 S Raymond Ave Fullerton (92831) ***(P-4504)***
South Coast Village, Santa Ana *Also called Edwards Theatres Circuit Inc* ***(P-17837)***
South Coast Water District (PA) D 949 499-4555
31592 West St Laguna Beach (92651) ***(P-6121)***

Mergent e-mail: customerrelations@mergent.com
1436
2020 Directory of California
Wholesalers and Services Companies
(P-0000) Products & Services Section entry number
(PA)=Parent Co (HQ)=Headquarters (DH)=Div Headquarters

South Coast Westin Hotel Co......D......714 540-2500
686 Anton Blvd Costa Mesa (92626) ***(P-12947)***
South County Housing Corp (PA)......E......510 582-1460
16500 Monterey St Ste 120 Morgan Hill (95037) ***(P-11462)***
South County Orthopedic Specia......D......949 586-3200
24331 El Toro Rd Ste 200 Laguna Hills (92637) ***(P-19409)***
South Feather Water & Pwr Agcy (PA)......D......530 533-4578
2310 Oro Quincy Hwy Oroville (95966) ***(P-6373)***
South Gate Care Centers, South Gate *Also called Far West Inc* ***(P-19910)***
South Gate Dental Group, South Gate *Also called Castle Dental* ***(P-19606)***
South Hills Country Club......D......626 339-1231
2655 S Citrus St West Covina (91791) ***(P-18577)***
South Market Child Care Inc......D......415 820-3500
790 Folsom St San Francisco (94107) ***(P-23789)***
South Pasadena San Marino YMCA, South Pasadena *Also called Young Mens Chrstn Assn of La* ***(P-24750)***
South San Jquin Irrigation Dst......D......209 249-4600
11011 E Highway 120 Manteca (95336) ***(P-6122)***
South Seas Imports, Compton *Also called M M Fab Inc* ***(P-8001)***
South Tahoe Public Utility Dst......C......530 544-6474
1275 Meadow Crest Dr South Lake Tahoe (96150) ***(P-6138)***
South Tahoe Refuse Co......D......530 541-5105
2140 Ruth Ave South Lake Tahoe (96150) ***(P-6286)***
South Valley Almond Co LLC......C......661 391-9000
15443 Beech Ave Wasco (93280) ***(P-8682)***
South Valley Farms, Wasco *Also called South Valley Almond Co LLC* ***(P-8682)***
South Valley Plumbing Inc......C......408 265-5566
3750 Charter Park Dr F San Jose (95136) ***(P-2286)***
South Valley School District, Fountain Valley *Also called Fountain Valley School Dst* ***(P-13929)***
South West Sun Solar Inc......E......714 582-3909
13752 Harbor Blvd Garden Grove (92843) ***(P-7438)***
Southbay Sndblst & Tank Clg......D......619 238-8338
3589 Dalbergia St San Diego (92113) ***(P-17546)***
SOUTHBAY TEEN CHALLENGE, Santa Clara *Also called Teen Challenge Norwestcal Nev* ***(P-23498)***
Southbay Website Design LLC......D......310 370-4043
1601 Pcf Cast Hwy Ste 290 Hermosa Beach (90254) ***(P-15816)***
Southbourne Inc......C......415 781-5555
340 Stockton St San Francisco (94108) ***(P-12948)***
Southcoast Dyeing & Finishing, Santa Ana *Also called Chroma Systems* ***(P-13265)***
Southcoast Welding & Mfg LLC......B......619 429-1337
2591 Faivre St Ste 1 Chula Vista (91911) ***(P-17475)***
Southeast Area Social Services......E......562 946-2237
10400 Pioneer Blvd Ste 8 Santa Fe Springs (90670) ***(P-23476)***
Southeast Fresno Rad LP......C......559 443-8400
1331 Fulton St Fresno (93721) ***(P-27218)***
SOUTHEAST INDUSTRIES, Downey *Also called ARC Los Angles Orange Counties* ***(P-23562)***
Southeastern Westminster, Westminster *Also called Southern California Edison Co* ***(P-5944)***
Southern CA Hlth & Rhbltn Prg......C......310 631-8004
2610 Industry Way Ste A Lynwood (90262) ***(P-19410)***
Southern Cal Appraisal Co, Burbank *Also called Sca Enterprises Inc* ***(P-17047)***
Southern Cal Blldog Rescue Inc......E......714 381-7691
2219 N Spurgeon St Santa Ana (92706) ***(P-24874)***
Southern Cal Maid Svc Crpt Clg......D......310 675-0585
14909 Crenshaw Blvd # 209 Gardena (90249) ***(P-14055)***
Southern Cal Orthopedics, La Mirada *Also called Healthpointe Medical Group Inc* ***(P-19006)***
Southern Cal Orthpd Inst LP......D......805 497-7015
375 Rolling Oaks Dr Thousand Oaks (91361) ***(P-19411)***
Southern Cal Orthpd Inst LP......C......818 901-6600
6815 Noble Ave Frnt Frnt Van Nuys (91405) ***(P-19412)***
Southern Cal Orthpd Inst LP......D......818 901-6600
6815 Noble Ave Ste 112 Westlake Village (91361) ***(P-19413)***
Southern Cal Pipe Trades ADM, Los Angeles *Also called Southern Cal Pipe Trades ADM* ***(P-11817)***
Southern Cal Pipe Trades ADM (PA)......D......213 385-6161
501 Shatto Pl Ste 500 Los Angeles (90020) ***(P-11817)***
Southern Cal Prmnnte Med Group......D......949 262-5780
6 Willard Irvine (92604) ***(P-19414)***
Southern Cal Prmnnte Med Group......D......800 272-3500
13652 Cantara St Panorama City (91402) ***(P-10048)***
Southern Cal Prmnnte Med Group......D......858 974-1000
5855 Copley Dr Ste 250 San Diego (92111) ***(P-10049)***
Southern Cal Prmnnte Med Group......D......661 398-5085
3501 Stockdale Hwy Bakersfield (93309) ***(P-19415)***
Southern Cal Prmnnte Med Group......D......619 528-5000
4647 Zion Ave San Diego (92120) ***(P-19416)***
Southern Cal Prmnnte Med Group......B......866 984-7483
10800 Magnolia Ave Riverside (92505) ***(P-10050)***
Southern Cal Prmnnte Med Group......D......310 604-5700
3830 Martin L King Jr Blv Lynwood (90262) ***(P-19417)***
Southern Cal Prmnnte Med Group......D......661 290-3100
26415 Carl Boyer Dr Santa Clarita (91350) ***(P-21205)***
Southern Cal Prmnnte Med Group......D......323 857-2000
6041 Cadillac Ave Los Angeles (90034) ***(P-19418)***
Southern Cal Prmnnte Med Group......D......800 780-1230
25825 Vermont Ave Harbor City (90710) ***(P-19419)***
Southern Cal Prmnnte Med Group......E......909 427-5000
9961 Sierra Ave Fontana (92335) ***(P-21206)***
Southern Cal Prmnnte Med Group......D......323 783-5455
4841 Hollywood Blvd Los Angeles (90027) ***(P-19420)***
Southern Cal Prmnnte Med Group......D......626 960-4844
1511 W Garvey Ave N West Covina (91790) ***(P-10051)***
Southern Cal Prmnnte Med Group......D......714 734-4500
17542 17th St Ste 300 Tustin (92780) ***(P-10052)***
Southern Cal Prmnnte Med Group......B......323 783-4893
4760 W Sunset Blvd Los Angeles (90027) ***(P-19421)***
Southern Cal Prmnnte Med Group (PA)......D......626 405-5704
393 Walnut Dr Pasadena (91107) ***(P-10053)***
Southern Cal Prmnnte Med Group......E......909 370-2501
789 E Cooley Dr Colton (92324) ***(P-19422)***
Southern Cal Prmnnte Med Group......E......714 841-7293
18081 Beach Blvd Huntington Beach (92648) ***(P-19423)***
Southern Cal Prmnnte Med Group......E......619 528-5000
1630 E Main St El Cajon (92021) ***(P-19424)***
Southern Cal Prmnnte Med Group......E......714 279-4675
411 N Lakeview Ave Anaheim (92807) ***(P-19425)***
Southern Cal Prmnnte Med Group......E......949 234-2139
30400 Camino Capistrano San Juan Capistrano (92675) ***(P-19426)***
Southern Cal Prmnnte Med Group......E......714 685-3520
22550 Savi Ranch Pkwy Yorba Linda (92887) ***(P-19427)***
Southern Cal Prmnnte Med Group......D......714 967-4760
1900 E 4th St Santa Ana (92705) ***(P-19428)***
Southern Cal Prmnnte Med Group......E......619 516-6000
4405 Vandever Ave San Diego (92120) ***(P-19429)***
Southern Cal Prmnnte Med Group......E......760 839-7200
732 N Broadway Escondido (92025) ***(P-19430)***
Southern Cal Prmnnte Med Group......E......909 394-2505
1255 W Arrow Hwy San Dimas (91773) ***(P-10054)***
Southern Cal Prmnnte Med Group......E......323 562-6459
7825 Atlantic Ave Cudahy (90201) ***(P-19431)***
Southern Cal Prmnnte Med Group......E......818 592-3038
21263 Erwin St Woodland Hills (91367) ***(P-19432)***
Southern Cal Prmnnte Med Group......E......661 222-2150
27107 Tourney Rd Santa Clarita (91355) ***(P-19433)***
Southern Cal Prmnnte Med Group......A......619 528-5000
6860 Avenida Encinas Carlsbad (92011) ***(P-10055)***
Southern Cal Prmnnte Med Group......A......562 657-2200
9353 Imprl Hwy Grdn Med Downey (90242) ***(P-10056)***
Southern Cal Prmnnte Med Group......B......949 376-8619
23781 Maquina Mission Viejo (92691) ***(P-22326)***
Southern Cal Prmnnte Med Group......D......661 334-2020
5055 California Ave Bakersfield (93309) ***(P-19434)***
Southern Cal Spcialty Care Inc......D......626 339-5451
845 N Lark Ellen Ave West Covina (91791) ***(P-21207)***
Southern Cal Spcialty Care Inc......C......714 564-7800
1901 College Ave Santa Ana (92706) ***(P-21208)***
Southern Cal Spcialty Care Inc (HQ)......D......562 944-1900
14900 Imperial Hwy La Mirada (90638) ***(P-21209)***
Southern Cal Stone Ctr LLC......D......818 784-8975
5400 Balboa Blvd Ste 111 Encino (91316) ***(P-19435)***
Southern Cal Tele & Enrgy, Temecula *Also called Southern California Tele Co* ***(P-5473)***
Southern Calif Mtl Hdlg Co, Northridge *Also called Southern California Mtl Hdlg* ***(P-7591)***
Southern California / Hawa Reg, El Centro *Also called Securitas SEC Svcs USA Inc* ***(P-16414)***
Southern California / Hawa Reg, Goleta *Also called Securitas SEC Svcs USA Inc* ***(P-16419)***
Southern California / Hawa Reg, Pomona *Also called Securitas SEC Svcs USA Inc* ***(P-16425)***
Southern California / Hawa Reg, Commerce *Also called Securitas SEC Svcs USA Inc* ***(P-16426)***
Southern California / Hawa Reg, Los Angeles *Also called Securitas SEC Svcs USA Inc* ***(P-16427)***
Southern California / Hawa Reg, Long Beach *Also called Securitas SEC Svcs USA Inc* ***(P-16428)***
Southern California / Hawa Reg, Victorville *Also called Securitas SEC Svcs USA Inc* ***(P-16431)***
Southern California Alcohol An (PA)......D......562 923-4545
11500 Paramount Blvd Downey (90241) ***(P-22129)***
Southern California Car Transf......D......858 586-0006
11139 Roxboro Rd San Diego (92131) ***(P-5141)***
Southern California Carriers, Heber *Also called C S Transport Inc* ***(P-3859)***
Southern California Cen, Long Beach *Also called Memor Ortho Surgic Group A M* ***(P-19190)***
Southern California Document, Brea *Also called Document Proc Solutions Inc* ***(P-15751)***
Southern California Edison Co (HQ)......A......626 302-1212
2244 Walnut Grove Ave Rosemead (91770) ***(P-5925)***
Southern California Edison Co......C......626 543-8081
4900 Rivergrade Rd 2b1 Irwindale (91706) ***(P-5926)***
Southern California Edison Co......C......559 893-3611
54205 Mt Poplar Ave Big Creek (93605) ***(P-5927)***
Southern California Edison Co......D......626 303-8480
1440 S California Ave Monrovia (91016) ***(P-5928)***
Southern California Edison Co......C......760 873-0715
4000 Bishop Creek Rd Bishop (93514) ***(P-5929)***
Southern California Edison Co......C......714 934-0838
14799 Chestnut St Westminster (92683) ***(P-5930)***
Southern California Edison Co......C......559 893-2037
55481 Mt Poplar Big Creek (93605) ***(P-5931)***
Southern California Edison Co......C......626 302-5101
8380 Klingerman St Rosemead (91770) ***(P-5932)***
Southern California Edison Co......C......626 543-6093
4900 Rivergrade Rd Baldwin Park (91706) ***(P-5933)***
Southern California Edison Co......D......714 870-3225
1851 W Valencia Dr Fullerton (92833) ***(P-5934)***
Southern California Edison Co......A......949 368-2881
14300 Mesa Rd San Clemente (92672) ***(P-5935)***
Southern California Edison Co......C......626 302-1212
2131 Walnut Grove Ave Rosemead (91770) ***(P-5936)***
Southern California Edison Co......C......714 973-5481
1241 S Grand Ave Santa Ana (92705) ***(P-5937)***
Southern California Edison Co......C......818 999-1880
3589 Foothill Dr Thousand Oaks (91361) ***(P-5938)***
Southern California Edison Co......E......626 815-7296
6000 N Irwindale Ave A Irwindale (91702) ***(P-5939)***
Southern California Edison Co......D......909 469-0251
265 N East End Ave Pomona (91767) ***(P-5940)***

A L P H A B E T I C

Employee Codes: A=Over 500 employees, B=251-500 C=101-250, D=51-100, E=50
2020 Directory of California Wholesalers and Services Companies
© Mergent Inc. 1-800-342-5647
1437

Southern California Edison Co.......D.......714 895-0488
1515 Walnut Grove Ave Rosemead (91770) ***(P-5941)***
Southern California Edison Co.......C.......310 608-5029
1924 E Cashdan St Compton (90220) ***(P-5942)***
Southern California Edison Co.......D.......805 683-5291
103 Love Pl Goleta (93117) ***(P-5943)***
Southern California Edison Co.......B.......714 895-0420
7300 Fenwick Ln Westminster (92683) ***(P-5944)***
Southern California Edison Co.......C.......949 587-5416
14155 Bake Pkwy Irvine (92618) ***(P-5945)***
Southern California Edison Co.......C.......626 633-3070
6042 N Irwindale Ave A Irwindale (91702) ***(P-5946)***
Southern California Edison Co.......C.......714 895-0163
7333 Bolsa Ave Westminster (92683) ***(P-5947)***
Southern California Edison Co.......D.......626 814-4212
13025 Los Angeles St Irwindale (91706) ***(P-5948)***
Southern California Edison Co.......C.......909 592-3757
800 W Cienega Ave San Dimas (91773) ***(P-5949)***
Southern California Edison Co.......D.......562 903-3191
9901 Geary Ave Santa Fe Springs (90670) ***(P-5950)***
Southern California Edison Co.......B.......562 491-3803
125 Elm Ave Long Beach (90802) ***(P-5951)***
Southern California Edison Co.......C.......760 951-3172
12353 Hesperia Rd Victorville (92395) ***(P-5952)***
Southern California Edison Co.......C.......626 302-0530
1515 Walnut Grove Ave Rosemead (91770) ***(P-5953)***
Southern California Fleet Svc.......E.......951 272-8655
6726 Nicolett St Riverside (92504) ***(P-17347)***
Southern California Gas Co (HQ).......C.......213 244-1200
555 W 5th St Los Angeles (90013) ***(P-5974)***
Southern California Gas Co.......D.......714 634-7221
1 Liberty Aliso Viejo (92656) ***(P-5975)***
Southern California Gas Co.......E.......661 399-4431
1510 N Chester Ave Bakersfield (93308) ***(P-5976)***
Southern California Gas Co.......B.......213 244-1200
1801 S Atlantic Blvd Monterey Park (91754) ***(P-5977)***
Southern California Gas Co.......B.......909 335-7802
1981 W Lugonia Ave Redlands (92374) ***(P-5978)***
Southern California Gas Co.......D.......213 244-1200
920 S Stimson Ave City of Industry (91745) ***(P-5979)***
Southern California Gas Co.......D.......213 244-1200
25200 Trumble Rd Romoland (92585) ***(P-5980)***
Southern California Gas Co.......D.......323 881-3587
333 E Main St Ste J Alhambra (91801) ***(P-5981)***
Southern California Gas Co.......D.......562 803-3341
6738 Bright Ave Whittier (90601) ***(P-5982)***
Southern California Gas Co.......D.......310 823-7945
8141 Gulana Ave Venice (90293) ***(P-5983)***
Southern California Gas Co.......C.......909 335-7941
155 S G St San Bernardino (92410) ***(P-5984)***
Southern California Gas Co.......C.......213 244-1200
1600 Corporate Center Dr Monterey Park (91754) ***(P-5985)***
Southern California Gas Co.......E.......562 803-7453
9240 Firestone Blvd Downey (90241) ***(P-5986)***
Southern California Gas Co.......A.......909 305-8297
1050 Overland Ct San Dimas (91773) ***(P-5987)***
Southern California Gas Co.......D.......800 427-2200
23130 Valencia Blvd Valencia (91355) ***(P-5988)***
Southern California Gas Co.......B.......818 701-2592
9400 Oakdale Ave Chatsworth (91311) ***(P-5966)***
Southern California Gas Tower.......B.......213 244-1200
555 W 5th St Los Angeles (90013) ***(P-5989)***
Southern California Golf Assn (PA).......D.......818 980-3630
3740 Cahuenga Blvd North Hollywood (91604) ***(P-24365)***
Southern California Institute.......D.......562 826-8139
5901 E 7th St 151 Long Beach (90822) ***(P-26031)***
Southern California Mar Assn.......D.......714 850-4004
3333 Fairview Rd Costa Mesa (92626) ***(P-17348)***
Southern California Mkt Area, Los Angeles *Also called Veritiv Operating Company **(P-7909)***
Southern California Mkt Area, Commerce *Also called Veritiv Operating Company **(P-7910)***
Southern California Mtl Hdlg.......D.......805 650-6000
19755 Bahama St Northridge (91324) ***(P-7591)***
Southern California Mtl Hdlg.......D.......818 349-1220
8124 Deering Ave Canoga Park (91304) ***(P-7592)***
Southern California Mtl Hdlg (HQ).......C.......562 949-1006
12393 Slauson Ave Whittier (90606) ***(P-7593)***
Southern California Physicia.......D.......858 824-7000
6760 Top Gun St Ste 100 San Diego (92121) ***(P-26402)***
SOUTHERN CALIFORNIA PIPE TRADE, Los Angeles *Also called Defined Contribution Trust Fun **(P-11781)***
Southern California Regional, Indio *Also called Granite Construction Company **(P-1715)***
Southern California Tele Co (PA).......D.......951 693-1880
27515 Enterprise Cir W Temecula (92590) ***(P-5473)***
Southern Clfrn Edsn - Prvt CHR, Rosemead *Also called Southern California Edison Co **(P-5936)***
Southern Contracting Company.......C.......760 744-0760
559 N Twin Oaks Valley Rd San Marcos (92069) ***(P-2643)***
Southern Counties Oil Co (PA).......D.......714 744-7140
1800 W Katella Ave # 400 Orange (92867) ***(P-8716)***
Southern Counties Oil Co.......E.......408 251-0811
2075 Alum Rock Ave San Jose (95116) ***(P-8735)***
Southern Fresh Prod Provs Inc.......D.......562 236-2784
11954 Washington Blvd Whittier (90606) ***(P-8524)***
Southern Glazers Wine.......B.......510 477-5500
33321 Dowe Ave Union City (94587) ***(P-8816)***
Southern Glazers Wine.......E.......951 274-2420
723 Palmyrita Ave Riverside (92507) ***(P-8817)***
Southern Glazers Wine.......C.......858 537-3912
10730 Scripps Ranch Blvd San Diego (92131) ***(P-8818)***
Southern Glazers Wine.......D.......408 750-3540
2320 Kruse Dr San Jose (95131) ***(P-8819)***
Southern Glazers Wine.......B.......562 926-2000
17101 Valley View Ave Cerritos (90703) ***(P-8820)***
Southern Hmbldt Cmnty Dst Hosp.......D.......707 923-3921
733 Cedar St Garberville (95542) ***(P-21210)***
Southern Humboldt Cmnty Clinic, Garberville *Also called Southern Hmbldt Cmnty Dst Hosp **(P-21210)***
Southern Humboldt Comm Hlth Cr.......D.......707 923-3925
733 Cedar St Garberville (95542) ***(P-21211)***
Southern Implants Inc.......C.......949 273-8505
5 Holland Ste 209 Irvine (92618) ***(P-26403)***
Southern Indian Health Council (PA).......D.......619 445-1188
4058 Willows Rd Alpine (91901) ***(P-19436)***
Southern Inyo Healthcare Dst.......C.......760 876-5501
501 E Locust St Lone Pine (93545) ***(P-21212)***
Southern Mnterey Cnty Mem Hosp (PA).......B.......831 385-6000
300 Canal St King City (93930) ***(P-21213)***
Southern Mnterey Cnty Mem Hosp.......C.......831 674-0112
467 El Camino Real Greenfield (93927) ***(P-21214)***
Southern Mntrey Cnty Labor Sup, Greenfield *Also called Southern Mntrrey Cnty Lbor Sup **(P-647)***
Southern Mntrrey Cnty Lbor Sup.......D.......831 674-2727
44 El Camino Real Unit A Greenfield (93927) ***(P-647)***
Southern Mono Healthcare Dst.......B.......760 934-3311
85 Sierra Park Rd Mammoth Lakes (93546) ***(P-21215)***
Southern Pacific Railroad, Bakersfield *Also called Union Pacific Railroad Company **(P-3516)***
Southern Regional Office, Bakersfield *Also called San Joaquin Val UNI Air Pol **(P-27202)***
Southern Sierra Medical Clinic, Ridgecrest *Also called Ridgecrest Regional Hospital **(P-21136)***
Southgate Glass & Screen Inc (PA).......E.......916 476-8396
6852 Franklin Blvd Sacramento (95823) ***(P-6727)***
Southgate Glass & Screen Inc.......E.......916 476-8396
6199 Warehouse Way Sacramento (95826) ***(P-6728)***
Southgate Recreation & Pk Dst.......E.......916 421-7275
7320 Florin Mall Dr Sacramento (95823) ***(P-23477)***
Southland Arthritis Osteo.......E.......951 672-1866
949 Calhoun Pl Ste F Hemet (92543) ***(P-19437)***
Southland Care, San Juan Capistrano *Also called Ensign Southland LLC **(P-19890)***
Southland Credit Union (PA).......D.......562 862-6831
10701 Los Alamitos Blvd Los Alamitos (90720) ***(P-9406)***
Southland Credit Union.......D.......562 862-6831
8545 Florence Ave Downey (90240) ***(P-9407)***
Southland Electric Inc.......D.......858 634-5050
4950 Greencraig Ln San Diego (92123) ***(P-2644)***
Southland Industries (PA).......E.......800 613-6240
12131 Western Ave Garden Grove (92841) ***(P-2287)***
Southland Integrated Svcs Inc (PA).......D.......714 558-6009
1618 W 1st St Santa Ana (92703) ***(P-24228)***
Southland Lutheran Home, Norwalk *Also called Front Porch Communities & Svcs **(P-20561)***
Southland Paving Inc.......D.......760 747-6895
361 N Hale Ave Escondido (92029) ***(P-3220)***
Southland Rgonal Assn Realtors (PA).......D.......818 786-2110
7232 Balboa Blvd Van Nuys (91406) ***(P-24366)***
Southland Steel, Newport Beach *Also called Fallon Land Company Inc **(P-7065)***
Southland Technology Inc.......D.......858 694-0932
8053 Vickers St San Diego (92111) ***(P-6900)***
Southland Transit Inc (PA).......C.......626 258-1310
3650 Rockwell Ave El Monte (91731) ***(P-3725)***
Southland Transit Co, Baldwin Park *Also called San Gabriel Transit Inc **(P-3748)***
Southtown Industrial Park.......E.......909 947-3768
1701 S Bon View Ave 104 Ontario (91761) ***(P-10657)***
Southwest Airlines Co.......D.......510 563-1000
1 Airport Dr Ste 25 Oakland (94621) ***(P-4682)***
Southwest Airlines Co.......D.......310 665-5700
100 World Way Ste 328 Los Angeles (90045) ***(P-4683)***
Southwest Airlines Co.......C.......510 563-1234
10 Alan Shepard Way Oakland (94621) ***(P-4684)***
Southwest Construction Co Inc.......D.......760 728-4460
2909 Rainbow Valley Blvd Fallbrook (92028) ***(P-3221)***
Southwest Contractors (PA).......C.......661 588-0484
3235 Unicorn Rd Bakersfield (93308) ***(P-1914)***
Southwest Convalesant, Hawthorne *Also called Windsor Gardens **(P-20395)***
Southwest Dealer Services Inc.......C.......925 753-0696
1001 G St Ste 113 Sacramento (95814) ***(P-17065)***
Southwest Express LLC.......D.......949 474-5038
1720 E Garry Ave Ste 107 Santa Ana (92705) ***(P-3938)***
Southwest Fsheries Science Ctr, La Jolla *Also called National Marine Fisheries Svc **(P-25802)***
Southwest Gas Corporation.......D.......760 951-4000
13471 Mariposa Rd Victorville (92395) ***(P-5990)***
Southwest General Contrs Inc.......E.......760 480-8747
912 S Andreasen Dr # 101 Escondido (92029) ***(P-7494)***
Southwest Healthcare Sys Aux.......E.......800 404-6627
38977 Sky Canyon Dr # 200 Murrieta (92563) ***(P-21216)***
Southwest Healthcare Sys Aux (HQ).......B.......951 696-6000
25500 Medical Center Dr Murrieta (92562) ***(P-21217)***
Southwest Inspection and Tstg.......D.......562 941-2990
441 Commercial Way La Habra (90631) ***(P-17066)***
Southwest Inspection Testing, La Habra *Also called Southwest Inspection and Tstg **(P-17066)***
Southwest Landscape Inc.......D.......714 545-1084
2205 S Standard Ave Santa Ana (92707) ***(P-910)***
Southwest Rgnal Cncil Crpnters (PA).......E.......213 385-1457
533 S Fremont Ave Fl 10 Los Angeles (90071) ***(P-2982)***
Southwest Traders Incorporated.......D.......209 462-1607
4747 Frontier Way Stockton (95215) ***(P-8261)***

Southwest Traders Incorporated (PA) ....C....951 699-7800
27565 Diaz Rd Temecula (92590) ***(P-8262)***
Southwest Transportation Agcy, Caruthers *Also called Fresno Cnty Sprntndent Schools* ***(P-3815)***
Southwest YMCA, Saratoga *Also called YMCA of Silicon Valley* ***(P-24891)***
Southwestern Orthpd Med Corp ....E....562 803-0600
15901 Hawthorne Blvd Lawndale (90260) ***(P-19438)***
Southwestern Yacht Club Inc ....E....619 222-0438
2702 Qualtrough St San Diego (92106) ***(P-18578)***
Southwind Foods LLC (PA) ....D....323 262-8222
20644 S Fordyce Ave Carson (90810) ***(P-8391)***
Southwire Company LLC ....D....909 989-2888
9199 Cleveland Ave # 100 Rancho Cucamonga (91730) ***(P-7187)***
Sovereign Health, Rancho Mirage *Also called Dual Diagnosis Trtmnt Ctr Inc* ***(P-22234)***
Sovereign Health of California, Los Angeles *Also called Dual Diagnosis Trtmnt Ctr Inc* ***(P-21525)***
Sovereign Health of California, San Clemente *Also called Dual Diagnosis Trtmnt Ctr Inc* ***(P-22020)***
SP McClenahan Co ....D....650 326-8781
1 Arastradero Rd Portola Valley (94028) ***(P-945)***
Sp Plus Corporation ....D....213 488-3100
3470 Wilshire Blvd # 400 Los Angeles (90010) ***(P-17276)***
Spa At Club Sport, San Ramon *Also called Clubsport San Ramon LLC* ***(P-18133)***
Spa Cas Palmas ....E....760 836-3106
41000 Bob Hope Dr Rancho Mirage (92270) ***(P-18197)***
Spa Dreams ....D....818 298-1120
6419 Hesperia Ave Reseda (91335) ***(P-18198)***
Spa Havens LP ....C....760 945-2055
29402 Spa Haven Way Vista (92084) ***(P-18199)***
Spa Las Palmas of Marriot Intl, Rancho Mirage *Also called Spa Cas Palmas* ***(P-18197)***
Spa Partners Inc ....E....707 942-5789
1457 Lincoln Ave Calistoga (94515) ***(P-18200)***
Spa Resort Casino, Palm Springs *Also called Agua Clnte Band Chilla Indians* ***(P-11996)***
Spa Resort Casino (PA) ....A....888 999-1995
401 E Amado Rd Palm Springs (92262) ***(P-12949)***
Space Age Metal Products Inc ....C....310 539-5500
23605 Telo Ave Torrance (90505) ***(P-6901)***
Space Systems Division, El Segundo *Also called Orbital Sciences Corporation* ***(P-25806)***
Space Systems/Loral LLC (HQ) ....D....650 852-7320
3825 Fabian Way Palo Alto (94303) ***(P-5801)***
Space Systems/Loral LLC ....C....650 852-4000
1140 Hamilton Ct Menlo Park (94025) ***(P-4505)***
Spacer.com, Mountain View *Also called 500 Startups Management Co LLC* ***(P-11882)***
Spacetone Acoustics Inc ....E....925 931-0749
1051 Serpentine Ln # 300 Pleasanton (94566) ***(P-2860)***
Spalding Srgcl Ctr of Bvrly Hl ....C....949 863-0022
27520 Hawthorne Blvd # 176 Rllng HLS Est (90274) ***(P-19439)***
Span Construction & Engrg Inc (PA) ....D....559 661-1111
1841 Howard Rd Madera (93637) ***(P-1608)***
Spanish Hills Country Club (PA) ....C....805 389-1644
999 Crestview Ave Camarillo (93010) ***(P-18579)***
Spanish Trils Girl Scout Cncil ....E....909 627-2609
5007 Center St Chino (91710) ***(P-23478)***
Spare-Time Inc ....D....916 983-9180
820 Halidon Way Folsom (95630) ***(P-18580)***
Spare-Time Inc ....D....916 782-2600
2501 Eureka Rd Roseville (95661) ***(P-18581)***
Spare-Time Inc ....C....209 371-0241
429 W Lockeford St Lodi (95240) ***(P-18042)***
Spare-Time Inc ....E....916 638-7001
2201 Gold Rush Dr Gold River (95670) ***(P-18582)***
Spare-Time Inc ....D....916 649-0909
2450 Natomas Park Dr Sacramento (95833) ***(P-18201)***
Spare-Time Inc ....D....916 859-5910
9570 Racquet Ct Elk Grove (95758) ***(P-18583)***
Spark Compass, Los Angeles *Also called Total Cmmnicator Solutions Inc* ***(P-15524)***
Sparkle Uniform & Linen Svc, Bakersfield *Also called Richard K Newman and Assoc Inc* ***(P-13241)***
Sparkletts, Irwindale *Also called Ds Services of America Inc* ***(P-8573)***
Sparta Consulting Inc ....B....916 985-0300
111 Woodmere Rd Ste 200 Folsom (95630) ***(P-16117)***
Sparxent Inc (PA) ....E....949 222-2287
65 Enterprise Aliso Viejo (92656) ***(P-15696)***
Spc Building Services, Riverside *Also called J M V B Inc* ***(P-2360)***
Spca La, Los Angeles *Also called Society For The Prevention of* ***(P-24869)***
Spe Go Holdings Inc ....E....858 638-0672
16422 N Woodson Dr Ramona (92065) ***(P-18300)***
Spearman Clubs Inc (PA) ....E....949 496-2070
23500 Clubhouse Dr Laguna Niguel (92677) ***(P-18762)***
Spears Manufacturing Co (PA) ....C....818 364-1611
15853 Olden St Sylmar (91342) ***(P-7508)***
Spec Personnel LLC ....C....408 727-8000
1900 La Fytte St Unit 125 Santa Clara (95050) ***(P-14424)***
Spec Services Inc ....C....714 963-8077
10540 Talbert Ave 100e Fountain Valley (92708) ***(P-25313)***
Special Care, San Diego *Also called RAC & Associates* ***(P-14090)***
Special Dispatch Cal Inc ....D....510 713-0300
8328 Central Ave Newark (94560) ***(P-4133)***
Special Dispatch Cal Inc (PA) ....D....714 521-8200
16330 Phoebe Ave La Mirada (90638) ***(P-4233)***
Special Events, Livermore *Also called Pinamar LLC* ***(P-14191)***
Special Events, Livermore *Also called High Summit LLC* ***(P-17355)***
Special Events Staffing ....A....626 296-6771
1015 N Lake Ave Ste 205 Pasadena (91104) ***(P-14425)***
Special Home Needs ....D....408 985-8666
1440 Jackson St Santa Clara (95050) ***(P-20459)***
Special Needs Network ....E....323 291-7100
4401 Crenshaw Blvd # 215 Los Angeles (90043) ***(P-21496)***
Special Service Contrs Inc ....D....805 227-1081
3580 Airport Rd Paso Robles (93446) ***(P-3469)***
Special Service For Groups Inc ....D....310 323-6887
19401 S Vt Ave Ste A200 Torrance (90502) ***(P-24229)***
Special Service For Groups Inc (PA) ....A....213 368-1888
905 E 8th St Los Angeles (90021) ***(P-23641)***
Special Service For Groups Inc ....D....213 620-5713
470 E 3rd St Ste D Los Angeles (90013) ***(P-24230)***
Special Service For Groups Ssg, Los Angeles *Also called Special Service For Groups Inc* ***(P-23641)***
Specialized Elevator Svcs LLC ....D....562 407-1200
14320 Iseli Rd Santa Fe Springs (90670) ***(P-7594)***
Specialized Landscape MGT Svcs ....D....805 520-7590
4212 Peast Los Angeles Simi Valley (93063) ***(P-911)***
Specialized Laundry Svcs Inc ....C....510 487-8297
33485 Western Ave Union City (94587) ***(P-13311)***
Specialty Center, Ridgecrest *Also called Ridgecrest Regional Hospital* ***(P-19339)***
Specialty Construction Inc ....D....805 543-1706
645 Clarion Ct San Luis Obispo (93401) ***(P-2645)***
Specialty Equipment Mkt Assn (PA) ....D....909 396-0289
1575 Valley Vista Dr Diamond Bar (91765) ***(P-24367)***
Specialty Fibres LLC (PA) ....D....925 934-8700
3201 Dnville Blvd Ste 265 Alamo (94507) ***(P-7776)***
Specialty Laboratories Inc (HQ) ....A....661 799-6543
27027 Tourney Rd Valencia (91355) ***(P-21593)***
Specialty Merchandise Corp (PA) ....E....805 578-5500
4100 Guardian St Ste 112 Simi Valley (93063) ***(P-9013)***
Specialty Minerals Inc ....C....760 248-5300
6565 Meridian Rd Lucerne Valley (92356) ***(P-1051)***
Specialty Produce, San Diego *Also called Tomatoes Extraordinaire Inc* ***(P-8530)***
Specialty Risk Services Inc ....D....714 674-1000
1 Pointe Dr Ste 220 Brea (92821) ***(P-10496)***
Specialty Risk Services Inc ....C....877 809-9478
6140 Stoneridge Mall Rd # 245 Pleasanton (94588) ***(P-10497)***
Specialty Sealing, Anaheim *Also called Boyd Corporation* ***(P-7629)***
Specialty Services, Arcadia *Also called Andover Maintenance Inc* ***(P-13864)***
Specialty Solid Waste & Recycl, Santa Clara *Also called Bay Counties Waste Svcs Inc* ***(P-6158)***
Specialty Steel Service Co Inc (HQ) ....D....916 771-4737
3300 Douglas Blvd Ste 128 Roseville (95661) ***(P-7105)***
Specialty Surgical Centers ....E....949 341-3499
15825 Laguna Canyon Rd # 200 Irvine (92618) ***(P-19440)***
Specialty Team Plastering Inc ....C....805 966-3858
4652 Vintage Ranch Ln Santa Barbara (93110) ***(P-2861)***
Specilty Srgical Ctr Encino LP ....D....310 659-6333
16501 Ventura Blvd # 103 Encino (91436) ***(P-19441)***
Specilzed Foster Care Pasadena, Pasadena *Also called County of Los Angeles* ***(P-22215)***
Specimen Contracting, Sunland *Also called Brightview Tree Company* ***(P-955)***
Spectacor Management Group ....B....562 436-3636
300 E Ocean Blvd Long Beach (90802) ***(P-10658)***
Spectra, Santa Clara *Also called Spec Personnel LLC* ***(P-14424)***
Spectra Company ....C....909 599-0760
2510 Supply St Pomona (91767) ***(P-2729)***
Spectra I California ....D....310 835-0808
21818 S Wilmington Ave # 402 Carson (90810) ***(P-2646)***
Spectra Industrial Electric, Carson *Also called Spectra I California* ***(P-2646)***
Spectra Premium (usa) Corp ....D....951 653-0640
2220 Almond Ave Redlands (92374) ***(P-6470)***
Spectrum Abatement, Orange *Also called United Spectrum Inc* ***(P-3483)***
Spectrum Community Services (PA) ....D....510 881-0300
2617 Barrington Ct Hayward (94545) ***(P-23479)***
Spectrum Credit Union ....C....510 251-6000
500 12th St Ste 200 Oakland (94607) ***(P-9354)***
Spectrum Equipment LLC ....D....760 599-8849
2505 Commerce Way Vista (92081) ***(P-8919)***
Spectrum Floral Service, Vista *Also called Spectrum Equipment LLC* ***(P-8919)***
Spectrum Hotel Group LLC ....D....949 471-8888
90 Pacifica Irvine (92618) ***(P-12950)***
Spectrum Hotel Group LLC ....D....949 471-8888
90 Pacifica Irvine (92618) ***(P-12951)***
Spectrum Information Svcs LLC (PA) ....D....949 752-7070
16 Technology Dr Ste 107 Irvine (92618) ***(P-13739)***
Spectrum MGT Holdg Co LLC ....D....714 657-1040
6021 Katella Ave Ste 100 Cypress (90630) ***(P-5740)***
Spectrum MGT Holdg Co LLC ....D....951 260-3143
4077 W Stetson Ave Hemet (92545) ***(P-5741)***
Spectrum MGT Holdg Co LLC ....D....626 857-1075
1041 E Route 66 Glendora (91740) ***(P-5742)***
Spectrum MGT Holdg Co LLC ....D....951 587-8660
27555 Ynez Rd Ste 203 Temecula (92591) ***(P-5743)***
Spectrum MGT Holdg Co LLC ....D....909 918-6972
1078 E Hospitality Ln D San Bernardino (92408) ***(P-5744)***
Spectrum MGT Holdg Co LLC ....D....562 677-0228
17777 Center Court Dr N Cerritos (90703) ***(P-5745)***
Spectrum MGT Holdg Co LLC ....D....714 871-2643
1565 S Harbor Blvd Fullerton (92832) ***(P-5746)***
Spectrum MGT Holdg Co LLC ....D....562 372-4008
350 Stonewood St Downey (90241) ***(P-5747)***
Spectrum MGT Holdg Co LLC ....D....818 700-6126
9260 Topanga Canyon Blvd Chatsworth (91311) ***(P-5748)***
Spectrum MGT Holdg Co LLC ....C....424 529-6011
500 Lakewood Center Mall Lakewood (90712) ***(P-5749)***
Spectrum MGT Holdg Co LLC ....C....714 657-1060
6021 Katella Ave Ste 100 Cypress (90630) ***(P-5750)***
Spectrum MGT Holdg Co LLC ....D....714 903-4000
12040 Western Ave Garden Grove (92841) ***(P-5751)***

ALPHABETIC

Spectrum MGT Holdg Co LLC .... D 310 647-3000
550 Continental Blvd # 250 El Segundo (90245) (P-5752)
Spectrum MGT Holdg Co LLC .... D 909 821-8159
1500 Auto Center Dr Ontario (91761) (P-5753)
Spectrum MGT Holdg Co LLC .... D 714 414-1431
3430 E Miraloma Ave Anaheim (92806) (P-5754)
Spectrum MGT Holdg Co LLC .... D 951 571-8738
12625 Frederick St F10 Moreno Valley (92553) (P-5755)
Spectrum Prof Staffing Inc .... C 800 644-1150
13520 Evening Creek Dr N # 300 San Diego (92128) (P-14567)
Spectrum Security Services Inc .... D 714 542-9600
1633 E 4th St Ste 238 Santa Ana (92701) (P-16453)
Spectrum Security Services Inc (PA) .... C 619 669-6660
13967 Campo Rd Ste 101 Jamul (91935) (P-16564)
Speedway Sonoma LLC .... D 707 938-8448
Hwy 37 N Sonoma (95476) (P-18090)
Speedy Locksmith .... D 760 439-5000
429 Avnida De La Estrella San Clemente (92672) (P-17547)
Spencer Building Maintenance .... B 916 922-1900
10457 Old Placerville Rd Sacramento (95827) (P-14056)
Spencer Recovery Centers Inc (PA) .... D 949 376-3705
1316 S Coast Hwy Laguna Beach (92651) (P-22130)
Sperasoft Inc .... A 408 715-6615
2033 Gateway Pl Ste 500 San Jose (95110) (P-15120)
Sperry Van Ness, Los Angeles Also called Svn International Corp (P-11471)
Spf Capital Real Estate LLC .... D 310 519-8200
601 S Palos Verdes St San Pedro (90731) (P-12952)
Sph-Irvine LLC .... E 949 833-1432
18952 Macarthur Blvd # 103 Irvine (92612) (P-19442)
Sphere Institute .... C 650 558-3980
500 Airport Blvd Ste 340 Burlingame (94010) (P-25945)
Spherion Staffing Group, Redding Also called Sfn Group Inc (P-14566)
Spicers Paper Inc (HQ) .... C 562 698-1199
12310 Slauson Ave Santa Fe Springs (90670) (P-7848)
Spiess Construction Co Inc .... D 805 937-5859
201 S Broadway St Ste 140 Orcutt (93455) (P-1915)
Spike Technologies Inc .... E 408 410-0624
2386 Lacey Dr Milpitas (95035) (P-15697)
Spinecare Medical Group Inc .... E 650 985-7500
455 Hickey Blvd Ste 310 Daly City (94015) (P-19443)
Spiniello Companies .... D 909 629-1000
2650 Pomona Blvd Pomona (91768) (P-1916)
Spinning, Venice Also called Mad Dogg Athletics Inc (P-8089)
Spinning Spur Wind Three LLC .... A 858 521-3319
15445 Innovation Dr San Diego (92128) (P-5954)
Spira-Loc, El Cajon Also called University Mechanical & (P-2308)
Spiral Technology Inc .... D 661 723-3148
229 E Avenue K8 Ste 105 Lancaster (93535) (P-25314)
Spire Concessions LLC .... D 818 843-6000
2500 N Hollywood Way Burbank (91505) (P-12953)
Spire Global Inc (PA) .... D 415 356-3400
575 Florida St Ste 150 San Francisco (94110) (P-15888)
Spireon Inc (PA) .... C 800 557-1449
16802 Aston Irvine (92606) (P-4234)
Spiritual Direction .... E 650 952-9456
164 San Luis Ave San Bruno (94066) (P-23480)
Splash Fast Lube, Salinas Also called Gieg Chevron LLC (P-17375)
Splash Swim School Inc .... E 925 838-7946
2411 Old Crow Canyon Rd San Ramon (94583) (P-18763)
Splunk Inc (PA) .... E 415 848-8400
270 Brannan St San Francisco (94107) (P-15505)
Sport Center Fitness Inc .... D 310 376-9443
819 N Harbor Dr Redondo Beach (90277) (P-18202)
Sports Club of El Dorado, Shingle Springs Also called Salutary Sports Clubs Inc (P-18189)
Sports Office, Oakland Also called City of Oakland (P-18661)
Sportsmens Lodge Hotel LLC .... C 818 769-4700
12825 Ventura Blvd Studio City (91604) (P-12954)
Sportvision Inc .... E 510 736-2925
6657 Kaiser Dr Fremont (94555) (P-17676)
Spot Free Car Wash, Escondido Also called In & Out Car Wash Inc (P-17376)
Spotcues Inc .... A 408 435-2700
1975 W El Cmno Real 301 Mountain View (94040) (P-6902)
Spotlight 29 Casino, Coachella Also called 29 Palms Enterprises Corp (P-18613)
Spr Op Co Inc .... C 510 232-5030
70 W Ohio Ave Ste H Richmond (94804) (P-11694)
Spreadtrum Cmmncations USA Inc .... D 858 546-0895
10180 Telesis Ct Ste 500 San Diego (92121) (P-25837)
Sprig Electric Co .... D 408 298-3134
65 Oak Grove St San Francisco (94107) (P-2647)
Sprig Electric Co (PA) .... D 408 298-3134
1860 S 10th St San Jose (95112) (P-2648)
Spring Hl Mnor Cnvlescent Hosp, Grass Valley Also called Springhill Manor Rehabilitatio (P-20690)
Spring Lake Village, Santa Rosa Also called Covia Communities (P-23887)
Spring Valley Lake Country CLB .... D 760 245-5356
13229 Spring Valley Pkwy Victorville (92395) (P-18584)
Spring Valley Post Acute LLC .... C 760 245-6477
14973 Hesperia Rd Victorville (92395) (P-20268)
Springboard, Los Angeles Also called Evolve Media Holdings LLC (P-13505)
Springboard Solutions LLC .... C 951 779-7739
4351 Latham St Riverside (92501) (P-27219)
Springhill Manor Rehabilitatio .... E 530 273-7247
355 Joerschke Dr Grass Valley (95945) (P-20690)
Springhill Suites, Atascadero Also called Atascadero Hotel Partners LLC (P-12023)
Springhill Suites, San Diego Also called Marriott International Inc (P-12585)
Springhill Suites, Anaheim Also called M6 Dev LLC (P-12570)
Springml Inc .... D 916 316-1566
6200 Stoneridge Mall Rd Pleasanton (94588) (P-16118)

Springs Ambulance Service Inc .... D 760 883-5000
1111 Montalvo Way Palm Springs (92262) (P-3726)
Springs Club Inc .... D 760 328-0254
1 Duke Dr Rancho Mirage (92270) (P-18585)
Springs Country Club, The, Rancho Mirage Also called Springs Club Inc (P-18585)
Sprint, Anaheim Also called Arch Telecom Inc (P-5152)
Sprint Communications Co LP .... E 818 755-7100
111 Unversal Hollywood Dr Universal City (91608) (P-5474)
Sprint Communications Co LP .... D 909 382-6030
1505 E Enterprise Dr San Bernardino (92408) (P-5475)
Sprint Corporation .... B 949 748-3353
6591 Irvine Center Dr # 100 Irvine (92618) (P-5271)
Sprouts 252, San Pedro Also called Sprouts Farmers Market Inc (P-8263)
Sprouts Farmers Market Inc .... C 888 577-7688
280 De Berry St Colton (92324) (P-4506)
Sprouts Farmers Market Inc .... D 310 831-7836
820 N Western Ave San Pedro (90732) (P-8263)
Spruce Grove Inc (PA) .... D 714 546-4255
3719 S Plaza Dr Santa Ana (92704) (P-10817)
Spruce Technology Inc .... D 925 415-8160
3516 Browntail Way San Ramon (94582) (P-15121)
Spsv Entertainment LLC .... D 909 744-9373
28950 State Highway 18 Skyforest (92385) (P-18010)
Spurr Co., Paso Robles Also called Dave Spurr Excavating Inc (P-3311)
Spus7 125 Cambridgepark LP .... C 213 683-4200
515 S Flower St Ste 3100 Los Angeles (90071) (P-11463)
Spus7 150 Cambridgepark LP .... C 213 683-4200
515 S Flower St Ste 3100 Los Angeles (90071) (P-11464)
Spus7 235 Pine LP .... D 231 683-4200
235 Pine St Ste 125 San Francisco (94104) (P-11761)
Spus7 Miami Acc LP .... E 213 683-4200
515 S Flower St Ste 3100 Los Angeles (90071) (P-11762)
Spycher Brothers, Turlock Also called Select Harvest Usa LLC (P-8681)
Spyglass Hill Community Assn .... E 949 855-1800
39 Argonaut Ste 100 Aliso Viejo (92656) (P-24664)
Sqa Services Inc .... B 800 333-6180
550 Silver Spur Rd # 300 Rllng HLS Est (90275) (P-26827)
Squab Producers Calif Inc .... D 209 537-4744
409 Primo Way Modesto (95358) (P-8335)
Squar Milner Peterson (PA) .... C 949 222-2999
18500 Von Karman Ave # 10 Irvine (92612) (P-25683)
Squar Milner, Irvine Also called Squar Milner Peterson (P-25683)
Square Inc (PA) .... E 415 375-3176
1455 Market St Ste 600 San Francisco (94103) (P-15506)
Square Enix Inc .... C 310 846-0400
999 N Pacific Coast Hwy # 3 El Segundo (90245) (P-6903)
Squaretrade Inc (HQ) .... C 415 541-1000
600 Harrison St Ste 400 San Francisco (94107) (P-10236)
Squaw Creek Associates LLC .... A 530 581-6624
400 Squaw Creek Rd Alpine Meadows (96146) (P-12955)
Squaw Valley Development Co (HQ) .... D 530 452-6985
1960 Squaw Valley Rd Olympic Valley (96146) (P-12956)
Squaw Valley Ski, Olympic Valley Also called Squaw Valley Development Co (P-12956)
Squaw Valley Ski Corporation (HQ) .... D 530 583-6985
1960 Squaw Valley Rd Olympic Valley (96146) (P-12957)
Squire Patton Boggs (us) LLP .... D 213 624-2500
555 S Flower St Ste 3100 Los Angeles (90071) (P-22831)
Squire Patton Boggs (us) LLP .... C 415 954-0334
275 Battery St Ste 2600 San Francisco (94111) (P-22832)
SR Bray LLC .... E 951 436-2920
2750 N Perris Blvd Perris (92571) (P-14200)
SR Bray LLC (PA) .... E 714 765-7551
1210 N Red Gum St Anaheim (92806) (P-2649)
SR Freeman Inc .... D 408 364-2200
2380 S Bascom Ave Ste 200 Campbell (95008) (P-2983)
Sra Oss Inc .... C 408 855-8200
5201 Great America Pkwy # 419 Santa Clara (95054) (P-15507)
Srax Inc (PA) .... D 323 694-9800
456 Seaton St Los Angeles (90013) (P-13580)
Srcsd, Sacramento Also called Sacramento Reg Co Sanit Dist (P-6355)
Srd Engineering Inc .... D 714 630-2480
3578 E Enterprise Dr Anaheim (92807) (P-1917)
Srg Management Inc .... C 858 792-9300
500 Stevens Ave Ste 100 Solana Beach (92075) (P-26404)
Srht Property Mgmt Co .... D 213 683-0522
1317 E 7th St Los Angeles (90021) (P-26405)
SRI International (PA) .... A 650 859-2000
333 Ravenswood Ave Menlo Park (94025) (P-26032)
SRI International .... C 805 542-9330
4111 Broad St Ste 220 San Luis Obispo (93401) (P-26033)
SRK Global Consulting .... D 310 295-2524
7225 Crescent Park W # 255 Los Angeles (90094) (P-16119)
Srm Alliance Hospital Services (PA) .... B 707 778-1111
400 N Mcdowell Blvd Petaluma (94954) (P-21218)
SRS Consulting Inc .... D 510 252-0625
39465 Paseo Padre P Fremont (94538) (P-16120)
SS Heritage Inn Ontario LLC .... D 909 937-5000
3595 E Guasti Rd Ontario (91761) (P-12958)
SS Hert Trucking Inc (PA) .... E 760 248-9327
33924 Old Woman Sprng Rd Lucerne Valley (92356) (P-4134)
Ss Skikos Incorporated .... D 707 575-3000
1289 Sebastopol Rd Santa Rosa (95407) (P-4235)
Ss Travel, San Francisco Also called San Francisco Travel Assn (P-17044)
SS&c Advent, San Francisco Also called Advent Software Inc (P-14621)
Ss8 Networks Inc (PA) .... C 408 894-8400
750 Tasman Dr Milpitas (95035) (P-5802)
Ssa Containers Inc .... D 206 623-0304
1521 Pier J Ave Long Beach (90802) (P-4623)

Mergent e-mail: customerrelations@mergent.com
1440
2020 Directory of California
Wholesalers and Services Companies
(P-0000) Products & Services Section entry number
(PA)=Parent Co (HQ)=Headquarters (DH)=Div Headquarters

Ssa Marine Inc ... E ... 562 983-1001
1521 Pier J Ave Long Beach (90802) ***(P-4624)***
Ssae 16 Professionals LLP ... D ... 866 480-9485
3419 E Chapman Ave # 334 Orange (92869) ***(P-25684)***
SSC Carmichael Operating Co LP ... D ... 916 485-4793
3630 Mission Ave Carmichael (95608) ***(P-20269)***
SSC Construction Inc ... C ... 951 278-1177
4195 Chino Hills Pkwy Chino Hills (91709) ***(P-25315)***
SSC Newport Beach Oper Co LP ... C ... 949 642-8044
466 Flagship Rd Newport Beach (92663) ***(P-20270)***
SSC Oakland Excell Oper Co LP ... D ... 510 261-5200
3025 High St Oakland (94619) ***(P-20271)***
SSC Pittsburg Operating Co LP ... A ... 925 427-4444
2351 Loveridge Rd Pittsburg (94565) ***(P-20691)***
SSC San Jose Operating Co LP ... D ... 408 249-0344
340 Northlake Dr San Jose (95117) ***(P-20272)***
Ssd Systems, Anaheim *Also called Security Signal Devices Inc* ***(P-16560)***
SSE Merchandise, San Jose *Also called Sharks Sports & Entrmt LLC* ***(P-18080)***
Ssf Imported Auto Parts LLC ... D ... 310 782-8859
21175 Main St Ste A Carson (90745) ***(P-6471)***
Ssf Imported Auto Parts LLC (HQ) ... D ... 800 203-9287
466 Forbes Blvd South San Francisco (94080) ***(P-6472)***
Ssi, Stockton *Also called Super Store Industries* ***(P-8653)***
Ssi, Rocklin *Also called Surveillance Systems* ***(P-7350)***
Ssi, Valley Center *Also called Survival Systems Intl Inc* ***(P-17549)***
Ssi, San Luis Obispo *Also called Sealant Systems International* ***(P-6489)***
Ssjid, Manteca *Also called South San Jquin Irrigation Dst* ***(P-6122)***
Ssl, Palo Alto *Also called Space Systems/Loral LLC* ***(P-5801)***
Ssl Robotics LLC (HQ) ... D ... 626 296-1373
1250 Lincoln Ave Ste 100 Pasadena (91103) ***(P-25316)***
Ssl Robotics LLC ... D ... 626 296-1373
1250 Lincoln Ave Ste 100 Pasadena (91103) ***(P-25317)***
Ssl Robotics LLC ... C ... 626 296-1373
4398 Corporate Center Dr Los Alamitos (90720) ***(P-25318)***
Ssmb Pacific Holding Co Inc (HQ) ... D ... 510 836-6100
1755 Adams Ave San Leandro (94577) ***(P-6409)***
Ssmb Pacific Holding Co Inc ... D ... 530 222-1212
20769 Industry Rd Anderson (96007) ***(P-6410)***
Ssmb Pacific Holding Co Inc ... D ... 916 371-3372
707 Display Way Sacramento (95838) ***(P-6411)***
SSPCA, Sacramento *Also called The For Sacramento Society* ***(P-24878)***
SST, Newark *Also called Shotspotter Inc* ***(P-15497)***
Sstmas Y Aranda Eqpos Hdrlicos ... E ... 619 245-4502
280 Campillo St Ste L Calexico (92231) ***(P-7595)***
Ssw, Palm Springs *Also called S S W Mechanical Cnstr Inc* ***(P-2262)***
St Andrews Children Center ... E ... 949 651-0198
4400 Barranca Pkwy Irvine (92604) ***(P-23790)***
St Andrews Health Care, Los Angeles *Also called Washington Enterprises 3 LLC* ***(P-20370)***
ST ANNE'S HOME, San Francisco *Also called Little Sisters of Poor* ***(P-23975)***
St Annes Maternity Home ... C ... 213 381-2931
155 N Occidental Blvd Los Angeles (90026) ***(P-24083)***
St Anthony Foundation (PA) ... E ... 415 241-2600
150 Golden Gate Ave San Francisco (94102) ***(P-23481)***
St Baldricks Foundation Inc (PA) ... D ... 626 792-8247
1333 S Mayflower Ave Monrovia (91016) ***(P-24425)***
St Barnbas Snior Ctr Los Angle ... D ... 213 388-4444
675 S Carondelet St Los Angeles (90057) ***(P-23482)***
St Denis Electric Inc ... E ... 805 343-9999
734 Ralcoa Way Arroyo Grande (93420) ***(P-2650)***
St Elizabeth Community Hosp (HQ) ... D ... 530 529-7760
2550 Sster Mary Clumba Dr Red Bluff (96080) ***(P-21219)***
St Francis Electric Inc ... C ... 510 639-0639
975 Carden St San Leandro (94577) ***(P-2651)***
St Francis Electric LLC ... C ... 510 639-0639
975 Carden St San Leandro (94577) ***(P-2652)***
St Francis Extended Care Inc ... D ... 510 785-3630
718 Bartlett Ave Hayward (94541) ***(P-20692)***
St Francis Hts Convalescent ... D ... 650 755-9515
35 Escuela Dr Daly City (94015) ***(P-20693)***
St Francis Medical Center, Redwood City *Also called Verity Health System Cal Inc* ***(P-21356)***
St Francis Medical Center (HQ) ... C ... 310 900-8900
3630 E Imperial Hwy Lynwood (90262) ***(P-19444)***
St Francis Pavillion, Daly City *Also called Forte Enterprises Inc* ***(P-26232)***
St Francis Yacht Club ... C ... 415 563-6363
700 Marina Blvd San Francisco (94123) ***(P-18586)***
St George Logistics, Compton *Also called Patina Freight Inc* ***(P-5023)***
St Helena Hospital Clearlake, Clearlake *Also called Advintist Hlth Clearlake Hosp* ***(P-20735)***
St Helena Hospital (HQ) ... A ... 707 963-3611
10 Woodland Rd Saint Helena (94574) ***(P-21220)***
St Helena Hospital Clearlake, Clearlake *Also called Adventist Health System/West* ***(P-18791)***
St John's Health Centre, Santa Monica *Also called Saint Jhns Hlth Ctr Foundation* ***(P-21144)***
St Johns Regional Medical Ctr, Oxnard *Also called Dignity Health* ***(P-20852)***
St Johns Retirement Village ... C ... 530 662-9674
135 Woodland Ave Woodland (95695) ***(P-20694)***
St Johns Well Child (PA) ... D ... 323 541-1600
808 W 58th St Los Angeles (90037) ***(P-19632)***
St Joseph Center ... D ... 310 396-6468
204 Hampton Dr Venice (90291) ***(P-23483)***
St Joseph Community Home Care ... D ... 209 478-9547
7400 Shoreline Dr Ste 4 Stockton (95219) ***(P-21870)***
St Joseph Health Per Care Svcs ... D ... 800 365-1110
1315 Corona Pointe Ct Corona (92879) ***(P-21871)***
St Joseph Health System ... D ... 714 992-3000
101 E Valencia Mesa Dr Fullerton (92835) ***(P-21221)***
St Joseph Health System ... E ... 707 443-9371
2280 Harrison Ave Ste B Eureka (95501) ***(P-19445)***
St Joseph Health System ... E ... 707 778-2505
400 N Mcdowell Blvd Fl 1 Petaluma (94954) ***(P-21222)***
St Joseph Health System Home ... A ... 714 712-9500
200 W Center St Promenade Anaheim (92805) ***(P-21872)***
St Joseph Heritage Healthcare ... E ... 949 365-2492
27800 Medical Center Rd Mission Viejo (92691) ***(P-21223)***
St Joseph Heritage Med Group (PA) ... C ... 714 633-1011
2212 E 4th St Ste 201 Santa Ana (92705) ***(P-21224)***
St Joseph Home Health Network (HQ) ... D ... 714 712-9500
441 College Ave Santa Rosa (95401) ***(P-21873)***
St Joseph Home Health Network ... E ... 714 712-9559
200 W Center St Promenade Anaheim (92805) ***(P-21874)***
St Joseph Hospice ... D ... 714 712-7100
200 W Center St Promenade Anaheim (92805) ***(P-23484)***
St Joseph Hospital (PA) ... D ... 707 445-8121
2700 Dolbeer St Eureka (95501) ***(P-21225)***
St Joseph Hospital ... A ... 707 268-0190
2752 Harrison Ave Ste A Eureka (95501) ***(P-21226)***
St Joseph Hospital of Eureka ... A ... 707 445-8121
2700 Dolbeer St Eureka (95501) ***(P-21227)***
St Joseph Hospital of Orange (HQ) ... A ... 714 633-9111
1100 W Stewart Dr Orange (92868) ***(P-21228)***
St Joseph Hospital of Orange ... D ... 714 771-8037
1100 W Stewart Dr Orange (92868) ***(P-21229)***
St Joseph Surgery Center LP ... D ... 209 467-6316
1800 N California St # 1 Stockton (95204) ***(P-19446)***
St Josephs Med Ctr Stockton ... A ... 209 943-2000
1800 N California St Stockton (95204) ***(P-21230)***
St Josephs Medical Center ... C ... 209 943-2000
1800 N California St Stockton (95204) ***(P-21231)***
St Jsephs Regional Hsing Corp (PA) ... B ... 209 956-3400
3400 Wagner Heights Rd Stockton (95209) ***(P-10818)***
St Jude Heritage Medical Group ... C ... 714 528-4211
4300 Rose Dr Yorba Linda (92886) ***(P-19447)***
St Jude Hospital (HQ) ... A ... 714 871-3280
101 E Valencia Mesa Dr Fullerton (92835) ***(P-21232)***
St Jude Hospital ... C ... 714 578-8544
279 Imperial Hwy Ste 770 Fullerton (92835) ***(P-21233)***
St Jude Hospital ... A ... 714 992-3057
101 E Valencia Mesa Dr Fullerton (92835) ***(P-21234)***
St Jude Hospital Yorba Linda ... C ... 714 665-1797
11420 Warner Ave Fountain Valley (92708) ***(P-19448)***
ST JUDE MEDICAL CENTER, Fullerton *Also called St Jude Hospital* ***(P-21232)***
St Jude Medical Ctr Purch Dept, Fullerton *Also called St Jude Hospital* ***(P-21234)***
St Louis Rams, Agoura Hills *Also called Los Angeles Rams LLC* ***(P-18070)***
St Luke Hlthcr & Rehab Ctr LL ... D ... 707 725-4467
2321 Newburg Rd Fortuna (95540) ***(P-20273)***
St Madeleine Sophies Center ... D ... 619 442-5129
2119 E Madison Ave El Cajon (92019) ***(P-23642)***
St Mary Medical Center (HQ) ... A ... 562 491-9000
1050 Linden Ave Long Beach (90813) ***(P-21235)***
St Mary Medical Center (PA) ... A ... 760 242-2311
18300 Us Highway 18 Apple Valley (92307) ***(P-21236)***
ST MARY'S SCHOOL OF NURSING, Long Beach *Also called St Mary Medical Center* ***(P-21235)***
St Marys Med Ctr Foundation ... A ... 415 668-1000
450 Stanyan St San Francisco (94117) ***(P-21237)***
St Michael Convalescent Hosp ... D ... 510 782-8424
25919 Gading Rd Hayward (94544) ***(P-20274)***
St Paul's Towers, Oakland *Also called Covia Communities* ***(P-23885)***
St Paul's Villa, National City *Also called St Pauls Episcopal Home Inc* ***(P-24086)***
St Pauls Episcopal Home Inc ... D ... 619 239-2097
2635 2nd Ave Ofc San Diego (92103) ***(P-24084)***
St Pauls Episcopal Home Inc ... D ... 619 239-8687
235 Nutmeg St San Diego (92103) ***(P-24085)***
St Pauls Episcopal Home Inc ... D ... 619 232-2996
2700 E 4th St National City (91950) ***(P-24086)***
St Regis Resort Monarch Beach, Dana Point *Also called Cph Monarch Hotel LLC* ***(P-12186)***
St Rose Hospital, Hayward *Also called Hayward Sisters Hospital* ***(P-20900)***
St Vincent De Paul, Oakland *Also called District Council DC* ***(P-23195)***
St Vincent De Paul of La, Los Angeles *Also called Society of St Vincent De* ***(P-24871)***
St Vincent De Paul Vlg Inc ... C ... 619 233-8500
28225 Driza Mission Viejo (92692) ***(P-24875)***
ST VINCENT HEALTH CARE, Pasadena *Also called Vincent Hayley Enterprises* ***(P-20717)***
St Vincent Senior Citizn Nutr (PA) ... D ... 213 484-7775
2131 W 3rd St Los Angeles (90057) ***(P-24426)***
St Vncent De Paul Bltmore Inc ... C ... 916 485-3482
3100 Norris Ave Sacramento (95821) ***(P-23485)***
St. Edna Sb-Cute Rhbltion Ctr, Santa Ana *Also called Covenant Care California LLC* ***(P-19841)***
St. Francis Medical Center, Lynwood *Also called Verity Health System Cal Inc* ***(P-21361)***
St. Johns Pleasant Valley Hosp, Camarillo *Also called Dignity Health* ***(P-20850)***
St. Louise Regional Hospital, Gilroy *Also called Verity Health System Cal Inc* ***(P-21359)***
St. Mary's Medical Center, San Francisco *Also called Dignity Health* ***(P-20853)***
STA, Thousand Palms *Also called Sunline Transit Agency* ***(P-3767)***
Stackla Inc ... D ... 415 789-3304
33 New Mont San Francisco (94105) ***(P-15508)***
Stadtner Co Inc ... E ... 415 752-2850
3112 Geary Blvd San Francisco (94118) ***(P-2653)***
Staff Assistance Inc (PA) ... B ... 818 894-7879
72 Moody Ct Ste 100 Thousand Oaks (91360) ***(P-14426)***
Staff Assistance Inc ... B ... 805 371-9980
72 Moody Ct Ste 100 Thousand Oaks (91360) ***(P-14427)***
Staff Pro Inc ... C ... 619 544-1774
675 Convention Way San Diego (92101) ***(P-16454)***
Staff Pro Inc (PA) ... A ... 714 230-7200
1400 N Harbor Blvd # 700 Fullerton (92835) ***(P-16565)***

Employee Codes: A=Over 500 employees, B=251-500
C=101-250, D=51-100, E=50
2020 Directory of California
Wholesalers and Services Companies
© Mergent Inc. 1-800-342-5647
1441

Staff Today Incorporated ....C....800 928-5561
212 E Rowland St 313 Covina (91723) ***(P-14568)***
Staffchex Inc ....A....818 709-6100
20537 Devonshire St Chatsworth (91311) ***(P-14428)***
Staffing Home Care, San Bruno *Also called Staffing Specialists Intl* ***(P-21875)***
Staffing Solutions, Santa Ana *Also called L&T Staffing Inc* ***(P-14320)***
Staffing Solutions Inc ....D....408 980-9000
2142 Bering Dr San Jose (95131) ***(P-14429)***
Staffing Specialists Intl ....E....650 737-0777
2598 Olympic Dr San Bruno (94066) ***(P-21875)***
Stafford-King-Wiese Architects, Sacramento *Also called Coact Designworks* ***(P-25428)***
Staffrehab ....B....888 835-0894
5000 Birch St Newport Beach (92660) ***(P-22131)***
Stage 4 Solutions Incorporated ....E....408 868-9739
19200 Portos Dr Saratoga (95070) ***(P-26828)***
Stage II Design & Production, Corte Madera *Also called Stage II Inc* ***(P-17067)***
Stage II Inc ....E....415 285-8400
21 Channel Dr Corte Madera (94925) ***(P-17067)***
Stage Right Production Svcs, Agoura *Also called Up Stage Inc* ***(P-17700)***
Stagecoach Vineyards ....D....707 255-5459
1345 Hestia Way NAPA (94558) ***(P-164)***
Stagnaro Brothers Seafood Inc ....D....831 423-1188
320 Washington St Santa Cruz (95060) ***(P-8392)***
Stainless Stl Fabricators Inc ....D....714 739-9904
15120 Desman Rd La Mirada (90638) ***(P-7596)***
Stalker Software Inc ....E....415 569-2280
125 Park Pl Ste 210 Richmond (94801) ***(P-15509)***
Stamos Capital Partners LP ....D....650 233-5000
2498 Sand Hill Rd Menlo Park (94025) ***(P-11741)***
Stamoules Produce Co, Mendota *Also called S Stamoules Inc* ***(P-537)***
Stamoules Produce Company, Mendota *Also called S & S Ranch Inc* ***(P-440)***
Stampscom Inc (PA) ....C....310 482-5800
1990 E Grand Ave El Segundo (90245) ***(P-13740)***
Stan Farm, Modesto *Also called Stanislaus Farm Supply Company* ***(P-8859)***
Stan Tashman & Associates Inc ....A....310 460-7600
8675 Wash Blvd Ste 203 Culver City (90232) ***(P-26406)***
Stan Winston Inc ....D....818 782-0870
340 Parkside Dr San Fernando (91340) ***(P-17765)***
Stan Winston Studio, San Fernando *Also called Stan Winston Inc* ***(P-17765)***
Stand 8, Long Beach *Also called Talent & Acquisition LLC* ***(P-15141)***
Stand For Fmlies Free Volence ....D....510 964-7109
3220 Blume Dr San Pablo (94806) ***(P-23486)***
Standard Cattle LLC ....D....559 693-1977
8105a S Lassen Ave San Joaquin (93660) ***(P-600)***
Standard Chartered Bank ....C....626 639-8000
601 S Figueroa St # 2775 Los Angeles (90017) ***(P-9240)***
Standard Drywall Inc (HQ) ....B....619 443-7034
9902 Channel Rd Lakeside (92040) ***(P-2862)***
Standard Hollywood Lessee LLC ....C....323 822-3102
8300 W Sunset Blvd Los Angeles (90069) ***(P-12959)***
Standard Hollywood, The, Los Angeles *Also called Standard Hollywood Lessee LLC* ***(P-12959)***
Standard Hotel, The, Los Angeles *Also called 550 Flower St Operations LLC* ***(P-11985)***
Standard Industries Inc ....E....209 242-5000
3301 Navone Rd Stockton (95215) ***(P-6720)***
Standard Industries Inc ....D....661 387-1110
6505 S Zerker Rd Shafter (93263) ***(P-6721)***
Standard Iron & Metals Co ....E....510 535-0222
4525 San Leandro St Oakland (94601) ***(P-7777)***
Standard Pacific Capital LLC ....E....415 352-7100
101 California St Fl 36 San Francisco (94111) ***(P-9751)***
Standard Pacific Homes, Carlsbad *Also called Calatlantic Group Inc* ***(P-1093)***
Standard Poors Fincl Svcs LLC ....E....415 371-5000
1 California St Fl 31 San Francisco (94111) ***(P-9849)***
Standard The, Los Angeles *Also called Hollywood Standard LLC* ***(P-12377)***
Standard-Southern Corporation ....D....213 624-1831
400 S Central Ave Los Angeles (90013) ***(P-4352)***
Standard-Southern Corporation ....C....213 624-1831
440 S Central Ave Los Angeles (90013) ***(P-4353)***
Standard-Southern Corporation ....D....213 624-1831
715 E 4th St Los Angeles (90013) ***(P-4354)***
Standardbearer Insur Co Ltd ....B....949 487-9500
27101 Puerta Real Ste 450 Mission Viejo (92691) ***(P-20275)***
STANFORD & LATHROP MEMORIAL HO, Sacramento *Also called Stanford Youth Solutions* ***(P-24231)***
Stanford Alumni Association, Stanford *Also called Leland Stanford Junior Univ* ***(P-24582)***
Stanford Cancer Center S Bay, San Jose *Also called Stanford Health Care* ***(P-21239)***
Stanford Court Hotel, San Francisco *Also called Pine & Powell Partners LLC* ***(P-12755)***
Stanford Court Nursing Center, La Mesa *Also called Life Gnerations Healthcare LLC* ***(P-20080)***
Stanford Crt Nrsing Cntr-Sntee, Santee *Also called Life Gnerations Healthcare LLC* ***(P-20614)***
Stanford Federal Credit Union (PA) ....D....650 725-1000
1860 Embarcadero Rd # 200 Palo Alto (94303) ***(P-9355)***
Stanford Health Care ....A....650 723-4000
300 Pasteur Dr Stanford (94305) ***(P-21238)***
Stanford Health Care ....A....408 426-4900
2589 Samaritan Dr San Jose (95124) ***(P-21239)***
Stanford Health Care (HQ) ....A....650 723-4000
300 Pasteur Dr Stanford (94305) ***(P-21240)***
Stanford Health Care ....A....650 736-7844
3375 Hillview Ave Palo Alto (94304) ***(P-21241)***
Stanford Health Care Primary ....D....650 723-6963
211 Quarry Rd Fl 3 Palo Alto (94304) ***(P-19449)***
Stanford Health Services, Palo Alto *Also called Stanford Health Care Primary* ***(P-19449)***
Stanford Hospital and Clinics ....A....650 213-8360
1510 Page Mill Rd Ste 2 Palo Alto (94304) ***(P-21242)***
Stanford Hospitals and Clinics, Palo Alto *Also called Leland Stanford Junior Univ* ***(P-21000)***
Stanford Hotels Corporation ....C....408 330-0001
4949 Great America Pkwy Santa Clara (95054) ***(P-12960)***
Stanford Hotels Corporation (PA) ....E....415 398-3333
433 California St Ste 700 San Francisco (94104) ***(P-12961)***
Stanford Law Schl Off Fncl Aid ....D....650 723-9247
Crown Quadrangle 559 Stanford (94305) ***(P-17068)***
STANFORD LINEAR ACCELERATOR CE, Stanford *Also called Stanford Univ Med Ctr Aux* ***(P-23487)***
Stanford Management Company ....D....650 721-2200
635 Knight Way Stanford (94305) ***(P-26407)***
Stanford Medical Center, Stanford *Also called Stanford Health Care* ***(P-21240)***
Stanford Medical Center, Palo Alto *Also called Leland Stanford Junior Univ* ***(P-21001)***
Stanford Park Hotel ....C....650 322-1234
100 El Camino Real Menlo Park (94025) ***(P-12962)***
Stanford Sierra Camp & Lodge, South Lake Tahoe *Also called Saa Sierra Programs LLC* ***(P-24635)***
Stanford Transportation Inc ....D....661 302-3288
10201 Alondra Dr Bakersfield (93311) ***(P-3939)***
Stanford Univ Earth Secinces, Stanford *Also called Leland Stanford Junior Univ* ***(P-26007)***
Stanford Univ Frman Spgli Inst ....C....650 723-8681
616 Jane Stanford Way Stanford (94305) ***(P-26034)***
Stanford Univ Med Ctr Aux ....B....650 723-6636
300 Pasteur Dr Stanford (94305) ***(P-23487)***
Stanford University, Stanford *Also called Leland Stanford Junior Univ* ***(P-21003)***
Stanford University, Stanford *Also called Leland Stanford Junior Univ* ***(P-21004)***
Stanford University Med Ctr, Palo Alto *Also called Leland Stanford Junior Univ* ***(P-21002)***
Stanford University Medical, Stanford *Also called Leland Stanford Junior Univ* ***(P-21005)***
Stanford Youth Solutions (PA) ....D....916 344-0199
8912 Volunteer Ln Sacramento (95826) ***(P-24231)***
Stanislaus County Police ....C....209 529-9121
1325 Beverly Dr Modesto (95351) ***(P-23488)***
Stanislaus Farm Supply Company (PA) ....D....209 538-7070
624 E Service Rd Modesto (95358) ***(P-8859)***
Stanislaus Medical Center, Modesto *Also called County of Stanislaus* ***(P-20821)***
STANISLAUS SURGICAL CENTER, Modesto *Also called Stanislaus Surgical Hosp LLC* ***(P-21243)***
Stanislaus Surgical Hosp LLC (PA) ....C....209 572-2700
1421 Oakdale Rd Modesto (95355) ***(P-21243)***
Stanisluas County Mental Hlth, Modesto *Also called County of Stanislaus* ***(P-22010)***
Stanley M Kirkpatrick MD ....E....858 966-5855
3020 Childrens Way San Diego (92123) ***(P-19450)***
Stanley Pest Control, South El Monte *Also called Statewide Pest Control Co Inc* ***(P-13828)***
Stanley R Klein MD Facs Inc ....E....310 373-6864
23451 Madison St Ste 300 Torrance (90505) ***(P-19451)***
Stanley Steemer Carpet Cleaner, San Diego *Also called Colt Services Inc* ***(P-13266)***
Stanley Steemer of Los Angles (PA) ....D....626 791-9400
841 W Foothill Blvd Azusa (91702) ***(P-13270)***
Stansbury Hm Preservation Assn ....E....530 895-3848
307 W 5th St Chico (95928) ***(P-24294)***
Stantec Arch & Engrg PC ....C....949 923-6000
38 Technology Dr Ste 100 Irvine (92618) ***(P-25319)***
Stantec Architecture Inc ....C....949 923-6000
38 Technology Dr Irvine (92618) ***(P-25501)***
Stantec Architecture Inc ....D....626 796-9141
300 N Lake Ave Ste 400 Pasadena (91101) ***(P-25502)***
Stantec Architecture Inc ....D....415 882-9500
100 California St # 1000 San Francisco (94111) ***(P-25320)***
Stantec Consulting Svcs Inc ....D....916 773-8100
3875 Atherton Rd Rocklin (95765) ***(P-25503)***
Stantec Consulting Svcs Inc ....C....925 627-4500
1340 Treat Blvd Ste 525 Walnut Creek (94597) ***(P-25321)***
Stantec Consulting Svcs Inc ....D....805 963-9532
111 E Victoria St Santa Barbara (93101) ***(P-25322)***
Stantec Consulting Svcs Inc ....D....626 796-9141
300 N Lake Ave Ste 400 Pasadena (91101) ***(P-25323)***
Stantec Consulting Svcs Inc ....C....949 923-6000
38 Technology Dr Ste 100 Irvine (92618) ***(P-25504)***
Stantec Consulting Svcs Inc ....E....916 924-8844
3301 C St Ste 1900 Sacramento (95816) ***(P-25324)***
Stantec Consulting Svcs Inc ....D....415 882-9500
100 California St # 1000 San Francisco (94111) ***(P-25325)***
Stantec Energy & Resources Inc (HQ) ....C....661 396-3770
5500 Ming Ave Ste 410 Bakersfield (93309) ***(P-25527)***
Stantec Energy & Resources Inc ....C....925 627-4508
1340 Treat Blvd Ste 525 Walnut Creek (94597) ***(P-25528)***
Stantec Holdings Del III Inc ....C....661 396-3770
5500 Ming Ave Ste 300 Bakersfield (93309) ***(P-11695)***
Stantec Oil and Gas, Bakersfield *Also called Stantec Holdings Del III Inc* ***(P-11695)***
Stantru Reinforcing Steel, Fontana *Also called Stantru Resources Inc* ***(P-1380)***
Stantru Resources Inc ....D....909 587-1441
11175 Redwood Ave Fontana (92337) ***(P-1380)***
Stapleton - Spence Packing Co (PA) ....D....408 297-8815
1900 State Highway 99 Gridley (95948) ***(P-8646)***
Star & Crescent Boat Company (PA) ....E....619 234-4111
1311 1st St Coronado (92118) ***(P-4608)***
Star - Lite Electric, Chatsworth *Also called Mj Star-Lite Inc* ***(P-2555)***
Star Brite Building Maint ....B....562 988-2829
2688 Dawson Ave Long Beach (90755) ***(P-14057)***
Star Fabrics Inc (PA) ....D....213 688-2871
1440 Walnut St Los Angeles (90011) ***(P-8013)***
Star Fisheries ....D....310 549-4992
841 Watson Ave Wilmington (90744) ***(P-8393)***
Star Fisheries (PA) ....D....310 832-8395
222 W 6th St Ste 500 San Pedro (90731) ***(P-8394)***

Mergent e-mail: customerrelations@mergent.com
1442
2020 Directory of California
Wholesalers and Services Companies
(P-0000) Products & Services Section entry number
(PA)=Parent Co (HQ)=Headquarters (DH)=Div Headquarters

Star H-R....A....707 265-9911
1822 Jefferson St NAPA (94559) ***(P-14430)***
Star H-R....A....707 894-4404
105 E 1st St Cloverdale (95425) ***(P-14431)***
Star H-R (PA)....D....707 762-4447
3820 Cypress Dr Ste 2 Petaluma (94954) ***(P-14569)***
Star Laundry Services Inc....D....619 572-1009
3410 Main St San Diego (92113) ***(P-13325)***
Star Lax LLC....C....310 642-4500
150 S Doheny Dr Beverly Hills (90211) ***(P-17223)***
Star Nail International, Valencia *Also called Star Nail Products Inc* ***(P-7984)***
Star Nail Products Inc....D....661 257-3376
29120 Avenue Paine Valencia (91355) ***(P-7984)***
Star of California....D....805 379-1401
299 W Hillcrest Dr Thousand Oaks (91360) ***(P-22327)***
Star of California....C....805 466-1638
8834 Morro Rd Atascadero (93422) ***(P-22328)***
Star of California (PA)....C....805 644-7823
4880 Market St Ventura (93003) ***(P-22329)***
Star One Credit Union (PA)....C....408 543-5202
1306 Bordeaux Dr Sunnyvale (94089) ***(P-9356)***
Star Protection Agency CA, Oakland *Also called Star Protection Agency LLC* ***(P-16455)***
Star Protection Agency LLC....C....510 635-1732
8201 Edgewater Dr Ste 102 Oakland (94621) ***(P-16455)***
Star Real Estate South County....C....949 389-0004
26711 Aliso Creek Rd 200a Aliso Viejo (92656) ***(P-11465)***
Star Scrap Metal Company Inc....D....562 921-5045
1509 S Bluff Rd Montebello (90640) ***(P-6287)***
Star Services, San Diego *Also called Star Laundry Services Inc* ***(P-13325)***
Star Staffing, Petaluma *Also called Star H-R* ***(P-14569)***
Star View Adolescent Center....D....310 373-4556
4025 W 226th St Torrance (90505) ***(P-21427)***
Star View Chldrn Fmly Srvcs....D....310 868-5379
1085 W Victoria St Compton (90220) ***(P-23489)***
Starcity Properties Inc....D....415 918-2224
1020 Kearny St San Francisco (94133) ***(P-10659)***
Stargate Digital, South Pasadena *Also called Stargate Films Inc* ***(P-17677)***
Stargate Films Inc....D....626 403-8403
1001 El Centro St South Pasadena (91030) ***(P-17677)***
Stark Services....D....818 985-2003
12444 Victory Blvd # 300 North Hollywood (91606) ***(P-15817)***
Starlight Corporation (PA)....C....858 509-9006
2100 Palomar Airpt Rd # 2 Carlsbad (92011) ***(P-3609)***
Starlight Educational Center, Westminster *Also called Westview Services Inc* ***(P-23656)***
Starlight International Ltd LP....D....562 439-5740
38 Saint Joseph Ave Long Beach (90803) ***(P-7985)***
Starlight Management Group....D....408 334-7456
1355 N 4th St San Jose (95112) ***(P-12963)***
Starline Tours Hollywood Inc....D....323 262-1114
2130 S Tubeway Ave Commerce (90040) ***(P-4866)***
Starline Tours Hollywood Inc (PA)....D....323 463-3333
6801 Hollywood Blvd # 221 Los Angeles (90028) ***(P-4867)***
Starpoint Property MGT LLC....C....310 247-0550
450 N Roxbury Dr Ste 1050 Beverly Hills (90210) ***(P-11466)***
Starpoint Surgery Center, Irvine *Also called Sph-Irvine LLC* ***(P-19442)***
Stars, San Leandro *Also called Subacute Trtmnt Adolescnt Reha* ***(P-22133)***
Stars Recreation Center LP....E....707 455-7827
155 Browns Valley Pkwy Vacaville (95688) ***(P-18043)***
Startel Corporation (PA)....D....949 863-8700
16 Goodyear B-125 Irvine (92618) ***(P-15122)***
Startup Farms Intl LLC....B....510 440-0110
45690 Northport Loop E Fremont (94538) ***(P-15123)***
Starvista....C....650 591-9623
610 Elm St Ste 212 San Carlos (94070) ***(P-23490)***
Starwest Botanicals Inc (PA)....D....916 638-8100
161 Main Ave Sacramento (95838) ***(P-8647)***
Starwood Hotel....D....310 641-7740
5990 Green Valley Cir Culver City (90230) ***(P-12964)***
Starwood Hotels & Resorts, Costa Mesa *Also called South Coast Westin Hotel Co* ***(P-12947)***
Starwood Hotels & Resorts, Culver City *Also called Starwood Hotel* ***(P-12964)***
Starwood Hotels & Resorts....C....909 484-2018
10480 4th St Rancho Cucamonga (91730) ***(P-12965)***
Starwood Hotels & Resorts....D....650 692-6363
401 E Millbrae Ave Millbrae (94030) ***(P-12966)***
Starwood Hotels & Resorts....C....415 284-4000
125 3rd St San Francisco (94103) ***(P-12967)***
Starwood Hotels & Resorts....C....619 239-2200
910 Broadway Cir San Diego (92101) ***(P-12968)***
Starwood Htls & Rsrts Wrldwde....B....415 397-7000
335 Powell St San Francisco (94102) ***(P-12969)***
Starwood Htls & Rsrts Wrldwde....C....310 208-8765
930 Hilgard Ave Los Angeles (90024) ***(P-12970)***
Starwood Htls & Rsrts Wrldwde....D....415 777-5300
181 3rd St San Francisco (94103) ***(P-12971)***
Starwood Htls & Rsrts Wrldwde....A....213 624-1000
404 S Figueroa St Los Angeles (90071) ***(P-12972)***
Starwood Htls & Rsrts Wrldwde....C....415 479-8800
1010 Northgate Dr San Rafael (94903) ***(P-12973)***
Starwood Htls & Rsrts Wrldwde....B....760 328-5955
71333 Dinah Shore Dr Rancho Mirage (92270) ***(P-12974)***
Starwood Htls & Rsrts Wrldwde....C....415 512-1111
2 New Montgomery St San Francisco (94105) ***(P-12975)***
Starwood Htls & Rsrts Wrldwde....C....323 798-1300
6250 Hollywood Blvd Los Angeles (90028) ***(P-12976)***
Starwood Htls & Rsrts Wrldwde....C....909 622-2220
601 W Mckinley Ave Pomona (91768) ***(P-12977)***
Starwood Htls & Rsrts Wrldwde....D....619 239-9600
1617 1st Ave San Diego (92101) ***(P-12978)***

Starzz Management Services (PA)....D....510 632-5533
528 Stonehaven Ct Hayward (94544) ***(P-26408)***
Stat Registry Service, Long Beach *Also called Code America Inc* ***(P-14249)***
State Bar of California (PA)....B....415 538-2000
180 Howard St Fl Grnd San Francisco (94105) ***(P-24427)***
State Compensation Insur Fund (PA)....D....888 782-8338
333 Bush St Fl 8 San Francisco (94104) ***(P-10129)***
State Compensation Insur Fund....B....714 565-5000
1750 E 4th St Fl 3 Santa Ana (92705) ***(P-10130)***
State Compensation Insur Fund....C....661 664-4000
9801 Camino Media Ste 101 Bakersfield (93311) ***(P-10131)***
State Compensation Insur Fund....C....510 577-3000
2955 Peralta Oaks Ct Oakland (94605) ***(P-10132)***
State Compensation Insur Fund....C....888 782-8338
333 W San Carlos St # 950 San Jose (95110) ***(P-10133)***
State Compensation Insur Fund....C....888 782-8338
364 Knollcrest Dr Redding (96002) ***(P-10134)***
State Compensation Insur Fund....B....888 782-8338
10105 Pacific Hgts Blvd San Diego (92121) ***(P-10135)***
State Compensation Insur Fund....B....559 433-2700
10 E Rver Pk Pl E Ste 110 Fresno (93720) ***(P-10136)***
State Compensation Insur Fund....C....213 576-7335
655 N Central Ave Ste 200 Glendale (91203) ***(P-10137)***
State Compensation Insur Fund....C....323 266-5551
655 N Central Ave Ste 200 Glendale (91203) ***(P-10138)***
State Compensation Insur Fund....C....888 782-8338
3247 W March Ln Ste 110 Stockton (95219) ***(P-10139)***
State Compensation Insur Fund....C....888 782-8338
655 N Central Ave Ste 200 Glendale (91203) ***(P-10140)***
State Compensation Insur Fund....B....916 924-5100
2275 Gateway Oaks Dr Sacramento (95833) ***(P-10141)***
State Compensation Insur Fund....D....707 443-9721
800 W Harris St Ste 37 Eureka (95503) ***(P-10142)***
State Compensation Insur Fund....C....888 782-8338
6301 Day St Riverside (92507) ***(P-10143)***
State Compensation Insur Fund....B....888 782-8338
2901 N Ventura Rd Ste 100 Oxnard (93036) ***(P-9914)***
State Compensation Insur Fund....C....925 523-5000
5880 Owens Dr Pleasanton (94588) ***(P-10144)***
State Compensation Insur Fund....C....888 782-8338
5890 Owens Dr Pleasanton (94588) ***(P-10145)***
State Compensation Insur Fund....C....323 266-5000
900 Corporate Center Dr Monterey Park (91754) ***(P-10146)***
State Farm Fire and Cslty Co....D....559 625-4330
5127 W Walnut Ave Visalia (93277) ***(P-10498)***
State Farm Fire and Cslty Co....B....707 588-6011
6400 State Farm Dr Rohnert Park (94928) ***(P-10499)***
State Farm Insurance, Los Angeles *Also called State Farm Mutl Auto Insur Co* ***(P-10500)***
State Farm Insurance, Encino *Also called State Farm Mutl Auto Insur Co* ***(P-10501)***
State Farm Insurance, Visalia *Also called State Farm Fire and Cslty Co* ***(P-10498)***
State Farm Insurance, Agoura Hills *Also called State Farm Mutl Auto Insur Co* ***(P-10502)***
State Farm Insurance, Pinole *Also called State Farm Mutl Auto Insur Co* ***(P-10503)***
State Farm Insurance, Long Beach *Also called State Farm Mutl Auto Insur Co* ***(P-10504)***
State Farm Insurance, Fontana *Also called State Farm Mutl Auto Insur Co* ***(P-10505)***
State Farm Insurance, Bakersfield *Also called State Farm Mutl Auto Insur Co* ***(P-10506)***
State Farm Insurance, San Mateo *Also called State Farm Mutl Auto Insur Co* ***(P-10507)***
State Farm Insurance, Bakersfield *Also called State Farm Mutl Auto Insur Co* ***(P-10508)***
State Farm Insurance, Oakhurst *Also called State Farm Mutl Auto Insur Co* ***(P-10509)***
State Farm Insurance, Woodland Hills *Also called State Farm Mutl Auto Insur Co* ***(P-10510)***
State Farm Insurance, Pacific Palisades *Also called State Farm Mutl Auto Insur Co* ***(P-10511)***
State Farm Insurance, Los Angeles *Also called State Farm Mutl Auto Insur Co* ***(P-10512)***
State Farm Insurance, Bakersfield *Also called State Farm Mutl Auto Insur Co* ***(P-10513)***
State Farm Insurance, Rohnert Park *Also called State Farm Fire and Cslty Co* ***(P-10499)***
State Farm Mutl Auto Insur Co....B....309 766-2311
12122 S Halldale Ave # 200 Los Angeles (90047) ***(P-10500)***
State Farm Mutl Auto Insur Co....D....818 849-5126
16656 Ventura Blvd # 203 Encino (91436) ***(P-10501)***
State Farm Mutl Auto Insur Co....D....818 597-4300
30125 Agoura Rd Ste 200 Agoura Hills (91301) ***(P-10502)***
State Farm Mutl Auto Insur Co....D....510 222-1102
1558 Fitzgerald Dr Pinole (94564) ***(P-10503)***
State Farm Mutl Auto Insur Co....D....310 632-9810
1705 E 10th St Apt 201 Long Beach (90813) ***(P-10504)***
State Farm Mutl Auto Insur Co....D....909 349-2050
17122 Slover Ave Ste 106 Fontana (92337) ***(P-10505)***
State Farm Mutl Auto Insur Co....D....661 324-4077
2019 24th St Bakersfield (93301) ***(P-10506)***
State Farm Mutl Auto Insur Co....D....650 345-3571
2555 Flores St Ste 175 San Mateo (94403) ***(P-10507)***
State Farm Mutl Auto Insur Co....D....309 766-2311
900 Old River Rd 400 Bakersfield (93311) ***(P-10508)***
State Farm Mutl Auto Insur Co....D....559 683-3467
40315 Junction Dr Ste A Oakhurst (93644) ***(P-10509)***
State Farm Mutl Auto Insur Co....D....818 887-1060
5345 Fallbrook Ave Woodland Hills (91367) ***(P-10510)***
State Farm Mutl Auto Insur Co....D....310 454-0349
845 Via De La Paz Ste 12 Pacific Palisades (90272) ***(P-10511)***
State Farm Mutl Auto Insur Co....D....323 852-6868
8040 W 3rd St Los Angeles (90048) ***(P-10512)***
State Farm Mutl Auto Insur Co....D....661 664-9663
4600 Ashe Rd Ste 308 Bakersfield (93313) ***(P-10513)***
STATE FUND, San Francisco *Also called State Compensation Insur Fund* ***(P-10129)***
State Fund Office, Glendale *Also called State Compensation Insur Fund* ***(P-10137)***
State Group LLC....B....949 612-2879
77 Turnstone Irvine (92618) ***(P-26829)***
State Pipe & Supply Inc (HQ)....D....909 877-9999
183 S Cedar Ave Rialto (92376) ***(P-7106)***

ALPHABETIC

Employee Codes: A=Over 500 employees, B=251-500
C=101-250, D=51-100, E=50
2020 Directory of California
Wholesalers and Services Companies
© Mergent Inc. 1-800-342-5647
1443

State Preschool, Alhambra *Also called Options For Learning* ***(P-23763)***
State Preschool......E......925 473-4380
950 El Pueblo Ave Pittsburg (94565) ***(P-23791)***
State Roofing Systems Inc......D......510 317-1477
15444 Hesperian Blvd San Leandro (94578) ***(P-3099)***
States Drawer Box Spc LLC......D......714 744-4247
1482 N Batavia St Orange (92867) ***(P-6659)***
States Logistics Services Inc......D......714 523-1276
7221 Cate Dr Buena Park (90621) ***(P-5056)***
States Logistics Services Inc......C......714 523-1276
7151 Cate Dr Buena Park (90621) ***(P-4507)***
States Logistics Services Inc (PA)......C......714 521-6520
5650 Dolly Ave Buena Park (90621) ***(P-4508)***
Statewide, Sacramento *Also called Domus Construction & Design* ***(P-1117)***
Statewide Cnstr Sweeping Inc......E......510 683-9584
45945 Warm Springs Blvd Fremont (94539) ***(P-6357)***
Statewide Pest Control Co Inc (PA)......C......626 443-2847
2555 Loma Ave South El Monte (91733) ***(P-13828)***
Station Venture Operations LP......D......619 231-3939
9680 Granite Ridge Dr San Diego (92123) ***(P-5648)***
Stations, San Jose *Also called Andrian Inc* ***(P-3376)***
Status Medical Management, Modesto *Also called Pegasus Risk Management Inc* ***(P-10452)***
Stavatti Industries Ltd......D......651 238-5369
1443 S Gage St San Bernardino (92408) ***(P-971)***
Staybridge Suites, San Diego *Also called Six Continents Hotels Inc* ***(P-12938)***
Staybridge Suites, Sunnyvale *Also called Hpt Trs Ihg-2 Inc* ***(P-12421)***
STC Netcom Inc (PA)......D......951 685-8181
11611 Industry Ave Fontana (92337) ***(P-2654)***
Steadfast Management Co Inc......C......714 542-2229
15520 Tustin Village Way Tustin (92780) ***(P-10819)***
Steel House Inc......C......310 773-3331
3644 Eastham Dr Culver City (90232) ***(P-13581)***
Steelcase Inc......B......619 671-1040
7510 Airway Rd Ste 7 San Diego (92154) ***(P-6531)***
Steele Canyon Golf Club Corp (PA)......D......619 441-6900
3199 Stonefield Dr Jamul (91935) ***(P-18301)***
Steele Cis LLC......B......415 692-5000
1 Sansome St Ste 3500 San Francisco (94104) ***(P-22833)***
Steele Corp SEC Advisory Svcs, San Francisco *Also called Firstcall* ***(P-16273)***
Steelpoint Capital Partners LP......D......858 764-8700
2081 Faraday Ave Carlsbad (92008) ***(P-11956)***
Steelriver Infrastructure Fund (HQ)......C......415 291-2200
1 Letterman Dr Bldg C San Francisco (94129) ***(P-5991)***
Steeltech Construction Svcs......D......714 630-2890
4081 E La Palma Ave Ste G Anaheim (92807) ***(P-1381)***
Steelwave Inc (PA)......C......650 571-2200
999 Baker Way Ste 200 San Mateo (94404) ***(P-11605)***
Steelwave Inc......C......949 863-0390
3335 Susan St Ste 100 Costa Mesa (92626) ***(P-11606)***
Steelwave LLC......A......650 571-2200
999 Baker Way Ste 200 San Mateo (94404) ***(P-11607)***
Stefan Merli Plastering Co Inc (PA)......D......310 323-0404
1230 W 130th St Gardena (90247) ***(P-3222)***
Steger Inc......E......714 974-4383
1938 N Batavia St Ste L Orange (92865) ***(P-2396)***
Stein & Lubin LLP......E......415 981-0550
600 Montgomery St Fl 14 San Francisco (94111) ***(P-22834)***
Steinberg Architects, San Jose *Also called Steinberg Hart* ***(P-25505)***
Steinberg Hart (PA)......D......408 295-5446
125 S Market St Ste 110 San Jose (95113) ***(P-25505)***
Steiny and Company Inc (PA)......D......213 382-2331
221 N Ardmore Ave Los Angeles (90004) ***(P-2655)***
Stella Technology Incorporated......D......402 350-1681
6203 San Ignacio Ave # 100 San Jose (95119) ***(P-16121)***
Stellar Distributing Inc......B......559 664-8400
21801 Ave Ste 16 Madera (93637) ***(P-8525)***
Stellar Microelectronics Inc......C......661 775-3500
9340 Owensmouth Ave Chatsworth (91311) ***(P-7345)***
Stellartech Research Corp (PA)......D......408 331-3134
560 Cottonwood Dr Milpitas (95035) ***(P-25838)***
Step, Sacramento *Also called Stratgies To Empwer People Inc* ***(P-20460)***
Step House Recovery, Fountain Valley *Also called Stephouse Recovery Center* ***(P-23491)***
Step Up On Second Street Inc (PA)......D......310 394-6889
1328 2nd St Ofc Santa Monica (90401) ***(P-21876)***
Stephen B Meisel MD PC......E......310 828-8843
2811 Wilshire Blvd # 900 Santa Monica (90403) ***(P-19452)***
Stephen B Meisel MD A Med Corp (HQ)......D......310 828-8843
2811 Wilshire Blvd # 900 Santa Monica (90403) ***(P-19453)***
Stephouse Recovery Center......D......714 394-3494
10529 Slater Ave Fountain Valley (92708) ***(P-23491)***
Stepping Stn Grwth Ctr Fr Chld......D......510 568-3331
311 Macarthur Blvd San Leandro (94577) ***(P-23643)***
Steptoe & Johnson LLP......E......213 439-9400
633 W 5th St Fl 7 Los Angeles (90071) ***(P-22835)***
Steren Electronics Intl LLC (PA)......D......800 266-3333
6910 Carroll Rd Ste 200 San Diego (92121) ***(P-7346)***
Stereo D LLC......B......818 861-3100
3355 W Empire Ave Fl 1 Burbank (91504) ***(P-17766)***
Stereod, Burbank *Also called Stereo D LLC* ***(P-17766)***
Stericycle Comm Solutions Inc......D......888 370-6711
2255 Watt Ave Ste 50 Sacramento (95825) ***(P-17069)***
Stericycle Comm Solutions Inc......E......714 991-9595
612 S Harbor Blvd Anaheim (92805) ***(P-17070)***
Stericycles Envmtl Solutions, Rancho Cordova *Also called General Environmental* ***(P-16796)***
Sterling Asset Management, Fairfield *Also called Community Housing Opport* ***(P-26188)***
Sterling Brand, San Francisco *Also called Sterling Consulting Group LLC* ***(P-26830)***
Sterling Building Services, Anaheim *Also called Danlil Enterprise Inc* ***(P-13912)***
Sterling Collision Center LLC (PA)......D......714 259-1111
1111 Bell Ave Ste A Tustin (92780) ***(P-17312)***
Sterling Consulting Group LLC......D......415 248-7900
55 Union St Fl 3 San Francisco (94111) ***(P-26830)***
Sterling Court, San Mateo *Also called Fifty Peninsula Partners* ***(P-10727)***
Sterling Dry Cleaners, Los Angeles *Also called Sterling Westwood Inc* ***(P-13260)***
Sterling Hsa Inc......E......800 617-4729
475 14th St Ste 120 Oakland (94612) ***(P-17071)***
Sterling Inn, Victorville *Also called Sterling-Ase Ltd Partnership* ***(P-10820)***
Sterling Mktg & Fincl Corp......E......209 593-1140
4660 Spyres Way Ste 1 Modesto (95356) ***(P-26831)***
Sterling Pacific Meat Company, Commerce *Also called Interstate Meat & Provision* ***(P-8287)***
Sterling Plumbing Inc......D......714 641-5480
3111 W Central Ave Santa Ana (92704) ***(P-2288)***
Sterling Senior Communities, Temecula *Also called MBK Senior Living LLC* ***(P-20631)***
Sterling Westwood Inc......D......310 287-2431
3405 Overland Ave Los Angeles (90034) ***(P-13260)***
Sterling-Ase Ltd Partnership......C......760 951-9507
17738 Francesca Rd Victorville (92395) ***(P-10820)***
Steuber Corporation (PA)......D......310 632-8255
20425 S Susana Rd Long Beach (90810) ***(P-6932)***
Steve and Beth Chaput......E......909 596-9994
1025 Sentinel Dr Ste 103 La Verne (91750) ***(P-14058)***
Steve Beattie Inc......D......310 454-1786
1766 Westridge Rd Los Angeles (90049) ***(P-2397)***
Steve Beattie Painting, Los Angeles *Also called Steve Beattie Inc* ***(P-2397)***
Steve Duich Inc......E......619 444-6118
1369 N Magnolia Ave El Cajon (92020) ***(P-3223)***
Steve Manning Construction Inc......D......530 222-0810
5211 Churn Creek Rd Redding (96002) ***(P-1792)***
Steve Roberson......D......562 927-2626
7825 Florence Ave Downey (90240) ***(P-11467)***
Steve Silver Productions Inc......D......415 421-4284
678 Green St Ste 2 San Francisco (94133) ***(P-17948)***
Steven Engineering Inc......C......650 588-9200
230 Ryan Way South San Francisco (94080) ***(P-7188)***
Steven G Fogg MD......D......559 449-5010
1360 E Herndon Ave # 401 Fresno (93720) ***(P-19454)***
Steven Global Freight Services, Redondo Beach *Also called Stevens Global Logistics Inc* ***(P-5057)***
Steven N Ledson......D......707 537-3810
7335 Sonoma Hwy Santa Rosa (95409) ***(P-1200)***
Steven P Abelow MD......D......530 544-8033
2311 Lake Tahoe Blvd South Lake Tahoe (96150) ***(P-19455)***
Steven Rubinstein MD, Sunnyvale *Also called Palo Alto Medical Foundation* ***(P-19263)***
Steven Snyder, Hollister *Also called Hollister Process Service* ***(P-16831)***
Stevens Creek Quarry Inc (PA)......D......408 253-2512
12100 Stevens Canyon Rd Cupertino (95014) ***(P-1793)***
Stevens Global Logistics Inc (PA)......D......310 216-5645
3700 Redondo Beach Ave Redondo Beach (90278) ***(P-5057)***
Stewardship Company LLC......C......831 620-6700
1 Rancho San Carlos Rd Carmel (93923) ***(P-26409)***
Stewart Enterprises Inc......E......858 453-2121
5600 Carroll Canyon Rd San Diego (92121) ***(P-13380)***
Stewart Title California Inc (HQ)......C......619 692-1600
7676 Hazard Center Dr # 1400 San Diego (92108) ***(P-10201)***
Stewart Title California Inc......C......818 502-2700
525 N Brand Blvd Ste 200 Glendale (91203) ***(P-10202)***
Stila Styles, Jurupa Valley *Also called Geodis Logistics LLC* ***(P-4420)***
Stjohn God Rtirement Care Ctr......C......323 731-0641
2468 S St Andrews Pl Los Angeles (90018) ***(P-20276)***
Stk International Inc......D......310 720-1277
6160 Peach Tree St Compton (90220) ***(P-7743)***
Stmicroelectronics Inc......C......408 452-8585
2755 Great America Way Santa Clara (95054) ***(P-7347)***
Stockbridge/Sbe Holdings LLC......A......323 655-8000
5900 Wilshire Blvd # 3100 Los Angeles (90036) ***(P-12979)***
Stockcross Financial Svcs Inc (HQ)......E......800 993-2015
9464 Wilshire Blvd Beverly Hills (90212) ***(P-9752)***
Stockdale Country Club......D......661 832-0310
7001 Stockdale Hwy Bakersfield (93309) ***(P-18587)***
Stockdale Medical Offices, Bakersfield *Also called Kaiser Foundation Hospitals* ***(P-20954)***
Stocker & Allaire Inc......E......831 375-1890
21 Mandeville Ct Monterey (93940) ***(P-1201)***
Stockham Construction Inc......B......707 664-0945
475 Portal St Cotati (94931) ***(P-2984)***
Stockmar Industrial, Long Beach *Also called Elite Craftsman* ***(P-13917)***
Stockton Cardiology Medical Gr......D......209 824-1555
1148 Norman Dr Ste 3 Manteca (95336) ***(P-19456)***
Stockton Cardiology Medical Gr (PA)......E......209 994-5750
415 E Harding Way Ste D Stockton (95204) ***(P-19457)***
Stockton Congregational Home......D......209 466-4341
1319 N Madison St Ofc Stockton (95202) ***(P-24087)***
Stockton District Office, Stockton *Also called State Compensation Insur Fund* ***(P-10139)***
Stockton Edson Healthcare Corp......D......209 948-8762
1630 N Edison St Stockton (95204) ***(P-20695)***
Stockton Hilton Hotel, Stockton *Also called Stockton Hotel Ltd* ***(P-12980)***
Stockton Hotel Ltd......C......209 957-9090
2323 Grand Canal Blvd Stockton (95207) ***(P-12980)***
Stockton Orthpd Med Group Inc......E......209 948-1641
2545 W Hammer Ln Stockton (95209) ***(P-19458)***
Stockton Port District......D......209 946-0246
2201 W Washington St # 13 Stockton (95203) ***(P-4625)***
Stockton Scavengers Assn, Stockton *Also called USA Waste of California Inc* ***(P-3949)***
STOLLWOOD CONVALESCENT HOSPITA, Woodland *Also called St Johns Retirement Village* ***(P-20694)***
Stommel Inc (PA)......E......916 646-6626
4707 Northgate Blvd Sacramento (95834) ***(P-2656)***

Mergent e-mail: customerrelations@mergent.com
1444
2020 Directory of California
Wholesalers and Services Companies
(P-0000) Products & Services Section entry number
(PA)=Parent Co (HQ)=Headquarters (DH)=Div Headquarters

Stomper Co Inc D 510 574-0570
3135 Diablo Ave Hayward (94545) ***(P-3353)***
Stone & Youngberg LLC (PA) C 415 445-2300
1 Ferry Plz San Francisco (94111) ***(P-9753)***
Stone Blue Inc D 323 277-0008
2501 E 28th St Vernon (90058) ***(P-13312)***
Stone Entertainment, Costa Mesa *Also called Volcom LLC* ***(P-17155)***
Stone Land Company (PA) C 559 947-3185
28521 Nevada Ave Stratford (93266) ***(P-16)***
Stone Ranch, Stratford *Also called Stone Land Company* ***(P-16)***
Stonebrae LP D 510 728-7878
222 Country Club Dr Hayward (94542) ***(P-18588)***
Stonebridge McWhinney LLC E 714 703-8800
11747 Harbor Blvd Garden Grove (92840) ***(P-12981)***
Stonebrook Convalescent Center C 925 689-7457
4367 Concord Blvd Concord (94521) ***(P-20277)***
Stonebrook Health Care Center, Concord *Also called Stonebrook Convalescent Center* ***(P-20277)***
Stoneland, North Hollywood *Also called Arriaga Usa Inc* ***(P-6670)***
Stoneridge Creek Pleasanton, Pleasanton *Also called Conti Life Comm Plea LLC* ***(P-16716)***
Stoneriver Inc B 714 705-8227
770 The Cy Dr S Ste 5000 Orange (92868) ***(P-15124)***
Stonesfair Financial Corp D 650 347-0442
577 Airport Blvd Ste 700 Burlingame (94010) ***(P-10821)***
Stonesfair Management LLC (PA) D 650 401-3810
577 Airport Blvd Ste 700 Burlingame (94010) ***(P-11468)***
Stonetree Golf LLC E 415 209-6744
9 Stonetree Ln Novato (94945) ***(P-18302)***
Stonetree Management, Novato *Also called Stonetree Golf LLC* ***(P-18302)***
Stonewood Ctr Mall Office, Downey *Also called Macerich Company* ***(P-10617)***
Stop Hop Center, Carson *Also called Anschutz So Calif Sports Compl* ***(P-18050)***
Storage West, Los Angeles *Also called Laaco Ltd* ***(P-10876)***
Store & Online, City of Industry *Also called Solestage Inc* ***(P-15694)***
Store 17, Moorpark *Also called Prudential Overall Supply* ***(P-13238)***
Storer Transportation Service (PA) B 209 521-8250
3519 Mcdonald Ave Modesto (95358) ***(P-3771)***
Storer Travel Service, Modesto *Also called Storer Transportation Service* ***(P-3771)***
Stormgeo (HQ) C 408 731-8600
140 Kifer Ct Sunnyvale (94086) ***(P-27306)***
Storquest Self Storage (HQ) D 310 451-2130
201 Wilshire Blvd Ste 102 Santa Monica (90401) ***(P-4509)***
Story Teller, Universal City *Also called Amblin/Reliance Holding Co LLC* ***(P-17572)***
Stradling Yocca Carlson & Raut (PA) C 949 725-4000
660 Newport Center Dr # 1600 Newport Beach (92660) ***(P-22836)***
Stradling Yocca Carlson & Raut C 916 449-2350
500 Capitol Mall Sacramento (95814) ***(P-22837)***
Straight Edge, Windsor *Also called Robert A Hall* ***(P-14559)***
Straight Lander Inc D 323 337-9075
8335 W Sunset Blvd # 320 Los Angeles (90069) ***(P-26410)***
Straight Line Roofing & Cnstr E 530 672-9995
3811 Dividend Dr Ste A Shingle Springs (95682) ***(P-3100)***
Strands Finance, San Mateo *Also called Strands Labs Inc* ***(P-15126)***
Strands Inc A Delaware Corp E 541 753-4426
999 Baker Way Ste 430 San Mateo (94404) ***(P-15125)***
Strands Labs Inc E 415 398-4333
999 Baker Way Ste 430 San Mateo (94404) ***(P-15126)***
Strata Information Group Inc D 619 296-0170
3935 Harney St Ste 203 San Diego (92110) ***(P-16122)***
Stratacare Llc C 949 743-1200
17838 Gillette Ave Ste D Irvine (92614) ***(P-15127)***
Strategic Bus Insights Inc (PA) D 650 859-4600
333 Ravenswood Ave Menlo Park (94025) ***(P-26832)***
Strategic Financial Group E 949 622-7200
18191 Von Karman Ave # 100 Irvine (92612) ***(P-10514)***
Strategic Insights Inc D 858 452-7500
9191 Towne Centre Dr # 401 San Diego (92122) ***(P-15510)***
Strategic Materials Inc D 323 887-6831
7000 Bandini Blvd Commerce (90040) ***(P-6288)***
Strategic Mechanical Inc C 559 291-1952
4661 E Commerce Ave Fresno (93725) ***(P-2289)***
Strategic Operations Inc C 858 244-0559
4705 Ruffin Rd San Diego (92123) ***(P-17072)***
Strategic Property Management D 619 295-2211
2055 3rd Ave Ste 200 San Diego (92101) ***(P-11469)***
Strategic Secuirty Services, Fremont *Also called Strategic Security Services* ***(P-16456)***
Strategic Security Services C 510 623-2355
48521 Warm Springs Blvd # 302 Fremont (94539) ***(P-16456)***
Strategic Staffing Svcs Inc B 818 248-0049
35 N Lake Ave Ste 140 Pasadena (91101) ***(P-26833)***
Strategies For Change (PA) D 916 395-3552
4343 Williamsbourgh Dr Sacramento (95823) ***(P-22132)***
Strategy Companion Corp D 714 460-8398
3240 El Camino Real # 120 Irvine (92602) ***(P-15511)***
Stratford, San Mateo *Also called Raiser Senior Services LLC* ***(P-24037)***
Stratford School Inc D 408 371-3020
220 Kensington Way Los Gatos (95032) ***(P-23792)***
Stratford School Inc (PA) E 650 493-1151
870 N California Ave Palo Alto (94303) ***(P-23793)***
Stratgies To Empwer People Inc (PA) D 916 679-1527
2330 Glendale Ln Sacramento (95825) ***(P-20460)***
Stratham Homes Inc D 949 833-1554
2201 Dupont Dr Ste 300 Irvine (92612) ***(P-1274)***
Straub - Brutoco A Joint Ventr C 760 414-9000
202 W College St Ste 201 Fallbrook (92028) ***(P-1317)***
Straub Distributing Co Ltd (PA) C 714 779-4000
4633 E La Palma Ave Anaheim (92807) ***(P-8792)***
Strawberry Farms Golf Club, Irvine *Also called Sand Canyon LLC* ***(P-18293)***
Strawberry Farms Golf Club LLC D 949 551-2560
11 Strawberry Farm Rd Irvine (92612) ***(P-18303)***
Streamline Construction, Grass Valley *Also called JM Streamline Inc* ***(P-1512)***
Streamline Finishes Inc D 949 600-8964
26429 Rancho Pkwy S # 140 Lake Forest (92630) ***(P-1609)***
Streamray Inc B 408 745-5449
910 E Hamilton Ave Fl 6 Campbell (95008) ***(P-18011)***
Streamvector Inc C 415 870-8395
4701 Patrick Henry Dr # 2 Santa Clara (95054) ***(P-15128)***
Strech Plastics Incorporated E 951 922-2224
900 John St Ste J Banning (92220) ***(P-7700)***
Street and Sewer Yard Corp E 650 696-7260
1361 N Carolan Ave Burlingame (94010) ***(P-6139)***
Street Maintenance Department, Encinitas *Also called City of Encinitas* ***(P-1681)***
Street Sidewalks St Tree Maint, Chino *Also called City of Chino* ***(P-6340)***
Streets Street Tree Inquiries, Oxnard *Also called City of Oxnard* ***(P-18325)***
Stress Relief Services D 760 241-7472
12603 Mariposa Rd Victorville (92395) ***(P-12982)***
Stretto (PA) D 949 222-1212
5 Peters Canyon Rd # 200 Irvine (92606) ***(P-22838)***
Strevus Inc D 415 704-8182
455 Market St Ste 1670 San Francisco (94105) ***(P-15512)***
Stria, Bakersfield *Also called Technosocialworkcom LLC* ***(P-15824)***
Striim Inc E 425 894-1998
575 Middlefield Rd Palo Alto (94301) ***(P-15129)***
Strikes Unlimited Inc D 916 626-3600
5681 Lonetree Blvd Rocklin (95765) ***(P-18044)***
Striking Distance Studios Inc E 925 355-5131
2430 Cmino Rmon Ste 122s San Ramon (94583) ***(P-18012)***
Stripe Inc A 888 963-8955
510 Townsend St San Francisco (94103) ***(P-15698)***
Stripe Payments Company, San Francisco *Also called Stripe Inc* ***(P-15698)***
Strivr Labs Inc D 650 656-9987
90 Middlefield Rd Ste 101 Menlo Park (94025) ***(P-15130)***
Strlng Path Medcl Corp E 562 799-8900
3030 Old Ranch Pkwy # 430 Seal Beach (90740) ***(P-17428)***
Stronghold Engineering Inc (PA) C 951 684-9303
2000 Market St Riverside (92501) ***(P-1610)***
Stroock & Stroock & Lavan LLP C 310 556-5800
2029 Century Park E # 1800 Los Angeles (90067) ***(P-22839)***
Structural Integrity Assoc Inc (PA) D 408 978-8200
5215 Hellyer Ave Ste 210 San Jose (95138) ***(P-25326)***
Structure Cast, Bakersfield *Also called Golden Empire Concrete Pdts* ***(P-3151)***
Structures West Inc D 760 737-2349
300 W Grand Ave Ste 201 Escondido (92025) ***(P-3224)***
Stu Segall Productions Inc C 858 974-8988
4705 Ruffin Rd San Diego (92123) ***(P-17678)***
Stuart C. Gildred Family YMCA, Santa Ynez *Also called Channel Islands Young Mens Ch* ***(P-24519)***
Stuart Lovett D 510 444-0790
350 30th St Ste 208 Oakland (94609) ***(P-19459)***
Stuart Rental Company, Milpitas *Also called Ohana Partners Inc* ***(P-14185)***
Stubhub Inc (HQ) C 415 222-8400
199 Fremont St Fl 4 San Francisco (94105) ***(P-15818)***
Stubhub.com, San Francisco *Also called Stubhub Inc* ***(P-15818)***
Stucco Works Inc B 916 383-6699
5451 Whse Way Ste 105 Sacramento (95826) ***(P-2398)***
Student Government Associat C 949 824-5547
D200 Student Center Irvine (92697) ***(P-4837)***
Student Health Services, San Jose *Also called San Jose State University* ***(P-19362)***
Student Transportation America, San Jose *Also called Student Trnsp Amer Inc* ***(P-3727)***
Student Transportation America, Santa Maria *Also called Santa Barbara Trnsp Corp* ***(P-3823)***
Student Trnsp Amer Inc D 408 998-8275
1540 S 7th St San Jose (95112) ***(P-3727)***
Student Un San Jose State Univ D 408 924-6405
211 S. 9th Street San Jose (95192) ***(P-24876)***
Student Union Building, San Jose *Also called Student Un San Jose State Univ* ***(P-24876)***
Student Works Painting, Irvine *Also called S W P T X Inc* ***(P-2391)***
Student Works Painting Inc B 714 564-7900
1682 Langley Ave Irvine (92614) ***(P-2399)***
Students of Associated D 916 278-6216
6000 J St Sacramento (95819) ***(P-23794)***
Studio 71 LP C 323 370-1500
8383 Wilshire Blvd Ste 10 Beverly Hills (90211) ***(P-13634)***
Studio Royale, Culver City *Also called GK Management Co Inc* ***(P-10734)***
Study Tapes D 909 792-0111
1341 Pine Knoll Cres Redlands (92373) ***(P-17679)***
Study US Research Inst Inc D 213 840-9575
1335 N La Brea Ave 2-205 Los Angeles (90028) ***(P-26035)***
Stumbaugh & Associates Inc (PA) D 818 240-1627
3303 N San Fernando Blvd Burbank (91504) ***(P-3470)***
Sturdy Oil Company D 831 970-9897
721 Vertin Ave Salinas (93901) ***(P-8736)***
Sturgeon & Son, Bakersfield *Also called Sturgeon Services Intl Inc* ***(P-11696)***
Sturgeon Services Intl, Santa Maria *Also called Sturgeon Son Grading & Pav Inc* ***(P-25327)***
Sturgeon Services Intl Inc (PA) E 661 322-4408
3511 Gilmore Ave Bakersfield (93308) ***(P-11696)***
Sturgeon Son Grading & Pav Inc (PA) C 661 322-4408
3511 Gilmore Ave Bakersfield (93308) ***(P-3329)***
Sturgeon Son Grading & Pav Inc C 805 938-0618
6516 Cat Canyon Rd Santa Maria (93454) ***(P-25327)***
Stussy Inc D 949 474-9255
17426 Daimler St Irvine (92614) ***(P-8047)***
Stutman Treister Glatt Prof Co, Los Angeles *Also called Stutman Trster Glatt Prof Corp* ***(P-22840)***

ALPHABETIC

Employee Codes: A=Over 500 employees, B=251-500
C=101-250, D=51-100, E=50
2020 Directory of California
Wholesalers and Services Companies
© Mergent Inc. 1-800-342-5647
1445

Stutman Trster Glatt Prof Corp.....D.....310 228-5600
1901 Avenue Of The Los Angeles (90067) ***(P-22840)***
Stv Architects Inc.....D.....213 482-9444
1055 W 7th St Ste 3150 Los Angeles (90017) ***(P-25506)***
Stx Wireless Operations LLC.....A.....858 882-6000
5887 Copley Dr San Diego (92111) ***(P-5272)***
Sub-Acute Saratoga Hospital, Saratoga *Also called Progressive Sub-Acute Care* ***(P-21488)***
Subacute Chld Hosp Cal Inc.....D.....408 558-3644
3777 S Bascom Ave Campbell (95008) ***(P-21497)***
Subacute Trtmnt Adolescnt Reha (PA).....D.....510 352-9200
545 Estudillo Ave San Leandro (94577) ***(P-22133)***
Success Strategies Inst Inc.....D.....949 721-6808
6 Hutton Cntre Dr Ste 700 Santa Ana (92707) ***(P-23644)***
Successfactorscom Inc.....D.....650 645-2000
2000 Alameda De Las Pulga San Mateo (94403) ***(P-15131)***
Successor Agency To The Norco, Norco *Also called City of Norco* ***(P-27030)***
Successor To San Francisco.....D.....415 749-2400
1 S Van Ness Ave Fl 5 San Francisco (94103) ***(P-27220)***
Suddath Relo Sys of No CA.....D.....408 288-3030
2055 S 7th St San Jose (95112) ***(P-4135)***
Suddath Relocation Systems of.....E.....904 858-1273
2020 S 10th St San Jose (95112) ***(P-4136)***
Sudhakar Company International.....D.....909 879-2933
1450 N Fitzgerald Ave Rialto (92376) ***(P-1794)***
Suds Car Wash Inc.....E.....916 673-6300
4620 Post St El Dorado Hills (95762) ***(P-17398)***
Suez Wts Systems Usa Inc.....D.....408 360-5900
5900 Silvercreek Vly Rd San Jose (95138) ***(P-7439)***
Sufi, Fremont *Also called Startup Farms Intl LLC* ***(P-15123)***
Sugar Bowl Corporation.....D.....530 426-9000
629 Sugar Bowl Rd Norden (95724) ***(P-12983)***
Sugar Foods Corporation.....C.....818 768-7900
9500 El Dorado Ave Sun Valley (91352) ***(P-17073)***
Sugar Foods Corporation.....D.....818 768-7900
9500 El Dorado Ave Sun Valley (91352) ***(P-17074)***
Sugar Transport of The NW.....D.....209 931-3587
5463 Cherokee Rd Stockton (95215) ***(P-4137)***
Sugar Workers Local 1.....B.....510 787-1676
641 Loring Ave Crockett (94525) ***(P-24466)***
Sugarcrm Inc (PA).....C.....408 454-6900
10050 N Wolfe Rd Sw2130 Cupertino (95014) ***(P-15132)***
Suissa Miller Advertising LLC.....D.....310 392-9666
8687 Melrose Ave West Hollywood (90069) ***(P-13582)***
SUISUN REDEVELOPMENT AGENCY, Suisun City *Also called Redevelopment Agency of The Ci* ***(P-27186)***
Suja Juice, Oceanside *Also called Suja Life LLC* ***(P-8648)***
Suja Life LLC.....C.....855 879-7852
3831 Ocean Ranch Blvd Oceanside (92056) ***(P-8648)***
Sukut Construction LLC.....D.....714 540-5351
4010 W Chandler Ave Santa Ana (92704) ***(P-1918)***
Sukut Construction Inc.....D.....714 540-5351
4010 W Chandler Ave Santa Ana (92704) ***(P-3330)***
Sullinovo.....C.....619 260-1432
2750 Womble Rd Ste 100 San Diego (92106) ***(P-6358)***
Sullivan & Cromwell LLP.....D.....310 712-6600
1888 Century Park E # 2100 Los Angeles (90067) ***(P-22841)***
Sullivan Moving & Storage (HQ).....E.....858 874-2600
5704 Copley Dr San Diego (92111) ***(P-4138)***
Sullivancurtismonroe Insurance (PA).....C.....800 427-3253
1920 Main St Ste 600 Irvine (92614) ***(P-26834)***
Sully Miller Contracting, Brea *Also called United Rock Products Corp* ***(P-1805)***
Sully-Miller Contracting Co (HQ).....C.....714 578-9600
135 S State College Blvd # 400 Brea (92821) ***(P-1795)***
Sulzer Electro-Mechanical Serv.....E.....909 825-7971
620 S Rancho Ave Colton (92324) ***(P-17477)***
Sulzer Tower Field Svc Cal Inc.....D.....918 447-7676
18711 S Broadwick St Compton (90220) ***(P-26411)***
Suma Fruit Intl USA Inc.....E.....559 875-5000
1810 Academy Ave Sanger (93657) ***(P-543)***
Sumitomo Electric Device Innov.....D.....408 232-9500
2355 Zanker Rd San Jose (95131) ***(P-7348)***
Sumitomo Rubber North Amer Inc (HQ).....D.....909 466-1116
8656 Haven Ave Rancho Cucamonga (91730) ***(P-6490)***
Summer Crest Apartments, National City *Also called Plaza Manor Preservation LP* ***(P-11361)***
Summer House Inc (PA).....D.....530 662-8493
206 5th St Woodland (95695) ***(P-24088)***
Summer Systems Inc.....D.....661 257-4419
28942 Hancock Pkwy Valencia (91355) ***(P-1611)***
Summerfield Suites By Hyatt, Belmont *Also called Island Hospitality MGT LLC* ***(P-12483)***
Summerhill Construction Co.....E.....925 244-7520
3000 Executive Pkwy # 450 San Ramon (94583) ***(P-1202)***
Summerhill Homes, San Ramon *Also called Summerhill Construction Co* ***(P-1202)***
Summerville At Hazel Creek LLC.....A.....916 988-7901
6125 Hazel Ave Orangevale (95662) ***(P-24089)***
Summerville Senior Living Inc.....D.....562 943-3724
10615 Jordan Rd Whittier (90603) ***(P-10822)***
Summerville Senior Living Inc.....D.....818 341-2552
20801 Devonshire St Chatsworth (91311) ***(P-10823)***
Summit Building Services Inc.....D.....925 827-9500
1128 Willow Pass Ct Concord (94520) ***(P-14059)***
Summit Electric, Santa Rosa *Also called Summit Technology Group Inc* ***(P-2657)***
Summit Hr Worldwide Inc.....D.....408 884-7100
220 Main St Ste 208a San Jose (95112) ***(P-26835)***
Summit Technology Group Inc.....E.....707 542-4773
2450c Bluebell Dr Ste C Santa Rosa (95403) ***(P-2657)***
Summitpointe Golf Club, Milpitas *Also called American Golf Corporation* ***(P-18369)***

Summitview Child Treatment Ctr.....E.....530 644-2412
5036 Sunrey Rd Placerville (95667) ***(P-24090)***
Sumo Logic Inc.....B.....650 810-8700
305 Main St Fl 3 Redwood City (94063) ***(P-15133)***
SUN & SAIL CLUB, Lake Forest *Also called Lake Forest Ll Master Homeown* ***(P-24576)***
Sun America, Los Angeles *Also called American Intl Group Inc* ***(P-10227)***
Sun and Sands Enterprises LLC (PA).....D.....760 399-4278
86705 Avenue 54 Ste A Coachella (92236) ***(P-79)***
Sun Basket Inc (PA).....C.....408 669-4418
1170 Olinder Ct San Jose (95122) ***(P-23492)***
Sun Chlorella USA Corp.....D.....310 891-0600
3305 Kashiwa St Torrance (90505) ***(P-8649)***
Sun City Palm Dsert Cmnty Assn (PA).....D.....760 200-2100
38180 Del Webb Blvd Palm Desert (92211) ***(P-24665)***
Sun City Rsvlle Cmnty Assn Inc (PA).....C.....916 774-3880
7050 Del Webb Blvd Roseville (95747) ***(P-18304)***
Sun Coast Gen Insur Agcy Inc.....D.....949 768-1132
23042 Mill Creek Dr Laguna Hills (92653) ***(P-10515)***
Sun Coast Merchandise Corp.....C.....323 720-9700
6315 Bandini Blvd Commerce (90040) ***(P-7837)***
Sun Diego Charter, National City *Also called Sureride Charter Inc* ***(P-3782)***
Sun Electric LP.....D.....714 210-3744
2101 S Yale St Ste B Santa Ana (92704) ***(P-2658)***
Sun Express, Fontana *Also called Hanks Inc* ***(P-3890)***
Sun Haven Care Inc.....D.....714 870-0060
201 E Bastanchury Rd Fullerton (92835) ***(P-20278)***
Sun Healthcare Group Inc (HQ).....B.....949 255-7100
27442 Portola Pkwy # 200 Foothill Ranch (92610) ***(P-19460)***
Sun Hill Properties Inc (HQ).....B.....818 506-2500
555 Unversal Hollywood Dr Universal City (91608) ***(P-12984)***
Sun Innovations Inc.....E.....510 573-3913
43241 Osgood Rd Fremont (94539) ***(P-25839)***
Sun Lakes Cntry Club Hmeownrs.....D.....951 845-2135
850 Country Club Dr Banning (92220) ***(P-24666)***
Sun Lakes Country Club, Banning *Also called Professional Community MGT Cal* ***(P-11371)***
Sun Light & Power.....D.....510 845-2997
1035 Folger Ave Berkeley (94710) ***(P-17075)***
Sun Maid Growers, Kingsburg *Also called Sun-Maid Growers California* ***(P-8652)***
Sun Mar Health Care, Rosemead *Also called Sun Mar Management Services* ***(P-26413)***
Sun Mar Management Service, Monterey Park *Also called Monterey Pk Convalescent Hosp* ***(P-20634)***
SUN MAR MANAGEMENT SERVICES, Anaheim *Also called Sun Mar Nursing Center Inc* ***(P-20696)***
Sun Mar Management Services.....D.....909 822-8066
7509 Laurel Ave Fontana (92336) ***(P-26412)***
Sun Mar Management Services.....D.....626 288-8353
3136 Del Mar Ave Rosemead (91770) ***(P-26413)***
Sun Mar Management Services.....D.....818 352-1454
7660 Wyngate St Tujunga (91042) ***(P-26414)***
Sun Mar Management Services.....D.....951 687-3842
8171 Magnolia Ave Riverside (92504) ***(P-20279)***
Sun Mar Nursing Center Inc.....D.....714 776-1720
1720 W Orange Ave Anaheim (92804) ***(P-20696)***
Sun Microsystems, Santa Clara *Also called Oracle America Inc* ***(P-15437)***
Sun Microsystems, Pleasanton *Also called Oracle America Inc* ***(P-15440)***
Sun Microsystems, San Diego *Also called Oracle America Inc* ***(P-15441)***
Sun Microsystems, Santa Clara *Also called Oracle America Inc* ***(P-15442)***
Sun Oaks Tennis & Fitness, Redding *Also called Walsh Group Inc* ***(P-18210)***
Sun Pacific Cold Storage, Bakersfield *Also called Exeter Packers Inc* ***(P-4346)***
Sun Pacific Farming, Bakersfield *Also called 7th Standard Ranch Company* ***(P-115)***
Sun Pacific Farming, Bakersfield *Also called Sun Pacific Marketing Coop Inc* ***(P-8526)***
Sun Pacific Farming Coop Inc (PA).....B.....559 592-7121
1250 E Myer Ave Exeter (93221) ***(P-683)***
Sun Pacific Maricopa.....B.....661 847-1015
31452 Old River Rd Bakersfield (93311) ***(P-544)***
Sun Pacific Marketing Coop Inc.....A.....213 612-9957
33502 Lerdo Hwy Bakersfield (93308) ***(P-26836)***
Sun Pacific Marketing Coop Inc.....B.....661 847-1015
31452 Old River Rd Bakersfield (93311) ***(P-8526)***
Sun Pacific Packers, Exeter *Also called Exeter Packers Inc* ***(P-485)***
Sun Pharmaceuticals Inc.....C.....858 380-8865
13718 Sorbonne Ct San Diego (92128) ***(P-25840)***
Sun Rich Fresh Foods USA Inc (HQ).....D.....951 735-3800
515 E Rincon St Corona (92879) ***(P-545)***
Sun Ten Labs Liquidation Co.....D.....949 587-0509
9250 Jeronimo Rd Irvine (92618) ***(P-8650)***
Sun Valley Dairy, Sun Valley *Also called Svd Inc* ***(P-8324)***
Sun Valley Group Inc (PA).....B.....707 822-2885
3160 Upper Bay Rd Arcata (95521) ***(P-283)***
Sun Villa Inc.....C.....559 784-6644
350 N Villa St Porterville (93257) ***(P-20280)***
Sun West Mortgage Company Inc (PA).....D.....800 453-7884
6131 Orangethorpe Ave # 500 Buena Park (90620) ***(P-9605)***
Sun West Wild Rice Facility.....E.....530 868-5188
Vance Ave Biggs (95917) ***(P-7)***
Sun World International Inc (PA).....A.....661 392-5000
16351 Driver Rd Bakersfield (93308) ***(P-546)***
Sun World International LLC.....B.....661 392-5000
5701 Truxtun Ave Ste 200 Bakersfield (93309) ***(P-361)***
Sun World International Inc.....B.....760 398-9300
52200 Industrial Way Coachella (92236) ***(P-547)***
Sun-Air Convalescent Hospital, Panorama City *Also called Panorama Madows Nursing Ctr LP* ***(P-20185)***
Sun-Maid Growers California (PA).....A.....559 897-6235
13525 S Bethel Ave Kingsburg (93631) ***(P-8651)***
Sun-Maid Growers California.....B.....559 897-8900
15628 E Nebraska Ave Kingsburg (93631) ***(P-8652)***

Mergent e-mail: customerrelations@mergent.com 2020 Directory of California (P-0000) Products & Services Section entry number
1446 Wholesalers and Services Companies (PA)=Parent Co (HQ)=Headquarters (DH)=Div Headquarters

Sun-Maid Growers California......E......800 752-9277
4683 Chabot Dr Ste 100 Pleasanton (94588) ***(P-165)***
SunAmerica Hsng Fnd 1071......C......310 772-6000
1 Sun America Ctr Fl 36 Los Angeles (90067) ***(P-10660)***
SunAmerica Inc (HQ)......A......310 772-6000
1 Sun America Ctr Fl 38 Los Angeles (90067) ***(P-9417)***
SunAmerica Investments Inc (HQ)......D......310 772-6000
1 Sun America Ctr Fl 37 Los Angeles (90067) ***(P-26415)***
SunAmerica Investments Inc.......C......310 772-6000
1 Sun America Ctr Fl 38 Los Angeles (90067) ***(P-11742)***
SunAmerica Life Insurance Co (HQ)......D......310 772-6000
1 Sun America Ctr Fl 36 Los Angeles (90067) ***(P-9888)***
Sunbelt Controls Inc......D......626 610-2340
735 N Todd Ave Azusa (91702) ***(P-2290)***
Sunbelt Controls Inc......E......925 660-3900
4511 Willow Rd Ste 4 Pleasanton (94588) ***(P-17448)***
Sunbelt Towing Inc (PA)......D......619 297-8697
4370 Pacific Hwy San Diego (92110) ***(P-17429)***
Sunberry Growers LLC......A......805 922-9888
710 La Guardia St Ste A Salinas (93905) ***(P-8527)***
Sunbrdge Care Ctr - Bellflower, Bellflower *Also called Rebecca Terley* ***(P-20210)***
Sunbridge Brittany Rehab Centr......C......916 484-1393
3900 Garfield Ave Carmichael (95608) ***(P-20281)***
Sunbridge Care Ctr - Grnd Ter, Grand Terrace *Also called Grand Terrace Care Center* ***(P-19982)***
Sunbridge Care Ctr For Downey, Downey *Also called Sunbridge Healthcare LLC* ***(P-20463)***
Sunbridge Care Entps W Inc......D......559 897-5881
1101 Stroud Ave Kingsburg (93631) ***(P-20282)***
Sunbridge Care Entps W LLC......A......559 897-5881
1101 Stroud Ave Kingsburg (93631) ***(P-20283)***
Sunbridge Elmhaven Care Center, Stockton *Also called Sunbridge Healthcare LLC* ***(P-20285)***
Sunbridge Harbor View......C......562 989-9907
490 W 14th St Long Beach (90813) ***(P-20284)***
Sunbridge Healthcare LLC......D......209 477-4817
6940 Pacific Ave Stockton (95207) ***(P-20285)***
Sunbridge Healthcare LLC......D......530 934-2834
320 N Crawford St Willows (95988) ***(P-20461)***
Sunbridge Healthcare LLC......C......562 981-9392
850 E Wardlow Rd Long Beach (90807) ***(P-20462)***
Sunbridge Healthcare LLC......C......562 869-2567
9300 Telegraph Rd Downey (90240) ***(P-20463)***
Sunbridge Healthcare LLC......D......510 352-2211
14766 Washington Ave San Leandro (94578) ***(P-20464)***
Sunburst Shutters Cal Inc (PA)......D......714 997-0800
1037 S Melrose St Ste B Placentia (92870) ***(P-6660)***
Suncrest Nurseries Inc......D......831 728-2595
400 Casserly Rd Watsonville (95076) ***(P-8920)***
Sundance Construction Inc......C......714 437-0802
3500 W Lake Center Dr B Santa Ana (92704) ***(P-2985)***
Sundance Financial Inc......E......619 298-9877
2505 Congress St Ste 220 San Diego (92110) ***(P-11608)***
Sundance Natural Foods Company......E......760 945-9898
2231 Willowbrook Dr Oceanside (92056) ***(P-225)***
Sunday Bazaar Inc......D......415 621-0764
495 Barneveld Ave San Francisco (94124) ***(P-6585)***
Sundt Construction, Sacramento *Also called Halstead Partnership* ***(P-10605)***
Sunergy California LLC......E......916 550-5370
4801 Urbani Ave McClellan (95652) ***(P-7440)***
Sunfoods LLC (HQ)......D......530 661-1923
1620 E Kentucky Ave Woodland (95776) ***(P-8264)***
Sungevity, Oakland *Also called Solar Spectrum LLC* ***(P-2279)***
Sunharbor Management LLC......E......760 356-1262
708 E 5th St Holtville (92250) ***(P-24091)***
Suning Cmmerce R D Ctr USA Inc......D......650 834-9800
845 Page Mill Rd Palo Alto (94304) ***(P-25946)***
Suning USA, Palo Alto *Also called Suning Cmmerce R D Ctr USA Inc* ***(P-25946)***
Sunkist Enterprises......D......650 347-3900
1308 Rollins Rd Burlingame (94010) ***(P-7408)***
Sunkist Growers Inc (PA)......C......661 290-8900
27770 Entertainment Dr Valencia (91355) ***(P-8528)***
Sunkist Growers Inc......C......909 983-9811
531 W Poplar Ave Tipton (93272) ***(P-548)***
Sunkist Growers Inc......C......559 752-4256
531 W Poplar Ave Tipton (93272) ***(P-549)***
Sunland Insurance Agency......A......559 251-7861
4961 E Kings Canyon Rd Fresno (93727) ***(P-10516)***
Sunland Scaffold......D......951 595-9402
24885 Whitewood Rd # 106 Murrieta (92563) ***(P-3471)***
Sunland Shutters, Long Beach *Also called Ta Chen International Inc* ***(P-7107)***
Sunline Transit Agency......C......760 972-4059
790 Vine Ave Coachella (92236) ***(P-3728)***
Sunline Transit Agency (PA)......C......760 343-3456
32505 Harry Oliver Trl Thousand Palms (92276) ***(P-3767)***
Sunlit Gardens, Murrieta *Also called Alta Loma Assisted Living LLC* ***(P-22905)***
Sunny Cal Adhc Inc......D......626 307-7772
8450 Valley Blvd Ste 121b Rosemead (91770) ***(P-23493)***
Sunny Hills-Palladium LLC (PA)......E......626 304-0310
2500 E Foothill Blvd 50 West Covina (91791) ***(P-11470)***
Sunny Retirement Home......C......408 454-5600
22445 Cupertino Rd Cupertino (95014) ***(P-20697)***
Sunny Rose Glen LLC......D......951 679-3355
29620 Bradley Rd Sun City (92586) ***(P-24092)***
Sunny View Care Center, Los Angeles *Also called Longwood Management Corp* ***(P-20617)***
Sunnyside Convalescent Hosp, Fresno *Also called R Fellen Inc* ***(P-20207)***
Sunnyside Country Club......D......559 255-6871
5704 E Butler Ave Fresno (93727) ***(P-18589)***
Sunnyside Gardens......D......408 730-4070
1025 Carson Dr Sunnyvale (94086) ***(P-24093)***
Sunnyside Resort......D......530 583-7200
1850 W Lake Blvd Tahoe City (96145) ***(P-12985)***
Sunnyside Rhblttion Nrsing Ctr......C......310 320-4130
22617 S Vermont Ave Torrance (90502) ***(P-20286)***
Sunnyslope Tree Farm Inc......D......714 532-1440
1545 N Glassell St Orange (92867) ***(P-8921)***
Sunnyslope Trees, Orange *Also called Sunnyslope Tree Farm Inc* ***(P-8921)***
Sunnyvale Fluid Sys Tech Inc......E......510 933-2500
3393 W Warren Ave Fremont (94538) ***(P-7659)***
Sunnyvale Health Care, Sunnyvale *Also called Sunnyvale Healthcare Center* ***(P-20287)***
Sunnyvale Healthcare Center......D......408 245-8070
1291 S Bernardo Ave Sunnyvale (94087) ***(P-20287)***
Sunnyvale Sof-X Owner L P......E......408 542-8264
1100 N Mathilda Ave Sunnyvale (94089) ***(P-12986)***
Sunol Valley Golf Course, Pleasanton *Also called Sunol Vly Golf & Recreation Co* ***(P-18305)***
Sunol Vly Golf & Recreation Co......D......925 862-2404
5117 Mount Tam Cir Pleasanton (94588) ***(P-18305)***
Sunplus HM Care - Pleasant Hl, Pleasant Hill *Also called Accentcare Home Health Cal Inc* ***(P-21630)***
Sunplus HM Hlth - Newport Bch, Newport Beach *Also called Accentcare Home Health Cal Inc* ***(P-21634)***
Sunplus Home Care - Ontario, Ontario *Also called Accentcare Home Health Cal Inc* ***(P-21632)***
Sunplus Home Care - San Diego, San Diego *Also called Accentcare Home Health Cal Inc* ***(P-21633)***
Sunpower By Green Convergence, Valencia *Also called Green Convergence* ***(P-7428)***
Sunpower Corporation Systems (HQ)......D......510 260-8200
1414 Hrbour Way S Ste 190 Richmond (94804) ***(P-2291)***
Sunpro Solar Inc......D......951 678-7733
34859 Frederick St # 101 Wildomar (92595) ***(P-2292)***
Sunray Healthcare Center, Los Angeles *Also called Kf Sunray LLC* ***(P-20607)***
Sunridge Care & Rehabilitation, Salinas *Also called Helios Healthcare LLC* ***(P-20011)***
Sunridge Farms, Royal Oaks *Also called Falcon Trading Company* ***(P-8575)***
Sunridge Nurseries Inc......D......661 363-8463
441 Vineland Rd Bakersfield (93307) ***(P-442)***
Sunrise Assistd Lving of Wlnt, Walnut Creek *Also called Sunrise Senior Living LLC* ***(P-20307)***
Sunrise Asssted Lving San Mteo, San Mateo *Also called Sunrise Senior Living Inc* ***(P-20292)***
Sunrise At Alta Loma, Rancho Cucamonga *Also called Sunrise Senior Living Inc* ***(P-20289)***
Sunrise At Bonita, Chula Vista *Also called Sunrise Senior Living LLC* ***(P-20313)***
Sunrise At La Costa, Carlsbad *Also called Sunrise Senior Living LLC* ***(P-20312)***
Sunrise At Raincross Village, Riverside *Also called Sunrise Senior Living LLC* ***(P-20328)***
Sunrise At Sterling Canyon, Valencia *Also called Sunrise Senior Living Inc* ***(P-20296)***
Sunrise Brands LLC (PA)......E......323 780-8250
801 S Figueroa St # 2500 Los Angeles (90017) ***(P-8112)***
Sunrise Company, Palm Desert *Also called Sunrise Desert Partners* ***(P-11610)***
Sunrise Convalescent Hospital, Pasadena *Also called D & C Care Center Inc* ***(P-20543)***
Sunrise Delivery Service Inc......D......323 464-5121
13351 Riverside Dr 672d Sherman Oaks (91423) ***(P-4280)***
Sunrise Desert Partners......D......760 404-1280
300 Eagle Cir Palm Desert (92211) ***(P-11609)***
Sunrise Desert Partners (PA)......C......760 772-7227
300 Eagle Dance Cir Palm Desert (92211) ***(P-11610)***
Sunrise Farms LLC......D......707 778-6450
395 Liberty Rd Petaluma (94952) ***(P-8336)***
Sunrise Food Ministry......D......916 965-5431
5901 San Juan Ave Citrus Heights (95610) ***(P-23494)***
Sunrise Growers Inc (HQ)......B......714 630-2170
701 W Kimberly Ave # 210 Placentia (92870) ***(P-8529)***
Sunrise Growers-Frozsun Foods, Placentia *Also called Sunrise Growers Inc* ***(P-8529)***
Sunrise of Beverly Hills, Beverly Hills *Also called Sunrise Senior Living Inc* ***(P-20298)***
Sunrise of Carmichael, Carmichael *Also called Sunrise Senior Living Inc* ***(P-20303)***
Sunrise of Danville, Danville *Also called Sunrise Senior Living LLC* ***(P-20306)***
Sunrise of Fresno, Fresno *Also called Sunrise Senior Living LLC* ***(P-20319)***
Sunrise of Hemet, Hemet *Also called Sunrise Senior Living LLC* ***(P-20325)***
Sunrise of Hermosa Beach, Hermosa Beach *Also called Sunrise Senior Living LLC* ***(P-20311)***
Sunrise of La Palma, La Palma *Also called Sunrise Senior Living LLC* ***(P-20320)***
Sunrise of Mission Viejo, Mission Viejo *Also called Sunrise Senior Living LLC* ***(P-20310)***
Sunrise of Monterey, Monterey *Also called Sunrise Senior Living Inc* ***(P-20304)***
Sunrise of Oakland Hills, Oakland *Also called Sunrise Senior Living LLC* ***(P-20309)***
Sunrise of Palm Springs, Palm Springs *Also called Sunrise Senior Living LLC* ***(P-20322)***
Sunrise of Palo Alto, Beverly Hills *Also called Sunrise Senior Living Inc* ***(P-20295)***
Sunrise of Petaluma, Petaluma *Also called Sunrise Senior Living Inc* ***(P-20291)***
Sunrise of Petaluma......D......707 776-2885
815 Wood Sorrel Dr Petaluma (94954) ***(P-20288)***
Sunrise of Playa Vista, Los Angeles *Also called Sunrise Senior Living Inc* ***(P-20299)***
Sunrise of Rocklin, Rocklin *Also called Sunrise Senior Living LLC* ***(P-20326)***
Sunrise of Sacramento, Sacramento *Also called Sunrise Senior Living LLC* ***(P-20314)***
Sunrise of Santa Rosa, Santa Rosa *Also called Sunrise Senior Living Inc* ***(P-20305)***
Sunrise of Studio City, Studio City *Also called Sunrise Senior Living LLC* ***(P-20318)***
Sunrise of Sunnyvale, Sunnyvale *Also called Sunrise Senior Living LLC* ***(P-20316)***
Sunrise of Westlake Village, Westlake Village *Also called Sunrise Senior Living LLC* ***(P-20317)***
Sunrise of Woodland Hills, Encino *Also called Sunrise Senior Living Inc* ***(P-20294)***
Sunrise Plumbing & Mech Inc......E......562 424-0332
7581 Hazard Ave Ste C Westminster (92683) ***(P-2293)***
Sunrise Produce Company, Fullerton *Also called Loewy Enterprises* ***(P-8497)***

Employee Codes: A=Over 500 employees, B=251-500
C=101-250, D=51-100, E=50
2020 Directory of California
Wholesalers and Services Companies
© Mergent Inc. 1-800-342-5647
1447

Sunrise Ranch........D.......805 488-0813
3623 Etting Rd Oxnard (93033) ***(P-284)***
Sunrise Retirement Villa, Roseville *Also called Sign of Dove* ***(P-10813)***
Sunrise Retirement Villa........D.......916 786-3277
707 Sunrise Ave Ofc Roseville (95661) ***(P-10824)***
Sunrise Senior Living Inc........D.......909 941-3001
9519 Baseline Rd Rancho Cucamonga (91730) ***(P-20289)***
Sunrise Senior Living Inc........D.......760 340-5999
72201 Country Club Dr Palm Desert (92210) ***(P-20290)***
Sunrise Senior Living Inc........D.......707 776-2885
815 Wood Sorrel Dr Petaluma (94954) ***(P-20291)***
Sunrise Senior Living Inc........D.......650 558-8555
955 S El Camino Real San Mateo (94402) ***(P-20292)***
Sunrise Senior Living Inc........D.......562 594-5788
3840 Lampson Ave Seal Beach (90740) ***(P-20293)***
Sunrise Senior Living Inc........E.......818 346-9046
5501 Newcastle Ave # 130 Encino (91316) ***(P-20294)***
Sunrise Senior Living Inc........D.......650 326-1108
201 N Crescent Dr Apt 503 Beverly Hills (90210) ***(P-20295)***
Sunrise Senior Living Inc........D.......661 253-3551
25815 Mcbean Pkwy Ofc Valencia (91355) ***(P-20296)***
Sunrise Senior Living Inc........D.......949 234-3000
25421 Sea Bluffs Dr Dana Point (92629) ***(P-20297)***
Sunrise Senior Living Inc........D.......310 274-4479
201 N Crescent Dr Beverly Hills (90210) ***(P-20298)***
Sunrise Senior Living Inc........D.......310 437-7178
5555 Playa Vista Dr Los Angeles (90094) ***(P-20299)***
Sunrise Senior Living Inc........D.......415 664-6264
1601 19th Ave San Francisco (94122) ***(P-20300)***
Sunrise Senior Living Inc........D.......408 223-1312
4855 San Felipe Rd San Jose (95135) ***(P-20301)***
Sunrise Senior Living Inc........D.......949 581-6111
24552 Paseo De Valencia Laguna Hills (92653) ***(P-20302)***
Sunrise Senior Living Inc........D.......916 485-4500
5451 Fair Oaks Blvd Carmichael (95608) ***(P-20303)***
Sunrise Senior Living Inc........D.......831 643-2400
1110 Carmelo St Monterey (93940) ***(P-20304)***
Sunrise Senior Living Inc........E.......707 575-7503
3250 Chanate Rd Ofc Santa Rosa (95404) ***(P-20305)***
Sunrise Senior Living LLC........D.......925 309-4178
1027 Diablo Rd Danville (94526) ***(P-20306)***
Sunrise Senior Living LLC........E.......925 932-3500
2175 Ygnacio Valley Rd Walnut Creek (94598) ***(P-20307)***
Sunrise Senior Living LLC........D.......818 886-1616
17650 Devonshire St Northridge (91325) ***(P-20308)***
Sunrise Senior Living LLC........D.......510 531-7190
11889 Skyline Blvd Oakland (94619) ***(P-20309)***
Sunrise Senior Living LLC........D.......949 582-2010
26151 Country Club Dr Mission Viejo (92691) ***(P-20310)***
Sunrise Senior Living LLC........E.......310 937-0959
1837 Pacific Coast Hwy Hermosa Beach (90254) ***(P-20311)***
Sunrise Senior Living LLC........D.......760 930-0060
7020 Manzanita St Carlsbad (92011) ***(P-20312)***
Sunrise Senior Living LLC........D.......619 470-2220
3302 Bonita Rd Chula Vista (91910) ***(P-20313)***
Sunrise Senior Living LLC........E.......916 486-0200
345 Munroe St Sacramento (95825) ***(P-20314)***
Sunrise Senior Living LLC........D.......303 410-0500
530 Water St Fl 5 Oakland (94607) ***(P-20315)***
Sunrise Senior Living LLC........D.......408 749-8600
633 S Knickerbocker Dr # 263 Sunnyvale (94087) ***(P-20316)***
Sunrise Senior Living LLC........D.......805 557-1100
3101 Townsgate Rd Westlake Village (91361) ***(P-20317)***
Sunrise Senior Living LLC........D.......818 505-8484
4610 Coldwater Canyon Ave Studio City (91604) ***(P-20318)***
Sunrise Senior Living LLC........D.......559 325-8170
7444 N Cedar Ave Fresno (93720) ***(P-20319)***
Sunrise Senior Living LLC........D.......714 739-8111
5321 La Palma Ave Fl 2 La Palma (90623) ***(P-20320)***
Sunrise Senior Living LLC........D.......949 248-8855
31741 Rancho Viejo Rd San Juan Capistrano (92675) ***(P-20321)***
Sunrise Senior Living LLC........D.......760 322-3444
1780 E Baristo Rd Palm Springs (92262) ***(P-20322)***
Sunrise Senior Living LLC........D.......650 654-9700
1301 Ralston Ave Ste A Belmont (94002) ***(P-20323)***
Sunrise Senior Living LLC........D.......805 388-8086
6000 Santa Rosa Rd Ofc Camarillo (93012) ***(P-20324)***
Sunrise Senior Living LLC........D.......951 929-5988
1177 S Palm Ave Hemet (92543) ***(P-20325)***
Sunrise Senior Living LLC........D.......916 632-3003
6100 Sierra College Blvd Rocklin (95677) ***(P-20326)***
Sunrise Senior Living LLC........D.......760 346-5420
41505 Carlotta Dr Palm Desert (92211) ***(P-20327)***
Sunrise Senior Living LLC........D.......951 785-1200
5232 Central Ave Riverside (92504) ***(P-20328)***
Sunrise Villa Ctr Head Start, Wasco *Also called Community Action Partnr Kern* ***(P-24154)***
Sunrize Staging Inc........D.......760 743-2043
1326 Mission Rd Escondido (92029) ***(P-3472)***
Sunrun Installation Svcs Inc........A.......408 746-3062
575 Dado St San Jose (95131) ***(P-2294)***
Sunrun Installation Svcs Inc (HQ)........C.......415 580-6900
775 Fiero Ln Ste 200 San Luis Obispo (93401) ***(P-2295)***
Sunscape Eyewear Inc........D.......949 553-0590
17526 Von Karman Ave A Irvine (92614) ***(P-7838)***
Sunset Aviation LLC (PA)........E.......707 775-2786
201 1st St Ste 307 Petaluma (94952) ***(P-4795)***
Sunset Building Maintnace Inc........E.......408 727-3408
1920 Lafayette St Ste E Santa Clara (95050) ***(P-14060)***
Sunset Building Maintenance, Santa Clara *Also called Sunset Building Maintance Inc* ***(P-14060)***
Sunset Development Company, San Ramon *Also called Annabel Investment Company* ***(P-11541)***
Sunset Hills Country Club, Thousand Oaks *Also called American Golf Corporation* ***(P-18358)***
Sunset Landscape Maintenance........D.......949 455-4636
27201 Burbank El Toro (92610) ***(P-912)***
Sunset Linen Service, Santa Rosa *Also called City Towel & Dust Service Inc* ***(P-13219)***
Sunset Manor Convalescent Hosp, El Monte *Also called Gibralter Convalescent Hosp* ***(P-20570)***
Sunset Moulding Co........D.......530 695-3379
2200 Paseo Rd Live Oak (95953) ***(P-6661)***
Sunset Neighborhood Beacon Ctr, San Francisco *Also called Aspiranet* ***(P-23823)***
Sunset Pet Hospital Inc (PA)........D.......916 967-7768
7751 Sunset Ave Fair Oaks (95628) ***(P-585)***
Sunset Property Services, Irvine *Also called Jonset Corporation* ***(P-6350)***
Sunset Scavenger Company........B.......415 330-1300
250 Executive Park Blvd # 2100 San Francisco (94134) ***(P-6289)***
Sunset Station, Los Angeles *Also called Passprt Accept Fclty Los Angel* ***(P-16986)***
Sunset Tower Hotel LLC........D.......323 654-7100
8358 W Sunset Blvd Los Angeles (90069) ***(P-12987)***
Sunshine Communications Inc........C.......619 448-7600
350 Cypress Ln Ste D El Cajon (92020) ***(P-2659)***
Sunshine Floral Inc........D.......805 684-1177
4595 Foothill Rd Carpinteria (93013) ***(P-8922)***
Sunshine Floral LLC........D.......805 982-8822
1070 S Rice Ave Ste 1 Oxnard (93033) ***(P-8923)***
Sunshine Metal Clad Inc........D.......661 366-0575
7201 Edison Hwy Bakersfield (93307) ***(P-2863)***
Sunshine Midtown LLC........E.......602 604-4900
631 W Katella Ave Anaheim (92802) ***(P-12988)***
Sunshine Villa Assisted Living, Santa Cruz *Also called Regent Assisted Living Inc* ***(P-24046)***
Sunstone Center Crt Lessee Inc........C.......949 382-4000
200 Spectrum Center Dr # 21 Irvine (92618) ***(P-12989)***
Sunstone Durante LLC........C.......858 792-5200
15575 Jimmy Durante Blvd Del Mar (92014) ***(P-12990)***
Sunstone Hotel Investors LLC........C.......714 739-8500
14299 Firestone Blvd La Mirada (90638) ***(P-12991)***
Sunstone Hotel Investors LLC........C.......661 267-6587
39375 5th St W Palmdale (93551) ***(P-12992)***
Sunstone Hotel Investors LLC........D.......310 830-9200
2 Civic Plaza Dr Carson (90745) ***(P-12993)***
Sunstone Hotel Investors LLC........D.......619 239-6171
1617 1st Ave Ste 16 San Diego (92101) ***(P-12994)***
Sunstone Hotel Investors LLC........D.......707 253-8600
3425 Solano Ave NAPA (94558) ***(P-12995)***
Sunstone Hotel Investors LLC........C.......714 635-5000
1752 S Clementine St Anaheim (92802) ***(P-12996)***
Sunstone Hotel Investors LLC (PA)........D.......949 330-4000
200 Spectrum Dr Fl 21 Irvine (92618) ***(P-11957)***
Sunstone Hotel Investors LLC........C.......310 215-1000
9801 Airport Blvd Los Angeles (90045) ***(P-12997)***
Sunstone Hotel Investors LLC........C.......310 649-1400
6161 W Century Blvd Los Angeles (90045) ***(P-12998)***
Sunstone Hotel Management Inc........C.......951 784-8000
3400 Market St Riverside (92501) ***(P-12999)***
Sunstone Hotel Properties Inc........D.......310 228-4100
1177 S Beverly Dr Los Angeles (90035) ***(P-13000)***
Sunstone Hotel Properties Inc........D.......310 546-7627
1700 N Sepulveda Blvd Manhattan Beach (90266) ***(P-13001)***
Sunstone Hotel Properties Inc (HQ)........C.......949 330-4000
120 Vantis Dr Ste 350 Aliso Viejo (92656) ***(P-13002)***
Sunstone Ocean Lessee Inc........B.......949 382-4000
200 Spectrum Center Dr # 2100 Irvine (92618) ***(P-13003)***
Sunstone Top Gun LLC........D.......858 453-0400
4550 La Jolla Village Dr San Diego (92122) ***(P-13004)***
Sunstone Top Gun Lessee Inc........C.......949 330-4000
4550 La Jolla Village Dr San Diego (92122) ***(P-13005)***
Sunsystem Technology LLC (PA)........D.......916 671-3351
2731 Citrus Rd Ste D Rancho Cordova (95742) ***(P-25841)***
Suntreat Packing & Shipping Co, Lindsay *Also called Acmpc California 3 LLC* ***(P-184)***
Suntreat Pkg Shipg A Ltd Prtnr........C.......559 562-4991
391 Oxford Ave Lindsay (93247) ***(P-5099)***
Sunvair Aerospace Group Inc (PA)........D.......661 294-3777
29145 The Old Rd Valencia (91355) ***(P-17548)***
Sunwest Bank (HQ)........E.......714 730-4441
2050 Main St Fl 3 Irvine (92614) ***(P-9241)***
Sunwest Electric Inc........C.......714 630-8700
3064 E Miraloma Ave Anaheim (92806) ***(P-2660)***
Super 8 Motel, San Francisco *Also called Chirag Hospitality Inc* ***(P-12140)***
Super 8 Motel, Bakersfield *Also called Tiburon Hospitality LLC* ***(P-13023)***
Super Care Inc........D.......760 245-2034
12176 Industrial Blvd Victorville (92395) ***(P-7008)***
Super Garden Centers Inc........E.......818 348-9266
7659 Topanga Canyon Blvd Canoga Park (91304) ***(P-8924)***
Super Shuttle, Sun Valley *Also called Arcadia Transit Inc* ***(P-3524)***
Super Store Industries........B.......209 858-3365
2800 W March Ln Ste 210 Stockton (95219) ***(P-8653)***
Super Talent Technology Corp........A.......408 957-8133
2077 N Capitol Ave San Jose (95132) ***(P-6904)***
Superbalife International LLC........D.......310 553-7400
1171 S Robertson Blvd # 525 Los Angeles (90035) ***(P-7986)***
Superclean America, Palm Springs *Also called Joseph Dipuzo* ***(P-13185)***
Supercuts, Folsom *Also called Dager Corporation* ***(P-13337)***
Supercuts Administrative Office (PA)........C.......760 753-5543
7750 El Cmino Real Ste 2g Carlsbad (92009) ***(P-13360)***
Superhero App LLC........D.......562 341-0784
1517 W Carson St Apt 11 Torrance (90501) ***(P-17076)***
Superior Automatic Sprnklr Co........D.......408 946-7272
4378 Enterprise St Fremont (94538) ***(P-2296)***

Mergent e-mail: customerrelations@mergent.com
1448
2020 Directory of California
Wholesalers and Services Companies
(P-0000) Products & Services Section entry number
(PA)=Parent Co (HQ)=Headquarters (DH)=Div Headquarters

ALPHABETIC SECTION Sutter Health

Superior Cattle Feeders LLC (PA)....D....760 348-2218
551 S Industrial Ave Calipatria (92233) ***(P-378)***
Superior Communications Inc (PA)....C....877 522-4727
5027 Irwindale Ave # 900 Irwindale (91706) ***(P-7349)***
Superior Construction Inc....D....951 808-8780
265 N Joy St Corona (92879) ***(P-1203)***
Superior Contracting Corp....E....831 757-1089
45 N Main St Salinas (93901) ***(P-2864)***
Superior Court Unit, Fresno *Also called County of Fresno* ***(P-22434)***
Superior Elec Mech & Plbg Inc....B....909 357-9400
8613 Helms Ave Rancho Cucamonga (91730) ***(P-2661)***
Superior Envmtl Svcs Inc....E....619 462-7079
6383 Lake Arrowhead Dr San Diego (92119) ***(P-14061)***
Superior Foods Inc....D....831 728-3691
275 Westgate Dr Watsonville (95076) ***(P-8303)***
Superior Foods Companies, The, Watsonville *Also called Superior Foods Inc* ***(P-8303)***
Superior Fruit LLC....C....805 485-2519
4324 E Vineyard Ave Oxnard (93036) ***(P-112)***
Superior Gunite (PA)....C....818 896-9199
12306 Van Nuys Blvd Sylmar (91342) ***(P-3225)***
Superior Masonry Walls Ltd....D....909 370-1800
300 W Olive St Ste A Colton (92324) ***(P-2730)***
Superior Paving Company Inc....D....951 739-9200
1880 N Delilah St Corona (92879) ***(P-1796)***
Superior Pntg Drywall Fnshings, Carmichael *Also called H B J Corporation* ***(P-2794)***
Superior Seafood Co, Los Angeles *Also called PLD Enterprises Inc* ***(P-8383)***
Superior Seafood Co, San Pedro *Also called PLD Enterprises Inc* ***(P-8384)***
Superior Services, Oceanside *Also called Superior Support Services Inc* ***(P-26416)***
Superior Sod I LP....C....909 923-5068
17821 17th St Ste 165 Tustin (92780) ***(P-285)***
Superior Support Services Inc....B....559 458-0507
702 Civic Center Dr Oceanside (92054) ***(P-26416)***
Superior Tile Co, San Leandro *Also called TRM Corporation* ***(P-2912)***
Superior Truck Lines Inc....E....559 924-6418
527 F St Lemoore (93245) ***(P-4139)***
Superior Truck Lines Inc (PA)....D....209 862-9430
1457 Main St Ste A Newman (95360) ***(P-4140)***
Superior Vision Services Inc (PA)....D....800 507-3800
11090 White Rock Rd Rancho Cordova (95670) ***(P-10057)***
Superior Wall Systems Inc....B....714 278-0000
1232 E Orangethorpe Ave Fullerton (92831) ***(P-2865)***
Supershuttle International Inc....C....909 944-2606
9559 Center Ave Ste F Rancho Cucamonga (91730) ***(P-3610)***
Supershuttle International Inc....D....916 648-2500
3100 Northgate Blvd Sacramento (95833) ***(P-3611)***
Supershuttle Los Angeles Inc....C....310 222-5500
531 Van Ness Ave Torrance (90501) ***(P-3612)***
Supershuttle Orange County Inc....B....310 222-5500
531 Van Ness Ave Torrance (90501) ***(P-3613)***
Supershuttle Sacramento, Sacramento *Also called Supershuttle International Inc* ***(P-3611)***
Supervalu, Commerce *Also called Unified Grocers Inc* ***(P-4520)***
Supply Change Services, Sacramento *Also called Sacramento Municpl Utility Dst* ***(P-5916)***
Support For Family LLC....D....877 916-9111
1333 Howe Ave Ste 206 Sacramento (95825) ***(P-23495)***
Support For Home Inc....E....530 792-8484
1333 Howe Ave Ste 206 Sacramento (95825) ***(P-1204)***
Supportcom Inc (PA)....D....650 556-9440
1200 Crossman Ave Ste 210 Sunnyvale (94089) ***(P-15819)***
SUPPORTED LIVING SERVICES, NAPA *Also called Bayberry Inc* ***(P-20412)***
Supra National Express Inc....D....310 549-7105
1411 E Watson Center Rd Carson (90745) ***(P-5058)***
Supreme Court United States....C....619 557-7149
101 W Broadway Ste 700 San Diego (92101) ***(P-23496)***
Supreme Security Services Inc....D....760 415-7399
3517 Cameo Dr Unit 84 Oceanside (92056) ***(P-16457)***
Sure Forming Systems Inc....E....562 598-6348
10602 Humbolt St Los Alamitos (90720) ***(P-3226)***
Sure Haven Inc....A....949 467-9213
1730 Pomona Ave Ste 3 Costa Mesa (92627) ***(P-21498)***
Sure Haven Addiction Treatment, Costa Mesa *Also called Sure Haven Inc* ***(P-21498)***
Sureco Hlth Lf Insur Agcy Inc....D....866 235-5515
201 E Sndpinte Dr Ste 600 Santa Ana (92707) ***(P-10517)***
Sureride Charter Inc....C....619 336-9200
522 W 8th St National City (91950) ***(P-3782)***
Surety West Logistics Inc....D....800 761-2551
980 9th St Fl 16 Sacramento (95814) ***(P-5059)***
Surety West Transportation, Sacramento *Also called Surety West Logistics Inc* ***(P-5059)***
Surf Sand Hotel, Laguna Beach *Also called JC Resorts LLC* ***(P-26270)***
Surface Pumps Inc (PA)....D....661 393-1545
3301 Unicorn Rd Bakersfield (93308) ***(P-7597)***
SURFSIDE RACE PLACE AT DEL MAR, Del Mar *Also called Del Mar Thoroughbred Club* ***(P-18084)***
Surgener Electric Inc....D....661 399-3321
1406 N Chester Ave Bakersfield (93308) ***(P-2662)***
Surgery Center of Alta Bates (HQ)....A....510 204-4444
2450 Ashby Ave Berkeley (94705) ***(P-21244)***
Surgery Center of Alta Bates....E....510 204-4411
2001 Dwight Way Berkeley (94704) ***(P-19461)***
Surgery Center of Alta Bates....D....510 204-1591
2001 Dwight Way Berkeley (94704) ***(P-19462)***
Surgery Center of Health South, Oakland *Also called EBSC LP* ***(P-18964)***
Surgical Care Affiliate....E....916 529-4590
2450 Venture Oaks Way # 120 Sacramento (95833) ***(P-25685)***
Surgical Staff Inc....C....916 444-4424
1523 G St Sacramento (95814) ***(P-14570)***
Surplus Line Association Cal....D....415 434-4900
12667 Alcosta Blvd # 450 San Ramon (94583) ***(P-24368)***
Surprise Valley Hlth Care Dst....D....530 279-6111
741 N Main St Cedarville (96104) ***(P-21245)***
Surveillance Systems....E....800 508-6981
4465 Granite Dr Ste 700 Rocklin (95677) ***(P-7350)***
Survey Junkie, Glendale *Also called Disqo Inc* ***(P-25888)***
Surveymonkey Inc (HQ)....D....650 543-8400
1 Curiosity Way San Mateo (94403) ***(P-15820)***
Surveysavvy.com, San Diego *Also called Luth Research Inc* ***(P-25921)***
Survival Insurance Inc....C....818 565-1584
2550 N Hollywood Way # 120 Burbank (91505) ***(P-10518)***
Survival Insurance Brkg A Cal, Burbank *Also called Survival Insurance Inc* ***(P-10518)***
Survival Systems Intl Inc (PA)....D....760 749-6800
34140 Valley Center Rd Valley Center (92082) ***(P-17549)***
Survivalcave Inc....E....800 719-7650
10620 Treena St Ste 230 San Diego (92131) ***(P-8654)***
Sustainable Agriculture, Rancho Dominguez *Also called Seeds of Change Inc* ***(P-8857)***
Sutter Alhambra Surgery Center, Elk Grove *Also called Sutter Health* ***(P-21263)***
Sutter Amador Hospital, Jackson *Also called Sutter Valley Hospitals* ***(P-21296)***
Sutter Amador Hospital Lab, Jackson *Also called Sutter Hlth Scrmnto Sierra Reg* ***(P-19488)***
Sutter Auburn Faith Hospital, Auburn *Also called Sutter Health* ***(P-22134)***
Sutter Bay Hospitals (HQ)....A....415 600-6000
633 Folsom St Fl 5 San Francisco (94107) ***(P-21246)***
SUTTER C H S, Novato *Also called Sutter West Bay Hospitals* ***(P-21298)***
SUTTER C H S, Lakeport *Also called Sutter Lakeside Hospital* ***(P-21291)***
SUTTER C H S, Sacramento *Also called Sutter Health* ***(P-21272)***
SUTTER C H S, Crescent City *Also called Sutter Coast Hospital* ***(P-21248)***
Sutter Central Vly Hospitals (HQ)....C....209 526-4500
1700 Coffee Rd Modesto (95355) ***(P-21247)***
Sutter Central Vly Hospitals....E....209 526-4500
1700 Coffee Rd Modesto (95355) ***(P-4747)***
Sutter Club Inc....D....916 442-0456
1220 9th St Sacramento (95814) ***(P-24667)***
Sutter Coast Hospital (HQ)....C....707 464-8511
800 E Washington Blvd Crescent City (95531) ***(P-21248)***
Sutter Davis Hospital, Davis *Also called Sutter Hlth Scrmnto Sierra Reg* ***(P-21286)***
Sutter Delta Medical Ctr Aux....D....925 779-7200
3901 Lone Tree Way Antioch (94509) ***(P-21249)***
Sutter Elk Grove Surgery Ctr, Elk Grove *Also called Sutter Health* ***(P-21266)***
Sutter Gould Med Foundation (PA)....E....209 948-5940
600 Coffee Rd Modesto (95355) ***(P-19463)***
Sutter Health, Santa Rosa *Also called Santa Rosa Surgery Center LP* ***(P-21166)***
SUTTER HEALTH, Sacramento *Also called Sutter Valley Med Foundation* ***(P-21297)***
Sutter Health....C....530 747-0389
2068 John Jones Rd # 100 Davis (95616) ***(P-19464)***
Sutter Health....B....916 733-1025
1625 Stockton Blvd # 207 Sacramento (95816) ***(P-21250)***
Sutter Health....B....916 797-4725
2 Medical Plaza Dr Roseville (95661) ***(P-21251)***
Sutter Health....D....925 371-3800
2950 Collier Canyon Rd Livermore (94551) ***(P-22330)***
Sutter Health....B....415 600-7034
P.O. Box 7999 San Francisco (94120) ***(P-21252)***
Sutter Health....B....650 853-2975
795 El Camino Real Palo Alto (94301) ***(P-19465)***
Sutter Health....C....916 733-9588
1020 29th St Ste 600 Sacramento (95816) ***(P-21253)***
Sutter Health....B....408 524-5952
2734 El Camino Real Santa Clara (95051) ***(P-21254)***
Sutter Health....B....530 757-5111
2000 Sutter Pl Davis (95616) ***(P-21255)***
Sutter Health....B....415 600-3311
633 Folsom St Fl 5 San Francisco (94107) ***(P-26837)***
Sutter Health....A....925 779-7273
3901 Lone Tree Way Antioch (94509) ***(P-21256)***
Sutter Health....B....415 345-0100
3468 California St San Francisco (94118) ***(P-21257)***
Sutter Health....C....209 366-2007
1335 S Fairmont Ave Lodi (95240) ***(P-21258)***
Sutter Health....C....209 223-5445
100 Mission Blvd Jackson (95642) ***(P-19466)***
Sutter Health....C....415 731-6300
595 Buckingham Way # 515 San Francisco (94132) ***(P-21259)***
Sutter Health....C....415 600-0110
1375 Sutter St Ste 406 San Francisco (94109) ***(P-21260)***
Sutter Health....C....831 458-6310
1301 Mission St Santa Cruz (95060) ***(P-24668)***
Sutter Health....C....916 797-4715
3 Medical Plaza Dr # 100 Roseville (95661) ***(P-19467)***
Sutter Health....C....530 750-5904
2030 Sutter Pl Ste 1000 Davis (95616) ***(P-21261)***
Sutter Health....C....916 691-5900
8170 Laguna Blvd Ste 210 Elk Grove (95758) ***(P-19468)***
Sutter Health....C....707 535-5600
110 Stony Point Rd # 200 Santa Rosa (95401) ***(P-21262)***
Sutter Health....B....916 455-8137
8170 Laguna Blvd Ste 103 Elk Grove (95758) ***(P-21263)***
Sutter Health....A....415 600-1020
2340 Clay St Rm 121 San Francisco (94115) ***(P-21264)***
Sutter Health....C....707 263-6885
5196 Hill Rd E Ste 300 Lakeport (95453) ***(P-19469)***
Sutter Health....C....916 262-9400
2725 Capitol Ave Sacramento (95816) ***(P-19470)***
Sutter Health....B....916 566-4819
2880 Gateway Oaks Dr # 220 Sacramento (95833) ***(P-21265)***
Sutter Health....B....831 458-6272
2950 Research Park Dr Soquel (95073) ***(P-24669)***
Sutter Health....A....916 544-5423
8200 Laguna Blvd Elk Grove (95758) ***(P-21266)***

ALPHABETIC

Employee Codes: A=Over 500 employees, B=251-500
C=101-250, D=51-100, E=50
2020 Directory of California
Wholesalers and Services Companies
© Mergent Inc. 1-800-342-5647
1449

Sutter Health ....C....209 827-4866
520 W I St Los Banos (93635) ***(P-24670)***
Sutter Health ....C....707 263-3520
5150 Hill Rd Ste E Lakeport (95453) ***(P-19643)***
Sutter Health ....C....415 600-0140
1375 Sutter St Ste 208 San Francisco (94109) ***(P-21267)***
Sutter Health ....A....415 600-4280
2015 Steiner St Fl 1 San Francisco (94115) ***(P-21268)***
Sutter Health ....C....415 897-8495
100 Rowland Way Ste 210 Novato (94945) ***(P-21269)***
Sutter Health ....C....408 523-3900
360 Dardanelli Ln Ste 2d Los Gatos (95032) ***(P-24671)***
Sutter Health ....B....916 262-9414
2725 Capitol Ave Dept 304 Sacramento (95816) ***(P-19471)***
Sutter Health ....A....916 646-8300
1500 Expo Pkwy Sacramento (95815) ***(P-19472)***
Sutter Health ....B....510 547-2244
3875 Telegraph Ave Oakland (94609) ***(P-19473)***
Sutter Health ....B....916 887-0000
2825 Capitol Ave Sacramento (95816) ***(P-21270)***
Sutter Health ....C....510 869-8777
3000 Telegraph Ave Oakland (94609) ***(P-21271)***
Sutter Health (PA) ....A....916 733-8800
2200 River Plaza Dr Sacramento (95833) ***(P-21272)***
Sutter Health ....B....530 406-5600
475 Pioneer Ave Ste 400 Woodland (95776) ***(P-21273)***
Sutter Health ....C....209 524-1211
600 Coffee Rd Modesto (95355) ***(P-21274)***
Sutter Health ....D....916 454-8200
3707 Schriever Ave Mather (95655) ***(P-20329)***
Sutter Health ....C....530 406-5600
475 Pioneer Ave Ste 100 Woodland (95776) ***(P-19474)***
Sutter Health ....C....209 538-1733
2516 E Whitmore Ave Ceres (95307) ***(P-21275)***
Sutter Health ....C....209 522-0146
3612 Dale Rd Modesto (95356) ***(P-19475)***
Sutter Health ....B....916 691-5900
8170 Laguna Blvd Ste 220 Elk Grove (95758) ***(P-21276)***
Sutter Health ....C....650 262-4262
50 S San Mateo Dr Ste 470 San Mateo (94401) ***(P-19476)***
Sutter Health ....B....805 966-1600
25 W Micheltorena St Santa Barbara (93101) ***(P-21277)***
Sutter Health ....E....831 477-3600
2880 Soquel Ave Ste 10 Santa Cruz (95062) ***(P-21278)***
Sutter Health ....C....209 334-3333
999 S Fairmont Ave # 200 Lodi (95240) ***(P-19477)***
Sutter Health ....C....408 733-4380
325 N Mathilda Ave Sunnyvale (94085) ***(P-19478)***
Sutter Health ....C....707 263-6885
5196 Hill Rd E Ste 300 Lakeport (95453) ***(P-19479)***
Sutter Health ....B....707 545-2255
4702 Hoen Ave Santa Rosa (95405) ***(P-21279)***
Sutter Health ....C....650 853-2904
795 El Camino Real Palo Alto (94301) ***(P-19480)***
Sutter Health ....D....916 784-2277
1640 E Roseville Pkwy Roseville (95661) ***(P-21594)***
Sutter Health ....D....916 451-3344
3161 L St Sacramento (95816) ***(P-19481)***
Sutter Health ....C....916 453-5955
1020 29th St Ste 570b Sacramento (95816) ***(P-21280)***
Sutter Health ....C....415 600-6000
3555 Cesar Chavez San Francisco (94110) ***(P-19482)***
Sutter Health ....C....510 618-5200
1651 Alvarado St San Leandro (94577) ***(P-20465)***
Sutter Health ....C....530 749-3585
969 Plumas St Ste 103116 Yuba City (95991) ***(P-19483)***
Sutter Health ....C....916 731-5672
P.O. Box 160100 Sacramento (95816) ***(P-21281)***
Sutter Health ....D....916 797-4700
3 Medical Plaza Dr # 100 Roseville (95661) ***(P-19484)***
Sutter Health ....C....831 458-5500
2880 Soquel Ave Santa Cruz (95062) ***(P-24672)***
Sutter Health ....C....707 523-7253
2449 Summerfield Rd Santa Rosa (95405) ***(P-21282)***
Sutter Health ....C....916 262-9456
2725 Capitol Ave Dept 404 Sacramento (95816) ***(P-19485)***
Sutter Health ....C....530 750-5888
2030 Sutter Pl Ste 1300 Davis (95616) ***(P-21283)***
Sutter Health ....C....415 602-5380
100 Rowland Way Novato (94945) ***(P-21284)***
Sutter Health ....A....530 888-4500
11775 Education St # 201 Auburn (95602) ***(P-22134)***
Sutter Health ....C....916 286-6665
1025 Atlantic Ave Ste 100 Alameda (94501) ***(P-24673)***
Sutter Health At Work ....D....916 565-8607
1014 N Market Blvd Ste 20 Sacramento (95834) ***(P-19486)***
Sutter Hlth At Work - Natomas, Sacramento *Also called Sutter Health At Work* ***(P-19486)***
Sutter Hlth Rhabilitation Svcs ....D....916 733-3040
2801 L St Fl 3 Sacramento (95816) ***(P-23497)***
Sutter Hlth Scrmnto Sierra Reg ....A....530 747-5010
2030 Sutter Pl Ste 2000 Davis (95616) ***(P-19487)***
Sutter Hlth Scrmnto Sierra Reg ....A....209 223-7540
100 Mission Blvd Jackson (95642) ***(P-19488)***
Sutter Hlth Scrmnto Sierra Reg ....A....916 733-7080
701 Howe Ave Ste F20 Sacramento (95825) ***(P-22331)***
Sutter Hlth Scrmnto Sierra Reg (HQ) ....B....916 733-8800
2200 River Plaza Dr Sacramento (95833) ***(P-21285)***
Sutter Hlth Scrmnto Sierra Reg ....B....530 756-6440
2000 Sutter Pl Davis (95616) ***(P-21286)***
Sutter Hlth Scrmnto Sierra Reg ....B....916 454-2222
5151 F St Sacramento (95819) ***(P-21287)***
Sutter Hlth Scrmnto Sierra Reg ....D....916 446-3100
1234 U St Sacramento (95818) ***(P-21288)***
Sutter Hlth Scrmnto Sierra Reg ....A....916 781-1000
1 Medical Plaza Dr Roseville (95661) ***(P-21289)***
Sutter Hlth Scrmnto Sierra Reg ....A....916 733-3095
2800 L St Sacramento (95816) ***(P-21290)***
Sutter Hlth Scrmnto Sierra Reg ....A....530 406-5616
475 Pioneer Ave Ste 100 Woodland (95776) ***(P-19489)***
Sutter Lakeside Hospital (HQ) ....B....707 262-5000
5176 Hill Rd E Lakeport (95453) ***(P-21291)***
Sutter Maternity & Surgery Ctr ....C....831 477-2200
2900 Chanticleer Ave Santa Cruz (95065) ***(P-21292)***
Sutter Medical Center, Sacramento *Also called Sutter Health* ***(P-21270)***
Sutter Medical Center, Sacramento *Also called Sutter Hlth Scrmnto Sierra Reg* ***(P-21290)***
Sutter Medical Center, Woodland *Also called Sutter Hlth Scrmnto Sierra Reg* ***(P-19489)***
Sutter Medical Ctr Sacramento, Sacramento *Also called Sutter Hlth Rhabilitation Svcs* ***(P-23497)***
Sutter Medical Foundation ....A....916 924-7764
1014 N Market Blvd Ste 20 Sacramento (95834) ***(P-19696)***
Sutter Memorial Hospital, Sacramento *Also called Sutter Hlth Scrmnto Sierra Reg* ***(P-21285)***
Sutter Memorial Hospital, Sacramento *Also called Sutter Hlth Scrmnto Sierra Reg* ***(P-21287)***
Sutter N Med Group A Prof Corp (PA) ....D....530 749-3661
969 Plumas St Ste 205 Yuba City (95991) ***(P-19490)***
Sutter North Med Foundation (PA) ....C....530 741-1300
969 Plumas St Yuba City (95991) ***(P-19491)***
Sutter North Med Foundation ....D....530 749-3635
480 Plumas Blvd Yuba City (95991) ***(P-19492)***
Sutter North Med Foundation ....D....530 675-1245
16911 Willow Glen Rd Brownsville (95919) ***(P-19493)***
Sutter North Med Foundation ....D....530 749-3450
400 Plumas Blvd Ste 115 Yuba City (95991) ***(P-19494)***
Sutter Occupational Hlth Svcs, Roseville *Also called Sutter Health* ***(P-19484)***
Sutter Pacific Med Foundation, San Francisco *Also called Sutter Health* ***(P-21260)***
Sutter Pacific Med Foundation, Lakeport *Also called Sutter Health* ***(P-19479)***
Sutter Pacific Med Foundation, Santa Rosa *Also called Sutter Health* ***(P-21279)***
Sutter Physician Services (HQ) ....A....916 854-6600
10470 Old Placerville Rd Sacramento (95827) ***(P-26838)***
Sutter Regional Med Foundation ....D....707 551-3616
127 Hospital Dr Ste 102 Vallejo (94589) ***(P-24674)***
Sutter Regional Med Foundation ....D....707 454-5800
770 Mason St Vacaville (95688) ***(P-19495)***
Sutter Roseville Medical Ctr, Roseville *Also called Sutter Hlth Scrmnto Sierra Reg* ***(P-21289)***
Sutter Roseville Medical Ctr ....A....916 781-1000
1 Medical Plaza Dr Roseville (95661) ***(P-21293)***
Sutter Rsvlle Med Ctr Fndation ....A....916 781-1000
1 Medical Plaza Dr Roseville (95661) ***(P-21294)***
Sutter Senior Care, Sacramento *Also called Sutter Hlth Scrmnto Sierra Reg* ***(P-21288)***
Sutter Surgical Hospital N Vly ....C....530 749-5700
455 Plumas Blvd Yuba City (95991) ***(P-21295)***
Sutter Valley Hospitals (HQ) ....B....209 223-7500
200 Mission Blvd Jackson (95642) ***(P-21296)***
Sutter Valley Med Foundation (PA) ....A....916 887-7122
2700 Gateway Oaks Dr Sacramento (95833) ***(P-21297)***
Sutter Vsiting Nurse Assn Hosp, Concord *Also called Sutter Vsting Nrse Assn Hspice* ***(P-21879)***
Sutter Vsting Nrse Assn Hspice ....D....415 600-6200
1625 Van Ness Ave San Francisco (94109) ***(P-21877)***
Sutter Vsting Nrse Assn Hspice (HQ) ....E....866 652-9178
1900 Powell St Ste 300 Emeryville (94608) ***(P-21878)***
Sutter Vsting Nrse Assn Hspice ....D....510 618-5277
1651 Alvarado St San Leandro (94577) ***(P-20330)***
Sutter Vsting Nrse Assn Hspice ....D....925 677-4250
5099 Commercial Cir # 20594520 Concord (94520) ***(P-21879)***
Sutter West Bay Hospitals (HQ) ....B....415 209-1300
180 Rowland Way Novato (94945) ***(P-21298)***
Sutter West Foundation, Davis *Also called Sutter Hlth Scrmnto Sierra Reg* ***(P-19487)***
Sutter Yuba Mental Health Svcs, Yuba City *Also called County of Sutter* ***(P-22011)***
Suttles Plumbing & Mech Corp ....D....818 718-9779
2267 Agate Ct Simi Valley (93065) ***(P-2297)***
Suttter North Home Health, Yuba City *Also called Sutter North Med Foundation* ***(P-19494)***
Svb Financial Group (PA) ....C....408 654-7400
3003 Tasman Dr Santa Clara (95054) ***(P-9242)***
Svcf, Mountain View *Also called Silicon Vly Cmnty Foundation* ***(P-24660)***
Svd Inc ....D....818 504-1775
8088 San Fernando Rd Sun Valley (91352) ***(P-8324)***
Svi Lax LLC ....D....310 281-0300
5933 W Century Blvd Los Angeles (90045) ***(P-13006)***
Svmc Precision Orthopedics, Salinas *Also called Salinas Valley Memorial Hlthca* ***(P-21491)***
Svmk Inc ....A....503 225-1202
3050 S Delaware St San Mateo (94403) ***(P-15134)***
Svn International Corp ....D....310 979-0800
11999 San Vicente Blvd # 215 Los Angeles (90049) ***(P-11471)***
Swa Group (PA) ....C....415 332-5100
2200 Bridgeway Sausalito (94965) ***(P-766)***
Swagbucks, El Segundo *Also called Prodege LLC* ***(P-15034)***
Swagelok Northern California, Fremont *Also called Sunnyvale Fluid Sys Tech Inc* ***(P-7659)***
Swaminatha Mahadevan MD ....D....650 723-6576
701 Welch Rd Bldg C Palo Alto (94304) ***(P-19496)***
Swan Engineering Inc ....D....916 474-5299
4470 Yankee Hill Rd # 200 Rocklin (95677) ***(P-3331)***
Swander Pace Capital LLC (PA) ....A....415 477-8500
101 Mission St Ste 1900 San Francisco (94105) ***(P-26839)***
Swann Communications USA Inc ....D....562 777-2551
12636 Clark St Santa Fe Springs (90670) ***(P-7351)***
Swanson Farms ....D....209 667-2002
5213 W Main St Turlock (95380) ***(P-417)***

Swanton Berry Farms Inc .... E 831 425-8919
25 Swanton Rd Davenport (95017) *(P-362)*
Swatfame Inc (PA) .... B 626 961-7928
16425 Gale Ave City of Industry (91745) *(P-8113)*
Swayzer A-1 Sanitizing, Carson *Also called Swayzers Incorporated* *(P-14062)*
Swayzers Incorporated .... D 323 979-7223
1663 E Del Amo Blvd Carson (90746) *(P-14062)*
Swca Incorporated .... D 626 240-0587
51 W Dayton St Ste 100 Pasadena (91105) *(P-27221)*
Swca Environmental Consultants, Pasadena *Also called Swca Incorporated* *(P-27221)*
Sweda Company LLC .... C 626 357-9999
17411 E Valley Blvd City of Industry (91744) *(P-7793)*
Sweetwater Authority (PA) .... C 619 422-8395
505 Garrett Ave Chula Vista (91910) *(P-6123)*
Sweetwater Gardens Inc .... E 707 937-4140
955 Ukiah Mendocino (95460) *(P-18203)*
Sweis Inc (PA) .... C 310 375-0558
23760 Hawthorne Blvd Torrance (90505) *(P-7682)*
Swell Athletic Club GP .... D 805 964-7762
5800 Cathedral Oaks Rd Goleta (93117) *(P-18590)*
Swenson Developers and Contrs, San Jose *Also called Santa Clara Valley Corporation* *(P-14037)*
Swenson, Barry Builder, San Jose *Also called Green Valley Corporation* *(P-1486)*
Swinerton Bldrs Pacific R .... D 619 954-8011
16798 W Bernardo Dr San Diego (92127) *(P-1612)*
Swinerton Builders, San Diego *Also called Solv Inc* *(P-15503)*
Swinerton Builders (HQ) .... C 415 421-2980
260 Townsend St Fl 3 San Francisco (94107) *(P-1382)*
Swinerton Builders .... D 213 896-3400
865 S Figueroa St # 3000 Los Angeles (90017) *(P-1613)*
Swinerton Builders .... D 858 622-4040
16798 W Bernardo Dr San Diego (92127) *(P-1383)*
Swinerton Builders Hc .... D 916 383-4825
15 Business Park Way # 101 Sacramento (95828) *(P-1614)*
Swinerton Builders Inc .... D 925 602-6400
2300 Clayton Rd Ste 800 Concord (94520) *(P-1205)*
Swinerton Incorporated .... D 925 689-2336
2300 Clayton Rd Ste 800 Concord (94520) *(P-1275)*
Swinerton Incorporated (PA) .... C 415 421-2980
260 Townsend St San Francisco (94107) *(P-1615)*
SWINERTON MANAGEMENT & CONSULTING, San Francisco *Also called Swinerton Builders* *(P-1382)*
Swinford Electric Inc .... E 714 578-8888
1150 E Elm Ave Fullerton (92831) *(P-2663)*
Swirl Inc .... D 415 276-8300
101 Montgomery St Ste 200 San Francisco (94129) *(P-13583)*
Swirl McGarrybowen, San Francisco *Also called Swirl Inc* *(P-13583)*
Swiss Hotel Group Inc .... D 707 938-2884
18 W Spain St Sonoma (95476) *(P-13007)*
Swiss Port Corp .... B 310 417-0258
11001 Aviation Blvd Los Angeles (90045) *(P-26956)*
Swissport, Los Angeles *Also called Swiss Port Corp* *(P-26956)*
Swissport Cargo Services LP .... A 310 910-9541
11001 Aviation Blvd Los Angeles (90045) *(P-4796)*
Swissport Fueling Inc .... C 510 562-1701
1 Edward White Way Oakland (94621) *(P-8737)*
Swissport Usa Inc .... C 650 821-6220
San Francisco Intl Arprt San Francisco (94128) *(P-4797)*
Swissport Usa Inc .... B 310 345-1986
7025 W Imperial Hwy Los Angeles (90045) *(P-4798)*
Swissport Usa Inc .... C 571 214-7068
Delta Cargo Bldg 612 San Francisco (94128) *(P-4799)*
Swissport Usa Inc .... B 310 910-9560
11001 Aviation Blvd Los Angeles (90045) *(P-4800)*
Switchfly Inc (PA) .... C 415 541-9100
500 3rd St Ste 440 San Francisco (94107) *(P-6905)*
Sws, Fullerton *Also called Superior Wall Systems Inc* *(P-2865)*
Swt Stockton, Temecula *Also called Southwest Traders Incorporated* *(P-8262)*
Swvp Del Mar Hotel LLC .... C 858 481-5900
11915 El Camino Real San Diego (92130) *(P-13008)*
Swvp Westlake LLC .... C 805 557-1234
880 S Westlake Blvd Westlake Village (91361) *(P-13009)*
Syapse Inc .... C 650 924-1461
303 2nd St Ste N500 San Francisco (94107) *(P-15513)*
Syar Industries Inc .... D 707 643-3261
885 Lake Herman Rd Vallejo (94591) *(P-1052)*
Syar Industries Inc .... D 707 433-3366
13666 Healdsburg Ave Healdsburg (95448) *(P-6697)*
Sycamore Cc Inc .... D 760 451-3700
3742 Flowerwood Ln Fallbrook (92028) *(P-18591)*
Sycamore Cogeneration Co (PA) .... C 661 615-4630
1546 China Grade Loop Bakersfield (93308) *(P-5955)*
SYCAMORE COURT APT, Newport Beach *Also called 10632 Bolsa Avenue LP* *(P-10676)*
Sycamore Mineral Spring Resort .... D 805 595-7302
1215 Avila Beach Dr San Luis Obispo (93405) *(P-13010)*
Sycamore Park Care Center LLC .... D 323 223-3441
4585 N Figueroa St Los Angeles (90065) *(P-20698)*
SYCAMORE PARK CONVALESCENT HOSPITAL, Los Angeles *Also called Sycamore Park Care Center LLC* *(P-20698)*
Sycamores School, Altadena *Also called Pasadena Chld Training Soc* *(P-24023)*
Sycuan Casino .... A 619 445-6002
5459 Casino Way El Cajon (92019) *(P-18764)*
Sycuan Resort and Casino, El Cajon *Also called Sycuan Casino* *(P-18764)*
Sydata Inc .... C 760 444-4368
6494 Weathers Pl Ste 100 San Diego (92121) *(P-5476)*
Sydell Hotels LLC .... D 213 381-7411
3515 Wilshire Blvd Los Angeles (90010) *(P-13011)*

Sygma Network Inc .... C 661 723-0405
46905 47th St W Lancaster (93536) *(P-8655)*
Sygma Network Inc .... C 209 932-5300
3741 Gold River Ln Stockton (95215) *(P-8265)*
Sygma Network, The, Sun Valley *Also called Sugar Foods Corporation* *(P-17073)*
Sylmar Hlth Rehabilitation Ctr, Sylmar *Also called Sylmar Hlth Rehabilitation Ctr* *(P-21428)*
Sylmar Hlth Rehabilitation Ctr, Sylmar *Also called Golden State Health Ctrs Inc* *(P-21411)*
Sylmar Hlth Rehabilitation Ctr 818 834-5082
12220 Foothill Blvd Sylmar (91342) *(P-21428)*
Sylmark Group, Van Nuys *Also called Sylmark Inc* *(P-26417)*
Sylmark Inc (PA) .... D 818 217-2000
7821 Orion Ave Ste 200 Van Nuys (91406) *(P-26417)*
Sylvester Roofing Company Inc (PA) .... E 760 743-0048
2593 Auto Park Way Escondido (92029) *(P-3101)*
Symitar Systems Inc 619 542-6700
8985 Balboa Ave San Diego (92123) *(P-15135)*
Symphony Comm Svcs LLC (PA) .... D 650 733-6660
1117 California Ave Palo Alto (94304) *(P-27307)*
Synagro West LLC .... D 650 652-6531
1499 Bayshore Hwy Ste 111 Burlingame (94010) *(P-27222)*
Synarc Reiscdronate, Newark *Also called Bioclinca* *(P-25721)*
Synarc's, Newark *Also called Bioclinca* *(P-14675)*
Synchronoss Technologies Inc .... B 800 575-7606
60 S Market St Ste 700 San Jose (95113) *(P-2664)*
Synctruck LLC .... C 415 425-0447
415 Darrell Rd Hillsborough (94010) *(P-4281)*
Synectic Solutions Inc (PA) .... D 805 483-4800
1701 Pacific Ave Ste 260 Oxnard (93033) *(P-16123)*
Synergex International Corp .... D 916 635-7300
2355 Gold Meadow Way # 200 Gold River (95670) *(P-15514)*
Synergy Companies, Hayward *Also called Eagle Systems Intl Inc* *(P-2121)*
Synergy Environmental, Hayward *Also called American Synergy Asbestos Remo* *(P-3372)*
Synergy Health North Amer Inc .... D 562 428-5858
2240 E Artesia Blvd Long Beach (90805) *(P-13242)*
Synermed .... D 213 626-4556
711 W College St Fl 4 Los Angeles (90012) *(P-26418)*
Synermed .... C 216 406-2845
1200 Corp Ctr Dr Ste 200 Monterey Park (91754) *(P-19497)*
Syngenta Seeds Inc .... E 408 847-4242
5653 Monterey Frontage Rd Gilroy (95020) *(P-8860)*
Syniverse Technologies LLC .... C 408 324-1830
181 Metro Dr Ste 450 San Jose (95110) *(P-16124)*
Synnex Corporation .... D 909 923-8900
3655 E Philadelphia St Ontario (91761) *(P-4510)*
Synnexxus LLC .... E 714 933-4500
20251 Sw Acacia St # 200 Newport Beach (92660) *(P-22842)*
Synopsys Inc (PA) .... B 650 584-5000
690 E Middlefield Rd Mountain View (94043) *(P-15515)*
Synopsys Inc .... D 626 795-9101
199 S Los Robles Ave # 400 Pasadena (91101) *(P-15516)*
Synoptek Inc (PA) .... D 949 241-8600
19520 Jamboree Rd Ste 110 Irvine (92612) *(P-16125)*
Synplicity Inc (HQ) .... C 650 584-5000
690 E Middlefield Rd Mountain View (94043) *(P-15517)*
Syntelesys Inc .... E 323 859-2160
2550 Corp Pl Ste C108 Monterey Park (91754) *(P-17439)*
Synteract Inc (HQ) .... B 760 268-8200
5909 Sea Otter Pl Ste 100 Carlsbad (92010) *(P-25842)*
Synteracthcr, Carlsbad *Also called Synteract Inc* *(P-25842)*
Synteracthcr Corporation (HQ) .... B 760 268-8200
5909 Sea Otter Pl Ste 100 Carlsbad (92010) *(P-25843)*
Synteracthcr Holdings Corp (PA) .... B 760 268-8200
5909 Sea Otter Pl Ste 100 Carlsbad (92010) *(P-25844)*
Synthetic Genomics Inc (HQ) .... C 858 754-2900
11149 N Torrey Pines Rd La Jolla (92037) *(P-25845)*
Syntiro Healthcare Services (PA) .... C 949 923-3438
7 Technology Dr Irvine (92618) *(P-26419)*
Sypartners LLC (HQ) .... D 415 536-6600
475 Brannan St Ste 100 San Francisco (94107) *(P-27223)*
Sysco Central California Inc .... B 209 527-7700
136 Mariposa Rd Modesto (95354) *(P-8266)*
Sysco Labs, San Mateo *Also called Cake Corporation* *(P-14699)*
Sysco Los Angeles Inc .... A 909 595-9595
20701 Currier Rd Walnut (91789) *(P-8267)*
Sysco Riverside Inc .... B 951 601-5300
15750 Meridian Pkwy Riverside (92518) *(P-8268)*
Sysco Sacramento Inc .... B 916 275-2714
7062 Pacific Ave Pleasant Grove (95668) *(P-8269)*
Sysco San Diego Inc .... B 858 513-7300
12180 Kirkham Rd Poway (92064) *(P-8270)*
Sysco San Francisco Inc .... A 510 226-3000
5900 Stewart Ave Fremont (94538) *(P-8271)*
Sysco Ventura Inc .... B 805 205-7000
3100 Sturgis Rd Oxnard (93030) *(P-8272)*
Sysdig Inc (PA) .... D 415 872-9473
85 2nd St Ste 800 San Francisco (94105) *(P-15136)*
Sysintelli Inc .... C 858 271-1600
9466 Black Mountain Rd # 200 San Diego (92126) *(P-15137)*
Syska & Hennessy Engineers Inc .... D 310 312-0200
800 Crprate Pnte Ste 200 Culver City (90230) *(P-25328)*
Sysorex USA (HQ) .... D 415 389-7500
101 Larkspur Landing Cir # 120 Larkspur (94939) *(P-15699)*
Syspro Impact Software Inc .... C 714 437-1000
959 S Coast Dr Ste 100 Costa Mesa (92626) *(P-6906)*
Systech Integrators Inc .... D 408 441-2700
2050 Gateway Pl San Jose (95110) *(P-16126)*
Systech Solutions (PA) .... D 818 550-9690
500 N Brand Blvd Ste 1900 Glendale (91203) *(P-15138)*
Systechs, Orange *Also called Cruz Modular Inc* *(P-4202)*

Employee Codes: A=Over 500 employees, B=251-500
C=101-250, D=51-100, E=50

2020 Directory of California
Wholesalers and Services Companies

© Mergent Inc. 1-800-342-5647

1451

System Integrators Inc (HQ) ....C....916 830-2400
1740 N Market Blvd Sacramento (95834) ***(P-15700)***

Systems America Public Sector, Pleasanton *Also called Tryfacta Inc* ***(P-15165)***

Systems and Software Entps LLC (HQ) ....D....714 854-8600
2929 E Imperial Hwy # 170 Brea (92821) ***(P-15139)***

Systems Application & Tech Inc ....D....805 487-7373
1000 Town Center Dr # 110 Oxnard (93036) ***(P-25329)***

Systems Experience Inc ....D....310 215-9000
6033 W Century Blvd # 820 Los Angeles (90045) ***(P-27224)***

Systems Paving Inc (PA) ....D....949 263-8301
1570 Brookhollow Dr Santa Ana (92705) ***(P-1797)***

Syzygy Technologies Inc ....D....619 297-0970
1272 Calpella Ct Chula Vista (91913) ***(P-25330)***

T & P Farms ....D....530 476-3038
1241 Putnam Way Arbuckle (95912) ***(P-3)***

T & R Painting & Drywall, Van Nuys *Also called Touch-Up Inc* ***(P-2870)***

T & R Painting Construction ....C....818 779-3800
7116 Valjean Ave Van Nuys (91406) ***(P-2400)***

T & T Solutions Inc ....D....818 676-1786
7018 Owensmouth Ave # 201 Canoga Park (91303) ***(P-16127)***

T & T Truck & Crane Service, Ventura *Also called Offshore Crane & Service Co* ***(P-14108)***

T & T Trucking Inc (PA) ....C....800 692-3457
11396 N Hwy 99 Lodi (95240) ***(P-4141)***

T - Y Nursery Inc ....C....760 742-2151
15335 Highway 76 Pauma Valley (92061) ***(P-8925)***

T and D Communications Inc (PA) ....D....510 824-0010
6761 Sierra Ct Ste F Dublin (94568) ***(P-15140)***

T and M Agricultural Svcs LLC ....C....707 963-3330
493 Dowdell Ln Saint Helena (94574) ***(P-684)***

T B Penick & Sons Inc ....C....951 719-1492
41892 Enterprise Cir S Temecula (92590) ***(P-1206)***

T B Penick & Sons Inc (PA) ....C....858 558-1800
15435 Innovation Dr # 100 San Diego (92128) ***(P-1384)***

T Boyer Company ....E....949 642-2431
1656 Babcock St Costa Mesa (92627) ***(P-2665)***

T C Construction Company Inc ....C....619 448-4560
10540 Prospect Ave Santee (92071) ***(P-1919)***

T C H P Inc ....D....951 687-7330
11162 Palm Terrace Ln Riverside (92505) ***(P-20331)***

T C I, Redondo Beach *Also called Transportation Concept Inc* ***(P-3614)***

T C P, Santa Monica *Also called Tennenbaum Capitl Partners LLC* ***(P-11962)***

T C R Limited Partnership ....C....310 645-1881
5440 W Century Blvd Los Angeles (90045) ***(P-17224)***

T C W Realty Fund VI ....C....213 683-4200
515 S Flower St Fl 31 Los Angeles (90071) ***(P-11877)***

T D R, Turlock *Also called Turlock Dairy & Rfrgn Inc* ***(P-7511)***

T F Louderback Inc (PA) ....C....510 965-6120
700 National Ct Richmond (94804) ***(P-8793)***

T G T Enterprises Inc ....C....858 413-0300
12650 Danielson Ct Poway (92064) ***(P-13741)***

T I C Hotels Inc ....D....619 238-7577
555 W Ash St San Diego (92101) ***(P-13012)***

T I C Hotels Inc ....D....805 773-4671
2555 Price St Pismo Beach (93449) ***(P-13013)***

T I D, Turlock *Also called Turlock Irrigation District* ***(P-6374)***

T L Fabrications LP ....D....562 802-3980
2921 E Coronado St Anaheim (92806) ***(P-3286)***

T M B, San Fernando *Also called Jme Inc* ***(P-7158)***

T M Cobb Company ....D....916 381-7330
8490 Rovana Cir Sacramento (95828) ***(P-6662)***

T M I, San Diego *Also called Toward Maximum Independence* ***(P-23505)***

T M Mian & Associates Inc ....D....818 591-2300
24150 Park Sorrento Calabasas (91302) ***(P-13014)***

T M Mian & Associates Inc ....D....805 983-8600
2000 Solar Dr Oxnard (93036) ***(P-13015)***

T M S, Campbell *Also called Telecmmnctons MGT Slutions Inc* ***(P-2669)***

T McGee Electric Inc ....D....909 591-6461
2390 S Reservoir St Pomona (91766) ***(P-2666)***

T Points Inc ....E....323 846-9176
350 W Mrtn Lthr King Jr Los Angeles (90037) ***(P-13326)***

T R L, Rancho Cucamonga *Also called TRL Systems Incorporated* ***(P-2676)***

T Royal Management (PA) ....D....559 447-9887
7419 N Cedar Ave Ste 102 Fresno (93720) ***(P-11472)***

T T Miyasaka Inc ....B....831 722-3871
209 Riverside Rd Watsonville (95076) ***(P-113)***

T U D, Sonora *Also called Tuolumne Utilities District* ***(P-6124)***

T W R Framing ....D....951 279-2000
1661 Railroad St Corona (92880) ***(P-14432)***

T Y Lin International (HQ) ....D....415 291-3700
345 California St # 2300 San Francisco (94104) ***(P-25331)***

T Y R, Seal Beach *Also called Tyr Sport Inc* ***(P-8116)***

T&C Roofing Inc ....D....925 513-8463
2155 Elkins Way Ste H Brentwood (94513) ***(P-3102)***

T-12 Three LLC ....B....619 702-3000
207 5th Ave San Diego (92101) ***(P-13016)***

T-Force Inc (PA) ....D....949 208-1527
4695 Macarthur Ct Newport Beach (92660) ***(P-27225)***

T-Mobile Usa Inc ....C....510 797-8290
4095 Mowry Ave Fremont (94538) ***(P-5273)***

T-Mobile Usa Inc ....C....209 529-0539
2225 Plaza Pkwy Ste I1b Modesto (95350) ***(P-5274)***

T-Mobile Usa Inc ....C....415 440-5370
900 Van Ness Ave Ste 1 San Francisco (94109) ***(P-5275)***

T-N-T Grading, Escondido *Also called TNT Grading Inc* ***(P-1800)***

T.C.A.H, Sonora *Also called Watch Resources Inc* ***(P-23540)***

T.com Ontario Fc T-9479, Ontario *Also called Target Corporation* ***(P-4513)***

T.S.c, Altadena *Also called Tom Sawyer Camps Inc* ***(P-23799)***

T/O Printing, Westlake Village *Also called Thousand Oaks Prtg & Spc Inc* ***(P-17094)***

T2d Media, El Monte *Also called Dang Quinten* ***(P-5783)***

T3 Direct, Modesto *Also called Sterling Mktg & Fincl Corp* ***(P-26831)***

T3w Business Solutions Inc ....D....619 298-0888
3921 Ampudia St San Diego (92110) ***(P-26420)***

Ta Chen International Inc (HQ) ....C....562 808-8000
5855 Obispo Ave Long Beach (90805) ***(P-7107)***

TA Industries Inc (PA) ....D....562 466-1000
11130 Bloomfield Ave Santa Fe Springs (90670) ***(P-7441)***

Ta-Kai Home Care Inc ....D....714 393-4586
22349 La Palma Ave # 105 Yorba Linda (92887) ***(P-21880)***

Taber Company Inc ....D....714 543-7100
1442 Ritchey St Santa Ana (92705) ***(P-6663)***

Table Community Foudation ....D....209 951-1753
3201 W Benjamin Holt Dr Stockton (95219) ***(P-24675)***

Table Mountain Casino ....A....559 822-7777
8184 Table Mountain Rd Friant (93626) ***(P-13017)***

Tabletops Unlimited Inc (PA) ....D....310 549-6000
23000 Avalon Blvd Carson (90745) ***(P-6586)***

Tabula Inc ....D....408 986-9140
1100 La Avenida St Ste A Mountain View (94043) ***(P-7352)***

TAC Rbo, Sacramento *Also called Surgical Care Affiliate* ***(P-25685)***

Tacer, Van Nuys *Also called Town & Country Event Rentals* ***(P-14203)***

Tachi Palace Hotel & Casino ....A....559 924-7751
17225 Jersey Ave Lemoore (93245) ***(P-13018)***

Tachyon Inc ....E....858 882-8108
9339 Carroll Park Dr # 150 San Diego (92121) ***(P-5477)***

Tacori By B & T Jewelers, Glendale *Also called Tacori Enterprises* ***(P-7794)***

Tacori Enterprises ....D....818 863-1536
1736 Gardena Ave Glendale (91204) ***(P-7794)***

Tactical Engrg & Analis Inc (PA) ....C....858 573-9869
6050 Santo Rd Ste 250 San Diego (92124) ***(P-16128)***

Tactical Lgistic Solutions Inc ....D....909 464-2813
13799 Monte Vista Ave Chino (91710) ***(P-4511)***

Tactical Telesolutions Inc ....C....415 788-8808
2121 N Calif Blvd Ste 260 Walnut Creek (94596) ***(P-17077)***

Tactivos Inc ....D....415 687-2501
303 2nd St Ste S200 San Francisco (94107) ***(P-5478)***

Tad Group LLC ....C....949 476-3601
5000 Birch St Ste 3000 Newport Beach (92660) ***(P-16566)***

Tad Pgs Inc ....D....571 451-2428
10805 Holder St Ste 250 Cypress (90630) ***(P-14571)***

Tae Technologies Inc (PA) ....C....949 830-2117
19631 Pauling Foothill Ranch (92610) ***(P-25846)***

Taft College Children Center ....E....661 763-7850
29 Emmons Park Dr Taft (93268) ***(P-23795)***

Taft Correctional Institution, Taft *Also called Geo Group Inc* ***(P-26943)***

Taft Electric Company (PA) ....C....805 642-0121
1694 Eastman Ave Ventura (93003) ***(P-2667)***

Taft Production Company ....D....661 765-7194
950 Petroleum Club Rd Taft (93268) ***(P-975)***

Tahoe Beach & Ski Club ....D....530 541-6220
3601 Lake Tahoe Blvd South Lake Tahoe (96150) ***(P-13019)***

Tahoe Donner Association ....C....530 587-9437
12790 Northwoods Blvd Truckee (96161) ***(P-24676)***

Tahoe Donner Golf Course Inc ....D....530 587-9455
11509 Northwoods Blvd Truckee (96161) ***(P-18306)***

Tahoe Forest Hospital District ....D....530 582-7488
10710 Donner Pass Rd Truckee (96161) ***(P-19498)***

Tahoe Forest Hospital District ....C....530 582-3277
10956 Donner Paca Rd Truckee (96161) ***(P-21299)***

Tahoe Forest Hospital District (PA) ....B....530 587-6011
10121 Pine Ave Truckee (96161) ***(P-21300)***

Tahoe Lake Partners LLC ....D....707 255-9890
855 Bordeaux Way Ste 200 NAPA (94558) ***(P-11611)***

Tahoe Seasons Resort Time Inte ....C....530 541-6700
3901 Saddle Rd South Lake Tahoe (96150) ***(P-11473)***

Tahoe Trcke Unfd Sch Dis Fincn ....D....530 582-7630
11725 Donner Past Rd Truckee (96160) ***(P-27226)***

Tahoe Workx, Truckee *Also called Tahoe Forest Hospital District* ***(P-21299)***

Tahoe-Truckee Sanitation Agcy ....D....530 587-2525
13720 Butterfield Dr Truckee (96161) ***(P-6140)***

Tai Seng Entertainment, South San Francisco *Also called U-2 Home Entertainment Inc* ***(P-7358)***

Tailbroom Media Grop, North Hollywood *Also called Pilgrim Operations LLC* ***(P-6736)***

Tailored Living Choices LLC ....C....707 259-0526
1957 Sierra Ave NAPA (94558) ***(P-3473)***

Tait Environmental Svcs Inc (PA) ....D....714 560-8200
701 Parkcenter Dr Santa Ana (92705) ***(P-3474)***

Takara Bio Usa Inc ....C....650 919-7300
1290 Terra Bella Ave Mountain View (94043) ***(P-25847)***

Takeda California Inc ....C....858 622-8528
10410 Science Center Dr San Diego (92121) ***(P-26036)***

Takenaka Partners LLC (PA) ....E....213 593-4011
801 S Figueroa St Ste 620 Los Angeles (90017) ***(P-9754)***

Takeuchi Financial Services ....D....706 693-3600
475 Sansome St San Francisco (94111) ***(P-17078)***

Talari Networks Inc (PA) ....D....408 689-0400
4230 Leonard Stocking Dr Santa Clara (95054) ***(P-15701)***

Talbot Insurance & Fincl Svcs, Santa Barbara *Also called Caesar and Seider Insur Svcs* ***(P-10306)***

Talco Plastics Inc (PA) ....D....951 531-2000
1000 W Rincon St Corona (92880) ***(P-6290)***

Talega Golf Club, San Clemente *Also called Heritage Golf Group LLC* ***(P-18253)***

Talend Inc (HQ) ....C....650 539-3200
800 Bridge Pkwy Ste 200 Redwood City (94065) ***(P-15702)***

Talent & Acquisition LLC ....C....213 742-1972
100 W Broadway Ste 650 Long Beach (90802) ***(P-15141)***

Talent Space Inc ....D....408 330-1900
1650 The Alameda San Jose (95126) ***(P-14433)***

Mergent e-mail: customerrelations@mergent.com 2020 Directory of California (P-0000) Products & Services Section entry number
1452 Wholesalers and Services Companies (PA)=Parent Co (HQ)=Headquarters (DH)=Div Headquarters

Talentburst Inc ... C ... 415 813-4011
575 Market St Ste 3025 San Francisco (94105) ***(P-17079)***

Talentscale LLC ... D ... 951 744-0053
31805 Temecula Pkwy 204 Temecula (92592) ***(P-25332)***

Talentwave, Foster City *Also called Ic Compliance LLC* ***(P-14864)***

Talix Inc ... D ... 628 220-3885
660 3rd St Ste 302 San Francisco (94107) ***(P-15518)***

Tall Pony Productions Inc ... C ... 310 456-7495
300 Loma Metisse Rd Malibu (90265) ***(P-17680)***

Taller Technologies, San Francisco *Also called Quadriga Inc* ***(P-15042)***

Talley & Associates, Santa Fe Springs *Also called Talley Inc* ***(P-7353)***

Talley Farms ... C ... 805 489-2508
2900 Lopez Dr Arroyo Grande (93420) ***(P-550)***

Talley Inc (PA) ... C ... 562 906-8000
12976 Sandoval St Santa Fe Springs (90670) ***(P-7353)***

Talley Transportation ... D ... 559 673-9013
12325 Road 29 Madera (93638) ***(P-3940)***

Talon Executive Services Inc ... E ... 714 434-7476
151 Kalmus Dr Ste A103 Costa Mesa (92626) ***(P-16567)***

Talon International Inc (PA) ... D ... 818 444-4100
21900 Burbank Blvd # 270 Woodland Hills (91367) ***(P-8014)***

Tama Trading Company ... D ... 213 748-8262
1920 E 20th St Vernon (90058) ***(P-8656)***

Tamal Pais, Greenbrae *Also called Northern California Presbyteri* ***(P-20643)***

TAMALPAIS, Greenbrae *Also called Ross Valley Homes Inc* ***(P-20450)***

Tamalpais Creek, Novato *Also called Atria Senior Living Inc* ***(P-23828)***

Tamarack Bch Condo Owners Assn ... E ... 760 729-3500
3200 Carlsbad Blvd Carlsbad (92008) ***(P-24677)***

Tammi R James MD ... E ... 916 383-6783
7273 14th Ave Ste 120b Sacramento (95820) ***(P-19499)***

Tamtron Corporation (HQ) ... D ... 408 323-3303
6203 San Ignacio Ave # 110 San Jose (95119) ***(P-15142)***

Tan Jay-Nygard Outlet Store, Gardena *Also called Nygard Inc* ***(P-8104)***

Tanaka Farms ... D ... 949 653-2100
5380 University Dr Irvine (92612) ***(P-8657)***

Tangoe Us Inc ... D ... 858 452-6800
9920 Pcf Hts Blvd Ste 200 San Diego (92121) ***(P-15519)***

Tanimura & Antle, Salinas *Also called Plant Tape Usa Inc* ***(P-439)***

Tanimura & Antle Inc ... B ... 831 424-6100
4401 Foxdale St Baldwin Park (91706) ***(P-551)***

Tanimura & Antle Inc ... D ... 805 483-2358
761 Commercial Ave Oxnard (93030) ***(P-4512)***

Tanimura Antle Fresh Foods Inc (PA) ... D ... 831 455-2950
1 Harris Rd Salinas (93908) ***(P-80)***

Tanimura Brothers ... D ... 831 424-0841
81 Hitchcock Rd Salinas (93908) ***(P-9755)***

Tanner Mainstain Blatt & Gly ... D ... 310 446-2700
10866 Wilshire Blvd Fl 10 Los Angeles (90024) ***(P-25686)***

Tano Capital LLC ... E ... 650 212-0330
1 Franklin Pkwy San Mateo (94403) ***(P-11958)***

Tantra Lake Partners LP ... C ... 949 756-5959
18802 Bardeen Ave Irvine (92612) ***(P-10825)***

Tanvex Biopharma Usa Inc (PA) ... D ... 858 210-4100
10394 Pacific Center Ct San Diego (92121) ***(P-25848)***

Tao Mechanical Ltd ... E ... 925 447-5220
136 Wright Brothers Ave Livermore (94551) ***(P-2298)***

Taos Mountain LLC (PA) ... B ... 408 324-2800
121 Daggett Dr San Jose (95134) ***(P-16129)***

Tap Operating Co LLC ... A ... 310 900-5500
400 W Artesia Blvd Compton (90220) ***(P-6473)***

Tap Ram Reinforcing Inc ... D ... 562 484-0859
11658 Excelsior Dr Norwalk (90650) ***(P-3287)***

Tap Worldwide LLC (PA) ... C ... 310 900-5500
400 W Artesia Blvd Compton (90220) ***(P-6474)***

Tapestry Solutions Inc (HQ) ... C ... 858 503-1990
5643 Copley Dr San Diego (92111) ***(P-15143)***

Tapia Brothers Co, Maywood *Also called Tapia Enterprises Inc* ***(P-8273)***

Tapia Enterprises Inc (PA) ... D ... 323 560-7415
6067 District Blvd Maywood (90270) ***(P-8273)***

Tapjoy Inc (PA) ... D ... 415 766-6900
353 Sacramento St Ste 600 San Francisco (94111) ***(P-13584)***

Tara, Lomita *Also called Torrance Amateur Rdo Assn Inc* ***(P-24879)***

Tarana Wireless Inc ... C ... 510 868-3359
2105 Martin Luther King Berkeley (94704) ***(P-5276)***

Tarbel Realtors, Murrieta *Also called F M Tarbell Co* ***(P-11123)***

Tarbell Financial Corporation ... D ... 909 335-0750
1440 Industrial Park Ave Redlands (92374) ***(P-11474)***

Tarbell Financial Corporation (PA) ... D ... 714 972-0988
1403 N Tustin Ave Ste 380 Santa Ana (92705) ***(P-9647)***

Tarbell Realtors, Anaheim *Also called F M Tarbell Co* ***(P-11124)***

Tarbell Realtors, Anaheim *Also called F M Tarbell Co* ***(P-11125)***

Tarbell Realtors, Santa Ana *Also called F M Tarbell Co* ***(P-11126)***

Tarbell Realtors, Corona *Also called F M Tarbell Co* ***(P-11127)***

Tarbell Realtors, Laguna Hills *Also called F M Tarbell Co* ***(P-11128)***

Tarbell Realtors, Menifee *Also called F M Tarbell Co* ***(P-11129)***

Tarbell Realtors, Temecula *Also called F M Tarbell Co* ***(P-11130)***

Tarbell Realtors, Irvine *Also called F M Tarbell Co* ***(P-11131)***

Tarbell Realtors, Palm Desert *Also called F M Tarbell Co* ***(P-11133)***

Tarbell Realtors, Upland *Also called F M Tarbell Co* ***(P-11134)***

Target Corporation ... C ... 909 937-5500
1505 S Haven Ave Ontario (91761) ***(P-4513)***

Target Corporation ... B ... 909 355-6000
14750 Miller Ave Fontana (92336) ***(P-4514)***

Target Corporation ... B ... 530 666-3705
2050 E Beamer St Woodland (95776) ***(P-4515)***

Target Cw, San Diego *Also called Wmbe Payrolling Inc* ***(P-14453)***

Target Specialty Products, Santa Fe Springs *Also called Rentokil North America Inc* ***(P-8855)***

Target Specialty Products, Santa Fe Springs *Also called Western Exterminator Company* ***(P-13835)***

Targus International LLC (PA) ... C ... 714 765-5555
1211 N Miller St Anaheim (92806) ***(P-9014)***

Tariff Building Associates LP (PA) ... D ... 415 397-5572
222 Kearny St Ste 200 San Francisco (94108) ***(P-10661)***

Tarpy Heating & Air ... E ... 619 485-3311
9723 Roe Dr Santee (92071) ***(P-2299)***

Tarpy Plumbing Heating and Air, Santee *Also called Tarpy Heating & Air* ***(P-2299)***

Tarra Landscape, Oakland *Also called Tree Sculpture Group* ***(P-914)***

Tarrant Apparel Group ... C ... 323 780-8250
801 S Figueroa St # 2500 Los Angeles (90017) ***(P-8114)***

Tarsadia Hotels, Newport Beach *Also called Uka LLC* ***(P-13050)***

Tarsco Holdings LLC ... C ... 562 869-0200
11905 Regentview Ave Downey (90241) ***(P-17550)***

Tarzana Treatment Centers Inc ... C ... 818 654-3815
422 W Rancho Vista Blvd C280 Palmdale (93551) ***(P-22135)***

Tarzana Treatment Centers Inc (PA) ... C ... 818 996-1051
18646 Oxnard St Tarzana (91356) ***(P-22136)***

Tarzana Treatment Centers Inc ... C ... 562 428-4111
5190 Atlantic Ave Lakewood (90805) ***(P-22137)***

Tarzana Treatment Centers Inc ... E ... 562 218-1868
2101 Magnolia Ave Long Beach (90806) ***(P-22138)***

Tarzana Treatment Centers Inc ... D ... 661 726-2630
44447 10th St W Lancaster (93534) ***(P-22139)***

Tarzana Treatment Ctr, Lancaster *Also called Tarzana Treatment Centers Inc* ***(P-22139)***

Tarzana Trtmnt Ctrs LNG Bch O, Lakewood *Also called Tarzana Treatment Centers Inc* ***(P-22137)***

Task Force For Reg Autostaff, Monrovia *Also called Trap* ***(P-17105)***

Taskus Inc (PA) ... D ... 888 400-8275
3221 Donald Douglas Santa Monica (90405) ***(P-15821)***

Taslimi Construction Co Inc ... D ... 310 447-3000
1805 Colorado Ave Santa Monica (90404) ***(P-1616)***

Tasser Technologies Inc ... D ... 408 364-0373
43252 Christy St Fremont (94538) ***(P-27227)***

Tasteful Selections LLC ... D ... 661 588-1053
13003 Di Giorgio Rd Arvin (93203) ***(P-8658)***

Tata America Intl Corp ... D ... 408 569-5845
5201 Great America Pkwy # 400 Santa Clara (95054) ***(P-16130)***

Tata Communications Amer Inc ... D ... 650 262-0004
700 Airport Blvd Ste 100 Burlingame (94010) ***(P-17080)***

Tata Consulting Services, Santa Clara *Also called Tata America Intl Corp* ***(P-16130)***

Tate Neurological Surgery, Redding *Also called James D Tate MD* ***(P-19029)***

Taulia Inc (PA) ... D ... 415 376-8280
250 Montgomery St Ste 400 San Francisco (94104) ***(P-15144)***

Tavant Technologies Inc (PA) ... C ... 408 519-5400
3965 Freedom Cir Ste 750 Santa Clara (95054) ***(P-15145)***

Tawa Services Inc (PA) ... B ... 714 521-8899
6338 Regio Ave Buena Park (90620) ***(P-8659)***

Tax and Financial Group, Newport Beach *Also called R Mc Closkey Insurance Agency* ***(P-10473)***

Tax Compliance Inc ... D ... 858 547-4100
10089 Willow Creek Rd # 300 San Diego (92131) ***(P-15146)***

Tax Credit Co LLC ... C ... 323 927-0752
6255 W Sunset Blvd # 2200 Los Angeles (90028) ***(P-13393)***

Tax Problem Center, Los Angeles *Also called Authority Tax Services LLC* ***(P-16637)***

Tax Resolution Services, Co, Calabasas *Also called Danerica Enterprises Inc* ***(P-13417)***

Tax Rise Inc ... D ... 877 697-4732
19900 Macarthur Blvd Irvine (92612) ***(P-17081)***

Taxaudit.com, Folsom *Also called Taxresources Inc* ***(P-25687)***

Taxresources Inc (PA) ... C ... 877 369-7827
600 Coolidge Dr Ste 300 Folsom (95630) ***(P-25687)***

Taylor & Assoc Architects Inc (PA) ... E ... 949 574-1325
17850 Fitch Irvine (92614) ***(P-25507)***

Taylor Bailey Inc ... D ... 707 967-8090
355 Lafata St Ste E Saint Helena (94574) ***(P-1617)***

Taylor Communications Inc ... D ... 925 245-6420
5775 Brisa St Livermore (94550) ***(P-4577)***

Taylor Design, Irvine *Also called Taylor & Assoc Architects Inc* ***(P-25507)***

Taylor Farms, San Juan Bautista *Also called Earthbound Farm LLC* ***(P-483)***

Taylor Farms California Inc (HQ) ... E ... 831 754-0471
150 Main St Ste 500 Salinas (93901) ***(P-552)***

Taylor Fresh Foods Inc (PA) ... C ... 831 676-9023
150 Main St Ste 400 Salinas (93901) ***(P-553)***

Taylor Morrison California LLC ... C ... 949 341-1200
100 Spectrum Center Dr # 1450 Irvine (92618) ***(P-11612)***

Taylor Structures Inc ... D ... 707 499-6870
905 Cotting Ln Ste 100 Vacaville (95688) ***(P-1618)***

Taylored Services LLC (HQ) ... D ... 909 510-4800
1495 E Locust St Ontario (91761) ***(P-4516)***

Taylored Services Holdings LLC (HQ) ... D ... 909 510-4800
1495 E Locust St Ontario (91761) ***(P-4517)***

Taylored Svcs Parent Co Inc (PA) ... D ... 909 510-4800
1495 E Locust St Ontario (91761) ***(P-5060)***

Tbc - Boring Company ... D ... 425 495-4215
12200 Crenshaw Blvd Hawthorne (90250) ***(P-3475)***

TBG Insurance Services Corp ... B ... 310 203-8770
100 N Pacific Coast Hwy # 50 El Segundo (90245) ***(P-10519)***

Tbwa Chiat/Day Inc ... D ... 310 305-5000
5353 Grosvenor Blvd Los Angeles (90066) ***(P-17082)***

Tbwa Worldwide Inc ... C ... 310 305-4400
1017 16th St Apt C Santa Monica (90403) ***(P-13585)***

Tc Property Mgt A Californi ... D ... 530 666-5799
1224 Cottonwood St Ofc Woodland (95695) ***(P-11959)***

Tcal, San Diego *Also called Takeda California Inc* ***(P-26036)***

Employee Codes: A=Over 500 employees, B=251-500
C=101-250, D=51-100, E=50
2020 Directory of California
Wholesalers and Services Companies
© Mergent Inc. 1-800-342-5647
1453

Tcb Industrial Inc (PA) C 209 571-0569
2955 Farrar Ave Modesto (95354) ***(P-1385)***
Tccsc, Los Angeles *Also called Tessie Clvland Cmnty Svcs Corp* ***(P-23501)***
Tcg Builders Inc E 408 321-6450
890 N Mccarthy Blvd # 100 Milpitas (95035) ***(P-1619)***
Tcg Capital Management LP C 310 633-2900
1733 Ocean Ave Ste 300 Santa Monica (90401) ***(P-11960)***
Tcg Software Services Inc E 714 665-6200
320 Commerce Ste 200 Irvine (92602) ***(P-15147)***
TCI Aluminum/North Inc D 510 786-3750
2353 Davis Ave Hayward (94545) ***(P-7108)***
Tcm Group LLC E 909 527-8580
3130 Inland Empire Blvd Ontario (91764) ***(P-26421)***
Tcmi Inc (PA) E 650 614-8200
250 Middlefield Rd Menlo Park (94025) ***(P-11961)***
Tcp Global Corporation D 858 909-2110
6695 Rasha St San Diego (92121) ***(P-8946)***
Tct Circuit Supply Inc D 714 644-9700
560 S Melrose St Placentia (92870) ***(P-7660)***
Tcv Management 2004 LLC E 650 614-8200
528 Ramona St Palo Alto (94301) ***(P-26422)***
Tcw Funds Management Inc A 213 244-0000
865 S Figueroa St # 2100 Los Angeles (90017) ***(P-9756)***
Tcw Group Inc (PA) B 213 244-0000
865 S Figueroa St # 1800 Los Angeles (90017) ***(P-9850)***
Tcw Value Added Ltd Partnr D 213 244-0000
865 S Figueroa St Los Angeles (90017) ***(P-11818)***
TD Desert Dev Ltd Partnr (HQ) C 760 777-1001
81570 Carboneras La Quinta (92253) ***(P-11613)***
Tdic, Sacramento *Also called Dentists Insurance Company* ***(P-10339)***
Tdk-Lambda Americas Inc C 619 575-4400
401 Mile Of Cars Way # 3 National City (91950) ***(P-7354)***
TDS, Hornitos *Also called Hornitos Telephone Co* ***(P-5417)***
Teale Data Center, Rancho Cordova *Also called Technology Services Cal Dept* ***(P-15823)***
Tealium Inc (PA) D 858 779-1344
11095 Torreyana Rd Fl 2 San Diego (92121) ***(P-15822)***
Team Dykspra (PA) D 951 898-6482
2315 California Ave Corona (92881) ***(P-17399)***
Team Finish Inc D 714 671-9190
155 Arovista Cir Ste A Brea (92821) ***(P-3227)***
Team Ghilotti Inc E 707 763-8700
2531 Petaluma Blvd S Petaluma (94952) ***(P-1798)***
Team Makena LLC (PA) D 949 474-1753
27051 Towne Centre Dr # 180 Foothill Ranch (92610) ***(P-7009)***
Team One, Los Angeles *Also called Team-One Emplyment Spclsts LLC* ***(P-14434)***
Team Post-Op Inc (HQ) D 949 253-5500
17256 Red Hill Ave Irvine (92614) ***(P-7010)***
Team Power Forklift, Fair Oaks *Also called Clarklift-West Inc* ***(P-7537)***
Team Risk MGT Strategies LLC A 877 767-8728
3131 Camino Del Rio N # 650 San Diego (92108) ***(P-27228)***
Team San Jose A 408 295-9600
408 Almaden Blvd San Jose (95110) ***(P-17083)***
Team Services, Burbank *Also called The Team Companies LLC* ***(P-25688)***
Team Spirit Realty Inc E 714 562-0404
6301 Beach Blvd Ste 225 Buena Park (90621) ***(P-11475)***
Team Superstores, Vallejo *Also called Teamross Inc* ***(P-17349)***
Team Tomato, Norwalk *Also called Lj Distributors Inc* ***(P-8496)***
Team Truck Dismantling Inc D 951 685-6744
3760 Pyrite St Riverside (92509) ***(P-6497)***
Team West Contracting Corp D 951 340-3426
2733 S Vista Ave Bloomington (92316) ***(P-1995)***
Team-One Emplyment Spclsts LLC A 310 481-4480
2999 Overland Ave Ste 212 Los Angeles (90064) ***(P-14434)***
Teamross Inc D 707 643-9000
301 Auto Mall Pkwy Vallejo (94591) ***(P-17349)***
Tecan Sp Inc D 626 962-0010
14180 Live Oak Ave Baldwin Park (91706) ***(P-7035)***
Tech Flex Package E 323 241-1800
12624 Daphne Ave Hawthorne (90250) ***(P-13800)***
Tech Knowledge Associates LLC D 714 735-3810
1 Centerpointe Dr Ste 200 La Palma (90623) ***(P-17551)***
Tech Museum of Innovation (PA) D 408 795-6116
201 S Market St San Jose (95113) ***(P-24295)***
Tech Museum of Innovation D 408 795-6168
145 W San Carlos St San Jose (95113) ***(P-24296)***
Tech Packaging Inc D 909 243-7047
9545 Santa Anita Ave A Rancho Cucamonga (91730) ***(P-17084)***
Tech Soup, San Francisco *Also called Techsoup Global* ***(P-24678)***
Tech Systems Inc C 714 523-5404
7372 Walnut Ave Ste J Buena Park (90620) ***(P-7355)***
Tech Town Inc E 818 621-2744
1157 N Brand Blvd Glendale (91202) ***(P-15148)***
Tech-Ed Networks Inc C 916 784-2005
10000 Allantown Dr # 175 Roseville (95678) ***(P-16131)***
Techaisle LLC E 408 253-4416
5053 Doyle Rd Ste 105 San Jose (95129) ***(P-25947)***
Techcon, Morgan Hill *Also called Monument Construction Inc* ***(P-872)***
Techexcel Inc (PA) D 925 871-3900
3675 Mt Diablo Blvd # 200 Lafayette (94549) ***(P-15149)***
Techflow Inc (PA) C 858 412-8000
9889 Willow Creek Rd San Diego (92131) ***(P-26957)***
Technclor Crative Svcs USA Inc (HQ) B 818 260-3800
6040 W Sunset Blvd Los Angeles (90028) ***(P-17767)***
Technclor Crative Svcs USA Inc C 323 467-1244
6040 W Sunset Blvd Los Angeles (90028) ***(P-17768)***
Technclor Vdocassette Mich Inc (HQ) B 805 445-1122
3233 Mission Oaks Blvd Camarillo (93012) ***(P-17769)***
Technical America Inc D 951 272-9540
301 N Smith Ave Corona (92880) ***(P-25333)***
Technical Services, Mountain View *Also called Northrop Grumman Systems Corp* ***(P-15663)***
Technical Temps Inc D 408 956-8256
1096 Pecten Ct Milpitas (95035) ***(P-14435)***
Technicolor Inc B 818 260-4577
2255 N Ontario St Ste 180 Burbank (91504) ***(P-16584)***
Technicolor Inc (HQ) D 805 445-1122
3233 Mission Oaks Blvd Camarillo (93012) ***(P-17770)***
Technicolor - Funimation Ent, Calexico *Also called Technicolor HM Entrmt Svcs Inc* ***(P-17771)***
Technicolor HM Entrmt Svcs Inc B 760 357-3372
1778 Zinetta Rd Ste F Calexico (92231) ***(P-17771)***
Technicolor HM Entrmt Svcs Inc B 909 974-2016
5491 E Philadelphia St Ontario (91761) ***(P-17772)***
Technicolor HM Entrmt Svcs Inc (HQ) B 805 445-1122
3233 Mission Oaks Blvd Camarillo (93012) ***(P-17773)***
Technicolor Hollywood, Los Angeles *Also called Technicolor Thomson Group* ***(P-17774)***
Technicolor Lab, Burbank *Also called Technicolor Inc* ***(P-16584)***
Technicolor New Media Inc E 818 480-5100
250 E Olive Ave Ste 300 Burbank (91502) ***(P-17681)***
Technicolor Thomson Group A 323 817-6600
6040 W Sunset Blvd Los Angeles (90028) ***(P-17774)***
Technicolor Thomson Group B 818 260-3600
2255 N Ontario St Ste 100 Burbank (91504) ***(P-17775)***
Technicolor Thomson Group B 909 974-2222
5491 E Philadelphia St Ontario (91761) ***(P-17776)***
Technicolor Thomson Group A 805 445-1122
3301 Mission Oaks Blvd Camarillo (93012) ***(P-17777)***
Technicolor Video Service, Camarillo *Also called Technclor Vdocassette Mich Inc* ***(P-17769)***
Technicolor Video Services, Camarillo *Also called Technicolor HM Entrmt Svcs Inc* ***(P-17773)***
Technicon Design Corporation C 949 218-1300
26522 La Alameda Ste 150 Mission Viejo (92691) ***(P-17085)***
Techno Coatings Inc C 714 774-4671
795 Debra St Anaheim (92805) ***(P-1620)***
TECHNOLOGENT, Irvine *Also called Thomas Gallaway Corporation* ***(P-15154)***
Technology Associates EC Inc D 760 765-5275
3129 Tiger Run Ct Ste 206 Carlsbad (92010) ***(P-26840)***
Technology Credit Union D 408 467-2382
1562 S Bascom Ave San Jose (95125) ***(P-9408)***
Technology Credit Union D 408 467-2385
43848 Pcf Commons Blvd Fremont (94538) ***(P-9409)***
Technology Credit Union (PA) C 408 451-9111
2010 N 1st St Ste 200 San Jose (95131) ***(P-9410)***
Technology Credit Union D 650 326-6445
490 California Ave Palo Alto (94306) ***(P-9411)***
Technology Crossover Ventures, Menlo Park *Also called Tcmi Inc* ***(P-11961)***
Technology Services Cal Dept C 916 464-3747
3101 Gold Camp Dr Rancho Cordova (95670) ***(P-16132)***
Technology Services Cal Dept E 916 464-3747
10860 Gold Center Dr # 100 Rancho Cordova (95670) ***(P-15823)***
Technology Services Cal Dept (HQ) D 916 319-9223
1325 J St Ste 1600 Sacramento (95814) ***(P-16133)***
Technosocialworkcom LLC D 661 617-6601
4300 Resnik Ct Unit 103 Bakersfield (93313) ***(P-15824)***
Techsoup Global (PA) C 800 659-3579
435 Brannan St Ste 100 San Francisco (94107) ***(P-24678)***
Techstyles Sportswear, Hayward *Also called Bruml Management LLC* ***(P-8059)***
Tecolote Research Inc C 310 640-4700
2120 E Grand Ave Ste 200 El Segundo (90245) ***(P-26841)***
Tecta America Southern Cal Inc D 714 973-6233
1217 E Wakeham Ave Santa Ana (92705) ***(P-3103)***
Tectura Corporation (PA) E 650 273-4249
951 Old County Rd 2-317 Belmont (94002) ***(P-16134)***
Ted Cooper/Cooper Industries E 408 358-3060
P.O. Box 36007 San Jose (95158) ***(P-913)***
Ted Fisher Head Start, Huntington Beach *Also called Orange County Head Start* ***(P-23767)***
Ted Ford Jones Inc (PA) C 714 521-3110
6211 Beach Blvd Buena Park (90621) ***(P-17350)***
Ted Levine Drum Co (PA) D 626 579-1084
1817 Chico Ave South El Monte (91733) ***(P-17552)***
Teecom D 510 337-2800
1333 Broadway Ste 601 Oakland (94612) ***(P-25334)***
Teen Challenge Norwestcal Nev D 408 703-2001
390 Mathew St Santa Clara (95050) ***(P-23498)***
Teg Staffing Inc A 619 260-2000
2355 Northside Dr Ste 200 San Diego (92108) ***(P-14436)***
Tegile Systems Inc C 510 791-7900
7999 Gateway Blvd Ste 120 Newark (94560) ***(P-25849)***
Tegp Inc A 619 584-3408
2375 Northside Dr Ste 360 San Diego (92108) ***(P-14572)***
Tegtmeier Associates Inc D 530 872-7700
6701 Clark Rd Paradise (95969) ***(P-10662)***
Tehachapi Vly Healthcare Dst (PA) C 661 750-4848
305 S Robinson St Tehachapi (93561) ***(P-21301)***
Tehama Golf Club LLC D 831 622-2200
4 Tehama Carmel (93923) ***(P-18592)***
Teichert Construction, Sacramento *Also called A Teichert & Son Inc* ***(P-6668)***
Teichert/Great Lakes E&I JV D 916 484-3011
3500 American River Dr Sacramento (95864) ***(P-1996)***
Teixeira Farms Inc C 805 928-3801
2600 Bonita Lateral Rd Santa Maria (93458) ***(P-81)***
Tejon Ranch Co (PA) D 661 248-3000
4436 Lebec Rd Lebec (93243) ***(P-180)***
Tekever Corporation D 408 730-2617
5201 Great America Pkwy Santa Clara (95054) ***(P-15520)***
Tektetco D 707 822-9000
5251 Ericson Way Arcata (95521) ***(P-1386)***
Tekworks, Poway *Also called Paladin Technologies Inc* ***(P-16979)***
Tekworks Inc D 877 835-9675
12742 Knott St Garden Grove (92841) ***(P-5479)***

Tekworks Inc ....C....858 668-1705
13000 Gregg St Ste B Poway (92064) *(P-27229)*
Tel Tech Plus Inc ....E....760 510-1323
393 Enterprise St San Marcos (92078) *(P-2668)*
Telacu, Commerce *Also called East Los Angeles Community Un (P-9480)*
Telacu Industries Inc (HQ) ....E....323 721-1655
5400 E Olympic Blvd # 300 Commerce (90022) *(P-11614)*
Telaflora LLC ....B....310 231-9199
11444 W Olympic Blvd Fl 4 Los Angeles (90064) *(P-8926)*
Tele-Car Courier Service, Los Angeles *Also called Tele-Car Couriers Inc (P-4282)*
Tele-Car Couriers Inc ....D....877 910-1313
4035 Eagle Rock Blvd Los Angeles (90065) *(P-4282)*
Tele-Direct Communications ....D....916 348-2170
4741 Madison Ave Ste 200 Sacramento (95841) *(P-17086)*
Tele-Interpreters LLC ....B....800 811-7881
1 Lower Ragsdale Dr # 2 Monterey (93940) *(P-17087)*
Telecare Corporation ....D....714 361-6760
275 Baker St Costa Mesa (92626) *(P-21429)*
Telecare Corporation ....D....510 895-5502
2050 Fairmont Dr San Leandro (94578) *(P-21430)*
Telecare Corporation ....D....760 245-8837
16460 Victor St Victorville (92395) *(P-21431)*
Telecare Corporation ....D....619 275-8000
1675 Morena Blvd Ste 100 San Diego (92110) *(P-21432)*
Telecare Corporation ....D....562 630-8672
6060 N Paramount Blvd Long Beach (90805) *(P-21433)*
Telecare Corporation ....C....562 634-9534
6060 N Paramount Blvd Long Beach (90805) *(P-21434)*
Telecare Corporation ....C....510 261-9191
1451 28th Ave Oakland (94601) *(P-21435)*
Telecare Corporation ....C....510 582-7676
494 Blossom Way Hayward (94541) *(P-21436)*
Telecare Corporation ....C....510 352-9690
15200 Foothill Blvd San Leandro (94578) *(P-21437)*
Telecare Corporation ....D....619 692-8225
3851 Rosecrans St San Diego (92110) *(P-21438)*
Telecare Corporation ....D....805 383-3669
1756 S Lewis Rd Camarillo (93012) *(P-21439)*
Telecare Corporation ....C....650 367-1890
200 Edmonds Rd Redwood City (94062) *(P-21440)*
Telecare Corporation ....C....510 337-7950
1080 Marina Village Pkwy # 100 Alameda (94501) *(P-21441)*
Telecare Corporation ....C....562 633-5111
8835 Vans St Paramount (90723) *(P-21442)*
Telecare Corporation ....D....650 817-9070
300 Harbor Blvd E Belmont (94002) *(P-21443)*
Telecare Corporation ....C....510 535-5115
2633 E 27th St Oakland (94601) *(P-21444)*
Telecare Fsp, Belmont *Also called Telecare Corporation (P-21443)*
Telecare La Step Down ....E....562 216-4900
4335 Atlantic Ave Long Beach (90807) *(P-22140)*
Telecare Las Posadas ....D....805 383-3669
1756 S Lewis Rd Camarillo (93012) *(P-22141)*
Telecmmnctons MGT Slutions Inc ....D....408 866-5495
570 Division St Campbell (95008) *(P-2669)*
Telecntric Communications Intl ....D....562 906-2555
12070 Telg Rd Ste 107 Santa Fe Springs (90670) *(P-17088)*
Telecom Evolutions LLC ....E....818 264-4400
9221 Corbin Ave Ste 260 Northridge (91324) *(P-17089)*
Telecom Inc ....D....510 873-8283
2201 Broadway Ste 103 Oakland (94612) *(P-17090)*
Telecom Technology Svcs Inc ....C....925 224-7812
7901 Stoneridge Dr # 500 Pleasanton (94588) *(P-27230)*
Telecommunications Dept, Salinas *Also called County of Monterey (P-16722)*
Telecommunications Division, Sacramento *Also called General Services Cal Dept (P-25100)*
Telecontact Resource Services, Riverbank *Also called Econtactlive Inc (P-16760)*
Teledyne Scentific Imaging LLC ....C....805 373-4979
5212 Verdugo Way Camarillo (93012) *(P-25850)*
Teledyne Scentific Imaging LLC (HQ) ....C....805 373-4545
1049 Camino Dos Rios Thousand Oaks (91360) *(P-25851)*
Teledyne Scientific Company, Thousand Oaks *Also called Teledyne Scentific Imaging LLC (P-25851)*
Telegraph Hill Partners Invest (PA) ....E....415 765-6980
360 Post St Ste 601 San Francisco (94108) *(P-26842)*
Teleinterpreters, Monterey *Also called Language Line Services Inc (P-16884)*
Telemarketing, Fresno *Also called Fowler Packing Company Inc (P-491)*
Telemedicine Corp ....E....888 472-2853
8920 Wilshire Blvd # 310 Beverly Hills (90211) *(P-22332)*
Telenet Voip Inc ....D....310 253-9000
850 N Park View Dr El Segundo (90245) *(P-17465)*
Telepictures, Burbank *Also called Warner Bros Transatlantic Inc (P-17798)*
Teleplan Service Solutions Inc ....D....916 677-4500
8875 Washington Blvd B Roseville (95678) *(P-15926)*
Telescape, Los Angeles *Also called Truconnect Communications Inc (P-5483)*
Telesis Community Credit Union (PA) ....D....818 885-1226
9301 Winnetka Ave Chatsworth (91311) *(P-9357)*
Telesis Onion Co (PA) ....C....559 884-2441
3265 W Figarden Dr Fresno (93711) *(P-82)*
Telesis Onion Co ....E....559 884-2441
21484 S Colusa Five Points (93624) *(P-554)*
Telestar Consulting Inc ....E....310 748-0008
519 N Alta Dr Beverly Hills (90210) *(P-26843)*
Telestream LLC (PA) ....C....530 470-1300
848 Gold Flat Rd Nevada City (95959) *(P-15150)*
Telesys Software ....E....650 522-9922
1900 S Norfolk St Ste 221 San Mateo (94403) *(P-15151)*
Teletrac Inc (HQ) ....D....714 897-0877
7391 Lincoln Way Garden Grove (92841) *(P-5803)*
Television Academy, North Hollywood *Also called Academy TV Arts Scnces Fndtion (P-24374)*
Television Games Network, Los Angeles *Also called Ods Technologies LP (P-5641)*
Telfer Oil Company (PA) ....D....925 228-1515
211 Foster St Martinez (94553) *(P-1799)*
Telisimo International Corp ....B....619 325-1593
2330 Shelter Island Dr 210a San Diego (92106) *(P-5480)*
Tell Steel Inc ....D....562 435-4826
2345 W 17th St Long Beach (90813) *(P-7109)*
Telstar Instruments (PA) ....D....925 671-2888
1717 Solano Way Ste 34 Concord (94520) *(P-2670)*
Temalpakh Inc ....D....760 770-5778
979 S Gene Autry Trl Palm Springs (92264) *(P-1621)*
Temarry Recycling Inc ....D....619 270-9453
476 Tecate Rd Tecate (91980) *(P-6291)*
Temco, Laguna Beach *Also called C & B Delivery Services (P-4377)*
Temco Logistics, Laguna Beach *Also called Home Express Delivery Svc LLC (P-4967)*
Temecula 24 Hour Care, Temecula *Also called Responsible Med Solutions Corp (P-19332)*
Temecula Stadium Cinemas 15, Temecula *Also called Edwards Theatres Circuit Inc (P-17841)*
Temecula Valley Drywall Inc ....D....951 600-1742
41228 Raintree Ct Murrieta (92562) *(P-2866)*
Temecula Valley Unified School ....B....951 695-7110
40516 Roripaugh Rd Temecula (92591) *(P-3824)*
Temeku Hills, Temecula *Also called McMillin Communities Inc (P-18267)*
Temp Unlimited LLC ....D....562 860-3340
11306 183rd St Ste 301 Cerritos (90703) *(P-14573)*
Tempest Telecom Solutions LLC (PA) ....D....805 879-4800
136 W Canon Perdido St # 100 Santa Barbara (93101) *(P-27231)*
Temple City Convalescent Hosp, Temple City *Also called Fran-Jom Inc (P-20555)*
Temple City Youth Dev Fund ....D....626 548-5085
6415 N Muscatel Ave San Gabriel (91775) *(P-24679)*
Temple Israel of Hollywood (PA) ....D....323 876-8330
7300 Hollywood Blvd Los Angeles (90046) *(P-13381)*
Temple Park Convalescent Hosp ....D....213 380-2035
2411 W Temple St Los Angeles (90026) *(P-20699)*
Templo Calvario Cmnty Dev Corp ....D....714 543-3711
2501 W 5th St Santa Ana (92703) *(P-24232)*
Temporary Plant Cleaners, Martinez *Also called Plant Maintenance Inc (P-14545)*
Temporary Staffing Union ....A....714 728-5186
19800 Macarthur Blvd Irvine (92612) *(P-24467)*
Ten Enthusiast Network LLC ....C....714 709-9021
1821 E Dyer Rd Ste 150 Santa Ana (92705) *(P-8878)*
TEN ENTHUSIAST NETWORK, LLC, Santa Ana *Also called Ten Enthusiast Network LLC (P-8878)*
Ten Publishing Media LLC (PA) ....C....310 531-9900
831 S Douglas St Ste 100 El Segundo (90245) *(P-17778)*
Ten-X, San Mateo *Also called Auctioncom LLC (P-10926)*
Ten-X, Newport Beach *Also called Auctioncom LLC (P-10927)*
Ten-X LLC ....B....800 793-6107
1301 Shoreway Rd Ste 425 Belmont (94002) *(P-11476)*
Tenaya Lodge, Fish Camp *Also called DNC Prks Resorts At Tenaya Inc (P-12218)*
Tender Home Healthcare Inc ....D....323 466-2345
3550 Wilshire Blvd # 700 Los Angeles (90010) *(P-21881)*
Tenderloin Housing Clinic Inc ....C....415 771-2427
472 Turk St San Francisco (94102) *(P-22333)*
Tenderloin Housing Clinic Inc (PA) ....C....415 771-9850
126 Hyde St San Francisco (94102) *(P-11477)*
Tenet, Palm Springs *Also called Desert Regional Med Ctr Inc (P-20827)*
TENET, Santa Ana *Also called French Park Care Center (P-19925)*
TENET, Modesto *Also called Doctors Med Ctr Modesto Inc (P-20859)*
Tenet, Palm Springs *Also called Desert Regional Med Ctr Inc (P-21468)*
Tenet Health System Hospital, Manteca *Also called Tenet Healthsystem Medical (P-21305)*
Tenet Health Systems Norris ....B....323 865-3000
1441 Eastlake Ave Los Angeles (90089) *(P-21302)*
Tenet Healthsystem Medical ....A....714 966-8191
13032 Earlham St Santa Ana (92705) *(P-21303)*
Tenet Healthsystem Medical ....B....925 275-8303
414 Cliffside Dr Danville (94526) *(P-19500)*
Tenet Healthsystem Medical ....A....562 531-2550
3700 South St Lakewood (90712) *(P-19501)*
Tenet Healthsystem Medical ....A....562 531-2550
16331 Arthur St Cerritos (90703) *(P-21304)*
Tenet Healthsystem Medical ....C....619 426-6310
330 Moss St Chula Vista (91911) *(P-21445)*
Tenet Healthsystem Medical ....B....209 823-3111
1205 E North St Manteca (95336) *(P-21305)*
Tenet Healthsystem Medical ....A....714 428-6800
1400 S Duglaca Rd Ste 250 Anaheim (92806) *(P-21306)*
Tenet Healthsystem Medical ....D....530 222-1992
475 Knollcrest Dr Redding (96002) *(P-21882)*
Tenet Healthsystem Medical ....A....805 546-7698
3751 Katella Ave Los Alamitos (90720) *(P-19502)*
Tenet Healthsystem Medical ....B....714 993-2000
1301 N Rose Dr Placentia (92870) *(P-21499)*
Tenet Healthsystem Medical ....D....562 493-9581
1661 Golden Rain Rd Seal Beach (90740) *(P-19503)*
Tenet Healthsystem Medical ....A....408 378-6131
815 Pollard Rd Los Gatos (95032) *(P-21307)*
Tennenbaum Capitl Partners LLC (HQ) ....D....310 566-1000
2951 28th St Ste 1000 Santa Monica (90405) *(P-11962)*
Tennis Channel Inc (HQ) ....D....310 392-1920
2850 Ocean Park Blvd # 150 Santa Monica (90405) *(P-17949)*
Tennis Everyone Incorporated ....D....415 897-2185
351 San Andreas Dr Novato (94945) *(P-18593)*
Tennyson Electric Inc ....E....925 606-1038
7275 National Dr Livermore (94550) *(P-2671)*

Employee Codes: A=Over 500 employees, B=251-500
C=101-250, D=51-100, E=50
2020 Directory of California
Wholesalers and Services Companies
© Mergent Inc. 1-800-342-5647
1455

Tenpo Hardware, Ontario *Also called Ameriwest Industries Inc* ***(P-7379)***
Tensilica Inc (HQ)....D....408 986-8000
3393 Octavius Dr Santa Clara (95054) ***(P-11834)***
Teraburst Networks Inc....E....408 400-4100
1289 Anvilwood Ave Sunnyvale (94089) ***(P-5804)***
Teris LLC....E....619 231-3282
600 W Broadway Ste 300 San Diego (92101) ***(P-15825)***
Teris-Bay Area LLC....D....650 213-9922
2455 Faber Pl Ste 200 Palo Alto (94303) ***(P-22843)***
Terix Computer Service, Santa Clara *Also called Tusa Inc* ***(P-15930)***
Terkensha Associates Inc....D....916 922-9868
811 Grand Ave Ste D Sacramento (95838) ***(P-23499)***
Terminix Intl Co Ltd Partnr....E....818 972-2037
3055 N California St Burbank (91504) ***(P-13829)***
Terminix Intl Co Ltd Partnr....D....925 460-5063
6678 Owens Dr Ste 100 Pleasanton (94588) ***(P-13830)***
Terminix Intl Co Ltd Partnr....E....909 332-2479
649 S Waterman Ave Ste A San Bernardino (92408) ***(P-13831)***
Terminix Intl Co Ltd Partnr....D....818 361-1191
21113 Superior St Chatsworth (91311) ***(P-13832)***
Tero Tek International Inc (PA)....D....661 725-1135
1408 S Lexington St Delano (93215) ***(P-25335)***
Terra Coastal Properties Inc....E....310 457-2534
23405 Pacific Coast Hwy Malibu (90265) ***(P-11478)***
Terra Firma Farm Corp....E....530 795-2473
4713 Baker Rd Winters (95694) ***(P-83)***
Terra Firma Farms, Winters *Also called Terra Firma Farm Corp* ***(P-83)***
Terra Firma Landscape Company, San Diego *Also called L A Swikard Inc* ***(P-843)***
Terra Linda Farms 1....E....559 867-3400
17625 S Marks Ave Riverdale (93656) ***(P-363)***
Terra Nova Counseling (PA)....D....916 344-0249
5750 Sunrise Blvd Ste 100 Citrus Heights (95610) ***(P-23500)***
Terra Pacific Landscape (HQ)....D....714 567-0177
1627 E Wilshire Ave Santa Ana (92705) ***(P-767)***
Terra Vista Management, San Diego *Also called Terra Vista Management Inc* ***(P-11479)***
Terra Vista Management Inc....C....858 581-4200
2211 Pacific Beach Dr San Diego (92109) ***(P-11479)***
Terracare Associates LLC....D....925 374-0060
921 Arnold Dr Martinez (94553) ***(P-26844)***
Terrace View Care Center, Fullerton *Also called Sun Haven Care Inc* ***(P-20278)***
Terraces At Par Marino, Pasadena *Also called Diversified Health Svcs Del* ***(P-23904)***
TERRACES AT SQUAW PEAK, Pleasanton *Also called Humangood* ***(P-20598)***
Terraces of Los Gatos Agei, Los Gatos *Also called American Baptist Homes of West* ***(P-20489)***
Terraces of Roseville, The, Roseville *Also called Westmont Living Inc* ***(P-24115)***
Terraces Retirement Community....C....530 894-1010
2850 Sierra Sunrise Ter Chico (95928) ***(P-24094)***
Terracina Meadows Apts....E....916 419-0925
4500 Tynebourne St F105 Sacramento (95834) ***(P-10826)***
Terranea Resort, Rancho Palos Verdes *Also called Long Point Development LLC* ***(P-12563)***
Terranomics, Burlingame *Also called Cushman & Wakefield Inc* ***(P-11082)***
Terranova Ranch Inc....E....559 866-5644
16729 W Floral Ave Helm (93627) ***(P-364)***
Terre Du Soleil Ltd....B....707 963-1211
180 Rutherford Hill Rd Rutherford (94573) ***(P-13020)***
Terry Hines & Assoc, Burbank *Also called GL Nemirow Inc* ***(P-13511)***
Terry Meyer....D....408 723-3300
1712 Meridian Ave Ste C San Jose (95125) ***(P-11480)***
Terry Tuell Concrete Inc....D....559 431-0812
287 W Fallbrook Ave # 105 Fresno (93711) ***(P-3228)***
Tesancia La Jlla Ht Spa Resort, La Jolla *Also called Destination Residences LLC* ***(P-13419)***
Teserra (PA)....B....760 340-9000
86100 Avenue 54 Coachella (92236) ***(P-3476)***
Tesi Investment Company LLC....D....619 224-3254
5005 N Harbor Dr San Diego (92106) ***(P-13021)***
Tessie Clvland Cmnty Svcs Corp....D....323 586-7333
8019 Compton Ave Ste 219 Los Angeles (90001) ***(P-23501)***
Test-Rite Products Corp (HQ)....D....909 605-9899
1900 Burgundy Pl Ontario (91761) ***(P-6587)***
Testamerica Laboratories Inc....C....949 261-1022
17461 Derian Ave Ste 100 Irvine (92614) ***(P-26109)***
Testamerica Laboratories Inc....D....916 373-5600
880 Riverside Pkwy West Sacramento (95605) ***(P-26110)***
Testequity LLC (PA)....C....805 498-9933
6100 Condor Dr Moorpark (93021) ***(P-17466)***
Testing and Selection, Sacramento *Also called Justice California Department* ***(P-27104)***
Testing Engineers San Diego, San Diego *Also called San Diego Testing Engineers* ***(P-25297)***
Teter LLP (PA)....E....559 437-0887
7535 N Palm Ave Ste 201 Fresno (93711) ***(P-25336)***
Tetra Tech Inc....D....619 525-7188
1230 Columbia St Ste 1000 San Diego (92101) ***(P-26845)***
Tetra Tech Inc....D....805 739-2600
3201 Airpark Dr Ste 108 Santa Maria (93455) ***(P-27232)***
Tetra Tech Inc....D....949 263-0846
17885 Von Karman Ave # 500 Irvine (92614) ***(P-25337)***
Tetra Tech Inc....D....949 809-5000
17885 Von Karman Ave # 500 Irvine (92614) ***(P-25338)***
Tetra Tech Bas Inc (HQ)....D....909 860-7777
21700 Copley Dr Ste 200 Diamond Bar (91765) ***(P-25339)***
Tetra Tech Dpk, San Francisco *Also called Dpk Consulting* ***(P-26586)***
Tetra Tech Ec Inc....D....619 234-8690
1230 Columbia St Ste 750 San Diego (92101) ***(P-25340)***
Tetra Tech Ec Inc....A....916 852-8300
2969 Prospect Park Dr # 100 Rancho Cordova (95670) ***(P-27233)***
Tetra Tech Engrg & Arch Svcs, Irvine *Also called Tetra Tech Inc* ***(P-25338)***
Tetra Tech Executive Svcs Inc....C....626 470-2400
3475 E Foothill Blvd Pasadena (91107) ***(P-14437)***
Tetra Tech Nus Inc....D....412 921-7090
3475 E Foothill Blvd Pasadena (91107) ***(P-27234)***
Tetra Tech Technical Services....C....626 351-4664
3475 E Foothill Blvd Fl 3 Pasadena (91107) ***(P-25341)***
Teutonic Holdings LLC....C....818 264-4400
9221 Corbin Ave Ste 260 Northridge (91324) ***(P-15889)***
Texas Farm, Santa Fe Springs *Also called Seaboard Corporation* ***(P-383)***
Texas Home Health America LP (PA)....D....972 201-3800
1455 Auto Center Dr # 200 Ontario (91761) ***(P-21883)***
Texas Instruments Sunnyvale....E....408 541-9900
165 Gibraltar Ct Sunnyvale (94089) ***(P-17091)***
Textainer Equipment Mgt US Ltd (HQ)....D....415 434-0551
650 California St Fl 16 San Francisco (94108) ***(P-14201)***
Textainer Group Holdings Ltd (HQ)....D....415 434-0551
650 California St Fl 16 San Francisco (94108) ***(P-26423)***
Textaner Eqp Income Fund II LP....D....415 434-0551
650 California St Fl 16 San Francisco (94108) ***(P-14202)***
Textplus Inc....D....424 272-0296
13160 Mindanao Way # 200 Marina Del Rey (90292) ***(P-5277)***
Textron Aviation Inc....D....916 929-5656
5850 Citation Way Sacramento (95837) ***(P-4801)***
Texture Specialties Inc....E....559 904-6047
295 Mccreary Ave Hanford (93230) ***(P-3288)***
Texxis Limited....D....213 631-3547
400 Spectrum Center Dr # 1 Irvine (92618) ***(P-15152)***
Tf Courier Inc....D....916 379-0708
8331 Demetre Ave Sacramento (95828) ***(P-4283)***
Tf Courier Inc....D....888 541-2965
7130 Miramar Rd Ste 400 San Diego (92121) ***(P-4284)***
Tf Courier Inc....D....714 888-1452
2051 Raymer Ave Ste A Fullerton (92833) ***(P-4285)***
Tf Courier Inc....D....214 560-9000
21760 Garcia Ln City of Industry (91789) ***(P-4286)***
Tgcon Inc (HQ)....D....925 449-5764
50 Contractors St Livermore (94551) ***(P-25342)***
Tharp Truck Rental Inc (PA)....C....559 782-5800
15243 Road 192 Porterville (93257) ***(P-17553)***
Tharpe & Howell (PA)....D....818 205-9955
15250 Ventura Blvd Fl 9 Sherman Oaks (91403) ***(P-22844)***
Thc - Orange County Inc....C....310 642-0325
5525 W Slauson Ave Los Angeles (90056) ***(P-21308)***
The Bay Club Hotel and Marina, San Diego *Also called Bay Club Hotel and Marina A C* ***(P-12045)***
The Boardwalk, El Cajon *Also called Newport Diversified Inc* ***(P-16948)***
The Broadmoore, San Francisco *Also called Broadmoor Hotel* ***(P-12091)***
The Charles Schwab Trust Co (HQ)....E....415 371-0518
425 Market St Fl 7 San Francisco (94105) ***(P-9757)***
The David Lcile Pckard Fndtion....D....650 917-7167
300 2nd St Los Altos (94022) ***(P-24877)***
The Designory Inc (HQ)....C....562 624-0200
211 E Ocean Blvd Ste 100 Long Beach (90802) ***(P-13801)***
The Eberly Company, Beverly Hills *Also called Charles & Cynthia Eberly Inc* ***(P-10710)***
The Executive Office of....D....916 322-2318
1400 10th St Rm 100 Sacramento (95814) ***(P-25852)***
The For Califo Cente....C....760 839-4138
340 N Escondido Blvd Escondido (92025) ***(P-24297)***
The For Sacramento Society....D....916 383-7387
6201 Florin Perkins Rd Sacramento (95828) ***(P-24878)***
The For Valley Resource Center (PA)....E....951 766-8659
1285 N Santa Fe St Hemet (92543) ***(P-23645)***
The For Work Training Center....E....530 534-1112
1811 Kusel Rd Oroville (95966) ***(P-23646)***
The Golf Club of California, Fallbrook *Also called Sycamore Cc Inc* ***(P-18591)***
The Goodwin Company, Garden Grove *Also called Goodwin Ammonia Company* ***(P-4422)***
The Gray-Line Tours Company....C....323 463-3333
6541 Hollywood Blvd Los Angeles (90028) ***(P-4868)***
The Lodge At Torrey Pines, La Jolla *Also called Bh Partn A Calif Limit Partne* ***(P-12068)***
The Messenger Company, San Diego *Also called San Diego Messenger Inc* ***(P-4279)***
The National Food Lab LLC....C....925 828-1440
365 N Canyons Pkwy # 201 Livermore (94551) ***(P-26037)***
The Newly Wed, Culver City *Also called Avoca Productions Inc* ***(P-17580)***
The Orthopedic Institute of....A....213 977-2010
616 Witmer St Los Angeles (90017) ***(P-19504)***
The Peninsula Beverly Hills, Beverly Hills *Also called Hong Kong & Shanghai Hotels* ***(P-12382)***
The Pines Ltd....C....619 447-1880
1423 E Washington Ave El Cajon (92019) ***(P-10827)***
The Redwoods A Cmnty Seniors....C....415 383-2741
40 Camino Alto Ofc Mill Valley (94941) ***(P-24095)***
The Residence, Encino *Also called Actual Reality Pictures Inc* ***(P-10891)***
The Sterling Hotel, Sacramento *Also called Elizabethan Inn Associates LP* ***(P-12245)***
The Team Companies LLC (PA)....D....818 558-3261
901 W Alameda Ave Ste 100 Burbank (91506) ***(P-25688)***
The Teecor Group Inc....D....213 632-2350
1450 S Burlington Ave Los Angeles (90006) ***(P-3477)***
The Tristaff Group, San Diego *Also called Garich Inc* ***(P-14287)***
The Valley Club of Montecito....E....805 969-2215
1901 E Valley Rd Santa Barbara (93108) ***(P-18594)***
The Valley Inn, Holtville *Also called Sunharbor Management LLC* ***(P-24091)***
The Villa Florence Hotel, San Francisco *Also called Florence Villa Hotel* ***(P-12269)***
The Woodbridge Golf Cntry CLB....D....209 369-2371
800 E Woodbridge Rd Woodbridge (95258) ***(P-18595)***
Theat and Arts Found of San Di....C....858 623-3366
2910 La Jolla Village Dr La Jolla (92093) ***(P-24680)***
Thefloorstore/Flor Stor, Laguna Hills *Also called Tom Ray Industries Inc* ***(P-6590)***
Thera Home Care, Redwood City *Also called Zb Rehab Staffing Inc* ***(P-14598)***

Therapak LLC (HQ)..........D......909 267-2000
651 Wharton Dr Claremont (91711) *(P-7011)*
Therapeutic Associates Inc..........D......818 748-4900
181 S Buena Vista St Burbank (91505) *(P-21500)*
Therapeutic Associates Inc..........D......818 843-5111
Saint Joseph Hospital Burbank (91505) *(P-19697)*
Therapeutic Pathways Inc..........D......916 489-1376
2775 Cottage Way Ste 8 Sacramento (95825) *(P-19698)*
Therapy & Rehabilitation Ctrs, Simi Valley *Also called Simi Vly Hosp & Hlth Care Svcs (P-19695)*
Therapy For Kids Inc..........E......714 870-6116
233 Orangefair Mall Fullerton (92832) *(P-19699)*
Therapy In Your Home O TP TS..........D......408 358-0201
147 Vista Del Monte Los Gatos (95030) *(P-21884)*
Therm Pacific, Commerce *Also called Hkf Inc (P-7451)*
Therma Holdings LLC..........E......626 446-1854
2390 Bateman Ave Duarte (91010) *(P-2300)*
Thermal Air, Anaheim *Also called General Engineering Wstn Inc (P-2144)*
Thermal Engrg Intl USA Inc (HQ)..........D......323 726-0641
18000 Studebaker Rd # 400 Cerritos (90703) *(P-25343)*
Thermal Mechanical..........D......408 988-8744
425 Aldo Ave Santa Clara (95054) *(P-2301)*
Thermalair Inc (HQ)..........D......714 630-3200
1140 N Red Gum St Anaheim (92806) *(P-2302)*
Thermo Power Industries..........E......562 799-0087
10570 Humbolt St Los Alamitos (90720) *(P-2867)*
THETRADEDESK, Ventura *Also called Trade Desk Inc (P-15160)*
Thiara Sukhwant..........E......530 673-1581
1537 Atkinson Ct Yuba City (95993) *(P-443)*
Thiara Orchards, Yuba City *Also called Thiara Sukhwant (P-443)*
Thiel Capital LLC (PA)..........D......323 990-2030
9200 W Sunset Blvd # 1110 West Hollywood (90069) *(P-26846)*
Think Together..........A......562 236-3835
12016 Telegraph Rd Santa Fe Springs (90670) *(P-18204)*
Think Together..........A......909 723-1400
202 E Airport Dr Ste 200 San Bernardino (92408) *(P-23796)*
Think Together..........A......626 373-2311
800 S Barranca Ave # 120 Covina (91723) *(P-23797)*
Think Together..........A......951 571-9944
22620 Goldencrest Dr # 104 Moreno Valley (92553) *(P-23798)*
Thinkom Solutions Inc..........C......310 371-5486
4881 W 145th St Hawthorne (90250) *(P-5805)*
Thinkwell Design & Prod Inc..........C......818 333-3444
2710 Media Center Dr Los Angeles (90065) *(P-17779)*
Thinkwell Design & Productions, Los Angeles *Also called Thinkwell Design & Prod Inc (P-17779)*
Thinkwell Group Inc..........D......818 333-3444
2710 Media Center Dr Los Angeles (90065) *(P-17950)*
Third & Mission Associates LLC..........E......415 341-8457
680 Mission St San Francisco (94105) *(P-11481)*
Thirdwave Technology Services..........E......310 563-2160
4054 Del Rey Ave Ste 207 Marina Del Rey (90292) *(P-15927)*
Thismoment Inc..........C......415 200-4730
690 Market St Unit 1101 San Francisco (94104) *(P-15153)*
Thoits Insurance Service Inc..........D......408 792-5400
444 Castro St Ste 200 Mountain View (94041) *(P-10520)*
Thom Sharon & G Enterprises..........E......530 226-8350
2620 Larkspur Ln Ste N Redding (96002) *(P-21885)*
Thoma Bravo LLC..........B......415 263-3660
600 Montgomery St Fl 32 San Francisco (94111) *(P-11963)*
Thoma Electric Co, San Luis Obispo *Also called Thoma Electric Inc (P-2672)*
Thoma Electric Inc..........D......805 543-3850
3562 Empleo St Ste C San Luis Obispo (93401) *(P-2672)*
Thomas Crane and Trckg Co Inc..........E......562 592-2837
18851 Stewart Ln Huntington Beach (92648) *(P-1997)*
Thomas Doll & Company, Walnut Creek *Also called Thomas Wirig Doll & Co Cpas (P-25689)*
Thomas Edward Companies (PA)..........C......310 859-9366
9950 Santa Monica Blvd Beverly Hills (90212) *(P-13022)*
Thomas Gallaway Corporation (PA)..........D......949 716-9500
100 Spectrum Center Dr # 700 Irvine (92618) *(P-15154)*
Thomas J Hoban (PA)..........E......619 442-1665
215 W Lexington Ave El Cajon (92020) *(P-11482)*
Thomas Kinkade Company, The, Morgan Hill *Also called Pacific Metro LLC (P-8994)*
Thomas M Obinson Jr..........D......559 432-6200
7480 N Palm Ave Ste 101 Fresno (93711) *(P-11483)*
Thomas Mark & Company Inc (PA)..........C......408 453-5373
2833 Junction Ave Ste 110 San Jose (95134) *(P-25344)*
Thomas Weisel Partners LLC (HQ)..........B......415 364-2500
1 Montgomery St Ste 3700 San Francisco (94104) *(P-9758)*
Thomas Wirig Doll & Co Cpas..........D......925 939-2500
165 Lennon Ln Ste 200 Walnut Creek (94598) *(P-25689)*
Thomason Tractor Co California..........E......559 659-2039
985 12th St Firebaugh (93622) *(P-7509)*
Thompson & Colegate LLP..........E......951 682-5550
3610 14th St Lowr Riverside (92501) *(P-22845)*
Thompson & Rich Crane Service..........E......209 465-3161
2373 E Mariposa Rd Stockton (95205) *(P-17092)*
Thompson Builders Corporation..........C......415 456-8972
250 Bel Marin Keys Blvd A Novato (94949) *(P-1276)*
Thompson Building Materials, Orange *Also called Valori Sand & Gravel Company (P-6701)*
Thompson Building Materials, Fontana *Also called Valori Sand & Gravel Company (P-6702)*
Thompson Building Mtls Inc..........E......619 287-9410
6618 Federal Blvd Lemon Grove (91945) *(P-6698)*
Thompson Cnstr Sup Door Frame, Corona *Also called Fennel Inc (P-2933)*
Thompson Coburn LLP..........B......310 282-2500
2029 Century Park E # 1900 Los Angeles (90067) *(P-22846)*
Thompson Family Farms LLC..........E......714 848-7536
16478 Beach Blvd Ste 391 Westminster (92683) *(P-365)*
Thomson Reuters (markets) LLC..........D......415 677-2500
1 Sansome St San Francisco (94104) *(P-17093)*
Thor Group Inc (PA)..........E......310 727-1777
318 Avenue I Ste 167 Redondo Beach (90277) *(P-14438)*
Thoreau Janitorial Svcs Inc..........C......310 822-8017
5120 W Goldleaf Cir # 10 Los Angeles (90056) *(P-14063)*
Thoreau Services Nationwide, Los Angeles *Also called Thoreau Janitorial Svcs Inc (P-14063)*
Thornton Tomasetti Inc..........D......415 365-6900
301 Howard St Ste 1030 San Francisco (94105) *(P-25345)*
Thoro—Packaging (HQ)..........D......951 278-2100
1467 Davril Cir Corona (92880) *(P-9015)*
Thorpe Design Inc..........D......925 634-0787
410 Beatrice St Ct Ste A Brentwood (94513) *(P-2303)*
Thorsens Inc..........D......209 524-5296
2310 N Walnut Rd Turlock (95382) *(P-3104)*
Thorsens Plumbing & AC, Turlock *Also called Thorsens Inc (P-3104)*
Thorsnes Bartolotta & McGuire..........D......619 236-9363
2550 5th Ave Ste 1100 San Diego (92103) *(P-22847)*
Thosand Oaks 145 Hodencamp, Thousand Oaks *Also called Kaiser Foundation Hospitals (P-19100)*
Thoughtful Asia Limited, Sherman Oaks *Also called Thoughtful Media Group Inc (P-13635)*
Thoughtful Media Group Inc..........D......818 465-7500
14724 Ventura Blvd # 1110 Sherman Oaks (91403) *(P-13635)*
Thoughtspot Inc..........B......800 508-7008
910 Hermosa Ct Sunnyvale (94085) *(P-15521)*
Thousand Oaks 322 E Thousand, Thousand Oaks *Also called Kaiser Foundation Hospitals (P-19102)*
Thousand Oaks Prtg & Spc Inc..........C......818 706-8330
5334 Sterling Center Dr Westlake Village (91361) *(P-17094)*
Thousand Oaks Service Center, Thousand Oaks *Also called Southern California Edison Co (P-5938)*
Thousand Oaks Surgical Hosp LP..........D......805 777-7750
401 Rolling Oaks Dr Thousand Oaks (91361) *(P-21309)*
Thousand Trails Inc..........E......209 962-0100
31191 Hardin Flat Rd Groveland (95321) *(P-13165)*
Thousandeyes Inc (PA)..........D......415 513-4526
201 Mission St Ste 1700 San Francisco (94105) *(P-15522)*
Threatmetrix Inc..........C......408 200-5700
160 W Santa Clara St # 1400 San Jose (95113) *(P-15155)*
Three D Electric, Benicia *Also called Western Sun Enterprises Inc (P-2695)*
Three Rivers Golf Course, Lawndale *Also called Alondra Golf Course Inc (P-18215)*
Three Sons Inc..........D......562 801-4100
5201 Industry Ave Pico Rivera (90660) *(P-8421)*
Three Way Logistics Inc (PA)..........D......408 748-3929
42505 Christy St Fremont (94538) *(P-5061)*
Threesixty Group, Irvine *Also called Merchsource LLC (P-7738)*
Threshold Digital Research Lab..........E......310 452-8885
1649 11th St Santa Monica (90404) *(P-26847)*
Threshold Technologies Inc..........D......909 606-1666
8352 Kimball Ave Bldg F35 Chino (91708) *(P-4802)*
Thrifty Car Rental, Newport Beach *Also called Thrifty Rent-A-Car System Inc (P-17226)*
Thrifty Car Rental, Los Angeles *Also called T C R Limited Partnership (P-17224)*
Thrifty Car Rental..........C......877 283-0898
780 Mcdonnell Rd Ste 1 San Francisco (94128) *(P-17225)*
Thrifty Rent-A-Car System Inc..........E......949 757-0659
3500 Irvine Ave Newport Beach (92660) *(P-17226)*
Thrive Support Services Inc..........E......925 682-2273
900 Court St Martinez (94553) *(P-21886)*
Thunder Group Inc (PA)..........E......626 935-1605
780 Nogales St Ste C City of Industry (91748) *(P-6588)*
Thunder Mountain Enterprises (PA)..........D......916 381-3400
9335 Elder Creek Rd Sacramento (95829) *(P-3478)*
Thunder Valley Casino, Lincoln *Also called United Auburn Indian Community (P-13051)*
Thunderbird Country Club..........D......760 328-2161
70737 Country Club Dr Rancho Mirage (92270) *(P-18596)*
Thurston Martin H DDS Ms..........E......858 676-5010
11616 Iberia Pl San Diego (92128) *(P-19633)*
Thyde Inc (PA)..........C......951 817-2300
300 El Sobrante Rd Corona (92879) *(P-17095)*
Thyssenkrupp Elevator Corp..........D......510 476-1900
14400 Catalina St San Leandro (94577) *(P-7598)*
Thyssenkrupp Elevator Corp..........E......510 476-1900
30984 Santana St Hayward (94544) *(P-17554)*
Thyssenkrupp Elevator Corp..........D......619 596-7220
1965 Gillespie Way # 101 El Cajon (92020) *(P-7599)*
Thyssenkrupp Elevator Corp..........D......818 847-2568
2850 N California St Burbank (91504) *(P-7600)*
Thyssenkrupp Elevator Corp..........E......323 278-9888
16290 Shoemaker Ave Cerritos (90703) *(P-17555)*
TI Gotham Inc..........D......415 982-5000
2 Embarcadero Ctr # 1900 San Francisco (94111) *(P-13636)*
TI Gotham Inc..........C......310 268-7200
11766 Wilshire Blvd # 1700 Los Angeles (90025) *(P-13637)*
TI Limited LLC (PA)..........D......323 877-5991
20335 Ventura Blvd Woodland Hills (91364) *(P-15523)*
Tibco Software Inc..........D......650 846-1000
3307 Hillview Ave Palo Alto (94304) *(P-15703)*
Tibco Software Inc (HQ)..........C......650 846-1000
3307 Hillview Ave Palo Alto (94304) *(P-15156)*
Tiburcio Vasquez Hlth Ctr Inc (PA)..........E......510 471-5880
33255 9th St Union City (94587) *(P-19505)*
Tiburcio Vasquez Hlth Ctr Inc..........D......510 471-5907
22331 Mission Blvd Hayward (94541) *(P-19506)*
Tiburon Hospitality LLC..........C......661 322-1012
901 Real Rd Bakersfield (93309) *(P-13023)*
Tiburon Hotel LLC..........D......415 435-5996
1651 Tiburon Blvd Belvedere Tiburon (94920) *(P-13024)*

A L P H A B E T I C

Tiburon Peninsula Club Inc ....E....415 789-7900
1600 Mar West St Belvedere Tiburon (94920) ***(P-18597)***
Tic, Panorama City *Also called Import Collection* ***(P-8979)***
Tic Hotels Inc....E....619 238-7577
555 W Ash St San Diego (92101) ***(P-13025)***
Tic World-Wide Corp....D....619 233-7500
555 W Ash St San Diego (92101) ***(P-13026)***
Tic Worldwide, San Diego *Also called Tic Hotels Inc* ***(P-13025)***
Tice Oaks Apartments, Walnut Creek *Also called Mp Tice Oaks Associates A CA* ***(P-11306)***
Ticketmaster Entertainment LLC....A....800 653-8000
8800 W Sunset Blvd West Hollywood (90069) ***(P-18765)***
Tickets.com, Inc., Costa Mesa *Also called Ticketscom LLC* ***(P-17951)***
Ticketscom LLC (HQ)....E....714 327-5400
535 Anton Blvd Ste 250 Costa Mesa (92626) ***(P-17951)***
Ticketswest, Irvine *Also called Paciolan LLC* ***(P-15469)***
Ticketweb LLC....E....415 901-0210
685 Market St Ste 200 San Francisco (94105) ***(P-18766)***
Ticor Title Company California....E....951 509-0211
4210 Riverwalk Pkwy # 200 Riverside (92505) ***(P-10203)***
Ticor Title Insurance Company (HQ)....C....616 302-3121
131 N El Molino Ave Pasadena (91101) ***(P-10204)***
Tidavater Inc....C....818 848-4151
2107 W Alameda Ave Burbank (91506) ***(P-17096)***
Tidebreak Inc....D....650 289-9869
958 San Leandro Ave # 500 Mountain View (94043) ***(P-6907)***
Tides Inc (PA)....C....415 561-6400
1014 Torney Ave Ste 1 San Francisco (94129) ***(P-24233)***
Tides Center....C....415 359-9401
124 Turk St San Francisco (94102) ***(P-13027)***
Tides Network....D....415 561-6400
The Prsdio 1014 Trney Ave San Francisco (94129) ***(P-24234)***
Tides Shared Spaces, San Francisco *Also called Tides Inc* ***(P-24233)***
Tidwell Excav Acquisition Inc....D....805 647-4707
1691 Los Angeles Ave Ventura (93004) ***(P-3332)***
Tierra Del Oro Girl Scout Cnsl....D....916 452-9174
6601 Elvas Ave Sacramento (95819) ***(P-24681)***
Tierra Del Sol Foundation (PA)....D....818 352-1419
9919 Sunland Blvd Sunland (91040) ***(P-24096)***
Tierra Del Sol Foundation....D....909 626-8301
250 W 1st St Ste 120 Claremont (91711) ***(P-18767)***
Tierra Del Soul, Claremont *Also called Tierra Del Sol Foundation* ***(P-18767)***
Tierra Oaks Golf Club Inc....D....530 275-0795
19700 La Crescenta Dr Redding (96003) ***(P-18598)***
Tierra Rejada Golf Course, Moorpark *Also called Donovan Bros Golf LLC* ***(P-18242)***
Tifanny Mulhearn Realtors, Cerritos *Also called Mulhearn Realtors Inc* ***(P-11307)***
Tiffany Dale Inc (PA)....D....714 739-2700
14765 Industry Cir La Mirada (90638) ***(P-6589)***
Tiffanys Liu....D....415 644-0846
9465 Wilshire Blvd Beverly Hills (90212) ***(P-23502)***
Tiger Electric Inc (PA)....D....714 529-8061
650 N Berry St Brea (92821) ***(P-2673)***
Tiger Lines LLC (HQ)....D....209 334-4100
927 Black Diamond Way Lodi (95240) ***(P-4142)***
Tigerconnect Inc....E....310 401-1820
2110 Broadway Santa Monica (90404) ***(P-16135)***
Tiktok Inc (HQ)....C....844 523-3993
1920 Olympic Blvd Santa Monica (90404) ***(P-15157)***
Tile West Inc (PA)....D....415 382-7550
11 Hamilton Dr Novato (94949) ***(P-2911)***
Tiller Constructors Partnr Inc....D....714 771-5600
306 W Katella Ave Ste A Orange (92867) ***(P-1622)***
Tillster Inc (PA)....D....858 784-0800
5959 Cornerstone Ct W # 100 San Diego (92121) ***(P-16136)***
Tim Hofer Inc....C....559 732-6676
148 N Akers St Visalia (93291) ***(P-14064)***
Tim Mello Construction....E....530 205-8588
464 Lamarque Ct Grass Valley (95945) ***(P-1207)***
Tim Paxins Pacific Excavation....E....916 686-2800
9796 Kent St Elk Grove (95624) ***(P-3333)***
TIMBER CREEK GOLF COURSE, Roseville *Also called Sun City Rsvlle Cmnty Assn Inc* ***(P-18304)***
Timber Ridge At Eureka, Eureka *Also called Western Living Concepts Inc* ***(P-24113)***
Timber Works Construction Inc....C....916 786-6666
7031 Roseville Rd Ste A Sacramento (95842) ***(P-1208)***
Timberlake Painting, Murrieta *Also called Temecula Valley Drywall Inc* ***(P-2866)***
Timco, Fontana *Also called Tst Inc* ***(P-3944)***
Time and Alarm Systems (PA)....D....951 685-1761
3828 Wacker Dr Jurupa Valley (91752) ***(P-2674)***
Time Financial Services, Woodland Hills *Also called Ramkade Insurance Services* ***(P-10474)***
Time Warner, Burbank *Also called Historic TW Inc* ***(P-17617)***
Time Warner, Temecula *Also called Spectrum MGT Holdg Co LLC* ***(P-5743)***
Time Warner, San Bernardino *Also called Spectrum MGT Holdg Co LLC* ***(P-5744)***
Time Warner, Lancaster *Also called Warner Media LLC* ***(P-5771)***
Time Warner, Simi Valley *Also called Warner Media LLC* ***(P-5772)***
Time Warner, Cypress *Also called Spectrum MGT Holdg Co LLC* ***(P-5750)***
Time Warner, Garden Grove *Also called Spectrum MGT Holdg Co LLC* ***(P-5751)***
Time Warner, El Segundo *Also called Spectrum MGT Holdg Co LLC* ***(P-5752)***
Time Warner, Anaheim *Also called Spectrum MGT Holdg Co LLC* ***(P-5754)***
Time Warner Cable Entps LLC....D....818 972-0808
3500 W Olive Ave Ste 1000 Burbank (91505) ***(P-5756)***
Time Warner Cable Entps LLC....C....323 993-7076
1438 N Gower St Los Angeles (90028) ***(P-5757)***
Time Warner Cable Entps LLC....A....469 665-7735
550 Continental Blvd # 250 El Segundo (90245) ***(P-5758)***
Time Warner Cable Entps LLC....C....818 953-3283
3300 Warner Blvd Burbank (91505) ***(P-5759)***
Time Warner Cable Inc....D....619 346-4573
3051 Clairemont Dr San Diego (92117) ***(P-5760)***
Time Warner Cable Inc....D....888 892-2253
118 N 8th St Santa Paula (93060) ***(P-5761)***
Time Warner Cable Inc....D....805 214-1353
2323 Teller Rd Newbury Park (91320) ***(P-5762)***
Time Warner Cable Inc....B....858 695-3220
10450 Pacific Center Ct San Diego (92121) ***(P-5763)***
Time Warner Cable Inc....D....951 306-3117
660 W Acacia Ave Hemet (92543) ***(P-5764)***
Time Warner Cable Inc....D....626 705-7482
15255 Salt Lake Ave City of Industry (91745) ***(P-5765)***
Time Warner Cable Inc....B....323 993-8000
900 N Cahuenga Blvd Los Angeles (90038) ***(P-5766)***
Time Warner Cable Inc....B....858 695-3110
8949 Ware Ct San Diego (92121) ***(P-5767)***
Time Warner Cable Inc....D....760 335-4800
313 N 8th St El Centro (92243) ***(P-5768)***
Time Warner Media Sales, Cypress *Also called Spectrum MGT Holdg Co LLC* ***(P-5740)***
Timec Acquisitions Inc (HQ)....A....707 642-2222
155 Corporate Pl Vallejo (94590) ***(P-1998)***
Timec Companies Inc (HQ)....B....707 642-2222
155 Corporate Pl Vallejo (94590) ***(P-1999)***
Timelogic, Carlsbad *Also called Active Motif Inc* ***(P-25696)***
Timeshare Compliance, Aliso Viejo *Also called Pandora Marketing LLC* ***(P-26756)***
Timmerman Starlite Trckg Inc....D....209 538-1706
3955 Starlite Dr Ceres (95307) ***(P-4143)***
Tinco Sheet Metal Inc....C....323 263-0511
958 N Eastern Ave Los Angeles (90063) ***(P-3105)***
Tintri Inc....B....650 810-8200
303 Ravendale Dr Mountain View (94043) ***(P-15890)***
Tire Centers West LLC....C....909 854-1200
10516 Commerce Way # 875 Fontana (92337) ***(P-6491)***
Tireco Inc (PA)....C....310 767-7990
500 W 190th St Ste 100 Gardena (90248) ***(P-6492)***
Tishman Construction Corp Cal....D....213 542-6400
444 S Flower St Ste 2500 Los Angeles (90071) ***(P-26424)***
Titan Pulse Sciences Division, San Leandro *Also called Engility LLC* ***(P-25054)***
Titan Solar, Woodland Hills *Also called Memeged Tevuot Shemesh* ***(P-2199)***
Title Boy, Venice *Also called Prologue Films* ***(P-13795)***
Title Records Inc....D....818 767-9610
8926 Sunland Blvd Sun Valley (91352) ***(P-11536)***
Tivo Corporation (PA)....D....408 519-9100
2160 Gold St San Jose (95002) ***(P-11835)***
Tivo Corporation....D....303 273-7800
2233 N Ontario St Ste 200 Burbank (91504) ***(P-15826)***
Tj Cross Engineers Inc....C....661 831-8782
200 New Stine Rd Ste 270 Bakersfield (93309) ***(P-25346)***
Tjd LLC....C....209 357-3420
1685 Shaffer Rd Atwater (95301) ***(P-20700)***
Tka, La Palma *Also called Tech Knowledge Associates LLC* ***(P-17551)***
TLC of Bay Area Inc....D....408 988-7667
991 Clyde Ave Santa Clara (95054) ***(P-20332)***
TLC Services Group Inc (PA)....D....714 541-5415
1600 E 4th St Ste 340 Santa Ana (92701) ***(P-14439)***
Tlcs Inc....D....916 441-0123
650 Howe Ave Ste 400 Sacramento (95825) ***(P-23503)***
Tlg, Newark *Also called Lancashire Group Incorporated* ***(P-26670)***
Tm Financial Forensics LLC (PA)....E....415 692-6350
2 Embarcadero Ctr # 2510 San Francisco (94111) ***(P-27235)***
Tm Motion Picture Eqp Rentals, Sylmar *Also called Mbs Equipment Company* ***(P-17749)***
TMI, San Jose *Also called Traffic Management Inc* ***(P-17101)***
Tmp Worldwide Advertising & Co....D....818 539-2000
330 N Brand Blvd Ste 1050 Glendale (91203) ***(P-13586)***
Tms America, Torrance *Also called Total Management Svcs Amer Inc* ***(P-14440)***
TMT Industries Inc....D....909 493-3441
14774 Jurupa Ave Fontana (92337) ***(P-4144)***
Tmw Marketing, Brea *Also called Alta Resources Corp* ***(P-16615)***
Tmx Aerospace....C....562 215-4410
12821 Carmenita Rd Unit F Santa Fe Springs (90670) ***(P-7110)***
Tmx Engineering LLC....D....714 641-5884
2141 S Standard Ave Santa Ana (92707) ***(P-25347)***
Tnci Operating Company LLC (HQ)....D....800 800-8400
114 E Haley St Ste I Santa Barbara (93101) ***(P-5481)***
TNT Express Worldwide, Los Angeles *Also called TNT USA Inc* ***(P-4727)***
TNT Grading Inc....D....760 736-4054
529 W 4th Ave B Escondido (92025) ***(P-1800)***
TNT Originals, Burbank *Also called Turner Broadcasting System Inc* ***(P-17687)***
TNT USA Inc....D....310 242-9700
8500 Osage Ave Los Angeles (90045) ***(P-4727)***
TO HELP EVERYONE HEALTH AND WE, Los Angeles *Also called Clinic Inc* ***(P-18899)***
Toad 1350....E....951 369-1350
2030 Iowa Ave Ste A Riverside (92507) ***(P-5566)***
Tobin Lucks, Woodland Hills *Also called Joseph C Sansone Company* ***(P-22597)***
Todays Hotel Corporation (PA)....C....415 441-4000
1500 Van Ness Ave San Francisco (94109) ***(P-13028)***
Todays Vi LLC....D....909 980-2200
4760 Mills Cir Ontario (91764) ***(P-13029)***
Todda Merger Sub Inc....D....323 644-3720
443 N Varney St Burbank (91502) ***(P-13587)***
Tofasco of America Inc (PA)....D....909 392-8282
1661 Fairplex Dr La Verne (91750) ***(P-26425)***
Toiyabe Indian Health Prj Inc (PA)....C....760 873-8461
250 N See Vee Ln Bishop (93514) ***(P-19634)***
Tokai Intl Holdings Inc (PA)....E....909 930-5000
2055 S Haven Ave Ontario (91761) ***(P-11697)***
Tokio Marine Management Inc....C....626 568-7600
800 E Colorado Blvd Ste 8 Pasadena (91101) ***(P-10521)***

Mergent e-mail: customerrelations@mergent.com
1458
2020 Directory of California
Wholesalers and Services Companies
(P-0000) Products & Services Section entry number
(PA)=Parent Co (HQ)=Headquarters (DH)=Div Headquarters

ALPHABETIC SECTION
Touchofmodern Inc

Toll Brothers Inc ....D....925 855-0260
6800 Koll Center Pkwy # 320 Pleasanton (94566) ***(P-1209)***
Toll Brothers Division Office, Pleasanton *Also called Toll Brothers Inc* ***(P-1209)***
Toll Global Fwdg Scs USA Inc ....D....951 360-8310
3355 Dulles Dr Jurupa Valley (91752) ***(P-5062)***
Tollfreeforwarding.com, Los Angeles *Also called Ifncom Inc* ***(P-5423)***
Tollhouse Hotel, Los Gatos *Also called Trevi Partners A Calif LP* ***(P-13038)***
Tom Dreher Sales Inc ....D....562 355-4074
2021 W 17th St Long Beach (90813) ***(P-6933)***
Tom Ferry Your Coach, Santa Ana *Also called Success Strategies Inst Inc* ***(P-23644)***
Tom Hom Investment Corp ....D....858 456-5000
7660 Fay Ave Ste H La Jolla (92037) ***(P-10663)***
Tom Malloy Corporation (PA) ....E....310 327-5554
206 N Central Ave Compton (90220) ***(P-7495)***
Tom Ray, Sacramento *Also called T M Cobb Company* ***(P-6662)***
Tom Ray Industries Inc ....D....949 380-8333
23182 Alcalde Dr Ste G Laguna Hills (92653) ***(P-6590)***
Tom Sawyer Camps Inc ....C....626 794-1156
707 W Woodbury Rd Ste F Altadena (91001) ***(P-23799)***
Tomarco Contractor Spc Inc (PA) ....D....714 523-1771
14848 Northam St La Mirada (90638) ***(P-7409)***
Tomarco Fastening Systems, La Mirada *Also called Tomarco Contractor Spc Inc* ***(P-7409)***
Tomas Jewelry, Arcata *Also called Toucan Inc* ***(P-7795)***
Tomatoes Extraordinaire Inc ....C....619 295-3172
1929 Hancock St Ste 150 San Diego (92110) ***(P-8530)***
Tommy Bahama Group Inc ....C....805 482-8868
610 Ventura Blvd Ste 1340 Camarillo (93010) ***(P-17097)***
Tommy Bahama Group Inc ....C....415 737-0400
1720 Redwood Hwy Spc A019 Corte Madera (94925) ***(P-17098)***
Tommy Gun Plastering Inc ....D....909 795-9966
944 4th St Calimesa (92320) ***(P-2868)***
Tomra Recycling Network, Rancho Cucamonga *Also called Replanet LLC* ***(P-6255)***
Tonal Systems Inc ....D....855 698-6625
325 Vermont St San Francisco (94103) ***(P-18768)***
Tone Framing Inc ....E....951 304-0303
1821 Winterwarm Dr Fallbrook (92028) ***(P-2986)***
Toner Supply USA Inc ....E....818 504-6540
8055 Lankershim Blvd # 11 North Hollywood (91605) ***(P-6908)***
Toni & Guy Hairdressing (PA) ....E....949 721-1666
1177 Newport Center Dr Newport Beach (92660) ***(P-13361)***
Tonner Hills Hsing Partners LP ....E....949 263-8676
17701 Cowan Ste 200 Irvine (92614) ***(P-1277)***
Tonopah Solar Energy LLC ....D....310 315-2200
520 Broadway Fl 6 Santa Monica (90401) ***(P-2304)***
Tony Gomez Tree Service ....D....619 593-1552
700 N Johnson Ave Ste H El Cajon (92020) ***(P-946)***
Tony La Russas Animal RES Fnd ....D....925 256-1273
2890 Mitchell Dr Walnut Creek (94598) ***(P-586)***
Tony Marquez Pool Plst Inc ....D....818 833-5872
14960 Foothill Blvd Sylmar (91342) ***(P-2869)***
Tony R Crisalli Inc ....E....951 727-0110
3468 Campbell St Riverside (92509) ***(P-14115)***
Tonys Express Inc (PA) ....C....909 427-8700
10613 Jasmine St Fontana (92337) ***(P-4518)***
Tonys Fine Foods (HQ) ....B....916 374-4000
3575 Reed Ave West Sacramento (95605) ***(P-4519)***
Too Good Gourmet Inc (PA) ....D....510 317-8150
2380 Grant Ave San Lorenzo (94580) ***(P-8660)***
Toolwire Inc ....D....925 227-8500
7031 Koll Center Pkwy # 220 Pleasanton (94566) ***(P-15158)***
Toolworks Inc ....B....510 649-1322
3075 Adeline St Ste 230 Berkeley (94703) ***(P-23504)***
Toolworks Inc (PA) ....B....415 733-0990
25 Kearny St Ste 400 San Francisco (94108) ***(P-23647)***
Top Finance Company, Chatsworth *Also called Platinum Group Companies Inc* ***(P-11687)***
Top of Market ....B....619 234-4867
750 N Harbor Dr San Diego (92101) ***(P-26426)***
Top Priority Couriers Inc (PA) ....D....951 781-1000
1257 Columbia Ave Ste D1 Riverside (92507) ***(P-4287)***
Top Seed Tennis Academy Inc ....D....818 222-2782
23400 Park Sorrento Calabasas (91302) ***(P-18769)***
Top Tier Consulting ....D....818 338-2121
21550 Oxnard St Fl 3 Woodland Hills (91367) ***(P-26848)***
Topa Berkeley Ltd ....D....310 203-9199
1800 Avenue Of The Stars Los Angeles (90067) ***(P-11484)***
Topa Insurance Company (HQ) ....D....310 201-0451
1800 Ave Of Stars # 1200 Los Angeles (90067) ***(P-10237)***
Topa Management Company (PA) ....C....310 203-9199
1800 Avenue Of The Stars # 1400 Los Angeles (90067) ***(P-10664)***
Topanga Productions Inc ....E....310 244-4000
10202 Wash Blvd Ste 1132 Culver City (90232) ***(P-17682)***
Topanga Villas Company ....D....818 884-8017
5807 Topanga Canyon Blvd Woodland Hills (91367) ***(P-10828)***
Topbuild Services Group Corp ....D....408 882-0411
1341 Old Oakland Rd San Jose (95112) ***(P-3479)***
Topco Sales, Simi Valley *Also called Wsm Investments LLC* ***(P-11839)***
Topdown Consulting Inc ....D....888 644-8445
530 Divisadero St Ste 310 San Francisco (94117) ***(P-26849)***
Topgolf Media LLC (HQ) ....D....214 377-0615
100 California St Ste 650 San Francisco (94111) ***(P-18770)***
Topica Inc ....D....415 344-0800
1 Post St Ste 875 San Francisco (94104) ***(P-5482)***
Topocean Consolidation Service (PA) ....C....562 908-1688
2727 Workman Mill Rd City of Industry (90601) ***(P-5063)***
Tops Auto Parks, Los Angeles *Also called Paramunt Contrs Developers Inc* ***(P-11348)***
Topson Downs California Inc (PA) ....C....310 558-0300
3840 Watseka Ave Culver City (90232) ***(P-8115)***
Topstar Floral Inc ....E....805 984-7972
4255 W Gonzales Rd Oxnard (93036) ***(P-286)***
Topwin Corporation (PA) ....D....310 325-2255
1808 Abalone Ave Torrance (90501) ***(P-8048)***
Toro Enterprises Inc ....D....805 483-4515
2101 Ventura Blvd Oxnard (93036) ***(P-1801)***
Toro Nursery Inc ....D....310 715-1982
17585 Crenshaw Blvd Torrance (90504) ***(P-8927)***
Torrance Amateur Rdo Assn Inc ....E....310 245-0989
2162 248th St Lomita (90717) ***(P-24879)***
Torrance Care Center West Inc ....C....310 370-4561
4333 Torrance Blvd Torrance (90503) ***(P-20333)***
Torrance Health Assn Inc (PA) ....A....310 325-9110
3330 Lomita Blvd Torrance (90505) ***(P-21310)***
Torrance Marriott Hotel, Torrance *Also called Xld Group LLC* ***(P-13129)***
Torrance Memorial Medical Ctr (HQ) ....A....310 325-9110
3330 Lomita Blvd Torrance (90505) ***(P-21311)***
Torrance Surgery Center LP ....A....310 986-2005
23560 Crenshaw Blvd # 104 Torrance (90505) ***(P-19507)***
Torres Construction Corp (PA) ....D....323 257-7460
1370 N El Molino Ave Pasadena (91104) ***(P-1387)***
Torres Fence Co Inc ....E....559 237-4141
2357 S Orange Ave Fresno (93725) ***(P-3480)***
Torres General Inc ....D....619 448-8900
9484 Mission Park Pl Santee (92071) ***(P-1210)***
Torres-Martinez ....C....760 395-1200
3089 Norm Niver Rd Thermal (92274) ***(P-13030)***
Torrey Aat Point LLC ....D....858 350-2600
11455 El Camino Real San Diego (92130) ***(P-11878)***
Torrey Pines Bank (HQ) ....C....858 523-4600
12220 El Camino Real # 200 San Diego (92130) ***(P-9243)***
Toscana, Palm Desert *Also called Sunrise Desert Partners* ***(P-11609)***
Toscana Country Club, Palm Desert *Also called Toscana Homes LP* ***(P-1278)***
Toscana Country Club Inc ....C....760 404-1444
76009 Via Club Villa Indian Wells (92210) ***(P-18599)***
Toscana Homes LP ....E....760 772-7227
300 Eagle Dance Cir Palm Desert (92211) ***(P-1278)***
Toscana Land LLC ....D....760 772-7200
300 Eagle Dance Cir Palm Desert (92211) ***(P-11615)***
Toshiba Amer Bus Solutions Inc (HQ) ....B....949 462-6000
25530 Commercentre Dr Lake Forest (92630) ***(P-6774)***
Toshiba Bus Solutions USA Inc (HQ) ....C....949 462-6000
9740 Irvine Blvd Irvine (92618) ***(P-17467)***
Toshiba Education Center ....D....949 583-3000
9740 Irvine Blvd Irvine (92618) ***(P-25948)***
Toshiba Memory America, Inc., San Jose *Also called Kioxia America Inc* ***(P-7288)***
Tosoh Bioscience Inc ....D....650 615-4970
6000 Shoreline Ct Ste 101 South San Francisco (94080) ***(P-7012)***
Tosoh USA, South San Francisco *Also called Tosoh Bioscience Inc* ***(P-7012)***
Total Airport Services LLC ....D....650 358-0144
3537 Branson Dr San Mateo (94403) ***(P-4803)***
Total Building Care Inc ....D....562 467-8333
21228 Norwalk Blvd Hawaiian Gardens (90716) ***(P-1623)***
TOTAL CLEAN, La Verne *Also called Haaker Equipment Company* ***(P-6398)***
Total Cmmnicator Solutions Inc ....D....619 277-1488
11150 Santa Monica Blvd # 600 Los Angeles (90025) ***(P-15524)***
Total Education Solutions Inc (PA) ....E....323 341-5580
625 Fair Oaks Ave Ste 300 South Pasadena (91030) ***(P-27236)***
Total Hr Management, Pasadena *Also called Strategic Staffing Svcs Inc* ***(P-26833)***
Total Immersion, Los Angeles *Also called Dfusion Software Inc* ***(P-14762)***
Total Intermodal Services Inc (PA) ....E....562 427-6300
2396 E Sepulveda Blvd Long Beach (90810) ***(P-4626)***
Total Management Svcs Amer Inc ....E....310 328-0867
21151 S Wstn Ave Ste 139 Torrance (90501) ***(P-14440)***
Total Professional Network ....D....213 382-5550
3946 Wilshire Blvd Los Angeles (90010) ***(P-14441)***
Total Quality Maintenance Inc ....C....650 846-4700
895 Commercial St Palo Alto (94303) ***(P-14065)***
Total Renal Care Inc ....E....925 737-0120
5720 Stoneridge Mall Rd # 160 Pleasanton (94588) ***(P-21938)***
Total Renal Care Inc ....D....949 930-6882
15271 Laguna Canyon Rd Irvine (92618) ***(P-21939)***
Total Renal Care Inc ....A....707 556-3637
125 Corporate Pl Ste C Vallejo (94590) ***(P-21940)***
Total Renal Care Inc ....D....760 947-7405
14135 Main St Ste 501 Hesperia (92345) ***(P-21941)***
Total Tire Recycling, Sacramento *Also called AAA Signs Inc* ***(P-17316)***
Total Trnsp Logistics Inc ....D....951 360-9521
4325 Etiwanda Ave Ste A Jurupa Valley (91752) ***(P-4145)***
Total Vision LLC ....C....949 652-7242
27271 Las Ramblas 200a Mission Viejo (92691) ***(P-19651)***
Total Waste Systems, Santa Rosa *Also called Novato Disposal Service Inc* ***(P-6228)***
Total Woman ....D....714 993-6003
860 N Rose Dr Placentia (92870) ***(P-18205)***
Total-Western Inc ....D....661 589-5200
2811 Fruitvale Ave Ste A Bakersfield (93308) ***(P-1279)***
Total-Western Inc (HQ) ....E....562 220-1450
8049 Somerset Blvd Paramount (90723) ***(P-1046)***
Totally Kids Rhbilitation Hosp, Loma Linda *Also called Mountain View Child Care Inc* ***(P-21053)***
Totally Kids Spcalty Hlth Care, Sun Valley *Also called Mountain View Child Care Inc* ***(P-23754)***
Totten Tubes Inc (PA) ....D....626 812-0220
500 W Danlee St Azusa (91702) ***(P-7111)***
Toucan Inc (PA) ....D....707 822-6662
824 L St Ste 6 Arcata (95521) ***(P-7795)***
Touch-Up Inc ....C....818 994-6166
7116 Valjean Ave Van Nuys (91406) ***(P-2870)***
Touchofmodern Inc ....C....888 868-1232
30063 Ahern Ave Union City (94587) ***(P-17099)***

ALPHABETIC

Employee Codes: A=Over 500 employees, B=251-500
C=101-250, D=51-100, E=50
2020 Directory of California
Wholesalers and Services Companies
© Mergent Inc. 1-800-342-5647
1459

Touchstone Television Prod LLC (PA).....E.....323 671-5116
500 S Buena Vista St Burbank (91521) ***(P-17683)***
Tough2beat Auto Sales, Granada Hills *Also called Errama Trucking Company Inc* ***(P-4009)***
Tour Master, Calabasas Hills *Also called Helmet House Inc* ***(P-8032)***
Tourcoach Transportation, Commerce *Also called Screamline Investment Corp* ***(P-4865)***
Tournesol Siteworks LLC (PA).....D.....800 542-2282
2930 Faber St Union City (94587) ***(P-3481)***
Toward Maximum Independence (PA).....C.....858 467-0600
4740 Murphy Canyon Rd # 300 San Diego (92123) ***(P-23505)***
Towbes Group Inc (PA).....D.....805 962-2121
21 E Victoria St Ste 200 Santa Barbara (93101) ***(P-11616)***
Tower Car Wash, San Francisco *Also called Vladigor Investment Inc* ***(P-17402)***
Tower Energy Group (PA).....D.....310 538-8000
1983 W 190th St Ste 100 Torrance (90504) ***(P-8738)***
Tower Glass Inc.....D.....619 596-6199
9570 Pathway St Ste A Santee (92071) ***(P-3299)***
Tower Hematology Oncology Medi.....D.....310 888-8680
9090 Wilshire Blvd # 200 Beverly Hills (90211) ***(P-19508)***
Tower Park Marina, Lodi *Also called Westrec Marina Management Inc* ***(P-4637)***
Tower St John Imaging, Los Angeles *Also called Santa Mnica Wlshire Imging LLC* ***(P-21584)***
Tower- Imaging Roxanne, Beverly Hills *Also called Beverly Radiology Med Group* ***(P-18839)***
Towmaster Tire & Wheel, Anaheim *Also called Greenball Corp* ***(P-6487)***
Town & Country Event Rentals (PA).....B.....818 908-4211
7725 Airport Bus Pkwy Van Nuys (91406) ***(P-14203)***
Town & Country Event Rentals.....B.....805 770-5729
1 N Calle Cesar Chavez # 7 Santa Barbara (93103) ***(P-17100)***
Town & Country Manor of The Ch.....C.....714 547-7581
555 E Memory Ln Ofc Ofc Santa Ana (92706) ***(P-20334)***
Town & Country Roofing, Brentwood *Also called T&C Roofing Inc* ***(P-3102)***
Town and Country Hotel, San Diego *Also called Hotel Circle Property LLC* ***(P-12403)***
Town Cats Morgan Hill Rescue.....E.....408 779-5761
195 San Pedro Ave Ste B Morgan Hill (95037) ***(P-608)***
Town of Danville.....C.....925 314-3400
420 Front St Danville (94526) ***(P-18771)***
Towne Inc.....D.....714 540-3095
3441 W Macarthur Blvd Santa Ana (92704) ***(P-13742)***
Towne Advertising, Santa Ana *Also called Towne Inc* ***(P-13742)***
Towne Construction Inc.....D.....619 390-4557
12115 Lakeside Ave Lakeside (92040) ***(P-2871)***
TownePlace Suites.....D.....408 370-4510
700 E Campbell Ave Campbell (95008) ***(P-13031)***
TownePlace Suites By Marriott, Campbell *Also called TownePlace Suites* ***(P-13031)***
Towns End Studios LLC.....A.....415 802-7936
699 8th St San Francisco (94103) ***(P-15159)***
Toyo Tire USA Corp.....E.....562 431-6502
2151 S Vintage Ave Ontario (91761) ***(P-6493)***
Toyon Research Corporation (PA).....D.....805 968-6787
6800 Cortona Dr Goleta (93117) ***(P-25348)***
Toyota Logistics Services.....B.....562 437-6767
785 Edison Ave Long Beach (90813) ***(P-17430)***
Toyota Research Institute Inc.....D.....703 231-6680
4440 El Camino Real Los Altos (94022) ***(P-26038)***
Toyota-Lift of Los Angeles, Santa Fe Springs *Also called Rebas Inc* ***(P-7586)***
Toyota-Sunnyvale Inc (PA).....C.....408 245-6640
898 W El Camino Real Sunnyvale (94087) ***(P-17351)***
Toyotalift Inc (PA).....E.....619 562-5438
1850 John Towers Ave El Cajon (92020) ***(P-7601)***
TPC Stonebrea, Hayward *Also called Stonebrae LP* ***(P-18588)***
Tpd Dell Dios.....E.....760 741-2888
1817 Avenida Del Diablo Escondido (92029) ***(P-23506)***
Tpg La Commerce LLC.....D.....401 946-4600
5757 Telegraph Rd Commerce (90040) ***(P-13032)***
Tpg Reflections II LLC.....D.....213 613-1900
444 S Flower St Ste 600 Los Angeles (90071) ***(P-10829)***
Tpg Sixth Street Partners LLC.....C.....415 743-1500
345 California St Ste 330 San Francisco (94104) ***(P-9851)***
Tpg/Calstrs, Los Angeles *Also called Tpg Reflections II LLC* ***(P-10829)***
Tps Aviation Inc (PA).....D.....510 475-1010
1515 Crocker Ave Hayward (94544) ***(P-7701)***
Tps Parking Management LLC.....D.....310 846-4747
9101 S Sepulveda Blvd Los Angeles (90045) ***(P-17277)***
Tpx Communications, Los Angeles *Also called US Telepacific Corp* ***(P-5485)***
Tr Big Sur Management LLC.....E.....831 667-4212
48123 Highway 1 Big Sur (93920) ***(P-13033)***
Tr Warner Center LP.....B.....818 887-4800
21850 Oxnard St Woodland Hills (91367) ***(P-13034)***
Trace3 LLC (PA).....D.....949 333-2300
7565 Irvine Center Dr Irvine (92618) ***(P-26850)***
Tracy Bancshares Inc.....D.....209 836-5111
1003 N Central Ave Tracy (95376) ***(P-9286)***
Tracy Dlta Solid Waste Mgt Inc.....D.....209 835-0601
30703 S Macarthur Dr Tracy (95377) ***(P-6292)***
Tracy Industries, Ontario *Also called Genuine Parts Distributors* ***(P-6441)***
Tracy Interfaith Ministries.....D.....209 836-5424
311 W Grant Line Rd Tracy (95376) ***(P-23507)***
Tracy Medical Offices, Tracy *Also called Kaiser Foundation Hospitals* ***(P-19051)***
Tracy Sutter Community Hosp.....B.....209 835-1500
1420 N Tracy Blvd Tracy (95376) ***(P-21312)***
Tracy Trujillo MD.....E.....925 838-6511
200 Porter Dr Ste 300 San Ramon (94583) ***(P-19509)***
Trade Desk Inc (PA).....C.....805 585-3434
42 N Chestnut St Ventura (93001) ***(P-15160)***
Trade Services E2002-031, El Monte *Also called Wells Fargo Bank National Assn* ***(P-9135)***
Trade Shift APS, San Francisco *Also called Tradeshift Inc* ***(P-15704)***
Tradebeam Inc.....D.....650 653-4800
303 Twin Dolphin Dr # 600 Redwood City (94065) ***(P-16137)***
Tradecom Med Transcription Inc.....C.....408 225-9200
363 Piercy Rd San Jose (95138) ***(P-7013)***
Trademark Concrete Systems (PA).....E.....714 970-8200
4015 Via Pescador Camarillo (93012) ***(P-3229)***
Trader Joe Fontana Warehouse, Fontana *Also called World Class Distribution Inc* ***(P-4551)***
Tradeshift Holdings Inc (HQ).....D.....800 381-3585
221 Main St Ste 250 San Francisco (94105) ***(P-11698)***
Tradeshift Inc (HQ).....D.....800 381-3585
612 Howard St Ste 100 San Francisco (94105) ***(P-15704)***
Tradesmen International LLC.....D.....949 588-3280
15500 Rockfield Blvd Irvine (92618) ***(P-26427)***
Tradewind Seafood Inc.....E.....805 483-8555
1505 Mountain View Ave Oxnard (93030) ***(P-8395)***
Tradewinds Lodge (PA).....D.....707 964-4761
400 S Main St Fort Bragg (95437) ***(P-13035)***
Tradewinds Lodge Partnership, Sacramento *Also called Tradewinds Partnership* ***(P-13036)***
Tradewinds Partnership.....D.....916 333-5239
2920 Arden Way Ste F1 Sacramento (95825) ***(P-13036)***
Trading Financial Capital, Los Angeles *Also called Trading Financial Credit LLC* ***(P-9472)***
Trading Financial Credit LLC (PA).....E.....213 375-3113
3055 Wilshire Blvd # 530 Los Angeles (90010) ***(P-9472)***
TRADITION GOLF CLUB, La Quinta *Also called Chapman Golf Development LLC* ***(P-18419)***
Tradition Golf Club Associates.....D.....760 564-3355
78505 Avenue 52 La Quinta (92253) ***(P-18307)***
Traditions Golf LLC.....D.....408 323-5200
23600 Mckean Rd San Jose (95141) ***(P-18308)***
Traffic Management Inc.....D.....562 264-2353
1244 S Claudina St Anaheim (92805) ***(P-26428)***
Traffic Management Inc.....D.....415 370-7916
8399 Edgewater Dr Oakland (94621) ***(P-26429)***
Traffic Management Inc.....E.....877 763-5999
690 Quinn Ave San Jose (95112) ***(P-17101)***
Traffic Management Inc (PA).....C.....562 595-4278
2435 Lemon Ave Signal Hill (90755) ***(P-17102)***
Traffic Tech Inc.....C.....800 396-2531
910 Hale Pl Ste 100 Chula Vista (91914) ***(P-5064)***
Trail Lines Inc.....D.....562 758-6980
9415 Sorensen Ave Santa Fe Springs (90670) ***(P-3941)***
Trailer Park Inc.....D.....831 462-3271
4300 Soquel Dr Spc 90 Soquel (95073) ***(P-13166)***
Trailer Park Inc.....D.....310 845-8400
6922 Hollywood Blvd # 1200 Los Angeles (90028) ***(P-13588)***
Trailer Park Inc (PA).....D.....310 845-3000
6922 Hollywood Blvd Fl 12 Los Angeles (90028) ***(P-13589)***
Traina Dried Fruit Inc.....C.....209 892-5472
337 1/2 Lemon Ave Patterson (95363) ***(P-8661)***
Traina Foods, Patterson *Also called Traina Dried Fruit Inc* ***(P-8661)***
Training Toward Self Reliance.....E.....916 442-8877
1446 Ethan Way 101 Sacramento (95825) ***(P-23508)***
Trak Microwave Corporation.....C.....805 267-0100
375 Conejo Ridge Ave Thousand Oaks (91361) ***(P-7356)***
Traliant LLC.....D.....323 774-1325
1600 Rosecrans Ave Manhattan Beach (90266) ***(P-16138)***
Trams Inc (HQ).....D.....310 641-8726
5777 W Century Blvd # 1200 Los Angeles (90045) ***(P-15705)***
Trandes Corp.....E.....858 522-7021
4669 Murphy Canyon Rd # 102 San Diego (92123) ***(P-25349)***
Trandes Corp.....E.....619 524-2235
4297 Pacific Hwy Bldg 2 San Diego (92110) ***(P-25350)***
Trane US Inc.....D.....916 577-1100
4145 Delmar Ave Ste 2 Rocklin (95677) ***(P-7457)***
Tranquility Incorporated.....C.....925 825-4280
1050 San Miguel Rd Concord (94518) ***(P-20701)***
Tranquilmoney Inc.....D.....800 979-6739
5823 Ruddy Duck Ct Stockton (95207) ***(P-6909)***
Trans Globe Lighting, Valencia *Also called Bel Air Lighting Inc* ***(P-7129)***
Trans West Investigations Inc.....D.....213 381-1500
3255 Wilshire Blvd Los Angeles (90010) ***(P-16458)***
Trans World Maintenance Inc.....D.....650 455-2450
1590 Rollins Rd Millbrae (94030) ***(P-2401)***
Trans-Pak Incorporated.....C.....310 618-6937
2601 S Garnsey St Santa Ana (92707) ***(P-17103)***
Trans-West Security Svcs Inc.....B.....661 381-2900
8503 Crippen St Bakersfield (93311) ***(P-16459)***
Transamerica Cbo I Inc.....D.....415 983-4000
600 Montgomery St Fl 16 San Francisco (94111) ***(P-9852)***
Transamerica Finance Corp.....D.....714 778-5100
1731 W Medical Center Dr Anaheim (92801) ***(P-9889)***
Transamerica Intl Holdings.....C.....415 983-4000
600 Montgomery St Fl 16 San Francisco (94111) ***(P-11699)***
Transamerican Auto Parts, Chula Vista *Also called Poison Spyder Customs Inc* ***(P-17423)***
Transbay Fire Protection Inc (PA).....E.....925 846-9484
2182 Rheem Dr Pleasanton (94588) ***(P-3365)***
Transcendent Security Services.....E.....562 850-3313
3553 Atl Ave Ste 1197 Long Beach (90807) ***(P-16460)***
Transdev Services Inc.....B.....626 357-7912
5640 Peck Rd Arcadia (91006) ***(P-3729)***
Transforce Inc.....E.....209 952-2573
965 E Yosemite Ave Ste 7 Manteca (95336) ***(P-14574)***
Transiris Corporation.....D.....650 303-3495
555 Airport Blvd Ste 325 Burlingame (94010) ***(P-26851)***
Transit Air Cargo Inc.....D.....714 571-0393
2204 E 4th St Santa Ana (92705) ***(P-5065)***
Transitional Assistance Dept, Yucca Valley *Also called County of San Bernardino* ***(P-23142)***
Transitions - Mental Hlth Assn (PA).....D.....805 540-6500
784 High St San Luis Obispo (93401) ***(P-22142)***
TransMontaigne PDT Svcs LLC.....B.....415 576-2000
555 California St # 2100 San Francisco (94104) ***(P-5142)***

Mergent e-mail: customerrelations@mergent.com
1460
2020 Directory of California
Wholesalers and Services Companies
(P-0000) Products & Services Section entry number
(PA)=Parent Co (HQ)=Headquarters (DH)=Div Headquarters

Transmrcan Mling Flfllment Inc ......D......760 745-5343
355 State Pl Escondido (92029) ***(P-13743)***
Transpac, Vacaville *Also called Valyria LLC* ***(P-6597)***
Transpacific Management Svc ......D......714 285-2626
15661 Red Hill Ave # 205 Tustin (92780) ***(P-11485)***
Transpak Inc (PA) ......C......408 254-0500
520 Marburg Way San Jose (95133) ***(P-17104)***
Transpak Inc ......D......858 292-9094
8710 Avenida De La Fuente # 1 San Diego (92154) ***(P-5100)***
Transpak Los Angeles, Santa Ana *Also called Trans-Pak Incorporated* ***(P-17103)***
Transphorm Inc (PA) ......D......805 456-1300
115 Castilian Dr Goleta (93117) ***(P-25853)***
Transport Express Inc ......D......310 898-2000
19801 S Santa Fe Ave Compton (90221) ***(P-4236)***
Transportation, Lodi *Also called Lodi Unified School District* ***(P-3818)***
Transportation Bureau, Los Angeles *Also called County of Los Angeles* ***(P-5112)***
Transportation California Dept ......C......707 762-6641
611 Payran St Petaluma (94952) ***(P-1802)***
Transportation California Dept ......C......707 428-2031
2019 W Texas St Fairfield (94533) ***(P-1803)***
Transportation California Dept ......C......562 692-0823
1940 Workman Mill Rd Whittier (90601) ***(P-1804)***
Transportation Chrtr Svcs Inc ......E......714 396-0346
1931 N Batavia St Orange (92865) ***(P-3783)***
Transportation Concept Inc ......D......323 268-2202
1521 Kingsdale Ave Redondo Beach (90278) ***(P-3614)***
Transportation Department, Berkeley *Also called Berkeley Unified School Dst* ***(P-3787)***
Transportation Department, Sacramento *Also called Elk Grove Unified School Dst* ***(P-3799)***
Transportation Department, Long Beach *Also called Long Beach Unified School Dst* ***(P-3819)***
Transportation Dept, Ukiah *Also called County of Mendocino* ***(P-1693)***
Transportation Management LLC ......E......310 524-1555
880 Apollo St Ste 235 El Segundo (90245) ***(P-3942)***
Transprttion Corridor Agencies, Irvine *Also called San Joaquin Hills Transporttn* ***(P-1784)***
Transtar Automotive, Van Nuys *Also called Transtar Industries Inc* ***(P-6475)***
Transtar Industries Inc ......E......818 785-2000
15010 Calvert St Van Nuys (91411) ***(P-6475)***
Transtech Engineers Inc (PA) ......D......909 595-8599
13367 Benson Ave Chino (91710) ***(P-25351)***
Transwest San Diego LLC ......B......858 450-0707
6066 Miramar Rd San Diego (92121) ***(P-4237)***
Transwestern Corp Pointe LLC ......D......310 642-1001
600 Crprate Pinte Ste 250 Culver City (90230) ***(P-11486)***
Tranzeal Inc ......E......408 834-8711
2107 N 1st St Ste 500 San Jose (95131) ***(P-26852)***
Trap ......D......626 572-5610
1833 S Mountain Ave Monrovia (91016) ***(P-17105)***
Trapac LLC (HQ) ......E......310 513-1572
630 W Harry Bridges Blvd Wilmington (90744) ***(P-4627)***
Travel Store ......D......714 529-1947
633 S Brea Blvd Brea (92821) ***(P-4838)***
Travel Store (PA) ......D......310 575-5540
11601 Wilshire Blvd Los Angeles (90025) ***(P-4839)***
Travel Syndicate ......D......818 297-9979
350 S Beverly Dr Ste 170 Beverly Hills (90212) ***(P-4840)***
Travelers Club Luggage Inc ......D......714 523-8808
5911 Fresca Dr La Palma (90623) ***(P-7839)***
Travelers Indemnity Company ......C......909 612-3000
21688 Gateway Center Dr # 300 Diamond Bar (91765) ***(P-10522)***
Travelers Insurance, Diamond Bar *Also called Travelers Indemnity Company* ***(P-10522)***
Travelers Insurance, Walnut Creek *Also called Travelers Property Cslty Corp* ***(P-10523)***
Travelers Property Cslty Corp ......B......925 945-4000
401 Lennon Ln Walnut Creek (94598) ***(P-10523)***
Travelmasters Inc ......E......916 722-1648
8350 Auburn Blvd Ste 200 Citrus Heights (95610) ***(P-4841)***
Travelstore, Los Angeles *Also called Travel Store* ***(P-4839)***
Travelzoo Usa Inc ......D......650 316-6956
800 W El Camino Re Mountain View (94040) ***(P-13638)***
Travers Tree Service Inc ......E......310 545-5816
1811 Lomita Blvd Lomita (90717) ***(P-947)***
Travis Credit Union ......B......707 449-4000
1300 E Covell Blvd Davis (95616) ***(P-9358)***
Travis Credit Union ......B......800 877-8328
1796 Tuolumne St Vallejo (94589) ***(P-9359)***
Travis Credit Union ......B......800 877-8328
2095 Diamond Blvd Ste 115 Concord (94520) ***(P-9360)***
Travis Credit Union ......B......800 877-8328
3263 Claremont Way NAPA (94558) ***(P-9361)***
Travis Credit Union (PA) ......B......707 449-4000
1 Travis Way Vacaville (95687) ***(P-9362)***
Travis Credit Union ......B......916 443-1446
1515 K St Sacramento (95814) ***(P-9363)***
Travis Credit Union ......B......209 723-0732
1194 W Olive Ave Merced (95348) ***(P-9364)***
Travis Credit Union ......B......707 449-4000
11 Cernon St Vacaville (95688) ***(P-9365)***
Travis Credit Union ......B......707 449-4000
2570 N Texas St Fairfield (94533) ***(P-9366)***
Travis Credit Union ......B......800 877-8328
1372 E Main St Woodland (95776) ***(P-9367)***
Travis Credit Union ......B......707 449-4000
2020 Harbison Dr Vacaville (95687) ***(P-9368)***
Travis James Watts ......C......209 810-6159
9631 Harvey Rd Galt (95632) ***(P-366)***
TRC Pleasanton Dialysis Cntr, Pleasanton *Also called Total Renal Care Inc* ***(P-21938)***
TRC Solutions Inc (HQ) ......C......949 753-0101
9685 Research Dr Ste 100 Irvine (92618) ***(P-27237)***
Trcf Redondo LLC ......E......310 536-1209
2430 Marine Ave Redondo Beach (90278) ***(P-13037)***
Treadwell & Rollo Inc (HQ) ......E......415 955-9040
555 Montgomery St # 1300 San Francisco (94111) ***(P-25352)***
Treasure Data Inc ......D......866 899-5386
2565 Leghorn St Mountain View (94043) ***(P-15161)***
Treasurer/Tax Collector, Alturas *Also called County of Modoc* ***(P-16721)***
Treasury Wine Estates Americas ......C......805 237-6000
7000 E Highway 46 Paso Robles (93446) ***(P-166)***
Tredence Inc (PA) ......C......408 819-2336
1900 Camden Ave Ste 66 San Jose (95124) ***(P-25949)***
Tree Sculpture Group ......D......510 562-4000
463 Roland Way Oakland (94621) ***(P-914)***
Treebeard Landscape Inc ......D......619 697-8302
9917 Campo Rd Spring Valley (91977) ***(P-915)***
Treefrog Developments Inc ......D......619 324-7755
15110 Ave Of Science San Diego (92128) ***(P-7840)***
Treeline Staffing ......E......415 819-7195
100 Broadway San Francisco (94111) ***(P-14442)***
Treepeople Inc ......E......818 753-4600
12601 Mulholland Dr Beverly Hills (90210) ***(P-948)***
Trees Apartments LLC ......D......408 848-6400
7030 Eigleberry St Gilroy (95020) ***(P-10830)***
Trellisware Technologies Inc ......D......858 753-1600
10641 Scripps Summit Ct # 100 San Diego (92131) ***(P-5278)***
Trench Shoring Company, Compton *Also called Tom Malloy Corporation* ***(P-7495)***
Trend Micro Incorporated ......D......408 257-1500
10101 N De Anza Blvd Cupertino (95014) ***(P-6910)***
Trendex Corporation ......D......818 407-9600
9353 Eton Ave Chatsworth (91311) ***(P-1624)***
Trendnet Inc (PA) ......D......310 961-5500
20675 Manhattan Pl Torrance (90501) ***(P-6911)***
Trendsettah Usa Inc ......D......888 775-4881
1420 S Highland Ave L203 Fullerton (92832) ***(P-7841)***
Trendshift LLC ......D......866 644-8877
13274 Fiji Way Ste 250 Marina Del Rey (90292) ***(P-15162)***
Trendsource Inc ......D......619 718-7467
4891 Pacific Hwy Ste 200 San Diego (92110) ***(P-25950)***
Trepco Imports & Dist Ltd ......E......619 690-7999
11860 Cmnty Rd Ste 150 Poway (92064) ***(P-8943)***
Tressler LLP ......D......949 336-1200
2 Park Plz Ste 1050 Irvine (92614) ***(P-22848)***
Trestles Holdings LLC ......D......707 778-8686
450 Hayes Ln Petaluma (94952) ***(P-11700)***
Trevi Partners A Calif LP ......D......408 395-7070
140 S Santa Cruz Ave Los Gatos (95030) ***(P-13038)***
Trevi Partners A Calif LP (HQ) ......D......925 828-7750
6680 Regional St Dublin (94568) ***(P-13039)***
Trevi Partners A Calif LP ......D......831 624-1841
3665 Rio Rd Carmel (93923) ***(P-13040)***
Trevi Partners A Calif LP (PA) ......C......925 225-4000
5955 Coronado Ln Pleasanton (94588) ***(P-13041)***
Trex Partners LLC ......C......858 646-5300
10455 Pacific Center Ct San Diego (92121) ***(P-11701)***
Trg Inc ......D......310 396-6750
1350 Abbot Kinney Blvd # 101 Venice (90291) ***(P-11487)***
Tri - Star Win Coverings Inc ......E......818 718-3188
19555 Prairie St Northridge (91324) ***(P-6591)***
Tri Ced Community Recycling, Union City *Also called Tri-City Economic Dev Corp* ***(P-6293)***
Tri City Emergency Med Group ......E......760 439-1963
5050 Avenida Encinas # 200 Carlsbad (92008) ***(P-25690)***
Tri City Mental Health Center ......D......909 784-3200
1900 Royalty Dr Pomona (91767) ***(P-22143)***
Tri City Orthopedic Sgy & Mdcl ......E......760 724-9000
3905 Waring Rd Oceanside (92056) ***(P-19510)***
Tri Counties Bank (HQ) ......D......530 898-0300
63 Constitution Dr Chico (95973) ***(P-9273)***
Tri Counties Bank ......C......650 583-8450
975 El Camino Real South San Francisco (94080) ***(P-9274)***
Tri Counties Bank ......D......530 478-6001
305 Railroad Ave Ste 1 Nevada City (95959) ***(P-9275)***
Tri County Regional Center ......D......805 485-3177
2220 E Gonzales Rd 210a Oxnard (93036) ***(P-19700)***
Tri County Respite Care Svc ......D......530 755-3500
1215 Plumas St Ste 1600 Yuba City (95991) ***(P-23509)***
Tri Pointe Group Inc (PA) ......D......949 438-1400
19540 Jamboree Rd Ste 300 Irvine (92612) ***(P-1318)***
Tri Pointe Homes Inc (HQ) ......C......949 438-1400
19520 Jamboree Rd Ste 300 Irvine (92612) ***(P-1280)***
Tri Tool Inc (PA) ......C......916 288-6100
3041 Sunrise Blvd Rancho Cordova (95742) ***(P-7602)***
Tri Valley Vegetable Harvstg ......D......805 928-2727
123 N Depot St Santa Maria (93458) ***(P-460)***
Tri Valley Wholesale, Fairfield *Also called Tri-Valley Supply Inc* ***(P-6722)***
Tri-Ad Actuaries Inc ......C......760 743-7555
221 W Crest St Ste 300 Escondido (92025) ***(P-10524)***
Tri-City Economic Dev Corp ......D......510 429-8030
33377 Western Ave Union City (94587) ***(P-6293)***
Tri-City Health Center (PA) ......C......510 770-8040
39500 Liberty St Fremont (94538) ***(P-19511)***
Tri-City Home Care Services ......C......760 940-5800
2095 W Vista Way Ste 220 Vista (92083) ***(P-21313)***
Tri-City Hospital District (PA) ......A......760 724-8411
4002 Vista Way Oceanside (92056) ***(P-21314)***
Tri-City Medical Center, Oceanside *Also called Tri-City Hospital District* ***(P-21314)***
Tri-Counties Association F (PA) ......C......805 962-7881
520 E Montecito St Santa Barbara (93103) ***(P-23510)***
Tri-Counties Association F ......C......805 922-4640
1234 Fairway Dr A Santa Maria (93455) ***(P-24428)***
Tri-Counties Blood Bank, San Luis Obispo *Also called Vitalant* ***(P-22337)***

Employee Codes: A=Over 500 employees, B=251-500
C=101-250, D=51-100, E=50
2020 Directory of California
Wholesalers and Services Companies
© Mergent Inc. 1-800-342-5647
1461

TRI-COUNTIES REGIONAL CENTER, Santa Barbara *Also called Tri-Counties Association F* ***(P-23510)***
Tri-Marine Fish Company LLC...D.......310 547-1144
220 Cannery St San Pedro (90731) ***(P-8396)***
Tri-Marine Fishing MGT LLC...E.......310 547-1144
220 Cannery St San Pedro (90731) ***(P-26430)***
Tri-Mountain, Irwindale *Also called Mountain Gear Corporation* ***(P-8040)***
Tri-Power Group Inc...D.......925 583-8200
617 N Mary Ave Sunnyvale (94085) ***(P-5806)***
Tri-Signal Integration Inc (PA)...D.......818 566-8558
15853 Monte St Ste 101 Sylmar (91342) ***(P-2675)***
Tri-Star Ccw Management L P...D.......310 322-0999
1985 E Grand Ave El Segundo (90245) ***(P-13042)***
Tri-Star Drywall Lp...D.......559 299-9858
2479 Burgan Ave Clovis (93611) ***(P-2872)***
Tri-State AG Inc...D.......209 364-6185
47375 W Dakota Ave Firebaugh (93622) ***(P-6360)***
Tri-Tech Logistics LLC...C.......855 373-7049
3230 E Imperial Hwy # 140 Brea (92821) ***(P-5066)***
Tri-Tech Restoration Co Inc...D.......818 565-3900
3301 N San Fernando Blvd Burbank (91504) ***(P-1388)***
Tri-Union Seafoods LLC (HQ)...D.......858 558-9662
2150 E Grand Ave El Segundo (90245) ***(P-8397)***
Tri-Valley Supply Inc (PA)...D.......707 469-7470
1705 Enterprise Dr Fairfield (94533) ***(P-6722)***
Tri-West Ltd (PA)...C.......562 692-9166
12005 Pike St Santa Fe Springs (90670) ***(P-6592)***
Triad Broadcasting Company (PA)...C.......831 655-6350
2511 Garden Rd Ste A104 Monterey (93940) ***(P-5567)***
Triad Homes Assoc...D.......760 873-4273
873 N Main St Ste 150 Bishop (93514) ***(P-25353)***
Triad Properties...D.......805 648-5008
995 Riverside St Ventura (93001) ***(P-10665)***
Triad-Holmes Associates, Bishop *Also called Triad Homes Assoc* ***(P-25353)***
Triage Consulting Group (PA)...B.......415 512-9400
221 Main St Ste 1100 San Francisco (94105) ***(P-26853)***
Triage Entertainment LLC...D.......310 417-4800
6701 Center Dr W Ste 300 Los Angeles (90045) ***(P-17684)***
Triage Partners LLC...D.......562 634-0058
15717 Texaco Ave Paramount (90723) ***(P-16139)***
Triangle Distributing Co (PA)...C.......562 699-3424
12065 Pike St Santa Fe Springs (90670) ***(P-8794)***
Triangle Distributing Co...D.......760 347-4052
82851 Avenue 45 Indio (92201) ***(P-8795)***
Trianz Inc (HQ)...C.......408 387-5800
2350 Mission College Blvd Santa Clara (95054) ***(P-16140)***
Tribal Tektet, Arcata *Also called Tektetco* ***(P-1386)***
Tribeworx LLC...D.......800 949-3432
4 San Joaquin Plz Ste 150 Newport Beach (92660) ***(P-15525)***
Tricks Gymnastic Inc (PA)...D.......916 791-4496
4070 Cavitt Stallman Rd Granite Bay (95746) ***(P-18772)***
Trico Bancshares...D.......707 476-0981
2844 F St Eureka (95501) ***(P-9244)***
Tricom Management Inc...C.......714 630-2029
4025 E La Palma Ave # 101 Anaheim (92807) ***(P-26431)***
Tricor America Inc...D.......310 676-0800
12441 Eucalyptus Ave 7 Hawthorne (90250) ***(P-5067)***
Tricor America Inc...C.......916 371-1704
1690 Cebrian St West Sacramento (95691) ***(P-4288)***
Tricor America Inc...C.......510 293-3960
3149 Diablo Ave Hayward (94545) ***(P-4728)***
Tricor California, West Sacramento *Also called Tricor America Inc* ***(P-4288)***
Tricor Entertainment Inc...C.......626 282-5184
1613 Chelsea Rd San Marino (91108) ***(P-17685)***
Tricor International...D.......650 877-3678
717 Airport Blvd South San Francisco (94080) ***(P-5068)***
Tricorp Construction Inc (PA)...D.......916 779-8010
1030 G St Sacramento (95814) ***(P-1625)***
Tricorp Hearn Construction, Sacramento *Also called Tricorp Construction Inc* ***(P-1625)***
Trident Dental Labratories, Hawthorne *Also called Trident Labs LLC* ***(P-21615)***
Trident Labs LLC...C.......310 915-9121
12000 Aviation Blvd Hawthorne (90250) ***(P-21615)***
Tridentcare Imaging, San Leandro *Also called Community MBL Diagnostics LLC* ***(P-21514)***
Trifacta Inc (PA)...D.......415 429-7570
575 Market St Ste 1100 San Francisco (94105) ***(P-16141)***
Trifecta Clinical, Los Angeles *Also called Trifecta Multimedia LLC* ***(P-16142)***
Trifecta Multimedia LLC (PA)...E.......626 355-1303
725 S Figueroa St # 4050 Los Angeles (90017) ***(P-16142)***
Trigild International Inc...D.......619 295-6886
2151 Hotel Cir S San Diego (92108) ***(P-13043)***
Trilar Management Group...C.......951 925-2021
1025 S Gilbert St Hemet (92543) ***(P-26432)***
Trilink Biotechnologies LLC...C.......800 863-6801
10770 Wtridge Cir Ste 200 San Diego (92121) ***(P-25854)***
Trilliant Incorporated...D.......650 204-5050
1100 Island Dr Ste 201 Redwood City (94065) ***(P-27238)***
Trilliant Networks Inc (PA)...D.......650 204-5050
1100 Island Dr Ste 201 Redwood City (94065) ***(P-17106)***
Trilogy Day Spa, Manhattan Beach *Also called Trilogy Squaw Spa LLC* ***(P-13362)***
Trilogy Financial Services Inc (PA)...C.......714 843-9977
17011 Beach Blvd Ste 800 Huntington Beach (92647) ***(P-17107)***
Trilogy Financial Services Inc...E.......858 755-6696
12520 High Bluff Dr # 140 San Diego (92130) ***(P-17108)***
Trilogy Golf At La Quinta...D.......760 771-0707
60151 Trilogy Pkwy La Quinta (92253) ***(P-18309)***
Trilogy Plumbing Inc...C.......714 441-2952
1525 S Sinclair St Anaheim (92806) ***(P-2305)***
Trilogy Realty Group Inc...D.......937 206-0725
2025 N Mantle Ln Santa Ana (92705) ***(P-11488)***
Trilogy Rio Vista...D.......707 374-1100
1200 Clubhouse Dr Rio Vista (94571) ***(P-1389)***
Trilogy Squaw Spa LLC...E.......310 760-0044
451 Manhattan Beach Blvd Manhattan Beach (90266) ***(P-13362)***
Trim Tech Industries Inc...E.......408 573-4514
1724 Ringwood Ave San Jose (95131) ***(P-6664)***
Trimarine Fish Group, San Pedro *Also called Tri-Marine Fishing MGT LLC* ***(P-26430)***
Trimark Associates Inc...D.......916 357-5970
2365 Iron Point Rd # 100 Folsom (95630) ***(P-27239)***
Trimark Orange County, Irvine *Also called Trimark Raygal LLC* ***(P-17109)***
Trimark Raygal LLC...C.......949 474-1000
210 Commerce Irvine (92602) ***(P-17109)***
Trimont Land Company (HQ)...B.......530 562-1010
5001 Northstar Dr Truckee (96161) ***(P-11489)***
Trinet Group Inc (PA)...C.......510 352-5000
1 Park Pl Ste 600 Dublin (94568) ***(P-14443)***
Trinity Brdcstg Netwrk Inc...C.......714 665-3619
2442 Michelle Dr Tustin (92780) ***(P-5649)***
Trinity Broadcasting Network, Tustin *Also called Trinity Christian Center of SA* ***(P-5650)***
Trinity Building Services...B.......650 873-2121
430 N Canal St Ste 2 South San Francisco (94080) ***(P-14066)***
Trinity Capital Corporation (HQ)...D.......415 956-5174
475 Sansome St Fl 19 San Francisco (94111) ***(P-9510)***
Trinity Care & Nutria, Cerritos *Also called Trinitycare LLC* ***(P-21888)***
Trinity Christian Center of SA (PA)...C.......714 665-3619
2442 Michelle Dr Tustin (92780) ***(P-5650)***
Trinity Christn Ctr Santa Ana, Tustin *Also called Trinity Brdcstg Netwrk Inc* ***(P-5649)***
Trinity Fresh Distribution LLC...D.......916 714-7368
8200 Berry Ave Ste 140 Sacramento (95828) ***(P-8662)***
Trinity Fruit Packing Company...C.......559 743-3913
18700 E South Ave Reedley (93654) ***(P-555)***
Trinity Health Systems...D.......818 983-0103
13400 Sherman Way North Hollywood (91605) ***(P-20702)***
Trinity Health Systems...D.......562 437-2797
723 E 9th St Long Beach (90813) ***(P-20335)***
Trinity Health Systems (PA)...D.......626 960-1971
14318 Ohio St Baldwin Park (91706) ***(P-20336)***
Trinity Home Care, Torrance *Also called Providence Health System* ***(P-21845)***
Trinity Home Health Svcs Inc...D.......559 450-5112
6729 N Willow Ave Ste 103 Fresno (93710) ***(P-21887)***
Trinity Hospital, Weaverville *Also called Mountain Comm Hlth Cre Dist* ***(P-21051)***
Trinity Hospital, Weaverville *Also called Mountain Comm Hlth Cre Dist* ***(P-21052)***
Trinity Packing Company Inc (PA)...B.......559 433-3785
18700 E South Ave Reedley (93654) ***(P-17110)***
Trinity Packing Company Inc...B.......559 743-3913
7612 S Reed Ave Reedley (93654) ***(P-17111)***
Trinity Plaza, Richmond *Also called Macdonald Housing Partners LP* ***(P-11263)***
Trinity Technology Group Inc...D.......916 779-0201
2015 J St Ste 105 Sacramento (95811) ***(P-15706)***
Trinity Youth Services (PA)...D.......909 980-4755
201 N Indian Hill Blvd # 201 Claremont (91711) ***(P-24097)***
Trinitycare LLC (PA)...D.......818 709-4221
13030 Alondra Blvd Cerritos (90703) ***(P-21888)***
Trinus Corporation...E.......818 246-1143
225 S Lake Ave Ste 1080 Pasadena (91101) ***(P-15163)***
Triple A, Walnut Creek *Also called California State Automobile* ***(P-10079)***
Triple B Forwarders, Carson *Also called Triple B Forwarders Inc* ***(P-5069)***
Triple B Forwarders Inc (PA)...C.......310 604-5840
1511 Glenn Curtiss St Carson (90746) ***(P-5069)***
Triple E Trucking...E.......661 834-0071
1215 E White Ln Bakersfield (93307) ***(P-3943)***
Triple R Transportation Inc...D.......661 725-6494
978 Rd 192 Delano (93215) ***(P-3730)***
Triple Ring Technologies Inc...E.......510 592-3000
39655 Eureka Dr Newark (94560) ***(P-26854)***
Triple-E Machinery Moving Inc...D.......626 444-1137
3301 Gilman Rd El Monte (91732) ***(P-4146)***
Tristaff Group, Fallbrook *Also called Garich Inc* ***(P-14288)***
Tristar Insurance Group Inc (PA)...A.......562 495-6600
100 Oceangate Ste 700 Long Beach (90802) ***(P-10147)***
Tristar Risk Management...D.......714 543-0700
203 N Golden Circle Dr # 200 Santa Ana (92705) ***(P-10525)***
Tristar Television Music Inc...E.......310 244-4000
10202 Washington Blvd Culver City (90232) ***(P-17952)***
Tristart Risk Management, Long Beach *Also called Tristar Insurance Group Inc* ***(P-10147)***
Triton Logistics Corporation...D.......619 822-8832
706 Steffy Rd Ramona (92065) ***(P-5070)***
Triton Management Services LLC...D.......760 431-9911
1000 Aviara Dr Ste 300 Carlsbad (92011) ***(P-26433)***
Triton Media Group LLC (PA)...A.......323 290-6900
15303 Ventura Blvd # 1500 Sherman Oaks (91403) ***(P-5568)***
Triton Media Group LLC...D.......661 294-9000
8935 Lindblade St Culver City (90232) ***(P-5569)***
Triton Structural Concrete Inc...C.......858 866-2450
15435 Innovation Dr # 100 San Diego (92128) ***(P-1626)***
Triton Tower Inc (PA)...D.......916 375-8546
3200 Jefferson Blvd West Sacramento (95691) ***(P-1920)***
Triumph Protection Group Inc...C.......800 224-0286
853 Cotting Ct Ste D Vacaville (95688) ***(P-16461)***
Triunfo Public Facilities Corp...D.......805 658-4605
1001 Partridge Dr Ventura (93003) ***(P-6013)***
Trius Trucking Inc...D.......559 834-4000
4692 E Lincoln Ave Fowler (93625) ***(P-4147)***
Trivad Inc...C.......650 286-1086
1350 Bayshore Hwy Ste 450 Burlingame (94010) ***(P-6912)***
Triways Inc...D.......951 361-4840
11201 Iberia St Ste B Jurupa Valley (91752) ***(P-4148)***

Mergent e-mail: customerrelations@mergent.com
1462
2020 Directory of California
Wholesalers and Services Companies
(P-0000) Products & Services Section entry number
(PA)=Parent Co (HQ)=Headquarters (DH)=Div Headquarters

TRL Systems Incorporated..........D.....909 390-8392
9531 Milliken Ave Rancho Cucamonga (91730) ***(P-2676)***
TRM Corporation (PA)..........D.....510 895-2700
2378 Polvorosa Ave San Leandro (94577) ***(P-2912)***
Trojan Professional Svcs Inc..........D.....714 816-7169
4410 Cerritos Ave Los Alamitos (90720) ***(P-15891)***
Troon Golf LLC..........C.....760 346-4653
44500 Indian Wells Ln Indian Wells (92210) ***(P-26434)***
Troop Real Estate Inc..........D.....805 402-3028
4165 E Thousand Oaks Blvd # 100 Westlake Village (91362) ***(P-11490)***
Troop Real Estate Inc (PA)..........D.....805 581-3200
3200 E Los Angeles Ave # 18 Simi Valley (93065) ***(P-11491)***
Trope & Trope, Los Angeles *Also called Trope and Trope LLP* ***(P-22849)***
Trope and Trope LLP..........D.....323 879-2726
12121 Wilshire Blvd # 801 Los Angeles (90025) ***(P-22849)***
Tropical Plaza Nursery Inc..........D.....714 998-4100
9642 Santiago Blvd Villa Park (92867) ***(P-916)***
Trotta Associates..........D.....310 306-6866
13160 Mindanao Way # 100 Marina Del Rey (90292) ***(P-25951)***
Troutman Sanders LLP..........D.....858 509-6000
11682 El Camino Real # 400 San Diego (92130) ***(P-22850)***
Troutman Sanders LLP..........D.....415 477-5700
580 California St # 1100 San Francisco (94104) ***(P-22851)***
Trowbridge Enterprises (PA)..........D.....831 476-3815
2606 Chanticleer Ave Santa Cruz (95065) ***(P-7867)***
Troy Lee Designs LLC (PA)..........D.....951 371-5219
155 E Rincon St Corona (92879) ***(P-7721)***
Troyer Contracting Company Inc..........D.....562 944-6452
10122 Freeman Ave Santa Fe Springs (90670) ***(P-3482)***
Troygould PC..........D.....310 553-4441
1801 Century Park E # 1600 Los Angeles (90067) ***(P-22852)***
Trs Staffing Solutions, Aliso Viejo *Also called Fluor Corporation* ***(P-25075)***
Tru Green Landcare Inc..........B.....602 276-4311
5248 Governor Dr San Diego (92122) ***(P-917)***
Tru Green-Chemlawn, Riverside *Also called Trugreen Limited Partnership* ***(P-918)***
Truaire, Santa Fe Springs *Also called TA Industries Inc* ***(P-7441)***
Truck Terminal, Bakersfield *Also called Pan Pacific Petroleum Co Inc* ***(P-4109)***
Truck Tub International Inc..........D.....805 474-8680
P.O. Box 2111 Pismo Beach (93448) ***(P-17400)***
Truck Underwriters Association (HQ)..........A.....323 932-3200
4680 Wilshire Blvd Los Angeles (90010) ***(P-24429)***
Truck Underwriters Association..........A.....323 932-3200
6303 Owensmouth Ave Fl 1 Woodland Hills (91367) ***(P-9890)***
Truckee Dnner Rcreation Pk Dst..........D.....530 582-7720
10981 Truckee Way Truckee (96161) ***(P-18773)***
Truckee Donner Pub Utly Dist F..........D.....530 587-3896
11570 Donner Pass Rd Truckee (96161) ***(P-5956)***
TRUCKEE DONNER PUD, Truckee *Also called Truckee Donner Pub Utly Dist F* ***(P-5956)***
Truckee High School, Truckee *Also called Tahoe Trcke Unfd Sch Dis Fincn* ***(P-27226)***
Truconnect Communications Inc (PA)..........C.....512 919-2641
1149 S Hill St Ste 400 Los Angeles (90015) ***(P-5483)***
True Air Mechanical Inc..........C.....888 316-0642
4 Faraday Irvine (92618) ***(P-2306)***
True Home Heating and AC, Irvine *Also called True Air Mechanical Inc* ***(P-2306)***
True Religion Brand Jeans, Manhattan Beach *Also called Guru Denim LLC* ***(P-8074)***
True Wrld Fods Los Angeles LLC..........D.....323 846-3300
4200 S Alameda St Vernon (90058) ***(P-8398)***
True Wrld Fods San Frncsco LLC..........D.....510 352-8140
1815 Williams St San Leandro (94577) ***(P-8399)***
Truebeck Construction Inc (PA)..........D.....650 227-1957
951 Mariners San Mateo (94404) ***(P-1627)***
Trueblue Inc..........C.....530 755-3291
1362 Colusa Hwy Yuba City (95993) ***(P-14575)***
Trueblue Inc..........E.....805 963-5370
123 E Carrillo St Santa Barbara (93101) ***(P-14576)***
Trueblue Skilled Trade Group, Santa Ana *Also called TLC Services Group Inc* ***(P-14439)***
Truecar Inc..........B.....415 821-8270
140 New Montgomery St # 2400 San Francisco (94105) ***(P-6412)***
Truecar Inc..........D.....800 200-2000
1401 Ocean Ave Ste 300 Santa Monica (90401) ***(P-13456)***
Truecar Inc (PA)..........E.....800 200-2000
120 Broadway Ste 200 Santa Monica (90401) ***(P-15164)***
Truesdail Laboratories Inc..........E.....714 730-6239
3337 Michelson Dr Irvine (92612) ***(P-25855)***
Truform Construction Corp..........E.....714 630-7447
1041 N Shepard St Anaheim (92806) ***(P-2987)***
Trugreen, Santa Ana *Also called Landcare USA LLC* ***(P-845)***
Trugreen, Escondido *Also called Landcare USA LLC* ***(P-846)***
Trugreen, Simi Valley *Also called Landcare USA LLC* ***(P-847)***
Trugreen, Gardena *Also called Landcare USA LLC* ***(P-852)***
Trugreen, Rancho Cordova *Also called Landcare USA LLC* ***(P-853)***
Trugreen, San Diego *Also called Landcare USA LLC* ***(P-854)***
Trugreen, Canoga Park *Also called Landcare USA LLC* ***(P-855)***
Trugreen, San Jose *Also called Landcare USA LLC* ***(P-856)***
Trugreen Limited Partnership..........E.....951 231-2760
1130 Palmyrita Ave # 300 Riverside (92507) ***(P-918)***
Trugreen Lndcare Michael Bogan, Santa Fe Springs *Also called Landcare USA LLC* ***(P-849)***
Trulia Inc (HQ)..........B.....415 648-4358
535 Mission St Fl 7 San Francisco (94105) ***(P-15827)***
Trumpia, Anaheim *Also called Docircle Inc* ***(P-5394)***
Trust Automation Inc..........D.....805 544-0761
143 Suburban Rd Ste 100 San Luis Obispo (93401) ***(P-25354)***
Trust Employee ADM & MGT, San Diego *Also called Team Risk MGT Strategies LLC* ***(P-27228)***
Trust For Cnsrvtion Innovation..........D.....415 421-3774
405 14th St Ste 164 Oakland (94612) ***(P-27240)***

Trustarc Inc..........D.....415 520-3400
835 Market St Ste 800 San Francisco (94103) ***(P-16143)***
Truste, San Francisco *Also called Trustarc Inc* ***(P-16143)***
Trustee Corps, Irvine *Also called Mtc Financial Inc* ***(P-11804)***
Truthmd LLC..........D.....949 637-4296
32932 Pacific Coast Hwy Dana Point (92629) ***(P-16144)***
Truvida Recovery..........D.....949 283-4679
23726 Birtcher Dr Lake Forest (92630) ***(P-22144)***
Tryad Service Corporation..........D.....661 391-1524
5900 E Lerdo Hwy Shafter (93263) ***(P-1047)***
Tryfacta Inc..........B.....408 419-9200
4637 Chabot Dr Ste 100 Pleasanton (94588) ***(P-15165)***
Trz Holdings II Inc..........B.....213 955-7170
725 S Figueroa St # 1850 Los Angeles (90017) ***(P-11492)***
Tscm Corporation..........D.....714 841-1988
17791 Jamestown Ln Huntington Beach (92647) ***(P-14067)***
Tsg, San Diego *Also called Socal Services Inc* ***(P-14422)***
Tsmc North America (HQ)..........C.....408 382-8000
2851 Junction Ave San Jose (95134) ***(P-26855)***
Tst Inc..........D.....310 835-0115
11601 Etiwanda Ave Fontana (92337) ***(P-3944)***
Tst Inc..........D.....909 590-1098
11601 Etiwanda Ave Fontana (92337) ***(P-7778)***
Tsu Corporate Services, North Hollywood *Also called Toner Supply USA Inc* ***(P-6908)***
Ttg Engineers..........D.....714 490-5555
222 S Harbor Blvd Ste 800 Anaheim (92805) ***(P-25355)***
Ttg Engineers (PA)..........C.....626 463-2800
300 N Lake Ave Fl 14 Pasadena (91101) ***(P-25356)***
TTI, Milpitas *Also called Technical Temps Inc* ***(P-14435)***
Tti Inc..........D.....408 414-1450
188 Martinvale Ln San Jose (95119) ***(P-7357)***
TTI Technologies, Exeter *Also called Exeter Engineering Inc* ***(P-484)***
Ttp-US, San Marcos *Also called Tel Tech Plus Inc* ***(P-2668)***
Tts, Pleasanton *Also called Telecom Technology Svcs Inc* ***(P-27230)***
TTSA, Truckee *Also called Tahoe-Truckee Sanitation Agcy* ***(P-6140)***
Ttsi, Rancho Dominguez *Also called Premium Trnsp Svcs Inc* ***(P-4474)***
TTSR, Sacramento *Also called Training Toward Self Reliance* ***(P-23508)***
TTT West Coast Inc..........C.....818 972-0500
3000 W Alameda Ave # 125 Burbank (91505) ***(P-17686)***
Ttx Company..........B.....951 685-0158
10800 San Sevaine Way Jurupa Valley (91752) ***(P-5143)***
Tubemogul Inc..........D.....510 653-0126
1250 53rd St Ste 1 Emeryville (94608) ***(P-15526)***
Tucker Distributors..........E.....714 970-5742
5380 E Hunter Ave Anaheim (92807) ***(P-7458)***
Tucker Electric Corporation..........E.....818 426-7645
3365 Chestnut Ln Santa Rosa Valley (93012) ***(P-2677)***
Tucker Electrical, Santa Rosa Valley *Also called Tucker Electric Corporation* ***(P-2677)***
Tucker Ellis LLP..........D.....213 430-3400
1000 Wilshire Blvd # 1800 Los Angeles (90017) ***(P-22853)***
Tucker Sheet Metal Distr, Anaheim *Also called Tucker Distributors* ***(P-7458)***
Tucker Technology Inc..........D.....510 836-0422
300 Frnk H Ogw Plz 208 Oakland (94612) ***(P-2678)***
Tucoemas Federal Credit Union (PA)..........D.....559 737-5900
5222 W Cypress Ave Visalia (93277) ***(P-9369)***
Tucoemas Federal Credit Union..........D.....559 429-7094
2300 W Whitendale Ave Visalia (93277) ***(P-9370)***
Tucson Hotels LP..........B.....510 658-9300
1800 Powell St Oakland (94608) ***(P-13044)***
Tucson Hotels LP..........C.....916 446-0100
300 J St Sacramento (95814) ***(P-13045)***
Tucson Hotels LP..........C.....916 446-0100
300 J St Sacramento (95814) ***(P-13046)***
Tucson Hotels LP..........C.....831 393-1115
1441 Canyon Del Rey Blvd Seaside (93955) ***(P-13047)***
Tudor Cnstr & Restoration, Elk Grove *Also called Bennathon Corp* ***(P-1420)***
Tuftex Carpet Mills, Santa Fe Springs *Also called Shaw Industries Group Inc* ***(P-6581)***
Tulare Cnty Chld Care Home Edu..........D.....559 651-0247
7000 W Doe Ave Ste C Visalia (93291) ***(P-23800)***
TULARE DISTRICT HOSPITAL, Tulare *Also called Tulare Local Health Care Dst* ***(P-21315)***
Tulare Local Health Care Dst..........A.....559 685-3462
869 N Cherry St Tulare (93274) ***(P-21315)***
Tulare Nrsing Rhbilitation Ctr, Tulare *Also called Tulare Nrsing Rhblitation Hosp* ***(P-20337)***
Tulare Nrsing Rhblitation Hosp..........C.....559 686-8581
680 E Merritt Ave Tulare (93274) ***(P-20337)***
Tulare Regional Medical Center..........D.....559 688-0821
869 N Cherry St Tulare (93274) ***(P-21316)***
Tule River Indian Hlth Ctr Inc..........D.....559 784-2316
380 N Reservation Rd Porterville (93257) ***(P-22145)***
Tuls Cattle, Tulare *Also called M & T Calf Ranch* ***(P-379)***
Tulsa Street Pta CA Cngrss of, Granada Hills *Also called Los Angeles Unified School Dst* ***(P-24588)***
Tum Yeto Inc..........E.....619 232-7523
2001 Commercial St San Diego (92113) ***(P-7722)***
Tumbleweed Day Camp, Los Angeles *Also called Tumbleweed Educational Entps* ***(P-18774)***
Tumbleweed Educational Entps..........C.....310 444-3232
1024 Hanley Ave Los Angeles (90049) ***(P-18774)***
Tumi Inc..........D.....408 244-6512
333 Santana Row Apt 230 San Jose (95128) ***(P-7842)***
Tunari Corp Inc..........D.....650 249-6740
2755 Campus Dr Ste 300 San Mateo (94403) ***(P-15166)***
Tunein Inc..........C.....650 319-7100
210 King St Fl 3 San Francisco (94107) ***(P-5570)***
Tuolomne Cnty Bhvrl Hlth, Sonora *Also called Kingsview Corp* ***(P-22057)***
Tuolumne City Inv Grp II LP..........E.....209 928-1567
18402 Tuolumne Rd Apt 31 Tuolumne (95379) ***(P-10831)***

A
L
P
H
A
B
E
T
I
C

Employee Codes: A=Over 500 employees, B=251-500
C=101-250, D=51-100, E=50
2020 Directory of California
Wholesalers and Services Companies
© Mergent Inc. 1-800-342-5647
1463

Tuolumne Cy Senior Apartments, Tuolumne *Also called Tuolumne City Inv Grp II LP* ***(P-10831)***
Tuolumne Me-Wuk Indian ....D....209 928-5400
18880 Cherry Valley Blvd Tuolumne (95379) ***(P-19512)***
Tuolumne Mewuk Indian Health, Tuolumne *Also called Tuolumne Me-Wuk Indian* ***(P-19512)***
Tuolumne Utilities District ....D....209 532-5536
18885 Nugget Blvd Sonora (95370) ***(P-6124)***
Tupaz Day Care Services Inc ....D....408 377-1622
3015 Union Ave San Jose (95124) ***(P-23511)***
Tupaz Homes LLC ....D....408 377-1622
2038 Biarritz Pl San Jose (95138) ***(P-1211)***
Turbine Repair Services LLC (PA) ....D....909 947-2256
1838 E Cedar St Ontario (91761) ***(P-17556)***
Turbo Data Systems Inc (PA) ....E....714 573-5757
18302 Irvine Blvd Ste 200 Tustin (92780) ***(P-15828)***
Turbotax, San Diego *Also called Intuit Inc* ***(P-15369)***
Turelk Inc ....D....858 633-8085
11622 El Camino Real # 100 San Diego (92130) ***(P-1628)***
Turelk Inc (PA) ....C....310 835-3736
3700 Santa Fe Ave Ste 200 Long Beach (90810) ***(P-1629)***
Turelk San Diego, San Diego *Also called Turelk Inc* ***(P-1628)***
Turf Star Inc ....D....760 772-3575
79253 Country Club Dr Bermuda Dunes (92203) ***(P-7510)***
Turfstar, Bermuda Dunes *Also called Turf Star Inc* ***(P-7510)***
Turk & Eddy Associates LP ....D....415 474-6524
201 Eddy St San Francisco (94102) ***(P-10832)***
Turkey Creek Golf Club, Lincoln *Also called Clubcorp Usa Inc* ***(P-18233)***
Turlock Dairy & Rfrgn Inc ....D....209 667-6455
1819 S Walnut Rd Turlock (95380) ***(P-7511)***
Turlock Diagnostic Center, Turlock *Also called Emanuel Medical Center Inc* ***(P-20869)***
Turlock Fruit Co (PA) ....E....209 634-7207
500 S Tully Rd Turlock (95380) ***(P-8531)***
Turlock Irrigation District (PA) ....C....209 883-8222
333 E Canal Dr Turlock (95380) ***(P-24468)***
Turlock Irrigation District ....B....209 883-8300
901 N Broadway Turlock (95380) ***(P-6374)***
Turlock Nrsing Rhabilation Ctr, Turlock *Also called Covenant Care California LLC* ***(P-19837)***
Turn Around Communications Inc ....C....626 443-2400
4400 Temple City Blvd A El Monte (91731) ***(P-1921)***
Turn Behavioral Hlth Svcs Inc ....D....559 264-7521
2550 W Clinton Ave Fresno (93705) ***(P-22146)***
Turn Inc (HQ) ....C....650 353-4399
901 Marshall St Ste 200 Redwood City (94063) ***(P-13663)***
TURNABOUT SHOP, El Cerrito *Also called Berkeley Clinic Auxuillary* ***(P-24807)***
Turner Broadcasting System Inc ....E....818 977-5452
3500 W Olive Ave Ste 1500 Burbank (91505) ***(P-17687)***
Turner Broadcasting System Inc ....D....310 788-6767
1888 Century Park E # 1200 Los Angeles (90067) ***(P-5571)***
Turner Construction Company ....B....714 940-9000
1900 S State College Blvd # 200 Anaheim (92806) ***(P-1630)***
Turner Construction Company ....D....213 891-3000
555 S Flower St Ste 4220 Los Angeles (90071) ***(P-1212)***
Turner Construction Company ....D....916 444-4421
2500 Venture Oaks Way # 200 Sacramento (95833) ***(P-1631)***
Turner Construction Company ....E....510 267-8100
300 Frank H Ogawa Plz # 510 Oakland (94612) ***(P-1632)***
Turner Construction Company ....D....415 705-8900
311 California St Ste 450 San Francisco (94104) ***(P-1633)***
Turner Construction Company ....D....858 320-4040
15378 Ave Of Science # 100 San Diego (92128) ***(P-1634)***
Turner Dockworth, San Francisco *Also called Destination Moon LP* ***(P-13781)***
Turner Security Systems Inc ....C....559 486-3466
120 W Shields Ave Fresno (93705) ***(P-16462)***
Turner Techtronics Inc ....C....949 724-1339
17845 Sky Park Cir Irvine (92614) ***(P-15928)***
Turner Techtronics Inc (PA) ....C....818 973-1060
7675 N San Fernando Rd Burbank (91505) ***(P-15929)***
Turning Point Central Cal Inc ....E....559 627-1490
711 N Court St Visalia (93291) ***(P-23512)***
Turning Point Cmnty Programs ....D....916 393-1222
4600 47th Ave Ste 111 Sacramento (95824) ***(P-24098)***
Turning Point For God ....D....619 258-3600
10007 Riverford Rd Lakeside (92040) ***(P-17953)***
Turning Point I S A, Sacramento *Also called Turning Point Cmnty Programs* ***(P-24098)***
Turning Point Ministries, Lakeside *Also called Turning Point For God* ***(P-17953)***
Turnupseed Electric Service ....D....559 686-1541
1580 S K St Tulare (93274) ***(P-2679)***
Turtle Bay Exploration Park ....E....530 243-4282
1335 Arboretum Dr Ste A Redding (96003) ***(P-24298)***
Turtle Entertainment America ....E....818 861-7315
1212 Chestnut St Burbank (91506) ***(P-18013)***
Turtle Rock Cdc, Irvine *Also called Child Development Incorporated* ***(P-23694)***
Tusa Inc (PA) ....C....888 848-3749
986 Walsh Ave Santa Clara (95050) ***(P-15930)***
Tuscan Inn, San Francisco *Also called Kms Fishermans Wharf LP* ***(P-12519)***
Tuscan Inn, San Francisco *Also called Kimpton Hotel & Rest Group LLC* ***(P-12511)***
Tuscan Inn, San Francisco *Also called 425 North Point Street LLC* ***(P-11980)***
Tustin Care Center Corp ....D....714 832-6780
1051 Bryan Ave Tustin (92780) ***(P-20466)***
Tustin Executive Center, Tustin *Also called Southern Cal Prmnnte Med Group* ***(P-10052)***
Tustin Hcnda Memory Care Cmnty, Tustin *Also called Silverado Senior Living Inc* ***(P-24074)***
Tustin Ranch Golf Club, Tustin *Also called Crown Golf Properties LP* ***(P-26574)***
Tustin Ranch Golf Club, Tustin *Also called Sanyo Foods Corp America* ***(P-18563)***
Tustin Ranch Medical Offices, Tustin *Also called Kaiser Foundation Hospitals* ***(P-19103)***
Tutera Group Inc ....D....209 223-2231
811 Court St Jackson (95642) ***(P-20338)***
Tutor Perini Corporation (PA) ....C....818 362-8391
15901 Olden St Sylmar (91342) ***(P-1635)***
Tutor Perini/Zachry/Parsons ....D....559 385-7025
1401 Fulton St Ste 400 Fresno (93721) ***(P-2000)***
Tutor-Saliba Corporation (HQ) ....D....818 362-8391
15901 Olden St Sylmar (91342) ***(P-1636)***
Tuttle Family Enterprises Inc ....B....818 534-2566
21020 Superior St Chatsworth (91311) ***(P-14068)***
TV Group, San Diego *Also called Panasonic Corp North America* ***(P-7212)***
TV Guide Entrmt Group LLC ....D....310 360-1441
2700 Colorado Ave Ste 200 Santa Monica (90404) ***(P-7220)***
Tvb (usa) Inc (HQ) ....E....562 345-9871
15411 Blackburn Ave Norwalk (90650) ***(P-5769)***
Tvgla, Culver City *Also called Visionaire Group Inc* ***(P-13595)***
Tvguide.com, Playa Vista *Also called Pop Media Networks LLC* ***(P-17997)***
TW Holdings Inc ....A....858 217-8750
10805 Rncho Brnrdo Rd Ste San Diego (92127) ***(P-18206)***
TW Security Corp (HQ) ....C....949 932-1000
5 Park Plz Ste 400 Irvine (92614) ***(P-6913)***
TW Services Inc ....B....714 441-2400
2751 E Chapman Ave # 204 Fullerton (92831) ***(P-5144)***
Twain Harte Horsemen ....D....209 586-4841
23580 View Ln Columbia (95310) ***(P-24682)***
Twdc Enterprises 18 Corp ....B....818 754-6921
P.O. Box 4410 Anaheim (92803) ***(P-5651)***
Twdc Enterprises 18 Corp ....B....818 544-5009
532 Paula Ave Glendale (91201) ***(P-5652)***
Twdc Enterprises 18 Corp ....B....818 295-3134
914 N Victory Blvd Burbank (91502) ***(P-5653)***
Twdc Enterprises 18 Corp ....D....818 560-1268
121 E Buena Vista Burbank (91521) ***(P-5654)***
Twdc Enterprises 18 Corp ....A....818 567-5590
3900 W Alameda Ave Rm 845 Burbank (91505) ***(P-18014)***
Twdc Enterprises 18 Corp ....A....818 544-6500
1133 Flower St Glendale (91201) ***(P-5655)***
Twdc Enterprises 18 Corp ....C....818 553-7333
650 S Buenavista St Burbank (91501) ***(P-18342)***
Twdc Enterprises 18 Corp ....C....714 781-4278
1598 S Harbor Blvd Anaheim (92802) ***(P-13048)***
Twdc Enterprises 18 Corp ....B....818 460-6655
500 S Buena Vista St Burbank (91521) ***(P-5656)***
Twdc Enterprises 18 Corp ....A....818 560-1000
500 S Buena Vista St Burbank (91521) ***(P-5657)***
Twdc Enterprises 18 Corp (HQ) ....A....818 560-1000
500 S Buena Vista St Burbank (91521) ***(P-5658)***
Twdc Enterprises 18 Corp ....C....818 553-4222
601 Circle Seven Dr Glendale (91201) ***(P-17688)***
Twdc Enterprises 18 Corp ....B....818 560-1000
350 S Buena Vista St Burbank (91521) ***(P-5659)***
Twelve Bridges Golf Club, Lincoln *Also called Crstb Partners LLC* ***(P-18238)***
Twentieth Century Fox Home E (HQ) ....A....310 369-1000
10201 W Pico Blvd Los Angeles (90064) ***(P-17689)***
Twentieth Cntury Fox Film Corp (HQ) ....D....310 369-1000
10201 W Pico Blvd Los Angeles (90064) ***(P-17690)***
Twentieth Cntury Fox Intl Corp (HQ) ....B....310 969-5300
10201 W Pico Blvd Bldg 1 Los Angeles (90064) ***(P-17792)***
Twenty Mile Productions LLC ....C....412 251-0767
11833 Miss Ave Ste 101 Los Angeles (90025) ***(P-18015)***
Twenty4seven Hotels Corp ....B....949 734-6400
520 Newport Center Dr # 520 Newport Beach (92660) ***(P-26435)***
TWI- Techno West Inc ....D....714 635-4070
1391 S Allec St Anaheim (92805) ***(P-2402)***
Twilight Haven ....D....559 251-8417
1717 S Winery Ave Fresno (93727) ***(P-20339)***
Twilio Inc (PA) ....C....415 390-2337
375 Beale St Ste 300 San Francisco (94105) ***(P-5279)***
Twin Cities Community Hosp Inc ....B....805 434-3500
1100 Las Tablas Rd Templeton (93465) ***(P-19513)***
Twin Med LLC (PA) ....D....323 582-9900
11333 Greenstone Ave Santa Fe Springs (90670) ***(P-7014)***
Twin Oaks Nrsing Rhblttion Ctr, Chico *Also called Evergreen At Chico LLC* ***(P-19899)***
Twin Oaks Power LP (HQ) ....D....619 696-2034
101 Ash St Hq10b San Diego (92101) ***(P-5957)***
Twining Inc (PA) ....D....562 426-3355
2883 E Spring St Ste 300 Long Beach (90806) ***(P-26111)***
Twining Inc ....D....562 426-3355
3310 E Airport Way Long Beach (90806) ***(P-26112)***
Twining Laboratories, Long Beach *Also called Twining Inc* ***(P-26111)***
Twist Bioscience Corporation ....C....800 719-0671
455 Mssion Bay Blvd S S 5 San Francisco (94158) ***(P-25856)***
Two Harbors Enterprises Inc ....D....310 510-2000
150 Metropole Ave Avalon (90704) ***(P-3615)***
Two Jinn Inc (PA) ....D....760 431-9911
1000 Aviara Dr Ste 300 Carlsbad (92011) ***(P-17112)***
Two Palms Nursing Center Inc (PA) ....E....626 798-8991
2637 E Washington Blvd Pasadena (91107) ***(P-20703)***
Two Palms Nursing Center Inc ....D....626 796-1103
150 Bellefontaine St Pasadena (91105) ***(P-20704)***
Two Rivers Demolition Inc ....D....916 638-6775
2620 Mercantile Dr 100 Rancho Cordova (95742) ***(P-3354)***
Two Roads Prof Resources Inc ....C....714 901-3804
5122 Bolsa Ave Ste 112 Huntington Beach (92649) ***(P-14577)***
TWR Enterprises Inc ....C....951 279-2000
1661 Railroad St Corona (92880) ***(P-2988)***
Ty Investment Inc ....D....619 448-4242
1015 21st St Unit A Santa Monica (90403) ***(P-18600)***
Tyan Inc ....D....818 785-5831
1500 Glenoaks Blvd San Fernando (91340) ***(P-16463)***
Tyan Computer Corporation ....D....510 651-8868
3288 Laurelview Ct Fremont (94538) ***(P-6914)***

Tyler Bluff Wind Project LLC ....A....888 903-6926
15445 Innovation Dr San Diego (92128) *(P-5958)*
Tyler Palmieri Wiener ....D....949 851-9400
1900 Main St Ste 700 Irvine (92614) *(P-22854)*
Tylie Jones & Associates Inc (PA) ....E....818 955-7600
58 E Santa Anita Ave Burbank (91502) *(P-17113)*
TYlin Intl Group Ltd (PA) ....C....415 291-3700
345 California St Fl 23 San Francisco (94104) *(P-25357)*
Tyme Maidu Tribe-Berry Creek ....A....530 538-4560
4020 Olive Hwy Oroville (95966) *(P-13049)*
Tyr Sport Inc ....D....562 430-1380
1790 Apollo Ct Seal Beach (90740) *(P-8116)*
Tz Holdings LP ....A....949 719-2200
567 San Nicolas Dr # 120 Newport Beach (92660) *(P-15527)*
Tzippy Care Inc ....D....323 737-7778
2190 W Adams Blvd Los Angeles (90018) *(P-20705)*
U A L, Irvine *Also called United Agribusiness League (P-24369)*
U B C 200, Beverly Hills *Also called Mufg Union Bank National Assn (P-9106)*
U C Health Systems, Sacramento *Also called U C Med Humn Rsrces Aplcat Svc (P-21317)*
U C I Distribution Plus, Pasadena *Also called United Couriers Inc (P-4695)*
U C L A Dermatology, Los Angeles *Also called Gary Lask (P-18993)*
U C Med Humn Rsrces Aplcat Svc ....D....916 734-5916
2730 Stockton Blvd # 21002500 Sacramento (95817) *(P-21317)*
U C P-UNITED CEREBAL PALSY ASS, Fresno *Also called United Crbrl Plsy of Cntrl CA (P-24235)*
U F C Pension Trust Fund, Cypress *Also called Cal Southern United Food (P-10208)*
U Gym LLC ....D....951 808-3850
470 N Mckinley St Corona (92879) *(P-18207)*
U Gym LLC (PA) ....D....714 668-0911
1501 Quail St Ste 100 Newport Beach (92660) *(P-18208)*
U S ARMY CORPS OF ENGINEERS, Sacramento *Also called US Army Corps of Engineers (P-25376)*
U S ARMY CORPS OF ENGINEERS, Los Angeles *Also called US Army Corps of Engineers (P-25377)*
U S Army Corps of Engineers ....D....916 557-7491
1645 Riverbank Rd West Sacramento (95605) *(P-25358)*
U S Army Corps of Engineers ....D....916 649-0133
2194 Ascot Ave Rio Linda (95673) *(P-25359)*
U S Army Corps of Engineers ....D....916 925-7001
3900 Roseville Rd North Highlands (95660) *(P-25360)*
U S Army Corps of Engineers ....D....415 289-3067
2100 Bridgeway Sausalito (94965) *(P-25361)*
U S Foods, Fullerton *Also called US Foods Inc (P-8279)*
U S GOVERNMENT, Tulelake *Also called Lava Beds National Monuments (P-24844)*
U S Mbile Wrless Cmmunications (PA) ....D....858 537-0709
8300 Juniper Creek Ln # 100 San Diego (92126) *(P-5280)*
U S Merchant Services, Newport Beach *Also called Montrenes Financial Svcs Inc (P-16931)*
U S Office & Industry Supply, Van Nuys *Also called Nat Sim Corp (P-7860)*
U S Perma Inc ....E....408 436-0600
1696 Rogers Ave San Jose (95112) *(P-2913)*
U S Private Protection SEC Inc ....C....310 301-0010
5555 Inglewood Blvd # 205 Culver City (90230) *(P-16464)*
U S Weatherford L P ....D....661 589-9483
2815 Fruitvale Ave Bakersfield (93308) *(P-1048)*
U S Xpress Inc ....C....760 768-6707
363 Nina Lee Rd Calexico (92231) *(P-4149)*
U T L A, Los Angeles *Also called United Teachers-Los Angeles (P-24471)*
U W G Northern California Div, Stockton *Also called Unified Grocers Inc (P-4522)*
U W G Southern California Div, Los Angeles *Also called Unified Grocers Inc (P-4521)*
U-2 Home Entertainment Inc ....E....650 871-8118
170 S Spruce Ave Ste 200 South San Francisco (94080) *(P-7358)*
U-Dub Productions, Palm Desert *Also called Desert Television LLC (P-5594)*
U-Haul Co of California (HQ) ....C....800 528-0463
44511 S Grimmer Blvd Fremont (94538) *(P-17190)*
U. S. Grant Hotel, San Diego *Also called American Prprty-Mnagement Corp (P-12004)*
U.S. Healthworks Medical Group, Valencia *Also called US Healthworks Inc (P-19536)*
U.S. Trading Company, Hayward *Also called Ustov Inc (P-8281)*
Ua Galaxy Los Cerritos ....D....562 865-6499
4900 E 4th St Ontario (91764) *(P-17867)*
Ua Galaxy Los Cerritos 33, Ontario *Also called Ua Galaxy Los Cerritos (P-17867)*
Uaw-Lbor Emplyment Trning Corp ....C....323 730-7900
3965 S Vermont Ave Los Angeles (90037) *(P-14444)*
Uaw-Lbor Emplyment Trning Corp (PA) ....C....562 989-7700
11010 Artesia Blvd # 100 Cerritos (90703) *(P-14445)*
Uber Technologies Inc (PA) ....A....415 612-8582
1455 Market St Fl 4 San Francisco (94103) *(P-3731)*
Uber Technologies Inc ....C....832 610-0359
900 Arastradero Rd Bldg B Palo Alto (94304) *(P-3751)*
Ubi Soft Entertainment ....D....415 547-4000
625 3rd St Fl 3 San Francisco (94107) *(P-18016)*
Ubics Inc ....C....415 289-1400
1050 Bridgeway Sausalito (94965) *(P-15167)*
Ubiquity, San Francisco *Also called Decimal Inc (P-16740)*
UBS Financial Services Inc ....C....213 972-1511
777 S Figueroa St # 5100 Los Angeles (90017) *(P-9759)*
UBS Financial Services Inc ....D....310 274-8441
131 S Rodeo Dr Ste 200 Beverly Hills (90212) *(P-9760)*
UBS Financial Services Inc ....C....619 236-0460
600 W Broadway Ste 2100 San Diego (92101) *(P-9761)*
UBS Financial Services Inc ....C....415 954-6700
1 California St Ste 2000 San Francisco (94111) *(P-9762)*
UBS Financial Services Inc ....C....949 760-5308
888 San Clemente Dr # 300 Newport Beach (92660) *(P-9763)*
UBS Financial Services Inc ....E....916 648-7200
1610 Arden Way Ste 200 Sacramento (95815) *(P-9764)*
UBS Financial Services Inc ....D....415 398-6400
555 California St # 4650 San Francisco (94104) *(P-9765)*
UBS Financial Services Inc ....E....408 282-8402
50 W San Fernando St Fl 8 San Jose (95113) *(P-17114)*
UBS Financial Services Inc ....E....951 684-6300
3801 University Ave # 300 Riverside (92501) *(P-17115)*
UBS Financial Services Inc ....D....858 454-9181
1200 Prospect St Ste 100 La Jolla (92037) *(P-17116)*
UBS Financial Services Inc ....E....626 449-1501
200 S Los Robles Ave # 600 Pasadena (91101) *(P-17117)*
UBS Securities LLC ....D....415 352-5650
555 California St # 4650 San Francisco (94104) *(P-9766)*
Uc David Home Care Services, Sacramento *Also called Ucd Mc Home Care Services (P-26436)*
Uc Davis Health System (PA) ....D....916 734-1000
4610 X St Sacramento (95817) *(P-21318)*
Uc Davis Medical Center, Sacramento *Also called University California Davis (P-21340)*
Uc Irvine Hlth Rgonal Burn Ctr, Orange *Also called University California Irvine (P-19529)*
Uc Irvine Medical Center, Orange *Also called University California Irvine (P-21342)*
Uc Regents ....D....310 301-8777
300 Medical Plaza Los Angeles (90095) *(P-19514)*
Uc Riverside RES Economic Dev, Riverside *Also called University Cal Riverside (P-25952)*
Uca General Insurance, Cypress *Also called United Chinese American Genera (P-10527)*
Ucc Direct Services Inc ....D....818 662-4100
330 N Brand Blvd Ste 700 Glendale (91203) *(P-15829)*
UCCR, Petaluma *Also called United Cmps Cnfrences Retreats (P-13153)*
Ucd Mc Home Care Services ....C....916 734-2458
3630 Business Dr Sacramento (95820) *(P-26436)*
UCI Construction Inc ....D....661 587-0192
3900 Fruitvale Ave Bakersfield (93308) *(P-25362)*
UCI Family Health Center, Santa Ana *Also called University California Irvine (P-19530)*
Ucla Bookstore, Los Angeles *Also called Associated Students UCLA (P-24135)*
Ucla Copy Services ....E....310 794-6371
555 Westwood Plz Ste B Los Angeles (90095) *(P-13767)*
Ucla Foundation ....B....310 794-3193
10920 Wilshire Blvd # 200 Los Angeles (90024) *(P-11772)*
Ucla Health System ....D....310 825-9111
757 Westwood Plz Los Angeles (90095) *(P-21319)*
Ucla Health System Auxiliary ....A....310 267-4327
10920 Wilshire Blvd Los Angeles (90024) *(P-21889)*
Ucla Healthcare ....D....310 319-4560
1821 Wilshire Blvd Fl 6 Santa Monica (90403) *(P-21320)*
Ucla Marina Center ....D....310 825-3671
111 Deneve Dr Los Angeles (90095) *(P-18775)*
Ucla Mdcn SC Phrmclgy, Los Angeles *Also called Associated Students UCLA (P-18827)*
Ucla Medical Center, Los Angeles *Also called University Cal Los Angeles (P-21330)*
Ucla Medical Center, Sylmar *Also called University Cal Los Angeles (P-21331)*
Ucla Nrpsychtric Bhvioral Hlth, Los Angeles *Also called Uc Regents (P-19514)*
Ucla Primary Care Westlake, Westlake Village *Also called University Cal Los Angeles (P-19525)*
Ucp Dronfield North, Sylmar *Also called United Cp/S Chldrns Fndn La (P-20707)*
Ucp Work Inc (PA) ....D....805 566-9000
5320 Carpinteria Ave G Carpinteria (93013) *(P-23648)*
Ucr Botany and Plant Sciences ....D....951 827-5133
3401 Watkins Dr Riverside (92507) *(P-11773)*
Ucsd Healthcare ....D....858 657-7105
355 Dickinson St 340 San Diego (92103) *(P-22334)*
Ucsd Thornton Hospital, La Jolla *Also called University Cal San Diego (P-21335)*
Ucsf Aids Health Project ....D....415 476-6445
1930 Market St San Francisco (94102) *(P-23513)*
Ucsf Benioff Chld Hosp Oakland, Oakland *Also called Childrens Hospotal & Research (P-20784)*
Ucsf Dental Center-Buchanan, San Francisco *Also called University Cal San Francisco (P-19635)*
Ucsf Medical Center, San Francisco *Also called University Cal San Francisco (P-19526)*
Ucsf Medical Center At Mt Zion, San Francisco *Also called University Cal San Francisco (P-21338)*
UDC, Anaheim *Also called Universal Dust Collector (P-1390)*
Ue Authority Co ....D....800 466-4178
225 Broadway Ste 2200 San Diego (92101) *(P-13590)*
Uec, Cypress *Also called United Exchange Corp (P-17119)*
Ufc Gym, Newport Beach *Also called U Gym LLC (P-18208)*
Ufcw & Employers Trust LLC (PA) ....C....800 552-2400
1000 Burnett Ave Ste 110 Concord (94520) *(P-11819)*
Ufcw Local 770, Los Angeles *Also called United Food and Commercial (P-24470)*
UFS International LLC ....C....714 713-6311
10775 Bus Ctr Dr 100 Cypress (90630) *(P-17118)*
Ugm Citatah Inc (PA) ....C....562 921-9549
13220 Cambridge St Santa Fe Springs (90670) *(P-6699)*
Ugmc, Santa Fe Springs *Also called Ugm Citatah Inc (P-6699)*
Uhc of California (HQ) ....A....714 952-1121
5995 Plaza Dr Cypress (90630) *(P-10058)*
Uhp Healthcare, Inglewood *Also called Watts Health Foundation Inc (P-20470)*
UHS, Chino *Also called Canyon Ridge Hospital Inc (P-21393)*
UHS, Torrance *Also called Del AMO Hospital Inc (P-21409)*
UHS Surgical Services, Sun Valley *Also called PRI Medical Technologies Inc (P-6997)*
Uhs-Corona Inc (HQ) ....A....951 737-4343
800 S Main St Corona (92882) *(P-21321)*
Uhs-Corona Inc ....C....951 736-7200
730 Magnolia Ave Corona (92879) *(P-22147)*
Uiprojects, Costa Mesa *Also called United Infrstrcture Prjcts Inc (P-25363)*
Uka LLC ....E....949 610-8000
620 Newport Center Dr # 1400 Newport Beach (92660) *(P-13050)*

ALPHABETIC

Employee Codes: A=Over 500 employees, B=251-500
C=101-250, D=51-100, E=50
2020 Directory of California
Wholesalers and Services Companies
© Mergent Inc. 1-800-342-5647
1465

Ukiah Adventist Hospital (HQ)......B......707 462-3111
275 Hospital Dr Ukiah (95482) ***(P-21322)***
Ukiah Adventist Hospital......C......707 462-3111
1120 S Dora St Ukiah (95482) ***(P-21323)***
Ukiah Convalescent Hospital, Ukiah *Also called Berryman Health Inc* ***(P-20505)***
Ukiah Valley Medical Center, Ukiah *Also called Ukiah Adventist Hospital* ***(P-21322)***
Ukiah Vly Assn For Hbilitation (PA)......D......707 468-8824
990 S Dora St Ukiah (95482) ***(P-23649)***
Uline Inc......D......909 605-7090
2950 Jurupa St Ontario (91761) ***(P-9016)***
Ulta Beauty Inc......C......858 376-4574
11485 Carmel Mountain Rd San Diego (92128) ***(P-13363)***
Ulta Salon Cosmt Fragrance Inc......C......661 664-1402
9000 Ming Ave Bakersfield (93311) ***(P-13364)***
Ultimate Communication Systems, Anaheim *Also called Rjb Enterprises Inc* ***(P-2616)***
Ultimate Construction Inc......C......562 633-3389
8811 Alonzo Blvd Long Beach (90805) ***(P-2989)***
Ultimate Creations LLC......D......559 221-4936
516 W Shaw Ave Ste 200 Fresno (93704) ***(P-11964)***
ULTIMATE DEMO, Pomona *Also called Ultimate Removal Inc* ***(P-3355)***
Ultimate Landscaping MGT......D......714 502-9711
700 E Sycamore St Anaheim (92805) ***(P-919)***
Ultimate Maintenance Svcs Inc......E......310 542-1474
4237 Redondo Beach Blvd Lawndale (90260) ***(P-14069)***
Ultimate Removal Inc......C......909 524-0800
2168 Pomona Blvd Pomona (91768) ***(P-3355)***
Ultimate Staffing Services, Orange *Also called Roth Staffing Companies LP* ***(P-14561)***
Ultimo Software Solutions Inc......C......408 943-1490
33268 Central Ave 2 Union City (94587) ***(P-15168)***
Ultra Mobile, Costa Mesa *Also called Uvnv Inc* ***(P-5487)***
Ultra Solutions LLC......E......909 628-1778
1137 E Philadelphia St Ontario (91761) ***(P-7015)***
Ultradot Media......D......562 906-0737
9908 Bell Ranch Dr Santa Fe Springs (90670) ***(P-13639)***
Ultraex LLC......D......510 723-3760
2633 Barrington Ct Hayward (94545) ***(P-4289)***
Ultraex Inc......D......800 882-1000
2633 Barrington Ct Hayward (94545) ***(P-4729)***
Ultralink LLC......C......714 427-5500
535 Anton Blvd Ste 200 Costa Mesa (92626) ***(P-9891)***
Ultrasigns Electrical Advg, San Diego *Also called Jones Sign Co Inc* ***(P-6927)***
Ultraviolet Devices Inc......D......661 295-8140
26145 Technology Dr Valencia (91355) ***(P-7459)***
Ultrex Management Services (PA)......D......805 783-1234
712 Fiero Ln Ste 33 San Luis Obispo (93401) ***(P-6775)***
Uma Enterprises Inc (PA)......C......310 631-1166
350 W Apra St Compton (90220) ***(P-6593)***
Umi of Huntington Beach, Huntington Beach *Also called United Medical Imaging Inc* ***(P-19517)***
Umina Bros Inc (PA)......D......213 622-9206
1601 E Olympic Blvd # 403 Los Angeles (90021) ***(P-8532)***
Umpqua Bank......D......818 385-1362
16501 Ventura Blvd Encino (91436) ***(P-9120)***
Umpqua Bank......D......619 668-5159
7777 Alvarado Rd Ste 515 La Mesa (91942) ***(P-9245)***
Ums Banking, Glendale *Also called United Merchant Svcs Cal Inc* ***(P-6776)***
UNAC/UHCP, San Dimas *Also called Associations of United Nurses* ***(P-24435)***
Unchained Labs (PA)......C......925 587-9800
6870 Koll Center Pkwy # 20 Pleasanton (94566) ***(P-21595)***
Uncle Credit Union (PA)......D......925 447-5001
2100 Las Positas Ct Livermore (94551) ***(P-9371)***
Undc, Sacramento *Also called Universal Network Dev Corp* ***(P-27241)***
Underground Cnstr Co Inc......C......707 746-8800
5145 Industrial Way Benicia (94510) ***(P-5999)***
Underground Elephant, San Diego *Also called Ue Authority Co* ***(P-13590)***
Underwriters Laboratories Inc......B......248 427-5300
455 E Trimble Rd San Jose (95131) ***(P-26113)***
Underwriters Laboratories Inc......C......408 754-6500
4510 Riding Club Ct Hayward (94542) ***(P-26114)***
Underwriters Laboratories Inc......C......408 493-9910
2191 Zanker Rd San Jose (95131) ***(P-26115)***
Unfi, Rocklin *Also called United Natural Foods West Inc* ***(P-4525)***
UNI Hosiery Co Inc (PA)......C......213 228-0100
1911 E Olympic Blvd Los Angeles (90021) ***(P-8049)***
Unical Aviation Inc (PA)......C......909 348-1700
680 S Lemon Ave City of Industry (91789) ***(P-4804)***
Unical Enterprises Inc......D......626 965-5588
16960 Gale Ave City of Industry (91745) ***(P-6915)***
Unifax Insurance Systems Inc......D......818 591-9800
26050 Mureau Rd Fl 2 Calabasas (91302) ***(P-10526)***
Unified Aircraft Services Inc (PA)......D......909 877-0535
1571 S Lilac Ave Bloomington (92316) ***(P-5101)***
Unified Grocers Inc (HQ)......A......323 264-5200
5200 Sheila St Commerce (90040) ***(P-4520)***
Unified Grocers Inc......D......323 232-6124
457 E Martin Luther King Los Angeles (90011) ***(P-4521)***
Unified Grocers Inc......C......209 931-1990
1990 Piccoli Rd Stockton (95215) ***(P-4522)***
Unified Grocers Inc......D......323 264-5200
455 N Canyons Pkwy Livermore (94551) ***(P-8274)***
Unified Inv Programs Inc (PA)......D......310 782-1878
2368 Torrance Blvd # 200 Torrance (90501) ***(P-22335)***
Unified Teldata Inc......D......415 888-8940
126 Neider Ln Mill Valley (94941) ***(P-7359)***
Unified Valet Parking Inc......D......818 822-5807
99 S Chester Ave Fl 2 Pasadena (91106) ***(P-17278)***
Unifirst Corporation......E......209 941-8364
819 N Hunter St Stockton (95202) ***(P-13313)***
Unifirst Corporation......E......916 929-3766
4630 Beloit Dr Ste 40 Sacramento (95838) ***(P-13243)***
Unifirst Corporation......D......619 263-6116
4041 Market St San Diego (92102) ***(P-13314)***
Unifirst Corporation......C......909 390-8670
700 Etiwanda Ave Ste C Ontario (91761) ***(P-13315)***
Unifirst Corporation......D......408 297-8101
2016 Zanker Rd San Jose (95131) ***(P-13316)***
Uniform Accessories, Northridge *Also called Rashman Corporation* ***(P-7000)***
Unify Financial Federal Cr Un (PA)......D......310 536-5000
1899 Western Way Ste 100 Torrance (90501) ***(P-9372)***
Uniglobe Travel Planner, Irvine *Also called Uniglobe Travel West Inc* ***(P-4842)***
Uniglobe Travel West Inc (PA)......D......949 623-9000
18662 Macarthur Blvd # 100 Irvine (92612) ***(P-4842)***
Unigro, San Bernardino *Also called L & L Nursery Supply Inc* ***(P-8843)***
Unilab Corporation (HQ)......B......818 737-6000
8401 Fallbrook Ave West Hills (91304) ***(P-21596)***
Unilab Corporation......B......408 927-8331
6475 Camden Ave Ste 104 San Jose (95120) ***(P-21597)***
Union 76, Los Angeles *Also called Kim Chong* ***(P-16870)***
Union Asphalt Inc......D......805 922-3551
1625 E Donovan Rd Santa Maria (93454) ***(P-3945)***
Union Bank, Los Angeles *Also called Bank of Tokyo Ltd* ***(P-9249)***
Union Building Maintenance, Commerce *Also called Uniserve Facilities Svcs Corp* ***(P-14070)***
Union City Medical Offices, Union City *Also called Kaiser Foundation Hospitals* ***(P-19052)***
Union Pacific, Delano *Also called Loup Logistics Company* ***(P-4985)***
Union Pacific Corporation......A......916 789-5311
9451 Atkinson St Ste 100 Roseville (95747) ***(P-3509)***
Union Pacific Lines, Long Beach *Also called Union Pacific Railroad Company* ***(P-3517)***
Union Pacific Railroad Company......D......805 286-5851
999 Paso Robles St Paso Robles (93446) ***(P-3510)***
Union Pacific Railroad Company......C......559 443-2244
3135 N Weber Ave Fresno (93705) ***(P-3511)***
Union Pacific Railroad Company......D......909 685-2710
2000 S Sycamore Ave Bloomington (92316) ***(P-3512)***
Union Pacific Railroad Company......D......916 789-5930
9391 Atkinson St Ste 100 Roseville (95747) ***(P-3513)***
Union Pacific Railroad Company......D......213 446-1900
4341 E Washington Blvd Commerce (90023) ***(P-3514)***
Union Pacific Railroad Company......C......916 789-6055
10031 Fthlls Blvd Ste 200 Roseville (95747) ***(P-3515)***
Union Pacific Railroad Company......D......661 321-4604
730 Sumner St Bakersfield (93305) ***(P-3516)***
Union Pacific Railroad Company......B......562 490-7000
2401 E Sepulveda Blvd Long Beach (90810) ***(P-3517)***
Union Pan Asian Communities (PA)......D......619 232-6454
1031 25th St San Diego (92102) ***(P-23514)***
Union Sanitary District......C......510 477-7500
5072 Benson Rd Union City (94587) ***(P-6141)***
Union Supply Company, Rancho Dominguez *Also called Union Supply Group Inc* ***(P-8275)***
Union Supply Group Inc (PA)......C......310 603-8899
2301 E Pacifica Pl Rancho Dominguez (90220) ***(P-8275)***
Union Technology Corp......E......323 266-6871
718 Monterey Pass Rd Monterey Park (91754) ***(P-7360)***
Unique Carpets Ltd......D......951 352-8125
7360 Jurupa Ave Riverside (92504) ***(P-6594)***
Unique Scaffold, Concord *Also called Ernie & Sons Scaffolding* ***(P-3402)***
Unis LLC (PA)......C......909 839-2600
218 Machlin Ct Ste A Walnut (91789) ***(P-5071)***
Unis LLC......D......310 747-7388
19914 S Via Baron Rancho Dominguez (90220) ***(P-4523)***
Uniserve Facilities Svcs Corp (PA)......A......213 533-1000
2363 S Atlantic Blvd Commerce (90040) ***(P-14070)***
Uniserve Facilities Svcs Corp......A......310 440-6747
1200 Getty Center Dr Los Angeles (90049) ***(P-14071)***
Unish Corporation......E......408 708-9300
4300 Stevens Creek Blvd # 126 San Jose (95129) ***(P-16145)***
Unison, San Francisco *Also called Real Estate Equity Exchange* ***(P-9598)***
Unison Electric......E......714 375-5915
16652 Gemini Ln Huntington Beach (92647) ***(P-2680)***
Unisource Discovery LLC (PA)......D......888 248-0020
625 The City Dr S Ste 303 Orange (92868) ***(P-22855)***
Unisource Maint Sup Systems, La Palma *Also called Veritiv Operating Company* ***(P-7911)***
Unisource Packaging Inc......C......925 227-6000
4225 Hacienda Dr Ste A Pleasanton (94588) ***(P-7904)***
Unisource Solutions Inc (PA)......C......562 654-3500
8350 Rex Rd Pico Rivera (90660) ***(P-6532)***
Unisys Corporation......A......949 380-5000
9701 Jeronimo Rd Ste 100 Irvine (92618) ***(P-15169)***
Unitas Global LLC (PA)......D......213 785-6200
453 S Spring St Ste 201 Los Angeles (90013) ***(P-15830)***
Unitd Van Lines Agnt, Hayward *Also called Chipman Corporation* ***(P-3986)***
Unite Eurotherapy Inc......D......760 585-1800
2870 Whiptail Loop Carlsbad (92010) ***(P-7987)***
United Administrative Services, San Jose *Also called Chelbay Schuler & Chelbay* ***(P-10213)***
United Administrative Services......C......408 288-4400
6800 Santa Teresa Blvd # 100 San Jose (95119) ***(P-10225)***
United Agribusiness League (PA)......E......800 223-4590
54 Corporate Park Irvine (92606) ***(P-24369)***
United Airlines Inc......C......650 634-4209
United Airlines Mnt Optnb San Francisco (94128) ***(P-4685)***
United Airlines Inc......C......650 634-2468
2435 Whitman Way San Bruno (94066) ***(P-4686)***
United Airlines Inc......C......916 877-3002
6850 Airport Blvd Ste 34 Sacramento (95837) ***(P-4878)***
United Airlines Inc......C......310 342-8086
6018 Avion Dr Los Angeles (90045) ***(P-4687)***

United Airlines Inc ......D......650 634-7800
Maintenance Operation Ctr San Francisco (94128) ***(P-4688)***
United Airlines Inc ......C......619 692-3310
3835 N Harbor Dr Ste 115 San Diego (92101) ***(P-4689)***
United Airlines Inc ......B......310 258-3319
7300 World Way W Rm 144 Los Angeles (90045) ***(P-4690)***
United Airlines Inc ......C......650 634-4469
San Francisco Intl Arprt San Francisco (94128) ***(P-4691)***
United Airlines Inc ......D......760 778-5690
3400 E Tahquitz Cyn 17 Palm Springs (92262) ***(P-4692)***
United Airlines Inc ......C......650 634-2772
545 Mcdonald Rd 68305 San Francisco (94128) ***(P-4693)***
United Airlines Inc ......D......650 634-2085
800 S Arprt Blvd Bldg 84 San Francisco (94128) ***(P-4694)***
United American Indian Involve (PA) ......D......213 202-3970
1125 W 6th St Ste 103 Los Angeles (90017) ***(P-22148)***
United Artists Productions Inc ......C......310 449-3000
10250 Constellation Blvd # 19 Los Angeles (90067) ***(P-17793)***
United Artists Television Corp ......C......310 449-3000
10250 Constellation Blvd # 27 Los Angeles (90067) ***(P-17794)***
United Auburn Indian Community ......A......916 408-7777
1200 Athens Ave Lincoln (95648) ***(P-13051)***
United Behavioral Health ......C......925 246-1343
2300 Clayton Rd Ste 1000 Concord (94520) ***(P-10059)***
United Behavioral Health ......D......619 641-6800
3111 Cmino Del Rio N 50 San Diego (92108) ***(P-26437)***
United Behavioral Health (HQ) ......C......415 547-1403
425 Market St Fl 18 San Francisco (94105) ***(P-26438)***
United Biosource LLC ......D......415 293-1340
303 2nd St Ste S700 San Francisco (94107) ***(P-685)***
United Blood Services Ventura, San Luis Obispo *Also called Vitalant* ***(P-22336)***
United Blood Svcs Centl Coast, Ventura *Also called Vitalant* ***(P-22338)***
United Brothers Concrete Inc ......C......760 346-1013
41905 Boardwalk Ste K Palm Desert (92211) ***(P-3230)***
United Building Maint Inc ......C......916 772-8101
8211 Sierra College Blvd Roseville (95661) ***(P-14072)***
United Building Services, Santa Ana *Also called Ponderosa Builders Inc* ***(P-14012)***
United California Glass & Door ......D......415 824-8500
745 Cesar Chavez San Francisco (94124) ***(P-17557)***
United California Realty Inc ......D......760 949-4040
12829 Bear Valley Rd Victorville (92392) ***(P-11493)***
United Care Homes, City of Industry *Also called Pruitthealth Inc* ***(P-20664)***
United Cerebral Palsy Assoc ......C......949 333-6400
980 Roosevelt Ste 100 Irvine (92620) ***(P-23515)***
United Cerebral Palsy Assoc (PA) ......C......209 956-0290
333 W Benjamin Holt Dr # 1 Stockton (95207) ***(P-24430)***
United Cerebral Palsy Assoc ......C......209 956-0290
333 W Benjamin Holt Dr # 1 Stockton (95207) ***(P-21501)***
United Cerebral Palsy Assoc of ......D......805 543-2039
3620 Sacramento Dr # 201 San Luis Obispo (93401) ***(P-3732)***
United Chinese American Genera (PA) ......D......714 228-7800
6363 Katella Ave Cypress (90630) ***(P-10527)***
United Cmps Cnfrences Retreats (PA) ......D......707 762-3220
1304 Sthpint Blvd Ste 200 Petaluma (94954) ***(P-13153)***
United Com Serve ......D......530 790-3000
1260 Williams Way Yuba City (95991) ***(P-20340)***
United Consortium, Valencia *Also called CC Wellness LLC* ***(P-7934)***
United Convalescent Facilities ......D......626 629-6950
230 E Adams Blvd Los Angeles (90011) ***(P-20706)***
United Couriers Inc (HQ) ......C......213 383-3611
3280 E Foothill Blvd Pasadena (91107) ***(P-4695)***
United Cp/S Chldrns Fndn La ......E......805 494-1141
2170 N Westlake Blvd 22 Westlake Village (91362) ***(P-23516)***
United Cp/S Chldrns Fndn La ......D......818 364-5911
13272 Dronfield Ave Sylmar (91342) ***(P-20707)***
United Cp/S Chldrns Fndn La ......C......818 998-8755
11051 Old Snta Susna Pass Chatsworth (91311) ***(P-24099)***
United Cp/S Chldrns Fndn La ......D......323 737-0303
2628 Brighton Ave Los Angeles (90018) ***(P-23517)***
United Cpitl Fncl Advisers LLC ......D......949 999-8500
620 Nwport Ctr Dr Ste 500 Newport Beach (92660) ***(P-9853)***
United Crbral Plsy Assn San De (PA) ......E......858 571-7803
8525 Gibbs Dr Ste 209 San Diego (92123) ***(P-23518)***
United Crbrl Plsy of Cntrl CA (PA) ......E......559 221-8272
4224 N Cedar Ave Fresno (93726) ***(P-24235)***
United Development Group Inc ......E......858 244-0900
2805 Dickens St Ste 103 San Diego (92106) ***(P-11617)***
United Exchange Corp (PA) ......D......562 977-4500
5836 Corp Ave Ste 200 Cypress (90630) ***(P-17119)***
United Express Messengers Inc ......D......310 261-2000
1801 Century Park E # 520 Los Angeles (90067) ***(P-17120)***
United Fabricare Supply Inc (PA) ......D......310 886-3790
1237 W Walnut St Compton (90220) ***(P-7683)***
United Fabrics Intl Inc ......D......213 749-8200
1723 S Central Ave Los Angeles (90021) ***(P-8015)***
United Facilities Inc ......E......209 839-8051
25451 Mountain House Pkwy Tracy (95377) ***(P-5072)***
United Facilities Inc ......E......951 685-7030
11618 Mulberry Ave Fontana (92337) ***(P-4524)***
United Facility Solutions Inc ......B......310 743-3000
16835 Algonquin St # 429 Huntington Beach (92649) ***(P-16465)***
United Family Care Inc ......C......909 874-1679
8110 Mango Ave Ste 104 Fontana (92335) ***(P-19515)***
United Farm Workers America (PA) ......C......661 822-5571
29700 Wdford Tehachapi Rd Keene (93531) ***(P-24469)***
United Floral Exchange Inc ......D......760 597-1940
2834 La Mirada Dr Ste B Vista (92081) ***(P-8928)***
United Food and Commercial (PA) ......D......213 487-7070
630 Shatto Pl Ste 300 Los Angeles (90005) ***(P-24470)***

United Hauling Corp ......D......626 358-9417
2620 Buena Vista St Duarte (91010) ***(P-17191)***
United Health Ctrs San Joaquin (PA) ......D......559 646-6618
3875 W Beechwood Ave Fresno (93711) ***(P-22149)***
United Health Ctrs San Joaquin ......D......559 834-1568
106 E Main St Fowler (93625) ***(P-22150)***
United Health Ctrs San Joaquin ......D......559 626-4031
445 11th St Orange Cove (93646) ***(P-22151)***
United Health Systems Inc ......C......530 662-9161
124 Walnut St Woodland (95695) ***(P-20341)***
United Imaging, Woodland Hills *Also called United Ribbon Company Inc* ***(P-6777)***
United Ind Taxi Drivers (PA) ......D......323 462-1088
900 N Alvarado St Los Angeles (90026) ***(P-3752)***
United Independent Taxi Co ......E......213 385-2227
900 N Alvarado St Los Angeles (90026) ***(P-3753)***
United Indian Health Svcs Inc (PA) ......C......707 825-5000
1600 Weeot Way Arcata (95521) ***(P-19516)***
United Infrstrcture Prjcts Inc ......D......949 310-0092
1041 W 18th St Ste B104 Costa Mesa (92627) ***(P-25363)***
United Innovation Services Inc ......D......510 322-8922
1057 Hoskins Ln San Ramon (94582) ***(P-26856)***
United Insurance Company ......E......323 869-9381
5601 E Slauson Ave # 105 Commerce (90040) ***(P-10528)***
United International, Novato *Also called Cellmark Inc* ***(P-7802)***
United Landscape Resource Inc ......D......530 671-1029
5411 Colusa Hwy Yuba City (95993) ***(P-920)***
United Marble & Granite Inc ......D......408 347-3300
2163 Martin Ave Santa Clara (95050) ***(P-6700)***
United Material Handling Inc ......D......951 657-4900
23900 Brodiaea Ave Moreno Valley (92553) ***(P-7603)***
United Medical Imaging Inc ......D......714 843-6255
16161 Gothard St Ste C Huntington Beach (92647) ***(P-19517)***
United Medical Management Inc ......C......909 886-5291
1680 N Waterman Ave San Bernardino (92404) ***(P-20708)***
United Merchant Svcs Cal Inc ......D......818 246-6767
750 Fairmont Ave Ste 201 Glendale (91203) ***(P-6776)***
United Mfg Assembly Inc ......D......510 490-1065
44169 Fremont Blvd Fremont (94538) ***(P-26116)***
United Natural Foods Inc ......C......831 462-5870
2450 17th Ave Ste 250 Santa Cruz (95062) ***(P-8663)***
United Natural Foods West Inc (HQ) ......B......916 625-4100
1101 Sunset Blvd Rocklin (95765) ***(P-4525)***
United Network Info Svcs, Walnut *Also called Unis LLC* ***(P-5071)***
United Owners Services, Anaheim *Also called Tricom Management Inc* ***(P-26431)***
United Pacific Waste ......D......562 699-7600
4334 San Gbriel Rver Pkwy Pico Rivera (90660) ***(P-6294)***
United Paradyne Corporation ......D......805 734-2359
P.O. Box 5368 Santa Barbara (93150) ***(P-26439)***
United Parcel Service Inc ......B......949 643-6634
22 Brookline Aliso Viejo (92656) ***(P-17121)***
United Parcel Service Inc ......A......760 241-5540
14592 Palmdale Rd Victorville (92392) ***(P-17122)***
United Parcel Service Inc ......D......800 742-5877
12745 Arroyo St Sylmar (91342) ***(P-4290)***
United Parcel Service Inc ......A......626 280-8012
201 W Garvey Ave Ste 102 Monterey Park (91754) ***(P-17123)***
United Parcel Service Inc ......A......818 735-0945
4607 Lakeview Canyon Rd Westlake Village (91361) ***(P-17124)***
United Parcel Service Inc ......C......650 737-3737
657 Forbes Blvd South San Francisco (94080) ***(P-4291)***
United Parcel Service Inc OH ......D......858 541-2336
160 W Main St El Centro (92243) ***(P-4292)***
United Parcel Service Inc OH ......B......760 325-1762
650 N Commercial Rd Palm Springs (92262) ***(P-4293)***
United Parcel Service Inc OH ......A......678 339-3171
3331 Industrial Dr Ste C Santa Rosa (95403) ***(P-17125)***
United Parcel Service Inc OH ......C......510 262-2338
1601 Atlas Rd Richmond (94806) ***(P-4294)***
United Parcel Service Inc OH ......C......831 758-9112
1139 Madison Ln Salinas (93907) ***(P-4295)***
United Parcel Service Inc OH ......D......800 742-5877
2800 W 227th St Torrance (90505) ***(P-4296)***
United Parcel Service Inc OH ......B......323 837-1220
2747 Vail Ave Commerce (90040) ***(P-17126)***
United Parcel Service Inc OH ......D......530 365-7850
6845 Eastside Rd Anderson (96007) ***(P-4297)***
United Parcel Service Inc OH ......C......760 872-7661
2915 N Sierra Hwy Bishop (93514) ***(P-4298)***
United Parcel Service Inc OH ......C......707 864-8200
5000 W Cordelia Rd Fairfield (94534) ***(P-4299)***
United Parcel Service Inc OH ......C......800 742-5877
1400 Hil Mor Dr Ceres (95307) ***(P-4300)***
United Parcel Service Inc OH ......C......916 373-4076
1380 Shore St West Sacramento (95691) ***(P-4301)***
United Parcel Service Inc OH ......C......707 224-1205
2531 Napa Valley Corp Dr NAPA (94558) ***(P-4302)***
United Parcel Service Inc OH ......D......916 373-4089
128 Shore St Sacramento (95829) ***(P-4303)***
United Parcel Service Inc OH ......B......323 260-8957
3333 S Downey Rd Vernon (90058) ***(P-4730)***
United Parcel Service Inc OH ......B......310 217-2646
17115 S Western Ave Gardena (90247) ***(P-4304)***
United Parcel Service Inc OH ......B......408 291-2942
1999 S 7th St San Jose (95112) ***(P-4305)***
United Parcel Service Inc OH ......C......951 928-5221
25283 Sherman Rd Sun City (92585) ***(P-4731)***
United Parcel Service Inc OH ......C......209 944-5932
1724 Wawona St Manteca (95337) ***(P-4732)***
United Parcel Service Inc OH ......C......415 252-4564
2222 17th St San Francisco (94103) ***(P-4306)***

A L P H A B E T I C

United Parcel Service Inc OH ....C....707 252-4560
1012 Sterling St Vallejo (94591) ***(P-4307)***
United Parcel Service Inc OH ....C....858 455-8800
6060 Cornerstone Ct W San Diego (92121) ***(P-17127)***
United Parcel Service Inc OH ....C....310 474-0019
10690 Santa Monica Blvd Los Angeles (90025) ***(P-4308)***
United Parcel Service Inc OH ....C....949 643-6595
22 Brookline Aliso Viejo (92656) ***(P-4309)***
United Parcel Service Inc OH ....A....909 974-7250
3221 E Jurupa Ontario (91764) ***(P-17128)***
United Parcel Service Inc OH ....C....909 974-7190
Ontario Airport Ontario (91758) ***(P-4733)***
United Parcel Service Inc OH ....C....800 828-8264
290 W Avenue L Lancaster (93534) ***(P-4310)***
United Parcel Service Inc OH ....C....404 828-6000
16000 Arminta St Van Nuys (91406) ***(P-4311)***
United Parcel Service Inc OH ....C....909 279-5111
7925 Ronson Rd San Diego (92111) ***(P-4312)***
United Parcel Service Inc OH ....C....510 813-5662
8400 Pardee Dr Oakland (94621) ***(P-4313)***
United Parcel Service Inc OH ....B....800 742-5877
1746 D St South Lake Tahoe (96150) ***(P-17129)***
United Parcel Service Inc OH ....C....562 404-3236
13233 Moore St Cerritos (90703) ***(P-4314)***
United Parcel Service Inc OH ....C....707 468-5481
259 Cherry St Ukiah (95482) ***(P-4315)***
United Parcel Service Inc OH ....C....831 757-6294
6 Upper Ragsdale Dr Monterey (93940) ***(P-4316)***
United Parcel Service Inc OH ....C....801 973-3400
3601 Sacramento Dr San Luis Obispo (93401) ***(P-4317)***
United Parcel Service Inc OH ....C....925 689-6584
1970 Olivera Rd Concord (94520) ***(P-4318)***
United Parcel Service Inc OH ....C....805 964-7848
505 Pine Ave Goleta (93117) ***(P-4319)***
United Parcel Service Inc OH ....C....805 922-7851
309 Cooley Ln Santa Maria (93455) ***(P-4320)***
United Parcel Service Inc OH ....C....209 736-0878
2342 Gun Club Rd Angels Camp (95222) ***(P-4321)***
United Parcel Service Inc OH ....C....805 375-1832
1501 Rancho Conejo Blvd Newbury Park (91320) ***(P-4322)***
United Parcel Service Inc OH ....A....323 729-6762
3000 E Washington Blvd Los Angeles (90023) ***(P-4323)***
United Parcel Service Inc OH ....C....619 482-8119
2300 Boswell Ct Chula Vista (91914) ***(P-4324)***
United Parcel Service Inc OH ....C....831 425-1054
251 Sylvania Ave Santa Cruz (95060) ***(P-4325)***
United Parcel Service Inc OH ....D....909 974-7000
3140 Jurupa St Ontario (91761) ***(P-4326)***
United Parcel Service Inc OH ....C....800 833-9943
4500 Norris Canyon Rd San Ramon (94583) ***(P-4327)***
United Parcel Service Inc OH ....B....951 749-3400
11811 Landon Dr Eastvale (91752) ***(P-17130)***
United Parcel Service Inc OH ....C....805 642-6784
2559 Palma Dr Ventura (93003) ***(P-4328)***
United Parcel Service Inc OH ....B....800 742-5877
48921 Warm Springs Blvd Fremont (94539) ***(P-17131)***
United Parcel Service Inc OH ....C....626 814-6216
1100 Baldwin Park Blvd Baldwin Park (91706) ***(P-4329)***
United Parcel Service Inc OH ....C....916 857-0311
3930 Kristi Ct Sacramento (95827) ***(P-4330)***
United Parcel Service Inc OH ....B....866 553-1069
91 W Easy St Simi Valley (93065) ***(P-17132)***
United Paving Company, Corona *Also called Superior Paving Company Inc* ***(P-1796)***
United Petrochemicals Inc ....D....949 629-8736
3000 W Macarthur Blvd # 300 Santa Ana (92704) ***(P-8709)***
United Power Contractors Inc ....C....760 735-8028
405 Maple St Ste A-103 Ramona (92065) ***(P-1922)***
United Pumping Service Inc ....D....626 961-9326
14000 Valley Blvd City of Industry (91746) ***(P-3946)***
United Refrigeration Inc ....D....310 204-2500
3573a Hayden Ave Culver City (90232) ***(P-7465)***
United Rentals North Amer Inc ....D....209 948-9500
2911 E Fremont St Stockton (95205) ***(P-14204)***
United Rentals North Amer Inc ....C....562 695-0748
3455 San Gbriel Rver Pkwy Pico Rivera (90660) ***(P-14205)***
United Ribbon Company Inc ....D....818 716-1515
21201 Oxnard St Woodland Hills (91367) ***(P-6777)***
United Riggers & Erectors Inc (PA) ....C....909 978-0400
4188 Valley Blvd Walnut (91789) ***(P-3366)***
United Road Towing Inc ....D....909 923-6100
1516 S Bon View Ave Ontario (91761) ***(P-17431)***
United Road Towing Inc ....D....909 798-4863
945 W Brockton Ave Redlands (92374) ***(P-17432)***
United Rock Products Corp ....D....714 578-9600
135 S State College Blvd # 400 Brea (92821) ***(P-1805)***
United Seal Coating Slurryseal ....D....805 563-4922
3463 State St Ste 522 Santa Barbara (93105) ***(P-1637)***
United Service Tech Inc ....D....714 224-1406
21801 Cactus Ave Ste A Riverside (92518) ***(P-17558)***
United Site Services Cal Inc (PA) ....D....626 462-9110
242 Live Oak Ave Irwindale (91706) ***(P-14206)***
United Site Services Cal Inc ....C....408 295-2263
3408 Hillcap Ave San Jose (95136) ***(P-14207)***
United Site Services Cal Inc ....E....707 747-2810
1 Oak Rd Benicia (94510) ***(P-6295)***
United Spectrum Inc ....E....714 283-1010
1910 N Lime St Orange (92865) ***(P-3483)***
United States Attorneys ....C....213 894-2400
300 N Los Angeles St Lbby Los Angeles (90012) ***(P-22856)***
United States Cold Storage Cal, Bakersfield *Also called United States Cold Storage Inc* ***(P-4355)***
United States Cold Storage Inc ....D....661 832-2653
6501 District Blvd Bakersfield (93313) ***(P-4355)***
United States Cold Storage Inc ....E....559 686-1110
810 E Continental Ave Tulare (93274) ***(P-4356)***
United States Cold Storage Inc ....E....559 237-6145
2003 S Cherry Ave Fresno (93721) ***(P-4357)***
United States Cold Storage Inc ....E....209 835-2653
1400 N Macarthur Dr Ste A Tracy (95376) ***(P-4358)***
United States Dept of Energy ....A....510 486-4000
1 Cyclotron Rd Berkeley (94720) ***(P-26039)***
United States Dept of Energy ....A....510 486-4936
1 Cyclotron Rd Berkeley (94720) ***(P-25857)***
United States Dept of Energy ....A....925 422-1100
7000 East Ave Livermore (94550) ***(P-25858)***
United States Dept of Navy ....C....619 524-1069
32444 Echo Ln Fl 3 San Diego (92147) ***(P-14578)***
United States Dept of Navy ....A....559 998-4201
937 Vista Pl Lemoore (93245) ***(P-21324)***
United States Dept of Navy ....A....619 532-6397
8808 Balboa Ave San Diego (92123) ***(P-19518)***
United States Dept of Navy ....A....619 532-8953
34800 Bob Wilson Dr # 409 San Diego (92134) ***(P-19519)***
United States Dept of Navy ....B....619 556-8210
2310 Craven St San Diego (92136) ***(P-19520)***
United States Dept of Navy ....A....559 998-4481
Bldg 937 Franklin Ave Lemoore (93246) ***(P-21325)***
United States Dept of Navy ....A....619 532-6400
34800 Bob Wilson Dr San Diego (92134) ***(P-21326)***
United States Dept of Navy ....B....760 830-2190
Us Naval Hosp Bldg 1145 Twentynine Palms (92278) ***(P-21327)***
United States Dept of Navy ....A....805 982-6392
162 1st St Port Hueneme (93043) ***(P-19521)***
United States Dept of Navy ....E....619 532-1897
937 N Harbor Dr San Diego (92132) ***(P-25859)***
United States Dept of Navy ....B....559 998-2894
937 Franklin Blvd Lemoore (93246) ***(P-21328)***
United States Dept of Navy ....A....619 532-7400
34730 Bob Wilson Dr San Diego (92134) ***(P-19522)***
United States Dept of Navy ....A....805 982-6370
162 1st St Bldg 1402 Port Hueneme (93043) ***(P-19523)***
United States Dept of Navy ....A....619 767-6592
4170 Norman Scott Rd San Diego (92136) ***(P-19524)***
United States Dept of Navy ....D....831 656-4613
7 Grace Hopper Ave Stop 2 Monterey (93943) ***(P-25860)***
United States Fdral Prbatn, San Jose *Also called Adminstrtive Office of US Crts* ***(P-22895)***
United States Fire Insur Co ....D....213 797-3100
777 S Figueroa St # 1500 Los Angeles (90017) ***(P-10529)***
United States Info Systems Inc ....C....845 353-9224
7621 Galilee Rd Roseville (95678) ***(P-2681)***
United States Marines Youth Fd ....D....805 967-7990
90 La Venta Dr Santa Barbara (93110) ***(P-24683)***
United States Pipe Fndry LLC ....C....510 441-5810
1295 Whipple Rd Union City (94587) ***(P-4811)***
United States Pony Clubs ....D....916 791-1223
7010 Hidden Valley Pl Granite Bay (95746) ***(P-18601)***
United States Probation Office, San Diego *Also called Adminstrtive Office of US Crts* ***(P-22896)***
United States Technical Svcs ....C....714 374-6300
16541 Gothard St Ste 214 Huntington Beach (92647) ***(P-16146)***
United Stationers, City of Industry *Also called Essendant Co* ***(P-7856)***
United Sttes Bowl Congress Inc ....D....530 527-9049
12895 Arbor Ln Red Bluff (96080) ***(P-24880)***
United Sttes Intrmdal Svcs LLC ....D....209 341-4045
502 E Whitmore Ave Modesto (95358) ***(P-5073)***
United Sttes Olympic Committee ....E....619 656-1500
2800 Olympic Pkwy Chula Vista (91915) ***(P-18081)***
United Svcs Amer Federal Cr Un (PA) ....D....858 831-8100
9999 Willow Creek Rd San Diego (92131) ***(P-9373)***
United Talent Agency LLC ....B....310 385-2800
1880 Century Park E # 711 Los Angeles (90067) ***(P-26857)***
United Taxi San Fernando Vly, Los Angeles *Also called United Ind Taxi Drivers* ***(P-3752)***
United Teachers-Los Angeles ....D....213 487-5560
3303 Wilshire Blvd Fl 10 Los Angeles (90010) ***(P-24471)***
United Technologies, Anaheim *Also called Otis Elevator Company* ***(P-17521)***
United Technologies Corp ....D....951 351-5400
8200 Arlington Ave Riverside (92503) ***(P-25364)***
United Temp Services Inc ....D....408 472-4309
694 Albanese Cir San Jose (95111) ***(P-14446)***
United Van Lines, San Diego *Also called Sullivan Moving & Storage* ***(P-4138)***
United Van Lines, Fontana *Also called McCollisters Trnsp Group Inc* ***(P-4091)***
United Way Inc (PA) ....D....213 808-6220
1150 S Olive St Ste T500 Los Angeles (90015) ***(P-24236)***
United Way of Bay Area (PA) ....D....415 808-4300
550 Kearny St Ste 1000 San Francisco (94108) ***(P-23519)***
UNITED WAY OF GREATER LOS ANGE, Los Angeles *Also called United Way Inc* ***(P-24236)***
UNITED WAY, THE, San Francisco *Also called United Way of Bay Area* ***(P-23519)***
Unitedhealth Group Inc ....B....714 969-9050
7891 Moonmist Cir Huntington Beach (92648) ***(P-10060)***
Unitedhealth Group Inc ....D....952 936-1300
5701 Katella Ave Cypress (90630) ***(P-10061)***
Unitedhealth Group Inc ....B....530 879-8251
2080 E 20th St Chico (95928) ***(P-10062)***
Unitek Inc ....D....510 623-8544
41350 Christy St Fremont (94538) ***(P-15707)***
Unitek Information Systems Inc (PA) ....D....510 249-1060
4670 Auto Mall Pkwy Fremont (94538) ***(P-16147)***
Unitek It Education, Fremont *Also called Unitek Information Systems Inc* ***(P-16147)***

Mergent e-mail: customerrelations@mergent.com
1468
2020 Directory of California
Wholesalers and Services Companies
(P-0000) Products & Services Section entry number
(PA)=Parent Co (HQ)=Headquarters (DH)=Div Headquarters

Unity Biotechnology Inc......C......650 416-1192
3280 Byshore Blvd Ste 100 Brisbane (94005) ***(P-25861)***
Unity Care Group......D......408 971-9822
1400 Parkmoor Ave Ste 115 San Jose (95126) ***(P-23520)***
Unity Courier Service Inc (PA)......C......323 255-9800
3231 Fletcher Dr Los Angeles (90065) ***(P-4331)***
Unity Courier Service Inc......D......510 568-8890
1132 Beecher St San Leandro (94577) ***(P-17133)***
Unity SEC & Protective Svc......D......323 695-7234
619 E Washington Blvd Pasadena (91104) ***(P-16466)***
Unity Software Inc (HQ)......E......415 848-2533
30 3rd St San Francisco (94103) ***(P-15170)***
Unity Technologies, San Francisco *Also called Unity Software Inc* ***(P-15170)***
Univar Solutions USA Inc......C......323 727-7005
2600 Garfield Ave Commerce (90040) ***(P-8710)***
Univar Solutions USA Inc......D......408 435-8649
2256 Junction Ave San Jose (95131) ***(P-8711)***
Univers of Calif San Diego Hs......A......619 543-3713
200 W Arbor Dr 8201 San Diego (92103) ***(P-21329)***
Universal Accounts Inc......D......626 356-7900
690 E Green St Ste 300 Pasadena (91101) ***(P-13701)***
Universal Asphalt Co Inc......E......562 941-0201
10610 Painter Ave Santa Fe Springs (90670) ***(P-1806)***
Universal Bank (PA)......D......626 854-2818
3455 S Nogales St Fl 2 West Covina (91792) ***(P-9287)***
Universal Bldg Svcs & Sup Co (PA)......C......510 527-1078
3120 Pierce St Richmond (94804) ***(P-14073)***
Universal Bldg Svcs & Sup Co......C......925 934-5533
421 N Buchanan Cir Pacheco (94553) ***(P-14074)***
Universal Bldg Svcs & Sup Co......C......408 995-5111
430 Roberson Ln San Jose (95112) ***(P-14075)***
Universal Building Maint LLC (HQ)......A......714 619-9700
1551 N Tustin Ave Ste 650 Santa Ana (92705) ***(P-14076)***
Universal Card Inc......B......949 861-4000
9012 Research Dr Ste 200 Irvine (92618) ***(P-17134)***
Universal Care Inc (PA)......B......562 424-6200
19762 Macarthur Blvd # 100 Irvine (92612) ***(P-22152)***
Universal City, Santa Monica *Also called Universal Studios Company LLC* ***(P-17699)***
Universal City Studios LLC (HQ)......D......800 864-8377
100 Universal City Plz Universal City (91608) ***(P-17691)***
Universal Creative, Universal City *Also called Universal City Studios LLC* ***(P-17691)***
Universal Custom Farming Co, Tranquillity *Also called Don Gragnani Farms* ***(P-314)***
Universal Cylinder Exch Inc......D......714 744-1036
692 N Cypress St Ste B Orange (92867) ***(P-27308)***
Universal Dust Collector (PA)......D......714 630-8588
1041 N Kraemer Pl Anaheim (92806) ***(P-1390)***
Universal Framing Products, Santa Clarita *Also called Universal Wood Moulding Inc* ***(P-6595)***
Universal General Builders......D......650 591-3104
871 Industrial Rd Ste A San Carlos (94070) ***(P-25365)***
Universal Home Care Inc......C......323 653-9222
151 N San Vicente Blvd Beverly Hills (90211) ***(P-21890)***
Universal Limousine & Trnsp Co......D......916 361-5466
9944 Mills Station Rd C Sacramento (95827) ***(P-3733)***
Universal McCann, San Francisco *Also called McCann World Group Inc* ***(P-13538)***
Universal Mus Group Hldngs Inc......A......317 871-0319
21301 Burbank Blvd # 100 Woodland Hills (91367) ***(P-7843)***
Universal Mus Investments Inc (HQ)......D......818 577-4700
2220 Colorado Ave Santa Monica (90404) ***(P-17135)***
Universal Music Group Inc (HQ)......D......310 865-4000
2220 Colorado Ave Santa Monica (90404) ***(P-17136)***
Universal Music Group Inc......D......310 865-4000
2220 Colorado Ave Santa Monica (90404) ***(P-18017)***
Universal Music Group Inc......E......818 286-4000
10 Universal City Plz Universal City (91608) ***(P-17137)***
Universal Network Dev Corp (PA)......D......916 475-1200
2555 3rd St Ste 112 Sacramento (95818) ***(P-27241)***
Universal Network Exchange, Burbank *Also called Unx Inc A Delaware Corp* ***(P-15171)***
Universal Packg Systems Inc......C......909 517-2442
14570 Monte Vista Ave Chino (91710) ***(P-4526)***
Universal Paragon Corporation (PA)......B......415 468-6676
150 Executive Park Blvd # 4000 San Francisco (94134) ***(P-13052)***
Universal Protection Svc LP......D......805 496-4401
2415 San Ramon Vly Blvd San Ramon (94583) ***(P-16467)***
Universal Protection Svc LP......D......562 981-5700
340 Golden Shore Ste 100 Long Beach (90802) ***(P-16468)***
Universal Protection Svc LP......D......818 227-1240
21300 Victory Blvd # 230 Woodland Hills (91367) ***(P-16469)***
Universal Protection Svc LP (HQ)......C......714 619-9700
1551 N Tustin Ave Ste 650 Santa Ana (92705) ***(P-16470)***
Universal Protection Svc LP......C......415 759-5056
1208 Vicente St San Francisco (94116) ***(P-16471)***
Universal Self Storage......E......951 206-5263
25980 Barton Rd Loma Linda (92354) ***(P-4527)***
Universal Services America LP (HQ)......D......714 619-9700
1551 N Tustin Ave Fl 6 Santa Ana (92705) ***(P-16472)***
Universal Site Services Inc......D......916 635-1122
3174 Luyung Dr Ste 3 Rancho Cordova (95742) ***(P-14077)***
Universal Site Services Inc (PA)......D......800 647-9337
760 E Capitol Ave Milpitas (95035) ***(P-14078)***
Universal Space Lines Inc......D......215 328-9130
1501 Quail St Ste 102 Newport Beach (92660) ***(P-25366)***
Universal Stdios Licensing LLC......C......818 695-1273
100 Universal City Plz Universal City (91608) ***(P-11836)***
Universal Studios Inc......C......818 262-4301
1295 Los Angeles St Ste 1 Glendale (91204) ***(P-17692)***
Universal Studios Inc......D......818 753-0000
4123 Lankershim Blvd North Hollywood (91602) ***(P-17693)***
Universal Studios Inc......C......818 777-2351
3900 Lankershim Blvd Studio City (91604) ***(P-17694)***
Universal Studios Company LLC......B......818 622-4455
1000 Univ Studio Blvd 2 Universal City (91608) ***(P-17695)***
Universal Studios Company LLC (HQ)......C......818 777-1000
100 Universal City Plz North Hollywood (91608) ***(P-17696)***
Universal Studios Company LLC......C......818 777-1000
100 Universal City Plz # 3 Universal City (91608) ***(P-17697)***
Universal Studios Company LLC......C......310 235-4749
2440 S Sepulveda Blvd # 100 Los Angeles (90064) ***(P-17698)***
Universal Studios Company LLC......D......310 865-5000
2220 Colorado Ave Santa Monica (90404) ***(P-17699)***
Universal Wilkes Co Inc (PA)......D......626 839-2022
2899 Agoura Rd Ste 114 City of Industry (91715) ***(P-4528)***
Universal Wood Moulding Inc (PA)......D......661 362-6262
21139 Centre Pointe Pkwy Santa Clarita (91350) ***(P-6595)***
Universe Holdings Dev Co LLC......E......310 785-0077
350 S Beverly Dr Ste 210 Beverly Hills (90212) ***(P-11494)***
University Art Center Inc (PA)......D......650 328-3500
2550 El Camino Real Redwood City (94061) ***(P-17559)***
UNIVERSITY BOOKSTORE, Los Angeles *Also called California State Univ Aux Svcs* ***(P-26171)***
University Business Ctr Assoc......D......601 354-3555
5425 Hollister Ave # 160 Santa Barbara (93111) ***(P-10666)***
University Cal Los Angeles......E......310 794-2284
1100 Glendon Ave Ste 850 Los Angeles (90024) ***(P-26040)***
University Cal Los Angeles......E......805 494-6920
1250 Avanta Dr Ste 207 Westlake Village (91361) ***(P-19525)***
University Cal Los Angeles......A......310 825-0640
200 Ucla Medical Plz Los Angeles (90095) ***(P-21330)***
University Cal Los Angeles......A......818 364-1555
14445 Olive View Dr Sylmar (91342) ***(P-21331)***
University Cal Los Angeles......A......310 319-4000
1225 15th St Santa Monica (90404) ***(P-21332)***
University Cal Los Angeles......A......310 825-9111
757 Westwood Plz Los Angeles (90095) ***(P-21333)***
University Cal Riverside......D......951 827-4801
1160 University Ave Riverside (92507) ***(P-25952)***
University Cal San Diego......A......619 543-6654
200 W Arbor Dr Frnt San Diego (92103) ***(P-21334)***
University Cal San Diego......B......858 534-5000
10100 Hopkins Dr La Jolla (92093) ***(P-15831)***
University Cal San Diego......B......858 657-7000
9300 Campus Point Dr La Jolla (92037) ***(P-21335)***
University Cal San Francisco......D......415 476-9000
500 Parnassus Ave San Francisco (94143) ***(P-26041)***
University Cal San Francisco......A......415 476-7000
401 Parnassus Ave San Francisco (94143) ***(P-21336)***
University Cal San Francisco......E......415 476-1611
400 Parnassus Ave A633 San Francisco (94143) ***(P-21337)***
University Cal San Francisco......D......415 353-3155
3330 Geary Blvd San Francisco (94118) ***(P-19526)***
University Cal San Francisco......D......510 987-0700
616 Forbes Blvd South San Francisco (94080) ***(P-4529)***
University Cal San Francisco......B......415 567-6600
1600 Divisadero St San Francisco (94143) ***(P-21338)***
University Cal San Francisco......E......415 476-5608
100 Buchanan St San Francisco (94102) ***(P-19635)***
University California Davis......E......916 734-2846
2315 Stockton Blvd # 6309 Sacramento (95817) ***(P-19527)***
University California Davis......A......916 734-3141
4400 V St Sacramento (95817) ***(P-21339)***
University California Davis......C......530 752-2300
Student House Ctr Davis (95616) ***(P-19528)***
University California Davis......A......916 734-2011
2450 48th St Ste 2401 Sacramento (95817) ***(P-21340)***
University California Davis......A......916 734-5113
4150 V St Ste 1200 Sacramento (95817) ***(P-21341)***
University California Irvine......A......714 456-6170
101 The City Dr S Bldg 1a Orange (92868) ***(P-19529)***
University California Irvine......D......714 480-2443
800 N Main St Santa Ana (92701) ***(P-19530)***
University California Irvine......E......949 646-2267
1640 Newport Blvd Ste 340 Costa Mesa (92627) ***(P-19531)***
University California Irvine......A......714 456-6011
101 The City Dr S Orange (92868) ***(P-21342)***
University California Irvine......D......949 824-2819
2220 Engineering Gateway Irvine (92697) ***(P-25862)***
University California Irvine......A......714 456-5558
200 S Manchester Ave # 400 Orange (92868) ***(P-21343)***
University California Berkeley......A......510 495-2490
5885 Hollis St Emeryville (94608) ***(P-26042)***
University California Berkeley......B......510 642-2000
2222 Bancroft Way Berkeley (94720) ***(P-19532)***
University Credit Union......C......310 477-6628
1500 S Sepulveda Blvd Los Angeles (90025) ***(P-9374)***
University Head Neck Surgeons, Orange *Also called Roger L Crumley MD Inc* ***(P-19344)***
University Health Services, Berkeley *Also called University California Berkeley* ***(P-19532)***
University Lease, Irvine *Also called California First National Bank* ***(P-9250)***
University Marelich Mech Inc......C......714 632-2600
1000 N Kraemer Pl Anaheim (92806) ***(P-2307)***
University Mechanical & (HQ)......C......619 956-2500
1168 Fesler St El Cajon (92020) ***(P-2308)***
University of CA Office, Oakland *Also called C/O Uc San Francisco* ***(P-26167)***
University of Pacific......A......209 946-2030
1040 E Stadium Dr Stockton (95204) ***(P-18776)***
University Park Healthcare Ctr, Los Angeles *Also called United Convalescent Facilities* ***(P-20706)***
University Retirement Cmnty, Davis *Also called Pacific Retirement Svcs Inc* ***(P-24019)***

ALPHABETIC

Employee Codes: A=Over 500 employees, B=251-500
C=101-250, D=51-100, E=50
2020 Directory of California
Wholesalers and Services Companies
© Mergent Inc. 1-800-342-5647
1469

University Sequoia, Fresno *Also called Sunnyside Country Club* **(P-18589)**
University Southern California ....C......213 740-4694
  3737 Watt Way Fl 3 Los Angeles (90089) **(P-21344)**
University Southern California ....D......626 457-4240
  1000 S Fremont Ave Unit 7 Alhambra (91803) **(P-25863)**
University Southern California ....A......323 442-8500
  1500 San Pablo St Los Angeles (90033) **(P-21345)**
University Southern California ....D......213 743-5339
  849 W 34th St Ste 208 Los Angeles (90089) **(P-19533)**
University Stdnt Un Cal State ....B......818 677-2251
  18111 Nordhoff St Northridge (91330) **(P-24684)**
University Student Union Inc ....C......323 343-2450
  5151 State University Dr Los Angeles (90032) **(P-17138)**
Univision 67, Monterey *Also called Entravsion Communications Corp* **(P-5596)**
Univision Communications Inc ....C......818 484-7399
  655 N Central Ave # 2500 Glendale (91203) **(P-5572)**
Univision Radio Inc ....E......559 430-8500
  601 W Univision Plz Fresno (93704) **(P-5573)**
Univision Television Group Inc ....D......559 222-2121
  601 W Univision Plz Fresno (93704) **(P-5660)**
Univision Television Group Inc ....D......415 538-8000
  1940 Zanker Rd San Jose (95112) **(P-5661)**
Univision Television Group Inc ....E......858 576-1919
  5770 Ruffin Rd San Diego (92123) **(P-5662)**
Uniwell Corporation ....C......714 522-7000
  7000 Beach Blvd Buena Park (90620) **(P-13053)**
Uniwell Corporation ....D......559 268-1000
  2233 Ventura St Fresno (93721) **(P-11618)**
Uniwell Fresno Hotel LLC ....D......559 268-1000
  2233 Ventura St Fresno (93721) **(P-13054)**
Uniworld Boutique River Cruise, Encino *Also called Uniworld River Cruises Inc* **(P-4843)**
Uniworld River Cruises Inc ....C......818 382-2322
  17323 Ventura Blvd # 300 Encino (91316) **(P-4843)**
Unknown, Carlsbad *Also called Bomel Construction Co Inc* **(P-1334)**
Unknown, Susanville *Also called Golden 1 Credit Union* **(P-9396)**
Unlimited SEC Specialists Inc ....E......877 310-4877
  13636 Ventura Blvd # 206 Sherman Oaks (91423) **(P-16473)**
UNUM Life Insurance Co Amer ....C......818 291-4739
  655 N Central Ave Glendale (91203) **(P-10530)**
Unumprovident, Glendale *Also called UNUM Life Insurance Co Amer* **(P-10530)**
Unx Inc A Delaware Corp ....D......818 333-3300
  175 E Olive Ave Fl 2 Burbank (91502) **(P-15171)**
Unyeway Inc ....D......619 562-6330
  11440 Riverside Dr Ste D Lakeside (92040) **(P-23650)**
Up Stage Inc ....E......818 879-8781
  30757 Canwood St Agoura (91301) **(P-17700)**
UPAC, San Diego *Also called Union Pan Asian Communities* **(P-23514)**
Upham Hotel ....E......805 962-0058
  1404 De La Vina St # 93101 Santa Barbara (93101) **(P-13055)**
Upland Community Care Inc ....D......909 985-1903
  1221 E Arrow Hwy Upland (91786) **(P-20709)**
Upland Rehabilitation Care Ctr, Upland *Also called Upland Community Care Inc* **(P-20709)**
Uplift Family Services (PA) ....D......408 379-3790
  251 Llewellyn Ave Campbell (95008) **(P-23521)**
Uplift Family Services ....D......408 379-3790
  499 Loma Alta Ave Los Gatos (95030) **(P-22153)**
UPS, El Centro *Also called United Parcel Service Inc OH* **(P-4292)**
UPS, Palm Springs *Also called United Parcel Service Inc OH* **(P-4293)**
UPS, Santa Rosa *Also called United Parcel Service Inc OH* **(P-17125)**
UPS, Richmond *Also called United Parcel Service Inc OH* **(P-4294)**
UPS, Salinas *Also called United Parcel Service Inc OH* **(P-4295)**
UPS, Torrance *Also called United Parcel Service Inc OH* **(P-4296)**
UPS, Commerce *Also called United Parcel Service Inc OH* **(P-17126)**
UPS, Anderson *Also called United Parcel Service Inc OH* **(P-4297)**
UPS, Bishop *Also called United Parcel Service Inc OH* **(P-4298)**
UPS, Fairfield *Also called United Parcel Service Inc OH* **(P-4299)**
UPS, Ceres *Also called United Parcel Service Inc OH* **(P-4300)**
UPS, West Sacramento *Also called United Parcel Service Inc OH* **(P-4301)**
UPS, Aliso Viejo *Also called United Parcel Service Inc* **(P-17121)**
UPS, NAPA *Also called United Parcel Service Inc OH* **(P-4302)**
UPS, Sacramento *Also called United Parcel Service Inc OH* **(P-4303)**
UPS, Vernon *Also called United Parcel Service Inc OH* **(P-4730)**
UPS, Gardena *Also called United Parcel Service Inc OH* **(P-4304)**
UPS, San Jose *Also called United Parcel Service Inc OH* **(P-4305)**
UPS, Sun City *Also called United Parcel Service Inc OH* **(P-4731)**
UPS, Manteca *Also called United Parcel Service Inc OH* **(P-4732)**
UPS, Vallejo *Also called United Parcel Service Inc OH* **(P-4307)**
UPS, San Diego *Also called United Parcel Service Inc OH* **(P-17127)**
UPS, Los Angeles *Also called United Parcel Service Inc OH* **(P-4308)**
UPS, Aliso Viejo *Also called United Parcel Service Inc OH* **(P-4309)**
UPS, Ontario *Also called United Parcel Service Inc OH* **(P-17128)**
UPS, Ontario *Also called United Parcel Service Inc OH* **(P-4733)**
UPS, Victorville *Also called United Parcel Service Inc* **(P-17122)**
UPS, Sylmar *Also called United Parcel Service Inc* **(P-4290)**
UPS, Lancaster *Also called United Parcel Service Inc OH* **(P-4310)**
UPS, Van Nuys *Also called United Parcel Service Inc OH* **(P-4311)**
UPS, San Diego *Also called United Parcel Service Inc OH* **(P-4312)**
UPS, Oakland *Also called United Parcel Service Inc OH* **(P-4313)**
UPS, South Lake Tahoe *Also called United Parcel Service Inc OH* **(P-17129)**
UPS, Cerritos *Also called United Parcel Service Inc OH* **(P-4314)**
UPS, Monterey Park *Also called United Parcel Service Inc* **(P-17123)**
UPS, Ukiah *Also called United Parcel Service Inc OH* **(P-4315)**
UPS, Westlake Village *Also called United Parcel Service Inc* **(P-17124)**

UPS, Monterey *Also called United Parcel Service Inc OH* **(P-4316)**
UPS, San Luis Obispo *Also called United Parcel Service Inc OH* **(P-4317)**
UPS, Concord *Also called United Parcel Service Inc OH* **(P-4318)**
UPS, Goleta *Also called United Parcel Service Inc OH* **(P-4319)**
UPS, Santa Maria *Also called United Parcel Service Inc OH* **(P-4320)**
UPS, Angels Camp *Also called United Parcel Service Inc OH* **(P-4321)**
UPS, Newbury Park *Also called United Parcel Service Inc OH* **(P-4322)**
UPS, Los Angeles *Also called United Parcel Service Inc OH* **(P-4323)**
UPS, South San Francisco *Also called United Parcel Service Inc* **(P-4291)**
UPS, Chula Vista *Also called United Parcel Service Inc OH* **(P-4324)**
UPS, Santa Cruz *Also called United Parcel Service Inc OH* **(P-4325)**
UPS, Ontario *Also called United Parcel Service Inc OH* **(P-4326)**
UPS, San Ramon *Also called United Parcel Service Inc OH* **(P-4327)**
UPS, Eastvale *Also called United Parcel Service Inc OH* **(P-17130)**
UPS, Ventura *Also called United Parcel Service Inc OH* **(P-4328)**
UPS, Fremont *Also called United Parcel Service Inc OH* **(P-17131)**
UPS, Baldwin Park *Also called United Parcel Service Inc OH* **(P-4329)**
UPS, Sacramento *Also called United Parcel Service Inc OH* **(P-4330)**
UPS, Simi Valley *Also called United Parcel Service Inc OH* **(P-17132)**
UPS Freight, Pico Rivera *Also called UPS Ground Freight Inc* **(P-4156)**
UPS Freight Services Inc ....D......909 879-7400
  2650 S Willow Ave Bloomington (92316) **(P-4150)**
UPS Ground Freight Inc ....D......559 445-9010
  4587 S Chestnut Ave Fresno (93725) **(P-4151)**
UPS Ground Freight Inc ....D......661 395-9500
  600 Williams St Bakersfield (93305) **(P-4152)**
UPS Ground Freight Inc ....D......209 858-5095
  1444 Lathrop Rd Lathrop (95330) **(P-4153)**
UPS Ground Freight Inc ....D......707 526-1910
  7 College Ave Santa Rosa (95401) **(P-4154)**
UPS Ground Freight Inc ....D......408 400-0595
  925 Morse Ave Sunnyvale (94089) **(P-4155)**
UPS Ground Freight Inc ....D......562 801-1300
  7754 Paramount Blvd Pico Rivera (90660) **(P-4156)**
UPS Ground Freight Inc ....D......916 371-9101
  900 E St West Sacramento (95605) **(P-4157)**
UPS Ground Freight Inc ....D......866 372-5619
  650 S Acacia Ave Fullerton (92831) **(P-4158)**
UPS Store Inc (HQ) ....C......858 455-8800
  6060 Cornerstone Ct W San Diego (92121) **(P-17139)**
UPS Supply Chain Solutions Inc ....A......650 635-2693
  550-3 Eccles Ave San Francisco (94101) **(P-5074)**
UPS Supply Chain Solutions Inc ....C......310 404-2719
  19701 Hamilton Ave # 250 Torrance (90502) **(P-5075)**
UPS Supply Chain Solutions Inc ....E......650 875-8300
  455 Forbes Blvd South San Francisco (94080) **(P-5076)**
UPS Supply Chain Solutions Inc ....E......415 775-6644
  601 Van Neca Ave Ste E San Francisco (94102) **(P-5077)**
UPS Worldwide Logistics Inc ....C......310 673-7661
  3600 W Century Blvd Inglewood (90303) **(P-5078)**
Upstanding LLC ....C......949 788-9900
  440 Exchange Ste 100 Irvine (92602) **(P-15528)**
Upstrem Inc ....D......858 229-2979
  1253 University Ave # 1003 San Diego (92103) **(P-26858)**
Upwind Blade Solutions Inc ....C......866 927-3142
  2869 Historic Decatur Rd # 100 San Diego (92106) **(P-17560)**
Upwork Global Inc ....E......650 316-7500
  2625 Augustine Dr Ste 601 Santa Clara (95054) **(P-24431)**
Uquality Automotive Pdts Corp (PA) ....E......562 282-2888
  16411 Shoemaker Ave Cerritos (90703) **(P-6476)**
Urata & Sons Concrete Inc ....C......916 638-5364
  3430 Luyung Dr Rancho Cordova (95742) **(P-3231)**
Urata & Sons Concrete LLC ....D......916 638-5364
  3430 Luyung Dr Rancho Cordova (95742) **(P-3232)**
Urban Commons Queensway LLC ....A......562 499-1611
  1126 Queens Hwy Long Beach (90802) **(P-13056)**
Urban Corps of San Diego ....C......619 235-6884
  3127 Jefferson St San Diego (92110) **(P-23651)**
Urban Group, The, Santa Barbara *Also called Parsons Group Inc* **(P-10795)**
Urban Painting Inc ....D......415 485-1130
  40 Lisbon St San Rafael (94901) **(P-2403)**
Urban Plates - Playa Vista, Playa Vista *Also called Urban Plates LLC* **(P-18777)**
Urban Plates LLC ....D......424 256-7274
  12746 W Jefferson Blvd # 3140 Playa Vista (90094) **(P-18777)**
Urban Services YMCA, Oakland *Also called Young MNS Chrstn Assn of E Bay* **(P-24762)**
Urban Sony Service Center, Irvine *Also called Sony Electronics Inc* **(P-17670)**
Urban Trading Software Inc ....E......877 633-6171
  21227 Foothill Blvd Hayward (94541) **(P-15529)**
Urgent Care-Selma Dst Hosp, Selma *Also called Adventist Health Selma* **(P-20730)**
Uribe Trucking Inc ....C......805 483-1125
  542 Flynn Rd Camarillo (93012) **(P-4238)**
Urology Assoc of Cen Cal ....D......559 321-2800
  7014 N Whitney Ave Ste A Fresno (93720) **(P-19534)**
URS Group Inc ....C......510 893-3600
  1333 Broadway Oakland (94612) **(P-25367)**
URS Group Inc ....D......213 996-2200
  915 Wilshire Blvd Ste 700 Los Angeles (90017) **(P-25368)**
URS Group Inc ....D......213 996-2200
  915 Wilshire Blvd Ste 700 Los Angeles (90017) **(P-25369)**
URS Group Inc ....D......925 446-3800
  300 Lakeside Dr Ste 400 Oakland (94612) **(P-25370)**
URS Group Inc ....D......805 964-6010
  130 Robin Hill Rd Ste 100 Santa Barbara (93117) **(P-25371)**
URS Group Inc ....D......916 679-2000
  2020 L St Ste 400 Sacramento (95811) **(P-25508)**

URS Group Inc ....D....408 297-9585
100 W San Fernando St # 200 San Jose (95113) ***(P-25372)***
URS Group Inc ....C....916 679-2000
2870 Gateway Oaks Dr # 300 Sacramento (95833) ***(P-25373)***
URS Holdings Inc (HQ) ....B....415 774-2700
600 Montgomery St Fl 25 San Francisco (94111) ***(P-25374)***
URS-Gei Joint Venture ....E....510 874-3051
1333 Broadway Ste 800 Oakland (94612) ***(P-25375)***
US 3, Santa Ana *Also called Utility Systems Science* ***(P-15175)***
US Advisor LLC ....D....707 253-9953
600 Trancas St NAPA (94558) ***(P-11879)***
US Airforce Band of Golden W ....E....707 424-2263
551 Waldron St Bldg 240 Travis Afb (94535) ***(P-18018)***
US Airways, San Diego *Also called American Airlines Inc* ***(P-4655)***
US Airways, Los Angeles *Also called American Airlines Inc* ***(P-4656)***
US Army Corps of Engineers ....A....916 557-7490
1325 J St Frnt Sacramento (95814) ***(P-25376)***
US Army Corps of Engineers ....A....213 452-3967
915 Wilshire Blvd Ste 930 Los Angeles (90017) ***(P-25377)***
US Bank, Los Alamitos *Also called US Bank National Association* ***(P-9121)***
US Bank, San Diego *Also called US Bank National Association* ***(P-9122)***
US Bank National Association ....E....562 795-7520
10021 Bloomfield St Los Alamitos (90720) ***(P-9121)***
US Bank National Association ....D....619 744-2140
1420 Kettner Blvd Ste 101 San Diego (92101) ***(P-9122)***
US Bankcard Services Inc ....D....888 888-8872
17171 Gale Ave Ste 110 City of Industry (91745) ***(P-17140)***
US Best Repair Service Inc ....C....888 750-2378
2004 Mcgaw Ave Irvine (92614) ***(P-1213)***
US Best Repairs, Irvine *Also called US Best Repair Service Inc* ***(P-1213)***
US Blanks, Vernon *Also called LA Brands LLC* ***(P-8036)***
US Carenet Services LLC ....E....408 378-6131
815 Pollard Rd Los Gatos (95032) ***(P-21891)***
US Credit Bancorp Inc ....D....310 829-2112
851 20th St Santa Monica (90403) ***(P-9606)***
US Data Management LLC (PA) ....D....888 231-0816
535 Chapala St Santa Barbara (93101) ***(P-16148)***
US Dept of Air Force ....D....661 277-3432
5 Seller Ave Bldg 3000 Edwards (93524) ***(P-18209)***
US Dept of the Air Force ....C....661 277-3030
35 N Wolfe Ave Edwards (93524) ***(P-5807)***
US Dept of the Air Force ....B....530 634-4839
15301 Warren Shingle Rd Marysville (95903) ***(P-21346)***
US Dept of the Air Force ....D....661 275-5410
10 E Saturn Dr Edwards (93524) ***(P-25864)***
US Dept of the Air Force ....D....530 634-4738
15301 Warren Shingle Rd Beale Afb (95903) ***(P-19535)***
US Elogistics Service Corp ....D....732 357-6665
1521 E Francis St Ontario (91761) ***(P-4530)***
US Elogistics Service Corp ....D....732 881-6606
13725 Pipeline Ave Chino (91710) ***(P-4531)***
US Family Care, Rialto *Also called Caremark Rx Inc* ***(P-18869)***
US Family Care, Hesperia *Also called Caremark Rx LLC* ***(P-18870)***
US Foods Inc ....C....951 256-2400
1283 Sherborn St Ste 102 Corona (92879) ***(P-8276)***
US Foods Inc ....B....760 599-6200
1201 Park Center Dr Vista (92081) ***(P-9017)***
US Foods Inc ....C....800 888-3147
1283 Sherborn St Ste 102 Corona (92879) ***(P-8664)***
US Foods Inc ....B....925 606-3525
300 Lawrence Dr Frnt Livermore (94551) ***(P-8277)***
US Foods Inc ....C....951 582-8500
1283 Sherborn St Ste 102 Corona (92879) ***(P-8665)***
US Foods Inc ....C....714 670-3500
15155 Northam St La Mirada (90638) ***(P-8278)***
US Foods Inc ....E....714 670-3500
392 W Walnut Ave Fullerton (92832) ***(P-8279)***
US Foods Inc ....C....714 449-9990
700 S Raymond Ave Fullerton (92831) ***(P-8666)***
US Foods Inc ....C....209 572-2882
4300 Finch Rd Modesto (95357) ***(P-8667)***
US Foods Inc ....C....714 449-2880
1415 N Raymond Ave Anaheim (92801) ***(P-8668)***
US Foods Inc ....C....714 670-3500
15155 Northam St La Mirada (90638) ***(P-8669)***
US Foods Inc ....C....619 474-6525
1240 W 28th St National City (91950) ***(P-8670)***
US Foods Inc ....C....951 256-2400
1283 Sherborn St Ste 102 Corona (92879) ***(P-8671)***
US Grant Hotel Ventures LLC ....D....619 744-2007
326 Broadway San Diego (92101) ***(P-13057)***
US Green Building Council - ....D....818 621-4880
2879 Breezy Meadow Ln Corona (92883) ***(P-11774)***
US GREEN BUILDING COUNCIL INLA, Corona *Also called US Green Building Council - **(P-11774)***
US Healthworks Inc (HQ) ....D....661 678-2300
28035 Avenue Stanford Valencia (91355) ***(P-19536)***
US Home, Corona *Also called US Home Corporation* ***(P-1319)***
US Home Corporation ....E....951 817-3500
980 Montecito Dr 302 Corona (92879) ***(P-1319)***
US Hotel and Resort MGT Inc ....D....949 650-2988
2544 Newport Blvd Costa Mesa (92627) ***(P-13058)***
US Interactive Delaware ....C....408 863-7500
1270 Oakmead Pkwy Ste 318 Sunnyvale (94085) ***(P-13591)***
US International Media LLC (PA) ....D....310 482-6700
3415 S Sepulveda Blvd # 800 Los Angeles (90034) ***(P-13664)***
US Interstate Distrg Inc ....C....818 678-4592
21621 Nordhoff St Chatsworth (91311) ***(P-5484)***
US Investigations Services LLC (HQ) ....A....724 458-1750
3349 Michelson Dr Ste 150 Irvine (92612) ***(P-16474)***
US Lines LLC (HQ) ....D....714 751-3333
3501 Jamboree Rd Ste 300 Newport Beach (92660) ***(P-24370)***
US Loan Auditors LLC ....D....916 248-8625
7485 Rush Rver Dr Ste 710 Sacramento (95831) ***(P-25691)***
US Metro Group Inc ....A....213 382-6435
605 S Wilton Pl Los Angeles (90005) ***(P-14079)***
US Naval Medical Clinical Lab, Port Hueneme *Also called United States Dept of Navy* ***(P-19521)***
US Outdoor, Los Angeles *Also called US International Media LLC* ***(P-13664)***
US Probation, San Diego *Also called Supreme Court United States* ***(P-23496)***
US Property Group Inc ....E....559 227-1901
1901 E Shields Ave # 203 Fresno (93726) ***(P-10667)***
US Real Estate Services Inc ....D....949 598-9920
25520 Commercentre Dr # 1 Lake Forest (92630) ***(P-11495)***
US Skillserve Inc (PA) ....A....562 930-0777
4115 E Broadway Ste A Long Beach (90803) ***(P-26440)***
US Skillserve Inc ....C....909 621-4751
9620 Fremont Ave Montclair (91763) ***(P-20342)***
US Small Cpitl Value Portfolio ....D....310 395-8005
1299 Ocean Ave Ste 150 Santa Monica (90401) ***(P-11743)***
US Telepacific Corp (HQ) ....E....866 699-8242
515 S Flower St Ste 4500 Los Angeles (90071) ***(P-5485)***
US Tournament Golf Ltd Lblty ....E....909 987-6695
5464 Topaz St Rancho Cucamonga (91701) ***(P-26859)***
USA Bouquet LLC ....D....800 878-9909
2834 La Mirada Dr Ste B Vista (92081) ***(P-8929)***
USA Federal Credit Union, San Diego *Also called United Svcs Amer Federal Cr Un* ***(P-9373)***
USA Multifamily Management ....C....916 773-6060
3200 Douglas Blvd Ste 200 Roseville (95661) ***(P-11496)***
USA Properties Fund Inc (PA) ....D....916 773-6060
3200 Douglas Blvd Ste 200 Roseville (95661) ***(P-11619)***
USA Staffing Inc ....D....805 269-2677
505 Higuera St San Luis Obispo (93401) ***(P-14579)***
USA Transport Inc ....E....559 783-3563
12191 Violet Rd Adelanto (92301) ***(P-4239)***
USA Travel Services LLC ....A....207 899-8803
714 Washington Blvd Marina Del Rey (90292) ***(P-24881)***
USA Truck Inc ....D....909 334-1406
5861 Pine Ave Ste A-2 Chino Hills (91709) ***(P-4159)***
USA Valet Parking LLC ....E....916 792-1055
980 9th St Ste 1620 Sacramento (95814) ***(P-13457)***
USA Waste of California Inc ....D....559 741-1766
26951 Road 140 Visalia (93292) ***(P-6296)***
USA Waste of California Inc ....D....916 379-0500
8491 Fruitridge Rd Sacramento (95826) ***(P-6297)***
USA Waste of California Inc ....D....818 252-3112
9081 Tujunga Ave Sun Valley (91352) ***(P-6298)***
USA Waste of California Inc (HQ) ....C....916 387-1400
11931 Foundation Pl # 200 Gold River (95670) ***(P-6299)***
USA Waste of California Inc ....C....916 379-2611
8761 Younger Creek Dr Sacramento (95828) ***(P-3947)***
USA Waste of California Inc ....C....831 384-4860
11240 Commercial Pkwy Castroville (95012) ***(P-3948)***
USA Waste of California Inc ....E....209 946-5721
1240 Navy Dr Stockton (95206) ***(P-3949)***
USA Waste of California Inc ....D....800 423-9986
800 S Temescal St Corona (92879) ***(P-6300)***
USA Waste of California Inc ....E....530 274-3090
13083 Grass Valley Ave Grass Valley (95945) ***(P-3950)***
USA Waste of California Inc ....D....831 384-5000
29331 Pacific St Hayward (94544) ***(P-6301)***
USA Waste of California Inc ....D....626 856-1285
13970 Live Oak Ave Baldwin Park (91706) ***(P-6302)***
USA Waste of California Inc ....D....805 466-3636
8740 Pueblo Ave Ste B Atascadero (93422) ***(P-6303)***
USA Waste of California Inc ....D....619 596-5117
1001 W Bradley Ave El Cajon (92020) ***(P-6304)***
USA Waste of California Inc ....D....909 590-1793
13793 Redwood St Chino (91710) ***(P-6305)***
USA Waste of California Inc ....D....559 834-9151
4333 E Jefferson Ave Fresno (93725) ***(P-6306)***
USA Waste of California Inc ....D....310 830-7100
1970 E 213th St Long Beach (90810) ***(P-6307)***
USA Waste of California Inc ....D....310 763-8500
407 E El Segundo Blvd Compton (90222) ***(P-6308)***
USA Waste of California Inc ....D....530 877-2777
951 American Way Paradise (95969) ***(P-6309)***
USA Waste of California Inc ....D....831 754-2500
1120 Madison Ln Salinas (93907) ***(P-6310)***
USA Waste of California Inc ....D....559 834-4070
10725 W Goshen Ave Visalia (93291) ***(P-6311)***
USA Waste of California Inc ....D....661 259-2398
25772 Springbrook Ave Santa Clarita (91350) ***(P-6312)***
USA Waste of California Inc ....D....714 637-3010
1800 S Grand Ave Santa Ana (92705) ***(P-6313)***
Usaco Service Corp ....C....562 483-8747
16205 Distribution Way Cerritos (90703) ***(P-17468)***
Usag Ansbach Financial MGT Div ....D....210 466-1376
420 Montgomery St San Francisco (94104) ***(P-26441)***
Usag Rheinland Pfalz Fincl MGT ....D....210 466-1376
420 Montgomery St San Francisco (94104) ***(P-26442)***
Usag Vicenza Italy Dmwr F M D ....D....210 466-1376
420 Montgomery St San Francisco (94104) ***(P-26443)***
Usag Wiesbaden Fincl MGT Div ....D....210 466-1376
420 Montgomery St San Francisco (94104) ***(P-26444)***
Usas Express International ....D....310 645-2313
420 Hindry Ave Ste G Inglewood (90301) ***(P-5079)***

ALPHABETIC

Employee Codes: A=Over 500 employees, B=251-500
C=101-250, D=51-100, E=50
2020 Directory of California
Wholesalers and Services Companies
© Mergent Inc. 1-800-342-5647
1471

Usc Care Medical Group Inc ....D....323 442-5100
1510 San Pablo St Ste 649 Los Angeles (90033) ***(P-21347)***
Usc Credit Union ....D....213 821-7100
3720 S Flower St Los Angeles (90089) ***(P-9375)***
Usc Emergency Medicine Assoc ....D....323 226-6667
1200 N State St Ste 1011 Los Angeles (90033) ***(P-19537)***
Usc Institute For Neuroimaging ....C....323 442-7246
2001 N Soto St Ste 102 Los Angeles (90032) ***(P-19538)***
Usc MARk& Mary Steven Neuro, Los Angeles *Also called Usc Institute For Neuroimaging* ***(P-19538)***
Usc Shoah Fndn Inst For Visual ....D....213 740-6001
650 W 35th St Ste 114 Los Angeles (90089) ***(P-24882)***
Usc Srgcal Edcatn RES Fndation, Los Angeles *Also called Usc Surgeons Incorporated* ***(P-19539)***
Usc Student Health Center, Los Angeles *Also called University Southern California* ***(P-19533)***
Usc Surgeons Incorporated ....C....323 442-5910
1510 San Pablo St Ste 514 Los Angeles (90033) ***(P-19539)***
Usc University Hospital, Los Angeles *Also called University Southern California* ***(P-21345)***
Usc Verdugo Hills Hospital LLC ....A....818 790-7100
1812 Verdugo Blvd Glendale (91208) ***(P-21348)***
Usc Vrdugo Hlls Hosp Fundation (PA) ....B....800 872-2273
1812 Verdugo Blvd Glendale (91208) ***(P-21349)***
Uscb Inc ....D....213 387-6181
3535 Wilshire Blvd # 700 Los Angeles (90010) ***(P-13702)***
Uscb Inc (PA) ....C....213 985-2111
355 S Grand Ave Ste 3200 Los Angeles (90071) ***(P-13703)***
Uscb America, Los Angeles *Also called Uscb Inc* ***(P-13703)***
Uscf Caps Department Medicine, San Francisco *Also called University Cal San Francisco* ***(P-26041)***
Usd, Union City *Also called Union Sanitary District* ***(P-6141)***
USDA Forest Service ....D....951 680-1560
4955 Canyon Crest Dr Riverside (92507) ***(P-25865)***
USDA Forest Service ....D....530 626-1546
100 Forni Rd Placerville (95667) ***(P-967)***
Usdm Life Science, Santa Barbara *Also called US Data Management LLC* ***(P-16148)***
User Zoom Inc ....D....408 533-8619
10 Almaden Blvd Ste 250 San Jose (95113) ***(P-15172)***
USF Import FWD Wh 4150, Corona *Also called US Foods Inc* ***(P-8671)***
USF Reddaway Inc ....C....562 923-0648
11937 Regentview Ave Downey (90241) ***(P-4160)***
USF-La Mirada 4150, La Mirada *Also called US Foods Inc* ***(P-8669)***
Usfi Inc ....D....310 768-1937
110 W Walnut St 221 Gardena (90248) ***(P-8280)***
USG Interiors LLC ....D....209 466-4636
2575 Loomis Rd Stockton (95205) ***(P-6665)***
Ushio America Inc (HQ) ....D....714 236-8600
5440 Cerritos Ave Cypress (90630) ***(P-7189)***
USI Insurance Services Nat ....D....925 988-1700
1350 Treat Blvd Ste 550 Walnut Creek (94597) ***(P-10531)***
USI Insurance Services Nat Inc ....D....707 769-2900
1039a N Mcdowell Blvd Petaluma (94954) ***(P-10532)***
USI Insurance Services Nat Inc ....D....559 666-2001
5200 N Palm Ave Ste 114 Fresno (93704) ***(P-10533)***
USI Insurance Services Nat Inc ....C....213 253-6700
777 S Figueroa St # 2100 Los Angeles (90017) ***(P-10534)***
USI Insurance Services Nat Inc ....C....916 589-8000
10940 White Rock Rd Rancho Cordova (95670) ***(P-10535)***
USI Insurance Services Nat Inc ....C....628 201-9001
201 Mission St Ste 1100 San Francisco (94105) ***(P-10536)***
USI of Southern California Ins ....E....818 251-3000
21700 Oxnard St Ste 1200 Woodland Hills (91367) ***(P-10537)***
USI South Coast ....D....949 790-9200
29a Technology Dr 200 Irvine (92618) ***(P-10538)***
Usis, Irvine *Also called US Investigations Services LLC* ***(P-16474)***
Usko Expedite Inc ....E....916 233-4455
11290 Point East Dr # 110 Rancho Cordova (95742) ***(P-5080)***
Usl, Newport Beach *Also called Universal Space Lines Inc* ***(P-25366)***
USS Cal Builders Inc ....C....714 828-4882
8051 Main St Stanton (90680) ***(P-1638)***
UST Global Inc (PA) ....D....949 716-8757
5 Polaris Way Aliso Viejo (92656) ***(P-15173)***
Ustov Inc ....E....510 781-1818
21118 Cabot Blvd Hayward (94545) ***(P-8281)***
Ustream Inc ....D....415 489-9400
410 Townsend St Fl 4 San Francisco (94107) ***(P-5486)***
Usts, Huntington Beach *Also called United States Technical Svcs* ***(P-16146)***
Utah Pacific Construction Co ....E....951 677-9876
40940 Eleanora Way Murrieta (92562) ***(P-1923)***
Utblo Inc ....C....562 493-3664
11061 Los Alamitos Blvd Los Alamitos (90720) ***(P-11702)***
UTC Aerospace Systems, Riverside *Also called United Technologies Corp* ***(P-25364)***
UTC Fire SEC Americas Corp Inc ....D....949 737-7800
2955 Red Hill Ave Ste 100 Costa Mesa (92626) ***(P-15174)***
Utc, Mas, Costa Mesa *Also called UTC Fire SEC Americas Corp Inc* ***(P-15174)***
Utdi, Mill Valley *Also called Unified Teldata Inc* ***(P-7359)***
Uti Leak Seekers ....D....323 724-0081
1398 Monterey Pass Rd Monterey Park (91754) ***(P-1924)***
Uti Underground Technology, Monterey Park *Also called Uti Leak Seekers* ***(P-1924)***
Utility Systems Science (PA) ....D....714 542-1004
601 Parkcenter Dr Ste 209 Santa Ana (92705) ***(P-15175)***
Utility Trailer Sales of S CA (PA) ....D....877 275-4887
15567 Valley Blvd Fontana (92335) ***(P-6413)***
Utility Tree Service LLC (HQ) ....E....530 226-0330
1884 Keystone Ct Ste A Redding (96003) ***(P-949)***
Utility Tree Service, Inc., Redding *Also called Utility Tree Service LLC* ***(P-949)***
Utility Tree Services, Goleta *Also called Asplundh Tree Expert Co* ***(P-932)***
Utility Trlr Sls of Centl Cal ....E....559 237-2001
2680 S East Ave Fresno (93706) ***(P-7604)***
Utopia Lighting, Compton *Also called Pacific Lighting Mfr Inc* ***(P-7175)***
Utopia Lighting, Rancho Dominguez *Also called Pacific Lighting Mfr Inc* ***(P-7176)***
Uvnv Inc (PA) ....C....888 777-0446
1550 Scenic Ave Ste 100 Costa Mesa (92626) ***(P-5487)***
Uyematsu Inc ....D....831 724-2200
1004 E Lake Ave Watsonville (95076) ***(P-114)***
V & L Produce Inc ....C....323 589-3125
2550 E 25th St Vernon (90058) ***(P-8533)***
V A Anderson Enterprises Inc (PA) ....D....714 990-6100
400 Atlas St Brea (92821) ***(P-17141)***
V A Anderson Enterprises Inc ....D....925 866-6150
2680 Bishop Dr Ste 140 San Ramon (94583) ***(P-13768)***
V and V Farms, Lodi *Also called Jose Vramontes* ***(P-341)***
V B Z, Richgrove *Also called Vincent B Zaninovich Sons Inc* ***(P-168)***
V Development Inc ....D....925 634-8890
550 Harvest Park Dr Ste A Brentwood (94513) ***(P-1281)***
V G Carelli International Corp ....E....310 247-8410
1 Park Plz Ste 600 Irvine (92614) ***(P-17142)***
V G Pacific Equities, Los Angeles *Also called Pacific Equities Captl* ***(P-10881)***
V G S, Salinas *Also called Vegetable Growers Supply Co* ***(P-9018)***
V N A & Hospice Southern Calif, San Bernardino *Also called Vna Hospice & Pllatve Cre S CA* ***(P-21907)***
V P H, Van Nuys *Also called Valley Presbyterian Hospital* ***(P-21354)***
V S N F Inc ....D....916 452-6631
2120 Stockton Blvd Sacramento (95817) ***(P-20343)***
V S S, West Sacramento *Also called Vss International Inc* ***(P-1808)***
V Sangiacomo & Sons ....C....707 938-5503
21543 Broadway Sonoma (95476) ***(P-167)***
V Troth Inc ....D....661 948-4646
1801 W Avenue K Ste 101 Lancaster (93534) ***(P-11497)***
V Vcc Havens, Vista *Also called Vista Valley Country Club* ***(P-18608)***
V&V Farm Labor Contractor ....E....209 599-4834
18396 S Wagner Ave Ripon (95366) ***(P-367)***
V-Tek Systems Corporation ....D....909 396-5355
21045 Ridge Park Dr Yorba Linda (92886) ***(P-15708)***
V3 Electric Inc ....C....916 597-2627
4925 Rj Mathews Pkwy 100 El Dorado Hills (95762) ***(P-5959)***
VA Hospital, Fresno *Also called Veterans Health Administration* ***(P-21362)***
VA HSR&d Center of Excellence, North Hills *Also called Veterans Health Administration* ***(P-19575)***
Vaca Valley Hospital, Vacaville *Also called Northbay Healthcare Group* ***(P-21060)***
Vacation and Holiday Benefit F ....D....213 385-6161
501 Shatto Pl Fl 5 Los Angeles (90020) ***(P-11820)***
Vacation Interval Realty, Newport Beach *Also called Pacific Monarch Resorts Inc* ***(P-11336)***
Vacaville Condolescent and Reh ....C....707 449-8000
585 Nut Tree Ct Vacaville (95687) ***(P-14580)***
Vacaville Medical Center, Vacaville *Also called Kaiser Foundation Hospitals* ***(P-19050)***
Vacaville Psychiatric Program, Vacaville *Also called Mental Health California Dept* ***(P-21420)***
Vacavlle Cnvalescent Rehab Ctr ....C....707 449-8000
585 Nut Tree Ct Vacaville (95687) ***(P-20710)***
Vaco San Diego LLC ....D....858 642-0000
4250 Executive Sq Ste 750 La Jolla (92037) ***(P-14447)***
Vadnais Trenchless Svcs Inc ....D....858 550-1460
2130 La Mirada Dr Vista (92081) ***(P-1925)***
Vagabond Inns, El Segundo *Also called Rpd Hotels 18 LLC* ***(P-12848)***
Vagaro Inc ....D....800 919-0157
4120 Dublin Blvd Ste 250 Dublin (94568) ***(P-15176)***
Val-Pro Inc ....D....213 689-0844
1661 Mcgarry St Los Angeles (90021) ***(P-8534)***
Valadon Hotel LLC ....D....310 854-1114
8822 Cynthia St West Hollywood (90069) ***(P-13059)***
Valassis Communications Inc ....D....714 751-4006
1575 Corporate Dr Costa Mesa (92626) ***(P-13592)***
Valassis Direct Mail Inc ....D....510 505-6500
6955 Mowry Ave Newark (94560) ***(P-13744)***
Valco Construction, Bakersfield *Also called Gilliam & Sons Inc* ***(P-3316)***
Vale Healthcare Center, San Pablo *Also called Mariner Health Care Inc* ***(P-20109)***
Vale Healthcare Center, San Pablo *Also called Grancare LLC* ***(P-19980)***
Valeant Biomedicals Inc (HQ) ....D....949 461-6000
1 Enterprise Aliso Viejo (92656) ***(P-8712)***
Valencia Bros Inc ....D....760 353-2168
257 Maple Ave El Centro (92243) ***(P-3233)***
Valencia Brothers Concrete, El Centro *Also called Valencia Bros Inc* ***(P-3233)***
Valencia Country Club, Valencia *Also called Heritage Golf Group Inc* ***(P-18252)***
VALENCIA GARDENS HEALTH CARE CENTER, Riverside *Also called Riverside Care Inc* ***(P-20217)***
Valencia Health Care Inc ....D....661 254-2425
23801 Newhall Ave Newhall (91321) ***(P-20711)***
Valencia Tree Landscape ....E....805 965-4244
321 N Quarantina St Santa Barbara (93103) ***(P-768)***
Valente Concrete ....D....951 279-2221
255 Benjamin Dr Corona (92879) ***(P-3234)***
Valentine Corporation ....E....415 453-3732
111 Pelican Way San Rafael (94901) ***(P-3484)***
Valero Labor, Woodland *Also called Oscar Valero* ***(P-352)***
Valet Parking Svc A Cal Partnr (PA) ....A....323 465-5873
6933 Hollywood Blvd Los Angeles (90028) ***(P-17279)***
Valet Services, Bell Gardens *Also called Anitsa Inc* ***(P-13178)***
Valetor Inc ....E....323 654-1271
8359 Santa Monica Blvd Los Angeles (90069) ***(P-13261)***
Valew Welding & Fabrication, Adelanto *Also called Hayes Welding Inc* ***(P-17473)***
Valgenesis Inc ....E....510 445-0505
395 Oyster Point Blvd # 228 South San Francisco (94080) ***(P-6916)***

Mergent e-mail: customerrelations@mergent.com
1472
2020 Directory of California
Wholesalers and Services Companies
(P-0000) Products & Services Section entry number
(PA)=Parent Co (HQ)=Headquarters (DH)=Div Headquarters

Validus Group Inc..........D.......949 457-7606
1 Orchard Ste 210 Lake Forest (92630) ***(P-14448)***
Valin Corporation (PA)..........D.......408 730-9850
5225 Hellyer Ave Ste 220 San Jose (95138) ***(P-7605)***
Valle Vista Convalescent Hosp, Escondido *Also called Covenant Care California LLC* ***(P-19840)***
Valle Vsta Cnvlescent Hosp Inc..........D.......760 745-1288
1025 W 2nd Ave Escondido (92025) ***(P-20712)***
Vallejo Flood and Waste..........D.......707 644-8949
450 Ryder St Vallejo (94590) ***(P-27242)***
Vallejo Garbage & Recycling, Vallejo *Also called Recology Vallejo* ***(P-6250)***
Valley Aggregate Transport Inc..........D.......530 821-2600
753 N George Wash Blvd Yuba City (95993) ***(P-3951)***
Valley Air District, Fresno *Also called San Joaquin Val UNI Air Pol* ***(P-27201)***
Valley Base Materials, Westlake Village *Also called Security Paving Company Inc* ***(P-1785)***
Valley Bulk Inc..........D.......760 843-0574
17649 Turner Rd Victorville (92394) ***(P-4161)***
Valley Can..........E.......916 273-4890
921 11th St Ste 220 Sacramento (95814) ***(P-24237)***
Valley Care Center, Porterville *Also called Wescordon Incorporated* ***(P-20375)***
Valley Care Health System, The, Pleasanton *Also called Hospital Cmmttee For The Lvrmr* ***(P-26256)***
Valley Care Olive View Med Ctr, Sylmar *Also called Olive View-Ucla Medical Center* ***(P-19239)***
Valley Careidence Opco LLC..........D.......559 784-8371
661 W Poplar Ave Porterville (93257) ***(P-20344)***
Valley Center Municipal..........D.......760 735-4500
29300 Valley Center Rd Valley Center (92082) ***(P-6125)***
Valley Center Municpl Wtr Dst..........D.......760 735-4500
29300 Valley Center Rd Valley Center (92082) ***(P-6142)***
Valley Child Guidance Clinic, Palmdale *Also called Child and Family Guidance Ctr* ***(P-21977)***
Valley Childrens Healthcare..........A.......559 353-3000
9300 Valley Childrens Pl Madera (93636) ***(P-19540)***
Valley Childrens Hospital..........C.......559 353-6425
9300 Valley Childrens Pl Madera (93636) ***(P-21350)***
Valley Childrens Hospital (PA)..........A.......559 353-3000
9300 Valley Childrens Pl Madera (93636) ***(P-21351)***
Valley Clark Plbg & Htg Co Inc (PA)..........D.......818 782-1047
7640 Gloria Ave Ste L Van Nuys (91406) ***(P-2309)***
Valley Cmnty Counseling Svcs (PA)..........D.......209 956-4240
6707 Embarcadero Dr Stockton (95219) ***(P-23522)***
Valley Communications Inc (PA)..........D.......916 349-7300
6921 Roseville Rd Sacramento (95842) ***(P-2682)***
Valley Community Health Center, Pleasanton *Also called Center Cnslng Edctn & Crisis* ***(P-22977)***
Valley Community Healthcare..........B.......818 763-8836
6801 Coldwater Canyon Ave 1b North Hollywood (91605) ***(P-19541)***
Valley Convalescent Hospital, Watsonville *Also called West Coast Hospitals Inc* ***(P-20720)***
Valley Detriot Diesel, Bakersfield *Also called Valley Power Systems Inc* ***(P-7606)***
Valley Drive-In Theatre, Santa Maria *Also called Cal Gran Theatres LLC* ***(P-17822)***
Valley Eye Center Group, Van Nuys *Also called George M Rajacich MD PC* ***(P-18995)***
Valley Farm Management Inc..........D.......831 678-1592
37500 Foothill Rd Soledad (93960) ***(P-686)***
Valley Fig Growers, Pleasanton *Also called Sun-Maid Growers California* ***(P-165)***
Valley Fig Growers..........E.......559 237-3893
2028 S 3rd St Fresno (93702) ***(P-556)***
Valley First Credit Union (PA)..........D.......209 549-8511
1419 J St Modesto (95354) ***(P-9376)***
Valley Flowers Inc..........D.......805 684-6651
3920 Via Real Carpinteria (93013) ***(P-8930)***
Valley Fresh Foods Inc..........D.......209 669-5600
3600 E Linwood Ave Turlock (95380) ***(P-413)***
Valley Fresh Foods Inc..........D.......209 669-5510
1220 Hall Rd Denair (95316) ***(P-414)***
Valley Garbage Rubbish Co Inc..........D.......805 614-1131
1850 W Betteravia Rd Santa Maria (93455) ***(P-6314)***
Valley Health Care Systems Inc..........C.......916 505-4112
1300 National Dr Ste 140 Sacramento (95834) ***(P-14449)***
Valley Healthcare, San Bernardino *Also called United Medical Management Inc* ***(P-20708)***
Valley Healthcare Center LLC..........D.......559 251-7161
4840 E Tulare Ave Fresno (93727) ***(P-20345)***
Valley Healthcare Center LLC..........C.......559 251-7161
4840 E Tulare Ave Fresno (93727) ***(P-20346)***
Valley Healthcare Staffing, Sacramento *Also called Valley Health Care Systems Inc* ***(P-14449)***
Valley Hospital Medical Center (HQ)..........B.......818 885-8500
18300 Roscoe Blvd Northridge (91325) ***(P-21352)***
Valley House Care Center, Santa Clara *Also called TLC of Bay Area Inc* ***(P-20332)***
Valley Hunt Club..........D.......626 793-7134
520 S Orange Grove Blvd Pasadena (91105) ***(P-24685)***
Valley Industrial X-Ra..........C.......661 399-8497
3700 Pegasus Dr Ste 100 Bakersfield (93308) ***(P-26117)***
Valley Inventory Service Inc..........D.......707 422-6050
1180 Horizon Dr Ste B Fairfield (94533) ***(P-17143)***
Valley Labor Service Inc..........D.......559 591-5591
39678 Road 84 Dinuba (93618) ***(P-14450)***
Valley Landscaping & Maint Inc..........C.......209 334-3659
12900 N Lwer Scramento Rd Lodi (95242) ***(P-921)***
Valley Light Industries Inc..........C.......626 337-6200
5360 Irwindale Ave Baldwin Park (91706) ***(P-23652)***
Valley Management Services..........B.......626 333-1243
425 S Hacienda Blvd City of Industry (91745) ***(P-26445)***
Valley Med Ctr Billing Dept, San Jose *Also called Santa Clara County of* ***(P-25673)***
Valley Medical Group of Lompoc..........D.......805 736-1253
136 N 3rd St Lompoc (93436) ***(P-19542)***
Valley Medical Oncology (PA)..........D.......925 734-8130
5725 W Las Psts Blvd # 100 Pleasanton (94588) ***(P-21353)***
Valley Medical Trnsp LLC..........D.......760 501-8929
43612 Jackson St Ste 4 Indio (92201) ***(P-3734)***
Valley Milk LLC..........D.......209 410-6701
400 N Washington Rd Turlock (95380) ***(P-404)***
Valley Molding & Frame, North Hollywood *Also called Valley Wholesale Supply Corp* ***(P-6596)***
Valley Moon Fre Prtct Dist..........D.......707 996-2102
630 2nd St W Sonoma (95476) ***(P-17144)***
Valley Mtn Regional Ctr Inc (PA)..........C.......209 473-0951
702 N Aurora St Stockton (95202) ***(P-23523)***
Valley Mtn Regional Ctr Inc..........D.......209 529-2626
1620 Cummins Dr Modesto (95358) ***(P-24100)***
Valley Northamerican, Concord *Also called Valley Relocation and Storage* ***(P-4240)***
Valley Nurses..........D.......714 549-2512
1450 W 9th St Pomona (91766) ***(P-19701)***
Valley Oak Dental Group..........D.......209 823-9341
1507 W Yosemite Ave Manteca (95337) ***(P-19636)***
VALLEY OASIS SHELTER, Lancaster *Also called Antelope Vly Dom Vlnce Council* ***(P-22917)***
Valley Ob Gyn Medical Group..........E.......909 580-6333
400 N Pepper Ave Fl 6 Colton (92324) ***(P-19543)***
Valley of California, Inc., Concord *Also called Coldwell Bnkr Residential Brkg* ***(P-11045)***
Valley of Sun Cosmetics LLC..........C.......310 327-9062
535 Patrice Pl Gardena (90248) ***(P-7988)***
Valley of The Sun Labs, Gardena *Also called Valley of Sun Cosmetics LLC* ***(P-7988)***
Valley Pacific Concrete Inc..........C.......951 672-6151
27580 Tabb Ln Menifee (92584) ***(P-3235)***
Valley Pacific Petro Svcs Inc..........C.......661 746-7737
9521 Enos Ln Bakersfield (93314) ***(P-8739)***
Valley Palms Convalescent Hosp, North Hollywood *Also called Trinity Health Systems* ***(P-20702)***
Valley Peterbilt, Stockton *Also called Interstate Truck Center LLC* ***(P-6402)***
Valley Physical Theraphy, Escondido *Also called Physical Therapy Hand Ctrs Inc* ***(P-19685)***
Valley Physicians Alliance LLC..........D.......559 538-3000
9300 Valley Childrens Pl Madera (93636) ***(P-26446)***
Valley Pinte Nursing Rehab Ctr..........E.......510 538-8464
20090 Stanton Ave Castro Valley (94546) ***(P-24101)***
Valley Power System, City of Industry *Also called Valley Management Services* ***(P-26445)***
Valley Power Systems Inc..........E.......661 325-9001
4000 Rosedale Hwy Bakersfield (93308) ***(P-7606)***
Valley Presbyterian Hospital..........A.......818 782-6600
15107 Vanowen St Van Nuys (91405) ***(P-21354)***
Valley Pride Inc..........D.......760 398-1353
86120 Tyler Ln Coachella (92236) ***(P-461)***
Valley Pride Inc (PA)..........B.......831 633-5883
10855 Ocean Mist Pkwy D Castroville (95012) ***(P-648)***
Valley Process Systems Inc..........D.......408 261-1277
3567 Benton St Ste 341 Santa Clara (95051) ***(P-2310)***
Valley Properties Inc..........D.......818 360-3430
10324 Balboa Blvd Lbby Granada Hills (91344) ***(P-10668)***
Valley Radiology Consultants (PA)..........D.......619 797-8248
6185 Paseo Del Norte # 110 Carlsbad (92011) ***(P-21598)***
Valley Relocation and Storage (PA)..........C.......925 230-2025
5000 Marsh Dr Concord (94520) ***(P-4240)***
Valley Republic Bank..........D.......661 371-2000
5000 California Ave # 110 Bakersfield (93309) ***(P-9246)***
Valley Rsrce Ctr For Retarded..........D.......951 766-8659
1285 N Santa Fe St Hemet (92543) ***(P-24238)***
Valley Rubber & Gasket, Sacramento *Also called Lewis-Goetz and Company Inc* ***(P-7639)***
Valley Sheet Metal Co, Marysville *Also called Frank M Booth Inc* ***(P-25083)***
Valley Skilled Nursing Care, Sacramento *Also called V S N F Inc* ***(P-20343)***
Valley Stre Frnt Jwsh Fmly Svc, North Hollywood *Also called Jewish Family Svc Los Angeles* ***(P-23296)***
Valley Sun Mechanical Cnstr..........D.......661 321-9070
4205 Atlas Ct Bakersfield (93308) ***(P-3485)***
Valley Sweet LLC..........D.......559 686-3381
222 N Garden St Ste 400 Visalia (93291) ***(P-4359)***
Valley Teen Ranch..........D.......559 437-1144
2610 W Shaw Ln Ste 105 Fresno (93711) ***(P-24102)***
Valley Toxicology Service Inc..........D.......916 371-5440
2401 Port St West Sacramento (95691) ***(P-21599)***
Valley Unique Electric Inc..........D.......559 237-4795
75 Park Creek Dr Ste 101 Clovis (93611) ***(P-2683)***
Valley US Inc..........D.......408 260-7342
888 Saratoga Ave Ste 201 San Jose (95129) ***(P-16149)***
Valley View Care Center, Riverbank *Also called Valley West Health Care Inc* ***(P-20349)***
Valley View Casino, Valley Center *Also called San Psqual Band Mssion Indians* ***(P-12879)***
Valley View Casino, Valley Center *Also called San Psqual Csino Dev Group Inc* ***(P-12880)***
Valley View Skilled Nursing, Ukiah *Also called Horizon West Healthcare Inc* ***(P-20023)***
Valley View Sklled Nursing Ctr..........D.......707 462-1436
1162 S Dora St Ukiah (95482) ***(P-20347)***
VALLEY VILLAGE, Santa Clara *Also called Church of Vly Rtrment Hmes Inc* ***(P-23866)***
Valley Village (PA)..........D.......818 587-9450
20830 Sherman Way Winnetka (91306) ***(P-24103)***
Valley Vista Nursing and Trans..........C.......818 763-6275
6120 Vineland Ave North Hollywood (91606) ***(P-20348)***
Valley Water Proofing Inc..........D.......408 985-7701
825 Civic Center Dr Ste 6 Santa Clara (95050) ***(P-3486)***
Valley West Care Center, Williams *Also called Valley West Health Care Inc* ***(P-20713)***
Valley West Health Care Inc (PA)..........D.......530 473-5321
1224 E St Williams (95987) ***(P-20713)***
Valley West Health Care Inc..........D.......209 869-2569
2649 Topeka St Riverbank (95367) ***(P-20349)***
Valley Wholesale Drug Co LLC..........D.......209 466-0131
1401 W Fremont St Stockton (95203) ***(P-7989)***
Valley Wholesale Supply Corp (PA)..........D.......818 769-5656
10708 Vanowen St North Hollywood (91605) ***(P-6596)***

Employee Codes: A=Over 500 employees, B=251-500
C=101-250, D=51-100, E=50
2020 Directory of California
Wholesalers and Services Companies
© Mergent Inc. 1-800-342-5647
1473

Valley Wide Beverage Company, Fresno *Also called Fresno Beverage Company Inc* ***(P-8762)***
Valley Wide Recreation Pk Dst (PA) ....D....951 654-1505
901 W Esplanade Ave San Jacinto (92582) ***(P-18778)***
Valley-HI Country Club ....E....916 684-2120
9595 Franklin Blvd Elk Grove (95758) ***(P-18602)***
Valleycare Health, Livermore *Also called Valleycare Hospital Corp* ***(P-19544)***
VALLEYCARE HEALTH SYSTEM, Livermore *Also called Hospital Cmmttee For The Lvrmr* ***(P-26257)***
Valleycare Hospital Corp (HQ) ....D....925 447-7000
1111 E Stanley Blvd Livermore (94550) ***(P-19544)***
Valleycrest Ldscp Maint Vcc ....E....800 466-8510
24121 Ventura Blvd Calabasas (91302) ***(P-769)***
Valleywide Construction Inc ....C....559 834-6212
284 W Lester Ave Clovis (93619) ***(P-1214)***
Valori Sand & Gravel Company (PA) ....D....714 637-0104
141 W Taft Ave Orange (92865) ***(P-6701)***
Valori Sand & Gravel Company ....C....909 350-3000
11027 Cherry Ave Fontana (92337) ***(P-6702)***
Vals Plumbing and Heating Inc ....D....831 424-1633
413 Front St Salinas (93901) ***(P-2311)***
Valtox Laboratories, West Sacramento *Also called Valley Toxicology Service Inc* ***(P-21599)***
Valuation Concepts LLC ....D....818 812-6233
16350 Ventura Blvd D140 Encino (91436) ***(P-11498)***
Value Options-V B H, Cypress *Also called Valueoptions of California* ***(P-10539)***
Value-Centered Solutions Inc ....E....925 332-0555
2300 Stanwell Dr Ste A Concord (94520) ***(P-26860)***
Valueoptions of California ....C....800 228-1286
5665 Plaza Dr Ste 400 Cypress (90630) ***(P-10539)***
Valverde Construction Inc ....D....562 906-1826
10936 Shoemaker Ave Santa Fe Springs (90670) ***(P-1926)***
Valvoline Instant Oil Change, Santa Fe Springs *Also called Valvoline International Inc* ***(P-17433)***
Valvoline International Inc ....E....562 906-6200
9520 John St Santa Fe Springs (90670) ***(P-17433)***
Valyria LLC (HQ) ....D....707 452-0600
1050 Aviator Dr Vacaville (95688) ***(P-6597)***
Van Acker Cnstr Assoc Inc ....C....415 383-5589
1060 Redwood Hwy Frntg Rd Mill Valley (94941) ***(P-1215)***
Van Beurden Insurance Svcs Inc (PA) ....D....559 634-7125
1600 Draper St Kingsburg (93631) ***(P-10540)***
Van Daele Development Corp ....C....951 354-6800
2900 Adams St Ste C25 Riverside (92504) ***(P-1320)***
Van Daele Homes, Riverside *Also called Van Daele Development Corp* ***(P-1320)***
Van De Pol Enterprises Inc (PA) ....D....209 465-3421
4895 S Airport Way Stockton (95206) ***(P-8740)***
Van Dyk Tank Lines Inc ....E....951 682-5000
1800 S Riverside Ave Colton (92324) ***(P-3952)***
Van Etten Suzumoto Becket LLP ....D....310 315-8284
1620 26th St Ste 6000n Santa Monica (90404) ***(P-26861)***
Van Groningen & Sons Inc ....B....209 982-5248
15100 Jack Tone Rd Manteca (95336) ***(P-368)***
Van Grow Jack S MD ....E....714 564-3300
1140 W La Veta Ave # 640 Orange (92868) ***(P-19545)***
Van Horn Youth Center, Riverside *Also called County of Riverside* ***(P-23137)***
Van Inn II Inc (PA) ....D....510 548-6600
25 Avenida De Orinda Orinda (94563) ***(P-20350)***
Van King & Storage Inc ....D....562 921-0555
13535 Larwin Cir Santa Fe Springs (90670) ***(P-4162)***
Van Ness Hotel Inc ....D....415 673-4711
1050 Van Ness Ave San Francisco (94109) ***(P-13060)***
Van Nuys Airport, Van Nuys *Also called City of Los Angeles* ***(P-4759)***
Van Nuys Care Center Inc ....D....818 343-0700
16955 Vanowen St Van Nuys (91406) ***(P-20714)***
Van Nuys Community Hospital, Van Nuys *Also called Alta Healthcare System LLC* ***(P-24124)***
Van Nuys Health Care Center, Van Nuys *Also called Five Star Qulty Care-CA II LLC* ***(P-19918)***
Van Sark Inc ....D....415 362-5888
1255 Battery St Ste 200 San Francisco (94111) ***(P-6533)***
Van Torrance & Storage Company (PA) ....D....562 567-2100
12128 Burke St Santa Fe Springs (90670) ***(P-4241)***
Vanalden Ave School, Reseda *Also called West Valley Family YMCA* ***(P-23802)***
Vance Corporation ....E....909 355-4333
17761 Slover Ave Bloomington (92316) ***(P-1807)***
Vancrest Construction Corp ....E....323 256-0011
7171 N Figueroa St Los Angeles (90042) ***(P-1639)***
Vander Weerd General Cnstr ....D....559 688-1099
837 Commercial Ave Tulare (93274) ***(P-3334)***
Vandorpe Chou Associates Inc ....E....714 978-9780
1845 W Orangewood Ave # 210 Orange (92868) ***(P-25378)***
Vangard Concept Offices, San Jose *Also called Business Furn Solutions Inc* ***(P-6508)***
Vanguard Legato, San Leandro *Also called Vanguard Legato A Cal Corp* ***(P-6534)***
Vanguard Legato A Cal Corp ....D....510 351-3333
2121 Williams St San Leandro (94577) ***(P-6534)***
Vanguard Lgistics Svcs USA Inc (HQ) ....D....310 637-3700
2665 E Del Amo Blvd E Rncho Dmngz (90221) ***(P-4532)***
Vanguard Lgistics Svcs USA Inc (HQ) ....D....310 847-3000
5000 Arprt Plz Dr Ste 200 Long Beach (90815) ***(P-5081)***
Vanguard Lgistics Svcs USA Inc ....D....310 637-3700
2665 E Del Amo Blvd Compton (90221) ***(P-4533)***
Vanguard Resources Corp ....D....858 336-7147
13816 Fontanelle Pl San Diego (92128) ***(P-26958)***
Vanir Construction MGT Inc (PA) ....D....916 444-3700
4540 Duckhorn Dr Ste 300 Sacramento (95834) ***(P-26447)***
Vanpike Inc (PA) ....D....858 453-1331
6336 Greenwich Dr Ste 100 San Diego (92122) ***(P-14581)***
Vantage Company, Orange *Also called W Corporation* ***(P-27254)***
Vantage Oncology LLC (HQ) ....B....310 335-4000
1500 Rosecrans Ave # 400 Manhattan Beach (90266) ***(P-19546)***
Vantage Oncology Inc ....D....310 335-4000
1500 Rosecrans Ave # 400 Manhattan Beach (90266) ***(P-19547)***
Vantage Plaster & Drywall ....D....760 345-3622
79607 Country Club Dr Bermuda Dunes (92203) ***(P-2873)***
Vantagepoint Capital Partners, San Bruno *Also called Vantagepoint Management Inc* ***(P-11966)***
Vantagepoint Capital Partners (PA) ....D....650 866-3100
1111 Bayhill Dr Ste 220 San Bruno (94066) ***(P-11965)***
Vantagepoint Management Inc (PA) ....D....650 866-3100
1111 Bayhill Dr Ste 220 San Bruno (94066) ***(P-11966)***
Vantagepoint Venture Partners ....D....650 866-3100
1001 Bayhill Dr Ste 300 San Bruno (94066) ***(P-11744)***
Vaquero Energy Incorporated ....E....661 363-7240
15545 Hermosa Rd Bakersfield (93307) ***(P-992)***
Vaquero Farms Inc (PA) ....D....209 476-0002
24591 Silver Cloud Ct # 100 Monterey (93940) ***(P-84)***
Vaquero Farms Inc ....D....559 659-2790
43405 W Panoche Rd Firebaugh (93622) ***(P-369)***
Variations In Stone Inc ....D....949 438-8337
360 La Perle Pl Costa Mesa (92627) ***(P-2731)***
Varis LLC ....D....916 294-0860
3915 Security Park Dr B Rancho Cordova (95742) ***(P-26862)***
Varis LLC (PA) ....C....916 294-0860
9245 Sierra College Blvd Roseville (95661) ***(P-26863)***
Varner Family Ltd Partnership (PA) ....D....661 399-1163
5900 E Lerdo Hwy Shafter (93263) ***(P-11821)***
Varsity Contractors Inc ....D....949 586-8283
24155 Laguna Hills Mall Laguna Hills (92653) ***(P-14080)***
Vasindas Around The Clock Care ....E....661 395-5820
5251 Office Park Dr # 403 Bakersfield (93309) ***(P-24104)***
Vasko Electric Inc ....D....916 568-7700
4300 Astoria St Sacramento (95838) ***(P-2684)***
Vasona Management Inc ....B....510 352-8728
13949 Doolittle Dr San Leandro (94577) ***(P-10833)***
Vasona Management Inc ....D....510 413-0091
37390 Central Mont Pl Fremont (94538) ***(P-1216)***
Vasonic Construction, Fremont *Also called Vasona Management Inc* ***(P-1216)***
Vasquez Brothers Inc ....D....831 678-8894
157 Kidder St Soledad (93960) ***(P-557)***
Vastek Inc ....C....925 948-5701
1230 Columbia St Ste 1180 San Diego (92101) ***(P-17145)***
Vasto Valle Farms, Huron *Also called Dick Anderson & Sons Farming* ***(P-313)***
Vat Incorporated (HQ) ....E....781 935-1446
655 River Oaks Pkwy San Jose (95134) ***(P-7661)***
Vauche Bank Berkshire Mortgage, Irvine *Also called Berkshire Mortgage Fin Corp* ***(P-9528)***
Vaughn Weedman Inc (PA) ....C....425 481-0919
550 S Hope St Ste 1675 Los Angeles (90071) ***(P-922)***
Vaxaville Medical Offices, Vacaville *Also called Kaiser Foundation Hospitals* ***(P-9973)***
Vaya, San Diego *Also called Vietnms-Mrcan Yuth Alance Corp* ***(P-24692)***
Vayan Marketing Group LLC ....E....310 943-4990
10877 Wilshire Blvd Fl 12 Los Angeles (90024) ***(P-26864)***
Vb Golf LLC ....D....650 573-7888
2401 E 3rd Ave Foster City (94404) ***(P-18310)***
Vbp Orange, San Francisco *Also called Venables/Bell & Partners LLC* ***(P-13593)***
VCA Animal Hospitals Inc ....E....650 631-7400
501 Laurel St San Carlos (94070) ***(P-587)***
VCA Animal Hospitals Inc ....D....760 431-2273
2310 Faraday Ave Carlsbad (92008) ***(P-588)***
VCA Animal Hospitals Inc (HQ) ....C....310 571-6500
12401 W Olympic Blvd Los Angeles (90064) ***(P-589)***
VCA Antech Inc ....B....310 207-0781
12401 W Olympic Blvd Los Angeles (90064) ***(P-590)***
VCA Clfrnia Vtrnary Spcialists, Carlsbad *Also called VCA Animal Hospitals Inc* ***(P-588)***
VCA Code Group ....E....714 363-4700
1845 W Orangewood Ave # 210 Orange (92868) ***(P-25379)***
VCA Desert Animal Hospitals ....D....760 778-9999
4299 E Ramon Rd Palm Springs (92264) ***(P-591)***
VCA Engineering, Orange *Also called Vandorpe Chou Associates Inc* ***(P-25378)***
VCA Holly Street, San Carlos *Also called VCA Animal Hospitals Inc* ***(P-587)***
VCA Inc ....D....310 473-2951
1818 S Sepulveda Blvd Los Angeles (90025) ***(P-592)***
VCA Inc ....D....530 224-2200
2505 Hilltop Dr Redding (96002) ***(P-593)***
VCA TLC Animal Hospital, Los Angeles *Also called VCA Animal Hospitals Inc* ***(P-589)***
VCA-Asher Animal Hospital, Redding *Also called VCA Inc* ***(P-593)***
Vcall, Beverly Hills *Also called Mediaplatform Inc* ***(P-17632)***
Vci Construction LLC (HQ) ....D....909 946-0905
1921 W 11th St Ste A Upland (91786) ***(P-1927)***
Vci Event Technology Inc ....C....714 772-2002
1261 S Simpson Cir Anaheim (92806) ***(P-14208)***
Vcomply Technologies Inc ....D....650 319-8842
808 N Hampton Dr Palo Alto (94303) ***(P-15177)***
Veatch Carlson Grogan & Nelson ....E....213 381-2861
1055 Wilshire Blvd Fl 11 Los Angeles (90017) ***(P-22857)***
Veba Administrators Inc ....E....310 577-1444
4640 Admiralty Way Fl 9 Marina Del Rey (90292) ***(P-10541)***
Vector Resources Inc (PA) ....C....310 436-1000
20917 Higgins Ct Torrance (90501) ***(P-2685)***
Vector Resources Inc ....E....858 546-1014
9808 Waples St San Diego (92121) ***(P-25380)***
Vector Security Inc ....D....323 224-6700
5411 Valley Blvd Los Angeles (90032) ***(P-2686)***
Vector Talent II LLC ....A....415 293-5000
1 Market St Ste 2300 San Francisco (94105) ***(P-11763)***
Vector USA, San Diego *Also called Vector Resources Inc* ***(P-25380)***
Vectorusa, Torrance *Also called Vector Resources Inc* ***(P-2685)***

Mergent e-mail: customerrelations@mergent.com
1474
2020 Directory of California
Wholesalers and Services Companies
(P-0000) Products & Services Section entry number
(PA)=Parent Co (HQ)=Headquarters (DH)=Div Headquarters

Veeva Systems Inc (PA)..........C.......925 452-6500
4280 Hacienda Dr Pleasanton (94588) ***(P-15530)***
Veg-Fresh Farms LLC..........C.......800 422-5535
1400 W Rincon St Corona (92880) ***(P-8535)***
Veg-Land Inc..........E.......714 871-6712
1518 E Valencia Dr Fullerton (92831) ***(P-4335)***
Vegatek Corporation..........D.......949 502-0090
470 Wald Ste 100 Irvine (92618) ***(P-15178)***
Vegetable Growers Supply Co (PA)..........E.......831 759-4600
1360 Merrill St Salinas (93901) ***(P-9018)***
Vegiworks Inc..........D.......415 643-8686
2101 Jerrold Ave San Francisco (94124) ***(P-8536)***
Vehicle Accessory Center LLC..........D.......909 987-8237
10863 Jersey Blvd # 101 Rancho Cucamonga (91730) ***(P-6477)***
Velapoint LLC..........D.......877 434-1904
16802 Aston Irvine (92606) ***(P-10542)***
Velazquez Packing Inc..........D.......805 735-6477
124 N I St Lompoc (93436) ***(P-649)***
Veldhuis Dairy, Winton *Also called P H Ranch Inc* ***(P-403)***
Velocious Technologies Inc..........D.......650 434-7118
6520 N Irwindale Ave A Irwindale (91702) ***(P-15179)***
Velocitel Rf Inc..........C.......949 809-4999
2415 Campus Dr Ste 200 Irvine (92612) ***(P-25381)***
Velocity Commercial Capitl LLC..........E.......818 532-3700
30699 Russell Ranch Rd Westlake Village (91362) ***(P-11499)***
Velocity Tech Solutions Inc..........D.......949 417-0260
111 Pacifica Ste 320 Irvine (92618) ***(P-15832)***
Venables/Bell & Partners LLC..........C.......415 288-3300
201 Post St Fl 2 San Francisco (94108) ***(P-13593)***
Venco Western Inc (PA)..........C.......805 981-2400
2400 Eastman Ave Oxnard (93030) ***(P-923)***
Vendini Inc (PA)..........D.......415 693-9611
55 Francisco St Ste 350 San Francisco (94133) ***(P-15180)***
Vendor Direct Solutions LLC..........C.......213 362-5622
515 S Figueroa St # 1900 Los Angeles (90071) ***(P-26448)***
Venegas Farming LLC..........E.......805 529-5038
8002 Balcom Canyon Rd Somis (93066) ***(P-650)***
Vengroff Williams & Assoc Inc..........C.......714 889-6200
2099 S State College Blvd # 300 Anaheim (92806) ***(P-13704)***
Venice Family Clinic (PA)..........D.......310 664-7703
604 Rose Ave Venice (90291) ***(P-19548)***
Venida Packing Company..........C.......559 592-2816
19823 Avenue 300 Exeter (93221) ***(P-5102)***
Ventage Senior Housing..........E.......949 631-3555
4000 Hilaria Way Newport Beach (92663) ***(P-10834)***
Ventana Inn & Spa, Big Sur *Also called 48123 CA Investors LLC* ***(P-11982)***
Ventrum LLC..........D.......510 304-0852
2033 Gateway Pl Ste 500 San Jose (95110) ***(P-16150)***
Ventu Park LLC..........D.......805 716-4200
495 N Ventu Park Rd Thousand Oaks (91320) ***(P-13061)***
Ventura Beach Marriott Hotel, Ventura *Also called Kingledon Inc* ***(P-12514)***
Ventura Cnty Council On Aging..........D.......805 986-1424
4917 S Rose Ave Oxnard (93033) ***(P-23524)***
Ventura Cnty Human Srvce, Oxnard *Also called County of Ventura* ***(P-23716)***
Ventura County Credit Union (PA)..........D.......805 477-4000
2575 Vista Del Mar Dr Ventura (93001) ***(P-9377)***
Ventura County Fire Department..........E.......805 389-9710
165 Durley Ave Camarillo (93010) ***(P-24686)***
Ventura County Hematology (PA)..........E.......805 485-8709
1700 N Rose Ave Ste 320 Oxnard (93030) ***(P-19549)***
Ventura County Lemon Coops..........D.......805 385-3345
P.O. Box 6986 Oxnard (93031) ***(P-558)***
Ventura County Medical Center..........D.......805 933-8600
845 N 10th St Ste 3 Santa Paula (93060) ***(P-19550)***
Ventura County Medical Center (PA)..........C.......805 652-6000
3291 Loma Vista Rd Ventura (93003) ***(P-19551)***
Ventura County Medical Center..........D.......805 652-6201
3291 Loma Vista Rd # 343 Ventura (93003) ***(P-19552)***
Ventura County Office Educatn..........D.......805 495-7037
1379 Oakridge Ct Thousand Oaks (91362) ***(P-24687)***
Ventura Family YMCA, Ventura *Also called Channel Islands Young Mens Ch* ***(P-24518)***
Ventura Hsptality Partners LLC..........C.......805 648-2100
450 Harbor Blvd Ventura (93001) ***(P-13062)***
Ventura Medical Management LLC..........B.......805 477-6220
2601 E Main St Ventura (93003) ***(P-26449)***
Ventura Pacific Co, Ventura *Also called Ventura County Lemon Coops* ***(P-558)***
Ventura Streets Dept..........D.......805 652-4515
336 San Jon Rd Ventura (93001) ***(P-1217)***
Ventura Transfer Company (PA)..........D.......310 549-1660
2418 E 223rd St Long Beach (90810) ***(P-4163)***
Ventura Yuth Crrctional Fcilty, Camarillo *Also called Juvenile Justice Division Cal* ***(P-26278)***
Venture Design Services Inc..........D.......707 524-8368
451 Aviation Blvd Ste 215 Santa Rosa (95403) ***(P-17146)***
Venture Lath and Plaster, North Highlands *Also called Rick H Hitch Plastering Inc* ***(P-2851)***
Venture Pacific Tools Inc..........D.......949 475-5505
17152 Daimler St Irvine (92614) ***(P-7410)***
Venus Group Inc..........D.......949 609-1299
25861 Wright Foothill Ranch (92610) ***(P-6598)***
Venus Textiles, Foothill Ranch *Also called Venus Group Inc* ***(P-6598)***
Ver Sales Inc (PA)..........D.......818 567-3000
2509 N Naomi St Burbank (91504) ***(P-7112)***
Veracyte Inc..........C.......650 243-6300
6000 Shoreline Ct Ste 300 South San Francisco (94080) ***(P-21600)***
Verance Corporation..........D.......858 202-2800
10089 Willow Creek Rd San Diego (92131) ***(P-25953)***
Verasa Management LLC..........D.......707 257-1800
1314 Mckinstry St NAPA (94559) ***(P-13063)***
Verdugo Hills Medical Assoc, Glendale *Also called Verdugo Hills Urgent Care Mg* ***(P-19553)***
Verdugo Hills Urgent Care Mg..........D.......818 241-4331
544 N Glendale Ave Glendale (91206) ***(P-19553)***
Verdugo Mental Health..........D.......818 244-7257
1540 E Colorado St Glendale (91205) ***(P-22154)***
Verdugo Vista Healthcare Ctr, La Crescenta *Also called Mariner Health Care Inc* ***(P-20123)***
Verdugo Vly Convalescent Hosp, Montrose *Also called Great Wstn Cnvlescent Hosp Inc* ***(P-20584)***
Veridiam Allied Swiss..........D.......760 941-1702
4645 North Ave Oceanside (92056) ***(P-27243)***
Verifi Inc..........D.......323 655-5789
8391 Beverly Blvd Ste 310 Los Angeles (90048) ***(P-26865)***
Verifone Inc..........D.......916 408-4900
1401 Aviation Blvd Lincoln (95648) ***(P-4534)***
Verinata Health Inc..........D.......650 632-1680
200 Lincoln Centre Dr Foster City (94404) ***(P-25866)***
Verint, Santa Clara *Also called Kana Software Inc* ***(P-15375)***
Verint Americas Inc..........D.......408 830-5400
2250 Walsh Ave Ste 120 Santa Clara (95050) ***(P-15181)***
Veritable Vegetable Inc..........D.......415 641-3500
1100 Cesar Chavez San Francisco (94124) ***(P-8537)***
Veritas Health Services Inc..........A.......909 464-8600
5451 Walnut Ave Chino (91710) ***(P-21355)***
Veritas Media Group LLC..........E.......510 867-4699
1111 Broadway Ste 300 Oakland (94607) ***(P-26866)***
Veritas Technologies LLC (HQ)..........C.......866 837-4827
2625 Augustine Dr Santa Clara (95054) ***(P-15182)***
Veritas US Inc..........C.......650 933-1000
500 E Middlefield Rd Mountain View (94043) ***(P-15183)***
Veritiv Operating Company..........C.......925 245-6075
7337 Las Positas Rd Livermore (94551) ***(P-7607)***
Veritiv Operating Company..........D.......559 268-0467
4395 S Minnewawa Ave # 101 Fresno (93725) ***(P-7905)***
Veritiv Operating Company..........D.......714 690-4000
15005 Northam St La Mirada (90638) ***(P-7906)***
Veritiv Operating Company..........D.......916 283-2160
1701 National Dr Ste 110 Sacramento (95834) ***(P-7907)***
Veritiv Operating Company..........D.......415 586-9160
345 Schwerin St San Francisco (94134) ***(P-7908)***
Veritiv Operating Company..........C.......310 527-3000
13217 S Figueroa St Los Angeles (90061) ***(P-7909)***
Veritiv Operating Company..........C.......323 725-3700
2600 Commerce Way Commerce (90040) ***(P-7910)***
Veritiv Operating Company..........B.......714 690-6600
20 Centerpointe Dr # 130 La Palma (90623) ***(P-7911)***
Veritone Inc (PA)..........D.......888 507-1737
575 Anton Blvd Ste 900 Costa Mesa (92626) ***(P-15833)***
Veritxt/Clfornia Reporting LLC..........E.......714 432-1711
20 Corporate Park Irvine (92606) ***(P-13806)***
Verity Health System Cal Inc..........B.......310 900-8900
203 Redwood Shores Pkwy Redwood City (94065) ***(P-21356)***
Verity Health System Cal Inc..........C.......408 947-2500
2105 Forest Ave San Jose (95128) ***(P-21357)***
Verity Health System Cal Inc..........C.......650 551-6507
203 Redwood Shores Pkwy # 700 Redwood City (94065) ***(P-21358)***
Verity Health System Cal Inc..........C.......408 848-2000
9400 N Name Uno Gilroy (95020) ***(P-21359)***
Verity Health System Cal Inc..........D.......310 900-2000
3680 E Imperial Hwy # 306 Lynwood (90262) ***(P-21360)***
Verity Health System Cal Inc..........A.......310 900-8900
3630 E Imperial Hwy Lynwood (90262) ***(P-21361)***
Verity Medical Foundation (HQ)..........D.......408 278-3000
400 Race St San Jose (95126) ***(P-19554)***
Verizon, Indio *Also called Frontier California Inc* ***(P-5402)***
Verizon, Costa Mesa *Also called Cellco Partnership* ***(P-5207)***
Verizon, Roseville *Also called Cellco Partnership* ***(P-5209)***
Verizon, Santa Maria *Also called Frontier California Inc* ***(P-5403)***
Verizon, Irvine *Also called Cellco Partnership* ***(P-5210)***
Verizon, Bakersfield *Also called Cellco Partnership* ***(P-5211)***
Verizon, Carlsbad *Also called Cellco Partnership* ***(P-5212)***
Verizon, Cerritos *Also called Cellco Partnership* ***(P-5213)***
Verizon, Corona *Also called Cellco Partnership* ***(P-5214)***
Verizon, San Fernando *Also called Frontier California Inc* ***(P-5404)***
Verizon, Manteca *Also called Frontier California Inc* ***(P-5405)***
Verizon, San Francisco *Also called Cellco Partnership* ***(P-5243)***
Verizon, Westlake Village *Also called Frontier California Inc* ***(P-5406)***
Verizon, Exeter *Also called Frontier California Inc* ***(P-5407)***
Verizon, San Luis Obispo *Also called Cellco Partnership* ***(P-5248)***
Verizon, Fresno *Also called Frontier California Inc* ***(P-5259)***
Verizon Bus Netwrk Svcs Inc..........C.......916 779-5600
11080 White Rock Rd # 100 Rancho Cordova (95670) ***(P-5488)***
Verizon Bus Netwrk Svcs Inc..........C.......916 569-5999
1740 Creekside Oaks 200 Sacramento (95833) ***(P-5489)***
Verizon Bus Netwrk Svcs Inc..........D.......510 497-2500
4340 Solar Way Fremont (94538) ***(P-15906)***
Verizon Business, Los Angeles *Also called MCI Communications Svcs Inc* ***(P-5435)***
Verizon Communications Inc..........C.......805 390-5417
2801 Townsgate Rd Ste 300 Westlake Village (91361) ***(P-17147)***
Verizon Communications Inc..........B.......310 319-6148
2943 Exposition Blvd Santa Monica (90404) ***(P-5490)***
Verizon Connect Nwf Inc..........D.......858 450-3245
9868 Scranton Rd Ste 1000 San Diego (92121) ***(P-15184)***
Verizon Connect Telo Inc (HQ)..........C.......949 389-5500
20 Enterprise Ste 100 Aliso Viejo (92656) ***(P-15834)***
Verizon Digital Media Svcs Inc (HQ)..........C.......310 396-7400
13031 W Jefferson Blvd # 900 Los Angeles (90094) ***(P-16151)***
Verizon Network Integration..........C.......562 903-7953
12905 Los Nietos Rd Santa Fe Springs (90670) ***(P-5491)***

Verizon Wireless, Beaumont *Also called Cellco Partnership* **(P-5200)**
Verizon Wireless, Monterey *Also called Cellco Partnership* **(P-5201)**
Verizon Wireless, Orange *Also called Cellco Partnership* **(P-5202)**
Verizon Wireless, Brentwood *Also called Cellco Partnership* **(P-5203)**
Verizon Wireless, Riverside *Also called Cellco Partnership* **(P-5204)**
Verizon Wireless, Fresno *Also called Cellco Partnership* **(P-5206)**
Verizon Wireless, Eastvale *Also called Cellco Partnership* **(P-5208)**
Verizon Wireless, Fremont *Also called Cellco Partnership* **(P-5215)**
Verizon Wireless, Burbank *Also called Cellco Partnership* **(P-5219)**
Verizon Wireless, Milpitas *Also called Cellco Partnership* **(P-5220)**
Verizon Wireless, San Francisco *Also called Cellco Partnership* **(P-5221)**
Verizon Wireless, Oakland *Also called Cellco Partnership* **(P-5223)**
Verizon Wireless, Los Angeles *Also called Cellco Partnership* **(P-5224)**
Verizon Wireless, Downey *Also called Cellco Partnership* **(P-5225)**
Verizon Wireless, Clovis *Also called Cellco Partnership* **(P-5226)**
Verizon Wireless, Palmdale *Also called Cellco Partnership* **(P-5227)**
Verizon Wireless, Huntington Beach *Also called Cellco Partnership* **(P-5228)**
Verizon Wireless, Los Angeles *Also called Cellco Partnership* **(P-5229)**
Verizon Wireless, Modesto *Also called Cellco Partnership* **(P-5230)**
Verizon Wireless, Los Angeles *Also called Cellco Partnership* **(P-5231)**
Verizon Wireless, Carson *Also called Cellco Partnership* **(P-5232)**
Verizon Wireless, Hollywood *Also called Cellco Partnership* **(P-5233)**
Verizon Wireless, San Francisco *Also called Cellco Partnership* **(P-5234)**
Verizon Wireless, Union City *Also called Cellco Partnership* **(P-5235)**
Verizon Wireless, Valencia *Also called Cellco Partnership* **(P-5236)**
Verizon Wireless, Cypress *Also called Cellco Partnership* **(P-5237)**
Verizon Wireless, El Centro *Also called Cellco Partnership* **(P-5238)**
Verizon Wireless, Simi Valley *Also called Cellco Partnership* **(P-5239)**
Verizon Wireless, Santa Cruz *Also called Cellco Partnership* **(P-5240)**
Verizon Wireless, San Bernardino *Also called Cellco Partnership* **(P-5241)**
Verizon Wireless, Citrus Heights *Also called Cellco Partnership* **(P-5242)**
Verizon Wireless, Santa Barbara *Also called Cellco Partnership* **(P-5244)**
Verizon Wireless, Santa Rosa *Also called Cellco Partnership* **(P-5245)**
Verizon Wireless, Palo Alto *Also called Cellco Partnership* **(P-5247)**
Verizon Wireless, Irvine *Also called 4g Wireless Inc* **(P-5148)**
Verizon Wireless, Santa Ana *Also called Cellco Partnership* **(P-5249)**
Verizon Wireless, Commerce *Also called Cellco Partnership* **(P-5250)**
Verizon Wireless (PA) ....E......949 286-7000
   15505 Sand Canyon Ave Irvine (92618) **(P-5281)**
Verizon Wireless Premium Ret, Carlsbad *Also called 4g Wireless Inc* **(P-5290)**
Verizon Wreless Authorized Ret, Bell *Also called 4g Wireless Inc* **(P-5285)**
Verizon Wireless Authorized Ret, Dublin *Also called 4g Wireless Inc* **(P-5286)**
Verizon Wireless Authorized Ret, Los Angeles *Also called 4g Wireless Inc* **(P-5287)**
Verizon Wireless Authorized Ret, Los Angeles *Also called 4g Wireless Inc* **(P-5288)**
Verizon Wireless Authorized Ret, Escondido *Also called 4g Wireless Inc* **(P-5289)**
Verizon Wireless Authorized Ret, Perris *Also called 4g Wireless Inc* **(P-5291)**
Verizon Wireless Authorized Ret, Redondo Beach *Also called 4g Wireless Inc* **(P-5292)**
Verizon Wireless Authorized Ret, Long Beach *Also called 4g Wireless Inc* **(P-5293)**
Vermeer Pacific, Sacramento *Also called Rdo Vermeer LLC* **(P-7490)**
Vermont Care Center, Torrance *Also called Geri-Care II Inc* **(P-20568)**
Vernon Autoparts Inc ....D......323 249-7545
   1559 W 134th St Gardena (90249) **(P-17358)**
Vernon Central Warehouse Inc ....C......323 234-2200
   2050 E 38th St Vernon (90058) **(P-4242)**
Vernon Security Inc ....D......562 790-8993
   15317 Parmnt Blvd Ste 201 Paramount (90723) **(P-16475)**
Vernon Transportation Company, Stockton *Also called John Aguilar & Company Inc* **(P-3900)**
Vernon Truck Wash Inc ....C......323 267-0706
   3308 Bandini Blvd Vernon (90058) **(P-17401)**
Vernon Warehouse Co, Vernon *Also called Vernon Central Warehouse Inc* **(P-4242)**
Veros Credit LLC (PA) ....D......714 415-6185
   2333 N Broadway Ste 400 Santa Ana (92706) **(P-9494)**
Versa Engineering & Tech Inc (PA) ....D......925 405-4505
   1320 Willow Pass Rd # 500 Concord (94520) **(P-25382)**
Versa Products Inc (PA) ....D......310 353-7100
   14105 Avalon Blvd Los Angeles (90061) **(P-6535)**
Versacheck, San Diego *Also called G7 Productivity Systems* **(P-15334)**
Versant Health, Rancho Cordova *Also called Superior Vision Services Inc* **(P-10057)**
Versatables.com, Los Angeles *Also called Versa Products Inc* **(P-6535)**
Vertex Coatings Inc ....D......909 923-5795
   1291 W State St Ontario (91762) **(P-2404)**
Vertex Phrmctcals San Dego LLC (HQ) ....B......858 404-6600
   3215 Merryfield Row San Diego (92121) **(P-25867)**
Vertical Search Works Inc ....D......212 967-9502
   1808 Aston Ave Ste 170 Carlsbad (92008) **(P-13594)**
Verticalresponse Inc ....C......866 683-7842
   550 Kearny St Ste 710 San Francisco (94108) **(P-26867)**
Vertisystem Inc ....C......510 794-8099
   39300 Civic Center Dr # 160 Fremont (94538) **(P-15709)**
Verve Music Group, Santa Monica *Also called Universal Music Group Inc* **(P-18017)**
Very Important Pet Vaccine Svc, Windsor *Also called Happy Pet Co* **(P-578)**
Vesta Luxury Home Staging, Vernon *Also called Showroom Interiors LLC* **(P-14197)**
Vestek Systems Inc (HQ) ....D......415 344-6000
   425 Market St Fl 6 San Francisco (94105) **(P-15892)**
Veterans Affairs Cal Dept ....C......530 224-3300
   3400 Knighton Rd Redding (96002) **(P-20351)**
Veterans Affairs Cal Dept ....B......916 653-2535
   1227 O St Ste 105 Sacramento (95814) **(P-27244)**
Veterans Affairs Testing Off, Sacramento *Also called Veterans Affairs Cal Dept* **(P-27244)**

Veterans EZ Info Inc ....C......866 839-1329
   1901 1st Ave Ste 192 San Diego (92101) **(P-27245)**
Veterans Health Administration ....B......858 552-7525
   3350 La Jolla Village Dr San Diego (92161) **(P-19637)**
Veterans Health Administration ....B......707 562-8200
   Walnut Ave Bldg 201 Vallejo (94589) **(P-19555)**
Veterans Health Administration ....A......310 478-3711
   11301 Wilshire Blvd Los Angeles (90073) **(P-19556)**
Veterans Health Administration ....A......559 225-6100
   2615 E Clinton Ave Fresno (93703) **(P-21362)**
Veterans Health Administration ....B......805 543-1233
   1288 Morro St Ste 200 San Luis Obispo (93401) **(P-19557)**
Veterans Health Administration ....B......916 366-5427
   10535 Hospital Way Mather (95655) **(P-19558)**
Veterans Health Administration ....A......559 225-6100
   2615 E Clinton Ave Fresno (93703) **(P-19559)**
Veterans Health Administration ....B......530 226-7555
   351 Hartnell Ave Redding (96002) **(P-19560)**
Veterans Health Administration ....A......650 493-5000
   3801 Miranda Ave Bldg 101 Palo Alto (94304) **(P-19561)**
Veterans Health Administration ....B......510 267-7820
   2221 Martin Luther King J Oakland (94612) **(P-19562)**
Veterans Health Administration ....D......415 750-2009
   4150 Clement St 6205 San Francisco (94121) **(P-19563)**
Veterans Health Administration ....B......530 879-5000
   280 Cohasset Rd Chico (95926) **(P-19564)**
Veterans Health Administration ....B......707 570-3800
   3315 Chanate Rd Santa Rosa (95404) **(P-19565)**
Veterans Health Administration ....B......619 409-1600
   835 Third Ave Chula Vista (91911) **(P-19566)**
Veterans Health Administration ....B......760 745-2000
   815 E Pennsylvania Ave Escondido (92025) **(P-19567)**
Veterans Health Administration ....B......805 983-6384
   250 Citrus Grove Ln # 250 Oxnard (93036) **(P-19568)**
Veterans Health Administration ....B......619 400-5000
   8810 Rio San Diego Dr San Diego (92108) **(P-19569)**
Veterans Health Administration ....A......818 891-7711
   16111 Plummer St North Hills (91343) **(P-19570)**
Veterans Health Administration ....B......916 843-7000
   10535 Hospital Way Mather (95655) **(P-19571)**
Veterans Health Administration ....B......925 447-2560
   4951 Arroyo Rd Livermore (94550) **(P-19572)**
Veterans Health Administration ....A......909 825-7084
   11201 Benton St Loma Linda (92357) **(P-19573)**
Veterans Health Administration ....A......650 614-9997
   795 Willow Rd Menlo Park (94025) **(P-19574)**
Veterans Health Administration ....D......818 895-9449
   16111 Plummer St North Hills (91343) **(P-19575)**
Veterans Health Administration ....C......714 780-5400
   1801 W Romneya Dr Ste 303 Anaheim (92801) **(P-19576)**
Veterans Health Administration ....E......661 632-1871
   1801 Westwind Dr Bakersfield (93301) **(P-19577)**
Veterans Health Administration ....C......213 253-2677
   351 E Temple St Los Angeles (90012) **(P-19578)**
Veterans Health Administration ....B......661 323-8387
   1110 Golden Valley Fwy Bakersfield (93301) **(P-19579)**
Veterans Home Cal - Fresno ....D......559 493-4400
   2811 W California Ave Fresno (93706) **(P-20352)**
Veterans Medical Research Fund ....C......858 642-3080
   3350 La Jolla Village Dr San Diego (92161) **(P-24688)**
Veterans Village of San Diego, San Diego *Also called Vietnam Veterans of San Diego* **(P-24691)**
Veterinary Centers America VCA, Los Angeles *Also called Vicar Operating Inc* **(P-596)**
Veterinary Pharmaceuticals Inc ....D......559 582-6800
   13159 Hanford Armona Rd Hanford (93230) **(P-7990)**
Veterinary Practice Assoc Inc ....C......949 833-9020
   10435 Sorrento Valley Rd San Diego (92121) **(P-22155)**
Veterinary Service Inc ....D......951 328-4900
   935 Palmyrita Ave Riverside (92507) **(P-7016)**
Veterinary Specialty Hospital, San Diego *Also called Veterinary Practice Assoc Inc* **(P-22155)**
Veterinary Surgical Associates ....D......650 696-8196
   251 N Amphlett Blvd San Mateo (94401) **(P-19580)**
Veterinary Surgical Associates (PA) ....C......925 827-1777
   1410 Monu Blvd Ste 100 Concord (94520) **(P-594)**
Veternary Med Srgcal Group Inc ....D......805 339-2290
   2199 Sperry Ave Ventura (93003) **(P-595)**
Vetronix Crpration/Bosch Group, Santa Barbara *Also called Vetronix Sales Corporation* **(P-6478)**
Vetronix Sales Corporation ....D......805 966-2000
   2030 Alameda Padre Serra Santa Barbara (93103) **(P-6478)**
Vexillum Inc ....C......916 218-3815
   10636 Industrial Ave Roseville (95678) **(P-5960)**
Vfs Fire Protection Services, Orange *Also called Bernel Inc* **(P-2073)**
VFW Post 6476 ....C......909 754-3828
   1789 N 8th St Colton (92324) **(P-24689)**
Vh Property Corp ....B......310 303-3210
   1 Ocean Trl Rancho Palos Verdes (90275) **(P-18311)**
VI At Palo Alto, Palo Alto *Also called Cc-Palo Alto Inc* **(P-20416)**
Via Adventures Inc (PA) ....E......209 384-1315
   300 Grogan Ave Merced (95341) **(P-3784)**
Via Care Cmnty Hlth Ctr Inc ....D......323 268-9191
   507 S Atlantic Blvd Los Angeles (90022) **(P-19581)**
Via Charter Lines, Merced *Also called Via Adventures Inc* **(P-3784)**
Via Communications Inc ....C......510 687-4650
   940 Mission Ct Fremont (94539) **(P-25868)**
Via Embedded Store, Fremont *Also called Via Technologies Inc* **(P-7361)**
Via Magazine, San Francisco *Also called CA Ste Atom Assoc Intr-Ins Bur* **(P-10075)**
Via Technologies Inc ....C......510 683-3300
   940 Mission Ct Fremont (94539) **(P-7361)**

Via Trading Corporation...D...877 202-3616
2520 Industry Way Lynwood (90262) ***(P-9019)***
Via Verde Country Club, San Dimas *Also called San Dimas Golf Inc* ***(P-18553)***
Viacom Consumer Products Inc...E...323 956-5634
5555 Melrose Ave Los Angeles (90038) ***(P-11837)***
Viacom Networks...A...310 752-8000
1575 N Gower St Ste 100 Los Angeles (90028) ***(P-17701)***
Viacyte Inc...D...858 455-3708
3550 General Atomics Ct B2-503 San Diego (92121) ***(P-26043)***
Viad Corp...D...562 370-1500
5560 Katella Ave Cypress (90630) ***(P-17148)***
Vian Enterprises Inc...E...530 885-1997
1501 Industrial Dr Auburn (95603) ***(P-17149)***
Viant, Irvine *Also called Interactive Media Holdings* ***(P-13526)***
Viant Technology LLC (HQ)...C...949 861-8888
2722 Michelson Dr Ste 100 Irvine (92612) ***(P-13665)***
Viant US, Irvine *Also called Viant Technology LLC* ***(P-13665)***
Viaworld Advanced Products...D...408 597-7051
920 Saratoga Ave Ste 103 San Jose (95129) ***(P-7411)***
Vibra Healthcare LLC...D...559 325-5601
1315 Shaw Ave Ste 102 Clovis (93612) ***(P-21363)***
Vibra Healthcare LLC...C...530 246-9000
2801 Eureka Way Redding (96001) ***(P-21364)***
Vibra Healthcare LLC...D...559 436-3600
7173 N Sharon Ave Fresno (93720) ***(P-21365)***
Vibra Healthcare LLC...C...619 260-8300
555 Washington St San Diego (92103) ***(P-21366)***
Vibra Hospital Northern Cal, Redding *Also called Vibra Healthcare LLC* ***(P-21364)***
Vibra Hospital of San Diego, San Diego *Also called Vibra Healthcare LLC* ***(P-21366)***
Vibra Hospital Sacramento LLC...C...916 351-9151
330 Montrose Dr Folsom (95630) ***(P-21502)***
Vibra Hospital San Diego LLC...D...619 260-8300
555 Washington St San Diego (92103) ***(P-21367)***
Vibrantcare Outpatient Rehab (PA)...D...916 782-1212
2270 Douglas Blvd Ste 216 Roseville (95661) ***(P-22156)***
Vicar Operating Inc (HQ)...C...310 571-6500
12401 W Olympic Blvd Los Angeles (90064) ***(P-596)***
Viceroy Santa Monica, Santa Monica *Also called Seaside Hotel Lessee Inc* ***(P-17051)***
Vickie Lobello...D...805 750-2327
1333 S Mayflower Ave 40 Simi Valley (93063) ***(P-24883)***
Vicor Inc...D...510 621-2000
855 Marina Bay Pkwy # 100 Richmond (94804) ***(P-15710)***
Victor Cmnty Support Svcs Inc...C...530 273-2244
900 E Main St Ste 201 Grass Valley (95945) ***(P-27309)***
Victor Cmnty Support Svcs Inc (PA)...B...530 893-0758
1360 E Lassen Ave Chico (95973) ***(P-22157)***
Victor Treatment Centers Inc...C...707 360-1509
341 Irwin Ln Santa Rosa (95401) ***(P-24105)***
Victor Valley Moose Lodge No...C...760 244-1808
10230 E Ave Hesperia (92345) ***(P-24690)***
Victoria Care Center...D...805 642-1736
5445 Everglades St Ventura (93003) ***(P-20353)***
Victoria Island Farms...D...209 465-5609
16021 E Hwy 4 Holt (95234) ***(P-370)***
Victoria Place Community Assn...D...909 981-4131
195 N Euclid Ave Upland (91786) ***(P-24884)***
Victoria Post Acute Care...C...619 440-5005
654 S Anza St El Cajon (92020) ***(P-20715)***
Victorian Inn, Monterey *Also called Columbia Hospitality Inc* ***(P-12164)***
Victorvlle Trsure Holdings LLC...D...760 245-6565
15494 Palmdale Rd Victorville (92392) ***(P-13064)***
Victory Foam Inc (PA)...D...949 474-0690
3 Holland Irvine (92618) ***(P-9020)***
Victory Pharma Inc...C...858 720-4500
11682 El Camino Real # 250 San Diego (92130) ***(P-7991)***
Victory Studio, Burbank *Also called Warner Bros Entertainment Inc* ***(P-17710)***
Victus Group Inc...C...559 429-8080
2350 W Shaw Ave Fresno (93711) ***(P-26450)***
Vid, Vista *Also called Vista Irrigation District* ***(P-6375)***
Vida Health Inc...D...408 203-7959
100 Montgomery St Ste 750 San Francisco (94104) ***(P-15185)***
Vidal Sassoon Salon, Beverly Hills *Also called Regis Corporation* ***(P-13356)***
Vident...D...714 221-6700
22705 Savi Ranch Pkwy # 100 Yorba Linda (92887) ***(P-7017)***
Video Sensing Division, Tustin *Also called Canon Medical Systems USA Inc* ***(P-6956)***
Video Vice Data Communications...B...714 897-6300
12681 Pala Dr Garden Grove (92841) ***(P-5808)***
Videocam, Anaheim *Also called Vci Event Technology Inc* ***(P-14208)***
Vidhwan Inc (PA)...C...408 289-8200
2 N Market St Ste 400 San Jose (95113) ***(P-26868)***
Vidhwan Inc...C...408 521-0167
2 N Market St Ste 410 San Jose (95113) ***(P-15186)***
Viele & Sons Inc...D...714 447-3663
1820 E Valencia Dr Fullerton (92831) ***(P-8282)***
Viele & Sons Instnl Groc, Fullerton *Also called Viele & Sons Inc* ***(P-8282)***
Vienna Convalescent Hospital...C...209 368-7141
800 S Ham Ln Lodi (95242) ***(P-20354)***
Vietnam Veterans of San Diego (PA)...D...619 497-0142
4141 Pacific Hwy San Diego (92110) ***(P-24691)***
VIETNAMESE COMMUNITY OF ORANGE, Santa Ana *Also called Southland Integrated Svcs Inc* ***(P-24228)***
Vietnms-Mrcan Yuth Alance Corp...E...619 320-8292
7968 Arjons Dr Ste 109 San Diego (92126) ***(P-24692)***
View Heights Convalescent Hosp, Los Angeles *Also called Amada Enterprises Inc* ***(P-19719)***
VIEW PARK CONVALESCENT CENTER, Los Angeles *Also called Burlington Convalescent Hosp* ***(P-19766)***
View Park Convalescent Center, Los Angeles *Also called Burlington Convalescent Hosp* ***(P-19767)***
Viewray Technologies Inc...D...650 252-0920
815 E Middlefield Rd Mountain View (94043) ***(P-7018)***
Viewsonic Corporation (PA)...C...909 444-8888
10 Pointe Dr Ste 200 Brea (92821) ***(P-6917)***
Vignolo Farms Inc...C...661 393-1431
33342 Dresser Ave Bakersfield (93308) ***(P-17)***
Viharas Group Inc...D...310 537-6700
1919 W Artesia Blvd Compton (90220) ***(P-11745)***
Viking Demolition, Glendale *Also called Viking Equipment Corp* ***(P-3356)***
Viking Equipment Corp...D...818 500-9447
540 W Windsor Rd Glendale (91204) ***(P-3356)***
Viking Ocean Cruises, Woodland Hills *Also called Viking River Cruises Inc* ***(P-4844)***
Viking Office Products Inc (HQ)...B...562 490-1000
3366 E Willow St Signal Hill (90755) ***(P-7868)***
Viking River Cruises Inc (HQ)...D...818 227-1234
5700 Canoga Ave Ste 200 Woodland Hills (91367) ***(P-4844)***
Vila Construction Co...D...510 236-9111
590 S 33rd St Richmond (94804) ***(P-1640)***
Villa Balboa Community Assoc...D...949 450-1515
22 Mauchly Irvine (92618) ***(P-24693)***
Villa Convalescent Hosp Inc...D...951 689-5788
8965 Magnolia Ave Riverside (92503) ***(P-20355)***
Villa Del Rey Retirement Inn, Escondido *Also called Emeritus Corporation* ***(P-10719)***
Villa Fairmont Mental Hlth Ctr, San Leandro *Also called Telecare Corporation* ***(P-21437)***
Villa Gardens, Pasadena *Also called Front Porch Communities* ***(P-23933)***
Villa La Esperanza LP...D...805 781-3088
3533 Empleo St San Luis Obispo (93401) ***(P-1321)***
VILLA LAS PALMAS HEALTHCARE CE, El Cajon *Also called Jeffrey Pine Holdings LLC* ***(P-20036)***
Villa Las Posas, Camarillo *Also called Atria Senior Living Inc* ***(P-23825)***
Villa Maria Care Center, Long Beach *Also called Trinity Health Systems* ***(P-20335)***
Villa Maria Care Center, Baldwin Park *Also called Trinity Health Systems* ***(P-20336)***
Villa Marin Homeowners Assn...C...415 499-8711
100 Thorndale Dr San Rafael (94903) ***(P-24694)***
Villa Mrin Rtrement Residences, San Rafael *Also called Villa Marin Homeowners Assn* ***(P-24694)***
Villa Oaks Convalescent Homes, Pasadena *Also called Voch Inc* ***(P-20719)***
Villa Pacific Contractors Inc...E...714 850-1640
3303 Harbor Blvd Ste D6 Costa Mesa (92626) ***(P-2732)***
Villa Park Orchards Assn (PA)...B...805 524-0411
960 3rd St Fillmore (93015) ***(P-559)***
Villa Park Trucking, Fillmore *Also called Villa Park Orchards Assn* ***(P-559)***
Villa Paseo Palms, Paso Robles *Also called Villa Paseo Senior Residences* ***(P-10835)***
Villa Paseo Senior Residences...D...805 227-4588
2818 Ramada Dr Paso Robles (93446) ***(P-10835)***
VILLA RANCHO BERNARDO CARE CEN, San Diego *Also called Villa Rancho Brno Hlth Cr LLC* ***(P-20356)***
Villa Rancho Brno Hlth Cr LLC...C...858 672-3900
15720 Bernardo Center Dr San Diego (92127) ***(P-20356)***
Villa Real Inc...D...209 460-5069
421 S El Dorado St Ste D1 Stockton (95203) ***(P-27246)***
Villa Sclabrini Retirement Ctr, Sun Valley *Also called Fathers of St Charles* ***(P-10725)***
Villa Serena Healthcare Center...D...562 437-2797
723 E 9th St Long Beach (90813) ***(P-20357)***
Villa Serra Corporation...D...831 754-5532
1320 Padre Dr Apt 103 Salinas (93901) ***(P-10836)***
Villa Siena...D...650 961-6484
1855 Miramonte Ave 117 Mountain View (94040) ***(P-20716)***
Villa Theresa Mobile Home Park, San Jose *Also called Barbaccia Properties* ***(P-10862)***
Villa Valencia Health Care Ctr, Laguna Hills *Also called Sunrise Senior Living Inc* ***(P-20302)***
Village 8, Westlake Village *Also called WF Cinema Holdings LP* ***(P-17869)***
Village At Granite Bay...D...916 789-0326
8550 Barton Rd Granite Bay (95746) ***(P-24106)***
Village At Northridge...C...818 514-4497
9222 Corbin Ave Northridge (91324) ***(P-24107)***
Village At Sydney Creek, San Luis Obispo *Also called Village Pacific Mgt Group* ***(P-20358)***
Village At Sydney Creek, San Luis Obispo *Also called Village Pacific Mgt Group* ***(P-20359)***
Village Club...E...619 425-3333
429 Broadway Chula Vista (91910) ***(P-18779)***
Village Glen Apartments...D...626 963-4575
633 S Pasadena Ave Apt 45 Glendora (91740) ***(P-10837)***
Village Integrated Svc Agcy, Long Beach *Also called Mental Health Amer Los Angeles* ***(P-23338)***
Village Nurseries Whl LLC (PA)...E...714 279-3100
1589 N Main St Orange (92867) ***(P-8931)***
Village Nurseries Whl LLC...B...916 993-2292
6901 Bradshaw Rd Sacramento (95829) ***(P-8932)***
Village Nurseries Whl LLC...C...951 657-3940
20099 Santa Rosa Mine Rd Perris (92570) ***(P-8933)***
Village Pacific Mgt Group...D...805 543-2350
1234 Laurel Ln San Luis Obispo (93401) ***(P-20358)***
Village Pacific Mgt Group (PA)...D...805 543-2300
55 Broad St San Luis Obispo (93405) ***(P-20359)***
Village Rdshow Entrmt Group US...E...310 867-8000
9268 W 3rd St Beverly Hills (90210) ***(P-17702)***
Village Square Healthcare Ctr, San Marcos *Also called San Marcos Operating Co LP* ***(P-20235)***
Village Square Nursing Center...C...760 471-2986
1586 W San Marcos Blvd San Marcos (92078) ***(P-20360)***
Village The, San Juan Capistrano *Also called Freedom Properties-Hemet LLC* ***(P-10593)***
Village West Health Center, Riverside *Also called Air Force Village West Inc* ***(P-19712)***
Village West Yacht Club...D...209 478-8992
6633 Embarcadero Dr Stockton (95219) ***(P-18603)***

Employee Codes: A=Over 500 employees, B=251-500
C=101-250, D=51-100, E=50
2020 Directory of California
Wholesalers and Services Companies
© Mergent Inc. 1-800-342-5647
1477

Villagecraft Quality Furn, Santa Monica *Also called Century Finance Incorporated* ***(P-9537)***
Villages Golf and Country Club......C......408 274-4400
5000 Cribari Ln San Jose (95135) ***(P-18604)***
Villages, The, San Jose *Also called Villages Golf and Country Club* ***(P-18604)***
Villageway Management Inc......D......949 450-1515
23041 Ave De La Carlta # 270 Laguna Hills (92653) ***(P-11500)***
Villageway Property Management, Laguna Hills *Also called Villageway Management Inc* ***(P-11500)***
Villagio Inn & Spa LLC......C......707 944-8877
6481 Washington St Yountville (94599) ***(P-13065)***
Villara Corporation (PA)......B......916 646-2700
4700 Lang Ave McClellan (95652) ***(P-2312)***
Villara Corporation......E......707 863-8222
5005 Fulton Dr Ste F Fairfield (94534) ***(P-3106)***
Villara Corporation......D......209 824-1082
332 E Wetmore St Manteca (95337) ***(P-2313)***
Villas De Carlsbad Ltd A Cali (PA)......C......858 565-4424
9619 Chesapeake Dr # 103 San Diego (92123) ***(P-24108)***
Villas De Carlsbad Ltd A Cali......E......760 434-7116
3500 Lake Blvd Oceanside (92056) ***(P-24109)***
Vimark Inc......D......707 857-3588
19500 Geyserville Ave Geyserville (95441) ***(P-687)***
Vimark Vineyards, Geyserville *Also called Vimark Inc* ***(P-687)***
Vimo Inc (PA)......D......650 618-4600
1305 Terra Bella Ave Mountain View (94043) ***(P-27247)***
Vin Dibona Productions, Los Angeles *Also called Cara Communications Corp* ***(P-17589)***
Vina Holdings Inc......D......714 622-5334
13800 Arizona St Westminster (92683) ***(P-21892)***
Vince Solutions (PA)......D......510 432-0852
3910 Riverbend Ter Fremont (94555) ***(P-26869)***
Vincent B Zaninovich Sons Inc......A......661 720-9031
20715 Ave 8 Richgrove (93261) ***(P-168)***
Vincent Contractors Inc......B......714 693-1726
4501 E La Palma Ave # 200 Anaheim (92807) ***(P-2733)***
Vincent Hayley Enterprises......D......626 398-8182
1810 N Fair Oaks Ave Pasadena (91103) ***(P-20717)***
Vincent Huang & Associates LLC (PA)......D......909 861-9600
1550 Valley Vista Dr Diamond Bar (91765) ***(P-5492)***
Vincent V Zaninovich & Sons......D......661 849-2613
2480 E Washington St Earlimart (93219) ***(P-169)***
Vinculums Services Inc......C......949 783-3552
10 Pasteur Ste 100 Irvine (92618) ***(P-27248)***
Vindicia Inc......C......650 264-4700
2988 Campus Dr Ste 300 San Mateo (94403) ***(P-15531)***
Vindra Inc......D......707 994-7738
3805 Dexter Ln Clearlake (95422) ***(P-20361)***
Vine Transit, NAPA *Also called City of NAPA* ***(P-3757)***
Vino Farms Inc (PA)......E......209 334-6975
1377 E Lodi Ave Lodi (95240) ***(P-688)***
Vino Farms Inc......D......707 433-8241
10651 Eastside Rd Healdsburg (95448) ***(P-689)***
Vino Farms Inc......C......916 775-4095
51375 S Netherlands Rd Clarksburg (95612) ***(P-371)***
Vino Farms LLC......A......209 334-6975
1377 E Lodi Ave Lodi (95240) ***(P-8821)***
Vinod Kumar MD......D......661 324-4100
5020 Commerce Dr Bakersfield (93309) ***(P-19582)***
Vinson & Elkins LLP......C......650 617-8400
1841 Page Mill Rd Fl 2 Palo Alto (94304) ***(P-22858)***
Vintage Associates Inc......C......760 772-3673
78755 Darby Rd Bermuda Dunes (92203) ***(P-924)***
Vintage Club......D......760 340-0500
75001 Vintage Dr W Indian Wells (92210) ***(P-18605)***
Vintage Club Master Assn Inc......D......760 340-0500
75001 Vintage Dr W Indian Wells (92210) ***(P-24695)***
Vintage Design LLC (HQ)......D......949 900-5400
25200 Commercentre Dr Lake Forest (92630) ***(P-3019)***
Vintage Estates of Hayward, Hayward *Also called St Michael Convalescent Hosp* ***(P-20274)***
Vintage Faire Nrsng Rhbltn, Modesto *Also called Covenant Care California LLC* ***(P-20538)***
VINTAGE GARDENS, Fresno *Also called Central Cal Nikkei Foundation* ***(P-23858)***
Vintage Golden Gate, San Francisco *Also called Avalon Golden Gate LLC* ***(P-23833)***
Vintage Nursery, Bermuda Dunes *Also called Vintage Associates Inc* ***(P-924)***
Vintage Production California, Bakersfield *Also called California Resources Prod Corp* ***(P-984)***
Vintage Senior Housing LLC......B......805 583-3500
5300 E Los Angeles Ave Simi Valley (93063) ***(P-10838)***
Vintage Senior Living Corp......D......949 364-6210
27783 Center Dr Mission Viejo (92692) ***(P-10839)***
Vintage Senior Management Inc......A......818 954-9500
2721 W Willow St Burbank (91505) ***(P-23525)***
Vintage Senior Management Inc......A......707 595-0009
91 Napa Rd Sonoma (95476) ***(P-10840)***
Vintage Silver Creek, San Jose *Also called Sunrise Senior Living Inc* ***(P-20301)***
Vintage Simi Hills, Simi Valley *Also called Vintage Senior Housing LLC* ***(P-10838)***
Vintners Golf Club......E......707 944-1992
7901 Solano Ave Yountville (94599) ***(P-18312)***
Vintners Inn......D......707 575-7350
4350 Barnes Rd Santa Rosa (95403) ***(P-13066)***
Vintrust Inc......E......877 846-8787
38 Keyes Ave Ste 200 San Francisco (94129) ***(P-4578)***
Vinwood Cellars Inc......E......707 857-4011
18700 Geyserville Ave Geyserville (95441) ***(P-8822)***
VIP, Folsom *Also called Visionary Integration* ***(P-11703)***
VIP Tours of California Inc......D......310 216-7507
1419 E Maple Ave El Segundo (90245) ***(P-4869)***
VIP Transport Inc......E......951 272-3700
2703 Wardlow Rd Corona (92882) ***(P-4164)***

Vipstore USA Co......B......626 934-7880
13674 Star Ruby Ave Eastvale (92880) ***(P-9021)***
Virco Inc (HQ)......D......310 533-0474
2027 Harpers Way Torrance (90501) ***(P-6536)***
Virga Investment Property......C......530 755-4409
430 S George Wash Blvd Yuba City (95993) ***(P-10669)***
Virgil Convalescent Hospital, Los Angeles *Also called Virgil Sntrium Cnvlescent Hosp* ***(P-20362)***
Virgil Sntrium Cnvlescent Hosp......C......323 665-5793
975 N Virgil Ave Los Angeles (90029) ***(P-20362)***
Virgin America Inc (HQ)......C......877 359-8474
555 Airport Blvd Burlingame (94010) ***(P-4696)***
Virgin Fish Inc (PA)......C......310 391-6161
1000 Corporate Pointe # 150 Culver City (90230) ***(P-3735)***
Virgin Galactic LLC (HQ)......D......562 384-4400
16555 Spcship Landing Way Mojave (93501) ***(P-5145)***
Virginia Country Club......C......562 427-0924
4602 N Virginia Rd Long Beach (90807) ***(P-18606)***
Virginia Hardwood Company (PA)......D......626 815-0540
1000 W Foothill Blvd Azusa (91702) ***(P-6666)***
Virginia Sarabian......E......559 493-2900
2816 S Leonard Ave Sanger (93657) ***(P-217)***
Virident Systems Inc......C......408 573-5000
1745 Tech Dr Ste 700 San Jose (95110) ***(P-25869)***
Virtium LLC......D......949 888-2444
30052 Tomas Rcho STA Marg (92688) ***(P-16152)***
Virtual Instruments Corp (PA)......D......408 579-4000
2331 Zanker Rd San Jose (95131) ***(P-16153)***
Visage Imaging Inc......D......858 345-4410
12625 High Bluff Dr # 205 San Diego (92130) ***(P-13458)***
Visalia Convention Center, Visalia *Also called City of Visalia* ***(P-16702)***
Visalia Country Club......D......559 734-3733
625 N Ranch St Visalia (93291) ***(P-18607)***
Visalia Medical Clinic Inc (PA)......B......559 733-5222
5400 W Hillsdale Ave Visalia (93291) ***(P-19583)***
Visalia Unified School Dst......C......559 730-7871
801 N Mooney Blvd Visalia (93291) ***(P-23526)***
Visalia Youth Services, Visalia *Also called Turning Point Central Cal Inc* ***(P-23512)***
Visby Medical Inc......D......408 650-8878
625 River Oaks Pkwy San Jose (95134) ***(P-25870)***
Viscamar LLC......D......559 636-1111
300 S Court St Visalia (93291) ***(P-13067)***
Viscent Orthpd Solutions LLC (HQ)......E......214 501-0180
2885 Loker Ave E Carlsbad (92010) ***(P-19584)***
Viscira LLC......D......415 848-8010
200 Vallejo St San Francisco (94111) ***(P-6918)***
Visio Integ Profe LLC (HQ)......D......916 985-9625
80 Iron Point Cir Ste 100 Folsom (95630) ***(P-26870)***
Vision Care Center (PA)......D......559 486-2000
7075 N Sharon Ave Fresno (93720) ***(P-19585)***
Vision Care Center Central Cal, Fresno *Also called Vision Care Center* ***(P-19585)***
Vision Fund International, Monrovia *Also called World Vision International* ***(P-24890)***
VISION FUND INTERNATIONAL, Monrovia *Also called Visionfund International* ***(P-17150)***
Vision Realty Managements, Beverly Hills *Also called Starpoint Property MGT LLC* ***(P-11466)***
Vision Service Plan (PA)......A......916 851-5000
3333 Quality Dr Rancho Cordova (95670) ***(P-10063)***
Vision Solutions Inc (PA)......D......949 253-6500
15300 Barranca Pkwy # 100 Irvine (92618) ***(P-15187)***
Vision Solutions Inc......D......949 253-6500
15300 Barranca Pkwy # 100 Irvine (92618) ***(P-16154)***
Vision To Learn......E......800 485-9196
11611 San Vicente Blvd # 500 Los Angeles (90049) ***(P-24885)***
Visionaire Group Inc......D......310 823-1800
400 Crprate Pinte Ste 700 Culver City (90230) ***(P-13595)***
Visionary Integration (PA)......D......916 985-9625
80 Iron Point Cir Ste 100 Folsom (95630) ***(P-11703)***
Visionary Intgrtion Prfssonals, Folsom *Also called Visio Integ Profe LLC* ***(P-26870)***
Visionfund International......D......626 303-8811
800 W Chestnut Ave Monrovia (91016) ***(P-17150)***
Visions Unlimited (PA)......C......916 394-0800
6833 Stockton Blvd # 485 Sacramento (95823) ***(P-22158)***
Visionstar Inc......D......213 387-3700
3435 Wilsh Blvd Ste 2120 Los Angeles (90010) ***(P-26871)***
Visit Anaheim, Anaheim *Also called Anaheim/Orange Cnty Visitor Bu* ***(P-16623)***
Visiting Angels, Chino *Also called Angels In Motion LLC* ***(P-21666)***
Visiting Angels Riverside Cnty, Riverside *Also called Roberts & Associates Inc* ***(P-21854)***
Visiting Care & Companions Inc......D......805 690-6202
509 E Montecito St # 200 Santa Barbara (93103) ***(P-21893)***
Visiting Nrse Assn Orange Cnty (PA)......D......949 263-4700
2520 Redhill Ave Santa Ana (92705) ***(P-21894)***
VISITING NURSE & HOSPICE CARE, Santa Barbara *Also called Visiting Nurse & Hospice Care* ***(P-24432)***
Visiting Nurse & Hospice Care (PA)......C......805 965-5555
509 E Montecito St # 200 Santa Barbara (93103) ***(P-24432)***
Visiting Nurse Associ......D......909 621-3961
150 W 1st St Ste 176 Claremont (91711) ***(P-21895)***
Visiting Nurse Association......D......831 385-1014
5 Lower Ragsdle Dr 102 Monterey (93940) ***(P-21896)***
Visiting Nurse Association of (HQ)......D......831 477-2600
2880 Soquel Ave Ste 10 Santa Cruz (95062) ***(P-21897)***
Visitng Nurse Assn Inlnd CNT (PA)......A......951 413-1200
6235 River Crest Dr Ste L Riverside (92507) ***(P-21898)***
Visitng Nurse Assn Inlnd CNT......C......760 346-3982
42600 Cook St Ste 202 Palm Desert (92211) ***(P-21899)***
Visitor Services & Facilities, San Jose *Also called City of San Jose* ***(P-24305)***
Visiworks Software, El Dorado Hills *Also called Dorado Software Inc* ***(P-14770)***
Visor, San Francisco *Also called Hatfield Inc* ***(P-13390)***

Vista Anglina Hsing Prtners LP ....E....213 482-4718
418 E Edgeware Rd Los Angeles (90026) *(P-11501)*
Vista Behavioral Health Inc ....D....800 992-0901
5900 Brockton Ave Riverside (92506) *(P-21446)*
Vista Care Group LLC (PA) ....D....760 295-3900
1863 Devon Pl Vista (92084) *(P-23527)*
Vista Community Clinic ....D....951 245-2735
30195 Fraser Dr Lake Elsinore (92530) *(P-19586)*
Vista Community Clinic (PA) ....B....760 631-5000
1000 Vale Terrace Dr Vista (92084) *(P-19644)*
Vista Community Clinic ....E....760 631-5030
134 Grapevine Rd Vista (92083) *(P-19645)*
Vista Cove Care Center At Long ....D....562 426-4461
3401 Cedar Ave Long Beach (90807) *(P-20363)*
Vista Cove Care Ctr - Rialto ....D....909 877-1361
1471 S Riverside Ave Rialto (92376) *(P-20364)*
Vista Del Mar Child Fmly Svcs ....B....310 836-1223
1533 Euclid St Santa Monica (90404) *(P-24110)*
Vista Del Mar Health Centers, Vista *Also called Life Care Centers America Inc (P-20613)*
Vista Gardens, Vista *Also called Vista Care Group LLC (P-23527)*
Vista Hill Foundation ....D....619 266-0166
4125 Alpha St San Diego (92113) *(P-23528)*
Vista Hill Foundation (PA) ....E....585 514-5100
8910 Clairemont Mesa Blvd San Diego (92123) *(P-24433)*
Vista Home Health Service Inc ....D....818 701-1877
343 E Palmdale Blvd Ste 4 Palmdale (93550) *(P-21900)*
Vista Hospital Riverside, Rancho Cucamonga *Also called Perris Valley Cmnty Hosp LLC (P-21091)*
Vista Hospital San Gabriel Vly, Baldwin Park *Also called Vista Specialty Hosp Cal LP (P-21368)*
Vista Irrigation District ....D....760 597-3100
1391 Engineer St Vista (92081) *(P-6375)*
Vista Knoll Inc ....D....760 630-2273
2000 Westwood Rd Vista (92083) *(P-20365)*
Vista Knoll Spclzed Care Fclty, Vista *Also called Vista Woods Health Assoc LLC (P-20367)*
VISTA PACIFICA CONVALESCENT CE, Riverside *Also called Vista Pacifica Enterprises Inc (P-20366)*
Vista Pacifica Enterprises Inc (PA) ....C....951 682-4833
3662 Pacific Ave Riverside (92509) *(P-20366)*
Vista Pacifica Enterprises Inc ....C....951 682-4867
3662 Pacific Ave Riverside (92509) *(P-20718)*
Vista Pcifica Convalescent Ctr, Riverside *Also called Vista Pacifica Enterprises Inc (P-20718)*
Vista Specialty Hosp Cal LP ....C....626 388-2700
14148 Francisquito Ave Baldwin Park (91706) *(P-21368)*
Vista Specialty Hosp Riverside, Perris *Also called Perris Valley Cmnty Hosp LLC (P-21090)*
Vista Steel Co Inc ....E....805 653-1189
331 W Lewis St Ventura (93001) *(P-2001)*
Vista Valencia Group Inc ....E....661 255-4600
25545 Via Paladar Valencia (91355) *(P-11502)*
Vista Valley Country Club ....D....760 758-2800
29354 Vista Valley Dr Vista (92084) *(P-18608)*
Vista Verde Farms ....E....661 720-9733
11251 Melcher Rd Delano (93215) *(P-8672)*
Vista Verde Farms Inc ....D....559 992-3111
7124 Whitley Ave Corcoran (93212) *(P-444)*
Vista Woods Health Assoc LLC ....C....760 630-2273
2000 Westwood Rd Vista (92083) *(P-20367)*
Vistage International Inc (PA) ....C....858 523-6800
4840 Eastgate Mall San Diego (92121) *(P-26872)*
Vistancia Marketing LLC ....D....909 594-9500
655 Brea Canyon Rd Walnut (91789) *(P-26873)*
Visual Concepts Entertainment ....C....415 479-3634
10 Hamilton Landing Novato (94949) *(P-15188)*
Visual Pak San Diego LLC ....C....847 689-1000
2320 Paseo De Las Ave 2 San Diego (92154) *(P-17151)*
Visualon Inc ....C....408 645-6618
2590 N 1st St Ste 100 San Jose (95131) *(P-15532)*
Vita North America, Yorba Linda *Also called Vident (P-7017)*
Vital Express Inc ....E....330 777-5450
4000 Macarthur Blvd Ste 6 Newport Beach (92660) *(P-5146)*
Vital Farmland Holdings LLC ....D....415 465-2400
3 Corte Las Casas Belvedere Tiburon (94920) *(P-17152)*
Vitalant ....D....805 543-1077
4119 Broad St Ste 100 San Luis Obispo (93401) *(P-22336)*
Vitalant ....D....831 751-1993
4119 Broad St Ste 100 San Luis Obispo (93401) *(P-22337)*
Vitalant ....D....805 654-1603
2223 Eastman Ave Ste A Ventura (93003) *(P-22338)*
Vitalant Research Institute ....E....650 697-4034
111 Rollins Rd Millbrae (94030) *(P-22339)*
Vitalant Research Institute (PA) ....C....415 567-6400
270 Masonic Ave San Francisco (94118) *(P-22340)*
Vitalant Research Institute ....D....707 462-1754
620 Kings Ct Ste 110 Ukiah (95482) *(P-22341)*
Vitalant Research Institute ....E....707 428-6001
1325 Gateway Blvd Ste C1 Fairfield (94533) *(P-22342)*
Vitas Healthcare Corp Cal ....D....408 964-6800
670 N Mccarthy Blcvd 220 Milpitas (95035) *(P-21901)*
Vitas Healthcare Corp Cal ....D....916 925-7010
2710 Gateway Oaks Dr # 100 Sacramento (95833) *(P-21902)*
Vitas Healthcare Corp Cal ....D....925 930-9373
355 Lennon Ln Ste 150 Walnut Creek (94598) *(P-20467)*
Vitas Healthcare Corp Cal ....C....909 386-6000
7888 Mission Grove Pkwy S Riverside (92508) *(P-21903)*
Vitas Healthcare Corp Cal ....D....626 918-2273
1343 N Grand Ave Ste 100 Covina (91724) *(P-20468)*
Vitas Healthcare Corp Cal ....D....310 324-2273
990 W 190th St Ste 550 Torrance (90502) *(P-21904)*
Vitas Healthcare Corp Cal ....D....818 760-2273
16830 Ventura Blvd # 315 Encino (91436) *(P-21905)*
Vitas Healthcare Corporation ....D....805 437-2100
333 N Lantana St Ste 124 Camarillo (93010) *(P-20469)*
Vitas Innovative Hospice Care, Milpitas *Also called Vitas Healthcare Corp Cal (P-21901)*
Vitas Innovative Hospice Care, Riverside *Also called Vitas Healthcare Corp Cal (P-21903)*
Vitas Innovative Hospice Care, Encino *Also called Vitas Healthcare Corp Cal (P-21905)*
Vitco Distributors Inc ....D....909 355-1300
715 E California St Ontario (91761) *(P-7912)*
Vitco Food Service, Ontario *Also called Vitco Distributors Inc (P-7912)*
Vitesse LLC ....A....650 543-4800
1601 Willow Rd Menlo Park (94025) *(P-15835)*
Vitran Logistics Inc ....D....909 972-3100
1000 S Cucamonga Ave Ontario (91761) *(P-4535)*
Vitreo Retinal Medical Group, Chico *Also called Retinal Consultants Inc (P-19333)*
Vitro LLC ....D....619 234-0408
2305 Historic Decatur Rd # 205 San Diego (92106) *(P-13596)*
Vitrorobertson LLC ....D....619 234-0408
2305 Historic Decatur Rd San Diego (92106) *(P-13597)*
Vituity, Emeryville *Also called Cep America LLC (P-18888)*
Viva Group Inc ....D....310 449-6400
11766 Wilshire Blvd # 300 Los Angeles (90025) *(P-10841)*
Viva International, Belvedere Tiburon *Also called Marcolin USA Inc (P-7023)*
Viva Life Science Inc ....D....949 645-6100
350 Paularino Ave Costa Mesa (92626) *(P-7992)*
Viva Soma Lessee Inc ....A....415 974-6400
50 3rd St San Francisco (94103) *(P-26451)*
Vivente 1 Inc ....D....408 279-2706
2400 Enborg Ln San Jose (95128) *(P-10860)*
Vivente 2 Inc ....D....408 279-2706
5347 Dent Ave San Jose (95118) *(P-10861)*
Vivid Solution ....D....310 498-2559
5959 W Century Blvd Los Angeles (90045) *(P-17153)*
Vivopools LLC ....D....888 702-8486
245 W Foothill Blvd Monrovia (91016) *(P-17154)*
Vladigor Investment Inc ....D....415 558-9274
1601 Mission St San Francisco (94103) *(P-17402)*
Vlot Brothers, Chowchilla *Also called Case Vlott Cattle (P-386)*
Vlot Brothers Dairy, Chowchilla *Also called Vlot Brothers Trucking Co Inc (P-405)*
Vlot Brothers Trucking Co Inc ....D....559 665-7399
3197 Avenue 21 Chowchilla (93610) *(P-405)*
Vm Services Inc ....E....714 678-5200
1051 S East St Anaheim (92805) *(P-15189)*
Vm Services Inc (HQ) ....C....510 744-3720
6701 Mowry Ave Newark (94560) *(P-15190)*
Vmbc, Aliso Viejo *Also called Voice Mail Broadcasting Corp (P-15836)*
Vmsg, Ventura *Also called Veternary Med Srgcal Group Inc (P-595)*
Vmware Inc (HQ) ....C....650 427-5000
3401 Hillview Ave Palo Alto (94304) *(P-15533)*
Vmware Inc ....C....650 812-8200
3305 Hillview Ave Palo Alto (94304) *(P-15191)*
Vn Home Health Care LP ....D....408 998-0550
2528 Qume Dr Ste 7 San Jose (95131) *(P-21906)*
Vna Home Health Systems, Santa Ana *Also called Visiting Nrse Assn Orange Cnty (P-21894)*
Vna Hospice & Pllatve Cre S CA ....C....909 384-0737
412 E Vanderbilt Way San Bernardino (92408) *(P-21907)*
Vna Hospice & Pllatve Cre S CA (PA) ....B....909 624-3574
412 E Vanderbilt Way San Bernardino (92408) *(P-21908)*
Vna Private Duty Care, Claremont *Also called Visiting Nurse Associ (P-21895)*
Vna Private Duty Care, San Bernardino *Also called Vna Hospice & Pllatve Cre S CA (P-21908)*
Vnahnc, Emeryville *Also called Sutter Vsting Nrse Assn Hspice (P-21878)*
Vnaic, Riverside *Also called Visitng Nurse Assn Inlnd CNT (P-21898)*
Vocational Imprv Program Inc (PA) ....C....909 483-5924
9210 Rochester Ave Rancho Cucamonga (91730) *(P-23653)*
Vocational Visions ....C....949 837-7280
26041 Pala Mission Viejo (92691) *(P-23654)*
Voch Inc ....D....626 798-1111
1920 N Fair Oaks Ave Pasadena (91103) *(P-20719)*
Voice Mail Broadcasting Corp ....D....714 437-0600
5 Columbia Aliso Viejo (92656) *(P-15836)*
Voice Smart Networks LLC ....E....619 857-4638
10920 Via Frontera # 410 San Diego (92127) *(P-27249)*
Voit Commercial Brokerage, Irvine *Also called Voit Development Manager Inc (P-11620)*
Voit Development Manager Inc ....D....949 851-5110
2020 Main St Ste 100 Irvine (92614) *(P-11620)*
Voit Real Estate Services Lp ....C....949 644-8648
101 Shipyard Way Ste A Newport Beach (92663) *(P-11503)*
Volcano Communications Company (PA) ....D....209 296-7502
20000 State Highway 88 Pine Grove (95665) *(P-5493)*
Volcano Telephone Co., Pine Grove *Also called Volcano Vision Inc (P-5770)*
Volcano Telephone Company, Pine Grove *Also called Volcano Communications Company (P-5493)*
Volcano Vision Inc ....C....209 296-2288
20000 State Highway 88 Pine Grove (95665) *(P-5770)*
Volcom LLC ....C....949 646-2175
1725 Monrovia Ave Costa Mesa (92627) *(P-8050)*
Volcom LLC (PA) ....C....949 646-2175
1740 Monrovia Ave Costa Mesa (92627) *(P-17155)*
Voloagri Inc ....C....805 547-9391
3424 Roberto Ct San Luis Obispo (93401) *(P-8861)*
Volt Management Corp ....C....310 316-8523
19191 S Vt Ave Ste 950 Torrance (90502) *(P-14582)*
Volt Management Corp ....B....714 921-7460
2411 N Glassell St Orange (92865) *(P-14583)*
Volt Management Corp ....C....714 879-9330
1400 N Harbor Blvd # 103 Fullerton (92835) *(P-14584)*

ALPHABETIC

Employee Codes: A=Over 500 employees, B=251-500
C=101-250, D=51-100, E=50
2020 Directory of California
Wholesalers and Services Companies
© Mergent Inc. 1-800-342-5647
1479

Volt Management Corp...C.......858 576-3140
7676 Hazard Center Dr # 1000 San Diego (92108) ***(P-14585)***
Volt Management Corp...C.......858 578-0920
7676 Hazard Center Dr # 1000 San Diego (92108) ***(P-14586)***
Volt Management Corp...C.......559 435-1255
7330 N Palm Ave Ste 105 Fresno (93711) ***(P-14587)***
Volt Management Corp...C.......714 921-8800
2401 N Glassell St Orange (92865) ***(P-14588)***
Volt Management Corp...D.......916 923-0454
1544 Eureka Rd Ste 150 Roseville (95661) ***(P-14589)***
Volt Management Corp...D.......951 789-8133
1650 Iowa Ave Ste 140 Riverside (92507) ***(P-14590)***
Volt Management Corp...C.......209 952-5627
3558 Deer Park Dr 2 Stockton (95219) ***(P-14591)***
Volt Management Corp...C.......805 485-0506
1701 Solar Dr Ste 145 Oxnard (93030) ***(P-14592)***
Volt Telecom Group, Corona *Also called Volt Telecom Group Inc* ***(P-27250)***
Volt Telecom Group, Corona *Also called Volt Telecom Group Inc* ***(P-27251)***
Volt Telecom Group Inc...E.......800 548-6602
218 Helicopter Cir Corona (92880) ***(P-27250)***
Volt Telecom Group Inc...C.......951 493-8900
218 Helicopter Cir Corona (92880) ***(P-27251)***
Volt Temporary Services, Orange *Also called Volt Management Corp* ***(P-14583)***
Volt Workforce Solutions, Torrance *Also called Volt Management Corp* ***(P-14582)***
Volt Workforce Solutions, Fullerton *Also called Volt Management Corp* ***(P-14584)***
Volt Workforce Solutions, San Diego *Also called Volt Management Corp* ***(P-14585)***
Volt Workforce Solutions, San Diego *Also called Volt Management Corp* ***(P-14586)***
Volt Workforce Solutions, Fresno *Also called Volt Management Corp* ***(P-14587)***
Volt Workforce Solutions, Orange *Also called Volt Management Corp* ***(P-14588)***
Volt Workforce Solutions, Roseville *Also called Volt Management Corp* ***(P-14589)***
Volt Workforce Solutions, Riverside *Also called Volt Management Corp* ***(P-14590)***
Volt Workforce Solutions, Stockton *Also called Volt Management Corp* ***(P-14591)***
Volt Workforce Solutions, Oxnard *Also called Volt Management Corp* ***(P-14592)***
Volta Charging LLC...D.......415 735-5169
155 De Haro St San Francisco (94103) ***(P-13610)***
Volume Services Inc...D.......415 972-1500
24 Willie Mays Plz San Francisco (94107) ***(P-18780)***
Volume Services Inc...D.......323 644-6038
5333 Zoo Dr Los Angeles (90027) ***(P-18781)***
Volume Services Inc...D.......619 525-5800
111 W Harbor Dr San Diego (92101) ***(P-18782)***
VOLUNTEER CENTER ORANGE COUNTY, Santa Ana *Also called Oneoc* ***(P-24852)***
Volunteers America Head Start, San Fernando *Also called Child Care Resource Center Inc* ***(P-23689)***
Volunteers of Amer Los Angeles...C.......818 764-8722
11512 Valerio St North Hollywood (91605) ***(P-23529)***
Volunteers of Amer Los Angeles...C.......818 834-9097
10896 Lehigh Ave Pacoima (91331) ***(P-23530)***
Volunteers of Amer Los Angeles...C.......323 780-3770
522 N Dangler Ave Los Angeles (90022) ***(P-23531)***
Volunteers of Amer Los Angeles...C.......626 337-9878
1760 W Cameron Ave # 104 West Covina (91790) ***(P-23532)***
Volunteers of Amer Los Angeles...D.......661 290-2829
25141 Avenida Rondel Valencia (91355) ***(P-23533)***
Volunteers of Amer Los Angeles...C.......818 352-5974
10819 Plainview Ave Tujunga (91042) ***(P-23534)***
Volunteers of Amer Los Angeles...D.......714 426-9834
2100 N Broadway Ste 300 Santa Ana (92706) ***(P-23535)***
Volunteers of Amer Los Angeles...C.......818 769-3617
6724 Tujunga Ave North Hollywood (91606) ***(P-23536)***
Volunteers of Amer Los Angeles...E.......818 506-0597
11243 Kittridge St North Hollywood (91606) ***(P-23537)***
Volunteers of Amer Los Angeles...C.......818 834-8957
12550 Van Nuys Blvd Pacoima (91331) ***(P-23538)***
Volunteers of America Greater (PA)...D.......916 265-3400
3434 Marconi Ave Ste A Sacramento (95821) ***(P-23539)***
Vormetric Inc (HQ)...D.......408 433-6000
2860 Junction Ave San Jose (95134) ***(P-16155)***
Vorwaller & Brooks Inc...D.......760 262-6300
72182 Corporate Way Thousand Palms (92276) ***(P-1218)***
Voter Precinct Voter Reg Off, Norwalk *Also called County of Los Angeles* ***(P-15742)***
Votum Staffing Inc...B.......310 499-4902
515 W Whittier Blvd Montebello (90640) ***(P-14451)***
Vox Network Solutions Inc...C.......650 989-1000
8000 Marina Blvd Ste 130 Brisbane (94005) ***(P-27252)***
Voxify Inc...D.......510 545-3011
1151 Marina Village Pkwy Alameda (94501) ***(P-15192)***
Voyage Auto Inc...D.......917 588-1249
844 E Charleston Rd Palo Alto (94303) ***(P-3736)***
Vpet Usa Inc (PA)...D.......909 605-1668
12925 Marlay Ave Fontana (92337) ***(P-8686)***
Vpm Management Inc...C.......949 863-1500
2400 Main St Ste 201 Irvine (92614) ***(P-26452)***
Vps Companies Inc (PA)...E.......831 724-7551
310 Walker St Watsonville (95076) ***(P-8304)***
Vps Companies Inc...E.......831 633-4011
13526 Blackie Rd Castroville (95012) ***(P-8305)***
VSC Sports Inc...D.......415 820-3525
750 Folsom St San Francisco (94107) ***(P-27253)***
Vsp Holding Company Inc...D.......916 851-5000
3333 Quality Dr Rancho Cordova (95670) ***(P-10064)***
Vss Compressor Service, Paramount *Also called Vss Sales Inc* ***(P-17561)***
Vss International Inc (HQ)...D.......916 373-1500
3785 Channel Dr West Sacramento (95691) ***(P-1808)***
Vss Monitoring Inc (HQ)...C.......408 585-6800
178 E Tasman Dr San Jose (95134) ***(P-5494)***
Vss Sales Inc (PA)...D.......562 630-0606
16220 Garfield Ave Paramount (90723) ***(P-17561)***
VT Milcom Inc...D.......619 424-9024
1660 Logan Ave Ste 2 San Diego (92113) ***(P-25383)***
Vtc Enterprises (PA)...B.......805 928-5000
2445 A St Santa Maria (93455) ***(P-23655)***
Vubiquity Inc...C.......818 526-5000
15301 Ventura Blvd Bldg E Sherman Oaks (91403) ***(P-17795)***
Vucovich Inc (PA)...D.......559 486-8020
4288 S Bagley Ave Fresno (93725) ***(P-7512)***
Vvd Comuunications, Garden Grove *Also called Video Vice Data Communications* ***(P-5808)***
Vwi Concord LLC...C.......925 827-2000
1970 Diamond Blvd Concord (94520) ***(P-13068)***
Vwise Inc...D.......949 716-1276
85 Enterprise Ste 320 Aliso Viejo (92656) ***(P-15193)***
VWR International LLC...E.......714 220-2615
6609 Mount Whitney Dr Buena Park (90620) ***(P-7036)***
VWR Scientific, Buena Park *Also called VWR International LLC* ***(P-7036)***
Vxi Global Solutions LLC (PA)...A.......213 739-4720
220 W 1st St Fl 3 Los Angeles (90012) ***(P-17156)***
Vyborny Vineyard Management...D.......707 944-9135
7327 Silverado Trl Rutherford (94573) ***(P-690)***
Vyshnavi Information Techn...C.......408 454-6218
2603 Camino Ramon Ste 200 San Ramon (94583) ***(P-15194)***
W A Rasic Cnstr Co Inc (PA)...C.......562 928-6111
4150 Long Beach Blvd Long Beach (90807) ***(P-1928)***
W B Starr Inc...D.......949 770-8835
20602 Canada Rd Lake Forest (92630) ***(P-925)***
W Bradley Electric Inc...C.......650 701-1502
501 Seaport Ct Ste 103a Redwood City (94063) ***(P-2687)***
W Bradley Electric Inc (PA)...E.......415 898-1400
90 Hill Rd Novato (94945) ***(P-2688)***
W Brown & Assc Property & Csu...D.......949 851-2060
19000 Macarthur Blvd Irvine (92612) ***(P-10543)***
W C I, Hollister *Also called Woltcom Inc* ***(P-2697)***
W Corporation...C.......714 532-8800
1643 W Orange Grove Ave Orange (92868) ***(P-27254)***
W Diamond Supply Co (HQ)...D.......909 859-8939
19321 E Walnut Dr N City of Industry (91748) ***(P-6599)***
W F Hayward Co...D.......530 303-3030
629 Main St Ste 101 Placerville (95667) ***(P-2874)***
W G A, Irvine *Also called Western Growers Association* ***(P-24372)***
W G B, Tustin *Also called Wood Gutmann Bogart Insur Brkg* ***(P-10554)***
W G Warranty and Insur Svcs, Calabasas *Also called All Motorists Insurance Agency* ***(P-10245)***
W H C Inc...D.......916 927-9300
2240 Northrop Ave Sacramento (95825) ***(P-20368)***
W I C, Sutter Creek *Also called Resource Connection of Amador* ***(P-23411)***
W I S, Moreno Valley *Also called Retail Services Wis Corp* ***(P-17021)***
W L Butler Construction Inc (PA)...E.......650 361-1270
735 Shasta St Redwood City (94063) ***(P-1641)***
W L Hickey Sons Inc...C.......408 736-4938
930 E California Ave Sunnyvale (94085) ***(P-2314)***
W Los Angeles...B.......310 208-8765
930 Hilgard Ave Los Angeles (90024) ***(P-13069)***
W M Klorman Construction Corp...D.......818 591-5969
23047 Ventura Blvd Fl 2 Woodland Hills (91364) ***(P-1642)***
W M Lyles Co (HQ)...C.......559 441-1900
1210 W Olive Ave Fresno (93728) ***(P-1929)***
W M Lyles Co...E.......661 387-1600
2810 Unicorn Rd Bakersfield (93308) ***(P-25384)***
W O R K, Carpinteria *Also called Ucp Work Inc* ***(P-23648)***
W R Hambrecht Co Inc (PA)...D.......415 551-8600
Bay 3 Pier 1 San Francisco (94111) ***(P-9767)***
W S B & Associates Inc...D.......510 444-6266
150 Executive Park Blvd # 4700 San Francisco (94134) ***(P-16476)***
W S B & Associates Inc...C.......415 864-3510
150 Executive Park Blvd # 4700 San Francisco (94134) ***(P-16477)***
W San Diego Hotel, San Diego *Also called Rp Scs Wsd Hotel LLC* ***(P-12844)***
W Scott Bllard Dsign Arch Inc...E.......323 386-4740
1800 Century Park E # 600 Los Angeles (90067) ***(P-17157)***
W Why W Enterprises Inc...D.......626 969-4292
2671 Pomona Blvd Pomona (91768) ***(P-4243)***
W-Bel Age LLC...D.......310 854-1111
1020 N San Vicente Blvd West Hollywood (90069) ***(P-13070)***
W-Emerald LLC...C.......619 239-4500
400 W Broadway San Diego (92101) ***(P-13071)***
W2005 New Cntury Ht Prtflio LP...D.......408 745-6000
1100 N Mathilda Ave Sunnyvale (94089) ***(P-13072)***
W2005 Wyn Hotels LP...D.......323 887-8100
5757 Telegraph Rd Commerce (90040) ***(P-13073)***
Wachovia A Division Wells F...A.......415 571-2832
420 Montgomery St San Francisco (94104) ***(P-9123)***
Wad Productions Inc...D.......818 260-5673
3500 W Olive Ave Ste 1000 Burbank (91505) ***(P-17703)***
Waddell & Reed Inc...D.......714 437-7510
695 Town Center Dr # 200 Costa Mesa (92626) ***(P-9768)***
Wade & Lowe A Prof Corp (PA)...D.......909 483-6700
3200 Inland Empire Blvd # 160 Ontario (91764) ***(P-22859)***
Wagan Corporation...E.......510 471-9221
31088 San Clemente St Hayward (94544) ***(P-6479)***
Wageworks Inc (HQ)...C.......650 577-5200
1100 Park Pl 4 San Mateo (94403) ***(P-26874)***
Waggoners Trucking...D.......800 999-9097
801 Mcwane Blvd Port Hueneme (93043) ***(P-4165)***
Wagner Construction Co (PA)...C.......619 873-2160
12512 Ca 67 Lakeside (92040) ***(P-3236)***
Wagner Financials, Manhattan Beach *Also called GBS Financial Corp* ***(P-16793)***
Wagner Heights Nursing & Rehab, Stockton *Also called Covenant Care California LLC* ***(P-19827)***

Mergent e-mail: customerrelations@mergent.com 2020 Directory of California (P-0000) Products & Services Section entry number
1480 Wholesalers and Services Companies (PA)=Parent Co (HQ)=Headquarters (DH)=Div Headquarters

Wags & Wiggles Dog Daycare LLC (PA)...D...949 635-9655
23171 Arroyo Vis Rcho STA Marg (92688) ***(P-609)***

Wah Hung Intl McHy Inc...D...323 263-3513
800 Monterey Pass Rd Monterey Park (91754) ***(P-6414)***

Waldberg Inc...D...818 843-0004
14455 Ventura Blvd Fl 3 Sherman Oaks (91423) ***(P-13640)***

Walk Through Video, McClellan *Also called Villara Corporation* ***(P-2312)***

Walker & Dunlop Inc...D...301 215-5500
12100 Wilshire Blvd # 1500 Los Angeles (90025) ***(P-9607)***

Walker & Zanger Inc (PA)...D...818 280-8300
16719 Schoenborn St North Hills (91343) ***(P-6703)***

Walker Advertising LLC...E...310 519-4050
20101 Hamilton Ave # 300 Torrance (90502) ***(P-13598)***

Walker Communications Inc...D...707 421-1300
521 Railroad Ave Suisun City (94585) ***(P-2689)***

Walkme Inc (PA)...D...855 492-5563
525 Market St Lbby San Francisco (94105) ***(P-15195)***

Walkup Melodia Kelly...E...415 981-7210
650 California St Fl 26 San Francisco (94108) ***(P-22860)***

Walkup Law Office, San Francisco *Also called Walkup Melodia Kelly* ***(P-22860)***

Wall Systems Inc...D...805 523-9091
11975 Discovery Ct Moorpark (93021) ***(P-2875)***

Wall Tech, Diamond Bar *Also called March International Inc* ***(P-1974)***

Wallace-Kuhl & Associates, West Sacramento *Also called River Cy Geoprofessionals Inc* ***(P-25287)***

Wallace-Kuhl Investments LLC (PA)...D...916 372-1434
3050 Industrial Blvd West Sacramento (95691) ***(P-25385)***

Wallis Fashions Inc...C...510 763-8018
1100 8th Ave Oakland (94606) ***(P-17158)***

Wally Park, Los Angeles *Also called Lrw Investments LLC* ***(P-17263)***

Walmart Inc...B...909 349-3600
13550 Valley Blvd Fontana (92335) ***(P-4536)***

Walmart Inc...B...760 961-6300
21101 Johnson Rd Apple Valley (92307) ***(P-4537)***

Walmart Inc...A...530 529-0916
10815 Highway 99w Red Bluff (96080) ***(P-4538)***

Walmart Inc...B...951 681-7256
4250 Hamner Ave Eastvale (91752) ***(P-4539)***

Walmart Inc...B...559 783-1109
1300 S F St Porterville (93257) ***(P-4540)***

Walnut Country, Concord *Also called Cowell Homeowners Association* ***(P-24528)***

Walnut Creek Active Club, Walnut Creek *Also called 24 Hour Fitness Usa Inc* ***(P-18111)***

Walnut Creek Embassy Suites, Walnut Creek *Also called Ashford Trs Nickel LLC* ***(P-12022)***

Walnut Creek Spt & Fitnes CLB, Walnut Creek *Also called Olympic Investors Ltd* ***(P-18523)***

Walnut Manor Care Center, Anaheim *Also called Front Porch Communities* ***(P-20556)***

Walnut Valley Unified Schl Dst...D...909 595-1261
880 S Lemon Ave Walnut (91789) ***(P-24886)***

Walnut Valley Water District...D...909 595-7554
271 Brea Canyon Rd Walnut (91789) ***(P-6126)***

Walnut Whtney Cnvalescent Hosp...C...916 488-8601
3529 Walnut Ave Carmichael (95608) ***(P-20369)***

Walnut Whtney Convalecent Hosp, Carmichael *Also called Horizon West Inc* ***(P-20020)***

Walong Marketing Inc (PA)...D...714 670-8899
6281 Regio Ave Buena Park (90620) ***(P-8673)***

Walpert Center, Hayward *Also called ARC of Alameda County* ***(P-23564)***

Walsh Group Inc...D...530 221-4405
3135 Agassi Ln Redding (96002) ***(P-18210)***

Walsworth Franklin & Bevins, Orange *Also called Walswrth Frnklin Bevins McCall* ***(P-22861)***

Walswrth Frnklin Bevins McCall (PA)...D...714 634-2522
1 City Blvd W Ste 500 Orange (92868) ***(P-22861)***

Walt Disney Company...D...916 780-1470
8265 Sierra College Blvd # 21 Roseville (95661) ***(P-5574)***

Walt Disney Family Museum...D...415 345-6800
104 Montgomery St San Francisco (94129) ***(P-24299)***

Walt Disney Imagineering (HQ)...A...818 544-6500
1401 Flower St Glendale (91201) ***(P-17780)***

Walt Disney Pictures...B...818 409-2200
811 Sonora Ave Glendale (91201) ***(P-17781)***

Walt Disney Pictures and TV...D...818 560-1000
500 S Buena Vista St Burbank (91521) ***(P-17800)***

Walt Disney Records Direct (HQ)...A...818 560-1000
500 S Buena Vista St Burbank (91521) ***(P-17704)***

Walt Disney Studios, Burbank *Also called Twdc Enterprises 18 Corp* ***(P-5659)***

Walter & Wolf, Fremont *Also called Walters & Wolf Glass Company* ***(P-3300)***

Walter Anderson Plumbing Inc...C...619 449-7646
1830 John Towers Ave El Cajon (92020) ***(P-2315)***

Walter E McGuire RE Inc...C...650 348-0222
360 Primrose Rd Burlingame (94010) ***(P-11504)***

Walter E McGuire RE Inc (PA)...B...415 929-1500
2001 Lombard St San Francisco (94123) ***(P-11505)***

Walter E McGuire RE Inc...E...415 296-0123
17 Bluxome St San Francisco (94107) ***(P-11506)***

Walter J Conn & Associates...D...213 683-0500
800 W 6th St Ste 600 Los Angeles (90017) ***(P-25509)***

Walters & Wolf Glass Company (PA)...C...510 490-1115
41450 Boscell Rd Fremont (94538) ***(P-3300)***

Walters & Wolf Interiors (PA)...D...415 243-9400
41450 Boscell Rd Fremont (94538) ***(P-2990)***

Walters Family Partnership...C...760 320-6868
400 E Tahquitz Canyon Way Palm Springs (92262) ***(P-13074)***

Walters Wholesale Electric Co (HQ)...E...562 988-3100
2825 Temple Ave Signal Hill (90755) ***(P-7190)***

Walters Wholesale Electric Co...C...714 784-1900
200 N Berry St Brea (92821) ***(P-7191)***

Walton Construction Inc...D...909 267-7777
358 E Foothill Blvd # 100 San Dimas (91773) ***(P-1282)***

Walton Construction Services, San Dimas *Also called Walton Construction Inc* ***(P-1282)***

Walton Electric Corporation...D...909 981-5051
755 N Central Ave Upland (91786) ***(P-2690)***

Walton Engineering Inc...D...916 372-1888
3900 Commerce Dr West Sacramento (95691) ***(P-3487)***

Walz Group LLC (HQ)...C...951 491-6800
27398 Via Industria Temecula (92590) ***(P-15196)***

Walz Postal Solutions, Temecula *Also called Walz Group LLC* ***(P-15196)***

Wamc Company Inc (PA)...D...858 454-2753
7420 Clairemont Mesa Blvd San Diego (92111) ***(P-10842)***

Wannajob Inc...D...562 426-5272
2710 Saint Louis Ave Signal Hill (90755) ***(P-14593)***

War Memorial Prfrmg Art Ctr, San Francisco *Also called City & County of San Francisco* ***(P-17899)***

Ward Enterprises...B...209 358-0445
2679 Buhach Rd Atwater (95301) ***(P-14081)***

Ward, E B, Brisbane *Also called Edward B Ward & Company Inc* ***(P-7446)***

Wardens Office Inc (PA)...D...949 916-5771
4101 Technology Dr Modesto (95356) ***(P-7869)***

Wardlow 2 LP (PA)...D...562 432-8066
333 S Grand Ave Ste 4070 Los Angeles (90071) ***(P-17562)***

Ware Disposal Inc...C...714 834-0234
1451 Manhattan Ave Fullerton (92831) ***(P-6315)***

Ware Malcomb (PA)...C...949 660-9128
110 Edison Pl Irvine (92618) ***(P-25510)***

Warehouse, San Bernardino *Also called San Bernardino City Unf School* ***(P-4498)***

Warehouse, Lancaster *Also called Michaels Stores Inc* ***(P-4450)***

Warehouse and Distribution, Jurupa Valley *Also called Triways Inc* ***(P-4148)***

Warfighter & Family Services...D...619 556-7168
2375 Recreation Way San Diego (92136) ***(P-17159)***

Warfighter & Family Services C, San Diego *Also called Warfighter & Family Services* ***(P-17159)***

Warmington Homes (PA)...C...714 434-4435
3090 Pullman St Costa Mesa (92626) ***(P-1322)***

Warmington Homes...D...949 679-3100
15615 Alton Pkwy Ste 150 Irvine (92618) ***(P-1323)***

Warmington Homes...C...925 866-6700
2400 Camino Ramon Ste 234 San Ramon (94583) ***(P-1324)***

Warmington Residental, San Ramon *Also called Warmington Homes* ***(P-1324)***

Warmington Residential Cal Inc...C...714 557-5511
3090 Pullman St Costa Mesa (92626) ***(P-1219)***

Warner Bros Consumer Pdts Inc (HQ)...C...818 954-7980
4001 W Olive Ave Burbank (91505) ***(P-27255)***

Warner Bros Distributing Inc...C...818 954-6000
4000 Warner Blvd Bldg 154 Burbank (91522) ***(P-26453)***

Warner Bros Domestic TV Dist, Burbank *Also called Warner Bros Entertainment Inc* ***(P-17708)***

Warner Bros Entertainment Inc...C...818 954-1817
4000 Warner Blvd Burbank (91522) ***(P-17705)***

Warner Bros Entertainment Inc...B...818 954-7232
4000 W Alameda Ave Burbank (91505) ***(P-17706)***

Warner Bros Entertainment Inc...C...818 954-3000
4000 Warner Blvd Burbank (91522) ***(P-17707)***

Warner Bros Entertainment Inc...C...818 954-5301
4000 Warner Blvd Bldg 118 Burbank (91522) ***(P-17708)***

Warner Bros Entertainment Inc...C...818 954-6000
4000 Warner Blvd Burbank (91522) ***(P-17709)***

Warner Bros Entertainment Inc (HQ)...A...818 954-6000
4000 Warner Blvd Burbank (91522) ***(P-17710)***

Warner Bros Entertainment Inc...C...818 954-3000
15301 Ventura Blvd Sherman Oaks (91403) ***(P-17711)***

Warner Bros Entertainment Inc...C...818 954-2181
4000 Warner Blvd Bldg 30 Burbank (91522) ***(P-17712)***

Warner Bros Home Entrmt Inc (HQ)...D...818 954-6000
4000 Warner Blvd Bldg 160 Burbank (91522) ***(P-17713)***

Warner Bros Intl TV Dist Inc...D...818 954-6000
4000 Warner Blvd Burbank (91522) ***(P-17714)***

Warner Bros Records Inc (HQ)...B...818 846-9090
777 S Santa Fe Ave Los Angeles (90021) ***(P-17160)***

Warner Bros Studio Facilities, Burbank *Also called Warner Bros Entertainment Inc* ***(P-17707)***

Warner Bros Transatlantic Inc (HQ)...A...818 977-0018
4000 Warner Blvd Burbank (91522) ***(P-17796)***

Warner Bros Transatlantic Inc...A...818 977-6384
3300 W Olive Ave Ste 200 Burbank (91505) ***(P-17797)***

Warner Bros Transatlantic Inc...A...818 972-0777
3500 W Olive Ave Ste 1000 Burbank (91505) ***(P-17798)***

Warner Bros. Legal Department, Burbank *Also called Warner Bros Entertainment Inc* ***(P-17706)***

Warner Bros. Paint Department, Burbank *Also called Warner Bros Entertainment Inc* ***(P-17705)***

Warner Center Marriott Hotel, Woodland Hills *Also called Tr Warner Center LP* ***(P-13034)***

Warner Media LLC...D...661 344-1546
2014 W Avenue K Lancaster (93536) ***(P-5771)***

Warner Media LLC...D...805 421-4467
2650 Tapo Canyon Rd Simi Valley (93063) ***(P-5772)***

Warner Pacific Insur Svcs Inc (PA)...C...408 298-4049
32110 Agoura Rd Westlake Village (91361) ***(P-10544)***

Warner Villa, Woodland Hills *Also called Topanga Villas Company* ***(P-10828)***

Warren Auto De Mexico LLC...D...858 794-7947
517 S Cedros Ave Solana Beach (92075) ***(P-9022)***

Warren Distributing Inc (PA)...D...562 789-3360
8737 Dice Rd Santa Fe Springs (90670) ***(P-6480)***

Warren Drye Kelley...D...310 712-6100
10100 Santa Monica Blvd # 1050 Los Angeles (90067) ***(P-22862)***

Warren E & P, Long Beach *Also called Warren E&P Inc* ***(P-8741)***

Warren E&P Inc...D...877 587-9494
400 Oceangate Ste 200 Long Beach (90802) ***(P-8741)***

Warren Knox Roofing, Santa Cruz *Also called Forever Firewood Inc* ***(P-3055)***

Employee Codes: A=Over 500 employees, B=251-500
C=101-250, D=51-100, E=50
2020 Directory of California
Wholesalers and Services Companies
© Mergent Inc. 1-800-342-5647
1481

Warren Security Systems Inc .... E 415 456-7034
1305 Francisco Blvd E San Rafael (94901) *(P-16568)*
Warrior Custom Golf Inc (PA) .... C 949 699-2499
15 Mason Irvine (92618) *(P-7723)*
Warrior Golf, Irvine *Also called Warrior Custom Golf Inc (P-7723)*
Warwick California Corporation .... D 415 992-3809
490 Geary St San Francisco (94102) *(P-13075)*
Warwick Hotel San Francisco, San Francisco *Also called Warwick California Corporation (P-13075)*
Wash Mltfmily Ldry Systems LLC (PA) .... C 310 643-8491
100 N Pacific Coast Hwy El Segundo (90245) *(P-13252)*
Washington Enterprises 3 LLC .... D 323 731-0861
2300 W Washington Blvd Los Angeles (90018) *(P-20370)*
Washington Group, Del Mar *Also called Aecom Energy & Cnstr Inc (P-1656)*
Washington Inn LLC .... D 310 821-4455
737 Washington Blvd Marina Del Rey (90292) *(P-13076)*
Washington Inventory Service (HQ) .... C 858 565-8111
9265 Sky Park Ct Ste 100 San Diego (92123) *(P-17161)*
Washington Inventory Service .... D 619 461-8198
7150 El Cajon Blvd San Diego (92115) *(P-17162)*
Washington Iron Works, Gardena *Also called Washington Orna Ir Works Inc (P-3488)*
Washington Mutual, Studio City *Also called Jpmorgan Chase Bank Nat Assn (P-9265)*
Washington Orna Ir Works Inc (PA) .... D 310 327-8660
17926 S Broadway Gardena (90248) *(P-3488)*
Washington Otptent Surgery Ctr, Fremont *Also called Washington Outpatient (P-21369)*
Washington Outpatient .... D 510 791-5374
2299 Mowry Ave Fl 1 Fremont (94538) *(P-21369)*
Wasser Filtration Inc .... D 714 525-0630
1215 N Fee Ana St Anaheim (92807) *(P-7608)*
Wasserman Comden & Casselman (PA) .... D 323 872-0995
5567 Reseda Blvd Ste 330 Tarzana (91356) *(P-22863)*
Wasserman Media Group LLC (PA) .... C 310 407-0200
10900 Wilshire Blvd Fl 12 Los Angeles (90024) *(P-26875)*
Waste Connections, Diamond Springs *Also called County of El Dorado (P-6189)*
Waste Connections Cal Inc .... C 408 752-8530
301 Carl Rd Sunnyvale (94089) *(P-6316)*
Waste Connections Cal Inc (HQ) .... C 408 282-4400
1333 Oakland Rd San Jose (95112) *(P-6317)*
Waste Management, Visalia *Also called USA Waste of California Inc (P-6296)*
Waste Management, Gold River *Also called USA Waste of California Inc (P-6299)*
Waste Management, Castroville *Also called Ajax Portable Services (P-14124)*
Waste Management, Atascadero *Also called USA Waste of California Inc (P-6303)*
Waste Management, El Cajon *Also called USA Waste of California Inc (P-6304)*
Waste Management, Chino *Also called USA Waste of California Inc (P-6305)*
Waste Management Cal Inc (HQ) .... C 877 836-6526
9081 Tujunga Ave Sun Valley (91352) *(P-6318)*
Waste Management Cal Inc .... D 619 596-5100
1001 W Bradley Ave El Cajon (92020) *(P-6319)*
Waste Management Cal Inc .... D 661 947-7197
1200 W City Ranch Rd Palmdale (93551) *(P-6320)*
Waste Management Cal Inc .... D 760 439-2824
2141 Oceanside Blvd Oceanside (92054) *(P-6321)*
Waste Management Nevada County, Grass Valley *Also called USA Waste of California Inc (P-3950)*
Waste Management Orange County, Santa Ana *Also called USA Waste of California Inc (P-6313)*
Waste Management Recycling .... D 818 767-6180
9227 Tujunga Ave Sun Valley (91352) *(P-3953)*
Waste Managment, Corning *Also called Andersncttonwood Disposal Svcs (P-3849)*
Waste Mgt Collectn & Recycl .... C 626 960-7551
5701 S Eastrn Ave Ste 300 Commerce (90040) *(P-6322)*
Waste Mgt Collectn & Recycl .... C 925 935-8900
2658 N Main St Walnut Creek (94597) *(P-3954)*
Waste Mgt Collectn & Recycl .... D 831 768-9505
1340 W Beach St Watsonville (95076) *(P-6323)*
Waste MGT Collectn & Recycl .... D 707 462-0210
219 Pudding Creek Rd Fort Bragg (95437) *(P-6324)*
Waste MGT Collectn & Recycl .... D 909 242-0421
17700 Indian St Moreno Valley (92551) *(P-6325)*
Waste MGT Collectn & Recycl .... D 707 462-0210
450 Orr Springs Rd Ukiah (95482) *(P-6326)*
Waste MGT Collectn Recycl Inc .... C 951 242-0421
17700 Indian St Moreno Valley (92551) *(P-6327)*
Waste MGT Collectn Recycl Inc .... B 714 637-3010
1800 S Grand Ave Santa Ana (92705) *(P-14116)*
Waste MGT Collectn Recycl Inc .... D 949 451-2600
16122 Construction Cir E Irvine (92606) *(P-6328)*
Waste MGT of Alameda Cnty (HQ) .... A 510 613-8710
172 98th Ave Oakland (94603) *(P-6329)*
Waste MGT of Alameda Cnty .... D 510 638-2303
2615 Davis St San Leandro (94577) *(P-6330)*
Waste MGT of Alameda Cnty .... C 951 280-5471
800 S Temescal St Corona (92879) *(P-6331)*
Wastexperts Incorporated .... D 925 484-1057
901 Howe Rd Martinez (94553) *(P-26454)*
Watch Resources Inc (PA) .... D 209 533-0510
12801 Cabezut Rd Sonora (95370) *(P-23540)*
Watchit Media Inc .... C 702 740-1700
655 Montgomery St # 1000 San Francisco (94111) *(P-17715)*
Watchpoint Logistics Inc .... C 650 871-4747
50 Tanforan Ave South San Francisco (94080) *(P-5082)*
Water & Power Department, Long Beach *Also called County of Los Angeles (P-6041)*
Water & Sewer Service .... D 925 828-8524
7051 Dublin Blvd Dublin (94568) *(P-1930)*
Water Course Way, Palo Alto *Also called Watercourse Way (P-13459)*
Water Division, Fresno *Also called City of Fresno (P-6030)*
Water Drops Express Carwash, Santa Monica *Also called Alisam Oxnard Operating (P-10563)*
Water Emergency Dispatch, Long Beach *Also called City of Long Beach (P-6033)*
Water Heaters Only Inc .... D 650 368-9998
3620 Haven Ave Redwood City (94063) *(P-7221)*
Water Quality Control Plant, Palo Alto *Also called City of Palo Alto (P-16698)*
Water Resources Cal Dept .... D 916 574-1423
3310 El Cmino Ave Ste 200 Sacramento (95821) *(P-26044)*
Water Resources Cal Dept .... E 916 324-3812
1416 9th St Rm 1225 Sacramento (95814) *(P-15893)*
Water Resources Control Bd Cal .... D 619 521-3010
2375 Northside Dr Ste 100 San Diego (92108) *(P-24371)*
Water Resources Division, Livermore *Also called City of Livermore (P-1954)*
Water Supply, Vacaville *Also called County of Solano (P-6044)*
Water Svcs Operations & Repr, Oxnard *Also called City of Oxnard (P-6035)*
Watercourse Way .... C 650 462-2000
165 Channing Ave Palo Alto (94301) *(P-13459)*
Waterfall Resort .... D 805 879-3780
5951 Encina Rd Ste 207 Goleta (93117) *(P-13077)*
Waterfront Hotel LLC .... B 714 845-8000
21100 Pacific Coast Hwy Huntington Beach (92648) *(P-13078)*
Waterfront Plaza Hotel LLC .... D 510 836-3800
10 Washington St Oakland (94607) *(P-13079)*
Waterhill Ltd .... E 626 369-6828
140 N Orange Ave City of Industry (91744) *(P-6537)*
Waterhouse Management Corp .... C 916 772-4918
500 Giuseppe Ct Ste 2 Roseville (95678) *(P-10865)*
Waterline Data Science Inc .... D 650 868-4409
615 National Ave Ste 100 Mountain View (94043) *(P-15197)*
Waterman Convalescent Hospital .... C 951 681-2200
6401 33rd St Riverside (92509) *(P-21503)*
Waterman Convalescent Hospital (PA) .... C 909 882-1215
1850 N Waterman Ave San Bernardino (92404) *(P-20371)*
Watermark Rtrment Cmmnties Inc .... D 760 346-5420
41505 Carlotta Dr Palm Desert (92211) *(P-20372)*
Watermark Rtrment Cmmnties Inc .... D 858 597-8000
3890 Nobel Dr San Diego (92122) *(P-11507)*
Waters Edge Inc .... C 510 748-4300
2401 Blanding Ave Alameda (94501) *(P-20373)*
Waters Edge Lodge .... E 510 769-6264
801 Island Dr Apt 267 Alameda (94502) *(P-24111)*
Waters Edge Nursing Home, Alameda *Also called Waters Edge Inc (P-20373)*
Waters Moving & Storage Inc .... D 925 372-0914
37 Bridgehead Rd Martinez (94553) *(P-4244)*
Waterworks Park, Redding *Also called Yanaco Inc (P-18343)*
Waterworld USA, Concord *Also called Parc Management LLC (P-18734)*
Waterworld USA, Sacramento *Also called Six Flags Entertainment Corp (P-18341)*
Watg, Irvine *Also called Wimberly Allison Tong Goo Inc (P-25515)*
Watkin & Bortolussi Inc .... D 415 453-4675
726 Alfred Nobel Dr Hercules (94547) *(P-926)*
Watkins Construction Co Inc .... D 661 763-5395
112 E Cedar St Taft (93268) *(P-1931)*
Watlow Electric Mfg Co .... D 408 776-6646
6781 Via Del Oro San Jose (95119) *(P-25386)*
Watson Carton .... D 408 979-9618
4178 Ross Ave San Jose (95124) *(P-24239)*
Watson Cogeneration Co Inc .... D 310 816-8100
22850 Wilmington Ave Carson (90745) *(P-5961)*
Watson Contractors Inc .... D 916 481-6293
3185 Longview Dr Sacramento (95821) *(P-1391)*
Watsonville Coast Produce Inc .... C 831 722-3851
275 Kearney Ext Frnt Watsonville (95076) *(P-8538)*
Watsonville Community Hospital, Watsonville *Also called Halsen Healthcare LLC (P-20897)*
Watsonville Health Clinic, Watsonville *Also called Santa Cruz County of (P-19368)*
Watsonville Nursing Center, Watsonville *Also called CF Watsonville East LLC (P-19794)*
Watsonville Post Acute Center, Watsonville *Also called CF Watsonville LLC (P-19793)*
Watsonville Post Acute Center, Watsonville *Also called CF Watsonville West LLC (P-19795)*
Watt Commercial Properties, Santa Monica *Also called Watt Properties Inc (P-11621)*
Watt Properties Inc (PA) .... D 310 314-2430
2716 Ocean Park Blvd # 2025 Santa Monica (90405) *(P-11621)*
Watts Health Center, Los Angeles *Also called Watts Health Foundation Inc (P-11822)*
Watts Health Foundation Inc (HQ) .... B 310 424-2220
3405 W Imperial Hwy # 304 Inglewood (90303) *(P-20470)*
Watts Health Foundation Inc .... B 323 357-6688
10300 Compton Ave Los Angeles (90002) *(P-11822)*
Watts Healthcare Corporation .... C 323 241-1780
700 W Imperial Hwy Los Angeles (90044) *(P-19587)*
Watts Healthcare Corporation (PA) .... C 323 564-4331
10300 Compton Ave Los Angeles (90002) *(P-19588)*
Watts Labor Community Action .... C 323 563-5639
4142 Palmwood Dr Apt 11 Los Angeles (90008) *(P-23541)*
Wave Plastic Surgery Ctr Inc .... C 626 964-7788
18433 Colima Rd La Puente (91748) *(P-19589)*
Wave Plastic Surgery Ctr Inc .... B 626 898-9711
400 N Santa Anita Ave Arcadia (91006) *(P-21370)*
Wave Plstic Srgery Ctr Arcadia, Arcadia *Also called Wave Plastic Surgery Ctr Inc (P-21370)*
Wavestrong Inc .... D 925 549-2882
5674 Stoneridge Dr # 225 Pleasanton (94588) *(P-15711)*
Wawanesa General Insurance Co .... B 619 285-6020
9050 Friars Rd Ste 200 San Diego (92108) *(P-10148)*
Wawansea General Insurance, San Diego *Also called Wawanesa General Insurance Co (P-10148)*
Wawona Packing Co LLC (PA) .... D 559 528-4000
12133 Avenue 408 Cutler (93615) *(P-560)*
Wawona Packing Co LLC .... B 559 528-4699
12133 Avenue 408 Cutler (93615) *(P-17163)*

Mergent e-mail: customerrelations@mergent.com
1482
2020 Directory of California
Wholesalers and Services Companies
(P-0000) Products & Services Section entry number
(PA)=Parent Co (HQ)=Headquarters (DH)=Div Headquarters

Waxies Enterprises Inc .... C 909 942-3100
905 Wineville Ave Ontario (91764) ***(P-7684)***
Waxies Enterprises Inc .... E 925 454-2900
901 N Canyon Pkwy Livermore (94551) ***(P-7685)***
Way Cool Homecare Inc .... E 619 444-3200
900 N Cuyamaca St Ste 201 El Cajon (92020) ***(P-21909)***
Wayforward Technologies Inc .... E 661 286-2769
28738 The Old Rd Valencia (91355) ***(P-15198)***
Wayne E Swisher Cem Contr Inc .... D 925 757-3660
2620 E 18th St Antioch (94509) ***(P-3237)***
Wayne Maples Plumbing & Htg .... D 707 445-2500
317 W Cedar St Eureka (95501) ***(P-2316)***
Wayne Perry Inc (PA) .... C 714 826-0352
8281 Commonwealth Ave Buena Park (90621) ***(P-3489)***
Wayne Provision Co Inc (PA) .... D 323 277-5888
5030 Gifford Ave Vernon (90058) ***(P-8422)***
Wayne R Kidder .... D 805 967-6993
915 Via Los Padres Santa Barbara (93111) ***(P-19590)***
Wb Electric Inc .... D 408 842-7911
30611 Road 400 Coarsegold (93614) ***(P-2691)***
Wca, Los Angeles *Also called West Coast Ambulance Corp* ***(P-3737)***
Wcco Holdings Inc .... B 800 421-6150
6913 W Acco St Montebello (90640) ***(P-11704)***
Wcct Global Inc (PA) .... D 714 668-1500
5630 Cerritos Ave Cypress (90630) ***(P-26045)***
Wcg World, San Francisco *Also called Weisscomm Group Ltd* ***(P-27256)***
WCIRB, Oakland *Also called Workers Compensation* ***(P-10151)***
WCO Hotels Inc (HQ) .... D 323 636-3251
1150 W Magic Way Anaheim (92802) ***(P-13080)***
WD Partners Inc .... E 949 753-7676
16808 Armstrong Ave # 100 Irvine (92606) ***(P-25511)***
Wdc Explrtion Wells Holdg Corp .... C 916 419-6043
1300 National Dr Ste 140 Sacramento (95834) ***(P-1932)***
Wdi, Santa Fe Springs *Also called Warren Distributing Inc* ***(P-6480)***
Wdm Group, San Diego *Also called White Digital Media Inc* ***(P-8879)***
Wdpt Film Distribution LLC .... C 818 560-1000
500 S Buena Vista St Burbank (91521) ***(P-7362)***
We Care Day Care & Pre School .... D 209 832-4072
1790 Sequoia Blvd Tracy (95376) ***(P-23801)***
We Pack It All, Duarte *Also called Bershtel Enterprises LLC* ***(P-16649)***
We Team Security Firm Inc .... D 800 745-9051
12655 W Jefferson Blvd Los Angeles (90066) ***(P-16478)***
Wealth Educators Inc .... C 310 623-9145
5209 Wilshire Blvd Los Angeles (90036) ***(P-26455)***
Wealthtv, San Diego *Also called Herring Broadcasting Company* ***(P-5611)***
Weatherford International LLC .... D 805 781-3580
1880 Santa Barbara Ave # 220 San Luis Obispo (93401) ***(P-1049)***
Weatherford International LLC .... D 661 587-9753
21728 Rosedale Hwy Bakersfield (93314) ***(P-1050)***
Weave, Sacramento *Also called WEAVE Incorporated* ***(P-14594)***
WEAVE Incorporated (PA) .... D 916 448-2321
1900 K St Ste 200 Sacramento (95811) ***(P-14594)***
Webasto Charging Systems Inc (HQ) .... D 626 415-4000
1333 S Mayflower Ave # 100 Monrovia (91016) ***(P-6481)***
Webb Sunrise Inc .... E 619 220-7050
3320 Kemper St Ste 201 San Diego (92110) ***(P-9023)***
Webcor Builders, Alameda *Also called Webcor Construction LP* ***(P-1643)***
Webcor Construction LP (HQ) .... D 415 978-1000
1751 Harbor Bay Pkwy # 200 Alameda (94502) ***(P-1643)***
Weber Distribution LLC .... B 909 335-8800
1651 California St Ste A Redlands (92374) ***(P-4541)***
Weber Distribution LLC (PA) .... B 855 469-3237
13530 Rosecrans Ave Santa Fe Springs (90670) ***(P-4360)***
Weber Distribution Cwo, Rancho Cucamonga *Also called Weber Distribution Warehouses* ***(P-4542)***
Weber Distribution Warehouses .... E 909 481-1600
9345 Santa Anita Ave B Rancho Cucamonga (91730) ***(P-4542)***
Weber Distribution Warehouses .... E 562 404-9996
15301 Shoemaker Ave Norwalk (90650) ***(P-4543)***
Weber Logistics, Santa Fe Springs *Also called Weber Distribution LLC* ***(P-4360)***
Weber Shandwick .... D 415 262-5600
600 Battery St Fl 1 San Francisco (94111) ***(P-26925)***
Webers Quality Meats Inc .... D 510 635-9892
990 Carden St San Leandro (94577) ***(P-8423)***
Webex.com, San Jose *Also called Cisco Webex LLC* ***(P-16695)***
Webly Systems Inc .... E 888 444-6400
2603 Camino Ramon Ste 200 San Ramon (94583) ***(P-17164)***
Webpass Inc .... D 415 233-4100
267 8th St San Francisco (94103) ***(P-5495)***
Webster Investment Management, San Francisco *Also called Forward Management LLC* ***(P-9816)***
Webyog Inc .... C 408 512-1434
2900 Gordon Ave 100-7p Santa Clara (95051) ***(P-15199)***
Weckworth Construction Co Inc .... D 916 939-6636
3941 Park Dr Ste 20-373 El Dorado Hills (95762) ***(P-2692)***
Weckworth Electric Company, El Dorado Hills *Also called Weckworth Construction Co Inc* ***(P-2692)***
Weco - Us.ca. El Centro, El Centro *Also called Wilbur-Ellis Company LLC* ***(P-8865)***
Weco Aerospace Systems, Lincoln *Also called Weygandt & Associates* ***(P-17564)***
Weco Aerospace Systems, Lincoln *Also called Gdsa-Lincoln Inc* ***(P-17456)***
Wedbush Securities Inc (HQ) .... B 213 688-8000
1000 Wilshire Blvd # 800 Los Angeles (90017) ***(P-9769)***
Wedgewood Hspitality Group Inc .... E 951 491-8110
43385 Business Park Dr Temecula (92590) ***(P-13460)***
Wedgewood Inc (PA) .... D 310 640-3070
2015 Manhattan Beach Blvd # 100 Redondo Beach (90278) ***(P-11967)***
Weeks Drilling and Pump Co (PA) .... E 707 823-3184
6100 Highway 12 Sebastopol (95472) ***(P-2317)***
WEI-Chuan USA Inc (PA) .... C 626 225-7168
6655 Garfield Ave Bell Gardens (90201) ***(P-8306)***
Weil Gotshal & Manges LLP .... C 650 802-3000
201 Redwood Shors Pkwy Redwood City (94065) ***(P-22864)***
Weinberg Roger & Resenfeld (PA) .... D 510 337-1001
1001 Marina Village Pkwy # 200 Alameda (94501) ***(P-22865)***
Weingart Center Association .... C 213 622-6359
566 S San Pedro St Los Angeles (90013) ***(P-23542)***
Weingart Center For Homeless, Los Angeles *Also called Weingart Center Association* ***(P-23542)***
Weingart-Lakewood Family YMCA, Lakewood *Also called Young Mens Chrstn Assc Gr L B* ***(P-24745)***
Weinstein Company LLC .... D 424 204-4800
9100 Wilshire Blvd 700w Beverly Hills (90212) ***(P-17716)***
Weinstein Construction Corp .... E 818 782-4000
15102 Raymer St Van Nuys (91405) ***(P-1644)***
Weintraub Tobin Chediak .... E 310 858-7888
9665 Wilshire Blvd # 900 Beverly Hills (90212) ***(P-22866)***
Weintraub Tobin Chediak (PA) .... E 916 558-6000
400 Capitol Mall Fl 11 Sacramento (95814) ***(P-22867)***
Weiss Associates, Emeryville *Also called Aguatierra Associates Inc* ***(P-26928)***
Weisscomm Group Ltd (PA) .... D 415 362-5018
50 Francisco St Ste 400 San Francisco (94133) ***(P-27256)***
Weitz & Luxenberg PC .... D 310 247-0921
1880 Century Park E # 700 Los Angeles (90067) ***(P-22868)***
Welcome Baby, Anaheim *Also called Orange County Child Abuse* ***(P-23366)***
Welcome Group Management LLC .... D 310 378-6666
300 S Court St Visalia (93291) ***(P-13081)***
Weldlogic Inc .... D 805 375-1670
2651 Lavery Ct Newbury Park (91320) ***(P-17476)***
Welfare Administration, Oroville *Also called County of Butte* ***(P-23060)***
Welfare Department, Sonora *Also called County of Tuolumne* ***(P-23177)***
Welfare Dept, Pomona *Also called City of Pomona* ***(P-24145)***
Welfare Dept Warehouse, Oroville *Also called County of Butte* ***(P-23061)***
Welk Group Inc (PA) .... B 760 749-3000
8860 Lawrence Welk Dr Escondido (92026) ***(P-13082)***
Welk Music Group, Escondido *Also called Welk Group Inc* ***(P-13082)***
Welk Resort Center, San Marcos *Also called Welk Resort Group Inc* ***(P-11508)***
Welk Resort Group Inc (PA) .... E 760 652-4913
300 Rancheros Dr Ste 450 San Marcos (92069) ***(P-11508)***
Welker Bros, Milpitas *Also called H V Welker Co Inc* ***(P-3003)***
Well Being Group Inc .... D 559 432-3737
7075 N Howard St Ste 102 Fresno (93720) ***(P-21910)***
Well Within Spa .... D 831 458-9355
417 Cedar St Santa Cruz (95060) ***(P-3490)***
Wellhead Electric Company Inc .... E 916 447-5171
650 Bercut Dr Ste C Sacramento (95811) ***(P-5962)***
Wellington, The, Laguna Hills *Also called Birtcher/Aetna Laguna Hills* ***(P-10697)***
Wellmade Products, Merced *Also called WLMD* ***(P-3494)***
Wells & Bennett Realtors (PA) .... D 510 531-7000
1451 Leimert Blvd Oakland (94602) ***(P-11509)***
Wells Capital Management Inc (HQ) .... E 415 396-8000
525 Market St Fl 10 San Francisco (94105) ***(P-9854)***
Wells Fargo & Company (PA) .... C 866 249-3302
420 Montgomery St Frnt San Francisco (94104) ***(P-9124)***
Wells Fargo Advisors, Los Angeles *Also called Wells Fargo Clearing Svcs LLC* ***(P-9770)***
Wells Fargo Advisors, San Francisco *Also called Wells Fargo Clearing Svcs LLC* ***(P-9771)***
Wells Fargo Advisors, La Jolla *Also called Wells Fargo Clearing Svcs LLC* ***(P-9772)***
Wells Fargo Advisors, Seal Beach *Also called Wells Fargo Clearing Svcs LLC* ***(P-9773)***
Wells Fargo Advisors, Woodland Hills *Also called Wells Fargo Clearing Svcs LLC* ***(P-9774)***
Wells Fargo Bank Ltd .... D 213 253-6227
333 S Grand Ave Ste 500 Los Angeles (90071) ***(P-9125)***
Wells Fargo Bank NA .... C 213 628-2251
333 S Hope St Ste D100 Los Angeles (90071) ***(P-9126)***
Wells Fargo Bank National Assn .... E 818 766-7172
10225 Riverside Dr Toluca Lake (91602) ***(P-9127)***
Wells Fargo Bank National Assn .... E 415 396-6267
120 Kearny St Ste 1750 San Francisco (94108) ***(P-9128)***
Wells Fargo Bank National Assn .... D 415 396-6161
1 Montgomery St Ste 200 San Francisco (94104) ***(P-9129)***
Wells Fargo Bank National Assn .... D 209 578-6810
1120 K St Modesto (95354) ***(P-9130)***
Wells Fargo Bank National Assn .... E 408 998-3714
2170 Tully Rd San Jose (95122) ***(P-9131)***
Wells Fargo Bank National Assn .... D 858 622-6958
4365 Executive Dr Fl 18 San Diego (92121) ***(P-9132)***
Wells Fargo Bank National Assn .... D 707 259-5552
901 Main St NAPA (94559) ***(P-9133)***
Wells Fargo Bank National Assn .... D 925 746-3718
1655 Grant St Concord (94520) ***(P-9134)***
Wells Fargo Bank National Assn .... B 626 312-3006
9000 Flair Dr Fl 3 El Monte (91731) ***(P-9135)***
Wells Fargo Bank National Assn .... A 858 454-0362
7714 Girard Ave La Jolla (92037) ***(P-9136)***
Wells Fargo Bank National Assn .... D 916 724-2982
5007 Foothills Blvd Roseville (95747) ***(P-9137)***
Wells Fargo Bank National Assn .... E 408 378-8155
60 W Hamilton Ave Campbell (95008) ***(P-9138)***
Wells Fargo Bank National Assn .... B 415 777-9497
100 Spear St Ste 100 # 100 San Francisco (94105) ***(P-9139)***
Wells Fargo Bank National Assn .... B 916 774-2249
1620 E Roseville Pkwy Roseville (95661) ***(P-9140)***
Wells Fargo Bank National Assn .... C 626 573-6452
3440 Flair Dr El Monte (91731) ***(P-9141)***

ALPHABETIC

Employee Codes: A=Over 500 employees, B=251-500
C=101-250, D=51-100, E=50
2020 Directory of California
Wholesalers and Services Companies
© Mergent Inc. 1-800-342-5647
1483

Wells Fargo Bank National Assn......E......510 276-0875
16000 Hesperian Blvd San Lorenzo (94580) ***(P-9142)***
Wells Fargo Bank National Assn......D......510 792-3512
39265 Paseo Padre Pkwy Fremont (94538) ***(P-9143)***
Wells Fargo Bank National Assn......D......510 266-0595
950 Southland Dr Hayward (94545) ***(P-9144)***
Wells Fargo Bank National Assn......E......916 440-4570
2301 Watt Ave Sacramento (95825) ***(P-9145)***
Wells Fargo Bank National Assn......D......925 463-1983
5798 Stoneridge Mall Rd Pleasanton (94588) ***(P-9146)***
Wells Fargo Bank National Assn......D......310 831-0632
28350 S Western Ave Rancho Palos Verdes (90275) ***(P-9147)***
Wells Fargo Bank National Assn......E......415 222-1360
464 California St San Francisco (94104) ***(P-9148)***
Wells Fargo Bank National Assn......C......415 222-6834
455 Market Fremont (94536) ***(P-9149)***
Wells Fargo Bank National Assn......D......805 541-0143
665 Marsh St San Luis Obispo (93401) ***(P-9150)***
Wells Fargo Bank National Assn......A......415 394-4021
420 Montgomery St Fl 6 San Francisco (94104) ***(P-9151)***
Wells Fargo Bank National Assn......D......510 530-3095
2220 Mountain Blvd # 160 Oakland (94611) ***(P-9152)***
Wells Fargo Bank National Assn......E......562 924-1616
18712 Gridley Rd Cerritos (90703) ***(P-9153)***
Wells Fargo Bank National Assn......B......510 745-5025
3440 Walnut Ave Fl 3 Fremont (94538) ***(P-9154)***
Wells Fargo Bank National Assn......C......310 285-5817
433 N Camden Dr Ste 1200 Beverly Hills (90210) ***(P-9155)***
Wells Fargo Capital Fin LLC (HQ)......D......310 453-7300
2450 Colo Ave Ste 3000w Santa Monica (90404) ***(P-9511)***
Wells Fargo Clearing Svcs LLC......E......213 486-5200
777 S Figueroa St # 4700 Los Angeles (90017) ***(P-9770)***
Wells Fargo Clearing Svcs LLC......C......415 291-1200
555 California St # 2300 San Francisco (94104) ***(P-9771)***
Wells Fargo Clearing Svcs LLC......E......858 456-7706
888 Prospect St Ste 220 La Jolla (92037) ***(P-9772)***
Wells Fargo Clearing Svcs LLC......E......562 594-1220
3020 Old Ranch Pkwy # 190 Seal Beach (90740) ***(P-9773)***
Wells Fargo Clearing Svcs LLC......D......818 226-2222
5820 Canoga Ave Ste 100 Woodland Hills (91367) ***(P-9774)***
Wells Fargo Coml Dist Fin LLC......D......916 636-2020
3100 Zinfandel Dr Ste 255 Rancho Cordova (95670) ***(P-9495)***
Wells Fargo Home Mortgage Inc......E......916 782-2221
3010 Lava Ridge Ct # 150 Roseville (95661) ***(P-9608)***
Wells Fargo Home Mortgage Inc......B......760 603-7000
5540 Fermi Ct Fl 2002 Carlsbad (92008) ***(P-9609)***
Wells Fargo Intl Bond CIT......C......415 396-4943
525 Market St Fl 10 San Francisco (94105) ***(P-11746)***
Wells Hse Hspice Fundation Inc......D......714 952-3795
245 Cherry Ave Long Beach (90802) ***(P-20374)***
Wellspace Health (PA)......D......916 325-5556
1820 J St Sacramento (95811) ***(P-22159)***
Welltower Inc......B......760 436-4122
144 W D St Ste 202 Encinitas (92024) ***(P-11510)***
Wendel Rosen LLP (PA)......C......510 834-6600
1111 Broadway Ste 2400 Oakland (94607) ***(P-22869)***
Wendt Landscape Services Inc......D......949 589-8680
29714 Avenida De Las Rancho Santa Margari (92688) ***(P-927)***
Wendy's, Modesto *Also called Pacwend III Inc* ***(P-26344)***
Wentworth Hauser & Violich Inc......D......415 981-6911
301 Battery St Fl 4 San Francisco (94111) ***(P-9855)***
Wenzlau Engineering Inc......D......310 604-3400
2950 E Harcourt St Compton (90221) ***(P-7363)***
WERM Investments LLC......E......213 627-8070
14242 Ventura Blvd # 212 Sherman Oaks (91423) ***(P-18019)***
Wermers Multi-Family Corp......C......858 535-1475
5120 Shoreham Pl Ste 150 San Diego (92122) ***(P-1283)***
Werner Enterprises Inc......E......909 823-5803
10251 Calabash Ave Fontana (92335) ***(P-4166)***
Wesco Aircraft, Valencia *Also called Falcon Aerospace Holdings LLC* ***(P-26228)***
Wesco Aircraft Hardware Corp (HQ)......B......661 775-7200
24911 Avenue Stanford Valencia (91355) ***(P-7702)***
Wesco Aircraft Hardware Corp......B......661 775-7200
27727 Avenue Scott Valencia (91355) ***(P-7703)***
Wesco Aircraft Holdings Inc (PA)......D......661 775-7200
24911 Avenue Stanford Valencia (91355) ***(P-26456)***
Wescom Central Credit Union (PA)......B......888 493-7266
123 S Marengo Ave Pasadena (91101) ***(P-9412)***
Wescom Holdings LLC (HQ)......D......888 493-7266
123 S Marengo Ave Pasadena (91101) ***(P-10545)***
Wescon Technology Inc......C......408 727-8818
4699 Old Ironsides Dr # 290 Santa Clara (95054) ***(P-15712)***
Wescordon Incorporated (PA)......C......559 784-8371
661 W Poplar Ave Porterville (93257) ***(P-20375)***
Weslar Inc......D......661 702-1362
28310 Constellation Rd Valencia (91355) ***(P-2991)***
Weslend Financial, Santa Ana *Also called Lenox Financial Mortgage Corp* ***(P-9573)***
Wesley Palms, San Diego *Also called Front Porch Communities* ***(P-10730)***
West Air Inc......D......559 454-7843
5005 E Andersen Ave Fresno (93727) ***(P-4734)***
West Anaheim Care Center, Anaheim *Also called Mark & Fred Enterprises* ***(P-20125)***
WEST ANAHEIM MEDICAL CENTER, Anaheim *Also called Prime Healthcare Anaheim LLC* ***(P-21107)***
West Cast Fire Integration Inc......D......909 824-7980
1474 Miller Dr Colton (92324) ***(P-16569)***
West Cntinela Vly Care Ctr Inc......D......310 674-3216
950 S Flower St Inglewood (90301) ***(P-20376)***
West Coast AC Co Inc......C......619 561-8000
1155 Pioneer Way Ste 101 El Cajon (92020) ***(P-2318)***
West Coast Aggregate Supply......E......760 342-7598
92500 Airport Blvd Thermal (92274) ***(P-1059)***
West Coast Air Conditioning, Oxnard *Also called Gmh Inc* ***(P-17446)***
West Coast Ambulance Corp......C......310 435-1862
6739 S Victoria Ave Los Angeles (90043) ***(P-3737)***
West Coast Arborists Inc......C......805 671-5092
11405 Nardo St Ventura (93004) ***(P-950)***
West Coast Arborists Inc......C......858 566-4204
8163 Commercial St La Mesa (91942) ***(P-1220)***
West Coast Arborists Inc......E......909 783-6544
21718 Walnut Ave Grand Terrace (92313) ***(P-951)***
West Coast Aviation Svcs LLC (PA)......E......949 852-8340
19711 Campus Dr Ste 200 Santa Ana (92707) ***(P-26876)***
West Coast Charters, Santa Ana *Also called West Coast Aviation Svcs LLC* ***(P-26876)***
West Coast Childrens Center......E......510 269-9030
545 Ashbury Ave El Cerrito (94530) ***(P-19591)***
West Coast Construction, Riverside *Also called Perry Coast Construction Inc* ***(P-1565)***
West Coast Consulting LLC......C......949 250-4102
9233 Research Dr Ste 200 Irvine (92618) ***(P-15534)***
West Coast Contractors Inc......C......541 267-7689
2320 Courage Dr Ste 111 Fairfield (94533) ***(P-1645)***
West Coast Coupon Inc......E......818 341-2400
9400 Oso Ave Chatsworth (91311) ***(P-13666)***
West Coast Drywall & Co Inc......B......951 778-3592
1610 W Linden St Riverside (92507) ***(P-2876)***
West Coast Firestopping Inc......D......714 935-1104
1130 W Trenton Ave Orange (92867) ***(P-3491)***
West Coast Grape Farming Inc......A......209 538-3131
800 E Keyes Rd Ceres (95307) ***(P-691)***
West Coast Hospitals Inc......D......831 722-3581
919 Freedom Blvd Watsonville (95076) ***(P-20720)***
West Coast Interiors Inc......A......951 778-3592
1610 W Linden St Riverside (92507) ***(P-2405)***
West Coast Legal Service Inc......E......408 938-6520
1245 S Winchester Blvd # 208 San Jose (95128) ***(P-17165)***
West Coast Ltg & Enrgy Inc......D......951 296-0680
18550 Minthorn St Lake Elsinore (92530) ***(P-2693)***
West Coast Mailing & Dist, San Diego *Also called Mopar Enterprises* ***(P-13732)***
West Coast Maintenance Inc......D......310 324-2511
16312 S Main St Gardena (90248) ***(P-14082)***
West Coast Materials, Buena Park *Also called West Coast Sand and Gravel Inc* ***(P-6704)***
West Coast Painting, Riverside *Also called West Coast Interiors Inc* ***(P-2405)***
West Coast Physical Therapy, Laguna Niguel *Also called Mission Internal Med Group Inc* ***(P-19198)***
West Coast Prime Meats LLC......C......714 255-8560
344 Cliffwood Park St Brea (92821) ***(P-8424)***
West Coast Radiology Center, Santa Ana *Also called Santa Ana Radiology Center* ***(P-19365)***
West Coast Rags, Long Beach *Also called Coastal Closeouts Inc* ***(P-16709)***
West Coast Sand and Gravel Inc (PA)......D......714 522-0282
7282 Orangethorpe Ave Buena Park (90621) ***(P-6704)***
West Coast Santa Cruz Hotel, Santa Cruz *Also called Santa Cruz Hotel Associates* ***(P-12885)***
West Coast Storm Inc (PA)......E......909 890-5700
9701 Wilshire Blvd # 1000 Beverly Hills (90212) ***(P-26959)***
West Coast Turf (PA)......E......760 340-7300
42540 Melanie Pl Palm Desert (92211) ***(P-287)***
West Cotton AG Management Inc......C......559 945-2511
15900 W Dorris Huron (93234) ***(P-692)***
West Countra Costa Youth Svcs (PA)......D......510 412-5647
263 S 20th St Richmond (94804) ***(P-23543)***
West County Resource Recovery......E......510 231-4200
101 Pittsburg Ave Richmond (94801) ***(P-6332)***
West County Trnsp Agcy......C......707 206-9988
367 W Robles Ave Santa Rosa (95407) ***(P-3616)***
West Covina Lanes, West Covina *Also called Bowlero Corp* ***(P-18026)***
West Covina Medical Clinic Inc (PA)......C......626 960-8614
1500 W West Covina Pkwy West Covina (91790) ***(P-19592)***
WEST COVINA PHYSICAL THERAPY, West Covina *Also called Doctors Hospital W Covina Inc* ***(P-20858)***
West Dermatology Med MGT Inc......C......909 793-3000
400 Newport Center Dr # 702 Newport Beach (92660) ***(P-19593)***
West End Yung MNS Christn Assn......D......909 477-2780
1257 E D St Ontario (91764) ***(P-24696)***
West Escondido Healthcare LLC......D......760 746-0303
201 N Fig St Escondido (92025) ***(P-20377)***
West Flower Growers......D......805 488-0814
3623 Etting Rd Oxnard (93033) ***(P-288)***
West Health Care, Bonita *Also called Paradise Valley Hospital* ***(P-21084)***
West Hills Construction Inc......E......800 515-5270
423 Jenks Cir Ste 101 Corona (92880) ***(P-1392)***
West Hills Golf Associates......E......714 528-6400
1800 Carbon Canyon Rd Chino Hills (91709) ***(P-18609)***
West Hollywood Sport Club, West Hollywood *Also called 24 Hour Fitness Usa Inc* ***(P-18098)***
West Hotel Partners LP (PA)......C......310 477-3593
11828 La Grange Ave 200 Los Angeles (90025) ***(P-13083)***
West Hotel Partners LP......C......408 947-4450
300 Almaden Blvd San Jose (95110) ***(P-13084)***
West Inn & Suites LLC......D......760 448-4500
4970 Avenida Encinas Carlsbad (92008) ***(P-13085)***
West Lake Touchless Car Wash......E......650 992-5344
223 87th St Daly City (94015) ***(P-17403)***
West Los Angeles V A Med Ctr, Los Angeles *Also called Veterans Health Administration* ***(P-19556)***
West Medions, San Leandro *Also called KMA Emergency Services Inc* ***(P-3692)***
WEST OAKLAND HEALTH CENTER, Oakland *Also called West Oakland Health Council* ***(P-22160)***

Mergent e-mail: customerrelations@mergent.com 2020 Directory of California (P-0000) Products & Services Section entry number
1484 Wholesalers and Services Companies (PA)=Parent Co (HQ)=Headquarters (DH)=Div Headquarters

West Oakland Health Council (PA)..............C.......510 835-9610
700 Adeline St Oakland (94607) ***(P-22160)***
West Pacific Medical Lab, Santa Fe Springs *Also called California Lab Sciences LLC* ***(P-21509)***
West Pacific Medical Lab LLC (PA)..............D.......818 773-9771
10200 Pioneer Blvd # 500 Santa Fe Springs (90670) ***(P-21601)***
West Pico Distributors LLC..............D.......323 586-9050
5201 S Downey Rd Vernon (90058) ***(P-8283)***
West Pico Foods Inc..............C.......323 586-9050
5201 S Downey Rd Vernon (90058) ***(P-8307)***
West Publishing Corporation..............C.......424 243-2100
800 Crprate Pinte Ste 150 Culver City (90230) ***(P-15713)***
West Riverside Veterinary Hosp..............E.......951 686-2242
5488 Mission Blvd Riverside (92509) ***(P-597)***
West Safety Solutions Corp..............E.......514 340-3314
3009 Douglas Blvd Ste 300 Roseville (95661) ***(P-17166)***
West San Crlos Ht Partners LLC..............D.......408 998-0400
282 Almaden Blvd San Jose (95113) ***(P-13086)***
West Side District Hospital..............C.......805 763-4211
110 E North St Taft (93268) ***(P-21371)***
West Side Rehab Corporation..............C.......323 231-4174
1755 Kings Way Los Angeles (90069) ***(P-10670)***
West States Skanska Inc..............C.......970 565-4903
1995 Agua Mansa Rd Riverside (92509) ***(P-1933)***
West Valley Area Squad Club..............C.......818 888-0980
5825 De Soto Ave Woodland Hills (91367) ***(P-24240)***
West Valley Christian Academy, Tracy *Also called We Care Day Care & Pre School* ***(P-23801)***
West Valley Cnstr - Stockton, Stockton *Also called West Valley Cnstr Co Inc* ***(P-1935)***
West Valley Cnstr Co Inc (PA)..............C.......408 371-5510
580 E Mcglincy Ln Campbell (95008) ***(P-1934)***
West Valley Cnstr Co Inc..............D.......209 943-6812
2655 E Miner Ave Ste A Stockton (95205) ***(P-1935)***
West Valley Engineering Inc..............D.......925 416-9707
3875 Hopyard Rd Ste 130 Pleasanton (94588) ***(P-14452)***
West Valley Engineering Inc (PA)..............D.......408 735-1420
390 Potrero Ave Sunnyvale (94085) ***(P-14595)***
West Valley Family YMCA..............C.......818 774-2840
18810 Vanowen St Reseda (91335) ***(P-23802)***
West Valley Jewish Cmnty Ctr..............D.......818 348-0048
22622 Vanowen St Canoga Park (91307) ***(P-18783)***
West Valley M R F, Fontana *Also called West Valley Manufacturing LLC* ***(P-6333)***
West Valley Manufacturing LLC..............C.......909 899-5501
13373 Napa St Fontana (92335) ***(P-6333)***
West Valley Staffing Group, Sunnyvale *Also called West Valley Engineering Inc* ***(P-14595)***
West Ventura Family Care Ctr..............D.......805 641-5620
133 W Santa Clara St Ventura (93001) ***(P-19594)***
West Ville Palm Desert..............E.......760 346-2121
72840 Highway 111 Ste 115 Palm Desert (92260) ***(P-10671)***
West Yost & Associates Inc (PA)..............D.......530 756-5905
2020 Res Pk Dr Ste 100 Davis (95618) ***(P-25387)***
West-Spec Partners..............E.......818 725-7000
20525 Nordhoff St Ste 42 Chatsworth (91311) ***(P-7662)***
Westair Gas and Equipment, San Diego *Also called Laboratory Specialty Gases* ***(P-7555)***
Westair Gases & Equipment Inc..............D.......619 474-0079
2300 Haffley Ave National City (91950) ***(P-7609)***
Westair Gases & Equipment Inc (PA)..............E.......866 937-8247
2506 Market St San Diego (92102) ***(P-7610)***
Westar Capital Assoc II LLC..............A.......714 481-5160
949 S Coast Dr Costa Mesa (92626) ***(P-11968)***
Westar Manufacturing Inc..............D.......562 633-0581
13217 Laureldale Ave Downey (90242) ***(P-3492)***
Westar Marine Services, San Francisco *Also called Cross Link Inc* ***(P-4629)***
Westates Mechanical Corp Inc..............D.......510 635-9830
2566 Barrington Ct Hayward (94545) ***(P-2319)***
Westcal Management, Carmichael *Also called Pacific Cities Management Inc* ***(P-11332)***
Westcare California Inc (HQ)..............D.......559 251-4800
1900 N Gateway Blvd 100 Fresno (93727) ***(P-24112)***
Westchester Emerson Cmnty, Los Angeles *Also called Los Angeles Unified School Dst* ***(P-23324)***
Westcoast Childrens Clinic..............C.......510 269-9030
3301 E 12th St Ste 259 Oakland (94601) ***(P-22161)***
Westcoast Medial Imaging, Los Angeles *Also called Larchmont Radiology Med Group* ***(P-19151)***
Westcoast Performance Pdts USA..............D.......714 630-4411
3100 E Coronado St Anaheim (92806) ***(P-11880)***
Westcoe Escrow Division, Riverside *Also called Westcoe Realtors Inc* ***(P-11511)***
Westcoe Realtors Inc..............D.......951 784-2500
7191 Magnolia Ave Riverside (92504) ***(P-11511)***
Westcor Construction of Cal..............C.......909 796-8900
2351 W Lugonia Ave Ste D Redlands (92374) ***(P-1221)***
Westcore Croydon, San Diego *Also called Westcore Delta LLC* ***(P-11969)***
Westcore Delta LLC..............D.......858 625-4100
4350 La Jolla Village Dr # 900 San Diego (92122) ***(P-11969)***
Westech Systems Inc..............D.......559 298-5237
827 Jefferson Ave Clovis (93612) ***(P-2694)***
Wested..............D.......510 302-4200
300 Lakeside Dr Fl 25th Oakland (94612) ***(P-26046)***
Wested..............D.......415 289-2300
180 Harbor Dr Ste 112 Sausalito (94965) ***(P-26047)***
Wested (PA)..............C.......415 565-3000
730 Harrison St Ste 500 San Francisco (94107) ***(P-26048)***
Western Air & Refrigeration, Seal Beach *Also called Limbach Company LP* ***(P-2186)***
Western Alliance Bank, Oakland *Also called Porrey Pines Bank Inc* ***(P-9117)***
Western Alliance Bank..............D.......408 423-8500
55 Almaden Blvd Ste 200 San Jose (95113) ***(P-9247)***
Western Alliance Bank..............D.......415 230-4834
455 Market St Ste 1050 San Francisco (94105) ***(P-9276)***
Western Alliance Bank..............D.......949 222-0855
7545 Irvine Center Dr # 200 Irvine (92618) ***(P-9277)***
Western Allied Mechanical Inc..............C.......650 326-8290
1180 Obrien Dr Menlo Park (94025) ***(P-2320)***
Western Allied Service Company..............B.......562 941-3243
12046 Florence Ave Santa Fe Springs (90670) ***(P-17449)***
Western America Properties LLC..............D.......310 374-4381
111 N Sepulveda Blvd # 330 Manhattan Beach (90266) ***(P-11512)***
Western Area Security Services, Burbank *Also called Callan Management Corporation* ***(P-16501)***
Western Asset Core Plus..............D.......626 844-9400
385 E Colorado Blvd Pasadena (91101) ***(P-11747)***
Western Asset MGT Co LLC (HQ)..............E.......626 844-9265
385 E Colorado Blvd # 250 Pasadena (91101) ***(P-11748)***
Western Asset Mrtg Capitl Corp..............A.......626 844-9400
385 E Colorado Blvd Pasadena (91101) ***(P-11881)***
Western Building Materials Co (PA)..............D.......559 454-8500
4620 E Olive Ave Fresno (93702) ***(P-2877)***
Western City Magazine, Sacramento *Also called League of California Cities* ***(P-26915)***
Western Communications, Newbury Park *Also called Hearst Communications Inc* ***(P-5727)***
Western Concrete Pumping Inc (PA)..............D.......760 598-7855
2181 La Mirada Dr Vista (92081) ***(P-3238)***
Western Convalescent Hospital, Los Angeles *Also called Tzippy Care Inc* ***(P-20705)***
Western Convelescence, Los Angeles *Also called Longwood Management Corp* ***(P-20619)***
Western Costume Leasing..............D.......818 760-0900
11041 Vanowen St North Hollywood (91605) ***(P-13461)***
Western Dental Services Inc (HQ)..............B.......714 480-3000
530 S Main St Ste 600 Orange (92868) ***(P-19638)***
Western Dental Services Inc..............E.......562 461-1180
17660 Lakewood Blvd Bellflower (90706) ***(P-22162)***
Western Division Regional Off, Long Beach *Also called Southern California Edison Co* ***(P-5951)***
Western Drug Medical Supply, Stockton *Also called H and H Drug Stores Inc* ***(P-7817)***
Western Energy Services Corp..............C.......403 984-5916
3430 Getty St Bakersfield (93308) ***(P-14117)***
Western Exterminator Company..............D.......310 274-9244
3333 W Temple St Los Angeles (90026) ***(P-13833)***
Western Exterminator Company..............E.......310 835-3513
1985 W Wardlow Rd Long Beach (90810) ***(P-13834)***
Western Exterminator Company..............D.......562 802-2238
15415 Marquardt Ave Santa Fe Springs (90670) ***(P-13835)***
Western Feld Invstigations Inc (PA)..............D.......800 999-9589
405 W Foothill Blvd # 204 Claremont (91711) ***(P-15894)***
Western Freight Carrier Inc..............D.......909 357-1011
13819 Slover Ave Fontana (92337) ***(P-5083)***
Western General Holding Co (PA)..............C.......818 880-9070
5230 Las Virgenes Rd # 100 Calabasas (91302) ***(P-10149)***
Western General Insurance Co..............C.......818 880-9070
5230 Las Virgenes Rd Calabasas (91302) ***(P-10150)***
Western Growers Association (PA)..............C.......949 863-1000
15525 Sand Canyon Ave Irvine (92618) ***(P-24372)***
Western Health Advantage..............D.......916 567-1950
2349 Gateway Oaks Dr # 100 Sacramento (95833) ***(P-9915)***
Western Health Resources..............E.......559 537-2860
440 Greenfield Ave Ste B Hanford (93230) ***(P-26877)***
Western Healthcare Center, Colton *Also called Western Healthcare Management* ***(P-20378)***
Western Healthcare Management..............C.......909 824-1530
1700 E Washington St Colton (92324) ***(P-20378)***
Western Hills Country Club, Chino Hills *Also called West Hills Golf Associates* ***(P-18609)***
Western Hills Golf & Cntry CLB, Chino *Also called Donovan Golf Courses MGT* ***(P-18243)***
Western Homes, Fresno *Also called Lassley Enterprises Inc* ***(P-10754)***
Western Insulfoam, Chino *Also called Carlisle Construction Mtls Inc* ***(P-6712)***
Western Living Concepts Inc (PA)..............E.......707 443-3000
2740 Timber Ridge Ln Ofc Eureka (95503) ***(P-24113)***
Western Magnesite Inc..............E.......818 255-1150
11927 Sherman Rd Unit 1 North Hollywood (91605) ***(P-3493)***
Western Meat Processors Inc..............E.......760 355-1175
502 E Barioni Blvd Imperial (92251) ***(P-381)***
Western Med Assoc Med Group (PA)..............D.......831 475-1111
1595 Soquel Dr Ste 330 Santa Cruz (95065) ***(P-19595)***
Western Med Center-Santa Ana, Santa Ana *Also called Western Medical Center Aux* ***(P-21372)***
Western Medical Center Aux (HQ)..............C.......714 835-3555
1301 N Tustin Ave Santa Ana (92705) ***(P-21372)***
Western Medical Management LLC..............E.......949 260-6575
3333 Michelson Dr Ste 735 Irvine (92612) ***(P-26457)***
Western Messenger Service Inc..............C.......415 487-4229
75 Columbia Sq San Francisco (94103) ***(P-3955)***
Western Milling LLC (HQ)..............C.......559 302-1000
31120 West St Goshen (93227) ***(P-8862)***
Western Mutual Insurance Co (PA)..............D.......949 724-9402
2172 Dupont Dr Ste 220 Irvine (92612) ***(P-10546)***
Western National Contractors..............D.......949 862-6200
8 Executive Cir Irvine (92614) ***(P-26458)***
Western National Properties (PA)..............C.......949 862-6200
8 Executive Cir Irvine (92614) ***(P-1284)***
Western National Securities (PA)..............C.......949 862-6200
8 Executive Cir Irvine (92614) ***(P-11513)***
Western Nevada Supply Co..............C.......530 582-5009
10990 Industrial Way A Truckee (96161) ***(P-7442)***
Western Oil & Spreading, Martinez *Also called Telfer Oil Company* ***(P-1799)***
Western Oilfields Supply Co (PA)..............C.......661 399-9124
3404 State Rd Bakersfield (93308) ***(P-14209)***
Western Operations, Rancho Cucamonga *Also called Gentex Corporation* ***(P-25757)***
Western Operations Center, Westlake Village *Also called Securitas SEC Svcs USA Inc* ***(P-16417)***

ALPHABETIC

Employee Codes: A=Over 500 employees, B=251-500
C=101-250, D=51-100, E=50
2020 Directory of California
Wholesalers and Services Companies
© Mergent Inc. 1-800-342-5647
1485

Western Overseas Corporation (PA) ...E...562 985-0616
10731 Walker St Ste B Cypress (90630) ***(P-5084)***

Western Pacific Distrg LLC ...C...714 974-6837
341 W Meats Ave Orange (92865) ***(P-6705)***

Western Paving Contractors Inc ...D...626 338-7889
15533 Arrow Hwy Irwindale (91706) ***(P-1809)***

Western PCF Crane & Eqp LLC (HQ) ...D...562 286-6618
8600 Calabash Ave Fontana (92335) ***(P-14118)***

Western Precooling Systems ...D...805 486-6371
761 Commercial Ave Oxnard (93030) ***(P-14210)***

Western Pump Inc (PA) ...D...619 239-9988
3235 F St San Diego (92102) ***(P-17563)***

Western Region, Milpitas *Also called Xcerra Corporation* ***(P-7366)***

Western Regional Delivery Svc, Fullerton *Also called South Coast Trnsp & Dist Inc* ***(P-4504)***

Western Regional Office, Rancho Cordova *Also called Ducks Unlimited Inc* ***(P-24537)***

Western Rim Constructors Inc ...E...760 489-4328
621 S Andreasen Dr Ste B Escondido (92029) ***(P-1810)***

Western Rim Pipeline, Lakeside *Also called A M Ortega Construction Inc* ***(P-2408)***

Western Roofing Service, San Leandro *Also called Roofing Constructors Inc* ***(P-3096)***

Western Slope Health Care, Placerville *Also called Western Slope Health Center* ***(P-20379)***

Western Slope Health Center ...D...530 622-6842
3280 Washington St Placerville (95667) ***(P-20379)***

Western Star Nurseries LLC ...E...209 744-2552
9394 Robson Rd Galt (95632) ***(P-8934)***

Western Star Trnsp LLC ...C...310 605-1300
1065 E Walnut St Carson (90746) ***(P-4167)***

Western States Affiliate, Los Angeles *Also called American Heart Association Inc* ***(P-24376)***

Western States Fire Protection ...D...562 279-0770
3720 Industry Ave Ste 107 Lakewood (90712) ***(P-2321)***

Western States Fire Protection ...D...916 924-1631
4740 Northgate Blvd # 150 Sacramento (95834) ***(P-2322)***

Western Sun Enterprises Inc ...C...707 748-2542
4690 E 2nd St Ste 4 Benicia (94510) ***(P-2695)***

Western Tear-Off & Disposal ...D...626 443-9984
10920 Grand Ave Temple City (91780) ***(P-3107)***

Western Towing, San Diego *Also called Sunbelt Towing Inc* ***(P-17429)***

Western Transit Systems Inc ...D...949 515-0188
13591 Harbor Blvd Garden Grove (92843) ***(P-3754)***

Western United Insurance Co ...C...800 959-9842
3349 Michelson Dr Ste 100 Irvine (92612) ***(P-10547)***

Western Waste Services, Temple City *Also called Western Tear-Off & Disposal* ***(P-3107)***

Western Wine Services Inc (PA) ...D...800 999-8463
880 Hanna Dr American Canyon (94503) ***(P-4544)***

Westfield LLC (HQ) ...B...813 926-4600
2049 Century Park E # 4000 Los Angeles (90067) ***(P-10672)***

Westfield America Inc (HQ) ...C...310 478-4456
2049 Century Park E Fl 41 Los Angeles (90067) ***(P-10673)***

Westfield America Ltd Partnr ...D...310 478-4456
2049 Century Park E Fl 41 Los Angeles (90067) ***(P-11622)***

Westfield America Ltd Partnr ...B...310 277-3898
2049 Century Park E # 4100 Los Angeles (90067) ***(P-10674)***

Westgage Grdn Convalescent Ctr, Visalia *Also called Far West Inc* ***(P-20552)***

Westgate Cnstr & Maint Inc ...D...707 208-5763
5045 Fulton Dr Ste D Fairfield (94534) ***(P-1646)***

Westgate Gardens Care Center ...C...559 733-0901
4525 W Tulare Ave Visalia (93277) ***(P-20380)***

Westgate Hotel, San Diego *Also called Sinclair Companies* ***(P-12929)***

Westgroup Kona Kai LLC ...D...619 221-8000
1551 Shelter Island Dr San Diego (92106) ***(P-18610)***

Westgroup San Diego Associates ...B...858 274-4630
1404 Vacation Rd San Diego (92109) ***(P-13087)***

Westin Bonaventure Ht & Suites, Los Angeles *Also called Interstate Hotels Resorts Inc* ***(P-12474)***

Westin Desert Willow ...D...760 636-7003
75 Willow Ridge Palm Desert (92260) ***(P-13088)***

Westin Long Beach Hotel, The, Long Beach *Also called Noble/Utah Long Beach LLC* ***(P-12649)***

Westin Los Angeles Airport, Los Angeles *Also called Host Hotels & Resorts LP* ***(P-12396)***

Westin Pasadena, The, Pasadena *Also called Brookfield Dtla Fund Office* ***(P-12094)***

Westin San Diego, San Diego *Also called Diamondrock San Dego Tnant LLC* ***(P-12209)***

Westin San Diego, San Diego *Also called W-Emerald LLC* ***(P-13071)***

Westin St. Francis, The, San Francisco *Also called Dtrs St Francis LLC* ***(P-12233)***

Westlake Christian Terrace - E, Oakland *Also called Christian Church Homes* ***(P-11015)***

Westlake Development Group LLC (PA) ...D...650 579-1010
520 S El Camino Real # 900 San Mateo (94402) ***(P-10675)***

Westlake Development Group LLC ...D...650 579-1010
520 El Camino Real Fl 9 Belmont (94002) ***(P-26459)***

Westlake Financial Services, Los Angeles *Also called Westlake Services LLC* ***(P-9512)***

Westlake Health Care Center ...C...805 494-1233
1101 Crenshaw Blvd Los Angeles (90019) ***(P-20381)***

Westlake Nail Spa ...D...650 994-7777
233 Lake Merced Blvd Daly City (94015) ***(P-18211)***

Westlake Properties Inc ...C...818 889-0230
31943 Agoura Rd Westlake Village (91361) ***(P-13089)***

Westlake Realty Group Inc (PA) ...D...650 579-1010
520 S El Camino Real # 900 San Mateo (94402) ***(P-11514)***

Westlake Services LLC (PA) ...C...323 692-8800
4751 Wilshire Blvd # 100 Los Angeles (90010) ***(P-9512)***

Westlake Village Apartments, Daly City *Also called Gerson Baker & Associates* ***(P-10733)***

Westlake Village Golf Course, Westlake Village *Also called Pyj V A California Ltd Partnr* ***(P-18284)***

Westlake Village Inn, Westlake Village *Also called Westlake Properties Inc* ***(P-13089)***

Westland Floral, Carpinteria *Also called Westland Orchids Inc* ***(P-8936)***

Westland Flral Carpinteria Inc ...E...805 684-4011
1400 Cravens Ln Carpinteria (93013) ***(P-8935)***

Westland Hotel Corporation ...E...209 931-3131
4219 E Waterloo Rd Stockton (95215) ***(P-13090)***

Westland Orchids Inc ...E...805 684-1436
1400 Cravens Ln Carpinteria (93013) ***(P-8936)***

Westland Trailer Mfg, Lodi *Also called Bjj Company LLC* ***(P-3977)***

Westliving Management LLC (PA) ...D...760 602-5850
5800 Armada Dr Ste 100 Carlsbad (92008) ***(P-24114)***

Westmed Ambulance ...D...510 401-5420
14275 Wicks Blvd San Leandro (94577) ***(P-3738)***

Westmed Ambulance Inc ...C...310 456-3830
3872 Las Flores Canyon Rd Malibu (90265) ***(P-3739)***

Westmed Ambulance Inc ...B...310 219-1779
2537 Old San Pasqual Rd Escondido (92027) ***(P-3740)***

Westminster Gardens ...D...626 359-2571
1420 Santo Domingo Ave Duarte (91010) ***(P-20721)***

Westminster Housing Parteners ...E...714 891-3000
8140 13th St Westminster (92683) ***(P-11515)***

Westminster Woods Camp & Confe ...E...707 874-2426
6510 Bohemian Hwy Occidental (95465) ***(P-13154)***

Westmont Living Inc ...B...916 786-3277
707 Sunrise Ave Roseville (95661) ***(P-24115)***

Westmont Living Inc (PA) ...C...858 456-1233
7660 Fay Ave Ste N La Jolla (92037) ***(P-24116)***

Weston Solutions Inc ...D...760 795-6900
5817 Dryden Pl Ste 101 Carlsbad (92008) ***(P-27257)***

Westpac Materials, Orange *Also called Western Pacific Distrg LLC* ***(P-6705)***

Westpoint Marketing Intl Inc ...D...323 233-0233
5901 Avalon Blvd Los Angeles (90003) ***(P-17167)***

Westport Capital Partners LLC ...D...310 294-1234
2121 Rosecrans Ave # 4325 El Segundo (90245) ***(P-11970)***

Westpost Berkeley LLC ...D...510 548-7920
200 Marina Blvd Berkeley (94710) ***(P-13091)***

Westrec Marina Management Inc ...D...209 369-1041
14900 W Highway 12 Frnt Lodi (95242) ***(P-4637)***

Westridge Golf Inc ...D...562 690-4200
1400 S La Habra Hills Dr La Habra (90631) ***(P-18313)***

Westrux International Inc ...D...909 825-5121
2200 E Steel Rd Colton (92324) ***(P-5085)***

Westside Jewish Cmnty Ctr Inc (PA) ...A...323 938-2531
5870 W Olympic Blvd Los Angeles (90036) ***(P-24241)***

Westside Lodge ...E...415 864-1515
120 Page St San Francisco (94102) ***(P-24242)***

Westside Security Patrol, Bakersfield *Also called M & S Security Services Inc* ***(P-16346)***

Weststar Cinemas Inc ...D...323 461-3331
6801 Hollywood Blvd # 335 Los Angeles (90028) ***(P-17868)***

Weststar Marine Services Inc ...C...415 495-3191
50 Pier San Francisco (94158) ***(P-4640)***

Westview Cmnty Arts Program, Anaheim *Also called Westview Services Inc* ***(P-20383)***

Westview Healh Care Center ...C...530 885-7511
12225 Shale Ridge Ln Auburn (95602) ***(P-20382)***

Westview Services Inc ...C...714 956-4199
1701 S Euclid St Ste E Anaheim (92802) ***(P-20383)***

Westview Services Inc ...D...951 343-2356
11728 Magnolia Ave Ste D Riverside (92503) ***(P-27310)***

Westview Services Inc ...D...714 879-3980
626 W Commonwealth Ave Fullerton (92832) ***(P-23544)***

Westview Services Inc ...D...714 418-2090
9421 Edinger Ave Westminster (92683) ***(P-23656)***

Westward Hospitality MGT ...D...510 548-7920
200 Marina Blvd Berkeley (94710) ***(P-13092)***

Westwind Communications, Bakersfield *Also called Kbak TV Channel 29 CBS* ***(P-5616)***

Westwind Engineering Inc ...C...310 831-3454
553 N Pcfc Cst Hwy B179 Redondo Beach (90277) ***(P-25388)***

Westwind Engineering Inc ...D...310 831-3454
553 N Pcf Coastte B179 B Redondo Beach (90277) ***(P-25389)***

Westwind Equity Investors, Newport Beach *Also called Windjammer Capital Invstr III* ***(P-9775)***

Westwind Manor Resort Assn ...D...214 618-7200
15 Mason Ste A Irvine (92618) ***(P-26460)***

Westwind Media, Burbank *Also called Westwind Studios LLC* ***(P-17718)***

Westwind Media Inc ...D...818 972-9000
100 W Alameda Ave Burbank (91502) ***(P-17717)***

Westwind Studios LLC ...E...818 972-9000
100 W Alameda Ave Burbank (91502) ***(P-17718)***

Westwood Express Messenger Svc, Los Angeles *Also called Express Group Inc* ***(P-4251)***

Westwood Healthcare Center LP ...D...310 826-0821
12121 Santa Monica Blvd Los Angeles (90025) ***(P-20384)***

Westwood Insurance Agency (HQ) ...D...818 990-9715
8407 Fllbrook Ave Ste 200 Canoga Park (91304) ***(P-10548)***

Westwood Marquis Hotel & Grdns, Los Angeles *Also called W Los Angeles* ***(P-13069)***

Wet (PA) ...C...818 769-6200
10847 Sherman Way Sun Valley (91352) ***(P-17168)***

Wetherby Asset Management ...D...415 399-9159
580 California St Fl 8 San Francisco (94104) ***(P-9856)***

Wetransfer Corporation ...D...626 626-5565
2116 Zeno Pl Venice (90291) ***(P-15200)***

Wetzel & Sons Moving and Stor ...D...818 890-0992
12400 Osborne St Pacoima (91331) ***(P-4245)***

Wetzel Trucking, Pacoima *Also called Wetzel & Sons Moving and Stor* ***(P-4245)***

Weyerhaeuser Company ...D...562 983-6589
800 Pier T Ave Long Beach (90802) ***(P-960)***

Weyerhaeuser Company ...D...909 877-6100
17400 Slover Ave Fontana (92337) ***(P-6667)***

Weygandt & Associates ...E...916 543-0431
1501 Avi Blvd Ste 100 Lincoln (95648) ***(P-17564)***

Weyrick Pacific, Templeton *Also called Pacific Coast Supply LLC* ***(P-6639)***

WF Cinema Holdings LP ...E...805 379-8966
180 Promenade Way Ste R Westlake Village (91362) ***(P-17869)***

WF Cinema Holdings LP ....A....818 784-6266
3500 W Olive Ave Ste 890 Burbank (91505) ***(P-17870)***
Wfc Holdings LLC (HQ) ....C....415 396-7392
420 Montgomery St San Francisco (94104) ***(P-9156)***
Wfg National Title Insur Co (PA) ....B....818 476-4000
700 N Brand Blvd Ste 1100 Glendale (91203) ***(P-10205)***
Wfs, Los Angeles *Also called Worldwide Flight Services Inc* ***(P-4807)***
Wg, Santa Fe Springs *Also called Ethosenergy Field Services LLC* ***(P-1020)***
Wga West Inc ....D....323 782-4512
7000 W 3rd St Los Angeles (90048) ***(P-13641)***
Wgg Enterprises Inc ....C....626 442-5493
11340 Stewart St El Monte (91731) ***(P-2878)***
Whalen Medical Corporation (PA) ....E....213 622-6010
1000 S Hope St Ste 101 Los Angeles (90015) ***(P-23545)***
Whaling Bar & Grill, La Jolla *Also called Lav Hotel Corp* ***(P-12539)***
Wham-O Inc ....D....818 963-4200
6301 Owensmouth Ave # 700 Woodland Hills (91367) ***(P-7744)***
Whatever It Takes Inc ....E....760 329-6000
10805 Palm Dr Desert Hot Springs (92240) ***(P-13093)***
Whb Corporation ....A....213 624-1011
506 S Grand Ave Los Angeles (90071) ***(P-13094)***
Wheatland School District ....D....530 633-3135
100 Wheatland Park Dr Wheatland (95692) ***(P-11516)***
Wheatland Wind Project LLC ....A....888 903-6926
15445 Innovation Dr San Diego (92128) ***(P-5963)***
Wheel of Fortune, Culver City *Also called Quadra Productions Inc* ***(P-17656)***
Wheeler and Company, Cupertino *Also called Max Sportsters Inc* ***(P-26309)***
Wheelhouse Credit Union (PA) ....D....619 297-4835
9212 Balboa Ave San Diego (92123) ***(P-9413)***
Whgca LLC ....C....916 922-4700
2200 Harvard St Sacramento (95815) ***(P-13095)***
Whiskey Girl ....D....619 236-1616
702 5th Ave San Diego (92101) ***(P-26461)***
Whistlestop, San Rafael *Also called Marin Snior Crdnting Cncil Inc* ***(P-23329)***
White and Day, Torrance *Also called Light Hse Memorials Receptions* ***(P-13371)***
White Blossom Care Center, San Jose *Also called Plum Healthcare Group LLC* ***(P-20201)***
White Cap 24, Fairfield *Also called Hd Supply Construction Supply* ***(P-7393)***
White Cap 35, San Jose *Also called Hd Supply Construction Supply* ***(P-7394)***
White Cap Construction Supply ....A....949 794-5300
1815 Ritchey St Santa Ana (92705) ***(P-7496)***
White Digital Media Inc ....C....760 827-7800
3394 Carmel Mountain Rd # 250 San Diego (92121) ***(P-8879)***
White Hills Vineyard Ranc ....D....805 934-1986
8385 Graciosa Rd Santa Maria (93455) ***(P-693)***
White House Properties, Encino *Also called Schweizer Rena* ***(P-11440)***
White House Sales, Sacramento *Also called Chem Quip Inc* ***(P-7706)***
White Memorial Med Group Inc (PA) ....D....323 987-1300
1701 E Cesar E Chavez Ave # 510 Los Angeles (90033) ***(P-19596)***
White Memorial Medical Center (HQ) ....A....323 268-5000
1720 E Cesar E Chavez Ave Los Angeles (90033) ***(P-21373)***
White Rabbit Partners Inc ....C....310 975-1450
9000 W Sunset Blvd West Hollywood (90069) ***(P-24117)***
White Sands of La Jolla Clinic, La Jolla *Also called Cal Southern Presbt Homes* ***(P-23843)***
Whitefield Medical Lab & Rdlgy, Pomona *Also called Whitefield Medical Lab Inc* ***(P-21602)***
Whitefield Medical Lab Inc (PA) ....E....909 625-2114
764 Indigo Ct Ste A Pomona (91767) ***(P-21602)***
Whitegold Solutions Inc ....E....415 456-4493
43 Fernwood Way Ste 210 San Rafael (94901) ***(P-16156)***
Whitehat Security Inc ....D....408 343-8300
1741 Tech Dr Ste 300 San Jose (95110) ***(P-16157)***
Whiting Concrete Construction, Rancho Murieta *Also called Whiting Construction Inc* ***(P-3239)***
Whiting Construction Inc ....D....916 354-2756
7281 Lone Pine Dr Rancho Murieta (95683) ***(P-3239)***
Whiting-Turner Contracting Co ....E....949 863-0800
250 Commerce Ste 150 Irvine (92602) ***(P-1647)***
Whitmire Distribution, Valencia *Also called Cardinal Health Inc* ***(P-7933)***
Whittier Active Club, Whittier *Also called 24 Hour Fitness Usa Inc* ***(P-18110)***
Whittier City Community Svcs, Whittier *Also called City of Whittier* ***(P-23016)***
Whittier Equipment Rentals ....D....562 863-0641
11832 Bloomfield Ave Santa Fe Springs (90670) ***(P-1936)***
Whittier Grand Hotel, Whittier *Also called Ghg Properties LLC* ***(P-12295)***
Whittier Hills Health Care Ctr, Whittier *Also called Ensign Group Inc* ***(P-19884)***
Whittier Hospital Med Ctr Inc ....C....562 945-3561
9080 Colima Rd Whittier (90605) ***(P-21374)***
Whittier Inst For Diabetes ....D....877 944-8843
10140 Campus Point Dr San Diego (92121) ***(P-26049)***
Whittier Service Center, Santa Fe Springs *Also called Southern California Edison Co* ***(P-5950)***
Who Dat Nation Trnsp LLC ....D....760 403-7237
13186 Rincon Rd Apple Valley (92308) ***(P-5147)***
Whole Foods Market Cal Inc ....C....916 488-2800
4315 Arden Way Sacramento (95864) ***(P-4545)***
Whole Foods Market Cal Inc ....C....559 241-0300
650 W Shaw Ave Fresno (93704) ***(P-4546)***
Wholesale Air-Time Inc ....E....951 693-1880
27515 Enterprise Cir W Temecula (92590) ***(P-5496)***
Wholesale Fuels Inc ....D....661 327-4900
2200 E Brundage Ln Bakersfield (93307) ***(P-8742)***
Wholesale Solar Inc ....D....800 472-1142
412 N Mount Shasta Blvd Mount Shasta (96067) ***(P-2323)***
Wl Spa LLC ....E....213 487-2700
2700 Wilshire Blvd Los Angeles (90057) ***(P-18212)***
Wic, Torrance *Also called Public Hlth Fndation Entps Inc* ***(P-24628)***
Wic, Bakersfield *Also called Public Health California Dept* ***(P-19318)***
Wic, El Monte *Also called Public Hlth Fndation Entps Inc* ***(P-22305)***
Wicoro Inc (HQ) ....E....626 962-4489
919 N Sunset Ave West Covina (91790) ***(P-20722)***
Wideorbit Inc (PA) ....D....415 675-6700
1160 Battery St Ste 300 San Francisco (94111) ***(P-15201)***
Wiemar Distributors Inc ....D....213 747-7036
1953 S Alameda St Los Angeles (90058) ***(P-8539)***
Wier Construction Corporation ....E....760 743-6776
16884 Old Survey Rd Escondido (92025) ***(P-1648)***
Wightman Enterprises Inc ....D....916 961-2959
8017 Sacramento St Fair Oaks (95628) ***(P-14596)***
Wikimedia Foundation Inc ....C....415 839-6885
1 Montgomery St Ste 1600 San Francisco (94104) ***(P-24887)***
Wilbur Packing Company Inc ....B....530 671-4911
1500 Eager Rd Live Oak (95953) ***(P-561)***
Wilbur-Ellis Company LLC ....D....559 866-5667
12550 S Colorado Ave Helm (93627) ***(P-8863)***
Wilbur-Ellis Company LLC (HQ) ....B....415 772-4000
345 California St Fl 27 San Francisco (94104) ***(P-8864)***
Wilbur-Ellis Company LLC ....D....760 352-2847
45 Danenberg Dr El Centro (92243) ***(P-8865)***
Wild Electric Incorporated ....D....559 251-7770
4626 E Olive Ave Fresno (93702) ***(P-2696)***
Wild Goose Storage Inc ....D....530 846-7350
2780 W Liberty Rd Gridley (95948) ***(P-5967)***
Wild Karma Inc ....B....510 639-9088
2365 Hagen Oaks Dr Alamo (94507) ***(P-20385)***
Wild Palms Hotel & Bar, Sunnyvale *Also called Joie De Vivre Hospitality Inc* ***(P-12491)***
Wildenradt-Mcmurray Inc ....D....510 835-5500
568 7th St San Francisco (94103) ***(P-7412)***
WILDHAVEN RANCH, Cedar Glen *Also called San Bernardino Mtns Wildlife* ***(P-423)***
Wildlife Waystation ....E....818 899-5201
14831 Lttle Tjunga Cyn Rd Sylmar (91342) ***(P-24888)***
Wildomar Medical Offices, Wildomar *Also called Kaiser Foundation Hospitals* ***(P-20955)***
Wildwood Express ....E....559 805-3237
12416 Swanson Ave Kingsburg (93631) ***(P-4168)***
Wilkie Masonry Inc ....E....916 652-0118
4016 Hunter Oaks Ln Loomis (95650) ***(P-2734)***
Will Perkins Inc ....C....213 270-8400
617 W 7th St Fl 12 Los Angeles (90017) ***(P-25512)***
Will Perkins Inc ....D....415 856-3000
2 Bryant St Ste 300 San Francisco (94105) ***(P-25513)***
Willamette Valley Trtmnt Ctr, Cupertino *Also called CRC Health Corporate* ***(P-22015)***
Willdan Group Inc (PA) ....C....800 424-9144
2401 E Katella Ave # 300 Anaheim (92806) ***(P-25390)***
William Brammer ....C....760 746-6006
20505 San Pasqual Rd Escondido (92025) ***(P-8540)***
William C Arterberry ....D....760 728-9096
40147 Calle Roxanne Fallbrook (92028) ***(P-226)***
William E Heinselman ....E....916 920-0220
3303 Luyung Dr Rancho Cordova (95742) ***(P-25391)***
William H Warden III MD ....D....562 424-6666
2760 Atlantic Ave Long Beach (90806) ***(P-19597)***
William Hzmlhlch Archtects Inc ....D....949 250-0607
2850 Redhill Ave Ste 200 Santa Ana (92705) ***(P-25514)***
William L Lyon & Assoc Inc (PA) ....A....916 978-4200
3640 American River Dr Sacramento (95864) ***(P-26462)***
William L Lyon & Assoc Inc ....D....916 447-7878
2801 J St Sacramento (95816) ***(P-11517)***
William L Lyon & Assoc Inc ....D....916 535-0356
8814 Madison Ave Fair Oaks (95628) ***(P-11518)***
William Love Swimming Pool, Compton *Also called City of Compton* ***(P-18652)***
William Lyon Homes (PA) ....C....949 833-3600
4695 Macarthur Ct Ste 800 Newport Beach (92660) ***(P-1325)***
William Lyon Homes Inc (HQ) ....D....949 833-3600
4695 Macarthur Ct Ste 800 Newport Beach (92660) ***(P-1326)***
William McGann MD ....D....415 221-0665
1 Shrader St Ste 650 San Francisco (94117) ***(P-19598)***
William Morris Agency, Los Angeles *Also called William Morris Endeavor* ***(P-17954)***
William Morris Consulting, Beverly Hills *Also called William Morris Endeavor* ***(P-17955)***
William Morris Endeavor ....B....310 285-9000
2624 Military Ave Los Angeles (90064) ***(P-17954)***
William Morris Endeavor ....B....310 285-9000
9601 Wilshire Blvd Fl 3 Beverly Hills (90210) ***(P-17955)***
William Mrris Endvor Entrmt FN (HQ) ....C....310 285-9000
9601 Wilshire Blvd Fl 3 Beverly Hills (90210) ***(P-17956)***
William S Hart Pony & Softball ....D....661 254-9780
23437 Valencia Blvd Valencia (91355) ***(P-27258)***
William Warren Group Inc (PA) ....D....310 451-2130
201 Wilshire Blvd Ste 102 Santa Monica (90401) ***(P-17192)***
William Warren Properties Inc ....D....310 454-1500
201 Wilshire Blvd Ste 102 Santa Monica (90401) ***(P-10843)***
Williams & Sons Masonry Inc ....D....619 443-1751
8531 Winter Gardens Blvd A Lakeside (92040) ***(P-2735)***
Williams Adley & Company L L P (PA) ....D....510 893-8114
7677 Oakport St Ste 1000 Oakland (94621) ***(P-25692)***
Williams Keller Realty ....D....916 774-6700
7005 Boardwalk Dr Granite Bay (95746) ***(P-11519)***
Williams Tank Lines (PA) ....D....209 944-5613
1477 Tillie Lewis Dr Stockton (95206) ***(P-4169)***
Williamson Enterprises Inc ....D....310 822-6615
721 Washington Blvd Marina Del Rey (90292) ***(P-17313)***
Willis Allen Real Estate (PA) ....E....858 459-4033
1131 Wall St La Jolla (92037) ***(P-11520)***
Willis Allen Real Estate ....E....858 756-2444
6024 Pasco Delicias Rancho Santa Fe (92067) ***(P-11521)***
Willis Insurance Svcs Cal Inc ....E....858 678-2000
4250 Executive Sq Ste 250 La Jolla (92037) ***(P-9892)***
Willis Towers Watson, San Francisco *Also called Wtw Delaware Holdings LLC* ***(P-26882)***
Willis Towers Watson, San Diego *Also called Wtw Delaware Holdings LLC* ***(P-26883)***

ALPHABETIC

Employee Codes: A=Over 500 employees, B=251-500
C=101-250, D=51-100, E=50
2020 Directory of California
Wholesalers and Services Companies
© Mergent Inc. 1-800-342-5647
1487

Willits Hospital Inc.......B.......707 459-6801
1 Marcela Dr Willits (95490) ***(P-21375)***
Willits Perpetual LLC.......D.......818 668-6800
21600 Oxnard St Woodland Hills (91367) ***(P-17169)***
Willits Seniors Inc.......D.......707 459-6826
1501 Baechtel Rd Willits (95490) ***(P-23546)***
Willmark Cmmnties Univ Vlg Inc (PA).......D.......858 271-0582
9948 Hibert St Ste 210 San Diego (92131) ***(P-10844)***
Willow Creek Care Center, Clovis *Also called Willow Creek Halthcare Ctr LLC* ***(P-20387)***
Willow Creek Halthcare Ctr LLC.......A.......559 323-6200
650 W Alluvial Ave Clovis (93611) ***(P-20386)***
Willow Creek Halthcare Ctr LLC.......D.......559 323-6200
650 W Alluvial Ave Clovis (93611) ***(P-20387)***
Willow Creek Treatment Center, Santa Rosa *Also called Victor Treatment Centers Inc* ***(P-24105)***
Willow Farms LLC.......D.......805 647-0720
9452 Telephone Rd Pmb 142 Ventura (93004) ***(P-372)***
Willow Garage Inc.......D.......650 322-2584
921 E Charleston Rd Palo Alto (94303) ***(P-25871)***
Willow Glen Hsing Partners LP.......E.......408 267-7252
465 Willow Glen Way # 100 San Jose (95125) ***(P-11522)***
Willow Glen Villa, San Jose *Also called Atria Senior Living Inc* ***(P-23827)***
Willow Glen Villa A.......D.......408 266-1660
1660 Gaton Dr San Jose (95125) ***(P-10845)***
Willow Pass Healthcare Center, Concord *Also called Kissito Health Case Inc* ***(P-21800)***
Willow Pass Hlth Care Ctr Inc.......D.......925 689-9222
3318 Willow Pass Rd Concord (94519) ***(P-21911)***
Willow Rock Center, San Leandro *Also called Telecare Corporation* ***(P-21430)***
Willow Sprngs Alzhmrs Spcl Cr.......E.......530 242-0654
191 Churn Creek Rd Redding (96003) ***(P-24118)***
WILLOW TREE CONVALESCENT HOSPI, Oakland *Also called Willow Tree Nursing Center* ***(P-20723)***
Willow Tree Nursing Center, Oakland *Also called Covenant Care California LLC* ***(P-19830)***
Willow Tree Nursing Center.......D.......510 261-2628
2124 57th Ave Oakland (94621) ***(P-20723)***
Willows Care Rhabilitation Ctr, Willows *Also called Sunbridge Healthcare LLC* ***(P-20461)***
Wilmark Development, San Diego *Also called Wilmark Management Services* ***(P-11523)***
Wilmark Management Services (PA).......D.......858 271-0583
9948 Hibert St Ste 210 San Diego (92131) ***(P-11523)***
Wilmay Inc.......D.......805 524-2603
893 Oak Ave Fillmore (93015) ***(P-17170)***
Wilmer Cutler Pick Hale Dorr.......C.......213 443-5300
350 S Grand Ave Ste 2100 Los Angeles (90071) ***(P-22870)***
Wilmington Schll Bys & Grls CL, Wilmington *Also called Boys and Girls Clubs of The La* ***(P-24491)***
Wilmon Corporation.......D.......951 685-7474
8951 Granite Hill Dr Riverside (92509) ***(P-20388)***
Wilmor & Sons Plumbing & Cnstr.......D.......916 381-9114
8510 Thys Ct Sacramento (95828) ***(P-2324)***
Wilshire Animal Hospital.......E.......310 828-4587
2421 Wilshire Blvd Santa Monica (90403) ***(P-598)***
Wilshire Associates Inc (PA).......C.......310 451-3051
1299 Ocean Ave Ste 700 Santa Monica (90401) ***(P-26878)***
Wilshire Center Dental Group.......E.......213 386-3336
3932 Wilshire Blvd # 102 Los Angeles (90010) ***(P-19639)***
Wilshire Consumer Credit.......E.......323 692-8585
4751 Wilshire Blvd Los Angeles (90010) ***(P-9473)***
Wilshire Country Club.......D.......323 934-6050
301 N Rossmore Ave Los Angeles (90004) ***(P-18611)***
Wilshire Health and Cmnty Svcs.......D.......805 434-3035
290 Heather Ct Templeton (93465) ***(P-20724)***
Wilshire Health and Cmnty Svcs.......D.......805 484-2777
903 Carmen Dr Camarillo (93010) ***(P-24119)***
Wilshire Hlth & Cmnty Svcs Inc.......D.......310 679-9732
11630 Grevillea Ave Hawthorne (90250) ***(P-20725)***
Wilshire Hlth & Cmnty Svcs Inc.......D.......559 582-4414
851 Leslie Ln Hanford (93230) ***(P-20726)***
Wilshire Insurance Company.......E.......661 940-7300
1206 W Avenue J Ste 100 Lancaster (93534) ***(P-10549)***
Wilshire Nursing & Rehab, Templeton *Also called Wilshire Health and Cmnty Svcs* ***(P-20724)***
Wilson Elser Moskowitz.......D.......213 443-5100
555 S Flower St Ste 2900 Los Angeles (90071) ***(P-22871)***
Wilson Hampton Pntg Contrs Inc.......D.......714 772-5091
1524 W Mable St Anaheim (92802) ***(P-2406)***
Wilson Sonsini Goodrich & Rosa.......C.......858 350-2300
12235 El Camino Real # 200 San Diego (92130) ***(P-22872)***
Wilson Sonsini Goodrich & Rosa.......B.......650 353-6352
633 W 5th St Ste 1540 Los Angeles (90071) ***(P-22873)***
Wilson Sonsini Goodrich & Rosa (PA).......A.......650 493-9300
650 Page Mill Rd Palo Alto (94304) ***(P-22874)***
Wilson Sonsini Goodrich & Rosa.......D.......415 947-2000
1 Market Plz Fl 33 San Francisco (94105) ***(P-22875)***
Wilson Stephen Construction Co, Anaheim *Also called S W Construction Inc* ***(P-2973)***
Wilson Supply, Compton *Also called Dnow LP* ***(P-4562)***
Wilson Turner Kosmo LLP.......D.......619 236-9600
402 W Broadway Ste 1600 San Diego (92101) ***(P-22876)***
Wimberly Allison Tong Goo Inc.......D.......949 574-8500
300 Spectrum Center Dr # 500 Irvine (92618) ***(P-25515)***
Wimer Construction.......E.......818 848-0400
10855 Wimer Country Rd Sunland (91040) ***(P-1649)***
Win River Hotel Corporation.......E.......530 226-5111
5050 Bechelli Ln Redding (96002) ***(P-13096)***
Win Time Ltd (PA).......C.......858 695-2300
9335 Kearny Mesa Rd San Diego (92126) ***(P-13097)***
Win-River Resort & Casino.......B.......530 243-3377
2100 Redding Rancheria Rd Redding (96001) ***(P-13098)***
Winbond Electronics Corp Amer.......D.......408 943-6666
2727 N 1st St San Jose (95134) ***(P-7364)***
Wincere Inc.......C.......408 841-4355
2350 Mission College Blvd # 290 Santa Clara (95054) ***(P-16158)***
Winchester Mystery House LLC.......D.......408 247-2101
525 S Winchester Blvd San Jose (95128) ***(P-18784)***
Winco Dwl Industries Co, La Mirada *Also called Winco Industries Company* ***(P-7686)***
Winco Foods LLC.......D.......209 556-6040
4400 Crows Landing Rd Modesto (95358) ***(P-4547)***
Winco Industries Company.......E.......562 926-5600
14950 Valley View Ave La Mirada (90638) ***(P-7686)***
Wind River Enterprises Inc.......D.......707 864-1040
250 Dittmer Rd Fairfield (94534) ***(P-6415)***
Wind River Systems Inc (HQ).......C.......510 748-4100
500 Wind River Way Alameda (94501) ***(P-15535)***
Wind River Systems Inc.......D.......858 824-3100
10505 Sorrento Valley Rd San Diego (92121) ***(P-15536)***
Windermere Real Estate East.......D.......760 568-2568
71691 Highway 111 Rancho Mirage (92270) ***(P-11524)***
Windes Inc (PA).......D.......562 435-1191
111 W Ocean Blvd Ste 22 Long Beach (90802) ***(P-25693)***
Windflower Holdings LLC.......D.......707 263-6101
625 16th St Lakeport (95453) ***(P-20389)***
Windham At Saint Agnes.......D.......559 449-8070
1100 E Spruce Ave Ofc Fresno (93720) ***(P-10846)***
Windjammer Capital Invstr III.......A.......949 706-9989
610 Newport Center Dr # 1100 Newport Beach (92660) ***(P-9775)***
Windrow Earth Transport Inc.......E.......909 355-5531
14032 Santa Ana Ave Fontana (92337) ***(P-2002)***
Windsor Anaheim Healthcare (PA).......B.......714 826-8950
3415 W Ball Rd Anaheim (92804) ***(P-20390)***
Windsor Capital Group Inc.......D.......805 988-0627
2101 W Vineyard Ave Oxnard (93036) ***(P-13099)***
Windsor Capital Group Inc.......D.......310 566-1100
3250 Ocean Park Blvd # 350 Santa Monica (90405) ***(P-13100)***
Windsor Capital Group Inc.......D.......310 566-1100
3250 Ocean Park Blvd # 350 Santa Monica (90405) ***(P-13101)***
Windsor Capital Group Inc.......D.......209 577-3825
3250 Ocean Park Blvd # 350 Santa Monica (90405) ***(P-13102)***
Windsor Capital Group Inc.......D.......209 577-3825
3250 Ocean Park Blvd # 350 Santa Monica (90405) ***(P-13103)***
Windsor Capital Group Inc.......D.......714 990-6000
900 E Birch St Brea (92821) ***(P-13104)***
Windsor Capital Group Inc.......D.......951 676-5656
29345 Rancho California Temecula (92591) ***(P-13105)***
Windsor Capital Group Inc.......D.......310 566-1100
3250 Ocean Park Blvd # 350 Santa Monica (90405) ***(P-13106)***
Windsor Capital Group Inc.......D.......310 566-1100
3250 Ocean Park Blvd # 350 Santa Monica (90405) ***(P-13107)***
Windsor Capital Group Inc.......D.......714 241-3800
1325 E Dyer Rd Santa Ana (92705) ***(P-13108)***
Windsor Capital Group Inc.......D.......951 276-1200
1510 University Ave Riverside (92507) ***(P-13109)***
Windsor Capital Holet Group, Sacramento *Also called Recp/Wndsor Scramento Ventr LP* ***(P-12796)***
Windsor Convalescent.......C.......925 689-2266
3806 Clayton Rd Concord (94521) ***(P-20391)***
Windsor Convalescent.......C.......510 793-7222
2400 Parkside Dr Fremont (94536) ***(P-20392)***
Windsor Convalescent.......C.......831 424-0687
637 E Romie Ln Salinas (93901) ***(P-20393)***
Windsor Court/Stratford Place, Westminster *Also called Westminster Housing Parteners* ***(P-11515)***
Windsor Garden Conv Ctr Hwthrn, Hawthorne *Also called Sandhurst Convales Grp Ltd A* ***(P-20239)***
Windsor Gardens, Salinas *Also called Windsor Convalescent* ***(P-20393)***
Windsor Gardens.......D.......562 422-9219
4333 Torrance Blvd Torrance (90503) ***(P-20394)***
Windsor Gardens.......D.......310 675-3304
13922 Cerise Ave Hawthorne (90250) ***(P-20395)***
Windsor Gardens Convalescnt, National City *Also called Windsor Healthcare Management* ***(P-20398)***
Windsor Gardens Convalescnt.......D.......323 937-5466
915 Crenshaw Blvd Los Angeles (90019) ***(P-20396)***
Windsor Gardens Hea, North Hollywood *Also called Mariner Health Care Inc* ***(P-20122)***
WINDSOR GARDENS OF FULLERTON, Fullerton *Also called Windsor Gardns Healthcare Cntr* ***(P-20397)***
Windsor Gardens of Long Beach, Torrance *Also called Windsor Gardens* ***(P-20394)***
Windsor Gardns Healthcare Cntr.......C.......714 871-6020
245 E Wilshire Ave Fullerton (92832) ***(P-20397)***
Windsor Golf Club Inc.......D.......707 838-7888
1340 19th Hole Dr Windsor (95492) ***(P-18314)***
Windsor Grdns Cnvlescent Ctr A, Anaheim *Also called Windsor Anaheim Healthcare* ***(P-20390)***
Windsor Healthcare Management.......C.......619 474-6741
220 E 24th St National City (91950) ***(P-20398)***
Windsor Manor, Glendale *Also called Cal Southern Presbt Homes* ***(P-10704)***
WINDSOR MANOR REHABILITATION CENTER OF CO, Concord *Also called Windsor Convalescent* ***(P-20391)***
Windsor Monterey Care Ctr LLC.......D.......831 373-2731
1575 Skyline Dr Monterey (93940) ***(P-20399)***
Windsor Palms Care Ctr Artesia, Artesia *Also called Windsor Twin Palms Hlthcare* ***(P-20402)***
Windsor Park Care Ctr Fremont, Fremont *Also called Windsor Convalescent* ***(P-20392)***
Windsor Post Acute Care Center, Hayward *Also called S&F Management Company LLC* ***(P-22310)***
Windsor Rdge Rhbltion Ctr LLC.......D.......831 449-1515
350 Iris Dr Salinas (93906) ***(P-20400)***

Mergent e-mail: customerrelations@mergent.com
1488
2020 Directory of California
Wholesalers and Services Companies
(P-0000) Products & Services Section entry number
(PA)=Parent Co (HQ)=Headquarters (DH)=Div Headquarters

Windsor Sacramento Estates, Sacramento *Also called S&F Management Company LLC* ***(P-23419)***
Windsor Skyline Care Ctr LLC....D....831 449-5496
348 Iris Dr Salinas (93906) ***(P-20401)***
Windsor Twin Palms Hlthcare....C....562 865-0271
11900 Artesia Blvd Artesia (90701) ***(P-20402)***
Windsor Vallejo Care Center, Vallejo *Also called Helios Healthcare LLC* ***(P-20590)***
Windstar Capital Advisors....C....310 505-3720
10940 Wilshire Blvd # 2300 Los Angeles (90024) ***(P-9857)***
Windwalker Security Patrol Inc....D....209 333-3953
23987 Nw Frontage Rd Acampo (95220) ***(P-16479)***
Windy City Wire and Connectivi....C....510 284-3956
8024 Central Ave Newark (94560) ***(P-7113)***
Wine Country Party & Events, Torrance *Also called Bright Event Rentals LLC* ***(P-14133)***
Wine Dept, Los Angeles *Also called Youngs Market Company LLC* ***(P-8830)***
Wine Group Inc....D....559 638-3511
2916 S Reed Ave Sanger (93657) ***(P-8823)***
Wine Warehouse, Commerce *Also called Ben Myerson Candy Co Inc* ***(P-8799)***
Wine Warehouse, Richmond *Also called Ben Myerson Candy Co Inc* ***(P-8800)***
Winegard Energy Inc....D....559 441-0243
2885 S Chestnut Ave Fresno (93725) ***(P-2879)***
Winegard Energy Inc....D....661 393-9467
2159 Zeus Ct Bakersfield (93308) ***(P-2880)***
Winegardner Masonry Inc....E....909 795-9711
32147 Dunlap Blvd Ste A Yucaipa (92399) ***(P-2736)***
Winery Exchange Inc (PA)....E....415 382-6900
500 Redwood Blvd Ste 200 Novato (94947) ***(P-8824)***
Winfield Construction, Emeryville *Also called Alpha-Winfield Contractors Inc* ***(P-1076)***
Wing Aviation LLC....C....650 224-1198
3400 Hillview Ave Bldg 4 Palo Alto (94304) ***(P-4735)***
Wing Aviation LLC....D....650 260-8170
100 Mayfield Ave Mountain View (94043) ***(P-4736)***
Wingert Grebing Brubaker & Jus....D....619 232-8151
600 W Broadway Ste 1200 San Diego (92101) ***(P-22877)***
Winiarski Management Inc....D....707 944-2020
5766 Silverado Trl NAPA (94558) ***(P-8825)***
Winmax Systems Corporation....C....408 894-9000
1900 Mccarthy Blvd # 301 Milpitas (95035) ***(P-15202)***
Winnarainbow Inc (PA)....E....510 525-4304
1301 Henry St Berkeley (94709) ***(P-13155)***
Winners Only Inc....C....760 599-0300
1365 Park Center Dr Vista (92081) ***(P-6538)***
Winning Performance Pdts Inc....E....818 367-1041
13010 Bradley Ave Sylmar (91342) ***(P-17171)***
Winnresidential Ltd Partnr....B....559 435-3434
2350 W Shaw Ave Ste 148 Fresno (93711) ***(P-17193)***
Winnresidential Ltd Partnr....B....559 665-9600
255 Washington Rd Chowchilla (93610) ***(P-10847)***
Winsor House Compalessant....D....707 448-6458
101 S Orchard Ave Vacaville (95688) ***(P-20403)***
Winsor House Convalescent Hosp, Vacaville *Also called Winsor House Compalessant* ***(P-20403)***
Winston & Strawn LLP....B....650 858-6500
275 Middlefield Rd # 205 Menlo Park (94025) ***(P-22878)***
Winter Care Center Sacramento....C....916 922-8855
501 Jessie Ave Sacramento (95838) ***(P-20404)***
Winterthur U S Holdings Inc....C....213 228-0281
888 S Figueroa St Ste 570 Los Angeles (90017) ***(P-10550)***
Winton Irland Strom Green Insu (PA)....D....209 667-0995
627 E Canal Dr Turlock (95380) ***(P-10551)***
Winton-Ireland, Strom and Gr, Turlock *Also called Winton Irland Strom Green Insu* ***(P-10551)***
Winward International Inc (PA)....D....510 487-8686
42760 Albrae St Fremont (94538) ***(P-8937)***
Winward Silks, Fremont *Also called Winward International Inc* ***(P-8937)***
Winzler & Kelly....D....707 523-1010
2235 Mercury Way Ste 150 Santa Rosa (95407) ***(P-25392)***
Wipfli LLP....D....510 768-0066
505 14th St Ste 1220 Oakland (94612) ***(P-26879)***
Wipli HFS Consultants, Oakland *Also called Wipfli LLP* ***(P-26879)***
Wired Rite Electric, Burbank *Also called Grc Electric Inc* ***(P-2502)***
Wireless Lines, Los Angeles *Also called Cellular Palace Inc* ***(P-7249)***
Wirtz Qulty Installations Inc....D....858 569-3816
7932 Armour St San Diego (92111) ***(P-2737)***
Wirtz Tile & Stone Inc....D....858 569-3816
7932 Armour St San Diego (92111) ***(P-3020)***
Wis, San Diego *Also called Washington Inventory Service* ***(P-17161)***
Wis, San Diego *Also called Washington Inventory Service* ***(P-17162)***
Wisdom University....D....415 259-7122
35 Miller Ave Mill Valley (94941) ***(P-24889)***
Wise Commerce Inc....D....855 469-4737
1730 S El Camino Real # 500 San Mateo (94402) ***(P-15203)***
Wish I Ah Care Center Inc....C....559 855-2211
1665 M St Fresno (93721) ***(P-20405)***
Wish-Ah Skilled, Fresno *Also called Wish-I-Ah Skilled Nursing* ***(P-20407)***
Wish-I-Ah Hlthcre & Wellness....D....559 855-2211
1665 M St Fresno (93721) ***(P-20406)***
Wish-I-Ah Skilled Nursing....C....949 285-8859
1665 M St Fresno (93721) ***(P-20407)***
Wismettac Asian Foods Inc (HQ)....C....562 802-1900
13409 Orden Dr Santa Fe Springs (90670) ***(P-8284)***
Wismettac Fresh Fish, Santa Fe Springs *Also called Wismettac Asian Foods Inc* ***(P-8284)***
Withrow Cattle....D....916 780-0364
5301 Pleasant Grove Rd Pleasant Grove (95668) ***(P-406)***
Withrow Dairy, Pleasant Grove *Also called Withrow Cattle* ***(P-406)***
Withrow Phrm & Hlth Spc Lab....D....323 721-4281
2235 Via Puerta Unit A Laguna Woods (92637) ***(P-7993)***

Wj Newport LLC....C....949 476-2001
4500 Macarthur Blvd Newport Beach (92660) ***(P-13110)***
Wjbradley Mortgage Capital, Newport Beach *Also called Emery Financial Inc* ***(P-9623)***
Wjc Trapp Elementary Pta....E....909 820-7914
2750 N Riverside Ave Rialto (92377) ***(P-24697)***
WL Butler Inc....C....650 361-1270
1629 Main St Redwood City (94063) ***(P-1285)***
Wlcac, Los Angeles *Also called Watts Labor Community Action* ***(P-23541)***
WLMD....C....209 723-9120
1715 Kibby Rd Merced (95341) ***(P-3494)***
Wm B Saleh Co....D....559 255-2046
1364 N Jackson Ave Fresno (93703) ***(P-2407)***
Wm Bolthouse Farms Inc (HQ)....A....661 366-7209
7200 E Brundage Ln Bakersfield (93307) ***(P-85)***
Wm Healthcare Solutions Inc....D....713 328-7350
4280 Bandini Blvd Vernon (90058) ***(P-6334)***
WM LYLES CO, Fresno *Also called American Paving Co* ***(P-1662)***
WM LYLES CO, Fresno *Also called W M Lyles Co* ***(P-1929)***
Wm Michael Stemler Inc (PA)....C....209 948-8483
3244 Brookside Rd Ste 200 Stockton (95219) ***(P-10552)***
Wm Michael Stemler Inc....C....559 228-4144
7110 N Fresno St Ste 350 Fresno (93720) ***(P-10553)***
Wm ONeill Lath and Plst Corp....E....408 329-1413
1261 Birchwood Dr Sunnyvale (94089) ***(P-2881)***
Wm Recycle America LLC....D....562 948-3888
8405 Loch Lomond Dr Pico Rivera (90660) ***(P-6335)***
Wm S Hart Pony & Softball, Valencia *Also called William S Hart Pony & Softball* ***(P-27258)***
Wm Vandergeest Landscape Care....D....714 545-8432
3342 W Castor St Santa Ana (92704) ***(P-928)***
Wm Wireless Inc....E....562 633-9288
6723 N Paramount Blvd Long Beach (90805) ***(P-5282)***
Wmbe Payrolling Inc....C....858 810-3000
9475 Chesapeake Dr Ste A San Diego (92123) ***(P-14453)***
Wme Bi LLC....D....877 592-2472
17075 Camino San Diego (92127) ***(P-15537)***
Wmk Office San Diego LLC (PA)....D....858 569-4700
4780 Estgate Mall Ste 100 San Diego (92121) ***(P-6539)***
Wmk Sacramento LLC....C....916 929-8855
2001 Point West Way Sacramento (95815) ***(P-13111)***
WMS Transportation, Ventura *Also called Sam Hill & Sons Inc* ***(P-1908)***
Wnc Housing LP....E....714 662-5565
17782 Sky Park Cir Irvine (92614) ***(P-11971)***
Wolf Firm A Law Corporation....D....949 720-9200
2955 Main St Ste 200 Irvine (92614) ***(P-22879)***
Wolfe & Associates, Santa Barbara *Also called Ronald L Wolfe & Assoc Inc* ***(P-11429)***
Wolfe Engineering, Inc., San Jose *Also called Jabil Silver Creek Inc* ***(P-17474)***
Wolfe Trucking Inc....C....818 376-6960
7131 Valjean Ave Van Nuys (91406) ***(P-4170)***
Wolfsen Incorporated....C....209 827-7700
1269 W I St Los Banos (93635) ***(P-18)***
Wolt Com Inc....B....940 271-4703
2300 Tech Pkwy Ste 8 Hollister (95023) ***(P-14454)***
Woltcom, Hollister *Also called Wolt Com Inc* ***(P-14454)***
Woltcom Inc....C....831 638-4900
2300 Tech Pkwy Ste 8 Hollister (95023) ***(P-2697)***
Womble Bond Dickinson (us) LLP....C....408 720-8300
1841 Page Mill Rd Fl 2 Palo Alto (94304) ***(P-22880)***
Women Health Center (PA)....D....530 891-1917
1469 Humboldt Rd Ste 200 Chico (95928) ***(P-22163)***
Women Obsttrcts Gynocology Ctr, Laguna Hills *Also called Orange Coast Wns Med Group Inc* ***(P-19248)***
Women' S Health, French Camp *Also called Healthy Beginnings French Camp* ***(P-19007)***
Women's Health Center, Colusa *Also called Colusa Regional Medical Center* ***(P-26187)***
Women's Health Center, Merced *Also called Golden Valley Health Centers* ***(P-22033)***
Women's Imaging Center, Redding *Also called MD Imaging Inc A Prof Med Corp* ***(P-19180)***
Womens Center-Youth Fmly Svcs (PA)....C....209 941-2611
620 N San Joaquin St Stockton (95202) ***(P-23547)***
Womens Transitional Living Ctr....E....714 992-1939
P.O. Box 916 Fullerton (92836) ***(P-23657)***
Wonderful Agency....A....310 966-8600
11444 W Olympic Blvd # 210 Los Angeles (90064) ***(P-13599)***
Wonderful Citrus Packing LLC....D....559 798-3100
36445 Road 172 Visalia (93292) ***(P-562)***
Wonderful Citrus Packing LLC (HQ)....B....661 720-2400
1901 S Lexington St Delano (93215) ***(P-563)***
Wonderful Citrus Packing LLC....D....805 988-1456
710 Del Norte Blvd Oxnard (93030) ***(P-564)***
Wonderful Company LLC....B....661 720-2400
1901 S Lexington St Delano (93215) ***(P-196)***
Wonderful Company LLC....A....559 781-7438
5001 California Ave Bakersfield (93309) ***(P-565)***
Wonderful Company LLC....A....661 720-2609
11444 W Olympic Blvd # 210 Los Angeles (90064) ***(P-566)***
Wonderful Company LLC....A....661 399-4456
6801 E Lerdo Hwy Shafter (93263) ***(P-567)***
Wonderful Orchards LLC (HQ)....C....661 399-4456
6801 E Lerdo Hwy Shafter (93263) ***(P-181)***
Wonderful Orchards LLC....C....661 797-6400
13646 Highway 33 Lost Hills (93249) ***(P-182)***
Wonderfulpistachiosandalmonds, Lost Hills *Also called Wonderful Orchards LLC* ***(P-182)***
Wonderland Music Company Inc....D....818 840-1671
500 S Buena Vista St Burbank (91521) ***(P-11838)***
Wondertreats Inc....B....209 521-8881
2200 Lapham Dr Modesto (95354) ***(P-9024)***
Wonderware, Lake Forest *Also called Aveva Software LLC* ***(P-15562)***
Wonderware Corporation (HQ)....B....949 727-3200
26561 Rancho Pkwy S Lake Forest (92630) ***(P-6919)***

Wonolo Inc ....D....415 766-7692
535 Mission St Fl 14 San Francisco (94105) *(P-14455)*
Wood Bros Inc ....D....559 924-7715
14147 18th Ave Lemoore (93245) *(P-2003)*
Wood Castle Construction Inc ....E....626 966-8600
770 W Golden Grove Way Covina (91722) *(P-1222)*
Wood Environment & ....D....949 642-0245
3560 Hyland Ave 100 Costa Mesa (92626) *(P-25393)*
Wood Environment & ....C....510 663-4100
180 Grand Ave Fl 11 Oakland (94612) *(P-25394)*
Wood Environment & ....D....323 889-5300
6001 Rickenbacker Rd Commerce (90040) *(P-25395)*
Wood Gutmann Bogart Insur Brkg ....D....714 505-7000
15901 Red Hill Ave # 100 Tustin (92780) *(P-10554)*
Wood Ranch Golf Club, Simi Valley *Also called American Golf Corporation (P-18218)*
Wood Rodgers Inc (PA) ....C....916 341-7760
3301 C St Ste 100b Sacramento (95816) *(P-25396)*
Wood Smith Henning Berman LLP (PA) ....E....310 481-7600
10960 Wilshire Blvd Fl 18 Los Angeles (90024) *(P-22881)*
Woodbine Lgacy/Playa Owner LLC ....D....678 292-4962
6161 W Centinela Ave Culver City (90230) *(P-13112)*
Woodbridge Glass Inc ....C....714 838-4444
14321 Myford Rd Tustin (92780) *(P-3301)*
Woodbridge Village Association ....D....949 786-1800
31 Creek Rd Irvine (92604) *(P-24698)*
Wooden Valley Farms, Fairfield *Also called Lanza Vineyards Inc (P-145)*
Woodfin Suite Hotels LLC ....A....858 314-7910
12555 High Bluff Dr # 330 San Diego (92130) *(P-13113)*
Woodland Care Center LLC ....D....818 881-4540
7120 Corbin Ave Reseda (91335) *(P-20727)*
Woodland Healthcare ....D....530 756-2364
2660 W Covell Blvd Davis (95616) *(P-21376)*
Woodland Healthcare ....C....530 668-2600
1207 Fairchild Ct Woodland (95695) *(P-21377)*
Woodland Jint Unified Schl Dst ....E....530 662-0201
25 Matmor Rd Woodland (95776) *(P-3825)*
Woodland Lfyett Sklled Nursing, Lafayette *Also called Independent Quality Care Inc (P-20602)*
Woodland Lfytte Cnvlscent Hosp, San Ramon *Also called Independent Quality Care Inc (P-20600)*
Woodland Park Retirement Hotel, Pomona *Also called Longwood Management Corp (P-10761)*
Woodland Residential Services ....D....530 419-0059
1381 E Gum Ave Woodland (95776) *(P-10848)*
Woodland Swim Team Bosters CLB ....D....530 662-9783
155 West St Woodland (95695) *(P-24699)*
Woodley Lakes Golf Course ....D....818 780-6886
6331 Woodley Ave Van Nuys (91406) *(P-18315)*
Woodmont Real Estate Svcs LP ....B....707 569-0582
3883 Airway Dr Santa Rosa (95403) *(P-27311)*
Woodmont Realty Advisors Inc ....D....650 592-3960
1050 Ralston Ave Belmont (94002) *(P-10226)*
Woodroe Place, Hayward *Also called Bay Area Community Svcs Inc (P-10851)*
Woodruff Spradlin & Smart ....D....714 558-7000
555 Anton Blvd Ste 1200 Costa Mesa (92626) *(P-22882)*
Woodruff Convalescent Center, Duarte *Also called Estrella Inc (P-19897)*
Woodruff-Sawyer & Co (PA) ....C....415 391-2141
50 California St Fl 12 San Francisco (94111) *(P-10555)*
Woods Electric Company, Santa Fe Springs *Also called Harris L Woods Elec Contr (P-2510)*
Woods Maintenance Services Inc ....C....818 764-2515
7250 Coldwater Canyon Ave North Hollywood (91605) *(P-3495)*
Woodside Group Inc ....E....209 579-2030
3509 Coffee Rd Ste D10 Modesto (95355) *(P-9610)*
Woodside Healthcare Center, Sacramento *Also called W H C Inc (P-20368)*
Woodspear Properties (PA) ....E....760 761-4340
810 Los Vallecitos Blvd # 214 San Marcos (92069) *(P-10849)*
Woodspur Farming LLC ....D....760 398-9480
59111 Grapefruit Blvd Thermal (92274) *(P-373)*
Woolf Enterprises, Huron *Also called California Valley Land Co Inc (P-434)*
Woolf Farming Co Cal Inc ....A....559 945-9292
7041 N Van Ness Blvd Fresno (93711) *(P-374)*
Wor International Inc ....E....626 812-8888
15612 1st St Irwindale (91706) *(P-8051)*
Word & Brown Insurance ....C....714 567-4398
721 S Parker St Ste 200 Orange (92868) *(P-26463)*
Word and Brown, Orange *Also called Omega Insurance Services (P-10446)*
Word and Brown Hearing Ctr, Orange *Also called Providence Speech Hearing Ctr (P-22103)*
Wordsmart Corporation ....D....858 565-8068
10025 Mesa Rim Rd San Diego (92121) *(P-15538)*
Work Force Services Inc ....C....661 327-5019
300 Truxtun Ave Bakersfield (93301) *(P-14597)*
Work Force Staffing, Bakersfield *Also called Work Force Services Inc (P-14597)*
Work Truck Solutions Inc ....D....855 987-4544
2485 Notre Dame Blvd Chico (95928) *(P-16159)*
Work2fture - Yuth Training Ctr, San Jose *Also called Work2future Foundation (P-23658)*
Work2future - Gilroy Job Ctr, Gilroy *Also called Work2future Foundation (P-23660)*
Work2future Foundation ....C....408 794-1234
2072 Lucretia Ave San Jose (95122) *(P-23658)*
Work2future Foundation ....C....408 216-6202
1901 Zanker Rd San Jose (95112) *(P-23659)*
Work2future Foundation ....C....408 758-3477
379 Tomkins Ct Gilroy (95020) *(P-23660)*
Workcare Inc ....C....714 978-7488
300 S Harbor Blvd Ste 600 Anaheim (92805) *(P-26960)*
Workday Inc (PA) ....C....925 951-9000
6110 Stoneridge Mall Rd Pleasanton (94588) *(P-15204)*
Workers Compensation (PA) ....C....888 229-2472
1221 Broadway Ste 900 Oakland (94612) *(P-10151)*
Workforce, Santa Cruz *Also called His Manna Inc (P-26636)*
Workforce Dev Bd Solano Cnty, Fairfield *Also called Private Industry Cncl Slno Cty (P-14363)*
Workforce Development Bureau, Long Beach *Also called Career Transition Center (P-23575)*
Workforce Enterprises Wfe Inc ....E....909 718-8915
800 N Haven Ave Ste 330 Ontario (91764) *(P-14456)*
Workforce Investment- Admin, Merced *Also called County of Merced (P-23586)*
Workforce Resource Center, Santa Maria *Also called Employment Dev Cal Dept (P-14273)*
Workforcelogic ....D....707 939-4300
425 California St San Francisco (94104) *(P-15205)*
Working Assets Long Distance, San Francisco *Also called Credo Mobile Inc (P-5386)*
Working With Autism ....D....818 501-4240
16530 Ventura Blvd # 310 Encino (91436) *(P-22164)*
Workmens Auto Insurance Co ....D....213 742-8700
714 W Olympic Blvd # 800 Los Angeles (90015) *(P-10152)*
Workrite Uniform Company Inc (HQ) ....B....805 483-0175
1701 Lombard St Ste 200 Oxnard (93030) *(P-13317)*
Works Floor & Wall, The, Palm Springs *Also called Temalpakh Inc (P-1621)*
Workshare Technology Inc ....C....415 590-7700
650 California St Fl 7 San Francisco (94108) *(P-15539)*
World Class Distribution Inc ....C....909 574-4140
2121 Boeing Way Stockton (95206) *(P-4548)*
World Class Distribution Inc ....C....909 574-4140
800 S Shamrock Ave Monrovia (91016) *(P-4549)*
World Class Distribution Inc ....D....909 574-4140
343 S Lena Rd San Bernardino (92408) *(P-4550)*
World Class Distribution Inc (PA) ....D....909 574-4140
10288 Calabash Ave Fontana (92335) *(P-4551)*
World Famous San Diego Zoo, San Diego *Also called Zoological Society San Diego (P-24316)*
World For US, San Diego *Also called Mirnavseh Inc (P-14939)*
World Mark By Trend West, Oceanside *Also called World Mark of Oceanside (P-13114)*
World Mark of Oceanside ....D....760 721-0890
1301 Carmelo Dr Oceanside (92054) *(P-13114)*
World Market, Alameda *Also called Cost Plus Management Svcs Inc (P-26193)*
World Private Security Inc ....C....818 894-1800
16921 Parthenia St # 201 Northridge (91343) *(P-16480)*
World Service West ....C....310 538-7000
1812 W 135th St Gardena (90249) *(P-4805)*
World Trade Ctr Ht Assoc Ltd ....C....562 983-3400
701 W Ocean Blvd Long Beach (90831) *(P-13115)*
World Tuned Radio, Oceanside *Also called CK Enterprises Inc (P-16704)*
World Variety Produce Inc ....B....800 588-0151
5325 S Soto St Vernon (90058) *(P-8541)*
World Vision International (HQ) ....C....626 303-8811
800 W Chestnut Ave Monrovia (91016) *(P-24890)*
World Wide Technology LLC ....E....310 537-8335
1165 W Walnut St Compton (90220) *(P-6920)*
Worldlink East, Los Angeles *Also called Worldlink LLC (P-17172)*
Worldlink LLC (PA) ....D....323 866-5900
6100 Wilshire Blvd # 1400 Los Angeles (90048) *(P-17172)*
Worldmark By Wyndham, Anaheim *Also called Dolphins Cove Resort Ltd (P-12223)*
Worldsite.ws, Carlsbad *Also called Global Domains International (P-5412)*
Worldstage Inc (PA) ....D....714 508-1858
1111 Bell Ave Ste A Tustin (92780) *(P-26464)*
Worldway Airmail Center, Los Angeles *Also called Lax International Service Ctr (P-16886)*
Worldwide Flight Services Inc ....C....310 646-7510
5908 Avion Dr Los Angeles (90045) *(P-4806)*
Worldwide Flight Services Inc ....C....310 342-7830
5758 W Century Blvd Los Angeles (90045) *(P-4807)*
Worldwide Ground Transportatio ....D....408 727-0000
651 Aldo Ave Santa Clara (95054) *(P-3741)*
Worldwide Holdings Inc (PA) ....D....213 236-4500
725 S Figueroa St # 1900 Los Angeles (90017) *(P-10556)*
Worldwide Intgrted Rsurces Inc ....D....323 838-8938
7171 Telegraph Rd Montebello (90640) *(P-7687)*
Worldwide Produce, Los Angeles *Also called Green Farms Inc (P-8484)*
Worldwide Produce, Los Angeles *Also called Green Farms California LLC (P-8485)*
Worldwide Security Associates (HQ) ....B....310 743-3000
10311 S La Cienega Blvd Los Angeles (90045) *(P-16481)*
Worldwind Services LLC ....D....661 822-4877
915 Tehachapi Wllw Spgs Tehachapi (93561) *(P-2698)*
Worley Field Services Inc ....C....949 224-7585
2600 Michelson Dr Ste 500 Irvine (92612) *(P-2004)*
Worleyparsons Group Inc ....B....626 803-9000
181 W Huntington Dr 100 Monrovia (91016) *(P-25397)*
Worleyparsons Group Inc ....B....610 855-2000
721 Charles E Young Dr S Los Angeles (90095) *(P-25398)*
Worleyparsons Group Inc ....B....626 440-7000
100 W Walnut Pasadena (91101) *(P-25399)*
Worth Magazine, Malibu *Also called Curtco Publishing LLC (P-13618)*
Worxsitehr Insur Solutions Inc ....D....877 479-3591
5000 Parkway Calabasas # 302 Calabasas (91302) *(P-10557)*
Would You Rather - Season 1, Burbank *Also called A Its Laugh Productions Inc (P-17565)*
Woundco Holdings Inc ....B....310 551-0101
10877 Wilshire Blvd Los Angeles (90024) *(P-14091)*
Wovexx Holdings Inc (HQ) ....D....310 424-2080
10381 Jefferson Blvd Culver City (90232) *(P-5809)*
Wow Party Rental Inc ....D....714 367-3380
14575 Firestone Blvd La Mirada (90638) *(P-14211)*
Wp Electric Communications Inc ....E....909 606-3510
14198 Albers Way Chino (91710) *(P-2699)*
Wpcs Intrntional-Suisun Cy Inc ....D....916 624-1300
2208 Srra Madows Dr Ste B Rocklin (95677) *(P-2700)*
Wpromote LLC (PA) ....D....310 421-4844
2100 E Grand Ave Fl 1 El Segundo (90245) *(P-26880)*

Wr Chavez Company, Poway *Also called Wr Chavez Construction Inc* ***(P-1650)***
Wr Chavez Construction Inc.....D.....858 375-2100
12125 Kear Pl Ste A Poway (92064) ***(P-1650)***
WR Forde Associates Inc.....D.....510 215-9338
984 Hensley St Richmond (94801) ***(P-1811)***
Wrap News Inc.....E.....424 248-0612
2260 S Centinela Ave # 150 Los Angeles (90064) ***(P-16577)***
Wrap, The, Los Angeles *Also called Wrap News Inc* ***(P-16577)***
Wright Finlay & Zak LLP.....D.....949 477-5050
4665 Macarthur Ct Ste 200 Newport Beach (92660) ***(P-22883)***
Wright Broadband Group Inc.....D.....858 362-0380
4413 La Jolla Village Dr San Diego (92122) ***(P-27259)***
Wright Contracting EPA, Santa Rosa *Also called Wright Contracting LLC* ***(P-1651)***
Wright Contracting LLC.....D.....707 528-1172
3020 Dutton Ave Santa Rosa (95407) ***(P-1651)***
Wright Institute.....E.....510 841-9230
2728 Durant Ave Berkeley (94704) ***(P-19702)***
Writers Guild America West Inc.....C.....323 951-4000
7000 W 3rd St Los Angeles (90048) ***(P-24472)***
Writing Company, Culver City *Also called Social Studies School Service* ***(P-7034)***
Wrs, Woodland *Also called Woodland Residential Services* ***(P-10848)***
Ws Hdm LLC.....D.....858 792-5200
15575 Jimmy Durante Blvd Del Mar (92014) ***(P-13116)***
Ws Mmv Hotel LLC.....D.....619 692-3800
8757 Rio San Diego Dr San Diego (92108) ***(P-13117)***
Wsa Group Inc (PA).....E.....310 743-3000
19208 S Vermont Ave 200 Gardena (90248) ***(P-16482)***
Wsd Engineering Inc.....E.....619 954-7850
9245 Sky Park Ct Ste 105 San Diego (92123) ***(P-2701)***
WSH&b, Los Angeles *Also called Wood Smith Henning Berman LLP* ***(P-22881)***
Wsm Investments LLC.....C.....818 332-4600
3990b Heritage Oak Ct Simi Valley (93063) ***(P-11839)***
Wsp USA Buildings Inc.....C.....415 398-3833
425 Market St Fl 17 San Francisco (94105) ***(P-25400)***
Wsp USA Inc.....D.....714 973-4880
1100 W Town And Cntry 2 Orange (92868) ***(P-25401)***
Wsp USA Inc.....D.....909 427-9166
16689 Foothill Blvd Fontana (92335) ***(P-26881)***
Wsp USA Inc.....E.....212 465-5000
444 S Flower St Ste 800 Los Angeles (90071) ***(P-25402)***
Wsp USA Inc.....C.....415 243-4600
425 Market St Fl 17 San Francisco (94105) ***(P-25403)***
Wsp USA Inc.....D.....909 888-1106
451 E Vanderbilt Way # 200 San Bernardino (92408) ***(P-25404)***
WTLC, Fullerton *Also called Womens Transitional Living Ctr* ***(P-23657)***
Wtw Delaware Holdings LLC.....C.....415 733-4100
345 California St Fl 15 San Francisco (94104) ***(P-26882)***
Wtw Delaware Holdings LLC.....D.....858 523-5500
10955 Vista Sorrento Pkwy # 300 San Diego (92130) ***(P-26883)***
Wu Yee Child Care Center, San Francisco *Also called Wu Yee Childrens Services* ***(P-27312)***
Wu Yee Childrens Services.....D.....415 677-0100
880 Clay St San Francisco (94108) ***(P-23803)***
Wu Yee Childrens Services.....D.....415 677-0100
831 Broadway San Francisco (94133) ***(P-27312)***
Wurldtech Security Tech Ltd.....D.....604 669-6674
2623 Camino Ramon San Ramon (94583) ***(P-7365)***
Wurms Janitorial Service Inc.....D.....951 582-0003
544 Bateman Cir Corona (92880) ***(P-14083)***
Wurzel Landscape Maintenance.....E.....818 762-8653
3214 Oakdell Rd Studio City (91604) ***(P-929)***
WW Grainger Inc.....C.....408 432-8200
2261 Ringwood Ave San Jose (95131) ***(P-7192)***
WW Grainger Inc.....C.....951 727-2300
4700 Hamner Ave Eastvale (91752) ***(P-7663)***
Ww Lbv Inc.....C.....818 707-1220
30100 Agoura Rd Agoura Hills (91301) ***(P-13118)***
Ww San Diego Harbor Island LLC.....C.....619 291-6700
1960 Harbor Island Dr San Diego (92101) ***(P-13119)***
Wwl Vehicle Svcs Americas Inc.....C.....310 835-8806
500 E Water St Wilmington (90744) ***(P-4552)***
Wx Brands, Novato *Also called Winery Exchange Inc* ***(P-8824)***
Wyle Information Systems LLC.....B.....310 563-6800
970 W 190th St Ste 890 Torrance (90502) ***(P-15837)***
Wyndgate Technologies.....D.....916 404-8400
4925 Robert J Mathews Pkw El Dorado Hills (95762) ***(P-16160)***
Wyndham Anaheim Garden Grove, Garden Grove *Also called Ohi Resort Hotels LLC* ***(P-12665)***
Wyndham Canterbury At, San Francisco *Also called Canterbury Hotel Corp* ***(P-12112)***
Wyndham Garden Fresno Airport, Fresno *Also called Fresno Airport Hotels LLC* ***(P-12284)***
Wyndham Garden Hotel, Commerce *Also called Wyndham International Inc* ***(P-13124)***
Wyndham Garden Pierpont Inn, Ventura *Also called Fpl LLC* ***(P-12281)***
Wyndham Garden San Jose Arprt, San Jose *Also called Starlight Management Group* ***(P-12963)***
Wyndham Hotels & Resorts, Carmel *Also called Wyndham International Inc* ***(P-13123)***
Wyndham Hotels & Resorts, Fullerton *Also called Anaheim Park Hotel* ***(P-12008)***
Wyndham Hotels & Resorts, Belmont *Also called Wyndham International Inc* ***(P-13126)***
Wyndham Hotels & Resorts, San Jose *Also called Wyndham International Inc* ***(P-13127)***
Wyndham International Inc.....C.....714 992-1700
222 W Houston Ave Fullerton (92832) ***(P-13120)***
Wyndham International Inc.....C.....760 322-6000
888 E Tahquitz Canyon Way Palm Springs (92262) ***(P-13121)***
Wyndham International Inc.....C.....619 239-4500
400 W Broadway San Diego (92101) ***(P-13122)***
Wyndham International Inc.....C.....831 625-9500
1 Old Ranch Rd Carmel (93923) ***(P-13123)***
Wyndham International Inc.....D.....323 887-4331
5757 Telegraph Rd Commerce (90040) ***(P-13124)***
Wyndham International Inc.....D.....714 751-5100
3350 Ave Of The Arts Costa Mesa (92626) ***(P-13125)***
Wyndham International Inc.....E.....650 591-8600
400 Concourse Dr Belmont (94002) ***(P-13126)***
Wyndham International Inc.....C.....408 451-3050
1350 N 1st St San Jose (95112) ***(P-13127)***
Wyndham Irvine Orange.....D.....949 863-1999
17941 Von Karman Ave Irvine (92614) ***(P-26465)***
Wyndham San Dego At Emrald Plz, San Diego *Also called Wyndham International Inc* ***(P-13122)***
Wyndham San Jose, San Diego *Also called Pacifica San Jose LP* ***(P-12703)***
Wynne Systems Inc (HQ).....D.....949 224-6300
2601 Main St Ste 270 Irvine (92614) ***(P-15206)***
Wynwood At The Palms, Loma Linda *Also called Brookdale Senior Living Commun* ***(P-10700)***
X Prize Foundation Inc.....E.....310 741-4880
800 Crprate Pinte Ste 350 Culver City (90230) ***(P-24243)***
X-Act Finish & Trim Inc.....D.....951 582-9229
248 Glider Cir Corona (92880) ***(P-2992)***
X3 Management Services Inc.....D.....760 597-9336
2128 Auto Park Way Escondido (92029) ***(P-27260)***
Xactly Corporation (HQ).....C.....408 977-3132
505 S Market St San Jose (95113) ***(P-15207)***
Xad Inc.....C.....650 386-6867
189 Bernardo Ave Ste 100 Mountain View (94043) ***(P-26884)***
Xanterra Parks & Resorts Inc.....C.....760 786-2345
Hwy 190 Death Valley (92328) ***(P-13128)***
Xantrion Incorporated.....E.....510 272-4701
651 Thomas L Berkley Way Oakland (94612) ***(P-16161)***
Xap Corporation (PA).....E.....310 743-0450
600 Crprate Pinte Ste 220 Culver City (90230) ***(P-15208)***
Xavient Digital LLC.....A.....805 955-4111
21700 Oxnard St Ste 1700 Woodland Hills (91367) ***(P-15540)***
Xavient Info Systems Inc, Woodland Hills *Also called Xavient Digital LLC* ***(P-15540)***
Xavor Corporation.....D.....949 529-7372
300 Spectrum Center Dr # 400 Irvine (92618) ***(P-16162)***
Xceed Financial Credit Union (PA).....D.....800 932-8222
888 N Nash St El Segundo (90245) ***(P-9378)***
XCEL Mechanical Systems Inc.....C.....310 660-0090
1710 W 130th St Gardena (90249) ***(P-2325)***
Xcelmobility Inc.....D.....650 320-1728
2225 E Byshore Rd Ste 200 Palo Alto (94303) ***(P-15541)***
Xcerra Corporation.....C.....408 635-4300
880 N Mccarthy Blvd # 100 Milpitas (95035) ***(P-7366)***
Xcite Steps Corp.....C.....858 722-1948
3978 Sorrento Valley Blvd # 100 San Diego (92121) ***(P-20471)***
Xcommerce Inc (HQ).....D.....310 954-8012
3640 Holdrege Ave Los Angeles (90016) ***(P-16163)***
Xdbs Corporation.....D.....302 566-3006
3501 Jack Northrop Ave Hawthorne (90250) ***(P-25954)***
Xdbsb2b, Hawthorne *Also called Xdbs Corporation* ***(P-25954)***
Xdimensional Technologies Inc.....D.....714 672-8960
145 S State College Blvd # 160 Brea (92821) ***(P-15714)***
Xerox Corporation.....D.....818 848-8676
914 S Victory Blvd Burbank (91502) ***(P-6778)***
Xerox Corporation.....D.....310 526-3940
2118 Wilshire Blvd Santa Monica (90403) ***(P-6779)***
Xerox Corporation.....D.....650 813-6787
478 Ferne Ave Palo Alto (94306) ***(P-6780)***
Xerox Corporation.....C.....650 813-7138
3333 Coyote Hill Rd Palo Alto (94304) ***(P-6781)***
Xerox Education Services LLC (HQ).....D.....310 830-9847
2277 E 220th St Long Beach (90810) ***(P-6782)***
Xi Enterprise Inc.....D.....661 266-3200
2140 E Palmdale Blvd Palmdale (93550) ***(P-18213)***
Xin Xin Construction Inc.....D.....945 560-9511
6701 Koll Center Pkwy Pleasanton (94566) ***(P-1223)***
Xl Construction Corporation.....D.....916 282-2900
1810 13th St Ste 110 Sacramento (95811) ***(P-1224)***
Xl Construction Corporation (PA).....C.....408 240-6000
851 Buckeye Ct Milpitas (95035) ***(P-1652)***
Xl Fire Protection Co (PA).....D.....714 554-6132
3022 N Hesperian St Santa Ana (92706) ***(P-2326)***
Xl Specialty Insurance Corp.....D.....925 942-6142
1340 Treat Blvd Walnut Creek (94597) ***(P-10167)***
Xl Staffing Inc.....C.....619 579-0442
450 Fletcher Pkwy Ste 204 El Cajon (92020) ***(P-14457)***
Xld Group LLC.....D.....310 316-3636
3635 Fashion Way Torrance (90503) ***(P-13129)***
Xmultiple Technologies.....A.....805 579-1100
1919 Williams St Ste 325 Simi Valley (93065) ***(P-7367)***
Xobee Networks Inc.....D.....559 579-1300
7910 N Ingram Ave Ste 101 Fresno (93711) ***(P-5497)***
Xojet Inc (PA).....D.....650 594-6300
2000 Sierra Point Pkwy # 200 Brisbane (94005) ***(P-4808)***
Xoom Corporation.....C.....415 777-4800
425 Market St Ste 1200 San Francisco (94105) ***(P-9442)***
Xoriant Corporation (PA).....C.....408 743-4400
1248 Reamwood Ave Sunnyvale (94089) ***(P-16164)***
Xoxo, City of Industry *Also called Kellwood Company LLC* ***(P-8084)***
Xp Power LLC.....D.....209 267-1630
11383 Prospect Dr Jackson (95642) ***(P-7368)***
Xp Power LLC (HQ).....D.....408 732-7777
990 Benecia Ave Sunnyvale (94085) ***(P-7369)***
Xp Systems Corporation (HQ).....C.....805 532-9100
405 Science Dr Moorpark (93021) ***(P-15715)***
Xpo Enterprise Services Inc.....C.....916 399-8291
3810 Hill Rd Lakeport (95453) ***(P-4171)***

ALPHABETIC

Employee Codes: A=Over 500 employees, B=251-500
C=101-250, D=51-100, E=50
2020 Directory of California
Wholesalers and Services Companies
© Mergent Inc. 1-800-342-5647
1491

Xpo Logistics Freight Inc ....D.......209 983-8285
5475 S Airport Way Stockton (95206) ***(P-4172)***

Xpo Logistics Freight Inc ....D.......408 435-3876
2171 Otoole Ave San Jose (95131) ***(P-4173)***

Xpo Logistics Freight Inc ....E.......858 569-8921
4965 Convoy St San Diego (92111) ***(P-4174)***

Xpo Logistics Freight Inc ....D.......559 485-1164
4195 E Central Ave Fresno (93725) ***(P-4175)***

Xpo Logistics Freight Inc ....D.......831 758-8874
787 Airport Blvd Salinas (93901) ***(P-4176)***

Xpo Logistics Freight Inc ....C.......818 890-2095
12466 Montague St Pacoima (91331) ***(P-4177)***

Xpo Logistics Freight Inc ....D.......714 282-7717
2102 N Batavia St Orange (92865) ***(P-4178)***

Xpo Logistics Freight Inc ....C.......916 399-8291
3516 Kiessig Ave Sacramento (95823) ***(P-4179)***

Xpo Logistics Freight Inc ....D.......949 581-9030
20697 Prism Pl Lake Forest (92630) ***(P-4180)***

Xpo Logistics Freight Inc ....C.......213 744-0664
1955 E Washington Blvd Los Angeles (90021) ***(P-4181)***

Xpo Logistics Freight Inc ....D.......760 922-8538
12555 Mesa Dr Blythe (92225) ***(P-4182)***

Xpo Logistics Freight Inc ....D.......707 584-0211
4095 S Moorland Ave Santa Rosa (95407) ***(P-4183)***

Xpo Logistics Freight Inc ....C.......510 785-6920
2200 Claremont Ct Hayward (94545) ***(P-4184)***

Xpo Logistics Freight Inc ....C.......951 685-1244
13364 Marlay Ave Fontana (92337) ***(P-4185)***

Xpo Logistics Freight Inc ....C.......562 946-8331
12903 Lakeland Rd Santa Fe Springs (90670) ***(P-4186)***

Xpo Logistics Supply Chain Inc ....C.......559 408-7951
3825 S Willow Ave Fresno (93725) ***(P-5086)***

Xpo Logistics Supply Chain Inc ....D.......909 518-2095
26525 Pioneer Ave Redlands (92374) ***(P-5087)***

Xpo Logistics Supply Chain Inc ....C.......909 975-6300
5200a E Airport Dr Ontario (91761) ***(P-5088)***

Xqawesome Inc ....C.......949 929-9622
20 Mason Ln Ladera Ranch (92694) ***(P-23661)***

Xtra Department Inc ....D.......562 462-3800
12631 Imperial Hwy F106 Santa Fe Springs (90670) ***(P-26466)***

Xtraplus Corporation ....D.......510 897-1890
39889 Eureka Dr Newark (94560) ***(P-6921)***

Xtreme Security Services Inc ....E.......909 390-6818
337 N Vineyard Ave # 210 Ontario (91764) ***(P-16483)***

Xyka Inc ....E.......408 340-1923
5201 Great America Pkwy # 320 Santa Clara (95054) ***(P-15209)***

Y & R, San Francisco *Also called Young & Rubicam Inc* ***(P-13600)***

Y & S Auto Body Shop, San Pedro *Also called Y & S Enterprises Inc* ***(P-17314)***

Y & S Enterprises Inc (PA) ....E.......310 548-1120
1441 N Gaffey St San Pedro (90731) ***(P-17314)***

Y M C A, Berkeley *Also called Young MNS Chrstn Assn of E Bay* ***(P-23806)***

Y M C A Childcare Resource Ser, Oceanside *Also called YMCA of San Diego County* ***(P-24705)***

Y M C A Los Cerritos, Bellflower *Also called Young Mens Chrstn Assc Gr L B* ***(P-24744)***

Y M C A Metro Clinic, Berkeley *Also called Young MNS Chrstn Assn of E Bay* ***(P-24767)***

Y M C A The, Long Beach *Also called Young Mens Chrstn Assc Gr L B* ***(P-24748)***

Y W C A of Sonoma County ....E.......707 546-9922
811 3rd St Ste 100 Santa Rosa (95404) ***(P-24700)***

Y, THE, San Diego *Also called YMCA of San Diego County* ***(P-24707)***

Yale/Chase Eqp & Svcs Inc (PA) ....C.......562 463-8000
2615 Pellissier Pl City of Industry (90601) ***(P-7611)***

Yaley Enterprises Inc ....E.......530 365-5252
7664 Avianca Dr Redding (96002) ***(P-7844)***

Yamaha Corporation of America (HQ) ....B.......714 522-9011
6600 Orangethorpe Ave Buena Park (90620) ***(P-7845)***

Yamaha Music Corporation U S A, Buena Park *Also called Yamaha Corporation of America* ***(P-7845)***

Yamamoto of Orient Inc (HQ) ....C.......909 594-7356
122 Voyager St Pomona (91768) ***(P-8674)***

Yamamotoyama of America, Pomona *Also called Yamamoto of Orient Inc* ***(P-8674)***

Yammer Inc ....C.......415 796-7400
410 Townsend St San Francisco (94107) ***(P-16165)***

Yanaco Inc ....C.......530 246-9550
151 N Boulder Dr Redding (96003) ***(P-18343)***

Yancey Roofing, Sacramento *Also called Gudgel Roofing Inc* ***(P-3060)***

Yang C Park ....D.......408 260-8066
3703 Payne Ave San Jose (95117) ***(P-14458)***

Yapstone Inc (PA) ....C.......866 289-5977
2121 N Calif Blvd Ste 400 Walnut Creek (94596) ***(P-17173)***

Yardi Systems Inc (PA) ....B.......805 699-2040
430 S Fairview Ave Santa Barbara (93117) ***(P-15210)***

Yaskawa America Inc ....C.......408 748-4400
4101 Burton Dr Santa Clara (95054) ***(P-7193)***

Yates & Associates, Santa Ana *Also called Scottish American Insurance* ***(P-10484)***

YC Cable Usa Inc (HQ) ....D.......510 824-2788
44061 Nobel Dr Fremont (94538) ***(P-17174)***

Ycg LLC ....D.......760 230-8016
566 Shanas Ln Encinitas (92024) ***(P-27261)***

Ycusd, Yuba City *Also called Yuba City Unified School* ***(P-24244)***

Ydesign Group LLC (PA) ....E.......866 842-6209
1850 Mt Diablo Blvd # 210 Walnut Creek (94596) ***(P-7194)***

Year Round Landscape Maint Inc ....E.......909 597-7734
15189 Sierra Bonita Ln Chino (91710) ***(P-930)***

Yee Yuen Linen Service, Los Angeles *Also called Yuen Yee Laundry & Cleaners* ***(P-13184)***

Yefllow Shttle Vtrans Sdan Svc, San Leandro *Also called A-Para Transit Corp* ***(P-3518)***

Yellow Cab Company Penninsula ....C.......408 739-1234
7013 Realm Dr Ste A San Jose (95119) ***(P-3755)***

Yellow Cab Cooperative Inc ....D.......415 333-3333
55 New Montgomery St # 208 San Francisco (94105) ***(P-3756)***

Yellow Cabs, San Jose *Also called Yellow Cab Company Penninsula* ***(P-3755)***

Yellow Jacket Drlg Svcs LLC ....D.......909 989-8563
9460 Lucas Ranch Rd Rancho Cucamonga (91730) ***(P-3246)***

Yellow Radio Service, San Diego *Also called Administrative Services SD* ***(P-3743)***

Yellow Transportation, Hayward *Also called Yrc Inc* ***(P-4187)***

Yellow Transportation, Gardena *Also called Yrc Inc* ***(P-4188)***

Yellow Transportation, Tracy *Also called Yrc Inc* ***(P-4191)***

Yellowpagescom LLC (HQ) ....B.......818 937-5500
611 N Brand Blvd Ste 500 Glendale (91203) ***(P-17175)***

Yelp Inc (PA) ....D.......415 908-3801
140 New Montgomery St # 900 San Francisco (94105) ***(P-15895)***

Yes Videocom Inc (PA) ....B.......408 907-7600
2805 Bowers Ave Ste 230 Santa Clara (95051) ***(P-17719)***

Yeshiva Rau Isacsohn Academy ....C.......323 549-3170
540 N La Brea Ave Los Angeles (90036) ***(P-23804)***

Yeshivath Torath Emeth Academy, Los Angeles *Also called Yeshiva Rau Isacsohn Academy* ***(P-23804)***

Yew Bio-Pharm Group Inc ....D.......626 401-9588
9460 Telstar Ave Ste 6 El Monte (91731) ***(P-961)***

Yf Art Holdings Gp LLC ....A.......678 441-1400
9130 W Sunset Blvd Los Angeles (90069) ***(P-11705)***

Yhb Long Beach LLC ....D.......562 597-4401
2640 N Lakewood Blvd Long Beach (90815) ***(P-13130)***

Yhb San Francisco LLC ....D.......415 421-7500
85 5th St San Francisco (94103) ***(P-13131)***

Yliving, Walnut Creek *Also called Ydesign Group LLC* ***(P-7194)***

YMCA, Burbank *Also called Young Mens Christian* ***(P-24727)***

YMCA, Los Angeles *Also called Young MNS Chrstn Assn Mtro Los* ***(P-24761)***

YMCA, San Francisco *Also called Young Mens Christian Assoc SF* ***(P-24737)***

YMCA, Fullerton *Also called Young Mens Chrstn Assn Orange* ***(P-24758)***

YMCA, San Francisco *Also called Bayview Hunters Point Y M C A* ***(P-24479)***

YMCA Child Care Resource Svcs, San Diego *Also called YMCA of San Diego County* ***(P-24713)***

YMCA Crescenta-Canada, La Canada *Also called Crescenta-Canada YMCA* ***(P-24530)***

YMCA Glb Grant, Long Beach *Also called Young Mens Chrstn Assc Gr L B* ***(P-24747)***

YMCA Head Start, Berkeley *Also called Young MNS Chrstn Assn of E Bay* ***(P-24768)***

YMCA Metro La Summit Park, Valencia *Also called Young Mens Chrstn Assn of La* ***(P-24752)***

YMCA Metro La-52nd St School, Los Angeles *Also called Los Angeles Unified School Dst* ***(P-24587)***

YMCA of East Bay, Oakland *Also called Young MNS Chrstn Assn of E Bay* ***(P-24765)***

YMCA of East Valley (PA) ....C.......909 798-9622
500 E Citrus Ave Redlands (92373) ***(P-24701)***

YMCA of East Valley ....E.......909 881-9622
808 E 21st St San Bernardino (92404) ***(P-24702)***

YMCA of East Valley ....E.......909 425-9622
7793 Central Ave Highland (92346) ***(P-24703)***

YMCA of North Orange County ....D.......714 879-9622
2000 Youth Way Fullerton (92835) ***(P-24704)***

YMCA of San Diego County ....D.......760 754-6042
1310 Union Plaza Ct # 200 Oceanside (92054) ***(P-24705)***

YMCA of San Diego County ....C.......858 453-3483
8355 Cliffridge Ave La Jolla (92037) ***(P-24706)***

YMCA of San Diego County (PA) ....C.......858 292-9622
3708 Ruffin Rd San Diego (92123) ***(P-24707)***

YMCA of San Diego County ....B.......760 745-7490
1050 N Broadway Escondido (92026) ***(P-24708)***

YMCA of San Diego County ....D.......619 464-1323
8881 Dallas St La Mesa (91942) ***(P-24709)***

YMCA of San Diego County ....D.......858 292-4034
200 Saxony Rd Encinitas (92024) ***(P-24710)***

YMCA of San Diego County ....D.......619 281-8313
2927 Meade Ave San Diego (92116) ***(P-24711)***

YMCA of San Diego County ....D.......619 226-8888
2150 Beryl St Ste 18 San Diego (92109) ***(P-24712)***

YMCA of San Diego County ....C.......619 521-3055
3333 Camino Del Rio S # 120 San Diego (92108) ***(P-24713)***

YMCA of San Diego County ....E.......760 765-0642
4761 Pine Hills Rd Julian (92036) ***(P-24714)***

YMCA of San Diego County ....C.......619 298-3576
5505 Friars Rd San Diego (92110) ***(P-24715)***

YMCA of San Diego County ....D.......619 449-9622
10123 Riverwalk Dr Santee (92071) ***(P-24716)***

YMCA of San Diego County ....D.......760 758-0808
4701 Mesa Dr Oceanside (92056) ***(P-24717)***

YMCA of San Diego County ....D.......760 757-8270
333 Garrison St Oceanside (92054) ***(P-24718)***

YMCA of San Francisco, San Francisco *Also called Young Mens Christian Assoc SF* ***(P-24735)***

YMCA of San Joaquin County ....D.......209 472-9622
2105 W March Ln Ste 1 Stockton (95207) ***(P-24719)***

YMCA of Santa Clara Valley, San Jose *Also called YMCA of Silicon Valley* ***(P-24724)***

YMCA of Silicon Valley (PA) ....D.......408 351-6400
80 Saratoga Ave Santa Clara (95051) ***(P-24720)***

YMCA of Silicon Valley ....B.......650 493-9622
1922 The Alameda Ste 300 San Jose (95126) ***(P-24721)***

YMCA of Silicon Valley ....C.......408 298-1717
1717 The Alameda San Jose (95126) ***(P-24722)***

YMCA of Silicon Valley ....B.......650 969-9622
2400 Grant Rd Mountain View (94040) ***(P-24723)***

YMCA of Silicon Valley ....D.......408 226-9622
5632 Santa Teresa Blvd San Jose (95123) ***(P-24724)***

YMCA of Silicon Valley ....C.......408 370-1877
13500 Quito Rd Saratoga (95070) ***(P-24891)***

Mergent e-mail: customerrelations@mergent.com
1492
2020 Directory of California
Wholesalers and Services Companies
(P-0000) Products & Services Section entry number
(PA)=Parent Co (HQ)=Headquarters (DH)=Div Headquarters

YMCA of The Mid-Peninsula Inc ....B....650 493-9622
1922 The Alameda Ste 300 San Jose (95126) ***(P-24725)***
YMCA of Westchester, Los Angeles *Also called Young Mens Chrstn Assn of La* ***(P-24751)***
YMCA Overnight Camp, Julian *Also called YMCA of San Diego County* ***(P-24714)***
YMCA Pre School Hillview, Richmond *Also called Young MNS Chrstn Assn of E Bay* ***(P-24770)***
YMCA Youth & Family Service, San Rafael *Also called Young Mens Christian Assnsf* ***(P-24729)***
YMCA Youth & Family Services, San Diego *Also called YMCA of San Diego County* ***(P-24711)***
Ymcasf, San Rafael *Also called Young Mens Christian Assoc SF* ***(P-24740)***
Yodlee Inc (HQ) ....C....650 980-3600
3600 Bridge Pkwy Ste 200 Redwood City (94065) ***(P-26885)***
Yoga Works Inc (HQ) ....E....310 664-6470
5780 Uplander Way Culver City (90230) ***(P-18214)***
Yogaworks, Culver City *Also called Yoga Works Inc* ***(P-18214)***
Yogaworks Inc (PA) ....D....310 664-6470
5780 Uplander Way Culver City (90230) ***(P-18785)***
Yokohl Valley Packing, Lindsay *Also called Lindsay Fruit Company LLC* ***(P-16893)***
Yolo Hospice Inc (PA) ....D....530 758-5566
1909 Galileo Ct Ste A Davis (95618) ***(P-21912)***
Yorba Bena Ice Skting Bowl Ctr, San Francisco *Also called VSC Sports Inc* ***(P-27253)***
Yorba Linda Country Club, Yorba Linda *Also called American Golf Corporation* ***(P-18362)***
Yorba Linda Medical Offices, Yorba Linda *Also called Kaiser Foundation Hospitals* ***(P-19115)***
Yorba Park Medical Group, Santa Ana *Also called St Joseph Heritage Med Group* ***(P-21224)***
Yorba Properties Corp ....D....714 777-5112
20459 Yorba Linda Blvd Yorba Linda (92886) ***(P-11525)***
York Hlthcare Wllness Cntre LP ....D....323 254-3407
6071 York Blvd Los Angeles (90042) ***(P-23548)***
Yosemite Capital Mangagement, Tustin *Also called Hmwc Cpas & Business Advisors* ***(P-25607)***
Yosemite Concession Services, Yosemite Ntpk *Also called DNC Prks Rsrts At Yosemite Inc* ***(P-12219)***
Yosemite Farm Credit Aca (PA) ....D....209 667-2366
806 W Monte Vista Ave Turlock (95382) ***(P-9451)***
Yosemite Lakes Owners Assn ....D....559 658-7466
30250 Yosemite Springs Pk Coarsegold (93614) ***(P-24726)***
Yosemite Management Group LLC (PA) ....D....209 379-2817
11128 Hwy 140 El Portal (95318) ***(P-13132)***
Yosemite Meat Company Inc ....D....209 524-5117
601 Zeff Rd Modesto (95351) ***(P-8425)***
Yosh Enterprises Inc ....B....408 287-4411
675 E Gish Rd San Jose (95112) ***(P-16484)***
Yoshimura Research & Dev Amer ....D....909 628-4722
5420 Daniels St Ste A Chino (91710) ***(P-6482)***
You Consulting Group, Encinitas *Also called Ycg LLC* ***(P-27261)***
You Technology LLC ....D....650 624-3800
2001 Junipero Serra Blvd # 400 Daly City (94014) ***(P-15211)***
Youappi Inc ....D....646 854-3390
2 Embarcadero Ctr # 2310 San Francisco (94111) ***(P-26886)***
Young & Rubicam Inc ....C....415 882-0600
303 2nd St Ste N300 San Francisco (94107) ***(P-13600)***
Young Bae Fashions Inc ....D....323 583-8684
4811 Hampton St Vernon (90058) ***(P-8117)***
Young Brdcstg of San Francisco ....C....415 441-4444
900 Front St San Francisco (94111) ***(P-5663)***
Young Communications, San Francisco *Also called Young Electric Co* ***(P-2702)***
Young Dowlin L ....E....760 397-4104
101 Clay St San Francisco (94111) ***(P-197)***
Young Electric Co ....C....415 648-3355
195 Erie St San Francisco (94103) ***(P-2702)***
Young Mens Christian (PA) ....C....818 845-8551
321 E Magnolia Blvd Burbank (91502) ***(P-24727)***
Young Mens Christian Assn, South Pasadena *Also called Young Mens Chrstn Assn of La* ***(P-24756)***
Young Mens Christian Assnsf ....D....415 447-9622
63 Funston Ave San Francisco (94129) ***(P-24728)***
Young Mens Christian Assnsf ....C....415 459-9622
1115 3rd St San Rafael (94901) ***(P-24729)***
Young Mens Christian Asso ....D....805 583-5338
3200 Cochran St Simi Valley (93065) ***(P-18786)***
Young Mens Christian Asso ....D....805 523-7613
4031 N Moorpark Rd Thousand Oaks (91360) ***(P-24730)***
Young Mens Christian Assoc (PA) ....B....714 635-9622
240 S Euclid St Anaheim (92802) ***(P-24731)***
Young Mens Christian Assoc SF ....D....415 831-4093
680 18th Ave San Francisco (94121) ***(P-24732)***
Young Mens Christian Assoc SF ....D....415 447-9602
57 Post St San Francisco (94104) ***(P-24733)***
Young Mens Christian Assoc SF ....C....650 286-9622
1877 S Grant St San Mateo (94402) ***(P-24734)***
Young Mens Christian Assoc SF (PA) ....E....415 777-9622
50 California St Ste 650 San Francisco (94111) ***(P-24735)***
Young Mens Christian Assoc SF ....D....415 666-9622
360 18th Ave San Francisco (94121) ***(P-24736)***
Young Mens Christian Assoc SF ....D....415 957-9622
169 Steuart St San Francisco (94105) ***(P-24737)***
Young Mens Christian Assoc SF ....D....415 885-0460
246 Eddy St San Francisco (94102) ***(P-24738)***
Young Mens Christian Assoc SF ....D....415 883-9622
3 Hamilton Landing # 140 Novato (94949) ***(P-24739)***
Young Mens Christian Assoc SF ....B....415 492-9622
1500 Los Gamos Dr San Rafael (94903) ***(P-24740)***
Young Mens Christian Associat ....D....562 624-2376
525 E 7th St Long Beach (90813) ***(P-24741)***
Young Mens Chrstn Assc Gr L B ....D....562 272-4884
4116 South St Lakewood (90712) ***(P-24742)***
Young Mens Chrstn Assc Gr L B ....B....562 596-3394
1720 N Bellflower Blvd Long Beach (90815) ***(P-24743)***
Young Mens Chrstn Assc Gr L B ....D....562 925-1292
15530 Woodruff Ave Bellflower (90706) ***(P-24744)***
Young Mens Chrstn Assc Gr L B ....C....562 425-7431
5835 Carson St Lakewood (90713) ***(P-24745)***
Young Mens Chrstn Assc Gr L B ....D....562 423-0491
4949 Atlantic Ave Long Beach (90805) ***(P-24746)***
Young Mens Chrstn Assc Gr L B ....D....562 423-0491
4949 Atlantic Ave Long Beach (90805) ***(P-24747)***
Young Mens Chrstn Assc Gr L B ....D....562 633-0106
6125 Coke Ave Long Beach (90805) ***(P-24748)***
Young Mens Chrstn Assn of La ....E....818 989-3800
6901 Lennox Ave Van Nuys (91405) ***(P-24749)***
Young Mens Chrstn Assn of La ....D....626 799-9119
1605 Garfield Ave South Pasadena (91030) ***(P-24750)***
Young Mens Chrstn Assn of La ....E....310 216-9036
8015 S Sepulveda Blvd Los Angeles (90045) ***(P-24751)***
Young Mens Chrstn Assn of La ....C....661 253-3593
26147 Mcbean Pkwy Valencia (91355) ***(P-24752)***
Young Mens Chrstn Assn of La ....C....562 862-4201
11531 Downey Ave Downey (90241) ***(P-23549)***
Young Mens Chrstn Assn of La ....C....323 467-4161
1553 N Shrader Blvd Los Angeles (90028) ***(P-24753)***
Young Mens Chrstn Assn of La ....D....562 862-4201
11531 Downey Ave Downey (90241) ***(P-24754)***
Young Mens Chrstn Assn of La ....D....818 763-5126
5142 Tujunga Ave North Hollywood (91601) ***(P-23805)***
Young Mens Chrstn Assn of La ....D....213 624-2348
401 S Hope St Los Angeles (90071) ***(P-24755)***
Young Mens Chrstn Assn of La ....D....323 682-2147
1605 Garfield Ave South Pasadena (91030) ***(P-24756)***
Young Mens Chrstn Assn Orange ....D....949 642-9990
2300 University Dr Newport Beach (92660) ***(P-24757)***
Young Mens Chrstn Assn Orange ....D....714 879-9622
2000 Youth Way Fullerton (92835) ***(P-24758)***
Young Mens Chrstn Assn Orange ....D....949 859-9622
27341 Trabuco Cir Mission Viejo (92692) ***(P-24759)***
Young Mens Chrstn Assoc Gndl ....D....818 484-8256
140 N Louise St Glendale (91206) ***(P-24760)***
Young MNS Chrstn Assn Mtro Los (PA) ....D....213 380-6448
625 S New Hampshire Ave Los Angeles (90005) ***(P-24761)***
Young MNS Chrstn Assn of E Bay ....D....510 654-9622
3265 Market St Oakland (94608) ***(P-24762)***
Young MNS Chrstn Assn of E Bay ....D....925 687-8900
350 Civic Dr Pleasant Hill (94523) ***(P-24763)***
Young MNS Chrstn Assn of E Bay ....A....925 609-7971
1705 Thornwood Dr Concord (94521) ***(P-24764)***
Young MNS Chrstn Assn of E Bay ....A....510 451-8039
2350 Broadway Oakland (94612) ***(P-24765)***
Young MNS Chrstn Assn of E Bay ....D....510 601-8674
4727 San Pablo Ave Emeryville (94608) ***(P-24766)***
Young MNS Chrstn Assn of E Bay ....D....510 486-8400
2111 Mrtn Lthr King Jr Wa Berkeley (94704) ***(P-24767)***
Young MNS Chrstn Assn of E Bay ....D....510 848-9092
2009 10th St Berkeley (94710) ***(P-24768)***
Young MNS Chrstn Assn of E Bay ....C....510 848-9622
2001 Allston Way Berkeley (94704) ***(P-24769)***
Young MNS Chrstn Assn of E Bay ....A....510 223-7070
3800 Clark Rd Richmond (94803) ***(P-24770)***
Young MNS Chrstn Assn of E Bay ....D....510 526-2146
1130 Oxford St Berkeley (94707) ***(P-24771)***
Young MNS Chrstn Assn of E Bay ....A....510 644-6290
2241 Russell St Berkeley (94705) ***(P-23806)***
Young MNS Chrstn Assn of E Bay ....B....510 412-5647
263 S 20th St Richmond (94804) ***(P-24772)***
Young MNS Chrstn Assn of E Bay ....C....510 222-9622
4300 Lakeside Dr Richmond (94806) ***(P-24773)***
Young MNS Chrstn Assn of E Bay ....D....510 848-6800
2001 Allston Way Berkeley (94704) ***(P-24774)***
Young MNS Chrstn Assn of E Bay ....D....510 559-2090
1422 San Pablo Ave Berkeley (94702) ***(P-24775)***
Young Realtors ....D....805 497-0947
971 S Westlake Blvd # 100 Westlake Village (91361) ***(P-11526)***
Young Systems Corporation ....D....562 921-2256
13125 Midway Pl Cerritos (90703) ***(P-6783)***
Young Womens Christian Assoc ....C....323 295-4280
2501 W Vernon Ave Los Angeles (90008) ***(P-24776)***
Young Womens Christian Associ ....D....408 295-4011
375 S 3rd St San Jose (95112) ***(P-24777)***
Young's Nursery, San Francisco *Also called Young Dowlin L* ***(P-197)***
Youngs Holdings Inc (PA) ....D....714 368-4615
14402 Franklin Ave Tustin (92780) ***(P-8826)***
Youngs Market Company LLC (HQ) ....B....800 317-6150
14402 Franklin Ave Tustin (92780) ***(P-8827)***
Youngs Market Company LLC ....D....408 782-3121
850 Jarvis Dr Morgan Hill (95037) ***(P-8828)***
Youngs Market Company LLC ....B....510 475-2200
5100 Franklin Dr Pleasanton (94588) ***(P-8829)***
Youngs Market Company LLC ....B....213 629-3929
500 S Central Ave Los Angeles (90013) ***(P-8830)***
Youngs Market Company LLC ....D....707 584-5170
256 Sutton Pl Ste 106 Santa Rosa (95407) ***(P-8831)***
Youngs Market Company LLC ....E....916 617-4402
3620 Industrial Blvd # 10 West Sacramento (95691) ***(P-8832)***
Your Executive Solutions ....A....562 388-4150
9054 Slauson Ave Pico Rivera (90660) ***(P-14459)***
Your Man Tours Inc ....D....513 772-4411
100 N Pacific Coast Hwy # 1700 El Segundo (90245) ***(P-24892)***
Your Man Tours Merger Inc (HQ) ....D....310 649-3820
100 N Pacific Coast Hwy # 1700 El Segundo (90245) ***(P-4870)***

Your Man Tours, Inc., El Segundo *Also called Your Man Tours Merger Inc* ***(P-4870)***
Your Way Fumigation Inc..........D.......951 699-9116
41880 Kalmia St Ste 170 Murrieta (92562) ***(P-13836)***
Yourpeople Inc..........A.......888 249-3263
50 Beale St San Francisco (94105) ***(P-15542)***
YOUTH DEVELOPMENT CENTER, Harbor City *Also called South Bay Bright Future Inc* ***(P-24082)***
Youth For Change..........D.......530 605-1520
2400 Washington Ave Redding (96001) ***(P-23550)***
Youth For Change (PA)..........C.......530 877-8187
5538 Skyway Paradise (95969) ***(P-23551)***
Youth For Change..........D.......530 538-8347
2185 Baldwin Ave Oroville (95966) ***(P-23552)***
Youth Homes Incorporated (PA)..........D.......925 933-2627
3480 Buskirk Ave Ste 210 Pleasant Hill (94523) ***(P-24120)***
Youth Homes Incorporated..........D.......925 933-2627
1159 Everett Ct Concord (94518) ***(P-24121)***
Yrc Freight, Adelanto *Also called Yrc Inc* ***(P-4189)***
Yrc Inc..........D.......510 783-7010
25555 Clawiter Rd Hayward (94545) ***(P-4187)***
Yrc Inc..........C.......310 404-2221
15400 S Main St Gardena (90248) ***(P-4188)***
Yrc Inc..........D.......760 246-0031
17401 Adelanto Rd Adelanto (92301) ***(P-4189)***
Yrc Inc..........D.......916 371-4555
3210 52nd Ave Sacramento (95823) ***(P-4190)***
Yrc Inc..........C.......209 833-1300
1535 E Pescadero Ave Tracy (95304) ***(P-4191)***
Yrc Worldwide Inc..........D.......650 952-1112
201 Haskins Way South San Francisco (94080) ***(P-4192)***
YREKA EMPLOYMENT SERVICES, Mount Shasta *Also called Siskiyou Opportunity Center* ***(P-23637)***
Ytech, Monterey Park *Also called Syntelesys Inc* ***(P-17439)***
Ytel Inc..........D.......800 382-4913
94 Icon Foothill Ranch (92610) ***(P-5498)***
Yti, San Pedro *Also called Yusen Terminals LLC* ***(P-4628)***
Yub Inc..........C.......650 265-7316
520 Logue Ave Mountain View (94043) ***(P-13601)***
Yuba City Nursing & Rehab LLC..........D.......530 671-0550
1220 Plumas St Yuba City (95991) ***(P-20408)***
Yuba City Post-Acute, Yuba City *Also called Guava Holdings LLC* ***(P-21475)***
Yuba City Racquet Club Inc..........D.......530 673-6900
825 Jones Rd Yuba City (95991) ***(P-18612)***
Yuba City Unified School..........A.......530 822-7601
750 N Palora Ave Yuba City (95991) ***(P-24244)***
Yuba Community College Dst..........D.......530 788-0973
2088 N Beale Rd Marysville (95901) ***(P-23553)***
Yuba County Planning Dept, Marysville *Also called County of Yuba* ***(P-11555)***
Yuba County Probation Dept, Marysville *Also called County of Yuba* ***(P-23183)***
Yubico Inc..........C.......408 774-4064
530 Lytton Ave Ste 301 Palo Alto (94301) ***(P-6784)***
Yucaipa Companies LLC (PA)..........C.......310 789-7200
9130 W Sunset Blvd Los Angeles (90069) ***(P-27262)***
Yucaipa Valley Water District (PA)..........D.......909 797-5117
12770 2nd St Yucaipa (92399) ***(P-6127)***
Yue Feng Inc..........D.......310 253-9795
145 S Fairfax Ave Los Angeles (90036) ***(P-23554)***
Yuen Yee Laundry & Cleaners..........D.......323 734-7205
2575 S Normandie Ave Los Angeles (90007) ***(P-13184)***
Yuja Inc..........C.......888 257-2278
84 W Santa Clara St # 690 San Jose (95113) ***(P-15543)***
Yukevich / Cvanaugh A Law Corp (PA)..........D.......213 362-7777
355 S Grand Ave Fl 15 Los Angeles (90071) ***(P-22884)***
Yuma Lakes Resort, Earp *Also called Colorado River Adventures Inc* ***(P-13159)***
Yume Inc (HQ)..........D.......650 591-9400
601 Montgomery St # 1600 San Francisco (94111) ***(P-13602)***
Yuneec USA Inc..........D.......855 284-8888
9227 Haven Ave Ste 210 Rancho Cucamonga (91730) ***(P-7370)***
Yupana Inc..........E.......925 482-0657
5039 Commercial Cir Ste J Concord (94520) ***(P-25405)***
Yusen Logistics Americas Inc..........C.......310 518-3008
2417 E Carson St Ste 100 Carson (90810) ***(P-5089)***
Yusen Terminals LLC (HQ)..........D.......310 548-8000
701 New Dock St San Pedro (90731) ***(P-4628)***
YWCA, Santa Rosa *Also called Y W C A of Sonoma County* ***(P-24700)***
YWCA Contra Costa/Sacramento (PA)..........D.......925 372-4213
1320 Arnold Dr Ste 170 Martinez (94553) ***(P-23555)***
YWCA SILICON VALLEY, San Jose *Also called Young Womens Christian Associ* ***(P-24777)***
Z & M Associates Inc..........D.......408 996-8100
1601 S Danza Blvd Ste 150 Cupertino (95014) ***(P-11527)***
Z Garcia Farm Labor, Arvin *Also called Edwardo Z Garcia* ***(P-616)***
Z J'S Auto Body, Clovis *Also called Pk Autobody Inc* ***(P-17301)***
Z Microsystems, San Diego *Also called Zmicro Inc* ***(P-15717)***
Z Valet & Shuttle Service, Los Angeles *Also called Z Valet Inc* ***(P-13462)***
Z Valet Inc..........C.......323 954-3700
4221 Wilshire Blvd 170-11 Los Angeles (90010) ***(P-13462)***
Z-Best Concrete Inc..........D.......951 774-1870
2575 Main St Riverside (92501) ***(P-3240)***
Z57 Inc (HQ)..........D.......858 623-5577
10045 Mesa Rim Rd San Diego (92121) ***(P-13603)***
Zabin Industries Inc (PA)..........D.......213 749-1215
3957 S Hill St Ste A Los Angeles (90037) ***(P-8016)***
Zadaonet..........D.......650 556-6377
685 Scofield Ave Apt 22 East Palo Alto (94303) ***(P-5499)***
Zaharoni Holdings..........E.......310 297-9722
5400 W Rosecrans Ave Lowr Hawthorne (90250) ***(P-26467)***
Zambezi LLC..........D.......310 450-6800
10441 Jefferson Blvd Culver City (90232) ***(P-13667)***
Zanker Road Landfill, San Jose *Also called Zanker Road Resource MGT Ltd* ***(P-6336)***
Zanker Road Resource MGT Ltd..........D.......408 457-1189
675 Los Esteros Rd San Jose (95134) ***(P-6336)***
Zantos Living Trust, Anaheim *Also called Westcoast Performance Pdts USA* ***(P-11880)***
Zastrow Construction Inc..........C.......323 478-1956
3267 Verdugo Rd Los Angeles (90065) ***(P-1286)***
Zayo Group LLC..........D.......707 284-4000
3700 Old Redwood Hwy Santa Rosa (95403) ***(P-17176)***
Zb Rehab Staffing Inc..........D.......650 396-2207
650 El Camino Real Ste O Redwood City (94063) ***(P-14598)***
Zeeto Media, San Diego *Also called Zeetogroup LLC* ***(P-13604)***
Zeetogroup LLC..........D.......888 771-9194
925 B St Fl 5 San Diego (92101) ***(P-13604)***
Zefr Inc..........C.......310 392-3555
4101 Redwood Ave Los Angeles (90066) ***(P-17720)***
Zeiter Eye Medical Group Inc (PA)..........D.......209 366-0446
255 E Weber Ave Stockton (95202) ***(P-19599)***
Zell Associates Inc (PA)..........D.......408 978-1950
1777 Hamilton Ave # 1250 San Jose (95125) ***(P-9776)***
Zelle LLP..........E.......415 693-0700
44 Montgomery St Ste 3400 San Francisco (94104) ***(P-22885)***
Zellerbach Rehearsal Hall, San Francisco *Also called City & County of San Francisco* ***(P-17898)***
Zemarc Corporation (PA)..........E.......323 721-5598
6431 Flotilla St Commerce (90040) ***(P-7612)***
Zend Technologies Usa Inc..........C.......408 253-8800
19200 Stevens Creek Blvd # 100 Cupertino (95014) ***(P-15212)***
Zendesk Inc (PA)..........C.......415 418-7506
1019 Market St San Francisco (94103) ***(P-15544)***
Zenefits, San Francisco *Also called Yourpeople Inc* ***(P-15542)***
Zenith A Fairfax Company, The, Woodland Hills *Also called Zenith Insurance Company* ***(P-10153)***
Zenith Health Care..........D.......626 578-0460
245 S El Molino Ave Pasadena (91101) ***(P-11528)***
Zenith Infotech Limited..........C.......510 687-1943
39675 Cedar Blvd Ste 240b Newark (94560) ***(P-15716)***
Zenith Insurance Company (HQ)..........B.......818 713-1000
21255 Califa St Woodland Hills (91367) ***(P-10153)***
Zenith Insurance Company..........D.......619 299-6252
7676 Hazard Center Dr # 1200 San Diego (92108) ***(P-10154)***
Zenith Insurance Company..........D.......925 460-0600
4460 Rosewood Dr Ste 300 Pleasanton (94588) ***(P-9893)***
Zenith Talent Corporation..........C.......844 467-2300
3315 San Felipe Rd Ste 37 San Jose (95135) ***(P-14460)***
Zenpayroll Inc (PA)..........C.......800 936-0383
525 20th St San Francisco (94107) ***(P-15545)***
Zentek Corporation..........D.......916 749-3610
3031 Stnfrd Rnch Rd 2 Rocklin (95765) ***(P-15213)***
Zephyr Partners Re-LLC..........E.......858 558-3650
700 2nd St Encinitas (92024) ***(P-11529)***
Zephyr Real Estate, San Francisco *Also called Dppm Inc* ***(P-11102)***
Zephyr River Expeditions Inc..........D.......800 431-3636
22517 Parrotts Ferry Rd Columbia (95310) ***(P-18787)***
Zephyr White Water Expeditions, Columbia *Also called Zephyr River Expeditions Inc* ***(P-18787)***
Zerep Management Corporation..........D.......626 961-6291
17445 Railroad St City of Industry (91748) ***(P-6337)***
Zero Energy Contracting LLC..........D.......626 701-3180
13850 Cerritos Corporate Cerritos (90703) ***(P-2327)***
Zero Waste Solutions Inc..........C.......925 270-3339
1850 Gateway Blvd # 1030 Concord (94520) ***(P-26961)***
Zettler Components Inc (PA)..........C.......949 831-5000
75 Columbia Orange (92868) ***(P-7371)***
Zeus Living, San Francisco *Also called Egomotion Corp* ***(P-11111)***
Zhg Inc..........D.......831 394-3321
2600 Sand Dunes Dr Monterey (93940) ***(P-13133)***
Zieve Brodnax & Steele LLP (PA)..........C.......714 848-7920
30 Corporate Park Ste 450 Irvine (92606) ***(P-22886)***
Ziffren B B F G-L S&C Fnd..........C.......310 552-3388
1801 Century Park W Los Angeles (90067) ***(P-22887)***
Zignal Labs Inc..........D.......415 683-7871
600 California St Fl 18 San Francisco (94108) ***(P-15214)***
Zikakis Auto Holdings LLC..........E.......805 736-4595
1224 N H St Lompoc (93436) ***(P-17315)***
Zillionaire Empress Danielle B..........A.......310 461-9923
8549 Wilshire Blvd # 817 Beverly Hills (90211) ***(P-11749)***
Zillow Group Inc..........A.......415 836-6760
4100 Redwood Rd Oakland (94619) ***(P-15838)***
Zim Industries Inc..........D.......661 393-9661
7212 Fruitvale Ave Bakersfield (93308) ***(P-3247)***
Zimmer Gnsul Frsca Partnr Amer, Los Angeles *Also called Zimmer Gunsul* ***(P-25516)***
Zimmer Gunsul..........D.......213 617-1901
515 S Flower St Ste 3700 Los Angeles (90071) ***(P-25516)***
Zimmerman Roofing Inc..........D.......916 454-3667
3675 R St Sacramento (95816) ***(P-3108)***
Zinio Systems Inc..........D.......415 494-2700
114 Sansome St Fl 4 San Francisco (94104) ***(P-15546)***
Zions Bancorporation Nat Assn..........D.......626 445-5355
1130 S Baldwin Ave Arcadia (91007) ***(P-9157)***
Zions Bancorporation Nat Assn..........D.......415 524-1200
1451 Solano Ave Albany (94706) ***(P-9158)***
Zions Bancorporation Nat Assn..........C.......909 581-1680
9590 Foothill Blvd Rancho Cucamonga (91730) ***(P-9159)***
Zions Bancorporation Nat Assn..........E.......858 793-7400
11622 El Camino Real San Diego (92130) ***(P-9160)***
Zions Bancorporation Nat Assn..........D.......619 521-5800
6313 Mission Gorge Rd San Diego (92120) ***(P-9161)***
Zions Bancorporation Nat Assn..........C.......310 258-9300
100 Crprate Pinte Ste 110 Culver City (90230) ***(P-9162)***

Mergent e-mail: customerrelations@mergent.com
1494
2020 Directory of California
Wholesalers and Services Companies
(P-0000) Products & Services Section entry number
(PA)=Parent Co (HQ)=Headquarters (DH)=Div Headquarters

Ziontech Solutions Inc ....D......408 434-6001
 1900 Mccarthy Blvd # 415 Milpitas (95035) **(P-16166)**
Zipline International Inc ....C......415 993-0604
 529 Railroad Ave South San Francisco (94080) **(P-26887)**
Zippy Usa Inc ....D......949 366-9525
 1 Morgan Irvine (92618) **(P-7195)**
Ziprecruiter Inc ....A......800 557-9015
 604 Arizona Ave Santa Monica (90401) **(P-26888)**
Zipzoomfly, Newark *Also called Xtraplus Corporation* **(P-6921)**
Zks Real Estate Partners LLC ....E......925 934-2000
 2355 N Main St Walnut Creek (94596) **(P-13134)**
Zl Technologies Inc (PA) ....D......408 240-8989
 860 N Mccarthy Blvd # 100 Milpitas (95035) **(P-15215)**
Zmicro Inc (PA) ....D......858 831-7000
 9820 Summers Ridge Rd San Diego (92121) **(P-15717)**
Zmodo Technology Corp Ltd ....A......217 903-5673
 17870 Castleton St # 200 City of Industry (91748) **(P-7372)**
Zodax LP (PA) ....D......818 785-5626
 14040 Arminta St Panorama City (91402) **(P-6600)**
Zodiac Inflight Innovations US, Brea *Also called Systems and Software Entps LLC* **(P-15139)**
Zoe Holding Company Inc ....C......916 646-3100
 2143 Hurley Way Sacramento (95825) **(P-14461)**
Zoe Holding Company Inc ....C......415 421-4900
 44 Montgomery St San Francisco (94104) **(P-27313)**
Zohar Construction Inc ....D......818 609-7473
 4272 Pasadero Pl Tarzana (91356) **(P-1225)**
Zoic Inc ....C......310 838-0770
 3582 Eastham Dr Culver City (90232) **(P-17721)**
Zoic Studios, Culver City *Also called Zoic Inc* **(P-17721)**
Zonare Medical Systems Inc ....D......650 230-2800
 420 Bernardo Ave Mountain View (94043) **(P-26050)**
Zone24x7 Inc (PA) ....B......408 268-8589
 3150 Almaden Expy Ste 234 San Jose (95118) **(P-15216)**
Zonneveld Dairies Inc ....D......559 923-4546
 1560 Cerini Ave Laton (93242) **(P-407)**
Zonneveld Farms ....D......559 923-4546
 1560 Cerini Ave Laton (93242) **(P-408)**
Zoological Society San Diego (PA) ....A......619 231-1515
 2920 Zoo Dr San Diego (92101) **(P-24316)**
Zoological Society San Diego ....A......760 747-8702
 15500 San Pasqual Vly Rd Escondido (92027) **(P-24317)**

Zoological Society San Diego......................................A......619 744-3325
 2920 Zoo Dr San Diego (92101) **(P-24318)**
Zoom Video Communications Inc (PA) ....C......888 799-9666
 55 Almaden Blvd Fl 6 San Jose (95113) **(P-15217)**
Zoosk Inc (HQ) ....D......415 728-9543
 989 Market St Fl 5 San Francisco (94103) **(P-5500)**
Zs Associates Inc ....D......805 413-5900
 2535 W Hillcrest Dr # 100 Thousand Oaks (91320) **(P-26889)**
Zs Associates Inc ....D......650 762-7800
 400 S El Camino Real # 1500 San Mateo (94402) **(P-17177)**
Zs Associates Inc ....D......858 677-2200
 4365 Executive Dr # 1530 San Diego (92121) **(P-26890)**
Zscaler Inc (PA) ....C......408 533-0288
 110 Rose Orchard Way San Jose (95134) **(P-15218)**
Zspace Inc ....D......408 498-4050
 2728 Orchard Pkwy San Jose (95134) **(P-7196)**
Zumwalt Construction Inc ....D......559 252-1000
 5520 E Lamona Ave Fresno (93727) **(P-1653)**
Zurich American Insurance Co.....................................D......213 270-0600
 777 S Figueroa St Ste 400 Los Angeles (90017) **(P-10155)**
Zurich American Insurance Co.....................................C......415 538-7100
 525 Market St Ste 2900 San Francisco (94105) **(P-10156)**
Zvents Inc ....E......408 376-7346
 199 Fremont St Fl 4 San Francisco (94105) **(P-13605)**
Zwicker & Associates PC ....C......925 689-7070
 1320 Willow Paca Rd 730 Concord (94520) **(P-22888)**
Zws/ABS Joint Venture LLC ....D......510 461-1433
 39899 Balentine Dr # 200 Newark (94560) **(P-14084)**
Zyme Solutions Inc (PA) ....D......650 585-2258
 240 Twin Dolphin Dr Ste D Redwood City (94065) **(P-15896)**
Zymergen Inc (PA) ....D......415 801-8073
 5980 Horton St Ste 105 Emeryville (94608) **(P-25872)**
Zymo Research Corp (PA) ....D......949 679-1190
 17062 Murphy Ave Irvine (92614) **(P-25873)**
Zynga Inc (PA) ....C......855 449-9642
 699 8th St San Francisco (94103) **(P-15839)**
Zyrion Inc ....D......408 524-7424
 440 N Wolfe Rd Sunnyvale (94085) **(P-15547)**
Zyxel Communications Inc ....D......714 632-0882
 1130 N Miller St Anaheim (92806) **(P-5501)**

A
L
P
H
A
B
E
T
I
C

Employee Codes: A=Over 500 employees, B=251-500
C=101-250, D=51-100, E=50

2020 Directory of California
Wholesalers and Services Companies

© Mergent Inc. 1-800-342-5647

1495

COUNTY/CITY CROSS-REFERENCE INDEX

Alameda
Alameda
Albany
Berkeley
Castro Valley
Dublin
Emeryville
Fremont
Hayward
Livermore
Newark
Oakland
Piedmont
Pleasanton
San Leandro
San Lorenzo
Sunol
Union City

Alpine
Kirkwood

Amador
Ione
Jackson
Pine Grove
Pioneer
Plymouth
Sutter Creek

Butte
Biggs
Chico
Durham
Forest Ranch
Gridley
Oroville
Paradise

Calaveras
Angels Camp
Arnold
Bear Valley
Copperopolis
Murphys
San Andreas
Valley Springs

Colusa
Arbuckle
Colusa
Williams

Contra Costa
Alamo
Antioch
Bay Point
Brentwood
Byron
Clayton
Concord
Crockett
Danville
Diablo
El Cerrito
El Sobrante
Hercules
Lafayette
Martinez
Moraga

Oakley
Orinda
Pacheco
Pinole
Pittsburg
Pleasant Hill
Point Richmond
Richmond
San Pablo
San Ramon
Walnut Creek

Del Norte
Crescent City
Smith River

El Dorado
Cameron Park
Camino
Diamond Springs
El Dorado
El Dorado Hills
Garden Valley
Kelsey
Lotus
Placerville
Shingle Springs
South Lake Tahoe
Twin Bridges

Fresno
Auberry
Big Creek
Caruthers
Clovis
Coalinga
Del Rey
Firebaugh
Five Points
Fowler
Fresno
Friant
Helm
Huron
Kerman
Kingsburg
Lakeshore
Laton
Mendota
Miramonte
Orange Cove
Parlier
Reedley
Riverdale
San Joaquin
Sanger
Selma
Tranquillity

Glenn
Orland
Willows

Humboldt
Arcata
Bayside
Blue Lake
Eureka
Fortuna
Garberville

Hoopa
Korbel
Loleta
McKinleyville
Scotia
Trinidad
Willow Creek

Imperial
Brawley
Calexico
Calipatria
El Centro
Heber
Holtville
Imperial
Winterhaven

Inyo
Bishop
Death Valley
Independence
Little Lake
Lone Pine

Kern
Arvin
Bakersfield
Boron
Buttonwillow
Caliente
California City
Delano
Edison
Edwards
Edwards Afb
Keene
Kernville
Lake Isabella
Lamont
Lebec
Lost Hills
Maricopa
Mc Farland
Mc Kittrick
Mojave
Ridgecrest
Rosamond
Shafter
Taft
Tehachapi
Wasco

Kings
Avenal
Corcoran
Hanford
Kettleman City
Lemoore
Stratford

Lake
Clearlake
Hidden Valley Lake
Kelseyville
Lakeport
Lower Lake
Middletown

Lassen
Herlong

Susanville

Los Angeles
Acton
Agoura
Agoura Hills
Agua Dulce
Alhambra
Altadena
Arcadia
Arleta
Artesia
Avalon
Azusa
Baldwin Park
Bell
Bell Gardens
Bellflower
Beverly Hills
Burbank
Calabasas
Calabasas Hills
Canoga Park
Canyon Country
Carson
Cerritos
Chatsworth
City of Industry
Claremont
Commerce
Compton
Covina
Cudahy
Culver City
Diamond Bar
Downey
Duarte
E Rncho Dmngz
El Monte
El Segundo
Encino
Gardena
Glendale
Glendora
Granada Hills
Hacienda Heights
Harbor City
Hawaiian Gardens
Hawthorne
Hermosa Beach
Hollywood
Huntington Park
Inglewood
Irwindale
La Canada
La Canada Flintridge
La Crescenta
La Mirada
La Puente
La Verne
Lake View Terrace
Lakewood
Lancaster
Lawndale
Littlerock
Llano
Lomita
Long Beach

Los Angeles
Lynwood
Malibu
Manhattan Beach
Marina Del Rey
Maywood
Mission Hills
Monrovia
Montebello
Monterey Park
Montrose
Newhall
North Hills
North Hollywood
Northridge
Norwalk
Pacific Palisades
Pacoima
Palmdale
Palos Verdes Estates
Palos Verdes Peninsu
Panorama City
Paramount
Pasadena
Pico Rivera
Playa Del Rey
Playa Vista
Pls Vrds Pnsl
Pomona
Porter Ranch
Rancho Dominguez
Rancho Palos Verdes
Redondo Beach
Reseda
Rllng HLS Est
Rosemead
San Dimas
San Fernando
San Gabriel
San Marino
San Pedro
Santa Clarita
Santa Fe Springs
Santa Monica
Saugus
Sherman Oaks
Sherwood Forest
Signal Hill
South El Monte
South Gate
South Pasadena
Stevenson Ranch
Studio City
Sun Valley
Sunland
Sylmar
Tarzana
Temple City
Toluca Lake
Topanga
Torrance
Tujunga
Universal City
Valencia
Valley Village
Van Nuys
Venice

Vernon
View Park
Walnut
West Covina
West Hills
West Hollywood
Whittier
Wilmington
Winnetka
Woodland Hills

Madera

Bass Lake
Chowchilla
Coarsegold
Madera
North Fork
Oakhurst

Marin

Belvedere
Belvedere Tiburon
Bolinas
Corte Madera
Fairfax
Greenbrae
Kentfield
Larkspur
Marshall
Mill Valley
Novato
Point Reyes Station
Ross
San Geronimo
San Quentin
San Rafael
Sausalito

Mariposa

El Portal
Fish Camp
Hornitos
Mariposa
Yosemite Ntpk

Mendocino

Albion
Calpella
Caspar
Covelo
Fort Bragg
Gualala
Hopland
Little River
Mendocino
Point Arena
Potter Valley
Redwood Valley
Ukiah
Willits

Merced

Atwater
Ballico
Delhi
Dos Palos
Gustine
Le Grand
Livingston
Los Banos
Merced
Snelling
Stevinson

Winton

Modoc

Alturas
Cedarville

Mono

Mammoth Lakes
Topaz

Monterey

Aromas
Big Sur
Carmel
Carmel Valley
Castroville
Chualar
Gonzales
Greenfield
King City
Marina
Monterey
Moss Landing
Pacific Grove
Pebble Beach
Salinas
San Ardo
Seaside
Soledad

Napa

American Canyon
Angwin
Calistoga
NAPA
Rutherford
Saint Helena
Yountville

Nevada

Grass Valley
Nevada City
Norden
Penn Valley
Soda Springs
Truckee

Orange

Aliso Viejo
Anaheim
Brea
Buena Park
Capistrano Beach
Corona Del Mar
Costa Mesa
Cypress
Dana Point
El Toro
Foothill Ranch
Fountain Valley
Fullerton
Garden Grove
Huntington Beach
Irvine
La Habra
La Habra Heights
La Palma
Ladera Ranch
Laguna Beach
Laguna Hills
Laguna Niguel
Laguna Woods
Lake Forest

Los Alamitos
Mission Viejo
Newport Beach
Newport Coast
Orange
Placentia
Rancho Santa Margari
Rcho STA Marg
San Clemente
San Juan Capistrano
Santa Ana
Seal Beach
Silverado
Stanton
Trabuco Canyon
Tustin
Villa Park
Westminster
Yorba Linda

Placer

Alpine Meadows
Alta
Auburn
Granite Bay
Homewood
Kings Beach
Lincoln
Loomis
Olympic Valley
Penryn
Rocklin
Roseville
Tahoe City

Plumas

Chester
Greenville
Portola
Quincy

Riverside

Anza
Banning
Beaumont
Bermuda Dunes
Blythe
Cabazon
Calimesa
Canyon Lake
Cathedral City
Cherry Valley
Coachella
Corona
Desert Hot Springs
Eastvale
Hemet
Homeland
Idyllwild
Indian Wells
Indio
Jurupa Valley
La Quinta
Lake Elsinore
Mecca
Menifee
Mira Loma
Moreno Valley
Murrieta
Norco
North Palm Springs
Palm Desert

Palm Springs
Perris
Rancho Mirage
Riverside
Romoland
San Jacinto
Sun City
Temecula
Thermal
Thousand Palms
Wildomar
Winchester

Sacramento

Antelope
Carmichael
Citrus Heights
Courtland
Elk Grove
Fair Oaks
Folsom
Galt
Gold River
Isleton
Mather
McClellan
North Highlands
Orangevale
Rancho Cordova
Rancho Murieta
Rio Linda
Sacramento
Walnut Grove

San Benito

Hollister
San Juan Bautista

San Bernardino

Adelanto
Alta Loma
Apple Valley
Barstow
Big Bear City
Big Bear Lake
Bloomington
Blue Jay
Cedar Glen
Chino
Chino Hills
Colton
Earp
Etiwanda
Fontana
Fort Irwin
Grand Terrace
Helendale
Hesperia
Highland
Hinkley
Lake Arrowhead
Loma Linda
Lucerne Valley
Lytle Creek
Mentone
Montclair
Mountain Pass
Needles
Nipton
Oak Hills
Ontario
Parker Dam

Patton
Rancho Cucamonga
Redlands
Rialto
San Bernardino
Skyforest
Trona
Twentynine Palms
Upland
Victorville
Wrightwood
Yucaipa
Yucca Valley

San Diego

Alpine
Bonita
Bonsall
Borrego Springs
Boulevard
Camp Pendleton
Campo
Cardiff
Carlsbad
Chula Vista
Coronado
Del Mar
El Cajon
Encinitas
Escondido
Fallbrook
Imperial Beach
Jamul
Julian
La Jolla
La Mesa
Lakeside
Lemon Grove
National City
Oceanside
Pala
Pauma Valley
Potrero
Poway
Ramona
Rancho Santa Fe
San Diego
San Marcos
San Ysidro
Santee
Solana Beach
Spring Valley
Tecate
Valley Center
Vista

San Francisco

San Francisco

San Joaquin

Acampo
Escalon
Farmington
French Camp
Holt
Lathrop
Linden
Lodi
Manteca
Ripon
Stockton
Tracy

Woodbridge

San Luis Obispo

Arroyo Grande
Atascadero
Avila Beach
Cambria
Grover Beach
Los Osos
Morro Bay
Nipomo
Oceano
Paso Robles
Pismo Beach
San Luis Obispo
San Simeon
Shell Beach
Templeton

San Mateo

Atherton
Belmont
Brisbane
Burlingame
Colma
Daly City
El Granada
Emerald Hills
Foster City
Half Moon Bay
Hillsborough
Menlo Park
Millbrae
Moss Beach
Pacifica
Pescadero
Portola Valley
Portola Vally
Redwood City
San Bruno
San Carlos
San Francisco
San Mateo
South San Francisco
Woodside

Santa Barbara

Buellton

Carpinteria
Goleta
Guadalupe
Lompoc
Orcutt
Santa Barbara
Santa Maria
Santa Ynez
Solvang
Vandenberg Afb

Santa Clara

Alviso
Campbell
Cupertino
East Palo Alto
Gilroy
Los Altos
Los Altos Hills
Los Gatos
Milpitas
Moffett Field
Monte Sereno
Morgan Hill
Mountain View
Palo Alto
San Jose
San Martin
Santa Clara
Saratoga
Stanford
Sunnyvale

Santa Cruz

Aptos
Boulder Creek
Capitola
Davenport
Felton
Mount Hermon
Royal Oaks
Santa Cruz
Scotts Valley
Soquel
Watsonville

Shasta

Anderson

Burney
Cottonwood
Palo Cedro
Redding

Sierra

Loyalton

Siskiyou

Edgewood
Etna
Happy Camp
Macdoel
Mount Shasta
Tulelake
Weed
Yreka

Solano

Benicia
Dixon
Fairfield
Rio Vista
Suisun City
Travis Afb
Vacaville
Vallejo

Sonoma

Bodega Bay
Cazadero
Cloverdale
Cotati
Fulton
Geyserville
Glen Ellen
Guerneville
Healdsburg
Kenwood
Occidental
Petaluma
Rohnert Park
Santa Rosa
Sebastopol
Sonoma
Windsor

Stanislaus

Ceres

Denair
Hickman
Hughson
Keyes
La Grange
Modesto
Newman
Oakdale
Patterson
Riverbank
Turlock
Waterford

Sutter

Live Oak
Meridian
Pleasant Grove
Yuba City

Tehama

Corning
Red Bluff
Vina

Trinity

Weaverville

Tulare

Cutler
Dinuba
Earlimart
Exeter
Goshen
Ivanhoe
Kings Canyon Nationa
Lindsay
Orosi
Porterville
Richgrove
Strathmore
Terra Bella
Tipton
Traver
Tulare
Visalia
Woodlake

Tuolumne

Columbia

Groveland
Jamestown
Pinecrest
Sonora
Tuolumne

Ventura

Agoura Hills
Camarillo
Fillmore
Moorpark
Newbury Park
Oak View
Ojai
Oxnard
Piru
Port Hueneme
Santa Paula
Santa Rosa Valley
Simi Valley
Somis
Thousand Oaks
Ventura
Westlake Village

Yolo

Brooks
Clarksburg
Davis
El Macero
Esparto
Knights Landing
West Sacramento
Winters
Woodland

Yuba

Beale Afb
Brownsville
Marysville
Olivehurst
Wheatland

GEOGRAPHIC SECTION

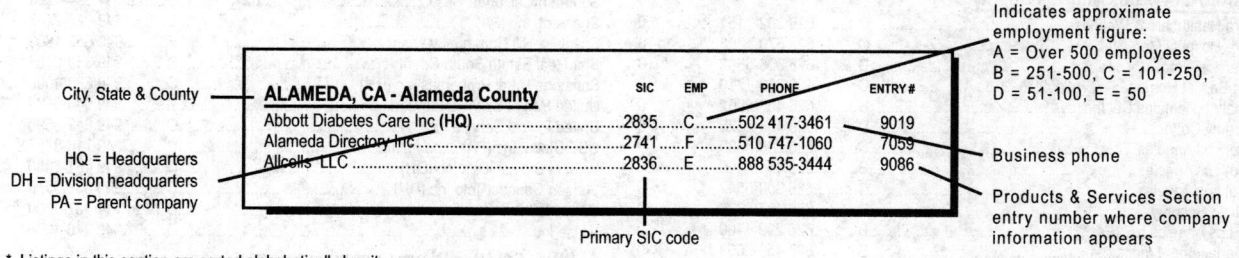

City, State & County → **ALAMEDA, CA - Alameda County**

	SIC	EMP	PHONE	ENTRY #
Abbott Diabetes Care Inc **(HQ)**	2835	C	502 417-3461	9019
Alameda Directory Inc	2741	F	510 747-1060	7059
Allcells LLC	2836	E	888 535-3444	9086

Indicates approximate employment figure:
A = Over 500 employees
B = 251-500, C = 101-250,
D = 51-100, E = 50

HQ = Headquarters
DH = Division headquarters
PA = Parent company

Business phone

Products & Services Section entry number where company information appears

Primary SIC code

* Listings in this section are sorted alphabetically by city.
* Listings within each city are sorted alphabetically by company name.

ACAMPO, CA - San Joaquin County

	SIC	EMP	PHONE	ENTRY #
JJ Rios Farm Services Inc		D	209 333-7467	0
Langetwins Inc		D	209 339-4055	0
Nestor Enterprises LLC		E	209 727-5711	0
Windwalker Security Patrol Inc		D	209 333-3953	0

ACTON, CA - Los Angeles County

	SIC	EMP	PHONE	ENTRY #
County of Los Angeles		D	661 223-8700	0
Dedication & Everlasting Love		D	661 269-4010	0
Delta Rescue Inc		D	661 269-4010	0

ADELANTO, CA - San Bernardino County

	SIC	EMP	PHONE	ENTRY #
Centerline Wood Products		D	760 246-4530	0
Cwp Cabinets Inc		C	760 246-4530	0
Geo Group Inc		D	760 246-1171	0
Hayes Welding Inc **(PA)**		D	760 246-4878	0
S E C C Corporation		D	760 246-6218	0
South Capitol Cottage		D	951 662-3026	0
USA Transport Inc		E	559 783-3563	0
Yrc Inc		D	760 246-0031	0

AGOURA, CA - Los Angeles County

	SIC	EMP	PHONE	ENTRY #
Abraham Jsha Hschl Dy Schl Wst		D	818 707-2365	0
Joni and Friends **(PA)**		D	818 707-5664	0
Up Stage Inc		E	818 879-8781	0

AGOURA HILLS, CA - Los Angeles County

	SIC	EMP	PHONE	ENTRY #
Allstate Technologies Inc **(PA)**		D	818 889-7600	0
Amcal Communities Inc		E	818 706-0694	0
Amh Portfolio One LLC		C	480 921-4600	0
Davidson Hotel Partners Lp		C	818 707-1220	0
Ess		D	888 303-6424	0
First Student Inc		D	818 707-2082	0
International Bus Mchs Corp		D	914 499-1900	0
James H Cowan & Associates Inc		D	310 457-2574	0
Los Angeles Rams LLC **(PA)**		D	314 982-7267	0
Meadowbrook Senior Living		D	818 991-3544	0
Mjd Construction Corp		D	818 575-9864	0
Motor Vehicle Software Corp **(PA)**		D	818 706-1949	0
National Everclean Svcs Inc		D	877 532-5326	0
National Veterinary Assoc Inc **(PA)**		C	805 777-7722	0
Novalogic Inc **(PA)**		D	818 880-1997	0
Pennymac Corp		C	818 878-8416	0
Private Nat Mrtg Accptance LLC **(HQ)**		A	818 224-7401	0
Quality Home Loans		D	818 206-6600	0
Regency Theatres Inc		E	818 224-3825	0
Sequoia Concepts Inc		D	818 409-6000	0
State Farm Mutl Auto Insur Co		D	818 597-4300	0
Ww Lbv Inc		C	818 707-1220	0
Coldwell Bankers Residential **(PA)**		D	818 575-2660	0

AGUA DULCE, CA - Los Angeles County

	SIC	EMP	PHONE	ENTRY #
Petrelli Electric Inc		D	661 268-7312	0

ALAMEDA, CA - Alameda County

	SIC	EMP	PHONE	ENTRY #
Abb/Con-Cise Optical Group LLC		D	800 852-8089	0
Abb/Con-Cise Optical Group LLC		D	510 483-9400	0
Absolutdata Technologies Inc		D	510 748-9922	0
Adrienne Mattos Swim Schl Inc **(PA)**		E	866 633-4147	0
Alameda Alliance For Health		C	510 747-4555	0
Alameda Bureau Elec Imprv Corp **(HQ)**		D	510 748-3902	0
Alameda Family Services		D	510 629-6300	0
Alameda Hlthcare & Wellnss Ctr		D	510 523-8857	0
Allcells LLC		D	510 521-2600	0
American Cancer Soc Cal Div **(PA)**		D	510 893-7900	0

	SIC	EMP	PHONE	ENTRY #
Asterias Biotherapeutics Inc		D	510 456-3800	0
Bay Marine & Indus Sup LLC		E	510 337-9122	0
Bay View Rhbilitation Hosp LLC		D	510 521-5600	0
Bladium Inc **(PA)**		C	510 814-4999	0
Chipman Corporation **(PA)**		E	510 748-8700	0
City Alameda Health Care Corp		A	510 522-3700	0
Commodore Dining Cruises Inc **(PA)**		D	510 337-9000	0
Cost Plus Management Svcs Inc **(DH)**		D	510 893-7300	0
Delphi Productions Inc **(PA)**		C	510 748-7494	0
Diehard Security Solutions Inc		C	510 995-8450	0
Elder Care Alliance Camarillo		D	510 769-2700	0
Elder Care Alliance San Rafael		D	510 769-2700	0
Embarcadero Systems Corp		C	510 749-7400	0
Family Stations Inc **(PA)**		D	510 568-6200	0
Frito-Lay North America Inc		D	510 769-5000	0
Garfield Nursing Home Inc		C	510 582-7676	0
Girl Scouts Northern Cal **(PA)**		D	510 562-8470	0
Global 360 Inc		C	510 263-4800	0
Harbor Bay Club Inc		D	510 521-5414	0
Health Educ Economic Devlpmnt		D	510 604-6143	0
International Union of Operati		C	510 748-7400	0
Kaiser Foundation Hospitals		C	510 752-1190	0
Kindred Nursing Centers W LLC		D	510 521-5600	0
Maintenance Service For The Cy		D	510 865-3778	0
Mariner Square Athletic Inc		D	510 523-8011	0
Mbh Architects Inc		C	510 865-8663	0
McGuire and Hester **(PA)**		B	510 632-7676	0
Metaswitch Networks		E	415 513-1500	0
NRC Environmental Services Inc **(DH)**		D	510 749-1390	0
Polarion Software Inc		D	877 572-4005	0
Ports America Inc		D	510 749-7400	0
San Francisco Bay AR Tran Assn		C	510 501-5318	0
Semifreddis Inc **(PA)**		C	510 596-9930	0
Shoreline S Intermediate Care		D	510 523-8857	0
Snelling Employment LLC		D	510 769-4400	0
Sutter Health		C	916 286-6665	0
Telecare Corporation		C	510 337-7950	0
Voxify Inc		D	510 545-3011	0
Waters Edge Inc		C	510 748-4300	0
Waters Edge Lodge		E	510 769-6264	0
Webcor Construction LP **(DH)**		D	415 978-1000	0
Weinberg Roger & Resenfeld **(PA)**		D	510 337-1001	0
Wind River Systems Inc **(HQ)**		C	510 748-4100	0

ALAMO, CA - Contra Costa County

	SIC	EMP	PHONE	ENTRY #
Bailey & Dutton **(PA)**		D	925 838-1460	0
Beta Healthcare Group **(PA)**		D	925 838-6070	0
Cintas Corporation		D	925 743-1745	0
Edgewood Properties **(PA)**		D	925 838-2847	0
Hospice and Palliative Care		D	925 945-8924	0
John Muir Physician Network		E	925 838-4633	0
Lendus LLC		A	925 295-9300	0
Lendusa LLC **(PA)**		D	925 295-9300	0
Round Hill Country Club		C	925 934-8211	0
Round Hill Country Club		E	925 934-8211	0
Specialty Fibres LLC **(PA)**		D	925 934-8700	0
Wild Karma Inc		B	510 639-9088	0

ALBANY, CA - Alameda County

	SIC	EMP	PHONE	ENTRY #
Pacific Racing Association		C	510 559-7300	0
Paladin Home Care		E	510 526-2273	0
Reichert Lengfeld Ltd Partnr		D	510 845-1077	0
Zions Bancorporation Nat Assn		D	415 524-1200	0

GEOGRAPHIC

	SIC	EMP	PHONE	ENTRY #

ALBION, CA - Mendocino County

	SIC	EMP	PHONE	ENTRY #
Albion River Inn Incorporated		D	707 937-1919	0

ALHAMBRA, CA - Los Angeles County

	SIC	EMP	PHONE	ENTRY #
Alhambra Healthcare & Wellness		D	626 282-3151	0
Alhambra Hospital Med Ctr LP		C	626 570-1606	0
AT&T Services Inc		B	626 308-8582	0
Atherton Baptist Homes		C	626 863-1710	0
Bio-Mdcal Applications Cal Inc		E	626 457-9002	0
City Security Co Inc		D	626 458-2325	0
County of Los Angeles		C	626 299-5300	0
County of Los Angeles		B	626 458-4000	0
County of Los Angeles		C	626 308-5542	0
Drew Chain Security Corp		D	626 457-8626	0
Eastern Los Angeles RE **(PA)**		B	626 299-4700	0
Ethos Management Inc		E	626 456-3669	0
Evikecom Inc		D	626 286-0360	0
FB Corporation		C	626 300-0880	0
I Lan Systems Inc		D	626 304-9021	0
Interviewing Service Amer Inc		D	626 979-4140	0
Inveserve Corporation		D	626 458-3435	0
Network Medical Management Inc		C	626 282-0288	0
Options For Learning		C	626 308-2411	0
Orora North America		C	626 284-9524	0
Pacific Ventures Ltd		C	626 576-0737	0
Serfin Funds Transfer **(PA)**		D	626 457-3070	0
Silverado Senior Living Inc		E	626 872-3941	0
Southern California Gas Co		D	323 881-3587	0
University Southern California		D	626 457-4240	0

ALISO VIEJO, CA - Orange County

	SIC	EMP	PHONE	ENTRY #
AAA Accounting Services		D	949 791-7368	0
Aliso Viejo Golf Club Inc		C	949 598-9200	0
All Hnds Crwash Dtail Ctr Lube		D	949 716-3600	0
Ambry Genetics Corporation **(DH)**		D	949 900-5500	0
American Zettler Inc **(HQ)**		D	949 831-5000	0
Apex Parks Group LLC		D	210 341-6663	0
Basketball Marketing Co Inc		D	610 249-2255	0
Bearing Engineers Inc **(PA)**		D	949 586-7442	0
By Wind Inc		D	949 385-6219	0
Clarient Diagnostic Svcs Inc		B	888 443-3310	0
Concerto Healthcare Inc **(PA)**		D	949 537-3400	0
Covenant Care California LLC **(HQ)**		E	949 349-1200	0
Covenant Care Indiana Inc **(DH)**		D	949 349-1200	0
Cox Communications Inc		D	949 716-2020	0
Cresse Mark School of Baseball		D	714 892-6145	0
Datallegro Inc		D	949 680-3000	0
Diageo North America Inc		D	949 421-3974	0
Don Juan Avila Elementary Pta		D	949 349-9452	0
Efuel LLC		D	949 330-7145	0
Facility Services Partners		D	949 480-4090	0
First Team RE - Orange Cnty		C	949 389-0004	0
Fluor Corporation		D	949 349-2000	0
Fluor Daniel Construction Co **(DH)**		B	949 349-2000	0
Fluor Enterprises Inc		D	469 398-7000	0
Fluor Enterprises Inc		C	949 349-2000	0
Fluor Industrial Services Inc		A	949 439-2000	0
Fluor Plant Services Intl Inc		D	949 349-2000	0
Fluoramec LLC **(HQ)**		E	949 349-2000	0
Geo Telecom		D	949 362-0921	0
Glenwood Village Cmnty Assn		D	949 855-1800	0
Hcs Holdco LLC **(DH)**		C	949 349-1200	0
International Litigation Svcs		E	888 313-4457	0
Ipayables Inc **(PA)**		D	949 215-9122	0
JMJ Financial Group **(PA)**		E	949 340-6336	0
Kaiser Foundation Hospitals		C	949 425-3150	0
L & O Aliso Viejo		D	949 643-6700	0
LMC Hollywood Highland		B	949 448-1600	0
Malibu Castle		E	210 341-6663	0
Marsh & McLennan Agency LLC		D	949 544-8460	0
Metagenics Inc **(DH)**		D	949 366-0818	0
NC Interactive LLC		D	512 623-8700	0
Nelson Bros Property MGT Inc		C	949 916-7300	0
New Home Company Inc **(PA)**		D	949 382-7800	0
Onsite Health Inc **(PA)**		D	949 305-2253	0
Pacific Crossing LLC		C	949 679-2588	0
Pacifica Hotel Company **(HQ)**		E	805 957-0095	0
Pandora Marketing LLC		D	800 705-6856	0
Quest Software Inc **(HQ)**		A	949 754-8000	0
Quest Software Inc		D	949 754-8000	0
Real Estate Digital LLC		C	800 234-2139	0
Remedytemp Inc **(DH)**		C	949 425-7600	0
Retronix International Inc		D	949 388-6930	0
Rxsight Inc		E	949 521-7830	0
Safeguard Health Entps Inc **(HQ)**		B	800 880-1800	0
Seabreeze Management Co Inc **(PA)**		D	949 855-1800	0

	SIC	EMP	PHONE	ENTRY #
Sequoia Environmental Svcs Inc		D	949 480-4742	0
Shea Properties MGT Co Inc		B	949 389-7000	0
Siliconsystems Inc		D	949 900-9400	0
Southern California Gas Co		D	714 634-7221	0
Sparxent Inc **(PA)**		E	949 222-2287	0
Spyglass Hill Community Assn		E	949 855-1800	0
Star Real Estate South County		C	949 389-0004	0
Sunstone Hotel Properties Inc **(DH)**		C	949 330-4000	0
United Parcel Service Inc		B	949 643-6634	0
United Parcel Service Inc OH		C	949 643-6595	0
UST Global Inc **(PA)**		D	949 716-8757	0
Valeant Biomedicals Inc **(DH)**		D	949 461-6000	0
Verizon Connect Telo Inc **(DH)**		C	949 389-5500	0
Voice Mail Broadcasting Corp		D	714 437-0600	0
Vwise Inc		D	949 716-1276	0

ALPINE, CA - San Diego County

	SIC	EMP	PHONE	ENTRY #
Abhe & Svoboda Inc		D	619 659-1320	0
Alpine Convalescent Center Inc		D	619 659-3120	0
Pacific Southwest Cnstr & Eqp.		D	619 445-5190	0
R A Schreiber Plumbing		E	619 659-3101	0
Southern Indian Health Council **(PA)**		D	619 445-1188	0

ALPINE MEADOWS, CA - Placer County

	SIC	EMP	PHONE	ENTRY #
Alpine Meadows Ski Area		E	530 583-4232	0
Squaw Creek Associates LLC		A	530 581-6624	0

ALTA, CA - Placer County

	SIC	EMP	PHONE	ENTRY #
Pacific Gas and Electric Co		D	530 389-2202	0

ALTA LOMA, CA - San Bernardino County

	SIC	EMP	PHONE	ENTRY #
Expreal Inc		D	909 373-4400	0
Inland Empire RE Solutions		D	909 476-1000	0

ALTADENA, CA - Los Angeles County

	SIC	EMP	PHONE	ENTRY #
Altadena Town and Country Club		D	626 345-9088	0
Cutting Edge Protection I		E	949 307-1596	0
D C Golf A CA Partnership		E	626 797-3821	0
Five Acres-The Boys & Girls &		B	626 798-6793	0
Life Line Screening Amer Ltd		B	626 797-9774	0
Mallcraft Inc		E	626 765-9100	0
Marcos Auto Body Inc **(PA)**		D	626 286-5691	0
Pasadena Chld Training Soc		C	626 798-0853	0
Tom Sawyer Camps Inc		C	626 794-1156	0

ALTURAS, CA - Modoc County

	SIC	EMP	PHONE	ENTRY #
County of Modoc		C	530 233-6223	0
County of Modoc		D	530 233-6501	0
County of Modoc		C	530 233-3416	0
County of Modoc		D	530 233-6400	0
Ed Staub & Sons Petroleum Inc		D	530 233-2610	0
Last Frontier Healthcare Dst		C	530 233-5131	0

ALVISO, CA - Santa Clara County

	SIC	EMP	PHONE	ENTRY #
Acme Building Maintenance Co **(DH)**		D	408 263-5911	0
Bayscape Management Inc		D	408 288-2940	0

AMERICAN CANYON, CA - Napa County

	SIC	EMP	PHONE	ENTRY #
Bvk Gaming Inc		D	707 644-8853	0
Comcast Corporation		D	707 266-7584	0
Eagle Vnes Vnyrds Golf CLB LLC		D	707 257-4470	0
Ghilotti Construction Co Inc		C	707 556-9145	0
Medical Receivables Solutions		E	707 980-6733	0
R E Maher Inc		D	707 642-3907	0
Western Wine Services Inc **(PA)**		D	800 999-8463	0

ANAHEIM, CA - Orange County

	SIC	EMP	PHONE	ENTRY #
1135 N Leisure Ct Inc		C	714 772-1353	0
24 Hour Fitness Usa Inc		E	714 525-9924	0
3067 Orange Avenue LLC		C	714 827-2440	0
5 Day Business Forms Mfg Inc **(PA)**		D	213 623-3577	0
5 Day Business Forms Mfg Inc		D	714 632-8674	0
A & R Wholesale Distrs Inc		D	714 777-7742	0
A S I Corporation		C	714 526-5533	0
Aat Kings Tours USA Inc		D	714 456-0505	0
Above Hlth HM Care Sltions LLC		D	714 585-2185	0
Advantage Mailing LLC **(PA)**		C	714 538-3881	0
Advantage-Crown Sls & Mktg LLC **(DH)**		A	714 780-3000	0
Adventure City Inc		D	714 821-3311	0
Aecom Global II LLC		D	415 774-2700	0
Agire Mortgage Corporation		E	714 564-5821	0
Air Mechanical Inc		D	714 995-3947	0
Albd Electric and Cable		D	949 440-1216	0
Aldoc Inc		D	714 836-8477	0
Alexanders Grand Salon		D	714 282-6438	0
Aliantel Inc		D	714 829-1650	0
Alsco Inc		D	714 774-4165	0
Alstyle AP & Activewear MGT Co **(HQ)**		A	714 765-0400	0

Mergent email: customerrelations@mergent.com

1502

2020 Directory of California
Wholesalers and Services Companies

(P-0000) Products & Services Section entry number
(PA)=Parent Co (HQ)=Headquarters (DH)=Div Headquarters

	SIC	EMP	PHONE	ENTRY #
Altamed Health Services Corp		C	714 635-0593	0
Altamed Health Services Corp		B	714 780-5690	0
Altura Comm Solutions LLC (DH)		D	714 948-8400	0
American Leak Detection Inc		E	714 836-8477	0
American Multi-Cinema Inc		E	714 630-2410	0
American Technologies Inc (PA)		C	714 283-9990	0
Americold Logistics LLC		D	678 441-1468	0
Amisub (irvine Regional Hospi)		A	949 916-7556	0
Ampco Contracting Inc		C	949 955-2255	0
Anaheim Arena Management LLC		C	714 704-2400	0
Anaheim Arts Council		C	714 868-6094	0
Anaheim Ducks Hockey Club LLC (PA)		D	714 940-2900	0
Anaheim First Fmly Dntl Group		D	714 999-5050	0
Anaheim Global Medical Center		B	714 533-6220	0
Anaheim Harbor Medical Group (PA)		C	714 533-4511	0
Anaheim Hills Auto Body Inc		D	714 632-8266	0
Anaheim Hotel LLC		C	714 750-1811	0
Anaheim Ice		D	714 535-7465	0
Anaheim Medical Center		D	714 774-1450	0
Anaheim Park Inn and Camelot		D	714 635-7275	0
Anaheim Plaza Hotel Inc		D	714 772-5900	0
Anaheim Regional Medical Ctr		A	714 774-1450	0
Anaheim Regional Medical Ctr		B	714 999-3847	0
Anaheim Regional Medical Ctr (PA)		D	714 774-1450	0
Anaheim/Orange Cnty Visitor Bu (PA)		D	714 765-8888	0
Angels Baseball LP (PA)		A	714 940-2000	0
Arch Telecom Inc (PA)		D	714 312-2724	0
Ardcore Senior Living		D	714 974-2226	0
Arizona Tile LLC		D	714 978-6403	0
Assocted Gstrntrlogy Med Group (PA)		D	714 778-1300	0
AST Sportswear Inc		B	714 223-2030	0
AT&T Corp		D	714 284-3818	0
AT&T Corp		D	714 666-5504	0
AT&T Services Inc		C	210 886-4922	0
AT&T Services Inc		C	714 259-4441	0
Atrium Door & Win Co Ariz Inc		B	714 693-0601	0
Avalon Building Maintenance (PA)		D	714 693-2407	0
B & B Specialties Inc		D	714 985-3075	0
Badalian Enterprises Inc		D	714 635-4082	0
Bcp Systems Inc		D	714 202-3900	0
Behavioral Health Works Inc		D	800 249-1266	0
Bell Pipe & Supply Co		E	714 772-3200	0
Benchmaster Furniture LLC		B	714 414-0240	0
Best Interiors Inc (PA)		D	714 490-7999	0
Best Western Stovalls Inn		E	714 776-4800	0
Best Western Stovalls Inn (PA)		C	714 956-4430	0
Borbon Incorporated		C	714 994-0170	0
Boyd Corporation		D	714 777-5995	0
Bpo Management Services Inc (PA)		D	714 972-2670	0
Brady Company/Los Angeles Inc		D	714 533-9850	0
Bridgford Marketing Company (DH)		D	714 526-5533	0
Broughton Hospitality Group (PA)		D	714 908-4237	0
Brownco Construction Co Inc		D	714 935-9600	0
Buena Vista Care Center Inc		D	714 535-7264	0
Bunzl Distribution Cal LLC (DH)		D	714 688-1900	0
Cal Mutual Inc		D	888 700-4650	0
Cal-State Auto Parts Inc (PA)		C	714 630-5950	0
California Private Trnsp Co LP		D	714 637-9191	0
California Safety Agency		E	866 994-6990	0
Califrnia Auto Dalers Exch LLC		B	714 996-2400	0
Care Ambulance Service Inc		A	714 828-7750	0
Carmel Architectural Sales		D	714 630-7221	0
Carrington Mrtg Holdings LLC		C	888 267-0584	0
Cbre Inc		D	714 939-2100	0
Challenger Industries Inc		D	714 630-4344	0
Cinema City Theaters		E	714 970-0865	0
Cintas Corporation		D	714 646-2550	0
Cintas Corporation No 2		D	714 288-8400	0
City of Anaheim		B	714 704-2400	0
Clinica Sagrado Corazon		E	714 491-7777	0
Clp Resources Inc		D	714 300-0510	0
Coach Usa Inc		D	714 978-8855	0
Comfort California Inc		D	714 750-3131	0
Conestoga Hotel		D	714 535-0300	0
Consolidated Design West Inc		D	714 999-1476	0
Construction Customer Service		E	714 701-1858	0
Contiki US Holdings Inc		D	714 935-0808	0
Control AC Svc Corp		D	714 777-8600	0
Coordnted Dlvry Instltion Inc		D	714 501-4040	0
Country Villa Service Corp (PA)		D	310 574-3733	0
County of Orange		D	714 937-4500	0
Coventry Court Health Center		C	714 636-2800	0
Credit Union Southern Cal		D	562 698-8326	0
Crocker Group LLC		D	714 221-5621	0
Crossmark Inc		D	714 464-6318	0
D/K Mechanical Contractors Inc		C	714 970-0180	0
Danlil Enterprise Inc		D	714 776-7705	0
Danny Ryan Precision Contg Inc		D	949 642-6664	0
Development Resource Cons Inc (PA)		D	714 685-6860	0
Disney Enterprises Inc		A	714 778-6600	0
Disney Enterprises Inc		B	714 999-0990	0
Disneyland International		B	714 956-6746	0
Disneyland International (DH)		C	714 781-4565	0
Diversified Clinical Services		D	714 579-8400	0
Dkn Hotel LLC		D	714 535-0300	0
Dma Greencare Contracting Inc		E	714 630-9470	0
Docircle Inc		E	415 484-4221	0
Dolphins Cove Resort Ltd		D	714 980-0830	0
Donahue Schriber Rlty Group LP		D	714 283-3535	0
Doubltree Suites By Hilton LLC		D	714 750-3000	0
Driver Spg		E	855 300-4774	0
DSV Solutions LLC		D	714 630-0110	0
Econo Air Conditioning Inc		E	714 630-3090	0
Ecotech Rfrgn & Hvac Inc		D	888 833-8100	0
Edge Mortgage Advisory Co LLC		D	714 564-5800	0
Edward Thomas Companies		D	714 782-7500	0
Eht Esan LLC		D	714 632-1221	0
Eleganza Tiles Inc (PA)		D	714 224-1700	0
Emerald Landscape Services		D	714 844-2200	0
Emercon Construction Inc (PA)		D	714 630-9615	0
Emery Smith Laboratories Inc		D	714 238-6133	0
Empi Inc		D	714 446-9606	0
Eps Corporate Holdings Inc		C	714 635-3131	0
Etherwan Systems Inc		D	714 779-3800	0
Eviholder Products LLC (HQ)		E	714 490-7878	0
Exactax Inc (PA)		D	714 284-4802	0
Express Messenger Systems Inc		D	949 235-1400	0
F M Tarbell Co		D	714 772-8990	0
F M Tarbell Co		E	714 637-7240	0
Family Tree Produce Inc		C	714 693-5688	0
Fci Lender Services Inc		C	800 931-2424	0
Fedex Freight Corporation		C	714 996-8720	0
Fedex Ground Package Sys Inc		C	800 463-3339	0
Fedex Ground Package Sys Inc		C	800 463-3339	0
Fenceworks Inc		D	714 238-0091	0
Filyn Corporation		C	714 632-0225	0
First Team RE - Orange Cnty		D	714 974-9191	0
Fjs Inc		C	714 905-1050	0
Fkc Partners A Cal Ltd Partnr		E	714 528-9864	0
Flawless Vape Wholesale Dist		D	714 768-7928	0
Fortress Holding Group LLC		D	714 202-8710	0
Frank Gates Service Company		D	800 994-4611	0
Freeman Audio Visual LLC		C	714 254-3400	0
Freeman Expositions LLC		C	714 254-3400	0
Freight Management Inc		D	714 632-1440	0
Front Porch Communities		C	714 776-7150	0
G4s Justice Services LLC		C	800 589-6003	0
G4s Secure Solutions USA Inc		C	714 939-4900	0
GBS Linens Inc (PA)		D	714 778-6448	0
General Engineering Wstn Inc (PA)		D	714 630-3200	0
Go-Staff Inc		A	657 242-9350	0
Golden State Water Company		D	714 535-7711	0
Greenball Corp (PA)		E	714 782-3060	0
Hacienda Rehabilitation & Heal (PA)		C	714 778-0221	0
Harbor Villa Care Center		D	714 635-8131	0
Harris Freeman & Co Inc (PA)		B	714 765-1190	0
Hba Incorporated		D	714 635-8602	0
Healthcare Partners LLC		D	714 995-1000	0
HI Anaheim LLC		D	714 533-1500	0
Highland Lumber Sales Inc		D	714 778-2293	0
Hob Entertainment LLC		C	714 778-2583	0
Hoffman Southwest Corp		E	714 630-0404	0
Holiday Garden SF Corp		E	714 533-3555	0
Holiday Inn & Suites Annaheim		D	714 535-0300	0
House Seven Gables RE Inc		D	714 282-0306	0
Howard Johnson (PA)		C	714 776-6120	0
Hpt Trs Ihg-2 Inc		D	714 748-7777	0
Hunter Easterday Corporation		C	714 238-3400	0
Infinity Drywall Contg Inc		D	714 634-2255	0
International Missing Persons		D	714 827-1947	0
Interstate Electronics Corp		A	714 758-0500	0
J & J Productions Incorporated		E	714 535-0951	0
J B Bostick Company Inc (PA)		D	714 238-2121	0
Jan Pro Clg Systems Sthern Cal		E	714 220-0500	0
Jetro Cash and Carry Entps LLC		C	714 666-8211	0
Kaiser Foundation Hospitals		C	714 279-4675	0
Kaiser Foundation Hospitals		A	888 988-2800	0
Kaiser Foundation Hospitals		A	888 988-2800	0
Kaiser Foundation Hospitals		D	714 284-6634	0
Kapl Inc		B	714 991-9543	0

Employment Codes: A=Over 500 employees, B=251-500,
C=101-250, D=51-100, E=50

2020 Directory of California
Wholesalers and Services Companies

© Mergent Inc. 1-800-342-5647

1503

GEOGRAPHIC

	SIC	EMP	PHONE	ENTRY #
Karcher Environmental Inc **(PA)**		C	714 385-1490	0
KCS Electric Inc		D	623 551-1500	0
Keenan Hopkins Suder & Stowell **(PA)**		D	714 695-3670	0
Keenan Hopkins Suder & Stowell		D	714 695-3670	0
Ken Real Estate Lease Ltd		D	714 778-1700	0
Ken Starr Inc		D	714 632-8789	0
Kinetic Systems Inc		E	949 502-4856	0
Kinsbursky Bros Supply Inc **(PA)**		D	714 738-8516	0
Kisco Senior Living LLC		D	714 872-9785	0
Kml Enterprises Career Dev LLC		C	714 221-3100	0
L&G Cable Construction		D	714 630-6174	0
La Palma Care Center		D	714 772-7480	0
LARK Industries Inc **(HQ)**		C	714 701-4200	0
Legacy Farms LLC		C	714 736-1800	0
Leisure Care LLC		E	714 974-1616	0
Lindley Fire Protection Co		D	714 535-5761	0
Liquidity Services Inc		D	714 738-6446	0
Lobel Financial Corporation **(PA)**		D	714 995-3333	0
Long Swimming Pool Steel Inc		D	714 524-8172	0
Longust Distributing LLC		E	480 820-6244	0
Lyons Security Service Inc		D	714 401-4850	0
M6 Dev LLC		E	714 533-2101	0
Machining Time Savers Inc		D	714 635-7373	0
Makar Anaheim LLC		A	714 740-4431	0
Malco Maintenance Inc		D	714 630-0194	0
Malco Services Inc		D	714 630-0194	0
Marina Landscape Maint Inc		B	714 939-6600	0
Mark & Fred Enterprises		D	714 821-1993	0
Marketing Professionals Inc		B	714 578-0500	0
Matrix Surfaces Inc		D	714 696-5449	0
Mc Graw Commercial Insur Svc		D	714 939-9875	0
McCormack Roofng Constrctn & E		D	714 777-4040	0
Merical LLC **(PA)**		D	714 238-7225	0
Millennium Transportation Inc		D	714 956-7882	0
Morphotrak LLC **(DH)**		D	714 238-2000	0
Motive Energy Inc **(PA)**		D	714 888-2525	0
Mowery Thomason Inc		C	714 666-1717	0
Moyes Custom Furniture Inc		E	714 729-0234	0
Msl Electric Inc		D	714 693-4837	0
Murrietta Circuits		D	714 970-2430	0
Nail Emporium		E	714 779-9889	0
Nations Direct Lender & In		C	800 969-7779	0
Nazzareno Electric Co Inc		D	714 712-4744	0
Newport Hotel Capital LLC		C	714 758-0900	0
Nicholas Lane Contractors Inc		B	714 630-7630	0
Nor-Cal Beverage Co Inc		C	714 526-8600	0
North American Client Svcs Inc **(PA)**		C	949 240-2423	0
Northwest Hotel Corporation **(PA)**		D	714 776-6120	0
Npl Anaheim Investments LLC		D	714 750-2010	0
Oasis Brands Inc		D	540 658-2830	0
Orange Cast Title Southern Cal		D	714 822-3211	0
Orange Cnty Adult Achvment Ctr		C	714 744-5301	0
Orange Cnty Conservation Corps		D	714 451-1301	0
Orange Coast Building Services		D	714 453-6300	0
Orange County Child Abuse		D	714 543-4333	0
Orange County Head Start		C	714 761-4967	0
Otis Elevator Company		E	714 758-9593	0
Outside Lines Inc		E	714 637-4747	0
Overhead Door Corporation		D	714 680-0600	0
Pacific Coast Equipment Co Inc **(PA)**		E	714 630-5957	0
Pacific Coast Nursery Inc		D	714 630-4868	0
Pacific Coast Sightseeing Tour		C	714 507-1157	0
Pacific Contours Corporation **(PA)**		D	714 693-1260	0
Pacific Design Directions Inc		E	714 685-7766	0
Pacific Utlity Instllation Inc		D	714 970-6430	0
Paglia & Associates Cnstr		D	714 982-5151	0
Paragon Industries Inc		D	714 778-8453	0
Park Hotels & Resorts Inc		D	714 632-1221	0
Paseo Vlg Hsing Partners LP		E	714 991-9172	0
Paulus Engineering Inc		D	714 632-3322	0
Peacock Stes Resort Ltd Partnr		D	714 535-8255	0
Performance Contracting Inc		D	913 310-7120	0
Petersen-Dean Inc		C	714 629-9670	0
Phg Engineering Services LLC		D	714 283-8288	0
Pinner Construction Co Inc **(PA)**		D	714 490-4000	0
Platinum Protection Group Inc		D	800 824-1097	0
Ponderosa Electric Inc		D	949 253-3100	0
Portofino Inn & Suites Anaheim		A	714 782-7600	0
Power Engineers Incorporated		D	714 507-2700	0
Power Plus LLC		D	714 507-1881	0
Power Plus Solutions Corp		E	714 507-1881	0
Premier Commercial Bancorp		D	714 978-2400	0
Prime Healthcare Anaheim LLC		A	714 827-3000	0
Quantum Bhvioral Solutions Inc		D	626 531-6999	0
Ramada Plaza Ht Anaheim Resort		C	714 991-6868	0
Ray W Choi		D	714 783-1000	0
Residence Inn By Marriott		D	714 533-3555	0
Resident Group Services Inc **(PA)**		C	714 630-5300	0
Residential Fire Systems Inc		D	714 666-8450	0
Restaurant Depot LLC		C	714 666-9205	0
Retriev Technologies Inc **(PA)**		D	714 738-8516	0
Rjb Enterprises Inc		E	714 484-3101	0
Rosendin Electric Inc		A	714 739-1334	0
Roy Miller Freight Lines LLC **(PA)**		D	714 632-5511	0
Rvtlzation Anaheim II Partners		D	714 520-4041	0
S W Construction Inc		C	714 978-7871	0
San Marino Plastering Inc		A	714 693-7840	0
San-Mar Construction Co Inc		C	714 693-5400	0
Scholastic Book Fairs Inc		D	714 237-1100	0
Security Signal Devices Inc **(PA)**		E	800 888-0444	0
Select Data Inc		C	714 577-1000	0
Self Serve Auto Dismantlers **(PA)**		C	714 630-8901	0
Sentinel Offender Services LLC **(PA)**		D	949 453-1550	0
Service 1st Electrical Svcs		E	714 630-9699	0
Shamrock Supply Company Inc **(PA)**		D	714 575-1800	0
So Cal Land Maintenance Inc		D	714 231-1454	0
Solaris Paper Inc **(PA)**		D	562 653-1680	0
Source Rfrgn & Hvac Inc **(DH)**		C	714 578-2300	0
South Coast Mechanical Inc		D	714 738-6644	0
Southern Cal Prmnnte Med Group		E	714 279-4675	0
Spectrum MGT Holdg Co LLC		D	714 414-1431	0
SR Bray LLC **(PA)**		E	714 765-7551	0
Srd Engineering Inc		D	714 630-2480	0
St Joseph Health System Home		A	714 712-9500	0
St Joseph Home Health Network		E	714 712-9559	0
St Joseph Hospice		D	714 712-7100	0
Steeltech Construction Svcs		D	714 630-2890	0
Stericycle Comm Solutions Inc		E	714 991-9595	0
Straub Distributing Co Ltd **(PA)**		C	714 779-4000	0
Sun Mar Nursing Center Inc		D	714 776-1720	0
Sunshine Midtown LLC		E	602 604-4900	0
Sunstone Hotel Investors LLC		C	714 635-5000	0
Sunwest Electric Inc		C	714 630-8700	0
T L Fabrications LP		C	562 802-3980	0
Targus International LLC **(PA)**		D	714 765-5555	0
Techno Coatings Inc		C	714 774-4671	0
Tenet Healthsystem Medical		A	714 428-6800	0
Thermalair Inc **(HQ)**		D	714 630-3200	0
Traffic Management Inc		D	562 264-2353	0
Transamerica Finance Corp		D	714 778-5100	0
Tricom Management Inc		C	714 630-2029	0
Trilogy Plumbing Inc		C	714 441-2952	0
Truform Construction Corp		E	714 630-7447	0
Ttg Engineers		D	714 490-5555	0
Tucker Distributors		E	714 970-5742	0
Turner Construction Company		B	714 940-9000	0
Twdc Enterprises 18 Corp		B	818 754-6921	0
Twdc Enterprises 18 Corp		C	714 781-4278	0
TWI- Techno West Inc			714 635-4070	0
Ultimate Landscaping MGT		D	714 502-9711	0
Universal Dust Collector **(PA)**		D	714 630-8588	0
University Marelich Mech Inc		C	714 632-2600	0
US Foods Inc		C	714 449-2880	0
Vci Event Technology Inc		C	714 772-2002	0
Vengroff Williams & Assoc Inc		C	714 889-6200	0
Veterans Health Administration		C	714 780-5400	0
Vincent Contractors Inc		B	714 693-1726	0
Vm Services Inc		E	714 678-5200	0
Wasser Filtration Inc		D	714 525-0630	0
WCO Hotels Inc **(DH)**		D	323 636-3251	0
Westcoast Performance Pdts USA		D	714 630-4411	0
Westview Services Inc		C	714 956-4199	0
Willdan Group Inc **(PA)**		C	800 424-9144	0
Wilson Hampton Pntg Contrs Inc		D	714 772-5091	0
Windsor Anaheim Healthcare **(PA)**		B	714 826-8950	0
Workcare Inc		C	714 978-7488	0
Young Mens Christian Assoc **(PA)**		B	714 635-9622	0
Zyxel Communications Inc		D	714 632-0882	0

ANDERSON, CA - Shasta County

	SIC	EMP	PHONE	ENTRY #
Bettendorf Enterprises Inc		D	530 365-1937	0
Davey Tree Surgery Company		D	530 378-2674	0
Linkus Enterprises LLC **(PA)**		C	530 229-9197	0
Oak River Rehabilitation		C	530 365-0025	0
Ssmb Pacific Holding Co Inc		D	530 222-1212	0
United Parcel Service Inc OH		D	530 365-7850	0

ANGELS CAMP, CA - Calaveras County

	SIC	EMP	PHONE	ENTRY #
Motherlode Investors LLC		D	209 736-8112	0
United Parcel Service Inc OH		C	209 736-0878	0

Mergent email: customerrelations@mergent.com
1504　　　　　　　　　　2020 Directory of California　　　　(P-0000) Products & Services Section entry number
　　　　　　　　　　Wholesalers and Services Companies　　(PA)=Parent Co (HQ)=Headquarters (DH)=Div Headquarters

	SIC	EMP	PHONE	ENTRY #

ANGWIN, CA - Napa County

Hermitage Hlthcr Mnkn Mnr		C	410 651-0011	0

ANTELOPE, CA - Sacramento County

Leavy Brothers Incorporated		D	916 773-5636	0
Sacramento Prestige Gunite Inc		E	916 723-0404	0
Skyva Construction Inc		E	916 726-4999	0

ANTIOCH, CA - Contra Costa County

Antioch Public Golf Corp		D	925 706-4220	0
Antioch Rotary Club		E	925 757-1800	0
AT&T Corp		D	925 776-1200	0
Banister Electrical Inc		D	925 778-7801	0
Better Homes and Gardens Mason		D	925 776-2740	0
Black Diamond Electric Inc		D	925 777-3440	0
City of Antioch		D	925 779-6950	0
Contra Costa ARC		D	925 755-4925	0
Contra Costa Newspapers Inc		E	925 757-2525	0
First Student Inc		C	925 754-4878	0
Freschi Air Systems Inc		D	925 827-9761	0
Halo		E	925 473-4642	0
Jamm Management LLC		E	510 437-5200	0
Kaiser Foundation Hospitals		C	925 813-6500	0
Kaiser Foundation Hospitals		D	925 779-5000	0
Kie-Con Inc		D	925 754-9494	0
Kiewit Infrastructure West Co		E	925 754-9494	0
Lone Tree Convalescent Hosp		D	925 754-0470	0
Mason-Mcduffie Real Estate Inc		D	925 776-2740	0
Montrose Environmental Corp		B	925 680-4300	0
Norcal Care Centers Inc		D	925 757-8787	0
NRG Energy Inc		D	913 689-3904	0
Peace Keepers Private Security		D	925 978-4140	0
Permanente Medical Group Inc		D	925 813-6149	0
Roddy Ranch Pbc LLC		D	925 978-4653	0
Sutter Delta Medical Ctr Aux		D	925 779-7200	0
Sutter Health		A	925 779-7273	0
Wayne E Swisher Cem Contr Inc		D	925 757-3660	0

ANZA, CA - Riverside County

Cahuilla Creek Rest & Casino		C	951 763-1200	0

APPLE VALLEY, CA - San Bernardino County

8520 Western Ave Inc		C	714 828-8222	0
Alpha Connection Group Home		D	760 247-6370	0
Apple Valley Golf Club		C	760 242-3653	0
Apple Vlley/ Vctrvlle Cnsrtium		D	760 240-7000	0
Automobile Club Southern Cal		C	760 247-4110	0
Front Porch Communities & Svcs		D	760 240-5051	0
High Desert Partnership		B	760 946-5414	0
Northfield Medical Inc		C	248 268-2500	0
Reliable Nursing Solutions		D	760 946-9191	0
St Mary Medical Center (PA)		A	760 242-2311	0
Walmart Inc		B	760 961-6300	0
Who Dat Nation Trnsp LLC		D	760 403-7237	0

APTOS, CA - Santa Cruz County

Aegis Senior Communities LLC		E	831 684-2700	0
American Golf Corporation		D	831 688-3213	0
Cabrillo College Children Ctr		D	831 479-6352	0
Dignity Health Med Foundation		D	831 535-1560	0
Easter Seals Central Cal		B	831 684-2166	0
Enlighticare Inc		D	831 750-3546	0
First Alarm (PA)		C	831 476-1111	0
Golden West Hotel Partnership (PA)		D	619 233-7594	0
Parkhurst Terrace		D	831 685-0800	0
Santa Cruz Montessori School		E	831 476-1646	0
Seacliff Inn Inc		D	831 661-4671	0
Seascape Resort Ltd A Calif		B	831 662-7120	0

ARBUCKLE, CA - Colusa County

Alsco - Geyer Irrigation Inc		D	530 476-2253	0
T & P Farms		D	530 476-3038	0

ARCADIA, CA - Los Angeles County

365 Delivery Inc		D	818 815-5005	0
American Home Alarms Inc		C	888 531-5065	0
American Plus Bank (PA)		E	626 821-9188	0
Andover Maintenance Inc		D	626 254-1651	0
Arcadia Convalescent Hosp Inc (PA)		C	323 681-1504	0
Arcadia Gardens MGT Corp		D	626 574-8571	0
Arroyo Insurance Services Inc (PA)		E	626 799-9532	0
Avantra Real Estate Services		E	626 357-7028	0
Capitol LLC (PA)		B	626 445-0402	0
Century 21 Ludecke Inc (PA)		D	626 445-0123	0
Chen Dvid MD Dgnstc Med Group		C	626 566-3900	0
Childrens Hospital Los Angeles		C	626 795-7177	0
City of Arcadia		B	626 574-5435	0
Coldwell Banker Residential RE		D	626 445-5500	0
Commercial Roofing Systems Inc		D	626 359-5354	0
Community Housing Options		D	626 359-3300	0
Country Villa Service Corp		D	626 445-2421	0
County of Los Angeles		E	626 821-5858	0
Ego Inc		C	626 447-0296	0
Foothill Federal Credit Union (PA)		E	626 445-0950	0
Forta (PA)		D	626 446-7027	0
Fumai Industrial Inc		D	626 272-1788	0
Gar Enterprises (PA)		D	626 574-1175	0
George Fasching		E	626 446-0654	0
Goodrich Lax A Cal Ltd Partnr		D	626 254-9988	0
Long Dragon Realty Co Inc		C	626 309-7999	0
Los Angeles Turf Club Inc (DH)		C	626 574-6330	0
Los Angles Arbretum Foundation		D	626 821-3222	0
Mednax Inc		E	626 574-3050	0
Methodist Hosp Southern Cal (PA)		A	626 898-8000	0
Methodist Hospital of S CA		D	626 574-3755	0
MWH Americas Inc		D	626 796-9141	0
N A Tomatobank		D	626 759-9200	0
Park Hotels & Resorts Inc		C	626 445-8525	0
Post Alarm Systems (PA)		D	626 446-7159	0
Samuel Son & Co (usa) Inc		E	323 722-0300	0
Santa Anita Associates (PA)		D	626 447-2764	0
Transdev Services Inc		B	626 357-7912	0
Wave Plastic Surgery Ctr Inc		B	626 898-9711	0
Zions Bancorporation Nat Assn		D	626 445-5355	0

ARCATA, CA - Humboldt County

American Hospital Mgt Corp (PA)		B	707 822-3621	0
Aquatic Designing Inc		E	707 822-4629	0
Danco Builders		D	707 822-9000	0
Danco Communities		D	707 822-9000	0
Healthsport Ltd A Ltd Partnr (PA)		C	707 822-3488	0
Humboldt State University Spon		D	707 826-4189	0
McCullough Construction Inc		D	707 825-1014	0
North Coast Fabricators Inc		E	707 822-4629	0
Northcountry Clinic		D	707 822-2481	0
Open Door Community Hlth Ctrs		D	707 826-8610	0
Open Door Community Hlth Ctrs (PA)		D	707 826-8642	0
Sun Valley Group Inc (PA)		B	707 822-2885	0
Tektetco		D	707 822-9000	0
Toucan Inc (PA)		D	707 822-6662	0
United Indian Health Svcs Inc (PA)		C	707 825-5000	0

ARLETA, CA - Los Angeles County

Lexington Scenery & Props Inc		C	818 768-5768	0

ARNOLD, CA - Calaveras County

Sequoia Wood Country Club		D	209 795-1000	0

AROMAS, CA - Monterey County

Driscolls Inc		E	831 763-5100	0
Granite Rock Co		C	831 768-2330	0
Granite Rock Co		C	831 392-3780	0
Granite Rock Co		D	831 768-2300	0
Jal Berry Farms LLC		E	831 763-7200	0

ARROYO GRANDE, CA - San Luis Obispo County

Ameri-Kleen		C	805 546-0706	0
Bill Papich Construction Inc		E	805 489-9420	0
Community Action Partnership		C	805 489-4026	0
Compass Health Inc		D	805 489-8137	0
Cypress Ridge Golf Course		E	805 474-7979	0
Dignity Health		D	805 489-4261	0
Dignity Health		B	805 473-7626	0
Greenheart Farms Inc (PA)		D	805 481-2234	0
Jk Consultants		E	209 532-7772	0
Life Steps Foundation Inc		C	805 474-8431	0
Papich Construction Co Inc (PA)		C	805 473-3016	0
Sierra Pacific Mortgage Co Inc		D	805 489-6060	0
Smart & Final Stores Inc		B	805 574-1599	0
St Denis Electric Inc		E	805 343-9999	0
Talley Farms		C	805 489-2508	0

ARTESIA, CA - Los Angeles County

Artesia Christian Home Inc		C	562 865-5218	0
Aspen Healthcare Corporation (PA)		D	562 888-6371	0
County of Los Angeles		E	562 402-0688	0
E R G Home Health Provider		D	562 403-1070	0
Edwards Theatres Circuit Inc		D	562 403-1133	0
I Wmi		B	562 977-4906	0
New Cingular Wireless Svcs Inc		D	562 924-0000	0
South Asian Help Referral Agcy		E	562 402-4132	0
Windsor Twin Palms Hlthcare		C	562 865-0271	0

ARVIN, CA - Kern County

Arvin-Edison Water Storage Dst (PA)		E	661 854-5573	0

G E O G R A P H I C

	SIC	EMP	PHONE	ENTRY #
Edwardo Z Garcia		C	661 854-5414	0
Evergreen Health Care LLC		D	661 854-4475	0
Granite Construction Company		D	661 854-3051	0
Grimmway Enterprises Inc		D	661 854-6240	0
Grimmway Enterprises Inc		B	661 854-6250	0
Grimmway Enterprises Inc		D	661 854-6200	0
Kern Ridge Growers LLC		B	661 854-3141	0
Tasteful Selections LLC		D	661 588-1053	0

ATASCADERO, CA - San Luis Obispo County

	SIC	EMP	PHONE	ENTRY #
Atascadero Hotel Partners LLC		D	805 462-3500	0
Califrnia Dept State Hospitals		A	805 468-2000	0
Califronia Department of State		A	805 468-2501	0
Compass Health Inc		D	805 466-9254	0
Kennedy Athletic Club (PA)		D	805 466-6775	0
Meridian Holdings		D	805 539-2752	0
Options Family of Services		E	805 462-8544	0
Star of California		C	805 466-1638	0
USA Waste of California Inc		D	805 466-3636	0

ATHERTON, CA - San Mateo County

	SIC	EMP	PHONE	ENTRY #
Matched Caregivers Inc		C	408 560-2382	0
Menlo Circus Club		D	650 322-4616	0
Menlo Park-Atherton Education (PA)		D	650 325-0100	0

ATWATER, CA - Merced County

	SIC	EMP	PHONE	ENTRY #
Castle Family Health Ctrs Inc (PA)		D	209 381-2000	0
Central Counties		D	209 356-0355	0
Gallo Cattle Co A Ltd Partnr		B	209 394-7984	0
Gino/Giuseppe Inc		C	209 358-0556	0
Kings View		E	209 357-0321	0
Tjd LLC		C	209 357-3420	0
Ward Enterprises		B	209 358-0445	0

AUBERRY, CA - Fresno County

	SIC	EMP	PHONE	ENTRY #
Mono Wind Casino		D	559 855-4350	0
Pacific Gas and Electric Co		E	559 855-6112	0

AUBURN, CA - Placer County

	SIC	EMP	PHONE	ENTRY #
American Medical Response Inc		E	530 887-9440	0
Andregg Geomatics		D	530 885-7072	0
Armstrong Mfg & Engrg Inc		D	530 888-6262	0
Auburn Oaks Care Center		D	650 949-7777	0
Auburn Old Town Gallery		D	530 887-9150	0
Auburn Placer Disposal Service		D	530 885-3735	0
California Envmtl Systems Inc		D	530 820-3693	0
Century Commercial Service		E	530 823-1004	0
Chapa-De Indian Health (PA)		D	530 887-2800	0
Coldwell Bnkr Residential Brkg		D	530 823-7653	0
Congrgtnal Ch Retirement Cmnty		D	530 823-6131	0
County of Placer		D	530 886-1870	0
County of Placer		D	530 889-7215	0
County of Placer		D	530 889-7500	0
County of Placer		C	530 823-4300	0
County of Placer		C	530 889-7900	0
Court House Athletic Club (PA)		D	530 885-1964	0
Decker Landscaping Inc		D	916 652-1780	0
East Hall Investors Inc		D	530 328-1900	0
Foothill Oaks Care Center Inc		D	530 888-6257	0
Horizon West Inc		D	530 889-8122	0
Horizon West Healthcare Inc		D	530 885-7511	0
Interior Specialists Inc		D	530 885-0632	0
Lake of The Pines Association		E	530 268-1141	0
Madera Convalescent Hospital		D	530 885-7051	0
Miltenyi Biotec Inc (HQ)		D	530 745-2800	0
Pacific Gas and Electric Co		E	530 889-3102	0
Placer Co Bar Association (PA)		B	916 557-9181	0
Placer County ADM Svcs		C	530 886-5401	0
Placer County Water Agency (PA)		D	530 823-4850	0
Placer County- Adult Sys Care		D	530 886-2974	0
Pride Industries		C	530 888-0331	0
Retirement Housing Foundation		C	530 823-6131	0
Riskalyze Inc		C	530 748-1660	0
Sierra West Construction Inc		E	530 268-7614	0
Smart & Final Stores Inc		C	530 823-1205	0
Sutter Health		A	530 888-4500	0
Vian Enterprises Inc		E	530 885-1997	0
Westview Healh Care Center		C	530 885-7511	0

AVALON, CA - Los Angeles County

	SIC	EMP	PHONE	ENTRY #
Catalina Business Entps Inc		E	310 510-1600	0
Catalina Glassbottom Boat Inc		D	310 510-2888	0
Santa Catalina Island Company (PA)		D	310 510-2000	0
Two Harbors Enterprises Inc		D	310 510-2000	0

AVENAL, CA - Kings County

	SIC	EMP	PHONE	ENTRY #
Prison Industry Authority-Pia		D	559 386-6060	0

AVILA BEACH, CA - San Luis Obispo County

	SIC	EMP	PHONE	ENTRY #
Pacific Gas and Electric Co		A	805 506-5280	0

AZUSA, CA - Los Angeles County

	SIC	EMP	PHONE	ENTRY #
Artistic Entrmt Svcs LLC		D	626 334-9388	0
Buena Vista Food Products Inc (DH)		C	626 815-8859	0
California Pediatric Fmly Svcs		D	626 812-0055	0
David L Amador Inc		D	626 334-2011	0
Direct Pack Inc		D	626 380-2360	0
Hanson Distributing Company (PA)		C	626 224-9800	0
Heidi Corporation		D	626 333-6317	0
Heppner Hardwoods Inc		D	626 969-7983	0
Monrovia Nursery Company (PA)		A	626 334-9321	0
Morris National Inc (HQ)		D	626 385-2000	0
Murrieta Gardens Senior Living		D	951 600-7676	0
Oj Insulation LP (PA)		C	626 812-6070	0
Precise Enterprises LLC		E	818 599-6450	0
Rain Bird Distribution Corp		D	626 963-9311	0
RES-Care California Inc		E	626 334-7862	0
Richard Wilson Wellington		D	626 812-7881	0
San Gabriel Valley Water Assn		D	626 815-1305	0
Seracada		E	626 486-0800	0
Silverado Senior Living Inc		D	626 650-9891	0
Smart & Final Stores Inc		B	626 334-5189	0
Stanley Steemer of Los Angles (PA)		D	626 791-9400	0
Sunbelt Controls Inc		D	626 610-2340	0
Totten Tubes Inc (PA)		D	626 812-0220	0
Virginia Hardwood Company (PA)		D	626 815-0540	0

BAKERSFIELD, CA - Kern County

	SIC	EMP	PHONE	ENTRY #
7th Standard Ranch Company		B	661 399-0416	0
A-C Electric Company (PA)		E	661 410-0000	0
A-C Electric Company		D	661 633-5368	0
Accelerated Envmtl Svcs Inc		D	661 765-4003	0
Account Control Technology Inc		E	661 395-5702	0
Advance Beverage Co Inc		D	661 833-3783	0
Advanced Cleanup Tech Inc (PA)		C	310 763-1423	0
Aecom		C	661 266-0802	0
Aera Energy LLC (HQ)		A	661 665-5000	0
Ag-Wise Enterprises Inc (PA)		C	661 325-1567	0
Agape In Home Care Inc		E	661 835-0364	0
Agri-Mix Transport Inc		C	661 833-6280	0
Alaidandrew Corporation		D	661 334-2200	0
Allpro Industry Solutions LLC		E	661 854-3613	0
American Baptist Homes of West		C	661 834-0620	0
Ameripride Services Inc		C	661 324-7941	0
AMF Bowling Centers Inc		E	661 324-4966	0
Ancon Marine		D	310 952-8160	0
Anthony Vineyards Inc (PA)		E	661 858-6211	0
Asbury Transportation Co		D	661 327-2271	0
AT&T Services Inc		C	661 398-2000	0
AT&T Services Inc		B	661 327-6030	0
Automobile Club Southern Cal		E	661 327-4661	0
B & B Surplus Inc (PA)		D	661 589-0381	0
Baker Hughes A GE Company LLC		D	661 387-1010	0
Baker Hughes A GE Company LLC		D	800 229-7447	0
Baker Petrolite LLC		D	661 325-4138	0
Bakersfield Assc Rrtd Ctzns		C	661 834-2272	0
Bakersfield Country Club		D	661 871-4000	0
Bakersfield Family Med Group		D	661 846-3605	0
Bakersfield Healthcare		D	661 872-2121	0
Bakersfield Kitchen & Bath		D	661 836-2284	0
Bakersfield Memorial Hospital		A	661 327-1792	0
Bakersfield Symphony Orch		D	661 323-7928	0
Baymarr Constructors Inc		D	661 395-1676	0
Bc Laboratories Inc		C	661 327-4911	0
Beautitudes Beauty Supply LLC		D	800 830-6076	0
Behavioral H Bakersfield		C	661 398-1800	0
Berry Petroleum Company LLC (HQ)		D	661 616-3900	0
Better Way Services		D	661 326-6444	0
Biomat Usa Inc		D	661 863-0621	0
Bolthouse Farms		A	661 366-7205	0
Boys Girls Clubs of Kern Cnty		D	661 325-3730	0
Braden Partners LP A Calif		D	661 632-1979	0
Braun Electric Company Inc (HQ)		E	661 633-1451	0
Bright House Networks LLC		D	661 634-2200	0
Brown Armstrong Accntancy Corp		D	661 324-4971	0
Burtch Trucking Inc		D	661 399-1736	0
Buttonwillow Warehouse Co Inc (HQ)		D	661 695-6500	0
Califia Farms LLC		D	661 679-1000	0
California Physicians Service		C	661 631-2277	0
California Resources Prod Corp (HQ)		C	661 869-8000	0
California Water Service Co		D	661 396-2400	0
Califrnia Rsrces Elk Hills LLC		B	661 412-5000	0
Cameron West Coast Inc		D	661 837-4980	0
Car Wash Partners Inc		C	661 837-9485	0

Mergent email: customerrelations@mergent.com
1506
2020 Directory of California
Wholesalers and Services Companies
(P-0000) Products & Services Section entry number
(PA)=Parent Co (HQ)=Headquarters (DH)=Div Headquarters

	SIC	EMP	PHONE	ENTRY #
Castle & Cooke California Inc		E	661 664-6500	0
Cbizmhm LLC		E	661 325-7500	0
Cellco Partnership		D	661 827-8728	0
Central Cardiology Med Clinic		C	661 395-0000	0
Centre For Neuro Skills (PA)		C	661 872-3408	0
Century Hlth Staffing Svcs Inc		C	661 322-0606	0
Cfp Designs Inc		D	661 903-8940	0
Cintas Corporation No 3		D	661 282-4300	0
Citizens Business Bank		D	661 281-0300	0
City of Bakersfield		C	661 852-7300	0
CL Knox Inc		D	661 837-0477	0
Clifford & Brown A Prof Corp		D	661 322-6023	0
Clinica Sierra Vista		E	661 326-6490	0
Clinica Sierra Vista (PA)		D	661 635-3050	0
CMA Fire Protection (PA)		D	661 322-9344	0
Cni Thl Propco Fe LLC		D	661 325-9700	0
Community Action Partnr Kern		D	661 336-0317	0
Community Action Partnr Kern		D	661 366-5953	0
Community Action Partnr Kern (PA)		E	661 336-5236	0
Construction Specialty Svc Inc		D	661 864-7573	0
Contra Costa Electric Inc		C	661 322-4036	0
Core-Mark International Inc		C	661 366-2673	0
Core-Mark International Inc		C	661 366-2673	0
County of Kern		A	661 868-4100	0
County of Kern		D	661 392-2010	0
County of Kern		D	661 336-6800	0
County of Kern		E	661 868-8360	0
County of Kern		A	661 326-2054	0
County of Kern		A	661 631-6346	0
County of Kern		D	661 363-8910	0
County of Kern		D	661 868-2000	0
Crestwood Behavioral Hlth Inc		D	661 363-8127	0
Crestwood Behavioral Hlth Inc		C	661 363-6711	0
Crystal Organic Farms LLC		B	661 845-5200	0
Csub Nursing Class of 2006		D	408 219-5914	0
CW Welding Service Inc		D	661 399-5422	0
Days Inn Bakersfield		C	661 324-6666	0
Dennis Hyde Construction Inc		D	661 393-1077	0
Dhv Industries Inc		D	661 392-8948	0
Diaz Plastering Inc		D	661 244-8228	0
Dignity Health		D	661 832-8300	0
Dignity Health		E	661 663-6767	0
Dignity Health		C	661 632-5279	0
Dignity Health		B	661 632-5000	0
Diversified Utility Svcs Inc		B	661 325-3212	0
Don Kinzel Construction Inc		D	661 322-9105	0
Donald Valpredo Farming Inc		D	661 858-2245	0
Dv Custom Farming LLC		D	661 858-2888	0
E & B Ntral Resources Mgt Corp (PA)		D	661 679-1714	0
E and B Natural Resources		D	661 679-1700	0
Elysium Jennings LLC		C	661 679-1700	0
Encompass Health Corporation		C	661 323-5500	0
Engineered Well Svc Intl Inc		C	866 913-6283	0
Esparza Enterprises Inc		D	661 831-0002	0
Esparza Enterprises Inc		A	661 631-0347	0
Esparza Enterprises Inc		B	661 631-0347	0
Esys Energy Control Company		D	661 833-1902	0
Evergreen At Lakeport LLC		D	661 871-3133	0
Excalibur Well Services Corp (PA)		D	661 589-5338	0
Exeter Packers Inc		C	661 399-0416	0
Fisher Communications Inc		D	661 327-7955	0
Flyers Energy LLC		B	661 321-9961	0
Freeport-Mcmoran Oil & Gas LLC		D	661 322-7600	0
Frito-Lay North America Inc		C	661 328-6034	0
Frito-Lay North America Inc		E	661 835-0347	0
Frontier Mechanical Inc		D	661 589-6203	0
G4s Secure Solutions (usa)		C	661 834-3454	0
Garcia Roofing Inc		E	661 325-5736	0
Gentiva Hospice		C	661 324-1232	0
Gilliam & Sons Inc		D	661 589-0913	0
Giumarra Vineyards Corporation		D	661 395-7071	0
Glenn E Porter		E	661 615-1500	0
Glenwood Gardens		B	661 587-0221	0
Golden Empire Concrete Pdts		D	661 833-4490	0
Golden Empire Mortgage Inc (PA)		D	661 328-1600	0
Golden Empire Mortgage Inc (PA)		D	661 328-1600	0
Golden Empire Transit District (PA)		C	661 869-2438	0
Golden Living LLC		D	661 323-2894	0
Golden State Drilling Inc		D	661 589-0730	0
Good Samaritan Hospital		B	661 399-4461	0
Goodwill Inds S Centl Cal		E	661 377-0191	0
Gottstein Contracting Corp		D	661 322-8934	0
Granite Construction Company		C	661 399-3361	0
Grant Construction Inc		C	661 588-4586	0
Grayson Service Inc		C	661 589-5444	0
Grimmway Enterprises Inc		C	661 845-5200	0
Gringteam Inc		C	661 426-7919	0
Guardsmark LLC		C	661 325-5906	0
Guinn Corporation		D	661 325-6109	0
H F Cox Inc (PA)		D	661 366-3236	0
H P Sears Co Inc		D	661 325-5981	0
Hall Ambulance Service Inc		D	661 322-8741	0
Hall Ambulance Service Inc (PA)		D	661 322-8741	0
Halliburton Company		D	661 393-8111	0
Heart Hospital of Bk LLC		B	661 316-6000	0
Henrietta Weill Memorial Child (PA)		D	661 322-1021	0
Herc Rentals Inc		C	661 392-3661	0
Hillcrest Sheet Metal Inc		D	661 335-1500	0
Hills Wldg & Engrg Contr Inc		D	661 746-5400	0
Hoffman Hospice of The Valley		D	661 410-1010	0
Houchin Blood Services		D	661 327-8541	0
Hps Mechanical Inc (PA)		C	661 397-2121	0
Hps Plumbing Service Inc		B	661 324-2121	0
Hunting Energy Services Inc		D	661 633-4272	0
Innovative Engrg Systems Inc (PA)		D	661 381-7800	0
J G Boswell Company		C	661 327-7721	0
Jamison Childrens Home		D	661 334-3500	0
Jims Steel Supply LLC		E	661 324-6514	0
Jims Supply Co Inc (PA)		D	661 616-6977	0
K S Fabrication & Machine Inc		C	661 617-1700	0
Kaiser Foundation Hospitals		A	877 524-7373	0
Kaiser Foundation Hospitals		B	661 395-3000	0
Kaiser Foundation Hospitals		A	877 524-7373	0
Kaiser Foundation Hospitals		A	661 337-7160	0
Kaiser Foundation Hospitals		A	877 524-7373	0
Kaiser Foundation Hospitals		A	877 524-7373	0
Kaiser Foundation Hospitals		E	661 398-5011	0
Kaiser Foundation Hospitals		C	661 334-2020	0
Kbak TV Channel 29 CBS		D	661 327-7955	0
Kearn Alternative Care Inc (PA)		B	661 631-2036	0
Kern Alternative Care Inc		C	661 631-2036	0
Kern Around Clock Foundation		E	661 324-3221	0
Kern Cnty Mntal Hlth Child Sys		D	661 868-8300	0
Kern County Hospital Authority		A	661 326-2102	0
Kern County Water Agency		D	661 634-1512	0
Kern Federal Credit Union		D	661 327-9461	0
Kern Health Systems Inc		D	661 664-5000	0
Kern Member Insurance Services		E	661 327-9461	0
Kern Rdlgy Imaging Systems Inc (PA)		C	661 326-9600	0
Kern Regional Center (PA)		C	661 327-8531	0
Kern River Co Generation Co		D	661 392-2663	0
Kern Schools Federal Credit Un (PA)		D	661 833-7900	0
Kern Security Corporation		D	661 363-6874	0
Kern Steel Fabrication Inc (PA)		C	661 327-9588	0
Kindred Healthcare Operating		C	661 872-2121	0
Kirschenman Enterprises Inc		D	661 366-5736	0
Klassen Corporation (PA)		C	661 327-0875	0
Klein Denatale Goldner Et Al (PA)		D	661 401-7755	0
KS Industries LP (PA)		A	661 617-1700	0
Ksi Engineering Inc		E	661 617-1700	0
Latara Enterprise Inc		D	661 665-9780	0
Laztrans Inc		E	661 833-3783	0
Linnco LLC		A	661 616-3900	0
LS Farms LLC		B	661 792-3192	0
Lutrel Trucking Inc		D	661 397-9756	0
M & S Security Services Inc		D	661 397-9616	0
Managed Care Systems Kern Cnty		D	661 716-7100	0
Maple Dairy LP		D	661 396-9600	0
Mechanical Industries Inc		E	661 634-9477	0
Mega Farm Labor Services Inc		C	661 229-8077	0
Mercies Home (PA)		E	661 832-3424	0
Mercy HM Svcs A Cal Ltd Partnr		C	661 632-5234	0
Mistras Group Inc		D	661 829-1192	0
Mmi Services Inc		C	661 589-9366	0
Moreland PCF Snoqualmie LLC		D	661 322-1081	0
Morgan Stanley & Co LLC		D	661 663-8100	0
Mp Environmental Services Inc (PA)		C	800 458-3036	0
Nabors Well Services Co		C	661 588-6140	0
Nabors Well Services Co		D	661 589-3970	0
Nabors Well Services Co		D	661 392-7668	0
National Mentor Inc		E	661 387-1000	0
Nations Petroleum Cal LLC		D	661 387-6402	0
Ned E Dunphy		D	661 395-1000	0
Nestle Ice Cream Company		A	661 398-3500	0
New Advances For People Disabi		D	661 327-0188	0
Newport Hospitality Group Inc		C	661 323-1900	0
Newport Television LLC		D	661 283-1700	0
Oakdale Heights Senior Living		E	661 663-9671	0
Oldenkamp Trucking Inc (PA)		D	661 833-3400	0
Olive Knolls Christian School		D	661 393-3566	0

GEOGRAPHIC

	SIC	EMP	PHONE	ENTRY #
Olympus Power LLC		C	661 393-6885	0
Omni Family Health **(PA)**		D	661 459-1900	0
Opal Fry and Son		E	661 858-2523	0
Optimal Health Services Inc		D	661 393-4483	0
Optimal Hospice Foundation		C	661 716-4000	0
OXY USA Inc		C	661 869-8000	0
Pacific Gas and Electric Co		D	661 398-5918	0
Pacific Process Systems Inc **(PA)**		D	661 321-9681	0
Pan Pacific Petroleum Co Inc		D	661 589-3200	0
Panama-Buena Vista Un Schl Dst		C	661 397-2205	0
Panama-Buena Vista Un Schl Dst		D	661 831-7879	0
Panorama Park Apts		E	661 325-4047	0
Parkview Jlian Cnvlescent Hosp		C	661 831-9150	0
Pavletich Elc Cmmnications Inc **(PA)**		D	661 589-9473	0
PCL Industrial Services Inc		B	661 832-3995	0
Pearce Industries Inc		D	661 695-3420	0
Penney Lawn Service Inc		D	661 587-4788	0
Perez Contracting LLC		C	661 399-2700	0
Physicians Automated Lab Inc **(DH)**		D	661 325-0744	0
Preferred Brokers Inc **(PA)**		D	661 836-2345	0
Progauge Technologies Inc		E	661 392-9600	0
Pros Incorporated		D	661 589-5400	0
Prosoft Technology Inc **(HQ)**		D	661 716-5100	0
Public Health California Dept		C	661 835-4668	0
Pyramid Produce Inc		C	661 366-5736	0
Quinn Company		D	661 393-5800	0
Quinn Group Inc		D	661 393-5800	0
R Stanley Security Service		D	661 634-9283	0
Rainbow Ranches Inc		C	661 858-2266	0
Ramsgate Engineering Inc		D	661 392-0050	0
Re/Max		E	661 616-4040	0
Re/Max Magic		E	661 616-4040	0
Regent Assisted Living Inc		E	661 663-8400	0
Rgis LLC		D	661 827-9195	0
Rhino Ready Mix Trucking Inc **(PA)**		E	661 679-3643	0
Richard K Newman and Assoc Inc **(PA)**		E	661 634-1130	0
Rio Bravo Ranch Shop		E	661 872-5050	0
Rncmba Inc		C	661 395-1700	0
Robert Heely Construction LP **(PA)**		B	661 617-1400	0
S A Camp Companies **(PA)**		D	661 399-4451	0
S A Camp Pump Company		E	661 399-2976	0
SA Recycling LLC		D	661 327-3559	0
San Dimas Medical Group Inc		D	661 663-4800	0
San Joaquin Community Hospital **(PA)**		A	661 395-3000	0
San Joaquin Val UNI Air Pol		D	209 497-1000	0
Sandrini Farms		D	661 792-3192	0
Schlumberger Technology Corp		D	661 864-4750	0
Seven Oaks Country Club		C	661 664-6404	0
Sierra International McHy LLC		D	661 327-7073	0
Sierra Recycling & Dem Inc		D	661 327-7073	0
Sierra Transport Inc		D	661 399-0246	0
Silla Automotive LLC		D	661 392-8880	0
Simmons Construction Inc		E	661 636-1321	0
Sippi Anne Riverside Ranch LLP		E	661 871-9697	0
Soli-Bond Inc		E	661 631-1633	0
Southern Cal Prmnnte Med Group		D	661 398-5085	0
Southern Cal Prmnnte Med Group		D	661 334-2020	0
Southern California Gas Co		E	661 399-4431	0
Southwest Contractors **(PA)**		C	661 588-0484	0
Stanford Transportation Inc		D	661 302-3288	0
Stantec Energy & Resources Inc **(HQ)**		C	661 396-3770	0
Stantec Holdings Del III Inc		C	661 396-3770	0
State Compensation Insur Fund		C	661 664-4000	0
State Farm Mutl Auto Insur Co		D	661 324-4077	0
State Farm Mutl Auto Insur Co		D	309 766-2311	0
State Farm Mutl Auto Insur Co		D	661 664-9663	0
Stockdale Country Club		D	661 832-0310	0
Sturgeon Services Intl Inc **(PA)**		E	661 322-4408	0
Sturgeon Son Grading & Pav Inc **(PA)**		E	661 322-4408	0
Sun Pacific Maricopa		B	661 847-1015	0
Sun Pacific Marketing Coop Inc		A	213 612-9957	0
Sun Pacific Marketing Coop Inc		B	661 847-1015	0
Sun World International Inc **(PA)**		A	661 392-5000	0
Sun World International LLC		B	661 392-5000	0
Sunridge Nurseries Inc		D	661 363-8463	0
Sunshine Metal Clad Inc		D	661 366-0575	0
Surface Pumps Inc **(PA)**		D	661 393-1545	0
Surgener Electric Inc		D	661 399-3321	0
Sycamore Cogeneration Co **(PA)**		D	661 615-4630	0
Technosocialworkcom LLC		D	661 617-6601	0
Tiburon Hospitality LLC		C	661 322-1012	0
Tj Cross Engineers Inc		D	661 831-8782	0
Total-Western Inc		D	661 589-5200	0
Trans-West Security Svcs Inc		B	661 381-2900	0
Triple E Trucking		E	661 834-0071	0
U S Weatherford L P		D	661 589-9483	0
UCI Construction Inc		D	661 587-0192	0
Ulta Salon Cosmt Fragrance Inc		C	661 664-1402	0
Union Pacific Railroad Company		D	661 321-4604	0
United States Cold Storage Inc		D	661 832-2653	0
UPS Ground Freight Inc		D	661 395-9500	0
Valley Industrial X-Ra		C	661 399-8497	0
Valley Pacific Petro Svcs Inc		C	661 746-7737	0
Valley Power Systems Inc		E	661 325-9001	0
Valley Republic Bank		D	661 371-2000	0
Valley Sun Mechanical Cnstr		D	661 321-9070	0
Vaquero Energy Incorporated		E	661 363-7240	0
Vasindas Around The Clock Care		E	661 395-5820	0
Veterans Health Administration		E	661 632-1871	0
Veterans Health Administration		C	661 323-8387	0
Vignolo Farms Inc		D	661 393-1431	0
Vinod Kumar MD		D	661 324-4100	0
W M Lyles Co		E	661 387-1600	0
Weatherford International LLC		D	661 587-9753	0
Western Energy Services Corp		C	403 984-5916	0
Western Oilfields Supply Co **(PA)**		C	661 399-9124	0
Wholesale Fuels Inc		D	661 327-4900	0
Winegard Energy Inc		D	661 393-9467	0
Wm Bolthouse Farms Inc **(HQ)**		A	661 366-7209	0
Wonderful Company LLC		A	559 781-7438	0
Work Force Services Inc		C	661 327-5019	0
Zim Industries Inc		D	661 393-9661	0

BALDWIN PARK, CA - Los Angeles County

	SIC	EMP	PHONE	ENTRY #
All Direct Mail Services Inc		C	818 833-7773	0
All Star Automotive Products		D	626 960-5164	0
American Kal Enterprises Inc **(PA)**		E	626 338-7308	0
American Mzhou Dngpo Group Inc		D	626 820-9239	0
Baldwin Hospitality LLC		D	626 962-6000	0
California Lighting Sales Inc **(PA)**		D	626 775-6000	0
Cbre Inc		B	626 814-7900	0
Cedarwood-Young Company **(PA)**		C	626 962-4047	0
Cedarwood-Young Company		D	626 962-4047	0
County of Los Angeles		C	626 337-1277	0
Crowner Sheet Metal Pdts Inc		E	626 960-4971	0
First Avenue Inc		D	626 856-2076	0
G K Tool Corp		D	626 338-7300	0
Garden View Care Center Inc		D	626 962-7095	0
Golden State Habilitation Conv **(PA)**		B	626 962-3274	0
Gr8 Care Inc		D	626 337-7229	0
Haynes Building Service LLC		C	626 359-6100	0
Ideal Transit Inc		E	626 448-2690	0
Kaiser Foundation Hospitals		A	626 851-1011	0
Lighting Technologies Intl LLC		C	626 480-0755	0
Nichols Lumber & Hardware Co		D	626 960-4802	0
Nr 2 Group Inc		E	626 251-6681	0
Ols Hotels & Resorts LLC		A	626 962-6000	0
Phoenix Satellite TV US Inc		E	626 388-1188	0
Physical Rhbltation Netwrk LLC		C	646 430-2300	0
San Gabriel Transit Inc		D	626 430-3650	0
SCE Federal Credit Union **(PA)**		D	626 960-6888	0
Sierra View Care Holdings LLC		D	626 960-1971	0
Southern California Edison Co		C	626 543-6093	0
Tanimura & Antle Inc		B	831 424-6100	0
Tecan Sp Inc		D	626 962-0010	0
Trinity Health Systems **(PA)**		D	626 960-1971	0
United Parcel Service Inc OH		C	626 814-6216	0
USA Waste of California Inc		D	626 856-1285	0
Valley Light Industries Inc		C	626 337-6200	0
Vista Specialty Hosp Cal LP		C	626 388-2700	0

BALLICO, CA - Merced County

	SIC	EMP	PHONE	ENTRY #
Hilltop Ranch Inc		C	209 874-1875	0

BANNING, CA - Riverside County

	SIC	EMP	PHONE	ENTRY #
Bho LLC		E	951 845-2220	0
Cancer Federation Inc **(PA)**		C	951 849-4325	0
Ferrees Group Home Inc		D	951 849-1927	0
Green Thumb Produce Inc		C	951 849-4711	0
H E L P Inc		D	951 922-2305	0
Professional Community MGT Cal		E	951 845-2191	0
Riverside-San Bernardino		A	951 849-4761	0
San Gorgonio Memorial Hospital **(PA)**		C	951 845-1121	0
Strech Plastics Incorporated		E	951 922-2224	0
Sun Lakes Cntry Club Hmeownrs		D	951 845-2135	0

BARSTOW, CA - San Bernardino County

	SIC	EMP	PHONE	ENTRY #
Barstow Redevelopment Agency		C	760 256-3531	0
Bnsf Railway Company		C	760 255-7803	0
Burrtec Waste Group Inc		D	760 256-2730	0
Darensburg Roghair & Renier		E	760 256-6891	0
Economy Inn		E	760 256-5601	0

Mergent email: customerrelations@mergent.com
1508

2020 Directory of California
Wholesalers and Services Companies

(P-0000) Products & Services Section entry number
(PA)=Parent Co (HQ)=Headquarters (DH)=Div Headquarters

	SIC	EMP	PHONE	ENTRY #
Golden Empire Mortgage Inc		D	760 256-3593	0
Hentrel Greathouse Foundation		D	302 513-4056	0
Hospital of Barstow Inc		C	760 256-1761	0
Kbrwyle Tech Solutions LLC		C	760 255-8322	0
Latara Enterprise Inc		D	760 256-3450	0
Life Care Centers America Inc		B	760 252-2515	0
Little Sisters Truck Wash Inc		D	760 253-2277	0

BASS LAKE, CA - Madera County

	SIC	EMP	PHONE	ENTRY #
Basslake LLC		D	559 642-3121	0
Home Away Inc		D	559 642-3121	0

BAY POINT, CA - Contra Costa County

	SIC	EMP	PHONE	ENTRY #
Ambrose Recreation & Park Dst		D	925 458-1601	0
Caribbean South Amercn Council		E	925 709-3433	0
Henkel US Operations Corp		C	925 458-8086	0
K & S Towing & Transport		D	925 709-0759	0

BAYSIDE, CA - Humboldt County

	SIC	EMP	PHONE	ENTRY #
O A Outfitting Inc		D	707 498-2917	0

BEALE AFB, CA - Yuba County

	SIC	EMP	PHONE	ENTRY #
US Dept of the Air Force		D	530 634-4738	0

BEAR VALLEY, CA - Calaveras County

	SIC	EMP	PHONE	ENTRY #
Bear Valley Ski Co		B	209 753-2301	0

BEAUMONT, CA - Riverside County

	SIC	EMP	PHONE	ENTRY #
Anderson Chrnesky Strl Stl Inc		D	951 769-5700	0
Arrow USA		D	951 845-6144	0
Beaumont Unified School Dst		A	951 845-3010	0
California Oak Valley Golf		E	951 769-9771	0
Cellco Partnership		D	951 769-0985	0
Charlee Family Care		D	951 845-3588	0
Childhelp Inc		C	951 845-6737	0
David-Kleis II LLC		D	951 845-3125	0
Kpu Roofing		E	909 586-2531	0

BELL, CA - Los Angeles County

	SIC	EMP	PHONE	ENTRY #
4g Wireless Inc		D	562 928-2972	0
Affiliated Temporary Help		B	323 771-1383	0
Briarcrest Nursing Center Inc		C	562 927-2641	0
City of Bell		D	323 773-1596	0
El Aviso Magazine		B	323 586-9199	0
Fam LLC		D	323 888-7755	0
Human Services Association (PA)		D	562 806-5400	0
Jwch Institute Inc		D	323 562-5813	0
Leonid M Glosman DDS A D		C	323 560-4514	0
Omega Moulding West LLC		C	323 261-3510	0
Perrin Bernard Supowitz LLC (PA)		D	323 981-2800	0

BELL GARDENS, CA - Los Angeles County

	SIC	EMP	PHONE	ENTRY #
Anitsa Inc		C	213 237-0533	0
Auchante Inc		D	562 231-1880	0
Bell Gardens Bicycle Club Inc		A	562 806-4646	0
Bicycle Casino LP		A	562 806-4646	0
Del Rio Sanitarium Inc		C	562 927-6586	0
WEI-Chuan USA Inc (PA)		C	626 225-7168	0

BELLFLOWER, CA - Los Angeles County

	SIC	EMP	PHONE	ENTRY #
Advent Securities Investments (PA)		E	562 920-5467	0
Bio-Mdcal Applications Cal Inc		D	562 920-2070	0
Empire Enterprises Inc		C	562 529-2676	0
Empire Transportation		B	562 529-2676	0
Habitat For Humanity of Greate		E	310 323-4663	0
Harbor Health Care Inc		C	562 866-7054	0
Hollywood Sports Park LLC		D	562 867-9600	0
Jwch Institute Inc		D	562 867-7999	0
Kaiser Foundation Hospitals		D	562 461-3084	0
Leroy Durbin		D	562 531-2001	0
Life Care Centers America Inc		D	562 867-1761	0
Produce Company		D	310 508-7760	0
Rebecca Terley		D	562 925-4252	0
Western Dental Services Inc		E	562 461-1180	0
Young Mens Chrstn Assc Gr L B		D	562 925-1292	0

BELMONT, CA - San Mateo County

	SIC	EMP	PHONE	ENTRY #
Anita Borg Inst For Women Tech		D	650 236-4756	0
Belmont Oaks Academy		D	650 593-6175	0
County of San Mateo		C	650 802-6470	0
Cw Healthcare Inc		E	510 636-9000	0
Island Hospitality MGT LLC		D	650 591-8600	0
Nikon Precision Inc (DH)		C	650 508-4674	0
Oracle Systems Corporation		B	650 654-7606	0
Pacific Gas and Electric Co		B	650 592-9411	0
Ringcentral Inc (PA)		D	650 472-4100	0
Silverado Senior Living Inc		D	650 226-8017	0
Sunrise Senior Living LLC		D	650 654-9700	0
Tectura Corporation (PA)		E	650 273-4249	0

	SIC	EMP	PHONE	ENTRY #
Telecare Corporation		D	650 817-9070	0
Ten-X LLC		B	800 793-6107	0
Westlake Development Group LLC		D	650 579-1010	0
Woodmont Realty Advisors Inc		D	650 592-3960	0
Wyndham International Inc		E	650 591-8600	0

BELVEDERE, CA - Marin County

	SIC	EMP	PHONE	ENTRY #
Pacific Union Co		D	415 789-8686	0

BELVEDERE TIBURON, CA - Marin County

	SIC	EMP	PHONE	ENTRY #
1651 Tiburon Hotel LLC		D	401 946-4600	0
Accenture LLP		C	415 537-5860	0
Digital Foundry Inc		E	415 789-1600	0
Magave Tequila Inc		E	415 515-3536	0
Marcolin USA Inc		D	415 383-6348	0
Marin Cnvlscent Rhbltton Hosp		D	415 435-4554	0
Melissa Bradley RE Inc		D	415 435-2705	0
Pharmacy Temps Inc		E	415 459-5211	0
Tiburon Hotel LLC		D	415 435-5996	0
Tiburon Peninsula Club Inc		E	415 789-7900	0
Vital Farmland Holdings LLC		D	415 465-2400	0

BENICIA, CA - Solano County

	SIC	EMP	PHONE	ENTRY #
1-800 Radiator & A/C (PA)		D	707 747-7400	0
All-Points Petroleum LLC		D	707 745-1116	0
American Civil Const		D	707 746-8028	0
American Civil Constrs LLC		C	707 746-8028	0
Americas Lemonade Stand Inc		C	707 745-1274	0
Anthony Trevino		D	707 747-4776	0
Awt Construction Group Inc		D	707 746-7500	0
Benicia Plumbing Inc		D	707 745-2930	0
Biagi Bros Inc		D	707 745-8115	0
C E Toland & Son		C	707 747-1000	0
Califrnia Erctors Bay Area Inc		C	707 746-1990	0
Clean Harbors Envmtl Svcs Inc		D	707 747-6699	0
Clean Hrbors Es Indus Svcs Inc		D	707 745-1581	0
Csu Holding Company		E	707 746-0353	0
Durkee Drayage Company		D	510 970-7550	0
Edgewater Plumbing of Benicia		E	707 747-9204	0
F3 and Associates Inc (PA)		D	707 748-4300	0
Fedex Ground Package Sys Inc		D	800 463-3339	0
Flatiron West Inc		C	707 742-6000	0
Henry Wine Group LLC (HQ)		B	707 745-8500	0
Herc Rentals Inc		E	707 747-4444	0
High End Development Inc		D	925 687-2540	0
Innovel Solutions Inc		D	707 748-1940	0
Inter-Rail Trnspt Nshville LLC		D	707 746-1695	0
J P Consulting		E	707 747-4800	0
Mistras Group Inc		E	707 746-5870	0
Plan-It Interactive Inc (PA)		E	707 752-6010	0
Ponder Environmental Svcs Inc (PA)		D	707 748-7775	0
Safway Services LP		E	707 745-2000	0
Solano Pacific Corporation		D	707 745-6000	0
Underground Cnstr Co Inc		C	707 746-8800	0
United Site Services Cal Inc		E	707 747-2810	0
Western Sun Enterprises Inc		C	707 748-2542	0

BERKELEY, CA - Alameda County

	SIC	EMP	PHONE	ENTRY #
A T Associates Inc		E	510 649-6670	0
Ala Costa Center Program For (PA)		D	510 527-2550	0
Altcare Cedar Creek LLC		D	510 527-7282	0
Andrew M Jordan Inc		D	510 999-6000	0
Annies Homegrown Inc		D	510 558-7500	0
Backroads (PA)		D	510 527-1555	0
Barra LLC (HQ)		B	510 548-5442	0
Bay Area Hispn Inst Advancmnt		D	510 525-1463	0
Berkeley 75 Hsing Partners LP		E	510 705-1488	0
Berkeley Cement Inc		C	510 525-8175	0
Berkeley Student Coop Inc		D	510 848-1936	0
Berkeley Symphony Orchestra		E	510 841-2800	0
Berkeley Unified School Dst		E	510 644-6182	0
Boykin Mgt Co Ltd Lblty Co		B	510 548-7920	0
California Alumni Association (PA)		E	510 900-8225	0
California Shakespeare Theater		C	510 548-3422	0
Chaparral Foundation		D	510 848-8774	0
City of Berkeley		A	510 981-6750	0
Claremont Ht Prpts Ltd Partnr		A	510 843-3000	0
Community Partners Intl		C	510 225-9676	0
DSM Biomedical Inc		C	510 841-8800	0
Earth Island Institute Inc		D	510 859-9100	0
Els		E	510 549-2929	0
Fmr LLC		C	800 225-6447	0
Gtxcel Inc		D	800 609-8994	0
Homegrown Natural Foods Inc		D	510 558-7500	0
Hornblower Yachts LLC		E	916 446-1185	0
Hotel Durant A Ltd Partnership		D	510 845-8981	0
Icygen LLC		D	510 540-7122	0

Employment Codes: A=Over 500 employees, B=251-500,
C=101-250, D=51-100, E=50

2020 Directory of California
Wholesalers and Services Companies

© Mergent Inc. 1-800-342-5647

1509

	SIC	EMP	PHONE	ENTRY #
Inclusive Cmnty Resources LLC		C	510 981-8115	0
Institute For Eductl Therapy		E	831 457-1207	0
International House		C	510 642-9490	0
Internet-Journals LLC		D	510 665-1200	0
Interntional Cmpt Science Inst		E	510 643-9153	0
Interstate Hotels Resorts Inc		D	510 843-3000	0
ISI Inspection Services Inc **(PA)**		D	510 900-2101	0
Jewish Fmly & Cmnty Svcs E Bay **(PA)**		D	510 704-7475	0
L J Kruse Co		D	510 644-0260	0
Lifelong Medical Care **(PA)**		E	510 704-6010	0
Mason-Mcduffie Real Estate Inc		D	510 705-8611	0
McKesson Corporation		D	510 666-0854	0
Moore Iacofano Goltsman Inc **(PA)**		D	510 845-7549	0
New Bridge Foundation Inc		D	510 548-7270	0
New Bridge Foundation Inc		D	510 548-7270	0
O C Jones & Sons Inc **(PA)**		C	510 526-3424	0
O C Sailing Club Inc		D	510 843-4200	0
Outfront Media LLC		D	510 527-3350	0
Partners For Community Access		D	510 558-6700	0
Permanente Medical Group Inc		D	510 559-5119	0
Permanente Medical Group Inc		D	510 559-5338	0
Pillsbury Winthrop Shaw		C	415 983-1865	0
Research Triangle Institute		D	510 849-4942	0
Ripple Foods Pbc		D	510 269-2563	0
Sanhyd Inc		D	510 843-2131	0
Satellite First Communities LP **(PA)**		D	510 647-0700	0
Shattuck Health Care Inc		D	510 665-2800	0
Sigma Kappa Sorority		D	510 540-9142	0
Sun Light & Power		D	510 845-2997	0
Surgery Center of Alta Bates **(HQ)**		A	510 204-4444	0
Surgery Center of Alta Bates		E	510 204-4411	0
Surgery Center of Alta Bates		D	510 204-1591	0
Tarana Wireless Inc		C	510 868-3359	0
Toolworks Inc		B	510 649-1322	0
United States Dept of Energy		A	510 486-4000	0
United States Dept of Energy		A	510 486-4936	0
University California Berkeley		B	510 642-2000	0
Westpost Berkeley LLC		D	510 548-7920	0
Westward Hospitality MGT		D	510 548-7920	0
Winnarainbow Inc **(PA)**		E	510 525-4304	0
Wright Institute		E	510 841-9230	0
Young MNS Chrstn Assn of E Bay		D	510 486-8400	0
Young MNS Chrstn Assn of E Bay		D	510 848-9092	0
Young MNS Chrstn Assn of E Bay		C	510 848-9622	0
Young MNS Chrstn Assn of E Bay		D	510 526-2146	0
Young MNS Chrstn Assn of E Bay		A	510 644-6290	0
Young MNS Chrstn Assn of E Bay		D	510 848-6800	0
Young MNS Chrstn Assn of E Bay		D	510 559-2090	0

BERMUDA DUNES, CA - Riverside County

	SIC	EMP	PHONE	ENTRY #
Bermuda Dunes Country Club		E	760 360-2481	0
Bermuda Dunes Learning Ctr Inc		E	760 772-7127	0
Cockrell Electric Inc		D	760 864-6233	0
Desert Cncpts Ldscpg Maint Inc		C	760 200-9007	0
Earth Systems Southwest **(HQ)**		D	760 345-1588	0
Hort Tech Inc		C	760 360-9000	0
James Monroe School Pto		E	760 772-4130	0
KDI Elements		C	760 345-9933	0
Turf Star Inc		D	760 772-3575	0
Vantage Plaster & Drywall		D	760 345-3622	0
Vintage Associates Inc		C	760 772-3673	0

BEVERLY HILLS, CA - Los Angeles County

	SIC	EMP	PHONE	ENTRY #
Academy Foundation **(HQ)**		D	310 247-3000	0
Academy Mpic Arts & Sciences **(PA)**		D	310 247-3000	0
Active Lawyers Referral Svc		D	310 247-0425	0
Advance Building Maintenance		B	310 247-0077	0
Aeroflot Russian Airlines		D	323 272-4861	0
Agency For Performing Arts Inc **(PA)**		D	310 557-9049	0
American Corporation		D	310 274-1800	0
American Health Connection		A	424 226-0420	0
Amtrow Group Inc		D	310 557-0857	0
Anderson Associates Staffing **(PA)**		C	323 930-3170	0
APA Incorporated		C	310 888-4200	0
Baker Winokur		D	310 248-6169	0
Beauty Recognized LP		D	310 278-7646	0
Beck International Inc		B	310 281-2980	0
Belvedere Hotel Partnership		B	310 551-2888	0
Belvedere Partnership		B	310 551-2888	0
Bentley Health Care Inc		D	310 967-3300	0
Beverly Hills Lingual Inst		E	323 651-5000	0
Beverly Hills Polc Ofcrs Assoc		D	310 288-1755	0
Beverly Radiology Med Group **(PA)**		C	310 975-1500	0
Bhrac LLC		D	310 862-1933	0
Bloom Hergott Diemer Cook LLC		D	310 859-6800	0
Brillstein Entrmt Partners LLC **(PA)**		B	310 205-5100	0

	SIC	EMP	PHONE	ENTRY #
Bwr Public Relations		D	310 248-6100	0
Canessa Investments N V		E	310 273-8543	0
Cardivsclr Mdcl Grp of Sthrn		E	310 278-3400	0
Casden Builders LLC		E	310 274-5553	0
Casden Company LLC		D	310 274-5553	0
Casewise Systems Inc **(DH)**		D	424 284-4101	0
Cedars-Sinai Medical Center		C	310 385-3400	0
Charles & Cynthia Eberly Inc		D	323 937-6468	0
City of Beverly Hills		B	310 285-2552	0
Coldwell Bnkr Residential Brkg		D	310 273-3113	0
Collective MGT Group LLC		C	323 655-8585	0
Condor Productions LLC		D	310 449-3000	0
Cznd Inc		D	323 378-6505	0
Defy Media LLC		D	310 360-4141	0
Douglas Elliman Real Estate		E	310 595-3888	0
E H Summit Inc		D	310 273-0300	0
Finn Holding Corporation **(PA)**		A	310 712-1850	0
G Katen Partners Ltd Lblty Co		A	424 354-3241	0
Gang Tyre Ramer & Brown Inc		E	310 777-7158	0
Gersh Agency Inc **(PA)**		D	310 274-6611	0
Ggwh LLC		E	310 786-1700	0
Global Horizons Inc		B	310 234-8475	0
Gores Group LLC **(PA)**		D	310 209-3010	0
Granite Escrow Services		D	310 288-0110	0
Griffin Slr Management Inc		D	310 270-4031	0
Hair Fashion Inc		D	310 274-0851	0
Hilltop Securities Inc		E	800 765-2200	0
Honeymoon Real Estate LP		D	310 277-5221	0
Hong Kong & Shanghai Hotels		D	310 551-2888	0
Hyatt Vacation Ownership Inc		D	310 285-0990	0
Insomniac Inc		D	323 874-7020	0
Insomniac Holdings LLC		C	310 867-7041	0
Kate Somerville Holdings LLC		D	323 655-4170	0
Keller Wllams Rlty Bvrly Hills		D	310 432-6400	0
Kennedy-Wilson Inc **(PA)**		C	310 887-6400	0
Kpmg LLP		E	310 273-2770	0
La Peer Surgery Center LLC		D	310 360-9119	0
Lfk Law		D	310 300-8464	0
Linden Crest Surgery Center		D	310 601-3900	0
Live Nation Entertainment Inc		D	323 462-4785	0
Live Nation Entertainment Inc **(PA)**		C	800 653-8000	0
Live Nation Worldwide Inc		A	310 867-7000	0
M L Stern & Co LLC **(DH)**		C	323 658-4400	0
Magic Workforce Solutions LLC		A	310 246-6153	0
Marcus Buckingham Company		D	323 302-9810	0
Massachusetts Mutl Lf Insur Co		D	323 965-6339	0
Mayer Associates		D	310 274-5553	0
Mediaplatform Inc		D	310 909-8410	0
Medical Group Bverly Hills Inc **(PA)**		E	310 385-3200	0
Medical Group Bverly Hills Inc		E	310 247-4646	0
Metro-Goldwyn-Mayer Inc **(DH)**		B	310 449-3000	0
MGM and Ua Services Company		A	310 449-3000	0
Montage Hotels & Resorts LLC		B	310 499-4199	0
Morgan Stanley & Co LLC		C	310 285-4800	0
Mufg Union Bank National Assn		D	310 550-6522	0
N S B N Investments Llc		D	310 273-2501	0
Nelson Shelton & Associates		C	310 271-2229	0
Next Management LLC		E	323 782-0038	0
Nextpoint Inc **(PA)**		D	310 360-5904	0
Nourmand & Associates		E	310 274-4000	0
Omninet Twin Towers Gp LLC		E	310 300-4100	0
Omninet Twin Towers LP		E	310 300-4100	0
Orion Pictures Corporation		A	310 449-3000	0
Paradigm Music LLC **(PA)**		D	310 288-8000	0
Park Hotels & Resorts Inc		C	310 415-3340	0
Participant Channel Inc		D	310 550-7715	0
Participant Media LLC **(PA)**		D	310 550-5100	0
Playboy Enterprises Inc **(PA)**		D	310 424-1800	0
Porter Ranch Development Co		D	323 655-7330	0
Premier Exec Solutions Inc		E	310 989-9925	0
Project Boat Holdings LLC		A	310 712-1850	0
Project Skyline Intermediate H		A	310 712-1850	0
Promote Media LP		D	323 433-7950	0
Protected Outcomes Corporation		D	203 540-9565	0
Protravel International LLC		D	310 271-9566	0
Pse Holding LLC **(HQ)**		B	248 377-0165	0
Radnet Management Inc		D	323 549-3000	0
Raffles Lrmitage Beverly Hills		C	310 278-3344	0
Raines Law Group LLP		E	310 440-4100	0
Rbc Capital Markets LLC		E	310 273-7600	0
Regent LP **(PA)**		D	310 299-4100	0
Regis Corporation		E	310 274-8791	0
Revel Travel Service Inc		D	310 553-5555	0
Rodeo Realty Inc **(PA)**		D	818 349-9997	0
S J S Link International Inc **(PA)**		E	310 860-7666	0

Mergent email: customerrelations@mergent.com
1510

2020 Directory of California
Wholesalers and Services Companies

(P-0000) Products & Services Section entry number
(PA)=Parent Co (HQ)=Headquarters (DH)=Div Headquarters

	SIC	EMP	PHONE	ENTRY #
Sajahtera Inc		A	310 276-2251	0
Shapell Industries LLC (HQ)		D	323 655-7330	0
Skidmore Owings & Merrill LLP		C	310 651-9924	0
Skin Health Experts Medic		D	310 623-6869	0
Sony Music Entertainment Inc		C	310 272-2555	0
SOS Security LLC		D	310 859-8248	0
Star Lax LLC		C	310 642-4500	0
Starpoint Property MGT LLC		C	310 247-0550	0
Stockcross Financial Svcs Inc (DH)		E	800 993-2015	0
Studio 71 LP		C	323 370-1500	0
Sunrise Senior Living Inc		D	650 326-1108	0
Sunrise Senior Living Inc		D	310 274-4479	0
Telemedicine Corp		E	888 472-2853	0
Telestar Consulting Inc		E	310 748-0008	0
Thomas Edward Companies (PA)		C	310 859-9366	0
Tiffanys Liu		D	415 644-0846	0
Tower Hematology Oncology Medi		D	310 888-8680	0
Travel Syndicate		D	818 297-9979	0
Treepeople Inc		E	818 753-4600	0
UBS Financial Services Inc		D	310 274-8441	0
Universal Home Care Inc		C	323 653-9222	0
Universe Holdings Dev Co LLC		E	310 785-0077	0
Village Rdshow Entrmt Group US		D	310 867-8000	0
Weinstein Company LLC		D	424 204-4800	0
Weintraub Tobin Chediak		E	310 858-7888	0
Wells Fargo Bank National Assn		C	310 285-5817	0
West Coast Storm Inc (PA)		E	909 890-5700	0
William Morris Endeavor		B	310 285-9000	0
William Mrris Endvor Entrmt FN (HQ)		C	310 285-9000	0
Zillionaire Empress Danielle B.		A	310 461-9923	0

BIG BEAR CITY, CA - San Bernardino County

	SIC	EMP	PHONE	ENTRY #
Big Bear City Cmnty Svcs Dst (PA)		D	909 585-2565	0
Snow Summit Ski Corporation		B	909 585-2517	0

BIG BEAR LAKE, CA - San Bernardino County

	SIC	EMP	PHONE	ENTRY #
Bear Vly Cmnty Healthcare Dst (PA)		C	909 866-6501	0
Golden State Water Company		E	909 866-4678	0
Pacific Snow Valley Resort LLC		D	909 866-3121	0
Snow Summit Ski Corporation (PA)		C	909 866-5766	0

BIG CREEK, CA - Fresno County

	SIC	EMP	PHONE	ENTRY #
Southern California Edison Co		C	559 893-3611	0
Southern California Edison Co		C	559 893-2037	0

BIG SUR, CA - Monterey County

	SIC	EMP	PHONE	ENTRY #
48123 CA Investors LLC		C	831 667-2331	0
Tr Big Sur Management LLC		E	831 667-4212	0

BIGGS, CA - Butte County

	SIC	EMP	PHONE	ENTRY #
Chuck Jones Flying Service (PA)		E	530 868-5798	0
Red Top Rice Growers		E	530 868-5975	0
Sun West Wild Rice Facility		E	530 868-5188	0

BISHOP, CA - Inyo County

	SIC	EMP	PHONE	ENTRY #
Bishop Paiute Gaming Corp		C	760 872-6005	0
Bishop Waste Disposal Inc		E	760 872-6561	0
Eastern Sierra Transit Auth		E	760 872-1901	0
Fedex Freight Corporation		D	760 873-8655	0
Fedex Ground Package Sys Inc		C	800 463-3339	0
High Country Lumber Inc (PA)		E	760 873-5874	0
Inyo Mono Advcts Fr Cmmnty Act (PA)		D	760 873-8557	0
Northern Inyo Healthcare Dst		B	760 873-5811	0
SCE Eastern Hydro Division		E	760 873-0767	0
Southern California Edison Co		C	760 873-0715	0
Toiyabe Indian Health Prj Inc (PA)		C	760 873-8461	0
Triad Homes Assoc		D	760 873-4273	0
United Parcel Service Inc OH		C	760 872-7661	0

BLOOMINGTON, CA - San Bernardino County

	SIC	EMP	PHONE	ENTRY #
Accurate Delivery Systems Inc		D	951 823-8870	0
C M C Steel Fabricators Inc		D	909 873-3060	0
Calmex Engineering Inc		D	909 546-1311	0
Chiro Inc (PA)		D	909 879-1160	0
Empire Oil Co		D	909 877-0226	0
Fedex Ground Package Sys Inc		A	800 463-3339	0
Flyers Energy LLC		C	909 877-2441	0
Ftdi West Inc		D	909 473-1111	0
Inland Valley Cnstr Co Inc		D	909 875-2112	0
Kinder Mrgan Enrgy Partners LP		E	909 873-5100	0
Lineage Logistics Holdings LLC		A	909 874-1200	0
MCM Construction Inc		D	909 875-0533	0
Optimum Inc (PA)		E	909 990-0767	0
Pacific Steel Group		C	858 449-7219	0
Revchem Composites Inc (PA)		D	909 877-8477	0
Roberts Lumber Sales Inc		D	909 350-9164	0
Social Science Service Center		D	909 421-7120	0
Team West Contracting Corp		D	951 340-3426	0

	SIC	EMP	PHONE	ENTRY #
Unified Aircraft Services Inc (PA)		D	909 877-0535	0
Union Pacific Railroad Company		D	909 685-2710	0
UPS Freight Services Inc		D	909 879-7400	0
Vance Corporation		E	909 355-4333	0

BLUE JAY, CA - San Bernardino County

	SIC	EMP	PHONE	ENTRY #
Alpine Camp Conference Ctr Inc		D	909 337-6287	0
Cbsrr Inc		D	909 336-2131	0

BLUE LAKE, CA - Humboldt County

	SIC	EMP	PHONE	ENTRY #
Blue Lake Casino		E	707 668-5101	0

BLYTHE, CA - Riverside County

	SIC	EMP	PHONE	ENTRY #
Aztec Harvesting		A	760 922-7348	0
Barnes and Berger		E	760 922-6136	0
Blythe Nursing Care Center		D	760 922-8176	0
Fisher Ranch LLC		D	760 922-4151	0
Hayday Farms Inc		D	760 922-4713	0
Palo Verde Health Care Dst		C	760 922-4115	0
Palo Verde Hospital Assn		C	760 922-4115	0
Palo Verde Irrigation District		D	760 922-3144	0
Xpo Logistics Freight Inc		D	760 922-8538	0

BODEGA BAY, CA - Sonoma County

	SIC	EMP	PHONE	ENTRY #
Bbcert		E	480 220-3799	0
Bodega Harbour Homeowners Assn		D	707 875-3519	0
NAPA Valley Lodge LP		D	707 875-3525	0

BOLINAS, CA - Marin County

	SIC	EMP	PHONE	ENTRY #
Commonweal		D	415 868-0970	0

BONITA, CA - San Diego County

	SIC	EMP	PHONE	ENTRY #
Child Development Assoc Inc (PA)		E	619 427-4411	0
Crockett & Coinc		D	619 267-1103	0
John Collins Co Inc		D	818 227-2190	0
Kaiser Foundation Hospitals		D	619 409-6405	0
Paradise Valley Hospital		D	619 472-7474	0

BONSALL, CA - San Diego County

	SIC	EMP	PHONE	ENTRY #
Cunningham Group Inc		D	303 295-1982	0

BORON, CA - Kern County

	SIC	EMP	PHONE	ENTRY #
Kjc Operating Company		C	760 762-5562	0
Rio Tinto Minerals Inc		C	760 762-7121	0

BORREGO SPRINGS, CA - San Diego County

	SIC	EMP	PHONE	ENTRY #
Borrego Cmnty Hlth Foundation (PA)		C	760 767-5051	0
Rams Hill Country Club		D	760 767-4259	0

BOULDER CREEK, CA - Santa Cruz County

	SIC	EMP	PHONE	ENTRY #
Easter Seals Inc		D	831 338-3383	0
San Lorenzo Valley Water Dst (PA)		E	831 338-2153	0

BOULEVARD, CA - San Diego County

	SIC	EMP	PHONE	ENTRY #
La Posta Casino		C	619 824-4100	0

BRAWLEY, CA - Imperial County

	SIC	EMP	PHONE	ENTRY #
Border Valley Trading Ltd		D	760 344-6700	0
Border Valley Trading Ltd		D	760 344-6700	0
Brandt Co Inc (PA)		D	760 344-3430	0
Clinicas De Slud Del Peblo Inc (PA)		D	760 344-9951	0
Clinicas De Slud Del Peblo Inc.		D	760 344-6471	0
Dacare Inc (PA)		D	760 344-4654	0
Esparza Enterprises Inc		B	760 344-2031	0
Grimmway Enterprises Inc		C	760 344-0204	0
Irby Construction Company		D	760 344-4478	0
Kelomar Inc		C	760 344-5253	0
Michael W Morgan		E	760 344-5253	0
Pacific Sun Labor		D	760 556-5085	0
Pioneers Mem Healthcare Dst (PA)		A	760 351-3333	0
Planters Hay Inc		D	760 344-0620	0
Rothfleisch Ranches Inc.		D	760 344-1819	0
Royal Convalescent Hospital		D	760 344-5431	0

BREA, CA - Orange County

	SIC	EMP	PHONE	ENTRY #
Acosta Inc.		C	714 988-1500	0
Aer Technologies Inc		B	714 871-7357	0
Air Treatment Corporation (PA)		D	909 869-7975	0
Albertsons LLC		A	714 990-8200	0
Allan Automatic Sprinkler Corp.		D	714 993-9500	0
Alta Resources Corp		D	800 424-9378	0
American Financial Network Inc (PA)		C	909 606-3905	0
American Sanitary Supply Inc		E	714 632-3010	0
Americold Logistics LLC		A	714 993-3533	0
Anatec International Inc (HQ)		D	949 498-3350	0
Apollo Electric		D	714 256-8414	0
Bank America National Assn		D	949 414-8451	0
Beazer Homes Holdings Corp		D	714 285-2900	0
Bergman Kprs LLC (PA)		C	714 924-7000	0
Blaine Convention Services Inc.		A	714 522-8270	0

Employment Codes: A=Over 500 employees, B=251-500,
C=101-250, D=51-100, E=50

2020 Directory of California
Wholesalers and Services Companies

© Mergent Inc. 1-800-342-5647

1511

GEOGRAPHIC

	SIC	EMP	PHONE	ENTRY #
Brookdale Brea		E	714 706-9968	0
Burns & McDonnell Inc		D	714 256-1595	0
California Automobile Insur Co (HQ)		A	714 232-8669	0
City of Brea		D	714 990-7650	0
Cmre Financial Services Inc		B	714 528-3200	0
CNA Financial Corporation		C	714 255-2200	0
Contact Security Inc		C	714 572-6760	0
Contract Services Group Inc		C	714 582-1800	0
Cosco Fire Protection Inc		C	714 989-1800	0
Diversfied Cmmnctions Svcs Inc		D	562 696-9660	0
Document Proc Solutions Inc (PA)		D	714 482-2060	0
Emergency Ambulance Service		D	714 990-1331	0
Evangelical Christian Cr Un		C	714 671-5700	0
Evangelical Christian Cr Un (PA)		D	714 671-5700	0
Evga Corporation (PA)		E	714 528-4500	0
Fit Electronics Inc (HQ)		C	714 988-9388	0
Glen Ivy Hot Springs		D	714 990-2090	0
Griffith Company (PA)		D	714 984-5500	0
Hon Hai Precision Indust Ltd		D	714 988-9388	0
International Code Council Inc		D	562 699-0541	0
Isys Solutions Inc		D	714 521-7656	0
Jdf Construction Inc		E	714 526-1120	0
Kaiser Foundation Hospitals		D	714 672-5100	0
Kindred Healthcare Oper Inc		D	714 529-6842	0
Kirkhill Aircraft Parts Co (PA)		C	323 216-9136	0
Kprs Construction Services Inc (PA)		D	714 672-0800	0
Leidos Inc		D	714 257-6400	0
Leidos Engineering LLC		D	714 257-6400	0
Louis Wurth and Company (DH)		D	714 529-1771	0
Mddr Inc		C	714 792-1993	0
Mercury Casualty Company (HQ)		A	323 937-1060	0
Mercury Insurance Company		D	714 671-6700	0
Mercury Insurance Company		D	714 255-5000	0
Merrill Lynch Pierce Fenner		D	714 257-4400	0
Monoprice Inc (HQ)		C	909 989-6887	0
Nevell Group Inc (PA)		D	714 579-7501	0
New Dream Network LLC (PA)		D	626 644-9466	0
New York Life Insurance Co		D	714 255-5100	0
Norcal Inc		C	714 224-3949	0
Norcal Inc		C	714 224-3949	0
Northstar Dem & Remediation LP (DH)		C	714 672-3500	0
Orora Packaging Solutions		D	714 984-2300	0
Otb Acquisition LLC		C	520 458-0540	0
P B C Pavers Inc		D	714 278-0488	0
Pacific Western Sales (PA)		D	714 572-6730	0
Park Hotels & Resorts Inc		D	714 990-6000	0
Peterson Bros Contruction Inc		A	714 278-0488	0
Plannet Consulting LLC		D	714 982-5800	0
Premier Medical Transport Inc		D	888 353-9556	0
Priority Building Services LLC (PA)		D	714 255-2940	0
Questus Inc (PA)		E	415 677-5719	0
Radiometer America Inc (HQ)		C	800 736-0600	0
Renal Treatment Ctrs - Cal Inc		D	714 990-0110	0
Sears Roebuck and Co		D	714 256-7328	0
Solugenix Corporation (PA)		E	866 749-7658	0
Specialty Risk Services Inc		D	714 674-1000	0
Sully-Miller Contracting Co (DH)		C	714 578-9600	0
Systems and Software Entps LLC (HQ)		D	714 854-8600	0
Team Finish Inc		D	714 671-9190	0
Tiger Electric Inc (PA)		D	714 529-8061	0
Travel Store		D	714 529-1947	0
Tri-Tech Logistics LLC		C	855 373-7049	0
United Rock Products Corp		D	714 578-9600	0
V A Anderson Enterprises Inc (PA)		D	714 990-6100	0
Viewsonic Corporation (PA)		C	909 444-8888	0
Walters Wholesale Electric Co		D	714 784-1900	0
West Coast Prime Meats LLC		C	714 255-8560	0
Windsor Capital Group Inc		D	714 990-6000	0
Xdimensional Technologies Inc		D	714 672-8960	0

BRENTWOOD, CA - Contra Costa County

	SIC	EMP	PHONE	ENTRY #
Avalon Staffing LLC		D	925 626-7138	0
Banyan Solutions Inc		D	650 766-9338	0
Bay Standard Inc		D	925 634-1181	0
Cellco Partnership		C	925 626-3480	0
Ellison Framing Inc		C	925 516-9269	0
Groundworks Inc		D	925 513-0300	0
Hot Line Construction Inc		B	925 634-9333	0
New York Life Insurance Co		D	925 809-7020	0
Nines Restaurant		D	925 516-3413	0
Pacific Communications Assoc.		E	925 634-1203	0
Premier Floor Care Inc (PA)		C	925 679-4901	0
Robert Cecchini Inc		D	925 634-4400	0
Rodda Electric Inc (PA)		D	925 240-6024	0
T&C Roofing Inc		D	925 513-8463	0
Thorpe Design Inc		D	925 634-0787	0

	SIC	EMP	PHONE	ENTRY #
V Development Inc		D	925 634-8890	0

BRISBANE, CA - San Mateo County

	SIC	EMP	PHONE	ENTRY #
Bi-Rite Restaurant Sup Co Inc		B	415 656-0187	0
Caredx Inc (PA)		C	415 287-2300	0
Childcare Careers LLC		A	650 372-0211	0
Covenant Aviation Security LLC		A	650 219-3473	0
Dhl Supply Chain (usa)		C	415 531-0596	0
Edward B Ward & Company Inc (DH)		E	415 330-6600	0
Expeditors Intl Wash Inc		E	415 657-3600	0
F W Spencer & Son Inc		C	415 468-5000	0
Fedex Corporation		E	415 657-0403	0
Frito-Lay North America Inc		D	415 467-1860	0
Johnson Cntrls SEC Sltions LLC		D	650 634-9000	0
Kinder Mrgan Lqds Trminals LLC		D	415 467-8107	0
Ktsf Channel 26		E	415 467-6397	0
Kuehne + Nagel Inc		E	415 656-4100	0
Lincoln Television Inc		D	415 468-2626	0
Michaael S Hensley		C	650 692-7007	0
Netease Information Tech Corp		D	415 612-7866	0
Norman S Wright Mech Eqp Corp (PA)		D	415 467-7600	0
Nsw Real Estate Holdings LLC		D	415 467-7600	0
Oakville Produce Partners LLC		C	415 647-2991	0
Pitney Bowes Presort Svcs Inc		D	415 468-1660	0
Progressive Corporation		D	440 461-5000	0
Sage Hospitality Resources LLC		D	650 589-1600	0
Unity Biotechnology Inc		C	650 416-1192	0
Vox Network Solutions Inc		C	650 989-1000	0
Xojet Inc (PA)		D	650 594-6300	0

BROOKS, CA - Yolo County

	SIC	EMP	PHONE	ENTRY #
Cache Creek Casino Resort		A	530 796-3118	0

BROWNSVILLE, CA - Yuba County

	SIC	EMP	PHONE	ENTRY #
Sutter North Med Foundation		D	530 675-1245	0

BUELLTON, CA - Santa Barbara County

	SIC	EMP	PHONE	ENTRY #
American Medical Response Inc		C	805 688-6550	0
Kang Family Partners LLC		C	805 688-1000	0

BUENA PARK, CA - Orange County

	SIC	EMP	PHONE	ENTRY #
A J Parent Company Inc (PA)		D	714 521-1100	0
AAA Network Solutions Inc		D	714 484-2711	0
Access Business Group Intl LLC		C	800 879-2732	0
Amada America Inc (HQ)		D	714 739-2111	0
Amada Capital Corporation		D	714 739-2111	0
American Wht Mssn In Sthrn		D	714 522-4599	0
AT&T Services Inc		D	714 992-3359	0
AT&T Services Inc		C	510 732-0830	0
Automatic Data Processing Inc		C	714 690-7000	0
Beach and La Mirada Car Wash		E	714 994-1099	0
Bitech-Ace A Joint Venture		D	714 521-1477	0
Buena Park Medical Group Inc (PA)		D	714 994-5290	0
Buena Park Police Association		D	714 562-3901	0
Cal Fresco LLC		C	714 690-7700	0
Cambium Business Group Inc (PA)		C	714 670-1171	0
Center of Rehabilitation		C	714 826-2330	0
Communications Supply Corp		D	714 670-7711	0
Continental Exch Solutions Inc		D	562 345-2100	0
Continental Exch Solutions Inc (HQ)		C	714 522-7044	0
ECB Corp (PA)		C	714 385-8900	0
Edco Disposal Corporation Inc		D	714 522-3577	0
Fibertron Corporation		D	714 670-7711	0
Fueling and Service Tech Inc		D	714 523-0194	0
Golden Hotel LLC		D	714 739-5600	0
Hochiki America Corporation		C	714 522-2246	0
Houdini Inc		C	714 228-4406	0
Islamic Relief USA		D	714 676-1300	0
Knotts Berry Farm LLC		C	714 995-1111	0
Korean Community Services Inc		E	714 527-6561	0
Krikorian Premiere Theatre LLC		C	626 305-7469	0
Matesta Corporation		D	949 874-6052	0
Noritsu America Corporation (HQ)		C	714 521-9040	0
Onesource Distributors LLC		D	714 685-5378	0
Openpopcom Inc (PA)		D	714 249-7044	0
Orora North America		D	714 562-6002	0
Orora Packaging Solutions (HQ)		D	714 562-6000	0
Pacific Chemical Dist Corp (HQ)		D	714 521-7161	0
Park Hotels & Resorts Inc		D	714 739-5600	0
Partners Information Tech Inc (HQ)		D	714 736-4487	0
Primary Freight Services Inc (PA)		D	310 635-3000	0
Royal Crest Building Maint		E	714 562-5034	0
States Logistics Services Inc		D	714 523-1276	0
States Logistics Services Inc		D	714 523-1276	0
States Logistics Services Inc (PA)		C	714 521-6520	0
Sun West Mortgage Company Inc (PA)		D	800 453-7884	0
Tawa Services Inc (PA)		B	714 521-8899	0

Mergent email: customerrelations@mergent.com
1512

2020 Directory of California
Wholesalers and Services Companies

(P-0000) Products & Services Section entry number
(PA)=Parent Co (HQ)=Headquarters (DH)=Div Headquarters

	SIC	EMP	PHONE	ENTRY #
Team Spirit Realty Inc		E	714 562-0404	0
Tech Systems Inc		C	714 523-5404	0
Ted Ford Jones Inc (PA)		C	714 521-3110	0
Uniwell Corporation		C	714 522-7000	0
VWR International LLC		E	714 220-2615	0
Walong Marketing Inc (PA)		D	714 670-8899	0
Wayne Perry Inc (PA)		C	714 826-0352	0
West Coast Sand and Gravel Inc (PA)		D	714 522-0282	0
Yamaha Corporation of America (HQ)		B	714 522-9011	0

BURBANK, CA - Los Angeles County

	SIC	EMP	PHONE	ENTRY #
24 Hour Fitness Usa Inc		E	818 531-0257	0
A Its Laugh Productions Inc		D	818 848-8787	0
A-1 Hospice Care Inc		D	818 237-2700	0
ABC Cable Networks Group		C	818 560-4365	0
ABC Cable Networks Group (DH)		C	818 460-7477	0
ABC Family Worldwide Inc (DH)		B	818 560-1000	0
ABC Signature Studios Inc		D	818 569-7500	0
Access Hollywood		C	818 840-4444	0
Ace Industrial Supply Inc (PA)		D	818 252-1981	0
ACT Lighting Inc		A	818 707-0884	0
Adcom Interactive Media Inc		D	800 296-7104	0
Allianz Globl Risks US Insur (DH)		D	818 260-7500	0
Allianz Underwriters Insur Co		D	818 260-7500	0
Amberfin Limited		E	818 768-8948	0
American Multi-Cinema Inc		D	818 953-4020	0
and Syndicated Productions Inc		D	818 308-5200	0
Andrews International Inc		C	818 260-9586	0
Andrews International Inc (PA)		A	818 487-4060	0
Ane Productions Inc		D	818 972-0777	0
Angeles Los Equestrian Center		C	818 840-9063	0
Aramark Unf & Career AP LLC		D	818 973-3700	0
Aramark Unf & Career AP LLC (DH)		C	818 973-3700	0
Ardwin Inc		C	818 767-7777	0
Artesia Healthcare Inc		D	818 843-1771	0
Atlas Digital LLC (PA)		D	323 762-2626	0
Avis Rent A Car System Inc		D	818 566-3001	0
AWH Burbank Hotel LLC		C	813 843-6000	0
Belmont Village LP		D	818 972-2405	0
Blufocus Inc		D	818 294-7695	0
Bonanza Productions Inc		A	818 954-4212	0
Borrmann Metal Center (PA)		D	818 846-7171	0
Boulevard Entertainment Inc		C	818 840-6969	0
Bryant Ranch Prepack		E	818 764-7225	0
Buena Vista International Inc (DH)		E	818 560-1000	0
Buena Vista Television (DH)		D	818 560-1878	0
Burbank Dental Laboratory Inc		C	818 841-2256	0
Burbank Television Entps LLC		C	818 954-6000	0
Bvs Entertainment Inc (DH)		E	818 460-6917	0
C D Payroll Inc		D	818 848-1562	0
Callan Management Corporation		B	818 846-2215	0
Cast & Crew Payroll LLC (PA)		D	818 848-6022	0
CBS Interactive Inc		C	415 344-1813	0
Cellco Partnership		D	818 842-2722	0
Chase Credit Systems Inc		D	818 762-6262	0
Check Disc Labs		D	818 847-2255	0
Cheque Guard Inc		D	818 563-9335	0
CIT Bank NA		D	818 525-3760	0
Citizens Business Bank		D	818 843-0707	0
City of Burbank		B	818 238-3550	0
Clp Resources Inc		D	818 260-9190	0
Cmp Film & Design Burbank LLC		D	818 729-0800	0
Come Land Maint Svc Co Inc		A	818 567-2455	0
Commodity Resource Envmtl Inc (PA)		D	818 843-2811	0
Consolidated Elec Distrs Inc		D	626 345-0000	0
County of Los Angeles		C	818 557-4164	0
Crime Finders Inc		D	877 999-3203	0
Crossroads Live Inc		D	818 247-0400	0
Cw Network LLC (PA)		D	818 977-2500	0
Deluxe Entrmt Svcs Group Inc (PA)		D	818 565-3600	0
Deluxe Laboratories Inc (DH)		A	323 462-6171	0
Deluxe Media Services		B	818 526-3700	0
Disney Enterprises Inc (DH)		C	818 560-1000	0
Disney Enterprises Inc		B	818 560-3692	0
Disney Incorporated (DH)		C	818 560-1000	0
Disney Interactive Studios Inc		C	818 553-5000	0
Disney Interfinance Corp		B	818 560-1000	0
Disney Regional Entrmt Inc (DH)		C	818 560-1000	0
Edgewise Media Services Inc (PA)		D	714 919-2020	0
Electrosonic Inc (DH)		C	818 333-3600	0
Emerson Elementary		D	818 558-5419	0
Emmis Communications Corp		C	818 238-6705	0
Enbio Corp		C	818 953-9976	0
Entertainment Partners Inc (PA)		B	818 955-6000	0
Eon Innovative Technology Inc		C	213 381-0061	0
Esc Entertainment Inc		C	818 954-1018	0

	SIC	EMP	PHONE	ENTRY #
Estrella Communications Inc		D	818 260-5700	0
Facey Medical Foundation		C	818 861-7831	0
Fact Foundation		D	818 729-8105	0
Final Film		D	323 467-0700	0
Firemans Fund Insurance Co		C	818 953-6533	0
Foto-Kem Industries Inc (PA)		B	818 846-3102	0
Foto-Kem Industries Inc		B	818 846-3102	0
Frasco (PA)		D	818 848-3888	0
Front Porch Communities & Svcs		D	818 729-8100	0
Gat - Arln Ground Support Inc		C	818 847-9127	0
Gentle Giant Studios Inc		D	818 504-3555	0
GL Nemirow Inc		D	818 562-9433	0
Global Entertainment Inds Inc		D	818 567-0000	0
Global Service Resources Inc		D	800 679-7658	0
Grc Electric Inc		D	818 242-9891	0
Guardsmark LLC		C	818 841-0288	0
Hertz Corporation		E	818 997-0414	0
Hertz Corporation		D	818 569-6900	0
Historic TW Inc		E	818 954-3096	0
Iheartcommunications Inc		D	818 846-0029	0
IKEA Purchasing Svcs US Inc		B	818 841-3500	0
Image IV Systems Inc (PA)		D	323 849-3049	0
Information Tech Partners Inc		D	800 789-7487	0
International Fmly Entrmt Inc (DH)		C	818 560-1000	0
J H Maddocks Photography		D	818 842-7150	0
Jake Hey Incorporated		C	323 856-5280	0
Jetblue Airways Corporation		D	718 286-7900	0
Jim & Doug Carters Automotive		E	818 842-5702	0
Johnson Cntrls SEC Sltions LLC		C	818 428-6669	0
JP Allen Inc		B	818 841-4770	0
JP Allen Extended Stay		E	818 841-4770	0
Kan-Di-Ki LLC (HQ)		C	818 549-1880	0
Kaza Azteca America Inc		C	818 241-5400	0
Kcetlink (PA)		C	714 241-4100	0
Kpwr Inc		D	818 953-4200	0
Lakeside Golf Club		D	818 984-0601	0
Lawyers Title Company (HQ)		E	818 767-0425	0
Lbi Media Inc		A	818 729-5316	0
Le Bleu Chateau Inc		E	818 843-3141	0
Le Crochet By Saro Inc (PA)		E	818 846-3314	0
Liberman Broadcasting Inc (PA)		D	818 729-5300	0
Liberman Broadcasting Inc		E	323 461-9300	0
Library Associates LLC		B	626 529-6786	0
Logix Federal Credit Union (PA)		C	888 718-5328	0
Loop Media Inc		D	650 704-7409	0
Los Angeles Equestrian Center		D	818 840-9063	0
Louie Almeida & Settler (PA)		D	818 461-9559	0
M-N-Z Janitorial Services Inc		C	323 851-4115	0
Mel Bernie and Company Inc (PA)		C	818 841-1928	0
Mel Bernie and Company Inc		C	818 841-1928	0
Mis Sciences Corp		C	818 847-0213	0
Modern Videofilm Inc (PA)		C	818 840-1700	0
NBC Universal Inc		C	818 260-5746	0
New Deal Studios Inc		D	310 578-9929	0
Nova Skilled Home Health Inc		C	323 658-6232	0
NW Entertainment Inc (PA)		C	818 295-5000	0
One K Studios LLC		E	818 531-3800	0
Outlook Amusements Inc		C	818 433-3800	0
P Murphy & Associates Inc		C	818 841-2002	0
Pacific Homes Foundation		D	818 729-8106	0
PHF II Burbank LLC		D	818 843-6000	0
Pixelogic Media Partners LLC		C	818 861-2001	0
Playboy Entrmt Group Inc (HQ)		C	323 276-4000	0
Point360		D	818 556-5700	0
Power 106 Radio		D	818 953-4200	0
Prdctions N Fremantle Amer Inc (DH)		D	818 748-1100	0
Producer -Writers Guild		D	818 846-1015	0
Providence Health & Services F		A	818 843-5111	0
Providence Health System		A	818 843-5111	0
Providence Health System		C	818 846-8141	0
Rgis LLC		C	248 651-2511	0
Roundabout Entertainment Inc		D	818 842-9300	0
Rudy Carrillo Drywall Inc		D	818 841-2011	0
Ryan Herco Products Corp (DH)		D	818 841-1141	0
Sag- Aftra Federal		D	818 562-3400	0
Sca Enterprises Inc (PA)		D	818 845-7621	0
Science of Skincare LLC		D	818 254-7961	0
Screen Actors Guild - American		C	818 954-9400	0
Secure Net Alliance		E	818 848-4900	0
Shadkor Inc		D	818 953-4627	0
Shamrock Plus Inc		E	818 845-4444	0
Shc Burbank II LLC		C	818 843-6000	0
Smart & Final Stores Inc		B	818 954-8631	0
Spire Concessions LLC		D	818 843-6000	0
Stereo D LLC		B	818 861-3100	0

GEOGRAPHIC

Employment Codes: A=Over 500 employees, B=251-500,
C=101-250, D=51-100, E=50

2020 Directory of California
Wholesalers and Services Companies

© Mergent Inc. 1-800-342-5647

1513

	SIC	EMP	PHONE	ENTRY #
Stumbaugh & Associates Inc **(PA)**		D	818 240-1627	0
Survival Insurance Inc		C	818 565-1584	0
Technicolor Inc		B	818 260-4577	0
Technicolor New Media Inc		E	818 480-5100	0
Technicolor Thomson Group		B	818 260-3600	0
Terminix Intl Co Ltd Partnr		E	818 972-2037	0
The Team Companies LLC **(PA)**		D	818 558-3261	0
Therapeutic Associates Inc		B	818 748-4900	0
Therapeutic Associates Inc		D	818 843-5111	0
Thyssenkrupp Elevator Corp		D	818 847-2568	0
Tidavater Inc		C	818 848-4151	0
Time Warner Cable Entps LLC		D	818 972-0808	0
Time Warner Cable Entps LLC		C	818 953-3283	0
Tivo Corporation		D	303 273-7800	0
Todda Merger Sub Inc		D	323 644-3720	0
Touchstone Television Prod LLC **(PA)**		E	323 671-5116	0
Tri-Tech Restoration Co Inc		D	818 565-3900	0
TTT West Coast Inc		C	818 972-0500	0
Turner Broadcasting System Inc		E	818 977-5452	0
Turner Techtronics Inc **(PA)**		C	818 973-1060	0
Turtle Entertainment America		E	818 861-7315	0
Twdc Enterprises 18 Corp		B	818 295-3134	0
Twdc Enterprises 18 Corp		D	818 560-1268	0
Twdc Enterprises 18 Corp		A	818 567-5590	0
Twdc Enterprises 18 Corp		C	818 553-7333	0
Twdc Enterprises 18 Corp		B	818 460-6655	0
Twdc Enterprises 18 Corp		A	818 560-1000	0
Twdc Enterprises 18 Corp **(HQ)**		A	818 560-1000	0
Twdc Enterprises 18 Corp		B	818 560-1000	0
Tylie Jones & Associates Inc **(PA)**		E	818 955-7600	0
Unx Inc A Delaware Corp		D	818 333-3300	0
Ver Sales Inc **(PA)**		B	818 567-3000	0
Vintage Senior Management Inc		A	818 954-9500	0
Wad Productions Inc		D	818 260-5673	0
Walt Disney Pictures and TV		D	818 560-1000	0
Walt Disney Records Direct **(DH)**		A	818 560-1000	0
Warner Bros Consumer Pdts Inc **(DH)**		C	818 954-7980	0
Warner Bros Distributing Inc		C	818 954-6000	0
Warner Bros Entertainment Inc		C	818 954-1817	0
Warner Bros Entertainment Inc		B	818 954-7232	0
Warner Bros Entertainment Inc		C	818 954-3000	0
Warner Bros Entertainment Inc		C	818 954-5301	0
Warner Bros Entertainment Inc		C	818 954-6000	0
Warner Bros Entertainment Inc **(DH)**		A	818 954-6000	0
Warner Bros Entertainment Inc		C	818 954-2181	0
Warner Bros Home Entrmt Inc **(DH)**		D	818 954-6000	0
Warner Bros Intl TV Dist Inc		D	818 954-6000	0
Warner Bros Transatlantic Inc **(DH)**		A	818 977-0018	0
Warner Bros Transatlantic Inc		A	818 977-6384	0
Warner Bros Transatlantic Inc		A	818 972-0777	0
Wdpt Film Distribution LLC		C	818 560-1000	0
Westwind Media Inc		D	818 972-9000	0
Westwind Studios LLC		E	818 972-9000	0
WF Cinema Holdings LP		A	818 784-6266	0
Wonderland Music Company Inc		D	818 840-1671	0
Xerox Corporation		D	818 848-8676	0
Young Mens Christian **(PA)**		C	818 845-8551	0

BURLINGAME, CA - San Mateo County

	SIC	EMP	PHONE	ENTRY #
24 Hour Fitness Usa Inc		E	650 343-7922	0
Abx Engineering Inc		D	650 552-2300	0
Acumen LLC		C	650 558-8882	0
Airline Coach Service Inc **(PA)**		D	650 697-7733	0
Alain Pinel Realtors Inc		D	650 375-1111	0
Allen Drywall & Associates		D	650 579-0664	0
Amato Industries Incorporated		D	650 697-5548	0
American Carequest Inc **(PA)**		D	415 885-3324	0
American Med		C	650 235-1333	0
American Medical Response		D	650 235-1333	0
AMS Relocation Incorporated		D	650 697-3530	0
AT&T Services Inc		C	650 579-5266	0
Burlingame Senior Care LLC		B	650 692-3758	0
California Teachers Assn **(PA)**		C	650 697-1400	0
Carr Mc Clellan Ingersoll Thom **(PA)**		D	650 342-9600	0
City of Burlingame		E	650 558-7670	0
Coldwell Bnkr Residential Brkg		D	650 558-4200	0
Comcast Corporation		D	650 689-5392	0
Crystal Springs Golf Partners		E	650 342-4188	0
Cushman & Wakefield Inc		E	650 347-3700	0
Disney Construction Inc		D	650 689-5149	0
Djont Operations LLC		D	650 342-4600	0
Environmental Chemical Corp **(PA)**		D	650 347-1555	0
Epitomics Inc **(HQ)**		D	650 583-6688	0
Gringteam Inc		D	650 344-5500	0
Guardsmark LLC		C	650 685-2400	0
Guardsmark LLC		C	650 652-9130	0

	SIC	EMP	PHONE	ENTRY #
Hamilton Partners		D	650 347-8800	0
Hanergy Holding America Inc		B	650 288-3722	0
Harbor View Hotels Inc		D	650 340-8500	0
Hcr Manorcare		D	419 252-5743	0
Host Hotels & Resorts LP		D	650 347-1234	0
Host Hotels & Resorts LP		D	650 692-9100	0
Iasco **(PA)**		B	707 252-3522	0
Jacobs Consultancy Inc		D	650 579-7722	0
Jbs International Inc		D	650 373-4900	0
Jeremiah Phillips LLC		C	650 697-7733	0
Kindred Healthcare Operating		B	650 697-1865	0
Kotobuki-Ya Inc		D	650 344-7955	0
Ksi Corp		D	650 952-0815	0
M H Podell Company **(PA)**		D	415 296-8800	0
Marriott International Inc		C	650 692-9100	0
Mid-Peninsula Roofing Inc		D	650 375-7850	0
Morgan Stanley & Co LLC		D	650 340-6550	0
OH My Green Inc		D	650 989-8181	0
Oritz Corporation **(PA)**		C	650 692-8000	0
Palcare Inc		E	650 340-1289	0
Park Hotels & Resorts Inc		C	650 342-4600	0
Partners Advctes For Rmrkble C		D	650 312-0730	0
Peninsula Womens Health **(PA)**		E	650 692-3818	0
Personal Protective Svcs Inc **(PA)**		D	650 344-3302	0
Prime Time Athletic Club Inc		D	650 204-3662	0
Pro Unlimited Inc		E	650 344-1099	0
Provident Mrtg Cpitl Assoc Inc		A	650 652-1300	0
Purcell-Murray Company Inc **(PA)**		D	415 468-6620	0
Randstad Professionals Us LLC		C	650 343-5111	0
Renesas Electronics Amer Inc		A	408 588-6750	0
Robert Meuschke Company Inc		D	650 342-3993	0
Safway Services LP		E	650 652-9255	0
Sage Software Inc		C	650 579-3628	0
San Mateo Healthcare & Wellnes		D	650 692-3758	0
Sky Chefs Inc		C	650 652-7886	0
Sphere Institute		C	650 558-3980	0
Stonesfair Financial Corp		D	650 347-0442	0
Stonesfair Management LLC **(PA)**		D	650 401-3810	0
Street and Sewer Yard Corp		E	650 696-7260	0
Sunkist Enterprises		D	650 347-3900	0
Synagro West LLC		D	650 652-6531	0
Tata Communications Amer Inc		D	650 262-0004	0
Transiris Corporation		D	650 303-3495	0
Trivad Inc		C	650 286-1086	0
Virgin America Inc **(HQ)**		C	877 359-8474	0
Walter E McGuire RE Inc		C	650 348-0222	0

BURNEY, CA - Shasta County

	SIC	EMP	PHONE	ENTRY #
Dicalite Minerals Corp **(HQ)**		D	530 335-5451	0
Hat Creek Cnstr & Mtls Inc **(PA)**		E	530 335-5501	0
Pit River Health Service Inc **(PA)**		D	530 335-3651	0
Pit River Tribal Council		D	530 335-3651	0
Pit River Tribal Council		D	530 335-2334	0

BUTTONWILLOW, CA - Kern County

	SIC	EMP	PHONE	ENTRY #
Choice Hotels Intl Inc		D	661 764-5207	0

BYRON, CA - Contra Costa County

	SIC	EMP	PHONE	ENTRY #
D & D Ready Mix Inc		D	209 627-7224	0
G3 Enterprises Inc		D	209 341-3441	0
New Discovery Inc		D	925 783-6613	0
New Discovery Inc		D	925 634-0505	0
Pacific Coast Ldscp MGT Inc		D	925 513-2310	0
San Luis Dlta-Mendota Wtr Auth		D	209 835-2593	0
Simoni & Massoni Farms		E	925 634-2304	0

CABAZON, CA - Riverside County

	SIC	EMP	PHONE	ENTRY #
Casino Morongo		D	951 849-3080	0
Matich Corporation		E	951 849-8280	0

CALABASAS, CA - Los Angeles County

	SIC	EMP	PHONE	ENTRY #
23627 Calabasas Road LLC		D	818 222-5300	0
Abbyson Living Corp		B	805 465-5500	0
Able Cable Inc **(PA)**		C	818 223-3600	0
AIA Holdings Inc **(PA)**		D	818 222-4999	0
All Motorists Insurance Agency		C	818 880-9070	0
Amawaterways LLC **(PA)**		C	800 626-0126	0
American Travel Solutions LLC		D	818 359-6514	0
Anchor Loans LP		C	310 395-0010	0
Arcs Commercial Mortgage Co LP **(DH)**		C	818 676-3274	0
Asgn Incorporated **(PA)**		C	818 878-7900	0
Atlas Database Software Corp **(PA)**		D	818 340-7080	0
Avanquest North America LLC **(HQ)**		D	818 591-9600	0
Boys and Girls Club		E	818 225-8406	0
Brightview Companies LLC **(DH)**		C	818 223-8500	0
Brightview Golf Maint Inc **(DH)**		D	818 223-8500	0
Brightview Landscape Dev Inc **(DH)**		E	818 223-8500	0

2020 Directory of California
Wholesalers and Services Companies

(P-0000) Products & Services Section entry number
(PA)=Parent Co (HQ)=Headquarters (DH)=Div Headquarters

	SIC	EMP	PHONE	ENTRY #
Calabasas Country Club		D	818 222-8111	0
Cartel Marketing Inc		C	818 483-1130	0
Center For Civic Education (PA)		D	818 591-9321	0
Coldwell Bnkr Residential Brkg		D	818 222-0023	0
Countrywide Capital Mkts LLC (DH)		C	818 225-3000	0
Countrywide Financial Corp (HQ)		A	818 225-3000	0
Countrywide Securities Corp		B	818 225-3000	0
Custom Tours Inc		D	310 274-8819	0
Danerica Enterprises		D	818 774-1813	0
David Shield Security Inc		D	310 849-4950	0
Davis Research LLC		C	818 591-2408	0
Dts Inc (HQ)		C	818 436-1000	0
Endocrine Sciences Inc		D	818 880-8040	0
Exterior Solutions Inc		D	310 400-3510	0
Galaxy Building Systems Inc		C	818 340-6557	0
Grant & Weber (PA)		D	818 878-7700	0
Hearthstone Inc		D	818 385-0005	0
Idrive Inc		C	818 594-5972	0
Informa Research Services Inc (HQ)		C	818 880-8877	0
Knight-Calabasas LLC (PA)		D	818 222-3200	0
Lantz Security Systems Inc		C	818 871-0193	0
Las Virgenes Municipal Wtr Dst		C	818 251-2100	0
Litigtion Rsrces of America-CA (PA)		D	818 878-9227	0
M S E Enterprises Inc (PA)		D	818 223-3500	0
Marcus & Millichap Inc (PA)		D	818 212-2250	0
Marcus & Millichap Capitl Corp		E	818 212-2250	0
Marcus Millichap Reis Nev Inc		D	650 494-1400	0
Marcus Mllchap RE Inv Svcs Inc (HQ)		E	818 212-2250	0
Monte Nido Holdings LLC		C	818 457-9958	0
Mrca Fire Division		E	818 880-4752	0
New View Landscape Inc		D	818 222-8972	0
Nowher Partners LLC		D	818 857-3366	0
Prolifics Inc (DH)		B	212 267-7722	0
Prolifics Testing Inc		D	925 485-9535	0
Quantum Solutions Inc		E	818 577-4555	0
Rainbow Camp Inc		E	310 456-3066	0
Red Peak Group LLC		D	818 222-7762	0
Rodeo Realty Inc		D	818 657-4609	0
Rpmc Inc (PA)		D	818 222-7762	0
Sedgwick Claims MGT Svcs Inc		C	818 591-9444	0
Small Business Advertising Inc		E	818 262-8923	0
T M Mian & Associates Inc		D	818 591-2300	0
Top Seed Tennis Academy Inc		D	818 222-2782	0
Unifax Insurance Systems Inc		D	818 591-9800	0
Valleycrest Ldscp Maint Vcc		E	800 466-8510	0
Western General Holding Co (PA)		D	818 880-9070	0
Western General Insurance Co		C	818 880-9070	0
Worxsitehr Insur Solutions Inc		D	877 479-3591	0

CALABASAS HILLS, CA - Los Angeles County

	SIC	EMP	PHONE	ENTRY #
Helmet House Inc (PA)		D	800 421-7247	0

CALEXICO, CA - Imperial County

	SIC	EMP	PHONE	ENTRY #
Adventures In Hospitality Inc		D	760 356-2806	0
ARC - Imperial Valley		D	760 768-1944	0
California Super Market		D	760 357-3065	0
Coppel Corporation		D	760 357-3707	0
Martech Medical Products Inc		D	215 256-8833	0
R L Jones-San Diego Inc (PA)		D	760 357-3177	0
R L Jones-San Diego Inc		D	760 357-0140	0
Sstmas Y Aranda Eqpos Hdrlicos		E	619 245-4502	0
Technicolor HM Entrmt Svcs Inc		B	760 357-3372	0
U S Xpress Inc		C	760 768-6707	0

CALIENTE, CA - Kern County

	SIC	EMP	PHONE	ENTRY #
James McCutcheon		E	661 867-1810	0

CALIFORNIA CITY, CA - Kern County

	SIC	EMP	PHONE	ENTRY #
Corecivic Inc		C	760 373-1764	0

CALIMESA, CA - Riverside County

	SIC	EMP	PHONE	ENTRY #
Tommy Gun Plastering Inc		D	909 795-9966	0

CALIPATRIA, CA - Imperial County

	SIC	EMP	PHONE	ENTRY #
Brandt Co Inc		D	760 348-2295	0
Calenergy LLC		B	402 231-1527	0
Superior Cattle Feeders LLC (PA)		D	760 348-2218	0

CALISTOGA, CA - Napa County

	SIC	EMP	PHONE	ENTRY #
Calistoga Spa Inc		D	707 942-6269	0
Mv Hospitality Inc		E	707 942-6877	0
Schramsberg Vineyards Company		D	707 942-4558	0
Spa Partners Inc		E	707 942-5789	0

CALPELLA, CA - Mendocino County

	SIC	EMP	PHONE	ENTRY #
Mendocino Forest Pdts Co LLC		D	707 485-6800	0
Mendocino Forest Pdts Co LLC		D	707 620-2961	0

CAMARILLO, CA - Ventura County

	SIC	EMP	PHONE	ENTRY #
Aecom C&E Inc		D	805 388-3775	0
Affiliated Communications Inc		E	805 650-4949	0
Airport Connection Inc		C	805 389-8196	0
All Control Cleaning Inc		D	805 987-4210	0
American Airlines Inc		D	805 988-0407	0
Applied Engineering MGT Corp		C	805 484-1909	0
Arconix/Usa Inc		D	805 388-2525	0
AT&T Corp		D	805 445-6562	0
Atria Senior Living Inc		D	805 482-9771	0
Automatic Data Processing Inc		C	805 383-8630	0
Boskovich Farms Inc		B	805 987-1443	0
C & C Boats Inc		E	805 445-9456	0
Camarillo Healthcare Center		C	805 482-9805	0
Camarillo Ranch Foundation		D	805 389-8182	0
Casa Pacifica Centers (PA)		C	805 482-3260	0
Central Courier LLC		D	805 654-1045	0
Central Purchasing LLC (PA)		B	800 444-3353	0
Channel Islands Young Mens Ch		D	805 484-0423	0
CIT Bank NA		D	805 465-1053	0
Coastal Grading and Excavating		E	805 445-6433	0
County of Ventura		B	805 654-5529	0
Data Exchange Corporation (PA)		B	805 388-1711	0
DB Roberts Inc		D	805 988-4882	0
Delicate Productions Inc (PA)		D	415 484-1174	0
Dex Corporation		C	805 388-1711	0
Dial Security (PA)		C	805 389-6700	0
Dignity Health		B	805 384-8071	0
Dignity Health		C	805 389-5800	0
DP Technology Corp (PA)		D	805 388-6000	0
Eurasia Power LLC		E	805 383-1234	0
Golden State Medical Sup Inc		C	805 477-9866	0
Golden State Medical Supply		D	805 477-8966	0
Holthouse Carlin Van Trigt LLP		D	805 374-8555	0
Institute For Applied Behavior		C	805 987-5886	0
Interface Community (PA)		D	805 485-6114	0
Jpmorgan Chase Bank Nat Assn		C	805 482-2902	0
Juvenile Justice Division Cal		B	805 485-7951	0
Kaiser Foundation Hospitals		A	888 515-3500	0
Las Posas Club Inc		D	805 482-1811	0
Las Posas Country Club		D	805 482-4518	0
Leisure Village Association		D	805 484-2861	0
Logix Development Corporation		D	888 505-6449	0
Market Scan Info Systems Inc (PA)		C	805 823-4258	0
Meathead Movers Inc		D	805 437-5100	0
Michael Baker Jr Inc		D	805 383-3373	0
Nallatech Inc		D	805 383-8997	0
Northrop Grumman Systems Corp		D	805 987-9739	0
Oasis Technology Inc		D	805 445-4833	0
Odu-Usa Inc (HQ)		D	805 484-0540	0
Omniupdate Inc		D	805 484-9400	0
Pacific Earth Resources (PA)		D	805 986-8277	0
People Creating Success Inc		C	805 644-9480	0
Research Management Cons Inc (PA)		D	805 987-5538	0
Rincon Pacific LLC		D	805 986-8806	0
Saalex Corp (PA)		C	805 482-1070	0
Salem Media Group Inc (PA)		D	805 987-0400	0
Solimar Farms Inc		E	805 986-8806	0
Spanish Hills Country Club (PA)		C	805 389-1644	0
Sunrise Senior Living LLC		D	805 388-8086	0
Technclor Vdocassette Mich Inc (DH)		B	805 445-1122	0
Technicolor Inc (DH)		D	805 445-1122	0
Technicolor HM Entrmt Svcs Inc (HQ)		B	805 445-1122	0
Technicolor Thomson Group		A	805 445-1122	0
Telecare Corporation		D	805 383-3669	0
Telecare Las Posadas		D	805 383-3669	0
Teledyne Scientific Imaging LLC		C	805 373-4979	0
Tommy Bahama Group Inc		C	805 482-8868	0
Trademark Concrete Systems (PA)		E	714 970-8200	0
Uribe Trucking Inc		C	805 483-1125	0
Ventura County Fire Department		E	805 389-9710	0
Vitas Healthcare Corporation		D	805 437-2100	0
Wilshire Health and Cmnty Svcs		D	805 484-2777	0

CAMBRIA, CA - San Luis Obispo County

	SIC	EMP	PHONE	ENTRY #
Moonstone Management Corp (PA)		C	805 927-4200	0
Pacific Cambria Inc		D	805 927-6114	0

CAMERON PARK, CA - El Dorado County

	SIC	EMP	PHONE	ENTRY #
Americas Flood Services Inc		D	916 636-9460	0
Cameron Park Country Club Inc		D	530 672-9840	0
Hemington Landscape Svcs Inc		D	530 677-9290	0
McClone Construction Company		C	559 431-9411	0

CAMINO, CA - El Dorado County

	SIC	EMP	PHONE	ENTRY #
McMillen Jacobs Associates Inc		D	530 497-5407	0

GEOGRAPHIC

Employment Codes: A=Over 500 employees, B=251-500,
C=101-250, D=51-100, E=50

2020 Directory of California
Wholesalers and Services Companies

© Mergent Inc. 1-800-342-5647

1515

	SIC	EMP	PHONE	ENTRY #

CAMP PENDLETON, CA - San Diego County

	SIC	EMP	PHONE	ENTRY #
Lion-Vallen Ltd Partnership		E	760 385-4885	0
Marine Corps United States		E	760 430-4709	0

CAMPBELL, CA - Santa Clara County

	SIC	EMP	PHONE	ENTRY #
Adorno Construction Inc		D	408 369-8675	0
Aicent Inc		C	408 324-1316	0
B C C S Inc (PA)		D	408 379-5500	0
Barracuda Networks Inc (HQ)		C	408 342-5400	0
Bio-Reference Laboratories Inc		C	408 341-8600	0
Bitglass Inc (PA)		D	408 337-0190	0
Calibuilder Construction Inc		E	408 832-2337	0
Campbell Hhg Hotel Dev LLP		D	408 626-9590	0
Cape Clear Software Inc		D	408 879-7365	0
Cem Builders Inc		E	408 395-1490	0
Century 21 Alpha LLC		D	408 369-2000	0
Charles Culberson Inc		C	650 335-4730	0
Classic Car Wash Inc (PA)		C	408 371-2414	0
Comglobal Systems Inc (DH)		D	619 321-6000	0
Daleys Drywall and Taping Inc		A	408 378-9500	0
Dentistat Inc		C	408 376-0336	0
Douglas Ross Construction Inc		D	408 429-7700	0
Duran Human Capital Partners		E	408 540-0070	0
Durham School Services L P		C	408 377-6655	0
Farmers Group Inc		E	408 557-1100	0
Fernandes & Sons Gen Contrs		D	408 626-9090	0
Fierce Wombat Games Inc		E	408 745-5400	0
Groupware Technology Inc (PA)		E	408 540-0090	0
Kaiser Foundation Hospitals		D	408 871-6500	0
Largo Concrete Inc		A	408 874-2500	0
LLP Moss Adams		C	408 369-2400	0
Martina Landscape Inc		D	408 871-8800	0
Masudas Landscape Services		D	408 379-7100	0
Maxonic Inc		D	408 739-4900	0
Merrill Gardens LLC		D	408 370-6431	0
Mission Vlla Alzhmers Rsidence		E	408 559-8301	0
Netnow		B	408 370-0425	0
Netpolarity Inc		B	408 971-1100	0
Odyssey Healthcare Inc		D	408 626-4868	0
On-Site Manager Inc (HQ)		E	866 266-7483	0
Online Technical Services Inc (PA)		E	408 378-1100	0
OSI Engineering Inc		C	408 550-2800	0
Panzura Inc		D	408 457-8504	0
Perspecta Engineering Inc		D	408 961-3250	0
Saama Technologies Inc (PA)		C	408 371-1900	0
Sandis Civil Engineers (PA)		D	408 636-0900	0
Senior Living Solutions LLC		C	408 385-1835	0
Silver Creek Home Owners		E	408 559-1977	0
Skyhigh Networks Inc (DH)		D	408 564-0278	0
SR Freeman Inc		D	408 364-2200	0
Streamray Inc		B	408 745-5449	0
Subacute Chld Hosp Cal Inc		D	408 558-3644	0
Telecmmnctons MGT Slutions Inc		D	408 866-5495	0
TownePlace Suites		D	408 370-4510	0
Uplift Family Services (PA)		E	408 379-3790	0
Wells Fargo Bank National Assn		E	408 378-8155	0
West Valley Cnstr Co Inc (PA)		C	408 371-5510	0

CAMPO, CA - San Diego County

	SIC	EMP	PHONE	ENTRY #
Campo Band Missions Indians		B	619 938-6000	0

CANOGA PARK, CA - Los Angeles County

	SIC	EMP	PHONE	ENTRY #
24 Hour Fitness Usa Inc		D	818 887-2582	0
24-7 Caregivers Registry Inc		C	800 687-8066	0
A Yafa Pen Company		E	818 704-8888	0
Aegis Treatment Centers LLC (PA)		D	818 206-0360	0
American Landscape		C	818 999-2041	0
American Landscape Management (PA)		B	818 999-2041	0
Apn Business Resources Inc		C	818 717-9980	0
Azimc Investments Inc		C	818 678-1200	0
Bay Clubs Inc		D	818 884-5034	0
Bubbla Inc		B	818 884-2000	0
Buyers Consultation Svc Inc (PA)		D	818 341-4820	0
Canoga Park Fitness LLC		E	818 884-5034	0
Canoga Park Worksource Center		E	818 596-4448	0
Catholic Charities of La Inc		C	818 883-6015	0
Cixta Enterprises Inc		C	818 346-1665	0
Computrition Inc (HQ)		D	818 961-3999	0
Golden State West Valley		C	818 348-8422	0
Green Thumb International Inc		C	818 340-6400	0
Heritage Landscape Inc		C	818 999-2041	0
Hmi Associates Inc		C	818 887-6800	0
Jones & Jones MGT Group Inc		C	818 594-0019	0
Landcare USA LLC		C	818 346-7552	0
Mailmark Enterprises LLC		E	818 407-0660	0
Mark Land Electric Inc		D	818 883-5110	0

	SIC	EMP	PHONE	ENTRY #
New Start Home Health Care Inc		C	818 665-7898	0
Northeast Valley Health Corp		D	818 340-3570	0
NRG Clean Power Inc		E	818 444-2020	0
One Call Medical Inc		D	818 346-8700	0
Richard Huetter Inc		D	818 700-8001	0
Right Choice In-Home Care Inc		A	818 836-6001	0
Rte Enterprises Inc		D	818 999-5300	0
Shield Security Inc		C	818 239-5800	0
Software Dynamics Incorporated		C	818 992-3299	0
Southern California Mtl Hdlg		D	818 349-1220	0
Super Garden Centers Inc		E	818 348-9266	0
T & T Solutions Inc		D	818 676-1786	0
West Valley Jewish Cmnty Ctr		D	818 348-0048	0
Westwood Insurance Agency (DH)		D	818 990-9715	0

CANYON COUNTRY, CA - Los Angeles County

	SIC	EMP	PHONE	ENTRY #
County of Los Angeles		D	661 298-3406	0
Design Masonry Inc		D	661 252-2784	0
Jencor Door and Trim Inc		E	661 251-8161	0

CANYON LAKE, CA - Riverside County

	SIC	EMP	PHONE	ENTRY #
A Caregiver LLC		E	951 676-4190	0
Canyon Lk Property Owners Assn		D	951 244-6841	0
Cbabr Inc (PA)		D	951 640-7056	0
Chan Family Partnership LP		D	626 322-7132	0
My Choice Inhome Care LLC		D	951 244-8770	0

CAPISTRANO BEACH, CA - Orange County

	SIC	EMP	PHONE	ENTRY #
Capistrano Beach Extended		D	949 496-5786	0
Golden Living LLC		D	949 496-5786	0
National Rtrement Partners Inc (PA)		D	949 488-8726	0
Soto Company Inc		D	949 493-9403	0

CAPITOLA, CA - Santa Cruz County

	SIC	EMP	PHONE	ENTRY #
AT&T Corp		D	831 465-6771	0
Bay Federal Credit Union (PA)		C	831 479-6000	0
CA Ste Atom Assoc Intr-Ins Bur		D	831 824-9128	0
Coldwell Bnkr Residential Brkg		D	831 462-9000	0
Covenant Care LLC		C	831 476-0770	0
Housing Athrty of The Cnty of		D	831 454-9455	0
Profile of Santa Cruz		D	831 479-0393	0

CARDIFF, CA - San Diego County

	SIC	EMP	PHONE	ENTRY #
2807 Dev LLC		D	510 319-7820	0

CARLSBAD, CA - San Diego County

	SIC	EMP	PHONE	ENTRY #
24 Hour Fitness Usa Inc		D	760 918-4790	0
24 Hour Fitness Usa Inc		D	760 602-5001	0
4g Wireless Inc		D	760 828-2543	0
Abtech Technologies Inc		D	760 827-5100	0
Active Motif Inc (PA)		D	760 431-1263	0
Adicio Inc		D	760 602-9502	0
Advanced Commercial Corporatio		C	760 431-8500	0
Alogent Holdings Inc		D	760 410-9000	0
Arnel Development Company			760 599-6111	0
Aviara Fsrc Associates Limited		A	760 603-6800	0
Aviara Resort Associates (HQ)		D	760 448-1234	0
Bergelectric Corp (PA)		C	760 638-2374	0
Bomel Construction Co Inc		C	760 431-6360	0
Brehm Communities (PA)		D	760 448-2420	0
Brehm Communities (PA)		D	760 448-2420	0
Brightview Landscapes LLC		D	760 438-3551	0
Buffini & Company (PA)		C	760 827-2100	0
Business Intelligence		E	858 452-8200	0
Buzztime Inc		C	760 476-1976	0
By Referral Only Inc		D	760 707-1300	0
Calatlantic Group Inc		C	760 602-6824	0
Calatlantic Group Inc		D	760 931-4414	0
California Bistro At Fo		D	760 603-3700	0
Callaway Golf Ball Oprtons Inc (HQ)		A	760 931-1771	0
Canon Solutions America Inc		D	760 438-6990	0
Carlsbad Firefighters Assn		D	760 729-3730	0
Carlsbad Inn Vactn Condo Ownrs		D	760 434-7542	0
Carlsbad Municipal Water Dst		E	760 438-2722	0
Carlsbad Surgery Center LLC		E	760 448-2488	0
Carollo Engineers Inc		C	858 505-1020	0
CAV Inc		D	760 729-5199	0
CDM SMITH INC		D	760 438-7755	0
Cellco Partnership		D	760 720-8400	0
Cellmatics		E	760 602-4423	0
Chopra Cntre For Wll-Being LLC		D	760 494-1600	0
Cierra Wireless		C	760 476-8700	0
Clark Richardson and Biskup		D	760 496-3714	0
Coast Environmental Inc		D	760 929-9570	0
Coast Waste Management		C	760 753-9412	0
Cofa Media Group LLC		D	877 293-2007	0
Colorescience Inc		C	866 426-5673	0

Mergent email: customerrelations@mergent.com

1516

2020 Directory of California
Wholesalers and Services Companies

(P-0000) Products & Services Section entry number
(PA)=Parent Co (HQ)=Headquarters (DH)=Div Headquarters

	SIC	EMP	PHONE	ENTRY #
Community Interface Services		D	760 729-3866	0
Continuing Lf Communities LLC (PA)		D	760 704-6400	0
Corporate Visions Inc		D	760 458-0914	0
Deepak Chopra LLC		E	760 494-1600	0
Demaria Landtech		E	858 481-5500	0
Dennis Group Inc		D	858 847-9633	0
Electronic Entrmt Design & RES		D	760 579-7100	0
Ems Construction Inc		D	858 679-8292	0
Encina Wastewater Authority		D	760 438-3941	0
Enviance Inc (HQ)		D	760 496-0200	0
Fashioncraft Floors Inc (PA)		E	714 255-8400	0
Federal Express Corporation		C	800 463-3339	0
Ferguson Salon Management		E	760 434-4141	0
Ferguson Salon Management Inc		E	760 434-5008	0
First Community Bancorp		D	858 756-3023	0
Fmt Consultants LLC (PA)		D	844 369-4593	0
Four Seasons Resort Aviara		D	760 603-6900	0
Franconnect LLC		C	760 720-5354	0
Front Porch Communities		C	760 729-4983	0
Genoptix (PA)		C	760 268-6200	0
Genoptix Inc		B	760 268-6200	0
Glenview Assisted Living LLP		E	760 704-6800	0
Global Domains International		E	760 602-3000	0
Grand Pacific Carlsbad Ht LP		B	760 827-2400	0
Grand Pacific Resorts Inc		C	760 431-8500	0
Grand Pacific Resorts Inc (PA)		C	760 431-8500	0
Grand Pacific Resorts Svcs LP		C	760 431-8500	0
H M Electronics Inc (PA)		B	858 535-6000	0
Havas Edge LLC (PA)		D	760 929-0041	0
Hay House Inc (PA)		D	760 431-7695	0
Hilton Garden Inns MGT LLC		C	760 476-0800	0
Hit Portfolio II NTC Trs LP		D	760 431-9399	0
Hyatt Coporation As Agent of B		E	760 603-6851	0
Ibis Biosciences Inc		C	760 476-3200	0
Integral Senior Living LLC (PA)		C	760 547-2863	0
Interior Specialists Inc (HQ)		D	760 929-6700	0
Interstate Hotels Resorts Inc		D	760 476-0800	0
Intravas Inc		D	760 650-4040	0
Ipitek Inc		D	760 438-1010	0
Jazzercise Inc (PA)		D	760 476-1750	0
Jefferson California Congress		D	760 331-5500	0
Jenny Craig Inc (PA)		C	760 696-4000	0
Jenny Craig Wght Loss Ctrs Inc (HQ)		C	760 696-4000	0
Jet Source Inc		D	760 438-0877	0
Kaiser Foundation Hospitals		C	760 931-4228	0
Kendal Floral Supply LLC (PA)		D	760 431-4910	0
La Costa Limousine (PA)		D	760 438-4455	0
Lassens Ali Leads Club (PA)		D	760 434-3761	0
Lawinfocom Inc		D	800 397-3743	0
Lc Trs Inc		A	760 438-9111	0
Legend Films		B	858 793-4420	0
Legoland California LLC		B	760 918-5346	0
Lg Display America Inc		E	760 692-0900	0
Mardx Diagnostics Inc		D	760 929-0500	0
Marriott International Inc		D	760 431-9399	0
Medsphere Systems Corporation (PA)		D	760 692-3700	0
National Assn Mus Mrchants Inc		D	760 438-8001	0
Navigate Biopharma Svcs Inc		C	866 992-4939	0
Nobelbiz Inc		D	760 405-0105	0
North Coast Home Care Inc		D	760 260-8700	0
Nossaman LLP		D	760 918-0500	0
Ntent Inc		D	760 930-7600	0
NTN Buzztime Inc (PA)		D	760 438-7400	0
Omni La Costa Resort & Spa LLC		E	760 438-9111	0
Optumrx Inc		B	760 804-2399	0
Ostendo Technologies Inc (PA)		D	760 710-3003	0
Pacific Western Bank		D	760 918-2469	0
Pavigym America Corp		D	858 414-8624	0
Physical Rhbltation Netwrk LLC (PA)		D	760 931-8310	0
Planet Group Inc		D	402 491-3560	0
Prana Living LLC (HQ)		D	866 915-6457	0
Premiere Financial		D	760 518-5034	0
Prescott Companies (PA)		C	760 634-4700	0
Prescription Solutions		A	760 804-2370	0
Proficio Inc (PA)		E	800 779-5042	0
Providence Seminars Inc		D	760 827-2100	0
Pta CA Cong Prents Kelley Schl		E	760 331-5800	0
Pulse-Link Inc		D	760 448-4690	0
Purism Spc		E	415 555-1212	0
Q-Free America Inc		D	855 737-3387	0
Quality Childrens Services (PA)		C	760 942-3433	0
R Q Construction Inc		C	760 631-7707	0
Rancho Leonero Resort		E	760 438-2905	0
Really Likeable People Inc		E	760 431-5577	0
Registry Network Inc (PA)		C	760 966-3700	0

	SIC	EMP	PHONE	ENTRY #
Rialto Bioenergy Facility LLC		C	760 436-8870	0
Richard Realty Group Inc		D	760 603-8377	0
Riolo Transportation Inc		C	760 729-4405	0
Rockstar San Diego		C	760 929-0700	0
Rowan Incorporated		D	760 692-0700	0
RPI Carlsbad LP		C	760 729-6183	0
Rq Construction LLC		C	760 631-7707	0
Safeop Surgical Inc		D	760 494-6752	0
Sambreel Services LLC		E	760 266-5090	0
San Diego Gas & Electric Co		A	760 438-6200	0
Search Engine Optimization Inc		D	760 929-0039	0
Sendx Medical Inc (DH)		D	760 930-6300	0
Sethi Management		C	760 692-5288	0
Sierra Wireless America Inc (HQ)		D	760 444-5650	0
Smart & Final Stores Inc		B	760 434-2449	0
Sound Technologies Inc		D	760 918-9626	0
Source 44 LLC		C	877 916-6337	0
Southern Cal Prmnnte Med Group		A	619 528-5000	0
Starlight Corporation (PA)		C	858 509-9006	0
Steelpoint Capital Partners LP		D	858 764-8700	0
Sunrise Senior Living LLC		D	760 930-0060	0
Supercuts Admnistrative Office (PA)		C	760 753-5543	0
Synteract Inc (DH)		B	760 268-8200	0
Synteracthcr Corporation (HQ)		B	760 268-8200	0
Synteracthcr Holdings Corp (PA)		B	760 268-8200	0
Tamarack Bch Condo Owners Assn		E	760 729-3500	0
Technology Associates EC Inc		D	760 765-5275	0
Tri City Emergency Med Group		E	760 439-1963	0
Triton Management Services LLC		D	760 431-9911	0
Two Jinn Inc (PA)		D	760 431-9911	0
Unite Eurotherapy Inc		D	760 585-1800	0
Valley Radiology Consultants (PA)		E	619 797-8248	0
VCA Animal Hospitals Inc		D	760 431-2273	0
Vertical Search Works Inc		D	212 967-9502	0
Viscent Orthpd Solutions LLC (DH)		E	214 501-0180	0
Wells Fargo Home Mortgage Inc		B	760 603-7000	0
West Inn & Suites LLC		D	760 448-4500	0
Westliving Management LLC (PA)		D	760 602-5850	0
Weston Solutions Inc		D	760 795-6900	0

CARMEL, CA - Monterey County

	SIC	EMP	PHONE	ENTRY #
Alain Pinel Realtors		D	831 622-1040	0
B S I Holdings Inc		A	831 622-1840	0
Bayview Properties Inc		D	831 624-1841	0
Carmel Valley Ranch		C	831 625-9500	0
Carmel Vly Mrtg Borrower LLC		C	831 625-9500	0
Highlands Inn Inc		C	831 620-1234	0
Highlands Inn Investors II LP		B	831 624-3801	0
Kagan Capital Management Inc		D	831 624-1536	0
Mission Ranch Inc		E	831 624-6436	0
Monterey Pacific Inc (PA)		E	831 678-4845	0
Northern CA Cngrgtnl Rtmt		C	831 624-1281	0
Preserve Golf Club Inc		E	831 620-6871	0
Quail Lodge Inc		C	831 624-1581	0
Santa Lucia Preserve Company		C	831 620-6760	0
Stewardship Company LLC		C	831 620-6700	0
Tehama Golf Club LLC		C	831 622-2200	0
Trevi Partners A Calif LP		D	831 624-1841	0
Wyndham International Inc		C	831 625-9500	0

CARMEL VALLEY, CA - Monterey County

	SIC	EMP	PHONE	ENTRY #
Douglas Ranch LLC		E	949 500-7009	0
Keller Williams Realty		D	831 622-6200	0

CARMICHAEL, CA - Sacramento County

	SIC	EMP	PHONE	ENTRY #
Acct Holdings LLC		A	916 971-1981	0
AEgis of Carmichael		D	916 972-1313	0
Aegis Senior Communities LLC		B	916 972-1313	0
Atria Senior Living Inc		D	916 488-5722	0
Cal Sierra Construction Inc		D	916 416-7901	0
Capital Eye Medical Group		D	916 241-9378	0
Carmichael Care Inc		C	916 483-8103	0
Carmichael Recreation & Pk Dst		C	916 485-5322	0
Crestwood Behavioral Hlth Inc		C	916 977-0949	0
Diez & Leis RE Group Inc		D	916 487-4287	0
Dignity Health		A	916 537-5151	0
Dignity Health		A	916 537-5000	0
Eskaton (PA)		A	916 334-0296	0
Eskaton Properties Inc		A	916 974-2060	0
Eskaton Properties Inc		D	916 331-8513	0
Eskaton Properties Inc (PA)		A	916 334-0810	0
Eskaton Properties Inc		A	916 974-2000	0
Fairwood Associates Apts		D	916 944-0152	0
H B J Corporation		D	707 333-7066	0
Helios Healthcare LLC		C	916 482-0465	0
Horizon West Inc		C	916 488-8601	0

	SIC	EMP	PHONE	ENTRY #
Mission Oaks Recreation Pk Dst		D	916 488-2810	0
Pacific Cities Management Inc **(PA)**		D	916 348-1188	0
Smart & Final Stores Inc		B	916 486-6315	0
SSC Carmichael Operating Co LP		D	916 485-4793	0
Sunbridge Brittany Rehab Centr		D	916 484-1393	0
Sunrise Senior Living Inc		D	916 485-4500	0
Walnut Whtney Cnvalescent Hosp		C	916 488-8601	0

CARPINTERIA, CA - Santa Barbara County

	SIC	EMP	PHONE	ENTRY #
Agilent Technologies Inc		C	805 566-6655	0
Beacon West Energy Group LLC		D	805 816-2790	0
Brand Flower Farms Inc **(PA)**		D	805 684-5531	0
Carpinteria Motor Inn Inc		E	805 684-0473	0
CP Opco LLC		D	805 566-3566	0
Gallup & Stribling Orchids LLC		E	805 684-1998	0
Jimenez Nursery Inc		D	805 684-7955	0
Johannes Flowers Inc		D	805 684-5686	0
Myriad Flowers International		D	805 684-8079	0
Normans Nursery Inc		B	805 684-5442	0
Ocean Breeze International		D	805 684-1747	0
Plan Member Financial Corp		D	800 874-6910	0
Procore Technologies Inc **(PA)**		A	866 477-6267	0
Smart & Final Stores Inc		B	805 566-2174	0
Sunshine Floral Inc		D	805 684-1177	0
Ucp Work Inc **(PA)**		D	805 566-9000	0
Valley Flowers Inc		D	805 684-6651	0
Westland Flral Carpinteria Inc		E	805 684-4011	0
Westland Orchids Inc		E	805 684-1436	0

CARSON, CA - Los Angeles County

	SIC	EMP	PHONE	ENTRY #
4as Trucking		E	424 308-9563	0
Agility Logistics Corp		D	310 507-6700	0
Alameda Corridor Engrg Team		D	310 816-0460	0
Alliedbarton Security Svcs LLC		C	310 324-1219	0
Ampam Parks Mechanical Inc		A	310 835-1532	0
Anheuser-Busch LLC		C	310 761-4600	0
Anschutz So Calif Sports Compl		C	310 630-2000	0
Apw International Inc		C	310 884-5003	0
Apw Knox-Seeman Warehouse Inc **(HQ)**		D	310 604-4373	0
Aramark Services Inc		D	310 635-5000	0
Ashland LLC		D	310 223-3505	0
AT&T Corp		D	310 225-3028	0
Auto Parts Warehouse Inc **(PA)**		E	800 913-6119	0
Bakkavor Foods Usa Inc **(DH)**		B	704 522-1977	0
Boeing Distribution Svcs Inc		D	310 900-1300	0
BP West Coast Products LLC		B	310 816-8787	0
BP West Coast Products LLC		C	310 549-6204	0
Calko Transport Company Inc		D	310 816-0602	0
Carson Operating Company LLC		D	310 830-9200	0
Carson Senior Assisted Living		D	310 830-4010	0
Cellco Partnership		D	310 329-9325	0
Cintas Corporation No 2		D	310 635-8713	0
Cirrus Enterprises LLC		D	310 204-6159	0
City Fashion Express Inc		D	310 223-1010	0
City of Carson		D	310 835-0212	0
Clay Dunn Enterprises Inc		C	310 549-1698	0
Clipper Corporation **(PA)**		E	310 533-8585	0
Color Spot Nurseries Inc		D	310 549-7470	0
County of Los Angeles		C	310 847-4400	0
County Santtn Dist 2 of La Co		B	310 830-2400	0
Custom Goods LLC **(PA)**		E	310 241-6700	0
Dependable Highway Express Inc		C	310 522-4111	0
Dmf Inc		D	323 934-7779	0
Durham School Services L P		D	310 767-5820	0
East Crson II Hsing Prtners LP		D	310 522-9606	0
Epson America Inc		C	562 290-5855	0
Fedex Ground Package Sys Inc		C	800 463-3339	0
Fortress Resources LLC **(HQ)**		D	562 633-9951	0
Grand View Geranium Grdns Inc		D	310 217-0490	0
H D Smith LLC		D	310 641-1885	0
H Rauvel Inc **(PA)**		D	310 604-0060	0
Hanjin Transportation Co Ltd		D	310 522-5030	0
Harvard Grand Inv Inc A Cal		D	310 513-7560	0
Hellmann Wrldwide Lgistics Inc		E	310 847-4600	0
Herc Rentals Inc		E	310 233-5000	0
Human Potential Cons LLC		D	310 756-1560	0
JB Dental Supply Co Inc **(PA)**		C	310 202-8855	0
Kaiser Foundation Hospitals		D	310 513-6707	0
Kinder Mrgan Enrgy Partners LP		E	310 518-7700	0
Kole Imports		D	310 834-0004	0
Liberty Mutual Insurance Co		C	781 740-1920	0
Long-Lok Fasteners Corporation		E	310 667-4200	0
Mainfreight Inc **(HQ)**		D	310 900-1974	0
Margate Construction Inc		C	310 830-8610	0
Merchants Bank California N A		D	310 549-4350	0
Mhx LLC		D	800 234-2098	0

	SIC	EMP	PHONE	ENTRY #
Nnr Global Logistics USA Inc		C	310 357-2100	0
North American Security Inc		B	310 630-4840	0
North Amrcn SEC Investigations		D	323 634-1911	0
Nova Ortho-Med Inc **(PA)**		E	310 352-3600	0
Pacifica Trucks LLC		D	310 549-1351	0
Phoenix Engineering Co Inc		D	310 532-1134	0
Porteous Enterprises Inc		C	310 549-9180	0
Quik Pick Express LLC		D	310 763-3000	0
Quik Pick Express LLC		D	310 763-3000	0
Schafer Bros Trnsf Pano Movers **(PA)**		D	310 835-7231	0
Scotts Labor Leasing Co Inc		D	310 835-8388	0
Secrom Inc		D	310 830-4010	0
Sony Electronics Inc		C	310 835-6121	0
South Bay Vocational Center		E	424 215-4589	0
Southwind Foods LLC **(PA)**		D	323 262-8222	0
Spectra I California		D	310 835-0808	0
Ssf Imported Auto Parts LLC		E	310 782-8859	0
Sunstone Hotel Investors LLC		D	310 830-9200	0
Supra National Express Inc		D	310 549-7105	0
Swayzers Incorporated		D	323 979-7223	0
Tabletops Unlimited Inc **(PA)**		D	310 549-6000	0
Triple B Forwarders Inc **(PA)**		C	310 604-5840	0
Watson Cogeneration Co Inc		D	310 816-8100	0
Western Star Trnsp LLC		D	310 605-1300	0
Yusen Logistics Americas Inc		C	310 518-3008	0

CARUTHERS, CA - Fresno County

	SIC	EMP	PHONE	ENTRY #
Charanjit Singh Batth		D	559 864-9421	0
Fresno Cnty Sprntndent Schools		D	559 644-1000	0
H & R Gunlund Ranches Inc		C	559 864-8186	0
Hammer Down Davila Cnstr		D	559 864-2001	0
Karam Bath		E	559 864-3868	0
Pacific Boring Incorporated		E	559 864-9444	0

CASPAR, CA - Mendocino County

	SIC	EMP	PHONE	ENTRY #
Caspar Community		E	707 964-4997	0

CASTRO VALLEY, CA - Alameda County

	SIC	EMP	PHONE	ENTRY #
American Building Service Inc		D	510 483-5120	0
Baywood Court **(PA)**		C	510 733-2102	0
Coldwell Bankers Residential		D	510 583-5400	0
East Bay Regional Park Dst		D	510 881-1833	0
Eden Labs Med Group Inc		E	510 537-1234	0
Mason-Mcduffie Real Estate Inc		D	510 886-7511	0
Mekwus Solar Energy		D	510 731-4134	0
Ras Management Inc **(PA)**		E	510 727-1800	0
Redwood Convalescent Hospital		D	510 537-8848	0
Solar Company Inc		D	510 888-9488	0
Valley Pinte Nursing Rehab Ctr		E	510 538-8464	0

CASTROVILLE, CA - Monterey County

	SIC	EMP	PHONE	ENTRY #
Ajax Portable Services		E	831 384-5000	0
Brady Company/Central Cal		C	831 633-3315	0
California Artichoke & Vegetab		D	831 633-2144	0
Giannas Baking Company		D	831 633-3700	0
National Custom Packing Inc		E	831 724-2026	0
Ocean Mist Farming Company **(PA)**		C	831 633-2144	0
Randazzo Enterprises Inc		D	831 633-4420	0
USA Waste of California Inc		C	831 384-4860	0
Valley Pride Inc **(PA)**		B	831 633-5883	0
Vps Companies Inc		E	831 633-4011	0

CATHEDRAL CITY, CA - Riverside County

	SIC	EMP	PHONE	ENTRY #
American Golf Corporation		D	702 431-2191	0
Big Lgue Dreams Consulting LLC		C	760 324-5600	0
Briar Golf LP		D	760 328-6571	0
Crystal Chrysler Plymuth Dodge		D	760 324-9375	0
Daniel Robert Knowlton		D	760 265-5293	0
Desert Princess Home		D	760 322-1655	0
Desert Prncess Homeowners Assn		D	760 322-1907	0
Heartland Payment Systems Inc		D	760 324-0133	0

CAZADERO, CA - Sonoma County

	SIC	EMP	PHONE	ENTRY #
Camp Royaneh Boy Scout		D	707 632-5291	0

CEDAR GLEN, CA - San Bernardino County

	SIC	EMP	PHONE	ENTRY #
San Bernardino Mtns Wildlife		E	909 226-6189	0

CEDARVILLE, CA - Modoc County

	SIC	EMP	PHONE	ENTRY #
Surprise Valley Hlth Care Dst		D	530 279-6111	0

CERES, CA - Stanislaus County

	SIC	EMP	PHONE	ENTRY #
Bertolottis Ceres Disposal		D	209 537-8000	0
Dan Avila and Sons		D	209 495-3899	0
Dbi Beverage Inc		D	209 524-2477	0
Exit Realty Consultants		C	209 484-8075	0
Irish Construction		D	209 576-8766	0
Mark One Corporation		E	209 537-4581	0

Mergent email: customerrelations@mergent.com
1518

2020 Directory of California
Wholesalers and Services Companies

(P-0000) Products & Services Section entry number
(PA)=Parent Co (HQ)=Headquarters (DH)=Div Headquarters

	SIC	EMP	PHONE	ENTRY #
Procter & Gamble Distrg LLC		B	209 538-3987	0
Ram Mechanical Inc		D	209 531-9155	0
Sutter Health		C	209 538-1733	0
Timmerman Starlite Trckg Inc		D	209 538-1706	0
United Parcel Service Inc OH		C	800 742-5877	0
West Coast Grape Farming Inc		A	209 538-3131	0

CERRITOS, CA - Los Angeles County

	SIC	EMP	PHONE	ENTRY #
A & D Hauling Services Inc		D	310 514-8969	0
All Care Industries Inc		D	562 623-4009	0
Amkotron Inc		D	562 921-3330	0
Apex Computer Systems Inc		D	562 926-6820	0
Aspen Youth Inc		D	562 567-5507	0
Astro Realty Inc		D	562 924-3381	0
Atkinson And Ly Rd & Rm Lw **(PA)**		C	562 653-3200	0
Auditboard Inc **(PA)**		E	877 769-5444	0
Auto Insurance Specialists LLC **(DH)**		C	562 345-6247	0
Avalon A Cerritos		E	562 865-9500	0
Axelacare Holdings Inc		A	714 522-8802	0
Biospace Inc		D	323 932-6503	0
Bunzl Usa Inc		D	314 997-5959	0
Calnetix Inc **(PA)**		C	562 293-1660	0
Caremore Health Plan **(HQ)**		D	562 622-2950	0
Cea-Pack Services Inc		C	562 407-0660	0
Cellco Partnership		D	562 809-5650	0
College Hospital Inc **(PA)**		B	562 924-9581	0
Community Family Guidance Ctr **(PA)**		D	562 865-6444	0
Complete Office California Inc		D	714 880-1222	0
Crest Financial Corporation **(DH)**		D	562 733-6500	0
David Levy Co Inc		E	562 404-9998	0
Faith Com Inc **(PA)**		D	562 719-9300	0
Firm A Chugh Professional Corp		D	562 229-1220	0
First Choice Bank **(HQ)**		D	562 345-9092	0
Global Med Services Inc		A	562 207-6970	0
Healthview Inc		D	562 468-0136	0
Hometown Buffet Inc		D	562 402-8307	0
Iron Mountain Info MGT LLC		D	714 526-0916	0
Kaiser Foundation Hospitals		A	800 823-4040	0
Management Trust Assn Inc		C	562 926-3372	0
Memorex Products Inc		D	562 653-2800	0
Microtek Lab Inc **(HQ)**		C	310 687-5823	0
Midway International Inc		E	562 921-2255	0
Mulhearn Realtors Inc		C	562 860-2443	0
O E C Shipg Los Angeles Inc		E	562 926-7186	0
Oocl (usa) Inc		D	562 499-2600	0
Pioneer Medical Group Inc		D	562 229-0902	0
Poliseek Ais Insur Sltions Inc		D	866 480-7335	0
Private Medical-Care Inc		C	562 924-8311	0
Razor USA LLC **(PA)**		D	562 345-6000	0
Royal Plywood Company LLC **(PA)**		D	562 404-2989	0
Secure One Data Solutions LLC		E	562 924-7056	0
Southern Glazers Wine		B	562 926-2000	0
Spectrum MGT Holdg Co LLC		D	562 677-0228	0
Temp Unlimited LLC		C	562 860-3340	0
Tenet Healthsystem Medical		A	562 531-2550	0
Thermal Engrg Intl USA Inc **(HQ)**		D	323 726-0641	0
Thyssenkrupp Elevator Corp		E	323 278-9888	0
Trinitycare LLC **(PA)**		D	818 709-4221	0
Uaw-Lbor Emplyment Trning Corp **(PA)**		C	562 989-7700	0
United Parcel Service Inc OH		C	562 404-3236	0
Uquality Automotive Pdts Corp **(PA)**		E	562 282-2888	0
Usaco Service Corp		D	562 483-8747	0
Wells Fargo Bank National Assn		E	562 924-1616	0
Young Systems Corporation		D	562 921-2256	0
Zero Energy Contracting LLC		D	626 701-3180	0

CHATSWORTH, CA - Los Angeles County

	SIC	EMP	PHONE	ENTRY #
A I T Development Corp		D	818 407-5533	0
Accunex Inc		E	818 882-5858	0
Adco Container Company		E	818 998-2565	0
All Tmperatures Controlled Inc		D	818 882-1478	0
Allsale Electric Inc		D	818 715-0181	0
Allstate Imaging Inc **(PA)**		D	818 678-4550	0
Atlantic Optical Co Inc		D	818 407-1890	0
Brewster Marble Co Inc		E	818 834-2195	0
Cbol Corporation		D	818 704-8200	0
Child Care Resource Center Inc **(PA)**		C	818 717-1000	0
Chubb US Holding Inc		C	818 428-3600	0
CIT Bank National Association		D	818 885-9065	0
Comet Electric Inc		C	818 340-0965	0
Cpcc Inc		D	818 882-3200	0
Crunch Fitness		D	805 522-5454	0
Delaware Electro Inds Inc **(PA)**		D	818 786-8111	0
Dolphin Imaging Systems LLC		E	818 435-1368	0
Eisenberg International Corp **(PA)**		D	818 365-8161	0
Eurodent Inc		D	818 832-1325	0

	SIC	EMP	PHONE	ENTRY #
Fromer Inc		D	818 341-3896	0
Genesis Tech Partners LLC		C	800 950-2647	0
Golden State Health Ctrs Inc		D	818 882-8233	0
Green Scene Landscape Inc		D	818 280-0420	0
Guardian National Inc		E	800 700-1467	0
Health Advocates LLC		B	818 995-9500	0
Joerns LLC **(HQ)**		C	800 966-6662	0
Kingdom Enterprise Films LLC		E	818 963-2513	0
Lennox Industries Inc		C	818 739-1616	0
Logistical Support LLC		C	818 341-3344	0
Los Angeles County MTA		C	213 922-6308	0
MGA Entertainment Inc **(PA)**		B	818 894-2525	0
Minilec Service Inc		E	818 341-1125	0
Mj Star-Lite Inc		E	818 717-0834	0
Multi-Pak Corporation		D	818 709-0508	0
National Notary Association		C	818 739-4071	0
NNA Insurance Services		C	818 739-4071	0
NNA Services		C	818 739-4071	0
Nna Services LLC		C	818 739-4071	0
Noble House Home Furn LLC **(PA)**		D	818 884-7059	0
OBryant Electric Inc		C	818 407-1986	0
On-Site Lasermedic Corporation **(PA)**		D	818 775-9111	0
Oncore Manufacturing LLC **(HQ)**		A	818 734-6500	0
Ontic Engineering and Mfg Inc **(HQ)**		B	818 678-6555	0
Pacific Toxicology Labs		D	818 598-3110	0
Patterson Dental Supply Inc		E	818 435-1368	0
Pd Liquidation Inc		C	818 772-0100	0
Piege Co **(PA)**		E	818 727-9100	0
Platinum Group Companies Inc **(PA)**		C	818 721-3800	0
Premier America Credit Union **(PA)**		C	818 772-4000	0
Primx Entertainment LLC		E	818 324-5229	0
Printing Technology Inc		C	818 576-9220	0
PS Development Corporation		D	818 340-0965	0
R M B Packaging Co Inc		E	818 998-0658	0
Rancho San Antonio Boys HM Inc **(PA)**		C	818 882-6400	0
Regency Enterprises Inc **(PA)**		B	818 901-0255	0
Retail Services Wis Corp		E	818 772-4969	0
Ricoh Usa Inc		E	818 294-8601	0
Sage Electric Company		D	818 718-9080	0
Service Genius Los Angeles Inc		D	818 200-3379	0
Seven One Inc **(PA)**		D	818 904-3435	0
Sexy Hair Concepts		C	800 848-3383	0
Silver Strand		E	818 701-9707	0
Sliding Door Company **(PA)**		D	818 997-7855	0
Southern California Gas Co		B	818 701-2592	0
Spectrum MGT Holdg Co LLC		D	818 700-6126	0
Staffchex Inc		A	818 709-6100	0
Stellar Microelectronics Inc		C	661 775-3500	0
Summerville Senior Living Inc		D	818 341-2552	0
Telesis Community Credit Union **(PA)**		C	818 885-1226	0
Terminix Intl Co Ltd Partnr		D	818 361-1191	0
Trendex Corporation		D	818 407-9600	0
Tuttle Family Enterprises Inc		B	818 534-2566	0
United Cp/S Chldrns Fndn La		C	818 998-8755	0
US Interstate Distrg Inc		C	818 678-4592	0
West Coast Coupon Inc		E	818 341-2400	0
West-Spec Partners		E	818 725-7000	0

CHERRY VALLEY, CA - Riverside County

	SIC	EMP	PHONE	ENTRY #
Little Peoples		D	951 849-1959	0

CHESTER, CA - Plumas County

	SIC	EMP	PHONE	ENTRY #
Chester Public Utility Dst		D	530 258-2171	0
Seneca Healthcare District		D	530 258-1977	0
Seneca Healthcare District **(PA)**		C	530 258-2151	0

CHICO, CA - Butte County

	SIC	EMP	PHONE	ENTRY #
11 Main Inc		C	530 892-9191	0
Addus Healthcare Inc		E	530 566-0405	0
Agreserves Inc		D	530 343-5365	0
Alternative Energy Systems Inc		D	530 345-6980	0
Ampla Health		D	530 342-4395	0
ARC of Butte County **(PA)**		C	530 891-5865	0
Associated Pension Cons Inc **(PA)**		D	530 343-4233	0
AT&T Corp		D	530 891-2025	0
Auctiva Corporation		D	530 894-7400	0
B A M I Inc		E	530 343-5678	0
Baney Corporation		D	530 899-9090	0
Bank America National Assn		D	530 891-7019	0
BCM Construction Company Inc		E	530 342-1722	0
Boys & Girls Clubs of N Vly		D	530 899-0335	0
Buildcom Inc		B	800 375-3403	0
Butte Home Health Inc		C	530 895-0462	0
Caldwell Ventures LLC		E	530 899-0814	0
California Vocations Inc		C	530 877-0937	0
Caminar		D	530 343-4421	0

GEOGRAPHIC

Employment Codes: A=Over 500 employees, B=251-500,
C=101-250, D=51-100, E=50

2020 Directory of California
Wholesalers and Services Companies

© Mergent Inc. 1-800-342-5647

1519

	SIC	EMP	PHONE	ENTRY #
Catamount Broadcasting of Chic (PA)		C	530 893-2424	0
Chico Area Recreation & Pk Dst (PA)		C	530 895-4711	0
Chico Csu		D	530 898-3917	0
Chico Electric Inc		D	530 891-1933	0
Chico Immdate Care Med Ctr Inc (PA)		E	530 891-1676	0
Chico State Enterprises		A	530 898-6811	0
Cloudpeople Global		E	530 591-7028	0
Community Action Agency of But (PA)		D	530 712-2600	0
County of Butte		B	530 891-2850	0
Cummings-Violich Inc		D	530 894-5494	0
Dfa of California		C	530 345-5077	0
Digital Path Inc		E	800 676-7284	0
Enloe Hospt-Phys Thrpy		C	530 891-7300	0
Enloe Medical Center		D	530 332-4111	0
Enloe Medical Center		B	530 332-7522	0
Enloe Medical Center		B	530 332-6050	0
Enloe Medical Center		C	530 332-6138	0
Enloe Medical Center		C	530 332-6400	0
Enloe Medical Center		B	530 332-6000	0
Evergreen At Chico LLC		C	530 342-4885	0
Fair Trade Corner Inc		E	530 566-1405	0
Far Northern Coordinating Coun		D	530 895-8633	0
Farmers International Inc		E	530 566-1405	0
Federal Express Corporation		C	800 463-3339	0
Fedex Ground Package Sys Inc		C	800 463-3339	0
First Responder Ems		C	530 897-6345	0
First Responder Ems Inc		D	530 897-6345	0
First Rsponder Emrgncy Med Svc		C	530 891-4357	0
Gas Transmission Systems Inc		C	530 893-6711	0
Golden Living LLC		D	530 343-6084	0
Gonzales Park LLC		C	530 343-8725	0
Helios Healthcare LLC		C	530 345-1306	0
Heritage One Carpentry Inc		C	530 345-6622	0
Hignell Incorporated		D	530 345-1965	0
Hmclause Inc		D	530 713-5838	0
Holdrege Kull Consultimg Engr		D	530 894-2487	0
Home Health Care Management		D	530 343-0727	0
Hotel Diamond		E	530 893-3100	0
Interwest Insurance Svcs LLC		D	530 895-1010	0
Jeff Stover Inc		D	530 345-9427	0
Mangrove Medical Group		E	530 345-0064	0
Mission Linen Supply		E	530 342-4110	0
Modern Building Inc		D	530 891-4533	0
Mooney Farms		E	530 899-2661	0
Morrison MGT Specialists Inc		D	530 332-7557	0
North State Radiology		E	530 898-0504	0
Northern Cal Adptive Lving Ctr (PA)		C	530 894-2726	0
Northern Cal Yuth Fmly Prgrams (PA)		D	530 893-2316	0
Northern Vly Indian Hlth Inc		D	530 896-9400	0
Nph Medical Services		D	530 899-2255	0
Pacific Gas and Electric Co		C	530 894-4739	0
Retinal Consultants Inc		D	530 899-2251	0
Rgis LLC		D	530 898-1055	0
Rhc Equipment LLC		E	530 892-1918	0
Riverside Cnvalescent Hosp Inc		D	530 343-5595	0
Riverside Health Care Corp (PA)		D	530 897-5100	0
Roy Carrington Inc		D	530 893-2100	0
RSC Associates Inc (PA)		C	530 893-8228	0
Selig Construction Corp		E	530 893-5898	0
Sierra Landscape & Maintenance		D	530 895-0263	0
Sourcecorp Bps Nthrn Cal Inc		D	530 893-7900	0
Stansbury Hm Preservation Assn		E	530 895-3848	0
Terraces Retirement Community		C	530 894-1010	0
Tri Counties Bank (HQ)		D	530 898-0300	0
Unitedhealth Group Inc		B	530 879-8251	0
Veterans Health Administration		B	530 879-5000	0
Victor Cmnty Support Svcs Inc (PA)		B	530 893-0758	0
Women Health Center (PA)		D	530 891-1917	0
Work Truck Solutions Inc		D	855 987-4544	0

CHINO, CA - San Bernardino County

	SIC	EMP	PHONE	ENTRY #
Acepex Management Corporation		B	909 591-1999	0
Advantage Pntg Solutions Inc		D	951 739-9204	0
Am-TEC Total Security Inc (PA)		D	909 573-4678	0
American Beef Packers Inc		C	909 628-4888	0
Angels In Motion LLC		D	909 590-9102	0
Applied P & Ch Laboratory Sout		D	909 590-1828	0
Arrow Wire & Cable Inc (PA)		E	909 282-1940	0
Aspects Furniture Mfg Inc		C	909 606-5806	0
Aviation Maintenance Group Inc		C	714 469-0515	0
Baronhr LLC		C	909 517-3800	0
Canyon Ridge Hospital Inc		C	909 590-3700	0
Carlisle Construction Mtls Inc		D	909 591-7425	0
Century 21 Home Realtors (PA)		D	909 591-0158	0
Chino Grading Inc		D	909 364-8667	0
Chino Medical Group Inc		D	909 591-6446	0

	SIC	EMP	PHONE	ENTRY #
Chino Valley Unified Schl Dst		D	909 627-9758	0
City of Chino		D	909 591-9843	0
Consolidated Plastics Corp (PA)		D	909 393-8222	0
Correctons Rhbltation Cal Dept		C	909 597-1821	0
Custom Bilt Holdings LLC		D	909 664-1587	0
DL Long Landscaping Inc		D	909 628-5531	0
Donovan Golf Courses MGT		E	714 528-6400	0
Duke Pacific Inc		D	909 591-0191	0
El Prado Golf Course LP		D	909 597-1751	0
Farmers Group Inc		D	909 839-2020	0
Fisher Scientific Company LLC		D	909 393-2100	0
Flatiron West Inc		E	909 597-8413	0
Foddrill Construction Corp		D	909 591-4095	0
Generation Construction Inc		C	909 923-2077	0
Gentek Media Inc		E	909 476-3818	0
Gilbert Service Corp		C	909 393-7575	0
Harrington Industrial Plas LLC (HQ)		D	909 597-8641	0
Inland Empire Utilities Agency (PA)		D	909 993-1600	0
Interior Experts General Bldrs		D	909 203-4922	0
June A Grothe Construction Inc		D	909 993-9393	0
Kaiser Foundation Hospitals		D	888 750-0036	0
Koury Engrg Tstg & Insptn		D	310 851-8685	0
McKesson Medical-Surgical Inc		D	800 767-6339	0
Mission Linen Supply		B	909 393-5589	0
Motivational Marketing Inc		C	909 517-2200	0
Motivational Marketing Inc		D	909 517-2200	0
Motivational Marketing Inc (PA)		D	909 517-2200	0
Navy Exchange Service Command		C	909 517-2640	0
Nexgrill Industries Inc (PA)		D	909 598-8799	0
Omnia Italian Design LLC		C	909 393-4400	0
Port Logistics Group Inc		D	909 539-0478	0
Port Logistics Group Inc		E	909 539-9773	0
Public Investment Corporation		C	310 451-5227	0
Quetico LLC (PA)		D	909 628-6200	0
R & B Reinforcing Steel Corp		D	909 591-1726	0
Ralison International Inc		E	909 393-0008	0
Redwood Products Chino Inc		D	909 923-5656	0
SA Recycling LLC		D	909 622-3337	0
Salem Christian Homes Inc (PA)		C	909 614-0575	0
Savant Construction Inc		D	909 614-4300	0
Schneider Electric Usa Inc		D	909 438-2295	0
Skate Enterprises Inc		D	562 924-0911	0
South Coast Childrens Soc Inc		C	909 364-9788	0
Spanish Trils Girl Scout Cncil		E	909 627-2609	0
Tactical Lgistic Solutions Inc		D	909 464-2813	0
Threshold Technologies Inc		D	909 606-1666	0
Transtech Engineers Inc (PA)		D	909 595-8599	0
Universal Packg Systems Inc		C	909 517-2442	0
US Elogistics Service Corp		D	732 881-6606	0
USA Waste of California Inc		D	909 590-1793	0
Veritas Health Services Inc		A	909 464-8600	0
Wp Electric Communications Inc		E	909 606-3510	0
Year Round Landscape Maint Inc		E	909 597-7734	0
Yoshimura Research & Dev Amer		D	909 628-4722	0

CHINO HILLS, CA - San Bernardino County

	SIC	EMP	PHONE	ENTRY #
American Financial Network Inc		D	909 287-7585	0
Bank America National Assn		D	909 393-3002	0
Bates Sample Case Company Inc		D	951 371-4922	0
Big Lgue Drams Chino Hills LLC		D	909 287-6900	0
Boys Republic (PA)		C	909 902-6690	0
Ch Market Center Inc		D	909 628-9100	0
Chino Valley Unified Schl Dst		D	909 590-2707	0
CIT Bank NA		D	909 631-2560	0
Flatiron Electric Group Inc		E	714 228-9631	0
Harkins Theatres Inc		D	909 627-8010	0
Jupiter Holding I Corp (HQ)		A	909 606-1416	0
Los Serranos Golf Club		C	909 597-1769	0
Optima Network Services Inc (DH)		D	305 599-1800	0
Prh Pro Inc		C	714 510-7226	0
SSC Construction Inc		C	951 278-1177	0
USA Truck Inc		D	909 334-1406	0
West Hills Golf Associates		E	714 528-6400	0

CHOWCHILLA, CA - Madera County

	SIC	EMP	PHONE	ENTRY #
Agriland Holding Inc		D	559 665-2100	0
Anderson Pump Company		D	559 665-4477	0
Avalon Care Ctr - Chwchlla LLC		D	559 665-4826	0
Case Vlott Cattle		E	559 665-7399	0
Chowchilla Mem Hlth Care Dst (PA)		D	559 665-3781	0
J & R Debenedetto Orchards Inc		D	559 665-1712	0
Madera Community Hospital		D	559 665-3768	0
Seaman Nurseries Inc		D	559 665-1860	0
Vlot Brothers Trucking Co Inc		D	559 665-7399	0
Winnresidential Ltd Partnr		B	559 665-9600	0

Mergent email: customerrelations@mergent.com
1520

2020 Directory of California
Wholesalers and Services Companies

(P-0000) Products & Services Section entry number
(PA)=Parent Co (HQ)=Headquarters (DH)=Div Headquarters

	SIC	EMP	PHONE	ENTRY #

CHUALAR, CA - Monterey County

	SIC	EMP	PHONE	ENTRY #
C & G Farms Inc		C	831 679-2978	0
P & P Agrilabor		D	831 679-2307	0

CHULA VISTA, CA - San Diego County

	SIC	EMP	PHONE	ENTRY #
24 Hour Fitness Usa Inc		D	619 425-6600	0
ARC Starlight Center		D	619 427-7524	0
Armando C Ibarra CPA		D	619 422-1348	0
At Your Svc Htg & Coolg LLC		D	602 550-6946	0
Bayview Hospital and Mental		C	619 426-6311	0
California American Water Co		D	619 656-2400	0
California Baking Company		B	619 591-8289	0
Call Center Services Intl LLC		D	858 427-8500	0
Care Plus North of San Diego		D	619 421-0807	0
Citibank National Association		C	619 870-0609	0
Citigroup Inc		D	619 498-3158	0
Community Health Group		C	800 224-7766	0
Coronado Financial Corp		E	619 946-1900	0
Cox Communications Cal LLC		B	619 263-9251	0
Culinary Hispanic Foods Inc		A	619 955-6101	0
Dirt Cheap Demolition Inc		E	619 426-9598	0
Econa Corp		E	619 722-6555	0
Episcopal Community		D	619 228-2800	0
FJ Willert Contracting Co		C	619 421-1980	0
Fredericka Manor		D	619 422-9271	0
Front Porch Communities		C	619 427-2777	0
George G Sharp Inc		D	619 425-4211	0
Global Exprnce Specialists Inc		C	619 498-6300	0
Gryphon Marine LLC		E	619 407-4010	0
Heartland Meat Company Inc		D	619 407-3668	0
Home Carpet Investment Inc (PA)		D	619 262-8040	0
J C Towing Inc		D	619 429-1492	0
Knight-Swift Trnsp Hldings Inc		D	619 671-0588	0
Loyda Yu Real Estate Inc		D	619 475-7777	0
McMillin RE & Mrtg Co Inc		D	619 422-4500	0
Metropolitan Area Advisory Com (PA)		D	619 426-3595	0
Metropolitan Area Advisory Com		C	619 420-8981	0
Nitai Partners Inc		D	855 879-2847	0
Pacific Coast Truck and Whse (PA)		E	619 661-5451	0
Pacific Spanish Network Inc		D	619 427-6323	0
Phoenix Intl Holdings Inc		C	619 207-0871	0
Plastiflex Company Inc (DH)		D	619 662-8792	0
Poison Spyder Customs Inc		A	951 849-5911	0
Prosciento Inc		C	619 427-1300	0
Quality Coast Incorporated		E	619 443-9192	0
Racelegal Com		E	619 265-8159	0
Rockland Builders Services Inc		D	619 592-9582	0
Samsung International Inc (DH)		E	619 671-6859	0
San Diego Country Club Inc		D	619 422-8895	0
San Diego Gas & Electric Co		C	800 411-7343	0
Scripps Health		C	619 862-6600	0
Scripps Health		A	619 691-7000	0
Sharp Chula Vista Medical Ctr		A	619 502-5800	0
Sharp Healthcare		D	858 499-2000	0
Sonora Trade Company Inc		D	619 878-5848	0
South Bay Community Services		C	619 420-3620	0
Southcoast Welding & Mfg LLC		B	619 429-1337	0
Sunrise Senior Living LLC		D	619 470-2220	0
Sweetwater Authority (PA)		D	619 422-8395	0
Syzygy Technologies Inc		D	619 297-0970	0
Tenet Healthsystem Medical		C	619 426-6310	0
Traffic Tech Inc		C	800 396-2531	0
United Parcel Service Inc OH		C	619 482-8119	0
United Sttes Olympic Committee		E	619 656-1500	0
Veterans Health Administration		B	619 409-1600	0
Village Club		E	619 425-3333	0

CITRUS HEIGHTS, CA - Sacramento County

	SIC	EMP	PHONE	ENTRY #
A Community For Peace		D	916 728-5613	0
Accountable Health Staff Inc		B	916 286-7667	0
Always Home Nursing Svc Inc		C	916 989-6420	0
Cellco Partnership		D	916 536-0440	0
Crossroads Diversfd Svcs Inc		D	916 676-2540	0
Cypress Garden At Citrus Hts		E	916 729-2722	0
Deacon Construction - Cal		D	916 969-0900	0
Deacon Holdings Inc (PA)		D	916 969-0900	0
Dignity Health		D	916 536-2420	0
Farmers Group Inc		D	916 727-4600	0
Hcr Manorcare Med Svcs Fla LLC		C	916 967-2929	0
Itc Srvice Group Acqsition LLC (DH)		E	877 370-4482	0
J R Roberts Corp (HQ)		D	916 729-5600	0
J R Roberts Enterprises Inc		C	916 729-5600	0
Kings Casino Management Corp		B	916 560-4405	0
L W Roth Insurance Agency		D	916 721-6273	0
Lifetouch Inc		D	916 535-7733	0
Office Depot Inc		D	916 927-0171	0

	SIC	EMP	PHONE	ENTRY #
Probe Information Services Inc		C	916 676-1826	0
Progrssive Employment Concepts (PA)		D	916 723-3112	0
SD Deacon Corp California		D	916 969-0900	0
Sunrise Food Ministry		D	916 965-5431	0
Terra Nova Counseling (PA)		D	916 344-0249	0
Travelmasters Inc		E	916 722-1648	0

CITY OF INDUSTRY, CA - Los Angeles County

	SIC	EMP	PHONE	ENTRY #
Abacus Business Capital Inc		E	909 594-8080	0
Acme Furniture Industry Inc (PA)		D	626 964-3456	0
Advanced Industrial Cmpt Inc (PA)		D	909 895-8989	0
Air Tiger Express (usa) Inc		E	626 965-8647	0
Airgas Safety Inc		D	562 699-5239	0
Alaska Diesel Electric		C	626 934-6211	0
Allfast Fastening Systems LLC		D	626 968-9388	0
Allied Entertainment Group Inc (PA)		A	626 330-0600	0
America Chung Nam (group) (PA)		C	909 839-8383	0
America Chung Nam LLC (HQ)		C	909 839-8383	0
American AC Distrs LLC		D	407 850-0147	0
American Ace International Co		D	626 937-6116	0
American Future Tech Corp		C	888 462-3899	0
American Multi-Cinema Inc		D	626 810-7949	0
American Paper & Plastics Inc		C	626 444-0000	0
Anning-Johnson Company		E	626 369-7131	0
Apw Construction Inc		D	626 855-1720	0
Arakelian Enterprises Inc		B	626 336-3636	0
Arakelian Enterprises Inc (PA)		B	626 336-3636	0
ARC Document Solutions Inc		D	626 333-7005	0
Arconic Global Fas & Rings Inc		B	626 968-3831	0
Ardmore Home Design Inc (PA)		E	626 333-1177	0
Articouture Inc		E	626 336-7299	0
Assa Abloy Rsdential Group Inc (HQ)		C	626 961-0413	0
Assa Abloy Rsdential Group Inc		B	626 369-4718	0
Boiling Point Rest Sca Inc		B	626 551-5181	0
California Access Scaffold LLC		D	310 324-3388	0
California Country Club		D	626 333-4571	0
California Steel and Tube LLC		C	626 968-5511	0
Carrara Marble Co Amer Inc (PA)		D	626 961-6010	0
Chefs Warehouse Westcoast LLC (HQ)		D	626 465-4200	0
China Yngxin Phrmceuticals Inc		A	626 581-9098	0
CIT Bank National Association		D	626 435-2000	0
Classic Distrg & Bev Group Inc		B	626 934-3700	0
Closet World Inc		B	626 855-0846	0
County of Los Angeles		B	562 908-8400	0
County of Los Angeles		C	626 854-4987	0
Cyberpower Inc		D	626 813-7730	0
D & D Wholesale Distrs Inc		D	626 333-2111	0
Dacor		D	626 961-2256	0
Dacor Holdings Inc		C	626 626-4461	0
Delta Creative Inc		C	800 423-4135	0
E-Sceptre Inc		D	888 350-8989	0
Eforcity Corp - Nfm		D	626 442-3168	0
El Encanto Healthcare & Rehab		C	626 336-1274	0
Elmco Sales Inc (PA)		D	626 855-4831	0
Elmco/Duddy Inc (HQ)		E	626 333-9942	0
Essendant Inc		C	626 961-0011	0
Estes Express Lines Inc		D	626 333-9090	0
Ettv America Corp		D	626 581-8899	0
Ever Win International Corp		E	626 810-8218	0
Federal Express Corporation		C	800 463-3339	0
Ferguson Enterprises Inc		D	626 965-0724	0
Finance America Mortgage LLC		B	562 478-4664	0
Fiserv Inc		D	909 595-9074	0
Forever Link International Inc		E	877 839-9899	0
Fortune Dynamic Inc		D	909 979-8318	0
Freshpoint Inc		C	626 855-1400	0
Freshpoint Southern Cal Inc		C	626 855-1400	0
Frito-Lay North America Inc		B	626 855-1300	0
Frize Corporation		D	800 834-2127	0
Furniture America Cal Inc (PA)		D	909 718-7276	0
Gale Lina Inc		D	909 595-8898	0
GBT Inc		D	626 854-9338	0
Gels Logistics Inc		D	909 610-2277	0
Golden Bridge Intl Group		D	626 968-8229	0
Graycon Inc		E	626 961-9640	0
Grifols Worldwide Operations		D	626 435-2600	0
Halbert Brothers Inc		D	626 913-1800	0
Haralambos Beverage Company (PA)		B	562 347-4300	0
Hikvision USA Inc (HQ)		C	909 895-0400	0
Home Organizers Inc		A	562 699-9945	0
J P Original Corp (PA)		D	626 839-4300	0
Kaiser Foundation Hospitals		A	562 463-4377	0
Kellwood Company LLC		C	626 934-4155	0
Klm Management Company		D	626 330-3479	0
Lasertech Computer Distr Inc		D	626 435-2800	0
Lee & Ro Inc (PA)		E	626 912-3391	0

Employment Codes: A=Over 500 employees, B=251-500,
C=101-250, D=51-100, E=50

2020 Directory of California
Wholesalers and Services Companies

© Mergent Inc. 1-800-342-5647

1521

GEOGRAPHIC

	SIC	EMP	PHONE	ENTRY #
Leon Chien Corp		D	626 964-8302	0
Los Altos Food Products Inc		C	626 330-6555	0
LTS Associate Inc (PA)		E	626 435-2838	0
MA Laboratories Inc		D	626 820-8988	0
Magnell Associate Inc (DH)		D	626 271-9700	0
Magnell Associate Inc		D	626 271-1580	0
Majestic Industry Hills LLC		B	626 810-4455	0
Markwins Beauty Products Inc		C	909 595-8898	0
Marquez Brothers Entps Inc		C	626 330-3310	0
Max Group Corporation (PA)		D	626 935-0050	0
Maxim Lighting		C	626 956-4200	0
Mercado Latino Inc (PA)		D	626 333-6862	0
Micro-Technology Concepts Inc		D	626 839-6800	0
Mohan Dialysis Center Industry		D	626 333-3801	0
Morrow-Meadows Corporation (PA)		A	858 974-3650	0
MSI Computer Corp (HQ)		D	626 913-0828	0
Mtc Worldwide Corp		D	626 839-6800	0
Mtm & Thomasville Co		D	626 934-1112	0
Nafta Shoes Inc		D	626 369-9681	0
New Century Media Corp		E	562 695-1000	0
New Century Science & Tech		D	626 581-5500	0
Oceanland Service Inc (PA)		D	626 573-8429	0
OTasty Foods Inc		D	626 330-1229	0
Par Engineering Inc		E	626 964-8700	0
Performance Food Group Inc		D	800 697-7662	0
Performance Sheets LLC		C	626 333-0195	0
Pilot Inc (PA)		D	626 937-6988	0
Potter Roemer LLC (HQ)		D	626 855-4890	0
Poundex Associates Corporation		D	909 444-5878	0
Prime Global Solutions Inc (PA)		D	800 424-7746	0
Private Label Pc LLC		C	626 965-8686	0
Pruitthealth Inc		E	626 810-5567	0
Public Hlth Fndation Entps Inc (PA)		C	800 201-7320	0
Quartz Logistics Inc		D	626 606-2001	0
Quest Components Inc		E	626 333-5858	0
Quinn Shepherd Machinery		B	562 463-6000	0
Qy Research Inc		D	626 295-2442	0
Rongcheng Trading LLC		E	626 338-1090	0
Rutland Tool & Supply Co (HQ)		D	562 566-5000	0
Snap-On Incorporated		D	626 965-0668	0
Solestage Inc		E	909 576-1309	0
Soto Provision Inc		D	626 458-4600	0
South Bay Freight System LLC (PA)		D	626 271-9800	0
Southern California Gas Co		D	213 244-1200	0
Swatfame Inc (PA)		B	626 961-7928	0
Sweda Company LLC		C	626 357-9999	0
Tf Courier Inc		D	214 560-9000	0
Thunder Group Inc (PA)		E	626 935-1605	0
Time Warner Cable Inc		D	626 705-7482	0
Topocean Consolidation Service (PA)		C	562 908-1688	0
Unical Aviation Inc (PA)		C	909 348-1700	0
Unical Enterprises Inc		D	626 965-5588	0
United Pumping Service Inc		D	626 961-9326	0
Universal Wilkes Co Inc (PA)		D	626 839-2022	0
US Bankcard Services Inc		D	888 888-8872	0
Valley Management Services		B	626 333-1243	0
W Diamond Supply Co (DH)		D	909 859-8939	0
Waterhill Ltd		E	626 369-6828	0
Yale/Chase Eqp & Svcs Inc (PA)		C	562 463-8000	0
Zerep Management Corporation		D	626 961-6291	0
Zmodo Technology Corp Ltd		A	217 903-5673	0

CLAREMONT, CA - Los Angeles County

	SIC	EMP	PHONE	ENTRY #
Atmc Incorporated (PA)		D	909 390-0470	0
Ben Bollinger Productions Inc		D	909 626-3296	0
Bluebridge Professional Svcs		D	909 625-6151	0
Citigroup Global Markets Inc		D	909 625-0781	0
Claremont Star LP		E	909 482-0124	0
Claremont Tennis Club		C	909 625-9515	0
Corey Nursery Co Inc (PA)		D	909 621-6886	0
Epitome Enterprises LLC		D	909 625-4728	0
Front Porch Communities		C	909 626-1227	0
Guillen Electric Company Inc		E	909 480-3915	0
HDR Engineering Inc		D	909 626-0967	0
Hotline Telecommunications (PA)		D	909 593-6575	0
Kaiser Foundation Hospitals		B	888 750-0036	0
Lovely Living Homecare		D	909 625-7999	0
Pilgrim Place In Claremont (PA)		C	909 399-5500	0
Pilgrim Place In Claremont		C	909 621-9581	0
Pomona College		C	909 621-8000	0
Pomona Valley Hospital Med Ctr		A	909 865-9104	0
Pomona Valley Hospital Med Ctr		D	909 621-7956	0
Pomona Valley Hospital Med Ctr		A	909 865-9977	0
Rancho Santa Ana Botanic Grdn		D	909 625-8767	0
Therapak LLC (DH)		D	909 267-2000	0
Tierra Del Sol Foundation		D	909 626-8301	0

	SIC	EMP	PHONE	ENTRY #
Trinity Youth Services (PA)		D	909 980-4755	0
Visiting Nurse Associ		D	909 621-3961	0
Western Feld Invstigations Inc (PA)		D	800 999-9589	0

CLARKSBURG, CA - Yolo County

	SIC	EMP	PHONE	ENTRY #
Vino Farms Inc		C	916 775-4095	0

CLAYTON, CA - Contra Costa County

	SIC	EMP	PHONE	ENTRY #
American Golf Corporation		D	925 672-9737	0

CLEARLAKE, CA - Lake County

	SIC	EMP	PHONE	ENTRY #
Adventist Health Clearlake (HQ)		B	707 994-6486	0
Adventist Health System/West		C	707 995-4888	0
Adventist Health System/West		E	707 995-4500	0
Adventist Health System/West		B	707 994-6486	0
Advintist Hlth Clearlake Hosp		B	707 994-6486	0
Vindra Inc		D	707 994-7738	0

CLOVERDALE, CA - Sonoma County

	SIC	EMP	PHONE	ENTRY #
Coppertower Family Medical Ctr		E	707 894-4229	0
Ensign Cloverdale LLC		D	707 894-5201	0
Pacific States Industries Inc		C	707 894-4242	0
Redwood Credit Union		D	800 479-7928	0
Star H-R		A	707 894-4404	0

CLOVIS, CA - Fresno County

	SIC	EMP	PHONE	ENTRY #
Agrian Inc (PA)		D	559 437-5700	0
Agriculture and Priority Pollu (PA)		E	559 275-2175	0
AT&T Corp		D	559 294-5431	0
Blair Engineering Inc (PA)		D	559 326-1400	0
Borunda Private SEC Patrol Inc		E	559 299-2662	0
Bowie Enterprises		D	559 292-6565	0
C2 Financial Corporation		C	559 824-2300	0
Cellco Partnership		D	559 325-1420	0
Central Valley Community Bank (HQ)		C	559 323-3384	0
Central Valley Indian Hlth Inc (PA)		D	559 299-2578	0
Clovis Custom Drywall Inc		E	559 297-7073	0
Clovis Unified School District		A	559 327-3900	0
County of Fresno		D	559 600-5127	0
Craftman Concrete		D	559 298-8864	0
Death Valley 49ers Inc		D	559 297-5691	0
Elite Landscaping Inc		C	559 292-7760	0
Floyd Johnston Cnstr Co Inc		D	559 299-7373	0
Fresno Cmnty Hosp & Med Ctr		D	559 324-4000	0
Generation Clovis LLC		C	559 297-4900	0
George Browns Sports Club (PA)		D	559 297-8656	0
Golden Living LLC		D	559 299-2591	0
Graham Concrete Cnstr Inc		D	559 292-6571	0
Guarantee Real Estate Corp		D	559 321-6040	0
Hodges Electric Inc		E	559 298-5533	0
J & L Vineyards		D	559 268-1627	0
Kaiser Foundation Hospitals		D	559 324-5100	0
Kings Credit Services		D	559 322-2550	0
Krazan & Associates (PA)		D	559 348-2200	0
Labor One Inc		D	559 430-4202	0
Ladell Inc		E	559 650-2000	0
New Vista Health Services (PA)		B	559 298-3236	0
Niacc-Avitech Technologies Inc (PA)		D	559 291-2500	0
Peachwood Medical Group Clovis		D	559 324-6200	0
Pk Autobody Inc		E	559 298-9691	0
Regent Assisted Living Inc		D	559 325-8400	0
Servi-Tech Controls Inc (PA)		D	559 264-6679	0
Smart & Final Stores Inc		B	559 297-9376	0
Tri-Star Drywall Lp		D	559 299-9858	0
Valley Unique Electric Inc		D	559 237-4795	0
Valleywide Construction Inc		C	559 834-6212	0
Vibra Healthcare LLC		D	559 325-5601	0
Westech Systems Inc		D	559 298-5237	0
Willow Creek Halthcare Ctr LLC		A	559 323-6200	0
Willow Creek Halthcare Ctr LLC		D	559 323-6200	0

COACHELLA, CA - Riverside County

	SIC	EMP	PHONE	ENTRY #
29 Palms Enterprises Corp		A	760 775-5566	0
Coachella Valley Water Dst (PA)		A	760 398-2651	0
Desert Valley Date Inc		E	760 398-0999	0
Downtown Metro		E	760 398-3310	0
Esparza Enterprises Inc		A	760 398-0349	0
L&D Farm Labor		E	760 408-6311	0
Primetime International Inc		D	760 399-4166	0
SA Recycling LLC		D	760 391-5591	0
Sun and Sands Enterprises LLC (PA)		D	760 399-4278	0
Sun World International Inc		B	760 398-9300	0
Sunline Transit Agency		C	760 972-4059	0
Teserra (PA)		B	760 340-9000	0
Valley Pride Inc		D	760 398-1353	0

COALINGA, CA - Fresno County

	SIC	EMP	PHONE	ENTRY #
Califrnia Dept State Hospitals		B	559 935-4300	0

Mergent email: customerrelations@mergent.com
1522

2020 Directory of California
Wholesalers and Services Companies

(P-0000) Products & Services Section entry number
(PA)=Parent Co (HQ)=Headquarters (DH)=Div Headquarters

	SIC	EMP	PHONE	ENTRY #
Coalinga Dstngished Cmnty Care		D	559 935-5939	0
Coalinga Regional Medical Cent		C	559 935-6400	0
Harris Farms Inc		E	559 884-2203	0
Harris Farms Inc		B	559 935-0717	0
Harris Farms Inc		C	559 884-2477	0
Harris Woolf Cal Almonds LLC		E	559 884-2147	0
Merchant Valley Corp		E	916 410-2021	0

COARSEGOLD, CA - Madera County

	SIC	EMP	PHONE	ENTRY #
Chukchansi Gold Resort Casino		A	866 794-6946	0
Wb Electric Inc		D	408 842-7911	0
Yosemite Lakes Owners Assn		D	559 658-7466	0

COLMA, CA - San Mateo County

	SIC	EMP	PHONE	ENTRY #
Cypress Funeral Services Inc		C	650 550-8808	0
Lucky Chances Inc		A	650 758-2237	0
Precision Auto Detailing LLC		D	650 992-9775	0

COLTON, CA - San Bernardino County

	SIC	EMP	PHONE	ENTRY #
A-Z Bus Sales Inc (PA)		D	951 781-7188	0
Arrowhead Regional Medical Ctr		A	909 580-1000	0
Bob Hubbard Horse Trnsp Inc (PA)		E	951 369-3770	0
Brithinee Electric		D	909 825-7971	0
C E P		D	909 580-1456	0
Cardinal Health Inc		D	909 824-1820	0
CBS Radio Inc		D	909 825-9525	0
Charter Hospice Colton LLC		C	909 825-2969	0
Coast2coast Public Safety LLC		E	833 262-7877	0
Colton Joint Unified Schl Dst		D	909 876-4240	0
Cornerstone Hospice Cal LLC		C	909 872-8100	0
County of San Bernardino		C	909 580-1000	0
Dish Factory Inc (PA)		D	213 687-9500	0
GATX Corporation		D	909 825-3043	0
Greenpath Recovery West Inc		D	909 954-0686	0
Inland Eye Inst Med Group Inc (PA)		D	909 825-3425	0
Kaiser Foundation Hospitals		A	909 427-5521	0
King Equipment LLC		D	909 986-5300	0
Medlin Development		E	909 825-5296	0
Pacific Vision Services Inc		D	909 824-6090	0
Premier Medical Trnsp Inc		D	909 433-3939	0
Reche Cyn Rhblitation Hlth Ctr		B	909 370-4411	0
Republic Services Inc		E	909 370-3377	0
SA Recycling LLC		D	909 825-1662	0
Sisters of Soul (sos) Youth		C	909 533-4889	0
Southern Cal Prmnnte Med Group		E	909 370-2501	0
Sprouts Farmers Market Inc		C	888 577-7688	0
Sulzer Electro-Mechanical Serv		E	909 825-7971	0
Superior Masonry Walls Ltd		D	909 370-1800	0
Valley Ob Gyn Medical Group		E	909 580-6333	0
Van Dyk Tank Lines Inc		E	951 682-5000	0
VFW Post 6476		C	909 754-3828	0
West Cast Fire Integration Inc		D	909 824-7980	0
Western Healthcare Management		C	909 824-1530	0
Westrux International Inc		D	909 825-5121	0

COLUMBIA, CA - Tuolumne County

	SIC	EMP	PHONE	ENTRY #
Twain Harte Horsemen		D	209 586-4841	0
Zephyr River Expeditions Inc		D	800 431-3636	0

COLUSA, CA - Colusa County

	SIC	EMP	PHONE	ENTRY #
Childrens Services		D	530 458-0300	0
Colusa Cnty Sbstnce Abuse Svcs		D	530 458-0520	0
Colusa Indian Cmnty Council		A	530 458-6572	0
Colusa Regional Medical Center		C	530 458-5821	0
New Colusa Indian Bingo		B	530 458-8844	0
Premier Mushrooms LP (PA)		C	530 458-2700	0
Premier Mushrooms LP		C	530 458-2700	0

COMMERCE, CA - Los Angeles County

	SIC	EMP	PHONE	ENTRY #
4 Earth Farms Inc (PA)		D	323 201-5800	0
99 Cents Only Stores LLC (HQ)		B	323 980-8145	0
Acco Engineered Systems Inc		D	323 727-7765	0
Acco Engineered Systems Inc		E	323 201-0931	0
Adj Products LLC (PA)		D	323 582-2650	0
Altamed Health Services Corp (PA)		C	323 725-8751	0
American De Rosa Lamparts LLC (PA)		D	800 777-4440	0
American Security Force Inc		C	323 722-8585	0
American Vanguard Corporation		C	323 264-3910	0
Arden-Mayfair Inc		E	310 638-2842	0
Associated Landscape		D	714 558-6100	0
Bayou Cinemas LP		D	213 235-2244	0
Bctc Corporation		D	323 888-9388	0
Ben Myerson Candy Co Inc (PA)		B	800 331-2829	0
Bnsf Railway Company		C	323 869-3002	0
Buy Fresh Produce Inc		D	323 796-0127	0
California Commerce Club Inc		A	323 721-2100	0
California Produce Wholsalers		E	562 776-5770	0

	SIC	EMP	PHONE	ENTRY #
Califrnia Intermodal Assoc Inc (PA)		D	323 562-7788	0
Cellco Partnership		D	323 725-9750	0
Celluphone LLC		D	323 727-9131	0
Century Snacks LLC		B	323 278-9578	0
Ceramic Decorating Company Inc		E	323 268-5135	0
Challenge Dairy Products Inc		E	323 724-3130	0
CIT Bank National Association		D	323 838-6881	0
City of Commerce		B	323 722-4805	0
Commerce Center Theatres		D	323 722-5577	0
County of Los Angeles		B	323 889-3405	0
D J American Supply Inc		C	323 582-2650	0
Dart International A Corp (HQ)		C	323 264-8746	0
Dart Warehouse Corporation (HQ)		B	323 264-1011	0
East Los Angeles Community Un (PA)		E	323 721-1655	0
East Los Angeles Mental Hlth		D	323 725-1337	0
EDS West LLC		D	323 887-7367	0
El Guapo Spices Inc (PA)		D	213 312-1300	0
Elkay Plastics Co Inc (PA)		D	323 722-7073	0
Ernest Packaging (PA)		C	800 233-7788	0
Express Messenger Systems Inc		D	323 725-2100	0
Farwest Insulation Contracting		E	310 634-2800	0
Fedex Smartpost Inc		D	323 888-8879	0
Fox Luggage Inc		D	323 588-1688	0
Gehr Development Corporation (HQ)		D	323 728-5558	0
Gibson Overseas Inc		A	323 832-8900	0
Grocers Specialty Company (DH)		E	323 264-5200	0
Haldeman Inc		D	323 726-7011	0
Hkf Inc		B	323 225-1318	0
Ineos Composites Us LLC		D	323 767-1300	0
Innovo Azteca Apparel Inc		D	323 837-3700	0
Interstate Electric Co Inc (PA)		D	323 724-0420	0
Interstate Meat & Provision		D	323 838-9400	0
Ivo Wall Experts Inc		D	323 246-4026	0
Iworks Us Inc		D	323 278-8363	0
Jfc International Inc (HQ)		C	323 721-6100	0
Jfc International Inc		C	323 721-6900	0
Justman Packaging & Display		D	323 728-8888	0
Malibu Design Group		E	323 271-1700	0
Maravilla Foundation (PA)		D	323 721-4162	0
Meridian Textiles Inc (PA)		D	323 869-5700	0
Mexican Amrcn Oprtnty Fndation		D	323 890-1555	0
Michelson Laboratories Inc (PA)		D	562 802-0553	0
Miken Sales Inc (PA)		D	323 266-2560	0
Milspec Industries Inc (DH)		D	213 680-9690	0
National Sales Corp		D	323 586-0200	0
Nora Lighting Inc		D	800 686-6672	0
Nurses Internet Staffing Svcs (PA)		C	323 720-9900	0
Parsec Inc		A	323 268-5011	0
Penny Lane Centers		C	323 318-9960	0
Pixior LLC (PA)		D	323 721-2221	0
Printing Inds Assn Suthern Cal		D	323 728-9500	0
Progressive Produce LLC (HQ)		D	323 890-8100	0
Prudential Overall Supply		D	323 724-4888	0
Prudential Overall Supply		D	323 722-0636	0
PWS Holdings LLC		C	323 721-8832	0
Ramcar Batteries Inc		E	323 726-1212	0
Reading Entertainment Inc (HQ)		D	213 235-2226	0
Rolled Steel Products Corp (PA)		D	323 723-8836	0
Ryan Shroads		E	310 936-5966	0
Screamline Investment Corp (PA)		C	323 201-0114	0
Securitas SEC Svcs USA Inc		D	323 832-9074	0
Seiu United Healthcare Workers		E	323 734-8399	0
Shims Bargain Inc		C	323 726-8800	0
Smart & Final Stores Inc (PA)		B	323 869-7500	0
Smart & Final Stores LLC (DH)		C	323 869-7500	0
Solemnity Personnel		E	323 718-3979	0
Starline Tours Hollywood Inc		D	323 262-1114	0
Strategic Materials Inc		D	323 887-6831	0
Sun Coast Merchandise Corp		C	323 720-9700	0
Telacu Industries Inc (HQ)		E	323 721-1655	0
Tpg La Commerce LLC		D	401 946-4600	0
Unified Grocers Inc (DH)		A	323 264-5200	0
Union Pacific Railroad Company		D	213 446-1900	0
Uniserve Facilities Svcs Corp (PA)		A	213 533-1000	0
United Insurance Company		E	323 869-9381	0
United Parcel Service Inc OH		B	323 837-1220	0
Univar Solutions USA Inc		C	323 727-7005	0
Veritiv Operating Company		C	323 725-3700	0
W2005 Wyn Hotels LP		D	323 887-8100	0
Waste Mgt Collectn & Recycl		C	626 960-7551	0
Wood Environment &		D	323 889-5300	0
Wyndham International Inc		D	323 887-4331	0
Zemarc Corporation (PA)		E	323 721-5598	0

COMPTON, CA - Los Angeles County

	SIC	EMP	PHONE	ENTRY #
Advanced Logistics MGT Inc		E	310 638-0715	0

Employment Codes: A=Over 500 employees, B=251-500,
C=101-250, D=51-100, E=50

2020 Directory of California
Wholesalers and Services Companies

© Mergent Inc. 1-800-342-5647

1523

GEOGRAPHIC

	SIC	EMP	PHONE	ENTRY #
Ajr Trucking Inc		C	562 989-9555	0
All Phase Business Supplies		E	310 631-1900	0
Apex Logistics Intl Inc **(PA)**		D	310 665-0288	0
Appliance Recycling Ctrs Amer		D	310 223-2800	0
Asbury Environmental Services **(PA)**		D	310 886-3400	0
Auto Expressions LLC		D	310 639-0666	0
Az/CFS West Inc		D	310 898-2090	0
Beauchamp Distributing Company		D	310 639-5320	0
Benettis Italia Inc		D	310 537-8036	0
Blake H Brown Inc **(DH)**		D	310 764-0110	0
Bst Enterprises Inc		D	310 638-1222	0
Cal-State Steel Corporation		C	310 632-2772	0
CCC Property Holdings LLC		C	310 609-1957	0
Celebrity Casinos Inc		B	310 631-3838	0
Cintas Corporation No 3		D	310 725-2850	0
City of Compton		D	310 635-3484	0
Colosseum Athletics Corp		D	310 667-8341	0
Concrete Tie Industries Inc **(PA)**		D	310 628-2328	0
Contractors Cargo Company **(PA)**		C	310 609-1957	0
Cordelia Lighting Inc		C	310 886-3490	0
County of Los Angeles		D	310 885-2100	0
County of Los Angeles		D	310 668-6845	0
County of Los Angeles		C	310 603-7483	0
County of Los Angeles		C	310 603-7271	0
County of Los Angeles		C	310 603-7311	0
County Santtn Dist 2 of La Co		D	310 638-1161	0
Crew Inc		D	310 608-6860	0
Decky Co Inc **(PA)**		D	310 608-2726	0
Demenno Kerdoon		C	310 537-7100	0
Demenno-Kerdoon		B	310 898-3848	0
Dependable Aircargo Ex Inc		C	310 537-2000	0
Dhx-Dependable Hawaiian Ex Inc **(PA)**		C	310 537-2000	0
Dna Specialty Inc		D	310 767-4070	0
Dnow LP		D	310 900-3900	0
Dti Inc		D	310 635-9002	0
Element Mtrls Tech HB Inc		D	310 632-8500	0
Evox Productions LLC **(PA)**		D	310 605-1400	0
Express Messenger Systems Inc		D	800 359-2959	0
F R T International Inc **(PA)**		C	310 604-8208	0
Florence Filter Corporation		D	310 637-1137	0
FNS Customs Brokers Inc		E	310 667-4880	0
General Petroleum Corporation **(DH)**		C	562 983-7300	0
Geodis Logistics LLC		D	310 604-8185	0
Global Mail Inc		C	310 735-0800	0
Gourmet Foods Inc **(PA)**		D	310 632-3300	0
Hydroprocessing Associates LLC		E	310 667-6456	0
Interstate Foods Inc		C	310 635-0426	0
JAM Industries Inc		D	310 254-0300	0
Kawai America Corporation **(HQ)**		E	310 631-1771	0
Knight Transportation Inc		C	888 549-7802	0
M M Fab Inc		D	310 763-3800	0
Mitsubishi Warehouse Cal Corp		D	310 886-5500	0
Monico Alloys Inc **(PA)**		D	310 928-0168	0
Nabors Well Services Co		D	310 639-7074	0
National Retail Trnsp Inc		D	310 605-3777	0
Newport Apparel Corporation **(PA)**		D	310 605-1900	0
Ocean Knight Shipping Inc		C	310 885-3388	0
Pacific Lighting Mfr Inc		C	310 327-7711	0
Pasha Group		C	310 735-0952	0
Patina Freight Inc		D	310 764-4395	0
Petrochem Insulation Inc		C	310 638-6663	0
Pitney Bowes Presort Svcs Inc		D	310 763-4615	0
Port Logistics Group Inc		D	310 669-2551	0
Progressive Trnsp Svcs Inc		D	510 268-3776	0
Purolator International Inc		D	888 511-4811	0
Quality Production Svcs Inc		D	310 406-3350	0
RPM Mechanical - A Joint Ventr		D	858 565-4131	0
Southern California Edison Co		C	310 608-5029	0
Star View Chldrn Fmly Srvcs		D	310 868-5379	0
Stk International Inc		D	310 720-1277	0
Sulzer Tower Field Svc Cal Inc		D	918 447-7676	0
Tap Operating Co LLC		A	310 900-5500	0
Tap Worldwide LLC **(PA)**		D	310 900-5500	0
Tom Malloy Corporation **(PA)**		E	310 327-5554	0
Transport Express Inc		D	310 898-2000	0
Uma Enterprises Inc **(PA)**		C	310 631-1166	0
United Fabricare Supply Inc **(PA)**		D	310 886-3790	0
USA Waste of California Inc		D	310 763-8500	0
Vanguard Lgistics Svcs USA Inc		D	310 637-3700	0
Viharas Group Inc		D	310 537-6700	0
Wenzlau Engineering Inc		D	310 604-3400	0
World Wide Technology LLC		E	310 537-8335	0

CONCORD, CA - Contra Costa County

	SIC	EMP	PHONE	ENTRY #
Admiral Security Services Inc		B	888 471-1128	0
ADT Security Corporation		E	925 251-9088	0

	SIC	EMP	PHONE	ENTRY #
Agostini and Associates Inc		E	925 691-7300	0
Albert D Seeno Cnstr Co Inc		D	925 671-7711	0
Albert McKnzie A Prof Law Corp		D	925 689-8000	0
American Brdge/Fluor Entps Inc		D	510 808-4623	0
American Medical Response		C	925 454-6000	0
American Medical Response Inc		C	925 602-1300	0
American National Red Cross		E	925 603-7400	0
Apria Healthcare LLC		D	925 827-8800	0
Aptim Corp		A	925 288-2011	0
Aramark Unf & Career AP LLC		D	925 827-3782	0
Ascent Services Group Inc		B	925 627-4900	0
Asrc Industrial Services LLC **(HQ)**		C	707 644-7455	0
Assetmark Inc **(HQ)**		E	925 521-1040	0
Assetmark Fincl Holdings Inc		A	925 521-2200	0
AT&T Corp		D	925 356-6204	0
AT&T Services Inc		D	925 671-1902	0
AT&T Services Inc		B	925 671-1059	0
Athens Insurance Service Inc		C	925 826-1000	0
Ausenco PSI LLC **(HQ)**		D	925 939-4420	0
Ausenco USA Inc **(PA)**		D	925 939-4420	0
Bay Alarm Company **(PA)**		D	925 935-1100	0
Bay Area Seating Service Inc		B	925 671-4000	0
Bay Area/Diablo Petroleum Co		C	925 228-2222	0
Bay Cities Pav & Grading Inc		C	925 687-6666	0
Bay Medic Transportation Inc		D	800 689-9511	0
Bayside Insulation & Cnstr		D	925 288-8960	0
Brenden Theatre Corporation **(PA)**		C	925 677-0462	0
Building Services/System Inc		D	925 688-1234	0
California Ticketscom Inc		C	925 671-4000	0
Carlton Senior Living Inc		D	925 935-1660	0
Carone & Company Inc		D	925 602-8800	0
CDM SMITH INC		D	617 452-6000	0
City of Concord		B	925 692-2400	0
City of Concord		D	925 686-6262	0
Clyde Miles Cnstr Co Inc		D	925 427-4473	0
Coldwell Bnkr Residential Brkg **(DH)**		D	925 275-3000	0
Comcast Corporation		B	925 271-9794	0
Compumail Information Svcs Inc		D	925 689-7100	0
Concord Hotel LLC		D	925 521-3751	0
Connexsys Engineering Inc		E	510 243-2050	0
Consumer Cr Cnsling Svc San Fr **(PA)**		D	888 456-2227	0
Contra Costa Vet Med Emrgcy CL		E	925 798-5830	0
Contra Costa Water District **(PA)**		C	925 688-8000	0
Cooper Vali & Associates Inc **(DH)**		D	510 446-8301	0
County of Contra Costa		D	925 646-5877	0
County of Contra Costa		E	925 646-5480	0
Courtyards At Pine Creek Inc		E	925 798-3900	0
Cowell Homeowners Association **(PA)**		D	925 825-0250	0
Customer Loyalty Builders Inc		D	888 478-7787	0
D A McCosker Construction Co		E	925 686-1780	0
D C Taylor Co		E	925 603-1100	0
Dave Calhoun and Assoc LLC		C	925 688-1234	0
Delta Personnel Services Inc		D	925 356-3034	0
Denova Home Sales Inc		B	925 852-0545	0
Dianne Adair Day Care Centers **(PA)**		D	925 429-3232	0
Edgewood Partners Insur Ctr		C	415 356-3900	0
Eichleay Inc **(PA)**		C	925 689-7000	0
Electric Tech Construction Inc		D	925 849-5324	0
Encore Inc		E	925 932-1033	0
Enterprise Roofing Service Inc		D	925 689-8100	0
Ernie & Sons Scaffolding		C	925 446-4442	0
Fidelity Nat HM Warranty Co		D	925 356-0194	0
First American Title Insur Co		D	925 356-7000	0
First American Title Insur Co		D	925 798-2800	0
First Student Inc		D	925 676-1976	0
Futures Explored		D	925 332-7183	0
General Electric Company		D	925 602-5950	0
Gilbane Aecom JV		D	925 946-3100	0
Gilbane Federal **(DH)**		C	925 946-3100	0
Gilbane Smcc LLC		D	925 946-3100	0
Goldman Avram		D	925 275-3000	0
Gonsalves & Santucci Inc **(PA)**		E	925 685-6799	0
Grappa Software Inc		D	925 818-4760	0
Harris & Associates Inc **(PA)**		D	925 827-4900	0
Jacobs Engineering Group Inc		D	925 356-3900	0
James C Jenkins Insur Svc Inc		C	925 798-3334	0
Janus Corporation **(PA)**		D	925 969-9200	0
John Muir Behavioral Hlth Ctr		C	925 674-5000	0
John Muir Health		A	925 692-5600	0
John Muir Health		A	925 682-8200	0
John Muir Physician Network		A	925 682-8200	0
John Muir Physician Network		A	925 674-2200	0
Jopari Solutions Inc		D	925 459-5200	0
Kindred Healthcare Oper Inc		C	925 692-5886	0
Kissito Health Case Inc		D	925 689-9222	0

	SIC	EMP	PHONE	ENTRY #
Kyocera Dcment Sltons Amer Inc		D	925 849-3300	0
Land Home Financial Svcs Inc **(PA)**		E	925 676-7038	0
Laughlin Falbo Levy Moresi LLP **(PA)**		D	510 628-0496	0
Leisure Planet		C	925 687-4386	0
Lemore Transportation Inc **(PA)**		D	925 689-6444	0
Lescure Company Inc		D	925 283-2528	0
McE Corporation **(PA)**		D	925 803-4111	0
Mike McCall Landscape Inc		C	925 363-8100	0
Mike Roses Auto Body Inc		E	925 686-1739	0
Montclair Hotels Mb LLC		D	925 687-5500	0
Mt Dblo Resource Recovery LLC		B	925 682-9113	0
New Way LLC		E	925 688-1520	0
Nextel Communications Inc		D	925 682-2355	0
Office Movers Inc		E	408 254-5010	0
Overmiller Inc		D	925 798-2122	0
Pace Inc		D	925 602-0900	0
Pacific Gas and Electric Co		D	925 676-0948	0
Pacific Gas and Electric Co		D	925 674-6305	0
Pacific Service Credit Union **(PA)**		D	888 858-6878	0
Pacificdental Benefits Inc **(PA)**		C	925 363-6000	0
Parc Management LLC		A	925 609-1364	0
Patriot Contract Services LLC		B	925 296-2000	0
Peppermill Casinos Inc		C	925 671-7711	0
Planned Prnthod Shst-Dblo Inc **(PA)**		E	925 676-0300	0
Precision Television Inc		D	925 825-5296	0
Ricoh Usa Inc		C	925 988-4000	0
Sears Roebuck and Co		D	925 246-1996	0
Seecon Built Homes Inc		D	925 671-7711	0
Service Hospitality LLC		D	925 566-8820	0
Shelter Inc **(PA)**		D	925 335-0698	0
Sierra Bay Contractors Inc		E	925 671-7711	0
Stonebrook Convalescent Center		C	925 689-7457	0
Summit Building Services Inc		D	925 827-9500	0
Sutter Vsting Nrse Assn Hspice		D	925 677-4250	0
Swinerton Builders Inc		D	925 602-6400	0
Swinerton Incorporated		D	925 689-2336	0
Telstar Instruments **(PA)**		D	925 671-2888	0
Tranquility Incorporated		C	925 825-4280	0
Travis Credit Union		B	800 877-8328	0
Ufcw & Employers Trust LLC **(PA)**		C	800 552-2400	0
United Behavioral Health		C	925 246-1343	0
United Parcel Service Inc OH		C	925 689-6584	0
Valley Relocation and Storage **(PA)**		C	925 230-2025	0
Value-Centered Solutions Inc		E	925 332-0555	0
Versa Engineering & Tech Inc **(PA)**		D	925 405-4505	0
Veterinary Surgical Associates **(PA)**		D	925 827-1777	0
Vwi Concord LLC		C	925 827-2000	0
Wells Fargo Bank National Assn		D	925 746-3718	0
Willow Pass Hlth Care Ctr Inc		D	925 689-9222	0
Windsor Convalescent		D	925 689-2266	0
Young MNS Chrstn Assn of E Bay		A	925 609-7971	0
Youth Homes Incorporated		D	925 933-2627	0
Yupana Inc		E	925 482-0657	0
Zero Waste Solutions Inc		C	925 270-3339	0
Zwicker & Associates PC		C	925 689-7070	0

COPPEROPOLIS, CA - Calaveras County

	SIC	EMP	PHONE	ENTRY #
Commercial Site Imprvs Inc		E	209 785-1920	0
Meridian Gold Inc		C	209 785-3222	0

CORCORAN, CA - Kings County

	SIC	EMP	PHONE	ENTRY #
Corcoran District Hospital		D	559 992-3300	0
Gilkey Farms Inc		D	559 992-2136	0
Hansen Equipment Company LLC		E	559 992-3111	0
Hansen Ranches		D	559 992-3111	0
J G Boswell Company		D	559 992-2141	0
J G Boswell Company		B	559 992-5141	0
Jason Proctor Trnsp Co		D	559 992-1767	0
Recreational Assn Corcoran		D	559 992-5171	0
Vista Verde Farms Inc		D	559 992-3111	0

CORNING, CA - Tehama County

	SIC	EMP	PHONE	ENTRY #
Andersncttonwood Disposal Svcs		D	530 824-4700	0
Omega Waste Management Inc		D	530 824-1890	0
Paskenta Band Nomlaki Indians		B	530 528-3500	0

CORONA, CA - Riverside County

	SIC	EMP	PHONE	ENTRY #
ABC School Equipment Inc		D	951 817-2200	0
Ability Counts Inc **(PA)**		D	951 734-6595	0
Acm Technologies Inc **(PA)**		D	951 738-9898	0
Ae & Associates LLC		D	951 278-3477	0
Agile Sourcing Partners Inc		C	951 279-4154	0
AK Constructors Inc		D	951 280-0269	0
All American Asphalt **(PA)**		D	951 736-7600	0
All American Asphalt		D	951 736-7617	0
All American Asphalt		C	951 736-7617	0
All American Service & Sups		D	951 736-3880	0

	SIC	EMP	PHONE	ENTRY #
Amec Fster Wheler E C Svcs Inc		C	951 273-7400	0
American Electric Supply Inc **(PA)**		D	951 734-7910	0
American Power SEC Svc Inc		D	866 974-9994	0
Amerisourcebergen Corporation		C	951 493-2339	0
Amerisourcebergen Drug Corp		C	951 371-2000	0
ARC Fastener Supply & Mfg		D	909 481-8171	0
Arizona Pipeline Company		C	951 270-3100	0
Auto Buyline Systems Inc **(PA)**		E	951 271-8999	0
Bbva USA		B	951 279-7071	0
Beador Construction Co Inc		D	951 674-7352	0
Bmb 1 LLC		D	951 272-6200	0
C & R Systems Inc **(PA)**		E	951 270-0255	0
Calatlantic Group Inc		D	951 898-5500	0
Cannon Fabrication Inc		D	951 278-1830	0
Canyon Insulation Inc		D	951 278-9200	0
Cellco Partnership		D	951 549-6400	0
Championship Golf Services Inc		C	951 272-4340	0
Chief Protective Services Inc		D	951 738-0881	0
Chilis 898 Corona		D	951 734-7275	0
City of Corona		C	951 279-3647	0
City of Corona		D	951 736-2266	0
Combustion Associates Inc		E	951 272-6999	0
Comcast Corporation		D	951 268-9378	0
Core-Mark Corona 2		E	800 622-1206	0
Corona Clipper Inc		D	951 737-6515	0
De La Torre Landscape & Maint		C	951 549-3525	0
Downs Fuel Transport Inc		E	951 256-8286	0
DR Horton Inc		E	951 272-9000	0
Eagle Glen Country Club LLC		D	951 272-4653	0
Ebs Concrete Inc		E	951 279-6869	0
Ebs General Engineering Inc		D	951 279-6869	0
Empire Demolition Inc		D	909 393-8300	0
Excel Landscape Inc		C	951 735-9650	0
Express Cable Communication		D	951 272-2029	0
F M Tarbell Co		D	951 280-6040	0
Fennel Inc		D	951 284-2020	0
Fire Sprinkler Systems Inc **(PA)**		D	800 915-3473	0
First Student Inc		C	951 736-3234	0
Fst Sand & Gravel Inc		E	951 277-8440	0
Green River Golf Corporation		D	714 970-8411	0
H & H Transportation LLC		D	951 817-2300	0
Halo Unlimted Inc		D	714 692-2270	0
Hardwood Creations **(PA)**		D	714 674-0527	0
Hillcrest Contracting Inc		D	951 273-9600	0
Hoffman Concrete Company Inc		E	951 372-8333	0
HP Communications Inc		C	951 572-1200	0
Infinity Plumbing Designs Inc		B	951 737-4436	0
JJ Mac Intyre Co Inc **(PA)**		C	951 898-4300	0
K&B Electric LLC		C	951 808-9501	0
K&B Engineering		C	951 808-9501	0
Kaiser Foundation Hospitals		D	866 984-7483	0
Kaiser Foundation Hospitals		A	866 984-7483	0
Kec Engineering		C	951 734-3010	0
La Steel Services Inc		E	951 393-2013	0
Laurence-Hovenier Inc		D	951 736-2990	0
LDI Mechanical Inc **(PA)**		C	951 340-9685	0
Lennar Homes Inc		D	951 739-0267	0
Lexani Wheel Corporation		D	951 808-4200	0
Live Media LLC		E	951 279-8877	0
M E Nollkamper Inc **(PA)**		E	951 737-9300	0
Management Trust Assn Inc		C	951 694-1758	0
Marie Cllender Wholesalers Inc		D	951 737-6760	0
Minka Lighting Inc **(PA)**		D	951 735-9220	0
Mission Ambulance Inc		C	951 272-2300	0
Monster Energy Company **(HQ)**		C	951 739-6200	0
More Truck Lines Inc		D	951 371-6673	0
MS Industrial Shtmtl Inc		C	951 272-6610	0
Multi Mechanical Inc		D	714 632-7404	0
Nep Group Inc		E	951 279-8877	0
NP Mechanical Inc		B	951 667-4220	0
Pacific Shores Masonry		E	951 371-8550	0
Pacwest Instrument Labs Inc		D	951 737-0790	0
Parcell Steel Corp **(PA)**		C	951 471-3200	0
Peaceful Hearts Home Care Inc		D	951 541-9343	0
Peoples Choice Staffing Inc		D	951 735-0550	0
Peppermint Ridge **(PA)**		D	951 273-7320	0
Ply Gem Pacific Windows Corp		D	951 272-1300	0
Preferred Insulation Contrs **(PA)**		D	951 735-3725	0
Primary Provider MGT Co Inc **(PA)**		C	951 280-7700	0
Pro Building Maintenance Inc		D	951 279-3386	0
Pro Group Inc		D	951 271-3000	0
Provident Group Crown Pnte LLC		D	951 737-7482	0
Quadramed Corporation		A	951 736-6290	0
Quality Wall Systems Inc		D	951 739-4409	0
R W Lyall & Company Inc **(DH)**		C	951 270-1500	0

Employment Codes: A=Over 500 employees, B=251-500,
C=101-250, D=51-100, E=50

2020 Directory of California
Wholesalers and Services Companies

© Mergent Inc. 1-800-342-5647

1525

GEOGRAPHIC

	SIC	EMP	PHONE	ENTRY #
Ranch House Doors Inc		D	951 278-2884	0
Reliable Interiors Inc		C	951 371-3390	0
Remax All Stars Realty		D	951 739-4000	0
Residence Inn By Marriott LLC		C	951 371-0107	0
RNA Ann Arbor Incorporated		D	877 762-7511	0
Rugby Laboratories Inc (DH)		D	951 270-1400	0
Ryland Hmes Inlnd Empire Cstmr		D	951 273-3473	0
Screenworks LLC		D	951 279-8877	0
Smart Energy Solar Inc		C	800 405-1978	0
So Cal Sandbags Inc		D	951 277-3404	0
South Coast Logistics		E	714 894-4744	0
St Joseph Health Per Care Svcs		D	800 365-1110	0
Sun Rich Fresh Foods USA Inc (HQ)		D	951 735-3800	0
Superior Construction Inc		D	951 808-8780	0
Superior Paving Company Inc		D	951 739-9200	0
T W R Framing		D	951 279-2000	0
Talco Plastics Inc (PA)		D	951 531-2000	0
Team Dykspra (PA)		D	951 898-6482	0
Technical America Inc		D	951 272-9540	0
Thoro—Packaging (DH)		D	951 278-2100	0
Thyde Inc (PA)		C	951 817-2300	0
Troy Lee Designs LLC (PA)		D	951 371-5219	0
TWR Enterprises Inc		C	951 279-2000	0
U Gym LLC		D	951 808-3850	0
Uhs-Corona Inc (HQ)		A	951 737-4343	0
Uhs-Corona Inc		C	951 736-7200	0
US Foods Inc		C	951 256-2400	0
US Foods Inc		C	800 888-3147	0
US Foods Inc		C	951 582-8500	0
US Foods Inc		C	951 256-2400	0
US Green Building Council -			818 621-4880	0
US Home Corporation		E	951 817-3500	0
USA Waste of California Inc		D	800 423-9986	0
Valente Concrete		D	951 279-2221	0
Veg-Fresh Farms LLC		C	800 422-5535	0
VIP Transport Inc		E	951 272-3700	0
Volt Telecom Group Inc		E	800 548-6602	0
Volt Telecom Group Inc		C	951 493-8900	0
Waste MGT of Alameda Cnty		C	951 280-5471	0
West Hills Construction Inc		E	800 515-5270	0
Wurms Janitorial Service Inc		D	951 582-0003	0
X-Act Finish & Trim Inc		D	951 582-9229	0

CORONA DEL MAR, CA - Orange County

	SIC	EMP	PHONE	ENTRY #
Anaheim Ducks Hockey Club LLC		D	714 940-2900	0
Balboa Yacht Club		D	949 673-3515	0
Broker Solutions Inc		D	800 450-2010	0
CIT Bank NA		D	949 675-2890	0
Crown Cove Senior Care Cmnty		D	949 760-2800	0
Delta Max		E	949 759-8529	0
Pacific Cleaning Service Inc		E	949 829-8790	0
Service Corp International		D	949 644-2700	0
Smart & Final Stores Inc		B	949 675-2396	0

CORONADO, CA - San Diego County

	SIC	EMP	PHONE	ENTRY #
51st St & 8th Ave Corp		A	619 424-4000	0
City of Coronado		D	619 522-7342	0
City of Coronado		D	619 522-7380	0
El Cordova Hotel		D	619 435-4131	0
Four Sisters Inns		C	619 437-1900	0
GK Management Co Inc		E	619 437-1777	0
Hotel Del Coronado LP		D	619 522-8011	0
Ksl Resorts Hotel Del Coronado		D	619 435-6611	0
L-O Coronado Hotel Inc		A	619 435-6611	0
Loews Corporation		B	619 424-4000	0
Mariner Systems Inc (PA)		D	305 266-7255	0
R3 Strategic Support Group Inc		D	800 418-2040	0
Smart & Final Stores Inc		B	619 522-2014	0
Star & Crescent Boat Company (PA)		E	619 234-4111	0

CORTE MADERA, CA - Marin County

	SIC	EMP	PHONE	ENTRY #
Alain Pinel Realtors Inc		D	415 755-1111	0
American Pacific Mortgage Corp		E	415 891-8706	0
Bay Clubs Inc		D	415 945-3000	0
Marin Municipal Water District (PA)		C	415 945-1455	0
Stage II Inc		E	415 285-8400	0
Tommy Bahama Group Inc		C	415 737-0400	0

COSTA MESA, CA - Orange County

	SIC	EMP	PHONE	ENTRY #
24 Hour Fitness Usa Inc		E	949 610-0651	0
24 Hour Fitness Usa Inc		D	949 650-3600	0
2ndgear LLC (DH)		C	714 702-1023	0
ABC Bus Inc		D	714 444-5888	0
Accent Service Company Inc		D	877 611-0131	0
Accredited Nursing Services		D	714 973-1234	0
Adopt-A-Highway Maintenance		C	800 200-0003	0
Advantage Ground Trnsp Corp		D	714 557-2465	0

	SIC	EMP	PHONE	ENTRY #
Alfreds Pictures Frames Inc		E	714 434-4838	0
Altametrics LLC		C	800 676-1281	0
Amen Clinics Inc A Med Corp (PA)		C	888 564-2700	0
American Reprographics Co LLC		C	714 751-2680	0
Americash		E	714 994-7554	0
Amica Mutual Insurance Company		D	877 972-6422	0
Andrew L Youngquist Cnstr Inc		D	949 862-5611	0
Arnel Interior Corp		B	714 481-5100	0
Auto Club Enterprises (PA)		A	714 850-5111	0
Automobile Club Southern Cal		B	213 741-3686	0
Automobile Club Southern Cal		C	714 885-1343	0
Ayres Group (PA)		D	714 540-6060	0
Balboa Capital Corporation (PA)		C	949 756-0800	0
Benco Dental Supply Co		D	714 424-0977	0
Benq America Corp (HQ)		D	714 559-4900	0
Boyd & Associates		C	714 835-5423	0
Bright Bristol Street LLC		D	714 557-3000	0
Brookfeld Sthland Holdings LLC		C	714 427-6868	0
Bunny Beach Swimwear Inc (PA)		D	949 336-6300	0
Caliber Bodyworks Texas Inc		D	714 436-5010	0
California Ticketscom Inc (DH)		D	714 327-5400	0
Califrnia Dept State Hospitals		A	714 957-5000	0
Canon Solutions America Inc		D	949 753-4200	0
Cardflex Inc		D	714 361-1900	0
Carecredit LLC		C	800 300-3046	0
Casanova Pndrill Pblicidad Inc (PA)		D	949 474-5001	0
Cellco Partnership		D	714 427-0733	0
Central Parking System Inc		D	714 751-2855	0
Chargers Footbaff Company LLC (PA)		D	619 280-2121	0
Coit Services Inc		E	949 760-0760	0
Competent Care Inc		D	714 545-4818	0
Cooksey Toolen Gage Duffy (PA)		D	714 431-1100	0
Countryside Inn-Corona LP		D	714 549-0300	0
County of Orange		C	949 252-5006	0
Creative Design Cons Inc (PA)		D	714 641-4868	0
Crisp Enterprises Inc (PA)		D	714 668-5955	0
Dechert LLP		C	949 442-6000	0
Deloitte & Touche LLP		A	714 436-7419	0
Developmental Svcs Cal Dept		A	714 957-5151	0
Donahue Schrber Rlty Group Inc (PA)		D	714 545-1400	0
Donahue Schriber Rlty Group LP (PA)		D	714 545-1400	0
Dwiw Inc		E	949 574-7147	0
Edward Straling		E	760 887-3673	0
Edwards Theatres Circuit Inc		D	714 428-0962	0
El Pollo Loco Holdings Inc (PA)		C	714 599-5000	0
Elite Tek Services Inc		D	714 881-5301	0
Empire Leasing Inc		D	949 646-7400	0
Ensign Group Inc		D	949 642-0387	0
Experian Info Solutions Inc (DH)		A	714 830-7000	0
Experian Mktg Solutions LLC		A	714 830-7000	0
Federal Express Corporation		D	800 463-3339	0
Flagstar Bancorp Inc		C	714 549-9100	0
Flat White Economy Inv USA LLC		C	949 344-5013	0
Food & Agriculture Cal Dept		A	714 751-3247	0
Food Sales West Inc (PA)		D	714 966-2900	0
Geek Squad Inc		D	714 434-0132	0
General Electric Company		C	714 434-4111	0
Golden Living LLC		D	949 642-0387	0
Hanley Wood Mkt Intelligence (HQ)		D	714 540-8500	0
HB Parkco Construction Inc (PA)		B	714 444-1441	0
Healthmarkets Inc		D	949 486-0600	0
Host Hotels & Resorts LP		D	714 957-5000	0
Human Options Inc		E	949 757-3635	0
Independent Options		D	714 434-1175	0
Innovative Cnstr Solutions		C	714 893-6366	0
Insight Investments LLC (HQ)		C	714 939-2300	0
Integrated Behavioral Hlth Inc		D	714 442-4150	0
International Bus Mchs Corp		B	714 327-3501	0
Jabez Building Services Inc		D	714 776-7705	0
JD Power (HQ)		D	714 621-6200	0
Jpmorgan Chase Bank Nat Assn		C	949 429-6071	0
K Line America Inc		E	714 861-5000	0
Koce-TV Foundation		D	714 241-4100	0
Kyocera International Inc		E	714 428-3600	0
Latham & Watkins LLP		C	714 540-1235	0
Lawrence B Bonas Company		D	714 668-5250	0
Livetime Software Inc		E	415 905-4009	0
Lombardy Holdings Inc (PA)		C	951 808-4550	0
Lz Management Group LLC		D	714 957-4061	0
Maersk Inc		D	714 428-5500	0
Manatt Phelps & Phillips LLP		E	714 371-2500	0
Materials Marketing		D	949 729-9881	0
Maxgen Energy Services Corp (DH)		D	714 908-5266	0
Medical Eye Services Inc		D	714 619-4660	0
Mesa Cnsld Wtr Dst Imprv Corp (PA)		D	949 631-1200	0

	SIC	EMP	PHONE	ENTRY #
Mesa Verde Convalescent Hosp	C		949 548-5584	0
Mesa Verde Country Club	C		714 549-0377	0
Mesa Verde Partners	D		714 540-7500	0
Michael Maguire & Associates	E		714 435-7500	0
Mobilitie Investments III LLC	C		877 999-7070	0
Moffatt & Nichol	D		657 261-2699	0
Morgan Lewis & Bockius LLP	C		949 399-7000	0
Mt Supply Inc (DH)	C		800 938-6658	0
Nader Mehr DDS Inc	D		562 634-2477	0
National Safety Services	E		714 679-9118	0
Nds Americas Inc (DH)	D		714 434-2100	0
Newma Garris Gilmo + Partne I	D		949 756-0818	0
North American Acceptance Corp	C		714 868-3195	0
Nwp Services Corporation (HQ)	C		949 253-2500	0
Olson & Assoc	D		714 878-6649	0
One Town Center Associates LLC	E		714 435-2100	0
Orange Cnty Sprntndent Schools	D		949 650-2506	0
Orange County Plst Co Inc	D		714 957-1971	0
Ovations Fanfare	D		714 708-1880	0
Pacific Mercantile Bank (HQ)	E		714 438-2500	0
Park Hotels & Resorts Inc	B		714 540-7000	0
Parkco Building Company	D		714 444-1441	0
Paul Hastings LLP	C		714 668-6200	0
Payoff Inc	D		949 430-0630	0
PDC Capital Group LLC	D		866 500-8550	0
Phelps United LLC	D		657 212-8050	0
Pivot Interiors Inc	D		949 988-5400	0
Planned Parenthood Federation	D		949 548-8830	0
Plexicor Inc (PA)	E		714 918-8700	0
Pmd Industries Inc	E		949 222-0999	0
Powerplant Mint Spcialists Inc	C		714 427-6900	0
Profit Recovery Partners LLC	D		949 851-2777	0
Remax Metro Inc	D		714 557-2544	0
Resources Connection Inc	D		714 430-6550	0
Rosanna Inc	C		714 751-5100	0
Rromeo Corporation	D		714 640-3800	0
Rutan & Tucker LLP (PA)	B		714 641-5100	0
Safe Harbor Treatment Cen	E		949 645-1026	0
Seaview Industries	E		714 957-5073	0
Secova Inc	C		714 384-0530	0
Secova Eservices Inc (HQ)	D		714 384-0655	0
Sheppard Mullin Richter	D		714 513-5100	0
Silverado Senior Living Inc	D		949 945-0189	0
Site Crew Inc	B		714 668-0100	0
Smith & Sons Investment Co	E		949 646-9648	0
Snell & Wilmer LLP	C		714 427-7000	0
Software Management Cons Inc	D		714 662-1841	0
Solopoint Solutions Inc	D		714 708-3639	0
South Coast Plaza LLC (PA)	D		714 546-0110	0
South Coast Plaza LLC	D		714 435-2000	0
South Coast Repertory Inc	D		714 708-5500	0
South Coast Westin Hotel Co	D		714 540-2500	0
Southern California Mar Assn	D		714 850-4004	0
Steelwave Inc	C		949 863-0390	0
Sure Haven Inc	A		949 467-9213	0
Syspro Impact Software Inc	C		714 437-1000	0
T Boyer Company	E		949 642-2431	0
Talon Executive Services Inc	E		714 434-7476	0
Telecare Corporation	D		714 361-6760	0
Ticketscom LLC (DH)	E		714 327-5400	0
Ultralink LLC	C		714 427-5500	0
United Infrstrcture Prjcts Inc	D		949 310-0092	0
University California Irvine	E		949 646-2267	0
US Hotel and Resort MGT Inc	D		949 650-2988	0
UTC Fire SEC Americas Corp Inc	D		949 737-7800	0
Uvnv Inc (PA)	D		888 777-0446	0
Valassis Communications Inc	D		714 751-4006	0
Variations In Stone Inc	D		949 438-8337	0
Veritone Inc (PA)	D		888 507-1737	0
Villa Pacific Contractors Inc	E		714 850-1640	0
Viva Life Science Inc	D		949 645-6100	0
Volcom LLC	C		949 646-2175	0
Volcom LLC (PA)	C		949 646-2175	0
Waddell & Reed Inc	D		714 437-7510	0
Warmington Homes (PA)	C		714 434-4435	0
Warmington Residential Cal Inc	C		714 557-5511	0
Westar Capital Assoc II LLC	A		714 481-5160	0
Wood Environment &	D		949 642-0245	0
Woodruff Spradlin & Smart	D		714 558-7000	0
Wyndham International Inc	D		714 751-5100	0

COTATI, CA - Sonoma County

	SIC	EMP	PHONE	ENTRY #
21st Century Health Club (PA)	D		707 795-0400	0
Mike Brown Electric Co	D		707 792-8100	0
Protransport-1 LLC (HQ)	A		707 975-2386	0
Stockham Construction Inc	B		707 664-0945	0

COTTONWOOD, CA - Shasta County

	SIC	EMP	PHONE	ENTRY #
All Pro Drywall	E		530 722-5182	0
County of Shasta	D		530 347-6276	0
Shasta Livestock Auction Yard	D		530 347-3793	0

COURTLAND, CA - Sacramento County

	SIC	EMP	PHONE	ENTRY #
Delta Breeze Farming Inc	C		916 775-2055	0

COVELO, CA - Mendocino County

	SIC	EMP	PHONE	ENTRY #
Covelo Indian Community Center	D		707 983-8478	0
Round Valley Indian Health Ctr	D		707 983-6182	0

COVINA, CA - Los Angeles County

	SIC	EMP	PHONE	ENTRY #
A-1 Event & Party Rentals	D		626 967-0500	0
Accu-Count Inventory Svcs Inc	D		805 231-6310	0
Acf Components & Fasteners Inc	D		949 833-0506	0
Altamed Health Services Corp	D		626 214-1480	0
American Multi-Cinema Inc	D		626 974-8624	0
Andrews International Inc	C		626 407-2290	0
Baltazar Construction Inc	E		626 339-8620	0
Bowlero Corp	D		626 339-1286	0
Briteworks Inc	D		626 337-0099	0
Cal Empire Engineering Inc	E		626 915-8030	0
Century 21 Masters	D		626 732-6184	0
Charter Behavioral Health Syst	D		626 966-1632	0
Christian Community Credit Un	D		800 347-2228	0
Citrus Valley Medical Ctr Inc	A		626 858-8515	0
Citrus Valley Medical Ctr Inc	A		626 331-7331	0
Citrus Vly Hlth Partners Inc	A		626 732-3100	0
Coldwell Banker Town & Country	D		626 966-3688	0
Covina Rehabilitation Center	C		626 967-3874	0
Cruz Hoffstetter LLC	D		626 915-5621	0
Cwf Inc	D		626 967-0500	0
Davita Magan Management Inc (DH)	C		626 331-6411	0
Emanate Hlth Intr-Cmmnity Hosp (PA)	A		626 331-7331	0
Golden Empire Mortgage Inc	D		626 967-3236	0
Grand Auto Care	E		626 331-8390	0
Home Capital Group	D		626 331-4213	0
Keller Williams Realty	D		626 384-2803	0
Lereta LLC (PA)	B		626 543-1765	0
Los Angeles Engineering Inc	C		626 869-1400	0
Masonic Homes of California	D		626 251-2200	0
Mohan Dialysis Ctr of Covina	D		626 859-2522	0
Outsource Testing Inc	D		909 592-8898	0
Park Hotels & Resorts Inc	D		626 915-3441	0
Rowland Convalescent Hosp Inc	D		626 967-2741	0
San Gabriel Childrens Ctr Inc	D		626 859-2089	0
Securitas SEC Svcs USA Inc	C		571 321-0913	0
Staff Today Incorporated	C		800 928-5561	0
Think Together	A		626 373-2311	0
Vitas Healthcare Corp Cal	D		626 918-2273	0
Wood Castle Construction Inc	E		626 966-8600	0

CRESCENT CITY, CA - Del Norte County

	SIC	EMP	PHONE	ENTRY #
County of Del Norte	C		707 464-3191	0
Del Norte Workforce Center	E		707 464-8347	0
Elk Valley Casino Inc	C		707 464-1020	0
Full Spectrum Services Inc	E		707 465-1460	0
Lantern of Crescent City LLC	D		949 445-1000	0
Leavitt Group Enterprises Inc	C		707 465-6508	0
North Shore Investment Inc	D		707 464-6151	0
Snoozie Shavings Inc (PA)	D		707 464-6186	0
Sutter Coast Hospital (HQ)	C		707 464-8511	0

CROCKETT, CA - Contra Costa County

	SIC	EMP	PHONE	ENTRY #
Sugar Workers Local 1	B		510 787-1676	0

CUDAHY, CA - Los Angeles County

	SIC	EMP	PHONE	ENTRY #
County of Los Angeles	C		323 560-5001	0
Kaiser Foundation Hospitals	D		323 562-6400	0
Mistras Group Inc	D		323 583-1653	0
Southern Cal Prmnnte Med Group	E		323 562-6459	0

CULVER CITY, CA - Los Angeles County

	SIC	EMP	PHONE	ENTRY #
A-1 Electric Service Co Inc	E		310 204-1077	0
Access Spclty Animal Hospitals	D		310 558-6100	0
Advanced Medical Reviews LLC	D		310 575-0900	0
Allies For Every Child Inc	D		310 846-4100	0
Alpine Interiors Corporation (PA)	D		310 390-7639	0
Anonymous Content LLC (PA)	D		310 558-6000	0
Avoca Productions Inc	D		310 244-4000	0
Cadforce Inc	A		310 876-1800	0
California Clinical Trials	C		310 945-1780	0
Carat N Amer Dntsu Ageis Ntwrk	C		310 255-1000	0
Carbon 38 Inc	D		888 723-5838	0
Century Wilshire Inc	D		310 558-9400	0
CIT Bank NA	D		310 390-7745	0

Employment Codes: A=Over 500 employees, B=251-500,
C=101-250, D=51-100, E=50

2020 Directory of California
Wholesalers and Services Companies

© Mergent Inc. 1-800-342-5647

1527

GEOGRAPHIC

	SIC	EMP	PHONE	ENTRY #
CIT Bank NA		D	310 559-7222	0
Clutter Inc **(PA)**		C	800 805-4023	0
Columbia Pictures Inds Inc **(DH)**		C	310 244-4000	0
Common Area Maint Svcs Inc **(PA)**		D	310 390-3552	0
Companion Hospice and		D	310 338-1257	0
Compulaw LLC		E	310 553-3355	0
Computer Consulting **(PA)**		A	310 568-5000	0
Cuningham Group Arch Inc		E	310 895-2200	0
D K Fortune & Associates Inc		C	310 391-7266	0
Daz Systems LLC **(DH)**		D	310 640-1300	0
Didi Hirsch Psychiatric Svc **(PA)**		C	310 390-6612	0
Digital Kitchen LLC		E	310 499-9255	0
Dual Diagnosis Trtmnt Ctr Inc		C	424 207-2220	0
Exceptional Chld Foundation		C	310 915-6606	0
Exceptional Chld Foundation **(PA)**		C	310 204-3300	0
Exodus Recovery **(PA)**		D	310 945-3350	0
Exodus Recovery Ctr At Brotman **(PA)**		D	310 253-9494	0
Force-Oakleaf LP		D	310 484-7000	0
Framestore Inc **(PA)**		E	310 975-7300	0
Gardner Neurologic Orthopedic		C	310 649-5824	0
Genex **(HQ)**		C	424 672-9500	0
GK Management Co Inc **(PA)**		C	310 204-2050	0
GK Management Co Inc		D	310 836-1812	0
Globecast America Incorporated **(DH)**		D	310 845-3900	0
Goldrich & Kest Industries LLC **(PA)**		A	310 204-2050	0
Goldrichkest **(PA)**		C	310 204-2050	0
Harel General Contractors Inc		E	310 558-8304	0
Hellmuth Obata & Kassabaum Inc		E	310 838-9555	0
Hok Group Inc		C	310 838-9555	0
Investment Tech Group Inc		C	310 216-6777	0
Ipsos Otx Corporation **(HQ)**		C	310 736-3400	0
Jeopardy Productions Inc		C	310 244-8855	0
Jesse Lee Group Inc		D	510 351-3700	0
Kovel/Fuller LLC		D	310 841-4444	0
Kpmg LLP		A	212 758-9700	0
L A Services Inc		E	310 838-0408	0
Lax Plaza Hotel		C	310 902-2202	0
Liveoffice LLC		D	877 253-2793	0
LMS Corporation		E	310 641-4222	0
Maker Studios Inc **(DH)**		D	310 606-2182	0
Marycrest Manor		D	310 838-2778	0
Max Leather		E	310 841-6990	0
Morphosis Architects		D	310 453-2247	0
Nantbioscience Inc		D	310 883-1300	0
Nanthealth Inc **(HQ)**		D	310 883-1300	0
Nantmobile LLC		C	310 883-7888	0
Nantworks LLC **(PA)**		D	310 883-1300	0
Nfl Properties LLC		B	310 840-4635	0
Office of Child Development		D	310 842-4230	0
Omelet LLC **(PA)**		D	213 427-6400	0
Oracle Corporation		B	310 258-7500	0
Oracle Systems Corporation		D	818 817-2900	0
Pacifica Hotel & Conference Ce		C	310 649-1776	0
Paychex Inc		D	310 338-7900	0
Pine Data Processing Inc		D	310 815-5700	0
Prestige Security Service Inc		B	310 670-5999	0
Prime Focus North America Inc **(PA)**		D	323 461-7887	0
Property Management Assoc Inc **(PA)**		C	323 295-2000	0
Psychemedics Corporation		D	310 216-7776	0
Punch Studio LLC **(PA)**		C	310 390-9900	0
Quadra Productions Inc		C	310 244-1234	0
Quadrix Information Tech Inc		E	424 603-2140	0
Reading International Inc **(PA)**		D	213 235-2240	0
Reliable Health Care Svcs Inc		E	310 397-2229	0
Rick Solomon Enterprises Inc **(PA)**		D	310 280-3700	0
Roman Cath Arch of Los Angels		E	310 836-5500	0
Scopely Inc **(PA)**		C	323 400-6618	0
Security Indust Spcialists Inc **(PA)**		C	310 215-5100	0
Servicon Systems Inc **(PA)**		A	310 204-5040	0
Social Studies School Service		D	310 839-2436	0
Solano County Mental Health		E	707 428-1131	0
Sony Pictures Entrmt Inc		B	310 840-8000	0
Sony Pictures Entrmt Inc		B	310 202-1234	0
Sony Pictures Entrmt Inc **(DH)**		A	310 244-4000	0
Sony Pictures Imageworks Inc		A	310 840-8000	0
Sony Pictures Television Inc **(DH)**		B	310 244-7625	0
Stan Tashman & Associates Inc		A	310 460-7600	0
Starwood Hotel		D	310 641-7000	0
Steel House Inc		C	310 773-3331	0
Syska & Hennessy Engineers Inc		D	310 312-0200	0
Topanga Productions Inc		E	310 244-4000	0
Topson Downs California Inc **(PA)**		D	310 558-0300	0
Transwestern Corp Pointe LLC		D	310 642-1001	0
Tristar Television Music Inc		E	310 244-4000	0
Triton Media Group LLC		D	661 294-9000	0
U S Private Protection SEC Inc		C	310 301-0010	0
United Refrigeration Inc		D	310 204-2500	0
Virgin Fish Inc **(PA)**		C	310 391-6161	0
Visionaire Group Inc		D	310 823-1800	0
West Publishing Corporation		C	424 243-2100	0
Woodbine Lgacy/Playa Owner LLC		D	678 292-4962	0
Wovexx Holdings Inc **(DH)**		D	310 424-2080	0
X Prize Foundation Inc		E	310 741-4880	0
Xap Corporation **(PA)**		E	310 743-0450	0
Yoga Works Inc **(HQ)**		E	310 664-6470	0
Yogaworks Inc **(PA)**		D	310 664-6470	0
Zambezi LLC		D	310 450-6800	0
Zions Bancorporation Nat Assn		C	310 258-9300	0
Zoic Inc		C	310 838-0770	0

CUPERTINO, CA - Santa Clara County

	SIC	EMP	PHONE	ENTRY #
California Dental Arts LLC		D	408 255-1020	0
Ch Cupertino Owner LLC		C	408 253-8900	0
Corinthian Intl Prkg Svcs Inc		B	408 867-7275	0
CRC Health Corporate **(DH)**		D	408 367-0044	0
CRC Health Group Inc **(HQ)**		D	877 272-8668	0
CRC Health LLC **(DH)**		D	877 272-8668	0
Cupertino Healthcare		D	408 253-9034	0
Cupertino Lessee LLC		C	908 253-8900	0
Digital Keystone Inc		E	650 938-7301	0
Digite Inc		C	408 418-3834	0
Ecrio Inc		D	408 973-7290	0
Esq Business Services Inc **(PA)**		D	925 734-9800	0
Ewing-Foley Inc **(PA)**		E	408 342-1201	0
Forge-Vidovich Motel Limited		D	408 996-7700	0
Forum Healthcare Center		C	650 944-0200	0
Ggec America Inc		D	714 750-2280	0
Howard Fischer Associates Inc		E	408 374-0580	0
Huawei Enterprise USA Inc		C	408 394-4295	0
Ice Center Enterprises LLC		D	510 604-8878	0
Lanwave Technology Inc		D	408 253-3883	0
Max Sportsters Inc		E	408 446-8330	0
Mist Systems Inc		C	408 326-0346	0
Panasonic Corp North America		C	408 861-3900	0
Pleasant View Convalescent Hos		C	408 253-9034	0
Rancho San Antonio Retirement		B	650 265-2637	0
Referral Realty Inc		D	408 996-8100	0
Silver Lake Partners II LP		D	408 454-4732	0
Stevens Creek Quarry Inc **(PA)**		D	408 253-2512	0
Sugarcrm Inc **(PA)**		C	408 454-6900	0
Sunny Retirement Home		C	408 454-5600	0
Trend Micro Incorporated		D	408 257-1500	0
Z & M Associates Inc		D	408 996-8100	0
Zend Technologies Usa Inc		C	408 253-8800	0

CUTLER, CA - Tulare County

	SIC	EMP	PHONE	ENTRY #
Penas Disposal Inc		D	559 528-3909	0
Wawona Packing Co LLC **(PA)**		D	559 528-4000	0
Wawona Packing Co LLC		B	559 528-4699	0

CYPRESS, CA - Orange County

	SIC	EMP	PHONE	ENTRY #
Alltrade Tools LLC		E	310 522-9008	0
American Honda Finance Corp		D	714 816-8110	0
Apple Eght Hospitality MGT Inc		D	714 827-1010	0
Asplundh Tree Expert LLC		C	714 893-2405	0
B2b Staffing Services Inc		B	714 243-4104	0
Barcott Frank A SEC Invstgtons		C	714 891-8556	0
Beacon Health Options Inc		C	714 763-2405	0
Brendan Tours **(PA)**		C	818 428-6000	0
Cal Southern United Food		C	714 220-2297	0
Caliber Capital Group LLC		A	714 507-1998	0
Cellco Partnership		D	714 899-4690	0
Christie Dgtal Systems USA Inc **(DH)**		D	714 527-7056	0
Clarion Corporation America **(HQ)**		D	310 327-9100	0
Consoldted Med Bo-Analysis Inc **(PA)**		D	714 657-7369	0
Cypress Ctr For Fmly Medicine		D	562 799-4801	0
Cypress Education Foundation		D	714 220-6900	0
Daiwa Corporation		D	562 375-6800	0
DAndrea Graphic Corportion		D	310 642-0260	0
Dean Goodman Inc		D	714 229-8999	0
Focus Diagnostics Inc		B	714 220-1900	0
Focus Technologies Holding Co		B	800 838-4548	0
Forest Lawn Memorial-Park Assn		D	714 828-3131	0
Fujifilm North America Corp		C	714 372-4200	0
Healthsmart Management Service		D	714 947-8600	0
Hoyu America Co		D	714 230-3000	0
Hybrid Promotions LLC **(PA)**		C	714 952-3866	0
J Perez Associates Inc **(PA)**		D	562 801-5397	0
Marriott International Inc		C	714 209-6586	0
Mercury Defense Systems Inc **(HQ)**		C	714 898-8200	0
Mitsubishi Electric Us Inc **(DH)**		C	714 220-2500	0

Mergent email: customerrelations@mergent.com
1528

2020 Directory of California
Wholesalers and Services Companies

(P-0000) Products & Services Section entry number
(PA)=Parent Co (HQ)=Headquarters (DH)=Div Headquarters

	SIC	EMP	PHONE	ENTRY #
Mitsubishi Motors Cr Amer Inc **(DH)**	B		714 799-4730	0
Money Mailer LLC **(PA)**	C		714 889-3800	0
Multiquip Inc **(DH)**	B		310 537-3700	0
New Air LLC	E		657 257-4349	0
Pacific Pioneer Insur Group **(PA)**	C		714 228-7888	0
Pacificare Health Systems LLC **(HQ)**	A		714 952-1121	0
Paragon Partners Ltd **(PA)**	D		714 379-3376	0
Pick-A-Part Auto Wrecking	D		559 485-3071	0
Plumbing Piping & Cnstr Inc	D		714 821-0490	0
Power Maintenance Services Inc	D		714 229-5900	0
Riphagen & Bullerdick Inc	E		714 763-2100	0
Scientific Applications & RES **(PA)**	D		714 828-1465	0
Siemens Industry Inc	C		714 761-2200	0
Siemens Product Life Mgmt Sftw	D		714 952-6500	0
Silliker Labs Group Inc	E		714 226-0000	0
Sitonit Seating Inc	C		714 995-4800	0
Spectrum MGT Holdg Co LLC	D		714 657-1040	0
Spectrum MGT Holdg Co LLC	D		714 657-1060	0
Tad Pgs Inc	D		571 451-2428	0
UFS International LLC	C		714 713-6311	0
Uhc of California **(DH)**	A		714 952-1121	0
United Chinese American Genera **(PA)**	D		714 228-7800	0
United Exchange Corp **(PA)**	D		562 977-4500	0
Unitedhealth Group Inc	D		952 936-1300	0
Ushio America Inc **(HQ)**	D		714 236-8600	0
Valueoptions of California	C		800 228-1286	0
Viad Corp	D		562 370-1500	0
Wcct Global Inc **(PA)**	D		714 668-1500	0
Western Overseas Corporation **(PA)**	E		562 985-0616	0

DALY CITY, CA - San Mateo County

	SIC	EMP	PHONE	ENTRY #
ABS-Cbn International **(DH)**	C		800 527-2820	0
American General Life Insur	D		650 994-6679	0
Bay Area Pdatric Med Group Inc **(PA)**	D		650 992-4200	0
Bdp Bowl Inc	E		650 878-0300	0
Casbn Investment Inc	D		650 991-2800	0
Catholic Chrts Cyo Archdiocs	E		650 757-2110	0
City of Daly City	D		650 991-8064	0
Forte Enterprises Inc **(PA)**	C		650 994-3200	0
Genesys Telecom Labs Inc **(HQ)**	B		650 466-1100	0
Gerson Baker & Associates	D		650 756-0959	0
Hillcrest Senior Housing Corp	C		650 757-1737	0
Kaiser Foundation Hospitals	D		650 301-5860	0
Lake Merced Golf & Country CLB	D		650 755-2233	0
Larry Blair Realtor	E		650 991-5267	0
Mission Villa LLC	D		650 756-1995	0
Nurse Providers Inc	A		650 992-8559	0
Olympic Club	C		415 404-4300	0
Oracle Systems Corporation	D		650 506-8648	0
Pacific Gas and Electric Co	D		650 755-1236	0
Permanente Medical Group Inc	D		650 301-5860	0
Reneson Hotels Inc **(PA)**	D		650 449-5353	0
Roman Catholic Archdiocese of	D		650 756-2060	0
San Mateo Cnty Pub Hlth Clinic	D		650 301-8600	0
Seton Medical Center **(HQ)**	A		650 992-4000	0
Seton Medical Center	D		650 992-4000	0
Spinecare Medical Group Inc	D		650 985-7500	0
St Francis Hts Convalescent	C		650 755-9515	0
West Lake Touchless Car Wash	E		650 992-5344	0
Westlake Nail Spa	D		650 994-7777	0
You Technology LLC	D		650 624-3800	0

DANA POINT, CA - Orange County

	SIC	EMP	PHONE	ENTRY #
Altera Real Estate	B		949 547-7351	0
Cph Monarch Hotel LLC	A		949 234-3200	0
Ergs Aim Hotel Realty LLC	D		949 661-1100	0
Gringteam Inc	D		949 661-1100	0
Mark R Eggen Construction Inc	E		949 661-2674	0
Monarch Beach Golf Links **(HQ)**	D		949 240-8247	0
Pangea Corporation	E		949 443-0666	0
Prutel Joint Venture	A		949 240-2000	0
Ritz-Carlton Hotel Company LLC	B		949 240-5020	0
Sunrise Senior Living Inc	D		949 234-3000	0
Truthmd LLC	D		949 637-4296	0

DANVILLE, CA - Contra Costa County

	SIC	EMP	PHONE	ENTRY #
Ameritac Inc **(PA)**	D		925 743-8398	0
Architrends Inc	D		925 648-8800	0
Bara Infoware Inc **(PA)**	D		925 790-0130	0
Bay Valley Medical Group Inc **(PA)**	D		510 785-5000	0
Blackhawk Country Club	D		925 736-6500	0
Braddock & Logan Group II LP	C		925 736-4000	0
Braddock & Logan Services Inc	D		925 736-4000	0
Brookfeld Bay Area Hldings LLC	D		925 743-8000	0
Cubix Construction Company **(PA)**	C		925 314-0770	0
Danville Long-Term Care Inc	D		925 837-4566	0

	SIC	EMP	PHONE	ENTRY #
Danville Village Skilled Nursn	D		925 837-4566	0
DW Morgan LLC	D		925 460-2700	0
Empire Realty Associates Inc	D		925 217-5000	0
James E Roberts-Obayashi Corp	C		925 820-0600	0
Meyers Research LLC	D		925 362-1028	0
Pacific Union Homes Inc **(PA)**	C		925 314-3800	0
Patelco Credit Union	D		925 785-9487	0
Reutlinger Community	C		925 964-2062	0
Sunrise Senior Living LLC	D		925 309-4178	0
Tenet Healthsystem Medical	B		925 275-8303	0
Town of Danville	C		925 314-3400	0

DAVENPORT, CA - Santa Cruz County

	SIC	EMP	PHONE	ENTRY #
Swanton Berry Farms Inc	E		831 425-8919	0

DAVIS, CA - Yolo County

	SIC	EMP	PHONE	ENTRY #
Brown and Caldwell	D		530 747-0650	0
Communicare Health Centers	C		530 758-2060	0
Covenant Care Courtyard LLC	D		530 756-1800	0
Cvf Capital Partners Inc	C		530 757-7004	0
Davis Community Clinic **(PA)**	C		530 758-2060	0
Doug Arnold Real Estate Inc	E		530 758-3080	0
Harpers Model Home Maintenance	D		916 335-0282	0
Hmclause Inc **(DH)**	C		800 320-4672	0
Hmclause Inc	D		530 747-3235	0
Ikes Landscaping & Maintenance	D		530 758-1698	0
Kaiser Foundation Hospitals	E		530 757-7100	0
Mariner Health Care Inc	C		530 756-1800	0
Novozymes Inc **(DH)**	D		530 757-8100	0
Novozymes Us Inc	A		530 757-8100	0
Pacific Gas and Electric Co	B		530 757-5803	0
Pacific Retirement Svcs Inc	C		530 753-1450	0
Schilling Robotics LLC	D		530 753-6718	0
Sciots Tract Association	D		530 753-5219	0
Sierra Railroad Company	D		530 554-2522	0
Sutter Health	C		530 747-0389	0
Sutter Health	B		530 757-5111	0
Sutter Health	C		530 750-5904	0
Sutter Health	D		530 750-5888	0
Sutter Hlth Scrmnto Sierra Reg	A		530 747-5010	0
Sutter Hlth Scrmnto Sierra Reg	B		530 756-6440	0
Travis Credit Union	B		707 449-4000	0
University California Davis	C		530 752-2300	0
West Yost & Associates Inc **(PA)**	D		530 756-5905	0
Woodland Healthcare	D		530 756-2364	0
Yolo Hospice Inc **(PA)**	D		530 758-5566	0

DEATH VALLEY, CA - Inyo County

	SIC	EMP	PHONE	ENTRY #
Xanterra Parks & Resorts Inc	C		760 786-2345	0

DEL MAR, CA - San Diego County

	SIC	EMP	PHONE	ENTRY #
Aecom Energy & Cnstr Inc	B		858 481-9502	0
Automobile Club Southern Cal	C		858 481-7181	0
Brightertech Incorporated	E		310 909-4940	0
Brookfield Homes of California	E		858 481-8500	0
Crest Beverage Company Inc	C		858 452-2300	0
Davidson Communities LLC **(PA)**	E		858 259-8500	0
Del Mar Thoroughbred Club	B		858 755-1141	0
Hive Tech Gurus Incorporated	E		323 445-1770	0
Humetrix Inc	E		858 259-8987	0
JP Morgan Securities LLC	D		310 201-2693	0
Lee Johnson	C		858 481-4411	0
Lhoberge Lessee Inc	C		858 259-1515	0
Liquid Investments Inc **(PA)**	C		858 509-8510	0
Mesa Distributing Coinc **(HQ)**	C		858 452-2300	0
Ramsey Real Estate Group	E		800 685-7734	0
Sunstone Durante LLC	C		858 792-5200	0
Ws Hdm LLC	D		858 792-5200	0

DEL REY, CA - Fresno County

	SIC	EMP	PHONE	ENTRY #
Chooljian & Sons Inc **(PA)**	D		559 888-2031	0

DELANO, CA - Kern County

	SIC	EMP	PHONE	ENTRY #
Cal Treehouse Almonds LLC	C		661 725-6334	0
City of Delano	E		661 721-3350	0
Coronel Construction Inc	D		661 725-4400	0
County of Kern	D		661 721-5134	0
Covanta Delano Inc	E		661 792-3067	0
Delano Dst Sklled Nrsing Fclty	C		661 720-2100	0
Hronis Inc A California Corp **(PA)**	D		661 725-2503	0
Innovel Solutions Inc	A		661 721-1000	0
Jorge Pimental Diaz	E		661 344-5139	0
Loup Logistics Company	C		661 370-4341	0
M Caratan Inc	C		661 725-2566	0
Monarch Nut Company LLC	C		661 725-6458	0
Munger Bros LLC	A		661 721-0390	0
P C A Farm Management LLC	A		661 720-2400	0

GEOGRAPHIC

	SIC	EMP	PHONE	ENTRY #
Pandol & Sons		E	661 725-3755	0
Proteus Inc		C	661 721-5800	0
Tero Tek International Inc (PA)		D	661 725-1135	0
Triple R Transportation Inc		D	661 725-6494	0
Vista Verde Farms		E	661 720-9733	0
Wonderful Citrus Packing LLC (HQ)		B	661 720-2400	0
Wonderful Company LLC		B	661 720-2400	0

DELHI, CA - Merced County

	SIC	EMP	PHONE	ENTRY #
Califrnia Psychtric Trnsitions		D	209 667-9304	0
Richard Swanson Inc		D	209 632-3883	0

DENAIR, CA - Stanislaus County

	SIC	EMP	PHONE	ENTRY #
Hamlow Ranches Inc.		E	209 632-2873	0
J Crecelius Inc		D	209 883-4826	0
Montpelier Orchards MGT Co Inc		E	209 883-4079	0
Valley Fresh Foods Inc		D	209 669-5510	0

DESERT HOT SPRINGS, CA - Riverside County

	SIC	EMP	PHONE	ENTRY #
Desert Hot Springs Real Proper		D	760 329-6000	0
Desert Springs Hotel		E	760 251-3399	0
Whatever It Takes Inc		E	760 329-6000	0

DIABLO, CA - Contra Costa County

	SIC	EMP	PHONE	ENTRY #
Diablo Country Club		D	925 837-4221	0
Diablo Country Club		E	925 837-4221	0

DIAMOND BAR, CA - Los Angeles County

	SIC	EMP	PHONE	ENTRY #
24-Hour Med Staffing Svcs LLC		C	909 895-8960	0
Allstate Insurance Company		A	909 612-5504	0
American Golf Corporation		A	909 861-5757	0
Avnet Inc		B	760 946-5030	0
Cdnetworks Inc (DH)		E	408 228-3379	0
E-N Realty II		C	909 597-1736	0
Futurenet Technologies Corp		C	909 396-4000	0
Graybar Electric Company Inc		C	909 451-4300	0
Insperity Inc		D	909 569-1000	0
Kaiser Foundation Hospitals		A	800 780-1277	0
Liferay Inc (PA)		D	877 543-3729	0
March International Inc		E	909 821-5128	0
Mitsuba Corporation		D	909 374-2631	0
Modrine Limited		D	213 269-5466	0
Motech Americas LLC		B	302 451-7500	0
Oak Creek LP		D	909 860-5440	0
Point of View Inc		D	909 860-0705	0
Residential Bancorp (PA)		D	330 499-8333	0
Schneider Electric Usa Inc		D	909 612-5400	0
Smart & Final Stores Inc		B	323 855-8434	0
South Coast Air Qulty MGT Dst (PA)		A	909 396-2000	0
Specialty Equipment Mkt Assn (PA)		D	909 396-0289	0
Tetra Tech Bas Inc (HQ)		D	909 860-7777	0
Travelers Indemnity Company		C	909 612-3000	0
Vincent Huang & Associates LLC (PA)		D	909 861-9600	0

DIAMOND SPRINGS, CA - El Dorado County

	SIC	EMP	PHONE	ENTRY #
Cook Cabinets Inc		D	530 621-0851	0
County of El Dorado		D	530 626-4141	0
Johnsen Construction Inc		D	530 642-2123	0
Snowline Hspc Eldorado Cnty		C	916 817-2338	0
Snowline Hspice El Dorado Cnty		C	530 621-7820	0

DINUBA, CA - Tulare County

	SIC	EMP	PHONE	ENTRY #
Adventist Health System		A	559 595-9890	0
College Operations LLC		E	559 353-0576	0
Dinuba Medical Clinic (PA)		D	559 591-1820	0
Fruit Patch Sales LLC		B	559 591-1170	0
Gillette Citrus Company		D	559 626-4236	0
Kaweah Delta Health Care Dst		C	559 591-5513	0
Mikaelian & Sons Inc		C	559 591-6324	0
New Covenant Care of Dinuba		D	559 591-3300	0
Patterson Dental Supply Inc		D	559 595-1450	0
Valley Labor Service Inc		D	559 591-5591	0

DIXON, CA - Solano County

	SIC	EMP	PHONE	ENTRY #
Button Transportation Inc		C	707 678-7434	0
Cardinal Health Inc		C	530 406-3600	0
Carlisle Construction Mtls Inc		D	707 678-6900	0
Century 21 Dstnctive Prpts Inc		D	707 678-9211	0
First Northern Bank of Dixon (HQ)		D	707 678-4422	0
John Stewart Company		D	707 676-5660	0
Mayoral Bros		B	707 693-9111	0
Recology Inc		D	916 379-3300	0

DOS PALOS, CA - Merced County

	SIC	EMP	PHONE	ENTRY #
Clark Bros Farming Inc		E	209 392-6144	0
Dos Palos Memorial Hosp Inc		D	209 392-6121	0

DOWNEY, CA - Los Angeles County

	SIC	EMP	PHONE	ENTRY #
American Financial Network Inc		D	562 861-1414	0

	SIC	EMP	PHONE	ENTRY #
ARC Los Angles Orange Counties (PA)		D	562 803-1556	0
AT&T Corp		D	562 923-3032	0
Cantamar Property MGT Inc		E	562 862-4470	0
Cellco Partnership		D	562 401-1045	0
Central Refill Pharmaceuticals		D	562 401-4214	0
Century 21 A Better Svc Rlty		D	562 287-0230	0
City of Downey		D	562 861-8211	0
Companion Hospice Care LLC		C	562 944-2711	0
Companion Hospice LLC		D	562 944-2711	0
Conrad A Cox		E	562 927-0033	0
County of Los Angeles		A	562 401-7088	0
Downey Community Health Center		C	562 862-6506	0
El Camino Children & Fmly Svcs		E	562 364-1258	0
Ensign Group Inc		D	562 923-9301	0
Farwest Corrosion Control Co (PA)		C	310 532-9524	0
Financial Partners Credit Un (PA)		D	562 904-3000	0
First Family Homes		E	562 862-7373	0
Healthcare Ctr of Downey LLC		C	562 869-0978	0
Intero Real Estate Svcs Inc		D	562 861-7242	0
Kaiser Foundation Hospitals		B	562 657-9000	0
Kaiser Foundation Hospitals		A	800 823-4040	0
Kaiser Foundation Hospitals		A	800 823-4040	0
Kaiser Foundation Hospitals		D	562 622-4190	0
Kpwr Radio LLC		C	562 745-2300	0
Lakewood Park Health Center (PA)		B	562 869-0978	0
Liberty Ambulance LLC		D	562 741-6230	0
Liberty Utilities Pk Wtr Corp (DH)		D	562 923-0711	0
Los Amigos Country Club Inc		D	562 923-9696	0
Los Angeles Cty Rnch Los Amgos		A	562 385-7111	0
Macerich Company		E	562 861-9233	0
Mental Hlth Cnvlscent Svcs Inc		B	562 869-0978	0
Meruelo Enterprises Inc (PA)		A	562 745-2300	0
Mike Campbell & Associates Ltd		A	626 369-3981	0
Newwest Mortgage Company		D	562 861-8393	0
Omniteam Inc		C	562 923-9660	0
Park Hotels & Resorts Inc		D	562 861-1900	0
Pih Health Hospital - Downey		A	562 698-0811	0
Pih Health Hospital - Whitti		A	562 904-5482	0
Pioneer Medical Group Inc		D	562 862-2775	0
Prestige Too Auto Body Inc		E	310 787-8852	0
Prudential 24 Hour Real Estate		D	562 861-7257	0
Ralphs Grocery Company		D	562 633-0830	0
Ralphs Grocery Company		D	562 869-2042	0
Rancho Los Amigos Nationa		B	562 401-7111	0
Rancho Los Amigos Nationa		A	562 401-7111	0
Rancho Los Amigos Nationa		B	562 401-7266	0
Rancho Los Amigos Nationa (PA)		D	562 401-7111	0
Rancho Research Institute		C	562 401-8111	0
Rockview Dairies Inc (PA)		E	562 927-5511	0
Rrm Construction Inc		E	562 440-3539	0
Sialic Contractors Corporation		D	562 803-9977	0
Southern Cal Prmnnte Med Group		A	562 657-2200	0
Southern California Alcohol An (PA)		D	562 923-4545	0
Southern California Gas Co		E	562 803-7453	0
Southland Credit Union		D	562 862-6831	0
Spectrum MGT Holdg Co LLC		D	562 372-4008	0
Steve Roberson		D	562 927-2626	0
Sunbridge Healthcare LLC		C	562 869-2567	0
Tarsco Holdings LLC		C	562 869-0200	0
USF Reddaway Inc		C	562 923-0648	0
Westar Manufacturing Inc		D	562 633-0581	0
Young Mens Chrstn Assn of La		C	562 862-4201	0
Young Mens Chrstn Assn of La		D	562 862-4201	0

DUARTE, CA - Los Angeles County

	SIC	EMP	PHONE	ENTRY #
Beckman Research Inst Hope		C	626 359-8111	0
Begroup		D	626 359-9371	0
Bershtel Enterprises LLC (PA)		C	626 301-9214	0
Cal Southern Presbt Homes		D	626 359-8141	0
Cal Southern Presbt Homes		C	626 357-1632	0
City Hope National Medical Ctr		A	626 256-4673	0
ESP Group Ltd		D	626 301-0280	0
Estrella Inc		C	562 925-6418	0
General Electric Company		C	626 359-7988	0
Kf Community Care LLC		C	626 357-3207	0
Maryvale Day Care Center		C	626 357-1514	0
Monrovia Convalescent Hospital		D	626 359-6618	0
Paris Blues Inc (PA)		D	310 605-2000	0
Royal Terrace Healthcare		D	626 256-4654	0
SA Recycling LLC		D	626 359-5815	0
Santa Teresita Inc (PA)		B	626 359-3243	0
Therma Holdings LLC		E	626 446-1854	0
United Hauling Corp		D	626 358-9417	0
Westminster Gardens		D	626 359-2571	0

Mergent email: customerrelations@mergent.com
1530

2020 Directory of California
Wholesalers and Services Companies

(P-0000) Products & Services Section entry number
(PA)=Parent Co (HQ)=Headquarters (DH)=Div Headquarters

	SIC	EMP	PHONE	ENTRY #

DUBLIN, CA - Alameda County

4g Wireless Inc		D	925 307-8990	0
AMS Electric Inc		D	925 961-1600	0
AT&T Corp		B	925 560-5011	0
Bay Area News Group E Bay LLC **(HQ)**		D	925 302-1683	0
Callidus Software Inc **(HQ)**		C	925 251-2200	0
Care Options Management Plans		C	925 551-3227	0
Challenge Dairy Products Inc **(HQ)**		D	925 828-6160	0
Corelynx Inc		C	877 267-3599	0
Corizon Health Inc		C	925 551-6500	0
Desilva Gates Construction LP **(PA)**		D	925 361-1380	0
Develpment Dimensions Intl Inc		B	925 361-4246	0
Dublin Hstrcal Prsrvation Assn		D	925 785-2898	0
Dublin San Ramon Services Dst **(PA)**		D	925 875-2276	0
Dublin Unified School District		C	925 415-2407	0
Epicor Software Corporation		C	925 361-9900	0
Franklin Tmpleton Inv Svcs LLC		C	925 875-2619	0
Gateway Landscape Cnstr Inc		D	925 875-0000	0
Gettler-Ryan Inc **(PA)**		D	925 551-7555	0
Lusardi Construction Co		C	925 829-1114	0
New Home Professionals		C	925 556-1555	0
Oracle Taleo LLC		A	925 452-3000	0
Pacific Sttes Envmtl Cntrs Inc		E	925 803-4333	0
Rakon America LLC		A	847 930-5100	0
Rgis LLC		D	925 829-2875	0
Saba Software Inc **(PA)**		D	877 722-2101	0
Sansa Technology LLC		E	866 204-3710	0
Service King Paint & Body LLC		C	925 301-8481	0
T and D Communications Inc **(PA)**		D	510 824-0010	0
Trevi Partners A Calif LP **(HQ)**		D	925 828-7750	0
Trinet Group Inc **(PA)**		C	510 352-5000	0
Vagaro Inc		D	800 919-0157	0
Water & Sewer Service		D	925 828-8524	0

DURHAM, CA - Butte County

Chico Produce Inc **(PA)**		C	530 893-0596	0
Fedex Ground Package Sys Inc		C	800 463-3339	0

E RNCHO DMNGZ, CA - Los Angeles County

Murray Plumbing and Htg Corp **(PA)**		A	310 637-1500	0
Vanguard Lgistics Svcs USA Inc **(DH)**		D	310 637-3700	0

EARLIMART, CA - Tulare County

Vincent V Zaninovich & Sons		D	661 849-2613	0

EARP, CA - San Bernardino County

Colorado River Adventures Inc **(PA)**		C	760 663-3737	0

EAST PALO ALTO, CA - Santa Clara County

Cintas Corporation No 3		D	650 589-4300	0
County of San Mateo		D	650 853-3139	0
Dla Piper LLP (us)		B	650 833-2000	0
Dla Piper LLP (us)		B	650 833-2000	0
Drew Health Foundation		E	650 328-1619	0
Duff & Phelps LLC		D	650 798-5500	0
East Palo Alto Hotel Dev Inc		C	650 566-1200	0
East Palo Alto Y M C A		E	650 328-9622	0
Facial Reconstructive Surgery		E	650 328-0511	0
Four Seasons Hotel Inc		A	650 566-1200	0
Greenberg Traurig LLP		D	650 328-8500	0
Hggc LLC **(PA)**		B	650 321-4910	0
Nutrition Parent LLC		A	650 321-4910	0
Ropes & Gray LLP		D	650 617-4000	0
Roto-Rooter Services Company		D	650 322-2366	0
South Cnty Cmmty Hlth Ctr Inc **(PA)**		D	650 330-7407	0
Zadaonet		D	650 556-6377	0

EASTVALE, CA - Riverside County

Cellco Partnership		D	951 361-1850	0
Dejuno Corporation		D	909 230-6744	0
DSC Logistics LLC		D	909 605-7233	0
Dz Trading Ltd		C	951 479-5700	0
Meiko America Inc		D	951 360-0281	0
Mentor Media (usa) Sup		D	909 930-0800	0
Smart & Final Stores Inc		C	909 773-1813	0
United Parcel Service Inc OH		B	951 749-3400	0
Vipstore USA Co		D	626 934-7880	0
Walmart Inc		B	951 681-7256	0
WW Grainger Inc		C	951 727-2300	0

EDGEWOOD, CA - Siskiyou County

Siskiyou Development Company		D	530 938-2731	0

EDISON, CA - Kern County

Giumarra Farms Inc		D	661 395-7000	0
Giumarra Vineyards Corporation **(PA)**		D	661 395-7000	0
Johnston Farms Fmly Ltd Partnr		D	661 366-3201	0
Kirschenman Enterprises Sls LP		B	661 366-5736	0
Kirschenman Packing Inc		C	661 366-5736	0

EDWARDS, CA - Kern County

Jt3 LLC		A	661 277-4900	0
US Dept of Air Force		D	661 277-3432	0
US Dept of the Air Force		C	661 277-3030	0
US Dept of the Air Force		D	661 275-5410	0

EDWARDS AFB, CA - Kern County

GE Aviation Systems LLC		C	661 277-7308	0

EL CAJON, CA - San Diego County

Aeromedevac Inc		D	619 284-7910	0
AJM Packaging Corporation		D	619 448-4007	0
American Residential Svcs LLC		D	858 292-4452	0
Anthony P Garofalo A Dental		D	619 440-0071	0
ARC of San Diego		C	619 448-2415	0
Artimex Iron Company Inc		C	619 444-3155	0
Automotive Service Council		D	800 810-4272	0
Baechler Investigative Svcs		D	619 464-5600	0
Builders Firstsource Inc		E	619 440-7711	0
C Team Construction Inc		D	619 579-6572	0
California Shtmtl Works Inc		C	619 562-7010	0
Cass Construction Inc **(PA)**		C	619 590-0929	0
Country Hills Health Care Inc		C	619 441-8745	0
Countywide Mech Systems Inc		C	619 449-9900	0
Cox Communications Cal LLC		B	619 562-9820	0
Demko Drywall & Demolition Co		E	619 590-0025	0
Division 8 Inc		E	619 741-7552	0
Edwards Theatres Circuit Inc		D	619 660-3460	0
El Cajon Motors **(PA)**		D	619 579-8888	0
Eldorado Care Center LP		B	619 440-1211	0
Eugene N Townsend		D	619 442-8807	0
Executive Protection Agency K-		E	619 442-5771	0
F R Ghianni Enterprises Inc		D	619 279-1073	0
Fox Factory Holding Corp		A	619 768-1800	0
G M A C-One Source Realty		D	619 405-6231	0
Gardner Pool Company Inc **(PA)**		D	619 593-8880	0
Global Check Service		D	619 449-5150	0
Granite Hills Healthcare		D	619 447-1020	0
Grossmont-Cuyamaca Community		D	619 644-7684	0
Hamann Construction		D	619 440-7424	0
Helix Water District		D	619 596-3860	0
Home Guiding Hands Corporation **(PA)**		B	619 938-2850	0
J P Witherow Roofing Company		D	619 297-4701	0
Jeffrey Pine Holdings LLC		D	619 442-0544	0
K T A Construction Inc		D	619 562-9464	0
Kaiser Foundation Hospitals		E	619 528-5000	0
Kaiser Foundation Hospitals		E	619 528-5000	0
Koch-Armstrong General Engrg		D	619 561-2005	0
Lexicon Consulting Inc **(PA)**		D	619 792-1530	0
Lundstrom & Associates Inc		E	619 641-5900	0
Madison Care Center LLC		D	619 444-1107	0
Magnolia Special Care Center		D	619 442-8826	0
McAlister Inst For Trtmnt Edca **(PA)**		C	619 442-0277	0
McClintock Enterprises Inc		D	619 579-5300	0
Nan McKay and Associates Inc		D	619 258-1855	0
National Pub Sfety SEC Svcs In		D	619 579-1660	0
Neighborhood Healthcare		D	619 440-2751	0
Newport Diversified Inc		D	619 449-7800	0
Our Lady of Grace P T G		E	619 466-0055	0
Pacific Production Plumbing **(PA)**		E	951 509-3100	0
Paradise Electric Inc		D	619 449-4141	0
Parkside Special Care Center		D	619 442-7744	0
Plum Healthcare Group LLC		C	619 873-2500	0
Professionals Choice Sport		D	619 873-1100	0
R D S Unlimited Inc		E	619 443-0221	0
S C Tile Company Inc		E	619 669-1575	0
San Diego Aerospace Museum		D	619 258-1221	0
Schilling Paradise Corp		C	619 449-4141	0
Seal Electric Inc		C	619 449-7323	0
Sears Roebuck and Co		D	619 590-3812	0
Sharp Healthcare		D	619 442-0844	0
Smart & Final Stores Inc		B	619 390-1738	0
Smart & Final Stores Inc		C	619 589-7000	0
Somerset Special Care Center		D	619 442-0245	0
Southern Cal Prmnnte Med Group		E	619 528-5000	0
St Madeleine Sophies Center		D	619 442-5129	0
Steve Duich Inc		E	619 444-6118	0
Sunshine Communications Inc		C	619 448-7600	0
Sycuan Casino		A	619 445-6002	0
The Pines Ltd		C	619 447-1880	0
Thomas J Hoban **(PA)**		E	619 442-1665	0
Thyssenkrupp Elevator Corp		D	619 596-7220	0
Tony Gomez Tree Service		D	619 593-1552	0
Toyotalift Inc **(PA)**		E	619 562-5438	0

	SIC	EMP	PHONE	ENTRY #
University Mechanical & (DH)		C	619 956-2500	0
USA Waste of California Inc		D	619 596-5117	0
Victoria Post Acute Care		C	619 440-5005	0
Walter Anderson Plumbing Inc		C	619 449-7646	0
Waste Management Cal Inc		C	619 596-5100	0
Way Cool Homecare Inc		E	619 444-3200	0
West Coast AC Co Inc		C	619 561-8000	0
XI Staffing Inc		C	619 579-0442	0

EL CENTRO, CA - Imperial County

	SIC	EMP	PHONE	ENTRY #
Accentcare Home Health		E	760 352-4022	0
All Star Seed (PA)		D	760 482-9400	0
ARC - Imperial Valley (PA)		D	760 352-0180	0
Canon Solutions America Inc		D	800 323-4827	0
Cellco Partnership		D	760 337-5508	0
Centene Chwp		D	760 482-5593	0
City of El Centro		C	760 337-4505	0
County of Imperial		C	760 482-4441	0
County of Imperial		D	760 336-3581	0
County of Imperial		D	760 482-4120	0
El Centro Regional Medical Ctr (PA)		A	760 339-7100	0
Granite Construction Inc		C	760 337-3030	0
Hay Kuhn Inc		E	760 353-0124	0
I N C Builders Inc		B	760 352-4200	0
Imperial County Behavioral HLT		E	760 482-2149	0
Imperial Irrigation District		D	760 339-9800	0
Noblesse Oblige Inc		D	760 353-3336	0
Original Sid Blackman Plbg Inc		D	760 352-3632	0
Securitas SEC Svcs USA Inc		C	760 353-8177	0
Time Warner Cable Inc		D	760 335-4800	0
United Parcel Service Inc OH		D	858 541-2336	0
Valencia Bros Inc		D	760 353-2168	0
Wilbur-Ellis Company LLC		D	760 352-2847	0

EL CERRITO, CA - Contra Costa County

	SIC	EMP	PHONE	ENTRY #
Berkeley Clinic Auxuillary		D	510 525-7844	0
Berkeley Country Club		D	510 233-7550	0
Shields Nursing Centers Inc		D	510 525-3212	0
West Coast Childrens Center		E	510 269-9030	0

EL DORADO, CA - El Dorado County

	SIC	EMP	PHONE	ENTRY #
Conforti Plumbing Inc		A	530 622-0202	0

EL DORADO HILLS, CA - El Dorado County

	SIC	EMP	PHONE	ENTRY #
Action Home Nursing Services		D	530 756-2600	0
Amdocs Inc		B	916 934-7000	0
Amdocs Bcs Inc		D	916 934-7000	0
Bayview Engrg & Cnstr Co Inc		D	916 939-8986	0
California Physicians Service		B	916 350-7800	0
CBS Maxpreps Inc		D	530 676-6440	0
Coldwell Bnkr Rsdntial RE Svcs		D	916 933-1155	0
Comerit Inc		C	888 556-5990	0
Consensus Orthopedics Inc		D	916 355-7123	0
Dorado Software Inc		D	916 673-1100	0
Dst Output California Inc		D	916 939-4617	0
El Dorado Hills County Wtr Dst		D	916 933-6623	0
Fortune Senior Enterprises		D	916 560-9100	0
Frank Gates Service Company		D	916 934-0812	0
G R Helm Inc		D	916 933-9697	0
Infinite Technologies Inc (PA)		D	916 987-3261	0
Marshall Medical Center		C	916 933-2273	0
O1 Communications Inc		D	888 444-1111	0
Patra Corporation (PA)		C	415 595-9987	0
Patrick K Willis Company Inc		B	800 398-6480	0
R Systems Inc (HQ)		D	916 939-9696	0
Response 1 Medical Staffing		D	916 932-0430	0
Roebbelen Construction Inc		D	916 939-4000	0
Roebbelen Contracting Inc		B	916 939-4000	0
School Innovations Achievement (PA)		D	916 933-2290	0
Securecom Inc		E	916 638-2855	0
Sequoia Insurance Company		D	916 933-9524	0
Serrano Associates LLC		D	916 939-3333	0
Serrano Country Club Inc		D	916 933-5005	0
Sierra Equipment Leasing Inc		E	925 676-7300	0
Suds Car Wash Inc		E	916 673-6300	0
V3 Electric Inc		C	916 939-6636	0
Weckworth Construction Co Inc		D	916 939-6636	0
Wyndgate Technologies		D	916 404-8400	0

EL GRANADA, CA - San Mateo County

	SIC	EMP	PHONE	ENTRY #
Indyne		D	805 606-0664	0
Range Generation Next LLC		E	310 647-9438	0

EL MACERO, CA - Yolo County

	SIC	EMP	PHONE	ENTRY #
El Macero Country Club Inc		D	530 753-3363	0

EL MONTE, CA - Los Angeles County

	SIC	EMP	PHONE	ENTRY #
Access Services		D	213 270-6000	0

	SIC	EMP	PHONE	ENTRY #
Ahm Gemch Inc		C	626 579-7777	0
Altamed Health Services Corp		C	323 889-7847	0
Atlanta Seafoods LLC		D	626 626-4900	0
Bangkit (usa) Inc		D	626 672-0888	0
California Schl Employees Assn		B	626 258-3300	0
Cathay Bank (HQ)		C	626 279-3698	0
Center Medical Company		E	626 575-7500	0
County of Los Angeles		C	626 575-4059	0
County of Los Angeles		D	626 455-4700	0
Dang Quinten		D	626 429-6332	0
Davita Medical Management LLC		D	626 444-0333	0
Driftwood Dairy Inc		C	626 444-9591	0
Eighty One Enterprise Inc		E	626 371-1980	0
El Monte Community Credit Un		D	626 444-0501	0
El Monte Convalescent Hospital		D	626 442-1500	0
ERs SEC Alarm Systems Inc		D	626 579-2525	0
Exterran Inc		D	626 455-0739	0
Firefighter Cancer Support Ntw		E	866 994-3276	0
First Student Inc		D	626 448-9446	0
Foundation For Early Childhood (PA)		D	626 572-5107	0
Georgia Atkison Snf LLC		C	626 444-2535	0
Gibralter Convalescent Hosp		D	626 443-9425	0
Hope Hse For Mltple Hndicapped (PA)		E	626 443-1313	0
Insul Acoustics Inc		C	323 686-2670	0
Integrated Parcel Network		B	714 278-6100	0
K T Lucky Co Inc		D	626 579-7272	0
Nijjar Realty Inc (PA)		C	626 575-0062	0
Optics Laboratory Inc		D	626 350-1926	0
Pacific Coast Drum Company		D	626 443-3096	0
Public Hlth Fndation Entps Inc		C	626 856-6618	0
Ramona Care Center Inc		C	626 442-5721	0
Rio Hondo Community Dev Corp		D	626 401-2784	0
S & S Rent-A-Fence Inc		D	818 896-7710	0
SA Recycling LLC		D	626 444-9530	0
Sabu Enterprises Inc		E	626 443-1351	0
San Gabriel Transit Inc (PA)		C	626 258-1310	0
San Gabriel Valley Water Co (PA)		C	626 448-6183	0
San Gbriel Vly Cnvlescent Hosp		D	626 401-1557	0
Southland Transit Inc (PA)		C	626 258-1310	0
Triple-E Machinery Moving Inc		D	626 444-1137	0
Turn Around Communications Inc		C	626 443-2400	0
Wells Fargo Bank National Assn		B	626 312-3006	0
Wells Fargo Bank National Assn		C	626 573-6452	0
Wgg Enterprises Inc		C	626 442-5493	0
Yew Bio-Pharm Group Inc		D	626 401-9588	0

EL PORTAL, CA - Mariposa County

	SIC	EMP	PHONE	ENTRY #
Yosemite Management Group LLC (PA)		D	209 379-2817	0

EL SEGUNDO, CA - Los Angeles County

	SIC	EMP	PHONE	ENTRY #
24hr Homecare LLC (PA)		D	310 906-3683	0
A-Mark Precious Metals Inc (PA)		D	310 587-1477	0
Accenture LLP		B	310 726-2700	0
Advantage Sales & Mktg Inc		C	310 321-6869	0
Aerospace Corporation (PA)		A	310 336-5000	0
After-Party2 Inc		D	310 535-3660	0
Air Force US Dept of		B	310 336-5000	0
Air New Zealand Limited		D	310 648-7000	0
Altech Services Inc		B	888 725-8324	0
American Golf Corporation (HQ)		C	310 664-4000	0
Asset Athene Management L P (HQ)		D	310 698-4444	0
Avanti Health System LLC		B	310 356-0550	0
Bear Nash Productions		D	310 428-5167	0
BMC Group Inc		D	310 321-5555	0
Boeing Satellite Systems		D	310 326-3100	0
Booz Allen Hamilton Inc		D	310 524-1557	0
Bshh II LLC		E	310 356-4587	0
BT Americas Inc		D	646 487-7400	0
California Physicians Service		C	310 744-2668	0
Carson Kurtzman Consultants (DH)		C	310 823-9000	0
Cathay Pacific Airways Limited		C	310 615-1113	0
Cbre Inc		C	310 363-4900	0
Century Pk Capitl Partners LLC (PA)		C	310 867-2210	0
Cetera Financial Group Inc (PA)		C	866 489-3100	0
Citigroup Global Markets Inc		D	310 727-9533	0
City National Bank		C	310 297-6606	0
Cls Trnsprttion Los Angles LLC (HQ)		C	310 414-8189	0
Continental 155 5th Corp		E	310 640-1520	0
Core Nutrition LLC		D	310 640-0500	0
Core Nutrition LLC		E	310 640-0500	0
Courtyard Management Corp		C	310 322-0700	0
David & Goliath LLC		C	310 445-5200	0
Davita Inc		D	310 536-2400	0
Davita Medical Management LLC (HQ)		A	310 354-4200	0
Dedicated Media Inc (PA)		D	310 524-9400	0
Dfds International Corporation		D	310 414-1516	0

2020 Directory of California
Wholesalers and Services Companies

(P-0000) Products & Services Section entry number
(PA)=Parent Co (HQ)=Headquarters (DH)=Div Headquarters

	SIC	EMP	PHONE	ENTRY #
Directv Inc.		B	888 388-4249	0
Directv Enterprises LLC		A	310 535-5000	0
Directv Group Holdings LLC (HQ)		C	310 964-5000	0
Directv Group Inc (DH)		C	310 964-5000	0
Directv International Inc (DH)		C	310 964-6460	0
Diverse Journeys Inc (PA)		D	310 643-7403	0
Doubletree By Hilton Hotel		C	310 322-0999	0
Edwards Technologies Inc.		D	310 536-7070	0
El Segundo Eductl Foundation		B	310 615-2650	0
Empire Chauffeur Service Ltd		C	310 414-8189	0
En Pointe Technologies Sls LLC		C	310 337-6151	0
Enterprise Services LLC		C	310 331-1074	0
Ernst & Young LLP		C	310 725-1764	0
Esaloncom LLC		D	866 550-2424	0
European Hotl Invstrs of CA		E	310 322-0999	0
Experian Info Solutions Inc.		C	310 343-6700	0
F&E Aircraft Maintenance (PA)		B	310 338-0063	0
Fc El Segundo LLC		D	702 439-7945	0
Federal Express Corporation		B	800 463-3339	0
Forsythe Technology LLC		C	424 217-6500	0
Frito-Lay North America Inc		E	310 322-5001	0
Fujitsu America Inc.		C	310 563-7000	0
Fujitsu Glovia Inc (HQ)		C	310 563-7000	0
Gbp Parent Corp (HQ)		A	424 254-9774	0
General Dynamics Info Tech Inc.		C	310 662-3202	0
Glovia Inc		C	310 563-7000	0
Governmentjobscom Inc		C	310 426-6304	0
Guthy-Renker LLC (PA)		D	760 773-9022	0
Hilton El Segundo LLC		D	310 726-0100	0
Hilton Garden Inns MGT LLC		D	310 726-0100	0
Hit Portfolio I NTC Trs LP		E	310 333-0888	0
Ibftech Inc		D	424 217-8010	0
Infineon Tech Americas Corp		A	310 726-8000	0
Infrascale Inc (PA)		D	310 878-2621	0
Inmotion Hosting Inc		E	888 321-4678	0
Internet Brands Inc (PA)		C	310 280-4000	0
Irise (PA)		D	800 556-0399	0
Ispace Inc		C	310 563-3800	0
Jackson Tull Chrtred Engineers		E	310 658-2132	0
Jalux Americas Inc (HQ)		E	310 524-1000	0
Japan Airlines Co Ltd		D	310 607-2305	0
Kellstrom Holding Corporation (PA)		D	561 222-7455	0
Kleinpartners Capital Corp		B	310 426-2055	0
Konami Digital Entrmt Inc (DH)		D	310 220-8100	0
Kyocera International Inc.		D	310 647-2805	0
L E Coppersmith Inc (PA)		D	310 607-8000	0
L E Coppersmith Inc.		D	310 607-8000	0
Leidos Inc.		C	310 524-3134	0
Login Consulting Services Inc		D	310 607-9091	0
Los Angeles Lakers Inc		C	310 426-6000	0
Los Angles Kings Hockey CLB LP		C	310 535-4502	0
Manduka LLC (HQ)		E	310 426-1495	0
Mantech International Corp		C	310 765-9324	0
Marketwire Inc (HQ)		D	310 765-3200	0
Matthews Retail Group Inc		D	866 889-0550	0
Michael Sullivan & Assoc LLP		C	310 337-4480	0
Nagra Usa Inc (HQ)		D	310 335-5225	0
National Air Cargo Inc		D	310 662-4766	0
National Planning Corporation		D	800 881-7174	0
Next Trucking Inc.		C	855 688-6398	0
Nippon Express USA Inc		D	310 535-7200	0
NRG El Segundo Operations Inc		D	310 615-6344	0
Oceanx LLC (HQ)		D	310 774-4088	0
Oracle Corporation		B	310 343-7405	0
Orbital Sciences Corporation		B	703 406-5000	0
Osata Enterprises Inc		D	888 445-6237	0
Pacific Aviation Corporation (PA)		C	310 646-4015	0
Pacific Theaters Inc		D	310 607-0007	0
Patterson Dental Supply Inc		D	310 426-3100	0
Pcm Sales Inc (DH)		C	310 354-5600	0
Peopleware Technical Resources		D	310 640-2406	0
Performance Team LLC (PA)		C	562 345-2200	0
Pinnacle Travel Services LLC		C	310 414-1787	0
Plumb Tech Inc.		D	310 322-4925	0
Primary Color Systems Corp		D	310 841-0250	0
Prodege LLC (PA)		D	310 294-9599	0
Professional Janitorial Svc		E	310 410-1452	0
Prologic Rdmption Slutions Inc (PA)		A	310 322-7774	0
Prosum Inc (PA)		D	310 426-0600	0
Pt Gaming LLC		A	323 260-5060	0
Q1media Inc.		D	512 388-2300	0
Quest Nutrition LLC (PA)		C	562 272-0180	0
Radica Enterprises Ltd		D	310 252-2000	0
Radiology Prtners Holdings LLC (PA)		D	424 290-8004	0
Rainier Financial Group LLC		E	310 335-9200	0

	SIC	EMP	PHONE	ENTRY #
Raytheon Command and Control		E	714 446-3232	0
Raytheon Company		C	310 647-9438	0
Residence Inn By Marriott LLC		C	310 333-0888	0
Rpd Hotels 18 LLC (PA)		A	213 746-1531	0
Rubicon B Hacienda LLC		D	424 290-5000	0
Rubicon B Hacienda LLC		D	424 290-5555	0
Saviynt Inc (PA)		C	310 641-1664	0
SC Harp El Segundo LLC		D	310 322-0999	0
Scope Seven LLC		D	310 220-3939	0
Securitas Critical Infrastruct.		A	310 426-3300	0
Sierra Systems Inc (PA)		C	310 536-6288	0
Singapore Airlines Limited		E	310 647-1922	0
Softscript Inc.		A	310 451-2110	0
Spectrum MGT Holdg Co LLC		D	310 647-3000	0
Square Enix Inc		C	310 846-0400	0
Stampscom Inc (PA)		C	310 482-5800	0
TBG Insurance Services Corp		B	310 203-8770	0
Tecolote Research Inc.		D	310 640-4700	0
Telenet Voip Inc		D	310 253-9000	0
Ten Publishing Media LLC (PA)		C	310 531-9900	0
Time Warner Cable Entps LLC		A	469 665-7735	0
Transportation Management LLC		E	310 524-1555	0
Tri-Star Ccw Management L P		D	310 322-0999	0
Tri-Union Seafoods LLC (DH)		D	858 558-9662	0
VIP Tours of California Inc		D	310 216-7507	0
Wash Mltfmily Ldry Systems LLC (PA)		C	310 643-8491	0
Westport Capital Partners LLC		E	310 294-1234	0
Wpromote LLC (PA)		D	310 421-4844	0
Xceed Financial Credit Union (PA)		D	800 932-8222	0
Your Man Tours Inc.		D	513 772-4411	0
Your Man Tours Merger Inc (DH)		D	310 649-3820	0

EL SOBRANTE, CA - Contra Costa County

	SIC	EMP	PHONE	ENTRY #
D & H Landscaping Inc.		D	510 223-6597	0
Greenridge Senior Care		C	510 758-9600	0
Ppm Real Estate Inc		D	510 758-5636	0

EL TORO, CA - Orange County

	SIC	EMP	PHONE	ENTRY #
Certainteed Gypsum Inc.		E	949 282-5300	0
Cohen Richard Ldscp & Cnstr		E	949 768-0599	0
Frito-Lay North America Inc		D	949 586-4644	0
Sunset Landscape Maintenance		D	949 455-4636	0

ELK GROVE, CA - Sacramento County

	SIC	EMP	PHONE	ENTRY #
Alldata LLC		D	916 684-5200	0
Banner Bank		D	916 685-6546	0
Bennathon Corp (PA)		D	916 405-2100	0
Bradshaw Veterinary Clinic		D	916 685-2494	0
Brookdale Senior Living Inc.		D	916 683-1881	0
California Family Health LLC		E	916 685-3355	0
Cardinal Health Inc.		C	916 372-9880	0
Carlton Senior Living Inc		E	916 714-2404	0
Comprehensive SEC Svcs Inc (PA)		D	916 683-3605	0
Concrete North Inc		D	209 745-7400	0
Cosumnes Community Svcs Dst		B	916 405-7150	0
County of Sacramento		C	916 874-1927	0
Customcare Home Hlth Svcs Inc		D	916 714-1155	0
Dominion International Inc.		D	916 683-9545	0
Elk Grove Adult Cmnty Training		D	916 431-3162	0
Emerald Site Services Inc		D	916 685-7211	0
Farmers Mrchants Bnk Centl Cal		D	916 394-3200	0
Future Energy Corporation (PA)		E	800 985-0733	0
Future Energy Corporation		D	916 685-4200	0
J & L Collections Services Inc		D	800 481-6006	0
Kaiser Foundation Hospitals		D	916 544-6000	0
Lifestyles Senior Housing Man		D	916 714-3755	0
Maritime Management		B	916 392-3000	0
Matheson Fast Freight Inc (HQ)		D	916 686-4600	0
Nugget Market Inc		D	916 226-2626	0
OC Communications Inc (PA)		C	916 686-3700	0
Pacific Excavation Inc		D	916 686-2800	0
Professional Bureau of Collect		D	916 685-3399	0
Provident Fincl Holdings Inc		D	916 709-3257	0
R & A Painting Inc.		D	916 688-3955	0
Rhodes Retail Services Inc		D	916 714-9233	0
River Oak Center For Children		D	916 226-2800	0
Sacramento Reg Co Sanit Dist		B	916 875-9000	0
Sacramento Yolo Cnty Mosquito		D	916 685-1022	0
Saia Motor Freight Line LLC		E	916 690-8417	0
Spare-Time Inc.		D	916 859-5910	0
Sutter Health		C	916 691-5900	0
Sutter Health		B	916 455-8137	0
Sutter Health		A	916 544-5423	0
Sutter Health		B	916 691-5900	0
Tim Paxins Pacific Excavation		E	916 686-2800	0
Valley-HI Country Club		E	916 684-2120	0

Employment Codes: A=Over 500 employees, B=251-500,
C=101-250, D=51-100, E=50

2020 Directory of California
Wholesalers and Services Companies

© Mergent Inc. 1-800-342-5647

1533

GEOGRAPHIC

	SIC	EMP	PHONE	ENTRY #

EMERALD HILLS, CA - San Mateo County

Company	SIC	EMP	PHONE	ENTRY #
Legion Industries		E	650 743-6358	0
Reynolds Cleaning Services Inc		C	650 599-0202	0

EMERYVILLE, CA - Alameda County

Company	SIC	EMP	PHONE	ENTRY #
Agilysys Inc		E	702 759-4879	0
Aguatierra Associates Inc (PA)		D	510 450-6000	0
Alpha-Winfield Contractors Inc		D	510 652-4712	0
Amyris Inc		D	510 597-4839	0
Amyris Fuels LLC		C	510 450-0761	0
APM Terminals Pacific Ltd		B	510 992-6430	0
Armstrong Installation Service		D	408 777-1234	0
Art Supply Enterprises Inc (PA)		C	510 428-9011	0
Barry Bishop		D	510 596-0888	0
Behavioral Intervention Assn		E	510 652-7445	0
Berkeley Lights Inc (PA)		D	510 898-1433	0
Berkeley Research Group LLC (PA)		C	510 285-3300	0
Bolt Threads Inc (PA)		D	415 279-5585	0
Broadmoor Hotel		D	415 673-8445	0
Cell Design Labs Inc		E	510 398-0501	0
Cep America LLC		D	510 350-2691	0
Chiron Corporation		D	510 655-8730	0
Clif Bar & Company (PA)		C	510 596-6300	0
E2 Consulting Engineers Inc		B	510 652-1164	0
Ernest Gallo Clinic & RES Ctr		D	510 985-3856	0
Exponential Interactive Inc (HQ)		D	510 250-5500	0
Federal Express Corporation		C	800 463-3339	0
Fort James Corporation		D	510 594-4900	0
Giampolini & Co		D	415 673-1236	0
Gracenote Inc (DH)		D	510 428-7200	0
Greenberg Inc (PA)		D	510 446-8200	0
Grill Recording Studio		D	510 531-4351	0
Leidos Inc		D	510 428-2550	0
Location Labs Inc		D	510 601-7012	0
Mobitv Inc		D	510 981-1303	0
Nmi Holdings Inc		B	855 530-6642	0
Onebody Inc		D	510 285-2000	0
Pacific Hotel Management LLC		C	510 547-7888	0
Pixar (DH)		A	510 922-3000	0
Ramboll Environ US Corporation		D	510 655-7400	0
Ratcliff Architects		D	510 899-6400	0
Real Estate America Inc		D	510 594-3100	0
Rlj Hgn Emeryville Lessee LP		D	510 658-9300	0
Rljhgn Emeryville Lessee LP		C	510 658-9300	0
Santen Incorporated		D	415 268-9100	0
Sutter Vsting Nrse Assn Hspice (HQ)		E	866 652-9178	0
Tubemogul Inc		D	510 653-0126	0
University California Berkeley		A	510 495-2490	0
Young MNS Chrstn Assn of E Bay		D	510 601-8674	0
Zymergen Inc (PA)		E	415 801-8073	0

ENCINITAS, CA - San Diego County

Company	SIC	EMP	PHONE	ENTRY #
Ad Results Media LLC		D	858 480-5223	0
Benex LLC		D	310 675-6200	0
Burtech Pipeline Incorporated		D	760 634-2822	0
Cielo Azul Inc		D	855 863-8503	0
City of Encinitas		E	760 633-2850	0
Cloudtrigger Inc		D	858 367-5272	0
Coldwell Banker		D	760 753-5616	0
Compass Real Estate LLC		A	760 979-5609	0
Dudek (PA)		D	760 942-5147	0
Express Companies Inc		E	760 944-1048	0
Five Star Senior Living Inc		E	760 479-1818	0
Hcr Manorcare Med Svcs Fla LLC		D	760 944-0331	0
J Robert Echter		E	760 436-0188	0
JC Resorts LLC		D	760 944-1936	0
New Earth Enterprises Inc		D	760 942-1298	0
Nixon Inc (PA)		D	760 944-0900	0
North Coast Presbyterian Ch		D	760 753-2535	0
Olivenhain Municipal Water Dst		D	760 753-6466	0
Perfect Workout Inc (PA)		D	949 943-7281	0
R N Priority Nursing Service		D	760 635-7776	0
Rancho Santa Fe Protective Svc		E	760 433-8887	0
San Diego Hebrew Homes (PA)		C	760 942-2695	0
Scripps Health		D	760 753-8413	0
Scripps Health		D	760 479-3900	0
Scripps Health		C	760 753-6501	0
Scripps Health		D	760 633-6915	0
Sethi Management Inc		D	760 652-4010	0
Silverado Senior Living Inc		D	760 270-9917	0
Welltower Inc		B	760 436-4122	0
Ycg LLC		D	760 230-8016	0
YMCA of San Diego County		D	858 292-4034	0
Zephyr Partners Re-LLC		E	858 558-3650	0

ENCINO, CA - Los Angeles County

Company	SIC	EMP	PHONE	ENTRY #
A-Able Inc (PA)		D	323 658-5779	0
Actual Reality Pictures Inc		E	818 325-8800	0
Adept Consumer Testing Inc		E	310 279-4600	0
Allen Edwards Beauty Salon (PA)		D	818 981-7711	0
Answer Financial Inc (HQ)		C	818 644-4000	0
Automobile Club Southern Cal		E	818 997-6230	0
Ballard Rosenberg Golper Sav (PA)		D	818 508-3700	0
Brite Media LLC		C	818 826-5790	0
Burkshire Has A Way Home Servc		D	818 501-4800	0
C M A Alliance		E	818 981-0800	0
Childrens Hospital Los Angeles		C	818 728-4930	0
CIT Bank NA		D	818 817-5320	0
Concrete Holding Co Cal Inc		B	818 788-4228	0
D3publisher of America Inc		D	310 268-0820	0
Dynata LLC		C	866 872-4006	0
Elizabeth Glaser Pedia		A	310 231-0400	0
Encino Center Car Wash Inc		E	818 788-6300	0
Encino Hospital Medical Center		B	818 995-5000	0
Encino Trzana Regional Med Ctr		B	818 995-5000	0
Graypay LLC		D	818 387-6735	0
Hemar Rousso & Heald L L P		E	818 501-3800	0
Holthouse Carlin Van Trigt LLP		D	818 849-3140	0
Ideal Brands Inc		E	213 489-5557	0
Integrted Spport Solutions Inc (PA)		B	818 787-2116	0
Israel Pops Orchestra		E	818 343-6450	0
Kramer-Wilson Company Inc (PA)		C	818 760-0880	0
Kravitz Investment Svcs Inc		D	818 995-6100	0
KSL Media Inc		C	212 468-3395	0
Life Alert Emergency Response (PA)		C	800 247-0000	0
Lmno Productions Inc		C	818 995-5555	0
Lodgen Lacher Golditch Sard		E	818 783-0570	0
Max Mri Imaging Inc (PA)		E	818 382-2220	0
Max/Mr Imaging Inc		D	818 382-2220	0
Merrill Lynch Pierce Fenner		E	818 528-7809	0
Nations Capital Group LLC		E	818 793-2050	0
Ols Hotels & Resorts LLC (PA)		A	818 905-8280	0
One Silver Serve Inc		E	818 995-6444	0
Orchard Horror Film LLC		E	212 203-6147	0
Orthopedic Consultants (PA)		E	818 788-7343	0
Pearlman Borska & Wax LLP (PA)		D	818 501-4343	0
Price Associates		E	818 995-9216	0
Price Law Group A Prof Corp (PA)		C	818 995-4540	0
Ralphs Grocery Company		C	818 345-6882	0
Reprints Desk Inc		D	310 477-0354	0
Republic Indemnity Co Amer (DH)		C	818 990-9860	0
Republic Indemnity Company Cal		C	818 990-9860	0
Research Solutions Inc (PA)		C	310 477-0354	0
Rodeo Realty Inc		D	818 285-3700	0
Schweizer Rena		D	818 501-7100	0
Southern Cal Stone Ctr LLC		D	818 784-8975	0
Specilty Srgical Ctr Encino LP		D	310 659-6333	0
State Farm Mutl Auto Insur Co		D	818 849-5126	0
Sunrise Senior Living Inc		E	818 346-9046	0
Umpqua Bank		D	818 385-1362	0
Uniworld River Cruises Inc		C	818 382-2322	0
Valuation Concepts LLC		D	818 812-6233	0
Vitas Healthcare Corp Cal		D	818 760-2273	0
Working With Autism		D	818 501-4240	0

ESCALON, CA - San Joaquin County

Company	SIC	EMP	PHONE	ENTRY #
Dan R Costa Inc		C	209 234-2004	0
Noralco Inc		C	209 551-4545	0

ESCONDIDO, CA - San Diego County

Company	SIC	EMP	PHONE	ENTRY #
20/20 Plumbing & Heating Inc		C	760 535-3101	0
4g Wireless Inc		D	760 705-7133	0
A & G Grove Service		D	760 728-5447	0
Airx Utility Surveyors Inc (PA)		D	760 480-2347	0
ARS National Services Inc (PA)		C	800 456-5053	0
ARS West LLC		D	760 480-6631	0
Associate Mechanical Contrs		D	760 294-3517	0
AT&T Services Inc		C	760 489-3519	0
AT&T Services Inc		B	760 489-3187	0
Baker Distributing Company LLC		D	760 708-4201	0
Bergelectric Corp		A	760 746-1003	0
Blanchard Training and Dev Inc (PA)		C	760 489-5005	0
Blanchardcoachingcom Inc		B	760 489-5005	0
Bmt Commercial Usa Inc (HQ)		C	760 737-3505	0
Borrego Cmnty Hlth Foundation		C	760 466-1080	0
Cal Southern Presbt Homes		C	760 747-4306	0
Cal Southern Presbt Homes		D	760 737-5110	0
Cal Southern Sound Image Inc (PA)		D	760 737-3900	0
California Healthcare		C	760 520-1333	0
Central State Pre-School		E	760 432-2499	0
Chicago Title & Escrow		E	760 746-3882	0

Mergent email: customerrelations@mergent.com
1534

2020 Directory of California
Wholesalers and Services Companies

(P-0000) Products & Services Section entry number
(PA)=Parent Co (HQ)=Headquarters (DH)=Div Headquarters

	SIC	EMP	PHONE	ENTRY #
Choa Hope LLC		E	712 277-4101	0
Christiansen Amusements Corp		D	760 735-8542	0
Concrete Concepts Inc		D	760 737-5470	0
Conrad Acceptance Corporation		E	760 735-5000	0
Conrad Credit Corporation		E	760 735-5000	0
Construction Tstg & Engrg Inc (PA)		D	760 746-4955	0
Covenant Care California LLC		E	760 745-1288	0
Davey Tree Surgery Company		D	760 975-0225	0
Eleven Western Builders Inc (PA)		C	760 796-6346	0
Elizabeth Hospice Inc (PA)		D	760 737-2050	0
Emeritus Corporation		E	760 741-3055	0
Ensign Group Inc		D	760 746-0303	0
Erickson-Hall Construction Co (PA)		D	760 796-7700	0
Garrick Motors Inc		C	760 489-2656	0
George Richard		D	619 805-6751	0
Graybill Medical Group Inc (PA)		C	866 228-2236	0
Green Guard Services Inc		D	619 488-1065	0
Henry Avocado Corporation (PA)		D	760 745-6632	0
Hidden Valley Mvg & Stor Inc (PA)		D	602 252-7800	0
Hmt Electric Inc		D	858 458-9771	0
In & Out Car Wash Inc		E	619 316-8492	0
Integrity Healthcare Services		D	760 432-9811	0
Interfaith Community Svcs Inc		D	760 489-6380	0
J & P Financial Inc (PA)		E	760 738-9000	0
JR Filanc Cnstr Co Inc (PA)		D	760 941-7130	0
Kaiser Foundation Hospitals		A	442 281-5000	0
Kaiser Foundation Hospitals		A	760 739-3000	0
Kaiser Foundation Hospitals		E	619 528-5000	0
Landcare USA LLC		D	760 747-1174	0
Las Villas Del Norte		D	760 741-1047	0
Laser Electric Inc (PA)		E	760 658-6626	0
Learning Services Corporation		E	760 746-3223	0
Legacy Partners Limited Inc		D	760 747-2711	0
Life Care Centers America Inc		C	760 741-6109	0
Marathon General Inc		D	760 738-9714	0
Master Design Drywall Inc		C	760 480-9001	0
Meadowbrook Village Christian		C	760 746-2500	0
Medley Communications Inc		D	760 294-4579	0
Mountain Meadow Mushrooms Inc		D	760 749-1201	0
Mountain Shadows Support Group (PA)		D	760 743-3714	0
Neighborhood Healthcare		C	760 737-6903	0
Neighborhood Healthcare (PA)		E	760 520-8372	0
Neighborhood Healthcare		D	760 737-2000	0
Oj Insulation LP		E	760 839-3200	0
Pacific Structures Cnstr Inc		E	740 480-4133	0
Pacific Western Bank		C	760 432-1350	0
Pacific Western Bank		D	760 432-1100	0
Pack & Crate Services Inc		E	760 737-6893	0
Palomar Fmly Cunseling Svc Inc (PA)		D	760 741-2660	0
Palomar Gem & Mineral Club		D	760 743-0809	0
Palomar Health		B	858 675-5360	0
Palomar Health (PA)		C	442 281-5000	0
Palomar Health		A	760 739-3000	0
Par Electrical Contractors Inc		D	760 291-1192	0
Physical Therapy Hand Ctrs Inc		E	760 233-9655	0
Pine Tree Lumber Company LP (PA)		D	760 745-0411	0
Pinery LLC		D	858 675-3575	0
Polestar Labs Inc		D	760 480-2600	0
Prowall Lath and Plaster		D	760 480-9001	0
Rapid Product Dev Group Inc		C	760 703-5770	0
Red Hawk Fire & SEC CA Inc		D	760 233-9787	0
Redwood Elderlink Scph		B	760 480-1030	0
Rio Vista Ventures LLC (PA)		D	760 480-8502	0
Rocky Coast Builders Inc		D	760 489-7770	0
Romero General Cnstr Corp		C	760 489-8412	0
Saber Plumbing Inc		D	760 480-5716	0
Salazar Labor Contracting		D	760 746-0805	0
San Diego County Water Auth		D	760 480-1991	0
Sbrm Inc (PA)		D	760 480-0208	0
Scripps Health		C	760 806-5700	0
Service Master Industries Inc		D	760 480-0208	0
Silverado Senior Living Inc		D	760 456-5137	0
Sound-Crete Contractors Inc		D	760 291-1240	0
Southern Cal Prmnnte Med Group		E	760 839-7200	0
Southland Paving Inc		D	760 747-6895	0
Southwest General Contrs Inc		E	760 480-8747	0
Structures West Inc		D	760 737-2349	0
Sunrize Staging Inc		D	760 743-2043	0
Sylvester Roofing Company Inc (PA)		E	760 743-0048	0
The For Califo Cente		C	760 839-4138	0
TNT Grading Inc		D	760 736-4054	0
Tpd Dell Dios		E	760 741-2888	0
Transmrcan Mling Flfilment Inc		D	760 745-5343	0
Tri-Ad Actuaries Inc		C	760 743-7555	0
Valle Vsta Cnvlescent Hosp Inc		D	760 745-1288	0

	SIC	EMP	PHONE	ENTRY #
Veterans Health Administration		B	760 745-2000	0
Welk Group Inc (PA)		B	760 749-3000	0
West Escondido Healthcare LLC		D	760 746-0303	0
Western Rim Constructors Inc		E	760 489-4328	0
Westmed Ambulance Inc		B	310 219-1779	0
Wier Construction Corporation		E	760 743-6776	0
William Brammer		C	760 746-6006	0
X3 Management Services Inc		D	760 597-9336	0
YMCA of San Diego County		B	760 745-7490	0
Zoological Society San Diego		A	760 747-8702	0

ESPARTO, CA - Yolo County

	SIC	EMP	PHONE	ENTRY #
Bz - Bee Pollination Inc		E	530 787-3044	0
R H Phillips Inc (HQ)		C	530 757-5557	0

ETIWANDA, CA - San Bernardino County

	SIC	EMP	PHONE	ENTRY #
C M C Steel Fabricators Inc		C	909 899-9993	0

ETNA, CA - Siskiyou County

	SIC	EMP	PHONE	ENTRY #
Etna Police Activities League		C	530 467-3400	0

EUREKA, CA - Humboldt County

	SIC	EMP	PHONE	ENTRY #
Best Western Bayshore Inn		E	707 268-8005	0
California Dept Transportation		B	707 445-6600	0
Changing Tides Family Services (PA)		D	707 444-8293	0
Coast Central Credit Union (PA)		C	707 445-8801	0
Correctons Rhbltation Cal Dept		D	707 445-6520	0
County of Humboldt		B	707 445-6180	0
County of Humboldt		C	707 476-4054	0
E G Ayers Distributing Inc		E	707 445-2077	0
Eureka Rehab & Wellness Center		D	707 445-3261	0
Forest Products Distrs Inc		D	707 443-7024	0
Fred H Lundblade Jr		D	707 442-8049	0
Ghd Inc		E	707 443-8326	0
Granada Healthcre & Rehab Cntr		D	707 443-1627	0
Humboldt Commnty Accss Resrc		D	707 443-7077	0
Humboldt Dog Obedience Group		E	707 444-3862	0
Humboldt Senior Resource Ctr (PA)		C	707 443-9747	0
Institute For Wildlife Studies		E	707 822-4258	0
Keenan & Associates		D	707 268-1616	0
Laco Associates (PA)		E	707 443-5054	0
McMurray & Sons Inc (PA)		D	707 443-3088	0
Mission Linen Supply		D	707 443-8681	0
Nor-Wall Inc (PA)		E	707 445-5445	0
North Coast Cleaning Services		E	707 269-0838	0
Pacific Choice Seafood Company		B	707 442-2981	0
Pacific Gas and Electric Co		D	707 444-0700	0
Pacific Rehabilitation & Wel		D	707 443-9767	0
Redwood Coast Regional		E	707 445-0893	0
Seaview Hlthcre & Rehab Ctr LL		D	707 443-5668	0
Securitas SEC Svcs USA Inc		D	707 445-5463	0
Security Nat Mstr Holdg Co LLC (PA)		C	707 442-2818	0
Shaw & Petersen Insurance Inc		E	707 443-0845	0
Shn Consulting Engin (PA)		D	707 441-8855	0
Six Rivers National Bank (HQ)		D	707 443-8400	0
Six Rivers Planned Parenthood		D	707 442-5700	0
St Joseph Health System		E	707 443-9371	0
St Joseph Hospital (PA)		D	707 445-8121	0
St Joseph Hospital		A	707 268-0190	0
St Joseph Hospital of Eureka		A	707 445-8121	0
State Compensation Insur Fund		D	707 443-9721	0
Trico Bancshares		D	707 476-0981	0
Wayne Maples Plumbing & Htg		D	707 445-2500	0
Western Living Concepts Inc (PA)		E	707 443-3000	0

EXETER, CA - Tulare County

	SIC	EMP	PHONE	ENTRY #
Badger Farming Company Inc		D	559 592-5520	0
Best Western International Inc		D	559 592-8118	0
Bowsmith Inc (PA)		D	559 592-9485	0
Exeter Engineering Inc		D	559 592-3161	0
Exeter Packers Inc (PA)		A	559 592-5168	0
Exeter-Ivanhoe Citrus Assn		D	559 592-3141	0
Farmers Insurance Exchange		B	559 594-4149	0
Frontier California Inc		D	559 592-2100	0
Kaweah Delta Health Care Dst		D	559 592-7128	0
Kaweah Dlta Hlth Care Dst Gild		D	559 592-7300	0
Randstad North America Inc		B	559 592-6700	0
Redding Tree Growers Corp		E	559 594-9299	0
San Joaquin Valley Railroad Co		C	559 592-1857	0
Sequoia Enterprises Inc		D	559 592-9455	0
Sequoia Orange Co Inc (PA)		D	559 592-9455	0
Sun Pacific Farming Coop Inc (PA)		B	559 592-7121	0
Venida Packing Company		C	559 592-2816	0

FAIR OAKS, CA - Sacramento County

	SIC	EMP	PHONE	ENTRY #
Atlaz Inc		D	415 671-6142	0
Burger Rhbilitation Systems Inc		D	916 863-5785	0

Employment Codes: A=Over 500 employees, B=251-500,
C=101-250, D=51-100, E=50

2020 Directory of California
Wholesalers and Services Companies

© Mergent Inc. 1-800-342-5647

1535

GEOGRAPHIC

	SIC	EMP	PHONE	ENTRY #
Clarklift-West Inc		C	916 381-5674	0
Coldwell Bnkr Residential Brkg		D	916 966-8200	0
Eskaton Properties Inc		C	916 965-4663	0
Lyon Realty		C	916 962-0111	0
North Ridge Country Club		D	916 967-5717	0
Sunset Pet Hospital Inc **(PA)**		D	916 967-7768	0
Wightman Enterprises Inc		D	916 961-2959	0
William L Lyon & Assoc Inc		D	916 535-0356	0

FAIRFAX, CA - Marin County

	SIC	EMP	PHONE	ENTRY #
Meadow Club		D	415 453-3274	

FAIRFIELD, CA - Solano County

	SIC	EMP	PHONE	ENTRY #
Aldea Inc		D	925 577-3102	0
Anheuser-Busch LLC		B	707 429-7595	0
AT&T Services Inc		B	707 428-2512	0
B R Funsten & Co		D	707 863-8300	0
Brand Services Inc		E	707 603-3400	0
Calbee North America LLC		E	707 427-2500	0
Caliber Home Loans Inc		B	707 432-1000	0
Century 21		E	707 429-2121	0
Certified Coatings Company		D	707 639-4414	0
City of Fairfield		C	707 428-7435	0
Coastal Select Insurance Co		E	707 863-3700	0
Community Housing Opport **(PA)**		E	530 757-4444	0
Community Housing Opport		E	707 759-6043	0
County of Solano		D	707 784-8400	0
County of Solano		C	707 784-7600	0
County of Solano		D	707 784-2080	0
Delta One Security Inc		D	707 425-9346	0
Directv Group Inc		C	707 452-7409	0
Fairfield Nursing & Rehab Ctr		D	707 425-0623	0
Fairfield-Suisun Sewer Dst		D	707 429-8930	0
First Priority Financial Inc		B	707 432-1000	0
Frank-Lin Distillers Pdts Ltd **(PA)**		C	408 259-8900	0
Frontier Title Co **(PA)**		E	707 427-5400	0
Gaw Van Male Smith Myers		D	707 425-1250	0
Geovera Holdings Inc **(PA)**		D	707 863-3700	0
Geovera Specialty Insurance Co		D	707 863-3700	0
Green Valley Country Club		D	707 864-1101	0
Hd Supply Construction Supply		D	707 863-8282	0
Hotel NAPA II Opco LP		E	707 863-0300	0
Jpmorgan Chase Bank Nat Assn		C	707 864-4700	0
Kaiser Foundation Hospitals		A	707 427-4000	0
Kiewit Corporation		D	707 439-7300	0
Laborers Funds Administrative **(PA)**		D	707 864-2800	0
Lanza Vineyards Inc		E	707 864-0730	0
Loyalton At Rancho Solano		D	707 425-3588	0
Meyer Corporation US		D	707 399-2100	0
Muehlhan Certifed Coatings Inc		C	707 639-4414	0
New Desserts Inc		D	415 780-6860	0
Northbay Healthcare Corp **(PA)**		C	707 646-5000	0
Northbay Healthcare Group **(PA)**		A	707 646-5000	0
Northern CA Retiredd Ofcrs		C	707 432-1200	0
Northstate Plastering Inc		D	707 207-0950	0
Pacific Gas and Electric Co		D	415 973-7000	0
Partnership Health Plan Cal		B	707 863-4100	0
Permanente Medical Group Inc		E	707 427-4000	0
Petersen-Dean Inc		E	707 469-7470	0
Petersen-Dean Commercial Inc		E	707 469-7470	0
Private Industry Cncl Slno Cty **(PA)**		E	707 864-3370	0
S & S Tool & Supply Inc **(HQ)**		D	925 313-0360	0
Solano Family & Chld Council		D	707 863-3950	0
Solano Garbage Company Inc		D	707 437-8900	0
Solano Gateway Realty Inc **(PA)**		D	707 422-1725	0
Transportation California Dept		C	707 428-2031	0
Travis Credit Union		B	707 449-4000	0
Tri-Valley Supply Inc **(PA)**		D	707 469-7470	0
United Parcel Service Inc OH		C	707 864-8200	0
Valley Inventory Service Inc		D	707 422-6050	0
Villara Corporation		E	707 863-8222	0
Vitalant Research Institute		E	707 428-6001	0
West Coast Contractors Inc		C	541 267-7689	0
Westgate Cnstr & Maint Inc		D	707 208-5763	0
Wind River Enterprises Inc		D	707 864-1040	0

FALLBROOK, CA - San Diego County

	SIC	EMP	PHONE	ENTRY #
Boys Club of Fallbrook Inc		D	760 728-5871	0
County of San Diego		D	866 262-9881	0
Crestwood Behavioral Hlth Inc		D	760 451-4165	0
Executive Landscape Inc		C	760 731-9036	0
Fallbrook Fire Protection Dst		D	760 723-2010	0
Fallbrook Public Utility Dst		D	760 728-1125	0
Fallbrook Sklled Nrsing Fcilty		D	760 728-2330	0
Garich Inc		A	951 302-4750	0
Garys Construction Inc		C	760 639-4456	0

	SIC	EMP	PHONE	ENTRY #
Hamilton Family Ranch		D	760 728-1358	0
Kendall Farms LP		E	760 731-0681	0
Little Sisters Truck Wash Inc **(PA)**		D	760 731-3170	0
N G A Associates		E	760 726-4015	0
New Visa Health Services Inc		B	760 723-0053	0
Olive Hill Greenhouses		D	760 728-4596	0
Pala Band of Mission Indians		C	760 207-2603	0
Pala Mesa Limited Partnership		C	760 728-5881	0
Petes Connection Inc		E	760 723-1972	0
Rainbow Municipal Water Dst		D	760 728-1178	0
Southwest Construction Co Inc		D	760 728-4460	0
Straub - Brutoco A Joint Ventr		C	760 414-9000	0
Sycamore Cc Inc		D	760 451-3700	0
Tone Framing Inc		E	951 304-0303	0
William C Arterberry		D	760 728-9096	0

FARMINGTON, CA - San Joaquin County

	SIC	EMP	PHONE	ENTRY #
Brightview Tree Company		D	209 886-5511	0

FELTON, CA - Santa Cruz County

	SIC	EMP	PHONE	ENTRY #
Cupertino Electric Inc		A	408 808-8260	0
Granite Construction Inc		D	831 335-3445	0

FILLMORE, CA - Ventura County

	SIC	EMP	PHONE	ENTRY #
Allied Avocados & Citrus Inc		D	805 625-7155	0
B & R Farm Labor Contractor		C	805 524-1346	0
Brightview Tree Company		C	714 546-7975	0
California Watercress Inc **(PA)**		D	805 524-4808	0
Fillmore Convalescent Ctr LLC		D	805 524-0083	0
Magana Labor Services Inc		C	805 524-0446	0
Moon Mountain Farms LLC		E	805 521-1742	0
Rotorcraft Support Inc		D	818 997-7667	0
Villa Park Orchards Assn **(PA)**		B	805 524-0411	0
Wilmay Inc		D	805 524-2603	0

FIREBAUGH, CA - Fresno County

	SIC	EMP	PHONE	ENTRY #
Empresas Del Bosque Inc		B	209 364-6428	0
Hall Company		D	209 364-0070	0
Hammonds Ranch Inc		D	209 364-6185	0
I S A Contracting Svcs Inc		A	559 659-1080	0
J & J Farms		E	559 659-1457	0
JR Simplot Company		E	559 659-2033	0
Oxford Farms Inc		E	559 659-3033	0
Panoche Water District		E	209 364-6136	0
R & N Packing Co		C	209 364-6101	0
Seasholtz John		C	559 659-3805	0
Thomason Tractor Co California		E	559 659-2039	0
Tri-State AG Inc		D	209 364-6185	0
Vaquero Farms Inc		D	559 659-2790	0

FISH CAMP, CA - Mariposa County

	SIC	EMP	PHONE	ENTRY #
DNC Prks Resorts At Tenaya Inc **(DH)**		D	877 247-9241	0

FIVE POINTS, CA - Fresno County

	SIC	EMP	PHONE	ENTRY #
ATI Machinery Inc		E	559 884-2471	0
Britz Fertilizers Inc		D	559 884-2421	0
Coelho West Custom Farming		D	559 884-2566	0
Nutrien AG Solutions Inc		E	559 884-6010	0
Telesis Onion Co		E	559 884-2441	0

FOLSOM, CA - Sacramento County

	SIC	EMP	PHONE	ENTRY #
24 Hour Fitness Usa Inc		E	916 984-1924	0
Agreeya Solutions Inc **(PA)**		D	916 294-0075	0
Benefit & Risk Management Svcs		C	916 467-1200	0
Brookdale Senior Living Inc		D	916 983-9300	0
Burger Physcl Therapy Svcs Inc **(HQ)**		C	916 983-5900	0
Burger Physical Therapy		E	916 983-5900	0
Burger Rhblitation Systems Inc **(PA)**		C	800 900-8491	0
Califrnia Ind Sys Oprator Corp		C	916 608-7000	0
Califrnia Ind Sys Oprator Corp **(PA)**		A	916 351-4400	0
Cellco Partnership		D	212 395-1000	0
Central Valley Community Bank		E	916 985-8700	0
Chicago Title Insurance Co		E	916 985-0300	0
City of Folsom		D	916 355-7285	0
Csac Excess Insurance Auth		D	916 850-7300	0
Dager Corporation **(PA)**		D	916 989-4229	0
Dignity Health		C	916 983-7400	0
Dignity Health		B	916 983-7400	0
Dignity Health		D	916 983-7988	0
Dokken Engineering **(PA)**		D	916 858-0642	0
Ea Consulting Inc		E	916 357-6767	0
Emergency Med Group of Folsom		D	916 983-7470	0
Erepublic Inc **(PA)**		C	916 932-1300	0
Eurofins Air Toxics LLC		D	916 985-1000	0
Flt Inc		C	916 355-1500	0
Folsom Recreation Corp		D	916 983-4411	0
FPI Management Inc **(PA)**		E	916 357-5300	0
Green Acres Nursery & Sup LLC		D	916 782-2273	0

	SIC	EMP	PHONE	ENTRY #
HDR Engineering Inc		D	916 817-4700	0
HDR/Cardno Entrix Joint Ventr		D	916 817-4700	0
Hoshall Corporation		E	916 987-1995	0
Inductive Automation LLC			800 266-7798	0
Kaiser Foundation Hospitals		A	916 986-4178	0
Kaiser Foundation Hospitals		C	916 817-5200	0
Kindred Healthcare Operating		C	916 351-9151	0
Kioxia America Inc		E	916 986-4707	0
Lake Natoma Lodging LP		D	916 351-1500	0
Liberty American Mortgage Corp (PA)		D	916 780-3000	0
Liberty Mutual Insurance Co		C	916 294-9518	0
Location Services LLC (PA)		D	800 588-0097	0
Lyon Real Estate		D	916 355-7000	0
Matthew Burns		D	209 676-4940	0
Maximus Inc		D	916 673-2175	0
Mercury Insurance Company		D	916 353-4859	0
Mercy HM Svcs A Cal Ltd Partnr		A	916 983-7400	0
Meridian Knwldge Solutions LLC (DH)		D	913 985-9625	0
Morton & Pitalo Inc (PA)		D	916 984-7621	0
Norcal Gold Inc		E	916 984-8778	0
Objective Systems Integrators (HQ)		E	916 467-1500	0
One Inc (PA)		D	866 343-6940	0
Powerschool Group LLC (HQ)		C	916 288-1636	0
Prairie City Commons LLC		D	916 458-0303	0
Precision Home Care LLC		D	916 749-4051	0
Related Technologies Inc		D	916 357-5900	0
Retail Pro International LLC (PA)		D	916 605-7200	0
Retail Services & Systems Inc		D	916 984-6923	0
Rjp Framing Inc		C	916 941-3934	0
Safe Credit Union (PA)		C	916 979-7233	0
Sierra Pacific Mortgage Co Inc (PA)		A	916 932-1700	0
Spare-Time Inc		D	916 983-9180	0
Sparta Consulting Inc		B	916 985-0300	0
Taxresources Inc (PA)		C	877 369-7827	0
Trimark Associates Inc		D	916 357-5970	0
Vibra Hospital Sacramento LLC		C	916 351-9151	0
Visio Integ Profe LLC (HQ)		D	916 985-9625	0
Visionary Integration (PA)		D	916 985-9625	0

FONTANA, CA - San Bernardino County

	SIC	EMP	PHONE	ENTRY #
ABF Freight System Inc		C	909 355-9805	0
Advanced Environmental Inc		E	909 356-9025	0
Advanced Sterlization		D	909 350-6987	0
American Asphalt South Inc		D	909 427-8276	0
American Bolt & Screw Mfg Corp (PA)		D	909 390-0522	0
AMS Paving Inc (PA)		E	909 357-0711	0
Anfinson Lumber Sales Inc (PA)		D	951 681-4707	0
Apex Bulk Commodities Inc		D	909 854-9991	0
Aqua-Serv Engineers Inc (HQ)		D	951 681-9696	0
B&B Industrial Services Inc (PA)		D	909 428-3167	0
Baby Trend Inc (HQ)		D	909 773-0018	0
Blackrock Logistics Inc		C	909 259-5357	0
Budway Enterprises Inc (PA)		D	909 463-0500	0
Burrtec Waste Industries Inc (HQ)		C	909 429-4200	0
California Speedway Corp		E	909 429-5000	0
Cattrac Construction Inc		D	909 355-1146	0
Central Reinforcing Corp		D	909 773-0840	0
Complete Logistics Company		C	909 427-9800	0
Conco Pumping		D	909 350-0503	0
Costco Wholesale Corporation		D	909 823-8270	0
Cox Automotive Inc		A	404 843-5000	0
CRST International Inc		C	909 829-1313	0
D W Powell Construction Inc		E	909 356-8880	0
Dalton Trucking Inc (PA)		D	909 823-0663	0
Daniel Gerard Worldwide Inc		D	951 361-1111	0
Desert Coastal Transport Inc (PA)		D	909 357-3395	0
Dhl Supply Chain (usa)		E	909 350-6976	0
Dispatch Transportation LLC		C	909 355-5531	0
Dispatch Trucking LLC (PA)		D	909 355-5531	0
DSV Solutions LLC		C	909 349-6100	0
Elegance Wood Products Inc		D	909 484-7676	0
Estes Express Lines Inc		D	909 427-9850	0
Express Contractors Inc		D	951 360-6500	0
Express Messenger Systems Inc		D	804 334-5000	0
Fedex Freight West Inc		B	909 357-3555	0
Finnco Services Incorporated		D	909 355-0707	0
Fontana Resources At Work		C	909 428-3833	0
Foundation Pile Inc		D	909 350-1584	0
Friends Group Express Inc		D	909 346-6816	0
General Motors LLC		D	951 361-6302	0
Hanks Inc		D	909 350-8365	0
Harrison Nichols Co Ltd		C	626 337-5020	0
Hartman Industries		D	909 428-0114	0
Hawk Transportation Inc		D	800 709-4295	0
Heartland Express Inc Iowa		E	319 626-3600	0
Hub Group Trucking Inc		B	909 770-8950	0

	SIC	EMP	PHONE	ENTRY #
Inland Cc Inc		C	909 355-1318	0
Inland Empire Utilities Agency		D	909 993-1600	0
Inland Kenworth (us) Inc (HQ)		C	909 823-9955	0
James Hardie Building Pdts Inc		C	909 355-6500	0
Jones Bold Security Inc		D	562 316-6552	0
Kaden Cash LLC		E	818 714-4665	0
Kaiser Foundation Hospitals		C	909 609-3800	0
Kaiser Foundation Hospitals		A	866 205-3595	0
Kaiser Foundation Hospitals		A	909 427-5000	0
Kaiser Foundation Hospitals		D	909 427-3910	0
Kds Printing and Packaging Inc		E	909 770-5400	0
Little Sisters Truck Wash Inc		D	909 549-1862	0
Los Angeles Truck Centers LLC		C	909 510-4000	0
Maxzone Vehicle Lighting Corp (HQ)		E	909 822-3288	0
McCollisters Trnsp Group Inc		D	909 428-5700	0
McGuire Contracting Inc		D	909 357-1200	0
Naumann/Hobbs Material		C	909 427-0125	0
Network Global Logistics LLC		C	888 285-7447	0
No Shnacks Inc		E	909 293-8747	0
Norco Ranch Inc (DH)		B	951 737-6735	0
NY Transport Inc		D	909 355-9832	0
Orwick Fresh Foods Inc		E	909 985-5604	0
Patrick Industries Inc		C	909 350-4440	0
Pointdirect Transport Inc		D	909 371-0837	0
Pro Loaders Inc (PA)		C	909 355-5531	0
Romark Logistics of California		D	909 356-5600	0
Salvation Army		E	323 263-1206	0
San Gabriel Valley Water Co		D	909 822-2201	0
Schneider National Inc		C	909 574-2165	0
Sierra Lakes Golf Club		D	909 350-2500	0
Slater Inc		D	909 822-6800	0
Southern Cal Prmnnte Med Group		E	909 427-5000	0
Stantru Resources Inc		D	909 587-1441	0
State Farm Mutl Auto Insur Co		D	909 349-2050	0
STC Netcom Inc (PA)		D	951 685-8181	0
Sun Mar Management Services		D	909 822-8066	0
Target Corporation		B	909 355-6000	0
Tire Centers West LLC		C	909 854-1200	0
TMT Industries Inc		D	909 493-3441	0
Tonys Express Inc (PA)		C	909 427-8700	0
Tst Inc		D	310 835-0115	0
Tst Inc		D	909 590-1098	0
United Facilities Inc		E	951 685-7030	0
United Family Care Inc		C	909 874-1679	0
Utility Trailer Sales of S CA (PA)		D	877 275-4887	0
Valori Sand & Gravel Company		C	909 350-3000	0
Vpet Usa Inc (PA)		D	909 605-1668	0
Walmart Inc		B	909 349-3600	0
Werner Enterprises Inc		E	909 823-5803	0
West Valley Manufacturing LLC		C	909 899-5501	0
Western Freight Carrier Inc		D	909 357-1011	0
Western PCF Crane & Eqp LLC (DH)		D	562 286-6618	0
Weyerhaeuser Company		D	909 877-6100	0
Windrow Earth Transport Inc		E	909 355-5531	0
World Class Distribution Inc (PA)		D	909 574-4140	0
Wsp USA Inc		D	909 427-9166	0
Xpo Logistics Freight Inc		C	951 685-1244	0

FOOTHILL RANCH, CA - Orange County

	SIC	EMP	PHONE	ENTRY #
Debisys Inc (PA)		D	949 699-1401	0
Frontech N Fujitsu Amer Inc (DH)		C	949 855-5500	0
Global Solutions Integration		D	949 307-1849	0
Guthy-Renker LLC		D	949 454-1400	0
Ibaset Federal Services LLC (PA)		D	949 598-5200	0
Image Options		C	949 586-7665	0
Kaiser Foundation Hospitals		A	800 922-2000	0
Loandepotcom LLC (PA)		A	888 337-6888	0
Mrt Inc		E	949 348-2292	0
Nth Degree Inc		E	714 734-4155	0
Professional Community MGT Cal (PA)		E	800 369-7260	0
Professional Community MGT Cal		D	949 768-7261	0
Sgii Inc		C	949 521-6161	0
Skilled Healthcare LLC (DH)		D	949 282-5800	0
Sun Healthcare Group Inc (DH)		B	949 255-7100	0
Tae Technologies Inc (PA)		C	949 830-2117	0
Team Makena LLC (PA)		D	949 474-1753	0
Venus Group Inc		D	949 609-1299	0
Ytel Inc		D	800 382-4913	0

FOREST RANCH, CA - Butte County

	SIC	EMP	PHONE	ENTRY #
Sierra Cascade Blueberries		E	530 894-8728	0

FORT BRAGG, CA - Mendocino County

	SIC	EMP	PHONE	ENTRY #
Caito Fisheries Inc (PA)		D	707 964-6368	0
Mendocino Coast Clinics Inc		D	707 964-1251	0
Mendocino Coast District Hosp (PA)		B	707 961-1234	0

Employment Codes: A=Over 500 employees, B=251-500, C=101-250, D=51-100, E=50

2020 Directory of California
Wholesalers and Services Companies

© Mergent Inc. 1-800-342-5647

1537

GEOGRAPHIC

	SIC	EMP	PHONE	ENTRY #
Mendocino Coast District Hosp		C	707 961-4736	0
Mendocino Transit Authority		D	707 462-1422	0
Redwood Coast Seniors Inc		D	707 964-0443	0
Sherwood Oaks Enterprises		D	707 964-6333	0
Tradewinds Lodge **(PA)**		D	707 964-4761	0
Waste MGT Collectn & Recycl		D	707 462-0210	0

FORT IRWIN, CA - San Bernardino County

	SIC	EMP	PHONE	ENTRY #
Dyncorp International LLC		D	817 224-8200	0
Family Mrale Wlfare Recreation		D	760 380-3493	0
Iap World Services Inc		B	760 380-6772	0
Leidos Inc		D	910 574-4597	0
Lockheed Martin Corporation		C	760 386-2572	0
Raytheon Company		B	760 386-2572	0

FORTUNA, CA - Humboldt County

	SIC	EMP	PHONE	ENTRY #
Reaching For Independence Inc		D	707 725-9010	0
Redwood Memorial Hosp Fortuna **(PA)**		C	707 725-7327	0
St Luke Hlthcr & Rehab Ctr LL		D	707 725-4467	0

FOSTER CITY, CA - San Mateo County

	SIC	EMP	PHONE	ENTRY #
Applied Underwriters Inc		E	415 656-5000	0
Arena Solutions Inc **(PA)**		D	650 513-3500	0
Arena Solutions Inc		E	978 988-3800	0
B B & K Fund Services Inc		D	650 571-5800	0
B B & K Holdings **(PA)**		E	650 571-5800	0
Bailard Inc **(HQ)**		E	650 571-5800	0
Bayshore Ambulance Inc **(PA)**		D	650 525-9700	0
Bertram Capital Management LLC		B	650 358-5000	0
Brightedge Technologies Inc **(PA)**		C	800 578-8023	0
City of Foster City		E	650 286-3380	0
Csg Consultants Inc **(PA)**		E	650 522-2500	0
Cybersource Corporation **(HQ)**		D	650 432-7350	0
Ecker Consumer Recruiting Inc		D	650 871-6800	0
Emeter Corporation		C	650 227-7770	0
Emove Express Company		D	650 377-0913	0
Founders Management II Corp		B	650 570-5700	0
Gridgain Systems Inc **(PA)**		D	650 241-2281	0
Hilton Garden In San Mateo		D	650 522-9000	0
Ic Compliance LLC **(PA)**		A	650 378-4150	0
International Bus Mchs Corp		B	800 426-4968	0
Legacy Prtners Residential Inc **(PA)**		C	650 571-2250	0
Menlo Gateway Inc		D	650 356-2900	0
Midpen Housing Corporation		D	650 356-2900	0
Midpen Resident Services Corp		B	650 356-2965	0
Oracle Corporation		B	650 678-3612	0
Pacific Partners MGT Svcs Inc		D	650 358-5804	0
Peninsula Jewish Community Ctr		C	650 212-7522	0
Peter H Mattson & Co Inc		D	650 356-2500	0
Qualys Inc **(PA)**		C	650 801-6100	0
Quinstreet Inc **(PA)**		E	650 578-7700	0
Sanzaru Games Inc		E	650 312-1000	0
Scientific Concepts Inc		B	650 578-1142	0
Sonifi Solutions Inc		C	650 752-1980	0
Sony Corporation of America		D	650 655-8000	0
Sony Interactive Entrmt LLC **(DH)**		C	310 981-1500	0
Vb Golf LLC		D	650 573-7888	0
Verinata Health Inc		D	650 632-1680	0

FOUNTAIN VALLEY, CA - Orange County

	SIC	EMP	PHONE	ENTRY #
B T B Events Inc		D	714 415-3313	0
Bell Private Security Inc		D	714 964-9381	0
Boys Girls CLB Huntington Vly **(PA)**		D	714 531-2582	0
Brightview Landscape Dev Inc		B	714 546-7975	0
Ceridian Tax Service Inc		D	714 963-1311	0
Command Security Corporation		C	714 557-9355	0
D-Link Systems Incorporated		C	714 885-6000	0
Edinger Medical Group Inc **(PA)**		C	714 965-2500	0
Forty Four Group LLC		D	949 407-6360	0
Fountain Valley Body Works M2		E	714 751-8812	0
Fountain Valley Regl Hospl		A	714 966-7200	0
Fountain Valley School Dst		D	714 668-5882	0
Hcr Manorcare Med Svcs Fla LLC		C	714 241-9800	0
His Passion Inc		E	800 760-6389	0
Hyundai Atver Tlmtics Amer Inc		D	949 381-6000	0
Hyundai Motor America **(HQ)**		B	714 965-3000	0
In Home Comfort and Care Inc		D	714 485-4120	0
Jmg Security Systems Inc		D	714 545-8882	0
Longwood Management Corp		D	714 962-5531	0
Memorial Healthtec Labratories		A	714 962-4677	0
Memorialcare Surgical Center A		D	714 369-1100	0
Mile Square Golf Course		C	714 962-5541	0
Mobis Parts America LLC **(HQ)**		D	786 515-1101	0
Norco Hills Car Wash		E	951 279-4398	0
Noritz America Corporation **(HQ)**		D	714 433-2905	0
Orange Coast Memorial Med Ctr **(HQ)**		D	714 378-7000	0
Orange County Sanitation **(PA)**		B	714 962-2411	0

	SIC	EMP	PHONE	ENTRY #
Orange County Water District		C	714 378-3200	0
Pacific Aquascape Inc		D	714 843-5734	0
Pan-Pacific Mechanical LLC **(PA)**		C	949 474-9170	0
Rcsn Inc		C	714 965-0244	0
Service King Holdings LLC		D	714 962-2600	0
Spec Services Inc		C	714 963-8077	0
St Jude Hospital Yorba Linda		C	714 665-1797	0
Stephouse Recovery Center		D	714 394-3494	0

FOWLER, CA - Fresno County

	SIC	EMP	PHONE	ENTRY #
Bedrosian Farms Inc		E	559 834-5981	0
Fowler Convalescent Hospital		E	559 834-2542	0
Fowler Labor Service Inc		B	559 834-3723	0
Gahvejian Enterprises Inc		E	559 834-5956	0
Golden Living LLC		D	559 834-2542	0
J B Hunt Transport Svcs Inc		A	559 834-3852	0
Kandarian Agri Enterprises		C	559 834-1501	0
Simonian Brothers Inc **(PA)**		D	559 834-5921	0
Trius Trucking Inc		D	559 834-4000	0
United Health Ctrs San Joaquin		D	559 834-1568	0

FREMONT, CA - Alameda County

	SIC	EMP	PHONE	ENTRY #
24 Hour Fitness Usa Inc		E	510 795-6666	0
Abode Services **(PA)**		D	510 657-7409	0
Ace Financial Services Inc		D	510 790-4600	0
Ace USA		D	510 790-4695	0
Actividentity Corporation		C	510 574-0100	0
Aegis Asssted Living Prpts LLC		E	510 739-1515	0
Aegis Senior Communities LLC		C	510 739-0909	0
Aer Electronics Inc **(PA)**		D	510 300-0500	0
Agama Solutions Inc		C	510 796-9300	0
Airgas Usa LLC		E	510 659-0162	0
Alameda County Water District **(PA)**		C	510 668-4200	0
Alertenterprise Inc		C	510 440-0840	0
Alom Technologies Corporation **(PA)**		C	510 360-3600	0
Amax Engineering Corporation **(PA)**		C	510 651-8886	0
American Bldg Maint Co of III		E	510 573-1618	0
American Portwell Tech Inc **(PA)**		D	510 403-3399	0
AMS Ventures Inc		D	301 980-5087	0
Anaspec Inc **(HQ)**		E	510 791-9560	0
Angioscore Inc		C	510 933-7900	0
Anka Behavioral Health Inc		C	510 494-1567	0
Apptivo Inc		C	650 906-1034	0
Arcsoft Inc **(PA)**		D	510 440-9901	0
Ashok Thummalachetty		C	510 687-9797	0
Asi Computer Technologies Inc **(PA)**		C	510 226-8000	0
Asus Computer International		C	510 739-3777	0
Atlas Security & Patrol Inc		E	510 791-7380	0
Avar Construction Inc		D	510 354-2000	0
Avar Construction Systems Inc **(PA)**		E	510 354-2000	0
Aver Information Inc		E	408 263-3828	0
AVI Systems Inc		B	415 915-2070	0
Bayside Interiors Inc **(PA)**		C	510 438-9171	0
BFI Waste Systems N Amer Inc		D	510 657-1350	0
Blocka Construction Inc		D	510 657-3686	0
By-The-Bay Investments Inc		B	510 793-2581	0
C & C Security Patrol Inc **(PA)**		C	510 713-1260	0
C J Health Services Inc		D	510 793-3000	0
Cal Coast Financial Inc		D	510 683-9850	0
Cancer Prevention Inst Cal **(PA)**		C	510 608-5000	0
Celestix Networks Inc		D	510 668-0700	0
Cellco Partnership		D	510 490-3800	0
Chrisp Company **(PA)**		D	510 656-2840	0
City of Fremont		C	510 791-4196	0
City of Fremont		C	510 494-4460	0
Club Sport of Fremont		C	510 226-8500	0
Cognitiveclouds Software Inc		D	415 234-3611	0
Coldwell Bnkr Residential Brkg		D	510 608-7600	0
Concentrix Corporation		D	510 668-3717	0
Concessionaires Urban Park		D	530 529-1596	0
Crestwood Behavioral Hlth Inc		C	510 651-1244	0
Crestwood Behavioral Hlth Inc		D	510 793-8383	0
CSC Covansys Corporation		C	510 304-3430	0
D F Rios Construction Inc		D	510 226-7467	0
Dcm Limited		D	510 494-2321	0
Dcm Technologies Inc		D	510 791-2182	0
Del Contes Landscaping Inc		D	510 353-6030	0
Delta America Ltd **(HQ)**		C	510 668-5100	0
Delta Electronics Americas Ltd **(DH)**		D	510 668-5100	0
DMS Facility Services Inc		A	510 656-9400	0
Droisys Inc		C	408 329-1761	0
Droisys Inc		D	407 610-0916	0
Dryco Construction Inc **(PA)**		C	510 438-6500	0
E & E Co Ltd **(PA)**		C	510 490-9788	0
Edata Solutions Inc		A	510 574-5380	0
Education California Dept		B	510 794-3666	0

Mergent email: customerrelations@mergent.com

1538

2020 Directory of California
Wholesalers and Services Companies

(P-0000) Products & Services Section entry number
(PA)=Parent Co (HQ)=Headquarters (DH)=Div Headquarters

	SIC	EMP	PHONE	ENTRY #
Elliott Laboratories Inc		E	510 440-9500	0
EMR Cpr LLC		B	408 471-6804	0
Enexus Global Inc		D	510 936-4044	0
Etouch Systems Corp		A	510 795-4800	0
Eurogentec North America Inc		C	510 791-9560	0
Everest Consulting Group Inc		D	510 494-8440	0
Forsys Inc		D	408 409-2567	0
Fremont Ambltory Srgery Ctr LP		D	510 456-4600	0
Fremont Bank **(HQ)**		C	510 505-5226	0
Fremont Candle Lighters		C	510 796-0595	0
Fremont Marriott		C	510 413-3700	0
Fremont Sports Inc		E	510 656-4411	0
Fremont Unified School Dst		D	510 657-0761	0
Genmark Automation **(HQ)**		D	510 897-3400	0
Globalways Inc **(PA)**		D	510 580-1974	0
Golden N-Life Diamite Intl Inc **(PA)**		D	510 651-0405	0
Greenbriar Management Company		D	510 497-8200	0
Growith Inc		D	805 650-6650	0
Homelegance Inc		D	510 933-6888	0
Hyve Solutions Corporation **(HQ)**		A	855 869-6873	0
Incalus Inc		E	510 209-4064	0
Infinity Nurses Care Inc		D	510 713-8892	0
Initek Soft Solutions LLC		D	209 309-0263	0
Instant Systems Inc		D	510 657-8100	0
Iron Systems Inc		C	408 943-8000	0
ISE Labs Inc **(DH)**		C	510 687-2500	0
ISS Facility Services Inc		B	650 593-9774	0
Ists Worldwide Inc		C	510 794-1400	0
Jiangsu Juwang Info Tech Co **(PA)**		D	510 967-3729	0
Jonce Thomas Construction Co		E	510 657-7171	0
Kaiser Foundation Hospitals		B	510 248-3000	0
Kidango **(PA)**		D	510 897-6900	0
Kidango Inc		D	510 494-9601	0
Kositch Enterprises Inc		D	510 657-4460	0
Kutir Corporation		E	510 402-4526	0
Land Services Landscape Contrs		D	510 656-8101	0
Leisure Sports Inc		C	510 226-8500	0
Lipman Insur Admnistrators Inc **(PA)**		D	510 796-4676	0
Loginext Solutions Inc		D	339 244-0380	0
Luxar Tech Inc		C	408 835-2551	0
Luxera Inc		E	510 456-7690	0
Magnum Drywall Inc		D	510 979-0420	0
Mariner Health Care Inc		D	510 792-3743	0
Marriott International Inc		C	510 413-3700	0
Med Staffing LLC		E	510 795-0114	0
Merrill Gardens		D	510 790-1645	0
Metabyte Inc		D	510 405-1117	0
Milan Corporation		E	510 656-6400	0
Milestone Technologies Inc **(PA)**		C	510 651-2454	0
Neptune Management Corporation		D	510 797-2269	0
Net Express		D	510 887-4395	0
Netversant - Silicon Vly Inc **(PA)**		C	510 771-1200	0
New Image Landscape Company		D	510 226-9191	0
Nextracker Inc **(DH)**		D	510 270-2500	0
Nisum Technologies Inc		A	714 579-7979	0
Novariant Inc **(PA)**		D	510 933-4800	0
NTS Technical Systems		E	510 578-3500	0
OES Equipment LLC **(PA)**		D	510 284-1900	0
On Lok Senior Health Services		E	510 249-2700	0
Onmycare LLC		D	510 858-2273	0
Oplink Communications LLC **(DH)**		D	510 933-7200	0
Overton Security Services Inc		E	510 791-7380	0
Pacific Gas and Electric Co		C	510 770-2025	0
Pacira Cryotech Inc		E	800 442-0989	0
Page Front Catering		D	408 406-8487	0
Pall Fortebio LLC		D	650 322-1360	0
Pape Material Handling Inc		D	510 659-4100	0
Park Cntl Care Rhbltation Ctr		D	510 797-5300	0
Penguin Computing Inc **(DH)**		D	415 954-2800	0
Permanente Medical Group Inc		D	510 248-3000	0
Phihong USA Corp **(HQ)**		D	510 445-0100	0
PJs Lumber Inc		C	510 743-5300	0
Ponyai Inc		C	650 281-4639	0
Priyo Inc		E	408 248-2507	0
Prospance Inc **(PA)**		D	925 415-2394	0
Prudential CA Realty		D	510 487-6088	0
Psychiatric Solutions Inc		C	510 796-1100	0
PW Stephens Envmtl Inc		D	510 651-9506	0
Pyramid Painting Inc		E	650 903-9791	0
Quadrant Components Inc		D	510 656-9988	0
Rahi Systems Inc **(PA)**		C	510 651-2205	0
Ravenswood Mangement Inc **(HQ)**		D	650 241-3661	0
Raymond Handling Concepts Corp **(DH)**		D	510 745-7500	0
Red Hawk Fire & SEC CA Inc		D	510 438-1300	0
Remax Active Realty		E	510 505-1660	0
Retirement Lf Care Communities		D	510 505-0555	0
RK Electric Inc		C	510 580-2850	0
Rk Logistics Group Inc		C	510 298-5128	0
Rk Logistics Group Inc **(PA)**		D	408 942-8107	0
S & M Moving Systems		D	510 497-2300	0
San Jose Arena Management LLC		C	510 623-7200	0
Sansei Gardens Inc		C	510 226-9191	0
Scholastic Book Fairs Inc		D	510 771-1700	0
Select Hotels Group LLC		E	510 623-6000	0
Seneca Family of Agencies		D	510 226-6180	0
Serrato-Mcdermott Inc		C	510 656-6233	0
Sierra Living Concepts Inc		D	510 402-4906	0
Sigmaways Inc		D	510 573-4208	0
Signature Building Maint Inc		D	408 377-8066	0
Smart Software Tstg Solutions		D	833 778-7872	0
Softsol Resources Inc **(HQ)**		D	510 824-2000	0
Sonata Software North Amer Inc **(HQ)**		D	510 791-7220	0
Sportvision Inc		E	510 736-2925	0
SRS Consulting Inc		D	510 252-0625	0
Startup Farms Intl LLC		B	510 440-0110	0
Statewide Cnstr Sweeping Inc		E	510 683-9584	0
Strategic Security Services		C	510 623-2355	0
Sun Innovations Inc		E	510 573-3913	0
Sunnyvale Fluid Sys Tech Inc		E	510 933-2500	0
Superior Automatic Sprnklr Co		D	408 946-7272	0
Sysco San Francisco Inc		A	510 226-3000	0
T-Mobile Usa Inc		C	510 797-8290	0
Tasser Technologies Inc		D	408 364-0373	0
Technology Credit Union		C	408 467-2385	0
Three Way Logistics Inc **(PA)**		D	408 748-3929	0
Tri-City Health Center **(PA)**		C	510 770-8040	0
Tyan Computer Corporation		D	510 651-8868	0
U-Haul Co of California **(DH)**		C	800 528-0463	0
United Mfg Assembly Inc		D	510 490-1065	0
United Parcel Service Inc OH		B	800 742-5877	0
Unitek Inc		D	510 623-8544	0
Unitek Information Systems Inc **(PA)**		D	510 249-1060	0
Vasona Management Inc		D	510 413-0091	0
Verizon Bus Netwrk Svcs Inc		D	510 497-2500	0
Vertisystem Inc		C	510 794-8099	0
Via Communications Inc		C	510 687-4650	0
Via Technologies Inc		D	510 683-3300	0
Vince Solutions **(PA)**		D	510 432-0852	0
Walters & Wolf Glass Company **(PA)**		C	510 490-1115	0
Walters & Wolf Interiors **(PA)**		D	415 243-9400	0
Washington Outpatient		D	510 791-5374	0
Wells Fargo Bank National Assn		D	510 792-3512	0
Wells Fargo Bank National Assn		C	415 222-6834	0
Wells Fargo Bank National Assn		B	510 745-5025	0
Windsor Convalescent		C	510 793-7222	0
Winward International Inc **(PA)**		D	510 487-8686	0
YC Cable Usa Inc **(HQ)**		D	510 824-2788	0

FRENCH CAMP, CA - San Joaquin County

	SIC	EMP	PHONE	ENTRY #
County of San Joaquin		D	209 468-6966	0
Fresno Truck Center		C	209 983-2400	0
Health Plan of San Joaquin		C	209 942-6300	0
Healthy Beginnings French Camp		D	209 468-6147	0
Interstate Con Pmpg Co Inc		D	209 983-3092	0
San Joaquin General Hospital		A	209 468-6000	0
Silva Trucking Inc		E	209 982-1114	0

FRESNO, CA - Fresno County

	SIC	EMP	PHONE	ENTRY #
A Colmenero Plastering Inc		D	559 435-3606	0
A J Excavation Inc		C	559 408-5908	0
Aaron Dowling Incorporated		D	559 432-4500	0
Absolute Urethane		E	877 471-3626	0
Activision Blizzard Inc		C	310 431-4000	0
Aecom Global II LLC		D	559 347-5669	0
Agri Valley Services		D	559 253-0104	0
All Commercial Landscape Svc		E	559 453-1670	0
Allen Spees Family Homes		E	559 432-3664	0
Alliant Educational Foundation		D	559 456-2777	0
Allied Electric Motor Svc Inc **(PA)**		D	559 486-4222	0
American All Risk Loss Adm		C	559 277-4960	0
American Baptist Homes of West		C	559 439-4770	0
American Fidelity Assurance Co		D	559 230-2107	0
American Paving Co		E	559 268-9886	0
Ameripride Services Inc		D	559 266-0627	0
Anthony Lambe		D	559 268-0709	0
Aramark Unf & Career AP LLC		D	559 291-6631	0
ARC Fresno/Madera Counties **(PA)**		D	559 226-6268	0
Archer-Daniels-Midland Company		D	559 233-6262	0
Arise LLC		D	559 485-0881	0
Arise Construction Inc		D	559 449-8989	0
Art Piccadilly Shaw LLC		D	559 375-7760	0

Employment Codes: A=Over 500 employees, B=251-500,
C=101-250, D=51-100, E=50

2020 Directory of California
Wholesalers and Services Companies

© Mergent Inc. 1-800-342-5647

1539

GEOGRAPHIC

	SIC	EMP	PHONE	ENTRY #
Art Piccadilly Shaw LLC		C	559 224-4200	0
Arthur J Gallagher & Co		D	559 436-0833	0
Ashwood Construction Inc		E	559 253-7240	0
Asist Inc		C	559 251-7701	0
AT&T Services Inc		C	559 454-3579	0
Automatic Leasing Inc		B	559 233-2444	0
B T & T Travel Inc		D	559 237-9410	0
Baker Mnock Jensen A Prof Corp		C	559 432-5400	0
Baloian Packing Co Inc (PA)		D	559 485-9200	0
Baloian Packing Co Inc		D	559 441-7043	0
Bank America National Assn		D	559 445-7731	0
BFI Waste Services LLC		D	559 275-1551	0
Bill Nlson Gen Engrg Cnstr Inc		D	559 439-1756	0
Bio-Mdical Applications Rl Inc		D	559 221-6311	0
Bowie Enterprises (PA)		D	559 227-6221	0
Bowie Enterprises		D	559 227-3400	0
Bradford Messenger Service		D	559 252-0775	0
Brix Group Inc (PA)		D	559 457-4700	0
Broder Bros Co		D	559 233-9900	0
BSK Associates		D	559 497-2888	0
Buckingham Property Management		D	559 322-1105	0
Burford Family Farming Co LP (PA)		C	559 431-0902	0
C&S Wholesale Grocers Inc		B	559 442-4700	0
Calif Stat Univ Fres Foun		D	559 278-0850	0
California Cancer Assctes		D	559 447-4949	0
California Coml Solar Inc		D	559 667-9200	0
California Eye Institute		C	559 449-5000	0
California Hlth Collaborative (PA)		D	559 221-6315	0
California HM For The Aged Inc		C	559 251-8414	0
Campos Family Farms LLC		D	559 275-3000	0
Cardinal Health Inc		D	559 448-0788	0
Cardiovascular Consultants Hea		D	559 432-4303	0
Carrollco Inc		E	559 396-3939	0
Carrolls LLC		D	800 559-4897	0
CBS Radio Inc		C	559 490-0106	0
Cellco Partnership		D	559 454-0803	0
Central Cal Nikkei Foundation		D	559 237-4006	0
Central California Blood Ctr		D	559 389-5433	0
Central California Blood Ctr		D	559 324-1211	0
Central California Blood Ctr (PA)		C	559 389-5433	0
Central California Ear Nose		E	559 432-3724	0
Central California Faculty Med (PA)		D	559 453-5200	0
Central Freight Lines Inc		D	559 233-5559	0
Central Unified School Dst		D	559 276-3185	0
Central Valley Cmnty Bancorp (PA)		C	559 298-1775	0
Central Valley Community Bank		C	559 298-1775	0
Central Vly Chld Svcs Netwrk		D	559 456-1100	0
Central Vly Yng MNS Chrn Assoc		E	559 225-9191	0
Century Adanalian & Vasquez		D	559 244-6000	0
Champagne Landscape Nurs Inc		D	559 277-8188	0
Change Healthcare Tech LLC		C	559 455-4000	0
Charles McMurray Co (PA)		C	559 292-5751	0
Charlies Enterprises		C	559 445-8600	0
Cherry Avenue Auction Inc		E	559 266-9856	0
Chicago Title Company		D	559 451-3700	0
Citigroup Global Markets Inc		E	559 438-2542	0
City of Fresno		B	559 621-7433	0
City of Fresno		D	559 621-5300	0
City of Fresno		D	559 445-8200	0
Claude Laval Corporation		D	559 255-1601	0
Clay Miranda Trucking Inc		D	559 275-6250	0
Clinica Sierra Vista		D	559 457-6900	0
Clinica Sierra Vista		D	559 457-5292	0
Club One Casino Inc		B	559 497-3000	0
Comcast Corporation		D	559 718-9917	0
Community Hospitals Centl Cal		C	559 459-2916	0
Community Hospitals Centl Cal (PA)		A	559 459-6000	0
Community Hospitals Centl Cal		A	559 459-6000	0
Community Integrated Work Prog		E	559 276-8564	0
Community Medical Center		C	559 222-7416	0
Community Medical Centers		D	559 320-2200	0
Community Medical Centers		D	559 447-4000	0
Comprehensive Youth Ser		D	559 229-3561	0
Congregation of Poor Sisters		D	559 237-3444	0
Conner Logistics Inc		D	888 939-4637	0
Contemporary Services Corp		C	559 225-9325	0
Copper River Country Club LP (PA)		D	559 434-5200	0
County of Fresno		D	559 600-3420	0
County of Fresno		D	559 600-3800	0
County of Fresno		D	559 600-3546	0
County of Fresno		D	559 600-4600	0
County of Fresno		D	559 600-3534	0
County of Fresno		C	559 600-3996	0
Covenant Care California LLC		C	559 251-8463	0
Crestwood Behavioral Hlth Inc		D	559 445-9094	0
Darden Architects Inc		D	559 448-8051	0
De Benedetto Farms Inc		D	559 276-2400	0
Decipher Inc (HQ)		D	559 436-6940	0
Deloitte & Touche LLP		D	559 449-6300	0
Diamond Intl Investment LLC		D	559 226-2200	0
Dibuduo Dfendis Insur Brks LLC (PA)		D	559 432-0222	0
Diversified Transport Systems		E	559 268-2760	0
Donaghy Sales Inc		C	559 486-0901	0
Donahue Schriber Rlty Group LP		D	714 545-1400	0
Donald P Dick AC Inc (PA)		D	559 255-1644	0
Douglas L Myovich Trucking Inc		D	559 233-8242	0
E & S Rsidential Care Svcs LLC		D	559 275-3555	0
East Bay Clarklift Inc		D	559 268-6621	0
Educational Employees Cr Un (PA)		C	559 437-7700	0
Educational Employees Cr Un		D	559 896-0222	0
Electric Motor Shop		D	559 233-1153	0
Electronic Recyclers		D	253 736-2627	0
Electronic Recyclers Intl Inc (PA)		C	800 374-3473	0
Elim Alzheimers & Rehab		D	559 320-2200	0
Elitecare Medical Staffing LLC		D	559 438-7700	0
Energy Experts International		C	559 449-1124	0
Enterprise Holdings Inc		D	559 261-9221	0
Environment Control		E	559 456-9791	0
Exceptnal Prents Unlimited Inc		C	559 229-2000	0
Express Messenger Systems Inc		D	559 277-4910	0
Eye Medical Clinic Fresno Inc		D	559 486-5000	0
Eye Q Vision Care (PA)		D	559 486-2000	0
F & F Contracting Inc		C	559 276-2418	0
Family Mdcine Rsidency Program		D	559 499-6450	0
Famous Software LLC (PA)		D	559 438-3600	0
Fedex Freight West Inc		C	559 266-0732	0
Ferguson Enterprises Inc		E	559 253-2900	0
Five Star Quality Care Inc		D	559 446-6226	0
Fort Wash Golf & Cntry CLB		D	559 434-1702	0
Fort Washington Parent Assoc		D	559 327-6600	0
Foster Poultry Farms		A	559 442-3771	0
Four CS Service Inc		D	559 237-3990	0
Fowler Packing Company Inc		C	559 834-5911	0
Freshko Produce Services Inc		C	559 497-7000	0
Fresno Airport Hotels LLC		D	559 252-3611	0
Fresno Auto Dealers Auction		C	559 268-8051	0
Fresno Beverage Company Inc		C	559 650-1500	0
Fresno Cmnty Hosp & Med Ctr (HQ)		A	559 459-3948	0
Fresno Cnty Economic Opportunt		A	559 263-1000	0
Fresno Cnty Economic Opportunt (PA)		A	559 263-1010	0
Fresno Cnty Economic Opportunt		B	559 263-1013	0
Fresno Cnty Economic Opportunt		D	559 485-3733	0
Fresno County Private Security		D	559 233-9800	0
Fresno County Rural Trnst Agcy (PA)		D	559 233-6789	0
Fresno Heart Hospital LLC		B	559 433-8000	0
Fresno Heritage Partners		E	559 446-6226	0
Fresno Hotel Partners LP		D	559 224-4040	0
Fresno Irrigation District		D	559 233-7161	0
Fresno Metro Flood Ctrl Dst		D	559 456-3292	0
Fresno Plumbing & Heating Inc (PA)		C	559 294-0200	0
Fresno Rescue Mission Inc (PA)		E	559 268-0839	0
Fresno Roofing Co Inc		D	559 255-8377	0
Fresno Skilled Nursing		D	559 486-5361	0
Fresno Surgery Center LP (PA)		C	559 431-8000	0
Fresno Truck Center		D	559 486-4310	0
Fresno Unified School District		C	559 457-3074	0
Fresnos Chaffee Zoo Corp		C	559 498-5910	0
Frito-Lay North America Inc		C	559 226-8153	0
Frontier California Inc		D	559 224-9222	0
Gateway Auto Sales & Lsg Inc		D	800 921-4336	0
Geil Enterprises Inc		C	559 495-3000	0
Gene A Garcia Construction		E	559 352-6173	0
General Coatings Corporation		C	559 495-4004	0
GLad Entertainment Inc (PA)		D	559 292-9000	0
Golden Cross Care II Inc		D	559 268-3023	0
Golden Living LLC		D	559 237-8377	0
Golden Living LLC		D	559 275-4785	0
Golden Living LLC		D	559 222-4807	0
Golden Living LLC		D	559 486-4433	0
Golden Living LLC		D	559 227-5383	0
Golden Living LLC		C	559 227-4063	0
Golden State Plastering		D	559 439-3920	0
Graham-Prewett Inc		E	559 291-3741	0
Granite Construction Company		C	559 441-5700	0
Granville Homes Inc		D	559 268-2000	0
Greyhound Lines Inc		D	559 268-1829	0
Guarantee Real Estate		E	559 650-6030	0
Guardsmark LLC		C	559 243-1217	0
Harris Construction Co Inc		C	559 251-0301	0
Health Comp Administrators (PA)		C	559 499-2450	0

Mergent email: customerrelations@mergent.com
1540

2020 Directory of California
Wholesalers and Services Companies

(P-0000) Products & Services Section entry number
(PA)=Parent Co (HQ)=Headquarters (DH)=Div Headquarters

	SIC	EMP	PHONE	ENTRY #
Healthcare California		D	559 243-9990	0
Healthcare Centre of Fresno		D	559 268-5361	0
Healthcomp		B	559 499-2450	0
HI Fresno Hospitality LLC		D	559 233-6650	0
Hinds Hospice (PA)		C	559 674-0407	0
Howe Electric Construction Inc		C	559 255-8992	0
Hub Intrntional Insur Svcs Inc		D	559 447-4600	0
Hydratech LLC (HQ)		D	559 233-0876	0
Iheartcommunications Inc		D	559 230-4300	0
Inland Star Dist Ctrs Inc (PA)		D	559 237-2052	0
Innovative Integrated Hlth Inc		C	949 228-5577	0
Intrade Industries Inc (PA)		D	559 274-9877	0
Ipsos Public Affairs Inc		C	559 451-2820	0
J & D Meat Company		C	559 445-1123	0
J M C International LLC		E	559 256-1300	0
J M Equipment Company Inc		E	559 233-0187	0
Jacks Car Wash 3		D	559 438-8201	0
James G Parker Insurance Assoc (PA)		D	559 222-7722	0
JMS Realtors Ltd (PA)		C	559 490-1500	0
Jorgensen & Sons Inc (PA)		C	559 268-6241	0
JR Simplot Company		C	559 439-3900	0
K W P H Enterprises		A	559 443-5900	0
Kaiser Foundation Hospitals		D	559 448-4555	0
Kaiser Foundation Hospitals		A	559 448-4500	0
Kaiser Foundation Hospitals		A	559 448-4500	0
Kaiser Radiology		D	559 448-5541	0
Karsyn Construction Inc		D	559 271-2900	0
Keisers Holdings LLC		D	559 265-4700	0
Kenyon Construction Inc		C	559 277-5645	0
Keolis Transit America Inc		D	559 621-5783	0
Kertel Communications Inc (HQ)		D	559 432-5800	0
Kfsn Television LLC		C	559 442-1170	0
Kftv		D	559 222-2121	0
Kimberlite Corporation (PA)		D	559 264-9730	0
Kings River Conservation Dst		D	559 237-5567	0
Kisco Senior Living LLC		D	559 449-8070	0
Kleinfelder Inc		D	559 486-0750	0
Kmph Fox 26		C	559 255-2600	0
Knight-Swift Trnsp Hldings Inc		D	559 441-0340	0
Kraft Heinz Foods Company		E	559 499-5300	0
Krm Risk Management Svcs Inc		D	559 277-4800	0
Kroeker Inc		C	559 237-3764	0
L A S Transportation Inc		B	559 264-6583	0
Labor Fnders of The Palm Bches		D	559 221-2023	0
Lang Richert & Patch		E	559 228-6700	0
Lassley Enterprises Inc		E	559 226-4300	0
Leisure Care LLC		D	559 434-1237	0
Lily Holdings LLC		D	559 222-4807	0
Linkus Enterprises LLC		B	559 256-6600	0
Lozano Smith LLP		C	559 431-5600	0
Lozano Smith A Prof Corp (PA)		D	559 431-5600	0
M & L Plumbing Co Inc		E	559 291-5525	0
Major Transportation Svcs Inc		E	559 485-5949	0
Manning Gardens Inc		E	559 834-2586	0
Manning Gardens Care Ctr Inc		E	559 834-2586	0
Matson Alarm Co Inc (PA)		E	559 438-8000	0
McCormick Barstow Shepprd Wayt (PA)		D	559 433-1300	0
McCutcheon Enterprises Inc		D	559 864-3200	0
Melos Plst Lthg & Drywall		D	559 237-0028	0
Mesa Energy Systems Inc		D	559 277-7900	0
Midland Express Credit LLC		D	800 961-3904	0
Millmens Local 1496		E	559 275-8676	0
Mirabella Farms Inc		D	559 237-4495	0
Mission Linen Supply		D	559 268-0647	0
Moore Twining Associates Inc (PA)		D	559 268-7021	0
Morgan Stanley & Co LLC		D	559 431-5900	0
Morrison MGT Specialists Inc		C	559 459-6449	0
Muniservices LLC (DH)		C	800 800-8181	0
Netafim Irrigation Inc (HQ)		C	559 453-6800	0
Nevocal Enterprises Inc		D	559 277-0700	0
New England Shtmtl Works Inc		C	559 268-7375	0
New York Life Insurance Co		D	559 447-3900	0
New York Life Insurance Co		D	559 447-3900	0
Newport Television LLC		C	559 761-0243	0
Nexstar Broadcasting Inc		C	559 222-2411	0
Nicole Pttrson Crt Rprting LLC		E	559 400-2407	0
Noble Credit Union (PA)		E	559 252-5000	0
Noia Residential Services Inc		D	559 485-5555	0
North Pt Hlth Wellness Ctr LLC		D	559 320-2200	0
North West Learning Center		E	559 228-3057	0
Northwest Medical Group Inc		D	559 271-6302	0
Northwest Physicians Med Group		D	559 271-6290	0
Olam Americas Inc (DH)		A	559 447-1390	0
Olam LLC		E	559 446-6420	0
Olam West Coast Inc (DH)		C	559 447-1390	0
Omni Womens Hlth Med Group Inc		D	559 441-4271	0
Organic Pastures Dairy Co LLC		E	559 846-9732	0
P K B Investments Inc		C	559 243-1224	0
Paccar Leasing Corporation		C	559 268-4344	0
Pacific Gas and Electric Co		B	559 263-7361	0
Pacific Grain & Foods LLC (PA)		C	559 276-2580	0
Pactiv LLC		C	559 251-7351	0
Pape Trucks Inc		D	559 268-4344	0
Park Inn By Radisson		D	559 226-2200	0
Park Inn By Readisson Fresno		D	559 226-2200	0
Patton Sheet Metal Works Inc		E	559 486-5222	0
Paychex Inc		D	559 432-1100	0
PDM Steel Service Centers		E	559 442-1410	0
Pearson Realty (PA)		D	559 432-6200	0
Penske Truck Leasing Co LP		E	559 268-7000	0
Permanente Medical Group Inc		D	559 448-4500	0
Piccadilly Hospitality LLC		E	559 348-5520	0
Pressed Juicery Inc		E	559 777-8900	0
Principal Financial Group Inc		D	559 261-2000	0
Producers Dairy Foods Inc (PA)		C	559 264-6583	0
Professional Exchange Svc		E	559 229-6249	0
Promesa Behavioral Health (PA)		C	559 439-5437	0
Protosource Corporation		D	559 490-8600	0
Prudential Overall Supply		C	559 264-8231	0
Quality Group Homes Inc (PA)		C	559 255-8519	0
Quest Diagnostics Incorporated		D	559 438-2893	0
Quiring Corporation		D	559 432-2800	0
Quiring General LLC		D	559 432-2800	0
R Fellen Inc		D	559 233-6248	0
Rainbow - Brite Indus Svcs LLC		E	559 925-2580	0
Randstad North America Inc		C	559 297-0054	0
Reading and Beyond		D	559 840-1068	0
Real Time Information Svcs Inc		E	559 222-6456	0
Recyclers I Electronic		D	317 522-1414	0
Rescue Children Inc		E	559 268-1123	0
Residence Inn By Marriott		D	559 222-8900	0
Rex More Elec Contrs Engineers		C	559 294-1300	0
Rincon Consultants Inc		C	559 228-9925	0
Riverside Nursery & Ldscp Inc		C	559 275-1891	0
Rollins Inc		D	559 292-8222	0
Royal Express Inc (PA)		C	559 272-3500	0
SA Recycling LLC		D	559 237-6677	0
Saint Agnes Med Providers Inc		D	559 435-2630	0
Saint Agnes Medical Center (HQ)		A	559 450-3000	0
Saladinos Inc (PA)		C	559 271-3700	0
San Joaquin Country Club		D	559 439-3483	0
San Joaquin Figs Inc		E	559 224-4492	0
San Joaquin Val UNI Air Pol (PA)		D	559 230-6000	0
San Joaquin Valley A P C D		D	559 230-6000	0
San Joaquin Valley Intergrp		E	559 856-0559	0
San Joaquin Valley Rehabili (HQ)		B	559 436-3600	0
Sante Health System Inc (PA)		D	559 228-5400	0
Scrip Advantage Inc		D	559 320-0052	0
Securitas SEC Svcs USA Inc		C	559 221-2302	0
Sierra Bancorp		D	559 449-8145	0
Sierra Pacific Development		D	559 256-1300	0
Sierra Pacific Ortho		C	559 256-5200	0
Signature Flight Support Corp		D	559 981-2490	0
Smart & Final Stores Inc		B	559 229-2944	0
Smartway Express Inc		C	559 272-3500	0
Smg Holdings Inc		B	559 445-8100	0
Social Vocational Services Inc		D	559 443-7119	0
Southeast Fresno Rad LP		C	559 443-8400	0
State Compensation Insur Fund		B	559 433-2700	0
Steven G Fogg MD		D	559 449-5010	0
Strategic Mechanical Inc		C	559 291-1952	0
Sunland Insurance Agency		A	559 251-7861	0
Sunnyside Country Club		D	559 255-6871	0
Sunrise Senior Living LLC		D	559 325-8170	0
T Royal Management (PA)		D	559 447-9887	0
Telesis Onion Co (PA)		C	559 884-2441	0
Terry Tuell Concrete Inc		E	559 431-0812	0
Teter LLP (PA)		E	559 437-0887	0
Thomas M Obinson Jr		D	559 432-6200	0
Torres Fence Co Inc		E	559 237-4141	0
Trinity Home Health Svcs Inc		D	559 450-5112	0
Turn Behavioral Hlth Svcs Inc		D	559 264-7521	0
Turner Security Systems Inc		C	559 486-3466	0
Tutor Perini/Zachry/Parsons		C	559 385-7025	0
Twilight Haven		D	559 251-8417	0
Ultimate Creations LLC		D	559 221-4936	0
Union Pacific Railroad Company		C	559 443-2244	0
United Crbrl Plsy of Cntrl CA (PA)		E	559 221-8272	0
United Health Ctrs San Joaquin (PA)		D	559 646-6618	0
United States Cold Storage Inc		E	559 237-6145	0

Employment Codes: A=Over 500 employees, B=251-500,
C=101-250, D=51-100, E=50

2020 Directory of California
Wholesalers and Services Companies

© Mergent Inc. 1-800-342-5647

1541

GEOGRAPHIC

	SIC	EMP	PHONE	ENTRY #
Univision Radio Inc		E	559 430-8500	0
Univision Television Group Inc		D	559 222-2121	0
Uniwell Corporation		D	559 268-1000	0
Uniwell Fresno Hotel LLC		D	559 268-1000	0
UPS Ground Freight Inc		D	559 445-9010	0
Urology Assoc of Cen Cal		D	559 321-2800	0
US Property Group Inc		E	559 227-1901	0
USA Waste of California Inc		D	559 834-9151	0
USI Insurance Services Nat Inc		D	559 666-2001	0
Utility Trlr Sls of Centl Cal		E	559 237-2001	0
Valley Fig Growers		E	559 237-3893	0
Valley Healthcare Center LLC		D	559 251-7161	0
Valley Healthcare Center LLC		C	559 251-7161	0
Valley Teen Ranch		D	559 437-1144	0
Veritiv Operating Company		D	559 268-0467	0
Veterans Health Administration		A	559 225-6100	0
Veterans Health Administration		A	559 225-6100	0
Veterans Home Cal - Fresno		D	559 493-4400	0
Vibra Healthcare LLC		D	559 436-3600	0
Victus Group Inc		C	559 429-8080	0
Vision Care Center **(PA)**		D	559 486-2000	0
Volt Management Corp		C	559 435-1255	0
Vucovich Inc **(PA)**		D	559 486-8020	0
W M Lyles Co **(HQ)**		D	559 441-1900	0
Well Being Group Inc		D	559 432-3737	0
West Air Inc		D	559 454-7843	0
Westcare California Inc **(HQ)**		D	559 251-4800	0
Western Building Materials Co **(PA)**		D	559 454-8500	0
Whole Foods Market Cal Inc		C	559 241-0300	0
Wild Electric Incorporated		D	559 251-7770	0
Windham At Saint Agnes		D	559 449-8070	0
Winegard Energy Inc		D	559 441-0243	0
Winnresidential Ltd Partnr		B	559 435-3434	0
Wish I Ah Care Center Inc		C	559 855-2211	0
Wish-I-Ah Hlthcre & Wellness		D	559 855-2211	0
Wish-I-Ah Skilled Nursing		C	949 285-8859	0
Wm B Saleh Co		D	559 255-2046	0
Wm Michael Stemler Inc		C	559 228-4144	0
Woolf Farming Co Cal Inc		A	559 945-9292	0
Xobee Networks Inc		D	559 579-1300	0
Xpo Logistics Freight Inc		D	559 485-1164	0
Xpo Logistics Supply Chain Inc		C	559 408-7951	0
Zumwalt Construction Inc		D	559 252-1000	0

FRIANT, CA - Fresno County

	SIC	EMP	PHONE	ENTRY #
Table Mountain Casino		A	559 822-7777	0

FULLERTON, CA - Orange County

	SIC	EMP	PHONE	ENTRY #
A1 Building Management Inc		C	714 447-3800	0
Achem Industry America Inc **(PA)**		D	562 802-0998	0
AJ Kirkwood & Associates Inc		C	714 505-1977	0
Alpha Swimming Pool & Spa		D	714 879-4667	0
American Golf Corporation		D	714 672-6800	0
American Multi-Cinema Inc		E	714 992-6961	0
AMS American Mech Svcs MD Inc		D	714 888-6820	0
Anaheim Park Hotel		C	714 992-1700	0
Anderson Air Conditioning LP		D	714 998-6850	0
Ans World Service Inc		D	714 441-2400	0
Arconic Global Fas & Rings Inc		D	714 871-1550	0
Bakery Ex Southern Cal LLC		D	714 446-9470	0
C & L Refrigeration Corp		C	800 901-4822	0
Cardservice International Inc		D	714 773-1778	0
Catalina Enterprise Inc		D	949 637-3091	0
Cellco Partnership		D	714 449-0715	0
City of Fullerton		C	714 738-6897	0
Corecare I I I		C	714 256-8000	0
Corecare V A Cal Ltd Partnr		C	714 256-1000	0
County of Orange		E	714 626-3700	0
Dunlap Property Group Inc		D	714 879-0111	0
Elliott Auto Supply Co Inc		D	310 527-2500	0
Excel Construction Svcs Inc **(PA)**		D	714 680-9200	0
Federal Express Corporation		C	800 463-3339	0
Florence Crittenton Services		B	714 680-9000	0
Geek Squad Inc		D	800 433-5778	0
Golden HI Elementary Schl Pta		E	714 447-7715	0
Gordon Lane Convalescent Hosp		D	714 879-7301	0
Harte Hanks Inc		D	210 829-9000	0
Harte-Hanks Direct Mail/Califo		D	714 738-5478	0
Healthcare Fullerton & Well		C	714 992-5701	0
Henry Bros Electronics Inc		C	714 525-4350	0
Hidden Villa Ranch Produce Inc		B	714 680-3447	0
Hot Dogger Tours Inc		C	714 988-4088	0
Huoyen International Inc		D	714 635-9000	0
Jcv Inc		E	714 871-2007	0
John G Shipley		D	714 626-2000	0
Loewy Enterprises		D	323 726-3838	0

	SIC	EMP	PHONE	ENTRY #
Merritt Hospitality LLC		C	714 738-7800	0
New Pride Tire Inc		E	310 631-7000	0
NTS Technical Systems		C	714 879-6110	0
Opus Bank		C	714 578-7500	0
Opus Inspection Inc		D	714 999-6727	0
Orange Pacific Plumbing Inc		D	714 992-4547	0
Orora Packaging Solutions		C	714 278-6000	0
Orora Packaging Solutions		D	714 773-0124	0
Prestige Sales II LLC		D	714 632-8020	0
Progressive Floor Covering Inc		E	714 213-8805	0
Quaker Oats Company		E	714 526-8800	0
Raytheon Command and Control **(HQ)**		A	714 446-3118	0
Real Estate Image Inc		C	714 502-3900	0
Rosary Academy Parent Council		D	714 879-6302	0
RPM Consolidated Services Inc **(PA)**		D	714 388-3500	0
Sage Behavior Services Inc		D	714 773-0077	0
Salon Lujon Inc		D	714 738-1882	0
South Coast Trnsp & Dist Inc **(PA)**		D	714 683-2300	0
Southern California Edison Co		D	714 870-3225	0
Spectrum MGT Holdg Co LLC		D	714 871-2643	0
St Joseph Health System		D	714 992-3000	0
St Jude Hospital **(DH)**		A	714 871-3280	0
St Jude Hospital		C	714 578-8544	0
St Jude Hospital		A	714 992-3057	0
Staff Pro Inc **(PA)**		A	714 230-7200	0
Sun Haven Care Inc		D	714 870-0060	0
Superior Wall Systems Inc		B	714 578-0000	0
Swinford Electric Inc		E	714 578-8888	0
Tf Courier Inc		D	714 888-1452	0
Therapy For Kids Inc		E	714 870-6116	0
Trendsettah Usa Inc		D	888 775-4881	0
TW Services Inc		B	714 441-2400	0
UPS Ground Freight Inc		D	866 372-5619	0
US Foods Inc		E	714 670-3500	0
US Foods Inc		C	714 449-9990	0
Veg-Land Inc		E	714 871-6712	0
Viele & Sons Inc		D	714 447-3663	0
Volt Management Corp		C	714 879-9330	0
Ware Disposal Inc		C	714 834-0234	0
Westview Services Inc		D	714 879-3980	0
Windsor Gardns Healthcare Cntr		C	714 871-6020	0
Womens Transitional Living Ctr		E	714 992-1939	0
Wyndham International Inc		A	714 992-1700	0
YMCA of North Orange County		D	714 879-9622	0
Young Mens Chrstn Assn Orange		D	714 879-9622	0

FULTON, CA - Sonoma County

	SIC	EMP	PHONE	ENTRY #
Bacchus Vineyard MGT LLC		D	707 837-8304	0

GALT, CA - Sacramento County

	SIC	EMP	PHONE	ENTRY #
Building Material Distrs Inc **(PA)**		C	209 745-3001	0
City of Galt		D	209 366-7180	0
Dry Creek Lath & Plaster Inc		D	209 367-8607	0
Eliseo Esparza Delgadillo		E	209 745-3937	0
Galt Joint Union School Dst		E	209 745-1546	0
Golden Living LLC		D	209 745-1537	0
Gonzales Salvador Labor Contrs		D	209 745-2223	0
Keb Keb Magic Clown		D	916 369-6054	0
Norogachi Construction Inc/CA		D	916 236-4201	0
Travis James Watts		C	209 810-6159	0
Western Star Nurseries LLC		E	209 744-2552	0

GARBERVILLE, CA - Humboldt County

	SIC	EMP	PHONE	ENTRY #
Southern Hmbldt Cmnty Dst Hosp		D	707 923-3921	0
Southern Humboldt Comm Hlth Cr		D	707 923-3925	0

GARDEN GROVE, CA - Orange County

	SIC	EMP	PHONE	ENTRY #
Aaron Thomas Company Inc **(PA)**		C	714 894-4468	0
Abbey-Properties LLC **(PA)**		D	562 435-2100	0
Accutherm Refrigeraton Inc		D	714 766-7800	0
Act Home Health Inc		D	714 560-0800	0
Acxiom Corporation		E	714 636-3093	0
AGR Group Inc		A	714 245-7151	0
Alta Care Center LLC		C	714 530-6322	0
Audio Visual MGT Solutions		D	714 590-8755	0
Bank America National Assn		E	714 973-8495	0
Best Valet Parking Corporation		D	800 708-2538	0
Boys Grls Clubs Grdn Grove Inc		C	714 537-8833	0
Buffalo Spot MGT Group LLC		C	949 354-0884	0
Chapman Hbr Sklled Nrsing Care		D	714 971-5517	0
Community Action Partnershi		C	714 897-6670	0
Compass Group Usa Inc		C	714 899-2520	0
Complete Relocation Svcs Inc		D	714 901-7411	0
Consoldted Med Bo-Analysis Inc		D	714 467-0240	0
Customfab Inc		C	714 891-9119	0
Dao Medical Group Inc		D	714 899-2000	0
Elrob Inc		D	714 230-6100	0

Mergent email: customerrelations@mergent.com
1542

2020 Directory of California
Wholesalers and Services Companies

(P-0000) Products & Services Section entry number
(PA)=Parent Co (HQ)=Headquarters (DH)=Div Headquarters

	SIC	EMP	PHONE	ENTRY #
Envise		D	714 901-5800	0
G Brothers Construction Inc		E	714 590-3070	0
Garden Grove Convales		C	714 638-9470	0
Garden Grove Unified Schl Dst		D	714 663-6437	0
Goodwin Ammonia Company		D	714 894-0531	0
Hansol Goldpoint LLC		D	714 594-5073	0
Harbor Suites LLC		E	714 703-8800	0
Hyatt Corporation		B	714 750-1234	0
Informative Research (PA)		E	714 638-2855	0
Janitorial Equipment Svcs Inc		D	951 205-8937	0
Kaiser Foundation Hospitals		D	714 741-3448	0
Kenneth Corp		A	714 537-5160	0
M M Direct Marketing Inc		B	714 265-4100	0
Mastroianni Family Entps Ltd		D	310 952-1700	0
Mitsubishi Electric Us Inc		D	714 934-5300	0
OfficeMax Incorporated		D	951 485-9353	0
Ohi Resort Hotels LLC		D	714 867-5555	0
Orange County Trnsp Auth		A	714 560-6282	0
Our Watch		D	714 622-5852	0
Pacific Exteriors Inc		D	714 265-1998	0
Pacific Haven Convalescent HM		D	714 534-1942	0
Pacific Rim Resources Srch		C	714 638-0307	0
Party Pantry Garden Room		E	714 899-0626	0
Pathfinder Health Inc		D	714 636-5649	0
Prime Health Care Svcs Grdn Gr		B	714 537-5160	0
Progressive Power Group Inc		E	714 899-2300	0
Protect-US		D	714 721-8127	0
R J Daum Construction Co (PA)		C	714 894-4300	0
RJ Allen Inc		D	714 539-1022	0
Schlumberger Technology Corp		D	714 379-7332	0
Sherton Grdn Grove Anheim S Ht		D	714 703-8400	0
South West Sun Solar		E	714 582-3909	0
Southland Industries (PA)		E	800 613-6240	0
Spectrum MGT Holdg Co LLC		D	714 903-4000	0
Stonebridge McWhinney LLC		E	714 703-8800	0
Tekworks Inc		D	877 835-9675	0
Teletrac Inc (HQ)		D	714 897-0877	0
Video Vice Data Communications		B	714 897-6300	0
Western Transit Systems Inc		D	949 515-0188	0

GARDEN VALLEY, CA - El Dorado County

	SIC	EMP	PHONE	ENTRY #
Buckland Vineyard Management		D	530 333-1534	0

GARDENA, CA - Los Angeles County

	SIC	EMP	PHONE	ENTRY #
Acme Metals & Steel Supply		D	310 329-2263	0
Acme Metals LLC		D	310 329-2263	0
Action Force Security		E	310 715-6053	0
Administrative Svcs Coop Inc		C	310 715-1968	0
American Guard Services Inc (PA)		B	310 645-6200	0
American Residential Svcs LLC		E	310 808-0279	0
AMG Construction Group		D	800 310-2609	0
Anvil Steel Corporation		D	310 329-5811	0
Arena Painting Contractors Inc		D	310 316-2446	0
Aries Filterworks		E	323 262-1600	0
Bank America National Assn		D	800 432-1000	0
Behavioral Health Services Inc (PA)		E	310 679-9031	0
Brentwood Medical Tech Corp		D	800 624-8950	0
Brightview Landscape Svcs Inc		C	310 327-8700	0
California Supply Inc (PA)		D	310 532-2500	0
California Waste Services LLC		C	310 538-5998	0
Canon Bus Solutions-West Inc		B	310 217-3000	0
Ceridian LLC		D	310 719-7481	0
Charles E Thomas Company Inc (PA)		D	310 323-6730	0
City of Gardena		D	310 324-1475	0
Classic Tile & Mosaic Inc (PA)		D	310 538-9605	0
Claud Townsley Inc		D	310 527-6770	0
Cleanstreet		C	310 329-3078	0
CM Laundry LLC		D	310 436-6170	0
Cns Logistics Inc		D	562 229-1133	0
Colich Sons		C	323 770-2920	0
Comprehensive Dist Svcs Inc		C	310 523-1546	0
Counseling and Research Assoc (PA)		C	310 715-2020	0
Disaster Rstrtion Prfssnals In		D	310 301-8030	0
Duggan & Associates Inc		D	323 965-1502	0
Eagle Security Service Inc		D	310 532-1626	0
El Dorado Enterprises Inc		A	310 719-9800	0
FARaday&future Inc		A	424 276-7616	0
Fedex Freight Corporation		B	310 323-5230	0
First Student Inc		D	310 769-2400	0
Gardena Flores Inc		D	310 323-4570	0
Gardena Hospital LP		A	310 532-4200	0
Gfk Custom Research LLC		C	310 527-2100	0
Gina B Ltd Inc		D	310 366-7926	0
Global Paratransit Inc		B	310 715-7550	0
Global Stainless Supply		B	310 525-1865	0
Greater South Bay Area HM Hlth		E	310 329-4835	0

	SIC	EMP	PHONE	ENTRY #
Guardsmark LLC		D	310 522-9603	0
Harbor Distributing LLC		B	310 538-5483	0
Health Care Investments Inc		C	310 323-3194	0
Houston Salem Inc		E	310 719-7004	0
JH Bryant Jr Inc (PA)		E	310 532-1840	0
Jilk Heavy Construction Inc		D	310 830-6323	0
Jk Imaging Ltd		D	310 755-6848	0
Jomar Industries Inc		E	323 770-0505	0
JS Real Estate Prpts Inc		D	310 856-6868	0
Jumpstart Games Inc		D	424 645-4311	0
Kaiser Foundation Hospitals		A	800 780-1230	0
Kaiser Foundation Hospitals		E	310 517-2956	0
Konica Minolta Business Soluti		E	310 214-6696	0
Landcare USA LLC		D	310 719-1008	0
Landcare USA LLC		C	310 354-1520	0
Legions Protective Svcs LLC		E	310 819-8881	0
Los Angeles Unified School Dst		E	310 808-1500	0
M&M Asseet Management Gnl		C	310 769-6669	0
Magnetika Inc (PA)		D	310 527-8100	0
Martin Bros/Marcowall Inc (PA)		C	310 532-5335	0
MGA Healthcare California Inc		E	310 324-5591	0
MGT Industries Inc		D	310 324-3152	0
Milestone Hospice		C	310 782-1177	0
Monark LP		D	310 769-6669	0
Mufg Union Bank National Assn		E	310 354-4700	0
Navigant Cymetrix Corporation		C	424 201-6300	0
New Crew Production Corp		C	323 234-8880	0
Nippon Travel Agency Amer Inc		D	310 768-1817	0
Nippon Travel Agency PCF Inc (DH)		D	310 768-0017	0
Northrop Grumman Federal Cr Un (PA)		D	310 808-4000	0
Nri Usa LLC		D	323 345-6456	0
Nygard Inc		D	310 776-8900	0
Oxgord Incorporated		C	800 221-0718	0
Peterson Hydraulics Inc (PA)		D	310 323-3155	0
Phoenix Textile Inc (PA)		D	310 715-7090	0
Premier Tile & Marble		D	310 516-1712	0
Ps2 (PA)		D	310 243-2980	0
Pulp Studio Incorporated		D	310 815-4999	0
R Haupt Roofing Construction		E	310 515-9709	0
Radford Alexander Corporation		D	310 523-2555	0
Radiant Services Corp (PA)		C	310 327-6300	0
Rancho California Landscaping		E	310 768-1680	0
Randall Mc-Anany Company		D	310 822-3344	0
Raymak Automotive Inc		E	310 329-8910	0
Republic Services Inc		D	310 527-6980	0
Roadex America Inc		D	310 878-9800	0
Schumacher Cargo Logistics Inc (PA)		D	562 408-6677	0
Secom International (PA)		D	310 641-1290	0
Servexo		E	323 527-9994	0
SMS Transportation		D	310 527-9200	0
SOS Metals Inc (DH)		C	310 217-8848	0
Southern Cal Maid Svc Crpt Clg		D	310 675-0585	0
Stefan Merli Plastering Co Inc (PA)		D	310 323-0404	0
Tireco Inc (PA)		C	310 767-7990	0
United Parcel Service Inc OH		B	310 217-2646	0
Usfi Inc		D	310 768-1937	0
Valley of Sun Cosmetics LLC		C	310 327-9062	0
Vernon Autoparts Inc		D	323 249-7545	0
Washington Orna Ir Works Inc (PA)		D	310 327-8660	0
West Coast Maintenance Inc		D	310 324-2511	0
World Service West		D	310 538-7000	0
Wsa Group Inc (PA)		E	310 743-3000	0
XCEL Mechanical Systems Inc		D	310 660-0090	0
Yrc Inc		C	310 404-2221	0

GEYSERVILLE, CA - Sonoma County

	SIC	EMP	PHONE	ENTRY #
Redwood Empire Vineyard Mgt		D	707 857-3401	0
River Rock Entertainment Auth		A	707 857-2777	0
Robert Young Family Ltd Partnr		D	707 433-3228	0
Vimark Inc		D	707 857-3588	0
Vinwood Cellars Inc		E	707 857-4011	0

GILROY, CA - Santa Clara County

	SIC	EMP	PHONE	ENTRY #
Advance Services Inc		A	408 767-2797	0
Aspen Grove Apartments LLC		D	408 848-6400	0
Bert E Jessup Transportation		D	408 848-3390	0
Christopher Ranch LLC (PA)		C	408 847-1100	0
Cleaning Services		E	408 778-9251	0
Communty Slns For Chldrn Fmls (PA)		D	408 779-2113	0
Countryside Mushrooms Inc		D	408 683-2748	0
Covenant Care California LLC		C	408 842-9311	0
Daleo Inc		D	408 846-9621	0
Eagle Ridge Golf Cntry CLB LLC		C	408 846-4531	0
G B Group Inc (PA)		D	408 848-8118	0
Gilroy Gardens Family Theme Pk		D	408 840-7100	0
Headstart Nursery Inc (PA)		D	408 842-3030	0

GEOGRAPHIC

	SIC	EMP	PHONE	ENTRY #
Infosoft Inc		D	408 659-4326	0
Intero Real Estate Services		D	408 848-8400	0
Learning Services Corporation		E	408 848-4379	0
Leonard Anthony Valenti Inc		D	408 848-9688	0
Mariner Health Care Inc		C	408 842-9311	0
Melo Concrete Construction		D	408 842-3484	0
Nestle Usa Inc		C	408 846-6892	0
Noah Concrete Corporation		D	408 842-7211	0
Odd Fellow-Rebekah Chld HM Cal **(PA)**		D	408 846-2100	0
Oj Insulation LP		D	408 842-6315	0
PSI Fire		E	408 842-9308	0
Recology South Valley **(HQ)**		D	408 842-3358	0
Renn Transportation Inc		D	408 842-3545	0
Rfid Textile Services Inc		D	408 840-7504	0
Rush Order Inc **(PA)**		E	408 848-3525	0
Saint Louise Hospital		B	408 848-2000	0
Syngenta Seeds Inc		E	408 847-4242	0
Trees Apartments LLC		D	408 848-6400	0
Verity Health System Cal Inc		C	408 848-2000	0
Work2future Foundation		C	408 758-3477	0

GLEN ELLEN, CA - Sonoma County

	SIC	EMP	PHONE	ENTRY #
Servico Building Maint Co		D	707 935-1224	0

GLENDALE, CA - Los Angeles County

	SIC	EMP	PHONE	ENTRY #
24 Hour Fitness Usa Inc		D	818 247-4334	0
A J R Trucking Inc		D	562 989-9555	0
Abc Inc		B	818 863-7801	0
Across Systems Inc		D	877 922-7677	0
Adventist Health System/West		E	818 409-8540	0
Amco Foods Inc		B	818 247-4716	0
American Realty Centre Inc		D	323 666-6111	0
Amgen Distribution Inc		D	760 989-4424	0
ARC Document Solutions Inc		C	818 242-6555	0
Armenian Amrcn Cuncil On Aging		E	818 241-8690	0
Arthur J Gallagher & Co		C	818 539-2000	0
Assign Corporation		C	818 247-7100	0
Atkinson-Baker Inc **(PA)**		C	818 551-7300	0
Automated Systems America Inc		D	877 500-0002	0
Avery Corp		C	626 304-2000	0
Bank America National Assn		D	800 432-1000	0
Bartholomew Barry & Associates		D	818 543-4000	0
Begroup **(PA)**		D	818 638-4563	0
Buena Ventura Care Center Inc		D	818 247-4476	0
Bunim-Murray Productions		D	818 756-5100	0
Cal Southern Presbt Homes **(PA)**		D	818 247-0420	0
Cal Southern Presbt Homes		C	818 244-7219	0
Cal Southern Presbt Homes		D	818 247-0420	0
California Credit Union **(PA)**		C	818 291-6700	0
Califrnia Insur Guarantee Assn		C	818 844-4300	0
Camble Center		D	818 242-2434	0
Caroline Promotions Inc		D	818 507-7666	0
Caspian Commercial Plbg Inc		D	818 649-2500	0
Cbre Inc		D	818 502-6700	0
Cellco Partnership		D	818 500-7779	0
Chandler Convalescent Hospital		D	818 240-1610	0
Chicago Title and Trust Co		E	818 548-0222	0
Childrens Hospital Los Angeles		C	323 361-2215	0
Cigna Healthcare Cal Inc **(DH)**		B	818 500-6262	0
Cinovation Inc		D	818 246-3160	0
CIT Bank NA		D	818 502-8400	0
Citadel Environmental Svcs Inc **(PA)**		E	818 246-2707	0
City of Glendale		D	818 548-3945	0
City of Glendale		D	818 548-3950	0
City of Glendale		B	818 548-3300	0
City of Glendale		E	818 548-3980	0
City of Glendale		C	818 548-2011	0
Coinmach Corporation **(PA)**		D	818 637-4300	0
Comprehensive Community Health **(PA)**		E	818 265-2264	0
Compspec Inc		D	818 551-4200	0
Country Villa Service Corp		D	818 246-5516	0
Countrywide Home Loans Inc		D	818 550-8700	0
CT Lien Solution		C	818 662-4100	0
Dish Network Corporation		E	818 334-8740	0
Disney Interactive Studios Inc		C	818 560-1000	0
Disney Research Pittsburgh		D	412 623-1800	0
Disqo Inc		D	818 459-4330	0
Dma Claims Inc **(PA)**		D	323 342-6800	0
Dma Claims Inc		D	323 342-6800	0
Drinks Holdings Inc		D	310 441-8400	0
Durini Luis Carlos Estrada		E	502 474-3112	0
Dwa Holdings LLC **(HQ)**		D	818 695-5000	0
Dwa Nova LLC		D	818 695-5000	0
E Z Staffing Inc **(PA)**		B	818 845-2500	0
Easter Seals Southern Cal Inc		D	818 551-0128	0
Emeritus Corporation		E	818 246-7457	0

	SIC	EMP	PHONE	ENTRY #
Equity Title Company **(DH)**		D	818 291-4400	0
Front Porch Communities **(PA)**		D	818 729-8100	0
General Networks Corporation		D	818 249-1962	0
Ggis Insurance Services Inc		C	818 553-2110	0
Glendale Adventist Medical Ctr		E	818 409-8379	0
Glendale Adventist Medical Ctr **(HQ)**		A	818 409-8000	0
Glendale Associates Ltd		D	818 246-6737	0
Glendale Eye Medical Group		D	818 956-1010	0
Glendale Eye Medical Group **(PA)**		D	818 956-1010	0
Glendale Healthcare Center		D	818 246-5516	0
Glenoaks Convalescent Hosp LP		D	818 240-4300	0
Global Asylum Incorporated		E	323 850-1214	0
Global Exprnce Specialists Inc		D	818 638-5959	0
Goway Travel Inc		D	800 810-3687	0
Granville Glendale Inc		D	818 550-0472	0
Griffith Pk Rhbltation Ctr LLC		D	818 845-8507	0
Gsa Design Inc		C	818 241-2558	0
H L Moe Co Inc **(PA)**		C	818 572-2100	0
Health Data Vision Inc **(PA)**		D	866 969-3222	0
Health Net California Inc		C	818 543-9037	0
Hemodialysis Inc **(PA)**		C	818 500-8736	0
Howroyd-Wright Emplymnt Agcy **(HQ)**		C	818 240-8688	0
Howroyd-Wright Emplymnt Agcy		D	818 240-8688	0
Hutchinson & Bloodgood LLP **(PA)**		C	818 637-5000	0
Insite Digestive Health Care		D	626 817-2900	0
Institute For Multicultural		D	818 240-4311	0
Interstate Rhbltation Svcs LLC		C	818 244-5656	0
Jimmys Fashions		E	818 790-8932	0
Johnson & Johnson Pistaccios		E	818 242-7853	0
JP Allen Extended Stay **(PA)**		C	818 956-0202	0
Kaiser Foundation Hospitals		A	800 954-8000	0
Kaiser Foundation Hospitals		E	818 552-3000	0
Kennard Development Group		D	818 241-0800	0
Kradjian Importing Company Inc **(PA)**		D	818 502-1313	0
Ksm Healthcare Inc		D	818 242-1183	0
Legalzoomcom Inc **(DH)**		B	323 962-8600	0
Longwood Management Corp		D	818 246-7174	0
Los Angeles Federal Credit Un **(PA)**		D	818 242-8640	0
Lounge 22 LLC **(PA)**		D	818 502-0700	0
Mader News Inc		D	818 551-5000	0
Mariner Health Care Inc		C	818 246-5677	0
Modern Videofilm Inc		C	818 637-6800	0
Mv Transportation Inc		D	818 409-3387	0
Neopets Inc		E	818 551-4338	0
New York Life Insurance Co		D	818 662-7500	0
Next Venture Inc		D	818 637-2888	0
Nurses Tuch HM Hlth Prvder Inc		E	818 500-4877	0
Oakmont Country Club		C	818 542-4260	0
Oel/Hhh Inc		D	818 246-6050	0
Old Republic Title Company		A	818 240-1936	0
Pacific Coast Title Company		D	818 244-5273	0
Parexel International Corp		C	818 254-7076	0
Patterson Ritner Lockwood **(PA)**		D	818 241-8001	0
PCL Construction Services Inc		D	818 246-3481	0
Pegasus Home Health Care A CA		D	818 551-1932	0
Pegasus Maritime Inc		D	714 728-8565	0
Pinnacle Electrical Svcs Inc		D	818 241-6009	0
Pinnacle Networking Svcs Inc		D	818 241-6009	0
Prestige Preschools Inc **(PA)**		D	818 957-1170	0
Primary Critical Care Medical		C	818 847-9950	0
Principal Financial Group Inc		D	818 243-7141	0
PS Business Parks Inc **(PA)**		D	818 244-8080	0
PS Business Parks LP		D	818 244-8080	0
PS Partners III Ltd		C	818 244-8080	0
Public Storage **(PA)**		C	818 244-8080	0
Public Storage Prpts IV Ltd		D	818 244-8080	0
Public Storage Prpts Xviii Inc		D	818 244-8080	0
Ralphs Grocery Company		C	818 549-0035	0
Real Good Food Company LLC		C	909 744-0073	0
RES-Care Inc		C	818 637-7727	0
Rev Enterprises		E	818 551-7111	0
Rose International Inc		C	636 812-4000	0
Safeco Insurance Company Amer		C	818 956-4250	0
Salem Media Group Inc		D	818 956-5254	0
Search Agency Inc **(PA)**		D	310 582-5700	0
Servicetitan Inc **(PA)**		D	855 899-0970	0
Smg Holdings Inc		D	310 432-2893	0
Sodexo Inc		D	818 952-2201	0
Software Management Cons Inc **(PA)**		B	818 240-3177	0
State Compensation Insur Fund		C	213 576-7335	0
State Compensation Insur Fund		C	323 266-5551	0
State Compensation Insur Fund		B	888 782-8338	0
Stewart Title California Inc		C	818 502-2700	0
Systech Solutions Inc **(PA)**		D	818 550-9690	0
Tacori Enterprises		D	818 863-1536	0

Mergent email: customerrelations@mergent.com
1544

2020 Directory of California
Wholesalers and Services Companies

(P-0000) Products & Services Section entry number
(PA)=Parent Co (HQ)=Headquarters (DH)=Div Headquarters

	SIC	EMP	PHONE	ENTRY #
Tech Town Inc		E	818 621-2744	0
Tmp Worldwide Advertising & Co		D	818 539-2000	0
Twdc Enterprises 18 Corp		B	818 544-5009	0
Twdc Enterprises 18 Corp		A	818 544-6500	0
Twdc Enterprises 18 Corp		C	818 553-4222	0
Ucc Direct Services Inc		D	818 662-4100	0
United Merchant Svcs Cal Inc		D	818 246-6767	0
Universal Studios Inc		C	818 262-4301	0
Univision Communications Inc		C	818 484-7399	0
UNUM Life Insurance Co Amer		D	818 291-4739	0
Usc Verdugo Hills Hospital LLC		A	818 790-7100	0
Usc Vrdugo Hlls Hosp Foundation (PA)		B	800 872-2273	0
Verdugo Hills Urgent Care Mg		D	818 241-4331	0
Verdugo Mental Health		D	818 244-7257	0
Viking Equipment Corp		D	818 500-9447	0
Walt Disney Imagineering (DH)		A	818 544-6500	0
Walt Disney Pictures		B	818 409-2200	0
Wfg National Title Insur Co (PA)		B	818 476-4000	0
Yellowpagescom LLC (HQ)		B	818 937-5500	0
Young Mens Chrstn Assoc Gndl		D	818 484-8256	0

GLENDORA, CA - Los Angeles County

	SIC	EMP	PHONE	ENTRY #
Americas Christian Credit Un (PA)		D	626 208-5400	0
Automobile Club Southern Cal		E	626 963-8531	0
Building Elctronic Contrls Inc (PA)		E	909 305-1600	0
Care Unlimited Health Systems		D	626 332-3767	0
Cliftonlarsonallen LLP		D	626 857-7300	0
Community Convalescent Hospita		D	626 963-6091	0
CPC Services Inc		D	626 852-6200	0
East Valley Glendora Hosp LLC		B	626 852-5000	0
Foothill Hsptl-Mrris L Jhnston (PA)		D	626 857-3145	0
Glendora Country Club		D	626 335-4051	0
Harbor Glen Care Center		D	626 963-7531	0
Home Care of America Inc		D	626 309-7696	0
National Hot Rod Association (PA)		C	626 914-4761	0
National Link Incorporated		D	909 670-1900	0
Oakdale Memorial Park (PA)		D	626 335-0281	0
Seidner-Miller Automotive Inc		E	909 394-3500	0
Spectrum MGT Holdg Co LLC		D	626 857-1075	0
Village Glen Apartments		D	626 963-4575	0

GOLD RIVER, CA - Sacramento County

	SIC	EMP	PHONE	ENTRY #
California Dept Fish Wildlife		C	916 358-2900	0
Centene Corporation		C	314 505-6689	0
Ehealthinsurance Services Inc		C	916 608-6101	0
Eskaton		D	916 852-7900	0
Hartford Fire Insurance Co		B	916 294-1000	0
Health Net California Inc		B	916 935-3520	0
Practice Wares Inc		E	916 526-2674	0
Premier Pools and Spas Lp (PA)		D	916 852-0223	0
Salu Beauty Inc		D	916 475-1400	0
Spare-Time Inc		E	916 638-7001	0
Synergex International Corp		D	916 635-7300	0
USA Waste of California Inc (HQ)		C	916 387-1400	0

GOLETA, CA - Santa Barbara County

	SIC	EMP	PHONE	ENTRY #
6500 Hllister Ave Partners LLC		D	805 722-1362	0
Aecom Global II LLC		D	805 692-0600	0
Appfolio Inc (PA)		C	805 364-6093	0
Asplundh Tree Expert Co		D	805 964-9216	0
AT&T Corp		D	805 562-0121	0
Bardex Corporation		D	805 964-7747	0
Community Action Commsn Santa (PA)		E	805 964-8857	0
Community West Bank		D	805 692-5821	0
Cottage Health System		A	805 967-3411	0
Deployable Space Systems Inc		E	805 722-8090	0
Devereux Foundation		B	805 968-2525	0
Devereux Foundation		B	805 968-2525	0
Ergomotion Inc		D	805 979-9400	0
Flir Commercial Systems Inc (HQ)		B	805 964-9797	0
Gamma PHI Beta Sorority Inc		D	805 968-4221	0
Givens John		D	805 964-4477	0
Glen Annie Golf Club		D	805 968-6400	0
Goleta Hhg Hotel Dev LP		D	805 562-5996	0
Icrco Inc (PA)		E	310 921-9559	0
Intercontinental Hotels Group		C	805 964-6241	0
Intouch Technologies Inc (PA)		D	805 562-8686	0
Juniper Networks Inc		D	805 880-2000	0
Khp III Goleta LLC		D	805 964-6241	0
Kitson Landscape MGT Inc		D	805 681-9460	0
L3 Maripro Inc		D	805 683-3881	0
Las Cumbres Observatory Global		E	805 880-1600	0
Lastline Inc		C	805 456-7075	0
Millenium Athletic Club LLc		D	805 562-3845	0
One Call Plumber Goleta		D	805 284-0441	0
Raytheon Company		D	805 562-2941	0

	SIC	EMP	PHONE	ENTRY #
Santa Barbara Airbus		D	805 964-7759	0
Santa Barbara Trnsp Corp (HQ)		D	805 681-8355	0
Schulte Ranches		D	805 563-0821	0
Securitas SEC Svcs USA Inc		C	805 967-8987	0
Sitestuff Yardi Systems I (PA)		I	805 966-3666	0
Southern California Edison Co		D	805 683-5291	0
Swell Athletic Club GP		D	805 964-7762	0
Toyon Research Corporation (PA)		D	805 968-6787	0
Transphorm Inc (PA)		D	805 456-1300	0
United Parcel Service Inc OH		C	805 964-7848	0
Waterfall Resort		D	805 879-3780	0

GONZALES, CA - Monterey County

	SIC	EMP	PHONE	ENTRY #
Alicia Arroyo Inc		C	831 675-2850	0
Bulmaro Castro Contractors		C	831 675-2927	0
Granite Construction Inc		D	831 763-5595	0
L & J Farms Caraccioli LLC		E	831 675-7901	0
Mann Packing Co Inc		D	831 245-0814	0
RC Packing LLC		B	831 675-0308	0
Silva Farms LLC (PA)		B	831 675-2327	0

GOSHEN, CA - Tulare County

	SIC	EMP	PHONE	ENTRY #
Western Milling LLC (HQ)		C	559 302-1000	0

GRANADA HILLS, CA - Los Angeles County

	SIC	EMP	PHONE	ENTRY #
A Cori Partnership		D	818 368-2802	0
Aegis Senior Communities LLC		D	818 363-3373	0
Atlas Security Inc		E	323 876-1401	0
Brad Watkins Masonry Inc		D	818 360-3796	0
C21 Peak		C	818 363-1717	0
Errama Trucking Company Inc		E	818 381-3341	0
Global Work Group LLC		D	424 220-9994	0
Granada Hlls Convalescent Hosp		D	818 891-1745	0
Jag Framing Inc		E	818 822-7110	0
James I Miller		E	818 363-7444	0
Kaiser Foundation Hospitals		A	818 832-7200	0
Longwood Management Corp		D	818 360-1864	0
Los Angeles Unified School Dst		C	818 363-5061	0
Medical Investment Co		C	818 360-1003	0
Metropolitan Water District		D	818 368-3731	0
Park Regency Inc		D	818 363-6116	0
PS National Inc		B	818 366-1300	0
San Fernando City of Inc		D	818 832-2400	0
Siracusa Enterprises Inc		D	818 831-1130	0
Valley Properties Inc		D	818 360-3430	0

GRAND TERRACE, CA - San Bernardino County

	SIC	EMP	PHONE	ENTRY #
Grand Terrace Care Center		D	909 825-5221	0
Keystone NPS LLC (DH)		D	909 633-6354	0
Riverside-San Bernardino (PA)		C	909 864-1097	0
West Coast Arborists Inc		E	909 783-6544	0

GRANITE BAY, CA - Placer County

	SIC	EMP	PHONE	ENTRY #
Allen L Bender Inc		C	916 372-2190	0
Bushnell Gardens		D	916 791-4199	0
C & C Construction Inc		E	916 434-5280	0
Granite Bay Golf Club		C	916 791-5379	0
Green Valley Security Inc		D	916 797-4058	0
Tricks Gymnastic Inc (PA)		D	916 791-4496	0
United States Pony Clubs		D	916 791-1223	0
Village At Granite Bay		D	916 789-0326	0
Williams Keller Realty		D	916 774-6700	0

GRASS VALLEY, CA - Nevada County

	SIC	EMP	PHONE	ENTRY #
Alta Sierra Country Club Inc		E	530 273-2041	0
Beam Vacuums California Inc		E	916 564-3279	0
Blue Eagle Contracting Inc		D	530 272-0287	0
Briarpatch Coop Nev Cnty Inc		D	530 272-5333	0
Byers Enterprises Inc		D	530 272-7777	0
Durham School Services L P		D	530 273-7282	0
Golden Empire Convalescent Hos		C	530 273-1316	0
Grass Valley LLC		D	530 273-1055	0
Hansen Bros Enterprises (PA)		D	530 273-3100	0
Hospice of Foothills (PA)		D	530 272-5739	0
JM Streamline Inc		D	530 272-6806	0
Meadow View Manor Inc		D	530 272-2273	0
Networked Insurance Agents LLC		C	800 682-8476	0
Nevada County Behavioral Hlth		E	530 265-1450	0
Nevada Irrigation District (PA)		C	530 273-6185	0
Pacific Gas and Electric Co		C	530 477-3245	0
Pride Industries		D	530 477-1832	0
Robert W Baird & Co Inc		A	530 271-3000	0
Sierra Nevada Memorial Hm Care		D	530 274-6350	0
Springhill Manor Rehabilitatio		E	530 273-7247	0
Tim Mello Construction		E	530 205-8588	0
USA Waste of California Inc		E	530 274-3090	0
Victor Cmnty Support Svcs Inc		C	530 273-2244	0

Employment Codes: A=Over 500 employees, B=251-500,
C=101-250, D=51-100, E=50

2020 Directory of California
Wholesalers and Services Companies

© Mergent Inc. 1-800-342-5647

1545

G E O G R A P H I C

	SIC	EMP	PHONE	ENTRY #

GREENBRAE, CA - Marin County

County of Marin		D	415 448-1500	0
Northern California Presbyteri		D	415 464-1767	0
Ocadian Care Centers LLC		D	415 461-9700	0
Petroleum Sales Inc		D	415 256-1600	0
Ross Valley Homes Inc		D	415 461-2300	0

GREENFIELD, CA - Monterey County

Azcona Harvesting LLC		C	831 674-2526	0
Neil Bassetti Farms		E	831 674-2040	0
Southern Mnterey Cnty Mem Hosp		C	831 674-0112	0
Southern Mntrrey Cnty Lbor Sup		D	831 674-2727	0

GREENVILLE, CA - Plumas County

Indian Valley Health Care Dist		D	530 284-7191	0

GRIDLEY, CA - Butte County

Gridley Packing Inc		C	530 846-3753	0
Hovlid Skilled Nursing		E	530 846-9065	0
Orchard Hospital		C	530 846-9000	0
Stapleton - Spence Packing Co **(PA)**		D	408 297-8815	0
Wild Goose Storage Inc		D	530 846-7350	0

GROVELAND, CA - Tuolumne County

Evergreen Dstntion Hldings LLC		D	209 379-2606	0
Pine Mountain Lake Association **(PA)**		C	209 962-4080	0
Thousand Trails Inc		E	209 962-0100	0

GROVER BEACH, CA - San Luis Obispo County

Regatta Tropicals Ltd **(PA)**		D	805 473-1320	0
Truck Tub International Inc		D	805 474-8680	0

GUADALUPE, CA - Santa Barbara County

Byrd Harvest Inc		B	805 343-1608	0
Community Action Commsn Santa		C	805 343-0615	0
Freitas Brothers		E	805 343-3134	0

GUALALA, CA - Mendocino County

Redwood Coast Medical Services **(PA)**		E	707 884-1721	0

GUERNEVILLE, CA - Sonoma County

Dawn Ranch Lodge & Rd Hse Rest		D	707 869-0656	0
Russian River Health Center		E	707 869-2849	0

GUSTINE, CA - Merced County

Andersen Nut Company		E	209 854-6820	0

HACIENDA HEIGHTS, CA - Los Angeles County

Berkshire Hattaway Home Servcs		D	626 913-2808	0
Care Associates Inc		D	626 330-4048	0
Courtyard By Marriott		D	626 965-1700	0
CSX Corporation		C	626 336-1377	0
Good Deal Insurance Services		D	626 275-6795	0

HALF MOON BAY, CA - San Mateo County

Bay City Flower Co **(PA)**		B	650 726-5535	0
Bay City Flower Co		C	650 712-8147	0
Bre Diamond Hotel LLC		C	650 712-7000	0
Coastside Senior Housing Limit		E	415 355-7100	0
Coldwell Banker		E	650 726-1100	0
Giusti Farms LLC		E	650 726-9221	0
Half Moon Bay Lodge		E	650 726-9000	0
Harbor Fuel Dock		D	650 726-4419	0
Home Helpers San Mateo County		D	650 532-3122	0
Lesley Foundation		D	650 726-4888	0
Ocean Colony Partners LLC		C	650 726-5764	0
Ocean Links Corporation		D	650 726-1800	0
Pacific Beach House LLC **(PA)**		D	650 712-0220	0
Pacifica Hotel Company		E	650 726-9000	0
Rocket Farms Inc **(PA)**		C	800 227-5229	0

HANFORD, CA - Kings County

All Health Services Corp **(PA)**		D	559 583-9101	0
City Hanford Public Imprv Corp		C	559 585-2550	0
County of Kings		C	559 584-1411	0
County of Kings		C	559 852-4316	0
Danell Bros Inc		D	559 582-1251	0
Danell Custom Harvesting LLC		C	559 582-1251	0
Educational Employees Cr Un		E	559 587-4460	0
Family Healthcare Network		C	559 582-2013	0
Hacienda Rehabilitation & Heal		C	559 582-9221	0
Hanford Community Hospital **(HQ)**		A	559 582-9000	0
Hanford Joint Un High Schl Dst		D	559 583-5905	0
High Plains Ranch LLC **(PA)**		C	559 583-1277	0
Kings Community Action O **(PA)**		E	559 582-4386	0
Kings Rehabilitation Center **(PA)**		D	559 582-9234	0
Kings View		D	559 582-9307	0
Marquez Brothers Intl Inc		C	559 584-8000	0
Mission Medical Entps Inc		C	559 582-2871	0

Mission Medical Entps Inc		D	559 582-4414	0
Randstad North America Inc		C	559 582-2700	0
Smith Residential Care Fcilty **(PA)**		D	559 584-8451	0
Texture Specialties		E	559 904-6047	0
Veterinary Pharmaceuticals Inc		D	559 582-6800	0
Western Health Resources		E	559 537-2860	0
Wilshire Hlth & Cmnty Svcs Inc		D	559 582-4414	0

HAPPY CAMP, CA - Siskiyou County

Happy Camp Chamber Commerce		E	530 493-2900	0

HARBOR CITY, CA - Los Angeles County

Bennett Enterprises A CA		D	310 534-3543	0
Del AMO Insurance Services		D	310 534-3444	0
Kaiser Foundation Hospitals		A	310 325-5111	0
South Bay Bright Future Inc **(PA)**		D	310 891-0096	0
Southern Cal Prmnnte Med Group		D	800 780-1230	0

HAWAIIAN GARDENS, CA - Los Angeles County

Hawaiian Gardens Casino		A	562 860-5887	0
Howard Contracting Inc		E	562 596-2969	0
Richmond Plastering Inc		E	562 924-4202	0
Total Building Care Inc		D	562 467-8333	0

HAWTHORNE, CA - Los Angeles County

2300 West El Secundo LP		D	310 769-6669	0
7days Inc		C	424 255-5872	0
Argon Enterprises Inc		D	310 349-8777	0
Blue Chip Moving and Stor Inc		D	323 463-6888	0
Calhot Illinios LLC		C	310 536-9800	0
Expeditors Intl Wash Inc		D	310 343-6401	0
Federal Express Corporation		C	800 463-3339	0
Hawthorne Healthcare		D	310 679-9732	0
Inspectorate America Corp		C	800 424-0099	0
Longwood Management Corp		C	310 679-1461	0
Marriott International Inc		C	310 725-9696	0
Pb Car Movers		D	310 283-2741	0
Roofing Supply Group LLC		D	424 269-7330	0
Sandhurst Convales Grp Ltd A		E	310 675-3304	0
Schnierow Dental Care		E	310 377-6453	0
Seems Plumbing Co Inc		E	310 297-4969	0
Servicon Systems Inc		A	310 970-0700	0
Skyone Federal Credit Union **(PA)**		D	310 491-7500	0
South Bay Rgonal Pub Comm Auth		E	310 973-1802	0
Tbc - Boring Company		D	425 495-4215	0
Tech Flex Package		E	323 241-1800	0
Thinkom Solutions Inc		C	310 371-5486	0
Tricor America Inc		D	310 676-0800	0
Trident Labs LLC		C	310 915-9121	0
Wilshire Hlth & Cmnty Svcs Inc		D	310 679-9732	0
Windsor Gardens		D	310 675-3304	0
Xdbs Corporation		D	302 566-3006	0
Zaharoni Holdings		E	310 297-9722	0

HAYWARD, CA - Alameda County

24 Hour Fitness Usa Inc		D	510 264-3275	0
American Asp Repr Rsrfcing Inc **(PA)**		D	510 723-0280	0
American Residential Svcs LLC		D	510 657-7601	0
American Synergy Asbestos Remo		D	510 444-2333	0
American Technologies Inc		D	510 429-5000	0
Ameriflight LLC		D	510 569-6000	0
Andrew Chekene Enterprises Inc		C	650 588-1001	0
Anning-Johnson Company		C	510 670-0100	0
Aramark Unf & Career AP LLC		D	510 487-1855	0
Arborwell Inc **(PA)**		D	510 881-4260	0
ARC of Alameda County		C	510 582-8151	0
Arcus Biosciences Inc		C	510 694-6200	0
Aurora Algae Inc		D	510 266-5000	0
Axis Services Inc		C	510 732-6111	0
Bassard Convalescent & Med Hm **(PA)**		D	510 537-6700	0
Bay Area Community Svcs Inc		C	510 537-1688	0
Bay Area Concrete LLC		D	510 294-0220	0
Bess Testlab Inc		E	408 988-0101	0
Big Joe California North Inc **(PA)**		C	510 785-6900	0
Bigham Taylor Roofing Corp		D	510 886-0197	0
Blue River Seafood Inc		E	510 300-6800	0
Boyett Construction Inc **(PA)**		D	510 264-9100	0
Brightview Landscape Svcs Inc		E	510 487-4826	0
Brook Furniture Rental Inc		E	510 487-4440	0
Bruml Management LLC		E	800 733-3629	0
California Golden Realty		A	408 822-6000	0
California Hydronics Corp **(PA)**		E	510 293-1993	0
Casa Sandoval LLC		D	510 727-1700	0
Cell-Crete Corporation		D	510 471-7257	0
Centimark Corporation		C	510 921-5500	0
Chapel of Chimes **(DH)**		D	510 471-3363	0
Chipman Corporation		D	510 748-8787	0

	SIC	EMP	PHONE	ENTRY #
Cintas Corporation No 3		D	510 352-6330	0
Classic Soft Trim Inc		D	510 782-4911	0
Cnet Technology Corporation (HQ)		C	408 392-9966	0
Comcast Corporation		D	510 266-3200	0
Commercial Rfrgn Spcalists LLC (HQ)		C	510 784-8990	0
Community Child Care Counci Al (PA)		D	510 582-2182	0
Community Integrated Work Prog		E	510 487-9768	0
Control Air North Inc		D	510 441-1800	0
Controlled Contamination Svcs		D	510 728-1106	0
Core-Mark International Inc		C	510 487-3000	0
County of Alameda		B	510 670-5455	0
County of Alameda		E	510 670-5700	0
Cox Automotive Inc		B	510 786-4500	0
Custom Commercial Dry Clrs Inc (PA)		E	510 723-1000	0
D S P Service Inc		E	510 782-2200	0
D W Nicholson Corporation (PA)		C	510 887-0900	0
Dhl Supply Chain (usa)		D	510 784-7360	0
Dt Floormasters Inc		D	510 476-1000	0
Durham School Services L P		C	510 887-6005	0
E W C H Inc		D	510 783-4811	0
Eagle Systems Intl Inc		B	510 259-1700	0
Earle M Jorgensen Company		D	510 487-2700	0
Early Transportation Services		D	510 324-1119	0
Eden Area Regnl Occupational P		D	510 293-2900	0
Eden Housing Inc (PA)		D	510 582-1460	0
Eden Housing Management Inc (PA)		E	510 582-1460	0
Eden West Rehabilitation		D	510 783-4811	0
Fba Inc (PA)		E	510 265-1888	0
Fedex Freight Corporation		B	510 895-0440	0
Felson Companies Inc		D	510 538-1150	0
Foam Distributors Incorporated		D	510 441-8377	0
Forensic Analytical Spc Inc (PA)		C	510 887-8828	0
Gallo Sales Company Inc (DH)		D	510 476-5000	0
Gco Inc (PA)		E	510 786-3333	0
Gel Pak LLC		D	510 576-2220	0
Glen Alpine Building Svcs Inc		D	510 582-7400	0
Gourmet Foods		D	510 887-0340	0
H U S D Maintenance Operation		D	510 784-2666	0
Hayward Area Recreation Pkdist		E	510 317-2300	0
Hayward Area Recreation Pkdist		D	510 881-6750	0
Hayward Police Officers Assn		D	510 293-7207	0
Hayward Sisters Hospital (HQ)		A	510 264-4000	0
HEs Transportation Svcs Inc		E	510 783-6100	0
Hillsdale Group LP		D	510 538-3866	0
Intarcia Therapeutics Inc		D	510 782-7800	0
Jagpreet Enterprises LLC		C	510 336-8376	0
Johnson Cntrls SEC Sltions LLC		D	510 246-2862	0
Jon K Takata Corporation (PA)		D	510 315-5400	0
Kaiser Foundation Hospitals		D	510 454-1000	0
Kaiser Foundation Hospitals		A	510 678-4000	0
Katherine Bousson		D	510 582-1166	0
Keeco LLC (PA)		D	510 324-8800	0
Kissito Health Care Inc		D	510 582-8311	0
Kuehne + Nagel Inc		D	510 785-0555	0
Kwan Wo Ironworks Inc		C	415 822-9628	0
LBC Mundial Corporation (DH)		D	650 873-0750	0
Leggett & Platt Incorporated		D	510 487-8063	0
Lifetouch Nat Schl Studios Inc		E	510 293-1818	0
Marelich Mechanical Co Inc (HQ)		D	510 785-5500	0
Mariner Health Care Inc		D	510 538-4424	0
Mariner Health Care Inc		C	510 785-2880	0
Metric Equipment Sales Inc		D	510 264-0887	0
Monument Security Inc		C	510 430-3540	0
Mygrant Glass Company Inc (PA)		E	510 785-4360	0
Nor-Cal Moving Services (PA)		C	510 371-4942	0
Northstar Contg Group Inc (DH)		D	510 491-1330	0
Oakhurst Industries Inc		D	510 265-2400	0
Omnicare Inc		D	510 293-9663	0
Pacheco Brothers Gardening Inc (PA)		D	510 732-6330	0
Pacific Cheese Co (PA)		D	510 784-8800	0
Pacific Gas and Electric Co		B	510 784-3253	0
Predicine Inc		E	650 300-2188	0
Pulse Biosciences Inc		D	510 906-4600	0
R F Macdonald Co (PA)		D	510 784-0110	0
R2g Enterprises Inc		D	510 489-6218	0
Restec Contractors Inc		D	510 670-0100	0
Ripcord Inc		D	408 838-7446	0
RJS & Associates Inc		D	510 670-9111	0
Rural/Metro Corporation		C	510 266-0885	0
S&F Management Company LLC		A	310 385-1088	0
Safeco Door & Hardware Inc		D	510 429-4768	0
Serpico Landscaping Inc		E	510 293-0341	0
Siemens Industry Inc		B	510 783-6000	0
Siemens Industry Inc		C	510 783-6000	0
Signet Testing Labs Inc (HQ)		E	510 887-8484	0

	SIC	EMP	PHONE	ENTRY #
Solcom Inc		B	510 940-2490	0
SOS Security Incorporated		C	510 782-4900	0
Spectrum Community Services (PA)		D	510 881-0300	0
St Francis Extended Care Inc		D	510 785-3630	0
St Michael Convalescent Hosp		D	510 782-8424	0
Starzz Management Services (PA)		D	510 632-5533	0
Stomper Co Inc		D	510 574-0570	0
Stonebrae LP		D	510 728-7878	0
TCI Aluminum/North Inc		D	510 786-3750	0
Telecare Corporation		C	510 582-7676	0
Thyssenkrupp Elevator Corp		E	510 476-1900	0
Tiburcio Vasquez Hlth Ctr Inc		D	510 471-5907	0
Tps Aviation Inc (PA)		D	510 475-1010	0
Tricor America Inc		D	510 293-3960	0
Ultraex LLC		D	510 723-3760	0
Ultraex Inc		D	800 882-1000	0
Underwriters Laboratories Inc		C	408 754-6500	0
Urban Trading Software Inc		E	877 633-6171	0
USA Waste of California Inc		D	831 384-5000	0
Ustov Inc		E	510 781-1818	0
Wagan Corporation		E	510 471-9221	0
Wells Fargo Bank National Assn		D	510 266-0595	0
Westates Mechanical Corp Inc		D	510 635-9830	0
Xpo Logistics Freight Inc		C	510 785-6920	0
Yrc Inc		D	510 783-7010	0

HEALDSBURG, CA - Sonoma County

	SIC	EMP	PHONE	ENTRY #
Alliance Medical Center Inc		D	707 431-8234	0
Clendenen Vineyard MGT LLC		D	707 473-0881	0
Corporate Soul LLC		B	707 431-7781	0
E & J Gallo Winery		D	707 431-5400	0
E & M Electric and McHy Inc (PA)		E	707 433-5578	0
Encore Events Rentals Inc		D	707 431-3500	0
H2 Hotel LLC		D	707 431-2202	0
Healdsburg Dist Hosp Rehab Svc		D	707 433-9150	0
Hotel Healdsburg (PA)		D	707 431-2800	0
Hotel Healdsburg		D	707 922-5399	0
Klein Foods Inc		D	707 431-1533	0
Madrona Mnr Wine Cntry Inn		D	707 433-4231	0
North Sonoma County Hosp Dst		D	707 431-6500	0
Scheid Vineyards Inc		C	707 433-1858	0
Social Finance Inc		A	707 473-9889	0
Syar Industries Inc		D	707 433-3366	0
Vino Farms Inc		D	707 433-8241	0

HEBER, CA - Imperial County

	SIC	EMP	PHONE	ENTRY #
C S Transport Inc		D	760 666-5661	0
Ormat Nevada Inc		E	760 353-8200	0
Ralph Collazo Packing Inc		D	760 353-0856	0

HELENDALE, CA - San Bernardino County

	SIC	EMP	PHONE	ENTRY #
Silver Lakes Association		D	760 245-1606	0

HELM, CA - Fresno County

	SIC	EMP	PHONE	ENTRY #
Terranova Ranch Inc		E	559 866-5644	0
Wilbur-Ellis Company LLC		D	559 866-5667	0

HEMET, CA - Riverside County

	SIC	EMP	PHONE	ENTRY #
American Medical Response Inc		C	951 765-3900	0
Anka Behavioral Health Inc		C	951 929-2744	0
Apex Healthcare Med Ctr (PA)		D	951 765-0700	0
Bank America National Assn		E	951 929-8614	0
Brookdale Senior Living Inc		D	951 744-9861	0
Caring Companions Home		D	951 765-1441	0
Casa-Pacifica Inc		B	951 658-3369	0
Casa-Pacifica Inc		D	951 766-5116	0
Devonshire Care Center LLC		D	951 925-2571	0
Hcr Manorcare Med Svcs Fla LLC		C	951 925-9171	0
Hemet Unified School District		C	951 765-2550	0
Hemet Valley Imaging Med Group (PA)		D	951 925-6537	0
Johnre Care LLC		D	951 658-6374	0
Lake Hemet Municipal Wtr Dst (PA)		D	951 927-1816	0
Lpsh Holdings Inc		A	951 926-1176	0
Meadowbrook Convalescent Hosp		D	951 658-2293	0
Miramonte Enterprises LLC		C	951 658-9441	0
Pama Management Co		E	951 929-0340	0
Physicians For Healthy Hospita (HQ)		C	951 652-2811	0
Physicians For Healthy Hospita		D	951 652-2811	0
Primerica Life Insurance Co		C	951 652-6190	0
Ramona Community Services Corp (HQ)		B	951 658-9288	0
Ramona Rehabilitation and Post		D	951 652-0011	0
Southland Arthritis Osteo		E	951 672-1866	0
Spectrum MGT Holdg Co LLC		D	951 260-3143	0
Sunrise Senior Living LLC		D	951 929-5988	0
The For Valley Resource Center (PA)		E	951 766-8659	0
Time Warner Cable Inc		D	951 306-3117	0
Trilar Management Group		C	951 925-2021	0

Employment Codes: A=Over 500 employees, B=251-500,
C=101-250, D=51-100, E=50

2020 Directory of California
Wholesalers and Services Companies

© Mergent Inc. 1-800-342-5647

1547

	SIC	EMP	PHONE	ENTRY #
Valley Rsrce Ctr For Retarded		D	951 766-8659	0

HERCULES, CA - Contra Costa County

	SIC	EMP	PHONE	ENTRY #
Blize Healthcare Cal Inc		D	800 343-2549	0
City Mechanical Inc		D	510 724-9088	0
Hercules Fitness		E	510 724-2900	0
Mechanics Bank		D	510 741-7545	0
Security Pacific RE Brkg		D	510 245-9901	0
Shields Nursing Centers Inc (PA)		C	510 724-9911	0
Watkin & Bortolussi Inc.		D	415 453-4675	0

HERLONG, CA - Lassen County

	SIC	EMP	PHONE	ENTRY #
Aecom Global II LLC		D	530 827-2406	0

HERMOSA BEACH, CA - Los Angeles County

	SIC	EMP	PHONE	ENTRY #
24 Hour Fitness Worldwide Inc		E	310 374-4524	0
All Environmental Inc		C	310 798-4255	0
AT&T Corp.		D	310 303-3888	0
Gps Flyers		D	951 588-7777	0
Liminex Inc		C	424 529-6960	0
Marlin Equity Partners LLC (PA)		D	310 364-0100	0
Marlin Equity Partners III LP (PA)		D	310 364-0100	0
Perverted Jstice Fundation Inc		C	310 910-9380	0
Pickleback Nola LLC		E	504 605-0911	0
Southbay Website Design LLC		D	310 370-4043	0
Sunrise Senior Living LLC		D	310 937-0959	0

HESPERIA, CA - San Bernardino County

	SIC	EMP	PHONE	ENTRY #
Arizona Pipeline Company (PA)		B	760 244-8212	0
Ascon Recycling Co		C	760 948-1538	0
Best Way Disposal Co Inc		D	760 244-9773	0
Caremark Rx LLC		D	760 948-6606	0
Desert Recycling Inc.		E	760 948-3122	0
Foremost Healthcare Centers		D	760 244-5579	0
Foremost Operations LLC		E	760 244-5579	0
Hannaknapp Realty Inc		D	760 244-8557	0
High Dsert Ptent Care Svcs LLC		D	760 956-4150	0
Jesse Alexander Transport		D	760 669-0379	0
Lake Arrowhead Cmnty Svcs Dst		E	909 337-6395	0
Ortiz Asphalt Paving Inc		D	951 966-7060	0
Total Renal Care Inc		D	760 947-7405	0
Victor Valley Moose Lodge No		C	760 244-1808	0

HICKMAN, CA - Stanislaus County

	SIC	EMP	PHONE	ENTRY #
Dave Wilson Nursery Inc (PA)		E	209 874-1821	0
Foster Dairy Farms		C	209 874-9605	0
Frantz Wholesale Nursery LLC		C	209 874-1459	0

HIDDEN VALLEY LAKE, CA - Lake County

	SIC	EMP	PHONE	ENTRY #
Hidden Valley Lake Association (PA)		D	707 987-3146	0

HIGHLAND, CA - San Bernardino County

	SIC	EMP	PHONE	ENTRY #
Cedar Holdings LLC		D	909 862-0611	0
Century 21 Showcase Inc		D	909 936-9334	0
County of San Bernardino		E	909 425-0785	0
East Valley Water District		D	909 889-9501	0
Immanuel Baptist Cruch		D	909 862-6641	0
Kcb Towers Inc		D	909 862-0322	0
Kindred Healthcare Oper Inc		C	909 862-0611	0
San Manuel Indian Bingo Casino (PA)		A	909 864-5050	0
YMCA of East Valley		E	909 425-9622	0

HILLSBOROUGH, CA - San Mateo County

	SIC	EMP	PHONE	ENTRY #
Burlingame Country Club		D	650 696-8100	0
Camaro Cleaners Corp (PA)		D	650 343-4296	0
John Plane Construction Inc		C	415 468-0555	0
Synctruck LLC		C	415 425-0447	0

HINKLEY, CA - San Bernardino County

	SIC	EMP	PHONE	ENTRY #
Luz Solar Partners Ix		D	760 762-3113	0

HOLLISTER, CA - San Benito County

	SIC	EMP	PHONE	ENTRY #
Alpha Teknova Inc		D	831 637-1100	0
American Electrical Svcs Inc		C	831 638-1737	0
American Medical Response Inc		C	831 636-9391	0
Bhandal Bros Inc		E	831 728-2691	0
Bhandal Bros Trucking Inc		D	831 728-2691	0
Chamberlains Children Ctr Inc		D	831 636-2121	0
Guerra Nut Shelling Company		D	831 637-4471	0
Hollister Process Service		E	831 634-1479	0
Icu Eyewear Inc		D	831 637-9300	0
Infinity Staffing Service		B	831 638-0360	0
R and R Labor Inc		B	831 638-0290	0
San Benito Health Care Dst (PA)		B	831 637-5711	0
San Benito Htg & Shtmtl Inc.		D	831 637-1112	0
San Juan Oaks LLC		D	831 636-6113	0
Wolt Com Inc		B	940 271-4703	0
Woltcom Inc.		C	831 638-4900	0

HOLLYWOOD, CA - Los Angeles County

	SIC	EMP	PHONE	ENTRY #
Battery Marketing Inc		D	323 467-7267	0
Car Park Inc		C	323 462-6060	0
Cellco Partnership		D	323 465-0640	0
Deep Focus Inc		A	323 790-5340	0
Loews Hollywood Hotel LLC		B	323 450-2235	0

HOLT, CA - San Joaquin County

	SIC	EMP	PHONE	ENTRY #
Victoria Island Farms		D	209 465-5609	0

HOLTVILLE, CA - Imperial County

	SIC	EMP	PHONE	ENTRY #
Black Dog Farms of California		C	760 356-2951	0
Five Star Packing LLC		A	760 356-4103	0
Grimmway Farms		D	760 356-2513	0
John Grizzle Farming		E	760 356-4381	0
Ormesa LLC		D	760 356-3020	0
Sunharbor Management LLC		E	760 356-1262	0

HOMELAND, CA - Riverside County

	SIC	EMP	PHONE	ENTRY #
Harvest V Citizens Patrol		C	951 926-9763	0

HOMEWOOD, CA - Placer County

	SIC	EMP	PHONE	ENTRY #
Homewood Village Resorts LLC		E	530 525-2992	0

HOOPA, CA - Humboldt County

	SIC	EMP	PHONE	ENTRY #
Klma W Medical Center		D	530 625-4114	0

HOPLAND, CA - Mendocino County

	SIC	EMP	PHONE	ENTRY #
Hopland Band Pomo Indians Inc		C	707 744-1395	0
Hopland Band Pomo Indians Inc (PA)		D	707 472-2100	0

HORNITOS, CA - Mariposa County

	SIC	EMP	PHONE	ENTRY #
Hornitos Telephone Co		D	608 831-1000	0

HUGHSON, CA - Stanislaus County

	SIC	EMP	PHONE	ENTRY #
Alderwoods (delaware) Inc		E	209 883-0411	0
Community Hospice Inc		E	209 578-6380	0
Duarte Nursery Inc (PA)		B	209 531-0351	0
Grower Direct Nut Company Inc		E	209 883-4890	0
Lakewood Mem Pk Fnrl Svcs Inc		E	209 883-4465	0
Samaritan Village Inc		C	209 883-3212	0

HUNTINGTON BEACH, CA - Orange County

	SIC	EMP	PHONE	ENTRY #
2nd Floor Main Street Concepts		E	714 969-9000	0
A Growing Concern Landscapes		D	714 843-5137	0
Ace Parking Management Inc		D	714 845-8000	0
AES Huntington Beach LLC		E	714 374-1476	0
Aire-Rite AC & Rfrgn Inc.		D	714 895-2338	0
Alltek Company U S A Inc		E	714 375-9785	0
American Golf Corporation		D	714 536-8866	0
American Golf Corporation		D	714 846-1364	0
Americare Medservices Inc		C	310 632-1141	0
AMG Huntington Beach LLC		E	714 894-9802	0
Applied Computer Solutions (HQ)		D	714 861-2200	0
Aramark Facility Services LLC		E	714 372-0683	0
AT&T Corp.		D	714 965-4685	0
Baker Hghes Olfld Oprtions LLC		D	714 893-8511	0
Baker Hughes A GE Company LLC		D	714 893-8511	0
Bartco Lighting Inc.		D	714 230-3200	0
BJs Restaurant Operations Co		C	714 500-2440	0
Burleigh Point Ltd (DH)		C	949 428-3200	0
Captured Sea Inc		D	714 856-3358	0
Careworks Health Services		D	949 859-4700	0
Cellco Partnership		D	714 847-8799	0
Centene Corporation		D	714 934-3373	0
Child Development Incorporated		B	714 842-4064	0
Childrens Hospital Los Angeles		B	714 841-4990	0
Cinemark Usa Inc.		D	714 373-4573	0
Clarendon Specialty Fas Inc		D	714 842-2603	0
Coastal Traffic Systems Inc		D	714 641-3744	0
Coastline Cnstr & Awng Co Inc		D	714 891-9798	0
Cogar International Enrgy Corp (PA)		E	626 494-8157	0
Confie Seguros Inc (HQ)		D	714 252-2500	0
Confie Seguros Holdings II Co (PA)		C	714 252-2649	0
Critchfeld Mech Inc Sthern Cal		D	949 390-2900	0
Dix Metals Inc.		D	714 677-0777	0
Douglas Fir Holdings LLC		C	714 842-5551	0
Element Mtrls Tech HB Inc (DH)		D	714 892-1961	0
First Team RE - Orange Cnty		D	714 965-2244	0
Flw Inc		D	714 751-7512	0
Freeway Insurance (PA)		C	714 252-2500	0
Friedman Professional Mgt Co		D	714 842-1426	0
Galkos Construction Inc (PA)		D	714 373-8545	0
GBI Tile & Stone Inc (PA)		E	949 567-1880	0
Geosyntec Consultants Inc		D	714 969-0800	0
Glen Beverly Laboratories Inc		D	714 848-5777	0
Grani Installation Inc (PA)		D	714 898-0441	0
Guardian Health Care Services		D	714 375-1110	0

Mergent email: customerrelations@mergent.com
1548

2020 Directory of California
Wholesalers and Services Companies

(P-0000) Products & Services Section entry number
(PA)=Parent Co (HQ)=Headquarters (DH)=Div Headquarters

	SIC	EMP	PHONE	ENTRY #
Harbor Distributing LLC (HQ)		C	714 933-2400	0
HB Healthcare Associates LLC		D	714 887-0144	0
Hobbs Herder Advertising		D	800 999-6090	0
Horsemen Inc		D	714 847-4243	0
House Seven Gables RE Inc		D	714 500-3300	0
House Seven Gables RE Inc		D	714 754-6262	0
Huntington Bch Cnvlescent Hosp		B	714 847-3515	0
I Hot Leads		D	714 960-8028	0
Ics Professional Services Inc		C	714 868-3900	0
Innocean Wrldwide Americas LLC (HQ)		D	714 861-5200	0
K W K Trucking Inc		C	714 791-7928	0
Kings Seafood Company LLC		D	714 793-1177	0
Landmark Health LLC (PA)		D	253 394-2566	0
Managed Health Network		A	714 934-5519	0
Marblewest Inc		E	714 847-6472	0
MCB-Cjs LLC		D	714 230-3600	0
Merrill Gardens LLC		D	714 842-6569	0
Michaelson Connor & Boul (PA)		D	714 230-3600	0
Mortgage Fax Inc		D	714 899-2656	0
Nakase Brothers Wholesale Nurs (PA)		D	949 855-4388	0
Netball America Inc		E	888 221-3650	0
New Port Orthopedic Institute		D	949 722-5071	0
No Ordinary Moments Inc		C	714 848-3800	0
Nuvision Fincl Federal Cr Un (PA)		C	714 375-8000	0
Orange County Head Start		E	714 241-8920	0
Orange County Sanitation		C	714 962-2411	0
Pachinko World Inc		C	714 895-7772	0
Pacific City Hotel LLC		B	714 698-6100	0
Paul Maurer Company		D	714 231-8241	0
Portermatt Electric Inc		D	714 596-8788	0
Precise Fit Limited One LLC		B	310 824-1800	0
Primal Elements Inc		D	714 899-0757	0
Prime Hlthcare Hntngton Bch		B	714 843-5000	0
PW Stephens Envmtl Inc (PA)		D	714 892-2028	0
Pyro-Comm Systems Inc (PA)		C	714 902-8000	0
R C Hotels Inc		D	714 891-0123	0
Rainbow Disposal Co Inc (HQ)		C	714 847-3581	0
Rainbow Transfer Recycling		C	714 847-5818	0
RC Wendt Painting Inc		C	714 960-2700	0
Reliable Wholesale Lumber Inc (PA)		D	714 848-8222	0
Restaurant Depot		E	714 378-3535	0
Restaurant Depot LLC		E	714 378-3535	0
Ricoh Usa Inc		E	714 396-0568	0
Russell Fisher Partnership		E	714 842-4453	0
Russell Fisher Partnership (PA)		E	909 930-5420	0
Sea Breeze Health Care Inc		C	714 847-9671	0
Shekinah Inc		E	714 475-5460	0
Sho-Air International Inc (PA)		E	949 476-9111	0
Skyhill Financial Inc		D	714 657-3938	0
Skynet USA Asset MGT Inc		E	702 969-5599	0
Soroptmist Intl Huntington Bch		E	714 271-9305	0
Southern Cal Prmnnte Med Group		E	714 841-7293	0
Thomas Crane and Trckg Co Inc		E	562 592-2837	0
Trilogy Financial Services Inc (PA)		D	714 843-9977	0
Tscm Corporation		D	714 841-1988	0
Two Roads Prof Resources Inc		C	714 901-3804	0
Unison Electric		E	714 375-5915	0
United Facility Solutions Inc		B	310 743-3000	0
United Medical Imaging Inc		D	714 843-6255	0
United States Technical Svcs		C	714 374-6300	0
Unitedhealth Group Inc		B	714 969-9050	0
Waterfront Hotel LLC		B	714 845-8000	0

HUNTINGTON PARK, CA - Los Angeles County

	SIC	EMP	PHONE	ENTRY #
Aircraft Xray Laboratories Inc		D	323 587-4141	0
All Care Medical Group Inc		D	408 278-3550	0
AT&T Corp		D	323 589-7045	0
Chhp Management LLC		D	323 583-1931	0
Covenant Care California LLC		C	323 589-5941	0
D2j Inc		D	323 589-1374	0
Huntington Pk Police League		D	323 584-6254	0
Living Opportunities MGT Co		C	323 589-5956	0
Mexican Amrcn Oprtnty Fndation		E	323 588-7320	0
Powerhouse Realty Inc		D	323 562-7777	0
Prajin 1 Stop Distributors Inc (PA)		E	323 395-5302	0
Saroyan Lumber Company Inc (PA)		D	800 624-9309	0

HURON, CA - Fresno County

	SIC	EMP	PHONE	ENTRY #
California Valley Land Co Inc (PA)		D	559 945-9292	0
Dick Anderson & Sons Farming		C	559 945-2511	0
Dole Fresh Vegetables Inc		D	559 945-2591	0
Dresick Farms Inc (PA)		D	559 945-2513	0
Royal Packing Dcf		D	559 945-2537	0
West Cotton AG Management Inc		C	559 945-2511	0

IDYLLWILD, CA - Riverside County

	SIC	EMP	PHONE	ENTRY #
Guided Discoveries Inc		E	951 659-6062	0

IMPERIAL, CA - Imperial County

	SIC	EMP	PHONE	ENTRY #
County of Imperial		D	760 355-1748	0
Empire Southwest LLC		B	760 545-6200	0
Imperial Irrigation District (PA)		A	800 303-7756	0
Imperial Irrigation District		B	760 339-9220	0
Nutrien AG Solutions Inc		D	760 355-1133	0
Western Meat Processors Inc		E	760 355-1175	0

IMPERIAL BEACH, CA - San Diego County

	SIC	EMP	PHONE	ENTRY #
Boys & Girls Clubs South Cnty		D	619 424-2266	0
Comprhnsive Trning Systems Inc		E	619 424-6650	0
Intervec Phoenix Travel Club		C	828 728-5287	0
Jpmorgan Chase Bank Nat Assn		E	619 424-8197	0

INDEPENDENCE, CA - Inyo County

	SIC	EMP	PHONE	ENTRY #
Eastern California Museum (PA)		B	760 878-0292	0
Los Angeles Dept Wtr & Pwr		A	760 878-2156	0
Sheriffs Offices		D	760 878-0383	0

INDIAN WELLS, CA - Riverside County

	SIC	EMP	PHONE	ENTRY #
Coldwell Bnkr Residential Brkg		D	760 771-5454	0
Dhccnp		D	760 340-4646	0
El Dorado Country Club		C	760 346-8081	0
Hyatt Corporation		B	760 341-1000	0
Indian Wells Country Club Inc		D	760 345-2561	0
Indian Wells Resort Hotel		E	760 345-6466	0
Lh Indian Wells Operating LLC		C	760 341-2200	0
Renaissance Hotel MGT Co LLC		A	760 773-4444	0
Renaissnce Esmralda Resort Spa		D	760 773-4444	0
Reserve Club		D	760 674-2222	0
Toscana Country Club Inc		C	760 404-1444	0
Troon Golf LLC		C	760 346-4653	0
Vintage Club		D	760 340-0500	0
Vintage Club Master Assn Inc		D	760 340-0500	0

INDIO, CA - Riverside County

	SIC	EMP	PHONE	ENTRY #
Coachella Vly Rescue Mission		E	760 347-3512	0
Commercial Lighting Inds Inc		D	800 755-0155	0
County of Riverside		D	760 863-8283	0
County of Riverside		D	760 863-7600	0
County of Riverside		D	760 863-8247	0
Desert Recreation District (PA)		D	760 347-3484	0
Easia Golf Investment LLC		D	760 775-2000	0
East Valley Tourist Dev Auth		A	760 342-5000	0
Fc Landscape Inc		D	760 347-6600	0
Frontier California Inc		D	760 342-0500	0
Granite Construction Company		B	760 775-7500	0
HMS Agricultural Corporation		D	760 347-2335	0
Indio Hlthcare Wllness Ctr LLC		D	760 347-6000	0
JB Finish Inc		D	760 342-6300	0
John F Kennedy Memorial Hosp		A	760 347-6191	0
Kaiser Foundation Hospitals		A	866 984-7483	0
Kirkpatrick Ldscpg Svcs Inc		C	760 347-6926	0
Lb Hills Golf Club LLC		D	760 775-2000	0
Marthas Village & Kitchen		D	760 347-4741	0
Oasis Mental Health Trtmnt Ctr		C	760 863-8609	0
P H B Contracting Inc		D	760 347-7290	0
Plantation Golf Club Inc		D	760 775-3688	0
Triangle Distributing Co		D	760 347-4052	0
Valley Medical Trnsp LLC		D	760 501-8929	0

INGLEWOOD, CA - Los Angeles County

	SIC	EMP	PHONE	ENTRY #
Aero Port Services Inc (PA)		D	310 623-8230	0
Air-Sea Forwarders Inc (PA)		D	310 216-1616	0
Alamo Rental (us) Inc		D	310 649-2242	0
American Eagle Protctve Svcs		D	310 412-0019	0
American Nursing Home MGT Inc		D	310 672-1012	0
American Service Industries		D	323 779-4000	0
Ao Freight Corporation (PA)		E	310 419-8833	0
Apollo Couriers Inc (PA)		D	310 337-0377	0
Beckett Enterprise		E	310 686-3817	0
Big 5 Sporting Goods Corp		B	323 755-2663	0
California Credit Union		D	310 671-1080	0
Centinela Skilled Nursing and		D	310 674-3216	0
Centinela Sklld Nrsng & Wllnss		D	310 674-3216	0
Centinela Valley Care Center		C	310 674-3216	0
Century Skill Care		D	310 672-1012	0
Cfhs Holdings Inc		A	310 673-4660	0
City of Inglewood		D	310 412-5370	0
CP Opco LLC (HQ)		A	310 966-4900	0
Dedicated Dental Systems Inc		D	661 397-5513	0
Dolphin Hkg Ltd (PA)		D	310 215-3356	0
Eldorado Community Service Ctr		D	424 227-7971	0
Forum Enterprises Inc		E	310 330-7300	0

GEOGRAPHIC

Name	SIC	EMP	PHONE	ENTRY #
Holiday Meat & Provision Corp		C	310 674-0541	0
Inglewood Meadows Kbs LP		D	310 820-4888	0
Inglewood Unified School Dst		D	310 419-2691	0
Interdent Inc **(HQ)**		D	310 765-2400	0
Interdent Service Corporation **(DH)**		E	310 765-2400	0
Kaiser Foundation Hospitals		B	310 419-3303	0
Lemonlight Media Inc		D	310 402-0275	0
Mariner Health Care Inc		C	310 677-9114	0
Motel 6 Operating LP		D	310 419-1234	0
Prime Healthcare Centinela LLC		A	310 673-4660	0
Prime International Security		D	310 670-4565	0
RHO Chem LLC **(DH)**		E	323 776-6234	0
Royal Airline Linen Inc		D	310 677-9885	0
Sea-Air International Inc		D	310 338-0778	0
Security Indust Spcialists Inc		C	323 924-9147	0
Smith Coleman Inc		D	310 671-8271	0
UPS Worldwide Logistics Inc		C	310 673-7661	0
Usas Express International		D	310 645-2313	0
Watts Health Foundation Inc **(HQ)**		B	310 424-2220	0
West Cntinela Vly Care Ctr Inc		D	310 674-3216	0

IONE, CA - Amador County

Name	SIC	EMP	PHONE	ENTRY #
Concessionaires Urban Park		E	209 763-5121	0
Concessionaires Urban Park		D	209 763-5166	0
Parks and Recreation Cal Dept		E	209 763-5121	0

IRVINE, CA - Orange County

Name	SIC	EMP	PHONE	ENTRY #
1105 Media Inc		C	949 265-1520	0
3d Infotech **(PA)**		E	949 988-0200	0
4g Wireless Inc **(PA)**		C	949 748-6100	0
5 Arches LLC		D	949 387-8092	0
7 Layers Inc		D	949 716-6512	0
A & H Communications Inc		C	949 250-4555	0
A Buchalter Professional Corp		D	714 549-5150	0
ABS Consulting Inc		D	714 734-4242	0
Absg Consulting Inc		D	714 734-4242	0
Accretive Solutions Inc **(HQ)**		A	312 994-4600	0
Accurate Background LLC **(PA)**		B	800 784-3911	0
Ace Parking Management Inc		C	949 727-1470	0
Action Property Management Inc **(PA)**		D	949 450-0202	0
Activision Blizzard Inc		D	949 955-1380	0
Adams Streeter Civil Engineers		D	949 474-2330	0
Advantage Sales & Mktg Inc **(PA)**		C	949 797-2900	0
Advantage Sales & Mktg LLC **(HQ)**		C	949 797-2900	0
Agendia Inc		C	949 540-6300	0
Agility Holdings Inc **(DH)**		D	714 617-6300	0
Ahtna-CDM JV		E	714 824-3470	0
Ahtna-CDM Smith JV		D	714 824-3471	0
Aids Svcs Fndation Orange Cnty		D	949 809-5700	0
Albertsons LLC		B	949 855-2465	0
Alcone Marketing Group Inc **(HQ)**		D	949 595-5322	0
All Counties Courier Inc		C	714 599-9300	0
All Environmental Inc		D	949 752-9300	0
Allen Matkins Leck Gmble		D	949 553-1313	0
Alliance Healthcare Svcs Inc **(DH)**		C	949 242-5300	0
Alorica Inc **(PA)**		A	949 527-4600	0
Alphaeon Corporation **(HQ)**		D	949 284-4555	0
Alton Irvine Inc		D	949 428-4141	0
American Express Travel		D	949 453-7123	0
American Funds Service Company		E	949 975-5000	0
American Golf Corporation		C	949 786-1224	0
American Interbanc Mrtg LLC		E	714 957-9430	0
American Liberty Capital Corp		D	949 623-0288	0
American Medical Tech Inc		D	949 553-0359	0
Americor Funding Inc		C	866 333-8686	0
Ameripath Mortgage Corporation		C	949 753-9211	0
Ampronix Inc		D	949 273-8000	0
Ancca Corporation		D	949 553-0084	0
Anderson & Howard Electric Inc		C	949 250-4555	0
Andrew Lauren Company Inc		D	949 861-4222	0
Anduril Industries Inc **(PA)**		D	949 891-1607	0
Anheuser-Busch LLC		C	949 263-9270	0
Apex Parks Group LLC **(PA)**		C	949 349-8461	0
Applied Geokinetics		D	949 502-5353	0
Aptim Corp		D	949 261-6441	0
Arbitech LLC		D	949 376-6650	0
Arcules Inc		D	949 439-0053	0
Argent Management Co LLC		D	949 777-4070	0
Aria Group Incorporated		D	949 475-2915	0
Arthur J Gallagher & Co		E	949 349-9800	0
Artistic Maintenance Inc		C	949 733-8690	0
Ashley Home Care Services LLC		E	323 286-2831	0
Ashley Management Group		E	949 754-3120	0
Asics America Corporation **(HQ)**		C	949 453-8888	0
Aspect Software Inc		E	408 595-5002	0
Assi Security **(PA)**		D	949 955-0244	0

Name	SIC	EMP	PHONE	ENTRY #
AT&T Corp		D	949 559-1457	0
AT&T Corp		D	949 622-8240	0
AT&T Datacomm LLC		E	714 675-9752	0
Aten Technology Inc		D	949 428-1111	0
Atkinson Construction Inc		B	303 410-2540	0
Atlas Hospitality Group		D	949 622-3400	0
Atria Senior Living Inc		D	949 786-5665	0
Auctioncom Inc		C	800 499-6199	0
Auctioncom LLC **(PA)**		D	949 859-2777	0
Automatic Data Processing Inc		C	949 751-0360	0
Autoweb Inc **(PA)**		C	949 225-4500	0
Avalonbay Communities Inc		E	949 955-6200	0
Avaya Inc		C	949 225-5678	0
Avente Inc		E	844 385-1556	0
Avnet Inc		C	949 789-4100	0
Axiom Memory Solutions Inc		D	949 581-1450	0
Axonics Modulation Tech Inc		D	949 396-6322	0
Ayco Company LP		C	949 955-1544	0
Aztec Engineering Group Inc		D	951 471-6190	0
Balt USA LLC		D	949 788-1443	0
BDS Marketing LLC **(DH)**		C	800 234-4237	0
Beacon Resources LLC		E	949 955-1773	0
Bear Stearns Companies LLC		A	949 856-8300	0
Bergelectric Corp		D	949 250-7005	0
Berger Kahn **(PA)**		D	949 474-1880	0
Berkshire Mortgage Fin Corp		D	949 754-6300	0
Best Best & Krieger LLP		E	949 263-2600	0
Best Life and Health Insur Co		D	949 253-4080	0
Bgrs Relocation Inc **(DH)**		D	949 794-7900	0
Bigrentz Inc		D	855 999-5438	0
Black & Veatch Corporation		E	913 458-2000	0
Black Knght RE Data Sltons LLC **(DH)**		A	626 808-9000	0
Blb Resources Inc **(PA)**		C	949 261-9155	0
Blizzard Entertainment Inc **(HQ)**		D	949 955-1380	0
Bogart Construction Inc		D	949 453-1400	0
Bomel Construction Co Inc **(PA)**		D	714 921-1660	0
Brady Vorwerck Rydr & Cspno **(PA)**		D	480 456-9888	0
Brandrep LLC		E	800 405-7119	0
Brer Affiliates LLC **(DH)**		C	949 794-7900	0
Bridgwter Consulting Group Inc		D	949 535-1755	0
Brinderson LP **(HQ)**		C	714 466-7100	0
Brinderson LP		D	714 466-7100	0
Brooker Associates		D	949 559-4877	0
Brown and Streza LLP		D	949 453-2900	0
Bryan Cave Lighton Paisner LLP		D	949 223-7000	0
C T Corporation System		D	925 287-9801	0
Cal Southern Presbt Homes		C	949 854-9500	0
Calatlantic Group Inc		D	949 789-1600	0
Calatlantic Group Inc		D	949 789-1600	0
Calico Building Services Inc		C	949 380-8700	0
California First National Bank		D	949 255-0500	0
California Limousines		D	949 581-7531	0
California Pacific Homes Inc **(PA)**		D	949 833-6000	0
Cannon Cochran MGT Svcs Inc		D	949 474-6500	0
Canon USA Inc		B	949 753-4000	0
Cap Diagnostics LLC		D	714 966-1221	0
Cape Environmental MGT Inc		B	949 236-3000	0
Capital Group Companies Inc		B	949 975-5000	0
Capital Research and MGT Co		D	949 975-5000	0
Carfinance Capital LLC		A	888 227-9555	0
Carothers Dsnte Frdnberger LLP **(PA)**		D	949 622-1661	0
Carpenter Fund Manager Gp LLC		C	949 261-8888	0
CDM SMITH INC		D	949 752-5452	0
Cellco Partnership		A	949 286-7000	0
Center For Autism &		E	949 203-8872	0
Centex Homes Inc		C	949 453-0113	0
Cfp Fire Protection Inc		D	949 727-3277	0
Cgtech **(PA)**		E	949 753-1050	0
Chambers Group Inc		E	949 261-5414	0
Child Development Incorporated		A	949 854-5060	0
Childrens Hospital Orange Cnty		A	949 387-2586	0
Cie Digital Labs LLC **(PA)**		D	949 381-6200	0
Citigroup Global Markets Inc		D	949 955-7500	0
Citigroup Inc		D	949 726-5124	0
City of Irvine		D	949 724-7600	0
City of Irvine		D	949 724-7740	0
City of Irvine		D	949 724-7101	0
City of Irvine		D	949 724-6900	0
CK Franchising Inc **(DH)**		D	800 498-8144	0
Clark Cnstr Group-California		B	714 754-0764	0
Clark Cnstr Grup-California LP		B	714 429-9779	0
Clearpath Lending		C	949 502-3577	0
Cloudvirga Inc		D	949 662-2944	0
Coast To Coast Bus Eqp Inc **(PA)**		D	949 457-7300	0
Cofiroute Usa LLC		C	949 754-0198	0

Mergent email: customerrelations@mergent.com

1550

2020 Directory of California
Wholesalers and Services Companies

(P-0000) Products & Services Section entry number
(PA)=Parent Co (HQ)=Headquarters (DH)=Div Headquarters

	SIC	EMP	PHONE	ENTRY #
Commerce Velocity LLC		E	949 756-8950	0
Commercial Landscape Svc		D	949 660-8655	0
Commonwealth Equity Svcs LLP		D	949 336-6440	0
Commonwealth Land Title Co		D	949 460-4500	0
Connect Your Home LLC		D	949 777-0100	0
Connotate Technologies Inc		E	949 270-1916	0
Consoldted Fire Protection LLC (HQ)		A	949 727-3277	0
Consumer Portfolio Svcs Inc		C	949 788-5695	0
Consumer Portfolio Svcs Inc		D	949 753-6800	0
Contec Microelectronics USA		D	949 250-4025	0
Corelogic Inc		E	714 250-6400	0
Corelogic Credco LLC (HQ)		C	949 214-1000	0
Corner Products Company		D	800 876-8889	0
Corporate Risk Hldings III Inc		A	949 428-5839	0
Corvel Corporation (PA)		C	949 851-1473	0
Corvel Enterprise Comp Inc		C	949 851-1473	0
Council On Aging - S Cali Inc		D	714 479-0107	0
Courtney Inc (PA)		D	949 222-2050	0
Courtyard Management Corp		D	949 453-1033	0
Cox Communications		D	949 546-1000	0
Creative Maintenance Systems		D	949 852-2871	0
Crescent Staffing Inc (PA)		C	949 724-0304	0
Crestmont Capital LLC		C	800 949-0401	0
Crowell & Moring LLP		E	949 263-8400	0
Ctpartners Exec Search Inc		D	949 754-2821	0
Cushman & Wakefield Cal Inc		E	949 474-4004	0
Custom Business Solutions Inc (PA)		D	949 380-7674	0
Customer Srvc Dlvry Pltfrm Crp		E	717 896-8489	0
Cwpfl Inc		E	714 564-7900	0
Cybercoders Inc		C	949 885-5151	0
Cylance Inc (DH)		C	949 375-3380	0
D P S Inc		D	714 564-7900	0
Dal-Tile Corporation		D	949 260-0488	0
Database Marketing Group Inc		B	714 727-0800	0
Davita Inc		B	949 930-4400	0
Deacon Corp		D	949 222-9060	0
Decision Ready Solutions Inc		E	949 400-1126	0
Decision Toolbox Inc		D	562 377-5600	0
Delta Galil USA Inc		D	949 296-0380	0
Denken Solutions Inc		C	949 630-5263	0
Developers Surety Indemnity Co (DH)		D	949 263-3300	0
Dharne & Company		D	949 293-5675	0
Digital Map Products Inc		D	949 333-5111	0
Dkn Hotel LLC (PA)		B	714 427-4320	0
DOT Leasing Company		C	949 474-1100	0
Duke Energy Corporation		C	949 727-7434	0
Dyntek Inc (PA)		D	949 271-6700	0
Dzyne Technologies Inc		E	703 454-0704	0
Edison Capital		C	909 594-3789	0
Edwards Lifesciences LLC (HQ)		A	949 250-2500	0
Edwards Theatres Circuit Inc		A	949 854-8811	0
Egs Financial Care Inc (DH)		B	877 217-4423	0
Elevate Property Services LP		E	562 219-2101	0
Elite Security Services Inc		B	949 222-2203	0
Empcc Inc		D	714 564-7900	0
Eon Reality Inc (PA)		E	949 460-2000	0
Equinox-76th Street Inc		D	949 296-1700	0
Equinox-76th Street Inc		B	949 975-8400	0
Equistar Irvine Company LLC		B	949 833-3331	0
Ernst & Young LLP		B	949 794-2300	0
Ernst & Young LLP		C	949 838-3300	0
Es Engineering Inc		D	714 919-6500	0
Es Engineering Services LLC		D	949 988-3500	0
Essex Properties LLC		D	949 798-8100	0
European Hotl Invstrs of CA (PA)		D	949 474-7368	0
Eveg Inc		E	844 221-3359	0
Evisions Inc (PA)		D	949 833-1384	0
Eworkplace Solutions Inc		C	949 583-1646	0
Experian Info Solutions Inc		C	949 567-3731	0
Exult Inc		A	949 856-8800	0
F M Tarbell Co		D	949 559-8451	0
Fao ROC Holdings LLC		D	949 900-6501	0
Far West Management Corp (PA)		D	949 863-1757	0
Federal Express Corporation		B	800 463-3339	0
Federal Express Corporation		D	949 862-4500	0
Fedex Freight Corporation		D	800 706-1687	0
Fehr & Peers		D	949 308-6300	0
Festival Fun Parks LLC		D	949 559-8336	0
Ficcadenti Waggoner & Castle S (PA)		D	949 474-0502	0
Fieldstone Communities Inc (PA)		C	949 790-5400	0
Finance America LLC (HQ)		C	949 440-1000	0
First Amercn Prof RE Svcs Inc		C	714 250-1400	0
First Team RE - Orange Cnty (PA)		C	888 236-1943	0
Firstservice Residential (HQ)		C	949 448-6000	0
Fisher & Paykel Healthcare Inc		C	949 453-4000	0
Fisher & Phillips LLP		D	949 851-2424	0
Flagship Credit Acceptance LLC		C	949 748-7172	0
Fluor Enterprises Inc		D	949 349-2000	0
Fnc Inc		D	714 866-1099	0
Footh The / Easte Trans Corri		D	949 754-3400	0
Ford Motor Company		B	949 341-5800	0
Ford Motor Land Dev Corp		B	949 242-6606	0
Fostering Executive Leadership		D	949 651-6250	0
Foundation Lead Group LLC		D	877 477-2311	0
Fox Head Inc (PA)		C	888 369-7223	0
Fragomen Del Rey Bernse		D	949 660-3504	0
Francisco Emilio Assoc Law Off		D	949 474-2222	0
Frank D Yelian MD PC		E	949 788-1133	0
Full Circle Wireless Inc		E	949 783-7979	0
Fuscoe Engineering Inc (PA)		D	949 474-1960	0
GA Services LLC		E	949 752-6515	0
Gabe Inc		D	949 679-2727	0
Gallup Inc		E	949 474-2700	0
Gdr Group Inc		D	949 453-8818	0
Genea Energy Partners Inc		D	714 694-0536	0
General Electric Company		C	949 838-3043	0
General Tool Inc		D	949 261-2322	0
Georg Fischer LLC (DH)		D	714 731-8800	0
Getac Inc		D	949 681-2900	0
Ghost Management Group LLC		C	949 870-1400	0
Gibson Dunn & Crutcher LLP		C	949 451-3800	0
Gkk Corporation (PA)		D	949 250-1500	0
Global Debt Management LLC (PA)		D	949 825-7800	0
Global Eagle Entertainment Inc		C	949 608-8700	0
Global Language Solutions LLC		D	949 798-1400	0
Glovis America Inc (HQ)		D	714 435-2960	0
Go2 Systems Inc		D	949 553-0800	0
Golden Hotels Ltd Partnership		C	949 833-2770	0
Goodman North America LLC		D	949 407-0100	0
Gordian Medical Inc		B	714 556-0200	0
Gordon Rees Scully Mansukhani		D	949 255-6950	0
Gradient Engineers Inc		D	949 477-0555	0
Greenberg Traurig LLP		D	949 732-6500	0
Greens Group Inc		D	949 829-4902	0
Griffin Technology LLC (HQ)		D	949 250-4929	0
Hallmark Rehabilitation GP LLC		A	949 282-5900	0
Hardesty LLC (PA)		E	949 407-6625	0
Harmony Escrow Inc		D	949 474-1134	0
Harris & Associates Inc		D	949 655-3900	0
HDR Engineering Inc		C	714 730-2300	0
Healthcare MGT Partners LLC		B	949 263-8620	0
Healthpeak Properties Inc (PA)		D	949 407-0700	0
Healthquest Laboratories Inc (PA)		D	714 418-5867	0
Hensel Phelps Construction Co		C	949 852-0111	0
Heritage Indemnity Company		D	303 987-5500	0
Hireright LLC (HQ)		C	949 428-5800	0
Holthouse Carlin Van Trigt LLP		D	714 361-7600	0
Home Franchise Concepts LLC (PA)		D	949 404-1100	0
Horiba Americas Holding Inc (HQ)		A	949 250-4811	0
HPM Construction LLC		D	949 474-9170	0
Huitt - Zollars Inc		E	949 988-5815	0
Human Options Inc (PA)		D	949 737-5242	0
Hunsaker & Assoc Irvine Inc (PA)		D	949 583-1010	0
Hwmm (HQ)		D	949 581-1144	0
Hyatt Corporation		B	949 975-1234	0
Hyland Software Inc		D	949 242-3100	0
Hyundai Capital America (DH)		D	714 965-3000	0
Icat Logistics Inc		D	310 884-5923	0
Icf Jones & Stokes Inc		D	949 333-6600	0
Idexx Reference Labs Inc		E	949 477-2840	0
Ignite Health LLC (PA)		C	949 862-3200	0
Illuminate Education Inc (PA)		D	949 656-3133	0
Impac Mortgage Corp		B	949 475-3600	0
Impac Mortgage Holdings Inc (PA)		A	949 475-3600	0
Impac Secured Assets Corp		C	949 475-3600	0
Indemnity Company California (DH)		D	949 263-3300	0
Ingram Micro Inc (HQ)		A	714 566-1000	0
Inhouseit Inc		D	949 660-5655	0
Insituform Technologies LLC		E	714 724-2324	0
Integrus LLC		D	714 547-9500	0
Interactive Media Holdings (DH)		D	949 861-8888	0
Intercontinental Hotels Group		C	949 863-1999	0
Intercontinental Hotels Group		D	949 863-1999	0
Interior Office Solutions Inc (PA)		E	949 724-9444	0
International Toy Inc		E	949 333-3777	0
Interstate Hotels Resorts Inc		C	949 833-9999	0
Interwall Dev Systems Inc		D	949 553-9102	0
Intratek Computer Inc		C	949 334-4200	0
Ipass Inc		D	650 232-4100	0
Irvine APT Communities LP (HQ)		C	949 720-5600	0

Employment Codes: A=Over 500 employees, B=251-500,
C=101-250, D=51-100, E=50

2020 Directory of California
Wholesalers and Services Companies

© Mergent Inc. 1-800-342-5647

1551

	SIC	EMP	PHONE	ENTRY #
Irvine Company LLC		D	949 653-5300	0
Irvine Ranch Water District **(PA)**		C	949 453-5300	0
Irvine Ranch Water District		C	949 453-5300	0
Irvine Technology Corporation		C	714 445-2624	0
Irvine Unified School Distict		D	949 936-5300	0
Irvine Valencia Growers		D	949 936-8000	0
Isotis Orthobiologics Inc		C	949 595-8710	0
Ixos Software Inc **(PA)**		D	949 784-8000	0
J Baron Inc		D	949 451-1200	0
J5 Infrastructure Partners LLC		D	949 299-5258	0
Jackson Demarco Tidus Peter **(PA)**		D	949 752-8585	0
Jacobs Engineering Group Inc		D	949 224-7585	0
Jacobs Project Management Co		D	949 224-7695	0
Jacobus Consulting Inc		E	949 727-0720	0
James R Glidewell Dental		A	800 411-9723	0
Jeff Tracy Inc		E	949 582-0877	0
Jelight Company Inc		D	949 380-8774	0
Jet Health Inc **(PA)**		A	949 356-6525	0
Jetsuite **(PA)**		D	949 892-4300	0
JF Shea Construction Inc		D	949 526-8792	0
Jnr Inc		D	949 476-2788	0
Johnson Cntrls SEC Sltions LLC		C	714 223-2300	0
Jones Day Limited Partnership		D	949 851-3939	0
Jones Lang Lsalle Americas Inc		D	949 296-3600	0
Jonset Corporation		D	949 551-5151	0
K Hovnanian Companies Cal Inc **(HQ)**		D	714 368-4500	0
Kaiser Foundation Hospitals		C	949 262-5780	0
Kaiser Foundation Hospitals		B	949 932-5000	0
Kasdan Smnds Riley Vaughan LLP **(PA)**		D	949 851-9000	0
Keating Dental Arts Inc		C	949 955-2100	0
Keystone PCF Property MGT Inc **(PA)**		D	949 833-2600	0
Kieckhafer Schiffer & Co LLP **(PA)**		E	949 250-3900	0
Kite Electric Inc		C	949 380-7471	0
Knobbe Martens Olson Bear LLP **(PA)**		B	949 760-0404	0
Koeller Nbker Crlson Hluck LLP **(PA)**		C	949 864-3400	0
Kofax Inc **(PA)**		B	949 783-1000	0
Kore1 Inc		D	949 706-6990	0
Kronos Incorporated		D	800 580-7374	0
Ktgy Group Inc **(PA)**		D	949 851-2133	0
L S A Associates Inc **(PA)**		D	949 553-0666	0
La Jolla Group Inc **(PA)**		D	949 428-2800	0
Landmark Event Staffing		A	714 293-4248	0
Lawyers Title Insurance Corp		D	949 223-5575	0
Lba Inc **(PA)**		D	949 833-0400	0
Lba Realty Fund III - III LLC		D	949 833-0400	0
Lba Realty LLC **(PA)**		E	949 833-0400	0
Lba Rlty Fund I-Company IV LLC		D	949 955-9321	0
Lee & Associates Coml RE Svcs **(PA)**		E	949 727-1200	0
Legacy Prtners Residential Inc		B	949 930-6600	0
Leighton and Associates Inc **(PA)**		D	949 250-1421	0
Lennar Corporation		D	949 349-8000	0
Lennar Homes California Inc **(DH)**		C	949 349-8000	0
Liberty Dental Plan Cal Inc		B	949 223-0007	0
Liberty Dental Plan Nevada Inc		D	888 703-6999	0
Lineage Logistics Holdings LLC **(PA)**		C	800 678-7271	0
Linksys LLC **(DH)**		B	949 270-8500	0
Livescribe Inc		E	503 290-4029	0
LLP Moss Adams		E	949 221-4000	0
Loan Administration Netwrk Inc		D	949 752-5246	0
Local Corporation **(PA)**		D	949 784-0800	0
LPA Inc **(PA)**		C	949 261-1001	0
Luther Burbank Corporation		D	949 428-8043	0
M F Salta Co Inc **(PA)**		D	562 421-2512	0
Malcolm & Cisneros A Law Corp		C	949 252-1039	0
Managed Homecare Inc		E	951 341-0782	0
Marriott International Inc		B	949 724-3606	0
Maruchan Inc		D	949 789-2300	0
Mazda Research & Dev of N Amer		D	949 852-8898	0
MBK Real Estate Companies		E	949 789-8300	0
MBK Real Estate Ltd A Calfor **(HQ)**		D	949 789-8300	0
McDermott Will & Emery LLP		D	949 757-7165	0
McKinley Equipment Corporation **(PA)**		D	800 770-6094	0
McLane Foodservice Dist Inc		D	714 863-0163	0
Mds Consulting **(PA)**		D	949 251-8821	0
Mechanics Bank		B	855 272-2886	0
Medata Inc **(PA)**		D	714 918-1310	0
Medterra Cbd LLC		D	800 971-1288	0
Mercer (us) Inc		D	949 222-1300	0
Merchsource LLC **(PA)**		D	800 374-2744	0
Merrill Lynch Pierce Fenner		D	949 859-2900	0
Mesa Energy Systems Inc **(HQ)**		C	949 460-0460	0
Mesa Properties GP		D	949 857-1905	0
Mhh Holdings Inc		C	949 651-9903	0
Michael Madden Co Inc		D	800 834-6248	0
Microsoft Corporation		C	949 263-3000	0

	SIC	EMP	PHONE	ENTRY #
Mind Research Institute		C	949 345-8700	0
Mirion Technologies Gds Inc **(HQ)**		C	949 419-1000	0
Mission Energy Holding Company		A	949 752-5588	0
Mission Hills Mortgage Corp **(HQ)**		C	714 972-3832	0
Mjp Empire Inc **(PA)**		B	714 564-7900	0
Mobilenet Services Inc **(PA)**		C	949 951-4444	0
Mobilityware LLC **(PA)**		D	949 788-9900	0
Monarch Healthcare A Medical **(HQ)**		D	949 923-3200	0
Montage Hotels & Resorts LLC **(PA)**		A	949 715-5002	0
Montrose Envmtl Group Inc **(PA)**		D	949 988-3500	0
Montrose Water and Sustainabil		D	949 988-3500	0
Morgan Stanley		C	949 809-1200	0
Mtc Financial Inc		E	949 252-8300	0
Murtaugh Myer Nlson Trglia LLP		D	949 794-4000	0
Mve + Partners Inc **(PA)**		D	949 809-3388	0
N2 Acquisition Company Inc		D	714 942-3563	0
Nationwide Funding LLC		E	949 679-3600	0
Netapp Inc		C	949 754-6600	0
Neudesic LLC **(PA)**		C	949 754-4500	0
Neuintel LLC **(PA)**		D	949 625-6117	0
New First Fincl Resources LLC		C	949 223-2160	0
New Vista Behavioral Hlth LLC		D	949 284-0095	0
New York Life Insurance Co		D	949 797-2400	0
Newport Meat Southern Cal Inc		C	949 399-4200	0
Newport Pacific Capital Co Inc **(PA)**		C	949 852-5575	0
Newton Softed Inc		E	949 396-6192	0
Nexgenix Inc **(PA)**		B	714 665-6240	0
Nextgen Healthcare Inc **(PA)**		D	949 255-2600	0
Nextgen Healthcare Info System **(HQ)**		D	949 255-2600	0
Nihon Kohden America Inc **(HQ)**		D	949 580-1555	0
Nikken Global Inc **(HQ)**		D	949 789-2000	0
Ninyo & Moore Geotechnical		D	949 753-7070	0
Nitto Avecia Pharma Svcs Inc **(DH)**		C	949 951-4425	0
Nnn Realty Investors LLC		B	714 667-8252	0
North Amercn Science Assoc Inc		D	949 951-3110	0
Northstar Technology Corp **(PA)**		C	949 788-0738	0
Nossaman LLP		E	949 833-7800	0
Novare Nat Settlement Svc LLC		E	714 352-4088	0
NRLL LLC		E	949 768-7777	0
Nrp Holding Co Inc **(PA)**		C	949 583-1000	0
Ntrust Infotech Inc		D	562 207-1600	0
NW Manor Community Partners LP		D	714 662-5565	0
Ocmbc Inc		D	714 479-0999	0
One 3 Two Inc		C	949 596-8400	0
Operation Technology Inc **(PA)**		D	949 462-0100	0
Optima Mortgage Corporation		D	714 389-4650	0
Optumrx Inc **(DH)**		B	714 825-3600	0
Ora Pacific Regional Field Off		D	949 608-2907	0
Oracle Corp		A	650 506-7000	0
Oracle Systems Corporation		D	949 224-1000	0
Oracle Systems Corporation		B	949 623-9460	0
Orange County Produce LLC		D	949 451-0880	0
Orangepeople LLC		D	949 535-1308	0
Orchard Holdings Group Inc		C	949 502-8300	0
Ortiz Enterprises Incorporated **(PA)**		D	949 753-1414	0
OSI Digital Inc		E	949 724-8300	0
Owl Companies **(PA)**		A	949 797-2000	0
Owl Education and Training		A	949 797-2000	0
Pacific Dental Services LLC **(PA)**		B	714 845-8500	0
Pacific Pharma Inc		A	714 246-4600	0
Pacific Premier Bank **(HQ)**		C	714 431-4000	0
Pacific Symphony		D	714 755-5788	0
Paciolan LLC **(DH)**		D	866 722-4652	0
Palumbo Lawyers LLP **(PA)**		D	949 442-0300	0
Pan American Bank Fsb		B	949 224-1917	0
Panattoni Development Co Inc **(PA)**		D	916 381-1561	0
Paramount Equity Mortgage LLC		C	916 290-9999	0
Park Hotels & Resorts Inc		C	949 553-8332	0
Passco Companies LLC **(PA)**		D	949 442-1000	0
Pathway Capital Management LP **(PA)**		D	949 622-1000	0
Patric Communications Inc **(PA)**		C	619 579-2898	0
Patron Solutions LLC		C	949 823-1700	0
Payne & Fears LLP **(PA)**		D	949 851-1101	0
Pennymac Financial Svcs Inc		A	949 341-0020	0
Pension Administrators Inc **(PA)**		C	949 253-4080	0
Peoples Choice Home **(PA)**		D	949 494-6167	0
Philips Medical Systems Clevel		D	949 699-2300	0
Physician Weblink of Cal **(HQ)**		D	949 923-3201	0
Post Modern Edit LLC **(PA)**		D	949 608-8700	0
Precept Inc **(DH)**		D	949 955-1430	0
Prelude Systems Inc		D	949 208-7126	0
Premier Office Centers LLC **(PA)**		E	949 253-4616	0
Pricewaterhousecoopers LLP		B	949 437-5200	0
Primecare Quality HM Care Inc		D	949 681-3515	0
Projections Unlimited Inc **(PA)**		E	714 544-2700	0

Mergent email: customerrelations@mergent.com

1552

2020 Directory of California
Wholesalers and Services Companies

(P-0000) Products & Services Section entry number
(PA)=Parent Co (HQ)=Headquarters (DH)=Div Headquarters

	SIC	EMP	PHONE	ENTRY #
Proove Medical Labs Inc		C	949 427-5303	0
Propath Inc		E	949 341-8000	0
Prudential Insur Co of Amer		E	949 440-5300	0
Prudential Overall Supply (PA)		D	949 250-4855	0
Pts Advance		C	949 268-4000	0
Quadion LLC		A	714 546-0994	0
Quest Group (PA)		D	949 585-0111	0
Quest Intl Monitor Svc Inc (PA)		D	949 581-9900	0
R & K Interests Inc (PA)		D	949 900-6160	0
Racquet Club of Irvine		D	949 786-3000	0
Railpros Inc (PA)		D	714 734-8765	0
Railpros Field Services		E	877 315-0513	0
Ramboll Environ US Corporation		D	949 261-5151	0
Ramboll US Corporation		E	949 798-3604	0
Rand Technology LLC (PA)		D	949 255-5700	0
Ranscapes Inc		E	866 883-9297	0
Redhill Group Inc		D	949 752-5900	0
Rels LLC		A	949 214-1000	0
Renal Treatment Ctrs - Cal Inc		D	949 930-6882	0
Renovo Solutions LLC		B	714 599-7969	0
Renwood Realtytrac LLC (PA)		D	949 502-8300	0
Residence Mutual Insurance Co		D	949 724-9402	0
Residnce Inn By Mrriott Irvine		D	949 380-3000	0
Resolve Systems LLC (PA)		D	949 325-0120	0
Resources Connection Inc (PA)		A	714 430-6400	0
Resources Connection LLC (HQ)		D	714 430-6400	0
Result Group Inc		D	480 777-7130	0
Ricoh Usa Inc		D	949 225-2300	0
Rimrock High Income Plus Fund		E	949 381-7800	0
Robert Half International Inc.		D	949 476-3199	0
Robert Kinsella Inc		D	949 453-9533	0
Rockefeller Group Dev Corp		D	949 468-1800	0
Roland Dga Corporation (HQ)		C	949 727-2100	0
Rose International Inc.		E	636 812-4000	0
RSM US LLP		D	949 255-6500	0
Rushmore Loan MGT Svcs LLC (PA)		A	949 727-4798	0
Ryland Homes of Texas Inc		C	805 367-3800	0
S E O P Inc		C	949 682-7906	0
S K & A Information Svcs Inc (DH)		D	949 476-2051	0
S W P T X Inc		C	714 564-7900	0
Safe-Guard Products Intl LLC		D	800 742-7896	0
Sage Software Inc		D	949 753-1222	0
Sage Software Holdings Inc (HQ)		B	866 530-7243	0
San Joaquin Hills Transprttn (PA)		D	949 754-3400	0
Sand Canyon Corporation (HQ)		D	949 727-9425	0
Sand Canyon LLC		D	949 551-2560	0
Savala Equipment Company Inc (PA)		D	949 552-1859	0
Savoy Contractors Group Inc		C	949 753-1919	0
SBE Contracting		E	714 544-5066	0
Sea Breeze Financial Services (PA)		E	949 223-9700	0
Sean P OConnor		D	949 851-7323	0
Second Harvest Food		D	949 653-2900	0
Secureauth Corporation (PA)		D	949 777-6959	0
Sema Inc (PA)		D	949 830-1400	0
Sema Construction Inc		D	949 330-4300	0
Sentinel Monitoring Corp (HQ)		C	949 453-1550	0
Seven Resorts Inc (PA)		B	949 588-7100	0
Sfn Group Inc		D	949 727-8500	0
Shady Canyon Golf Club Inc		D	949 856-7000	0
Shiftpixy Inc		D	949 207-7184	0
Shimano North Amer Holdg Inc (HQ)		C	949 951-5003	0
Shoffeitt Pipeline Inc		D	949 581-1600	0
Signature Resources Insurance		D	949 930-2400	0
Silverado Energy Company		B	949 752-5588	0
Silverado Senior Living Inc (PA)		D	949 240-7200	0
Silverado Senior Living Holdin		A	949 240-7200	0
Singerlewak LLP		D	949 261-8600	0
Sitelite Holdings Inc		C	949 265-6200	0
Smart Energy Systems LLC (PA)		C	909 703-9609	0
Smart Energy Systems LLC		C	909 703-9609	0
Smart Systems Technologies (PA)		D	949 367-9375	0
SMC Networks Inc (HQ)		D	949 679-8029	0
Smile Brands Group Inc (PA)		D	714 668-1300	0
Snyder Langston L P		D	949 863-9200	0
Sony Electronics Inc		C	714 508-7634	0
Southern Cal Prmnnte Med Group		D	949 262-5780	0
Southern California Edison Co		C	949 587-5416	0
Southern Implants Inc		D	949 273-8505	0
Specialty Surgical Centers		E	949 341-3499	0
Spectrum Hotel Group LLC		D	949 471-8888	0
Spectrum Hotel Group LLC		D	949 471-8888	0
Spectrum Information Svcs LLC (PA)		D	949 752-7070	0
Sph-Irvine LLC.		E	949 833-1432	0
Spireon Inc (PA)		C	800 557-1449	0
Sprint Corporation		B	949 748-3353	0
Squar Milner Peterson (PA)		C	949 222-2999	0
St Andrews Children Center		E	949 651-0198	0
Stantec Arch & Engrg PC		C	949 923-6000	0
Stantec Architecture Inc		C	949 923-6000	0
Stantec Consulting Svcs Inc		C	949 923-6000	0
Startel Corporation		D	949 863-8700	0
State Group LLC		B	949 612-2879	0
Stratacare Llc		C	949 743-1200	0
Strategic Financial Group		E	949 622-7200	0
Strategy Companion Corp		D	714 460-8398	0
Stratham Homes Inc		D	949 833-1554	0
Strawberry Farms Golf Club LLC		D	949 551-2560	0
Stretto (PA)		D	949 222-1212	0
Student Government Associat		C	949 824-5547	0
Student Works Painting Inc		B	714 564-7900	0
Stussy Inc		D	949 474-9255	0
Sullivancurtismonroe Insurance (PA)		C	800 427-3253	0
Sun Ten Labs Liquidation Co		D	949 587-0509	0
Sunscape Eyewear Inc		D	949 553-0590	0
Sunstone Center Crt Lessee Inc		C	949 382-4000	0
Sunstone Hotel Investors LLC (PA)		D	949 330-4000	0
Sunstone Ocean Lessee Inc		B	949 382-4000	0
Sunwest Bank (DH)		E	714 730-4441	0
Synoptek Inc (PA)		D	949 241-8600	0
Syntiro Healthcare Services (PA)		C	949 923-3438	0
Tanaka Farms		C	949 653-2100	0
Tantra Lake Partners LP		C	949 756-5959	0
Tax Rise Inc		D	877 697-4732	0
Taylor & Assoc Architects Inc (PA)		E	949 574-1325	0
Taylor Morrison California LLC		C	949 341-1200	0
Tcg Software Services Inc		E	714 665-6200	0
Team Post-Op Inc (DH)		D	949 253-5500	0
Temporary Staffing Union		A	714 728-5186	0
Testamerica Laboratories Inc		C	949 261-1022	0
Tetra Tech Inc		D	949 263-0846	0
Tetra Tech Inc		D	949 809-5000	0
Texxis Limited		D	213 631-3547	0
Thomas Gallaway Corporation (PA)		D	949 716-9500	0
Tonner Hills Hsing Partners LP		E	949 263-8676	0
Toshiba Bus Solutions USA Inc (DH)		C	949 462-6000	0
Toshiba Education Center		C	949 583-3000	0
Total Renal Care Inc		D	949 930-6882	0
Trace3 LLC (PA)		D	949 333-2300	0
Tradesmen International LLC		D	949 588-3280	0
TRC Solutions Inc (DH)		C	949 753-0101	0
Tressler LLP		D	949 336-1200	0
Tri Pointe Group Inc (PA)		D	949 438-1400	0
Tri Pointe Homes Inc (HQ)		C	949 438-1400	0
Trimark Raygal LLC		C	949 474-1000	0
True Air Mechanical Inc		C	888 316-0642	0
Truesdail Laboratories Inc		E	714 730-6239	0
Turner Techtronics Inc		C	949 724-1339	0
TW Security Corp (DH)		C	949 932-1000	0
Tyler Palmieri Wiener		D	949 851-9400	0
Uniglobe Travel West Inc (PA)		D	949 623-9000	0
Unisys Corporation		A	949 380-5000	0
United Agribusiness League (PA)		E	800 223-4590	0
United Cerebral Palsy Assoc		C	949 333-6400	0
Universal Card Inc		B	949 861-4000	0
Universal Care Inc (PA)		B	562 424-6200	0
University California Irvine		D	949 824-2819	0
Upstanding LLC		C	949 788-9900	0
US Best Repair Service Inc.		C	888 750-2378	0
US Investigations Services LLC (HQ)		A	724 458-1750	0
USI South Coast		D	949 790-9200	0
V G Carelli International Corp.		E	310 247-8410	0
Vegatek Corporation		D	949 502-0090	0
Velapoint LLC		D	877 434-1904	0
Velocitel Rf Inc		C	949 809-4999	0
Velocity Tech Solutions Inc		D	949 417-0260	0
Venture Pacific Tools Inc		D	949 475-5505	0
Veritxt/Clfornia Reporting LLC		E	714 432-1711	0
Verizon Wireless (PA)		E	949 286-7000	0
Viant Technology LLC (DH)		C	949 861-8888	0
Victory Foam Inc (PA)		D	949 474-0690	0
Villa Balboa Community Assoc		D	949 450-1515	0
Vinculums Services Inc		C	949 783-3552	0
Vision Solutions Inc (PA)		D	949 253-6500	0
Vision Solutions Inc.		D	949 253-6500	0
Voit Development Manager Inc		D	949 851-5110	0
Vpm Management Inc		C	949 863-1500	0
W Brown & Assc Property & Csu		D	949 851-2060	0
Ware Malcomb (PA)		D	949 660-9128	0
Warmington Homes		D	949 679-3100	0
Warrior Custom Golf Inc (PA)		C	949 699-2499	0

Employment Codes: A=Over 500 employees, B=251-500,
C=101-250, D=51-100, E=50

2020 Directory of California
Wholesalers and Services Companies

© Mergent Inc. 1-800-342-5647

1553

G
E
O
G
R
A
P
H
I
C

	SIC	EMP	PHONE	ENTRY #
Waste MGT Collectn Recycl Inc		D	949 451-2600	0
WD Partners Inc		E	949 753-7676	0
West Coast Consulting LLC		C	949 250-4102	0
Western Alliance Bank		D	949 222-0855	0
Western Growers Association (PA)		C	949 863-1000	0
Western Medical Management LLC		E	949 260-6575	0
Western Mutual Insurance Co (PA)		D	949 724-9402	0
Western National Contractors		D	949 862-6200	0
Western National Properties (PA)		D	949 862-6200	0
Western National Securities (PA)		C	949 862-6200	0
Western United Insurance Co		C	800 959-9842	0
Westwind Manor Resort Assn		D	214 618-7200	0
Whiting-Turner Contracting Co		E	949 863-0800	0
Wimberly Allison Tong Goo Inc		D	949 574-8500	0
Wnc Housing LP		E	714 662-5565	0
Wolf Firm A Law Corporation		D	949 720-9200	0
Woodbridge Village Association		D	949 786-1800	0
Worley Field Services Inc		C	949 224-7585	0
Wyndham Irvine Orange		D	949 863-1999	0
Wynne Systems Inc (DH)		D	949 224-6300	0
Xavor Corporation		D	949 529-7372	0
Zieve Brodnax & Steele LLP (PA)		C	714 848-7920	0
Zippy Usa Inc		D	949 366-9525	0
Zymo Research Corp (PA)		D	949 679-1190	0

IRWINDALE, CA - Los Angeles County

	SIC	EMP	PHONE	ENTRY #
Agritec International Ltd		E	626 812-7200	0
American Med		B	626 633-4600	0
AP Express LLC		D	562 236-2250	0
Arminak & Associates LLC		C	626 358-4804	0
Best Overnite Express Inc (PA)		C	626 256-6340	0
Brightview Companies LLC		C	626 574-3940	0
Calibre International LLC (PA)		C	626 969-4660	0
Central Garden & Pet Company		D	626 334-9301	0
Church & Larsen Inc		C	626 303-8741	0
Ds Services of America Inc		C	626 472-7201	0
East San Gbriel Vly Consortium		D	626 960-3964	0
Eggleston Youth Centers Inc (PA)		D	626 480-8107	0
Essilor Laboratories Amer Inc		D	626 969-6181	0
Health Valley Foods Inc		B	626 334-3241	0
Mariposa Landscapes Inc (PA)		D	626 960-0196	0
Metro One Telecom Inc		C	626 337-8100	0
Mountain Gear Corporation		C	626 851-2488	0
Neovia Logistics Dist LP		C	626 359-4500	0
Pacific Wine Distributors Inc		D	626 471-9997	0
Phfe Wic Program		C	626 856-6650	0
Pierre Landscape Inc		C	626 587-2121	0
Public Hlth Fndation Entps Inc		C	626 856-6600	0
Service Solutions Group LLC		D	626 960-9390	0
Sinecera Inc		C	626 962-1087	0
Southern California Edison Co		C	626 543-8081	0
Southern California Edison Co		E	626 815-7296	0
Southern California Edison Co		C	626 633-3070	0
Southern California Edison Co		D	626 814-4212	0
Superior Communications Inc (PA)		C	877 522-4727	0
United Site Services Cal Inc (PA)		D	626 462-9110	0
Velocious Technologies Inc		D	650 434-7118	0
Western Paving Contractors Inc		D	626 338-7889	0
Wor International Inc		E	626 812-8888	0

ISLETON, CA - Sacramento County

	SIC	EMP	PHONE	ENTRY #
Kay Dix Inc		E	916 776-1701	0

IVANHOE, CA - Tulare County

	SIC	EMP	PHONE	ENTRY #
Family Healthcare Network		C	559 798-1877	0
Klink Citrus Association		C	559 798-1881	0

JACKSON, CA - Amador County

	SIC	EMP	PHONE	ENTRY #
Amador Tlmne Cmnty Action Agcy (PA)		C	209 296-2785	0
Amador-Tolumne Cmnty Resources		D	209 223-1485	0
AT&T Services Inc		D	209 223-0012	0
Farms of Amador		D	209 257-0112	0
Sita Ram LLC		D	209 223-0211	0
Sutter Health		C	209 223-5445	0
Sutter Hlth Scrmnto Sierra Reg		A	209 223-7540	0
Sutter Valley Hospitals (HQ)		B	209 223-7500	0
Tutera Group Inc		D	209 223-2231	0
Xp Power LLC		D	209 267-1630	0

JAMESTOWN, CA - Tuolumne County

	SIC	EMP	PHONE	ENTRY #
Chicken Ranch Bingo & Casino		C	209 984-3000	0
Condor Earth Technologies Inc		D	209 984-4593	0
Diestel Turkey Ranch		C	209 984-0826	0

JAMUL, CA - San Diego County

	SIC	EMP	PHONE	ENTRY #
Poltex Company Inc		D	619 669-1846	0
Spectrum Security Services Inc (PA)		C	619 669-6660	0

	SIC	EMP	PHONE	ENTRY #
Steele Canyon Golf Club Corp (PA)		D	619 441-6900	0

JULIAN, CA - San Diego County

	SIC	EMP	PHONE	ENTRY #
Borrego Cmnty Hlth Foundation		C	760 765-1223	0
YMCA of San Diego County		E	760 765-0642	0

JURUPA VALLEY, CA - Riverside County

	SIC	EMP	PHONE	ENTRY #
Adesa Corporation LLC		E	951 361-9400	0
Big League Dreams Jurupa LLC		D	951 685-6900	0
C P S Express (HQ)		D	951 685-1041	0
Ceva Logistics US Inc		E	951 332-3202	0
Charles Komar & Sons Inc		B	951 934-1377	0
Complete Food Service Inc		D	951 685-8490	0
Costco Wholesale Corporation		B	951 361-3606	0
Deluxe Auto Carriers Inc		D	909 746-0900	0
Galassos Bakery (PA)		C	951 360-1211	0
Geodis Logistics LLC		D	951 571-2481	0
Hino Motors Mfg USA Inc		C	951 727-0286	0
Home Depot USA Inc		C	951 361-1235	0
J G Haddy Sales Co Inc (PA)		C	951 685-4100	0
Knight-Swift Trnsp Hldings Inc		D	951 360-0130	0
Le Vecke Corporation (PA)		D	951 681-8600	0
Lineage Logistics LLC		E	951 360-7970	0
Olivet International Inc (PA)		D	951 681-8888	0
Optimum Con Fundations USA Inc		D	877 212-7994	0
Pavement Recycling Systems Inc (PA)		C	951 682-1091	0
Professional Cabinet Solutions		C	909 614-2900	0
S P Richards Company		D	951 681-3114	0
Time and Alarm Systems (PA)		D	951 685-1761	0
Toll Global Fwdg Scs USA Inc		D	951 360-8310	0
Total Trnsp Logistics Inc		D	951 360-9521	0
Triways Inc		D	951 361-4840	0
Ttx Company		B	951 685-0158	0

KEENE, CA - Kern County

	SIC	EMP	PHONE	ENTRY #
United Farm Workers America (PA)		C	661 822-5571	0

KELSEY, CA - El Dorado County

	SIC	EMP	PHONE	ENTRY #
California Teachers Assn		D	530 622-8013	0
Califrnia Frnsic Med Group Inc		D	530 573-3035	0

KELSEYVILLE, CA - Lake County

	SIC	EMP	PHONE	ENTRY #
BT Holdings Inc		E	707 279-4317	0

KENTFIELD, CA - Marin County

	SIC	EMP	PHONE	ENTRY #
1125 Sir Francis Drake Bouleva		C	415 456-9680	0
Marin General Hospital		A	415 925-7000	0

KENWOOD, CA - Sonoma County

	SIC	EMP	PHONE	ENTRY #
Arthur Kunde & Sons Inc		E	707 833-5501	0
Dirt Farmer & Co Inc		D	707 833-2054	0
Palo Alto Vineyard MGT LLC		D	707 996-7725	0

KERMAN, CA - Fresno County

	SIC	EMP	PHONE	ENTRY #
Acemi Nursery Inc		D	559 842-7766	0
Hall AG Enterprises Inc		C	559 846-7360	0
Hall Management Corp		A	559 846-7382	0
Kerman Telephone Co		D	559 846-4954	0
Kermantelnet Internet Service		D	559 842-2223	0
Sebastian Enterprises Inc (PA)		D	559 946-4954	0

KERNVILLE, CA - Kern County

	SIC	EMP	PHONE	ENTRY #
Eagle Rafting		C	760 376-3648	0

KETTLEMAN CITY, CA - Kings County

	SIC	EMP	PHONE	ENTRY #
Chemical Waste Management Inc		D	559 386-9711	0
Keenan Farms Inc		D	559 945-1400	0

KEYES, CA - Stanislaus County

	SIC	EMP	PHONE	ENTRY #
A L Gilbert Company		D	209 537-0766	0

KING CITY, CA - Monterey County

	SIC	EMP	PHONE	ENTRY #
Anthony Harvesting Inc		C	831 385-6460	0
El Camino Labor LLC		D	831 809-9537	0
Fresh Farms Inc		E	831 385-3285	0
L A Hearne Company (PA)		D	831 385-5441	0
Rava Ranches Inc		E	831 385-3285	0
San Bernabe Vineyards		D	831 385-4897	0
Southern Mntrey Cnty Mem Hosp (PA)		B	831 385-6000	0

KINGS BEACH, CA - Placer County

	SIC	EMP	PHONE	ENTRY #
Robert Morken Construction		E	530 386-1512	0

KINGS CANYON NATIONA, CA - Tulare County

	SIC	EMP	PHONE	ENTRY #
Montecito Sequoia Inc		D	559 565-3388	0

KINGSBURG, CA - Fresno County

	SIC	EMP	PHONE	ENTRY #
Cheema Logistics		D	559 702-1444	0
Design Machine and Mfg		E	559 897-7374	0
Enns Packing Company Inc		E	559 897-7700	0
Jeff W Boldt Farms		D	559 318-6690	0

Mergent email: customerrelations@mergent.com
1554

2020 Directory of California
Wholesalers and Services Companies

(P-0000) Products & Services Section entry number
(PA)=Parent Co (HQ)=Headquarters (DH)=Div Headquarters

	SIC	EMP	PHONE	ENTRY #
Kingsburg Apple Packers Inc		B	559 897-5132	0
Kingsburg Apple Partners LP		D	559 897-5132	0
Mike Jensen Farms		C	559 897-4192	0
Peterson Family Inc		D	559 897-5064	0
Sun-Maid Growers California (PA)		A	559 897-6235	0
Sun-Maid Growers California		B	559 897-8900	0
Sunbridge Care Entps W Inc		D	559 897-5881	0
Sunbridge Care Entps W LLC		D	559 897-5881	0
Van Beurden Insurance Svcs Inc (PA)		D	559 634-7125	0
Wildwood Express		E	559 805-3237	0

KIRKWOOD, CA - Alpine County

	SIC	EMP	PHONE	ENTRY #
Mountain Springs Kirkwood LLC		C	209 258-6000	0

KNIGHTS LANDING, CA - Yolo County

	SIC	EMP	PHONE	ENTRY #
Cattail Farms Inc		D	916 207-6580	0

KORBEL, CA - Humboldt County

	SIC	EMP	PHONE	ENTRY #
Green Diamond Resource Company		D	707 668-4400	0

LA CANADA, CA - Los Angeles County

	SIC	EMP	PHONE	ENTRY #
Child Educational Center		D	818 354-3418	0
Crescenta-Canada YMCA (PA)		B	818 790-0123	0
Dilbeck Inc (PA)		D	818 790-6774	0
La Canada Flintridge Cntry CLB		D	818 790-0611	0

LA CANADA FLINTRIDGE, CA - Los Angeles County

	SIC	EMP	PHONE	ENTRY #
Allen Lund Company LLC (HQ)		D	818 790-8412	0
Allen Lund Corporation (PA)		E	818 790-8412	0
Cal Tech Emplyees Fderal Cr Un (PA)		D	818 952-4444	0
California Peo Home		D	626 300-0400	0
Holmes Body Shop Inc (PA)		D	626 795-6447	0
J&R Fleet Services LLC		D	909 820-7000	0

LA CRESCENTA, CA - Los Angeles County

	SIC	EMP	PHONE	ENTRY #
Angel Care Home Health Inc		E	818 248-8811	0
Century 21 Crest		D	818 248-9100	0
Dilbeck Inc		D	818 248-2248	0
EAM Enterprises Inc (PA)		B	818 248-9100	0
Mariner Health Care Inc		D	818 957-0850	0
Neardata Inc		D	818 249-2469	0

LA GRANGE, CA - Stanislaus County

	SIC	EMP	PHONE	ENTRY #
Green Tree Nursery		E	209 874-9100	0

LA HABRA, CA - Orange County

	SIC	EMP	PHONE	ENTRY #
Add2net Inc (PA)		E	714 521-8150	0
Albertsons LLC		D	714 578-4670	0
American First Credit Union (PA)		D	562 691-1112	0
Applied Language Solutions LLC		C	800 579-5010	0
City of La Habra		E	562 905-9708	0
Corner Bakery Store		E	714 459-1420	0
Haircutters		D	562 690-2217	0
Infinity Metals Inc		E	562 697-8826	0
Jayasinghe Medical Group Inc (PA)		D	562 267-7000	0
JKB Corporation		E	562 905-3477	0
JWdangelo Company Inc		E	562 690-1000	0
Life Care Centers America Inc		D	562 690-0852	0
Mary and Friends		C	562 691-1575	0
Ob Usa Inc		C	213 465-4876	0
Peerless Maintenance Service		B	714 871-3380	0
Quail Engineering Inc		D	714 636-0612	0
Seasons		D	562 691-1200	0
Shinsuke Clifford Yamamoto		D	714 992-5783	0
Southwest Inspection and Tstg		D	562 941-2990	0
Westridge Golf Inc		D	562 690-4200	0

LA HABRA HEIGHTS, CA - Orange County

	SIC	EMP	PHONE	ENTRY #
Hacienda Golf Club		D	562 694-1081	0
R Navarro Landscape Services		D	562 690-6414	0

LA JOLLA, CA - San Diego County

	SIC	EMP	PHONE	ENTRY #
A Ursgi-Bmdc Joint Venture		D	858 812-9292	0
Advance Health Solutions LLC		D	858 876-0136	0
Aegis Software Inc		D	858 551-1652	0
Altium LLC		D	800 544-4186	0
Bartell Hotels		D	858 453-5500	0
Bh Partn A Calif Limit Partne		D	858 453-4420	0
Birch Aquarium At Scripps		E	858 534-4109	0
Cal Southern Presbt Homes		C	858 454-4201	0
Chateau La Jolla Inn		E	858 459-4451	0
Citigroup Global Markets Inc		D	858 456-9400	0
Cloisters of La Jolla Inc		D	858 459-4361	0
Covenant Care La Jolla LLC		C	858 453-5810	0
Cripts Health Care		E	858 554-8646	0
CSS Holdings Inc		D	888 884-9224	0
Destination Residences LLC		B	858 550-1000	0
Dewhurst & Associates		D	858 456-5345	0
Fargo Colonial LLC		D	858 454-2181	0

	SIC	EMP	PHONE	ENTRY #
Front Porch Communities		D	858 454-2151	0
Gary Mary W Wireless Hlth Inst		E	858 412-8600	0
Geneohm Sciences Inc		C	201 847-5824	0
Glaxosmithkline LLC		E	858 260-5900	0
Hensel Phelps Construction Co		D	619 544-6828	0
Host Healthcare Inc		A	858 999-3579	0
Hotel La Jolla		D	858 459-0261	0
Impact Assessment Inc		D	858 459-0142	0
J Craig Venter Institute Inc (PA)		B	301 795-7000	0
Joshua J Bodenstadt CPA A Prof		E	858 642-5050	0
La Jolla Bch & Tennis CLB Inc (PA)		C	858 454-7126	0
La Jolla Bch & Tennis CLB Inc		C	858 459-8271	0
La Jolla Country Club Inc		C	858 454-9601	0
La Jolla Cove Hotel & Motel		D	858 459-2621	0
La Jolla Inst For Immunology		B	858 752-6500	0
La Jolla Nurses Home Care		C	858 454-9339	0
La Jolla Orthopaedic		D	858 657-0055	0
Lav Hotel Corp		C	858 454-0771	0
Lavine Lofgren Morris Engelb		E	858 455-1200	0
Lawrence Family Jewish Commu (PA)		C	858 362-1144	0
Leidos Inc		B	858 826-6000	0
Machintel Corporation		D	617 517-3090	0
Marriott International Inc		B	858 587-1414	0
Merrill Lynch Pierce Fenner		D	858 456-3600	0
Mfw Partners		D	858 454-8857	0
Mountain-Pacific Financial (PA)		D	858 456-8420	0
National Marine Fisheries Svc		C	858 546-7081	0
North County Ob-Gyn Med Group		E	858 453-0753	0
Northwestern Mutl Fincl Netwrk (PA)		C	619 234-3111	0
Palomar Holdings Inc		D	619 567-5290	0
Park Hotels & Resorts Inc		E	858 450-4569	0
Professional Health Tech		D	858 449-1599	0
Robert Half International Inc		D	888 744-9202	0
Sanford Burnham Prebys Medical (PA)		A	858 795-5000	0
Scripps Clinic Carmel Valley		B	858 554-8096	0
Scripps Clinic Medical Group		B	858 554-9606	0
Scripps Dialasys Inc (PA)		E	619 453-9070	0
Scripps Health		B	858 455-9100	0
Scripps Health		C	800 727-4777	0
Scripps Health		C	858 452-1279	0
Scripps Health		B	858 458-5100	0
Scripps Health		C	858 626-5200	0
Scripps Health		B	858 626-6150	0
Scripps Health		C	858 554-8892	0
Scripps Health		C	858 554-9489	0
Scripps Health		C	858 626-4123	0
Scripps Health		C	858 652-5504	0
Scripps Research Institute		D	858 242-1000	0
Scripps Research Institute (PA)		C	858 784-1000	0
Sk Sanctuary Day Spa Salon LLC		E	858 459-2400	0
Synthetic Genomics Inc (DH)		C	858 754-2900	0
Theat and Arts Found of San Di		C	858 623-3366	0
Tom Hom Investment Corp		D	858 456-5000	0
UBS Financial Services Inc		D	858 454-9181	0
University Cal San Diego		B	858 534-5000	0
University Cal San Diego		B	858 657-7000	0
Vaco San Diego LLC		D	858 642-0000	0
Wells Fargo Bank National Assn		A	858 454-0362	0
Wells Fargo Clearing Svcs LLC		E	858 456-7706	0
Westmont Living Inc (PA)		C	858 456-1233	0
Willis Allen Real Estate (PA)		E	858 459-4033	0
Willis Insurance Svcs Cal Inc		E	858 678-2000	0
YMCA of San Diego County		C	858 453-3483	0

LA MESA, CA - San Diego County

	SIC	EMP	PHONE	ENTRY #
Abbood Zeyad		E	619 212-2820	0
Age Advantage HM Care Svcs		D	619 449-5900	0
Anthonys Fish Grotto		D	619 713-1853	0
Automobile Club Southern Cal		D	619 464-7001	0
Brady Company/San Diego Inc		B	619 462-2600	0
Brady Socal Incorporated		D	619 462-2600	0
Cal West General Engrg Inc		E	619 469-5811	0
California Coast Credit Union		D	858 495-1600	0
Center Glass Co No 3		E	619 469-6181	0
City of La Mesa		E	619 667-1450	0
Coldwell Banker		D	619 460-6600	0
Community Living Services LLC		E	619 921-3136	0
Comprehensive Autism Ctr Inc		D	951 813-4035	0
Davis Framing Inc		E	619 463-2394	0
Excel Home Health Inc		E	619 460-6622	0
Grossmont Hospital Corporation (HQ)		A	619 740-6000	0
Grossmont Hospital Corporation		C	619 667-1900	0
Grossmont Shopping Center Co		D	619 465-2900	0
Healthcare Group		C	619 463-0281	0
Helix Healthcare Inc		B	619 465-4411	0
Helm Management Co (PA)		D	619 589-6222	0

Employment Codes: A=Over 500 employees, B=251-500,
C=101-250, D=51-100, E=50

2020 Directory of California
Wholesalers and Services Companies

© Mergent Inc. 1-800-342-5647

1555

GEOGRAPHIC

	SIC	EMP	PHONE	ENTRY #
Home Instead Senior Care		E	619 460-6222	0
Kaiser Foundation Hospitals		A	619 528-5000	0
Kaiser Foundation Hospitals		E	619 528-5000	0
Kensington Agency Inc		E	619 280-6993	0
La Mesa Intml Mdc Mdcl Gr		E	619 460-4050	0
La Mesa Lions Club		D	619 469-9988	0
Life Gnerations Healthcare LLC		C	619 460-2330	0
Perry & Shaw Inc		D	619 390-6500	0
Pvcc Inc **(PA)**		D	619 463-0404	0
Razavi Corporation		D	619 465-8010	0
San Diego Mortgage & RE		E	619 334-7779	0
Scripps Health		D	619 670-5400	0
Senior Care Inc		C	619 928-5644	0
Sharp Healthcare		D	619 460-6200	0
Umpqua Bank		D	619 668-5159	0
West Coast Arborists Inc		E	858 566-4204	0
YMCA of San Diego County		D	619 464-1323	0

LA MIRADA, CA - Los Angeles County

	SIC	EMP	PHONE	ENTRY #
American Financial Network Inc		D	562 926-2401	0
American Golf Corporation		D	562 943-7123	0
B S A Partners		D	714 523-2800	0
Bravo Tech Inc		E	714 230-8333	0
CHG Security Inc		E	562 284-6260	0
Dynamex Operations West Inc		E	714 994-1615	0
E T Horn Company **(PA)**		D	714 523-8050	0
Eagle High Reach Equipment LLC		D	619 265-2637	0
Estes Express Lines Inc		C	714 994-3770	0
Far East Broadcasting Co Inc		D	562 947-4651	0
Georgia-Pacific LLC		D	562 926-8888	0
Green Wave Ingredients Inc		E	562 207-9770	0
Healthpointe Medical Group Inc **(PA)**		D	714 956-2663	0
Life Care Centers America Inc		C	562 947-8691	0
Life Care Centers America Inc		C	562 943-7156	0
Makita USA Inc **(HQ)**		C	714 522-8088	0
Mejico Express Inc **(PA)**		C	714 690-8300	0
Nittany Lion Landscaping Inc		D	714 635-1788	0
Northeast Protective Svcs Inc		D	800 577-0899	0
Norwalk La Mirada Unif		D	714 521-0970	0
Physical Distribution Svc Inc **(PA)**		D	323 881-0886	0
Precision Relocation Inc		C	714 690-9344	0
Reliance Steel & Aluminum Co		C	714 736-4800	0
Southern Cal Spcialty Care Inc **(DH)**		D	562 944-1900	0
Special Dispatch Cal Inc **(PA)**		D	714 521-8200	0
Stainless Stl Fabricators Inc		D	714 739-9904	0
Sunstone Hotel Investors LLC		C	714 739-8500	0
Tiffany Dale Inc **(PA)**		D	714 739-2700	0
Tomarco Contractor Spc Inc **(PA)**		D	714 523-1771	0
US Foods Inc		D	714 670-3500	0
US Foods Inc		C	714 670-3500	0
Veritiv Operating Company		D	714 690-4000	0
Winco Industries Company		E	562 926-5600	0
Wow Party Rental Inc		D	714 367-3380	0

LA PALMA, CA - Orange County

	SIC	EMP	PHONE	ENTRY #
Applecare Medical MGT LLC		C	714 443-4507	0
Arco Envmtl Remediation LLC		D	714 523-5674	0
Automatic Data Processing Inc		D	714 994-2000	0
Commercial Carriers Insur Agcy		C	562 404-4900	0
Dr Fresh LLC		D	714 690-1573	0
Kaiser Foundation Hospitals		E	714 562-3420	0
La Palma Hospital Medical Ctr		B	714 670-7400	0
Parsons Corporation		C	714 562-5725	0
Slade Gorton & Co Inc		D	714 676-4200	0
Sunrise Senior Living LLC		D	714 739-8111	0
Tech Knowledge Associates LLC		D	714 735-3810	0
Travelers Club Luggage Inc		D	714 523-8808	0
Veritiv Operating Company		B	714 690-6600	0

LA PUENTE, CA - Los Angeles County

	SIC	EMP	PHONE	ENTRY #
Alert Insulation Company Inc		D	626 961-9113	0
Apw Construction Inc **(PA)**		D	626 820-0812	0
Arrow Disposal Services Inc		E	626 336-2255	0
Athens Disposal Company Inc **(PA)**		B	626 336-3636	0
Cacique Inc		C	626 961-3399	0
Cal-Lift Inc		D	562 566-1400	0
Ldla Clothing LLC		D	323 312-2805	0
Plaza De La Raza Child Develop **(PA)**		D	562 776-1301	0
Powell Works Inc		B	909 861-6699	0
San Gabriel Vly Training Ctr **(PA)**		D	626 330-3185	0
Smart & Final Stores Inc		B	626 330-2495	0
Wave Plastic Surgery Ctr Inc		D	626 964-7788	0

LA QUINTA, CA - Riverside County

	SIC	EMP	PHONE	ENTRY #
Adams Learning Center		E	760 777-4260	0
Cartwright Termite & Pest Cntrl		E	760 771-6091	0
Chapman Golf Development LLC		D	760 564-8723	0

	SIC	EMP	PHONE	ENTRY #
CIT Bank NA		D	760 771-3498	0
Deser Sands Unifi Schoo Distr		D	760 777-4200	0
Hideaway Club		A	760 777-7400	0
Imperial Irrigation District		C	760 398-5811	0
Interiors By Linda		E	760 341-9651	0
Ksl II Mngement Operations LLC		D	760 564-8000	0
La Quinta Country Club		D	760 564-4151	0
Lqr Property LLC		D	760 564-4111	0
Madison Club Owners Assn		C	760 777-9320	0
Professional Golf MGT LLC		D	760 564-0804	0
Silver Rock Resort Golf Club		D	760 777-8884	0
TD Desert Dev Ltd Partnr **(HQ)**		D	760 777-1001	0
Tradition Golf Club Associates		D	760 564-3355	0
Trilogy Golf At La Quinta		D	760 771-0707	0

LA VERNE, CA - Los Angeles County

	SIC	EMP	PHONE	ENTRY #
Alquest Technologies Inc		D	909 592-8708	0
American Eagle Services Inc		D	574 859-2055	0
Automobile Club Southern Cal		C	909 392-1444	0
Brethren Hillcrest Homes		C	909 593-4917	0
David and Margaret Home Inc		C	909 596-5921	0
Haaker Equipment Company **(PA)**		D	909 542-0800	0
Haynes Family Programs Inc		C	909 593-2581	0
J C French & Company		D	909 596-1423	0
Jet Delivery Inc **(PA)**		D	800 716-7177	0
Mass Electric Construction Co		D	800 933-6322	0
Metropolitan Water District		B	909 593-7474	0
Onemain Holdings Inc		D	909 392-5578	0
Peter Kiewit Sons Inc		C	909 962-6001	0
Steve and Beth Chaput		E	909 596-9994	0
Tofasco of America Inc **(PA)**		D	909 392-8282	0

LADERA RANCH, CA - Orange County

	SIC	EMP	PHONE	ENTRY #
AT&T Corp		D	949 364-4052	0
Dustin Hoke		D	949 347-8670	0
Xqawesome Inc		C	949 929-9622	0

LAFAYETTE, CA - Contra Costa County

	SIC	EMP	PHONE	ENTRY #
Advanced Acoustics		E	925 299-0515	0
Arthur J Gallagher & Co		E	925 299-1112	0
Civicactions Inc		D	510 408-7510	0
Clubsport San Ramon LLC		C	925 283-4000	0
Ep Wealth Advisors LLC		D	925 283-2201	0
Independent Quality Care Inc		D	925 284-5544	0
Murphy McKay & Associates Inc		E	925 283-9555	0
Optimum Solutions Group LLC		C	415 954-7100	0
Prestige Car Wash Lafayette LP		E	925 283-1190	0
Techexcel Inc **(PA)**		D	925 871-3900	0

LAGUNA BEACH, CA - Orange County

	SIC	EMP	PHONE	ENTRY #
Baja Life Online Partners		E	949 376-4619	0
C & B Delivery Services		D	909 623-4708	0
Esolar Inc **(DH)**		D	818 303-9500	0
Festival of Arts Laguna Beach		D	949 494-1145	0
Home Express Delivery Svc LLC		A	949 715-9844	0
JC Resorts LLC		B	949 376-2779	0
Laguna Bch Golf Bnglow Vlg LLC		E	949 499-2271	0
Laguna Bch Golf Bnglow Vlg LLC		D	949 499-2271	0
Laguna Playhouse **(PA)**		C	949 497-2787	0
Landmark Hotels LLC		C	949 640-5040	0
Moshun Group LLC		D	855 258-2220	0
National Film Laboratories		C	323 466-0281	0
Pacific Housing Management **(PA)**		D	714 508-1777	0
Seaside Laguna Inn & Suites		D	949 494-9717	0
South Coast Water District **(PA)**		D	949 499-4555	0
Spencer Recovery Centers Inc **(PA)**		D	949 376-3705	0

LAGUNA HILLS, CA - Orange County

	SIC	EMP	PHONE	ENTRY #
Altec Products Inc **(PA)**		D	949 727-1248	0
American Capital Group Inc		D	949 271-5800	0
Automobile Club Southern Cal		E	949 951-1400	0
Bel Esprit Builders Inc		E	949 709-3500	0
Birtcher/Aetna Laguna Hills		D	949 458-2311	0
Blytheco LLC		E	813 854-3388	0
Care Plus Home Care Inc		C	949 716-2273	0
Care Plus Nursing Services Inc		C	949 600-7194	0
Cirrus Health II LP		C	949 855-0562	0
Dva Renal Healthcare Inc		D	949 588-9211	0
F M Tarbell Co		E	949 830-6030	0
Factory R D		E	949 900-3460	0
Gate Three Healthcare LLC		C	949 770-3348	0
Groundwork Open Source Inc		D	415 992-4500	0
Hardrock Tile & Marble Inc		D	714 282-1766	0
Harvest Small Business Fin LLC		D	949 446-8683	0
Herren Enterprises Inc		D	949 951-1666	0
Hillview Acres		D	714 694-2828	0
Hines Nurseries LLC		D	602 254-2831	0

Mergent email: customerrelations@mergent.com
1556

2020 Directory of California
Wholesalers and Services Companies

(P-0000) Products & Services Section entry number
(PA)=Parent Co (HQ)=Headquarters (DH)=Div Headquarters

	SIC	EMP	PHONE	ENTRY #
Jamboree Realty Corp **(PA)**		C	949 380-0300	0
Kennedy Pipeline Company		D	949 380-8363	0
Laguna Hills Hotel Dev Ventr		D	949 586-5000	0
Laguna Woods Golf Club		E	949 597-4336	0
Magarro Farms		C	949 859-6506	0
Mednax Inc		C	949 587-9037	0
Metron-Athene Inc **(PA)**		D	949 588-5757	0
Muller-Ing-Gateway LLC		D	951 687-2900	0
Nms Data Inc		E	949 472-2700	0
Nvision Laser Eye Centers Inc		D	949 951-1457	0
Orange Coast Wns Med Group Inc **(PA)**		D	949 829-5500	0
Parallax Capital Partners **(PA)**		D	949 296-4800	0
Professional Community MGT Cal		C	949 597-4200	0
Rakworx Inc		C	949 215-1362	0
Rye Electric Inc		E	949 441-0545	0
Saddle Corp **(PA)**		D	949 589-3422	0
Saddleback Memorial Med Ctr **(HQ)**		A	949 837-4500	0
Saddleback Memorial Med Ctr		D	949 452-3405	0
South County Orthopedic Specia		D	949 586-3200	0
Sun Coast Gen Insur Agcy Inc		D	949 768-1132	0
Sunrise Senior Living Inc		D	949 581-6111	0
Tom Ray Industries Inc		D	949 380-8333	0
Varsity Contractors Inc		D	949 586-8283	0
Villageway Management Inc		D	949 450-1515	0

LAGUNA NIGUEL, CA - Orange County

	SIC	EMP	PHONE	ENTRY #
Aegis Senior Communities LLC		E	949 496-8080	0
Bitfone Corporation **(PA)**		E	949 234-7000	0
California Title Company **(PA)**		D	949 582-8709	0
E Tradeshowgirlscom		D	949 661-4177	0
Enterprise Rent-A-Car		D	949 373-9350	0
First Team RE - Orange Cnty		C	949 240-7979	0
Focus 360 Inc		D	949 234-0008	0
Irvine Pharmaceutical Svcs Inc		D	949 439-6677	0
Jdr Engineering Cons Inc		C	949 495-2063	0
Mission Internal Med Group Inc		C	949 364-3605	0
Moulton Niguel Water **(PA)**		D	949 831-2500	0
Pacific Line Clean-Up Inc		C	949 348-0245	0
Pacific Monarch Resorts Inc		D	949 228-1396	0
Rancho Niguel Dental Group		E	949 249-4180	0
Spearman Clubs Inc **(PA)**		E	949 496-2070	0

LAGUNA WOODS, CA - Orange County

	SIC	EMP	PHONE	ENTRY #
Countryside Inn-Corona LP		D	949 588-0131	0
Laguna Woods Village		A	949 597-4267	0
Professional Community MGT Cal		C	949 206-0580	0
Rainbow Realty Corporation		D	949 770-9626	0
Withrow Phrm & Hlth Spc Lab		D	323 721-4281	0

LAKE ARROWHEAD, CA - San Bernardino County

	SIC	EMP	PHONE	ENTRY #
Lake Arrwhead Rsort Oprtor Inc **(HQ)**		C	909 336-1511	0
Mountains Community Hosp Fndtn		D	909 336-3651	0
RE Max All Cities Lk Arrowhead		E	909 337-6111	0

LAKE ELSINORE, CA - Riverside County

	SIC	EMP	PHONE	ENTRY #
AAA Restoration Inc		E	951 471-5828	0
Chief Trnsp & Engrg Contrs Inc		D	951 258-6607	0
County of Riverside		D	951 245-3060	0
Division Three Cnstr Svcs		D	951 609-3043	0
Edje-Enterprises		D	951 245-7070	0
Elsinore Vly Municpl Wtr Dst **(PA)**		D	951 674-3146	0
F M Tarbell Co		E	951 471-5333	0
Gbc Concrete Masnry Cnstr Inc		C	951 245-2355	0
Hakes Sash & Door Inc		C	951 674-2414	0
JD Miller Construction Inc		E	951 471-3513	0
Lake Elsinore Unified Schl Dst		D	951 253-7091	0
Near-Cal Corp		E	951 245-5400	0
Onemain Holdings Inc		D	951 245-5029	0
Pacific Clay Products Inc		C	661 857-1401	0
Perfection Glass Inc		E	951 674-0240	0
Prime Communications LP		D	951 253-3304	0
Sci Inc		D	951 245-7511	0
Service Transport Inc		D	951 403-3464	0
Vista Community Clinic		D	951 245-2735	0
West Coast Ltg & Enrgy Inc		D	951 296-0680	0

LAKE FOREST, CA - Orange County

	SIC	EMP	PHONE	ENTRY #
24 Hour Fitness Usa Inc		D	949 830-4213	0
AMF Bowling Centers Inc		E	949 770-0055	0
Apria Healthcare Group Inc **(PA)**		B	949 639-2000	0
Apria Healthcare LLC **(HQ)**		B	949 639-2000	0
Arb Inc **(HQ)**		C	949 598-9242	0
Atria Senior Living Inc		D	805 370-5400	0
Aveva Software LLC **(DH)**		B	949 727-3200	0
Beech Street Corporation **(DH)**		B	949 672-1000	0
Chapel Funding Corporation		C	949 580-1800	0
Cloudradiant Corp **(PA)**		C	408 256-1527	0

	SIC	EMP	PHONE	ENTRY #
Commercial Indus Design Co Inc		D	949 273-6199	0
Digital Networks Group Inc		D	949 428-6333	0
Dove Ceilings Inc **(PA)**		E	949 597-1794	0
El Toro Water Distr Public Fac **(PA)**		D	949 837-1662	0
Environmental Resolutions Inc		B	949 457-8950	0
Environments For Learning Inc **(PA)**		D	949 855-5630	0
Freedom Village Healthcare Ctr		D	949 472-4733	0
Golden West Custom WD Shutters		E	949 951-0600	0
Great Destinations Inc		D	949 667-9401	0
Gypsum Contractors Inc		E	949 340-9100	0
Hardy & Harper Inc		E	714 444-1851	0
Heinaman Contract Glazing Inc **(PA)**		E	949 587-0266	0
Infor (us) Inc		C	678 319-8000	0
Inspiria Inc **(PA)**		D	949 206-0606	0
Insulectro **(PA)**		D	949 587-3200	0
Intertek Testing Svcs Inc		D	949 448-4100	0
Intertek Testing Svcs NA Inc		D	949 349-1684	0
Itek Services Inc		D	949 770-4835	0
Lake Forest LI Master Homeown		D	949 586-0860	0
Life Care Centers America Inc		C	949 380-9380	0
Mike Rovner Construction Inc		C	949 458-1562	0
Molly Maid		E	949 367-8000	0
Nakase Brothers Wholesale Nurs		C	949 855-4388	0
Natures Image Inc		D	949 680-4400	0
Nelson Moving & Storage Inc		E	949 582-0380	0
Olive US Bidco Inc **(DH)**		E	800 662-1711	0
Panasonic		C	949 581-0661	0
Panasonic Avionics Corporation		D	949 472-2376	0
Panasonic Avionics Corporation **(DH)**		B	949 672-2000	0
Parsons Government Svcs Inc **(HQ)**		D	949 768-8161	0
Performance Building Services		C	949 364-4364	0
Quantum Technologies Inc		C	949 399-4500	0
Ses LLC		A	949 727-3200	0
Share Our Selves Corporation		D	949 609-8199	0
Solutions 2 Go LLC		D	949 825-7700	0
Streamline Finishes Inc		D	949 600-8964	0
Toshiba Amer Bus Solutions Inc **(HQ)**		B	949 462-6000	0
Truvida Recovery		D	949 283-4679	0
US Real Estate Services Inc		D	949 598-9920	0
Validus Group Inc		E	949 457-7606	0
Vintage Design LLC **(HQ)**		D	949 900-5400	0
W B Starr Inc		D	949 770-8835	0
Wonderware Corporation **(DH)**		B	949 727-3200	0
Xpo Logistics Freight Inc		D	949 581-9030	0

LAKE ISABELLA, CA - Kern County

	SIC	EMP	PHONE	ENTRY #
Kern River Tours Inc		D	760 379-4616	0

LAKE VIEW TERRACE, CA - Los Angeles County

	SIC	EMP	PHONE	ENTRY #
Phoenix Houses Los Angeles Inc		D	818 686-3000	0

LAKEPORT, CA - Lake County

	SIC	EMP	PHONE	ENTRY #
ABC Phones North Carolina Inc		D	707 263-3959	0
County Lake Health Services		D	707 263-1090	0
Evergreen At Lakeport LLC **(PA)**		D	707 263-6382	0
Konocti Vista Casino **(PA)**		C	707 262-1900	0
Lake Cnty Trbal Hlth Cnsortium		D	707 263-8382	0
People Services Inc **(PA)**		D	707 263-3810	0
Sequoia Senior Solutions Inc		D	707 263-3070	0
Sutter Health		C	707 263-6885	0
Sutter Health		D	707 263-3520	0
Sutter Health		C	707 263-6885	0
Sutter Lakeside Hospital **(HQ)**		B	707 262-5000	0
Windflower Holdings LLC		D	707 263-6101	0
Xpo Enterprise Services Inc		C	916 399-8291	0

LAKESHORE, CA - Fresno County

	SIC	EMP	PHONE	ENTRY #
China Peak Mountain Resort LLC		D	559 233-2500	0

LAKESIDE, CA - San Diego County

	SIC	EMP	PHONE	ENTRY #
A M Ortega Construction Inc **(PA)**		C	619 390-1988	0
Barona Creek Golf Club		D	619 387-7018	0
Barona Resort & Casino		A	619 443-2300	0
Buds & Son Trucking Inc		D	619 443-4200	0
Burner Sheet Metal LLC **(HQ)**		E	619 938-9727	0
Clauss Construction		D	619 390-4940	0
Global Power Group Inc **(PA)**		D	619 579-1221	0
Lakeside Fire Protection Dst		D	619 390-2350	0
Lakeside Tax & Financial Svcs		D	619 561-2681	0
LLC Brewer Crane		D	619 390-8252	0
Marathon Construction Corp		D	619 276-4401	0
Marco Crane & Rigging Co		D	619 938-8080	0
Minshew Brothers Stl Cnstr Inc		C	619 561-5700	0
Neighborhood Healthcare		D	619 390-9975	0
Nicholas Grant Corporation		C	619 390-3900	0
Pacific Green Landscape Inc **(PA)**		C	619 390-1546	0
Rdo Construction Equipment Co		D	619 443-3758	0

GEOGRAPHIC

	SIC	EMP	PHONE	ENTRY #
Standard Drywall Inc **(HQ)**		B	619 443-7034	0
Towne Construction Inc		D	619 390-4557	0
Turning Point For God		D	619 258-3600	0
Unyeway Inc		D	619 562-6330	0
Wagner Construction Co **(PA)**		C	619 873-2160	0
Williams & Sons Masonry Inc		D	619 443-1751	0

LAKEWOOD, CA - Los Angeles County

	SIC	EMP	PHONE	ENTRY #
Admiral Home Health Inc		D	562 421-0777	0
American Golf Corporation		E	562 421-0550	0
Berro Management		D	562 432-3444	0
Cal Bowl Enterprises LLC		B	562 421-8448	0
Caremore Medical Group Inc		B	562 622-2900	0
Center For Dscovery Adoloscent		E	562 425-6404	0
Contractor Warehouse		D	562 633-1428	0
County of Los Angeles		B	562 497-3500	0
Discovery Practice Management		E	562 425-6404	0
Lakewood Cerritos Dental Ctr		D	562 860-0388	0
Nationwide Theatres Corp		D	562 421-8448	0
Pacific Theaters Inc		D	562 634-1183	0
Spectrum MGT Holdg Co LLC		C	424 529-6011	0
Tarzana Treatment Centers Inc		C	562 428-4111	0
Tenet Healthsystem Medical		A	562 531-2550	0
Western States Fire Protection		D	562 279-0770	0
Young Mens Chrstn Assc Gr L B		D	562 272-4884	0
Young Mens Chrstn Assc Gr L B		C	562 425-7431	0

LAMONT, CA - Kern County

	SIC	EMP	PHONE	ENTRY #
Community Action Partnr Kern		D	661 845-3901	0
Grimmway Enterprises Inc		B	661 845-3758	0
Maxco Supply Inc		D	559 646-6700	0

LANCASTER, CA - Los Angeles County

	SIC	EMP	PHONE	ENTRY #
Allied Risk Management Inc		D	661 305-0455	0
American Med Rspnse Sthern Cal		A	661 945-9310	0
Antelope Valley Foundation		E	661 945-7290	0
Antelope Valley Hospital Inc		D	661 949-1550	0
Antelope Valley Hospital Inc		C	661 726-6180	0
Antelope Valley Hospital Inc **(PA)**		A	661 949-5000	0
Antelope Valley Medical Group		E	661 945-2783	0
Antelope Vly Dom Vlnce Council **(PA)**		D	661 723-7772	0
Antelope Vly Retirement HM Inc		B	661 948-7501	0
Antelope Vly Retirement HM Inc		C	661 949-5524	0
Antelope Vly Schl Trnsp Agcy		C	661 945-3621	0
BDR Industries Inc **(PA)**		D	661 940-8554	0
C D R Enterprises Inc		D	661 940-0344	0
California Traffic Safety Inst		C	661 940-1907	0
Counseling and Research Assoc		D	661 726-5500	0
County of Los Angeles		B	661 940-4181	0
County of Los Angeles		C	661 948-2320	0
County of Los Angeles		D	661 723-6088	0
County of Los Angeles		D	661 524-2005	0
Daniel O Mongiano MD A PR		E	661 951-9195	0
Desert Haven Enterprises Inc		A	661 948-8402	0
Easter Seals Southern Cal Inc		E	661 723-3414	0
Esna Corporation		D	661 206-6010	0
Excel Contractors Inc		D	661 942-6944	0
Frito-Lay North America Inc		D	661 951-1399	0
Gene Wheeler Farms Inc		C	661 942-2100	0
Go Get Em Inc		D	702 985-5637	0
Granite Construction Company		C	661 726-4447	0
Hartwig Realty Inc **(PA)**		D	661 948-8424	0
High Desert Med Corp A Med Grp **(PA)**		C	661 945-5984	0
High Desert Phoenix		E	661 547-5630	0
Iheartcommunications Inc		D	661 942-1268	0
Kaiser Foundation Hospitals		C	661 726-2500	0
Kaiser Foundation Hospitals		B	661 949-5000	0
Kaiser Foundation Hospitals		D	661 951-0070	0
Keolis Transit America Inc		D	661 341-3910	0
La County High Desert Hlth Sys		B	661 945-8461	0
Lancaster Comm Srvcs Fndtn		D	661 723-6230	0
Lancaster Crdlgy Med Group Inc **(PA)**		D	661 726-3058	0
Lancaster Jethawks		D	661 726-5400	0
Lantz Security Systems Inc **(PA)**		D	661 949-3565	0
Linda Verde School		E	661 942-0431	0
Metropolitan Dst Private SEC		D	661 942-3999	0
Michaels Stores Inc		C	661 951-3500	0
Nibbelink Masonry Cnstr Corp		D	661 948-7859	0
North La County Regional Ctr		D	661 945-6761	0
Opsec Specialized Protection		D	661 942-3999	0
Penny Lane Centers		C	661 274-0770	0
Rich Meiers Landscaping Inc **(PA)**		D	661 723-2220	0
SA Recycling LLC		D	661 723-1383	0
Sarah Elizabeth Treusdell		E	661 949-0131	0
Spiral Technology Inc		D	661 723-3148	0
Sygma Network Inc		C	661 723-0405	0

	SIC	EMP	PHONE	ENTRY #
Tarzana Treatment Centers Inc		D	661 726-2630	0
United Parcel Service Inc OH		C	800 828-8264	0
V Troth Inc		D	661 948-4646	0
Warner Media LLC		D	661 344-1546	0
Wilshire Insurance Company		E	661 940-7300	0

LARKSPUR, CA - Marin County

	SIC	EMP	PHONE	ENTRY #
All California Mortgage Inc **(PA)**		D	415 925-5225	0
Courtyard By Marriott		D	415 925-1800	0
Golden Gate		D	415 455-2000	0
Hospice By Bay **(PA)**		C	415 927-2273	0
Lilien LLC **(HQ)**		E	415 389-7500	0
ONeill Beverages Co LLC **(PA)**		D	844 825-6600	0
Sysorex USA **(HQ)**		D	415 389-7500	0

LATHROP, CA - San Joaquin County

	SIC	EMP	PHONE	ENTRY #
Cen Cal Plastering Inc		B	209 981-5265	0
Crosslink Prof Tax Sltions LLC **(PA)**		D	800 345-4337	0
Cunha Draying Inc		D	209 858-1400	0
Elma Electronic Inc		E	209 858-2411	0
Global Building Services Inc		A	209 858-9501	0
Home Depot USA Inc		D	209 858-9243	0
J C Penney Purchasing Corp		C	209 858-9463	0
Knight-Swift Trnsp Hldings Inc		D	209 858-1630	0
Mid Valley Plastering Inc		B	209 858-9766	0
Performant Recovery Inc		D	209 858-3500	0
UPS Ground Freight Inc		D	209 858-5095	0

LATON, CA - Fresno County

	SIC	EMP	PHONE	ENTRY #
Zonneveld Dairies Inc		D	559 923-4546	0
Zonneveld Farms		D	559 923-4546	0

LAWNDALE, CA - Los Angeles County

	SIC	EMP	PHONE	ENTRY #
Advanced Veterinary Care Ctr		D	310 542-8018	0
Alondra Golf Course Inc		D	310 217-9915	0
McCarthy Framing Construction		D	310 219-3038	0
Southwestern Orthpd Med Corp		E	562 803-0600	0
Ultimate Maintenance Svcs Inc		E	310 542-1474	0

LE GRAND, CA - Merced County

	SIC	EMP	PHONE	ENTRY #
J Marchini & Son Inc		D	559 665-2944	0
Marchini Inc		E	209 389-4566	0

LEBEC, CA - Kern County

	SIC	EMP	PHONE	ENTRY #
Schneider National Inc		C	661 858-1031	0
Tejon Ranch Co **(PA)**		D	661 248-3000	0

LEMON GROVE, CA - San Diego County

	SIC	EMP	PHONE	ENTRY #
Aztec Landscaping Inc **(PA)**		C	619 464-3303	0
Developmental Svcs Continuum		D	619 460-7333	0
Monte Vista Retirement Lodge		D	619 465-1331	0
Pacific Sthwest Structures Inc		C	619 469-2323	0
San Diego Recyling Inc		B	619 287-7555	0
Thompson Building Mtls Inc		E	619 287-9410	0

LEMOORE, CA - Kings County

	SIC	EMP	PHONE	ENTRY #
City of Lemoore		E	559 924-6744	0
R & D Leasing Inc		D	559 924-1276	0
Santa Rosa Rnchria Gaming Comm		D	559 924-6948	0
Superior Truck Lines Inc		E	559 924-6418	0
Tachi Palace Hotel & Casino		A	559 924-7751	0
United States Dept of Navy		A	559 998-4201	0
United States Dept of Navy		A	559 998-4481	0
United States Dept of Navy		B	559 998-2894	0
Wood Bros Inc		D	559 924-7715	0

LINCOLN, CA - Placer County

	SIC	EMP	PHONE	ENTRY #
B Z Plumbing Company Inc		C	916 645-1600	0
Calhoun Construction Inc		C	916 434-8356	0
Catta Verdera Country Club		D	916 645-7200	0
Clubcorp Usa Inc		E	916 434-9100	0
Crstb Partners LLC		D	916 645-7200	0
Gdsa-Lincoln Inc **(PA)**		D	916 645-8961	0
Gold Hill Grange No 326		D	916 645-3605	0
Kaiser Foundation Hospitals		A	916 543-5153	0
Lincoln Hills Golf Club		E	916 543-9200	0
Raylee Electric		E	916 408-7556	0
Rocklin Power Investors LP		D	916 645-3383	0
United Auburn Indian Community		A	916 408-7777	0
Verifone Inc		D	916 408-4900	0
Weygandt & Associates		E	916 543-0431	0

LINDEN, CA - San Joaquin County

	SIC	EMP	PHONE	ENTRY #
Duarte Nursery Inc		B	209 887-3409	0
Normans Nursery Inc		C	209 887-2033	0

LINDSAY, CA - Tulare County

	SIC	EMP	PHONE	ENTRY #
Acmpc California 3 LLC		C	559 591-6140	0
Cal Citrus Packing Co		D	559 562-2536	0

	SIC	EMP	PHONE	ENTRY #
California Silver-Agriculture		E	559 562-3795	0
Friant Water Users Association		D	559 562-6305	0
Lindsay Fruit Company LLC		D	559 562-1327	0
Lo Bue Bros Inc		C	559 562-6367	0
Padilla Farm Labor Inc		D	559 562-1166	0
Sheldon Ranches		D	559 562-3978	0
Suntreat Pkg Shipg A Ltd Prtnr		C	559 562-4991	0

LITTLE LAKE, CA - Inyo County

	SIC	EMP	PHONE	ENTRY #
Cgp Holdings LLC		D	760 764-1300	0
Coso Operating Company LLC		D	760 764-1300	0

LITTLE RIVER, CA - Mendocino County

	SIC	EMP	PHONE	ENTRY #
Little River Inn Inc		D	707 937-5942	0

LITTLEROCK, CA - Los Angeles County

	SIC	EMP	PHONE	ENTRY #
Harrison Inventory Services		E	661 269-9220	0

LIVE OAK, CA - Sutter County

	SIC	EMP	PHONE	ENTRY #
Malloy Orchards Inc		C	530 695-1861	0
Micheli Farms Inc		E	530 695-9022	0
Smith Ranch		E	530 695-2521	0
Sunset Moulding Co		D	530 695-3379	0
Wilbur Packing Company Inc		B	530 671-4911	0

LIVERMORE, CA - Alameda County

	SIC	EMP	PHONE	ENTRY #
Access Info MGT Shred Svcs LLC		C	925 461-5352	0
Aeronautical Radio Inc		D	925 294-8400	0
All-Guard Alarm Systems Inc (PA)		D	800 255-4273	0
Altamont Infrastructure Co		D	925 245-5500	0
American Med		C	510 895-7600	0
Amsnet Inc (PA)		E	925 245-6100	0
Aqua Gunite Inc		E	408 271-2782	0
Aragon Commercial Ldscpg Inc		D	408 998-0600	0
Architectural GL & Alum Co Inc (PA)		C	925 583-2460	0
Brock LLC (PA)		D	925 371-2184	0
Califrnias Gnite Pool Plst Inc		D	925 960-9500	0
Care Solution Associates LLC		D	925 443-1000	0
Cattlemens		D	925 447-1224	0
City of Livermore		E	925 960-8100	0
Clark Pest Ctrl Stockton Inc		D	925 449-6203	0
CMS Llnl		E	925 422-5584	0
Comcast of California/Colo		D	925 424-0273	0
Cosco Fire Protection Inc		D	925 455-2751	0
Country Builders Inc		C	925 373-1020	0
Coventina-Gse Jv LLC		E	813 509-0669	0
Custom Product Dev Corp		D	925 960-0577	0
Davey Tree Surgery Company (HQ)		A	925 443-1723	0
Eurofins Food		A	609 452-4440	0
Evans Brothers Inc (PA)		D	925 443-0225	0
Fault Line Plumbing		E	925 443-6450	0
Fbd Vanguard Construction Inc		C	925 245-1300	0
Fields Construction Services		D	925 294-8183	0
Goodfellow Bros California LLC		B	925 245-2111	0
Green Ridge Services LLC		D	925 245-5500	0
GSe Construction Company Inc (PA)		C	925 447-0292	0
Harris Rebar Northern Cal Inc		C	925 373-0733	0
Haskell Company (inc)		C	925 960-1815	0
High Summit LLC		E	925 605-2900	0
Hilton Garden Inns MGT LLC		E	925 292-2000	0
Hospital Cmmttee For The Lvrmr		A	925 447-7000	0
J & M Inc		D	925 724-0300	0
J Redfern Inc		C	925 371-3300	0
Jacobs Engineering Group Inc		D	925 423-7564	0
JF Shea Construction Inc		C	925 245-3660	0
Jpa Landscape & Cnstr Inc		D	925 960-9602	0
Kenyon Construction Inc		B	925 371-8102	0
Kier & Wright Civil ENGrs&srvy		E	925 245-8788	0
Kindred Healthcare Oper Inc		D	925 443-1800	0
Kinetics Mechanical Svc Inc		D	925 245-6200	0
Lanlogic Inc (HQ)		E	925 273-2300	0
Lbf Enterprises (PA)		D	925 461-7171	0
Livermore Area Rcration Pk Dst		C	925 373-5700	0
Livermore Area Rcration Pk Dst (PA)		B	925 373-5700	0
Livermore Snior Lving Assoc LP		E	925 371-2300	0
Livermore Valley Tennis Club		D	925 443-7700	0
LJ Walch Co Inc		D	925 449-9252	0
McGrath Rentcorp		D	925 606-9200	0
McGrath Rentcorp		C	877 221-2813	0
McGrath Rentcorp (PA)		C	925 606-9200	0
Mike Champlin		D	925 961-1004	0
Mthuron Inc		E	925 932-4101	0
National Security Tech LLC		D	925 960-2500	0
North Valley Construction Inc		D	925 373-1246	0
Pacific Gas and Electric Co		D	925 373-2623	0
Packaging Innovators LLC		D	925 371-2000	0
Pen-Cal Administrators Inc		D	925 251-3400	0

	SIC	EMP	PHONE	ENTRY #
Performance Contracting Inc		E	925 273-3800	0
Performance Food Group Inc		D	925 456-8664	0
Performant Financial Corp (PA)		D	925 960-4800	0
Performant Recovery Inc (HQ)		C	209 858-3994	0
Performant Technologies		B	925 960-4800	0
Permanente Medical Group Inc		D	925 243-2600	0
Peterson Painting Inc		B	925 455-5864	0
Pinamar LLC		D	925 243-8979	0
Point One Elec Systems Inc		D	925 667-2935	0
Poppy Ridge Inc		D	925 456-8229	0
Prevent Life Safety Svcs Inc		E	925 667-2088	0
Produce Exchange Incorporated (DH)		D	925 454-8700	0
Pta California Cong P A S Elem		E	925 606-4700	0
Puronics Retail Services Inc		D	925 456-7000	0
Republic Svcs Vsco Rd Landfill		E	925 447-0491	0
Seaside Rfrigerated Trnspt Inc (PA)		E	510 732-0472	0
Selex Inc (PA)		D	707 836-8836	0
Sidjon Corporation		D	925 606-6135	0
Smp Construction & Maint Inc (PA)		D	925 961-9012	0
Sosa Granite & Marble Inc		D	925 373-7675	0
Sutter Health		D	925 371-3800	0
Tao Mechanical Ltd		E	925 447-5220	0
Taylor Communications Inc		D	925 245-6420	0
Tennyson Electric Inc		E	925 606-1038	0
Tgcon Inc (HQ)		D	925 449-5764	0
The National Food Lab LLC		C	925 828-1440	0
Uncle Credit Union (PA)		D	925 447-5001	0
Unified Grocers Inc		D	323 264-5200	0
United States Dept of Energy		A	925 422-1100	0
US Foods Inc		B	925 606-3525	0
Valleycare Hospital Corp (DH)		D	925 447-7000	0
Veritiv Operating Company		C	925 245-6075	0
Veterans Health Administration		B	925 447-2560	0
Waxies Enterprises Inc		E	925 454-2900	0

LIVINGSTON, CA - Merced County

	SIC	EMP	PHONE	ENTRY #
E & J Gallo Winery		D	209 394-6271	0
Foster Poultry Farms		A	209 394-7901	0
Livingston Community Health		C	209 394-7913	0
Quail H Farms LLC		A	209 394-8001	0

LLANO, CA - Los Angeles County

	SIC	EMP	PHONE	ENTRY #
Crystal Aire Country Club Golf		E	661 944-2112	0

LODI, CA - San Joaquin County

	SIC	EMP	PHONE	ENTRY #
Alexander Delu		D	209 334-6660	0
Anka Behavioral Health Inc		C	209 982-4697	0
Bjj Company LLC (PA)		D	209 941-8361	0
Boething Treeland Farms Inc		C	209 727-3741	0
California Fruit Exchange LLC (PA)		D	209 334-2988	0
City Rise Inc (PA)		C	209 333-0807	0
Clark Pest Ctrl Stockton Inc (HQ)		D	209 368-7152	0
Crescent Court Nursing Home		E	209 367-7400	0
Diede Construction Inc		D	209 369-8255	0
ED Safety Services Inc		C	209 333-0807	0
Evergreen Company Inc		D	916 257-5994	0
F & H Construction (PA)		D	209 931-3738	0
Ford Construction Company Inc		D	209 333-1116	0
Frank C Alegre Trucking Inc (PA)		C	209 334-2112	0
Golden Living LLC		D	209 368-0693	0
Greg H Carpenter Concrete Inc		E	209 367-4224	0
Gross Convalescent Hospital		D	209 334-3760	0
J Rivera Associates Inc		D	415 617-5660	0
John H Kautz Farms		E	209 334-4786	0
Jose Vramontes		E	209 810-5384	0
Lockeford Spring Golf Course (PA)		C	209 333-6275	0
Lodi Development Inc		E	209 367-7600	0
Lodi Memorial Hosp Assn Inc (HQ)		A	209 334-3411	0
Lodi Memorial Hosp Assn Inc		E	209 339-7583	0
Lodi Memorial Hosp Assn Inc		C	209 333-3100	0
Lodi Unified School District		D	209 331-7181	0
Lodi Unified School District		C	209 331-7169	0
Mv Transportation Inc		D	209 339-1972	0
Odyssey Landscaping Co Inc		D	209 369-6197	0
Pacific Coast Producers		B	209 365-9982	0
R DS For Healthcare		E	209 333-2115	0
Rdr Builders LP		D	209 368-7561	0
River Maid Land Co A Cal Ll (PA)		B	209 369-3586	0
Schryver Med Sls & Mktg LLC		D	303 459-8150	0
Sg Personnel LLC		D	209 369-3018	0
Spare-Time Inc		C	209 371-0241	0
Sutter Health		C	209 366-2007	0
Sutter Health		C	209 334-3333	0
T & T Trucking Inc (PA)		C	800 692-3457	0
Tiger Lines LLC (HQ)		D	209 334-4100	0
Valley Landscaping & Maint Inc		C	209 334-3659	0

Employment Codes: A=Over 500 employees, B=251-500,
C=101-250, D=51-100, E=50

GEOGRAPHIC

	SIC	EMP	PHONE	ENTRY #
Vienna Convalescent Hospital		C	209 368-7141	0
Vino Farms Inc (PA)		E	209 334-6975	0
Vino Farms LLC		A	209 334-6975	0
Westrec Marina Management Inc		D	209 369-1041	0

LOLETA, CA - Humboldt County

	SIC	EMP	PHONE	ENTRY #
Bear River Casino		B	707 733-9644	0

LOMA LINDA, CA - San Bernardino County

	SIC	EMP	PHONE	ENTRY #
ABI Document Support Svcs LLC		D	909 793-0613	0
Brookdale Senior Living Commun		D	909 796-5421	0
Chancellor Hlth Care Cal I Inc (PA)		D	909 796-0235	0
Faculty Physcans Srgeons Llusm		D	909 558-4000	0
Heritage Health Care Inc		C	909 796-0216	0
Laren D Tan MD		D	909 558-4444	0
Linda Loma Univ Hlth Care (HQ)		D	909 558-2806	0
Linda Loma Univ Hlth Care		C	909 558-2851	0
Linda Loma Univ Hlth Care (PA)		A	909 558-4729	0
Linda Loma Univ Hlth Care		C	909 558-2840	0
Loma Linda University Med Ctr		C	909 558-2100	0
Loma Linda University Med Ctr (DH)		A	909 558-4000	0
Loma Linda University Med Ctr		C	909 558-8244	0
Loma Linda University Med Ctr		C	909 558-4216	0
Loma Linda University Med Ctr		C	909 558-3096	0
Loma Linda University Med Ctr		C	909 796-0167	0
Mountain View Child Care Inc (PA)		B	909 796-6915	0
South Coast Childrens Soc Inc		C	909 478-3377	0
Universal Self Storage		E	951 206-5263	0
Veterans Health Administration		A	909 825-7084	0

LOMITA, CA - Los Angeles County

	SIC	EMP	PHONE	ENTRY #
Aaxis Pharmaceuticals Inc		C	424 263-5294	0
City of Lomita		E	310 325-9830	0
Industry Events		E	310 834-3422	0
Kaiser Foundation Hospitals		A	310 325-6542	0
Kaiser Foundation Hospitals		C	424 251-7000	0
Lomita Verde Inc		D	310 325-1970	0
Long Beach Investment Group		E	562 595-7277	0
Torrance Amateur Rdo Assn Inc		C	310 245-0989	0
Travers Tree Service Inc		E	310 545-5816	0

LOMPOC, CA - Santa Barbara County

	SIC	EMP	PHONE	ENTRY #
Affordable Hsing Key Partners		D	805 736-3423	0
Air Force US Dept of		D	805 606-5355	0
Carnahan Occupational Therapy		E	805 737-1604	0
Channel Islands Young Mens Ch		D	805 736-3483	0
Coasthills Credit Union (PA)		D	805 733-7600	0
Family Service Agency		E	805 735-4376	0
Ghc of Lompoc LLC		C	805 735-4010	0
Imerys Minerals California Inc		B	805 736-1221	0
Imerys Minerals California Inc (DH)		D	805 736-1221	0
Jay Fisher Farms Inc		E	805 735-1598	0
Kbrwyle Tech Solutions LLC		B	805 734-2982	0
Life Optons Vctnal Rsource Ctr (PA)		C	805 735-3428	0
Lompoc Valley Medical Center		C	805 735-9229	0
Lompoc Valley Medical Center (PA)		B	805 737-3300	0
Lompoc Valley Medical Center		C	805 736-3466	0
Ocean View Flowers LLC		C	800 736-5608	0
Santa Barbara County of		C	805 737-7080	0
Santa Barbara Farms LLC (PA)		D	805 736-9776	0
Valley Medical Group of Lompoc		D	805 736-1253	0
Velazquez Packing Inc		D	805 735-6477	0
Zikakis Auto Holdings LLC		E	805 736-4595	0

LONE PINE, CA - Inyo County

	SIC	EMP	PHONE	ENTRY #
Southern Inyo Healthcare Dst		C	760 876-5501	0

LONG BEACH, CA - Los Angeles County

	SIC	EMP	PHONE	ENTRY #
1130 W La Palma Ave Inc		D	562 930-0777	0
4g Wireless Inc		D	562 432-7744	0
A-Throne Co Inc		D	562 981-1197	0
Abbey Management Company LLC		D	562 243-2100	0
Abilty First		D	562 426-6161	0
Ace Relocation Systems Inc		E	310 632-2800	0
Acom Solutions Inc (PA)		E	562 424-7899	0
Advanced Medical MGT Inc		D	562 766-2000	0
Advertising Consultants Inc (PA)		C	310 233-2750	0
Advocacy For Respect and Ch (PA)		D	562 597-7716	0
Aecom Global II LLC		D	310 343-6977	0
AES Alamitos LLC		D	562 493-7891	0
AES Southland LLC		D	562 430-8685	0
Agilon Health Inc		D	562 256-3800	0
Air Rutter International LLC		E	855 359-2576	0
Alamitos-Belmont Rehab Inc		C	562 434-8421	0
Alpert & Alpert Iron & Met Inc		E	562 624-8833	0
Als Services Usa Corp		D	562 597-3932	0
American Corporate SEC Inc (PA)		D	562 216-7440	0

	SIC	EMP	PHONE	ENTRY #
American Golf Corporation		E	562 494-4424	0
American Textile Maint Co		D	562 438-7656	0
American Textile Maint Co		D	562 438-1126	0
American Textile Maint Co		C	562 424-1607	0
AON Consulting Inc		D	562 496-2888	0
APL Logistics Ltd		C	310 548-8700	0
Apriso Corporation		C	562 951-8000	0
Aquarium of Pacific		D	562 590-3100	0
Aquarium of Pacific (PA)		C	562 590-3100	0
Argus Management Company LLC		B	562 299-5200	0
Armada Trucking Group Inc		D	800 620-8592	0
Arts and Services For Disabled		E	562 377-0302	0
Associated Students California		B	562 985-4994	0
Atlantic Express Trnsp		C	562 997-6868	0
Atlantic Mem Healthcare Assoc (PA)		C	562 424-8101	0
Auto Ins Spcialists-Long Beach		D	562 496-2888	0
Bank America National Assn		E	562 624-4330	0
Behavioral Health Services Inc		D	562 599-4194	0
Belmont Athletic Club		D	562 438-3816	0
Bragg Investment Company Inc (PA)		A	562 984-2400	0
Bret Boylan Property Mgt		E	562 437-7886	0
Brittany House LLC		D	562 421-4717	0
Brittney House		D	562 421-4717	0
C O T S Inc (PA)		D	714 751-5466	0
C S I Patrol Services		D	562 981-8988	0
California Broadcast Ctr LLC		C	310 233-2425	0
California Repertory Company		E	562 985-7891	0
California Resources Corp		D	562 624-3400	0
California Traffic Control		D	562 595-7575	0
Califrnia Rsurces Long Bch Inc		C	562 624-3204	0
Cambodian Association America (PA)		E	562 988-1863	0
Camp Fire USA Long Beach Cncl		E	562 421-2725	0
Career Transition Center		C	562 570-9675	0
Careonsite Inc (PA)		E	562 437-0831	0
Casey Company (PA)		C	562 436-9685	0
Catalina Channel Express Inc		C	562 435-8686	0
CE Allencompany Inc		E	562 989-6100	0
Century 21 Landmark Properties		E	562 422-0911	0
Charter Cmmnctons Oprating LLC		B	310 971-4001	0
Childnet Youth & Fmly Svcs Inc (PA)		C	562 498-5500	0
Childnet Youth & Fmly Svcs Inc		D	562 492-9983	0
Childrens Clinic serving Chl		B	562 264-4638	0
Chlb LLC		C	562 997-2000	0
Choura Venue Services		D	562 426-0555	0
Circle Marina Car Wash Inc		E	562 494-4698	0
CIT Bank NA		D	562 433-0972	0
Citadel Security Inc		C	562 248-2300	0
City of Long Beach		C	562 570-2828	0
City of Long Beach		D	562 570-5423	0
City of Long Beach		C	562 570-2890	0
City of Long Beach		C	562 570-2000	0
City of Long Beach		D	562 570-2600	0
City of Long Beach		B	562 436-3636	0
City of Long Beach		D	562 570-6919	0
City of Long Beach		B	562 570-6383	0
City of Long Beach		E	562 570-2390	0
Cloudstaff LLC (PA)		D	888 551-5339	0
Cmac Construction Company		D	562 435-5611	0
Coast Carwash LP		E	562 961-5555	0
Coastal Alliance Holdings Inc		C	562 370-1000	0
Coastal Closeouts		D	323 589-7900	0
Coastal Cmnty Senior Care LLC		C	562 596-4884	0
Code America Inc		D	562 502-7365	0
Cogent Financial Group		D	562 985-1388	0
College Park Realty Inc		E	562 982-0300	0
Comcast Corporation		D	800 240-3640	0
Commercial Protective Svcs Inc		A	310 515-5290	0
Compulink Management Ctr Inc		C	562 988-1688	0
Conservation Corps Long Beach		C	562 986-1249	0
Continental Graphics Corp (HQ)		C	714 503-4200	0
Continental Graphics Corp		A	714 503-4200	0
Corridor Recycling Inc		D	310 835-3849	0
Cosco Agencies (los Angeles) (DH)		D	213 689-6700	0
Country Villa Blmnt Hght Hlth		D	562 597-8817	0
Country Villa Service Corp		C	562 597-8817	0
County of Los Angeles		C	213 367-3176	0
County of Los Angeles		C	562 599-9000	0
Covenant Care California LLC		D	562 427-7493	0
Covenant Industries Inc		D	951 808-3708	0
CPS Security Solutions Inc (PA)		D	310 818-1030	0
Crane Co		C	562 426-2531	0
Daylight Transport LLC (PA)		D	310 507-8200	0
Demler Armstrong & Rowland LLP		E	562 597-0029	0
Denso Pdts & Svcs Americas Inc (DH)		C	310 834-6352	0
Dhs Member Services		E	562 595-5151	0

Mergent email: customerrelations@mergent.com

1560

2020 Directory of California
Wholesalers and Services Companies

(P-0000) Products & Services Section entry number
(PA)=Parent Co (HQ)=Headquarters (DH)=Div Headquarters

	SIC	EMP	PHONE	ENTRY #
Dignity Health		A	562 491-9000	0
Douglas W Jackson MD		D	562 424-6666	0
Dream Home Care Inc		D	562 595-9021	0
Duthie Electric Service Corp		E	562 790-1772	0
Easy Care Mso LLC		C	562 676-9600	0
Ecamsecure		D	888 246-0556	0
Edge Systems LLC (PA)		C	800 603-4996	0
Edgewater Convalescent Hosp		D	562 434-0974	0
Eichleay Inc		C	562 256-8600	0
Elements Behavioral Health Inc (PA)		C	562 741-6470	0
Elite Craftsman (PA)		C	562 989-3511	0
Envent Corporation (PA)		D	562 997-9465	0
Epcm Prof Svc Partners LLC		D	562 936-1000	0
Eric D Feldman MD Inc		E	562 424-6666	0
Erp Integrated Solutions Inc		D	562 425-7800	0
Fabric Barn		C	562 494-3450	0
Family Plg Assoc Med Group		D	562 595-5653	0
Family Plg Assoc Med Group (PA)		D	213 738-7283	0
Farmers Merchants Bnk Long Bch (HQ)		C	562 437-0011	0
Federal Express Corporation		D	800 463-3339	0
Federal Express Corporation		C	562 522-4014	0
Fire and Police		E	562 961-0066	0
First Team RE - Orange Cnty		D	562 346-5088	0
First Transit Inc		D	310 515-8270	0
Foasberg Laundry & Clrs Inc (PA)		D	562 426-7345	0
Forest Lawn Memorial-Park Assn		D	562 424-1631	0
Formula One Systems Inc (HQ)		D	562 424-7899	0
Foss Maritime Co Inc		D	562 435-0171	0
Foss Maritime Company Llc		C	562 435-0171	0
Free Conferencing Corporation		C	562 437-1411	0
Fresenius Med Care Long Beach		E	562 432-4444	0
Garcia Juarez Construction Inc (PA)		D	951 657-3535	0
Goodwill Srvng The Ppl of Sthr (PA)		D	562 435-3411	0
Greater Alarm Company Inc (DH)		D	949 474-0555	0
Guidance Center (PA)		C	562 595-1159	0
Gulfstream Aerospace Corp GA		A	562 420-1818	0
Hanjin Shipping Co Ltd		A	201 291-4600	0
Harbor Diesel and Eqp Inc		D	562 591-5665	0
Healthcare Partners LLC		D	562 304-2100	0
Healthcare Partners LLC		D	562 429-2473	0
Healthcare Partners LLC		B	562 988-7000	0
Healthcare Services Group Inc		A	562 494-7939	0
Healthsmart Pacific Inc (PA)		A	562 595-1911	0
HEI Long Beach LLC		C	562 983-3400	0
Hellmann Wrldwide Lgistics Inc		D	310 847-4600	0
HFS Concepts 4 Inc		E	562 424-1720	0
Hillcrest Cnvalescent Hosp Inc		C	323 636-3462	0
Hospitlity Fcsed Solutions Inc		D	562 424-1720	0
Howard John		D	562 425-4232	0
Howard CDM		E	562 427-4124	0
Human Touch LLC		D	562 426-8700	0
Hutchison Corporation		D	310 763-7991	0
Hyatt Corporation		B	562 432-0161	0
ICI Enterprises Inc		D	562 989-7715	0
Intelsat US LLC		C	310 525-5500	0
Intercommunity Care Centers		C	562 427-8915	0
International Garment Finisher		D	562 983-7400	0
International Trnsp Svc (HQ)		C	562 435-7781	0
Intertrend Communications Inc		D	562 733-1888	0
Intex Recreation Corp		D	310 549-1846	0
Intex Recreation Corp (PA)		D	310 549-5400	0
Intex Recreation Corp		C	310 549-5400	0
Iqa Solutions Inc		D	562 420-1000	0
Jacobs Civil Inc		D	310 847-2500	0
Jacobs Engineering Group Inc		D	310 847-2500	0
Jewish Community Ctr Long Bch		D	562 426-7601	0
Jfe Shoji Trade America Inc (HQ)		D	562 637-3500	0
Jvckenwood USA Corporation (HQ)		C	310 639-9000	0
Kazarian/Jewett Inc		E	562 594-5927	0
Keesal Young Logan A Prof Corp (PA)		D	562 436-2000	0
Kenny Pabst		E	562 439-2147	0
Kevcomp Inc		D	562 423-3028	0
Kindercare Learning Ctrs LLC		D	562 961-8882	0
Kirkhill Rubber Company		D	562 803-1117	0
Km Industrial Inc		D	562 786-6200	0
Kpff Inc		D	562 437-9100	0
L A Cstm AP & Promotions Inc (PA)		D	562 595-1770	0
Laugh Factory Inc		C	562 495-2844	0
Lawndale Hlthcare Wllness Ctr		D	310 679-3344	0
Lb Funding LLC		D	562 983-3400	0
Ld Products Inc		C	562 986-6940	0
Life Steps Foundation Inc		D	562 436-0751	0
Lite Solar Corp		C	562 256-1249	0
Long Bch Museum Art Foundation		D	562 439-2119	0
Long Beach Behavioral Health U		D	310 221-6336	0

	SIC	EMP	PHONE	ENTRY #
Long Beach Care Center Inc		C	562 426-6141	0
Long Beach Cmnty Action Partnr		C	562 216-4600	0
Long Beach Cmnty College Dst		A	562 938-4291	0
Long Beach Day Nursery (PA)		D	562 421-1488	0
Long Beach Day Nursery		E	562 421-1488	0
Long Beach Memorial Med Ctr (HQ)		A	562 933-2000	0
Long Beach Public Trnsp Co		B	562 591-2301	0
Long Beach Public Trnsp Co (PA)		A	562 591-8753	0
Long Beach Public Trnsp Co		D	562 591-8753	0
Long Beach Unified School Dst		A	562 491-1281	0
Long Beach Unified School Dst		D	562 426-6176	0
Long Beach Unified School Dst		C	562 997-7550	0
Long Beach Unified School Dst		A	562 493-3596	0
Long Beach Yacht Club		D	562 598-9401	0
Longwood Management Corp		C	562 432-5751	0
Loofs Lite A Line		E	562 436-2978	0
M O Dion & Sons Inc (PA)		D	562 432-3946	0
M P O Inc (HQ)		D	562 628-1007	0
M4 Wind Services Inc		D	562 981-7797	0
Macro-Pro Inc (PA)		C	562 595-0900	0
Maintenance Staff Inc		A	562 493-3982	0
Mangan Inc (PA)		D	310 835-8080	0
Maritzcx Research LLC		A	310 525-1300	0
Marlora Investments LLC		D	562 494-3311	0
Marriott International Inc		C	562 425-5210	0
Matrix Environmental Inc		D	562 236-2704	0
Matrix Industries Inc		B	562 236-2700	0
Matus International Inc		C	562 435-5200	0
Med-Legal LLC		C	626 653-5160	0
Medasend Biomedical Inc (PA)		C	800 200-3581	0
Memor Ortho Surgic Group A M		D	562 424-6666	0
Memorial Counseling Assoc Inc		D	562 961-0155	0
Memorial Psychiatric Hlth Svcs		E	562 494-9243	0
Mental Health Amer Los Angeles		D	562 437-6717	0
Mercedes-Benz RE		E	310 547-6086	0
Merritt Hospitality LLC		C	562 983-3400	0
Metropower Inc		D	562 305-9617	0
Michael McCarthy		E	310 800-5367	0
Mida Industries Inc		C	562 616-1020	0
Midnite Air Corp (HQ)		D	310 910-9199	0
Milco Constructors Inc		E	562 595-1977	0
Mistras Group Inc		D	562 597-3932	0
Moffatt & Nichol		D	562 426-9551	0
Molina Healthcare Inc		B	888 562-5442	0
Molina Healthcare Inc		B	310 221-3031	0
Molina Healthcare Inc (PA)		A	562 435-3666	0
Molina Healthcare Inc		B	562 435-3666	0
Molina Healthcare California		C	800 526-8196	0
Molina Healthcare of Californi		A	562 435-3666	0
Motion Theory Inc		C	310 396-9433	0
Muni-Fed Energy Inc		E	714 321-3346	0
Museum of Latin American Art		E	562 437-1689	0
Neonatal Medical Assoc Inc		B	562 933-8100	0
New Alliance Insurance Brokers		E	424 205-6700	0
Nhca Inc		C	310 519-8200	0
Noble/Utah Long Beach LLC		C	562 436-3000	0
NRC Environmental Services Inc		D	562 432-1304	0
Ocean Blue Envmtl Svcs Inc (PA)		D	562 624-4120	0
Olive Crest		D	562 216-8841	0
Olympix Fitness LLC		D	562 366-4600	0
Onewest Bank NA		D	562 433-0971	0
Oocl (usa) Inc		D	562 499-2600	0
Opex Communications Inc		E	562 968-5420	0
Oshyn Inc		D	213 483-1770	0
Overland Pacific & Cutler LLC (PA)		D	800 400-7356	0
P2s Inc		C	562 497-2999	0
Pacific Care Inc		D	562 494-6500	0
Pacific Gtwy Wrkfrce Prtnr Inc		D	562 570-3700	0
Pacific Occptnal Medicine Svcs		E	562 997-2290	0
Pacific Palms Healthcare Inc		D	562 436-0791	0
Pacific Shores Med Group Inc (PA)		D	562 590-0345	0
Palm Harbor Residency LP		C	562 595-4551	0
Palmcrest Grand Care Ctr Inc		D	562 595-4551	0
Palp Inc		C	562 595-5841	0
Parwood Preservation LP		D	562 531-7880	0
Pbi-Birkenwald Market Eqp Inc (PA)		E	562 595-4785	0
Penske Truck Leasing Co LP		D	310 327-3116	0
Perona Langer Beck A Prof Corp		D	562 426-6155	0
Platt Security Systems Inc		C	562 986-4484	0
Polar Tankers Inc (DH)		D	562 388-1400	0
Porchlight Inc		D	562 989-5100	0
Port of Long Bch Employees CLB		B	562 590-4102	0
Posca Brothers Dental Lab		D	562 427-1811	0
Pponext Inc		B	888 446-6098	0
Praxair Inc		D	562 427-0099	0

Employment Codes: A=Over 500 employees, B=251-500,
C=101-250, D=51-100, E=50

2020 Directory of California
Wholesalers and Services Companies

© Mergent Inc. 1-800-342-5647

1561

GEOGRAPHIC

	SIC	EMP	PHONE	ENTRY #
Preferred Construction Co Inc		D	714 630-3004	0
Premier Insite Group Inc		D	562 741-5018	0
Premier Nursing Services Inc **(PA)**		A	562 437-4313	0
Prindle Decker & Amaro LLP **(PA)**		D	562 436-3946	0
PSC Industrial Outsourcing LP		D	562 997-6000	0
Qualfax Inc		D	562 988-1272	0
Queensbay Hotel LLC **(PA)**		C	562 628-0625	0
Queensbay Hotel LLC		D	562 481-3910	0
R & B Realty Group LP		A	310 478-1021	0
R G Vanderweil Engineers LLP		C	562 256-8623	0
R L Klein & Associates		D	562 427-5577	0
Rance King Properties Inc **(PA)**		C	562 240-1000	0
Rdc-S111 Inc **(PA)**		D	562 628-8000	0
Recon Refractory & Cnstr Inc		E	562 988-7981	0
Recovery Place Inc		D	954 200-8308	0
Redbarn Pet Products Inc **(PA)**		C	562 495-7315	0
Regency Oaks Care Center		D	562 498-3368	0
Rehabilitation California Dept		E	562 422-8325	0
Residence Inn By Marriott LLC		C	562 595-0909	0
Resource Environmental Inc		D	562 468-7000	0
Restaurant Depot LLC		D	562 634-6771	0
Retirement Housing Foundation **(PA)**		D	562 257-5100	0
Reynolds Health Industries		D	562 591-7621	0
Rmd Group Inc		B	562 866-9288	0
RMS Foundation Inc		A	562 435-3511	0
Ronald J Lemieux Assoc Law Off		D	562 375-0095	0
Roux Associates Inc		D	562 446-8600	0
Ruffin Hotel Corp of Cal		B	562 425-5210	0
Runa Hr Holdings Inc		D	562 883-3546	0
Safe Refuge		D	562 987-5722	0
Save Queen LLC		B	562 435-3511	0
Scan California Management Co		A	562 989-5100	0
Scan Group **(PA)**		B	562 308-2733	0
Securitas SEC Svcs USA Inc		C	562 427-2737	0
Senior Care **(PA)**		A	562 989-5100	0
Senior Care		D	562 492-9878	0
Shelton Construction Company		D	714 903-7853	0
Shield Security Inc		B	562 283-1100	0
Shimadzu Precision Instrs Inc **(DH)**		D	562 420-6226	0
Shipco Transport Inc		D	562 295-2900	0
Signature Flight Support Corp		D	562 997-0700	0
Smart & Final Stores Inc		B	562 438-0450	0
Smg Holdings LLC		D	562 499-7611	0
Southern California Edison Co		B	562 491-3803	0
Southern California Institute		D	562 826-8139	0
Spectacor Management Group		B	562 436-3636	0
Ssa Containers Inc		D	206 623-0304	0
Ssa Marine Inc		E	562 983-1001	0
St Mary Medical Center **(DH)**		A	562 491-9000	0
Star Brite Building Maint		B	562 988-2829	0
Starlight International Ltd LP		D	562 439-5740	0
State Farm Mutl Auto Insur Co		D	310 632-9810	0
Steuber Corporation **(PA)**		D	310 632-8255	0
Sunbridge Harbor View		C	562 989-9097	0
Sunbridge Healthcare LLC		D	562 981-9392	0
Synergy Health North Amer Inc		D	562 428-5858	0
Ta Chen International Inc **(HQ)**		C	562 808-8000	0
Talent & Acquisition LLC		C	213 742-1972	0
Tarzana Treatment Centers Inc		E	562 218-1868	0
Telecare Corporation		D	562 630-8672	0
Telecare Corporation		C	562 634-9534	0
Telecare La Step Down		E	562 216-4900	0
Tell Steel Inc		D	562 435-4826	0
The Designory Inc **(HQ)**		C	562 624-0200	0
Tom Dreher Sales Inc		D	562 355-4074	0
Total Intermodal Services Inc **(PA)**		E	562 427-6300	0
Toyota Logistics Services		B	562 437-6767	0
Transcendent Security Services		E	562 850-3313	0
Trinity Health Systems		D	562 347-2797	0
Tristar Insurance Group Inc **(PA)**		A	562 495-6600	0
Turelk Inc **(PA)**		C	310 835-3736	0
Twining Inc **(PA)**		D	562 426-3355	0
Twining Inc		D	562 426-3355	0
Ultimate Construction Inc		D	562 633-3389	0
Union Pacific Railroad Company		B	562 490-7000	0
Universal Protection Svc LP		D	562 981-5700	0
Urban Commons Queensway LLC		A	562 499-1611	0
US Skillserve Inc **(PA)**		A	562 930-0777	0
USA Waste of California Inc		D	310 830-7100	0
Vanguard Lgistics Svcs USA Inc **(HQ)**		D	310 847-3000	0
Ventura Transfer Company **(PA)**		D	310 549-5961	0
Villa Serena Healthcare Center		D	562 437-2797	0
Virginia Country Club		C	562 427-0924	0
Vista Cove Care Center At Long		D	562 426-4461	0
W A Rasic Cnstr Co Inc **(PA)**		C	562 928-6111	0

	SIC	EMP	PHONE	ENTRY #
Warren E&P Inc		D	877 587-9494	0
Wells Hse Hspice Fundation Inc		D	714 952-3795	0
Western Exterminator Company		E	310 835-3513	0
Weyerhaeuser Company		D	562 983-6589	0
William H Warden III MD		D	562 424-6666	0
Windes Inc **(PA)**		D	562 435-1191	0
Wm Wireless Inc		E	562 633-9288	0
World Trade Ctr Ht Assoc Ltd		D	562 983-3400	0
Xerox Education Services LLC **(DH)**		D	310 830-9847	0
Yhb Long Beach LLC		D	562 597-4401	0
Young Mens Christian Associat		D	562 624-2376	0
Young Mens Chrstn Assc Gr L B		B	562 596-3394	0
Young Mens Chrstn Assc Gr L B		D	562 423-0491	0
Young Mens Chrstn Assc Gr L B		D	562 423-0491	0
Young Mens Chrstn Assc Gr L B		D	562 633-0106	0

LOOMIS, CA - Placer County

	SIC	EMP	PHONE	ENTRY #
Abshear Landscape Development		E	916 660-1617	0
Jls Environmental Services Inc		D	916 660-1525	0
McCuen Construction Inc **(PA)**		E	916 652-7824	0
Online Communications Inc		C	916 652-7253	0
Wilkie Masonry Inc		E	916 652-0118	0

LOS ALAMITOS, CA - Orange County

	SIC	EMP	PHONE	ENTRY #
Advantage Plumbing Group Inc		D	714 898-6020	0
Alamitos Enterprises LLC **(PA)**		D	562 596-1827	0
Apfeld & Neal Insurance Svcs		E	714 821-7041	0
Barrys Security Services Inc		C	562 493-7007	0
Carol Electric Company Inc		D	562 431-1870	0
College Park Realty Inc **(PA)**		C	562 594-6753	0
Dynalectric Company		C	714 236-2242	0
Friedas Inc		D	714 826-6100	0
Fruit Guys		D	714 826-2993	0
General Services Cal Dept		D	562 342-7212	0
Goodman Group Inc		D	562 596-5561	0
Katella Properties		C	562 596-5561	0
Kdc Inc **(HQ)**		C	714 828-7000	0
Lakewood South Car Wash LLC		E	562 430-4975	0
Los Alamitos Medical Ctr Inc **(HQ)**		A	714 826-6400	0
Los Almtos Hmodialysis Ctr Inc		D	562 426-8881	0
Marinow Harry MD Facs Inc		E	562 430-3561	0
Mggb Inc		C	714 226-0520	0
Millie and Severson Inc		D	562 493-3611	0
Mulligan Limited **(PA)**		D	714 484-6799	0
Severson Group Incorporated **(PA)**		D	562 493-3611	0
Southland Credit Union **(PA)**		D	562 862-6831	0
Ssl Robotics LLC		C	626 296-1373	0
Sure Forming Systems Inc		E	562 598-6348	0
Tenet Healthsystem Medical		A	805 546-7698	0
Thermo Power Industries		E	562 799-0087	0
Trojan Professional Svcs Inc		D	714 816-7169	0
US Bank National Association		E	562 795-7520	0
Utblo Inc		C	562 493-3664	0

LOS ALTOS, CA - Santa Clara County

	SIC	EMP	PHONE	ENTRY #
Adobe Animal Hospital Inc		D	650 948-9661	0
Alain Pinel Realtors Inc		D	650 941-1111	0
American Baptist Homes of West		C	650 948-8291	0
Cerebras Systems Inc		C	650 933-4980	0
Comity Designs Inc		D	415 967-1530	0
Covenant Care California LLC		C	650 941-5255	0
Guardsmark LLC		D	800 238-5878	0
Institute On Aging		C	510 536-3377	0
Iqtalent Partners LLC		D	888 501-4787	0
Kisco Senior Living LLC		E	650 948-7337	0
Los Altos Golf and Country CLB		D	650 947-3100	0
Midpeninsul Rgnl Opn Sp		D	650 691-1200	0
Mw2 Consulting LLC		D	408 573-6310	0
Netcube Systems Inc		D	650 862-7858	0
Older Adults Care Management **(PA)**		C	650 329-1411	0
Palo Alto Medical Foundation		D	650 254-5200	0
Portworx Inc		D	650 386-0766	0
R J Dailey Construction Co		D	650 948-5196	0
Robertson Piper Management LLC		C	650 625-8333	0
Roman Cthlic Bishp of San Jose		A	833 304-0763	0
The David Lcile Pckard Fndtion		D	650 917-7167	0
Toyota Research Institute Inc		D	703 231-6680	0

LOS ALTOS HILLS, CA - Santa Clara County

	SIC	EMP	PHONE	ENTRY #
Footh-De Anza Commun Colleg Di		D	650 949-7260	0
Idea Travel Company		A	650 948-0207	0
Impulsa Bus Accelerator LLC		C	650 924-5010	0

LOS ANGELES, CA - Los Angeles County

	SIC	EMP	PHONE	ENTRY #
120 South Los Angeles Street H		D	213 629-1200	0
1755 Efm 1 LLC		D	323 231-4174	0
180la LLC		C	310 382-1400	0

2020 Directory of California
Wholesalers and Services Companies

(P-0000) Products & Services Section entry number
(PA)=Parent Co (HQ)=Headquarters (DH)=Div Headquarters

	SIC	EMP	PHONE	ENTRY #
24 Hour Fitness Usa Inc		D	310 553-7600	0
3dna Corp (PA)		D	213 394-4623	0
417 Stockton St LLC		D	323 327-9656	0
4g Wireless Inc		D	310 429-9048	0
4g Wireless Inc		D	323 679-9991	0
5 Design Inc		D	323 308-3558	0
550 Flower St Operations LLC		C	213 892-8080	0
6417 Selma Hotel LLC		C	323 844-6417	0
711 Hope LP		C	213 365-5000	0
800 Degrees LLC		E	310 443-1911	0
834 W Arrow Highway LP		D	213 355-1024	0
901 West Olympic Blvd LP		D	347 992-5707	0
A Buchalter Professional Corp (PA)		C	213 891-0700	0
A Community of Friends		D	213 480-0809	0
A F Gilmore Company		D	323 939-1191	0
A Filml Inc		D	213 977-8600	0
A M S Partnership (PA)		D	310 312-6698	0
A S E C International Inc		A	803 939-4809	0
A Touch of Kindness		D	323 997-6500	0
A World Fit For Kids		C	213 387-7712	0
A&E Television Networks LLC		C	310 201-6015	0
AA Autmtive Personnel Svcs Inc		C	310 914-3012	0
Aaaza Inc		D	213 380-8333	0
Abba Bail Bonds (PA)		E	213 680-1400	0
ABC Cable Networks Group		C	323 860-5900	0
Abilityfirst		D	213 748-7309	0
ABM Distributors Inc		D	310 401-0434	0
ABM Industries Incorporated		E	323 720-4020	0
ABM Janitorial Services Inc		A	213 384-0600	0
Abode Communities		C	213 629-2702	0
Absolute Towing-Hollenbeck Div		E	323 225-9294	0
Access Finance Inc		E	310 826-4000	0
Accor Corp		C	310 278-5444	0
Accurate Courier Services Inc		D	310 481-3937	0
Accurate Services Inc		C	323 906-1000	0
Ace Beverage Co		D	323 266-6238	0
Acetech Construction Inc		E	213 637-4702	0
Aceteck Roofing Co Inc		E	323 231-6060	0
Aci International (PA)		D	310 889-3400	0
ACS Security Industries Inc		D	310 475-9016	0
Action Property Management Inc		C	800 400-2284	0
Adcolony Inc		D	650 625-1262	0
Added Value LLC (DH)		C	323 254-4326	0
Adee Plumbing and Heating Inc (PA)		D	323 296-8787	0
Adeste Program Company		B	213 251-3551	0
Adexa Inc (PA)		E	310 642-2100	0
Adir International LLC		D	213 386-4412	0
Adlink Cable Advertising LLC		C	310 477-3994	0
Admiralty Partners Inc		D	310 471-3772	0
Advanced Digital Services Inc (PA)		D	323 962-8585	0
Advantage Produce Inc		E	213 627-2777	0
Aecom (PA)		C	213 593-8000	0
Aecom C&E Inc		C	213 593-8100	0
Aecom E&C Holdings Inc (DH)		D	213 593-8000	0
Aecom Energy & Cnstr Inc (DH)		C	213 593-8100	0
Aecom Global II LLC (HQ)		D	213 593-8100	0
Aecom Global II LLC		C	213 996-2200	0
Aecom Services Inc (HQ)		C	213 593-8000	0
Aecom Technical Services Inc (HQ)		D	213 593-8000	0
Aecom Usa Inc		C	213 330-7200	0
Aecom Usa Inc		B	213 593-8000	0
AEG Global Partnerships LLC		C	213 763-7700	0
AEG Management Lacc LLC		C	213 741-1151	0
AEG Presents LLC (DH)		C	323 930-5700	0
Aegis Ambulance Service Inc (PA)		D	626 685-9410	0
Aero-Engines Inc		D	323 663-3961	0
Aerotransporte De Carge Union		B	310 649-0069	0
Aesthetic Maintenance Corp		E	213 353-1525	0
Aetna Health California Inc (DH)		C	925 543-9223	0
African American Unity Center		D	323 789-7300	0
Aftershock La Studios Inc		D	650 450-9660	0
AG Facilities Operations LLC		A	323 651-1808	0
Agencycom LLC		B	415 817-3800	0
Aids Project Los Angeles (PA)		D	213 201-1600	0
Air Lease Corporation (PA)		D	310 553-0555	0
Airgas Usa LLC		D	323 568-2244	0
Airpush Inc		C	877 944-2490	0
Ajit Healthcare Inc		D	213 484-0510	0
Akin Gump Strauss		D	310 229-1000	0
Alameda Produce Market LLC		D	213 221-3400	0
Alaska Airlines Inc		C	310 925-2409	0
Alchemy Communications Inc		D	310 568-0700	0
Alexandria Care Center LLC		C	323 660-1800	0
All Area Plumbing Inc		C	323 939-9990	0
All Nation Security Svcs Inc (PA)		C	213 769-4510	0

	SIC	EMP	PHONE	ENTRY #
Allaquaria LLC		D	310 645-1107	0
Allbright Group La LLC		E	310 402-3570	0
Alldayeveryday Productions LLC		E	323 556-6200	0
Allen Matkins Leck Gmble (PA)		B	213 622-5555	0
Alliance For Housing & Healing (PA)		D	323 344-4885	0
Alliance Ground Intl LLC		D	310 646-2446	0
Alliancebernstein LP		D	310 286-6000	0
Alliedbarton Security Svcs LLC		B	800 418-6423	0
Allstate Construction Co		E	310 652-6942	0
Allzone Management Svcs Inc		B	213 291-8879	0
Alpha Source Inc		E	424 270-9600	0
Alsco Co		C	323 465-5111	0
Alston & Bird LLP		C	213 626-8830	0
Alta Healthcare System LLC (HQ)		C	323 267-0477	0
Alta Hospitals System LLC		C	323 267-0477	0
Alta Hospitals System LLC (HQ)		C	310 943-4500	0
Altamed Health Services Corp		D	323 980-4466	0
Altamed Health Services Corp		C	323 276-0267	0
Altamed Health Services Corp		E	323 980-4000	0
Altegra Health		D	310 776-4001	0
Altoon Partners LLP (PA)		D	213 225-1900	0
Altour International Inc		C	310 571-6000	0
Altour International Inc (PA)		D	310 571-6000	0
Alzheimers Greater Los Angeles		D	323 938-3379	0
Amada Enterprises		C	323 757-1881	0
Amanecer Cmnty Counseling Svc		D	213 481-7464	0
Ambulnz Co LLC		D	877 311-5555	0
Amcap Fund Inc		B	213 486-9200	0
American Airlines Inc		C	310 215-7054	0
American Airlines Inc		D	213 935-6045	0
American Airlines Inc		C	310 646-3013	0
American Care Givers Westwood		D	310 208-8005	0
American Contrs Indemnity Co (DH)		C	213 330-1309	0
American Funds Distrs Inc (DH)		C	213 486-9200	0
American Heart Association Inc		E	213 291-7000	0
American Home Assurance Co		B	213 689-3500	0
American Intl Group Inc		B	213 689-3500	0
American Multi-Cinema Inc		E	310 228-5500	0
American Mutual Fund Inc		C	213 486-9200	0
American National Red Cross		D	310 445-9900	0
American Realty Advisors		D	818 545-1152	0
American Red Cross La Chapter (PA)		C	310 445-9900	0
American Reprographics Co LLC		D	213 745-3145	0
American Tax Solutions		E	323 306-7032	0
American Textile Maint Co		E	213 749-4433	0
American Textile Maint Co		C	323 735-1661	0
American Voice Mail Inc (PA)		E	310 478-4949	0
Americantours Intl LLC (HQ)		C	310 641-9953	0
Amgreen Solar & Electric Inc		E	213 388-5647	0
Amgreen Solutions Inc		E	213 388-5647	0
AMS - Exotic LLC		D	213 612-5888	0
Analytic US Market Neutral Off		D	213 688-3015	0
Andersen Tax LLC		C	213 593-2300	0
Anderson Kayne Capital		B	800 231-7414	0
Anderson Kayne Inv MGT Inc (PA)		D	310 556-2721	0
Anderson McPharlin Conners LLP (PA)		D	213 688-0080	0
Angeles Home Health Care Inc		C	213 487-5131	0
Angelus Western Ppr Fibers Inc		D	213 623-9221	0
Anschutz Entrmt Group Inc (HQ)		C	213 337-5052	0
Anschutz Film Group		A	310 887-1000	0
AON Consulting Inc		D	818 506-4300	0
AON Risk Svcs Companies Inc		D	213 630-3200	0
Apla Health & Wellness		D	213 201-1546	0
App Wholesale LLC		B	323 980-3746	0
Appetize Technologies Inc		C	877 559-4225	0
Apumac LLC		C	888 248-7775	0
Aramark Facility Services LLC		C	213 740-8968	0
Aramark Services Inc		D	323 587-7661	0
Aramark Spt & Entrmt Group LLC		D	213 740-1224	0
Aramark Unf & Career AP LLC		C	323 266-0555	0
ARC Mid-Cities Inc		C	310 329-9272	0
Arclight Cinema Company		C	323 464-1465	0
Arden Realty Inc (HQ)		D	310 966-2600	0
Arent Fox LLP		C	213 629-7400	0
Ares Management Corporation (PA)		C	310 201-4100	0
Ares Management LLC (HQ)		C	310 201-4100	0
Ares Management LLC		C	310 201-4100	0
Arinwine Arcft Maint Svcs LLC		C	310 338-0063	0
Armand Hammer Museum		C	310 443-7000	0
Armanino LLP		C	310 478-4148	0
Arnies Supplies Service Ltd		D	323 263-1696	0
Arnold Porter Kaye Scholer LLP		C	310 788-1000	0
Aroma Spa & Sports LLC		D	213 387-2111	0
Arthrtis Fundation PCF Reg Inc		E	323 954-5760	0
Artist Silva Management LLC (PA)		C	323 856-8222	0

Employment Codes: A=Over 500 employees, B=251-500, C=101-250, D=51-100, E=50

2020 Directory of California
Wholesalers and Services Companies

© Mergent Inc. 1-800-342-5647

1563

GEOGRAPHIC

	SIC	EMP	PHONE	ENTRY #
Artwear Inc		E	310 217-1393	0
Arup North America Limited		C	310 578-4182	0
Arya Group Inc		E	310 446-7000	0
Arya Ice Cream Distrg Co Inc		D	323 234-2994	0
Asbestos Instant Response Inc		C	323 733-0508	0
Ascot Hotel LP		C	310 476-6411	0
Asia Pacific Capital		D	213 628-8800	0
Asian PCF Hlth Care Ventr Inc **(PA)**		C	323 644-3880	0
Assist 65 Plus		E	323 557-4426	0
Associated Entrmt Releasing **(PA)**		E	323 934-7044	0
Associated Press		D	213 626-1200	0
Associated Students UCLA **(PA)**		B	310 825-4321	0
Associated Students UCLA		C	310 794-0242	0
Associated Students UCLA		A	310 825-9451	0
AT&T Corp		D	310 473-3649	0
AT&T Corp		D	213 787-0055	0
AT&T Corp		D	310 659-7600	0
AT&T Corp		D	213 787-0055	0
AT&T Services Inc		A	213 975-4089	0
AT&T Services Inc		E	213 741-3111	0
AT&T Services Inc		B	323 468-6813	0
Athicon		E	213 454-0662	0
Attn Inc		C	323 413-2878	0
Aurora Resurgence Fund LP		A	310 551-0101	0
Authority Tax Services LLC		D	213 486-5135	0
Authorized Taxi Cab		D	323 776-5324	0
Automatic Data Processing Inc		D	800 225-5237	0
Automobile Club Southern Cal **(PA)**		C	213 741-3686	0
Autry Museum of American West		C	323 667-2000	0
Avida Caregivers Inc		A	323 498-1500	0
Axa Advisors LLC		D	213 251-1600	0
Axaio Industries LLC		E	323 504-1074	0
Axminster Medical Group Inc **(PA)**		D	310 670-3255	0
B F Management		D	323 931-7776	0
B H Premier Inc **(PA)**		D	310 286-2004	0
Babyfirst Americas LLC		D	310 442-9853	0
Bachelor Productions Inc		D	310 567-9249	0
Bain & Company Inc		D	310 229-3000	0
Baker Keener & Nahra		E	213 241-0900	0
Baker & Hostetler LLP		D	310 820-8800	0
Ballard Spahr LLP		D	424 204-4400	0
Bamko Inc		C	310 470-5859	0
Banamex USA Bancorp **(DH)**		D	310 203-3440	0
Banc California National Assn		E	310 286-0710	0
Bank America National Assn		D	310 384-4562	0
Bank Leumi USA		D	323 966-4700	0
Bank of Hope		E	213 389-5550	0
Bank of Hope **(HQ)**		C	213 639-1700	0
Bank of Tokyo Ltd		A	213 488-3700	0
Barclays Capital Inc		C	310 481-4100	0
Barlow Group **(PA)**		C	213 250-4200	0
Barlow Respiratory Hospital **(PA)**		C	213 250-4200	0
Barnes & Thornburg LLP		C	310 284-3880	0
Becker Interiors Ltd		E	323 469-1908	0
Behringer Harvard Wilshire Blv		D	310 475-8711	0
Beitler & Associates Inc **(PA)**		C	310 820-2955	0
Bel-Air Country Club		C	310 472-9563	0
Belmont Village LP		E	323 874-7711	0
Bender/Helper Impact Inc **(PA)**		D	310 473-4147	0
Beres Consulting		D	310 476-9941	0
Berg Lacquer Co **(PA)**		D	323 261-8114	0
Bestway Recycling Company Inc **(PA)**		D	323 588-8157	0
Bet Tzedek		D	323 939-0506	0
Beverly Blvd Leaseco LLC		D	310 278-5444	0
Beverly Hills Country Club		C	310 836-4400	0
Beverly Hills Luxury Hotel LLC		B	310 274-9999	0
Beverly Sunstone Hills LLC		D	310 228-4100	0
Beverly West Health Care Inc		D	323 938-2451	0
Beverlywood Realty Inc		E	310 836-8322	0
Big3 Basketball LLC		D	213 417-2013	0
Biomat Usa Inc **(DH)**		E	323 225-2221	0
Bird Mrlla Bxer Wlpert A Prof		D	310 201-2100	0
Blackstone Consulting Inc **(PA)**		C	310 826-4389	0
Blair Television Inc		D	714 537-5923	0
Blank Rome LLP		D	424 239-3400	0
Blc Residential Care Inc		D	310 722-7541	0
Bloom David Law Offices of		E	323 938-5248	0
Bls Lmsine Svc Los Angeles Inc		B	323 644-7166	0
BLT & Associates Inc		C	323 860-4000	0
Blue Cross & Blue Shield Mich		C	323 782-3046	0
Blue Lagoon Textile Inc		E	213 590-4545	0
Blue Planet International Inc		E	323 526-9999	0
Blx Group LLC		D	213 612-2400	0
Blx Group LLC **(PA)**		D	213 612-2200	0
Bonne Bridge Muell Okeef & **(PA)**		D	213 480-1900	0
Bonneville International Corp		E	323 634-1800	0
Bonnie Brae Cnvlscent Hosp Inc **(PA)**		D	213 483-8144	0
Booz Allen Hamilton Inc		D	310 297-2100	0
Booz Allen Hamilton Inc		D	213 620-1900	0
Boston Consulting Group Inc		D	213 621-2772	0
Braille Institute America Inc **(PA)**		C	323 663-1111	0
Breitbart News Network LLC		D	424 371-0585	0
Breitburn GP LLC		A	213 225-5900	0
Brentwood Bmdical RES Inst Inc		C	310 312-1554	0
Brentwood Country Club		C	310 451-8011	0
Brier Oak On Sunset LLC		C	323 663-3951	0
Brinks Incorporated		C	818 503-8630	0
Brinks Incorporated		E	323 262-2646	0
Brisam Lax (de) LLC		D	310 649-5151	0
Broadreach Capitl Partners LLC		A	310 691-5760	0
Broadview Inc		E	323 221-9174	0
Brookfield Dtla Fund Office		D	213 626-3300	0
Browning Apartments		E	213 252-8847	0
Bsm UNI		E	213 626-2557	0
Buck Global LLC		D	310 282-8232	0
Buckingham Affrdbl Aprtmnts LP		D	424 273-6162	0
Buena Ventura Care Center Inc **(PA)**		D	323 268-0106	0
Bungalow 16 Entertainment LLC		E	310 226-7870	0
Bunker Hill Club Inc		D	213 620-9662	0
Burke Williams & Sorensen LLP **(PA)**		D	213 236-0600	0
Burlington Convalescent Hosp **(PA)**		D	213 381-5585	0
Burlington Convalescent Hosp		D	323 295-7737	0
Burn 60 LLC		E	310 476-5656	0
Burton-Way House Ltd A CA		C	310 273-2222	0
Burton-Way House Ltd A CA **(PA)**		E	310 552-6623	0
Busa Servicing Inc **(DH)**		C	310 203-3400	0
BV General Inc		D	323 651-0043	0
C&C Jewelry Mfg Inc		D	213 623-6800	0
C-Air International Inc		D	310 695-3400	0
Caa Sports LLC **(HQ)**		D	424 288-2000	0
Caffeine Productions		D	323 860-8111	0
Cal Southern Assn Governments **(PA)**		C	213 236-1800	0
Caliber Holdings Corporation		D	323 913-4000	0
Califia Farms LLC **(PA)**		E	213 694-4667	0
California Assn Realtors Inc **(PA)**		C	213 739-8200	0
California Club		C	213 622-1391	0
California Cmnty Foundation **(PA)**		D	213 413-4130	0
California Credit Union		D	213 975-1254	0
California Cryobank LLC **(PA)**		D	310 496-5691	0
California Endowment **(PA)**		D	213 928-8800	0
California Fair Plan Assn		D	213 487-0111	0
California Pav Grading Co Inc		D	323 372-5920	0
California Rain Company Inc		D	213 623-6061	0
California State Univ Aux Svcs		A	323 343-2531	0
California Suncare Inc		D	310 578-4400	0
Califrnia Hosp Med Ctr Fndtion		A	213 748-2411	0
Califrnia Scnce Ctr Foundation		B	213 744-2545	0
Call To Action LLC **(PA)**		D	310 996-7200	0
Callisonrtkl Inc		C	213 627-7373	0
Callisonrtkl Inc		C	213 633-6000	0
Camp Bow Wow Franchising Inc		D	310 571-6500	0
Candleberry Properties LP		E	323 852-7000	0
Canton Food Co Inc		C	213 688-7707	0
Cantor Fitzgerald L P		D	310 282-6500	0
Canvas Worldwide LLC		C	424 303-4300	0
Canyon Partners Incorporated **(HQ)**		D	310 272-1000	0
Cap-Mpt **(PA)**		C	213 473-8600	0
Capital Brands LLC **(HQ)**		D	310 996-7200	0
Capital Brands Dist LLC		D	310 996-7200	0
Capital Drywall LP		C	909 599-6818	0
Capital Group Companies Inc		B	310 996-6238	0
Capital Group Companies Inc **(PA)**		A	213 486-9200	0
Capital Guardian Trust Company **(HQ)**		D	213 486-9200	0
Capital Research and MGT Co **(HQ)**		B	213 486-9200	0
Capitol Records		A	213 462-6252	0
Capnet Financial Services Inc **(PA)**		D	877 980-0558	0
Captain Marketing Inc		D	310 402-9709	0
Cara Communications Corp		E	310 442-5600	0
Career Group Inc **(PA)**		A	310 277-8188	0
Carleton Booker Marketing Inc		D	510 999-1682	0
Carmichael International Svc **(DH)**		D	213 353-0800	0
Carpenters Southwest ADM Corp **(PA)**		D	213 386-8590	0
Caruso MGT Ltd A Cal Ltd Prtnr		D	323 900-8100	0
Casa Dscanso Convalescent Hosp		C	323 225-5991	0
Catasys Inc **(PA)**		C	310 444-4300	0
Catchpoint Systems Inc		C	646 727-4557	0
Cathay Bank		B	213 687-1300	0
Cathay Bank		D	213 896-0098	0
Cathedral Center of St Paul		D	213 482-2040	0
Catholic Charities of La Inc **(PA)**		D	213 251-3400	0

Mergent email: customerrelations@mergent.com

1564

2020 Directory of California
Wholesalers and Services Companies

(P-0000) Products & Services Section entry number
(PA)=Parent Co (HQ)=Headquarters (DH)=Div Headquarters

	SIC	EMP	PHONE	ENTRY #
Catholic Charities of La Inc		D	213 251-3400	0
CB Richard Ellis RE Svcs LLC		D	213 613-3333	0
CB Richard Ellis Strategic Par		D	213 614-6862	0
CB Richard Ellis Strtgc Prtnrs		D	213 683-4200	0
Cbest Inc		D	310 445-2378	0
Cbre Inc **(HQ)**		C	213 613-3333	0
Cbre Inc		D	310 550-2500	0
Cbre Global Investors LLC **(DH)**		D	213 683-4200	0
Cbre Group Inc **(PA)**		C	213 613-3333	0
Cbre Services Inc		D	213 613-3333	0
CBS Broadcasting Inc		D	323 575-2345	0
CBS Corporation		D	323 575-2345	0
Cdsnet LLC		D	310 981-9500	0
Cecico Inc		D	323 269-7000	0
Cedars-Sinai Medical Center		C	310 824-3664	0
Cedars-Sinai Medical Center		C	310 423-3849	0
Cedars-Sinai Medical Center		A	323 866-8483	0
Cellco Partnership		D	213 380-2299	0
Cellco Partnership		D	310 659-0775	0
Cellco Partnership		D	213 738-9771	0
Cellular Palace Inc		D	310 278-2007	0
Cels Enterprises Inc **(PA)**		D	310 838-2103	0
Center Thtre Group Los Angeles **(PA)**		C	213 972-7344	0
Centerfield Media Holdings LLC **(PA)**		C	310 341-4420	0
Centurion Security Inc		C	818 755-0202	0
Century 21 Beverlywood Realty		D	310 836-8321	0
Century City Primary Care		E	310 553-3189	0
Century Plaza Garage		C	310 226-7495	0
Century Properties Owners Assn		E	310 272-8580	0
Certified Aviation Svcs LLC		D	310 338-1224	0
Cha Hollywood Medical Ctr LP **(PA)**		A	213 413-3000	0
Chain & Charm Inc		D	213 683-1039	0
Chance Group LLC		E	310 343-3766	0
Charles Dunn Co Inc		C	213 481-1800	0
Charles Dunn RE Svcs Inc **(PA)**		D	213 270-6200	0
Charles Schwab Corporation		C	714 385-6000	0
Charter Realty Group Inc **(PA)**		D	310 826-3174	0
Chase Care Center Inc		C	323 935-8490	0
Chicago Title Company		D	213 488-4375	0
Childrens Bureau Southern Cal **(PA)**		C	213 342-0100	0
Childrens Hospital Los Angeles		C	323 361-2153	0
Childrens Hospital Los Angeles **(PA)**		D	323 660-2450	0
Childrens Hospital Los Angeles		B	323 361-2119	0
Childrens Hospital Los Angeles		B	323 361-2751	0
Childrens Hospital Los Angeles		D	323 660-2450	0
Childrens Hospital Los Angeles		C	323 361-5702	0
Childrens Inst Los Angeles		A	213 383-2765	0
Childrens Inst Los Angeles **(PA)**		A	213 385-5100	0
Childrens Institute Inc		D	323 541-9368	0
Childrens Institute Inc **(PA)**		C	213 385-5100	0
China Airlines Ltd **(HQ)**		D	310 646-4233	0
Chinatown Service Center **(PA)**		C	213 808-1700	0
Chinese Laundry Inc		E	310 945-3299	0
Chiquita Brands Intl Inc		D	213 488-0925	0
Chodorow De Castro West		D	310 478-2541	0
Christmas Bonus Fund of The Pl		D	213 385-6161	0
Chrome River Technologies Inc **(PA)**		D	323 857-5800	0
Chsp Trs Los Angeles LLC		D	213 624-0000	0
Church of Jsus Chrst of Ld STS		C	323 268-7281	0
Churchill MGT Group Corp		E	877 937-7110	0
Cim Group LP **(PA)**		D	323 860-4900	0
Cinelease Inc **(HQ)**		E	855 441-5500	0
Cinepolis Luxury Cinemas		D	323 556-6340	0
Cinnabar		C	818 842-8190	0
Cinnabar California Inc		D	818 842-8190	0
CIT Bank NA		D	310 475-4594	0
CIT Bank NA		D	310 477-0546	0
CIT Bank National Association		D	310 820-9650	0
Citigroup Global Markets Inc		C	213 486-8811	0
City National Bank **(DH)**		B	310 888-6000	0
City National SEC Svcs Inc		D	310 641-6666	0
City of Los Angeles		A	213 978-0259	0
City of Los Angeles		C	213 473-6872	0
City of Los Angeles		D	213 473-0800	0
City of Los Angeles		D	213 485-4282	0
City of Los Angeles		D	213 202-5500	0
City of Los Angeles		D	213 847-2799	0
City of Los Angeles		D	213 978-8100	0
City of Los Angeles		E	323 467-7193	0
CJ America Inc **(HQ)**		D	213 427-5566	0
Clare Matrix		D	310 478-6006	0
Classic Protection Inc		E	213 742-1238	0
Clearview Capital LLC		A	310 806-9555	0
Cliftonlarsonallen LLP		D	310 273-2501	0
Clinic Inc		D	323 730-1920	0
Clinica Msr Oscar A Romero **(PA)**		D	213 989-7700	0
Clinica Popular Medical Group		E	213 381-7175	0
Clinics On Demand Inc		D	310 709-7355	0
Cloudtech Incorporated		C	213 230-2616	0
Club Assist North America Inc **(DH)**		D	213 388-4333	0
Club Assist US LLC		C	213 388-4333	0
CMI Management Inc		C	323 465-8044	0
Cnn America Inc		D	323 993-5000	0
Coast Citrus Distributors		C	213 955-3444	0
Coast Produce Company **(PA)**		D	213 955-4900	0
Cohen Brown MGT Group Inc **(PA)**		D	310 966-1001	0
Cohnreznick LLP		E	310 477-3722	0
Collins Avenue LLC		E	323 930-6633	0
Colony Capital Inc **(PA)**		E	310 282-8820	0
Colony Management Inc		D	310 282-8820	0
Comcast Cble Cmmunications LLC		E	310 216-3500	0
Comcast Cble Cmmunications LLC		C	310 216-3686	0
Comcast Corporation		D	323 993-8000	0
Command Security Corporation		A	310 981-4530	0
Commercial Coating Company Inc		D	323 256-1331	0
Commercial Property Management **(PA)**		D	213 739-2000	0
Commodity Forwarders Inc **(DH)**		C	310 348-8855	0
Community College Foundation		E	213 427-6910	0
Community Partners **(PA)**		D	213 346-3200	0
Community Redevelopment Agency **(PA)**		C	213 977-1600	0
Complex Studios		E	310 477-1938	0
Comprehensive Cmnty Hlth Ctr		C	323 344-4144	0
Concession Management Svcs Inc		C	310 846-5830	0
Confido LLC		A	310 361-8558	0
Constellation Newenergy Inc		D	213 576-6001	0
Coopertive Amrcn Physcians Inc **(PA)**		D	213 473-8600	0
Cordoba Corporation		D	213 895-0224	0
Cornerstone Research Inc		D	213 553-2500	0
Corporate Building Svcs Inc		C	213 252-0999	0
Corridor Capital LLC **(PA)**		C	310 442-7000	0
Country Villa East LP		C	323 939-3184	0
Country Villa Service Corp		C	323 666-1544	0
Country Villa Service Corp		C	323 734-1101	0
Country Villa Service Corp		C	310 574-3733	0
Country Villa Service Corp		D	323 734-9122	0
Country Villa Terrace **(PA)**		D	323 653-3980	0
Country Villa Terrace		E	323 939-3184	0
County of Los Angeles		D	213 739-2360	0
County of Los Angeles		C	213 974-0515	0
County of Los Angeles		A	213 974-7284	0
County of Los Angeles		C	310 668-4545	0
County of Los Angeles		D	323 226-8611	0
County of Los Angeles		C	323 897-6187	0
County of Los Angeles		C	323 226-8998	0
County of Los Angeles		A	213 922-6210	0
County of Los Angeles		C	323 267-2136	0
County of Los Angeles **(PA)**		C	213 974-9331	0
County of Los Angeles		A	213 240-8412	0
County of Los Angeles		D	323 769-7800	0
County of Los Angeles		C	323 226-8511	0
County of Los Angeles		A	323 226-3468	0
County of Los Angeles		D	213 351-5600	0
County of Los Angeles		C	323 727-1639	0
County of Los Angeles		B	213 744-5601	0
County of Los Angeles		D	213 351-7800	0
County of Los Angeles		A	562 940-4324	0
County of Los Angeles		C	323 226-6021	0
County of Los Angeles		D	323 857-6000	0
County of Los Angeles		C	323 730-3507	0
County of Los Angeles		C	213 974-2811	0
County of Los Angeles		D	323 780-2185	0
County of Los Angeles		A	213 351-7257	0
County of Los Angeles		D	323 586-6469	0
County of Los Angeles		C	626 458-1700	0
County of Los Angeles		C	323 267-2771	0
County of Los Angeles		B	213 473-6100	0
County of Los Angeles		D	213 974-4561	0
County of Los Angeles		C	213 974-8301	0
Courtyard By Marriott/Lax		D	310 981-2350	0
Covenant House California		D	323 461-3131	0
Covington & Burling LLP		B	424 332-4800	0
Cox Castle & Nicholson LLP **(PA)**		C	310 284-2200	0
CP Opco LLC		D	209 524-1966	0
CP Opco LLC		D	310 966-4900	0
Create Music Group Inc		D	310 623-0696	0
Creative Artists Agency LLC **(PA)**		A	424 288-2000	0
Creative Channel Services LLC **(HQ)**		D	310 482-6500	0
Creative Circle LLC **(DH)**		D	323 930-2333	0
Credit Ssse Securities USA LLC		D	213 253-2600	0
Crenshaw YMCA		D	323 290-9113	0

GEOGRAPHIC

	SIC	EMP	PHONE	ENTRY #
Crestline Hotels & Resorts Inc		C	213 629-1200	0
Crestline Hotels & Resorts LLC		D	213 624-0000	0
Crew Creative Advertising LLC		C	310 451-3225	0
Crime Impact Security Patrol		D	323 296-6406	0
Crown Building Maintenance Co		E	213 765-7800	0
Crown Energy Services Inc		A	213 765-7800	0
Crown Transportation Inc		D	310 737-0888	0
Crowne Plaza Lax LLC		C	310 258-1321	0
Crystal Cruises LLC (DH)		C	310 785-9300	0
Crystal Stairs Inc (PA)		B	323 299-8998	0
Crystal Valet Parking Inc		D	323 663-7275	0
Culinary Services America Inc		E	323 965-7582	0
Culver West Health Center LLC		D	310 390-9506	0
Cumulus Intrmdate Holdings Inc		D	310 840-4900	0
Curatel LLC		B	213 427-7411	0
Custom Hotel LLC		D	310 645-0400	0
Cyberdefender Corporation		B	323 449-0774	0
Cybrex Consulting Inc		D	513 999-2109	0
DA Davidson & Co		B	213 620-1850	0
Daily Journal Corporation		E	213 229-5500	0
Dailylook Inc		D	888 888-6645	0
Daiwa House California Inc		B	310 228-5675	0
Daniel J Edelman Inc		D	323 857-9100	0
Daniel J Edelman Inc		D	323 857-9100	0
Danning Gill Damnd Kollitz LLP		D	310 277-0077	0
Daqri LLC (PA)		D	213 375-8830	0
Davalan Sales Inc		C	213 623-2500	0
David Evans Enterprises Inc		A	213 337-3680	0
Davie Brown Entertainment Inc		D	310 979-1980	0
Davis Wright Tremaine LLP		D	213 633-6800	0
Daviselen Advertising Inc (PA)		C	213 688-7000	0
Decurion Corporation (PA)		D	310 659-9432	0
Defined Contribution Trust Fun		D	213 385-6161	0
Deloitte & Touche LLP		A	213 688-0800	0
Deloitte & Touche LLP		C	213 688-0800	0
Delta Air Lines Inc		D	310 646-9614	0
Delta Air Lines Inc		D	323 417-7374	0
Delta Floral Distributors Inc		C	323 751-8116	0
Deluxe Digital Dist Inc		E	818 260-6202	0
Deluxe Media Services LLC		A	323 462-6171	0
Dentons US LLP		C	213 623-9300	0
Dentons US LLP		C	213 688-1000	0
Dependable Highway Express Inc (PA)		B	323 526-2200	0
Design Collection Inc		D	323 277-9200	0
Desmond Mail Delivery Service		D	323 262-1085	0
Destination Shuttle Svcs LLC		C	310 338-9466	0
Deutsch La Inc		D	310 862-3000	0
Deutsche Bank National Tr Co (DH)		D	213 620-8200	0
Dfusion Software Inc		E	323 617-5577	0
Dianas Mexican Food Pdts Inc		D	323 758-4845	0
Digital Domain 30 Inc (PA)		B	310 314-2800	0
Digital Media Management LLC		D	323 378-6505	0
Dignity Health		B	213 484-7111	0
Dignity Health		A	213 748-2411	0
Direct Partners Inc (HQ)		D	310 482-4200	0
Directors Guild America Inc (PA)		C	310 289-2000	0
Disability Rights California		D	213 213-8000	0
Discovery Communications Inc (PA)		B	310 975-5906	0
Diversified RE Packaging Corp		A	310 855-1946	0
Diversified Transportation LLC		D	310 981-9500	0
Dla Piper LLP (us)		B	213 330-7700	0
Dla Piper LLP (us)		C	310 595-3000	0
Dlr Group Inc		C	626 796-8230	0
Dlr Group Inc (HQ)		C	213 800-9400	0
Docler Media LLC (DH)		D	424 777-3999	0
Document Technologies LLC		D	213 892-9000	0
Dominguez Firm Inc		D	213 388-7788	0
Donald T Sterling Corporation		D	310 275-5575	0
Double G Productions Ltd		D	310 479-0978	0
Doubleline Capital LP		C	213 633-8200	0
Drew Child Dev Corp Inc (PA)		C	323 249-2950	0
Drinker Biddle & Reath LLP		C	310 229-1282	0
Dti Services Inc (PA)		D	213 670-1100	0
Dual Diagnosis Trtmnt Ctr Inc		C	424 289-9031	0
Duckpunk Productions Inc		D	310 836-3818	0
Duff & Phelps LLC		D	213 270-2300	0
Dx Holdings LLC		A	323 462-6171	0
Dya Assoc		D	323 364-4270	0
Dykema Gossett PLLC		D	213 457-1800	0
E & C Fashion Inc		B	323 262-0099	0
E H Summit LLC (PA)		D	310 476-6571	0
E L Payne Heating Company		E	310 275-5331	0
E-Times Corporation Ltd		B	213 452-6720	0
Ea Mobile Inc		B	310 754-7125	0
Earle M Jorgensen Company		D	323 567-1122	0
Earth Technology Corp USA		A	213 593-8000	0
Earthbound Productions LLC		D	504 734-3337	0
East L A Remarkable Citizens (PA)		D	323 223-3079	0
Eastside Group Corporation		C	213 368-9777	0
Eaton Aerospace LLC		B	818 409-0200	0
EC Group Inc (PA)		D	310 815-2700	0
Eclipse Berry Farms LLC		D	310 207-7879	0
Economic Dev Corp of La County		E	213 622-4300	0
Edge Financial Inc		E	323 857-5809	0
Edge Logistics Services Corp		A	424 320-5300	0
Edgemine Inc		C	323 267-8222	0
Efilm LLC		C	323 463-7041	0
Eharmony Inc (HQ)		C	424 258-1199	0
Ejm Kyrene LLC (PA)		E	310 278-1830	0
El Al Israel Airlines Ltd		C	323 852-1252	0
El Pas-Los Angles Lmsne Ex Inc		E	213 623-2323	0
Eladh LP		D	323 268-5514	0
Elevator Equipment Corporation (PA)		D	323 245-0147	0
Elijah Textiles Inc		D	310 666-3443	0
Elite Information Group Inc (DH)		B	323 642-5200	0
Emerald Trans Los Angeles LLC		E	323 277-2500	0
Emerik Hotel Corp		D	213 748-1291	0
Emery Smith Laboratories Inc		C	213 745-5333	0
Emmi Inc		D	213 622-7234	0
Emmis Publishing Corporation		D	323 801-0100	0
Emp III Inc		D	323 231-4174	0
Emser International LLC (PA)		D	323 650-2000	0
End-Time Message & Support		E	323 756-6252	0
Engineerai Corp		E	650 721-1158	0
Englekirk Institutional Inc (PA)		E	323 733-2640	0
Englekirk Structural Engineers (PA)		E	323 733-6673	0
Engstrom Lipscomb and Lack A (PA)		D	310 552-3800	0
Entertainment & Sports Today		D	213 388-9050	0
Entertinment Studios Media Inc (PA)		D	310 277-3500	0
Entravsion Communications Corp		D	323 900-6100	0
Epstein Becker & Green PC		D	310 556-8861	0
Equator LLC (HQ)		C	310 469-9500	0
Equicare Medical Supply Inc		D	213 385-1715	0
Eric Jones Customs Brokerage		E	310 348-3777	0
Ernst & Young LLP		A	213 977-3200	0
Espn Inc		B	212 456-7439	0
Essense		A	323 202-4650	0
Essential Access Health (PA)		D	213 386-5614	0
Ethiopian World Federation		E	323 844-1826	0
Evergreen Cleaning Systems Inc		E	213 386-3260	0
Evgo Services LLC		D	310 954-2900	0
Evolve Growth Initiatives LLC		E	424 281-5000	0
Evolve Media Holdings LLC (PA)		C	310 449-1890	0
Evoq Properties Inc		D	213 988-8890	0
Excellence Ventures Inc		D	323 262-6800	0
Exceptional Chld Foundation		C	213 748-3556	0
Express Group Inc (PA)		D	310 474-5999	0
F O C Electronics Corporation		E	213 625-5775	0
Facter Direct Ltd		C	323 634-1999	0
Fame Assistance Corporation		D	323 373-7720	0
Far East Home Care Inc		A	949 673-3100	0
Farmers Group Inc		D	213 615-2500	0
Farmers Group Inc		D	818 249-3000	0
Farmers Insurance Fed Cred UNI (PA)		D	323 209-6000	0
Faze Clan Inc		D	818 538-5204	0
Fc Metropolitan Lofts Inc		D	213 488-0010	0
Fcs Medical Corporation		D	323 317-9200	0
Fcti Inc (PA)		D	310 405-0022	0
Federal Deposit Insurance Corp		C	323 545-9260	0
Federal Express Corporation		D	800 463-3339	0
Federal Rsrve Bnk San Frncisco		A	213 683-2300	0
Fedex Office & Print Svcs Inc		E	213 892-1700	0
Fei Enterprises Inc		E	323 937-0856	0
Fifth & Sunset Enterprises LLC		D	310 979-0212	0
Fiji Water Company LLC (HQ)		E	310 966-5700	0
Film Payroll Services Inc (PA)		D	310 440-9600	0
Fire Insurance Exchange (PA)		A	323 932-3200	0
Firefighters First Credit Un (PA)		C	323 254-1100	0
First Capitol Consulting Inc		D	213 382-1115	0
First Choice Bank		D	213 617-0082	0
First City Credit Union (PA)		C	213 482-3477	0
First Entertainment Credit Un (PA)		D	323 851-3673	0
First Fire Systems Inc (PA)		D	310 559-0900	0
First Legal Support Svcs LLC (PA)		D	213 250-1111	0
First Regional Bancorp		B	310 552-1776	0
First Republic Bank		C	213 239-8883	0
First Republic Bank		D	310 712-1888	0
Five Star Transportation Inc		E	310 348-0820	0
Floorgate Inc		D	323 478-2000	0
Foley & Lardner LLP		C	213 972-4500	0

Mergent email: customerrelations@mergent.com
1566
2020 Directory of California
Wholesalers and Services Companies
(P-0000) Products & Services Section entry number
(PA)=Parent Co (HQ)=Headquarters (DH)=Div Headquarters

	SIC	EMP	PHONE	ENTRY #
Fonda & Frazer LLP **(PA)**		D	310 553-3320	0
Forest Lawn Memorial-Park Assn		D	323 254-7251	0
Fortress Investment Group LLC		D	310 228-3030	0
Fortuna Enterprises LP		B	310 410-4000	0
Four Points By Sheraton		D	310 645-4600	0
Fox Inc **(DH)**		A	310 369-1000	0
Fox Animation Studios Inc		B	323 857-8800	0
Fox Broadcasting Company **(HQ)**		C	310 369-1000	0
Fox BSB Holdco Inc		A	323 224-1500	0
Fox Latin American Channel LLC		B	305 774-4167	0
Fox Networks Group Inc		C	310 369-5104	0
Fox Networks Group Inc **(DH)**		D	310 369-9369	0
Fox Rent A Car Inc **(PA)**		E	310 342-5155	0
Fox Sports Productions Inc		A	310 369-1000	0
Fox Television Stations Inc **(HQ)**		B	310 584-2000	0
Fragomen Del Rey Bernse		E	310 820-3322	0
Frandzel Share Robins Bloom Lc		D	323 852-1000	0
Fred Leeds Properties		E	310 826-2466	0
Freeman Freeman & Smiley **(PA)**		D	310 398-6100	0
Freshology Inc		B	818 847-1888	0
Friends of The Los Angeles		C	323 653-0440	0
Front Line MGT Group Inc		D	310 209-3100	0
Front Porch Communities		C	323 661-1128	0
Fti Consulting Inc		D	213 689-1200	0
Fuel Cycle Inc **(PA)**		D	323 556-5400	0
Fuel TV		D	310 444-8564	0
Full Throttle Energy Company		C	323 474-8417	0
Fulwider and Patton LLP		D	310 824-5555	0
Fund Services Advisors Inc		E	213 612-2196	0
Futuredontics Inc **(HQ)**		D	310 215-6400	0
Fx Networks LLC		C	310 369-1000	0
Fyeo Apparel Inc		E	213 278-0435	0
G B & P Citrus Co Inc **(PA)**		D	213 312-1380	0
G J Sullivan Co Inc		D	213 626-1000	0
G M Floral Company		E	213 489-7055	0
G4s Secure Solutions (usa)		B	323 938-9100	0
Gabriella Foundation		D	213 365-2491	0
Gaju Market Corporation		C	213 382-9444	0
Gamefly Holdings LLC **(PA)**		C	310 568-8224	0
Garda CL West Inc **(DH)**		B	213 383-3611	0
Garden Crest Convalesce		D	323 663-8281	0
Garden Grove Advanced Imaging		B	310 445-2800	0
Garment Industry Laundry		C	323 752-8335	0
Gartner Inc		D	310 479-2108	0
Gary Lask		D	310 825-0631	0
Gateway Security Inc		A	310 410-0790	0
Gateways Hosp Mental Hlth Ctr		D	323 644-2026	0
Gateways Hosp Mental Hlth Ctr **(PA)**		D	323 644-2000	0
Gehry Partners LLP		C	310 482-3000	0
Gelfand Rennert & Feldman LLP **(PA)**		C	310 553-1707	0
General Services Cal Dept		D	213 897-3995	0
General Services Cal Dept		D	213 897-2241	0
Genesis Healthcare Corporation		D	310 391-8266	0
Genesis Healthcare LLC		C	323 461-9961	0
Gentlecare Transport Inc		D	323 662-8777	0
Gentry Group LLC		E	310 968-5399	0
Genzyme Corporation		C	310 482-5000	0
Getty Images Inc		D	323 202-4200	0
Gibbs Giden Locher		D	310 552-3400	0
Gibson Dunn & Crutcher LLP **(PA)**		B	213 229-7000	0
Gibson Dunn & Crutcher LLP		D	310 552-8500	0
Gilbert Klly Crwley Jnnett LLP **(PA)**		D	213 615-7000	0
Gils Distributing Service		C	213 627-0539	0
Gipson Hoffman & Pancione A		D	310 556-4660	0
Girardi & Keese **(PA)**		D	213 977-0211	0
Girardi and Keefe		D	213 489-5330	0
Girl Scuts Greater Los Angeles **(PA)**		C	626 677-2200	0
Giroux Glass Inc **(PA)**		C	213 747-7406	0
Giumarra Bros Fruit Co Inc **(PA)**		D	213 627-2900	0
Glaser Weil Fink Jacobs **(PA)**		C	310 553-3000	0
Global Management Company LLC		D	323 261-8114	0
Global Nurses Online Inc		D	310 306-2760	0
Global Reach 18 Inc **(PA)**		D	310 203-5850	0
Godigital Media Group LLC		D	310 853-7940	0
Gold Derby Media LLC		D	310 321-5000	0
Gold Parent LP		A	310 954-0440	0
Golden International		A	213 628-1388	0
Golden State Mutl Lf Insur Co **(PA)**		D	713 526-4361	0
Goldman Sachs & Co		C	310 407-5700	0
Goldstar Hlthcr Cntr of Chtswr		C	818 882-8233	0
Gonzalez Barba Enterprises		E	323 233-7995	0
Good Samaritan Hospital Aux		A	213 977-2121	0
Goodwin Procter LLP		D	213 426-2500	0
Gordon Edelstein Krepack Gr		E	213 739-7000	0
Gordon Rees Scully Mansukhani		D	213 576-5000	0
Gores Norment Holdings Inc		C	310 209-3010	0
Grand Park Convalescent Hosp		C	213 382-7315	0
Grand Performances		D	213 687-2190	0
Grandpoint Capital Inc		C	213 542-4410	0
Grant Thornton LLP		E	213 627-1717	0
Grant Thornton LLP		D	213 627-1717	0
Great American Insurance Co		D	323 937-8600	0
Great American Insurance Co		C	213 430-4300	0
Great Western Bancorp Inc		B	213 622-1895	0
Greater Los Ang **(PA)**		D	213 413-4400	0
Greater Los Angeles Agency		D	323 478-8000	0
Greater Los Angeles Zoo Assn		D	323 644-4200	0
Green Equity Investors III L P		A	310 954-0444	0
Green Equity Investors IV LP **(PA)**		A	310 954-0444	0
Green Farms Inc		B	858 831-7701	0
Green Farms California LLC **(PA)**		C	213 747-4411	0
Green Glusk Field Clama & Mach		C	310 553-3610	0
Green Hasson & Janks LLP		C	310 873-1600	0
Greenberg Traurig LLP		D	310 586-7708	0
Greenland US Consulting Inc		D	213 362-9300	0
Greenway Arts Alliance Inc		D	323 655-7679	0
Greybor Medical Transportation		E	213 250-4444	0
Greyhound Lines Inc		B	213 629-8400	0
Grifols Biologicals LLC		B	323 255-2221	0
Grifols Diagnstc Solutions Inc **(HQ)**		C	323 225-2221	0
Grifols Shared Svcs N Amer Inc **(HQ)**		C	323 225-2221	0
Grill On The Alley The Inc		A	323 856-5530	0
Grosslight Insurance Inc		D	310 473-9611	0
Gruen Associates		D	323 937-4270	0
Gs Foods Group		B	310 806-9780	0
Gsa Des Plaines LLC		D	310 557-5100	0
Guardian Eagle Security Inc		B	888 990-0002	0
Guardian Rehabilitation Hosp		D	323 930-4815	0
Guardians of The Los Angeles		D	310 479-2468	0
Guardsmark LLC		C	310 287-3103	0
Guardsmark LLC		C	818 841-0288	0
Guardsmark LLC		C	818 841-0288	0
Gursey Schneider & Co LLC **(PA)**		D	310 552-0960	0
Gva Enterprises Inc **(PA)**		D	213 484-0510	0
Gva Enterprises Inc		D	213 484-0784	0
Gvs Italy		D	424 382-4343	0
H & K Abouaf Corporation		D	310 393-1282	0
H D S I Managment		E	323 231-1104	0
H2 Wellness Incorporated		D	310 362-1888	0
Haight Brown & Bonesteel LLP **(PA)**		D	213 542-8000	0
Hall Windsor		D	213 383-1547	0
Hamburger Home		D	213 637-5000	0
Hamburger Home **(PA)**		D	323 876-0550	0
Hana Commercial Finance Inc		D	213 240-1234	0
Hana Financial Inc **(PA)**		D	213 240-1234	0
Hancock Pk Rhblitation Ctr LLC		C	323 937-4860	0
Hanil Development Inc		E	213 387-0111	0
Hanin Federal Credit Union **(PA)**		E	213 368-9000	0
Hanmi Bank **(HQ)**		C	213 382-2200	0
Hannam Chain USA Inc **(PA)**		C	213 382-2922	0
Harris Stockwell **(PA)**		E	310 277-6669	0
Harrys Auto Body Inc		D	323 933-4600	0
Hartford Fire Insurance Co		C	213 452-5179	0
Harvest Sensations LLC **(PA)**		D	213 895-6968	0
Hatchbeauty Products LLC **(PA)**		D	310 396-7070	0
Hathaway Resource Center		E	323 837-0838	0
Hathaway-Sycamores Chld Fam Sv		D	323 257-9600	0
Hawaiian Airlines Inc		D	310 417-1677	0
Hawkins Brown USA Inc		B	310 600-2695	0
Hazens Investment LLC		B	310 642-1111	0
HDR Architecture Inc		D	626 584-1700	0
HDR Engineering Inc		C	626 584-1700	0
Hdsi Management Inc **(PA)**		D	323 231-1104	0
Health Link Medi Van		D	310 981-9500	0
Height Brown and Bonesteel		D	213 241-0900	0
Helloworld Travel Svcs USA Inc		D	310 535-1000	0
Here Films		E	310 806-4288	0
Highland Park Skilled Nursing		D	323 254-6125	0
Hill Farrer & Burrill		D	213 620-0460	0
Hillcrest Country Club		C	310 553-8911	0
Hinerfeld-Ward Inc		D	310 842-7929	0
Hinshaw & Culbertson LLP		D	213 680-2800	0
Hirsh Inc		E	213 622-9441	0
Historical Soc Centinela Vly		B	310 649-6272	0
Hks Inc		D	310 788-9700	0
Hntb Corporation		D	213 403-1000	0
Hob Entertainment LLC **(DH)**		C	323 769-4600	0
Holland & Knight LLP		D	213 896-2400	0
Holland Flower Market Inc **(PA)**		D	213 627-9900	0
Hollywood Community Hospital M		C	323 462-2271	0

Employment Codes: A=Over 500 employees, B=251-500,
C=101-250, D=51-100, E=50

2020 Directory of California
Wholesalers and Services Companies

© Mergent Inc. 1-800-342-5647

1567

GEOGRAPHIC

Company	SIC	EMP	PHONE	ENTRY #
Hollywood Medical Center LP		A	213 413-3000	0
Hollywood Mental Health Center		D	323 769-6100	0
Hollywood Rntals Prod Svcs LLC (PA)		D	818 407-7800	0
Hollywood Standard LLC		C	323 822-3111	0
Holthouse Carlin Van Trigt LLP (PA)		C	310 477-5551	0
Homeboy Industries (PA)		B	323 526-1254	0
Homeland Housewares LLC		D	310 996-7200	0
Hong Kong & Shanghai Banking		D	213 626-2460	0
Honk Technologies Inc		D	800 979-3162	0
Horizon Media Inc		B	310 282-0909	0
Hospital Assn Southern Cal (PA)		D	213 347-2002	0
Host Hotels & Resorts LP		D	310 216-5858	0
Houlihan Lokey Inc (PA)		B	310 788-5200	0
Howard Building Corporation (PA)		C	213 683-1850	0
Hpt Trs Ihg-2 Inc		D	310 642-7500	0
Hsbc Business Credit (usa)		D	213 553-8089	0
Hsbc Finance Corporation		C	213 628-8167	0
Hudson Pacific Properties Inc (PA)		D	310 445-5700	0
Hueston Hennigan LLP		D	213 788-4340	0
Hulu LLC		C	888 631-4858	0
Humnit Hotel At Lax LLC		D	424 702-1234	0
Hunton Andrews Kurth LLP		D	213 532-2000	0
Hustle Digital Inc		E	310 882-2680	0
Hwn Mariposa Associates LLC		D	310 478-8757	0
Hyatt Corporation		C	323 656-1234	0
Hyatt Corporation		B	312 750-1234	0
Hyde Park Convalescent Hosp		E	323 753-1354	0
Hyperloop Technologies Inc (PA)		D	213 800-3270	0
Hyrecar Inc		D	888 688-6769	0
Hyrian LLC		C	212 590-2567	0
I D Property Corporation		C	213 625-0100	0
I Mean It Creative Inc		E	310 287-1000	0
Ibi Group A California Partnr		D	213 769-0011	0
Ibisworld Inc (DH)		D	800 330-3772	0
Icarus Fuel Services US Corp		D	310 417-0124	0
Icon Exposure Inc		D	323 933-1666	0
Ideal Program Services Inc		D	323 296-2255	0
IDS Real Estate Group (PA)		D	213 627-9937	0
Ifncom Inc (PA)		D	213 452-1505	0
Ignition Creative LLC		D	310 315-6300	0
Ihg Management (maryland) LLC		C	310 642-7500	0
Imaging Technologies Group LLC		E	310 638-2500	0
Imax Corporation (HQ)		D	310 255-5559	0
Imperial Capital Group LLC (PA)		D	310 246-3700	0
Imperial Capital LLC (PA)		D	310 246-3700	0
Imperial Mridian Companies Inc		D	310 447-3460	0
Imperial Parking Industries (PA)		D	323 651-5588	0
Infinity Broadcasting Corp Cal		D	323 936-5784	0
Infinity Care of East LA		D	323 261-8108	0
Institute For Applied Behavior (PA)		C	310 649-0499	0
Integrated Decision Systems		D	310 954-5530	0
Integrated Trnsp Svcs Inc		D	310 553-6060	0
Interbake Foods LLC		D	213 484-8161	0
Intercare Therapy Inc		C	323 866-1880	0
Interior Office Solutions Inc		E	310 726-9067	0
Interlink		C	310 734-1499	0
International Creative Mgt Inc (HQ)		C	310 550-4000	0
International Creative MGT Inc		C	310 550-4000	0
International Design Services		D	323 662-3963	0
International Fdn For Korea Un		B	213 550-2182	0
International Inst Los Angeles (PA)		D	323 224-3800	0
International Marine Pdts Inc (HQ)		E	213 893-6123	0
International Media Group Inc		D	310 478-1818	0
International Medical Corps (PA)		D	310 826-7800	0
Internet Corp For Assigned Nam (PA)		C	310 823-9358	0
Interstate Hotels Resorts Inc		D	213 617-1133	0
Interstate Hotels Resorts Inc		B	213 624-1000	0
Intrado Corporation		C	310 481-7878	0
Intrepid Inv Bankers LLC		A	310 478-9000	0
Investors Capital MGT Group		B	310 553-5175	0
Irell & Manella LLP (PA)		B	310 277-1010	0
Irp Lax Hotel LLC		C	310 645-4600	0
Irwin Naturals		D	310 306-3636	0
Israel Discount Bank New York		C	213 861-6440	0
Ivie McNeill Wyatt A Prof Law		E	213 489-0028	0
Ivy Realty		E	213 386-8888	0
Iw Group (PA)		D	310 289-5500	0
J Alexander Investments Inc (PA)		D	213 687-8400	0
J Brand Holdings LLC		D	212 228-8181	0
J C Entertainment Ltg Svcs Inc		D	818 252-7481	0
J H Synder Co LLC		D	323 857-5546	0
J M Carden Sprinkler Co Inc		D	323 258-8300	0
J P H Consulting Inc (PA)		E	323 934-5660	0
J P H Consulting Inc		C	323 934-5660	0
J Paul Getty Trust		D	310 440-7325	0
J2 Cloud Services LLC (HQ)		D	323 860-9200	0
J2 Global Inc (PA)		C	323 860-9200	0
Jack Engle & Co (PA)		D	323 589-8111	0
Jack Morton Worldwide Inc		D	310 967-2400	0
Jack Nadel Inc (PA)		D	310 815-2600	0
Jackoway Tyreman Wertheimer Au		D	310 553-0305	0
Jackson Lewis PC		D	213 689-0404	0
Jacobs Engineering Group Inc		C	213 362-4336	0
Jalmar Properties Inc (PA)		E	310 207-8481	0
Jameson Properties Co Inc		E	213 487-3770	0
Jarrow Formulas Inc (PA)		D	310 204-6936	0
JE Williams Trucking Inc		E	406 248-7397	0
Jean Mart Inc		D	323 752-7775	0
Jeffer Mngels Btlr Mtchell LLP (PA)		C	310 203-8080	0
Jefferies LLC		D	310 445-1199	0
Jenkins Gales & Martinez Inc		D	310 645-0561	0
Jetro Cash and Carry Entps LLC		D	323 964-1200	0
Jewish Cmnty Fndn of (PA)		C	323 761-8700	0
Jewish Family Svc Los Angeles (PA)		D	323 761-8800	0
Jewish Family Svc Los Angeles		E	323 937-5900	0
Jewish Vocational Services (PA)		E	323 761-8888	0
Jhp Produce Inc		D	213 627-1093	0
Jim Henson Company Inc (PA)		D	323 856-6680	0
Jj Grand Hotel		D	213 383-3000	0
John Hancock Life Insur Co USA (DH)		A	213 689-0813	0
John Stewart Company		E	213 787-2700	0
Johnson Fain Inc		C	323 224-6000	0
Jonathan Club (PA)		B	213 624-0881	0
Jones Lang La Salle		D	213 239-6000	0
Jules and Associates Inc		D	213 362-5600	0
Julio Gonzalez		D	310 310-4055	0
Jwmcc Limited Partnership		B	310 277-1234	0
K A Associates Inc		C	310 556-2721	0
K&L Gates LLP		E	310 552-5000	0
Kaa Design Group Inc		D	310 821-1400	0
Kaiser Foundation Hospitals		D	323 783-4011	0
Kaiser Foundation Hospitals		A	323 857-2000	0
Kaiser Foundation Hospitals		D	800 954-8000	0
Kaiser Foundation Hospitals		D	800 954-8000	0
Kaiser Foundation Hospitals		E	323 881-5516	0
Kaiser Foundation Hospitals		C	323 298-3300	0
Kaiser Foundation Hospitals		C	213 580-7200	0
Kajima Construction Svcs Inc		E	323 269-0020	0
Kal Krishnan Consulting Svcs (PA)		D	510 893-3500	0
Kash Apparel LLC		D	213 747-8885	0
Katten Muchin Rosenman LLP		C	310 788-4498	0
Katten Muchin Rosenman LLP		C	310 788-4400	0
Katz Media Group Inc		D	323 966-5000	0
Kaufman and Broad Limited		C	310 231-4000	0
Kava Holdings Inc (DH)		C	310 472-1211	0
Kayne Anderson Rudni		D	310 229-9260	0
KB Home (PA)		D	310 231-4000	0
KB Home Coastal Inc		D	310 231-4000	0
KB Home Grater Los Angeles Inc (HQ)		D	310 231-4000	0
Kbsa Inc		D	310 231-4000	0
Keck Hospital of Usc		D	800 872-2273	0
Kedren Community Hlth Ctr Inc		C	323 524-0634	0
Kedren Community Hlth Ctr Inc (PA)		D	323 233-0425	0
Keiro Nursing Home		C	323 276-5700	0
Keiro Services		B	213 873-5700	0
Kelley Drye & Warren LLP		C	310 712-6100	0
Kennedy Care Center		C	323 651-0043	0
Kenneth Brdwick Intr Dsgns Inc		D	310 274-9999	0
Keolis Transit America Inc (DH)		E	310 981-9500	0
Kerlan-Jobe Orthopedic Clinic (PA)		D	310 665-7200	0
Ketchum Incorporated		D	310 437-2600	0
Kf Sunray LLC		D	323 734-2171	0
Kfco Inc		C	310 441-2483	0
Kilroy Realty Corporation (PA)		D	310 481-8400	0
Kim Chong		D	323 521-4700	0
Kimco Staffing Services Inc		A	310 622-1616	0
Kindred Healthcare Operating		B	310 642-0325	0
King Hlmes Pterno Soriano LLP		E	310 282-8989	0
Kings Pawnshop		D	213 383-5555	0
Kintetsu Enterprises		D	213 687-2000	0
Kintetsu Enterprises Co Amer		D	213 617-2000	0
Kl Cutting Service Inc		C	213 742-9001	0
Km Fresno Investors LLC		E	323 556-6600	0
Knet TV		E	323 469-5638	0
Knit Generation Group Inc		D	213 221-5081	0
Kommonwealth Inc		E	310 278-7328	0
Koram Insurance Center Inc		D	323 660-1000	0
Korean Air Lines Co Ltd		C	310 646-4866	0
Korean Airlines		C	310 417-5294	0
Korean Airlines Co Ltd		C	310 410-2000	0

2020 Directory of California
Wholesalers and Services Companies

(P-0000) Products & Services Section entry number
(PA)=Parent Co (HQ)=Headquarters (DH)=Div Headquarters

	SIC	EMP	PHONE	ENTRY #
Korean Airlines Co Ltd	D		213 484-1900	0
Korean Health Education **(PA)**	D		213 427-4000	0
Koreatown Youth and Cmnty Ctr **(PA)**	D		213 365-7400	0
Korn Ferry **(PA)**	C		310 552-1834	0
Kos-USA	D		213 747-2591	0
Kpff Inc	C		310 665-1536	0
Kpmg LLP	D		703 286-8175	0
Ktgy Group Inc	E		310 394-2625	0
Kusc Radio	E		213 225-7400	0
Kxp Advantage Services LLC **(PA)**	C		424 320-5300	0
L & T Meat Co	D		323 262-2815	0
L and R Auto Parks Inc	D		213 784-3018	0
L J Trucking USA	D		323 469-9663	0
L R Investment Company	D		213 627-8211	0
La 1000 Santa Fe LLC	C		213 205-1000	0
La Asociacion Nacional Pro Per	B		213 202-5900	0
La Cienega Associates	D		310 854-0071	0
La Follette Johnson De Haas **(PA)**	D		213 426-3600	0
La Hotel Venture LLC	B		213 617-1133	0
La Inc Convention Vistors Bur	D		213 236-2301	0
La Laser Center Pc Cpmc	D		310 446-4400	0
La Live Properties LLC	E		213 763-7700	0
LA Sports Properties Inc	C		213 742-7500	0
La Vida Mltispecialty Med Ctrs	D		213 765-7500	0
Laaco Ltd **(PA)**	C		213 622-1254	0
Ladas & Parry LLP	E		323 934-2300	0
Laguna Country Mart Ltd Inc	E		310 826-5635	0
Lakewood Manor North Inc	D		213 380-9175	0
Lamp Inc	D		213 488-9559	0
Language Weaver Inc	D		310 437-7300	0
Larchmont Radiology Med Group	D		213 483-5953	0
Lasr Inc	D		877 591-9979	0
Latham & Watkins LLP **(PA)**	A		213 485-1234	0
Latham & Watkins LLP	D		213 891-7108	0
Latham & Watkins LLP	C		213 891-1200	0
Lathrop & Gage LLP	D		310 789-4600	0
Lax Hospitality LP	C		310 670-9000	0
Lax Hotel Ventures LLC	E		310 645-4600	0
Lax International Service Ctr	D		310 337-8764	0
LAX Wheel Refinishing Inc	D		323 269-1484	0
Lax-C Inc	E		323 343-9000	0
Lear Capital Inc	D		310 571-0190	0
Led Global LLC	D		917 921-4315	0
Legacy Partners Hollywood	D		949 930-7706	0
Legend3d Inc	D		858 793-4420	0
LEK Consulting LLC	D		310 209-9800	0
Lendlease US Construction Inc	D		213 430-4660	0
Lenlyn Limited Which Will Do B **(HQ)**	D		310 417-3432	0
Leo A Daly Company	D		213 627-9300	0
Level Four Business MGT LLC	E		310 914-1600	0
Levy Prmium Fdsrvice Ltd Prtnr	D		213 742-7867	0
Lewis Brsbois Bsgard Smith LLP **(PA)**	A		213 250-1800	0
Libsource LLC	C		323 852-1083	0
Lieberman RES Worldwide LLC **(PA)**	C		310 553-0550	0
Lifesigns Now Inc **(PA)**	B		323 550-4210	0
Lifetime Entrmt Svcs LLC	D		310 556-7500	0
Lighthouse Healthcare Ctr LLC	D		323 564-4461	0
Liner LLP	C		310 500-3500	0
Linne Entertainment LLC	E		213 425-1146	0
Linquest Corporation **(PA)**	D		323 924-1600	0
Lippin Group Inc **(PA)**	E		323 965-1990	0
Little Citizens Schools Inc	D		323 732-1212	0
Live Nation Entertainment Inc	D		213 639-6178	0
Live Nation Worldwide Inc	C		323 966-5066	0
Livhome Inc **(PA)**	A		800 807-5854	0
LLP Mayer Brown	C		213 229-9500	0
LLP Moss Adams	D		310 477-0450	0
LLP Robins Kaplan	D		310 552-0130	0
Lmb Mortgage Services Inc **(HQ)**	C		310 348-6800	0
Local Initiative Health Author	A		213 694-1250	0
Lockton Companies LLC- Pacifi **(HQ)**	B		213 689-0500	0
Loeb & Loeb LLP **(PA)**	C		310 282-2000	0
Longwood Management Corp	D		323 735-5146	0
Longwood Management Corp	D		323 737-7778	0
Longwood Management Corp	D		213 382-8461	0
Longwood Management Corp	E		323 933-1560	0
Longwood Manor	C		323 935-1157	0
Lookout Productions LLC	C		310 408-5687	0
Los Angeles Airport Peace Offc	B		310 242-5218	0
Los Angeles Athletic Club Inc	C		213 625-2211	0
Los Angeles Cardiology Assoc **(PA)**	D		213 977-0419	0
Los Angeles Chmber Orchstra	D		213 622-7001	0
Los Angeles Cnty Dev Svc Fndtn	C		213 383-1300	0
Los Angeles Cnty Mseum of Art	D		323 857-6000	0
Los Angeles Conven and Exh	B		213 741-1151	0

	SIC	EMP	PHONE	ENTRY #
Los Angeles Country Club	C		310 276-6104	0
Los Angeles County Bar Assn **(PA)**	D		213 627-2727	0
Los Angeles County MTA	C		213 922-5887	0
Los Angeles County MTA	C		213 922-6301	0
Los Angeles County MTA	B		213 922-6203	0
Los Angeles County MTA	C		213 922-6202	0
Los Angeles County MTA **(PA)**	A		323 466-3876	0
Los Angeles County MTA	A		213 922-6207	0
Los Angeles County MTA	B		213 533-1506	0
Los Angeles County MTA	C		213 922-5012	0
Los Angeles County MTA	A		213 244-6783	0
Los Angeles County MTA	C		213 626-4455	0
Los Angeles Dept Wtr & Pwr	A		323 256-8079	0
Los Angeles Dept Wtr & Pwr **(PA)**	C		213 367-4211	0
Los Angeles Dept Wtr & Pwr	D		213 367-4211	0
Los Angeles Dept Wtr & Pwr	C		213 367-5706	0
Los Angeles Dodgers LLC	A		323 224-1507	0
Los Angeles Free Clinic **(PA)**	B		323 653-8622	0
Los Angeles Free Clinic	D		323 653-8622	0
Los Angeles Lgbt Center **(PA)**	C		323 993-7618	0
Los Angeles Mem Coliseum Comm	B		213 747-7111	0
Los Angeles Mission Inc **(PA)**	D		213 629-1227	0
Los Angeles Organizing	E		310 407-0539	0
Los Angeles Orphans Home Soc **(HQ)**	C		323 463-2119	0
Los Angeles Philharmonic Assn **(PA)**	A		213 972-7300	0
Los Angeles Police Command	B		877 275-5273	0
Los Angeles Rubber Company **(PA)**	D		323 263-4131	0
Los Angeles SEC National **(PA)**	E		323 651-2930	0
Los Angeles Senior Citizen	D		310 271-9670	0
Los Angeles Unified School Dst	C		213 485-3691	0
Los Angeles Unified School Dst	C		323 753-3175	0
Los Angeles Unified School Dst	D		323 939-7322	0
Los Angeles Unified School Dst	A		213 847-6911	0
Los Angeles Unified School Dst	C		310 258-2000	0
Los Angeles World Airports **(PA)**	C		310 646-7911	0
Los Angles Area Chmber Cmmerce	D		213 580-7500	0
Los Angles Child Gdance Clinic **(PA)**	C		323 373-2400	0
Los Angles Clippers Foundation	D		213 742-7555	0
Los Angles Cnty Employees Assn	D		213 368-8660	0
Los Angles Kings Hockey CLB LP **(PA)**	C		888 546-4752	0
Los Angles Trism Convention Bd **(PA)**	D		213 624-7300	0
Los Angles Universal Preschool	C		213 416-1200	0
Lotus Communications Corp **(PA)**	C		323 512-2225	0
Lotus Interworks Inc	C		310 442-3330	0
Louis Luskin & Sons Inc	C		323 938-5142	0
Lowcom LLC	C		213 408-0080	0
Lowe Enterprises Inc	C		310 820-6661	0
Lowe Enterprises Inc **(PA)**	C		310 820-6661	0
Lowe Enterprises Inc	C		310 820-6661	0
Lowe Enterprises RE Group	D		310 820-6661	0
Loyola Marymount University	D		310 338-2866	0
Lq Management LLC	C		310 645-2200	0
Lrw Investments LLC	D		310 337-1944	0
Lucky Strike Entertainment LLC	D		818 933-3752	0
Lufthnsa Crgo Aktngesellschaft	C		310 242-2500	0
Lumina Healthcare LLC **(PA)**	D		888 958-6462	0
Lusive Decor	E		323 227-9207	0
Lynberg & Watkins A Prof Corp **(PA)**	E		213 624-8700	0
M & S Acquisition Corporation **(PA)**	C		213 385-1515	0
M Arthur Gensler Jr Assoc Inc	C		213 927-3600	0
M-E Engineers Inc	D		310 842-8700	0
Macdonald Mott Group Inc	D		323 903-4100	0
Macerich Company	D		310 474-5940	0
Made In USA Foundation Inc	E		310 623-3872	0
Mafab Inc **(PA)**	D		714 893-0551	0
Magnolia Ventures Ltd	D		213 389-6900	0
Management Tech Consulting LLC	D		323 851-5008	0
Manchster Mnor Cnvlescent Hosp	D		323 753-1789	0
Mandalay Sports Entrmt LLC **(PA)**	D		323 549-4300	0
Manning Kass Ellrod Ram Trestr **(PA)**	C		213 624-6900	0
Manufacturers Bank **(HQ)**	C		213 489-6200	0
Marcum LLP	D		310 432-7400	0
Mariner Health Care Inc	D		323 665-1185	0
Marland Co LP	E		213 614-6171	0
Marmol Radziner	D		310 826-6222	0
Marriott International Inc	A		310 641-5700	0
Marriott International Inc	C		213 284-3862	0
Marsh & McLennan Companies Inc	D		213 346-5555	0
Martin AC Partners Inc	C		213 683-1900	0
Martin Associates Group Inc **(PA)**	D		213 483-6490	0
Martin Lther King/Drew Med Ctr	D		310 773-4926	0
Massage Place	C		310 204-3004	0
Matrix Aviation Services Inc	C		310 337-3037	0
Maxim Healthcare Services Inc	C		866 465-5678	0
Maxim Healthcare Services Inc	C		323 937-9410	0

Employment Codes: A=Over 500 employees, B=251-500,
C=101-250, D=51-100, E=50

2020 Directory of California
Wholesalers and Services Companies

© Mergent Inc. 1-800-342-5647

1569

GEOGRAPHIC

Company	SIC	EMP	PHONE	ENTRY #
Mayesh Wholesale Florist Inc (PA)		E	310 342-0980	0
Mayfair Hotel		D	213 484-9789	0
McDermott Will & Emery LLP		C	310 277-4110	0
McGuirewoods LLP		C	310 315-8200	0
MCI Communications Svcs Inc		C	213 625-1005	0
McKinsey & Company Inc		E	424 249-1000	0
McKool Smith Hennigan		D	213 694-1200	0
Mechanical Drives Co (PA)		C	323 263-4131	0
Med-Life Ambulance Services		D	818 242-1785	0
Mediabrands Worldwide Inc		B	323 370-8000	0
Medical Management Cons Inc (PA)		E	310 659-3835	0
Medical Support Services		D	323 860-7994	0
Mellano & Co (PA)		B	213 622-0796	0
Memco Holdings Inc		C	310 277-0057	0
Memory To Go		D	310 446-0111	0
Mendelsohn/Zien Advg LLC		D	310 444-1990	0
Mercer (us) Inc		C	213 346-2200	0
Mercury Air Cargo Inc (HQ)		C	310 258-6100	0
Mercury General Corporation (PA)		D	323 937-1060	0
Mercury Insurance Company (HQ)		C	323 937-1060	0
Mercury Insurance Services LLC		A	323 937-1060	0
Mercury Mailing Systems Inc		C	323 730-0307	0
Merlot Film Productions Inc		C	323 575-2906	0
Merrill Lynch Pierce Fenner		C	310 407-3900	0
Metrolux Theatres		D	310 858-2800	0
Metropolis Hotel MGT LLC		C	213 683-4855	0
Mgh Corporation		E	323 754-1408	0
Michael A Meczka		E	310 670-4824	0
Mid Rckland Imging Prtners Inc (HQ)		E	310 445-2800	0
Mid Wilshire Health Care Ctr		D	213 483-9921	0
Mid-Cities Association Inc (PA)		D	310 537-4510	0
Midnight Mission (PA)		D	213 624-9258	0
Midnite Air Corp		E	310 330-2300	0
Midway Motors		D	310 649-5549	0
Midway Rent A Car Inc		D	310 445-4355	0
Milbank Tweed Hdley McCloy LLP		C	424 386-4000	0
Millennia Holdings Inc		D	213 252-1230	0
Miniluxe Inc		D	424 442-1630	0
Minority Aids Project Inc		D	323 936-4949	0
Mintie Corporation (PA)		D	323 225-4111	0
Miramax Film Ny LLC (HQ)		D	310 409-4321	0
Mission Beverage Co (HQ)		C	323 266-6238	0
Mitchell Silberberg Knupp LLP (PA)		C	310 312-2000	0
Mitsui & Co (usa) Inc		D	213 896-1100	0
Miyako Hotels		D	213 617-2000	0
Moaddel Law Firm APC		E	323 999-5099	0
Mocean LLC		C	310 481-0808	0
Modern Button Company of Cal		E	213 747-7431	0
Monarch Landscape Holdings LLC (PA)		C	213 816-1750	0
Monarchy Diamond Inc		B	213 924-1161	0
Morgan Lewis & Bockius LLP		C	213 612-2500	0
Morgan Lewis & Bockius LLP		C	213 612-2500	0
Morgan Creek Productions (PA)		D	310 432-4848	0
Morgan Services Inc		D	213 485-9666	0
Morgans Hotel Group MGT LLC		C	323 650-8999	0
Morris Polich & Purdy LLP (PA)		D	213 891-9100	0
Morrison & Foerster LLP		C	213 892-5200	0
Mortgage Capital Assoc Inc		D	310 477-6877	0
Mortgage Capital Partners Inc		D	310 295-2900	0
Mpower Communications Corp (DH)		D	866 699-8242	0
Ms Bubbles Inc (PA)		D	323 544-0300	0
MSS Nurses Registry Inc		D	323 467-5717	0
Mufg Bank Ltd		D	213 488-3700	0
Mufg Union Bank Foundation		A	213 236-5000	0
Mufg Union Bank National Assn		E	213 972-5500	0
Mufg Union Bank National Assn		D	213 312-4500	0
Muir-Chase Plumbing Co Inc		D	818 500-1940	0
Mulholland SEC & Patrol Inc		B	818 755-0202	0
Mulroses Usa Inc		D	213 489-1761	0
Munger Tolles & Olson LLP		C	213 683-9100	0
Munger Tolles Olson Foundation (PA)		B	213 683-9100	0
Murchison & Cumming LLP (PA)		D	213 623-7400	0
Murphy OBrien Inc		D	310 453-2539	0
Museum Associates		B	323 857-6172	0
Museum of Contemporary Art (PA)		D	213 626-6222	0
Musick Peeler & Garrett LLP (PA)		C	213 629-7600	0
Mutesix Group Inc		C	310 215-3467	0
Mutual Trading Co Inc (HQ)		D	213 626-9458	0
Mv Medical Management		D	323 257-7637	0
Myers & Sons Construction LP		D	424 227-3285	0
Mystic Inc (PA)		D	213 746-8538	0
Mza Events Inc (PA)		E	213 201-1348	0
Nadel Inc (PA)		D	310 826-2100	0
National Cble Cmmnications LLC		D	310 231-0745	0
National Ecnomic RES Assoc Inc		D	213 346-3000	0
National Research Group Inc		B	323 817-2000	0
Nationwide Legal LLC (PA)		D	213 249-9999	0
Nationwide Theatres Corp (HQ)		D	310 657-8420	0
Natural History Museum of Los		B	213 763-3442	0
Navigant Consulting Inc		D	213 452-4516	0
NBBJ LP		E	213 243-3333	0
Nederlander of California Inc		E	323 468-1700	0
Ner Precious Metals Inc		D	310 367-3179	0
Netflix Productions LLC		C	323 960-3457	0
Network Automation Inc		E	213 738-1700	0
Network Management Group Inc (PA)		C	323 263-2632	0
Neuberg Nuberg Importers Group		E	800 832-2742	0
New Directions Inc (PA)		D	310 914-4045	0
New Dream Network LLC		D	323 375-3842	0
New Economics For Women (PA)		D	213 483-2060	0
New Figueroa Hotel Inc		D	213 627-8971	0
New Regency Productions Inc (PA)		D	310 369-8300	0
New Vista Health Services		C	310 477-5501	0
New York Life Insurance Co		E	323 782-3000	0
Newsways Services Inc		C	323 258-6000	0
Nexstar Digital LLC		D	310 971-9300	0
Nextel Communications Inc		D	323 290-2400	0
Nexus Healthcare Solutions Inc		E	310 448-2693	0
Ngs Group Inc		D	323 735-1700	0
Nhn Global Inc (PA)		C	424 672-1177	0
Nielsen Company (us) LLC		B	323 817-2000	0
Nielsen Company (us) LLC		D	323 462-0050	0
Nixon Peabody LLP		D	213 629-6000	0
Northeast Community Clinic		D	323 373-9400	0
Northern Trust Company		E	310 282-3800	0
Nossaman LLP (PA)		D	213 612-7800	0
Notellage Corporation		E	323 257-8151	0
Nowcom Corporation		D	323 938-6449	0
Nrea-TRC 711 LLC		C	213 488-3500	0
Nri Usa LLC (PA)		B	323 345-6456	0
Ntt Data Services Corporation		D	310 342-3200	0
Nuevo Amnecer Latino Chld Svcs (PA)		D	323 720-9951	0
Numero Uno Market		D	323 231-9403	0
Numero Uno Market		D	213 381-1734	0
O & S Holdings LLC		E	310 207-8600	0
Oak Paper Products Co Inc (PA)		C	323 268-0507	0
Oaks Diagnostics Inc (PA)		D	310 855-0035	0
Oaktree Capital Management LP (DH)		C	213 830-6300	0
Oaktree Holdings Inc		A	213 830-6300	0
Oaktree Real Estate Opportunit		A	213 830-6300	0
Oaktree Strategic Income LLC		A	213 830-6300	0
Oberman Tivoli & Pickert Inc		C	310 440-9600	0
Oblong Industries Inc (HQ)		C	213 683-8863	0
Ocean Breeze Manufacturing		D	323 586-8760	0
Ocean Group Inc (PA)		D	213 622-3677	0
Ocm Real Estate Opportunities		A	213 830-6300	0
Odesus Inc (PA)		D	310 473-4600	0
Ods Technologies LP		C	310 242-9400	0
Olympia Convalescent Hospital		C	213 487-3000	0
Olympia Health Care LLC		A	323 938-3161	0
Olympus Adhc Inc		E	310 572-7272	0
Omega/Cinema Props Inc		D	323 466-8201	0
OMelveny & Myers LLP (PA)		A	213 430-6000	0
OMelveny & Myers LLP		C	310 553-6700	0
Omni Hotels Corporation		C	213 617-3300	0
On Central Realty Inc		B	323 543-8500	0
One Legal Inc		D	213 617-1212	0
One Rock Capital Partners LLC		D	213 292-5870	0
Onelegacy (PA)		D	213 625-0665	0
Oneunited Bank		D	323 295-3381	0
Onsite Consulting LLC		D	323 401-3190	0
Op Bancorp		C	213 892-9999	0
Ore-Cal Corp (PA)		D	213 623-8493	0
Organic & Sustainable Buty Inc		E	310 815-8201	0
Organztion Amrcn Kdaly Edctors		E	310 441-3555	0
Orrick Hrrington Sutcliffe LLP		C	213 629-2020	0
Orthopaedic Hospital (PA)		C	213 742-1000	0
Otis Elevator Company		E	323 342-4500	0
Otts Asia		D	562 259-3447	0
Overseenet (PA)		C	213 408-0080	0
Oxford Palace Hotel		D	213 382-7756	0
P-Wave Holdings LLC		A	310 209-3010	0
P8ge Consulting Inc		E	310 666-2301	0
Pachulski Stang Zehl Jones LLP (PA)		D	310 277-6910	0
Pacific Asian Consortm Emplymn		D	213 989-3228	0
Pacific Asian Consortm Emplymn (PA)		C	213 353-3982	0
Pacific Capital Companies LLC		C	800 583-3015	0
Pacific Equities Captl		D	310 477-5300	0
Pacific Health Corporation		B	714 619-7797	0
Pacific Indemnity Company		B	213 622-2334	0

Mergent email: customerrelations@mergent.com
1570

2020 Directory of California
Wholesalers and Services Companies

(P-0000) Products & Services Section entry number
(PA)=Parent Co (HQ)=Headquarters (DH)=Div Headquarters

	SIC	EMP	PHONE	ENTRY #
Pacific Paper Converting Inc **(PA)**		D	323 888-1330	0
Pacific Premier Bank		D	213 626-0085	0
Pacific Theaters Inc **(PA)**		C	310 657-8420	0
Pacific Theatres Entrmt Corp **(HQ)**		D	310 659-9432	0
Pacific Trellis Fruit LLC **(PA)**		C	323 859-9600	0
Pacific Western Bank		C	213 430-7000	0
Pacific Western Bank		E	310 996-9100	0
Pacifica Hosts Inc		C	310 670-9000	0
Packard Realty Inc		D	310 649-5151	0
Paladin Realty Partners LLC **(PA)**		E	310 914-2410	0
Pamc Ltd **(PA)**		A	213 624-8411	0
Panasonic Corp North America		C	323 436-3500	0
Para Los Ninos		D	213 623-3942	0
Paracelsus Los Angeles Comm		C	323 267-0477	0
Paragon Textiles Inc		D	310 323-7500	0
Paramount Pictures Corporation **(HQ)**		C	323 956-5000	0
Paramount Television Service		A	323 956-5000	0
Paramunt Contrs Developers Inc		E	323 464-7050	0
Park Hotels & Resorts Inc		C	310 410-4000	0
Park n Fly Inc		D	310 417-3566	0
Parker Milliken Clark OHar		D	818 784-8087	0
Parker Stanbury LLP **(PA)**		D	619 528-1259	0
Parking Company of America		D	562 862-2118	0
Parking Concepts Inc		E	310 208-1611	0
Parking Concepts Inc		E	213 746-5764	0
Parking Concepts Inc		E	213 623-2661	0
Parking Network Inc		C	213 613-1500	0
Parsec Inc		D	323 276-3116	0
Pasadena Model Railroad Club		D	323 222-1718	0
Passprt Accept Fclty Los Angel		D	323 460-4811	0
Pathstone Family Office LLC		C	888 750-7284	0
Pathways La **(PA)**		E	213 427-2700	0
Patriot Communications LLC **(PA)**		D	888 833-4711	0
Paul Hastings LLP **(PA)**		C	213 683-6000	0
Payden and Rygel **(PA)**		C	213 625-1900	0
Pbms Inc		D	213 386-2552	0
Pcs Property Managmnt LLC		C	310 231-1000	0
PDQ Enterprises Inc		D	818 504-4900	0
Peach Inc		C	323 654-2333	0
Pediatric & Family Medical Ctr		C	213 342-3325	0
Pegasus Squire Inc		D	866 208-6837	0
Penny Roofing Company		E	323 731-5424	0
Penske Media Corporation **(PA)**		D	310 321-5000	0
Penske Truck Leasing Co LP		E	213 628-1255	0
People Assisting Homeless		C	323 644-2216	0
Performing Arts Center of La C		C	213 972-7211	0
Pexs International Inc		C	626 365-6706	0
Phenomenon Mktg & Entrmt LLC **(PA)**		D	323 648-4000	0
Philippine Airlines		D	310 646-1981	0
Philmont Management Inc		D	213 380-0159	0
Phoenix Textile Inc		D	213 239-9640	0
Pico Cleaner Inc **(PA)**		D	310 274-2431	0
Pico Rents Inc		D	310 275-9431	0
Pillsbury Winthrop Shaw		C	213 488-7100	0
Pircher Nichols & Meeks **(PA)**		D	310 201-0132	0
Pixelmags Inc		D	310 598-7303	0
Pixi Inc		D	310 670-7767	0
Planned Parenthood Los Angeles **(PA)**		D	213 284-3200	0
Plasma Collection Centers Inc		C	323 441-7720	0
Playa Proper Jv LLC		D	310 645-0400	0
Plaza De La Raza Child Develop		D	323 224-1788	0
Plb Management LLC		E	323 549-5400	0
PLD Enterprises Inc		D	213 626-4444	0
Plh Aviation Services Inc		E	310 417-0124	0
Pmk-Bnc Inc **(PA)**		C	310 854-0455	0
Pmk-Bnc Inc		E	310 854-4800	0
Point360 **(PA)**		D	818 565-1400	0
Polsinelli PC		D	310 556-1801	0
Pomwonderful LLC **(DH)**		C	310 966-5800	0
Post Group Inc **(PA)**		C	323 462-2300	0
Preciseq Inc		D	310 709-6094	0
Prg Parking Century LLC		D	310 642-0947	0
Prime Administration LLC		A	323 549-7155	0
Pro-Wash Inc		D	323 756-6000	0
Professional Produce		D	323 277-1550	0
Professional Security Cons **(PA)**		C	310 207-7729	0
Proland Property Managment LLC **(PA)**		D	213 738-8175	0
Promo Shop Inc **(PA)**		D	310 821-1780	0
Proskauer Rose LLP		D	310 557-2900	0
Prospect Enterprises Inc **(PA)**		C	213 599-5700	0
Prospect Medical Holdings Inc **(PA)**		D	310 943-4500	0
Protiviti Inc		D	213 327-1400	0
Prototypes Centers For Innov		C	213 542-3838	0
Proven Solutions Inc		D	310 933-4544	0
PS Arts		E	310 586-1017	0
Psomas **(PA)**		C	213 223-1400	0
Public Communications Svcs Inc		C	310 231-1000	0
Public Counsel		D	213 385-2977	0
Public Health California Dept		C	213 620-6160	0
Public Hlth Fndation Entps Inc		C	323 261-6188	0
Public Hlth Fndation Entps Inc		C	323 263-0262	0
Public Hlth Fndation Entps Inc		C	323 733-9381	0
Public Security Inc		E	323 293-9884	0
Qre Operating LLC		C	213 225-5900	0
Quake City Casuals Inc		C	213 746-0540	0
Qualified Blling Cllctions LLC		C	323 556-3470	0
Quantum Bhvioral Solutions Inc **(PA)**		D	626 531-6999	0
Queen of Angels Hollywood Pres		A	213 413-3000	0
Queenscare Health Centers		D	323 780-4510	0
Queenscare Health Centers		D	323 644-6180	0
Quick Systems Inc		E	702 530-3574	0
Quigly-Simpson Heppelwhite Inc		C	310 996-5800	0
Quinn Emanuel Urquhart **(PA)**		B	213 443-3000	0
R & B Realty Group		D	323 851-3450	0
R & R Electric		E	310 785-0288	0
R F R Corporation		D	800 346-7663	0
R W Zant Co **(PA)**		D	323 980-5457	0
Radar Medical Systems Inc		D	440 337-9521	0
Radiology Department Cal Hosp		E	213 742-5840	0
Radisson Hotel At Usc		C	213 748-4141	0
Radix Textile Inc		D	323 234-1667	0
Radlax Gateway Hotel LLC		B	310 670-9000	0
Radleys		E	310 765-2223	0
Radnet Inc **(PA)**		C	310 445-2800	0
Raleigh Enterprises Inc **(PA)**		C	310 899-8900	0
Raleigh Enterprises Inc		C	323 466-3111	0
Ralphs Grocery Company		A	310 637-1101	0
Ramcast Ornamental Sup Co Inc **(PA)**		C	323 585-1625	0
Ramsey-Shilling Residential RE		D	323 851-5512	0
Rapp Worldwide Inc		D	310 563-7200	0
Rayv Inc		E	310 600-2959	0
Rbb Architects Inc **(PA)**		D	310 479-1473	0
Reaume and Associates Inc		D	310 398-5768	0
Red Hawk Fire & SEC CA Inc **(DH)**		D	818 683-1500	0
Red Hawk Fire & Security LLC		D	323 276-3100	0
Reed Smith LLP		C	213 457-8000	0
Regent Worldwide Sales LLC		E	310 806-4288	0
Rehabltion Cntre of Bvrly Hlls		C	323 782-1500	0
Reliance Steel & Aluminum Co **(PA)**		D	213 687-7700	0
Religious Technology Center		D	323 663-3258	0
Relx Inc		D	213 627-1130	0
Remington Hotel Corporation		D	310 553-6561	0
Renaissance Hotel MGT Co LLC		B	310 337-2800	0
Resolution Economics Group LLC **(PA)**		D	310 275-9137	0
Restaurant Depot LLC		C	323 964-1220	0
Revenue Frontier LLC		C	310 584-9200	0
Revolt Media and Tv LLC		C	323 645-3000	0
Rey-Crest Roofg Waterproofing		C	323 257-9329	0
Rheumatology Diagnostics Lab		D	310 253-5455	0
Richard J Metz MD Inc		E	310 553-3189	0
Richards Watson & Gershon PC **(PA)**		C	213 626-8484	0
Richards Group Inc		C	214 891-5700	0
Riot Games Inc **(DH)**		C	310 207-1444	0
Rnc Capital Management LLC		D	310 477-6543	0
Robert Consl Englekirk Strctrl **(PA)**		C	323 733-6673	0
Robert Half International Inc		D	800 356-1994	0
Robert Kaufman Co Inc		E	310 538-3482	0
Rock-It Cargo USA LLC		D	215 947-5400	0
Rock-It Cargo USA LLC		D	310 410-0935	0
Rocket Smog Inc		D	310 390-7664	0
Rockport ADM Svcs LLC **(PA)**		D	323 330-6500	0
Rodeo Realty Inc		D	310 873-0100	0
Rodgers Security Service Inc		D	310 684-3016	0
Rogers Poultry Co		D	800 585-0802	0
Roland Corporation US **(HQ)**		C	323 890-3700	0
Romex Textiles Inc **(PA)**		E	213 749-9090	0
Roosevelt Hotel LLC		C	323 466-7000	0
Rosano Partners		E	213 802-0300	0
Rp Realty Partners LLC		E	310 667-6990	0
Rrt Enterprises LP		B	323 653-1521	0
Rubicon Project Inc **(PA)**		C	310 207-0272	0
Ruby Creek Resources Inc		E	212 671-0404	0
Rutherford Co Inc **(PA)**		D	323 666-5284	0
S W K Properties LLC **(PA)**		C	213 383-9204	0
SA Recycling LLC		D	323 564-5601	0
Saatchi & Saatchi N Amer Inc		C	310 437-2500	0
Saban Brands LLC **(HQ)**		C	310 557-5230	0
Saban Films LLC		D	310 203-5850	0
Sac International Steel Inc **(PA)**		D	323 232-2467	0
Saehan Bank **(PA)**		E	213 368-7700	0

Employment Codes: A=Over 500 employees, B=251-500,
C=101-250, D=51-100, E=50

2020 Directory of California
Wholesalers and Services Companies

© Mergent Inc. 1-800-342-5647

1571

GEOGRAPHIC

	SIC	EMP	PHONE	ENTRY #
Sag-Aftra Foundation		E	323 549-6708	0
Saint Justin Education Fu		D	323 221-3400	0
Salt of Earth Productions Inc		C	818 399-1860	0
Saltzburg Ray & Bergman LLP		C	310 481-6700	0
Salvation Army		D	213 553-3273	0
Salvation Army		E	213 484-0772	0
Sam Jung USA Inc		D	323 231-0811	0
Samaritan Imaging Center		A	213 977-2140	0
Santa Mnica Wlshire Imging LLC		E	323 549-3055	0
Santa Monica Bay Physicians He (PA)		D	310 417-5900	0
Santa Monica Express Inc		D	310 458-6000	0
Santee Systems Services II		D	323 445-0044	0
Santee Systems Services II LL		E	323 445-0044	0
Sbb Roofing Inc (PA)		C	323 254-2888	0
Scalelab LLC (DH)		E	310 526-7524	0
Schaefer Ambulance Service Inc		B	323 468-1642	0
Schindler Elevator Corporation		D	310 785-9775	0
Schirmer Fire Protection Eng		D	213 630-2020	0
Schmidt Phyllis MD Corporation		A	213 613-1163	0
SCI Real Estate Invstments LLC		D	310 361-8588	0
Scottel Voice & Data Inc		C	310 737-7300	0
Scv Facilities Services		D	310 803-4588	0
SDI Media USA Inc (DH)		D	323 602-5455	0
Sea Win Inc		E	213 688-2899	0
Season Produce Co Inc		B	213 689-0008	0
Seaworld Global Logistics		B	310 208-9488	0
Secret Charm LLC (PA)		C	213 742-7744	0
Secure Nursing Service Inc		B	213 736-6771	0
Securitas SEC Svcs USA Inc		C	213 580-8825	0
Securitech Security Services		C	213 387-5050	0
Seiu Local 2015		C	213 985-0384	0
Seiu Local 721		D	213 368-8660	0
Senior Keiro Health Care		D	323 263-9651	0
Sentinel Acqstion Holdings Inc		A	310 201-4100	0
Serrano Covalescent Hospital		D	323 465-2106	0
Service Parking Corporation		D	323 851-2416	0
ServiceMaster Company LLC		D	760 298-7001	0
Seven Licensing Company LLC		D	323 881-0308	0
Seyfarth Shaw LLP		C	213 270-9600	0
Seyfarth Shaw LLP		C	310 277-7200	0
Shadow Animation LLC		E	323 466-7771	0
Shapiro-Gilman-Shandler Co (PA)		C	213 593-1200	0
Sharon Care Center LLC		C	323 655-2023	0
Sharp Guard Services Inc		A	213 739-1900	0
Shawmut Woodworking & Sup Inc		C	323 602-1000	0
Shed Media US Inc		D	323 904-4680	0
Sheppard Mullin Richter (PA)		B	213 620-1780	0
Sheppard Mullin Richter		D	310 228-3700	0
Sheraton LLC		B	310 642-1111	0
Shields For Families (PA)		D	323 242-5000	0
Shilpark Paint Corporation (PA)		D	323 732-7093	0
Showa Marine Inc (PA)		D	213 627-4091	0
Sia Engineering (usa) Inc		D	310 693-7108	0
Signature Consultants LLC		D	310 229-5731	0
Silv Communication Inc		D	213 381-7999	0
Silver Cinemas Acquisition Co (HQ)		D	310 473-6701	0
Silver Fredman A Prof Law Corp		E	310 556-2356	0
Silverado Senior Living Inc		D	323 984-7313	0
Simpson & Simpson		D	213 736-6664	0
Sinai Temple		C	323 469-6000	0
Singerlewak LLP (PA)		C	310 477-3924	0
Sisters of Nzareth Los Angeles		D	310 839-2361	0
Sitrick Brincko Group LLC		D	310 788-2850	0
Six Continents Hotels Inc		D	213 748-1291	0
Six Point Harness		E	323 462-3344	0
Skadden Arps Slate Meagher & F		C	213 687-5000	0
Skanska-Rados A Joint Venture		D	213 978-0600	0
Skidmore Owings & Merrill LLP		C	213 996-8366	0
Skilled Healthcare LLC		D	323 663-3951	0
Skirball Cultural Center		C	310 440-4500	0
Sky Zone LLC (HQ)		D	310 734-0300	0
Skyline Healthcare & Wellness		D	323 665-1185	0
Skypower Holdings LLC		C	323 860-4900	0
SM 10000 Property LLC		D	305 374-5700	0
Smart & Final Stores Inc		B	323 549-9586	0
Smith-Emery Company (PA)		D	213 745-5312	0
SMS Transportation Svcs Inc		C	213 489-5367	0
Smuk Inc		C	323 904-4680	0
Sobel Ross H Law Offices		E	310 788-8995	0
Sobol Philip A MD P C Inc		E	310 649-5894	0
Society For The Prevention of (PA)		D	888 772-2521	0
Society of St Vincent De (PA)		D	323 226-9445	0
Sola Impact Fund II LP		E	323 306-4648	0
Sola Impact Fund II LP		E	323 306-4648	0
Sola Impact Fund II LP		E	323 306-4648	0

	SIC	EMP	PHONE	ENTRY #
Sola Impact Fund II LP		E	323 306-4648	0
Sola Impact Fund II LP		E	323 306-4648	0
Sola Rentals Inc		E	323 306-4648	0
Solheim Lutheran Home		C	323 257-7518	0
Solver Inc		E	310 691-5300	0
Sonicocom Inc		D	213 291-0475	0
Sony Pictures Entrmt Inc		B	310 244-3558	0
Sony Pictures Studios Inc		B	310 244-4000	0
South Bay Senior Services Inc		D	310 338-8558	0
South Bay Vlla Preservation LP		D	310 516-7325	0
South Baylo University		C	213 387-2414	0
South Central Family Hlth Ctr		D	323 908-4200	0
South Central Los (PA)		C	213 744-7000	0
South China Sheet Metal Inc		D	323 225-1522	0
South Cntl Heatlh & Rehab Prog		D	323 751-2677	0
Southern Cal Pipe Trades ADM (PA)		D	213 385-6161	0
Southern Cal Prmnnte Med Group		D	323 857-2000	0
Southern Cal Prmnnte Med Group		D	323 783-5455	0
Southern Cal Prmnnte Med Group		B	323 783-4893	0
Southern California Gas Co (DH)		C	213 244-1200	0
Southern California Gas Tower		B	213 244-1200	0
Southwest Airlines Co		D	310 665-5700	0
Southwest Rgnal Cncil Crpnters (PA)		E	213 385-1457	0
Sp Plus Corporation		D	213 488-3100	0
Special Needs Network		E	323 291-7100	0
Special Service For Groups Inc (PA)		A	213 368-1888	0
Special Service For Groups Inc		D	213 620-5713	0
Spus7 125 Cambridgepark LP		C	213 683-4200	0
Spus7 150 Cambridgepark LP		C	213 683-4200	0
Spus7 Miami Acc LP		E	213 683-4200	0
Squire Patton Boggs (us) LLP		D	213 624-2500	0
Srax Inc (PA)		D	323 694-9800	0
Srht Property Mgmt Co		D	213 683-0522	0
SRK Global Consulting		D	310 295-2524	0
St Annes Maternity Home		C	213 381-2931	0
St Barnbas Snior Ctr Los Angle		D	213 388-4444	0
St Johns Well Child (PA)		D	323 541-1600	0
St Vincent Senior Citizn Nutr (PA)		D	213 484-7775	0
Standard Chartered Bank		E	626 683-8000	0
Standard Hollywood Lessee LLC		C	323 822-3102	0
Standard-Southern Corporation		D	213 624-1831	0
Standard-Southern Corporation		C	213 624-1831	0
Standard-Southern Corporation		D	213 624-1831	0
Star Fabrics Inc (PA)		D	213 688-2871	0
Starline Tours Hollywood Inc (PA)		D	323 463-3333	0
Starwood Htls & Rsrts Wrldwde		C	310 208-8765	0
Starwood Htls & Rsrts Wrldwde		A	213 624-1000	0
Starwood Htls & Rsrts Wrldwde		C	323 798-1300	0
State Farm Mutl Auto Insur Co		B	309 766-2311	0
State Farm Mutl Auto Insur Co		D	323 852-6868	0
Steiny and Company Inc (PA)		D	213 382-2331	0
Steptoe & Johnson LLP		E	213 439-9400	0
Sterling Westwood Inc		D	310 287-2431	0
Steve Beattie Inc		D	310 454-1786	0
Stjohn God Rtirement Care Ctr		C	323 731-0641	0
Stockbridge/Sbe Holdings LLC		A	323 655-8000	0
Straight Lander Inc		D	323 337-9075	0
Stroock & Stroock & Lavan LLP		C	310 556-5800	0
Study US Research Inst Inc		D	213 840-9575	0
Stutman Trster Glatt Prof Corp		D	310 228-5600	0
Stv Architects Inc		D	213 482-9444	0
Sullivan & Cromwell LLP		C	310 712-6600	0
SunAmerica Hsng Fnd 1071		C	310 772-6000	0
SunAmerica Inc (HQ)		A	310 772-6000	0
SunAmerica Investments Inc (DH)		D	310 772-6000	0
SunAmerica Investments Inc		C	310 772-6000	0
SunAmerica Life Insurance Co (DH)		C	310 772-6000	0
Sunrise Brands LLC (PA)		E	323 780-8250	0
Sunrise Senior Living Inc		D	310 437-7178	0
Sunset Tower Hotel LLC		C	323 654-7100	0
Sunstone Hotel Investors LLC		C	310 215-1000	0
Sunstone Hotel Investors LLC		C	310 649-1400	0
Sunstone Hotel Properties Inc		D	310 228-4100	0
Superbalife International LLC		D	310 553-7400	0
Svi Lax LLC		D	310 281-0300	0
Svn International Corp		D	310 979-0800	0
Swinerton Builders		D	213 896-3400	0
Swiss Port Corp		B	310 417-0258	0
Swissport Cargo Services LP		A	310 910-9541	0
Swissport Usa Inc		B	310 345-1986	0
Swissport Usa Inc		B	310 910-9560	0
Sycamore Park Care Center LLC		D	323 223-3441	0
Sydell Hotels LLC		C	213 381-7411	0
Synermed		D	213 626-4556	0
Systems Experience Inc		D	310 215-9000	0

Mergent email: customerrelations@mergent.com
1572

2020 Directory of California
Wholesalers and Services Companies

(P-0000) Products & Services Section entry number
(PA)=Parent Co (HQ)=Headquarters (DH)=Div Headquarters

Company	SIC	EMP	PHONE	ENTRY #
T C R Limited Partnership		C	310 645-1881	0
T C W Realty Fund VI		C	213 683-4200	0
T Points Inc		E	323 846-9176	0
Takenaka Partners LLC (PA)		E	213 593-4011	0
Tanner Mainstain Blatt & Gly		D	310 446-2700	0
Tarrant Apparel Group		C	323 780-8250	0
Tax Credit Co LLC		C	323 927-0752	0
Tbwa Chiat/Day Inc		D	310 305-5000	0
Tcw Funds Management Inc		A	213 244-0000	0
Tcw Group Inc (PA)		B	213 244-0000	0
Tcw Value Added Ltd Partnr		D	213 244-0000	0
Team-One Emplyment Spclsts LLC		A	310 481-4480	0
Technclor Crative Svcs USA Inc (DH)		B	818 260-3800	0
Technclor Crative Svcs USA Inc		C	323 467-1244	0
Technicolor Thomson Group		A	323 817-6600	0
Telaflora LLC		B	310 231-9199	0
Tele-Car Couriers Inc		D	877 910-1313	0
Temple Israel of Hollywood (PA)		D	323 876-8330	0
Temple Park Convalescent Hosp		D	213 380-2035	0
Tender Home Healthcare Inc		D	323 466-2345	0
Tenet Health Systems Norris		B	323 865-3000	0
Tessie Clvland Cmnty Svcs Corp		D	323 586-7333	0
Thc - Orange County Inc		C	310 642-0325	0
The Gray-Line Tours Company		C	323 463-3333	0
The Orthopedic Institute of		A	213 977-2010	0
The Teecor Group Inc		D	213 632-2350	0
Thinkwell Design & Prod Inc		C	818 333-3444	0
Thinkwell Group Inc		D	818 333-3444	0
Thompson Coburn LLP		B	310 282-2500	0
Thoreau Janitorial Svcs Inc		C	310 822-8017	0
TI Gotham Inc		C	310 268-7200	0
Time Warner Cable Entps LLC		C	323 993-7076	0
Time Warner Cable Inc		B	323 993-8000	0
Tinco Sheet Metal Inc		C	323 263-0511	0
Tishman Construction Corp Cal		D	213 542-6400	0
TNT USA Inc		D	310 242-9700	0
Topa Berkeley Ltd		D	310 203-9199	0
Topa Insurance Company (HQ)		D	310 201-0451	0
Topa Management Company (PA)		D	310 203-9199	0
Total Cmmnicator Solutions Inc		D	619 277-1488	0
Total Professional Network		D	213 382-5550	0
Tpg Reflections II LLC		D	213 613-1900	0
Tps Parking Management LLC		D	310 846-4747	0
Trading Financial Credit LLC (PA)		E	213 375-3113	0
Trailer Park Inc		D	310 845-8400	0
Trailer Park Inc (PA)		D	310 845-3000	0
Trams Inc (DH)		D	310 641-8726	0
Trans West Investigations Inc		D	213 381-1500	0
Travel Store (PA)		D	310 575-5540	0
Triage Entertainment LLC		D	310 417-4800	0
Trifecta Multimedia LLC (PA)		E	626 355-1303	0
Trope and Trope LLP		D	323 879-2726	0
Troygould PC		D	310 553-4441	0
Truck Underwriters Association (DH)		A	323 932-3200	0
Truconnect Communications Inc (PA)		C	512 919-2641	0
Trz Holdings II Inc		B	213 955-7170	0
Tucker Ellis LLP		D	213 430-3400	0
Tumbleweed Educational Entps		C	310 444-3232	0
Turner Broadcasting System Inc		D	310 788-6767	0
Turner Construction Company		D	213 891-3000	0
Twentieth Century Fox Home E (DH)		A	310 369-1000	0
Twentieth Cntury Fox Film Corp (DH)		D	310 369-1000	0
Twentieth Cntury Fox Intl Corp (DH)		C	310 969-5300	0
Twenty Mile Productions LLC		D	412 251-0767	0
Tzippy Care Inc		D	323 737-7778	0
Uaw-Lbor Emplyment Trning Corp		C	323 730-7900	0
UBS Financial Services Inc		D	213 972-1511	0
Uc Regents		D	310 301-8777	0
Ucla Copy Services		E	310 794-6371	0
Ucla Foundation		B	310 794-3193	0
Ucla Health System		D	310 825-9111	0
Ucla Health System Auxiliary		A	310 267-4327	0
Ucla Marina Center		D	310 825-3671	0
Umina Bros Inc (PA)		D	213 622-9206	0
UNI Hosiery Co Inc (PA)		C	213 228-0100	0
Unified Grocers Inc		D	323 232-6124	0
Uniserve Facilities Svcs Corp		A	310 440-6747	0
Unitas Global LLC (PA)		D	213 785-6200	0
United Airlines Inc		C	310 342-8086	0
United Airlines Inc		B	310 258-3319	0
United American Indian Involve (PA)		D	213 202-3970	0
United Artists Productions Inc		C	310 449-3000	0
United Artists Television Corp		C	310 449-3000	0
United Convalescent Facilities		D	626 629-6950	0
United Cp/S Chldrns Fndn La		D	323 737-0303	0
United Express Messengers Inc		D	310 261-2000	0
United Fabrics Intl Inc		D	213 749-8200	0
United Food and Commercial (PA)		D	213 487-7070	0
United Ind Taxi Drivers (PA)		D	323 462-1088	0
United Independent Taxi Co		E	213 385-2227	0
United Parcel Service Inc OH		C	310 474-0019	0
United Parcel Service Inc OH		A	323 729-6762	0
United States Attorneys		C	213 894-2400	0
United States Fire Insur Co		D	213 797-3100	0
United Talent Agency LLC		B	310 385-2800	0
United Teachers-Los Angeles		D	213 487-5560	0
United Way Inc (PA)		D	213 808-6220	0
Unity Courier Service Inc (PA)		C	323 255-9800	0
Universal Studios Company LLC		C	310 235-4749	0
University Cal Los Angeles		E	310 794-2284	0
University Cal Los Angeles		A	310 825-0640	0
University Cal Los Angeles		A	310 825-9111	0
University Credit Union		C	310 477-6628	0
University Southern California		C	213 740-4694	0
University Southern California		A	323 442-8500	0
University Southern California		D	213 743-5339	0
University Student Union Inc		C	323 343-2450	0
URS Group Inc		D	213 996-2200	0
URS Group Inc		D	213 996-2200	0
US Army Corps of Engineers		A	213 452-3967	0
US International Media LLC (PA)		D	310 482-6700	0
US Metro Group Inc		A	213 382-6435	0
US Telepacific Corp (HQ)		E	866 699-8242	0
Usc Care Medical Group Inc		D	323 442-5100	0
Usc Credit Union		D	213 821-7100	0
Usc Emergency Medicine Assoc		D	323 226-6667	0
Usc Institute For Neuroimaging		C	323 442-7246	0
Usc Shoah Fndn Inst For Visual		C	213 740-6001	0
Usc Surgeons Incorporated		C	323 442-5910	0
Uscb Inc		D	213 387-6181	0
Uscb Inc (PA)		C	213 985-2111	0
USI Insurance Services Nat Inc		C	213 253-6700	0
Vacation and Holiday Benefit F		D	213 385-6161	0
Val-Pro Inc		D	213 689-0844	0
Valet Parking Svc A Cal Partnr (PA)		A	323 465-5873	0
Valetor Inc		E	323 654-1271	0
Vancrest Construction Corp		E	323 256-0011	0
Vaughn Weedman Inc (PA)		C	425 481-0919	0
Vayan Marketing Group LLC		E	310 943-4990	0
VCA Animal Hospitals Inc (DH)		C	310 571-6500	0
VCA Antech Inc		B	310 207-0781	0
VCA Inc		D	310 473-2951	0
Veatch Carlson Grogan & Nelson		E	213 381-2861	0
Vector Security Inc		D	323 224-6700	0
Vendor Direct Solutions LLC		C	213 362-5622	0
Verifi Inc		D	323 655-5789	0
Veritiv Operating Company		C	310 527-3000	0
Verizon Digital Media Svcs Inc (HQ)		D	310 396-7400	0
Versa Products Inc (PA)		D	310 353-7100	0
Veterans Health Administration		A	310 478-3711	0
Veterans Health Administration		C	213 253-2677	0
Via Care Cmnty Hlth Ctr Inc		D	323 268-9191	0
Viacom Consumer Products Inc		E	323 956-5634	0
Viacom Networks		A	310 752-8000	0
Vicar Operating Inc (DH)		C	310 571-6500	0
Virgil Sntrium Cnvlescent Hosp		C	323 665-5793	0
Vision To Learn		E	800 485-9196	0
Visionstar Inc		D	213 387-3700	0
Vista Anglina Hsing Prtners LP		E	213 482-4718	0
Viva Group Inc		D	310 449-6400	0
Vivid Solution		D	310 498-2559	0
Volume Services Inc		D	323 644-6038	0
Volunteers of Amer Los Angeles		C	323 780-3770	0
Vxi Global Solutions LLC (PA)		A	213 739-4720	0
W Los Angeles		B	310 208-8765	0
W Scott Bllard Dsign Arch Inc		E	323 386-4740	0
Walker & Dunlop Inc		D	301 215-5500	0
Walter J Conn & Associates		D	213 683-0500	0
Wardlow 2 LP (PA)		D	562 432-8066	0
Warner Bros Records Inc (DH)		B	818 846-9090	0
Warren Drye Kelley		D	310 712-6100	0
Washington Enterprises 3 LLC		D	323 731-0861	0
Wasserman Media Group LLC (PA)		C	310 407-0200	0
Watts Health Foundation Inc		B	323 357-6688	0
Watts Healthcare Corporation		C	323 241-1780	0
Watts Healthcare Corporation (PA)		C	323 564-4331	0
Watts Labor Community Action		C	323 563-5639	0
We Team Security Firm Inc		D	800 745-9051	0
Wealth Educators Inc		C	310 623-9145	0
Wedbush Securities Inc (HQ)		B	213 688-8000	0

Employment Codes: A=Over 500 employees, B=251-500, C=101-250, D=51-100, E=50

2020 Directory of California
Wholesalers and Services Companies

© Mergent Inc. 1-800-342-5647
1573

GEOGRAPHIC

	SIC	EMP	PHONE	ENTRY #
Weingart Center Association		C	213 622-6359	0
Weitz & Luxenberg PC		D	310 247-0921	0
Wells Fargo Bank Ltd		D	213 253-6227	0
Wells Fargo Bank NA		C	213 628-2251	0
Wells Fargo Clearing Svcs LLC		E	213 486-5200	0
West Coast Ambulance Corp		C	310 435-1862	0
West Hotel Partners LP **(PA)**		C	310 477-3593	0
West Side Rehab Corporation		C	323 231-4174	0
Western Exterminator Company		D	310 274-9244	0
Westfield LLC **(DH)**		B	813 926-4600	0
Westfield America Inc **(HQ)**		C	310 478-4456	0
Westfield America Ltd Partnr		D	310 478-4456	0
Westfield America Ltd Partnr		B	310 277-3898	0
Westlake Health Care Center		C	805 494-1233	0
Westlake Services LLC **(PA)**		C	323 692-8800	0
Westpoint Marketing Intl Inc		D	323 233-0233	0
Westside Jewish Cmnty Ctr Inc **(PA)**		A	323 938-2531	0
Weststar Cinemas Inc		D	323 461-3331	0
Westwood Healthcare Center LP		D	310 826-0821	0
Wga West Inc		D	323 782-4512	0
Whalen Medical Corporation **(PA)**		E	213 622-6010	0
Whb Corporation		A	213 624-1011	0
White Memorial Med Group Inc **(PA)**		D	323 987-1300	0
White Memorial Medical Center **(HQ)**		A	323 268-5000	0
WI Spa LLC		E	213 487-2700	0
Wiemar Distributors Inc		D	213 747-7036	0
Will Perkins Inc		C	213 270-8400	0
William Morris Endeavor		B	310 285-9000	0
Wilmer Cutler Pick Hale Dorr		C	213 443-5300	0
Wilshire Center Dental Group		E	213 386-3336	0
Wilshire Consumer Credit		E	323 692-8585	0
Wilshire Country Club		D	323 934-6050	0
Wilson Elser Moskowitz		D	213 443-5100	0
Wilson Sonsini Goodrich & Rosa		B	650 493-6352	0
Windsor Gardens Convalescnt		D	323 937-5466	0
Windstar Capital Advisors		C	310 505-3720	0
Winterthur U S Holdings Inc		C	213 228-0281	0
Wonderful Agency		A	310 966-8600	0
Wonderful Company LLC		A	661 720-2609	0
Wood Smith Henning Berman LLP **(PA)**		E	310 481-7600	0
Workmens Auto Insurance Co		D	213 742-8700	0
Worldlink LLC **(PA)**		D	323 866-5900	0
Worldwide Flight Services Inc		C	310 646-7510	0
Worldwide Flight Services Inc		C	310 342-7830	0
Worldwide Holdings Inc **(PA)**		D	213 236-4500	0
Worldwide Security Associates **(HQ)**		B	310 743-3000	0
Worleyparsons Group Inc		B	610 855-2000	0
Woundco Holdings Inc		B	310 551-0101	0
Wrap News Inc		E	424 248-0612	0
Writers Guild America West Inc		C	323 951-4000	0
Wsp USA Inc		E	212 465-5000	0
Xcommerce Inc **(HQ)**		D	310 954-8012	0
Xpo Logistics Freight Inc		C	213 744-0664	0
Yeshiva Rau Isacsohn Academy		C	323 549-3170	0
Yf Art Holdings Gp LLC		A	678 441-1400	0
York Hlthcare Wllness Cntre LP		D	323 254-3407	0
Young Mens Chrstn Assn of La		E	310 216-9036	0
Young Mens Chrstn Assn of La		D	323 467-4161	0
Young Mens Chrstn Assn of La		D	213 624-2348	0
Young MNS Chrstn Assn Mtro Los **(PA)**		D	213 380-6448	0
Young Womens Christian Assoc		C	323 295-4280	0
Youngs Market Company LLC		B	213 629-3929	0
Yucaipa Companies LLC **(PA)**		C	310 789-7200	0
Yue Feng Inc		D	310 253-9795	0
Yuen Yee Laundry & Cleaners		D	323 734-7205	0
Yukevich / Cvanaugh A Law Corp **(PA)**		D	213 362-7777	0
Z Valet Inc		C	323 954-3700	0
Zabin Industries Inc **(PA)**		D	213 749-1215	0
Zastrow Construction Inc		C	323 478-1956	0
Zefr Inc		C	310 392-3555	0
Ziffren B B F G-L S&C Fnd		C	310 552-3388	0
Zimmer Gunsul		D	213 617-1901	0
Zurich American Insurance Co		C	213 270-0600	0

LOS BANOS, CA - Merced County

	SIC	EMP	PHONE	ENTRY #
Al Barcellos Et		E	209 826-2636	0
Bowles Farming Co Inc		E	209 827-3000	0
David Santos Farming		D	209 826-1065	0
Facilities Operation and Trnsp		E	209 826-1936	0
Kings View Work Experience Ctr		E	209 826-8118	0
McElvany Inc		D	209 826-1102	0
New Bthny Rsdntl CRE&sklld		D	209 827-8933	0
Para & Palli Inc		D	209 826-0790	0
Ranchwood Contractors Inc		D	209 826-6200	0
Sutter Health		C	209 827-4866	0
Wolfsen Incorporated		C	209 827-7700	0

LOS GATOS, CA - Santa Clara County

	SIC	EMP	PHONE	ENTRY #
Accel Biotech LLC		D	408 354-1700	0
Addison-Penzak Jewish Communit		C	408 358-3636	0
Alain Pinel Realtors Inc		D	408 358-1111	0
American Baptist Homes of West		C	408 357-1100	0
Audrey Adams MD		E	408 354-2114	0
Auto World Car Wash LLC		A	408 345-6532	0
Butter Paddle		D	408 395-1678	0
Calvary Baptist Ch Los Gatos		D	408 356-5126	0
Coldwell Bnkr Rsdential RE LLC		D	408 355-1500	0
Courtside Tennis Club		D	408 395-7111	0
Episcopal Senior Communities		C	408 354-0211	0
Golden Living LLC		D	408 356-8136	0
Golden Living LLC		D	408 356-9151	0
Good Samaritan Hospital LP		C	408 356-4111	0
Infogain Corporation **(PA)**		C	408 355-6000	0
Inner Circle Entertainment		D	415 693-1900	0
Intellicus Tech Pvt Ltd		D	408 213-3314	0
Joie De Vivre Hospitality LLC		A	408 335-1700	0
La Rinconada Country Club Inc **(PA)**		D	408 395-4181	0
Los Gatos Senior Living LLC		E	408 356-9146	0
NC Fit Inc		D	408 910-6748	0
Netflix Inc		A	408 540-3700	0
Netline Corporation **(PA)**		D	408 374-4200	0
Roku Inc **(PA)**		B	408 556-9040	0
SA Photonics Inc		D	408 560-3500	0
Sanco Pipelines Incorporated		E	408 377-2793	0
Santa Clara County of		C	408 355-2200	0
Santa Clara Valley Water		D	408 395-8121	0
Sierra Nevada Corporation		C	408 395-2004	0
Sierra Weatherization Co Inc		D	408 354-1900	0
Stratford School Inc		D	408 371-3020	0
Sutter Health		C	408 523-3900	0
Tenet Healthsystem Medical		A	408 378-6131	0
Therapy In Your Home O TP TS		D	408 358-0201	0
Trevi Partners A Calif LP		D	408 395-7070	0
Uplift Family Services		D	408 379-3790	0
US Carenet Services LLC		E	408 378-6131	0

LOS OSOS, CA - San Luis Obispo County

	SIC	EMP	PHONE	ENTRY #
Rantec Power Systems Inc **(HQ)**		D	805 596-6000	0

LOST HILLS, CA - Kern County

	SIC	EMP	PHONE	ENTRY #
Roll Properties Intl Inc		C	661 797-6500	0
Wonderful Orchards LLC		C	661 797-6400	0

LOTUS, CA - El Dorado County

	SIC	EMP	PHONE	ENTRY #
Adventure Connection Inc		D	530 626-7385	0

LOWER LAKE, CA - Lake County

	SIC	EMP	PHONE	ENTRY #
Barrick Gold Corporation		D	707 995-6070	0
Epidendio Construction Inc		E	707 994-5100	0

LOYALTON, CA - Sierra County

	SIC	EMP	PHONE	ENTRY #
Eastern Plumas Health Care		D	530 993-1225	0

LUCERNE VALLEY, CA - San Bernardino County

	SIC	EMP	PHONE	ENTRY #
Specialty Minerals Inc		C	760 248-5300	0
SS Hert Trucking Inc **(PA)**		E	760 248-9327	0

LYNWOOD, CA - Los Angeles County

	SIC	EMP	PHONE	ENTRY #
ADM Furniture Inc		D	310 762-2800	0
Country Villa Service Corp		D	310 537-2500	0
Kaiser Foundation Hospitals		A	310 604-5700	0
Legacy Frames		D	310 537-4210	0
Marlinda Management Inc **(PA)**		C	310 631-6122	0
Midas Express Los Angeles Inc		C	310 609-0366	0
South Cntl Heatlh & Rehab Prog		D	310 667-4070	0
Southern CA Hlth & Rhbltn Prg		C	310 631-8004	0
Southern Cal Prmnnte Med Group		D	310 604-5700	0
St Francis Medical Center **(HQ)**		C	310 900-8900	0
Verity Health System Cal Inc		D	310 900-2000	0
Verity Health System Cal Inc		A	310 900-8900	0
Via Trading Corporation		D	877 202-3616	0

LYTLE CREEK, CA - San Bernardino County

	SIC	EMP	PHONE	ENTRY #
Burlingame Industries Inc		C	909 887-7038	0

MACDOEL, CA - Siskiyou County

	SIC	EMP	PHONE	ENTRY #
Plant Sciences Inc		E	530 398-4042	0

MADERA, CA - Madera County

	SIC	EMP	PHONE	ENTRY #
Agri-World Cooperative		E	559 673-1306	0
Avalon Care Ctr - Madera LLC		D	559 673-9278	0
Berry & Berry Inc **(PA)**		D	559 674-2491	0
Camarena Health		D	559 664-4000	0
Comcast Corporation		D	559 474-4194	0
Community Action Prtnrshp **(PA)**		C	559 673-9173	0

Mergent email: customerrelations@mergent.com
1574

2020 Directory of California
Wholesalers and Services Companies

(P-0000) Products & Services Section entry number
(PA)=Parent Co (HQ)=Headquarters (DH)=Div Headquarters

	SIC	EMP	PHONE	ENTRY #
Costa View Farms		E	559 675-3131	0
County of Los Angeles		C	559 675-7739	0
County of Madera		D	559 675-7811	0
Eurodrip USA Inc		D	559 674-2670	0
First Student Inc		C	559 661-7433	0
Fresno-Madera Federal Land		D	559 674-2437	0
Golden Living LLC		D	559 673-9278	0
Iest Family Farms		D	559 674-9417	0
Kronos Foods Corp		D	559 674-4445	0
Lamanuzzi & Pantaleo LLC (PA)		C	559 432-3170	0
Lion Raisins Inc		C	559 662-8686	0
Madera Cnty Bhvioral Hlth Svcs		C	559 673-3508	0
Madera Community Hospital		C	559 675-5530	0
Madera Community Hospital (PA)		B	559 675-5555	0
Madera Convalescent Hospital (PA)		C	559 673-9228	0
Madera Private Security Patrol		D	559 662-1546	0
Mid Valley Labor Services Inc		B	559 661-6390	0
Our Huse Rsdntial Care Ctr Inc		E	559 674-8670	0
Pediatric Physical Rehab Clnc		E	559 353-6130	0
Ready Roast Nut Company LLC (PA)		D	559 661-1696	0
Resource Rfrral Child Care Dev		E	559 673-9173	0
Richard Iest Dairy Inc		D	559 673-2635	0
S & J Ranches LLC		D	559 437-2600	0
Span Construction & Engrg Inc (PA)		D	559 661-1111	0
Stellar Distributing Inc		B	559 664-8400	0
Talley Transportation		D	559 673-9013	0
Valley Childrens Healthcare		A	559 353-3000	0
Valley Childrens Hospital		C	559 353-6425	0
Valley Childrens Hospital (PA)		A	559 353-3000	0
Valley Physicians Alliance LLC		D	559 538-3000	0

MALIBU, CA - Los Angeles County

	SIC	EMP	PHONE	ENTRY #
California Fuji International		E	818 889-6680	0
Creating Arts Company		E	310 804-0223	0
Curtco Publishing LLC (PA)		C	310 589-7700	0
Dun & Bradstreet Emerging (DH)		C	310 456-8271	0
Fitness Ridge Malibu LLC		D	818 874-1300	0
Grasshopper House LLC		C	310 589-2880	0
Hrl Laboratories LLC		B	310 317-5000	0
Las Vegas Intrntnl Tours		C	323 960-0300	0
Malibu Conference Center Inc		B	818 889-6440	0
Malibu Realty Inc		E	310 457-5124	0
Marmalade LLC		E	310 317-4242	0
Mbipch LLC		D	310 456-6444	0
Parks and Recreation Cal Dept		D	310 456-8432	0
Phifactor Technologies LLC		D	424 234-9494	0
Pritchett Rapf and Associates		D	310 456-6771	0
Sobaliving Llc		E	800 595-3803	0
Sothebys Intl Rlty Inc		E	310 456-6431	0
Tall Pony Productions Inc		C	310 456-7495	0
Terra Coastal Properties Inc		E	310 457-2534	0
Westmed Ambulance Inc		C	310 456-3830	0

MAMMOTH LAKES, CA - Mono County

	SIC	EMP	PHONE	ENTRY #
Horizons 4 Condominiums Inc		D	760 934-6779	0
Mammoth Mountain Lake Corp		B	760 934-2571	0
Mammoth Mountain Ski Area LLC (DH)		B	760 934-2571	0
Snowcreek Property Management		E	760 934-3333	0
Southern Mono Healthcare Dst		B	760 934-3311	0

MANHATTAN BEACH, CA - Los Angeles County

	SIC	EMP	PHONE	ENTRY #
1334 Partners LP		D	310 546-5656	0
Access To Loans For Learning		E	310 979-4700	0
Adventureplex		E	310 546-7708	0
CIT Bank NA		C	310 727-5660	0
Comstock Crosser Assoc Dev Inc		E	310 546-5781	0
Dalaklis McKeown Entertainment		D	310 545-0120	0
Ebc Inc (PA)		D	310 753-6407	0
Emergent Medical Associates (PA)		D	310 379-2134	0
Frys Electronics Inc		C	310 364-3797	0
GBS Financial Corp		D	310 937-0073	0
Global Holdings Inc		C	818 905-6000	0
Guru Denim LLC (DH)		C	323 266-3072	0
Host Hotels & Resorts LP		D	310 546-7511	0
Human Touch Home Health		C	424 247-8165	0
Indigo Hospitality Management		E	310 787-7795	0
Investlinc Group LLC (PA)		D	310 997-0580	0
Jag Professional Services Inc		C	310 945-5648	0
Kinecta Federal Credit Union (PA)		C	310 643-5400	0
Pancreatic Cancr Actn Netwrk I (PA)		C	310 725-0025	0
Re/Max Beach Cities Realty Mar		C	310 376-2225	0
Solartis LLC		C	310 251-4861	0
Sunstone Hotel Properties Inc		D	310 546-7627	0
Traliant LLC		C	323 774-1325	0
Trilogy Squaw Spa LLC		E	310 760-0044	0
Vantage Oncology LLC (HQ)		B	310 335-4000	0

	SIC	EMP	PHONE	ENTRY #
Vantage Oncology Inc		D	310 335-4000	0
Western America Properties LLC		D	310 374-4381	0

MANTECA, CA - San Joaquin County

	SIC	EMP	PHONE	ENTRY #
1st Light Energy Inc (PA)		E	209 824-5500	0
American Crane Rental Inc		D	209 838-8815	0
B R Funsten & Co		D	209 825-5375	0
Bay Area Cnstr Framers Inc		C	925 454-8514	0
Bbva USA		B	209 239-1381	0
Clearpath Management Group Inc (PA)		B	209 239-8700	0
Clearpath Workforce MGT Inc		B	209 239-8700	0
Cool Roofing Systems (PA)		D	209 825-0818	0
Doctors Hospital Manteca Inc		B	209 823-3111	0
Ford Motor Company		C	209 824-6600	0
Frontier California Inc		C	209 239-4128	0
J M Equipment Company Inc (PA)		D	209 522-3271	0
Kaiser Foundation Hospitals		A	209 825-3700	0
Kaiser Manteca Medical Office		C	209 825-3700	0
Kamps Company		C	209 823-8924	0
Karma Inc		C	209 239-1222	0
Merrill Gardens LLC		D	209 823-0164	0
Pgande		E	209 942-1745	0
Priority 1 Warehousing Inc (PA)		D	209 824-8876	0
Propane Transport Service Inc		D	209 823-8005	0
S K S Enterprises Inc (PA)		D	209 599-4095	0
South San Jquin Irrigation Dst		D	209 249-4600	0
Stockton Cardiology Medical Gr		D	209 824-1555	0
Tenet Healthsystem Medical		B	209 823-3111	0
Transforce Inc		E	209 952-2573	0
United Parcel Service Inc OH		C	209 944-5932	0
Valley Oak Dental Group		D	209 823-9341	0
Van Groningen & Sons Inc		B	209 982-5248	0
Villara Corporation		D	209 824-1082	0

MARICOPA, CA - Kern County

	SIC	EMP	PHONE	ENTRY #
Aera Energy LLC		D	661 665-3200	0
Luis Esparza Services Inc		B	661 766-2344	0

MARINA, CA - Monterey County

	SIC	EMP	PHONE	ENTRY #
American Medical Response Inc		C	831 718-9555	0
Collins Electrical Company Inc		D	831 384-0114	0
Monterey Rgional Waste MGT Dst		C	831 384-5313	0

MARINA DEL REY, CA - Los Angeles County

	SIC	EMP	PHONE	ENTRY #
Al Anwa USA Incorporated		C	310 301-2000	0
ARINC Incorporated		D	310 301-9040	0
Calatlantic Group Inc		D	310 821-9843	0
Can-Do		D	646 228-7049	0
Cfhs Holdings Inc		A	310 823-8911	0
Cfhs Holdings Inc		A	310 448-7800	0
CIT Bank National Association		D	310 577-6142	0
Diagnostic and Interventio		D	310 574-0400	0
Executive Network Entps Inc (PA)		D	310 447-2759	0
Fastxchange Inc		E	310 827-2445	0
Fedex Office & Print Svcs Inc		E	310 827-2297	0
Four Medica Inc		D	310 348-4100	0
Gebbs Software Intl Inc		D	201 207-0088	0
Guidance Solutions Inc		E	310 754-4000	0
Host Hotels & Resorts LP		D	310 301-3000	0
Iconic Collective LLC		D	877 930-0409	0
International Mgt Systems		D	310 822-2022	0
Laaco Ltd		D	310 823-4567	0
Liquidate Direct LLC		E	800 750-7617	0
Marina Auto Body Shop Inc		E	310 822-6615	0
Marina City Club LP A Cali		C	310 822-0611	0
Modern Parking Inc		D	310 821-1081	0
Post Modern Edit LLC		E	310 396-7375	0
R & B Realty Group		D	310 751-4545	0
Regional Investment & MGT LLC		E	310 821-1945	0
Ritz-Carlton Marina Del Rey		D	310 823-1700	0
Skylar Film Studios LLC		C	424 653-8902	0
Sony Dadc New Mdia Sltions Inc		C	310 760-8500	0
Textplus Inc		D	424 272-0296	0
Thirdwave Technology Services		E	310 563-2160	0
Trendshift LLC		D	866 644-8877	0
Trotta Associates		D	310 306-6866	0
USA Travel Services LLC		A	207 899-8803	0
Veba Administrators Inc		E	310 577-1444	0
Washington Inn LLC		D	310 821-4455	0
Williamson Enterprises Inc		D	310 822-6615	0

MARIPOSA, CA - Mariposa County

	SIC	EMP	PHONE	ENTRY #
John C Fremont Healthcare Dst		C	209 966-3631	0

MARSHALL, CA - Marin County

	SIC	EMP	PHONE	ENTRY #
Nicks Cove Inc		D	415 663-1033	0

Employment Codes: A=Over 500 employees, B=251-500,
C=101-250, D=51-100, E=50

2020 Directory of California
Wholesalers and Services Companies

© Mergent Inc. 1-800-342-5647

1575

	SIC	EMP	PHONE	ENTRY #
MARTINEZ, CA - Contra Costa County				
Alhambra Convalescent Hosp LLC		D	925 228-2020	0
Baja Construction Co Inc **(PA)**		D	925 229-0732	0
Bay Area/Diablo Petroleum Co **(HQ)**		C	925 228-2222	0
Braddock & Logan Inc		D	925 229-1747	0
Brightview Landscape Svcs Inc		D	925 957-8831	0
Careosite Inc		D	562 437-0381	0
Central Contra Costa Sanit		D	925 228-9500	0
Contra Costa Electric Inc **(DH)**		B	925 229-4250	0
County of Contra Costa		C	925 313-4000	0
County of Contra Costa		C	925 313-2000	0
County of Contra Costa		C	866 901-3212	0
County of Contra Costa		C	925 370-5000	0
Dynalectric Company		C	415 487-4700	0
Dynamic Maintenance Svcs Inc		D	925 228-7434	0
Engineering/Remdtn Rsrcs Grp **(PA)**		D	925 839-2200	0
Gregg Drilling LLC		D	925 313-5800	0
Gregg Drilling & Testing Inc		D	925 313-5800	0
Kaiser Foundation Hospitals		C	925 372-1000	0
Legacy and Nursing Rehab		D	925 228-8383	0
Molinas Pntg Wallcovering Inc		D	925 228-7487	0
Nalco Company LLC		D	925 957-9720	0
Parsons Government Svcs Inc		D	925 313-3217	0
Permanente Medical Group Inc		D	925 372-1000	0
Plant Maintenance Inc		C	925 228-3285	0
Power Engineers Incorporated		D	925 372-9284	0
R M Harris Company Inc		D	925 335-3000	0
RE Milano Plumbing Corp		E	925 500-1372	0
Schetter Electric Inc		C	925 228-2424	0
Telfer Oil Company **(PA)**		D	925 228-1515	0
Terracare Associates LLC		D	925 374-0060	0
Thrive Support Services Inc		E	925 682-2273	0
Wastexperts Incorporated		D	925 484-1057	0
Waters Moving & Storage Inc		D	925 372-0914	0
YWCA Contra Costa/Sacramento **(PA)**		D	925 372-4213	0
MARYSVILLE, CA - Yuba County				
Advantage Framing Solutions		E	530 742-7660	0
Alliance Wall Systems Inc		E	530 740-7800	0
Childrens Protective Services		D	530 749-6311	0
County of Yuba		D	530 749-5470	0
County of Yuba		D	530 749-7550	0
Frank M Booth Inc **(PA)**		D	530 742-7134	0
Fremont Hospital		A	530 751-4000	0
Marysvlle Nrsing Rehab Ctr LLC		D	530 742-7311	0
Melon Holdings LLC		D	530 742-7311	0
Peach Tree Healthcare		D	530 749-3242	0
Recology Yuba-Sutter		D	530 743-6933	0
Rideout Memorial Hospital **(HQ)**		A	530 749-4416	0
US Dept of the Air Force		D	530 634-4839	0
Yuba Community College Dst		D	530 788-0973	0
MATHER, CA - Sacramento County				
Bloodsource Inc **(PA)**		B	916 456-1500	0
Mather Aviation LLC **(PA)**		D	916 364-4711	0
Reynen & Bardis Construction **(PA)**		C	916 366-3665	0
Sutter Health		D	916 454-8200	0
Veterans Health Administration		B	916 366-5427	0
Veterans Health Administration		B	916 843-7000	0
MAYWOOD, CA - Los Angeles County				
Food Express Inc		E	323 589-1417	0
Jack H Caldwell & Sons Inc		D	323 589-4008	0
Keeney Truck Lines Inc		E	323 589-3231	0
Los Angeles Job Corps		C	213 748-0135	0
Maywood Healthcare Wellness Ctr		E	323 560-0720	0
R G Canning Enterprises Inc		C	323 560-7469	0
Tapia Enterprises Inc **(PA)**		D	323 560-7415	0
MC FARLAND, CA - Kern County				
A G Hacienda Incorporated		B	661 792-2418	0
Armando Gonzalez Contracting		B	661 792-3785	0
Community Action Partnr Kern		D	661 792-1066	0
Etchegaray Farms LLC		E	661 393-0920	0
Flores Labor Contracting		B	661 792-3061	0
Geo Group Inc		C	661 792-2731	0
Jakov P Dulcich & Sons		C	661 792-6360	0
Renteria Santiago J Farm Labo		C	661 792-0052	0
MC KITTRICK, CA - Kern County				
Dwaynes Engineering & Cnstr		D	661 762-7261	0
MCCLELLAN, CA - Sacramento County				
AAR Manufacturing Inc		D	916 830-7011	0
AAR Manufacturing Inc		D	800 422-2213	0
Califrnia Shock Truma A Rescue **(PA)**		D	916 921-4000	0
Global Blue Dvbe Inc		D	916 632-2583	0
Lionsgate Ht & Conference Ctr		D	916 643-6222	0
Mansion Hospitality Services		D	916 643-6222	0
McClellan Business Park LLC		D	916 965-7100	0
McClellan Facilities Svcs LLC		D	916 965-7100	0
McClellan Hospitality Svcs LLC		D	916 965-7100	0
Monument Security Inc **(PA)**		C	916 564-4234	0
Sbm Management Services LP		B	866 855-2211	0
Sbm Site Services LLC **(PA)**		A	916 922-7600	0
Siemens Mobility Inc		D	916 621-2700	0
Sunergy California LLC		E	916 550-5370	0
Villara Corporation **(PA)**		B	916 646-2700	0
MCKINLEYVILLE, CA - Humboldt County				
Kernen Construction		D	707 826-8686	0
MECCA, CA - Riverside County				
Richard Bagdasarian Inc		D	760 396-2168	0
MENDOCINO, CA - Mendocino County				
Big River Ltd-Design		D	707 937-5615	0
Mendocino Hotel & Resort Corp		D	707 937-0511	0
Sweetwater Gardens Inc		E	707 937-4140	0
MENDOTA, CA - Fresno County				
Pomwonderful LLC		D	310 966-5800	0
S & S Ranch Inc		D	559 655-3491	0
S Stamoules Inc		A	559 655-9777	0
MENIFEE, CA - Riverside County				
Bedon Construction Inc		D	951 246-9005	0
F M Tarbell Co		D	951 301-5932	0
Mackenzie Landscape A Cal Corp		D	951 679-5477	0
Pro Structural Inc		D	951 526-2010	0
Valley Pacific Concrete Inc		C	951 672-6151	0
MENLO PARK, CA - San Mateo County				
Alain Pinel Realtors Inc		D	650 462-1111	0
Allstate Research and Plg Ctr		D	650 833-6200	0
American Cancer Soc Cal Div		D	650 325-8939	0
Atrium Capital Corp		A	650 233-7878	0
Avitas Systems Inc		D	650 233-3900	0
Barclays Capital Inc		D	650 289-6000	0
Bodega Bay Associates		D	650 330-8888	0
Boys & Girls CLB of Peninsula		D	650 322-6255	0
Burr Pilger Mayer Inc		E	650 855-6800	0
Cal Care Inc		C	650 325-8600	0
Caprion Proteomics USA LLC		E	650 776-3676	0
Carr & Ferrell		D	650 812-3400	0
Carr & Ferrell LLP **(PA)**		D	650 812-3400	0
Cataphora Inc **(PA)**		D	650 622-9840	0
Citigroup Global Markets Inc		C	650 926-7600	0
Coldwell Banker		D	650 324-4456	0
Cornerstone Research Inc **(PA)**		D	650 853-1660	0
Critchfield Mechanical Inc		B	650 321-7801	0
D E Shaw Valence LLC		C	650 926-9460	0
Exponent Inc **(PA)**		C	650 326-9400	0
Facebook Inc **(PA)**		A	650 543-4800	0
First Republic Bank		C	650 233-8880	0
First Republic Bank		C	650 470-8888	0
Gachina Landscape MGT Inc		B	650 853-0400	0
Hewlett Wlliam Flora Fndation		D	650 234-4500	0
Hines Interests Ltd Partnr		C	650 518-6139	0
Intuit Inc		C	650 944-6000	0
Katerra Inc **(PA)**		D	650 422-3572	0
Kind Homecare Inc		D	888 885-5463	0
Kleiner Prkins Cfeld Byers LLC **(PA)**		C	650 233-2750	0
Kohlberg Kravis Roberts Co LP		D	650 233-6560	0
Kranz & Assoc Holdings LLC		D	650 854-4400	0
Lafayette Park Hotel Corp **(PA)**		B	650 330-8888	0
Latham & Watkins LLP		C	650 328-4600	0
Lifemoves **(PA)**		E	650 685-5880	0
Lovazzano Mechanical Inc		D	650 367-6216	0
Lucile Salter Packard Chil		C	650 736-2142	0
Merrill Lynch Pierce Fenner		D	650 473-7888	0
Merrill Lynch Pierce Fenner		C	650 473-7888	0
Morningside Corecare Assoc LP		C	650 854-5600	0
Novo Construction Inc **(PA)**		C	650 701-1500	0
Nuance Communications Inc		C	650 847-0000	0
Oak Hill Capital Partners LP		A	650 234-0500	0
OMelveny & Myers LLP		C	650 473-2600	0
Orrick Hrrington Sutcliffe LLP		C	650 614-7400	0
Orrick Hrrington Sutcliffe LLP		C	650 614-7454	0
Pan-Pacific Mechanical LLC		A	650 561-8810	0
Peninsula Volunteers Inc **(PA)**		E	650 326-0665	0
Peninsula World Travel LLC **(PA)**		E	650 328-2030	0
Personalis Inc		C	650 752-1300	0
Protiviti Inc **(HQ)**		D	650 234-6000	0

2020 Directory of California
Wholesalers and Services Companies

(P-0000) Products & Services Section entry number
(PA)=Parent Co (HQ)=Headquarters (DH)=Div Headquarters

	SIC	EMP	PHONE	ENTRY #
Quicken Inc		C	650 564-3399	0
Robert Half International Inc **(PA)**		D	650 234-6000	0
Robert Half International Inc.		D	650 234-6000	0
Robert Half International Inc.		D	650 234-6000	0
Robert Half International Inc.		D	650 234-6000	0
S R I C B I		D	650 859-4865	0
Sequoia Capital Operations LLC		D	650 854-3927	0
Silver Lake Partners LP **(PA)**		D	650 233-8120	0
Space Systems/Loral LLC		C	650 852-4000	0
SRI International **(PA)**		A	650 859-2000	0
Stamos Capital Partners LP		D	650 233-5000	0
Stanford Park Hotel		C	650 322-1234	0
Strategic Bus Insights Inc **(PA)**		D	650 859-4600	0
Strivr Labs Inc		D	650 656-9987	0
Tcmi Inc **(PA)**		E	650 614-8200	0
Veterans Health Administration		A	650 614-9997	0
Vitesse LLC		D	650 543-4800	0
Western Allied Mechanical Inc		C	650 326-8290	0
Winston & Strawn LLP		B	650 858-6500	0

MENTONE, CA - San Bernardino County

	SIC	EMP	PHONE	ENTRY #
International Paving Svcs Inc		D	909 794-2101	0
Nice Avenue LLC		D	909 794-1189	0

MERCED, CA - Merced County

	SIC	EMP	PHONE	ENTRY #
Avalon Care Cen		D	209 723-1056	0
Avalon Care Center - Merced		D	209 722-6231	0
Bear Creek Manor		E	209 723-4674	0
Bloodsource Inc.		D	209 724-0428	0
Central Valley Concrete Inc **(PA)**		C	209 723-8846	0
CF Merced La Sierra LLC		D	209 723-4224	0
Country Villa Service Corp		D	209 723-2911	0
County of Merced		C	209 724-2000	0
Culver-Melin Enterprises		D	209 726-9182	0
Dedicated Management Group LLC		C	209 385-0694	0
Fuentes Farms Ag Inc		B	209 722-7201	0
Golden Living LLC		D	209 722-6231	0
Golden Valley Health Centers **(PA)**		A	209 383-1848	0
Golden Valley Health Centers		A	209 383-5871	0
Guardco Security Services		D	209 723-4273	0
Holiday Inn Express Merced		D	209 383-0333	0
Madera Convalescent Hospital		D	209 723-8814	0
Madera Convalescent Hospital		C	209 723-2911	0
Mater Misericordiae Hospital **(PA)**		A	209 564-5000	0
McLane/Pacific Inc		B	209 725-2500	0
Merced Irrigation District **(PA)**		E	209 722-5761	0
Merced Irrigation District		C	209 722-2719	0
Merced School Employees F C U **(PA)**		D	209 383-5550	0
Merced Transportation Company		D	209 384-2575	0
Mercy HM Svcs A Cal Ltd Partnr		B	209 564-4200	0
N & S Tractor Co **(PA)**		D	209 383-5888	0
Paul Pietrzyk		E	209 726-5034	0
Promesa Behavioral Health		D	209 725-3114	0
Travis Credit Union		B	209 723-0732	0
Via Adventures Inc **(PA)**		E	209 384-1315	0
WLMD		C	209 723-9120	0

MERIDIAN, CA - Sutter County

	SIC	EMP	PHONE	ENTRY #
Colusa Produce Corporation		D	530 696-0121	0

MIDDLETOWN, CA - Lake County

	SIC	EMP	PHONE	ENTRY #
Cpn Wild Horse Geothermal LLC		B	707 431-6229	0
Gr Hardester LLC		C	707 987-2325	0
Heart Consciousness Church **(PA)**		C	707 987-2477	0
Northern California Power Agcy		D	707 987-2381	0

MILL VALLEY, CA - Marin County

	SIC	EMP	PHONE	ENTRY #
Advantis Global Inc **(PA)**		C	415 850-1500	0
Adventres Rlling Cross-Country		C	415 332-5075	0
City of Mill Valley		E	415 383-1370	0
City of Mill Valley		C	415 388-4033	0
First Marin Realty Inc		D	415 383-9393	0
First Republic Bank		C	415 389-0880	0
Kabler Construction Svcs Inc		E	415 888-8812	0
Marin Horizon School Inc		E	415 388-8408	0
S & P Company **(PA)**		D	415 332-0550	0
Sequoia Residential Funding		D	415 389-7373	0
The Redwoods A Cmnty Seniors		D	415 383-2741	0
Unified Teldata Inc		D	415 888-8940	0
Van Acker Cnstr Assoc Inc		C	415 383-5589	0
Wisdom University		D	415 259-7122	0

MILLBRAE, CA - San Mateo County

	SIC	EMP	PHONE	ENTRY #
A & C Health Care Services Inc		C	650 689-5784	0
El Rancho Motel Inc		C	650 588-8500	0
Hillsdale Group LP		E	650 742-9150	0
Magnolia of Millbrae Inc		D	650 697-7700	0

	SIC	EMP	PHONE	ENTRY #
Millbrae Serra Sanitarium		C	650 697-8386	0
Millbrae Wcp Hotel II LLC		E	650 443-5500	0
Starwood Hotels & Resorts		D	650 692-6363	0
Trans World Maintenance Inc		D	650 455-2450	0
Vitalant Research Institute		E	650 697-4034	0

MILPITAS, CA - Santa Clara County

	SIC	EMP	PHONE	ENTRY #
3k Technologies LLC		C	408 716-5900	0
Abbyy USA Software House Inc **(DH)**		C	408 457-9777	0
Abzooba Inc		C	650 453-8760	0
Advantech Corporation **(HQ)**		C	408 519-3800	0
Aerohive Networks Inc **(HQ)**		C	408 510-6100	0
American Golf Corporation		E	408 262-8813	0
Anjaneyap Inc.		D	408 922-9690	0
Arena Stuart Rentals Inc		C	408 856-3232	0
Automatic Data Processing Inc		B	408 876-6600	0
B H R Operations LLC		D	408 321-9500	0
B T Mancini Co Inc **(PA)**		B	408 942-7900	0
Bizcom Electronics Inc **(HQ)**		C	408 262-7877	0
Bottomley Distributing Co Inc		D	408 945-0660	0
Boys & Girls Club Silicon Vly		D	408 957-9685	0
Bre Select Hotels Oper LLC		D	408 719-1313	0
Bright Horizons Chld Ctrs LLC		C	408 853-2196	0
Browning-Ferris Industries LLC		D	408 262-1401	0
Cellco Partnership		D	408 263-1960	0
Cetecom Inc		D	408 586-6200	0
Cg2 Inc		D	407 737-8800	0
Clement Support Services Inc		D	408 227-1171	0
Cni Thl Ops LLC		C	510 623-2355	0
Command Security Corporation		C	408 943-0600	0
Composite Software LLC **(HQ)**		D	800 553-6387	0
Coyote Creek Consulting Inc		C	408 383-9200	0
Creative Labs Inc **(DH)**		C	408 428-6600	0
Custom Drywall Inc		D	408 263-1616	0
Decision Minds		C	408 309-8051	0
Devcon Construction Inc **(PA)**		B	408 942-8200	0
Dga Services Inc **(PA)**		D	408 232-4800	0
Elo Touch Solutions Inc **(HQ)**		D	408 597-8000	0
Enquero Inc		D	408 406-3203	0
Estuate Inc		D	408 946-0002	0
Fieldserver Technologies		E	408 262-2299	0
Fireeye Inc **(PA)**		C	408 321-6800	0
First Call Nursing Svcs Inc		C	408 262-1533	0
Flextronics Intl USA Inc		C	408 576-6769	0
Fresh Lifelines For Youth Inc		D	408 263-2600	0
H V Welker Co Inc		D	408 263-4400	0
Haworth Inc		D	408 262-6400	0
Homefrst Svcs Santa Clara Cnty		C	408 539-2100	0
Humane Society Silicon Valley		D	408 262-2133	0
Idc Technologies Inc **(PA)**		D	408 376-0212	0
Igenex Inc		E	650 424-1191	0
Interntional Disposal Corp Cal		D	408 945-2802	0
Iron Mountain Fulfillment **(HQ)**		E	408 945-1600	0
Jag Software Inc.		D	408 262-0572	0
Kaiser Foundation Hospitals		E	408 945-2900	0
Knights of Columbus		D	408 262-6609	0
Lightwaves 2020 Inc.		E	408 503-8888	0
Lite-On Inc **(HQ)**		E	408 946-4873	0
Lite-On Sales and Dist Inc		D	510 687-1800	0
Macronix America Inc **(HQ)**		D	408 262-8887	0
Mega Professional Intl		D	408 946-1500	0
Nanolab Technologies Inc **(PA)**		D	408 433-3320	0
New Solar Incorporated		E	888 886-0103	0
Nikewoman		E	408 942-6457	0
Northland Control Systems Inc **(PA)**		C	510 226-1015	0
NTS It Care Inc.		D	408 480-4083	0
Ohana Partners Inc **(PA)**		D	408 856-3232	0
Pacific Gas and Electric Co		D	408 945-6215	0
Park Hotels & Resorts Inc		D	408 942-0400	0
Permanente Medical Group Inc		D	408 945-2900	0
Preston Pipelines Inc **(PA)**		C	408 262-1418	0
Promise Technology Inc		D	408 228-1400	0
Prudential Overall Supply		D	408 719-0886	0
R S Software India Limited		D	408 382-1200	0
R&M USA Inc		D	408 945-6626	0
Reading Partners		D	408 945-5720	0
Saint-Joseph Home Health		E	408 244-5488	0
Sankara Eye Foundation USA		D	408 456-0555	0
Semi **(PA)**		C	408 943-6900	0
SGS North America Inc		D	408 588-0200	0
SJ Distributors Inc **(PA)**		D	888 988-2328	0
Smart & Final Stores Inc.		B	408 941-9642	0
Sonicwall Inc **(PA)**		C	888 557-6642	0
Spike Networks Inc		E	408 410-0624	0
Ss8 Networks Inc **(PA)**		C	408 894-8400	0
Stellartech Research Corp **(PA)**		D	408 331-3134	0

Employment Codes: A=Over 500 employees, B=251-500,
C=101-250, D=51-100, E=50

2020 Directory of California
Wholesalers and Services Companies

© Mergent Inc. 1-800-342-5647

1577

GEOGRAPHIC

	SIC	EMP	PHONE	ENTRY #
Tcg Builders Inc		E	408 321-6450	0
Technical Temps Inc		D	408 956-8256	0
Universal Site Services Inc **(PA)**		D	800 647-9337	0
Vitas Healthcare Corp Cal		D	408 964-6800	0
Winmax Systems Corporation		C	408 894-9000	0
Xcerra Corporation		C	408 635-4300	0
XI Construction Corporation **(PA)**		C	408 240-6000	0
Ziontech Solutions Inc		D	408 434-6001	0
ZI Technologies Inc **(PA)**		D	408 240-8989	0

MIRA LOMA, CA - Riverside County

	SIC	EMP	PHONE	ENTRY #
Act Fulfillment Inc		C	909 930-9083	0

MIRAMONTE, CA - Fresno County

	SIC	EMP	PHONE	ENTRY #
Hume Lake Christian Camps Inc		D	559 305-7770	0

MISSION HILLS, CA - Los Angeles County

	SIC	EMP	PHONE	ENTRY #
Accentcare Home Health Cal Inc		E	818 528-8855	0
Ararat Home of Los Angeles		C	818 837-1800	0
Best Friends Animal Society		B	818 643-3989	0
Clean King Laundry Systems Inc		E	818 363-5500	0
Ecola Services Inc		D	818 920-7301	0
El Nido Family Centers **(PA)**		C	818 830-3646	0
Facey Medical Foundation **(PA)**		C	818 365-9531	0
Facey Medical Foundation		C	818 837-5677	0
Facey Medical Foundation		C	818 365-9531	0
Greater Valley Medical Group **(PA)**		B	818 838-4500	0
Hemodialysis Inc		E	818 365-6961	0
Jade Inc		D	818 365-7137	0
Kaiser Foundation Hospitals		D	888 778-5000	0
Laboratory Corporation America		D	818 361-7089	0
National Business Group Inc **(PA)**		D	818 221-6000	0
National Cnstr Rentals Inc **(HQ)**		D	818 221-6000	0
Providence Health & Svcs - Ore		B	818 365-8051	0
Providence Health System		A	818 898-4530	0
Providence Health System		A	818 898-4561	0
Providence Holy Cross **(PA)**		D	818 365-8051	0
RLCS Inc **(PA)**		D	818 898-1164	0

MISSION VIEJO, CA - Orange County

	SIC	EMP	PHONE	ENTRY #
Associated Realtors		D	949 813-1888	0
Auxiliary of Mission		D	949 364-1400	0
Black Dot Wireless LLC		D	949 502-3800	0
Centex Homes Inc		C	949 453-0113	0
CIT Bank NA		D	949 347-7014	0
Coldwell Banker Residential **(DH)**		D	949 837-5700	0
Coldwell Banker Residential RE **(DH)**		B	949 367-1800	0
Community Orthopedic Medical		D	949 348-4000	0
Cs Concrete Solutions Inc		D	949 285-3122	0
Disruptive Visions LLC		D	949 502-3800	0
Edwards Theatres Circuit Inc		D	949 582-4078	0
Ensign Services Inc		D	949 487-9500	0
Fimac Inc		D	949 359-6100	0
Fitness International LLC		E	949 421-6082	0
Foundstone Inc		D	949 297-5600	0
Golda & I Chocolatiers Inc		D	949 660-9581	0
Goldcoast Liquidating LLC		D	949 461-7170	0
Greenleaf Paper Products		D	949 348-0048	0
Hoffman Southwest Corp **(PA)**		D	949 380-4161	0
Home Instead Senior Care		E	949 347-6767	0
Jewish Home For The Aging of O		C	949 364-0010	0
Lake Mission Viejo Association		D	949 770-1313	0
Lauras House		D	949 361-3775	0
Law Enforcement Officers Inc		C	855 477-3536	0
Mimg Medical Management LLC		D	949 282-1600	0
Mission Hosp Regional Med Ctr **(PA)**		A	949 364-1400	0
Mission Internal Med Group Inc		C	949 364-3570	0
Mission Viejo Country Club		C	949 582-1550	0
Olympus America Inc		D	949 466-3548	0
Orange County Royale Convlscnt		D	949 458-6346	0
Paydarfar Industries Inc		D	949 481-3267	0
Philip DAmato Racing LLC		D	949 830-7027	0
Planned Prnthood Mar Monte Inc		D	949 768-3643	0
Prestige Auto Collision Inc		D	949 470-6031	0
Quest Diagnostics Incorporated		B	949 728-4235	0
Rock Canyon Healthcare Inc		C	719 404-1000	0
Saddleback Vly		D	949 586-1234	0
Smart & Final Stores Inc		B	949 581-1212	0
Southern Cal Prmnnte Med Group		B	949 376-8619	0
St Joseph Heritage Healthcare		E	949 365-2492	0
St Vincent De Paul Vlg Inc		B	619 233-8500	0
Standardbearer Insur Co Ltd		B	949 487-9500	0
Sunrise Senior Living LLC		D	949 582-2010	0
Technicon Design Corporation		C	949 218-1300	0
Total Vision LLC		C	949 652-7242	0
Vintage Senior Living Corp.		D	949 364-6210	0
Vocational Visions		C	949 837-7280	0

	SIC	EMP	PHONE	ENTRY #
Young Mens Chrstn Assn Orange		D	949 859-9622	0

MODESTO, CA - Stanislaus County

	SIC	EMP	PHONE	ENTRY #
Addus Healthcare Inc		D	209 526-8451	0
Aderholt Specialty Company Inc		D	209 526-2000	0
Almond Board of California		E	209 549-8262	0
Aramark Unf & Career AP LLC		D	209 368-9785	0
Arete Hotels LLC		D	209 602-7952	0
Avalon Care Center - Modesto		D	209 526-1775	0
Avalon Care Ctr - Modesto LLC		D	209 529-0516	0
Basic Resources Inc **(PA)**		E	209 521-9771	0
Beard Land & Investment Co **(PA)**		C	209 524-4631	0
Beaver Dam Health Care Center		D	209 529-0516	0
Bethel Retirement Community		D	209 577-1901	0
Beyer Park Villas LLC		D	209 236-1900	0
BJs Restaurants Inc		C	209 526-8850	0
Blue Diamond Growers		C	209 545-6221	0
Brenden Theatre Corporation		D	209 491-7770	0
C & S Draperies Inc.		C	209 466-5371	0
C L Bryant Inc		C	209 566-5000	0
Califrnia Frnsic Med Group Inc		C	209 525-5670	0
Cellco Partnership		D	209 543-6500	0
Central Valley Autism Project		D	209 521-4791	0
Central Valley Party Supply		E	209 569-0399	0
Central Vly Specialty Hosp Inc		D	209 248-7700	0
Charles Fenley Enterprises		E	209 523-2832	0
Childrens Crisis Cntr Stanisls		D	209 577-4413	0
Clark Pest Ctrl Stockton Inc		D	209 524-6384	0
Comcast Corporation		D	209 222-3656	0
Community Hospice Inc **(PA)**		C	209 578-6300	0
County of Stanislaus		A	209 525-7000	0
County of Stanislaus		D	209 558-8828	0
County of Stanislaus		C	209 567-4120	0
County of Stanislaus		C	209 558-7377	0
County of Stanislaus		C	209 558-9675	0
County of Stanislaus		D	209 525-6225	0
County of Stanislaus		C	209 525-7423	0
County of Stanislaus		D	209 558-2500	0
County of Stanislaus		C	209 558-2100	0
County of Stanislaus		C	209 525-5400	0
Covenant Care California LLC		D	209 521-2094	0
Crestwood Behavioral Hlth Inc		C	209 526-8050	0
Curtis Legal Group A Professi		E	209 521-1800	0
D A Wood Construction Inc		D	209 491-4970	0
D C Vient Inc **(PA)**		B	209 578-1224	0
Dal-Tile Corporation		D	209 543-0924	0
Del Rio Golf & Country Club		C	209 341-2414	0
Delta Blood Bank		D	209 943-3830	0
Dependable Highway Express Inc		D	209 342-0184	0
Doctors Med Ctr Modesto Inc **(HQ)**		D	209 578-1211	0
DOT Foods Inc		C	209 581-9090	0
Eastside Management Co Inc		D	209 578-9852	0
Ed Rocha Livestock Trnsp Inc		D	209 538-1302	0
English Oaks Convalescent		C	209 577-1001	0
Enviro Tech Chemical Svcs Inc **(PA)**		C	209 581-9576	0
Fellowship Homes Inc		C	209 529-4950	0
Fig Holdings LLC		D	209 524-4817	0
Foster Dairy Farms **(PA)**		A	209 576-3400	0
Foster Dairy Products Distrg **(PA)**		A	209 576-3400	0
Frito-Lay North America Inc.		C	209 544-5424	0
G3 Enterprises Inc **(PA)**		C	209 341-7515	0
G3 Enterprises Inc.		D	209 341-4045	0
General Petroleum Corporation		D	209 537-1056	0
Golden Living LLC		C	209 548-0318	0
Graham Packaging Company LP		C	209 572-5187	0
Gringteam Inc		B	209 526-6000	0
Grover Landscape Services Inc		D	209 545-4401	0
Hamilton and Dillon Elc Inc		D	209 529-6292	0
Howard Training Center **(PA)**		D	209 538-2431	0
Industrial Automtn Group LLC		D	209 579-7527	0
Kaiser Foundation Hospitals		A	209 735-5000	0
Kaiser Foundation Hospitals		A	209 735-5000	0
Kaiser Foundation Hospitals		D	855 268-4096	0
Kaiser Foundation Hospitals		D	209 557-1000	0
Khatri Inc		E	209 576-1481	0
Kissito Health Case Inc		C	209 524-4817	0
Kiwanis International Inc		D	209 578-1448	0
McHenry Bowl Inc		E	209 571-2695	0
McHenry Medical Group Inc		D	209 577-3388	0
Medamerica Billing Svcs Inc **(HQ)**		D	209 491-7710	0
Medex Pratice Solutions Inc		D	209 845-1346	0
Mocse Federal Credit Union		D	209 572-3600	0
Modesto & Empire Traction Co **(HQ)**		D	209 524-4631	0
Modesto Court Room Inc		D	209 577-1060	0
Modesto Hospitality LLC		C	209 526-6000	0
Modesto Hospitality Lessee LLC		D	209 526-6000	0

Mergent email: customerrelations@mergent.com
1578

2020 Directory of California
Wholesalers and Services Companies

(P-0000) Products & Services Section entry number
(PA)=Parent Co (HQ)=Headquarters (DH)=Div Headquarters

	SIC	EMP	PHONE	ENTRY #
Modesto Industrial Elec Co Inc **(PA)**		C	209 527-2800	0
Modesto Irrigation District		B	209 526-7563	0
Modesto Irrigation District **(PA)**		C	209 526-7337	0
Modesto Irrigation District		B	209 526-7373	0
Modesto Wstewater Trtmnt Plant		D	209 577-5300	0
Montpelier Nut Company Inc **(PA)**		C	209 566-9084	0
Mtc Distributing **(PA)**		C	209 523-6449	0
Muscolino Inventory Svc Inc		E	209 576-8469	0
Mve Inc **(PA)**		D	209 526-4214	0
Ontel Security Services Inc		D	209 521-0200	0
Pacific Gas and Electric Co		E	209 576-6636	0
Pacwend III Inc		D	209 577-6690	0
Paratransit Incorporated		C	209 522-2300	0
Pegasus Risk Management Inc **(PA)**		D	209 574-2800	0
Pepsi-Cola Metro Btlg Co Inc		C	209 557-5100	0
Permanente Medical Group Inc		D	209 735-5000	0
Provident Care Inc		C	209 578-1210	0
Radnet Management Inc		D	209 524-6800	0
Regent Assisted Living Inc		D	209 491-0800	0
Riverside Health Care Corp		D	209 523-5667	0
S&F Management Company Inc		A	209 846-9744	0
Salon-Salon		D	209 571-3500	0
Satellite Healthcare Inc		D	209 578-0691	0
Sawyers Heating & AC		D	209 416-7700	0
Scotts Plant Service Co		D	209 545-0903	0
Seca Eqp Removal & Dismantle		E	209 543-1600	0
Sierra Pacific Dist Svcs Inc **(PA)**		D	209 572-2882	0
Sintex Security Services Inc		D	209 543-9044	0
Slakey Brothers Inc		E	209 556-1100	0
Solecon Industrial Contrs Inc		D	209 572-7390	0
Squab Producers Calif Inc		D	209 537-4744	0
Stanislaus County Police		D	209 529-9121	0
Stanislaus Farm Supply Company **(PA)**		D	209 538-7070	0
Stanislaus Surgical Hosp LLC **(PA)**		C	209 572-2700	0
Sterling Mktg & Fincl Corp		E	209 593-1140	0
Storer Transportation Service **(PA)**		B	209 521-8250	0
Sutter Central Vly Hospitals **(HQ)**		D	209 526-4500	0
Sutter Central Vly Hospitals		E	209 526-4500	0
Sutter Gould Med Foundation **(PA)**		E	209 948-5940	0
Sutter Health		D	209 524-1211	0
Sutter Health		C	209 522-0146	0
Sysco Central California Inc		B	209 527-7700	0
T-Mobile Usa Inc		C	209 529-0539	0
Tcb Industrial Inc **(PA)**		C	209 571-0569	0
United Sttes Intrmdal Svcs LLC		D	209 341-4045	0
US Foods Inc		C	209 572-2882	0
Valley First Credit Union **(PA)**		D	209 549-8511	0
Valley Mtn Regional Ctr Inc		D	209 529-2626	0
Wardens Office Inc **(PA)**		D	949 916-5771	0
Wells Fargo Bank National Assn		D	209 578-6810	0
Winco Foods LLC		D	209 556-6040	0
Wondertreats Inc		B	209 521-8881	0
Woodside Group Inc		E	209 579-2030	0
Yosemite Meat Company Inc		D	209 524-5117	0

MOFFETT FIELD, CA - Santa Clara County

	SIC	EMP	PHONE	ENTRY #
Bay Area Envmtl Res Inst		D	707 938-9387	0
Millennium Engrg Integration		D	703 413-7750	0

MOJAVE, CA - Kern County

	SIC	EMP	PHONE	ENTRY #
Bae Systems Tech Sol Srvc Inc		D	661 816-3474	0
Golden Queen Mining Co LLC		C	661 824-4300	0
La Department Water and Power		D	661 824-7900	0
Ridgetop Energy LLC		E	661 822-2400	0
Virgin Galactic LLC **(DH)**		D	562 384-4400	0

MONROVIA, CA - Los Angeles County

	SIC	EMP	PHONE	ENTRY #
Adams & Barnes Inc		E	626 358-1858	0
Alakor Healthcare LLC		C	626 408-9800	0
Amatel Inc **(PA)**		E	323 801-0199	0
Arch Bay Holdings LLC		D	949 679-2400	0
California Business Bureau Inc **(PA)**		C	626 303-1515	0
Country Villa Service Corp		C	626 358-4547	0
Creative Housing & Svcs LLC		C	626 403-5454	0
Ctour Holiday LLC		B	323 261-8811	0
Federal Deposit Insurance Corp		E	626 359-7152	0
Garden View Inc		E	626 303-4043	0
H C Olsen Cnstr Co Inc		D	626 359-8900	0
Imperial Project Inc		D	310 671-3263	0
Kentmaster Mfg Co Inc **(PA)**		E	626 359-8888	0
Leekilpatrick Management Inc		D	818 500-9631	0
Linear Industries Ltd **(PA)**		D	626 303-1130	0
M T M & M Inc		D	626 445-2922	0
Monrovia Health Center		D	626 256-1600	0
MWH Americas Inc		C	626 386-1100	0
Parasoft Corporation **(PA)**		E	626 256-3680	0

	SIC	EMP	PHONE	ENTRY #
Pih Health Hospital - Whitti		B	626 357-6876	0
R B International Inc **(PA)**		E	626 357-7652	0
Renew Health Group LLC		E	310 625-2838	0
Sage Hospitality Resources LLC		D	626 357-5211	0
Santa Anita Family Young		D	626 359-9244	0
Southern California Edison Co		D	626 303-8480	0
St Baldricks Foundation Inc **(PA)**		D	626 792-8247	0
Trap		C	626 572-5610	0
Visionfund International		D	626 303-8811	0
Vivopools LLC		D	888 702-8486	0
Webasto Charging Systems Inc **(DH)**		D	626 415-4000	0
World Class Distribution Inc		C	909 574-4140	0
World Vision International **(HQ)**		C	626 303-8811	0
Worleyparsons Group Inc		B	626 803-9000	0

MONTCLAIR, CA - San Bernardino County

	SIC	EMP	PHONE	ENTRY #
A Plus Senior Care Inc		E	909 989-2563	0
Acepex Management Corporation		C	909 625-6900	0
Aragon Construction Inc		D	909 621-2200	0
Cls Landscape Management Inc		B	909 628-3005	0
Community Convalescent Center		D	909 621-4751	0
Converse Inc		D	909 625-6655	0
Cramer Painting Inc		E	909 397-5770	0
E M S Trading Inc		E	909 581-7800	0
Foundation For Dance Education		D	909 482-1590	0
Medicrest of California 1		D	909 626-1294	0
Mission Drive-In Theatre Co		D	909 465-9219	0
Omnitrans Inc		C	909 379-7100	0
Oparc **(PA)**		E	909 982-4090	0
Pomona Valley Motorcycles Inc		D	909 981-9500	0
Pomona Valley Workshop **(PA)**		D	909 624-3555	0
Prime Healthcare Svcs III LLC **(DH)**		C	909 625-5411	0
US Skillserve Inc		C	909 621-4751	0

MONTE SERENO, CA - Santa Clara County

	SIC	EMP	PHONE	ENTRY #
El Camino Surgery Center LLC		D	650 961-1200	0

MONTEBELLO, CA - Los Angeles County

	SIC	EMP	PHONE	ENTRY #
2253 Apparel Inc **(PA)**		D	323 837-9800	0
Allied Building Products Corp		D	323 721-9011	0
American Multi-Cinema Inc		E	323 722-4583	0
AMF Bowling Centers Inc		E	323 728-9161	0
Beverly Community Hosp Assn		B	323 889-2452	0
Beverly Community Hosp Assn **(PA)**		C	323 726-1222	0
Beverly Community Hosp Assn		A	323 725-1519	0
Care Ambulance Service Inc		B	323 838-0542	0
Davita Medical Management LLC		D	323 720-1144	0
Eastwestproto Inc		C	888 535-5728	0
Fast Deer Bus Chrtr Incrprtion		D	323 201-8988	0
Ford Motor Company		C	323 267-6121	0
Honolulu Freight Service **(PA)**		E	323 887-6777	0
Hubbard Iron Doors Inc		E	323 724-6500	0
Katzkin Leather Inc **(PA)**		C	323 725-1243	0
Lockheed Martin Government Ser		E	323 721-6979	0
Marquez Brothers Intl Inc		D	323 722-8103	0
Mexican Amrcn Oprtnty Fndation **(PA)**		D	323 890-9600	0
Montebello School Transportion		D	323 887-7900	0
Montebello Transit		C	323 887-4600	0
Montebello Unified School		D	323 887-2140	0
Old Dominion Freight Line Inc		C	323 725-3400	0
Orora Packaging Solutions		C	323 832-2000	0
Paladin Eastside Services Inc		D	323 890-0180	0
SA Recycling LLC		D	323 723-8327	0
Source Logistics Center Corp		C	323 887-3884	0
Star Scrap Metal Company Inc		D	562 921-5045	0
Votum Staffing Inc		B	310 499-4902	0
Wcco Holdings Inc		B	800 421-6150	0
Worldwide Intgrted Rsurces Inc		D	323 838-8938	0

MONTEREY, CA - Monterey County

	SIC	EMP	PHONE	ENTRY #
1000 Aguajito Op Co LLC		D	831 373-6141	0
Aramark Spt & Entrmt Group LLC		D	831 648-9809	0
AT&T Corp		D	831 642-0100	0
AT&T Services Inc		D	831 394-2690	0
AT&T Services Inc		D	831 649-2029	0
Augustine Consulting Inc **(PA)**		D	831 920-1754	0
Ave Maria Convalescent Hosp		D	831 373-1216	0
Bayview Properties Inc **(PA)**		D	831 394-3321	0
Bayview Properties Inc		D	831 655-7650	0
California Capital Insur Co **(PA)**		D	831 233-5500	0
Casa Munras Hotel LLC		D	831 375-2411	0
Cellco Partnership		D	831 644-0858	0
Central Coast Cmnty Hlth Care		D	831 372-6668	0
Central Coast Cmnty Hlth Care		B	831 648-8800	0
Central Coast Vna & Hospice **(PA)**		E	831 372-6668	0
Classic Park Lane Partnership		D	831 373-0101	0
Classic Riverdale Inc		D	831 373-0101	0

Employment Codes: A=Over 500 employees, B=251-500,
C=101-250, D=51-100, E=50

2020 Directory of California
Wholesalers and Services Companies

© Mergent Inc. 1-800-342-5647

1579

GEOGRAPHIC

	SIC	EMP	PHONE	ENTRY #
Classic Rsdence Mgt Ltd Partnr		D	831 373-0101	0
Clum Morford Distributing (PA)		D	831 333-1100	0
Columbia Hospitality Inc		C	831 646-8900	0
Columbia Hospitality Inc		D	831 373-5700	0
Columbia Hospitality Inc		E	831 373-8000	0
Comcast Corporation		D	831 657-6095	0
Community Care Inc		D	831 645-1434	0
Custom House Hotel LP		D	831 649-4511	0
Cypress Halthcare Partners LLC (PA)		E	831 649-1000	0
Data Recognition Corporation		E	831 393-0700	0
Del Mar French Laundry		E	831 375-9597	0
DMC Construction Incorporated		D	831 656-1600	0
Entravsion Communications Corp		E	831 333-9736	0
Excelligence Learning Corp		D	800 482-5846	0
Federal Express Corporation		D	800 463-3339	0
First Alarm		A	831 649-1111	0
Granite Construction Inc		D	831 657-1700	0
Hospital of Community (HQ)		A	831 624-5311	0
Hyatt Corporation		B	831 372-1234	0
Hyatt Hotels Management Corp		B	831 372-1234	0
Language Line Services Inc (DH)		D	800 752-6096	0
Mangold Property Management		D	831 372-1338	0
Marriott International Inc		C	831 649-4234	0
Michael Bruington		E	831 663-1772	0
Montage Health		A	831 625-4821	0
Montage Health (PA)		A	831 625-4830	0
Monterey Bay Aqar Foundation (PA)		B	831 648-4800	0
Monterey Credit Union (PA)		D	831 647-1000	0
Monterey Dental Group		D	831 373-3068	0
Monterey One Water (PA)		D	831 372-3367	0
Monterey Peninsula Dntl Group		D	831 373-3068	0
Monterey Peninsula Hospital		E	831 373-0924	0
Monterey Pines Sklld Nursg Fac		D	831 373-3716	0
Monterey Plaza Ht Ltd Partnr		B	800 334-3999	0
Ocean Park Hotels Inc		C	831 373-3048	0
P Monterey LP		D	831 250-6159	0
Pacific Gas and Electric Co		E	831 648-3231	0
Pacific Parking & Valet LLC		C	831 646-0426	0
Pater Digintas Inc		D	831 624-1875	0
Portfolio Hotels & Resorts LLC		E	831 375-2411	0
Pro Act LLC		D	831 655-4250	0
Product Development Corp (PA)		C	831 333-1100	0
Robert Half International Inc		D	831 241-9042	0
Salinas Valley Memorial Hlthca		B	831 884-5048	0
Sequoia Insurance Company (DH)		D	831 655-9612	0
Stocker & Allaire Inc		E	831 375-1890	0
Sunrise Senior Living Inc		D	831 643-2400	0
Tele-Interpreters LLC		B	800 811-7881	0
Triad Broadcasting Company (PA)		C	831 655-6350	0
United Parcel Service Inc OH		C	831 757-6294	0
United States Dept of Navy		D	831 656-4613	0
Vaquero Farms Inc (PA)		D	209 476-0002	0
Visiting Nurse Association		D	831 385-1014	0
Windsor Monterey Care Ctr LLC		D	831 373-2731	0
Zhg Inc		D	831 394-3321	0

MONTEREY PARK, CA - Los Angeles County

	SIC	EMP	PHONE	ENTRY #
Ahmc Garfield Medical Ctr LP		C	626 573-2222	0
American Multi-Cinema Inc		D	626 407-0240	0
American Reprographics Co LLC		D	626 289-5021	0
Arroyo Developmental Services		D	626 307-2240	0
Care 1st Health Plan (PA)		C	323 889-6638	0
Cathay Bank		D	626 588-1911	0
Childrens Law Center Cal (PA)		C	323 980-8700	0
City of Monterey Park		D	626 307-1388	0
County of Los Angeles		C	323 265-1804	0
East West Bank		D	626 280-1688	0
Guard-Systems Inc		B	323 881-6715	0
Heritage Manor Inc		C	626 573-3141	0
Innovations Building Svcs LLC		D	323 787-6068	0
JC Foodservice Inc (PA)		D	626 299-3800	0
Lincoln Plaza Hotel Inc		D	626 571-8818	0
Merchants Building Maint Co (PA)		D	323 881-6701	0
Merchants Building Maint Co		C	323 881-8902	0
Monterey Park Hospital		C	626 570-9000	0
Monterey Pk Convalescent Hosp		D	626 280-0280	0
Ntt Data Inc		D	213 228-2500	0
Roque Development and Inv		D	626 427-9077	0
Southern California Gas Co		B	213 244-1200	0
Southern California Gas Co		C	213 244-1200	0
State Compensation Insur Fund		C	323 266-5000	0
Synermed		C	216 406-2845	0
Syntelesys Inc		E	323 859-2160	0
Union Technology Corp		D	323 266-6871	0
United Parcel Service Inc		A	626 280-8012	0
Uti Leak Seekers		D	323 724-0081	0

	SIC	EMP	PHONE	ENTRY #
Wah Hung Intl McHy Inc		D	323 263-3513	0

MONTROSE, CA - Los Angeles County

	SIC	EMP	PHONE	ENTRY #
Golden Living LLC		D	818 249-3925	0
Great Wstn Cnvlescent Hosp Inc		C	818 248-6856	0

MOORPARK, CA - Ventura County

	SIC	EMP	PHONE	ENTRY #
Ace Floor Co Inc		D	866 522-4500	0
Cimatron Gibbs LLC		D	805 523-0004	0
Citrus North Venture		D	256 428-2000	0
City of Moorpark		D	805 517-6261	0
Donovan Bros Golf LLC		D	805 531-9300	0
Dynalectric Company		C	805 517-1253	0
EBM Janitorial Services Inc		D	805 523-3700	0
Fiserv Inc		D	805 532-9100	0
Gemmm Corp		D	805 267-2700	0
Harold Jones Landscape Inc		E	805 582-7443	0
Joy Senior Inc		C	805 577-0926	0
Kretek International Inc (DH)		D	805 531-8888	0
Malibu Canyon Ldscp & Maint		D	805 523-2676	0
Marine Holding US Corp		A	805 529-2000	0
Muranaka Farm		C	805 529-0201	0
Ned L Webster Concrete Cnstr		D	805 529-4900	0
Pacific Rim Realty Group		E	805 553-9562	0
Pindler & Pindler Inc (PA)		D	805 531-9090	0
Pom Medical LLC		D	805 306-2105	0
Prudential Overall Supply		D	805 529-0833	0
Testequity LLC (PA)		C	805 498-9933	0
Wall Systems Inc		D	805 523-9091	0
Xp Systems Corporation (HQ)		C	805 532-9100	0

MORAGA, CA - Contra Costa County

	SIC	EMP	PHONE	ENTRY #
Engineered Forest Products LLC		D	925 376-0881	0
Moraga Cntry CLB Hmowners Assn		D	925 376-2200	0
Pioneer Health Care Services		C	925 631-9100	0
Ptac Don L Rhee Elem Sch R Pta		D	925 376-4441	0

MORENO VALLEY, CA - Riverside County

	SIC	EMP	PHONE	ENTRY #
Atsugi Kokusai Kanko USA Inc		D	951 924-4444	0
Bluegill Technologies LLC		D	877 765-2770	0
Community Health Systems Inc		C	951 571-2300	0
County of Riverside		D	951 486-4000	0
County of Riverside		B	951 486-4000	0
Glacier House Franchisee LLC		E	951 455-3644	0
Integrted Care Communities Inc		E	951 243-3837	0
Kaiser Foundation Hospitals		E	951 601-6174	0
Kaiser Foundation Hospitals		B	951 243-0811	0
National Construction & Maint		E	909 888-7042	0
National Lgal Studies Inst Inc		E	951 653-4240	0
Parenthood of Planned		D	951 222-3101	0
Plaza Hand Carwash Inc		E	951 697-4420	0
Retail Services Wis Corp		D	951 653-1472	0
Ritchie Plumbing Inc		C	949 709-7575	0
Riverside University Health		A	951 486-4000	0
Spectrum MGT Holdg Co LLC		D	951 571-8738	0
Think Together		A	951 571-9944	0
United Material Handling Inc		D	951 657-4900	0
Waste MGT Collectn & Recycl		D	909 242-0421	0
Waste MGT Collectn Recycl Inc		C	951 242-0421	0

MORGAN HILL, CA - Santa Clara County

	SIC	EMP	PHONE	ENTRY #
Anritsu Americas Sales Company		A	408 778-2000	0
Aragen Bioscience Inc		E	408 779-1700	0
Cal Color Growers LLC		D	408 778-0835	0
Child Development Incorporated (PA)		E	408 556-7300	0
City of Morgan Hill		D	408 776-7333	0
Continuing Development Inc (PA)		D	408 556-7300	0
Coyote Creek Golf Club		D	408 463-1400	0
Dae-IL Usa Inc		D	559 651-5170	0
Del Monaco Specialty Foods Inc		D	408 500-4100	0
Fresh Pick Produce		E	408 315-4612	0
George Chiala Farms Inc		C	408 778-0562	0
Hillview Convalescent Hospital		E	408 779-3633	0
Institute LLC		E	408 782-7101	0
Irish Construction		D	408 612-8440	0
K R Anderson Inc (PA)		D	408 825-1800	0
Kawahara Nursery Inc		C	408 779-2400	0
Medallion Landscape MGT Inc (PA)		D	408 782-7500	0
Micro-Mechanics Inc		E	408 779-2927	0
Monterey Mushrooms Inc		B	408 779-4191	0
Monument Construction Inc		D	408 778-1350	0
Operating Engineers Loca		C	408 782-9803	0
Pacific Metro LLC (PA)		B	408 201-5000	0
Prism Electronics Corp (PA)		E	408 778-7050	0
Psynergy Programs Inc		D	408 776-0422	0
Reinhardt Roofing Inc		D	510 713-7014	0
Royal Oaks Enterprises Inc		E	408 779-2362	0

Mergent email: customerrelations@mergent.com
1580

2020 Directory of California
Wholesalers and Services Companies

(P-0000) Products & Services Section entry number
(PA)=Parent Co (HQ)=Headquarters (DH)=Div Headquarters

	SIC	EMP	PHONE	ENTRY #
Sakata Seed America Inc **(HQ)**		D	408 778-7758	0
Santa Clara County of		D	408 201-7600	0
South County Housing Corp **(PA)**		E	510 582-1460	0
Town Cats Morgan Hill Rescue		E	408 779-5761	0
Youngs Market Company LLC		D	408 782-3121	0

MORRO BAY, CA - San Luis Obispo County

	SIC	EMP	PHONE	ENTRY #
Compass Health Inc		C	805 772-7372	0
Mission Linen Supply		E	805 772-4451	0
Morro Bay Public Works		D	805 772-6261	0
Smile Housing Corporation		D	805 772-6066	0

MOSS BEACH, CA - San Mateo County

	SIC	EMP	PHONE	ENTRY #
Friends Fitzgerald Mar Reserve		D	650 728-3584	0
Seton Medical Center		C	650 563-7100	0

MOSS LANDING, CA - Monterey County

	SIC	EMP	PHONE	ENTRY #
Capurro Marketing LLC		D	831 728-1767	0
Dobler & Sons LLC		B	831 724-6727	0
Dynegy Marketing & Trade LLC		D	831 633-6700	0
Dynegy Moss Landing LLC		D	831 633-6618	0
Monterey Bay Aquarium RES Inst		C	831 775-1700	0
Moss Landing Marine Labs		C	831 771-4400	0

MOUNT HERMON, CA - Santa Cruz County

	SIC	EMP	PHONE	ENTRY #
Mount Hermon Association Inc **(PA)**		D	831 335-4466	0

MOUNT SHASTA, CA - Siskiyou County

	SIC	EMP	PHONE	ENTRY #
County of Siskiyou		D	530 918-7200	0
Mercy HM Svcs A Cal Ltd Partnr		B	530 926-6111	0
Siskiyou Lake Golf Resort Inc		C	530 926-3030	0
Siskiyou Opportunity Center **(PA)**		C	530 926-4698	0
Wholesale Solar Inc		D	800 472-1142	0

MOUNTAIN PASS, CA - San Bernardino County

	SIC	EMP	PHONE	ENTRY #
Chevron Mining Inc		B	760 856-7625	0
Mp Mine Operations LLC		C	702 277-0848	0

MOUNTAIN VIEW, CA - Santa Clara County

	SIC	EMP	PHONE	ENTRY #
24 Hour Fitness Usa Inc		E	650 941-2268	0
500 Startups Management Co LLC		C	650 743-4738	0
Acetld Solar		C	800 241-6030	0
Achievo Corporation **(PA)**		D	925 498-8864	0
Addepar Inc **(PA)**		D	855 464-6268	0
Aera Technology Inc **(PA)**		D	408 524-2222	0
Alphabet Inc **(PA)**		D	650 253-0000	0
American Century Inv MGT Inc		C	650 965-8300	0
Apigee Corporation		B	408 343-7300	0
Apteligent Inc		D	415 371-1402	0
Assure Consulting Inc		D	650 966-1967	0
AT&T Corp		D	415 276-0039	0
AT&T Services Inc		C	650 960-2255	0
Atrenta Inc **(HQ)**		D	408 453-3333	0
Axcient Inc **(HQ)**		D	650 314-7300	0
Balboa Enterprises Inc		C	650 961-6161	0
Bella Terra Technologies Inc		D	650 316-6660	0
Bionetics Corporation		E	650 604-5327	0
Blue Coat LLC		A	408 220-2200	0
Blue Coat Systems LLC **(HQ)**		D	650 527-8000	0
Boeing Company		B	650 316-3732	0
CA Ste Atom Assoc Intr-Ins Bur		D	650 623-3200	0
Camino Real Group LLC		E	650 964-1700	0
Chronicle LLC **(HQ)**		D	650 214-5199	0
Churchill Downs Incorporated		A	502 638-3879	0
Clearwell Systems Inc		C	877 253-2793	0
Coherent Inc		D	408 764-4000	0
Computer History Museum		D	650 810-1010	0
Coursera Inc **(PA)**		D	650 963-9884	0
Covenant Care California LLC		D	650 964-0543	0
Cumulus Networks Inc **(PA)**		C	650 383-6700	0
Cushman & Wakefield Inc		E	408 664-5403	0
Devxcom Inc		E	650 390-6553	0
Dg Architects Inc **(PA)**		D	650 943-1660	0
Driveai Inc		C	408 693-0765	0
Egnyte Inc **(PA)**		D	650 968-4018	0
El Camino Hospital		C	650 988-7444	0
El Camino Hospital		D	650 940-7310	0
El Camino Hospital Auxiliary		A	650 940-7214	0
Elasticsearch Inc **(HQ)**		D	650 458-2620	0
Fenwick & West LLP **(PA)**		B	650 988-8500	0
General Dynamics Advanced Info		A	650 966-2000	0
Gigya Inc **(HQ)**		D	650 353-7230	0
Google Fiber Inc **(DH)**		D	650 253-0000	0
Google International LLC **(DH)**		D	650 253-0000	0
Google LLC **(HQ)**		C	650 253-0000	0
Google Payment Corp		E	650 253-0000	0
Group Avantica Inc		B	650 248-9678	0
Harman Cnncted Svcs Holdg Corp **(DH)**		D	650 623-9400	0

	SIC	EMP	PHONE	ENTRY #
Healthpocket Inc		D	800 984-8015	0
Hypergrid Inc **(PA)**		D	650 316-5524	0
Iap World Services Inc		D	650 604-0451	0
Intellisync Corporation **(HQ)**		D	650 625-2185	0
Intuit Inc **(PA)**		D	650 944-6000	0
Intuit Inc		C	650 944-6000	0
Intuit Inc		C	650 944-6000	0
Kaiser Foundation Hospitals		C	650 903-3000	0
Kaiser Med Clinic		C	650 903-2103	0
Khan Academy Inc		D	650 336-5426	0
Livongo Health Inc **(PA)**		E	866 435-5643	0
Lozano Inc		C	650 941-0590	0
Mednax Inc		C	650 625-0127	0
Microsoft Corporation		D	650 964-7200	0
Mindsource Inc		D	650 314-6400	0
Mobileiron Inc **(PA)**		C	650 919-8100	0
Moog Inc		D	650 210-9000	0
Mozilla Corporation **(HQ)**		A	650 903-0800	0
Mozilla Foundation **(PA)**		A	650 903-0800	0
Mp Shoreline Assoc Ltd Partnr		E	650 966-1327	0
Neuropace Inc		D	650 237-2700	0
Northrop Grumman Systems Corp		C	650 604-6056	0
OGrady Paving Inc		C	650 966-1926	0
Parkinsons Institute		D	800 786-2958	0
Perkstreet Financial Inc		E	978 801-1177	0
Planprescriber Inc		B	650 584-2700	0
Polaris Building Maintenance		D	650 964-9400	0
Polaris Wireless Inc		E	408 492-8900	0
Project Consulting Specialists		E	650 265-2400	0
Quotient Technology Inc **(PA)**		C	650 605-4600	0
Quova Inc		D	650 965-2898	0
Redis Labs Inc		D	415 930-9666	0
Rhythmone LLC		D	650 961-9024	0
Samsung Electronics Amer Inc		A	650 210-1000	0
Samsung Research America Inc **(DH)**		E	408 544-5700	0
Sectek Inc		D	650 604-1785	0
Seedif Inc		E	408 930-3446	0
Sequoia Retail Systems Inc **(DH)**		D	650 237-9000	0
Service By Medallion		B	650 625-1010	0
Seti Institute		C	650 961-6633	0
Siemens AG		C	650 969-9112	0
Siemens Med Solutions USA Inc		B	650 694-5747	0
Silicon Vly Cmnty Foundation		C	650 450-5400	0
Soaprojects Inc **(PA)**		D	650 960-9900	0
Spotcues Inc		A	408 435-2700	0
Synopsys Inc **(PA)**		B	650 584-5000	0
Synplicity Inc **(HQ)**		C	650 584-5000	0
Tabula Inc		D	408 986-9140	0
Takara Bio Usa Inc		C	650 919-7300	0
Thoits Insurance Service Inc		D	408 792-5400	0
Tidebreak Inc		D	650 289-9869	0
Tintri Inc		B	650 810-8200	0
Travelzoo Usa Inc		D	650 316-6956	0
Treasure Data Inc		D	866 899-5386	0
Veritas US Inc		C	650 933-1000	0
Vieway Technologies Inc		D	650 252-0920	0
Villa Siena		D	650 961-6484	0
Vimo Inc **(PA)**		D	650 618-4600	0
Waterline Data Science Inc		D	650 868-4409	0
Wing Aviation LLC		D	650 260-8170	0
Xad Inc		C	650 386-6867	0
YMCA of Silicon Valley		B	650 969-9622	0
Yub Inc		C	650 265-7316	0
Zonare Medical Systems Inc		D	650 230-2800	0

MURPHYS, CA - Calaveras County

	SIC	EMP	PHONE	ENTRY #
Kautz Vineyards Inc **(PA)**		D	209 728-1251	0

MURRIETA, CA - Riverside County

	SIC	EMP	PHONE	ENTRY #
Alta Loma Assisted Living LLC		D	909 481-2600	0
Bear Creek Golf Club Inc		D	951 677-8621	0
Bear Creek Partners LLC		D	951 677-8621	0
Bowlero Corp		E	951 698-2202	0
Carson Capital Corp **(PA)**		D	951 684-9585	0
Community Health Network LLC		D	951 265-8281	0
Elite Enfrcment SEC Sltons Inc		E	866 354-8308	0
F M Tarbell Co		D	951 677-3565	0
Faith Quality Auto Body Inc		D	951 698-8215	0
First American Card Service		E	951 677-8720	0
Glare Technology Usa Inc		C	909 437-6999	0
Golden Living LLC		D	951 600-4640	0
Goodman Manufacturing Co LP		B	951 304-7402	0
Hospice of Valleys SC **(PA)**		D	951 200-7800	0
Inzunza Real Estate		D	951 544-8801	0
Jpi Development Group Inc		D	951 973-7680	0
Legacy Tile and Stone Inc		E	951 296-1096	0

GEOGRAPHIC

Employment Codes: A=Over 500 employees, B=251-500,
C=101-250, D=51-100, E=50

2020 Directory of California
Wholesalers and Services Companies

© Mergent Inc. 1-800-342-5647

1581

	SIC	EMP	PHONE	ENTRY #
Monique Suraci		D	951 677-8111	0
Mulligan Ltd A Cal Ltd Partnr		D	951 696-9696	0
My Kids Dentist		B	951 600-1062	0
National Bus Investigations		D	951 677-3500	0
Oak Grove Inst Foundation Inc (PA)		B	951 677-5599	0
Ptac Rail Ranch Elem School		D	951 696-1404	0
Rancho Physical Therapy Inc (PA)		D	951 696-9353	0
Reading International Inc		E	951 696-7045	0
Real Goods Solar Inc		C	951 304-3301	0
Ron D & Shelley N Horn		E	559 834-2118	0
S I J Inc		E	951 304-9444	0
Sanborn Theatres Inc		D	909 296-9728	0
Scga Golf Course MGT Inc		D	951 677-7446	0
SI Inc		E	951 304-9444	0
Skywest Airlines Inc		D	951 600-9181	0
South Coast Piering Inc		D	800 922-2488	0
Southwest Healthcare Sys Aux		D	800 404-6627	0
Southwest Healthcare Sys Aux (HQ)		B	951 696-6000	0
Sunland Scaffold		D	951 595-9402	0
Temecula Valley Drywall Inc		D	951 600-1742	0
Utah Pacific Construction Co		E	951 677-9876	0
Your Way Fumigation Inc		D	951 699-9116	0

NAPA, CA - Napa County

	SIC	EMP	PHONE	ENTRY #
Allworth Financial LP		D	888 577-2489	0
Back Street Fitness Inc		E	707 254-7200	0
Barrel Ten Quarter Circle Inc		B	707 265-4000	0
Bayberry Inc (PA)		D	707 252-5587	0
Beaver Dam Health Care Center		D	707 255-6060	0
Bell Products Inc		D	707 255-1811	0
California Odd Fellows (PA)		D	707 257-7885	0
California Odd Fellows		D	707 257-7885	0
Califrnia Dept State Hospitals		A	707 253-5000	0
Carneros Inn LLC		B	707 299-4880	0
Cello & Maudru Cnstr Co Inc		D	707 257-0454	0
Chardonnay/ Club Shakespeare		D	707 257-1900	0
City of NAPA		E	707 255-7631	0
Collabria Care		D	707 258-9080	0
Comcast Corporation		D	707 266-7012	0
County of NAPA		B	707 253-4625	0
County of NAPA		E	707 253-4361	0
County of NAPA		B	707 253-4461	0
Crimson Wine Group Ltd (PA)		C	800 486-0503	0
Doctors Company Foundation		A	800 421-2368	0
Doctors Company Insurance Svcs		B	707 226-0100	0
Doctors Management Company (HQ)		C	707 226-0100	0
DOD Constructors A JV		D	707 265-1100	0
DOD Fueling Constructors A JV		D	707 265-1100	0
DOD Marine Constructors A JV		D	707 265-1100	0
Dolce International / NAPA LLC		B	707 257-0200	0
Domaine Carneros Ltd		D	707 257-0101	0
Folio Wine Company LLC (PA)		C	707 254-9885	0
Folio Wine Company LLC		D	707 256-2757	0
GD Nielson Construction Inc		D	707 253-8774	0
GF Carneros Tenant LLC		E	707 299-4900	0
IA Lodging NAPA Solano Trs LLC		C	707 253-8600	0
Kaiser Foundation Hospitals		D	707 258-2500	0
La Tavola LLC (PA)		D	707 257-3358	0
LLP Moss Adams		D	707 224-4001	0
Lodgeworks LP		D	707 690-9800	0
Melissa Bradley RE Inc		D	707 258-3900	0
Meritage Resort LLC		B	707 251-1900	0
NAPA Es Leasing LLC		C	707 253-9540	0
NAPA Golf Associates LLC		D	707 257-1900	0
NAPA Nursing Center Inc		C	707 257-0931	0
NAPA Sanitation District		E	707 254-9231	0
NAPA Sunrise Rotary Club Inc		D	707 257-9564	0
NAPA Valley Country Club		D	707 252-1111	0
NAPA Valley PSI Inc		D	707 255-0177	0
NAPA Valley Wine Train LLC (HQ)		C	707 253-2160	0
Napastyle Inc (PA)		E	707 251-5100	0
North Bay Developmental (PA)		D	707 256-1224	0
Nova ATL Elc A Joint Ventr		D	707 265-1100	0
Nova Brink A Joint Venture		D	707 265-1100	0
Nova Group Inc (HQ)		C	707 265-1100	0
Nova Lane Constructors A JV		D	707 265-1100	0
Nova-Cpf Inc		C	707 257-3200	0
Nova/Tic Gov Proj JV		C	707 257-3200	0
Ole Health		E	707 254-1770	0
On The Move		E	707 251-9432	0
Park Hotels & Resorts Inc		D	707 253-9540	0
Peck & Hiller Company		D	707 258-8800	0
Pina Vineyard Management LLC		E	707 944-2229	0
Piners Nursing Home Inc		D	707 224-7925	0
Queen of Valley Medical Center (DH)		A	707 252-4411	0
Retreat & Conference Center		E	707 252-3810	0

	SIC	EMP	PHONE	ENTRY #
Seguin Mreau NAPA Coperage Inc		D	707 252-3408	0
Sheehan Construction Inc		B	707 603-2610	0
Silverado Resort and Spa		A	707 257-0200	0
Silverado Rsort Svcs Group LLC		B	707 257-0200	0
Stagecoach Vineyards		D	707 255-5459	0
Star H-R		A	707 265-9911	0
Sunstone Hotel Investors LLC		D	707 253-8600	0
Tahoe Lake Partners LLC		D	707 255-9890	0
Tailored Living Choices LLC		C	707 259-0526	0
Travis Credit Union		B	800 877-8328	0
United Parcel Service Inc OH		C	707 224-1205	0
US Advisor LLC		D	707 253-9953	0
Verasa Management LLC		D	707 257-1800	0
Wells Fargo Bank National Assn		D	707 259-5552	0
Winiarski Management Inc		D	707 944-2020	0

NATIONAL CITY, CA - San Diego County

	SIC	EMP	PHONE	ENTRY #
Builders Firstsource Inc		E	619 425-6660	0
Castle Manor Inc		D	619 791-7900	0
Centro De Salud De La		D	619 477-0165	0
Centro De Salud De La Comuni		D	619 336-2300	0
Del Mar Holding LLC		A	313 659-7300	0
Ehmcke Sheet Metal Corp		D	619 477-6484	0
Epsilon Systems Solutions Inc		E	619 474-3252	0
Fornaca Inc (PA)		C	866 308-9461	0
Framing Associates Inc		E	619 336-9991	0
Greenwalds Autobody Frameworks (PA)		D	619 477-2600	0
Hardisty Construction Administ		D	619 245-6828	0
Harvest Meat Company Inc (HQ)		D	619 477-0185	0
Horizons Adult Day Health Care		D	619 474-1822	0
Imaginative Horizons Inc		D	619 477-1176	0
Kmea (PA)		D	619 399-5900	0
Maniflo Money Exchange Inc		D	619 434-7200	0
McKinley Plaza LLC		D	619 405-6307	0
Motivational Systems Inc (PA)		D	619 474-8246	0
Nms Management Inc		D	619 425-0440	0
Paradise Vly Hlth Care Ctr Inc		D	619 470-6700	0
Plaza Manor Preservation LP		A	619 475-2125	0
San Diego Unified Port Dst		C	619 686-6200	0
San Diego-Imperial		D	619 336-6600	0
Sand Dollar Holdings Inc (PA)		D	619 477-0185	0
Six Continents Hotels Inc		D	619 474-2800	0
South Bay Sand Blasting and Ta		D	619 238-8338	0
St Pauls Episcopal Home Inc		D	619 232-2996	0
Sureride Charter Inc		D	619 336-9200	0
Tdk-Lambda Americas Inc		C	619 575-4400	0
US Foods Inc		C	619 474-6525	0
Westair Gases & Equipment Inc		D	619 474-0079	0
Windsor Healthcare Management		C	619 474-6741	0

NEEDLES, CA - San Bernardino County

	SIC	EMP	PHONE	ENTRY #
Colorado River Medical Center		D	760 326-4531	0
Havasu Landing Casino (PA)		D	760 858-5380	0
International Assoc of Machini		E	760 326-7048	0
Legacy Lifepoint Health Inc		C	760 326-7100	0

NEVADA CITY, CA - Nevada County

	SIC	EMP	PHONE	ENTRY #
Milhous Feed		C	530 292-3242	0
Mountain Valley Child and Fami		C	530 265-9057	0
Northern Queen Inc		D	530 265-4492	0
Patrick Dean Bryan		D	530 273-5484	0
Robinson & Sons		D	530 265-5844	0
Telestream LLC (PA)		C	530 470-1300	0
Tri Counties Bank		D	530 478-6001	0

NEWARK, CA - Alameda County

	SIC	EMP	PHONE	ENTRY #
Advanced Cell Diagnostics Inc		D	510 576-8800	0
Alliance Bay Funding Inc		D	510 742-6600	0
America Shredding		D	702 262-3607	0
Apn Software Services Inc (PA)		D	510 623-5050	0
Bay Advanced Technologies LLC		D	510 857-0900	0
Bioclinca (PA)		C	415 817-8900	0
Bioclinca		E	503 284-3334	0
Biomed Realty Trust Inc		D	510 505-0932	0
Cargill Incorporated		C	510 797-1820	0
Central Business Solutions Inc		D	510 573-5500	0
Courtesy Security Inc		D	888 572-5545	0
D&A Enterprises Inc		B	510 445-1600	0
Dna Twopointo Inc		D	650 853-8347	0
Elitegroup Cmpt Systems Inc		C	510 226-7333	0
Everest Silicon Valley MGT LP		D	510 494-8800	0
Fitness 2000 Inc		E	510 791-2481	0
Hardage Hospitality LLC		E	510 795-1200	0
Innovated Packaging Company		C	510 713-3560	0
Integrated Pkg & Crating Svcs		E	510 745-8180	0
Intelliswift Software Inc (PA)		C	510 490-9240	0
Itrenew Inc (HQ)		E	408 744-9600	0

(P-0000) Products & Services Section entry number
(PA)=Parent Co (HQ)=Headquarters (DH)=Div Headquarters

	SIC	EMP	PHONE	ENTRY #
Javelin Logistics Company Inc	C		800 577-1060	0
Javelin Logistics Corporation (PA)	E		510 795-7287	0
Lancashire Group Incorporated	B		510 792-9384	0
Marriott International Inc	C		510 657-4600	0
Membrane Technology & RES Inc	D		650 328-2228	0
Mickwee Group Inc	D		510 651-5527	0
Mission Linen Supply	D		510 996-3416	0
Moving Solutions Inc	C		408 920-0110	0
Mshift Inc	E		408 437-2740	0
Nefab Packaging West LLC	D		408 678-2516	0
Newark Courtyard By Marriott	D		510 792-5200	0
Oak Harbor Freight Lines Inc	D		510 608-8841	0
Oatey Supply Chain Svcs Inc	E		510 797-4677	0
Palo Alto Egg and Food Svc Co	E		510 456-2420	0
Payment Processing Inc	C		510 795-2290	0
Perlegen Sciences Inc	C		650 625-4500	0
Risk Management Solutions Inc (DH)	C		510 505-2500	0
Roseryan Inc	D		510 456-3056	0
Second Chance Inc (PA)	E		510 792-4357	0
Shotspotter Inc	D		510 794-3100	0
Special Dispatch Cal Inc	D		510 713-0300	0
Tegile Systems Inc	C		510 791-7900	0
Triple Ring Technologies Inc	E		510 592-3000	0
Valassis Direct Mail Inc	D		510 505-6500	0
Vm Services Inc (DH)	C		510 744-3720	0
Windy City Wire and Connectivi	C		510 284-3956	0
Xtraplus Corporation	D		510 897-1890	0
Zenith Infotech Limited	C		510 687-1943	0
Zws/ABS Joint Venture LLC	D		510 461-1433	0

NEWBURY PARK, CA - Ventura County

	SIC	EMP	PHONE	ENTRY #
Area Housing Authority (PA)	E		805 480-9991	0
Carnegie Agency Inc	E		805 445-1470	0
Compulink Business Systems Inc (PA)	D		805 446-2050	0
Conejo Pacific Technologies	D		805 498-5315	0
Giant Bicycle Inc (DH)	D		805 267-4600	0
Graymeta Inc	E		855 202-2270	0
Hawaiian Hotels & Resorts Inc	D		805 480-0052	0
Hearst Communications Inc	B		805 375-3121	0
Isolutecom Inc (PA)	E		805 498-6259	0
Mary Hlth SCK Cnvlscnt &NRsng	D		805 498-3644	0
McKesson Medical-Surgical Inc	D		805 375-8800	0
Perillo Industries Inc	E		805 498-9838	0
Time Warner Cable Inc	D		805 214-1353	0
United Parcel Service Inc OH	C		805 375-1832	0
Weldlogic Inc	D		805 375-1670	0

NEWHALL, CA - Los Angeles County

	SIC	EMP	PHONE	ENTRY #
Calex Engineering Inc	D		661 254-1866	0
Hollenbeck Palms	C		323 263-6195	0
N V Landscape Inc	D		661 286-8888	0
Santa Clarita Athletic Club	D		661 255-3365	0
Valencia Health Care Inc	D		661 254-2425	0

NEWMAN, CA - Stanislaus County

	SIC	EMP	PHONE	ENTRY #
Avalon Care Ctr - Newman LLC	D		209 862-2862	0
Cerutti Bros Inc	D		209 862-2249	0
Dimare Enterprises Inc (PA)	C		209 827-2900	0
Golden Living LLC	D		209 862-2862	0
Superior Truck Lines Inc (PA)	D		209 862-9430	0

NEWPORT BEACH, CA - Orange County

	SIC	EMP	PHONE	ENTRY #
10632 Bolsa Avenue LP	D		949 673-1221	0
A White and Yellow Cab Inc	C		714 258-1000	0
Absolute Return Portfolio	A		800 800-7646	0
Accelerize Inc	D		949 515-2166	0
Accentcare Home Health Cal Inc	D		949 250-0133	0
Alamo Rental (us) Inc	E		949 852-0403	0
Alight (us) LLC	C		949 725-4500	0
Alliant Insurance Services Inc (PA)	C		949 756-0271	0
Allied Lube Texas LP (PA)	D		949 486-4008	0
Amarik Properties Inc (PA)	D		714 505-5200	0
Ambassador Gaming Inc	D		714 969-8730	0
America Consulting Group LLC	C		714 390-3105	0
Andersonpenna Partners Inc (HQ)	D		949 428-1500	0
Anne M Kent MD	D		949 650-7100	0
Applebee Leasing Inc	D		818 612-6218	0
Auctioncom LLC	D		949 609-5376	0
Avalon At Newport LLC	D		949 631-3555	0
Balboa Bay Club Inc (HQ)	B		949 645-5000	0
Barcelo Enterprises Inc	D		760 728-3444	0
Bassenian/Lagoni Architects	D		949 553-9100	0
Beacon Accounting Resources LLC	E		949 981-5946	0
Beacon Healthcare Services	D		949 650-9750	0
Beauty Barrage LLC	C		949 771-3399	0
Ben Bennett Inc (PA)	C		949 209-9712	0
Big Canyon Country Club	C		949 644-5404	0

	SIC	EMP	PHONE	ENTRY #
Bremer Whyte Brown Omeara LLP (PA)	E		949 221-1000	0
Buchanan Fund I LLC	D		949 721-1414	0
Buchanan Street Partners LP	D		949 721-1414	0
C B Coast Newport Properties	D		949 644-1600	0
Call & Jensen APC	E		949 717-3000	0
Canadian Imperial Bank	D		949 759-4718	0
Cbre Global Investors LLC	B		949 725-8500	0
Cemak Trucking Inc (PA)	D		949 253-2800	0
Centurion Security Svcs Inc (PA)	D		949 474-0444	0
Childrens Hospital Orange Cnty	A		949 631-2062	0
Citivest Inc	D		949 474-0440	0
Citizens Business Bank	D		949 440-5200	0
Clean Energy	A		949 437-1000	0
Clean Energy Fuels Corp (PA)	C		949 437-1000	0
Community Cllbrtive Chrtr Schl	D		949 387-7822	0
Compass Real Estate LLC	B		949 945-8176	0
Conversionpoint Holdings Inc	D		888 706-6764	0
Core Realty Holdings LLC (PA)	D		949 863-1031	0
Core Realty Holdings MGT Inc	D		949 863-1031	0
Cws Apartment Homes LLC (PA)	B		949 640-4000	0
Dansk Enterprises Inc	D		714 751-0347	0
Dentons US LLP	C		949 732-3700	0
Donald Lucky LLC	C		949 752-0647	0
Downtown SD Ventures LLC	D		619 231-9200	0
Dpr Construction A Gen Partnr	E		949 955-3771	0
Dream Home Estates Inc	E		949 415-4646	0
Edwards Theatres Circuit Inc (DH)	C		949 640-4600	0
Emery Financial Inc	D		949 219-0640	0
Entrepreneurial Capital Corp	C		949 809-3900	0
ESA P Prtfolio Oper Lessee LLC	E		949 851-2711	0
Eureka Realty Partners Inc (PA)	B		949 224-4100	0
Fallon Land Company Inc	E		213 880-1279	0
Festival Fun Parks LLC	C		954 921-1411	0
Fidelity National Fincl Inc	D		949 622-5000	0
First Team RE - Orange Cnty	D		949 759-5747	0
Five Star Quality Care Inc	C		949 642-8044	0
FMC Financial Group (PA)	D		949 225-9369	0
Global Risk MGT Solutions LLC	C		949 759-8500	0
Greystar Management Svcs LP	A		949 705-0010	0
Harbor Health Systems LLC	D		949 273-7020	0
Health Information Partners	D		949 261-5000	0
Healthcare Cost Solutions Inc	D		949 721-2795	0
Heat Waves LLC	C		323 753-8441	0
Hoag Memorial Hospital Presbt (PA)	A		949 764-4624	0
Host Hotels & Resorts LP	D		949 640-4000	0
Host Hotels & Resorts LP	D		949 854-4500	0
Houalla Enterprises Ltd	D		949 515-4350	0
Hyatt Corporation	B		949 729-1234	0
International Bay Clubs LLC (PA)	B		949 645-5000	0
Internet Booking Agencycom Inc	B		949 673-7707	0
Interstate Hotels Resorts Inc	D		949 783-2500	0
Irell & Manella LLP	D		949 760-0991	0
Iron Mountain Incorporated	D		562 345-6900	0
Irvine Eastgate Office II LLC	A		949 720-2000	0
James R Glidewell Dental (PA)	A		949 440-2600	0
Jeffrey Rome & Associates	D		949 760-3929	0
Jwc Construction Inc	E		949 252-2107	0
Kalpana LLC (PA)	B		949 610-8200	0
Ko Holdings LLC	D		949 629-3044	0
Koll Management Services Inc	A		949 833-3030	0
Kollwood Golf Operating LP	B		949 833-3025	0
La Habra Villa	D		714 529-1697	0
Labmed Partners	E		949 242-9925	0
Lbs Financial Credit Union	D		714 893-5111	0
Lee Hong Degerman Kang	D		949 250-9954	0
Lee & Associates Realty Group	E		949 724-1000	0
Leisure Care Inc	D		949 645-6833	0
Lennar Partners of Los Angeles (PA)	E		949 885-8500	0
Lionakis	C		949 955-1919	0
LLP Locke Lord	D		949 423-2100	0
Lyon Promenade LLC	E		949 252-9101	0
M Arthur Gensler Jr Assoc Inc	D		949 863-9434	0
Makar Properties LLC (PA)	A		949 255-1100	0
Marriotts Newport Coast Villa	D		949 464-6000	0
Marwit Capital Partners II LP (PA)	B		949 861-3636	0
McCarthy Bldg Companies Inc	B		949 851-8383	0
McCarthy Bldg Companies Inc	B		949 851-8383	0
MDE Semiconductor Inc	D		760 564-8656	0
Merrill Lynch Pierce Fenner	C		949 467-3760	0
Mesa Management Inc	D		949 851-0995	0
Message Broadcast LLC	E		949 428-3111	0
Meyer Properties Corp (PA)	D		949 862-0500	0
Mf Services Company LLC (HQ)	D		949 474-5800	0
Mig Management Services LLC	D		949 474-5800	0
Mobilitie Services LLC	B		877 999-7070	0

Employment Codes: A=Over 500 employees, B=251-500,
C=101-250, D=51-100, E=50

2020 Directory of California
Wholesalers and Services Companies

© Mergent Inc. 1-800-342-5647

1583

GEOGRAPHIC

	SIC	EMP	PHONE	ENTRY #
Montrenes Financial Svcs Inc		D	562 795-0450	0
Morgan Stanley		D	949 760-2440	0
Mscsoftware Corporation (HQ)		C	714 540-8900	0
Mscsoftware Corporation.		B	714 540-8900	0
Mulechain Inc		E	888 456-8881	0
Multipoint Wireless LLC		E	714 262-4172	0
National Liquidators		E	949 631-6715	0
National Therapeutic Svcs Inc (PA)		D	866 311-0003	0
Newmark & Company RE Inc.		C	949 608-2000	0
Newmeyer & Dillion LLP (PA)		C	949 854-7000	0
Newport Beach Country Club Inc		D	949 644-9550	0
Newport Beach Orthopedic Inst		D	949 722-7038	0
Newport Beach Surgery Ctr LLC		C	949 631-0988	0
Newport Diagnostic Center Inc (PA)		D	949 760-3025	0
Newport Fmly Mdcne/A Med Group		D	949 644-1025	0
Newport Harbor Radiology Assoc		D	949 721-8191	0
Oc Accessories LLC		D	949 229-2410	0
Olen Commercial Realty Corp		B	949 644-6536	0
Olen Residential Realty Corp (HQ)		D	949 644-6536	0
OMelveny & Myers LLP		C	949 760-9600	0
Pacific Bay Properties (PA)		E	949 440-7200	0
Pacific Club (PA)		D	949 955-1123	0
Pacific Hotel Management Inc		C	949 608-1091	0
Pacific Investment MGT Co LLC (DH)		C	949 720-6000	0
Pacific Life & Annuity Company		A	949 219-3011	0
Pacific Monarch Resorts Inc (PA)		D	949 609-2400	0
Pacific Select Distributors		D	949 219-3011	0
Palace Entertainment Inc (DH)		E	949 261-0404	0
Park Newport Ltd (PA)		D	949 644-1900	0
Pimco Funds Distribution Co		B	949 720-4761	0
Pimco Mortgage Income Tr Inc		B	949 720-6000	0
Pyramid Peak Corporation		D	949 769-8600	0
Qw Media International LLC		E	949 200-4616	0
R Mc Closkey Insurance Agency		C	949 223-8100	0
Research Affiliates Capital LP		D	949 325-8700	0
Research Affiliates LLC		D	949 325-8700	0
Riverside Research Institute		E	949 631-0107	0
Roth Capital Partners LLC (PA)		D	800 678-9147	0
RSI Insurance Brokers Inc (DH)		E	714 546-6616	0
Sagepoint Financial Inc		B	949 756-1462	0
Scicon Technologies Corp		D	949 252-1341	0
Signature Services		D	949 851-9391	0
Sleepy Giant Entertainment Inc.		C	949 464-7986	0
Sleepy Giant Entertainment Inc.		C	714 460-4113	0
Solve Healthcare Corporation (PA)		D	949 891-0300	0
Sound Mind and Body Inc		C	206 547-2706	0
SSC Newport Beach Oper Co LP		C	949 642-8044	0
Staffrehab		B	888 835-0894	0
Stradling Yocca Carlson & Raut (PA)		C	949 725-4000	0
Synnexxus LLC		E	714 933-4900	0
T-Force Inc (PA)		D	949 208-1527	0
Tad Group LLC		C	949 476-3601	0
Thrifty Rent-A-Car System Inc		E	949 757-0659	0
Toni & Guy Hairdressing (PA)		E	949 721-1666	0
Tribeworx LLC		D	800 949-3432	0
Twenty4seven Hotels Corp		B	949 734-6400	0
Tz Holdings LP		A	949 719-2200	0
U Gym LLC (PA)		C	714 668-0911	0
UBS Financial Services Inc		C	949 760-5308	0
Uka LLC		E	949 610-8000	0
United Cpitl Fncl Advisers LLC		D	949 999-8500	0
Universal Space Lines Inc		D	215 328-9130	0
US Lines LLC (DH)		D	714 751-3333	0
Ventage Senior Housing		E	949 631-3555	0
Vital Express Inc		E	330 777-5450	0
Voit Real Estate Services Lp		C	949 644-8648	0
West Dermatology Med MGT Inc		C	909 793-3000	0
William Lyon Homes (PA)		C	949 833-3600	0
William Lyon Homes Inc (HQ)		C	949 833-3600	0
Windjammer Capital Invstr III		A	949 706-9989	0
Wj Newport LLC		C	949 476-2001	0
Wright Finlay & Zak LLP		D	949 477-5050	0
Young Mens Chrstn Assn Orange		D	949 642-9990	0

NEWPORT COAST, CA - Orange County

	SIC	EMP	PHONE	ENTRY #
Concert Golf Partners LLC		A	949 715-0602	0
Pricemetrix Usa Inc		E	714 357-6192	0
Resort At Pelican Hill LLC		C	949 467-6800	0

NIPOMO, CA - San Luis Obispo County

	SIC	EMP	PHONE	ENTRY #
American Golf Corporation		D	805 343-1214	0
Community Health Centers (PA)		D	805 929-3211	0
Integrity Management Svcs Inc		C	805 238-0905	0
Jj Fisher Construction Inc		D	805 723-5220	0
L J T Flowers Inc		D	805 310-6036	0
Pre Con Industries Inc		E	805 481-7305	0

NIPTON, CA - San Bernardino County

	SIC	EMP	PHONE	ENTRY #
Primm Valley Golf Club		D	702 679-5509	0

NORCO, CA - Riverside County

	SIC	EMP	PHONE	ENTRY #
Anna Corporation		E	951 736-6037	0
Bonanza Plumbing Inc (PA)		D	951 360-8262	0
Cal West Underground Inc		D	951 371-6775	0
Cal-West Nurseries Inc		C	951 270-0667	0
Car Spa Inc.		E	951 279-1422	0
City of Norco		D	951 270-5632	0
City of Norco.		D	951 270-5617	0
Clima-Tech Inc.		D	909 613-5513	0
County of Riverside		E	951 272-5400	0
CSRA Systems & Solutions LLC		E	951 735-3300	0
F J Hoover Plumbing Inc		D	951 360-8262	0
Guy Yocom Construction Inc (PA)		C	951 284-3456	0
Hampton Inn Norco Corona North		D	951 279-1111	0
Hci Inc (HQ)		B	951 520-4200	0
Industrial Masonry Inc		D	951 284-0251	0
Janus Corporation		E	951 479-0700	0
JIT Corporation		D	805 238-5000	0
Kerdus Plastering Inc		C	951 272-6720	0
Luberski Inc		D	951 271-3866	0
Norco Fire Department		A	951 737-8097	0
North Orange Coast Pntg Inc		D	951 279-2694	0
Royal West Drywall Inc		D	951 271-4600	0

NORDEN, CA - Nevada County

	SIC	EMP	PHONE	ENTRY #
Sugar Bowl Corporation		D	530 426-9000	0

NORTH FORK, CA - Madera County

	SIC	EMP	PHONE	ENTRY #
Mono Nation		D	559 877-2450	0

NORTH HIGHLANDS, CA - Sacramento County

	SIC	EMP	PHONE	ENTRY #
AAA Drain Patrol		E	916 348-3098	0
BMC Stock Holdings Inc		B	916 481-5030	0
Capital City Drywall Inc		D	916 331-9200	0
Eagle Lath & Plaster Inc		D	916 925-1435	0
Energetic Pntg & Drywall Inc (PA)		C	916 488-8455	0
Heritage 1 Window and Building		D	916 481-5030	0
Heritage Interests LLC (PA)		D	916 481-5030	0
Heritage One Door and Building		D	916 481-5030	0
Homeq Servicing Corporation (DH)		A	916 339-6192	0
Kenyon Construction Inc		C	916 514-9502	0
Lund Construction Co.		C	916 344-5800	0
Lund Equipment LP		E	916 344-5800	0
MCM Construction Inc (PA)		D	916 334-1221	0
Mission Courier Inc		D	916 484-1992	0
Pacific Coast Supply LLC		C	916 481-2220	0
Pacific Coast Supply LLC (HQ)		C	916 971-2301	0
Paragon Coml Bldg Maint Inc		D	916 344-8801	0
Pride Industries		D	916 334-5415	0
Quest Discovery Services Inc		D	916 483-7030	0
Recycling Industries Inc		D	916 452-3961	0
Rick H Hitch Plastering Inc		C	916 334-3591	0
Security Contractor Svcs Inc (PA)		D	916 338-4200	0
Sierra Select Distributors Inc.		D	916 483-9295	0
U S Army Corps of Engineers		D	916 925-7001	0

NORTH HILLS, CA - Los Angeles County

	SIC	EMP	PHONE	ENTRY #
Brentwood Cmmncations Intl Inc		E	818 333-3680	0
Dynamo Aviation Inc		D	818 785-9561	0
Living Colors Inc		D	818 893-5068	0
Penny Lane Centers (PA)		B	818 892-3423	0
Penny Lane Centers.		C	818 892-3423	0
Penny Lane Centers.		C	818 892-3423	0
Penny Lane Centers.		C	818 892-1112	0
Penny Lane Centers.		C	818 892-3423	0
Plummer Vlg Preservation LP		D	818 891-0646	0
Prn Ambulance LLC.		B	818 810-3600	0
Veterans Health Administration		A	818 891-7711	0
Veterans Health Administration		D	818 895-9449	0
Walker & Zanger Inc (PA)		D	818 280-8300	0

NORTH HOLLYWOOD, CA - Los Angeles County

	SIC	EMP	PHONE	ENTRY #
1658 Camden LLC		E	818 769-1944	0
51 Minds Entertainment LLC		D	323 466-9200	0
Academy TV Arts Scnces Fndtion		D	818 754-2800	0
Advanced Cable Technologies		E	818 262-6484	0
Albany Inventory Services		E	818 986-5705	0
Alpha Systems Fire Protection		E	323 227-0700	0
Ambulnz Health LLC		B	877 311-5555	0
Andy Gump Inc.		D	818 255-0650	0
Arriaga Usa Inc.		D	818 982-9559	0
Arriaga Usa Inc (PA)		D	818 982-9559	0
AT&T Corp.		D	818 506-9118	0
Bento Box Entertainment LLC		B	818 333-7700	0

2020 Directory of California
Wholesalers and Services Companies

(P-0000) Products & Services Section entry number
(PA)=Parent Co (HQ)=Headquarters (DH)=Div Headquarters

Company	SIC	EMP	PHONE	ENTRY #
Break Floor Productions LLC (PA)		E	818 432-1234	0
California Credit Union		D	818 291-5434	0
Cats USA Inc		D	818 506-1000	0
CB Associates Inc		E	424 777-8214	0
Center For Autism Related Svcs		E	323 850-7177	0
Century National Properties (PA)		D	818 760-0880	0
Century Theatres Inc		D	818 508-1943	0
Chapman/Leonard Studio Eqp Inc (PA)		C	323 877-5309	0
Circulating Air Inc (PA)		D	818 764-0530	0
City Moving Inc		E	888 794-8808	0
Coastal Tile Inc		D	818 988-6134	0
Coldwater Care Center LLC		D	818 766-6105	0
Core Bts Inc		D	818 766-2400	0
Cri-Help Inc (PA)		C	818 985-8323	0
Emergency Technologies Inc		D	818 765-4421	0
Eqal Inc		C	818 276-6300	0
Four Seasons Healthcare		D	818 985-1814	0
Hillsdale Group LP		D	818 623-2170	0
Hollywood Health System Inc		D	323 662-3731	0
Hollywood Spa Inc		E	323 464-0445	0
Horizon Actuarial Services LLC		D	818 691-2000	0
Iaa Inc		D	818 487-2222	0
IPC Healthcare Inc (DH)		C	888 447-2362	0
Jackson Shrub Supply Inc		D	818 982-0100	0
Japanese Assistance Netwrk Inc		B	818 505-6080	0
JC Party Rentals Inc		D	818 765-4819	0
Jessica Cosmetics Intl Inc		D	818 759-1050	0
Jewish Family Svc Los Angeles		D	818 984-0276	0
Kaiser Foundation Hospitals		A	888 778-5000	0
Kaiser Foundation Hospitals		D	818 503-7082	0
Landscape Support Services		D	818 475-0680	0
M Gaw Inc		D	818 503-7997	0
Mariner Health Care Inc		D	818 985-5990	0
Mark Herzog & Company Inc		D	818 762-4640	0
Messenger Express (PA)		C	213 614-0475	0
Midway Rent A Car Inc		E	818 985-9770	0
Mikado Hotels Inc		E	818 763-9141	0
Morigon Technologies LLC		E	818 764-8880	0
O P I Products Inc (HQ)		B	818 759-8688	0
On-Scene Security Services Inc		C	661 263-2343	0
PCL Construction Services Inc		C	818 509-7816	0
Pie Town Productions Inc		C	818 255-9300	0
Pierce Brothers (DH)		D	818 763-9121	0
Pilgrim Operations LLC		B	818 478-4500	0
Power Generation Entps Inc		C	818 484-8550	0
Protection Specialists		B	818 503-1306	0
Rio Vista Development Company (PA)		C	818 980-8000	0
Rodin & Co Inc		D	818 358-3427	0
Sada Systems Inc		C	818 766-2400	0
Silverscreen Healthcare Inc		D	818 763-8247	0
SLC Operating Ltd Partnership		B	818 980-1212	0
Southern California Golf Assn (PA)		D	818 980-3630	0
Stark Services		D	818 985-2003	0
Toner Supply USA Inc		E	818 504-6540	0
Trinity Health Systems		D	818 983-0103	0
Universal Studios Inc		D	818 753-0000	0
Universal Studios Company LLC (DH)		C	818 777-1000	0
Valley Community Healthcare		B	818 763-8836	0
Valley Vista Nursing and Trans		D	818 763-6275	0
Valley Wholesale Supply Corp (PA)		D	818 769-5656	0
Volunteers of Amer Los Angeles		C	818 764-8722	0
Volunteers of Amer Los Angeles		D	818 769-3617	0
Volunteers of Amer Los Angeles		E	818 506-0597	0
Western Costume Leasing		D	818 760-0900	0
Western Magnesite Inc		E	818 255-1150	0
Woods Maintenance Services Inc		C	818 764-2515	0
Young Mens Chrstn Assn of La		D	818 763-5126	0

NORTH PALM SPRINGS, CA - Riverside County

Company	SIC	EMP	PHONE	ENTRY #
Lloyd Pest Control Co		D	951 232-9687	0

NORTHRIDGE, CA - Los Angeles County

Company	SIC	EMP	PHONE	ENTRY #
Alliant Tchsystems Oprtons LLC		B	818 887-8195	0
Apex Group		C	818 885-0513	0
Arete Associates (PA)		C	818 885-2200	0
Assisted Home Recovery Inc (PA)		C	818 894-8117	0
Automobile Club Southern Cal		D	818 993-1616	0
Bellis Steel Company Inc (PA)		D	818 886-5601	0
California Survey Res Svcs		C	818 780-2777	0
Cardiomart Inc		E	310 572-6724	0
Child and Family Guidance Ctr (PA)		C	818 739-5140	0
Child and Family Guidance Ctr		E	818 830-0200	0
Choosing Independence Inc		D	818 257-0323	0
Contemporary Services Corp (PA)		D	818 885-5150	0
Discount Tire Ctr		D	818 993-4758	0
Eminence Home Health Care Inc		E	818 830-7113	0

Company	SIC	EMP	PHONE	ENTRY #
Extreme Telecom Inc		C	818 902-4821	0
First Nationwide Mortgage Corp		C	818 209-3134	0
Friends of Family		E	818 988-4430	0
Hemacare Corporation (PA)		C	877 310-0717	0
Ikano Communications Inc (PA)		D	801 924-0900	0
Lakeside Systems Inc		A	866 654-3471	0
M K H Inc		D	818 882-9274	0
Mikuni American Corporation (HQ)		D	310 676-0522	0
Move Inc		C	818 701-0012	0
MSC Chatsworth		D	818 718-7696	0
Musclebound Inc (PA)		B	818 349-0123	0
National Center On Deafness		D	818 677-2054	0
Northrop Grumman Innovation		D	818 887-8100	0
Northwest Excavating Inc		D	818 349-5861	0
Omega Security Services & Cons		D	818 831-1100	0
Pacific Theaters		D	818 501-5121	0
PHI Delta Theta Inc		E	818 885-9940	0
Pinnacle Estate Properties (PA)		C	818 993-4707	0
Porter Valley Country Club		C	818 360-1071	0
Production Special Events Svcs		E	818 831-5326	0
Prudential Amrcn Rlty A Cal LP		E	818 993-8900	0
Rashman Corporation		D	818 993-3030	0
Regal Medical Group Inc (PA)		D	818 654-3400	0
Retail Services Wis Corp		D	818 407-2680	0
Rodeo Realty Inc		D	818 349-9997	0
Ryder Integrated Logistics Inc		E	818 701-9332	0
San Frnndo Vly Intrfth Cuncil		C	818 885-5220	0
Securitas SEC Svcs USA Inc		C	818 891-0458	0
Shapell Industries LLC		E	818 366-1132	0
Smart & Final Stores Inc		B	818 368-6409	0
Southern California Mtl Hdlg		D	805 650-6000	0
Sunrise Senior Living LLC		D	818 886-1616	0
Telecom Evolutions LLC		E	818 264-4400	0
Teutonic Holdings LLC		C	818 264-4400	0
Tri - Star Win Coverings Inc		E	818 718-3188	0
University Stdnt Un Cal State		B	818 677-2251	0
Valley Hospital Medical Center (DH)		B	818 885-8500	0
Village At Northridge		C	818 514-4497	0
World Private Security Inc		C	818 894-1800	0

NORWALK, CA - Los Angeles County

Company	SIC	EMP	PHONE	ENTRY #
American Multi-Cinema Inc		E	562 864-6206	0
Aquirecorps Norwalk Auto Auctn		C	562 864-7464	0
Coast Plaza Doctors Hospital (PA)		D	562 868-3751	0
County of Los Angeles		A	562 462-2094	0
County of Los Angeles		C	562 807-7860	0
Cph Hospital Management LLC		A	562 838-3751	0
El Clasificado (PA)		D	323 837-4095	0
Elena Villa Healthcare Center		D	562 868-0591	0
Faro Services Inc		C	562 483-7799	0
Front Porch Communities & Svcs		C	562 868-9761	0
Granville Hotel Corp		C	562 863-5555	0
Joes Sweeping Inc		D	562 929-4344	0
Jwch Institute Inc		C	562 281-0306	0
Kaiser Foundation Hospitals		A	562 807-6100	0
Life Care Centers America Inc		D	562 921-6624	0
Lj Distributors Inc		D	562 229-7660	0
Norwalk Community Hospital		D	562 863-4763	0
Norwalk Meadows Nursing Ctr LP		D	562 864-2541	0
Norwalk Transit System		D	562 929-5550	0
Pedestal Capital II LLC		D	562 863-5555	0
Personnel Plus Inc (PA)		C	562 712-5490	0
Tap Ram Reinforcing Inc		D	562 484-0859	0
Tvb (usa) Inc (DH)		E	562 345-9871	0
Weber Distribution Warehouses		E	562 404-9996	0

NOVATO, CA - Marin County

Company	SIC	EMP	PHONE	ENTRY #
Activision Blizzard Inc		C	415 881-9100	0
Atria Senior Living Inc		E	415 892-0944	0
Automatic Data Processing Inc		C	415 899-7300	0
Bank of Marin Bancorp (PA)		C	415 763-4520	0
Bear Flag Marketing Corp		C	415 899-7060	0
Birkenstock Usa Lp (DH)		C	415 884-3200	0
Brayton Purcell APC (PA)		C	415 898-1555	0
Buck Inst For RES On Aging (PA)		C	415 209-2000	0
Cellmark Inc (DH)		D	415 927-1700	0
Charles Schwab Corporation		D	415 294-3503	0
Charming Trim & Packaging		A	415 302-7021	0
Comet Building Maintenance Inc		D	415 383-1035	0
County of Marin		A	415 499-7060	0
Drivesavers Inc		D	415 382-2000	0
Griffin Group LLC (PA)		C	415 892-4569	0
Horizon Pharmaceutical LLC (HQ)		D	415 408-6200	0
Indian Valley Golf Club Inc		E	415 897-1118	0
Interntnal Prnsrance Assoc LLC		E	415 223-5548	0
Jaylaneentertainment Corp		D	707 820-2773	0

Employment Codes: A=Over 500 employees, B=251-500,
C=101-250, D=51-100, E=50

2020 Directory of California
Wholesalers and Services Companies

© Mergent Inc. 1-800-342-5647

1585

GEOGRAPHIC

	SIC	EMP	PHONE	ENTRY #
Kaiser Foundation Hospitals		E	415 899-7400	0
King Security Services Inc		A	415 556-5464	0
L & L Logic and Logistics LP		E	707 795-2475	0
Marin Community Clinic		D	415 448-1500	0
Marin Country Club Inc		D	415 382-6700	0
Marin County Sart Program		D	415 892-1628	0
Marin Humane Society		D	415 883-4621	0
Melissa Bradley RE Inc		D	415 209-1000	0
Navitas LLC		E	415 883-8116	0
North Bay Childrens Center **(PA)**		D	415 883-6222	0
North Marin Water District **(PA)**		E	415 897-4133	0
Novato Fire Protection Dist		D	415 878-2690	0
Novato Healthcare Center LLC		C	415 897-6161	0
Pacific Inptient Med Group Inc		D	415 485-8824	0
Permanente Medical Group Inc		D	415 209-2444	0
Permanente Medical Group Inc		D	415 899-7400	0
Radiant Logic Inc **(PA)**		D	415 209-6800	0
Scene7 Inc		D	415 506-6000	0
Stonetree Golf LLC		E	415 209-6744	0
Sutter Health		C	415 897-8495	0
Sutter Health		D	415 602-5380	0
Sutter West Bay Hospitals **(HQ)**		B	415 209-1300	0
Tennis Everyone Incorporated		D	415 897-2185	0
Thompson Builders Corporation		C	415 456-8972	0
Tile West Inc **(PA)**		D	415 382-7550	0
Visual Concepts Entertainment		C	415 479-3634	0
W Bradley Electric Inc **(PA)**		E	415 898-1400	0
Winery Exchange Inc **(PA)**		E	415 382-6200	0
Young Mens Christian Assoc SF		D	415 883-9622	0

OAK HILLS, CA - San Bernardino County

	SIC	EMP	PHONE	ENTRY #
Double Eagle Trnsp Corp		C	760 956-3770	0
Little Sisters Truck Wash Inc		D	760 947-4448	0

OAK VIEW, CA - Ventura County

	SIC	EMP	PHONE	ENTRY #
Casablanca Alzheimers Resid		D	805 649-5143	0

OAKDALE, CA - Stanislaus County

	SIC	EMP	PHONE	ENTRY #
Alldrin Brothers Inc		E	855 667-4231	0
Amerine Systems Incorporated		E	209 847-5968	0
Central Valley AG Trnspt Inc		E	209 544-9246	0
Damrell Nelson Schrimp Pall		E	209 848-3500	0
Gcu Trucking Inc		D	209 845-2117	0
Gilton Resource Recovery		D	209 527-3781	0
Gilton Solid Waste MGT Inc		C	209 527-3781	0
Mozingo Construction Inc		E	209 848-0160	0
Oak Valley Hospital District **(DH)**		B	209 847-3011	0
Oakdale Golf and Country Club		D	209 847-2984	0
Oakdale Irrgtion Dst Fing Corp		D	209 847-0341	0
Premier Valley Inc A Cal Corp **(PA)**		D	209 847-6111	0
Ross F Carroll Inc		E	209 848-5959	0

OAKHURST, CA - Madera County

	SIC	EMP	PHONE	ENTRY #
Associated Koi Clubs America		D	949 650-5225	0
Camarena Health		D	559 642-6724	0
Kaiser Foundation Hospitals		D	559 658-8388	0
Oakhurst Skilled Nursing Welln		D	559 683-2244	0
Sierra Masonic Association		D	559 683-7713	0
Sierra Tel Cmmunications Group		D	559 683-7777	0
Sierra Tel Cmmunications Group **(PA)**		D	559 683-4611	0
Sierra Telephone Company Inc		C	559 683-4611	0
State Farm Mutl Auto Insur Co		D	559 683-3467	0

OAKLAND, CA - Alameda County

	SIC	EMP	PHONE	ENTRY #
A T Associates Inc		D	510 261-8564	0
ABC Security Service Inc **(PA)**		C	510 436-0666	0
ABF Freight System Inc		D	510 533-8575	0
ABM Facility Services Inc **(DH)**		D	510 251-0381	0
Absg Consulting Inc		E	510 508-6289	0
Ace Parking Management Inc		D	510 589-2313	0
Ace Parking Management Inc		D	510 272-9788	0
Ace Parking Management Inc		C	510 251-0509	0
Aecom Technical Services Inc		C	510 834-4304	0
Aecom-TSE Joint Venture		D	510 285-6639	0
Alameda Cnty Cmnty Fd Bnk Inc		D	510 635-3663	0
Alameda County Employees Retir		D	510 628-3000	0
Alameda Health System **(PA)**		D	510 437-4800	0
Alameda-Contra Costa Trnst Dst **(PA)**		A	510 891-4777	0
Alameda-Contra Costa Trnst Dst		C	510 577-8816	0
Alaska Airlines Inc		D	510 577-5813	0
Alliance For Safety & Justice		D	209 507-6882	0
Allied Fire Protection		C	510 533-5516	0
Altenheim Inc		D	510 530-4013	0
Alton Management Corporation **(PA)**		D	510 663-0177	0
American Automobile Assctn		C	510 350-2042	0
American Baptist Homes of West		C	510 654-7172	0
American National Red Cross		C	510 594-5100	0

	SIC	EMP	PHONE	ENTRY #
American President Lines LLC		D	510 272-3990	0
Aperian Global Inc **(PA)**		D	628 222-3773	0
Aramark Unf & Career AP LLC		C	510 835-9285	0
Asian Community Mental Hlth Bd		D	510 869-6000	0
Asian Health Services		D	510 986-0601	0
Asian Health Services **(PA)**		C	510 986-6800	0
AT&T Services Inc		C	510 645-7684	0
Athletics Investment Group LLC **(PA)**		C	510 638-4900	0
Avis Rent A Car System Inc		D	510 577-6360	0
B&C Transit Inc **(PA)**		D	510 483-3560	0
Balfour Beatty Cnstr LLC		C	510 903-2060	0
Bay Alarm Company		D	510 452-3211	0
Bay Area Community Svcs Inc **(PA)**		E	510 613-0330	0
Belcampo Group Inc **(PA)**		D	510 250-7810	0
Beneficial State Bank **(HQ)**		D	510 550-8420	0
Berry & Berry Law Firm		D	510 250-0200	0
Bonita House Inc		D	510 923-0180	0
Boornazian Jensen & Garthe A		D	510 834-4350	0
Brightcurrent Inc		D	877 896-3306	0
Brilliance Investment LLC		D	510 568-1880	0
Brita Products Company		D	510 271-7000	0
Broadway Mech - Contrs Inc		C	510 746-4000	0
Brown Tland Physcn Svcs Orgnzt **(PA)**		B	415 972-4162	0
Burnham Brown A Prof Corp		C	510 444-6800	0
C/O Uc San Francisco **(PA)**		C	858 534-7323	0
California Cereal Products Inc **(PA)**		D	510 452-4500	0
California Child Care Resourc		E	510 658-0381	0
California Motorcycle Club		D	510 534-6222	0
California Nurses Association **(PA)**		D	510 273-2200	0
California Waste Solutions Inc		D	408 292-0830	0
Califrnia Leag Cnsrvtion Vters **(PA)**		D	510 271-0900	0
Califrnia-Nevada Methdst Homes		D	510 835-5511	0
Carpenter Fnds Admnstrtive Off		D	510 633-0333	0
Cartridge Family Inc		C	510 658-0400	0
Cass Inc **(PA)**		C	510 893-6476	0
Catholic Charities of The Dioc **(PA)**		D	510 768-3100	0
Cellco Partnership		D	510 267-0731	0
Center For Elders Independence		C	510 433-1150	0
Center To Promote Healthcare A **(PA)**		D	510 834-1300	0
Central Parking Corporation		D	510 832-7227	0
Cgi Technologies Solutions Inc		D	510 238-5300	0
Ch2m Hill Inc		C	510 604-4144	0
Charles Pankow Bldrs Ltd A Cal		B	510 893-5170	0
Chevron Federal Credit Union **(PA)**		D	888 884-4630	0
Childrens Hosp Okland Res Inst		D	510 450-7600	0
Childrens Hospotal & Research **(PA)**		A	510 428-3000	0
Christian Church Homes		B	510 893-2998	0
Christopher Ransom LLC		D	510 345-9144	0
Cim/Oakland City Center LLC		D	510 451-4000	0
City of Oakland		B	510 238-6796	0
City of Oakland		E	510 238-3494	0
City of Oakland		E	510 268-9000	0
Civicorps		C	510 992-7800	0
Claremont Country Club		D	510 653-6789	0
Claremont House Incorporated		D	510 658-9266	0
Clorox Services Company **(HQ)**		D	510 271-7000	0
College Track		C	510 834-3295	0
Computer Sciences Corporation		D	510 645-3000	0
Condon-Johnson & Assoc Inc **(PA)**		E	510 636-2100	0
Conservation Society Cal		D	510 632-9525	0
Consolidated Cleaning Services		D	510 663-2585	0
County of Alameda		D	510 271-5138	0
Covenant Care California LLC		D	510 261-2628	0
Covia Communities		C	510 835-4700	0
Creative Energy Foods Inc		D	510 638-8668	0
Crucible		C	510 444-0919	0
Custom Alloy Scrap Sales Inc **(HQ)**		E	510 893-6476	0
David Darroch		D	510 835-9100	0
Destiny Arts Center		E	510 597-1619	0
District Council DC **(PA)**		D	510 638-7600	0
Dnv GL Energy Insights USA Inc		E	510 891-0446	0
Donahue Gallager Woods LLP **(PA)**		D	415 381-4161	0
Dorado Network Systems Corp		C	650 227-7300	0
Dreyers Grand Ice Cream Hold **(DH)**		C	510 652-8187	0
East Bay Asian Local Dev Corp		C	510 267-1917	0
East Bay Asian Youth Center		E	510 533-1092	0
East Bay Community Foundation		D	510 836-3223	0
East Bay Foundation Grad Med		D	510 437-4197	0
East Bay Municpl Utilty Distr		D	866 403-2683	0
East Bay Municpl Utilty Distr **(PA)**		A	866 403-2683	0
East Bay Municpl Utilty Distr		D	510 287-0760	0
East Bay Municpl Utilty Distr		D	866 403-2683	0
EBSC LP		D	510 547-2244	0
Encompass Health Corporation		D	510 547-2244	0
Engie Services US Inc **(HQ)**		D	844 678-3772	0

Mergent email: customerrelations@mergent.com
1586

2020 Directory of California
Wholesalers and Services Companies

(P-0000) Products & Services Section entry number
(PA)=Parent Co (HQ)=Headquarters (DH)=Div Headquarters

	SIC	EMP	PHONE	ENTRY #
Environmental Health Hazard		D	510 622-3200	0
Fair Trade USA		C	510 663-5260	0
Family Bridges Inc		C	510 839-2270	0
Family Paths Inc (PA)		D	510 893-9230	0
Family Support Services (PA)		D	510 834-2443	0
Federal Express Corporation		B	510 382-2344	0
Federal Express Corporation		C	510 465-5209	0
Federal Express Corporation		D	800 463-3339	0
Fidelity Roof Company (PA)		D	510 547-6330	0
First Place For Youth (PA)		E	510 272-0979	0
First Transit Inc		D	510 535-9192	0
First Transit Inc		D	510 437-8990	0
Fitzgrald Abbott Beardsley LLP		D	510 451-1300	0
Fluid Inc (DH)		D	877 343-3240	0
Flurish Inc		D	855 253-6387	0
Fruitvale Long Term Care LLC		D	510 261-5613	0
Future State		D	925 956-4200	0
Gallagher Properties Inc (PA)		D	510 261-0466	0
General Services Cal Dept		D	510 622-3101	0
George E Masker Inc		D	510 568-1206	0
Geosyntec Consultants Inc		E	510 836-3034	0
Golden State Warriors LLC		D	510 986-2200	0
Green Planet 21 Inc (PA)		E	510 873-8777	0
Grubb Co Inc		D	510 339-0400	0
GSC Logistics Inc (PA)		C	510 844-3700	0
Gt Nexus Inc (HQ)		D	510 808-2222	0
Guardsmark LLC		C	510 562-7606	0
H2c2 & Associates Inc (PA)		E	510 562-6181	0
Hanna Brophy Mac Lean Mc Ale (PA)		E	510 839-1180	0
Hans Technologies Inc		D	510 464-8018	0
Health Care Workers Union (PA)		C	510 251-1250	0
Health Net California Inc		B	510 465-9600	0
Herc Rentals Inc		C	510 633-2040	0
High Street Hand Car Wash Inc		D	510 536-4333	0
Highcom Security Services		D	510 893-7600	0
Hntb-Gerwick JV		D	510 839-8972	0
Homewood Suites Management LLC		E	510 663-2700	0
Horizon Beverage Company		D	800 332-8358	0
Horizon Beverage Company LP		D	510 465-2212	0
Hospice & Home Health of E Bay		D	510 632-4390	0
IAC Publishing LLC		D	510 985-7400	0
IAC Search & Media Inc (HQ)		C	510 985-7400	0
Imperial Parking (us) LLC		E	510 382-2140	0
Independent Quality Care Inc		D	510 836-3677	0
Intelliguard Security Services		C	510 547-7656	0
Itron Inc		A	510 844-2800	0
Jacobs Project Management Co		D	510 457-2436	0
Jaqui Foundation Inc		E	510 562-4721	0
Jetblue Airways Corporation		D	510 381-1369	0
K G O T V News Bureau		D	510 451-4772	0
Kaiser Foundation Hospital		E	510 752-6295	0
Kaiser Foundation Hospitals		A	510 752-1000	0
Kaiser Foundation Hospitals (HQ)		C	510 271-6611	0
Kaiser Foundation Hospitals		A	510 752-1000	0
Kaiser Foundation Hospitals		D	510 752-7864	0
Kaiser Foundation Hospitals		A	510 987-1000	0
Kaiser Foundation Hospitals		B	510 891-3400	0
Kaiser Foundation Hospitals		D	510 251-0121	0
Kaiser Fundation Hlth Plan Inc (PA)		B	510 271-5800	0
Kaiser Fundation Hlth Plan Inc		D	510 752-7644	0
Kaiser Fundation Hlth Plan Inc		D	510 987-2255	0
Kaiser Group Holdings Inc		D	510 419-6000	0
Kaiser Hlth Plan Asset MGT Inc		E	510 271-5910	0
Kaiser Permanente		D	510 450-2109	0
Kaiserair Inc (PA)		C	510 569-9622	0
Katten Muchin Rosenman LLP		C	415 360-5444	0
Kazan McClain Satterley &		C	877 995-6372	0
Kids Overcoming LLC		D	415 748-8052	0
Kiewit Infrastructure West Co		D	510 452-1400	0
Ktgy Group Inc		E	510 463-2097	0
Ktvu Partnership Inc		C	510 834-1212	0
La Clinica De La Raza Inc		C	510 535-6300	0
La Clinica De La Raza Inc		B	510 535-4700	0
La Clinica De La Raza Inc		B	510 535-6200	0
Lake Merritt Hotel Associates		E	510 832-2300	0
Lake Mrritt Healthcare Ctr LLC		D	510 227-1806	0
Lapham Company Inc		D	510 531-6000	0
Lazar Landscape Design & Cnstr		D	510 444-5195	0
Leidos Inc		D	510 466-7138	0
Lincoln (PA)		D	510 273-4700	0
Lion Creek Senior Housing Part		D	510 878-9120	0
LN Curtis and Sons (PA)		D	510 839-5111	0
Lucid Design Group Inc		D	510 907-0400	0
M Arthur Gensler Jr Assoc Inc		C	510 625-7400	0
Magnetic Imaging Affilates		D	510 204-1820	0
Mariner Health Care Inc		D	510 261-5200	0
Marriott Foundation For People		D	510 834-4700	0
Mason-Mcduffie Real Estate Inc		D	510 834-2010	0
Matson Navigation Company Inc (HQ)		C	510 628-4000	0
Mbh Enterprises Inc		D	510 302-6680	0
Medical Insurance Exchange Cal		D	510 596-4935	0
Meditab Software Inc		C	510 632-2021	0
Menke & Associates Inc (PA)		D	415 362-5200	0
Mercy Retirement and Care Ctr		C	510 534-8540	0
Meyers Nave Riback Silver &		C	510 351-4300	0
Michael Baker Intl Inc		D	510 879-0950	0
Moc Products Company Inc		D	510 635-1230	0
Moffatt & Nichol		E	510 645-1238	0
Monarch Place Piedmont LLC		C	510 658-9266	0
Monterey Mechanical Co (PA)		E	510 632-3173	0
Morgan Stanley & Co LLC		D	510 839-8080	0
Mufg Union Bank National Assn		D	510 891-2495	0
Multivision Inc (DH)		D	510 740-5600	0
Museum of Childrens Art		E	510 465-8770	0
Nancy Smith Construction Inc		E	510 923-1671	0
National Rental (us) Inc		D	510 877-4507	0
Native American Health Ctr Inc (PA)		D	510 535-4400	0
Navis Holdings LLC		C	510 267-5000	0
Noble Tower Preservation LP		D	510 444-5228	0
North Star Emergency Svcs Inc		D	510 452-3400	0
Northgate Ter Cmnty Partner LP		E	510 465-9346	0
Nt Sunset Inc		E	510 420-3772	0
O C Jones & Sons Inc		D	510 663-6911	0
Oakland Healthcare & Wellness		C	323 330-6572	0
Oakland Mrtime Spport Svcs Inc		E	510 868-1005	0
Oakland Museum of California		D	510 318-8400	0
Oakland Private Industry Counc		D	510 768-4400	0
Oakland Public Education Fund		D	510 221-6968	0
Oakland Renaissance Associates		D	510 451-4000	0
Oakland Renaissance Associates		B	510 451-4000	0
Oakland Unified School Dst		D	510 729-7775	0
Oakland Unified School Dst		C	510 535-2717	0
Ocadian Care Centers LLC		D	510 832-3222	0
Officeworks Inc		D	510 444-2161	0
Otis Elevator Intl Inc		D	510 874-5129	0
Pacific Gas and Electric Co		D	510 450-5744	0
Pacific Union Intl Inc		B	510 338-1379	0
Pacific Union Residential Brkg		D	510 339-6460	0
Pandora Media LLC (DH)		C	510 451-4100	0
Paradigm Staffing Solutions		E	510 663-7860	0
Paramount Theatre of Arts Inc		D	510 893-2300	0
Park Hotels & Resorts Inc		C	510 635-5000	0
Park Plaza Hotel		E	510 635-5300	0
Pasha Hawaii Trnspt Lines LLC		D	510 271-1400	0
Pasta Shop (PA)		D	510 250-6005	0
Paylocity Holding Corporation		B	847 956-4850	0
Peace Action West (PA)		E	510 830-3600	0
Permanente Federation LLC		D	510 625-6920	0
Permanente Kaiser Intl (HQ)		C	510 271-5910	0
Permanente Medical Group Inc		D	510 752-1000	0
Permanente Medical Group Inc (DH)		B	866 858-2226	0
Permanente Medical Group Inc		D	510 625-6262	0
Permanente Medical Group Inc		D	510 752-1190	0
Phillips & Assoc Law Offs PC		D	510 464-8040	0
Playworks Education Energized (PA)		E	510 893-4180	0
Porrey Pines Bank Inc		B	510 899-7500	0
Port Dept City of Oakland (PA)		B	510 627-1100	0
Port Dept City of Oakland		C	510 563-3300	0
Prevention Institute		D	510 444-4133	0
Proactive Bus Solutions Inc		C	510 302-0120	0
Professional Technical SEC Svcs		B	510 645-9200	0
Providence Health & Svcs - Ore		B	510 444-0839	0
Public Health Institute (PA)		D	510 285-5500	0
Purple Communications Inc		C	510 268-0120	0
Ramsell Public Health Rx LLC		D	510 587-2600	0
Rcc Facility Incorporated		D	510 658-2041	0
Restaurant Depot LLC		C	510 628-0600	0
Ricoh Usa Inc		E	510 839-6399	0
Rmt Landscape Contractors Inc		E	510 568-3208	0
Robert Half MGT Resources		E	510 271-0910	0
San Francisco Bay Area Rapid		E	510 464-6000	0
San Francisco Bay Area Rapid		D	510 834-1297	0
San Francisco Bay Area Rapid		C	510 464-6126	0
San Francisco Bay Area Rapid		A	510 286-2893	0
San Francisco Bay Area Rapid		D	510 464-7000	0
San Francisco Bay Area Rapid		C	510 464-6000	0
San Frncsco Bay Area Rpid Trns (PA)		B	510 464-6000	0
Schnitzer Steel Industries Inc		D	510 444-3919	0
Sea West Cast Gard Fdral Cr Un (PA)		D	510 568-4100	0
Sea-Logix LLC		D	510 271-1400	0

Employment Codes: A=Over 500 employees, B=251-500,
C=101-250, D=51-100, E=50

2020 Directory of California
Wholesalers and Services Companies

© Mergent Inc. 1-800-342-5647

1587

GEOGRAPHIC

	SIC	EMP	PHONE	ENTRY #
Security Central Inc		D	510 652-2477	0
Sedgwick Claims MGT Svcs Inc		D	510 302-3000	0
SEIU Local 1021		C	510 350-9811	0
Seiu United Healthcare Workers (PA)		C	510 251-1250	0
Service King Holdings LLC		C	510 562-9650	0
Shimmick Construction Co Inc (HQ)		C	510 777-5000	0
Sierra Club (PA)		C	415 977-5500	0
Silverado Contractors Inc (PA)		D	510 658-9960	0
Society of St Vincent (PA)		D	510 638-7600	0
Solar Spectrum LLC		B	844 777-6527	0
Southwest Airlines Co		D	510 563-1000	0
Southwest Airlines Co		C	510 563-1234	0
Spectrum Credit Union		D	510 251-6000	0
SSC Oakland Excell Oper Co LP		D	510 261-5200	0
Standard Iron & Metals Co		E	510 535-0222	0
Star Protection Agency LLC		C	510 635-1732	0
State Compensation Insur Fund		C	510 577-3000	0
Sterling Hsa Inc		E	800 617-4729	0
Stuart Lovett		D	510 444-0790	0
Sunrise Senior Living LLC		D	510 531-7190	0
Sunrise Senior Living LLC		D	303 410-0500	0
Sutter Health		B	510 547-2244	0
Sutter Health		C	510 869-8777	0
Swissport Fueling Inc		D	510 562-1701	0
Teecom		D	510 337-2800	0
Telecare Corporation		C	510 261-9191	0
Telecare Corporation		D	510 535-5115	0
Telecom Inc		D	510 873-8283	0
Traffic Management Inc		D	415 370-7916	0
Tree Sculpture Group		D	510 562-4000	0
Trust For Cnsrvtion Innovation		D	415 421-3774	0
Tucker Technology Inc		D	510 836-0422	0
Tucson Hotels LP		B	510 658-9300	0
Turner Construction Company		E	510 267-8100	0
United Parcel Service Inc OH		C	510 813-5662	0
URS Group Inc		D	510 893-3600	0
URS Group Inc		D	925 446-3800	0
URS-Gei Joint Venture		E	510 874-3051	0
Veritas Media Group LLC		D	510 867-4699	0
Veterans Health Administration		B	510 267-7820	0
Wallis Fashions Inc.		C	510 763-8018	0
Waste MGT of Alameda Cnty (HQ)		A	510 613-8710	0
Waterfront Plaza Hotel LLC		D	510 836-3800	0
Wells & Bennett Realtors (PA)		D	510 531-7000	0
Wells Fargo Bank National Assn		D	510 530-3095	0
Wendel Rosen LLP (PA)		C	510 834-6600	0
West Oakland Health Council (PA)		C	510 835-9610	0
Westcoast Childrens Clinic		C	510 269-9030	0
Wested		D	510 302-4200	0
Williams Adley & Company L L P (PA)		D	510 893-8114	0
Willow Tree Nursing Center		D	510 261-2628	0
Wipfli LLP		D	510 768-0066	0
Wood Environment &		D	510 663-4100	0
Workers Compensation (PA)		C	888 229-2472	0
Xantrion Incorporated		E	510 272-4701	0
Young MNS Chrstn Assn of E Bay		D	510 654-9622	0
Young MNS Chrstn Assn of E Bay		A	510 451-8039	0
Zillow Group Inc		A	415 836-6760	0

OAKLEY, CA - Contra Costa County

	SIC	EMP	PHONE	ENTRY #
Coldwell Banker Amaral & Assoc		D	925 439-7400	0
Contra Costa Water District		D	925 383-2576	0
Flordo Oakley Hall		C	925 625-4076	0
Foundation Constructors Inc (PA)		D	925 754-6633	0
Oakley Union School District		D	925 625-5060	0

OCCIDENTAL, CA - Sonoma County

	SIC	EMP	PHONE	ENTRY #
Alliance Rdwods Cnfrnce Grunds		D	707 874-3507	0
Westminster Woods Camp & Confe		E	707 874-2426	0

OCEANO, CA - San Luis Obispo County

	SIC	EMP	PHONE	ENTRY #
Phelan & Taylor Produce Co		C	805 489-2413	0

OCEANSIDE, CA - San Diego County

	SIC	EMP	PHONE	ENTRY #
Aegis Asssted Living Prpts LLC		D	760 806-3600	0
Allied Swiss Limited		C	760 941-1702	0
American Golf Corporation		D	760 757-2100	0
AT&T Services Inc		C	760 722-7261	0
Bergensons Property Svcs Inc		A	760 631-5111	0
Boral Roofing LLC		C	760 967-0827	0
Business and Support Services		B	760 725-5187	0
Business and Support Services		E	760 725-2817	0
Central Indiana Hdwr Co Inc (PA)		D	317 558-5700	0
Cinemastar Luxury Theaters		B	760 945-2500	0
CK Enterprises Inc		D	760 967-8863	0
County of San Diego		C	760 754-3456	0
Cox Automotive Inc		B	760 754-3600	0

	SIC	EMP	PHONE	ENTRY #
Cox California Telcom LLC		C	760 966-0447	0
E R I T Inc (PA)		D	760 433-6024	0
E R I T Inc.		C	760 721-1706	0
El Camino Rental		E	760 722-7368	0
Frontwave Credit Union (PA)		C	760 430-7511	0
Future Energy Corporation		D	760 477-9700	0
Go-Staff Inc		A	760 730-8520	0
Goodwill Inds San Diego Cnty		C	760 806-7670	0
Impact Solutions LLC		E	760 231-0450	0
La Cantina Doors Inc		E	888 221-0141	0
Laconstructora Co Inc		E	760 439-7686	0
Marine Corps United States		A	760 725-1304	0
McAlister Institute For Treat		D	760 726-4451	0
Mellano & Co		C	760 433-9550	0
Mission Linen Supply		C	760 757-9099	0
Mold Testing and Inspection		D	760 643-1834	0
Monterey Financial Svcs Inc (PA)		C	760 639-3500	0
Nitto Denko Technical Corp		D	760 435-7011	0
North Coast Surgery Center		D	760 940-0997	0
North County Transit District (PA)		D	760 966-6500	0
Ocean Holiday LP		D	760 231-7000	0
Oceans Eleven Casino		B	760 439-6988	0
Oceanside Lifeguards		D	760 435-4500	0
OConnell Landscape Maint Inc		E	760 630-4963	0
Panoramic Doors LLC		D	760 722-1300	0
Pardee Tree Nursery		D	760 630-5400	0
Peopleready Inc		E	760 643-4980	0
Primeco Painting & Cnstr		D	760 967-8278	0
R & R Profession		C	760 754-9020	0
Rancho Del Oro Ldscp Maint Inc		D	760 726-0215	0
S and R Towing Inc (PA)		E	760 722-6686	0
Sadie Rose Baking Co		D	619 718-9532	0
San Diego Coastl Med Group Inc		C	760 901-5259	0
Scripps Health		C	760 901-5200	0
Service Corp International		D	760 754-6600	0
Shieldx Networks Inc		E	760 724-2700	0
Smart & Final Stores LLC		D	760 726-7274	0
Suja Life LLC		C	855 879-7852	0
Sundance Natural Foods Company		E	760 945-9898	0
Superior Support Services Inc.		B	559 458-0507	0
Supreme Security Services Inc		D	760 415-7399	0
Tri City Orthopedic Sgy & Mdcl		E	760 724-9000	0
Tri-City Hospital District (PA)		A	760 724-8411	0
Veridiam Allied Swiss		D	760 941-1702	0
Villas De Carlsbad Ltd A Cali		E	760 434-7116	0
Waste Management Cal Inc		D	760 439-2824	0
World Mark of Oceanside		D	760 721-0890	0
YMCA of San Diego County		D	760 754-6042	0
YMCA of San Diego County		D	760 758-0808	0
YMCA of San Diego County		D	760 757-8270	0

OJAI, CA - Ventura County

	SIC	EMP	PHONE	ENTRY #
ARC of Ventura County Inc		D	805 650-8611	0
Coldwell Banker Property Shop		D	805 646-7288	0
Community Memorial Health Sys		C	805 646-1401	0
Gables of Ojai LLC		D	805 646-1446	0
Hotrollergirl Productions		D	530 521-2745	0
Krishnamurti Foundation Amer (PA)		D	805 646-2726	0
Mf Daily Oxnard Ranch Partnr		E	805 646-5633	0
Ojai Valley Inn Golf Course		A	805 646-2420	0
Ovis Llc		A	805 646-5511	0

OLIVEHURST, CA - Yuba County

	SIC	EMP	PHONE	ENTRY #
Ampla Health		D	530 743-4614	0
Lindhurst Dental Clinic		E	530 743-4614	0
Naumes Inc		E	530 743-2055	0
Nordic Industries Inc		D	530 742-7124	0
Nordic/Great Lakes E&I JV		D	530 742-7124	0
Rodgz Farm Labor Contg LLC		D	530 329-8403	0
Shoei Foods USA Inc		D	530 742-7866	0

OLYMPIC VALLEY, CA - Placer County

	SIC	EMP	PHONE	ENTRY #
Cncml A California Ltd Partnr		D	530 583-1578	0
Squaw Valley Development Co (HQ)		D	530 452-6985	0
Squaw Valley Ski Corporation (DH)		D	530 583-6985	0

ONTARIO, CA - San Bernardino County

	SIC	EMP	PHONE	ENTRY #
3M Company		C	909 974-3004	0
A-1 Delivery Co		D	909 444-1220	0
Accentcare Home Health Cal Inc		D	909 605-7000	0
Access Info Holdings LLC		A	909 459-1417	0
ACI Construction Company Inc		E	909 391-4477	0
Adminsure Inc		C	909 718-1200	0
Aecom Technical Services Inc.		D	909 554-5000	0
Air Control Systems Inc		E	909 786-4230	0
Alaska Airlines Inc		D	800 426-0333	0
AMC Entertainment Inc		E	909 476-1288	0

(P-0000) Products & Services Section entry number
(PA)=Parent Co (HQ)=Headquarters (DH)=Div Headquarters

Company	SIC	EMP	PHONE	ENTRY #
American Business Bank		D	909 919-2040	0
American Financial Network Inc			951 582-2655	0
Americold Logistics LLC		E	909 390-4950	0
Ameriwest Industries Inc		E	909 930-1898	0
Artistic Maintenance Inc		D	909 390-5156	0
AT&T Corp		D	909 930-6508	0
Atchesons Express Inc		E	714 808-9199	0
Automotive Tstg & Dev Svcs Inc **(PA)**		C	909 390-1100	0
Avis Rent A Car System Inc		D	909 974-2192	0
AZ Countertops Inc		E	909 983-5386	0
B Braun Medical Inc		A	909 906-7575	0
Beauty 21 Cosmetics Inc		C	909 945-2220	0
Behavoral Autism Therapies LLC **(PA)**		D	909 483-5000	0
Bella Vista Healthcare Center		D	909 985-2731	0
Biagi Bros Inc		C	909 390-6910	0
Bio-Med Services Inc		D	909 235-4400	0
Blumenthal Distributing Inc **(PA)**		D	909 930-2000	0
Boshart Automotive Tstg Svcs		D	909 466-1602	0
BP Industries Incorporated		D	909 481-0227	0
C E B M Inc		E	909 975-4440	0
CA Station Management Inc		C	909 245-6251	0
Calico Brands Inc		E	909 930-5000	0
Canon Solutions America Inc		D	909 390-7400	0
Cardinal Health Inc		D	909 605-0900	0
CAT Logistics Inc		D	909 390-1920	0
Cbre Inc		D	909 418-2000	0
Celestica LLC		B	909 418-6986	0
Centimark Corporation		E	909 652-2600	0
Chino Valley Sawdust Inc		D	909 947-5983	0
Chino-Pacific Warehouse Corp **(PA)**		D	909 545-8100	0
Cintas Corporation No 3		C	909 930-9096	0
Cintas Corporation No 3		D	909 390-4912	0
Citizens Business Bank **(HQ)**		C	909 980-4030	0
Coastal Pacific Fd Distrs Inc		C	909 947-2066	0
Comfort Systems Usa Inc		D	909 390-6677	0
Concord Foods Inc **(PA)**		D	909 975-2000	0
Contemporary Services Corp		D	909 740-3834	0
Converse Inc		D	909 974-5695	0
Country Inn &SUite By Carlson		E	909 937-6000	0
CU Direct Corporation **(PA)**		C	909 481-2300	0
Customized Dist Svcs Inc		D	909 947-0084	0
Dal-Tile Corporation		D	909 390-7000	0
Damao Luggage Intl Inc		A	909 923-6531	0
David Evans and Associates Inc		E	909 481-5750	0
Dependable Highway Express Inc		D	909 923-0065	0
Directv LLC		D	909 509-4790	0
Dirt Cheap Inc **(PA)**		E	909 230-6330	0
Distribution Alternatives Inc		D	909 673-1000	0
Diversity Bus Solutions Inc		C	909 395-0243	0
Dlt Growers Inc		E	909 947-8198	0
Dominos Pizza LLC		C	909 390-1990	0
Dpi Specialty Foods West Inc **(DH)**		C	909 975-1019	0
Dt Ontrio Ht Prtners Lssee LLC		B	909 937-0900	0
Edc Service Corporation		D	909 390-4747	0
Emser Tile LLC		D	909 974-1600	0
F M Tarbell Co		D	951 270-1022	0
F R T International Inc		C	909 390-4892	0
Federal Express Corporation		B	800 463-3339	0
Federal Express Corporation		D	909 390-3237	0
Fedex Sup Chain Dist Sys Inc		E	909 605-9210	0
Foland Group Inc		D	909 930-9900	0
Fortune Avenue Foods Inc		D	909 930-5989	0
Fruit Growers Supply Company		D	909 390-0190	0
Fullmer Construction		C	909 947-9467	0
Gardner Trucking Inc **(HQ)**		B	909 563-5606	0
General Electric Company		B	909 605-7603	0
Genuine Parts Distributors		D	562 692-9034	0
Gold Star Foods Inc **(HQ)**		D	909 843-9600	0
Gregg Electric Inc		C	909 983-1794	0
Grove Lumber & Bldg Sups Inc **(PA)**		C	909 947-0277	0
Guard-Systems Inc		B	909 947-5400	0
Hci Systems Inc **(PA)**		E	909 628-7773	0
HHS Communications Inc		D	909 230-5170	0
HMC Group **(HQ)**		C	909 989-9979	0
HMC Group		C	909 980-8058	0
Hospital Business Services Inc		C	909 235-4400	0
Hub Construction Spc Inc		E	909 947-4669	0
Hub Group Trucking Inc		C	951 693-9813	0
Iapmo Research and Testing Inc **(HQ)**		D	909 472-4100	0
Impact Logistics		E	909 937-9035	0
Inland Christian Home Inc		C	909 395-9322	0
Inland Empire Chapter-Assn of		D	512 478-9000	0
Innovel Solutions Inc		D	909 605-1446	0
Inqbrands Inc		D	909 390-7788	0
Intercontinental Hotels Group		C	909 930-5555	0
International Assoc of Plmbng **(PA)**		D	909 472-4100	0
International City Mrtg Inc		D	909 944-7361	0
Island Hospitality MGT LLC		E	909 937-6788	0
Jack Jones Trucking Inc		D	909 456-2500	0
Jacobs Engineering Group Inc		D	909 974-2700	0
Jcm Engineering Corp		D	909 923-3730	0
Jeeva Corp		D	909 238-4073	0
Kaiser Foundation Hospitals		A	909 724-5000	0
Kaiser Foundation Hospitals		D	888 750-0036	0
Keystone Automotive Inds Inc		D	909 986-4586	0
Kf Ontario Healthcare LLC		E	909 984-6713	0
Kindred Healthcare Oper Inc		B	909 391-0333	0
Lanting Hay Dealer Inc		D	909 563-5601	0
Las Vegas / LA Express Inc **(PA)**		C	909 972-3100	0
Lee & Assoc Comm Real Est Svcs		E	909 989-7771	0
Liberty Hardware Mfg Corp		D	909 605-2300	0
Liberty Mutual Insurance Co		D	909 476-6688	0
Los Angeles World Airports		D	909 544-5490	0
Main Street Fibers Inc		D	909 986-6310	0
Mazar Corp		D	909 292-8269	0
McIntyre Company **(PA)**		D	909 962-6322	0
Menifee Management Corp			951 672-4824	0
Menzies Aviation (texas) Inc		D	909 937-3998	0
Michael Baker Intl Inc		E	909 974-4900	0
Mills Corporation		D	909 484-8300	0
Mission Landscape Service		D	909 947-7290	0
Mondelez Global LLC		D	909 605-0140	0
Myers Power Products Inc **(PA)**		C	909 923-1800	0
NAFTA Distributors		E	909 605-7515	0
National General Insurance Co		D	909 944-8085	0
Nationwide Trans Inc **(PA)**		D	909 355-3211	0
Nordstrom Inc		B	909 390-1040	0
North American Med MGT Cal Inc **(DH)**		D	909 605-8000	0
Nvision Laser Eye Centers Inc **(PA)**		D	909 605-1975	0
Oakley Inc		D	951 685-0038	0
Ontario Convention Center Corp		C	909 937-3000	0
Ontario Health Educatn Co Inc		E	951 817-8553	0
Ontario Montclar Sch Dist Food		D	909 930-6360	0
Ontario Refrigeration Svc Inc **(PA)**		D	909 984-2771	0
Oregon PCF Bldg Pdts Maple Inc		C	909 627-4043	0
Otto International Inc **(PA)**		D	909 937-1998	0
Owens & Minor Inc		D	909 944-2100	0
Pacific Metals Group LLC		E	909 218-8889	0
Pacific Rebar Inc		D	909 984-7199	0
Park Hotels & Resorts Inc		D	909 980-3420	0
Park Hotels & Resorts Inc		C	909 980-0400	0
Patton Sales Corp **(PA)**		C	909 988-0661	0
Penske Logistics LLC		D	800 529-6531	0
Pentel of America Ltd		E	909 975-2200	0
Prize Proz		E	909 509-8600	0
Pro-Med Hlth Care Administrator		D	909 932-1045	0
R & B Wholesale Distrs Inc **(PA)**		C	909 230-5400	0
R F Metro Services Inc **(PA)**		D	909 230-4920	0
Rahf IV Grove LP		E	216 621-6060	0
Raymond Handling Solutions Inc		D	909 930-9399	0
RDM Electric Co Inc **(PA)**		D	909 591-0990	0
Redlands Employment Services		B	951 688-0083	0
Residence Inn By Marriott LLC		C	909 937-6788	0
Ridgeside Construction Inc		D	909 218-7593	0
Rosen Electronics LLC		D	951 898-9808	0
Ruby Industrial Tech LLC		E	909 390-7919	0
Ruuhwa Dann and Associates Inc		D	909 467-4800	0
San Dimas Luggage Company		D	909 510-8820	0
Sears Roebuck and Co		C	909 390-4210	0
Securitas SEC Svcs USA Inc		D	909 974-3160	0
Sedgwick CMS Holdings Inc		A	909 477-5500	0
Shii LLC		E	909 354-8000	0
Sigmanet Inc **(HQ)**		C	909 230-7500	0
Signal 88 LLC		A	714 713-5306	0
Smg Food and Beverage LLC **(PA)**		D	909 937-3000	0
Solar Link International Inc		C	909 605-7789	0
Southtown Industrial Park		E	909 947-3768	0
Spectrum MGT Holdg Co LLC		D	909 821-8159	0
SS Heritage Inn Ontario LLC		D	909 937-5000	0
Synnex Corporation		D	909 923-8900	0
Target Corporation		D	909 937-5500	0
Taylored Services LLC **(DH)**		D	909 510-4800	0
Taylored Services Holdings LLC **(HQ)**		D	909 510-4800	0
Taylored Svcs Parent Co Inc **(PA)**		D	909 510-4800	0
Tcm Group LLC		E	909 527-8580	0
Technicolor HM Entrmt Svcs Inc		B	909 974-2016	0
Technicolor Thomson Group		D	909 974-2222	0
Test-Rite Products Corp **(DH)**		D	909 605-9899	0
Texas Home Health America LP **(PA)**		D	972 201-3800	0
Todays Vi LLC		D	909 980-2200	0

Employment Codes: A=Over 500 employees, B=251-500,
C=101-250, D=51-100, E=50

2020 Directory of California
Wholesalers and Services Companies

© Mergent Inc. 1-800-342-5647

1589

GEOGRAPHIC

Company	SIC	EMP	PHONE	ENTRY #
Tokai Intl Holdings Inc (PA)		E	909 930-5000	0
Toyo Tire USA Corp		E	562 431-6502	0
Turbine Repair Services LLC (PA)		D	909 947-2256	0
Ua Galaxy Los Cerritos		D	562 865-6499	0
Uline Inc		D	909 605-7090	0
Ultra Solutions LLC		E	909 628-1778	0
Unifirst Corporation		C	909 390-8670	0
United Parcel Service Inc OH		A	909 974-7250	0
United Parcel Service Inc OH		C	909 974-7190	0
United Parcel Service Inc OH		C	909 974-7000	0
United Road Towing Inc		D	909 923-6100	0
US Elogistics Service Corp		D	732 357-6665	0
Vertex Coatings Inc		D	909 923-5795	0
Vitco Distributors Inc		D	909 355-1300	0
Vitran Logistics Inc		D	909 972-3100	0
Wade & Lowe A Prof Corp (PA)		D	909 483-6700	0
Waxies Enterprises Inc		C	909 942-3100	0
West End Yung MNS Christn Assn		D	909 477-2780	0
Workforce Enterprises Wfe Inc		E	909 718-8915	0
Xpo Logistics Supply Chain Inc		D	909 975-6300	0
Xtreme Security Services Inc		E	909 390-6818	0

ORANGE, CA - Orange County

Company	SIC	EMP	PHONE	ENTRY #
ABF Freight System Inc		E	714 974-2485	0
Access Dental Plan (PA)		D	916 922-5000	0
Ademco Inc		E	714 283-0110	0
Aecom Usa Inc		D	714 567-2501	0
Alan Smith Pool Plastering Inc		D	714 628-9494	0
Alignment Health Plan		D	323 728-7232	0
Alignment Healthcare USA LLC (PA)		D	844 310-2247	0
All Seasons Framing Corp		E	714 634-2324	0
All-Pro Remodeling		D	714 288-1314	0
Alliedbarton Security Svcs LLC		C	626 213-3100	0
Alliedbarton Security Svcs LLC		C	714 260-0805	0
American Advisors Group (PA)		E	866 948-0003	0
American Contractors Inc		D	714 282-5700	0
American Intgrted Rsources Inc		D	714 921-4100	0
American Multi-Cinema Inc		D	714 769-4288	0
American Residential Svcs LLC		D	714 634-1826	0
Ameripride Services Inc		E	714 385-8991	0
Ameriquest Capital Corporation (PA)		B	714 564-0600	0
Amerisourcebergen Corporation		C	714 704-4407	0
Amerisourcebergen Corporation		C	610 727-7000	0
Amerisourcebergen Corporation		C	714 704-4407	0
Anaheim Ca LLC		D	714 634-4500	0
Arbormed Inc (PA)		C	714 689-1500	0
Architects Orange		C	714 639-9860	0
Ashunya Inc		D	714 385-1900	0
Atc Services Inc		B	213 593-8100	0
Avanti Agency Corporation		B	714 935-0900	0
B C Rentals LLC (HQ)		D	714 974-1190	0
Bapko Metal Inc		D	714 639-9380	0
Barnett Customer Management		E	714 747-7908	0
Beks Acquisition Inc		E	714 744-2990	0
Bergen Brunswig Drug Company		A	714 385-4000	0
Bernel Inc		C	714 778-6070	0
Boyle Engineering Corporation		D	714 543-5274	0
Cal/Pac Paintings & Coatings		D	714 628-1514	0
Calnev Pipe Line LLC		C	714 560-4400	0
Cashcall Inc		A	949 752-4600	0
Cdsrvs LLC		D	714 912-8353	0
Cellco Partnership		D	714 921-5130	0
Center For Indvdual and Fam Th		D	714 558-9266	0
Chapman Global Medical Center		B	714 633-0011	0
Childrens Healthcare Cal		A	714 997-3000	0
Childrens Healthcare Cal (PA)		A	714 997-3000	0
Childrens Hospital Orange Cnty (PA)		A	714 997-3000	0
Childrens Hospital Orange Cnty		A	949 365-2416	0
Choc Health Alliance		D	714 565-5100	0
Choic Admini Insur Servi		B	714 542-4200	0
Cik Power Distributors LLC		D	714 938-0297	0
Cirtech Inc		E	714 921-0860	0
Citigroup Inc		D	714 938-0748	0
City of Orange		D	714 744-7264	0
City of Orange		D	714 744-7272	0
City Orange Police Assn Inc		C	714 457-5340	0
Cleveland Marble LP		E	714 998-3280	0
Cmf Inc		D	714 637-2409	0
Coastal Building Services Inc		B	714 775-2855	0
Cobb Waterblasting Inc		C	714 769-2622	0
Colonial Home Care Svcs Inc		C	714 289-7220	0
Companion Home Hlth & Hospice		D	714 560-8177	0
Comppartners Inc		D	949 253-3111	0
Conexis Bneft Admnistrators LP (HQ)		C	714 835-5006	0
Cornerstone Family Svcs LLC		D	714 744-3800	0
County of Orange		C	714 704-8000	0
County of Orange		D	714 935-6435	0
County Whl Elc Co Los Angeles		D	714 633-3801	0
Cruz Modular Inc (PA)		D	714 283-2890	0
De Par Inc		D	714 771-6900	0
Destination Science LLC		C	714 289-9100	0
Doctors of Affiliated		D	714 539-3100	0
Dynamic Auto Images Inc		B	714 981-4367	0
Electronic Commerce LLC		D	800 770-5520	0
Elite Nursing Services Inc		E	714 919-7898	0
Elliott Auto Supply Co Inc		E	800 278-6394	0
Emergency Medicine Specialist		D	714 543-8911	0
Enterprise Rent-A-Car (DH)		D	657 221-4400	0
Ergs Aim Hotel Realty LLC		D	714 938-1111	0
ESA P Prtfolio Oper Lessee LLC		D	714 639-8608	0
Fedex Freight Corporation		E	714 637-9346	0
Ford Plastering Inc		B	714 921-0624	0
Frick Paper Company		C	323 726-8200	0
Geek Squad Inc		D	714 938-0380	0
General Coatings Corporation		C	858 587-1277	0
General Underground		C	714 632-8646	0
Handyman Connection		E	714 288-0077	0
Harvest Landscape Entps Inc		C	714 693-8100	0
Hill Brothers Chemical Company (PA)		C	714 998-8800	0
Hit Portfolio II Trs LLC		C	714 938-1111	0
Holmes & Narver Inc (HQ)		C	714 567-2400	0
Inductors Inc		E	949 623-2460	0
Interior Electric Incorporated		D	714 771-9098	0
Intrado Corporation		C	949 294-2801	0
Jack P Selman		D	714 639-9860	0
Jezowski & Markel Contrs Inc		C	714 978-2222	0
John Jory Corporation (PA)		B	714 279-7901	0
K & S Air Conditioning Inc		C	714 685-0077	0
K T W Productions Inc		A	714 685-0428	0
Kaiser Foundation Hospitals		D	714 748-7622	0
Kaiser Foundation Hospitals		D	888 988-2800	0
Kings Seafood Company LLC		D	714 771-6655	0
Kondaur Capital Corporation (PA)		C	714 352-2038	0
Larkin Leasing Inc		D	714 528-3232	0
Leaf Commercial Capital Inc		E	866 219-7924	0
Leonard Chaidez Inc		B	714 279-8173	0
Liberty Debt Relief LLC		D	800 756-8447	0
Liberty Mutual Insurance Co		C	714 937-1400	0
Lonestar Sierra LLC		C	866 575-5680	0
Lres Corporation (PA)		D	714 520-5737	0
Lucky Strike Entertainment LLC		D	248 374-3420	0
M S International Inc (PA)		B	714 685-7500	0
Madden Corporation		D	714 922-1670	0
Main Street Specialty Surgery		D	714 704-1900	0
Maintech Incorporated		C	714 921-8000	0
Mark 1 Mortgage Corporation (PA)		E	714 752-5700	0
Marne Construction Inc		D	714 935-0995	0
Martin Integrated Systems		D	714 998-9100	0
MB Coatings Inc		E	714 625-2118	0
Medical Specialties Managers		C	714 571-5000	0
Merical LLC		D	714 685-0977	0
Merical LLC		C	714 283-9551	0
Meyer Coatings Inc		E	714 467-4600	0
Miller Environmental Inc		C	714 385-0099	0
Mx Courier Systems Inc		E	714 288-8622	0
Nestle Waters North Amer Inc		C	714 532-6220	0
Newport Ch International LLC (PA)		D	714 572-8881	0
Nexinfo Solutions Inc		E	714 368-1452	0
Omega Insurance Services		E	714 973-0311	0
Optisource Technologies Inc		E	714 288-0825	0
Orange Coast Masonry Acquisit		D	714 538-4386	0
Orange County Health Auth		B	714 246-8500	0
Orange County Trnsp Auth (PA)		B	714 636-7433	0
Orange County Trnsp Auth		A	714 999-1726	0
Orange Healthcare & Wellness		C	714 633-3568	0
P & D Consultants Inc (HQ)		E	714 835-4447	0
P H S Management Group (PA)		E	714 547-7551	0
Padilla Construction Company		C	714 685-8500	0
Pavilion Surgery Center LLC		D	714 744-8850	0
Pentron Clinical Tech LLC		D	203 265-7397	0
Planned Parenthood/Orange and (PA)		C	714 633-6373	0
Platinum Strands Salon		D	714 532-2633	0
Providence Speech Hearing Ctr		E	714 639-4990	0
Raymond Group (PA)		C	714 771-7670	0
Red Hawk Fire & SEC CA Inc		C	714 685-8100	0
Red Pointe Roofing LP (PA)		D	714 685-0010	0
Rehabltation Inst Southern Cal (PA)		C	714 633-7400	0
Retail Services Wis Corp		D	714 347-3431	0
Rfid Textile Services Inc		C	714 998-6109	0
Rick Hamm Construction Inc		D	714 532-0815	0
Rika Corporation		D	949 830-9050	0

2020 Directory of California
Wholesalers and Services Companies

(P-0000) Products & Services Section entry number
(PA)=Parent Co (HQ)=Headquarters (DH)=Div Headquarters

	SIC	EMP	PHONE	ENTRY #
Rio		C	714 633-7400	0
RJ Noble Company **(PA)**		C	714 637-1550	0
Roger L Crumley MD Inc		E	714 456-5750	0
Roth Staffing Companies LP **(PA)**		D	714 939-8600	0
SA Recycling LLC **(PA)**		D	714 632-2000	0
Sanders & Wohrman Corporation		C	714 919-0446	0
Sas Institute Inc		D	949 250-9999	0
Schryver Med Sls & Mktg LLC		D	303 459-8160	0
Securitas Critical Infrastruct		A	310 817-2177	0
Sfpp LP **(DH)**		C	714 560-4400	0
Signature Flooring Inc		D	714 558-9200	0
Solari Enterprises Inc		D	714 282-2520	0
Southern Counties Oil Co **(PA)**		C	714 744-7140	0
Ssae 16 Professionals LLP		D	866 480-9485	0
St Joseph Hospital of Orange **(DH)**		A	714 633-9111	0
St Joseph Hospital of Orange		D	714 771-8037	0
States Drawer Box Spc LLC		D	714 744-4247	0
Steger Inc		E	714 974-4383	0
Stoneriver Inc		B	714 705-8227	0
Sunnyslope Tree Farm Inc		D	714 532-1440	0
Tiller Constructors Partnr Inc		D	714 771-5600	0
Transportation Chrtr Svcs Inc		E	714 396-0346	0
Unisource Discovery LLC **(PA)**		D	888 248-0020	0
United Spectrum Inc		E	714 283-1010	0
Universal Cylinder Exch Inc		D	714 744-1036	0
University California Irvine		A	714 456-6170	0
University California Irvine		A	714 456-6011	0
University California Irvine		A	714 456-5558	0
Valori Sand & Gravel Company **(PA)**		D	714 637-0104	0
Van Grow Jack S MD		E	714 564-3300	0
Vandorpe Chou Associates Inc		E	714 978-9780	0
VCA Code Group		E	714 363-4700	0
Village Nurseries Whl LLC **(PA)**		E	714 279-3100	0
Volt Management Corp		B	714 921-7460	0
Volt Management Corp		C	714 921-8800	0
W Corporation		C	714 532-8800	0
Walswrth Frnklin Bevins McCall **(PA)**		D	714 634-2522	0
West Coast Firestopping Inc		D	714 935-1104	0
Western Dental Services Inc **(HQ)**		D	714 480-3000	0
Western Pacific Distrg LLC		C	714 974-6837	0
Word & Brown Insurance		C	714 567-4398	0
Wsp USA Inc		D	714 973-4880	0
Xpo Logistics Freight Inc		D	714 282-7717	0
Zettler Components Inc **(PA)**		C	949 831-5000	0

ORANGE COVE, CA - Fresno County

	SIC	EMP	PHONE	ENTRY #
Booth Ranches LLC		D	559 626-4472	0
Cecelia Packing Corporation		C	559 626-5000	0
Nnncc Ranch		D	559 626-4890	0
United Health Ctrs San Joaquin		D	559 626-4031	0

ORANGEVALE, CA - Sacramento County

	SIC	EMP	PHONE	ENTRY #
Fountainwood Residential Care		D	916 988-2200	0
MA Steiner Construction Inc		D	916 988-6300	0
Summerville At Hazel Creek LLC		A	916 988-7901	0

ORCUTT, CA - Santa Barbara County

	SIC	EMP	PHONE	ENTRY #
Orcutt Lions Club		D	805 937-0158	0
Spiess Construction Co Inc		D	805 937-5859	0

ORINDA, CA - Contra Costa County

	SIC	EMP	PHONE	ENTRY #
Agemark Corporation **(PA)**		D	925 257-4671	0
First Republic Bank		C	925 254-8993	0
Miramnte High Schl Parents CLB		C	925 280-3965	0
Orinda Convalescent Hospital		D	925 254-6500	0
Orinda Country Club		D	925 254-4313	0
Van Inn II Inc **(PA)**		D	510 548-6600	0

ORLAND, CA - Glenn County

	SIC	EMP	PHONE	ENTRY #
Glenn County Office Education		D	530 865-1145	0
Honey Olivarez Bees Inc		D	530 865-0298	0
Lassen Land Co		E	530 865-7676	0
Omega Walnut Inc		E	530 865-0136	0
Pacific Gas and Electric Co		C	530 865-4461	0

OROSI, CA - Tulare County

	SIC	EMP	PHONE	ENTRY #
Abe-El Produce		B	559 528-3030	0
Mountain View AG Services Inc		A	559 528-6004	0

OROVILLE, CA - Butte County

	SIC	EMP	PHONE	ENTRY #
1000 Executive Parkway LLC		C	530 533-7335	0
Artists of River Town		D	530 534-7690	0
County of Butte		C	530 538-7661	0
County of Butte		A	530 538-7572	0
County of Butte		B	530 538-6802	0
County of Butte		A	530 538-7711	0
Evergreen At Oroville LLC		D	530 533-7335	0
Feather Rver Recreation Pk Dst		D	530 533-2011	0

	SIC	EMP	PHONE	ENTRY #
Mooretown Rancheria		B	530 533-3885	0
Mooretown Rancheria **(PA)**		E	530 533-3625	0
Orohealth Corporation		A	530 534-9183	0
Oroville Hospital		D	530 538-8700	0
Oroville Internal Meds Group		E	530 538-3171	0
Pacific Gas and Electric Co		C	530 532-4093	0
Peter J Wolk MD		E	530 534-6517	0
Recology Inc		D	530 533-5868	0
Shadowbrook Health Care Inc		E	530 534-1353	0
South Feather Water & Pwr Agcy **(PA)**		D	530 533-4578	0
The For Work Training Center		E	530 534-1112	0
Tyme Maidu Tribe-Berry Creek		A	530 534-4560	0
Youth For Change		D	530 538-8347	0

OXNARD, CA - Ventura County

	SIC	EMP	PHONE	ENTRY #
AG Rx **(PA)**		D	805 487-0696	0
Alliedbarton Security Svcs LLC		D	805 983-1204	0
Apria Healthcare LLC		C	805 278-6700	0
Aptos Berry Farms Inc		D	831 726-3256	0
Arizona Channel Isla		D	480 788-0755	0
Ava Enterprises Inc		E	805 988-0192	0
Ayala Drywall		E	805 487-3392	0
Blois Construction Inc		C	805 485-0011	0
Boskovich Farms Inc **(PA)**		C	805 487-2299	0
Boyd & Associates		D	805 988-8298	0
California Resources Prod Corp		D	805 483-8017	0
Channel Islnds Vegetable Farms **(PA)**		D	805 984-1910	0
Child Development Resources of **(PA)**		C	805 485-7878	0
Chiquita Fresh North Amer LLC		B	954 924-5642	0
City Impact Inc		D	805 983-3636	0
City of Oxnard		D	805 385-8019	0
City of Oxnard		D	805 385-8136	0
City of Oxnard		D	805 385-7950	0
City of Oxnard		D	805 983-4653	0
Clinicas Del Camino Real Inc		D	805 487-5351	0
Coalition For Family Harmony		D	805 983-6014	0
Conroy Farms Inc		B	805 981-0537	0
County of Ventura		C	805 385-8654	0
County of Ventura		E	805 240-2701	0
Courtyard Oxnard		D	805 988-3600	0
Covenant Care California LLC		C	805 488-3696	0
Covenant Players **(PA)**		C	805 486-7155	0
Deardorff-Jackson Co		E	805 487-7801	0
Dignity Health		A	805 988-2500	0
Dw Berry Farms LLC		B	805 795-8403	0
Etchandy Farms LLC		D	805 983-4700	0
Fame Systems Inc		E	805 485-0808	0
Family Circle Inc		D	805 385-4180	0
Federal Express Corporation		D	800 463-3339	0
Fedex Ground Package Sys Inc		D	800 463-3339	0
Fresh Venture Farms LLC		D	805 754-4449	0
G P M M Money Centers Inc		E	619 288-7607	0
Gama Berry Farms LLC		D	805 483-1000	0
Geek Squad Inc		D	805 278-9555	0
Gibbs International Inc **(PA)**		C	805 485-0551	0
Gill Transport LLC		B	805 240-1979	0
Gills Onions LLC		D	805 240-1983	0
Glenwood Corporation		D	805 983-0305	0
Gmh Inc		E	805 485-1410	0
Golden Living LLC		D	805 983-0305	0
Grolink Plant Company Inc **(PA)**		C	805 984-7958	0
H & F Grain Farms LLC		D	805 754-4449	0
HE Julien & Associates Inc		E	805 488-8342	0
High Tide and Green Grass Inc		D	805 981-8722	0
ICI Services Corporation		B	805 988-3210	0
Insurance Services Amercn LLC		D	805 981-2220	0
Js Hospitality Group LLC		D	805 988-3600	0
Jsl Technologies Inc		B	805 985-7700	0
Kaiser Foundation Hospitals		A	888 515-3500	0
Kaiser Foundation Hospitals		A	805 988-6300	0
Kindred Healthcare Oper Inc		D	805 487-7840	0
Koxr Spanish Radio		E	805 487-0444	0
Labaya Beachcomber LP		C	805 278-6688	0
Marathon Land Inc **(PA)**		C	805 488-3585	0
Mariz Berry Farms		C	805 981-9908	0
Maxim Healthcare Services Inc		A	805 278-4593	0
Merrill Lynch Pierce Fenner		C	800 964-5182	0
Milwood Healthcare Inc		D	626 274-4345	0
Mission Linen Supply		C	805 485-6794	0
Mission Produce Inc		C	805 981-3650	0
New York Life Insurance Co		E	805 656-4598	0
Nordman Cormany Hair & Compton		C	805 485-1000	0
Oceanview Produce Company		C	805 488-6401	0
Olde Thompson LLC		C	805 983-0388	0
Oxnard Manor Healthcare Ctr LP		D	805 983-0324	0
Oxnard Perfrmn Arts & Convtn		E	805 486-2424	0

Employment Codes: A=Over 500 employees, B=251-500, C=101-250, D=51-100, E=50

2020 Directory of California
Wholesalers and Services Companies

© Mergent Inc. 1-800-342-5647

1591

GEOGRAPHIC

	SIC	EMP	PHONE	ENTRY #
Pacific Coast Produce Inc		E	805 240-3385	0
Pacific Labor Services Inc		E	805 488-4625	0
Pleasant Valley Flowers Inc		B	805 986-2776	0
Pratt Industries Inc		E	805 483-5331	0
Primal Nutrition LLC		E	310 317-4414	0
Pyramid Flowers Inc		C	805 382-8070	0
Quinn Company		D	805 485-2171	0
Quinn Group Inc		D	805 485-2171	0
Ramco Enterprises LP		A	805 486-9328	0
Recp Cy Oxnard LLC		D	805 604-7527	0
Recp RI Oxnard LLC		C	805 278-2200	0
Republic Services		D	805 385-8060	0
Rescue Mission Alliance (PA)		D	805 487-1234	0
Rescue Mission Alliance		E	805 201-4341	0
River Ridge Farms Inc		D	805 647-6880	0
River Ridge Golf Club		B	805 981-8724	0
SA Recycling LLC		D	805 486-7525	0
Safeguard Business Systems Inc		C	805 486-9769	0
San Miguel Produce Inc		B	805 488-0981	0
Santa Rosa Berry Farms LLC		B	805 981-3060	0
Saticoy Lemon Association		E	805 654-6543	0
Scarborough Farms Inc		C	805 483-9113	0
Scorpion Athc Booster CLB Inc		E	805 482-2005	0
Sea View Medical Group Inc		D	805 373-5781	0
Seaboard Produce Distrs Inc		D	805 981-8001	0
Seminis Inc (DH)		B	805 485-7317	0
Seminis Vegetable Seeds Inc (DH)		A	855 733-3834	0
State Compensation Insur Fund		B	888 782-8338	0
Sunrise Ranch		D	805 488-0813	0
Sunshine Floral LLC		D	805 982-8822	0
Superior Fruit LLC		C	805 485-2519	0
Synectic Solutions Inc (PA)		D	805 483-4800	0
Sysco Ventura Inc		B	805 205-7000	0
Systems Application & Tech Inc		D	805 487-7373	0
T M Mian & Associates Inc		D	805 983-8600	0
Tanimura & Antle Inc		D	805 483-2358	0
Topstar Floral Inc		E	805 984-7972	0
Toro Enterprises Inc		D	805 483-4515	0
Tradewind Seafood Inc		E	805 483-8555	0
Tri County Regional Center		D	805 485-3177	0
Venco Western Inc (PA)		C	805 981-2400	0
Ventura Cnty Council On Aging		D	805 986-1424	0
Ventura County Hematology (PA)		E	805 485-8709	0
Veterans Health Administration		B	805 983-6384	0
Volt Management Corp		C	805 485-0506	0
West Flower Growers		D	805 488-0814	0
Western Precooling Systems		D	805 486-6371	0
Windsor Capital Group Inc		D	805 988-0627	0
Wonderful Citrus Packing LLC		D	805 988-1456	0
Workrite Uniform Company Inc (DH)		B	805 483-0175	0

PACHECO, CA - Contra Costa County

	SIC	EMP	PHONE	ENTRY #
Hertz Corporation		D	925 680-0316	0
Pleasant HI Byshore Dspsal Inc		C	925 685-4711	0
Universal Bldg Svcs & Sup Co		C	925 934-5533	0

PACIFIC GROVE, CA - Monterey County

	SIC	EMP	PHONE	ENTRY #
Aramark Services Inc		C	831 372-8016	0
Covia Communities		D	831 373-3111	0
Gateway Ctr of Monterey Cnty (PA)		D	831 372-8002	0
K&M Construction		D	831 643-2819	0
Pacific Grove Aslmar Oper Corp		C	831 372-8016	0
Pacific Grove Cnvalescent Hosp		D	831 375-2695	0
Rotary CLB PCF Grove Char Fund		D	831 372-3877	0

PACIFIC PALISADES, CA - Los Angeles County

	SIC	EMP	PHONE	ENTRY #
Atria Senior Living Inc		D	310 573-9545	0
Bel-Air Bay Club Ltd		C	310 230-4700	0
Fusionzone Automotive Inc		E	888 576-1136	0
Get Heal Inc		D	310 528-4957	0
Lighthouse Capital Funding		E	310 230-8335	0
Palisades Optimist Foundation		D	310 454-4111	0
Santa Monica Bay Physcians		C	310 459-2363	0
State Farm Mutl Auto Insur Co		D	310 454-0349	0

PACIFICA, CA - San Mateo County

	SIC	EMP	PHONE	ENTRY #
Cal-Pacific Construction Inc		E	650 557-1238	0
City of Pacifica-Vallemar		D	650 738-7466	0
Little Giant Bldg Maint Inc		C	415 508-0282	0
Ortega Elementary Pto		D	650 738-6670	0
Pacific Engineering Builders		D	650 557-1238	0
Pacifica Care Center		C	650 355-5622	0
Pacifica Linda Mar Inc		D	650 359-4800	0
Pyramid Alternatives Inc (PA)		E	650 355-8787	0

PACOIMA, CA - Los Angeles County

	SIC	EMP	PHONE	ENTRY #
County of Los Angeles		C	818 896-1903	0

	SIC	EMP	PHONE	ENTRY #
CPI Luxury Group		D	818 249-9888	0
Global Emergency Road Svc LLC		E	818 518-1166	0
Gonzalez Management Co Inc		D	818 485-0596	0
Hillview Mental Health Center		D	818 896-1161	0
Hope of Valley Rescue Mission		D	818 392-0020	0
Looney Bins Inc (PA)		D	818 485-8200	0
Northeast Valley Health Corp		D	818 896-0531	0
Phillips Plywood Co Inc		D	818 897-7736	0
Scenic Route Inc		E	818 896-6006	0
Volunteers of Amer Los Angeles		C	818 834-9097	0
Volunteers of Amer Los Angeles		C	818 834-8957	0
Wetzel & Sons Moving and Stor		D	818 890-0992	0
Xpo Logistics Freight Inc		C	818 890-2095	0

PALA, CA - San Diego County

	SIC	EMP	PHONE	ENTRY #
Pala Casino Spa & Resort		A	760 510-5100	0

PALM DESERT, CA - Riverside County

	SIC	EMP	PHONE	ENTRY #
Ambiente Enterprises Inc		C	760 674-1905	0
American Golf Corporation		E	760 568-9311	0
Atria Senior Living Inc		D	760 341-0890	0
Bank America National Assn		C	760 636-7500	0
Bighorn Golf Club		C	760 773-2468	0
California Closet Co O		D	760 773-4784	0
CJ Construction & Dev Inc		D	760 247-6868	0
Claro Pool Services Inc		D	760 341-3377	0
Coachella Valley Water Dst		C	760 398-2651	0
Coachella Valley Water Dst		C	760 398-2651	0
Coldwell Bnkr Residential Brkg		D	760 776-9898	0
Cora Constructors Inc		E	760 674-3201	0
Cove Electric Inc		D	760 568-9924	0
Danny Mahagna Shapprie		E	760 341-5070	0
Dave Williams Plbg & Elec Inc		C	760 296-1397	0
Desert Falls Country Club Inc		D	760 340-5646	0
Desert Resort Management		D	760 831-0172	0
Desert Television LLC		D	760 343-5700	0
Desert Willow Golf Resort Inc		C	760 346-0015	0
Desertarc		B	760 346-1611	0
Destination Residences LLC		E	760 346-4647	0
Dlo Enterprises Inc		D	760 346-8033	0
Emerald Brook LLC		E	760 345-4770	0
Enterprise Rent-A-Car		D	760 772-0281	0
Entravsion Communications Corp		D	760 568-3636	0
F M Tarbell Co		E	760 346-7405	0
First Team RE - Orange Cnty		D	760 340-9911	0
Friends of Cultural Center Inc		D	760 346-6505	0
Gary Cardiff Enterprises Inc		D	760 568-1403	0
Host Hotels & Resorts LP		D	760 341-2211	0
Kaiser Foundation Hospitals		A	800 777-1256	0
Kaiser Foundation Hospitals		A	866 984-7483	0
Kaiser Foundation Hospitals		D	760 360-1475	0
Lakes Country Club Assn Inc (PA)		B	760 568-4321	0
Leighton Group Inc		C	760 776-4192	0
Living Desert		C	760 346-5694	0
Marrakesh Management Corp		E	760 568-2688	0
Marriott Rsrts Hspitality Corp		D	760 779-1200	0
Marriotts Shadow Ridge		D	760 674-2600	0
Oasis Palm Dsert Hmowners Assn		D	760 345-5661	0
Odyssey Healthcare Inc		E	760 674-0066	0
Oj Insulation LP		D	760 200-4343	0
Olive Crest		D	760 341-8507	0
Palm Desert Greens Association		D	760 346-8005	0
Palm Dsert Rcrtl Fclities Corp		D	760 346-0015	0
Paul Williams Tile Co Inc		D	760 772-7440	0
Platinum Landscape Inc		C	760 200-3673	0
Premier Residential Svcs LLC		D	760 773-4081	0
Quarry At La Quinta Inc (PA)		D	760 777-1100	0
Renova Energy Corp		E	760 568-3413	0
Residence Inn By Marriott LLC		C	760 776-0050	0
Resort Parking Services Inc		C	760 328-4041	0
Securitas SEC Svcs USA Inc		C	559 221-2302	0
Shamrock-Hostmark Palm Desrt		D	760 340-6600	0
Sun City Palm Dsert Cmnty Assn (PA)		D	760 200-2100	0
Sunrise Desert Partners		D	760 404-1280	0
Sunrise Desert Partners (PA)		C	760 772-7227	0
Sunrise Senior Living Inc		D	760 340-5999	0
Sunrise Senior Living LLC		D	760 346-5420	0
Toscana Homes LP		E	760 772-7227	0
Toscana Land LLC		D	760 772-7200	0
United Brothers Concrete Inc		C	760 346-1013	0
Visitng Nurse Assn Inlnd CNT		C	760 346-3982	0
Watermark Rtrment Cmmnties Inc		D	760 346-5420	0
West Coast Turf (PA)		E	760 340-7300	0
West Ville Palm Desert		E	760 346-2121	0
Westin Desert Willow		D	760 636-7003	0

Mergent email: customerrelations@mergent.com
1592

2020 Directory of California
Wholesalers and Services Companies

(P-0000) Products & Services Section entry number
(PA)=Parent Co (HQ)=Headquarters (DH)=Div Headquarters

PALM SPRINGS, CA - Riverside County

	SIC	EMP	PHONE	ENTRY #
A & A Home Care Services		D	760 416-6769	0
A A A Five Star Adventures		E	760 320-1500	0
Agua Caliente Development Auth		D	760 699-6800	0
Agua Clnte Band Chilla Indians (PA)		C	760 699-6800	0
Agua Clnte Band Chilla Indians		A	800 854-1279	0
American Medical Response Inc		D	760 883-5000	0
Angel View Inc		E	760 322-2440	0
Brudvik Inc (PA)		D	760 320-4429	0
California Nursing and Rehab		D	760 325-2937	0
Cardinal Health Inc		D	951 360-2199	0
City of Palm Springs		D	760 318-3800	0
Cnrc LLC		D	760 325-2937	0
Coldwell Bnkr Residential Brkg		D	760 325-4500	0
Colony Palms Hotel LLC		D	760 969-1800	0
County of Riverside Department		D	760 320-1048	0
Crestline Hotels & Resorts LLC		D	760 322-6000	0
Desert Aids Project (PA)		D	760 323-2118	0
Desert Air Conditioning Inc		E	760 323-3383	0
Desert Arts Center		D	760 323-7973	0
Desert Medical Group Inc (PA)		D	760 320-8814	0
Desert Medical Group Inc		C	760 323-8657	0
Desert Regional Med Ctr Inc (HQ)		A	760 323-6511	0
Desert Regional Med Ctr Inc		C	760 323-6640	0
Desert Water Agency Fing Corp		D	760 323-4971	0
Diamond Resorts LLC		D	760 866-1800	0
Ensign Palm I LLC		D	760 323-2638	0
Federal Express Corporation		C	800 463-3339	0
First Student Inc		D	760 320-4659	0
Five Star Quality Care Inc		D	760 327-8541	0
HHC Trs Portsmouth LLC		D	760 322-6000	0
Hilton Resort Palm Springs		C	760 320-6868	0
Hyatt Hotels Management Corp		C	760 322-9000	0
Interstate Hotels Resorts Inc		C	760 322-7000	0
Jack Parker Corp		C	760 770-5000	0
Joseph Dipuzo		E	760 325-1200	0
Kaiser Foundation Hospitals		D	866 370-1942	0
Kings Garden LLC		D	760 275-4969	0
Kittridge Hotels & Resorts LLC		D	760 325-9676	0
Loandepotcom LLC		A	760 797-6000	0
M C Builder Corp		E	760 323-8010	0
Morrison MGT Specialists Inc		D	760 323-6296	0
Mount San Jacinto Win Pk Auth		D	760 325-1449	0
Palm Springs Art Museum Inc		D	760 322-4800	0
Palm Springs Disposal Services		D	760 327-1351	0
R P S Resort Corp		C	760 327-8311	0
Remington Hotel Corporation		D	760 322-6000	0
Riviera Reincarnate LLC		D	760 327-8311	0
S S W Mechanical Cnstr Inc		C	760 327-1481	0
Seven Lakes Hm Assn Cntry CLB		E	760 328-2695	0
Smg Holdings Inc		D	760 325-6611	0
Smoke Tree Inc		D	760 327-1221	0
Spa Resort Casino (PA)		A	888 999-1995	0
Springs Ambulance Service Inc.		D	760 883-5000	0
Sunrise Senior Living LLC		D	760 322-3444	0
Temalpakh Inc		D	760 770-5778	0
United Airlines Inc		D	760 778-5690	0
United Parcel Service Inc OH		B	760 325-1762	0
VCA Desert Animal Hospitals		D	760 778-9999	0
Walters Family Partnership		D	760 320-6868	0
Wyndham International Inc		C	760 322-6000	0

PALMDALE, CA - Los Angeles County

	SIC	EMP	PHONE	ENTRY #
Antelope Valley Country Club		C	661 947-3142	0
Antelope Valley Mall		D	661 266-9150	0
Antelope Valley Recycling		D	661 945-5944	0
Cellco Partnership		D	661 274-2112	0
Child and Family Guidance Ctr		D	661 265-8627	0
Child Care Resource Center Inc		E	661 723-3246	0
City of Palmdale		C	661 267-5338	0
Colsa Corporation		D	661 273-3859	0
County of Los Angeles		C	661 947-7173	0
Csi Electrical Contractors Inc		D	661 723-0869	0
Delta Scientific Corporation (PA)		C	661 575-1100	0
Forest City Rental Prpts Corp		D	661 266-9150	0
Jacobs Engineering Group Inc		D	661 275-5685	0
Lou Bozigian		D	661 948-4737	0
Palmdale Center For Pain MGT		E	661 267-6876	0
Palmdale Resort Inc		D	661 947-8055	0
Palmdale Water District		D	661 947-4111	0
Palmdale Womans Club		D	661 266-3008	0
Penny Lane Centers		C	818 892-3423	0
People Creating Success Inc		D	661 225-9700	0
Primerica Life Insurance Co		C	661 947-9070	0
Smart & Final Stores Inc		B	661 722-6210	0

	SIC	EMP	PHONE	ENTRY #
Sunstone Hotel Investors LLC		C	661 267-6587	0
Tarzana Treatment Centers Inc		C	818 654-3815	0
Vista Home Health Service Inc		D	818 701-1877	0
Waste Management Cal Inc		D	661 947-7197	0
Xi Enterprise Inc		D	661 266-3200	0

PALO ALTO, CA - Santa Clara County

	SIC	EMP	PHONE	ENTRY #
4290 El Camino Properties LP		C	650 857-0787	0
Abilities United (PA)		D	650 494-0550	0
Actian Corporation (PA)		D	650 587-5500	0
Activehours Inc		C	650 272-4083	0
Adaptive Insghts LLC A Workday (HQ)		C	650 528-7500	0
Adara Inc (PA)		D	408 876-6360	0
Affymax Research Institute		E	650 812-8700	0
Alain Pinel Realtors Inc		C	650 323-1111	0
Arable Corporation		D	650 331-1401	0
Ariba Inc (DH)		C	650 849-4000	0
Arnold Porter Kaye Scholer LLP		C	650 319-4500	0
Autonomic LLC (PA)		D	650 823-1806	0
Avenidas (PA)		D	650 289-5400	0
Azumio Inc (PA)		C	719 310-3774	0
Baker & McKenzie LLP		C	650 856-2400	0
Beauty Bazar Inc		D	650 326-8522	0
Beneficent Technology Inc		E	650 644-3400	0
Bex Portfolio LLC		D	650 494-3700	0
Billcom Inc		C	650 353-3301	0
Bml Works Na LLC		D	650 268-8305	0
Bpr Properties Berkeley LLC		C	650 424-1400	0
Broadrach Cpitl Prtners Fund I		A	650 331-2500	0
Broadreach Capitl Partners LLC (PA)		A	650 331-2500	0
Bytedance Inc		D	844 523-3993	0
California Land Mgt Svcs Corp (PA)		E	650 322-1181	0
Cambridge Design Partnr Inc		D	650 387-7812	0
Cardic Arithmias		E	650 617-8100	0
Cc-Palo Alto Inc		C	650 853-5000	0
Cellco Partnership		D	650 323-6127	0
Channing House		D	650 327-0950	0
City of Palo Alto		D	650 329-2598	0
Cloudera Inc (PA)		C	650 362-0488	0
Community Housing Inc		E	650 328-3300	0
Convrgd Data Tech Inc		C	650 461-4488	0
Cooley LLP (PA)		B	650 843-5000	0
Cooley LLP		C	650 843-5124	0
Covenant Care California LLC		D	415 327-0511	0
Datasafe Inc		E	650 875-3800	0
Declara Inc		D	650 800-7695	0
Dentons US LLP		D	650 798-0300	0
Dlight Design Inc		A	415 872-6136	0
Document Technologies LLC		D	650 485-2705	0
E3 Healthcare Management LLC		D	650 324-0600	0
Electric Power RES Inst Inc (PA)		A	650 855-2000	0
End To End Analytics LLC		D	650 331-9659	0
Eprisolutions Inc		D	650 855-8900	0
Ernst & Young LLP		C	650 496-1600	0
Essential Products Inc		D	650 300-0000	0
F-Secure Inc		E	888 432-8233	0
Family & Children Services		D	650 326-6576	0
Ferrado Garden Court LLC		D	650 543-2224	0
Fiorano Software Inc		D	650 326-1136	0
Foley & Lardner LLP		C	650 856-3700	0
Garden Court Hotel		D	650 322-9000	0
Genomic Health Inc		B	650 269-0545	0
Genpact LLC		E	203 690-9308	0
Gibson Dunn & Crutcher LLP		C	650 849-5300	0
Gordon Betty Moore Foundation		D	650 213-3000	0
Gordon E Btty I More Fundation		D	650 213-3000	0
Harris Mycfo Inc		D	480 348-7725	0
Haynes and Boone LLP		D	650 687-8800	0
Henderson Finnegan Farabow		D	650 849-6600	0
Hercules Capital Inc (PA)		D	650 289-3060	0
Hewlett Packard		A	650 857-1501	0
Houzz Inc (PA)		D	650 326-3000	0
Hyatt Hotels Management Corp		B	650 352-1234	0
Ideo LP (PA)		B	650 289-3400	0
Insignia Environmental		D	650 321-6787	0
Instabug Inc		D	650 422-9555	0
Instart Logic Inc (PA)		D	888 418-5044	0
Insulation Sources Inc (PA)		D	650 856-8378	0
Intapp Inc (DH)		D	650 852-0400	0
Integral Development Corp (PA)		C	650 424-4500	0
Intellectual Ventures LLC		B	650 941-1330	0
Jewish Family and Chld Svcs		D	650 931-1860	0
Jewish Family and Chld Svcs		D	650 688-3030	0
Joguru Inc		D	855 526-4332	0
Jones Day Limited Partnership		D	650 739-3939	0
Kawela One LLC		D	650 843-5000	0

GEOGRAPHIC

Name	SIC	EMP	PHONE	ENTRY #
Leland Stanford Junior Univ		C	650 723-6254	0
Leland Stanford Junior Univ		E	650 723-2997	0
Leland Stanford Junior Univ		B	650 723-7546	0
Leland Stanford Junior Univ		A	650 725-2377	0
Leland Stanford Junior Univ		A	650 723-4000	0
Leland Stanford Junior Univ		D	650 725-4416	0
Leland Stanford Junior Univ		A	650 725-4617	0
Leland Stanford Junior Univ		D	650 723-4733	0
LLP Mayer Brown		A	650 331-2000	0
Lowenstein Sandler LLP		E	650 433-5800	0
Lucideus Inc		C	650 843-0988	0
Lucile Packard Childrens Hosp		D	650 321-2545	0
Lucile Salter Packard Chil (PA)		D	650 497-8000	0
Luminar Technologies Inc		D	650 849-8797	0
Machine Zone Inc (PA)		D	650 320-1678	0
Map Energy LLC		D	650 324-9095	0
Marcus Millichap Corp RE Svcs (HQ)		D	650 391-1700	0
Maximus Holdings Inc		A	650 935-9500	0
McKinsey & Company Inc		D	650 494-6262	0
Menlo Security Inc (PA)		D	650 614-1705	0
Merrill Lynch Pierce Fenner		D	650 842-2440	0
Metricstream Inc (PA)		C	650 620-2900	0
Metricus Inc		C	650 328-2500	0
Morgan Lewis & Bockius LLP		D	650 843-4000	0
Morrison & Foerster LLP		B	650 813-5600	0
Movocash Inc		E	650 722-3990	0
My Ally Inc		D	650 387-9118	0
Nest Labs Inc		D	855 469-6378	0
Norwest Venture Partners VI LP		D	650 289-2243	0
Npario Inc		D	650 461-9696	0
Nuevacare LLC		D	650 396-3596	0
Oak Creek Apartments		E	650 327-1600	0
Odyssey Telecorp Inc		C	650 470-7550	0
Oshman Family Jewish Cmnty Ctr		C	650 223-8700	0
Pacific Hotel Dev Ventr LP		C	650 347-8260	0
Pacific Hotel Management LLC		B	650 328-2800	0
Pacific Specialty Insurance Co		E	800 303-5000	0
Packard Childrens Hlth Aliance		D	650 497-8000	0
Packard Medical Group Inc		D	650 724-3637	0
Pahc Apartments Inc		E	650 321-9709	0
Palantir Technologies Inc (PA)		C	650 815-0200	0
Palantir Usg Inc (HQ)		C	650 815-0200	0
Palmetto Hospitality		D	650 843-0795	0
Palo Alto Commons		D	650 320-8626	0
Palo Alto Family Y M C A		E	650 856-9622	0
Palo Alto Hills Golf An		D	650 948-1800	0
Palo Alto Medical Clinic		D	650 321-4121	0
Palo Alto Medical Foundation (HQ)		A	650 321-4121	0
Palo Alto Medical Foundation		E	650 326-8120	0
Palo Alto Research Center Inc		C	650 812-4000	0
Palo Alto Vterans Inst For RES		C	650 858-3970	0
Paul Hastings LLP		C	650 320-1800	0
Paycycle Inc		D	866 729-2925	0
Perkins Coie LLP		C	415 725-1313	0
Pillsbury Winthrop Shaw		C	650 233-4500	0
Plume Design Inc		D	408 498-5512	0
Precision Ideo Inc		B	650 688-3400	0
Primerica Life Insurance Co		C	650 323-2554	0
R H O Capital Partners Inc		E	650 463-0300	0
Robert Half International Inc		D	650 812-9790	0
Rubrik Inc (PA)		D	650 300-5862	0
Sap Labs LLC		D	650 849-4000	0
Sap Labs LLC (DH)		B	650 849-4000	0
Science Exchange Inc (PA)		D	562 665-8978	0
Sharethis Inc (PA)		E	650 641-0191	0
Shopping Center Mgt Corp		D	650 617-8234	0
Sidley Austin LLP		D	650 565-7000	0
Simpson Thacher & Bartlett LLP		C	650 251-5000	0
Sitetracker Inc		D	408 838-9419	0
Skoll Foundation		E	650 331-1031	0
Skype Inc		D	650 493-7900	0
Space Systems/Loral LLC (DH)		D	650 852-7320	0
Stanford Federal Credit Union (PA)		D	650 725-1000	0
Stanford Health Care		A	650 736-7844	0
Stanford Health Care Primary		D	650 723-6963	0
Stanford Hospital and Clinics		A	650 213-8360	0
Stratford School Inc (PA)		E	650 493-1151	0
Striim Inc		E	425 894-1998	0
Suning Cmmerce R D Ctr USA Inc		D	650 834-9800	0
Sutter Health		B	650 853-2975	0
Sutter Health		C	650 853-2904	0
Swaminatha Mahadevan MD		D	650 723-6576	0
Symphony Comm Svcs LLC (PA)		D	650 733-6660	0
Tcv Management 2004 LLC		E	650 614-8200	0
Technology Credit Union		D	650 326-6445	0
Teris-Bay Area LLC		D	650 213-9922	0
Tibco Software Inc		D	650 846-1000	0
Tibco Software Inc (HQ)		C	650 846-1000	0
Total Quality Maintenance Inc		C	650 846-4700	0
Uber Technologies Inc		C	832 610-0359	0
Vcomply Technologies Inc		D	650 319-8842	0
Veterans Health Administration		A	650 493-5000	0
Vinson & Elkins LLP		C	650 617-8400	0
Vmware Inc (DH)		C	650 427-5000	0
Vmware Inc		C	650 812-8200	0
Voyage Auto Inc		D	917 588-1249	0
Watercourse Way		D	650 462-2000	0
Willow Garage Inc		D	650 322-2584	0
Wilson Sonsini Goodrich & Rosa (PA)		A	650 493-9300	0
Wing Aviation LLC		C	650 224-1198	0
Womble Bond Dickinson (us) LLP		C	408 720-8300	0
Xcelmobility Inc		D	650 320-1728	0
Xerox Corporation		D	650 813-6787	0
Xerox Corporation		D	650 813-7138	0
Yubico Inc		C	408 774-4064	0

PALO CEDRO, CA - Shasta County

Name	SIC	EMP	PHONE	ENTRY #
Rotary International		D	530 547-5272	

PALOS VERDES ESTATES, CA - Los Angeles County

Name	SIC	EMP	PHONE	ENTRY #
Malaga Financial Corporation (PA)		D	310 375-9000	0
Palos Verdes Beach & Athc CLB		D	310 375-8777	0
Plantasia Inc		D	310 375-0387	0

PALOS VERDES PENINSU, CA - Los Angeles County

Name	SIC	EMP	PHONE	ENTRY #
County of Los Angeles		B	310 222-2401	0

PANORAMA CITY, CA - Los Angeles County

Name	SIC	EMP	PHONE	ENTRY #
American Protection Group Inc (PA)		C	818 279-2433	0
Creative Technology Group Inc (DH)		D	818 779-2400	0
Deanco Healthcare LLC		A	818 787-2222	0
E2 Corp		D	818 904-5660	0
Ensign Group Inc		C	818 893-6385	0
Golden Living LLC		D	818 893-6385	0
Import Collection (PA)		D	818 782-3060	0
Kaiser Foundation Hospitals		A	818 375-2000	0
Kaiser Foundation Hospitals		A	818 375-2028	0
Panorama Madows Nursing Ctr LP		D	818 894-5707	0
Qmadix Inc		D	818 988-4300	0
Rahf IV Casa Panorama LP		E	216 621-6060	0
Southern Cal Prmnnte Med Group		D	800 272-3500	0
Zodax LP (PA)		D	818 785-5626	0

PARADISE, CA - Butte County

Name	SIC	EMP	PHONE	ENTRY #
Adventist Health System/West		D	530 872-3378	0
Butte Primary Care Med Group		D	530 877-0762	0
Tegtmeier Associates Inc.		D	530 872-7700	0
USA Waste of California Inc		D	530 877-2777	0
Youth For Change (PA)		C	530 877-8187	0

PARAMOUNT, CA - Los Angeles County

Name	SIC	EMP	PHONE	ENTRY #
Advanced Industrial Svcs Inc		D	562 940-8305	0
Aramark Unf & Career AP LLC		D	323 774-4216	0
Asphalt Management Inc.		E	562 630-6811	0
Aylesva Inc		C	562 688-0592	0
Braun Linen Service Inc (PA)		C	909 623-2678	0
Calmet Inc (PA)		C	323 721-8120	0
Cfr Rinkens LLC (PA)		D	310 639-7725	0
Cnet Express		C	949 357-5475	0
Cort Business Services Corp		D	562 582-1515	0
Don Brandel Plumbing Inc		E	562 408-0400	0
Goldenpark LLC		D	562 863-5555	0
M & J Seafood Company Inc		D	562 529-2786	0
MB Herzog Electric Inc		C	562 531-2002	0
Modern Dev Co A Ltd Partnr		D	949 646-6400	0
Mountain Valley Express Co Inc		C	562 630-5500	0
Mv Transportation Inc		D	562 790-8642	0
Paramunt Cnvalescent Group Inc		D	562 634-6895	0
Paramunt Madows Nursing Ctr LP		D	562 531-0990	0
Premier Mailing Inc		E	562 408-2134	0
Reliable Energy Management Inc		D	562 984-5511	0
Schaefer Mary-Judith		D	562 634-3164	0
Telecare Corporation		C	562 633-5111	0
Total-Western Inc (HQ)		E	562 220-1450	0
Triage Partners LLC		D	562 634-0058	0
Vernon Security Inc		D	562 790-8993	0
Vss Sales Inc (PA)		D	562 630-0606	0

PARKER DAM, CA - San Bernardino County

Name	SIC	EMP	PHONE	ENTRY #
Black Meadow Landing		D	760 663-4901	0

PARLIER, CA - Fresno County

Name	SIC	EMP	PHONE	ENTRY #
Custom Produce Sales (PA)		C	559 254-5800	0

Mergent email: customerrelations@mergent.com
1594

2020 Directory of California
Wholesalers and Services Companies

(P-0000) Products & Services Section entry number
(PA)=Parent Co (HQ)=Headquarters (DH)=Div Headquarters

	SIC	EMP	PHONE	ENTRY #
Kozuki Farming Inc		D	559 646-2652	0
Maxco Supply Inc **(PA)**		C	559 646-8449	0
ONeill Beverages Co LLC		C	559 638-3544	0

PASADENA, CA - Los Angeles County

	SIC	EMP	PHONE	ENTRY #
24 Hour Fitness Usa Inc		D	626 795-7121	0
A P H Technological Consulting		E	626 796-0331	0
Aah Hudson LP		A	626 794-9179	0
Ab/SW 70 S Lake Owner LLC		E	650 571-2200	0
Access Pacific Inc		E	626 792-0616	0
Accredited Nursing Services		D	626 573-1234	0
Algos Inc A Medical Corp **(PA)**		D	626 696-1400	0
American General Design		E	626 304-0800	0
American Multi-Cinema Inc		E	626 585-8900	0
American Multimedia TV USA		D	626 466-1038	0
Annandale Golf Club		C	626 796-6125	0
AON Consulting Inc		D	626 683-5200	0
Are- Maryland No 31 LLC		E	626 578-0777	0
Arroyo Seco Medical Group **(PA)**		D	626 795-7556	0
Art & Logic Inc		D	818 500-1933	0
AT&T Corp		D	626 396-0100	0
Atk Space Systems Inc		D	626 351-0205	0
Aurora Las Encinas LLC		C	626 795-9901	0
Avicena LLC **(PA)**		D	626 344-9665	0
Ayzenberg Group Inc		D	626 584-4070	0
B Jacqueline and Assoc Inc		B	626 844-1400	0
Blue Chip Stamps		A	626 585-6700	0
Bluebeam Inc **(PA)**		C	626 788-4100	0
Boston Brick & Stone Inc		E	626 269-2622	0
Brighton Convalescent Center		D	626 798-9124	0
Brookfield Dtla Fund Office		D	626 792-2727	0
C W Driver Incorporated **(PA)**		D	626 351-8800	0
California Convalescent Hosptl		D	626 793-5114	0
California Credits Group LLC		E	626 584-9800	0
California Institute Tech		A	818 354-9154	0
California Institute Tech		C	626 395-8700	0
California Institute Tech		D	626 395-8200	0
California Linen Services		D	626 564-4576	0
Camellia Gardens Care Ctr		D	626 798-6777	0
Carnegie Institution Wash		D	626 577-1122	0
Casecentral Inc **(DH)**		D	415 989-2300	0
Century 21 Golden Realty **(PA)**		D	626 797-6680	0
Charles Pankow Bldrs Ltd A Cal **(PA)**		E	626 304-1190	0
CIT Bank NA **(HQ)**		D	626 859-5400	0
Citizens Business Bank		E	626 577-1700	0
City of Pasadena		D	626 744-4311	0
City of Pasadena		D	626 543-4708	0
Community Hlth Alance Pasadena **(PA)**		D	626 398-6300	0
Congress Med Surgery Ctr LLC		D	626 396-8100	0
County of Los Angeles		C	626 356-5281	0
County of Los Angeles		D	626 229-3825	0
County of Los Angeles		D	626 356-5281	0
Cpo Commerce LLC		D	626 585-3600	0
D & C Care Center Inc		D	626 798-1175	0
Dallas Union Hotel Inc		C	626 356-1000	0
David Ross Inc		D	323 684-7673	0
Dilbeck Inc		D	626 584-0101	0
Discoverorg Data LLC		D	360 783-6924	0
Diversified Health Svcs Del		E	626 798-6753	0
Dowling Advisory Group		D	626 319-1369	0
Dy-Dee Service Pasadena Inc		D	626 792-6183	0
Dydee Service of Pasedena		D	626 240-0115	0
E Z Data Inc **(HQ)**		D	626 585-3505	0
East West Bank **(HQ)**		A	626 768-6000	0
Econnections Inc		C	626 307-6200	0
Electric Svc & Sup Co Pasadena		D	626 795-8641	0
Emmis Communications Corp		C	626 484-4440	0
Employee Benefits Security ADM		D	626 229-1000	0
Energy Innovations Inc		C	626 585-6900	0
Environmental Science Assoc		B	626 204-6170	0
Fed Air Security Corporation		D	626 535-2200	0
Financial Healthcare Services		E	626 356-7950	0
First Foundation Inc		D	626 993-1300	0
Founders Healthcare LLC		D	626 683-5401	0
Front Porch Communities		D	626 796-8162	0
Further Products Inc		E	323 839-1246	0
Garda CL West Inc		D	800 883-8305	0
Gates of Spain Wibel		E	626 441-3078	0
Gem Transitional Care Center		D	626 737-0560	0
Gemalto Cogent Inc **(DH)**		E	626 325-9600	0
Glenn Building Services Inc		D	626 398-8000	0
Golden Cross Care Inc		C	626 791-1948	0
Golds Gym International Inc		D	626 304-1133	0
Gonzalez/Goodale Architects		D	626 568-1428	0
Good Works LLC		D	626 584-8130	0
Grandcare Health Services LLC **(PA)**		C	866 554-2447	0
Green Dot Corporation **(PA)**		D	626 765-2000	0
Greensoft Technology Inc		C	323 254-5961	0
Grizzard Cmmncations Group Inc		D	818 543-1315	0
Gs1 Group Inc		D	626 510-6384	0
Gsg Associates Inc		D	626 585-1808	0
Guidance Software Inc **(HQ)**		C	626 229-9191	0
Hahn & Hahn LLP		D	626 796-9123	0
Hathaway-Sycamores Chld Fam Sv **(PA)**		D	626 395-7100	0
Heilwell Gad MD		D	626 817-4747	0
Hertz Claim Management Corp		D	626 296-4760	0
Hillsides		B	323 254-2274	0
Holthouse Carlin Van Trigt LLP		D	626 243-5100	0
Hunt Ortmann Palffy Nieves		E	626 440-5200	0
Huntington Ambltry Surg Ctr		E	626 229-8999	0
Huntington Care LLC		B	877 405-6990	0
Huntington Med Res Institutes		D	626 397-5804	0
Huntington Otptent Surgery Ctr		D	626 535-2434	0
Huntington Reprodctve Ctr Inc **(PA)**		E	626 204-9699	0
Idealab Holdings LLC **(PA)**		A	626 585-6900	0
Imagescan Inc		D	626 844-2050	0
Integro USA Inc		E	626 795-9000	0
Inter-Con Investigators Inc		D	626 535-2200	0
Inter-Con Security Systems Inc **(PA)**		C	626 535-2200	0
Interntional Un Oper Engineers		E	626 792-2519	0
Interprsnal Dvlpmntal Fclttors		D	626 793-8967	0
Invitation Homes Inc		D	805 372-2900	0
Ion Media Networks Inc		E	818 953-7193	0
Ironwrker Emplyees Beneft Corp		D	626 792-7337	0
Jacobs Atcs Fema A Joint Ventr		D	571 218-1115	0
Jacobs Engineering Company		A	626 449-2171	0
Jacobs Engineering Group Inc		D	626 578-3500	0
Jacobs Engineering Inc **(HQ)**		C	626 578-3500	0
Jacobs International Ltd Inc		B	626 578-3500	0
Jpmorgan Chase Bank Nat Assn		D	626 795-5177	0
Jurlique Hlistic Skin Care Inc **(PA)**		E	914 998-8800	0
Kaiser Foundation Hospitals		E	626 405-5000	0
Kaiser Foundation Hospitals		E	626 440-5639	0
Kaiser Foundation Hospitals		B	626 440-5659	0
Kids Klub Care Centers Inc **(PA)**		D	626 795-2600	0
Kidspace A Prticipatory Museum		D	626 449-9144	0
Kinemetrics Inc **(DH)**		D	626 795-2220	0
La Asociacion Nacional Pro Per **(PA)**		A	626 564-1988	0
Land Design Consultants Inc		D	626 578-7000	0
Langham Hotels Pacific Corp		D	617 451-1900	0
Law Crossing **(PA)**		D	626 243-1801	0
Law School Financial Inc		C	626 243-1800	0
Legacy Healthcare Center LLC		D	626 798-0558	0
Lender Processing Services Inc		D	626 808-9000	0
Linden Optometry A Prof Corp		D	323 681-5678	0
Los Angeles Cnty Emp Retiremnt **(PA)**		B	626 564-6000	0
M-S Cash Drawer Corporation **(PA)**		D	626 792-2111	0
Madison Radiology Med Group		D	626 793-8189	0
Marianne Frostig Center **(PA)**		E	626 791-1255	0
Maxim Planning Group		D	818 425-4343	0
Merrill Lynch Pierce Fenner		D	626 304-1596	0
Merrill Lynch Pierce Fenner		D	626 844-8500	0
Mhh Holdings Inc		C	626 744-9370	0
Monte Vista Grove Homes		D	626 796-6135	0
Morgan Stanley		D	626 405-9313	0
Msj Healthcare LLC		E	818 244-8446	0
Msla Management LLC		C	626 824-6020	0
Myers Capital Partners LLC		E	626 568-1398	0
Myinternetservicescom LLC		D	213 256-0575	0
Norton Simon Museum		D	626 449-6840	0
Nrt Commercial Utah LLC		D	626 449-5222	0
Odona Central Security Inc		C	323 728-8818	0
Old Republic Contractors Ins		D	626 683-5200	0
Openx Technologies Inc **(DH)**		D	855 673-6948	0
Operating Engineers Funds Inc **(PA)**		C	866 400-5200	0
Pacific Clinics Foundation		D	626 796-3453	0
Pacific Huntington Hotel Corp		A	626 568-3900	0
Pacific Program/Design Managem		D	626 440-2000	0
Pacifica Services Inc		D	626 405-0131	0
Pardee Homes **(DH)**		D	310 955-3100	0
Park Hotels & Resorts Inc		C	626 577-1000	0
Park Marino Convalescent Ctr		E	626 463-4105	0
Parsons Constructors Inc		A	626 440-2000	0
Parsons Engrg Science Inc **(DH)**		B	626 440-2000	0
Parsons Government Svcs Inc **(HQ)**		B	626 440-2000	0
Parsons Gvrnment Svcs Intl Inc		B	626 440-6000	0
Parsons Project Services Inc		C	626 440-4000	0
Parsons Services Company		A	626 440-2000	0
Parsons Technical Services Inc		D	626 440-3998	0
Parsons Wtr Infrastructure Inc		A	626 440-7000	0
Pasadena Baking Co		E	626 796-5093	0

Employment Codes: A=Over 500 employees, B=251-500,
C=101-250, D=51-100, E=50

2020 Directory of California
Wholesalers and Services Companies

© Mergent Inc. 1-800-342-5647

1595

GEOGRAPHIC

	SIC	EMP	PHONE	ENTRY #
Pasadena Billing Associates		D	626 795-6596	0
Pasadena Center Operating Co		C	626 795-9311	0
Pasadena Child Dev Assoc Inc		D	626 793-7350	0
Pasadena Child Development Ass		D	626 793-7350	0
Pasadena Cyto Pathology Lab		B	626 397-8616	0
Pasadena Hospital Assn Ltd		D	626 397-3322	0
Pasadena Hotel Dev Ventr LP		D	626 449-4000	0
Pasadena Humane Society		D	626 792-7151	0
Pasadena Madows Nursing Ctr LP		D	626 796-1103	0
Pasadena Rbles Acquisition LLC		D	626 577-1000	0
Pasta Piccinini Inc		D	626 798-0841	0
Permits Today LLC		D	626 585-2931	0
Physician Assoc San Gabriel		C	626 817-8300	0
PNC Bank National Association		D	626 432-4500	0
PNC Bank National Association		D	626 351-2211	0
Pollard Crnert Crwford Stevens		E	626 793-4440	0
Prima Royale Enterprises Ltd		D	626 960-8388	0
Prime Clinical Systems (PA)		D	626 449-1705	0
Principles Inc (PA)		D	323 681-2575	0
Ptsi Managed Services Inc		D	626 440-3118	0
Ralphs Grocery Company		D	626 793-7480	0
Real Property Systems Inc		C	760 243-1143	0
Regency Park Senior Living Inc		D	626 396-4911	0
Regency Park Senior Living Inc		D	626 578-0460	0
Restaurant Depot LLC		C	626 744-0204	0
Robert C Hamilton		D	626 794-4103	0
Robert Half International Inc		D	626 463-2037	0
Rose Bowl Aquatics Center		C	626 564-0330	0
Rosemary Childrens Services (PA)		C	626 844-3033	0
Roughan Associates At Linc		E	626 351-0991	0
Rt Pasad Hotel Partners LP		C	626 403-7600	0
Saiful/Bouquet Con Stru Eng (PA)		D	626 304-2616	0
Sedgwick Claims MGT Svcs Inc		D	626 568-1415	0
Seville Construction Svcs Inc		D	626 204-0800	0
Shriners Hspitals For Children		B	213 388-3151	0
Sierra Lobo Inc		C	626 510-6340	0
Sigma Investment Holdings LLC		E	626 398-3098	0
Slch Inc (PA)		E	626 798-0558	0
Smith Brothers Restaurant Inc		D	626 577-2400	0
Southern Cal Prmnnte Med Group (PA)		D	626 405-5704	0
Special Events Staffing		A	626 296-6771	0
Ssl Robotics LLC (DH)		D	626 296-1373	0
Ssl Robotics LLC		D	626 296-1373	0
Stantec Architecture Inc		D	626 796-9141	0
Stantec Consulting Svcs Inc		D	626 796-9141	0
Strategic Staffing Svcs Inc		B	818 248-0049	0
Swca Incorporated		D	626 240-0587	0
Synopsys Inc		D	626 795-9101	0
Tetra Tech Executive Svcs Inc		D	626 470-2400	0
Tetra Tech Nus Inc		D	412 921-7090	0
Tetra Tech Technical Services		C	626 351-4664	0
Ticor Title Insurance Company (DH)		C	616 302-3121	0
Tokio Marine Management Inc		C	626 568-7600	0
Torres Construction Corp (PA)		D	323 257-7460	0
Trinus Corporation		E	818 246-1143	0
Ttg Engineers (PA)		C	626 463-2800	0
Two Palms Nursing Center Inc (PA)		E	626 798-8991	0
Two Palms Nursing Center Inc		D	626 796-1103	0
UBS Financial Services Inc		E	626 449-1501	0
Unified Valet Parking Inc		D	818 822-5807	0
United Couriers Inc (DH)		C	213 383-3611	0
Unity SEC & Protective Svc		D	323 695-7234	0
Universal Accounts Inc		D	626 356-7900	0
Valley Hunt Club		D	626 793-7134	0
Vincent Hayley Enterprises		D	626 398-8182	0
Voch Inc		D	626 798-1111	0
Wescom Central Credit Union (PA)		B	888 493-7266	0
Wescom Holdings LLC (HQ)		D	888 493-7266	0
Western Asset Core Plus		D	626 844-9400	0
Western Asset MGT Co LLC (HQ)		E	626 844-9265	0
Western Asset Mrtg Capitl Corp		A	626 844-9400	0
Worleyparsons Group Inc		B	626 440-7000	0
Zenith Health Care		D	626 578-0460	0

PASO ROBLES, CA - San Luis Obispo County

	SIC	EMP	PHONE	ENTRY #
Ameripride Services Inc		D	805 239-9449	0
AT&T Services Inc		C	805 237-9503	0
Ayres - Paso Robles LP		C	714 850-0409	0
Boneso Brothers Cnstr Inc		D	805 227-4450	0
Cellco Partnership		D	805 237-8200	0
County of Los Angeles		C	805 237-3110	0
Dave Spurr Excavating Inc		E	805 238-0834	0
Emeritus Corporation		E	805 239-1313	0
Iqms (HQ)		C	805 227-1122	0
Marsh Consulting Group		D	239 433-5500	0
Mge Underground Inc		D	805 238-3510	0

	SIC	EMP	PHONE	ENTRY #
Michael Dusi Trucking Inc		D	805 237-9499	0
Omega 2 Alpha Services LLC		D	805 610-2249	0
Paso Robles Inn LLC		D	805 238-2660	0
Paso Robles Tank Inc (PA)		D	805 227-1641	0
Pearce Services LLC (HQ)		E	805 237-7480	0
RE Max Parkside Real Estate		D	805 239-3310	0
Smart & Final Stores Inc		B	805 237-0323	0
Special Service Contrs Inc		D	805 227-1081	0
Treasury Wine Estates Americas		C	805 237-6000	0
Union Pacific Railroad Company		D	805 286-5851	0
Villa Paseo Senior Residences		D	805 227-4588	0

PATTERSON, CA - Stanislaus County

	SIC	EMP	PHONE	ENTRY #
Del Puerto Health Care Dst		D	209 892-9100	0
Designed MBL Systems Inds Inc		C	209 892-6298	0
Diablo Grande Ltd Partnership		D	209 892-7421	0
Lucich Santos Farms		C	209 892-6500	0
Traina Dried Fruit Inc		C	209 892-5472	0

PATTON, CA - San Bernardino County

	SIC	EMP	PHONE	ENTRY #
Califrnia Dept State Hospitals		A	909 425-7000	0

PAUMA VALLEY, CA - San Diego County

	SIC	EMP	PHONE	ENTRY #
Pauma Band of Mission Indians		B	760 742-2177	0
Pauma Valley Country Club		D	760 742-1230	0
T - Y Nursery Inc		C	760 742-2151	0

PEBBLE BEACH, CA - Monterey County

	SIC	EMP	PHONE	ENTRY #
California Golf Association		D	831 625-4653	0
Czech Commerce Ltd		D	831 649-4633	0
I Cypress Company (PA)		D	831 647-7500	0
Lone Cypress Company LLC		A	831 624-3811	0
Lone Cypress Company LLC		D	831 625-8507	0
Monterey Peninsula Country CLB		C	831 373-1556	0
Poppy Hills Inc		D	831 625-1513	0

PENN VALLEY, CA - Nevada County

	SIC	EMP	PHONE	ENTRY #
Lake Wildwood Association		C	530 432-1152	0

PENRYN, CA - Placer County

	SIC	EMP	PHONE	ENTRY #
Sinclair Concrete		D	916 663-0303	0

PERRIS, CA - Riverside County

	SIC	EMP	PHONE	ENTRY #
4g Wireless Inc		D	951 210-7980	0
American Airlines Group Inc		A	310 251-9184	0
Basic Occpational Training Ctr		C	951 657-8028	0
Big Lgue Dreams Consulting LLC		C	619 846-8855	0
County of Riverside		D	951 443-2262	0
Dropzone Waterpark		C	951 210-1600	0
Eastern Municipal Water Dst (PA)		B	951 928-3777	0
Eastern Municipal Water Dst		C	951 657-7469	0
Global Plastics Inc		C	951 657-5466	0
Griswold Industries		D	951 657-1718	0
Herca Telecomm Services Inc		D	951 940-5941	0
Integrity Rebar Placers		C	951 696-6843	0
Jeff Carpenter Inc		D	951 657-5115	0
Mamco Inc (PA)		C	951 776-9300	0
Pacific Hydrotech Corporation		C	951 943-8803	0
Pacific Restoration Group Inc		E	951 940-6069	0
Perris Valley Cmnty Hosp LLC (PA)		B	951 436-5000	0
Perris Vly Skydiving Schl Inc		E	951 657-1664	0
Proprocess Corporation		D	800 624-6717	0
Silver Creek Industries Inc		C	951 943-5393	0
SR Bray LLC		E	951 436-2920	0
Village Nurseries Whl LLC		C	951 657-3940	0

PESCADERO, CA - San Mateo County

	SIC	EMP	PHONE	ENTRY #
Joie De Vivre Hospitality LLC		D	650 879-1100	0
King-Reynolds Ventures LLC		D	650 879-2136	0
Pescadero Conservation Aliance		E	650 879-1441	0

PETALUMA, CA - Sonoma County

	SIC	EMP	PHONE	ENTRY #
AB Closing Corporation		D	707 766-1777	0
Allianz Globl Risks US Insur		B	415 899-3758	0
Allianz Reinsurance Amer Inc		D	415 899-2000	0
Allianz Technology America Inc		C	415 899-2713	0
American Insurance Company Inc		A	415 899-2000	0
Arntz Builders Inc		E	415 382-1188	0
Associated Indemnity Corp		A	415 899-2000	0
Braden Partners LP A Calif (HQ)		D	415 893-1518	0
Clover-Stornetta Farms Inc (PA)		D	707 769-3282	0
Club One At Petaluma		D	707 766-8080	0
County Engineers Assn Cal		D	707 762-3492	0
Courseco Inc (PA)		A	707 763-0335	0
Crocodile Bay Lodge		C	707 559-7990	0
Crosscheck Inc (PA)		C	707 665-2100	0
Evergreen At Petaluma LLC		C	707 763-6887	0
Exchange Bank		D	707 762-5555	0

Mergent email: customerrelations@mergent.com
1596

2020 Directory of California
Wholesalers and Services Companies

(P-0000) Products & Services Section entry number
(PA)=Parent Co (HQ)=Headquarters (DH)=Div Headquarters

	SIC	EMP	PHONE	ENTRY #
Federal Express Corporation		D	800 463-3339	0
Fedex Freight West Inc		E	707 778-3191	0
Firemans Fund Insurance Co (HQ)		A	415 899-2000	0
First California Mrtg Co II		D	415 209-0910	0
Fishman Supply Company		D	707 763-8161	0
Golden Living LLC		D	707 763-4109	0
Incom Mechanical Inc		D	707 586-0511	0
Intelisys Inc		D	800 615-8330	0
Kaiser Foundation Hospitals		E	707 765-3900	0
Legacy Marketing Group (PA)		C	707 778-8638	0
Midstate Construction Corp		D	707 762-3200	0
Morris Distributing Inc		D	707 769-7294	0
National Surety Corporation		A	415 899-2000	0
NMN Construction Inc		D	707 763-6981	0
North Bay Construction Inc		D	707 283-0093	0
Oak Knoll Convalescent Center		D	707 778-8686	0
Optio Solutions LLC		C	800 360-2827	0
Pacific Gas and Electric Co		E	707 765-5118	0
Permanente Medical Group Inc		D	707 765-3900	0
Petaluma Health Center Inc		B	707 559-7500	0
Photo TLC Inc		C	415 462-0010	0
Point Reyes Bird Observator		D	415 868-0371	0
Point Reyes Bird Observatory		D	707 781-2555	0
Praetorian USA		D	707 780-8020	0
Pure Luxury Limousine Service		C	800 626-5466	0
Redwood Building Maint Co		D	707 782-9100	0
Reichardt Duck Farm Inc		D	707 762-6314	0
Rooster Run Golf Club Inc		E	707 778-1211	0
San Frncsco North/Petaluma KOA		E	707 763-1492	0
Securitas SEC Svcs USA Inc		C	707 586-1393	0
Soligent Distribution LLC (HQ)		D	707 992-3100	0
Sonoma Hotel Partners LP		D	707 283-2888	0
Sonoma Technology Inc		D	707 665-9900	0
Srm Alliance Hospital Services (PA)		B	707 778-1111	0
St Joseph Health System		E	707 778-2505	0
Star H-R (PA)		D	707 762-4447	0
Sunrise Farms LLC		D	707 778-6450	0
Sunrise of Petaluma		D	707 776-2885	0
Sunrise Senior Living Inc		D	707 776-2885	0
Sunset Aviation LLC (PA)		E	707 775-2786	0
Team Ghilotti Inc		E	707 763-8700	0
Transportation California Dept		C	707 762-6641	0
Trestles Holdings LLC		D	707 778-8686	0
United Cmps Cnfrences Retreats (PA)		D	707 762-3220	0
USI Insurance Services Nat Inc		D	707 769-2900	0

PICO RIVERA, CA - Los Angeles County

	SIC	EMP	PHONE	ENTRY #
ABF Freight System Inc		E	323 773-2580	0
Altamed Health Services Corp		D	562 949-8717	0
Amini Innovation Corp		C	562 222-2500	0
AP Express International LLC		D	562 236-2250	0
Aurora World Inc		C	562 205-1222	0
California Hispanic Com		C	562 942-9625	0
Century 21 Excellence		E	562 948-4553	0
Chalmers Corporation		D	562 948-4850	0
Cintas Corporation No 3		C	562 368-3200	0
Daniels Western Meat Packers		D	562 948-2254	0
Fedex Office & Print Svcs Inc		D	562 942-1953	0
Grm Information MGT Services		E	562 373-9000	0
Grm Information MGT Svcs Inc		D	562 373-9000	0
Herb Thyme Farm Inc		D	603 542-3690	0
Howards Appliances Inc		D	626 288-4010	0
Ionics Altrpure Wtr Crparation		D	562 948-2188	0
Jjj Floor Covering Inc (PA)		D	562 692-9008	0
Krikorian Premiere Theatre LLC		C	562 205-3456	0
L I Metal Systems		E	562 948-5950	0
Level 9 Security Services		E	562 949-7180	0
Los Angeles Unified School Dst		D	562 654-9007	0
Lucky Installations		E	562 948-5950	0
Manhole Adjusting Contrs Inc		E	323 725-1387	0
Mariner Health Care Inc		D	562 942-7019	0
Noble Rents Inc		D	855 767-4424	0
Pacific Logistics Corp (PA)		C	562 478-4700	0
Partschannel Inc		E	562 654-3400	0
Public Hlth Fndation Entps Inc		C	562 801-2323	0
Rivera Sanitarium Inc		D	562 949-2591	0
Riviera Nursing & Conva		C	562 806-2576	0
Santa Teresa Conv Hospital		D	562 948-1961	0
Sectran Security Incorporated (PA)		C	562 948-1446	0
Three Sons Inc		D	562 801-4100	0
Unisource Solutions Inc (PA)		D	562 654-3500	0
United Pacific Waste		D	562 699-7600	0
United Rentals North Amer Inc		C	562 695-0748	0
UPS Ground Freight Inc		D	562 801-1300	0
Wm Recycle America LLC		D	562 948-3888	0
Your Executive Solutions		A	562 388-4150	0

PIEDMONT, CA - Alameda County

	SIC	EMP	PHONE	ENTRY #
Boyscout of America		D	510 547-4493	0
Linda Beach Coop Pre-School		E	510 547-4432	0

PINE GROVE, CA - Amador County

	SIC	EMP	PHONE	ENTRY #
Volcano Communications Company (PA)		D	209 296-7502	0
Volcano Vision Inc		C	209 296-2288	0

PINECREST, CA - Tuolumne County

	SIC	EMP	PHONE	ENTRY #
Dodge Ridge Corporation		B	209 536-5300	0

PINOLE, CA - Contra Costa County

	SIC	EMP	PHONE	ENTRY #
Cameron International Corp		D	510 928-1480	0
Geek Squad Inc		D	800 433-5778	0
Kaiser Foundation Hospitals		A	510 243-4000	0
Pathway To Choices Inc		D	510 724-9044	0
Pinole Assisted Living Cmnty		D	510 758-1122	0
Pinole Senior Center		D	510 724-9800	0
State Farm Mutl Auto Insur Co		D	510 222-1102	0

PIONEER, CA - Amador County

	SIC	EMP	PHONE	ENTRY #
Pacific Gas and Electric Co		D	209 295-2651	0

PIRU, CA - Ventura County

	SIC	EMP	PHONE	ENTRY #
La Verne Nursery Inc		D	805 521-0111	0

PISMO BEACH, CA - San Luis Obispo County

	SIC	EMP	PHONE	ENTRY #
Castlblack Pismo Bch Owner LLC		E	805 773-6020	0
Castleblack Owner Holdings LLC		E	805 773-6020	0
Pismo Beach Athletic Club		E	805 773-3011	0
Pismo Coast Village Inc		D	805 773-1811	0
T I C Hotels Inc		D	805 773-4671	0

PITTSBURG, CA - Contra Costa County

	SIC	EMP	PHONE	ENTRY #
A T Associates Inc (PA)		D	925 808-6540	0
Arb Inc		E	925 432-3649	0
Chrome Deposit Corp		D	925 432-4507	0
Comcast Corporation		D	925 432-0500	0
Concord Iron Works Inc		E	925 432-0136	0
Durham School Services L P		C	925 686-3391	0
First Baptist Head Start		D	925 473-2000	0
G&K Services LLC		E	925 427-4401	0
Hydrochem LLC		D	925 432-1749	0
La Clinica De La Raza Inc		B	925 431-1250	0
Lincoln Child Center Inc		C	925 521-1270	0
McCampbell Analytical Inc		D	925 252-9262	0
Pacific Gas and Electric Co		B	925 757-2000	0
Pittsburg Care Center Ltd		E	925 432-3831	0
Pittsburg Skilled Nursing		D	925 808-6540	0
Ravig Inc		D	925 526-1234	0
Redwood Painting Co Inc		C	925 432-4500	0
Rfid Corporation		C	925 473-9978	0
SSC Pittsburg Operating Co LP		A	925 427-4444	0
State Preschool		E	925 473-4380	0

PLACENTIA, CA - Orange County

	SIC	EMP	PHONE	ENTRY #
Alta Vista Country Club LLC		D	714 524-1591	0
Bejac Corporation (PA)		D	714 528-6224	0
City Service Contracting Inc (PA)		D	714 632-6610	0
Customline Professional		B	714 996-1333	0
Elljay Acoustics Inc		D	714 961-1173	0
Facility Solutions Group Inc		D	714 993-3966	0
GD Heil Inc		C	714 687-9100	0
Hardy Window Company (PA)		C	714 996-1807	0
Interface Rehab Inc		A	714 646-8300	0
Linda Placentia-Yorba		D	714 985-8775	0
Linda Yorba Water District (PA)		D	714 701-3000	0
Micon Construction Cal Inc		D	714 666-0203	0
Osscim Inc		E	714 680-0015	0
Premier Auto W Covina LLC		D	626 858-7202	0
Residence Inn By Marriott		D	714 996-0555	0
SGF Produce Holding Corp		B	714 630-6292	0
So California Ventures Ltd		D	714 524-0021	0
Sunburst Shutters Cal Inc (PA)		D	714 997-0800	0
Sunrise Growers Inc (HQ)		B	714 630-2170	0
Tct Circuit Supply Inc		D	714 644-9700	0
Tenet Healthsystem Medical		B	714 993-2000	0
Total Woman		D	714 993-6003	0

PLACERVILLE, CA - El Dorado County

	SIC	EMP	PHONE	ENTRY #
Centene Corporation		D	530 626-5773	0
Consortm On Reachng Excellnce		E	510 540-4200	0
County of El Dorado		D	530 621-6210	0
County of El Dorado		D	530 621-5845	0
County of El Dorado		D	530 642-7130	0
El Dorado County Health Dept		D	530 621-6100	0
El Dorado Irrigation District		B	530 622-4513	0
El Dorado Savings Bank (PA)		D	530 622-1492	0

GEOGRAPHIC

	SIC	EMP	PHONE	ENTRY #
El Dorado Water & Shower Svc		E	530 622-8995	0
Elder Options (PA)		E	530 626-6939	0
ERA Realty Center		D	530 295-2900	0
Gladiolus Holdings LLC		D	530 622-3400	0
Gold Country Health Center Inc (PA)		C	530 621-1100	0
Hangtown Knnel CLB Plcrvlle CA		D	530 622-4867	0
Harmony Home Health LLC		D	916 933-9777	0
Innovative Education MGT Inc (PA)		D	530 295-3566	0
Lyon Realty		D	530 295-4444	0
Marshall Medical Center (PA)		A	530 622-1441	0
Mother Lode Rehabilit		C	530 622-4848	0
NPS Marketing		B	916 941-5510	0
Pacific Gas and Electric Co		D	530 621-7237	0
Placervlle Pnes Cnvlscent Hosp		C	530 622-3400	0
Progress House Inc (PA)		D	530 626-9240	0
Quality In-Hmecare Specialists		D	530 303-3477	0
Shingle Sprng Trbal Gming Auth		A	530 677-7000	0
Summitview Child Treatment Ctr		E	530 644-2412	0
USDA Forest Service		D	530 626-1546	0
W F Hayward Co		D	530 303-3030	0
Western Slope Health Center		D	530 622-6842	0

PLAYA DEL REY, CA - Los Angeles County

	SIC	EMP	PHONE	ENTRY #
Automate Parking Inc		D	310 674-3396	0
Los Angeles Dept Wtr & Pwr		D	310 524-8500	0
Parking Concepts Inc		D	310 322-5008	0

PLAYA VISTA, CA - Los Angeles County

	SIC	EMP	PHONE	ENTRY #
1on1 LLC		E	310 448-5376	0
72andsunny LLC		D	310 215-9009	0
Avongard Products USa Ltd		E	310 319-2300	0
Belkin International Inc (DH)		B	310 751-5100	0
Chownow Inc		D	888 707-2469	0
Fullscreen Inc (HQ)		E	310 202-3333	0
Gehry Technologies Inc (HQ)		E	310 862-1200	0
Kelton Research LLC (PA)		D	310 479-4040	0
Linksys LLC		C	310 751-5100	0
Lmb Opco LLC		D	310 348-6800	0
Media Temple Inc		C	877 578-4000	0
Microsoft Corporation		D	213 806-7300	0
Phelps Group		E	310 752-4400	0
Pop Media Networks LLC (DH)		D	323 856-4000	0
Ryot Corp		D	323 356-1787	0
Urban Plates LLC		D	424 256-7274	0

PLEASANT GROVE, CA - Sutter County

	SIC	EMP	PHONE	ENTRY #
Holt of California (HQ)		C	916 991-8200	0
Sysco Sacramento Inc		B	916 275-2714	0
Withrow Cattle		D	916 780-0364	0

PLEASANT HILL, CA - Contra Costa County

	SIC	EMP	PHONE	ENTRY #
Accentcare Home Health Cal Inc		D	925 356-6066	0
Aegis Senior Communities LLC		D	925 588-7030	0
Anka Behavioral Health Inc (PA)		C	925 825-4700	0
Ascendantfx Capital USA Inc		D	201 633-4667	0
AT&T Corp		D	925 603-9476	0
Brighter Beginnings (PA)		D	510 903-7503	0
Buildings Iot Inc (PA)		D	800 800-7126	0
Carlton Senior Living		D	925 935-1001	0
Choice In Aging (PA)		D	925 682-6330	0
Contra Costa Country Club		D	925 798-7135	0
Courtyard Management Corp		E	925 691-1444	0
Crestwood Behavioral Hlth Inc		D	925 938-8050	0
Diablo Vly College Foundation (PA)		C	925 685-1230	0
Dreamctchers Empwerment Netwrk		C	925 935-5630	0
East Bay Connection Inc		E	925 609-1920	0
John Muir Health		A	925 952-2887	0
John Muir Physician Network		A	925 685-0843	0
Mark Scott Construction Inc (PA)		E	925 944-0502	0
Maxim Services Ltd Inc		D	925 969-1907	0
Mc Namara Dodge Ney Beatt (PA)		D	925 939-5330	0
Quest Diagnostics Incorporated		B	925 687-2514	0
Residence Inn By Marriott LLC		C	925 689-1010	0
Solo W-2 Inc		D	925 680-0200	0
Young MNS Chrstn Assn of E Bay		D	925 687-8900	0
Youth Homes Incorporated (PA)		D	925 933-2627	0

PLEASANTON, CA - Alameda County

	SIC	EMP	PHONE	ENTRY #
1st United Services Credit Un (PA)		D	800 649-0193	0
2dream Inc		D	650 943-2366	0
314e Corporation (PA)		C	510 371-6736	0
ABM Elctrcal Ltg Solutions Inc		D	408 399-3030	0
ABM Janitorial Services Inc		B	925 924-0270	0
Accurate Firestop Inc		C	510 886-1169	0
Acosta Inc		D	925 600-3500	0
Advantage Sales & Marketing		C	925 463-5600	0
Advantage Sales & Mktg LLC		D	925 463-5600	0

	SIC	EMP	PHONE	ENTRY #
Aegis Enterprises Inc		D	925 417-5550	0
Alain Pinel Realtors Inc		D	925 251-1111	0
Alameda County AG Fair Assn		D	925 426-7600	0
Alliance Information Technolog (PA)		D	925 462-9787	0
American Baptist Homes of West (HQ)		D	925 924-7100	0
American Property Management		C	925 463-8000	0
Anixter Inc		E	925 469-8500	0
AOC Technologies Inc		B	925 875-0808	0
Axis Community Health Inc		D	925 462-1755	0
Bay Vista Senior Housing		C	925 924-7100	0
Black Tie Transportation LLC		C	925 847-0747	0
Blackhawk Network Inc (DH)		A	925 226-9990	0
Blackhawk Network Holdings Inc (HQ)		B	925 226-9990	0
Bodhtree Solutions Inc		C	844 409-0510	0
Boeing Company		D	925 398-7664	0
Bricsnet FM America Inc		D	202 756-1840	0
Brightview Landscape Svcs Inc		D	925 924-8900	0
Buxton Consulting		D	925 467-0700	0
Calatlantic Group Inc		E	925 847-8700	0
Caliber Home Loans Inc		D	925 417-3491	0
California and Nevada IBEW/Nec		D	925 828-6322	0
Califrnia Yuth Soccer Assn Inc		D	925 426-5437	0
Can-AM Plumbing Inc		C	925 846-1833	0
Carnegie Mellon University		C	412 268-3818	0
Castlewood Country Club		D	925 846-2871	0
Ce2 Kleinfelder JV		D	925 463-7301	0
Center Cnslng Edctn & Crisis		D	925 462-1755	0
Citimortgage Inc		E	925 730-3800	0
CJ Model Home Maintenance Inc		D	925 485-3280	0
Cognix Automation Inc		E	925 464-8822	0
Commerce West Insurance Co		D	925 730-6400	0
Config Consultants LLC		E	844 226-6344	0
Construction Testing Services (PA)		E	925 462-5151	0
Conti Life Comm Plea LLC		D	925 227-6800	0
Convergint Technologies LLC		E	510 300-2800	0
Convo Communications LLC		C	925 227-5500	0
Corporate Visions Inc (PA)		D	415 464-4400	0
Covad Communications Group Inc (DH)		C	408 952-6400	0
Crossmark Inc		B	925 463-3555	0
Cs-Pleasanton LLC		B	925 463-2822	0
Dahlin Group Inc (PA)		D	925 251-7200	0
Dan Lofgren		D	925 846-6632	0
Deloitte & Touche LLP		C	415 782-4020	0
Devcool Inc		D	408 372-4313	0
Dimension Data North Amer Inc		D	925 226-8378	0
Dublin San Ramon Services Dst		D	925 846-4565	0
E-Loan Inc (DH)		A	925 847-6200	0
Elavon Inc		B	925 734-8939	0
Ellie Mae Inc (HQ)		C	855 224-8572	0
Em Eagle Purchaser LLC (PA)		A	855 224-8572	0
Ernst & Young LLP		C	925 734-6388	0
Et Capital Solar Partners USA		E	925 460-9898	0
Evidentio Inc (HQ)		D	855 933-1337	0
Excel Building Services LLC		A	925 474-1080	0
Federal Express Corporation		D	800 463-3339	0
Ford Motor Company		D	925 351-6205	0
Fusion Cloud Company LLC (DH)		D	925 201-2500	0
Gatan Inc (HQ)		D	925 463-0200	0
Glass Pak Inc		D	707 207-0400	0
Global Software Resources Inc (PA)		E	925 249-2200	0
Gtt Communications (mp) Inc (DH)		C	925 201-2500	0
Guardian Computer Support		C	925 251-8800	0
Guardsmark LLC		B	925 484-4412	0
Hitachi High Tech Amer Inc		D	925 218-2800	0
Hospital Cmmttee For The Lvrmr (DH)		B	925 847-3000	0
Humangood (PA)		D	602 906-4024	0
Impact Group LLC		D	925 327-7322	0
Jpmorgan Xign Corporation		D	925 469-9446	0
Kaiser Foundation Hospitals		B	925 598-2799	0
Kaiser Foundation Hospitals		B	925 847-5000	0
Kaiser Fundation Hlth Plan Inc		D	510 271-5800	0
Kiewit Infrastructure West Co		D	925 462-1088	0
Kleinfelder Inc		D	925 484-1700	0
Kraft Heinz Foods Company		D	925 469-0057	0
Mackay Smps Cvil Engineers Inc (PA)		D	925 416-1790	0
Martin ATI-AC Inc (PA)		D	925 648-8800	0
Mason-Mcduffie Real Estate Inc		D	925 734-5000	0
Maxplore Technologies Inc		D	925 621-1400	0
McLane Foodservice Dist Inc		D	252 985-7200	0
McM Partners Inc		D	925 463-9500	0
Megapath Inc (PA)		D	877 611-6342	0
Mission Peak Orthopedics		D	510 797-3933	0
North American Title Co Inc		D	925 399-3000	0
Nucompass Mobility Svcs Inc (PA)		D	925 734-3434	0
Oc IV A California LP		E	925 734-5800	0

2020 Directory of California
Wholesalers and Services Companies

(P-0000) Products & Services Section entry number
(PA)=Parent Co (HQ)=Headquarters (DH)=Div Headquarters

	SIC	EMP	PHONE	ENTRY #
On-Time AC & Htg Inc (PA)		C	925 598-1911	0
Oracle America Inc		D	925 694-3314	0
Oracle Corporation		B	877 767-2253	0
Oracle Systems Corporation		B	925 694-3000	0
Patelco Credit Union (PA)		C	800 358-8228	0
Philips Hlthcare Infrmtics Inc (DH)		C	650 293-2300	0
Pleasant Canyon Hotel Inc		E	925 847-0535	0
Pleasanton Project Owner LLC		D	925 847-7592	0
Plex Systems Inc		D	248 391-8001	0
Proctoru Inc		B	205 870-8122	0
Product Quality Partners Inc		D	925 484-6491	0
Psinapse Technology Ltd		D	925 225-0400	0
Pulte Home Company LLC		D	925 249-3200	0
Pyramid Advisors Ltd Partnr		D	925 847-6000	0
Quality Auto Craft Inc		A	925 426-0120	0
Rs Calibration Services Inc		E	925 462-4217	0
Ruby Hill Golf Club LLC		D	925 417-5840	0
S&J Stadtler Inc		B	925 847-8900	0
Sabah International Inc (HQ)		D	925 463-0431	0
Safe America Credit Union (PA)		D	925 734-4111	0
Schneider Electric Usa Inc		D	925 462-0986	0
Servicemax Inc (PA)		D	925 965-7859	0
Sheraton LLC		B	925 463-3330	0
Shooter & Butts Inc		E	925 460-5155	0
Signature Properties Inc		D	925 463-1122	0
Simbol Inc		D	925 226-7400	0
Simpson Strong-Tie Intl Inc		D	925 560-9000	0
Six Continents Hotels Inc		D	925 847-6000	0
Smartzip Analytics Inc		D	855 661-1064	0
Spacetone Acoustics Inc		E	925 931-0749	0
Specialty Risk Services Inc		C	877 809-9478	0
Springml Inc		D	916 316-1566	0
State Compensation Insur Fund		C	925 523-5000	0
State Compensation Insur Fund		C	888 782-8338	0
Sun-Maid Growers California		E	800 752-9277	0
Sunbelt Controls Inc		E	925 660-3900	0
Sunol Vly Golf & Recreation Co		D	925 862-2404	0
Telecom Technology Svcs Inc		C	925 224-7812	0
Terminix Intl Co Ltd Partnr		C	925 460-5063	0
Toll Brothers Inc		D	925 855-0260	0
Toolwire Inc		D	925 227-8500	0
Total Renal Care Inc		E	925 737-0120	0
Transbay Fire Protection Inc (PA)		E	925 846-9484	0
Trevi Partners A Calif LP (PA)		C	925 225-4000	0
Tryfacta Inc		B	408 419-9200	0
Unchained Labs (PA)		C	925 587-9800	0
Unisource Packaging Inc		C	925 227-6000	0
Valley Medical Oncology (PA)		D	925 734-8130	0
Veeva Systems Inc (PA)		C	925 452-6500	0
Wavestrong Inc		D	925 549-2882	0
Wells Fargo Bank National Assn		D	925 463-1983	0
West Valley Engineering Inc		D	925 416-9707	0
Workday Inc (PA)		C	925 951-9000	0
Xin Xin Construction Inc		D	945 560-9511	0
Youngs Market Company LLC		B	510 475-2200	0
Zenith Insurance Company		C	925 460-0600	0

PLS VRDS PNSL, CA - Los Angeles County

	SIC	EMP	PHONE	ENTRY #
Aichinger International Inc		D	310 375-1533	0
Episcopal Communities & Servic		D	310 544-2204	0

PLYMOUTH, CA - Amador County

	SIC	EMP	PHONE	ENTRY #
Borjon Iscander		C	209 245-6289	0

POINT ARENA, CA - Mendocino County

	SIC	EMP	PHONE	ENTRY #
Manchester Band Pomo Indians		D	707 882-2788	0

POINT REYES STATION, CA - Marin County

	SIC	EMP	PHONE	ENTRY #
Pacific Slope Tree Coop Inc		E	415 663-1300	0

POINT RICHMOND, CA - Contra Costa County

	SIC	EMP	PHONE	ENTRY #
Hartmann Studios Inc		C	510 232-5030	0

POMONA, CA - Los Angeles County

	SIC	EMP	PHONE	ENTRY #
American National Red Cross		A	909 859-7006	0
Anka Behavioral Health Inc		C	909 622-8217	0
Behavioral Health Services Inc		D	909 865-2336	0
Braun Linen Service Inc		D	909 623-2678	0
Cal Poly Pomona Foundation Inc (PA)		A	909 869-2950	0
Cape Robbin Inc		E	626 810-8080	0
Casa Colin Comprehensive		A	909 596-7733	0
Casa Colina Inc (PA)		C	909 596-7733	0
Casa Colina Hospital and Cente (HQ)		B	909 596-7733	0
Centrescapes Inc		D	909 392-3303	0
Chino Valley Healthcare Center		D	909 628-1245	0
Circle Wood Services Inc		D	909 784-0733	0
City of Pomona		B	909 397-5506	0

	SIC	EMP	PHONE	ENTRY #
City of Pomona		C	909 620-2361	0
Coan Construction Co Inc		D	909 868-6812	0
Commercial Door Company Inc		D	714 529-2179	0
Continental Agency Inc (PA)		D	909 595-8884	0
Coptic Clinics		D	562 900-2692	0
Country Oaks Partners LLC		D	909 622-1067	0
County of Los Angeles		C	909 620-3330	0
County of Los Angeles		C	909 469-4500	0
Dedicated Fleet Systems Inc (PA)		D	909 590-8209	0
DJ Scheffler Inc (PA)		E	909 595-2924	0
Eastman Music Company (PA)		D	909 868-1777	0
Fairplex Enterprises Inc		D	909 623-3111	0
Ferguson Enterprises Inc		C	909 364-8700	0
Ferguson Fire Fabrication Inc (DH)		D	909 517-3085	0
Frank S Smith Masonry Inc		D	909 468-0525	0
Furniture Trnsp Systems		D	909 869-1200	0
Genesis Healthcare Corporation		E	909 622-1069	0
Genesis Healthcare Corporation		C	909 628-6024	0
Healthright 360		D	909 624-1233	0
Henkels & McCoy Inc		B	909 517-3011	0
Henkels & McCoy Inc		C	909 590-8419	0
Howard Roofing Company Inc		D	909 622-5598	0
Hsbc Finance Corporation		A	909 623-3355	0
Inland Valley Partners LLC		D	909 623-7100	0
Inter Valley Pool Supply Inc		D	626 969-5657	0
Inter-Valley Health Plan Inc		D	909 623-6333	0
J & E Private Security Corp		D	909 594-1111	0
Jeff Kerber Pool Plst Inc		B	909 465-0677	0
K K W Trucking Inc (PA)		D	909 869-1200	0
Keith T Kusunis MD		D	909 469-9494	0
Landmark Medical Services Inc		D	909 593-2585	0
Latara Enterprise Inc (PA)		C	909 623-9301	0
LDI Transportation Inc		D	909 620-7001	0
Lee Jennings Target Ex Inc (PA)		C	909 868-1040	0
Lexmar Distribution Inc		C	909 620-7001	0
Longwood Management Corp		D	818 884-7100	0
Los Angeles County Fair Assn (PA)		D	909 623-3111	0
Master Disposal Co		E	626 444-6789	0
Merchants Building Maint Co		C	909 622-8260	0
Mission Series Inc		E	714 736-1000	0
MJB Partners LLC		D	909 623-2481	0
Murcor Inc		C	909 623-4001	0
Myers Tire Supply Dist Inc		D	602 233-1037	0
Norac Additives LLC		D	909 321-5952	0
NW Packaging LLC (PA)		D	909 706-3627	0
PHD Marketing Inc		D	909 620-1000	0
Pomona Community Health Center		D	909 630-7927	0
Pomona Housing Partners LP		E	909 622-1010	0
Pomona Valley Hospital Med Ctr (PA)		A	909 865-9500	0
Pomona Valley Hospital Med Ctr		C	909 865-9700	0
Quest Discovery Services Inc		D	310 769-5557	0
Rfid Textile Services Inc		D	909 623-5135	0
Rwp Transfer Inc		E	909 868-6882	0
San Gabriel/Pomona Valleys		B	909 620-7722	0
Securitas SEC Svcs USA Inc		C	909 865-4356	0
Siemens Industry Inc		D	909 627-6141	0
Southern California Edison Co		D	909 469-0251	0
Spectra Company		D	909 599-0760	0
Spiniello Companies		D	909 629-1000	0
Starwood Htls & Rsrts Wrldwde		C	909 622-2220	0
T McGee Electric Inc		D	909 591-6461	0
Tri City Mental Health Center		D	909 784-3200	0
Ultimate Removal Inc		C	909 524-0800	0
Valley Nurses		D	714 549-2512	0
W Why W Enterprises Inc		D	626 969-4292	0
Whitefield Medical Lab Inc (PA)		E	909 625-2114	0
Yamamoto of Orient Inc (HQ)		C	909 594-7356	0

PORT HUENEME, CA - Ventura County

	SIC	EMP	PHONE	ENTRY #
Advantedge Technology Inc		D	805 488-0405	0
Alion Science and Tech Corp		D	805 488-8761	0
Interntional Longshore Whse Un		D	805 488-2944	0
Oxnard Beach Hotel LP		E	805 488-6560	0
Pride Industries		C	805 985-8481	0
United States Dept of Navy		A	805 982-6392	0
United States Dept of Navy		A	805 982-6370	0
Waggoners Trucking		D	800 999-9097	0

PORTER RANCH, CA - Los Angeles County

	SIC	EMP	PHONE	ENTRY #
American Technical Svcs Inc		D	951 372-9664	0
Coast To Coast Realty		D	818 360-2609	0
Infogen Labs Inc		D	818 825-5024	0

PORTERVILLE, CA - Tulare County

	SIC	EMP	PHONE	ENTRY #
Baird-Neece Packing Corp		C	559 784-3393	0
Bank of Sierra (HQ)		C	559 782-4300	0

GEOGRAPHIC

	SIC	EMP	PHONE	ENTRY #
Developmental Svcs Cal Dept		A	559 782-2222	0
E M Tharp Inc **(PA)**		D	559 782-5800	0
E W Merritt Farms **(PA)**		D	559 784-8916	0
Exeter Packers Inc		C	559 784-8820	0
Family Healthcare Network		C	559 781-7242	0
Fern Oaks Frms A Cal Gen Prtnr		E	559 684-8220	0
Foster Farms LLC		B	559 793-5501	0
Gaithers Family Home		E	559 781-0301	0
Good Shepherd Lutheran Hm of W **(PA)**		D	559 791-2000	0
Mitch Brown Construction Inc		D	559 781-6389	0
Moyles Central Vly Hlth Care		C	559 782-1509	0
Nuvi Global		A	559 306-2646	0
Propak Logistics Inc		C	559 782-8696	0
R & G Enterprises		C	559 781-1351	0
Raul V Acevedo		E	559 791-1304	0
River Island Country Club Inc		D	559 781-2917	0
Salvador Martinez		C	559 781-5150	0
Sierra Valley Rehab Center		C	559 784-7375	0
Sierra View Dst Hosp Leag Inc **(PA)**		C	559 784-1110	0
Sierra View Local Hospital Dst		B	559 781-7877	0
Sun Villa Inc		C	559 784-6644	0
Tharp Truck Rental Inc **(PA)**		C	559 782-5800	0
Tule River Indian Hlth Ctr Inc		D	559 784-2316	0
Valley Careidence Opco LLC		D	559 784-8371	0
Walmart Inc		B	559 783-1109	0
Wescordon Incorporated **(PA)**		C	559 784-8371	0

PORTOLA, CA - Plumas County

	SIC	EMP	PHONE	ENTRY #
R Joy Inc		D	530 832-5760	0

PORTOLA VALLEY, CA - San Mateo County

	SIC	EMP	PHONE	ENTRY #
Boething Treeland Farms Inc		A	650 851-4770	0
Intuit Inc		C	650 944-2840	0
McClenahan Pest Control Inc		E	650 326-8781	0
Pointspeed Inc		D	650 638-3720	0
SP McClenahan Co		D	650 326-8781	0

PORTOLA VALLY, CA - San Mateo County

	SIC	EMP	PHONE	ENTRY #
Semans Communications **(PA)**		D	650 529-9984	0

POTRERO, CA - San Diego County

	SIC	EMP	PHONE	ENTRY #
Rancho De Sus Ninos Inc		D	619 661-9232	0

POTTER VALLEY, CA - Mendocino County

	SIC	EMP	PHONE	ENTRY #
McFadden Farm		E	707 743-1122	0

POWAY, CA - San Diego County

	SIC	EMP	PHONE	ENTRY #
American Golf Corporation		E	760 737-9762	0
Arch Health Partners Inc **(HQ)**		D	858 675-3100	0
Bay City Equipment Inds Inc		D	619 938-8200	0
BCM Customer Service		D	858 679-5757	0
Benchmark Landscape		C	858 513-7190	0
Body Beautiful Car Wash Inc		D	858 748-4400	0
Braswells Villa Monte Vista		C	858 487-6242	0
Brieck Restoration Inc		E	858 679-9928	0
Califrnia Crtive Solutions Inc **(PA)**		D	858 208-4143	0
Centre Care Management Co LLC		C	858 613-6255	0
Champion Investment Corp **(PA)**		D	917 712-7807	0
Chef Works Inc **(PA)**		C	858 643-5600	0
Climatec LLC		E	858 391-7000	0
Community Dev Inst Head Start		D	858 668-2985	0
Concrete Images International		D	858 676-1253	0
Corodata Corporation **(PA)**		D	858 748-1100	0
Corovan Corporation **(PA)**		D	858 762-8100	0
Corovan Moving & Storage Co **(HQ)**		D	858 748-1100	0
D and D Concrete Cnstr Inc		D	619 518-9737	0
Decision Sciences Intl Corp		D	858 571-1900	0
Demcon Concrete Contrs Inc		D	858 748-5090	0
Diazyme Laboratories Inc		D	858 455-4768	0
Eappraiseit LLC **(PA)**		D	800 281-6200	0
Electronic Control Systems LLC		C	858 513-1911	0
Floaties Swim School LLC		C	877 277-7946	0
Geico General Insurance Co		B	858 848-8200	0
Generation Contracting & Emerg		E	858 679-9928	0
Hubb Systems LLC		D	510 865-9100	0
Ickler Electric Corporation		E	858 486-1585	0
Information Systems Labs Inc **(PA)**		E	858 535-9680	0
Jinx Inc **(PA)**		D	888 546-9266	0
Kiewit Infrastructure West Co		D	360 693-1478	0
Law Offices of Thomas W		D	858 883-2000	0
Lorber Greenfield & Polito LLP **(PA)**		D	858 486-6757	0
Maderas Golf Club		D	858 451-8100	0
Mutual Trading Co Inc		E	858 748-9458	0
Paladin Technologies Inc		C	858 668-1705	0
Palomar Health		B	858 613-4000	0
Pkl Services Inc		C	858 679-1755	0
Pomerado Operations LLC		D	858 487-6242	0

	SIC	EMP	PHONE	ENTRY #
Prestige Concrete		D	858 679-2772	0
Provoast Automation Controls **(PA)**		D	858 748-2237	0
Quality Reinforcing Inc		D	858 748-8400	0
Richmond Engineering Co Inc		C	800 589-7058	0
Rutledge Claims Management Inc		D	858 883-2000	0
San Diego Bay Area Elc Inc		D	858 748-2060	0
Smart & Final Stores Inc		A	858 748-0101	0
Sysco San Diego Inc		B	858 513-7300	0
T G T Enterprises Inc		C	858 413-0300	0
Tekworks Inc		C	858 668-1705	0
Trepco Imports & Dist Ltd		E	619 690-7999	0
Wr Chavez Construction Inc		D	858 375-2100	0

QUINCY, CA - Plumas County

	SIC	EMP	PHONE	ENTRY #
Artimisa & Co		D	530 283-3700	0
Plumas District Hospital **(PA)**		C	530 283-2121	0
Plumas District Hospital		C	530 283-0650	0
Plumas Rural Services		D	530 283-2725	0
Sierra Cscade Fmly Opprtnities **(PA)**		C	530 283-1242	0

RAMONA, CA - San Diego County

	SIC	EMP	PHONE	ENTRY #
Burch Construction Company Inc		E	760 788-9370	0
Famous Ramona Water Inc		E	760 789-0174	0
Innovative Drywall Systems Inc		D	760 743-0331	0
Prudential California Realty		D	858 487-3520	0
San Diego Country Estates Assn		C	760 789-3788	0
Spe Go Holdings Inc		E	858 638-0672	0
Triton Logistics Corporation		D	619 822-8832	0
United Power Contractors Inc		C	760 735-8028	0

RANCHO CORDOVA, CA - Sacramento County

	SIC	EMP	PHONE	ENTRY #
A B C D Associates		C	916 363-4843	0
ABI Document Support Svcs LLC		E	909 793-0613	0
Accentcare HM Hlth Scrmnto Inc		D	916 852-5888	0
AmeriGas Propane LP		D	916 852-7400	0
AT&T Services Inc		C	916 638-6096	0
Bergelectric Corp		D	916 636-1880	0
Bissell Brothers Janitorial		D	916 635-1852	0
Capital Engineering Cons Inc **(PA)**		D	916 851-3500	0
CBA Site Services Inc		D	925 754-7633	0
Clark Pest Ctrl Stockton Inc		E	916 635-7770	0
Corelogic Inc		D	916 431-2146	0
Courtyard Management Corp		E	916 638-3800	0
D7 Roofing Services Inc		D	916 447-2175	0
Dignity Health		C	916 851-2153	0
Dignity Health		E	916 851-3800	0
Dignity Health Med Foundation		A	916 379-2840	0
Dignity Health Med Foundation **(DH)**		C	916 379-2840	0
Ducks Unlimited Inc		E	916 852-2000	0
Educational Credit MGT Corp		B	800 367-1590	0
Enterprise Services LLC		A	916 636-1000	0
Fine Chemicals Holdings Corp		B	916 357-6880	0
Franklin Tmpleton Inv Svcs LLC		C	650 312-2000	0
Franklin Tmpleton Inv Svcs LLC **(DH)**		A	916 463-1500	0
Gei Consultants Inc		D	916 631-4500	0
General Electric Company		C	916 286-8020	0
General Environmental		D	916 351-0980	0
General Pool & Spa Supply Inc **(PA)**		D	916 853-2401	0
Harelson Mechanical Inc		D	916 386-2586	0
Health Net Federal Svcs LLC **(DH)**		A	916 935-5000	0
Heritage Community Credit Un		E	916 364-1700	0
Home Instead Senior Care		D	916 920-2273	0
Infor (us) Inc		C	916 921-0883	0
Infor Public Sector Inc **(DH)**		C	916 921-0883	0
Jason Mechanical Inc		E	916 638-8763	0
Judson Enterprises Inc **(PA)**		B	916 596-6721	0
Kaiser Foundation Hospitals		E	916 631-3088	0
Keenan & Associates		D	916 858-2981	0
Kleinfelder Inc		D	916 366-1701	0
Landcare USA LLC		D	916 635-0936	0
Lennar Homes Inc		C	916 517-4950	0
LLP Moss Adams		D	916 503-8100	0
Lyle Company		D	916 266-7000	0
Maximus Inc		D	916 364-6610	0
McKesson Corporation		D	916 636-8700	0
Michael Baker Intl Inc		D	916 361-8384	0
Mitchell Jones Concrete Inc		C	916 638-6870	0
Nehemiah Construction Inc		E	707 746-6815	0
Nevada Republic Electric N Inc		C	916 294-0140	0
Nightingale Vantagemed Corp **(HQ)**		D	916 638-4744	0
North State Elec Contrs Inc		D	916 572-0571	0
Pacific Coast Companies Inc		C	916 631-6500	0
Permanente Medical Group Inc		C	916 631-3000	0
Pick Pull Auto Dismantling Inc **(HQ)**		E	916 689-2000	0
PR Rancho Hotel LLC		D	916 638-4141	0
Presidio Hotel Group LLC		D	916 631-7500	0

2020 Directory of California
Wholesalers and Services Companies

(P-0000) Products & Services Section entry number
(PA)=Parent Co (HQ)=Headquarters (DH)=Div Headquarters

	SIC	EMP	PHONE	ENTRY #
Rci Electric Inc	D		916 858-8000	0
Ricoh Usa Inc	D		916 638-3333	0
River City Auto Recovery Inc	D		916 851-1100	0
Ron Nurss Inc	D		916 631-9761	0
Russell Mechanical Inc	D		916 635-2522	0
Scott Silva Concrete Inc	D		916 859-0593	0
Select Hotels Group LLC	E		916 638-4141	0
Sierra PCF HM & Comfort Inc	D		916 638-0543	0
Sunsystem Technology LLC **(PA)**	D		916 671-3351	0
Superior Vision Services Inc **(PA)**	D		800 507-3800	0
Technology Services Cal Dept	C		916 464-3747	0
Technology Services Cal Dept	E		916 464-3747	0
Tetra Tech Ec Inc	A		916 852-8300	0
Tri Tool Inc **(PA)**	C		916 288-6100	0
Two Rivers Demolition Inc	D		916 638-6775	0
Universal Site Services Inc	D		916 635-1122	0
Urata & Sons Concrete Inc	C		916 638-5364	0
Urata & Sons Concrete LLC	D		916 638-5364	0
USI Insurance Services Nat Inc	D		916 589-8000	0
Usko Expedite Inc	E		916 233-4455	0
Varis LLC	D		916 294-0860	0
Verizon Bus Netwrk Svcs Inc	C		916 779-5600	0
Vision Service Plan **(PA)**	A		916 851-5000	0
Vsp Holding Company Inc	D		916 851-5000	0
Wells Fargo Coml Dist Fin LLC	D		916 636-2020	0
William E Heinselman	E		916 920-0220	0

RANCHO CUCAMONGA, CA - San Bernardino County

	SIC	EMP	PHONE	ENTRY #
24 Hour Fitness Usa Inc	D		909 944-1000	0
ABM Janitorial Services Inc	C		909 987-3700	0
ABM Office Solutions Inc	D		909 527-8145	0
Adrianas Insurance Svcs Inc **(PA)**	D		909 291-4040	0
Allmark Inc **(PA)**	D		909 989-7556	0
Aloft Ontario-Rancho Cucamonga	D		909 484-2018	0
American Med	C		909 948-1714	0
Arrowhead Central Credit Union **(PA)**	B		866 212-4333	0
Artic Mechanical Inc **(PA)**	D		909 980-2539	0
Assistnce Leag of Fthill Cmmnt	D		909 987-2813	0
AT&T Corp	D		909 646-9644	0
Atlas Testing Laboratories Inc	E		909 373-4130	0
Automatic Data Processing Inc	C		800 225-5237	0
Automobile Club Southern Cal	B		909 477-8600	0
Automobile Club Southern Cal	C		909 980-0233	0
Bear Vly Fbrcators Stl Sup Inc	D		760 247-5381	0
Bowlero Corp	E		909 945-9392	0
Bradshaw International Inc **(HQ)**	B		909 476-3884	0
Branlyn Prominence Inc **(PA)**	D		909 476-9030	0
Bunzl Retail Services LLC	D		909 476-2457	0
C A Hofmann Construction Inc	E		909 484-5888	0
Ccna Vons Athletes For Life	D		805 453-2499	0
CDM Constructors Inc	D		909 579-3500	0
Century 21 Home Realtors	D		909 980-8000	0
Cerenzia Foods Inc	D		909 989-4000	0
Childrens Btq At Stevens Hope	E		909 256-0100	0
Collection Technology Inc	D		800 743-4284	0
Commercial Metals Company	B		909 899-9993	0
Corvel Corporation	C		909 257-3700	0
County of San Bernardino	D		909 945-4000	0
CU Cooperative Systems Inc **(PA)**	B		909 948-2500	0
Cucamonga Valley Water Dst	D		909 987-2591	0
Davis Brothers Framing Inc	C		909 944-4899	0
Eide Bailly LLP	B		909 466-4410	0
Empire Estates Inc	D		909 980-3100	0
Etiwanda Historical Society	D		909 899-8432	0
Evolution Fresh Inc **(HQ)**	D		800 794-9986	0
Excellnce of Inland Empire Inc	C		909 758-4311	0
Falken Tire Holdings Inc	D		800 723-2553	0
Fox Transportation Inc **(PA)**	D		909 291-4646	0
Gamut Construction Company Inc	D		909 948-0500	0
General Coatings Corporation	C		909 204-4150	0
General Micro Systems Inc **(PA)**	D		909 980-4863	0
General Motors LLC	D		800 521-7300	0
Gentex Corporation	D		909 481-7667	0
Giti Tire (usa) Ltd **(DH)**	D		909 527-8800	0
Hibshman Trading Corporation	D		909 581-1800	0
Hoffman Southwest Corp	D		909 397-0567	0
Honeyville Inc	D		909 980-9500	0
Infinity Svc Group Inc A Cal C	D		909 466-6237	0
Inland Empire Health Plan **(PA)**	A		909 890-2000	0
Inland Empire Utilities Agency	D		909 993-1755	0
J B Hunt Transport Inc	C		909 466-5361	0
JB Upland Ltd Liability Co	E		909 944-5456	0
Jett Pro Line Maintenance Inc **(PA)**	D		909 980-0552	0
Jones/Covey Group Incorporated	D		888 972-7581	0
Just Mortgage Inc	C		562 908-5000	0
Kaiser Foundation Hospitals	A		888 750-0036	0

	SIC	EMP	PHONE	ENTRY #
Knd Development 55 LLC	D		909 581-6400	0
L & R Distributors Inc	B		909 980-3807	0
Ledesma & Meyer Cnstr Co Inc	D		909 297-1100	0
Ledesma & Meyer Dev Inc	D		909 476-0590	0
Lexxiom Inc	B		909 581-7313	0
M & G Jewelers Inc	D		909 989-2929	0
Majestic Terminal Services Inc	D		909 390-1210	0
Majesty One Properties Inc	D		909 980-8000	0
McGuire Talent Inc	D		909 527-7006	0
McLane Foodservice Dist Inc	C		909 484-6100	0
Miracle Home Health Agency	E		562 653-0668	0
Msblous LLC	D		909 929-9689	0
National Cmnty Renaissance Cal **(PA)**	D		909 483-2444	0
National Community Renaissance **(PA)**	D		909 483-2444	0
National Mentor Inc	D		909 483-2505	0
Nationwide Guard Services Inc	D		909 608-1112	0
Network Intgrtion Partners Inc	D		909 919-2800	0
New Legend Inc	C		855 210-2300	0
Newco Distributors Inc	D		909 291-2240	0
Nongshim America Inc **(HQ)**	C		909 481-3698	0
Novatime Technology Inc **(HQ)**	D		909 895-8100	0
NRG California South LP	D		909 899-7241	0
Pacific Cycle Inc	E		909 481-5613	0
Par Electrical Contractors Inc	D		909 854-2880	0
Paradise Building Services	C		909 399-0707	0
Penwal Industries Inc	D		909 466-1555	0
Perris Valley Cmnty Hosp LLC	C		909 581-6400	0
Priority One Med Trnspt Inc **(PA)**	D		909 948-4400	0
Professnl Elec Cnstr Svcs Inc	D		909 373-4100	0
Promed Hlth Care Admnistrators	D		909 932-1045	0
Puratos Corporation	D		909 484-1312	0
R M A Group Inc **(PA)**	D		909 980-6096	0
Rancho Ccamonga Cmnty Hosp LLC	C		909 581-6400	0
Rancho Pacific Electric Inc	E		909 476-1022	0
Red Hill Country Club	D		909 982-1358	0
Replanet LLC	D		951 892-3079	0
Rwc Enterprises Inc	E		909 373-4100	0
Ryder Truck Rental Inc	D		909 980-3137	0
San Antonio Community Hospital	E		909 948-8000	0
Sheraton LLC	B		909 204-6100	0
Sherman Security	C		909 941-4167	0
Smith International Inc	C		909 906-7900	0
Southwire Company LLC	D		909 989-2888	0
Starwood Hotels & Resorts	C		909 484-2018	0
Sumitomo Rubber North Amer Inc **(HQ)**	D		909 466-1116	0
Sunrise Senior Living Inc	D		909 941-3001	0
Superior Elec Mech & Plbg Inc	B		909 357-9400	0
Supershuttle International Inc	C		909 944-2606	0
Tech Packaging Inc	D		909 243-7047	0
TRL Systems Incorporated	D		909 390-8392	0
US Tournament Golf Ltd Lblty	E		909 987-6695	0
Vehicle Accessory Center LLC	D		909 987-8237	0
Vocational Imprv Program Inc **(PA)**	C		909 483-5924	0
Weber Distribution Warehouses	E		909 481-1600	0
Yellow Jacket Drlg Svcs LLC	D		909 989-8563	0
Yuneec USA Inc	D		855 284-8888	0
Zions Bancorporation Nat Assn	C		909 581-1680	0

RANCHO DOMINGUEZ, CA - Los Angeles County

	SIC	EMP	PHONE	ENTRY #
Advanced Fresh Concepts Corp **(PA)**	D		310 604-3630	0
Afc Distribution Corp	E		310 604-3630	0
Allied High Tech Products Inc	D		310 635-2466	0
Calpipe Industries LLC **(HQ)**	C		562 803-4388	0
Cds Moving Equipment Inc **(PA)**	D		310 631-1100	0
Eco Flow Transportation LLC	D		310 816-0260	0
Heavy Load Transfer LLC	D		310 816-0260	0
Iap West Inc	D		310 667-9720	0
Kw International Inc	D		310 747-1380	0
Kw International Inc	B		213 703-6914	0
Mariak Industries Inc	B		310 661-4400	0
Mover Services Inc	E		310 868-5143	0
Neway Packaging Corp **(PA)**	D		602 454-9000	0
Nippon Ex Nec Lgstics Amer Inc	D		310 604-6100	0
Pacific Lighting Mfr Inc	D		310 327-7711	0
Premium Trnsp Svcs Inc **(PA)**	D		310 816-0260	0
R R Donnelley & Sons Company	E		310 784-8485	0
Samsung Electronics Amer Inc	D		310 537-7000	0
Seeds of Change Inc	D		310 764-7700	0
Soc Pathology Med Group Inc	D		310 225-3244	0
Union Supply Group Inc **(PA)**	C		310 603-8899	0
Unis LLC	D		310 747-7388	0

RANCHO MIRAGE, CA - Riverside County

	SIC	EMP	PHONE	ENTRY #
Agua Clnte Band Chilla Indians	A		760 321-2000	0
Annenberg Foundation Trust **(PA)**	D		760 202-2222	0
Betty Ford Center **(HQ)**	C		760 773-4100	0

Employment Codes: A=Over 500 employees, B=251-500,
C=101-250, D=51-100, E=50

2020 Directory of California
Wholesalers and Services Companies

© Mergent Inc. 1-800-342-5647

1601

GEOGRAPHIC

	SIC	EMP	PHONE	ENTRY #
Blx Group Inc		D	760 776-6622	0
Brookdale Senior Living Inc		D	760 346-7772	0
Charlie W Shaeffer Jr MD		D	760 346-0642	0
Childrens Museum of Desert		E	760 321-0602	0
Club of Sunrise Country		D	760 328-6549	0
Community Blood Bank Inc		D	760 773-4190	0
Country Villa Rancho		C	760 340-0053	0
Country Villa Service Corp		D	760 340-0053	0
Desert Cardiology Consultants		D	760 346-0642	0
Desert Orthopdc Center A Mdcl **(PA)**		D	760 568-2684	0
Dual Diagnosis Trtmnt Ctr Inc		C	949 324-4531	0
Eisenhower Medical Center **(PA)**		A	760 340-3911	0
Janet K Hartzler MD		D	760 340-3937	0
Mission Hills Country Club Inc		C	760 324-9400	0
Mission Hills Senior Living		D	760 770-7737	0
Morningside Community Assn		D	760 328-3323	0
Omni Hotels Corporation		B	760 568-2727	0
Outpatnt Eye Srgry Ctr of Dsrt		E	760 340-3937	0
Protect-For-Less Security Svcs		E	760 343-1192	0
Ritz-Carlton Hotel Company LLC		B	760 321-8282	0
Ritz-Carlton Hotel Company LLC		B	760 321-8282	0
Spa Cas Palmas		E	760 836-3106	0
Springs Club Inc		D	760 328-6549	0
Starwood Htls & Rsrts Wrldwde		B	760 328-5955	0
Thunderbird Country Club		D	760 328-2161	0
Windermere Real Estate East		D	760 568-2568	0

RANCHO MURIETA, CA - Sacramento County

	SIC	EMP	PHONE	ENTRY #
Energy Store of California Inc		D	916 825-8751	0
Rancho Murieta Country Club		D	916 354-2400	0
Whiting Construction Inc		D	916 354-2756	0

RANCHO PALOS VERDES, CA - Los Angeles County

	SIC	EMP	PHONE	ENTRY #
American Golf Corporation		D	310 377-7370	0
Artists Studio Gallery		D	424 206-9902	0
Belmont Village LP		D	310 377-9977	0
Carpet Solutions		E	310 886-3800	0
CIT Bank National Association		D	310 265-1656	0
Inman Spinosa & Buchan Inc		D	310 519-1080	0
Long Point Development LLC		A	310 265-2800	0
Los Verdes MNS Golf Cntry CLB		E	310 377-7370	0
Normandie Club LP		A	310 352-3486	0
Re/Max Plos Vrdes Rlty / Exces		E	310 541-5224	0
Salvation Army **(HQ)**		C	562 491-8496	0
Vh Property Corp		B	310 303-3210	0
Wells Fargo Bank National Assn		D	310 831-0632	0

RANCHO SANTA FE, CA - San Diego County

	SIC	EMP	PHONE	ENTRY #
A W Properties West LLC		D	858 832-1462	0
Bridges Club At Rancho SA		C	858 759-7200	0
Clubcorp Usa Inc		C	858 756-2471	0
Crosby National Golf Club LLC		D	858 756-6310	0
Del Mar Country Club Inc		D	858 759-5500	0
Fairbanks Ranch Cntry CLB Inc		C	858 259-8811	0
Farms Golf Club Inc		D	858 756-5585	0
First National Bank		B	858 756-3023	0
HCC Investors LLC		C	858 759-7200	0
Helen Woodward Animal Center **(PA)**		D	858 756-4117	0
Huntington Hotel Company		D	858 756-1131	0
Pacific Western Bank		B	858 756-3023	0
Rancho Santa Fe Association A		D	858 756-1182	0
Rancho Valencia Resort		D	858 756-1123	0
Willis Allen Real Estate		E	858 756-2444	0

RANCHO SANTA MARGARI, CA - Orange County

	SIC	EMP	PHONE	ENTRY #
Aliso Mechanical Incorporated		C	949 544-1601	0
Foundation 9 Entertainment Inc **(PA)**		C	949 698-1500	0
Jct Company LLC		E	949 589-2021	0
Safe Harbor Intl Relief		E	949 858-6786	0
Wendt Landscape Services Inc		E	949 589-8680	0

RCHO STA MARG, CA - Orange County

	SIC	EMP	PHONE	ENTRY #
C-21 Super Stars		D	949 389-1600	0
Capital Invstmnts Vntures Corp **(PA)**		C	949 858-0647	0
Fakouri Electrical Engrg Inc		D	949 888-2400	0
Hackney Electric Inc **(PA)**		D	949 264-4000	0
Jipc Management Inc		A	949 916-2000	0
Kisco Senior Living LLC		D	949 888-2250	0
Murano Group		D	949 409-1079	0
Nucourse Distribution Inc		D	866 655-4366	0
Padi Americas Inc		C	949 858-7234	0
Park Landscape Maintenance **(PA)**		B	949 546-8300	0
Park West Rescom Inc		C	949 546-8300	0
Santa Margarita Water District **(PA)**		D	949 459-6400	0
Sarco Inc		E	949 888-5548	0
Virtium LLC		D	949 888-2444	0
Wags & Wiggles Dog Daycare LLC **(PA)**		D	949 635-9655	0

RED BLUFF, CA - Tehama County

	SIC	EMP	PHONE	ENTRY #
Bio Industries Inc		E	530 529-3290	0
Brentwood Skill Nursng & Rehab		D	530 527-2046	0
Business Connections		D	530 527-6229	0
Concessionaires Urban Park **(PA)**		B	530 529-1512	0
County of Tehama		C	530 527-5631	0
County of Tehama		D	530 527-4052	0
Lassen Hse Assisted Living LLC		E	530 529-2900	0
Lassen Medical Group Inc **(PA)**		D	530 527-0414	0
Pactiv LLC		D	530 529-3340	0
St Elizabeth Community Hosp **(DH)**		D	530 529-7760	0
United Sttes Bowl Congress Inc		D	530 527-9049	0
Walmart Inc		A	530 529-0916	0

REDDING, CA - Shasta County

	SIC	EMP	PHONE	ENTRY #
Addus Healthcare Inc		D	530 247-0858	0
Airgas Inc		B	530 241-1544	0
Alexandria Clayton		E	530 262-5961	0
Ameripride Services Inc		E	530 242-0564	0
Aramark Unf & Career AP LLC		D	530 241-6433	0
Best Western Hilltop Inn		E	530 221-6100	0
Big Lgue Dreams Consulting LLC		C	530 223-1177	0
Bridge Bay Resort & Marina		D	530 275-3021	0
California Oregon Broadcasting **(HQ)**		D	530 243-7777	0
California Physicians Service		C	530 351-6115	0
Califrnia Physcn Reimbursement		D	530 241-0473	0
Cardinal Health Inc		D	530 225-8735	0
Care Options Management Plans **(PA)**		D	530 242-8580	0
CB C&C Properties/Comm Di Inc		D	530 221-7551	0
Charter Cmmnctons Oprating LLC		E	530 241-7352	0
Class Act Hair & Nail Salon		D	530 223-3442	0
Copper Ridge Care Center		C	530 222-2273	0
County of Shasta		D	530 225-5000	0
County of Shasta		D	530 225-5554	0
County of Shasta		D	530 245-6300	0
County of Shasta		E	530 225-2999	0
Crestwood Behavioral Hlth Inc		D	530 221-0976	0
David Civalier MD Inc		E	530 244-4034	0
Dignity Health		C	530 225-6345	0
Donor Network West		D	510 418-0336	0
Far Northern Coordinating Coun **(PA)**		D	530 222-4791	0
Federal Express Corporation		C	800 463-3339	0
Fedex Ground Package Sys Inc		E	800 463-3339	0
Foothill Distributing Co Inc		C	530 243-3932	0
Forestry and Fire Protection		C	530 225-2418	0
Golden Living LLC		D	530 241-6756	0
Honolua Bay Holdings LLC		E	530 243-6317	0
Interim Assisited Care of Nort		D	530 722-1530	0
Interim Hlthcare Nthrn Cal Inc **(PA)**		B	530 221-1300	0
James D Tate MD		D	530 225-8710	0
JF Shea Construction Inc		E	530 246-4292	0
Kaidan Hospitality LP		D	530 221-8700	0
Kindred Nursing Centers W LLC		C	530 243-6317	0
Knot Wedding Wire		E	530 242-1621	0
Ku Kyoung		C	510 582-2765	0
Lassen Canyon Nursery Inc **(PA)**		C	530 223-1075	0
MD Imaging Inc A Prof Med Corp		D	530 243-1249	0
Medical Home Specialists Inc		C	530 226-5517	0
Merchants Bank of Commerce **(HQ)**		D	530 224-7355	0
Mercy Foundation North		D	530 247-3424	0
Mercy HM Svcs A Cal Ltd Partnr **(DH)**		A	530 225-6000	0
Mercy HM Svcs A Cal Ltd Partnr		B	530 225-6000	0
Mercy HM Svcs A Cal Ltd Partnr		D	530 245-4070	0
Meyers Earthwork Inc		D	530 365-8858	0
Muse Concrete Contractors Inc		D	530 226-5151	0
Nichols Melburg Rossetto Assoc **(PA)**		E	530 222-3300	0
North State Security Inc		D	530 243-0295	0
Northern California Hlth Care		D	530 223-2332	0
Northern California Rehab		C	530 246-9000	0
Northern Valley Catholic Socia		C	530 241-0552	0
Northstar Senior Living Inc		A	530 242-8300	0
Ocadian Care Centers LLC		C	530 246-9000	0
Pacific Gas and Electric Co		D	530 365-7672	0
Parenthood of Planned		D	530 351-7100	0
Patients Hospital		D	530 225-8700	0
Peerless Building Maint Inc		D	530 222-6369	0
Pre-Employcom		D	800 300-1821	0
Pre-Employcom		D	800 300-1821	0
Prime Healthcare Services		A	530 244-5400	0
Prime Healthcare Servs Sh		A	530 244-5458	0
Redding Aero Enterprises Inc		D	530 224-2300	0
Redding Drywall Systems Inc		E	530 222-8767	0
Redding Family Medicine Assoc		D	530 244-4907	0
Redding Pathologists Lab		D	530 225-8050	0
Redding Rancheria **(PA)**		D	530 225-8979	0

Mergent email: customerrelations@mergent.com

1602

2020 Directory of California
Wholesalers and Services Companies

(P-0000) Products & Services Section entry number
(PA)=Parent Co (HQ)=Headquarters (DH)=Div Headquarters

	SIC	EMP	PHONE	ENTRY #
Redding Rancheria		D	530 224-2700	0
Remi Vista Inc (PA)		C	530 245-5805	0
Riverview Golf and Country CLB		D	530 224-2254	0
Roy E Ladd Inc		E	530 241-6102	0
Sac River Outfitters		D	530 275-3500	0
Securitas SEC Svcs USA Inc		D	530 245-0256	0
Sfn Group Inc		C	530 222-3434	0
Shasta Convalescent Center		C	530 222-3630	0
Shasta County Head Start Child (PA)		E	530 241-1036	0
Shasta Lake Resorts LP		D	209 785-3300	0
Sheraton Redding Hotel		D	530 364-2800	0
Sierra Oaks Senior Living		D	530 241-5100	0
State Compensation Insur Fund		C	888 782-8338	0
Steve Manning Construction Inc		D	530 222-0810	0
Tenet Healthsystem Medical		D	530 222-1992	0
Thom Sharon & G Enterprises		E	530 226-8350	0
Tierra Oaks Golf Club Inc		D	530 275-0795	0
Turtle Bay Exploration Park		E	530 243-4282	0
Utility Tree Service LLC (DH)		E	530 226-0330	0
VCA Inc		D	530 224-2200	0
Veterans Affairs Cal Dept		C	530 224-3300	0
Veterans Health Administration		B	530 226-7555	0
Vibra Healthcare LLC		D	530 246-9000	0
Walsh Group Inc		D	530 221-4405	0
Willow Sprngs Alzhmrs Spcl Cr		E	530 242-0654	0
Win River Hotel Corporation		E	530 226-5111	0
Win-River Resort & Casino		B	530 243-3377	0
Yaley Enterprises Inc		E	530 365-5252	0
Yanaco Inc		C	530 246-9550	0
Youth For Change		D	530 605-1520	0

REDLANDS, CA - San Bernardino County

	SIC	EMP	PHONE	ENTRY #
ABI Attorneys Service Inc (PA)		D	909 793-0613	0
Ach Mechanical Contractors Inc		D	909 307-2850	0
AG Redlands LLC		C	909 793-2678	0
American Baptist Homes of West		C	909 335-3077	0
American Baptist Homes of West		C	909 793-1233	0
American Med		D	909 793-7676	0
Ash Holdings LLC		D	909 793-2609	0
Assistance League of Redlands		C	909 792-2675	0
Beaver Medical Clinic Inc (PA)		C	909 793-3311	0
Becton Dickinson and Company		D	909 748-7300	0
Bon Appetit Management Co		C	909 748-8970	0
Braswell Col Care Redlands CA		C	909 792-6050	0
Central Svc Ctr & Exec Offs		E	909 307-6555	0
Citigroup Inc		D	909 335-0547	0
City of Redlands (PA)		D	909 798-7531	0
City of Redlands		E	909 798-7525	0
Coldwell Banker RE Corp		C	909 792-4147	0
Countryside Inn-Corona LP		E	909 335-9024	0
David Ollis Landscape Dev Inc		E	909 307-1911	0
DSC Logistics Inc		D	909 363-4354	0
Enerpath Services Inc		C	909 335-1699	0
Epic Management LP (PA)		C	909 799-1818	0
First American Title Insur Co		C	909 889-0311	0
Geodis Logistics LLC		D	909 801-3145	0
Girl Scuts San Grgonio Council (PA)		D	909 307-6555	0
Harvest Facility Holdings LP		D	909 793-8691	0
Hr Mission Commons Fc 5183		D	909 793-8691	0
Hydro Tek Systems Inc		D	909 799-9222	0
Inland Hlth Org of So Cal (DH)		E	909 335-7171	0
Jonbec Care Incorporated (PA)		D	909 798-4003	0
Kaiser Foundation Hospitals		D	888 750-0036	0
Kuehne + Nagel Inc		C	909 574-2300	0
L Lyon Distributing Inc		E	909 798-7129	0
Larry Jacinto Construction Inc		D	909 794-2151	0
Larry Jacinto Farming Inc		D	909 794-2276	0
Layne Christensen Company		C	909 390-2833	0
Lois Lauer Realty		C	909 748-7000	0
Loma Linda University		D	909 558-6422	0
Loma Linda University Med Ctr		B	909 558-9275	0
Loma Linda Vet Association For		D	909 583-6250	0
M Block & Sons Inc		C	909 335-6684	0
Mountain Top Comm Svcs LLC		E	909 798-4400	0
Mountain West Financial Inc (PA)		B	909 793-1500	0
Option One Home Med Eqp Inc		C	909 478-5413	0
P & R Paper Supply Co Inc (PA)		C	909 389-1811	0
Performance Team Frt Sys Inc		C	424 358-6943	0
Performance Team LLC		B	801 301-1732	0
Plum Healthcare Group LLC		D	909 793-2609	0
Plumbing Systems West Inc		D	909 794-3823	0
Prime-Line Products Company (DH)		B	909 887-8118	0
Pro-Craft Construction Inc		C	909 790-5222	0
R J M Construction Inc		E	909 794-8853	0
Redlands Cmnty Hosp Foundation		C	909 793-1382	0
Redlands Community Hospital (PA)		D	909 335-5500	0

	SIC	EMP	PHONE	ENTRY #
Redlands Country Club		D	909 793-2661	0
Redlands Foothill Groves		E	909 793-2164	0
Redlands Ford Inc		E	909 793-3211	0
RHS Corp		A	909 335-5500	0
Safely Home		D	909 370-0343	0
Silverscreen Healthcare Inc		C	909 793-1382	0
Soren McAdam Christianson LLP		D	909 798-2222	0
Southern California Gas Co		B	909 335-7802	0
Spectra Premium (usa) Corp		D	951 653-0640	0
Study Tapes		D	909 792-0111	0
Tarbell Financial Corporation		D	909 335-0750	0
United Road Towing Inc		D	909 798-4863	0
Weber Distribution LLC		B	909 335-8800	0
Westcor Construction of Cal		C	909 796-8900	0
Xpo Logistics Supply Chain Inc		D	909 518-2095	0
YMCA of East Valley (PA)		C	909 798-9622	0

REDONDO BEACH, CA - Los Angeles County

	SIC	EMP	PHONE	ENTRY #
4g Wireless Inc		D	310 376-2299	0
Aamcom LLC		E	310 318-8100	0
Axiom Home Warranty LLC		C	844 562-9466	0
Beach Cities Health District		C	310 374-3426	0
Beachsports Inc		E	310 372-2202	0
Bicara Ltd		B	310 316-6222	0
Catalina Events Inc		E	310 925-6986	0
Cmp Wellness LLC		D	323 697-8808	0
Corporate Production Designs		E	310 937-9663	0
Craft Resources Inc		C	310 937-3744	0
D & W LLC		D	310 345-0075	0
Dsd Trucking Inc (PA)		D	310 338-3395	0
Fire Safe Systems Inc		D	310 542-0585	0
Heartland Payment Systems LLC		D	424 247-8521	0
Hpt Trs Ihg-2 Inc		B	310 318-8888	0
K & P Janitorial Services		D	310 540-8878	0
Leidos Inc		D	310 791-9671	0
Leight Sales Co Inc		D	310 223-1000	0
Map Cargo Global Logistics (PA)		D	310 297-8300	0
Max Sommers Real Estate		D	310 560-1499	0
Muscle Improvement Inc		E	310 374-5522	0
NBC Consulting Inc		D	310 798-5000	0
Nzg Specialties Inc (PA)		D	310 216-7575	0
Portofino Hotel Partners LP		C	310 379-8481	0
Reign Accessories Inc		E	310 297-6400	0
Riviera Finance of Texas Inc (PA)		C	310 540-3993	0
Scat Enterprises Inc		D	310 370-5501	0
Silverado Senior Living Inc		D	424 257-6418	0
Smart & Final Stores Inc		B	323 497-8528	0
Sport Center Fitness Inc		D	310 376-9443	0
Stevens Global Logistics Inc (PA)		D	310 216-5645	0
Thor Group Inc (PA)		E	310 727-1777	0
Transportation Concept Inc		D	323 268-2202	0
Trcf Redondo LLC		E	310 536-1209	0
Wedgewood Inc (PA)		D	310 640-3070	0
Westwind Engineering Inc		C	310 831-3454	0
Westwind Engineering Inc		D	310 831-3454	0

REDWOOD CITY, CA - San Mateo County

	SIC	EMP	PHONE	ENTRY #
ABC Bus Inc		D	650 368-3364	0
Accor Bus & Leisure N Amer LLC		C	650 598-9000	0
Acxiom Corporation		D	650 356-3400	0
Adaptive Spectrum and Signal A		D	650 264-2667	0
Alliances MGT Consulting Inc		E	650 780-0466	0
Amobee Inc (DH)		C	650 353-4399	0
Anomali Incorporated		C	408 800-4050	0
Ascend Clinical LLC (PA)		C	800 800-5655	0
AT&T Corp		C	650 780-1005	0
Automatic Data Processing Inc		C	800 225-5237	0
Barnard Bessac Joint Venture		D	650 212-8957	0
Bay Brokerage Inc		E	650 413-1721	0
Bay Clubs Inc		D	650 593-1112	0
Betterworks Systems Inc		D	650 656-9013	0
Bkf Engineers (PA)		C	650 482-6300	0
Bluevine Capital Inc		D	888 216-9619	0
Box Inc (PA)		C	877 729-4269	0
Broadvision Inc (PA)		D	650 331-1000	0
Brookdale Lving Cmmunities Inc		D	650 366-3900	0
Buildingminds Inc		E	973 397-6510	0
C3ai Inc (PA)		C	650 503-2200	0
California State Automobile		D	650 572-5600	0
Care 2		D	650 622-0860	0
Chapel of Chimes		D	650 349-4411	0
Child Care Coordinating Counsi		E	650 517-1400	0
Clp Resources Inc		C	650 261-2100	0
Coherus Biosciences Inc (PA)		D	650 649-3530	0
Community Gatepath		C	650 259-8500	0
Coretechs Staffing Inc		D	650 363-7960	0

Employment Codes: A=Over 500 employees, B=251-500,
C=101-250, D=51-100, E=50

2020 Directory of California
Wholesalers and Services Companies

© Mergent Inc. 1-800-342-5647

1603

GEOGRAPHIC

	SIC	EMP	PHONE	ENTRY #
County of San Mateo		C	650 599-7336	0
County of San Mateo		C	650 363-4915	0
County of San Mateo		E	650 363-4343	0
County of San Mateo		C	650 363-4548	0
County of San Mateo		D	650 363-1910	0
County of San Mateo		D	650 363-4020	0
County of San Mateo		C	650 363-4244	0
Covington & Burling LLP		C	650 632-4700	0
Crystal Dynamics Inc **(DH)**		D	650 421-7600	0
Cyara Solutions Corp		C	650 549-8522	0
Delphix Corp **(PA)**		E	650 494-1645	0
Des Architects + Engineers Inc		C	650 364-6453	0
Digital Insight Corporation **(HQ)**		C	818 879-1010	0
Diva Systems Corporation		C	650 779-3000	0
Dpr Construction Inc **(PA)**		A	650 474-1450	0
Dpr Construction A Gen Partnr **(HQ)**		A	650 474-1450	0
El Concilio San Mateo Cnty Inc		E	650 373-1080	0
Electronic Arts Inc **(PA)**		B	650 628-1500	0
Equilar Inc		C	877 441-6090	0
Equinix Inc **(PA)**		C	650 598-6000	0
Equinix (us) Enterprises Inc **(HQ)**		D	650 598-6363	0
Ernst & Young LLP		C	650 802-4500	0
Evernote Corporation **(PA)**		C	650 216-7700	0
Festival Fun Parks LLC		E	949 261-0404	0
Fish & Richardson PC		D	650 839-5070	0
Flo Health Inc		D	510 303-9307	0
French Redwood Inc		C	650 598-9000	0
Genium Inc		E	415 935-3593	0
Genomic Health Inc **(PA)**		C	650 556-9300	0
Genomic Health Inc		B	650 556-9300	0
Glint Inc		D	650 817-7240	0
Goodwill Industrs of San Franc		D	650 556-9709	0
Granite Rock Co		B	650 869-3370	0
Green Again Ldscpg & Con Inc		D	650 368-9304	0
Guardant Health Inc **(PA)**		B	855 698-8887	0
Gunderson Dettmer Stough Ville **(PA)**		C	650 321-2400	0
Heartflow Inc **(PA)**		D	650 241-1221	0
Heartland Payment Systems LLC		D	650 678-2824	0
I2c Inc		B	650 593-5400	0
Imperva Inc **(HQ)**		C	650 345-9000	0
Inflection Risk Solutions LLC		E	650 618-9910	0
Informatica LLC **(PA)**		C	650 385-5000	0
Interana Inc		D	650 569-1122	0
Ipass Inc **(HQ)**		C	650 232-4100	0
Isheriff Inc		C	650 412-4300	0
Itco Solutions Inc		B	650 367-0514	0
Kainos Home & Training Ctr		E	650 361-1355	0
Kaiser Foundation Hospitals		A	650 299-2000	0
Kaspick & Co LLC **(DH)**		D	650 585-4100	0
Keenan & Associates		D	650 306-6500	0
Lastline Inc **(PA)**		E	805 456-7075	0
Lydia C Gonzalez		E	650 299-4707	0
Mid-Peninsula Tyrella Corp **(PA)**		D	650 299-8000	0
Motiga Inc		D	425 748-8509	0
Multiven Inc		E	408 828-2715	0
Oracle America Inc		D	800 633-0584	0
Oracle Corporation **(PA)**		A	650 506-7000	0
Oracle Systems Corporation		B	650 506-0300	0
Oracle Systems Corporation **(HQ)**		A	650 506-7000	0
Origin Systems Inc		B	650 628-1500	0
Paxata Inc		D	650 542-7897	0
Perfect World Entrmt Inc		C	650 590-7700	0
Permanente Medical Group Inc		D	650 299-2000	0
Permanente Medical Group Inc		D	650 299-2015	0
Permanente Medical Group Inc		D	650 598-2852	0
Photo Holdings LLC		A	650 610-5200	0
Picture It On Canvas Inc		D	858 679-1200	0
Plug & Play LLC		D	650 722-2195	0
Provident Credit Union **(PA)**		C	650 508-0300	0
Pubmatic Inc **(PA)**		D	650 351-9162	0
Quantbiome Inc		E	408 421-0315	0
Quinn Emanuel Urquhart		D	650 801-5000	0
Reputationcom Inc **(PA)**		C	650 381-3056	0
Revolution Medicines Inc **(PA)**		D	650 481-6801	0
Ropers Majeski Kohn Bentley **(PA)**		D	650 364-8200	0
Ruiz Janitorial Co Inc		E	650 222-2078	0
S J Amoroso Cnstr Co Inc **(PA)**		B	650 654-1900	0
San Mateo Credit Union **(PA)**		D	650 363-1725	0
Seiler LLP **(PA)**		C	650 365-4646	0
Selligent Inc **(HQ)**		D	650 421-4255	0
Senior Companions At Home		E	650 364-1265	0
Sequoia Adrc LP		D	650 364-5504	0
Sequoia Health Services **(DH)**		D	650 369-5811	0
Shopkick Inc		D	650 763-8727	0
Shutterfly Inc **(PA)**		C	650 610-5200	0

	SIC	EMP	PHONE	ENTRY #
Silicon Valley Clean Water		D	650 591-7121	0
Sizmek Dsp Inc **(DH)**		C	650 595-1300	0
Skire Inc		D	650 289-2600	0
Sumo Logic Inc		B	650 810-8700	0
Talend Inc **(HQ)**		C	650 539-3200	0
Telecare Corporation		C	650 367-1890	0
Tradebeam Inc		D	650 653-4800	0
Trilliant Incorporated		D	650 204-5050	0
Trilliant Networks Inc **(PA)**		D	650 204-5050	0
Turn Inc **(DH)**		C	650 353-4399	0
University Art Center Inc **(PA)**		D	650 328-3500	0
Verity Health System Cal Inc		B	310 900-8900	0
Verity Health System Cal Inc		D	650 551-6507	0
W Bradley Electric Inc		C	650 701-1502	0
W L Butler Construction Inc **(PA)**		E	650 361-1270	0
Water Heaters Only Inc		D	650 368-9998	0
Weil Gotshal & Manges LLP		C	650 802-3000	0
WL Butler Inc		C	650 361-1270	0
Yodlee Inc **(HQ)**		C	650 980-3600	0
Zb Rehab Staffing Inc		D	650 396-2207	0
Zyme Solutions Inc **(PA)**		D	650 585-2258	0

REDWOOD VALLEY, CA - Mendocino County

	SIC	EMP	PHONE	ENTRY #
Consolidated Tribal Health Prj		D	707 485-5115	0
Redwood Valley Industrial Park		D	707 485-8766	0

REEDLEY, CA - Fresno County

	SIC	EMP	PHONE	ENTRY #
Beaver Dam Health Care Center		D	559 638-3577	0
Cal Packing & Storage LP		D	559 638-2929	0
Moonlight Packing Corporation		A	559 638-7799	0
Moonlight Packing Corporation **(PA)**		C	559 638-7799	0
Moya Juan Farm Labor Services		C	559 638-9498	0
Paragon Health & Rehab CT		E	559 638-3578	0
Rio Vista Ventures LLC		E	559 897-6730	0
Sierra View Homes		C	559 637-2256	0
Trinity Fruit Packing Company		C	559 743-3913	0
Trinity Packing Company Inc **(PA)**		B	559 433-3785	0
Trinity Packing Company Inc		B	559 743-3913	0

RESEDA, CA - Los Angeles County

	SIC	EMP	PHONE	ENTRY #
Advanced Bioservices LLC **(PA)**		D	818 342-0100	0
Alumatec Inc		D	818 609-7460	0
Auto Body Management Inc		E	818 888-7654	0
Chase Group Llc		D	818 708-3533	0
Fabulous & Company LLC		E	818 261-7242	0
GK Management Co Inc		D	818 705-8834	0
Honda R&D Americas Inc		E	818 345-7922	0
Longwood Management Corp		D	818 881-7414	0
Los Angles Jewish HM For Aging **(PA)**		A	818 774-3000	0
Los Angles Jewish HM For Aging		B	818 774-3000	0
Mid Vlley Racquetball Athc CLB		C	818 705-6500	0
Moore Foundations Inc		E	818 698-4737	0
Spa Dreams		D	818 298-1120	0
West Valley Family YMCA		C	818 774-2840	0
Woodland Care Center LLC		D	818 881-4540	0

RIALTO, CA - San Bernardino County

	SIC	EMP	PHONE	ENTRY #
B & B Plastics Recyclers Inc **(PA)**		D	909 829-3606	0
Burlingame Industries Inc **(PA)**		D	909 355-7000	0
Caremark Rx Inc		D	909 822-1164	0
Confire J P A		D	909 356-2375	0
Crestview Cnvalescent Hosp Inc		C	909 877-1361	0
Geodis Logistics LLC		D	909 240-6298	0
Guitar Center Holdings Inc		E	818 735-8800	0
Hazmat Tsdf Inc **(PA)**		D	909 873-4141	0
Mercy Air Tri-County LLC		C	909 829-1051	0
Mesa Counselling		E	909 421-9301	0
Molina Healthcare Inc		C	909 546-7116	0
Ptr Group Inc		E	951 965-1822	0
Robert Clapper Cnstr Svcs Inc		D	909 829-3688	0
Sierra Lathing Company Inc		C	909 421-0211	0
Simple Luxuries LLC		E	310 627-6514	0
So-Cal Strl Stl Fbrication Inc		E	909 877-1299	0
State Pipe & Supply Inc **(DH)**		D	909 877-9999	0
Sudhakar Company International		D	909 879-2933	0
Vista Cove Care Ctr - Rialto		D	909 877-1361	0
Wjc Trapp Elementary Pta		E	909 820-7914	0

RICHGROVE, CA - Tulare County

	SIC	EMP	PHONE	ENTRY #
Famous Vineyards LLC		D	661 392-5000	0
Vincent B Zaninovich Sons Inc		A	661 720-9031	0

RICHMOND, CA - Contra Costa County

	SIC	EMP	PHONE	ENTRY #
Alsco Inc		D	510 237-9634	0
Alta Vista Solutions		C	510 594-0510	0
Alten Construction Inc		D	510 234-4200	0
Ameripride Services Inc		E	800 748-6178	0

Mergent email: customerrelations@mergent.com
1604

2020 Directory of California
Wholesalers and Services Companies

(P-0000) Products & Services Section entry number
(PA)=Parent Co (HQ)=Headquarters (DH)=Div Headquarters

	SIC	EMP	PHONE	ENTRY #
Aquatic Science Center		E	510 746-7334	0
AT&T Corp		D	510 965-9714	0
Bay Area Beverage Co		C	510 965-6120	0
Bay Area Distributing Coinc		E	510 232-8554	0
Bay Cities Crane & Rigging Inc (PA)		E	510 232-7222	0
Bay City Mechanical Inc		C	510 233-7000	0
Ben Myerson Candy Co Inc		D	510 236-2233	0
BP West Coast Products LLC		B	510 231-4724	0
Brand Services LLC		D	510 231-9640	0
C Overaa & Co (PA)		C	510 234-0926	0
Califrnia Atism Foundation Inc (PA)		C	510 758-0433	0
Cardinal Health Inc		D	510 232-2030	0
Century Theatres Inc		D	510 758-9626	0
Chevron Energy Technology Co (HQ)		D	510 242-5059	0
Chevron Investor Inc		D	510 242-3000	0
City of Richmond		D	510 620-6788	0
Contra Costa ARC		D	510 233-7303	0
Ctc Food International Inc (PA)		E	650 873-7600	0
Dahl-Beck Electric Co		D	510 237-2325	0
Department Health Care Svcs		D	510 412-3700	0
Diversified Health Svcs Del (PA)		C	510 231-6200	0
East Bay Municipl Utilty Distr		C	866 403-2683	0
Ecology Control Industries		D	510 235-1393	0
First Student Inc		D	510 237-6677	0
Foss Maritime Company		D	510 307-4271	0
Gardeners Guild Inc		C	415 457-0400	0
Hotel Mac Restaurant Inc		E	510 233-0576	0
Hydrox Properties Xii LLC		D	510 262-7200	0
Inter-Rail Trnspt Nshville LLC		D	510 231-2744	0
Kaiser Foundation Hospitals		B	510 307-1500	0
Levin-Richmond Terminal Corp		D	510 232-4422	0
Macdonald Housing Partners LP		E	510 620-0865	0
New Ngc Inc		E	510 234-6745	0
Oliver & Company Inc		D	510 412-9090	0
Pacific Hotel Management LLC		D	510 262-0700	0
Palecek Imports Inc (PA)		D	510 236-7730	0
Permanente Medical Group Inc		D	510 231-5406	0
Public Health California Dept		C	510 412-1502	0
Richmond Country Club		D	510 231-2241	0
Richmond Rescue Mission (PA)		D	510 215-4555	0
Richmond Sanitary Service Inc (HQ)		C	510 262-7100	0
Richmond Wholesale Meat Co		D	510 233-5111	0
Rubber Dust Inc (PA)		D	510 237-6344	0
Rubicon Enterprises Inc		C	510 235-1516	0
Rubicon Programs Incorporated (PA)		D	510 235-1516	0
S P R E Inc		D	510 222-8340	0
San Francisco Bay Area Rapid		C	510 233-6848	0
San Francisco Bay Area Rapid		D	510 233-7444	0
Sangamo Therapeutics Inc (PA)		C	510 970-6000	0
Sims Group USA Corporation (DH)		D	510 412-5300	0
Sims Group USA Corporation		D	510 236-0606	0
Siteworks Landscape Inc		C	510 843-0409	0
Spr Op Co Inc		C	510 232-5030	0
Stalker Software Inc		E	415 569-2280	0
Sunpower Corporation Systems (DH)		C	510 260-8200	0
T F Louderback Inc (PA)		C	510 965-6120	0
United Parcel Service Inc OH		C	510 262-2338	0
Universal Bldg Svcs & Sup Co (PA)		D	510 527-1078	0
Vicor Inc		D	510 621-2000	0
Vila Construction Co		D	510 236-9111	0
West Countra Costa Youth Svcs (PA)		D	510 412-5647	0
West County Resource Recovery		E	510 231-4200	0
WR Forde Associates Inc		D	510 215-9338	0
Young MNS Chrstn Assn of E Bay		A	510 223-7070	0
Young MNS Chrstn Assn of E Bay		B	510 412-5647	0
Young MNS Chrstn Assn of E Bay		C	510 222-9622	0

RIDGECREST, CA - Kern County

	SIC	EMP	PHONE	ENTRY #
Altaone Federal Credit Union (PA)		C	760 371-7000	0
Community Action Partnr Kern		C	760 371-1469	0
Desert Area Resources Training		D	760 375-8494	0
Drummond Medical Group Inc		C	760 446-4571	0
Golden Living LLC		D	760 446-3591	0
Great Western Hotels Corp		E	760 446-6543	0
Jacobs Technology Inc		C	760 446-1549	0
L3 Technologies Inc		D	760 375-0390	0
Leidos Inc		B	858 826-7670	0
Navy Exchange Service Command		D	760 939-8681	0
New Directions Tech Inc (PA)		D	760 384-2444	0
Peekay Investments Prpts LLC		E	714 403-1923	0
Poulin Corporation (PA)		D	760 375-6531	0
Ridgecrest Regional Hospital		B	760 499-7260	0
Ridgecrest Regional Hospital (PA)		D	760 446-3551	0

RIO LINDA, CA - Sacramento County

	SIC	EMP	PHONE	ENTRY #
KRC Builders Incorporated		D	916 417-1200	0

	SIC	EMP	PHONE	ENTRY #
U S Army Corps of Engineers		D	916 649-0133	0

RIO VISTA, CA - Solano County

	SIC	EMP	PHONE	ENTRY #
California Vegetable Spc Inc		D	707 374-2111	0
Lindsay Transportation		C	707 374-6800	0
Paul Graham Drilling & Svc Co		C	707 374-5123	0
Trilogy Rio Vista		D	707 374-1100	0

RIPON, CA - San Joaquin County

	SIC	EMP	PHONE	ENTRY #
Brocchini Farms Inc		E	209 599-4229	0
Cheema Freightlines LLC		D	209 599-0777	0
Fishers Nursery		D	209 599-3412	0
Gico Management		D	209 599-7131	0
Lassen Canyon Nursery Inc		D	209 599-7777	0
Nulaid Foods Inc (PA)		D	209 599-2121	0
Nushake Inc		D	209 239-8616	0
V&V Farm Labor Contractor		E	209 599-4834	0

RIVERBANK, CA - Stanislaus County

	SIC	EMP	PHONE	ENTRY #
Econtactlive Inc		D	209 548-4300	0
LMC West Inc		E	209 869-0144	0
Onemain Holdings Inc		D	209 869-8030	0
Valley West Health Care Inc		D	209 869-2569	0

RIVERDALE, CA - Fresno County

	SIC	EMP	PHONE	ENTRY #
Ayala Corporation		C	559 867-5700	0
Linda Terra Farms (PA)		C	559 867-3473	0
Maddox Dairy LLC		D	559 866-5308	0
Maddox Dairy A Ltd Partnership (PA)		D	559 867-3545	0
Maddox Dairy A Ltd Partnership		E	559 867-4457	0
Maddox Farms		D	559 866-5308	0
Terra Linda Farms 1		E	559 867-3400	0

RIVERSIDE, CA - Riverside County

	SIC	EMP	PHONE	ENTRY #
20/20 Plumbing & Heating Inc (PA)		D	951 396-2020	0
A F V W Health Center		B	951 697-2025	0
A-Check America Inc (PA)		C	951 750-1501	0
Ace Cash Express Inc		C	951 509-3506	0
Adkison Engineers Inc		C	951 688-0241	0
Adventist Media Center Inc (PA)		D	805 955-7777	0
Air Force Village West Inc		B	951 697-2000	0
Albert A Webb Associates (PA)		C	951 686-1070	0
Allied Steel Co Inc		D	951 241-7000	0
Alta Vista Healthcare and Well		C	951 688-8200	0
Altura Credit Union (PA)		D	888 883-7228	0
Always There Live In Care LLC		D	888 606-8880	0
American Dntl Partners of Cal		C	951 689-5031	0
American Medical Response (DH)		D	951 782-5200	0
American Reprographics Co LLC		D	951 686-0530	0
American Residential Svcs LLC		C	951 341-9371	0
Anheuser-Busch LLC		C	951 782-3935	0
Apria Healthcare LLC		D	951 320-1100	0
Arakelian Enterprises Inc		C	951 342-3300	0
Aramark Unf & Career AP LLC		D	951 274-9622	0
Arthur J Gallagher & Co		D	800 217-9800	0
AT&T Corp		D	951 275-8801	0
AT&T Services Inc		C	951 369-2282	0
Automobile Club Southern Cal		D	951 684-4250	0
B & B Nurseries Inc		D	951 352-8383	0
Babcock Laboratories Inc		D	951 653-3351	0
Banquet Facilities		E	951 360-2081	0
Barrys Security Services Inc (PA)		D	951 789-7575	0
Bedrock Company		D	951 273-1931	0
Behavioral Health Resources		C	951 275-8400	0
Bens Asphalt & Maint Co Inc		E	951 248-1103	0
Best Best & Krieger LLP (PA)		C	951 686-1450	0
Big 5 Corp		B	951 774-1600	0
Bio-Mdcal Applications Cal Inc		D	951 343-7700	0
Bledsoe Masonry Inc		D	951 360-6140	0
Bright Expectations Inc		D	951 360-2070	0
Bx Construction LLC		D	951 509-9412	0
California Citrus Cooperative		D	951 683-4045	0
Canyon Crest Country Club Inc		D	951 274-7900	0
Career Dev Inst For Excptnl		E	951 337-3678	0
Carolyn E Wylie Center		D	951 683-5193	0
Ceed Security Corp		E	951 222-2233	0
Cellco Partnership		D	951 697-3035	0
Champion Electric Inc		D	951 276-9619	0
Citibank National Association		C	800 627-3999	0
City National Bank		E	951 276-8800	0
City of Riverside		D	951 346-4700	0
Community Care & Rehab Ctr LLC		D	951 680-6500	0
Community Connect (PA)		D	951 686-4402	0
Complete Coach Works (HQ)		B	951 682-2500	0
Corona - College Heights Ora		B	951 359-6451	0
Corporate Alnce Strategies Inc		C	877 777-7487	0
County of Riverside		C	951 955-6000	0

Employment Codes: A=Over 500 employees, B=251-500,
C=101-250, D=51-100, E=50

2020 Directory of California
Wholesalers and Services Companies

© Mergent Inc. 1-800-342-5647

1605

GEOGRAPHIC

Company	SIC	EMP	PHONE	ENTRY #
County of Riverside		D	951 955-0840	0
County of Riverside		B	951 358-5306	0
County of Riverside		D	951 358-6000	0
County of Riverside		C	951 955-3100	0
County of Riverside		D	951 275-8783	0
County of Riverside		D	951 697-4699	0
County of Riverside		E	951 486-7700	0
County of Riverside		A	951 955-0905	0
County of Riverside		D	951 358-4415	0
County of Riverside		B	951 955-4800	0
County of Riverside		D	951 955-3100	0
County of Riverside Department (PA)		D	951 358-5000	0
Cove Builders Inc		C	714 436-2973	0
Cox Automotive Inc		B	951 689-6000	0
Craftsman Lath and Plaster Inc		B	951 685-9922	0
Crest Steel Corporation			310 830-2651	0
Cross Country Healthcare Inc		C	951 786-7683	0
Cypress Gardens Convalescent H		C	951 688-3643	0
Del Mar Plastering Inc		D	951 343-5955	0
Digiquest Corp		E	951 776-4344	0
Dmcg Inc (PA)		D	951 683-9685	0
Doctors Hospital Riverside LLC (PA)		E	951 354-7404	0
Dynamic Plumbing Commercial		D	951 343-1200	0
Edwards Theatres Circuit Inc		D	951 361-1917	0
Elias Elliott Lampasi Fehn (PA)		D	951 689-5031	0
Elite Electric		D	951 681-5811	0
Empire Company LLC		D	951 742-5273	0
Encore Senior Living III LLC		D	951 360-1616	0
Entrepreneurial Hospitality		C	951 346-4700	0
Erlanger Distribution Ctr Inc		E	951 784-5147	0
Etairos Consulting		E	844 219-7027	0
Far West Electric Inc		D	909 684-8661	0
Fencecorp Inc (HQ)		B	951 686-3170	0
Fenceworks Inc (PA)		C	951 788-5620	0
Festival Fun Parks LLC		D	951 785-3000	0
FS Commercial Landscape Inc (PA)		D	951 360-7070	0
G4s Secure Solutions (usa)		B	951 341-3000	0
Ghossain & Truelock Entps Inc		D	951 781-9345	0
Gless Ranch Inc (PA)		E	951 780-8458	0
Gonzales Painting Corp		D	951 214-6400	0
Guardsmark LLC		B	909 989-5345	0
Haider Spine Ctr Med Group Inc		E	951 413-0200	0
Hal Hays Construction Inc (PA)		C	951 788-0703	0
Hamblins Bdy Pnt Frame Sp Inc		D	951 689-8440	0
Harbor Pipe and Steel Inc		C	951 369-3990	0
Herman Weissker Inc (HQ)		C	951 826-8800	0
High-Light Electric Inc		D	951 352-9646	0
Historic Mission Inn Corp		B	951 784-0300	0
Honey Flower Holdings LLC		C	951 351-2800	0
Hy-Tech Tile Inc		C	951 788-0550	0
Hyatt Corporation		B	909 240-9526	0
Iheartcommunications Inc		D	951 684-1992	0
Index Fresh Inc (PA)		D	909 877-0999	0
Inland Inspections Consulting		E	951 697-1000	0
J Ginger Masonry LP (PA)		B	951 688-5050	0
J M V B Inc		D	714 288-9797	0
Jaguar Computer Systems Inc		E	951 273-7950	0
James McMinn Inc		E	909 514-1231	0
John L Ginger Masonry Inc		D	951 688-5050	0
Johnson Cntrls SEC Sltions LLC		D	951 787-0420	0
Johnson Machinery Co (PA)		C	951 686-4560	0
Kadena Pacific Inc		E	951 990-7865	0
Kaiser Foundation Hospitals		A	951 248-4000	0
Kaiser Foundation Hospitals		A	866 984-7483	0
Kaiser Foundation Hospitals		A	951 353-2000	0
Kana Pipeline Inc		D	714 986-1400	0
Keenan & Associates		D	951 788-0330	0
Keller Williams Realty		E	951 215-0787	0
Kindred Healthcare Operating		D	951 688-8200	0
Kleinfelder Inc		D	951 801-3681	0
Knollwood Psychiatric and Chem		D	951 275-8400	0
Liberty Landscaping Inc (PA)		C	951 683-2999	0
Lozano Plumbing Services Inc		C	951 683-4840	0
M & M Plumbing Inc		D	951 354-5388	0
Magnolia Rhbltiton Nursing Ctr		D	951 688-4321	0
Main Electric Supply Co LLC		D	951 784-2900	0
McKesson Corporation		D	951 686-3575	0
Metropolitan Water District		E	951 688-5672	0
Metropolitan Water District		D	951 780-1511	0
Mfi Recovery Center (PA)		C	951 683-6596	0
Mgb Construction Inc		C	951 342-0303	0
ML Electricworks Inc		D	951 687-5078	0
Morgan Truck Body LLC		D	951 689-0800	0
Mount Rbdoux Convalescent Hosp		C	951 681-2200	0
National Paving Company Inc		D	951 369-1332	0
Neal Trucking Inc		D	951 685-5048	0
New York Life Insurance Co		D	951 354-2094	0
Officeworks Inc		D	951 784-2534	0
Olive Grove Retirement Resort		D	951 687-2241	0
Onrad Inc		D	800 848-5876	0
Opendoor Labs Inc		D	888 352-7075	0
Pacific Strucframe LLC		D	951 405-8536	0
Pacific Tank Lines Inc		D	951 680-1900	0
Parkview Cmnty Hosp Med Ctr		A	951 354-7404	0
Paychex Inc		E	951 682-6100	0
Peggs Company Inc (PA)		D	253 584-9548	0
Pepsi-Cola Metro Btlg Co Inc		B	951 697-3200	0
Perry Coast Construction Inc		C	951 774-0677	0
Pharmerica Long-Term Care LLC		D	951 784-1616	0
Pinnacle Rvrside Hspitality LP		D	951 784-8000	0
Plan-It Life Inc		D	951 742-7561	0
Ppc Enterprises Inc		C	951 354-5402	0
Precise Distribution Inc		E	951 367-1037	0
Professnal Cmmnctons Netwrk LP (PA)		E	951 275-9149	0
Provident Savings Bank (HQ)		D	951 782-6177	0
Provident Savings Bank		D	951 686-6060	0
Provident Savings Bank LLC		D	951 686-6060	0
Prudential Overall Supply		D	951 687-0440	0
Psychiatric Solutions Inc		C	951 789-4405	0
R&S Carpet Services Inc		D	909 740-6645	0
Raincross Hospitality Corp (PA)		D	951 346-4700	0
Rancho Jurupa Park		E	951 684-7032	0
Rdo Construction Equipment Co		D	951 778-3700	0
Real Estate California Dept		D	951 715-0130	0
Realty One Group Inc		D	951 565-8105	0
Recycler Core Company Inc		D	951 276-1687	0
Regional Connector Constrs		E	951 368-6400	0
Reid & Helly		D	951 682-1771	0
Rhf Plymouth Tower		D	951 248-0456	0
Rls Electrical Contrs Inc		D	951 688-8049	0
Riverside Care Inc		C	951 683-7111	0
Riverside Cmnty Hlth Systems (DH)		D	951 788-3000	0
Riverside County Flood Control		D	951 955-1200	0
Riverside Dialysis Center		E	951 682-2700	0
Riverside Equities LLC		D	951 688-2222	0
Riverside Healthcare System LP		A	951 788-3000	0
Riverside Medical Clinic Inc		B	951 683-6370	0
Riverside Medical Clinic Inc (PA)		B	951 683-6370	0
Riverside Sanitarium LLC		D	951 684-7701	0
Riverside Scrap Ir & Met Corp (PA)		E	951 686-2120	0
Riverside Transit Agency (PA)		B	951 565-5000	0
Riverside University Health (PA)		D	951 358-5000	0
Robert Half International Inc		D	951 779-9081	0
Roberts & Associates Inc		D	951 727-4357	0
Rogan Building Services Inc		E	951 248-1261	0
Roy E Whitehead Inc		D	951 682-1490	0
Santana Concrete		D	909 421-2218	0
Secure Transportation Company		D	951 737-7300	0
Security California Bancorp		D	951 368-2265	0
Silverado Framing & Cnstr		D	951 352-1100	0
Skanska USA Civil West Rocky M (DH)		D	970 565-8000	0
Skanska USA Civil W Cal Dst Inc (DH)		A	951 684-5360	0
Sky Scan Satelite Systems		D	909 322-1393	0
Solcius LLC		B	951 772-0030	0
South Coast Concrete Cnstr		E	951 351-7777	0
South Coast Health Wellness		E	951 686-9001	0
Southern Cal Prmnnte Med Group		B	866 984-7483	0
Southern California Fleet Svc		E	951 272-8655	0
Southern Glazers Wine		E	951 274-2420	0
Springboard Solutions LLC		D	951 779-7300	0
State Compensation Insur Fund		C	888 782-8338	0
Stronghold Engineering Inc (PA)		C	951 684-9303	0
Sun Mar Management Services		D	951 687-3842	0
Sunrise Senior Living LLC		D	951 785-1200	0
Sunstone Hotel Management Inc		C	951 784-8000	0
Sysco Riverside Inc		B	951 601-5300	0
T C H P Inc		D	951 687-7330	0
Team Truck Dismantling Inc		D	951 685-6744	0
Thompson & Colegate LLP		E	951 682-5550	0
Ticor Title Company California		E	951 509-0211	0
Toad 1350		E	951 369-1350	0
Tony R Crisalli Inc		E	951 727-0110	0
Top Priority Couriers Inc (PA)		D	951 781-1000	0
Trugreen Limited Partnership		E	951 231-2760	0
UBS Financial Services Inc		E	951 684-6300	0
Ucr Botany and Plant Sciences		D	951 827-5133	0
Unique Carpets Ltd		D	951 352-8125	0
United Service Tech Inc		D	714 224-1406	0
United Technologies Corp		D	951 351-5400	0
University Cal Riverside		D	951 827-4801	0

	SIC	EMP	PHONE	ENTRY #
USDA Forest Service		D	951 680-1560	0
Van Daele Development Corp		C	951 354-6800	0
Veterinary Service Inc		D	951 328-4900	0
Villa Convalescent Hosp Inc		D	951 689-5788	0
Visitng Nurse Assn Inlnd CNT **(PA)**		A	951 413-1200	0
Vista Behavioral Health Inc			800 992-0901	0
Vista Pacifica Enterprises Inc **(PA)**		C	951 682-4833	0
Vista Pacifica Enterprises Inc		C	951 682-4867	0
Vitas Healthcare Corp Cal		D	909 386-6000	0
Volt Management Corp		D	951 789-8133	0
Waterman Convalescent Hospital		C	951 681-2200	0
West Coast Drywall & Co Inc		B	951 778-3592	0
West Coast Interiors		A	951 778-3592	0
West Riverside Veterinary Hosp		E	951 686-2242	0
West States Skanska Inc		C	970 565-4903	0
Westcoe Realtors Inc		D	951 784-2500	0
Westview Services Inc		D	951 343-2356	0
Wilmon Corporation		D	951 685-7474	0
Windsor Capital Group Inc		D	951 276-1200	0
Z-Best Concrete Inc		D	951 774-1870	0

RLLNG HLS EST, CA - Los Angeles County

	SIC	EMP	PHONE	ENTRY #
Citigroup Global Markets Inc		D	310 544-3600	0
Cox California Telcom LLC		D	310 377-1800	0
Das Global Capital Corp		D	702 967-1688	0
Dincloud Inc		D	310 929-1101	0
Jack Kramer Club		E	310 326-4404	0
Metropolitan Water District		A	310 832-6106	0
Natural Health Trends Corp		D	310 541-0888	0
Regal Cinemas Inc		D	310 544-3042	0
Rolling Hlls Esttes Tennis CLB		E	310 541-4585	0
Seatech Consulting Group Inc		E	310 356-6828	0
Spalding Srgcl Ctr of Bvrly Hl		C	949 863-0022	0
Sqa Services Inc		B	800 333-6180	0

ROCKLIN, CA - Placer County

	SIC	EMP	PHONE	ENTRY #
Ace Hardware Corporation		B	916 435-4567	0
American Hlthcare ADM Svcs Inc		B	916 773-7227	0
Brower Mechanical Inc		D	530 749-0808	0
Builders & Tradesmens		D	916 772-9200	0
Builders & Tradesmens Insur		D	916 772-9200	0
Data Control Corporation		D	916 774-4000	0
Ecorp Consulting Inc **(PA)**		D	916 782-9100	0
Educational Media Foundation **(PA)**		C	916 251-1600	0
Federal Express Corporation			800 463-3339	0
Financial Pacific Insurance Co		D	916 630-5000	0
First Technology Federal Cr Un		C	855 855-8805	0
Great Lakes E & I/ Inquip JV		D	805 687-2007	0
Habitat Rstration Sciences Inc		E	916 408-2990	0
Horizon West Healthcare Inc **(HQ)**		D	916 624-6230	0
Infinity Energy Inc		C	916 474-4723	0
Jemtown Inc		E	916 315-0555	0
Jkf Auto Service Inc		D	916 315-0555	0
JR Perce Plbg Inc Sacramento		C	916 434-9554	0
Kitchen Mart Inc		D	916 315-3535	0
Kniesels Auto Collision Center		E	916 315-8888	0
L&H Airco LLC		D	916 677-1000	0
La Voie & Sons Construction		E	916 408-6900	0
Marksys LLC		D	916 745-4883	0
Marksys Holdings LLC		D	916 745-4883	0
Oracle Corporation		B	916 435-8342	0
Oracle Corporation		B	916 315-3500	0
Pacific Secured Equities Inc		B	916 677-2500	0
Precision Medical Products Inc		D	573 474-9302	0
Quality Telecom Consultants **(PA)**		D	916 315-0500	0
Road Safety Inc		C	916 543-4600	0
Rruff-Rocklin Residents Unite		E	415 806-2778	0
SE Scher Corporation		B	916 632-1363	0
Security On-Site Services Inc		D	916 988-6500	0
Sierra View Landscape Inc		E	916 408-2990	0
SMA Solar Technology Amer LLC **(HQ)**		D	916 625-0870	0
Sonoran Roofing Inc		C	916 624-1080	0
Stantec Consulting Svcs Inc		D	916 773-8100	0
Strikes Unlimited Inc		D	916 626-3600	0
Sunrise Senior Living LLC		D	916 632-3003	0
Surveillance Systems		E	800 508-6981	0
Swan Engineering Inc		D	916 474-5299	0
Trane US Inc		D	916 577-1100	0
United Natural Foods West Inc **(HQ)**		B	916 625-4100	0
Wpcs Intrntional-Suisun Cy Inc		D	916 624-1300	0
Zentek Corporation		D	916 749-3610	0

ROHNERT PARK, CA - Sonoma County

	SIC	EMP	PHONE	ENTRY #
24 Hour Fitness Usa Inc		E	707 536-0048	0
Animal Care Center		D	707 584-4343	0
Artizen Incorporated		C	650 261-9400	0
Calif Institute Human Ser		D	707 664-2416	0
Catati Rohnert Park Inc		E	707 792-4531	0
Codding Construction Co		E	707 795-3550	0
Cve Nb Contracting Group Inc		E	707 584-1900	0
Exchange Bank		B	707 524-3000	0
Federted Indans Grton Rncheria		A	707 588-7100	0
Herc Rentals Inc		D	707 586-6491	0
Kaiser Foundation Hospitals		D	707 206-3000	0
Kisco Senior Living LLC		D	707 585-1800	0
Lemo USA Inc		D	707 206-3700	0
Merrill Gardens LLC		D	707 585-7878	0
North Bay Eye Assoc A Med Corp		D	707 206-0849	0
OHagin Manufacturing LLC		E	707 872-3620	0
OHagins Inc		D	707 303-3660	0
Pace Supply Corp **(PA)**		D	707 755-2499	0
Pennacchio Tile Inc		D	707 586-8858	0
Red Condor Inc		D	707 569-7419	0
State Farm Fire and Cslty Co		B	707 588-6011	0

ROMOLAND, CA - Riverside County

	SIC	EMP	PHONE	ENTRY #
Southern California Gas Co		D	213 244-1200	0

ROSAMOND, CA - Kern County

	SIC	EMP	PHONE	ENTRY #
Catalina Solar Lessee LLC		A	888 903-6926	0

ROSEMEAD, CA - Los Angeles County

	SIC	EMP	PHONE	ENTRY #
Anka Behavioral Health Inc		D	626 573-5902	0
Cathay Bank		C	626 452-1582	0
Del Mar Convalescent Hospital		D	626 288-8353	0
Doubletree Hotel		D	323 722-8800	0
Durham School Services L P		C	626 573-3769	0
Edison International **(PA)**		D	626 302-2222	0
Edison Mssion Midwest Holdings		A	626 302-2222	0
Ensign Group Inc		D	626 607-2400	0
Herald Christian Health Center **(PA)**		D	626 286-8700	0
Irish Communication Company **(DH)**		D	626 288-6170	0
Irish Construction **(HQ)**		C	626 288-8530	0
K&I International Trade Inc		E	312 766-1848	0
Landcare USA LLC		D	310 354-1520	0
Longwood Management Corp		D	626 280-2293	0
Longwood Management Corp		C	626 280-4820	0
Los Angeles Orphan Asylum Inc		C	323 283-9311	0
Maryvale		D	626 280-6510	0
Maryvale Day Care Center **(PA)**		D	626 280-6511	0
Monterey Healthcare & Wellness		D	626 280-3220	0
Psychiatric Solutions Inc		C	626 286-1191	0
Southern California Edison Co **(HQ)**		A	626 302-1212	0
Southern California Edison Co		C	626 302-5101	0
Southern California Edison Co		C	626 302-1212	0
Southern California Edison Co		D	714 895-0488	0
Southern California Edison Co		C	626 302-0530	0
Sun Mar Management Services		D	626 288-8353	0
Sunny Cal Adhc Inc		D	626 307-7772	0

ROSEVILLE, CA - Placer County

	SIC	EMP	PHONE	ENTRY #
10up Inc		D	888 571-7130	0
Aardvark Staffing Inc		E	916 774-7115	0
Abcsp LLC		C	855 470-2273	0
Abso		C	800 943-2589	0
Advanced Ipm		E	916 759-1570	0
American Pacific Mortgage Corp **(PA)**		C	916 960-1325	0
Atria Senior Living Inc		D	916 786-7200	0
Cal Consolated Communications		D	916 786-6141	0
California Rural Indian Health		D	916 437-0104	0
California Sun Centers Inc		D	916 789-9767	0
Cellco Partnership		D	916 786-6151	0
Century 21 Haley & Associates		D	916 782-1500	0
Century Theatres Inc		D	916 797-3466	0
Chicago Title Insurance Co		B	916 783-7195	0
Claims Management Inc		C	916 631-1250	0
Clark & Sullivan Builders Inc		C	916 338-7707	0
CLC Incorporated **(PA)**		E	916 789-7600	0
Clearcapitalcom Inc		D	530 582-5011	0
Clearcaptions LLC		E	866 868-8695	0
Cliftonlarsonallen LLP		B	916 784-7800	0
Clp Resources Inc		D	916 788-0300	0
Cokeva Inc		C	916 462-6001	0
Coldwell Banker RE Corp		E	408 981-7200	0
Coleman Chavez & Assoc LLP		D	916 787-2310	0
Crocus Holdings LLC		D	916 782-1238	0
D Augustine & Associates		D	916 774-9600	0
Denios Roseville Farmers		D	916 782-2704	0
Dignity Health Med Foundation		D	916 787-0404	0
Directapps Inc **(PA)**		D	916 787-2200	0
Dwayne Nash Industries Inc		D	916 253-1900	0
Dynamic Staffing Inc **(PA)**		D	916 773-3900	0
Enterprise Rent-A-Car Compan **(DH)**		E	916 787-4500	0

Employment Codes: A=Over 500 employees, B=251-500,
C=101-250, D=51-100, E=50

2020 Directory of California
Wholesalers and Services Companies

© Mergent Inc. 1-800-342-5647

1607

GEOGRAPHIC

	SIC	EMP	PHONE	ENTRY #
Erickson Construction LP		C	916 774-1100	0
Ernst & Young LLP		C	916 218-1900	0
Eskaton Properties Inc		D	916 334-0810	0
Esl Technologies Inc		B	916 677-4500	0
Federal Deposit Insurance Corp		C	916 789-8580	0
First Data Hardware Svcs Inc		B	916 632-7600	0
Flexcare LLC		A	866 564-3589	0
Flintco Pacific Inc		D	916 757-1000	0
Fmr LLC		C	916 784-3649	0
Fraternal Order Eagles 1582		C	916 782-2694	0
Genuent Usa LLC		D	916 772-3700	0
Global Touchpoints Inc		D	916 878-5954	0
Golden State Collision Centers		D	916 772-1666	0
Horizon West Healthcare Inc		C	916 782-1238	0
Huppe Landscape Company Inc **(HQ)**		D	916 784-7666	0
Industrial Container Services		D	916 781-2775	0
Intech Mechanical Company LLC		C	916 797-4900	0
Intercare Specialty Risk Ins **(PA)**		D	916 757-1200	0
Interwest Insurance Svcs LLC		D	916 784-1008	0
Iptor Supply Chain Systems USA **(DH)**		B	916 542-2820	0
Kaiser Foundation Hospitals		C	916 746-3937	0
Kaiser Foundation Hospitals		C	916 784-4000	0
Kaiser Foundation Hospitals		C	916 784-4050	0
Kaiser Foundation Hospitals		A	916 784-4000	0
Lancaster Burns Cnstr Inc		C	916 624-8404	0
Med-Data Incorporated		D	916 771-1362	0
Merchant Valley Corporation		C	916 786-7227	0
Nations First Capital LLC		C	855 396-3600	0
Neptune Management Corporation		D	916 771-5300	0
New York Life Insurance Co		D	916 774-6200	0
Nortech Waste LLC		C	916 645-5230	0
Northern California Power Agcy **(PA)**		D	916 781-3636	0
Olivieri Enterprises LP		C	916 791-7857	0
Patterson Dental Supply Inc		D	916 780-5100	0
Permanente Medical Group Inc		B	916 784-4000	0
Pinnacle Builders Inc		B	916 372-5000	0
Pinnacle Telecom Inc **(PA)**		E	916 426-1000	0
Polycomp Administrative Svcs		E	916 773-3480	0
Precision Framing Inc		B	916 791-7464	0
Pride Industries **(PA)**		C	916 788-2100	0
Production Framing Inc		D	916 978-2843	0
Production Framing Systems Inc **(PA)**		C	916 978-2888	0
Project Go Incorporated		E	916 782-3443	0
Psomas		D	916 788-8122	0
Quest Media & Supplies Inc **(PA)**		D	916 338-7070	0
Reeve-Knight Construction Inc		D	916 786-5112	0
River Rock Equipment LLC		D	916 791-1609	0
Roseville Sportworld Inc		D	916 783-8550	0
Roseville Towne Place Suites		D	916 782-2232	0
Rountree Plumbing and Htg Inc		D	650 298-0300	0
S P Thomas Co of Northern Cal **(PA)**		B	916 786-2040	0
Safe Credit Union		E	916 979-7233	0
Sedgwick Claims MGT Svcs Inc		B	916 771-2900	0
Sierra Care Rehabilitation Ctr		D	916 782-3188	0
Sierra Hills Care Center Inc		D	916 782-7007	0
Sierra View Country Club		D	916 782-3741	0
Sign of Dove		D	916 786-3277	0
Spare-Time Inc		D	916 782-2600	0
Specialty Steel Service Co Inc **(HQ)**		D	916 771-4737	0
Sun City Rsvlle Cmnty Assn Inc **(PA)**		C	916 774-3880	0
Sunrise Retirement Villa		D	916 786-3277	0
Sutter Health		B	916 797-4725	0
Sutter Health		D	916 797-4715	0
Sutter Health		D	916 784-2277	0
Sutter Health		D	916 797-4700	0
Sutter Hlth Scrmnto Sierra Reg		A	916 781-1000	0
Sutter Roseville Medical Ctr		D	916 781-1000	0
Sutter Rsvlle Med Ctr Fndation		A	916 781-1000	0
Tech-Ed Networks Inc		C	916 784-2005	0
Teleplan Service Solutions Inc		B	916 677-4500	0
Union Pacific Corporation		A	916 789-5311	0
Union Pacific Railroad Company		D	916 789-5930	0
Union Pacific Railroad Company		C	916 789-6055	0
United Building Maint Inc		C	916 772-8101	0
United States Info Systems Inc		C	845 353-9224	0
USA Multifamily Management		C	916 773-6060	0
USA Properties Fund Inc **(PA)**		D	916 773-6060	0
Varis LLC **(PA)**		C	916 294-0860	0
Vexillum Inc		E	916 218-3815	0
Vibrantcare Outpatient Rehab **(PA)**		D	916 782-1212	0
Volt Management Corp		D	916 923-0454	0
Walt Disney Company		D	916 780-1470	0
Waterhouse Management Corp		C	916 772-4918	0
Wells Fargo Bank National Assn		D	916 724-2982	0
Wells Fargo Bank National Assn		B	916 774-2249	0

	SIC	EMP	PHONE	ENTRY #
Wells Fargo Home Mortgage Inc		E	916 782-2221	0
West Safety Solutions Corp		E	514 340-3314	0
Westmont Living Inc		B	916 786-3277	0

ROSS, CA - Marin County

	SIC	EMP	PHONE	ENTRY #
Pacific Union Intl Inc		B	415 461-8686	0

ROYAL OAKS, CA - Santa Cruz County

	SIC	EMP	PHONE	ENTRY #
Falcon Trading Company **(PA)**		C	831 786-7000	0
Gino Rinaldi Inc		D	831 761-0195	0
Kelvin Hildebrand Inc		E	831 768-9104	0
Monterey Mushrooms Inc		A	831 728-8300	0

RUTHERFORD, CA - Napa County

	SIC	EMP	PHONE	ENTRY #
Amer Zoetrope Research LLC		C	707 963-9230	0
Terre Du Soleil Ltd		B	707 963-1211	0
Vyborny Vineyard Management		D	707 944-9135	0

SACRAMENTO, CA - Sacramento County

	SIC	EMP	PHONE	ENTRY #
15th & L Investors LLC		D	916 267-6805	0
A Meissners Hhld & Indus Svc		D	916 920-2121	0
A Teichert & Son Inc **(HQ)**		C	916 484-3011	0
A1 Protective Services LLC		E	916 421-3000	0
AAA Signs Inc		D	916 568-3456	0
Abacus Service Corporation		B	916 288-8948	0
ABF Freight System Inc		D	916 428-3531	0
Accenture LLP		C	916 557-2200	0
Access Info MGT Shred Svcs LLC		D	925 461-5352	0
Ace High Entertainnment LLC		E	916 243-5515	0
Adesa Corporation LLC		C	916 388-8899	0
Administrative Systems Inc		D	916 563-1121	0
Advanced HM Hlth & Hospice Inc		D	916 978-0744	0
Advanced Home Health Inc		D	916 978-0744	0
Aecom Global II LLC		B	916 679-2000	0
Aecom Global II LLC		D	916 679-8700	0
Aecom Technology Corporation		D	916 414-5800	0
Agamerica Fcb **(PA)**		D	651 282-8800	0
Air Systems Service & Cnstr		C	916 368-0336	0
Airco Mechanical Inc **(PA)**		C	916 381-4523	0
Alcal Glass Systems Inc		D	916 929-3100	0
Alcal Specialty Contg Inc **(DH)**		D	916 929-3100	0
Alliedbarton Security Svcs LLC		C	916 489-8280	0
Alsco Inc		D	916 454-5545	0
Alston Construction Co Inc **(PA)**		D	916 340-2400	0
Amador Stage Lines Inc		C	916 444-7880	0
American Building Supply Inc **(HQ)**		C	916 503-4100	0
American Institute Research		B	916 286-8800	0
American Medical Response		B	916 563-0600	0
American Patriot Security		D	916 706-2449	0
American Reprographics Co LLC		D	916 443-1322	0
American Water Works Co Inc		D	916 568-4236	0
Amerisourcebergen Drug Corp		C	916 830-4500	0
Anixter Inc		D	916 563-7560	0
AON Consulting Inc		D	800 558-0655	0
Apexcare Inc **(PA)**		A	916 924-9111	0
Apple Hospitality Reit Inc		D	916 568-5400	0
Applewood Care Center		E	916 446-2506	0
Apria Healthcare LLC		C	530 677-2713	0
Aramark Unf & Career AP LLC		B	916 286-4100	0
Aramark Uniform Services		D	916 286-4100	0
Arden Hills Country Club Inc		D	916 482-6111	0
Arraycon LLC **(PA)**		E	916 925-0201	0
Arreolas Complete Ldscp Svc		E	916 387-6777	0
Asbury Pk Nrsing Rhbltition Ctr		C	916 649-2000	0
Asian Community Center of Sac **(PA)**		C	916 394-6399	0
Assuredpartners Inc		D	916 443-0200	0
AT&T Corp		B	916 830-5000	0
AT&T Services Inc		C	916 972-2248	0
AT&T Services Inc		D	916 453-6267	0
AT&T Services Inc		C	916 972-2423	0
Atlas Disposal Industries LLC		D	916 455-2800	0
Atrium Finance I LP		D	916 446-0100	0
Auburn Constructors LLC		D	916 924-0344	0
Avis Rent A Car System Inc		C	916 922-5601	0
Azalea Holdings LLC		D	916 452-3592	0
B B & T Management Corp		C	916 428-8060	0
Baco Realty Corporation		D	916 974-9898	0
Bagatelos Glass Systems Inc **(PA)**		D	916 364-3600	0
Bank America National Assn		C	916 326-3161	0
Barnum & Celillo Electric Inc **(PA)**		D	916 646-4661	0
Bayer Protective Services Inc		C	916 486-5800	0
Benetech Inc **(PA)**		D	916 484-6811	0
Benetech Inc		E	916 484-6811	0
BEST Consulting Inc		E	916 448-2050	0
Bickmore and Associates Inc **(DH)**		D	916 244-1100	0
Bloodsource Inc		E	916 488-1701	0
Bohm Law Group Inc **(PA)**		E	916 927-5574	0

Mergent email: customerrelations@mergent.com

1608

2020 Directory of California
Wholesalers and Services Companies

(P-0000) Products & Services Section entry number
(PA)=Parent Co (HQ)=Headquarters (DH)=Div Headquarters

Company	SIC	EMP	PHONE	ENTRY #
Bradford & Barthel LLP **(PA)**		C	916 569-0790	0
Briarwood Health Care Inc		E	916 383-2741	0
Brightview Landscape Svcs Inc		D	916 381-2800	0
Brinks Incorporated		C	916 452-5279	0
Broadway Sacramento **(PA)**		C	916 446-5880	0
Brunswick Corner Partnership		E	916 649-7500	0
Buzz Oates Management Services		E	916 381-3843	0
C & S Wholesale Grocers Inc		B	916 383-5275	0
C A H H S		D	916 552-7507	0
Cali Hsg Finance Agcy		D	916 326-8627	0
California American Water Co		E	916 568-4216	0
California Association O **(PA)**		D	916 443-7401	0
California Chamber Commerce **(PA)**		D	916 444-6670	0
California Cmplte CNT Cnsus		D	916 852-2020	0
California Dental Association **(PA)**		C	916 443-0505	0
California Govrnmnt Opr Agncy		A	800 228-5453	0
California Health Benefit Exch		D	916 228-8210	0
California Medical Association **(PA)**		D	916 444-5532	0
California Pavement Maint Inc		C	916 381-8033	0
California Public Emplyees Ret		C	916 795-3000	0
California Public Emplyees Ret **(DH)**		A	916 795-3000	0
Califrnia High Speed Rail Auth		D	916 324-1541	0
Califrnia Hlth Humn Srvcs Agcy		B	916 739-7640	0
Califrnia State Employees Assn **(PA)**		B	916 444-8134	0
Calstars		E	916 445-0211	0
Calvey Incorporated		D	916 681-4800	0
Cambria Solutions Inc **(PA)**		C	916 326-4446	0
Capital Athletic Club Inc		D	916 442-3927	0
Capital Commercial Flrg Inc		E	916 569-1960	0
Capital Public Radio Inc		E	916 278-8900	0
Capitol Casino		C	916 446-0700	0
Capitol Corporate Services		E	916 444-6787	0
Capitol Regency LLC		B	916 443-1234	0
Careability Health Svcs Corp		D	916 479-8554	0
Cares Community Health		C	916 443-3299	0
Carescope LLC		D	916 780-1384	0
Carlton Senior Living Inc		D	916 971-4800	0
Carrier Corporation		E	916 928-9500	0
Cathedral Pioneer Church Homes **(PA)**		D	916 442-4906	0
Cbre Inc		D	916 446-6800	0
CBS Radio Inc		D	916 923-6800	0
Central Anesthesia Service		D	916 481-6800	0
Central Freight Lines Inc		D	800 782-5036	0
Central Parking System Inc		D	916 441-1074	0
Ceva Freight LLC		C	916 379-6000	0
Cgl Companies LLC		D	916 678-7890	0
Ch2m Hill Inc		E	916 920-0300	0
Ch2m Hill Constructors Inc		B	916 920-0212	0
Channel 40 Inc		C	916 454-4422	0
Chem Quip Inc		D	800 821-1678	0
Chemical Dependency Recovery		C	916 482-1132	0
Child Action Inc **(PA)**		B	916 369-4460	0
Childrens Recvg Hm Sacramento		C	916 482-2370	0
Choice Medical Group Inc		D	916 483-2885	0
Church of Jsus Chrst of Ld STS		D	916 482-1480	0
Cinemark Usa Inc		D	916 922-4241	0
Cintas Corporation No 3		C	916 419-8519	0
Citigroup Global Markets Inc		E	916 567-2056	0
Clark Pest Ctrl Stockton Inc		D	916 925-7000	0
Cleanrite Inc		D	916 381-1321	0
Coact Designworks		E	916 930-5900	0
Coldwell Banker		D	916 447-5900	0
Colliers Intl Prperty Cons Inc		D	916 929-5999	0
Columbia Woodlake LLC		D	206 728-9063	0
Comcast Corporation		D	916 459-2964	0
Comcast Corporation		B	916 830-6790	0
Confi-Chek Inc **(PA)**		D	800 718-8997	0
Consultnts In Edctl Per Skills **(PA)**		D	916 348-1890	0
Cook Realty Inc		C	916 451-6702	0
Cooperative Personnel Services **(PA)**		C	916 263-3600	0
Core-Mark International Inc		D	509 535-9768	0
Corporation Service Company		D	302 636-5400	0
Correctons Rhbltation Cal Dept		C	916 358-2319	0
County of Sacramento		B	916 874-7752	0
County of Sacramento		D	916 875-2711	0
County of Sacramento		D	916 875-0900	0
County of Sacramento		D	916 874-0746	0
County of Sacramento		D	916 363-8383	0
County of Sacramento		B	916 874-0912	0
County of Sacramento		C	916 875-4467	0
Covenant Care California LLC		D	916 391-6011	0
Creative Design Interiors Inc **(PA)**		D	916 641-1121	0
Crestwood Behavioral Hlth Inc		C	916 452-1431	0
Crocker Art Museum Association		D	916 808-7000	0
Crossroads Facility Svcs Inc		D	916 568-5230	0
Crown Building Maintenance Co		A	916 920-9556	0
Cuneo Black Ward Missler A Law		E	916 363-8822	0
Cusa AWC LLC		E	916 423-4000	0
Cy Sac Operator LLC		D	916 455-6800	0
D & J Plumbing Inc		D	916 922-4888	0
Dal Cais Inc		D	916 381-8080	0
Dave Gross Enterprises Inc		D	916 388-2000	0
DC Transport Inc		D	916 438-0888	0
Dealertrack Collte Manag Servi		C	916 368-5300	0
Del Paso Country Club		E	916 489-3681	0
Delegata Corporation		D	916 609-5400	0
Delta Dental of California		A	916 853-7373	0
Dentists Insurance Company **(HQ)**		C	916 443-4567	0
Desilva Gates Construction LP		C	916 386-9708	0
Develop Disabilities Svc Org		D	916 973-1951	0
Developmental Disabilities **(PA)**		D	916 456-5166	0
Dialysis Clinic Inc		E	916 453-0803	0
Diepenbrock Elkin LLP		D	916 492-5000	0
Dignity Health		E	916 681-1600	0
Dignity Health		C	916 667-0000	0
Dignity Health		C	916 423-5940	0
Dignity Health		A	916 453-4545	0
Dignity Health		C	916 453-4453	0
Dignity Health Med Foundation		D	916 681-6300	0
Dimare Fresh		B	916 921-6302	0
Disability Rights California **(PA)**		D	916 488-9950	0
Dominguez Landscape Svcs Inc		D	916 381-8855	0
Domus Construction & Design		E	916 381-7500	0
Dongalen Enterprises Inc **(PA)**		E	916 422-3110	0
Doumit Communication Inc		D	916 362-3519	0
Downey Brand LLP **(PA)**		C	916 444-1000	0
Dpr Construction A Gen Partnr		B	916 568-3434	0
Dreyer Bbich Bccola Cllham LLP		E	916 379-3500	0
Drywall Works Inc		D	916 383-6667	0
Easter Seal Soc Superior Cal **(PA)**		D	916 485-6711	0
Easun Inc		C	916 929-8855	0
Eclipse Solutions Inc		D	916 565-8090	0
Edaw Inc		D	916 414-5800	0
Edward E Straine CPA		E	916 646-6464	0
Ehealthwirecom Inc		C	916 924-8092	0
Elegant Surfaces		D	209 823-9388	0
Elica Health Centers		D	916 454-2345	0
Elite Power Inc		D	916 739-1580	0
Elizabethan Inn Associates LP		D	916 448-1300	0
Elk Grove Unified School Dst		C	916 686-7733	0
Elliott Benson Market Research		E	916 325-1670	0
Els Investments		C	916 388-0308	0
Employment Dev Cal Dept		A	916 654-7867	0
Energy Salvage Inc		E	916 737-8640	0
Entercom Communications Corp		C	916 766-5000	0
Entercom Communications Corp		C	916 334-7777	0
Enterprise Rent-A-Car Compan		D	916 576-3164	0
Entravsion Communications Corp		E	916 646-4000	0
Entravsion Communications Corp		E	916 648-6029	0
Environmental Protection Agcy		C	916 324-7572	0
Environmental Systems Research		D	916 448-2412	0
Eskaton Lodge		E	916 789-0326	0
Eskaton Properties Inc		C	916 393-2550	0
Essendant Co		C	916 344-6707	0
Essex Property Trust Inc		D	916 381-0345	0
Ethan Conrad Properties Inc **(PA)**		D	916 779-1000	0
Eugene Burger Management Corp		C	916 443-6637	0
Excel Managed Care Disa		C	916 944-7185	0
Express Messenger Systems Inc		E	916 921-6016	0
Federal Express Corporation		D	916 361-5500	0
Federico Beauty Institute		E	916 929-4242	0
First US Community Credit Un **(PA)**		D	916 576-5700	0
Fischer Tile and Marble Inc		C	916 452-1426	0
Foundtion For Cal Cmnty Cllges **(PA)**		C	916 325-4300	0
Frank Carson Ldscp & Maint Inc		C	916 856-5400	0
Frys Electronics Inc		B	916 286-5800	0
Fusion Real Estate Network Inc		D	916 448-3174	0
G&K Services LLC		D	916 381-5500	0
Gat - Arln Ground Support Inc		B	916 923-2349	0
Gccfc 2005-Gg5 Y St Ltd Partnr		D	916 455-6800	0
Geico Corporation		C	707 448-7172	0
General Prod A Cal Ltd Partnr **(PA)**		C	916 441-6431	0
General Services Cal Dept		C	916 845-4942	0
General Services Cal Dept		B	916 657-9960	0
General Services Cal Dept		A	916 445-4566	0
Girl Scouts Heart Central Cal		C	916 452-9181	0
Gold Country Management Inc		D	916 929-3003	0
Golden 1 Credit Union **(PA)**		B	916 732-2900	0
Golden Coast Cnstr Restoration		E	916 955-7461	0
Golden Pond LP		E	916 369-8967	0

2020 Directory of California
Wholesalers and Services Companies

	SIC	EMP	PHONE	ENTRY #
Gordon & Schwenkmeyer Inc		D	916 569-1740	0
Gordon Rees Scully Mansukhani		D	916 830-6900	0
Granite Construction Company		D	916 855-4400	0
Granite Construction Inc		D	916 855-4495	0
Greater Sacramento Sur		D	916 929-7229	0
Gringteam Inc		B	916 929-8855	0
Growing Company Inc		D	916 379-9088	0
Gudgel Roofing Inc		E	916 387-6900	0
Guild Mortgage Company		E	916 486-6257	0
H & D Electric		B	916 332-0794	0
H C C S Inc		D	916 454-5752	0
Halstead Partnership		D	916 830-8000	0
Hammel Green & Abrahamson Inc		D	916 787-5100	0
Hank Fisher Properties Inc		C	916 447-4444	0
Hank Fisher Properties Inc		D	916 921-1970	0
Hanson Bridgett LLP		E	916 442-3333	0
Harold E Nutter Inc (PA)		D	916 334-4343	0
Harris & Sloan Consulting		E	916 921-2800	0
HDR Engineering Inc		D	916 564-4214	0
Health By Design		E	916 974-3322	0
Heartland Payment Systems LLC		D	916 844-9548	0
Helping Hearts Foundation Inc		D	916 368-7200	0
Hendrickson Truck Lines Inc		C	916 387-9614	0
Hendrickson Trucking Inc		B	916 387-9614	0
Henwood Energy Services Inc (DH)		D	916 955-6031	0
Heritage Community Credit Un (PA)		E	916 364-1700	0
Hilary A Brodie MD PHD		D	916 734-3744	0
Honeywell International Inc		D	916 923-7851	0
Horizon West Inc		D	916 331-4590	0
Howe Community Center		E	916 927-3802	0
Hub Intrntional Insur Svcs Inc		D	916 974-7400	0
Humboldt Dev LLC		D	213 295-2890	0
Hunt Convenience Stores LLC		E	916 383-4868	0
Hurley Construction Inc		D	916 446-7599	0
Huttig Building Products Inc		D	916 383-3721	0
Hylton Security Inc		C	916 442-1000	0
Iconic Chronicles Magazine LLC		D	707 712-2097	0
Iheartcommunications Inc		C	916 929-5325	0
Iheartcommunications Inc		D	916 929-5325	0
Inland Business Machines Inc (DH)		D	916 928-0770	0
Inter-State Oil Co (PA)		D	916 457-6572	0
Internal Mdcine Rsdncy Affairs		D	916 734-7080	0
Interntional Un Oper Engineers (PA)		D	916 444-6880	0
Interstate Fuel Systems Inc		D	916 457-6572	0
Interstate Hotels Resorts Inc		C	916 922-4700	0
Interwest Insurance Svcs LLC (PA)		C	916 488-3100	0
Iunlimited Incorporated		D	916 218-6198	0
Iuoe Sttonary Engineers Lcl 39		E	916 928-0399	0
J and J Wall Baking Co Inc		D	916 381-1410	0
J B Company		D	916 929-3003	0
Jackson Construction (PA)		E	916 381-8113	0
Jarka Enterprises Inc		D	916 491-6180	0
Jensen Enterprises Inc		D	916 992-8301	0
Jerry S Powell MD		D	916 734-5959	0
Jetro Cash and Carry Entps LLC		D	916 492-2305	0
JJR Enterprises Inc (PA)		D	916 363-2666	0
Jma Investments Ltd		D	916 685-1355	0
John F Otto Inc		D	916 441-6870	0
John Jackson Masonry		D	916 381-8021	0
John Stewart Company		C	415 345-4400	0
Juniper Networks Inc		D	916 503-1593	0
Justice California Department		A	916 324-5039	0
Kaiser Foundation Hospitals		D	916 973-5000	0
Kaiser Foundation Hospitals		A	916 688-2000	0
Kaiser Foundation Hospitals		C	916 525-6300	0
Khanna Entps - Il Ltd Partnr		C	916 338-5800	0
Kindred Healthcare Oper Inc		C	916 454-5752	0
Kindred Healthcare Oper LLC		C	916 457-6521	0
Kings Arena Ltd Partnership		D	916 928-0000	0
Kojenov Arkadi Nilovich		E	916 718-1790	0
Kpmg LLP		C	916 448-4700	0
Kronick Moskovitz Tiedemann (PA)		D	916 321-4500	0
Kvie Inc (PA)		D	916 929-5843	0
Kxtv Inc		D	916 441-2345	0
La Familia Counseling Center		D	916 452-3601	0
Landmark Healthcare Svcs Inc (DH)		C	800 638-4557	0
Lawnman II Inc		D	916 739-1420	0
Lawson Mechanical Contractors (PA)		D	916 381-5000	0
LDI Mechanical Inc		E	916 361-3925	0
League of California Cities (PA)		D	916 658-8200	0
Leidos Inc		B	916 974-8800	0
Leo A Daly Company		D	916 564-3259	0
Lewis-Goetz and Company Inc		D	916 366-9340	0
Lexisnexis Courtlink Inc		C	425 974-5000	0
Liberty Mutual Insurance Co		B	916 564-1792	0
Lighthouse Living Services (PA)		D	916 454-4381	0
Lionakis (PA)		C	916 558-1901	0
LLP Downey Brand		D	775 329-5900	0
Loomis Armored Us LLC		D	916 441-1091	0
Lpa Insurance Agency Inc		D	916 286-7850	0
Lpas Inc		D	916 443-0335	0
Lukenbill Enterprises		D	916 454-2400	0
Lumens LLC (HQ)		D	916 444-5585	0
Luppen and Hawley Inc		C	916 456-7831	0
Lupton Excavation Inc		D	916 387-1104	0
Lyon Realty (PA)		A	916 574-8800	0
Lyons Security Service Inc		D	916 925-9667	0
M K S Construction Inc		C	916 446-2521	0
Macdonald Mott LLC		D	916 399-0580	0
Macias Gini & OConnell LLP (PA)		D	916 928-4600	0
Macys Inc		D	916 373-0333	0
Mariner Health Care Inc		C	916 422-4825	0
Mariner Health Care Inc		C	916 481-5500	0
Mark Diversified Inc		E	916 923-6275	0
Mark H Leibenhaut MD		E	916 454-6600	0
Mark III Construction Inc (PA)		D	916 381-8080	0
Markstein Bev Co Sacramento		C	916 920-3911	0
Marquee Fire Protection (PA)		D	916 641-7997	0
Marques Pipeline Inc		E	916 923-3434	0
Marticus Electric Inc		D	916 368-2186	0
Martin Brothers Construction (PA)		D	916 386-1600	0
Matheny Sars Linkert Jaime LLP		D	916 978-3434	0
Matheson Fast Freight Inc		D	209 342-0184	0
Matheson Trucking Inc (PA)		E	916 685-2330	0
May-Han Electric Inc		D	916 929-0150	0
McClatchy Company		A	916 321-1941	0
McWong Envmtl & Enrgy Group		E	916 371-8080	0
Medical Couriers Inc		D	916 452-5700	0
Medstar LLC		D	916 669-0550	0
Mek Norwood Pines LLC		E	916 922-7177	0
Mercy HM Svcs A Cal Ltd Partnr		A	916 453-4545	0
Mercy Housing California Xxvi		D	916 414-4400	0
Meringcarson Holdings (PA)		D	916 441-0571	0
Mission Linen Supply		C	916 423-3179	0
Mission Linen Supply		C	916 423-3135	0
Montessori Learning Commons (PA)		D	916 444-7786	0
Morgan Stanley & Co LLC		E	916 444-8041	0
Morton Golf LLC		D	916 481-4653	0
Mounting Systems Inc		D	916 374-8872	0
Mueller Pet Medical Center		E	916 428-9202	0
Mutual Assist Network Del Paso (PA)		E	916 927-7694	0
Myers & Sons Construction LP (PA)		C	916 283-9950	0
National Security Industries		B	916 779-0640	0
Nehemiah Progressive Housing D		D	916 231-1999	0
New West Partitions		C	916 456-8365	0
Nissan North America Inc		D	916 920-4712	0
Nmi Industrial Holdings Inc		D	916 635-7030	0
North Wind Cnstr Svcs LLC		D	916 333-3015	0
Northern California Inalliance (PA)		C	916 381-1300	0
Northwest Staffing Resources		A	916 960-2668	0
Nv5 Inc (DH)		D	916 641-9100	0
Nv5 Inc		D	916 641-9100	0
Oates Buzz Enterprises		D	916 381-3600	0
Office of The Legislative Coun		B	916 341-8708	0
Office of The Legislative Coun		A	916 445-3796	0
Ogilvy Pub Rltons Wrldwide Inc		D	916 231-7700	0
Oleander Holdings LLC		D	916 331-4990	0
Opendoor Labs Inc		D	888 352-7075	0
Oregon PCF Bldg Pdts Calif Inc		D	916 381-8051	0
Original Petes Pizza Inc		E	916 442-6770	0
Orrick Hrrington Sutcliffe LLP		D	916 447-9200	0
Owen & Company		D	916 993-2700	0
Pacific Civil & Strl Cons LLC		E	916 421-1000	0
Pacific Coast Trnsp Svcs Inc		E	916 266-5300	0
Pacific Fresh Sea Food Company (HQ)		C	916 419-5500	0
Pacific Frnsic Psychlgy Assoc		D	925 253-3111	0
Pacific Gas and Electric Co		C	916 923-7007	0
Pacific Gas and Electric Co		C	916 275-2763	0
Pacific Legal Foundation (PA)		E	916 419-7111	0
Pacific Sea Food Co Inc		D	916 419-5500	0
Pacific West Lath & Plaster		E	916 387-5773	0
Pacifica Hosts Inc		C	619 296-9000	0
Paladin Prtction Spcalists Inc		D	916 331-3175	0
Pape Machinery Inc		D	916 922-7181	0
Parasec Incorporated (PA)		D	916 576-7000	0
Paratransit Incorporated (PA)		C	916 429-2009	0
Parc Specialty Contractors		D	916 992-5405	0
Parker Landscape Dev Inc		E	916 383-4071	0
Parsons Brnckrhoff Hldings Inc		D	916 567-2500	0
Patricks Construction Clean-Up		D	916 452-5495	0

Mergent email: customerrelations@mergent.com
1610

2020 Directory of California
Wholesalers and Services Companies

(P-0000) Products & Services Section entry number
(PA)=Parent Co (HQ)=Headquarters (DH)=Div Headquarters

	SIC	EMP	PHONE	ENTRY #
PDQ Automatic Transm Parts Inc		D	916 681-7701	0
Performance Tech Partners LLC		C	800 787-4143	0
Performance Warehouse Co		D	916 920-2221	0
Permanente Medical Group Inc		D	916 688-2055	0
Perry-Smith LLP		D	916 441-1000	0
Personlzed Hmcare Hmmaker Agcy		D	916 979-4975	0
Pinelands Preservation Inc		D	609 703-0359	0
Pinsetters Inc		D	916 488-7545	0
Pioneer Towers Rhf Partners LP		E	916 443-6548	0
Planned Parenthood Federation		D	916 446-5247	0
Presidio Hotel Group LLC (PA)		C	707 429-6000	0
Pricewaterhousecoopers LLP		D	916 930-8100	0
Pride Industries		C	916 649-9499	0
Primrose Alzheimers Living		D	916 392-3510	0
Procida Landscape Inc		C	916 387-5296	0
Professnal Ldscp Solutions Inc		E	916 424-3815	0
Protege Builders Inc		E	916 825-8478	0
Prs/Roebbelen JV		E	916 641-0324	0
Psychiatric Solutions Inc		C	916 288-0300	0
Psychiatric Solutions Inc		D	916 489-3336	0
Public Consulting Group Inc		D	916 565-8090	0
Public Employees Retirement		B	916 795-3400	0
Public Health Institute		C	916 285-1231	0
Pulmonary Medicine Assoc		D	916 733-5040	0
Quality Group Homes Inc		C	916 930-0066	0
Quality Inv Prpts Scrmento LLC		D	916 679-2100	0
Ragingwire Data Centers Inc (HQ)		B	916 286-3000	0
Raleys		B	916 928-0575	0
Ram Commercial Enterprises Inc		E	916 429-1205	0
Rcb Corporation (PA)		D	916 567-2600	0
Rdo Vermeer LLC		D	916 643-0999	0
Reading International Inc		C	916 442-0985	0
Recp/Wndsor Scramento Ventr LP		D	916 455-6800	0
Refrigeration Solutions LLC		C	916 281-2000	0
Regal Cinemas Inc		D	916 419-0205	0
Remax Gold		D	916 609-2800	0
Republic Electric Inc		D	916 294-0140	0
Republic Electric West Inc		D	916 294-0140	0
Rescue Concrete Inc		D	916 852-2400	0
Research of America		C	916 443-4722	0
Retail Services Wis Corp		C	916 485-3427	0
Retinal Consultants Inc (PA)		E	916 454-4861	0
Rex Moore Group Inc		B	916 372-1300	0
Rex More Elec Contrs Engineers (PA)		A	916 372-1300	0
Rex More Elec Contrs Engineers		D	510 785-1300	0
Rgis LLC		D	916 387-9692	0
River City Bank (HQ)		C	916 567-2600	0
River Oak Center For Children (PA)		C	916 609-5100	0
River Oak Center For Children		D	916 550-5600	0
Riverside Health Care Corp		D	916 446-2506	0
Royal Plywood Company LLC		D	916 426-3292	0
Runyon Saltzman Inc		D	916 446-9900	0
S L H C C Inc		E	916 457-6521	0
S&F Management Company LLC		A	916 922-8855	0
S&W Seed Company (PA)		D	559 884-2535	0
Saccani Distributing Company		D	916 441-0213	0
Sacramento Area Sewer District (PA)		B	916 876-6000	0
Sacramento Childrens Home		D	916 927-5059	0
Sacramento Childrens Home (PA)		D	916 452-3981	0
Sacramento Chinese Community S		C	916 442-4228	0
Sacramento County Off Educatn		E	916 875-0300	0
Sacramento County Water Agency		D	916 874-6851	0
Sacramento Credit Union (PA)		D	916 444-6070	0
Sacramento Cy Unified Schl Dst (PA)		B	916 643-7400	0
Sacramento Ear Nose & Throat (PA)		D	916 736-3399	0
Sacramento Employement & Train		C	916 263-3800	0
Sacramento Employement & Train (PA)		D	916 263-3800	0
Sacramento Harness Association		D	916 239-4040	0
Sacramento Heart and Cardiovas (PA)		D	916 830-2000	0
Sacramento Hotel Partners LLC		D	916 326-5000	0
Sacramento Loaves & Fishes (PA)		D	916 446-0874	0
Sacramento Municpl Utility Dst (PA)		A	916 452-3211	0
Sacramento Municpl Utility Dst		A	916 452-3211	0
Sacramento Municpl Utility Dst		A	916 452-3211	0
Sacramento Municpl Utility Dst		D	916 732-5155	0
Sacramento Municpl Utility Dst		B	916 732-5616	0
Sacramento Operating Co LP		C	916 422-4825	0
Sacramento Reg Co Sanit Dist (PA)		A	916 876-6000	0
Sacramento Regional Trnst Dist (PA)		A	916 726-2877	0
Sacramento Regional Trnst Dist		C	916 321-2800	0
Sacramento Regional Trnst Dist		C	916 869-8611	0
Sacramento Suburban Water Dst		D	916 972-7171	0
Sacramento Suburban Water Dst		D	916 972-7171	0
Sacramento Theatrical Ltg Ltd		D	916 447-3258	0
Sacramento Zoological Society		E	916 808-5888	0
Sacramnto Forty Niner Trvl Plz		C	916 927-4774	0
Sacramnto Mtro A Qulty MGT Dst		D	916 874-4800	0
Sacramnto Ntiv Amercn Hlth Ctr		D	916 341-0575	0
Sacromento Eductn Readng Lions		E	916 228-2219	0
Safelite Fulfillment Inc		D	916 442-4715	0
Saia Inc		C	916 483-8331	0
Saint Claires Nursing Ctr LLC		C	916 392-4440	0
Salvation Army		D	916 441-5137	0
Sandwich Spot (PA)		D	916 492-2613	0
Santos Legacy Builders LLC		D	916 439-2777	0
Scandia Sports Inc		E	916 331-5757	0
Schetter Electric Inc (PA)		D	916 446-2521	0
Schetter Electric LLC		D	916 446-2521	0
Schools Financial Credit Union (PA)		C	916 569-5400	0
Scott A Porter Prof Corp		D	916 929-1481	0
Securitas SEC Svcs USA Inc		C	916 564-2009	0
Securitas SEC Svcs USA Inc		C	916 569-4500	0
Sedgwick Claims MGT Svcs Inc		D	916 568-7394	0
Sheraton LLC		B	916 447-1700	0
Shermn-Lehr Cstm Tile Wrks Inc		D	916 386-0417	0
Shri Sidhi Vinayaka Hotel Inc		C	855 922-5252	0
Shriners Hspitals For Children		B	916 453-2050	0
Sierra Bookkeeping & Tax Svc		D	916 349-7610	0
Sierra Forever Families		D	916 368-5114	0
Sierra Waste Transport Inc		E	916 386-9937	0
Simas Floor Co Inc (PA)		C	916 452-4933	0
Singley Enterprises (PA)		E	866 890-1776	0
Sitoa		D	916 444-0008	0
Six Flags Entertainment Corp		B	916 924-3747	0
Sky Park Gardens Assisted		D	916 422-5650	0
Skyles Insurance Agency		E	916 361-9585	0
Skyslope Inc		D	916 833-2390	0
Southgate Glass & Screen Inc (PA)		E	916 476-8396	0
Southgate Glass & Screen Inc		E	916 476-8396	0
Southgate Recreation & Pk Dst		E	916 421-7275	0
Southwest Dealer Services Inc		C	925 753-0696	0
Spare-Time Inc		D	916 649-0909	0
Spencer Building Maintenance		B	916 922-1900	0
Ssmb Pacific Holding Co Inc		D	916 371-3372	0
St Vncent De Paul Bltmore Inc		C	916 485-3482	0
Stanford Youth Solutions (PA)		D	916 344-0199	0
Stantec Consulting Svcs Inc		E	916 924-8844	0
Starwest Botanicals Inc (PA)		D	916 638-8100	0
State Compensation Insur Fund		B	916 924-5100	0
Stericycle Comm Solutions Inc		D	888 370-6711	0
Stommel Inc (PA)		E	916 646-6626	0
Stradling Yocca Carlson & Raut		C	916 449-2350	0
Strategies For Change (PA)		D	916 395-3552	0
Stratgies To Empwer People Inc (PA)		D	916 679-1527	0
Stucco Works Inc		B	916 383-6699	0
Students of Associated		D	916 278-6216	0
Sunrise Senior Living LLC		E	916 486-0200	0
Supershuttle International Inc		D	916 648-2500	0
Support For Family LLC		D	877 916-9111	0
Support For Home Inc		E	530 792-8464	0
Surety West Logistics Inc		D	800 761-2551	0
Surgical Care Affiliate		E	916 529-4590	0
Surgical Staff Inc		C	916 444-4424	0
Sutter Club Inc		D	916 442-0456	0
Sutter Health		B	916 733-1025	0
Sutter Health		C	916 733-9588	0
Sutter Health		C	916 262-9400	0
Sutter Health		B	916 566-4819	0
Sutter Health		B	916 262-9414	0
Sutter Health		A	916 646-8300	0
Sutter Health		B	916 887-0000	0
Sutter Health (PA)		A	916 733-8800	0
Sutter Health		C	916 451-3344	0
Sutter Health		C	916 453-5955	0
Sutter Health		C	916 731-5672	0
Sutter Health		C	916 262-9456	0
Sutter Health At Work		D	916 565-8607	0
Sutter Hlth Rhabilitation Svcs		D	916 733-3040	0
Sutter Hlth Scrmnto Sierra Reg		A	916 733-7080	0
Sutter Hlth Scrmnto Sierra Reg (HQ)		B	916 733-8800	0
Sutter Hlth Scrmnto Sierra Reg		B	916 454-2222	0
Sutter Hlth Scrmnto Sierra Reg		D	916 446-3100	0
Sutter Hlth Scrmnto Sierra Reg		D	916 733-3095	0
Sutter Medical Foundation		A	916 924-7764	0
Sutter Physician Services (HQ)		A	916 854-6600	0
Sutter Valley Med Foundation (PA)		A	916 887-7122	0
Swinerton Builders Hc		C	916 383-4825	0
System Integrators Inc (HQ)		C	916 830-2400	0
T M Cobb Company		D	916 381-7330	0
Tammi R James MD		E	916 383-6783	0

Employment Codes: A=Over 500 employees, B=251-500, C=101-250, D=51-100, E=50

2020 Directory of California
Wholesalers and Services Companies

© Mergent Inc. 1-800-342-5647

1611

GEOGRAPHIC

	SIC	EMP	PHONE	ENTRY #
Technology Services Cal Dept **(DH)**		D	916 319-9223	0
Teichert/Great Lakes E&I JV		D	916 484-3011	0
Tele-Direct Communications		D	916 348-2170	0
Terkensha Associates Inc		D	916 922-9868	0
Terracina Meadows Apts		E	916 419-0925	0
Textron Aviation Inc		D	916 929-5656	0
Tf Courier Inc		D	916 379-0708	0
The Executive Office of		D	916 322-2318	0
The For Sacramento Society		D	916 383-7387	0
Therapeutic Pathways Inc		D	916 489-1376	0
Thunder Mountain Enterprises **(PA)**		D	916 381-3400	0
Tierra Del Oro Girl Scout Cnsl		D	916 452-9174	0
Timber Works Construction Inc		C	916 786-6666	0
Tlcs Inc		D	916 441-0123	0
Tradewinds Partnership		D	916 333-5239	0
Training Toward Self Reliance		E	916 442-8877	0
Travis Credit Union		B	916 443-1446	0
Tricorp Construction Inc **(PA)**		D	916 779-8010	0
Trinity Fresh Distribution LLC		D	916 714-7368	0
Trinity Technology Group Inc		D	916 779-0201	0
Tucson Hotels LP		C	916 446-0100	0
Tucson Hotels LP		C	916 446-0100	0
Turner Construction Company		D	916 444-4421	0
Turning Point Cmnty Programs		D	916 393-1222	0
U C Med Humn Rsrces Aplcat Svc		D	916 734-5916	0
UBS Financial Services Inc		E	916 648-7200	0
Uc Davis Health System **(PA)**		D	916 734-1000	0
Ucd Mc Home Care Services		C	916 734-2458	0
Unifirst Corporation		E	916 929-3766	0
United Airlines Inc		C	916 877-3002	0
United Parcel Service Inc OH		D	916 373-4089	0
United Parcel Service Inc OH		C	916 857-0311	0
Universal Limousine & Trnsp Co		D	916 361-5466	0
Universal Network Dev Corp **(PA)**		D	916 475-1200	0
University California Davis		E	916 734-2846	0
University California Davis		A	916 734-3141	0
University California Davis		A	916 734-2011	0
University California Davis		A	916 734-5113	0
URS Group Inc		D	916 679-2000	0
URS Group Inc		C	916 679-2000	0
US Army Corps of Engineers		A	916 557-7490	0
US Loan Auditors LLC		D	916 248-8625	0
USA Valet Parking LLC		E	916 792-1055	0
USA Waste of California Inc		D	916 379-0500	0
USA Waste of California Inc		C	916 379-2611	0
V S N F Inc		D	916 452-6631	0
Valley Can		E	916 273-4890	0
Valley Communications Inc **(PA)**		D	916 349-7300	0
Valley Health Care Systems Inc		C	916 505-4112	0
Vanir Construction MGT Inc **(PA)**		D	916 444-3700	0
Vasko Electric Inc		D	916 568-7700	0
Veritiv Operating Company		D	916 283-2160	0
Verizon Bus Netwrk Svcs Inc		C	916 569-5999	0
Veterans Affairs Cal Dept		B	916 653-2535	0
Village Nurseries Whl LLC		B	916 993-2292	0
Visions Unlimited **(PA)**		C	916 394-0800	0
Vitas Healthcare Corp Cal		D	916 925-7010	0
Volunteers of America Greater **(PA)**		D	916 265-3400	0
W H C Inc		D	916 927-9300	0
Water Resources Cal Dept		D	916 574-1423	0
Water Resources Cal Dept		E	916 324-3812	0
Watson Contractors Inc		D	916 481-6293	0
Wdc Explrtion Wells Holdg Corp		C	916 419-6043	0
WEAVE Incorporated **(PA)**		D	916 448-2321	0
Weintraub Tobin Chediak **(PA)**		E	916 558-6000	0
Wellhead Electric Company Inc		E	916 447-5171	0
Wells Fargo Bank National Assn		E	916 440-4570	0
Wellspace Health **(PA)**		D	916 325-5556	0
Western Health Advantage		D	916 567-1950	0
Western States Fire Protection		D	916 924-1631	0
Whgca LLC		C	916 922-4700	0
Whole Foods Market Cal Inc		C	916 488-2800	0
William L Lyon & Assoc Inc **(PA)**		A	916 978-4200	0
William L Lyon & Assoc Inc		D	916 447-7878	0
Wilmor & Sons Plumbing & Cnstr		D	916 381-9114	0
Winter Care Center Sacramento		C	916 922-8855	0
Wmk Sacramento LLC		E	916 929-8855	0
Wood Rodgers Inc **(PA)**		C	916 341-7760	0
Xl Construction Corporation		D	916 282-2900	0
Xpo Logistics Freight Inc		C	916 399-8291	0
Yrc Inc		D	916 371-4555	0
Zimmerman Roofing Inc		D	916 454-3667	0
Zoe Holding Company Inc		C	916 646-3100	0

SAINT HELENA, CA - Napa County

	SIC	EMP	PHONE	ENTRY #
Jack Neal & Son Inc		C	707 963-7303	0

	SIC	EMP	PHONE	ENTRY #
Mitchell Vineyards LLC		D	707 963-7050	0
Nissen Vineyard Services Inc		D	707 963-3480	0
Rios Farming Company LLC		C	707 965-2587	0
Silverado Orchards **(PA)**		D	707 963-1461	0
St Helena Hospital **(HQ)**		A	707 963-3611	0
T and M Agricultural Svcs LLC		C	707 963-3330	0
Taylor Bailey Inc		D	707 967-8090	0

SALINAS, CA - Monterey County

	SIC	EMP	PHONE	ENTRY #
Adobe Packing Company **(PA)**		C	831 753-6195	0
American Farms LLC		D	831 424-1815	0
Americold Logistics LLC		E	831 424-1537	0
Ameripride Services Inc		E	800 882-5326	0
ASset Private Security Inc		D	831 809-9779	0
BFI Waste Systems N Amer Inc		D	831 775-3850	0
Blazer Wilkinson LP		B	831 455-3700	0
Califrnia Frnsic Med Group Inc		C	831 755-3886	0
Carmel Valley Packing Inc		C	831 771-8860	0
Central Coast Cooling LLC		D	831 422-7265	0
Central Coast Vna & Hospice		D	831 758-8243	0
Christensen & Giannini LLC		D	831 449-2494	0
Church Brothers LLC **(PA)**		D	831 796-1000	0
City of Salinas		D	831 758-7233	0
Corral De Tierra Country Club		D	831 484-1325	0
Corral Del Tierra		D	831 372-6244	0
County of Monterey		D	831 755-4944	0
County of Monterey		D	831 755-5027	0
County of Monterey		E	831 755-4500	0
County of Monterey		A	831 755-4201	0
County of Monterey		E	831 769-8800	0
County of Monterey		B	831 755-3700	0
County of Monterey		A	831 755-8500	0
County of Monterey		C	831 755-3782	0
County of Monterey		B	831 755-4800	0
DArrigo Broscoof California **(PA)**		E	831 455-4500	0
Dassels Petroleum Inc		E	831 636-5100	0
Elioco Produce Inc		C	831 424-5450	0
Employnet Inc		A	831 233-9999	0
Foothill Estates Inc		D	831 422-7819	0
Fresh Leaf Farms LLC **(DH)**		E	831 422-7405	0
Gieg Chevron LLC		D	831 755-8000	0
Growers Company Inc		D	831 424-3850	0
Growers Express LLC **(PA)**		C	831 757-9951	0
Growers Street Cooling LLC		D	831 424-2929	0
Growers Transplanting Inc **(HQ)**		D	831 449-3440	0
Guardsmark LLC		C	831 769-8981	0
Hearst Stations Inc		D	831 758-8888	0
Helios Healthcare LLC		D	831 449-1515	0
Henry Hibino Farms		D	831 757-3081	0
Higard Farms LLC		D	831 753-5982	0
Hilltown Packing Co Inc		B	831 784-1931	0
Hope Services		D	831 455-4940	0
Interim Inc		C	831 754-3838	0
J Waters Inc		D	866 424-1946	0
Jensco Inc		E	831 422-7819	0
Jlg Harvesting Inc		B	831 422-7871	0
Kindred Healthcare Oper LLC		C	831 424-8072	0
Kysmet Security & Patrol Inc		E	831 710-2425	0
Mann Packing Co Inc **(DH)**		B	831 422-7405	0
Mann Packing Co Inc		D	831 796-2670	0
Massolo Trucking LLC **(PA)**		E	831 424-7205	0
Matsui Nursery Inc **(PA)**		D	831 422-6433	0
Mechanics Bank		C	831 422-6642	0
Mission Linen Supply		D	831 424-1707	0
Mission Linen Supply		C	831 424-1753	0
Monterey County Office Educatn		D	831 755-0324	0
Monterey-Salinas Transit Corp		C	831 754-2804	0
Mv Transportation Inc		C	831 373-1395	0
Natividad Medical Center		A	831 755-4111	0
Newstar Fresh Foods LLC		D	831 758-7800	0
Newstar Fresh Foods LLC **(PA)**		C	888 782-7220	0
Noland Hamerly Etienne **(PA)**		E	831 372-7525	0
Nunes Company Inc **(PA)**		E	831 751-7510	0
Nunes Cooling Inc		E	831 751-7510	0
Nutrien AG Solutions Inc		D	831 757-5391	0
Odd Fellow-Rebekah Chld HM Cal		D	831 775-0348	0
Old Republic Title Company		E	831 757-8051	0
Pacific Intl Vgetable Mktg Inc **(PA)**		D	831 422-3745	0
Pemer Packing Co Inc		A	831 758-8586	0
Planned Parenthood Mar Monte **(PA)**		D	831 373-1709	0
Plant Tape Usa Inc **(HQ)**		E	831 455-2255	0
Porter Construction Co Inc		C	831 455-3020	0
Pre Con Industries Inc		E	805 345-3147	0
Premium Packing Inc		C	831 443-6855	0
Quinn Group Inc		A	831 758-8461	0
Quinn Lift Inc		D	831 758-4086	0

Mergent email: customerrelations@mergent.com
1612

2020 Directory of California
Wholesalers and Services Companies

(P-0000) Products & Services Section entry number
(PA)=Parent Co (HQ)=Headquarters (DH)=Div Headquarters

	SIC	EMP	PHONE	ENTRY #
Rancho Salinas Packing Inc		C	831 758-3624	0
Red Blossom Sales Inc		A	831 751-9169	0
Reegs Inc		D	831 455-7931	0
Rh Framing Inc		C	831 759-8860	0
River Ranch Fresh Foods LLC (HQ)		B	831 758-1390	0
Rocket Farms Herbs Inc		B	562 340-5108	0
S&P Global Inc		C	831 393-6044	0
Salinas Med Mngt Srvcs Org Inc		D	831 751-7070	0
Salinas Valley Medical Clinic		B	831 424-7389	0
Salinas Valley Memorial Hlthca (PA)		D	831 757-4333	0
Salinas Valley Memorial Hlthca		B	831 757-3041	0
Salinas Valley Memorial Hlthca		B	831 755-7880	0
Scheid Vineyards Inc (PA)		D	831 455-9990	0
Schubert Nursery (PA)		D	831 753-0144	0
Securitas SEC Svcs USA Inc		C	831 444-9607	0
Seed Dynamics Inc		D	831 424-1177	0
Sg Personnel LLC		B	831 444-0523	0
SMD Logistics Inc		C	831 758-5300	0
Sturdy Oil Company		D	831 970-9897	0
Sunberry Growers LLC		A	805 922-9888	0
Superior Contracting Corp		E	831 757-1089	0
Tanimura Antle Fresh Foods Inc (PA)		D	831 455-2950	0
Tanimura Brothers		D	831 424-0841	0
Taylor Farms California Inc (HQ)		E	831 754-0471	0
Taylor Fresh Foods Inc (PA)		C	831 676-9023	0
United Parcel Service Inc OH		C	831 758-9112	0
USA Waste of California Inc		D	831 754-2500	0
Vals Plumbing and Heating Inc		D	831 424-1633	0
Vegetable Growers Supply Co (PA)		E	831 759-4600	0
Villa Serra Corporation		D	831 754-5532	0
Windsor Convalescent		C	831 424-0687	0
Windsor Rdge Rhbltttion Ctr LLC		D	831 449-1515	0
Windsor Skyline Care Ctr LLC		D	831 449-5496	0
Xpo Logistics Freight Inc		D	831 758-8874	0

SAN ANDREAS, CA - Calaveras County

	SIC	EMP	PHONE	ENTRY #
Avalon Care Center		C	209 754-3823	0
Calaveras County Water Dst		D	209 754-3543	0
County of Calaveras		D	209 754-6402	0
Dignity Health		C	209 754-3521	0
Mark Twain Medical Center (DH)		C	209 754-3521	0
Mark Twain Medical Center		B	209 754-1487	0
Resource Connection of Amador (PA)		D	209 754-3114	0
Rite of Pass Athl Trai Cent		C	209 736-4500	0

SAN ARDO, CA - Monterey County

	SIC	EMP	PHONE	ENTRY #
PSC Industrial Outsourcing LP		D	831 627-2595	0

SAN BERNARDINO, CA - San Bernardino County

	SIC	EMP	PHONE	ENTRY #
Alliance Fc		E	909 784-0005	0
Allied Building Products Corp		E	909 796-6926	0
American Force Private SEC Inc		D	909 384-9820	0
Arrowhead Convalescent Home		D	909 886-4731	0
Association For Retarded		D	909 884-6484	0
AT&T Corp		D	909 381-7729	0
Aviation & Defense Inc		C	909 382-3487	0
Baron Pool Plst Sthern Cal Inc		D	909 792-8891	0
Barrett Business Services Inc		A	909 890-3633	0
Bear Trucking Inc		D	909 799-1616	0
Blood Bank of San Bernardino A (HQ)		C	909 885-6503	0
Bnsf Railway Company		C	909 386-4148	0
Brennan Electric Inc		C	909 772-2263	0
Brickley Construction Co Inc		E	909 888-2010	0
Budget Electrical Contrs Inc		D	909 381-2646	0
California Title Co Nthrn Cal		C	909 825-8800	0
Care Tech Inc		D	909 882-2965	0
Caston Inc		D	909 381-1619	0
Cellco Partnership		D	909 381-0576	0
CMC Steel Fabricators Inc		D	909 713-1130	0
Community Action Prtnship Sb C		D	909 723-1500	0
Community Hosp San Bernardino (DH)		B	909 887-6333	0
Copier Source Inc (PA)		D	909 890-4040	0
Cornerstone Medical Group		E	909 890-4353	0
Correctons Rhbltation Cal Dept		D	909 806-3516	0
County of San Bernardino		D	909 891-3300	0
County of San Bernardino		D	909 387-5455	0
County of San Bernardino		D	909 387-2363	0
County of San Bernardino		D	909 387-0535	0
County of San Bernardino		C	909 386-8818	0
D M Electric Inc		D	909 888-8639	0
Daart Engineering Company Inc		D	909 888-8696	0
Del Rosa Villa Inc		D	909 885-3261	0
Dish Network Corporation		D	909 381-4767	0
DSC Logistics LLC		B	540 377-2302	0
Eagle Systems Inc		C	909 386-4343	0

	SIC	EMP	PHONE	ENTRY #
Empire Disposal LLC		E	909 797-9125	0
Far West Inc		D	909 884-4781	0
Fedex Freight Corporation		D	909 887-3970	0
First Hotels International Inc		C	909 884-9364	0
First Student Inc		D	909 383-1640	0
First Student Inc		D	909 383-7104	0
Fischer Inc		D	909 881-2910	0
Garda CL West Inc		E	909 574-2676	0
Gate City Beverage Distrs (PA)		B	909 799-0281	0
Gresham Savage Nolan & Tilden (PA)		D	619 794-0050	0
Help For The Hurting Inc		D	909 796-4222	0
Hillcrest Care Inc		D	909 882-2965	0
Hub Construction Spc Inc (PA)		E	909 889-0161	0
Inland Bhavioral Hlth Svcs Inc (PA)		D	909 881-6146	0
Inland Cnties Regional Ctr Inc (PA)		C	909 890-3000	0
Inland Empire Health Plan		B	866 228-4347	0
Inland Empre 66ers Bsebll CLB		C	909 888-9922	0
Institute For Bhvoral Hlth Inc		B	909 289-1041	0
Iron Workers Local 433		E	909 884-5500	0
J G Golfing Enterprises Inc		E	909 885-2414	0
Jenco Productions Inc (PA)		C	909 381-9453	0
Job Options Incorporated		A	909 890-4612	0
Kaiser Foundation Hospitals		D	888 750-0036	0
Kohls Corporation		B	909 382-4300	0
Konica Minolta Business Soluti		D	909 824-2000	0
L & L Nursery Supply Inc (PA)		C	909 591-0461	0
Legacy Vulcan LLC		E	909 875-1150	0
Lewis Brsbois Bsgard Smith LLP		E	909 387-1130	0
Llu Advntist Hlth Sciences Ctr		D	909 558-4386	0
Lucky Farms Inc		D	909 799-6688	0
Marna Health Services Inc		D	909 882-2965	0
Matich Corporation (PA)		D	909 382-7400	0
Maxim Healthcare Services Inc		B	951 684-4148	0
Medina Concrete Construction		E	909 474-9640	0
Metropolitan Water District		E	909 890-3776	0
Michael P Byko DDS A Prof Corp (PA)		D	909 888-7817	0
Michael Reyes		C	909 444-0120	0
Midnight Auto Recycling LLC		E	909 884-5308	0
NTS Technical Systems		D	909 863-5150	0
Omnitrans Inc		B	909 383-1680	0
On Trac Overhead Door Co Inc		E	909 799-8555	0
Original Mowbrays Tree Svc Inc (PA)		C	909 383-7009	0
Pacific Airworks Group LLC		D	909 815-7012	0
Pathway Inc		D	909 890-1070	0
Plott Management Co		D	909 883-0288	0
Property Insight		C	909 876-6505	0
Roofing Wholesale Co Inc		D	909 825-8440	0
S&E Gourmet Cuts Inc		C	909 370-0155	0
Sac Health System (PA)		D	909 382-7100	0
Safety Security Patrol LLC		D	909 888-7778	0
Salvation Army		D	909 889-9605	0
Sample Tile and Stone Inc		D	951 776-8562	0
San Bernardino California City (PA)		B	909 384-7272	0
San Bernardino California City		D	909 384-5111	0
San Bernardino Care Company		C	909 884-4781	0
San Bernardino City Unf School		D	909 388-6137	0
San Bernardino City Unf School		D	909 388-6100	0
San Bernardino City Unf School		D	909 388-6307	0
San Bernardino City Unf School		D	909 881-8000	0
San Bernardino Hilton (HQ)		C	909 889-0133	0
San Bernardino Med Group Inc (PA)		C	909 883-8611	0
San Bernardino Symphony		D	909 381-5388	0
San Brnrdino Pub Emplyees Assn		E	909 386-1260	0
Scdrg Inc		D	818 874-0830	0
Soffietti Co		D	909 907-2277	0
Southern California Gas Co		C	909 335-7941	0
Spectrum MGT Holdg Co LLC		D	909 918-6972	0
Sprint Communications Co LP		D	909 382-6030	0
Stavatti Industries Ltd		D	651 238-5369	0
Terminix Intl Co Ltd Partnr		E	909 332-2479	0
Think Together		A	909 723-1400	0
United Medical Management Inc		C	909 886-5291	0
Vna Hospice & Plltve Cre S CA		D	909 384-0737	0
Vna Hospice & Plltve Cre S CA (PA)		B	909 624-3574	0
Waterman Convalescent Hospital (PA)		C	909 882-1215	0
World Class Distribution Inc		D	909 574-4140	0
Wsp USA Inc		D	909 888-1106	0
YMCA of East Valley		E	909 881-9622	0

SAN BRUNO, CA - San Mateo County

	SIC	EMP	PHONE	ENTRY #
Airport Parking Service Inc		D	650 875-6655	0
Artichoke Joes Inc		B	650 589-8812	0
Epixel Solutions		D	650 616-4488	0
Honeywell International Inc		D	650 918-3229	0
Kaiser Foundation Hospitals		D	650 742-2100	0
Ksi Corp (PA)		D	650 952-0815	0

Employment Codes: A=Over 500 employees, B=251-500,
C=101-250, D=51-100, E=50

2020 Directory of California
Wholesalers and Services Companies

© Mergent Inc. 1-800-342-5647

1613

	SIC	EMP	PHONE	ENTRY #
La Petite Baleen Inc		D	650 588-7665	0
Ohl LLC		C	650 872-3399	0
Permanente Medical Group Inc		D	650 742-2100	0
Premier Source LLC		D	415 349-2010	0
Provident Funding Assoc LP (PA)		E	650 652-1300	0
Qumu Inc (HQ)		D	650 396-8530	0
Responsys Inc (DH)		D	650 745-1700	0
Sapho Inc		D	650 597-2746	0
Spiritual Direction		E	650 952-9456	0
Staffing Specialists Intl		E	650 737-0777	0
United Airlines Inc		C	650 634-2468	0
Vantagepoint Capital Partners (PA)		D	650 866-3100	0
Vantagepoint Management Inc (PA)		D	650 866-3100	0
Vantagepoint Venture Partners		D	650 866-3100	0

SAN CARLOS, CA - San Mateo County

	SIC	EMP	PHONE	ENTRY #
A G Paceman Inc		D	650 592-7282	0
Broadway By Bay		C	650 579-5565	0
Check Point Software Tech Inc (HQ)		C	650 628-2000	0
Coldwell Banker		D	650 596-5400	0
Commercial Mechanical Svc Inc (PA)		E	650 610-8440	0
D & J Tile Company Inc		D	650 632-4000	0
Duckys of San Carlos Inc		E	650 637-1301	0
Emagined Security Inc		E	415 944-2977	0
Fbn Inputs LLC		D	844 200-3276	0
George P Johnson Company		C	650 226-0600	0
Helix Holdings I LLC		D	415 805-3360	0
Helix Opco LLC		D	415 805-3360	0
Inside Source Inc (PA)		D	650 508-9101	0
Lifestreet Corporation		D	650 508-2220	0
Lyngso Garden Materials Inc		E	650 364-1730	0
Marklogic Corporation (PA)		D	650 655-2300	0
Maxx Metals Inc		D	650 654-1500	0
Natera Inc (PA)		C	650 249-9090	0
Oportun Financial Corporation (PA)		A	650 810-8823	0
Peninsula Crrdor Jint Pwers Bd		C	650 508-6200	0
Peninsula Custom Homes Inc		D	650 574-0241	0
Professional Insur Assoc Inc (PA)		E	650 592-7333	0
Recology San Mateo County		D	650 595-3900	0
Revjet		C	650 508-2215	0
Ruby Burma Investment LLC		D	650 590-0545	0
Rudolph and Sletten Inc (HQ)		D	650 216-3600	0
San Mateo County Transit Dst (PA)		D	650 508-6200	0
San Mateo County Transit Dst		C	650 508-6412	0
Sb Product Group LLC		C	650 562-8221	0
Starvista		C	650 591-9623	0
Universal General Builders		D	650 591-3104	0
VCA Animal Hospitals Inc		E	650 631-7400	0

SAN CLEMENTE, CA - Orange County

	SIC	EMP	PHONE	ENTRY #
Advanced Mp Technology LLC (DH)		C	800 492-3113	0
Asociacon De Bomberos Del Esta		D	949 355-4249	0
Bemus Landscape Inc		B	714 557-7910	0
Brad Rambo & Associates Inc (PA)		D	949 366-9911	0
Buyefficient LLC		D	949 382-3129	0
Dealersocket Inc (PA)		D	949 900-0300	0
Dual Diagnosis Trtmnt Ctr Inc (PA)		D	949 276-5553	0
Evolution Hospitality LLC (PA)		D	949 325-1350	0
GCI Construction Inc		E	714 957-0233	0
Golf Investment LLC (PA)		D	949 498-6604	0
HCA Inc		D	949 496-1122	0
Heritage Golf Group LLC		D	949 369-6226	0
Internet Marketing Assn Inc		D	949 443-9300	0
Julius Steve Construction Inc		E	949 369-7820	0
Keenan & Associates		D	949 940-1760	0
Leaf Communications Inc		D	949 388-0192	0
Matsushita International Corp (PA)		D	949 498-1000	0
Metagenics Inc		D	800 692-9400	0
Pacific Golf & Country Club		D	949 498-6604	0
Partner Hero Inc		E	888 968-2767	0
Rainbow Sandals Inc		E	949 276-4431	0
Regenesis Bioremediation Pdts (PA)		E	949 366-8000	0
Sambazon Inc (PA)		D	877 726-2296	0
San Clemente Medical Ctr LLC		B	949 496-1122	0
San Clemente Villas By Sea		D	949 489-3400	0
San Diego Gas & Electric Co		E	949 361-8090	0
Southern California Edison Co		A	949 368-2881	0
Speedy Locksmith		D	760 439-5000	0

SAN DIEGO, CA - San Diego County

	SIC	EMP	PHONE	ENTRY #
1111 6th Ave LLC		D	312 283-3683	0
1835 Columbia Street LP		D	619 564-3993	0
24 Hour Elevator Inc		D	858 279-8900	0
24 Hour Fitness Usa Inc		E	619 294-2424	0
24 Hour Fitness Usa Inc		E	858 538-4400	0
5th Avenue Partners LLC		B	619 515-3000	0

	SIC	EMP	PHONE	ENTRY #
8110 Aero Holding LLC		C	858 277-8888	0
A & D Fire Protection Inc		D	619 258-7697	0
A C Rentals LLC		E	858 271-8571	0
A Caos Medical Corporation		D	800 362-2731	0
A J Esprit		E	619 223-8171	0
A O Reed & Co		B	858 565-4131	0
A-Star Staffing Inc		C	619 574-7600	0
Aat Torrey Reserve 6 LLC		D	858 350-2600	0
Aba Holdings LLC		C	858 565-4131	0
Abacus Data Systems Inc (HQ)		D	858 452-4280	0
ABC Home Health Care Llc		C	858 455-5000	0
Accentcare Inc		A	858 576-7410	0
Accentcare Home Health Cal Inc		C	858 576-7410	0
Accenture Federal Services LLC		C	619 574-2400	0
Access Nurses Inc		D	858 458-4400	0
Accumen Inc (PA)		D	858 777-8160	0
Ace Parking Management Inc		C	858 552-0237	0
Ace Parking Management Inc (PA)		E	619 233-6624	0
Ace Parking Management Inc		D	619 232-1234	0
Ace Relocation Systems Inc (PA)		B	858 677-5500	0
Acea Biosciences Inc		D	858 724-0928	0
Achates Power Inc		D	858 535-9920	0
Acon Laboratories Inc (PA)		B	858 875-8000	0
Activcare Living Inc (PA)		C	858 565-4424	0
Adaptamed LLC		C	877 478-7773	0
Adesa Corporation LLC		C	619 661-5565	0
Adler Dev LLC		D	707 229-3162	0
Administrative Services SD		E	619 398-2314	0
Adminstrtive Office of US Crts		C	619 557-6650	0
Advanced Rehabilitation Tech		D	858 621-5959	0
Advanced Rsrvation Systems Inc		D	619 501-7000	0
Advanced Test Equipment Corp		D	858 558-6500	0
Aecom Technical Services Inc		D	619 610-7600	0
Aewestjv		E	619 233-1023	0
Affinity Auto Programs Inc		D	858 643-9324	0
Affinity Development Group Inc		C	858 643-9324	0
Affordable Engrg Svcs Inc		D	973 890-8915	0
Age Concerns Inc		B	619 544-1622	0
AIG Direct Insurance Svcs Inc		B	858 309-3000	0
Air Express Intl USA Inc		E	858 578-9602	0
Airgas Inc		C	858 279-8200	0
Airgas Usa LLC		C	858 279-8200	0
AJW Restoration Services LLC		E	858 429-5641	0
Akela Pharma Inc		E	512 391-3525	0
Aldridge Pite LLP		C	858 750-7700	0
All Star Glass Inc (PA)		E	619 275-3343	0
All Star Maintenance Inc		D	858 259-0900	0
All System Personnel Mgmt		E	858 674-4090	0
All Valley Home Hlth Care Inc		D	619 276-8001	0
Allegis Residential Svcs Inc		D	858 430-5700	0
Allied Gardens Towing Inc (HQ)		D	619 563-4060	0
Alliedbarton Security Svcs LLC		B	858 874-8200	0
Allstar Commercial Cleaning		E	858 715-0500	0
Alorica Customer Care Inc		A	619 298-7103	0
Alpha Mechanical Inc		D	858 278-3500	0
Alpha Mechanical Inc (PA)		D	858 278-3500	0
Alsco Inc		C	619 234-7291	0
Alta-Dena Certified Dairy LLC		D	858 292-6930	0
Alvarado Hospital LLC (DH)		D	619 287-3270	0
Alvizia Landscape Co LLC		C	619 661-6557	0
Amber Financial Group LLC (PA)		C	858 487-7209	0
America West Airlines Inc		C	619 231-7340	0
American Airlines Inc		E	619 574-0615	0
American Assets Trust Inc (PA)		D	858 350-2600	0
American Electronic Warfare As		D	858 524-6119	0
American Freightways LP		D	866 326-5902	0
American Institute of Aeronaut		D	619 545-3736	0
American Internet Mortgage Inc		C	888 411-4246	0
American Intl Group Inc		C	619 682-4058	0
American Medical Response Inc		C	858 492-3500	0
American Multi-Cinema Inc		E	619 296-0370	0
American Multi-Cinema Inc		D	619 296-2737	0
American National Red Cross		D	858 309-1200	0
American Nwland Communities LP (PA)		E	858 455-7503	0
American Prprty-Mnagement Corp		C	619 232-3121	0
American Red Cross San Diego (PA)		C	858 309-1200	0
American Residential Svcs LLC		D	858 457-5547	0
American Spclty Hlth Group Inc		B	858 754-2000	0
American Specialty Health Inc (PA)		C	858 754-2000	0
American Technologies Inc		D	858 530-2400	0
Amn Healthcare Inc (HQ)		C	858 792-0711	0
Amn Healthcare Services Inc		A	858 792-0711	0
Amn Healthcare Services Inc (PA)		C	866 871-8519	0
Anchor General Insurance Agcy		C	858 527-3600	0
Andrew and Williamson Sales Co (PA)		D	619 661-6000	0

Mergent email: customerrelations@mergent.com
1614

2020 Directory of California
Wholesalers and Services Companies

(P-0000) Products & Services Section entry number
(PA)=Parent Co (HQ)=Headquarters (DH)=Div Headquarters

	SIC	EMP	PHONE	ENTRY #		SIC	EMP	PHONE	ENTRY #
Andrew M Golden MD		D	619 528-5342	0	Blue Box Opco LLC **(DH)**		D	800 840-4916	0
Anesthesia Service Med Group		E	858 277-4767	0	Bmr 21 Erie St LLC		D	858 485-9840	0
Anixter Inc		D	800 854-2088	0	Bmv Direct II LP		D	858 485-9840	0
Anova Food LLC		D	813 902-9003	0	Bonded Inc **(PA)**		D	858 576-8400	0
Apex Mechanical Systems Inc		D	858 536-8700	0	Booz Allen Hamilton Inc		D	619 725-6500	0
Appfolio Inc		A	866 648-1536	0	Boykin Mgt Co Ltd Lblty Co		E	619 299-6633	0
Apple Nine Hospitality MGT		D	858 573-0700	0	Bps Bioscience Inc		E	858 202-1401	0
Applied Molecular Evolution **(HQ)**		E	858 597-4990	0	Brady Gce II		D	858 496-0500	0
Apria Healthcare LLC		D	858 653-6800	0	Braemar Partnership		B	858 488-1081	0
Aquaclean Janitorial		D	858 537-9090	0	Brandes Inv Partners Inc **(PA)**		C	858 755-0239	0
Aramark Unf & Career AP LLC		C	858 550-5200	0	Bridge Group Hh Inc		C	858 455-5000	0
ARC of San Diego **(PA)**		C	619 685-1175	0	Bright Event Rentals LLC		A	858 496-9700	0
Archer Western Contractors LLC		D	858 715-7200	0	Brightcloud Inc		C	858 652-4803	0
Armed Forces Officials Assn		E	858 672-1438	0	Brighton Gardens Inc		D	858 259-2222	0
Arrowhead Gen Insur Agcy Inc **(DH)**		C	619 881-8600	0	Brighton Health Alliance **(PA)**		D	619 461-0376	0
Arrowhead Management Company **(DH)**		D	619 881-8733	0	Brighton Place San Diego		C	619 263-2166	0
Artiano Shinoff Abed **(PA)**		D	619 232-3122	0	Brightview Landscape Dev Inc		B	858 458-9900	0
Ashford Trs Nickel LLC		D	619 260-0111	0	Brightview Landscape Svcs Inc		C	858 458-1900	0
ASI Hastings Inc		C	619 590-9300	0	Brinks Incorporated		C	619 263-6615	0
Asset Management Tr Svcs LLC		D	858 457-2202	0	Bristol Hotel		D	619 232-6141	0
Asset Marketing Systems Insu		D	888 303-8755	0	Broadcast Co of Americas LLC **(PA)**		D	858 453-0658	0
Associated General Contract		D	858 558-0739	0	Broadway Typewriter Co Inc		D	800 998-9199	0
Associated Students San Diego **(PA)**		A	619 594-0234	0	Brokerage Lgstics Slutions Inc		D	619 671-0276	0
Assocted Third Pty Admnstrtors		C	619 358-8140	0	Brown and Caldwell		D	858 514-8822	0
At Your Home Familycare		C	858 625-0406	0	Bullup Inc		E	566 997-2543	0
AT&T Corp		D	858 693-0815	0	Business and Support Services		A	858 577-1061	0
AT&T Services Inc		C	619 515-5100	0	Butterwick Dr Kimberly Jane MD		D	858 657-1002	0
AT&T Services Inc		C	858 886-2762	0	Bycor General Contractors Inc		D	858 587-1901	0
AT&T Services Inc		B	858 495-3907	0	Byrom-Davey Inc		E	858 513-7199	0
Ata Engineering Inc **(PA)**		D	858 480-2000	0	C N L Hotel Del Partners LP		A	619 522-8299	0
Atk Space Systems Inc		B	858 621-5700	0	C2 Financial Corporation		C	858 220-2112	0
Atkins North America Inc		D	858 874-1810	0	Cableconn Industries Inc		D	858 571-7111	0
Atlas Construction Supply Inc **(PA)**		D	858 277-2100	0	Cabrillo Gen Insur Agcy Inc		D	858 244-0550	0
Atlas General Insur Svcs LLC		C	858 529-6700	0	Caci Inc - Federal		E	619 881-6000	0
Audatex North America Inc **(DH)**		C	858 946-1900	0	Cactus Recycling Inc **(PA)**		C	619 661-1283	0
Aurora Behavioral Health Care		C	858 487-3200	0	Cal Pinnacle Mltary Cmmunities		D	619 764-5087	0
Aurora Healthcare Inc		E	858 487-3200	0	Calderon Building Maintenance		D	619 269-5940	0
Ausgar Technologies Inc		C	855 428-7427	0	California Air Cartage Inc **(PA)**		D	619 291-8544	0
Austin Veum Rbbins Prtners Inc **(PA)**		D	619 231-1960	0	California Club Lucky Lady		E	619 287-6690	0
Autism Otrach Southern Cal LLC		D	619 795-9925	0	California Coast Credit Union **(PA)**		D	858 495-1600	0
Automatic Data Processing Inc		D	619 293-4800	0	California Coast Credit Union		C	858 495-1600	0
Automation Engrg Systems Inc		D	858 967-8650	0	California Comfort Systems USA		B	858 564-1100	0
Avia Tech LLC		D	858 777-5000	0	California Marine Cleaning Inc **(PA)**		C	619 231-8788	0
Aviva Systems Biology Corp **(PA)**		D	858 552-6979	0	California Schools Veba		D	888 276-0250	0
Avnet Inc		B	858 385-7500	0	California Title Company		D	619 516-5227	0
Awarepoint Corporation **(PA)**		D	858 345-5000	0	California-American Water Co **(HQ)**		D	619 446-4760	0
Axa Advisors LLC		D	619 239-0018	0	Califrnia Frnsic Med Group Inc		D	858 694-4960	0
Axa Equitable Life Insur Co		D	858 552-1234	0	Califrnia Rgional Intranet Inc		D	858 974-5080	0
Axos Clearing LLC **(HQ)**		A	858 350-6200	0	Calpine Energy Solutions LLC **(DH)**		D	877 273-6772	0
Aya Healthcare Inc **(PA)**		C	858 458-4410	0	Calworks Partnr Conference		E	858 292-2900	0
Babcock & Brown Elec MGT LLC		C	858 587-5820	0	Cameron Intrstate Pipeline LLC		C	619 696-3110	0
Bahia Sternwheelers Inc		E	858 539-7720	0	Canji Inc		D	858 597-0177	0
Bainbridge Inc **(PA)**		D	858 638-1800	0	Canteen Vending - San Diego		D	619 527-1900	0
Baja Freight Forwarders Inc **(PA)**		D	619 671-3100	0	Capital Plus Financial Corp		E	619 744-1900	0
Bakbone Software Inc **(DH)**		D	858 450-9009	0	Captiva Software Corporation **(DH)**		D	858 320-1000	0
Baker & Taylor LLC		C	858 457-2500	0	Cardinal Health 200 LLC		C	951 686-8900	0
Bald Eagle Security Svcs Inc		D	619 230-0022	0	Cardinal Point Captains Inc		D	760 438-7361	0
Balfour Beatty Cnstr LLC		D	858 635-7400	0	Care Medical Trnsp Inc		D	858 653-4520	0
Banner Bank		E	619 243-7900	0	Carefusion Solutions LLC **(DH)**		A	858 617-2100	0
Barrett Business Services Inc		A	858 314-1100	0	Carolina Trucking Inc **(PA)**		E	619 661-1554	0
Bartell Hotels		D	619 291-6700	0	Carrier Johnson **(PA)**		D	619 236-9462	0
Bartell Hotels		C	619 224-3411	0	Casa De Las Campanas Inc **(PA)**		C	858 451-9152	0
Bartell Hotels		C	619 222-6440	0	Casas - Comprehensive		D	858 292-2900	0
Bartell Hotels		E	858 581-3500	0	Casas International Brkg Inc **(PA)**		D	619 661-6162	0
Bartell Hotels		D	619 222-0561	0	Cask Technologies LLC **(PA)**		D	888 418-7067	0
Bay City Television Inc **(PA)**		D	858 279-6666	0	Caster Family Enterprises Inc		C	619 287-8893	0
Bay Club Hotel and Marina A C		D	619 224-8888	0	Catalent San Diego Inc		C	858 805-6383	0
Bdo Usa LLP		D	858 404-9200	0	Catalina Solar 2 LLC		A	888 903-6926	0
Being Fit Inc **(PA)**		D	858 549-3456	0	Catholic Charities Diocese San		E	619 287-9454	0
Being Fit Inc		D	858 483-9294	0	Cbiz Mayor Hoffman Mechan **(PA)**		D	858 795-2000	0
Belmont Village LP		D	858 486-5020	0	Cbre Inc		C	858 546-4600	0
Belville Enterprises Inc		D	858 652-6960	0	Celgene Corporation		E	858 677-0034	0
Ben F Smith Inc		C	858 271-4320	0	Cellco Partnership		D	858 625-7751	0
Berger Inc		E	858 547-0075	0	Cement Cutting Inc		D	619 296-9592	0
Berkshire Hathaway Homestates		D	619 686-8424	0	Center For Autsm Rsrch Evltn		C	858 444-8823	0
Bernardo Hts Healthcare Inc		D	858 673-0101	0	Center For Sustainable Energy		D	858 244-1177	0
Beston Development		D	619 232-6315	0	Central Garden & Pet Company		D	858 695-0743	0
Bh Partn A Calif Limit Partne **(PA)**		B	858 539-7635	0	Centro De Salud De La Comuni **(PA)**		D	619 428-4463	0
Bill Howe Plumbing Inc		D	800 245-5469	0	Century 21 Able Inc		D	858 450-2100	0
Binding Site Inc **(PA)**		D	858 453-9177	0	Certified Air Conditioning Inc		D	858 292-5740	0
Biocept Inc		D	858 320-8200	0	Certona Corporation		C	858 369-3888	0
Biomed Realty LP **(HQ)**		E	858 485-9840	0	Chaduxtt JV		D	619 525-7188	0
Biomedicure LLC		D	858 586-1888	0	Chadwick Center For Children &		E	858 966-5814	0
Biosite Inc		D	510 683-9063	0	Champion Signs Incorporated		D	858 751-2900	0
Biotheranostics Inc **(PA)**		D	877 886-6739	0	Charles Schwab Corporation		E	858 523-2454	0

Employment Codes: A=Over 500 employees, B=251-500,
C=101-250, D=51-100, E=50

2020 Directory of California
Wholesalers and Services Companies

© Mergent Inc. 1-800-342-5647

1615

GEOGRAPHIC

	SIC	EMP	PHONE	ENTRY #
Chatmeter Inc		D	619 795-6262	0
Chicago Title Company		C	619 230-6340	0
Children of Rainbow Inc (PA)		C	619 615-0652	0
Children of The Rainbow Head		C	619 266-7311	0
Childrens Angelcare Aid Intl		C	619 795-6234	0
Childrens Specialist of San D (PA)		B	858 576-1700	0
Christian and Wakefield (PA)		D	619 236-1555	0
Chromalloy San Diego Corp		C	858 877-2800	0
Chubb US Holding Inc		C	619 563-2400	0
Cibus Global Ltd		C	858 450-0008	0
CIC Research Inc		D	858 637-4000	0
Cintas Corporation No 3		C	619 239-1001	0
Cintiva Financial Corporation			877 246-8482	0
Citigroup Global Markets Inc		D	858 597-7777	0
City Leasing & Rentals		C	619 276-6171	0
City National Bank		D	619 645-6100	0
City of San Diego		E	619 533-3012	0
City of San Diego		D	619 533-6518	0
Citywide Plumbing Heating		E	619 231-2022	0
Clairemont Healthcare		D	858 278-4750	0
Clean Enviroment		D	619 521-0543	0
Clearbalance Holdings LLC		E	858 535-0870	0
Clinapps Inc		D	858 866-0228	0
Clinicomp International Inc (PA)		D	858 546-8202	0
Closingcorp Inc		D	858 551-1500	0
CMC Steel Fabricators Inc (DH)		E	858 737-7700	0
CNA Surety Corporation		D	619 682-3550	0
Co-Production Intl Inc		A	619 429-4344	0
Coast Citrus Distributors (PA)		D	619 661-7950	0
Coastal Transport Co Inc		D	619 584-1055	0
Coffman Specialties Inc (PA)		C	858 536-3100	0
Cohn Wholesale Fruit & Grocery (PA)		C	619 528-1113	0
Colliers Intl Prperty Cons Inc		E	858 455-1515	0
Collwood Ter Stellar Care Inc		D	619 287-2920	0
Colrich Communities Inc		D	858 350-7672	0
Colt Services Inc		D	858 271-9910	0
Commercial Finance & L		D	858 866-8525	0
Communction Wirg Spcalists Inc		D	858 278-4545	0
Community Clinics Hlth Netwrk		E	619 542-4300	0
Competitive Edge RES Comm Inc		D	619 702-2372	0
Competitor Group Events Inc		E	858 450-6510	0
Comprehensive Enviro		E	619 294-9400	0
Comps Inc		C	858 658-0576	0
Computer Proc Unlimited Inc		D	858 530-0875	0
Conam Management Corporation (PA)		C	858 614-7200	0
Concerro (DH)		E	858 882-8500	0
Considine & Considine An Acco		D	619 231-1977	0
Consolidated Elec Distrs Inc		D	858 268-1020	0
Contrlled Cntmination Svcs LLC		C	888 263-9886	0
Cooley LLP		C	858 550-6000	0
Cordial Experience Inc		D	619 793-9787	0
Corecivic Inc		C	619 661-9119	0
Corelation Inc		C	619 876-5074	0
Corinthian Title Company Inc		D	619 299-4800	0
Correctional Services Corp LLC		D	858 566-9816	0
Cortel Inc		D	650 703-7217	0
Cosco Fire Protection Inc		D	858 444-2000	0
Costar Group Inc		C	858 452-4900	0
County of San Diego		D	858 694-5141	0
County of San Diego		D	760 967-4621	0
County of San Diego		D	619 515-8202	0
County of San Diego		D	619 531-4040	0
County of San Diego		E	858 505-6423	0
County of San Diego		E	858 505-6423	0
County of San Diego		B	858 616-5989	0
County of San Diego		D	619 236-2191	0
County of San Diego		D	858 694-2895	0
County of San Diego		B	619 692-8200	0
County of San Diego		D	619 563-2765	0
County of San Diego		D	619 531-4521	0
County of San Diego		C	619 236-8725	0
County Sandiego Dept Chldspprt		B	619 578-6660	0
Courtyard By Marriott		D	619 291-5720	0
Courtyard-Central		D	858 573-0700	0
Covance Inc		D	858 352-2300	0
Cox Communications Inc		D	858 715-4500	0
Cox Communications Cal LLC		B	619 262-1122	0
CP Opco LLC		D	858 496-9700	0
CPM Ltd Inc (PA)		A	619 237-9900	0
Crash Inc		D	619 297-5131	0
Crash Inc Short Term I		E	619 282-7274	0
Crestline Funding Corporation		E	949 863-8600	0
Cricket Communications LLC (DH)		D	858 882-6000	0
Cricket Indiana Property Co		D	858 587-2648	0
Crown Building Maintenance Co		C	858 560-5785	0
Crown Plaza SD		D	619 297-1101	0
Csi Financial Services LLC		E	858 200-9200	0
CSRA LLC		A	619 225-2600	0
Cubic Corporation		A	858 277-6780	0
Cusa Gcbs LLC		D	619 266-7365	0
Customzed Svcs Admnstrtors Inc		C	858 810-2004	0
Cutting Edge Drywall Inc		E	858 408-0870	0
Cy Gaslamp LLC		D	619 544-1004	0
D & K Engineering (PA)		C	858 451-8999	0
Dal-Tile Corporation		D	858 571-0283	0
Davenport Development Corp		E	858 300-3333	0
Davis Trucking LLC (PA)		E	619 229-9997	0
Daw Industries Inc		E	858 622-4955	0
Daybreak Game Company LLC		B	858 239-0500	0
Daymark Realty Advisors Inc		B	714 975-2999	0
De Anza Campland LLC (PA)		D	858 581-4200	0
De Anza Land & Leisure Corp		E	619 423-2727	0
Decipher Corp		D	888 975-4540	0
Dehart Inc		D	858 695-0882	0
Del Rey Systems and Tech Inc (PA)		D	858 874-8992	0
Delimex Holdings Inc		A	619 210-2700	0
Deloitte & Touche LLP		C	619 232-6500	0
Delta Dental of California		B	619 683-2549	0
Delta-T Group Inc		B	619 543-0556	0
Dentons US LLP		D	619 595-5400	0
Dentons US LLP		B	619 236-1414	0
Diamondrock San Dego Tnant LLC		B	619 239-9600	0
Dietz Glmor Chazen A Prof Corp (PA)		D	858 565-0269	0
Digital Operative Inc		E	310 630-0072	0
Digitalmojo Inc		D	800 413-5916	0
Dimension Development Two LLC		D	858 485-9250	0
Dish Network Service LLC		E	858 452-2239	0
Distinctive Concrete Inc		E	858 277-9707	0
Dla Piper LLP (us)		D	858 677-1400	0
DMS Facility Services LLC		C	858 560-4191	0
Donahue Schriber Rlty Group LP		D	858 793-5757	0
Doubletree By Hilton Hotel		D	619 881-6900	0
Downtown San Diego Partnr Inc (PA)		D	619 234-0201	0
Downtown San Diego Partnr Inc		D	619 234-8900	0
Dpr Construction A Gen Partnr		B	858 646-0757	0
Drain Patrol		D	858 560-1137	0
Dreamscape Ldscp & Maint Inc		E	619 583-4439	0
Duckor Spradling Metzger		D	619 209-3000	0
Dynalectric Company		B	858 712-4700	0
Dyncorp		C	619 522-2222	0
Eastern Goldfields Inc		C	619 497-2555	0
Eastrdge Prsonnel of Las Vegas (PA)		E	619 260-2000	0
Edaw Inc		D	619 233-1454	0
Edf Msschstts Spnsor Mmber LLC		A	888 903-6926	0
Edf Renewables Inc (PA)		D	858 521-3300	0
Edf Renewables Services Inc (HQ)		D	858 521-3575	0
Edf Rnwbles Asset Holdings Inc		A	888 903-6926	0
Edmin Open Systems Inc (PA)		D	858 712-9341	0
Edwards Theatres Circuit Inc		D	858 653-7716	0
Einstein Industries Inc		C	858 459-1182	0
El Cajon Plumbing & Htg Sup Co		E	619 449-7300	0
Elavon Inc		A	954 776-7990	0
Electra Owners Assoc		C	619 236-3310	0
Elevate Credit Inc		C	817 928-1500	0
Elite Maintenance Services Inc		D	619 516-7000	0
Elite Show Services Inc		A	619 574-1589	0
Elk Hills Power LLC		C	661 763-2730	0
Embassy Suites Management LLC		C	858 453-0400	0
Emcor Fclities Svcs N Amer Inc		C	858 712-4700	0
Emerald Connect LLC (HQ)		D	800 233-2834	0
Emergent Travel Health Inc		E	858 450-9595	0
Emeritus Corporation		E	858 292-8044	0
Employment & Community Options		C	858 565-9870	0
Empyr Incorporated		D	888 664-5669	0
Encore Capital Group Inc (PA)		C	877 445-4581	0
Encore Semi Inc		D	858 225-4993	0
Engility LLC		C	858 552-9500	0
Enginring Sftwr Sys Sltons Inc (PA)		D	619 338-0380	0
Enterprise Rent-A-Car		D	619 297-0311	0
Enterprise Services LLC		B	619 817-3851	0
Envoy Air Inc		E	619 260-9069	0
Epic Sciences Inc		D	858 356-6610	0
Epicenter Live Inc		C	424 235-4835	0
Eplica Inc (PA)		C	619 260-2000	0
Eplica Corporate Services Inc		A	619 282-1400	0
Epsilon Mission Solutions Inc		D	619 702-1700	0
Epsilon Systems Solutions Inc		D	619 702-1700	0
Epsilon Systems Solutions Inc (PA)		D	619 702-1700	0
Equitable Variable Lf Insur Co		D	619 239-0018	0
Ernst & Young LLP		C	858 535-7200	0

Mergent email: customerrelations@mergent.com
1616

2020 Directory of California
Wholesalers and Services Companies

(P-0000) Products & Services Section entry number
(PA)=Parent Co (HQ)=Headquarters (DH)=Div Headquarters

	SIC	EMP	PHONE	ENTRY #
Escalate Inc **(DH)**		B	858 457-3888	0
Eset LLC **(HQ)**		D	619 876-5400	0
Esquire Landscape Inc		E	858 530-2949	0
Etc Building & Design Inc **(PA)**		C	858 554-1150	0
Evotek Inc **(PA)**		D	858 362-5083	0
EW Scripps Company		C	619 237-1010	0
Examone World Wide Inc		D	619 299-3926	0
Exp US Services Inc		D	858 597-0555	0
Expeditors Intl Wash Inc		D	619 710-1900	0
Exprescom LLC		D	619 271-0531	0
EZ Acceptance Inc		C	858 278-8351	0
Fairfield Development Inc **(PA)**		C	858 457-2123	0
Faith Jones & Associates Inc **(PA)**		D	619 297-9601	0
Falconwood Inc		D	619 297-9080	0
Family Hlth Ctrs San Diego Inc **(PA)**		D	619 515-2303	0
Federal Dfenders San Diego Inc **(PA)**		D	619 234-8467	0
Federal Express Corporation		C	800 463-3339	0
Federal Express Corporation		C	800 463-3339	0
Fedex Freight Corporation		D	619 710-0268	0
Fedex Ground Package Sys Inc		C	800 463-3339	0
Fedex Ground Package Sys Inc		C	800 463-3339	0
Fenton Scripps Landing LLC		D	858 586-0206	0
Ferguson Enterprises Inc		D	619 515-0300	0
Ferring Research Institute Inc		D	858 657-1400	0
Fieldstone Communities Inc		E	858 546-8226	0
Fieno Inc		D	760 352-2996	0
Figi Acquisition Company LLC		C	800 678-3444	0
Firemans Fund Insurance Co		C	858 492-3019	0
First Allied Securities Inc **(HQ)**		D	619 702-9600	0
First American Title Insur Co		C	619 238-1776	0
First National Bank **(PA)**		D	619 233-5588	0
First Republic Bank		D	619 238-9088	0
Firstat Nursing Services Inc		C	619 220-7600	0
Fish & Richardson PC		C	858 678-5070	0
Fitness International LLC		E	858 550-5912	0
Five Star Parking-San Diego		C	619 235-4500	0
Five Star Quality Care Inc		B	858 673-6300	0
Fmg Suite LLC **(PA)**		E	888 364-1260	0
Foley & Lardner LLP		D	858 847-6700	0
Forensic Analytical		D	858 859-3322	0
Forward Slope Incorporated		D	619 299-4400	0
Foshay Electric Coinc		D	858 277-7676	0
Foster Wheeler Energy Svcs Inc		E	800 500-1993	0
Fragomen Del Rey Bernse		D	858 793-1600	0
Frank Sciarrino Marble G		D	858 695-8030	0
Friendemic LLC		D	855 880-6337	0
Front Porch Communities		B	858 274-4110	0
Fuji Food Products Inc		C	619 268-3118	0
G & L Penasquitos Inc		D	858 538-0802	0
G2 Software Systems Inc		C	619 222-8025	0
G4s Secure Solutions USA Inc		A	619 295-2394	0
G5 Global Partners Ix LLC		D	619 291-6500	0
G7 Productivity Systems		D	858 675-1095	0
Gafcon Inc **(PA)**		D	858 875-0010	0
Garich Inc **(PA)**		B	858 453-1331	0
Garrad Hassan America Inc **(DH)**		D	858 836-3370	0
Gary R Edwards Inc		D	619 299-8700	0
Gaslamp Hotel Management Inc		C	619 234-0977	0
General Atomics **(HQ)**		A	858 455-2810	0
General Atomics		D	858 676-7100	0
General Atomics		C	858 455-4000	0
General Coatings Corporation **(PA)**		D	858 587-1277	0
General Dynamics Info Tech Inc		E	619 881-8989	0
Genesis Healthcare Partners PC		D	619 230-0400	0
Genesis Healthcare Partners PC **(PA)**		C	858 810-7200	0
Gentiva Health Services Inc		B	858 565-2499	0
Gentry Associates LLC		D	619 291-0999	0
Geocon Consultants Inc **(PA)**		D	858 558-6900	0
Geocon Incorporated		D	858 558-6900	0
Gerwend Enterprises Inc		C	619 254-5018	0
Girl Scts Sn Diego-Imprl Cncl **(PA)**		D	619 610-0751	0
Gkk Corporation		D	619 398-0215	0
Glenn A Rick Engrg & Dev Co **(PA)**		C	619 291-0708	0
Global Dev Strategies Inc		D	858 408-1173	0
GMI Building Services Inc		D	858 279-6262	0
Gms Janitorial Services Inc		D	858 569-6009	0
Goforth & Marti **(PA)**		D	951 684-0870	0
Gold Coast Design Inc		D	619 574-0111	0
Golden Eagle Insurance Corp **(DH)**		C	619 744-6000	0
Golden Hour Data Systems Inc		C	858 768-2500	0
Goodman Manufacturing Co LP		B	858 569-1715	0
Gordon Rees Scully Mansukhani		D	619 696-6700	0
Gordon Rees Scully Mansukhani		D	415 986-5900	0
Grand Del Mar Resort LP		A	858 314-2000	0
Grant Thornton LLP		C	858 704-8000	0
Greater San Diego AC Co Inc		C	619 469-7818	0
Greencycle US Holding Inc		D	858 677-0884	0
Greenwood Holdings LLC		D	619 299-6633	0
Gringteam Inc		C	858 485-4145	0
Gringteam Inc		B	619 297-5466	0
Grisworld Real Estate MGT **(PA)**		D	858 597-6100	0
GS Levine Insurance Svcs Inc		D	858 481-8692	0
Guaranteed Rate Inc		C	760 310-6008	0
Guard Management Inc		A	858 279-8282	0
Guardsmark LLC		D	858 499-0025	0
H & R Accounts Inc		D	619 819-8844	0
H C T Inc		B	619 224-1234	0
Hampstead Lafayette Hotel LLC		E	619 296-2101	0
Handlery Hotels Inc		C	415 781-4550	0
Harbor View Hotel Ventures LLC		D	619 239-6800	0
Hardage Hospitality LLC **(PA)**		D	858 314-7910	0
Harmonium Inc **(PA)**		C	858 684-3080	0
Harper Construction Co Inc **(PA)**		D	619 233-7900	0
Harvey Inc		C	858 769-4000	0
Havas Formula LLC		D	619 234-0345	0
Hawthorne Machinery Co **(PA)**		D	858 674-7000	0
Hawthorne Machinery Co **(HQ)**		D	858 674-7000	0
Hawthorne Machinery Co		D	858 674-7000	0
Hawthorne Machinery Co		D	858 974-6800	0
Hazard Construction Company		D	858 587-3600	0
HDR Engineering Inc		D	619 231-4865	0
HDR Engineering Inc		E	858 712-8400	0
HDR Environmental Ope		D	858 712-8400	0
Healthstream Inc		C	800 733-8737	0
HEI Mission Valley LP		C	619 299-2729	0
Hensel Phelps Construction Co		D	858 266-7979	0
Herring Broadcasting Company		E	858 270-6900	0
Herring Networks Inc		C	858 270-6900	0
Herzog Contracting Corp		B	619 849-6990	0
HG Fenton Company		D	619 400-0120	0
Hhlp San Diego Lessee LLC		D	619 446-3000	0
Higgs Fletcher & Mack Llp		C	619 236-1551	0
High Ridge Wind LLC		A	888 903-6926	0
Hii Fleet Support Group LLC		B	858 522-6319	0
Historical Properties Inc **(PA)**		D	619 230-8417	0
Hitachi Vantara Corporation		C	858 537-3000	0
Hob Entertainment LLC		C	619 299-2583	0
Holiday Inn Rncho Bernardo LLC		D	858 485-6530	0
Home Instead Senior Care		D	858 277-3722	0
Hornblower Yachts Inc		C	619 686-8700	0
Hornblower Yachts Inc		C	619 234-8687	0
Host Hotels & Resorts Inc		C	619 232-1234	0
Host Hotels & Resorts LP		D	619 692-3800	0
Host Hotels & Resorts LP		D	619 291-2900	0
Host International Inc		C	619 231-5100	0
Hotel Circle Inn & Suites		E	619 851-6800	0
Hotel Circle Property LLC		B	619 291-7131	0
Hotel Managers Group Llc		B	858 673-1534	0
HP Inc		B	858 924-5117	0
Hronopoulos		E	619 237-6161	0
Hst Lessee Boston LLC		D	619 692-2255	0
Hst Lessee San Diego LP		B	619 291-2900	0
Hubbell Lighting Inc		B	619 946-1800	0
Hubbs-Sea World Research Inst **(PA)**		D	619 226-3870	0
Hudson Ranch Power I LLC		D	858 509-0150	0
Huntleigh USA Corporation		D	619 231-8111	0
Hyatt Corporation		C	619 849-1234	0
Hyatt Hotels Management Corp		B	858 552-1234	0
Icw Group Holdings Inc **(PA)**		D	858 350-2400	0
Icw Valencia LLC		D	858 350-2600	0
ID Analytics LLC		C	858 312-6200	0
Idun Pharmaceuticals Inc		E	858 622-3000	0
Igo Medical Group A Med Corp **(PA)**		D	858 455-7520	0
Iheartcommunications Inc		B	858 522-5547	0
Iheartcommunications Inc		D	858 292-2000	0
Imageware Systems Inc		D	858 673-8600	0
Imaging Hlthcare Spcalists LLC		D	619 229-2299	0
Imaging Hlthcare Spcalists LLC **(PA)**		D	619 295-9729	0
IMS Recycling Services Inc **(PA)**		D	619 231-2521	0
Independa Inc		E	800 815-7829	0
Independent Options Inc		C	858 598-5260	0
Indevia Accounting Inc		D	858 450-2981	0
Indus Technology Inc		C	619 299-2555	0
Indyme Solutions LLC		E	858 268-0717	0
Ingenium Technologies Corp		D	858 227-4422	0
Innovasystems Intl LLC		D	619 955-5890	0
Innovasystems Intl LLC **(PA)**		D	619 756-6500	0
Innovtive Emplyee Slutions Inc		A	858 715-5100	0
Inova Diagnostics Inc **(HQ)**		B	858 586-9900	0
Inseego North America LLC **(HQ)**		D	541 685-9045	0

GEOGRAPHIC

	SIC	EMP	PHONE	ENTRY #		SIC	EMP	PHONE	ENTRY #
Insurance Company of West (HQ)		C	858 350-2400	0	Laboratory Specialty Gases		C	619 234-6060	0
Integrits Corporation (PA)		E	858 300-1600	0	Landcare USA LLC		C	858 453-1755	0
Inter Con Security Inc		E	619 523-0291	0	Largo Concrete Inc		C	619 356-2142	0
Intercontinental Hotels Group		D	619 727-4000	0	Latham & Watkins LLP		C	858 523-5400	0
Interlab Inc		E	619 302-3095	0	Lawyers Title Company		D	858 650-3900	0
International Indus Pk Inc		D	858 623-9000	0	Ledcor CMI Inc		D	602 595-3017	0
Interntional Pet Sups Dist Inc		D	858 453-7845	0	Ledcor Management Services Inc		E	858 527-6400	0
Interntnal Rscue Committee Inc		D	619 641-7510	0	Legal Recovery Law Offices Inc		D	619 275-4001	0
Interstate Btry San Diego Inc		E	858 790-8244	0	Leidos Inc		B	858 826-5552	0
Interstate Electronics Corp		D	858 552-9500	0	Leidos Inc		C	858 535-4499	0
Intertek USA Inc		D	858 558-2599	0	Leidos Inc		C	703 676-4300	0
Intuit Inc		B	858 215-8000	0	Leidos Inc		C	858 826-9416	0
Ips Group Inc (PA)		D	858 404-0607	0	Leidos Inc		D	858 826-6616	0
Isaac Fair Corporation		D	858 369-8000	0	Leidos Inc		D	858 826-6000	0
Iserve Residential Lending LLC		D	858 486-4169	0	Leidos Inc		C	858 826-7129	0
J B Hunt Transport Svcs Inc		A	619 230-0054	0	Leidos Engineering LLC		D	858 826-6000	0
J D L Motor Express		E	619 232-6136	0	Leidos Engrg & Sciences LLC		D	619 542-3130	0
J Gelt Corporation		E	619 424-8181	0	Lenore John & Co (PA)		C	619 232-6136	0
J Harris Sim Inc (PA)		D	858 437-0190	0	Leonards Carpet Service Inc		E	858 453-9525	0
J W Floor Covering Inc (PA)		C	858 536-8565	0	Lewis Brsbois Bsgard Smith LLP		D	619 233-1006	0
J5th LLC		D	619 487-1200	0	Lho Mssion Bay Rsie Lessee Inc		B	619 276-4010	0
Ja Automation & Control LLC		E	619 661-2591	0	Liberty Station Hhg Hotel LP		D	619 221-1900	0
Jackson & Blanc		C	858 831-7900	0	Liberty Station Hhg Hotel LP		D	619 222-0500	0
Jacobs Cshman San Diego Fd Bnk		D	858 527-1419	0	Life Cycle Engineering Inc		D	619 785-5990	0
Jacobs Project Management Co		D	619 687-0110	0	Lifetouch Portrait Studios Inc		E	858 693-9197	0
Jaynes Corporation California		C	619 233-4080	0	Lightbridge Hospice LLC (PA)		D	858 458-2992	0
JC Resorts Inn		D	858 487-0700	0	Lincoln Mariners Assoc Ltd		E	619 225-1473	0
Jck Hotels LLC		E	858 635-5566	0	Linda Vista Manor Inc		C	858 278-8121	0
Jelem LLC		E	858 457-2202	0	Lindbergh Parking Inc		C	619 291-1508	0
Jetblue Airways Corporation		D	619 725-0807	0	LLP Moss Adams		D	858 627-1400	0
Jetmore Wind LLC		A	888 903-6926	0	Local Media San Diego LLC		D	858 888-7000	0
Jewish Family Svc San Diego (PA)		D	858 637-3000	0	Locator Services Inc		C	619 229-6100	0
Joe Canpagna		D	619 222-0555	0	Lockheed Martin Orincon Corp (HQ)		C	858 455-5530	0
Johnson Cntrls SEC Sltions LLC		C	561 988-3600	0	Locums Unlimited LLC		B	619 550-3763	0
Jones Day Limited Partnership		D	858 314-1200	0	Logility Inc		D	858 565-4238	0
Jones Sign Co Inc		C	858 569-1400	0	Loma Riviera Community Assn		D	619 224-1313	0
Jr Construction Inc		D	858 505-4760	0	Loomis Armored Us LLC		D	619 232-5106	0
Juan Lopez		D	619 428-3138	0	Lpl Holdings Inc (HQ)		C	858 450-9606	0
June Group LLC		D	858 450-4290	0	Luth Research Inc (PA)		B	619 234-5884	0
K Tech Security & Protect Svc		C	619 858-5832	0	Lynup Corporation		D	858 207-4610	0
Ka Management Inc		D	858 404-6080	0	M4dev LLC		D	619 696-6300	0
Kaiser Foundation Hospitals		B	619 662-5107	0	Mabie Marketing Group Inc		C	858 279-5585	0
Kaiser Foundation Hospitals		D	619 542-7210	0	Magnesite Specialties Inc		E	858 578-4186	0
Kaiser Foundation Hospitals		A	619 528-5888	0	Magnus Security		E	619 546-7789	0
Kaiser Foundation Hospitals		D	619 528-2583	0	Management Trust Assn Inc		C	858 547-4373	0
Kaiser Foundation Hospitals		D	619 528-5000	0	Manas Hospitality LLC		E	619 298-1291	0
Kaiser Foundation Hospitals		D	619 528-5000	0	Manchester Grand Resorts LP		A	619 232-1234	0
Kaiser Foundation Hospitals		A	858 847-3500	0	Mantech International Corp		C	858 492-9938	0
Kaiser Foundation Hospitals		A	858 502-1350	0	Mantech Systems Engrg Corp		D	858 292-9000	0
Kaiser Foundation Hospitals		C	858 573-0090	0	Mapp Digital Us LLC		C	619 295-1856	0
Kaiser Foundation Hospitals		B	619 641-4663	0	Marika Group Inc		D	858 537-5300	0
Kalpana LLC		C	619 543-9000	0	Marine Band San Diego		E	619 524-1754	0
Kbm Fclity Sltons Holdings LLC		B	858 467-0202	0	Mariner LLC		C	858 795-2100	0
Kesari Hospitality LLC		D	619 298-1291	0	Marlin Alliance Inc		E	619 450-1717	0
Kforce Inc		D	858 550-1645	0	Marriott International Inc		C	858 523-1700	0
Khp II San Diego Hotel LLC (PA)		D	619 515-3000	0	Marriott International Inc		D	619 831-0225	0
Kidder Mathews LLC		C	858 509-1200	0	Marriott International Inc		D	619 831-0200	0
Kifm Smooth Jazz 981 Inc		D	619 297-3698	0	Marsh & McLennan Agency LLC		C	858 457-3414	0
Kimball Tirey & St John LLP (PA)		D	619 234-1690	0	Martinez Farms Inc		B	619 661-6571	0
Kimley-Horn and Associates Inc		D	619 234-9411	0	Mason-West Inc		E	619 226-8253	0
Kinder Mrgan Lqds Trminals LLC		D	619 283-6511	0	MAT Parcel Express Inc (PA)		D	619 849-9600	0
Kindred Healthcare Oper LLC		C	502 596-7300	0	Mbp Land LLC		D	619 291-5720	0
Kineticom Inc (PA)		D	619 330-3100	0	McAfee Inc		D	858 967-2342	0
Kings Inn Hotel San Diego		D	619 297-2231	0	McKesson Ptent Care Sltons Inc (HQ)		D	412 507-0077	0
Kintera Inc (HQ)		D	858 795-3000	0	McKinnon Broadcasting Company (HQ)		C	858 571-5151	0
Kleinfelder Inc (HQ)		D	619 831-4600	0	McKinnon Publishing Company		A	858 571-5151	0
Kleinfelder Associates		A	619 831-4600	0	McKowskis Maint Systems Inc		D	619 269-4600	0
Knobbe Martens Olson Bear LLP		D	858 707-4000	0	McMillin Companies LLC (PA)		D	619 477-4117	0
Knox Attorney Service Inc (PA)		C	619 233-9700	0	McMillin Construction Svcs LP		E	619 477-4170	0
Koam Engineering Systems Inc		C	858 292-0922	0	McMillin Management Svcs LP (HQ)		C	619 477-4117	0
Kobey Corporation Inc (PA)		C	619 523-2700	0	MCR Printing and Packg Corp		C	619 488-3012	0
Kpmg LLP		C	858 750-7100	0	Mea Digital Worx LLC		E	619 238-8923	0
Kratos Rt Logic Inc		D	858 812-7300	0	Meals-On-Wheels Grtr Sn Diego (PA)		D	619 260-6110	0
Kratos Tech Trning Sltions Inc (HQ)		D	858 812-7300	0	Media All Stars Inc		D	858 300-9600	0
Kswb Inc		D	858 492-9269	0	Medical Management Cons Inc		A	858 587-0609	0
Kyriba Corp (PA)		E	858 210-3560	0	Medical Transcription Billing		A	800 869-3700	0
L & W Supply Corporation		E	858 627-0811	0	Medimpact Hlthcare Systems Inc (HQ)		A	858 566-2727	0
L A Swikard Inc		C	858 408-3700	0	Mental Health Systems Inc (PA)		D	858 573-2600	0
L C C H Associates Inc		E	858 565-4424	0	Merchants Building Maint Co		B	858 455-0163	0
La Jolla Pharmaceutical Co (PA)		C	858 207-4264	0	Mercury Insurance Company		D	858 694-4100	0
La Jolla Village Towers 500		D	858 646-7700	0	Meridian Rack & Pinion Inc		C	858 587-8777	0
La Maestra Family Clinic Inc		D	619 280-4213	0	Merit Technologies LLC		D	858 623-9800	0
La Maestra Family Clinic Inc		D	619 501-1235	0	Merrill Gardens LLC		D	619 961-4990	0
La Maestra Family Clinic Inc (PA)		C	619 584-1612	0	Merrill Lynch Pierce Fenner		C	619 699-3700	0
La Puerta		E	619 696-3466	0	Merritt Hawkins & Assoc LLC (HQ)		C	858 792-0711	0

Mergent email: customerrelations@mergent.com
1618

2020 Directory of California
Wholesalers and Services Companies

(P-0000) Products & Services Section entry number
(PA)=Parent Co (HQ)=Headquarters (DH)=Div Headquarters

	SIC	EMP	PHONE	ENTRY #		SIC	EMP	PHONE	ENTRY #
Merry X-Ray Chemical Corp (PA)		C	858 565-4472	0	Oracle America Inc		D	858 625-5044	0
Message Center Communication		E	858 974-7419	0	Oracle Corporation		C	858 202-0648	0
Messenger Express		D	858 550-1400	0	Overseas Service Corporation		D	858 408-0751	0
Metron Incorporated		E	858 792-8904	0	P J J Enterprises Inc		D	619 232-6136	0
Metropolitan Area Advisory Com		B	619 255-7284	0	Pacific Building Group		D	858 552-0600	0
MHS Customer Service Inc		D	858 695-2151	0	Pacific Building Group (PA)		C	858 552-0600	0
Michael Baker Intl Inc		D	858 453-3602	0	Pacific Composite Mtls Inc		E	310 956-5357	0
Michael S Duffy Sr Do Inc		D	619 461-3717	0	Pacific Event Productions Inc (PA)		C	858 458-9908	0
Microconstants Inc		E	858 652-4600	0	Pacific Gas Turbine Center LLC		C	858 877-2910	0
Microsoft Corporation		D	619 849-5872	0	Pacific Maritime Group Inc (PA)		C	619 533-7932	0
Midland Credit Management Inc (HQ)		A	877 240-2377	0	Pacific Medical Buildings LP		D	858 794-1900	0
Millennium Health LLC		B	877 451-3534	0	Pacific Rim Mech Contrs Inc (PA)		B	858 974-6500	0
Milo Wind Project LLC		D	888 903-6926	0	Pacific Western Bank		D	858 436-3500	0
Mindlance Inc		C	858 433-9298	0	Pacifica Companies LLC (PA)		D	619 296-9000	0
Mintz Levin Cohn Ferris GL		D	858 314-1500	0	Pacifica Hotel Company		C	619 221-8000	0
Miramar Ford Truck Sales Inc		D	619 272-5340	0	Pacifica Katie Avenue LLC		C	619 296-9000	0
Miramar Transportation Inc		D	858 693-0071	0	Pacifica San Jose LP		C	619 296-9000	0
Mirnavseh Inc		D	858 335-2470	0	Pacira Pharmaceuticals Inc		C	858 625-2424	0
Mirum Inc		C	619 237-5552	0	Packaging Manufacturing Inc		C	619 498-9199	0
Mission Federal Credit Union (PA)		A	858 546-2184	0	Packard Hospitality Group LLC		C	877 247-4305	0
Mission Federal Services LLC (PA)		C	858 524-2850	0	Packetvideo Corporation (HQ)		D	858 731-5300	0
Mission Hills Healthcare Inc		D	619 297-4086	0	Padres LP		A	619 795-5000	0
Mission Hills Post Acute Care		D	619 297-4484	0	Pan Pcfic Htels Rsrts Amer Inc		B	619 239-4500	0
Mission Valley Ht Operator Inc		D	619 291-5720	0	Pan-Pacific Mechanical LLC		C	858 764-2464	0
Mission Valley Hts Surgery Ctr		D	619 291-3737	0	Panasonic Corp North America		E	619 661-1134	0
Mitchell International Inc (HQ)		C	858 368-7000	0	Panasonic Corp North America		D	619 661-1134	0
Mlim Holdings LLC		A	619 299-3131	0	Paradigm Information Services		D	858 693-6115	0
Molina Healthcare Inc		B	858 614-1580	0	Paradise Lessee Inc		B	858 274-4630	0
Montesquieu Corp		D	877 705-5669	0	Paramount Export Company		D	858 452-8101	0
Mopar Enterprises		D	858 492-1123	0	Parenthood of Planned (PA)		D	619 881-4500	0
Morgan Stanley		E	858 597-7777	0	Park Hotels & Resorts Inc		B	619 276-4010	0
Morgan Stanley & Co LLC		D	619 236-1331	0	Parma Management Co Inc		E	858 457-4999	0
Morrison & Foerster LLP		C	858 720-5100	0	Parpro Holdings Co Ltd		C	619 498-9004	0
Mosaic		D	858 397-2261	0	Parron-Hall Corporation		D	858 268-1212	0
Motorola Mobility LLC		D	858 455-1500	0	Parsons Government Svcs Inc		B	619 685-0085	0
Mr Copy Inc (DH)		D	858 573-6300	0	Partners Risk Specialists		E	619 326-0840	0
Mrs Gochs Natural Fd Mkts Inc		C	619 294-2800	0	Patenaude & Felix A Prof Corp (PA)		D	858 244-7600	0
Mufg Union Bank National Assn		D	619 230-4666	0	Patientsafe Solutions Inc (PA)		D	858 746-3100	0
Multimodal Esquer Inc		D	619 710-0477	0	Paul Hastings LLP		D	858 458-3000	0
Museum Cntmprary Art San Diego		D	858 454-3541	0	Paychex Inc		D	858 547-2920	0
Musicmatch Inc		C	858 485-4300	0	Paychex Benefit Tech Inc		C	800 322-7292	0
My Office Inc		D	858 549-6700	0	Pbp Hotel LLC		D	619 881-6900	0
Narven Enterprises Inc		D	619 239-2261	0	PCI Collections Inc		B	619 595-3114	0
National Air Inc		C	619 299-2500	0	Pegasus Building Svcs Co Inc		C	858 444-2290	0
National Railroad Pass Corp		C	619 239-9989	0	Pegasus Building Svcs Co Inc (PA)		C	858 444-2290	0
Nationl Medcl Assn Comp Health		D	619 231-9300	0	Penske Automotive Group Inc		C	858 430-2320	0
Naval Coating Inc		D	619 234-8366	0	Perfect Bar LLC		D	866 628-8548	0
Naval Fac Eng Cmmd SW Wrkng CA		D	619 532-1158	0	Performance Designed Pdts LLC (HQ)		D	323 234-9911	0
Neighborhood House Association		D	619 262-8199	0	Petco Animal Supplies Inc (DH)		B	858 453-7845	0
Neighborhood House Association (PA)		B	858 715-2642	0	Petti Kohn Ingrassia & L PR Co		D	310 649-5772	0
Neighborhood House Association		E	619 527-1287	0	Pfizer Inc		A	858 622-3000	0
Neighborhood House Association		D	619 263-7761	0	Phamatech Incorporated		C	858 643-5555	0
Neil Dymott Frank McFall		C	619 238-1712	0	Phone Ware Inc		B	858 530-8550	0
Nerys Logistics Inc		C	619 616-2124	0	Physician Management Group Inc		C	858 309-6300	0
Nestwise LLC		B	855 444-6378	0	Pillsbury Winthrop Shaw		D	858 509-4000	0
New Bi US Gaming LLC		D	858 592-2472	0	Pinnacle 1617 LLC		E	619 239-9600	0
New Childrens Museum		D	619 233-8792	0	Plaza Home Mortgage Inc (PA)		E	858 346-1200	0
New Day Staffing Inc		C	619 481-5400	0	Plaza Home Mortgage Inc		C	714 508-6406	0
New Way Landscape & Tree Svcs		C	858 505-8300	0	Point Loma Convalescent Hosp		C	619 224-4141	0
New York Life Insurance Co		C	858 623-8600	0	Point Loma Rhblitation Ctr LLC		C	619 224-4141	0
Newland Group Inc (PA)		E	858 455-7503	0	Polexis Inc		D	858 812-7300	0
Newland Real Estate Group LLC (HQ)		D	858 455-7503	0	Polypeptide Labs San Diego LLC		D	858 408-0808	0
Next Image Medical Inc (PA)		D	858 847-9185	0	Poor Sisters of Nazareth of SA		D	619 563-0480	0
Nielsen Company (us) LLC		C	858 677-9542	0	Precision Toxicology LLC		D	800 635-6901	0
Ninyo & Moore Geotechnical (PA)		D	858 576-1000	0	Predicate Logic Inc (PA)		B	858 715-0100	0
Nnj Services Inc		C	858 550-7900	0	Preferred Employers Insur Co		D	619 688-3900	0
Noiro West LLC		C	619 819-6620	0	Preferred Hlthcare Rgistry Inc		C	800 787-6787	0
Norman Industrial Mtls Inc		E	858 277-8200	0	Preferred Valet Parking LLC		E	619 233-7275	0
Northrop Grumman Systems Corp		B	858 514-0400	0	Premier Dealer Services Inc		D	858 810-1700	0
Northrop Grumman Systems Corp		A	858 592-3000	0	Premier Hlthcare Solutions Inc		B	858 569-8629	0
Nphase LLC		D	312 577-1650	0	Premier Management Company		E	619 582-5168	0
Nu Flow America Inc (PA)		D	619 275-9130	0	Presidio Components Inc		C	858 578-9390	0
Nurlogic Design Inc (DH)		D	858 455-7570	0	Pricewaterhousecoopers LLP		B	858 677-2400	0
Nursefinders LLC (HQ)		C	858 314-7427	0	Primero Systems Incorporated		D	866 426-0779	0
Nv5 Inc		C	858 385-0500	0	Priority Building Services LLC		B	858 695-1326	0
Oak Valley Hotel LLC		D	619 297-1101	0	Pro Specialties Group Inc		D	858 541-1100	0
Oasis Repower LLC		A	888 903-6926	0	Professional Maint Systems Inc		A	619 276-1150	0
Odyssey Healthcare Inc		D	858 565-2499	0	Proform Interior Cnstr Inc		D	619 881-0041	0
Old Globe Theatre		B	619 234-5623	0	Progenity Inc (PA)		C	760 494-1555	0
Old Town Fmly Hospitality Corp		C	619 246-8010	0	Progressive Computing LLC		D	858 707-0707	0
Old Town Trlley Turs San Diego		D	619 298-8687	0	Project Concern International (PA)		D	858 279-9690	0
Olivermcmillan LLC (DH)		D	619 321-1111	0	Project Design Consultants		D	619 235-6471	0
Omni Hotels Corporation		B	619 231-6664	0	Project Management Institute		D	760 458-6198	0
Onsolve LLC		D	858 724-1200	0	Property Management Cons (PA)		E	858 485-9811	0
Operation Samahan Inc		C	619 477-4451	0	Propulsion Controls Engrg (PA)		D	619 235-0961	0

Employment Codes: A=Over 500 employees, B=251-500,
C=101-250, D=51-100, E=50

2020 Directory of California
Wholesalers and Services Companies

© Mergent Inc. 1-800-342-5647

1619

GEOGRAPHIC

Company	SIC	EMP	PHONE	ENTRY #
Protec Association Services (PA)		C	858 569-1080	0
Psychiatric Ctrs At San Diego (PA)		D	619 528-4600	0
Ptac Carmel Valley Mid School		D	858 481-8221	0
Qualcomm International Inc (HQ)		A	858 587-1121	0
Quality Claims Management Corp		C	619 450-8600	0
Quality Loan Service Corp		B	619 645-7711	0
Quality Plus Auto Parts Inc		E	619 424-9991	0
Quartus Engineering Inc (PA)		D	858 875-6000	0
R & V Management Corporation		D	619 429-3305	0
RAC & Associates		D	858 694-5800	0
Radiation Medical Group Inc (PA)		E	619 220-4100	0
Rady Childrens Hosp & Hlth Ctr (PA)		A	858 576-1700	0
Rady Chld Hospital-San Diego (HQ)		A	858 576-1700	0
Rady Chld Hospital-San Diego		D	858 966-5833	0
Rain Bird Corporation		D	619 661-4493	0
Rancho Bernardo Golf Club		D	858 487-1134	0
Rancho Bernardo Partners Ltd		C	858 451-6600	0
Randstad Technologies LLC		D	619 798-7300	0
Raphaels Party Rentals Inc (PA)		C	858 444-1692	0
Raytheon Company		C	858 455-9741	0
RB Anglers Club		D	858 487-6484	0
Reading International Inc		D	858 207-2606	0
Realtor Sfr Green		E	858 488-4090	0
Recon Environmental Inc (PA)		D	619 308-9333	0
Redwood Bridge Club		D	619 296-4274	0
Redwood Healthcare Staffing		D	619 238-4180	0
Regency Hill Associates		D	619 281-5200	0
Regulus Therapeutics Inc		D	858 202-6300	0
Relational Investors LLC		D	858 704-3333	0
Relationedge LLC		C	858 451-4665	0
Reliant Services Group LLC		C	877 850-0998	0
Renovate America Inc		C	858 605-5333	0
Renty LLC		E	858 560-0066	0
Reputation Impression LLC		D	858 633-4500	0
Rescue Agency Pub Benefit LLC (PA)		D	619 231-7555	0
Residence Inn By Marriott		D	858 673-1900	0
Residence Inn By Marriott LLC		D	858 587-1770	0
Residence Inn By Marriott LLC		C	858 278-2100	0
Residntial Alzheimers Care Inc		C	858 565-4424	0
Resort Procomm Inc		D	858 866-6280	0
Resource Management Group Inc (PA)		D	858 677-0884	0
Rett Inc		D	619 231-0403	0
Reuben H Fleet Science Center		C	619 238-1233	0
Reyes Holdings LLC		B	858 452-2300	0
Rhino Building Services Inc		C	858 455-1440	0
Riosoft Holdings Inc		E	858 529-5005	0
Robbins Geller Rudman Dowd LLP (PA)		B	619 231-1058	0
Robert Cromeans Salon (PA)		E	858 270-9975	0
Robinsn Clgne Rsn Shpr Dvs Inc		D	619 338-4060	0
Rore Inc (PA)		D	858 404-7393	0
Rosemont Media LLC		E	858 200-0044	0
Rossin Steel Inc		C	619 656-9200	0
Royal Hospitality Incorporated		D	858 278-0800	0
Rp Scs Wsd Hotel LLC		D	619 398-3020	0
RPC Old Town Avenue Owner LLC		D	619 299-7400	0
RPC Old Town Jefferson		D	619 725-4221	0
Rt San Diego LLC		E	858 278-2100	0
Rt Sd-Denver LP		E	858 278-2100	0
Rural/Metro San Diego Inc		D	619 280-6060	0
Rx Pro Health LLC		A	858 369-4050	0
SA Recycling LLC		D	619 238-6740	0
SA Recycling LLC		D	714 632-2000	0
Sackett National Holdings Inc		C	866 834-6242	0
Salvation Army		D	858 279-1100	0
Salvation Army Ray & Joan		B	619 287-5762	0
San Dego Cnty Rgnal Arprt Auth (PA)		D	619 400-2400	0
San Dego Cnty Rgnal Arprt Auth		C	619 400-2404	0
San Dego Cnvntion Ctr Corp Inc (PA)		D	619 525-5000	0
San Dego Mrrott Marquis Marina		E	301 380-3000	0
San Dego Soc of Ntural History		D	619 232-3821	0
San Diego Arcft Carier Museum		C	619 544-9600	0
San Diego Assn Governments (PA)		B	619 699-1900	0
San Diego Blood Bank (PA)		C	619 296-6393	0
San Diego Car Accident Lawyers		E	858 201-4178	0
San Diego Cemetery Assn		C	858 453-2121	0
San Diego Center For Children (PA)		D	858 277-9550	0
San Diego Community Hsing Corp		C	619 527-4633	0
San Diego Composites Inc		D	858 751-0450	0
San Diego County Credit Union (PA)		C	877 732-2848	0
San Diego County Employees Ret		D	619 515-6800	0
San Diego County Water Auth (PA)		B	858 522-6600	0
San Diego Family Care (PA)		D	858 279-0925	0
San Diego Family Care		C	619 563-0250	0
San Diego Farah Partners		E	619 239-2261	0
San Diego Gas & Electric Co (DH)		C	619 696-2000	0
San Diego Gas & Electric Co		C	619 699-1018	0
San Diego Gulls Hockey CLB LLC		D	619 359-4700	0
San Diego Hbr Excursions Inc		D	619 234-4111	0
San Diego Hospice		A	619 688-1600	0
San Diego Hotel Company LLC		C	619 696-0234	0
San Diego Hotel Lease LLC		C	619 446-3000	0
San Diego Humane Soc & Spca		D	619 299-7012	0
San Diego Imaging - Chula Vist (PA)		D	858 565-0950	0
San Diego Land Systems		E	858 558-0542	0
San Diego Lesbian Gay Bisexu		E	619 692-2077	0
San Diego Lessee LLC		C	619 297-5466	0
San Diego Med Svcs Entp LLC		B	619 280-6060	0
San Diego Messenger Inc		E	858 514-8866	0
San Diego Metro Trnst Sys		A	619 231-1466	0
San Diego Opera Association (PA)		E	619 232-7636	0
San Diego Orthopaedic Associat		C	619 299-8500	0
San Diego Pathologists Medical		C	619 297-4012	0
San Diego Rescue Mission Inc (PA)		D	619 819-1880	0
San Diego Services LLC		C	858 654-0102	0
San Diego Symphony Orchestra		C	619 235-0800	0
San Diego Testing Engineers		D	858 715-5800	0
San Diego Theatres Inc		C	619 615-4000	0
San Diego Tourism Authority (PA)		D	619 232-3101	0
San Diego Transit Corporation (PA)		A	619 238-0100	0
San Diego Trolley Inc		B	619 595-4933	0
San Diego Unified Port Dst		C	619 686-6585	0
San Diego Unified Port Dst (PA)		C	619 686-6200	0
San Diego Unified School Dst		D	619 266-4500	0
San Diego Youth Services Inc (PA)		D	619 221-8600	0
San Diego-Imperial Counties De (PA)		B	858 576-2996	0
Sandm San Dego Mrriott Del Mar		A	858 523-1700	0
Santaluz Club Inc		C	858 759-3120	0
Saturn Electric Inc		E	858 271-4100	0
SC Wright Construction Inc		B	619 698-6909	0
Scalematrix Holdings Inc		D	888 349-9994	0
Schmidt Fire Protection Co Inc		D	858 279-6122	0
Schroff Inc		C	858 740-2400	0
Schroff Inc		C	858 740-2400	0
Schryver Med Sls & Mktg LLC		D	303 459-8160	0
Science Applications Intl Corp		D	703 676-4300	0
Science Applications Intl Corp		A	858 826-3061	0
Scilex Holding Company (HQ)		D	858 203-4100	0
Scilex Pharmaceuticals Inc (DH)		D	949 441-2270	0
Scripps Clinic		C	858 794-1250	0
Scripps Clinic Foundation		A	858 554-9000	0
Scripps Health		D	858 622-9076	0
Scripps Health		D	858 294-8111	0
Scripps Health		C	858 678-6966	0
Scripps Health		C	858 657-4218	0
Scripps Health		B	858 271-9770	0
Scripps Health		B	619 245-2350	0
Scripps Health		C	858 882-8350	0
Scripps Health (PA)		A	800 727-4777	0
Scripps Health		B	619 294-8111	0
Scripps Health		D	858 764-3000	0
Scripps Health		D	858 784-5888	0
Scripps Health		C	858 794-0160	0
Scripps Mercy Hospital		D	619 294-8111	0
Scripps Ranch Recreation Club (PA)		D	858 271-6222	0
Scst Inc (HQ)		D	619 280-4321	0
SD Hotel Circle LLC		D	619 881-6800	0
SD Sports MDCne&fmly Hlth Cntr		D	619 229-3910	0
SD Stadium Hotel LLC		D	858 278-9300	0
SE San Diego Hotel LLC		D	619 515-3000	0
SE Scher Corporation		A	858 546-8300	0
Seacoast Commerce Bank (HQ)		D	858 432-7000	0
Sealaska Envmtl Svcs LLC		D	619 564-8329	0
Search Optics LLC (PA)		D	858 678-0707	0
Sears Home Imprv Pdts Inc		D	858 790-7721	0
Secure Transportation Co Inc		C	858 790-3958	0
Securitas Critical Infrastruct		A	858 560-0448	0
Securitas Electronic SEC Inc		D	858 812-7349	0
Securitas SEC Svcs USA Inc		C	619 641-0049	0
Security On-Demand Inc		E	858 563-5655	0
Seismic Software Inc (PA)		D	855 466-8748	0
Seltzer Caplan McMahon (PA)		C	619 685-3003	0
Semantic Ai Inc (PA)		D	619 222-4050	0
Sempra Energy (PA)		A	619 696-2000	0
Sempra Energy		A	619 696-2000	0
Sempra Energy Global Entps		A	619 696-2000	0
Sempra Energy International (HQ)		A	619 696-2000	0
Senior Care Inc		C	619 817-8855	0
Senomyx Inc		D	858 646-8300	0
Sentek Consulting Inc		C	619 543-9550	0
Sequenom Inc (HQ)		D	858 202-9000	0

	SIC	EMP	PHONE	ENTRY #
Sequenom Center For Molecular		B	858 202-9051	0
Sequoia Consultants Inc		D	858 345-1544	0
Serco Inc		C	858 569-8979	0
Servi-Tek Inc		B	858 638-7735	0
Service King Holdings LLC		C	619 219-3927	0
Seven Seas Associates LLC		C	619 291-1300	0
Sharp Chula Vista Medical Ctr		D	858 499-5150	0
Sharp Community Medical Group		C	858 499-4525	0
Sharp Health Plan		D	858 499-8300	0
Sharp Healthcare		C	619 398-2988	0
Sharp Healthcare		D	619 284-1400	0
Sharp Healthcare		D	858 939-5434	0
Sharp Healthcare		D	619 297-0008	0
Sharp Healthcare		C	619 446-1575	0
Sharp Healthcare		D	858 653-6100	0
Sharp Healthcare		C	858 627-5152	0
Sharp Healthcare		D	858 541-4850	0
Sharp Healthcare		D	858 616-8411	0
Sharp Healthcare		D	800 827-4277	0
Sharp Healthcare		D	858 616-8200	0
Sharp Mary Birch H		D	858 939-3400	0
Sharp McDonald Center		A	858 637-6920	0
Sharp Memorial Hospital (HQ)		A	858 939-3636	0
Sharp Memorial Hospital		C	858 278-4110	0
SHe Manages Properties Inc (PA)		D	619 291-6300	0
Shelter Pointe LLC		C	619 221-8000	0
Sheppard Mullin Richter		D	619 338-6500	0
Sheraton Htl San Diego Msn Vly		D	619 321-4602	0
Sherwood Mechanical Inc		D	858 679-3000	0
Shinwoo P&C Usa Inc (PA)		A	619 407-7164	0
Shopcore Properties LP (DH)		D	858 613-1800	0
Shoreline Land Care Inc		D	858 560-8555	0
Show Call Productions Inc		B	619 602-0656	0
Siemens Industry Inc		D	858 693-8711	0
Simplex Time Recorder LLC		D	858 740-0100	0
Simpson Delmore and Greene LLP (PA)		E	619 515-1194	0
Sinclair Companies		C	619 238-1818	0
Six Continents Hotels Inc		D	619 232-3861	0
Six Continents Hotels Inc		D	619 795-4000	0
Skylight Halthcare Systems Inc		D	858 523-3700	0
Slate Creek Wind Project LLC		A	888 903-6926	0
Smart & Final Stores Inc		B	619 291-1842	0
Smart & Final Stores Inc		D	858 578-7343	0
Smart & Final Stores LLC		D	858 268-2400	0
Smart & Final Stores LLC		D	858 270-8200	0
Smart & Final Stores LLC		D	619 523-3640	0
Smart & Final Stores LLC		D	619 291-8287	0
Smartdrive Systems Inc (PA)		D	858 225-5550	0
Socal Services Inc		C	858 453-1331	0
Socal Sportsnet LLC		A	619 795-5000	0
Social Advocates For Y		C	619 283-9624	0
Soft Hq Holdings LLC		E	858 658-9200	0
Soleil Communications LLC		D	619 624-2888	0
Solimar Systems Inc (PA)		D	619 849-2800	0
Solomon Ward Sdnwurm Smith LLP		D	619 231-0303	0
Solpac Inc		C	619 296-6247	0
Solpac Construction Inc		C	619 296-6247	0
Solute (PA)		D	619 224-2810	0
Solv Inc		C	858 622-4040	0
Sorrento Therapeutics Inc (PA)		C	858 203-4100	0
Souldriver Lessee Inc		D	619 819-9500	0
Southbay Sndblst & Tank Clg		D	619 238-8338	0
Southern Cal Prmnnte Med Group		D	858 974-1000	0
Southern Cal Prmnnte Med Group		D	619 528-5000	0
Southern Cal Prmnnte Med Group		E	619 516-6000	0
Southern California Car Transf		D	858 586-0006	0
Southern California Physicia		D	858 824-7000	0
Southern Glazers Wine		C	858 537-3912	0
Southland Electric Inc		D	858 634-5050	0
Southland Technology Inc		D	858 694-0932	0
Southwestern Yacht Club Inc		E	619 222-0438	0
Spectrum Prof Staffing Inc		C	800 644-1150	0
Spinning Spur Wind Three LLC		A	858 521-3319	0
Spreadtrum Cmmncations USA Inc		D	858 546-0895	0
St Pauls Episcopal Home Inc		D	619 239-2097	0
St Pauls Episcopal Home Inc		D	619 239-8687	0
Staff Pro Inc		C	619 544-1774	0
Stanley M Kirkpatrick MD		E	858 966-5855	0
Star Laundry Services Inc		D	619 572-1009	0
Starwood Hotels & Resorts		C	619 239-2200	0
Starwood Htls & Rsrts Wrldwde		D	619 239-9600	0
State Compensation Insur Fund		B	888 782-8338	0
Station Venture Operations LP		D	619 231-3939	0
Steelcase Inc		B	619 671-1040	0
Steren Electronics Intl LLC (PA)		D	800 266-3333	0
Stewart Enterprises Inc		E	858 453-2121	0
Stewart Title California Inc (DH)		C	619 692-1600	0
Strata Information Group Inc		D	619 296-0170	0
Strategic Insights Inc		D	858 452-7500	0
Strategic Operations Inc		C	858 244-0559	0
Strategic Property Management		D	619 295-2211	0
Stu Segall Productions Inc		C	858 974-8988	0
Stx Wireless Operations LLC		A	858 882-6000	0
Sullinovo		C	619 260-1432	0
Sullivan Moving & Storage (HQ)		E	858 874-2600	0
Sun Pharmaceuticals Inc		C	858 380-8865	0
Sunbelt Towing Inc (PA)		D	619 297-8697	0
Sundance Financial Inc		E	619 298-9877	0
Sunstone Hotel Investors LLC		D	619 239-6171	0
Sunstone Top Gun LLC		D	858 453-0400	0
Sunstone Top Gun Lessee Inc		D	949 330-4000	0
Superior Envmtl Svcs Inc		E	619 462-7079	0
Supreme Court United States		C	619 557-7149	0
Survivalcave Inc		E	800 719-7650	0
Swinerton Bldrs Pacific R		D	619 954-8011	0
Swinerton Builders		D	858 622-4040	0
Swwp Del Mar Hotel LLC		C	858 481-5900	0
Sydata Inc		C	760 444-4368	0
Symitar Systems Inc		C	619 542-6700	0
Sysintelli Inc		C	858 271-1600	0
T B Penick & Sons Inc (PA)		C	858 558-1800	0
T I C Hotels Inc		D	619 238-7577	0
T-12 Three LLC		B	619 702-3000	0
T3w Business Solutions Inc		D	619 298-0888	0
Tachyon Inc		E	858 882-8108	0
Tactical Engrg & Analis Inc (PA)		C	858 573-9869	0
Takeda California Inc		C	858 622-8528	0
Tangoe Us Inc		D	858 452-6800	0
Tanvex Biopharma Usa Inc (PA)		D	858 210-4100	0
Tapestry Solutions Inc (HQ)		A	858 503-1990	0
Tax Compliance Inc		D	858 547-4100	0
Tcp Global Corporation		D	858 909-2110	0
Tealium Inc (PA)		D	858 779-1344	0
Team Risk MGT Strategies LLC		A	877 767-8728	0
Techflow Inc (PA)		C	858 412-8000	0
Teg Staffing Inc		A	619 260-2000	0
Tegp Inc		A	619 584-3408	0
Telecare Corporation		D	619 275-8000	0
Telecare Corporation		D	619 692-8225	0
Telisimo International Corp		B	619 325-1593	0
Teris LLC		E	619 231-3282	0
Terra Vista Management Inc		C	858 581-4200	0
Tesi Investment Company LLC		D	619 224-3254	0
Tetra Tech Inc		D	619 525-7188	0
Tetra Tech Ec Inc		D	619 234-8690	0
Tf Courier Inc		D	888 541-2965	0
Thorsnes Bartolotta & McGuire		D	619 236-9363	0
Thurston Martin H DDS Ms		E	858 676-5010	0
Tic Hotels Inc		E	619 238-7577	0
Tic World-Wide Corp		D	619 233-7500	0
Tillster Inc (PA)		D	858 784-0800	0
Time Warner Cable Inc		D	619 346-4573	0
Time Warner Cable Inc		B	858 695-3220	0
Time Warner Cable Inc		B	858 695-3110	0
Tomatoes Extraordinaire Inc		C	619 295-3172	0
Top of Market		B	619 234-4867	0
Torrey Aat Point LLC		D	858 350-2600	0
Torrey Pines Bank (HQ)		C	858 523-4600	0
Toward Maximum Independence (PA)		D	858 467-0600	0
Trandes Corp		E	858 522-7021	0
Trandes Corp		E	619 524-2235	0
Transpak Inc		D	858 292-9094	0
Transwest San Diego LLC		B	858 450-0707	0
Treefrog Developments Inc		D	619 324-7755	0
Trellisware Technologies Inc		D	858 753-1600	0
Trendsource Inc		C	619 718-7467	0
Trex Partners LLC		C	858 646-5300	0
Trigild International Inc		D	619 295-6886	0
Trilink Biotechnologies LLC		C	800 863-6601	0
Trilogy Financial Services Inc		E	858 755-6696	0
Triton Structural Concrete Inc		C	858 866-2450	0
Troutman Sanders LLP		D	858 509-6000	0
Tru Green Landcare Inc		B	602 276-4311	0
Tum Yeto Inc		E	619 232-7523	0
Turelk Inc		D	858 633-8085	0
Turner Construction Company		D	858 320-4040	0
TW Holdings Inc		A	858 217-7803	0
Twin Oaks Power LP (HQ)		D	619 696-2034	0
Tyler Bluff Wind Project LLC		A	888 903-6926	0
U S Mbile Wrless Cmmunications (PA)		D	858 537-0709	0

GEOGRAPHIC

Company	SIC	EMP	PHONE	ENTRY #
UBS Financial Services Inc		C	619 236-0460	0
Ucsd Healthcare		D	858 657-7105	0
Ue Authority Co		D	800 466-4178	0
Ulta Beauty Inc		C	858 376-4574	0
Unifirst Corporation		C	619 263-6116	0
Union Pan Asian Communities (PA)		D	619 232-6454	0
United Airlines Inc		C	619 692-3310	0
United Behavioral Health		D	619 641-6800	0
United Crbral Plsy Assn San De (PA)		E	858 571-7803	0
United Development Group Inc		E	858 244-0900	0
United Parcel Service Inc OH		C	858 455-8800	0
United Parcel Service Inc OH		C	909 279-5111	0
United States Dept of Navy		C	619 524-1069	0
United States Dept of Navy		A	619 532-6397	0
United States Dept of Navy		A	619 532-8953	0
United States Dept of Navy		B	619 556-8210	0
United States Dept of Navy		A	619 532-6400	0
United States Dept of Navy		E	619 532-1897	0
United States Dept of Navy		A	619 532-7400	0
United States Dept of Navy		A	619 767-6592	0
United Svcs Amer Federal Cr Un (PA)		D	858 831-8100	0
Univers of Calif San Diego Hs		A	619 543-3713	0
University Cal San Diego		A	619 543-6654	0
Univision Television Group Inc		E	858 576-1919	0
UPS Store Inc (HQ)		C	858 455-8800	0
Upstrem Inc		D	858 229-2979	0
Upwind Blade Solutions Inc		C	866 927-3142	0
Urban Corps of San Diego		C	619 235-6884	0
US Bank National Association		D	619 744-2140	0
US Grant Hotel Ventures LLC		D	619 744-2007	0
Vanguard Resources Corp		D	858 336-7147	0
Vanpike Inc (PA)		D	858 453-1331	0
Vastek Inc		C	925 948-5701	0
Vector Resources Inc		E	858 546-1014	0
Verance Corporation		D	858 202-2800	0
Verizon Connect Nwf Inc		C	858 450-3245	0
Vertex Phrmctcals San Dego LLC (HQ)		C	858 404-6600	0
Veterans EZ Info Inc		C	866 839-1329	0
Veterans Health Administration		B	858 552-7525	0
Veterans Health Administration		B	619 400-5000	0
Veterans Medical Research Fund		C	858 642-3080	0
Veterinary Practice Assoc Inc		C	949 833-9020	0
Viacyte Inc		D	858 455-3708	0
Vibra Healthcare LLC		D	619 260-8300	0
Vibra Hospital San Diego LLC		D	619 260-8300	0
Victory Pharma Inc		C	858 720-4500	0
Vietnam Veterans of San Diego		D	619 497-0142	0
Vietnms-Mrcan Yuth Alance Corp		D	619 320-8292	0
Villa Rancho Brno Hlth Cr LLC		C	858 672-3900	0
Villas De Carlsbad Ltd A Cali (PA)		C	858 565-4424	0
Visage Imaging Inc		D	858 345-4410	0
Vista Hill Foundation		D	619 266-0166	0
Vista Hill Foundation (PA)		E	585 514-5100	0
Vistage International Inc (PA)		C	858 523-6800	0
Visual Pak San Diego LLC		D	847 689-1000	0
Vitro LLC		D	619 234-0408	0
Vitrorobertson LLC		D	619 234-0408	0
Voice Smart Networks LLC		E	619 857-4638	0
Volt Management Corp		D	858 576-3140	0
Volt Management Corp		C	858 578-0920	0
Volume Services Inc		D	619 525-5800	0
VT Milcom Inc		D	619 424-9024	0
W-Emerald LLC		D	619 239-4500	0
Wamc Company Inc (PA)		D	858 454-2753	0
Warfighter & Family Services		D	619 556-7168	0
Washington Inventory Service (DH)		C	858 565-8111	0
Washington Inventory Service		D	619 461-8198	0
Water Resources Control Bd Cal		D	619 521-3010	0
Watermark Rtrment Cmmnties Inc		D	858 597-8000	0
Wawanesa General Insurance Co		B	619 285-6020	0
Webb Sunrise Inc		E	619 220-7050	0
Wells Fargo Bank National Assn		D	858 622-6958	0
Wermers Multi-Family Corp		C	858 535-1475	0
Westair Gases & Equipment Inc (PA)		E	866 937-8247	0
Westcore Delta LLC		D	858 625-4100	0
Western Pump Inc (PA)		D	619 239-9988	0
Westgroup Kona Kai LLC		D	619 221-8000	0
Westgroup San Diego Associates		B	858 274-4630	0
Wheatland Wind Project LLC		A	888 903-6926	0
Wheelhouse Credit Union (PA)		D	619 297-4835	0
Whiskey Girl		D	619 236-1616	0
White Digital Media Inc		C	760 827-7800	0
Whittier Inst For Diabetes		D	877 944-8843	0
Willmark Cmmnties Univ Vlg Inc (PA)		D	858 271-0582	0
Wilmark Management Services (PA)		D	858 271-0583	0

Company	SIC	EMP	PHONE	ENTRY #
Wilson Sonsini Goodrich & Rosa		C	858 350-2300	0
Wilson Turner Kosmo LLP		D	619 236-9600	0
Win Time Ltd (PA)		C	858 695-2300	0
Wind River Systems Inc		D	858 824-3100	0
Wingert Grebing Brubaker & Jus		D	619 232-8151	0
Wirtz Qulty Installations Inc		D	858 569-3816	0
Wirtz Tile & Stone Inc		D	858 569-3816	0
Wmbe Payrolling Inc		C	858 810-3000	0
Wme Bi LLC		D	877 592-2472	0
Wmk Office San Diego LLC (PA)		D	858 569-4700	0
Woodfin Suite Hotels LLC		A	858 314-7910	0
Wordsmart Corporation		D	858 565-8068	0
Wright Broadband Group Inc		D	858 362-0380	0
Ws Mmv Hotel LLC		D	619 692-3800	0
Wsd Engineering Inc		E	619 954-7850	0
Wtw Delaware Holdings LLC		D	858 523-5500	0
Ww San Diego Harbor Island LLC		C	619 291-6700	0
Wyndham International Inc		C	619 239-4500	0
Xcite Steps Corp		C	858 722-1948	0
Xpo Logistics Freight Inc		E	858 569-8921	0
YMCA of San Diego County (PA)		C	858 292-9622	0
YMCA of San Diego County		D	619 281-8313	0
YMCA of San Diego County Inc		D	619 226-8888	0
YMCA of San Diego County		C	619 521-3055	0
YMCA of San Diego County		C	619 298-3576	0
Z57 Inc (DH)		D	858 623-5577	0
Zeetogroup LLC		D	888 771-9194	0
Zenith Insurance Company		D	619 299-6252	0
Zions Bancorporation Nat Assn		E	858 793-7400	0
Zions Bancorporation Nat Assn		D	619 521-5800	0
Zmicro Inc (PA)		D	858 831-7000	0
Zoological Society San Diego (PA)		A	619 231-1515	0
Zoological Society San Diego		A	619 744-3325	0
Zs Associates Inc		D	858 677-2200	0

SAN DIMAS, CA - Los Angeles County

Company	SIC	EMP	PHONE	ENTRY #
AON Consulting Inc		D	800 815-1823	0
Associations of United Nurses (PA)		D	909 599-8622	0
AT&T Corp		D	626 912-0600	0
Automatic Data Processing Inc		C	909 592-6411	0
Automatic Data Processing Inc		C	800 225-5237	0
Christian Community Credit Un (PA)		D	626 915-7551	0
Custom Cooler Inc (HQ)		D	909 592-1111	0
Davita Magan Management Inc		D	909 592-9712	0
Festival Fun Parks LLC		A	909 802-2200	0
Golden State Water Company (HQ)		D	909 394-3600	0
Golden State Water Company		D	909 394-3600	0
I P S Services Inc		D	909 305-0250	0
Imobile LLC		B	909 599-8822	0
Kaiser Foundation Hospitals		D	909 394-2530	0
L Barrios and Associates Inc		E	909 592-5893	0
Legal Solutions Holdings Inc		C	800 244-3495	0
McKinley Childrens Center Inc (PA)		D	909 599-1227	0
McKinley Home Foundation		D	909 599-1227	0
ML Prior Inc		C	626 653-5160	0
National Credit Industries Inc		D	626 967-4355	0
New York Life Insurance Co		D	909 305-6500	0
Om Food Sejal Enterprises Inc		D	626 712-3138	0
Pacific Systems Interiors Inc		C	310 436-6820	0
Pacific W Space Cmmnctions Inc		D	909 592-4321	0
Prime Healthcare-San Dimas LLC		B	909 599-6811	0
Progressive Corporation		D	626 232-1540	0
Qtc Management Inc (DH)		C	800 260-1515	0
Qtc Mdcal Group Inc A Med Corp		A	800 260-1515	0
San Dimas Golf Inc		D	909 599-8486	0
San Dimas Retirement Center (PA)		D	909 599-8441	0
Second Image National LLC (PA)		C	800 229-7477	0
Smart & Final Stores Inc		B	909 592-2190	0
Southern Cal Prmnnte Med Group		E	909 394-2505	0
Southern California Edison Co		C	909 592-3757	0
Southern California Gas Co		A	909 305-8297	0
Walton Construction Inc		D	909 267-7777	0

SAN FERNANDO, CA - Los Angeles County

Company	SIC	EMP	PHONE	ENTRY #
All State Association Inc		C	877 425-2558	0
Bank America National Assn		D	818 898-3033	0
Bernards Builders Inc		B	818 898-1521	0
Bernards Inc		D	818 898-1521	0
Brightview Landscape Dev Inc		D	818 838-4700	0
Cacho Landscape Maintenance Co		E	818 365-0773	0
Child Care Resource Center Inc		B	818 837-0097	0
County of Los Angeles		C	818 837-6969	0
Environments Plus (PA)		D	866 865-8120	0
First Student Inc		B	818 896-0333	0
Frontier California Inc		C	818 365-0542	0
Jme Inc (PA)		C	201 896-8600	0

Mergent email: customerrelations@mergent.com
1622

2020 Directory of California
Wholesalers and Services Companies

(P-0000) Products & Services Section entry number
(PA)=Parent Co (HQ)=Headquarters (DH)=Div Headquarters

	SIC	EMP	PHONE	ENTRY #
Mv Transportation Inc		D	323 666-0856	0
Northeast Valley Health Corp **(PA)**		D	818 898-1388	0
Northeast Valley Health Corp		D	818 365-8086	0
Prg (california) Inc		E	818 252-2600	0
Stan Winston Inc		D	818 782-0870	0
Tyan Inc		D	818 785-5831	0

SAN FRANCISCO, CA - San Francisco County

	SIC	EMP	PHONE	ENTRY #
1life Healthcare Inc		D	415 644-5265	0
3vr Security Inc		D	415 513-4577	0
425 North Point Street LLC		D	800 648-4626	0
42nd Street Moon		E	415 255-8207	0
495 Geary LLC		C	415 775-4700	0
500 Startups Incubator LLC		C	415 974-6343	0
A Ruiz Cnstr Co & Assoc Inc		E	415 647-4010	0
A Smwm California Corporation		D	415 546-0400	0
A T Kearney Inc		D	415 490-4000	0
A1 Protective Services Inc		D	415 467-7200	0
ABB Enterprise Software Inc		C	415 527-2850	0
ABC Cable Networks Group		C	415 954-7911	0
ABS Capital Partners III LP		D	415 617-2800	0
Accenture LLP		B	415 537-5000	0
Access Public Relations LLC		D	415 904-7070	0
Accor Services US LLC **(HQ)**		A	415 772-5000	0
Accountants 4 Contract		D	415 781-8644	0
Ace Parking Management Inc		D	415 421-8800	0
Active Wellness LLC		A	415 741-3300	0
Addiction RES & Trtmnt Inc		D	415 928-7800	0
Adg Corporation		E	415 864-4090	0
Adivo Associates LLC		D	415 992-1449	0
Adobe Inc		A	415 832-2000	0
Advantage Workforce Svcs LLC		C	415 212-6464	0
Advent Software Inc **(HQ)**		C	415 543-7696	0
Aecom Global II LLC		D	415 774-2700	0
Aero Technologies Inc		E	415 314-7479	0
Aetna Health California Inc		D	415 645-8200	0
Air France (air Nationale)		D	415 877-0179	0
Airbnb Inc **(PA)**		A	415 800-5959	0
Airco Mechanical Inc		C	415 982-4726	0
Akin Gump Strauss Hauer & Fel		C	415 765-9500	0
Akqa Inc **(HQ)**		B	415 645-9400	0
Alain Pinel Realtors Inc		C	415 814-6690	0
Alcatraz Cruises LLC		C	415 981-7625	0
Alegrecare Inc		B	415 974-3530	0
All Hallows Preservation LP		A	415 285-3909	0
Allen Matkins Leck Gmble		D	415 837-1515	0
Allied Medical Service of Cal		E	415 931-1400	0
Almavia of San Francisco		D	415 337-1339	0
Alois LLC		C	215 297-4492	0
Alsco Inc		D	415 648-9266	0
Alta Equipment Leasing Company		D	415 875-1000	0
Alvarez & Marsal Holdings LLC		C	415 490-2300	0
Amber Holdings Inc		A	415 765-6500	0
AMD Trading Company Inc		C	415 391-0601	0
American Academy of Opthalmlgy **(PA)**		C	415 561-8500	0
American Bldg Maint Co-West **(HQ)**		A	415 733-4000	0
American Building Maint Co NY		A	415 733-4000	0
American Conservatory		D	415 749-2228	0
American Conservatory		D	415 749-2228	0
American Gen Lf Insur Co Del		B	415 836-2700	0
American Legal Copy-Or LLC		D	415 777-4449	0
American Marketing Systems Inc		D	800 747-7784	0
American Medical Response		D	415 922-9400	0
American National Red Cross		D	415 427-8134	0
Ammunition LLC		D	415 632-1170	0
Amoeba Music Inc		D	415 831-1200	0
Amour Vert Inc		D	650 388-4284	0
Amplify Education Inc		D	562 209-7875	0
Amzn Mobile LLC		B	925 348-4580	0
Anaplan Inc **(PA)**		C	415 742-8199	0
Anderson Rowe & Buckley Inc		C	415 282-1625	0
Animoto LLC		D	415 987-3139	0
Annie App Inc **(DH)**		D	844 277-2664	0
Anvil Builders Inc		C	415 285-5000	0
AON Benfield Fac Inc		C	415 486-6900	0
AON Consulting Inc		D	800 283-1667	0
AON Consulting Inc		C	415 486-6226	0
AON Consulting & Insur Svcs		D	415 486-7500	0
Apic Hotels Group LLC **(HQ)**		D	415 692-1502	0
Appdirect Inc **(PA)**		D	415 852-3924	0
Appdynamics Inc **(HQ)**		C	415 442-8400	0
Appsflyer Ltd		D	415 636-9430	0
AR Preservation LP		D	415 776-2151	0
Aramark Unf & Career AP LLC		C	415 244-8332	0
Arb Inc		E	415 206-1015	0
ARC Document Solutions Inc		E	415 495-8700	0
ARC San Francisco **(PA)**		C	415 255-7200	0
Archetype Consulting Inc		D	888 644-8445	0
Arctouch LLC		C	415 944-2000	0
Argonaut Hotel		C	415 563-0800	0
Aria Systems Inc **(PA)**		D	415 852-7250	0
Arlene Keller MD		E	415 923-3598	0
Arnold & Porter LLP		B	818 788-8081	0
Arnold & Porter PC		B	415 434-1600	0
Arnold Palmer Golf MGT LLC		D	415 561-4670	0
Arriba Juntos **(PA)**		D	415 487-3240	0
Arroyo & Coates Inc		D	415 445-7800	0
Arthur J Gallagher & Co		C	415 546-9300	0
Arup North America Limited **(DH)**		C	415 957-9445	0
Asana Inc **(PA)**		D	415 525-3888	0
Ascendify Corporation		E	415 528-5503	0
Asia Foundation **(PA)**		D	415 982-4640	0
Asian Art Museum Found San Fra		C	415 581-3500	0
Aspen Apts I		D	415 673-5879	0
Aspiranet		D	415 759-3690	0
Aspiriant LLC		E	415 371-7800	0
AT&T Corp		D	415 970-8520	0
AT&T Corp		A	415 442-2600	0
AT&T Corp		C	415 442-5900	0
AT&T Services Inc		C	415 545-9051	0
AT&T Services Inc		D	415 545-9058	0
AT&T Services Inc		B	415 394-3000	0
AT&T Services Inc		C	415 774-1957	0
Atel Capital Group **(PA)**		D	800 543-2835	0
Atel Corporation		D	415 989-8800	0
Atkins North America Inc		E	916 325-4800	0
Atlassian Inc **(DH)**		C	415 701-1110	0
Aura Financial Corporation		D	415 391-2431	0
Autodesk Inc		D	415 356-0700	0
Automatic Data Processing Inc		E	800 225-5237	0
Automattic Inc		D	877 273-3049	0
Avalon Golden Gate LLC		D	415 664-6264	0
Axa Advisors LLC		D	415 276-2100	0
Ayoob & Peery Plumbing Co Inc		D	415 550-0975	0
B F C Inc		C	415 495-3085	0
Ba Leasing & Capital Corp **(DH)**		C	415 765-1804	0
Baart Behavioral Hlth Svcs Inc		D	415 928-7800	0
Baart Community Healthcare		D	415 928-7800	0
Baaz Inc		D	408 621-6912	0
Bain & Company Inc		C	415 627-1000	0
Baker & McKenzie LLP		C	415 576-3000	0
Baker Places Inc		C	415 503-3137	0
Baker Places Inc **(PA)**		C	415 864-4655	0
Banc America Lsg & Capitl LLC **(DH)**		C	415 765-7349	0
Bank America National Assn		E	800 432-1000	0
Bank America National Assn		C	415 913-5891	0
Bank of New York Mellon Corp		D	415 399-4450	0
Bank of Orient **(HQ)**		D	415 338-0668	0
BANK OF THE WEST **(HQ)**		A	415 765-4800	0
Bankamerica Financial Inc		A	415 622-3521	0
Bar Architects		D	415 293-5700	0
Bar Asscation of San Francisco **(PA)**		C	415 982-1600	0
Barger & Wolen LLP		E	415 434-2800	0
Barrett SF		E	415 986-2960	0
Bartko Zankel Tarrant & Mil		D	415 956-1900	0
Bauers Intelligent Trnsp Inc **(PA)**		C	415 522-1212	0
Bavaria Holdings Inc		A	415 418-2900	0
Bay Area Air Quality **(PA)**		C	415 749-4900	0
Bay Area Video Coalition Inc		D	415 861-3282	0
Bay Bread LLC		D	415 440-0356	0
Bay Club Golden Gateway LLC		E	415 616-8800	0
Bay Club Holdings III LLC		D	415 433-2936	0
Bay Grove Capital Group LLC **(PA)**		E	415 229-7953	0
Bay West Shwplace Invstors LLC **(PA)**		D	415 490-5800	0
Bayorg		D	415 623-5300	0
Bayspring Medical Group A Pro		E	415 674-2600	0
Bayview Hunters Point Foundati **(PA)**		D	415 468-5100	0
Bayview Hunters Point Y M C A		D	415 822-7728	0
Bayview Preservation LP		A	415 285-7344	0
Bbam Arcft Holdings 137 Labuan		D	415 267-1600	0
Bbam US LP		B	415 267-1600	0
BBDO Worldwide Inc		D	415 808-6200	0
Bcci Construction Company **(DH)**		C	415 817-5100	0
Bdo Usa LLP		C	415 397-7900	0
Beats Music LLC		D	415 590-5104	0
Bechtel Capital MGT Corp		A	415 768-1234	0
Bechtel Global Energy Inc		A	415 768-1234	0
Beresford Corporation		C	415 981-7386	0
Beresford Corporation		D	415 673-9900	0
Berkshire Hathaway Homestates **(HQ)**		C	415 433-1650	0
Best Western Hotel Tomo		E	415 921-4000	0

	SIC	EMP	PHONE	ENTRY #
Big Health Inc		D	415 867-3473	0
Billing Services Plus DBA Apex		D	415 604-3515	0
Birst Inc		B	415 766-4800	0
Bitalign Inc		D	415 395-9525	0
Bite Communications LLC **(HQ)**		D	415 365-0222	0
Bittorrent Inc		E	408 641-4219	0
Black Bear Security Services		C	415 559-5159	0
Blackrock Funds III		D	415 597-2000	0
Blackrock Global Investors		A	415 670-2000	0
Blackrock Holdco 2 Inc		A	415 678-2000	0
Blackrock Instnl Tr Nat Assn **(HQ)**		A	415 597-2000	0
Blackstone Technology Group **(PA)**		D	415 837-1400	0
Bleacher Report Inc		D	415 777-5505	0
Bleacher Report Inc		C	415 777-5505	0
Bloomberg LP		D	415 912-2960	0
Blue and Gold Fleet		D	415 705-8200	0
Blue Bus Tours LLC		C	415 353-5310	0
Bmr Apps Inc		D	954 651-1412	0
Bohemian Club **(PA)**		C	415 885-2440	0
Bongmi Inc		E	415 823-8595	0
Bonhams Bttrflds Actneers Corp **(DH)**		D	415 861-7500	0
Bonhams Corporation		C	415 861-7500	0
Bonneville International Corp		E	415 777-0965	0
Bossa Nova Robotics Inc **(HQ)**		C	415 234-5136	0
Boston Properties Ltd Partnr		D	415 772-0700	0
Boutique Air Inc **(PA)**		D	415 449-0505	0
Bpaz Holdings 18 LLC		D	972 354-6250	0
Bpaz Holdings 2 LLC		E	972 354-6250	0
Bpaz Holdings 6 LLC		D	415 295-8080	0
Bpm LLP **(PA)**		D	415 421-5757	0
Bracket Global LLC		D	415 293-1340	0
Brad S Miller		C	415 986-5400	0
Brafton Incorporated		D	617 206-3040	0
Brandnet Inc		D	415 216-4152	0
Bre/Japantown Owner LLC		D	415 922-3200	0
Bridge Housing Acquisition		D	415 989-1111	0
Bridge Housing Corporation **(PA)**		D	415 989-1111	0
Brience Inc **(DH)**		D	415 974-5300	0
Brighterion Inc		D	415 986-5600	0
Broadmoor Hotel **(PA)**		C	415 776-7034	0
Broadmoor Hotel		D	415 673-2511	0
Broadreach Capitl Partners LLC		A	415 354-4640	0
Brown & Toland Medical Group		C	415 752-8038	0
Bryan Cave Lighton Paisner LLP		E	415 675-3400	0
Btig LLC **(PA)**		D	415 248-2200	0
Build Group Inc **(PA)**		C	415 367-9399	0
Burr Pilger Mayer Inc **(PA)**		C	415 421-5757	0
Business For Scial Rspnsbility **(PA)**		D	415 984-3200	0
Business Services Network		D	415 282-8161	0
Bynd LLC		D	415 944-2293	0
CA Ste Atom Assoc Intr-Ins Bur		A	415 565-2012	0
Cadreon LLC		C	415 262-5900	0
Cahill Contractors Inc **(PA)**		D	415 986-0600	0
Cahill Contractors LLC		D	415 986-0600	0
Cai International Inc **(PA)**		C	415 788-0100	0
California Academy Sciences **(PA)**		A	415 379-8000	0
California Childcare Resource **(PA)**		D	415 882-0234	0
California Dept Rehabilitation		D	415 904-7100	0
California Pacific CA		E	415 345-0940	0
California Pacific Medical Ctr		D	415 600-1378	0
California Parking Company **(PA)**		D	415 781-4896	0
California Physicians Service **(PA)**		A	415 229-5000	0
California Shellfish Co Inc		B	707 542-9490	0
Califrnia PCF Med Ctr Fndation **(PA)**		D	415 600-4400	0
Callan LLC **(PA)**		C	415 974-5060	0
Campaign Monitor USA Inc		D	888 533-8098	0
Canon Solutions America Inc		D	415 743-7300	0
Canterbury Hotel Corp		C	415 345-3200	0
Capcom Entertainment Inc		D	650 350-6500	0
Capcom U S A Inc **(HQ)**		C	650 350-6500	0
Capgemini America Inc		D	415 796-6777	0
Capital Group Companies Inc		B	213 486-1698	0
Carat		D	415 541-2700	0
Carbonfive Incorporated		D	415 546-0500	0
Caritas Management Corporation		D	415 647-7191	0
Carlton Hotel Properties LP		D	415 673-0242	0
Carmel Partners Inc **(PA)**		C	415 273-2900	0
Carroll Burdick Mc Donough LLP **(PA)**		C	415 989-5900	0
Casey Securities Inc **(PA)**		D	415 544-5030	0
Cassidy Trly Prop MGT Sn Frncs		D	415 781-8100	0
Castlight Health Inc **(PA)**		C	415 829-1400	0
Catholic Chrts Cyo Archdiocs		D	415 743-0017	0
Catholic Chrts Cyo Archdiocs		D	415 405-2000	0
Catholic Chrts Cyo Archdiocs		D	415 334-5550	0
Catholic Chrts Cyo Archdiocs		D	415 553-8700	0
Catholic Chrts Cyo Archdiocs **(PA)**		D	415 972-1200	0
Cb-1 Hotel		D	415 633-3838	0
CBS Broadcasting Inc		B	415 765-0928	0
CBS Broadcasting Inc		D	415 765-4097	0
CBS Corporation		D	415 765-4000	0
CBS Interactive Inc **(DH)**		A	415 344-2000	0
CBS Radio Inc		D	415 765-4097	0
Cdc San Francisco LLC		D	415 616-6512	0
Celerity Consulting Group Inc **(PA)**		D	415 986-8850	0
Cellco Partnership		D	415 402-0640	0
Cellco Partnership		D	415 695-8400	0
Cellco Partnership		D	415 351-1700	0
Central Gardens Inc		C	415 567-2967	0
Cesar Chavez Student Center		C	415 338-7362	0
Cesars Productions		E	415 821-1156	0
Cfgi LLC		C	415 670-9041	0
Changeorg Inc		C	415 817-1840	0
Charles Schwab & Co Inc **(HQ)**		D	415 636-7000	0
Charles Schwab Corporation **(PA)**		D	415 667-7000	0
Charolais Care V Inc		D	415 921-5038	0
Chesapeake Lodging Trust		D	415 296-2900	0
Chikpea Inc		E	888 342-3828	0
Childrens Creativity Museum		D	415 820-3320	0
Childrens Cuncil San Francisco **(PA)**		D	415 343-3378	0
Childrens Day School		E	415 861-5432	0
Chinese Cnsld Benevolent Assn		D	415 982-6000	0
Chinese Hospital Association **(PA)**		B	415 982-2400	0
Chirag Hospitality Inc		D	415 922-0244	0
Chong Partners Architecher Inc		C	613 995-8210	0
Chronicle Broadcasting Co		B	415 561-8000	0
Chsp Trs Fisherman Wharf LLC		C	415 563-1234	0
Chubb US Holding Inc		D	415 547-4400	0
Cigna Healthcare Cal Inc		C	415 374-2500	0
Citibank FSB **(HQ)**		B	415 627-6000	0
Citibank National Association		A	415 431-6940	0
Citigroup Inc		D	415 617-8524	0
City & County of San Francisco		C	415 553-1706	0
City & County of San Francisco		D	415 621-6600	0
City & County of San Francisco		C	415 621-6600	0
City & County of San Francisco		A	415 551-3000	0
City & County of San Francisco		D	415 581-3500	0
City & County of San Francisco		A	415 206-8000	0
City & County of San Francisco		C	415 557-4713	0
City & County of San Francisco		C	415 554-4700	0
City & County of San Francisco		C	415 553-1752	0
City & County of San Francisco		D	415 753-7561	0
City & County of San Francisco		D	415 554-4799	0
City Club LLC		D	415 362-2480	0
City Impact		E	415 292-1770	0
Clean Power Finance Inc		C	899 525-2123	0
Clean-A-Rama Maint Svc LLC		D	415 495-5298	0
Clearesult Consulting Inc		D	415 848-1250	0
Clearslide Inc **(DH)**		D	877 360-3366	0
Click Labs Inc		A	415 658-5227	0
Climate Corporation **(DH)**		D	415 363-0500	0
Cloudflare Inc **(PA)**		C	888 993-5273	0
Clp Resources Inc		E	415 508-0910	0
Club Quarters San Francisco		D	415 268-3606	0
Clyde & Co US LLP		D	415 365-9800	0
CM Wind Down Topco Inc		D	415 995-6800	0
Cnet Networks Inc		A	415 344-2000	0
CNX Media Inc		D	415 229-8300	0
Code For America Labs Inc		D	415 625-9633	0
Cognifit Inc		D	646 340-1740	0
Coinbase Inc **(PA)**		D	415 275-2890	0
Coldwell Bnkr Residential Brkg		D	415 447-8800	0
Collabrus Inc		C	415 288-1826	0
Collectivehealth Inc		B	650 376-3804	0
Collier Warehouse Inc		E	415 920-9720	0
Colliers International		D	415 788-3100	0
Comca Sport Net Bay Area		C	415 896-2557	0
Comcast Cble Cmmunications LLC		C	415 715-0524	0
Comcast Corporation		D	415 665-5507	0
Comfort California Inc		E	415 928-5000	0
Compass Family Services		D	415 644-0504	0
Compass Family Services		D	415 644-0504	0
Compass Family Services		D	415 644-0504	0
Computacenter Fusionstorm Inc		C	415 623-2626	0
Computer Resources Group Inc		C	415 398-3535	0
Condor Trading LP		A	415 248-2200	0
Conduit Inc		C	650 340-1550	0
Conrad Imports Inc		D	415 626-3303	0
Conservation Liquidation		D	415 676-5000	0
Consumer Loan Underlying		C	415 767-4105	0
Cooley LLP		D	415 693-2000	0

Mergent email: customerrelations@mergent.com
1624

2020 Directory of California
Wholesalers and Services Companies

(P-0000) Products & Services Section entry number
(PA)=Parent Co (HQ)=Headquarters (DH)=Div Headquarters

	SIC	EMP	PHONE	ENTRY #
Cooper Pugeda Management Inc		E	415 543-6251	0
Cooper White & Cooper LLP (PA)		C	415 433-1900	0
Copper Crm Inc (PA)		C	415 231-6360	0
Corelogic Inc		E	714 250-6400	0
Coreos LLC		D	888 733-4281	0
Cornell Companies Inc		E	415 346-9769	0
Cornerstone Cnsulting Tech Inc		E	415 705-7800	0
Cornerstone Hotel Management (DH)		D	415 397-5572	0
Cornerstone Research Inc		D	415 229-8100	0
Corportion of Fine Arts Mseums		C	415 750-3600	0
Corportion of Fine Arts Mseums		C	415 750-3600	0
Corportion of Fine Arts Mseums (PA)		C	415 750-3600	0
Costless Maintenance Svcs Co		D	415 550-8819	0
Coveo Software Corp		D	800 635-5476	0
Coverity LLC (HQ)		D	415 321-5200	0
Covia Communities		C	415 776-0500	0
Covington & Burling LLP		E	415 591-6000	0
Craftworks Rest Breweries Inc		C	415 292-5800	0
Crane Acquisition Inc		D	415 922-1666	0
Creativebug LLC		C	415 325-5926	0
Credit Karma Inc (PA)		C	415 510-5059	0
Credit Suisse (usa) Inc		D	415 249-2100	0
Credit Suisse (usa) Inc		E	415 678-3940	0
Credo Mobile Inc		C	415 369-2000	0
Creedence Lessee LLC		D	415 561-1100	0
Crestline Hotels & Resorts LLC		C	415 775-7555	0
Cross Link Inc		D	415 495-3191	0
Crosscap Media Services Inc (PA)		D	415 217-8860	0
Crowell & Moring LLP		D	415 986-2800	0
Crown Building Maintenance Co		B	303 680-3713	0
Crunch LLC		C	415 495-1939	0
Cupertino Electric Inc		D	415 970-3400	0
Current Tv LLC		D	415 995-8328	0
Cusa FI LLC		C	415 642-9400	0
Cushman & Wakefield Cal Inc (DH)		C	408 275-6730	0
Cutler Group LP		E	415 645-6745	0
Cvpartners Inc (HQ)		C	415 543-8600	0
Cyber Policy		C	877 626-9991	0
Cybernet Entertainment LLC (PA)		D	415 865-0230	0
Cypress Creek Renewables LLC		D	415 306-5300	0
Cypress Security LLC (PA)		D	866 345-1277	0
Daniel J Edelman Inc		D	415 222-9944	0
Dannis Wlver Klley A Prof Corp (PA)		D	415 543-4111	0
Databricks Inc (PA)		D	415 494-7672	0
Datameer Inc (PA)		D	650 286-9100	0
Davis Wright Tremaine LLP		D	415 276-6500	0
Davis Ziff Publishing Inc		C	415 551-4800	0
Dcp Jl Triton Sf LLC		E	844 808-0290	0
DDB Worldwide		C	415 732-3600	0
Dechert LLP		E	415 262-4500	0
Decimal Inc		D	855 980-6612	0
Deem Inc (DH)		D	415 590-8300	0
Degenkolb Engineers (PA)		C	415 392-6952	0
Delancey Street Foundation (PA)		B	415 957-9800	0
Deloitte & Touche LLP		B	415 783-4000	0
Deloitte Consulting LLP			510 251-4400	0
Deloitte Tax LLP		B	415 783-4000	0
Delta Dental of California (PA)		B	415 972-8300	0
Delta Project Management Inc		D	415 590-3202	0
Demandbase Inc		B	415 683-2660	0
Dena Corp		D	415 375-3170	0
Dentons US LLP		C	415 882-5000	0
Destination Moon LP		D	415 675-7777	0
Deutsche Bank Tr Co Americas		C	415 617-4200	0
Deutsche Inv MGT Americas Inc		E	415 648-9408	0
Dewolf Realty Co Inc		D	415 221-2032	0
Dhap Digital Inc		D	415 962-4900	0
Dhl Express (usa) Inc		D	415 826-7338	0
Dietrich Post Co Inc		E	510 596-0080	0
Digital Realty Trust Inc (PA)		C	415 738-6500	0
Digital Realty Trust LP (HQ)		A	415 738-6500	0
Digitalist USA Ltd		A	949 278-1354	0
Digitalthink Inc (DH)		D	415 625-4000	0
Dignity Health		B	415 438-5500	0
Dignity Health (HQ)		B	415 438-5500	0
Dignity Health		A	415 668-1000	0
Directorate of Mwr Fmd Usag		D	210 466-1376	0
Discount Builders Supply		D	415 285-2800	0
Docker Inc (PA)		D	800 764-4847	0
Doctor On Demand Inc		D	415 935-4447	0
Document Technologies LLC		D	415 495-4100	0
Docusign Inc (PA)		B	415 489-4940	0
Dodge & Cox		C	415 981-1710	0
Dolby Labs Licensing Corp		C	415 558-0200	0
Doremus & Company		E	415 273-7800	0

	SIC	EMP	PHONE	ENTRY #
Doubledutch Inc (PA)		D	800 748-9024	0
Dpk Consulting		D	415 495-7772	0
Dppm Inc		D	415 695-7707	0
Drinker Biddle & Reath LLP		C	415 591-7500	0
Dropbox Inc (PA)		C	415 857-6800	0
Dtrs St Francis LLC		A	415 397-7000	0
Duane Morris LLP		D	415 957-3000	0
Duff & Phelps LLC		D	415 693-5300	0
Dun & Bradstreet Inc		D	925 216-2493	0
Dunhill Worldwide		A	415 814-6006	0
Earls Organic		D	415 824-7419	0
East West Bank		C	415 391-8912	0
Eastrdge Prsonnel of Las Vegas		D	415 248-2567	0
Eco Bay Services Inc		D	415 643-7777	0
Edaw Inc (HQ)		C	415 955-2800	0
Edgewood Ctr For Childrens (PA)		B	415 681-3211	0
Edgewood Partners Insur Ctr (HQ)		D	415 356-3900	0
Efront Financial Solutions Inc		D	415 653-3239	0
Egomotion Corp (PA)		E	415 849-4662	0
Eileen Nottoli		D	415 837-1515	0
Eis Group Inc		C	415 402-2622	0
Elaine Null		D	415 345-4428	0
Elastic Projects Inc		D	415 857-1593	0
Eleven Inc		C	415 707-1111	0
Elizabeth Larson		D	415 409-7300	0
Ellation Inc (PA)		D	415 796-3560	0
Embarcadero Inn Associates		C	415 495-2100	0
Embassador Private Securities		D	415 822-8811	0
Emerge Digital Inc		D	415 839-5055	0
Emergent Ventures Intl Inc		D	415 655-6617	0
Emotiv Systems Inc		E	415 503-3601	0
Encore Cnsmr Capitl Fund II LP (PA)		D	415 296-9850	0
Encore Fund LP		D	415 676-4000	0
Enertis Solar Inc		E	415 400-5271	0
Entangled Ventures LLC (PA)		D	415 795-2767	0
Entercom Communications Corp		D	610 660-5610	0
Environmental Science Assoc (PA)		D	415 896-5900	0
Envivio Inc		C	650 243-2700	0
Envoy Comm		D	415 787-7871	0
Episcopal Comm Svc San Fran (PA)		C	415 487-3300	0
Equal Access International		D	415 561-4884	0
Equinox Holdings Inc		B	415 243-0492	0
Equinox-76th Street Inc		D	398-0747	0
Ernst & Young LLP		D	415 894-8000	0
Ernst & Young LLP		A	415 894-8000	0
Esurance Insurance Svcs Inc (HQ)		C	415 875-4500	0
Eventbrite Inc (PA)		B	415 692-7779	0
Everest Wtrprfing Rstrtion Inc		D	415 282-9800	0
Everwise Corporation		D	888 250-6219	0
Evidera Archimedes Inc		D	415 490-0400	0
Evolent Health Inc		B	571 389-6000	0
Execushield Inc		D	415 508-0825	0
Executives Outlet Inc		C	415 433-6044	0
Exigen (usa) Inc (PA)		A	415 402-2600	0
Exploratorium		B	415 528-4462	0
Express Messenger Systems Inc		D	415 495-7300	0
F50 League LLC		E	415 939-4076	0
Family Svc Agcy San Francisco (PA)		D	415 474-7310	0
Farallon Capital Partners LP (PA)		C	415 421-2132	0
Fastly Inc (PA)		C	844 432-7859	0
Fcb Worldwide Inc		A	415 820-8545	0
Federal Deposit Insurance Corp		C	415 546-0160	0
Federal Express Corporation		C	800 463-3339	0
Federal Hm Ln Bnk San Frncisco (PA)		B	415 616-1000	0
Federal Insurance Company		D	415 273-6300	0
Federal Rsrve Bnk San Frncisco (HQ)		A	415 974-2000	0
Fenton Communications Inc		E	415 255-1946	0
Fenty Beauty LLC		C	818 973-2709	0
Fenwick & West LLP		C	415 875-2300	0
Ferguson Enterprises Inc		D	408 441-7276	0
Figure Eight Technologies Inc		D	415 471-1920	0
Fillmore Marketplace LP		E	415 921-6514	0
Financialforcecom Inc (DH)		D	866 743-2220	0
Finastra Merchant Services Inc (PA)		D	415 277-9900	0
Fine Line Group Inc		E	415 777-4070	0
First Databank Inc		D	650 588-5454	0
First Page Sage LLC		D	415 624-3526	0
First Republic Bank		D	415 392-1400	0
First Republic Bank		D	415 392-3888	0
First Republic Bank		D	415 564-8881	0
First Republic Bank		D	415 487-0888	0
First Republic Bank		C	415 975-3877	0
First Republic Bank (PA)		B	415 392-1400	0
First Student Inc		B	415 647-9012	0
Firstcall (PA)		C	415 781-4300	0

Employment Codes: A=Over 500 employees, B=251-500,
C=101-250, D=51-100, E=50

2020 Directory of California
Wholesalers and Services Companies

© Mergent Inc. 1-800-342-5647

1625

GEOGRAPHIC

	SIC	EMP	PHONE	ENTRY #
Fleischman Field Research Inc		C	415 398-4140	0
Fleishman-Hillard Inc		E	415 318-4000	0
Flexport Inc (PA)		D	415 231-5252	0
Flickr Inc		E	650 265-0396	0
Florence Villa Hotel		C	415 397-7700	0
Florence Villa Hotel LLC		D	415 397-7700	0
Flynn Properties Inc		E	415 835-0225	0
Foley & Lardner LLP		D	415 434-4484	0
Forex Capital Markets LLC		D	415 343-4874	0
Forgerock Inc (PA)		D	415 599-1100	0
Forgerock US Inc (HQ)		D	415 599-1100	0
Formation Inc		D	650 257-2277	0
Fort Mason Center		D	415 345-7500	0
Fortress Investment Group LLC		D	415 284-7400	0
Forward Management LLC		D	415 869-6300	0
Four Seasons Hotel Inc		A	415 633-3441	0
Fox Rothschild LLP		D	415 539-3336	0
France Telecom RES & Dev LLC		D	415 284-9765	0
Franciscan Lines Inc		E	415 642-9400	0
Francisco Partners LP (HQ)		D	415 418-2900	0
Francisco Partners MGT LP (PA)		E	415 418-2900	0
Frank Rimerman & Co LLP		D	415 439-1144	0
Franklin Electric Co Inc		A	415 467-2693	0
Free Stream Media Corp (PA)		E	415 854-0073	0
Fremont Group LLC (PA)		E	415 284-8880	0
Fremont Mutual Funds Inc		D	800 548-4539	0
Fremont Properties Inc		E	415 284-8500	0
Fremont Realty Capital LP		D	415 284-8665	0
Frog Design Inc (DH)		D	415 442-4804	0
Frontapp Inc		D	415 680-3048	0
Fti Consulting Inc		D	415 283-4200	0
Ftv Management Company LP		C	415 291-8164	0
Fundbox Inc		C	415 509-1343	0
Funding Circle Usa Inc		D	855 385-5356	0
Fuse Project LLC		D	415 908-1492	0
G2 Direct and Digital		E	415 421-1000	0
G4s Secure Solutions USA Inc		C	415 591-0780	0
Galleria Park Associates LLC		D	415 781-3060	0
Gastroenterology Division		E	415 206-8823	0
Geary Darling Lessee Inc		C	415 292-0100	0
Genstar Capital LP		A	415 834-2350	0
Geographic Expeditions Inc		D	415 922-0448	0
Getaround Inc (PA)		D	866 438-2768	0
Getfeedback Inc		D	888 684-8821	0
Gfk Custom Research LLC		D	415 398-2812	0
Ggc Administration LLC		A	415 983-2700	0
GI GP IV LLC (PA)		E	415 688-4800	0
Giant Creative Strategy Llc		C	415 655-5200	0
Gibson Dunn & Crutcher LLP		C	415 393-8200	0
Gic Real Estate Inc (HQ)		D	415 229-1800	0
Giga Omni Media Inc		D	415 974-6355	0
Gigster Inc		C	941 888-4447	0
Gigsurf Inc		B	415 894-2445	0
Gilbert LLP		D	415 646-4002	0
Gingerio Inc		C	408 455-0574	0
Gitlab Inc		A	408 569-3035	0
Glass Lewis & Co LLC (HQ)		D	415 678-4110	0
Global USA Green Card		A	415 915-4151	0
Glu Mobile Inc (PA)		C	415 800-6100	0
GM Cruise LLC (HQ)		D	415 335-4097	0
Go West Holdings LLC		D	888 670-0080	0
Go West Tours Inc (PA)		E	415 837-0154	0
Gobig Inc		E	415 513-3029	0
Golden Bear Rest Assn LLC		E	415 227-8660	0
Golden Gate Brdg Hwy & Transpo (PA)		C	415 921-5858	0
Golden Gate Capitol		B	415 983-2700	0
Golden Gate Nat Prks Cnsrvancy		C	415 440-4068	0
Golden Gate Nat Prks Cnsrvancy (PA)		D	415 561-3000	0
Golden Gate Regional Ctr Inc (PA)		C	415 546-9222	0
Golden Gate Scnic Stmship Corp		E	415 901-5249	0
Golden Living LLC		D	415 563-0565	0
Goldman Sachs & Co		C	415 393-7500	0
Good Eggs Inc (PA)		C	415 483-7344	0
Goodby Slverstein Partners Inc		C	415 392-0669	0
Gordon Rees Scully Mansukhani (PA)		B	415 986-5900	0
Gould Evans P C		D	415 503-1411	0
Grand View Research Inc		E	415 349-0058	0
Granite Solutions Groupe Inc		D	415 963-3999	0
Grant Thornton LLP		D	415 986-3900	0
Great American Music Hall		E	415 885-0750	0
Gree International Inc		C	415 409-5200	0
Gree International Entrmt Inc		C	415 409-5200	0
Green Tortoise Adventure Trvl		D	415 834-1000	0
Greenberg Traurig LLP		D	415 655-1300	0
Greene Rdvsky Maloney Share LP		D	415 981-1400	0
Greentree Property MGT Inc		E	415 347-8600	0
Guardsmark LLC		B	415 956-6070	0
Guidebook Inc (PA)		D	650 319-7233	0
H&R Block Inc		E	415 441-2666	0
Habenicht & Howlett A Corp		D	415 824-7040	0
Hackerone Inc (PA)		B	415 891-0777	0
Hall Capital Partners LLC (PA)		D	415 288-0544	0
Hamilton Families		D	415 409-2100	0
Handlery Hotels Inc		C	415 781-7800	0
Hands-On Mobile Americas Inc (PA)		E	415 580-6400	0
Hanson Bridgett LLP (PA)		B	415 543-2055	0
Harley Ellis Devereaux Corp		D	415 981-2345	0
Harrison Drywall Inc		E	415 821-9584	0
Hart Howerton Ltd (PA)		D	415 439-2200	0
Hartford Casualty Insurance Co		A	415 836-4800	0
Hassard Bonnington LLP (PA)		D	415 288-9800	0
Hatfield Inc		E	415 802-8635	0
Hathaway Dinwiddie Cnstr Co		B	415 986-2718	0
Hathaway Dinwiddie Cnstr Group (PA)		B	415 986-2718	0
Hawaii Parent Corp		B	415 263-3660	0
HDR Architecture Inc		D	415 546-4242	0
HDR Engineering Inc		D	415 546-4200	0
Hearsay Social Inc (PA)		D	888 990-3777	0
Heartland Payment Systems Inc		D	415 518-4810	0
Hebrew Home For Aged Disabled		A	415 334-2500	0
Heffernan Insurance Brokers		E	800 829-9996	0
Hellmuth Obata & Kassabaum Inc (DH)		C	415 243-0555	0
Henry Broadcasting Co		E	415 285-1133	0
Henry J Kaiser Fmly Foundation (PA)		C	650 854-9400	0
Herrero Builders Incorporated (PA)		C	415 824-7675	0
High Fidelity Inc		D	415 862-4434	0
Highmark Capital Management		D	800 582-4734	0
Hill & Knowlton Strategies LLC		D	415 281-7120	0
Hilton San Francisco Fincl Dst		D	415 433-6600	0
Hines Gs Properties Inc		E	415 982-6200	0
Hinttech Inc		C	415 874-3200	0
Hired Inc (PA)		E	415 813-4987	0
Hirschfeld Kraemer LLP (PA)		E	415 835-9000	0
Hks Architects Inc		E	415 356-3800	0
Hok Group Inc		C	415 243-0555	0
Holland & Knight LLP		E	415 743-6900	0
Holzmueller Corporation		E	415 826-8383	0
Homebridge Inc		B	415 255-2079	0
Homeless Prenatal Program		E	415 546-6756	0
Homestar Systems Inc		D	415 694-6000	0
Honeybook Inc		D	770 403-9234	0
Hood & Strong LLP (PA)		D	415 781-0793	0
Horn Group Inc		E	415 905-4000	0
Hornberger Worstell Assoc Inc		E	415 391-1080	0
Hornblower Group Inc		B	415 635-2210	0
Hornblower Yachts LLC (PA)		C	415 788-8866	0
Host Hotels & Resorts Inc		C	415 775-7555	0
Host Hotels & Resorts LP		D	415 896-1600	0
Hotel Nikko San Francisco Inc		B	415 394-1111	0
Hotel Tonight Inc (PA)		D	800 208-2949	0
Hotel Whitcomb		D	415 626-8000	0
Hotwire Inc		C	415 343-8400	0
House of Air LLC		D	415 345-9675	0
Howard Hughes Medical Inst		C	415 476-9668	0
Htec Group Inc (PA)		D	650 949-4880	0
Humanitycom Inc		E	415 230-0108	0
Hunton Andrews Kurth LLP		D	415 975-3700	0
Huntsman Architectural Group (PA)		D	415 394-1212	0
Huskies Lessee LLC		B	415 392-7755	0
Hvsf Transition LLC		D	415 477-1999	0
Hyatt Corporation		B	415 848-6050	0
Hyatt Corporation		A	415 788-1234	0
Hyatt Corporation		A	415 788-1234	0
Ic BP III Holdings Xii LLC		D	415 549-5054	0
Ic BP III Holdings Xv LLC		E	415 273-4250	0
Ideo LP		D	415 615-5000	0
Ifwe Inc (HQ)		D	415 946-1850	0
Iheartcommunications Inc		B	415 975-5555	0
Ihms (sf) LLC		C	415 781-5555	0
Impact Destinations & Events		E	415 766-4170	0
Imperial Parking (us) LLC		A	415 495-3909	0
Indus Corporation		D	415 202-1830	0
Indus Light & Magic (vanco) LL		D	415 292-4671	0
Industrial Grwth Partners V LP		C	415 882-4550	0
Influxdata Inc		C	415 295-1901	0
Ingenio Inc		C	415 248-4000	0
Ingenio LLC		D	415 992-8218	0
Inkling Systems Inc		D	415 975-4420	0
Insideview Technologies Inc		C	415 728-9309	0
Institute For Health & Healing		E	415 600-3503	0

2020 Directory of California
Wholesalers and Services Companies

(P-0000) Products & Services Section entry number
(PA)=Parent Co (HQ)=Headquarters (DH)=Div Headquarters

Company	SIC	EMP	PHONE	ENTRY #
Institute For One World Health		E	650 392-2510	0
Institute On Aging		C	415 600-2690	0
Institute On Aging (PA)		D	415 750-4101	0
Insurance Services Office Inc		B	415 874-4361	0
Integrated Clg Solutions Inc		E	415 821-6757	0
Intercom Inc		B	831 920-7088	0
Intercontinental Hotels		C	415 616-6500	0
Intercontinental Hotels Group		C	415 626-6103	0
Intercontinental Hotels Group		C	415 398-8900	0
Intercontinental Hotels Group		B	415 771-9000	0
Intercontinental Hotels Group		E	415 409-4600	0
International Bus Mchs Corp		C	415 545-4747	0
Internet Archive		C	415 561-6767	0
Internet Escrow Services Inc		D	888 511-8600	0
Interpacific Group Inc		A	415 442-0711	0
Interstate Hotels Resorts Inc		C	415 362-5500	0
Invitae Corporation (PA)		C	415 374-7782	0
Ironclad Inc		D	818 404-2777	0
Ita Group Inc		C	415 277-3200	0
J Walter Thompson USA LLC		D	415 268-5555	0
Jackson Lewis PC		E	415 394-9400	0
Japanese Cmnty Youth Council (PA)		D	415 202-7905	0
Jeffer Mngels Btlr Mtchell LLP		D	415 398-8080	0
Jetro Cash and Carry Entps LLC		D	415 920-2888	0
Jewis Vocational & Counseling		D	415 391-3600	0
Jewish Community Fedrtn San Fr (PA)		D	415 777-0411	0
Jewish Family and Chld Svcs (PA)		D	415 449-1200	0
Jewish Senior Living Group		D	415 562-2600	0
Jh Capital Partners LP		E	415 364-0300	0
Jiff Inc (HQ)		B	415 829-1400	0
Jillians San Francisco CA		D	415 369-6100	0
Jmp Securities LLC (DH)		D	415 835-8900	0
Jmt Charitable Foundation		D	415 974-6000	0
Jn Projects Inc		D	415 766-0273	0
John Paul USA (PA)		C	415 905-6088	0
John Stewart Company (PA)		D	415 345-4400	0
Joie De Vivre Hospitality LLC (PA)		E	415 835-0300	0
Joie De Vivre Hospitality LLC		D	415 986-2000	0
Jones Day Limited Partnership		D	415 626-3939	0
Jones Lang Lasalle Inc		C	415 395-4900	0
Joseph Cozza Salon Inc (PA)		D	415 433-3030	0
Joyent Inc		C	415 400-0600	0
Joyride Coffee Distrs LLC		D	718 841-7206	0
Jumpshot Inc		D	415 212-9250	0
Jumpstart Digital Mktg Inc (DH)		D	415 844-6336	0
K&L Gates LLP		D	415 882-8200	0
Kabam Inc (HQ)		D	604 256-0054	0
Kaiser Foundation Hospitals		D	415 833-2616	0
Kaiser Foundation Hospitals		A	415 833-2000	0
Kaiser Foundation Hospitals		C	415 833-9688	0
Kaiser Foundation Hospitals		A	415 833-2000	0
Kaiser Med Security Services		D	415 833-3683	0
Kallidus Inc		D	877 554-2176	0
Kcbs News Radio 74		D	415 765-4112	0
Keep Truckin Inc (PA)		E	855 434-3564	0
Keker Van Nest & Peters LLP		D	415 391-5400	0
Kennedy/Jenks Consultants Inc (PA)		D	415 243-2150	0
Kenshoo Inc (HQ)		C	877 536-7462	0
Ketchum Incorporated		D	415 984-6100	0
Keystone Strategy LLC		D	877 419-2623	0
Kfi		E	415 956-9812	0
Kgo Television Inc		C	415 954-7777	0
Khoros LLC (PA)		D	415 757-3100	0
Kid Stock Inc		D	415 753-3737	0
Kimpton Hotel & Rest Group LLC		D	415 885-2500	0
Kimpton Hotel & Rest Group LLC (HQ)		D	415 397-5572	0
Kimpton Hotel & Rest Group LLC		D	415 561-1100	0
Kimpton Hotel & Rest Group LLC		D	415 561-1111	0
Kimpton Hotel & Rest Group LLC		D	415 292-0100	0
Kindred Healthcare Oper LLC		D	415 922-5085	0
Kindred Healthcare Oper LLC		C	415 566-1200	0
Kindred Nursing Centers W LLC		C	415 673-8405	0
King & Spalding LLP		B	415 318-1200	0
Kipp Foundation		D	415 399-1556	0
Kirkland & Ellis LLP		C	415 439-1400	0
Kisco Senior Living LLC		D	415 664-6264	0
KMD Architects (PA)		D	415 398-5191	0
Kms Fishermans Wharf LP		D	415 561-1100	0
Kong Inc		E	415 754-9283	0
Kountable Inc		D	310 613-5481	0
Kpff Inc		D	415 989-1004	0
Kpisoft Inc		D	415 439-5228	0
Kpmg LLP		E	415 963-5100	0
Kqed Inc (PA)		B	415 864-2000	0
Kraft & Kennedy Inc		D	415 956-4000	0
L-O Soma Hotel Inc		B	415 974-6400	0
La Salle Apartments		D	415 647-0607	0
Landor Associates Intl Ltd (DH)		D	415 365-1700	0
Lateral Designs Inc		D	415 847-6618	0
Latham & Watkins LLP		D	415 391-0600	0
Lawson Roofing Co Inc		D	415 285-1661	0
Leadstack Inc		D	628 200-3063	0
Lee Burkhart Liu Inc		D	415 580-6740	0
Leemah Electronics Inc		C	415 394-1288	0
Leerink Partners LLC		D	800 778-1164	0
Legend Merchant Group Inc		E	415 957-9555	0
Legion Corporation		D	415 829-7307	0
Lendingclub Asset MGT LLC		B	415 632-5600	0
Lendingclub Corporation (PA)		B	415 632-5600	0
Level-It Installations Ltd		E	604 942-2022	0
Lever Inc		D	415 458-2731	0
Levin and Simes		E	415 426-3000	0
Lewis & Taylor LLC		C	415 781-3496	0
Lewis Brsbois Bsgard Smith LLP		C	415 362-2580	0
Lewis PR Inc (DH)		D	415 432-2400	0
Liberty Mutual Insurance Co		C	415 957-1175	0
Licensale Inc		D	604 681-6888	0
Lieff Cabraser Heimann & (PA)		D	415 788-0245	0
Lightbend Inc		D	877 989-7372	0
Linardos Enterprises Inc		D	415 644-0827	0
Linden Research Inc		B	415 243-9000	0
Little Sisters of Poor		C	415 751-6510	0
Littler Mendelson PC (PA)		B	415 433-1940	0
Littlethings Inc		D	917 364-9277	0
Live Nation Merchandise Inc (HQ)		E	415 247-7400	0
Livevox Inc (PA)		D	415 671-6000	0
LLP Downey Brand		D	415 848-4800	0
LLP Locke Lord		C	415 318-8800	0
LLP Moss Adams		C	415 956-1500	0
Lockheed Martin Corporation		C	415 402-0406	0
Long & Levit LLP		E	415 397-2222	0
Lookout Inc (PA)		C	650 241-2358	0
Low Ball & Lynch A Prof Corp (PA)		D	415 981-6630	0
Loyal3 Holdings Inc		D	415 981-0700	0
Lucasfilm Ltd LLC (DH)		C	415 623-1000	0
Lumetra Healthcare Solutions		E	415 677-2000	0
Luxor Cabs Inc		D	415 282-4141	0
Lyft Inc (PA)		B	844 250-2773	0
Lynch Gilardi & Grummer LLP		E	415 397-2800	0
M & H Realty Partners LP		D	415 693-9000	0
M Arthur Gensler Jr Assoc Inc (PA)		B	415 433-3700	0
M T C Holdings Inc (DH)		E	912 651-4400	0
Macarthur Transit Community		C	415 989-1111	0
Macfarlane Partners LLC (PA)		D	415 356-2500	0
Macqurie Arcft Lsg Svcs US Inc		D	415 829-6600	0
Malcolm Drilling Company Inc (PA)		C	415 901-4400	0
Maplebear Inc (PA)		D	888 246-7822	0
Marcum LLP		D	415 543-6900	0
Marcus & Millichap Real Estate		E	415 391-9220	0
Mariadb Usa Inc		D	847 562-9000	0
Marin Software Incorporated (PA)		C	415 399-2580	0
Marines Memorial Association		C	415 673-6672	0
Marketbridge Corp		D	240 752-1800	0
Marketwatch Inc (DH)		D	415 439-6400	0
Markmonitor Holdings Inc		B	415 278-8400	0
Markmonitor Inc (DH)		B	415 278-8400	0
Maroevich OShea & Coghlan		D	415 957-0600	0
Marriot Courtyard		E	415 775-1103	0
Marriott International Inc		D	415 947-0700	0
Marsh & McLennan Agency LLC		D	415 243-4160	0
Marsh USA Inc		D	415 743-8000	0
Mason Street Opco LLC		A	415 772-5000	0
Masonic Homes of California (PA)		B	415 776-7000	0
Massdrop Inc (PA)		D	415 340-2999	0
Matrix Resources Inc		C	415 644-0642	0
Maverick Hotel Partners LLC		B	415 655-9526	0
Maximus Real Estate Partners		D	415 584-4832	0
Maxson Young Assoc Inc		C	415 228-6400	0
Maynard Cooper & Gale PC		C	415 704-7433	0
Mazzetti Inc (PA)		E	415 362-3266	0
McCann World Group Inc (PA)		D	415 262-5500	0
McCann-Erickson Corporation (HQ)		D	415 348-5600	0
McCann-Erickson Usa Inc		C	415 262-5600	0
McKinsey & Company Inc		B	415 981-0250	0
McMillan Data Cmmnications Inc		D	415 826-5100	0
McMillan Electric		B	415 826-5100	0
MD P Foundation Inc		C	415 552-0240	0
Meals On Whels San Frncsco Inc		E	415 920-1111	0
Meany Wilson L P		E	415 905-5300	0
Medallia Inc (PA)		C	650 321-3000	0

G
E
O
G
R
A
P
H
I
C

	SIC	EMP	PHONE	ENTRY #		SIC	EMP	PHONE	ENTRY #
Mediabrands Worldwide Inc (HQ)		A	212 605-7000	0	Nvision Laser Eye Centers Inc		D	415 421-8667	0
Mekanism Inc (PA)		E	415 908-4000	0	Nyse Arca Inc		B	415 393-4000	0
Meltwater News US Inc (DH)		D	415 829-5900	0	Obscura Digital Incorporated		E	415 227-9979	0
Mercer (us) Inc		C	415 743-8700	0	Ocean Park Health Center		E	415 753-8100	0
Merchant Services Inc (PA)		B	817 725-0900	0	Odc (PA)		D	415 863-6606	0
Mercy Hsing California Xxxiv		D	415 503-0816	0	Odc Theater		D	415 863-6606	0
Meridian Industrial Trust		D	415 281-3900	0	Ogletree Deakins Nash Smoak		D	415 442-4810	0
Meridian Management Group		C	415 434-9700	0	Okabe International Inc (PA)		E	415 921-0808	0
Merlin Securities LLC		E	415 848-0269	0	Okta Inc (PA)		C	888 722-7871	0
Merrill Lynch Pierce Fenner		E	415 274-7000	0	Olympic Club		D	415 676-1412	0
Metromile Inc (PA)		D	888 244-1702	0	Olympic Club (PA)		C	415 345-5100	0
Metropolitan Club		D	415 673-0600	0	OMelveny & Myers LLP		C	415 984-8700	0
Metropolitan Elec Cnstr Inc		B	415 642-3000	0	Omni Hotels Corporation		B	415 677-9494	0
Metropolitan Life Insur Co		B	415 536-1065	0	On Lok Inc		D	415 292-8888	0
Metropolitan Trnsp Comm (PA)		C	415 778-6700	0	On Lok Senior Health Services (PA)		A	415 292-8888	0
Micro Holding Corp		A	415 788-5111	0	On24 Inc (PA)		B	877 202-9599	0
Micromenders Inc (PA)		D	415 344-0917	0	Onboardiq Inc		E	480 433-1197	0
Microsoft Corporation		C	415 972-6400	0	One Embarcadero Center Venture		D	415 772-0700	0
Mile Post Properties LLC		D	415 673-4711	0	One Heart World Which Will Do		D	415 379-4762	0
Milliman Inc		E	415 403-1333	0	One Medical Group Inc (PA)		D	415 578-3100	0
Minami Tamaki LLP		E	415 788-9000	0	One Medical Group Inc		D	415 529-4522	0
Mindfull Body		D	415 931-2639	0	One Medical Group Inc		D	212 530-2288	0
Minimalisms Inc		D	415 309-3108	0	One Nob Hill Associates LLC		D	415 392-3434	0
Mission Lane LLC		C	408 505-3081	0	One Workplace L Ferrari LLC		E	415 357-2200	0
Mission Linen Supply		C	510 429-7305	0	One10 LLC		D	415 398-3534	0
Mission Neighborhood Hlth Ctr (PA)		C	415 552-3870	0	One10 LLC		D	415 844-2200	0
Mission Pets Inc		E	415 904-9914	0	Opendoor Labs Inc (PA)		D	415 510-7213	0
Mission Stuart Ht Partners LLC		C	415 278-3700	0	Opentable Inc (HQ)		C	415 344-4200	0
Mitchell Engineering		E	415 227-1040	0	Opentv Inc (DH)		C	415 962-5000	0
Mixpanel Inc (PA)		D	415 688-4001	0	Opswat Inc (PA)		D	415 590-7300	0
Mizuho Securities USA Inc		D	415 268-5500	0	Optimizely Inc (PA)		B	415 376-4598	0
Mobpartner Inc		D	650 300-6388	0	Opus 2 International Inc		E	888 960-3117	0
Moffitt H C Hospital		C	415 476-1000	0	Oracle America Inc		D	415 908-3609	0
Monroe Residence Club		D	415 771-9119	0	Oracle Corporation		C	415 402-7200	0
Moov Corporation		C	877 666-8932	0	Orange Silicon Valley		D	415 243-1500	0
Morgan Lewis & Bockius LLP		A	415 393-2000	0	Orchard International Group (PA)		D	415 362-8878	0
Morgan Lewis & Bockius LLP		B	415 442-1000	0	Organic Inc (HQ)		C	415 581-5300	0
Morgan Stanley & Co LLC		B	415 693-6000	0	Organic Holdings Inc		B	415 581-5300	0
Morgans Hotel Group MGT LLC		C	415 775-4700	0	Orrick Hrrington Sutcliffe LLP (PA)		C	415 773-5700	0
Morrison & Foerster LLP (PA)		C	415 268-7000	0	Osterhout Group Inc		E	415 644-4000	0
Morrison & Foerster LLP		C	415 268-7178	0	Otis Elevator Company		C	415 546-0880	0
Morrison & Foerster LLP		E	925 295-3300	0	Otr Global LLC		E	415 675-7660	0
Motion Math Inc		C	415 590-2961	0	Oum & Co LLP (PA)		D	415 434-3744	0
Mufg Union Bank National Assn (DH)		A	415 705-7000	0	Outcast Agency LLC		C	415 392-8282	0
Mulesoft Inc		A	415 229-2009	0	Pac-12 Enteprises LLC		C	415 580-4200	0
Munger Tolles Olson Foundation		E	415 512-4000	0	Pacific Aviation Corporation		C	650 821-1190	0
Murphy (PA)		E	415 788-1900	0	Pacific Bell Telephone Company (HQ)		A	415 542-9000	0
Mursion Inc (PA)		D	415 746-9631	0	Pacific CST Mar Fireman Oilers (PA)		D	415 362-4592	0
Mv Transportation Inc		C	415 206-7386	0	Pacific Eagle Holdings Corp		D	415 398-2473	0
MWH Americas Inc		D	415 430-1800	0	Pacific Energy Fuels Company		A	415 973-8200	0
Mxb Battery Operations LP		D	415 230-8000	0	Pacific Eye Associated Inc		D	415 923-3007	0
Mya Systems Inc		E	877 679-0952	0	Pacific Gas and Electric Co		D	415 972-5654	0
Mypointscom LLC (HQ)		D	415 615-1100	0	Pacific Gas and Electric Co (HQ)		A	415 973-7000	0
National Assn Ltr Carriers		B	415 362-0214	0	Pacific Gas and Electric Co		B	415 695-3513	0
National Council Negro Women		D	415 564-4153	0	Pacific Growth Equities LLC		D	415 274-6800	0
National Opinion Research Ctr		C	415 315-2000	0	Pacific Park Management		C	415 440-4840	0
Ncc Group Inc (HQ)		D	415 268-9300	0	Pacific Structures Inc (PA)		C	415 970-5434	0
Netsource Inc		D	415 831-3681	0	Pacific Union Club		D	415 775-1234	0
Nevin Levy LLP A Partnership		D	415 800-5770	0	Pacific Union Co		D	415 474-6600	0
New Civic Company Ltd		C	415 986-1668	0	Pacific Union RE Group (DH)		D	415 929-7100	0
New Paradigm Productions Inc (PA)		D	415 924-8000	0	Pacific Ygnacio Corporation		D	925 939-3275	0
New Relic Inc (PA)		D	650 777-7600	0	Pae Consulting Engineers Inc		D	503 226-2921	0
New York Life Insurance Co		E	415 393-6060	0	Paganini Electric Corporation		C	415 575-3900	0
Nexant Inc (PA)		D	415 369-1000	0	Pagerduty Inc (PA)		C	844 800-3889	0
Nexstar Broadcasting Inc		B	415 441-4444	0	Pantheon Systems Inc (PA)		C	855 927-9387	0
Nextdoorcom Inc		D		0	Paragon Real Estate Group		D	415 323-4066	0
Nextroll Inc (PA)		C	877 723-7655	0	Parallel Advisors LLC		D	866 627-6984	0
Nibbi Bros Associates Inc		C	415 863-1820	0	Parenthood of Planned		D	415 821-1282	0
Nielsen Mobile LLC (DH)		C	917 435-9301	0	Paribas Asset Management Inc		D	415 772-1300	0
Ning Trucking Inc		D	415 544-2531	0	Park Hotels & Resorts Inc		B	415 771-1400	0
Nisum Technologies Inc		A	714 619-7989	0	Park Hotels & Resorts Inc		B	415 392-8000	0
Nitro Software Inc		C	415 632-4894	0	Parkmerced Investors LLC		E	877 243-5544	0
Nixon Peabody LLP		C	415 984-8200	0	Parkside Lending LLC		D	415 771-3700	0
No More Dirt Inc		C	415 821-6757	0	Parsons Corporation		D	415 490-2400	0
Nob Hill Properties Inc		B	415 474-5400	0	Parthenon Capital LLC		A	415 913-3900	0
Nomura Securities Intl Inc		B	415 445-3831	0	Parthenon DCS Holdings LLC		A	925 960-4800	0
Noodle Analytics Inc		B	415 412-2139	0	Pattern Energy Group LP (PA)		B	415 283-4000	0
Norcal Mutual Insurance Co (PA)		B	415 397-9703	0	Pattern Renewables 2 LP (HQ)		C	415 283-4000	0
Norcal Painters Inc		B	415 566-6800	0	Paul Hastings LLP		C	415 856-7000	0
Northern California Institute		B	415 750-6954	0	Paystack Inc		D	415 941-8102	0
Northern California Presbyteri		B	415 922-9700	0	People Center Inc		E	781 661-1232	0
Nossaman LLP		E	415 398-3600	0	Peopleai Inc		D	888 997-3675	0
Novogradac & Company LLP		E	415 356-8000	0	Pereira & ODell LLC (PA)		D	415 284-9916	0
Nozomi Networks Inc (HQ)		D	800 314-6114	0	Perkins Coie LLP		E	415 344-7000	0
Nuna Incorporated		D	415 942-5200	0	Permanente Medical Group Inc		D	415 833-2000	0

2020 Directory of California
Wholesalers and Services Companies

Name	SIC	EMP	PHONE	ENTRY #
Permanente Medical Group Inc		C	415 833-2000	0
Perquest Inc		D	510 740-6300	0
Pets Unlimited		C	415 563-6700	0
PHF Ruby LLC		C	415 885-4700	0
Philippine Airlines Inc		C	415 217-3100	0
Philotic Inc		D	510 730-1740	0
Picsart Inc		D	415 757-6800	0
Pier 39 Limited Partnership (PA)		C	415 705-5500	0
Pillsbury Winthrop Shaw		D	415 983-1000	0
Pillsbury Winthrop Shaw		B	415 983-1075	0
Pine & Powell Partners LLC		D	415 989-3500	0
Pinterest Inc		C	415 400-4645	0
Pinterest Inc (PA)		C	415 617-5585	0
Pioneer Square Hotel Company		E	415 346-2323	0
Pivotal Software Inc (HQ)		C	415 777-4868	0
Plaid Inc (PA)		D	415 799-1354	0
Planet Labs Inc (PA)		D	415 829-3313	0
Plangrid Inc (HQ)		D	800 646-0796	0
Playwrights Foundation Inc		D	415 626-2176	0
Polaris Research & Development		D	415 777-3229	0
Pomeroy Rcrtion Rhbltation Ctr (PA)		C	415 665-4100	0
Post Street Renaissance		B	415 563-0303	0
Postman Inc		D	415 796-6470	0
Postmates Inc (PA)		D	800 882-6106	0
Powerreviews Oc LLC		D	415 315-9208	0
Practice Fusion Inc (DH)		C	415 346-7700	0
Praetorian Group (PA)		E	415 962-8310	0
PRC		D	415 777-0333	0
Presidio Wealth Management LLC		E	415 449-2500	0
Pricewaterhousecoopers LLP		B	415 498-5000	0
Primitive Logic Inc		D	415 391-8080	0
Prn LLC (HQ)		D	415 805-2525	0
Progress Foundation		D	415 553-3100	0
Progress Glass Co Inc (PA)		C	415 824-7040	0
Project Open Hand (PA)		D	415 292-3400	0
Prologis Inc (PA)		B	415 394-9000	0
Prologis LP (HQ)		B	415 394-9000	0
Prophet Brand Strategy (PA)		E	415 677-0909	0
Prosper Funding LLC		D	415 593-5400	0
Prosper Marketplace Inc (PA)		D	415 593-5400	0
Prudential California Realty		D	415 664-9400	0
Prudential Insur Co of Amer		D	415 398-7310	0
Prudential Insur Co of Amer		D	415 486-3050	0
Prudential Realty Corp		D	415 566-9800	0
Ps24 Inc		D	415 834-5105	0
Public Policy Institute Cal (PA)		D	415 291-4400	0
Pubnub Inc		D	415 223-7552	0
PWC STRategy& (us) LLC		C	415 498-5000	0
Quadriga Inc		D	650 270-6326	0
Quality Planning Corporation		D	415 369-0707	0
Quantcast Corporation (PA)		D	800 293-5706	0
Quest Software Inc		D	415 373-2222	0
Quicksilver Delivery Inc		D	415 431-1600	0
Quinn Emanuel Urquhart		E	415 875-6600	0
Quri Inc		E	415 413-0100	0
R & S Investments LLC		D	415 591-2700	0
Radisson Ht Fishermans Wharf		D	415 392-6700	0
Rainbow Wtrprofing Restoration		C	415 641-1578	0
Rainforest Qa Inc		D	650 866-1407	0
Randstad North America Inc		C	415 397-3384	0
Ranger Pipelines Incorporated		C	415 822-3700	0
RE Barren Ridge 1 LLC		C	415 675-1500	0
RE La Mesa LLC		D	415 675-1500	0
Real Estate Equity Exchange		D	415 992-4200	0
Rec Center		C	415 831-6818	0
Reciprocity Inc		E	415 851-8667	0
Recology Inc (PA)		D	415 875-1000	0
Recology Inc		D	415 330-1300	0
Recology Inc		D	415 970-1582	0
Recology Inc		C	415 330-1400	0
Recology San Francisco		D	415 468-1752	0
Recurve Inc		D	510 540-4860	0
Redfin Corporation		B	206 340-8794	0
Redwood Credit Union		D	800 479-7928	0
Reed Smith LLP		C	415 659-5964	0
Reed Smith LLP		C	415 543-8700	0
Reed Smith LLP		C	415 543-8700	0
Reliable Caregivers Inc		C	415 436-0100	0
Renaissance Hotel MGT Co LLC		C	415 989-3500	0
Reneson Hotels Inc		C	415 621-7001	0
Rentjuice Corporation		D	415 376-0369	0
Republic Indemnity Co Amer		D	415 981-3200	0
Resmex Partners LLC		E	415 440-2737	0
Respond 2 LLC		D	415 398-4200	0
Restaurant Depot LLC		C	415 920-2888	0
Retailnext Inc		C	408 298-2585	0
Revinate Inc		D	415 671-4703	0
Rfj Corporation		D	415 824-6890	0
Rhumbix Inc		D	435 764-3014	0
Rhythmone LLC (DH)		D	415 655-1450	0
Richard J Mendoza Inc		D	415 644-0180	0
Richmond Area Mlt-Services Inc		D	415 392-4453	0
Richmond Area Mlt-Services Inc		D	415 689-5662	0
Richmond Area Mlt-Services Inc		D	415 579-3021	0
Richmond Area Mlt-Services Inc (PA)		D	415 800-0699	0
Richmond Dst Neighborhood Ctr (PA)		D	415 751-6600	0
Ricoh Usa Inc		D	415 392-6850	0
Riivos Inc		D	415 813-1840	0
Ritz-Carlton Hotel Company LLC		B	415 781-9000	0
Ritz-Carlton Hotel Company LLC		B	415 773-6168	0
Riverbed Technology Inc (HQ)		D	415 247-8800	0
Riviera Partners LLC (PA)		D	877 748-4372	0
RMR Construction Company		C	415 647-0884	0
Robert Half International Inc		C	415 434-1900	0
Ropes & Gray LLP		B	415 315-6300	0
Rosendin Electric Inc		C	415 495-9300	0
Rosendin Electric Inc		A	415 495-9300	0
Rp/Kinetic Parc 55 Owner LLC		B	415 392-8000	0
Rpx Corporation (HQ)		D	866 779-7641	0
RSM US LLP		D	415 848-5300	0
Ruth Barajas		E	415 977-6949	0
Ryder Truck Rental Inc		C	415 285-0756	0
S F Auto Parts Whse Inc		D	415 255-0115	0
Saarman Construction Ltd		C	415 749-2700	0
Sagan Systems Inc		D	650 387-8485	0
Sage Group		D	415 512-8200	0
Salesforcecom Inc (PA)		A	415 901-7000	0
Salesforcecom/Foundation		C	800 667-6389	0
Salesian Boys and Girls Club		D	415 397-3068	0
Salon Media Group Inc (PA)		D	415 870-7566	0
Salt Lake Hotel Associates LP (PA)		C	415 397-5572	0
Salvation Army		D	415 643-8000	0
Salvation Army Glden State Div (PA)		D	415 553-3500	0
San Francisco City & County		D	415 695-5660	0
San Francisco Aids Foundation (PA)		D	415 487-3000	0
San Francisco Ballet Assn		C	415 865-2000	0
San Francisco City & County		D	415 356-2700	0
San Francisco City & County		D	415 356-2700	0
San Francisco City & County		C	415 550-4600	0
San Francisco City Clinic		D	415 487-5500	0
San Francisco Federal Cr Un (PA)		C	415 775-5377	0
San Francisco Fertility Ctrs		D	415 834-3000	0
San Francisco Food Bank		D	415 282-1900	0
San Francisco Foundation		D	415 733-8500	0
San Francisco Health Authority (PA)		D	415 615-4407	0
San Francisco Hotel Associates		D	415 392-4666	0
San Francisco Hotel Group LLC		C	415 276-9888	0
San Francisco Ladies Protecti		C	415 931-3136	0
San Francisco Meritime N H P		D	415 561-7000	0
San Francisco Opera Assn		A	415 861-4008	0
San Francisco Partclr Cncl Sct		D	415 255-3525	0
San Francisco Radio Assets LLC (DH)		D	415 216-1300	0
San Francisco Symphony Inc (PA)		B	415 552-8000	0
San Francisco Tennis Club		D	415 777-9000	0
San Francisco Travel Assn		D	415 974-6900	0
San Francisco Zoological Soc		C	415 753-7080	0
San Frncisco Incoming Svcs LLC (PA)		D	415 777-2288	0
San Frncsco Mrtime Nat Pk Assn (PA)		E	415 561-6662	0
Sauce Labs Inc (PA)		D	855 677-0011	0
Scale Ai Inc		D	617 803-5667	0
Scott Street Senior Housing Co		C	415 345-5083	0
Scribd Inc		D	415 896-9890	0
Securitas SEC Svcs USA Inc		C	510 568-6818	0
Seiler LLP		D	415 392-2123	0
Selectquote Insurance Services (PA)		D	415 543-7338	0
Self-Help For Elderly		D	415 391-3843	0
Self-Help For Elderly (PA)		C	415 677-7600	0
Sentient Technologies USA LLC		E	415 422-9886	0
Severson & Werson A Prof Corp		D	415 398-3344	0
Seyfarth Shaw LLP		D	415 397-2823	0
Sfd Partners LLC		B	415 392-7755	0
Sfi 2365 Iron Point LLC		E	415 395-9701	0
Sfi Carlsbad LLC		E	415 395-9701	0
Sfo Airporter Inc		D	415 495-3909	0
Sfusd Building Ground		D	415 695-5508	0
Sfusd Jrotc Brigade		D	415 242-2546	0
Sharespost Inc		D	800 279-7754	0
Shartsis Friese LLP		C	415 421-6500	0
Sheedy Drayage Co (PA)		D	415 648-7171	0
Shell Vacations LLC		D	415 441-7100	0

GEOGRAPHIC

	SIC	EMP	PHONE	ENTRY #
Shenyang Zhong Yi Tin-Plating		C	415 788-2280	0
Sheppard Mullin Richter		D	415 434-9100	0
Sheraton LLC		B	415 362-5500	0
Shift Technologies Inc		D	415 800-2038	0
Shook Hardy & Bacon LLP		D	415 544-1900	0
Shoppingcom Inc		C	650 616-6500	0
Shorenstein Company LLC		E	415 772-7000	0
Shorenstein Properties LLC (PA)		C	415 772-7000	0
Shoreview Preservation LP		D	415 647-6922	0
Showpad Inc (HQ)		B	415 800-2033	0
Sideman & Bancroft LLP		D	415 392-1960	0
Sift Science Inc		D	415 882-7709	0
Sight Machine Inc		D	888 461-5739	0
Signaldemand Inc		E	415 356-0800	0
Signature Consultants LLC		C	415 544-7510	0
Silicon Valley Sftwr Group LLC		E	844 946-7874	0
Silver Lake Partners II LP		C	415 293-4355	0
Simpler Postage Inc (PA)		D	408 915-0063	0
Simpson Gumpertz & Heger Inc		D	415 495-3700	0
Skidmore Owings & Merrill LLP		C	415 981-1555	0
Skyblue Sewing Manufacturing		E	415 777-9978	0
Skyline Commercial Interiors (PA)		D	415 908-1020	0
Slack Technologies Inc (PA)		C	415 902-5526	0
Smg Holdings Inc		C	650 738-8737	0
Smith-Emery San Francisco Inc		C	415 642-7326	0
Smithgroup Inc		D	415 227-0100	0
Smithgroup Inc		C	313 442-8351	0
Snapdocs Inc		E	415 967-0136	0
Soc/General Services/Bpm		D	415 703-5341	0
Social Finance Inc (PA)		C	415 612-8229	0
Socialize Inc		E	415 529-4019	0
Society For San Francisco		D	415 554-3000	0
Sodexo Management Inc		D	925 325-9657	0
Soiree Valet Parking Service		C	415 284-9700	0
Soma Surgicenter		E	415 641-6889	0
Sony Electronics Inc		B	415 833-4796	0
South Market Child Care Inc		D	415 820-3500	0
Southbourne Inc		C	415 781-5555	0
Spire Global Inc (PA)		D	415 356-3400	0
Splunk Inc (PA)		C	415 848-8400	0
Sprig Electric Co		D	408 298-3134	0
Spus7 235 Pine LP		D	231 683-4200	0
Square Inc (PA)		E	415 375-3176	0
Squaretrade Inc (DH)		C	415 541-1000	0
Squire Patton Boggs (us) LLP		C	415 954-0334	0
St Anthony Foundation (PA)		E	415 241-2600	0
St Francis Yacht Club		D	415 563-6363	0
St Marys Med Ctr Foundation		A	415 668-1000	0
Stackla Inc		D	415 789-3304	0
Stadtner Co Inc		E	415 752-2850	0
Standard Pacific Capital LLC		D	415 352-7100	0
Standard Poors Fincl Svcs LLC		E	415 371-5000	0
Stanford Hotels Corporation (PA)		E	415 398-3333	0
Stantec Architecture Inc		D	415 882-9500	0
Stantec Consulting Svcs Inc		D	415 882-9500	0
Starcity Properties Inc		D	415 918-2224	0
Starwood Hotels & Resorts		C	415 284-4000	0
Starwood Htls & Rsrts Wrldwde		B	415 397-7000	0
Starwood Htls & Rsrts Wrldwde		D	415 777-5300	0
Starwood Htls & Rsrts Wrldwde		C	415 512-1111	0
State Bar of California (PA)		B	415 538-2000	0
State Compensation Insur Fund (PA)		C	888 782-8338	0
Steele Cis LLC		B	415 692-5000	0
Steelriver Infrastructure Fund (HQ)		C	415 291-2200	0
Stein & Lubin LLP		E	415 981-0550	0
Sterling Consulting Group LLC		D	415 248-7900	0
Steve Silver Productions Inc		D	415 421-4284	0
Stone & Youngberg LLC (PA)		C	415 445-2300	0
Strevus Inc		D	415 704-8182	0
Stripe Inc		A	888 963-8955	0
Stubhub Inc (HQ)		D	415 222-8400	0
Successor To San Francisco		D	415 749-2400	0
Sunday Bazaar Inc		D	415 621-0764	0
Sunrise Senior Living Inc		D	415 664-6264	0
Sunset Scavenger Company		B	415 330-1300	0
Sutter Bay Hospitals (HQ)		A	415 600-6000	0
Sutter Health		B	415 600-7034	0
Sutter Health		B	415 600-3311	0
Sutter Health		B	415 345-0100	0
Sutter Health		C	415 731-6300	0
Sutter Health		C	415 600-0110	0
Sutter Health		A	415 600-1020	0
Sutter Health		C	415 600-0140	0
Sutter Health		A	415 600-4280	0
Sutter Health		C	415 600-6000	0
Sutter Vsting Nrse Assn Hspice		D	415 600-6200	0
Swander Pace Capital LLC (PA)		A	415 477-8500	0
Swinerton Builders (HQ)		C	415 421-2980	0
Swinerton Incorporated (PA)		C	415 421-2980	0
Swirl Inc		D	415 276-8300	0
Switchfly Inc (PA)		C	415 541-9100	0
Syapse Inc		C	650 924-1461	0
Sypartners LLC (HQ)		D	415 536-6600	0
Sysdig Inc (PA)		D	415 872-9473	0
T Y Lin International (HQ)		D	415 291-3700	0
T-Mobile Usa Inc		C	415 440-5370	0
Tactivos Inc		D	415 687-2501	0
Takeuchi Financial Services		D	706 693-3600	0
Talentburst Inc		C	415 813-4011	0
Talix Inc		D	628 220-3885	0
Tapjoy Inc (PA)		D	415 766-6900	0
Tariff Building Associates LP (PA)		D	415 397-5572	0
Taulia Inc (PA)		D	415 376-8280	0
Techsoup Global (PA)		C	800 659-3579	0
Telegraph Hill Partners Invest (PA)		E	415 765-6980	0
Tenderloin Housing Clinic Inc		C	415 771-2427	0
Tenderloin Housing Clinic Inc (PA)		C	415 771-9850	0
Textainer Equipment Mgt US Ltd (DH)		D	415 434-0551	0
Textainer Group Holdings Ltd (DH)		D	415 434-0551	0
Textaner Eqp Income Fund II LP		D	415 434-0551	0
The Charles Schwab Trust Co (HQ)		E	415 371-0518	0
Third & Mission Associates LLC		E	415 341-8457	0
Thismoment Inc		C	415 200-4730	0
Thoma Bravo LLC		B	415 263-3660	0
Thomas Weisel Partners LLC (DH)		B	415 364-2500	0
Thomson Reuters (markets) LLC		D	415 677-2500	0
Thornton Tomasetti Inc		D	415 365-6900	0
Thousandeyes Inc (PA)		D	415 513-4526	0
TI Gotham Inc		D	415 982-5000	0
Ticketweb LLC		E	415 901-0210	0
Tides Inc (PA)		C	415 561-6400	0
Tides Center		C	415 359-9401	0
Tides Network		D	415 561-6400	0
Tm Financial Forensics LLC (PA)		D	415 692-6350	0
Todays Hotel Corporation (PA)		C	415 441-4000	0
Tonal Systems Inc		D	855 698-6625	0
Toolworks Inc (PA)		B	415 733-0990	0
Topdown Consulting Inc		D	888 644-8445	0
Topgolf Media LLC (HQ)		D	214 377-0615	0
Topica Inc		D	415 344-0800	0
Towns End Studios LLC		A	415 802-7936	0
Tpg Sixth Street Partners LLC		C	415 743-1500	0
Tradeshift Holdings Inc (HQ)		D	800 381-3585	0
Tradeshift Inc (DH)		D	800 381-3585	0
Transamerica Cbo I Inc		D	415 983-4000	0
Transamerica Intl Holdings		C	415 983-4000	0
TransMontaigne PDT Svcs LLC		B	415 576-2000	0
Treadwell & Rollo Inc (DH)		E	415 955-9040	0
Treeline Staffing		E	415 819-7195	0
Triage Consulting Group (PA)		B	415 512-9400	0
Trifacta Inc (PA)		D	415 429-7570	0
Trinity Capital Corporation (DH)		D	415 956-5174	0
Troutman Sanders LLP		D	415 477-5700	0
Truecar Inc		B	415 821-8270	0
Trulia Inc (HQ)		B	415 648-4358	0
Trustarc Inc		D	415 520-3400	0
Tunein Inc		C	650 319-7100	0
Turk & Eddy Associates LP		D	415 474-6524	0
Turner Construction Company		D	415 705-8900	0
Twilio Inc (PA)		C	415 390-2337	0
Twist Bioscience Corporation		C	800 719-0671	0
TYlin Intl Group Ltd (PA)		C	415 291-3700	0
Uber Technologies Inc (PA)		A	415 612-8582	0
Ubi Soft Entertainment		D	415 547-4000	0
UBS Financial Services Inc		C	415 954-6700	0
UBS Financial Services Inc		D	415 398-6400	0
UBS Securities LLC		D	415 352-5650	0
Ucsf Aids Health Project		D	415 476-6445	0
United Behavioral Health (HQ)		C	415 547-1403	0
United Biosource LLC		D	415 293-1340	0
United California Glass & Door		D	415 824-8500	0
United Parcel Service Inc OH		C	415 252-4564	0
United Way of Bay Area (PA)		D	415 808-4300	0
Unity Software Inc (HQ)		E	415 848-2533	0
Universal Paragon Corporation (PA)		B	415 468-6676	0
Universal Protection Svc LP		C	415 759-5056	0
University Cal San Francisco		D	415 476-9000	0
University Cal San Francisco		A	415 476-7000	0
University Cal San Francisco		E	415 476-1611	0
University Cal San Francisco		D	415 353-3155	0

Mergent email: customerrelations@mergent.com
1630

2020 Directory of California
Wholesalers and Services Companies

(P-0000) Products & Services Section entry number
(PA)=Parent Co (HQ)=Headquarters (DH)=Div Headquarters

	SIC	EMP	PHONE	ENTRY #
University Cal San Francisco		B	415 567-6600	0
University Cal San Francisco		E	415 476-5608	0
UPS Supply Chain Solutions Inc		A	650 635-2693	0
UPS Supply Chain Solutions Inc		E	415 775-6644	0
URS Holdings Inc (DH)		B	415 774-2700	0
Usag Ansbach Financial MGT Div		D	210 466-1376	0
Usag Rheinland Pfalz Fincl MGT		D	210 466-1376	0
Usag Vicenza Italy Dmwr F M D		D	210 466-1376	0
Usag Wiesbaden Fincl MGT Div		D	210 466-1376	0
USI Insurance Services Nat Inc		C	628 201-9001	0
Ustream Inc		D	415 489-9400	0
Van Ness Hotel Inc		D	415 673-4711	0
Van Sark Inc		D	415 362-5888	0
Vector Talent II LLC		A	415 293-5000	0
Vegiworks Inc		D	415 643-8686	0
Venables/Bell & Partners LLC		C	415 288-3300	0
Vendini Inc (PA)		D	415 693-9611	0
Veritable Vegetable Inc		D	415 641-3500	0
Veritiv Operating Company		D	415 586-9160	0
Verticalresponse Inc		C	866 683-7842	0
Vestek Systems Inc (DH)		D	415 344-6000	0
Veterans Health Administration		D	415 750-2009	0
Vida Health Inc		D	408 203-7959	0
Vintrust Inc		E	877 846-8787	0
Viscira LLC		D	415 848-8010	0
Vitalant Research Institute (PA)		C	415 567-6400	0
Viva Soma Lessee Inc		A	415 974-6400	0
Vladigor Investment Inc		D	415 558-9274	0
Volta Charging LLC		D	415 735-5169	0
Volume Services Inc		D	415 972-1500	0
VSC Sports Inc		D	415 820-3525	0
W R Hambrecht Co Inc (PA)		D	415 551-8600	0
W S B & Associates Inc		D	510 444-6266	0
W S B & Associates Inc		C	415 864-3510	0
Wachovia A Division Wells F		A	415 571-2832	0
Walkme Inc (PA)		D	855 492-5563	0
Walkup Melodia Kelly		E	415 981-7210	0
Walt Disney Family Museum		D	415 345-6800	0
Walter E McGuire RE Inc (PA)		D	415 929-1500	0
Walter E McGuire RE Inc		E	415 296-0123	0
Warwick California Corporation		D	415 992-3809	0
Watchit Media Inc		C	702 740-1700	0
Weber Shandwick		D	415 262-5600	0
Webpass Inc		D	415 233-4100	0
Weisscomm Group Ltd (PA)		D	415 362-5018	0
Wells Capital Management Inc (DH)		E	415 396-8000	0
Wells Fargo & Company (PA)		C	866 249-3302	0
Wells Fargo Bank National Assn		E	415 396-6267	0
Wells Fargo Bank National Assn		D	415 396-6161	0
Wells Fargo Bank National Assn		B	415 777-9497	0
Wells Fargo Bank National Assn		E	415 222-1360	0
Wells Fargo Bank National Assn		A	415 394-4021	0
Wells Fargo Clearing Svcs LLC		C	415 291-1200	0
Wells Fargo Intl Bond CIT		C	415 396-4943	0
Wentworth Hauser & Violich Inc		D	415 981-6911	0
Wested (PA)		C	415 565-3000	0
Western Alliance Bank		D	415 230-4834	0
Western Messenger Service Inc		C	415 487-4229	0
Westside Lodge		E	415 864-1515	0
Weststar Marine Services Inc		C	415 495-3191	0
Wetherby Asset Management		D	415 399-9159	0
Wfc Holdings LLC (HQ)		C	415 396-7392	0
Wideorbit Inc (PA)		C	415 675-6700	0
Wikimedia Foundation Inc		C	415 839-6885	0
Wilbur-Ellis Company LLC (DH)		B	415 772-4000	0
Wildenradt-Mcmurray Inc		D	510 835-5500	0
Will Perkins Inc		D	415 856-3000	0
William McGann MD		D	415 221-0665	0
Wilson Sonsini Goodrich & Rosa		D	415 947-2000	0
Wonolo Inc		D	415 766-7692	0
Woodruff-Sawyer & Co (PA)		C	415 391-2141	0
Workforcelogic		D	707 939-4300	0
Workshare Technology Inc		C	415 590-7700	0
Wsp USA Buildings Inc		C	415 398-3833	0
Wsp USA Inc		C	415 243-4600	0
Wtw Delaware Holdings LLC		C	415 733-4100	0
Wu Yee Childrens Services		D	415 677-0100	0
Wu Yee Childrens Services		D	415 677-0100	0
Xoom Corporation		C	415 777-4800	0
Yammer Inc		C	415 796-7400	0
Yellow Cab Cooperative Inc		D	415 333-3333	0
Yelp Inc (PA)		D	415 908-3801	0
Yhb San Francisco LLC		D	415 421-7500	0
Youappi Inc		D	646 854-3390	0
Young & Rubicam Inc		C	415 882-0600	0

	SIC	EMP	PHONE	ENTRY #
Young Brdcstg of San Francisco		C	415 441-4444	0
Young Dowlin L		E	760 397-4104	0
Young Electric Co		C	415 648-3355	0
Young Mens Christian Assnsf		D	415 447-9622	0
Young Mens Christian Assoc SF		D	415 831-4093	0
Young Mens Christian Assoc SF		D	415 447-9602	0
Young Mens Christian Assoc SF (PA)		E	415 777-9622	0
Young Mens Christian Assoc SF		D	415 666-9622	0
Young Mens Christian Assoc SF		D	415 957-9622	0
Young Mens Christian Assoc SF		D	415 885-0460	0
Yourpeople Inc		A	888 249-3263	0
Yume Inc (DH)		D	650 591-9400	0
Zelle LLP		E	415 693-0700	0
Zendesk Inc (PA)		C	415 418-7506	0
Zenpayroll Inc (PA)		C	800 936-0383	0
Zignal Labs Inc		D	415 683-7871	0
Zinio Systems Inc		D	415 494-2700	0
Zoe Holding Company Inc		C	415 421-4900	0
Zoosk Inc (HQ)		D	415 728-9543	0
Zurich American Insurance Co		C	415 538-7100	0
Zvents Inc		E	408 376-7346	0
Zynga Inc (PA)		C	855 449-9642	0
Airport Commisions		A	650 821-5000	0
Alliance Ground Intl LLC		D	650 821-0855	0
American Airlines Inc		B	650 877-6000	0
Sfo Shuttle Bus Inc		C	650 877-0430	0
Signature Flight Support Corp		D	650 877-6800	0
Swissport Usa Inc		C	650 821-6220	0
Swissport Usa Inc		C	571 214-7068	0
Thrifty Car Rental		C	877 283-0898	0
United Airlines Inc		C	650 634-4209	0
United Airlines Inc		D	650 634-7800	0
United Airlines Inc		C	650 634-4469	0
United Airlines Inc		D	650 634-2772	0
United Airlines Inc		D	650 634-2085	0

SAN GABRIEL, CA - Los Angeles County

	SIC	EMP	PHONE	ENTRY #
Ahmc Healthcare Inc		A	626 248-3452	0
Alderwood Inc		D	626 289-4439	0
Cal Southern Services		D	626 281-5942	0
Country Villa Service Corp		C	626 285-2165	0
Facey Medical Foundation		D	626 576-0800	0
Fernview Convalescent Hospital		D	626 285-3131	0
Information & Referral Fed Los		D	626 350-1841	0
Life Care Centers America Inc		D	626 289-5365	0
Longwood Management Corp		D	626 289-3763	0
Normans Nursery Inc (PA)		E	626 285-9795	0
Park Cleaners Inc (PA)		D	626 281-5942	0
Park Hotels & Resorts Inc		C	626 270-2700	0
Pine Grove Healthcare		D	626 285-3131	0
Pta CA Cong Prents Emperor Sch		D	626 548-5084	0
San Gabriel Ambulatory Sugery		A	626 300-5300	0
San Gabriel Country Club		D	626 287-9671	0
San Gabriel Nursery and Flor (PA)		D	626 286-0787	0
San Gbriel Vly Med Ctr Fndtion		A	626 289-5454	0
San Marino Manor		E	626 446-5263	0
Temple City Youth Dev Fund		D	626 548-5085	0

SAN GERONIMO, CA - Marin County

	SIC	EMP	PHONE	ENTRY #
National Golf Properties LLC		D	415 488-4030	0

SAN JACINTO, CA - Riverside County

	SIC	EMP	PHONE	ENTRY #
Healthcare MGT Systems Inc		D	951 654-9347	0
Matthews International Corp		E	951 654-9123	0
Millenia Development		E	951 660-5691	0
Physicians For Healthy Hospita		C	951 652-2811	0
Riverside-San Bernardino		D	951 654-0803	0
Soboba Band Luiseno Indians		A	951 665-1000	0
Valley Wide Recreation Pk Dst (PA)		D	951 654-1505	0

SAN JOAQUIN, CA - Fresno County

	SIC	EMP	PHONE	ENTRY #
Standard Cattle LLC		D	559 693-1977	0

SAN JOSE, CA - Santa Clara County

	SIC	EMP	PHONE	ENTRY #
22nd Century Technologies Inc		C	866 537-9191	0
24 7ai Inc (PA)		C	650 385-2247	0
4 CS Council		C	408 487-0747	0
40 Hrs Inc		A	408 414-0158	0
4d Inc		C	408 557-4600	0
8x8 Inc (PA)		C	408 727-1885	0
A & A Mechanical Contractors		D	408 225-1321	0
A A A Furnace AC Co		D	408 293-4717	0
A Is For Apple Inc		C	877 991-0009	0
A10 Networks Inc (PA)		C	408 325-8668	0
Abbott Stringham An		D	408 377-8700	0
ABF Freight System Inc		E	408 435-8550	0
Able Exterminators Inc		D	408 251-6500	0

GEOGRAPHIC

	SIC	EMP	PHONE	ENTRY #
Accenture LLP		C	408 817-2100	0
Accenture LLP		C	650 213-2000	0
Ace Parking Management Inc		D	408 437-2185	0
Acer America Corporation **(DH)**		D	408 533-7700	0
Achiever Christian Pre-Schl &		E	408 264-2345	0
Acronics Systems Inc		D	408 432-0888	0
Action Day Nrseries Prmry Plus		E	408 266-8952	0
Adminstrtive Office of US Crts		D	510 535-5200	0
Adobe Inc **(PA)**		A	408 536-6000	0
Advent Group Ministries Inc		D	408 281-0708	0
Aecom Usa Inc		C	408 392-0670	0
Aeris Communications Inc **(PA)**		D	408 557-1900	0
Aerospace & Marine Intl		E	408 360-0440	0
Air Systems Inc.		A	408 280-1666	0
Airdrome Orchards Inc **(PA)**		E	408 297-6461	0
Airgas Usa LLC		D	408 998-6380	0
Alfa Tech Cnslting Engners Inc **(PA)**		D	408 487-1200	0
All Fab Prcsion Sheetmetal Inc		D	408 279-1099	0
All Seasons Homecare		D	408 378-0900	0
Alldragon International Inc		E	408 410-6248	0
Alliance Credit Union **(PA)**		D	408 445-3386	0
Allied Landscape Svcs S Inc		D	408 310-8476	0
Alliedbarton Security Svcs LLC		B	408 954-8274	0
Almaden Golf & Country Club		D	408 323-4812	0
Almaden Valley Athletic Club		D	408 445-4900	0
Alsco Inc		C	408 279-2345	0
American Airlines Inc		D	408 291-3800	0
American Cancer Soc Cal Div		E	408 265-5535	0
American Funding		E	408 269-4238	0
American Metal & Iron Inc		D	408 452-0777	0
American Residential Svcs LLC		D	650 856-1612	0
American Residential Svcs LLC		D	408 435-3810	0
American Tire Distributors		E	408 435-3340	0
Amtel Inc		E	408 615-0522	0
Andrian Inc		E	408 434-0730	0
AON Consulting Inc		D	408 321-2500	0
Aopen America Incorporated		D	408 586-1200	0
Apria Healthcare LLC		D	949 639-2163	0
Aptiv Digital LLC		D	818 295-6789	0
Apx Inc **(PA)**		E	408 517-2100	0
Aqualine Piping Inc		D	408 745-7100	0
Aquinas Corporation		C	408 248-7100	0
Aramark Spt & Entrmt Group LLC		C	408 999-5735	0
Aramark Unf & Career AP LLC		D	408 243-9824	0
Arcadia Management Service Co		E	408 286-4440	0
Ariosa Diagnostics Inc		C	408 229-7500	0
Asian Amercn Recovery Svcs Inc		C	408 271-3900	0
Associated Students Cdc		D	408 924-6988	0
AT&T Corp		D	408 729-8400	0
AT&T Corp		D	408 871-3870	0
AT&T Services Inc		C	408 554-3335	0
AT&T Services Inc		D	408 973-7504	0
Atlantic Aviation Svc		E	408 297-7552	0
Atria Senior Living Inc		D	408 266-1660	0
Automation Anywhere Inc **(PA)**		D	888 484-3535	0
Avnet Inc		D	408 501-3925	0
Bad Boys Bail Bonds Inc **(PA)**		D	408 298-3333	0
Bam Advisor Services LLC		D	800 366-7266	0
Barbaccia Properties		D	408 225-1010	0
Bay Area Surgical MGT LLC		E	408 297-3432	0
Baynote Inc		D	866 921-0919	0
Bea Systems Inc **(HQ)**		A	650 506-7000	0
Beacon Roofing Supply Inc		D	408 293-5947	0
Belmont Bruns Construction Inc		D	408 977-1708	0
Berryessa Union School Dst		D	408 923-1960	0
Bhatnagar Law Office		E	408 564-8051	0
Biarca Inc **(PA)**		D	408 564-4465	0
Biggs Cardosa Associates Inc **(PA)**		D	408 296-5515	0
Bill Brown Construction Co.		D	408 297-3738	0
Bill Brown Construction Co.		D	408 297-3738	0
Bizmatics Inc **(PA)**		C	408 873-3030	0
Blach Construction Company **(PA)**		D	408 244-7100	0
Blossom Valley Cnstr Inc		D	408 993-0766	0
Blue Jeans Network Inc **(PA)**		D	408 550-2828	0
Brandvia Alliance Inc **(PA)**		D	408 955-0500	0
Breakout Prison Outreach		D	408 702-2405	0
Brinks Incorporated		D	408 436-7717	0
Bristlecone Incorporated		A	650 386-4000	0
Brocade Cmmnctions Systems Inc		D	408 333-4300	0
Brookdale Lving Cmmunities Inc		C	408 445-7770	0
Burr Pilger Mayer Inc		E	408 961-6300	0
Business Furn Solutions Inc **(PA)**		D	408 325-3100	0
C & O Painting Inc		E	408 279-8011	0
C H Reynolds Electric Inc		B	408 436-9280	0
C R S Drywall Inc		D	408 998-4360	0
Cadence Design Systems Inc **(PA)**		A	408 943-1234	0
Cadent Inc		C	408 470-1000	0
Cadent Tech Inc **(HQ)**		D	408 642-6400	0
Caliber Bodyworks Texas Inc		D	408 972-0300	0
California Drywall Co **(PA)**		D	408 292-7500	0
California Schl Employees Assn **(PA)**		C	408 473-1000	0
California United Mech Inc **(PA)**		B	408 232-9000	0
California Waste Solutions Inc **(PA)**		D	510 832-8111	0
California Water Service Co **(HQ)**		C	408 367-8200	0
Cambium Networks Inc		C	847 640-3809	0
Careage Inc		E	408 238-9751	0
Carlton Senior Living Inc		C	408 972-1400	0
Casavina Foundation Corp		C	408 238-9751	0
Catholic Charities of Santa CL **(PA)**		C	408 468-0100	0
Cavendish Kinetics Inc		E	408 627-4504	0
Cbre Inc		D	408 453-7400	0
Cbsj Financial Corporation		D	408 792-4600	0
Ccintegration Inc **(PA)**		E	408 228-1314	0
Center For Employment Training **(PA)**		D	408 287-7924	0
Central Valley Clinic Inc.		E	408 885-5400	0
Ch2m Hill Inc		E	408 436-4936	0
Challenger Schools		D	408 723-0111	0
Chelbay Schuler & Chelbay **(PA)**		D	408 288-4400	0
Chester C Lehmann Co Inc **(PA)**		D	408 293-5818	0
Chicago Title Company		C	408 292-4212	0
Choices For Children **(PA)**		D	408 297-3295	0
Christian Counseling Centers		D	408 559-1115	0
Cintas Corporation No 2		D	408 262-6700	0
Ciphercloud Inc **(PA)**		D	408 519-6930	0
Cisco Ironport Systems LLC **(HQ)**		B	650 989-6500	0
Cisco Systems Capital Corp **(HQ)**		C	610 386-5870	0
Cisco Webex LLC **(PA)**		A	408 435-7000	0
City II Enterprises Inc		E	408 275-1200	0
City of San Jose		B	408 277-5277	0
City of San Jose		D	408 794-6400	0
City of San Jose		B	408 392-3600	0
City of San Jose		C	408 226-6765	0
Ckl Construction Inc		B	408 244-7042	0
Clarion Hotel San Jose Airport		D	408 453-5340	0
Classic Custom Vacations Inc		C	800 221-3949	0
Classic Parking Inc		A	408 278-1444	0
Classic Vacations LLC		C	800 221-3949	0
Cloudradiant Corp		A	408 256-1527	0
Coassure Inc		D	408 244-0400	0
Coast Insulation Contrs Inc **(DH)**		D	386 304-2222	0
Cohesity Inc **(PA)**		B	855 926-4374	0
Coldwell Banker Prof Group		D	408 383-1044	0
Coldwell Banker RE LLC		D	408 723-3300	0
Colliers Parrish Intl Inc		D	408 282-3800	0
Comcast Corporation		D	408 216-2878	0
Command Security Corporation		D	650 574-0911	0
Common Ground Ldscp MGT Inc.		E	408 278-9807	0
Commonwealth Central Credit Un **(PA)**		D	408 531-3100	0
Complete Genomics Inc		B	650 943-2800	0
Computer Task Group Inc		C	408 573-6070	0
Computer Task Group Inc.		B	800 992-5350	0
Corventis Inc **(PA)**		D	408 790-9300	0
County Building Materials Inc		D	408 274-4920	0
Creative Security Company Inc		B	408 295-2600	0
Crestwood Behavioral Hlth Inc		D	408 275-1067	0
Crunch LLC		D	650 257-8000	0
Cupertino Electric Inc **(PA)**		B	408 808-8000	0
Cws Utility Services Corp		B	408 367-8200	0
Dapcon Inc		D	408 573-7200	0
De Mattei Construction Inc		D	408 295-7516	0
Della Maggiore Tile Inc		D	408 286-3991	0
Deloitte & Touche LLP		B	408 704-4000	0
Deloitte Tax LLP		B	408 704-4000	0
DH Smith Company Inc		D	408 532-7617	0
Diablo Landscape Inc.		D	408 487-9620	0
Digex Inc.		E	408 468-5000	0
Dinyari Construction Inc		E	408 289-5400	0
Dma Claims Inc		D	800 649-7602	0
Doubletree By Hilton San Jose		D	408 453-4000	0
Doudell Trucking Company **(PA)**		C	408 263-7300	0
Dpr Construction A Gen Partnr		E	408 370-2322	0
Dtex Systems Inc.		E	408 418-3786	0
Durham School Services		D	408 448-0740	0
Eah Elena Gardens LP		B	415 295-8840	0
Echelon Security Inc.		D	408 436-8844	0
ECi Corporation A Corp Nev **(PA)**		D	408 941-9268	0
Econosoft Inc.		D	408 442-3663	0
Edges Electrical Group LLC **(HQ)**		D	408 293-5818	0
Edgewater Networks Inc		D	408 351-7200	0
Ees Residential Group Homes		D	408 265-8780	0

Mergent email: customerrelations@mergent.com

1632

2020 Directory of California
Wholesalers and Services Companies

(P-0000) Products & Services Section entry number
(PA)=Parent Co (HQ)=Headquarters (DH)=Div Headquarters

Company	SIC	EMP	PHONE	ENTRY #
Einfochips Inc (HQ)		D	408 496-1882	0
Ek Health Services Inc (PA)		D	408 973-0888	0
El Camino Hospital		C	650 940-7000	0
El Camino Hospital		C	650 988-4825	0
Empress Care Center		D	408 287-0616	0
Ensighten Inc (HQ)		D	650 249-4712	0
Epicentro Advertising Mktg Svc		E	408 453-0353	0
Eric Stark Interiors Inc		D	408 441-6136	0
Ericsson Inc		A	408 597-3600	0
Ernst & Young LLP		A	408 947-5500	0
Estes Express Lines Inc		E	408 286-3894	0
Etrigue Corporation		E	408 490-2900	0
European Paving Designs Inc		D	408 283-5230	0
Exis Inc		E	408 944-4600	0
Facility Masters Inc (PA)		B	408 436-9090	0
Fair Isaac Corporation (PA)		B	408 535-1500	0
Family and Children Services		D	408 292-9353	0
Fcs Software Solutions Limited		D	408 324-1203	0
Federal Express Corporation		C	800 463-3339	0
Fedex Ground Package Sys Inc		B	800 463-3339	0
Fertility & Reproductive		D	408 358-2500	0
First Alarm SEC & Patrol Inc (PA)		C	408 866-1111	0
First Technology Federal Cr Un (PA)		D	855 855-8805	0
Fluor Enterprises Inc		D	408 256-0853	0
Fluor Facility & Plant Svcs		C	408 256-1333	0
Fnti Fidelity Nat Tech Imagin		E	408 942-1780	0
Foothill Health Center Inc		C	408 729-4290	0
Force10 Networks Inc		A	800 289-3355	0
Forescout Technologies Inc (PA)		D	408 213-3191	0
Foundtion For Hispanic Educatn (PA)		D	408 585-5022	0
Four Points San Jose Downtown		D	408 282-8800	0
Fourth Street Bowl		E	408 453-5555	0
FPI Management Inc		C	408 267-3952	0
Frito-Lay North America Inc		D	559 312-8553	0
Frontiir Corporation		D	510 996-2071	0
Fujitsu America Inc		D	408 746-8419	0
Fusion Mphc Group Inc		C	408 324-1353	0
Fusionone Inc		D	408 282-1200	0
Gaia Interactive Inc		C	408 573-8800	0
Galli Produce Company		D	408 436-6100	0
Garden City Inc		A	408 244-3333	0
Gardner Family Hlth Netwrk Inc (PA)		E	408 457-7100	0
Gda Technologies Inc (HQ)		D	408 753-1191	0
General George W Sliney Basha		D	408 296-3423	0
George M Robinson & Co (PA)		D	510 632-7017	0
Giarretto Institute		E	408 453-7616	0
Gilbane Building Company		D	408 660-4400	0
Gilbane Building Company		D	408 660-4400	0
Glenrock Group		D	408 323-9900	0
Global Industry Analysts Inc		A	408 528-9966	0
Global Infotech Corporation		D	408 567-0600	0
Globallogic Inc (PA)		C	408 273-8900	0
Golden Living LLC		C	408 923-7232	0
Golden Living LLC		E	408 255-5555	0
Good Samaritan Hospital LP (DH)		A	408 559-2011	0
Goodwill of Silicon Valley (PA)		D	408 998-5774	0
Graham Contractors Inc		E	408 293-9516	0
Grand Intelligence LLC.		D	408 954-7368	0
Grant Thornton LLP		E	408 275-9000	0
Green Bits Inc		D	408 596-3341	0
Green Valley Corporation (PA)		E	408 287-0246	0
Greenbriar Homes Communities		D	510 497-8200	0
Greenwaste Recovery Inc		E	408 283-4804	0
Greystone Plastering Inc		D	408 298-5934	0
Gringteam Inc		B	408 453-4000	0
Guavus Inc (HQ)		D	650 243-3400	0
Gypsum Dry Wall Supply Co		E	408 993-9710	0
H M H Engineers		D	408 487-2200	0
H&H Resolution LLC		D	408 362-2293	0
Hacienda Invlved Parents Staff		D	408 535-6259	0
Harding Mktg Cmmunications Inc (PA)		D	408 345-4545	0
Hayes Mansion Conference Ctr		C	408 226-3200	0
HCA Inc		C	408 729-2801	0
Hd Supply Construction Supply		E	408 428-2000	0
Health & Rehabilitation Center		E	408 377-9275	0
Health Trust (PA)		C	408 513-8700	0
Heat Software Intermediate Inc		B	408 601-2800	0
Heavenly Construction Inc		D	408 723-4954	0
Hensel Phelps Construction Co		C	408 452-1800	0
Heritage Bank of Commerce (HQ)		C	408 947-6900	0
Herman Sanitarium		C	408 269-0701	0
Hetrosys LLC.		D	408 270-0240	0
Hewlett Packard Enterprise Co (PA)		C	650 687-5817	0
Hid Global Safe Inc		D	408 453-1008	0
Hoffman Agency (PA)		D	408 286-2611	0
Home Port Inc		D	408 377-4134	0
Homeguard Incorporated (PA)		D	408 993-1900	0
Hopkins & Carley A Law Corp (PA)		D	408 286-9800	0
Hospice of Valley (PA)		E	408 947-1233	0
Host International Inc		C	408 294-1702	0
Hsbc Finance Corporation		C	408 796-3600	0
Hyatt Corporation		B	408 453-3006	0
Hyatt Equities LLC		B	408 993-1234	0
Ice Delivery Systems Inc		C	408 640-4625	0
Ics Integrated Comm Systems		D	408 491-6000	0
Imerys Filtration Minerals Inc (DH)		E	805 562-0200	0
Immersion Medical Inc		D	408 467-1900	0
Incline Incorporated		C	408 454-1140	0
Incube Labs LLC (PA)		D	408 457-3700	0
Indian Hlth Ctr Snta Clara Vly		C	408 445-3400	0
Indosys Corporation		C	408 705-1953	0
Insite Digestive Health Care		C	408 471-2222	0
Inspira Inc		D	408 247-9500	0
International Bus Mchs Corp		A	408 463-2000	0
International Bus Mchs Corp		C	408 452-4800	0
International Bus Mchs Corp		B	408 927-1080	0
Intero Real Estate Svcs Inc		C	408 574-5000	0
Intero Real Estate Svcs Inc		E	408 558-3600	0
Invesmart Inc		D	408 961-2800	0
Iscs Inc		C	408 362-3000	0
Italent Corporation (PA)		C	408 496-6200	0
Itron Networked Solutions Inc (HQ)		B	669 770-4000	0
Ixsystems Inc (PA)		D	408 943-4100	0
J & J Air Conditioning Inc		D	408 920-0662	0
J T R Company Inc (PA)		D	408 975-7733	0
J T R Company Inc		E	408 293-3272	0
Jabil Silver Creek Inc (HQ)		C	669 255-2900	0
Jacobs Engineering Group Inc		D	408 436-4936	0
Jade Global Inc (PA)		D	408 899-7200	0
Jensen Corp Landscape Contr		C	408 446-4881	0
Jensen Corporate Holdings Inc (PA)		C	408 446-1118	0
Jensen Landscape Services Inc		C	408 446-1118	0
Jeppesen Dataplan Inc		C	408 961-2825	0
JF Shea Construction Inc		B	408 225-1475	0
John A Maida Enterprises		E	408 254-3100	0
John F Dmingue Attorney At Law		C	408 591-5180	0
Johns Dog Food Distributing		D	408 275-1943	0
Johnson Service Group Inc		A	408 728-9510	0
Josephines Prof Staffing (PA)		C	408 943-0111	0
Kaiser Foundation Hospitals		A	408 361-2100	0
Kaiser Foundation Hospitals		B	408 972-6010	0
Kaiser Foundation Hospitals		A	408 972-7000	0
Kaiser Foundation Hospitals		C	408 972-3000	0
Kaiser Foundation Hospitals		D	408 972-3376	0
Kaiser Foundation Hospitals		C	408 972-6700	0
Keenan & Associates		E	408 441-0754	0
Kinder Mrgan Lqds Trminals LLC		D	408 435-7399	0
Kioxia America Inc (DH)		C	408 526-2400	0
Koning & Associates Inc (PA)		E	408 265-3800	0
Kranem Corporation		C	650 319-6743	0
Krty Ltd A Cal Ltd Partnr		E	408 293-8030	0
Lab-Gistics LLC		C	650 309-2627	0
Labcyte Inc (DH)		D	408 747-2000	0
Landcare USA LLC.		D	408 727-4099	0
Landmark Protection Inc		B	408 293-6300	0
Lark Avenue Car Wash		D	408 371-2565	0
Lee Bros Foodservices Inc (PA)		C	408 275-0700	0
Leed International LLC		E	650 861-7883	0
Legacy Transportation Svcs Inc (PA)		C	408 294-9800	0
Lg Display America Inc (HQ)		D	408 350-0190	0
Liberty Healthcare of Oklahoma		D	408 532-7607	0
Lightbeam Power Company Gridle		D	800 696-7114	0
Lightbeam Pwr Gridley Main LLC		D	800 696-7114	0
Lims Inc		D	925 803-7795	0
Lincoln Glen Manor		C	408 267-1492	0
Liveworld Inc (PA)		D	800 301-9507	0
Loglogic Inc		C	408 215-5900	0
LPA Inc		C	408 780-7200	0
LSI - Silvercreek LLC		D	408 226-8080	0
Lynx Software Technologies Inc (PA)		D	408 979-3900	0
M Arthur Gensler Jr Assoc Inc		E	408 885-8100	0
M K Technical Services Inc		E	408 528-0401	0
Macdonald Mott LLC		D	408 321-5900	0
Magma Design Automation Inc (HQ)		B	408 565-7500	0
Magnus Tech Solutions Inc		D	408 963-0808	0
Mariner Health Care Inc		C	408 298-3950	0
Mariner Health Care Inc		D	408 377-9275	0
Marquez Brothers Advg Agcy		D	408 960-2700	0
Marquez Brothers Intl Inc (PA)		D	408 960-2700	0
Marsh USA Inc		D	408 467-5600	0

Employment Codes: A=Over 500 employees, B=251-500,
C=101-250, D=51-100, E=50

2020 Directory of California
Wholesalers and Services Companies

© Mergent Inc. 1-800-342-5647

1633

GEOGRAPHIC

	SIC	EMP	PHONE	ENTRY #		SIC	EMP	PHONE	ENTRY #
Maxim Healthcare Services Inc		C	408 914-7478	0	Pricewaterhousecoopers LLP		A	408 817-3700	0
McManis Faulkner A Prof Corp		E	408 279-8700	0	Procera Networks Inc **(HQ)**		D	510 230-2777	0
ME Fox & Company Inc		D	408 435-8510	0	Propel Software Corporation		C	408 571-6300	0
Meals On Wheels-The Health Tr		E	408 961-9870	0	Property Maintenance Company **(PA)**		C	408 297-7849	0
Mednax Inc		D	408 254-8257	0	Proxim Wireless Corporation		C	408 383-7600	0
Meriwest Credit Union **(PA)**		C	408 363-3200	0	Pulse Secure LLC **(HQ)**		D	408 372-9600	0
Merrill Lynch Pierce Fenner		E	408 283-3000	0	Q Analysts LLC **(PA)**		D	408 907-8500	0
MGM Drywall Inc		D	408 292-4085	0	Qal Affiliate Inc		E	408 238-5111	0
Mike Rovner Construction Inc		D	408 453-6070	0	Qct LLC		A	510 270-6111	0
Minerva Networks Inc **(PA)**		D	800 806-9594	0	Quail Hill Investments Inc		C	408 978-9000	0
Mission Truck Sales		D	408 436-2920	0	Quest Dgnstics Clncal Labs Inc		B	408 975-1015	0
Mobica US Inc		A	650 450-6654	0	R E Cuddie Co		E	408 998-1250	0
Mobile Hm Communities of Amer **(PA)**		C	408 279-5200	0	R L Safety Inc		E	408 557-0887	0
Mobilygen Corporation		D	408 601-1000	0	R-Bros Painting Inc		E	408 291-6820	0
Mochanin LLC		D	408 432-7259	0	Race Street Partners Inc **(PA)**		D	408 294-6161	0
Momentum For Mental Health		D	408 261-7777	0	Radius Product Development Inc		A	408 361-6000	0
Monster Mechanical Inc		E	408 727-8362	0	Radonich Corp		E	408 275-8888	0
Monterey Bay Masonry Inc		E	408 289-8295	0	Ranch Golf Club		D	408 270-0557	0
Morgan Stanley & Co LLC		D	408 947-2200	0	Rando AAA Hvac Inc		D	408 293-4717	0
Mt Eden Nursery Co Inc **(PA)**		E	408 213-5777	0	Rawitser Golf Shop Mike		E	408 441-4653	0
Mt Hamilton Grange		D	408 513-5528	0	Redseal Inc		D	408 641-2200	0
Nagarro Inc **(DH)**		D	408 436-6170	0	Resonate Inc **(PA)**		C	408 545-5500	0
ND Systems Inc		D	408 776-0085	0	Responselogix Inc		D	408 220-6505	0
Nds Surgical Imaging LLC		C	408 776-0085	0	Restaurant Depot LLC		C	408 344-0107	0
Neals Janitorial Service		E	408 271-9944	0	Retailnext Inc **(PA)**		D	408 884-2162	0
Netapp Inc		C	408 822-3803	0	RFI Enterprises Inc **(PA)**		D	408 298-5400	0
Netcontinuum Inc		D	408 961-5600	0	Rgis LLC		D	408 243-9141	0
Netenrich Inc **(PA)**		D	408 436-5900	0	Ricoh Usa Inc		D	408 436-1000	0
Netronix Integration Inc **(PA)**		D	408 573-1444	0	Robert Half International Inc		D	408 961-2975	0
New Age Electric Inc		D	408 279-8787	0	Robert Half International Inc		E	408 293-8611	0
New York Life Insurance Co		D	408 392-9782	0	Robinson and Wood Inc		D	408 298-7120	0
Nexsentio Inc		D	408 392-9249	0	Ron Filice Enterprises Inc		E	408 294-0477	0
Next Door Sltons To Dom Vlence		D	408 279-2962	0	Rosendin Electric Inc **(PA)**		A	408 286-2800	0
Nidek Incorporated		E	510 226-5700	0	Rosendin Electric Inc		A	408 321-2200	0
Nor-Cal Moving Services		D	408 954-1175	0	Rossi Hamerslough Reishchl &		D	408 244-4570	0
Normandin Auto Brokers		D	408 266-2824	0	Royal Coach Tours **(PA)**		C	408 279-4801	0
Northwest Landscape Maint Co		E	408 298-6489	0	Royalty Tours		E	408 279-4801	0
Nsg Technology Inc		B	408 547-8770	0	RSM US LLP		D	408 572-4440	0
Nu Horizons Electronics Corp		E	408 946-4154	0	Rural/Metro Corporation		C	888 876-0740	0
Nutanix Inc **(PA)**		A	408 216-8360	0	S J General Building Maint		D	408 392-0800	0
Nuvoton Technology Corp Amer		D	408 544-1718	0	Sage Intacct Inc **(HQ)**		E	408 878-0900	0
O C McDonald Co Inc		C	408 295-2182	0	Salas OBrien Engineers Inc **(PA)**		E	408 282-1500	0
Ocadian Care Centers LLC		E	408 295-2665	0	Samsung SDS America Inc		D	408 638-8800	0
OConnor Hospital		D	408 947-2929	0	Samsung Semiconductor Inc **(DH)**		C	408 544-4000	0
OConnor Hospital **(HQ)**		A	408 947-2500	0	San Andreas Regional Center **(PA)**		C	408 374-9960	0
OConnor Imaging Med Group Inc		D	408 947-2992	0	San Jose Airport Garden Hotel		D	408 793-3300	0
Oocl (usa) Inc		D	408 576-6543	0	San Jose Airport Hotel LLC		C	408 793-3939	0
Ooyala Inc **(HQ)**		D	650 961-3400	0	San Jose Chld Discovery Museum		D	408 298-5437	0
Opera San Jose Inc		D	408 437-4450	0	San Jose Conservation Corps		C	408 283-7171	0
Operatix Inc		D	408 332-5796	0	San Jose Country Club		D	408 258-4901	0
Oracle Corporation		B	408 276-3822	0	San Jose Fairmont Lessee LLC		B	408 998-1900	0
Oracle Corporation		B	408 390-8623	0	San Jose Medical Systems Lp		A	408 259-5000	0
Oracle Corporation		B	925 694-6258	0	San Jose Museum of Art Assn		D	408 271-6840	0
Outfront Media Inc		C	408 457-0111	0	San Jose Redevelopment Agency		D	408 535-8500	0
Outreach & Escort Inc **(PA)**		D	408 678-8585	0	San Jose Sharks LLC		C	408 999-6810	0
Pacific Groservice Inc		B	408 727-4826	0	San Jose Silicon Valley Cham		D	408 291-5250	0
Pacific West Security Inc		D	801 748-1034	0	San Jose State University		E	408 924-1000	0
Packet Design Inc		D	408 490-1000	0	San Jose Surgical Supply Inc **(PA)**		E	408 293-9033	0
Panasonic Corp North America		D	201 348-7000	0	San Jose Water Company **(HQ)**		C	408 288-5314	0
Pathway Society		E	408 244-1834	0	San Jose Water Company		C	408 298-0364	0
Paypal Inc **(HQ)**		C	877 981-2163	0	San Joses Healthcare & Well		D	408 295-2665	0
Paypal Holdings Inc **(PA)**		D	408 967-1000	0	Santa Clara County of		D	408 435-2000	0
Pds Tech Inc		A	408 916-4848	0	Santa Clara Cnty Fderal Cr Un **(PA)**		D	408 282-0700	0
Peninsula Family Service		D	650 403-4300	0	Santa Clara County of		A	408 792-2704	0
Penske Automotive Group Inc		E	408 293-7688	0	Santa Clara County of		C	408 885-7200	0
Permanente Medical Group Inc		D	408 972-6883	0	Santa Clara County of		E	408 885-6818	0
Pernixdata Inc		D	408 724-8413	0	Santa Clara County of		D	408 282-3200	0
Petalon Landscape MGT Inc		D	408 453-3998	0	Santa Clara County of		C	408 435-2111	0
Phase 3 Communications		D	408 946-9011	0	Santa Clara County of		C	408 885-7354	0
Physical Rehabilitation Netwrk		E	408 570-0510	0	Santa Clara Valley Corporation		D	408 947-1100	0
Piedmont Transfer & Storage		E	408 288-5600	0	Santa Clara Valley Medical Ctr		B	408 885-6300	0
Pillar Data Systems Inc		B	408 503-4000	0	Santa Clara Valley Medical Ctr		A	408 885-5730	0
Pittsburg Wholesale Groc Inc **(PA)**		C	916 372-7772	0	Santa Clara Valley Trnsp Auth **(PA)**		A	408 321-2300	0
Pivot Systems Inc		C	408 435-1000	0	Santa Clara Valley Trnsp Auth		C	408 321-5559	0
Pixim Inc		C	650 934-0550	0	Santa Clara Valley Trnsp Auth		B	408 321-5555	0
Planned Prnthood Mar Monte Inc		C	408 287-7529	0	Santa Clara Valley Water **(PA)**		A	408 265-2600	0
Planned Prnthood Mar Monte Inc **(PA)**		D	408 287-7532	0	Santa Teresa Golf Club		D	408 225-2650	0
Platinum Facilities Services		C	408 998-9004	0	Santana Row Hotel Partners LP		C	408 551-0010	0
Platinum Roofing Inc		D	408 280-5028	0	Saratoga Capital Inc		D	408 286-1000	0
Playmar Inc		D	408 324-1930	0	Sarpa-Feldman Enterprises Inc		D	408 982-1790	0
Playphone Inc		D	408 261-6200	0	Satellite Healthcare Inc **(PA)**		D	650 404-3600	0
Plda Inc		D	408 273-4528	0	Satellite Healthcare Inc		D	408 258-8720	0
Plum Healthcare Group LLC		D	408 998-8447	0	Scaleflux Inc		D	408 628-2291	0
Plx Technology Inc		C	408 435-7400	0	SCC ESA Dept of Risk Mgmt		D	408 441-4207	0
Polaris Networks Incorporated		D	408 625-7273	0	Schaper Construction Inc **(PA)**		D	408 437-0337	0

2020 Directory of California
Wholesalers and Services Companies

(P-0000) Products & Services Section entry number
(PA)=Parent Co (HQ)=Headquarters (DH)=Div Headquarters

	SIC	EMP	PHONE	ENTRY #
Schwager Davis Inc		C	408 281-9300	0
SE Scher Corporation		A	408 844-0772	0
Second Harvest Silicon Valley (PA)		C	408 266-8866	0
Service Workers Local 715 (PA)		D	408 678-3300	0
Sharks Sports & Entrmt LLC		A	408 287-7070	0
Sierra Lumber Co		C	408 286-7071	0
Sigma Networks Inc		C	408 876-4002	0
Significant Cleaning Svcs LLC		C	408 559-5959	0
Silicon Valley Hwang LLC		C	408 452-0200	0
Silicon Valley Mechanical Inc		D	408 943-0380	0
Silicon Vly Educatn Foundation		A	408 790-9400	0
Silicon Vly Mntrey Bay Cncil I (PA)		D	408 279-2086	0
Silicon Vly SEC & Patrol Inc (PA)		C	408 267-1539	0
Siliconware Usa Inc (DH)		E	408 573-5500	0
Silver Creek Vly Cntry CLB Inc		C	408 239-5775	0
Silver Shield Security		C	408 435-1111	0
Silverline Construction Inc		C	408 437-8810	0
SIM Investment Corporation		D	408 445-3310	0
Sims Group USA Corporation		D	408 494-4242	0
Sjb Child Development Centers (PA)		C	408 538-0200	0
Sjsu Foundation		A	408 924-1410	0
SJW Group (PA)		B	408 279-7800	0
Sk Hynix America Inc (HQ)		D	408 232-8000	0
Skybox Security Inc (PA)		D	408 441-8060	0
Skylite Networks		D	403 934-9349	0
Slakey Brothers Inc		E	408 494-0460	0
Smart & Final Stores Inc		B	408 251-0109	0
Smashon Inc		E	855 762-7466	0
SMC Corporation of America		E	408 943-9600	0
Sofa Holdco Dev LLC		D	847 713-0680	0
Soleeva Energy Inc		D	408 396-4954	0
Somansa Technologies Inc		D	408 297-1234	0
Sony Biotechnology Inc		E	408 352-4257	0
Sourcewise		D	408 350-3200	0
South Bay Airport Shuttle		D	408 225-4444	0
South Bay Regl Public Safety T		E	408 270-6494	0
South Bay Senior Solutions Inc		D	408 370-6360	0
South Valley Plumbing Inc		C	408 265-5566	0
Southern Counties Oil Co		E	408 251-0811	0
Southern Glazers Wine		D	408 750-3540	0
Sperasoft Inc		B	408 715-6615	0
Sprig Electric Co (PA)		C	408 298-3134	0
SSC San Jose Operating Co LP		D	408 249-0344	0
Staffing Solutions Inc		D	408 980-9000	0
Stanford Health Care		A	408 426-4900	0
Starlight Management Group		D	408 334-7456	0
State Compensation Insur Fund		C	888 782-8338	0
Steinberg Hart (PA)		D	408 295-5446	0
Stella Technology Incorporated		D	402 350-1681	0
Structural Integrity Assoc Inc (PA)		D	408 978-8200	0
Student Trnsp Amer Inc		D	408 998-8275	0
Student Un San Jose State Univ		D	408 924-6405	0
Suddath Relo Sys of No CA		D	408 288-3030	0
Suddath Relocation Systems of		E	904 858-1273	0
Suez Wts Systems Usa Inc		D	408 360-5900	0
Sumitomo Electric Device Innov		D	408 232-9500	0
Summit Hr Worldwide Inc		D	408 884-7100	0
Sun Basket Inc (PA)		D	408 669-4418	0
Sunrise Senior Living Inc		D	408 223-1312	0
Sunrun Installation Svcs Inc		A	408 746-3062	0
Super Talent Technology Corp		A	408 957-8133	0
Synchronoss Technologies Inc		B	800 575-7606	0
Syniverse Technologies LLC		C	408 324-1830	0
Systech Integrators Inc		C	408 441-2700	0
Talent Space Inc		D	408 330-1900	0
Tamtron Corporation (DH)		D	408 323-3303	0
Taos Mountain LLC (PA)		B	408 324-2800	0
Team San Jose		A	408 295-9600	0
Tech Museum of Innovation (PA)		D	408 795-6116	0
Tech Museum of Innovation		D	408 795-6168	0
Techaisle LLC		E	408 253-4416	0
Technology Credit Union		D	408 467-2382	0
Technology Credit Union (PA)		C	408 451-9111	0
Ted Cooper/Cooper Industries		E	408 358-3060	0
Terry Meyer		D	408 723-3300	0
Thomas Mark & Company Inc (PA)		C	408 453-5373	0
Threatmetrix Inc		C	408 200-5700	0
Tivo Corporation (PA)		D	408 519-9100	0
Topbuild Services Group Corp		D	408 882-0411	0
Tradecom Med Transcription Inc		C	408 225-9200	0
Traditions Golf LLC		D	408 323-5200	0
Traffic Management Inc		E	877 763-5999	0
Transpak Inc (PA)		C	408 254-0500	0
Tranzeal Inc		E	408 834-8711	0
Tredence Inc (PA)		C	408 819-2336	0

	SIC	EMP	PHONE	ENTRY #
Trim Tech Industries Inc		E	408 573-4514	0
Tsmc North America (HQ)		C	408 382-8000	0
Tti Inc		D	408 414-1450	0
Tumi Inc		D	408 244-6512	0
Tupaz Day Care Services Inc		D	408 377-1622	0
Tupaz Homes LLC		D	408 377-1622	0
U S Perma Inc		E	408 436-0600	0
UBS Financial Services Inc		E	408 282-8402	0
Underwriters Laboratories Inc		B	248 427-5300	0
Underwriters Laboratories Inc		C	408 493-9910	0
Unifirst Corporation		D	408 297-8101	0
Unilab Corporation		B	408 927-8331	0
Unish Corporation		E	408 708-9300	0
United Administrative Services		C	408 288-4400	0
United Parcel Service Inc OH		B	408 291-2942	0
United Site Services Cal Inc		C	408 295-2263	0
United Temp Services Inc		D	408 472-4309	0
Unity Care Group		D	408 971-9822	0
Univar Solutions USA Inc		D	408 435-8649	0
Universal Bldg Svcs & Sup Co		C	408 995-5111	0
Univision Television Group Inc		D	415 538-8000	0
URS Group Inc		D	408 297-9585	0
User Zoom Inc		D	408 533-8619	0
Valin Corporation (PA)		D	408 730-9850	0
Valley US Inc		D	408 260-7342	0
Vat Incorporated (DH)		E	781 935-1446	0
Ventrum Inc		D	510 304-0852	0
Verity Health System Cal Inc		C	408 947-2500	0
Verity Medical Foundation (HQ)		D	408 278-3000	0
Viaworld Advanced Products		D	408 597-7051	0
Vidhwan Inc (PA)		C	408 289-8200	0
Vidhwan Inc		C	408 521-0167	0
Villages Golf and Country Club		C	408 274-4400	0
Virident Systems Inc		C	408 573-5000	0
Virtual Instruments Corp (PA)		D	408 579-4000	0
Visby Medical Inc		D	408 650-8878	0
Visualon Inc		C	408 645-6618	0
Vivente 1 Inc		D	408 279-2706	0
Vivente 2 Inc		D	408 279-2706	0
Vn Home Health Care LP		D	408 998-0550	0
Vormetric Inc (HQ)		D	408 433-6000	0
Vss Monitoring Inc (HQ)		C	408 585-6800	0
Waste Connections Cal Inc (DH)		C	408 282-4400	0
Watlow Electric Mfg Co		D	408 776-6646	0
Watson Carton		D	408 979-9618	0
Wells Fargo Bank National Assn		E	408 998-3714	0
West Coast Legal Service Inc		E	408 938-6520	0
West Hotel Partners LP		C	408 947-4450	0
West San Crlos Ht Partners LLC		C	408 998-0400	0
Western Alliance Bank		D	408 423-8500	0
Whitehat Security Inc		D	408 343-8300	0
Willow Glen Hsing Partners LP		E	408 267-7252	0
Willow Glen Villa A		C	408 266-1660	0
Winbond Electronics Corp Amer		D	408 943-6666	0
Winchester Mystery House LLC		D	408 247-2101	0
Work2future Foundation		C	408 794-1234	0
Work2future Foundation		C	408 216-6202	0
WW Grainger Inc		C	408 432-8200	0
Wyndham International Inc		C	408 451-3050	0
Xactly Corporation (HQ)		C	408 977-3132	0
Xpo Logistics Freight Inc		D	408 435-3876	0
Yang C Park		D	408 260-8066	0
Yellow Cab Company Penninsula		C	408 739-1234	0
YMCA of Silicon Valley		B	650 493-9622	0
YMCA of Silicon Valley		C	408 298-1717	0
YMCA of Silicon Valley		D	408 226-9622	0
YMCA of The Mid-Peninsula Inc		D	650 493-9622	0
Yosh Enterprises Inc		B	408 287-4411	0
Young Womens Christian Associ		D	408 295-4011	0
Yuja Inc		C	888 257-2278	0
Zanker Road Resource MGT Ltd		D	408 457-1189	0
Zell Associates Inc (PA)		D	408 978-1950	0
Zenith Talent Corporation		C	844 467-2300	0
Zone24x7 Inc (PA)		B	408 268-8589	0
Zoom Video Communications Inc (PA)		C	888 799-9666	0
Zscaler Inc (PA)		C	408 533-0288	0
Zspace Inc		D	408 498-4050	0

SAN JUAN BAUTISTA, CA - San Benito County

	SIC	EMP	PHONE	ENTRY #
Anthony Botelho		D	831 623-4228	0
Christopher Ranch LLC		D	831 636-8722	0
Earthbound Farm LLC (DH)		A	831 623-7880	0
Seminis Inc		D	831 623-4554	0

SAN JUAN CAPISTRANO, CA - Orange County

	SIC	EMP	PHONE	ENTRY #
Action Sports Retailer		D	949 226-5744	0

Employment Codes: A=Over 500 employees, B=251-500,
C=101-250, D=51-100, E=50

2020 Directory of California
Wholesalers and Services Companies

© Mergent Inc. 1-800-342-5647

1635

GEOGRAPHIC

	SIC	EMP	PHONE	ENTRY #
Atria Senior Living Inc		C	949 661-1220	0
Birtcher Andrson Investors LLC		E	949 545-0526	0
Carparts Technologies		C	949 488-8860	0
Cox Communications Inc		C	949 240-1212	0
Diamondpeo LLC		C	714 728-5186	0
Emerald Expositions LLC (HQ)		B	949 226-5700	0
Ensign Southland LLC		C	949 487-9500	0
Enterprise Rent A Car		C	949 240-7000	0
Freedom Properties-Hemet LLC		E	949 489-0430	0
Ip Access International		E	949 655-1000	0
Kaiser Foundation Hospitals		D	888 988-2800	0
Marbella Country Club		C	949 248-3700	0
Marbella Golf & Country Club		C	949 248-3700	0
Medusind Solutions Inc (HQ)		A	949 240-8895	0
Merit Logistics LLC		A	949 481-0685	0
Nichols Inst Reference Labs (DH)		A	949 728-4000	0
Pioneer Sands LLC		D	949 728-0171	0
Rancho Mission Viejo LLC (PA)		D	949 240-3363	0
San Juan Golf Inc		E	949 493-1167	0
Solag Incorporated		D	949 728-1206	0
Southern Cal Prmnnte Med Group		E	949 234-2139	0
Sunrise Senior Living LLC		D	949 248-8855	0

SAN LEANDRO, CA - Alameda County

	SIC	EMP	PHONE	ENTRY #
14766 Wash Ave Operations LLC		A	510 352-2211	0
A-Para Transit Corp		C	510 562-5500	0
Aa/Acme Locksmiths Inc		D	510 483-6584	0
Acco Engineered Systems Inc		C	510 346-4300	0
Alameda County Industries Inc		E	510 357-7282	0
Alco Iron & Metal Co (PA)		D	510 562-1107	0
Alemeda County Industries LLC		D	510 357-7282	0
All Saintsidence Opco LLC		D	510 481-3200	0
American Medical Response Inc		C	415 794-9204	0
American Residential Svcs LLC		D	510 729-6227	0
Apple Inns Inc		E	510 895-1311	0
Apria Healthcare LLC		D	510 346-4000	0
ARC of Alameda County (PA)		C	510 357-3569	0
Avis Rent A Car System Inc		C	510 562-8828	0
Bae Sys Sierra Detroit Allison (DH)		D	510 635-8991	0
Bay Area Installations Inc (PA)		D	510 895-8196	0
Bluewater Envmtl Svcs Inc		D	510 346-8800	0
Buckeye Fire Equipment Company		B	510 483-1815	0
Carlton Senior Living		D	510 636-0660	0
Carrier Corporation		B	510 347-2000	0
Cinemark Usa Inc		D	510 276-9684	0
Cintas Corporation No 3		E	510 352-6330	0
Cnh Industrial America LLC		E	510 351-2015	0
Coast Counties Truck & Eqp Co		D	510 568-6933	0
Community MBL Diagnostics LLC		D	925 516-6851	0
Continental Western Corp (PA)		E	510 352-3133	0
County of Alameda		C	510 481-4141	0
Crossroad Services Inc		B	714 728-3915	0
Cummins Pacific LLC		B	510 351-6101	0
Dal-Tile Corporation		D	510 357-6197	0
Datapark Inc		D	510 483-7275	0
Dependable Highway Express Inc		E	510 357-2223	0
Dependable Highway Express Inc		D	510 357-2223	0
Dhx-Dependable Hawaiian Ex Inc		C	510 686-2600	0
Dunbar Armored Inc		D	510 569-7400	0
East Bay Innovations		D	510 618-1580	0
Engility LLC		C	510 357-4610	0
Estes Express Lines Inc		D	510 635-0165	0
Fayaka Airways Inc		C	800 771-5489	0
Federal Express Corporation		D	510 347-2430	0
Fedex Freight West Inc		D	650 244-9522	0
Fidelity Home Energy Inc (PA)		D	858 220-7784	0
Frank Ghiglione Inc (PA)		C	510 483-7000	0
Frank Ghiglione Inc		D	510 483-2063	0
Galena Equipment Rental LLC		E	510 638-8100	0
H A Bowen Electric Inc		D	510 483-0500	0
Hilton Garden Inn		D	510 346-5533	0
Independent Electric Sup Inc (DH)		C	510 877-9850	0
J R Pierce Plumbing Company		D	510 483-5473	0
K/P LLC		E	510 614-7800	0
Kaimanu Outrigger Canoe Club		D	510 895-0435	0
Kaiser Foundation Hospitals		A	510 454-1000	0
Kindred Healthcare Oper Inc		B	510 357-8300	0
Kissito Health Case Inc		D	510 357-4015	0
KMA Emergency Services Inc		D	510 614-1420	0
Koffler Elec Mech Apprts Repai		D	510 567-0630	0
Kp LLC		C	510 346-0729	0
L3 Applied Technologies Inc		C	510 577-7100	0
Laboratory Corporation America		B	510 635-4555	0
Landmark Event Staffing		A	510 632-9000	0
Marymount Villa LLC		D	510 895-5007	0
McIntyre		D	510 614-5890	0

	SIC	EMP	PHONE	ENTRY #
Medical Couriers Inc		D	650 872-1144	0
Monarch Bay Golf Resort		D	510 895-2162	0
Mv Transportation Inc		C	510 351-1603	0
N V Heathorn Inc		D	510 569-9100	0
Nan Fang Dist Group Inc		D	510 297-5382	0
Osisoft LLC (PA)		B	510 297-5800	0
Pacific Coast Container Inc (PA)		C	510 346-6100	0
Penhall Company		D	510 357-8810	0
Permanente Medical Group Inc		D	510 454-1000	0
Peterson Machinery Co (PA)		D	541 302-9199	0
R & S Erection Incorporated (PA)		D	510 483-3710	0
Ransome Company		E	510 686-9900	0
Regional Center of E Bay Inc		C	510 618-6100	0
Roofing Constructors Inc		C	415 648-6472	0
Royal Ambulance		C	510 568-6161	0
Royal Investigation Patrol Inc		D	510 352-6800	0
Saia Motor Freight Line LLC		D	510 347-6890	0
San Francisco Bay Area Councl		D	510 577-9000	0
San Leandro Healthcare Center		D	510 357-4015	0
San Leandro Hospital LP		B	510 357-6500	0
San Leandro Surgery Center Lt		D	510 276-2800	0
Schryver Med Sls & Mktg LLC		C	303 371-0073	0
Service Lathing Company		E	510 483-9732	0
Silman Venture Corporation (PA)		D	510 347-4800	0
Ssmb Pacific Holding Co Inc (HQ)		D	510 836-6100	0
St Francis Electric Inc		D	510 639-0639	0
St Francis Electric LLC		C	510 639-0639	0
State Roofing Systems Inc		D	510 317-1477	0
Stepping Stn Grwth Ctr Fr Chld		D	510 568-3331	0
Subacute Trtmnt Adolescnt Reha (PA)		D	510 352-9200	0
Sunbridge Healthcare LLC		D	510 352-2211	0
Sutter Health		C	510 618-5200	0
Sutter Vsting Nrse Assn Hspice		D	510 618-5277	0
Telecare Corporation		D	510 895-5502	0
Telecare Corporation		C	510 352-9690	0
Thyssenkrupp Elevator Corp		D	510 476-1900	0
TRM Corporation (PA)		D	510 895-2700	0
True Wrld Fods San Frncsco LLC		D	510 352-8140	0
Unity Courier Service Inc		D	510 568-8890	0
Vanguard Legato A Cal Corp		D	510 351-3333	0
Vasona Management Inc		B	510 352-8728	0
Waste MGT of Alameda Cnty		D	510 638-2303	0
Webers Quality Meats Inc		D	510 635-9892	0
Westmed Ambulance		D	510 401-5420	0

SAN LORENZO, CA - Alameda County

	SIC	EMP	PHONE	ENTRY #
Directv Group Inc		C	510 481-1324	0
Echo Landscape		D	510 481-8614	0
Oakland Pallet Company Inc (PA)		D	510 278-1291	0
Too Good Gourmet Inc (PA)		D	510 317-8150	0
Wells Fargo Bank National Assn		E	510 276-0875	0

SAN LUIS OBISPO, CA - San Luis Obispo County

	SIC	EMP	PHONE	ENTRY #
American West Worldwide Ex Inc		E	805 926-2800	0
American West Worldwide Ex Inc (PA)		D	800 788-4534	0
Amir Ahmad MD		D	805 545-8100	0
Amk Foodservices Inc		C	805 544-7600	0
Associated Students Inc (PA)		D	805 756-1281	0
Associated Students Inc		D	805 756-1281	0
Aviation Consultants Inc (PA)		D	805 548-1300	0
Bank of Sierra		D	805 541-0400	0
Bayshore Healthcare Inc		C	805 544-5100	0
Boeing Company		D	805 606-6340	0
Cal Poly Corporation		D	805 756-1587	0
Cal Poly Corporation		C	805 756-1131	0
Cannon Corporation (PA)		D	805 544-7407	0
Cellco Partnership		D	805 549-6260	0
Community Action Partnership		B	805 541-4122	0
Community Action Partnership (PA)		D	805 544-4355	0
Compass Health Inc		D	805 543-0210	0
Correctons Rhbltation Cal Dept		A	805 547-7900	0
County of San Luis Obispo		D	805 781-5437	0
County of San Luis Obispo		C	805 781-4700	0
County of San Luis Obispo		B	805 781-1864	0
County of San Luis Obispo		D	805 781-5258	0
Courtyard By Marriott		D	805 786-4200	0
Drug & Alcohol Services of		D	805 781-4275	0
Experts Exchange LLC		D	805 787-0603	0
Family Care Network Inc (PA)		C	805 503-6240	0
First American Title Insur Co		E	805 543-8900	0
French Hosp Med Ctr Foundation (DH)		B	805 543-5353	0
Gentiva Health Services Inc		D	805 549-0801	0
Harvest Management Sub LLC		A	805 543-0187	0
Kci Environmental Inc		E	805 543-3311	0
Kennedy Club Fitness		D	805 781-3488	0
King Ventures		C	805 544-4444	0

Mergent email: customerrelations@mergent.com

1636

2020 Directory of California
Wholesalers and Services Companies

(P-0000) Products & Services Section entry number
(PA)=Parent Co (HQ)=Headquarters (DH)=Div Headquarters

	SIC	EMP	PHONE	ENTRY #
Ksby Communications LLC		D	805 541-6666	0
Life Steps Foundation Inc		D	805 549-0150	0
Lindamood-Bell Lrng Processes (PA)		C	805 541-3836	0
Martin Resorts Inc (PA)		B	805 545-7900	0
Meathead Movers Inc (PA)		D	805 544-6328	0
Merrill Lynch Pierce Fenner		E	661 802-0764	0
Mindbody Inc (PA)		C	877 755-4279	0
Morris Grritano Insur Agcy Inc		D	805 543-6887	0
National Assn Ltr Carriers		B	805 543-7329	0
Nipomo Dial A Ride		D	805 929-2881	0
Ocean View Manor LP		D	805 781-3088	0
Oddworld Inhabitants Inc		D	805 503-3000	0
Pain Management Specialists PC		E	805 544-7246	0
Pathpoint		D	805 782-8890	0
Pickford Realty Inc		D	805 782-6000	0
Q S San Luis Obispo LP		E	805 541-5001	0
Rew Inc		D	805 541-1308	0
Rrm Design Group (PA)		D	805 439-0442	0
San Luis Obispo Ambulance Service Inc		C	805 543-2626	0
San Luis Obispo County YMCA (PA)		D	805 543-8235	0
San Luis Obispo Golf		C	805 543-3400	0
San Luis Obispo Regional		D	805 781-4465	0
Sealant Systems International		D	805 489-0490	0
Sesloc Federal Credit Union (PA)		D	805 543-1816	0
Sierra Vista Hospital Inc (HQ)		A	805 546-7600	0
Specialty Construction Inc		D	805 543-1706	0
SRI International		C	805 542-9330	0
Sunrun Installation Svcs Inc (HQ)		C	415 580-6900	0
Sycamore Mineral Spring Resort		D	805 595-7302	0
Thoma Electric Inc		D	805 543-3850	0
Transitions - Mental Hlth Assn (PA)		D	805 540-6500	0
Trust Automation Inc		D	805 544-0761	0
Ultrex Management Services (PA)		D	805 783-1234	0
United Cerebral Palsy Assoc of		D	805 543-2039	0
United Parcel Service Inc OH		D	801 973-3400	0
USA Staffing Inc		D	805 269-2677	0
Veterans Health Administration		B	805 543-1233	0
Villa La Esperanza LP		D	805 781-3088	0
Village Pacific Mgt Group		D	805 543-2350	0
Village Pacific Mgt Group (PA)		D	805 543-2300	0
Vitalant		D	805 543-1077	0
Vitalant		D	831 751-1993	0
Voloagri Inc		C	805 547-9391	0
Weatherford International LLC		D	805 781-3580	0
Wells Fargo Bank National Assn		D	805 541-0143	0

SAN MARCOS, CA - San Diego County

	SIC	EMP	PHONE	ENTRY #
American Concrete		D	760 471-9907	0
American Homes Trust		D	619 694-7821	0
Americare Hlth Retirement Inc		D	760 744-4484	0
Associated Students Inc		E	760 750-4990	0
AT&T Corp		D	760 752-3273	0
Birth Choice of San Marco		D	760 744-1313	0
Care Choice Health Systems Inc		D	760 798-4508	0
Casa De Amparo (PA)		D	760 754-5500	0
Chateau Lake San Marcos Homeow		D	760 471-0083	0
Chatham Inc		E	800 222-2002	0
Citizens Development Corp (PA)		D	760 744-0120	0
Community Catalysts California		E	760 471-3700	0
Corkys Pest Control Inc		D	760 432-8801	0
Diamond Environmental Svcs LP		D	760 744-7191	0
Doose Landscape Incorporated		D	760 591-4500	0
Duke Financial Co Inc		C	858 694-1215	0
Edco Waste & Recycl Svcs Inc (HQ)		D	760 744-2700	0
Edwards Theatres Circuit Inc		D	760 471-3734	0
Fresh Origins LLC		B	760 736-4072	0
Golden Door Properties LLC		C	760 744-5777	0
Hollandia Dairy Inc (PA)		C	760 744-3222	0
Home Improvement Company Inc		E	760 744-4840	0
Iron Law Inc (PA)		D	844 476-6529	0
Kindred Healthcare Oper LLC		C	760 471-2986	0
KRC Equipment LLC		D	760 744-1036	0
Kros-Wise Inc		C	619 607-2899	0
La Provence Inc		D	760 736-3299	0
M Bar C Construction Inc		D	760 744-4131	0
Markstein Beverage Co		C	760 744-9100	0
Naumann/Hobbs Material		C	858 207-6274	0
North County Health Prj Inc (PA)		C	760 736-6755	0
Olympus Building Services Inc		A	760 750-4629	0
Orora North America		D	760 510-7170	0
Orora North America		D	760 510-7000	0
Paramount Trnsp Systems Inc (PA)		E	760 510-7979	0
Plant Source Inc		E	760 743-7743	0
Plum Healthcare Group LLC (PA)		D	760 471-0388	0
Primary Care Assod Med Group (PA)		D	760 471-7505	0
Rancho Physical Therapy Inc		C	760 752-1011	0

	SIC	EMP	PHONE	ENTRY #
Rehab West Inc		E	619 518-3710	0
Rose Thompson Company		D	760 736-6020	0
San Diego-Imperial Counties De		D	760 736-1200	0
San Marcos Caterers Inc		D	760 744-0120	0
San Marcos Operating Co LP		D	760 471-2986	0
Shasta Landscaping Inc		D	760 744-6551	0
Southern Contracting Company		C	760 744-0760	0
Tel Tech Plus Inc		E	760 510-1323	0
Village Square Nursing Center		C	760 471-2986	0
Welk Resort Group Inc (PA)		E	760 652-4913	0
Woodspear Properties (PA)		E	760 761-4340	0

SAN MARINO, CA - Los Angeles County

	SIC	EMP	PHONE	ENTRY #
D&D Equipment Rental LLC		E	562 903-9333	0
Tricor Entertainment Inc		C	626 282-5184	0

SAN MARTIN, CA - Santa Clara County

	SIC	EMP	PHONE	ENTRY #
Cordevalle Golf Club LLC		C	408 695-4500	0

SAN MATEO, CA - San Mateo County

	SIC	EMP	PHONE	ENTRY #
AAA Travel		E	650 572-5600	0
Aauw Action Fund Inc		D	650 574-9160	0
Abd Insurance & Fincl Svcs Inc (PA)		D	650 488-8565	0
Aceva Technologies Inc		C	650 227-5500	0
Addus Healthcare Inc		B	650 638-7943	0
AF Software Holdings Inc		B	888 317-3395	0
AF Software Parent Inc		B	888 317-3395	0
Alain Pinel Realtors Inc		D	650 548-1111	0
Alienvault LLC (DH)		D	650 713-3333	0
Allegis Group Inc		C	650 425-6950	0
Allen Lund Company LLC		D	650 358-9454	0
Alliance Hospital Services		E	650 697-6900	0
Altura Comm Solutions LLC		D	650 513-5100	0
Andreini & Company (PA)		D	650 573-1111	0
Apttus Corporation (PA)		C	650 445-7700	0
Archives Management Corp (PA)		C	650 544-2200	0
Aryaka Networks Inc (PA)		C	408 273-8420	0
Assista Hlthcare Prfssnals LLC		C	650 393-4293	0
Atrium Plaza LLC		C	650 653-6000	0
Auctioncom LLC		C	949 609-5376	0
Barrett Business Services Inc		A	650 653-7588	0
Bay Area Senior Services Inc		C	650 579-5500	0
Bay Meadows Racing Association		C	650 573-4500	0
Borland Software Corporation		D	650 286-1900	0
C9 Edge Inc		D	650 561-7855	0
Cake Corporation		D	650 215-7777	0
California Casualty Mgt Co (HQ)		C	650 574-4000	0
California Envmtl Hlth Assn		D	650 363-4726	0
Califrnia CPA Edcatn Fundation		D	800 922-5272	0
Califrnia Cslty Indemnity Exch (PA)		C	650 574-4000	0
Camico Mutual Insurance Co (PA)		D	650 378-6874	0
Celigo Inc (PA)		E	650 579-0210	0
Cellarstone Inc (PA)		D	650 242-0008	0
Center For Learning and		B	800 538-8365	0
Cir		C	650 574-6900	0
City of San Mateo		D	650 522-7300	0
Clarizen Inc		D	866 502-9813	0
Coldwell Bnkr Residential Brkg		D	650 558-6800	0
County of San Mateo		C	650 312-5327	0
County of San Mateo		B	650 312-8887	0
County of San Mateo		D	650 372-8540	0
County of San Mateo		C	650 312-8803	0
Coupa Software Incorporated (PA)		C	650 931-3200	0
Cprime Inc (HQ)		D	650 931-1650	0
Daniel J Edelman Inc		D	650 762-2800	0
David D Bohannon Organization (PA)		D	650 345-8222	0
Demandtec LLC		B	914 499-1900	0
Device Anywhere		D	650 655-6400	0
Endorse Corp		A	617 470-8332	0
Engagio Inc		E	650 265-2264	0
Ero-Tech Corp		D	415 468-5600	0
Essex Property Trust Inc (PA)		C	650 655-7800	0
Fce Benefit Administrators Inc (PA)		C	650 341-0306	0
Fhar Fmly Hsing Adult Rsources		D	650 573-3341	0
Fifty Peninsula Partners		D	650 344-8210	0
First Student Inc		D	650 685-8245	0
Franklin Advisers Inc (HQ)		A	650 312-2000	0
Franklin Resources Inc (PA)		A	650 312-2000	0
Franklin Templeton Svcs LLC		A	650 312-3000	0
Freedom Financial Network LLC (PA)		C	650 393-6619	0
Gainsight Inc		B	888 623-8562	0
Gengo Inc		E	650 585-4390	0
Glenborough LLC (PA)		D	650 343-9300	0
Golden Gate Regional Ctr Inc		C	650 574-9232	0
Guidewire Software Inc (PA)		C	650 357-9100	0
HE Inc		D	650 794-1128	0

Employment Codes: A=Over 500 employees, B=251-500,
C=101-250, D=51-100, E=50

2020 Directory of California
Wholesalers and Services Companies

© Mergent Inc. 1-800-342-5647

1637

GEOGRAPHIC

	SIC	EMP	PHONE	ENTRY #
Inclin Inc		D	650 961-3422	0
Infogroup Inc		D	650 389-0700	0
Instill Corporation		C	650 645-2600	0
Institute For Humn Social Dev **(PA)**		C	650 871-5613	0
Intelpeer Cloud Cmmnctions LLC		C	650 525-9200	0
Ip International Inc		E	650 403-7800	0
Isearch Media LLC		D	415 358-0882	0
Island Hospitality MGT LLC		D	650 574-4700	0
Jobvite Inc **(PA)**		D	650 376-7200	0
John Gore Organization Inc		D	650 340-0469	0
Judy Madrigal & Associates Inc		A	650 873-3444	0
Kaiser Foundation Hospitals		A	650 358-7000	0
Kurt Meiswinkel Inc		E	650 344-7200	0
La Joie Jerry		E	650 375-1808	0
Lattice Engines Inc **(DH)**		D	877 460-0010	0
Lisi Inc **(PA)**		D	650 348-4131	0
Logictier Inc		C	650 235-6600	0
Marketo Inc **(DH)**		C	650 376-2300	0
Milestone Topco Inc **(HQ)**		A	650 376-2300	0
Mission Hospice & HM Care Inc **(PA)**		C	650 554-1000	0
Movoto LLC		D	888 766-8686	0
N Model Inc **(PA)**		C	650 610-4600	0
National Fncl Srvcs Cnsrtm LLC		D	650 572-2872	0
NC Interactive LLC		D	650 393-2200	0
Netsuite Inc **(DH)**		C	650 627-1000	0
New York Life Insurance Co		B	650 571-1220	0
Nursing & Rehab At Home		D	650 286-4272	0
Open Text Inc **(HQ)**		C	650 645-3000	0
Opya Inc		D	650 931-6300	0
Oracle Systems Corporation		C	650 506-6780	0
Pacific Hotel Management LLC **(PA)**		A	650 347-8260	0
Peninsula Community Foundation		D	650 358-9369	0
Peninsula Family Service **(PA)**		D	650 403-4300	0
People Science Inc		E	888 924-1004	0
Permanente Medical Group Inc		D	650 358-7000	0
Prometheus RE Group Inc **(PA)**		C	650 931-3400	0
Raiser Senior Services LLC		D	650 342-4106	0
Rapid Solutions Consulting LLC		E	415 226-1131	0
Reflektion Inc **(PA)**		D	650 293-0800	0
Research Libraries Group Inc		D	650 288-1288	0
Robert Half International Inc		E	650 574-8200	0
Roblox Corporation		B	888 858-2569	0
San Mateo Cnty Expo Fair Assn		E	650 574-3247	0
San Mateo County Community		D	650 574-6586	0
San Mateo Credit Union		C	650 363-1725	0
Satmetrix Systems Inc		D	650 227-8300	0
Scott Place Associates		D	650 345-8222	0
Securitas SEC Svcs USA Inc		C	650 358-1556	0
Sequoia Bnefits Insur Svcs LLC		D	650 369-0200	0
Snaplogic Inc **(PA)**		C	888 494-1570	0
Snowflake Inc **(PA)**		C	844 766-9355	0
Sociable Labs Inc		E	415 225-8740	0
Sonim Technologies Inc **(PA)**		D	650 378-8100	0
State Farm Mutl Auto Insur Co		D	650 345-3571	0
Steelwave Inc **(PA)**		C	650 571-2200	0
Steelwave LLC		A	650 571-2200	0
Strands Inc A Delaware Corp		E	541 753-4426	0
Strands Labs Inc		E	415 398-4333	0
Successfactorscom Inc		D	650 645-2000	0
Sunrise Senior Living Inc		D	650 558-8555	0
Surveymonkey Inc **(HQ)**		D	650 543-8400	0
Sutter Health		C	650 262-4262	0
Svmk Inc		A	503 225-1202	0
Tano Capital LLC		E	650 212-0330	0
Telesys Software		E	650 522-9922	0
Total Airport Services LLC		D	650 358-0144	0
Truebeck Construction Inc **(PA)**		D	650 227-1957	0
Tunari Corp Inc		D	650 249-6740	0
Veterinary Surgical Associates		D	650 696-8196	0
Vindicia Inc		C	650 264-4700	0
Wageworks Inc **(HQ)**		C	650 577-5200	0
Westlake Development Group LLC **(PA)**		D	650 579-1010	0
Westlake Realty Group Inc **(PA)**		D	650 579-1010	0
Wise Commerce Inc		D	855 469-4737	0
Young Mens Christian Assoc SF		C	650 286-9622	0
Zs Associates Inc		D	650 762-7800	0

SAN PABLO, CA - Contra Costa County

	SIC	EMP	PHONE	ENTRY #
Brookside Community Health Ctr **(PA)**		D	510 215-9092	0
C Overaa & Co		C	510 235-0540	0
Creekside Healthcare Ctr		E	510 235-5514	0
East Bay Nephrology		E	510 235-1057	0
Grancare LLC		D	510 232-5945	0
Lytton Rancheria		A	510 215-7888	0
Mariner Health Care Inc		C	510 232-5945	0
Promab Biotechnologies Inc		D	510 860-4615	0

	SIC	EMP	PHONE	ENTRY #
San Pablo Healthcare		C	510 235-3720	0
Stand For Fmlies Free Volence		D	510 964-7109	0

SAN PEDRO, CA - Los Angeles County

	SIC	EMP	PHONE	ENTRY #
Advent Resources Inc		D	310 241-1500	0
APM Terminals Pacific LLC		E	310 221-4000	0
APM Terminals Pacific LLC **(DH)**		C	704 571-2768	0
AT&T Corp		D	310 547-0400	0
Beach Cities Invest & Protctn		B	310 322-4724	0
Boys and Girls Clubs of The La **(PA)**		D	310 833-1322	0
Boys and Girls Clubs of The La		D	310 833-1322	0
Bridges At Sn Pdro Pnnsla Hspt		D	310 514-5359	0
Catalina Channel Express Inc **(HQ)**		B	310 519-7971	0
Catalina Channel Express Inc		C	562 495-3565	0
City of Los Angeles		C	310 732-7681	0
Comprehensive Child Dev Inc		D	310 514-4998	0
Exel Inc		D	310 832-3376	0
Fenix Marine Services Ltd		C	310 548-8877	0
Gs Brothers Inc **(PA)**		C	310 833-1369	0
Healthview Inc **(PA)**		C	310 547-3341	0
Isabel Garreton Inc **(PA)**		C	310 833-7768	0
Little Sisters The Poor of La		D	310 548-0625	0
Meristar San Pedro Hilton LLC		C	310 514-3344	0
Nippon Express USA Inc		D	310 532-6300	0
Performance Team Frt Sys Inc		D	310 241-4100	0
PLD Enterprises Inc **(PA)**		D	310 547-3366	0
Port of Los Angeles		D	310 732-3508	0
Procel Temporary Services Inc		B	310 372-0560	0
Proficient LLC		D	310 519-8200	0
Providence Health & Services S		D	310 832-3311	0
Providence Health System		A	310 832-3311	0
Providence Health System		D	310 514-5270	0
San Pedro Convalescent HM Inc		D	310 832-6431	0
Seacrest Convalescent Hosp Inc		D	310 833-3526	0
So Cal Ship Services		D	310 519-8411	0
Spf Capital Real Estate LLC		D	310 519-8200	0
Sprouts Farmers Market Inc		D	310 831-7836	0
Star Fisheries **(PA)**		D	310 832-8395	0
Tri-Marine Fish Company LLC		D	310 547-1144	0
Tri-Marine Fishing MGT LLC		E	310 547-1144	0
Y & S Enterprises Inc **(PA)**		E	310 548-1120	0
Yusen Terminals LLC **(DH)**		D	310 548-8000	0

SAN QUENTIN, CA - Marin County

	SIC	EMP	PHONE	ENTRY #
Distillery Inc		D	415 505-5446	0

SAN RAFAEL, CA - Marin County

	SIC	EMP	PHONE	ENTRY #
Adolph Gasser Inc		C	415 495-3852	0
Aldersly Retirement Center		D	415 453-9271	0
Arcadia Services Inc		D	248 352-7530	0
AT&T Corp		D	415 721-1470	0
Autodesk Inc **(PA)**		B	415 507-5000	0
Autodesk Inc		C	415 507-5000	0
Bank of Marin		D	415 472-2265	0
Bernard Osher Marin Jewish Com		C	415 444-8000	0
Buckelew Programs **(PA)**		C	415 457-6964	0
Cal-Coast Healthcare Inc		D	415 479-5149	0
Casa Allegra Community Svcs		D	415 499-1116	0
Catholic Chrts Cyo Archdiocs		B	415 507-2000	0
Center For Domestic Peace		E	415 457-2464	0
Center Point Inc **(PA)**		D	415 492-4444	0
Central Payment Co LLC		D	415 462-8335	0
CF San Rafael LLC		D	415 479-5161	0
Clp Resources Inc		E	415 446-7000	0
Comcast California Ix Inc		D	215 286-3345	0
Community Action Marin **(PA)**		B	415 485-1489	0
Community Action Marin		C	415 459-6330	0
County of Marin		B	415 499-6970	0
County of Marin		C	415 499-7877	0
De Mello Roofing Inc		D	415 456-0741	0
Dutra Dredging Company **(HQ)**		D	415 721-2131	0
Dutra Group **(PA)**		D	415 258-6876	0
Dutra Manson JV		D	415 258-6876	0
E C Wise Inc **(PA)**		D	415 355-9473	0
Eah Inc **(PA)**		D	415 258-1800	0
Edgewood Prtners Insur Ctr Inc		D	415 456-4323	0
Enterprise Events Group Inc		C	415 499-4444	0
Fair Isaac International Corp **(HQ)**		A	415 446-6000	0
Family Svcs Agcy Marin Cnty		D	415 491-5700	0
Frank Howard Allen Fincl Corp		D	415 456-3000	0
Ghilotti Bros Inc		B	415 454-7011	0
Gilardi & Co LLC		D	415 461-0410	0
Golden Gate Bridge High		A	415 457-3110	0
Golden Gate Nat Prks Cnsrvancy		D	415 785-4787	0
Guide Dogs For Blind Inc **(PA)**		C	415 499-4000	0
Herbs Pool Service Inc		D	415 479-4040	0

Mergent email: customerrelations@mergent.com
1638

2020 Directory of California
Wholesalers and Services Companies

(P-0000) Products & Services Section entry number
(PA)=Parent Co (HQ)=Headquarters (DH)=Div Headquarters

	SIC	EMP	PHONE	ENTRY #
Hospitality Ventures MGT LLC		D	415 499-9222	0
Icf Consulting Group Inc		A	703 934-3000	0
Independent Quality Care Inc		D	415 479-1230	0
Interactive Med Specialists		D	415 472-4204	0
Jacksons Hardware Inc		D	415 870-4083	0
Jerry Thompson & Sons Pntg Inc		C	415 454-1500	0
Kaiser Foundation Hospitals		A	415 444-2000	0
Kaiser Foundation Hospitals		D	415 444-3522	0
Kindred Nursing Centers W LLC		D	415 456-7170	0
Kisco Senior Living LLC		D	415 491-1935	0
Knight-Calabasas LLC		D	415 453-4940	0
Lifehouse Inc (PA)		B	415 472-2373	0
Managed Health Network (DH)		B	415 460-8168	0
Marin Airporter Inc (PA)		D	415 256-8833	0
Marin Clean Energy		D	415 464-6028	0
Marin Sanitary Service (PA)		D	415 456-2601	0
Marin Snior Crdnting Cncil Inc		D	415 454-0964	0
Mariner Health Care Inc		D	415 479-3610	0
Mhn Government Services LLC		C	916 294-4941	0
Michael B Mayock Inc		D	415 456-9306	0
Mighty Leaf Tea		D	415 491-2650	0
Mill Valley Refuse Service Inc		D	415 457-2287	0
Millsap Degnan & Assoc Inc		D	415 472-4244	0
Mountain Play Association		E	415 383-1100	0
Northgate Care Center		D	415 479-1230	0
Ocadian Care Centers LLC		D	415 499-1000	0
Pasha Group (PA)		B	415 927-6400	0
Pasha Hawaii Trnspt Lines LLC (PA)		C	415 927-6400	0
Penske Automotive Group Inc		E	415 492-1922	0
Permanente Medical Group Inc		D	415 444-2000	0
Petroleum Sales Inc (PA)		C	415 256-1600	0
Pf West LLC		C	415 479-9600	0
Phoenix American Incorporated (PA)		D	415 485-4500	0
Powerhouse Building Inc		D	415 446-0188	0
Quaker Pet Group Inc		D	415 721-7400	0
R C Roberts & Co (PA)		C	415 456-8600	0
Rafael Convalescent Hospital		C	415 479-3450	0
Redhorse Constructors Inc		C	415 492-2020	0
Richard Shames MD		D	415 388-0456	0
San Rafael Hillcrest LLC		D	415 479-8800	0
San Rafael Rock Quarry Inc (HQ)		D	415 459-7740	0
Sisters of Nazareth		D	415 479-8282	0
Starwood Htls & Rsrts Wrldwde		C	415 479-8800	0
Urban Painting Inc		D	415 485-1130	0
Valentine Corporation		E	415 453-3732	0
Villa Marin Homeowners Assn		D	415 499-8711	0
Warren Security Systems Inc		E	415 456-7034	0
Whitegold Solutions Inc		E	415 456-4493	0
Young Mens Christian Assnsf		C	415 459-9622	0
Young Mens Christian Assoc SF		B	415 492-9622	0

SAN RAMON, CA - Contra Costa County

	SIC	EMP	PHONE	ENTRY #
24 Hour Fitness Usa Inc (HQ)		C	925 543-3100	0
24 Hour Fitness Usa Inc		D	916 722-7588	0
24 Hour Fitness Worldwide Inc (PA)		D	925 543-3100	0
A D Bilich Inc		E	925 820-5557	0
A S A P Professional Services		D	800 303-2727	0
Accela Inc (PA)		C	925 659-3200	0
Accelon Inc		E	925 216-5735	0
Accountnow Inc		D	925 498-1800	0
Alexander Properties Company		E	925 866-0100	0
AMP Technologies LLC		C	877 442-2824	0
Annabel Investment Company		D	925 866-0100	0
Armanino LLP (PA)		D	925 790-2600	0
AT&T Corp		C	415 394-3000	0
AT&T Corp		D	925 327-7100	0
AT&T Corp		A	925 823-5388	0
AT&T Services Inc		D	925 901-9318	0
AT&T Services Inc		C	415 823-0993	0
Athoc Inc (DH)		D	925 242-5660	0
Atlas Lift Tech Inc		C	415 283-1804	0
Baco Realty Corporation		D	925 275-0100	0
Bay Area Techworkers (PA)		D	925 359-2200	0
Bishop Ranch Veterinary Center (PA)		D	925 743-9300	0
Blackberry Corporation (HQ)		D	972 650-6126	0
Bridges At Gale Ranch LLC		D	925 735-4253	0
Carlson Barbee & Gibson Inc		D	925 866-0322	0
Castro Valley Health Inc		C	510 690-1930	0
Cellco Partnership		D	925 743-9327	0
Clubsport San Ramon LLC (PA)		B	925 735-1182	0
Cmg Financial Services		D	925 983-3073	0
Cmg Mortgage Inc (PA)		B	619 554-1327	0
Commerce Home Mortgage Inc (HQ)		D	925 830-1500	0
Concessionaires Urban Park		D	530 529-1513	0
Donor Network West (PA)		C	925 480-3100	0
Ecifm Solutions Inc		D	925 830-1925	0

	SIC	EMP	PHONE	ENTRY #
Enpower Management Corp		E	925 244-1100	0
Express System Intermodal Inc		C	801 302-6625	0
Expressworks International LLC (PA)		C	925 244-0900	0
Ferreira Service Inc (PA)		D	925 831-9330	0
Five9 Inc (PA)		C	925 201-2000	0
G4s Secure Solutions (usa)		C	925 543-0008	0
GE Digital LLC (HQ)		D	925 242-6200	0
General Electric Company		D	925 242-6200	0
Good Technology Corporation (HQ)		C	408 352-9102	0
Gorilla Tech Americas Inc		D	925 365-1161	0
Greystone Homes Inc		C	925 242-0811	0
Hill Physicians Med Group Inc (PA)		B	800 445-5747	0
Hyatt Corporation		B	925 743-1882	0
Independent Quality Care Inc (PA)		D	925 855-0881	0
International Bus Mchs Corp		C	925 277-5000	0
Jaroth Inc		C	925 553-3650	0
Kaiser Foundation Hospitals		A	925 244-7600	0
KB Home South Bay Inc		C	925 983-2500	0
Kindercare Education LLC		D	925 824-0267	0
Legacy Mech & Enrgy Svcs Inc		D	925 820-6938	0
Lucile Salter Packard Chil		D	925 277-7550	0
Macdonald Mott Group Inc		D	925 469-8010	0
Mason McDuffie Mortgage Corp (PA)		D	925 242-4400	0
Millennial Brands LLC (PA)		D	866 938-4806	0
Mountain Retreat Incorporated		D	925 838-7780	0
Mt View Apartments LLC		D	925 866-8429	0
Native Sons Landscaping Inc		E	925 837-8175	0
Netpace Inc		D	925 543-7760	0
New York Life Insurance Co		D	415 999-9576	0
Old Republic HM Protection Inc		B	925 866-1500	0
Pacifica Reflections		E	925 275-9800	0
Parkway Apartments LLC		E	925 866-8429	0
Pinnacle Funding Group Inc		E	925 552-5302	0
Plus Group Inc		D	925 831-8551	0
Primed MGT Consulting Svcs Inc		B	925 327-6710	0
Procter & Gamble Distrg LLC		B	925 867-4900	0
Protiviti Inc		D	925 913-1000	0
Reproductive Science Center		D	925 867-1800	0
Robert Half International Inc		E	925 913-1000	0
Rose International Inc		C	636 812-4000	0
RW Lynch Co Inc (PA)		D	925 837-3877	0
Safe Security Inc		B	925 830-4777	0
San Ramon Regional Med Ctr LLC		A	925 275-9200	0
Seacastle Inc		D	925 480-3000	0
Security Alarm Fing Entps Inc		D	925 830-4786	0
Sirva Inc		C	925 824-3109	0
Splash Swim School Inc		E	925 838-7946	0
Spruce Technology Inc		D	925 415-8160	0
Striking Distance Studios Inc		E	925 355-5131	0
Summerhill Construction Co		E	925 244-7520	0
Surplus Line Association Cal		D	415 434-4900	0
Tracy Trujillo MD		E	925 838-6511	0
United Innovation Services Inc		D	510 322-8922	0
United Parcel Service Inc OH		C	800 833-9943	0
Universal Protection Svc LP		D	805 496-4401	0
V A Anderson Enterprises Inc		D	925 866-6150	0
Vyshnavi Information Techn		C	408 454-6218	0
Warmington Homes		C	925 866-6700	0
Webly Systems Inc		E	888 444-6400	0
Wurldtech Security Tech Ltd		D	604 669-6674	0

SAN SIMEON, CA - San Luis Obispo County

	SIC	EMP	PHONE	ENTRY #
Cavalier Inn Inc		D	805 927-4688	0
Cavalier Inn Incorporated		D	805 927-6444	0

SAN YSIDRO, CA - San Diego County

	SIC	EMP	PHONE	ENTRY #
San Ysidro School District		D	619 428-4424	0

SANGER, CA - Fresno County

	SIC	EMP	PHONE	ENTRY #
Cal Custom Tile		D	559 875-1460	0
Chooljian Bros Packing Co Inc		E	559 875-5501	0
Farmex Land Management Inc		C	559 875-7181	0
Gerawan Farming Partners Inc		B	559 787-8780	0
Golden Living LLC		D	559 875-6501	0
Gongs Market of Sanger Inc (PA)		E	559 875-5576	0
If Holding Inc (PA)		C	559 875-3354	0
Suma Fruit Intl USA Inc		E	559 875-5000	0
Virginia Sarabian		E	559 493-2900	0
Wine Group Inc		D	559 638-3511	0

SANTA ANA, CA - Orange County

	SIC	EMP	PHONE	ENTRY #
2100 Trust LLC (PA)		C	877 469-7344	0
5 Diamond Protection Inc		D	949 466-1367	0
Adtek Engineering Service		D	800 451-0782	0
Advanced Clnroom McRclean Corp		C	714 751-1152	0
Alan B Whitson Company Inc		A	949 955-1200	0
Allied Anesthesia Med Group		D	951 830-9816	0

Employment Codes: A=Over 500 employees, B=251-500,
C=101-250, D=51-100, E=50

2020 Directory of California
Wholesalers and Services Companies

© Mergent Inc. 1-800-342-5647

1639

Company	SIC	EMP	PHONE	ENTRY #
Allied Building Products Corp		E	714 647-9792	0
Aluminum Precision Pdts Inc (PA)		A	714 546-8125	0
Alvaradosmith A Prof Corp (PA)		C	714 852-6800	0
Alzheimers Care Since 1983		E	714 641-0959	0
AM Products Inc		E	714 662-4454	0
America West Airlines Inc		D	949 852-5471	0
American Airlines Inc		C	949 852-5470	0
American Concrete Cutting Inc		D	714 547-7181	0
American National Red Cross		E	714 481-5300	0
American-1 Airtight SEC Co		E	714 997-0605	0
Aramark Unf & Career AP LLC		D	714 545-4877	0
Architectural Coatings Inc		E	714 701-1360	0
Assurant Inc		B	714 571-3900	0
B-Per Electronic Inc		D	626 912-0600	0
Banc California National Assn (HQ)		D	877 770-2262	0
Banc of California Inc (PA)		C	855 361-2262	0
Barry McPherson Inc		C	425 343-5000	0
Beacon Sales Acquisition Inc		C	714 288-1974	0
Behr Process Sales Company		C	714 545-7101	0
Bizringer Inc		D	949 396-0162	0
Blind Childrens Lrng Ctr Inc		E	714 573-8888	0
Blower-Dempsay Corporation (PA)		C	714 481-3800	0
Brethren Inc		E	714 836-4800	0
Brightview Landscape Dev Inc		D	714 546-7843	0
Brightview Landscape Svcs Inc		D	714 546-7843	0
Bsnap LLC		D	657 269-4410	0
Bureau Veritas North Amer Inc		D	714 431-4400	0
California Anesthesia Asso Med		D	800 888-2186	0
Calspec Enterprises Inc (PA)		D	949 263-0779	0
Calvary Church Santa Ana Inc		C	714 973-4800	0
Carollo Engineers Inc		D	714 540-4300	0
Carrasco Heleo		D	714 639-1759	0
Cellco Partnership		D	714 775-0600	0
Celmol Inc		D	714 259-1000	0
Cemtek Environmental Inc		E	714 437-7100	0
Certified Trnsp Svcs Inc		D	714 835-8676	0
Chamson Management Inc		D	714 751-2400	0
Charles W Bowers Museum Corp		D	714 567-3600	0
Chroma Systems		D	714 557-8480	0
Clear World Communications		B	714 445-3900	0
Clinica Medica Familiar		D	714 541-0870	0
Collectors Universe Inc (PA)		D	949 567-1234	0
Colton Real Estate Group (PA)		D	949 475-4200	0
Concept Technology Inc		B	949 851-6550	0
Continental Currency Svcs Inc (HQ)		E	714 569-0300	0
Continental Currency Svcs Inc (PA)		D	714 569-0300	0
Contractors Flrg Svc Cal Inc		C	714 556-6100	0
County of Orange		E	714 834-8385	0
County of Orange		B	714 834-4000	0
County of Orange		E	714 567-7422	0
County of Orange		D	714 834-8899	0
County of Orange		A	714 834-6021	0
Covenant Care California LLC		C	714 554-9700	0
CP Opco LLC		D	714 540-6111	0
CRC Health Corporate		D	714 542-3581	0
Crown Building Maintenance Co		E	714 434-9494	0
Crown Facility Solutions		E	657 266-0821	0
Data Trace Info Svcs LLC (HQ)		D	714 250-6700	0
Debtmerica LLC		D	714 389-4200	0
Dekra-Lite Industries Inc		D	714 436-0705	0
Deutsche Bank National Tr Co		D	714 247-6000	0
Deutsche Bank National Tr Co		D	714 247-6054	0
Dgwb Inc		D	714 881-2300	0
Dgwb Ventures LLC		D	714 881-2308	0
Dhs Consulting LLC		C	714 276-1135	0
Discovery Scnce Ctr Ornge Cnty		D	866 552-2823	0
Dish Network Corporation		E	714 424-0503	0
DOT Printer Inc		E	949 752-7730	0
Duplo USA Corporation (PA)		D	949 752-8222	0
Durham School Services L P		C	714 542-8989	0
Edwards Theatres Circuit Inc		D	714 557-5701	0
Embee Processing LLC		B	714 546-9842	0
Empire Building Services Inc		D	714 836-7700	0
Ephonamationcom Inc		D	714 560-1000	0
Experian Corporation		A	714 830-7000	0
F M Tarbell Co (HQ)		C	714 972-0988	0
F R A L P		D	714 633-1442	0
Family Assessment Cnslng Edctn		E	714 447-9024	0
Financial Statement Svcs Inc (PA)		C	714 436-3326	0
First American Financial Corp (PA)		C	714 250-3000	0
First American Mortgage Svcs		B	714 250-4210	0
First American Title Company		A	714 250-3109	0
First American Title Insur Co (HQ)		C	800 854-3643	0
First American Title Insur Co		C	714 800-3000	0
First American Title Insur Co		A	714 250-4000	0
First American Trust Company (HQ)		D	714 560-7856	0
First Student Inc		D	714 850-7578	0
Fishel Company		D	714 668-9268	0
French Park Care Center		C	714 973-1656	0
Fresh Grill LLC		C	714 444-2126	0
G W Maintenance Inc (PA)		D	714 541-2211	0
Gamboa Service Inc		D	714 966-5325	0
Goodwill Inds Orange Cnty Cal		C	714 754-7808	0
Gps Painting Wallcovering Inc		C	714 730-8904	0
Grants Landscape Services Inc		D	714 444-1903	0
Gringteam Inc		D	714 825-3333	0
Guardsmark LLC (DH)		C	714 619-9700	0
Hart King Coldren A Prof Corp		D	714 432-8700	0
Harveys Industries Inc		D	714 277-4700	0
Health Resources Corp		B	714 754-5454	0
Healthcare Partners LLC		E	714 964-6229	0
Hirsch Electronics LLC		D	949 250-8888	0
Hntb Corporation		D	714 460-1600	0
Hntb Gerwick Water Solutions		D	714 460-1600	0
Hollins Schechter A Prof Corp		D	714 558-9119	0
Honeywell International Inc		C	714 796-7500	0
Hutchings Court Reporters LLC (PA)		E	702 314-7200	0
Idondemand Inc		B	415 200-4546	0
Intergro Rehab Service		D	714 901-4200	0
IPC (usa) Inc (HQ)		D	949 648-5600	0
IRC Technologies Inc (PA)		D	949 476-8626	0
Jhc Investment Inc		D	714 751-2400	0
Jmac Lending Inc		D	949 390-2688	0
John M Frank Construction Inc		D	714 210-3600	0
Johnson La Follette		D	714 558-7008	0
Kaiser Foundation Hospitals		A	714 223-2606	0
Kaiser Foundation Hospitals		D	888 988-2800	0
Kaiser Foundation Hospitals		E	714 967-4700	0
Kingspan Light & Air LLC		C	714 540-8950	0
Klein-Testan-Brundo		E	714 245-8888	0
Knox Services LLC (PA)		D	714 479-1650	0
Kya Services LLC		E	714 659-6476	0
L&T Staffing Inc (PA)		B	714 558-1821	0
La Boxing Franchise Corp		D	714 668-0911	0
Landcare USA LLC		D	949 559-7771	0
Landmark Services Inc		D	714 547-6308	0
Latham & Watkins LLP		B	714 755-8288	0
Lenox Financial Mortgage Corp		C	949 428-5100	0
Lisi Inc		D	714 460-5153	0
Lloyd Pest Control Co		E	714 979-6021	0
Loan Now		D	714 352-2250	0
M & A Mortgage Inc		D	714 560-1970	0
Macro-Z-Technology Company (PA)		D	714 564-1130	0
Madison Materials		D	714 664-0159	0
Main Electric Supply Co LLC (PA)		D	949 833-3052	0
Marriott International Inc		C	714 545-5261	0
Medical Network Inc		D	949 863-0022	0
Melmet Steven J Law Ofc		D	949 263-1000	0
Merchants Building Maint Co		B	714 973-9272	0
Mercy House Living Centers		D	714 836-7188	0
Metropro Road Services Inc (PA)		D	714 556-7600	0
Midori Landscape Inc		D	714 751-8792	0
Mission Ldscp Companies Inc		C	714 545-9962	0
Moms Orange County		E	714 972-2610	0
Montrose Envmtl Group Inc		A	714 332-8646	0
Moore Law Group A Prof Corp		D	714 431-2000	0
Moorefield Construction Inc (PA)		D	714 972-0700	0
Morgan Stanley & Co LLC		D	714 836-5181	0
Morris & Willner Partners		D	949 705-0682	0
Morrison Landscape		E	714 571-0455	0
Mpl Enterprises Inc		D	714 545-1717	0
Newmark & Company RE Inc		D	714 667-8252	0
Nieves Landscape Inc		C	714 835-7332	0
North River Ranch LLC		E	714 556-6244	0
NRG Power Inc		D	714 424-6484	0
Oc 405 Partners Joint Venture		D	858 251-2200	0
Oc Engineering		D	714 667-3212	0
OC Special Events SEC Inc		C	714 541-4111	0
Ocpw		A	714 955-0255	0
Odyssey Healthcare Inc		D	714 245-7420	0
Olive Crest (PA)		B	714 543-5437	0
Oneoc (PA)		D	714 953-5757	0
Optima Tax Relief LLC		C	714 361-4636	0
Orange Cnty Assn For Mntal HLT (PA)		D	714 547-7559	0
Orange Coast Title Company (PA)		D	714 558-2836	0
Orange County Cncl Bsa (PA)		D	714 546-4990	0
Orange County Employees Retir		D	714 558-6200	0
Orange County Head Start (PA)		D	714 241-8920	0
Orange County Health Care Agcy		D	714 568-5683	0
Orange County Royale Convlscnt (PA)		B	714 546-6450	0

Mergent email: customerrelations@mergent.com
1640

2020 Directory of California
Wholesalers and Services Companies

(P-0000) Products & Services Section entry number
(PA)=Parent Co (HQ)=Headquarters (DH)=Div Headquarters

	SIC	EMP	PHONE	ENTRY #
Orange County Services Inc	E		714 541-9753	0
Orange Countys Credit Union **(PA)**	C		714 755-5900	0
Orange Courier Inc	B		714 384-3600	0
Orangewood Foundation	D		714 619-0200	0
Orchid MPS	D		714 549-9203	0
Pacific Eastern Intl Pdts	D		714 538-3434	0
Pacific Foods & Dist Inc	D		714 547-0787	0
Pacific Rim Contractors Inc	D		714 641-7380	0
Pacific Rim Mech Contrs Inc	D		714 285-2600	0
Pacifica Hiorange LP	D		714 556-3838	0
Pacificare Dental	C		661 631-8613	0
Pacificare Health Plan Admin **(DH)**	B		714 825-5200	0
Partners Capital Group Inc **(PA)**	C		949 916-3900	0
Patrol Masters Inc	D		714 426-2526	0
Paul Hastings LLP	D		714 668-6200	0
Pds Tech Inc	D		214 647-9600	0
Phoenix House Orange County	D		714 953-9373	0
Pipe Restoration Inc	E		714 564-7600	0
Pipeline Restoration Plumbing	E		714 957-5836	0
Platinum Equity Partners Inc	D		714 444-3100	0
Ponderosa Builders Inc	A		714 434-9494	0
Pps Parking Inc	A		949 223-8707	0
PRC Builders Inc	D		949 529-7011	0
Prime Tech Cabinets Inc	C		949 757-4900	0
Prospect Medical Group Inc **(HQ)**	B		714 796-5900	0
Psomas	D		714 751-7373	0
Pta CA Cngrss of Parnts Tchrs	D		714 836-2700	0
Q S H Properties Inc	D		714 957-9200	0
Rainbow Home Care Services	D		714 544-8070	0
Ralph D Mitzel Inc	D		714 554-4745	0
Rbc Transport Dynamics Corp	C		203 267-7001	0
Reed Thomas Company Inc	D		714 558-7691	0
Reputation Management Cons Inc	D		949 682-7906	0
Rice Drywall Inc	D		714 543-5400	0
RPM Transportation Inc **(HQ)**	C		714 388-3500	0
S W K Properties LLC	D		714 481-6300	0
SA Recycling LLC	D		714 667-7898	0
Santa Ana City of	E		714 565-2600	0
Santa Ana Country Club	D		714 556-3000	0
Santa Ana Police Officers Assn	A		714 836-1211	0
Santa Ana Radiology Center	D		714 835-6055	0
Santa Ana Unified School Dst	D		714 431-1900	0
Satellite Management Co **(PA)**	C		714 558-2411	0
SBE Electrical Contracting Inc	D		714 544-5066	0
Schoolsfirst Federal Credit Un **(PA)**	B		714 258-4000	0
Scottish American Insurance **(PA)**	D		714 550-5050	0
Script To Screen Inc	D		714 558-3287	0
Service First Contractors	E		714 573-2200	0
ServiceMaster Company LLC	C		714 245-1465	0
Shield Security Inc **(DH)**	B		714 210-1501	0
Silverwood Landscape Cnstr Inc	E		714 427-6134	0
Skeffington Enterprises Inc	D		714 540-1700	0
Smart & Final Stores Inc	B		714 549-2362	0
South Coast Fencing Center	D		714 549-2946	0
South Coast Stone Paving	D		714 835-0258	0
Southern Cal Blldog Rescue Inc	E		714 381-7691	0
Southern Cal Prmnnte Med Group	D		714 967-4760	0
Southern Cal Spcialty Care Inc	C		714 564-7800	0
Southern California Edison Co	C		714 973-5481	0
Southland Integrated Svcs Inc **(PA)**	D		714 558-6009	0
Southwest Express LLC	D		949 474-5038	0
Southwest Landscape Inc	D		714 545-1084	0
Spectrum Security Services Inc	D		714 542-9600	0
Spruce Grove Inc **(PA)**	D		714 546-4255	0
St Joseph Heritage Med Group **(PA)**	C		714 633-1011	0
State Compensation Insur Fund	B		714 565-5000	0
Sterling Plumbing Inc	D		714 641-5480	0
Success Strategies Inst Inc	D		949 721-6808	0
Sukut Construction LLC	D		714 540-5351	0
Sukut Construction Inc	D		714 540-5351	0
Sun Electric LP	D		714 210-3744	0
Sundance Construction Inc	D		714 437-0802	0
Sureco Hlth Lf Insur Agcy Inc	D		866 235-5515	0
Systems Paving Inc **(PA)**	D		949 263-8301	0
Taber Company Inc	D		714 543-7100	0
Tait Environmental Svcs Inc **(PA)**	D		714 560-8200	0
Tarbell Financial Corporation **(PA)**	D		714 972-0988	0
Tecta America Southern Cal Inc	D		714 973-6233	0
Templo Calvario Cmnty Dev Corp	D		714 543-3711	0
Ten Enthusiast Network LLC	C		714 709-9021	0
Tenet Healthsystem Medical	A		714 966-8191	0
Terra Pacific Landscape **(HQ)**	D		714 567-1017	0
TLC Services Group Inc **(PA)**	D		714 541-5415	0
Tmx Engineering LLC	D		714 641-5884	0
Town & Country Manor of The Ch	C		714 547-7581	0
Towne Inc	D		714 540-3095	0
Trans-Pak Incorporated	C		310 618-6937	0
Transit Air Cargo Inc	D		714 571-0393	0
Trilogy Realty Group Inc	D		937 206-0725	0
Tristar Risk Management	D		714 543-0700	0
United Petrochemicals Inc	D		949 629-8736	0
Universal Building Maint LLC **(DH)**	A		714 619-9700	0
Universal Protection Svc LP **(HQ)**	C		714 619-9700	0
Universal Services America LP **(DH)**	A		714 619-9700	0
University California Irvine	D		714 480-2443	0
USA Waste of California Inc	D		714 637-3010	0
Utility Systems Science **(PA)**	D		714 542-1004	0
Veros Credit LLC **(PA)**	D		714 415-6185	0
Visiting Nrse Assn Orange Cnty **(PA)**	D		949 263-4700	0
Volunteers of Amer Los Angeles	D		714 426-9834	0
Waste MGT Collectn Recycl Inc	D		714 637-3010	0
West Coast Aviation Svcs LLC **(PA)**	E		949 852-8340	0
Western Medical Center Aux **(HQ)**	C		714 835-3555	0
White Cap Construction Supply	A		949 794-5300	0
William Hzmlhlch Archtects Inc	D		949 250-0607	0
Windsor Capital Group Inc	D		714 241-3800	0
Wm Vandergeest Landscape Care	D		714 545-8432	0
Xl Fire Protection Co **(PA)**	D		714 554-6132	0

SANTA BARBARA, CA - Santa Barbara County

	SIC	EMP	PHONE	ENTRY #
1260 Bb Property LLC	B		805 969-2261	0
Agilysys Inc	C		805 692-6339	0
American Indian Health & Svcs	E		805 681-7356	0
Anthem Inc	B		805 560-3520	0
Applied Research Assoc Inc	D		805 962-4810	0
Arcana Corporation	E		805 882-1305	0
Beach Motel Partners Ltd	D		800 755-0222	0
BFI Waste Systems N Amer Inc	D		805 965-5248	0
Birnam Wood Golf Club **(PA)**	D		805 969-2223	0
Blue Casa Communications	E		805 966-1669	0
Brightview Golf Maint Inc	E		805 968-6400	0
Butler America Holdings Inc **(PA)**	A		805 880-1978	0
Butler International Inc **(PA)**	C		805 882-2200	0
Butler Service Group Inc **(HQ)**	D		201 891-5312	0
Caesar and Seider Insur Svcs **(PA)**	D		805 682-2571	0
Caliber Home Loans Inc	D		805 883-6800	0
California Convalescent Hosp	D		805 682-1355	0
Cellco Partnership	D		805 569-2525	0
Channel Islands Young Mens Ch	C		805 687-7727	0
Channel Islands Young Mens Ch	D		805 969-3288	0
Chicago Title Insurance Co **(HQ)**	C		805 565-6900	0
Child Abuse Lstening Mediation	E		805 965-2376	0
Cicileo Landscapes	E		805 967-3939	0
Classified Advertising	D		805 564-5200	0
Cliff View Terrace Inc	D		805 682-7443	0
Coldwell Banker Premier Prpts	D		805 565-2200	0
Commission Junction LLC **(DH)**	D		805 730-8000	0
Cottage Care Center	C		805 682-7111	0
Cottage Health **(PA)**	A		805 682-7111	0
County of Santa Barbara Alcoho	D		805 681-4093	0
Covenant Care California LLC	C		805 964-4471	0
Cox Communications Inc	D		805 681-6600	0
Curvature LLC **(DH)**	B		800 230-6638	0
Dennis Allen Associates **(PA)**	D		805 884-8777	0
El Capitan Canyon LLC	D		805 685-3887	0
Employbridge LLC **(HQ)**	C		805 882-2200	0
Encina Pepper Tree Joint Ventr **(PA)**	D		805 687-5511	0
Evangelical Covenant Church	C		805 687-0701	0
Evans Hardy & Young Inc	E		805 963-5841	0
Family Svc Agcy Santa Barbara	D		805 965-1001	0
Fastclick Inc	D		805 689-9839	0
Fess Prker-Red Lion Gen Partnr	B		805 564-4333	0
Frank Schipper Construction Co	E		805 963-4359	0
Front Prch Cmmunities/Services	C		805 687-0793	0
Girls Rock Sb	D		805 861-8128	0
Gold Coast Surgery Center LLC	D		805 324-4555	0
Goleta Valley Cottage Hospital	B		805 681-6468	0
Granite Construction Company	C		805 964-9951	0
Green Hills Software LLC **(HQ)**	C		805 965-6044	0
H D G Associates	D		805 963-0744	0
Hillside House Inc	D		805 687-4818	0
Hub Intrntional Insur Svcs Inc	D		805 682-2571	0
International Alliance Thea	D		805 898-0442	0
JM Roofing Company Inc	D		805 966-3696	0
John Kenney Construction Inc	D		805 884-1579	0
Jordanos Inc **(PA)**	C		805 964-0611	0
Kenneth P Slaught Inc	E		805 962-8989	0
La Cumbre Country Club	D		805 687-2421	0
Lacolina Jr High CA Congress O	D		805 967-4506	0
Logicmonitor Inc **(PA)**	C		805 617-3884	0
Los Prietos Boys Camp	D		805 692-1750	0

Employment Codes: A=Over 500 employees, B=251-500,
C=101-250, D=51-100, E=50

2020 Directory of California
Wholesalers and Services Companies

© Mergent Inc. 1-800-342-5647

1641

	SIC	EMP	PHONE	ENTRY #		SIC	EMP	PHONE	ENTRY #
M Timm Development Inc **(PA)**		C	805 963-0358	0	Acalvio Technologies Inc		D	408 931-6160	0
Marborg Industries **(PA)**		B	805 963-1852	0	Access Systems Americas Inc		A	408 400-3000	0
Master Clean USA Inc		E	805 681-0950	0	Accion Labs Us Inc		A	408 970-9809	0
Meathead Movers Inc		D	805 966-6328	0	Ademco Inc		D	408 986-8200	0
Mentor Worldwide LLC		B	805 681-6000	0	Advance Staffing Inc		B	408 205-6154	0
Mercer Global Securities LLC		D	805 565-1681	0	Alpha Net Consulting LLC		D	408 330-0896	0
Mission Linen Supply		E	805 962-7687	0	Altaba Inc		C	408 349-5080	0
Mission Security and Patrol		D	805 899-3039	0	American Reprographics Co LLC		D	408 295-5770	0
MNS Engineers Inc **(PA)**		D	805 692-6921	0	Anderson PCF Engrg Cnstr Inc		D	408 970-9900	0
Modular Systems Inc		D	805 963-9350	0	Aramark Spt & Entrmt Group LLC		D	408 748-7030	0
Montecito Fire Protection Dst		E	805 969-7762	0	Aricent NA Inc **(DH)**		D	408 324-1800	0
Montecito Retirement Assn		B	805 969-8011	0	Aricent US Inc **(DH)**		E	408 329-7400	0
Morgans Hotel Group MGT LLC		D	805 969-2203	0	Asiainfo-Linkage Inc		A	408 970-9788	0
Mufg Union Bank National Assn		D	805 564-6410	0	AT&T Corp		D	408 980-2004	0
Mullen & Henzell LLP		E	805 966-1501	0	Atac **(PA)**		D	408 736-2822	0
Nevins-Adams Properties Inc **(PA)**		D	805 963-2884	0	Atypon Systems LLC **(PA)**		D	408 988-1240	0
New York Life Insurance Co		D	805 898-7625	0	Avaya Inc **(HQ)**		C	908 953-6000	0
Nhr Newco Holdings LLC **(HQ)**		D	805 964-9975	0	B A Technolinks Corporation		D	408 940-5921	0
One Call Plumber Santa Barbara		D	805 364-6337	0	Backweb Technologies Inc		E	408 933-1700	0
Pacific Building Maint Inc		D	805 969-5221	0	Bandai Namco Entrmt Amer Inc **(DH)**		C	408 235-2000	0
Pacific Centrex Services Inc		D	818 623-2300	0	Bay Clubs Inc		D	408 738-2582	0
Park Hotels & Resorts Inc		B	805 564-4333	0	Bay Counties Waste Svcs Inc		D	408 565-9900	0
Parsons Group Inc **(PA)**		D	805 564-3341	0	Big Switch Networks Inc **(PA)**		D	650 322-6510	0
People Creating Success Inc		C	805 692-5290	0	Bill Wilson Center **(PA)**		D	408 243-0222	0
Pitts & Bachmann Realtors Inc		D	805 963-1391	0	Biltmore Hotel		C	408 988-8411	0
Planned Prnthood Cal Cntl Cast **(PA)**		D	805 963-2445	0	Bramasol Inc		D	408 831-0046	0
Price Postel and Parma LLP		D	805 962-0011	0	Brillio LLC		A	800 317-0575	0
Qad Inc **(PA)**		C	805 566-6000	0	Buckles-Smith Electric Company **(PA)**		D	408 280-7777	0
R M Matovu Memorial		E	412 337-5975	0	Build Group Inc		D	408 986-8711	0
Real Time Staffing Services		D	805 882-2200	0	Burdick Painting		D	408 567-1330	0
Rightscale Inc **(PA)**		D	805 500-4164	0	Bytemobile Inc **(DH)**		B	408 327-7700	0
Rincon Technology Inc **(PA)**		E	805 684-8100	0	Ca Inc		C	800 225-5224	0
Ritz-Carlton Hotel Company LLC		A	805 968-0100	0	Calculi Corporation		E	408 970-0007	0
Roman Cath Arch of Los Angels		A	805 687-8811	0	California Eastern Labs Inc **(PA)**		D	408 919-2500	0
Ronald L Wolfe & Assoc Inc		E	805 964-6770	0	Cardiodx Inc		C	650 475-2788	0
S B C Senior Care Inc		D	805 560-6995	0	Cavisson Systems Inc		B	800 701-6125	0
San Marcos Kids Helpng Kids FN		C	800 659-6411	0	Cedar Fair LP		C	408 988-1776	0
Sansum Clinic **(PA)**		D	805 681-7700	0	Centrify Corporation **(PA)**		C	669 444-5200	0
Sansum Clinic		E	805 682-6507	0	Church of Vly Rtrment Hmes Inc		D	408 241-7750	0
Santa Barbara City of		D	805 962-6464	0	Citrix Systems Inc		D	408 790-8000	0
Santa Barbara City of		C	805 564-5485	0	City of Santa Clara		D	408 615-3770	0
Santa Barbara Cottage Hospital		A	805 569-7367	0	City of Santa Clara		E	408 615-2300	0
Santa Barbara Cottage Hospital **(PA)**		D	805 682-7111	0	City of Santa Clara		C	408 615-2046	0
Santa Barbara County of		B	805 882-3700	0	Claris International Inc **(HQ)**		C	408 987-7000	0
Santa Barbara County of		D	805 681-5100	0	Coast Personnel Services Inc **(PA)**		A	408 653-2100	0
Santa Barbara County of		D	805 884-1600	0	Coastal Paving Incorporated		D	408 988-5559	0
Santa Barbara County of		C	866 901-3212	0	Colortokens Inc		E	408 341-6030	0
Santa Barbara Fabricare Inc		E	805 963-6677	0	Community Home Partners LLC		D	408 985-5252	0
Santa Barbara Metro Trnst Dst **(PA)**		D	805 963-3364	0	Complete Millwork Services Inc		D	408 567-9664	0
Santa Barbara Museum		D	805 682-4711	0	Covenant Care California LLC		D	408 248-3736	0
Santa Barbara Museum of Art **(PA)**		D	805 963-4364	0	Cybercsi Inc		D	408 727-2900	0
Santa Barbara San Luis Obispo		C	800 421-2560	0	Dan Connolly Inc		D	408 241-0910	0
Santa Brbara Cttge Hsptl		B	805 569-7224	0	Data Domain LLC		A	408 980-4800	0
Santa Brbara Zlgcal Foundation		C	805 962-1673	0	Datastax Inc **(PA)**		C	650 389-6000	0
Select Temporaries LLC **(DH)**		D	805 882-2200	0	Decathlon Club Inc		C	408 738-2582	0
Smith Broadcasting Group Inc **(PA)**		C	805 965-0400	0	Dewmobile USA Inc		E	408 550-2818	0
Smith Broadcasting Group Inc		D	805 882-3933	0	Dialog Semiconductor Inc		C	408 327-8800	0
Solid Oak Software Inc **(PA)**		D	805 568-5415	0	Digital Guardian Inc		B	408 716-4200	0
Specialty Team Plastering Inc		C	805 966-3858	0	Dolan Concrete Construction		D	408 869-3250	0
Stantec Consulting Svcs Inc		D	805 963-9532	0	Eag Holdings LLC		A	408 530-3500	0
Sutter Health		B	805 966-1600	0	Ehealthinsurance Services Inc **(HQ)**		D	650 584-2700	0
Tempest Telecom Solutions LLC **(PA)**		D	805 879-4800	0	Elance Inc **(HQ)**		C	650 316-7500	0
The Valley Club of Montecito		E	805 969-2215	0	Elcor Electric Inc		C	408 986-1320	0
Tnci Operating Company LLC **(HQ)**		D	800 800-8400	0	Electric USA		E	800 921-1151	0
Towbes Group Inc **(PA)**		D	805 962-2121	0	Emagia Corporation		E	408 654-6575	0
Town & Country Event Rentals		B	805 770-5729	0	Embrane Inc		A	408 550-2700	0
Tri-Counties Association F **(PA)**		C	805 962-7881	0	Enterprise Solutions Inc		C	408 727-3627	0
Trueblue Inc		E	805 963-5370	0	Environmental Systems Inc **(PA)**		D	408 980-1711	0
United Paradyne Corporation		D	805 734-2359	0	Ericsson Inc		A	408 750-5000	0
United Seal Coating Slurryseal		D	805 563-4922	0	Eurofins Eag Engrg Science LLC **(DH)**		D	408 588-0050	0
United States Marines Youth Fd		D	805 967-7990	0	Extreme Networks Inc		D	630 288-3665	0
University Business Ctr Assoc		D	601 354-3555	0	Fast Pro Inc		D	408 566-0200	0
Upham Hotel		E	805 962-0058	0	Fedex Freight Corporation		E	408 988-2111	0
URS Group Inc		D	805 964-6010	0	Firm A Chugh Professional Corp		E	408 970-0100	0
US Data Management LLC **(PA)**		D	888 231-0816	0	Flair Building Services Inc		D	408 987-4040	0
Valencia Tree Landscape		E	805 965-4244	0	Forest Park Cabana Club		E	408 244-1884	0
Vetronix Sales Corporation		D	805 966-2000	0	Forty Niners Football Co LLC		D	408 562-4949	0
Visiting Care & Companions Inc		D	805 690-6202	0	Fragomen Del Rey Bernse		D	408 919-0600	0
Visiting Nurse & Hospice Care **(PA)**		C	805 965-5555	0	Frontech N Fujitsu Amer Inc		D	408 982-3697	0
Wayne R Kidder		D	805 967-6993	0	Fungible Inc		D	669 292-5522	0
Yardi Systems Inc **(PA)**		B	805 699-2040	0	Gigamon Inc **(HQ)**		D	408 831-4000	0

SANTA CLARA, CA - Santa Clara County

	SIC	EMP	PHONE	ENTRY #		SIC	EMP	PHONE	ENTRY #
2wire Inc **(DH)**		C	408 235-5500	0	Granite Construction Company		C	408 327-7000	0
6wind Usa Inc		D	408 816-1366	0	Hathaway Dinwiddie Cnstr Co		D	415 986-2718	0
A Mobile Development		C	415 350-4532	0	Hcl Finance Inc **(PA)**		C	408 845-9035	0
					Hertz Corporation		D	408 450-6025	0

Mergent email: customerrelations@mergent.com

1642

2020 Directory of California
Wholesalers and Services Companies

(P-0000) Products & Services Section entry number
(PA)=Parent Co (HQ)=Headquarters (DH)=Div Headquarters

	SIC	EMP	PHONE	ENTRY #
Hortonworks Inc (HQ)		A	408 916-4121	0
Hostmark Investors Ltd Partnr		C	408 330-0001	0
Hpt Trs Ihg-2 Inc		D	408 241-9305	0
Hudson Tchmart Cmmerce Ctr LLC		D	408 451-4440	0
Hyatt Regency Santa Clara		D	408 200-1234	0
Immigration Voice		D	408 204-2200	0
Impec Group Inc (PA)		D	408 330-9350	0
In Home Health Inc		C	408 986-8160	0
Innova Solutions Inc		A	408 889-2020	0
Innovative Silicon Inc		D	408 572-8700	0
Intel Media Inc		B	408 765-0063	0
Intellipro Group Inc		B	408 200-9891	0
International Bus Mchs Corp		A	408 850-8999	0
Ip Infusion Inc (HQ)		D	408 400-1900	0
Ironclad Security Services Inc		D	408 773-2800	0
J & J Acoustics Inc		C	408 275-9255	0
Jamcracker Inc		E	408 496-5500	0
Joseph J Albanese Inc		A	408 727-5700	0
Kaiser Foundation Hospitals		A	408 851-1000	0
Kana Software Inc (HQ)		D	650 614-8300	0
Kazeon Systems Inc		D	650 641-8100	0
Keypoint Credit Union (PA)		C	408 731-4100	0
KG Oldco Inc (HQ)		E	408 980-8550	0
Kno Inc		D	408 844-8120	0
Laxmi Group Inc		D	408 329-7733	0
Leantaas Inc		D	650 409-3501	0
Legrande Affaire Inc		D	408 988-4884	0
Lennar Homes California Inc		D	858 759-7200	0
Lombardo Diamnd Core Drlg Inc		D	408 727-7922	0
Lucid Vr Inc		D	408 391-0506	0
Malwarebytes Corporation		A	408 852-4336	0
Mapr Technologies Inc (PA)		B	408 914-2390	0
McAfee LLC (HQ)		C	888 847-8766	0
McAfee Finance 2 LLC		A	888 847-8766	0
McAfee Security LLC		A	866 622-3911	0
Memoryten Inc (PA)		D	408 516-4141	0
Microsoft Corporation		D	408 987-9608	0
Minimatics Inc (PA)		D	650 969-5630	0
Mission Trail Wste Systems Inc		D	408 727-5365	0
Mojo Networks Inc (PA)		C	650 961-1111	0
Moschip Semiconductor Tech USA		C	408 737-7141	0
Move Inc (HQ)		B	408 558-7100	0
Move Sales Inc (DH)		D	805 557-2300	0
Msr Hotels & Resorts Inc		D	408 496-6400	0
National Rental (us) Inc		D	408 492-0501	0
Navisite LLC		E	408 965-9000	0
Net Optics Inc		D	408 737-7777	0
Net4site LLC		D	408 427-3004	0
Netbase Solutions Inc (PA)		D	650 810-2100	0
Netskope Inc (PA)		D	800 979-6988	0
Ni Ki Cruz LLC		D	408 332-7616	0
Nominum Inc		E	650 381-6000	0
Norland Group		C	408 855-8255	0
O2 Micro Inc		D	408 987-5920	0
One Diversified LLC		D	408 969-1972	0
Onebill Software Inc		D	844 462-7638	0
Ontario Airport Hotel Corp		C	408 562-6709	0
Opallios Inc		E	408 769-4594	0
Oracle America Inc		C	408 276-4300	0
Oracle America Inc		C	408 276-3331	0
Oracle America Inc		C	408 276-7534	0
Oracle Corporation		B	408 421-2890	0
Oracle Corporation		B	408 276-5552	0
Oracle Corporation		B	650 506-9864	0
Owens Corning Sales LLC		B	408 235-1351	0
Pdf Solutions Inc (PA)		D	408 280-7900	0
PDM Steel Service Centers		D	408 988-3000	0
Persistent Systems Inc (HQ)		D	408 216-7010	0
Persistent Tlcom Solutions Inc		E	408 216-7010	0
Phase Matrix Inc		E	954 490-9429	0
Playspan LLC		E	408 617-9155	0
Posh Bagel Inc (PA)		D	408 980-8451	0
Pragiti Inc		D	408 689-7214	0
Priority Dispatch Service Inc		E	408 400-3860	0
Proactive Technical Svcs Inc		E	408 531-6040	0
Punctus Temporis Translations		E	510 309-0888	0
Recology Los Altos		D	650 961-8044	0
Redwood Electric Group Inc (PA)		A	707 451-7348	0
Restivo Enterprises		D	408 988-4884	0
Rivio Inc		E	408 653-4400	0
Robert A Bothman Inc (PA)		C	408 279-2277	0
Royal Glass Company Inc		D	408 969-0444	0
Sacramento Hotel Partners LLC (PA)		D	408 249-2500	0
Safeway Stores Incorporated		D	408 719-9460	0
San Francisco Forty Niners		D	408 562-4949	0
San Francisco Forty Niners (PA)		C	408 562-4949	0
San Jose Earthquakes MGT LLC		C	408 556-7700	0
Santa Clara Tenant Corp		D	408 496-6400	0
Santa Clara Vngard Booster CLB		E	408 727-5532	0
Santa Clara Womens Club		D	408 246-8000	0
Serene Ast LLC (HQ)		D	408 986-8544	0
Serrano Electric Inc		E	408 986-1570	0
Sharedata Inc		D	408 490-2500	0
Silicon Valley Bank (HQ)		A	408 654-7400	0
Silvaco Inc (PA)		D	408 567-1000	0
Simco Electronics (PA)		D	408 734-9750	0
Software Ag Inc		C	408 490-5300	0
Solidcore Systems Inc (DH)		D	408 387-8400	0
Solix Technologies Inc (PA)		D	408 654-6446	0
Sonic Solutions Holdings Inc		D	408 562-8400	0
Soundhound Inc (PA)		D	408 441-3200	0
South Bay Historical RR Soc		E	408 243-3969	0
Spec Personnel LLC		C	408 727-8000	0
Special Home Needs		D	408 985-8666	0
Sra Oss Inc		C	408 855-8200	0
Stanford Hotels Corporation		C	408 330-0001	0
Stmicroelectronics Inc		C	408 452-8585	0
Streamvector Inc		C	415 870-8395	0
Sunset Building Maintenance Inc		E	408 727-3408	0
Sutter Health		B	408 524-5952	0
Svb Financial Group (PA)		C	408 654-7400	0
Talari Networks Inc (PA)		D	408 689-0400	0
Tata America Intl Corp		D	408 569-5845	0
Tavant Technologies Inc (PA)		D	408 519-5400	0
Teen Challenge Norwestcal Nev		D	408 703-2001	0
Tekever Corporation		D	408 730-2617	0
Tensilica Inc (HQ)		D	408 986-8000	0
Thermal Mechanical		D	408 988-8744	0
TLC of Bay Area Inc		D	408 988-7667	0
Trianz Inc (HQ)		C	408 387-5800	0
Tusa Inc (PA)		C	888 848-3749	0
United Marble & Granite Inc		D	408 347-3300	0
Upwork Global Inc		E	650 316-7500	0
Valley Process Systems Inc		D	408 261-1277	0
Valley Water Proofing Inc		D	408 985-7701	0
Verint Americas Inc		D	408 830-5400	0
Veritas Technologies LLC (DH)		C	866 837-4827	0
Webyog Inc		C	408 512-1434	0
Wescon Technology Inc		C	408 727-8818	0
Wincere Inc		C	408 841-4355	0
Worldwide Ground Transportatio		D	408 727-0000	0
Xyka Inc		E	408 340-1923	0
Yaskawa America Inc		C	408 748-4400	0
Yes Videocom Inc (PA)		B	408 907-7600	0
YMCA of Silicon Valley (PA)		D	408 351-6400	0

SANTA CLARITA, CA - Los Angeles County

	SIC	EMP	PHONE	ENTRY #
American Health Services LLC		C	661 254-6630	0
Applied Companies		E	661 257-0090	0
AT&T Corp		D	661 297-1720	0
Broadspire Inc		D	213 785-8043	0
California Resources Corp (PA)		C	888 848-4754	0
Canon Recruiting Group LLC		B	661 252-7400	0
Castaic Lk Wtr Agcy Fing Corp		C	661 259-2737	0
Child & Family Center		C	661 259-9439	0
Community Therapies		E	661 945-7878	0
Curtiss-Wright Controls		C	661 257-4430	0
Curtiss-Wright Controls (DH)		C	661 702-1494	0
De Oliviera Concrete Inc		E	661 252-7522	0
Facey Medical Foundation		D	661 250-5225	0
Facey Medical Foundation		D	661 513-2100	0
Friendly Valley Recrtl Assn		E	661 252-3223	0
Gierahn Dry Wall Inc		E	661 257-7900	0
Henry Mayo Newhall Mem Hosp		B	661 253-8227	0
Hope of Valley Mission		E	661 673-5951	0
Kaiser Foundation Hospitals		A	888 750-5000	0
Kaiser Foundation Hospitals		D	661 222-2323	0
Los Angeles Residential Comm F		D	661 296-8636	0
Marathon Industries Inc		C	661 286-1520	0
Midwest Enviromental Control		C	661 255-0722	0
Mountasia Family Fun Center		D	661 253-4386	0
Mountasia of Santa Clarita		D	661 253-4386	0
NTS Technical Systems		C	661 259-8184	0
Oceanside Hlthcare Stfing Inc		C	213 503-7843	0
Partsearch Technologies Inc		E	661 257-7700	0
Paul Mitchell John Systems (PA)		D	310 248-3888	0
Petersen-Dean Inc		D	661 254-3322	0
Princess Cruise Lines Ltd		A	661 753-2197	0
Princess Cruise Lines Ltd (HQ)		A	661 753-0000	0
RE/Max of Valencia Inc (PA)		C	661 255-2650	0
Robinson Ranch Golf LLC		C	818 885-0599	0

Employment Codes: A=Over 500 employees, B=251-500,
C=101-250, D=51-100, E=50

2020 Directory of California
Wholesalers and Services Companies

© Mergent Inc. 1-800-342-5647

1643

GEOGRAPHIC

	SIC	EMP	PHONE	ENTRY #
S C Security Inc		E	661 251-6999	0
Santa Clarita City of		B	661 294-1287	0
Santa Clarita City of		B	661 284-1423	0
Santa Clarita Concrete		E	661 252-2012	0
Santa Clarita Health Care Assn (PA)		D	661 253-8000	0
Santa Clarita Interiors Inc		D	661 253-0861	0
Santa Clarita Valley Bldrs Inc		C	661 295-6722	0
Santa Clarita Valley Wtr Agcy		C	661 259-2737	0
Santa Clarita Vlly Cmmtt Aging		D	661 259-9444	0
Sheldon Mechanical Corporation		D	661 286-1361	0
Southern Cal Prmnnte Med Group		D	661 290-3100	0
Southern Cal Prmnnte Med Group		E	661 222-2150	0
Universal Wood Moulding Inc (PA)		D	661 362-6262	0
USA Waste of California Inc		D	661 259-2398	0

SANTA CRUZ, CA - Santa Cruz County

	SIC	EMP	PHONE	ENTRY #
(a) Tool Shed Inc (PA)		D	831 477-7133	0
7th Avenue Center LLC		D	831 476-1700	0
Alliance Member Services Inc		D	831 459-0980	0
American Medical Response		D	831 423-7030	0
Bastille Networks Inc		E	800 530-3341	0
Benchmark-Tech Corporation		C	831 475-5600	0
Bontadelli Inc		D	831 423-8572	0
California Certified Organic		D	831 423-2263	0
Camp Recovery Centers LLP		D	831 438-1868	0
Canyon View Capital Inc		D	831 480-6335	0
Cellco Partnership		D	831 421-0753	0
Chaminade Ltd		C	831 475-5600	0
Coldwell Bnkr Residential Brkg		D	831 420-2628	0
Cruz Veterinary Hospital		D	831 475-5400	0
David Lyng & Associates Inc		D	831 429-5700	0
Derjjan Associates Inc (PA)		C	831 423-4111	0
Dignity Health		A	831 462-7700	0
Dignity Health Med Foundation		D	831 475-8834	0
Dominican Hospital Foundation		C	831 457-7057	0
Dominican Hospital Foundation (DH)		C	831 462-7700	0
Dominican Oaks Corporation		D	831 462-6257	0
First American Title Insur Co (HQ)		A	714 250-3109	0
Forever Firewood Inc (PA)		E	831 461-0634	0
Friends Santa Cruz State Parks		D	831 429-1840	0
Front St Inc		C	831 420-0120	0
His Manna Inc		C	831 423-5515	0
Janus of Santa Cruz		D	831 462-1060	0
Lho Santa Cruz One Lesse Inc		C	831 475-5600	0
Lifespan Inc		D	831 469-4900	0
Mariner Health Care Inc		D	831 475-6323	0
Moose International Inc		C	831 438-1817	0
National Security Industries		B	831 425-2052	0
Nicholas B Macy Dvm		D	831 475-5400	0
Palo Alto Med Fndtion STA Cruz		A	831 458-5670	0
Performance Food Group Inc		C	831 462-4400	0
Pfyffer Associates Inc		E	831 423-8572	0
Regent Assisted Living Inc		D	831 459-8400	0
Rope Partner Inc		D	831 460-9448	0
Santa Cruz County of		D	831 454-2030	0
Santa Cruz County Symphony		E	831 462-0553	0
Santa Cruz Hotel Associates		C	831 426-4330	0
Santa Cruz Medical Foundation (HQ)		D	831 458-5537	0
Santa Cruz Metro Trnst Dst		D	831 469-1954	0
Santa Cruz Seaside Company (PA)		B	831 423-5590	0
Santa Cruz Westside Elc Inc		D	831 469-8888	0
Skills Center Inc (PA)		D	831 421-9900	0
Smartrevenuecom Inc		B	203 733-9156	0
Stagnaro Brothers Seafood Inc		C	831 423-1188	0
Sutter Health		D	831 458-6310	0
Sutter Health		E	831 477-3600	0
Sutter Health		D	831 458-5500	0
Sutter Maternity & Surgery Ctr		D	831 477-2200	0
Trowbridge Enterprises (PA)		D	831 476-3815	0
United Natural Foods Inc		C	831 462-5870	0
United Parcel Service Inc OH		C	831 425-1054	0
Visiting Nurse Association of (DH)		D	831 477-2600	0
Well Within Spa		D	831 458-9355	0
Western Med Assoc Med Group (PA)		D	831 475-1111	0

SANTA FE SPRINGS, CA - Los Angeles County

	SIC	EMP	PHONE	ENTRY #
All-City Management Svcs Inc		A	310 202-8284	0
Alliedbarton Security Svcs LLC		B	562 906-4800	0
B & E Convalescent Center Inc (PA)		D	562 923-9449	0
Barr Engineering Inc		D	562 944-1722	0
Bekins Moving Solutions Inc (PA)		D	562 356-9460	0
Brenntag Pacific Inc (DH)		C	562 903-9626	0
Cadnchev Inc		D	562 944-6422	0
California Lab Sciences LLC		B	562 758-6900	0
Coa Inc (PA)		C	562 944-7899	0
Coast Alum & Architectural Inc (PA)		C	562 946-6061	0

	SIC	EMP	PHONE	ENTRY #
Coast Iron & Steel Co		E	562 946-4421	0
Commodity Distribution Service		E	562 777-9969	0
County of Los Angeles		B	562 903-5000	0
Crescent Healthcare Inc (DH)		C	714 520-6300	0
Crown Fence Co		D	562 864-5177	0
Csi Electrical Contractors Inc (HQ)		C	562 946-0700	0
Custom Companies Inc		D	310 672-8800	0
Cypress Security LLC		D	562 222-4197	0
Dynamic Worldwide West Inc (PA)		C	562 407-1000	0
E Jordan Brookes Co Inc (PA)		D	562 968-2100	0
El Monte Rents Inc (HQ)		C	562 404-9300	0
Electric Sales Unlimited		E	562 463-8300	0
Ellison Machinery Co (DH)		D	562 949-8311	0
Ellison Technologies Inc		D	562 949-8311	0
Ethosenergy Field Services LLC (DH)		D	310 603-3523	0
Federal Express Corporation		D	800 463-3339	0
Field Foundation		E	562 921-3567	0
Fuji Food Products Inc (PA)		D	562 404-2590	0
Galleher LLC (PA)		C	562 944-8885	0
Gatehouse Msi LLC		E	562 623-3000	0
Georgia-Pacific LLC		B	562 861-6226	0
Great Amrcn Logistics Dist Inc		D	800 381-4527	0
Griffith Company		D	562 929-1128	0
Haringa Inc (PA)		D	800 499-9991	0
Harris L Woods Elec Contr		D	562 945-8751	0
Healthfirst Medical Group Inc (PA)		E	562 949-9328	0
Holbrook Construction Inc		D	714 523-1150	0
Horner-Halleher Holding Co (PA)		C	562 944-8885	0
Integrated Office Tech LLC (PA)		D	562 236-9200	0
Interntonal Win Treatments Inc (PA)		D	562 236-2120	0
Janus Et Cie (PA)		C	310 601-2908	0
Johnson Controls		C	562 405-3817	0
Jvc Americas Corp		D	562 463-8110	0
Kbl Group International Ltd		E	562 699-9995	0
Kemp Bros Construction Inc		E	562 236-5000	0
Key Air Cnditioning Contrs Inc		D	562 941-2233	0
Kiewit Corporation		D	907 222-9350	0
Kiewit Infrastructure West Co		C	562 946-1816	0
Kloeckner Metals Corporation		D	562 906-2020	0
Kloeckner Metals Corporation		E	562 906-2020	0
L Tech Network Services Inc		D	562 222-1121	0
LA Specialty Produce Co (PA)		B	562 741-2200	0
Lakin Tire West Incorporated (PA)		D	562 802-2752	0
Landcare USA LLC		D	714 936-9512	0
Larsen Supply Co (PA)		D	562 698-0731	0
Leed Electric Inc		D	562 270-9500	0
Masonry Concepts Inc		D	562 802-3700	0
Material Handling Supply Inc (HQ)		D	562 921-7715	0
Matt Construction Corporation (PA)		C	562 903-2277	0
Matt-Colombo A Joint Venture		D	562 903-2277	0
Maxon Lift Corporation		C	562 464-0099	0
McKesson Corporation		C	562 463-2100	0
MCP Industries Inc		D	562 944-5511	0
Memo Scaffolding Inc		D	562 404-8600	0
Mias Fashion Mfg Co Inc		B	562 906-1060	0
Millennia Stainless Inc		D	562 946-3545	0
Morrison Concrete Inc		E	562 802-1450	0
Nelson & Associates Inc		D	562 921-4423	0
Newport Diversified Inc		C	562 921-4359	0
Ninos Latino Unidos FSA		D	562 801-5454	0
Norman International Inc		D	562 946-0420	0
Northstar Contg Group Inc		D	714 639-7600	0
Oil Well Service Company (PA)		C	562 612-0600	0
Pacific Clinics		D	562 949-8455	0
Partitions Installation Inc		D	562 207-9868	0
Penny Lane Centers		C	562 903-4135	0
Peoples Care Inc		C	562 320-0174	0
Performance Team Frt Sys Inc		D	562 741-1300	0
Pro-Tech Design & Mfg Inc		D	562 207-1680	0
Production Delivery Svcs Inc		D	562 777-0060	0
Raymond Handling Solutions Inc (DH)		C	562 944-8067	0
Rebar Engineering Inc		C	562 946-2461	0
Rebas Inc		D	562 941-4155	0
Reliance Steel & Aluminum Co		D	562 695-0467	0
Reliance Steel & Aluminum Co		D	562 944-3322	0
Rentokil North America Inc		D	562 802-2238	0
Rockey Murata Landscaping		D	562 921-3210	0
Royal Paper Corp (PA)		D	562 903-9030	0
Ryder Truck Rental Inc		D	562 921-0033	0
S E Pipe Line Construction Co		D	562 868-9771	0
Scorpio Enterprises		D	562 946-9464	0
Seaboard Corporation		B	806 435-5935	0
Sequel Contractors Inc		E	562 802-7227	0
Sfadia Inc		D	323 622-1930	0
Shaw Industries Group Inc		B	562 921-7209	0

	SIC	EMP	PHONE	ENTRY #
Shoring Engineers		D	562 944-9331	0
Sohnen Barry As Co Trustee		E	562 946-3531	0
Sohnen Enterprises Inc (PA)		E	562 903-4957	0
Southeast Area Social Services		E	562 946-2237	0
Southern California Edison Co		D	562 903-3191	0
Specialized Elevator Svcs LLC		D	562 407-1200	0
Spicers Paper Inc (HQ)		C	562 698-1199	0
Swann Communications USA Inc		D	562 777-2551	0
TA Industries Inc (PA)		D	562 466-1000	0
Talley Inc (PA)		C	562 906-8000	0
Telecntric Communications Intl		D	562 906-2555	0
Think Together		A	562 236-3835	0
Tmx Aerospace		D	562 215-4410	0
Trail Lines Inc		D	562 758-6980	0
Tri-West Ltd (PA)		C	562 692-9166	0
Triangle Distributing Co (PA)		C	562 699-3424	0
Troyer Contracting Company Inc		D	562 944-6452	0
Twin Med LLC (PA)		D	323 582-9900	0
Ugm Citatah Inc (PA)		C	562 921-9549	0
Ultradot Media		D	562 906-0737	0
Universal Asphalt Co Inc		E	562 941-0201	0
Valverde Construction Inc		D	562 906-1826	0
Valvoline International Inc		E	562 906-6200	0
Van King & Storage Inc		D	562 921-0555	0
Van Torrance & Storage Company (PA)		D	562 567-2100	0
Verizon Network Integration		C	562 903-7953	0
Warren Distributing Inc (PA)		D	562 789-3360	0
Weber Distribution LLC (PA)		B	855 469-3237	0
West Pacific Medical Lab LLC (PA)		D	818 773-9771	0
Western Allied Service Company		B	562 941-3243	0
Western Exterminator Company		D	562 802-2238	0
Whittier Equipment Rentals		D	562 863-0641	0
Wismettac Asian Foods Inc (HQ)		C	562 802-1900	0
Xpo Logistics Freight Inc		C	562 946-8331	0
Xtra Department Inc		D	562 462-3800	0

SANTA MARIA, CA - Santa Barbara County

	SIC	EMP	PHONE	ENTRY #
Aardex Inc		D	805 928-7600	0
Agro-Jal Farms Inc		D	805 928-2682	0
Ais Construction Company		D	805 928-9467	0
Arbor Medical Group Inc (PA)		D	805 614-7591	0
Blackjack Farms De La Costa CN		C	805 347-1333	0
Boca Mesa Incorporated		D	805 934-9470	0
Brannon Inc		C	805 621-5000	0
Buona Terra Farming Co Inc		D	805 614-9229	0
Caci Nss Inc		C	703 841-7800	0
Cal Gran Theatres LLC		E	805 934-1582	0
Cardenas Bros Farming Company		D	805 928-1559	0
Central Coast Distributing LLC		D	805 922-2108	0
Certified Frt Logistics Inc (PA)		C	800 592-5906	0
CJJ Farming Inc		E	805 739-1723	0
Community Action Commsn Santa		B	805 614-0786	0
Community Action Commsn Santa		D	805 922-2243	0
Country Oaks Care Center Inc		D	805 922-6657	0
Darensberries LLC		C	805 937-8000	0
Diani Building Corp (PA)		D	805 925-9533	0
Dignity Health		B	805 739-3000	0
Dignity Health		D	805 739-3830	0
Dignity Health		C	805 739-3650	0
Dignity Health		A	805 739-3100	0
Eagle Resources Inc		D	805 922-0000	0
Edwards Theatres Circuit Inc		D	805 347-1164	0
Employment Dev Cal Dept		D	805 614-1550	0
Express Messenger Systems Inc		C	800 488-2829	0
Festival Fun Parks LLC		C	805 922-1574	0
First Transit		D	805 925-5254	0
Foothill Packing Inc		B	805 925-7900	0
Freshway Farms LLC		D	805 349-7170	0
Frey Farming & Tpsry Vineyards		D	805 937-1542	0
Frontier California Inc		D	805 925-0000	0
Glad-A-Way Gardens Inc		C	805 938-0569	0
Good Samaritan Shelter		D	805 346-8185	0
Greka Inc		D	805 347-8700	0
Greka Integrated Inc (PA)		C	805 347-8700	0
H & R Block Inc		D	805 349-9266	0
Hardy Diagnostics (PA)		B	805 346-2766	0
Hunter Realty Inc		D	805 346-8688	0
Hvi Cat Canyon Inc		C	805 621-5800	0
J&G Berry Farms LLC		C	831 750-9408	0
KG Berry Farms LLC		C	805 680-6751	0
Kimberly Care Center Inc		D	805 925-8877	0
Larrabee Brothrs Distribtng Co		D	805 922-2108	0
Laurel Labor Services Inc		D	805 928-0113	0
Los Dos Valles Harvstg & Pkg		D	805 739-1688	0
Meathead Movers		D	805 349-8000	0
Merrill Gardens LLC		D	805 310-4102	0
Mesa Vineyard Management Inc		D	805 925-7200	0
Mission Linen Supply		D	805 922-3579	0
New Hope Harvesting LLC		D	805 478-4469	0
Nursecore Management Svcs LLC		A	805 938-7660	0
Nutrien AG Solutions Inc		D	805 922-5848	0
PC Mechanical Inc		E	805 925-2888	0
Peoples Self-Help Housing Corp		D	805 349-9341	0
Plantel Nurseries Inc		B	805 349-8952	0
Premier Drywall		D	805 928-3397	0
Primus Group Inc (PA)		E	805 922-0055	0
Quinn Company		D	805 925-8611	0
Radisson Hotel Santa Maria		D	805 928-8000	0
Ramco Enterprises LP		A	805 922-9888	0
Rancho Laguna Farms LLC		D	805 925-7805	0
Red Blossom Sales Inc		B	805 349-9404	0
Safari Harvstg & Farming LLC		B	805 925-2600	0
Santa Barbara Cottage Hospital		C	805 346-7135	0
Santa Barbara County of		C	805 614-1550	0
Santa Barbara County of		E	805 346-7540	0
Santa Barbara Trnsp Co		D	805 928-0402	0
Santa Maria Hotel Corp		D	805 928-6000	0
Santa Maria Valley YMCA		C	805 937-8521	0
Segura Enterprises Inc		D	805 349-0550	0
Shepard Eye Center		E	805 925-2637	0
Skylstad-Schoelen Co Inc		D	805 349-0503	0
Social Advocates For Youth (PA)		E	805 928-1707	0
Sturgeon Son Grading & Pav Inc		D	805 938-0618	0
Teixeira Farms Inc		C	805 928-3801	0
Tetra Tech Inc		D	805 739-2600	0
Tri Valley Vegetable Harvstg		D	805 928-2727	0
Tri-Counties Association F		C	805 922-4640	0
Union Asphalt Inc		D	805 922-3551	0
United Parcel Service Inc OH		D	805 922-7851	0
Valley Garbage Rubbish Co Inc		D	805 614-1131	0
Vtc Enterprises (PA)		B	805 928-5000	0
White Hills Vineyard Ranc		D	805 934-1986	0

SANTA MONICA, CA - Los Angeles County

	SIC	EMP	PHONE	ENTRY #
19 Entertainment Worldwide LLC		D	310 777-1940	0
1nteger LLC		E	424 320-2977	0
24 Hour Fitness Usa Inc		D	310 450-4464	0
Accor Services US LLC		B	310 319-3122	0
Activision Blizzard Inc		C	310 581-4700	0
Activision Blizzard Inc (PA)		B	310 255-2000	0
Activision Publishing Inc (HQ)		A	310 255-2000	0
Air Force US Dept of		B	310 393-0411	0
Alisam Oxnard Operating		C	310 877-7179	0
American Retirement Corp		C	310 399-3227	0
Apex Machine Works Inc		D	310 393-5987	0
Arizona and 21st Corp		D	310 829-5377	0
Artisan Entertainment Inc		A	310 449-9200	0
Artisan Pictures Inc		C	310 449-9200	0
Attendant Care Referrals Inc		D	310 399-2904	0
Basis Worldwide		E	424 261-2354	0
Beach Club		D	310 395-3254	0
Beachbody LLC (PA)		B	310 883-9000	0
Bird Rides Inc (PA)		D	866 205-2442	0
Blue Devils Lessee LLC		C	310 399-9344	0
Box Bros Corp		E	310 394-8660	0
Boys Grls CLB Snta Monica Inc		D	310 361-8500	0
Bryan Cave Lighton Paisner LLP		C	310 576-2100	0
Businesscom Inc		D	310 586-4000	0
By The Blue Sea LLC		B	310 458-0030	0
C W Hotels Ltd		C	310 395-9700	0
C/O Uc San Francisco		D	310 794-1841	0
Caliber Bodyworks Texas Inc		D	310 392-7662	0
Callfire Inc		D	213 221-2289	0
Callison LLC		C	310 394-8460	0
Capital Oversight Inc (PA)		B	310 453-8000	0
Casestack LLC (HQ)		D	310 473-8885	0
CBS Television Distribution (PA)		A	310 264-3300	0
Cedar Management LLC		D	310 396-3100	0
Century Finance Incorporated		D	310 281-3081	0
Charles Schwab Corporation		D	310 752-9951	0
Childrens Hospital Los Angeles		C	310 820-8608	0
CIT Bank NA		D	310 452-3802	0
CIT Bank National Association		D	310 394-1640	0
CIT Bank National Association		D	310 829-4477	0
Clare Matrix (PA)		C	310 314-6200	0
Clare Foundation Inc		D	310 314-6200	0
Clearlake Capital Group LP (PA)		B	310 400-8800	0
Coastal Health Care Inc		D	310 828-5596	0
Colfin Esh Funding LLC		C	310 282-8820	0
Company 3 Inc		D	310 255-6600	0
Connexity Inc (HQ)		C	310 571-1235	0
Converse Inc		D	310 451-0314	0

Employment Codes: A=Over 500 employees, B=251-500,
C=101-250, D=51-100, E=50

2020 Directory of California
Wholesalers and Services Companies

© Mergent Inc. 1-800-342-5647

1645

GEOGRAPHIC

	SIC	EMP	PHONE	ENTRY #
Cornerstone Ondemand Inc **(PA)**		C	310 752-0200	0
Counter Brands LLC **(PA)**		D	310 828-0111	0
County of Los Angeles		D	310 266-3711	0
Cwgp Limited Partnership		D	310 395-9700	0
Cypress Creek Holdings LLC		D	310 581-6299	0
David King Convalescent Hosp		D	310 451-9706	0
Dcp Rights LLC		E	310 255-4600	0
Demand One Media LLC **(PA)**		C	310 656-6253	0
Disability Group Inc		B	310 829-5100	0
Douglas Emmett Realty Fund 199		D	310 255-7700	0
Dtrs Santa Monica LLC		B	310 458-6700	0
Ecompanies LLC		E	310 586-4000	0
Edmunds Holding Company **(PA)**		A	310 309-6300	0
Edmundscom Inc **(HQ)**		A	310 309-6300	0
Edward Thomas Hospitality Corp		B	310 458-0030	0
Ellie Fashion Group Inc		D	818 355-3812	0
Entitlement LLC		E	224 336-2669	0
Entravsion Communications Corp **(PA)**		C	310 447-3870	0
Epochcom LLC		C	310 664-5700	0
Et Whitehall Seascape LLC		C	310 581-5533	0
Executive Network Entps Inc		D	310 457-8822	0
Friends of Max Rose LLC		D	424 901-1260	0
Game Show Network LLC **(DH)**		D	310 255-6800	0
Genius Products Inc		D	310 453-1222	0
Georgian Hotel		D	310 395-9945	0
Glamour Industries Co		D	213 687-8600	0
Global Futures Exch & Trdg Co		D	818 996-0401	0
Global-Dining Inc California		C	310 576-9922	0
Good Shepherd Health Care Ce		D	310 451-4809	0
Greenspire LLC		E	310 477-7686	0
Grow Brains System Inc		E	310 428-6445	0
Gumbiner Savett Inc CPA		D	310 828-9798	0
Guthy-Renker LLC		D	310 581-6250	0
Hct Packaging Inc **(DH)**		C	310 260-7680	0
Hirsch/Bedner Intl Inc **(PA)**		D	310 829-9087	0
Home Box Office Inc		D	310 382-3000	0
Hulu LLC **(HQ)**		C	310 571-4700	0
Ice Data Services Inc		D	310 664-2500	0
Ice Specialty Entrmt Inc **(PA)**		C	310 899-3889	0
Imagestat Corporation		C	310 392-1100	0
Innovative Artists Talent Agny **(PA)**		D	310 656-0400	0
Inspire Energy Holdings LLC		C	866 403-2620	0
Jakks Sales Corporation		E	424 268-9444	0
John M Adams Jr MD		D	310 829-2663	0
John Wayne Institute For Ctr		C	310 449-5253	0
Jonathan Club		C	310 393-9245	0
K-Micro Inc		D	310 442-3200	0
Kcrw Foundation Inc		D	310 450-5183	0
Kfa LLP		D	310 399-7975	0
Kingcom(us) LLC **(HQ)**		C	424 744-5697	0
Kite Pharma Inc **(HQ)**		D	310 824-9999	0
Kor Hotel Groups Inc		D	310 309-8066	0
Les Kelley Family Health Ctr		D	310 319-4700	0
Lightcrest LLC		E	888 320-8495	0
Lions Gate Entertainment Inc **(HQ)**		D	310 449-9200	0
Lions Gate Films Inc		C	310 449-9200	0
Luma Pictures Inc		C	310 888-8738	0
M&C Hotel Interests Inc		D	310 399-9344	0
Macerich Company **(PA)**		D	310 394-6000	0
Maguire Properties Twr 17 LLC		D	310 857-1100	0
MBK Real Estate Ltd A Califor		E	310 399-3227	0
Media Vntures Entrmt Group LLC		E	310 260-3171	0
Medicl Imgng Ctr of Southrn CA		D	310 829-9788	0
Mens Apparel Guild In Cal Inc		D	310 857-7500	0
Mercury Insurance Company		D	310 451-4943	0
Method Studios LLC		D	310 434-6500	0
Milken Family Foundation		C	310 570-4800	0
Milken Institute		E	310 570-4600	0
Miller & Associates LLP		D	310 315-1100	0
Millward Brown LLC		E	310 309-3352	0
Morgan Stanley & Co LLC		D	310 319-5200	0
Morley Construction Company **(HQ)**		D	310 399-1600	0
MSC Service Co		D	310 399-1600	0
Msd Capital LP		D	310 458-3600	0
National Apartment Flrg LLC		D	800 773-6904	0
Natural Rsrces Def Council Inc		D	310 434-2300	0
Nms Properties Inc		D	310 475-7600	0
Ocean Avenue LLC		B	310 576-7777	0
Ocean Park Community Center		C	310 828-6717	0
Ogilvy & Mather Worldwide Inc		D	310 280-2200	0
Palisades Media Group Inc **(PA)**		D	310 564-5400	0
Patientpop Inc		D	844 487-8399	0
People Concern		C	310 883-1222	0
People Concern		C	310 450-0650	0
Perkins Coie LLP		D	310 788-9900	0
Perr & Knight Inc **(PA)**		D	310 230-9339	0
Pk Nevada LLC		E	310 255-0025	0
Platinum Clg Indianapolis LLC		B	310 584-8000	0
Porter Crispin & LLC Bogusky		C	305 859-2070	0
Postaer Rubin and Associates **(PA)**		C	310 394-4000	0
Providence St Johns Hlth Ctr		B	310 829-6562	0
Provident Financial Management		D	310 282-0477	0
Realdefense LLC		D	310 693-5935	0
Red Bull Distribution Co Inc **(HQ)**		D	916 515-3501	0
Red Interactive Agency LLC **(PA)**		D	310 399-4242	0
Reilly Worldwide Inc		E	310 449-4065	0
Remote Control Productions Inc **(PA)**		E	310 260-0171	0
Revolution Studios Dist Co LP **(PA)**		D	310 255-7000	0
Rick Weiss New Hope Apartments		E	310 395-1026	0
Right At Home		D	310 313-0600	0
Rightpoint Consulting LLC		C	310 451-4619	0
Rock Paper Scissors LLC		E	310 586-0600	0
Roscoe Real Estate Ltd Partnr		D	310 260-7500	0
Rustic Canyon Group LLC		D	310 998-8000	0
S F Broadcasting of Wisconsin		D	310 586-2410	0
Saint Jhns Hlth Ctr Foundation		C	310 315-6111	0
Saint Jhns Hlth Ctr Foundation		D	310 829-5511	0
Saint Jhns Hlth Ctr Foundation		B	310 829-8970	0
Santa Monica City of		B	310 451-5444	0
Santa Monica Amusements LLC		B	310 451-9641	0
Santa Monica Bay Womens Club		E	310 395-1308	0
Santa Monica City of		D	310 399-5865	0
Santa Monica City of		E	310 458-8551	0
Santa Monica Family YMCA		D	310 451-7387	0
Santa Monica Hotel Owner LLC		C	310 395-3332	0
Santa Monica Hsr Ltd Partnr		C	310 395-3332	0
Santa Monica Orthopedic **(PA)**		D	310 315-2018	0
Santa Monica Proper Jv LLC		D	310 620-9990	0
Santa Monica Seafood Company		C	310 393-5244	0
Seaside Hotel Lessee Inc		C	310 260-7500	0
Second Street Corporation		C	310 394-5454	0
Shore Hotel		D	310 458-1515	0
Snap Inc **(PA)**		C	310 399-3339	0
Society6 LLC		E	310 394-6400	0
Solarreserve LLC		D	310 315-2200	0
SOS Security Incorporated		C	310 392-9600	0
Step Up On Second Street Inc **(PA)**		D	310 394-6889	0
Stephen B Meisel MD PC		E	310 828-8843	0
Stephen B Meisel MD A Med Corp **(HQ)**		D	310 828-8843	0
Storquest Self Storage **(HQ)**		D	310 451-2130	0
Taskus Inc **(PA)**		D	888 400-8275	0
Taslimi Construction Co Inc		D	310 447-3000	0
Tbwa Worldwide Inc		C	310 305-4400	0
Tcg Capital Management LP		C	310 633-2900	0
Tennenbaum Capitl Partners LLC **(HQ)**		D	310 566-1000	0
Tennis Channel Inc **(HQ)**		D	310 392-1920	0
Threshold Digital Research Lab		E	310 452-8885	0
Tigerconnect Inc		E	310 401-1820	0
Tiktok Inc **(DH)**		C	844 523-3993	0
Tonopah Solar Energy LLC		D	310 315-2200	0
Truecar Inc		D	800 200-2000	0
Truecar Inc **(PA)**		E	800 200-2000	0
TV Guide Entrmt Group LLC		D	310 360-1441	0
Ty Investment Inc		D	619 448-4242	0
Ucla Healthcare		D	310 399-4560	0
Universal Mus Investments Inc **(HQ)**		D	818 577-4700	0
Universal Music Group Inc **(HQ)**		D	310 865-4000	0
Universal Music Group Inc		D	310 865-4000	0
Universal Studios Company LLC		D	310 865-5000	0
University Cal Los Angeles		A	310 319-4000	0
US Credit Bancorp Inc		D	310 829-2112	0
US Small Cpitl Value Portfolio		D	310 395-8005	0
Van Etten Suzumoto Becket LLP		D	310 315-8284	0
Verizon Communications Inc		B	310 319-6148	0
Vista Del Mar Child Fmly Svcs		B	310 836-1223	0
Watt Properties Inc **(PA)**		D	310 314-2430	0
Wells Fargo Capital Fin LLC **(DH)**		D	310 453-7300	0
William Warren Group Inc **(PA)**		D	310 451-2130	0
William Warren Properties Inc		D	310 454-1500	0
Wilshire Animal Hospital		E	310 828-4587	0
Wilshire Associates Inc **(PA)**		C	310 451-3051	0
Windsor Capital Group Inc		D	310 566-1100	0
Windsor Capital Group Inc		D	310 566-1100	0
Windsor Capital Group Inc		D	209 577-3825	0
Windsor Capital Group Inc		D	209 577-3825	0
Windsor Capital Group Inc		D	310 566-1100	0
Windsor Capital Group Inc		D	310 566-1100	0
Xerox Corporation		D	310 526-3940	0
Ziprecruiter Inc		A	800 557-9015	0

Mergent email: customerrelations@mergent.com

1646

2020 Directory of California
Wholesalers and Services Companies

(P-0000) Products & Services Section entry number
(PA)=Parent Co (HQ)=Headquarters (DH)=Div Headquarters

	SIC	EMP	PHONE	ENTRY #

SANTA PAULA, CA - Ventura County

Company	SIC	EMP	PHONE	ENTRY #
Calavo Growers Inc		D	805 525-5511	0
Coastal Harvesting Inc		B	805 525-6250	0
Fenceworks Inc		D	661 265-0082	0
Granite Construction Inc.		D	805 879-0033	0
Hayward Baker Inc		D	805 933-1331	0
Knights of Columbus		C	805 525-7810	0
Limoneira Company (PA)		C	805 525-5541	0
Marin Labor Services		D	805 525-7730	0
Raycon Construction Inc		E	805 525-5256	0
Rey Con Construction Inc		D	805 525-8134	0
Santa Clara Vly Job Career Ctr		D	805 933-8300	0
Saticoy Lemon Association (PA)		D	805 654-6500	0
Time Warner Cable Inc.		D	888 892-2253	0
Ventura County Medical Center		D	805 933-8600	0

SANTA ROSA, CA - Sonoma County

Company	SIC	EMP	PHONE	ENTRY #
Airport Club		C	707 528-2582	0
Alain Pinel Realtors Inc		D	707 636-3800	0
Allied Building Products Corp		E	707 584-7599	0
Alsco Inc		D	707 523-3311	0
Amaturo Sonoma Media Group LLC		D	707 543-0126	0
American Agcredit Flca (PA)		D	707 545-1200	0
American Automobile Assctn		D	707 566-4000	0
American Med Resp AmbInc Svc		D	707 536-0400	0
Apria Healthcare LLC		D	707 543-0979	0
Argonaut Constructors		C	707 542-4862	0
Ashley Ltc Inc		D	707 528-2100	0
AT&T Services Inc		D	707 545-5000	0
Atech Logistics Inc		C	707 526-1910	0
Atech Warehousing & Dist Inc (PA)		D	707 526-1910	0
Aurora Behavioral Health		D	707 800-7700	0
Balletto Ranch Inc (PA)		D	707 568-2455	0
Bavarian Lion Company Cal (PA)		C	707 545-8530	0
Blood Bank of Redwoods (PA)		C	707 545-1222	0
Boys Girls Clubs Sonoma-Marin		C	707 528-7977	0
Burbank Housing Dev Corp		C	707 526-9782	0
Burr Pilger Mayer		D	707 544-4078	0
California American Water Co		E	707 284-1717	0
California Human Dev Corp (PA)		D	707 523-1155	0
Canine Cmpnons For Indpendence (PA)		D	707 577-1700	0
Carlilemacy Inc		E	707 542-6451	0
Cellco Partnership		D	707 525-5010	0
Century 21 Les Ryan Realty		D	707 577-7777	0
City Towel & Dust Service Inc		E	707 542-0391	0
Claimremedi Inc		D	707 827-1274	0
Clp Resources Inc		E	707 569-0200	0
Community Chld Cre Cncl Sonoma (PA)		D	707 522-1413	0
Council On Aging Svcs For SRS (PA)		C	707 525-0143	0
County of Sonoma		D	707 565-4850	0
County of Sonoma		C	707 527-2911	0
County of Sonoma		C	707 565-2209	0
County of Sonoma		D	707 527-2641	0
County of Sonoma		D	707 527-2911	0
Covia Communities		B	707 538-8400	0
CPI International		D	707 521-6327	0
Creekside Cnvalescent Hosp Inc		C	707 544-7750	0
Creekside Rehab and Behavioral		C	707 524-7030	0
Dennett Tile & Stone Inc		E	707 541-3700	0
Deposition Sciences Inc		D	707 573-6700	0
Devincenzi Concrete Cnstr		E	707 568-4370	0
Driven Performance Brands Inc (PA)		D	707 544-4761	0
Drug Abuse Alternatives Center		E	707 571-2233	0
Dura Metrics Inc (PA)		D	707 546-5138	0
Ensign Group Inc		C	707 525-1250	0
Exchange Bank (PA)		C	707 524-3000	0
F Korbel & Bros		C	707 525-1875	0
Famand Inc		C	707 255-9295	0
Finley Swim Center		E	707 543-3760	0
First Alarm SEC & Patrol Inc		B	707 584-1110	0
Fountain Grove Golf & Athc CLB		D	707 701-3050	0
Fountaingrove Inn LLC		D	707 578-6101	0
Gallaher Construction Inc		E	707 535-3200	0
Ghd Inc		D	707 523-1010	0
Ghilotti Construction Co Inc (PA)		C	707 585-1221	0
Golden Living LLC		D	707 546-0471	0
Heartland Payment Systems LLC		D	707 338-0510	0
Hired Hands Inc		D	707 575-4700	0
Icon Design and Display Inc		D	707 284-3400	0
Individuals Now		D	707 544-3299	0
Inoxpa USA Inc		B	707 585-3900	0
Jackson Family Wines Inc		C	415 819-0301	0
Jlp Landscape Contracting		E	707 526-6285	0
Joe Lunardi Electric Inc		D	707 545-4755	0
Johnson Controls		D	707 578-3212	0
Johnson Controls Inc		D	707 546-3042	0
K G Walters Cnstr Co Inc		D	707 527-9968	0
Kaiser Foundation Hospitals		A	707 393-4000	0
Kaiser Foundation Hospitals		D	707 571-3835	0
Kaiser Foundation Hospitals		D	707 393-4033	0
Keith Development Corporation		E	707 528-8703	0
Klh Consulting Inc		D	707 575-9986	0
La Tortilla Factory Inc (PA)		B	707 586-4000	0
Landesign Cnstr & Maint Inc		D	707 578-2657	0
Loring Smart Roast Inc		D	707 526-7215	0
Luther Burbank Mem Foundation		D	707 546-3600	0
Luther Burbank Savings (HQ)		E	707 578-9216	0
Manor Bell L P		D	707 526-9782	0
Mark E Jacobson M D		D	707 571-4022	0
Mayacama Golf Club LLC		C	707 569-2900	0
Melissa Bradley RE Inc		D	707 536-0888	0
Mendocino Forest Pdts Co LLC (PA)		B	707 620-2961	0
Mission Car Wash		E	707 537-2040	0
Murphy-True Inc		D	707 576-7337	0
Neese Inc		E	707 544-4444	0
Noble Aew Vineyard Creek LLC		D	707 284-1234	0
Nordby Construction Co		E	707 526-4500	0
North American Cinemas Inc		D	707 571-1412	0
North Coast Fisheries LLC		D	707 579-0679	0
Northwest Insurance Agency		D	707 573-1300	0
Novato Disposal Service Inc (PA)		D	707 765-9995	0
Oakmont Golf Club Inc		D	707 538-2454	0
Occidental Cnty Sanitation Dst		D	707 547-1900	0
Optima Building Services Maint		D	707 586-6640	0
Orenda Center		D	707 565-7450	0
Pacific Gas and Electric Co		C	800 756-7243	0
Parenthood of Planned		D	707 527-7656	0
Pepsi-Cola Metro Btlg Co Inc		D	707 535-4560	0
Permanente Medical Group Inc		D	707 393-4000	0
Primrose Alzheimers Living (PA)		E	707 568-4355	0
Primrose Alzheimers Living		E	707 578-8360	0
Protective Business & Health		D	845 354-5372	0
Pw Jade LLC		D	707 843-5192	0
Realogy Holdings Corp.		B	707 284-1111	0
Recology Sonoma Marin		B	707 586-8261	0
Redwood Credit Union (PA)		C	707 545-4000	0
Redwood Empir		D	707 586-5533	0
Redwood Empire Ice Oprtons LLC (PA)		D	707 546-7147	0
Redwood Regional Medical Group (PA)		D	707 525-4080	0
Redwood Toxicology Lab Inc		C	707 577-7958	0
Richard Hancock Inc		E	707 528-4900	0
Roman Cthlic Bshp of Snta Rosa		C	707 528-8712	0
Saint Joseph Home Care Network		D	707 206-9124	0
Santa Rosa & Sonoma Co Real Es		E	707 524-1124	0
Santa Rosa Community Hlth Ctrs (PA)		C	707 547-2222	0
Santa Rosa Dental Group		D	707 545-0944	0
Santa Rosa Golf & Country Club		D	707 546-3485	0
Santa Rosa Memorial Hospital (DH)		A	707 546-3210	0
Santa Rosa Radiology Med Group (PA)		E	707 546-4062	0
Santa Rosa Surgery Center LP		D	707 575-5831	0
Santa Rosaidence Opco LLC		C	707 546-0471	0
Security One Inc.		D	800 778-3017	0
Sonoma County Airport Ex Inc		D	707 837-8700	0
Sonoma County Humane Society		E	707 542-0882	0
Sonoma County Indian Health PR (PA)		C	707 521-4545	0
Sonoma County Water Agency		C	707 526-5370	0
Sonoma Vly Cnty Sanitation Dst		C	707 547-1900	0
Sotoyome Medical Building LLC		D	707 525-4000	0
Ss Skikos Incorporated		D	707 575-3000	0
St Joseph Home Health Network (DH)		D	714 712-9500	0
Steven N Ledson		D	707 537-3810	0
Summit Technology Group Inc		E	707 542-4773	0
Sunrise Senior Living Inc		E	707 575-7503	0
Sutter Health		C	707 535-5600	0
Sutter Health		B	707 545-2255	0
Sutter Health		C	707 523-7253	0
United Parcel Service Inc OH		A	678 339-3171	0
UPS Ground Freight Inc		D	707 526-1910	0
Venture Design Services Inc		D	707 524-8368	0
Veterans Health Administration		B	707 570-3800	0
Victor Treatment Centers Inc.		C	707 360-1509	0
Vintners Inn		D	707 575-7350	0
West County Trnsp Agcy		C	707 206-9988	0
Winzler & Kelly		D	707 523-1010	0
Woodmont Real Estate Svcs LP		B	707 569-0582	0
Wright Contracting LLC		D	707 528-1172	0
Xpo Logistics Freight Inc		D	707 584-0211	0
Y W C A of Sonoma County		E	707 546-9922	0
Youngs Market Company LLC		B	707 584-5170	0
Zayo Group LLC		D	707 284-4000	0

GEOGRAPHIC

Employment Codes: A=Over 500 employees, B=251-500,
C=101-250, D=51-100, E=50

2020 Directory of California
Wholesalers and Services Companies

© Mergent Inc. 1-800-342-5647

1647

	SIC	EMP	PHONE	ENTRY #

SANTA ROSA VALLEY, CA - Ventura County

	SIC	EMP	PHONE	ENTRY #
Tucker Electric Corporation		E	818 426-7645	0

SANTA YNEZ, CA - Santa Barbara County

	SIC	EMP	PHONE	ENTRY #
Channel Islands Young Mens Ch		D	805 686-2037	0
Chumash Casino Resort (HQ)		C	805 686-0855	0

SANTEE, CA - San Diego County

	SIC	EMP	PHONE	ENTRY #
A&M Rinforcing Specialists Inc		E	619 334-6608	0
AT&T Corp		D	619 448-1798	0
Aztec Sheet Metal Inc		D	619 937-0005	0
C & M Transfer San Diego Inc		D	619 562-6111	0
Challenger Sheet Metal Inc		D	619 596-8040	0
County of San Diego		B	619 956-2800	0
Edgemoor Hospital		B	619 596-5500	0
Hd Supply Inc		D	800 431-3000	0
International Thermoproducts		E	619 562-7001	0
J Vitale Landscape & Maint		D	619 938-2435	0
Life Gnerations Healthcare LLC		D	619 449-5555	0
Pacific Western Bank		D	619 562-6400	0
Padre Dam Municipal Water Dst (PA)		D	619 258-4617	0
Ra Hughes Enterprises In		E	619 938-4880	0
Santee School District		D	619 956-5000	0
Santee Senior Retirement Com		C	619 955-0901	0
Scantibodies Clinical Lab Inc		E	866 249-1212	0
Smart & Final Stores Inc		B	619 449-2396	0
Soapy Joes Inc (PA)		D	619 660-1113	0
T C Construction Company Inc		C	619 448-4560	0
Tarpy Heating & Air		E	619 485-3311	0
Torres General Inc		D	619 448-8900	0
Tower Glass Inc		D	619 596-6199	0
YMCA of San Diego County		D	619 449-9622	0

SARATOGA, CA - Santa Clara County

	SIC	EMP	PHONE	ENTRY #
Action Day Nrseries Prmry Plus		D	408 370-0350	0
Club At Los Gatos Inc		D	408 867-5110	0
I Merit Inc		A	504 226-2427	0
Intero Real Estate Svcs Inc		D	408 741-1600	0
Montalvo Association		D	408 961-5800	0
Odd Fellows Home California		B	408 741-7100	0
Our Lady of Fatima Villa Inc		D	408 741-2950	0
Precious Enterprises Inc		D	408 265-2226	0
Preston Wynne Spa Inc		D	408 741-1750	0
Progressive Sub-Acute Care		C	408 378-8875	0
Saratoga Court Inc		D	408 866-1392	0
Stage 4 Solutions Incorporated		E	408 868-9739	0
YMCA of Silicon Valley		C	408 370-1877	0

SAUGUS, CA - Los Angeles County

	SIC	EMP	PHONE	ENTRY #
Desert Star Co		E	661 259-5848	0
Pleasantview Industries Inc		D	661 296-6700	0

SAUSALITO, CA - Marin County

	SIC	EMP	PHONE	ENTRY #
Bay Equity LLC (PA)		D	415 632-5150	0
Butler Shine Stern Prtners LLC		C	415 331-6049	0
Casa Madrona Hotel and Spa LLC		D	415 332-0502	0
Cavallo Point LLC (PA)		D	415 339-4700	0
Comcast Corporation		D	415 367-4153	0
County of Marin		B	415 332-6158	0
Gate Five Group LLC		E	415 339-9500	0
Marine Mammal Center (PA)		D	415 339-0430	0
Naturebridge		D	415 332-5771	0
Qlm Consulting Inc		E	415 331-9292	0
Swa Group (PA)		C	415 332-5100	0
U S Army Corps of Engineers		D	415 289-3067	0
Ubics Inc		C	415 289-1400	0
Wested		D	415 289-2300	0

SCOTIA, CA - Humboldt County

	SIC	EMP	PHONE	ENTRY #
Humboldt Redwood Company LLC (HQ)		B	707 764-4472	0

SCOTTS VALLEY, CA - Santa Cruz County

	SIC	EMP	PHONE	ENTRY #
Ava The Rabbit Haven Inc		D	831 600-7479	0
Bfp Fire Protection Inc		D	831 461-1100	0
Hospice of Santa Cruz County (PA)		D	831 430-3000	0
Inn At Scotts Valley LLC		D	831 440-1000	0
Intrado Interactive Svcs Corp		D	888 527-5225	0
MBK Real Estate Ltd A Calfor		D	831 438-7533	0
R W Garcia Co Inc (PA)		E	408 287-4616	0
Roi Communications Inc (PA)		E	831 430-0170	0

SEAL BEACH, CA - Orange County

	SIC	EMP	PHONE	ENTRY #
Autism Partnership Inc		D	562 431-9293	0
Country Villa Service Corp		D	562 598-2477	0
Countryside Inn-Corona LP		E	562 596-8330	0
Encore Aerospace LLC		D	562 344-1700	0
Farmers Merchants Bnk Long Bch		C	562 430-4724	0
First Team RE - Orange Cnty		C	562 596-9911	0

	SIC	EMP	PHONE	ENTRY #
Fisheries Resource Vlntr Corps		C	562 596-9261	0
Golden Living LLC		D	562 598-2477	0
Golden Rain Foundation		D	562 493-9581	0
Healthnet California Inc		D	562 598-4043	0
Kendrick Construction Services		D	562 546-0200	0
Limbach Company LP		C	714 653-7000	0
Madaluxe Group LLC (PA)		E	562 296-1055	0
Olson Company LLC (PA)		D	562 596-4770	0
Olson Urban Housing LLC		D	562 596-4770	0
Pasha Distribution Svcs LLC		D	714 889-2460	0
Premier Healthcare Svcs LLC (HQ)		D	626 204-7930	0
Saga Seal Co Ltd		C	562 493-7501	0
Samedan Oil Corporation		B	661 319-5038	0
Strlng Path Medcl Corp		E	562 799-8900	0
Sunrise Senior Living Inc		D	562 594-5788	0
Tenet Healthsystem Medical		D	562 493-9581	0
Tyr Sport Inc		D	562 430-1380	0
Wells Fargo Clearing Svcs LLC		E	562 594-1220	0

SEASIDE, CA - Monterey County

	SIC	EMP	PHONE	ENTRY #
Boys Girls Clubs Monterey Cnty (PA)		D	831 394-5171	0
Bsl Golf Corp		D	831 899-7271	0
County Monterey Social Svcs		D	831 899-8001	0
Morale Welfare Recreation Fund		C	831 242-6631	0
Sodexo Operations LLC		D	831 582-3838	0
Tucson Hotels LP		C	831 393-1115	0

SEBASTOPOL, CA - Sonoma County

	SIC	EMP	PHONE	ENTRY #
Apple Vly Cnvalescent Hosp Inc		C	707 823-7675	0
Camp Recovery Centers LP		A	707 823-3385	0
County of Sonoma		C	707 823-8511	0
Seaver International		D	707 291-4929	0
Weeks Drilling and Pump Co (PA)		E	707 823-3184	0

SELMA, CA - Fresno County

	SIC	EMP	PHONE	ENTRY #
Adventist Health Selma		B	559 891-1000	0
Amdal In-Home Care Inc		D	559 227-1701	0
Bethel Lutheran Home Inc		D	559 896-4900	0
Circle K Ranch		D	559 834-1571	0
Dragados/Flatiron Joint Ventr		D	559 847-5388	0
Jane McClurg		D	559 834-3080	0
Kaiser Foundation Hospitals		D	559 898-6000	0
Robert Alves Farms Inc		D	559 896-3309	0
Selma Portuguese Azorian Assn		E	559 896-2508	0
Serimian M S D L Ranch		E	559 896-1517	0

SHAFTER, CA - Kern County

	SIC	EMP	PHONE	ENTRY #
Baker Hghes Olfld Oprtions LLC		E	661 834-9654	0
Bps Supply Group (PA)		D	661 589-9141	0
Cummings Vacuum Service Inc		D	661 746-1786	0
Delmart Farms Inc		D	661 746-2148	0
Farm Pump & Irrigation Co Inc (PA)		D	661 589-6901	0
Garlic Company		C	661 393-4212	0
Grimmway Enterprises Inc		C	661 393-3320	0
Grimmway Enterprises Inc		B	661 399-0844	0
J D Rush Company Inc (HQ)		C	661 392-1900	0
Standard Industries Inc		D	661 387-1110	0
Tryad Service Corporation		C	661 391-1524	0
Varner Family Ltd Partnership (PA)		D	661 399-1163	0
Wonderful Company LLC		A	661 399-4456	0
Wonderful Orchards LLC (HQ)		C	661 399-4456	0

SHELL BEACH, CA - San Luis Obispo County

	SIC	EMP	PHONE	ENTRY #
Dolphin Bay Ht & Residence Inc		D	805 773-4300	0
La Bonne Vie Inc		D	805 773-5003	0

SHERMAN OAKS, CA - Los Angeles County

	SIC	EMP	PHONE	ENTRY #
Adhei Enterprises Inc		E	818 788-7680	0
American Solar Solution Inc		D	877 946-8855	0
Ansira Partners Inc		D	818 461-6100	0
Arclight Cinema Company		D	818 501-0753	0
Azubu North America Inc		E	310 759-9529	0
Barazani Outdoors Inc		D	818 701-6977	0
Baseline Consulting Group Inc		E	818 906-7638	0
Beating Wall Street Inc (PA)		D	818 332-9696	0
Blue Chip Inventory Service		D	818 461-1765	0
Branded Entrmt Netwrk Inc (PA)		C	310 342-1500	0
Bright Pharmaceutical Services		D	818 981-9100	0
Campanile II LP		B	323 939-6813	0
Care Inc		E	818 232-7940	0
Coldwell Banker RE Corp		D	818 995-2424	0
Crowe LLP		C	818 501-5200	0
Dynamic Home Care Service Inc (PA)		D	818 981-4446	0
Fedelity National Title Co Org		D	818 758-6849	0
Filmquest Pictures Corporation		C	818 905-1006	0
Frank N Magid Associates Inc		D	818 263-3300	0
Frank N Magid Associates Inc		C	818 263-3300	0

	SIC	EMP	PHONE	ENTRY #
Golden State Health Ctrs Inc **(PA)**		C	818 385-3200	0
Help Group West **(PA)**		C	818 781-0360	0
Highpoint Productions Inc		D	818 728-7600	0
Homebridge Financial Svcs Inc		A	818 981-0606	0
Ideal Products LLC		E	818 217-2574	0
Investors MGT Tr RE Group Inc **(PA)**		E	818 784-4700	0
Lucky Strike Entertainment LLC		C	818 933-0872	0
Malka Communications Group Inc		E	818 239-4431	0
Mega Appraisers Inc		A	818 246-7370	0
Metro Home Loan Inc		D	818 461-9840	0
Moss & Company Inc **(PA)**		D	310 453-0911	0
Motion Picture Assn Amer Inc **(PA)**		D	818 995-6600	0
Mpc Productions LLC		D	310 418-8115	0
Neurobrands LLC		C	310 393-6444	0
Nexcare Collaborative **(PA)**		E	818 907-0322	0
Organic Affinity LLC		D	801 870-7433	0
P& JP Brokerage LLC		E	310 801-9707	0
Pk Management LLC		B	818 808-0600	0
Premiere Radio Network Inc **(DH)**		C	818 377-5300	0
Prime Healthcare Services - Sh		A	818 981-7111	0
Prime Healthcare Svcs II LLC		B	818 981-7111	0
Project Six		D	818 781-0360	0
Prudential Insur Co of Amer		E	818 990-2122	0
Reel Security California Inc		D	818 928-4737	0
Refinery Av LLC		E	818 843-0004	0
Rodeo Realty Inc		D	818 986-7300	0
Royal Specialty Undwrt Inc		D	818 922-6700	0
Serviz Inc		D	818 381-4826	0
Seymour Gale & Associates		E	213 622-5361	0
Sherman Oaks Health System		D	818 981-7111	0
Silicon Valley Bank		D	818 382-2600	0
Sunrise Delivery Service Inc		D	323 464-5121	0
Tharpe & Howell **(PA)**		D	818 205-9955	0
Thoughtful Media Group Inc		D	818 465-7500	0
Triton Media Group LLC **(PA)**		A	323 290-6900	0
Unlimited SEC Specialists Inc		E	877 310-4877	0
Vubiquity Inc		C	818 526-5000	0
Waldberg Inc		D	818 843-0004	0
Warner Bros Entertainment Inc		E	818 954-3000	0
WERM Investments LLC		E	213 627-8070	0

SHERWOOD FOREST, CA - Los Angeles County

	SIC	EMP	PHONE	ENTRY #
Slade Industrial Landscape Inc		D	818 885-1916	0

SHINGLE SPRINGS, CA - El Dorado County

	SIC	EMP	PHONE	ENTRY #
County of El Dorado		C	530 621-5625	0
Salutary Sports Clubs Inc		E	530 677-5705	0
Straight Line Roofing & Cnstr		E	530 672-9995	0

SIGNAL HILL, CA - Los Angeles County

	SIC	EMP	PHONE	ENTRY #
2h Construction Inc		D	562 424-5567	0
American Tile Brick Veneer Inc		E	562 595-9293	0
Edco Disposal Corporation Inc **(PA)**		C	619 287-7555	0
Fenderscape Inc		C	562 988-2228	0
First American Team Realty Inc **(PA)**		C	562 427-7765	0
Goldsmith Construction Co Inc		E	562 595-5975	0
Gregg Drilling LLC **(PA)**		D	562 427-6899	0
Gregg Drilling & Testing Inc **(PA)**		D	562 427-6899	0
Intertek USA Inc		E	562 494-4999	0
John M Phillips LLC **(PA)**		E	562 595-7363	0
Lovco Construction Inc		C	562 595-1601	0
Nsv International Corp		D	562 438-3836	0
SCCH Inc		D	562 494-5188	0
Signal Health Police Dept		E	562 989-7200	0
Traffic Management Inc **(PA)**		C	562 595-4278	0
Viking Office Products Inc **(HQ)**		B	562 490-1000	0
Walters Wholesale Electric Co **(HQ)**		E	562 988-3100	0
Wannajob Inc		D	562 426-5272	0

SILVERADO, CA - Orange County

	SIC	EMP	PHONE	ENTRY #
Inside Outdoors Foundation		C	714 708-3885	0

SIMI VALLEY, CA - Ventura County

	SIC	EMP	PHONE	ENTRY #
Aerovironment Inc		D	626 357-9983	0
Aerovironment Inc		C	805 581-2187	0
American GNC Corporation		E	805 582-0582	0
American Golf Corporation		D	805 522-0803	0
American Golf Corporation		D	805 527-9663	0
American Technologies Inc		E	818 700-5060	0
American Vision Windows Inc		C	805 582-1833	0
Andwin Corporation **(PA)**		D	818 999-2828	0
Anjana Software Solutions Inc		D	805 583-0121	0
ARC Industries		D	805 520-0399	0
Arconic Global Fas & Rings Inc **(HQ)**		C	805 527-3600	0
AT&T Corp		D	805 583-9483	0
B & M Contractors Inc		D	805 581-5480	0
B S Hand & Sons Inc		E	818 983-1155	0

	SIC	EMP	PHONE	ENTRY #
Bank America National Assn		D	805 520-5100	0
Bestitcom Inc **(PA)**		D	602 667-5613	0
Big Sky Country Club LLC		D	805 522-4653	0
Boys & Girls Club Simi Vly Inc		E	805 527-4437	0
Cardservice International Inc		A	800 217-4622	0
Cellco Partnership		D	805 955-9035	0
CFS Tax Software		D	805 522-1157	0
Chase Group Llc		D	805 522-9155	0
Cobalt Construction Company		D	805 577-6222	0
Collectech Systems Inc **(DH)**		C	818 597-7500	0
Computerized Management		D	805 522-5999	0
Computerized Mgt Svcs Inc		D	805 522-5940	0
Daicel Safety Systems		C	805 387-1004	0
Dbi Services Inc		D	805 523-7114	0
Edwards Theatres Circuit Inc		D	805 526-4329	0
Engility LLC		A	703 633-8300	0
Facey Medical Foundation		C	805 206-2000	0
First & La Realty Corp **(PA)**		D	805 581-0021	0
Genesis Home Health Inc		E	805 520-7100	0
GI Industries		D	805 522-2150	0
Golden State Water Company		E	805 583-6400	0
Hewitt and Canfield Cnstr Inc		D	805 522-4426	0
Johnson Controls Inc		D	805 522-5555	0
Kaiser Foundation Hospitals		D	888 515-3500	0
Kidney Center Inc		C	805 433-7777	0
Kids N Things Inc **(PA)**		D	805 522-1011	0
Landcare USA LLC		C	805 520-9394	0
LBC Inc		D	805 581-1068	0
Mortgage Corp America Inc		D	805 582-2220	0
Nfp Property & Casualty Svcs		E	805 579-1900	0
North Star Building Maint Inc		D	805 518-0417	0
Official Police Garage Assn of		A	805 624-0572	0
Posada Royale Hotel & Suites		E	805 584-6300	0
PQL Inc **(PA)**		E	805 579-8279	0
PW Gillibrand Co Inc **(PA)**		D	805 526-2195	0
Qualitylogic Inc **(PA)**		C	805 531-9030	0
Rancho Simi Recreation Pk Dst **(PA)**		D	805 584-4400	0
Rand Medical Billing Inc		D	805 578-8300	0
Ronald Reagan Presidential		D	805 522-2977	0
Second Opinion Med Grp Inc		D	805 496-4315	0
Shopper Inc		B	805 527-6700	0
Sierra Vista Family Medical		D	805 582-4000	0
Simi Radiology & Imaging		D	805 522-5978	0
Simi Vly Hosp & Hlth Care Svcs **(HQ)**		C	805 955-6000	0
Simi West Inc		C	760 346-5502	0
Specialized Landscape MGT Svcs		D	805 520-7590	0
Specialty Merchandise Corp **(PA)**		E	805 578-5500	0
Suttles Plumbing & Mech Corp		D	818 718-9779	0
Troop Real Estate Inc **(PA)**		D	805 581-3200	0
United Parcel Service Inc OH		B	866 553-1069	0
Vickie Lobello		D	805 750-2327	0
Vintage Senior Housing LLC		B	805 583-3500	0
Warner Media LLC		D	805 421-4467	0
Wsm Investments LLC		C	818 332-4600	0
Xmultiple Technologies		A	805 579-1100	0
Young Mens Christian Asso		D	805 583-5338	0

SKYFOREST, CA - San Bernardino County

	SIC	EMP	PHONE	ENTRY #
Spsv Entertainment LLC		D	909 744-9373	0

SMITH RIVER, CA - Del Norte County

	SIC	EMP	PHONE	ENTRY #
Reservation Ranch **(PA)**		C	707 487-3516	0
Smith River Lucky 7 Casino		D	707 487-7777	0

SNELLING, CA - Merced County

	SIC	EMP	PHONE	ENTRY #
JS Homen Trucking Inc		D	209 723-9559	0

SODA SPRINGS, CA - Nevada County

	SIC	EMP	PHONE	ENTRY #
Boreal Ridge Corporation		C	530 426-1012	0
Royal Gorge Nordic Ski Resort **(PA)**		C	530 426-3871	0

SOLANA BEACH, CA - San Diego County

	SIC	EMP	PHONE	ENTRY #
Alg Inc		C	858 945-1312	0
All-Pro Bail Bonds Inc **(PA)**		D	858 481-1200	0
American Golf Corporation		C	858 755-6768	0
BNC Real Estate **(PA)**		B	858 481-3000	0
Boys Grls Clubs of San Deguito **(PA)**		D	858 755-9371	0
Carefield Solana LLC		E	858 259-5591	0
Child Development Center		E	858 794-7160	0
Daley & Heft Attorneys		E	858 755-5666	0
Daviselen Advertising Inc		D	858 847-0789	0
Healthfusion Holdings Inc **(HQ)**		D	858 523-2120	0
Merlin Global Services LLC		C	904 305-9559	0
National Insurance Housing		D	800 550-1911	0
Onehealth Solutions Inc		D	858 947-6333	0
Senior Resource Group LLC		E	858 519-0890	0
Smart & Final Stores LLC		D	858 350-7900	0

GEOGRAPHIC

	SIC	EMP	PHONE	ENTRY #
Srg Management LLC		C	858 792-9300	0
Warren Auto De Mexico LLC		D	858 794-7947	0

SOLEDAD, CA - Monterey County

	SIC	EMP	PHONE	ENTRY #
Costa Sons		E	831 678-0799	0
Dole Fresh Vegetables Inc		C	831 678-5030	0
Kvl Holdings Inc (PA)		E	831 678-2132	0
Robertas Labor Contracting		B	831 678-8176	0
Sandoval Brothers Inc		D	831 678-1465	0
Soledad Cmnty Hlth Care Dst		D	831 678-2462	0
Valley Farm Management Inc		D	831 678-1592	0
Vasquez Brothers Inc		D	831 678-8894	0

SOLVANG, CA - Santa Barbara County

	SIC	EMP	PHONE	ENTRY #
Alisal Properties (PA)		C	805 688-6411	0
Cottage Health		C	805 688-6432	0
MWH Americas Inc		D	805 683-2409	0
National Hospitality LLC		D	805 688-8000	0
Pacific Western Bank		C	805 688-6644	0
Santa Ynez Valley Cottage Hosp		D	805 688-6431	0

SOMIS, CA - Ventura County

	SIC	EMP	PHONE	ENTRY #
Coast Nurseries Inc (PA)		C	805 386-4253	0
Saticoy Country Club		D	805 647-1153	0
Venegas Farming LLC		E	805 529-5038	0

SONOMA, CA - Sonoma County

	SIC	EMP	PHONE	ENTRY #
Appellation Tours Inc		E	707 938-9390	0
Artisan Bakers		D	707 939-1765	0
AV Brands Inc		E	410 884-9463	0
Bright Event Rentals LLC		E	310 202-0011	0
Broderick Gen Enginnering Inc		E	707 996-7809	0
Clarbec Inc		E	707 996-4012	0
CP Opco LLC		D	707 253-2332	0
CP Opco LLC		D	650 652-0300	0
Credit Bureau NAPA County Inc		C	707 940-3000	0
Diageo North America Inc		D	707 939-6200	0
Emeritus Corporation		E	707 996-7101	0
Enterprise Vineyards		E	707 996-6513	0
Freixenet Usa Inc		D	707 996-7256	0
Golden Living LLC		D	707 938-1096	0
Grega Brooke Sra		E	707 938-3362	0
Marriott International Inc		C	707 935-6600	0
Merrill Gardens LLC		D	707 996-7101	0
North Counties Drywall Inc		E	707 996-0198	0
On My Own Indepedent Living		D	707 938-9156	0
Pacific Union Intl Inc		A	707 934-2300	0
Renaissance Hotel Holdings Inc		D	707 935-6600	0
Smisc Holdings LLC		E	707 938-8448	0
Sonoma Hotel Operator Inc		C	707 938-9000	0
Sonoma Valley Health Care Dst (PA)		B	707 935-5000	0
Sonoma Valley Womans Club		D	707 938-8313	0
Speedway Sonoma LLC		D	707 938-8448	0
Swiss Hotel Group Inc		D	707 938-2884	0
V Sangiacomo & Sons		C	707 938-5503	0
Valley Moon Fre Prtct Dist		D	707 996-2102	0
Vintage Senior Management Inc		A	707 595-0009	0

SONORA, CA - Tuolumne County

	SIC	EMP	PHONE	ENTRY #
Adventist Health Sonora (HQ)		A	209 532-5000	0
Aladdin Sonora Motor Inn		E	209 533-4971	0
Amador Tlmne Cmnty Action Agcy		E	209 533-1397	0
Avalon Care Ctr - Sonora LLC		C	209 533-2500	0
Condor Earth Technologies Inc (PA)		B	209 532-0361	0
County of Tuolumne		B	209 533-5561	0
County of Tuolumne		C	209 533-5711	0
Diestel Turkey Ranch (PA)		C	209 532-4950	0
Front Porch Inc (PA)		D	209 288-5500	0
Golden Living LLC		C	209 533-2500	0
Kingsview Corp		D	209 533-6245	0
Sonora Retirement Center Inc		E	209 588-0373	0
Tuolumne Utilities District		D	209 532-5536	0
Watch Resources Inc (PA)		D	209 533-0510	0

SOQUEL, CA - Santa Cruz County

	SIC	EMP	PHONE	ENTRY #
Balance4kids		D	831 464-8669	0
Bask Jewelry Inc		D	831 479-8849	0
Bay Photo Inc		C	831 475-6090	0
Federal Express Corporation		D	800 463-3339	0
Sutter Health		B	831 458-6272	0
Trailer Park Inc		D	831 462-3271	0

SOUTH EL MONTE, CA - Los Angeles County

	SIC	EMP	PHONE	ENTRY #
Ahmc Healthcare Inc		A	626 579-7777	0
American Wrecking Inc		D	626 350-8303	0
Bali Construction Inc		D	626 442-8003	0
California Med Response Inc		D	562 968-1818	0
Commonwealth International		E	626 279-9201	0

	SIC	EMP	PHONE	ENTRY #
Fresh Air Environmental Svcs		D	323 913-1965	0
Gama Contracting Services Inc		C	626 442-7200	0
Jetworld Inc		C	626 448-0150	0
Leader Industries Inc		C	626 575-0880	0
Lincoln Training Center and RE		D	626 442-0621	0
Out of Shell LLC		C	626 401-1923	0
Statewide Pest Control Co Inc (PA)		C	626 443-2847	0
Ted Levine Drum Co (PA)		D	626 579-1084	0

SOUTH GATE, CA - Los Angeles County

	SIC	EMP	PHONE	ENTRY #
AG Adriano Goldschmied Inc (PA)		D	323 357-1111	0
AT&T Corp		D	323 568-2006	0
Castle Dental		E	323 567-1227	0
Century 21 A Better Svc Rlty		D	562 806-1000	0
County of Los Angeles		D	562 861-0316	0
Dickson Testing Co Inc (DH)		D	562 862-8378	0
Eppink of California Inc		E	562 633-1275	0
Far West Inc		D	323 564-7761	0
Firma Plastic Co Inc		B	323 567-7767	0
Herbert Malarkey Roofing Co		D	562 806-8000	0
Interior Rmoval Specialist Inc		C	323 357-6900	0
Koos Manufacturing Inc		A	323 249-1000	0
Meribear Productions Inc		D	310 204-5353	0
Pan Pacific Petroleum Co Inc (PA)		B	562 928-0100	0
Pcs Mobile Solutions LLC		D	323 567-2490	0
Privilege International Inc		D	323 585-0777	0
Pws Inc (PA)		D	323 721-8832	0
Quality Carriers Inc		D	800 282-2031	0
Rick Studer		E	323 357-1720	0
Samuel J Piazza & Son Inc (PA)		D	323 357-1999	0
Scott Jacks DDS Inc		C	323 564-2444	0

SOUTH LAKE TAHOE, CA - El Dorado County

	SIC	EMP	PHONE	ENTRY #
Barton Hospital		A	530 543-5685	0
Belmont Corporation		D	530 542-1101	0
California Land Mgt Svcs Corp		C	530 544-5994	0
California Tahoe Conservancy		E	530 542-5580	0
City of South Lake Tahoe		D	530 542-6056	0
Healthcare Barton System (PA)		A	530 541-3420	0
Healthcare Barton System		A	530 543-5685	0
Lake Tahoe Secret Witness		D	530 541-6800	0
Liberty Utlties Clpeco Elc LLC		D	800 782-2506	0
Marriott Grand Residence		B	530 542-8400	0
Park Hotels & Resorts Inc		C	530 543-2126	0
Park Hotels & Resorts Inc		E	530 541-6122	0
Roppongi-Tahoe Lp A Californi		C	530 544-5400	0
Saa Sierra Programs LLC		D	530 541-1244	0
Soroptomist Intl Tahoe Sierra		E	530 573-1657	0
South Tahoe Public Utility Dst		C	530 544-6474	0
South Tahoe Refuse Co		D	530 541-5105	0
Steven P Abelow MD		D	530 544-8033	0
Tahoe Beach & Ski Club		D	530 541-6220	0
Tahoe Seasons Resort Time Inte		C	530 541-6700	0
United Parcel Service Inc OH		B	800 742-5877	0

SOUTH PASADENA, CA - Los Angeles County

	SIC	EMP	PHONE	ENTRY #
Cccc Growth Fund LLC		D	626 441-8770	0
Collins Cllins Muir Stwart LLP		E	626 243-1100	0
Hospice Cheers		D	626 799-2727	0
Priority One Credit Union (PA)		D	323 682-1999	0
Stargate Films Inc		D	626 403-8403	0
Total Education Solutions Inc (PA)		E	323 341-5580	0
Young Mens Chrstn Assn of La		D	626 799-9119	0
Young Mens Chrstn Assn of La		D	323 682-2147	0

SOUTH SAN FRANCISCO, CA - San Mateo County

	SIC	EMP	PHONE	ENTRY #
23andme Inc		C	510 381-7237	0
ABM Aviation Inc		B	650 872-5400	0
Abp Liquidating Corp		E	650 871-7689	0
Ageis Living		E	650 952-6100	0
Alector LLC (PA)		D	415 231-5660	0
Allogene Therapeutics Inc		C	650 457-2700	0
American Etc Inc		B	650 873-5353	0
Andrighetto Produce Inc		D	650 588-0930	0
Apria Healthcare LLC		D	650 588-9744	0
Aramark Unf & Career AP LLC		D	650 244-9332	0
Ashbury Market Inc		D	650 952-8889	0
Asian Amercn Recovery Svcs Inc (PA)		C	650 243-4888	0
Avis Rent A Car System Inc		D	650 616-0150	0
Balliet Bros Construction Corp		E	650 871-9000	0
California Cryobank Inc		B	650 635-1420	0
Califrnia Golf CLB San Frncsco		D	650 588-9021	0
Centra Freight Services Inc (PA)		B	650 873-8147	0
Coast Citrus Distributors		E	650 588-0707	0
Comfort Suites		D	650 589-7100	0
Comparenetworks Inc (PA)		D	650 873-9031	0
Complete Linen Svc		D	650 873-1221	0

Mergent email: customerrelations@mergent.com
1650

2020 Directory of California
Wholesalers and Services Companies

(P-0000) Products & Services Section entry number
(PA)=Parent Co (HQ)=Headquarters (DH)=Div Headquarters

	SIC	EMP	PHONE	ENTRY #
Cooper & Jackson Inc		C	408 437-2750	0
Crown Energy Services Inc		A	415 546-6534	0
Datasafe Inc **(PA)**		E	650 875-3800	0
Dbi Beverage San Francisco		C	415 643-9900	0
Decker Elc Co Inc Elec Contrs		C	650 635-1390	0
Discharge Resource Group		C	650 877-8111	0
Djont/Cmb Ssf Leasing LLC		D	650 589-3400	0
Double Day Office Services Inc		E	650 872-6600	0
Elan Drug Delivery Inc		D	770 531-8100	0
Emerald Cloud Lab Inc		D	650 257-7554	0
Expeditors Intl Wash Inc		C	919 489-7431	0
Fedex Ground Package Sys Inc		E	800 463-3339	0
Freeman Expositions LLC		D	650 878-6023	0
Geodis Wilson Usa Inc		C	650 692-9850	0
Grosvenor Properties Ltd		C	650 873-3200	0
Hertz Corporation		D	650 624-6391	0
Hoem & Associates Inc		D	650 871-5194	0
Imperial Parking (us) LLC		D	650 871-5423	0
Inter-City Cleaners		D	650 875-9200	0
Italfoods Inc		D	650 877-0724	0
Jacobs Farm/Del Cabo Inc		D	650 827-1133	0
Janssen Alzheimer Immunothera		D	650 794-2500	0
JMB Construction Inc		D	650 267-5300	0
Kaiser Foundation Hospitals		A	650 742-2000	0
L B C Holdings U S A Corp **(PA)**		C	650 873-0750	0
Larkspur Hsptality Dev MGT LLC		D	650 872-1515	0
Legalmatchcom **(PA)**		E	415 946-0800	0
Lehar Sales Co		D	510 465-3255	0
Lyell Immunopharma Inc		D	650 383-5381	0
Mad Dog Express Inc **(PA)**		D	650 588-1900	0
Master Roofing Systems Inc		D	415 407-4450	0
Matagrano Inc		C	650 829-4829	0
Medical Care Professionals		D	650 583-9898	0
Monster Inc **(PA)**		B	415 840-2000	0
Myriad Womens Health Inc		B	888 268-6795	0
Panalpina Inc		E	650 825-3036	0
Park Hotels & Resorts Inc		D	650 589-3400	0
Pathways Home Health		E	650 634-0133	0
Peeters Transportation Co		E	800 356-5877	0
Peking Handicraft Inc **(PA)**		C	650 871-3788	0
Peninou French Ldry & Clrs Inc **(PA)**		D	800 392-2532	0
Peninsula Family Service		D	650 952-6848	0
Pennisula Pthlogists Med Group		D	650 616-2940	0
Permanente Medical Group Inc		D	650 827-6500	0
Pribuss Engineering Inc		D	650 588-0447	0
Prothena Biosciences Inc		E	650 837-8550	0
Quality Systems Installations		D	650 875-9000	0
Raven Biotechnologies Inc		D	650 624-2600	0
San Mateo County Transit Dst		B	650 588-4860	0
San Mateo Health Commission		C	650 616-0050	0
Schenker Inc		C	650 745-3000	0
Seafus Corporation		E	415 584-6100	0
Sfo Airporter Inc **(PA)**		D	650 246-2734	0
Shaw Bakers LLC		D	650 273-1440	0
Ssf Imported Auto Parts LLC **(DH)**		D	800 203-9287	0
Steven Engineering Inc		C	650 588-9200	0
Tosoh Bioscience Inc		D	650 615-4970	0
Tri Counties Bank		D	650 583-8450	0
Tricor International		D	650 877-3678	0
Trinity Building Services		B	650 873-2121	0
U-2 Home Entertainment Inc		E	650 871-8118	0
United Parcel Service Inc		D	650 737-3737	0
University Cal San Francisco		D	510 987-0700	0
UPS Supply Chain Solutions Inc		E	650 875-8300	0
Valgenesis Inc		E	510 445-0505	0
Veracyte Inc		D	650 243-6300	0
Watchpoint Logistics Inc		C	650 871-4747	0
Yrc Worldwide Inc		D	650 952-1112	0
Zipline International Inc		C	415 993-0604	0

SPRING VALLEY, CA - San Diego County

	SIC	EMP	PHONE	ENTRY #
A Better Life Together Inc		D	619 741-1548	0
B-Spring Valley LLC		D	619 797-3991	0
Brighton Place East Inc		D	619 461-3222	0
Brightview Landscapes LLC		D	619 644-8584	0
Burns and Sons Trucking Inc		D	619 460-5394	0
Casper Company		C	619 589-6001	0
Commercial Indus Roofg Co Inc		D	619 465-3737	0
County of San Diego		D	619 479-1832	0
Covenant Rtirement Communities		D	619 479-4790	0
D A V Industries		D	619 337-9244	0
Evangelical Covenant Church		D	619 931-1114	0
Greenbrier Lawn Tree Exprt Co		D	619 469-8720	0
Irish Construction		D	619 713-1991	0
J&M Keystone Inc		D	619 466-9876	0
Layfield USA Corporation **(DH)**		D	619 562-1200	0

	SIC	EMP	PHONE	ENTRY #
Mt Miquel Covenant Village		C	619 479-4790	0
Otay Water District		C	619 670-2222	0
Pnc Inc		D	619 713-2278	0
Robinson Company Contrs Inc		D	619 697-6040	0
Smart & Final Stores Inc		C	619 668-9039	0
Socal Coatings Inc		E	619 660-5395	0
Treebeard Landscape Inc		D	619 697-8302	0

STANFORD, CA - Santa Clara County

	SIC	EMP	PHONE	ENTRY #
Associated Students Stanford **(PA)**		D	650 723-4331	0
General Electric Company		C	650 725-0516	0
Hoover Institution		C	650 723-0603	0
Howard Hughes Medical Inst		D	650 725-8252	0
Imperial Parking (us) LLC		E	650 724-4309	0
Leland Stanford Junior Univ		D	650 725-4868	0
Leland Stanford Junior Univ		D	650 723-7863	0
Leland Stanford Junior Univ		D	650 723-4150	0
Leland Stanford Junior Univ		C	650 723-2021	0
Leland Stanford Junior Univ		D	650 723-9633	0
Leland Stanford Junior Univ		C	650 723-0107	0
Leland Stanford Junior Univ		C	650 724-8899	0
Leland Stanford Junior Univ		A	650 725-2386	0
Leland Stanford Junior Univ		A	650 725-6127	0
Leland Stanford Junior Univ		D	650 723-0821	0
Leland Stanford Junior Univ		D	650 723-4000	0
Lucile Salter Packard Chil		C	650 723-5791	0
Palo Alto Community Child Care		D	650 855-9828	0
Stanford Health Care		A	650 723-4000	0
Stanford Health Care **(HQ)**		A	650 723-4000	0
Stanford Law Schl Off Fncl Aid		D	650 723-9247	0
Stanford Management Company		D	650 721-2200	0
Stanford Univ Frman Spgli Inst		C	650 723-8681	0
Stanford Univ Med Ctr Aux		B	650 723-6636	0

STANTON, CA - Orange County

	SIC	EMP	PHONE	ENTRY #
California Friends Homes		B	714 530-9100	0
Denver D Darling Inc		D	714 761-8299	0
Fang Inc		D	714 898-7785	0
Great Scott Tree Service Inc **(PA)**		C	714 826-1750	0
Haulaway Storage Cntrs Inc		A	800 826-9040	0
Johnson & Turner Painting Co		E	714 828-8282	0
Muth Development Co Inc		D	714 527-2239	0
USS Cal Builders Inc		C	714 828-4882	0

STEVENSON RANCH, CA - Los Angeles County

	SIC	EMP	PHONE	ENTRY #
AT&T Corp		D	661 799-0800	0
Century Bankcard Services		D	818 700-3100	0

STEVINSON, CA - Merced County

	SIC	EMP	PHONE	ENTRY #
Frank J Gomes Dairy A Califo		D	209 669-7978	0
James J Stevinson A Corp **(PA)**		E	209 632-1681	0

STOCKTON, CA - San Joaquin County

	SIC	EMP	PHONE	ENTRY #
3900 West Lane Bowl Inc		E	209 466-6100	0
A G Spanos Management Inc		E	209 478-7954	0
ABM Janitorial Services Inc		C	209 983-3923	0
AC Square Inc		C	650 293-2730	0
Ace Tomato Company Inc		D	209 982-0734	0
Acrt Pacific LLC		B	330 945-7500	0
Alsha Academy		D	310 908-1962	0
American Automobile Assctn		E	209 952-4100	0
American Building Supply Inc		D	209 941-8852	0
American Cstm Private SEC Inc		D	209 369-1200	0
American Golf Corporation		E	209 477-4653	0
American Medical Response West		B	209 948-5136	0
Ameripride Services Inc		E	209 982-0020	0
Anand Software Inc		D	209 287-1708	0
Apria Healthcare LLC		C	209 223-7727	0
Aryzta LLC		E	209 469-4920	0
Ashley Lane Cherry Orchards LP		E	209 546-0426	0
Auto Town Inc		D	209 473-2513	0
Bank of Stockton **(HQ)**		C	209 929-1600	0
Bbva USA		B	209 473-6925	0
Bbva USA		B	209 939-3288	0
Best Western Plus-Heritage Inn		E	209 474-3301	0
Bockmon & Woody Elc Co Inc		C	209 464-4878	0
Boretech Resrce Recovry Engine		E	209 373-2588	0
Borgens & Borgens Inc		D	209 547-2980	0
Brightview Companies LLC		C	209 993-9277	0
Brookside Country Club		D	209 956-6200	0
Burlingame Industries Inc		D	209 464-9001	0
California Guard Inc		D	209 465-8420	0
California Materials Inc		E	209 472-7422	0
California Security Cons		D	209 465-8420	0
California Water Service Co		D	209 547-7900	0
Caraustar Industries Inc		C	209 476-7710	0
Caremark Rx LLC		E	209 957-7050	0

Employment Codes: A=Over 500 employees, B=251-500,
C=101-250, D=51-100, E=50

2020 Directory of California
Wholesalers and Services Companies

© Mergent Inc. 1-800-342-5647

1651

GEOGRAPHIC

	SIC	EMP	PHONE	ENTRY #
Castlehill Properties Inc **(PA)**		D	209 472-9800	0
Catholic Charities Diocese **(PA)**		D	209 444-5900	0
Chicago Title Insurance Co		D	209 952-5500	0
Childrens Home of Stockton		D	209 466-0853	0
Clark Pest Ctrl Stockton Inc		E	209 474-3204	0
Coastal Pacific Fd Distrs Inc **(PA)**		C	909 947-2066	0
Collins Electrical Company Inc **(PA)**		C	209 466-3691	0
Comcast Corporation		D	209 955-6521	0
Comfort Air Inc		D	209 466-4601	0
Communication Svc For Deaf Inc		E	209 475-5000	0
Community Medical Centers Inc		D	209 944-4700	0
Community Medical Centers Inc **(PA)**		D	209 373-2800	0
County of San Joaquin		B	209 468-2601	0
County of San Joaquin		D	209 468-4100	0
County of San Joaquin		B	209 468-8750	0
County of San Joaquin		D	209 468-3021	0
County of San Joaquin		C	209 468-3500	0
Covenant Care California LLC		C	209 477-5252	0
Covey Auto Express Inc **(PA)**		C	253 826-0461	0
Cumulus Intrmdate Holdings Inc		C	209 766-5103	0
D S S Company		E	209 948-0302	0
Dameron Hospital Association **(PA)**		A	209 944-5550	0
Delta Blood Bank **(HQ)**		D	800 244-6794	0
Delta Hawkeye Security Inc		D	209 957-3333	0
Designers LLC **(PA)**		D	209 982-0600	0
Dfa of California		D	209 465-2289	0
Dignity Health		C	209 467-6430	0
Dignity Health		E	209 943-4663	0
Dorfman-Pacific Co **(HQ)**		C	209 982-1400	0
Dreamctchers Empwerment Netwrk **(PA)**		A	209 478-5291	0
Dreamctchers Empwerment Netwrk		D	209 477-4817	0
Dynamex Inc		D	209 464-7008	0
E D D 2100		D	209 941-6501	0
E J Williams Property MGT		D	209 473-4022	0
Ecs Refining Inc		C	209 774-5000	0
Embarcadero Homes Assn Inc		D	954 776-2611	0
Employment Training Academy		E	209 475-1529	0
Estes Express Lines Inc		D	209 982-1841	0
Exel N Amercn Logistics Inc		D	209 942-0102	0
Exel N Amercn Logistics Inc		D	209 932-2400	0
Express Messenger Systems Inc		D	209 234-8255	0
Express Messenger Systems Inc		D	209 234-8255	0
Family Resource & Referral Ctr		D	209 948-1553	0
Federal Express Corporation		E	800 463-3339	0
Fedex Freight Corporation		C	209 466-7726	0
First Alarm SEC & Patrol Inc		A	209 473-1110	0
First Student Inc		C	209 466-7737	0
Five Star Qulty Care-CA II LLC		C	209 466-2066	0
Five Star Senior Living Inc		E	209 951-6500	0
Franke Con J Electric Inc		D	209 462-0717	0
Friends Outside		D	209 955-0701	0
Frontier Land Companies		E	209 957-8112	0
Fsq Rio Las Palmas Business Tr		D	209 957-4711	0
Fuel Delivery Services Inc		D	209 751-2185	0
G and L Brock Cnstr Co Inc		D	209 931-3626	0
Golden Living LLC		D	707 546-0471	0
Golden Living LLC		D	209 466-3522	0
Golden State Lumber Inc		C	209 234-7700	0
Greyhound Lines Inc		E	209 466-3568	0
Groupe Development Associates		D	209 473-6000	0
Grupe Company **(PA)**		D	209 473-6000	0
Grupe Dev Companynorthern Cal		D	209 473-6000	0
Grupe Properties Co		E	209 956-7885	0
Guard Force Inc		E	951 233-0206	0
Guy Yocom Construction Inc		C	951 284-3456	0
H and H Drug Stores Inc		D	209 931-5200	0
Heritage Land Company Inc		E	209 444-1700	0
Holistic Approach Inc		D	209 956-7050	0
Holt of California		C	209 462-3660	0
Hospice of San Joaquin		D	209 957-3888	0
In Shape Management Company		B	209 472-2231	0
In-Shape Health Clubs LLC **(PA)**		E	209 472-2231	0
Inncal Incorporated **(PA)**		D	209 473-4667	0
Inreach Internet LLC **(HQ)**		D	888 467-3224	0
International Longshoremens		D	209 464-1827	0
Interstate Truck Center LLC **(PA)**		D	209 944-5821	0
Its Technologies Logistics LLC		D	209 460-6023	0
J & P Solari		D	209 931-1765	0
John Aguilar & Company Inc		D	209 546-0171	0
Jpmorgan Chase Bank Nat Assn		A	209 460-2888	0
Kaiser Foundation Hospitals		C	209 476-3101	0
Kenyon Construction Inc		D	209 462-4060	0
Kimberlite Corporation		D	209 948-2551	0
Kindred Nursing Centers W LLC		C	209 957-4539	0
Lafaltte Rhbilitation Care Ctr		D	209 466-2066	0
Lincoln School Bus Trnsp		D	209 953-8596	0
Lithia Motors Inc		E	209 956-1930	0
LLP Moss Adams		E	209 955-6100	0
Mariner Health Care Inc		C	209 466-2066	0
Mark Scott Construction Inc		D	209 982-0502	0
Martin-Brower Company LLC		C	209 466-2980	0
Maxim Crane Works LP		C	209 464-7635	0
Meadowood Hlth Rehabilitation		B	209 956-3444	0
Mexican Heritg Ctr Gallery Inc		D	209 969-9306	0
Mid State Steel Erection **(PA)**		D	209 464-9497	0
Midstate Barrier Inc		D	209 449-9565	0
Morada Produce Company LP		A	209 546-0426	0
Mountain Valley Express Co Inc **(PA)**		D	209 823-2168	0
Mv Transportation Inc		D	209 547-7879	0
New Stockton Poultry Inc		E	209 466-1952	0
OConner Woods A California		D	209 956-3400	0
OConnor Woods Housing Corp		D	209 956-3400	0
Pacific Coast Services Inc		A	209 956-2532	0
Pacific Gas and Electric Co		D	209 942-1523	0
Pacific Gas and Electric Co		D	209 942-1787	0
Pacific Metro Electric Inc		D	209 939-3222	0
Pacific State Bancorp		D	209 870-3214	0
Pacific Steel Group		D	707 297-8922	0
PDM Steel Service Centers		D	209 234-0548	0
Pearl Crop Inc **(PA)**		D	209 808-7575	0
Permanente Medical Group Inc		E	209 476-2000	0
Permanente Medical Group Inc		D	209 476-3737	0
Pinasco Plumbing & Heating Inc		E	209 463-7793	0
Progressive Services Inc		D	209 824-2837	0
Pw Fund B LP		D	916 379-3852	0
Reeve Trucking Company Inc **(PA)**		D	209 948-4061	0
Reliance Intermodal Inc		D	209 946-0200	0
Retirement Housing Foundation		D	209 466-4341	0
S&F Management Company LLC		A	209 466-0456	0
Salvation Army		D	209 466-3871	0
San Joaquin Cnty Aging & Commu		C	209 468-9455	0
San Joaquin Regional Trnst Dst		C	209 948-5566	0
Scan-Vino LLC **(PA)**		D	209 931-3570	0
Schuff Steel Company		D	209 938-0869	0
Securitas SEC Svcs USA Inc		C	209 943-1401	0
Sierra Health Services LLC		E	209 956-7725	0
Smg		B	209 937-7433	0
Southwest Traders Incorporated		D	209 462-1607	0
St Joseph Community Home Care		D	209 478-9547	0
St Joseph Surgery Center LP		D	209 467-6316	0
St Josephs Med Ctr Stockton		A	209 943-2000	0
St Josephs Medical Center		D	209 943-2000	0
St Jsephs Regional Hsing Corp **(PA)**		B	209 956-3400	0
Standard Industries Inc		E	209 242-5000	0
State Compensation Insur Fund		C	888 782-8338	0
Stockton Cardiology Medical Gr **(PA)**		E	209 994-5750	0
Stockton Congregational Home		D	209 466-4341	0
Stockton Edson Healthcare Corp		D	209 948-8762	0
Stockton Hotel Ltd		C	209 957-9090	0
Stockton Orthpd Med Group Inc		E	209 948-1641	0
Stockton Port District		D	209 946-0246	0
Sugar Transport of The NW		D	209 931-3587	0
Sunbridge Healthcare LLC		D	209 477-4817	0
Super Store Industries		B	209 858-3365	0
Sygma Network Inc		C	209 932-5300	0
Table Community Foudation		D	209 951-1753	0
Thompson & Rich Crane Service		E	209 465-3161	0
Tranquilmoney Inc		D	800 979-6739	0
Unified Grocers Inc		C	209 931-1990	0
Unifirst Corporation		E	209 941-8364	0
United Cerebral Palsy Assoc **(PA)**		D	209 956-0290	0
United Cerebral Palsy Assoc		C	209 956-0290	0
United Rentals North Amer Inc		D	209 948-9500	0
University of Pacific		A	209 946-2030	0
USA Waste of California Inc		E	209 946-5721	0
USG Interiors LLC		D	209 466-4636	0
Valley Cmnty Counseling Svcs **(PA)**		D	209 956-4240	0
Valley Mtn Regional Ctr Inc **(PA)**		C	209 473-0951	0
Valley Wholesale Drug Co LLC		D	209 466-0131	0
Van De Pol Enterprises Inc **(PA)**		D	209 465-3421	0
Villa Real Inc		D	209 460-5069	0
Village West Yacht Club		D	209 478-8992	0
Volt Management Corp		C	209 952-5627	0
West Valley Cnstr Co Inc		D	209 943-6812	0
Westland Hotel Corporation		E	209 931-3131	0
Williams Tank Lines **(PA)**		D	209 944-5613	0
Wm Michael Stemler Inc **(PA)**		C	209 948-8483	0
Womens Center-Youth Fmly Svcs **(PA)**		C	209 941-2611	0
World Class Distribution Inc		C	909 574-4140	0
Xpo Logistics Freight Inc		D	209 983-8285	0

Mergent email: customerrelations@mergent.com

1652

2020 Directory of California
Wholesalers and Services Companies

(P-0000) Products & Services Section entry number
(PA)=Parent Co (HQ)=Headquarters (DH)=Div Headquarters

Company	SIC	EMP	PHONE	ENTRY #
YMCA of San Joaquin County		D	209 472-9622	0
Zeiter Eye Medical Group Inc (PA)		D	209 366-0446	0

STRATFORD, CA - Kings County

Company	SIC	EMP	PHONE	ENTRY #
Crisp Warehouse Inc		D	559 947-9221	0
Stone Land Company (PA)		C	559 947-3185	0

STRATHMORE, CA - Tulare County

Company	SIC	EMP	PHONE	ENTRY #
Golden Valley Citrus Inc		D	559 568-1768	0
Lopez Harvesting		D	559 568-2553	0

STUDIO CITY, CA - Los Angeles County

Company	SIC	EMP	PHONE	ENTRY #
American Private Duty Inc		D	818 386-6358	0
Blayne Pacelli		D	310 383-6281	0
CBS Broadcasting Inc		B	818 655-2000	0
Commercial Prgrm Systems Inc (PA)		C	818 308-8560	0
Crown Media United States LLC (DH)		D	818 755-2400	0
Dpr Holdings LLC		E	323 761-9829	0
Dream Lounge Inc		A	213 688-7888	0
Edgebrook Productions Inc		D	818 766-6789	0
Enrichment Eductl Experiences		D	818 989-7509	0
Everett Mall 01 LLC		E	818 505-6777	0
Fort Hill Construction (PA)		D	323 656-7425	0
Gavin De Becker & Associates		C	818 760-4213	0
High Technology Video Inc		D	323 969-8822	0
Jpmorgan Chase Bank Nat Assn		E	818 763-7343	0
Longwood Management Corp		C	818 980-8200	0
Motion Pcture Hlth Wlfare Fund		C	818 769-0007	0
Motion Picture Industry Plans		C	818 769-0007	0
Music Collective LLC		E	818 508-3303	0
Northridge 07 A LLC		D	818 505-6777	0
Radford Studio Center Inc		B	818 655-5000	0
Ranch Hand Entertainment Inc		D	612 396-2632	0
Rodeo Realty Inc		D	818 308-8273	0
Sierra Vista 16 A LLC		E	818 505-6777	0
Sportsmens Lodge Hotel LLC		C	818 769-4700	0
Sunrise Senior Living LLC		D	818 505-8484	0
Universal Studios Inc		C	818 777-2351	0
Wurzel Landscape Maintenance		E	818 762-8653	0

SUISUN CITY, CA - Solano County

Company	SIC	EMP	PHONE	ENTRY #
Cement Mason Health & Welfare		D	707 864-3300	0
E B Stone & Son Inc		D	707 426-2500	0
Hal-Mar-Jac Enterprises		C	415 467-1470	0
Redevelopment Agency of The Ci		D	707 421-7309	0
Walker Communications Inc		D	707 421-1300	0

SUN CITY, CA - Riverside County

Company	SIC	EMP	PHONE	ENTRY #
Bbva USA		B	951 672-4829	0
Physicians For Healthy Hospita		B	951 679-8888	0
Sunny Rose Glen LLC		D	951 679-3355	0
United Parcel Service Inc OH		C	951 928-5221	0

SUN VALLEY, CA - Los Angeles County

Company	SIC	EMP	PHONE	ENTRY #
Aadlen Brothers Auto Wrecking (PA)		D	323 875-1400	0
Alcorn Fence Company (PA)		C	818 983-0650	0
Araco Enterprises LLC		B	818 767-0675	0
Arcadia Transit Inc		E	818 252-0630	0
Beacon Roofing Supply Inc		D	818 768-4661	0
Browning-Ferris Industries Inc		C	818 790-5410	0
Ceramic Tile Art Inc		D	818 767-9088	0
Coast To Coast Water Damage		E	818 255-3323	0
Crown Disposal Company Inc		C	818 767-0675	0
CSC Auto Salv Dismantling Inc		D	818 532-4624	0
Daybreak Care Center (PA)		E	818 504-6154	0
Dazian LLC		D	818 287-3800	0
Estes Express Lines Inc		D	818 504-4155	0
Express Messenger Systems Inc		C	818 504-9043	0
Fathers of St Charles		E	818 768-6500	0
Federal Express Corporation		C	800 463-3339	0
Fedex Freight Corporation		D	818 899-1141	0
Fedex Ground Package Sys Inc		D	800 463-3339	0
Hawker Pacific Aerospace		B	818 765-6201	0
JP Motorsports Inc		D	818 381-8313	0
LA Hydro-Jet Rooter Svc Inc		D	818 768-4225	0
Landco		D	818 612-0118	0
Los Angeles County MTA		B	213 922-6215	0
Los Angeles Dept Wtr & Pwr		A	213 367-1342	0
Mission Valley Bancorp		D	818 394-2300	0
Mountain View Child Care Inc		C	818 252-5863	0
Nicola International Inc		C	818 767-1133	0
Norman Industrial Mtls Inc (PA)		C	818 729-3333	0
Northeast Valley Health Corp		D	818 432-4400	0
Option Care Home Care Inc		D	818 351-3000	0
Pacific Pavingstone Inc		D	818 244-4000	0
Pacifica of Valley Corporation		A	818 767-3310	0
PBM Maintenance Corp		B	818 771-1100	0
Pena Grading & Demolition Inc		E	818 768-5202	0
PMC Leaders In Chemicals Inc (HQ)		C	818 896-1101	0
PRI Medical Technologies Inc (DH)		C	818 394-2800	0
Pro Ponds West Inc		D	818 244-4000	0
Quixote Studios LLC		E	818 252-7722	0
Rawlings Mechanical Corp (PA)		D	323 875-2040	0
Refrigeration Hdwr Sup Corp		E	818 768-3636	0
Reliable Carriers Inc		E	818 252-6400	0
REM Optical Company Inc		D	818 504-3950	0
Rose Brand Wipers Inc		D	818 505-6290	0
SA Recycling LLC		D	323 875-2520	0
San Gabriel Transit Inc		D	818 771-0374	0
Serra Community Med Clinic Inc		C	818 768-3000	0
Serra Medical Clinic Inc		C	818 768-3000	0
Smg Stone Company Inc		D	818 767-0000	0
Sugar Foods Corporation		C	818 768-7900	0
Sugar Foods Corporation		D	818 768-7900	0
Svd Inc		D	818 504-1775	0
Title Records Inc		D	818 767-9610	0
USA Waste of California Inc		D	818 252-3112	0
Waste Management Cal Inc (HQ)		C	877 836-6526	0
Waste Management Recycling		D	818 767-6180	0
Wet (PA)		C	818 769-6200	0

SUNLAND, CA - Los Angeles County

Company	SIC	EMP	PHONE	ENTRY #
Brightview Tree Company		C	818 951-5500	0
British American Communication		D	818 943-6111	0
New Vista Health Services		C	818 352-1421	0
P R N Convalescent Hospital		D	818 352-3158	0
Patriot Brokerage Inc		E	910 227-4142	0
Shadow Hlls Cnvlscent Hosp Inc		D	818 352-4438	0
Tierra Del Sol Foundation (PA)		D	818 352-1419	0
Wimer Construction		E	818 848-0400	0

SUNNYVALE, CA - Santa Clara County

Company	SIC	EMP	PHONE	ENTRY #
23andme Inc (PA)		C	650 961-7152	0
A 3 By Airbus LLC		C	650 815-1881	0
Aarki Inc (PA)		E	408 382-1180	0
Al-Tar Services Inc		D	866 522-3499	0
Alvarion Inc (HQ)		E	650 314-2500	0
AT&T Corp.		D	650 960-2313	0
Avenuesocial Inc		C	510 275-4485	0
Azul Systems Inc (PA)		D	650 230-6500	0
Backproject Corporation		D	408 730-1111	0
Baidu USA LLC		C	669 224-6400	0
Belmont Village LP		D	408 720-8498	0
Broadsoft Contact Center Inc		E	408 338-0900	0
Cashedge Inc		D	408 541-3900	0
Chelsio Communications Inc		C	408 962-3600	0
City of Sunnyvale		D	408 730-7451	0
City of Sunnyvale		C	408 730-7510	0
Clover Network Inc		D	650 210-7888	0
Coadna Holdings Inc		D	408 736-1100	0
Compvue Inc		D	408 892-9909	0
Comtel Systems Technology		D	408 543-5600	0
Contactual Inc		E	650 292-4408	0
Crowdstrike Inc (HQ)		C	888 512-8906	0
Crowdstrike Holdings Inc (PA)		C	888 512-8906	0
Cyphort Inc		E	408 841-4665	0
De Anza Square Shopping Center		D	408 738-4444	0
Drawbridge Inc		D	650 513-2323	0
Druva Inc (HQ)		D	650 241-3501	0
Edelman Financial Engines LLC (HQ)		C	408 498-6000	0
Egain Corporation (PA)		C	408 636-4500	0
Entco LLC (DH)		B	312 580-9100	0
Enterprise Signal Inc		D	877 256-8303	0
Eurofins Eag Mtls Science LLC (DH)		C	408 454-4600	0
Evergent Technologies Inc (PA)		B	408 718-5453	0
Exablox Corporation		D	408 773-8477	0
Executive Inn Inc		D	408 245-5330	0
Federal Express Corporation		D	800 463-3339	0
Fiserv Inc		D	408 242-3011	0
Fujitsu America Inc (DH)		B	408 746-6000	0
Fujitsu Computer Pdts Amer Inc (HQ)		B	800 626-4686	0
Fujitsu Electronics Amer Inc (DH)		D	408 737-5600	0
Fujitsu Laboratories Amer Inc (DH)		D	408 530-4500	0
Future Dial Incorporated		D	408 245-8880	0
Gener8 LLC		C	650 940-9898	0
Ghc of Sunnyvale LLC		D	408 738-4880	0
Guck Ariba		C	650 390-1445	0
Hcl America Inc (DH)		C	408 733-0480	0
Hcr Manorcare Med Svcs Fla LLC		D	408 735-7200	0
Headstrong Corporation		D	408 732-8700	0
Honeywell International Inc		E	408 962-2000	0
Horizon Technologies Inc		C	408 733-1530	0
Hpt Trs Ihg-2 Inc		E	408 745-1515	0

GEOGRAPHIC

Company	SIC	EMP	PHONE	ENTRY #
Idec Corporation (HQ)		D	408 747-0550	0
Illumio Inc		C	669 800-5000	0
Indium Software Inc		C	408 501-8844	0
Inko Industrial Corporation		D	408 830-1040	0
Innopath Software Inc (PA)		D	408 962-9200	0
Intermedia Holdings Inc (PA)		D	650 641-4000	0
Intertrust Technologies Corp (HQ)		C	408 616-1600	0
Ipolipo Inc		D	408 916-5290	0
Island Hospitality MGT LLC		E	408 720-1000	0
Island Hospitality MGT LLC		D	408 720-8893	0
Joie De Vivre Hospitality Inc		D	408 738-0500	0
Juniper Networks Inc		A	408 745-2000	0
Juniper Networks Inc		A	888 586-4737	0
K3 Dev LLC		D	408 733-7950	0
Kaiser Foundation Hospitals		A	408 851-1000	0
Level 10 Construction LP		C	408 747-5000	0
Linkedin Corporation (HQ)		C	650 687-3600	0
Luxn Inc		D	408 213-7437	0
Malibu It Labs LLC		D	408 650-6100	0
Manor Care Sunnyvale Ca LLC		D	408 735-7200	0
Matterport Inc (PA)		C	888 993-8990	0
MDE Electric Company Inc		E	408 738-8600	0
Microsoft Corporation		C	650 693-1009	0
Mlslistings Inc		D	408 874-0200	0
Mocana Corporation		D	415 617-0055	0
Moreno & Associates Inc		D	408 924-0353	0
Mp Morse Court Associates		D	408 734-9442	0
National Opinion Research Ctr		D	415 315-3800	0
Netapp Inc		C	408 822-3402	0
Netapp Inc		C	408 419-5301	0
Ooma Inc (PA)		C	650 566-6600	0
Opal Soft Inc		D	408 267-2211	0
Oracle Corporation		B	650 607-5402	0
Osram Opto Semiconductors Inc		D	408 588-3800	0
Osram Opto Semiconductors Inc (HQ)		E	408 962-3736	0
Palo Alto Medical Foundation		D	408 730-4390	0
Palo Alto Medical Foundation		D	408 524-5900	0
Panasas Inc (PA)		D	408 215-6800	0
Pareto Networks Inc		C	877 727-8020	0
Personagraph Corporation		D	408 616-1600	0
Pivotcloud Inc		E	408 475-6090	0
Polaris Home Care LLC		D	408 400-7020	0
Polyvore Inc		D	650 968-1195	0
Proofpoint Inc (PA)		C	408 517-4710	0
Qsolv Inc		C	408 429-0918	0
Qubera Solutions Inc		E	650 294-4460	0
Real-Time Innovations Inc		D	408 990-7400	0
Ruckus Wireless Inc (HQ)		C	650 265-4200	0
S R H H Inc		E	408 247-0800	0
SC Builders Inc (PA)		D	408 328-0688	0
Screen Spe Usa LLC (DH)		C	408 523-9140	0
Selvi-Vidovich LP		D	408 720-8500	0
Sendmail Inc		D	510 594-5400	0
Sensity Systems Inc (HQ)		D	408 841-4200	0
Silicon Valley Exec Netwrk		A	408 746-5803	0
Siliconsage Construction Inc		C	408 916-3205	0
Software AG Usa Inc		C	703 860-5050	0
Star One Credit Union (PA)		C	408 543-5202	0
Stormgeo (DH)		D	408 731-8600	0
Sunnyside Gardens		D	408 730-4070	0
Sunnyvale Healthcare Center		D	408 245-8070	0
Sunnyvale Sof-X Owner L P		E	408 542-8264	0
Sunrise Senior Living LLC		D	408 749-8600	0
Supportcom Inc (PA)		D	650 556-9440	0
Sutter Health		C	408 733-4380	0
Teraburst Networks Inc		E	408 400-4100	0
Texas Instruments Sunnyvale		E	408 541-9900	0
Thoughtspot Inc		B	800 508-7008	0
Toyota-Sunnyvale Inc (PA)		C	408 245-6640	0
Tri-Power Group Inc		D	925 583-8200	0
UPS Ground Freight Inc		D	408 400-0595	0
US Interactive Delaware		C	408 863-7500	0
W L Hickey Sons Inc		C	408 736-4938	0
W2005 New Cntury Ht Prtflio LP		D	408 745-6000	0
Waste Connections Cal Inc		C	408 752-8530	0
West Valley Engineering Inc (PA)		C	408 735-1420	0
Wm ONeill Lath and Plst Corp		E	408 329-1413	0
Xoriant Corporation (PA)		C	408 743-4400	0
Xp Power LLC (DH)		D	408 732-7777	0
Zyrion Inc		D	408 524-7424	0

SUNOL, CA - Alameda County

Company	SIC	EMP	PHONE	ENTRY #
Bamboo Pipeline Inc		E	925 862-1904	0
Brightview Tree Company		D	925 862-2485	0
Save Our Sunol		D	925 862-2263	0

SUSANVILLE, CA - Lassen County

Company	SIC	EMP	PHONE	ENTRY #
Banner Health		C	530 251-3147	0
Banner Lassen Medical Center		C	530 252-2000	0
Diamond Mountain Casino		C	530 252-1100	0
Golden 1 Credit Union		D	530 251-0205	0
Honey Lake Hospice Inc		D	530 257-3137	0
Northeastern Rur Hlth Clinics (PA)		D	530 251-5000	0
Sierra-Cascade Nursery Inc (PA)		B	530 254-6867	0

SUTTER CREEK, CA - Amador County

Company	SIC	EMP	PHONE	ENTRY #
Amador Water Agency		D	209 223-3018	0
American Legion Ambulance Svc		D	209 223-2963	0
Resource Connection of Amador		D	209 223-7685	0

SYLMAR, CA - Los Angeles County

Company	SIC	EMP	PHONE	ENTRY #
A A Gonzalez Inc		D	818 367-2242	0
Advanced Mnlythic Ceramics Inc		C	818 364-9800	0
Allied Beverage LLC		B	818 493-6400	0
Allied Company Holdings Inc (PA)		B	818 493-6400	0
Ambiance Transportation LLC		D	818 955-5757	0
American Residential Svcs LLC		D	818 833-6677	0
Aramark Unf & Career AP LLC		D	818 364-8272	0
Astoria Convalescent Hospital		C	818 367-5881	0
Becho Inc		D	818 362-8391	0
Canyon Properties III LLC		D	818 890-0430	0
County of Los Angeles		C	818 364-1555	0
County of Los Angeles		D	818 364-2011	0
Desert Mechanical Inc		A	702 873-7333	0
Fisk Electric Company		C	818 884-1166	0
Foothill Waste Reclamation Inc		D	818 897-5099	0
Garda CL Technical Svcs Inc		D	818 362-7011	0
Golden State Health Ctrs Inc		C	818 834-5082	0
Lopez Canyon Landfill		E	818 834-5122	0
Mbs Equipment Company (PA)		D	310 558-3100	0
Morrison MGT Specialists Inc		D	818 364-4219	0
Mountain View Cnvalescent Hosp		E	818 367-1033	0
Oak Springs Nursery Inc		D	818 367-5832	0
Olive View-Ucla Medical Center (PA)		D	818 364-1555	0
Olive View/Ucla Education &		D	818 364-3434	0
Quality Long Term Care Nev Inc		D	818 361-0191	0
Quinn Company		D	818 767-7171	0
Reyes Coca-Cola Bottling LLC		D	818 362-4307	0
Schindler Elevator Corporation		C	818 336-3000	0
Sigue Corporation (PA)		D	818 837-5939	0
Spears Manufacturing Co (PA)		C	818 364-1611	0
Superior Gunite (PA)		C	818 896-9199	0
Sylmar Hlth Rehabilitation Ctr		C	818 834-5082	0
Tony Marquez Pool Plst Inc		D	818 833-5872	0
Tri-Signal Integration Inc (PA)		D	818 566-8558	0
Tutor Perini Corporation (PA)		C	818 362-8391	0
Tutor-Saliba Corporation (HQ)		D	818 362-8391	0
United Cp/S Chldrns Fndn La		D	818 364-5911	0
United Parcel Service Inc		D	800 742-5877	0
University Cal Los Angeles		A	818 364-1555	0
Wildlife Waystation		E	818 899-5201	0
Winning Performance Pdts Inc		E	818 367-1041	0

TAFT, CA - Kern County

Company	SIC	EMP	PHONE	ENTRY #
Alloy Construction Inc		D	661 203-2592	0
Braun Electric Company Inc		C	661 763-1531	0
County of Kern		D	661 763-1535	0
County of Kern		E	661 763-4246	0
Gene Watson Construction A CA		A	661 763-5254	0
General Production Svc Cal Inc		C	661 765-5330	0
Geo Group Inc		B	661 763-2510	0
Jerry Melton & Sons Cnstr		D	661 765-5546	0
Mashburn Trnsp Svcs Inc		C	661 763-5724	0
Providence Service Corporation		E	661 765-7025	0
Taft College Children Center		E	661 763-7850	0
Taft Production Company		C	661 765-7194	0
Watkins Construction Co Inc		D	661 763-5395	0
West Side District Hospital		C	805 763-4211	0

TAHOE CITY, CA - Placer County

Company	SIC	EMP	PHONE	ENTRY #
Bruce Olson Construction Inc		D	530 581-1087	0
Granlibakken Management Co Ltd		D	800 543-3221	0
John Brink General Contractor		E	530 583-2005	0
Pepper Tree Inn		D	530 583-3711	0
Sunnyside Resort		D	530 583-7200	0

TARZANA, CA - Los Angeles County

Company	SIC	EMP	PHONE	ENTRY #
Advanced Critical Care Emerge		D	818 887-2262	0
Advanced Medical Placement		C	818 996-9812	0
Airey Enterprises LLC		C	818 530-3362	0
AMI-Hti Tarzana Encino Joint V		A	818 881-0800	0
Amisub of California Inc (DH)		A	818 881-0800	0
Attorney Recovery Systems Inc (PA)		D	818 774-1420	0

	SIC	EMP	PHONE	ENTRY #
Blue Sky Services Inc		D	818 609-8779	0
Braemar Country Club Inc		C	323 873-6880	0
Drum Security Service Inc		D	818 708-7914	0
El Caballero Country Club		C	818 654-3000	0
Enrich Financial Inc		D	818 237-2100	0
Guardnow Inc (PA)		E	877 482-7366	0
Institute For Applied Behavior		D	818 881-1933	0
JB Partners Group Inc		C	818 668-8201	0
National Organization of		D	800 489-0210	0
Nurturing Tots Inc		D	818 996-1602	0
Providence Tarzana Medical Ctr		A	818 881-0800	0
Shapp International Trdg Inc		C	818 348-3000	0
Sinanian Development Inc		D	818 996-9666	0
Tarzana Treatment Centers Inc (PA)		C	818 996-1051	0
Wasserman Comden & Casselman (PA)		D	323 872-0995	0
Zohar Construction Inc		D	818 609-7473	0

TECATE, CA - San Diego County

	SIC	EMP	PHONE	ENTRY #
Temarry Recycling Inc		D	619 270-9453	0

TEHACHAPI, CA - Kern County

	SIC	EMP	PHONE	ENTRY #
Bear Valley Springs Assn		C	661 821-5537	0
Galice Inc		D	323 731-8200	0
LLC Woodward West		C	661 822-7900	0
Pjbs Holdings Inc (PA)		D	661 822-5273	0
Selecta Products Inc (PA)		D	661 823-7050	0
Tehachapi Vly Healthcare Dst (PA)		C	661 750-4848	0
Worldwind Services LLC		D	661 822-4877	0

TEMECULA, CA - Riverside County

	SIC	EMP	PHONE	ENTRY #
ABC Child Care Inc (PA)		D	951 699-5251	0
Altaf Zahid Engineering Svcs		E	760 481-9072	0
Bank America National Assn		D	951 676-4114	0
Bbk Performance Inc		D	951 296-1771	0
Calavo Growers Inc		E	951 676-7331	0
Charles Schwab Corporation		C	951 587-2840	0
County of Riverside		D	951 600-6500	0
Eco Farm Field Inc		D	951 676-4047	0
Eco Farms Avocados Inc (PA)		C	951 694-3013	0
Eco Farms Sales Inc (PA)		E	951 694-3013	0
Edwards Theatres Circuit Inc		C	951 296-0144	0
F M Tarbell Co		C	951 303-0307	0
Fff Enterprises Inc (PA)		B	951 296-2500	0
Homeland Security Services Inc.		B	714 956-2200	0
Inland Erosion Control Svcs		D	951 301-8334	0
Inland Valley Business and Com		D	951 378-5316	0
Irri-Scape Construction Inc		D	951 694-6936	0
Kaiser Foundation Hospitals		D	866 984-7483	0
Kelly Moses Floors		E	951 296-5147	0
Lewis Brsbois Bsgard Smith LLP		D	951 252-6150	0
MBK Senior Living LLC		D	951 506-5555	0
McCusker Enterprises Inc		D	951 699-9777	0
McMillan Farm Management		C	951 676-2045	0
McMillin Communities Inc		A	951 506-3303	0
Medley Communications Inc (PA)		C	951 245-5200	0
Michael Baker Intl Inc		D	951 676-8042	0
Miles Construction Group Inc		E	951 260-2504	0
Neighborhood Healthcare		D	951 225-6400	0
Oreq Corporation		E	951 296-5076	0
Partners In Leadership LLC (HQ)		D	951 694-5596	0
Partners In Leadership Interme (PA)		D	951 506-6878	0
Pechanga Development Corp		A	951 695-4655	0
Peed Equipment Company		E	951 657-0900	0
Phs / Mwa (HQ)		E	950 695-1008	0
Plant Holdings Inc (HQ)		D	951 719-2100	0
Ponte Vineyard Inn		D	951 587-6688	0
Primerica Financial Svcs Inc		D	951 695-4325	0
Professional Hospital Sup Inc (HQ)		A	951 699-5000	0
Pslq Inc		D	951 795-4260	0
Raintree Systems Inc		D	951 252-9400	0
Rancho California Water Dst (PA)		C	951 296-6900	0
Rancho West Landscape		E	951 301-3979	0
Responsible Med Solutions Corp		D	951 308-0024	0
Richard Burns MD		D	951 296-9300	0
RR Donnelley & Sons Company		D	951 296-2890	0
Sears Roebuck and Co		D	951 719-3528	0
Securitas SEC Svcs USA Inc		C	951 676-3954	0
Sft Realty Galway Downs LLC		D	951 232-1880	0
Sierra Pacific Farms Inc (PA)		D	951 699-9980	0
Solex Contracting Inc		D	951 308-1706	0
Southern California Tele Co (PA)		D	951 693-1880	0
Southwest Traders Incorporated (PA)		C	951 699-7800	0
Spectrum MGT Holdg Co LLC		D	951 587-8660	0
T B Penick & Sons Inc		D	951 719-1492	0
Talentscale LLC		D	951 744-0053	0
Temecula Valley Unified School		B	951 695-7110	0

	SIC	EMP	PHONE	ENTRY #
Walz Group LLC (HQ)		C	951 491-6800	0
Wedgewood Hspitality Group Inc		E	951 491-8110	0
Wholesale Air-Time Inc		E	951 693-1880	0
Windsor Capital Group Inc		D	951 676-5656	0

TEMPLE CITY, CA - Los Angeles County

	SIC	EMP	PHONE	ENTRY #
Community Care Adhc Inc		D	626 614-8999	0
Fran-Jom Inc		D	626 443-3028	0
Golden State Health Ctrs Inc		C	626 579-0310	0
Santa Anita Convalescent Hospi		C	626 579-0310	0
Western Tear-Off & Disposal		D	626 443-9984	0

TEMPLETON, CA - San Luis Obispo County

	SIC	EMP	PHONE	ENTRY #
Aha Shoes Inc		D	805 434-9891	0
Grants Custom Cabinets		C	805 466-9680	0
Mesa Vineyard Management Inc (PA)		D	805 434-4100	0
Pacific Coast Supply LLC		D	805 434-4800	0
Pacific Gas and Electric Co		D	805 434-4418	0
Twin Cities Community Hosp Inc		B	805 434-3500	0
Wilshire Health and Cmnty Svcs		D	805 434-3035	0

TERRA BELLA, CA - Tulare County

	SIC	EMP	PHONE	ENTRY #
Setton Pstchio Terra Bella Inc (HQ)		D	559 535-6050	0
Sierra Forest Products		C	559 535-4893	0

THERMAL, CA - Riverside County

	SIC	EMP	PHONE	ENTRY #
Drake Larson Ranchs		C	760 399-5494	0
Golden Acres Farms		E	760 399-1923	0
Golden State Herbs (PA)		E	760 342-7117	0
Gomez Farm Labor Contg Inc		D	760 399-1994	0
Interntnal Pvment Slutions Inc		D	909 794-2101	0
James Fedor Masonry Inc		D	760 772-3036	0
Kono Farms Incorporated		C	760 397-7110	0
North Shore Greenhouses Inc		C	760 397-0400	0
Red Earth Casino		C	760 395-1200	0
Torres-Martinez		C	760 395-1200	0
West Coast Aggregate Supply		E	760 342-7598	0
Woodspur Farming LLC		D	760 398-9480	0

THOUSAND OAKS, CA - Ventura County

	SIC	EMP	PHONE	ENTRY #
A P R Inc		C	805 379-3400	0
American Golf Corporation		D	805 495-5407	0
American Services and Products		D	805 375-2858	0
Amgen Pharmaceuticals Inc		A	805 447-1000	0
Andrews International Inc		C	805 409-4160	0
Anthem Inc		B	805 231-0994	0
Bauer Hockey Inc		B	818 782-6445	0
Bead Society		C	805 495-2550	0
Bob Dillon Construction Inc		C	805 495-2607	0
Bright Horizons Chld Ctrs LLC		C	805 447-6793	0
California Kidney Med Group		D	805 497-7775	0
Calleguas Municipal Water Dict.		D	805 526-9323	0
Castlewood Treatment Ctr LLC (PA)		D	805 273-5217	0
Change Hlthcare Operations LLC		D	805 777-7773	0
Chase Group Llc (PA)		A	805 497-7330	0
Cigna Healthcare Cal Inc		C	805 230-8300	0
CIT Bank NA		D	805 379-5520	0
Citigroup Inc		D	805 557-0930	0
Conejo Valley Unified Schl Dst		B	805 496-9035	0
Countrywide Home Loans Inc (DH)		A	818 225-3000	0
Durham School Services L P		D	805 495-8338	0
Elms Sanitarium Inc		D	818 240-6720	0
Enhanced Landscape MGT Inc		D	805 557-2737	0
Fedex Office & Print Svcs Inc		E	805 379-1552	0
Floyd Skeren & Kelly LLP (PA)		D	818 206-9222	0
Gemmm Corp (PA)		D	805 496-0555	0
Kaiser Foundation Hospitals		A	888 515-3500	0
Kaiser Foundation Hospitals		A	888 515-3500	0
Kaiser Foundation Hospitals		D	888 515-3500	0
Kevin Persons Inc		E	805 371-8746	0
Los Robles Bank		D	805 373-6763	0
Los Robles Hospital & Med Ctr (DH)		D	805 497-2727	0
Management Trust Assn Inc		C	805 496-5514	0
Meathead Movers Inc		D	805 496-1416	0
Miramed Global Services Inc		A	805 277-1017	0
Mv Transportation Inc		D	805 557-7372	0
R T Framing Corporation		D	805 496-3985	0
Red Pocket Inc		D	888 993-3888	0
Retail Services & Systems Inc		D	805 494-0108	0
S A Cali-U Acoustics Inc		D	805 376-9300	0
Sherwood Country Club		C	805 496-3036	0
Sherwood Development Company (PA)		E	805 496-1833	0
Southern Cal Orthpd Inst LP		D	805 497-7015	0
Southern California Edison Co		C	818 999-1880	0
Staff Assistance Inc (PA)		B	818 894-7879	0
Staff Assistance Inc		B	805 371-9980	0
Star of California		D	805 379-1401	0

Employment Codes: A=Over 500 employees, B=251-500,
C=101-250, D=51-100, E=50

2020 Directory of California
Wholesalers and Services Companies

© Mergent Inc. 1-800-342-5647

1655

GEOGRAPHIC

	SIC	EMP	PHONE	ENTRY #
Teledyne Scentific Imaging LLC **(HQ)**		C	805 373-4545	0
Thousand Oaks Surgical Hosp LP		D	805 777-7750	0
Trak Microwave Corporation		C	805 267-0100	0
Ventu Park LLC		D	805 716-4200	0
Ventura County Office Educatn		D	805 495-7037	0
Young Mens Christian Asso		D	805 523-7613	0
Zs Associates Inc		D	805 413-5900	0

THOUSAND PALMS, CA - Riverside County

	SIC	EMP	PHONE	ENTRY #
CBS Corporation		D	760 343-5700	0
Club At Shnndoah Sprng Vlg Inc		E	760 343-3497	0
Gate City Beverage Distrs		B	760 775-5483	0
Gulf- California Broadcast Co		C	760 773-0342	0
Jacobsson Engrg Cnstr Inc		D	760 345-8700	0
Kincaid Industries Inc		C	760 343-5457	0
Little Sisters Truck Wash Inc		D	760 343-3448	0
Readylink Inc		D	760 343-7000	0
Readylink Healthcare		D	760 343-7000	0
San Val Corp **(PA)**		B	760 346-3999	0
Sunline Transit Agency **(PA)**		C	760 343-3456	0
Vorwaller & Brooks Inc		D	760 262-6300	0

TIPTON, CA - Tulare County

	SIC	EMP	PHONE	ENTRY #
Bosman Dairy LLC		C	559 752-7018	0
Mendes Calf Ranch		D	559 688-4708	0
Sunkist Growers Inc		C	909 983-9811	0
Sunkist Growers Inc		C	559 752-4256	0

TOLUCA LAKE, CA - Los Angeles County

	SIC	EMP	PHONE	ENTRY #
James B Branch Inc **(PA)**		E	818 765-3521	0
Wells Fargo Bank National Assn		E	818 766-7172	0

TOPANGA, CA - Los Angeles County

	SIC	EMP	PHONE	ENTRY #
Rock-It Cargo USA LLC		D	310 455-1900	0

TOPAZ, CA - Mono County

	SIC	EMP	PHONE	ENTRY #
Northern Mono Chamber Commerce		E	530 208-6078	0

TORRANCE, CA - Los Angeles County

	SIC	EMP	PHONE	ENTRY #
A L S Industries Inc		E	310 532-9262	0
ACS Communications Inc		D	310 767-2145	0
Act 1 Group Inc **(PA)**		D	310 532-1529	0
Aestiva Software Inc		E	310 697-0338	0
Ait Worldwide Logistics Inc		D	310 538-4383	0
All In One Inc		C	310 538-3374	0
All South Bay Central Office		D	310 618-1180	0
Allied Digital Services LLC **(HQ)**		C	310 431-2375	0
Allied Protection Services Inc		D	310 330-8314	0
Alpine Electronics America Inc		D	310 783-7391	0
Alpine Village		C	310 327-4384	0
American Honda Finance Corp **(DH)**		C	310 972-2239	0
American Honda Motor Co Inc **(HQ)**		A	310 783-2000	0
American Multi-Cinema Inc		C	310 326-5011	0
Ana Trading Corp USA **(DH)**		D	310 542-2500	0
Arconic Global Fas & Rings Inc		D	310 784-0700	0
Arconic Global Fas & Rings Inc		B	310 530-2220	0
Arconic Global Fas & Rings Inc		E	310 530-2220	0
Arconic Global Fas & Rings Inc		A	310 530-2220	0
Automobile Club Southern Cal		D	310 325-3111	0
Bankcard Services **(PA)**		D	213 365-1122	0
Bayco Financial Corporation **(PA)**		D	310 378-8181	0
Binex Line Corp **(PA)**		D	310 416-8600	0
Bioscreen Testing Services Inc **(DH)**		D	310 214-0043	0
Bowman and Brooke LLP		D	310 768-3068	0
BQE Software Inc		D	310 602-4020	0
Breast Diagnostic Center		E	310 517-4709	0
Breville Usa Inc		E	310 755-3000	0
Bright Event Rentals LLC **(PA)**		D	310 202-0011	0
Burdette De Cock Inc		C	310 542-0563	0
C H Robinson Intl Inc		D	310 763-6080	0
California Mfg Tech Consulting		D	310 263-3060	0
California Yacht Marina Inc **(PA)**		E	310 534-8436	0
CCH Incorporated		B	310 800-9800	0
Century 21 Amber Realty Inc		D	310 625-4363	0
Century 21 Exclusive Realtors		C	310 373-5252	0
Ceva Freight LLC		D	310 972-5500	0
Ceva Logistics LLC		B	310 223-6500	0
CH Robinson Freight Svcs Ltd		E	310 515-7755	0
Charles M Kamiya and Sons Inc		D	310 781-2066	0
Choura Events		D	310 320-6200	0
Citigroup Global Markets Inc		E	310 540-9511	0
City of Torrance		D	310 781-6901	0
Compex Legal Services Inc **(PA)**		C	310 782-1801	0
Contemporary Services Corp		D	310 320-8418	0
Continental Dntl Ceramics Inc		E	310 618-8821	0
County of Los Angeles		C	310 222-4220	0
County of Los Angeles		D	310 222-2357	0

	SIC	EMP	PHONE	ENTRY #
County of Los Angeles		C	310 222-3552	0
Credit Card Services Inc **(PA)**		D	213 365-1122	0
Crenshaw Bowling		E	310 326-5120	0
Ctc Group Inc **(DH)**		C	310 540-0500	0
Del AMO Construction		D	310 378-6203	0
Del AMO Diagnostic Center		E	310 316-2424	0
Del AMO Grdns Cnvlscnt Hosp &		D	310 378-4233	0
Del AMO Hospital Inc		B	310 530-1151	0
Delta Computer Consulting		C	310 541-9440	0
Dicaperl Corporation **(DH)**		D	610 667-6640	0
Divergent Technologies Inc		D	310 339-1186	0
Docmagic Inc		D	800 649-1362	0
DTM Services Inc **(PA)**		D	310 521-1200	0
Earlwood LLC		D	310 371-1228	0
Easy Ride Transportation		D	424 999-8830	0
Electronic Data Care Inc		D	310 791-2600	0
Emax Laboratories Inc		E	310 618-8889	0
Express Imaging Services Inc		D	888 846-8804	0
Ezcaretech USA Inc		B	424 558-3191	0
Fns Inc **(PA)**		D	661 615-2300	0
Freedom Staff Leasing Inc		B	310 834-6621	0
Frito-Lay North America Inc		C	310 224-5600	0
Fujitsu Ten Corp of America		C	310 327-2151	0
Gable House Inc		D	310 378-2265	0
Gdf Parent LLC		D	714 743-7209	0
Gebruder Weiss Inc		D	310 414-9300	0
Gerber Ambulance Company Inc		D	310 542-6464	0
Geri Care Inc		D	310 320-0961	0
Geri-Care II Inc		C	310 328-0812	0
Gky Dental Arts Inc **(PA)**		D	310 214-8007	0
Global Accents Inc		C	310 639-2600	0
Good Sports Plus Ltd		B	310 671-4400	0
Goodridge Usa Inc **(DH)**		D	310 533-1924	0
Harbor Building Services		D	310 320-2966	0
Harbor Developmental Disabilit		C	310 540-1711	0
Harbor-Cla Med Ctr Dept Srgery		D	310 222-2701	0
Harbor-Ucla Med Foundation Inc **(PA)**		B	310 222-5015	0
Holiday Inn Hotel Torrance		C	310 781-9100	0
Hunt Enterprises Inc		C	310 325-1496	0
I C Class Components Corp **(PA)**		D	310 539-5500	0
Imperial Cfs Inc		E	310 768-8188	0
Industrial Parts Depot LLC **(HQ)**		D	310 530-1900	0
Intercontinental Hotels Group		D	310 781-9100	0
Janet Hilton		D	310 851-7200	0
Jtb Americas Ltd **(HQ)**		D	310 303-3750	0
Kaiser Foundation Hospitals		D	800 780-1230	0
Keenan & Associates **(HQ)**		B	310 212-3344	0
Keller Williams Realty		B	310 375-3511	0
Kingdom Express Inc		D	310 258-0900	0
Kintetsu Enterprises Co Amer **(HQ)**		C	310 782-9300	0
Knowledge Holdings Inc **(PA)**		D	310 533-3400	0
Kobata Growers Inc **(PA)**		D	310 323-0662	0
Liberty Mutual Insurance Co		C	310 316-9428	0
Lifecare Systems Inc		C	310 540-7676	0
Light Hse Memorials Receptions **(PA)**		D	310 792-7599	0
Little Company Mary Hospital		A	310 540-7676	0
Long Beach Golden Sails Inc		D	562 596-1631	0
Longwood Management Inc		D	310 370-5828	0
Los Defensores Inc		E	310 519-4050	0
Mariner Health Care Inc		D	310 371-4628	0
Maritzcx Research LLC		D	310 783-4300	0
Mednax Inc		C	310 375-7172	0
Menemsha Development Group Inc **(PA)**		C	310 343-3430	0
Metroplex Theatres LLC		A	310 856-1270	0
Mighty Enterprises Inc		D	310 516-7478	0
Mishima Foods USA Inc **(PA)**		D	310 787-1533	0
Nippon Express USA Inc		E	310 532-6300	0
Nissin Intl Trnspt USA Inc **(HQ)**		E	310 222-8500	0
Organic Inc		D	310 543-4600	0
Oriental Motor USA Corporation **(DH)**		D	310 715-3300	0
Pacific Echo Inc		D	310 539-1822	0
Pacific Home Works Inc		C	310 781-3012	0
Panalpina Inc		D	310 819-4060	0
Partner Assessment Corporation **(PA)**		C	800 419-4923	0
Pediatric Therapy Network		D	310 328-0276	0
Pentel of America Ltd **(HQ)**		C	310 320-3831	0
Performance Team Frt Sys Inc		D	562 345-2200	0
Pharmaco Inc		D	310 328-3897	0
Physical Optics Corporation **(PA)**		D	310 320-3088	0
Physicians Choice HM Hlth Inc		E	310 793-1616	0
Pioneer Theatres Inc		C	310 532-8183	0
Platinum Empire Group Inc		C	310 821-5888	0
Polypeptide Laboratories Inc **(DH)**		D	310 782-3569	0
Proactive Risk Management Inc		D	213 840-8856	0
Providence Health System		C	310 543-5900	0

(P-0000) Products & Services Section entry number
(PA)=Parent Co (HQ)=Headquarters (DH)=Div Headquarters

	SIC	EMP	PHONE	ENTRY #
Providence Health System		C	310 370-5895	0
Providence Health System		C	310 370-5895	0
Providence Health System		C	310 303-6970	0
PS Environmental Svcs Inc		D	310 373-6259	0
PSC Industrial Outsourcing LP		C	310 325-1600	0
Pta California Congress of Par		C	310 328-3100	0
Public Hlth Fndation Entps Inc		C	310 320-5215	0
Quinstar Technology Inc		D	310 320-1111	0
R C I Enterprises Inc		E	310 370-5900	0
Resource Collection Inc		A	310 219-3272	0
Restaurant Depot LLC		D	310 516-7400	0
Riad Adoumie MD		D	310 373-6864	0
Rmi International Inc		D	310 781-6768	0
Roy Jorgensen Associates Inc		D	310 468-2478	0
Ryans Express Trnsp Svcs Inc (PA)		D	310 219-2960	0
Sakura Finetek USA Inc (HQ)		C	310 972-7800	0
Salson Logistics Inc		D	310 328-6800	0
Sanyo Denki America Inc (HQ)		D	310 783-5400	0
Securitas SEC Svcs USA Inc		C	310 787-0747	0
Securitas SEC Svcs USA Inc		C	714 385-9745	0
Shimadzu Precision Instrs Inc		D	310 217-8855	0
Silicon Prime Technologies Inc		E	310 279-0222	0
Simplehuman LLC (PA)		D	310 436-2250	0
Six Continents Hotels Inc		D	310 371-8525	0
Six Continents Hotels Inc		C	310 781-9100	0
Sonic Industries Inc		C	310 532-8382	0
South Bay Family Medical Group		D	310 378-2234	0
Space Age Metal Products Inc		C	310 539-5500	0
Special Service For Groups Inc		C	310 323-6887	0
Stanley R Klein MD Facs Inc		E	310 373-6864	0
Star View Adolescent Center		D	310 373-4556	0
Sun Chlorella USA Corp		D	310 891-0600	0
Sunnyside Rhblttion Nrsing Ctr		C	310 320-4130	0
Superhero App LLC		D	562 341-0784	0
Supershuttle Los Angeles Inc		C	310 222-5500	0
Supershuttle Orange County Inc		B	310 222-5500	0
Sweis Inc (PA)		C	310 375-0558	0
Topwin Corporation (PA)		D	310 325-2255	0
Toro Nursery Inc		D	310 715-1982	0
Torrance Care Center West Inc		C	310 370-4561	0
Torrance Health Assn Inc (PA)		A	310 325-9110	0
Torrance Memorial Medical Ctr (HQ)		A	310 325-9110	0
Torrance Surgery Center LP		D	310 986-2005	0
Total Management Svcs Amer Inc		E	310 328-0867	0
Tower Energy Group (PA)		D	310 538-8000	0
Trendnet Inc (PA)		D	310 961-5500	0
Unified Inv Programs Inc (PA)		D	310 782-1878	0
Unify Financial Federal Cr Un (PA)		D	310 536-5000	0
United Parcel Service Inc OH		D	800 742-5877	0
UPS Supply Chain Solutions Inc		C	310 404-2719	0
Vector Resources Inc (PA)		C	310 436-1000	0
Virco Inc (HQ)		D	310 533-0474	0
Vitas Healthcare Corp Cal		D	310 324-2273	0
Volt Management Corp.		C	310 316-8523	0
Walker Advertising LLC		E	310 519-4050	0
Windsor Gardens		D	562 422-9219	0
Wyle Information Systems LLC		B	310 563-6800	0
Xld Group LLC		D	310 316-3636	0

TRABUCO CANYON, CA - Orange County

	SIC	EMP	PHONE	ENTRY #
Coto De Caza Golf Club Inc		C	949 766-7886	0
Coto De Caza Golf Racquet CLB		C	949 858-4100	0
Davlor Company		D	949 244-9748	0

TRACY, CA - San Joaquin County

	SIC	EMP	PHONE	ENTRY #
American Engrg Contrs Inc		C	209 229-1591	0
Arconic Global Fas & Rings Inc		D	209 839-3005	0
Arnaudo Bros Transport Inc (PA)		D	209 835-0406	0
Boys & Girls Club of Tracy (PA)		E	209 832-2582	0
Cascade Logistics LLC		D	209 832-4205	0
Costco Wholesale Corporation		B	209 835-5222	0
DSC Logistics Inc		D	209 362-2232	0
Ed Thoming & Sons Inc		D	209 835-2792	0
Es3 LLC		E	209 832-4205	0
Faith Enterprises Inc		E	209 835-6034	0
Glassfab Tempering Svcs Inc (PA)		D	209 229-1060	0
Green Valley Trnsp Corp		E	209 836-5192	0
Imobile LLC		B	209 833-6757	0
In-Shape Health Clubs LLC		C	209 836-2504	0
Jesse Lee Group Inc		D	209 832-2273	0
Kaiser Foundation Hospitals		A	209 839-3200	0
Kaiser Foundation Hospitals		D	209 832-6339	0
McLane Company Inc		C	209 221-7500	0
Myra Investment and Dev Corp.		D	209 834-2343	0
Owens & Minor Inc		D	209 833-4600	0
Pacific Medical Inc (PA)		C	800 726-9180	0

	SIC	EMP	PHONE	ENTRY #
Safeway Stores Incorporated		B	209 833-4700	0
Tracy Bancshares Inc		D	209 836-5111	0
Tracy Dlta Solid Waste Mgt Inc		D	209 835-0601	0
Tracy Interfaith Ministries		D	209 836-5424	0
Tracy Sutter Community Hosp		B	209 835-1500	0
United Facilities Inc		E	209 839-8051	0
United States Cold Storage Inc		E	209 835-2653	0
We Care Day Care & Pre School		D	209 832-4072	0
Yrc Inc		C	209 833-1300	0

TRANQUILLITY, CA - Fresno County

	SIC	EMP	PHONE	ENTRY #
Don Gragnani Farms		D	559 693-4352	0

TRAVER, CA - Tulare County

	SIC	EMP	PHONE	ENTRY #
Foster Poultry Farms		A	559 457-6509	0

TRAVIS AFB, CA - Solano County

	SIC	EMP	PHONE	ENTRY #
US Airforce Band of Golden W		E	707 424-2263	0

TRINIDAD, CA - Humboldt County

	SIC	EMP	PHONE	ENTRY #
Cher-Ae Heights Indian Cmnty		C	707 677-3611	0

TRONA, CA - San Bernardino County

	SIC	EMP	PHONE	ENTRY #
Searles Valley Minerals Inc		A	760 372-2259	0

TRUCKEE, CA - Nevada County

	SIC	EMP	PHONE	ENTRY #
Bhr Trs Tahoe LLC		C	530 562-3045	0
Charles Schwab Corporation		D	530 448-8038	0
Clearcapitalcom Inc		C	530 550-2500	0
Hyatt Corporation		B	530 562-3900	0
Lahontan Golf Club		C	530 550-2400	0
Martis Camp Club		B	530 550-6000	0
Tahoe Donner Association		C	530 587-9437	0
Tahoe Donner Golf Course Inc		D	530 587-9455	0
Tahoe Forest Hospital District		D	530 582-7488	0
Tahoe Forest Hospital District		C	530 582-3277	0
Tahoe Forest Hospital District (PA)		B	530 587-6011	0
Tahoe Trcke Unfd Sch Dis Fincn		D	530 582-7630	0
Tahoe-Truckee Sanitation Agcy		D	530 587-2525	0
Trimont Land Company (DH)		B	530 562-1010	0
Truckee Dnner Rcreation Pk Dst		D	530 582-7720	0
Truckee Donner Pub Utly Dist F		D	530 587-3896	0
Western Nevada Supply Co		C	530 582-5009	0

TUJUNGA, CA - Los Angeles County

	SIC	EMP	PHONE	ENTRY #
Crescenta-Canada YMCA		E	818 352-3255	0
Oakview Convalescent Hospital		E	818 352-4426	0
Sun Mar Management Services		D	818 352-1454	0
Volunteers of Amer Los Angeles		C	818 352-5974	0

TULARE, CA - Tulare County

	SIC	EMP	PHONE	ENTRY #
Altura Centers For Health		D	559 686-9097	0
Amdal In-Home Care Inc (PA)		E	559 686-6611	0
Central California Tr		D	559 686-4973	0
City of Tulare		D	559 684-4200	0
Curti Family Inc		D	559 688-8323	0
Dan Freitas Electric		D	559 686-9572	0
Darrell L Green Inc		D	559 688-0686	0
Kings County Truck Lines (HQ)		C	559 686-2857	0
Kloeckner Metals Corporation		D	559 688-7980	0
Klx Inc		D	559 684-1037	0
M & T Calf Ranch		D	559 686-7663	0
Moyles Central Vly Hlth Care (PA)		B	559 688-0288	0
Moyles Health Care Inc		A	559 686-1601	0
Nielsens Creamery (PA)		D	559 686-4744	0
Porterville Sheltered Workshop		D	559 684-9168	0
SA Recycling LLC		D	559 688-0271	0
Tulare Local Health Care Dst		A	559 685-3462	0
Tulare Nrsing Rhblitation Hosp		C	559 686-8581	0
Tulare Regional Medical Center		D	559 688-0821	0
Turnupseed Electric Service		D	559 686-1541	0
United States Cold Storage Inc		E	559 686-1110	0
Vander Weerd General Cnstr		D	559 688-1099	0

TULELAKE, CA - Siskiyou County

	SIC	EMP	PHONE	ENTRY #
Lava Beds National Monuments		E	530 667-2282	0

TUOLUMNE, CA - Tuolumne County

	SIC	EMP	PHONE	ENTRY #
Black Oak Casino		D	209 928-9300	0
Silver Spur Christian Camp		D	209 928-4248	0
Tuolumne City Inv Grp II LP		E	209 928-1567	0
Tuolumne Me-Wuk Indian		D	209 928-5400	0

TURLOCK, CA - Stanislaus County

	SIC	EMP	PHONE	ENTRY #
American Medical Response Inc		C	209 567-4030	0
Aspiranet		D	209 669-2582	0
Aspiranet		D	209 667-0327	0
Associated Feed & Supply Co (PA)		C	209 667-2708	0
Central California Faculty Med		B	209 620-6937	0

GEOGRAPHIC

Employment Codes: A=Over 500 employees, B=251-500,
C=101-250, D=51-100, E=50

2020 Directory of California
Wholesalers and Services Companies

© Mergent Inc. 1-800-342-5647

1657

	SIC	EMP	PHONE	ENTRY #
Central Valley Cheese Inc		D	209 664-1080	0
Covenant Care California LLC		C	209 632-3821	0
Covenant Rtirement Communities		C	209 632-9976	0
Creative Alternatives		C	209 668-9361	0
Crimetek Security		B	209 668-6208	0
Emanuel Medical Center Inc		C	209 667-5600	0
Emanuel Medical Center Inc **(DH)**		A	209 667-4200	0
Emanuel Medical Center Inc		A	209 664-2520	0
Freshpoint Central California		C	209 216-0200	0
Funtopia Inc		D	510 246-3098	0
Gemperle Enterprises		D	209 667-2651	0
Humphrey Plumbing Inc		D	209 634-4626	0
Joe L Coelho Inc		E	209 667-2676	0
LJC Construction Inc		D	209 668-2700	0
Machado & Sons Cnstr Inc		E	209 632-5260	0
Mickey Wall Painting Inc		E	209 669-0557	0
Nelson & Sons Electric Inc		E	209 667-4343	0
Northern Rfrigerated Trnsp Inc **(PA)**		C	209 664-3800	0
PJs Lumber Inc		D	209 850-9444	0
Poppy State Express Inc		D	209 664-3950	0
Ruan		D	209 634-4928	0
Select Harvest Usa LLC **(PA)**		D	209 668-2471	0
Sodexo Management Inc		D	209 667-3634	0
Swanson Farms		D	209 667-2002	0
Thorsens Inc		D	209 524-5296	0
Turlock Dairy & Rfrgn Inc		D	209 667-6455	0
Turlock Fruit Co **(PA)**		E	209 634-7207	0
Turlock Irrigation District **(PA)**		C	209 883-8222	0
Turlock Irrigation District		B	209 883-8300	0
Valley Fresh Foods Inc		D	209 669-5600	0
Valley Milk LLC		D	209 410-6701	0
Winton Irland Strom Green Insu **(PA)**		D	209 667-0995	0
Yosemite Farm Credit Aca **(PA)**		D	209 667-2366	0

TUSTIN, CA - Orange County

	SIC	EMP	PHONE	ENTRY #
A P R Consulting Inc		A	714 544-3696	0
AB Cellular Holding LLC		A	562 468-6846	0
ABM Elctrcal Ltg Solutions Inc **(DH)**		D	866 226-2838	0
Absolute Exhibits Inc **(PA)**		D	714 685-2800	0
Advantage Waypoint LLC		D	717 424-4973	0
All Care Services Inc		D	714 669-1148	0
Alliance Funding Group		D	800 978-8817	0
Alta Hospitals System LLC		A	714 619-7700	0
Apollo Agencies Inc **(PA)**		D	714 832-2100	0
AT&T Corp		D	714 258-8290	0
Autocrib Inc		C	714 274-0400	0
Briggs Electric Inc **(PA)**		D	714 544-2500	0
Broker Solutions Inc **(PA)**		A	800 450-2010	0
Caliber Bodyworks Texas Inc		C	714 665-3905	0
Canon Medical Systems USA Inc **(DH)**		B	714 730-5000	0
Centrl Territrl Salvation Army		D	714 832-7100	0
Coastal International Inc **(PA)**		D	415 339-1700	0
Corland Companies **(PA)**		D	714 573-7780	0
Cosmopro West Inc		E	714 258-8301	0
Crown Golf Properties LP		C	714 730-1611	0
Day Star Fixtures		E	714 838-4613	0
Encompass Health Corporation		C	714 832-9200	0
Executive Personnel Services		B	714 310-9506	0
First Team RE - Orange Cnty		C	714 544-5456	0
Foundation Building Mtls Inc **(PA)**		D	714 380-3127	0
General Procurement Inc **(PA)**		D	949 679-7960	0
Hanford Hotels LLC		C	714 210-0400	0
Health South Tustin Rehab Hosp		C	714 832-9200	0
Hmwc Cpas & Business Advisors		D	714 505-9000	0
Hotel Adventures LLC		D	714 730-7717	0
I L S West Inc		E	714 505-7530	0
Innovative Medical Solutions		D	714 505-7070	0
Innovtive Scntfic Slutions Inc		D	714 508-8620	0
Internet Blueprint Inc		E	714 673-6000	0
Kaiser Foundation Hospitals		A	951 353-4000	0
Kaiser Foundation Hospitals		A	888 988-2800	0
Key Inn Ltd A Cal Ltd Partnr		E	714 832-3220	0
Kinship Center		D	714 979-2365	0
Ledra Brands Inc		D	714 259-9959	0
Logomark Inc		D	714 675-6100	0
Lsf9 Cypress Holdings LLC		A	714 380-3127	0
M & S Trading Inc		D	714 241-7190	0
Management Trust Assn Inc **(PA)**		D	714 285-2626	0
Oracle Corporation		C	713 654-0919	0
Orange County Dept Education		A	714 730-7301	0
Portellus Inc		D	949 250-9600	0
Pphm Inc		D	714 508-6100	0
Pramira Inc		C	800 678-1169	0
R Ranch Market		A	714 573-1182	0
RES-Care Inc		D	800 707-8781	0
RJN Investigations Inc		D	951 686-7638	0

	SIC	EMP	PHONE	ENTRY #
Sanyo Foods Corp America		C	714 730-1611	0
Schick Moving & Storage Co **(PA)**		D	714 731-5500	0
Shubin Services Inc		E	714 259-0908	0
Silverado Senior Living Inc		D	657 888-5752	0
Southern Cal Prmnnte Med Group		D	714 734-4500	0
Steadfast Management Co Inc		C	714 542-2229	0
Sterling Collision Center LLC **(PA)**		D	714 259-1111	0
Superior Sod I LP		C	909 923-5068	0
Transpacific Management Svc		D	714 285-2626	0
Trinity Brdcstg Netwrk Inc		C	714 665-3619	0
Trinity Christian Center of SA **(PA)**		C	714 665-3619	0
Turbo Data Systems Inc **(PA)**		E	714 573-5757	0
Tustin Care Center Corp		D	714 832-6780	0
Wood Gutmann Bogart Insur Brkg		D	714 505-7000	0
Woodbridge Glass Inc		C	714 838-4444	0
Worldstage Inc **(PA)**		D	714 508-1858	0
Youngs Holdings Inc **(PA)**		D	714 368-4615	0
Youngs Market Company LLC **(HQ)**		B	800 317-6150	0

TWENTYNINE PALMS, CA - San Bernardino County

	SIC	EMP	PHONE	ENTRY #
Business and Support Services		D	760 830-6873	0
Mark Clemons		C	760 361-1531	0
United States Dept of Navy		B	760 830-2190	0

TWIN BRIDGES, CA - El Dorado County

	SIC	EMP	PHONE	ENTRY #
Sierra At Taho Ski Resorts		E	530 659-7519	0

UKIAH, CA - Mendocino County

	SIC	EMP	PHONE	ENTRY #
Berryman Health Inc		D	707 462-8864	0
County of Mendocino		D	707 463-4363	0
County of Mendocino		B	707 463-2437	0
County of Mendocino		D	707 463-4363	0
County of Mendocino		C	707 463-4396	0
Fedex Ground Package Sys Inc		D	800 463-3339	0
Ford Street Project Inc		E	707 462-1934	0
Granite Construction Inc		D	707 467-4100	0
Hildreth Farm Incorporated		D	707 462-0648	0
Horizon West Healthcare Inc		D	707 462-1436	0
Lake County Home Loans		E	707 462-4000	0
Mendocino Cmnty Hlth Clnic Inc **(PA)**		C	707 468-1010	0
Mendocino Forest Pdts Co LLC		C	707 468-1431	0
National Veterinary Assoc Inc		D	707 462-8625	0
Redwood Coast Regional **(PA)**		D	707 462-3832	0
Redwood Community Services **(PA)**		C	707 467-2000	0
Redwood Empire Packing Inc		C	707 462-5521	0
Redwood Health Club **(PA)**		D	707 468-0441	0
Redwood Regional Medical Group		D	707 463-3636	0
Savings Bank Mendocino County **(PA)**		C	707 462-6613	0
Sequoia Senior Solutions Inc		D	707 621-9235	0
SERVPRO of Mendocino		E	707 462-3848	0
Ukiah Adventist Hospital **(HQ)**		B	707 462-3111	0
Ukiah Adventist Hospital		C	707 462-3111	0
Ukiah Vly Assn For Hbilitation **(PA)**		D	707 468-8824	0
United Parcel Service Inc OH		C	707 468-5481	0
Valley View Sklled Nursing Ctr		D	707 462-1436	0
Vitalant Research Institute		D	707 462-1754	0
Waste MGT Collectn & Recycl		D	707 462-0210	0

UNION CITY, CA - Alameda County

	SIC	EMP	PHONE	ENTRY #
AAA Restaurant Fire Ctrl Inc		D	510 786-9555	0
Anixter Inc		D	510 477-2400	0
Basquez Tiburcio Health Center		C	510 471-5907	0
Best Contracting Services Inc		D	510 886-7240	0
Buffalo Distribution		E	510 475-9810	0
Cal-West Concrete Cutting Inc **(PA)**		C	510 656-0253	0
Cellco Partnership		D	510 324-5740	0
Child Family & Cmnty Svcs Inc		D	510 796-9512	0
Corinthian Realty LLC		C	510 487-8653	0
CSC Serviceworks Holdings Inc		D	510 429-0900	0
Daylight Foods Inc		C	408 284-7300	0
Dust Networks Inc		D	510 400-2900	0
Emerald Packaging Inc		C	510 429-5700	0
Excel Moving Services		D	800 392-3596	0
Finezi Inc		D	510 790-4768	0
Forward Air Inc		E	415 570-6040	0
Freshpoint Inc		C	510 476-5900	0
Gcm Holding Corporation		B	510 475-0404	0
Genesis Logistics Inc		D	510 476-0790	0
Graybar Electric Company Inc		D	925 557-3000	0
Intero Real Estate Svcs Inc		D	510 489-8989	0
Interstate Hotels Resorts Inc		C	510 489-2200	0
Iron Mountain Incorporated		D	510 798-6387	0
JS International Shipg Corp **(PA)**		D	650 697-3963	0
Kaiser Foundation Hospitals		D	510 675-5777	0
Kaiser Foundation Hospitals		A	510 675-4010	0
Kaiser Foundation Hospitals		D	510 675-2170	0
Masonic Homes of California		B	510 441-3700	0

2020 Directory of California
Wholesalers and Services Companies

(P-0000) Products & Services Section entry number
(PA)=Parent Co (HQ)=Headquarters (DH)=Div Headquarters

	SIC	EMP	PHONE	ENTRY #
Mercado Latino Inc		E	510 475-5500	0
Oracle Corporation		B	510 471-6971	0
Orora Packaging Solutions		D	510 487-1211	0
Permanente Medical Group Inc		D	510 675-4010	0
Pregis LLC		E	510 404-1360	0
Purebeauty Inc		E	510 477-7950	0
Reliance Steel & Aluminum Co		D	510 476-4400	0
Rki Instruments Inc **(PA)**		D	510 441-5656	0
Southern Glazers Wine		B	510 477-5500	0
Specialized Laundry Svcs Inc		C	510 487-8297	0
Tiburcio Vasquez Hlth Ctr Inc **(PA)**		E	510 471-5880	0
Touchofmodern Inc		C	888 868-1232	0
Tournesol Siteworks LLC **(PA)**		D	800 542-2282	0
Tri-City Economic Dev Corp		D	510 429-8030	0
Ultimo Software Solutions Inc		C	408 943-1490	0
Union Sanitary District		C	510 477-7500	0
United States Pipe Fndry LLC		D	510 441-5810	0

UNIVERSAL CITY, CA - Los Angeles County

	SIC	EMP	PHONE	ENTRY #
Access Hollywood LLC		D	818 684-7000	0
Amblin/Reliance Holding Co LLC		D	818 733-6272	0
Dw Studios Productions LLC **(PA)**		E	818 733-9631	0
Hilton Los Angles Universal Cy		B	818 506-2500	0
Hilton Universal Hotel		D	818 506-2500	0
Latham & Watkins LLP		B	818 753-5000	0
Lh Universal Operating LLC		B	818 980-1212	0
NBC Subsidiary (knbc-Tv) LLC		C	818 684-5746	0
Shen Zhen New World II LLC		B	818 980-1212	0
Sprint Communications Co LP		E	818 755-7100	0
Sun Hill Properties Inc **(HQ)**		B	818 506-2500	0
Universal City Studios LLC **(DH)**		D	800 864-8377	0
Universal Music Group Inc		E	818 286-4000	0
Universal Stdios Licensing LLC		C	818 695-1273	0
Universal Studios Company LLC		B	818 622-4455	0
Universal Studios Company LLC		C	818 777-1000	0

UPLAND, CA - San Bernardino County

	SIC	EMP	PHONE	ENTRY #
Allied Prof Nursing Care		D	909 949-1066	0
Azalea & Rose Co		E	909 949-2442	0
B & L Consulting LLC		D	682 238-6994	0
Bms Parent Inc **(PA)**		D	909 981-2341	0
Bni Enterprises Inc		A	909 305-1818	0
C P Construction Co Inc		E	909 981-1091	0
California Ldscp & Design Inc		C	909 949-1601	0
California Skateparks		C	909 949-1601	0
Camstar International Inc		D	909 931-2540	0
Diamond Ridge Corporation		C	909 949-0605	0
F M Tarbell Co		C	909 982-8881	0
Firstsight Vision Services Inc **(DH)**		D	909 920-5008	0
Firstsrvice Rsidential Cal Inc **(DH)**		D	909 981-4131	0
Garrett J Gentry Gen Engrg Inc		D	909 693-3391	0
Golden Eagle Moving Svcs Inc		D	909 946-7655	0
Hamilton Brwart Insur Agcy LLC		D	909 920-3250	0
Hardcore Skateparks Inc		C	909 949-1601	0
Holliday Rock Co Inc **(PA)**		D	909 982-1553	0
Inland Empire Therapy Provider **(PA)**		D	909 985-7905	0
Inland Valley Drug & Alcohol **(PA)**		D	909 932-1069	0
Inland-Metro Services Inc		D	909 373-6810	0
JAS Pacific		C	909 605-7777	0
Kanopy Insurance Center LLC		C	877 513-2434	0
Largo Concrete Inc		A	909 981-7844	0
Lewis Companies **(PA)**		B	909 985-0971	0
Mgr Services Inc		D	909 981-4466	0
Mladen Buntich Cnstr Co Inc		D	909 920-9977	0
Mountain View Physical Therapy		D	909 949-6235	0
Paat & Kimmel Development Inc		D	909 315-8074	0
Perry Floor Systems Inc		D	909 949-1211	0
Re/Max LLC		E	303 770-5531	0
Reach Out West End		D	909 982-8641	0
San Antonio Regional Hospital **(PA)**		A	909 985-2811	0
Sapphire Softech Solutions LLC		D	888 357-5222	0
Sela Healthcare Inc **(PA)**		C	909 985-1981	0
Serec Entertainment LLC		E	626 893-0600	0
Shield Security Inc		B	909 920-1173	0
Sneary Construction Inc		E	909 982-1833	0
Soltis Golf Incorporated		D	909 822-7000	0
Upland Community Care Inc		D	909 985-1903	0
Vci Construction LLC **(HQ)**		D	909 946-0905	0
Victoria Place Community Assn		D	909 981-4131	0
Walton Electric Corporation		D	909 981-5051	0

VACAVILLE, CA - Solano County

	SIC	EMP	PHONE	ENTRY #
AFA Constrctn Grp/Cal Inc JV		D	707 446-7996	0
Allied Framers Inc		C	707 452-7050	0
Blue Mountain Cnstr Svcs Inc		C	800 889-2085	0
Brenden Theatre Corporation		D	707 469-0180	0

	SIC	EMP	PHONE	ENTRY #
Citadel Roofing & Solar		C	707 446-5500	0
City of Vacaville		D	707 449-6122	0
City of Vacaville		B	707 449-5170	0
Clark Pest Ctrl Stockton Inc		E	707 446-9748	0
Contemprary Hstrical Vhcl Assn		D	707 447-7266	0
County of Solano		D	707 451-6090	0
International Brthrhd of Elctr **(PA)**		D	707 452-2700	0
Kaiser Foundation Hospitals		A	707 624-4000	0
Kaiser Foundation Hospitals		E	707 624-4000	0
Kuic Inc		D	707 446-0200	0
Mariani Packing Co Inc **(PA)**		B	707 452-2800	0
Mark Garcia		D	707 446-4529	0
Master Drywall Inc		C	707 448-8659	0
Maximum Fitness LLC		E	707 447-0606	0
Mental Health California Dept		B	707 449-6504	0
Merrill Gardens LLC		D	707 447-7496	0
Mv Transportation Inc		D	707 446-5573	0
Navy Federal Credit Union		C	888 842-6328	0
No Barriers		D	707 451-1947	0
North Bay Distribution Inc		D	707 450-1219	0
North Bay Distribution Inc **(PA)**		D	707 452-9984	0
Northbay Healthcare Group		A	707 446-4000	0
Par Electrical Contractors Inc		D	707 693-1237	0
Recology Vacaville Solano		D	707 448-2945	0
Solano Irrigation District		D	707 448-6847	0
Stars Recreation Center LP		E	707 455-7827	0
Sutter Regional Med Foundation		D	707 454-5800	0
Taylor Structures Inc		D	707 499-6870	0
Travis Credit Union **(PA)**		B	707 449-4000	0
Travis Credit Union		D	707 449-4000	0
Travis Credit Union		B	707 449-4000	0
Triumph Protection Group Inc		C	800 224-0286	0
Vacaville Condolescent and Reh		C	707 449-8000	0
Vacavlle Cnvalescent Rehab Ctr		C	707 449-8000	0
Valyria LLC **(HQ)**		D	707 452-0600	0
Winsor House Compalessant		D	707 448-6458	0

VALENCIA, CA - Los Angeles County

	SIC	EMP	PHONE	ENTRY #
AAA Elctrcal Cmmunications Inc **(PA)**		C	800 892-4784	0
Academy Swim Club		D	661 702-8585	0
Adept Fasteners Inc **(PA)**		D	661 257-6600	0
Advanced Dcument Solutions Inc **(PA)**		E	661 251-0337	0
Advantage Media Services Inc		C	661 705-7588	0
Amerisourcebergen Drug Corp		C	661 257-6400	0
Applied Companies RE LLC		E	661 257-0090	0
Atk Audiotek		D	661 705-3700	0
Avita Medical Americas LLC		D	661 367-9170	0
AWI Acquisition Company **(PA)**		D	818 364-2333	0
Behavioral Learning Center Inc		D	661 254-7086	0
Bel Air Lighting Inc **(PA)**		C	818 768-5511	0
C A Rasmussen Inc **(PA)**		E	661 367-9040	0
California Strl Concepts Inc		C	661 257-6903	0
Cardinal Health Inc		C	661 295-6100	0
CC Wellness LLC **(HQ)**		D	661 295-1700	0
Cellco Partnership		D	661 286-2399	0
Cicoil LLC		D	661 295-1295	0
Cintas Corporation No 3		D	661 310-7400	0
Discoverready LLC		D	661 284-6401	0
Efs West		E	661 705-8200	0
Falcon Aerospace Holdings LLC		A	661 775-7200	0
Fdsi Logistics LLC		D	818 971-3300	0
Fidelity Security Services Inc		C	661 295-5007	0
Fpk Security Inc		B	661 702-9091	0
Global Building Services Inc **(PA)**		A	800 675-6643	0
Gothic Landscaping Inc **(PA)**		C	661 257-1266	0
Gothic Landscaping Inc		B	661 257-5085	0
Green Convergence **(PA)**		D	661 294-9495	0
Henry Mayo Newhall Mem Hlth		A	661 253-8000	0
Henry Mayo Newhall Mem Hosp		D	661 253-8112	0
Henry Mayo Newhall Mem Hosp		B	661 253-8400	0
Heritage Golf Group Inc		C	661 254-4401	0
Hoffman Texas Inc		E	661 257-9200	0
Hrd Aero Systems Inc		D	661 295-0670	0
Hrd Aero Systems Inc **(PA)**		D	661 295-0670	0
Hyatt Hotels Management Corp		C	661 799-1234	0
Ice Station Valencia L L C		D	661 775-8686	0
Image 2000 **(PA)**		E	818 781-2200	0
Iron Mountain Incorporated		D	661 775-9008	0
JT Wimsatt Contg Co Inc **(PA)**		D	661 775-8090	0
Jyg Concrete Construction Inc		C	661 607-0337	0
King Monster Inc		D	661 253-3000	0
Klm Orthotic Laboratories Inc		C	661 295-2600	0
Krg Technologies Inc		A	661 257-9967	0
Landscape Development Inc **(PA)**		B	661 295-1970	0
Magic Mountain LLC		B	661 255-4100	0
Market Tech Media Corporation		D	661 257-4745	0

Employment Codes: A=Over 500 employees, B=251-500,
C=101-250, D=51-100, E=50

2020 Directory of California
Wholesalers and Services Companies

© Mergent Inc. 1-800-342-5647

1659

	SIC	EMP	PHONE	ENTRY #
Mercury Insurance Company		D	661 291-6470	0
N Qiagen Amercn Holdings Inc (HQ)		C	800 426-8157	0
Novacap LLC		B	661 295-5920	0
Nutec Enterprises Inc		D	661 287-3200	0
Oakridge Landscape Inc (PA)		D	661 295-7228	0
Ocean Park Hotels Inc		D	661 284-3200	0
Ocean Park Hotels Mmex LLC		E	661 284-2101	0
Orange Health Solutions Inc		D	661 310-9333	0
Princess Cruises and Tours Inc (HQ)		A	206 336-6000	0
Pyramid Enterprises Inc (PA)		D	661 702-1420	0
Quest Dgnstics Clncal Labs Inc		B	661 964-6582	0
Realty Executives		C	661 286-8600	0
Regent Aerospace Corporation (PA)		C	661 257-3000	0
Rgis LLC		D	661 702-8987	0
Sage Staffing Consultants Inc (PA)		C	661 254-4026	0
Santa Clarita Medical Group		E	661 255-6802	0
Scicon Technologies Corp (PA)		D	661 295-8630	0
Scorpion Design LLC		A	661 702-0100	0
Shield-Denver Health Care Ctr (HQ)		C	661 294-4200	0
Southern California Gas Co		D	800 427-2200	0
Specialty Laboratories Inc (DH)		A	661 799-6543	0
Star Nail Products Inc		D	661 257-3376	0
Summer Systems Inc		D	661 257-4419	0
Sunkist Growers Inc (PA)		C	661 290-8900	0
Sunrise Senior Living Inc		D	661 253-3551	0
Sunvair Aerospace Group Inc (PA)		D	661 254-3777	0
Ultraviolet Devices Inc		D	661 295-8140	0
US Healthworks Inc (DH)		D	661 678-2300	0
Vista Valencia Group Inc		E	661 255-4600	0
Volunteers of Amer Los Angeles		D	661 290-2829	0
Wayforward Technologies Inc		E	661 286-2769	0
Wesco Aircraft Hardware Corp (HQ)		B	661 775-7200	0
Wesco Aircraft Hardware Corp		B	661 775-7200	0
Wesco Aircraft Holdings Inc (PA)		B	661 775-7200	0
Weslar Inc		D	661 702-1362	0
William S Hart Pony & Softball		D	661 254-9780	0
Young Mens Chrstn Assn of La		C	661 253-3593	0

VALLEJO, CA - Solano County

	SIC	EMP	PHONE	ENTRY #
California Maritime Acdmy		C	707 654-1000	0
City of Vallejo		B	707 644-4000	0
Crestwood Behavioral Hlth Inc		C	707 552-0215	0
Crestwood Behavioral Hlth Inc		D	707 558-1777	0
Crestwood Behavioral Hlth Inc		D	707 552-0215	0
Earthquake Protection Systems		D	707 644-5993	0
Emeritus Corporation		E	707 552-3336	0
Empres Financial Services LLC		D	707 643-2793	0
Execusheld Prtection Group LLC		D	707 439-6351	0
Getright Ventures Inc		D	510 402-4816	0
Greater Vallejo Recreation Dst		C	707 648-4600	0
H & R Block Inc		C	707 643-1856	0
Helios Healthcare LLC		C	707 644-7401	0
J B Laquindanum & Associates		D	707 648-0501	0
James-Timec International		E	707 642-2222	0
Jeffco Painting & Coating Inc		D	707 562-1900	0
Kaiser Foundation Hospitals		D	707 645-2720	0
Kaiser Foundation Hospitals		A	707 651-1000	0
La Clinica De La Raza Inc		B	707 556-8100	0
M F Maher Inc		D	707 552-2774	0
Medic Ambulance Service Inc (PA)		C	707 644-1761	0
Merrill Gardens LLC		D	707 553-2698	0
Michaels Trnsp Svc Inc		D	707 674-6013	0
Milestones Adult Dev Ctr		D	707 644-0464	0
Milestones of Development Inc		D	707 644-0496	0
Permanente Medical Group Inc		D	707 765-3930	0
R & R Maher Construction Co		E	707 552-0330	0
Recology Vallejo (HQ)		C	707 552-3110	0
San Pablo Lodge 43		D	707 642-1391	0
Sutter Regional Med Foundation		D	707 551-3616	0
Syar Industries Inc		D	707 643-3261	0
Teamross Inc		D	707 643-9000	0
Timec Acquisitions Inc (DH)		A	707 642-2222	0
Timec Companies Inc (DH)		B	707 642-2222	0
Total Renal Care Inc		A	707 556-3637	0
Travis Credit Union		B	800 877-8328	0
United Parcel Service Inc OH		C	707 252-4560	0
Vallejo Flood and Waste		D	707 644-8949	0
Veterans Health Administration		B	707 562-8200	0

VALLEY CENTER, CA - San Diego County

	SIC	EMP	PHONE	ENTRY #
Caesars Entrtnment Oprting Inc		A	760 751-3100	0
Hcal LLC		C	760 751-3100	0
Indian Health Council Inc (PA)		D	760 749-1410	0
San Psqual Band Mssion Indians		B	760 291-5500	0
San Psqual Csino Dev Group Inc		E	760 291-5500	0
Survival Systems Intl Inc (PA)		D	760 749-6800	0

	SIC	EMP	PHONE	ENTRY #
Valley Center Municipal		D	760 735-4500	0
Valley Center Municpl Wtr Dst		D	760 735-4500	0

VALLEY SPRINGS, CA - Calaveras County

	SIC	EMP	PHONE	ENTRY #
Bolin Builders Inc		E	209 772-9721	0

VALLEY VILLAGE, CA - Los Angeles County

	SIC	EMP	PHONE	ENTRY #
Afm & Sag-Aftra Intellectual		D	818 255-7980	0
Douglas Steel Supply Inc		D	323 587-7676	0
Executive Financial HM Ln Corp		E	818 285-5626	0
Naimies Beauty Center Inc (PA)		D	818 655-9933	0

VAN NUYS, CA - Los Angeles County

	SIC	EMP	PHONE	ENTRY #
1370 Realty Corp		C	818 817-0092	0
16700 Roscoe Associates LLC		D	818 989-2300	0
AG Air Conditioning & Htg Inc		E	818 988-5388	0
Airespring Inc		D	818 786-8990	0
Albert McKnzie A Prof Law Corp		D	818 650-6900	0
All Valley Washer Service Inc		D	818 787-1100	0
Allen Medical Group Inc		E	818 698-8444	0
Alta Healthcare System LLC		C	818 787-1511	0
Alta Hollywood Community Hsptl		C	818 787-1511	0
American Merchant Center Inc		D	818 947-1700	0
American Prof Ambulance Corp		C	818 996-2200	0
Apprentice & Journeymen Traini		D	818 464-4579	0
Apprentice & Journeymen Trn Tr		D	323 636-9871	0
Apu Inc (PA)		E	661 948-2880	0
ARC Document Solutions Inc		C	818 908-0222	0
Arrow Tools Fas & Saw Inc		E	818 780-1464	0
AT&T Corp		D	818 374-6458	0
AT&T Corp		D	818 373-6896	0
AT&T Corp		D	818 997-5998	0
Barazani Pave Stone Inc		C	818 701-6977	0
Berkley Vly Cnvlscent Hosp Inc		C	818 786-0020	0
Broadstreet Solar Inc		E	818 206-1464	0
C B B Z S Inc		D	818 908-1900	0
Caine & Weiner Company Inc (PA)		D	818 226-6000	0
California Contrs Sups Inc		D	818 785-8823	0
Carlisle Research Corporation		D	818 785-8677	0
Cbre Inc		D	818 907-4600	0
Century-National Insurance Co (HQ)		B	818 760-0880	0
Checker Cab Co		D	818 488-5088	0
City of Los Angeles		A	818 756-8022	0
City of Los Angeles		D	818 908-5950	0
Clay Lacy Aviation Inc (PA)		B	818 989-2900	0
Command International SEC Svcs		D	818 997-1666	0
County of Los Angeles		C	818 362-6437	0
County of Los Angeles		D	818 374-2000	0
County of Los Angeles		D	818 374-2406	0
Courtyard Plaza		E	818 780-5005	0
Dee Sign Co		D	818 904-3400	0
Dfs Flooring Inc (PA)		D	818 374-5200	0
Dsg Associates Inc		E	800 462-8765	0
E & S International Entps Inc (PA)		C	818 887-0700	0
Elite Aviation LLC		D	818 988-5387	0
Energy Enterprises USA Inc (PA)		D	424 339-0005	0
Exandal Corporation		C	818 705-9497	0
Factory 2-U Import Export Inc		D	323 587-9900	0
Ferguson Enterprises Inc		E	818 786-9720	0
Financial Information Network		D	818 782-0331	0
Five Star Qulty Care-CA II LLC		D	818 997-1841	0
Fusefx LLC		B	818 237-5052	0
George M Rajacich MD PC		E	818 787-2020	0
Golden Living LLC		D	805 494-4949	0
Grand Valley Health Care Ctr		C	818 786-3470	0
Grht Inc		D	323 873-6393	0
Grobstein Horwath & Co		D	818 501-5200	0
Hamburger Home		C	818 980-3200	0
Health Entps Lf Long Plan		B	818 654-0330	0
Helinet Aviation Services LLC (PA)		D	818 902-0229	0
Hi-TEC Sports Usa Inc (DH)		D	209 545-1111	0
Icon Media Direct Inc (PA)		D	818 995-6400	0
Incare Dme		D	818 582-1016	0
Industrial Media Inc		C	310 777-1940	0
Interviewing Service Amer LLC (PA)		C	818 989-1044	0
Jet Edge International LLC		D	818 442-0096	0
Keolis Transit America Inc		C	818 616-5254	0
L A Party Rents Inc		E	818 989-4300	0
Lees Maintenance Service Inc		B	818 988-6644	0
Longwood Management Corp		E	818 781-6348	0
Los Angeles Police Credit Un (PA)		D	818 787-6520	0
Los Angeles Unified School Dst		B	818 997-2640	0
Love Lifted US Youth Services		E	818 471-0594	0
M Network Television Inc		E	818 756-5150	0
M P M & Associates Inc		D	818 708-9676	0
Maguire Aviation Group LLC		E	818 989-2300	0

Mergent email: customerrelations@mergent.com
1660

2020 Directory of California
Wholesalers and Services Companies

(P-0000) Products & Services Section entry number
(PA)=Parent Co (HQ)=Headquarters (DH)=Div Headquarters

	SIC	EMP	PHONE	ENTRY #
ME and ME Inc		D	818 891-0197	0
Merabi & Sons LLC		C	818 817-0006	0
Mercury Messenger Service Inc		E	818 989-3115	0
Mesa Energy Systems Inc		C	818 756-0500	0
Microlease Inc (DH)		D	866 520-0200	0
Momentous Insurance Brkg Inc		D	818 933-2700	0
Moulton Logistics Management (PA)		D	818 997-1800	0
Mp Aero LLC		D	818 901-9828	0
Nat Sim Corp		D	818 705-3131	0
National Commercial Services		D	818 701-4400	0
Nep Group Inc		D	412 423-1354	0
Normand/Wlshire Rtrment Ht Inc		D	818 373-5429	0
North La County Regional Ctr (PA)		B	818 778-1900	0
Onegeneration (PA)		D	818 708-6625	0
Parkwood Landscape Maint Inc		D	818 988-9677	0
Pride Collision Centers Inc (PA)		D	818 909-0660	0
Primex Clinical Labs Inc (PA)		D	818 779-0496	0
Prudential Insur Co of Amer		D	818 901-0028	0
Regency Fire Protection Inc		D	818 982-0126	0
Reliable Gardens Inc		D	818 904-9801	0
Restaurant Depot LLC		C	818 376-7687	0
Richmond American Homes		E	818 908-3267	0
Rite Way Enterprises		E	818 376-6960	0
S D Property Management Inc		D	323 658-7990	0
S G D Enterprises		E	323 658-1047	0
San Fernando Valley Community (PA)		B	818 901-4830	0
Shalev Senior Living		E	818 780-4808	0
Sharf Woodward & Associates		D	818 989-2200	0
Signature Flight Support Corp		D	818 464-9500	0
Six Continents Hotels Inc		D	818 989-5010	0
SMA Builders Inc		E	818 994-8306	0
Southern Cal Orthpd Inst LP		C	818 901-6600	0
Southland Rgonal Assn Realtors (PA)		D	818 786-2110	0
Sylmark Inc (PA)		D	818 217-2000	0
T & R Painting Construction		C	818 779-3800	0
Touch-Up Inc		C	818 994-6166	0
Town & Country Event Rentals (PA)		B	818 908-4211	0
Transtar Industries Inc		E	818 785-2000	0
United Parcel Service Inc OH		C	404 828-6000	0
Valley Clark Plbg & Htg Co Inc (PA)		D	818 782-1047	0
Valley Presbyterian Hospital		A	818 782-6600	0
Van Nuys Care Center Inc		D	818 343-0700	0
Weinstein Construction Corp		E	818 782-4000	0
Wolfe Trucking Inc		E	818 376-6960	0
Woodley Lakes Golf Course		D	818 780-6886	0
Young Mens Chrstn Assn of La		E	818 989-3800	0

VANDENBERG AFB, CA - Santa Barbara County

	SIC	EMP	PHONE	ENTRY #
Indyne Inc		A	805 606-7225	0
Range Generation Next LLC		D	310 647-9438	0
Securitas Critical Infrastruct		A	805 685-1100	0

VENICE, CA - Los Angeles County

	SIC	EMP	PHONE	ENTRY #
1524 Abbot Kinney LLC		D	310 907-6517	0
Bully Pictures Inc (PA)		C	310 395-6500	0
DDB Worldwide		C	310 907-1500	0
Host Hotels & Resorts LP		D	310 823-1700	0
Intrinsik Envmtl Sciences Inc		D	310 392-6462	0
Los Angeles County MTA		C	310 392-8636	0
Mad Dogg Athletics Inc (PA)		D	310 823-7008	0
Outrigger Hotels Hawaii		D	310 301-2000	0
Parking Concepts Inc		D	310 821-1081	0
Partos Agency LLC		D	310 458-7800	0
Prologue Films (PA)		E	310 589-9090	0
Southern California Gas Co		D	310 823-7945	0
St Joseph Center		D	310 396-6468	0
Trg Inc		D	310 396-6750	0
Venice Family Clinic (PA)		D	310 664-7703	0
Wetransfer Corporation		D	626 626-5565	0

VENTURA, CA - Ventura County

	SIC	EMP	PHONE	ENTRY #
A M Ortega Construction Inc		D	951 360-1352	0
Agi Holding Corp (PA)		D	805 667-4100	0
Alsco Inc		D	805 650-6578	0
American Landscape Management		E	805 647-5077	0
ARC of Ventura County Inc		C	805 644-0880	0
Asplundh Tree Expert LLC		D	805 641-0528	0
Automobile Club Southern Cal		D	805 644-7171	0
Bentley-Simonson Inc		D	805 650-2794	0
Beverly Health Care Corp (PA)		D	805 642-1736	0
Boyd & Associates (PA)		C	818 752-1888	0
Brokaw Nursery LLC		D	805 647-2262	0
Buenaventura Medical Group (PA)		B	805 477-6004	0
Buenaventura Medical Group		D	805 477-6220	0
C D Lyon Construction Inc (PA)		D	805 653-0173	0
C J Vandergeest Ldscp Care Inc		D	805 650-0726	0

	SIC	EMP	PHONE	ENTRY #
Cabrillo Economic Dev Corp (PA)		D	805 659-3791	0
Califrnia Frnsic Med Group Inc		D	805 654-3343	0
Catholic Charities of Santa CL		D	805 643-4694	0
Channel Islands Young Mens Ch		C	805 484-0423	0
Clinicas Del Camino Real Inc (PA)		C	805 647-6322	0
Clocktower Inn		D	805 652-0141	0
Coastal View Hlthcare Ctr LLC		D	805 642-4101	0
Community Mem HSP/Sn Benua		D	805 652-5072	0
Cornell Corrections Cal Inc (DH)		B	805 644-8700	0
County of Ventura		C	805 654-2561	0
County of Ventura		D	805 654-3456	0
County of Ventura		D	805 654-3456	0
County of Ventura		A	805 652-6000	0
D S R Inc		D	805 275-0039	0
Dcor LLC (PA)		D	805 535-2000	0
Del Mar Seafoods Inc		D	805 850-0421	0
Dialysis Centers Ventura Cnty		D	805 658-9211	0
E & M Concrete Construction		D	805 658-2888	0
E J Harrison & Sons Inc		C	805 647-1414	0
E&S Financial Group Inc		D	805 644-1621	0
Evans/Sipes Inc (PA)		C	805 644-1242	0
Florida Beauty Flora Inc		C	805 642-1633	0
Fpl LLC		D	805 643-6144	0
G W Surfaces (PA)		C	805 642-5004	0
Golden Living LLC		D	805 642-1736	0
GPA Technologies Inc		D	805 643-7878	0
Hailwood Inc		D	805 487-4981	0
Harbor Island Hotel Group LP		D	805 658-1212	0
Help Unlmted Personnel Svc Inc		C	805 962-4646	0
Interact Pmti Inc (PA)		D	805 658-5600	0
J L S Concrete Pumping Inc		D	805 643-0766	0
Johnson Controls		D	805 642-0366	0
Kaiser Foundation Hospitals		D	888 515-3500	0
Kingledon Inc		C	805 643-6000	0
Kkzz 1590		E	805 289-1400	0
L A Fitness Intl LLC		D	805 289-9907	0
Livingston Mem Vna Hlth Corp		B	805 642-0239	0
Nabors Well Services Co		D	805 648-2731	0
Offshore Crane & Service Co (PA)		D	805 648-3348	0
Oilfield Electric Company		D	805 648-3131	0
Ojai Ambulance Inc		E	805 653-9111	0
Ost Trucks and Cranes Inc		D	805 643-9963	0
Pier Pont Hotel LP		E	805 643-6144	0
Pierpont Inn Inc		E	805 643-0245	0
Plowboy Landscapes Inc		D	805 643-4966	0
Registration Ctrl Systems Inc (PA)		D	805 654-0171	0
Retail Services Wis Corp		D	805 644-5422	0
Rgis LLC		D	805 644-0454	0
Sam Hill & Sons Inc		E	805 620-0828	0
Saticoy Lemon Association		D	805 654-6500	0
Securitas SEC Svcs USA Inc		C	805 650-6285	0
Sigma Services Inc (PA)		D	805 642-8377	0
SL Power Electronics Corp (PA)		D	800 235-5929	0
Smart & Final Stores Inc		B	805 647-4276	0
Snapdragon Place 1 LP		D	805 659-3791	0
Star of California (PA)		C	805 644-7823	0
Taft Electric Company (PA)		D	805 642-0121	0
Tidwell Excav Acquisition Inc		D	805 647-4707	0
Trade Desk Inc (PA)		D	805 585-3434	0
Triad Properties		D	805 648-5008	0
Triunfo Public Facilities Corp		D	805 658-4605	0
United Parcel Service Inc OH		C	805 642-6784	0
Ventura County Credit Union (PA)		D	805 477-4000	0
Ventura County Lemon Coops		D	805 385-3345	0
Ventura County Medical Center (PA)		C	805 652-6000	0
Ventura County Medical Center		D	805 652-6201	0
Ventura Hsptality Partners LLC		C	805 648-2100	0
Ventura Medical Management LLC		B	805 477-6220	0
Ventura Streets Dept		D	805 652-4515	0
Veternary Med Srgcal Group Inc		D	805 339-2290	0
Victoria Care Center		C	805 642-1736	0
Vista Steel Co Inc		E	805 653-1189	0
Vitalant		D	805 654-1603	0
West Coast Arborists Inc		C	805 671-5092	0
West Ventura Family Care Ctr		D	805 641-5620	0
Willow Farms LLC		D	805 647-0720	0

VERNON, CA - Los Angeles County

	SIC	EMP	PHONE	ENTRY #
A A A Packing and Shipping Inc		E	626 310-7787	0
Adir International LLC		C	213 639-7716	0
Americold Logistics LLC		D	323 581-0025	0
Bcbg Max Azria Group LLC		D	323 589-2224	0
Bnsf Railway Company		C	323 267-4133	0
California Farms Meat Co Inc		D	323 581-3663	0
California Transit Inc		D	323 234-8750	0
City Fibers Inc (PA)		D	323 583-1013	0

GEOGRAPHIC

	SIC	EMP	PHONE	ENTRY #
City Fibers Inc		D	323 583-1013	0
City of Los Angeles		D	213 485-4981	0
Claudia Richard Inc		D	323 264-3915	0
Collected Group Company LLC		E	323 277-3900	0
Comak Trading Inc A Cal Corp		C	323 261-3404	0
Completely Fresh Foods Inc		C	323 722-9136	0
Core-Mark International Inc		C	323 583-6531	0
Country Floors America LLC **(PA)**		D	310 657-0510	0
DOT-Line Transportation Inc		D	877 900-7768	0
Dutch LLC **(DH)**		C	323 277-3900	0
Famma Group Inc **(PA)**		D	323 826-9600	0
Fedex Freight Corporation		D	323 269-9800	0
Generational Properties Inc		B	323 583-3163	0
Golden West Trading Inc		C	323 581-3663	0
Gourmet Specialties Inc		D	323 587-1734	0
Greatwide Logistics Svcs LLC		D	323 268-7100	0
H & N Foods International Inc **(HQ)**		C	323 586-9300	0
Incremento Inc		D	213 624-7777	0
Indiev Inc		D	323 703-5720	0
Jordana Cosmetics LLC		D	310 730-4400	0
Joseph T Ryerson & Son Inc		D	323 267-6000	0
Karen Kane Inc **(PA)**		C	323 588-0000	0
Kellytoy Worldwide Inc		D	323 923-1300	0
Kenan Advantage Group Inc		D	323 582-3778	0
LA Brands LLC		E	323 234-5070	0
Lafayette Textile Inds LLC		D	323 264-2212	0
Lineage Logistics LLC		C	323 583-3163	0
Los Angeles Regional Food Bank		C	323 234-3030	0
Lymi Inc **(PA)**		D	213 434-2772	0
Macsei Industries Corporation		D	323 233-7864	0
Martys Cutting Inc		D	323 582-5758	0
Mola Inc		C	323 582-0088	0
Morgan Fabrics Corporation **(PA)**		D	323 583-9981	0
Natures Produce Company		D	323 235-4343	0
New Pride Corporation		D	323 584-6608	0
Nydj Apparel LLC		C	323 581-9040	0
Ocean Queen 87 Inc		E	323 585-1200	0
Orient Fisheries Inc		D	323 588-4185	0
Pacific American Fish Co Inc **(PA)**		B	323 319-1551	0
Pactiv Packaging Inc **(DH)**		D	323 513-9000	0
Palisades Ranch Inc		B	323 581-6161	0
Paradigm Industries Inc		D	310 965-1900	0
Preferred Frzr Svcs - Lbf LLC		D	323 263-8811	0
Rancho Foods Inc		D	323 585-0503	0
Red Chamber Co **(PA)**		B	323 234-9000	0
Reliance Steel & Aluminum Co		C	323 583-6111	0
Rggd Inc **(PA)**		D	323 581-6617	0
Rite-Way Meat Packers Inc		D	323 826-2144	0
Rogers Poultry Co **(PA)**		D	323 585-0802	0
Rose & Shore Inc		B	323 826-2144	0
Runway Liquidation LLC **(HQ)**		C	323 589-2224	0
Saia Motor Freight Line LLC		D	323 277-2880	0
Same Swim LLC		D	323 582-2588	0
Shason Inc **(PA)**		D	323 269-6666	0
Shims Bargain Inc **(PA)**		D	323 881-0099	0
Showroom Interiors LLC		C	323 348-1551	0
Simply Fresh Fruit Inc		D	323 586-0000	0
Soofer Co Inc		D	323 234-6666	0
Stone Blue Inc		D	323 277-0008	0
Tama Trading Company		D	213 748-8262	0
True Wrld Fods Los Angeles LLC		B	323 846-3300	0
United Parcel Service Inc OH		B	323 260-8957	0
V & L Produce Inc		C	323 589-3125	0
Vernon Central Warehouse Inc		C	323 234-2200	0
Vernon Truck Wash Inc		C	323 267-0706	0
Wayne Provision Co Inc **(PA)**		D	323 277-5888	0
West Pico Distributors LLC		D	323 586-9050	0
West Pico Foods LLC		C	323 586-9050	0
Wm Healthcare Solutions Inc		D	713 328-7350	0
World Variety Produce Inc		B	800 588-0151	0
Young Bae Fashions Inc		D	323 583-8684	0

VICTORVILLE, CA - San Bernardino County

	SIC	EMP	PHONE	ENTRY #
Branlyn Prominence Inc		C	760 843-5655	0
Cambrian Homecare Inc		D	760 955-2250	0
Cemex Cnstr Mtls PCF LLC		D	760 381-7600	0
Charter Cmmnctons Oprating LLC		D	760 452-8609	0
Coldwell Banker Home Source		D	760 684-8100	0
Comav Technical Services LLC		C	760 530-2400	0
County of San Bernardino		D	760 843-5100	0
Desert Valley Hospital Inc **(DH)**		D	760 241-8000	0
Desert Valley Med Group Inc **(PA)**		B	760 241-8000	0
Desert View Funeral Home		E	760 244-0007	0
E & T Foods Inc		B	760 843-7730	0
Faith Electric LLC		C	909 767-2682	0
Green Tree Capital LP		D	760 245-3461	0

	SIC	EMP	PHONE	ENTRY #
Hartwick & Hand Inc **(PA)**		D	760 245-1666	0
Heritage Medical Group		C	760 956-1286	0
Heritage Senior Care Inc		D	800 562-2734	0
In-Shape Health Clubs LLC		E	760 381-1200	0
Interntnal Arospc Coatings Inc		C	760 246-1651	0
Jamboor Medical Corporation		D	760 241-8063	0
Joseph A Foroosh Dental Corp **(PA)**		D	760 241-3336	0
Kaiser Foundation Hospitals		D	888 750-0036	0
Keller Williams Realty		D	760 951-5242	0
Knolls Convalescent Hospital **(PA)**		C	760 245-5361	0
Knolls Convalescent Hospital		D	760 245-6477	0
Knolls West Enterprise		D	760 245-0107	0
Knolls West Post Acute LLC		D	760 245-5361	0
L & S Investment Co Inc		D	760 245-3461	0
Landforce Express Corporation		C	760 843-7839	0
Lee-Victorville Hotel Corp		C	760 245-3461	0
Odyssey Healthcare Inc		D	760 241-7044	0
Peoples Care Inc		C	760 962-1900	0
Psomas		E	760 843-5700	0
Securitas SEC Svcs USA Inc		C	760 245-1915	0
Sonshine Collision Services		D	760 243-3185	0
Southern California Edison Co		C	760 951-3172	0
Southwest Gas Corporation		D	760 951-4000	0
Spring Valley Lake Country CLB		D	760 245-5356	0
Spring Valley Post Acute LLC		C	760 245-6477	0
Sterling-Ase Ltd Partnership		D	760 951-9507	0
Stress Relief Services		D	760 241-7472	0
Super Care Inc		D	760 245-2034	0
Telecare Corporation		D	760 245-8837	0
United California Realty Inc		D	760 949-4040	0
United Parcel Service Inc		A	760 241-5540	0
Valley Bulk Inc		D	760 843-0574	0
Victorvlle Trsure Holdings LLC		D	760 245-6565	0

VIEW PARK, CA - Los Angeles County

	SIC	EMP	PHONE	ENTRY #
Hathaway-Sycamores Chld Fam Sv		D	323 733-0322	0

VILLA PARK, CA - Orange County

	SIC	EMP	PHONE	ENTRY #
Tropical Plaza Nursery Inc		D	714 998-4100	0

VINA, CA - Tehama County

	SIC	EMP	PHONE	ENTRY #
Abbey of New Clairvaux **(PA)**		D	530 839-2161	0
Andersen & Sons Shelling Inc		D	530 839-2236	0

VISALIA, CA - Tulare County

	SIC	EMP	PHONE	ENTRY #
Able Industries Inc		D	559 651-8150	0
ABM Janitorial Services Inc		D	559 651-1612	0
Agriholding Inc **(PA)**		D	559 738-5880	0
Agsource Services LLC		E	559 735-9700	0
Allen Development Partners LLC **(PA)**		D	559 732-5425	0
American Incorporated		B	559 651-1776	0
Arthur J Gallagher & Co		D	559 733-1181	0
Bacci Glinn Physcl Therapy Inc		E	559 733-2247	0
Bank America National Assn		E	800 432-1000	0
Beethoven Holdings Inc		C	559 733-4100	0
Bethesda Lthran Cmmunities Inc		D	559 636-6300	0
Bowie Enterprises		D	559 732-2988	0
Boys Grls Clubs of Squoias Inc		D	559 592-4074	0
Centex Homes Inc		C	559 733-2717	0
Central Valley Community Bank		D	559 625-8733	0
Central Vly Regional Ctr Inc		C	559 738-2200	0
Chicago Title Insurance Co		D	559 733-3814	0
Cigna Healthcare Cal Inc		B	559 738-2000	0
City of Visalia		D	559 713-4000	0
Comcast Cble Cmmunications LLC		C	559 253-4050	0
Delta Nrsing Rhbilitation Hosp		D	559 625-4003	0
Donald Lawrence Fulbright Co		D	559 625-0762	0
E & M AG Svc Inc A Cal Corp		E	559 627-2724	0
Family Healthcare Network		C	559 734-1939	0
Family Services		E	559 741-7310	0
Family Services Tulare County		D	559 732-1970	0
Far West Inc		D	559 627-1241	0
Far West Inc		C	559 733-0901	0
Federal Express Corporation		C	800 463-3339	0
Financial Credit Network Inc **(PA)**		D	559 733-7550	0
Frito-Lay North America Inc		D	559 651-1334	0
GAF Holdings Inc		B	559 734-3333	0
Georgia-Pacific LLC		C	559 651-5500	0
Grosvenor Visalia Associates		D	559 651-5000	0
Heilind Electronics Inc		D	559 651-0168	0
Indian River Transport Co		B	209 664-0456	0
J & S Farm		D	559 308-0294	0
J A Contracting Inc		D	559 733-4865	0
Jacobs Tree Specialist Inc		E	559 639-7138	0
Kaweah Delta Health Care Dst **(PA)**		A	559 624-2000	0
Kaweah Dlta Hlth Care Dst Gild		C	559 624-3100	0
Kaweah Dlta Hlth Care Dst Gild		C	559 624-4800	0

Mergent email: customerrelations@mergent.com
1662

2020 Directory of California
Wholesalers and Services Companies

(P-0000) Products & Services Section entry number
(PA)=Parent Co (HQ)=Headquarters (DH)=Div Headquarters

	SIC	EMP	PHONE	ENTRY #
Keller Williams Realty Inc		D	559 733-4100	0
Kern 2008 Cmnty Partners LP		D	559 651-3559	0
L E Cooke Co		C	559 732-9146	0
Lamp Liter Associates		D	559 733-4328	0
Lawrence Tractor Coinc (PA)		D	559 734-7406	0
Los Osos Management Co Inc (PA)		D	559 733-4328	0
Michael SD Nagatini		D	559 738-7502	0
Mitchell Buckman Inc (PA)		D	559 733-1181	0
Morgan Kleppe & Nash		D	559 732-3436	0
OConnor Pest Control Visalia		D	559 366-4853	0
Orange Belt Stages (PA)		D	559 733-4408	0
Phillips Farms		E	559 798-1871	0
Pta California Congress of Par		E	559 622-3195	0
Quad Knopf Inc (PA)		E	559 733-0440	0
Quail Park Retirement Village		D	559 624-3500	0
Red One - PSI Joint Ventr LLC		E	559 772-8264	0
Robert Quintero Labor Contg		D	559 732-6954	0
Self Help Enterprises (PA)		D	559 651-1000	0
Sequoia Beverage Company LP		C	559 651-2444	0
State Farm Fire and Cslty Co		D	559 625-4330	0
Tim Hofer Inc		C	559 732-6676	0
Tucoemas Federal Credit Union (PA)		D	559 737-5900	0
Tucoemas Federal Credit Union		D	559 429-7094	0
Tulare Cnty Chld Care Home Edu		D	559 651-0247	0
Turning Point Central Cal Inc		E	559 627-1490	0
USA Waste of California Inc		D	559 741-1766	0
USA Waste of California Inc		D	559 834-4070	0
Valley Sweet LLC		D	559 686-3381	0
Visalia Country Club		D	559 734-3733	0
Visalia Medical Clinic Inc (PA)		B	559 733-5222	0
Visalia Unified School Dst		D	559 730-7871	0
Viscamar LLC		D	559 636-1111	0
Welcome Group Management LLC		D	310 378-6666	0
Westgate Gardens Care Center		C	559 733-0901	0
Wonderful Citrus Packing LLC		D	559 798-3100	0

VISTA, CA - San Diego County

	SIC	EMP	PHONE	ENTRY #
Access Biologicals LLC		D	760 931-8444	0
All-Pro Bail Bonds Inc		D	760 941-4100	0
Altman Specialty Plants LLC (PA)		A	800 348-4881	0
American Faucet Coatings Corp		E	760 598-5895	0
Apical Industries Inc		C	760 724-5300	0
Bent Tree Nursing Center Inc		C	760 945-3033	0
Caldwell Banker Inc		D	760 941-6888	0
Cassidy Medical Group Inc (PA)		E	760 630-5487	0
City of Vista		C	760 940-9283	0
Cols Inc		C	714 720-6100	0
Demaria Landtech Inc		E	858 481-5500	0
Deployment Solutions LLC		C	317 281-9682	0
Directed LLC		C	800 876-0800	0
Easyturf Inc (DH)		D	760 745-7026	0
Epitec Inc		A	760 650-2515	0
Exagen Diagnostics Inc		C	505 272-7966	0
Excel Mdular Scaffold Lsg Corp		A	760 598-0050	0
Experienced Home Care Registry		D	760 724-0880	0
Festival Fun Parks LLC		D	760 945-9474	0
Frito-Lay North America Inc		D	760 727-6022	0
Habitat Rstration Sciences Inc (PA)		D	760 479-4210	0
Heaviland Enterprises Inc (PA)		C	760 598-7065	0
HMS Construction Inc (PA)		D	760 727-9808	0
I Pwlc Inc		D	760 630-0231	0
Industrial Coml Systems Inc		C	760 300-4094	0
Jeld-Wen Inc		B	760 597-4201	0
Jwc Construction Inc (PA)		E	760 727-2494	0
Kids First Foundation		D	760 631-7550	0
Kids First Foundation		D	760 631-7550	0
Krikorian Premiere Theatre LLC		C	760 945-7469	0
Lee-Mar Aquarium & Pet Sups		D	760 727-1300	0
Leidos Inc		C	858 826-9090	0
Life Care Centers America Inc		C	760 724-8222	0
McCain Inc (DH)		C	760 727-8100	0
Meeting Services Inc		D	858 348-0100	0
Minegar Contracting Inc		E	760 598-5001	0
Neal Electric Corp (HQ)		D	858 513-2525	0
Neostyle Eyewear Corporation		D	760 305-4004	0
New Haven Youth Fmly Svcs Inc		C	760 630-4060	0
Novo Engineering Inc (PA)		D	760 598-6686	0
Off Duty Officers Inc		A	888 408-5900	0
Orion Construction Corporation		D	760 597-9660	0
Pac West Land Care Inc		D	760 630-0231	0
Pave-Tech Inc		E	760 727-8700	0
Pleasant Care of Vista		C	760 945-3033	0
Plug Connection Inc		D	760 631-0992	0
Ponto Nursery Inc		D	760 724-6003	0
Production Plus Plumbing Inc		C	760 597-0235	0
Prudential Overall Supply		D	760 727-7163	0

	SIC	EMP	PHONE	ENTRY #
Rancho Vista Health Center		C	760 941-1480	0
Ready America Inc (PA)		D	760 295-0234	0
Regency Centers LP		A	760 724-9795	0
Rescom Services Inc		D	760 930-3900	0
Roto Rooter Plumbing & Drain S		E	951 658-8541	0
Scripps Health		B	760 806-9263	0
Sharp Healthcare		D	760 806-5600	0
Sherpaul Corporation		D	760 639-6472	0
Sierra Pacific West Inc		D	760 599-0755	0
Smart & Final Stores Inc		B	760 732-1480	0
Sol Transportation Inc		E	760 720-4327	0
Spa Havens LP		C	760 945-2055	0
Spectrum Equipment LLC		D	760 599-8849	0
Tri-City Home Care Services		C	760 940-5800	0
United Floral Exchange Inc		D	760 597-1940	0
US Foods Inc		B	760 599-6200	0
USA Bouquet LLC		D	800 878-9909	0
Vadnais Trenchless Svcs Inc		D	858 550-1460	0
Vista Care Group LLC (PA)		D	760 295-3900	0
Vista Community Clinic (PA)		B	760 631-5000	0
Vista Community Clinic		E	760 631-5030	0
Vista Irrigation District		D	760 597-3100	0
Vista Knoll Inc		D	760 630-2273	0
Vista Valley Country Club		D	760 758-2800	0
Vista Woods Health Assoc LLC		C	760 630-2273	0
Western Concrete Pumping Inc (PA)		D	760 598-7855	0
Winners Only Inc		C	760 599-0300	0

WALNUT, CA - Los Angeles County

	SIC	EMP	PHONE	ENTRY #
Able Hands Inc		D	626 965-2233	0
Adesso Inc		C	909 839-2929	0
Ahg Inc		B	703 596-0111	0
Amerifreight Inc		A	909 839-2600	0
Bulk Transportation (PA)		D	909 594-2855	0
Caliber Bodyworks Texas Inc		E	909 598-1113	0
Capacity LLC		C	732 745-7770	0
Clarion Construction Inc		E	909 598-4060	0
Command Delivery Systems Inc (PA)		D	909 444-1475	0
Concept Enterprises Inc		D	626 968-8827	0
East Lion Corporation		E	626 912-1818	0
Emeritus Corporation		E	909 595-5030	0
Extra Express (cerritos) Inc		E	714 985-6000	0
Fiserv Inc		D	909 598-8700	0
Fiserv Inc		D	909 595-9074	0
Guesty Inc		C	415 244-0277	0
JF Shea Construction Inc		E	909 594-0998	0
Kelly Paper Company (HQ)		E	909 859-8200	0
M & R Joint Venture Electrical		D	909 598-7700	0
Markwins International Corp (PA)		C	909 595-8898	0
Nestle Dreyers Ice Cream Co		C	909 595-0677	0
Oparc		D	909 598-8055	0
Patina Freight Inc		C	909 444-1025	0
Ronsin Photocopy Inc (PA)		D	909 594-5995	0
Shea Homes Arizona Ltd Partnr		D	909 594-9500	0
Shea Homes At Montage LLC		D	909 594-9500	0
Shea Homes Lmtd Partnership A (HQ)		E	909 594-9500	0
Shea Homes Vantis LLC		D	909 594-9500	0
Shipbycom LLC		D	626 271-9800	0
Sysco Los Angeles Inc		A	909 595-9595	0
Unis LLC (PA)		C	909 839-2600	0
United Riggers & Erectors Inc (PA)		C	909 978-0400	0
Vistancia Marketing LLC		D	909 594-9500	0
Walnut Valley Unified Schl Dst		D	909 595-1261	0
Walnut Valley Water District		D	909 595-7554	0

WALNUT CREEK, CA - Contra Costa County

	SIC	EMP	PHONE	ENTRY #
24 Hour Fitness Usa Inc		D	925 930-7900	0
A F Evans Company Inc		D	925 937-1700	0
Advanced Software Design Inc		D	925 975-0691	0
Alliance Hospital Services (PA)		B	925 304-1107	0
Alliedbarton Security Svcs LLC		B	510 839-4041	0
Amen Clinics Inc A Med Corp		E	650 416-7830	0
American Automobile		D	925 279-2300	0
American Automobile Associatio		B	510 596-3669	0
American Financial Network Inc		D	925 705-7710	0
Amerit Fleet Solutions Inc (HQ)		D	877 512-6374	0
Anderson & Martella Inc		E	925 934-3831	0
Anesthesia Business Cons Inc		D	925 951-1366	0
Appery LLC		D	925 602-5504	0
Argonaut Kensington Associates		D	925 943-1121	0
Ashford Trs Nickel LLC (PA)		D	925 934-2500	0
AT&T Services Inc		B	510 836-6889	0
AT&T Services Inc		D	925 943-4383	0
Atria Senior Living Inc		D	925 938-6611	0
Axiom Global Technologies Inc		C	925 393-5800	0
Barcelon Associates MGT Corp		C	925 627-7000	0

Employment Codes: A=Over 500 employees, B=251-500, C=101-250, D=51-100, E=50

2020 Directory of California
Wholesalers and Services Companies

© Mergent Inc. 1-800-342-5647

1663

GEOGRAPHIC

	SIC	EMP	PHONE	ENTRY #
Bay Imaging Cons Med Group Inc (PA)		D	925 296-7150	0
Bay Medical Management LLC		C	925 296-7150	0
BDS Plumbing Inc		D	925 939-1004	0
Bentley Systems Incorporated		D	925 933-2525	0
Berding & Weil LLP (PA)		D	925 838-2090	0
Bowles & Verna		E	925 935-3300	0
Bpg Storage Solutions Inc		D	562 467-2000	0
Bridge Partners Inc (PA)		D	925 256-9448	0
Brosamer & Wall Inc		C	925 932-7900	0
Brosamer & Wall LLC		E	925 932-7900	0
Brown and Caldwell (PA)		C	925 937-9010	0
C C Connection Inc		D	925 937-0100	0
C2 Financial Corporation		C	925 938-1300	0
California Physicians Service		C	925 927-7419	0
California State Automobile (HQ)		A	925 287-7600	0
Carollo Engineers Inc (PA)		D	925 932-1710	0
Caswell Bay Inc		D	925 933-8181	0
Century Vision Developers Inc		E	925 588-7390	0
Clicksafetycom (HQ)		E	800 971-1080	0
Colliers Parrish Intl Inc		D	925 279-1050	0
Comerica Bank		D	925 941-1900	0
Compwest Insurance Company		C	415 593-5100	0
Concord Jet Service Inc		C	925 825-2980	0
Covia Affordable Communities		D	925 956-7400	0
Csaa Insurance Exchange (PA)		D	800 922-8228	0
Davidon Five Star Corp		D	925 945-8000	0
Diablo Realty Inc		E	925 933-9300	0
Engineered Soil Repairs Inc (PA)		D	408 297-2150	0
Erm-West Inc (DH)		D	925 946-0455	0
Exadel Inc (PA)		D	925 363-9510	0
Factory Mutual Insurance Co		C	925 934-2200	0
Fehr & Peers (PA)		D	925 977-3200	0
First Alarm SEC & Patrol Inc		B	925 295-1260	0
Fugro USA Land Inc		E	925 256-6070	0
Galloway Lucchese Everson		E	925 930-9090	0
Glaspy & Glaspy A Prof Corp			408 279-8844	0
Golden Rain Foundation (PA)		D	925 988-7700	0
Golden Rain Foundation		B	925 988-7800	0
Harvest Technical Service Inc		C	925 937-4874	0
Hcr Manorcare Med Svcs Fla LLC		C	925 274-1325	0
Hcr Manorcare Med Svcs Fla LLC		C	925 975-5000	0
HDR Engineering Inc		D	925 974-2500	0
Heartland Payment Systems LLC		C	925 360-3258	0
Holiday Garden Wc Corp		E	925 932-3332	0
Home Instead Senior Care		D	510 686-9940	0
Hospitlity Prch Group Intl LLC (PA)		D	925 949-5706	0
Interstate Hotels Resorts Inc		C	925 934-2500	0
Izt Mortgage Inc (PA)		E	925 946-1858	0
John Muir Health (HQ)		A	925 947-4449	0
John Muir Health		E	925 947-5300	0
John Muir Health		A	925 939-3000	0
John Muir Physician Network		A	925 952-2701	0
John Muir Physician Network (PA)		A	925 296-9700	0
John Muir Physician Network		B	925 939-3000	0
Kaiser Foundation Hospitals		A	925 906-2380	0
Kaiser Foundation Hospitals		A	925 295-4145	0
Kaiser Foundation Hospitals		A	925 295-4000	0
Kaiser Foundation Hospitals		A	925 906-2000	0
Kaiser Foundation Hospitals		A	925 926-3000	0
Kelleyamerit Holdings Inc (PA)		D	877 512-6374	0
Kilpatrick Twnsend Stckton LLP		C	925 472-5000	0
Kimco Staffing Services Inc		D	925 945-1444	0
Kpmg LLP		E	925 946-1300	0
Kugga Inc		D	925 639-0721	0
Leisure Sports Inc		B	925 938-3058	0
Lindsay Wildlife Museum		D	925 935-1978	0
Mackevision Corporation		C	248 656-6566	0
Malikco LLC		E	925 974-3555	0
Mason-Mcduffie Real Estate Inc		D	925 932-1000	0
Meals On Wheels Diablo Region (PA)		D	925 937-8311	0
Mechanics Bank (DH)		C	800 797-6324	0
Merrill Lynch Pierce Fenner		D	925 945-4800	0
Miller Starr & Regalia A Pro (PA)		D	925 935-9400	0
Moffatt & Nichol		E	925 944-5411	0
Mp Tice Oaks Associates A CA		D	650 356-2976	0
Muir Labs		B	925 947-3335	0
Muir Orthopedic Specialists		C	925 939-8585	0
Newport Group Inc (PA)		C	925 328-4540	0
Northern Cal Ret Clks-Emp Fund		C	925 746-7530	0
Olympic Investors Ltd		D	925 322-8996	0
One Planet Ops Inc (PA)		C	925 983-2800	0
Pacific Cast Bnkers Bancshares (PA)		D	415 399-1900	0
Pacific Coast Bankers Bank		D	415 399-1900	0
Permanente Medical Group Inc		D	925 906-2000	0
Professnal Creer Placementscom		E	415 615-0688	0
Qwest Corporation		D	925 974-4908	0
R R Donnelley & Sons Company		E	925 951-1320	0
Robert Half International Inc		D	925 930-7766	0
Savvius Inc (HQ)		D	925 937-3200	0
SEC Pac Inc		D	925 938-9200	0
Sequoia Surgical Center LP		E	925 935-6700	0
Signature Painting & Cnstr Inc		E	925 287-0444	0
Stantec Consulting Svcs Inc		C	925 627-4500	0
Stantec Energy & Resources Inc		C	925 627-4508	0
Sunrise Senior Living LLC		E	925 932-3500	0
Tactical Telesolutions Inc		C	415 788-8808	0
Thomas Wirig Doll & Co Cpas		D	925 939-2500	0
Tony La Russas Animal RES Fnd		D	925 256-1273	0
Travelers Property Cslty Corp		B	925 945-4000	0
USI Insurance Services Nat		D	925 988-1100	0
Vitas Healthcare Corp Cal		D	925 930-9373	0
Waste Mgt Collectn & Recycl		C	925 935-8900	0
XI Specialty Insurance Corp		E	925 942-6142	0
Yapstone Inc (PA)		C	866 289-5977	0
Ydesign Group LLC (PA)		E	866 842-6209	0
Zks Real Estate Partners LLC		E	925 934-2000	0

WALNUT GROVE, CA - Sacramento County

	SIC	EMP	PHONE	ENTRY #
Ryde Hotel LLC		E	916 776-1318	0

WASCO, CA - Kern County

	SIC	EMP	PHONE	ENTRY #
Community Action Partnr Kern		D	661 758-0129	0
Community Support Options Inc		C	661 758-5331	0
D J Farm Management		E	661 792-6222	0
Demler Egg Ranch		E	661 758-4577	0
R Mora Farm Labor		E	661 746-2858	0
South Valley Almond Co LLC		C	661 391-9000	0

WATERFORD, CA - Stanislaus County

	SIC	EMP	PHONE	ENTRY #
Frazier Nut Farms Inc		E	209 522-1406	0

WATSONVILLE, CA - Santa Cruz County

	SIC	EMP	PHONE	ENTRY #
3-Way Farms (PA)		E	831 722-0748	0
A & I Trucking Inc (PA)		E	831 763-7805	0
Amar Transportation Inc (PA)		C	831 728-8209	0
Ameri-Kleen		B	831 722-8888	0
California Pajarosa		D	831 722-6374	0
California Pajarosa Floral		E	831 722-6374	0
Camflor Inc		C	831 726-1330	0
CB North LLC		A	831 786-1642	0
CBS Farms LLC		E	831 724-0700	0
CF Watsonville LLC		D	831 724-7505	0
CF Watsonville East LLC		D	310 574-3733	0
CF Watsonville West LLC		D	831 724-7505	0
Community Action Brd of Snt Cr		E	831 724-0206	0
Community Bridges		C	831 724-2024	0
Couch Distributing Company Inc		C	831 724-0649	0
Driscolls Inc (PA)		D	831 424-0506	0
Driscolls Inc		D	800 871-3333	0
Edward J Kelly		C	831 724-0832	0
Elkhorn Berry Farms LLC		E	831 722-2472	0
Elyxir Distributing LLC		C	831 761-6400	0
Encompass Community Services		B	831 724-3885	0
Fedex Ground Package Sys Inc		D	800 463-3339	0
Field Fresh Farms LLC		D	831 722-1422	0
Fitz Fresh Inc		E	831 763-4440	0
G I L C Inc		E	831 724-1011	0
Granit-Bayashi 2 A Joint Ventr		E	831 724-1011	0
Granit-Bayashi 3 A Joint Ventr		E	831 724-1011	0
Granite Construction Company (HQ)		C	831 724-1011	0
Granite Construction Inc (PA)		C	831 724-1011	0
Granite Power Inc		B	831 724-1011	0
Granite Rock Co (PA)		D	831 768-2000	0
Greenwaste Recovery Inc (PA)		D	408 283-4800	0
Guy George		E	831 728-2410	0
Halsen Healthcare LLC		A	831 724-4741	0
Hospice of Santa Cruz County		D	831 430-3000	0
International Almond Exchange		E	831 728-4534	0
Jacobs Farm/Del Cabo Inc		C	831 460-3500	0
Kitayama Brothers Inc		D	831 722-8118	0
Maggiora Bros Drilling Inc (PA)		D	831 724-1338	0
Marty Franich Leasing Co		E	831 724-2463	0
Monte Vsta Mem Schlrship Assoc		E	831 722-8178	0
Monterey Bay Acadamy Laundry		D	831 728-1481	0
Monterey Bay Bouquet Acquisit		C	831 786-2700	0
Monterey Mushrooms Inc (PA)		E	831 763-5300	0
Morgan Farm LLC		D	831 726-5120	0
Oceanside Laundry LLC		D	831 722-4358	0
Pajaro Valley Prevntn & Studen		D	831 728-6445	0
Pt Logistics Inc		E	831 728-4535	0
Ramco Enterprises LP		A	831 722-3370	0
Rio Mesa Farms LLC		D	831 728-1965	0

	SIC	EMP	PHONE	ENTRY #
Salud Para La Gente	C		831 728-0222	0
Santa Cruz County of	E		831 763-8400	0
Santa Cruz Metro Trnst Dst	B		831 426-6080	0
Smith Gardens Inc	E		831 768-6300	0
Suncrest Nurseries Inc	D		831 728-2595	0
Superior Foods Inc	D		831 728-3691	0
T T Miyasaka Inc	B		831 722-3871	0
Uyematsu Inc	E		831 724-2200	0
Vps Companies Inc (PA)	E		831 724-7551	0
Waste Mgt Collectn & Recycl	D		831 768-9505	0
Watsonville Coast Produce Inc	C		831 722-3851	0
West Coast Hospitals Inc	D		831 722-3581	0

WEAVERVILLE, CA - Trinity County

	SIC	EMP	PHONE	ENTRY #
Mountain Comm Hlth Cre Dist	C		530 623-5541	0
Mountain Comm Hlth Cre Dist (PA)	C		530 623-5541	0

WEED, CA - Siskiyou County

	SIC	EMP	PHONE	ENTRY #
Lassen Canyon Nursery Inc	D		530 938-4720	0
Personnel Preference Inc	C		530 938-3909	0
Roseburg Forest Products Co	C		530 938-2721	0

WEST COVINA, CA - Los Angeles County

	SIC	EMP	PHONE	ENTRY #
Assisted Home Recovery Inc	D		626 915-5595	0
Beaver Dam Health Care Center	D		626 962-3368	0
Big Lgue Dreams Consulting LLC	C		626 839-1100	0
BKK Corporation (PA)	D		626 965-0911	0
Bowlero Corp	D		626 960-3636	0
Certified Nursing Registry Inc	C		626 912-1877	0
Citrus Valley Hospice	D		626 859-2263	0
Citrus Valley Medical Ctr Inc (PA)	A		626 962-4011	0
Citrus Valley Medical Ctr Inc	A		626 963-8411	0
Citrus Vly Hlth Partners Inc	A		626 962-4011	0
Clara Baldwin Stocker Home	E		626 962-7151	0
Concorde Battery Corp	C		626 813-1234	0
Covina Bowl Inc	D		626 339-1286	0
Doctors Hospital W Covina Inc	D		626 338-8481	0
East Valley Cmnty Hlth Ctr Inc (PA)	D		626 919-3402	0
Eastland Tower Partnership	E		626 858-2000	0
Foothill Transit Service Corp (PA)	D		626 967-3147	0
Futuro Infantil Hispano Ffa	E		626 339-1824	0
Harris & Ruth Painting Contg (PA)	D		626 960-4004	0
In Home Health Inc	D		419 254-7841	0
Jpmorgan Chase Bank Nat Assn	D		626 919-3129	0
Kaiser Foundation Hospitals	E		866 319-4269	0
Lead Staffing Corporation	C		800 928-5561	0
Lfp Ecommerce LLC	D		314 428-5069	0
Matrix Group International Inc	D		626 960-6205	0
Paul Calvo and Company	E		626 814-8000	0
Queen of Valley Hospital	A		626 962-4011	0
Regent Assisted Living Inc	D		626 332-3344	0
RM Galicia Inc	D		626 813-6200	0
Schoolwires Inc	D		626 974-7600	0
Solugenix Corporation	D		866 749-7658	0
South Hills Country Club	D		626 339-1231	0
Southern Cal Prmnnte Med Group	D		626 960-4844	0
Southern Cal Spcialty Care Inc	D		626 339-5451	0
Sunny Hills-Palladium LLC (PA)	E		626 304-0310	0
Universal Bank (PA)	D		626 854-2818	0
Volunteers of Amer Los Angeles	D		626 337-9878	0
West Covina Medical Clinic Inc (PA)	C		626 960-8614	0
Wicoro Inc (HQ)	E		626 962-4489	0

WEST HILLS, CA - Los Angeles County

	SIC	EMP	PHONE	ENTRY #
Benjamin Kurzban Son Ctrl Inc	E		347 227-3425	0
Boeing Company	E		818 466-8800	0
Canew Inc	D		818 703-5100	0
Care 4 U LLC	D		818 593-7911	0
Childrens Homes Southern Cal (PA)	E		818 592-2960	0
Damon Electrical	D		818 426-3450	0
Dlh Davinci LLC	D		818 703-5100	0
Electro Rent Corporation (HQ)	C		818 786-2525	0
Fiserv Inc	D		818 226-4400	0
Holman Family Counseling Inc (PA)	D		818 704-1444	0
Hvantage Technologies Inc	D		818 661-6301	0
Insite Digestive Health Care	D		818 346-9911	0
Leisure Care LLC	D		818 713-0900	0
Source Photonics Usa Inc (PA)	C		818 773-9044	0
Unilab Corporation (HQ)	B		818 737-6000	0

WEST HOLLYWOOD, CA - Los Angeles County

	SIC	EMP	PHONE	ENTRY #
24 Hour Fitness Usa Inc	E		310 652-7440	0
Alpha Soft Support LLC	D		857 219-5505	0
AT&T Corp	E		323 874-7000	0
Atlas Entertainment Inc	E		310 786-4900	0
Auto Club Enterprises	B		310 914-8500	0
Black & White TV Inc	E		310 855-1040	0

	SIC	EMP	PHONE	ENTRY #
Coldwer Banker Previews	C		310 278-9470	0
Cpe Hr Inc	D		310 270-9800	0
Cpe Peo Inc	D		310 385-1000	0
Crunch LLC	D		323 654-4550	0
Dailey & Associates	D		323 490-3847	0
Empoweredexpansions Corp (PA)	D		310 492-5988	0
Endemol	D		310 860-9914	0
Essex Property Trust Inc	E		323 461-9346	0
Funny or Die Inc	E		650 461-3929	0
Graphic Orb Inc	D		310 967-2350	0
Harpo Inc	D		312 633-1000	0
Harpo Productions Inc	C		312 633-1000	0
Hmbl LLC	C		323 656-8090	0
Hob Entertainment LLC	C		323 848-5100	0
Le Montrose Hotel	D		310 855-1115	0
Liveuniverse Inc	D		310 492-2200	0
Modern Hr Inc	B		310 270-9800	0
N Compass International Inc	C		323 785-1700	0
Neonroots LLC	C		310 907-9210	0
Ols Hotels & Resorts LP	C		310 855-1115	0
Operam Inc	D		855 673-7261	0
Outrigger Hotels Hawaii	D		323 491-9015	0
Own LLC	C		323 602-5500	0
Quixote Mm LLC	E		323 851-5030	0
Quixote Studios LLC (PA)	E		323 851-5030	0
Rsa Films Inc (PA)	D		310 659-1577	0
S&F Management Company LLC (PA)	C		310 385-1090	0
Snf Management	D		310 385-1090	0
Suissa Miller Advertising LLC	D		310 392-9666	0
Thiel Capital LLC (PA)	D		323 990-2030	0
Ticketmaster Entertainment LLC	A		800 653-8000	0
Valadon Hotel LLC	D		310 854-1114	0
W-Bel Age LLC	D		310 854-1111	0
White Rabbit Partners Inc	C		310 975-1450	0

WEST SACRAMENTO, CA - Yolo County

	SIC	EMP	PHONE	ENTRY #
A Csg-Nova Joint Venture	D		916 371-7303	0
ABM Janitorial Services Inc	B		916 374-1739	0
AEP Span Inc	D		916 372-0933	0
Ahtna Government Services Corp	D		916 372-2000	0
American Metals Corporation (HQ)	C		916 371-7700	0
ASC Profiles LLC (DH)	D		916 376-2800	0
AT&T Services Inc	C		916 376-2006	0
Aus Decking Inc	D		916 373-5320	0
Blazona Concrete Cnstr Inc	D		916 375-8337	0
Brown Construction Inc	D		916 374-8616	0
Burger Rhblitation Systems Inc	D		916 617-2400	0
Byteways Manufacturing Inc	B		916 453-1212	0
Califor State Teach Retire Sys (DH)	C		800 228-5453	0
California Chamber Commerce	D		916 928-3594	0
California Correctnl Peace Ofc (PA)	C		916 372-6060	0
California School Boards Assn	D		800 266-3382	0
California Sierra Express Inc	C		916 375-7070	0
Capay Incorporated (PA)	D		530 796-0730	0
Capital Beverage Company (PA)	C		916 371-8164	0
Cgi Technologies Solutions Inc	E		916 281-3200	0
Cirks Construction Inc	C		916 362-5460	0
Clark - Pacific Corporation (PA)	B		916 371-0305	0
Collins Electrical Company Inc	C		209 466-3691	0
Core-Mark Sacramento 2	E		866 791-4210	0
Creative Living Options Inc	C		916 372-2102	0
Dbi Beverage Sacramento (HQ)	D		916 373-5700	0
Dennis Blazona Construction	D		916 375-8337	0
Dependable Highway Express Inc	E		916 374-0782	0
Devine & Son Trucking Co Inc (PA)	C		559 486-7440	0
Farm Fresh To You (PA)	C		916 303-7145	0
Fredericksen Tank Lines Inc (PA)	D		916 371-4960	0
Frito-Lay North America Inc	C		916 372-5400	0
Harbor Distributing LLC	B		916 373-5700	0
Holt of California	C		916 373-4100	0
Idexx Reference Labs Inc	C		916 372-4200	0
Jacmar Ddc LLC	D		916 372-9795	0
Mac Arthur Co	D		916 226-5706	0
Marathon Staffing Solutions	D		978 649-6230	0
Nor-Cal Beverage Co Inc (PA)	B		916 372-0600	0
Nor-Cal Pipeline Services	D		530 673-3886	0
Nor-Cal Produce Inc	C		916 373-0830	0
Oak Harbor Freight Lines Inc	D		916 371-3960	0
Occupnl Urgnt Care Hlth Syst	A		916 374-4600	0
Pacific Gas and Electric Co	C		916 375-5005	0
Parts	D		916 371-3115	0
Pittsburg Wholesale Groc Inc	C		916 372-7772	0
Psi3g Inc	D		916 803-2879	0
Quad/Graphics Inc	C		916 371-9500	0
Redstone Print & Mail Inc	D		916 318-6450	0
River Bend Holdings LLC	C		916 371-1890	0

GEOGRAPHIC

Company	SIC	EMP	PHONE	ENTRY #
River Cy Basbal Inv Group LLC **(PA)**		D	916 376-4700	0
River Cy Geoprofessionals Inc		D	916 372-1434	0
Rural Cmnty Assistance Corp **(PA)**		D	916 447-2854	0
Sacramento River Cats Baseball		E	916 376-4700	0
Sacramento Television Stns Inc **(DH)**		C	916 374-1452	0
Sacramento-Yolo Port District		C	916 371-8000	0
Testamerica Laboratories Inc		D	916 373-5600	0
Tonys Fine Foods **(HQ)**		B	916 374-4000	0
Tricor America Inc		D	916 371-1704	0
Triton Tower Inc **(PA)**		D	916 375-8546	0
U S Army Corps of Engineers		D	916 557-7491	0
United Parcel Service Inc OH		C	916 373-4076	0
UPS Ground Freight Inc		D	916 371-9101	0
Valley Toxicology Service Inc		D	916 371-5440	0
Vss International Inc **(HQ)**		D	916 373-1500	0
Wallace-Kuhl Investments LLC **(PA)**		D	916 372-1434	0
Walton Engineering Inc		D	916 372-1888	0
Youngs Market Company LLC		E	916 617-4402	0

WESTLAKE VILLAGE, CA - Ventura County

Company	SIC	EMP	PHONE	ENTRY #
5 Nine Group Inc		C	805 880-2948	0
Adelson Testan Brundo Novel **(PA)**		E	805 604-1816	0
Allen Construction Inc		B	818 879-5334	0
Alston & Bird LLP		B	202 239-3673	0
Amgreen-Karena Ht Partnr Ltd **(PA)**		D	818 707-9494	0
Anthem Inc		A	562 622-2869	0
AP Global Inc		B	818 707-3167	0
Appraiser Loft LLC		E	858 832-8334	0
Bana Home Loan Servicing		A	213 345-7975	0
Bankcard USA Merchant Srvc		D	818 597-7000	0
Baxter Healthcare Corporation		A	805 372-3000	0
Blue Cross of California **(DH)**		C	805 557-6050	0
Burton-Way House Ltd A CA		C	805 214-8075	0
California Coml Inv Group Inc		E	805 495-8400	0
Callsource Inc **(PA)**		C	818 673-4700	0
Citibank National Association		C	805 497-7361	0
Coastal Radiation Oncology Med		D	805 494-4483	0
Conversant LLC **(HQ)**		C	818 575-4500	0
Cornerstone Healthcare Inc		C	805 777-1133	0
Country Floral Supply Inc **(PA)**		D	805 520-8026	0
Dennis M McCoy & Sons Inc		D	818 874-3872	0
Digital Insight Corporation		C	818 879-1010	0
Dilbeck Inc		E	805 379-1880	0
Dole Food Company Inc **(PA)**		C	818 874-4000	0
Dole Fresh Fruit Company **(HQ)**		B	818 874-4000	0
Dole Holding Company LLC		A	818 879-6600	0
Dole Holdings Inc **(PA)**		D	818 879-6600	0
Elite Airways LLC		C	805 496-3334	0
Ernst & Young LLP		D	805 778-7000	0
Frontier California Inc		A	805 372-6000	0
Frontier California Inc		D	805 372-6000	0
G4s Secure Solutions USA Inc		C	818 889-1113	0
Gemmm Corp		D	818 522-0740	0
General Home Medical Sup Inc		D	805 449-1559	0
Greystripe Incorporated		C	415 644-1702	0
Hanover Builders Inc		E	818 706-2279	0
High Road Program **(PA)**		D	805 497-8800	0
Intellirisk Management Corp		E	818 575-5400	0
Ipayment Inc **(DH)**		D	212 802-7200	0
Jackie Hoofring		E	818 961-7272	0
JD Power		B	805 418-8000	0
Jri Inc		E	818 706-2424	0
Lantz Security Systems Inc		B	805 496-5775	0
Mediaplex Inc **(DH)**		D	818 575-4500	0
Microfinancial Incorporated		C	805 367-8900	0
Move Co		C	805 557-2300	0
Mws Precision Wire Inds Inc		D	818 991-8553	0
National Builder Services Inc		D	714 634-7800	0
North Ranch Country Club		C	818 889-3531	0
Ownit Mortgage Solutions Inc		B	513 872-6922	0
Pacific Compensation Insur Co		C	818 575-8500	0
Pleasant Holidays LLC **(HQ)**		B	818 991-3390	0
Pmt Crdit Risk Trnsf Tr 2015-1		D	818 224-7028	0
Pmt Crdit Risk Trnsf Tr 2015-2		C	818 224-7442	0
Pmt Issuer Trust - Fmsr		D	818 224-7028	0
Pnmac Gmsr Issuer Trust		A	818 746-2271	0
Premium Rock Drywall Inc		D	818 676-3350	0
Pyj V A California Ltd Partnr		D	805 495-8437	0
Registry Monitoring Ins Srvcs		D	800 400-4924	0
Remax Olson		D	805 267-4929	0
Rwr Homes Inc **(PA)**		D	805 413-1792	0
Sdg Enterprises		D	805 777-7978	0
Securitas SEC Svcs USA Inc		B	818 706-6800	0
Securitas SEC Svcs USA Inc		C	818 706-6800	0
Security Paving Company Inc **(PA)**		D	818 362-9200	0
Select Home Care		D	805 777-3855	0

Company	SIC	EMP	PHONE	ENTRY #
Sky Court USA Inc		C	805 497-9991	0
Smart & Final Stores Inc		B	818 889-8253	0
Smith Bros Inc **(PA)**		D	805 449-2841	0
Southern Cal Orthpd Inst LP		D	818 901-6600	0
Sunrise Senior Living LLC		D	805 557-1100	0
Swvp Westlake LLC		C	805 557-1234	0
Thousand Oaks Prtg & Spc Inc		C	818 706-8330	0
Troop Real Estate Inc		D	805 402-3028	0
United Cp/S Chldrns Fndn La		E	805 494-1141	0
United Parcel Service Inc		A	818 735-0945	0
University Cal Los Angeles		E	805 494-6920	0
Velocity Commercial Capitl LLC		E	818 532-3700	0
Verizon Communications Inc		C	805 390-5417	0
Warner Pacific Insur Svcs Inc **(PA)**		C	408 298-4049	0
Westlake Properties Inc		C	818 889-0230	0
WF Cinema Holdings LP		E	805 379-8966	0
Young Realtors		D	805 497-0947	0

WESTMINSTER, CA - Orange County

Company	SIC	EMP	PHONE	ENTRY #
Abrazar Inc		D	714 893-3581	0
Anderson News LLC		D	714 892-7766	0
B & E Farms Inc		E	714 893-8166	0
Co D L Pham MD		E	714 531-2091	0
Consoldted Med Bo-Analysis Inc		D	714 657-7389	0
County of Orange		D	714 896-7188	0
County of Orange		D	714 896-7500	0
Edco Drywall Inc		E	714 799-9886	0
Extended Care Hosp Westminster		C	714 891-2769	0
Ferguson Enterprises Inc		C	714 893-1936	0
Helping Hands Sanctuary of Ida		D	714 892-6686	0
Inlog Inc		D	949 212-3867	0
Lbs Financial Credit Union **(PA)**		C	562 598-9007	0
Maxwell Petersen Associates		E	714 230-3150	0
National Fail Safe Inc		E	562 493-5447	0
New CAM Commerce Solutions LLC		D	714 338-0200	0
Orange County One Stop Center		D	714 241-4900	0
Pyramid Logistics Services Inc **(PA)**		D	714 903-2600	0
Snowbounders Ski Club		D	714 892-4897	0
Southern California Edison Co		C	714 934-0838	0
Southern California Edison Co		B	714 895-0420	0
Southern California Edison Co		C	714 895-0163	0
Sunrise Plumbing & Mech Inc		E	562 424-0332	0
Thompson Family Farms LLC		E	714 848-7536	0
Vina Holdings Inc		D	714 622-5334	0
Westminster Housing Parteners		E	714 891-3000	0
Westview Services Inc		D	714 418-2090	0

WHEATLAND, CA - Yuba County

Company	SIC	EMP	PHONE	ENTRY #
Northern California Inalliance		C	530 633-9695	0
Wheatland School District		D	530 633-3135	0

WHITTIER, CA - Los Angeles County

Company	SIC	EMP	PHONE	ENTRY #
24 Hour Fitness Usa Inc		D	562 943-3771	0
Ahmc Whittier Hosp Med Ctr LP		A	562 945-3561	0
Asian Rehabilitation Svc Inc **(PA)**		D	562 632-1141	0
Assocted Reproduction Svcs Inc		C	562 696-1181	0
Bright Health Physicians **(PA)**		C	562 947-8478	0
Caldwell Realty		D	562 907-5655	0
Capc Inc		C	562 693-8826	0
Cintas Corporation No 3		D	562 692-8741	0
City of Whittier		D	562 567-9446	0
Complete Landscape Care Inc		D	562 946-4441	0
Concept 7 Inc **(PA)**		D	714 966-9734	0
County of Los Angeles		C	562 908-3119	0
County of Los Angeles		C	562 945-2581	0
County Santtn Dist 2 of La Co **(PA)**		A	562 699-7411	0
County Santtn Dist 2 of La Co		D	562 699-5204	0
Credit Union Southern Cal **(PA)**		D	562 698-8326	0
Cypress College Foundation		D	714 484-7128	0
Del Rio Health Care Inc		C	562 947-5221	0
Ensign Group Inc		C	562 947-7817	0
Fedex Freight Corporation		B	800 288-0743	0
Freedom Painting Inc		E	562 696-0785	0
Friendly Hills Country Club		C	562 698-0331	0
General Transistor Corporation **(PA)**		D	310 578-7344	0
Ghg Properties LLC		D	562 945-8511	0
Gourmet India Food Company LLC		D	562 698-9763	0
Grand Supercenter Inc		D	562 318-3451	0
Helpline Youth Counseling **(PA)**		E	562 273-0722	0
Inclusion Services LLC		C	562 945-2000	0
Intercommunity Child		D	562 692-0383	0
Intercommunity Dialysis Svcs		E	562 696-1841	0
Interhealth Corp **(PA)**		A	562 698-0811	0
Interhealth Services Inc **(HQ)**		D	562 698-0811	0
International Home Mortgage		D	562 945-7753	0
J P Carroll Co Inc		D	323 660-9230	0

Mergent email: customerrelations@mergent.com
1666

2020 Directory of California
Wholesalers and Services Companies

(P-0000) Products & Services Section entry number
(PA)=Parent Co (HQ)=Headquarters (DH)=Div Headquarters

	SIC	EMP	PHONE	ENTRY #
John Shannon Mc Gee Co Inc		E	562 789-1777	0
Kaiser Foundation Hospitals		E	866 340-5974	0
League of Wmen Voters Whittier		E	562 947-5818	0
Longwood Management Corp		D	562 693-5240	0
Magnell Associate Inc		C	626 271-1420	0
Mercedes Diaz Homes Inc		D	562 945-4576	0
Merrill Gardens LLC		D	562 693-0505	0
NLc Enterprises Incorporated		E	562 693-3590	0
Oltmans Construction Co **(PA)**		D	562 948-4242	0
Oltmans Investment Company		E	562 948-4242	0
Orchard - Post Acute Care Ctr		A	562 693-7701	0
Pep Boys Manny Moe Jack of Cal		E	562 908-4400	0
Pih Health Hospital - Whittier **(PA)**		A	562 698-0811	0
Plaza De La Raza Child Develop		D	562 695-1070	0
Presbyterian Health Physicians		C	562 464-4717	0
Rio Hondo Education Consortium		C	562 945-0150	0
Rose Hills Company **(HQ)**		A	562 699-0921	0
Rose Hills Holdings Corp **(PA)**		B	562 699-0921	0
Rose Hills Mortuary Inc		A	562 699-0921	0
Sanitation Districts		A	562 908-4288	0
Sas Entertainment Partners Inc		E	213 400-1901	0
Smart & Final Stores Inc		B	562 907-7037	0
Southern California Gas Co		D	562 803-3341	0
Southern California Mtl Hdlg **(DH)**		C	562 949-1006	0
Southern Fresh Prod Provs Inc		C	562 236-2784	0
Summerville Senior Living Inc		D	562 943-3724	0
Transportation California Dept		C	562 692-0823	0
Whittier Hospital Med Ctr Inc		C	562 945-3561	0

WILDOMAR, CA - Riverside County

	SIC	EMP	PHONE	ENTRY #
Asr Constructors Inc		B	951 779-6580	0
Classic Installs Inc		D	951 678-9906	0
Coldwell Banker and Associates **(PA)**		D	951 304-2900	0
Diverscape Inc		D	951 245-1686	0
Heartland Payment Systems LLC		D	909 609-1836	0
Inland Vly Rgional Med Ctr Inc		A	951 677-1111	0
Kaiser Foundation Hospitals		E	951 353-2000	0
Kilcrew Productions		D	619 564-2080	0
Lake Elsinore Unified Schl Dst		C	951 253-7830	0
S Taylor Construction Inc		C	310 291-4505	0
Sunpro Solar Inc		D	951 678-7733	0

WILLIAMS, CA - Colusa County

	SIC	EMP	PHONE	ENTRY #
ACC-Gwg LLC		D	530 473-2827	0
Elvira Sandoval		C	530 473-5718	0
La Grande Farm		D	530 473-5923	0
Latham Pool Products Inc		E	530 473-5319	0
Valley West Health Care Inc **(PA)**		D	530 473-5321	0

WILLITS, CA - Mendocino County

	SIC	EMP	PHONE	ENTRY #
Brooktrails Lodge LLC		D	707 459-1596	0
Sherwood Valley Rancheria		D	707 459-7330	0
Shusters Transportation Inc		D	707 459-4131	0
Willits Hospital Inc		B	707 459-6801	0
Willits Seniors Inc		D	707 459-6826	0

WILLOW CREEK, CA - Humboldt County

	SIC	EMP	PHONE	ENTRY #
Northcoast Childrens Services		D	530 629-2283	0

WILLOWS, CA - Glenn County

	SIC	EMP	PHONE	ENTRY #
County of Glenn		D	530 934-6582	0
County of Glenn		C	530 934-6530	0
County of Glenn		C	530 934-6453	0
County of Glenn		C	530 934-6514	0
County of Glenn		D	530 934-6582	0
Glenn Cnty Humn Resource Agcy		C	530 934-6510	0
Glenn Cnty Plg Pub Works Agcy		D	530 934-6541	0
Glenn Medical Center Inc		D	530 934-4681	0
Glenn-Colusa Irrigation Dst **(PA)**		D	530 934-8881	0
Kumar Hotels Inc		D	530 934-8900	0
Sunbridge Healthcare LLC		D	530 934-2834	0

WILMINGTON, CA - Los Angeles County

	SIC	EMP	PHONE	ENTRY #
Ajc Sandblasting Inc		D	562 436-3606	0
American Integrated Svcs Inc **(PA)**		E	310 522-1168	0
Anderson Hay & Grain Co Inc		C	509 925-9818	0
Boys and Girls Clubs of The La		D	310 833-1322	0
Ccc2931 LLC		D	562 590-8591	0
City of Los Angeles		B	310 732-3550	0
Conglobal Industries LLC		D	310 518-2500	0
County of Los Angeles		D	310 518-8800	0
E Street Cold Logistics LLC **(PA)**		E	310 233-7300	0
Estes Express Lines Inc		D	310 549-7306	0
Fast Lane Transportation Inc **(PA)**		D	562 435-3000	0
Harbor Industrial Services		D	310 522-1193	0
Icpk Corporation		D	310 830-8020	0
Konoike-Pacific California Inc **(HQ)**		D	310 518-1000	0

	SIC	EMP	PHONE	ENTRY #
Los Angeles Unified School Dst		C	310 518-1128	0
Marine Technical Services Inc		D	310 549-8030	0
MCM Construction Inc		D	310 549-9207	0
Pacific Harbor Line Inc **(HQ)**		C	310 834-4594	0
Pacific Sea Food Co Inc		E	310 835-4343	0
Pasha Stevedoring Terminals LP		E	310 233-2006	0
Pasha Stevedoring Terminals LP		E	415 927-6353	0
Potential Industries Inc **(PA)**		C	310 807-4466	0
Praxair Inc		D	562 983-2100	0
Public Hlth Fndation Entps Inc		C	310 518-2835	0
South Bay Ctr For Counseling		D	310 414-2090	0
Star Fisheries		D	310 549-4992	0
Trapac LLC **(HQ)**		E	310 513-1572	0
Wwl Vehicle Svcs Americas Inc		C	310 835-8806	0

WINCHESTER, CA - Riverside County

	SIC	EMP	PHONE	ENTRY #
Help Hospitalized Veterans II		D	951 926-4500	0
Metropolitan Water District		D	951 926-7095	0
Metropolitan Water District		D	951 926-1501	0
Mind Dragon Inc		E	877 367-6060	0
Skywest Airlines Inc		D	951 926-9511	0

WINDSOR, CA - Sonoma County

	SIC	EMP	PHONE	ENTRY #
Cali Calmecac Language Academy		D	707 837-7747	0
Fedex Ground Package Sys Inc		C	800 463-3339	0
Happy Pet Co		E	707 586-8660	0
Landcare USA LLC		D	707 836-1460	0
North Bay Construction Inc		E	707 836-8500	0
Petersen Builders Inc		E	707 838-3035	0
Richards Grove Saralees Vinyrd		D	707 837-9200	0
Robert A Hall		D	707 837-8564	0
Selex Inc		D	707 836-8836	0
Shook & Waller Cnstr Inc		D	707 578-3933	0
Windsor Golf Club Inc		D	707 838-7888	0

WINNETKA, CA - Los Angeles County

	SIC	EMP	PHONE	ENTRY #
David W Golen		D	213 716-0706	0
Memon Aamir		E	818 339-8810	0
Valley Village **(PA)**		D	818 587-9450	0

WINTERHAVEN, CA - Imperial County

	SIC	EMP	PHONE	ENTRY #
Quechan Indian Tribe		B	760 572-2413	0

WINTERS, CA - Yolo County

	SIC	EMP	PHONE	ENTRY #
Button & Turkovich		D	530 795-2090	0
Mariani Nut Company Inc		D	530 795-2225	0
Terra Firma Farm Corp		E	530 795-2473	0

WINTON, CA - Merced County

	SIC	EMP	PHONE	ENTRY #
Cederlind Farms LP		D	209 606-8586	0
Central Valley Oprtnty Ctr Inc **(PA)**		C	209 357-0062	0
P H Ranch Inc		E	209 358-5111	0

WOODBRIDGE, CA - San Joaquin County

	SIC	EMP	PHONE	ENTRY #
The Woodbridge Golf Cntry CLB		D	209 369-2371	0

WOODLAKE, CA - Tulare County

	SIC	EMP	PHONE	ENTRY #
Gold Coast Farms LLC		E	559 564-6316	0
Peltzer Groves		E	559 804-0661	0
Pete Santellan		C	559 564-3748	0

WOODLAND, CA - Yolo County

	SIC	EMP	PHONE	ENTRY #
Alcohol DRG Program Yolo Cnty		E	530 666-8650	0
Apria Healthcare LLC		D	530 669-6441	0
AT&T Corp		D	530 661-7724	0
B E Giovannetti & Sons **(PA)**		E	530 662-1729	0
Broward Builders Inc		D	530 666-5635	0
Bunge Milling Inc		C	530 666-1691	0
Butterfield Electric Inc **(PA)**		C	530 666-2116	0
Campos Dmetrio Frm Labor Contr		D	530 662-4143	0
Child Development Incorporated		B	530 666-4822	0
City of Woodland		C	530 661-5878	0
City of Woodland		D	530 661-5962	0
City of Woodland		D	530 661-5961	0
County of Yolo		D	530 666-8630	0
CPI Econco Division **(DH)**		D	530 662-7553	0
Dignity Health		C	530 666-8828	0
E & E Co Ltd		A	530 669-5991	0
Half Moon Fruit & Produce Co **(PA)**		D	530 662-1727	0
Home Instead Senior Care		E	707 678-2005	0
Interpac Technologies Inc		D	530 662-6363	0
J H Meek & Sons Inc		E	530 662-1106	0
Joe Heidrick Enterprises Inc		E	530 662-2339	0
Liberty Packing Company LLC **(PA)**		C	209 826-7100	0
Mann Lake Ltd		E	530 662-4061	0
Monsanto Company		B	530 669-6224	0
Muller Ranch LLC		D	530 662-0105	0
North American Health Care		D	530 662-9193	0

Employment Codes: A=Over 500 employees, B=251-500,
C=101-250, D=51-100, E=50

2020 Directory of California
Wholesalers and Services Companies

© Mergent Inc. 1-800-342-5647

1667

GEOGRAPHIC

Company	SIC	EMP	PHONE	ENTRY #
Northern Vly Indian Hlth Inc		D	530 661-4400	0
Nugget Market Inc		C	530 662-5479	0
Omar Orozco		D	530 723-0849	0
Oscar Valero		E	530 668-4342	0
Palm Grdns Rsdntial Care Fclty		E	530 661-0574	0
Payne Brothers Ranches		D	530 662-2354	0
Rite Aid Drug Palace Inc		E	530 661-1800	0
Sierra Entertainment		E	530 666-9646	0
St Johns Retirement Village		C	530 662-9674	0
Summer House Inc (PA)		D	530 662-8493	0
Sunfoods LLC (HQ)		D	530 661-1923	0
Sutter Health		C	530 406-5600	0
Sutter Health		C	530 406-5600	0
Sutter Hlth Scrmnto Sierra Reg		A	530 406-5616	0
Target Corporation		B	530 666-3705	0
Tc Property Mgt A Californi		D	530 666-5799	0
Travis Credit Union		B	800 877-8328	0
United Health Systems Inc		C	530 662-9161	0
Woodland Healthcare		C	530 668-2600	0
Woodland Jint Unified Schl Dst		E	530 662-0201	0
Woodland Residential Services		D	530 419-0059	0
Woodland Swim Team Bosters CLB		D	530 662-9783	0

WOODLAND HILLS, CA - Los Angeles County

Company	SIC	EMP	PHONE	ENTRY #
21st Century Insurance Company (DH)		A	877 310-5687	0
21st Century Lf & Hlth Co Inc (PA)		A	818 887-4436	0
7410 Woodman Avenue LLC		D	805 496-4336	0
8020 Consulting LLC		E	818 523-3201	0
All Action Security Inc		D	800 482-7371	0
Alliant Asset MGT Co LLC (PA)		D	818 668-2805	0
Allied Industries Inc (PA)		C	800 605-5323	0
Amwins Insurance Brkg Cal LLC (HQ)		D	818 772-1774	0
AON Consulting Inc		D	562 345-4700	0
Arrow Electronics Inc		D	818 932-1022	0
Asana Integrated Medical Group		D	888 212-7545	0
Assertive Security Services &		A	818 888-2405	0
Associated Foreign Exch Inc (HQ)		D	888 307-2339	0
Assocted Fgn Exch Holdings Inc (PA)		D	818 386-2702	0
Automobile Club Southern Cal		E	818 883-2660	0
Avnet Inc		D	818 594-8310	0
B C Life & Health Insurance Co		D	818 703-2345	0
B Riley Financial Inc (PA)		C	818 884-3737	0
Bank America National Assn		D	818 577-2000	0
Benefitvision Inc		D	818 348-3100	0
Blackline Inc (PA)		D	818 223-9008	0
Blackline Systems Inc (HQ)		C	877 777-7750	0
Blh Construction Company		C	818 905-3837	0
Boething Treeland Farms Inc (PA)		D	818 883-1222	0
California Physicians Service		B	818 598-8000	0
California Preferred Bldrs Inc		E	818 402-3345	0
Canoga Hotel Corporation		C	818 595-1000	0
Center For Autism & (PA)		C	818 345-2345	0
Centrelink Insur & Fincl Svcs		D	818 587-2001	0
Child Development Institute		E	818 888-4559	0
Classmates Media Corporation		B	818 287-3600	0
Cohnreznick LLP		D	818 205-2600	0
Conduit Lngage Specialists Inc		C	859 299-3178	0
Corptax LLC		D	818 316-2400	0
Courtyard Management Corp		D	818 999-2200	0
Creative Events Enterprises		C	818 610-7000	0
Custom Design Co Inc		E	818 507-5959	0
Dassault Systemes Americas		C	818 999-2500	0
Digital Communications Network (PA)		D	818 227-3333	0
Dunn & Berger Inc		B	818 986-1234	0
Environmental Construction Inc		D	818 449-8920	0
Ev Ray Inc		E	818 346-5381	0
Factory Mutual Insurance Co		D	818 227-2200	0
Farmers Group Inc (HQ)		A	323 932-3200	0
Farmers Group Inc		A	805 583-7400	0
Farmers Insurance Exchange (DH)		A	323 932-3200	0
Federal Insurance Company		D	818 596-6100	0
Film Roman Llc		C	818 748-4000	0
Film Roman LLC		C	818 748-4000	0
First Interstate Security Inc		C	818 995-6664	0
Goetzman Group Inc (PA)		D	818 595-1112	0
Goldco Direct LLC		D	818 343-0186	0
Greystar Management Svcs LP		B	818 596-2180	0
Guarachi Wine Partners Inc		D	818 225-5100	0
Harris Direct		D	818 357-2040	0
Health Net LLC (HQ)		C	818 676-6000	0
HEI Hospitality LLC		C	818 887-4800	0
Hilton Woodland Hills & Towers		C	818 595-1000	0
Hsbc Finance Corporation		B	818 999-9175	0
IDS Inc		D	866 297-5757	0
Image Entertainment Inc (DH)		D	818 407-9100	0
Infinite Home Health Inc		D	818 888-7772	0

Company	SIC	EMP	PHONE	ENTRY #
Innovative Merch Solutions LLC		C	818 936-7800	0
Input 1 LLC		C	818 340-0030	0
Inter/Media Time Buying Corp (PA)		E	818 995-1455	0
Interstate Protective Services		D	818 995-6664	0
John Alden Life Insurance Co		D	818 595-7600	0
Joseph C Sansone Company (PA)		D	818 226-3400	0
Kaiser Foundation Hospitals		A	818 719-2000	0
Kaiser Foundation Hospitals		E	818 592-3100	0
Kaiser Foundation Hospitals			888 515-3500	0
Kellogg Andlson Accntancy Corp (PA)		D	818 971-5100	0
Kern Organization Inc		D	818 703-8775	0
Kpmg LLP		E	818 227-6900	0
Law Offices Berglund & Johnson (PA)		D	951 276-4783	0
Lewis Marenstein Wicke Sherwin		E	818 703-6000	0
Lifecare Assurance Company		D	818 887-4436	0
LLP Moss Adams		D	818 577-1822	0
Markel Corp		B	818 595-0600	0
Markel West Inc		E	818 595-0600	0
Mediscan Diagnostic Svcs LLC		D	818 758-4224	0
Medpoint Management		E	818 702-0100	0
Memeged Tevuot Shemesh (PA)		C	866 575-1211	0
Mid Century Insurance Company		C	323 932-7116	0
Motion Picture and TV Fund (PA)		A	818 876-1777	0
Mventix Inc (PA)		B	818 337-3747	0
Netapp Inc		C	818 227-5025	0
Network Telephone Services Inc (PA)		B	800 742-5687	0
Netzero Inc (DH)		C	805 418-2000	0
Neversoft Entertainment Inc		C	818 610-4100	0
New Mediscan II LLC		D	866 758-4224	0
Nmms Twin Peaks LLC		D	818 710-6100	0
Novastar Post Inc		D	323 467-5020	0
Omnikron Systems Inc		D	818 591-7890	0
Pacific Lodge Youth Services		C	818 347-1577	0
Pacific Protection Services		D	818 313-9369	0
Panavision Inc (PA)		B	818 316-1000	0
Physicians Choice LLC		D	818 340-9988	0
Pinnacle Contracting Corp		E	818 888-6548	0
Pro-Tek Consulting (PA)		C	805 807-5571	0
Prober & Raphael A Law Corp		D	818 227-0100	0
Propertyplus Insur Agcy Inc		A	818 432-2640	0
Pta CA Congress of Parents		E	818 340-6700	0
Qbi LLC (PA)		D	818 594-4900	0
Qualified Benefits Inc		E	818 594-4900	0
R & B Realty Group		D	818 710-5400	0
Ramkade Insurance Services		D	818 444-1340	0
Reachlocal Inc (HQ)		C	818 274-0260	0
Real Software Systems LLC (PA)		D	818 313-8000	0
Ricoh Usa Inc		D	213 629-1838	0
Ricoh Usa Inc		E	818 703-0265	0
Rodeo Realty Inc		D	818 999-2030	0
Russon Financial Services Inc		D	818 999-2800	0
Santa Mnica Mntins Trils Cncil		D	818 222-4531	0
Scherzer International Corp (PA)		D	818 227-2700	0
Singerlewak LLP		D	818 999-3924	0
Skyhigh Woodland Hills LLC		D	805 484-6300	0
Solar Energy LLC		D	818 449-5816	0
Southern Cal Prmnnte Med Group		E	818 592-3038	0
State Farm Mutl Auto Insur Co		D	818 887-1060	0
Talon International Inc (PA)		D	818 444-4100	0
TI Limited LLC (PA)		D	323 877-5991	0
Top Tier Consulting		D	818 338-2121	0
Topanga Villas Company		D	818 884-8017	0
Tr Warner Center LP		B	818 887-4800	0
Truck Underwriters Association		A	323 932-3200	0
United Ribbon Company Inc		D	818 716-1515	0
Universal Mus Group Hldngs Inc		A	317 871-0319	0
Universal Protection Svc LP		D	818 227-1240	0
USI of Southern California Ins		E	818 251-3000	0
Viking River Cruises Inc (HQ)		D	818 227-1234	0
W M Klorman Construction Corp		D	818 591-5969	0
Wells Fargo Clearing Svcs LLC		D	818 226-2222	0
West Valley Area Squad Club		C	818 888-0980	0
Wham-O Inc		D	818 963-4200	0
Willits Perpetual LLC		D	818 668-6800	0
Xavient Digital LLC		A	805 955-4111	0
Zenith Insurance Company (DH)		B	818 713-1000	0

WOODSIDE, CA - San Mateo County

Company	SIC	EMP	PHONE	ENTRY #
Ecullet Inc		D	650 493-7300	0
Filoli Center		D	650 364-8300	0
Menlo Country Club		E	650 369-2342	0
Skyline Consulting Group		C	650 529-3455	0

WRIGHTWOOD, CA - San Bernardino County

Company	SIC	EMP	PHONE	ENTRY #
MHRP Resort Inc		D	760 249-5808	0
Mountain High Resort Assoc LLC		A	760 249-5808	0

	SIC	EMP	PHONE	ENTRY #
YORBA LINDA, CA - Orange County				
AJ Oster West LLC		D	714 692-1000	0
Alliance Rvrside Hsptality LLC		E	949 229-3168	0
Ambreen Enterprises Inc		D	909 620-1339	0
American Golf Corporation		D	714 779-2461	0
American Transport Inc		D	714 567-8000	0
Black Gold Golf Club		D	714 961-0060	0
Brewsters Automotive Inc		D	714 528-4683	0
Coldwell Bnkr Residential Brkg		E	714 832-0020	0
Dsh West Inc		D	714 692-8777	0
Eastern Star Homes California **(PA)**		D	714 986-2380	0
First Team RE - Orange Cnty		D	714 223-2143	0
Food Management Associates Inc		E	714 694-2828	0
Force Framing Inc		E	714 970-3888	0
Hulk Construction		D	714 701-9458	0
IMG **(PA)**		E	714 974-1700	0
Kaiser Foundation Hospitals		E	714 685-3520	0
Loma Vista Nursery		D	714 779-5583	0
Metropolitan Water District		D	714 577-5031	0
Nasser Company Inc **(PA)**		D	714 279-2100	0
Professnl Rgistry Netwrk Corp		C	714 394-4071	0
Reeves Tractor Service Inc		D	714 692-4020	0
Southern Cal Prmnnte Med Group		E	714 685-3520	0
St Jude Heritage Medical Group		C	714 528-4211	0
Ta-Kai Home Care Inc		D	714 393-4586	0
V-Tek Systems Corporation		D	909 396-5355	0
Vident		D	714 221-6700	0
Yorba Properties Corp		D	714 777-5112	0
YOSEMITE NTPK, CA - Mariposa County				
DNC Prks Rsrts At Yosemite Inc		A	209 372-1001	0
YOUNTVILLE, CA - Napa County				
Bazan Mario AG Services & Vine		D	707 945-0718	0
Villagio Inn & Spa LLC		C	707 944-8877	0
Vintners Golf Club		E	707 944-1992	0
YREKA, CA - Siskiyou County				
Belcampo Group Inc		D	530 842-5200	0
County of Siskiyou		D	530 841-2700	0
RCO Reforesting Inc		E	530 842-7647	0
Siskiyou Hospital Inc		B	530 842-4121	0
YUBA CITY, CA - Sutter County				
Alta Cal Regional Ctr Inc		B	530 674-3070	0
Ampla Health **(PA)**		C	530 674-4261	0
AT&T Corp		D	530 822-2700	0
Bi Warehousing Inc		E	530 671-8787	0
Bi-County Ambulance Service		E	530 674-2780	0
Bianchi Ag Services Inc		D	530 923-7675	0
Butte Basin Management Co		E	530 674-2060	0
Butte-Yb-Stter Wtr Qlty Cltion		D	530 673-5131	0
Calpine Corporation		E	530 821-2075	0
County of Sutter		C	530 822-7250	0
E Center		C	530 634-1200	0
Express Personnel Services		D	530 671-9202	0
Freemont Rideout Health Group		D	530 671-2883	0
Frito-Lay North America Inc		C	530 671-7854	0
Gene M Accito		D	530 674-3179	0
Golden 1 Credit Union		C	877 465-3361	0
Guava Holdings LLC		E	530 671-0550	0
Hilbers Inc		D	530 673-2947	0
Lamon Construction Company Inc		E	530 671-1370	0
New Legend Inc		B	530 674-3100	0
Northgate Terrace Apts		D	530 671-2026	0
R B Spencer Inc		D	530 674-8307	0
Sacramento Packing Inc		B	530 671-4488	0
Sears Roebuck and Co		D	530 751-4628	0
Sierra Central Credit Union **(PA)**		D	530 671-3009	0
Sierra Gold Nurseries Inc		D	530 674-1145	0
Sutter Health		C	530 749-3585	0
Sutter N Med Group A Prof Corp **(PA)**		D	530 749-3661	0
Sutter North Med Foundation **(PA)**		C	530 741-1300	0
Sutter North Med Foundation		D	530 749-3635	0
Sutter North Med Foundation		D	530 749-3450	0
Sutter Surgical Hospital N Vly		C	530 749-5700	0
Thiara Sukhwant		E	530 673-1581	0
Tri County Respite Care Svc		D	530 755-3500	0
Trueblue Inc		C	530 755-3291	0
United Com Serve		D	530 790-3000	0
United Landscape Resource Inc		D	530 671-1029	0
Valley Aggregate Transport Inc		D	530 821-2600	0
Virga Investment Property		C	530 755-4409	0
Yuba City Nursing & Rehab LLC		D	530 671-0550	0
Yuba City Racquet Club Inc		D	530 673-6900	0
Yuba City Unified School		A	530 822-7601	0
YUCAIPA, CA - San Bernardino County				
B B G Management Group **(PA)**		D	909 797-9581	0
Braswells Yucaipa Valley C		D	909 795-2476	0
Calimesa Operations LLC		C	909 795-2421	0
Cedar Operations LLC		C	909 790-2273	0
Winegardner Masonry Inc		E	909 795-9711	0
Yucaipa Valley Water District **(PA)**		D	909 797-5117	0
YUCCA VALLEY, CA - San Bernardino County				
A & W Maintenance		D	310 619-8694	0
A-1 Elite Painting Inc		E	760 365-6702	0
Catalyst Development Corp		E	760 228-9653	0
County of San Bernardino		D	760 228-5234	0
Desert Manor Care Center LP		D	760 365-0717	0
Hi-Desert Mem Hlth Care Dst **(PA)**		D	760 820-9229	0

GEOGRAPHIC

Employment Codes: A=Over 500 employees, B=251-500,
C=101-250, D=51-100, E=50

2020 Directory of California
Wholesalers and Services Companies

© Mergent Inc. 1-800-342-5647

1669